VOX
ENGLISH
and
SPANISH
Learner's
Dictionary

NTC *NTC Publishing Group*

Library of Congress Cataloging-in-Publication Data

Vox English and Spanish learner's dictionary.
   p. cm. — (Vox dictionaries)
  ISBN 0-8442-7094-6 (hardcover)
  ISBN 0-658-00188-4 (paperback)
  1. English language—Dictionaries—Spanish. 2. Spanish language—
Dictionaries—English. I. Series.
  PC4640.V6915 1998
  463'.21—dc21
                 98-8398
                 CIP

Hardcover 5 6 7 8 9 0 FGR/FGR 1 0 9 8 7 6 5 4 3 2
Paperback 5 6 7 8 9 0 FGR/FGR 1 0 9 8 7 6 5 4 3

ISBN 0-8442-7094-6 (hardcover)
ISBN 0-658-00188-4 (paperback)

McGraw-Hill books are available at special quantity discounts to use as premiums and sales promotions, or for use in corporate training programs. For more information, please write to the Director of Special Sales, Professional Publishing, McGraw-Hill, Two Penn Plaza, New York, NY 10121-2298. Or contact your local bookstore.

This book is printed on acid-free paper.

How to consult this dictionary

American Spanish

blanket ['blæŋkɪt] **1** *n* manta, AM frazada. **2** (*layer*) capa, manto: *a blanket of snow*, una capa de nieve. – **3** *adj* (*overall*) general, global; (*unanimous*) unánime: *a blanket agreement*, un acuerdo global; *blanket condemnation*, una condena unánime. – **4** *t* cubrir con un manto: *the hills were blanketed with snow*, las colinas estaban cubiertas con un manto de nieve. **5** (*stifle rumours*) acallar. ● **to be a wet blanket**, ser un aguafiestas. ‖ **to be born on the wrong side of the blanket**, nacer fuera del matrimonio. ■ **blanket of fog**, banco de niebla. ‖ **blanket bath**, *lavado de un paciente en su cama.* ‖ **blanket bombing**, bombardeo masivo. ‖ **blanket insurance**, póliza de seguro a todo riesgo. ‖ **blanket stitch**, punto de festón.

Español de América

New part of speech

Cambio de categoría gramatical

Explanation where no translation exists

Explicación donde no hay traducción

ranslation with explanation

chaser ['tʃeɪsə'] *n* GB copa de licor *que se toma típicamente después de una cerveza;* US bebida suave *que se toma después de otra fuerte.*
chasm ['kæzəm] **1** *n* GEOG sima. **2** *fig* abismo.
chassis ['ʃæsɪ] *n* chasis *m.*
▲ *pl chassis.*

Traducción con explicación

Gender of translation

Género de la traducción

Irregular plural cross-referenced to singular

feet [fiːt] *npl* → **foot**.
feign [feɪn] *t* fingir, aparentar: *she feigned illness to get off school*, fingió estar enferma para no ir a la escuela.
feint [feɪnt] *n fml* (*fencing*) finta; (*boxing*) treta, estratagema.
feisty ['fiːstɪ] *adj* (*forceful*) batallador,-ra; (*irritable*) irritable.
▲ *comp feistier, superl feistiest.*
feline ['fiːlaɪn] **1** *adj* felino,-a. – **2** *n* felino.
fell[1] [fel] *adj* feroz, cruel.
● **at one fell swoop**, de un solo golpe.
fell[2] [fel] **1** *t* (*tree*) talar. **2** (*enemy*) derribar.
fell[3] [fel] *n* GEOG (*moorland*) páramo alto; (*hilly land*) monte *m*, colina.
fell[4] [fel] *pt* → **fall**.

Envío de plural irregular a singular

Context indicators

Indicadores de contexto

Homonymous headwords

Entradas homónimas

Irregularities or spelling difficulties

fez [fez] *n* fez *m.*
▲ *pl fezzes.*
fiancé [fɪ'ænseɪ] *n* prometido, novio.
fiancée [fɪ'ænseɪ] *n* prometida, novia.
fiasco [fɪ'æskəʊ] *n* fiasco, fracaso.
▲ *pl fiascos,* US *fiascoes.*
fib [fɪb] **1** *n fam* bola, trola. – **2** *i fam* contar bolas, contar trolas.
▲ (*verbo*) *pt & pp fibbed, ger fibbing.*
fibber ['fɪbə'] *n fam* trolero,-a, mentiroso,-a.

Irregularidades o dificultades ortográficas

American spelling referenced to British entry

molder ['məʊldə'] *i* US → **moulder**.
molding ['məʊldɪŋ] *n* US → **moulding**.
Moldova [mɒl'dəʊvə] *n* Moldova.
moldy ['məʊldɪ] *adj* US → **mouldy**.
▲ *comp moldier, superl moldiest.*
mole[1] [məʊl] *n* (*on skin*) lunar *m.*
mole[2] [məʊl] **1** *n* ZOOL topo. **2** *fam* (*spy*) topo *mf*, espía *mf.*

Envío de grafía americana a grafía británica

Register label

Etiqueta de registro lingüístico

Phonetic transcription

rift [rɪft] **1** *n* hendedura, grieta. **2** *fig* ruptura.
rig [rɪg] **1** *n* rig *m*, plataforma petrolífera. – **2** *t* MAR aparejar. **3** *fam* (*fix*) amañar.
◆ **to rig up** *t sep* improvisar.
▲ *pt & pp rigged, ger rigging.*
rigging ['rɪgɪŋ] *n* MAR aparejo, jarcia.

Transcripción fonética

Phrasal verb

Verbo preposicional

Guía para consultar este diccionario

Categoría gramatical de la entrada	**arabismo** *m* Arabic expression. **arabista** *mf* Arabist. **arabizar** *t* to arabize. ▲ *Conjugation model* [4], *like realizar.* **arácnido** *m* arachnid.
Ortografía del inglés americano	**arada** 1 *f* (*acción*) ploughing (US plowing). **2** (*tierra*) ploughed (US plowed) land. **arado** *m* plough (US plow). **arador** *m* ploughman (US plowman). **Aragón** *m* Aragon.

Part of speech of entry

American English spelling

Tecnicismo	**arranque** 1 *m* TÉC starting mechanism. **2** (*comienzo*) start. **3** *fig* (*arrebato*) outburst, fit: *un arranque de furia,* a fit of rage. **4** ARQ (*de escalera*) foot; (*de arco*) base. **5** (*decisión, valentía*) courage, determination. **6** (*ocurrencia ingeniosa*) joke, witticism. ● **en un arranque,** *fig* impulsively.
Nombres en construcciones fijas	■ **motor de arranque,** starter motor. ‖ **punto de arranque,** beginning. **arrapiezo** 1 *m* (*andrajo*) rag, tatter. **2** (*niño*) whippersnapper, urchin.
Explicación de hechos culturales	**arras** *fpl* 13 *coins given by bridegroom to bride during the wedding ceremony.*

Field label

Noun compounds

Explanation of cultural items

	ascensionista *mf* (*en globo*) balloonist; (*alpinista*) mountaineer. **ascenso** 1 *m* (*subida*) climb, ascent. **2** (*aumento*) rise (**de,** in). **3** (*promoción*) promotion. **ascensor** *m* lift, US elevator.
Traducción del inglés americano	**ascensorista** *mf* lift attendant, US elevator operator. **asceta** *mf* ascetic.

American English translation

Fraseología	**asco** *m* disgust, repugnance. ● **coger asco a algo,** to get sick of sth. ‖ **dar asco,** to be disgusting: *dejó la cocina que daba asco,* he left the kitchen in a terrible mess. ‖ **dar asco a algn.,** to make sb. sick: *me da asco ese sitio,* this place makes me feel sick, this place is disgusting. ‖ **estar hecho,-a un asco,** (*cosa*) to be filthy, look a real mess; (*persona*) to be filthy, be in a right state. ‖ **hacer ascos a algo,** to turn up one's nose at sth. ‖ **¡qué asco!,** how disgusting!, how revolting!
Elementos intercambiables	**ascua** *f* live coal. ● **arrimar el ascua a su sardina,** *fam* to look after number one. ‖ **estar en/sobre ascuas,** to be on tenterhooks. ‖ **tener a algn. sobre/en ascuas,** to keep sb. on tenterhooks. ▲ *Takes el in singular.*
Subentrada	**aseado,-a** 1 *pp* → **asear.** – 2 *adj* clean, neat, tidy. **asear** 1 *t* (*adecentar*) to clean, tidy up. – 2 **asearse,** *p* (*arreglarse*) to wash, get washed.

Idiomatic expressions

Interchangeable elements

Subentry

	cabalgada 1 *f* (*tropa*) troop of riders. **2** (*correría*) cavalry raid. **cabalgadura** 1 *f* (*bestia en que se cabalga*) mount. **2** (*bestia de carga*) beast of burden.
Régimen preposicional del verbo	**cabalgar** 1 *i* (*sobre un animal*) to ride (**en/sobre,** -): *cabalgó sobre un caballo blanco,* she rode a white horse. **2** (*sobre otra cosa*) to straddle (**sobre,** -), sit astride (**sobre,** -): *el niño cabalgaba sobre la silla,* the boy sat astride the chair. – 3 *t* to ride. **4** (*cubrir a una hembra*) to cover, mount.
Modelo de conjugación de verbo irregular	▲ *Conjugation model* [7], *like llegar.* **cabalgata** *f* cavalcade. ■ **la cabalgata de los Reyes Magos,** the procession of the Three Wise Men.

Prepositional complementa of verb

Conjugation model for irregular verb

Índice/Contents

Foreword

This totally new VOX *English and Spanish Learner's Dictionary*, the most recent addition to the extensive range of VOX dictionaries, has been compiled by a team of experienced lexicographers, translators, and language teachers who know the type of problem learners of Spanish come up against and are aware of their needs.

It presents a large amount of up-to-date information and pays special attention to current English and Spanish usage, both European and American varieties, formal and informal registers. It contains over 160,000 translations differentiated by bracketed context indicators and field labels which guide the user to the correct sense and help him to choose the right translation for a given context or express himself correctly in the foreign language.

The dictionary has been specially designed to be convenient and easy to use: the typography is clear, the layout simple and logical. First, in a numbered section, come all the basic translations of the headword; these are backed up by abundant examples of usage which clarify and illustrate those senses which present particular problems and show the user how the word is used in context. After this initial section come easy-to-find blocks of phrasal verbs, idiomatic expressions, and compound nouns and finally a grammatical note with valuable information on verb conjugation and irregularities, irregular plurals of nouns, comparatives and superlatives of adjectives, and, in general, any irregularity or spelling difficulty presented by the headword. The phrasal verb section distinguishes between separable and inseparable verbs and also contains examples of usage, as do the idiomatic expression and compound noun sections.

The headword list contains all the basic vocabulary the user will need as well as selected placenames, proper names, abbreviations, and acronyms. There are appendices with a summary of the grammar of each language, a table of English irregular verbs, and complete conjugation tables for Spanish verbs.

We are sure that the dictionary contains all the information the user needs, whether he be beginner, intermediate, or advanced, and is up-to-date, practical, and easy to consult—an indispensable tool not only in the classroom and the workplace, but also in the home, or indeed in any situation where there is interaction between these two important world languages.

Prólogo

Este VOX *English and Spanish Learner's Dictionary*, la más reciente adición a la extensa gama de diccionarios VOX, ha sido redactado completamente de nuevo por un equipo compuesto por experimentados lexicógrafos, traductores y profesores de idiomas que conocen a fondo los problemas que se le presentan al estudiante de inglés y saben cuáles son sus necesidades.

Contiene gran cantidad de información totalmente puesta al día y presta especial atención a los usos actuales del inglés y del español en sus variedades europea y americana, en los niveles tanto formal como coloquial. Ofrece más de 160 000 traducciones rigurosamente acotadas por el uso de indicadores de contexto y etiquetas de especialidad que guían al usuario a la acepción adecuada y le ayudan a escoger la traducción más idónea para cada contexto o a expresarse correctamente en el idioma extranjero.

El diccionario ha sido diseñado específicamente para que resulte de cómodo y fácil empleo: la tipografía es clara y la organización sencilla y lógica. Primero, en una sección numerada, aparecen todas las traducciones básicas de la voz; éstas se complementan con abundantes ejemplos de uso que aclaran e ilustran las acepciones que presentan problemas especiales y muestran al usuario cómo se emplea la palabra dentro de un contexto. A continuación de esta sección inicial, fácilmente localizables, vienen los bloques de *phrasal verbs* (verbos preposicionales ingleses), fraseología, sustantivos compuestos, y, al final, una nota gramatical con valiosa información sobre las irregularidades y la conjugación de los verbos, los plurales de los sustantivos, las formas comparativa y superlativa de los adjetivos y, en general, cualquier irregularidad o dificultad ortográfica de la entrada. La sección de los *phrasal verbs* distingue entre los llamados *separables* e *inseparables* y contiene también, al igual que las secciones de fraseología y sustantivos compuestos, ejemplos de uso.

El lemario abarca todo el léxico básico que necesitará el usuario, además de topónimos, nombres propios, abreviaturas y siglas. Hay también apéndices con un resumen de la gramática de ambos idiomas, una tabla de verbos irregulares ingleses y un cuadro completo de conjugación de los verbos españoles.

Estamos seguros de que este diccionario contiene toda la información que necesita el usuario, sea principiante, intermedio, o avanzado y que es actual, eficaz y fácil de consultar: una herramienta indispensable, no sólo en el aula y en el lugar de trabajo, sino también en el hogar o en cualquier situación donde haya interacción entre estas dos grandes lenguas de importancia mundial.

ENGLISH-SPANISH

Abbreviations used in this dictionary

abbr	abbreviation, acronym	*fpl*	feminine plural
adj	adjective	GB	British English
adv	adverb	*gen*	general
AER	aeronautics	GEOG	geography
AGR	agriculture	GEOL	geology
AM	American Spanish	*ger*	gerund
ANAT	anatomy	GRAM	grammar
ARCH	architecture	HIST	history
ART	art	*i*	intransitive verb
ASTROL	astrology	*indef art*	indefinite article
ASTRON	astronomy	*inf*	infinitive
AUTO	automobiles	*interj*	interjection
aux	auxiliary verb	*iron*	ironic
AV	aviation	JUR	law
BIOL	biology	LING	linguistics
BOT	botany	LIT	literature
CINEM	cinema	*m*	masculine
COMM	commerce	*m & f*	masculine or feminine
comp	comparative	MAR	maritime
COMPUT	computing	MATH	mathematics
conj	conjunction	MED	medicine
contr	contraction	METEOR	meteorology
CULIN	cookery	*mf*	masculine and feminine
CHEM	chemistry	MIL	military
def art	definite article	*mpl*	masculine plural
ECON	economy	MUS	music
EDUC	education	*n*	noun
ELEC	electricity	*npl*	plural noun
etc	etcetera	ORN	ornithology
euph	euphemistic	*os.*	oneself
f	feminine	*pej*	pejorative
fam	familiar	*pers*	person
fig	figurative	*phr*	phrase
FIN	finance	PHYS	physics
fml	formal	*pl*	plural

POL	politics	*subj*	subjunctive
pp	past participle	*superl*	superlative
pref	prefix	*symb*	symbol
prep	preposition	*t*	transitive verb
pres	present	*t insep*	inseparable transitive phrasal
pron	pronoun		verb
pt	past	*t sep*	separable transitive phrasal
RAD	radio		verb
REL	religion	TECH·	technical
sb.	somebody	THEAT	theatre
SEW	sewing	TV	television
sing	singular	US	American English
sl	slang	ZOOL	zoology
SP	sport	→	see
sth.	something	≈	approximately equivalent to

Gramatica inglesa

Fonética

Fonética

Todas las entradas inglesas en este diccionario llevan transcripción fonética basada en el sistema de la Asociación Fonética Internacional (AFI). He aquí una relación de los símbolos empleados. El símbolo ' delante de una sílaba indica que es ésta la acentuada.

Las consonantes

[p]-   pan [pæn], happy ['hæpɪ], slip [slɪp].
[b]-   big [bɪg], habit ['hæbɪt], stab [stæb].
[t]-   top [tɒp], sitting ['sɪtɪŋ], bit [bɪt].
[d]-   drip [drɪp], middle ['mɪdəl], rid [rɪd].
[k]-   card [kɑːd], maker ['meɪkəʳ], sock [sɒk].
[g]-   god [gɒd], mugger ['mʌgəʳ], dog [dɒg].
[tʃ]-   chap [tʃæp], hatchet ['hætʃɪt], beach [biːtʃ].
[dʒ]-   jack [dʒæk], digest [daɪ'dʒest], wage [weɪdʒ].
[f]-   wish [wɪʃ], coffee ['kɒfɪ], wife [waɪf].
[v]-   very ['verɪ], never ['nevəʳ], give [gɪv].
[θ]-   thing [θɪŋ], cathode ['kæθəʊd], filth [fɪlθ].
[ð]-   they [ðeɪ], father ['fɑːðəʳ], loathe [ləʊð].
[s]-   spit [spɪt], stencil ['stensəl], niece [niːs].
[z]-   zoo ['zuː], weasel ['wiːzəl], buzz [bʌz].
[ʃ]-   show [ʃəʊ], fascist [fæ'ʃɪst], gush [gʌʃ].
[ʒ]-   gigolo ['ʒɪgələʊ], pleasure ['pleʒəʳ], massage ['mæsɑːʒ].
[h]-   help [help], ahead [ə'hed].
[m]-   moon [muːn], common ['kɒmən], came [keɪm].
[n]-   nail [neɪl], counter ['kaʊntəʳ], shone [ʃɒn].
[ŋ]-   finger ['fɪŋgəʳ], sank [sæŋk], thing [θɪŋ].
[l]-   light [laɪt], illness ['ɪlnəs], bull [bʊl].
[r]-   rug [rʌg], merry ['merɪ].
[j]-   young [jʌŋ], university [juːnɪ'vɜːsɪtɪ], Europe ['jʊərəp].
[w]-   want [wɒnt], rewind [riː'waɪnd].
[x]-   loch [lɒx].
[ʳ]-   se llama "linking r" y se encuentra únicamente a final de palabra. Se pronuncia sólo cuando la palabra siguiente empieza por una vocal: mother and father ['mʌðər ən 'fɑːðəʳ].

Las vocales y los diptongos

[iː]-   sheep [ʃiːp], sea [siː], scene [siːn], field [fiːld].
[ɪ]-   ship [ʃɪp], pity ['pɪtɪ], roses ['rəʊzɪz], babies ['beɪbɪz], college ['kɒlɪdʒ].
[e]-   shed [ʃed], instead [ɪn'sted], any ['enɪ], bury ['berɪ], friend [frend].
[æ]-   fat [fæt], thank [θæŋk], plait [plæt].
[ɑː]-   rather ['rɑːðəʳ], car [kɑːʳ], heart [hɑːt], clerk [klɑːk], palm [pɑːm], aunt [ɑːnt].
[ɒ]-   lock [lɒk], wash [wɒʃ], trough [trɒf], because [bɪ'kɒz].
[ɔː]-   horse [hɔːs], straw [strɔː], fought [fɔːt], cause [kɔːz], fall [fɔːl], boar [bɔːʳ], door [dɔːʳ].
[ʊ]-   look [lʊk], pull [pʊl], woman ['wʊmən], should [ʃʊd].
[uː]-   loop [luːp], do [duː], soup [suːp], elude [ɪ'luːd], true [truː], shoe [ʃuː], few [fjuː].
[ʌ]-   cub [kʌb], ton [tʌn], young [jʌŋ], flood [flʌd], does [dʌz].
[ɜː]-   third [θɜːd], herd [hɜːd], heard [hɜːd], curl [kɜːl], word [wɜːd], journey ['dʒɜːnɪ].
[ə]-   actor ['æktəʳ], honour ['ɒnəʳ], about [ə'baʊt].
[ə]-   opcional. En algunos casos se pronuncia y en otros se omite: trifle ['traɪfəl].
[eɪ]-   cable ['keɪbəl], way [weɪ], plain [pleɪn], freight [freɪt], prey [preɪ], great [greɪt].
[əʊ]-   go [gəʊ], toad [təʊd], toe [təʊ], though [ðəʊ], snow [snəʊ].
[aɪ]-   lime [laɪm], thigh [θaɪ], height [haɪt], lie [laɪ], try [traɪ], either ['aɪðəʳ].
[aʊ]-   house [haʊs], cow [kaʊ].
[ɔɪ]-   toy [tɔɪ], soil [sɔɪl].
[ɪə]-   near [nɪəʳ], here [hɪəʳ], sheer [ʃɪəʳ], idea [aɪ'dɪə], museum [mjuː'zɪəm], weird [wɪəd], pierce [pɪəs].
[eə]-   hare [heəʳ], hair [heəʳ], wear [weəʳ].
[ʊə]-   pure [pjʊəʳ], during ['djʊərɪŋ], tourist ['tʊərɪst].

Ortografía

1. El sufijo -s/-es según la forma de la raíz.

a) Para formar la tercera persona del singular del presente de indicativo se añade -s al infinitivo, pero si el infinitivo acaba en -sh, -ch, -s, -x, -z y, a veces, -o, se añade -es. Lo mismo pasa cuando se añade s para formar el plural de los sustantivos. Véase también el apartado sobre los sustantivos.

wish	-	wishes	fix	-	fixes
teach	-	teaches	buzz	-	buzzes
kiss	-	kisses	go	-	goes

b) Si la raíz acaba en cualquier consonante + y, ésta se convierte en i y se añade -es. Pero si la y va precedida de una vocal no experimenta ningún cambio.

	fry	-	fries	worry	-	worries
pero	play	-	plays			

2. Cambios ortográficos en la raíz al añadir ciertos sufijos.

a) Para formar el gerundio o participio presente se añade -ing al infinitivo, pero si el infinitivo acaba en cualquier consonante + e, ésta desaparece. Si acaba en -ie esta combinación se convierte en y.

give	-	giving	die	-	dying
move	-	moving	lie	-	lying

b) Si se trata de una raíz monosílaba que acaba en una sola consonante precedida de una sola vocal, la consonante se duplica en los siguientes casos: al añadir
   -ing al verbo para formar el gerundio o participio presente
   -ed al verbo para formar el pasado simple
   -er al verbo para formar el agente,
   -er o -est al adjetivo para formar el comparativo y superlativo

	stab	-	stabbing	trek	-	trekked
	swim	-	swimming	clap	-	clapped
	run	-	runner	grin	-	grinned
pero	sleep	-	sleeping	look	-	looked
	pant	-	panting	grasp	-	grasped
	sad	-	sadder, saddest	hot	-	hotter, hottest
	wet	-	wetter, wettest	big	-	bigger, biggest
pero	cold	-	colder, coldest	cool	-	cooler, coolest
	dear	-	dearer, dearest	fast	-	faster, fastest

NB   Las consonantes y, w y x no se duplican.

c) También se duplica la consonante final de los verbos de más de una sílaba si el acento tónico recae en la última sílaba.

	begin	-	beginning	admit	-	admitted
	refer		referring			
pero	offer	-	offering	open	-	opened

Sin embargo, si la consonante final es l, ésta se duplica independientemente de donde recaiga el acento tónico. Véase también el apartado 4f.

travel	-	travelling	model	-	modelled

d) Si la raíz acaba en cualquier consonante + **y**, al añadir **-ed** a la raíz del verbo o **-er** o **-est** a la del adjetivo, la **y** se convierte en **i**.

      spy   -   **spied**   **carry**   -   **carried**

      pretty   -   **prettier, prettiest**

e) Si un adjetivo acaba en **-y**, al formar el adverbio añadiendo **-ly** la **y** se convierte en **i**.

      happy   -   **happily**   **gay**   -   **gaily**

3. Las contracciones

En inglés familiar el uso de las formas contractas de ciertos verbos en las que un apóstrofo ocupa el lugar de una letra suprimida es muy frecuente. He aquí una lista de las más usuales:

's	is, has	**'re**	are
've	have	**'d**	would, had
'm	am	**'ll**	will, shall
-n't	not	**can't**	cannot
won't	will not		

4. Diferencias ortográficas entre el inglés británico y el americano.

Hay varias diferencias entre la ortografía británica y la americana. Aquí se resumen las diferencias regulares, pero todas las formas diferentes constan en el cuerpo del diccionario. El punto de referencia es siempre el inglés británico.

a) Algunas palabras que acaban en **-tre** se escriben con **-ter** en el inglés americano.

      centre   -   **center**   **mitre**   -   **miter**
      theatre   -   **theater**

b) Algunas palabras que acaban en **-our** se escriben con **-or** en el inglés americano.

      harbour   -   **harbor**   **vapour**   -   **vapor**
      colour   -   **olor**

c) Algunas palabras que contienen el dígrafo **ae** en el ingles americano se escriben con **e**.

      mediaeval   -   **medieval**   **gynaecology**   -   **gynecology**

d) Algunas palabras que contienen el dígrafo **oe** en el ingles americano se escriben con **e**.

      manoeuvre   -   **maneuver**   **oestrogen**   -   **estrogen**

e) Algunas palabras que acaban en **-ogue** acaban en **-og** en el inglés americano.

      catalogue   -   **catalog**   **dialogue**   -   **dialog**

f) A pesar de lo expresado arriba en el apartado 2c, mientras que en el inglés británico una **l** final suele duplicarse independientemente de donde recaiga el acento tónico, en el inglés americano esta **l** solo se duplica si el acento recae en la última sílaba:

      travel   -   **traveled, traveling**

pero   **rebel**   -   **rebelled, rebelling**.

El artículo
El artículo indefinido
El artículo indefinido es **a** y es invariable: **a man, a young woman, a boy, a girl, a big dog, a tree, a planet**.

Delante de las palabras que empiecen por vocal, *a* se convierte en *an*: *an apple, an eagle, an easy test, an Indian, an untidy room*.
Sin embargo una palabra puede empezar por una vocal escrita y no empezar por sonido vocálico: esto ocurre con las palabras que empiezan por *eu-* y algunas de las que empiezan por *u-* (véanse las transcripciones fonéticas en el diccionario). En estos casos se usa *a* en vez de *an*: *a European, a euphemistic expression; a union, a university professor*.
Asimismo, si una *h* inicial se pronuncia se empleará *a*, si es muda *an*: *a house, a helpful person*, pero *an hour, an honest man*.

El artículo indefinido solo se pone delante de los sustantivos en singular.

a dog	un perro	*dogs*	unos perros
an eel	una angula	*eels*	unas angulas
an old house	una casa antigua	*old houses*	casas antiguas

El artículo definido
El artículo definido es *the* y es invariable. Sirve tanto para el singular como para el plural: *the man , the men, the woman, the women, the children, the earth, the sea*. Su pronunciación es [ðə], pero delante de las palabras que empiecen por un sonido vocálico se pronuncia [ðɪ].

El sustantivo
Género
En inglés, a diferencia del español, los sustantivos carecen de género gramatical y los artículos y adjetivos son invariables. Solo algunos nombres referentes a las personas tienen forma femenina y en algunos casos existen palabras diferentes para designar el varón y la hembra:

actor	*- actress*	*prince*	*- princess*	*host*	*- hostess*
king	*- queen*	*boy*	*- girl*	*son*	*- daughter*
cock	*- hen*	*bull*	*- cow*	*ram*	*- ewe*

El genitivo sajón
Para indicar la relación de poseedor/posesión en inglés se usa el llamado genitivo sajón, que consiste en añadir *'s* al poseedor y colocarlo delante de lo poseído. Funciona para las personas y también para los animales:

Lawrence's mother	la madre de Lawrence
the boy's bicycle	la bicicleta del chico
my teacher's glasses	las gafas de mi profesor
the government's policies	la política del gobierno
our dog's tail	la cola de nuestro perro

Si el poseedor está en plural y acaba en *-s*, en vez de añadir *'s* se añade únicamente el apóstrofo, pero si se trata de un plural irregular que no acaba en *-s* se añade *'s*:

the boys' bicycles	las bicicletas de los chicos
my parents' car	el coche de mis padres
your children's toys	los juguetes de tus niños
men's trousers	pantalones de caballero

Si el poseedor acaba en *-s* en el singular se suele añadir *'s*, aunque a algunos nombres extranjeros, antiguos o clásicos, se añade solo el apóstrofo:

Charles's wife	la mujer de Charles
Mrs Jones's house	la casa de la Sra. Jones
Cervantes' novels	las novelas de Cervantes
Aristophanes' plays	las obras de Aristófanes

Sustantivos contables e incontables
En inglés los sustantivos son contables o incontables. Los primeros pueden ser contados y, por tanto, pueden optar a tener singular y plural: *boy, boys*; *knife, knives*; *pencil, pencils* - es evidente que los chicos, cuchillos y lápices se pueden contar. Sin embargo, *electricity* es incontable, la electricidad no se puede contar.

Mientras que los contables pueden tener singular y plural, los incontables sólo tienen forma singular: *furniture, advice, news, information, health, chaos, honesty, peace*. No obstante, algunos de estos sustantivos incontables pueden contarse mediante el uso de *a piece of*:

furniture	los muebles	*a piece of furniture*	un mueble
advice	los consejos	*two pieces of advice*	dos consejos
news	las noticias	*three pieces of news*	tres noticias

Plurales irregulares

La mayoría de sustantivos en inglés son regulares y el plural se forma añadiendo *-s* (o *-es*, véase el apartado 1 de la sección de ortografía) a la forma del singular. Existen plurales irregulares y formas invariables, los cuales constan en el diccionario.

Los sustantivos que acaban en *-o* pueden formar el plural añadiendo *-s*, *-es*, o bien cualquiera de las dos. Para comprobar la forma correcta, véase la entrada.

Los sustantivos que acaban en *-f* pueden formar el plural añadiendo *-s*, cambiando la *f* en *v* y añadiendo *-es*, o bien de cualquiera de las dos maneras. Los que acaban en *-ff* siempre (salvo el caso de *staff* que también tiene un plural irregular) forman el plural añadiendo una sola *s*. Para comprobar la forma correcta, véase la entrada.

Los sustantivos que acaban en *-fe* suelen formar el plural en *-ves*, mientras que *safe* y los acabados en *-ffe* solo añaden una *-s*.

El pronombre
Cuadro de pronombres y adjetivos posesivos

pronombre sujeto	pronombre complemento directo/indirecto	adjetivo posesivo	pronombre posesivo	pronombre reflexivo
I	me	my	mine	myself
you	you	your	yours	yourself
he	him	his	his	himself
she	her	her	hers	herself
it	it	its	—	itself
we	us	our	ours	ourselves
you	you	your	yours	yourselves
they	them	their	theirs	themselves

Los pronombres sujeto

En inglés el pronombre sujeto debe figurar siempre:
> **I was very pleased to see him there**,

aunque en una misma frase no es preciso repetir el pronombre si el sujeto no varía:
> **She locked the door and then put the key in her pocket**.

Los pronombres de complemento directo/indirecto

El pronombre de complemento directo se coloca detrás del verbo que complementa:
> **She shot him; I washed and dried it**.

El pronombre de complemento indirecto, si acompaña un complemento directo que es un sustantivo, se coloca también detrás del verbo que complementa:
> **She made me a cake; I gave him the keys**,

pero cuando acompaña un complemento directo que es pronombre es más corriente usar las preposiciones **to** o **for**, nótese también el cambio de orden:
> **She made it for me; I gave them to him**.

El pronombre con función de complemento también se usa:
> 1 - detrás de una preposición:
> > **She goes out with him; Look at them**.
> 2 - detrás de **than** y **as ... as ...** en los comparativos:
> > **He's taller than her; She's as quick as him**.
> 3 - en inglés informal detrás del verbo **to be**:
> > **It's me, John; It wasn't me, it was him**.
> 4 - para respuestas cortas como:
> > **Who's got my pencil? —Me!**

Los adjetivos posesivos

Los adjetivos posesivos no varían según lo poseído sino según el poseedor:
> **my sister, my sisters; their friend, their friends**.

Los pronombres posesivos

Los pronombres posesivos se usan para sustituir la estructura adjetivo posesivo + nombre:
This is my car. Where's yours? (= *your car*); **His family is bigger than mine.** (= *my family*).

Los pronombres reflexivos

Los pronombres reflexivos se usan:

      1 - cuando el sujeto y el complemento del verbo son el mismo:
          I've hurt myself; Please help yourselves!

      2 - cuando se quiere remarcar que es una persona y no otra quien realiza la acción:
          If nobody will do it for me, I'll have to do it myself.

El pronombre impersonal

Como pronombre impersonal en inglés coloquial se usa **you**, mientras que en inglés formal se usa **one**:
You push this button if you want tea; You can't drive a car if you're under 17.
One must be sure before one makes such serious accusations.

El adjetivo
General

Los adjetivos en inglés son invariables y casi siempre van delante de los sustantivos: **an old man, an old woman; old men, old women.**

Pueden ir después de los siguientes verbos: **be, look, seem, appear, feel, taste, smell, sound.**

Si un sustantivo en una expresión numérica se usa como adjetivo, siempre va en singular: **a two-mile walk; an eight-hour day.**

El comparativo y el superlativo

Los comparativos se usan para comparar una o dos personas, cosas, etc. con otra u otras. Los superlativos se usan para comparar una persona o cosa de un grupo con dos o más personas o cosas del mismo grupo.

Añaden a la raíz **-er** para el comparativo y **-est** para el superlativo:
- los adjetivos de una sola sílaba:

big	*bigger*	*biggest*
cold	*colder*	*coldest*

- los de dos sílabas que acaban en **-y**:

pretty	*prettier*	*prettiest*

Forman el comparativo con **more** y el superlativo con **most**:
- la mayoría de los demás adjetivos de dos sílabas:

boring	*more boring*	*the most boring*

- los de tres sílabas y más:

beautiful	*more beautiful*	*the most beautiful*

Pueden formar el comparativo y superlativo de cualquiera de las dos maneras los adjetivos de dos sílabas acabados en **-er, -ure, -le** y **-ow** así como (entre otros) **common, quiet, tired, pleasant, handsome, stupid, cruel, wicked** y **polite**, aunque es más corriente la forma con **more** y **most**.

Son irregulares los siguientes:

good	*better*	*best*
bad	*worse*	*worst*
far	*farther/further*	*farther/furthest*

El adverbio
General

Los adverbios muy a menudo pueden formarse a partir de los adjetivos añadiendo **-ly**: **sad - sadly, quick - quickly, happy - happily, beautiful - beautifully.**

Si el adjetivo acaba en **-ly** esto no es posible: los adjetivos **lovely**, **friendly**, **ugly**, **lonely** y **silly**, entre otros, no tienen adverbio correspondiente.

En algunos casos esta formación de un adverbio conlleva cambios ortográficos, véase el apartado de ortografía.

Algunos adverbios tienen la misma forma que el adjetivo correspondiente: **hard**, **late**, **early**, **fast**, **far**, **much**, **little**, **high**, **low**, **near**.

Algunos adverbios cambian de sentido respecto al adjetivo al que corresponden:

hard = duro; duramente	**hardly** = apenas
late = tarde	**lately** = últimamente
near = cercano	**nearly** = casi
high = alto	**highly** = muy; muy favorablemente

Posición
Aunque los adverbios pueden ir al principio de la frase, la posición más frecuente es después del verbo y el complemento. Sin embargo hay ciertos adverbios que suelen ir delante del verbo (después del primer auxiliar si es un tiempo compuesto) y después del verbo **be**. Los más frecuentes de este grupo son **always**, **usually**, **generally**, **normally**, **often**, **sometimes**, **occasionally**, **seldom**, **rarely**, **never**, **almost**, **just**, **still**, **already** y **only**.

El comparativo y el superlativo
La regla general es como la de los adjetivos; los adverbios de dos o más sílabas anteponen siempre **more** para la comparación y **most** para el superlativo, y los de una sola sílaba añaden los sufijos **-er** para el comparativo y **-est** para el superlativo:

quickly	**more quickly**	**most quickly**
beautifully	**more beautifully**	**most beautifully**
fast	**faster**	**fastest**
hard	**harder**	**hardest**
near	**nearer**	**nearest**

pero

early	**earlier**	**earliest**

Son irregulares:

well	**better**	**best**
badly	**worse**	**worst**
little	**less**	**least**
much	**more**	**most**
far	**farther/further**	**farthest/furthest**
late	**later**	**last**

El verbo
Conjugación
La conjugación del verbo inglés es sencilla. La mayoría de los verbos ingleses son regulares y el pasado simple y participio pasado se forman añadiendo **-ed** a la raíz; solo **-d** si la raíz ya tiene **-e** final. El participio presente se forma añadiendo **-ing** a la raíz. Véase también la sección de ortografía.

Infinitivo	Pasado simple	Participio pasado	Participio presente
sail	**sailed**	**sailed**	**sailing**
grab	**grabbed**	**grabbed**	**grabbing**
kiss	**kissed**	**kissed**	**kissing**
waste	**wasted**	**wasted**	**wasting**

Pronunciación del pasado y participio pasado regulares
El sufijo **-ed** siempre se escribe igual, pero se pronuncia de tres maneras distintas según la pronunciación (fíjese en la transcripción fonética) de la raíz a la que se añade.

Se pronuncia [d] si la raíz acaba en una consonante sonora [b], [g], [dʒ], [v], [ð], [z], [ʒ], [m], [n], [ŋ] y [l] o cualquier vocal:

- **stabbed** [stabd], **begged** [begd], **opened** ['əʊpənd], **filled** [fɪld], **vetoed** ['viːtəʊd].

Se pronuncia [t] si la raíz acaba en una consonante sorda [p], [k], [tʃ], [f], [θ], [s], [ʃ]:
- *clapped* [klapt], *licked* [lɪkt], *kissed* [kɪst], *wished* [wɪʃt].

Se pronuncia [ɪd] si la raíz acaba en [t] o [d];
- *tasted* ['teɪstɪd], *defended* [dɪ'fendɪd].

Para los verbos irregulares véase la tabla al final de esta sección y las respectivas entradas.

Phrasal verbs

Los *phrasal verbs* o verbos preposicionales son muy numerosos en inglés. Al añadir una partícula adverbial o preposición a un verbo, se modifica o cambia totalmente el significado del verbo original.

put (poner)	*put out* (apagar)
turn (girar)	*turn on* (encender)

En este diccionario los *phrasal verbs* aparecen en una sección al final de la entrada, introducida por el símbolo ◆. Distinguimos tres categorías de *phrasal verbs*; los transitivos separables (*t sep*), los transitivos inseparables (*t insep*) y los intransitivos (*i*). Claro está, los intransitivos nunca llevan complemento directo, pero los transitivos sí lo llevan. La diferencia entre los transitivos inseparables y los separables es que en aquéllos el complemento no puede colocarse entre el verbo y la partícula:

The bigger boys were always picking on him - los chicos mayores siempre se metían con él

mientras que en éstos el complemento si es sustantivo puede ir detrás de la partícula o entre el verbo y la partícula, y si es promombre debe ir forzosamente entre el verbo y la partícula:

She picked up her umbrella o *She picked her umbrella up* - cogió su paraguas
She picked it up - lo cogió

La formación de los tiempos verbales

Presente simple

Tiene la misma forma que el infinitivo del verbo en todas las personas excepto en la tercera persona del singular, en la que se añade la terminación *-s* o *-es* (véase el apartado de ortografía):

I *sail*	we *sail*
you *sail*	you *sail*
he/she/it *sails*	they *sail*

Los verbos *to be* y *to have* son irregulares:

I *am*	we *are*	I *have*	we *have*
you *are*	you *are*	you *have*	you *have*
he/she/it *is*	they *are*	he/she/it *has*	they *have*

Presente continuo

Se forma del presente del verbo *to be* + el participio presente:

I am resting, you are painting etc.

Pretérito perfecto

Se forma del presente del verbo *to have* + el participio pasado:

He has arrived, they have just left etc.

Pretérito perfecto continuo

Se forma del presente del verbo *to have* + *been* + el participio presente:

I have been dreaming, we have been riding etc.

Pasado simple

Véase el principio de esta sección y la tabla de verbos irregulares. El verbo *to be* es irregular:

I was	we were
you were	you were
he/she/it was	they were

Pasado continuo

Se forma del pasado simple de *to be* + el participio presente:

It was raining, they were laughing, etc.

Pluscuamperfecto

Se forma del pasado simple de *to have* + el participio pasado:

I had lost my slippers, the dog had taken them etc.

Pluscuamperfecto continuo

Se forma del pasado simple de *to have* + *been* + el participio pasado:

He had been repairing his motorbike etc.

Futuro

Se forma de *will/shall* + el infinitivo. (Como norma general *will* se usa para todas las personas aunque, en el lenguaje formal, *shall* lo sustituye en la primera persona tanto del singular como del plural):

It will be here next week etc.

Futuro continuo

Se forma de *will/shall* + *be* + el participio presente:

They will be lying on the beach etc.

Futuro perfecto

Se forma de *will/shall* + *have* + participio pasado:

I will have finished in ten minutes etc.

Futuro perfecto continuo

Se forma de *will/shall* + *have* + *been* + participio presente:

We will have been living here for forty years etc.

Las oraciones condicionales

Aquí damos cuenta de los tres tipos básicos de oraciones condicionales del inglés, las llamadas reales, irreales e imposibles. Las construcciones 1) y 2) hacen referencia al presente y futuro mientras que 3) describe situaciones en el pasado.

1) Condicional real (first conditional)

If + presente simple	*will/shall* + infinitivo
If it snows this week,	*we will go skiing on Saturday*

2) Condicional irreal (second conditional)

If + pasado simple	*would* + infinitivo
If we had a corkscrew,	*we would be able to open the bottle*

3) Condicional imposible (third conditional)

If + pluscuamperfecto	*would have* + participio pasado
If you had run a little faster,	*you would have caught the train*

La voz pasiva

La voz pasiva es frecuente en inglés. Se forma de la siguiente manera: se invierten el sujeto y el complemento directo, se pone el verbo *be* en el mismo tiempo que el verbo en la frase activa seguido del participio pasado del verbo, y se coloca la partícula *by* delante del sujeto:

John broke the window	- *The window was broken by John*
Leeds United have beaten Stoke City	- *Stoke City have been beaten by Leeds United*

A menudo se emplea para dar más énfasis al complemento directo o cuando el sujeto no se conoce o no tiene mucha importancia:

The police will tow away your car	- *Your car will be towed away (by the police)*
Someone has stolen my pen	- *My pen has been stolen.*

El Imperativo

Tanto en singular como en plural, el imperativo se forma con el infinitivo sin *to*:

Shut up!; Open this door!; Give me my umbrella!

Las oraciones negativas se forman con *do not* (*don't*) + infinitivo:

Do not feed the animals!; Don't put your feet on the chair!

Se usa *let's* (*let us*) + infinitivo (sin *to*) como imperativo para la primera persona del plural o para hacer sugerencias:

Let's watch the other channel; Let's not quarrel *o* **Don't let's quarrel.**

La construcción de las frases negativas e interrogativas

Negativas

Los tiempos compuestos forman las frases negativas intercalando *not* después del verbo auxiliar:

He has finished	- *He has not finished*
It is raining	- *It is not raining*
She will see you later	- *She will not see you later*

En el presente simple la negación se forma empleando el infinitivo del verbo (que es invariable) junto con el verbo auxiliar *do* (*does* para la tercera persona singular) seguido de *not*:

He works on Saturdays	- *He does not work on Saturdays*
You make a lot of mistakes	- *You do not make a lot of mistakes*

Para el pasado simple el auxiliar *do/does* toma la forma del pasado *did* mientras que el verbo principal se mantiene en infinitivo:

He worked last Saturday	- *He did not work last Saturday*
You made a lot of mistakes	- *You did not make a lot of mistakes*

Interrogativas

En los tiempos compuestos se forman las frases interrogativas anteponiendo el verbo auxiliar al sujeto:

She is having a shower	- *Is she having a shower?*
We shall come to help you	- *Shall we come to help you?*

En el presente simple se forma empleando el infinitivo del verbo (que es invariable) junto con el verbo auxiliar *do* (*does* para la tercera persona singular) que se coloca antes del sujeto:

He works on Saturdays	- *Does he work on Saturdays?*
They eat fish	- *Do they eat fish?*

Para el pasado simple el auxiliar *do/does* toma la forma del pasado *did*:

He worked last Saturday	- *Did he work last Saturday?*
They ate all of it	- *Did they eat all of it?*

Tablas de verbos irregulares

Infinitivo	Pasado simple	Participio pasado
abide	abided/abode[1]	abided
arise	arose	arisen
awake	awoke	awaked/awoken
be	was/were	been
bear	bore	borne/born
beat	beat	beaten
become	became	become
befall	befell	befallen
beget	begot	begotten
begin	began	begun
behold	beheld	beheld
bend	bent	bent
bereave	bereft	bereft
beseech	besought/beseeched	besought/beseeched
beset	beset	beset
bet	bet/betted	bet/betted
bid	bid/bade	bid/bidden
bide	bode/bided	bided
bind	bound	bound
bite	bit	bitten
bleed	bled	bled
blow	blew	blown
break	broke	broken
breed	bred	bred
bring	brought	brought
broadcast	broadcast	broadcast
build	built	built
burn	burnt/burned	burnt/burned
burst	burst	burst
buy	bought	bought
cast	cast	cast
catch	caught	caught
chide	chided/chid	chid/chidden
choose	chose	chosen
cleave	cleft/cleaved/clove	cleft/cleaved/cloven
cling	clung	clung
clothe	clothed/clad	clothed/clad
come	came	come
cost	cost	cost
creep	crept	crept
crow	crowed/crew	crowed
cut	cut	cut
deal	dealt	dealt
dig	dug	dug
dive	dived, US dove	dived
do	did	done
draw	drew	drawn
dream	dreamed/dreamt	dreamed/dreamt
drink	drank	drunk
drive	drove	driven
dwell	dwelt/dwelled	dwelt/dwelled
eat	ate	eaten
fall	fell	fallen
feed	fed	fed
feel	felt	felt
fight	fought	fought
find	found	found

flee	fled	fled
fling	flung	flung
fly	flew	flown
forbear	forbore	forborne
forbid	forbade/forbad	forbidden
forecast	forecast/forecasted	forecast/forecasted
forego	forewent	foregone
foresee	foresaw	foreseen
foretell	foretold	foretold
forget	forgot	forgotten
forgive	forgave	forgiven
forgo	forwent	forgone
forsake	forsook	forsaken
forswear	forswore	forsworn
freeze	froze	frozen
gainsay	gainsaid	gainsaid
get	got	got, US gotten
gird	girded/girt[1]	girded/girt[1]
give	gave	given
go	went	gone
grind	ground	ground
grow	grew	grown
hamstring	hamstrung	hamstrung
hang	hung/hanged[1]	hung/hanged[1]
have	had	had
hear	heard	heard
heave	heaved/hove	heaved/hove
hew	hewed	hewed/hewn
hide	hid	hidden/hid
hit	hit	hit
hold	held	held
hurt	hurt	hurt
input	input	input
keep	kept	kept
kneel	knelt, US kneeled	knelt, US kneeled
knit	knit/knitted	knit/knitted
know	knew	known
lay	laid	laid
lead	led	led
lean	leant/leaned	leant/leaned
leap	leapt/leaped	leapt/leaped
learn	learnt/learned	learnt/learned
leave	left	left
lend	lent	lent
let	let	let
light	lighted/lit	lighted/lit
lose	lost	lost
make	made	made
mean	meant	meant
meet	met	met
mislay	mislaid	mislaid
mislead	misled	misled
misread	misread	misread
misspell	misspelled/misspelt	misspelled/misspelt
misspend	misspent	misspent
mistake	mistook	mistaken
misunderstand	misunderstood	misunderstood
mow	mowed	mowed/mown
offset	offset	offset
outbid	outbid	outbid
outdo	outdid	outdone
outgrow	outgrew	outgrown
outrun	outran	outrun
outshine	outshone	outshone

overbear	overbore	overborne
overcome	overcame	overcome
overdo	overdid	overdone
overhang	overhung	overhung
overhear	overheard	overheard
override	overrode	overridden
overrun	overran	overrun
oversee	oversaw	overseen
oversleep	overslept	overslept
overtake	overtook	overtaken
overthrow	overthrew	overthrown
pay	paid	paid
prove	proved	proved/proven
put	put	put
read	read	read
rebuild	rebuilt	rebuilt
recast	recast	recast
redo	redid	redone
re-lay	re-laid	re-laid
remake	remade	remade
rend	rent	rent
repay	repaid	repaid
rerun	reran	rerun
reset	reset	reset
retell	retold	retold
rewind	rewound	rewound
rewrite	rewrote	rewritten
rid	rid/ridded	rid/ridded
ride	rode	ridden
ring	rang	rung
rise	rose	risen
run	ran	run
saw	sawed	sawed/sawn
say	said	said
see	saw	seen
seek	sought	sought
sell	sold	sold
send	sent	sent
set	set	set
sew	sewed	sewed/sewn
shake	shook	shaken
shear	sheared	sheared/shorn
shed	shed	shed
shine	shone	shone
shoe	shod	shod
shoot	shot	shot
show	showed	shown/showed
shrink	shrank	shrunk
shut	shut	shut
sing	sang	sung
sink	sank	sunk
sit	sat	sat
slay	slew	slain
sleep	slept	slept
slide	slid	slid
sling	slung	slung
slink	slunk	slunk
slit	slit	slit
smell	smelled/smelt	smelled/smelt
smite	smote	smitten
sneak	sneaked, US snuck	sneaked, US snuck
sow	sowed	sowed/sown
speak	spoke	spoken
speed	speeded/sped	speeded/sped

spell	spelled/spelt	spelled/spelt
spend	spent	spent
spill	spilled/spilt	spilled/spilt
spin	spun/span	spun
spit	spat	spat
split	split	split
spoil	spoiled/spoilt	spoiled/spoilt
spread	spread	spread
spring	sprang	sprung
stand	stood	stood
steal	stole	stolen
stick	stuck	stuck
sting	stung	stung
stink	stank/stunk	stunk
strew	strewed	strewed/strewn
stride	strode	stridden
strike	struck	struck
string	strung	strung
strive	strove	striven
sublet	sublet	sublet
swear	swore	sworn
sweep	swept	swept
swell	swelled	swollen
swim	swam	swum
swing	swung	swung
take	took	taken
teach	taught	taught
tear	tore	torn
tell	told	told
think	thought	thought
thrive	throve/thrived	thrived/thriven
throw	threw	thrown
thrust	thrust	thrust
tread	trod	trodden/trod
undercut	undercut	undercut
undergo	underwent	undergone
understand	understood	understood
undertake	undertook	undertaken
underwrite	underwrote	underwritten
undo	undid	undone
unwind	unwound	unwound
uphold	upheld	upheld
upset	upset	upset
wake	woke	woken
waylay	waylaid	waylaid
wear	wore	worn
weave	wove	woven
wed	wedded/wed	wedded/wed
weep	wept	wept
wet	wetted/wet	wetted/wet
win	won	won
wind	wound	wound
withdraw	withdrew	withdrawn
withhold	withheld	withheld
withstand	withstood	withstood
wring	wrung	wrung
write	wrote	written

[1] Para la diferencia véase la entrada.

A

A, a [eɪ] **1** n (*the letter*) A, a. **2** MUS la.
● **from A to Z,** de la A a la Z, de cabo a rabo.
■ **A road,** carretera principal.

a [eɪ, *unstressed* ə] **1** *indef art* un, una: *a man and a woman,* un hombre y una mujer; *a boy with a big nose,* un chico con la nariz grande; *a leopard is faster than a lion,* los leopardos son más rápidos que los leones; *I think it's a Van Gogh,* creo que es un Van Gogh. **2** (*not translated*): *I'm a history teacher,* soy profesor de historia; *two and a half litres,* dos litros y medio; *what a lovely dress!,* ¡qué vestido más mono!; *what a mess!,* ¡vaya lío! **3** (*per*) por: *three times a week,* tres veces por semana; *£3 a kilo,* tres libras el kilo. **4** (*a certain*) un tal, una tal: *a Mr Fletcher would like to see you,* un tal Sr. Fletcher quiere verle.
▲ *Se usa delante de las palabras que empiezan con sonido no vocálico. Véase también* **an.**

A [æmp, 'æmpeəʳ] *symb* (*ampere*) amperio; (*symbol*) A.

AA¹ ['eɪ'eɪ] *abbr* (*Alcoholics Anonymous*) Alcohólicos Anónimos; (*abbreviation*) AA *mpl.*

AA² ['eɪ'eɪ] *abbr* GB (*Automobile Association*) automóvil club británico.

AAA¹ ['eɪ'eɪ'eɪ] *abbr* GB (*Amateur Athletic Association*) asociación atlética amateur.

AAA² ['eɪ'eɪ'eɪ] *abbr* US (*Automobile Association of America*) automóvil club de los Estados Unidos.

AB¹ ['eɪ'biː] *abbr* GB (*able-bodied seaman*) marinero de primera.

AB² ['eɪ'biː] *abbr* US → **BA.**

aback [ə'bæk] *adv* hacia atrás.
● **to be taken aback,** asombrarse, quedarse asombrado,-a.

abacus ['æbəkəs] *n* ábaco.

abaft [ə'bɑːft] **1** *adv* MAR (*direction*) a popa; (*position*) en popa. – **2** *prep* MAR detrás de.

abandon [ə'bændən] **1** *t* abandonar: *the car was abandoned at the side of the road,* el coche fue abandonado al lado de la carretera; *they abandoned the match because of the rain,* el partido se suspendió a causa de la lluvia; *they abandoned all hope of saving the patient,* abandonaron toda esperanza de salvar al paciente; *he gave the order to abandon ship,* dio orden de abandonar el barco. – **2** *n* desenfreno, abandono.

abandoned [ə'bændənd] **1** *adj* abandonado,-a. **2** (*immoral*) vicioso,-a, inmoral.

abandonment [ə'bændənmənt] *n* abandono.

abase [ə'beɪs] *t* to abase os., *phr* humillarse.

abasement [ə'beɪsmənt] *n* humillación *f.*

abashed [ə'bæʃt] *adj* (*embarrassed*) incómodo,-a; (*ashamed*) avergonzado,-a.

abate [ə'beɪt] **1** *i* (*gen*) reducirse; (*storm, anger*) amainar; (*wind*) cesar; (*pain*) ceder; (*flood waters*) descender. – **2** *t* (*reduce*) reducir; (*stop*) acabar con.

abatement [ə'beɪtmənt] *n* (*reduction*) reducción *f,* disminución *f;* (*stopping*) supresión *f.*

abattoir ['æbətwɑː'] *n* matadero.

abbess ['æbes] *n* abadesa.

abbey ['æbɪ] *n* abadía.

abbot ['æbət] *n* abad *m.*

abbreviate [ə'briːvɪeɪt] *t* abreviar.

abbreviation [əbriːvɪ'eɪʃən] **1** *n* (*shortening*) abreviación *f.* **2** (*shortened form*) abreviatura.

ABC¹ ['eɪ'biː'siː] *abbr* (*American Broadcasting Company*) compañía norteamericana de radiodifusión; (*abbreviation*) ABC *f.*

ABC² ['eɪ'biː'siː] *abbr* (*Australian Broadcasting Commission*) comisión *f* australiana de radiodifusión; (*abbreviation*) ABC *f.*

abdicate ['æbdɪkeɪt] **1** *t* abdicar: *he abdicated the throne,* abdicó el trono, abdicó la corona; *she abdicated all responsibility in the affair,* declinó toda responsabilidad en el asunto. – **2** *i* abdicar: *he abdicated in favour of his brother,* abdicó en su hermano.

abdication [æbdɪ'keɪʃən] *n* abdicación *f.*

abdomen ['æbdəmən] *n* abdomen *m.*

abdominal [æb'dɒmɪnəl] *adj* abdominal.

abduct [æb'dʌkt] *t* raptar, secuestrar.

abduction [æb'dʌkʃən] *n* rapto, secuestro.

abductor [æb'dʌktə'] *n* raptor,-ra, secuestrador,-ra.

abeam [ə'biːm] *adv* MAR por el través.

abed [ə'bed] *adv arch* en la cama.

aberrant [æ'berənt] *adj* aberrante, anormal.

aberration [æbə'reɪʃən] *n* aberración *f.*

abet [ə'bet] *t* incitar y ayudar: *the murderer was aided and abetted by his sister,* el asesino contó con la complicidad de su hermana.
▲ *pt & pp* **abetted,** *ger* **abetting.**

abeyance [ə'beɪəns] **in abeyance,** *adv phr* en desuso.

abhor [əb'hɔː'] *t* aborrecer, detestar.
▲ *pt & pp* **abhorred,** *ger* **abhorring.**

abhorrence [əb'hɒrəns] *n* aborrecimiento, odio.

abhorrent [əb'hɒrənt] *adj* aborrecible, detestable, odioso,-a: *I find it abhorrent,* lo detesto.

abide [ə'baɪd] **1** *t* (*bear, stand*) soportar, aguantar: *I can't abide that woman,* no aguanto a esa mujer. – **2** *i arch* (*dwell*) morar. **3** *arch* (*remain*) permanecer.
◆ **to abide by** *t insep* (*promise*) cumplir con; (*rules, decision*) acatar.
▲ *En 1 pt & pp* **abided;** *en 2 y 3* **abode** [ə'bəʊd].

abiding [ə'baɪdɪŋ] *adj* duradero,-a, perdurable, permanente.

ability [ə'bɪlɪtɪ] **1** *n* (*capability*) capacidad *f,* aptitud *f.* **2** (*talent*) talento.
● **to the best of one's ability,** lo mejor que uno puede.
▲ *pl* **abilities.**

abject ['æbdʒekt] **1** *adj* (*conditions*) abyecto,-a: *they live in abject poverty,* viven en la más abyecta miseria. **2** (*person*) despreciable, vil.

abjuration [æbdʒʊˈreɪʃən] *n* abjuración *f*.
abjure [æbˈdʒʊəˈ] *t* abjurar, abjurar de.
ablative [ˈæblətɪv] *n* ablativo.
ablaze [əˈbleɪz] *adj* ardiendo, en llamas.
● ablaze with light, *fig* resplandeciente de luz.
able [ˈeɪbəl] **1** *adj* que puede: *those able to escape did so*, aquéllos que podían se escaparon. **2** (*capable*) hábil, capaz, competente: *he's a very able administrator*, es un gestor muy competente.
● to be able to, poder: *we weren't able to go*, no pudimos ir; *will you be able to do it?*, ¿podrás hacerlo?
■ able seaman, marinero hecho.
able-bodied [eɪbəlˈbɒdɪd] *adj* sano,-a, robusto,-a.
ablution [əˈbluːʃən] *n* ablución *f*, lavatorio.
● to do one's ablutions, lavarse.
ably [ˈeɪblɪ] *adv* con habilidad, hábilmente.
ABM [ˈeɪˈbiːˈem] *abbr* (*anti-ballistic missile*) misil *m* antibalístico; (*abbreviation*) ABM *m*.
abnegation [æbnɪˈgeɪʃən] *n* abnegación *f*.
abnormal [æbˈnɔːməl] **1** *adj* (*not normal*) anormal. **2** (*unusual*) inusual.
abnormality [æbnɔːˈmælɪtɪ] *n* anormalidad *f*, anomalía.
▲ *pl* abnormalities.
abnormally [æbˈnɔːməlɪ] **1** *adv* anormalmente, de modo anormal. **2** (*unusually*) excepcionalmente.
aboard [əˈbɔːd] **1** *adv* (*ship*, *plane*) a bordo; (*train*) en el tren; (*bus*) en el autobús: *a coach with 45 people aboard plunged into the river Seine*, un autocar que llevaba 45 pasajeros se precipitó al río Sena. – **2** *prep* (*ship*, *plane*) a bordo de; (*train*, *bus*) en.
● to go aboard, (*ship*, *plane*) embarcar, subir a bordo; (*train*, *bus*) subir.
abode [əˈbəʊd] **1** *n fml* morada, domicilio. – **2** *pt & pp*
→ abide.
● of no fixed abode, sin domicilio fijo.
abolish [əˈbɒlɪʃ] **1** *t* abolir, suprimir. **2** *JUR* derogar.
abolition [æbəˈlɪʃən] **1** *n* abolición *f*, supresión *f*. **2** *JUR* derogación *f*.
abolitionist [æbəˈlɪʃənɪst] *n* abolicionista *mf*.
abominable [əˈbɒmɪnəbəl] *adj* abominable; (*terrible*) terrible, horrible.
■ the Abominable Snowman, el Yeti.
abominably [əˈbɒmɪnəblɪ] *adv* (*gen*) abominablemente; (*terribly*) terriblemente, horriblemente.
abominate [əˈbɒmɪneɪt] *t* abominar, aborrecer, detestar
abomination [əbɒmɪˈneɪʃən] *n* abominación *f*.
aboriginal [æbəˈrɪdʒɪnəl] **1** *adj* aborigen. – **2** *n* aborigen *mf*.
aborigine [æbəˈrɪdʒɪnɪ] *n* aborigen *mf*.
abort [əˈbɔːt] **1** *i* abortar. – **2** *t* (*pregnant woman*) hacer abortar. **3** (*mission, program, etc*) abortar.
abortion [əˈbɔːʃən] **1** *n* (*of pregnancy*) aborto. **2** (*of missión etc*) interrupción *f*.
● to have an abortion, abortar.
abortionist [əˈbɔːʃənɪst] *n* abortista *mf*.
abortive [əˈbɔːtɪv] *adj* fallido,-a.
abound [əˈbaʊnd] *i* abundar.
● to abound in/with, abundar en.
about [əˈbaʊt] **1** *prep* (*concerning*) sobre, acerca de: *to speak about* ..., hablar de ...; *what is the book about?*, ¿de qué trata el libro?; *what did you do about* ...?, ¿qué hiciste con ...?; *there's something odd about Jim*, Jim tiene algo de extraño; *a man came about the drains*, vino un hombre por lo de las alcantarillas. **2** (*showing where*) por,

en; (*around*) alrededor de: *he's somewhere about the house*, está por algún rincón de la casa; *he travels about the country*, viaja por todo el país; *there were bodies lying about the streets*, había cadáveres por las calles; *when I looked about me I saw that* ..., al mirar a mi alrededor vi que ... – **3** *adv* (*approximately*) alrededor de: *it cost about £500*, costó unas quinientas libras; *at about three o'clock*, a eso de las tres. **4** *fam* (*almost*) casi: *she's about finished*, está a punto de acabar; *I'm about ready*, me falta poquito; *it's about stopped raining*, ya casi no llueve. **5** (*near*) por aquí, por ahí: *there was nobody about*, no había nadie; *where's Jean? –she's somewhere about*, ¿dónde está Jean? –andará por aquí. **6** (*out of bed*) levantado,-a: *you were about early this morning*, te levantaste muy temprano esta mañana; *you'll soon be up and about again*, dentro de nada te pondrás bien. **7** (*in all directions*) de un lado a otro: *there were children running about all over the place*, había niños correteando por todas partes. **8 to be about,** (*around*) haber: *there are lots of forged notes about*, circulan muchos billetes falsos; *with the recession there's not much money about*, a causa de la crisis el dinero escasea; *there's a lot of flu about*, hay mucha gente con gripe.
● to be about to ..., estar a punto de ... ‖ how about + *noun*, ¿qué te parece + *sustantivo*?: *how about a pizza?*, ¿qué te parece una pizza? ‖ how about + *-ing*, ¿y si + *subj*?: *how about going to Paris*, ¿y si fuéramos a París? ‖ it's about time (that) + *past tense*, ya va siendo hora de que + *subj*. ‖ and about time too!, *fam* ¡ya era hora!
about-face [əbaʊtˈfeɪs] *n* → about-turn.
about-turn [əbaʊtˈtɜːn] **1** *n* MIL media vuelta. **2** *fig* cambio radical, cambio total (*de idea, opinión, postura, política, etc*): *the government performed a complete about-turn in its monetary policy*, el gobierno efectuó un cambio total en su política monetaria.
above [əˈbʌv] **1** *prep* (*higher than*) por encima de: *above our heads*, por encima de nuestras cabezas; *she is above suspicion*, está por encima de toda sospecha; *only the manager is above him*, sólo el gerente está por encima de él; *a captain is above a sargeant*, un capitán manda más que un sargento. **2** (*more than*) más de, más que: *above 5,000 people*, más de 5.000 personas; *those above the age of 65*, los mayores de 65 años; *the temperature is above 45 °C*, la temperatura supera los 45 °C; *I value your friendship above all else*, valoro tu amistad ante todo. **3** (*too good for*): *he can't have said that*, *he's above such things*, él no puede haberlo dicho, no es de ese tipo de gente; *he's not above taking bribes*, es muy capaz de aceptar un soborno. **4** (*up river from*) más arriba de: *there's a mill above the waterfall*, hay un molino más arriba de la cascada. – **5** *adv* arriba, en lo alto: *the palace, seen from above*, el palacio, visto desde arriba; *she gazed at the stars above*, contemplaba las estrellas allá en lo alto. **6** (*in writing*) arriba: *see above*, véase arriba.
● above all, sobre todo. ‖ above and beyond the call of duty, más allá de lo que exige el deber.
above-board [əbʌvˈbɔːd] *adj* legítimo,-a, legal.
above-mentioned [əbʌvˈmenʃənd] *adj* arriba mencionado,-a, arriba citado,-a.
Abp [ɑːtʃˈbɪʃəp] *abbr* (*Archbishop*) Arzobispo; (*abbreviation*) Arz., Arzpo.
abracadabra [æbrəkəˈdæbrə] *interj* ¡abracadabra!
abrade [əˈbreɪd] *t* raer, desgastar, erosionar.
abrasion [əˈbreɪʒən] *n* abrasión *f*.
abrasive [əˈbreɪsɪv] **1** *adj* (*substance*) abrasivo,-a. **2** (*person*) áspero,-a, arisco,-a, agresivo,-a; (*comment*) hiriente,-a. – **3** *n* abrasivo.

abrasively [ə'breɪsɪvlɪ] *adv* de manera áspera.
abrasiveness [ə'breɪsɪvnəs] 1 *n* (*of substance*) lo abrasivo. 2 (*of person*) aspereza, agresividad *f.*
abreast [ə'brest] *adv* de frente: *to walk four abreast,* caminar cuatro de frente.
● to keep abreast of, mantenerse al corriente de.
abridge [ə'brɪdʒ] *t* resumir, abreviar: *an abridged edition of "Hamlet",* una edición abreviada de "Hamlet".
abridgement [ə'brɪdʒmənt] *t* → **abridgment.**
abridgment [ə'brɪdʒmənt] *t* resumen *m,* abreviación *f.*
abroad [ə'brɔːd] 1 *adv* (*position*) en el extranjero; (*movement*) al extranjero: *she lives abroad,* vive en el extranjero; *to go abroad,* ir al extranjero. 2 *fml* (*everywhere*) por todas partes: *it is rumoured abroad that ...,* se rumorea por ahí que ... 3 *arch* fuera, fuera de casa: *she never ventures abroad after nightfall,* nunca se atreve a salir a la calle por la noche.
abrogate ['æbrəgeɪt] *t* abrogar.
abrogation ['æbrəgeɪʃən] *n* abrogación *f.*
abrupt [ə'brʌpt] 1 *adj* (*sudden*) repentino,-a. 2 (*rude*) brusco,-a, arisco,-a. 3 (*slope*) empinado,-a.
abruptly [ə'brʌptlɪ] 1 *adv* (*suddenly*) repentinamente, de repente. 2 (*rudely*) bruscamente, de manera arisca.
abruptness [ə'brʌptnəs] 1 *n* (*suddenness*) lo repentino. 2 (*rudeness*) brusquedad *f.* 3 (*of slope*) pendiente *f.*
abscess ['æbses] *n* (*gen*) absceso; (*on gum*) flemón *m.*
abscond [əb'skɒnd] *i* fugarse: *he absconded from boarding school with the headmaster's savings,* se fugó del internado con los ahorros del director.
abseil ['æbseɪl] *i* hacer rappel: *we abseiled down the cliff face,* bajamos por el acantilado haciendo rappel.
abseiling ['æbseɪlɪŋ] *n* rappel *m.*
absence ['æbsəns] 1 *n* (*of person*) ausencia: *in the manager's absence I am in charge,* en ausencia del jefe quien manda soy yo. 2 (*of thing*) falta, carencia.
● absence makes the heart grow fonder, la distancia ablanda el corazón.
■ absence of mind, despiste *m.*
absent ['æbsənt] 1 *adj* ausente: *John's been absent a lot recently,* John ha faltado mucho a clase últimamente. 2 (*expression*) distraído,-a. – 3 to absent os., ausentarse.
● absent without leave, ausente sin permiso.
▲ (*verbo*) [æb'sent].
absentee [æbsən'tiː] *n* ausente *mf.*
absenteeism [æbsən'tiːɪzəm] *n* absentismo.
absently ['æbsəntlɪ] *adv* distraídamente.
absent-minded [æbsənt'maɪndɪd] *adj* distraído,-a, despistado,-a.
absent-mindedly [æbsənt'maɪndɪdlɪ] *adv* distraídamente, despistadamente.
absent-mindedness [æbsənt'maɪndɪdnəs] *n* despiste *m.*
absinth ['æbsɪnθ] *n* → **absinthe.**
absinthe ['æbsɪnθ] *n* absenta, ajenjo.
absolute ['æbsəluːt] 1 *adj* (*gen*) absoluto,-a: *in absolute terms,* en términos absolutos. 2 (*total*) total: *there was absolute silence,* hubo silencio total; *it's the absolute truth,* es la pura verdad; *it's absolute rubbish,* es una perfecta tontería. 3 (*unlimited*) absoluto,-a: *he held absolute power over her,* ejercía un poder absoluto sobre ella. 4 (*irrefutable*) irrefutable, incontrovertible: *we have absolute proof,* tenemos pruebas incontrovertibles.
■ absolute majority, mayoría absoluta. ‖ absolute zero, cero absoluto.
absolutely [æbsə'luːtlɪ] 1 *adv* completamente, totalmente: *it's absolutely impossible,* es totalmente impo-

sible; *he's absolutely right,* tiene toda la razón; *that is absolutely forbidden,* eso está terminantemente prohibido. 2 (*used for emphasis*) absolutamente: *you've done absolutely nothing all day,* no has hecho absolutamente nada en todo el día; *it's absolutely pouring down,* está diluviando; *she absolutely refused to help us,* se negó rotundamente a ayudarnos. – 3 *interj* (*agreement*) ¡por supuesto!, ¡desde luego!: *I think we should sell. what about you John? –oh, absolutely!,* creo que deberíamos vender. ¿y tú John? –oh, ¡por supuesto!
absolution [æbsə'luːʃən] *n* absolución *f.*
absolutism ['æbsəluːtɪzəm] *n* absolutismo.
absolve [əb'zɒlv] *t* absolver: *he was absolved of/from all responsibility,* le absolvieron de toda responsabilidad.
absorb [əb'zɔːb] 1 *t* (*liquids etc*) absorber; (*shock*) amortiguar. 2 (*time*) ocupar. 3 *fig* (*ideas etc*) asimilar.
● to be absorbed in sth., estar absorto,-a en algo.
absorbent [əb'zɔːbənt] *adj* absorbente.
absorbing [əb'zɔːbɪŋ] *adj* absorbente, muy interesante.
absorption [əb'zɔːpʃən] *n* absorción *f.*
abstain [əb'steɪn] *i* abstenerse (**from,** de).
abstainer [æb'steɪnəʳ] *n* abstemio,-a.
abstemious [æb'stiːmɪəs] *adj* abstemio,-a, sobrio,-a.
abstemiousness [æb'stiːmɪəsnəs] *n* sobriedad *f.*
abstention [æb'stenʃən] *n* abstención *f.*
abstinence ['æbstɪnəns] *n* abstinencia.
abstinent ['æbstɪnənt] *adj* abstinente.
abstract ['æbstrækt] 1 *adj* (*not concrete*) abstracto,-a. – 2 *n* (*summary*) resumen *m.* – 3 *t* (*summarize*) resumir. 4 *euph* (*steal*) sustraer.
● in the abstract, en abstracto.
■ abstract noun, nombre *m* abstracto.
▲ (*verbo*) [æb'strækt].
abstracted [æb'stræktɪd] *adj* distraído,-a.
abstractedly [æb'stræktɪdlɪ] *adv* distraídamente.
abstraction [æb'strækʃən] 1 *n* abstracción *f.* 2 (*absentmindedness*) distracción *f,* ensimismamiento.
abstruse [əb'struːs] *adj* abstruso,-a, recóndito,-a.
abstruseness [əb'struːsnəs] *n* lo recóndito.
absurd [əb'sɜːd] *adj* absurdo,-a.
absurdity [əb'sɜːdɪtɪ] *n* disparate *m.*
▲ *pl* absurdities.
ABTA ['æbtə] *abbr* (*Association of British Travel Agents*) asociación de agentes de viajes británicos.
abundance [ə'bʌndəns] *n* abundancia.
abundant [ə'bʌndənt] *adj* abundante.
● to be abundant in sth., ser abundante en algo, abundar en algo.
abundantly [ə'bʌndəntlɪ] 1 *adv* abundantemente, en abundancia. 2 (*very*) muy: *he made his views abundantly clear,* expresó sus opiniones con toda claridad.
abuse [ə'bjuːs] 1 *n* (*verbal*) insultos *mpl*; (*physical*) malos tratos *mpl.* 2 (*misuse*) abuso. – 3 *t* (*verbally*) insultar; (*physically*) maltratar. 4 (*misuse*) abusar de.
▲ (*verbo*) [ə'bjuːz].
abusive [ə'bjuːsɪv] *adj* (*insulting*) injurioso,-a, insultante.
abut [ə'bʌt] *i* estar contiguo,-a.
● to abut on / about against, lindar con.
▲ *pt & pp* abutted, *ger* abutting.
abutting [ə'bʌtɪŋ] *adj* contiguo,-a, colindante.
abysmal [ə'bɪzməl] *adj fam* malísimo,-a, fatal.
abyss [ə'bɪs] *n* abismo.
Abyssinia [æbɪ'sɪnɪə] *n* Abisinia.
Abyssinian [æbɪ'sɪnɪən] 1 *adj* abisinio,-a. – 2 *n* abisinio,-a.

AC [ˈeɪˈsiː] *abbr* ELEC (*alternating current*) corriente *f* alterna; (*abbreviation*) CA *f*.

a/c [əˈkaʊnt] *abbr* FIN (*account*) cuenta; (*abbreviation*) cta.

acacia [əˈkeɪʃə] *n* acacia.

academic [ækəˈdemɪk] 1 *adj* (*gen*) académico,-a. 2 (*theoretical*) teórico: *it's a purely academic question*, es una cuestión puramente teórica. – 3 *n* (*scholar*) académico,-a; (*lecturer*) profesor,-ra universitario,-a.
■ **academic year**, año académico.

academically [ækəˈdemɪkəlɪ] *adv* intelectualmente: *he's not academically inclined*, no tiene grandes dotes intelectuales.

academician [əkædəˈmɪʃən] *n* académico,-a.

academy [əˈkædəmɪ] 1 *n* academia. 2 (*in Scotland*) instituto de enseñanza media.
▲ *pl* **academies**.

ACAS [ˈeɪkæs] *abbr* GB (*Advisory Conciliation and Arbitration Service*) *organismo independiente que arbitra en cuestiones laborales.*

accede [ækˈsiːd] 1 *i* *fml* (*agree*) acceder (**to**, a). 2 (*to throne*) ascender (**to**, a), subir (**to**, a); (*to position, office*) acceder (**to**, a).

accelerate [ækˈseləreɪt] 1 *t* acelerar. – 2 *i* acelerarse.

acceleration [əkseləˈreɪʃən] *n* aceleración *f*.

accelerator [əkˈseləreɪtəʳ] *n* acelerador *m*.

accent [ˈæksənt] 1 *n* acento. – 2 *t* acentuar.
▲ (*verbo*) [ækˈsent].

accentuate [ækˈsentʃʊeɪt] *t* acentuar.

accentuation [æksentʃʊˈeɪʃən] *n* acentuación *f*.

accept [əkˈsept] 1 *t* (*gift, offer, etc*) aceptar. 2 (*admit to be true*) admitir, aceptar: *I accept that this is true*, admito que esto es verdad; *I accept what you say, but ...*, acepto lo que dices, pero ...

acceptability [əkseptəˈbɪlɪtɪ] *n* (*satisfactory*) aceptabilidad *f*, admisibilidad *f*.

acceptable [əkˈseptəbəl] 1 *adj* (*satisfactory*) aceptable, admisible: *this sort of behaviour is not acceptable*, este comportamiento no es admisible. 2 (*welcome*) grato,-a.

acceptance [əkˈseptəns] 1 *n* (*act of accepting*) aceptación *f*. 2 (*approval*) acogida.

access [ˈækses] 1 *n* acceso. – 2 *t* COMPUT acceder a, entrar en.
■ **access code**, código de acceso. ‖ **access road**, carretera de acceso. ‖ **access time**, tiempo de acceso.

accessary [əkˈsesərɪ] *n* JUR → **accessory 2**.
▲ *pl* **accessaries**.

accessibility [æksesɪˈbɪlɪtɪ] *adj* accesibilidad *f*.

accessible [ækˈsesɪbəl] 1 *adj* accesible. 2 (*person*) asequible, tratable.

accession [ækˈseʃən] 1 *n* (*agreement*) asentimiento. 2 (*to throne*) advenimiento. 3 (*acquisition*) adquisición *f*.

accessory [ækˈsesərɪ] 1 *n* (*gadget*) accesorio. 2 JUR (*accomplice*) cómplice *mf*. – 3 **accessories**, *npl* (*bag, gloves etc*) complementos *mpl*.
■ **accessory after the fact**, cómplice *mf*. ‖ **accessory before the fact**, cómplice *mf* encubridor,-ra.
▲ *pl* **accessories**.

accidence [ˈæksɪdəns] *n* accidentes *mpl* gramaticales.

accident [ˈæksɪdənt] 1 *n* accidente *m*: *she had an accident*, tuvo un accidente; *I'm sorry, it was an accident*, lo siento, lo hice sin querer. 2 (*coincidence*) casualidad *f*: *it happened quite by accident*, fue una pura casualidad.
● **accidents will happen**, las cosas pasan, lo que tiene que pasar pasa. ‖ **by accident**, por casualidad. ‖ *it was more by accident than design*, sonó la flauta por casualidad.

■ **car accident**, accidente *m* de coche.

accidental [æksɪˈdentəl] *adj* fortuito,-a.
■ **accidental death**, muerte *f* por accidente.

accidentally [æksɪˈdentəlɪ] 1 *adv* (*by chance*) por casualidad. 2 (*unintentionally*) sin querer.

accident-prone [ˈæksɪdəntprəʊn] *adj* propenso,-a a los accidentes.

acclaim [əˈkleɪm] 1 *n* (*welcome*) aclamación *f*. 2 (*praise*) elogios *mpl*, alabanza. – 3 *t* (*welcome*) aclamar. 4 (*praise*) elogiar, alabar.

acclamation [æcləˈmeɪʃən] *n* aclamación *f*.

acclimate [əˈklaɪmət] *t-i* → **acclimatize**.

acclimation [æklaɪˈmeɪʃən] *n* US → **acclimatization**.

acclimatization [əklaɪmətaɪˈzeɪʃən] *n* aclimatación *f*.

acclimatize [əˈklaɪmətaɪz] 1 *t* aclimatar. – 2 *i* aclimatarse.

acclivity [əˈklɪvɪtɪ] *n* cuesta, pendiente *f*.
▲ *pl* **acclivities**.

accolade [ˈækəleɪd] 1 *n* (*award*) galardón *m*, premio. 2 (*praise*) elogio.

accommodate [əˈkɒmədeɪt] 1 *t* (*put up*) alojar: *we can accommodate you, we've got a spare room*, podemos alojarte, tenemos un dormitorio de sobra. 2 (*hold*) contener, tener capacidad para: *this hotel can accommodate 250 guests*, este hotel tiene capacidad para 250 personas. 3 (*adapt*) adaptar, acomodar: *it's difficult to accommodate oneself to new circumstances*, es difícil acomodarse a unas circunstancias nuevas. 4 (*supply*) facilitar, proporcionar: *we regret we are unable to accommodate you with a loan*, lamentamos no poder facilitarle el préstamo. 5 (*satisfy*) complacer: *they bent over backwards to accommodate us*, hicieron lo imposible para complacernos.

accommodating [əˈkɒmədeɪtɪŋ] *adj* complaciente, acomodadizo,-a.

accommodation [əkɒməˈdeɪʃən] 1 *n* (*lodging*) alojamiento. 2 (*agreement*) acuerdo; (*compromise*) compromiso. – 3 **accommodations**, *npl* US (*lodging*) alojamiento *m* *sing*; (*lodging and board*) alojamiento y pensión.

accompaniment [əˈkʌmpənɪmənt] *n* acompañamiento.
● **to the accompaniment of**, acompañado,-a de.

accompanist [əˈkʌmpənɪst] *n* acompañante *mf*.

accompany [əˈkʌmpənɪ] *t* acompañar: *she was accompanied by her mother*, iba acompañada de su madre.
▲ *pt & pp* **accompanied**, *ger* **accompanying**.

accomplice [əˈkɒmplɪs] *n* cómplice *mf*.

accomplish [əˈkɒmplɪʃ] 1 *t* (*achieve*) lograr, conseguir: *I don't think your protests will accomplish anything*, no creo que consigas nada con tus protestas. 2 (*carry out*) hacer, llevar a cabo: *they accomplished a great deal in a short time*, hicieron mucho en poco tiempo.

accomplished [əˈkɒmplɪʃt] *adj* cumplido,-a, consumado,-a.
■ **accomplished fact**, hecho consumado.

accomplishment [əˈkɒmplɪʃmənt] 1 *n* (*act of achieving*) realización *f*. 2 (*achievement*) logro. – 3 **accomplishments**, *npl* (*skills*) aptitudes *fpl*, dotes *mpl*, habilidades *fpl*.

accord [əˈkɔːd] 1 *n* (*agreement*) acuerdo. – 2 *t* (*award*) conceder, otorgar. – 3 *i* (*agree*) concordar.
● **in accord with**, de acuerdo con. ‖ **of one's own accord**, espontáneamente, por propia voluntad. ‖ **with one accord**, unánimemente.

accordance [əˈkɔːdəns] **in accordance with**, *prep* de acuerdo con.

according [ə'kɔːdɪŋ]. **1 according to,** *prep* según: *according to Philip/the paper/my watch,* según Philip/el periódico/mi reloj. **2** (*consistent with*) de acuerdo con: *it went according to plan,* salió tal como se había previsto; *we were paid according to our experience,* se nos pagó de acuerdo con nuestra experiencia. – **3 according as,** *adv fml* según si.

accordingly [ə'kɔːdɪŋlɪ] **1** *adv* (*appropriately*) en consecuencia, de conformidad: *you must examine your conscience and act accordingly,* debes reflexionar y actuar en consecuencia; *she works hard and is paid accordingly,* trabaja mucho y cobra conforme a sus esfuerzos. **2** (*therefore*) por consiguiente.

accordion [ə'kɔːdɪən] *n* acordeón *m*.

accost [ə'kɒst] *t* abordar, dirigirse a.

account [ə'kaʊnt] **1** *n* (*in bank*) cuenta: *my account is in the red,* mi cuenta está en números rojos. **2** (*report*) relación *f,* relato, informe *m: he gave us an account of his experiences,* nos contó sus experiencias; *Ted's account differs significantly from yours,* el relato de Ted difiere sensiblemente del tuyo. **3** (*importance*) importancia: *it is of no account,* no tiene importancia. – **4 accounts,** *npl* cuentas *fpl: who did these accounts?,* ¿quién ha hecho estas cuentas?; *I keep the accounts myself,* llevo las cuentas yo mismo.

◆ **to account for** *i* explicar.

● **by all accounts,** al decir de todos. ‖ **on account,** a cuenta. ‖ **on account of,** por, a causa de: *don't leave on my account,* no te vayas por mí. ‖ **on no account,** bajo ningún concepto. ‖ **on one's own account,** por su propia cuenta y riesgo. ‖ **there's no accounting for tastes,** sobre gustos no hay nada escrito. ‖ **to bring sb. to account, to call sb. to account,** pedir cuentas a algn. ‖ **to give a good account of os.,** quedar en buen lugar, quedar bien. ‖ **to take into account,** tener en cuenta. ‖ **to turn sth. to (good) account,** sacar (buen) provecho de algo.

■ **accounts department,** sección *f* de contabilidad.

accountability [əkaʊnə'bɪlɪtɪ] *n* responsabilidad *f.*

accountable [ə'kaʊntəbəl] *adj* responsable (**to,** ante): *I'm not accountable to you,* no tengo por qué darte explicaciones.

accountancy [ə'kaʊntənsɪ] *n* contabilidad *f.*

accountant [ə'kaʊntənt] *n* contable *mf.*

accounting [ə'kaʊntɪŋ] *n* contabilidad *f.*

accoutrements [ə'kuːtrəmənts] *npl* (*gen*) equipo; (*luggage*) equipaje *m.*

accredit [ə'kredɪt] **1** *t* (*gen*) autorizar, reconocer; (*diplomat*) acreditar: *an accredited representative of the company,* un representante autorizado de la empresa. **2** (*approve*) aprobar, homologar; (*certify*) certificar: *it said "accredited organically grown tomatoes",* ponía "garantizamos que estos tomates han sido cultivados biológicamente". **3** (*attribute*) atribuir: *she is accredited with several miracles,* se le atribuyen varios milagros.

accretion [ə'kriːʃən] *n* acumulación *f.*

accrue [ə'kruː] *i* FIN acumularse.

acct. [ə'kaʊnt] *abbr* FIN (*account*) cuenta; (*abbreviation*) cta.

accumulate [ə'kjuːmjʊleɪt] **1** *t* acumular. – **2** *i* acumularse.

accumulation [əkjuːmjʊ'leɪʃən] *n* acumulación *f.*

accumulative [ə'kjuːmjʊlətɪv] *adj* acumulativo,-a.

accumulator [ə'kjuːmjʊleɪtəʳ] *n* acumulador *m.*

accuracy ['ækjʊrəsɪ] **1** *n* (*of numbers, instrument, information*) exactitud *f,* precisión *f.* **2** (*of shot*) certeza. **3** (*of interpretation, translation*) fidelidad *f.*

accurate ['ækjʊrət] **1** *adj* (*numbers etc*) exacto,-a, preciso,-a. **2** (*instrument*) de precisión. **3** (*shot*) certero,-a. **4** (*information etc*) exacto,-a. **5** (*interpretation, translation*) fiel.

accursed [ə'kɜːsəd] *adj* maldito,-a.

accusation [ækjuː'zeɪʃən] *n* acusación *f: to bring an accusation against,* presentar una denuncia contra.

accusative [ə'kjuːzətɪv] **1** *adj* acusativo,-a. – **2** *n* acusativo.

accusatory [ə'kjuːzətərɪ] *adj* acusador,-ra.

accuse [ə'kjuːz] *t* acusar (**of,** de): *she was accused of lying,* la acusaron de mentir.

accused [ə'kjuːzd] **the accused,** *n* (*man*) el acusado; (*woman*) la acusada.

accuser [ə'kjuːzəʳ] *n* acusador,-ra.

accusingly [ə'kjuːzɪŋlɪ] *adv* (*tone*) con tono acusador; (*look*) con mirada acusadora.

accustom [ə'kʌstəm] *t* acostumbrar (**to,** a).

accustomed [ə'kʌstəmd] *adj* acostumbrado,-a (**to,** a).

● **to grow accustomed to sth.,** acostumbrarse a algo.

ace [eɪs] **1** *n* (*cards*) as *m.* **2** (*tennis*) ace *m.* **3** *fam* (*expert*) as *m.* – **4** *adj fam* fantástico,-a.

● **to have an ace up one's sleeve,** guardar un as en la manga. ‖ **within an ace of,** en un tris de, a dos dedos de.

acerbic [ə'sɜːbɪk] *adj* áspero,-a, desabrido,-a.

acerbity [ə'sɜːbɪtɪ] *n* aspereza.

acetate ['æsɪteɪt] *n* acetato.

acetic [ə'siːtɪk] *adj* acético,-a.

■ **acetic acid,** ácido acético.

acetone ['æsɪtəʊn] *n* acetona.

acetylene [ə'setɪliːn] *n* acetileno.

ache [eɪk] **1** *n* dolor *m.* – **2** *i* doler: *my head aches,* me duele la cabeza, tengo dolor de cabeza.

achievable [ə'tʃiːvəbəl] *adj* realizable, alcanzable.

achieve [ə'tʃiːv] **1** *t* (*finish*) realizar, llevar a cabo. **2** (*attain*) lograr, conseguir.

achievement [ə'tʃiːvmənt] **1** *n* (*completion*) realización *f.* **2** (*attainment*) logro. **3** (*feat*) hazaña, proeza.

■ **sense of achievement,** satisfacción *f.*

Achilles [ə'kɪliːz] *n* Aquiles.

■ **Achilles' heel,** *fig* talón *m* de Aquiles. ‖ **Achilles' tendon,** ANAT tendón *m* de Aquiles.

aching ['eɪkɪŋ] *adj* dolorido,-a.

achy ['eɪkɪ] *adj fam* dolorido,-a.

▲ *comp* **achier,** *superl* **achiest.**

acid ['æsɪd] **1** *adj* CHEM ácido,-a. **2** (*taste*) agrio,-a. **3** *fig* (*comment*) mordaz. – **4** *n* CHEM ácido,-a.

■ **acid rain,** lluvia ácida. ‖ **acid test,** prueba decisiva.

acidic [ə'sɪdɪk] *adj* ácido,-a.

acidify [ə'sɪdɪfaɪ] **1** *t* acidificar. – **2** *i* acidificarse.

▲ *pt & pp* **acidified,** *ger* **acidifying.**

acidity [ə'sɪdɪtɪ] *n* acidez *f.*

acidly ['æsɪdlɪ] *adv* con mordacidad, mordazmente.

acidulate [ə'sɪdjʊleɪt] *t* acidular.

acidulous [ə'sɪdjʊləs] **1** *adj* (*taste*) agrio,-a. **2** (*manner*) áspero,-a.

acknowledge [ək'nɒlɪdʒ] **1** *t* (*admit*) admitir: *to acknowledge defeat,* admitir la derrota. **2** (*recognize*) reconocer: *King Henry acknowledged Prince Arthur as his heir,* el rey Henry reconoció al príncipe Arthur como su heredero; *she's acknowledged to be the greatest living pianist,* se la considera la mejor pianista contemporánea. **3** (*an acquaintance*) saludar: *he walked straight past without even acknowledging me,* pasó a mi lado y

ni siquiera me saludó. **4** (*be thankful*) agradecer, expresar agradecimiento por.
● **to acknowledge receipt of,** acusar recibo de.
acknowledgement [ək'nɒlɪdʒmənt] **1** *n* (*admission*) admisión *f*: *to do that would be an acknowledgement of guilt,* hacer eso sería una admisión de culpa. **2** (*recognition*) reconocimiento: *in acknowledgement of your help,* en reconocimiento de tu ayuda. **3** (*thanks*) muestra de agradecimiento: *she stood up in acknowledgement of the audience's applause,* se puso de pie para mostrar su agradecimiento por los aplausos del público. **4** (*reply*) contestación *f*: *I received no acknowledgement of my CV,* no recibí respuesta a mi currículum; *I shouted, and one of them waved back in acknowledgement,* grité, y uno de ellos gesticuló en conformidad.
■ **acknowledgement of receipt,** acuse *m* de recibo.
acknowledgment [æk'nɒlɪdʒmənt] *n* → **acknowledgement**.
acme ['ækmɪ] *n* apogeo, colmo: *the acme of perfection,* el colmo de la perfección.
acne ['æknɪ] *n* acné *f*.
acolyte ['ækəlaɪt] **1** *n* REL acólito, monaguillo. **2** *fig* seguidor,-ra.
acorn ['eɪkɔːn] *n* bellota.
acoustic [ə'kuːstɪk] **1** *adj* acústico,-a. – **2** **acoustics,** *n* (*science*) acústica: *acoustics is the study of sound,* la acústica es el estudio del sonido. – **3** *npl* (*sound conditions*) acústica *f sing*: *the acoustics here are perfect,* la acústica aquí es perfecta.
acquaint [ə'kweɪnt] *t* informar (**with**, de): *he acquainted me with the facts,* me informó de los hechos.
● **to acquaint os. with sth.,** familiarizarse con algo. ‖ **to be acquainted with sb.,** conocer a algn, tener trato con algn. ‖ **to be acquainted with sth.,** conocer algo, tener conocimientos de algo.
acquaintance [ə'kweɪntəns] **1** *n* (*knowledge*) conocimiento, conocimientos *mpl*: *I have a slight acquaintance with physics,* tengo unos conocimientos rudimentarios de la física; *on closer acquaintance I find her fascinating,* conociéndola mejor, la encuentro fascinante. **2** (*friendship*) amistad *f*: *my acquaintance with the minister goes back to our school days,* mi amistad con el ministro remonta a nuestros días en la escuela. **3** (*person*) conocido,-a: *an acquaintance of mine,* una persona que conozco; *I don't know him well, he's just a nodding acquaintance,* no lo conozco bien, sólo para saludarlo.
● **to make sb.'s acquaintance,** conocer a algn.
acquiesce [ækwɪ'es] *i* consentir (**in**, en), conformarse (**in**, con).
acquiescence [ækwɪ'esəns] *n* conformidad *f*, aquiescencia.
acquiescent [ækwɪ'esənt] *adj* condescendiente, aquiescente.
acquire [ə'kwaɪəʳ] *t* adquirir.
● **it's an acquired taste,** es un gusto adquirido, es un gusto aprendido. ‖ **to acquire a taste for sth.,** tomarle gusto a algo.
acquisition [ækwɪ'zɪʃən] *n* adquisición *f*.
acquisitive [ə'kwɪzɪtɪv] *adj* codicioso,-a, acaparador,-ra.
acquit [ə'kwɪt] *t* absolver, declarar inocente.
● **to acquit os. well,** quedar en buen lugar, quedar bien, salir airoso,-a.
▲ *pt & pp* **acquitted,** *ger* **acquitting.**

acquittal [ə'kwɪtəl] *n* absolución *f*.
acre ['eɪkəʳ] *n* acre *m*.
▲ *Un* **acre** *equivale a 40,47 hectáreas.*
acreage ['eɪkərɪdʒ] *n* extensión *f* (*en acres*): *what's the acreage of your estate?,* ¿qué extensión tiene su finca?
acrid ['ækrɪd] **1** *adj* acre. **2** *fig* (*remark*) cáustico,-a; (*dispute*) enconado,-a.
acridity [æ'krɪdɪtɪ] *n* acritud *f*.
acrimonious [ækrɪ'məʊnɪəs] *adj* (*remark*) cáustico,-a; (*dispute*) enconado,-a, amargo,-a.
acrimony ['ækrɪmənɪ] *n* acritud *f*, aspereza.
acrobat ['ækrəbæt] *n* acróbata *mf*.
acrobatic [ækrə'bætɪk] **1** *adj* acrobático,-a. – **2** **acrobatics,** *npl* acrobacia *f sing*.
acronym ['ækrənɪm] *n* sigla.
acropolis [ə'krɒpəlɪs] *n* acrópolis *f*.
across [ə'krɒs] **1** *prep* (*movement*) a través de, de un lado a otro de: *to go across the road,* cruzar la carretera; *to swim across a river,* cruzar un río nadando/a nado; *to fly across the Atlantic,* sobrevolar el Atlántico; *he helped the old man across the road,* ayudó al viejo a cruzar la carretera. **2** (*position*) al otro lado de: *it's across the river,* está al otro lado del río; *they live across the road,* viven enfrente. – **3** *adv* de un lado a otro: *it's 4 metres across,* mide 4 metros de lado a lado; *he ran/swam across,* cruzó corriendo/nadando.
across-the-board [əkrɒsðə'bɔːd] **1** *adj* general, generalizado,-a: *7% across-the-board pay rises,* subidas de sueldo del 7% para todos. – **2** *adv* en general: *wages will rise 7% across-the-board,* los sueldos subirán un 7% en general.
acrostic [ə'krɒstɪk] **1** *adj* acróstico,-a. – **2** *n* acróstico.
acrylic [ə'krɪlɪk] *adj* acrílico,-a.
act [ækt] **1** *n* acto, acción *f*: *this is the act of a madman,* esto es la acción de un loco; *he's not responsible for his acts,* no es responsable de sus actos. **2** THEAT acto. **3** (*of parliament*) ley *f*. – **4** *i* (*do something*) actuar: *the police acted quickly on the information,* la policía actuó deprisa al recibir la información; *we must act immediately,* hemos de actuar inmediatamente; *Perry Mason acted for the widow in that case,* Perry Mason representó a la viuda en ese caso; *the drug acts on the heart muscles,* la droga actúa sobre los músculos del corazón. **5** (*behave*) portarse, comportarse: *she acts like a little girl,* se comporta como una niña; *she acted as if nothing had happened,* hizo como si no hubiera pasado nada; *how would you act if that happened to you?,* ¿qué harías tú si te pasara eso? **6** (*in theatre*) actuar, hacer teatro; (*in cinema*) actuar, hacer cine: *have you been acting a long time?,* ¿hace mucho que actúas? **7** (*pretend*) fingir: *she's not angry, she's just acting,* no está enfadada, sólo lo finge. – **8** *t* hacer el papel de: *she's acting (the part of) Portia,* ella hace el papel de Portia.
◆ **to act as** *t insep* hacer de: *I had to act as interpreter,* tuve que hacer de intérprete. ‖ **to act out** *t sep* llevar a cabo: *to act out one's fantasies,* llevar a cabo su fantasías. ‖ **to act up** *i* (*gen*) causar problemas; (*machine*) funcionar mal; (*child*) dar guerra; (*wound, injury*) doler.
● **to catch sb. in the act,** coger a algn. in fraganti, coger a algn. con las manos en la masa. ‖ **to get in on the act,** *fam* subirse al carro. ‖ **to get one's act together,** *fam* organizarse, espabilarse.
■ **act of God,** fuerza mayor. ‖ **the Acts of the Apostles,** los Hechos de los Apóstoles.
acting ['æktɪŋ] **1** *adj* en funciones, accidental: *the acting director chaired the ceremony,* el director accidental

presidió la ceremonia. – **2** n THEAT (*profession*) teatro: *I've never done any acting,* no he hecho nunca teatro. **3** (*performance*) interpretación *f,* actuación *f: the acting was awful,* la interpretación era malísima. **4** (*pretence*) comedia: *it's not for real, it's only acting,* no es de verdad, es pura comedia.

action ['ækʃən] **1** n (*gen*) acción *f: he's a man of action,* es un hombre de acción; *I like a film with plenty of action,* me gustan las películas con mucha acción. **2** (*intervention*) actuación *f: only the swift action of the firemen saved the building,* sólo la rápida actuación de los bomberos salvó el edificio; *we must take action now,* hemos de actuar ya; *the government is taking action to reduce inflation,* el gobierno está tomando medidas para frenar la inflación. **3** (*of film*) historia, acción *f: the action takes place in Bavaria,* la acción transcurre en Baviera. **4** MIL combate *m,* acción *f: five soldiers are missing in action in northern Bosnia,* han desaparecido cinco soldados en los combates del norte de Bosnia. **5** (*working*) funcionamiento: *the action of the lungs,* el funcionamiento de los pulmones. **6** (*mechanism*) mecanismo: *this gun has a very smooth action,* el mecanismo de esta pistola funciona muy bien. **7** JUR demanda.
● **actions speak louder than words,** hechos son amores y no buenas razones. ‖ **killed in action,** muerto,-a en combate. ‖ **out of action,** fuera de servicio. ‖ **to bring an action against sb.,** entablar una demanda contra algn. ‖ **to put out of action,** inutilizar.
■ **action replay,** repetición *f* de la jugada. ‖ **action stations,** zafarrancho de combate.

actionable ['ækʃənəbəl] adj justiciable.
action-packed ['ækʃənpækt] adj fam lleno,-a de acción.
activate ['æktɪveɪt] t activar.
activation [æktɪ'veɪʃən] n activación *f.*
active ['æktɪv] **1** adj activo,-a. **2** (*volcano*) en actividad. **3** (*energetic*) activo,-a, vivo,-a, vigoroso,-a.
● **to be on active service,** estar en servicio activo. ‖ **to take an active part in sth.,** participar activamente en algo.
■ **the active voice,** la voz activa.
actively ['æktɪvlɪ] adv activamente.
activist ['æktɪvɪst] n activista *mf.*
activity [æk'tɪvɪtɪ] n actividad *f.*
▲ pl **activities**.
actor ['æktər] n actor *m.*
actress ['æktrɪs] n actriz *f.*
actual ['æktʃuəl] adj real, verdadero,-a.
● **in actual fact,** en realidad.
actuality [æktʃu'ælɪtɪ] n realidad *f.*
actually ['æktjuəlɪ] **1** adv en realidad, realmente, de hecho: *I haven't actually decided what to do yet,* en realidad, todavía no he decidido qué hacer; *can I see you? —well, actually I'm rather busy,* ¿podría verte? —verás, es que estoy muy ocupada. **2** (*indicating surprise*) incluso, hasta: *she actually accused me of stealing her bag,* hasta me acusó de robarle el bolso.
actuarial [æktju'eərɪəl] adj actuarial.
actuary ['æktʃuərɪ] n actuario,-a de seguros.
▲ pl **actuaries**.
actuate ['æktʃueɪt] **1** t (*make work*) accionar. **2** (*motivate*) mover, impulsar: *he was actuated by a desire for revenge,* le impulsaba un deseo de venganza.
acuity [ə'kjuːɪtɪ] n agudeza.
acumen ['ækjumən] n perspicacia.
acupuncture ['ækjupʌnktʃə] n acupuntura.
acupuncturist ['ækjupʌnktʃərɪst] n acupunturista *mf.*

acute [ə'kjuːt] **1** adj (*gen*) agudo,-a. **2** (*illness, pain*) agudo,-a: *acute appendicitis,* apendicitis aguda. **3** (*angle*) agudo,-a. **4** (*hearing etc*) muy fino,-a, muy desarrollado,-a: *she has an acute sense of smell,* tiene el olfato muy fino. **5** (*mind*) perspicaz. **6** (*lack, shortage*) acusado,-a, grave.
acutely [ə'kjuːtlɪ] adv agudamente, intensamente.
● **to be acutely aware of sth.,** ser perfectamente consciente de algo.
acuteness [ə'kjuːtnəs] n (*gen*) agudeza; (*of mind*) perspicacia.
ad [æd] n fam anuncio.
AD ['eɪ'diː] abbr (**Anno Domini**) después de Cristo; (*abbreviation*) d.J.C.
adage ['ædɪdʒ] n adagio, refrán *m.*
adagio [ə'dɑːdʒɪəʊ] n adagio.
▲ pl **adagios**.
Adam ['ædəm] n Adán *m.*
● **I don't know him from Adam,** no lo conozco de nada.
■ **Adam's apple,** nuez *f* (de la garganta).
adamant ['ædəmənt] adj firme, inflexible.
adamantly ['ædəməntlɪ] adv inflexiblemente.
adapt [ə'dæpt] **1** t adaptar. – **2** i adaptarse.
adaptability [ədæptə'bɪlɪtɪ] n capacidad *f* para adaptarse.
adaptable [ə'dæptəbəl] adj (*person*) capaz de adaptarse.
● **to be adaptable,** ser adaptable, saber adaptarse.
adaptation [ædəp'teɪʃən] n adaptación *f.*
adapter [ə'dæptə] n ELEC → **adaptor**.
adaptor [ə'dæptə] n ELEC ladrón *m.*
Adc ['eɪ'diː'siː] abbr (**aide-de-camp**) edecán *m.*
add [æd] **1** t (*gen*) añadir, agregar: *"and don't tell anyone,"* he added, "y no se lo digas a nadie," añadió; *beat well and then add the flour,* batir bien y luego agregar la harina. **2** (*numbers*) sumar: *add these figures together,* suma estas cantidades; *overheads must be added to the cost,* los gastos generales han de sumarse al coste.
◆ **to add to** t insep aumentar: *the wind only added to our problems,* el viento no hizo más que aumentar nuestros problemas. ‖ **to add up 1** t sep (*numbers*) sumar. – **2** i fig cuadrar: *there's something funny going on; it doesn't add up,* pasa algo raro; es que no cuadra. ‖ **to add up to 1** t insep sumar: *what do these numbers add up to?,* ¿cuánto suman estas cifras? **2** fig significar, querer decir: *what does it all add up to?,* ¿qué quiere decir todo esto?
added ['ædɪd] adj añadido,-a, adicional.
addenda [ə'dendə] npl addenda *m* sing, adiciones *fpl.*
▲ sing **addendum** [ə'dendəm].
adder ['ædə] n ZOOL víbora.
addict ['ædɪkt] **1** n adicto,-a. **2** fam (*fanatic*) fanático,-a.
addicted [ə'dɪktɪd] adj adicto,-a.
addiction [ə'dɪkʃən] n adicción *f.*
addictive [ə'dɪktɪv] adj que crea adicción: *nicotine is addictive,* la nicotina crea adicción.
addition [ə'dɪʃən] **1** n adición *f,* añadidura. **2** MATH adición *f,* suma.
● **in addition to,** además de.
additional [ə'dɪʃənəl] adj adicional.
additive ['ædɪtɪv] n aditivo.
addled ['ædəld] **1** adj podrido,-a. **2** (*brain*) confuso,-a.
add-on ['ædɒn] n adicional *m.*
address [ə'dres] **1** n (*on letter*) dirección *f,* señas *fpl: is that your business address or your home address?,* ¿es

ésta su dirección profesional o particular? **2** (*speech*) discurso, alocución *f*. − **3** *t* (*tackle*) abordar: *the problem must be addressed soon,* habrá que abordar pronto el problema. **4** (*speak to*) dirigirse a: *the chairman addressed the board,* el presidente se dirigió al consejo. **5** (*use title etc*) llamar: *they addressed him as "your highness",* lo llamaron "su alteza"; *you will address me as "sir",* me llamarás "señor". **6** (*letter*) poner la dirección en: *the letter didn't arrive because it was wrongly addressed,* la carta no llegó porque llevaba la dirección mal puesta; *the letter was addressed to my mother,* la carta iba dirigida a mi madre. ● **to address os. to sb.,** dirigirse a algn. ‖ **to address os. to sth.,** aplicarse a algo. ■ **form of address,** tratamiento.

addressee [ædreˈsiː] *n* destinatario,-a.
adduce [əˈdjuːs] *t* aducir.
Adelaide [ˈædəleɪd] *n* Adelaida.
Aden [ˈeɪdən] *n* Adén.
adenoidal [ædəˈnɔɪdəl] *adj* gangoso,-a.
adenoids [ˈædənɔɪdz] *npl* adenoides *mpl,* vegetaciones *fpl.*
adept [ˈædept] **1** *adj* experto,-a, diestro,-a, ducho,-a. − **2** *n* experto,-a, perito,-a.
adequacy [ˈædɪkwəsɪ] **1** *n* (*in quantity*) suficiencia. **2** (*in quality*) calidad *f,* aceptabilidad *f.*
adequate [ˈædɪkwɪt] **1** *adj* (*enough*) suficiente. **2** (*satisfactory*) satisfactorio,-a.
adequately [ˈædɪkwətlɪ] **1** *adv* (*sufficiently*) suficientemente, bastante. **2** (*satisfactorily*) satisfactoriamente.
adhere [ədˈhɪəʳ] *i* (*stick*) adherirse, pegarse. ✦ **to adhere to 1** *t insep* (*cause*) adherirse a. **2** (*promise*) cumplir con. **3** (*belief*) aferrarse a, mantenerse fiel a. **4** (*rules*) observar, acatar.
adherence [ədˈhɪərəns] **1** *n* (*to cause*) adhesión *f.* **2** (*to promise*) cumplimiento. **3** (*to belief*) fidelidad *f.* **4** (*to rules*) observación *f.*
adherent [ədˈhɪərənt] **1** *adj* adherente. − **2** *n* (*supporter*) adherido,-a, partidario,-a.
adhesion [ədˈhiːʒən] **1** *n* (*sticking*) adherencia, adhesión *f.* **2** MED adherencia.
adhesive [ədˈhiːsɪv] **1** *adj* adhesivo,-a. − **2** *n* adhesivo.
ad hoc [ædˈhɒk] *adj* ad hoc.
adieu [əˈdjuː] *n* LIT adiós *m.*
ad infinitum [ædɪnfɪˈnaɪtəm] *adv* ad infinitum, a lo infinito.
adipose [ˈædɪpəʊz] *adj* adiposo,-a.
adjacent [əˈdʒeɪsənt] *adj* adyacente.
adjectival [ædʒɪkˈtaɪvəl] *adj* adjetival.
adjectivally [ædʒɪkˈtaɪvəlɪ] *adv* adjetivalmente.
adjective [ˈædʒɪktɪv] *n* adjetivo.
adjoin [əˈdʒɔɪn] **1** *t* lindar con. − **2** *i* colindar.
adjoining [əˈdʒɔɪnɪŋ] **1** *adj* (*building*) contiguo,-a. **2** (*land*) colindante.
adjourn [əˈdʒɜːn] **1** *t* aplazar, suspender: *they adjourned the meeting for two days,* aplazaron la reunión dos días. − **2** *i* suspenderse: *the court adjourned for lunch,* la sesión se suspendió para almorzar.
adjournment [əˈdʒɜːnmənt] *n* aplazamiento, suspensión *f.*
adjudge [əˈdʒʌdʒ] **1** *t* (*judge*) juzgar. **2** (*award*) adjudicar.
adjudicate [əˈdʒuːdɪkeɪt] *t* juzgar.
adjudication [ədʒuːdɪˈkeɪʃən] **1** *n* (*decision*) fallo. **2** (*awarding*) adjudicación *f.*
adjudicator [əˈdʒuːdɪkeɪtəʳ] *n* juez,-za, árbitro,-a.

adjunct [ˈædʒʌŋkt] *n* adjunto, accesorio.
adjure [əˈdʒʊəʳ] *t* ordenar.
adjust [əˈdʒʌst] **1** *t* ajustar, arreglar. − **2** *i* (*person*) adaptarse.
adjustable [əˈdʒʌstəbəl] *adj* regulable. ■ **adjustable spanner,** llave *f* inglesa.
adjusted [əˈdʒʌstɪd] *adj* equilibrado,-a: *a well adjusted person,* una persona bien equilibrada.
adjustment [əˈdʒʌstmənt] **1** *n* ajuste *m,* arreglo. **2** (*person*) adaptación *f.* **3** (*change*) cambio.
adjutant [ˈædʒʊtənt] *n* MIL ayudante *m.*
ad lib [ædˈlɪb] **1** *adj* (*without preparation*) improvisado,-a, espontáneo,-a. − **2** *adv* (*without preparation*) improvisadamente, espontáneamente. **3** (*freely*) a voluntad. − **4** *i* (*gen*) improvisar; (*actor*) meter morcillas.
Adm [ˈædmɪrəl] *abbr* (*Admiral*) Almirante; (*abbreviation*) Almte.
adman [ˈædmæn] *n* publicista *m.* ▲ *pl* **admen** [ˈædmen].
administer [ədˈmɪnɪstəʳ] **1** *t* (*control*) administrar. **2** (*give*) administrar, dar; (*laws, punishment*) aplicar.
administration [ədmɪnɪsˈtreɪʃən] **1** *n* administración *f.* **2** (*of law etc*) aplicación *f.*
administratively [ədˈmɪnɪstrətɪvlɪ] *adj* administrativamente.
administrative [ədˈmɪnɪstrətɪv] *adj* administrativo,-a.
administrator [ədˈmɪnɪstreɪtəʳ] *n* administrador,-ra.
admirable [ˈædmɪrəbəl] *adj* admirable.
admirably [ˈædmɪrəblɪ] *adv* de manera admirable, admirablemente.
admiral [ˈædmərəl] *n* almirante *m.* ■ **Admiral of the fleet,** Almirante *m* de la flota.
admiralty [ˈædmɪtəltɪ] *n* almirantazgo. ▲ *pl* **admiralties.**
admiration [ædmɪˈreɪʃən] *n* admiración *f: he is the admiration of all,* todos lo admiran.
admire [ədˈmaɪəʳ] *t* admirar.
admirer [ədˈmaɪərəʳ] *n* (*gen*) admirador,-ra; (*suitor*) pretendiente *mf.*
admiring [ədˈmaɪərɪŋ] **1** *adj* (*person*) que admira: *thousands of admiring fans,* miles de admiradores. **2** (*look*) de admiración.
admiringly [ədˈmaɪərɪŋlɪ] *adv* con admiración.
admissibility [ədmɪsɪˈbɪlɪtɪ] *adj* admisibilidad *f.*
admissible [ədˈmɪsɪbəl] *adj* admisible.
admission [ədˈmɪʃən] **1** *n* (*gen*) admisión *f;* (*to hospital*) ingreso. **2** (*price*) entrada. **3** (*acknowledgement*) reconocimiento; (*confession*) confesión *f.* ● **by one's own admission,** por confesión propia.
admit [ədˈmɪt] **1** *t* (*allow in*) admitir; (*to hospital*) ingresar: *she was admitted to St James' yesterday,* la ingresaron en el hospital de St James ayer. **2** (*acknowledge*) reconocer; (*confess*) confesar. ✦ **to admit of** *t insep* admitir. ● **to admit to defeat,** darse por vencido,-a. ‖ **to admit to doing sth.,** confesarse culpable de hacer algo. ▲ *pt & pp* **admitted,** *ger* **admitting.**
admittance [ədˈmɪtəns] *n* entrada. ● **"no admittance",** "prohibida la entrada".
admitted [ədˈmɪtɪd] *adv* confeso,-a, autoconfesado,-a.
admittedly [ədˈmɪtɪdlɪ] *adv* es verdad que, lo cierto es que.
admixture [ædˈmɪkstʃəʳ] **1** *n* (*mixture*) mezcla, admixtión *f.* **2** (*ingredient*) ingrediente *m,* componente *m.*
admonish [ədˈmɒnɪʃ] *t* amonestar.

admonishment [ədˈmɒnɪʃmənt] t → **admonition.**
admonition [ædməˈnɪʃən] n admonición f, amonestación f.
admonitory [ədˈmɒnɪtərɪ] adj admonitorio,-a.
ad nauseam [ædˈnɔːzɪæm] adv hasta la saciedad.
ado [əˈduː] n ajetreo, alboroto.
   ● **without further ado,** sin más preámbulos, sin más dilación. ‖ **much ado about nothing,** mucho ruido y pocas nueces.
adobe [əˈdəʊbɪ] n adobe m.
adolescence [ædəˈlesəns] n adolescencia.
adolescent [ædəˈlesənt] **1** adj adolescente. **2** adolescente mf.
adopt [əˈdɒpt] **1** t (gen) adoptar. **2** (accept) aceptar.
adoption [əˈdɒpʃən] n adopción f.
adoptive [əˈdɒptɪv] adj adoptivo,-a.
adorable [əˈdɔːrəbəl] adj adorable.
adoration [ædəˈreɪʃən] n adoración f.
adore [əˈdɔːʳ] t adorar: I simply adore that film, me encanta esa película.
adoring [əˈdɔːrɪŋ] **1** adj (person) que adora: from your adoring sister, Cynthia, de tu hermana, Cynthia, quien te adora. **2** (look) de adoración.
adorn [əˈdɔːn] t adornar.
adornment [əˈdɔːnmənt] n adorno.
adrenalin [əˈdrenəlɪn] n adrenalina.
Adriatic [eɪdrɪˈætɪk] adj adriático,-a.
   ■ **the Adriatic (Sea),** el (mar) Adriático.
adrift [əˈdrɪft] adj a la deriva.
   ● **to come adrift,** fam desengancharse, desprenderse, soltarse. ‖ **to go adrift,** (plans) irse a pique.
adroit [əˈdrɔɪt] adj diestro,-a, hábil.
adroitly [əˈdrɔɪtlɪ] adv hábilmente.
adsorb [ædˈzɔːb] t adsorber.
adsorbent [ædˈzɔːbənt] adj adsorbente.
adsorbtion [ædˈzɔːbʃən] n adsorbción f.
adulation [ædjuˈleɪʃən] n adulación f.
adulatory [ædjuˈleɪtərɪ] adj adulador,-ra.
adult [ˈædʌlt] **1** adj (gen) adulto,-a. **2** (legally) mayor de edad. **3** (film etc) para adultos. – **4** n (gen) adulto,-a. **5** (legally) mayor mf de edad.
   ■ **adult education,** educación f de adultos.
adulterate [əˈdʌltəreɪt] t adulterar.
adulteration [əˈdʌltəreɪʃən] n adulteración f.
adulterer [əˈdʌltərəʳ] n adúltero.
adulteress [əˈdʌltərɪs] n adúltera.
adulterous [əˈdʌltərəs] adj adúltero,-a.
adultery [əˈdʌltərɪ] n adulterio.
adulthood [ˈædʌlthʊd] n adultez f, mayoría de edad.
adumbrate [ˈædʌmbreɪt] **1** t (draw) esbozar, bosquejar. **2** (suggest) anunciar, presagiar.
advance [ədˈvɑːns] **1** n (movement) avance m. **2** (progress) adelanto, progreso, avance m. **3** (payment) anticipo. – **4** t (person, object) avanzar: he advanced all his troops, avanzó toda su tropa; advance the film a little, avanza un poco la película. **5** (theory) avanzar; (idea) proponer; (suggestion) hacer; (opinion) dar. **6** (money) anticipar, adelantar. **7** (price) aumentar, incrementar. **8** (cause, interests) favorecer, ayudar: this will advance the cause of peace, esto favorecerá la causa de la paz. **9** (date) adelantar: he wants to advance the date of the meeting to the 5th, quiere adelantar la fecha de la reunión al día cinco. – **10** i (move forward) avanzar: the enemy advanced slowly towards us, el enemigo avanzó lentamente hacia nosotros; as the days advanced our problems increased,

conforme pasaban los días nuestros problemas fueron creciendo. **11** (rise) subir: house prices continue to advance, el precio de la vivienda sigue en alza.
   ● **in advance,** (gen) antes; (rent etc) por adelantado: to pay in advance, pagar por adelantado; to know sth. in advance, saber algo de antemano; to let sb. know in advance, informar a algn. por adelantado; to book/prepare in advance, reservar/preparar con antelación. ‖ **in advance of,** antes de. ‖ **to make advances,** progresar. ‖ **to make advances to sb.,** (contact) establecer contacto con; (proposal) hacer una propuesta a; (sexually) insinuarse a algn.
   ■ **advance booking,** reserva anticipada. ‖ **advance guard,** avanzadilla. ‖ **advance notice,** previo aviso. ‖ **advance party,** avanzadilla. ‖ **advance payment,** pago anticipado. ‖ **advance warning,** previo aviso.
advanced [ədˈvɑːnst] adj avanzado,-a.
   ● **of advanced years,** de avanzada edad.
advancement [ədˈvɑːnsmənt] **1** n (promotion) ascenso, promoción f. **2** (encouragement) difusión f, promoción f.
advantage [ədˈvɑːntɪdʒ] **1** n ventaja. **2** (benefit) provecho.
   ● **to be to sb.'s advantage,** ir en beneficio de algn.; (person) aprovecharse de. ‖ **to take advantage of,** (thing) aprovechar; (person) aprovecharse de; (seduce) seducir: to take full advantage of sth., aprovechar algo al máximo. ‖ **to turn sth. to one's advantage,** sacar buen partido de algo.
advantageous [ædvənˈteɪdʒəs] adj ventajoso,-a, provechoso,-a.
advent [ˈædvənt] **1** n advenimiento, llegada. **2** Advent, Adviento.
adventitious [ædvənˈtɪʃəs] adj adventicio,-a.
adventure [ədˈventʃəʳ] n aventura.
   ■ **adventure playground,** parque m infantil.
adventurer [ədˈventʃərəʳ] n aventurero.
adventuress [ədˈventʃərɪs] n aventurera.
adventurous [ədˈventʃərəs] **1** adj aventurero,-a. **2** (risky) arriesgado,-a.
adverb [ˈædvɜːb] n adverbio.
adverbial [ædˈvɜːbɪəl] adj adverbial.
adverbially [ædˈvɜːbɪəlɪ] adv adverbialmente.
adversary [ˈædvəsərɪ] n adversario,-a.
   ▲ pl **adversaries.**
adverse [ˈædvɜːs] adj desfavorable: adverse weather conditions, condiciones meteorológicas adversas.
   ● **to have an adverse effect on,** influir negativamente en, afectar negativamente.
adversely [ˈædvɜːslɪ] adv desfavorablemente, negativamente.
adversity [ədˈvɜːsɪtɪ] n adversidad f.
   ▲ pl **adversities.**
advert [ˈædvɜːt] n fam anuncio.
advertise [ˈædvətaɪz] **1** t anunciar: I saw it advertised on the telly, lo vi anunciado en la tele; they're advertising for a painter, buscan un pintor. – **2** i hacer publicidad: if you don't advertise you never sell anything, si no se hace publicidad nunca se vende nada.
advertisement [ədˈvɜːtɪsmənt] **1** n anuncio. – **2** advertisements, npl (on television) publicidad f, anuncios mpl.
advertiser [ˈædvətaɪzəʳ] n anunciante mf.
advertising [ˈædvətaɪzɪŋ] n publicidad f: there's no cigarette advertising on television, no hay anuncios de tabaco en la televisión.
   ■ **advertising agency,** agencia de publicidad. ‖ **advertising campaign,** campaña publicitaria.

advice [əd'vaɪs] 1 *n* consejos *mpl*. 2 COMM aviso, nota: *we have not yet received advice of payment,* aún no hemos recibido la nota de pago.
● **to take/follow sb.'s advice,** seguir el consejo de algn. ‖ **to take legal advice,** consultar con un abogado.
■ **advice note,** nota de aviso, notificación *f*. ‖ **a piece of advice,** un consejo.
advisable [əd'vaɪzəbəl] *adj* aconsejable.
advisablility [əd'vaɪzəbɪlɪtɪ] *n* conveniencia.
advise [əd'vaɪz] 1 *t* aconsejar: *I advise you to see a specialist,* le aconsejo que vaya a ver a un especialista; *he advised me against selling it,* me aconsejó que no lo vendiera. 2 (*inform*) informar, comunicar: *please advise us of your policy number,* sírvanse comunicarnos su número de póliza.
advisedly [əd'vaɪzədlɪ] *adv* con conocimiento de causa.
adviser [əd'vaɪzəʳ] *n* consejero,-a.
advisor [əd'vaɪzəʳ] *n* consejero,-a.
advisory [əd'vaɪzərɪ] *adj* asesor,-ra, consultivo,-a: *he's acting in an advisory capacity only,* actúa únicamente en calidad de asesor.
advocacy ['ædvəkəsɪ] 1 *n* (*support*) defensa, apoyo: *his advocacy of majority rule cost him his liberty,* su defensa del gobierno de la mayoría le costó la libertad. 2 (*profession*) abogacía.
advocate ['ædvəkət] 1 *n* (*supporter*) partidario,-a. 2 (*lawyer*) abogado,-a defensor,-ra. – 3 *t* abogar por, propugnar.
▲ (*verbo*) ['ædvəkeɪt].
adze [ædz] *n* azuela.
Aegean [ɪ'dʒiːən] *adj* egeo,-a.
■ **the Aegean (Sea),** el (mar) Egeo.
aegis ['iːdʒɪs] **under the aegis of,** *phr* bajo el patrocinio de.
aeon ['iːən] *n* eón *m*.
aerate ['eəreɪt] *t* (*room*) airear, ventilar; (*liquid*) gasificar; (*blood*) oxigenar; (*soil*) airear.
aeration ['eəreɪʃən] *n* (*of room*) aireación *f*, ventilación *f*; (*of liquid*) gasificación *f*; (*of blood*) oxigenación *f*; (*of soil*) aireación *f*.
aerial ['eərɪəl] 1 *adj* aéreo,-a. – 2 *n* antena.
aerie ['eərɪ] *n* US aguilera.
aerobatics [eərə'bætɪks] 1 *n* (*sport*) acrobacia aérea. – 2 *npl* (*feats*) acrobacia *f sing* aérea, acrobacias *fpl* aéreas.
aerobics [eə'rəʊbɪks] *n* aerobic *m*, aeróbic *m*.
aerodrome ['eərədrəʊm] *n* aeródromo.
aerodynamic [eərəʊdaɪ'næmɪk] 1 *adj* aerodinámico,-a. – 2 **aerodynamics,** *n* aerodinámica.
aeronautic [eərə'nɔːtɪk] 1 *adj* aeronáutico,-a. – 2 **aeronautics,** *n* aeronáutica.
aeronautical [eərə'nɔːtɪkəl] *adj* aeronáutico,-a.
aeroplane ['eərəpleɪn] *n* aeroplano, avión *m*.
aerosol ['eərəsɒl] *n* aerosol *m*.
aerospace ['eərəʊspeɪs] *adj* aeroespacial.
aesthete ['ɪsθiːt] *n* esteta *mf*.
aesthetic [iːs'θetɪk] 1 *adj* estético,-a. – 2 **aesthetics,** *n* estética.
aesthetically [iːs'θetɪkəlɪ] *adv* estéticamente.
aetiology [iːtɪ'ɒledʒɪ] *n* etiología.
▲ *pl* **aetiologies.**
afar [ə'fɑːʳ] *adv* lejos.
● **from afar,** desde lejos.
affability [æfə'bɪlɪtɪ] *n* afabilidad *f*.
affable ['æfəbəl] *adj* afable.

affably ['æfəbəlɪ] *adv* afablemente.
affair [ə'feəʳ] 1 *n* (*matter*) asunto: *that's your affair,* eso es asunto tuyo. 2 (*case*) caso: *the Watergate affair,* el caso Watergate. 3 *fam* (*event*) acontecimiento; (*thing*) cosa: *the wedding was a high class affair,* la boda era un acontecimiento de mucha clase; *her dress was a wonderful affair with sequins and feathers,* su vestido era una cosa maravillosa con lentejuelas y plumas.
■ **affairs of state,** asuntos *mpl* de estado. ‖ **current affairs,** actualidad *f sing*. ‖ **state of affairs,** situación *f*.
affect [ə'fekt] 1 *t* (*gen*) afectar; (*negatively*) perjudicar: *does this decision affect me?,* ¿esta decisión me afecta?; *this could affect your chances of winning,* esto podría perjudicar tus posibilidades de ganar. 2 (*move*) conmover, impresionar: *the ceremony really affected her,* la ceremonia la conmovió. 3 (*feign*) fingir, afectar: *he affected indifference,* fingió indiferencia.
affectation [æfek'teɪʃən] *n* afectación *f*.
affected [ə'fektɪd] *adj* afectado,-a, falso,-a, fingido,-a.
affection [ə'fekʃən] *n* afecto, cariño.
● **to hold sb. in affection,** tener cariño a algn.
affectionate [ə'fekʃənət] *adj* afectuoso,-a, cariñoso,-a.
affectionately [ə'fekʃənətlɪ] *adv* afectuosamente, cariñosamente.
● **yours affectionately,** (*in letter*) un saludo cariñoso.
affidavit [æfɪ'deɪvɪt] *n* declaración *f* jurada, afidávit *m*.
affiliate [ə'fɪlɪət] *n* afiliado,-a.
affiliated [ə'fɪlɪeɪtɪd] *adj* afiliado,-a.
affiliation [əfɪlɪ'eɪʃən] *n* afiliación *f*.
affinity [ə'fɪnɪtɪ] *n* afinidad *f*.
▲ *pl* **affinities.**
affirm [ə'fɜːm] *t* afirmar, asegurar.
affirmation [æfə'meɪʃən] *n* afirmación *f*.
affirmative [ə'fɜːmətɪv] 1 *adj* afirmativo,-a. – 2 *n* afirmativo.
● **in the affirmative,** afirmativamente: *the answer was in the affirmative,* la respuesta fue afirmativa.
affirmatively [ə'fɜːmətɪvlɪ] *adv* afirmativamente.
affix [ə'fɪks] 1 *n* afijo. – 2 *t* pegar, añadir, fijar.
▲ (*verbo*) [ə'fɪks].
afflict [ə'flɪkt] *t* afligir.
● **to be afflicted with,** estar aquejado,-a de.
affliction [ə'flɪkʃən] *n* aflicción *f*.
affluence ['æfluəns] *n* riqueza, prosperidad *f*.
affluent ['æfluənt] *adj* rico,-a, próspero,-a.
afford [ə'fɔːd] 1 *t* permitirse, costear: *I can't afford to pay £750 for a coat,* no puedo (permitirme) pagar 750 libras por un abrigo; *how does she afford it?,* ¿cómo se lo costea?; *can you afford to reject his offer?,* ¿puedes permitirte el lujo de rechazar su oferta? 2 *fml* dar, proporcionar: *the shack afforded us shelter from the storm,* la cabaña nos abrigó de la tormenta.
▲ 1 generalmente con *can* o *be able.*
afforest [ə'fɒrɪst] *t* repoblar (de árboles).
afforestation [əfɒrɪ'steɪʃən] *n* repoblación *f* forestal.
affray [ə'freɪ] *n* reyerta, refriega.
affricate ['æfrɪkət] *n* africada *f*.
affront [ə'frʌnt] 1 *n* afrenta, insulto. – 2 *t* afrentar, insultar.
Afghan ['æfgæn] 1 *adj* afgano,-a. – 2 *n* (*person*) afgano,-a. 3 (*language*) afgano.
Afghanistan [æfgæni'stæn] *n* Afganistán *m*.
afield [ə'fiːld] *adv* lejos.
● **far afield,** lejos.
aflame [ə'fleɪm] *adj* en llamas.

AFL-CIO ['eɪ'ef'el'siː'aɪ'əʊ] *abbr* US (*American Federation of Labor and Congress of Industrial Organizations*) *federación norteamericana de organizaciones sindicales*.

afloat [ə'fləʊt] *adj* a flote.

afoot [ə'fʊt] *adv* en marcha, en proceso.
● **something's afoot**, se está tramando algo: *there's a scheme afoot to build a prison*, hay un proyecto para construir una cárcel.

aforementioned [əfɔː'menʃənd] *adj* arriba mencionado,-a, antedicho,-a, susodicho,-a.

aforesaid [ə'fɔːsed] *adj* → **aforementioned**.

aforethought [ə'fɔːθɔːt] **with malice aforethought**, *phr* JUR con premeditación.

afraid [ə'freɪd] *adj* temeroso,-a.
● **to be afraid**, (*frightened*) tener miedo; (*sorry*) temer, sentir, lamentar: *I'm afraid so/not*, me temo que sí/no; *I'm afraid Mr Gómez is out*, me temo que el Sr Gómez no está; *he's afraid to go to the dentist's*, le da miedo ir al dentista; *I'm afraid that you have cancer*, lamento decirle que tiene cáncer.

afresh [ə'freʃ] *adv* de nuevo.

Africa ['æfrɪkə] *n* Africa.
■ **South Africa**, Sudáfrica.

African ['æfrɪkən] **1** *adj* africano,-a. – **2** *n* africano,-a.
■ **South African**, sudafricano,-a.

Afrikaans [æfrɪ'kɑːns] *n* afrikaans *m*.

Afrikaner [æfrɪ'kɑːnəʳ] *n* afrikaner *mf*.

Afro ['æfrəʊ] *adj* (*hairstyle*) afro.

Afro-american [æfrəʊə'merɪkən] **1** *adj* afroamericano,-a. – **2** *n* afroamericano,-a.

aft [æft] *adv* (*position*) en popa; (*movement*) a popa.

after ['ɑːftəʳ] **1** *prep* (*time*) después de: *after class*, después de la clase; *after poisoning her he buried her*, después de envenenarla la enterró. **2** (*following*) detrás de: *we all went after the thief*, todos fuimos detrás del ladrón; *the police are after us*, la policía nos está persiguiendo. **3** (*wanting*) buscando: *what are you after?*, ¿qué pretendes?, ¿qué buscas?; *I've been after one of these things for ages*, hace tiempo que ando detrás de un chisme de estos. **4** (*in the style of*) al estilo de: *a painting after Gainsborough*, un cuadro al estilo de Gainsborough. **5** (*named because of*) por: *his name's Horace, after his grandfather*, se llama Horace por su abuelo. **6** US (*past*) y: *it's a quarter after four*, son las cuatro y cuarto. – **7** *adv* después: *the day after*, el día después. – **8** *conj* después que, después de que: *after he left, I went to bed*, después de que se marchara, me acosté. – **9** **afters**, *npl* GB *fam* postre *m*.

afterbirth ['ɑːftəbɜːθ] *n* placenta.

aftercare ['ɑːftəkeəʳ] *n* *ayuda prestada a una persona que acaba de salir del hospital o de la cárcel*.

after-effect ['ɑːftərɪfekt] *n* efecto secundario, secuela.

afterglow ['ɑːftəgləʊ] **1** *n* (*after sunset*) arrebol *m*. **2** (*feeling*) sensación *f* de bienestar.

afterlife ['ɑːftəlaɪf] *n* más allá *m*.

aftermath ['ɑːftəmɑːθ] *n* (*period*) período posterior; (*circumstances*) situación *f* posterior.
● **in the aftermath of the war**, después de la guerra, en la posguerra.

afternoon [ɑːftə'nuːn] **1** *n* tarde *f*: *in the afternoon*, por la tarde. – **2** **afternoons**, *adv* por la tarde.

after-sales service [ɑːftə'seɪlzsɜːvɪs] *n* servicio posventa.

aftershave ['ɑːftəʃeɪv] *n* loción *f* para después del afeitado.

aftertaste ['ɑːftəteɪst] *n* regusto, resabio.

afterthought ['ɑːftəθɔːt] *n* ocurrencia posterior, ocurrencia tardía.

afterwards ['ɑːftəwədz] *adv* después, luego.

again [ə'gen, ə'geɪn] **1** *prep* (*once more*) otra vez, de nuevo: *play me that song again*, tócame esa canción otra vez; *it's no good, write it again!*, no sirve ¡vuelve a escribirlo!, no sirve ¡escríbelo de nuevo!; *here he is again, Ken Dodd!*, de nuevo con ustedes, ¡Ken Dodd!; *we need half as much again*, necesitamos la mitad otra vez. – **2** *adv* (*in questions*): *where do you live again?*, ¿dónde has dicho que vives?; *what's the answer again?*, ¿cómo era la respuesta? **3** (*also*) también: *the next point is again rather a tricky one*, el próximo tema es también bastante peliagudo.
● **again and again**, repetidamente. ‖ **come again**, *fam* ¿cómo? ‖ **now and again**, de vez en cuando. ‖ **then again**, por otra parte.

against [ə'genst, ə'geɪnst] **1** *prep* (*gen*) contra: *against the wall*, contra la pared; *Leeds played against Liverpool*, Leeds jugó contra el Liverpool; *there's no evidence against her*, no hay pruebas contra ella; *I have nothing against him, but ...*, no tengo nada contra él, pero ...; *insurance against fire*, un seguro contra incendios. **2** (*opposed to*) en contra de: *it's against the law*, va en contra de la ley; *I am against the plan*, me opongo al plan; *I voted against the proposal*, voté en contra de la propuesta. **3** (*in contrast to*) respecto a, frente a: *the mark has risen against the peseta*, el marco ha subido frente a la peseta; *the black bear was clearly visible against the white snow*, el oso negro se veía claramente sobre el fondo blanco de la nieve.
● **to work against the clock**, trabajar contra reloj.

agape [ə'geɪp] *adj* boquiabierto,-a.

agate ['ægət] *n* ágata.

age [eɪdʒ] **1** *n* edad *f*: *at the age of sixty*, a los sesenta años; *children of school age*, niños de edad escolar; *men in the 40 to 50 age group are most at risk*, los hombres de los 40 a 50 años corren el mayor riesgo. – **2** *t* envejecer: *aged in oak barrels*, envejecido en barricas de roble. – **3** *i* envejecer: *he's aged since I last saw him*, ha envejecido desde la última vez que lo vi. – **4** **ages**, *npl fam* años *mpl*, siglos *mpl*: *I haven't seen you for ages*, hace años que no te veo; *it's ages since she left*, hace un rato largo que se marchó.
● **of age**, mayor de edad. ‖ **to come of age**, llegar a la mayoría de edad. ‖ **to look one's age**, representar la edad que uno tiene. ‖ **under age**, menor de edad.
■ **age of consent**, edad *f* núbil. ‖ **the Middle Ages**, la Edad *f* Media.

aged[1] ['eɪdʒd] *adj* de (tantos años de) edad: *a boy aged ten*, un muchacho de diez años; *she died aged only 43*, murió a la edad de sólo 43 años.

aged[2] ['eɪdʒɪd] *adj* viejo,-a, anciano,-a.
■ **the aged**, los ancianos *mpl*.

ageing ['eɪdʒɪŋ] **1** *adj* viejo,-a. – **2** *n* envejecimiento.

ageism ['eɪdʒɪzəm] *n* discriminación *contra la gente de edad avanzada*.

ageless ['eɪdʒləs] *adj* (*person*) siempre joven; (*thing*) eterno,-a, inmortal, imperecedero,-a.

agelong ['eɪdʒlɒŋ] *adj* ancestral.

agency ['eɪdʒənsɪ] **1** *n* (*commercial*) agencia: *a travel/advertising/employment agency*, una agencia de viajes/publicidad/empleo. **2** (*governmental etc*) organismo.
● **by the agency of**, mediante, por medio de, por la acción de.
▲ *pl* **agencies**.

agenda [ə'dʒendə] *n* orden *m* del día.

agent ['eɪdʒənt] 1 *n* (*gen*) agente *mf*; (*representative*) representante *mf*; (*of artist*) agente *mf*. 2 (*active ingredient*) agente *m*.

agent provocateur [æʒɒnprəvɒkə'tɜːʳ] *n* agente *m* provocador.
▲ *pl* **agents provocateurs** ['æʒɒn prəvɒkə'tɜːʳ].

age-old ['eɪdʒəʊld] *adj* ancestral.

agglomerate [ə'glɒməreɪt] 1 *t* aglomerar. – 2 *i* aglomerarse. – 3 *n* aglomerado.
▲ (*substantivo*) [ə'glɒmərət].

agglomeration [əglɒmə'reɪʃən] *n* aglomeración *f*.

agglutinate [ə'gluːtɪneɪt] 1 *t* aglutinar. – 2 *i* aglutinarse.

agglutination [əgluːtɪ'neɪʃən] *n* aglutinación *f*.

agglutinative [ə'gluːtɪnətɪv] *adj* aglutinante.

aggrandize [ə'grændaɪz] *t* agrandar.

aggrandizement [ə'grændɪzmənt] *t* agrandamiento.

aggravate ['ægrəveɪt] 1 *t* (*make worse*) agravar. 2 *fam* (*annoy*) irritar, molestar.

aggravating ['ægrəveɪtɪŋ] *adj fam* irritante, molesto,-a.

aggravation [ægrə'veɪʃən] 1 *n* (*worsening*) agravamiento. 2 (*annoyance*) exasperación *f*. 3 *fam* (*hassle*) follones *mpl*.

aggregate ['ægrɪgət] 1 *n* (*total*) total *m*, totalidad *f*, conjunto. 2 (*for concrete*) conglomerado. – 3 *adj* total, global. – 4 *t* agregar, reunir. – 5 *i* ascender a.
● **in the aggregate**, en conjunto. ‖ **on aggregate**, en conjunto.
▲ (*verbo*) ['ægrɪgeɪt].

aggression [ə'greʃən] 1 *n* (*act*) agresión *f*. 2 (*feeling*) agresividad *f*.

aggressive [ə'gresɪv] 1 *adj* (*gen*) agresivo,-a. 2 (*dynamic*) dinámico,-a, emprendedor,-ra.

aggressively [ə'gresɪvlɪ] *adv* agresivamente.

aggressiveness [ə'gresɪvnəs] *n* agresividad *f*.

aggressor [ə'gresəʳ] *n* agresor,-ra.

aggrieved [ə'griːvd] 1 *adj* ofendido,-a. 2 JUR dañado,-a, agraviado,-a.
● **to feel aggrieved**, ofenderse.

aggro ['ægrəʊ] *n fam* (*hassle*) follones *mpl*; (*violence*) violencia.

aghast [ə'gɑːst] *adj* horrorizado,-a: *she was aghast at the size of the bill*, se horrorizó al ver cuánto subía la factura.

agile ['ædʒaɪl] *adj* ágil.

agility [ə'dʒɪlɪtɪ] *n* agilidad *f*.

aging ['eɪdʒɪŋ] *adj* → **ageing**.

agism ['eɪdʒɪzəm] *n* → **ageism**.

agitate ['ædʒɪteɪt] 1 *t* (*shake*) agitar. 2 (*worry*) inquietar, perturbar.
● **to agitate for/against sth.**, hacer una campaña a favor de/en contra de algo.

agitated ['ædʒɪteɪtɪd] *adj* nervioso,-a.

agitation [ædʒɪ'teɪʃən] 1 *n* (*worry*) inquietud *f*, perturbación *f*: *she was in a state of great agitation*, estaba muy perturbada. 2 (*pressure*) presión *f*: *there has been a lot of agitation against the new prison*, ha habido mucha presión en contra de la nueva cárcel. 3 (*shaking*) agitación *f*.

agitator ['ædʒɪteɪtəʳ] 1 *n* (*person*) agitador,-ra. 2 (*machine*) agitador *m*.

aglow [ə'gləʊ] *adj* resplandeciente: *her face was aglow with happiness*, su cara resplandecía de alegría.

AGM ['eɪ'dʒiː'em] *abbr* (*annual general meeting*) junta general anual.

agnostic [æg'nɒstɪk] 1 *adj* agnóstico,-a. – 2 *n* agnóstico,-a.

agnosticism [æg'nɒstɪsɪzəm] *n* agnosticismo.

ago [ə'gəʊ] *adv* hace: *ten days ago*, hace diez días; *it happened a long time ago*, ocurrió hace mucho tiempo; *she arrived a short time ago*, ha llegado hace un ratito; *how long ago did you pass your driving test?*, ¿cuánto hace que te sacaste el carnet de conducir?

agog [ə'gɒg] *adj* anhelante, deseoso,-a: *they were all agog with expectation*, estaban todos anhelantes por la expectación.

agonize ['ægənaɪz] *i* agonizar, sufrir angustiosamente: *it was a terrible decision to have to make, how I agonized over it!*, era una decisión terriblemente difícil, ¡cómo sufrí!

agonized ['ægənaɪzd] *adj* agónico,-a, de gran dolor: *an agonized expression*, una mueca agónica.

agonizing ['ægənaɪzɪŋ] *adj* agónico,-a, angustioso,-a: *it was an agonizing decision*, fue una decisión agónica.

agony ['ægənɪ] 1 *n* (*pain*) dolor *m* muy agudo: *no drug could relieve her agony*, ninguna droga pudo aliviar su dolor; *I'm in agony with my knee*, me duele muchísimo la rodilla. 2 (*anguish*) angustia.
■ **agony aunt**, autora de un consultorio sentimental. ‖ **agony column**, consultorio sentimental.
▲ *pl* **agonies**.

agoraphobia [ægərə'fəʊbɪə] *n* agorafobia.

agoraphobic [ægərə'fəʊbɪk] 1 *adj* agorafóbico,-a. – 2 *n* agorafóbico,-a.

agrarian [ə'greərɪən] *adj* agrario,-a.

agree [ə'griː] 1 *i* (*be in agreement*) estar de acuerdo (**with**, con): *I agree entirely that ...*, estoy completamente de acuerdo en que ...; *do you agree with me?*, ¿estás de acuerdo conmigo? 2 (*reach an agreement*) ponerse de acuerdo (**on**, en): *I don't think we'll ever agree*, no creo que nos pongamos de acuerdo nunca; *we agreed not to say anything*, nos pusimos de acuerdo en no decir nada; *they can't agree on a name for the baby*, no se ponen de acuerdo en el nombre del bebé. 3 (*say yes*) acceder, consentir: *will he agree to our request?*, ¿accederá a nuestra petición?; *the minister has agreed to see the protesters*, el ministro ha consentido en recibir a los manifestantes. 4 (*square*) concordar, encajar: *the two men's stories don't agree*, las historias de los dos hombres no encajan. 5 (*food, climate etc.*) sentar bien (**with**, -): *the prawns didn't agree with me*, las gambas no me sentaron bien. – 6 *t* GRAM concordar (**with**, con). 7 (*accept as correct*) aceptar, aprobar: *the board agreed the economy measures*, el consejo aprobó las medidas de ahorro.
● *it was agreed that ...*, se acordó que ... ‖ **to agree to differ**, quedarse cada uno con su idea.

agreeable [ə'griːəbəl] 1 *adj* (*pleasant*) agradable. 2 (*in agreement*) conforme.

agreement [ə'griːmənt] 1 *n* acuerdo. 2 GRAM concordancia.
● **to be in agreement**, estar de acuerdo.

agricultural [ægrɪ'kʌltʃərəl] *adj* agrícola.
■ **agricultural college**, escuela de ingeniería agrícola. ‖ **agricultural expert**, ingeniero,-a técnico,-a agrícola.

agriculturalist [ægrɪ'kʌltʃərəlɪst] *n* → **agriculturist**.

agriculture ['ægrɪkʌltʃəʳ] *n* agricultura.

agriculturist [ægrɪ'kʌltʃərɪst] *n* agrónomo,-a.

agronomist [ə'grɒnəmɪst] *n* agrónomo,-a.

agronomy [ə'grɒnəmɪ] *n* agronomía.

aground [ə'graʊnd] **to run aground**, *adv* encallar, varar.

ah [ɑː] *interj* ¡ah!

aha [ɑːˈhɑː] *interj* ¡ajá!

ahead [əˈhed] *adv* (*in front*) delante: *there's a police checkpoint ahead,* hay un control de policía aquí delante; *Tom went on ahead to look for water,* Tom se adelantó por agua; *we are ahead of the others,* llevamos ventaja sobre los otros; *we are ahead of schedule,* vamos adelantados; *we finished ahead of schedule,* acabamos antes de lo previsto. ● **go ahead!,** ¡adelante! ‖ **to go ahead wth sth.,** llevar algo adelante. ‖ **to plan ahead,** planear para el futuro. ‖ **to think ahead,** pensar en el futuro.

ahem [əˈhem] *interj* ¡ejem!

ahoy [əˈhɔɪ] *interj* MAR: *ahoy there!,* ¡ah del barco!; *land ahoy!,* ¡tierra a la vista!; *ship ahoy!,* ¡barco a la vista!

AI¹ [ˈeɪˈaɪ] *abbr* (*artificial intelligence*) inteligencia artificial.

AI² [ˈeɪˈaɪ] *abbr* (*artificial insemination*) inseminación *f* artificial.

AI³ [ˈeɪˈaɪ] *abbr* (*Amnesty International*) Amnistía Internacional; (*abbreviation*) AI.

aid [eɪd] 1 *n* (*help*) ayuda; (*rescue*) auxilio: *with the aid of a knife,* con la ayuda de un cuchillo; *without the aid of a safety net,* sin la ayuda de la red. –2 *t* ayudar, auxiliar. ● **in aid of,** a beneficio de. ‖ **to go to sb.'s aid,** socorrer a algn., acudir en auxilio a algn. ‖ **what's all this in aid of?,** ¿a qué obedece todo esto? ■ **economic aid,** ayuda económica. ‖ **humanitarian aid,** ayuda humanitaria.

aide [eɪd] 1 *n* (*assistant*) ayudante *mf*. 2 MIL → **aide-de-camp**.

aide-de-camp [eɪddeˈkæm] *n* MIL edecán *m*, ayudante *mf* de campo.

AIDS [eɪdz] *n* sida *m*.

ail [eɪl] *t arch* afligir.

aileron [ˈeɪlərɒn] *n* alerón *m*.

ailing [ˈeɪlɪŋ] *adj* enfermo,-a.

ailment [ˈeɪlmənt] *n* dolencia, achaque *m*: *he's always complaining of some minor ailment or other,* siempre se está quejando de algún achaque.

aim [eɪm] 1 *n* (*marksmanship*) puntería: *his aim is good,* tiene buena puntería. 2 (*objective*) meta, objetivo: *what's your aim in life?,* ¿qué objetivo tienes en la vida? – 3 *t* (*gun*) apuntar: *aim the rifle at the target,* apunta el rifle a la diana; *don't aim at me,* no me apuntes a mí. 4 (*attack*) dirigir: *I aimed my punch at his nose, but I hit his shoulder,* dirigí el golpe a la cara, pero le di en el hombro; *this advertising campaign is aimed at smokers,* esta campaña publicitaria está dirigida a los fumadores. ● **to aim for sth.,** intentar conseguir algo: *he's aiming for the presidency,* va por la presidencia. ‖ **to aim to do sth.,** tener la intención de hacer algo, pretender hacer algo: *we're aiming to win,* vamos a ganar. ‖ **to aim high,** ser ambicioso,-a, apuntar alto. ‖ **to take aim,** apuntar. ‖ **to miss one's aim,** errar el tiro.

aimless [ˈeɪmləs] *adj* sin objetivo, sin propósito.

aimlessly [ˈeɪmləslɪ] *adv* sin rumbo fijo.

aimlessness [ˈeɪmləsnəs] *adv* falta de objetivo.

ain't [eɪnt] *contr fam* → **am not, is not, are not, has not, have not.**

air [eəʳ] 1 *n* aire *m*: *open the window, we need air in here,* abre la ventana, necesitamos aire; *they fly through the air,* vuelan por los aires. 2 (*feeling*) aire *m*: *there's an air of mystery about her,* tiene un aire de misterio. 3 (*affectation*) afectación *f*. 4 MUS aire *m*, tonada. – 5 *t* (*clothes*) airear, orear. 6 (*room*) ventilar. 7 (*opinions*) airear. 8 (*knowledge*) hacer alarde de.

● **by air,** (*send letter*) por avión; (*travel*) en avión. ‖ **(up) in the air,** sin decidir: *nothing's been decided yet, it's still up in the air,* todavía no hay nada decidido, aún está en el aire. ‖ **in the air,** en el ambiente: *there's mistrust in the air,* hay un ambiente de desconfianza. ‖ **to be walking on air,** estar en la gloria. ‖ **to clear the air,** aclarar una situación. ‖ **to put on airs,** presumir. ■ **air brake,** freno neumático. ‖ **air force,** fuerzas *fpl* aéreas. ‖ **air hostess,** azafata. ‖ **air lane,** ruta aérea. ‖ **air letter,** aerograma *m*. ‖ **air pocket,** bache *m*. ‖ **air pressure,** presión *f* atmosférica. ‖ **air raid,** ataque *m* aéreo. ‖ **air rifle,** escopeta de aire comprimido, escopeta de balines. ‖ **airs and graces,** presunción *f*. ‖ **air terminal,** terminal *f* aérea. ‖ **air traffic control,** control *m* aéreo. ‖ **air traffic controller,** controlador,-ra aéreo,-a. ‖ **fresh air,** aire *m* fresco.

airbag [ˈeəbæg] *n* airbag *m*.

airbase [ˈeəbeɪs] *n* base *f* aérea.

air-bed [ˈeəbed] *n* GB colchón *m* de aire.

airborne [ˈeəbɔːn] 1 *adj* (*troops*) aerotransportado,-a. 2 (*aircraft*) en el aire.

airbrush [ˈeəbrʌʃ] *n* aerógrafo.

airbus [ˈeəbʌs] *n* aerobús *m*.

air-conditioned [eəkənˈdɪʃənd] *adj* con aire acondicionado, refrigerado,-a.

air-conditioner [eəkənˈdɪʃənəʳ] *n* acondicionador *m* de aire.

air-conditioning [eəkənˈdɪʃənɪŋ] *n* aire *m* acondicionado.

air-cooled [ˈeəkuːld] *adj* refrigerado,-a por aire.

aircraft [ˈeəkrɑːft] *n* (*gen*) aeronave *f*; (*plane*) avión *m*. ▲ *pl* aircraft.

aircraft-carrier [ˈeəkrɑːftkærɪəʳ] *n* portaaeronaves *m inv*, portaaviones *m inv*.

aircraftman [ˈeəkrɑːftmən] *n* soldado del ejército del aire. ▲ *pl* aircraftmen [ˈeəkrɑːftmən].

aircraftwoman [ˈeəkrɑːftwumən] *n* soldado *f* del ejército del aire. ▲ *pl* aircraftwomen [ˈeəkrɑːftwɪmɪn].

aircrew [ˈeəkruː] *n* tripulación *f* (*de una aeronave*).

air-cushion [ˈeəkuʃən] *n* cojín *m* neumático.

airdrome [ˈeədrəum] *n* US aeródromo.

airfield [ˈeəfiːld] *n* campo de aviación.

airgun [ˈeəgʌn] *n* pistola de aire comprimido.

airily [ˈeərɪlɪ] *adv* despreocupadamente.

airing [ˈeərɪŋ] *n* ventilación *f*. ■ **airing cupboard,** *armario que aprovecha el calor de un termo de agua para secar la ropa.*

airless [ˈeələs] 1 *adj* (*in building*) mal ventilado,-a. 2 (*outside*) sin una brizna de viento.

airlift [ˈeəlɪft] 1 *n* puente *m* aéreo. – 2 *t* transportar por avión.

airline [ˈeəlaɪn] *n* línea aérea.

airliner [ˈeəlaɪnəʳ] *n* avión *m* de pasajeros (*grande*).

airmail [ˈeəmeɪl] 1 *n* correo aéreo. – 2 *t* enviar por correo aéreo.

airman [ˈeəmən] 1 *n* aviador *m*. 2 GB miembro de la fuerzas aéreas. ▲ *pl* airmen [ˈeəmən].

airplane [ˈeəpleɪn] *n* US aeroplano, avión *m*.

airport [ˈeəpɔːt] *n* aeropuerto.

air-raid [ˈeəreɪd] *adj* antiaéreo,-a. ■ **air-raid shelter,** refugio antiaéreo.

airship [ˈeəʃɪp] *n* dirigible *m*.

airsick ['eəsɪk] *adj* mareado,-a.
● **to be airsick,** marearse.
airsickness ['eəsɪknəs] *n* mareo.
● **to suffer from airsickness,** marearse.
airspace ['eəspeɪs] *n* espacio aéreo.
airspeed ['eəspiːd] *n* velocidad *f.*
airstrip ['eəstrɪp] *n* pista de aterrizaje.
airtight ['eətaɪt] *adj* hermético,-a.
airtime ['eətaɪm] *n* cobertura radiofónica: *his records get a lot of airtime,* sus discos se oyen mucho por la radio.
air-to-air [eətʊ'eəʳ] *adj* aire-aire: *they fired an air-to-air missile,* lanzaron un misil aire-aire.
airwaves ['eəweɪvz] *npl* ondas *fpl.*
airway ['eəweɪ] 1 *n (route)* ruta aérea, vía aérea. 2 *(airline)* línea aérea.
airworthiness ['eəwɜːðɪnəs] *n*: *the airworthiness of these planes is now in doubt,* ahora se duda de si estos aviones se encuentran en condiciones de volar.
airworthy ['eəwɜːðɪ] *adj* en condiciones de volar.
airy ['eərɪ] 1 *adj (ventilated)* bien ventilado,-a. 2 *(light)* ligero,-a. 3 *(insincere)* insincero,-a. 4 *(carefree)* despreocupado,-a.
▲ *comp* **airier,** *superl* **airiest.**
airy-fairy [eərɪ'feərɪ] *adj fam (project)* poco práctico,-a; *(person)* poco realista.
aisle [aɪl] 1 *n (in theatre, plane, etc)* pasillo. 2 *(in church)* nave *f* lateral.
aitch [eɪtʃ] *n* hache *f.*
ajar [ə'dʒɑːʳ] *adj* entreabierto,-a.
aka [eɪkeɪ'eɪ] *abbr (also known as)* alias.
akimbo [ə'kɪmbəʊ] *adv* en jarras.
akin [ə'kɪn] *adj* parecido,-a **(to,** a), semejante **(to,** a).
alabaster ['æləbɑːstəʳ] *n* alabastro.
à la carte [ɑːlɑː'kɑːt] 1 *adj* a la carta. – 2 *adv* a la carta.
alacrity [ə'lækrɪtɪ] *n* presteza.
alarm [ə'lɑːm] 1 *n (device)* alarma. 2 *(fear)* temor *m,* alarma. – 3 *t* alarmar, asustar.
● **to raise the alarm,** dar la alarma, dar la voz de alarma. ‖ **to sound the alarm,** dar la alarma, dar la voz de alarma.
■ **alarm clock,** despertador *m.*
alarmed [ə'lɑːmd] *adj* alarmado,-a: *there's no need to be alarmed,* no hay por qué alarmarse.
alarming [ə'lɑːmɪŋ] *adj* alarmante.
alarmingly [ə'lɑːmɪŋlɪ] *adv* de manera alarmante.
alarmist [ə'lɑːmɪst] *adj* alarmista.
alas [ə'lɑːs] *interj* ¡ay!, ¡ay de mí!
Alaska [ə'læskə] *n* Alaska.
Alaskan [ə'læskən] *adj* de Alaska.
Albania [æl'beɪnɪə] *n* albania.
Albanian [æl'beɪnɪən] 1 *adj* albanés,-esa. – 2 *n (person)* albanés,-esa. 3 *(language)* albanés *m.*
albatross ['ælbətrɒs] *n* albatros *m.*
albeit [ɔːl'biːɪt] *conj fml* aunque.
Alberta [æl'bɜːtə] *n* Alberta.
albino [æl'biːnəʊ] 1 *adj* albino,-a. – 2 *n* albino,-a.
▲ *pl* **albinos.**
album ['ælbəm] 1 *n (for stamps, photos, etc)* álbum *m.* 2 *(LP)* elepé *m.*
albumen ['ælbjʊmɪn, ʃ* æl'bjuːmən] 1 *n (white of egg)* clara de huevo. 2 *(in plants)* albumen *m.*
albumin ['ælbjʊmɪn, ʃ* æl'bjuːmən] *n* albúmina.
alchemist ['ælkəmɪst] *n* alquimista *mf.*
alchemy ['ælkəmɪ] *n* alquimia.

alcohol ['ælkəhɒl] *n* alcohol *m.*
alcohol-free ['ælkəhɒlfriː] *adj* sin alcohol.
alcoholic [ælkə'hɒlɪk] 1 *adj* alcohólico,-a. – 2 *n* alcohólico,-a.
alcoholism ['ælkəhɒlɪzəm] *n* alcoholismo.
alcove ['ælkəʊv] *n* hueco, hornacina, cavidad *f.*
alder ['ɔːldəʳ] *n* aliso.
alderman ['ɔːldəmən] *n* concejal,-la, edil *mf.*
▲ *pl* **aldermen** ['ɔːldəmən].
ale [eɪl] *n* cerveza.
alehouse ['eɪlhaʊs] *n arch* taberna.
alert [ə'lɜːt] 1 *adj (quick to act)* alerta, vigilante. 2 *(lively)* vivo,-a. – 3 *n* alarma. – 4 *t* alertar, avisar: *he alerted the officer to the danger,* alertó al oficial del peligro.
● **to be on the alert for sth.,** estar alerta por algo: *when on safari you must be alert for lions,* en un safari debes estar alerta por los leones. ‖ **to be alert to sth.,** ser consciente de algo: *we are alert to the danger,* somos conscientes del peligro.
Aleutian [ə'luːʃən] 1 *adj* aleutiano,-a. – 2 *n (person)* aleutiano,-a. 3 *(language)* aleutiano.
■ **Aleutian Islands,** islas *fpl* Aleutianas.
A-level ['eɪlevəl] *abbr* GB EDUC *(Advanced level)* ≈ Curso de Orientación Universitaria; *(abbreviation)* COU *m.*
Alexandria [ælɪg'zændrɪə] *n* Alejandría.
alfalfa [æl'fælfə] *n* alfalfa.
alfresco [æl'freskəʊ] 1 *adj* al aire libre. – 2 *adv* al aire libre.
algae ['ældʒiː] *npl* algas *fpl.*
▲ *sing* **alga** ['ælgə].
Algarve [æl'gɑːv] **the Algarve,** *n* el Algarve *m.*
algebra ['ældʒɪbrə] *n* álgebra.
algebraic [ældʒɪ'breɪɪk] *adj* algebraico,-a.
Algeria [æl'dʒɪərɪə] *n* Argelia.
Algerian [æl'dʒɪərɪən] 1 *adj* argelino,-a. – 2 *n* argelino,-a.
Algiers [æl'dʒɪəz] *n* Argel.
algorithm ['ælgərɪðəm] *n* algoritmo.
algorithmic [ælgə'rɪðmɪk] *adj* algorítmico,-a.
alias ['eɪlɪəs] 1 *adv* alias. – 2 *n* alias *m.*
alibi ['ælɪbaɪ] *n* coartada.
alien ['eɪlɪən] 1 *adj (foreign)* extranjero,-a. 2 *(extraterrestrial)* extraterrestre. 3 *(strange)* extraño,-a, ajeno,-a: *his ideas are alien to me,* sus ideas me son ajenas. – 4 *n (foreigner)* extranjero,-a. 5 *(extraterrestrial)* extraterrestre *mf.*
alienate ['eɪlɪəneɪt] 1 *t (estrange)* ganarse la antipatía de; *(reject)* marginar: *his policies have alienated many of his followers,* su política se ha ganado la antipatía de muchos de sus seguidores; *they feel alienated from society,* se sienten marginados por la sociedad. 2 JUR enajenar.
alienation [eɪlɪə'neɪʃən] *n (estrangement)* distanciamiento, alejamiento; *(rejection)* marginación *f.*
alight [ə'laɪt] 1 *adj* encendido,-a, ardiendo. – 2 *i fml* apearse.
◆ **to alight on** 1 *t insep (land on)* posarse en. 2 *(find)* encontrar por casualidad.
● **to catch alight,** incendiarse. ‖ **to set alight,** incendiar, prender fuego a.
align [ə'laɪn] 1 *t* alinear **(with,** con). – 2 *i* alinearse.
alignment [ə'laɪnmənt] *n* alineación *f.*
● **in alignment with,** alineado,-a con. ‖ **out of alignment with,** mal alineado,-a con.
alike [ə'laɪk] 1 *adj (the same)* iguales; *(similar)* parecidos,-as: *almost alike,* casi iguales; *they are alike in all respects,* son iguales en todo; *you're very much alike,* sois

muy parecidos. – **2** *adv* igual: *they dress alike,* visten igual; *we think alike,* pensamos igual; *men and women alike,* tanto hombres como mujeres, hombres y mujeres por igual.

alimentary [ælɪ'mentərɪ] *adj* alimenticio,-a.
■ alimentary canal, tubo digestivo.

alimony ['ælɪmənɪ] *n* pensión *f* alimenticia.

alive [ə'laɪv] **1** *adj* (*not dead*) vivo,-a: *they were buried alive,* fueron enterrados vivos; *the tradition is still very much alive,* la tradición sigue viva. **2** (*lively*) vivo,-a, vivaz.
● alive and kicking, vivo,-a y coleando. ‖ alive to sth., consciente de algo. ‖ alive with, lleno,-a de, infestado,-a de. ‖ look alive!, ¡espabílate!, ¡despabílate! ‖ to come alive, (*meeting etc*) animarse; (*narrative*) cobrar vida.

alkali ['ælkəlaɪ] *n* álcali *m*.

alkaline ['ælkəlaɪn] *adj* alcalino,-a.

alkalinity [ælkə'lɪnɪtɪ] *n* alcalinidad *f*.

all [ɔːl] **1** *adj* (*singular*) todo,-a; (*plural*) todos,-as: *all the money,* todo el dinero; *all the ink,* toda la tinta; *all the books,* todos los libros; *all the chairs,* todas las sillas; *all kinds of knives,* toda clase de cuchillos; *all day/month/year,* todo el día/mes/año; *all morning/afternoon/night/week,* toda la mañana/tarde/noche/semana. – **2** *pron* (*everything*) todo, la totalidad *f*: *all was lost in the fire,* se perdió todo en el incendio; *best of all were the acrobats,* lo mejor de todo fueron los acróbatas. **3** (*everybody*) todos *mpl,* todo el mundo: *a good time was had by all,* todos se lo pasaron bien; *all of them helped/they all helped,* ayudaron todos. – **4** *adv* completamente, totalmente: *you're all dirty!,* ¡estás todo sucio!; *she was dressed all in leather,* iba vestida toda de cuero.
● after all, (*despite everything*) después de todo; (*it must be remembered*) no hay que olvidarlo. ‖ all along, desde el principio. ‖ all but, casi. ‖ all in, (*tired*) agotado,-a, hecho,-a polvo; (*included*) todo incluido: *after the race I was all in,* después de la carrera estaba hecho polvo; *it's £235 all in,* son £235 todo incluido. ‖ all in all, en conjunto. ‖ all or nothing, todo o nada. ‖ all over, en todas partes: *he's been all over,* ha estado en todas partes; *I ache all over,* me duele todo el cuerpo; *I spilt wine all over my shirt,* me manché toda la camisa de vino; *that's Fred all over,* eso es típico de Fred. ‖ to be all over, acabar: *in ten minutes it was all over,* en diez minutos todo había acabado. ‖ all right, (*acceptable*) bien, bueno,-a, satisfactorio,-a; (*well, safe*) bien; (*accepting suggestion*) vale, bueno; (*calming, silencing*) vale; (*definitely*) seguro: *are you all right?,* ¿estás bien?; *the film's all right, but I've seen better ones,* era el filme, no está mal, pero las he visto mejores; *are you coming? –all right,* ¿te vienes? –vale; *all right, that's enough!,* ¡vale, basta ya!; *all right then this one all right,* era el flaco, estoy seguro. ‖ all the + *comp,* tanto + *adj/adv,* aún + *adj/adv*: *all the better,* tanto mejor; *this makes the situation all the more dangerous,* esto hace que la situación sea más peligrosa aún. ‖ all the same, igualmente, a pesar de todo. ‖ to be all the same to sb., dar lo mismo a algn. ‖ all the time, todo el rato, siempre. ‖ all told, en total. ‖ all too + *adj/adv,* demasiado + *adj/adv*: *it happens all too frequently,* pasa con demasiada frecuencia. ‖ at all, en absoluto: *I didn't like it at all,* no me gustó en absoluto; *nothing at all,* nada de nada. ‖ at all times, siempre. ‖ in all, en total. ‖ not at all, no hay de qué.
■ All Fools' Day, día 1 de abril, ≈ día de los Santos Inocentes. ‖ All Saints' Day, día *m* de Todos los Santos. ‖ All Souls' Day, día *m* los Fieles Difuntos.

Allah ['ælə] *n* Alá *m*.

allay [ə'leɪ] *t* calmar, apaciguar.

all-clear [ɔːl'klɪəʳ] *n* (*after danger*) señal *f* de fin de peligro; (*go-ahead*) luz *f* verde: *we've got the all-clear on the project,* nos han dicho que adelante con el proyecto.

allegation [ælə'geɪʃən] *n* acusación *f.*

allege [ə'ledʒ] *t* alegar.

alleged [ə'ledʒd] *adj* presunto,-a.

allegedly [ə'ledʒədlɪ] *adj* presuntamente.

allegiance [ə'liːdʒəns] *n* lealtad *f.*

allegorical [ælɪ'gɒrɪkəl] *adj* alegórico,-a.

allegory ['ælɪgərɪ] *n* alegoría *f.*
▲ *pl* allegories.

alleluia [ælɪ'luːjə] *interj* ¡aleluya!

allergen ['ælədʒən] *n* alérgeno.

allergic [ə'lɜːdʒɪk] *adj* alérgico,-a (**to**, a).
● to be allergic to sth., ser alérgico,-a a algo.

allergy ['ælədʒɪ] *n* alergia.
● to have an allergy to sth., tener alergia a algo.
▲ *pl* allergies.

alleviate [ə'liːvɪeɪt] *t* aliviar, mitigar.

alleviation [ə'liːvɪeɪʃən] *n* alivio.

alley ['ælɪ] *n* callejuela, callejón *m.*

alley-way ['ælɪweɪ] *n* callejuela, callejón *m.*

alliance [ə'laɪəns] *n* alianza.

allied ['ælaɪd] **1** *adj* POL aliado,-a. **2** (*related*) relacionado,-a, afín.

alligator ['ælɪgeɪtəʳ] *n* caimán *m.*

all-important [ɔːlɪm'pɔːtənt] *adj* vital, de suma importancia.

all-in [ɔːl'ɪn] *adj* (*price*) con todo incluido.
■ all-in wrestling, lucha libre.

alliteration [əlɪtə'reɪʃən] *n* aliteración *f.*

alliterative [ə'lɪtərətɪv] *adj* aliterado,-a.

all-night ['ɔːlnaɪt] *adj* (*lasting all night*) que dura toda la noche; (*open all night*) que no cierra en toda la noche.

allocate ['æləkeɪt] *t* (*money*) destinar; (*time, space, job, etc*) asignar: *they allocated £1M for the building of the bridge,* destinaron un millón de libras a la construcción del puente; *each settler was allocated land,* a cada colono se le asignaron tierras.

allocation [ælə'keɪʃən] **1** *n* (*distribution*) asignación *f;* (*of money*) distribución *f.* **2** (*gen*) lo asignado; (*money given*) cuota.

allot [ə'lɒt] *t* (*moner*) asignar; (*time, space, job, etc*) designar.
▲ *pt* & *pp* allotted, *ger* allotting.

allotment [ə'lɒtmənt] **1** *n* (*of time etc*) asignación *f;* (*of money*) distribución *f.* **2** (*gen*) lo asignado; (*money given*) cuota. **3** (*land*) huerto.

allow [ə'laʊ] **1** *t* (*permit*) permitir, dejar: *to allow sb. to sth.,* dejar/permitir que algn. haga algo; *dogs are not allowed in,* no se permite la entrada con perros; *this card allows you to travel free,* esta tarjeta te permite viajar gratis; *allow me!,* ¡permítame! **2** (*set aside*) conceder, dar, dejar: *you must allow at least £50 for the taxi fare,* tienes que contar con £50 como mínimo para el taxi; *he allowed us two hours to complete the test,* nos concedió dos horas para completar la prueba. **3** (*admit*) admitir, reconocer: *I allow that she tried hard, but ...,* admito que hizo un esfuerzo, pero ...
◆ to allow for *t insep* tener en cuenta: *allowing for possible errors,* teniendo en cuenta los posibles errores. ‖ to allow of *t insep* admitir: *this allows of only one explanation,* esto no admite más que una sola explicación.

allowance [ə'laʊəns] 1 n (from government) subsidio, prestación f. 2 (from employer) dietas fpl, asignación f. 3 (income tax) ganancias exentas de tributación. 4 US (pocket money) paga semanal.
● to make allowances for, (take into account) tener en cuenta; (be permissive) tener paciencia con.

alloy ['ælɔɪ] 1 n aleación f. – 2 t alear. 3 fml estropear.

all-powerful [ɔːl'paʊəfʊl] adj todopoderoso,-a.

all-purpose [ɔːl'pɜːpəs] adj multiusos.

all-round [ɔːl'raʊnd] adj completo,-a.

all-rounder [ɔːl'raʊndəʳ] n (gen) persona polifacética; (sportsperson) deportista mf completo,-a.

all-star ['ɔːlstɑːʳ] adj estelar: an all-star cast, un reparto estelar.

allude [ə'luːd] i aludir (to, a), hacer alusión (to, a).

allure [ə'ljʊəʳ] 1 n atractivo, encanto. – 2 t atraer, seducir.

alluring ['ælaɪ] adj seductor,-ra.

allusion [ə'luːʒən] n alusión f.

alluvial [ə'luːvɪəl] adj aluvial.

alluvium [ə'luːvɪəm] n aluvión m.
▲ pl alluviums o alluvia [ə'luvɪə].

ally ['ælaɪ] 1 n aliado,-a. – 2 t aliar (with, con). – 3 i aliarse (with, con).
▲ (sustantivo) pl allies; (verbo) pt & pp allied, ger allying.

almanac ['ɔːlmənæk] n almanaque m.

almanack ['ɔːlmənæk] n → almanac.

almighty [ɔːl'maɪtɪ] 1 adj todopoderoso,-a. – 2 the Almighty, n el Todopoderoso.

almond ['ɑːmənd] n almendra.
■ almond paste, mazapán m. || almond tree, almendro.

almoner ['ɑːmənəʳ] n limosnero.

almost ['ɔːlməʊst] adv casi: it weighs almost a kilo, pesa casi un kilo; he almost fell into the river, por poco cae al río; the potatoes are almost ready, les falta poco a las patatas.

alms [ɑːmz] npl limosna f sing, caridad f sing.

aloe ['æləʊ] 1 n áloe m. 2 aloes, áloe m.

aloft [ə'lɒft] 1 adv arriba, en lo alto. 2 MAR en la jarcia.

alone [ə'ləʊn] 1 adj (unaccompanied) solo,-a. – 2 adv (only) sólo, solamente: the King alone can save the country, sólo el Rey puede salvar al país.
● let alone, y mucho menos: he can't boil an egg, let alone make an omelette, no sabe cocer un huevo, y mucho menos hacer una tortilla. || to be alone in + ger, ser el/la único,-a que + verbo: you're not alone in thinking we've made a mistake, no eres el único que piensa que nos hemos equivocado. || to be alone with sb., estar a solas con algn. || to go it alone, ir por libre. || to leave sth. alone, no tocar algo. || to leave sb. alone, dejar a algn. en paz, dejar tranquilo,-a a algn.

along [ə'lɒŋ] 1 prep por: go along here and then turn left, ve por aquí y gira a la izquierda; we walked along the riverbank, caminamos por la orilla del río; there were crowds all along the royal route, había multitudes a lo largo de la ruta real. 2 (in) en: his office is along this corridor, su despacho está en este pasillo. – 3 adv adelante, hacia adelante: move along, please, circulen, por favor.
● along with, junto con. || come along, (sing) ven; (plural) venid; (including speaker) vamos.

alongside [ə'lɒŋsaɪd] 1 prep al lado de. – 2 adv al costado, al lado.
● to come alongside, ponerse a la misma altura.

aloof [ə'luːf] 1 adj distante. – 2 adv a distancia.

aloud [ə'laʊd] adv en voz alta.

alpaca [æl'pækə] n alpaca.

alpha ['ælfə] n alfa.
■ alpha and omega, alfa y omega. || alpha particle, partícula alfa. || alpha radiation, radiación f alfa. || alpha ray, rayo alfa.

alphabet ['ælfəbet] n alfabeto, abecedario.

alphabetical [ælfə'betɪkəl] adj alfabético,-a.
● in alphabetical order, por orden alfabético.

alphabetically [ælfə'betɪkəlɪ] adv alfabéticamente, por orden alfabético.

alphabetize ['ælfəbetaɪz] t ordenar alfabéticamente.

alphanumeric [ælfənjuː'merɪk] adj alfanumérico,-a.

alpine [ɪ'ælpaɪn] adj alpino,-a.

Alps ['ælps] the Alps, npl los Alpes mpl.

already [ɔːl'redɪ] adv ya: they've already left, ya se han ido.

alright [ɔːl'raɪt] 1 t (en) adv fam → all right.

Alsace [æl'sæs] n Alsacia.

Alsatian [æl'seɪʃən] 1 adj alsaciano,-a. – 2 n (person) alsaciano,-a. 3 (dog) pastor m alemán.

also ['ɔːlsəʊ] adv también.
● not only ..., but also ..., no sólo ..., sino también ...

also-ran ['ɔːlsəʊræn] 1 n (in race - horse) caballo no clasificado; (- dog) perro no clasificado. 2 (person) perdedor,-ra.

alt [ælttjuːd] abbr (altitude) altitud f; (abbreviation) alt.

altar ['ɔːltəʳ] n altar m.
■ altar boy, monaguillo.

altar-piece ['ɔːltəpiːs] n retablo.

alter ['ɔːltəʳ] 1 t (gen) cambiar; (clothes) arreglar. 2 us euph castrar. – 3 i cambiar, cambiarse: she's altered so much that you'll hardly recognize her, ha cambiado tanto que apenas la reconocerás.

alteration [ɔːltə'reɪʃən] 1 n modificación f. – 2 alterations, npl reformas fpl: we're having alterations done to the house, estamos haciendo reformas en casa.
● to make alterations to sth., modificar algo.

altercation [ɔːltə'keɪʃən] n altercado, disputa.

alter ego [æltər'iːgəʊ] n álter ego m.

alternate [ɔːl'tɜːnət] 1 adj alterno,-a: I go jogging on alternate days, hago footing un día sí y un día no. – 2 t alternar. – 3 i alternarse.
▲ (verbo) ['ɔːltɜːneɪt].

alternately [ɔːl'tɜːnətlɪ] adv alternativamente: the meetings are held alternately in Paris and Rome, las reuniones se celebran en París y Roma alternativamente.

alternating ['ɔːltɜːneɪtɪŋ] alternating current, n corriente f alterna.

alternative [ɔːl'tɜːnətɪv] 1 adj alternativo,-a, otro,-a: we had to make alternative arrangements, tuvimos que cambiar nuestros planes. – 2 n (option) opción f, alternativa.
● to have no alternative but to + inf, no tener otra alternativa que la de + inf, no tener más remedio que + inf.
■ alternative medicine, medicina alternativa.

alternatively [ɔːl'tɜːnətɪvlɪ] adv o bien, por otra parte.

alternator ['ɔːltəneɪtəʳ] n alternador m.

although [ɔːl'ðəʊ] conj aunque.

altimeter ['æltɪmiːtəʳ] n altímetro.

altitude ['æltɪtjuːd] n altitud f, altura.

alto ['æltəʊ] n (male) contralto m; (female) contralto f.
▲ pl altos.

altogether [ɔːltə'geðəʳ] 1 adv (completely) del todo. 2 (on the whole) en conjunto. 3 (in total) en total.

● in the altogether, *fam* en cueros.
altruism ['æltruɪzəm] *n* altruismo.
altruist ['æltruɪst] *n* altruista *mf.*
altruistic ['æltruɪstɪk] *adj* altruista.
alum ['æləm] *n* alumbre *m.*
aluminium [ælju'mɪnɪəm] *n* aluminio.
■ **aluminium foil**, papel *m* de aluminio, papel *m* de plata.
aluminum [ə'luːmɪnəm] *n* us aluminio.
alumna [ə'lʌmnə] *n* us ex-alumna.
▲ *pl* **alumnae** [ə'lʌmniː].
alumnus [ə'lʌmnəs] *n* us ex-alumno.
▲ *pl* **alumni** [ə'lʌmnaɪ].
alveolar [ælvɪ'əuləʳ] *adj* alveolar.
always ['ɔːlweɪz] *adv* siempre.
Alzheimer's disease ['æltshaɪməsdɪziːz] *n* enfermedad *f* de Alzheimer.
AM[1] ['eɪ'em] *abbr* RAD (*amplitude modulation*) modulación *f* de amplitud; (*abbreviation*) AM *f.*
AM[2] ['eɪ'em] *abbr* us → **MA**.
am [æm] 1[a] *pers sing pres* → **be**.
a.m. ['eɪ'em] *abbr* (*ante meridiem*) de la mañana.
amalgam [ə'mælgəm] *n* amalgama.
amalgamate [ə'mælgəmeɪt] 1 *t* (*metals*) amalgamar. **2** (*groups*) fusionar. **– 3** *i* (*metals*) amalgamarse. **4** (*groups*) fusionarse.
amalgamation [əmælgə'meɪʃən] *n* fusión *f.*
amanuensis [əmænju'ensɪs] *n* amanuense *mf.*
▲ *pl* **amanuenses** [əmænju'ensiːz].
amass [ə'mæs] *t* acumular.
amateur ['æmətəʳ] 1 *adj* aficionado,-a. **– 2** *n* aficionado,-a.
amateurish ['æmətərɪʃ] *adj* poco profesional, poco serio,-a, chapucero,-a.
amaze [ə'meɪz] *t* asombrar, pasmar.
amazed [ə'meɪzd] *adj* asombrado,-a, pasmado,-a.
amazement [ə'meɪzmənt] *n* asombro, pasmo.
amazing [ə'meɪzɪŋ] *adj* asombroso,-a, pasmoso,-a.
amazingly [ə'meɪzɪŋlɪ] *adv* asombrosamente.
amazon ['æməzən] 1 *n* (*warrior*) amazona. **2 the Amazon**, (*river*) el Amazonas *m.* **3** (*basin*) Amazonia.
■ **the Amazon jungle**, la selva amazónica. ‖ **the Amazon rain forest**, la selva amazónica.
Amazonian [æmə'zəunɪən] *adj* amazónico,-a.
ambassador [æm'bæsədəʳ] *n* embajador,-ra.
ambassadorial [æmbæsə'dɔːrɪəl] *adj* de embajador.
ambassadress [æm'bæsədrəs] *n* embajadora.
amber ['æmbəʳ] 1 *n* ámbar *m.* **– 2** *adj* ámbar.
ambergris ['æmbəgriːs] *n* ámbar *m* gris.
ambiance ['æmbɪəns] *n* ambiente *m.*
ambidextrous [æmbɪ'dekstrəs] *adj* ambidextro,-a.
ambience ['æmbɪəns] *n* ambiente *m.*
ambient ['æmbɪənt] *adj* ambiental.
ambiguity [æmbɪ'gjuːɪtɪ] *n* ambigüedad *f.*
▲ *pl* **ambiguities**.
ambiguous [æm'bɪgjuəs] *adj* ambiguo,-a.
ambiguously [æm'bɪgjuəslɪ] *adv* con ambigüedad.
ambiguousness [æm'bɪgjuəsnəs] *n* ambigüedad *f.*
ambit ['æmbɪt] *n* ámbito.
ambition [æm'bɪʃən] *n* ambición *f.*
ambitious [æm'bɪʃəs] *adj* ambicioso,-a.
ambitiously [æm'bɪʃəslɪ] *adv* ambiciosamente.
ambitiousness [æm'bɪʃəsnəs] *n* lo ambicioso.
ambivalence [æm'bɪvələns] *n* ambivalencia.

ambivalent [æm'bɪvələnt] *adj* ambivalente.
amble ['æmbəl] 1 *i* (*horse*) amblar. **2** (*person*) ir tranquilamente, ir sin prisa: *he ambled out of the room*, salió tranquilamente de la habitación.
● **at an amble**, a paso tranquilo.
ambulance ['æmbjuləns] *n* ambulancia.
■ **ambulance man**, ambulanciero. ‖ **ambulance woman**, ambulanciera.
ambush ['æmbuʃ] 1 *n* emboscada. **– 2** *t* poner una emboscada a.
ameba [ə'miːbə] *n* us → **amoeba**.
ameliorate [ə'miːlɪəreɪt] 1 *t* mejorar. **– 2** *i* mejorar.
amelioration [əmiːlɪə'reɪʃən] *n* mejora.
amen [ɑː'men] *interj* amén.
amenable [ə'miːnəbəl] *adj* tratable, bien dispuesto,-a: *he's amenable to reason*, es una persona razonable.
amend [ə'mend] 1 *t* (*law*) enmendar; (*error*) corregir. **– 2** *i* (*law*) enmendarse; (*error*) corregirse. **– 3 amends**, *npl* reparación *f sing*, compensación *f sing*: *to make amends to sb. for sth.*, compensar a algn. por algo.
amendment [ə'mendmənt] *n* enmienda.
amenities [ə'miːnɪtɪz] *npl* servicios *mpl*, prestaciones *fpl.*
America [ə'merɪkə] *n* América.
■ **Central America**, América Central, Centroamérica. ‖ **Latin America**, América Latina, Latinoamérica. ‖ **North America**, América del Norte, Norteamérica. ‖ **South America**, América del Sur, Sudamérica.
American [ə'merɪkən] 1 *adj* (*gen*) americano,-a. **2** (*from USA*) estadounidense. **– 3** *n* (*gen*) americano,-a. **4** (*from USA*) estadounidense *mf.*
■ **American dream**, sueño americano. ‖ **American football**, fútbol *m* americano. ‖ **American Indian**, amerindio,-a.
Americanism [ə'merɪkənɪzəm] *n* americanismo.
Americanization [əmerɪkənaɪ'zeɪʃən] *n* americanización *f.*
Americanize [ə'merɪkənaɪz] *t* americanizar.
Amerindian [æmə'rɪndɪən] 1 *adj* amerindio,-a. **– 2** *n* amerindio,-a.
amethyst ['æməθɪst] *n* amatista, ametista.
Amharic [æm'hærɪk] 1 *adj* amárico,-a. **– 2** *n* (*language*) amárico.
amiability [eɪmɪə'bɪlɪtɪ] *n* afabilidad *f*, amabilidad *f.*
amiable ['eɪmɪəbəl] *adj* afable, amable.
amiably ['eɪmɪəblɪ] *adv* afablemente, amablemente.
amicability [æmɪkə'bɪlɪtɪ] *n* amistosidad *f.*
amicable ['æmɪkəbəl] *adj* amistoso,-a, amigable.
amicably ['æmɪkəblɪ] *adv* amistosamente, amigablemente.
amid [ə'mɪd] *prep* en medio de, entre.
amidships [ə'mɪdʃɪps] *adv* en medio del barco.
amidst [ə'mɪdst] *prep* → **amid**.
amino acid [æmiːnəu'æsɪd] *n* aminoácido.
amiss [ə'mɪs] 1 *adv* mal. **– 2** *adj* mal.
● **to take amiss**, tomar a mal.
amity ['æmɪtɪ] *n* buenas relaciones *fpl.*
ammeter ['æmiːtəʳ] *n* amperímetro.
ammo ['æməu] *n fam* (*abbr of* **ammunition**) munición *f.*
ammonia [ə'məunɪ] *n* amoníaco, amoniaco.
ammunition [æmju'nɪʃən] 1 *n* municiones *fpl.* **2** *fig* (*arguments*) argumentos *mpl.*
■ **ammunition dump**, depósito de municiones.
amnesia [æm'niːzɪə] *n* amnesia.
amnesty ['æmnəstɪ] *n* amnistía.
▲ *pl* **amnesties**.

amoeba [æ'miːbə] *n* ameba.
▲ *pl* **amoebae** [ə'miːbiː].
amok [ə'mɒk] **to run amok,** *phr* volverse loco,-a y causar destrozos.
among [ə'mʌŋ] *prep* entre.
amongst [ə'mʌŋst] *prep* → **among**.
amoral [eɪ'mɒrəl] *adj* amoral.
amorous ['æmərəs] *adj* amoroso,-a.
amorously ['æmərəslɪ] *adv* amorosamente.
amorphous [ə'mɔːfəs] *adj* amorfo,-a.
amount [ə'maʊnt] *n* (*gen*) cantidad *f*; (*bill*) importe *m*: *the total amount is £234,* el importe total es de 234 libras.
◆ **to amount to** *t insep* ascender a; *fig* equivaler a.
amp ['æmp] *n* (*abbr of* **ampere**) amperio, ampere *m*.
amperage ['æmpərɪdʒ] *n* amperaje *m*.
ampere ['æmpeəʳ] *n* amperio, ampere *m*.
ampersand ['æmpəsænd] *n* el signo &.
amphetamine [æm'fetəmiːn] *n* anfetamina.
amphibian [æm'fɪbɪən] *n* anfibio.
amphibious [æm'fɪbɪəs] *adj* anfibio,-a.
amphitheater ['æmfɪθɪətəʳ] *n* US anfiteatro.
amphitheatre ['æmfɪθɪətəʳ] *n* anfiteatro.
ample ['æmpəl] **1** *adj* (*enough*) bastante. **2** (*plenty*) más que suficiente. **3** (*large, generous*) amplio,-a.
amplification [æmplɪfɪ'keɪʃən] **1** *n* (*of sound*) amplificación *f*. **2** (*of ststement*) ampliación *f*.
amplifier ['æmplɪfaɪəʳ] *n* amplificador *m*.
amplify ['æmplɪfaɪ] **1** *t* (*sound*) amplificar. **2** (*statement*) ampliar.
▲ *pt & pp* **amplified,** *ger* **amplifying**.
amplitude ['æmplɪtjuːd] *n* amplitud *f*.
amply ['æmplɪ] **1** *adv* (*enough*) suficientemente. **2** (*more than enough*) sobradamente. **3** (*generously*) ampliamente.
ampoule ['æmpuːl] *n* ampolla.
ampule ['æmpuːl] *n* US ampolla.
amputate ['æmpjʊteɪt] *t* amputar.
amputation [æmpjʊ'teɪʃən] *n* amputación *f*.
Amsterdam ['æmstədæm] *n* Amsterdam.
amuck [ə'mʌk] *adv* → **amok**.
amulet ['æmjʊlət] *n* amuleto.
amuse [ə'mjuːz] *t* entretener, divertir.
● **to amuse os.,** entretenerse. ‖ **to keep sb. amused,** entretener a algn.
amusement [ə'mjuːzmənt] **1** *n* (*enjoyment*) diversión *f*, entretenimiento. **2** (*pastime*) pasatiempo.
■ **amusement arcade,** salón *m* de juegos. ‖ **amusement park,** parque *m* de atracciones.
amusing [ə'mjuːzɪŋ] **1** *adj* (*fun*) entretenido,-a, divertido,-a. **2** (*funny*) gracioso,-a.
an [ən, æn] **1** *indef art* un, una. **2** (*per*) por.
▲ *Se usa delante de las palabras que empiezan por un sonido vocálico; Véase también* **a**.
anabolic steroid [ænəbɒlɪk'sterɔɪd] *n* esteroide *m* anabólico.
anachronism [ə'nækrənɪzəm] *n* anacronismo.
anachronistic [ənækrə'nɪstɪk] *adj* anacrónico,-a.
anaconda [ænə'kɒndə] *n* anaconda.
anaemia [ə'niːmɪə] *n* anemia.
anaemic [ə'niːmɪk] *adj* anémico,-a.
anaesthesia [ænəs'θiːzɪə] *n* anestesia.
anaesthetic [ænəs'θetɪk] **1** *adj* anestésico,-a. – **2** *n* anestésico.
anaesthetist [ə'niːsθətɪst] *n* anestesista *mf*.
anaesthetize [ə'niːsθətaɪz] *t* anestesiar.

anagram ['ænəgræm] *n* anagrama *m*.
anal ['eɪnəl] *adj* anal.
analgesic [ænəl'dʒiːzɪk] **1** *adj* analgésico,-a. – **2** *n* analgésico.
analog ['ænəlɒg] *adj-n* US → **analogue**.
analogous [ə'næləgəs] *adj* análogo,-a (**to/with,** a).
analogue ['ænəlɒg] **1** *adj* analógico,-a. – **2** *n* análogo.
analogy [ə'nælədʒɪ] *n* analogía, semejanza.
▲ *pl* **analogies**.
analyse ['ænəlaɪz] *t* analizar.
analysis [ə'nælɪsɪs] *n* análisis *m*.
▲ *pl* **analyses** [ə'nælɪsiːz].
analyst ['ænəlɪst] *n* analista *mf*.
anaphoric [ænə'fɒrɪk] *adj* anafórico,-a.
anarchic [æ'nɑːkɪk] *adj* anárquico,-a.
anarchical [æ'nɑːkɪkəl] *adj* anárquico,-a.
anarchist ['ænəkɪst] *n* anarquista *mf*.
anarchistic [ænə'kɪstɪk] *adj* anarquista.
anarchy ['ænəkɪ] *n* anarquía.
▲ *pl* **anarchies**.
anathema [ə'næθəmə] *n* anatema *m*.
● **to be anathema to sb.,** repugnar a algn.
anathematize [ə'næθəmətaɪz] *t* anatematizar.
anatomical [ænə'tɒmɪkəl] *adj* anatómico,-a.
anatomist [ə'nætənɪst] *n* anatomista *mf*.
anatomy [ə'nætəmɪ] *n* anatomía.
▲ *pl* **anatomies**.
ANC ['eɪ'en'siː] *abbr* (**African National Congress**) Congreso Nacional Africano; (*abbreviation*) CNA.
ancestor ['ænsəstəʳ] *n* antepasado.
ancestral [æn'sestrəl] *adj* ancestral.
■ **ancestral home,** casa solariega.
ancestry ['ænsəstrɪ] *n* ascendencia.
▲ *pl* **ancestries**.
anchor ['æŋkəʳ] **1** *n* (*of ship*) ancla, áncora. **2** *fig* sostén *m*. – **3** *t* (*ship*) anclar. **4** (*make secure*) sujetar. – **5** *i* anclar.
● **at anchor,** anclado,-a.
anchorage ['æŋkərɪdʒ] **1** *n* (*place*) fondeadero. **2** (*fee*) anclaje *m*.
anchorman ['æŋkəmæn] *n* TV presentador *m*.
▲ *pl* **anchormen** ['æŋkəmen].
anchorperson ['æŋkəpɜːsən] *n* TV (*man*) presentador *m*; (*woman*) presentadora.
anchorwoman ['æŋkəwʊmən] *n* TV presentadora.
▲ *pl* **anchorwomen** ['æŋkəwɪmɪn].
anchovy ['æntʃəvɪ] *n* (*salted*) anchoa; (*fresh*) boquerón *m*.
▲ *pl* **anchovies**.
ancient ['eɪnʃənt] **1** *adj* antiguo,-a; (*monument*) histórico,-a. **2** *fam* viejísimo,-a. – **3 the ancients,** *npl* los antiguos *mpl*.
■ **ancient history,** historia antigua.
ancillary [æn'sɪlərɪ] *adj* auxiliar.
and [ænd, *unstressed* and] **1** *conj* y; (*before i-* and *hi-*) e: *black and white,* blanco y negro; *opinions and ideas,* opiniones e ideas; *I hit him and he fell over,* le pegué y se cayó. **2** (*with infinitives*): *go and look for it,* ve a buscarlo; *try and start the car,* intenta arrancar el coche; *come and visit us,* ven a visitarnos; *wait and see what happens,* espera a ver lo que pasa. **3** (*expressing repetition, increase*): *it rained and rained,* no paró de llover; *it rained harder and harder,* llovía cada vez más fuerte; *it rained for hours and hours,* llovió durante horas y horas. **4** (*with numbers*): *a hundred and twenty,* ciento veinte; *two thousand and eighty four,* dos mil ochenta y cuatro; *five and a quarter inches,* cinco pulgadas y cuarto; *three and a*

half hours, tres horas y media. **5** (*in sums*) más: *four and six are ten,* cuatro más seis son diez.

Andalusia [ændə'luːzɪə] *n* Andalucía.

Andalusian [ændə'luːzɪən] **1** *adj* andaluz,-za. – **2** *n* (*person*) andaluz,-za. **3** (*dialect*) andaluz *m*.

Andean [æn'diːən, 'ændɪən] *adj* andino,-a.

Andes ['ændiːz] the Andes, *npl* los Andes *mpl*.

Andorra [æn'dɔːrə] *n* Andorra.

Andorran [æn'dɔːrən] **1** *adj* andorrano,-a. – **2** *n* andorrano,-a.

androgynous [æn'drɒdʒɪnəs] *adj* andrógino,-a.

android ['ændrɔɪd] *n* androide *m*.

anecdotal [ænɪk'dəʊtəl] *n* anecdótico,-a.

anecdote ['ænɪkdəʊt] *n* anécdota.

anemia [ə'niːmɪə] *n* US → **anaemia**.

anemic [ə'niːmɪk] *adj* US → **anaemic**.

anemometer [ænɪ'mɒmɪtəʳ] *n* anemómetro.

anemone [ə'neMƏnɪ] *n* ʙoт anémona.

aneroid ['ænərɔɪd] *adj* aneroide.

anesthesia [ænəs'θiːzɪə] *n* → **anaesthesia**.

anesthetic [ænəs'θetɪk] *adj-n* → **anaesthetic**.

anesthetist [ə'niːsθətɪst] *n* → **anaesthetist**.

anesthetize [ə'niːsθətaɪz] *t* → **anaesthetize**.

anew [ə'njuː] *adv* nuevamente, de nuevo, otra vez.

angel ['eɪndʒəl] **1** *n* ángel *m*. **2** (*kind person*) cielo, sol *m*; (*child*) angelito.

angelic [æn'dʒelɪk] *adj* angelical.

angelica [æn'dʒelɪkə] *n* angélica.

angelus ['ændʒələs] *n* ángelus *m*.

anger ['æŋgəʳ] **1** *n* cólera, ira, furia. – **2** *t* encolerizar, enojar, enfurecer.

angina [æn'dʒaɪnə] *n* angina de pecho.
  ▲ *También angina pectoris.*

angle¹ ['æŋgəl] **1** *n* ángulo. **2** (*point of view*) punto de vista, perspectiva. – **3** *t* (*slant*) sesgar.

angle² ['æŋgəl] *i* pescar, pescar con caña.
  ◆ to angle for *t insep* ir a la caza de, andar buscando: *he's angling for an invitation,* anda buscando que le inviten.

Angle ['æŋgəl] *n* anglo,-a.

angler ['æŋgləʳ] *n* pescador,-ra, pescador,-ra de caña.
  ■ angler fish, rape *m*.

Anglican ['æŋglɪkən] **1** *adj* anglicano,-a. – **2** *n* anglicano,-a.

anglicism ['æŋglɪsɪzəm] *n* anglicismo.

anglicize ['æŋglɪsaɪz] *t* anglicanizar.

angling ['æŋglɪŋ] *n* pesca, pesca con caña.

anglophile ['æŋgləʊfaɪl] **1** *adj* anglófilo,-a. – **2** *n* anglófilo,-a.

anglophilia [æŋgləʊ'fɪlɪə] *n* anglofilia.

anglophobe ['æŋgləʊfəʊb] **1** *adj* anglófobo,-a. – **2** *n* anglófobo,-a.

anglophobia [æŋgləʊ'fəʊbɪə] *n* anglofobia.

Anglo-Saxon ['æŋgləʊ'sæksən] **1** *adj* anglosajón,-ona. – **2** *n* (*person*) anglosajón,-ona. **3** (*language*) anglosajón *m*.

Angola [æŋ'gəʊlə] *n* Angola.

Angolan [æŋ'gəʊlən] **1** *adj* angoleño,-a. – **2** *n* angoleño,-a.

angora [æŋ'gɔːrə] **1** *n* (*yarn*) angora. **2** (*cat*) gato de angora; (*goat*) cabra de angora.

angrily ['æŋgrɪlɪ] *adv* furiosamente.

angry ['æŋgrɪ] **1** *adj* (*person*) enojado,-a, enfadado,-a: *she was angry about the delay,* estaba enfadada por el retraso. **2** (*wound*) inflamado,-a. **3** (*sky*) tormentoso,-a.

● to be angry with sb., estar enfadado,-a con algn. ‖ to get angry, enojarse, enfadarse.
  ▲ *comp* angrier, *superl* angriest.

angst [æŋst] *n* angustia.

anguish ['æŋgwɪʃ] *n* angustia.

anguished ['æŋgwɪʃt] *adj* angustiado,-a.

angular ['æŋgjʊləʳ] **1** *adj* (*with angles, of angles*) angular. **2** (*person*) anguloso,-a.

aniline ['ænɪlaɪn] *n* anilina.

animal ['ænɪməl] **1** *adj* animal. – **2** *n* animal *m*.
  ■ animal magnetism, magnetismo animal. ‖ animal rights, derechos *mpl* de los animales.

animate ['ænɪmət] **1** *adj* animado,-a, vivo,-a. – **2** *t* animar. **3** *fig* estimular.
  ▲ (*verbo*) ['ænɪmeɪt].

animated ['ænɪmeɪtɪd] *adj* animado,-a.

animation [ænɪ'meɪʃən] **1** *n* animación *f*. **2** (*life*) vida, marcha.

animator ['ænɪmeɪtəʳ] *n* animador,-ra.

animism ['ænɪmɪzəm] *n* animismo.

animist ['ænɪmɪst] **1** *adj* animista. – **2** *n* animista *mf*.

animosity [ænɪ'mɒsɪtɪ] *n* animosidad *f*.
  ▲ *pl animosities.*

animus ['ænɪməs] *n* animosidad *f*.

anise ['ænɪs] *n* anís *m*.

aniseed ['ænɪsiːd] *n* anís *m*.

Ankara ['æŋkərə] *n* Ankara.

ankh [æŋk] *n* cruz *f* ankh, ankh *f*.

ankle ['æŋkəl] *n* tobillo.

ankle-length ['æŋkəlleŋθ] *adj* hasta el tobillo.

anklet ['æŋklət] *n* ajorca.

annals ['ænəlz] *npl* anales *mpl*.

anneal [ə'niːl] *t* templar.

annex [ə'neks] **1** *t* anexar. – **2** *n* → **annexe**.

annexation [ænek'seɪʃən] *n* anexión *f*.

annexe ['æneks] *n* anexo, anejo.

annihilate [ə'naɪəleɪt] *t* aniquilar.

annihilation [ənaɪə'leɪʃən] *n* aniquilación *f*.

anniversary [ænɪ'vɜːsərɪ] *n* aniversario.
  ▲ *pl anniversaries.*

annotate ['ænəteɪt] *t* anotar.

annotated ['ænəteɪtɪd] *adj* (*edition*) crítico,-a.

annotation [ænə'teɪʃən] *n* anotación *f*.

announce [ə'naʊns] *t* (*event*) anunciar; (*fact*) anunciar, hacer saber, dar a conocer.

announcement [ə'naʊnsmənt] *n* anuncio.

announcer [ə'naʊnsəʳ] *n* ᴛᴠ ʀᴀᴅ presentador,-ra, locutor,-ra.

annoy [ə'nɔɪ] *t* molestar, fastidiar.

annoyance [ə'nɔɪəns] *n* molestia.

annoyed [ə'nɔɪd] *adj* enfadado,-a, enojado,-a.
  ● to get annoyed with sb., enfadarse con algn.

annoying [ə'nɔɪɪŋ] *adj* molesto,-a, enojoso,-a: *it's very annoying,* molesta mucho, da rabia.

annual ['ænjʊəl] **1** *adj* anual. – **2** *n* (*plant*) planta anual. **3** (*book*) anuario.

annually ['ænjʊəlɪ] *adv* anualmente.

annuity [ə'njuːɪtɪ] *n* renta vitalicia.
  ▲ *pl annuities.*

annul [ə'nʌl] *t* anular.
  ▲ *pt & pp annulled, ger annulling.*

annular ['ænjʊləʳ] *adj* anular.

annulment [ə'nʌlmənt] *n* anulación *f*.

Annunciation [ənʌnsɪ'eɪʃən] the Annunciation, *n* la Anunciación *f*.

anode ['ænəʊd] n ánodo.
anodyne ['ænədaɪn] 1 adj anodino,-a. – 2 n calmante m.
anoint [ə'nɔɪnt] t ungir.
anomalous [ə'nɒmələs] adj anómalo,-a.
anomaly [ə'nɒməlɪ] n anomalía.
▲ pl anomalies.
anon¹ [ə'nɒn] adv pronto.
anon² [ə'nɒn] adj (abbr of anonymous) anón.
anonymity [ænə'nɪmɪtɪ] n anonimidad f.
anonymous [ə'nɒnɪməs] adj anónimo,-a.
anonymously [ə'nɒnɪməslɪ] adv de manera anónima.
anopheles [ə'nɒfəliːz] n anofeles m.
anorak ['ænəræk] n anorak m.
anorectic [ænə'rektɪk] adj → **anorexic**.
anorexia [ænə'reksɪə] n anorexia.
■ anorexia nervosa, anorexia nervosa.
anorexic [ænə'reksɪk] adj anoréxico,-a.
another [ə'nʌðəʳ] 1 adj otro,-a: would you like another biscuit?, ¿quieres otra galleta?; we'll go there another day, iremos allí otro día; if you want one with a shower it'll be another £5, si quiere una con ducha serán cinco libras más. – 2 pron otro,-a: I loved her, but she married another, la quería, pero se casó con otro.
● at one time or another, en algún momento.
answer ['ɑːnsəʳ] 1 n (reply) respuesta, contestación f: his answer was correct, su respuesta fue correcta. 2 (solution) solución f: there's no answer to this problem, este problema no tiene solución. – 3 t (question) responder a, contestar a. 4 (door) abrir; (telephone) contestar a, coger. – 5 i (question) responder, contestar.
◆ to answer back 1 t sep replicar. – 2 i replicar. ‖ to answer for 1 t insep (guarantee) responder por, garantizar. 2 (accept responsibility) responder de. 3 (speak for) responder por, contestar por.
● in answer to, en respuesta a. ‖ to have a lot to answer for, tener mucha culpa. ‖ to answer to the name of ..., atender por ...
answerable ['ɑːnsərəbəl] adj responsable (to, ante) (for, de).
answering machine ['ɑːnsərɪŋməʃiːn] n contestador m automático.
answerphone ['ɑːnsəfəʊn] n contestador m automático.
ant [ænt] n hormiga.
■ ant hill, hormiguero.
antacid [ænt'æsɪd] 1 adj antiácido,-a. – 2 n antiácido.
antagonism [æn'tægənɪzəm] n antagonismo.
antagonist [æn'tægənɪst] n antagonista mf.
antagonistic [æntægə'nɪstɪk] adj hostil, antagónico,-a.
antagonize [æn'tægənaɪz] t enemistarse con.
Antarctic [ænt'ɑːktɪk] 1 adj antártico,-a. – 2 the Antarctic, n Antártida.
■ Antarctic Circle, Círculo antártico.
Antarctica [ænt'ɑːktɪkə] n Antártida.
ante ['æntɪ] 1 n apuesta. – 2 i hacer una apuesta.
anteater ['æntiːtəʳ] n oso hormiguero.
antecedent [æntɪ'siːdənt] 1 adj antecedente. – 2 n antecedente m.
antechamber ['æntɪtʃeɪmbəʳ] n antecámara.
antedate [æntɪ'deɪt] 1 t (predate) ser anterior a. 2 (put earlier date on) poner una fecha anterior a.
antediluvian [æntɪdɪ'luːvɪən] adj antediluviano,-a.
antelope ['æntɪləʊp] n antílope m.
antenatal [æntɪ'neɪtəl] adj prenatal.
■ antenatal clinic, centro de preparación al parto.

antenna [æn'tenə] 1 n ZOOL antena. 2 TV RAD antena.
▲ En 1 pl antennae [æn'teniː], en 2 pl antennas.
antepenultimate [æntɪpə'nʌltɪmət] adj antepenúltimo,-a.
anterior [æn'tɪərɪəʳ] adj anterior.
anteroom ['æntruːm] n antesala.
anthem ['ænθəm] n motete m.
anther ['ænθəʳ] n antera.
anthology [æn'θɒlədʒɪ] n antología.
▲ pl anthologies.
anthracite ['ænθrəsaɪt] n antracita.
anthrax ['ænθræks] n ántrax m.
anthropoid ['ænθrəpɔɪd] 1 adj antropoide. – 2 n antropoide m.
anthropological [ænθrəpə'lɒdʒɪkəl] adj antropológico,-a.
anthropologist [ænθrə'pɒlədʒɪst] n antropólogo,-a.
anthropology [ænθrə'pɒlədʒɪ] n antropología.
anthropomorphic [ænθrəpə'mɔːfɪk] 1 adj (religion) antropomórfico,-a. 2 (form) antropomorfo,-a.
anthropomorphism [ænθrəpə'mɔːfɪzəm] n antropomorfismo.
anti ['æntɪ] prep en contra de.
anti-aircraft [æntɪ'eəkrɑːft] adj antiaéreo,-a.
antiballistic missile [æntɪbəlɪstɪk'mɪsaɪl] n misil m antibalístico.
antibiotic [æntɪbaɪ'ɒtɪk] 1 adj antibiótico,-a. – 2 n antibiótico.
antibody ['æntɪbɒdɪ] n anticuerpo.
▲ pl antibodies.
anticipate [æn'tɪsɪpeɪt] 1 t (expect) esperar: it wasn't what I anticipated, no era lo que esperaba. 2 (get ahead of) adelantarse a: we wanted to be first, but the others anticipated us, quisimos ser los primeros, pero los otros se nos adelantaron. 3 (forsee) anticiparse a, prever: you should try to anticipate your opponent's next move, debes intentar anticiparte al movimiento de tu oponente.
anticipation [æntɪsɪ'peɪʃən] 1 n (expectation) expectación f. 2 (foresight) previsión f.
● in anticipation of, en previsión de.
anticlerical [æntɪ'klerɪkəl] adj anticlerical.
anticlericalism [æntɪ'klerɪkəlɪzm] n anticlericalismo.
anticlimactic [æntɪklaɪ'mæktɪk] adj decepcionante.
anticlimax [æntɪ'klaɪmæks] n anticlímax m.
anticlockwise [æntɪ'klɒkwaɪz] adj en el sentido contrario al de las agujas del reloj.
antics ['æntɪks] npl payasadas fpl.
anticyclone [æntɪ'saɪkləʊn] n anticiclón m.
antidepressant [æntɪdɪ'presənt] 1 adj antidepresivo,-a. – 2 n antidepresivo.
antidote ['æntɪdəʊt] n antídoto.
antifreeze ['æntɪfriːz] n anticongelante m.
antigen ['æntɪdʒen] n antígeno.
Antigua [æn'tiːgə] n Antigua.
Antiguan [æn'tiːgən] 1 adj antigüeño,-a. – 2 n antigüeño,-a.
antihero [æntɪhɪərəʊ] n antihéroe m.
▲ pl antiheroes.
antihistamine [æntɪ'hɪstəmiːn] n antihistamínico.
Antilles [æn'tɪliːz] npl Antillas fpl.
■ Greater Antilles, Grandes Antillas fpl. ‖ Lesser Antilles, Pequeñas Antillas fpl.
antilogarithm [æntɪ'lɒgərɪðəm] n antilogaritmo.
antimony ['æntɪmənɪ] n antimonio.
antinuclear [æntɪ'njuːklɪəʳ] adj antinuclear.

antioxidant [æntɪ'ɒksɪdənt] *n* antioxidante *m*.
antipathy [æn'tɪpəθɪ] *n* antipatía.
  ▲ *pl antipathies*.
antipersonnel [æntɪpɜːsə'nel] *adj* antipersonal.
antiperspirant [æntɪ'pɜːspɪrənt] *n* antiperspirante *m*.
antipodes [æn'tɪpədiːz] *npl* antípodas *fpl*.
  ■ the Antipodes, Australia y Nueva Zelanda.
antiquarian [æntɪ'kweərɪən] **1** *adj* de viejo: *an anti-quarian bookshop*, una librería de viejo. – **2** *n* anticuario,-a.
antiquated ['æntɪkweɪtɪd] *adj* anticuado,-a.
antique [æn'tiːk] **1** *adj* antiguo,-a. – **2** *n* antigüedad *f*.
antiquity [æn'tɪkwɪtɪ] *n* antigüedad *f*.
  ▲ *pl antiquities*.
anti-Semite [æntɪ'semaɪt] *n* antisemita *mf*.
anti-Semitic [æntɪsə'mɪtɪk] *adj* antisemita.
anti-Semitism [æntɪ'semɪtɪzəm] *n* antisemitismo.
antiseptic [æntɪ'septɪk] **1** *adj* antiséptico,-a. – **2** *n* anti-séptico.
antisocial [æntɪ'səʊʃəl] *adj* antisocial.
antistatic [æntɪ'stætɪk] *adj* antiestático,-a.
anti-tank [æntɪ'tæŋk] *adj* antitanque.
anti-terrorist [æntɪ'terərɪst] *adj* antiterrorista.
antithesis [æn'tɪθəsɪs] *n* antítesis *f*.
antitoxin [æntɪ'tɒksɪn] *n* antitoxina.
antlers ['æntləʳ] *npl* cornamenta *f sing*.
antonym ['æntənɪm] *n* antónimo.
Antwerp ['æntwɜːp] *n* Amberes.
anus ['eɪnəs] *n* ano.
anvil ['ænvɪl] *n* yunque *m*.
anxiety [æŋ'zaɪətɪ] **1** *n* (*concern*) preocupación *f*, ansiedad *f*; (*cause of concern*) preocupación *f*. **2** MED ansiedad *f*. **3** (*strong desire*) ansia, afán *m*.
  ▲ *pl anxieties*.
anxious ['æŋkʃəs] **1** *adj* (*worried*) preocupado,-a (**about**, por), inquieto,-a. **2** (*desirous*) ansioso,-a.
  ● to be anxious to do sth., desear hacer algo.
any ['enɪ] **1** *adj* (*in questions*) algún,-una: *are there any biscuits left?*, ¿queda alguna galleta?; *have you got any money/gloves?*, ¿tienes dinero/guantes? **2** (*negative*) ningún,-una: *he hasn't bought any milk/biscuits*, no ha comprado leche/galletas; *without any difficulty*, sin ninguna dificultad. **3** (*no matter which*) cualquier,-ra: *any fool knows that*, cualquier tonto sabe eso; *any old rag will do*, cualquier trapo sirve; *come round any time*, ven cuando quieras. – **4** *pron* (*in questions*) alguno,-a: *there are foxes round here, have you seen any?*, hay zorros por aquí, ¿has visto alguno?; *do you want any?*, ¿quieres?; *he's got lots of money, but does he ever spend any?*, tiene mucho dinero, pero ¿gasta algo alguna vez? **5** (*negative*) ninguno,-a: *they're very cheap, but I haven't sold any*, son muy baratos, pero no he vendido ninguno; *I asked for snails/caviar, but they hadn't got any*, pedí caracoles/caviar pero no tenían; *brandy?, there isn't any*, ¿coñac?, no hay. **6** (*no matter which*) cualquiera: *any of these books will do*, cualquiera de estos libros sirve. – **7** *adv*: *I don't work there any more*, ya no trabajo allí; *do you want any more?*, ¿quieres más?; *I can't work any faster*, no puedo trabajar más deprisa.
  ▲ En preguntas y frases negativas no se usa *any* sino *a* o *an* con los sustantivos contables en singular; en 7 (*adverbio*) generalmente no se traduce.
anybody ['enɪbɒdɪ] **1** *pron* (*in questions*) alguien: *has anybody seen my car?*, ¿ha visto alguien mi coche? **2** (*negative*) nadie: *there isn't anybody in the room*, no hay nadie en la sala. **3** (*no matter who*) cualquiera: *anybody would tell you the same*, cualquiera te diría lo mismo.

anyhow ['enɪhaʊ] **1** *adv* → **anyway**. **2** (*carelessly*) de cualquier forma, de cualquier manera.
anyone ['enɪwʌn] *pron* → **anybody**.
anyplace ['enɪpleɪs] *adv* US → **anywhere**.
anything ['enɪθɪŋ] **1** *pron* (*in questions*) algo, alguna cosa: *is there anything left?*, ¿queda algo? **2** (*negative*) nada: *there isn't anything left*, no queda nada. **3** (*no matter what*) cualquier cosa: *anything will do*, cualquier cosa sirve; *they can cost anything from £5 to £5000*, el precio va desde cinco libras a cinco mil.
anyway ['enɪweɪ] **1** *adv* (*in any case*) de todas formas, de todos modos: *they didn't invite me, but I didn't want to go anyway*, no me invitaron, pero de todas formas no quería ir. **2** (*all the same*) igual, de todos modos: *it was dear, but I bought it anyway*, era caro, pero lo compré igual; *I don't care if I'm not invited, I'm going anyway*, no me importa si no estoy invitada, voy de todos modos. **3** (*in conversation*) bueno, bueno pues, total, en cualquier caso: *anyway, as I was saying, ...*, bueno pues, como te decía, ...
anywhere ['enɪweəʳ] **1** *adv* (*in questions - situation*) en algún sitio, en alguna parte; (*- direction*) a algún sitio, a alguna parte: *have you seen my keys anywhere?*, ¿has visto mis llaves en alguna parte?; *are you going anywhere this weekend?*, ¿vas a algún sitio el fin de semana? **2** (*negative - situation*) en ningún sitio, en ninguna parte; (*- direction*) a ningún sitio, a ninguna parte: *I can't find him anywhere*, no lo encuentro en ninguna parte; *we're not going anywhere*, no vamos a ningún sitio. **3** (*no matter where - situation*) donde sea, en cualquier sitio; (*- direction*) a donde sea, a cualquier sitio: *I'd live anywhere as long as it's with you*, viviría en cualquier sitio mientras sea contigo; *she'd travel anywhere to see Bruce*, viajaría a cualquier sitio para ver a Bruce; *we'll eat anywhere you like*, comeremos donde tú quieras; *they can cost anywhere between £5 and £5000*, el precio va desde cinco libras a cinco mil.
aorta [eɪ'ɔːtə] *n* aorta.
apace [ə'peɪs] *adv* rápidamente.
apart [ə'pɑːt] **1** *adv* (*not together*) separado,-a; (*distant*) alejado,-a: *these nails are too far apart*, estos clavos están demasiado separados; *the villages are a long way apart*, los pueblos están alejados entre sí. **2** (*in pieces*) en piezas.
  ● apart from, aparte de. ‖ to fall apart, deshacerse. ‖ to live apart, vivir separados. ‖ to take apart, desarmar, desmontar. ‖ to tell apart, distinguir.
apartheid [ə'pɑːtheɪt] *n* apartheid *m*.
apartment [ə'pɑːtmənt] *n* piso, apartamento.
  ■ apartment block / apartment building, bloque *m* de pisos.
apathetic [æpə'θetɪk] *adj* apático,-a.
apathy ['æpəθɪ] *n* apatía.
ape [eɪp] **1** *n* simio. – **2** *t* imitar.
Appenines ['æpənaɪnz] the Appenines, *n* los (montes) Apeninos *mpl*.
aperitif [əperɪ'tiːf] *n* aperitivo.
aperture ['æpətjəʳ] *n* abertura.
apex ['eɪpeks] *n* ápice *m*; (*of triangle*) vértice *m*.
  ▲ *pl apexes o apices*.
APEX ['eɪpeks] *abbr* (*Advance Purchase Excursion*) APEX.
aphid ['eɪfɪd] *n* pulgón *m*.
aphorism ['æfərɪzm] *n* aforismo.
aphrodisiac [æfrə'dɪzɪæk] **1** *adj* afrodisíaco,-a. – **2** *n* afrodisíaco.
apiary ['eɪpɪərɪ] *n* colmenar *m*.
  ▲ *pl apiaries*.

apices ['eɪpɪsiːz] *npl* → **apex**.

apiece [ə'piːs] *adv* cada uno,-a: *she gave us three apiece,* nos dio tres a cada uno.

aplomb [ə'plɒm] *n* aplomo.

apocalypse [ə'pɒkəlɪps] *n* apocalipsis *m*.

apocalyptic [əpɒkə'lɪptɪk] *adj* apocalíptico,-a.

Apocrypha [ə'pɒkrɪfə] *n* textos *mpl* apócrifos.

apocryphal [ə'pɒkrɪfəl] *adj* imaginario,-a, inventado,-a.

apogee ['æpədʒiː] *n* apogeo.

apolitical [eɪpə'lɪtɪkəl] *adj* apolítico,-a.

apologetic [əpɒlə'dʒetɪk] *adj* compungido,-a, arrepentido,-a: *they were very apologetic about it,* se disculparon profusamente por lo ocurrido.

apologetically [əpɒlə'dʒetɪləlɪ] *adv* disculpándose.

apologize [ə'pɒlədʒaɪz] *i* disculparse, pedir perdón: *she apologized to the minister for making him wait,* se disculpó con el ministro por hacerlo esperar.

apology [ə'pɒlədʒɪ] **1** *n* (*for mistake*) disculpa: *I think I owe you an apology,* creo que debo pedirte disculpas. **2** *fml* (*of beliefs*) apología. **3** (*poor example*) remedo: *what an apology for a wedding cake,* vaya tarta nupcial más pobre.
● to offer one's apologies, disculparse.
▲ *pl* apologies.

apoplectic [æpə'plektɪk] **1** *adj* MED apoplético,-a. **2** (*angry*) furioso,-a.

apoplexy ['æpəpleksɪ] *n* apoplejía.
▲ *pl* apoplexies.

a posteriori [eɪpɒsterɪ'ɔːraɪ] *phr* a posteriori.

apostle [ə'pɒsəl] *n* apóstol *m*.

apostolic [æpə'stɒlɪk] *adj* apostólico,-a.

apostrophe [ə'pɒstrəfɪ] **1** *n* (*punctuation*) apóstrofo. **2** (*in rhetoric*) apóstrofe *m*.

apothecary [ə'pɒθəkərɪ] *n* apotecario,-a.
▲ *pl* apothecaries.

apotheosis [əpɒθɪ'əʊsɪs] *n* apoteosis *f*.

appal [ə'pɔːl] *t* horrorizar.
▲ *pt & pp* appalled, *ger* appalling.

Appalachians [æpə'leɪʃəns] the Appalachians, *n* los (montes) Apalaches *mpl*.

appall [ə'pɔːl] *t* US → **appal**.

appalling [ə'pɔːlɪŋ] **1** *adj* (*horrific*) horroroso,-a. **2** (*bad*) malísimo,-a.

appallingly [ə'pɔːlɪŋlɪ] *adv* (*horrific*) horriblemente, horrorosamente.

apparatus [æpə'reɪtəs] **1** *n* (*equipment*) aparatos *mpl*; (*piece of equipment*) aparato. **2** (*structure*) aparato.

apparel [ə'pærəl] *n* indumentaria.

apparent [ə'pærənt] **1** *adj* (*obvious*) evidente. **2** (*seeming*) aparente.

apparently [ə'pærəntlɪ] **1** *adv* (*obviously*) evidentemente. **2** (*seemingly*) aparentemente.

apparition [æpə'rɪʃən] *n* aparición *f*.

appeal [ə'piːl] **1** *n* (*request*) ruego, llamamiento; (*plea*) súplica. **2** (*for money*) campaña de recaudación de fondos. **3** (*attraction*) atractivo. **4** JUR apelación *f*. – **5** *i* (*request*) pedir, solicitar; (*plead*) suplicar: *she appealed for help,* pidió ayuda. **6** (*attract*) atraer: *it doesn't appeal to me,* no me atrae. **7** JUR apelar (**against,** -), recurrir (**against,** -): *they have decided to appeal against the sentence,* han decidido apelar la sentencia.

appealing [ə'piːlɪŋ] **1** *adj* (*moving*) suplicante. **2** (*attractive*) atrayente, atractivo,-a.

appealingly [ə'piːlɪŋlɪ] *adv* (*movingly*) de manera suplicante.

appear [ə'pɪəʳ] **1** *i* (*become visible*) aparecer. **2** (*before a court etc*) comparecer (**before,** ante). **3** (*on stage etc*) actuar. **4** (*seem*) parecer. **5** (*on TV, in film, in newspaper*) salir.
● so it appears / so it would appear, así parece.

appearance [ə'pɪərəns] **1** *n* (*becoming visible*) aparición *f*. **2** (*before a court etc*) comparecencia. **3** (*on stage*) actuación *f*. **4** (*look*) apariencia, aspecto.
● appearances can be deceptive, las apariencias engañan. ‖ to all appearances, por lo que parece (*parecía, etc*). ‖ to keep up appearances, guardar las apariencias. ‖ to put in an appearance, hacer acto de presencia.

appease [ə'piːz] *t* aplacar, calmar.

appeasement [ə'piːzmənt] *n* pacificación *f*.

append [ə'pend] *t* añadir (**to,** a).

appendage [ə'pendɪdʒ] *n* apéndice *m*, añadidura.

appendectomy [æpen'dektəmɪ] *n* apendicectomía.
▲ *pl* appendectomies.

appendicectomy [æpendɪ'sektəmɪ] *n* → **appendectomy**.
▲ *pl* appendicectomies.

appendices [ə'pendɪsiːz] *npl* → **appendix**.

appendicitis [əpendɪ'saɪtɪs] *n* apendicitis *f*.

appendix [ə'pendɪks] **1** *n* (*in book*) apéndice *m*. **2** MED apéndice *m*.
● to have one's appendix out, operarse de apendicitis.
▲ En *1* pl appendices; en *2* pl appendixes.

appertain [æpe'teɪn] *i* atañer (**to,** a).

appetite ['æpɪtaɪt] *n* apetito.

appetizer ['æpɪtaɪzəʳ] *n* aperitivo.

appetizing ['æpɪtaɪzɪŋ] *adj* apetitoso,-a.

applaud [ə'plɔːd] **1** *i* (*clap*) aplaudir. – **2** *t* (*clap*) aplaudir. **3** (*praise*) alabar.

applause [ə'plɔːz] *n* aplauso.

apple ['æpəl] *n* manzana.
● to be the apple of sb.'s eye, ser la niña de los ojos de algn.
■ apple green, verde *m* manzana. ‖ apple of discord, manzana de la discordia. ‖ apple pie, tarta de manzana. ‖ apple tree, manzano. ‖ cooking apple, manzana ácida. ‖ the Big Apple, Nueva York.

appliance [ə'plaɪəns] **1** *n* (*device*) aparato. **2** (*fire engine*) coche *m* de bomberos.

applicability [əplɪkə'bɪlɪtɪ] *n* aplicabilidad *f*.

applicable ['æplɪkəbəl] *adj* aplicable.

applicant ['æplɪkənt] *n* (*for job*) candidato,-a, aspirante *mf*, solicitante *mf*.

application [æplɪ'keɪʃən] **1** *n* (*for job*) solicitud *f*. **2** (*of ointment, theory, etc*) aplicación *f*. **3** (*effort*) diligencia.

applicator ['æplɪkaɪtəʳ] *n* aplicador *m*.

applied [ə'plaɪd] *adj* aplicado,-a.

apply [ə'plaɪ] **1** *t* (*ointment, theory, etc*) aplicar. – **2** *i* (*be true*) aplicarse, ser aplicable. **3** (*for job*) solicitar: *I applied for information,* pedí información.
● to apply os. to sth., aplicarse a algo, aplicarse en algo. ‖ to apply one's mind to sth., concentrarse en algo.
▲ *pt & pp* applied, *ger* applying.

appoint [ə'pɔɪnt] **1** *t* (*person for job*) nombrar. **2** (*day, date, etc*) fijar, señalar.

appointee [əpɔɪn'tiː] *n* persona nombrada.

appointment [ə'pɔɪntmənt] **1** *n* (*meeting - with lawyer etc*) cita; (- *with hairdresser, dentist, doctor*) hora: *she asked for an appointment with the doctor,* pidió hora con el médico; *he didn't keep the appointment,* no acudió a la cita. **2** (*person for job*) nombramiento.

apportion [ə'pɔːʃən] *t* repartir, distribuir.
● **to apportion blame to sb.**, echar la culpa a algn.
apportionment [ə'pɔːʃənmənt] *n* repartimiento, distribución *f.*
apposite ['æpəzɪt] *adj* apropiado,-a.
apposition [æpə'zɪʃən] *n* aposición *f.*
appraisal [ə'preɪzəl] *n* valoración, *f* evaluación *f.*
appraise [ə'preɪz] *t* valorar, evaluar.
appreciable [ə'priːʃəbəl] *adj* apreciable.
appreciably [ə'priːʃəblɪ] *adv* perceptiblemente, de manera apreciable.
appreciate [ə'priːʃɪeɪt] 1 *t* (*be thankful for*) agradecer. 2 (*understand*) entender, comprender. 3 (*value*) valorar, apreciar. – 4 *i* revalorizarse, valorizarse.
appreciation [əpriːʃɪ'eɪʃən] 1 *n* (*thanks*) agradecimiento, gratitud *f.* 2 (*understanding*) comprensión *f.* 3 (*appraisal*) evaluación *f.* 4 (*increase in value*) apreciación *f,* aumento en valor.
apprehend [æprɪ'hend] 1 *t* (*arrest*) detener, capturar. 2 (*understand*) comprender.
apprehension [æprɪ'henʃən] 1 *n* (*arrest*) detención *f,* captura. 2 (*fear*) aprensión *f,* temor *m,* recelo.
apprehensive [æprɪ'hensɪv] *adj* (*fearful*) aprensivo,-a, temeroso,-a, receloso,-a.
apprehensively [æprɪ'hensɪvlɪ] *adv* con aprensión.
apprentice [ə'prentɪs] *n* aprendiz,-za.
● **to apprentice sb. to sb.**, poner a algn. como aprendiz,-za con algn.: *he was apprenticed to a carpenter*, lo pusieron de aprendiz con un carpintero.
apprenticeship [ə'prentɪsʃɪp] *n* aprendizaje *m.*
apprise [ə'praɪz] *t* informar (**of**, de): *the minister must be apprised of this*, al ministro hay que informarlo de esto.
approach [ə'prəʊtʃ] 1 *n* (*coming near*) aproximación *f,* acercamiento; (*arrival*) llegada. 2 (*way in*) acceso, entrada. 3 (*to problem*) enfoque *m*: *we have to try a different approach to the problem*, deberíamos intentar un enfoque diferente del problema. – 4 *i* (*come near*) acercarse, aproximarse. – 5 *t* (*come near*) acercarse a, aproximarse a. 6 (*tackle - problem*) enfocar, abordar; (-*person*) dirigirse a.
● **to make approaches to sb.**, hacer propuestas a algn.
■ **approach road**, vía de acceso.
approachable [ə'prəʊtʃəbəl] 1 *adj* (*person*) tratable, accesible. 2 (*place*) accesible.
approaching [ə'prəʊtʃɪŋ] *adj* que se acerca.
approbation [æprə'beɪʃən] *n* aprobación *f.*
appropriate [ə'prəʊprɪət] 1 *adj* apropiado,-a, adecuado,-a, indicado,-a. – 2 *t* (*allocate*) asignar, destinar. 3 (*steal*) apropiarse de.
● **at the appropriate time**, en el momento oportuno.
▲ (*verbo*) [ə'prəʊprɪeɪt].
appropriation [əprəʊprɪ'eɪʃən] 1 *n* (*allocation*) asignación *f.* 2 (*sum of money*) partida. 3 (*seizure*) apropiación *f.*
approval [ə'pruːvəl] *n* aprobación *f,* visto bueno, beneplácito.
● **on approval**, a prueba. ‖ **to give one's approval**, dar el visto bueno. ‖ **to meet with sb.'s approval**, merecer la aprobación de algn.
approve [ə'pruːv] *t* aprobar, dar el visto bueno a.
◆ **to approve of** *t insep* aprobar, estar de acuerdo con, ver con buenos ojos.
approving [ə'pruːvɪŋ] *adj* de aprobación.
approvingly [ə'pruːvɪŋlɪ] *adv* con aprobación.
approx [ə'prɒks] 1 *abbr* (*approximate*) aproximado,-a. 2 (*approximately*) aproximadamente.

approximate [ə'prɒksɪmət] 1 *adj* aproximado,-a. – 2 *i* aproximarse (**to**, a).
▲ (*verbo*) [ə'prɒksɪmeɪt].
approximately [ə'prɒksɪmətlɪ] *adv* aproximadamente.
approximation [əprɒksɪ'meɪʃən] *n* aproximación *f.*
appurtenances [ə'pɜːtɪnənsɪz] 1 *npl* (*accessories*) accesorios *mpl.* 2 (*rights*) derechos *mpl,* privilegios *mpl.*
Apr ['eɪprɪl] *abbr* (*April*) abril.
après-ski [æpreɪ'skiː] 1 *n* après-ski *m.* – 2 *adj* de après-ski.
apricot ['eɪprɪkɒt] 1 *n* (*fruit*) albaricoque *m.* 2 (*colour*) color *m* asalmonado: *an apricot hat*, un sombrero de color asalmonado.
■ **apricot jam**, mermelada de albaricoque. ‖ **apricot tree**, albaricoquero.
April ['eɪprɪl] *n* abril *m.*
■ **April Fool**, inocente *mf.* ‖ **April Fool's Day**, el día 1 de abril (≈ día de los Santos Inocentes).
▲ *Véase también* May.
a priori [eɪpraɪ'ɔːraɪ] *phr* a priori.
apron ['eɪprən] 1 *n* (*garment - domestic*) delantal *m*; (-*workman's*) mandil *m.* 2 (*at airport*) pista de estacionamiento. 3 (*in theatre*) proscenio.
● **to be tied to sb.'s apron strings**, estar pegado,-a a las faldas de algn.
apropos ['æprəpəʊ] 1 *adj* oportuno,-a. – 2 **apropos of**, *prep* a propósito de.
apse [æps] *n* ábside *m.*
apt [æpt] 1 *adj* (*suitable*) apropiado,-a; (*remark*) acertado,-a. 2 (*liable to*) propenso,-a: *she's apt to faint*, es propensa a desmayarse.
APT ['eɪ'piː'tiː] *abbr* GB (*Advanced Passenger Train*) ≈ AVE *m.*
apt. [ə'pɑːtmənt] *abbr* (*apartment*) apartamento, piso.
aptitude ['æptɪtjuːd] *n* aptitud *f.*
■ **aptitude test**, prueba de aptitud.
aptly ['æptlɪ] *adv* adecuadamente, acertadamente.
aptness ['æptnəs] *n* lo acertado.
Aqualung ['ækwəlʌŋ] *n* escafandra autónoma.
▲ *Es marca registrada.*
aquamarine [ækwəmə'riːn] 1 *n* (*stone*) aguamarina. 2 (*colour*) color *m* aguamarina.
aquaplane ['ækwəpleɪn] 1 *n* esquí *m* acuático. – 2 *i* (*person*) hacer esquí acuático (*con un solo esquí*). 3 (*car*) patinar.
aquarium [ə'kweərɪəm] *n* acuario.
▲ *pl* aquaria *o* aquariums.
Aquarius [ə'kweərɪəs] *n* Acuario.
aquatic [ə'kwætɪk] *adj* acuático,-a.
aquatint ['ækwətɪnt] *n* aguatinta.
aqueduct ['ækwɪdʌkt] *n* acueducto.
aqueous ['ækwɪəs] *adj* (*like water*) acuoso.
aquiline ['ækwɪlaɪn] *adj* aguileño,-a.
Arab ['ærəb] 1 *adj* árabe. – 2 *n* (*person*) árabe *mf.*
arabesque [ærə'besk] *n* arabesco.
Arabia [ə'reɪbɪə] *n* Arabia.
Arabian [ə'reɪbɪən] 1 *adj* árabe, arábigo,-a. – 2 *n* árabe *mf.*
■ **Arabian Peninsula**, Península Arábiga. ‖ **Arabian Sea**, Mar *m* Arábigo. ‖ **the Arabian Nights**, las mil y una noches *fpl.*
Arabic ['ærəbɪk] 1 *adj* Árabe. – 2 *n* (*language*) Árabe *m.*
■ **arabic numerals**, números *mpl* arábigos. ‖ **gum Arabic**, goma arábiga.
Arabist ['ærəbɪst] *n* arabista *mf.*

arable ['ærəbəl] *adj* cultivable.
arachnid [ə'ræ knɪd] *n* arácnido.
Aragon ['ærəg n] *n* Aragón *m.*
Aragonese [æ əgə'niːz] **1** *adj* aragonés,-esa. – **2** *n* aragonés,-esa. – **3 the Aragonese,** *npl* los aragoneses *mpl.*
Aral ['ærəl] **Aral Sea,** *n* Mar *m* de Aral.
arbiter ['ɑːbɪtəʳ] *n* árbitro,-a.
arbitrarily [ɑːbɪ'trerəlɪ] *adv* arbitrariamente.
arbitrariness ['ɑːbɪtrərɪnəs] *n* arbitrariedad *f.*
arbitrary ['ɑːbɪtrərɪ] *adj* arbitrario,-a.
arbitrate ['ɑːbɪtreɪt] **1** *t* arbitrar. – **2** *i* arbitrar.
arbitration [ɑːbɪ'treɪʃən] *n* arbitraje *m.*
arbitrator ['ɑːbɪtreɪtəʳ] *n* árbitro,-a.
arbor ['ɑːbəʳ] *n* us → **arbour.**
arboretum [ɑːbə'riːtəm] *n* arboreto.
arbour ['ɑːbəʳ] *n* cenador *m.*
arc [ɑːk] **1** *n* arco. **2** ELEC arco voltaico.
arcade [ɑː'keɪd] *n* pasaje *m.*
  ■ **shopping arcade,** galerías *fpl* comerciales.
arcane [ɑː'keɪn] *adj* arcano,-a, misterioso,-a.
arch[1] [ɑːtʃ] **1** *n* ARCH arco; (*vault*) bóveda. **2** (*of foot*) empeine *m*: *he's got fallen arches,* tiene los pies planos. – **3** *t* (*back, eyebrows*) arquear, enarcar. **4** (*vault*) abovedar. – **5** *i* (*back, eyebrows*) arquearse. **6** (*vault*) formar bóveda.
arch[2] [ɑːtʃ] *adj* pícaro,-a.
archaeological [ɑːkɪə'lɒdʒɪkəl] *adj* arqueológico,-a.
archaeologist [ɑːkɪ'ɒlədʒɪst] *n* arqueólogo,-a.
archaeology [ɑːkɪ'ɒlədʒɪ] *n* arqueología.
archaic [ɑː'keɪɪk] *adj* arcaico,-a.
archaism ['ɑːkeɪɪzəm] *n* arcaísmo.
archangel [ɑː'keɪndʒəl] *n* arcángel *m.*
archbishop [ɑːtʃ'bɪʃəp] *n* arzobispo.
archbishopric [ɑːtʃ'bɪʃəprɪk] *n* arzobispado.
archdeacon [ɑːtʃ'diːkən] *n* archidiácono.
archdiocese [ɑːtʃ'daɪəsɪs] *n* archidiócesis *f.*
archduchess [ɑːtʃ'dʌtʃəs] *n* archiduquesa.
archduchy [ɑːtʃ'dʌtʃɪ] *n* archiducado.
  ▲ *pl* **archduchies.**
archduke [ɑːtʃ'djuːk] *n* archiduque *m.*
arch-enemy [ɑːtʃ'enəmɪ] *n* archienemigo,-a.
  ▲ *pl* **arch-enemies.**
archeological [ɑːkɪə'lɒdʒɪkəl] *adj* us → **archaeological.**
archeologist [ɑːkɪ'ɒlədʒɪst] *n* us → **archaeologist.**
archeology [ɑːkɪ'ɒlədʒɪ] *n* us → **archaeology.**
archer ['ɑːtʃəʳ] *n* arquero.
archery ['ɑːtʃərɪ] *n* tiro con arco.
archetypal [ɑːkɪ'taɪpəl] *adj* arquetípico,-a.
archetype ['ɑːkɪtaɪp] *n* arquetipo.
archipelago [ɑːkɪ'pelɪgəʊ] *n* archipiélago.
  ▲ *pl* **archipelagos** o **archipelagoes.**
architect ['ɑːkɪtekt] **1** *n* (*of buildings*) arquitecto,-a. **2** (*person responsible*) artífice *mf.*
architectural [ɑːkɪ'tektʃərəl] *adj* arquitectónico,-a.
architecture ['ɑːkɪtektʃəʳ] *n* arquitectura.
archives ['ɑːkaɪvz] *npl* archivo *m sing.*
archivist ['ɑːkaɪvɪst] *n* archivero,-a.
archway ['ɑːtʃweɪ] *n* arco.
Arctic ['ɑːktɪk] **1** *adj* ártico,-a. – **2 the Arctic,** *n* el Ártico.
  ■ **the Arctic Circle,** el Círculo Polar Ártico. ‖ **the Arctic Ocean,** el océano Ártico.
ardent ['ɑːdənt] *adj* apasionado,-a, fervoroso,-a.
ardently ['ɑːdəntlɪ] *adv* apasionadamente, fervorosamente.

ardor ['ɑːdəʳ] *n* us → **ardour.**
ardour ['ɑːdəʳ] *n* ardor *m.*
arduous ['ɑːdjʊəs] *adj* arduo,-a.
are [ɑːʳ, əʳ] 2nd *pers sing,* 1st, 2nd *and* 3rd *pers pl pres indic* → **be.**
area ['eərɪə] **1** *n* (*extent*) área, superficie *f*: *calculate the area of this rectangle,* calcula el área de este rectángulo; *the room has a floor area of 50 square metres,* la sala tiene una superficie de 50 metros cuadrados. **2** (*region*) región *f*; (*of town*) zona: *we live in a quiet area,* vivimos en una zona tranquila. **3** (*field*) campo.
arena [ə'riːnə] **1** *n* (*stadium*) estadio. **2** (*in amphitheatre*) arena. **3** *fig* ámbito.
aren't [ɑːnt] *contr* → **are not.**
Argentina [ɑːdʒən'tiːnə] *n* Argentina.
Argentine ['ɑːdʒəntaɪn] **1** *adj* argentino,-a. – **2 the Argentine,** *n* Argentina.
Argentinian [ɑːdʒən'tɪnɪən] **1** *adj* argentino,-a. – **2** *n* argentino,-a.
argon ['ɑːgɒn] *n* argón *m.*
argot ['ɑːgəʊ] *n* jerga.
arguable ['ɑːgjʊəbəl] *adj* discutible.
arguably ['ɑːgjʊəblɪ] *adv* posiblemente.
argue ['ɑːgjuː] **1** *i* (*quarrel*) discutir (**with,** con): *she's always arguing with her husband about politics,* siempre discute con su marido sobre política. **2** (*reason*) argüir, argumentar, sostener: *he argues that we should invest more,* sostiene que debemos invertir más. – **3** *t* (*present*) presentar, exponer.
  ◆ **to argue for** *t insep* abogar por, argumentar a favor de: *he argues for more investment,* aboga por una mayor inversión. ‖ **to argue against** *t insep* argumentar en contra de.
  ● **to argue the toss,** discutir, seguir discutiendo.
argument ['ɑːgjʊmənt] **1** *n* (*quarrel*) discusión *f*, disputa. **2** (*reasoning*) argumento.
  ● **for the sake of argument,** por decir algo. ‖ **to have an argument with sb.,** discutir con algn., tener una discusión con algn.
argumentation [ɑːgjʊmən'teɪʃən] *n* argumentación *f*, razonamiento.
argumentative [ɑːgjʊ'mentətɪv] *adj* que discute, que replica.
argy-bargy [ɑːdʒɪ'bɑːdʒɪ] *n* GB *fam* discusiones *fpl.*
aria ['ɑːrɪə] *n* aria.
arid ['ærɪd] *adj* árido,-a.
aridity [ə'rɪdɪtɪ] *n* aridez *f.*
Aries ['eəriːz] **1** *n* (*sign*) Aries *m.* **2** (*person*) Aries *mf.*
aright [ə'taɪt] *adv* bien.
arise [ə'raɪz] **1** *i* (*occur*) surgir (**from,** de). **2** *arch* (*get up*) levantarse; (*stand up*) ponerse de pie.
  ▲ *pt* **arose,** *pp* **arisen** [ə'rɪzən].
aristocracy [ærɪs'tɒkrəsɪ] *n* aristocracia.
  ▲ *pl* **aristocracies.**
aristocrat ['ærɪstəkræt, *ʲe* ə'rɪstəkræt] *n* aristócrata *mf.*
aristocratic [ærɪstə'krætɪk] *adj* aristocrático,-a.
arithmetic [ə'rɪθmətɪk] **1** *n* aritmética. – **2** *adj* aritmético,-a.
  ▲ (*adjetivo*) [ærɪθ'metɪk].
arithmetical [ærɪθ'metɪkəl] *adj* aritmético,-a.
  ■ **arithmetical progression,** progresión *f* aritmética.
arithmetician [ərɪθmə'tɪʃən] *n* aritmético,-a.
ark [ɑːk] *n* arca.
  ■ **Ark of the Covenant,** Arca de la alianza.
arm [ɑːm] **1** *n* ANAT brazo. **2** (*of coat etc*) manga. **3** (*of chair*) brazo. **4** (*of organization*) rama. – **5** *t* armar. – **6** *i* armarse.
  – **7 arms,** *npl* (*weapons*) armas *fpl.*

● **arm in arm**, cogidos,-as del brazo. ‖ **with open arms**, con los brazos abiertos. ‖ **to be up in arms about sth.**, estar furioso,-a por algo. ‖ **to keep sb. at arm's length**, mantener a algn. a distancia.
■ **arms control**, control *m* armamentístico. ‖ **arms race**, carrera armamentística.

armada [ɑːˈmɑːdə] *n* armada, flota.
■ **the Spanish Armada**, la Armada Invencible.

armadillo [ɑːməˈdɪləʊ] *n* armadillo.
▲ *pl armadillos*.

Armageddon [ɑːməˈgedən] *n* guerra del fin del mundo.

armaments [ˈɑːməmənts] *npl* armamentos *mpl*.

armature [ˈɑːmətʃə] *n* armadura.

armband [ˈɑːmbænd] **1** *n* MIL brazalete *m*. **2** (*for swimming*) flotador *m*.

armchair [ˈɑːmtʃeə'] *n* sillón *m*.

armed [ɑːmd] *adj* armado,-a.
● **armed to the teeth**, armado,-a hasta los dientes.
■ **armed forces**, fuerzas *fpl* armadas. ‖ **armed robbery**, robo a mano armada.

Armenia [ɑːˈmiːnɪə] *n* Armenia.

Armenian [ɑːˈmiːnɪən] **1** *adj* armenio,-a. – **2** *n* (*person*) armenio,-a. **3** (*language*) armenio.

armful [ˈɑːmfʊl] *n* brazada, brazado: *she came round with an armful of gladioli*, se presentó en casa con un montón de gladiolos.

armhole [ˈɑːmhəʊl] *n* sisa.

armistice [ˈɑːmɪstɪs] *n* armisticio.

armor [ˈɑːmə'] *n* US → **armour**.

armored [ˈɑːməd] *adj* US → **armoured**.

armorial [ɑːˈmɔːrɪəl] *adj* heráldico,-a.

armor-plated [ˈɑːməˈpleɪtɪd] *adj* → **armour-plated**.

armory [ˈɑːmərɪ] *n* US → **armoury**.
▲ *pl armories*.

armour [ˈɑːmə'] **1** *n* armadura. **2** (*on vehicle*) blindaje *m*.

armoured [ˈɑːməd] **1** *adj* (*column etc*) acorazado,-a. **2** (*vehicle*) blindado,-a.
■ **armoured car**, carro blindado.

armour-plated [ˈɑːməˈpleɪtɪd] *adj* blindado,-a, acorazado,-a.

armoury [ˈɑːmərɪ] *n* armería.
▲ *pl armouries*.

armpit [ˈɑːmpɪt] *n* sobaco, axila.

armrest [ˈɑːmrest] *n* brazo.

army [ˈɑːmɪ] *n* ejército.
● **to join the army**, alistarse en el ejército.
▲ *pl armies*.

aroma [əˈrəʊmə] *n* aroma *m*.

aromatherapist [ərəʊməˈθerəpɪst] *n* aromaterapeuta *mf*.

aromatherapy [ərəʊməˈθerəpɪ] *n* aromaterapia.

aromatic [ærəˈmætɪk] *adj* aromático,-a.

arose [əˈrəʊz] *pt* → **arise**.

around [əˈraʊnd] **1** *adv* (*near, in the area*) alrededor: *is there anybody around?*, ¿hay alguien cerca?; *don't leave your money around*, *put it away*, no dejes tu dinero por ahí, guárdalo; *have a look around*, echa un vistazo. **2** (*from place to place*): *they cycle around together*, van juntos en bicicleta; *he's been around*, *he knows what's what*, ha visto mundo, sabe de qué va la cosa. **3** (*available, in existence*): *£1 coins have been around for some time*, hace tiempo que circulan las monedas de una libra; *there isn't much fresh fruit around*, hay poca fruta fresca. **4** (*to face the opposite way*): *turn around please*, dése

la vuelta por favor. **5** (*approximately*) alrededor de: *it costs around £5,000*, cuesta unas cinco mil libras. – **6** *prep* (*near*): *there aren't many shops around here*, hay pocas tiendas por aquí. **7** (*all over*): *there were clothes around the room*, había ropa por toda la habitación. **8** (*in a circle or curve*) alrededor de: *they travelled around the world*, dieron la vuelta al mundo; *he put his arms around her*, la rodeó con los brazos. **9** (*at*) sobre, cerca de: *they came around seven*, vinieron sobre las siete.
● **around the corner**, a la vuelta de la esquina.

arousal [əˈraʊzəl] *n* excitación *f*.

arouse [əˈraʊz] **1** *t* (*awake*) despertar. **2** (*sexually*) excitar.

arpeggio [ɑːˈpedʒɪəʊ] *n* arpegio.
▲ *pl arpeggios*.

arr.[1] [əˈraɪvəl] *abbr* (*arrival*) llegada.

arr.[2] [əˈreɪndʒdbaɪ] *abbr* MUS (*arranged by*) con arreglos de.

arrange [əˈreɪndʒ] **1** *t* (*hair, flowers*) arreglar; (*furniture etc*) colocar, ordenar. **2** (*plan*) planear, organizar. **3** (*music*) arreglar. **4** (*marriage*) concertar. **5** (*agree on*) acordar: *we arranged a time for the meeting*, acordamos una hora para la reunión. **6** (*take care of*) arreglar, encargarse de: *they will arrange everything*, ellos se encargarán de todo. – **7** *i* hacer preparativos: *I'll arrange for a car for you*, les buscaré un coche; *we've arranged to have the house redecorated*, lo hemos arreglado para que nos redecoren la casa.
● **to arrange to do sth.**, quedar en hacer algo.

arrangement [əˈreɪndʒmənt] **1** *n* (*of flowers*) arreglo; arreglo floral. **2** (*agreement*) acuerdo, arreglo. **3** MUS arreglo. – **4 arrangements**, *npl* (*plans*) planes *mpl*; (*preparations*) preparativos *mpl*.
● **to make arrangements**, hacer los preparativos.

arrant [ˈærənt] *adj* total, absoluto,-a.

array [eˈreɪ] **1** *n* (*selection*) surtido. **2** (*series*) serie *f*. **3** COMPUT matriz *f*. – **4** *t* (*things*) disponer; (*soldiers*) formar.
● **in battle array**, en orden de batalla.

arrears [əˈrɪəz] *npl* atrasos *mpl*.
● **to be in arrears with sth.**, estar atrasado,-a con algo. ‖ **to be paid in arrears**, cobrar por períodos vencidos.

arrest [əˈrest] **1** *n* arresto, detención *f*. – **2** *t* arrestar, detener. **3** *fml* (*stop*) detener.
● **to arrest sb.'s attention**, llamar la atención a algn. ‖ **to be under arrest**, estar detenido,-a, estar bajo arresto. ‖ **to place sb. under arrest**, detener a algn.

arresting [əˈrestɪŋ] *adj* llamativo,-a.

arrival [əˈraɪvəl] *n* llegada.
■ **late arrival**, persona que llega tarde: *late arrivals will not be admitted*, no se permitirá la entrada a los que lleguen tarde. ‖ **new arrival**, (*person*) recién llegado,-a; (*baby*) recién nacido,-a.

arrive [əˈraɪv] **1** *i* llegar: *he arrived at work in a taxi*, llegó al trabajo en taxi; *she arrived home yesterday*, llegó a casa ayer; *I'll arrive in Paris in the evening*, llegaré a París por la tarde. **2** (*be born*) nacer.
◆ **to arrive at** *t insep* llegar a: *we can't arrive at a decision*, no llegamos a una decisión.

arrogance [ˈærəgəns] *n* arrogancia.

arrogant [ˈærəgənt] *adj* arrogante.

arrogantly [ˈærəgəntlɪ] *adv* con arrogancia.

arrogate [ˈærəgeɪt] *t* atribuir.
● **to arrogate sth. to os.**, arrogarse algo.

arrow [ˈærəʊ] *n* flecha.

arrowroot [ˈærəʊruːt] *n* arrurruz *m*.

arse [ɑːs] **1** *n* taboo (*part of body*) culo.
◆ **to arse about / arse around** *i* taboo hacer el idiota.

● **not to know one's arse from one's elbow**, *taboo* no tener ni puta idea.
arsehole [ˈɑːshəʊl] **1** *n taboo* (*anus*) ano. **2** *taboo* (*person*) gilipollas *mf*.
arselicker [ˈɑːslɪkəʳ] *n taboo* lameculos *mf*.
arsenal [ˈɑːsənəl] *n* arsenal *m*.
arsenic [ˈɑːsənɪk] *n* arsénico.
arson [ˈɑːsən] *n* incendio provocado.
arsonist [ˈɑːsənɪst] *n* incendiario,-a, pirómano,-a.
art[1] [ɑːt] **1** *n* (*painting etc*) arte *m*. **2** (*skill*) arte *m*, habilidad *f*. – **3 arts**, *npl* (*branch of knowledge*) letras *fpl*.
■ **art dealer**, marchante *m*. ‖ **art deco**, art deco *m*. ‖ **art exhibition**, exposición *f* de obras de arte. ‖ **art gallery**, (*museum*) pinacoteca; (*commercial*) galería de arte. ‖ **art nouveau**, art nouveau *m*, modernismo.
art[2] [ɑːt] 2ⁿᵈ *pers sing arch* → **be**.
artefact [ˈɑːtɪfækt] *n* artefacto.
arterial [ɑːˈtɪərɪəl] **1** *adj* ANAT arterial. **2** (*road*) principal, importante.
arteriosclerosis [ɑːtɪərəʊsklɪəˈrəʊsɪs] *n* arteriosclerosis *f*.
artery [ˈɑːtɪərɪ] *n* ANAT arteria.
▲ *pl* **arteries**.
artesian well [ɑːtiːzɪənˈwel] *n* pozo artesiano.
artful [ˈɑːtfʊl] *n* (*person*) ladino,-a, astuto,-a; (*thing*) ingenioso,-a.
arthritic [ɑːθˈrɪtɪk] *adj* artrítico,-a.
arthritis [ɑːθˈraɪtəs] *n* artritis *f*.
artichoke [ˈɑːtɪtʃəʊk] *n* alcachofa.
■ **globe artichoke**, alcachofa. ‖ **Jerusalem artichoke**, aguaturma, pataca.
article [ˈɑːtɪkəl] **1** *n* artículo. **2** LING artículo. – **3 articles**, *npl* contrato de aprendizaje.
● **to be articled to a firm of solicitors**, ser abogado,-a en prácticas con un gabinete de abogados.
■ **article of clothing**, prenda de vestir. ‖ **definite article**, artículo determinado. ‖ **indefinite article**, artículo indeterminado. ‖ **leading article**, editorial *m*.
articled clerk [ɑːtɪkəldˈklɑːk] *n* abogado,-a en prácticas.
articulate [ɑːˈtɪkjʊlət] **1** *adj* (*person*) que se expresa con facilidad; (*speech*) claro,-a. – **2** *t* articular. **3** (*pronounce*) pronunciar.
▲ (*verbo*) [ɑːˈtɪkjʊleɪt].
articulated [ɑːˈtɪkjʊleɪtɪd] *adj* articulado,-a.
■ **articulated lorry**, camión *m* articulado.
articulately [ɑːˈtɪkjʊlətlɪ] *adv* con fluidez, con elocuencia.
articulateness [ɑːˈtɪkjʊlətnəs] *n* fluidez *f*, elocuencia.
articulation [ɑːtɪkjuˈleɪʃən] **1** *n* (*of sound*) articulación *f*. **2** (*of idea*) expresión *f*. **3** (*joint*) articulación *f*.
artifact [ˈɑːtɪfækt] *n* US → **artefact**.
artifice [ˈɑːtɪfɪs] **1** *n* (*trick*) artificio. **2** (*cunning*) astucia.
artificer [ɑːˈtɪfɪsəʳ] *n* artificiero.
artificial [ɑːtɪˈfɪʃəl] **1** *adj* (*flowers, light, etc*) artificial. **2** (*limb*) ortopédico,-a; (*hair*) postizo,-a. **3** (*smile etc*) afectado,-a, fingido,-a.
■ **artificial insemination**, inseminación *f* artificial. ‖ **artificial intelligence**, inteligencia artificial. ‖ **artificial respiration**, respiración *f* artificial.
artificiality [ɑːtɪfɪʃɪˈælɪt] *n* artificialidad *f*.
artificially [ɑːtɪˈfɪʃəlɪ] *adv* de modo artificial.
artillery [ɑːˈtɪlərɪ] *n* artillería.
artisan [ˈɑːtɪzæn] *n* artesano,-a.
artist [ˈɑːtɪst] **1** *n* artista *mf*. **2** (*painter*) pintor,-ra.

artiste [ɑːˈtiːst] *n* artista *mf*.
artistic [ɑːˈtɪstɪk] *adj* artístico,-a.
artistry [ˈɑːtɪstrɪ] *n* maestría.
artless [ˈɑːtləs] *adj* ingenuo,-a, sencillo,-a.
artlessness [ˈɑːtləsnəs] *n* ingenuidad *f*, sencillez *f*.
artwork [ˈɑːtwɜːk] *n* ilustraciones *fpl*.
Aryan [ˈeərɪən] **1** *adj* ario,-a. – **2** *n* ario,-a.
as [æz, *unstressed* əz] **1** *prep* como: *he works as a clerk*, trabaja de oficinista; *she was dressed as a monkey*, iba disfrazada de mono; *as a child he was often ill*, de niño a menudo estuvo enfermo. – **2** *adv* (*in comparatives*): *this is not as good as his last film*, ésta no es tan buena como su última película; *eat as much as you like*, come tanto como quieras; *this is twice as expensive as the other*, éste es dos veces más caro que el otro. – **3** *conj* (*while*) mientras; (*when*) cuando: *as he painted, he whistled*, mientras pintaba, silbaba; *as I shut the door I realized I'd left the keys inside*, al cerrar la puerta me di cuenta de que había dejado las llaves dentro; *as he grew older he became more tolerant*, a medida que iba envejeciendo se volvía más tolerante. **4** (*because*) ya que, como: *as there were no seats we had to stand*, como no había asientos tuvimos que estar de pie. **5** (*although*) aunque: *tall as he was, he still couldn't reach the shelf*, aunque era alto no podía alcanzar el estante. **6** (*showing manner*): *everything is just as she left it*, todo está tal como ella lo dejó; *as I was saying, ...*, como decía, ...; *do as you are told!*, ¡haz lo que te dicen!; *as you all know, ...*, como ya sabéis todos, ... **7** (*and so too*) como, igual que: *she's colour-blind, as is her mother*, es daltónica, igual que su madre.
● **as against**, frente a, en comparación con. ‖ **as far as**, hasta. ‖ **as far as I know**, que yo sepa. ‖ **as far as I'm concerned**, por lo que a mí respecta. ‖ **as for**, en cuanto a. ‖ **as if**, como si. ‖ **as it is**, tal como están las cosas. ‖ **as it were**, por así decirlo. ‖ **as long as**, mientras. ‖ **as of**, desde. ‖ **as often as not**, las más de las veces. ‖ **as soon as**, tan pronto como. ‖ **as though**, como si. ‖ **as well as**, además de. ‖ **as yet**, hasta ahora, de momento.
ASA[1] [ˈeɪesˈeɪ] *abbr* US (*American Standards Association*) ASA.
ASA[2] [ˈeɪesˈeɪ] *abbr* GB (*Advertising Standards Authority*) organismo que regula la publicidad.
ASA[3] [ˈeɪesˈeɪ] *abbr* GB (*Amateur Swimming Association*) federación de natación amateur.
a.s.a.p. [ˈeɪesˈeɪpiː] *abbr* (*as soon as possible*) tan pronto como sea posible.
asbestos [æsˈbestəs] *n* amianto, asbesto.
asbestosis [æsbesˈtəʊsɪs] *n* asbestosis *f*.
ascend [əˈsend] **1** *t* ascender, subir a. – **2** *i* ascender, subir.
● **to ascend the throne**, subir al trono.
ascendancy [əˈsendənsɪ] *n* predominio, supremacía.
▲ *pl* **ascendancies**.
ascendant [əˈsendənt] *n* ascendiente *m*.
● **to be in the ascendant**, estar en auge.
ascendency [əˈsendənsɪ] *n* → **ascendancy**.
▲ *pl* **ascendencies**.
ascendent [əˈsendənt] *n* → **ascendant**.
ascension [əˈsenʃən] *n* ascensión *f*.
■ **Ascension Day**, Día *m* de la Ascensión. ‖ **Ascension Island**, Isla de la Ascensión.
ascent [əˈsent] **1** *n* (*slope*) subida. **2** (*climb*) ascensión *f*.
ascertain [æsəˈteɪn] *t* averiguar.
ascetic [əˈsetɪk] **1** *adj* ascético,-a. – **2** *n* asceta *mf*.

asceticism [ə'setɪsɪzəm] n ascetismo.
ASCII ['æski:] abbr (American standard code for information interchange) ASCII.
ascorbic acid [əskɔːbɪk'æsɪd] n ácido ascórbico.
ascribe [əs'kraɪb] t atribuir (**to**, a).
ascription [ə'skrɪpʃən] n atribución f.
ASEAN ['æsɪæn] abbr (Association of South East Asian Nations) Asociación f de Naciones del Sureste Asiático; (abbreviation) ASEAN.
asepsis [ə'sepsɪs] n asepsia.
aseptic [ə'septɪk] adj aséptico,-a.
asexual [eɪ'sekʃuəl] adj asexual.
asexuality [eɪsekʃu'lɪtɪ] n asexualidad f.
ash¹ [æʃ] 1 n ceniza. – 2 **ashes,** npl cenizas fpl.
■ **Ash Wednesday,** miércoles m de ceniza.
ash² [æʃ] n (tree) fresno; (wood) madera de fresno.
■ **ash tree,** fresno. ‖ **ash grove,** fresneda.
ASH [æʃ] abbr GB (Action on Smoking and Health) organización anti-tabaco.
ashamed [ə'ʃeɪmd] adj avergonzado,-a.
● **to be ashamed of ...,** avergonzarse de ..., tener vergüenza de ...
ashbin ['æʃbɪn] n US cubo de la basura.
ashcan ['æʃkæn] n US → **ashbin.**
ashen ['æʃən] adj pálido,-a.
ashore [ə'ʃɔːʳ] adv (position) en tierra; (movement) a tierra.
● **to go ashore,** desembarcar. ‖ **to put sb. ashore,** desembarcar a algn.
ashtray ['æʃtreɪ] n cenicero.
Asia ['eɪʃə, 'eɪʒə] n Asia.
■ **Asia Minor,** Asia Menor.
Asian ['eɪʃən, 'eɪʒən] 1 adj asiático,-a. – 2 n asiático,-a.
Asiatic [eɪʃɪ'ætɪk, eɪʒɪ'ætɪk] adj asiático,-a.
aside [ə'saɪd] 1 adv al lado, a un lado. – 2 n (comment - gen) inciso; (-in theatre) aparte m.
● **aside from,** aparte de. ‖ **to cast aside,** echar a un lado. ‖ **to set aside,** apartar, reservar. ‖ **to step aside,** apartarse. ‖ **to take sb. aside,** separar a algn. (del grupo) para hablar aparte.
asimilable [ə'sɪmɪləbəl] adj asimilable.
asinine ['æsɪnaɪn] adj estúpido,-a.
ask [ɑːsk] 1 t (inquire) preguntar: she asked me my name, preguntó mi nombre; ask any questions you like, pregunta lo que quieras; ask him what he wants, pregúntale qué quiere. 2 (request) pedir: we have to ask permission, debemos pedir permiso; I asked him to help me, le pedí que me ayudara. 3 (invite) invitar, convidar: we'll ask Peter to dinner, convidaremos a Peter a cenar; he asked her to go out with him, la invitó a salir con él; she asked me round to her flat, me invitó a su piso. – 4 i (inquire) preguntar: if you don't know, ask, si no lo sabes, pregúntalo. 5 (request) pedir: she asked to speak to the boss, pidió hablar con el jefe.
◆ **to ask after** t insep preguntar por: I saw Helen, she asked after you, vi a Helen, preguntó por ti. ‖ **to ask around** 1 i (inquire) preguntar por ahí. ‖ **to ask back** 1 t sep (invite home) invitar a casa. 2 (return invitation) devolver la invitación a. ‖ **to ask for** t insep (thing) pedir; (person) preguntar por: he asked for a wage rise, pidió un aumento de sueldo; there's a man on the phone asking for Terry, hay un señor al teléfono que pregunta por Terry. ‖ **to ask out** t sep invitar a salir.
● **to ask for it,** buscárselo. ‖ **to be asking for trouble,** estarse buscando problemas.
askance [əs'kæns] to look askance at, phr mirar con recelo.

askew [əs'kjuː] 1 adv de lado. – 2 adj ladeado,-a.
asleep [ə'sliːp] adj (person) dormido,-a; (leg etc) adormecido,-a: she fell asleep, se durmió.
asp [æsp] n áspid m.
asparagus [æs'pærəgəs] n (plant) espárrago; (shoots) espárragos mpl.
■ **asparagus fern,** esparraguera. ‖ **asparagus tips,** puntas fpl de espárrago.
aspect ['æspekt] 1 n (gen) aspecto. 2 (question) asunto, tema m, cuestión f: the public health aspect must not be forgotten, no debe olvidarse la cuestión de la salud pública. 3 (of building) orientación f: it has a west-facing aspect, está orientada al oeste.
aspen ['æspən] n álamo temblón.
asperity [æs'perɪtɪ] n aspereza.
aspersions [əs'pɜːʃənz] to cast aspersions on, phr poner en duda, poner en tela de juicio.
asphalt ['æsfælt] 1 n asfalto. – 2 t asfaltar.
asphyxia [æs'fɪksɪə] n asfixia.
asphyxiate [æs'fɪksɪeɪt] t asfixiar.
asphyxiating [æs'fɪksɪeɪtɪŋ] adj asfixiante, asfixiador,-ra.
asphyxiation [æsfɪksɪ'eɪʃən] t asfixia.
aspic ['æspɪk] n CULIN gelatina.
aspirant [əs'paɪərənt] n aspirante mf.
aspirate ['æspəreɪt] 1 t aspirar. – 2 n consonante f aspirada.
▲ (sustantivo) ['æspɪrət].
aspiration [æspə'reɪʃən] 1 n LING aspiración f. 2 (ambition) aspiración f, ambición f.
aspire [əs'paɪəʳ] i aspirar (**to**, a).
aspirin ['æspɪrɪn] n aspirina.
▲ Es marca registrada.
aspiring [ə'spaɪərɪŋ] adj aspirante: an aspiring musician, un aspirante a músico.
ass¹ [æs] n (animal) burro,-a, asno,-a; (person) burro,-a, imbécil mf.
● **to make an ass of os.,** quedar en ridículo.
ass² [æs] n US taboo culo.
assail [ə'seɪl] 1 t (physically) atacar. 2 (doubts, problems, etc) asaltar.
assailant [ə'seɪlənt] n atacante mf, agresor,-ra.
assassin [ə'sæsɪn] n asesino,-a.
assassinate [ə'sæsɪneɪt] t asesinar.
assassination [əsæsɪ'neɪʃən] n asesinato.
assault [ə'sɔːlt] 1 n MIL asalto, ataque m. 2 JUR agresión f. – 3 t JUR (gen) agredir; (sexually) abusar de.
■ **assault and battery,** lesiones fpl. ‖ **assault course,** pista americana. ‖ **assault craft,** lancha de combate. ‖ **assault rifle,** fusil m de asalto. ‖ **indecent assault,** abusos mpl deshonestos.
assay [ə'seɪ] 1 t ensayar. – 2 n ensayo.
assegai ['æsəgaɪ] n azagaya.
assemble [ə'sembəl] 1 t (bring together - people) reunir; (- things) reunir, juntar; (- facts etc) recopilar, recoger. 2 (put together) montar. 3 COMPUT ensamblar. – 4 i reunirse.
assembler [ə'sembləʳ] n ensamblador m.
assembly [ə'semblɪ] 1 n (meeting) reunión f. 2 (group, body) asamblea. 3 (in school) reunión de alumnos y profesores antes de iniciar las clases por la mañana. 4 TECH (putting together) montaje m; (unit) unidad f.
■ **assembly hall,** sala de actos. ‖ **assembly line,** cadena de montaje. ‖ **assembly language,** lenguaje m ensamblador. ‖ **assembly point,** punto de reunión. ‖

right of assembly, libertad *f* de reunión. ‖ **assembly plant**, planta de montaje. ‖ **National Assembly**, Asamblea Nacional.

assent [ə'sent] **1** *n* asentimiento. – **2** *i* asentir (**to**, a).

assert [ə'sɜːt] *t* (*declare*) aseverar, afirmar.
● **to assert os.**, imponerse. ‖ **to assert one's authority**, imponer su autoridad.

assertion [ə'sɜːʃən] **1** *n* (*statement*) aseveración *f*. **2** (*of authority etc*) reafirmación *f*.

assess [ə'ses] **1** *t* (*value*) tasar, valorar. **2** (*calculate*) calcular. **3** *fig* evaluar.

assessment [ə'sesmənt] **1** *n* (*valuation*) tasación *f*, valoración *f*. **2** (*calculation*) cálculo. **3** *fig* evaluación *f*.
■ **continuous assessment**, evaluación *f* continua.

assessor [ə'sesəʳ] **1** *n* (*advisor*) asesor,-ra. **2** (*of taxes*) tasador,-ra; (*of merits*) evaluador,-ra.

asset ['æset] **1** *n* (*quality*) calidad *f* positiva, ventaja. **2** (*person*) elemento valioso. – **3 assets**, *npl* COMM activo *m sing*.
■ **assets and liabilities**, positivo y activo. ‖ **capital assets**, activo fijo. ‖ **current assets**, activo realizable. ‖ **fixed assets**, activo inmovilizado. ‖ **liquid assets**, activo realizable. ‖ **personal assets**, bienes *mpl* muebles.

asset-stripping ['æsetstrɪpɪŋ] *n práctica de adquirir a bajo precio una empresa para liquidar sus activos y luego cerrarla.*

asseverate [ə'sevəreɪt] *t* aseverar.

asseveration [əsevə'reɪʃən] *n* aseveración *f*.

asshole ['æʃəʊl] *n* US *taboo* → **arsehole**.

assiduity [æsɪ'djuːɪtɪ] *n* diligencia, dedicación *f*.

assiduous [ə'sɪdjʊəs] *adj* diligente, dedicado,-a.

assiduously [ə'sɪdjʊəslɪ] *adv* diligentemente, con dedicación.

assign [ə'saɪn] **1** *t* (*thing to a person*) asignar, atribuir: *I was assigned a room on the ground floor,* me asignaron una habitación en la planta baja. **2** (*task to person*) asignar: *his boss assigns him all the minor tasks,* su jefe le asigna todas las tareas menores. **3** (*person - to place*) atribuir, transferir; (*- to group*) ceder: *three new warders were assigned to the prison,* transfirieron tres nuevos celadores a la prisión; *Spanish soldiers assigned to the peace-keeping force,* soldados españoles cedidos a la fuerza de paz. **4** (*role, value*) asignar: *first we assign a value to this variable,* primero asignamos un valor a esta variable; *the soldiers were assigned a peace-keeping role,* a los soldados se les asignó un papel pacificador. **5** (*property, rights*) ceder.

assignation [æsɪg'neɪʃən] *n* cita a escondidas.

assignee [æsaɪ'niː] *n* cesionario,-a.

assignment [ə'saɪnmənt] **1** *n* (*act of assigning*) asignación *f*. **2** (*mission*) misión *f*. **3** (*task*) tarea.

assimilate [ə'sɪmɪleɪt] **1** *t* asimilar. – **2** *i* asimilarse.

assimilation [əsɪmɪ'leɪʃən] *n* asimilación *f*.

assist [ə'sɪst] **1** *t* ayudar: *Tom will assist you with the preparations,* Tom te ayudará con los preparativos. – **2** *i* ayudar.
● **to assist the police with their enquiries**, prestar declaración ante la policía: *three men are assisting police in their enquiries,* tres hombres están siendo interrogados por la policía.

assistance [ə'sɪstəns] *n* ayuda.
● **to be of assistance**, ayudar. ‖ **to come to sb.'s assistance**, ayudar a algn.

assistant [ə'sɪstənt] **1** *n* (*helper*) ayudante *mf*. **2** (*in shop*) dependiente *mf*.

■ **assistant manager**, subdirector,-ra, director,-ra adjunto,-a.

assoc [ə'səʊsɪeɪʃən] **1** *abbr* (*association*) asociación *f*. **2** (*associated*) asociado,-a.
▲ En **2** [ə'səʊsɪeɪtɪd].

associate [ə'səʊʃɪət] **1** *adj* (*company*) asociado,-a. **2** (*member*) correspondiente. – **3** *n* (*partner*) socio,-a. – **4** *t* asociar. – **5** *i* relacionarse (**with**, con).
● **to be associated with sth.**, tener que ver con algo, estar relacionado,-a con algo.
■ **associate member**, miembro correspondiente.
▲ (*verbo*) [ə'səʊʃɪeɪt].

association [əsəʊsɪ'eɪʃən] *n* asociación *f*.
● **in association with**, en colaboración con.
■ **Association football**, fútbol *m*.

assonance ['æsənəns] *n* asonancia.

assorted [ə'sɔːtɪd] *adj* surtido,-a, variado,-a.

assortment [ə'sɔːtmənt] *n* surtido, variedad *f*.

asst. [ə'sɪstənt] *abbr* (*assistant*) ayudante *mf*; (*abbreviation*) ayte.

assuage [ə'sweɪdʒ] *t* saciar.

assume [ə'sjuːm] **1** *t* (*suppose*) suponer. **2** (*power, responsibility*) tomar, asumir. **3** (*attitude, expression*) adoptar.

assumption [ə'sʌmpʃən] **1** *n* (*supposition*) suposición *f*. **2** (*of power*) asunción *f*.
■ **the Assumption**, la Asunción *f*.

assurance [ə'ʃʊərəns] **1** *n* (*guarantee*) garantía. **2** (*confidence*) seguridad *f*, confianza. **3** (*insurance*) seguro.
■ **life assurance**, seguro de vida.

assure [ə'ʃʊəʳ] *t* asegurar.

assured [ə'ʃʊəd] **1** *adj* seguro,-a. – **2 the assured**, *n* (*man*) el asegurado; (*woman*) la asegurada.

assuredly [ə'ʃʊərədlɪ] *adv* con toda seguridad.

aster ['æstəʳ] *n* áster *m*.

asterisk ['æstərɪsk] *n* asterisco.

astern [ə'stɜːn] **1** *adv* (*towards stern*) a popa; (*at stern*) en popa. **2** (*sailing backwards*) atrás.

asteroid ['æstərɔɪd] *n* asteroide *m*.

asthma ['æsmə] *n* asma.

asthmatic [æs'mætɪk] **1** *adj* asmático,-a. – **2** *n* asmático,-a.

astigmatic [æstɪg'mætɪk] *adj* astigmático,-a.

astigmatism [ə'stɪgmətɪzəm] *n* astigmatismo.

astir [ə'stɜːʳ] **1** *adj arch* (*out of bed*) en pie. **2** (*excited*) en un estado de excitación, en ebullición.

astonish [əs'tɒnɪʃ] *t* asombrar, sorprender.

astonished [əs'tɒnɪʃt] *adj* asombrado,-a.

astonishing [əs'tɒnɪʃɪŋ] *adj* asombroso,-a, sorprendente.

astonishment [əs'tɒnɪʃmənt] *n* asombro.

astound [əs'taʊnd] *t* pasmar, asombrar.

astounded [əs'taʊnd] *adj* pasmado,-a, asombrado,-a.

astounding [ə'staʊndɪŋ] *adj* pasmoso,-a, asombroso,-a.

astrakhan [æstrə'kæn] *n* astracán *m*.

astral ['æstrəl] *adj* astral.

astray [ə'streɪ] *adv* extraviado,-a.
● **to go astray**, (*err*) descarriarse; (*be lost*) extraviarse. ‖ **to lead astray**, pervertir, llevar por el mal camino.

astride [ə'straɪd] *prep* a horcajadas sobre.

astringent [əs'trɪndʒənt] **1** *adj* astringente. – **2** *n* astringente *m*.

astrolabe ['æstrəleɪb] *n* astrolabio.

astrologer [əs'trɒlədʒəʳ] *n* astrólogo,-a.

astrological [æstrə'lɒdʒɪkəl] *adj* astrológico,-a.

astrology [əs'trɒlədʒɪ] n astrología.
astronaut ['æstrənɔːt] n astronauta mf.
astronautics [æstrə'nɔːtɪks] n astronáutica.
astronomer [əs'trɒnəməʳ] n astrónomo,-a.
astronomical [æstrə'nɒmɪkəl] n astronómico,-a.
astronomy [əs'trɒnəmɪ] n astronomía.
astrophysicist [æstrəʊ'fɪzɪsɪst] n astrofísico,-a.
astrophysics [æstrəʊ'fɪzɪks] n astrofísica.
Asturian [æ'stjʊərɪən] 1 adj asturiano,-a. – 2 n asturiano,-a.
Asturias [æ'stjʊərɪəs] n Asturias.
astute [əs'tjuːt] adj astuto,-a, sagaz.
astutely [əs'tjuːtlɪ] adv astutamente, sagazmente.
astuteness [əs'tjuːtnəs] n astucia, sagacidad f.
asunder [ə'sʌndəʳ] adv lit a trozos.
asylum [ə'saɪləm] 1 n (political) asilo, refugio. 2 (for mentally ill) manicomio.
■ **mental asylum**, manicomio.
asymmetric [æsɪ'metrɪk] adj asimétrico,-a.
■ **asymmetric bars**, barras fpl asimétricas.
asymmetrical [æsɪ'metrɪk] adj asimétrico,-a.
asynchronous [eɪ'sɪŋkrənəs] adj asíncrono,-a.
at [æt, unstressed ət] 1 prep (position) en, a: at the door, en la puerta; at home/school/work/church, en casa/el colegio/el trabajo/la iglesia; they're at Alyson's, están en casa de Alyson; she's at the dentist's, ha ido al dentista; at the foot of the stairs, al pie de la escalera; at the top of the mountain, en la cumbre de la montaña; at the bottom of the well, en el fondo del pozo. 2 (time) a: at two o'clock, a las dos; at night, por la noche; at midnight/noon, a medianoche/mediodía; at Christmas, en Navidad; at the age of 13, a los trece años; at the beginning/end, al principio/final. 3 (direction, violence) a, contra: she's always shouting at them, no para de gritarles; they're shooting at the minister, disparan contra el ministro; he threw a stone at me, me tiró una piedra. 4 (with numbers): at 50 miles an hour, a 50 millas la hora; we buy at £400 a ton and sell at £1000, compramos a cuatrocientas libras la tonelada y vendemos a mil; three at a time, de tres en tres; water boils at 100 degrees, el agua hierve a los 100 grados. 5 (state): he's at breakfast/lunch/dinner, está desayunando/comiendo/cenando; they were at war/peace, estaban en guerra/paz; men at work, hombres trabajando; they've been at it all day, han estado todo el día dale que te pego; those kids are at it again, esos críos han vuelto a empezar. 6 (ability): he's good at French, va bien en francés; she's bad at painting, no pinta bien; you're great at swimming, eres un fantástico nadador. – 7 adj (reaction, result): I'm surprised at you, me sorprendes; she was horrified/astounded at the sentence, quedó horrorizada/pasmada ante la sentencia; he blows his top at the slightest provocation, salta a la mínima; at the flick of a switch, con sólo tocar un botón.
● **at first**, al principio. ‖ **at last!**, ¡por fin! ‖ **at least**, por lo menos. ‖ **at most**, como máximo. ‖ **at the earliest**, lo más pronto. ‖ **at the latest**, como tarde, a lo más tardar. ‖ **at the moment**, ahora. ‖ **at worst**, en el peor de los casos.
atavism ['ætəvɪzəm] n atavismo.
atavistic [ætə'vɪstɪk] adj atávico,-a.
ate [et, eɪt] pt → **eat**.
atheism ['eɪθɪɪzəm] n ateísmo.
atheist ['eɪθɪɪst] n ateo,-a.
atheistic [eɪθɪ'ɪstɪk] adj ateo,-a.
Athenian [ə'θiːnɪən] 1 adj ateniense. – 2 n ateniense mf.

Athens ['æθənz] n Atenas.
athlete ['æθliːt] n atleta mf.
■ **athlete's foot**, pie m de atleta.
athletic [æθ'letɪk] 1 adj atlético,-a. 2 (sporty) deportista.
■ **athletic support**, suspensorio.
athletics [æθ'letɪks] n atletismo.
■ **athletics club**, club m de atletismo. ‖ **athletics meeting**, reunión f atlética.
Atlantic [ət'læntɪk] adj atlántico,-a.
■ **the Atlantic (Ocean)**, el (océano) Atlántico.
atlas ['ætləs] n atlas m inv.
Atlas ['ætləs] the Atlas Mountains, npl el Atlas m.
atmosphere ['ætməsfɪəʳ] 1 n atmósfera. 2 (ambience) ambiente m, atmósfera.
atmospheric [ætməs'ferɪk] 1 adj atmosférico,-a. – 2 atmospherics, npl parásitos mpl.
■ **atmospheric pressure**, presión f atmosférica.
atoll ['ætɒl] n atolón m.
atom ['ætəm] 1 n átomo. 2 fig ápice m, pizca.
■ **atom bomb**, bomba atómica.
atomic [ə'tɒmɪk] adj atómico,-a.
■ **atomic bomb**, bomba atómica. ‖ **atomic energy**, energía atómica. ‖ **atomic number**, número atómico. ‖ **atomic pile**, pila atómica. ‖ **atomic warfare**, guerra atómica. ‖ **atomic weight**, peso atómico.
atomize ['ætəmaɪz] t atomizar.
atomizer ['ætəmaɪzəʳ] n atomizador m.
atone [ə'təʊn] to atone for, i (sin) expiar; (crime) reparar.
atonement [ə'təʊnmənt] n (for sin) expiación f; (for crime) reparación f.
atrocious [ə'trəʊʃəs] 1 adj (cruel) atroz. 2 fam fatal, malísimo,-a.
atrocity [ə'trɒsɪtɪ] n atrocidad f.
▲ pl atrocities.
atrophy ['ætrəfɪ] 1 n atrofia. – 2 t atrofiar. – 3 i atrofiarse.
▲ (sustantivo) pl atrophies; (verbo) pt & pp atrophied, ger atrophying.
attach [ə'tætʃ] 1 t (fasten) sujetar. 2 (tie) atar. 3 (stick) pegar. 4 (document) adjuntar. 5 (person) agregar, destinar, adscribir.
● **to attach importance to**, considerar importante, dar importancia a.
attaché [ə'tæʃeɪ] n agregado,-a.
■ **attaché case**, maletín m. ‖ **military attaché**, agregado militar.
attached [ə'tætʃt] adj (document) adjunto,-a.
● **to be attached to**, tener cariño a. ‖ **to grow attached to**, coger cariño a, encariñarse con.
attachment [ə'tætʃmənt] 1 n TECH accesorio. 2 (fondness) cariño, apego.
attack [ə'tæk] 1 n (gen) ataque m; (terrorist) atentado. – 2 t (gen) atacar; (terrorist) atentar contra. 3 (task, problem) acometer; (person) agredir, atacar. – 4 i atacar.
● **on the attack**, atacando. ‖ **to come under attack**, ser atacado,-a. ‖ **to launch an attack on**, lanzar un ataque a.
attacker [ə'tækəʳ] n atacante mf, agresor,-ra.
attain [ə'teɪn] 1 t (goal) lograr. 2 (rank, age) llegar a.
attainable [ə'teɪnəbəl] adj alcanzable.
attainment [ə'teɪnmənt] 1 n (sth. achieved) logro. 2 (skill) talento.
attempt [ə'tempt] 1 n (try) intento, tentativa: he made an attempt at 4 metres, hizo un intento a 4 metros; I'll do it or die in the attempt, lo haré o moriré en el intento. – 2 t intentar.

attend 30

● **to make an attempt on sb.'s life,** atentar contra la vida de algn.

attend [ə'tend] **1** *t* (*be present at*) asistir a: *all her friends attended the funeral,* todos sus amigos asistieron al funeral. **2** (*care for*) atender, cuidar: *she is attended by a nurse,* la atiende una enfermera. **3** (*accompany*) acompañar. – **4** *i* (*be present*) asistir. **5** (*pay attention*) prestar atención.
◆ **to attend to 1** *t insep* ocuparse de. **2** (*in shop*) despachar.

attendance [ə'tendəns] **1** *n* (*being present*) asistencia. **2** (*people present*) asistentes *mpl.*
● **to be in attendance on,** (*accompany*) acompañar; (*tend to*) asistir a.

attendant [ə'tendənt] *n* (*in car park, museum*) vigilante *mf;* (*in cinema*) acomodador,-ra.

attention [ə'tenʃən] **1** *n* atención *f.* – **2** **attention!,** *interj* MIL ¡firmes!
● **for the attention of,** a la atención de. ‖ **to attract sb.'s attention,** llamar la atención a algn. ‖ **to bring sth. to sb.'s attention,** informar a algn. de algo, poner algo en conocimiento de algn. ‖ **to hold sb.'s attention,** mantener la atención de algn. ‖ **to pay attention,** prestar atención. ‖ **to stand to attention,** cuadrarse.

attentive [ə'tentɪv] **1** *adj* (*paying attention*) atento,-a. **2** (*helpful*) solícito,-a.

attentively [ə'tentɪvlɪ] *adv* con atención.

attentiveness [ə'tentɪvnəs] **1** *n* (*attention*) atención *f.* **2** (*helpfulness*) solicitud *f.*

attenuate [ə'tenjʊeɪt] *t* atenuar.

attenuating [ə'tenjʊeɪtɪŋ] *adj* atenuante.

attenuation [ətenjʊ'eɪʃən] *n* atenuación *f.*

attest [ə'test] *t* (*gen*) atestiguar; (*signature*) autentificar.
● **to attest to sth.,** atestiguar algo.

attic ['ætɪk] *n* desván *m.*

attire [ə'taɪə'] **1** *n* atuendo, atavío, vestido. – **2** *t* ataviar, vestir.

attitude ['ætɪtjuːd] **1** *n* (*way of thinking*) actitud *f: I take the attitude that ...,* para mí, ..., yo creo que ... **2** (*pose*) postura, pose *f.*
■ **attitude of mind,** estado de ánimo.

attn [fɔː'ðɪə'tenʃənʊv] *abbr* COM (*for the attention of*) a la atención de.

attorney [ə'tɜːnɪ] *n* US abogado,-a.
■ **Attorney General,** GB ≈ Ministro,-a de Justicia.

attract [ə'trækt] *t* atraer.
● **to attract attention,** llamar la atención. ‖ **to be attracted to sb.,** sentir atracción por algn.

attraction [ə'trækʃən] **1** *n* (*power*) atracción *f.* **2** (*thing*) atractivo: *it holds no attraction for me,* no me atrae. **3** (*incentive*) aliciente *m.*
■ **the main attraction,** (*gen*) el principal atractivo; (*in show*) el número fuerte. ‖ **tourist attraction,** atracción *f* turística.

attractive [ə'træktɪv] **1** *adj* (*person*) atractivo,-a. **2** (*offer*) interesante, tentador,-ra.

attractively [ə'træktɪvlɪ] *adv: our products are very attractively presented,* nuestros productos tienen una presentación muy atractiva; *she smiled at him attractively,* le dirigió una sonrisa atractiva.

attractiveness [ə'træktɪvnəs] *n* atractivo.

attributable [ə'trɪbjʊtəbəl] *adj* atribuible.

attribute ['ætrɪbjuːt] **1** *n* atributo. – **2** *t* atribuir.
▲ (*verbo*) [ə'trɪbjuːt].

attribution [ætrɪ'bjuːʃən] *n* atribución *f.*

attributive [ə'trɪbjʊtɪv] *adj* atributivo,-a.

attrition [ə'trɪʃən] *n* desgaste *m.*
■ **war of attrition,** guerra de desgaste.

attune [ə'tjuːn]. **1 to be attuned to,** *phr* estar en sintonía con, entender bien. – **2 to attune to,** *i* acostumbrarse a.

atypical [eɪ'tɪpɪkəl] *adj* atípico,-a.

atypically [eɪ'tɪpɪkəlɪ] *adv* atípicamente, de manera atípica.

aubergine ['əʊbəʒiːn] *n* berenjena.

auburn ['ɔːbən] *adj* castaño,-a.

auction ['ɔːkʃən] **1** *n* subasta. – **2** *t* subastar.
◆ **to auction off** *t sep* subastar.
● **at auction,** en subasta. ‖ **to put sth. up for auction,** subastar algo.
■ **auction room,** sala de subastas. ‖ **auction sale,** subasta.

auctioneer [ɔːkʃə'nɪə'] *n* subastador,-ra.

audacious [ɔː'deɪʃəs] **1** *adj* (*daring*) audaz, intrépido,-a. **2** (*rude*) descarado,-a, osado,-a.

audacity [ɔː'dæsɪtɪ] **1** *n* (*daring*) audacia, intrepidez *f.* **2** (*rudeness*) descaro, atrevimiento, osadía.

audibility [ɔːdɪ'bɪlɪtɪ] *n* audibilidad *f.*

audible ['ɔːdɪbəl] *adj* audible.

audibly ['ɔːdɪblɪ] *adv* de forma audible.

audience ['ɔːdɪəns] **1** *n* (*spectators*) público; (*to radio*) audiencia; (*to television*) telespectadores *mpl.* **2** (*interview*) audiencia.

audio frequency [ɔːdɪəʊ'friːkwənsɪ] *n* audiofrecuencia.

audiotape ['ɔːdɪəʊteɪp] *n* cinta de audio.

audio typist [ɔːdɪəʊ'taɪpɪst] *n* audiomecanógrafo,-a.

audio-visual [ɔːdɪəʊ'vɪzjʊəl] *adj* audiovisual.

audit ['ɔːdɪt] **1** *n* auditoría. – **2** *t* auditar.

audition [ɔː'dɪʃən] **1** *n* prueba. – **2** *t* hacer una prueba a. – **3** *i* hacer una prueba: *she auditioned for the part of Goneril,* hizo una prueba para el papel de Goneril.

auditor ['ɔːdɪtə'] *n* auditor,-ra.

auditorium [ɔːdɪ'tɔːrɪəm] *n* auditorio, sala.
▲ *pl* **auditoriums** *o* **auditoria** [ɔːdɪ'tɔːrɪə].

auditory ['ɔːdɪtərɪ] *adj* auditivo,-a.

au fait [əʊ'feɪ] **to be au fait with,** *phr* estar familiarizado,-a con.

Aug ['ɔːgəst] *abbr* (*August*) agosto.

auger ['ɔːgə'] *n* barrena.

aught [ɔːt] *pron arch* a cosa.
● **for aught I care,** por mí, por lo que a mí me importa. ‖ **for aught I know,** que yo sepa.

augment [ɔːg'ment] **1** *t fml* aumentar. – **2** *i fml* aumentarse.

augmentative [ɔːg'mentətɪv] *adj* aumentativo,-a.

au gratin [əʊ'grætæn] *adv* gratinado,-a.

augur ['ɔːgə'] *t* presagiar.
● **to augur well,** ser de buen agüero. ‖ **to augur ill,** ser de mal agüero.

august [ɔː'gʌst] *adj* augusto,-a.

August ['ɔːgəst] *n* agosto.
▲ *Véase también* May.

auld lang syne [ɔːldlæŋ'zaɪn] *n* canción popular escocesa que tradicionalmente se canta en Nochevieja.

aunt [ɑːnt] *n* tía.

auntie ['ɑːntɪ] *n fam* tía, tita.

aunty ['ɑːntɪ] *n fam* tía, tita.
▲ *pl* **aunties.**

au pair [əʊ'peə'] *n* au pair *f.*
■ **au pair girl,** au pair *f.*

aura [ɔːrə] *n* (*of person*) aura; (*of place*) sensación *f*.

aural ['ɔːrəl] *adj* auditivo,-a.
▲ A *veces se pronuncia* ['aurəl] *para distinguirlo de* oral.

aureola [ɔːrɪ'ələ] *n* → **aureole**.

aureole [ɔːrɪ'əʊl] *n* aureola.

auricle ['ɒrɪkəl] 1 *n* (*of heart*) aurícula. 2 (*of ear*) aurícula, pabellón *m* de la oreja.

auricular [ɒ'rɪkjʊləʳ] *adj* auricular.

aurora [ɔː'rɔːrə] *n* aurora.
■ aurora australis, aurora austral. ‖ aurora borealis, aurora boreal.

auscultate ['ɔːskʌlteɪt] *t* auscultar.

auscultation [ɔːskʌl'teɪʃən] *n* auscultación *f*.

auspices ['ɔːspɪsɪz] *npl* auspicios *mpl*: under the auspices of, bajo los auspicios de.

auspicious [ɔːs'pɪʃəs] *adj* (*start etc*) prometedor,-ra; (*occasion*) feliz.

Aussie ['ɒzɪ] 1 *adj fam* australiano,-a. – 2 *n fam* australiano,-a.

austere [ɒs'tɪəʳ] *adj* austero,-a.

austerity [ɒs'terɪtɪ] *n* austeridad *f*.

Australasia [ɒstrəl'eɪʒə] *n* Australasia.

Australasian [ɒstrəl'eɪʒən] 1 *adj* australasiano,-a. – 2 *n* australasiano,-a.

Australia [ɒ'streɪlɪə] *n* Australia.

Australian [ɒ'streɪlɪən] 1 *adj* australiano,-a. – 2 *n* (*person*) australiano,-a. 3 (*language*) australiano.

Austria ['ɒstrɪə] *n* Austria.

Austrian ['ɒstrɪən] 1 *adj* austríaco,-a, austriaco,-a. – 2 *n* austríaco,-a, austriaco,-a.

authentic [ɔː'θentɪk] *adj* auténtico,-a.

authenticate [ɔː'θentɪkeɪt] *t* autenticar, autentificar.

authentication [ɔːθentɪ'keɪʃən] *n* autenticación *f*.

authenticity [ɔːθen'tɪsɪtɪ] *n* autenticidad *f*.

author ['ɔːθəʳ] *n* autor,-ra, escritor,-ra.

authoress ['ɔːθərəs] *n* autora, escritora.

authoritarian [ɔːθɒrɪ'teərɪən] *adj* autoritario,-a.

authoritative [ɔː'θɒrɪtətɪv] 1 *adj* (*reliable*) autorizado,-a, fidedigno,-a. 2 (*authoritarian*) autoritario,-a.

authoritatively [ɔː'θɒrɪtətɪvlɪ] 1 *adv* (*reliably*) con autoridad. – 2 *adj* (*in authoritarian way*) autoritariamente.

authority [ɔː'θɒrɪtɪ] 1 *n* (*gen*) autoridad *f*. 2 (*permission*) autorización *f*, permiso. 3 (*expert*) autoridad *f*, experto: he's an authority on rabbit breeding, es una autoridad en cunicultura.
● to exercise one's authority, ejercer la autoridad. ‖ to have it on good authority that ..., saber de buena tinta que ...
■ the local authority, el ayuntamiento.
▲ *pl* authorities.

authorization [ɔːθəraɪ'zeɪʃən] *n* autorización *f*.

authorize ['ɔːθəraɪz] *t* autorizar.
■ the Authorized Version, *traducción inglesa de la Biblia publicada en 1611*.

authorship ['ɔːθəʃɪp] *n* autoría.

autism ['ɔːtɪzəm] *n* autismo.

autistic [ɔː'tɪstɪk] *adj* autista.

auto ['ɔːtəʊ] *n us fam* coche *m*.
▲ *pl* autos.

autobiographical [ɔːtəbaɪə'græfɪkəl] *adj* autobiográfico,-a.

autobiographic [ɔːtəbaɪə'græfɪk] *adj* autobiográfico,-a.

autobiography [ɔːtəbaɪ'ɒgrəfɪ] *n* autobiografía.
▲ *pl* autobiographies.

autocracy [ɔː'tɒkrəsɪ] *n* autocracia.
▲ *pl* autocracies.

autocrat ['ɔːtəkræt] *n* autócrata *mf*.

autocratic [ɔːtə'krætɪk] *adj* autocrático,-a.

autocross ['ɔːtəʊkrɒs] *n* autocross *m*.

Autocue ['ɔːtəʊkjuː] *n* teleapuntador *m*, teleprómpter *m*.

autograph ['ɔːtəgrɑːf] 1 *n* autógrafo. – 2 *t* autografiar.

automat ['ɔːtəʊmæt] *n us restaurante autoservicio*.

automata [ɔː'tɒmətə] *npl* → **automaton**.

automate ['ɔːtəmeɪt] *t* automatizar.

automatic [ɔːtə'mætɪk] 1 *adj* automático,-a. – 2 *n* (*car*) coche *m* automático. 3 (*gun*) automática. 4 (*washing machine*) lavadora automática.
■ automatic pilot, piloto automático: I'm on automatic pilot, tengo el piloto automático puesto.

automation [ɔːtə'meɪʃən] *n* automatización *f*.

automaton [ɔː'tɒmətən] 1 *n* (*robot*) autómata *m*. 2 (*person*) autómata *mf*.
▲ *pl* automatons *o* automata.

automobile ['ɔːtəməbiːl] *n* automóvil *m*, coche *m*.

automotive [ɔːtə'məʊtɪv] *adj* automovilístico,-a.

autonomous [ɔː'tɒnəməs] *adj* autónomo,-a.

autonomy [ɔː'tɒnəmɪ] *n* autonomía.
▲ *pl* autonomies.

autopsy ['ɔːtɒpsɪ] *n* autopsia.
▲ *pl* autopsies.

autosuggestion [ɔːtəʊsə'dʒestʃən] *n* autosugestión *f*.

autumn ['ɔːtəm] *n* otoño.

autumnal [ɔː'tʌmnəl] *adj* otoñal.

auxiliary [ɔːg'zɪljərɪ] 1 *adj* auxiliar. – 2 *n* auxiliar *m*, ayudante *mf*.
■ auxiliary verb, verbo auxiliar.
▲ (*sustantivo*) *pl* auxiliaries.

AV[1] [ɔːdɪəʊ'vɪzjʊəl] *abbr* (*audio-visual*) audiovisual.

AV[2] ['ɔːθəraɪzdvɜːʒən] *abbr* (*Authorized Version*) *traducción inglesa de la Biblia publicada en 1611*.

av. ['ævərɪdʒ] *abbr* (*average*) promedio.

avail [ə'veɪl] *i lit* servir: it avails little to plead, de poco sirve suplicar.
● to avail os. of, aprovecharse de. ‖ to no avail, en vano.

availability [əveɪlə'bɪlɪtɪ] *n* disponibilidad *f*.

available [ə'veɪləbəl] 1 *adj* (*thing*) disponible: it's available in four colours, lo hay en cuatro colores. 2 (*person*) libre, disponible.
● to make sth. available to sb., poner algo a disposición de algn.

avalanche ['ævəlɑːnʃ] *n* alud *m*; *fig* avalancha.

avant-garde [ævɒŋ'gɑːd] 1 *n* vanguardia. – 2 *adj* vanguardista.

avarice ['ævərɪs] *n* avaricia.

avaricious [ævə'rɪʃəs] *adj* avaro,-a.

Ave ['ævənjuː] *abbr* (*Avenue*) Avenida; (*abbreviation*) Av, Avda.

avenge [ə'vendʒ] *t* vengar.

avenger [ə'vendʒəʳ] *n* vengador,-ra.

avenue ['ævənjuː] 1 *n* (*street*) avenida. 2 (*means*) vía.

aver [ə'vɜːʳ] *t* asegurar.
▲ *pt & pp* averred, *ger* averring.

average ['ævərɪdʒ] 1 *n* promedio, media. – 2 *adj* medio,-a. 3 (*not special*) corriente, regular. – 4 *t* hacer un promedio de: I average 10 cigarettes a day, fumo un promedio de 10 cigarrillos al día. 5 (*calculate*) determinar el promedio de.
◆ to average out at *t insep* salir a una media de.
● above average, por encima de la media. ‖ below

average, por debajo de la media. ‖ **on average,** por término medio.

averse [ə'vɜːs] *adj* reacio,-a (**to,** a): *he's not averse to the occasional drink,* le gusta una copa de vez en cuando.

aversion [ə'vɜːʒən] **1** *n* (*hatred*) aversión *f*: *I have an aversion to cats,* odio los gatos. **2** (*thing hated*) bestia negra: *cats are my pet aversion,* lo que más odio son los gatos.

■ **aversion therapy,** terapia por aversión.

avert [ə'vɜːt] *t* (*avoid*) evitar.

● **to avert one's eyes,** apartar la vista.

aviary [ˈeɪvjərɪ] *n* pajarera.

▲ *pl* **aviaries**.

aviation [eɪvɪ'eɪʃən] *n* aviación *f*.

aviator [ˈeɪvɪeɪtə'] *n* aviador,-ra.

avid [ˈævɪd] *adj* ávido,-a.

avidity [ə'vɪdɪtɪ] *n* avidez *f*.

avidly [ˈævɪdlɪ] *adv* ávidamente.

avionics [eɪvɪ'ɒnɪks] *n* aviónica.

avocado [ævəˈkɑːdəʊ] **avocado / avocado pear,** *n* aguacate *m*.

▲ *pl* **avocados**.

avoid [ə'vɔɪd] **1** *t* evitar. **2** (*question*) eludir. **3** (*person*) esquivar.

avoidable [ə'vɔɪdəbəl] *adj* evitable.

avoirdupois [ævədə'pɔɪz] *n* sistema de pesos basado en la libra de 16 onzas usado en los países anglosajones.

avow [ə'vaʊ] *t* confesar, declarar.

avowal [ə'vaʊəl] *n* confesión *f*, declaración *f*.

avowed [ə'vaʊd] *adj* declarado,-a.

avowedly [ə'vaʊədlɪ] *adv* declaradamente.

await [ə'weɪt] *t fml* aguardar, esperar.

awake [ə'weɪk] **1** *adj* despierto,-a. – **2** *i* despertar. **3** despertarse.

● **to be awake to sth.,** ser consciente de algo.

▲ *pt* **awoke,** *pp* **awaked** *o* **awoken**.

awaken [ə'weɪkən] *t-i* → **awake**.

◆ **to awaken to** *t insep* darse cuenta de.

▲ *pt* **awakened,** *pp* **awoken**.

awakening [ə'weɪkənɪŋ] *n* despertar *m*: *a rude awakening,* un brusco y desagradable despertar.

award [ə'wɔːd] **1** *n* (*prize*) premio; (*medal*) condecoración *f*; (*trophy*) trofeo. **2** (*grant*) beca. **3** (*damages*) indemnización *f*. – **4** *t* (*prize, grant*) otorgar, conceder. **5** (*damages*) adjudicar.

aware [ə'weə'] **1** *adj* consciente: *I was not aware that you were invited,* no sabía que estabas invitado. **2** (*informed*) informado,-a, enterado,-a.

● **to be aware of,** ser consciente de. ‖ **to become aware of,** darse cuenta de.

awareness [ə'weənəs] *n* conciencia.

awash [ə'wɒʃ] *adj* inundado,-a (**with,** de).

away [ə'weɪ] **1** *adv* lejos, fuera, alejándose: *he lives 4 km away,* vive a 4 km (de aquí); *the wedding is 6 weeks away,* faltan 6 semanas para la boda; *she was away from school last week,* estuvo ausente del colegio la semana pasada; *Mr Korda is away on business,* el Sr Korda está fuera por negocios. **2** (*indicating continuity*): *they worked away all day,* trabajaron todo el día. **3** (*till nothing is left*): *she left the gas on and the milk boiled away,* dejó el gas encendido y la leche hirvió hasta evaporarse; *the straw blew away,* la paja se la llevó el viento; *she gave his things away,* regaló todas sus cosas. **4** *SP* en campo contrario: *we're playing Barnsley away next week,* la semana que viene jugamos contra Barnsley en su campo.

● **to be away,** estar fuera; (*from school*) estar ausente. ‖ **to go away,** irse, marcharse. ‖ **to put away,** guardar. ‖ **to run away,** irse corriendo.

awe [ɔː] *n* sobrecogimiento.

● **to fill with awe,** sobrecoger. ‖ **to stand in awe of sb.,** sentir mucho respeto hacia algn.

awe-inspiring [ˈɔːɪnspaɪərɪŋ] *adj* sobrecogedor,-ra, impresionante.

awesome [ˈɔːsʌm] *adj* imponente.

awestricken [ˈɔːstrɪkən] *adj* → **awestruck**.

awestruck [ˈɔːstrʌk] *adj* sobrecogido,-a.

awful [ˈɔːfʊl] **1** *adj* (*shocking*) atroz, horrible. **2** *fam* (*very bad*) fatal, horrible, espantoso,-a.

awfully [ˈɔːfʊlɪ] *adv fam* terriblemente.

awhile [ə'waɪl] *adv* un rato.

awkward [ˈɔːkwəd] **1** *adj* (*clumsy - person*) torpe; (- *expression*) poco elegante. **2** (*difficult*) difícil; (*uncooperative*) poco cooperativo,-a: *it's an awkward place to get to,* es difícil llegar hasta allí; *she enjoys being awkward and causing problems,* le gusta poner pegas y causar problemas. **3** (*embarrassing*) embarazoso,-a, delicado,-a: *it's an awkward situation,* es una situación delicada. **4** (*inconvenient*) inconveniente, inoportuno,-a: *it's a little awkward now, can you come back later?,* no es conveniente ahora mismo, ¿puedes volver después? **5** (*uncomfortable*) incómodo,-a.

■ **awkward customer,** tipo difícil.

awkwardly [ˈɔːkwədlɪ] **1** *adv* (*gen*) torpemente; (*express os.*) con poca elegancia. **2** (*in an embarrassing way*) incómodamente: *he smiled awkwardly trying to hide his embarrassment,* sonrió incómodamente para intentar ocultar su vergüenza.

awkwardness [ˈɔːkwədnəs] **1** *n* (*clumsiness - of person*) torpeza; (- *of espression*) poca elegancia. **2** (*difficulty*) dificultad *f*, lo difícil. **3** (*embarrassment*) incomodidad *f*: *his awkwardness was apparent to all,* su incomodidad era evidente a todos. **4** (*delicate nature*) lo delicado, lo embarazoso. **5** (*inconvenience*) lo inconveniente. **6** (*non-cooperation*) falta de cooperación.

awl [ɔːl] *n* lezna.

awning [ˈɔːnɪŋ] *n* toldo.

awoke [ə'wəʊk] *pt* → **awake**.

awoken [ə'wəʊkən] *pp* → **awake**.

awry [ə'raɪ] *adj* torcido,-a.

● **to go awry,** salir mal.

ax [æks] *n* → **axe**.

axe [æks] **1** *n* hacha. – **2** *t* (*reduce*) recortar. **3** (*dismiss*) despedir. **4** (*get rid of*) suprimir; (*cancel*) cancelar.

● **to get the axe,** ser despedido,-a. ‖ **to have an axe to grind,** tener intereses personales.

axiom [ˈæksɪəm] *n* axioma *m*.

axiomatic [æksɪə'mætɪk] *adj* axiomático,-a.

axis [ˈæksɪs] *n* eje *m*.

axle [ˈæksəl] *n* eje *m*.

ayatollah [aɪə'tɒlə] *n* ayatollah *m*.

aye [aɪ] **1** *adv* sí. – **2** *n* sí *m*.

● **the ayes have it,** gana el sí.

azalea [ə'zeɪlɪə] *n* azalea.

Azerbaijan [æzəbaɪ'dʒɑːn] *n* Azerbaiyán *m*.

Azerbaijani [æzəbaɪ'dʒɑːnɪ] **1** *adj* azerbaiyano,-a, azerí. – **2** *n* (*person*) azerbaiyano,-a, azerí *mf*. **3** (*language*) azerí *m*, azerbaiyano.

azimuth [ˈæzɪməθ] *n* acimut *m*.

Aztec [ˈæztek] **1** *adj* azteca. – **2** *n* (*person*) azteca *mf*. **3** (*language*) azteca *m*.

azure [ˈeɪʒə'] **1** *adj* azul celeste. – **2** *n* azul *m* celeste

B

B, b [biː] **1** *n* (*the letter*) B, b *f*. **2** MUS si *m*.
- **B movie**, película de la serie B. ‖ **B road**, carretera secundaria.

b [bɔːn] *abbr* (*born*) nacido,-a; (*abbreviation*) n.

BA [ˈbiːˈeɪ] *abbr* (*Bachelor of Arts*) licenciado,-a en letras.

baa [baː] **1** *i* balar. – **2** *n* balido.

babble [ˈbæbəl] **1** *i* (*excitedly*) barbullar. **2** (*meaninglessly*) balbucear. **3** (*gossip*) chismorrear. **4** (*stream*) murmurar. – **5** *t* (*say incoherently*) mascullar, farfullar. – **6** *n* (*confused voices*) murmullo, rumor *m*. **7** (*chatter*) cotorreo. **8** (*gossip*) chismorreo. **9** (*incoherent speech*) farfulla. **10** (*stream*) murmullo.

babbling [ˈbæbəlɪŋ] **1** *adj* (*stream*) murmullante. **2** (*talkative*) parlanchín,-ina. – **3** *n* → **babble**.

babe [beɪb] **1** *n* (*baby*) nene,-a, criatura. **2** US (*girl*) nena, chica.
- **babe in arms**, niño de pecho.

babel [ˈbeɪbəl] **Tower of Babel**, *n* torre *f* de Babel.

baboon [bəˈbuːn] *n* mandril *m*, babuino.

baby [ˈbeɪbɪ] **1** *n* bebé *m*. **2** (*young child*) niño,-a. **3** (*youngest son*) benjamín *m*. **4** (*of animal*) cría. **5** *fig* (*infantile person*) niño,-a: *don't be such a baby!*, ¡no seas niño! **6** (*brainchild*) invento. – **7** *t* (*pamper*) mimar.
- **to have a baby**, dar a luz, tener un niño. ‖ **to be left holding the baby**, pagar el pato. ‖ **to throw the baby out with the bath-water**, tirar las frutas frescas con las pochas. ‖ **it's your baby!**, ¡ya te las apañarás!
- **baby boom**, explosión *f* demográfica. ‖ **baby boomer**, persona nacida durante una explosión demográfica. ‖ **baby boy**, niño. ‖ **baby carriage**, US cochecito de niño. ‖ **baby farm**, US guardería infantil. ‖ **baby girl**, niña. ‖ **baby grand**, piano de media cola. ‖ **baby powder**, polvos *mpl* (de talco) para niños. ‖ **baby tooth**, diente *m* de leche.
- ▲ *pl* **babies**.

baby-battering [ˈbeɪbɪbætərɪŋ] *n* malos tratos *mpl* infantiles.

baby-faced [ˈbeɪbɪfeɪst] **1** *adj* con cara de niño. **2** (*without facial hair*) barbilampiño, imberbe.

babyhood [ˈbeɪbɪhʊd] *n* infancia.

babyish [ˈbeɪbɪʃ] **1** *adj* infantil, de niño. **2** (*immature*) pueril.

Babylon [ˈbæbɪlɒn] *n* Babilonia.

Babylonian [bæbɪˈləʊnɪən] **1** *adj* babilónico,-a. – **2** *n* (*person*) babilónico,-a. **3** (*language*) babilónico.

baby-minder [ˈbeɪbɪmaɪndə'] *n* niñera.

baby-scales [ˈbeɪbɪskeɪlz] *n* pesabebés *m*.

baby-sit [ˈbeɪbɪsɪt] *i* hacer de canguro, cuidar niños.
- ▲ *pt & pp* **baby-sat** [ˈbeɪbɪsæt], ger **baby-sitting**.

baby-sitter [ˈbeɪbɪsɪtə'] *n* canguro *mf*.

baby-sitting [ˈbeɪbɪsɪtɪŋ] *n* cuidado de los niños (*por un canguro*).

baby-walker [ˈbeɪbɪwɔːkə'] *n* andador *m*, tacataca *m*, tacatá *m*.

bachelor [ˈbætʃələ'] *n* soltero.
- **confirmed bachelor**, solterón *m*. ‖ **bachelor flat**, piso de soltero. ‖ **Bachelor of Arts**, licenciado,-a en letras. ‖ **Bachelor of Science**, licenciado,-a en ciencias. ‖ **Bachelor of Law**, licenciado,-a en derecho.

bacillus [bəˈsɪləs] *n* MED bacilo.
- ▲ *pl* **bacilli** [bəˈsɪlaɪ].

back [bæk] **1** *n* ANAT espalda. **2** (*of animal, book*) lomo. **3** (*of chair*) respaldo. **4** (*of hand*) dorso. **5** (*of knife, sword*) canto. **6** (*of coin, medal*) reverso. **7** (*of cheque*) dorso. **8** (*of stage, room, cupboard*) fondo. **9** SP (*player*) defensa *mf*; (*position*) defensa. – **10** *adj* trasero,-a, de atrás. – **11** *adv* (*at the rear*) atrás; (*towards the rear*) hacia atrás; (*time*) hace: *several years back*, hace varios años. – **12** *t* (*support*) apoyar, respaldar. **13** FIN financiar. **14** (*bet on*) apostar por.
- ◆ **to back away** *i* retirarse. ‖ **to back down** *i* claudicar, cejar. ‖ **to back off** *i* apartarse. ‖ **to back out** *i* volverse atrás. ‖ **to back up** *t sep* (*vehicle*) dar marcha atrás a; (*support*) apoyar.
- ● **back to back**, espalda con espalda. ‖ **back to front**, al revés. ‖ **to answer back**, replicar. ‖ **to be back**, estar de vuelta. ‖ **to be glad to see the back of sb.**, estar contento de haberse quitado a algn. de encima. ‖ **to break one's back**, deslomarse. ‖ **to carry on one's back**, llevar a cuestas. ‖ **to fall on one's back**, caerse de espaldas. ‖ **to have sb. on one's back**, tener a algn. encima. ‖ **to come back / go back**, volver. ‖ **to get sb.'s back up**, mosquear a algn. ‖ **to get off sb.'s back**, dejar de fastidiar a algn. ‖ **to hit back**, devolver el golpe; *fig* contestar a una acusación. ‖ **to have one's back to the wall**, *fig* estar entre la espada y la pared. ‖ **to lie on one's back**, estar acostado,-a boca arriba. ‖ **to give back**, devolver. ‖ **to put back**, volver a guardar en su sitio. ‖ **to put one's back into sth.**, arrimar el hombro. ‖ **to phone back**, volver a llamar. ‖ **to stand back**, apartarse. ‖ **to turn one's back on sb.**, volver la espalda a algn.
- ■ **back door**, puerta trasera. ‖ **back number**, número atrasado. ‖ **back pay**, atrasos *mpl*. ‖ **back row**, última fila. ‖ **back seat**, asiento de atrás. ‖ **back street**, callejuela. ‖ **back wheel**, rueda trasera. ‖ **short back and sides**, corte *m* de pelo casi al rape.

backache [ˈbækeɪk] *n* dolor *m* de espalda.

backbencher [bækˈbenʃə'] *n* POL diputado,-a (*que no forma parte del consejo de ministros*).

backbite [ˈbækbaɪt] *i* quejarse, protestar.
- ● **to backbite about sb.**, poner a algn. de vuelta y media.

backbiter [ˈbækbaɪtə'] *n* gruñón,-ona, pendenciero,-a.

backbiting [ˈbækbaɪtɪŋ] *n* murmuración *f*, refunfuño.

backbone [ˈbækbəʊn] **1** *n* ANAT columna vertebral, espinazo. **2** *fig* carácter *m*, aguante *m*. **3** (*chief support*) piedra angular.

backbreaking [ˈbækbreɪkɪŋ] *adj* (*work*) agotador,-ra, matador,-ra: *a backbreaking job*, un trabajo agotador.

backchat ['bæktʃæt] n GB fam impertinencia, réplicas fpl.
backcloth ['bækklɒθ] n telón m de fondo.
backcomb ['bækkəʊm] t cardar (el pelo).
backdate [bæk'deɪt] 1 t (document, agreement) retrodatar. 2 (make valid) dar efecto retroactivo a.
backdated [bæk'deɪtɪd] 1 adj (valid) con efecto retroactivo. 2 (document) antedatado,-a.
backdrop ['bækdrɒp] n telón m de fondo.
backer ['bækə'] 1 n FIN promotor,-ra. 2 (guarantor) fiador,-ra. 3 (supporter) partidario,-a.
backfire [bæk'faɪə'] 1 i fallar: our plan backfired, nos salió el tiro por la culata. 2 AUTO (engine) petardear. – 3 n AUTO petardeo.
backgammon ['bækgæmən] n chaquete m, tablas f.
background ['bækgraʊnd] 1 n fondo: he painted it on a black background, lo pintó sobre un fondo negro. 2 fig trasfondo, antecedentes mpl: the background to the strike, los antecedentes de la huelga. 3 (of photograph, picture) último plano. 4 fig (origins) orígenes mpl, antecedentes mpl: his background is completely unknown, sus antecedentes son una gran incógnita.
● to come from a humble background, ser de origen humilde. ‖ to have a criminal background, tener antecedentes penales. ‖ to stay in the background, mantenerse en segundo plano.
■ background information, información f previa. ‖ background knowledge, conocimientos mpl previos. ‖ background music, música de fondo. ‖ background noise, ruido de fondo.
backhand ['bækhænd] 1 n revés m. – 2 adj dado,-a con el dorso de la mano. 3 (tennis) del revés.
■ backhand shot, revés m.
backhanded [bæk'hændɪd] 1 adj dado,-a con el dorso de la mano. 2 (compliment) equívoco,-a.
backhander [bæk'hændə'] n fam soborno.
● to slip sb. a backhander, untar la mano a algn.
backing ['bækɪŋ] 1 n (support) apoyo, respaldo: he did it with the government's backing, lo hizo con el apoyo del gobierno. 2 (lining) entretela. 3 MUS acompañamiento.
backlash ['bæklæʃ] n reacción f violenta y repentina.
backlog ['bæklɒg] n acumulación f de trabajo, trabajos mpl pendientes.
backpack ['bækpæk] 1 n US mochila. – 2 i hacer de trotamundos: my sister's backpacking around Europe, mi hermana hace de trotamundos por toda Europa.
backpacker ['bækpækə'] n mochilero,-a, trotamundos mf.
backpacking ['bækpækɪŋ] n el viajar m como trotamundos: backpacking's become really popular, viajar como trotamundos se ha puesto muy de moda.
● to go backpacking, hacer de trotamundos.
backpedal ['bækpedəl] 1 i pedalear hacia atrás. 2 fig desdecirse.
▲ pt & pp backpedalled (US backpedaled), ger backpedalling (US backpedaling).
backrest ['bækrest] n respaldo.
back-seat ['bæksiːt] n asiento trasero.
● to take a back-seat, desempeñar un papel secundario.
■ back-seat driver, persona que importuna al conductor de un coche con consejos innecesarios.
backside [bæk'saɪd] n fam trasero.
● to tan sb.'s backside, zurrarle la badana a algn.
backslide ['bækslaɪd] i reincidir.
▲ pt & pp backslid ['bækslɪd].
backsliding ['bækslaɪdɪŋ] n reincidencia.

backstage [bæk'steɪdʒ] 1 n (area) bastidores mpl. 2 (dressing-rooms) camerinos mpl. – 3 adj de bastidores. – 4 adv entre bastidores: they met him backstage, le encontraron entre bastidores.
● to be backstage, estar entre bastidores.
■ backstage life, vida privada de los actores.
backstairs [bæk'steəz] 1 adj clandestino,-a, secreto,-a: a backstairs deal, un acuerdo clandestino. – 2 npl escalera de servicio.
backstreet ['bækstriːt] n callejuela m, calle f tranquila apartada del centro.
■ backstreet abortion, aborto ilegal. ‖ backstreet deals, negocios mpl sucios.
backstroke ['bækstrəʊk] n (swimming) espalda.
● to do the backstroke, nadar a espalda.
backtrack ['bæktræk] 1 i (retrace one's steps) desandar lo andado, volverse atrás. 2 (reverse opinion) desdecirse.
backup ['bækʌp] 1 n (moral support) apoyo, respaldo. 2 (reserve) reserva. 3 COMPUT copia de seguridad.
■ backup file, archivo de seguridad. ‖ backup services, servicios mpl auxiliares.
backward ['bækwəd] 1 adj hacia atrás: a backward movement, un movimiento hacia atrás. 2 (child) atrasado,-a. 3 (shy) tímido,-a. 4 (unassertive) modesto,-a. 5 (country) subdesarrollado,-a. – 6 adv → backwards.
● he's not backward at coming forward, no se corta ni un pelo.
backwardness ['bækwədnəs] 1 n (of child) atraso. 2 (shyness) timidez f. 3 (unassertiveness) modestia.
backwards ['bækwədz] 1 adv hacia atrás: she took a step backwards, dio un paso hacia atrás. 2 (the wrong way) al revés: he always does things backwards, siempre hace las cosas al revés.
● backwards and forwards, de acá para allá. ‖ a backwards and forwards motion, un vaivén. ‖ to move backwards, retroceder. ‖ to walk backwards, andar de espaldas. ‖ to fall backwards, caerse de espaldas. ‖ to know sth. backwards, saber algo al dedillo. ‖ to bend over backwards to do sth, hacer todo lo posible para hacer algo: he bent over backwards to help us, hizo todo lo posible para ayudarnos.
backwash ['bækwɒʃ] 1 n (wind, water) remolino. 2 fig repercusión f, eco.
backwater ['bækwɔːtə'] 1 n fig (remote place) lugar m apartado, remanso. 2 (peaceful place) sitio tranquilo. 3 (of water) brazo de río estancado.
■ cultural backwater, desierto cultural.
backyard [bæk'jɑːd] 1 n patio de atrás, AM traspatio. 2 US jardín m de atrás.
bacon ['beɪkən] n tocino, bacon m.
● to bring home the bacon, fam ganarse el pan. ‖ to save one's bacon, fam salvar el pellejo.
bacteria ['bæktɪərɪə] npl bacterias fpl.
▲ sing bacterium.
bacterial [bæk'tɪərɪəl] adj bacteriano,-a.
bactericide [bæk'tɪərɪsaɪd] n bactericida m.
bacteriological [bæktɪərɪə'lɒdʒɪkəl] adj bacteriológico,-a.
bacteriologist [bæktɪərɪ'ɒlədʒɪst] n bacteriólogo,-a.
bacteriology [bæktɪərɪ'ɒlədʒɪ] n bacteriología.
bacterium [bæk'tɪərɪəm] n bacteria.
▲ pl bacteria.
bad [bæd] 1 adj malo,-a; (before masc noun) mal: he made a bad decision, tomó una mala decisión; he arrived at a bad time, llegó en un mal momento. 2 (rotten) podrido,-a, pasado,-a. 3 (serious) grave: they had a bad ac-

● **to cause a ballyhoo,** armar un jaleo. ‖ **to make a great ballyhoo about sth.,** dar mucho bombo a algo.
balm [baːm] *n* bálsamo.
balmy ['baːmɪ] **1** *adj (weather)* suave. **2** *(soothing)* balsámico,-a.
▲ *comp balmier, superl balmiest.*
baloney [bə'ləʊnɪ] *n* us *sl* chorradas *fpl: it's a load of baloney,* es un rollo patatero.
balsam ['bɔːlsəm] *n* → **balm.**
Baltic ['bɔːltɪk] *adj* báltico,-a.
■ **the Baltic (Sea),** el (mar) Báltico.
balustrade [bælə'streɪd] *n* balaustrada, barandilla.
bamboo [bæm'buː] *n* bambú *m.*
bamboozle [bæm'buːzəl] **1** *t fam (cajole)* engatusar. **2** *(cheat)* engañar.
ban [bæn] **1** *n* prohibición *f,* interdicción *f.* – **2** *t* prohibir.
● **to ban sb. from doing sth.,** prohibirle a algn. que haga algo. ‖ **to ban sb. from driving,** retirarle el carnet a algn. ‖ **to ban a player,** suspender a un,-a jugador,-ra. ‖ **to impose/put a ban on sth.,** prohibir algo.
▲ *pt & pp* **banned,** *ger* **banning.**
banal [bə'naːl] **1** *adj (commonplace)* banal, trivial. **2** *(trite)* trillado,-a.
banality [bə'nælɪtɪ] *n* banalidad *f.*
▲ *pl* **banalities.**
banana [bə'naːnə] **1** *n (fruit)* plátano, banana. **2** *(tree)* bananero, ᴀᴍ banano.
● **to be bananas,** estar chiflado,-a. ‖ **to go bananas,** cogerle a uno un patatús.
■ **banana plantation,** platanal *m.* ‖ **banana republic,** república bananera. ‖ **banana skin,** *(gen)* piel *f* de plátano; *(blunder)* pifia. ‖ **banana split,** banana split *m,* postre *m* de helado y plátano con nata.
band [bænd] **1** *n* ᴍᴜꜱ banda; *(pop)* conjunto; *(jazz)* orquesta. **2** *(strip)* tira. **3** *(of hat)* cinta, cintillo. **4** *(around waist)* ceñidor *m,* faja. **5** *(around arm)* brazalete *m.* **6** *(wrapper)* faja. **7** *(stripe)* raya. **8** ᴘʜʏꜱ banda, frecuencia. **9** ᴛᴇᴄʜ correa. **10** *(youths)* pandilla; *(thieves)* banda.
● **to band together,** acuadrillarse, apiñarse.
■ **military band,** banda militar. ‖ **elastic band / rubber band,** goma elástica, goma. ‖ **frequency band,** banda de frecuencia.
bandage ['bændɪdʒ] **1** *n* venda, vendaje *m.* – **2** *t* vendar.
◆ **to bandage up** *t sep* vendar.
Band-Aid ['bændeɪd] *n* tirita.
▲ *Es marca registrada.*
B and B ['biːən'biː] *abbr (bed and breakfast)* casa de huéspedes que ofrece habitación y desayuno incluido.
bandit ['bændɪt] *n* bandido,-a.
bandmaster ['bændmaːstə'] *n* director *m* de una banda.
bandsman ['bændzmən] *n* ᴍᴜꜱ músico *m* que toca en una banda.
▲ *pl* **bandsmen** ['bændzmən].
bandstand ['bændstænd] *n* quiosco de música.
bandwagon ['bændwægən] **to jump on the bandwagon,** dar subirse al tren.
bandy¹ ['bændɪ] *adj (legs)* arqueado,-a: *he has bandy legs,* es estevado, tiene las piernas arqueadas.
bandy² ['bændɪ] *t* ꜱᴘ *(ball)* pasarse.
◆ **to bandy about** *t sep (story, information)* difundir.
● **to bandy sb.'s name about,** difamar algn., hablar mal de algn. ‖ **to bandy words with sb.,** discutir con algn.
▲ *pt & pp* **bandied,** *ger* **bandying.**

bandy-legged ['bændɪlegd] *adj* estevado,-a, patiestevado,-a.
bane [beɪn] **1** *n (cause of trouble)* perdición *f,* ruina. **2** *(poison)* veneno.
● **to be the bane of sb.'s life,** amargarle la vida a algn.
bang [bæŋ] **1** *n (blow)* golpe *m.* **2** *(noise)* ruido; *(of gun)* estampido; *(explosion)* estallido; *(of door)* portazo. **3** us flequillo. – **4** *t* golpear, dar golpes en: *don't bang the table!,* ¡no des golpes en la mesa! **5** *taboo (have sex with)* follar. – **6** *i* dar golpes: *the shutters were banging all night,* las persianas estuvieron dando golpes toda la noche. **7** *taboo (have sex with)* follar. – **8** *adv fam* justo: *bang in the middle,* justo en medio.
◆ **to bang about 1** *t sep* maltratar, destrozar. – **2** *i* moverse estrepitosamente. ‖ **to bang away on** *t insep (musical instrument)* aporrear. ‖ **to bang on** *i* machacar: *stop banging on!,* ¡no machaques! ‖ **to bang on about** *t insep* machacar en: *he's always banging on about his in-laws,* siempre machaca en el tema de sus suegros. ‖ **to bang out** *t sep (tune)* tocar con mucho ruido. ‖ **to bang up** *t sep* enchironar, meter en la cárcel: *they banged him up for ten years,* le enchironaron durante diez años.
● **bang on!,** *fam* ¡exacto! ‖ **bang go my chances!,** *fam* ¡mi gozo en un pozo! ‖ **to go bang,** hacer pum. ‖ **to go with a bang,** tener mucho éxito. ‖ **it's like banging your head against a brick wall,** es como machacar en hierro frío. ‖ **to bang the door,** dar un portazo. ‖ **to bang on a door,** dar golpes en una puerta. ‖ **to bang one's fist on the table,** dar un puñetazo en la mesa. ‖ **to bang against sth.,** dar un golpe contra algo. ‖ **to bang into sb. / sth.,** chocar contra algn. / algo. ‖ **to bang on a drum,** tocar un tambor. ‖ **to bang one's head,** darse un golpe en la cabeza. ‖ **to bang sb. on the head,** dar un coscorrón en la cabeza a algn.
banger ['bæŋə'] **1** *n (firework)* petardo. **2** ᴳʙ *fam (sausage)* salchicha. **3** *fam (car)* tartana, trasto.
Bangladesh [bæŋglə'deʃ] *n* Bangladesh.
Bangladeshi [bæŋglə'deʃɪ] **1** *adj* bangladesí. – **2** *n* bangladesí *mf.*
bangle ['bæŋgəl] *n* brazalete *m,* ajorca.
banish ['bænɪʃ] *t (expel)* desterrar: *they banished him from his homeland,* lo desterraron de su patria.
● **to banish sadness / worry / fear,** desterrar la tristeza / las preocupaciones / el miedo.
banishment ['bænɪʃmənt] *n* destierro, exilio.
banister ['bænɪstə'] *n* pasamanos *m,* barandilla.
banjo ['bændʒəʊ] *n* ᴍᴜꜱ banjo.
▲ *pl* **banjos** o **banjoes.**
bank¹ [bæŋk] **1** *n* ꜰɪɴ banco. – **2** *t (deposit money)* ingresar, depositar.
◆ **to bank on** *t insep* contar con.
● **to bank with,** tener una cuenta en.
■ **bank balance,** saldo. ‖ **bank card,** tarjeta bancaria. ‖ **bank charges,** cargos *mpl* de comisiones. ‖ **bank draft,** letra bancaria. ‖ **bank holiday,** ᴳʙ *(día)* festivo. ‖ **bank manager,** director,-ra de sucursal bancaria. ‖ **eye bank,** banco de ojos. ‖ **issuing bank,** banco emisor. ‖ **lending bank,** banco hipotecario. ‖ **loans bank,** banco hipotecario.
bank² [bæŋk] **1** *n (of river)* ribera; *(edge)* orilla: *on the banks of the Manzanares,* a orillas del Manzanares. **2** *(mound)* loma; *(embankment)* terraplén *m.* **3** *(slope)* pendiente *f.* **4** *(of cloud, fog)* banco. – **5** *t (soil, earth)* amontonar. **6** *(river)* encauzar.
bank³ [bæŋk] *n* ᴛᴇᴄʜ *(row, line)* batería: *a bank of lights,* una batería de luces.

bankbook ['bæŋkbʊk] *n* libreta de ahorro, cartilla de ahorro.

banker ['bæŋkə'] *n* banquero,-a.

banking ['bæŋkɪŋ] *n* banca.

banknote ['bæŋknəʊt] *n* billete *m* de banco.

bankroll ['bæŋkrəʊl] **1** *n* us fajo de billetes. **2** (*funds*) fondos *mpl*, recursos *mpl*. – **3** *t* *sl* dar apoyo financiero.

bankrupt ['bæŋkrʌpt] **1** *adj* quebrado,-a, insolvente. – **2** *n* quebrado,-a. – **3** *t* hacer quebrar, arruinar.
● to be declared bankrupt, declararse en quiebra. ‖ to go bankrupt, quebrar, hacer bancarrota. ‖ to bankrupt oneself, arruinarse.

bankruptcy ['bæŋkrʌptsɪ] *n* quiebra, bancarrota.
▲ *pl* bankruptcies.

banner ['bænə'] **1** *n* (*flag*) bandera. **2** (*placard*) pancarta. **3** (*pennant*) banderola. – **4** *adj* us excelente, de primera.
■ banner headlines, grandes titulares *mpl*.

bannister ['bænɪstə'] *n* → **banister**.

banns [bænz] *npl* amonestaciones *fpl*.
● to publish the banns, correr las amonestaciones.

banquet ['bæŋkwɪt] *n* banquete *m*.

banshee [bæn'ʃiː] *n* espíritu maligno irlandés que con sus gemidos anuncia la muerte.

bantam ['bæntəm] *n* gallina enana, gallina bantam.

bantamweight ['bæntəmweɪt] *n* (*boxing*) peso gallo.

banter ['bæntə'] **1** *n* bromas *fpl*, guasa *f*. – **2** *i* bromear, estar de guasa.

baptise [bæp'taɪz] *t* → **baptize**.

baptism ['bæptɪzəm] *n* bautismo.

baptismal [bæp'tɪzməl] *adj* bautismal.

Baptist ['bæptɪst] **1** *n* REL baptista *mf*. – **2** *adj* REL baptista.
■ Saint John the Baptist, San Juan Bautista.

baptistery ['bæptɪstrɪ] *n* baptisterio.
▲ *pl* baptisteries.

baptistry ['bæptɪstrɪ] *n* → **baptistery**.
▲ *pl* baptistries.

baptize [bæp'taɪz] *t* bautizar.

bar [bɑː'] **1** *n* (*iron, gold*) barra. **2** (*prison*) barrote *m*. **3** (*soap*) pastilla. **4** (*chocolate*) tableta. **5** (*on door*) tranca. **6** (*gymnastics*) barra. **7** (*obstacle*) obstáculo, traba. **8** (*counter*) barra, mostrador *m*. **9** (*room*) bar *m*. **10** (*of colour, light*) franja. **11** JUR (*in court*) tribunal *m*. – **12** *t* (*door*) atrancar; (*road, access*) cortar. **13** (*ban*) prohibir, vedar; (*from a place*) excluir, prohibir la entrada. **14** (*prevent*) impedir. – **15** *prep* excepto, salvo: *they all came, bar his parents*, acudieron todos, excepto sus padres. – **16** the Bar, *n* JUR el colegio de abogados.
● bar none, sin excepción. ‖ behind bars, entre rejas. ‖ to bar sb. from doing sth., prohibir a algn. que haga algo. ‖ to be called to the bar, ser admitido,-a al ejercicio de la abogacía. ‖ to summon to the bar, hacer comparecer delante del tribunal.
■ asymmetrical bars, barras *fpl* asimétricas. ‖ bar billiards, billar *m*. ‖ bar chart, gráfica estadística. ‖ bar line, MUS barra. ‖ colour bar, segregación *f* racial, apartheid *m*. ‖ heel bar, *establecimiento donde se repara el calzado en el acto*. ‖ horizontal bar, barra fija. ‖ parallel bars, barras *fpl* paralelas. ‖ snack bar, bar-restaurante *m*, snack bar *m*. ‖ the prisoner at the bar, el acusado, la acusada.
▲ *pt & pp* barred, *ger* barring.

barb [bɑːb] **1** *n* púa, lengüeta. **2** *fig* (*comment*) dardo.

Barbadian [bɑː'beɪdɪən] **1** *adj* de Barbados. – **2** *n* (*person*) nativo,-a de Barbados.

Barbados [bɑː'beɪdɒs] *n* Barbados.

barbarian [bɑː'beərɪən] **1** *adj* bárbaro,-a. – **2** *n* bárbaro,-a.

barbaric [bɑː'bærɪk] *adj* bárbaro,-a.

barbarity [bɑː'bærɪtɪ] *n* barbaridad *f*.
▲ *pl* barbarities.

barbarize ['bɑːbəraɪz] *t* barbarizar.

barbarous ['bɑːbərəs] *adj* bárbaro,-a.

Barbary ['bɑːbərɪ] *n* Berbería.
■ Barbary ape, macaco.

barbecue ['bɑːbəkjuː] **1** *n* (*appliance*) barbacoa; (*meal*) parrillada. – **2** *t* asar a la parrilla.
● to have a barbecue, hacer una parrillada.
■ barbecue sauce, salsa barbacoa.
▲ *ger* barbecuing.

barbed [bɑːbd] **1** *adj* con púas, punzante. **2** *fig* mordaz, incisivo,-a: *a barbed comment*, un comentario incisivo.
■ barbed wire, alambre *m* de púas.

barbel ['bɑːbəl] *n* (*fish*) barbo.

barbell ['bɑːbəl] *n* barra con pesas, haltera.

barber ['bɑːbə'] *n* barbero.
■ barber's shop, barbería.

barbershop ['bɑːbəʃɒp] *n* us barbería.

barbiturate [bɑː'bɪtʃərət] *n* barbitúrico.

bard [bɑːd] *n* bardo, vate *m*.
■ the Bard of Avon, William Shakespeare.

bare [beə'] **1** *adj* (*naked*) desnudo,-a; (*head*) descubierto,-a; (*feet*) descalzo,-a. **2** (*land*) raso,-a; (*tree, plant*) sin hojas. **3** (*empty*) vacío,-a; (*unfurnished*) sin muebles. **4** (*scant*) escaso,-a. **5** (*worn*) gastado,-a, raído,-a. – **6** *t* desnudar; (*uncover*) descubrir.
● to bare one's teeth, enseñar los dientes. ‖ to bare one's soul, desnudarse, revelar sus secretos más íntimos. ‖ to earn a bare living, ganar lo justo para vivir. ‖ to lay bare, poner al descubierto. ‖ with one's bare hands, con sus propias manos.
■ the bare essentials, lo imprescindible. ‖ the bare facts, los hechos *mpl* innegables. ‖ the bare minimum, lo justo. ‖ the bare truth, la pura verdad *f*.

bareback ['beəbæk] **1** *adj* a pelo: *bareback rider*, jinete que monta a pelo. – **2** *adv* a pelo.
● to ride bareback, montar a pelo.

barefaced ['beəfeɪst] *adj* descarado,-a.
■ barefaced cheek, morro, descaro: *he had the barefaced cheek to tell me I was wrong*, tuvo el morro de decirme que no tenía razón.

barefoot ['beəfʊt] **1** *adj* descalzo,-a. – **2** *adv* descalzo,-a: *she was barefoot*, iba descalza.

bareheaded [beə'hedɪd] *adj* con la cabeza descubierta, sin sombrero.

barelegged ['beəlegd] *adj* con las piernas desnudas, en pernetas.

barely ['beəlɪ] **1** *adv* apenas: *he can barely read*, apenas sabe leer. **2** (*scantily*) escasamente: *a barely furnished flat*, un piso escasamente amueblado.

bareness ['beənəs] *n* desnudez *f*. **2** *fig* lo escueto.

bargain ['bɑːgən] **1** *n* (*agreement*) trato, acuerdo. **2** (*good buy*) ganga, bicoca. – **3** *i* (*negotiate*) negociar. **4** (*haggle*) regatear.
◆ to bargain away *t sep* malbaratar, malvender: *he bargained away his property*, malbarató sus propiedades. ‖ to bargain for *t insep* contar con, esperar: *they hadn't bargained for rain*, no habían contado con la lluvia.
● to bargain with sb. for sth., negociar algo con algn.: *they bargained with the bosses for a pay rise*, negociaron un aumento de sueldo con la patronal. ‖ to

drive a hard **bargain,** imponer duras condiciones. ‖ **more than one bargained for,** más de lo que uno esperaba: *I only wanted a biscuit but they gave me a plateful, much more than I bargained for,* sólo quería una galleta, pero me dieron un plato entero, mucho más de lo que me esperaba; *he got more than he bargained for when he picked a fight with the boxer's brother,* cuando se metió con el hermano del boxeador, fue por lana y salió trasquilado. ‖ **to strike a bargain,** cerrar un acuerdo. ‖ **into the bargain,** además: *...and he got a free bottle of wine into the bargain,* ...y además le ofrecieron una botella de vino gratis.
■ **bargain basement,** sección *f* de oportunidades. ‖ **bargain offer,** oferta especial. ‖ **bargain price,** precio de oferta, precio de saldo.
bargaining ['bɑːgənɪŋ] **1** *n* COMM negociación *f.* **2** (*haggling*) regateo.
■ **free-collective bargaining,** negociaciones *fpl* colectivas.
barge [bɑːdʒ] **1** *n* gabarra, barcaza. – **2** *t* transportar en barcaza.
◆ **to barge around** *i* dar vueltas sin ton ni son. ‖ **to barge in** *i* entrar sin llamar: *he barged in,* entró sin llamar. ‖ **to barge into** *t insep* irrumpir en: *he barged into the bedroom,* irrumpió en el dormitorio.
● **to barge in on a conversation,** meter baza. ‖ **to barge one's way through the crowd,** abrirse paso entre la multitud a empujones.
bargee [bɑːˈdʒiː] *n* gabarrero.
baritone ['bærɪtəʊn] **1** *n* barítono. – **2** *adj* barítono.
barium ['beərɪʌm] *n* CHEM bario.
■ **barium meal,** sulfato de bario.
bark¹ [bɑːk] **1** *n* (*of dog*) ladrido. **2** (*cough*) tos *f* fuerte. – **3** *i* ladrar. – **4** *t* (*shout*) gritar: *he barked an order,* gritó una orden. – **5** *i* (*cough*) tener una tos fuerte.
● **to bark up the wrong tree,** tomar el rábano por las hojas. ‖ **his bark is worse than his bite,** perro ladrador poco mordedor.
bark² [bɑːk] *n* (*of tree*) corteza.
barking ['bɑːkɪŋ] *n* (*of dog*) ladrido.
● **to be barking mad,** estar como una cabra. ■ **a barking cough,** una tos *f* fuerte.
barley ['bɑːlɪ] *n* cebada.
■ **barley field,** cebadal *m.* ‖ **barley sugar,** *tipo de caramelo.* ‖ **barley water,** GB *bebida hecha de jarabe de frutas y cebada.*
barmaid ['bɑːmeɪd] *n* camarera.
barman ['bɑːmən] *n* camarero, barman *m.*
▲ *pl* **barmen** ['bɑːmen].
barmy ['bɑːmɪ] *adj fam* chiflado,-a, chalado,-a.
▲ *comp* **barmier;** *superl* **barmiest.**
barn [bɑːn] *n* (*for grain*) granero.
■ **barn dance,** baile *m* popular (*que tiene lugar en un granero*).
barnacle ['bɑːnəkəl] *n* percebe *m.*
■ **barnacle goose,** barnacla *m.*
barnstorm ['bɑːnstɔːm] **1** *i* recorrer áreas rurales representando obras de teatro. **2** US POL hacer campaña (*en áreas rurales*).
barnyard ['bɑːnjɑːd] *n* corral *m.*
barometer [bəˈrɒmɪtəʳ] *n* barómetro.
■ **aneroid barometer,** barómetro aneroide. ‖ **mercury barometer,** barómetro de mercurio. ‖ **recording barometer,** barómetro registrador.
barometric [bærəˈmetrɪk] *adj* barométrico,-a.
■ **barometric pressure,** presión *f* barométrica.

baron ['bærən] *n* barón *m.*
■ **drugs baron,** potentado de la droga. ‖ **oil baron,** magnate *m* del petróleo.
baroness ['bærənəs] *n* baronesa.
baronet ['bærənət] *n* baronet *m.*
baronial [bəˈrəʊnɪəl] **1** *adj* de barón. **2** señorial.
■ **baronial mansion,** casa señorial, mansión *f.*
baroque [bəˈrɒk] **1** *adj* barroco,-a. – **2** *n* barroco.
barque [bɑːk] *n* bricbarca.
barrack¹ ['bærək] *t* (*soldiers*) acuartelar.
barrack² ['bærək] *t* (*jeer*) abuchear.
barracking ['bærəkɪŋ] *n* acuartelamiento.
● **to give sb. a good barracking,** poner verde a algn.
barrack-room ['bærəkruːm] *n* dormitorio de tropa.
■ **barrack-room joke,** chiste *m* cuartelero. ‖ **barrack-room lawyer,** GB picapleitos *m.*
barracks ['bærəks] *npl* cuartel *m.*
● **to be confined to barracks,** estar bajo arresto en cuartel.
barracuda [bærəˈkuːdə] *n* barracuda.
barrage ['bærɑːʒ] **1** *n* (*dam*) presa, embalse *m.* **2** MIL barrera de fuego. **3** *fig* (*of questions*) aluvión *m.*
barrel ['bærəl] **1** *n* (*of beer*) barril *m;* (*of wine*) tonel *m,* cuba. **2** (*of gun*) cañón *m.* **3** (*of pen*) depósito. **4** TECH tambor *m.* – **5** *t* embarrilar, poner en barriles.
● **to scrape the bottom of the barrel,** utilizar algo como último recurso. ‖ **to have sb. over a barrel,** poner a algn. entre la espada y la pared.
▲ *pt & pp* **barrelled** (US **barreled**), *ger* **barrelling** (US **barreling**).
barrel-organ ['bærəlɔːgən] *n* MUS organillo.
barren ['bærən] **1** *adj* (*land, woman*) estéril. **2** (*meagre*) escaso,-a.
barrenness ['bærənnəs] *n* esterilidad *f.*
barricade [bærɪˈkeɪd] **1** *n* barricada. – **2** *t* poner barricadas en.
● **to storm the barricades,** asaltar las barricadas. ‖ **to barricade oneself in,** encerrarse a cal y canto.
barrier ['bærɪəʳ] **1** *n* barrera. **2** *fig* obstáculo.
■ **barrier reef,** banco de coral, arrecife *m.* ‖ **barrier cream,** crema dermoprotectora. ‖ **language barrier,** barrera de los idiomas. ‖ **class barrier,** barrera social, discriminación *f* social entre las clases. ‖ **a barrier to progress,** un obstáculo al progreso.
barrister ['bærɪstəʳ] *n* abogado,-a (*capacitado,-a para actuar en tribunales superiores*).
barrow ['bærəʊ] *n* (*wheelbarrow*) carretilla; (*for carrying goods*) carro.
■ **barrowboy,** vendedor *m* de frutas y verduras (*en un mercado*).
barstool ['bɑːstuːl] *n* taburete *m* de bar.
Bart. [bɑːt] *abbr* (*baronet*) baronet *m.*
bartender ['bɑːtendəʳ] *n* US camarero, barman *m.*
barter ['bɑːtəʳ] **1** *n* trueque *m.* – **2** *t* trocar.
basalt ['bæsɔːlt] *n* basalto.
base¹ [beɪs] **1** *n* (*gen*) base *f: a drink with a whisky base,* una bebida a base de whisky. **2** ARCH (*of column*) basa, base *f.* **3** (*of word*) raíz *f.* – **4** *t* basar: *the novel is based on real events,* la novela está basada en hechos reales. **5** MIL (*troops*) estacionar.
● **to be based in,** (*troops*) tener la base en: *they were based in Germany,* tenían su base en Alemania. ‖ **to get to first base,** superar el primer reto.
■ **airforce base,** base *f* aérea. ‖ **base rate,** tipo base. ‖ **base unit,** unidad *f* base. ‖ **military base,** base *f* militar. ‖ **naval base,** base *f* naval. ‖ **power base,** base *f* de operaciones.

base² [beɪs] **1** *adj* bajo,-a, vil. **2** (*metal*) común, de baja ley.

baseball ['beɪsbɔːl] *n* béisbol *m*.
■ **baseball bat,** bate *m*.

baseboard ['beɪsbɔːð] *n* US zócalo.

Basel ['bɑːzəl] *n* Basilea.

baseless ['beɪsləs] *adj* infundado,-a, sin fundamento.

baseline ['beɪslaɪn] **1** *n* SP (*tennis*) línea de saque; (*baseball*) línea de base. **2** (*surveying*) base *f.* **3** (*diagram*) línea cero. **4** ART punto de fuga.

basement ['beɪsmənt] *n* sótano.

baseness ['beɪsnəs] *n* vileza, bajeza.

bash [bæʃ] **1** *t fam* golpear, aporrear. – **2** *n fam* (*blow*) golpe *m.* **3** *fam* (*try*) intento. **4** *sl* (*party, social event*) jarana, juerga.
◆ **to bash about** *t sep* dar una paliza: *he really bashed him about,* le dio una buena paliza. ‖ **to bash down** *t sep* derribar, echar abajo: *they bashed the door down,* derribaron la puerta. ‖ **to bash in** *t sep* abollar: *he bashed his car in,* abolló su coche. ‖ **to bash into** *t insep* estrellarse contra: *he bashed into the car in front,* se estrelló contra el coche de delante.
● **to have a bash at sth.,** *fam* probar suerte con algo. ‖ **to bash sb.'s head in,** romperle la crisma a algn.

bashful ['bæʃfʊl] *adj* vergonzoso,-a, tímido,-a, modesto,-a.

bashfulness ['bæʃfʊlnəs] *n* vergüenza, timidez *f.*

basic ['beɪsɪk] **1** *adj* básico,-a. **2** (*elementary*) elemental, para principiantes: *basic English,* inglés elemental. – **3 the basics,** *npl* lo esencial.

BASIC ['beɪsɪk] *abbr* (*Beginner's All-purpose Symbolic Instruction Code*) código de instrucción simbólico omnivalente para principiantes; (*abbreviation*) BASIC.

basil ['bæzəl] *n* BOT albahaca.

basilica [bə'zɪlɪkə] *n* basílica.

basilisk ['bæzɪlɪsk] *n* basilisco.

basin ['beɪsən] **1** *n* (*bowl*) cuenco; (*washbowl*) palangana. **2** (*washbasin*) lavabo. **3** GEOG cuenca.

basis ['beɪsɪs] *n* base *f,* fundamento.
● **on a daily / weekly / monthly basis,** cada día / semana / mes. ‖ **on the basis of ...,** según indica (*indican etc*) ...: *on the basis of the evidence,* según indican las pruebas.
▲ *pl* **bases** ['beɪsɪːz].

bask [bɑːsk] *i* tumbarse al sol.
● **to bask in the sun,** tomar el sol. ‖ **to bask in reflected glory,** participar del éxito ajeno.

basket ['bɑːskɪt] **1** *n* cesta, cesto. **2** (*basketball*) canasta, cesta. **3** (*of balloon*) barquilla. **4** *sl* imbécil *mf,* capullo.
■ **basket case,** caso perdido.

basketball ['bɑːskɪtbɔːl] *n* baloncesto.

basketwork ['bɑːskɪtwɜːk] *n* cestería, mimbre *m & f.*

Basle [bɑːl] *n* → **Basel.**

Basque [bɑːsk] **1** *adj* vasco,-a. – **2** *n* (*person*) vasco,-a. **3** (*language*) vasco, eusquera *m,* euskera *m,* vascuence *m.*
■ **the Basque Country,** el País *m* Vasco, Euskadi *m.* ‖ **the Basque provinces,** (*in Spain*) las provincias *fpl* Vascongadas.

bas-relief [bæsrɪ'liːf] *n* bajo-relieve *m.*

bass¹ [beɪs] **1** *n* MUS (*singer*) bajo. **2** MUS (*notes*) graves *mpl.* **3** MUS (*guitar*) bajo. – **4** *adj* MUS bajo,-a.
■ **bass clef,** clave *f* de fa.

bass² [bæs] *n* (*fish*) róbalo, lubina; (*freshwater*) perca.

basset ['bæsɪt] *n* ZOOL perro basset.

bassoon [bə'suːn] *n* fagot *m.*

bassoonist [bə'suːnɪst] *n* fagotista *mf.*

bastard ['bɑːstəd] **1** *n* bastardo,-a. **2** *taboo* cabrón *m*: *poor bastard!,* ¡pobre desgraciado! – **3** *adj* ilegítimo,-a, bastardo,-a.

bastardize ['bɑːstədaɪz] **1** *t* (*debase*) corromper, degradar. **2** (*text, piece of work*) destrozar.

baste¹ [beɪst] *t* CULIN rociar, bañar.

baste² [beɪst] *t* SEW hilvanar.

baste³ [beɪst] *t* apalear, dar una paliza a.

bastion ['bæstɪən] *n* baluarte *m.*

bat¹ [bæt] *n* ZOOL murciélago.
● **like a bat out of hell,** a toda leche. ‖ **to be as blind as a bat,** no ver ni torta.
■ **old bat,** *fam* vieja bruja.

bat² [bæt] **1** *n* SP bate *m*; (*table tennis*) pala. – **2** *i* batear.
● **off one's own bat,** por su cuenta.
▲ *pt & pp* **batted,** *ger* **batting.**

bat³ [bæt] *t* pestañear.
● **without batting an eyelid,** sin inmutarse.
▲ *pt & pp* **batted,** *ger* **batting.**

batch [bætʃ] *n* (*gen*) lote *m,* remesa; (*of bread etc*) hornada.
■ **batch processing,** COMPUT procesamiento por lotes.

bated ['beɪtɪd] **with bated breath,** *phr* con ansiedad.

bath [bɑːθ] **1** *n* baño. **2** (*tub*) bañera. – **3** *t* bañar, dar un baño a. – **4** *i* bañarse. – **5 baths,** *npl* piscina *f sing* municipal.
● **to have a bath / take a bath,** bañarse. ‖ **to run a bath,** preparar un baño.
■ **bath gel,** gel *m* de baño. ‖ **bath mat,** alfombra de baño. ‖ **bath salts,** sales *fpl* de baño. ‖ **bath towel,** toalla de baño.

bathe [beɪð] **1** *t* MED (*cut, wound*) lavar. **2** (*eyes*) bañarse. **3** *fig* (*with light*) bañar. – **4** *i* (*in sea*) bañarse.

bather ['beɪðəʳ] *n* bañista *mf.*

bathing ['beɪðɪŋ] *n* baño.
● **"no bathing",** "prohibido bañarse".
■ **bathing costume / bathing suit,** traje *m* de baño.

bathos ['beɪθɒs] **1** *n* paso de lo sublime a lo trivial. **2** (*sentimentality*) sensiblería. **3** (*anticlimax*) decepción *f.*

bathrobe ['bɑːθrəʊb] *n* albornoz *m.*

bathroom ['bɑːθruːm] *n* cuarto de baño.

bathtub ['bɑːθtʌb] *n* US bañera.

batik [bə'tiːk] *n* batik *m.*

batman ['bætmæn] *n* MIL ordenanza *m.*
▲ *pl* **batmen** ['bætmen].

baton ['bætən, 'bætɒn] *n* (*truncheon*) porra. **2** MUS batuta. **3** SP testigo.

batsman ['bætsmən] *n* bateador *m.*
▲ *pl* **batsmen** ['bætsmən].

batswoman ['bætswʊmən] *n* bateadora *f.*
▲ *pl* **batswomen** ['bætswɪmɪn].

battalion [bə'tæljən] *n* batallón *m.*

batten¹ ['bætən] **1** *n* listón *m.* – **2** *t* listonar.
◆ **to batten down** *t sep* sujetar con listones.
● **to batten down the hatches,** atrancar las escotillas. ‖ **to batten on sb.,** prosperar a costa de algn.: *he battened on his family,* prosperó a costa de su familia.

batter¹ ['bætəʳ] *n* CULIN rebozado.
● **in batter,** rebozado,-a: *squid in batter,* calamares a la romana.

batter² ['bætəʳ] *t* (*person*) golpear, apalear; (*bruise*) magullar; (*object*) maltratar, estropear.
● **to batter sb. about,** dar una buena paliza a algn. ‖ **to batter at sth.,** golpear algo: *the police battered at the door,* la policía golpeó la puerta. ‖ **to batter sth. in,** echar algo abajo: *they had to batter the door in,* tuvieron que echar la puerta abajo. ‖ **to batter sb. to death,** matar a algn. a palos.

batter[3] ['bætəʳ] *n* SP (*baseball, cricket*) bateador,-ra.

battered[1] ['bætəd] *adj* CULIN rebozado,-a: *battered fish,* pescado rebozado.

battered[2] ['bætəd] **1** *adj* (*shabby, in bad repair*) estropeado,-a; (*carpet, coat*) raído,-a: *a pair of battered shoes,* un par de zapatos estropeados. **2** (*dented*) abollado,-a. **3** (*bruised*) lleno,-a de magulladuras.
■ **battered baby,** bebé *m* maltratado. ‖ **battered wife,** mujer *f* maltratada.

battering ['bætərɪŋ] *n* (*beating*) apaleamiento.
■ **battering ram,** ariete *m*.

battery ['bætərɪ] **1** *n* ELEC (*wet*) batería; (*dry*) pila. **2** MIL (*of artillery*) batería. **3** THEAT (*row of lights*) batería. **4** (*series*) batería: *the system includes a battery of questions,* el sistema incluye una batería de preguntas.
■ **battery farming,** cría intensiva de animales. ‖ **battery hen,** gallina de criadero.
▲ *pl* **batteries.**

battle ['bætəl] **1** *n* batalla, combate *m*. **2** *fig* lucha: *the battle for the party leadership has begun,* la lucha por el liderazgo del partido ya ha empezado. **– 3** *i* pelearse, batirse: *they battled for weeks,* se pelearon durante semanas.
◆ **to battle on** *i* seguir luchando.
● **in battle dress,** en uniforme de campaña. ‖ *that's half the battle, fig* ya hay medio camino andado. ‖ **to battle against sth.,** *fig* luchar contra algo: *he battled against the illness for years,* luchó contra la enfermedad durante años. ‖ **to battle for sth./sb.,** luchar por algo/algn.: *he's battling for human rights,* lucha por los derechos humanos. ‖ **to battle one's way through,** abrirse camino a empujones: *he had to battle his way through the crowd,* tuvo que abrirse camino entre la multitud a empujones. ‖ **to battle over sth.,** disputar algo a golpes. ‖ **to do battle for,** luchar por. ‖ **to do battle with,** librar batalla con. ‖ **to fight a battle,** luchar. ‖ **to fight a losing battle,** *fig* luchar por una causa perdida.
■ **battle of wits,** duelo de ingenio. ‖ **a battle of wills,** una lucha de voluntades. ‖ **battle cry,** grito de guerra.

battle-ax ['bætəlæks] *n* US → **battle-axe.**

battle-axe ['bætəlæks] **1** *n* hacha de combate. **2** *fig* bruja, arpía.

battlefield ['bætəlfiːld] *n* campo de batalla.

battlements ['bætəlmənts] *npl* ARCH almenas *fpl.*

battleship ['bætəlʃɪp] *n* acorazado.

batty ['bætɪ] *adj fam* chiflado,-a, chalado,-a.
▲ *comp* **battier,** *superl* **battiest.**

bauble ['bɔːbəl] **1** *n* (*trinket*) baratija. **2** (*Christmas decoration*) bola de Navidad.

baulk [bɔːk] *t* → **balk.**

Bavaria [bə'veərɪə] *n* Baviera.

Bavarian [bə'veərɪən] **1** *adj* bávaro,-a. **– 2** *n* bávaro,-a.

bawdy ['bɔːdɪ] *adj* obsceno,-a, grosero,-a: *she told us a bawdy joke,* nos contó un chiste verde.
■ **bawdy house,** *arch* mancebía.
▲ *comp* **bawdier,** *superl* **bawdiest.**

bawl [bɔːl] **1** *i* (*shout*) chillar, gritar. **2** (*weep loudly*) llorar a lágrima viva. **– 3** *t* gritar.
● **to bawl at sb.,** gritarle a algn. ‖ **to bawl out sb.'s name,** gritar el nombre de algn. ‖ **to bawl sb. out,** pegarle una bronca a algn.

bay[1] [beɪ] *n* GEOG bahía; (*large*) golfo.
■ **Bay of Biscay,** golfo de Vizcaya.

bay[2] [beɪ] *n* (*tree*) laurel *m*.
■ **bay leaf,** hoja de laurel.

bay[3] [beɪ] *i* (*howl*) aullar.
● **to bay at the moon,** ladrar a la luna. ‖ **to keep sth. / sb. at bay,** mantener algo / algn. a raya.

bay[4] [beɪ] **1** *n* ARCH (*recess*) hueco, nicho. **– 2** (*in factory*) nave *f*.
■ **parking bay,** área de aparcamiento. ‖ **sick bay,** enfermería. ‖ **bay window,** ventana saliente.

bay[5] [beɪ] **1** *adj* (*colour*) bayo. **– 2** *n* (*colour*) bayo. **3** (*horse*) caballo bayo.

bayonet ['beɪənət] **1** *n* MIL bayoneta. **– 2** *t* MIL pasar a la bayoneta.
■ **bayonet wound,** bayonetazo. ‖ **bayonet charge,** carga a la bayoneta.

bazaar [bə'zɑːʳ] **1** *n* (*eastern*) bazar *m*. **2** (*at church etc*) venta benéfica.

bazooka [bə'zuːkə] *n* MIL bazuca, lanzagranadas *m*.

BBC ['biː'biː'siː] *abbr* (*British Broadcasting Corporation*) compañía británica de radiofusión; (*abbreviation*) BBC *f*.

BC[1] ['biː'siː] *abbr* (*before Christ*) antes de Cristo, antes de Jesucristo; (*abbreviation*) a.d.C., a.d.J.C.

BC[2] ['biː'siː] *abbr* (*British Columbia*) Colombia Británica.

be [biː] **1** *i* (*permanent characteristic*) ser: *she's clever,* es inteligente; *he's blind,* es ciego; *I'm deaf,* soy sordo. **2** (*essential quality*) ser: *diamonds are hard,* los diamantes son duros. **3** (*nationality*) ser: *John's English,* John es inglés; *they are Japanese,* son japoneses. **4** (*occupation*) ser: *he's an engineer,* es ingeniero; *we are both teachers,* los dos somos profesores. **5** (*origin*) ser: *they are from York,* son de York. **6** (*ownership*) ser: *it's my pencil,* es mi lápiz. **7** (*authorship*) ser: *this painting is by Botero,* este cuadro es de Botero. **8** (*composition*) ser: *this cupboard is oak,* este armario es de roble. **9** (*use*) ser: *this product is for tiles,* este producto es para baldosas. **10** (*location*) estar: *Whitby is on the coast,* Whitby está en la costa. **11** (*temporary state*) estar: *your supper's cold,* tu cena está fría; *how are you?,* ¿cómo estás?; *you're a bit deaf today,* estás un poco sordo hoy; *prawns are cheap today,* las gambas están bien de precio hoy. **12** (*age*) tener: *Philip is 22,* Philip tiene 22 años. **13** (*price*) costar, valer: *a single ticket is £9.50,* un billete de ida cuesta £9.50. **14** tener: *he's hot/cold,* tiene calor/frío; *we're hungry/thirsty,* tenemos hambre/sed; *she's in a hurry,* tiene prisa; *he's right,* tiene razón. **– 15 be + *pres part*,** *aux* (*action in progress or near future*) estar: *it is raining,* está lloviendo; *he's working,* está trabajando; *the train is coming,* viene el tren; *I am going on Thursday,* iré el jueves; *she's meeting Mr Broddle tomorrow,* se reunirá con el señor Broddle mañana. **16 be + *pp*,** (*passive*) ser: *she was arrested at the border,* fue detenida en la frontera, la detuvieron en la frontera; *he's hated by everybody,* es odiado por todos, todos lo odian; *he was discharged,* fue dado de alta, lo dieron de alta; *the house has been sold,* la casa ha sido vendida, la casa se ha vendido, han vendido la casa; *he was given a clock,* le dieron un reloj; *thirty children were injured,* treinta niños fueron heridos, treinta niños resultaron heridos; *the two areas of the town are divided by a wall,* las dos zonas de la ciudad están divididas por un muro. **17 be + *to* + *inf*,** (*obligation*) deber, tener que: *you are not to come here again,* no debes volver aquí; *you are to do as I say,* tienes que hacer lo que yo te diga. **18** (*future*): *the King is to visit Egypt,* el Rey visitará Egipto. **– 19 there is / there are,** *phr* hay: *there's some wine in the bottle,* hay algo de vino en la botella; *there are two policemen following us,* hay dos policías que nos siguen; *is there much traffic,* ¿hay mucho tráfico? **20 there was / there were,** había: *there was no money,* no había dinero; *there were twenty five candles on the cake,* había veinticinco velas en la tarta; *were there many people?,* ¿había mucha gente? **21 there will be,** habrá: *there will be snow in the mountains,* habrá nieve en las montañas. **22 there would be,** habría: *there would be time to see the castle,* habría tiempo para ver el castillo; *if Mike came, there would be ten of us,* si viniera Mike, seríamos diez.

◆ **to be after** *i* querer, estar buscando: *what are you after?,* ¿que estás buscando? ‖ **to be off** *i* (*leave*) salir, marcharse; (*be stale, bad*) estar pasado,-a. ‖ **to be in** *1 i* (*at home*) estar en casa. **2** (*in fashion*) estar de moda. ‖ **to be out** *i* (*away*) no estar, estar fuera; (*published*) haber salido; (*extinguished*) estar apagado,-a, haberse apagado; (*unconscious*) estar sin conocimiento: *John's out at the moment,* John no está en estos momentos; *the record was out last week,* el disco salió la semana pasada; *the fire was out,* el fuego se había apagado; *when she was admitted she was out,* cuando la ingresaron estaba sin conocimiento. ‖ **to be away** *i* estar fuera. ‖ **to be back** *i* estar de vuelta, haber vuelto: *is Mr Robinson back?,* ¿ha vuelto el señor Robinson? ‖ **to be for** *t insep* ser partidario,-a de, estar a favor de. ‖ **to be in for** *t insep* estar a punto de tener: *he's in for a surprise,* le espera una sorpresa; *it looks as if we're in for snow,* parece que va a nevar. ‖ **to be over** *i* haber acabado, haber terminado: *the film's over,* la película ha acabado. ‖ **to be up** *i* (*out of bed*) estar levantado,-a. ‖ **to be up to** *1 i* (*capacitated*) estar a la altura de, ser apto,-a para: *he's not up to the job,* no está a la altura del trabajo. **2** (*doing*) hacer: *what are they up to?,* ¿qué están haciendo?

● **to be about to** + *inf,* estar para + *inf,* estar a punto de + *inf: the train is about to arrive,* el tren está a punto de llegar. ‖ **to be or not to be,** ser o no ser.

▲ *pres* 1ª *pers am,* 2ª *pers sing y todas del pl* **are,** 3ª *pers sing* **is;** *pt* 1ª *y* 3ª *pers sing* **was,** 2ª *pers sing y todas del pl;* *pp* **been.**

beach [biːtʃ] **1** *n* playa. – **2** *t* varar.
● **on the beach,** en la playa.
■ **beach hut,** caseta de playa. ‖ **beach umbrella,** sombrilla, quitasol *m.*

beachcomber ['biːtʃkəʊmə'] **1** *n* (*person*) raquero,-a. **2** (*wave*) ola.

beachhead ['biːtʃhed] *n* MIL cabeza de playa.

beachwear [biːtʃweə] *n* ropa de playa.

beacon ['biːkən] **1** *n* (*fire*) almenara. **2** AV MAR baliza. **3** (*lighthouse*) faro. **4** (*hill*) hacho.

bead [biːd] **1** *n* (*on rosary, necklace*) cuenta; (*glass*) abalorio: *a string of beads,* una sarta de cuentas. **2** (*of liquid*) gota: *a bead of sweat,* una gota de sudor.
● **to thread beads,** ensartar cuentas.

beading ['biːdɪŋ] *n* junquillo, tapajuntas *m.*

beady ['biːdɪ] *adj* (*eye*) pequeño,-a y brillante.
▲ *comp* **beadier,** *superl* **beadiest.**

beady-eyed [biːdɪ'aɪd] *adj* de ojos pequeños y brillantes.

beagle ['biːgəl] *n* beagle *m.*

beak[1] [biːk] **1** *n* pico. **2** *fam* (*nose*) nariz *f* ganchuda.

beak[2] [biːk] *n sl* (*magistrate*) juez,-za; (*teacher*) profe,-a.

beaker ['biːkə'] **1** *n* taza alta. **2** (*for measuring, playing dice*) cubilete *m.* **3** CHEM vaso de precipitación.

be-all ['biːɔːl] **the be-all and end-all,** *phr* la única cosa que importa, lo único que vale: *having possessions isn't the be-all and end-all in life,* hay más cosas en la vida que tener posesiones.

beam [biːm] **1** *n* (*wooden*) viga. **2** (*of light*) rayo. **3** (*width of ship*) manga. **4** (*smile*) sonrisa radiante. **5** PHYS haz *m.* – **6** *i* (*shine*) brillar. **7** (*smile*) sonreír. – **8** *t* irradiar, emitir.

● **to be broad in the beam,** ser ancho,-a de caderas.
■ **electron beam,** haz *m* de electrones.

beam-ends [biːm'endz] *npl* MAR cabezas *fpl* de los baos.
● **on her beam-ends,** MAR escorado,-a. ‖ **to be on one's beam ends,** estar sin un duro.

beaming ['biːmɪŋ] *adj* radiante, sonriente.

bean [biːn] **1** *n* (*vegetable*) alubia, judía, haba. **2** (*of coffee*) grano.
● **to be full of beans,** rebosar vitalidad. ‖ **to spill the beans,** descubrir el pastel. ‖ **not a bean,** GB ni un duro. ‖ **not to know beans about sth.,** US no saber ni jota de algo.
■ **bean curd,** tofu *m.* ‖ **bean shoot,** brote *m* de soja. ‖ **broad bean,** haba. ‖ **French bean,** judía verde. ‖ **green bean,** judía verde. ‖ **kidney bean,** frijol *m.* ‖ **runner bean,** judía verde. ‖ **string bean,** judía verde.

beanfeast ['biːnfiːst] *n fam* comilona.

beanpole ['biːnpəʊl] **1** *n* (*stick*) rodrigón *m,* rodriga. **2** *fam* (*person*) espárrago.
● **to be like a beanpole,** estar hecho,-a un espárrago.

beansprout ['biːnspraʊt] *n* brote *m* de soja.

bear[1] [beə'] **1** *n* ZOOL oso. **2** FIN bajista *mf,* especulador,-ra a la baja. **3** (*rough person*) bruto. – **4** *i* FIN vender al iniciarse una bajada de precios para volver a comprar luego a un precio más bajo.
● **to be like a bear with a sore head,** estar de un humor de perros.
■ **bear hug,** apretujón *m,* abrazo muy fuerte. ‖ **bear account,** posición *f* de vendedor. ‖ **bear cub,** ZOOL osezno. ‖ **grizzly bear,** oso pardo. ‖ **the Great Bear,** la Osa Mayor. ‖ **the Little Bear,** la Osa Menor.

bear[2] [beə'] **1** *t* (*carry*) llevar: *the officer bore the flag,* el oficial llevaba la bandera. **2** (*name, date*) llevar: *the document bore the date of the meeting,* el documento llevaba la fecha de la reunión. **3** (*show signs of*) mostrar, revelar: *the body bore no signs of violence,* el cadáver no mostraba señales de violencia. **4** (*weight*) soportar, aguantar; (*responsibility, cost*) asumir. **5** (*tolerate*) soportar, aguantar: *I can't bear him,* no lo soporto; *how do you bear the job?,* ¿cómo aguantas el trabajo? **6** (*fruit*) producir. **7** FIN (*interest*) devengar. **8** (*give birth*) tener, dar a luz: *she has borne a son,* ha tenido un niño; *her daughter was born deaf,* su hija nació sorda. – **9** *i* (*turn*) torcer a: *bear left at the next set of traffic lights,* tuerza hacia la izquierda al próximo semáforo.
◆ **to bear down** *t sep lit* vencer, derrotar. ‖ **to bear out** *t sep* confirmar, corroborar: *his wife bore out the facts,* su mujer confirmó los hechos. ‖ **to bear up** *i* ir tirando: *John's bearing up in spite of his problems,* John va tirando a pesar de sus problemas. ‖ **to bear with** *t insep* tener paciencia con.
● **to bear in mind,** tener presente. ‖ **to bear a grudge,** guardar rencor. ‖ **to bear a resemblance to,** parecerse a. ‖ **to bear hard on,** oprimir. ‖ **to bear witness to sth.,** ser testigo de algo. ‖ **to bear no relation to,** no tener nada que ver con: *the facts bear no relation to this case,* los hechos no tienen nada que ver con este caso. ‖ **to bring pressure to bear,** ejercer presión (**on,** a): *they brought pressure to bear on the government,* ejercieron presión sobre el gobierno. ‖ **it doesn't bear thinking about,** me da escalofríos nada más pensar en ello.
▲ *pt* **bore,** *pp* **borne.**

bearable ['beərəbəl] *adj* soportable, llevadero,-a.

beard [bɪəd] **1** *n* (*on face*) barba. **2** (*of corn*) arista, raspa. – **3** *t* (*oppose*) oponerse a. **4** (*challenge*) desafiar.
● **to beard the lion in his den,** entrar en el cubil de la fiera.

bearded ['bɪədɪd] *adj* barbudo,-a, con barba.
beardless ['bɪədləs] *adj* sin barba, imberbe.
bearer ['beərəʳ] **1** *n* (*of news, cheque, etc*) portador,-ra; (*of passport*) titular *mf*. **2** (*porter*) portador,-ra.
■ **bearer bond**, FIN título al portador.
beargarden ['beəgɑːdən] *n* casa de locos, la casa de Tócame Roque.
bearing ['beərɪŋ] **1** *n* (*posture*) porte *m*. **2** (*relevance*) relación *f*. **3** (*importance*) trascendencia. **4** TECH cojinete *m*. **5** ARCH soporte *m*, columna. **6** MAR orientación *f*.
● **to lose one's bearings,** desorientarse; *fig* perder el norte. ‖ **to have no bearing on,** no tener la menor influencia sobre: *the events had no bearing on his decision,* los acontecimientos no tenían la menor influencia sobre su decisión.
bearish ['beərɪʃ] *adj* FIN bajista.
■ **bearish tendency,** tendencia a la baja.
beast [biːst] **1** *n* bestia, animal *m*. **2** (*unpleasant person*) sinvergüenza *mf*.
■ **beast of burden,** bestia de carga.
beastly [biːstlɪ] **1** *adj* bestial. **2** (*unpleasant*) antipático,-a. **3** *sl* (*damn*) dichoso,-a, maldito,-a. **4** (*weather, job*) espantoso,-a, horroroso,-a.
● **to be beastly to sb.,** tratar a algn. a patadas.
▲ *comp* **beastlier,** *superl* **beastliest**.
beat [biːt] **1** *n* (*of heart*) latido. **2** (*noise*) golpe *m*, ruido; (*of rain*) tamborileo; (*of wings*) aleteo. **3** MUS ritmo. **4** (*of policeman*) ronda. – **5** *t* (*hit*) golpear; (*metals*) martillear; (*person*) azotar; (*drum*) tocar; (*wings*) batir. **6** CULIN batir. **7** (*defeat*) vencer, derrotar; (*in competition*) ganar: *he beat him by 10 points,* le ganó por diez puntos. **8** *fam* (*puzzle*) extrañar, dejar perplejo,-a: *the problem beats me,* el problema me deja perplejo. – **9** *i* (*heart*) latir. **10** (*wings*) batir. – **11** *adj fam* agotado,-a, rendido,-a: *he was beat after the match,* estaba rendido después del partido.
◆ **to beat back** *t sep* hacer retroceder: *they beat back the enemy,* hicieron retroceder al enemigo. ‖ **to beat down** **1** *t sep* (*door*) derribar, echar abajo. **2** (*price*) conseguir un precio más bajo: *I managed to beat him down to £20,* conseguí que me lo dejara en veinte libras. – **3** *i* (*sun*) hacer un sol de justicia; (*rain*) llover a cántaros. ‖ **to beat up** *t sep* dar una paliza a, vapulear.
● **to beat about the bush,** andarse por las ramas. ‖ **to beat against sth.,** golpear contra algo: *the hail beat against the shutters,* el granizo golpeaba contra las persianas. ‖ **to beat on sth.,** dar golpes en algo: *the bailiffs beat on the door,* los administradores dieron golpes en la puerta. ‖ **to beat time,** MUS llevar el compás. ‖ **to beat some sense into sb.,** meter un poco de sentido común en la cabeza de algn. ‖ **to beat sb. to it,** sentar la mano a algn. ‖ **to beat the record,** batir el récord. ‖ **to beat sb. to death,** matar a algn. a palos. ‖ **to beat sb.'s brains out,** romperle la crisma a algn. ‖ **beat it!,** ¡lárgate! ‖ **that beats everything!,** ¡esto es el colmo! ‖ **it beats me how ...,** no me cabe en la cabeza cómo ...
■ **off beat,** raro,-a, extraño,-a. ‖ **the beat generation,** la generación *f* de los beatniks.
▲ *pt* **beat** [biːt], pp **beaten**.
beaten ['biːtən] **1** *adj* (*defeated*) vencido,-a, derrotado,-a. **2** (*metal*) martillado,-a. **3** (*exhausted*) rendido,-a, agotado,-a.
● **off the beaten track,** apartado,-a, aislado,-a: *his house is a bit off the beaten track,* su casa está un poco apartada.
beater ['biːtəʳ] **1** *n* CULIN batidora. **2** (*in hunting*) ojeador,-ra.

beatification [bɪætɪfɪ'keɪʃən] *n* beatificación *f*.
beatify [bɪ'ætɪfaɪ] *t* beatificar.
▲ *pt & pp* **beatified,** *ger* **beatifying**.
beating ['biːtɪŋ] **1** *n* (*thrashing*) paliza. **2** (*defeat*) derrota. **3** (*of heart*) latidos *mpl*.
● **to give sb. a good beating,** dar una buena paliza a algn. ‖ **to take a beating,** sufrir una derrota.
beatitude [bɪ'ætɪtjuːd] *n* beatitud *f*.
■ **the Beatitudes,** las Bienaventuranzas.
beatnik ['biːtnɪk] *n* beatnik *mf*.
beau [bəʊ] **1** *n* galán *m*. **2** (*suitor*) pretendiente *m*.
▲ *pl* **beaux** [bəʊz] o **beau** [bəʊ].
beautician [bjuː'tɪʃən] *n* esteticista *mf*.
beautiful ['bjuːtɪfʊl] **1** *adj* (*person, object, place*) hermoso,-a, bonito,-a, precioso,-a; (*person*) guapo,-a: *a beautiful girl,* una chica hermosa, una chica guapa; *a beautiful place,* un sitio bonito; *a beautiful painting,* un cuadro precioso. **2** (*wonderful*) maravilloso,-a, magnífico,-a. **3** (*delicious*) delicioso,-a.
beautify ['bjuːtɪfaɪ] **1** *t* embellecer. – **2** *i* embellecerse.
▲ *pt & pp* **beautified,** *ger* **beautifying**.
beauty ['bjuːtɪ] **1** *n* belleza, hermosura: *a sculpture of great beauty,* una escultura de una gran belleza. **2** (*person*) belleza.
● **beauty is only skin deep,** las apariencias engañan. ‖ **that's a beauty!,** (*object*) ¡es una maravilla!; (*shot in game*) ¡qué golpe más bueno! ‖ **that's the beauty of it,** esto es el encanto que tiene. ‖ **to get one's beauty sleep,** dormir para estar guapo,-a.
■ **beauty consultant,** esteticista *mf*. ‖ **beauty contest,** concurso de belleza. ‖ **beauty cream,** crema de belleza. ‖ **beauty parlour,** sala de belleza. ‖ **beauty queen,** miss *f*, ganadora de un concurso de belleza. ‖ **beauty spot,** (*on face*) lunar *m*; (*place*) lugar *m* pintoresco. ‖ **beauty treatment,** tratamiento de belleza. ‖ **Beauty and the Beast,** la Bella y la Bestia.
▲ *pl* **beauties**.
beaver ['biːvəʳ] *n* castor *m*.
bebop ['biːbɒp] *n* MUS bebop *m*.
became [bɪ'keɪm] *pt* → **become**.
because [bɪ'kɒz] **1** *conj* porque: *she hasn't come because she's ill,* no ha venido porque está enferma. – **2** **because of,** *prep* a causa de: *they were late because of the snow,* llegaron tarde a causa de la nieve.
bechamel ['beɪʃəmel] *n* CULIN bechamel *f*, besamela.
beckon ['bekən] **1** *t* llamar con señas: *he beckoned the boy to come nearer,* llamó al niño con señas para que se acercase. – **2** *i fig* llamar, atraer: *the theatre world beckoned,* el mundo del teatro llamaba. **3** hacer señas: *to beckon to sb.,* hacer señas a algn.
become [bɪ'kʌm] **1** *i* (*with noun*) convertirse en, hacerse, llegar a ser: *to become a doctor/teacher,* hacerse médico,-a/maestro,-a; *to become friends,* hacerse amigos; *to become president,* llegar a la presidencia. **2** (*change into*) convertirse en, transformarse en: *chrysalises become butterflies,* las crisálidas se transforman en mariposas; *when he got married he became a different man,* cuando se casó se convirtió en otro hombre. **3** (*irrevocable state*) volverse; (*temporary state*) ponerse; (*involuntary state*) quedarse: *to become mad,* volverse loco,-a, enloquecer; *to become fat,* ponerse gordo,-a, engordar; *to become angry,* ponerse enfadado,-a, enfadarse; *to become sad,* ponerse triste, entristecerse; *to become deaf,* quedarse sordo,-a, ensordecer; *to become blind,* quedarse ciego,-a. – **4** *t dated* (*suit*) sentarle bien, favorecer: *that blouse becomes you,* esta blusa te favo-

rece. **5** dated (befit) ser propio,-a de, convenir: that kind of behaviour doesn't become you, ese tipo de comportamiento no te conviene.
● what has become of ...?, ¿qué ha sido de ...?: what has become of your sister?, ¿qué ha sido de tu hermana?
▲ pt **became**, pp **become**.

becoming [bɪˈkʌmɪŋ] **1** adj (dress etc) que sienta bien, favorecedor,-ra. **2** (behaviour, language) apropiado,-a.

bed [bed] **1** n cama. **2** (for animals) lecho. **3** (of flowers) arriate m, macizo. **4** (of river) lecho, cauce m; (of sea) fondo. **5** GEOL capa, yacimiento. – **6** t sl acostarse con.
◆ to **bed down** i (in camping) acostarse. ‖ to **bed out** t sep (plants) plantar en un arriate.
● to go to bed, acostarse. ‖ to put sb. to bed, acostar a algn. ‖ to put a newspaper to bed, fig terminar la redacción de un número. ‖ to take to one's bed, guardar cama. ‖ to make the bed, hacer la cama. ‖ to make one's bed and lie in it, quien mala cama hace en ella yace. ‖ to get out of bed on the wrong side, fam levantarse con el pie izquierdo.
■ bunk bed, litera. ‖ double bed, cama de matrimonio. ‖ single bed, cama individual. ‖ twin beds, camas fpl separadas. ‖ bed and board, pensión f completa. ‖ bed and breakfast, alojamiento con desayuno incluido. ‖ a bed of roses, fig un lecho de rosas.
▲ pt & pp **bedded**, ger **bedding**.

bedazzle [bɪˈdæzəl] t deslumbrar, encandilar.

bedbug [ˈbedbʌg] n chinche m & f.

bedclothes [ˈbedkləʊðz] npl ropa de cama.

bedding [ˈbedɪŋ] **1** n ropa de cama. **2** (for animals) lecho.

bedeck [bɪˈdek] t engalanar, adornar.

bedevil [bɪˈdevəl] **1** t (pester, bother) importunar, incomodar. **2** (confuse, bewilder) dejar perplejo,-a. **3** (with evil spirit) endiablar, endemoniar.
▲ pt & pp **bedevilled** (US bedeviled), ger **bedevilling** (US bedeviling).

bedfellow [ˈbedfeləʊ] n compañero,-a de viaje.
● to make strange bedfellows, hacer una extraña pareja.

bedhead [ˈbedhed] n cabecera de cama.

bedlam [ˈbedləm] **1** n (confusion) alboroto, jaleo. **2** dated manicomio.

Bedouin [ˈbeduɪn] **1** adj beduino,-a. **2** (wandering) nómada. – **3** n beduino,-a. **4** (wanderer) nómada mf.

bedpan [ˈbedpæn] n cuña, orinal m de cama.

bedpost [ˈbedpəʊst] n columna de la cama.

bedraggled [bɪˈdrægəld] adj desaliñado,-a.

bedridden [ˈbedrɪdən] adj postrado,-a en cama.

bedrock [ˈbedrɒk] **1** n GEOL roca de fondo. **2** fig fondo de la cuestión.
● to get down to bedrock, ir al grano.

bedroom [ˈbedruːm] n dormitorio, habitación f.
■ bedroom comedy, comedia de enredos. ‖ bedroom eyes, ojos mpl seductores. ‖ bedroom slippers, zapatillas. ‖ bedroom suite, mobiliario de dormitorio.

bedside [ˈbedsaɪd] n cabecera.
● to have a good bedside manner, tener buen trato con los enfermos.
■ bedside table, mesita de noche. ‖ bedside lamp, lámpara de noche.

bedsitter [bedˈsɪtəʳ] n estudio.

bedsore [ˈbedsɔː] n MED llaga, úlcera.

bedspread [ˈbedspred] n cubrecama.

bedstead [ˈbedsted] n armazón m de la cama.

bedtime [ˈbedtaɪm] n la hora de acostarse.

bed-wetting [ˈbedwetɪŋ] n MED enuresis f.

bee [biː] **1** n abeja. **2** US círculo de amigos.
● to be as busy as a bee, estar muy ocupado,-a. ‖ to have a bee in one's bonnet, fam tener una obsesión. ‖ to think one's the bees' knees, fam creerse el rey del mambo.
■ carpenter bee, abeja carpintera.

Beeb [biːb] the Beeb, n la BBC f.

beech [biːtʃ] n (wood) haya.
■ beech grove, hayal m, hayedo. ‖ beech tree, haya.

beechnut [ˈbiːtʃnʌt] n hayuco.

bee-eater [ˈbiːiːtəʳ] n abejaruco.

beef [biːf] **1** n (meat) carne f de buey, carne f de vaca. **2** (animal) buey m, vaca; (cattle) ganado vacuno. **3** US (complaint) queja. – **4** i fam quejarse: to beef about sth., quejarse de algo.
◆ to beef up t sep reforzar, impulsar.
■ beef tea, caldo de carne. ‖ bully beef, US carne f de vaca en conserva. ‖ corned beef, carne f de vaca en conserva.

beefburger [ˈbiːfbɜːgəʳ] n hamburguesa.

beefeater [ˈbiːfiːtəʳ] n alabardero de la Torre de Londres.

beefsteak [ˈbiːfsteɪk] n bistec m.

beefy [ˈbiːfɪ] adj cachas, fornido,-a.
▲ comp **beefier**, superl **beefiest**.

beehive [ˈbiːhaɪv] **1** n colmena. **2** (hairstyle) peinado crepado, peinado cardado.

bee-keeper [ˈbiːkiːpəʳ] n apicultor,-ra.

bee-keeping [ˈbiːkiːpɪŋ] n apicultura.

beeline [ˈbiːlaɪn] n línea recta.
● to make a beeline for sb./sth., ir derecho hacia algn./algo.

been [biːn, bɪn] pp → be.

beep [biːp] **1** n pitido. – **2** i pitar, tocar el pito.
● to beep the horn, tocar el claxon.

beer [bɪəʳ] n cerveza.
● life isn't all beer and skittles, la vida no es un lecho de rosas. ‖ to think no small beer of oneself, creerse muy importante.

beery [ˈbɪərɪ] **1** adj que huele a cerveza: he had beery breath, su aliento olía a cerveza. **2** (party) en que se bebe mucha cerveza.
▲ comp **beerier**, superl **beeriest**.

beeswax [ˈbiːzwæks] n cera de abejas.

beetle [ˈbiːtəl] n escarabajo.
◆ to beetle about i ir a toda prisa.

beetroot [ˈbiːtruːt] n remolacha.

befall [bɪˈfɔːl] **1** t lit acontecer a, suceder a: he never knew what had befallen her, nunca supo lo que le había sucedido. – **2** i acontecer.
▲ pt **befell**, pp **befallen**.

befallen [bɪˈfɔːlən] pp → befall.

befell [bɪˈfel] pt → befall.

befit [bɪˈfɪt] t lit convenir a, ser digno,-a de: such treatment doesn't befit a man of your station, semejantes tratos no son dignos de un hombre de su posición social.
▲ pt & pp **befitted**, ger **befitting**. Se usa únicamente en tercera persona.

befitting [bɪˈfɪtɪŋ] adj propio-a, digno,-a, conveniente.

before [bɪˈfɔːʳ] **1** prep (earlier) antes de: spring comes before summer, la primavera viene antes del verano; they arrived the night before the party, llegaron la noche antes de la fiesta. **2** (in front of) delante de; (in the presence of) ante; (for the attention of) ante: he's before me in the

queue, va delante de mi en la cola; *he appeared before the judge,* compareció ante el juez; *he presented the project before the committee,* presentó el proyecto ante el comité. **3** (*rather than*) antes que: *death before dishonour,* la muerte antes que la deshonra. **4** (*ahead*) por delante: *he's got all his life before him,* tiene toda su vida por delante. **5** (*first*) primero: *ladies before gentlemen,* las señoras primero. – **6** *conj* (*earlier than*) antes de + *inf,* antes de que + *subj*: *don't forget to say goodbye before you go,* no te olvides de despedirte antes de irte; *he left before we arrived,* se fue antes de que llegásemos nosotros. **7** (*rather than*) antes de + *inf*: *he would starve before he asked them for money,* preferiría morir de hambre antes de pedirles dinero. – **8** *adv* (*earlier*) antes: *he had arrived two hours before,* había llegado dos horas antes. **9** (*previous*) anterior: *the day before,* el día anterior. **10** (*already*) ya: *we've seen it before,* ya lo hemos visto. **11** (*position*) delante, por delante: *they were attacked before and behind,* les atacaron por delante y por detrás.
● **as never before,** como nunca. ‖ **Before Christ,** antes de Cristo. ‖ **before God,** ante Dios. ‖ **before long,** dentro de poco. ‖ **long before,** mucho antes de. ‖ **not long before,** poco antes de. ‖ **pride comes before a fall,** un exceso de orgullo conduce a la caída. ‖ **to put the cart before the horse,** empezar la casa por el tejado.
■ **the day before yesterday,** anteayer. ‖ **the one before,** el anterior, la anterior.
beforehand [bɪˈfɔːhænd] **1** *adv* (*earlier*) antes. **2** (*in advance*) de antemano, con antelación: *payment must be made a month beforehand,* los pagos deben efectuarse con un mes de antelación. **3** (*before*) antes: *they arrived two hours beforehand,* llegaron dos horas antes.
befriend [bɪˈfrend] *t* ofrecer su amistad a.
befuddled [bɪˈfʌdəld] *adj* aturdido,-a, atontado,-a,.
beg [beg] **1** *t* mendigar: *she begged some food from the shop,* mendigó algo de comida de la tienda. **2** (*ask for*) pedir: *she begged forgiveness,* pidió perdón. **3** *lit* (*beseech*) suplicar, rogar: *she begged him to help her,* le suplicó que le ayudara. – **4** *i* mendigar: *she spent all day begging in the streets,* pasó todo el día mendigando por las calles. **5** (*dog*) sentarse (*con las patas delanteras levantadas*).
◆ **to beg off** *i* us escabullirse.
● **I beg to differ,** no estoy de acuerdo. ‖ **to beg the question,** ser una petición de principio.
▲ *pt* & *pp* begged, *ger* begging.
began [bɪˈgæn] *pt →* **begin**.
beget [bɪˈget] *t* engendrar.
▲ *pt* begot, *pp* begotten, *ger* begetting.
beggar [ˈbegəʳ] **1** *n* mendigo,-a, pordiosero,-a. **2** *fam* tipo, individuo,-a: *he's a funny beggar,* es un tipo raro. – **3** *t* empobrecer, arruinar; *fig* hacer imposible.
● **beggars can't be choosers,** a caballo regalado no le mires el dentado. ‖ **to beggar description,** superar toda descripción.
beggarly [ˈbegəlɪ] *adj* pobre, miserable.
begging [ˈbegɪŋ] *n* mendigar *m*.
● **to go begging,** sobrar: *is this sandwich going begging?,* ¿sobra este bocadillo?, ¿no quiere nadie este bocadillo?
■ **begging bowl,** plato de las limosnas.
begin [bɪˈgɪn] **1** *t* empezar, comenzar: *he began his job on Monday,* comenzó el trabajo el lunes; *he began to feel ill,* empezó a sentirse mal; *he began working when he was sixteen,* empezó a trabajar cuando tenía die-

ciséis años. – **2** *i* empezar, comenzar: *the performance begins at nine,* la representación empieza a las nueve.
● **beginning from,** a partir de: *beginning from next week,* a partir de la semana que viene. ‖ **not to begin to ...,** estar lejos de ...: *he can't begin to compete with us,* está muy lejos de poder competir con nosotros. ‖ **to begin by** + *-ing,* empezar por + *inf,* empezar + *ger*: *he began by asking them some questions,* empezó por hacerles algunas preguntas. ‖ **to begin with,** (*firstly*) en primer lugar; (*take as starting point*) empezar con: *we're going to begin with the alphabet,* empezaremos con el alfabeto.
▲ *pt* began, *pp* begun, *ger* beginning.
beginner [bɪˈgɪnəʳ] *n* principiante *mf.*
■ **beginner's luck,** la suerte del principiante.
beginning [bɪˈgɪnɪŋ] **1** *n* principio, comienzo: *the beginning of the film,* el principio de la película. **2** (*cause*) origen *m,* causa: *the beginning of the quarrel,* la causa de la disputa. – **3 beginnings,** *npl* (*origins*) orígenes *mpl*: *he never discussed his humble beginnings,* nunca habló de sus orígenes humildes.
● **at the beginning of,** a principios de: *at the beginning of December,* a principios de diciembre. ‖ **from beginning to end,** desde el principio hasta el final. ‖ **the beginning of the end,** el principio del fin.
begone [bɪˈgɒn] *interj arch* ¡retiraos!
begonia [bɪˈgəʊnɪə] *n* BOT begonia.
begot [bɪˈgɒt] *pt →* **beget**.
begotten [bɪˈgɒtən] *pp →* **beget**.
begrudge [bɪˈgrʌdʒ] **1** *t* (*envy*) envidiar: *he begrudges him his success,* le envidia su éxito. **2** (*disapprove*) desaprobar, no ver con buenos ojos: *he begrudges what they have done,* no ve con buenos ojos lo que han hecho.
● **to begrudge doing sth.,** hacer algo a regañadientes, hacer algo de mala gana.
begrudgingly [bɪˈgrʌdʒɪŋlɪ] *adv* a regañadientes, de mala gana.
beguile [bɪˈgaɪl] **1** *t* (*seduce*) seducir, atraer; (*bewitch*) embrujar. **2** (*cheat*) engañar.
● **to beguile sb. into doing sth.,** engatusar a algn. para que haga algo.
beguiling [bɪˈgaɪlɪŋ] *adj* atractivo,-a, seductor,-ra.
begun [bɪˈgʌn] *pp →* **begin**.
behalf [bɪˈhɑːf] **on behalf of,** *phr* (*acting for*) en nombre de, de parte de; (*in favour of*) por, en favor de; (*for the benefit of*) para, en beneficio de: *he spoke on behalf of all those involved,* habló en nombre de todos los implicados; *he went to see her on my behalf,* fue de mi parte a verla; *she intervened on their behalf,* intervino por ellos; *a collection on behalf of the poor,* una colecta para los pobres.
behave [bɪˈheɪv] **1** *i* (*people*) comportarse, portarse. **2** (*equipment, machinery*) funcionar bien: *this computer won't behave,* este ordenador no funciona bien.
● **to behave os.,** comportarse, portarse bien: *behave yourselves while I'm away,* portaos bien mientras estoy fuera. ‖ **to behave badly,** comportarse mal, portarse mal: *they behaved badly at the party,* se portaron mal en la fiesta. ‖ **to behave towards sb.,** tratar a algn.: *I don't like how he behaves towards them,* no me gusta como les trata.
behavior [bɪˈheɪvjəʳ] *n* US *→* **behaviour**.
behavioral [bɪˈheɪvjərəl] *adj* US *→* **behavioural**.
behaviorism [bɪˈheɪvjərɪzəm] *n* US *→* **behaviourism**.
behaviorist [bɪˈheɪvjərɪst] *n* US *→* **behaviourist**.

behaviour [bɪˈheɪvjəʳ] 1 *n* (*of person*) conducta, comportamiento. 2 (*of equipment, machine*) funcionamiento. 3 (*treatment*) trato. 4 PHYS comportamiento.
● **to be on one's best behaviour,** comportarse de la mejor manera posible.
■ **behaviour therapy,** terapia de comportamiento.

behavioural [bɪˈheɪvjərəl] *adj* behaviorístico,-a, conductista.

behaviourism [bɪˈheɪvjərɪzəm] *n* behaviorismo, conductismo.

behaviourist [bɪˈheɪvjərɪst] *n* behaviorista *mf*, conductista *mf*.

behead [bɪˈhed] *t* decapitar, descabezar.

beheld [bɪˈheld] *pt & pp →* **behold**.

behest [bɪˈhest] *n lit* orden *m*, petición *f*.
● **at sb.'s behest,** por orden de, a petición de algn.: *he went at the King's behest,* fue por orden del rey.

behind [bɪˈhaɪnd] 1 *prep* detrás de: *he's over there behind that tree,* está allí detrás de ese árbol; *I don't know what's behind his statements,* no sé qué hay detrás de sus declaraciones. – 2 *adv* detrás, atrás: *look at all those people behind,* mira toda aquella gente que hay detrás. 3 (*late*) atrasado,-a: *she's behind with her mortgage payments,* está atrasada en el pago de la hipoteca. – 4 *n fam* (*buttocks*) trasero.
● **behind sb.'s back,** a espaldas de algn. ‖ **to be behind schedule,** estar atrasado,-a. ‖ **behind the scenes,** entre bastidores. ‖ **to be behind the times,** ser anticuado,-a. ‖ **to attack sb. from behind,** atacar a algn. por la espalda. ‖ **to leave behind,** (*person, thing, animal*) dejar algo; (*in competition*) dejar atrás: *when they went back to England they had to leave their dog behind,* cuando regresaron a Inglaterra tuvieron que dejar su perro; *he left the other athletes far behind,* dejo a los otros atletas muy atrás. ‖ **to fall behind,** quedarse atrás. ‖ **to put sth. behind one,** (*events, worries,*) olvidarse de algo, dejar de lado algo: *put your problems behind you!,* ¡olvídate de tus problemas! ‖ **to look behind,** mirar hacia atrás. ‖ **to stay behind,** quedarse: *he had to stay behind after school,* tuvo que quedarse después de la clase. ‖ **to be behind sb.,** *fig* apoyar a algn. ‖ **to be behind sth.,** *fig* ser el/la responsable de algo, estar detrás de algo.

behindhand [bɪˈhaɪndhænd] 1 *adv* en retraso, retrasado,-a: *he's behindhand with the payments,* está retrasado en los pagos. – 2 *adj* atrasado,-a, retrasado,-a.

behind-the-scenes [bɪhaɪndðəˈsiːnz] *adj* en secreto: *a behind-the-scenes investigation,* una investigación en secreto.

behold [bɪˈhəʊld] *t lit* contemplar, observar.
▲ *pt & pp* **beheld** [bɪˈheld].

beholden [bɪˈhəʊldən] **to be beholden to sb.,** *phr* estar bajo una obligación a algn.

beholder [bɪˈhəʊldəʳ] *n lit* observador,-ra.
● **beauty is in the eye of the beholder,** la belleza está en el que mira.

beige [beɪʒ] 1 *n* beige *m*. – 2 *adj* (de color) beige.

being [ˈbiːɪŋ] 1 *n* (*living thing*) ser *m*. 2 (*existence*) existencia.
● **being as,** ya que, puesto que: *being as they arrived late ...,* puesto que llegaron tarde ... ‖ **for the time being,** por ahora, de momento. ‖ **to bring into being,** llevar a cabo, crear. ‖ **to come into being,** nacer.
■ **human being,** ser *m* humano.

Beirut [beɪˈruːt] *n* Beirut.

Belarus [ˈbelərʌs] *n →* **Byelorussia**.

belated [bɪˈleɪtɪd] *adj fam* tardío,-a, atrasado,-a.

belay [bɪˈleɪ] *t* (*boat*) amarrar; (*rope in mountaineering*) asegurar, fijar.

belch [beltʃ] 1 *n* eructo. – 2 *i* eructar.
● **to belch (out),** vomitar, arrojar: *the burning building belched out smoke,* el edificio en llamas arrojaba humo.

beleaguer [bɪˈliːgəʳ] 1 *t* (*besiege*) sitiar, cercar. 2 (*harass*) perseguir, hostigar.

beleaguered [bɪˈliːgəd] 1 *adj* (*besieged*) sitiado,-a, cercado,-a. 2 (*harassed*) perseguido,-a, hostigado,-a.

belfry [ˈbelfrɪ] *n* campanario *m*.
● **to have bats in the belfry,** estar como una cabra.
▲ *pl* **belfries**.

Belgian [ˈbeldʒən] 1 *adj* belga. – 2 *n* belga *mf*.

Belgium [ˈbeldʒəm] *n* Bélgica.

Belgrade [belˈgreɪd] *n* Belgrado.

belief [bɪˈliːf] 1 *n* (*gen*) creencia: *his political beliefs,* sus creencias políticas. 2 (*opinion*) opinión *f*: *it is his belief that they are guilty,* en su opinión son culpables. 3 (*confidence*) confianza: *he has no belief in the legal system,* no tiene confianza en el sistema jurídico.
● **to the best of my belief,** que yo sepa. ‖ **it is my firm belief that,** creo firmemente que. ‖ **it is beyond belief,** parece mentira.

believable [bɪˈliːvəbəl] *adj* creíble, verosímil.

believe [bɪˈliːv] 1 *t* (*accept as true, think*) creer: *I don't believe you,* no te creo; *I think it's going to rain,* creo que va a llover. 2 (*suppose*) creer, suponer: *they believe he has left the country,* creen que ha abandonado el país. – 3 *i* creer (**in,** en): *we believe in God,* creemos en Dios; *she still believes in him,* todavía cree en él. 4 (*trust*) confiar (**in,** en): *they don't believe in the president anymore,* ya no confían en el presidente. 5 (*support, be in favour of*) ser partidario,-a (**in,** de): *they believe in free trade,* son partidarios del libre comercio. 6 REL tener fe.
● **it is believed that,** se cree que: *it is believed that they were caught in the avalanche,* se cree que se quedaron atrapados por el alud. ‖ **believe it or not,** por extraño que pueda parecer. ‖ **not to believe one's eyes,** no dar crédito a sus ojos. ‖ **you'd better believe it!,** ¡esto va en serio! ‖ **don't you believe it!,** ¡no te lo creas! ‖ **believe me!,** ¡créeme! ‖ **to make believe,** fingir.

believer [bɪˈliːvəʳ] 1 *n* creyente *mf*. 2 (*supporter*) partidario,-a.

belittle [bɪˈlɪtəl] *t* menospreciar, despreciar: *they belittled his contributions to the project,* despreciaron sus aportaciones al proyecto.
● **to belittle oneself,** rebajarse.

Belize [beˈliːz] *n* Belice.

Belizean [beˈliːzɪən] 1 *adj* belicense, beliceño,-a. – 2 *n* belicense *mf*, beliceño,-a.

bell[1] [bel] 1 *n* (*church etc*) campana. 2 (*handbell*) campanilla. 3 (*on bicycle, door, etc*) timbre *m*. 4 (*on toy, hat*) cascabel *m*. 5 (*cowbell*) cencerro *m*. 6 (*flower*) campanilla.
● **that rings a bell,** esto me suena. ‖ **to bell the cat,** poner el cascabel al gato. ‖ **to be saved by the bell,** salvarse por los pelos. ‖ **sound as a bell,** más sano,-a que una manzana. ‖ **to ring the bell,** tocar el timbre. ‖ **to give sb. a bell,** *fam* (*phone sb.*) dar un toque a algn.

bell[2] [bel] 1 *n* (*of stag*) bramido. – 2 *i* bramar.

belladonna [beləˈdɒnə] *n* BOT belladona.

bell-bottomed [belˈbɒtəmd] *adj* (*trousers*) acampanado,-a.

bell-bottoms [belˈbɒtəmz] *npl* pantalones *mpl* acampanados.

bellboy ['belbɔɪ] n botones m.
belle [bel] n (beautiful woman) belleza, beldad f.
● **the belle of the ball,** la reina del baile.
bellhop ['belhɒp] n us botones m.
bellicose ['belɪkəʊs] adj belicoso,-a, pendenciero,-a.
belligerence [bɪ'lɪdʒərəns] n beligerancia.
belligerent [bɪ'lɪdʒərənt] adj beligerante.
bell-jar ['beldʒɑː] n campana de cristal.
bellow ['beləʊ] 1 n bramido. – 2 i bramar. 3 fig vociferar.
– 4 bellows, npl fuelle m sing.
bell-pull ['belpʊl] n tirador m del timbre.
bell-push ['belpʊʃ] n botón m del timbre.
bell-ringer ['belrɪŋəʳ] n campanólogo,-a.
belly ['belɪ] 1 n (person) vientre m, barriga. 2 (animal) panza.
■ **belly laugh,** carcajada.
▲ pl bellies.
bellyache ['belɪeɪk] 1 n fam dolor m de barriga. – 2 i fam quejarse.
bellybutton ['belɪbʌtən] n fam ombligo.
bellyful ['belɪfʊl] n panzada, hartazgo.
● **to have had a bellyful of sth.,** estar hasta la coronilla de algo.
belong [bɪ'lɒŋ] 1 i pertenecer (**to,** a), ser (**to,** de): the house belongs to her, la casa la pertenece; this book belongs to him, este libro es de él. 2 (be a member of a club) ser socio,-a (**to,** de); (be a member of political party) ser miembro (**to,** de). 3 (have suitable qualities) ser apto,-a (**in,** para): he doesn't belong in this job, no es apto para este trabajo. 4 (fit specific environment) estar en su ambiente natural. 5 (be correctly placed) estar en su sitio, deber colocarse en: these files don't belong here, estos archivos no están en su sitio aquí; these books belong on that shelf, estos libros deben colocarse en aquel estante.
belongings [bɪ'lɒŋɪŋz] npl pertenencias fpl, bártulos mpl.
● **to pack up one's belongings,** liar el petate, preparar los bártulos.
beloved [bɪ'lʌvd] 1 adj querido,-a, amado,-a. – 2 n amado,-a.
▲ (sustantivo) [bɪ'lʌvɪd].
below [bɪ'ləʊ] 1 prep debajo de, bajo: my parents live in the flat below us, mis padres viven en el piso debajo de nosotros. 2 por debajo de (de): the drainage system runs below our house, la alcantarilla pasa por debajo de nuestra casa. 3 (lower than) bajo: temperatures are 5 degrees below freezing, las temperaturas están a 5 grados bajo cero. – 4 adv abajo: there are some protesters below in the street, hay unos manifestantes abajo en la calle. 5 de abajo: the old lady in the flat below, la anciana del piso de abajo.
● **below sea-level,** por debajo del nivel del mar. ‖ see below, véase abajo. ‖ that was a bit below the belt, fue un golpe bajo.
belt [belt] 1 n cinturón m. 2 TECH correa. 3 (area) zona. – 4 t fam (hit) arrear un tortazo.
◆ **to belt along** i fam a todo gas. ‖ **to belt up** i fam cerrar el pico.
■ **a blow below the belt,** un golpe m bajo. ‖ diving belt, cinturón m de lastre. ‖ industrial belt, zona industrial.
bemoan [bɪ'məʊn] t lamentar.
bemused [bɪ'mjuːzd] adj perplejo,-a.
bench [bentʃ] 1 n banco. 2 JUR tribunal m. 3 SP banquillo.
● **to be on the bench,** ser juez,-za.

■ **front benches,** GB POL escaños ocupados por los miembros del consejo de ministros. ‖ **back benches,** GB POL escaños de los diputados que no forman parte del consejo de ministros. ‖ **bench mark,** cota de referencia, punto de referencia. ‖ **bench mark test,** prueba patrón. ‖ **bench test,** prueba de banco.
bend [bend] 1 n (in road etc) curva. 2 (in pipe) ángulo. – 3 t doblar, curvar: he couldn't bend the iron bar, no consiguió doblar la barra de hierro. 4 (head) inclinar; (back) doblar, encorvar; (knee) doblar, flexionar: he couldn't bend his back after the accident, no pudo doblar la espalda tras el accidente. – 5 i doblarse, combarse: the legs of the chair bent when he sat down, las patas de la silla se combaron cuando se sentó. 6 (head) inclinarse; (back) encorvarse: his back had bent under the weight, se le había encorvado la espalda bajo el peso. 7 (road) torcer.
◆ **to bend down** i agacharse. ‖ **to bend over** i inclinarse.
● **to bend sth. back,** doblar algo hacia atrás. ‖ **to bend sth. straight,** enderezar algo. ‖ **to bend over backwards for sb.,** hacer todo lo posible por algn. ‖ **to be round the bend,** estar loco,-a perdido,-a. ‖ **to send sb. round the bend,** sacar a algn. de quicio. ‖ **to bend the rules for sb.,** hacer una excepción por algn. ‖ on bended knee, arrodillado,-a. ‖ "please do not bend", (on package) "no doblar".
■ **wide bend,** curva abierta.
▲ pt & pp bent [bent].
bender ['bendəʳ] **to go on a bender,** phr irse de juerga, irse de borrachera.
beneath [bɪ'niːθ] 1 prep bajo, debajo de: they sleep in the room beneath ours, duermen en la habitación debajo de la nuestra. 2 por debajo de: the underground line runs beneath our house, la línea de metro va por debajo de nuestra casa. 3 fig indigno,-a de, no digno,-a de: it's beneath you to behave like this, es indigno de ti comportarte de esta manera. – 4 adv de abajo: she lives in the flat beneath, vive en el piso de abajo.
● **to marry beneath oneself,** casarse con algn. de clase inferior.
Benedictine [benɪ'dɪktɪn] 1 adj benedictino,-a. – 2 n benedictino.
benediction [benɪ'dɪkʃən] n bendición f.
benefactor ['benɪfæktəʳ] n benefactor m.
benefactress ['benɪfæktrəs] n benefactora.
benefice ['benɪfɪs] n REL beneficio.
beneficent [bɪ'nefɪsənt] adj benefactor,-ra.
beneficial [benɪ'fɪʃəl] adj beneficioso,-a, provechoso,-a.
beneficiary [benɪ'fɪʃərɪ] n beneficiario,-a.
▲ pl beneficiaries.
benefit ['benɪfɪt] 1 n (advantage) beneficio, provecho. 2 (good) bien m. 3 (allowance) subsidio. 4 (charity performance) función f benéfica; (charity game) partido benéfico. – 5 t beneficiar: his actions benefitted the poor, sus acciones beneficiaron a los pobres. – 6 i beneficiarse (**from,** de): he benefitted from their help, se benefició de su ayuda.
● **to do sth. for sb.'s benefit,** hacer algo por el bien de algn. ‖ **to gain benefit from sth.,** sacar provecho de algo. ‖ **to reap the benefits of sth.,** sacar el máximo provecho de algo. ‖ **for the benefit of sb.,** en beneficio de algn. ‖ **to give sb. the benefit of the doubt,** dar a algn. el beneficio de la duda.
■ **benefit of clergy,** fuero eclesiástico.
▲ pt & pp benefitted, ger benefitting.
benevolence [bɪ'nevələns] n benevolencia.

benevolent [bɪ'nevələnt] *adj* benévolo,-a.
■ **benevolent society,** sociedad *f* benéfica.
Bengal [ben'gɔːl] *n* Bengala.
■ **Bay of Bengal,** golfo de Bengala.
Bengali [ben'gɔːlɪ] **1** *adj* bengalí. – **2** *n* (*person*) bengalí *mf.* **3** (*language*) bengalí *m.*
benificence [bɪ'nefɪsəns] *n* beneficencia.
benign [bɪ'naɪn] *adj* benigno,-a.
Benin ['benɪn] *n* Benín.
Beninese [benɪ'niːz] **1** *adj* benimeño,-a. – **2** *n* benimeño,-a. – **3 the Beninese,** *npl* los benimeños *mpl.*
bent [bent] **1** *pt & pp* → **bend.** – **2** *adj* torcido,-a, doblado,-a. **3** *sl* (*corrupt*) corrupto,-a. **4** *sl* (*homosexual*) de la acera de enfrente. – **5** *n* (*innate ability*) facilidad *f*, don *m*: *she's got a bent for maths,* tiene facilidad para las matemáticas.
● **to be bent on** + **-ing,** estar empeñado,-a en +*inf*: *he's bent on getting what he wants,* está empeñado en conseguir lo que quiere.
Benzedrine ['benzədriːn] *n* MED bencedrina.
benzene ['benziːn] *n* CHEM benceno.
benzine ['benziːn] *n* CHEM bencina.
bequeath [bɪ'kwiːð] *t* legar.
● **to bequeath sth. to sb.,** legar algo a algn.
bequest [bɪ'kwest] *n* legado.
berate [bɪ'reɪt] *t* reprender, regañar.
Berber ['bɜːbəʳ] **1** *adj* beréber, bereber. – **2** *n* (*person*) beréber *mf*, bereber *mf.* **3** (*languaje*) beréber *m*, bereber *m.*
bereave [bɪ'riːv] *t lit* privar: *the loss of his fortune had bereft him of all hope,* la pérdida de su fortuna le había privado de toda esperanza.
▲ *pt & pp* **bereft** [bɪ'reft].
bereaved [bɪ'riːvd] **1** *adj* desconsolado,-a, afligido,-a: *his bereaved wife,* su desconsolada esposa. – **2 the bereaved,** *npl* los afligidos *mpl*, la desconsolada familia.
bereavement [bɪ'riːvmənt] **1** *n* (*loss*) pérdida. **2** (*mourning*) duelo.
bereft [bɪ'reft] **1** *pt & pp* → **bereave.**
● **to be bereft of sth./sb.,** ser privado,-a de algo/algn.
beret ['bereɪ] *n* boina.
bergamot ['bɜːgəmɒt] **1** *n* (*fruit*) bergamota. **2** (*tree*) bergamoto, bergamote *m.*
beriberi [berɪ'berɪ] *n* MED beriberi *m.*
berk [bɜːk] *n fam* capullo.
Berlin [bɜː'lɪn] *n* Berlín.
Berliner [bɜː'lɪnəʳ] *n* berlinés,-esa.
Bermuda [bə'mjuːdə] *n* las Bermudas.
■ **Bermuda shorts,** bermudas *mpl.* ‖ **Bermuda grass,** grama, argentina. ‖ **Bermuda Triangle,** el triángulo de las Bermudas.
Bermudan [bə'mjuːdən] **1** *adj* de las Bermudas. – **2** *n* nativo,-a de las Bermudas.
Bern [bɜːn] *n* Berna.
berry ['berɪ] *n* baya.
▲ *pl* **berries.**
berserk [bə'zɜːk] *adj* enloquecido,-a.
● **to go berserk,** perder los estribos. ‖ **to drive sb. berserk,** sacar a algn. de quicio.
berth [bɜːθ] **1** *n* (*in harbour*) amarradero. **2** (*on ship*) camarote *m*, litera. – **3** *t* poner en dique. – **4** *i* atracar.
● **to give sb. a wide berth,** esquivar a algn.
beryl ['berəl] *n* GEOL berilo.
berylium [bə'rɪləm] *n* CHEM berilio.
beseech [bɪ'siːtʃ] *t lit* implorar, suplicar.
▲ *pt & pp* **besought** *o* **beseeched.**

beset [bɪ'set] **1** *t* (*attack, harass*) acosar, asaltar. **2** (*hem in, surround*) acorralar, cercar.
● **to be beset by worries/doubts,** estar acosado,-a por preocupaciones/dudas.
▲ *pt & pp* **beset** [bɪ'set], ger *besetting.*
beside [bɪ'saɪd] **1** *prep* al lado de: *they live beside the football stadium,* viven al lado del estadio de fútbol. **2** (*compared to*) frente a, comparado,-a con: *his contribution looks insignificant beside yours,* su aportación parece insignificante frente a la tuya.
● **to be beside os.,** estar fuera de sí. ‖ **to be beside os. with joy,** estar loco,-a de alegría. ‖ **that's beside the point,** esto no viene al caso.
besides [bɪ'saɪdz] **1** *prep* (*as well as*) además de, aparte de: *who was at the party besides your family and friends?,* ¿quién estaba en la fiesta además de tu familia y tus amigos?; *besides history, we have to study geography and maths,* además de historia, tenemos que estudiar geografía y matemáticas. – **2** *adv* además: *he's a swindler and a crook besides,* es un estafador y además es un ladrón.
besiege [bɪ'siːdʒ] **1** *t* MIL sitiar. **2** *fig* asediar, inundar.
besom ['biːzəm] *n* escoba.
besotted [bɪ'sɒtɪd] *adj* locamente enamorado,-a (**with,** de).
besought [bɪ'sɔːt] *pt & pp* → **beseech.**
bespatter [bɪ'spætəʳ] *t* salpicar (**with,** de): *the car bespattered him with mud,* el coche le salpicó de fango.
bespectacled [bɪ'spektəkəld] *adj* con gafas, que lleva gafas.
bespoke [bɪs'pəʊk] *adj* hecho,-a a la medida: *he wore a bespoke suit,* llevaba un traje hecho a la medida.
■ **bespoke tailor,** sastre *m* (*que confecciona ropa a medida*).
best [best] **1** *adj* (*superl of good*) mejor: *this is a selection of his best works,* es una muestra de sus mejores obras; *we need to find the best solution,* tenemos que encontrar la mejor solución. – **2** *adv* (*superl of well*) mejor: *he works best at night,* trabaja mejor por la noche. **3** (*to a greater extent*) más: *of all the girls she is the one he likes best,* de todas las chicas ella es la que le gusta más. – **4** *n* lo mejor: *the best is yet to come,* lo mejor aún queda por venir; *it's the best there is,* es lo mejor que hay. **5** (*person*) el mejor, la mejor: *she's the best in the class,* es la mejor de la clase. – **6** *t fam* ganar, vencer.
● **all the best!,** ¡que te vaya bien! ‖ **as best you can,** lo mejor que puedas. ‖ **at best,** en el mejor de los casos. ‖ **it is best that ...,** más vale que ...: *it's best that you leave home,* más vale que te marches de casa. ‖ **it's for the best,** más vale que sea así. ‖ **not to be at one's best,** no estar en forma, estar en baja forma. ‖ **to act for the best,** obrar con la mejor intención. ‖ **to be at one's best,** estar en su mejor momento. ‖ **to be the best of friends,** ser excelentes amigos. ‖ **to do one's best,** esmerarse, hacer lo mejor que uno puede. ‖ **to do sth. to the best of one's ability,** hacer algo lo mejor que uno puede. ‖ **to get the best of sb.,** imponerse a algn. ‖ **to get the best of sth.,** sacar mejor partido de algo. ‖ **to know what is best for one,** saber lo que más le conviene a uno. ‖ **to make the best of a bad job,** conformarse. ‖ **to the best of my knowledge,** que yo sepa. ‖ **with the best of them,** como él que más: *he can drink with the best of them,* él sabe beber como él que más.
■ **best man,** padrino de boda. ‖ **Sunday best,** galas *fpl* de domingo. ‖ **the best one,** el mejor, la mejor. ‖ **the best part of,** la mayor parte de.

bestial ['bestɪəl] *adj* bestial.

bestiality [bestɪ'ælɪtɪ] *n* bestialidad *f*.

bestow [bɪ'stəʊ] *t* (*honour, award*) otorgar (**on**, a); (*favour*) hacer (**on**, a); (*title*) conferir (**on**, a).

best-seller [best'selə'] *n* best-seller *m*, superventas *m*.

best-selling [best'selɪŋ] *adj* más vendido,-a: *this is the best-selling novel of the year,* esta es la novela más vendida del año.

bet [bet] **1** *n* apuesta. – **2** *t* apostar: *he bet twenty pounds on that horse,* apostó veinte libras a aquel caballo. – **3** *i* apostar: *how much do you want to bet?,* ¿cuánto quieres apostar? **4** (*feel sure*) estar seguro,-a, estar convencido,-a: *I bet they've missed their train,* estoy seguro de que han perdido el tren.
● **to make a bet,** hacer una apuesta. ‖ **I bet you can't do it!,** ¿a qué no puedes? ‖ **you bet!,** ¡ya lo creo! ‖ **your best bet is to...,** lo mejor que puedes hacer es...: *your best bet is to forget about it,* lo mejor que puedes hacer es olvidarte del asunto.
▲ *pt & pp* **bet** [bet] o **betted**, *ger* **betting**.

beta ['biːtə] *n* beta.
■ **beta rays,** rayos *mpl* beta.

beta-blocker ['biːtəblɒkə'] *n* MED betabloqueante *m*.

betel ['biːtəl] *n* (*plant*) betel *m*.
■ **betel nut,** areca.

bête-noir [bet'nwɑː'] *n* bestia negra.

Bethlehem ['beθlɪhem] *n* Belén.

betide [bɪ'taɪd] *t lit* acontecer, acaecer.
▲ *Se usa únicamente en tercera persona del singular.*

betray [bɪ'treɪ] **1** *t* traicionar: *he betrayed his friends,* traicionó a sus amigos. **2** (*secret*) revelar. **3** (*show signs of*) dejar ver, acusar. **4** (*deceive*) engañar. **5** (*trust*) defraudar.

betrayal [bɪ'treɪəl] **1** *n* traición *f*. **2** (*deceit*) engaño.

betrayer [bɪ'treɪə'] *n* traidor,-ra, traicionero,-a.

betroth [bɪ'trəʊð] *t* prometer en matrimonio.
● **to be betrothed,** contraer matrimonio, desposarse.

betrothal [bɪ'trəʊðəl] *n* enlace *m*, esponsales *mpl*.

betrothed [bɪ'trəʊðd] **1** *adj* prometido,-a. – **2** *n* prometido,-a.

better[1] ['betə'] **1** *adj* (*comp of good*) mejor: *his new novel is better than his last one,* su última novela es mejor que la anterior; *you won't find a better product,* no encontrarás un producto mejor. **2** (*more healthy*) mejor: *he's feeling better today,* hoy se encuentra mejor. – **3** *adv* (*comp of well*) mejor: *he works better than I do,* trabaja mejor que yo. **4** (*to a greater extent*) más: *I like this one better,* me gusta más éste. – **5** *n* el mejor, la mejor: *it's hard to decide who is the better of the two,* es difícil decidir quién es el mejor de los dos. – **6** *t* (*improve*) mejorar: *he has bettered his own working conditions,* ha mejorado sus condiciones de trabajo. **7** (*surpass*) superar: *he bettered his own record,* superó su propio récord. – **8 betters,** *npl* superiores *mpl*: *you must listen to your betters,* debes escuchar tus superiores.
● **to better os.,** mejorar su posición social. ‖ **better late than never,** más vale tarde que nunca. ‖ **so much the better,** tanto mejor. ‖ **for want of sth. better,** a falta de otra cosa mejor. ‖ **to be no better than,** no ser más que: *he's no better than a thief,* no es más que un ladrón. ‖ **to get better,** recuperarse, mejorarse. ‖ **to go one better,** hacer mejor todavía. ‖ **to like sth./sb. better,** preferir algo/a algn. ‖ **better and better,** cada vez mejor. ‖ **for better or for worse,** para lo bueno o para lo malo. ‖ **to be better off than sb.,** tener más dinero que algn. ‖ **to get the better of sb.,** llevar la ventaja a algn., salir ganando a algn. ‖ **the better part**

of, la mayor parte de. ‖ **you know better than me,** tú sabes más que yo.
■ **better feelings,** conciencia. ‖ **better half,** media naranja.

better[2] ['betə'] *n* apostante *mf*.

betterment ['betəmənt] *n* mejoría, mejora.

betting ['betɪŋ] *n* apuestas *fpl*.
● **what's the betting that he** (*she, it, etc*)**...?,** ,, ¿qué te apuestas a que ...?: *what's the betting that he arrives late?,* ¿qué te apuestas a que llega tarde?
■ **betting shop,** GB administración *f* de apuestas hípicas. ‖ **betting slip,** boleto de la quiniela hípica.

bettor ['betə'] *n* apostante *mf*.

between [bɪ'twiːn] **1** *prep* entre: *we broke down between London and Brighton,* se nos averió el coche entre Londres y Brighton; *choose a number between one and ten,* escoge un número entre uno y diez; *we fixed it between the four of us,* lo arreglamos entre los cuatro; *they shared the food between themselves,* se repartieron la comida; *is there a difference between a crocodile and an alligator?,* ¿hay alguna diferencia entre un cocodrilo y un caimán? – **2** (*in*) between, *adv* de en medio: *we could see the sea if it wasn't for the houses (in) between,* podríamos ver el mar si no fuera por las casas de en medio.
● **to tell the difference between A and B,** diferenciar A de B. ‖ **between the lines,** entre líneas. ‖ **between you and me,** entre tú y yo, en confianza. ‖ **between ourselves,** entre nosotros. ‖ **between times,** de vez en cuando. ‖ **between now and then,** de aquí a entonces. ‖ **in between,** en medio de, entre. ‖ **to be between the devil and the deep blue sea,** estar entre la espada y la pared. ‖ **to fall between two stools,** no saber a qué santo confesarse.

betwixt [bɪ'twɪkst] **1** *prep arch* entre. – **2** *adv arch* en medio.
● **betwixt and between,** *fam* ni chicha ni limonada.

bevel ['bevəl] **1** *n* bisel *m*, chaflán *m*. – **2** *t* biselar.
■ **bevel square,** falsa escuadra.
▲ *pt & pp* **bevelled** (us *beveled*), *ger* **bevelling** (us *beveling*).

bevel-edged [bevəl'edʒd] *adj* biselado,-a.

beverage ['bevərɪdʒ] *n* bebida.

bevvy ['bevɪ] **1** *n sl* (*drink*) trago, trinquis *m*: *fancy a bevvy?,* ¿te apetece un trago? – **2** *i sl* beber.
● **to get bevvied,** *sl* cogerse una curda.
▲ (*verbo*) *pt & pp* **bevvied**, *ger* **bevvying**; (*sustantivo*) *pl* **bevvies**.

bevy ['bevɪ] **1** *n* (*of birds*) bandada. **2** (*of women*) grupo: *a bevy of beauties,* un grupo de chicas guapas.
▲ *pl* **bevies**.

bewail [bɪ'weɪl] *t fml* lamentar.

beware [bɪ'weə'] **1** *i* tener cuidado (**of**, con): *beware of the dog!,* ¡cuidado con el perro! – **2** *interj* ¡ojo!, ¡cuidado!

bewilder [bɪ'wɪldə'] *t* desconcertar, dejar perplejo,-a.

bewildered [bɪ'wɪldəd] *adj* desconcertado,-a, perplejo,-a.

bewilderment [bɪ'wɪldəmənt] *n* desconcierto, perplejidad *f*, confusión *f*.

bewitch [bɪ'wɪtʃ] *t* hechizar, embrujar; *fig* hechizar, fascinar.

bewitching [bɪ'wɪtʃɪŋ] *adj* hechicero,-a, fascinante.

beyond [bɪ'jɒnd] **1** *prep* más allá de: *they live beyond the mountains,* viven más allá de las montañas. **2** (*outside*) fuera de: *it's beyond my jurisdiction,* está fuera de mi jurisdicción. – **3** *adv* más allá, más lejos: *the lake and*

the trees beyond, el lago y más allá los árboles. – **4** the beyond, *n* el más allá.
● **at the back of beyond,** en el quinto pino. ‖ **it's beyond belief,** parece mentira, es increíble. ‖ **it's beyond doubt,** es indudable, es seguro, no cabe duda. ‖ **it's beyond me,** no lo entiendo. ‖ **to be beyond a joke,** ser el colmo. ‖ **to be beyond help,** ser un caso perdido. ‖ **to live beyond one's means,** vivir por encima de sus posibilidades.

Bhutan [buːˈtɑːn] *n* Bhután.

Bhutanese [buːtæˈniːz] **1** *adj* bhutanés,-esa. – **2** *n* bhutanés,-esa. – **3** the Bhutanese, *npl* los bhutaneses *mpl.*

bias [ˈbaɪəs] **1** *n* (*prejudice*) parcialidad *f,* prejuicio. **2** (*inclination*) tendencia, predisposición *f.* **3** SP descentramiento. – **4** *t* predisponer, influenciar.
● **to be biased in favour of sth./sb.,** ser partidario,-a de algo/algn. ‖ **to be biased against sth./sb.,** tener prejuicio en contra de algo/algn. ‖ **to bias sb. against sth./sb.,** predisponer a algn. en contra de algo/algn. ‖ **on the bias,** al bies, al sesgo.
▲ *pt & pp biased o biassed, ger biasing o biassing.*

biased [ˈbaɪəst] *adj* parcial.

biassed [ˈbaɪəst] *adj* → **biased**.

bib [bɪb] **1** *n* (*for baby*) babero. **2** (*top of apron, overall*) peto.
● **to be in one's best bib and tucker,** ir de punta en blanco.

Bible [ˈbaɪbəl] *n* Biblia.
■ **the Holy Bible,** la Sagrada Biblia. ‖ **Bible basher,** fanático,-a religioso,-a. ‖ **the Bible belt,** *zona de los Estados Unidos y Canadá donde impera el fundamentalismo protestante.*

biblical [ˈbɪblɪkəl] *adj* bíblico,-a.

bibliographer [bɪblɪˈɒɡrəfəʳ] *n* bibliógrafo,-a.

bibliographic [bɪblɪəˈɡræfɪk] *adj* bibliográfico,-a.

bibliographical [bɪblɪəˈɡræfɪkəl] *adj* bibliográfico,-a.

bibliography [bɪblɪˈɒɡrəfɪ] *n* bibliografía.
▲ *pl bibliographies.*

bibliophile [ˈbɪblɪəfaɪl] *n* bibliófilo,-a.

bicameral [baɪˈkæmərəl] *adj* POL bicameral.

bicameralism [baɪˈkæmərəlɪzəm] *adj* POL bicameralismo.

bicarbonate [baɪˈkɑːbənət] *n* CHEM bicarbonato.
■ **bicarbonate of soda,** bicarbonato sódico.

bicentenary [baɪsenˈtiːnərɪ] *n* bicentenario.
▲ *pl bicentenaries.*

bicentennial [baɪsenˈtenɪəl] *n* US → **bicentenary**.

biceps [ˈbaɪseps] *n* bíceps *m.*

bicker [ˈbɪkəʳ] *i* discutir, porfiar.
● **to bicker over sth.,** porfiar sobre algo.

bickering [ˈbɪkərɪŋ] *n* discusión *f,* altercado: *that's enough bickering!,* ¡basta ya de discutir!

bicycle [ˈbaɪsɪkəl] *n* bicicleta.
● **to ride a bicycle,** montar en bicicleta.
■ **bicycle chain,** cadena de bicicleta. ‖ **bicycle clip,** pinza para ir en bicicleta. ‖ **bicycle pump,** bomba de bicicleta.

bid [bɪd] **1** *n* (*at auction*) puja: *he made a bid for the Chinese vase,* hizo una puja por el jarrón chino. **2** (*attempt*) intento: *a failed bid for freedom,* un intento fracasado por conseguir la libertad. **3** (*offer*) oferta: *his bid for the company was unsuccessful,* la oferta que hizo por la empresa fracasó. **4** (*in card game*) declaración *f.* – **5** *i* (*at auction*) pujar (**for,** por). **6** (*in card game*) declarar. – **7** *t* (*at auction*) pujar, hacer una oferta de: *he bid fifty pounds,* hizo una oferta de cincuenta libras. **8** *lit* (*ask*)

rogar: *I bid you go,* le ruego que se vaya. **9** *lit* (*order*) ordenar, mandar: *she bade him come,* le ordenó que viniera.
● **to put in a bid for sth.,** hacer una oferta por algo. ‖ **to bid sb. good-day,** *lit* dar a algn. los buenos días. ‖ **to bid sb. welcome,** *lit* dar la bienvenida a algn. ‖ **to bid sb. farewell,** *lit* despedirse de algn.
▲ *pt bid,* en **9** también *bade; pp bid,* en **9** también *bidden; ger bidding.*

bidder [ˈbɪdəʳ] *n* postor,-ra, licitador,-ra.
■ **highest bidder,** mayor postor,-ra. ‖ **successful bidder,** rematante *mf.*

bidding [ˈbɪdɪŋ] **1** *n* (*at auction*) puja, oferta: *the bidding opened at fifty pounds,* la primera oferta fue de cincuenta libras. **2** (*order*) orden *f.* **3** (*card game*) declaración *f.*
● **to do sb.'s bidding,** cumplir las órdenes de algn.

biddy [ˈbɪdɪ] old biddy, *n fam* vieja carca.
▲ *pl biddies.*

bide [baɪd] **to bide one's time,** *phr* esperar el momento oportuno.
▲ *pt bode* [bəʊd] *o bided, pp bided.*

bidet [ˈbiːdeɪ] *n* bidé *m.*

biennial [baɪˈenɪəl] **1** *adj* bienal. – **2** *n* bienal *f.*

bier [bɪə] *n* féretro.

biff [bɪf] **1** *n fam* bofetada. – **2** *t* pegar una bofetada.
● **to biff sb. about the ears,** dar un cachete a algn.

bifocal [baɪˈfəʊkəl] **1** *adj* bifocal. – **2** bifocals, *npl* lentes *fpl* bifocales.

big [bɪg] **1** *adj* (*size, importance*) grande; (*before sing noun*) gran: *a big car,* un coche grande; *a big day,* un gran día; *this skirt is too big for me,* esta falda me va grande. **2** (*older*) mayor: *my big brother,* mi hermano mayor.
● **to be too big for one's boots,** ser muy fanfarrón,-ona. ‖ **to be big with child,** *lit* estar encinta. ‖ **to go over big,** tener un gran éxito. ‖ **to talk big,** fanfarronear.
■ **the Big Apple,** Nueva York. ‖ **big bang theory,** teoría del big bang. ‖ **the Big Board,** US *fam* la bolsa de Nueva York. ‖ **big drum,** bombo. ‖ **big end,** cabeza de biela. ‖ **big game,** caza mayor. ‖ **big noise / big shot,** pez *m* gordo. ‖ **big talk,** fanfarronadas *fpl.* ‖ **big toe,** dedo gordo del pie. ‖ **big top,** carpa de circo. ‖ **big wheel,** noria.
▲ *comp bigger, superl biggest.*

bigamist [ˈbɪɡəmɪst] *n* bígamo,-a.

bigamous [ˈbɪɡəməs] *adj* bígamo,-a.

bigamy [ˈbɪɡəmɪ] *n* bigamia.

big-bellied [bɪɡˈbelɪd] *adj* barrigón,-ona, barrigudo,-a.

big-boned [bɪɡˈbəʊnd] *adj* huesudo,-a.

big-eared [bɪɡˈɪəd] *adj* orejudo,-a.

big-head [ˈbɪɡhed] *n* sabihondo,-a, creído,-a.

big-headed [bɪɡˈhedɪd] *adj* sabihondo,-a, creído,-a.

big-hearted [bɪɡˈhɑːtɪd] *adj* de buen corazón, generoso,-a.

bighorn [ˈbɪɡhɔːn] *n* ZOOL oveja de las Montañas Rocosas.

bight [baɪt] *n* GEOG ensenada, bahía.
■ **Great Australian Bight,** Gran Bahía Australiana.

bigmouth [ˈbɪɡmaʊθ] *n* bocazas *mf.*

bigot [ˈbɪɡət] *n* intolerante, fanático,-a.

bigoted [ˈbɪɡətɪd] *adj* intolerante, fanático,-a.

bigotry [ˈbɪɡətrɪ] *n* intolerancia, fanatismo.

big-sounding [bɪɡˈsaʊndɪŋ] *adj iron* rimbombante, altisonante.

bigwig [ˈbɪɡwɪɡ] *n fam* pez *m* gordo.

bike [baɪk] 1 *n fam* (*bicycle*) bici *f.* 2 (*motorcycle*) moto *f.*
● **on your bike!**, *fam* ¡vete a freír espárragos!
bikini [bɪ'kiːnɪ] *n* biquini *m*, bikini *m.*
bilabial [baɪ'leɪbɪəl] *adj* bilabial.
bilateral [baɪ'lætərəl] *adj* bilateral.
bilberry ['bɪlbərɪ] *n* arándano.
▲ *pl bilberries.*
bile [baɪl] *n* bilis *f,* hiel *f.*
■ **bile duct,** conducto biliar.
bilge [bɪldʒ] 1 *n* MAR (*inner*) sentina; (*outer*) pantoque *m.*
2 *fig* tonterías *fpl.*
■ **bilge block,** picadero del pantoque. ‖ **bilge keel,**
quilla de pantoque. ‖ **bilge water,** agua de sentina.
bilingual [baɪ'lɪŋgwəl] *adj* bilingüe.
bilingualism [baɪ'lɪŋgwəlɪzəm] *n* bilingüismo.
bilious ['bɪlɪəs] 1 *adj* MED bilioso,-a. 2 *fig* (*bad-tempered*)
malhumorado,-a.
bill[1] [bɪl] 1 *n* factura; (*in restaurant*) cuenta: *the electricity/*
telephone bill, la factura de la luz/del teléfono; *could we*
have the bill please?, ¿nos trae la cuenta por favor? 2
(*law*) proyecto de ley. 3 US (*banknote*) billete *m.* 4 (*poster*)
cartel *m.* 5 (*leaflet*) volante *m.* – 6 *t* facturar, pasar la
factura. 7 THEAT programar.
● **to fit the bill,** cumplir los requisitos. ‖ **to top the**
bill, THEAT encabezar el reparto. ‖ **to give sb. a clean**
bill of health, dar de alta a algn. ‖ **to run up a bill of**
..., contraer deudas de ...: *he's run up a bill of a thousand*
pounds, ha contraído deudas de mil libras. ‖ *"post no*
bills", "prohibido fijar carteles".
■ **bill of exchange,** letra de cambio. ‖ **bill of lading,**
conocimiento de embarque. ‖ **bill of sale,** escritura de
venta. ‖ **Bill of Rights,** declaración *f* de derechos. ‖ **bill**
of fare, lista de platos, carta.
bill[2] [bɪl] 1 *n* (*of bird*) pico. 2 (*headland*) cabo, promontorio.
● **to bill and coo,** acariciarse.
Bill [bɪl] *prn* (*William*) Guillermo.
■ **the Old Bill,** GB *sl* la bofia, la pasma.
billabong ['bɪləbɒŋ] *n* (*in Australia*) remanso.
billboard ['bɪlbɔːd] *n* US valla publicitaria.
billet ['bɪlɪt] 1 *n* MIL alojamiento, acuartelamiento. – 2 *t*
MIL alojar, acuartelar.
● **to be billetted in,** alojarse en.
▲ *pt & pp billetted, ger billetting.*
billet-doux [bɪlɪ'duː] *n* carta de amor.
▲ *pl billets-doux* [bɪl'duːz].
billfold ['bɪlfəʊld] *n* US billetero, cartera.
billhook ['bɪlhʊk] *n* podadera.
billiard ['bɪljəd] 1 *n adj* de billar: *a billiard player,* jugador
de billar. – 2 **billiards,** *n* billar *m.*
■ **billiard ball,** bola de billar. ‖ **billiard cue,** taco de
billar. ‖ **billiard table,** mesa de billar.
billing ['bɪlɪŋ] 1 *n* (*invoicing*) facturación *f.* 2 THEAT *orden*
de aparición en cartel.
● **to get top billing,** salir primero,-a en cartel.
billion ['bɪljən] 1 *n* GB billón *m.* 2 US mil millones *mpl.*
● **billions of,** *fig* un mogollón de, la tira de: *there were*
billions of people, había la tira de gente.
billionaire [bɪljə'neəʳ] *n* multimillonario,-a.
billow ['bɪləʊ] 1 *n* (*of water*) ola. 2 (*of smoke*) nube *f.* – 3
t (*sea*) ondear. 4 (*sail*) hincharse.
billowy ['bɪləʊɪ] 1 *adj* (*waves*) encrespado,-a; (*sea*) on-
doso,-a. 2 (*sail*) hinchado,-a.
billposter ['bɪlpəʊstəʳ] *n* cartelero,-a.
billsticker ['bɪlstɪkəʳ] *n* → **billposter.**
billycan ['bɪlɪkæn] *n* cazo.
billy-goat ['bɪlɪgəʊt] *n* macho cabrío.

billy-ho ['bɪlɪhəʊ] like billy-ho, *phr fam* a toda pastilla:
he ran like billy-ho, se fue corriendo a toda pastilla; *it's*
raining like billy-ho, llueven chuzos de punta.
billy-o ['bɪlɪəʊ] *n fam* → **billy-ho.**
bimbo ['bɪmbəʊ] *n fam pej* chica guapa pero tonta.
▲ *pl bimbos o bimboes.*
bimonthly [baɪ'mʌnθlɪ] 1 *adj* (*twice monthly*) bimensual.
2 (*every two months*) bimestral. – 3 *adv* (*twice monthly*) dos
veces al mes. 4 (*every two months*) cada dos meses. – 5
n (*twice monthly*) publicación *f* bimensual. 6 (*every two*
months) publicación *f* bimestral.
bin [bɪn] 1 *n* (*for rubbish*) cubo de la basura; (*for paper*)
papelera. 2 (*large container*) recipiente *m.* – 3 *t fam* (*throw*
away) tirar; (*reject plan, project, etc*) desechar, descartar.
■ **wine bin,** botellero.
▲ *pt & pp binned, ger binning.*
binary ['baɪnərɪ] *adj* binario,-a.
■ **binary code,** código binario. ‖ **binary element,** elemento binario. ‖ **binary fission,** bipartición *f.* ‖ **binary**
number, número binario. ‖ **binary star,** estrella bi-
naria, estrella doble.
bind [baɪnd] 1 *n fam* fastidio, molestia. – 2 *t* (*tie up*) atar;
(*cereals, corn*) agavillar. 3 CULIN (*sauce*) ligar. 4 (*book etc*)
encuadernar. 5 (*bandage*) vendar. 6 (*require*) obligar.
◆ **to bind up** *t sep* (*with bandage*) vendar. ‖ **to bind over**
t sep JUR obligar por ley a hacer algo: *they bound him over*
to keep the peace, lo obligaron por ley a mantener el
orden público.
▲ *pt & pp bound.*
binder ['baɪndəʳ] 1 *n* (*file*) carpeta. 2 (*of books*) encuadernador,-ra. 3 AGR (*machine*) agavilladora. 4 CHEM aglutinante *m.*
binding ['baɪndɪŋ] 1 *n* (*of book*) encuadernación *f.* 2 SEW
ribete *m.* 3 (*of skis*) fijación *f.* – 4 *adj* obligatorio,-a (**on,**
para): *an investment binding on all members,* una inversión obligatoria para todos los miembros. 5 que se
tiene que cumplir: *a binding agreement,* un compromiso que se tiene que cumplir.
bindweed ['baɪndwiːd] *n* BOT correhuela.
binge [bɪndʒ] 1 *n* (*drinking*) borrachera; (*eating*) atracón
m. – 2 *i* atiborrarse, hartarse de comida.
● **to go on a binge,** ir de farra.
bingo ['bɪŋgəʊ] *n* bingo.
● **to play bingo,** jugar al bingo.
■ **bingo card,** cartón *m* de bingo. ‖ **bingo hall,** bingo.
▲ *pl bingos.*
bin-liner ['bɪnlaɪnəʳ] *n* bolsa para la basura.
binocular [bɪ'nɒkjʊləʳ] 1 *adj* binocular. – 2 **binoculars,**
npl prismáticos *mpl*, gemelos *mpl.*
biochemical [baɪəʊ'kemɪkəl] *adj* bioquímico,-a.
biochemist [baɪəʊ'kemɪst] *n* bioquímico,-a.
biochemistry [baɪəʊ'kemɪstrɪ] *n* bioquímica.
biodegradable [baɪəʊdɪ'greɪdəbəl] *adj* biodegradable.
biofeedback [baɪəʊ'fiːdbæk] *n* biorretroacción *f.*
biographer [baɪ'ɒgrəfəʳ] *n* biógrafo,-a.
biographical [baɪə'græfɪkəl] *adj* biográfico,-a.
biography [baɪ'ɒgrəfɪ] *n* biografía.
▲ *pl biographies.*
biological [baɪə'lɒdʒɪkəl] *adj* biológico,-a.
biologist [baɪ'ɒlədʒɪst] *n* biólogo,-a.
biology [baɪ'ɒlədʒɪ] *n* biología.
biomechanics [baɪəʊmɪ'kæniks] *n* biomecánica.
bionic [baɪ'ɒnɪk] *adj* biónico,-a.
bionics [baɪ'ɒniks] *n* biónica.
biophysical [baɪəʊ'fɪzɪkəl] *adj* biofísico,-a.
biophysicist [baɪəʊ'fɪzɪsɪst] *n* biofísico,-a.

biophysics [baɪəʊ'fɪzɪks] *n* biofísica.
biopsy ['baɪɒpsɪ] *n* biopsia.
▲ *pl biopsies.*
biorhythm ['baɪərɪðəm] *n* biorritmo.
biosphere ['baɪəsfɪəʳ] *n* biosfera.
bipartisan [baɪ'pɑːtɪzən] *adj* POL de dos partidos políticos.
bipartite [baɪ'pɑːtaɪt] *adj* bipartito,-a.
biped ['baɪped] **1** *adj* bípedo,-a. – **2** *n* bípedo.
biplane ['baɪpleɪn] *n* AER biplano.
birch [bɜːtʃ] **1** *n* (*tree*) abedul *m*. **2** (*rod*) vara de abedul. – **3** *t* azotar.
bird [bɜːd] **1** *n* (*large*) ave *f*; (*small*) pájaro. **2** GB *sl* (*girl*) chica. **3** (*person*) tipo: *he's a funny old bird,* es un tipo raro; *he's a wily old bird,* es un viejo zorro.
● *a bird in the hand is worth two in the bush,* más vale pájaro en mano que ciento volando. ‖ **to kill two birds with one stone,** matar dos pájaros de un tiro. ‖ **a little bird told me,** me lo ha dicho un pajarito. ‖ **birds of a feather flock together,** Dios los cría y ellos se juntan. ‖ **to do bird,** *sl* estar en chirona. ‖ **to get the bird,** ser rechazado,-a.
■ **bird of ill-omen,** pájaro de mal agüero. ‖ **bird of paradise,** ave *f* del paraíso. ‖ **bird of passage,** ave *f* de paso. ‖ **bird of prey,** ave *f* de rapiña. ‖ **bird's nest,** nido de pájaro. ‖ **bird's nest soup,** sopa de nido de golondrina. ‖ **the birds and the bees,** *euph* la sexualidad.
birdbath ['bɜːdbɑːθ] *n* pila para pájaros.
birdbrain ['bɜːdbreɪn] *n* cabeza de chorlito.
birdcage ['bɜːdkeɪdʒ] *n* jaula de pájaro.
birdie ['bɜːdɪ] **1** *n* (*little bird*) pajarito. **2** (*in golf*) birdie *m*.
● **to score a birdie,** hacer menos uno: *Olazábal scored a birdie at the sixth hole,* Olazábal hizo menos uno en el hoyo seis. ‖ **watch the birdie!,** ¡mira el pajarito!
birdseed ['bɜːdsiːd] *n* BOT alpiste *m*.
bird's-eye view [bɜːdzaɪ'vjuː] *n* vista panorámica.
● **to get a bird's-eye view of sth.,** ver algo a vista de pájaro.
bird-watcher ['bɜːdwɒtʃəʳ] *n* ornitólogo,-a (*cuya afición es observar las aves*).
bird-watching ['bɜːdwɒtʃɪŋ] *n* ornitología (*como afición*).
biretta [bɪ'retə] *n* REL birrete *m*.
Biro ['baɪrəʊ] *n fam* boli *m*.
▲ *pl Biros. Es marca registrada.*
birth [bɜːθ] **1** *n* nacimiento: *he was present at his son's birth,* asistió al nacimiento de su hijo; *the birth of civilization,* el nacimiento de la civilización. **2** MED parto: *it was a difficult birth,* el parto fue difícil. **3** (*descent*) linaje *m*: *he is of noble birth,* es de linaje noble.
● **to give birth to,** (*child*) dar a luz a; (*fig*) dar lugar a. ‖ **to be of humble birth,** ser de origen humilde.
■ **birth certificate,** partida de nacimiento. ‖ **birth control,** control *m* de la natalidad.
birthday ['bɜːθdeɪ] *n* cumpleaños *m*: *it's my twenty-fifth birthday today,* hoy cumplo veinticinco años.
● **to be in one's birthday suit,** estar como Dios le trajo al mundo.
■ **birthday card,** tarjeta de cumpleaños, felicitación *f* de cumpleaños. ‖ **birthday party,** fiesta de cumpleaños. ‖ **birthday present,** regalo de cumpleaños.
birthmark ['bɜːθmɑːk] *n* mancha de nacimiento, antojo.
birthplace ['bɜːθpleɪs] *n* lugar *m* de nacimiento.
birthright ['bɜːθraɪt] *n* derechos *mpl* de nacimiento.

birthstone ['bɜːθstəʊn] *n* piedra preciosa correspondiente al mes de nacimiento o signo zodiacal.
Biscay ['bɪskeɪ] Bay of Biscay, *n* golfo de Vizcaya.
biscuit ['bɪskɪt] **1** *n* galleta. **2** (*ceramics*) porcelana mate. **3** (*colour*) beige *m*.
● **to take the biscuit,** ser el colmo.
bisect [baɪ'sekt] *t* MATH bisecar.
bisexual [baɪ'seksjʊəl] **1** *adj* bisexual. – **2** *n* bisexual *mf*.
bishop ['bɪʃəp] **1** *n* obispo. **2** (*chess*) alfil *m*.
bishopric ['bɪʃəprɪk] *n* obispado.
bismuth ['bɪzməθ] *n* CHEM bismuto.
bison ['baɪsən] *n* bisonte *m*.
bisque [biːsk] *n* sopa de marisco.
bistro ['biːstrəʊ] *n* pequeño restaurante *m*.
▲ *pl bistros.*
bisulfate [baɪ'sʌlfeɪt] *n* (*us*) → **bisulphate**.
bisulphate [baɪ'sʌlfeɪt] *n* CHEM bisulfato.
bit[1] [bɪt] **1** *n* (*small piece*) trozo, pedacito: *a bit of cheese,* un trozo de queso. **2** (*small amount*) poco: *they've only got a bit of money,* sólo tienen un poco de dinero; *he wants a bit of wine,* quiere un poco de vino. **3** *fam* (*time*) un poco, un ratito: *wait a bit,* espera un poco. **4** (*part of film, play, book*) parte *f*. **5** (*coin*) moneda: *a five-peseta bit,* una moneda de cinco pesetas. – **6** a bit, *adv fam* (*rather*) algo, un poco: *he's a bit tired,* está un poco cansado; *I'm a bit older than her,* soy un poco mayor que ella; *it's a bit warmer today,* hoy hace un poco más calor.
● **a bit of,** algo de: *he's got a bit of a headache,* tiene un ligero dolor de cabeza; *it's a bit of a problem,* es un problema bastante peliagudo; *she's a bit of a painter,* la pintura le sale bastante bien; *it's not a bit of use,* no sirve para nada en absoluto. ‖ **bit by bit,** poco a poco. ‖ **not a bit of it,** nada de eso. ‖ **quite a bit / a good bit,** *fam* bastante: *it's a good bit more expensive,* es bastante más caro. ‖ **that's a bit much,** esto ya es pasarse. ‖ **to be a bit of all right,** *fam* estar como un tren. ‖ **to come to bits,** hacerse pedazos, romperse. ‖ **to do one's bit,** aportar su granito de arena. ‖ **to go to bits,** *fig* ponerse histérico,-a. ‖ **to smash sth. to bits,** hacer algo añicos. ‖ **to take sth. to bits,** desmontar algo.
■ **a bit of advice,** un consejo. ‖ **a bit on the side,** *fam* un rollo, amante *mf*. ‖ **bit of stuff,** *fam* amante *mf*. ‖ **bit part,** papel *m* secundario. ‖ **bits and pieces,** trastos *mpl*, bártulos *mpl*.
bit[2] [bɪt] **1** *n* (*of bridle*) bocado. **2** (*of drill*) broca. **3** (*of brace*) barrena. **3** (*of key*) paletón *m*.
● **to take the bit between one's teeth,** coger el toro por los cuernos.
■ **brace and bit,** berbiquí *m* y barrena.
bit[3] [bɪt] *n* COMPUT bit *m*.
bit[4] [bɪt] *pt* → **bite**.
bitch [bɪtʃ] **1** *n* (*gen*) hembra; (*of dog*) perra. **2** *pej* (*woman*) bruja, lagarta. – **3** *i fam* quejarse.
● **to bitch about sb.,** poner a algn. a parir. ‖ **life's a bitch,** *sl* la vida es una mierda.
■ **son of a bitch,** *taboo* hijo de perra, hijo de puta.
bitchy ['bɪtʃɪ] *adj fam* malicioso,-a, rencoroso,-a.
▲ *comp bitchier, superl bitchiest.*
bite [baɪt] **1** *n* (*act*) mordisco. **2** (*of insect*) picadura. **3** (*of dog etc*) mordedura. **4** (*of food*) bocado. **5** (*incisiveness*) mordacidad *f*. **6** (*grip of wheel, cog*) agarre *m*. – **7** *t* morder: *the dog bit him in the leg,* el perro le mordió la pierna. **8** (*insect, snake*) picar. **9** (*grip*) agarrar. – **10** *i* morder: *be careful, it bites,* ten cuidado, que muerde. **11** (*insect, snake*) picar: *mosquitoes bite,* los mosquitos pican. **12**

(*fish*) picar. **13** (*grip*) agarrarse. **14** (*recession etc*) apretar, hacerse sentir, hacerse notar.

◆ **to bite off** *t sep* arrancar con los dientes: *he bit the top off,* arrancó la tapa con los dientes. ‖ **to bite through** *t insep* cortar de un mordisco: *he bit through the rope,* cortó la cuerda de un mordisco.

● **to have a bite,** probar bocado: *she hasn't had a bite all day,* no ha probado bocado en todo el día. ‖ **to bite the bullet,** apechugar. ‖ **to bite the dust,** morder el polvo. ‖ **to bite the hand that feeds one,** volverse en contra de su bienhechor. ‖ **to bite sb.'s head off,** echar un rapapolvo a algn. ‖ **to bite off more than one can chew,** abarcar demasiado. ‖ **to be bitten by sth.,** (*hobby, interest*) estar obsesionado,-a por algo. ‖ **what's bitten you?,** ¿qué mosca te ha picado? ‖ **once bitten twice shy,** gato escaldado del agua fría huye.

▲ *pt bit, pp bitten.*

biting ['baɪtɪŋ] *adj* (*wind*) cortante, penetrante; *fig* mordaz, socarrón,-ona.

bitten ['bɪtən] *pp* → **bite**.

bitter ['bɪtəʳ] **1** *adj* (*gen*) amargo,-a; (*fruit*) ácido,-a, agrio,-a. **2** (*weather*) glacial. **3** (*person*) amargado,-a. **4** (*fight*) enconado,-a. – **5** *n* cerveza amarga.

● **to carry on to the bitter end,** seguir hasta el final. ‖ **to feel bitter about sth.,** guardar rencor por algo.

bitterly ['bɪtəlɪ] **1** *adv* con amargura, amargamente: *she complained bitterly,* se quejó amargamente. **2** (*very*) muy: *it's bitterly cold,* hace un frío glacial; *she was bitterly disappointed,* estuvo terriblemente decepcionada.

bitterness ['bɪtənəs] **1** *n* (*gen*) amargura; (*of fruit*) acidez *f.* **2** (*of person*) amargura, rencor *m.* **3** (*of weather*) crudeza. **4** (*resentment*) rencor *m,* resentimiento.

bittersweet ['bɪtəswiːt] *adj* agridulce.

bitty ['bɪtɪ] *adj* fragmentario,-a, incompleto,-a.

▲ *comp bittier, superl bittiest.*

bitumen ['bɪtjʊmɪn] *n* betún *m.*

bituminous [bɪ'tjuːmɪnəs] *adj* bituminoso,-a, betuminoso,-a.

bivouac ['bɪvʊæk] **1** *n* vivaque *m.* – **2** *i* hacer vivaque.

▲ *pt & pp bivouacked, ger bivouacking.*

biweekly [baɪ'wiːklɪ] **1** *adj* (*twice weekly*) bisemanal. **2** (*fortnightly*) quincenal. – **3** *adv* (*twice weekly*) dos veces por semana. **4** (*fortnightly*) cada quincena. – **5** *n* (*twice weekly*) publicación *f* bisemanal. **6** (*fortnightly*) publicación *f* quincenal.

bizarre [bɪ'zɑːʳ] **1** *adj* raro,-a, extraño,-a. **2** (*eccentric*) estrafalario,-a, extravagante. **3** (*grotesque*) grotesco,-a.

blab [blæb] **1** *i fam* (*gossip*) cotillear, chismear. **2** *fam* (*talk constantly*) rajar, parlotear. **3** (*tell secret*) tirar de la manta, descubrir el pastel. **4** (*inform police*) chivar, soplar.

▲ *pt & pp blabbed* [blabd]*, ger blabbing* ['blabɪŋ]*.*

blabbermouth ['blæbəmaʊθ] **1** *n fam* (*talkative person*) cotorra. **2** (*informant*) chivato,-a, soplón,-ona.

black [blæk] **1** *adj* negro,-a. **2** (*gloomy*) aciago,-a, negro,-a. **3** (*dirty*) sucio,-a. **4** (*threatening*) amenazador,-ra. – **5** *n* (*colour*) negro. **6** (*person*) negro,-a. – **7** *t* (*make black*) ennegrecer. **8** (*boycott*) boicotear.

◆ **to black out 1** *t sep* (*windows of house*) tapar; (*electrical supply*) apagar el alumbrado. **2** (*cause power cut*) dejar sin luz, causar un apagón: *the heavy snow blacked out the town,* la fuerte nevada causó un apagón en todo el pueblo. – **3** *i* (*faint*) desmayarse, sufrir un desmayo.

● **black and white,** blanco y negro. ‖ **to put sth. down in black and white,** *fam* poner algo por escrito. ‖ **to black sb.'s eye,** ponerle a algn. el ojo amoratado. ‖ **to be in sb.'s black books,** estar en la lista negra de algn. ‖ **to give sb. a black look,** apuñalar a algn. con la mirada. ‖ **to look black,** no ser nada prometedor,-ra. ‖ **to wear black,** (*be in mourning*) estar de luto. ‖ **as black as pitch/coal/night,** negro,-a como el carbón.

■ **Black Africa,** Africa Negra. ‖ **black beetle,** cucaracha. ‖ **black belt,** SP cinturón *m* negro. ‖ **black box,** AV caja negra. ‖ **Black Country,** GB *zona industrial de la región central de Inglaterra.* ‖ **Black Death,** HIST peste *f* negra. ‖ **black diamonds,** *euph* carbón *m.* ‖ **black economy,** economía sumergida. ‖ **black eye,** ojo morado, ojo a la funerala. ‖ **Black Forest,** GEOG Selva Negra. ‖ **Black Forest gâteau,** tarta de la Selva Negra. ‖ **Black Friar,** fraile *m* dominico. ‖ **black hole,** agujero negro. ‖ **black humour,** humor *m* negro. ‖ **black ice,** hielo, verglás *m.* ‖ **black magic,** magia negra. ‖ **black mark,** mala nota. ‖ **black market,** mercado negro. ‖ **black marketeer,** estraperlista *mf.* ‖ **Black Maria,** *fam* furgón *m* de la policía. ‖ **Black power,** movimiento de poder negro. ‖ **black pepper,** CULIN pimienta negra. ‖ **black pudding,** CULIN morcilla. ‖ **Black Sea,** Mar Negro. ‖ **black sheep,** *fig* oveja negra. ‖ **black spot,** *fig* (*on road*) punto negro. ‖ **black velvet,** cóctel de champán y cerveza negra, black velvet *m.* ‖ **black widow,** ZOOL (*spider*) viuda negra.

black-and-blue [blækən'bluː] *adj* amoratado,-a.

blackball ['blækbɔːl] **1** *t* POL dar bola negra a un candidato, rechazar a un candidato en una votación. **2** (*ostracise*) excluir, rechazar.

blackberry ['blækbərɪ] *n* zarzamora, mora.

■ blackberry bush, zarza.

▲ *pl blackberries.*

blackbird ['blækbɜːd] *n* mirlo.

blackboard ['blækbɔːd] *n* pizarra.

blackcap ['blækkæp] *n* ORN curruca.

blackcurrant [blæk'kʌrənt] *n* grosella negra.

■ blackcurrant bush, grosellero negro, casis *m.*

blacken ['blækən] **1** *t* ennegrecer. **2** *fig* (*defame*) manchar: *they blackened his reputation,* mancharon su reputación.

blackguard ['blægɑːd] *n* truhán *m,* pillo.

blackhead ['blækhed] *n* espinilla.

blackish ['blækɪʃ] *adj* negruzco,-a.

blackjack[1] ['blækdʒæk] *n* (*card game*) veintiuna.

blackjack[2] ['blækdʒæk] *n* US (*bludgeon*) cachiporra.

blackjack[3] ['blækdʒæk] *n* (*pirate flag*) pabellón *m* pirata.

blackleg ['blækleg] **1** *n* esquirol *m.* – **2** *i* ser un esquirol.

▲ *pt & pp blacklegged, ger blacklegging.*

blacklist ['blæklɪst] **1** *n* lista negra. – **2** *t* poner en la lista negra.

blackmail ['blækmeɪl] **1** *n* chantaje *m.* – **2** *t* hacer chantaje a, chantajear: *they are still blackmailing him,* todavía le hacen chantaje.

● **to blackmail sb. into doing sth.,** chantajear a algn. para que haga algo: *they blackmailed him into going,* le chantajearon para que fuera.

blackmailer ['blækmeɪləʳ] *n* chantajista *mf.*

blackness ['blæknəs] **1** *n* negrura, oscuridad *f.* **2** (*black culture*) negritud *f.*

blackout ['blækaʊt] **1** *n* (*through electrical fault*) apagón *m*; (*in wartime*) oscurecimiento general de una ciudad. **2** (*fainting*) pérdida de conocimiento, desmayo.

Blackshirt ['blækʃɜːt] *n* HIST camisa *m* negra.

blacksmith ['blæksmɪθ] *n* herrero.

■ blacksmith's forge, herrería.

blackthorn ['blækθɔːn] *n* BOT endrino.

black-tie [ˈblæktaɪ] *adj* de etiqueta: *a black-tie dinner,* cena de etiqueta.
bladder [ˈblædəʳ] **1** *n* vejiga. **2** *(in tyre, football)* cámara de aire.
blade [bleɪd] **1** *n* *(of sword, knife, etc)* hoja. **2** *(of iceskate)* cuchilla. **3** *(of propeller, fan, oar, hoe)* pala. **4** *(of grass)* brizna. **5** *(of machine, guillotine)* cuchilla. **6** *dated* *(young man)* galán *m.*
blame [bleɪm] **1** *n* culpa. – **2** *t* culpar, echar la culpa a: *they blamed the wrong man,* culparon al hombre equivocado.
● **to be to blame,** tener la culpa: *I'm to blame,* soy el culpable, tengo la culpa, las culpa es mía. ‖ **to put the blame on,** echar la culpa a, inculpar a: *they always put the blame on me,* siempre me echan la culpa a mí. ‖ **to blame os.,** reprocharse: *there's no need for you to blame yourself,* no tienes por qué reprocharte. ‖ **you've only got yourself to blame,** tú te lo has buscado. ‖ **I don't blame you,** no me extraña: *I didn't want to go. –I don't blame you,* no quise ir. –No me extraña.
blameless [ˈbleɪmləs] **1** *adj* *(not guilty)* libre de culpa, inocente. **2** *(virtuous)* intachable.
blameworthy [ˈbleɪmwɜːðɪ] *adj* censurable, reprobable.
blanch [blɑːntʃ] **1** *t* CULIN escaldar. – **2** *i* palidecer.
blancmange [bləˈmɒnʒ] *n* CULIN manjar *m* blanco.
bland [blænd] *adj* soso,-a.
blandishments [ˈblændɪʃmənts] *n lit* halago, lisonja.
blank [blæŋk] **1** *adj* *(page etc)* en blanco. **2** *(look etc)* vacío,-a. **3** *(cassette, tape)* virgen. – **4** *n* *(on paper)* espacio en blanco. **5** *(bullet)* bala de fogueo. **6** *(coin, disc)* cospel *m.* – **7** *t* fingir no ver a, hacer como si no hubiera visto a: *I said hello but she just blanked me,* la saludé pero hizo como si no me hubiera visto.
◆ **to blank out** *t sep* tapar, esconder: *the clouds blanked out the sun,* las nubes taparon el sol.
● **my mind went blank,** me quedé en blanco. ‖ **to draw a blank,** *fam* no tener éxito.
■ **blank cartridge,** cartucho de fogueo. ‖ **blank cheque,** cheque *m* en blanco. ‖ **blank denial,** denegación *f* categórica. ‖ **blank refusal,** rotunda negativa. ‖ **blank verse,** verso blanco.
blanket [ˈblæŋkɪt] **1** *n* manta, AM frazada. **2** *(layer)* capa, manto: *a blanket of snow,* una capa de nieve. **3** *adj* *(overall)* general, global; *(unanimous)* unánime: *a blanket agreement,* un acuerdo global; *blanket condemnation,* una condena unánime. – **4** *t* cubrir con un manto: *the hills were blanketed with snow,* las colinas estaban cubiertas con un manto de nieve. **5** *(stifle rumours)* acallar.
● **to be a wet blanket,** ser un aguafiestas. ‖ **to be born on the wrong side of the blanket,** nacer fuera del matrimonio.
■ **blanket of fog,** banco de niebla. ‖ **blanket bath,** *lavado de un paciente en su cama.* ‖ **blanket bombing,** bombardeo masivo. ‖ **blanket insurance,** póliza de seguro a todo riesgo. ‖ **blanket stitch,** punto de festón.
blankly [ˈblæŋklɪ] *adv* con la mirada vacía, sin expresión.
blare [bleəʳ] **1** *n* *(loud noise)* estruendo, fragor *m.* **2** *(of trumpet)* trompetazo. – **3** *i* resonar, sonar.
◆ **to blare out** *i* sonar muy fuerte.
blarney [ˈblɑːnɪ] **1** *n fam* halago, coba. – **2** *t fam* dar coba.
blasé [ˈblɑːzeɪ] **1** *adj* indiferente, poco impresionado,-a. **2** *(satiated)* hastiado,-a.
● **to be blasé about sth.,** serle indiferente a algn.

algo: *he's blasé about the whole thing,* el asunto le es indiferente.
blaspheme [blæsˈfiːm] *i* blasfemar (**against,** contra).
blasphemer [blæsˈfiːməʳ] *n* blasfemo,-a, blasfemador,-ra.
blasphemous [ˈblæsfəməs] *adj* blasfemo,-a, blasfemador,-ra.
blasphemy [ˈblæsfəmɪ] *n* blasfemia.
▲ *pl* **blasphemies.**
blast [blɑːst] **1** *n* *(of wind)* ráfaga. **2** *(of water, air, etc)* chorro. **3** *(of horn)* toque *m.* **4** *(of trumpet)* trompetazo. **5** *(explosion)* explosión *f,* voladura. **6** *(shock wave)* onda expansiva. **7** *(reprimand)* bronca. – **8** *t (explode)* volar, hacer volar. **9** *(criticize)* criticar. **10** *(reprimand)* echar una bronca. **11** *(ruin, spoil)* echar a perder, dar al traste con: *they blasted her hopes,* dieron al traste con sus esperanzas. **12** *(shoot)* pegar un tiro a, disparar contra; *(wound)* herir en: *they blasted him,* le pegaron un tiro; *they blasted him in the leg,* le hirieron en la pierna. **13** *(shrivel, wither)* marchitar. – **14** *i (shoot)* disparar. – **15** *interj* ¡maldito sea!
◆ **to blast away on** *t insep (brass instrument)* tocar con estrépito. ‖ **to blast off** *i (rocket)* despegar.
● **to blast a hole in,** abrir con carga explosiva. ‖ **to get a blast out of sth.,** pasarlo bomba con algo. ‖ **at full blast,** a todo volumen.
■ **blast furnace,** alto horno. ‖ **blast hole,** agujero *(hecho por una explosión).*
blasted [ˈblɑːstɪd] *adj* maldito,-a, dichoso,-a.
blasting [ˈblɑːstɪŋ] *n* voladura, explosión *f.*
■ **blasting charge,** carga explosiva.
blast-off [ˈblɑːstɒf] *n (of rocket, missile)* despegue *m.*
blatancy [ˈbleɪtənsɪ] *n* descaro.
blatant [ˈbleɪtənt] **1** *adj* descarado,-a, flagrante: *a blatant abuse of power,* un abuso de poder descarado. **2** *(obtrusive)* llamativo,-a, intruso,-a.
blather [ˈblæðəʳ] **1** *n* chuminadas *fpl,* chorradas *fpl.* – **2** *i* decir chuminadas, decir chorradas.
blaze¹ [bleɪz] **1** *n (fire)* incendio. **2** *(flame)* llamarada. **3** *(of light)* resplandor *m.* **4** *(outburst)* arranque *m,* acceso. – **5** *i (fire)* arder. **6** *(sun)* brillar con fuerza. **7** *(light)* resplandecer.
◆ **to blaze away** *i* seguir disparando. ‖ **to blaze past** *i* pasar volando, ir disparado,-a.
● **to go like blazes,** ir a toda pastilla, ir a todo gas. ‖ **to be a blaze of colour,** estar resplandeciente de color. ‖ **to blaze with anger,** echar chispas. ‖ **in a blaze of publicity,** a bombo y platillo. ‖ **go to blazes!,** *fam* ¡vete a la porra! ‖ **what the blazes ...?,** *fam* ¿qué demonios ...?
blaze² [bleɪz] *n (on animal's face)* mancha blanca en la frente.
● **to blaze a trail,** abrir un camino.
blaze³ [bleɪz] *n (of trumpets)* fanfarria, toque *m* de trompeta.
blazer [ˈbleɪzəʳ] *n* americana de sport, blazer *m.*
blazing [ˈbleɪzɪŋ] **1** *adj (fire)* ardiente. **2** *(light)* brillante. **3** *(sun, heat)* abrasador,-ra. **4** *(argument)* violento,-a.
blazon [ˈbleɪzən] **1** *n* blasón *m.* – **2** *t* blasonar.
bleach [bliːtʃ] **1** *n* lejía. – **2** *t (whiten)* blanquear. **3** *(remove colour)* desteñir, decolorar. **4** *(hair)* decolorar. – **5** *i (whiten)* blanquearse. **6** *(lose colour)* desteñirse, descolorarse.
bleachers [ˈbliːtʃəʳz] *npl* US gradas *fpl.*
bleak [bliːk] **1** *adj (countryside)* desolado,-a. **2** *(weather)* desapacible. **3** *(future)* poco prometedor,-ra. **4** *(welcome, reception)* frío,-a.

bleary ['blɪərɪ] 1 adj (from tears) nubloso,-a. 2 (from tiredness) legañoso,-a.

▲ comp **blearier**, superl **bleariest**.

bleary-eyed ['blɪərɪ'aɪd] adj con los ojos legañosos.

bleat [bliːt] 1 n balido. – 2 i balar. 3 fig gimotear.

bled [bled] pt & pp → **bleed**.

bleed [bliːd] 1 i MED sangrar: his leg was bleeding, le sangraba la pierna. 2 (colour, dye) desteñirse: "wash separately as colour will bleed", "lavar por separado, se destiñe fácilmente". 3 (plant, tree) exudar, sudar. – 4 t MED sacar sangre, sangrar. 5 (cistern, radiator) sacar el agua. 6 (tree, plant) exudar, sudar.

● to bleed sb. dry, sacarle a algn. hasta el último céntimo. ‖ to bleed to death, morir desangrado,-a. ‖ my heart bleeds for you!, iron ¡te lo has buscado!

▲ pt & pp bled.

bleeder ['bliːdəʳ] n sl hijo,-a de tal, capullo m.

■ little bleeder, sl (naughty child) mocoso,-a.

bleeding ['bliːdɪŋ] 1 adj sangriento,-a. 2 sl (blasted) puñetero,-a. – 3 n MED sangría.

bleed-valve ['bliːdvælv] n TECH válvula de purga.

bleep [bliːp] 1 n pitido. – 2 i pitar. – 3 t localizar con un busca.

bleeper ['bliːpəʳ] n busca m, buscapersonas m.

blemish ['blemɪʃ] 1 n desperfecto, imperfección f. 2 (on fruit) maca. 3 fig mancha. 4 t (spoil) estropear, desmejorar. 5 fig (reputation) manchar, tiznar.

● without a blemish, fig intachable.

blench [blenʃ] 1 i (recoil) retroceder. 2 (flinch) pestañear, inmutarse: he didn't blench, no se inmutó.

blend [blend] 1 t mezcla, combinación f. – 2 t (mix) mezclar, combinar. 3 (match) matizar, armonizar. – 4 i mezclarse, combinarse. 5 armonizarse.

blender ['blendəʳ] n CULIN batidora, minipímer m.

bless [bles] t bendecir.

● to bless os., persignarse, santiguarse. ‖ bless you!, (on sneezing) ¡Jesús! ‖ bless my soul!, dated ¡Dios mío! ‖ well, I'll be blessed!, ¡caramba!

blessed ['blesɪd] 1 adj (holy) bendito,-a, santo,-a. 2 (content, happy) bienaventurado,-a: blessed are the pure in heart, bienaventurados los puros de corazón. 3 fam (damn) santo,-a; (more strongly) maldito,-a: the whole blessed day, todo el santo día; that blessed man, ese maldito hombre; every blessed day, todos los días; he doesn't know a blessed thing about it, no sabe ni jota de ello.

● blessed be thy name, bendito sea su nombre. ‖ of blessed memory, de feliz memoria.

■ Blessed Sacrament, Santísimo Sacramento.

blessing ['blesɪŋ] 1 n bendición f. 2 (advantage) beneficio, ventaja: the blessings of central heating, las ventajas de la calefacción central.

● to give the blessing, dar la bendición. ‖ to give one's blessing to sth./sb., dar su bendición a algo/algn.: they gave their blessing to the marriage, dieron su bendición al matrimonio. ‖ to be a blessing, ser una bendición: the rain was a blessing, la lluvia era una bendición. ‖ it's a blessing in disguise, no hay mal que por bien no venga. ‖ to count one's blessings, considerarse afortunado,-a. ‖ what a blessing!, ¡qué suerte!

blew [bluː] pt → **blow**.

blight [blaɪt] 1 n (mildew) tizón m, añublo. 2 fig (person) azote m; (calamity) plaga. – 3 t (mildew) atizonar, añublar. 4 fig (ruin, spoil) echar a perder, estropear: he blighted her life, le estropeó la vida. 5 (harm) perjudicar, dañar.

blighter ['blaɪtəʳ] 1 n fam (man) tipo, individuo. 2 fam (rogue) sinvergüenza m.

■ stupid blighter, cretino.

Blighty ['blaɪtɪ] n fam Inglaterra.

blimey ['blaɪmɪ] interj ¡jolines!, ¡caray!

blimp [blɪmp] 1 n reaccionario,-a, chauvinista mf.

blind [blaɪnd] 1 adj ciego,-a. – 2 n (on window) persiana. – 3 t cegar, dejar ciego,-a. 4 (dazzle) deslumbrar.

● blind in one eye, tuerto,-a. ‖ blind with jealousy, ciego,-a con los celos. ‖ blind with rage, ciego,-a de ira. ‖ in the kingdom of the blind the one eyed man is king, en el reino de los ciegos el tuerto es rey. ‖ it's a case of the blind leading the blind, fig tan ciego el uno como el otro. ‖ not to take a blind bit of notice, fig no hacer el menor caso. ‖ to bake blind, cocer sin el relleno. ‖ to be as blind as a bat, no ver ni torta. ‖ to be blind drunk, estar borracho,-a, como una cuba. ‖ to be blind to sth., estar inconsciente de algo, no darse cuenta de algo. ‖ to blind sb. with science, deslumbrar a algn. con sus conocimientos. ‖ to get blind drunk, ponerse ciego,-a, coger una tajada. ‖ to go blind, quedarse ciego,-a. ‖ to turn a blind eye, fig hacer la vista gorda, hacerse el sueco.

■ blind alley, callejón m sin salida. ‖ blind corner, curva sin visibilidad. ‖ blind date, cita a ciegas. ‖ blind man, ciego. ‖ blind woman, ciega. ‖ blind man's buff, el juego de la gallina ciega. ‖ blind spot, punto ciego.

blinder ['blaɪndəʳ] 1 n SP (game) partido excepcional; (shot) golpe m excepcional: Mike played a blinder, Mike tuvo un partido excepcional; his second goal was a blinder, su segundo gol fue increíble. – 2 blinders, npl US anteojeras fpl.

blindfold ['blaɪndfəʊld] 1 n venda. – 2 t vendar los ojos a. – 3 adv con los ojos vendados: I could do it blindfold, lo sabría hacer con los ojos vendados.

● to do sth. blindfold, fig hacer algo a ojos cerrados.

blindfolded ['blaɪndfəʊldɪd] adj con los ojos vendados.

blinding ['blaɪndɪŋ] 1 adj cegador,-ra, deslumbrante. – 2 n deslumbramiento.

blindly ['blaɪndlɪ] adv ciegamente, a ciegas.

● to go into sth. blindly, emprender algo sin reflexionar.

blindness ['blaɪndnəs] n ceguera.

blink [blɪŋk] 1 n parpadeo. 2 (gleam, glimmer) destello. – 3 i parpadear. 4 (gleam, glimmer) destellar.

● on the blink, fam averiado,-a.

blinkered ['blɪnkəd] adj fig estrecho,-a de miras.

blinkers ['blɪnkəz] npl anteojeras fpl.

blinking ['blɪŋkɪŋ] adj sl maldito,-a, puñetero,-a: the blinking phone won't work, este puñetero teléfono no va.

■ blinking idiot, tonto de remate.

blip [blɪp] 1 n (on radar screen) punto luminoso. 2 (noise) bip m.

bliss [blɪs] n felicidad f, dicha: it was bliss, fue maravilloso.

● what bliss!, ¡qué dicha!

blissful ['blɪsfʊl] adj feliz, dichoso,-a.

blister ['blɪstəʳ] 1 n (on skin) ampolla. 2 (on paint, surface) burbuja. – 3 t producir ampollas en. – 4 i ampollarse, formarse ampollas.

blistering ['blɪstərɪŋ] adj (heat) abrasador,-ra.

blithe [blaɪð] 1 adj lit alegre. 2 (indifferent) desinteresado,-a, indiferente.

blithering ['blɪðərɪŋ] blithering idiot, n imbécil mf.

blitz [blɪts] **1** *n* bombardeo masivo. – **2** *t* bombardear.
● **to have a blitz on sth.**, limpiar algo a fondo.
■ **the Blitz**, HIST *los bombardeos aéreos alemanes de ciudades británicas en los años* 1940-41.
blitzkrieg ['blɪtskriːg] *n* guerra relámpago.
blizzard ['blɪzəd] *n* tempestad *f* de nieve, ventisca.
bloated ['bləʊtɪd] *adj* hinchado,-a.
● **bloated with pride**, hinchado,-a de orgullo. ‖ **to become bloated**, abotagarse, hincharse.
bloater ['bləʊtə'] *n* arenque *m* ahumado.
blob [blɒb] **1** *n* (*drop*) gota. **2** (*smudge*) borrón *m*. **3** (*of colour*) mancha.
bloc [blɒk] *n* POL bloque *m*.
block [blɒk] **1** *n* bloque *m*: *a block of ice*, un bloque de hielo. **2** (*of wood, stone*) taco. **3** (*building*) edificio, bloque *m*. **4** (*group of buildings*) manzana: *it's three blocks away*, está a tres calles de aquí. **5** (*obstruction*) obstrucción *f*. – **6** *t* (*pipe etc*) obstruir, atascar: *he blocked the sink*, atascó el fregadero. **7** (*streets etc*) bloquear.
◆ **to block off** *t sep* (*street*) cortar. ‖ **to block out** *t sep* (*view, light*) tapar; (*erase memories*) borrar: *the building blocks out the light*, el edificio nos tapa la luz; *she's trying to block out the past*, intenta borrar el pasado. ‖ **to block up** *t sep* (*hole, window, door*) tapar.
● **to block the way**, cerrar el paso. ‖ **to become blocked**, obstruirse, atascarse. ‖ **to knock sb.'s block off**, romperle la crisma a algn. ‖ **to take a walk around the block**, dar una vuelta.
■ **block and tackle**, aparejo de poleas. ‖ **block letters**, mayúsculas *fpl*. ‖ **block of flats**, bloque *m* de pisos. ‖ **block operation**, COMPUT operación *f* de bloque. ‖ **block of seats**, grupo de asientos. ‖ **block booking**, reserva en grupo. ‖ **block vote**, voto por cabeza de delegación. ‖ **building blocks**, juego de construcción. ‖ **mental block**, bloqueo mental. ‖ **note block**, taco, bloc *m* de notas.
blockade [blɒ'keɪd] **1** *n* MIL bloqueo. – **2** *t* bloquear.
● **to lift a blockade**, levantar un bloqueo.
blockage ['blɒkɪdʒ] *n* obstrucción *f*, atasco.
blockbuster ['blɒkbʌstə'] **1** *n* fig (*novel*) best seller *m*, éxito de ventas. **2** fig (*film*) película de acción. **3** (*bomb*) bomba de demolición.
blockhead ['blɒkhed] *n* zoquete *mf*, tarugo.
blockhouse ['blɒkhaʊs] *n* MIL blocao, fortín *m*.
blocking ['blɒkɪŋ] *n* bloqueo, obstrucción *f*.
bloke [bləʊk] *n* GB fam tipo, tío.
blond [blɒnd] **1** *adj* rubio,-a. – **2** *n* rubio,-a.
▲ *Suele escribirse* **blonde** *cuando se refiere a una mujer.*
blonde [blɒnd] *adj-n* → **blond**.
blood [blʌd] **1** *n* sangre *f*. **2** (*ancestry*) parentesco, alcurnia.
● **in cold blood**, a sangre fría. ‖ **to make sb.'s blood boil**, freírle la sangre a algn. ‖ **to have blood on one's hands**, fig tener las manos manchadas de sangre. ‖ **to shed blood**, derramar sangre. ‖ **my blood ran cold**, se me heló la sangre. ‖ **it runs in his blood**, lo lleva en la sangre. ‖ **blood is thicker than water**, la sangre tira.
■ **bad blood**, mala sangre *f*. ‖ **blood bank**, banco de sangre *f*. ‖ **blood brother**, hermano de sangre. ‖ **blood cell**, glóbulo. ‖ **blood clot**, coágulo. ‖ **blood donor**, donante *mf* de sangre. ‖ **blood group**, grupo sanguíneo. ‖ **blood money**, dinero pagado a un asesino a sueldo. ‖ **blood orange**, sanguina. ‖ **blood plasma**, plasma sanguíneo. ‖ **blood pressure**, tensión *f* arterial. ‖ **blood relative**, pariente *mf* consanguíneo,-a. ‖

blood sausage, morcilla. ‖ **blood serum**, suero de sangre. ‖ **blood sugar**, MED glucemia. ‖ **blood test**, análisis *m* de sangre. ‖ **blood transfusion**, transfusión *f* de sangre. ‖ **blood vessel**, vaso sanguíneo. ‖ **high blood pressure**, tensión *f* alta. ‖ **low blood pressure**, tensión *f* baja. ‖ **one's own flesh and blood**, gente *f* de su propia sangre.
bloodbath ['blʌdbɑːθ] *n* matanza, masacre *f*.
bloodcurdling ['blʌdkɜːdəlɪŋ] *adj* horripilante, escalofriante.
bloodhound ['blʌdhaʊnd] *n* sabueso.
bloodless ['blʌdləs] **1** *adj* (*pale*) pálido,-a. **2** (*revolution etc*) incruento,-a, sin derramamiento de sangre.
bloodletting ['blʌdletɪŋ] *n* MED sangría.
blood-red ['blʌdred] **1** *n* rojo sangre. – **2** *adj* de color rojo sangre.
bloodshed ['blʌdʃed] *n* derramamiento de sangre.
bloodshot ['blʌdʃɒt] *adj* inyectado,-a de sangre.
bloodstain ['blʌdsteɪn] *n* mancha de sangre.
bloodstained ['blʌdsteɪnd] *adj* manchado,-a de sangre.
bloodstream ['blʌdstriːm] *n* corriente *f* sanguínea.
bloodsucker ['blʌdsʌkə'] *n* sanguijuela.
bloodthirsty ['blʌdθɜːstɪ] *adj* sanguinario,-a, ávido,-a de sangre.
▲ *comp* **bloodthirstier**, *superl* **bloodthirstiest**.
bloody ['blʌdɪ] **1** *adj* (*battle*) sangriento,-a. **2** sl (*damned*) puñetero,-a, mierda de: *the bloody car won't start*, este mierda de coche no arranca; *answer the bloody phone!*, ¡coge el teléfono, coño!
● **it's a bloody nuisance**, es un coñazo. ‖ **bloody hell!**, ¡hostia!
■ **Bloody Mary**, HIST María Tudor; (*drink*) bloody mary *m* (*vodka con zumo de tomate*).
▲ *comp* **bloodier**, *superl* **bloodiest**.
bloody-minded [blʌdɪ'maɪndɪd] **1** *adj* (*stubborn*) tozudo,-a, terco,-a. **2** (*bad-tempered*) de malas pulgas.
bloody-mindedness [blʌdɪ'maɪndɪdnəs] **1** *n* (*bad temper*) mal genio. **2** (*stubborness*) terquedad *f*.
bloom [bluːm] **1** *n* (*flower*) flor *f*. **2** (*on fruit*) pelusa. **3** (*freshness*) frescura, lozanía. – **4** *i* florecer.
● **to be in bloom**, estar en flor. ‖ **in the bloom of youth**, en la flor de la edad. ‖ **to burst into bloom**, florecer. ‖ **to take the bloom off sth.**, quitar la frescura de algo.
bloomer ['bluːmə'] *n* GB fam metedura de pata, pifia.
bloomers ['bluːməz] *npl* pololos *mpl*.
blooming ['bluːmɪŋ] **1** *adj* (*flower*) floreciente. **2** (*radiant*) radiante, resplandeciente: *she was blooming*, estaba radiante. **3** fam repajolero,-a, puñetero,-a: *this blooming radio*, esta puñetera radio.
blooper ['bluːpə] *n* US fam metedura de pata.
blossom ['blɒsəm] **1** *n* flor *f*. – **2** *i* florecer.
◆ **to blossom out** *i* alcanzar su plenitud.
● **to be in blossom**, florecer. ‖ **to blossom into**, fig convertirse en.
blot [blɒt] **1** *n* (*of ink*) borrón *m*; (*on reputation*) mancha: *the power station's a blot on the landscape*, la central eléctrica afea el paisaje. – **2** *t* (*stain*) manchar. **3** (*dry*) secar.
◆ **to blot out** *t sep* (*hide*) ocultar. **2** (*memory*) borrar.
▲ *pt & pp* **blotted**, *ger* **blotting**.
blotch [blɒtʃ] **1** *n* mancha. **3** *i* (*become stained*) mancharse. **3** (*skin*) salir manchas.
blotchy ['blɒtʃɪ] *adj* lleno,-a de manchas.
blotter ['blɒtə'] **1** *n* papel *m* secante. **2** US registro.
blotting-paper ['blɒtɪŋpeɪpə'] *n* papel *m* secante.

blotto ['blɒtəʊ] *adj fam* trompa.
blouse [blaʊz] *n* blusa.
blow[1] [bləʊ] *n* golpe *m*: *he suffered a blow to the head,* recibió un golpe en la cabeza; *her death was a severe blow,* su muerte fue un golpe muy duro; *a blow with the fist,* un puñetazo; *a blow with a hammer,* un martillazo; *a blow with an axe,* un hachazo.
● **to strike sb. a blow,** asestar un golpe a algn. ‖ **to come to blows,** llegar a las manos.
blow[2] [bləʊ] **1** *i* (*wind*) soplar. **2** (*instrument*) tocar, sonar; (*whistle*) pitar; (*horn*) sonar. **3** (*fuse*) fundirse. **4** (*tyre*) reventarse. **5** (*puff, pant*) jadear. – **6** *t* (*instrument*) tocar; (*whistle*) pitar; (*horn*) sonar. **7** *fam* (*money*) despilfarrar, malgastar.
◆ **to blow away 1** *t sep* arrastrar: *the wind blew away the leaves,* el viento arrastró las hojas. **2** *fam fig* mandar al otro barrio: *the gangsters blew him away,* los gángsters lo mandaron al otro barrio. – **3** *i* ser arrastrado,-a, ser llevado,-a. ‖ **to blow in** *t sep* derribar: *the gusts of wind blew in the door,* las ráfagas de viento derribaron la puerta. ‖ **to blow off** *i* (*lid, hat*) salir volando. ‖ **to blow out 1** *t sep* (*flame*) apagar; (*candle*) soplar. **2** (*cheeks*) hinchar. – **3** *i* (*candle, flame*) apagarse. **4** (*tyre*) reventarse. ‖ **to blow over 1** *t sep* derribar, echar a tierra: *the wind blew over the flowerpots,* el viento echó a tierra las macetas. – **2** *i* derrumbarse: *the hoardings blew over,* las vallas se derrumbaron. **3** (*storm*) amainar. **4** (*scandal*) olvidarse. ‖ **to blow up 1** *t sep* (*explode*) (hacer) volar: *they blew up the building,* hicieron volar el edificio. **2** (*inflate*) hinchar. **3** (*photograph*) ampliar. – **4** *i* (*explode*) explotar. **5** (*lose one's temper*) salirse de sus casillas.
● **blow you!,** *fam euph* ¡vete a hacer puñetas! ‖ **I'll be blowed!,** *arch* ¡válgame Dios! ‖ **to blow one's nose,** sonarse las narices. ‖ **to blow one's top,** perder los estribos. ‖ **to blow the lid off sth.,** desvelar algo: *he threatened to blow the lid off the affair,* amenazó con tirar de la manta. ‖ **to blow hot and cold,** vacilar, no saber qué hacer. ‖ **to blow sb.'s mind,** *fam* flipar a algn. ‖ **to blow it,** *fam* pifiarla, cagarla: *now you've blown it!,* ¡ahora la has cagado! ‖ **to be blown up with pride,** ser un,-a engreído,-a, estar henchido,-a de orgullo.
▲ *pt blew* [bluː], *pp blown* [bləʊn].
blow-by-blow ['bləʊbaɪ'bləʊ] *adj* con pelos y señales: *he gave us a blow-by-blow explanation of what happened,* nos explicó con pelos y señales lo que había sucedido.
blow-dry ['bləʊdraɪ] **1** *n* secado del pelo con secador. – **2** *t* secar el pelo con secador.
▲ (*verbo*) *pt & pp* blow-dried, *ger* blow-drying.
blower ['bləʊə'] **1** *n* (*glass worker*) soplador,-ra. **2** *fam* teléfono.
blowfly ['bləʊflaɪ] *n* zool moscarda de la carne.
▲ *pl* blowflies.
blowhole ['bləʊhəʊl] **1** *n* (*of whale*) orificio nasal. **2** (*hole, air vent*) respiradero.
blow-job ['bləʊdʒɒb] *n taboo* mamada.
● **to give sb. a blow-job,** *taboo* mamársela a algn.
blowlamp ['bləʊlæmp] *n* soplete *m*.
blown [bləʊn] *pp* → **blow**.
blowout ['bləʊaʊt] **1** *n* AUTO reventón *m*, pinchazo *m*. **2** *sl* comilona, atracón *m*.
blowpipe ['bləʊpaɪp] *n* cerbatana.
blowsy ['blaʊzɪ] *adj* → **blowzy**.
▲ *comp* blowsier, *superl* blowsiest.

blowtorch ['bləʊtɔːtʃ] *n* soplete *m*.
blow-up ['bləʊʌp] *n* (*photograph*) ampliación *f*.
blowy ['bləʊɪ] *adj* ventoso,-a.
▲ *comp* blowier, *superl* blowiest.
blowzy ['blaʊzɪ] **1** *adj* (*coarse*) basto,-a. **2** (*dishevelled*) desaliñado,-a.
▲ *comp* blowzier, *superl* blowziest.
blubber ['blʌbə'] **1** *n* grasa de ballena. – **2** *i* lloriquear.
bludgeon ['blʌdʒən] **1** *n* cachiporra. – **2** *t* aporrear.
blue [bluː] **1** *adj* azul. **2** (*sad*) triste. **3** (*depressed*) deprimido,-a. **4** (*obscene*) verde: *a blue joke,* un chiste verde. – **5** *n* azul *m*: *light/dark blue,* azul claro/oscuro. – **6** blues, *npl* MUS blues *m*. **7** the blues, la depresión *f*.
● **out of the blue,** como llovido del cielo. ‖ **to be blue with cold,** estar amoratado,-a de frío. ‖ **to have the blues,** estar deprimido,-a. ‖ **to say sth. until one is blue in the face,** repetir algo hasta la saciedad.
■ **blue baby,** MED bebé *m* cianótico. ‖ **blue blood,** sangre *f* azul. ‖ **blue mould,** moho. ‖ **blue movie,** película porno. ‖ **laundry blue,** azulete *m*, añil *m*.
bluebell ['bluːbel] *n* BOT campanilla.
blueberry ['bluːbərɪ] *n* BOT arándano.
▲ *pl* blueberries.
bluebird ['bluːbɜːd] *n* ORN azulejo.
blue-blooded ['bluːblʌdɪd] *adj* de sangre azul.
bluebottle ['bluːbɒtəl] *n* zool moscarda.
blue-chip ['bluːtʃɪp] *adj* FIN de rentabilidad segura: *blue-chip shares,* acciones de rentabilidad segura.
blue-collar ['bluːkɒlə'] *adj* obrero,-a.
■ **blue-collar worker,** obrero,-a de una fábrica.
blue-eyed ['bluːaɪd] *adj* de ojos azules.
■ **blue-eyed boy,** niño mimado, ojo derecho, niña de los ojos.
blueprint ['bluːprɪnt] **1** *n* cianotipo. **2** *fig* anteproyecto. – **3** *t* US (*project, plan*) elaborar, desarrollar.
blues [bluːz] *npl* → **blue**.
bluestocking ['bluːstɒkɪŋ] *n pej* marisabidilla *f*.
bluff[1] [blʌf] **1** *n* camelo, farol *m*, bluff *m*. – **2** *t* engañar a, hacer un bluff a. – **3** *i* tirarse un farol, fanfarronear, AM blofear.
● **to call sb.'s bluff,** hacer que algn. ponga las cartas boca arriba.
bluff[2] [blʌf] **1** *adj* (*blunt*) brusco,-a, que no tiene pelos en la lengua. **2** (*hearty*) campechano,-a. – **3** *n* (*cliff*) acantilado.
bluffer ['blʌfə'] *n* farolero,-a, AM blofeador,-ra.
bluish ['bluːɪʃ] *adj* azulado,-a.
blunder ['blʌndə'] **1** *n* plancha, metedura de pata. – **2** *i* meter la pata.
◆ **to blunder about** *i* andar a ciegas. ‖ **to blunder into** *t insep* tropezar con.
blunderbuss ['blʌndəbʌs] *n* trabuco *m* naranjero.
blunderer ['blʌndərə'] *n* gafe *m*, torpe *m*.
blunt [blʌnt] **1** *adj* (*knife*) desafilado,-a; (*pencil*) despuntado,-a. **2** *fig* (*person*) directo,-a, que no tiene pelos en la lengua. – **3** *t* desafilar, embotar; (*pencil*) despuntar.
■ **blunt angle,** MATH ángulo obtuso. ‖ **blunt instrument,** instrumento contundente.
bluntly ['blʌntlɪ] *adv* sin rodeos, sin andarse por las ramas.
bluntness ['blʌntnəs] **1** *n* (*of knife, weapon*) embotadura, (*of pencil*) despunte *m*, despuntadura. **2** *fig* brusquedad *f*, franqueza.
blur [blɜː'] **1** *n* borrón *m*, mancha. – **2** *t* (*make indistinct*) difuminar. – **3** *i* (*mark, stain*) emborronar, manchar. **4** (*become indistinct*) difuminarse.

● **to be a blur,** ser confuso,-a, quedar confuso,-a: *everything was a blur after the accident,* todo quedó confuso tras el accidente.

▲ *(verbo) pt & pp* **blurred,** *ger* **blurring.**

blurb [blɜːb] *n fam pej* información *f* publicitaria.

blurred [blɜːd] **1** *adj* borroso,-a. **2** *fig (memories)* vago,-a, confuso,-a.

blurt [blɜːt] **to blurt out,** *t* soltar bruscamente, espetar.

blush [blʌʃ] **1** *n* rubor *m,* sonrojo. – **2** *i* ruborizarse, sonrojarse.

● **to blush with embarrassment,** ponerse rojo,-a de vergüenza. ‖ **to make sb. blush,** hacer sonrojar a algn.

blusher ['blʌʃəʳ] *n* colorete *m.*

blushing ['blʌʃɪŋ] **1** *n* rubor *m,* sonrojo. – **2** *adj* ruborizado,-a, rojo,-a de vergüenza.

bluster ['blʌstəʳ] **1** *n* fanfarronadas *fpl.* – **2** *i* fanfarronear. **3** *(wind)* soplar con fuerza, bramar.

blustery ['blʌstərɪ] *adj (windy)* ventoso,-a.

boa ['bəuə] **1** *n* ZOOL boa. **2** BIOL *(feather stole)* boa *m.*

boar [bɔːʳ] *n* ZOOL verraco.

board [bɔːd] **1** *n (piece of wood)* tabla, tablero. **2** *(food)* comida, pensión *f.* **3** *(committee)* junta, consejo. – **4** *t (ship etc)* subirse a, embarcar en. – **5** *i (lodge)* alojarse; *(at school)* ser interno,-a.

◆ **to board up** *t sep (door, window)* entablar.

● **on board,** MAR a bordo. ‖ **above board,** *fig* en regla, legal. ‖ **across the board,** *fig* general, global. ‖ **to go by the board,** irse al traste. ‖ **to sweep the board,** *(be succesful)* arrasar; *(in competition)* llevarse todos los premios; *(in election)* conseguir la mayoría de los escaños. ‖ **to take on board,** *(responsibilty)* asumir; *(concept, idea)* abarcar. ‖ **to go back to the drawing board,** volver a empezar de cero.

■ **board and lodging,** alojamiento con comida incluida. ‖ **board of directors,** junta directiva. ‖ **board of trade,** US cámara de comercio.

boarder ['bɔːdəʳ] **1** *n (gen)* huésped *mf.* **2** *(at school)* interno,-a.

boardgame ['bɔːdɡeɪm] *n* juego de mesa.

boarding ['bɔːdɪŋ] **1** *n (ship, plane etc)* embarque *m.* **2** *(lodging)* pensión *f,* alojamiento.

■ **boarding card,** tarjeta de embarque. ‖ **boarding house,** casa de huéspedes. ‖ **boarding school,** internado.

boardroom ['bɔːdruːm] *n* sala de juntas.

boardsailing ['bɔːdseɪlɪŋ] *n* SP windsurf *m.*

boardwalk ['bɔːdwɔːk] *n* US paseo entablado, muelle *m* hecho de tablas de madera.

boast [bəust] **1** *n* jactancia. – **2** *i* jactarse **(about,** de); presumir **(about,** de): *he's always boasting (about his investments),* no deja de presumir (de sus inversiones). – **3** *t fig* presumir de: *the city boasts new roadways and facilities,* la ciudad presume de sus nuevas vías de circulación y equipamientos.

boaster ['bəustəʳ] *n* jactancioso,-a, presumido,-a.

boastful ['bəustful] *adj* jactancioso,-a, presumido,-a.

boasting ['bəustɪŋ] *n* fanfarronada *fpl,* jactancia.

boat [bəut] **1** *n* barco, nave *f; (small)* bote *m,* barca; *(large)* buque *m,* navío *m; (launch)* lancha. **2** *(for sauce, gravy)* salsera.

● **to burn one's boats,** quemar las naves. ‖ **to miss the boat,** perder el tren. ‖ **to push the boat out,** echar la casa por la ventana. ‖ **to rock the boat,** *fig* ser una influencia desestabilizadora.

■ **boat people,** refugiados vietnamitas *(que huyeron a bordo de barcas).* ‖ **boat race,** regata. ‖ **boat shoes,** náuticos *mpl.* ‖ **boat train,** tren *m* que enlaza con un barco. ‖ **cargo boat,** buque *m* de carga.

boatbuilder ['bəutbɪldəʳ] *n* constructor,-ra de barcos.

boater ['bəutəʳ] *n* canotié *m.*

boathouse ['bəuthaus] *n* cobertizo para embarcaciones.

boating ['bəutɪŋ] *n* ir en barca.

● **to go boating,** dar un paseo en barca.

boatload ['bəutləud] **1** *n* barcada. **2** *fam fig* montón *m: a boatload of tourists got off at Piccadilly,* un montón de turistas bajó en Piccadilly; *people came in boatloads,* vino la tira de gente.

boatman ['bəutmən] *n* barquero.

▲ *pl* **boatmen** ['bəutmen].

boatswain ['bəusən] *n* contramaestre *m.*

boatwoman ['bəutwumən] *n* barquera.

▲ *pl* **boatwomen** ['bəutwimin].

boatyard ['bəutjɑːd] *n* astillero.

bob[1] [bɒb] **1** *n (jerking movement)* sacudida; *(bouncing movement)* rebote *m.* **2** *(curtsy)* reverencia. – **3** *i (jerk)* moverse a sacudidas; *(bounce)* rebotar. **4** *(curtsy)* hacer una reverencia.

◆ **to bob about** *i (on water)* fluctuar, flotar; *(in air)* ondear. ‖ **to bob along** *i* balancearse. ‖ **to bob up 1** *i* aparecer de pronto. **2** *(in water)* salir a la superficie. ‖ **to bob down** *i* agacharse repentinamente.

▲ *(verbo) pt & pp* **bobbed,** *ger* **bobbing.**

bob[2] [bɒb] **1** *n (haircut)* pelo a lo chico. **2** *(bobsleigh)* bobsleigh *m.* – **3** *t (hair)* cortar a lo chico.

▲ *(verbo) pt & pp* **bobbed,** *ger* **bobbing.**

bob[3] [bɒb] *n fam* chelín *m.*

Bob [bɒb] *n (diminutive of Robert)* Roberto.

● **Bob's your uncle!,** ¡y listo!: *put it in the pan, boil for five minutes and Bob's your uncle!,* lo viertes en el cazo, lo hierves durante cinco minutos, ¡y listo!

bob-a-job ['bɒbədʒɒb] **bob-a-job week,** *n* GB *semana en que los scouts se dedican a hacer pequeñas tareas para la gente a cambio de dinero.*

bobbin ['bɒbɪn] *n (for textiles, wire etc.)* carrete *m,* bobina; *(for lace)* bolillo, palillo.

bobbin-lace ['bɒbɪnleɪs] *n* encaje *m* de bolillos.

bobby ['bɒbɪ] *n fam* poli *m.*

● **to be a bobby's job,** ser un chollo.

■ **bobby socks / bobby sox,** US calcetines *mpl* cortos.

▲ *pl* **bobbies.**

bobby-soxer ['bɒbɪsɒksəʳ] *n* US quinceañera.

bobsled ['bɒbsled] *n-i* US → **bobsleigh.**

bobsleigh ['bɒbsleɪ] **1** *n* bobsleigh *m.* – **2** *i* practicar el bobsleigh.

bobtail ['bɒbteɪl] **1** *adj* rabicorto,-a, descolado,-a. – **2** *n* animal *m* que tiene la cola cortada. **3** *(docked tail)* rabo cortado, cola cortada.

bode [bəud] **1** *pt* → **bide.** – **2** *t (foretell)* presagiar, augurar: *her predictions bode no good,* sus predicciones no presagiaban nada bueno.

● **to bode ill/well,** ser de buen/mal agüero.

bodice ['bɒdɪs] *n* corpiño.

bodily ['bɒdɪlɪ] **1** *adj* físico,-a, corporal. – **2** *adv (in person)* físicamente. **3** *(en masse)* como un solo hombre, en pleno.

■ **(grievous) bodily harm,** lesiones *fpl* corporales (graves).

body ['bɒdɪ] **1** *n* cuerpo. **2** *(corpse)* cadáver *m.* **3** *(organization)* organismo, entidad *f,* ente *m; (association)* agrupación *f: public body,* ente *m* público; *state body,* organismo estatal; *parliamentary body,* agrupación *f*

parlamentaria. **4** (*of wine*) cuerpo. **5** (*of people*) grupo, conjunto. **6** AUTO (*of car*) carrocería. **7** AV fuselaje *m*. **8** (*main part*) parte *f* principal, grueso: *the body of the play*, la parte principal de la obra.
● **to keep body and soul together**, hacer equilibrios para vivir. ‖ **in a body**, todos juntos, en pleno.
■ **body of opinion**, la opinión generalizada. ‖ **body of facts**, conjunto de hechos. ‖ **body of water**, masa de agua. ‖ **body bag**, bolsa hermética para cadáveres. ‖ **body clock**, reloj *m* interior. ‖ **body corporate**, cuerpo jurídico. ‖ **body count**, balance *m* de los muertos. ‖ **body language**, lenguaje *m* corporal. ‖ **body lotion**, loción *f* corporal. ‖ **body odour**, olor *m* corporal. ‖ the **body politic**, el estado. ‖ **body scanner**, escáner *m*. ‖ **body search**, cacheo. ‖ **body shop**, taller *m* de reparaciones.
▲ *pl* **bodies**.
body-blow ['bɒdɪbləʊ] *n* revés *m*.
● **to suffer a body-blow**, sufrir un revés.
body-builder ['bɒdɪbɪldə'] *n* SP culturista *mf*.
body-building ['bɒdɪbɪldɪŋ] *n* SP culturismo.
bodyguard ['bɒdɪgɑːd] *n* guardaespaldas *m*.
body-snatcher ['bɒdɪsnætʃə'] *n* profanador,-ra de tumbas.
bodystocking ['bɒdɪstɒkɪŋ] *n* malla.
bodywave ['bɒdɪweɪv] *n* peinado ondulado.
bodywork ['bɒdɪwɜːk] *n* AUTO carrocería.
Boer ['bəʊə] **1** *adj* bóer. – **2** *n* bóer *m*.
boffin ['bɒfɪn] *n* GB *fam* (*scientist*) científico,-a,; (*luminary*) lumbrera.
bog [bɒg] **1** *n* pantano, cenagal *m*. **2** *sl* (*toilet*) meódromo.
◆ **to bog down** *t sep* atascar.
● **to get bogged down**, atascarse, encallarse. ‖ **bog off!**, *sl* ¡vete a freír espárragos!
bogey[1] ['bəʊgɪ] **1** *n* (*spirit*) espíritu *m* maligno; (*goblin*) duende *m*. **2** *sl* moco.
bogey[2] ['bəʊgɪ] *n* (*in golf*) bogey *m*, golpe *m* más del par.
● **to score a bogey**, hacer más uno.
bogeyman ['bəʊgɪmæn] *n* coco, hombre *m* del saco.
▲ *pl* **bogeymen** ['bəʊgɪmen].
boggle ['bɒgəl] *i* sobresaltarse, quedarse boquiabierto,-a.
● **the mind boggles!**, ¡alucina!
boggy ['bɒgɪ] *adj* pantanoso,-a, cenagoso,-a.
▲ *comp* **boggier**, *superl* **boggiest**.
bogie ['bəʊgɪ] *n* GB bogie *m*, carretón *m*.
bogus ['bəʊgəs] **1** *adj* (*fake*) falso,-a, apócrifo,-a. **2** (*fictitious*) ficticio,-a. **3** (*sham*) simulado,-a, fingido,-a.
bogy ['bəʊgɪ] *n* → **bogey**[1].
▲ *pl* **bogies**.
Bohemia [bəʊ'hiːmɪə] *n* HIST Bohemia.
bohemian [bəʊ'hiːmɪən] **1** *adj* bohemio,-a: *they lived a a bohemian lifestyle*, llevaron una vida bohemia. – **2** *n* bohemio,-a.
Bohemian [bəʊ'hiːmɪən] **1** *adj* HIST bohemio,-a. – **2** *n* HIST bohemio,-a.
■ **Bohemian crystal**, cristal *m* de Bohemia.
boil[1] [bɔɪl] *n* MED furúnculo, forúnculo.
boil[2] [bɔɪl] **1** *t* (*liquid*) hervir; (*food*) hervir, cocer; (*egg*) pasar por agua, cocer. – **2** *i* (*liquid*) hervir; (*food*) hervir, cocerse. **3** *fig* (*undulate*, *seeth*) bullir.
◆ **to boil away** *i* evaporarse, reducirse. ‖ **to boil down** *to t insep fig* reducirse a: *the events boil down to the following*, los acontecimientos se reducen a lo siguiente. ‖ **to boil over** *i* (*liquid*) salirse, rebosar; (*become over-excited*) exaltarse.

● **to bring to the boil**, llevar a la ebullición. ‖ **to be on the boil**, estar hirviendo. ‖ **to come to the boil**, empezar a hervir. ‖ **to go off the boil**, (*literally*) dejar de hervir; (*figuratively*) perder las ganas. ‖ **to keep sth. on the boil**, (*literally*) mantener algo hirviendo; (*figuratively*) no dejar que algo se enfríe. ‖ **it makes my blood boil**, me da rabia. ‖ **to boil with rage**, estar hecho,-a una fiera.
boiled [bɔɪld] *adj* hervido,-a.
■ **boiled sweet**, GB caramelo con sabor a frutas.
boiler ['bɔɪlə'] **1** *n* caldera. **2** (*fowl*) gallina (*que sólo sirve para el caldo*).
■ **boiler suit**, (*overalls*) mono.
boilermaker ['bɔɪləmeɪkə'] *n* calderero.
boiler-room ['bɔɪləruːm] *n* sala de calderas.
boiling ['bɔɪlɪŋ] *adj* hirviendo, hirviente.
● **to be boiling (hot)**, hacer un calor achicharrante.
■ **boiling point**, punto de ebullición.
boisterous ['bɔɪstərəs] **1** *adj* (*noisy*, *rowdy*) bullicioso,-a, alborotador,-ra. **2** (*unruly*) revoltoso,-a. **3** (*exuberant*) exuberante. **4** (*weather*) borrascoso,-a; (*sea*) agitado,-a.
bold [bəʊld] **1** *adj* (*brave*) valiente. **2** (*daring*) audaz, atrevido,-a. **3** (*cheeky*) descarado,-a, fresco,-a. **4** (*vivid*) vivo,-a: *bold colours*, colores vivos. **5** (*print*) en negrita.
● **as bold as brass**, tan fresco,-a: *he went up to her as bold as brass*, se acercó a ella tan fresco. ‖ **to make so bold as to do sth.**, *lit* permitirse hacer algo: *if I may make so bold as to enquire*, si se me permite preguntar.
■ **bold features**, rasgos *mpl* marcados. ‖ **bold face**, negrita.
boldface ['bəʊldfeɪs] *adj* (*printing*) en negrita.
bold-faced ['bəʊldfeɪst] *adj* impudente, descarado,-a.
boldly ['bəʊldlɪ] **1** *adv* (*bravely*) con valentía, valientemente. **2** (*daringly*) audazmente, atrevidamente. **3** (*cheekily*) descaradamente.
boldness ['bəʊldnəs] **1** *n* (*courage*) valor *m*. **2** (*daring*) audacia. **3** (*cheek*) descaro.
bolero [bə'lɜːrəʊ] **1** *n* MUS bolero. **2** (*short jacket*) bolero.
▲ *pl* **boleros**; en **2** también ['bɒlərəʊ].
Bolivia [bə'lɪvɪə] *n* Bolivia.
Bolivian [bə'lɪvɪən] **1** *adj* boliviano,-a. – **2** *n* boliviano,-a.
bollard ['bɒlɑːd] **1** *n* MAR noray *m*. **2** AUTO (*on traffic island*, *roadside*) poste *m*.
bollocks ['bɒləks] **1** *npl taboo* (*testicles*) cojones *mpl*. **2** *taboo* (*nonsense*) gilipolleces *fpl*, chuminadas *fpl*. – **3** *interj taboo* ¡cojones!, ¡y un huevo!
boloney [bə'ləʊnɪ] **1** *n* US *sl* chorradas *fpl*. – **2** *interj sl* ¡una mierda!
Bolshevik ['bɒlʃəvɪk] **1** *adj* POL bolchevique. – **2** *n* POL bolchevique *mf*.
Bolshevism ['bɒlʃəvɪzəm] *n* POL bolchevismo.
Bolshevist ['bɒlʃəvɪst] *n-adj* → **bolchevik**.
bolshie ['bɒlʃɪ] **1** *adj* GB *fam* (*rebellious*) rebelde. **2** GB (*quarrelsome*) pendenciero,-a. **3** GB (*left-wing*) de izquierdas. – **4** *n* GB *fam* (*left-winger*) izquierdista *mf*.
bolshy ['bɒlʃɪ] *n-adj* GB *fam* → **bolshie**.
▲ (*sustantivo*) *pl* **bolshies**; (*adjetivo*) *comp* **bolshier**, *superl* **bolshiest**.
bolster ['bəʊlstə'] **1** *n* (*pillow*) cabezal *m*, travesaño. **2** TECH soporte *m*. – **3** *t* (*strengthen*) reforzar. **4** (*support*) apoyar.
◆ **to bolster up** *t sep* (*support*) apoyar; (*encourage*) animar, alentar.
bolt [bəʊlt] **1** *n* (*on door etc*) cerrojo; (*small*) pestillo. **2** (*screw*) perno, tornillo. **3** (*lightning*) rayo. – **4** *t* (*lock*) ce-

rrar con cerrojo, cerrar con pestillo. **5** (*screw*) sujetar con pernos, sujetar con tornillos. **6** *fam* (*food*) engullir. **– 7** *i* (*person*) escaparse; (*horse*) desbocarse.
◆ **to bolt in 1** *t sep* (*lock in*) encerrar echando el cerrojo: *she bolted him in,* lo encerró echando el cerrojo. **– 2** *i* (*rush in*) entrar de golpe. ‖ **to bolt out** *i* salir precipitadamente.
● **to bolt together,** unir con tornillos, unir con pernos. ‖ **bolt upright,** tieso,-a, rígido,-a. ‖ **to sit bolt upright,** incorporarse de repente. ‖ **to make a bolt for it,** darse a la fuga. ‖ **to make a bolt for sth.,** precipitarse hacia algo: *she made a bolt for the exit,* se precipitó hacia la salida. ‖ **to shoot one's bolt,** quemar su último cartucho. ‖ **like a bolt from the blue,** como una bomba.

bolt-hole ['bəʊlthəʊl] *n* escondrijo.

bomb [bɒm] **1** *n* bomba. **2** US (*failure*) fracaso. **– 3** *t* MIL bombardear; (*terrorist*) colocar una bomba en. **– 4** *i* US *fam* (*fail*) fracasar.
◆ **to bomb along** *i* ir a toda leche. ‖ **to bomb out** *t sep* (hacer) volar la casa: *the guerrillas bombed them out,* la guerrilla les voló la casa.
● **to cost a bomb,** costar un ojo de la cara. ‖ **to be worth a bomb,** valer un dineral. ‖ **to go down a bomb,** tener mucho éxito, arrasar. ‖ **to earn a bomb,** ganar un pastón. ‖ **to go like a bomb,** (*go smoothly*) marchar como una seda, ir sobre ruedas; (*go fast*) ir a toda pastilla.
■ **bomb attack,** bombardeo. ‖ **bomb bay,** compartimiento de bombas. ‖ **bomb crater,** cráter *m* de bomba. ‖ **bomb disposal,** desactivación *f* de bombas. ‖ **bomb disposal expert,** artificiero. ‖ **bomb scare,** aviso de bomba. ‖ **bomb squad,** brigada de bombas. ‖ **bomb threat,** amenaza de bomba.

bombard [bɒm'bɑːd] **1** *t* bombardear. **2** *fam fig* acosar (**with,** con), asediar (**with,** con): *they bombarded him with questions,* lo acosaron con preguntas.

bombardment [bɒm'bɑːdmənt] *n* bombardeo.

bombastic [bɒm'bæstɪk] *adj* rimbombante, ampuloso,-a.

bomber ['bɒmə'] **1** *n* MIL bombardero. **2** (*terrorist*) terrorista *mf* que coloca bombas.
■ **bomber jacket,** cazadora de aviador.

bombing ['bɒmɪŋ] **1** *n* MIL bombardeo. **2** (*terrorist act*) atentado con bomba.
■ **bombing raid,** ataque *m* aéreo.

bomb-proof ['bɒmpruːf] *adj* a prueba de bombas.

bombshell ['bɒmʃel] **1** *n fig* bomba: *the news came as a bombshell,* la noticia cayó como una bomba. **2** MIL (*artillery bomb*) obús *m*. **3** *fam* (*attractive woman*) mujer *f* explosiva: *blonde bombshell,* rubia explosiva.

bona fide [bəʊnə'faɪdɪ] *adj* genuino,-a, auténtico,-a.

bonanza [bə'nænzə] **1** *n* (*prosperity*) prosperidad *f*. **2** (*source of wealth*) mina. **3** (*run of good luck*) buena racha. **4** (*mineral deposit*) bonanza. **– 5** *adj* (*prosperous*) próspero,-a. **6** (*productive*) productivo,-a.

bonbon ['bɒnbɒn] *n* caramelo.

bonce [bɒns] *n fam* coco, mollera.

bond [bɒnd] **1** *n* (*link*) lazo, vínculo: *bonds of friendship,* vínculos de amistad. **2** FIN bono, obligación *f*. **3** JUR fianza. **4** (*agreement*) pacto, compromiso. **5** (*adhesion*) unión *f*. **– 6** *t* (*stick, join*) pegar, unir. **7** (*deposit in customs*) depositar. **– 8** *i* (*stick, join*) pegarse, unirse.
● **to be in bond,** estar en depósito.
■ **industrial bond,** obligación *f* industrial. ‖ **mortgage bond,** cédula hipotecaria. ‖ **municipal bond,** obligación *f* municipal. ‖ **convertible bond,** obliga-

ción *f* convertible. ‖ **Treasury bonds,** bonos del Tesoro.

bondage ['bɒndɪdʒ] *n* esclavitud *f*, servidumbre *f*.

bonded ['bɒndɪd] **1** *adj* (*goods*) en depósito. **2** (*debt*) avalado,-a, garantizado,-a. **3** (*material*) reforzado,-a.
■ **bonded warehouse,** almacén *m* de depósito.

bondholder ['bɒndhəʊldə'] *n* obligacionista *mf*.

bone [bəʊn] **1** *n* hueso. **2** (*of fish*) espina, raspa; (*of whale*) barba. **3** (*of corset*) ballena. **– 4** *t* (*meat*) deshuesar; (*fish*) quitar la espina. **5** (*corset*) emballenar. **– 6 bones,** *npl* (*remains*) huesos *mpl*, restos *mpl* mortales.
◆ **to bone up on** *t insep* empollar: *you'll have to bone up on your chemistry,* tendrás que empollar química.
● **to be as dry as a bone,** estar más seco,-a que una pasa. ‖ **to break every bone in one's body,** romperse todos los huesos. ‖ **to break every bone in sb.'s body,** molerle a algn. los huesos, no dejarle a algn. un hueso sano. ‖ **to have a bone to pick with sb.,** tener que ajustarle las cuentas a algn. ‖ **to work one's fingers to the bone,** trabajar como un esclavo. ‖ **to feel sth. in one's bones,** tener un presentimiento de algo. ‖ **to make no bones about it,** no andarse por las ramas. ‖ **to make no bones about doing sth.,** no vacilar en hacer algo. ‖ **to be a bag of bones,** estar en los huesos. ‖ **near the bone,** (*joke, humour*) verde, picante.
■ **bone of contention,** *fig* manzana de la discordia. ‖ **bone china,** porcelana, loza fina. ‖ **the bare bones,** lo esencial.

boned [bəʊnd] *adj* (*meat*) deshuesado,-a; (*fish*) sin espina.

bone-dry [bəʊn'draɪ] *adj* totalmente seco,-a.

bonehead ['bəʊnhed] *n* imbécil *mf*.

bone-idle [bəʊn'aɪdəl] *adj* holgazán,-ana, vago,-a.
● **to be bone-idle,** no rascar bola, ser un,-a vago,-a.

boner ['bəʊnə'] *n sl* pifia, plancha.

bonesetter ['bəʊnsetə'] *n* ensalmador,-ra.

boneshaker ['bəʊnʃeɪkə'] *n fam* (*car*) cacharro, trasto.

bonfire ['bɒnfaɪə'] *n* hoguera.
■ **bonfire night,** GB *la noche del cinco de noviembre; se celebra con hogueras y fuegos de artificio.*

bongo ['bɒŋgəʊ] *n* MUS bongó *m*.
▲ *pl* **bongos** o **bongoes**.

bonhomie ['bɒnhɒmiː] *n* campechanería, afabilidad *f*.

bonkers ['bɒŋkəz] *adj* GB *sl* chalado,-a.

Bonn [bɒn] *n* Bonn.

bonnet ['bɒnɪt] **1** *n* (*child's, woman's*) gorro, gorra. **2** (*maid's*) cofia. **3** AUTO capó *m*.

bonny ['bɒnɪ] *adj* hermoso,-a, lindo,-a.
▲ *comp* **bonnier,** *superl* **bonniest**.

bonsai ['bɒnsaɪ] *n* bonsai *m*.
▲ *pl* **bonsai** ['bɒnsaɪ].

bonus ['bəʊnəs] **1** *n* (*gratuity*) plus *m*, sobresueldo, prima. **2** (*benefit*) beneficio. **3** FIN (*extra dividend*) dividendo extraordinario. **– 4** *adj* extra, adicional.

bony ['bəʊnɪ] **1** *adj* (*thin*) esquelético,-a. **2** (*with a lot of bone*) huesudo,-a. **3** (*like bone*) óseo,-a. **4** (*meat*) lleno,-a de huesos; (*fish*) lleno,-a de espinas.
▲ *comp* **bonier,** *superl* **boniest**.

boo [buː] **1** *n* abucheo. **– 2** *t* abuchear: *they booed the actor,* abuchearon al actor. **– 3** *i* abuchear. **– 4** *interj* ¡bu!
● **he (she, etc) wouldn't say boo to a goose,** es un,-a miedica.
▲ (*verbo*) *pt & pp* **booed,** *ger* **booing**.

boob[1] [buːb] **1** *n fam* (*mistake*) metedura de pata, plancha. **– 2** *i* meter la pata, hacer una plancha.

● **to make a boob,** cometer una pifia.
boob² [buːb] *m fam* (*breast*) teta.
■ **boob tube,** camiseta-tubo *f*.
booboo ['buːbuː] *n →* **boob¹**.
▲ *pl* **booboos**.
booby ['buːbɪ] **1** *n* (*person*) bobo,-a. **2** ORN alcatraz *m*.
■ **booby hatch,** US *fam* manicomio. ‖ **booby prize,** premio de consolación, premio al peor. ‖ **booby trap,** (*bomb*) trampa explosiva; (*practical joke*) broma.
▲ *pl* **boobies**.
booby-trap ['buːbɪtræp] *t* colocar una trampa en.
▲ *pt* & *pp* **booby-trapped,** *ger* **booby-trapping**.
boogie ['buːgɪ] **1** *n fam* bugui *m*. **– 2** *t fam* menear el esqueleto.
boogie-woogie ['buːgɪwuːgɪ] *n* MUS bugui-bugui *m*.
boohoo [buːˈhuː] **1** *n* lloriqueo. **– 2** *interj* ¡ay! **– 3** *i* lloriquear.
▲ (*verbo*) *pt* & *pp* **boohooed,** *ger* **boohooing**.
book [buk] **1** *n* libro. **2** (*of tickets*) taco; (*of matches*) cajetilla. **– 3** *t* (*table, room, holiday*) reservar; (*entertainer, speaker*) contratar. **4** (*police*) multar; (*football*) advertir, amonestar. **– 5 books,** *npl* COMM libros *mpl*, cuentas *fpl*.
◆ **to book in 1** *t sep* (*in hotel*) hacer la reserva: *can you book me in next week?,* ¿me pueden hacer la reserva para la semana que viene? **– 2** *i* registrarse: *he booked in last night,* se registró anoche.
● **to be booked up,** (*hotel, restaurant*) estar completo; (*theatre, cinema*) no haber localidades. ‖ **to be a closed book to sb.,** *fig* estar muy pez en algo: *computing's a closed book to him,* está muy pez en la informática. ‖ **to be in sb.'s good books,** *fig* estar en buena relación con algn. ‖ **to be in sb.'s bad books,** *fig* estar en la lista negra de algn. ‖ **to bring sb. to book,** *fig* pedir cuentas a algn. ‖ **to go by the book,** *fig* proceder según las reglas. ‖ **to make a book,** registrar apuestas. ‖ **to read sb. like a book,** *fig* leer los pensamientos de algn. ‖ **to take a leaf out of sb.'s book,** *fig* tomar ejemplo de algn. ‖ **to throw the book at sb.,** *fig* castigar duramente a algn.: *they're going to throw the book at him,* se le va a caer el pelo. ‖ **in my book,** *fig* a mi parecer.
■ **address book,** libro de direcciones. ‖ **bank book,** libreta de ahorro. ‖ **book club,** círculo de lectores. ‖ **book lover,** bibliófilo,-a. ‖ **book token,** GB cheque *m* regalo (*para comprar libros*). ‖ **complaints book,** libro de reclamaciones. ‖ **exercise book,** cuaderno. ‖ **phone book,** listín *m*, guía telefónica. ‖ **savings book,** libreta de ahorro. ‖ **the good Book,** la Biblia.
bookable ['bukəbəl] *adj* que se puede reservar.
bookbinder ['bukbaɪndəʳ] *n* encuadernador,-ra.
bookbinding ['bukbaɪndɪŋ] *n* encuadernación *f*.
bookcase ['bukkeɪs] *n* librería, estantería.
bookend ['bukend] *n* sujetalibros *m*.
bookie ['bukɪ] *n fam* corredor,-ra de apuestas.
booking ['bukɪŋ] *n* (*table, room, holiday*) reserva *f*, reservación *f*; (*entertainer, speaker*) contratación *f*.
■ **booking clerk,** taquillero,-a de estación. ‖ **booking office,** taquilla.
bookish ['bukɪʃ] **1** *adj* (*fond of reading*) aficionado,-a a la lectura. **2** (*studious*) estudioso,-a. **3** (*literary*) literario,-a, culto,-a.
bookkeeper ['bukkiːpəʳ] *n* contable *mf*, tenedor,-ra de libros.
bookkeeping ['bukkiːpɪŋ] *n* contabilidad *f*, teneduría de libros.
booklet ['buklət] *n* folleto.

bookmaker ['bukmeɪkəʳ] *n* GB corredor,-ra de apuestas.
bookmark ['bukmɑːk] *n* punto de libro.
bookmobile ['bukməbiːl] *n* US biblioteca ambulante.
bookplate ['bukpleɪt] *n* ex libris *m*.
bookrest ['bukrest] *n* atril *m*.
bookseller ['bukseləʳ] *n* librero,-a.
bookshelf ['bukʃelf] **1** *n* estante *m* para libros. **– 2** **bookshelves,** *npl* estantería *f*.
▲ *pl* **bookshelves**.
bookshop ['bukʃɒp] *n* librería.
bookstall ['bukstɔːl] **1** *n* (*stand selling books*) quiosco, puesto de libros. **2** (*newsagent's*) quiosco, puesto de periódicos.
bookstand ['bukstænd] **1** *n* (*stall*) quiosco, puesto de periódicos. **2** (*bookrest*) atril *m*.
bookstore ['bukstɔːʳ] *n* US librería.
bookworm ['bukwɜːm] *n fig* ratón *m* de biblioteca.
boom¹ [buːm] **1** *n* (*noise*) estampido, retumbo. **– 2** *i* tronar, retumbar. **– 3** *interj* ¡bum! **– 4 to boom / boom out,** *i* (*voice*) resonar.
boom² [buːm] **1** *n* MAR botalón *m*. **2** (*of microphone*) jirafa. **3** (*of crane*) brazo. **4** (*barrier*) barrera.
■ **boom operator,** jirafista *mf*.
boom³ [buːm] **1** *n fig* (*prosperity, increase*) boom *m*, auge *m*. **– 2** *i* (*prosper*) estar en auge.
■ **boom town,** *ciudad que experimenta un boom económico*. ‖ **boom years,** años de prosperidad. ‖ **population boom,** explosión *f* demográfica.
boomerang ['buːməræŋ] **1** *n* bumerán *m*. **2** *fig* resultado contraproducente. **– 3 to boomerang on sb.,** *i* salirle a algn. el tiro por la culata.
booming ['buːmɪŋ] **1** *adj* (*noisy*) que truena, que retumba. **2** (*voice*) resonante. **3** (*prosperous*) próspero,-a, en auge.
boon [buːn] **1** *n* (*blessing*) bendición *f*. **2** (*advantage*) ventaja.
● **to be a boon to sb.,** ser muy provechoso,-a para algn.
boondocks ['buːndɒks] **out in the boondocks,** *phr* US allí donde Cristo perdió el gorro.
boor [buəʳ] *n* patán *m*.
boorish ['buərɪʃ] *adj* tosco,-a, zafio,-a.
boost [buːst] **1** *n* (*incentive*) incentivo, estímulo. **2** (*promotion*) promoción *f*, fomento. **3** (*increase*) aumento. **4** (*push up*) empujón *m* hacia arriba, empuje *m* hacia arriba. **– 5** *t* (*create an incentive*) incentivar, estimular. **6** (*promote*) promocionar, fomentar. **7** (*increase*) aumentar. **8** (*push up*) empujar hacia arriba. **9** ELEC aumentar el voltaje. **10** (*morale*) levantar.
● **to give sb. a boost,** (*raise spirits*) dar aliento a algn.; (*help up*) aupar a algn.
booster ['buːstəʳ] **1** *n* ELEC elevador *m* de voltaje. **2** RAD repetidor *m*. **3** TECH motor *m* auxiliar de propulsión.
■ **booster injection,** MED revacunación *f*.
boot [buːt] **1** *n* (*footwear*) bota. **2** GB (*of car*) maletero, portaequipajes *m*. **3** (*kick*) patada. **– 4** *t* (*kick*) dar una patada a. **5** COMPUT cargar el sistema operativo.
◆ **to boot out** *t sep* echar, echar a patadas.
● **to boot,** y además: *he was a good father to boot,* y además, era buen padre. ‖ **to be too big for one's boots,** ser un,-a creído,-a, ser un engreído,-a. ‖ **to be as tough as old boots,** (*food*) ser duro,-a como,-a, la suela de un zapato; (*person*) ser duro,-a de pelar. ‖ **to get the boot,** ser puesto,-a de patitas en la calle. ‖ **to give sb. the boot,** poner a algn. de patitas en la calle. ‖ **to lick sb.'s boots,** hacer la pelota a algn. ‖ **to put**

bootblack 62

the boot in, (*attack*) romperle la crisma a algn.; (*criticize severely*) poner a algn. a caldo. ‖ the boot is on the other foot, se han vuelto las tornas. ‖ I wouldn't like to be in his boots, no me gustaría estar en su pellejo.
bootblack ['buːtblæk] *n* US limpiabotas *m*, AM lustrabotas *m*.
bootee [buː'tiː] 1 *n* (*baby's*) calzado de punto. 2 (*lady's*) botín *m*.
booth [buːð] 1 *n* cabina. 2 (*at fair*) puesto.
■ telephone booth, locutorio.
bootlace ['buːtleɪs] *n* cordón *m*.
bootleg ['buːtleg] 1 *n* (*illegal recording*) grabación *f* pirata. – 2 *adj* (*alcohol*) de contrabando; (*recording*) pirata, ilegal. – 3 *i* (*smuggle alcohol*) pasar licor de contrabando. 4 (*manufacture alcohol*) fabricar licor de contrabando. 5 (*sell alcohol*) vender licor de contrabando. – 6 *t* (*record illegally*) hacer una grabación pirata de.
▲ *pt* & *pp* **bootlegged**, *ger* **bootlegging**.
bootlegger ['buːtlegə'] *n* contrabandista *mf* de licores.
bootlicker ['buːtlɪkə'] *n* pelotillero,-a.
booty ['buːtɪ] *n* botín *m*.
▲ *pl* **booties**.
booze [buːz] 1 *n fam* trinque *m*, alcohol *m*. – 2 *i fam* mamar.
● to go on the booze, irse de farra.
boozer ['buːzə'] 1 *n fam* (*person*) bebedor,-ra: *he's a bit of a boozer*, se da a la bebida. 2 (*pub*) bar *m*, tasca.
booze-up ['buːzʌp] *n fam* borrachera.
bop [bɒp] 1 *n fam* (*dance*) baile *m*. 2 *fam* (*thump*) cachete *m*. – 3 *i fam* (*dance*) bailar. – 4 *t fam* (*thump*) dar un cachete.
● to have a bop, mover el esqueleto.
▲ (*verbo*) *pt* & *pp* **bopped**, *ger* **bopping**.
boracic ['bəræsɪk] *adj* CHEM bórico,-a.
■ boracic acid, ácido bórico.
borage ['bɒrɪdʒ] *n* BOT borraja.
borax ['bɔːræks] *n* CHEM bórax *m*.
Bordeaux [bɔː'dəu] 1 *n* Burdeos. 2 (*wine*) vino de Burdeos.
border ['bɔːdə'] 1 *n* (*of country*) frontera. 2 (*edge*) borde *m*. 3 (*in sewing*) ribete *m*, orla. 4 (*of flowers, plants*) arriate *m*. – 5 *adj* fronterizo,-a: *border town*, pueblo fronterizo. – 6 *t* (*sew*) ribetear, orlar.
◆ to border on *t insep* lindar con; *fig* rayar en: *the settlement borders on the forest*, el campamento linda con el bosque; *this borders on the ridiculous*, esto raya en lo ridículo.
● to cross the border, cruzar la frontera.
■ the Borders, GB *zona fronteriza entre Inglaterra y Escocia*. ‖ Border collie, perro *m* pastor escocés.
borderland ['bɔːdəlænd] *n* área fronteriza.
borderline ['bɔːdəlaɪn] 1 *n* línea de demarcación. – 2 *adj* fronterizo,-a. 3 *fig* incierto,-a, dudoso,-a,: *a borderline case*, un caso dudoso.
bore[1] [bɔː'] *pt* → **bear**.
bore[2] [bɔː'] 1 *n* (*of gun*) ánima, alma; (*calibre*) calibre *m*. 2 (*hole*) taladro. – 3 *t* (*perforate*) perforar, taladrar, horadar. – 4 *i* perforar, taladrar, horadar.
● to bore a hole in, barrenar, abrir un agujero en.
bore[3] [bɔː'] 1 *n* (*person*) pelmazo,-a, pesado,-a, plasta *mf*; (*thing*) lata, rollo, tostón *m*: *that bloke's a real bore*, ese tío es un pelmazo; *what a bore!*, ¡vaya lata!; *don't be such a bore!*, ¡no seas tan plasta! – 2 *t* aburrir, fastidiar: *this job bores me*, este trabajo me aburre.
bored [bɔːd] *adj* aburrido,-a.
● to be bored stiff, aburrirse como una ostra. ‖ to get bored, aburrirse.

boredom ['bɔːdəm] *n* aburrimiento.
borehole ['bɔːhəul] *n* perforación *f*.
borer ['bɔːrə'] 1 *n* (*tool*) taladro, barrena. 2 (*machine*) taladradora. 3 ZOOL barrenillo.
boric ['bɔːrɪk] *adj* CHEM bórico,-a.
■ boric acid, ácido bórico.
boring ['bɔːrɪŋ] *adj* aburrido,-a.
born [bɔːn] *adj* nato,-a: *she's a born leader*, es una líder nata.
● to be born, nacer: *he was born in 1960*, nació en 1960. ‖ in all my born days, en mi vida. ‖ born and bred, de pura cepa: *she's Spanish born and bred*, es española de pura cepa. ‖ not to be born yesterday, *fig* no tener ni un pelo de tonto. ‖ to be born to be sth., nacer para ser algo: *he was born to be king*, nació para ser rey. ‖ to be born again, volver a nacer. ‖ he's English-born, es inglés de nacimiento.
■ the first-born, el/la primogénito,-a.
born-again ['bɔːnəgen] *adj* renacido,-a.
borne [bɔːn] *pp* → **bear**[2].
borough ['bʌrə] 1 *n* (*district*) barrio, distrito. 2 (*town, city*) ciudad *f*. 3 (*municipality*) municipio.
borrow ['bɒrəu] 1 *t* pedir prestado,-a, tomar prestado,-a: *he borrowed my suit*, me pidió el traje prestado; *I don't like borrowing things*, no me gusta pedir las cosas prestadas; *can I borrow your pen?*, ¿me dejas tu boli?; *you can borrow it if you like*, te lo presto si quieres. 2 (*appropriate, plagiarize*) apropiarse de, plagiar: *he borrowed all my ideas*, plagió todas mis ideas.
borrower ['bɒrəuə'] 1 *n persona que pide algo prestado*. 2 FIN prestatario,-a.
borstal ['bɔːstəl] *n* reformatorio, correccional *m* de menores.
bosh [bɒʃ] 1 *n sl* tonterías *fpl*. – 2 *interj* ¡tonterías!
Bosnia ['bɒznɪə] *n* Bosnia.
Bosnian ['bɒznɪən] 1 *adj* bosnio,-a. – 2 *n* bosnio,-a.
bosom ['buzəm] 1 *n* pecho. 2 (*centre*) seno: *in the bosom of the family*, en el seno de la familia.
■ bosom friend, amigo,-a del alma.
bosomy ['buzəmɪ] *adj* pechugón,-ona.
Bosphorus ['bɒsfərəs] *n* Bósforo *m*.
boss[1] [bɒs] 1 *n* jefe,-a. 2 (*of criminal organization*) capo.
◆ to boss around *t sep* mangonear.
boss[2] [bɒs] 1 *n* (*protuberance*) bulto, protuberancia. 2 ARCH crucería.
boss-eyed ['bɒsaɪd] *adj fam* bizco,-a.
bossy ['bɒsɪ] *adj* mandón,-ona.
▲ *comp* **bossier**, *superl* **bossiest**.
Bostonian [bɒs'təunɪən] 1 *adj* bostoniano,-a. – 2 *n* bostoniano,-a.
bosun ['bəusən] *n* MAR contramaestre *m*.
botanic [bə'tænɪk] *adj* botánico,-a.
botanical [bə'tænɪkəl] *adj* botánico,-a.
■ botanical gardens, jardín *m* botánico.
botanist ['bɒtənɪst] *n* botánico,-a.
botany ['bɒtənɪ] *n* botánica.
botch [bɒtʃ] 1 *n* chapuza. – 2 *t* (*repair badly*) chapucear, hacer una chapuza. 3 to botch (up), (*bungle*) pifiarla, fastidiarla.
● to make a botch of sth., chapucear algo, fastidiar algo.
botcher ['bɒtʃə'] *n* chapucero,-a.
both [bəuθ] 1 *adj* ambos,-as, los dos, las dos: *both films are interesting*, ambas películas son interesantes. – 2 *pron* ambos,-as, los dos, las dos: *both are boring*, los

dos son aburridos; *both of us,* nosotros,-as dos; *both of you,* vosotros,-as dos; *both of them,* los dos, las dos, ambos,-as. – **3** *adv* a la vez: *it's both cheap and good,* es bueno y barato a la vez.
● both ... and, tanto ... como: *both she and her sister are teachers,* tanto ella como su hermana son profesoras.

bother ['bɒðə^r] **1** *n* (*nuisance*) molestia, fastidio. **2** (*problems*) problemas *mpl.* – **3** *interj* GB ¡mecachis! – **4** *t* (*be a nuisance*) molestar, fastidiar. **5** (*worry*) preocupar. – **6** *i* (*take trouble*) molestarse: *he didn't even bother to ring,* ni se molestó en llamar. **7** (*worry*) preocuparse.
◆ to bother about *t insep* (*worry*) preocuparse por; (*take the trouble*) tomarse la molestia de: *don't bother about me, I'm all right,* no te preocupes por mí, estoy bien; *you needn't bother to phone for a cab, I'll walk,* no te tomes la molestia de llamar un taxi, voy andando.
● to give sb. bother, *fam* darle la lata a algn. ‖ to be no bother, no costar nada: *it's no bother to give you a lift,* no cuesta nada llevarte en coche.

bothersome ['bɒðəsəm] *adj* fastidioso,-a, latoso,-a.

Bothnia ['bɒθnɪə] *n* Botnia.
■ Gulf of Bothnia, golfo de Botnia.

Botswana [bɒt'swɑːnə] *n* Botswana.

Botswanan [bɒt'swɑːnən] **1** *adj* botswanés,-esa. – **2** *n* botswanés,-esa.

bottle ['bɒtəl] **1** *n* botella; (*small*) (*for baby*) biberón *m;* (*for gas*) bombona. **2** *sl* (*nerve*) agallas *fpl: she's got a lot of bottle,* tiene muchas agallas; *he's got no bottle,* no tiene agallas. – **3** *t* (*wine etc*) embotellar; (*fruit*) envasar.
◆ to bottle up *t sep* reprimir: *he always bottles up his emotions,* siempre reprime sus sentimientos. ‖ to bottle out *i* dar marcha atrás, acobardarse, rajarse: *when the moment of truth came, he bottled out,* en el momento de la verdad, dio marcha atrás.
● to hit the bottle, darse a la bebida.
■ bottle party, fiesta (*a la que cada invitado lleva su botella*). ‖ bottle rack, botellero.

bottle-bank ['bɒtəlbæŋk] *n* contenedor *m* para la recogida de vidrio usado.

bottlebrush ['bɒtəlbrʌʃ] *n* limpiabotellas *m.*

bottled ['bɒtəld] *adj* (*wine etc*) embotellado,-a; (*fruit*) envasado,-a.
■ bottled gas, gas *m* butano.

bottle-fed ['bɒtəlfed] *adj* criado,-a con biberón.

bottle-feed ['bɒtəlfiːd] *t* criar con biberón.
▲ *pt & pp* bottle-fed.

bottle-green [bɒtəl'griːn] **1** *n* verde *m* botella. – **2** *adj* de color verde botella.

bottleneck ['bɒtəlnek] *n fig* cuello de botella.

bottle-opener ['bɒtələupənə^r] *n* abrebotellas *m.*

bottler ['bɒtlə^r] *n* (*of wine etc.*) embotellador,-ra; (*of fruit*) envasador,-ra.

bottling ['bɒtəlɪŋ] *n* (*of wine etc*) embotellamiento; (*of fruit*) envase *m.*
■ bottling machine, (*for wine etc*) embotelladora; (*for fruit, jam etc*) envasadora. ‖ bottling plant, planta embotelladora.

bottom ['bɒtəm] **1** *n* (*of sea, box, garden, street, etc*) fondo; (*of bottle*) culo; (*of hill, steps, page*) pie *m;* (*of ship*) quilla. **2** (*of dress*) bajo; (*of trousers*) bajos *mpl.* **3** (*buttocks*) trasero, culo. **4** (*last*) último,-a: *he's bottom of the class,* es el último de la clase. **5** (*underneath*) parte *f* inferior, parte *f* de abajo. – **6** *adj* (*position*) de abajo: *the bottom shelf,* el estante de abajo. **7** (*number, result*) más bajo,-a: *the*

bottom score, la puntuación más baja. – **8** *t* (*chair*) poner fondo a. **9** (*ship*) hacer tocar fondo. – **10** *i* (*ship*) tocar fondo.
◆ to bottom on *t insep* (*theory, argument*) basarse en. ‖ to bottom out *i* ECON tocar fondo.
● at bottom, en el fondo: *at bottom he's not so bad,* en el fondo no es tan malo. ‖ bottoms up!, ¡salud! ‖ to be at the bottom of sth., *fig* estar detrás de algo, ser la causa de algo. ‖ to bet one's bottom dollar, apostar hasta el último céntimo. ‖ to get to the bottom of sth., *fig* llegar al fondo de algo. ‖ to go to the bottom, (*sink*) hundirse, irse al pique. ‖ to knock the bottom out of sth., *fig* echar por tierra algo.
■ bottom drawer, ajuar *m.* ‖ bottom gear, AUTO primera marcha. ‖ bottom line, (*in accounts*) balance *m;* (*result*) resultado final: *that's the bottom line!,* ¡esto es lo que hay!, ¡esto es así!; *the bottom line is that ...,* en resumidas cuentas ...

bottomless ['bɒtəmləs] *adj* sin fondo, insondable.

bottommost ['bɒtəmməust] *adj* inferior, último,-a: *the bottommost drawer,* el último cajón.

botulism ['bɒtjəlɪzəm] *n* MED botulismo.

boudoir ['buːdwɑː^r] *n* tocador *m.*

bougainvillea ['buːgənvɪljə] *n* BOT buganvilla.

bough [bau] *n* rama.

bought [bɔːt] *pt & pp →* buy.

bouillabaisse ['buːjəbeɪs] *n* CULIN bullabesa.

bouillon ['buːjɒn] *n* CULIN caldo.

boulder ['bəuldə^r] *n* canto rodado.

boulevard ['buːləvɑːd] *n* bulevar *m.*

bounce [bauns] **1** *n* (*of ball*) bote *m.* **2** *fig* (*energy*) vitalidad *f.* – **3** *i* (*ball*) rebotar, botar. – **4** *t* (*cheque*) ser rechazado por el banco. **5** (*ball*) hacer botar.
◆ to bounce back *i fig* recuperarse.

bouncer ['baunsə^r] *n sl* gorila *m.*

bouncing ['baunsɪŋ] **1** *adj* (*strong*) fuerte, robusto,-a. **2** (*healthy*) sano,-a. **3** (*boisterous*) bullicioso,-a.
● to be bouncing with health, rebosar de salud.

bouncy ['baunsɪ] **1** *adj* (*ball*) con rebota. **2** (*chair, mattress*) mullido,-a. **3** *fig* (*person*) lleno,-a de vigor, vital.
▲ *comp* bouncier, *superl* bounciest.

bound¹ [baund] **1** *pt & pp →* bind. – **2** *adj* (*tied*) atado,-a. **3** (*forced*) obligado,-a. **4** (*book*) encuadernado,-a.
● to be bound to, ser seguro que: *Susan's bound to win,* seguro que ganará Susan. ‖ to be duty bound to + *inf,* estar obligado,-a a + *inf: he was duty bound to visit her,* estaba obligado a visitarla. ‖ to be bound by contract, estar obligado,-a por contrato. ‖ to be bound up in sth., estar absorbido,-a por: *he's bound up in the project,* está absorbido por el proyecto. ‖ to be bound up with sth., estar vinculado,-a con algo: *he's bound up with the mafia,* está vinculado con la mafia.
▲ *pt & pp* bound.

bound² [baund] *adj* (*destined*) destinado,-a: *he knew he was bound to succeed,* sabía que estaba destinado a tener éxito.
● to be bound for, ir con destino, navegar con rumbo a: *the ship was bound for Southampton,* el barco navegaba con rumbo a Southampton. ‖ -bound, con rumbo a: *Paris-bound,* con rumbo a París.

bound³ [baund] **1** *n* (*jump*) salto, brinco. – **2** *i* saltar.
◆ to bound about *i* dar saltos, brincar.
● with a bound, de un salto, de un brinco: *he got out of bed with a bound,* se levantó de la cama de un salto.
‖ to bound into, entrar dando saltos: *the children*

bounded into the room, los niños entraron en la habitación dando saltos. || **to bound over,** saltar por encima de: *he bounded over the fence,* saltó por encima de la valla.

bound⁴ [baʊnd] *t* (*mark the boundary*) delimitar: *the Roman wall bounds the old quarter,* la muralla romana delimita el casco antiguo.

boundary ['baʊndərɪ] *n* límite *m*, frontera.
■ **boundary stone,** hito, mojón *m*.
▲ *pl boundaries.*

bounder ['baʊndəʳ] *n dated* canalla *m*, sinvergüenza *mf*.

boundless ['baʊndləs] *adj* sin límites, ilimitado,-a: *there are boundless possibilities,* las posibilidades son ilimitadas.

bounds [baʊndz] *npl* (*border*) frontera; (*boundary*) límites *mpl*.
● **out of bounds,** fuera de los límites, en zona prohibida. || **beyond the bounds of possibility,** más allá de los límites de la posibilidad.

bounteous ['baʊntɪəs] **1** *adj lit* generoso,-a. **2** *lit* (*abundant*) abundante.

bountiful ['baʊntɪfʊl] *adj* → **bounteous**.

bounty ['baʊntɪ] **1** *n* (*generosity*) generosidad *f*. **2** (*reward*) prima. **3** (*gift*) regalo.
▲ *pl bounties.*

bouquet [buːˈkeɪ] **1** *n* (*flowers*) ramo. **2** (*wine*) aroma *m*, buqué *m*. **3** (*compliment*) cumplido.
■ **bouquet garni,** ramito de hierbas.

bourbon ['bɜːbən] *n* bourbon *m*.

Bourbon ['bʊəbən] **1** *n* Borbón *m*. – **2** *adj* Borbónico,-a.

bourgeois ['bʊəʒwɑː] **1** *adj* burgués,-esa. – **2** *n* burgués,-esa.

bourgeoisie [bʊəʒwɑːˈziː] *n* burguesía.

bout [baʊt] **1** *n* (*period*) rato. **2** MED (*of flu, measles etc*) ataque *m*. **3** (*boxing*) encuentro.

boutique [buːˈtiːk] *n* boutique *f*, tienda.

bovine ['bəʊvaɪn] **1** *adj* bovino,-a, vacuno,-a. **2** *fig* (*dim, stupid*) torpe, lerdo,-a. – **3** *n* bovino.

bovver ['bɒvəʳ] *n sl* (*troublemaking*) camorra, jaleo.
● **to cause bovver,** armar jaleo.
■ **bovver boot,** *bota de suela gruesa que se asocia con los jóvenes camorristas.* || **bovver boy,** gamberro.

bow¹ [bəʊ] **1** *n* (*for arrows*) arco. **2** (*of violin*) arco. **3** (*knot*) lazo. – **4** *t* (*cause to bend*) arquear, doblar. – **5** *i* (*violin*) pasar el arco (por las cuerdas). **6** (*wall*) arquearse, combarse.
■ **bow saw,** sierra de arco.

bow² [baʊ] *n* MAR proa.
● **a shot across the bows,** un aviso.

bow³ [baʊ] **1** *n* (*with body*) reverencia. – **2** *t* inclinar: *he bowed his head,* inclinó la cabeza. – **3** *i* (*in respect*) inclinarse, hacer una reverencia. **4 to bow to,** *fig* (*submit*) someterse a: *he had to bow to their wishes,* tuvo que someterse a sus deseos.
◆ **to bow out** *i* (*withdraw*) retirarse: *he bowed out of the championship,* se retiró del campeonato.
● **to bow down,** inclinarse. || **to bow and scrape (to sb.),** hacer la pelota (a algn.).

bowdlerize ['baʊdləraɪz] *t* (*book etc*) expurgar.

bowed [baʊd] *adj* encorvado,-a.

bowel ['baʊəl] **1** *n* intestino. – **2 bowels,** *npl* (*entrails*) entrañas *fpl*.
● **the bowels of the earth,** las entrañas de la tierra.
■ **bowel movement,** evacuación *f* intestinal.

bower¹ ['baʊəʳ] *n* MAR (*anchor*) ancla de proa.

bower² ['baʊəʳ] *n* (*arbour*) cenador *m*, pérgola.

bowing¹ ['baʊɪŋ] *n* reverencia.

bowing² ['bəʊɪŋ] *n* (*of violin*) arqueada.

bowl¹ [bəʊl] **1** *n* (*for food etc*) cuenco, fuente *f*, bol *m*; (*for soup*) escudilla; (*large drinking bowl*) tazón *m*; (*small drinking bowl*) taza. **2** (*for washing*) palangana, barreño. **3** (*of toilet*) taza. **4** (*of pipe*) cazoleta. **5** (*of spoon*) cuenco. **6** US (*amphitheatre*) anfiteatro.

bowl² [bəʊl] **1** *n* (*ball*) bocha. – **2** *i* (*cricket*) lanzar la pelota.
◆ **to bowl along** *t insep* circular: *the car bowled along the road,* el coche circulaba por la carretera. || **to bowl over** *t sep* dejar pasmado,-a: *the news bowled him over,* la noticia lo dejo pasmado.

bow-legged [bəʊˈlegd, bəʊˈlegɪd] *adj* patizambo,-a, estevado,-a.

bowler¹ ['bəʊləʳ] *n* (*hat*) bombín *m*.

bowler² ['bəʊləʳ] **1** *n* (*cricket*) lanzador,-ra. **2** (*bowls player*) jugador,-ra de bochas.

bowling ['bəʊlɪŋ] *n* (*ten-pin*) bolos *mpl*; (*bowls*) las bochas.
● **to go bowling,** (*tenpin*) jugar a los bolos; (*bowls*) jugar a las bochas.
■ **bowling alley,** bolera. || **bowling green,** pista de bochas.

bowls [bəʊlz] *npl* (*game*) las bochas.
● **to play bowls,** jugar a las bochas.

bowsprit ['bəʊsprɪt] *n* MAR bauprés *m*.

bow-tie [bəʊˈtaɪ] *n* pajarita.

bow-wow ['baʊwaʊ] **1** *n* (*dog*) perrito. **2** (*barking noise*) guau guau *m*.

box¹ [bɒks] **1** *n* caja; (*large*) cajón *m*. **2** (*of matches*) cajetilla. **3** THEAT palco. **4** (*for sentry*) garita. **5** (*of coach*) pescante *m*. **6** (*in printing*) cajetín *m*. **7** GB *fam* (*telly*) tele *f*. **8** (*in baseball - pitcher's*) puesto del lanzador; (*- batter's*) puesto del bateador,-a; (*in football*) área del penalty. – **9** *t* meter en cajas, encajonar.
◆ **to box in** *t sep fig* (*vehicle*) bloquear la salida, impedir la salida: *a lorry had boxed him in,* un camión le había bloqueado la salida. || **to box off** *t sep* compartimentar: *they boxed off the room,* compartimentaron la habitación. || **to box up** *t sep* meter en cajas, embalar.
■ **box camera,** cámara de cajón. || **box girder,** viga de caja. || **box junction,** cruce *m* con parrilla. || **box number,** número de apartado de correos. || **box office,** taquilla. || **box spanner,** llave *f* de tubo. || **pencil box,** plumier *m*. || **post-office box,** apartado de correos.

box² [bɒks] *i* boxear.
● **a box on the ears,** un cachete. || **to box clever,** actuar de una forma astuta. || **to box sb.'s ears,** zurrarle la badana a algn.

box³ [bɒks] *n* BOT boj *m*.

boxcar ['bɒkskɑːʳ] *n* US furgón *m*.

boxer ['bɒksəʳ] **1** *n* boxeador,-ra. **2** (*dog*) bóxer *m*.

boxing ['bɒksɪŋ] *n* boxeo.
■ **Boxing Day,** GB *el día 26 de diciembre.* || **boxing gloves,** guantes *mpl* de boxeo. || **boxing ring,** ring *m*.

box-office ['bɒksɒfɪs] *adj* taquillero,-a, de taquilla: *his last film was a box-office success,* su última película fue un éxito de taquilla.

boxroom ['bɒksruːm] *n* GB trastero.

boxwood ['bɒkswʊd] **1** *n* boj *m*. – **2** *adj* de boj.

boy [bɔɪ] *n* (*baby*) niño; (*child*) chico, muchacho; (*youth*) joven *m*.
● **boy oh boy!,** ¡vaya, vaya! || **jobs for the boys,** amiguismo, enchufes *mpl*.
■ **boy scout,** scout *m*, explorador *m*. || **the boys,** *fam*

los colegas: *he had a night out with the boys yesterday,* se fue de farra con sus colegas anoche. || **the boys in blue,** *fam* la poli.

boycott ['bɔɪkɒt] 1 *n* boicoteo, boicot *m*. – 2 *t* boicotear.

boyfriend ['bɔɪfrend] 1 *n* (*fiancé*) novio. 2 (*male friend*) amigo.

boyhood ['bɔɪhʊd] 1 *n* infancia, niñez *f*. – 2 *adj* de la infancia: *a boyhood friend,* un amigo de la infancia.

boyish ['bɔɪɪʃ] *adj* muchachil, juvenil.

bra [brɑː] *n* sostén *m*, sujetador *m*.

brace [breɪs] 1 *n* (*clamp*) abrazadera. 2 ARCH (*support*) riostra. 3 (*drill*) berbiquí *m*. 4 (*on teeth*) aparato. 5 (*pair of game*) par *m*: *a brace of pheasants,* un par de faisanes. 6 MAR braza. 7 MUS corchete *m*. – 8 *t* (*fasten tightly*) tensar. 9 (*make steady*) estabilizar. 10 ARCH reforzar. 11 MAR (*rope, sail*) bracear. 12 (*invigorate*) dar vigor, tonificar. – 13 **braces,** *npl* tirantes *mpl*.
● **to brace os. for sth.,** prepararse para algo.
▲ (*sustantivo*) *pl* **braces,** *en* 6 **brace***.*

bracelet ['breɪslət] 1 *n* pulsera, brazalete *m*. 2 (*armband*) brazalete *m*. – 3 **bracelets,** *npl sl* (*handcuffs*) esposas *fpl*.

bracing ['breɪsɪŋ] *adj* (*wind, weather*) tonificante, vigorizador,-ra.

bracken ['brækən] *n* BOT helechos *mpl*.

bracket ['brækɪt] 1 *n* (*round*) paréntesis *m*. 2 (*for shelf*) escuadra *f*, soporte *m*. 3 (*group, category*) grupo, categoría *m*: *tax bracket,* banda impositiva. – 4 *t* (*put in brackets*) poner entre paréntesis. 5 (*classify*) clasificar. 6 (*group together*) agrupar.
■ **square bracket,** corchete *m*. || **curly bracket,** llave *f*.

brackish ['brækɪʃ] *adj* (*water*) salobre.

bradawl ['brædɔːl] *n* punzón *m*.

bradycardia [brædɪ'kɑːdɪə] *n* MED bradicardia.

brag [bræg] 1 *n* jactancia, fanfarria. – 2 *i* jactarse (**about,** de).
▲ (*verbo*) *pt & pp* **bragged,** *ger* **bragging***.*

braggart ['brægət] *n* fanfarrón,-ona.

Brahma ['brɑːmə] *n* REL Brahma *m*.

Brahman ['brɑːmən] 1 *n* REL brahmán *m*. 2 REL (*Hindu deity*) Brahma *m*.
▲ *pl* **brahmans***.*

Brahmin ['brɑːmɪn] 1 *n* REL brahmín *m*, brahmán *m*. 2 US lumbrera.

braid [breɪd] 1 *n* (*on clothing*) galón *m*. 2 (*plait*) trenza. – 3 *t* (*clothing*) galonear. 4 (*plait hair*) trenzar.

Braille [breɪl] *n* braille *m*.

brain [breɪn] 1 *n* ANAT cerebro, seso. – 2 **brains,** *npl* (*intellect*) cerebro, seso, inteligencia. 3 CULIN sesos *mpl*.
● **to blow one's brain out,** pegarse un tiro. || **to blow sb.'s brains out,** volar la tapa de los sesos a algn. || **to brain sb.,** *fam* partirle la cara a algn. || **to have brains,** ser un cerebro, ser inteligente. || **to have sth. on the brain,** estar obsesionado,-a con algo. || **to pick sb.'s brains,** hacer una consulta a algn.
■ **the brains,** (*instigator, originator*) el cerebro gris: *he was the brains behind the robbery,* era el cerebro gris del asalto. || **brain cell,** célula cerebral. || **brain death,** muerte *f* cerebral. || **brain drain,** fuga de cerebros. || **brain scan,** electroencefalograma *m*. || **brain scanner,** escáner *m* cerebral. || **brain teaser,** rompecocos *m*. || **brain tumour,** tumor *m* cerebral. || **brain trust,** US panel *m* de expertos. || **brains trust,** GB panel *m* de expertos. || **brain wave,** idea genial. || **electronic brain,** cerebro electrónico.

brainchild ['breɪntʃaɪld] *n* (*idea, invention, plan*) (propia) idea, (propio) invento, (propio) proyecto: *the new road*

network was his brainchild, la nueva red de carreteras fue su (propia) idea.
▲ *pl* **brainchildren** ['breɪntʃɪldrən]*.*

brain-dead ['breɪnded] *adj* clínicamente muerto,-a.

brainless ['breɪnləs] *adj* memo,-a, cretino,-a.

brainpower ['breɪnpaʊəʳ] *n* capacidad *f* intelectual.

brainstorm ['breɪnstɔːm] 1 *n* (*violent outburst*) telele *m*, ataque *m*, patatús *m*. 2 (*mental confusion*) cacao *m* mental, empanada mental. 3 US (*brainwave*) idea genial. 4 (*brainstorming*) reunión *f* creativa.
● **to have a brainstorm,** coger un patatús.

brainstorming ['breɪnstɔːmɪŋ] *n* reunión *f* creativa.

brainwash ['breɪnwɒʃ] *t* lavar el cerebro a, comer el coco a.

brainwashing ['breɪnwɒʃɪŋ] *n* lavado de cerebro, comida de coco.

brainy ['breɪnɪ] *adj fam* inteligente, sesudo,-a.
▲ *comp* **brainier,** *superl* **brainiest***.*

braise [breɪz] *t* CULIN freír y luego cocer a fuego lento.

brake[1] [breɪk] 1 *n* freno. – 2 *i* frenar: *the car skidded and the driver couldn't brake,* el coche derrapó y el conductor no pudo frenar. – 3 *t* frenar, hacer frenar.
● **to apply the brake** / **put on the brake,** frenar, echar el freno. || **to release the brake,** soltar el freno. || **to put a brake on sth./sb.,** *fig* poner trabas a algo/algn.
■ **back brake,** freno trasero. || **brake arm,** palanca del freno. || **brake axle,** árbol *m* del freno. || **brake band,** cinta del freno. || **brake block,** pastilla de freno. || **brake disc,** disco del freno. || **brake drum,** tambor *m* de freno. || **brake fluid,** líquido de freno. || **brake horsepower,** potencia al freno. || **brake lights,** luces *fpl* de frenado. || **brake lining,** forro del freno. || **brake pedal,** pedal *m* de freno. || **brake shaft,** árbol *m* del freno. || **brake shoe,** zapata del freno. || **foot brake,** freno de pedal. || **front brake,** freno delantero.

brake[2] [breɪk] *n* (*estate car*) furgoneta.

braking ['breɪkɪŋ] *n* frenado.

bramble ['bræmbəl] *n* BOT zarzamora, mora.
■ **bramble bush,** zarza. || **bramble patch,** zarzal *m*.

brambling ['bræmblɪŋ] *n* BOT pinzón *m* real.

bran [bræn] *n* salvado.

branch [brɑːntʃ] 1 *n* (*tree*) rama. 2 (*of family*) ramo. 3 (*road, railway*) ramal *m*; (*stream, river*) brazo *m*. 4 (*of shop*) sucursal *f*; (*of bank*) oficina, sucursal *f*. 5 (*field of science etc*) ramo. 6 (*of candleabra*) brazo. – 7 *i* (*road*) bifurcarse.
◆ **to branch off** *i* salir de la carretera. || **to branch out** *i* extender su campo de interés.
■ **branch line,** ramal *m*.

brand [brænd] 1 *n* marca: *he always buys that brand of jeans,* siempre compra aquella marca de tejanos. 2 (*type*) clase *f*, tipo: *a particular brand of humor,* un tipo de humor peculiar. 3 (*for livestock*) hierro de marcar. 4 (*piece of burning wood*) tea. 5 (*stigma*) estigma *m*. 6 AGR BOT (*blight*) tizón *m*. 7 *lit* (*sword*) hierro. – 8 *t* (*livestock*) marcar con un hierro candente.
● **to brand sb. sth.,** tildar a algn. de algo: *they branded him a thief,* lo tildaron de ladrón. || **to brand sth. as sth.,** calificar algo de algo: *they branded it a success,* lo calificaron de éxito.

Brandenburg ['brændənbɜːg] *n* Brandeburgo, Brandenburgo: *the Brandenburg Gate,* la puerta de Brandeburgo.

branding-iron ['brændɪŋaɪən] *n* (*for livestock*) hierro de marcar.

brandish ['brændɪʃ] *t* blandir.

brand-new [bræn'njuː] *adj* flamante.

brandy [ˈbrændɪ] *n* coñac *m*, brandy *m*.
▲ *pl* **brandies**.
brash [bræʃ] **1** *adj pej* (*ostentatious, showy*) ostentoso,-a,
rimbombante. **2** (*hasty, thoughtless*) irreflexivo,-a. **3** (*imprudent*) imprudente.
brass [brɑːs] **1** *n* latón *m*. **2** *sl* (*money*) pasta. **3** MUS metales *mpl*. **4** *fam fig* cara, jeta: *he had the brass to ask me for more money*, tuvo la cara de pedirme más dinero. –
5 *adj* de cobre.
● **to be brassed off**, *fam* estar cabreado,-a, estar mosca. ‖ **he's got a brass neck**, tiene mucho morro. ‖ **to get down to brass tacks**, ir al grano. ‖ **not a brass farthing**, *fam* ni un duro: *he hasn't got a brass farthing*, no tiene ni un duro.
■ **brass band**, banda (municipal). ‖ **top brass**, MIL altos mandos *mpl*.
brassiere [ˈbræzɪə'] *n* sujetador *m*, sostén *m*.
brass-monkeys [brɑːsˈmʌŋkɪz] **to be brass monkey(s)**, *phr sl* hacer un frío que pela.
brass-rubbing [ˈbrɑːsrʌbɪŋ] *n* calco de planchas.
● **to do brass-rubbings**, calcar planchas sobre un papel.
brassy [ˈbrɑːsɪ] **1** *adj* (*impudent*) descarado,-a, impudente. **2** (*ostentatious, showy*) ostentoso,-a, rimbombante. **3** (*vulgar, coarse*) grosero,-a, basto,-a. **4** (*made of brass*) de latón.
▲ *comp* **brassier**, *superl* **brassiest**.
brat [bræt] *n fam pej* mocoso,-a.
bravado [brəˈvɑːdəʊ] *n* baladronada, fanfarronada.
● **to do sth. with bravado**, hacer algo con audacia. ‖ **a piece of bravado**, una bravata.
brave [breɪv] **1** *adj* valiente. **– 3** *n* guerrero indio. **– 3** *t* (*defy*) desafiar. **4** (*confront*) afrontar, hacer frente a.
● **to brave death**, desafiar a la muerte. ‖ **to brave it out**, (*person under suspicion*) aguantar la tormenta: *the minister will have to brave it out*, el ministro tendrá que aguantar la tormenta. ‖ **to brave the elements**, aguantar el mal tiempo. ‖ **to put a brave face on**, poner a mal tiempo buena cara.
bravery [ˈbreɪvərɪ] *n* valentía.
bravo [brɑːˈvəʊ] *interj* ¡bravo!
brawl [brɔːl] **1** *n* reyerta, pelea. **– 2** *i* pelearse.
brawler [ˈbrɔːlə'] *n* peleador,-ra, alborotador,-ra.
brawn [brɔːn] **1** *n* (*muscular strength*) fuerza muscular. **2** (*muscle*) músculo. **3** CULIN carne *f* de cabeza de cerdo en gelatina.
brawny [ˈbrɔːnɪ] *adj* fornido,-a, musculoso,-a.
▲ *comp* **brawnier**, *superl* **brawniest**.
bray [breɪ] **1** *i* (*donkey, ass*) rebuznar. **– 2 to bray (out)**, *t* (*voice*) vociferar, anunciar a gritos.
braying [ˈbreɪɪŋ] **1** *n* rebuzno. **2** (*harsh laugh*) carcajada.
brazen [ˈbreɪzən] **1** *adj* desvergonzado,-a, descarado,-a.
● **to brazen it out**, aguantar las acusaciones con descaro.
brazen-faced [ˈbreɪzənfeɪst] *adj* desvergonzado,-a, descarado,-a.
brazier [ˈbreɪzɪə'] *n* brasero.
Brazil [brəˈzɪl] *n* el Brasil.
■ **Brazil nut**, BOT nuez *f* del Brasil.
Brazilian [brəˈzɪlɪən] **1** *adj* brasileño,-a. **– 2** *n* brasileño,-a.
breach [briːtʃ] **1** *n* (*opening*) brecha, abertura. **2** (*in promise, undertaking*) incumplimiento; (*in law*) violación *f*, infracción *f*. **4** (*in relationship*) ruptura. **– 5** *t* (*break a hole*) romper. **6** JUR violar, infringir. **7** MIL abrir brecha en.

● **to stand in the breach**, estar en la brecha. ‖ **to step into the breach**, hacer de suplente, acudir en sustitución.
■ **breach of contract**, incumplimiento de contrato. ‖ **breach of faith / breach of trust**, abuso de confianza. ‖ **breach of the peace**, alteración *f* del orden público. ‖ **breach of privilege**, POL abuso de privilegio parlamentario. ‖ **breach of promise**, incumplimiento de una promesa.
bread [bred] **1** *n* pan *m*. **2** *sl* (*money*) guita, pasta.
● **to be on bread and water**, estar a pan y agua. ‖ **to cast one's bread upon the water**, hacer el bien sin mirar a quién. ‖ **to earn one's bread and butter**, ganarse el pan. ‖ **to know which side one's bread is buttered**, saber lo que más le conviene a uno. ‖ **to take the bread out of sb.'s mouth**, quitarle el pan de la boca a algn. ‖ **man cannot live by bread alone**, no sólo de pan vive el hombre.
■ **bread and wine**, REL Eucaristía. ‖ **bread bin**, caja para guardar el pan. ‖ **bread sauce**, *salsa hecha con migas de pan, cebolla y leche*. ‖ **brown bread**, pan *m* moreno. ‖ **white bread**, pan *m* blanco. ‖ **communion bread**, pan *m* bendito. ‖ **fresh bread**, pan *m* tierno. ‖ **linseed bread**, pan *m* de linaza. ‖ **wholemeal bread**, pan *m* integral.
bread-and-butter [ˈbredənbʌtə'] *adj* (*commonplace*) rutinario,-a, corriente y moliente.
■ **a bread-and-butter letter**, carta de agradecimiento.
breadbasket [ˈbredbɑːskɪt] *n* panera.
breadboard [ˈbredbɔːd] *n* tabla (*para cortar el pan*).
breadcrumb [ˈbredkrʌm] **1** *n* miga de pan, migaja de pan. **– 2 breadcrumbs**, *npl* CULIN pan *m* rallado.
● **in breadcrumbs**, CULIN empanado,-a.
breadfruit [ˈbredfruːt] *n* BOT fruto del árbol del pan.
■ **breadfruit tree**, BOT árbol *m* del pan.
breadline [ˈbredlaɪn] *n* US *cola para recibir alimentos gratuitos*.
● **to live on the breadline**, vivir en la miseria.
breadth [bredθ] **1** *n* (*broadness*) ancho, anchura. **2** (*space*) extensión *f*, amplitud *f*.
■ **breadth of mind**, generosidad *f* de espíritu, largueza.
breadwinner [ˈbredwɪnə'] *n* el/la que gana el pan.
break [breɪk] **1** *n* (*in leg etc*) rotura. **2** (*in relationship*) ruptura. **3** (*in meeting*) descanso, pausa; (*in broadcast*) interrupción *f*; (*at school*) recreo. **4** SP (*billiards, snooker*) tacada. **5** METEOR (*in clouds*) claro; (*in weather*) cambio. **6** (*chance*) oportunidad *f*. **7** (*on stock exchange*) baja. **8** SP (*tennis*) break *m*. **9** MUS (*jazz*) break *m*. **10** (*in voice*) gallo. **– 11** *t* romper. **12** (*record*) batir. **13** (*promise, word*) faltar a. **14** (*law, contract*) violar, infringir. **15** (*news*) comunicar. **16** (*code*) descifrar. **17** (*mystery, case*) resolver. **18** (*fall*) amortiguar. **19** (*journey*) interrumpir. **20** (*tame*) domar. **21** ELEC (*circuit*) cortar, interrumpir. **– 22** *i* romperse. **23** (*storm*) estallar. **24** (*stock exchange*) bajar. **25** (*meeting, session*) parar. **26** (*disperse*) dispersarse. **27** (*voice*) cambiar. **28** (*health*) quebrantarse. **29** (*spot, abcess*) reventar. **30** (*waves*) romper, reventar.
◆ **to break away** *i* (*escape*) escaparse, darse a la fuga; (*leave family, job*) irse. ‖ **to break away from** *t insep* (*family, group*) romper con; (*athlete*) salir del pelotón. ‖ **to break down** **1** *t sep* (*door*) derribar, echar abajo. **2** (*resistance*) vencer. **3** (*analyse*) desglosar. **– 4** *i* (*car*) averiarse; (*driver*) tener una avería. **5** (*appliance*) estropearse. **6** (*health*) quebrantarse. **7** (*burst into tears*) romper a llorar. **8** (*talks, negotiations*) fracasar. ‖ **to break in** **1** *t sep*

(*animal*) domar. **- 2** *i* (*intervene*) intervenir. **3** (*force entry*) entrar por la fuerza. ‖ **to break into** *t insep* (*house*) entrar por la fuerza en, allanar; (*safe*) forzar. ‖ **to break off 1** *t sep* (*relationship*) romper. **2** (*discussions, negotiations*) interrumpir. **- 3** *i* (*discussions, negotiations*) interrumpirse. **4** (*become detached*) desprenderse. **5** (*stop talking*) detenerse. ‖ **to break out 1** *i* (*prisoners*) escaparse. **2** (*war, fire etc*) estallar. ‖ **to break through 1** *t insep* (*obstacle, fence*) atravesar, abrirse paso por. **2** (*sunlight*) atravesar. ‖ **to break up 1** *t sep* (*chair, table etc*) romper; (*ship, boat*) desguazar. **2** (*gathering, meeting*) disolver. **- 3** *i* (*marriage*) fracasar; (*couple*) separarse. **4** (*gathering, meeting*) disolverse. **5** (*school*) empezar las vacaciones. **6** US echarse a reír. ‖ **to break with** *t insep* (*friends, family*) romper con.
● **to break cover**, salir al descubierto. ‖ **to break even**, salir sin ganar ni perder. ‖ **to break free**, evadirse. ‖ **to break ground**, *fig* abrirse un nuevo camino. ‖ **to break sb.'s heart**, partir el corazón a algn. ‖ **to break into song**, ponerse a cantar. ‖ **to break it off**, terminar una relación. ‖ **to break the ice**, *fig* romper el hielo. ‖ **to break one's neck**, (*in fall etc*) desnucarse; (*make a great effort*) matarse. ‖ **to break one's word**, no cumplir su palabra. ‖ **to break open**, abrir forzando. ‖ **to break out in spots**, salirle a uno granos. ‖ **to break ranks**, MIL romper filas. ‖ **to break sb.'s neck**, *fig* (*assault*) romperle el hocico a algn. ‖ **to break the back of a job**, haber hecho la parte más difícil de un trabajo. ‖ **to break the bank**, hacer quebrar la banca. ‖ **to break a strike**, romper una huelga. ‖ **to break sth. to pieces**, hacer algo añicos. ‖ **to give sb. a break**, dar una oportunidad a algn. ‖ **to make a break for it**, intentar fugarse. ‖ **it's make or break time,** es la hora de la verdad. ‖ **to take a break,** tomarse una pausa, tomarse un descanso. ‖ **break it up!,** (*in fight*) ¡basta ya! ‖ **without a break,** sin descansar, sin parar. ‖ **at break of day,** al amanecer.
▲ (*verbo*) *pt* **broke,** *pp* **broken.**
breakable [ˈbreɪkəbəl] *adj* frágil, rompible.
breakage [ˈbreɪkɪdʒ] *n* rotura.
breakaway [ˈbreɪkəweɪ] **1** *adj* (*group, faction*) separatista, disidente. **- 2** *n* (*with group, faction*) ruptura.
break-dance [ˈbreɪkdɑːns] *n* hacer break-dance.
break-dancing [ˈbreɪkdɑːnsɪŋ] *n* MUS break-dance *m.*
breakdown [ˈbreɪkdaʊn] **1** *n* (*of car, machine*) avería. **2** MED crisis *f* nerviosa. **3** (*in negotiations*) ruptura. **4** (*chemical analysis*) análisis *m;* (*of accounts, expenses*) desglose *m.* **5** (*in negotiations*) fracaso.
■ **breakdown service,** (servicio de) asistencia en carretera. ‖ **breakdown van** / **breakdown truck,** grúa.
breaker [ˈbreɪkəʳ] **1** *n* MAR (*heavy wave*) cachón *m.* **2** (*of horse*) domador,-ra. **3** (*of cars, materials*) *persona que trabaja en un desguace.*
■ **breaker's yard,** desguace *m.*
breakfast [ˈbrekfəst] **1** *n* desayuno. **- 2** *i* desayunar.
● **to have breakfast,** desayunar.
■ **breakfast cereal,** cereales *mpl* (*para el desayuno*). ‖ **breakfast television,** televisión *f* matinal.
break-in [ˈbreɪkɪn] *n* entrada forzada.
breaking [ˈbreɪkɪŋ] **1** *n* (*of leg, object*) rotura. **2** (*of relationship*) ruptura.
■ **breaking point,** punto de ruptura. ‖ **breaking and entering,** JUR allanamiento de domicilio.
breakneck [ˈbreɪknek] **at breakneck speed,** *phr* a toda pastilla.
break-out [ˈbreɪkaʊt] *n* (*from prison*) fuga.
breakthrough [ˈbreɪkθruː] *n* avance *m* importante.

break-up [ˈbreɪkʌp] *n* (*of relationship, negotiations*) ruptura; (*of couple*) separación *f.*
breakwater [ˈbreɪkwɔːtəʳ] *n* rompeolas *m.*
bream [briːm] *n* ZOOL brema *f.*
breast [brest] **1** *n* (*chest*) pecho; (*of woman*) pecho, seno. **2** (*of chicken etc*) pechuga. **3** (*of armour*) peto. **4** (*of chimney*) antepecho.
● **to make a clean breast of it,** desembuchar.
breastbone [ˈbrestbəʊn] *n* ANAT esternón *m.*
breast-fed [ˈbrestfed] *adj* amamantado,-a, criado,-a a pecho.
breast-feed [ˈbrestfiːd] *t* amamantar, dar el pecho a.
▲ *pt* & *pp* **breast-fed.**
breast-feeding [ˈbrestfiːdɪŋ] *n* amamantamiento.
breaststroke [ˈbreststrəʊk] *n* (*swimming*) braza.
breath [breθ] **1** *n* (*of person*) aliento; (*of animal*) hálito. **2** (*of air*) soplo. **3** (*of perfume*) olor *m,* olorcillo. **4** (*life*) aliento, vida. **5** (*breathing*) resuello, respiración *f.* **6** (*of scandal*) rumor *m.*
● **out of breath,** sin aliento, sin resuello. ‖ **short of breath,** corto,-a de resuello. ‖ **under one's breath,** en voz baja. ‖ **a breath of fresh air,** un aire renovador. ‖ **in the next breath,** a continuación, inmediatamente después. ‖ **in the same breath,** todo a la vez, al mismo tiempo. ‖ **to catch one's breath,** (*restore breathing*) recobrar el aliento; (*with surprise*) quedarse atónito,-a. ‖ **to draw breath,** respirar, vivir. ‖ **to draw one's last breath,** exhalar el último suspiro. ‖ **to get one's breath back,** recobrar el aliento. ‖ **to take a deep breath,** respirar hondo. ‖ **to take one's breath away,** dejar pasmado,-a a uno.
■ **bad breath,** mal aliento, halitosis *f.* ‖ **breath of life,** cosa imprescindible, requisito indispensable. ‖ **breath test,** GB prueba del alcohol.
breathalyse [ˈbreθəlaɪz] *t* hacer la prueba del alcohol a.
Breathalyzer [ˈbreθəlaɪzəʳ] *n* GB alcoholímetro, alcohotest *m.*
▲ Es marca registrada.
breathe [briːð] **1** *t* (*air, etc*) respirar: *it's wonderful to breathe fresh air,* es maravilloso respirar aire puro; *they breathed in the fumes,* respiraron el humo tóxico. **- 2** *i* (*air, etc*) respirar: *it was impossible to breathe,* fue imposible respirar. **3** (*be alive*) respirar, vivir: *is he still breathing?,* ¿respira aún? **4** (*wine*) airear.
● **to breathe in,** aspirar. ‖ **to breathe out,** espirar. ‖ **don't breathe a word!,** ¡punto en boca! ‖ **not to breathe a word about,** no decir ni una palabra de. ‖ **to breathe air into,** (*balloon etc*) inflar soplando. ‖ **to breathe a sigh,** dar un suspiro. ‖ **to breathe one's last,** exhalar el último suspiro. ‖ **to breath new life into sth.,** infundir un espíritu nuevo a algo. ‖ **to breath down sb.'s neck,** no dejar a algn. a sol ni a sombra.
breather [ˈbriːðəʳ] *n* respiro, pausa.
● **to take a breather,** tomarse un respiro.
breathing [ˈbriːðɪŋ] *n* respiración *f.*
● **to give sb. breathing space,** *fig* dejar respirar a algn. ‖ **to need breathing space,** *fig* necesitar tiempo.
breathless [ˈbreθləs] *adj* sin aliento, jadeante.
breathtaking [ˈbreθteɪkɪŋ] **1** *adj* (*amazing*) impresionante: *the countryside was breathtaking,* el paisaje era impresionante. **2** (*exciting*) emocionante: *a breathtaking experience,* una experiencia emocionante.
bred [bred] *pt* & *pp* → **breed.**
breech [briːtʃ] *n* (*of gun*) recámara.
■ **breech birth,** parto invertido.

breeches ['brɪtʃɪz] 1 *npl* (*knee-length trousers*) calzones *mpl*. 2 *fam* (*trousers*) pantalones *mpl*.
■ **riding breeches,** pantalones *mpl* de montar.
breech-loading ['briːtʃləʊdɪŋ] *adj* (*gun*) de retrocarga.
breed [briːd] 1 *n* (*of animal*) raza; (*of plant*) variedad *f*. – 2 *t* (*animals*) criar. 3 *fig* (*cause*) engendrar, resultar en. – 4 *i* (*animals*) reproducirse. 5 (*disease*) propagarse, difundirse.
▲ *pt & pp* **bred**.
breeder ['briːdəʳ] 1 *n* (*of animals*) criador,-ra; (*of cattle*) ganadero,-a. 2 (*animal*) animal *m* criadero.
breeding ['briːdɪŋ] 1 *n* (*of animals*) cría; (*of plants*) propagación *f*. 2 (*social background*) clase *f*; (*manners*) modales *mpl*: *he lacks breeding,* le falta clase.
■ **breeding ground,** *fig* (*for germs, infection*) caldo de cultivo. ‖ **breeding place,** criadero. ‖ **breeding season,** época de la reproducción.
breeze [briːz] *n* METEOR brisa.
◆ **to breeze in** *i* entrar airosamente. ‖ **to breeze out** *i* salir airosamente. ‖ **to breeze through** *t insep* (*exam*) aprobar sin hacer ningún esfuerzo.
● **to be a breeze,** *fig* estar chupado,-a, ser pan comido.
breeze-block ['briːzblɒk] *n* bloque *m* de cemento.
breezy ['briːzɪ] *adj* METEOR ventoso,-a.
▲ *comp* **breezier,** *superl* **breeziest**.
Bren [bren] **Bren gun,** *n* MIL fusil *m* ametrallador.
brethren ['breðrən] *npl arch* hermanos *mpl*.
Breton ['bretɒn] 1 *adj* bretón,-ona. – 2 *n* (*person*) bretón,-ona. 3 (*language*) bretón *m*.
breve [briːv] 1 *n* MUS LING breve *f*. 2 REL (*papal letter*) breve *m*.
breviary ['briːvjərɪ] *n* REL breviario.
▲ *pl* **breviaries**.
brevity ['brevɪtɪ] *n fml* brevedad *f*.
brew [bruː] 1 *n* (*tea etc*) infusión *f*. 2 (*potion*) brebaje *m*. – 3 *t* (*beer*) elaborar. 4 (*tea etc*) preparar. – 5 *i* (*tea etc*) reposar. 6 (*storm*) prepararse, acercarse.
◆ **to brew up** *i* preparar el té.
● **there's trouble brewing,** corren malos vientos.
brewer ['bruːəʳ] *n* fabricante *mf* de cerveza.
■ **brewer's yeast,** levadura de cerveza.
brewery ['bruːərɪ] *n* fábrica de cerveza, cervecería.
▲ *pl* **breweries**.
brewing ['bruːɪŋ] *n* elaboración *f* de cerveza.
briar ['braɪəʳ] 1 *n* BOT (*heather*) brezo. 2 BOT (*briar-rose bush*) escaramujo.
■ **briar pipe,** pipa de brezo.
bribe [braɪb] 1 *n* soborno. – 2 *t* sobornar.
● **to take bribes,** dejarse sobornar. ‖ **to slip sb. a bribe,** untar la mano a algn.
bribery ['braɪbərɪ] *n* soborno.
bric-a-brac ['brɪkəbræk] *n* baratijas *fpl*.
brick [brɪk] 1 *n* ladrillo. 2 (*toy*) cubo (de madera). 3 *fam fig* (*person*) buena persona. – 4 *adj* de ladrillos: *a brick wall,* una pared de ladrillo. – 5 *t* enladrillar.
◆ **to brick up** *t sep* tapar con ladrillos.
● **to come down on sb. like a ton of bricks,** poner a algn. a caldo. ‖ **it's like talking to a brick wall,** es como hablar con la pared. ‖ **to drop a brick,** GB *fam* meter la pata.
brickbat ['brɪkbæt] *n* (*comment*) crítica.
brickie ['brɪkɪ] *n fam* albañil *m*.
bricklayer ['brɪkleɪəʳ] *n* albañil *m*.
brickwork ['brɪkwɜːk] *n* enladrillado *m*.
bridal ['braɪdəl] *adj* nupcial.
■ **bridal gown,** vestido de novia. ‖ **bridal suite,** suite *f* nupcial.

bride [braɪd] *n* novia, desposada.
● **the bride and groom,** los novios.
bridegroom ['braɪdgruːm] *n* novio, desposado.
bridesmaid ['braɪdzmeɪd] *n* dama de honor.
bridge [brɪdʒ] 1 *n* puente *m*. 2 (*of nose*) caballete *m*. 3 (*on ship*) puente *m* de mando. 4 (*game*) bridge *m*. – 5 *t* (*river*) tender un puente sobre.
● **to bridge the gap,** colmar un vacío. ‖ **we'll cross that bridge when we come to it,** nos ocuparemos del problema cuando surja.
■ **railway bridge,** puente *m* ferroviario. ‖ **rope bridge,** puente *m* de cuerdas. ‖ **stone-arch bridge,** puente *m* de arcos.
bridgehead ['brɪdʒhed] *n* MIL cabeza de puente.
bridging ['brɪdʒɪŋ] **bridging loan,** *n* ECON préstamo puente, préstamo provisional.
bridle ['braɪdəl] 1 *n* brida. – 2 *t* (*horse*) embridar. – 3 *i* mostrar desagrado (**at,** por).
brief [briːf] 1 *adj* (*short*) breve; (*concise*) conciso,-a; (*scanty*) diminuto,-a. – 2 *n* (*report*) informe *m*. 3 JUR expediente *m*. 4 MIL instrucciones *fpl*. – 5 *t* (*inform*) informar (**about,** sobre). 6 (*instruct*) dar instrucciones a.
● **in brief,** en resumen. ‖ **to hold a brief for,** JUR representar a.
briefcase ['briːfkeɪs] *n* maletín *m*, cartera.
briefing ['briːfɪŋ] *n* reunión *f* informativa, briefing *m*.
briefness ['briːfnəs] *n* brevedad *f*.
brier [braɪəʳ] *n-adj* → **briar**.
brig [brɪgə'dɪəʳ] *abbr* (*Brigadier*) General *m* de Brigada; (*abbreviation*) Gral. Brig.
brigade [brɪ'geɪd] 1 *n* MIL brigada. – 2 *t* MIL formar una brigada con.
brigadier [brɪgə'dɪəʳ] *n* GB general *m* de brigada.
brigand ['brɪgənd] *n* bandido, bandolero.
brigantine ['brɪgəntiːn] *n* MAR bergantín *m*.
bright [braɪt] 1 *adj* (*light, eyes, etc*) brillante. 2 METEOR (*sky, day*) claro,-a, despejado,-a; (*sunny*) soleado,-a, de sol. 3 (*colour*) vivo,-a. 4 (*future*) prometedor,-ra. 5 (*clever*) inteligente, listo,-a. 6 (*cheerful*) alegre, animado,-a.
● **to look on the bright side,** mirar el lado positivo de las cosas. ‖ **bright and early,** muy de mañana.
■ **the bright lights,** *fig* el atractivo de la gran ciudad. ‖ **bright spark,** *fig* listillo.
brighten ['braɪtən] *t* (*colour*) avivar.
◆ **to brighten up** 1 *t sep* METEOR despejar: *the sun brightened up the sky,* el sol despejó el cielo. 2 (*room, house*) dar un aspecto más alegre a: *a coat of paint will brighten up the lounge,* una mano de pintura dará un aspecto más alegre al salón. 3 (*enliven*) alegrar, animar: *he's guaranteed to brighten up the party,* seguro que animará la fiesta. – 4 *i* METEOR despejarse, aclarar, salir el sol. 5 (*person*) animarse.
brightness ['braɪtnəs] 1 *n* (*light*) luminosidad *f*. 2 (*of sun*) resplandor *m*. 3 (*of day*) claridad *f*. 4 (*of colour*) viveza. 5 (*cleverness*) inteligencia.
brill[1] [brɪl] *n* ZOOL (*fish*) rémol *m*.
brill[2] [brɪl] *adj fam* (*brilliant*) guay, chachi.
brilliance ['brɪljəns] *n* brillo, brillantez *f*.
brilliant ['brɪljənt] 1 *adj* (*light*) brillante, reluciente. 2 (*colour*) vivo,-a. 3 (*person*) brillante, genial. 4 *fam* estupendo,-a, fantástico,-a.
brilliantine ['brɪljəntiːn] *n* brillantina.
brim [brɪm] 1 *n* (*of cup, glass etc*) borde *m*. 2 (*of hat*) ala. – 3 *i* rebosar (**with,** de): *he was brimming with pride,* rebosaba de orgullo.
◆ **to brim over** *i* (*liquid*) rebosar, desbordarse. ‖ **to brim (over) with** *t insep* (*health, happiness*) rebosar de.

▲ *(verbo) pt & pp* brimmed, *ger* brimming.

brimstone ['brɪmstəʊn] **1** *n arch (sulphur)* azufre *m*. **2** brimstone (butterfly), ZOOL limonera.

● fire and brimstone, *fig* fuego del infierno.

brine [braɪn] *n* salmuera.

bring [brɪŋ] **1** *t* traer: *he brought his sister to the party,* trajo a su hermana a la fiesta. **2** *(lead)* llevar, conducir: *he was brought before the court,* fue llevado ante el tribunal; *this path brings you to the church,* este camino te lleva a la iglesia. **3** *(be sold for)* dar: *the Van Gogh is expected to bring over a million,* se espera que el Van Gogh dé más de un millón.

◆ to bring about *t sep (accident, change etc)* provocar, causar. ‖ to bring along *t sep (friend, colleague)* traer. ‖ to bring back **1** *t sep (book, record, etc)* devolver. **2** *(law, legislation)* volver a introducir. **3** *(past experience, childhood, etc)* recordar, hacer recordar. ‖ to bring down **1** *t sep (chair, book etc)* bajar. **2** *(door, house, government)* derribar. **3** *(prices, temperature)* hacer bajar. ‖ to bring forward **1** *t sep (meeting, appointment)* adelantar. **2** *(theme, question)* presentar, plantear. ‖ to bring in **1** *t sep (person)* hacer pasar. **2** *(coal, food etc into house)* traer. **3** *(law, legislation)* introducir. **4** *(yield)* rendir, producir. **5** JUR *(verdict)* emitir, pronunciar. **6** *(crowds)* atraer. ‖ to bring off *t sep (victory, result)* conseguir, lograr. ‖ to bring on *t sep (illness)* provocar. ‖ to bring out **1** *t sep (record)* sacar al mercado, sacar; *(book)* publicar. **2** *(talents, qualities)* sacar a relucir. ‖ to bring round **1** *t sep (persuade)* persuadir, convencer. **2** *(revive)* hacer volver en sí. ‖ to bring through *t sep (help survive)* ayudar a sobrevivir. ‖ to bring to *t sep* hacer volver en sí. ‖ to bring up **1** *t sep (chair, book etc)* subir. **2** *(child)* criar, educar. **3** *(subject, topic)* plantear. **4** *(vomit)* devolver.

● brought forward, COMM suma y sigue. ‖ to bring a charge against sb., JUR acusar a algn. ‖ to bring a complaint, hacer una reclamación. ‖ to bring nearer / bring closer, acercar. ‖ to bring nothing but trouble, no hacer más que causar problemas. ‖ to bring os. to do sth., armarse de suficiente valor para hacer algo: *he couldn't bring himself to do it,* no pudo armarse de suficiente valor para hacerlo. ‖ to bring sb. to their senses, hacer que algn. entre en razón: *let's see if that brings you to your senses,* a ver si esto se te hace entrar en razón. ‖ to bring sth. home to sb., hacer que algn. se dé cuenta de algo. ‖ to bring sth. into play, poner algo en juego. ‖ to bring sth. on os., buscárselo. ‖ to bring sth. to light, sacar algo a la luz. ‖ to bring sth. to mind, recordarle algo a algn.: *it brings his last film to mind,* me recuerda su última película. ‖ to bring the house down, THEAT hacer desternillarse de risa al público. ‖ to bring to a conclusion, llevar a una conclusión. ‖ to bring to bear, ejercer.

▲ *pt & pp* brought.

brink [brɪŋk] *n* borde *m*.

● on the brink of, a punto de, al borde de: *he's on the brink of bankruptcy,* está al borde de la quiebra.

brinkmanship ['brɪŋkmənʃɪp] *n* POL política en la cuerda floja.

briny ['braɪnɪ] **1** *adj (salty)* salobre, salado,-a. – **2** the briny, *n* GB *fam* el mar.

▲ *comp* brinier, *superl* briniest.

briquette [brɪ'ket] *n* briquet *f*.

brisk [brɪsk] **1** *adj (energetic)* enérgico,-a, vigoroso,-a. **2** *(invigorating)* vigorizador,-ra. **3** *(business, trade)* activo,-a.

● to go for a brisk walk, caminar a paso ligero.

briskness ['brɪsknəs] **1** *n (energy)* energía, vigor *m*. **2** *(of business, trade)* actividad *f*. **3** *(of walk)* ligereza.

bristle ['brɪsəl] **1** *n* cerda. – **2** *i (hair)* erizarse, ponerse de punta. **3** *(show annoyance)* mosquearse.

◆ to bristle with *t insep fig (difficulties, problems)* estar erizado,-a de.

Britain ['brɪtən] *n* Gran Bretaña.

■ Great Britain, Gran Bretaña.

British ['brɪtɪʃ] **1** *adj* británico,-a. – **2** the British, *npl* los británicos *mpl*.

● and the best of British (luck)!, *fam iron* ¡y buen provecho te haga!

■ British English, inglés *m* británico.

Britisher ['brɪtɪʃəʳ] *n* US británico,-a.

Briton ['brɪtən] *n* británico,-a.

Brittany ['brɪtənɪ] *n* Bretaña.

brittle ['brɪtəl] *adj* quebradizo,-a, frágil.

brittleness ['brɪtəlnəs] *n* fragilidad *f*.

broach [brəʊtʃ] **1** *n (drill bit)* broca. **2** *(roasting-spit)* espetón *m*. – **3** *t (subject, theme for discussion)* abordar.

broad [brɔːd] **1** *adj (street, avenue)* ancho,-a; *(surface, water, plateau)* extenso,-a. **2** *fig (field of study, debate)* amplio,-a. **3** *(measurement)* de ancho: *three metres broad,* tres metros de ancho. **4** *(general)* general: *a broad outline,* un esquema general; *in broad terms,* en términos generales. **5** *(main)* principal: *the broad facts,* los hechos principales. **6** *(explicit)* claro,-a: *a broad indication,* una clara indicación; *a broad hint,* una indirecta clara. **7** *(accent)* marcado,-a, cerrado,-a: *he spoke in broad Irish,* habló con un marcado acento irlandés. **8** *(smile)* abierto,-a. **9** *(vowel)* abierto,-a. – **10** *n* US *fam (woman)* tía, gachí *f*.

● in a broad sense, en sentido amplio. ‖ in the broadest sense of the word, en el sentido más amplio de la palabra.

■ a broad outline, un esquema general.

broadcast ['brɔːdkɑːst] **1** *n* RAD TV emisión *f*. – **2** *t* RAD TV emitir, transmitir. **3** *(make known)* difundir.

▲ *pt & pp* broadcast.

broadcaster ['brɔːdkɑːstəʳ] *n* locutor,-ra, presentador,-ra.

broadcasting ['brɔːdkɑːstɪŋ] **1** *n* RAD radiodifusión *f*. **2** TV transmisión *f*.

broaden ['brɔːdən] *t* ensanchar; *fig* ampliar.

◆ to broaden out *i* ensancharse.

● to broaden one's horizons, ampliar sus perspectivas.

broadly ['brɔːdlɪ] *adv* en términos generales.

broadly-based ['brɔːdlɪbeɪst] *adj* de base amplia.

broad-minded [brɔːd'maɪndɪd] *adj* liberal, tolerante.

broad-mindedness [brɔːd'maɪndɪdnəs] *n* tolerancia.

broadness ['brɔːdnəs] **1** *n* anchura. **2** *fig (of accent)* lo marcado, lo cerrado.

broadsheet ['brɔːdʃiːt] *n* periódico de gran formato.

broad-shouldered [brɔːd'ʃəʊldəd] *adj* ancho,-a de espaldas.

broadside ['brɔːdsaɪd] **1** *n* MAR *(gunfire)* andanada. **2** *fig (insult)* improperio, andanada verbal, lanzada. **3** MAR costado.

● broadside on, de costado.

broadsword ['brɔːdsɔːd] *n* sable *m*.

brocade [brə'keɪd] *n* brocado.

broccoli ['brɒkəlɪ] *n* brécol *m*, brócoli *m*.

brochette [brə'ʃet] *n* pincho, brocheta.

brochure ['brəʊʃəʳ] *n* folleto.

brogue[1] [brəʊg] *n (shoe)* zapato fuerte de suela gruesa.

brogue[2] [brəʊg] *n (Irish accent)* acento irlandés.

broil [brɔɪl] *t* US asar a la parrilla.

broiler ['brɔɪləʳ] 1 n CULIN pollo. 2 (gridiron) parrilla.
broke [brəʊk] 1 pt → **break**. – 2 adj fam sin un duro, sin blanca: *he's flat broke,* no tiene ni un duro.
● to go for broke, ir a por todas.
broken ['brəʊkən] 1 pp → **break**. – 2 adj (plate, window etc) roto,-a. 3 (machine) estropeado,-a. 4 (bone) fracturado,-a. 5 (person) destrozado,-a. 6 (health) quebrantado,-a. 7 (language) chapurreado,-a: *he speaks broken Spanish,* chapurrea el español. 8 (sleep, pattern) interrumpido, -a.
broken-down ['brəʊkəndaʊn] 1 adj (vehicle) estropeado,-a. 2 (building) desmoronado,-a. 3 (person) destrozado,-a.
broken-hearted [brəʊkən'hɑːtəd] adj desolado,-a, con el corazón destrozado.
broker ['brəʊkəʳ] n COMM (on Stock Exchange) corredor,-ra, agente mf de Bolsa; (middleman) intermediario,-a sin riesgo.
brokerage ['brəʊkərɪdʒ] n COMM corretaje m.
brolly ['brɒlɪ] n GB fam paraguas m.
▲ pl **brollies**.
bromide ['brəʊmaɪd] n CHEM bromuro.
bromine ['brəʊmaɪn] n CHEM bromo.
bronchial ['brɒŋkɪəl] adj ANAT bronquial.
■ bronchial tubes, ANAT bronquios mpl.
bronchitic [brɒn'kɪtɪk] adj MED bronquítico,-a.
bronchitis [brɒŋ'kaɪtəs] n MED bronquitis f.
bronze [brɒnz] 1 n (metal) bronce m. 2 (statue, sculpture) talla de bronce. 3 (colour) color m de bronce. – 4 adj (colour) de color de bronce, bronceado,-a. – 5 t (colour bronze) broncear. – 6 i (get a suntan) broncearse.
■ the Bronze Age, HIST la Edad del Bronce.
bronzed [brɒnzd] adj (suntanned) bronceado,-a.
brooch [brəʊtʃ] n broche m.
brood [bruːd] 1 n (birds) nidada. 2 fam fig (children) prole f. – 3 i (hen) empollar. 4 fig (worry) apurarse, preocuparse.
◆ to brood about t insep dar vueltas a: *stop brooding about it!,* ¡no le des más vueltas! ‖ to brood over t insep rumiar, reflexionar sobre.
■ brood hen, gallina clueca. ‖ brood mare, ZOOL yegua f de cría.
broody ['bruːdɪ] 1 adj (hen) clueco,-a. 2 (thoughtful) pensativo,-a. 3 (melancholy) melancólico,-a. 4 (depressed) deprimido,-a. 5 fam (woman) ansiosa de tener un hijo.
▲ comp **broodier**, superl **broodiest**.
brook [brʊk] n arroyo, riachuelo.
broom [bruːm] 1 n (for sweeping) escoba. 2 BOT hiniesta.
broomstick ['bruːmstɪk] 1 n (handle) palo de escoba. 2 (of witch) escoba.
Bros [brɒs] abbr (Brothers) Hermanos mpl; (abbreviation) Hnos: *Jones Bros.,* Hnos. Jones.
broth [brɒθ] n CULIN caldo.
brothel ['brɒθəl] n burdel m.
brothel-creeper ['brɒθəlkriːpəʳ] n fam zapato de ante de suela gruesa que se asocia con los rockeros.
brother ['brʌðəʳ] 1 n hermano. 2 (member of society, religious order etc) hermano. 3 US fam (friend) colega m, hermano, tío: *what's happening brother?,* ¿qué pasa colega?
■ brothers and sisters, hermanos mpl. ‖ older brother, hermano mayor. ‖ younger brother, hermano menor.
brotherhood ['brʌðəhʊd] n hermandad f, cofradía.
brother-in-law ['brʌðərɪnlɔː] n cuñado.
▲ pl **brothers-in-law** ['brʌðəzɪnlɔː].

brotherly ['brʌðəlɪ] adj fraternal.
■ brotherly love, amor m fraternal.
brought [brɔːt] pt & pp → **bring**.
brow [braʊ] 1 n (eyebrow) ceja. 2 (forehead) frente f. 3 (of hill) cresta.
browbeat ['braʊbiːt] t intimidar.
▲ pt browbeat, pp browbeaten ['braʊbiːtən].
brown [braʊn] 1 adj marrón. 2 (hair etc) castaño,-a. 3 (skin) moreno,-a. – 4 n marrón m. 5 (hair) castaño m. 6 (skin) color m moreno. – 7 t CULIN dorar. 8 (skin) poner moreno,-a, broncear. – 9 i CULIN quedarse dorado,-a, dorarse. 10 (tan) ponerse moreno,-a, broncearse.
◆ to brown off t sep fam fastidiar, molestar.
● to go brown, (in sun) ponerse moreno.
■ brown ale, cerveza negra. ‖ brown bear, oso pardo. ‖ brown rice, arroz m integral.
browned-off ['braʊndɒf] adj fam mosqueado,-a, fastidiado,-a.
● to be browned off, estar hasta la coronilla.
brownie ['braʊnɪ] n US CULIN pastel de chocolate y nueces.
Brownie ['braʊnɪ] n niña exploradora.
brownish ['braʊnɪʃ] 1 adj pardusco,-a. – 2 n color m pardusco.
brownout ['braʊnaʊt] n US apagón m parcial.
browse [braʊz] 1 i (grass) pacer; (leaves) ramonear. 2 (person in shop) mirar: *"Can I help you?" –"No, thanks, I'm just browsing",* "¿Le puedo ayudar en algo?" –"No gracias, sólo estoy mirando".
◆ to browse through t insep (book, magazine) hojear.
● to have a browse, (in shop) ir a echar un vistazo, entrar para mirar.
bruise [bruːz] 1 n morado, magulladura, contusión f. 2 (on fruit) magulladura, machucadura. – 3 t (body) magullar, contusionar. 4 (fruit) magullar, machucar. – 5 i (body) magullarse, salirle cardenales. 6 (fruit) magullarse.
bruised [bruːzd] adj magullado,-a.
bruiser ['bruːzəʳ] n fam gorila m, matón m.
brunch [brʌnʃ] n brunch m, (desayuno que se toma sobre las doce y sustituye al almuerzo).
Brunei [bruː'naɪ] n Brunei.
brunette [bruː'net] 1 n morena. – 2 adj moreno,-a.
brunt [brʌnt] n lo más duro, lo peor.
● to bear the brunt of, llevar el peso de, aguantar lo más recio de: *they bore the brunt of the bombing,* llevaron el peso de los bombardeos. ‖ the brunt of the work, el grueso del trabajo.
brush [brʌʃ] 1 n (for teeth, clothes, etc) cepillo. 2 (artist's) pincel m; (house painter's) brocha. 3 (fox's tail) hopo. 4 (undergrowth) maleza. 5 (unpleasant encounter) roce m: *he had a brush with the police,* tuvo un roce con la policía. – 6 t (gen) cepillar; (teeth) cepillar, limpiar, lavar. 7 (touch lightly) rozar: *he brushed the glass with his sleeve and knocked it off the table,* rozó la copa con la manga y la hizo caer de la mesa.
◆ to brush aside t sep (person, problem) dejar de lado. ‖ to brush away t sep (dirt, dust) quitar, limpiar. ‖ to brush off t sep (dust, dirt) quitar, limpiar. 2 (rebuff, snub a person) desairar. ‖ to brush over t sep (paint lightly) dar una ligera mano de pintura; (conceal) ocultar, encubrir: *he tried to brush over what had happened,* intentó ocultar lo que había sucedido. ‖ to brush up t sep (knowledge) refrescar, repasar.
● to brush up against, rozar al pasar.
brush-off ['brʌʃɒf] n (rebuff, snub) desaire m.
● to get the brush-off, aguantar un desaire. ‖ to give sb. the brush-off, quitar a algn. de encima.

brushstroke [ˈbrʌʃstrəʊk] n (of artist's brush) pincelada; (house painter's brush) brochazo.
brush-up [ˈbrʌʃʌp] to have a wash and brush-up, phr arreglarse.
brushwood [ˈbrʌʃwʊd] 1 n (twigs) broza. 2 (undergrowth) maleza.
brusque [brʌsk] adj brusco,-a, áspero,-a.
brusqueness [ˈbrʌsknəs] n brusquedad f.
Brussels [ˈbrʌsəlz] n Bruselas.
■ Brussels sprouts, coles fpl de Bruselas.
brutal [ˈbruːtəl] adj brutal, cruel.
brutality [bruːˈtælɪtɪ] n brutalidad f, crueldad f.
brute [bruːt] 1 n bruto,-a, bestia mf. – 2 adj brutal, bruto,-a.
■ brute force, fuerza bruta.
brutish [ˈbruːtɪʃ] 1 adj brutal, bestial. 2 (stupid) bruto,-a.
BSc [ˈbiːˈesˈsiː] abbr (Bachelor of Science) licenciado,-a en ciencias.
BSE [ˈbiːˈesˈiː] abbr (bovine spongiform encephalopathy) encefalopatía espongiforme bovina.
BSI [ˈbiːˈesˈaɪ] abbr (British Standards Institution) ≈ Aenor.
BST [ˈbiːˈesˈtiː] abbr (British Summer Time) hora británica de verano.
Bt [ˈbærənət] abbr (Baronet) baronet m.
BT [ˈbiːˈtiː] abbr (British Telecom) compañía británica de telecomunicaciones.
BTA [ˈbiːˈtiːˈeɪ] abbr (British Tourist Authority) organismo británico que regula el turismo.
BThu [ˈbiːtiːˈeɪtʃˈjuː] abbr (British Thermal Unit) → **btu**.
btu [ˈbiːˈtiːˈjuː] abbr (British Thermal Unit) unidad calorífica británica que equivale a 251,997 calorías.
bubble [ˈbʌbəl] 1 n (in liquid) burbuja; (of soap) pompa. – 2 i burbujear. 3 (boil) borbotear.
◆ to bubble over i (water, liquid) desbordarse, rebosar; (with happiness, emotion) rebosar de.
■ bubble bath, espuma de baño. ‖ bubble chamber, PHYS cámara de burbujas. ‖ bubble gum, chicle m de globos. ‖ bubble wrap, plástico burbujas.
bubble-and-squeak [ˈbʌbələnskwiːk] n plato hecho de col con patatas y, a veces, carne picada, todo frito.
bubbly [ˈbʌblɪ] 1 adj burbujeante, espumoso,-a. 2 (person) vivaz. – 3 n fam (champagne) champán m.
▲ comp bubblier, superl bubbliest.
bubonic [bjuːˈbɒnɪk] adj MED bubónico,-a.
■ bubonic plague, peste f bubónica.
buccaneer [bʌkəˈnɪəʳ] n bucanero.
Bucharest [buːkəˈrest] n Bucarest.
buck¹ [bʌk] 1 n (rabbit, hare) macho; (deer) ciervo; (goat) macho cabrío. 2 arch (young man) galán m, señorito. – 3 adj (animal) macho. – 4 i (horse) corcovear. – 5 t (rider) desarzonar. 6 US fig (system, authority) oponerse a, resistir a.
◆ to buck up 1 t sep fam dar ánimos a: he tried to buck her up, intentó darle ánimos: buck up!, ¡anímate!
● buck your ideas up!, ¡espabílate!
■ buck soldier, US soldado raso.
buck² [bʌk] n US fam dólar m.
● to make a fast buck, fam hacer dinero fácil. ‖ to pass the buck, fig escurrir el bulto. ‖ the buck stops here!, ¡se acabó!
■ Buck's Fizz, cóctel de champán y zumo de naranja.
bucket [ˈbʌkɪt] 1 n cubo. 2 (on dredger, waterwheel) canguilón m.
● to rain buckets, fam llover chuzos de punta. ‖ to cry

buckets, fam llorar a lágrima viva. ‖ to kick the bucket, fam palmarla, estirar la pata.
■ bucket seat, (in car) asiento envolvente.
bucketful [ˈbʌkɪtfʊl] n (contents) cubo (lleno): a bucketful of water, un cubo (lleno) de agua.
● by the bucketful, fam fig a punta pala: they sell them by the bucketful, los venden a punta pala.
bucket-shop [ˈbʌkɪtʃɒp] n agencia de viajes (que vende billetes a precios más bajos).
buckle [ˈbʌkəl] 1 n (on shoe, belt) hebilla. – 2 t (belt) abrochar. – 3 i (metal, object) torcerse, combarse. 4 (knees) doblarse.
◆ to buckle down i ponerse a trabajo en serio: come on, buckle down to it!, ¡venga, a trabajar!
buckshee [bʌkˈʃiː] 1 adj GB fam gratuito,-a. – 2 adv gratis, de balde.
buckshot [ˈbʌkʃɒt] n perdigón m.
buckskin [ˈbʌkskɪn] n ante m.
bucktooth [bʌkˈtuːθ] n diente m protuberante.
▲ pl buckteeth [bʌkˈtiːθ].
buckwheat [ˈbʌkwiːt] n BOT trigo sarraceno, alforfón m.
bucolic [bjuːˈkɒlɪk] adj bucólico,-a.
bud¹ [bʌd] 1 n (on tree, plant) brote m, yema; (of flower) botón m, capullo. – 2 i (trees, plants) echar brotes, brotar; (flower) empezar a echar flor.
● to be in bud, (tree, plant) estar en brote; (flower) estar a punto de florecer. ‖ to nip sth. in the bud, fig cortar algo a raíz.
▲ (verbo) pt & pp budded, ger budding.
bud² [bʌd] n US fam colega mf: hi bud!, ¡hola colega!
Budapest [buːdəˈpest] n Budapest.
Buddha [ˈbudə] n REL Buda m.
Buddhism [ˈbudɪzəm] n REL budismo m.
Buddhist [ˈbudɪst] 1 adj REL budista. 2 n REL budista mf.
budding [ˈbʌdɪŋ] adj en ciernes: he's a budding politician, es un político en ciernes.
buddy [ˈbʌdɪ] n US fam amigote m, colega mf.
▲ pl buddies.
budge [bʌdʒ] 1 t (move) mover: they couldn't budge the piano, no podían mover el piano. 2 (make change opinion) hacer cambiar de opinión: there's no way of budging him, no hay manera de hacerle cambiar de opinión. – 3 i (move) moverse: it won't budge, no se mueva. 4 (change opinion) cambiar de opinión: he won't budge, no cambiará de opinión.
◆ to budge up i (move over) moverse, echarse: budge up a bit!, ¡muévete un poco!, ¡hazme un poco de sitio a tu lado!
budgerigar [ˈbʌdʒərɪgaːʳ] n ZOOL periquito.
budget [ˈbʌdʒɪt] 1 n presupuesto: a budget of 2,000 pounds, un presupuesto de 2.000 libras. – 2 adj (good-value) bien de precio. – 3 to budget for, t presupuestar, hacer el presupuesto para: we'll have to budget for the coming year, tendremos que hacer el presupuesto para el año que viene.
● to be on a tight budget, tener fondos limitados.
■ budget account / budget plan, cuenta presupuestaria. ‖ the Budget, GB el presupuesto general del Estado.
budgetary [ˈbʌdʒɪtərɪ] adj presupuestario,-a.
budgie [ˈbʌdʒɪ] n ZOOL fam periquito.
buff [bʌf] 1 (leather) pief f de ante. 2 n (colour) color m de ante. 3 n (enthusiast) aficionado,-a: a theatre buff, un aficionado al teatro; a film buff, un cinéfilo. – 4 adj de color de ante. – 5 t (metal, floor etc) dar brillo a. 6 (leather) aterciopelar.

● **in the buff,** *fam* en pelotas.
buffalo ['bʌfələʊ] *n* ZOOL búfalo.
▲ *pl* **buffalo** o **buffaloes**.
buffer[1] ['bʌfəʳ] **1** *n* (*for train*) tope *m*. **2** COMPUT memoria intermedia. **3** CHEM regulador *m*.
■ **buffer state,** POL estado tapón.
buffer[2] ['bʌfəʳ] *n* GB *fam* (*old man*) carca *m*, carcamal *m*.
buffet[1] ['bʌfeɪ] **1** *n* (*bar*) bar *m*; (*at station*) bar *m*, cantina. **2** (*meal*) bufé *m* libre, bufé *m*. **3** (*sideboard*) aparador *m*.
■ **buffet car,** GB coche *m* comedor.
buffet[2] ['bʌfɪt] **1** *n* (*slap*) bofetada. – **2** *t* (*slap*) abofetear. **3** (*strike*) azotar, zarandear: *the wind buffeted the trees,* el viento azotaba los árboles.
buffoon [bə'fuːn] **1** *n* (*idiot*) payaso. **2** (*jester*) bufón *m*.
buffoonery ['bəfuːnəri] *n* payasada, bufonada.
bug [bʌg] **1** *n* (*insect*) bicho. **2** *fam* (*microbe*) microbio. **3** (*microphone*) micrófono oculto. **4** *fam* (*interest*) afición *f*. – **5** *t fam* ocultar micrófonos en. **6** US (*annoy*) molestar, fastidiar: *stop bugging me!,* ¡deja de fastidiarme!; *what's bugging her?,* ¿qué mosca le ha picado?
▲ *pt* & *pp* **bugged,** *ger* **bugging**.
bugbear ['bʌgbeəʳ] *n* bestia negra.
bugger ['bʌgəʳ] **1** *n* sodomita *m*. **2** *taboo* (*unpleasant person*) cabrón,-ona, puñetero,-a. **3** *taboo* (*specific person*) tipo, individuo; (*referring to child*) mocoso,-a, sinvergüenza *mf*: *funny bugger,* bicho raro; *poor bugger,* desgraciado,-a; *silly bugger,* gilipollas *mf*. **4** *taboo* (*job, thing*) coñazo. – **5** *interj taboo* ¡joder! – **6** *t* sodomizar.
◆ **to bugger about** *i taboo* hacer el gilipollas. ‖ **to bugger off** *i taboo* pirárselas. ‖ **to bugger up** *t sep taboo* joderla.
● **bugger all!,** *taboo* nada de nada. ‖ **bugger off!,** *taboo* ¡vete a la porra! ‖ **to be buggered,** *taboo* estar hecho,-a polvo. ‖ **not to give a bugger,** *taboo* importar un huevo: *I don't give a bugger,* me importa un huevo.
buggery ['bʌgəri] *n* sodomía.
buggy ['bʌgi] **1** *n* (*horse-drawn*) calesa. **2** (*open-top vehicle*) ≈ jeep *m*. **3** US (*pram*) cochecito (de bebé).
▲ *pl* **buggies**.
bugle ['bjuːgəl] **1** *n* MUS corneta, clarín *m*. – **2** *i* MUS tocar la corneta.
bugler ['bjuːgləʳ] *n* MUS corneta *mf*.
bug-ridden ['bʌgrɪdən] *adj* infestado,-a de bichos.
build [bɪld] **1** *n* (*physique*) constitución *f*, complexión *f*: *a strong build,* una complexión fuerte. – **2** *t* (*car, ship etc*) construir; (*house, block of flats etc*) construir, edificar.
◆ **to build in** *t sep* (*as part of structure*) incorporar: *they've built in an alarm system,* han incorporado un sistema de alarmas. ‖ **to build on** *t sep* (*extension, part of house*) añadir: *they're going to build an extra bedroom on,* van a añadir otro dormitorio. **2** *fig* (*base on, found*) basarse en, fundarse en: *their partnership is built on mutual trust,* su asociación se basa en la confianza mutua. – **3** *t insep* (*use profitably*) saber aprovechar: *we need to build on foreign investment,* tenemos que saber aprovechar la inversión exterior. ‖ **to build up** *t sep* (*business*) desarrollar; (*reputation*) establecer; (*sales*) aumentar; (*collection, objects*) reunir, acumular; (*speed*) coger. – **2** *i* (*business*) desarrollarse; (*reputation*) establecerse; (*sales, profits*) aumentarse; (*collection, objects*) acumularse.
● **tu build up one's hopes,** hacerse ilusiones.
▲ (*verbo*) *pt* & *pp* **built**.
builder ['bɪldəʳ] **1** *n* (*owner of company*) constructor,-ra. **2** (*bricklayer*) albañil *m*. **3** (*foreman*) maestro *m* de obras. **4** (*contractor*) contratista *mf*. **5** *fig* (*of company, state*) fundador,-ra.

■ **builder's,** empresa constructora. ‖ **builder's yard,** almacén *m* de materiales de construcción.
building ['bɪldɪŋ] **1** *n* edificio. **2** (*action*) construcción *f*, edificación *f*.
■ **building land,** terrenos *mpl* edificables. ‖ **building permit,** permiso de obras. ‖ **building site,** (*before construction*) solar *m*; (*during construction*) obra. ‖ **building society,** sociedad *f* hipotecaria. ‖ **the building industry / the building trade,** la construcción.
build-up ['bɪldʌp] **1** *n* (*increase*) aumento: *a build-up in pollution,* un aumento de la contaminación; *a build-up in tension,* un aumento de la tensión. **2** (*of gas*) acumulación *f*. **3** (*of troops*) concentración *f*. **4** (*of plot in film, play*) desarrollo. **5** (*favourable publicity*) bombo, publicidad *f*.
● **to give sth. big build-up,** (*film, concert, event*) anunciar algo a bombo y platillo.
built [bɪlt] *pt* & *pp* → **build**.
● **-built,** de construcción ..., de fabricación ...: *a Spanish-built rocket,* un cohete de construcción española.
built-in [bɪlt'ɪn] **1** *adj* (*as component*) incorporado,-a: *the telephone has a built-in answering machine,* el teléfono tiene contestador incorporado. **2** (*recessed*) empotrado,-a: *built-in cupboards,* armarios empotrados.
built-up [bɪlt'ʌp] *adj* urbanizado,-a.
■ **built-up area,** zona urbanizada.
Bujumbura ['budzəmbuərə] *n* Buyumbura.
bulb [bʌlb] **1** *n* BOT bulbo. **2** ELEC bombilla.
bulbous ['bʌlbəs] *adj* bulboso,-a.
Bulgaria [bʌl'geəriə] *n* Bulgaria.
Bulgarian [bʌl'geəriən] **1** *adj* búlgaro,-a. – **2** *n* (*person*) búlgaro,-a. **3** (*language*) búlgaro.
bulge [bʌldʒ] **1** *n* (*lump*) bulto; (*protuberance*) protuberancia. **2** (*in surface*) pandeo. – **3** *i* (*protrude*) sobresalir; (*eyes*) saltar: *his stomach bulges,* le sobresale la barriga; *his eyes bulged when he saw all the money,* se le saltaron los ojos al ver todo el dinero. **4** (*swell*) hincharse. **5** (*warp*) pandearse. **6** **to bulge with,** estar abultado,-a de: *his pockets were bulging with sweets,* sus bolsillos estaban abultados de caramelos.
bulging ['bʌldʒɪŋ] **1** *adj* (*lumpy, bulky*) abultado,-a. **2** (*eyes, features*) saltón,-ona. **3** (*swollen*) hinchado,-a. **4** (*surface*) pandeado,-a. – **5** *n* (*with bulk*) abultamiento. **6** (*swelling*) hinchazón *m*. **7** (*of wall, surface*) pandeo.
bulk [bʌlk] **1** *n* (*mass*) masa, bulto; (*amount, quantity*) volumen *m*, cantidad *f*. **2** (*object*) mole *f*. **3** (*weight of person*) peso. **4** (*greater part*) mayor parte *f*. **5** MAR carga.
◆ **to bulk out** *t sep* (*book, article*) hinchar, llenar de paja.
● **in bulk,** COMM (*loose*) a granel; (*in large quantities*) en grandes cantidades. ‖ **to break bulk,** desestibar. ‖ **to bulk large,** ocupar un lugar importante.
bulk-buying ['bʌlkbaɪɪŋ] *n* compra en grandes cantidades: *bulk-buying usually works out cheaper,* suele salir más barato comprar en grandes cantidades.
bulkhead ['bʌlkhed] *n* AV MAR mamparo.
bulkiness ['bʌlkinəs] *n* abultamiento, volumen *m*.
bulky ['bʌlki] *adj* abultado,-a, voluminoso,-a.
▲ *comp* **bulkier,** *superl* **bulkiest**.
bull[1] [bul] **1** *n* toro. **2** (*elephant, whale, etc*) macho. **3** COMM alcista *mf*. **4** GB *fam* (*target*) blanco, diana. – **5** *adj* (*elephant, whale, etc*) macho. **6** COMM FIN alcista, en alza. – **7** *t* COMM FIN provocar un alza en el precio de los valores, jugar al alza. – **8** *i* COMM FIN especular en el mercado para provocar un alza.
● **to be like a bull at a gate,** ser muy impetuoso,-a. ‖ **to be like a bull in a china shop,** ser un,-a manazas.

he's like a bull in a china shop, destroza lo que toca. ‖ **to take the bull by the horns,** coger el toro por los cuernos.

■ **the Bull,** ASTROL Tauro. ‖ **bull calf,** becerro. ‖ **fighting bull,** toro bravo, toro de lidia. ‖ **bull market,** FIN mercado alcista.

bull² [bʊl] *n* REL *(papal)* bula.

bull³ [bʊl] **(a load of old) bull,** *n sl (nonsense)* chorradas *fpl.*

● **to shoot the bull,** *sl* rajar, charlar.

bulldog ['bʊldɒg] **1** *n* buldog *m.* **2** *fig (person)* persona tenaz, persona porfiada.

■ **the bulldog breed,** los ingleses *(como arquetipos de tenacidad y coraje).* ‖ **bulldog clip,** clip *m* de pinza.

bulldoze ['bʊldəʊz] *t (dig)* excavar con un bulldozer; *(clear land)* allanar con un bulldozer; *(demolish)* derribar con un bulldozer.

● **to bulldoze sb. into doing sth.,** *fig* intimidar a algn. para que haga algo: *they bulldozed him into giving them the money,* lo intimidaron para que les diera el dinero. ‖ **to bulldoze one's way through,** *fig* abrirse paso a empujones. ‖ **to bulldoze one's way in,** *fig* entrar a empujones. ‖ **to bulldoze one's way into a conversation,** *fig* meter baza.

bulldozer ['bʊldəʊzəʳ] *n* bulldozer *m,* maquina excavadora.

bullet ['bʊlɪt] *n* bala.

● **to bite the bullet,** *fig* mostrar estoicismo.

■ **bullet hole,** agujero de bala. ‖ **bullet train,** tren *m* bala. ‖ **rubber bullet,** bala de goma. ‖ **plastic bullet,** bala de plástico.

bulletin ['bʊlɪtɪn] **1** *n (publication)* boletín *m.* **2** MED MIL parte *m.* **3** *(communiqué)* comunicado.

bulletin-board ['bʊlətɪnbɔːd] *n* US tablón *m* de anuncios.

bullet-proof ['bʊlɪtpruːf] *adj* antibalas.

■ **bullet-proof vest,** chaleco antibalas.

bullfight ['bʊlfaɪt] *n* corrida de toros, lidia.

● **to go to a bullfight,** ir a los toros.

bullfighter ['bʊlfaɪtəʳ] *n* torero,-a.

bullfighting ['bʊlfaɪtɪŋ] *n* los toros *mpl;* *(art)* tauromaquia.

bullfinch ['bʊlfɪntʃ] *n* ORN camachuelo.

bullfrog ['bʊlfrɒg] *n* ZOOL rana mugidora.

bullion ['bʊljən] *n (gold)* oro en lingotes; *(silver)* plata en lingotes.

bullish ['bʊlɪʃ] **1** *adj* COMM alcista, en alza. **2** *(optimistic)* optimista. **3** *(impetuous)* impetuoso,-a.

bullock ['bʊlək] *n* toro castrado, buey *m.*

bullring ['bʊlrɪŋ] *n* plaza de toros.

bull's-eye ['bʊlzaɪ] **1** *n (target)* diana. **2** *(score)* acierto. **3** MAR *(porthole)* portilla.

● **to score a bull's-eye,** dar en el blanco.

■ **bull's-eye glass,** vidrio de ojo de buey. ‖ **bull's-eye window,** ojo de buey.

bullshit ['bʊlʃɪt] **1** *n* taboo *(nonsense)* chorradas *fpl.* – **2** *t* taboo liar a algn. (con historias): *stop bullshitting me!,* ¡no me líes con tus historias! – **3** *i* taboo parir chorradas.

● **to talk bullshit,** taboo decir chorradas.

▲ *pt & pp* **bullshitted,** *ger* **bullshitting.**

bully¹ ['bʊlɪ] **1** *n* matón,-ona. – **2** *t (intimidate)* intimidar, atemorizar. **3** *(force, coerce)* coaccionar.

● **to bully sb. into doing sth.,** coaccionar a algn. para que haga algo: *they bullied him into going,* lo coaccionaron para que se fuera.

▲ *(sustantivo) pl* **bullies;** *(verbo) pt & pp* **bullied,** *ger* **bullying.**

bully² ['bʊlɪ] **1** *n* SP *(hockey)* saque *m* inicial. – **2** *i* SP *(hockey)* hacer el saque inicial.

▲ *(sustantivo) pl* **bullies;** *(verbo) pt & pp* **bullied,** *ger* **bullying.**

bully³ ['bʊlɪ] *adj* US estupendo,-a.

● **bully for you!,** *fam* ¡pues fíjate!

bully-beef ['bʊlɪbiːf] *n* carne *f* de vacuno en conserva.

bully-boy ['bʊlɪbɔɪ] *n* matón *m,* gorila *m.*

bullying ['bʊlɪɪŋ] **1** *n (intimidation)* amenazas *fpl,* intimidación *f.* **2** *(coercion)* coacción *f.*

bully-off ['bʊlɪɒf] **1** *n* SP *(hockey)* saque *m* inicial. – **2** *i* SP *(hockey)* hacer el saque inicial.

▲ *(sustantivo) pl* **bully-offs;** *(verbo) pt & pp* **bullied-off,** *ger* **bullying-off.**

bulrush ['bʊlrʌʃ] *n* BOT anea.

bulwark ['bʊlwɔːk] **1** *n (rampart)* baluarte *m.* **2** *(breakwater)* rompeolas *m.*

bum¹ [bʌm] *n* GB *fam (bottom)* culo.

bum² [bʌm] **1** *n* US *fam (tramp)* vagabundo,-a. **2** US *fam (idler)* vago,-a, holgazán-ana. **3** US *fam (wretch) (pobre)* desgraciado,-a. – **4** *adj* US *fam (faulty)* defectuoso,-a. **5** US *fam (shoddy)* de pacotilla, de mala calidad. **6** US *fam (useless object, information)* que no vale, inútil. – **7** *t fam (scrounge)* gorrear, sablear: *can I bum a cigarrette?,* ¿te puedo gorrear un pitillo?

◆ **to bum around 1** *t insep* US *fam (roam)* recorrer sin propósito fijo por, vagar por: *he's bumming around the States,* está vagando por los Estados Unidos. – **2** *i (roam)* ir de un sitio a otro sin rumbo. **3** US *fam (be idle)* rascarse la barriga, no rascar dos: *he just bums around all day,* pasa todo el día rascándose la barriga.

● **to bum sth. off sb.,** *fam* gorronear algo a algn. ‖ **to give sb. the bum's rush,** mandar a algn. a hacer puñetas. ‖ **to be on the bum,** US *fam* vivir de gorra.

■ **bum rap,** US *fam* acusación *f* falsa. ‖ **bum steer,** US *fam* información *f* falsa.

bumbag ['bʌmbæg] *n* riñonera *f.*

bumble ['bʌmbəl] **1** *i (blunder)* hacer una plancha. **2 to bumble (on),** *(speak incoherently)* farfullar.

◆ **to bumble along** *i* andar a tropezones.

bumblebee ['bʌmbəlbiː] *n* ZOOL abejorro.

bumbler ['bʌmbələʳ] *n* torpe *mf,* manazas *mf.*

bumbling ['bʌmbəlɪŋ] *adj* torpe, manazas.

bumf [bʌmf] *n* GB *fam* propaganda, papeleo.

bump [bʌmp] **1** *n (blow)* golpe *m,* batacazo. **2** *(collision)* choque *m,* colisión *f.* **3** *(on head)* chichón *m;* *(swelling)* hinchazón *m;* *(lump)* bulto. **4** *(dent)* abolladura. **5** *(on road)* bache *m.* **6** AER bache *m,* rebote *m.* – **7** *t* darse un golpe en: *he bumped his head,* se dio un golpe en la cabeza. **8** dar un golpe a: *he bumped me with his shopping trolley,* me dio un golpe con el carro de la compra. – **9** *i* chocar **(into,** con), topar **(into,** contra): *his car bumped into my moped,* su coche chocó con mi moto. **10** *(collide)* chocar, colisionar.

◆ **to bump along** *i (vehicle)* traquetear. ‖ **to bump into** *t insep fam* encontrar por casualidad, tropezar con. ‖ **to bump off** *t sep sl* cargar, liquidar. ‖ **to bump up** *t sep (prices)* aumentar.

● **with a bump,** dándose un batacazo, ¡catapún! ‖ **to bump sth. against/on sth.,** darse con algo contra algo: *she bumped her knee on the table,* se dio con la rodilla contra la mesa.

bumper ['bʌmpəʳ] **1** *n* parachoques *m.* – **2** *adj* abundante: *a bumper crop,* una cosecha abundante.

■ **bumper cars,** autochoques *mpl.* ‖ **bumper issue,** *(of magazine)* edición *f* especial.

bumper-to-bumper [ˈbʌmpətəˈbʌmpə˞] *adv* (*vehicles*) en caravana.
bumph [bʌmf] *n* GB *fam* → **bumf**.
bumpkin [ˈbʌmpkɪn] *n* paleto,-a, palurdo,-a.
bumptious [ˈbʌmtʃəs] *adj* presumido,-a, engreído,-a.
bumpy [ˈbʌmpɪ] **1** *adj* (*surface*) desigual, accidentado,-a. **2** (*road*) lleno,-a de baches. **3** (*journey*) con muchos baches; (*flight*) con turbulencias.
▲ *comp* **bumpier**, *superl* **bumpiest**.
bun [bʌn] **1** *n* (*bread*) panecillo; (*sweet*) bollo. **2** (*cake*) ma(g)dalena. **3** (*hair*) moño.
● **to have a bun in the oven**, *fam* (*be pregnant*) estar preñada, estar en estado.
bunch [bʌntʃ] **1** *n* manojo: *a bunch of leeks,* un manojo de puerros; *a bunch of keys,* un manojo de llaves. **2** (*flowers*) ramo. **3** (*fruit*) racimo: *a bunch of grapes/bananas,* un racimo de uvas/plátanos. **4** *fam* (*group of people*) grupo *m*; (*gang*) pandilla *f.* – **5** *t* atar en un manojo. – **6 bunches,** *npl* (*hair*) coletas *fpl.*
◆ **to bunch together** I *t sep* agrupar: *they bunched together all the 11 year-olds,* agruparon a todos los niños de 11 años. – **2** *i* apretujarse. ‖ **to bunch up** *i* (*sit close together*) apretujarse, estar apretujado,-a; (*make room*) hacer sitio: *they were bunched up on the sofa,* estaban apretujados en el sofá; *bunch up a bit!,* ¡hazme un poco de sitio!
● **to wear one's hair in bunches**, llevar coletas. ‖ **a whole bunch of,** *fam* un montón de, mogollón de: *there were a whole bunch of fans waiting for him,* hubo un montón de fans esperándole. ‖ **the best of the bunch**, lo mejor de lo mejor. ‖ **a bunch of fives,** *sl* un puñetazo.
bundle [ˈbʌndəl] **1** *n* (*clothes*) fardo, bulto. **2** (*wood*) haz *m.* **3** (*papers, banknotes*) fajo. **4** (*keys*) manojo. – **5** *t* atar en un fardo, atar en un bulto.
◆ **to bundle into** *t sep* (*push forcibly*) introducir a empujones, meter a empujones: *they bundled him into a taxi,* lo introdujeron a empujones en un taxi. ‖ **to bundle off** *t sep* echar, despachar: *they bundled them off the premises,* les echaron del local.
● **to be a bundle of nerves**, estar hecho,-a un manojo de nervios. ‖ **to go a bundle on sth.,** *fam* chiflarle a uno algo: *they go a bundle on second-hand clothes,* les chifla la ropa de segunda mano.
bung [bʌŋ] **1** *n* (*stopper*) tapón *m*; (*of barrel*) bitoque *m.* **2** GB SP (*bribe*) soborno *m.* – **3** *t* taponar. **4** GB *fam* (*put*) poner, meter: *bung it on the table,* ponlo encima de la mesa. **5** GB *fam* (*serve*) poner: *bung me another beer in here,* ponme otra cerveza aquí. **6** GB *fam* (*throw*) tirar: *bung it in the bin,* tíralo en la papelera.
◆ **to bung up** *t sep fam* atascar: *they've bunged up the drains,* han atascado el desagüe.
● **to be bunged up,** (*pipes, drains, etc*) estar atascado,-a; (*with cold, flu*) estar congestionado,-a. ‖ **to have a bunged up nose,** tener la nariz tapada.
bungalow [ˈbʌŋɡələʊ] *n* bungalow *m.*
bungee [ˈbʌndʒɪ] *n* correa elástica, goma.
■ **bungee jumping**, salto elástico.
bungle [ˈbʌŋɡəl] **1** *t* (*botch*) chapucear: *they bungled the job,* chapucearon el trabajo. **2** (*mess up*) pifiar: *they bungled the robbery,* pifiaron el atraco.
● **to bungle it,** pifiarla. ‖ **to make a bungle of sth.,** salir fatal algo a algn.: *he made a bungle of the exam,* el examen le salió fatal.
bungler [ˈbʌŋɡələ˞] *n* chapucero,-a.
bungling [ˈbʌŋɡəlɪŋ] **1** *n* (*clumsiness*) torpeza. – **2** *adj* (*clumsy*) torpe. **3** (*worker*) chapucero,-a.

bunion [ˈbʌnjən] *n* MED juanete *m.*
bunk[1] [bʌŋk] *n* (*bed*) litera.
bunk[2] [bʌŋk] *n* (*nonsense*) tonterías *fpl.*
bunk[3] [bʌŋk] **to do a bunk**, *phr* irse a la francesa, poner pies en polvorosa.
bunk-bed [ˈbʌŋkbed] *n* litera.
▲ *pl* **bunk-beds**.
bunker [ˈbʌŋkə˞] **1** *n* MIL búnker *m.* **2** (*golf*) búnker *m.* **3** (*for coal*) carbonera; (*on ship*) pañol *m* del carbón. – **4** *t* (*ship*) abastecer de carbón.
● **to be bunkered,** *fig* estar en un callejón sin salida.
bunkum [ˈbʌŋkəm] *n* tonterías *fpl*, desatinos *mpl.*
bunk-up [ˈbʌŋkʌp] **to give sb. a bunk-up,** *phr* aupar a algn.
bunny [ˈbʌnɪ] *n fam* conejito.
■ **bunny girl**, chica de club.
▲ *pl* **bunnies**.
bunting[1] [ˈbʌntɪŋ] *n* (*flags*) banderines *mpl.*
bunting[2] [ˈbʌntɪŋ] *n* (*bird*) escribano *m.*
buoy [bɔɪ] **1** *n* (*navegation mark*) boya, baliza. **2** (*lifebuoy*) boya salvavidas. – **3 to buoy (out),** *t* señalar con balizas, señalar con boyas, abalizar.
◆ **to buoy up 1** *t sep* mantener a flote. **2** *fig* dar aliento a, dar ánimos a: *she tried to buoy him up,* intentó darle ánimos.
buoyancy [ˈbɔɪənsɪ] **1** *n* flotabilidad *f.* **2** (*cheerfulness*) buen humor *m.* **3** (*optimism*) optimismo. **4** COMM FIN tendencia alcista.
buoyant [ˈbɔɪənt] **1** *adj* flotante. **2** (*cheerful*) animado,-a. **3** (*optimistic*) optimista. **4** COMM FIN con tendencia alcista.
burble [ˈbɜːbəl] **1** *n* (*incoherent speech*) murmullo. – **2** *i* (*speak incoherently*) murmullar, farfullar.
◆ **to burble on** *i* divagar.
burden [ˈbɜːdən] **1** *n* carga. – **2** *t* cargar.
● **to burden sb. with problems,** cargar a algn. con problemas: *he burdened her with his problems,* la cargó con sus problemas. ‖ **to be burdened with,** tener que cargar con: *he's burdened with responsibilities,* tiene que cargar con muchas responsabilidades. ‖ **to be a burden to sb.,** ser una carga para algn.
■ **burden of proof,** JUR carga de la prueba. ‖ **tax burden,** FIN gravamen *m.*
burdensome [ˈbɜːdənsəm] *adj* pesado,-a, oneroso,-a.
bureau [ˈbjʊərəʊ] **1** *n* (*desk*) escritorio. **2** US (*office*) oficina. **3** US (*agency*) agencia. **4** US (*chest of drawers*) cómoda *f.* **5** US POL departamento del estado.
■ **employment bureau,** oficina de empleo. ‖ **bureau de change,** oficina de cambio.
▲ *pl* **bureaus** o **bureaux** [ˈbjʊərəʊ].
bureaucracy [bjʊəˈrɒkrəsɪ] **1** *n* (*body, administration*) burocracia. **2** (*paperwork*) burocracia, papeleo.
▲ *pl* **bureaucracies**. En **2** es *invariable* es *invariable*.
bureaucrat [ˈbjʊərəkræt] *n* burócrata *mf.*
bureaucratic [bjʊərəˈkrætɪk] *adj* burocrático,-a.
burgeon [ˈbɜːdʒən] **1** *i lit* (*flower*) florecer; (*plant, tree*) retoñar. **2** *fig* (*talent, potential*) desarrollarse.
burgeoning [ˈbɜːdʒənɪŋ] **1** *adj lit* (*flower*) en flor; (*plant, tree*) en brote. **2** *fig* en ciernes: *a burgeoning poet,* un poeta en ciernes.
burger [ˈbɜːɡə˞] *n* hamburguesa.
burglar [ˈbɜːɡlə˞] *n* ladrón,-ona.
■ **burglar alarm,** alarma antirrobo.
burglarize [ˈbɜːɡləraɪz] *t* US → **burgle**.
burglar-proof [ˈbɜːɡləpruːf] *adj* antirrobo.
burglary [ˈbɜːɡlərɪ] *n* (*gen*) robo; JUR allanamiento de morada.

▲ *pl burglaries.*
burgle ['bɜːgəl] *t* robar: *they burgled his house,* entraron en su casa a robar.
Burgundian [bɜː'gʌndɪən] **1** *adj* borgoñón,-ona. – **2** *n* borgoñón,-ona.
Burgundy ['bɜːgəndɪ] **1** *n* Borgoña. **2** *(wine)* borgoña *m.*
burial ['berɪəl] *n* entierro.
■ **burial ground,** cementerio. ‖ **burial mound,** túmulo. ‖ **burial place,** lugar *m* de sepultura. ‖ **burial vault,** cripta.
Burkina-Faso [bɜːkiːnə'fæsəʊ] *n* Burkina Faso.
Burkinese [bɜːkɪ'niːz] **1** *adj* burkinés,-esa. – **2** *n* burkinés,-esa.
burlap ['bɜːlæp] *n* arpillera, harpillera.
burlesque [bɜː'lesk] **1** *n* parodia burlesca. **2** *(genre)* género burlesco, vodevil *m.* **3** US *(show)* revista. – **4** *adj* burlesco,-a, de vodevil. – **5** *t* parodiar.
burly ['bɜːlɪ] *adj* fornido,-a, corpulento,-a.
▲ *comp burlier, superl burliest.*
Burma ['bɜːmə] *n* Birmania.
Burmese [bɜː'miːz] **1** *adj* birmano,-a. – **2** *n* *(person)* birmano,-a. **3** *(language)* birmano. – **4** the Burmese, *npl* los birmanos *mpl.*
burn¹ [bɜːn] **1** *n* quemadura: *he suffered third-degree burns,* sufrió quemaduras de tercer grado. – **2** *t* quemar: *they burnt all the old magazines,* quemaron todas las revistas viejas. **3** *(coal)* quemar; *(fuel)* gastar, consumir. **5** *(food)* quemar: *he's burnt the toast,* se le han quemado las tostadas. **6** *(land, plants)* abrasar. **7** *(body)* incinerar. **8** MED *(cauterise)* cauterizar. **9** *(harden bricks)* cocer. **10** *(put to death)* quemar: *she was burnt at the stake,* la quemaron en la hoguera. – **11** *i* *(blaze, glow)* arder: *we saw the building burning from the rooftop,* vimos como ardía el edificio desde el terrado; *the building burnt for two days,* el edificio ardió durante dos días. **12** *(candle, light)* estar encendido,-a. **13** *(food)* quemarse: *the steak has burnt,* el bistec se ha quemado. **14** *fig* *(passion, rage, desire)* arder (**with,** de).
◆ **to burn away 1** *t sep* consumir: *the flames burnt part of door away,* las llamas consumieron parte de la puerta. – **2** *i* consumirse. **3** *(keep burning)* seguir quemando, seguir ardiendo. ‖ **to burn down 1** *t sep* incendiar, quemar totalmente: *they burnt the house down,* incendiaron la casa. – **2** *i* quemarse, quedarse totalmente destruido,-a por las llamas. ‖ **to burn off** *t sep* *(paint, varnish)* quitar (con soplete); *(calories)* quemar. ‖ **to burn out 1** *i* *(fire)* extinguirse. **2** *(fuse, bulb)* fundirse. **3** *fig* *(person)* quemarse; *(machine)* gastarse. ‖ **to burn up 1** *i* *(building, etc)* abrasarse, quedarse totalmente destruido,-a por las llamas. **2** *fig* *(with heat)* abrasarse de calor, achicharrarse. – **3** *t sep* *(fuel)* consumir.
● **to burn to a cinder,** calcinar, reducir a cenizas. ‖ **burn low,** no quemar bien. ‖ **to burn well,** quemar bien. ‖ **to burn one's boats,** *fig* quemar el último cartucho. ‖ **to burn the candle at both ends,** *fig* hacer de la noche día. ‖ **to burn one's fingers,** *fig* pillarse los dedos. ‖ **to burn the midnight oil,** *fig* quemarse las pestañas. ‖ **to burn a hole in sth.,** hacer un agujero en algo quemándolo. ‖ **to burn a hole in one's pocket,** *fig* quemarle a uno el bolsillo. ‖ **to be burned alive,** ser quemado,-a vivo,-a. ‖ **to get burnt,** quemarse: *if you touch it you'll get burnt,* si lo tocas te quemarás. ‖ **to have a burnt taste,** saber a quemado.
▲ *pt & pp burnt o burned* [bɜːnd].
burn² [bɜːn] *n* *(stream)* arroyo.
burner ['bɜːnə'] *n* *(on cooker, lamp)* quemador *m.*
● **to put sth. on the back burner,** aparcar algo, dejar algo aparcado.

■ **Bunsen burner,** mechero Bunsen.
burning ['bɜːnɪŋ] **1** *n* *(of waste, body)* incineración *f.* **2** *(of building)* incendio. **3** *(of skin)* quemadura. **4** *(sensation)* escozor *m.* – **5** *adj* *(on fire)* en llamas, ardiendo. **6** *(sun)* abrasador,-ra, de justicia; *(heat)* achicharrante. **7** *(desire, need)* ardiente.
● **to be burning hot,** hacer un calor achicharrante.
■ **burning issue / burning question,** cuestión *f* candente.
burnish ['bɜːnɪʃ] **1** *n* bruñido. – **2** *t* bruñir.
burnt [bɜːnt] *pt & pp* → **burn.**
burnt-out ['bɜːntaʊt] **1** *adj* *(building, car)* carbonizado,-a. **2** *fig* *(person)* quemado,-a, caduco,-a.
burp [bɜːp] **1** *n fam* eructo. – **2** *t fam* *(baby)* hacer eructar. – **3** *i fam* eructar.
burr [bɜː'] **1** *n* *(whirring)* zumbido, runrún *m.* **2** *(accent)* acento regional que pronuncia la "r" de forma gutural. **3** TECH *(rough edge)* rebaba. **4** TECH *(dental drill)* fresa. – **5** *i* *(whirr)* zumbar, runrunear. **6** *(accent)* pronunciar la "r" de forma gutural.
burrow ['bʌrəʊ] **1** *n* madriguera. – **2** *t* excavar, cavar. – **3** *i* excavar una madriguera.
● **to burrow into sth.,** *fig* investigar.
bursar ['bɜːsə'] **1** *n* *(at college, university)* tesorero,-a. **2** *(holder of scholarship)* bursario,-a.
bursary ['bɜːsərɪ] *n* *(scholarship)* beca.
▲ *pl bursaries.*
burst [bɜːst] **1** *n* *(of balloon, pipe)* reventón *m*; *(of tyre)* pinchazo, reventón *m.* **2** *(explosion)* estallido, explosión *f.* **3** *(of activity, anger)* arranque *m.* **4** *(of speed)* arrancada. **5** *(of applause)* salva. **6** *(of gunfire)* ráfaga. – **7** *t* *(balloon, pipe)* reventar; *(tyre)* pinchar, reventar. – **8** *i* *(balloon, pipe)* reventarse; *(tyre)* pincharse, reventarse.
◆ **to burst in** *i* entrar precipitadamente. ‖ **to burst into** *t insep* irrumpir en: *the police burst into the room,* la policía irrumpió en la habitación. ‖ **to burst open 1** *i* *(bud, flower)* abrirse. **2** *fig* abrirse de golpe: *the door burst open and they marched in,* la puerta se abrió de golpe y entraron. ‖ **to burst through 1** *t insep* *(cordon, barrier)* atravesar a empujones, romper. **2** *fig* *(sun)* brillar a través de: *the sun burst through the clouds,* el sol brilló a través de las nubes. – **3** *i* *(sun)* brillar repentinamente.
● **to burst forth,** *(water)* brotar, salir a chorro. ‖ **to burst into flames,** estallar en llamas. ‖ **to burst into song,** empezar a cantar. ‖ **to burst into tears,** echarse a llorar. ‖ **to burst out crying/laughing,** echarse a llorar/reír. ‖ **to burst its banks,** *(river)* salirse de madre.
▲ *pt & pp burst* [bɜːst].
bursting ['bɜːstɪŋ] *adj* muy lleno,-a, lleno,-a a rebosar.
● **to be bursting at the seams,** *fig* estar a tope. ‖ **to be bursting to do sth.,** reventar por hacer algo: *he was bursting to tell her,* reventaba por decírselo. ‖ **to be bursting with health,** rebosar de salud.
burton ['bɜːtən] **to go for a burton,** *phr* GB *fam* *(gen)* estropearse; *(hopes, plans)* ir al traste.
Burundi [bə'rʊndɪ] *n* Burundi.
Burundian [bə'rʊndɪən] **1** *n* burundés,-esa. – **2** *adj* burundés,-esa.
bury ['berɪ] **1** *t* enterrar: *they buried the treasure under that tree,* enterraron el tesoro bajo aquel árbol. **2** *(body)* sepultar, enterrar. **3** *fig* *(outlive)* enterrar: *she's buried five husbands,* ha enterrado a seis maridos.
● **to be buried,** recibir sepultura. ‖ **to be buried at sea,** recibir sepultura en el mar. ‖ **to be buried alive,** ser enterrado,-a vivo,-a. ‖ **to bury os. in ones' work,**

fig enfrascarse en el trabajo. ‖ **to bury one's face in one's hands,** *fig* taparse el rostro con las manos. ‖ **to be buried in thought,** *fig* estar ensimismado,-a.
▲ *pt & pp* **buried,** *ger* **burying**.

bus [bʌs] **1** *n* autobús *m*, bus *m*. **2** COMPUT bus *m*. – **3** *t* transportar en autobús, llevar en autobús: *they bus them to school,* les llevan a la escuela en autobús.
■ **bus conductor,** cobrador. ‖ **bus conductress,** cobradora. ‖ **bus lane,** carril *m* de autobuses. ‖ **bus route,** línea de autobuses. ‖ **bus shelter,** parada de autobús cubierta. ‖ **bus station,** estación *f* de autobuses. ‖ **bus stop,** parada de autobús.
▲ *(sustantivo)* *pl* buses, US *busses*; *(verbo)* *pt & pp* **bussed** *ger,* **bussing**.

busby ['bʌzbɪ] *n* GB MIL *gorro alto de piel negra.*
▲ *pl* **busbies**.

bush[1] [bʊʃ] **1** *n* *(plant)* arbusto. **2** *(land)* breña. – **3** bushes, *npl* *(thicket)* matorral *m,* maleza.
■ **the bush,** *(in Australia)* el monte. ‖ **bush telegraph,** radio macuto.

bush[2] [bʊʃ] **1** *n* TECH *(lining)* forro. – **2** *t* TECH forrar.

bush-baby ['bʊʃbeɪbɪ] *n* ZOOL lemúrido.
▲ *pl* **bush-babies**.

bushed [bʊʃt] **to be bushed,** *phr fam* estar hecho,-a polvo.

bushel ['bʊʃəl] *n* medida de capacidad para áridos.
▲ En Gran Bretaña equivale a 36,37 litros y en Estados Unidos a 35,24 litros.

Bushman ['bʊʃmən] **1** *n* *(person)* bosquimano,-a. **2** *(language)* bosquimano. – **3** *adj* bosquimano,-a.
▲ *pl* **Bushmen** ['bʊʃmən].

bushy ['bʊʃɪ] *adj* espeso,-a, tupido,-a.
● **to have bushy eyebrows,** ser cejudo,-a.
▲ *comp* **bushier,** *superl* **bushiest**.

busily ['bɪzɪlɪ] *adv* con afán.

business ['bɪznəs] **1** *n* *(commerce)* negocios *mpl:* *the business world,* el mundo de los negocios. **2** *(firm)* negocio, empresa: *he's got a small business on the coast,* tiene un pequeño negocio en la costa. **3** *(affair)* asunto, tema *m: I've got business to discuss with the manager,* tengo asuntos que tratar con el director; *it's none of your business,* no es asunto tuyo; *does he know about the business with the money?,* ¿se ha enterado del asunto del dinero?.
● **it's my** *(your, etc)* **business to ...,** me *(te, etc)* incumbe ...: *it's my business to investigate the case,* me incumbe investigar el caso. ‖ **to be away on business,** estar (fuera) de viaje. ‖ **to be big business,** ser un buen negocio. ‖ **to be in business,** dedicarse al mundo de los negocios. ‖ **to be the business,** *fam* molar, ser muy guay: *these shoes really are the business,* estos zapatos son muy guays. ‖ **to do business with sb.,** comerciar con algn., tener relaciones comerciales con algn. ‖ **to get down to business,** entrar en materia. ‖ **to go out of business,** quebrar. ‖ **to have no business to** + *inf,* no tener ningún derecho a + *inf: you had no business to tell him,* no tenías ningún derecho a decírselo. ‖ **to mean business,** ir en serio. ‖ **to put sb. out of business,** hacer que algn. quiebre. ‖ **to run a business,** llevar un negocio. ‖ **to send sb. about his** *(her, etc)* **business,** mandar a algn. de paseo. ‖ **to set up a business,** montar un negocio. ‖ **mind your own business!,** ¡no te metas donde no te llaman! ‖ **line of business,** profesión *f: what line of business are you in?,* ¿a qué te dedicas?. ‖ **business before pleasure,** primero es la obligación que la devoción. ‖ **business is business,** el negocio es el negocio.

■ **big business,** grandes negocios *mpl.* ‖ **business administration,** administración *f* de negocios. ‖ **business card,** tarjeta de visita, tarjeta comercial. ‖ **business centre,** centro de negocios. ‖ **business consultant,** asesor,-ra de empresas. ‖ **business consultancy,** asesoría de empresas. ‖ **business deal,** trato comercial. ‖ **business district,** área de negocios, zona comercial. ‖ **business hours,** horario comercial. ‖ **business of the day,** orden *m* del día. ‖ **business manager,** director,-ra de empresas. ‖ **business school,** escuela de negocios. ‖ **business studies,** estudios *mpl* empresariales, empresariales *mpl.* ‖ **business trip,** viaje *m* de negocios.

businesslike ['bɪznəslaɪk] **1** *adj* *(responsible)* formal, serio,-a. **2** *(systematic)* metódico,-a, sistemático,-a. **3** *(efficient)* eficaz. **4** *(practical)* práctico,-a.

businessman ['bɪznəsmən] *n* hombre *m* de negocios, empresario.
▲ *pl* **businessmen** ['bɪznəsmen].

businesswoman ['bɪznəswʊmən] *n* mujer *m* de negocios, empresaria.
▲ *pl* **businesswomen** ['bɪznəswɪmɪn].

busker ['bʌskə'] *n* GB músico callejero,-a.

busman ['bʌsmən] *n* conductor *m* de autobús.
■ **busman's holiday,** tiempo libre dedicado una actividad similar a la del trabajo habitual.

bust[1] [bʌst] **1** *n* *(bosom)* busto, pecho. **2** *(sculpture)* busto.

bust[2] [bʌst] **1** *n fam* *(bankruptcy)* quiebra, bancarrota. **2** *fam* *(police raid)* redada. – **3** *adj fam* *(broken)* roto,-a. **4** *(burst)* reventado,-a. **5** *fam* *(bankrupt)* en quiebra, arruinado,-a. – **6** *t fam* *(break)* romper. **7** *(burst)* reventar. **8** *fam* *(make bankrupt)* llevar a la quiebra. **9** *fam* *(raid)* organizar una redada en, registrar: *the police busted the club,* la policía organizó una redada en el club. **10** *fam* *(arrest)* pillar, pescar. – **11** *i* *(break)* romperse. **12** *(burst)* reventarse.
◆ **to bust up 1** *t sep fam* *(marriage, relationship)* romper. – **2** *i fam* *(marriage, relationship)* irse al traste.
● **to go bust,** *fam* quebrar.
▲ *pt & pp* **bust** o **busted**.

bustard ['bʌstəd] *n* ORN avutarda.

busted ['bʌstɪd] *adj* → **bust**[2].

bustle[1] ['bʌsəl] *n* bullicio, ajetreo: *the bustle of the city,* el bullicio de la gran ciudad.
◆ **to bustle about 1** *t insep* andar ajetreado,-a en: *she bustled about the kitchen,* andaba ajetreada en la cocina. – **2** *i* ir y venir, no parar: *she's always bustling about,* es que no para.
◆ **to bustle into** *t sep* introducir sin miramientos: *they bustled her into the court,* la introdujeron en el juzgado sin miramientos.

bustle[2] ['bʌsəl] *n* *(of skirt)* polizón *m.*

bustling ['bʌsəlɪŋ] **1** *adj* *(place)* bullicioso,-a. **2** *(person)* ajetreado,-a, activo,-a.

bust-up ['bʌstʌp] *n fam* riña, camorra.
● **to have a bust-up,** *fam* reñir.

busy ['bɪzɪ] **1** *adj* *(person)* ocupado,-a, atareado,-a. **2** *(street, place)* concurrido,-a. **3** *(day)* ajetreado,-a. **4** US *(telephone)* comunicando: *the line was busy,* estaba comunicando. – **5** *n fam* *(police officer)* poli *mf.*
● **to busy os. doing sth.,** ocuparse en hacer algo: *he busied himself washing the dishes,* se ocupó en fregar los platos. ‖ **to be busy doing sth.,** estar ocupado,-a en hacer algo: *she was busy revising her notes,* estaba ocupada en repasar los apuntes. ‖ **to be as busy as a bee,** estar que no para, estar muy ocupado,-a. ‖ **to get busy,** *fam* *(work)* ponerse a trabajar; *(hurry)* darse

prisa. ‖ **to keep os. busy,** mantenerse ocupado,-a. ‖ **to keep sb. busy,** mantener ocupado,-a algn.
■ **busy Lizzie,** ʙᴏᴛ alegría de la casa. ‖ **the busies,** *fam (police)* la poli, la pasma.
▲ *(verbo)* pt & pp **busied,** ger **busying**; *(adjetivo)* comp **busier,** superl **busiest**.

busybody ['bɪzɪbɒdɪ] *n* entremetido,-a, fisgón,-ona.
▲ *pl* **busybodies**.

but [bʌt] **1** *conj* pero: *it's cold, but dry,* hace frío, pero no llueve; *I'd like to, but I can't,* me gustaría, pero no puedo. **2** *(after negative)* sino: *not two, but three,* no dos, sino tres. **3** *(after negative with verb)* sino que: *she told him not to wait,* le dijo que no se esperara, sino que se fuera para casa. – **4** *adv (nada)* más que, no ... sino, solamente, sólo,: *he spoke nothing but the truth,* no dijo nada más que la verdad; *she is but three days old,* sólo tiene tres días; *he spoke to her but a few days ago,* sólo hace un par de días que habló con ella. – **5** *prep* excepto, salvo, menos: *everyone but me,* todos menos yo; *I can meet you any day but Friday,* te puedo ver cualquier día excepto el viernes; *he'll do anything except scrub the floor,* hará cualquier cosa salvo fregar el suelo. – **6** *n* pero: *there are no buts about it,* no hay pero que valga.
● **but for,** de no ser por, si no fuera por: *but for him, we would have failed,* de no ser por él, habríamos fracasado; *but for his help we would be bankrupt,* si no fuera por su ayuda estaríamos en la ruina. ‖ **had I but + pp ...,** si lo + *imperf subj* ...: *had I but known,* si lo hubiera sabido. ‖ **there is nothing for it but to + inf,** no hay más remedio que + *inf*: *there's nothing for it but to report him,* no hay más remedio que denunciarlo. ‖ **the last but one,** el/la penúltimo,-a.

butane ['bjuːteɪn] *n* ᴄʜᴇᴍ butano.
■ **butane bottle,** bombona (de butano). ‖ **butane gas,** gas *m* butano.

butcher ['bʊtʃəʳ] **1** *n* carnicero,-a. – **2** *t (meat)* matar. **3** *(massacre)* masacrar, hacer una carnicería con. **4** *fig (book, play)* destrozar.

butcher's ['bʊtʃəz] *n* carnicería.
● **to have a butcher's,** ɢʙ *fam* echar un vistazo. ‖ **give me a butcher's,** ɢʙ *fam* déjame ver.
■ **butcher's block,** tajo.

butchery ['bʊtʃərɪ] *n* carnicería.

butler ['bʌtləʳ] *n* mayordomo.

butt[1] [bʌt] **1** *n (with head)* cabezazo, topetazo. – **2** *t (goat, ram)* topetar, dar un topetazo; *(person)* dar un cabezazo. – **3** *i (goat, ram)* dar topetazos; *(person)* dar un cabezazo.
◆ **to butt into** *t insep* meterse en: *he butted into our conversation,* se metió en nuestra conversación. ‖ **to butt in** *i* meter baza.

butt[2] [bʌt] **1** *n (of rifle)* culata. **2** *(of cigarette)* colilla. **3** ᴜs *fam (bottom)* culo.
● **to work one's butt off,** ᴜs *fam* herniarse, romperse los cuernos.

butt[3] [bʌt] **1** *n (target)* blanco. – **2 butts,** *npl (shooting range)* campo de tiro.
● **to be the butt of sb.'s jokes,** ser el blanco de las bromas de algn.

butt[4] [bʌt] **1** *n (barrel)* tonel *m*. **2** *(for water)* aljibe *m*.

butter ['bʌtəʳ] **1** *n* mantequilla. – **2** *t* untar con mantequilla.
◆ **to butter up** *t sep fam* dar coba a.
● **to look as if butter wouldn't melt in one's mouth,** parecer no haber roto nunca un plato, parecer una mosquita muerta.
■ **butter dish,** mantequera. ‖ **butter knife,** cuchillo

para la mantequilla. ‖ **salted butter,** mantequilla con sal. ‖ **unsalted butter,** mantequilla sin sal.

butter-bean ['bʌtəbiːn] *n* judión *m*.

buttercup ['bʌtəkʌp] *n* ʙᴏᴛ botón *m* de oro, ranúnculo.

butterfingered ['bʌtəfɪŋgəd] *adj* manazas, torpe.

butterfingers ['bʌtəfɪŋgəz] *n* manazas *mf*, torpe *mf*.

butterfly ['bʌtəflaɪ] **1** *n* mariposa. **2** sᴘ *(swimming)* braza mariposa, mariposa.
● **to have butterflies in one's stomach,** *fig* sentir un cosquilleo en el estómago, estar nervioso,-a.
▲ *pl* **butterflies**.

buttermilk ['bʌtəmɪlk] *n* suero de la leche.

buttery ['bʌtərɪ] *adj* mantecoso,-a.

buttock ['bʌtək] **1** *n (of person)* nalga. **2** *(of animal)* anca. – **3 buttocks,** *npl (bottom)* trasero, nalgas *fpl*.

button ['bʌtən] **1** *n (on clothing, machine)* botón *m*; *(on doorbell)* pulsador *m*, botón *m*: *press the button,* pulse el botón. **2** ʙᴏᴛ *(bud)* botón *m*, yema. – **3** *i* abrocharse: *how does it button?,* ¿cómo se abrocha? – **4** *to* **button / button up,** *t* abrochar, abrocharse: *button (up) your coat,* abróchate el abrigo.
● **button your lip!,** ¡punto en boca!
■ **button nose,** nariz *f* chata. ‖ **button mushroom,** champiñón *m* pequeño.

buttonhole ['bʌtənhəʊl] **1** *n* ojal *m*. **2** *(flower)* flor *f* que se lleva en el ojal. – **3** *t fig* abordar y detener, enganchar: *I was buttonholed by two pollsters,* me engancharon dos encuestadores.

buttress ['bʌtrəs] **1** *n* ᴀʀᴄʜ contrafuerte *m*. – **2** *t* ᴀʀᴄʜ apuntalar.

butty ['bʌtɪ] *n fam* bocata *m*.
▲ *pl* **butties**.

buxom ['bʌksəm] **1** *adj (plump)* metida en carnes. – **2** *n (busty)* pechugona.

buy [baɪ] **1** *n* compra. – **2** *t* comprar: *they've just bought a new flat,* acaban de comprar un piso nuevo. **3** *(bribe)* sobornar. **4** *fam (accept, believe)* tragárselo: *he's so gullible he bought it,* es tan ingenuo que se lo tragó.
◆ **to buy back** *t sep* volver a comprar. ‖ **to buy off** *t sep* quitar a algn. de en medio pagándole, deshacerse de algn. pagándole: *he bought off the blackmailers,* se deshizo de los chantajistas pagándoles. ‖ **to buy into** *t insep* ꜰɪɴ comprar acciones de: *they bought into the business,* compraron acciones de la empresa. ‖ **to buy out** *t sep* comprar la parte de: *he bought out his brother,* compró la parte de su hermano. ‖ **to buy up** *t sep* comprar todas las existencias de: *he bought up the shop,* compró todas las existencias de la tienda.
● **to buy it,** *fam (die)* palmarla.
■ **a good buy,** una ganga.
▲ *pt & pp* **bought** [bɔːt].

buyer ['baɪəʳ] *n* comprador,-ra.
■ **buyer's market,** mercado favorable al comprador.

buying power ['baɪɪŋpaʊəʳ] *n* poder *m* adquisitivo.

buzz [bʌz] **1** *n* zumbido. **2** *(of voices)* murmullo. **3** *fam* telefonazo, toque *m*: *give me a buzz,* dame un toque. **4** *fam (thrill)* emoción *f*, sensación *f*. – **5** *i* zumbar.
◆ **to buzz around** *i (bee)* ir zumbando de un sitio a otro; *(person)* ir y venir, no parar.
● **to get a buzz out of sth.,** *fam* estar entusiasmado,-a por algo: *he really gets a buzz out of hang-gliding,* está entusiasmado por el ala delta. ‖ **buzz off!,** *fam* ¡lárgate!

buzzard ['bʌzəd] *n* ᴏʀɴ ratonero *m*.

buzzer ['bʌzəʳ] *n* zumbador *m*, timbre *m*.

buzzing ['bʌzɪŋ] *n* zumbido.

buzz-saw ['bʌzsɔː] *n* sierra circular.
buzz-word ['bʌzwɜːd] *n* palabra pegadiza, palabra que está de moda.
by [baɪ] **1** *prep* (*agent*) por: *painted by Constable*, pintado por Constable; *bought by a tycoon*, comprado por un magnate. **2** (*means*) por: *by air/road*, por avión/carretera; *by car/train*, en coche/tren; *by hand*, a mano; *by heart*, de memoria. **3** (*showing difference*) por: *I won by 3 points*, gané por tres puntos; *better by far*, muchísimo mejor. **4** (*not later than*) para: *I need it by ten*, lo necesito para las diez. **5** (*during*) de: *by day/night*, de día/noche. **6** (*near*) junto a, al lado de: *sit by me*, siéntate a mi lado. **7** (*according to*) según: *by the rules*, según las reglas. **8** (*measurements*) por: *6 metres by 4*, 6 metros por 4. **9** (*rate*) por: *paid by the hour*, pagado,-a por horas. **10** MATH por: *12 divided by 3*, 12 dividido por 3. **11** (*progression*) a: *day by day*, día a día; *little by little*, poco a poco. **12** (*in sets*) en: *two by two*, de dos en dos. **13** (*introducing gerund*): *you can find out by reading the papers*, te enterarás leyendo los periódicos. – **14** *adv* al lado, delante.
● to go by, pasar delante. ‖ by and by, con el tiempo. ‖ by the by, a propósito. ‖ by os., solo,-a.
bye [baɪ] *interj fam* ¡adiós!, ¡hasta luego!
bye-bye ['baɪbaɪ] *interj fam* ¡adiós!, ¡hasta luego!
● to say bye-bye, *fam* decir adiós. ‖ to go to bye-byes, ir a dormir, ir a la cama.
by-election ['baɪlekʃən] *n* POL elección *f* parcial.
Byelorussia [bjeləʊ'rʌʃə] *n* Bielorrusia.

Byelorussian [bjeləʊ'rʌʃən] **1** *adj* bielorruso,-a. – **2** *n* (*person*) bielorruso,-a. **3** (*language*) bielorruso.
bygone ['baɪɡɒn] **1** *adj* pasado,-a: *a bygone age*, tiempos pasados. – **2** *n* (*object*) antigualla.
● in bygone times, antiguamente. ‖ let bygones be bygones, lo pasado, pasado está.
by-law ['baɪlɔː] *n* ley *f* municipal.
bypass ['baɪpɑːs] **1** *n* AUTO variante *f*. **2** TECH tubo de desviación. **3** MED by-pass *m*. – **4** *t* (*traffic, road*) desviar. **5** (*avoid*) esquivar, evitar.
by-product ['baɪprɒdʌkt] **1** *n* subproducto, derivado. **2** *fig* consecuencia.
byre ['baɪə'] *n* establo.
by-road ['baɪrəʊd] *n* carretera secundaria.
bystander ['baɪstændə'] *n* espectador,-ra, curioso,-a.
byte [baɪt] *n* COMPUT byte *m*.
by-way ['baɪweɪ] **1** *n* (*road*) carretera secundaria. **2** (*remote path*) camino poco frecuentado.
byword ['baɪwɜːd] **1** *n* arquetipo, mayor *mf* exponente. **2** (*proverb*) refrán *m*, proverbio.
● to be a byword in, ser sinónimo de: *their products are a byword in luxury*, sus productos son sinónimo de lujo.
Byzantine [bɪ'zæntaɪn] **1** *n* HIST bizantino,-a. – **2** *adj* HIST bizantino,-a.
Byzantium [bɪ'zæntɪəm] *n* HIST Bizancio

C

C, c [siː] **1** *n* (*the letter*) C, c *f*. **2** MUS do.
c¹ [sent] *abbr* (*cent*) céntimo.
c² ['sɜːkə] *abbr* (*circa*) hacia; (*abbreviation*) h.
c³ ['kɒpɪraɪt] *abbr* (*copyright*) propiedad *f* literaria, copy-right *m*; (*abbreviation*) c.
c. ['sentʃərɪ] *abbr* (*century*) siglo; (*abbreviation*) s.: *c. 18 literature,* la literatura del s. XVIII.
c/a [karəntə'kaunt] *abbr* (*current account*) cuenta corrien-te; (*abbreviation*) c/c.
cab [kæb] **1** *n* (*taxi*) taxi *m*. **2** (*in vehicle*) cabina. **3** HIST ca-briolé *m*.
● to go by cab, ir en taxi.
■ cab driver, taxista *mf*. ‖ cab rank, parada de taxis.
cabaret ['kæbəreɪ] *n* cabaret *m*.
cabbage ['kæbɪdʒ] *n* col *f*, repollo, berza.
■ cabbage white, (*butterfly*) mariposa de la col.
cabbie ['kæbɪ] *n fam* taxista *mf*.
caber ['keɪbəʳ] *n* (*in Scotland*) tronco.
● tossing the caber, lanzamiento del tronco.
cabin ['kæbɪn] **1** *n* (*wooden house*) cabaña. **2** MAR camarote *m*. **3** AER cabina.
■ cabin boy, grumete *m*. ‖ cabin crew, personal *m* de cabina. ‖ cabin cruiser, yate *m* de motor.
cabinet ['kæbɪnət] **1** *n* (*furniture - gen*) armario; (*glass fronted*) vitrina. **2** POL gabinete *m* (ministerial), consejo de ministros.
■ cabinet meeting, consejo de ministros. ‖ cabinet minister, ministro,-a. ‖ cabinet reshuffle, remode-lación *f* ministerial, remodelación *f* del gobierno. ‖ cocktail cabinet, mueble bar *m*. ‖ shadow cabinet, gobierno en la sombra.
cabinet-maker ['kæbɪnətmeɪkəʳ] *n* ebanista *mf*.
cable ['keɪbəl] **1** *n* (*rope, wire*) cable *m*. **2** (*telegram*) cable *m*, cablegrama *m*, telegrama *m*. – **3** *t* (*message*) cable-grafiar, telegrafiar.
● to cable sb., enviar un cable a algn., telegrafiar a algn.
■ cable car, teleférico, telecabina. ‖ cable television, televisión *f* por cable.
caboodle [kə'buːdəl] **the whole caboodle,** *n* toda la pesca.
cacao [kə'kɑːəʊ] *n* BOT cacao.
cache [kæʃ] *n* escondrijo.
cack-handed [kæk'hændɪd] *adj fam* torpe, patoso,-a.
cackle ['kækəl] **1** *n* (*of hen*) cacareo. **2** (*of person*) risotada, carcajada. – **3** *i* (*of hen*) cacarear. **4** (*of person*) reírse a carcajadas, carcajearse.
cacophonous [kə'kɒfənəs] *adj* cacofónico,-a.
cacophony [kə'kɒfənɪ] *n* LING cacofonía.
cactus ['kæktəs] *n* cactus *m*.
▲ *pl cacti o cactuses.*
cad [kæd] *n* GB *fam dated* canalla *m*.
CAD [kæd] *abbr* (*computer-aided design*) diseño con ayu-da de ordenador.

cadaver [kə'deɪvəʳ] *n* MED cadáver *m*.
cadaverous [kə'dævərəs] *adj* cadavérico,-a.
CADCAM ['kædkæm] *abbr* (*computer-aided design and manufacture*) diseño y fabricación con ayuda de or-denador.
caddie ['kædɪ] **1** *n* (*in golf*) cadi *m*. – **2** *i* hacer de cadi (**for,** de).
■ caddie car / caddie cart, carrito de golf.
caddy ['kædɪ] *n* (*for tea*) cajita (para guardar el té), lata (para guardar el té).
▲ *pl caddies.*
cadence ['keɪdəns] *n* cadencia.
cadenza [kə'denzə] *n* MUS cadencia.
cadet [kə'det] *n* cadete *m*.
■ cadet school, escuela militar.
cadge [kædʒ] **1** *t fam* gorronear: *she's always cadging cigarettes,* siempre está gorroneando cigarrillos. – **2** *i fam* gorronear (**from/off,** a).
● to cadge a lift off sb., conseguir que algn. te lleve en coche: *I cadged a lift off Kathryn,* Kathryn me llevó en coche. ‖ to cadge money off sb., darle un sablazo a algn.
cadger ['kædʒəʳ] *n fam* gorrón,-ona.
cadmium ['kædmɪəm] *n* cadmio.
Caesarean [sɪ'zeərɪən] **Caesarean (section),** *n* cesá-rea.
● to have a Caesarean, hacerle a una la cesárea: *I had a Caesarean,* me hicieron la cesárea.
café ['kæfeɪ] *n* cafetería, café *m*.
cafeteria [kæfə'tɪərɪə] *n* (*in factory, college, etc*) cafetería, cantina; (*restaurant*) autoservicio, self-service *m*.
caffeine ['kæfiːn] *n* cafeína.
caftan ['kæftæn] *n* → **kaftan.**
cage [keɪdʒ] **1** *n* (*gen*) jaula. – **2** *t* enjaular.
● to feel caged in, sentirse enjaulado,-a.
cagey ['keɪdʒɪ] *adj fam* reservado,-a, cauteloso,-a, pre-cavido,-a: *she was very cagey about what happened at the meeting,* se mostró reacia a explicar lo que pasó en la reunión.
▲ *comp cagier; superl cagiest.*
cagoule [kə'guːl] *n* chubasquero, capelina.
cahoots [kə'huːts] **to be in cahoots with sb.,** *phr* estar confabulado,-a con algn., estar conchabado,-a con algn.
cairn [keən] *n* hito formado por piedras apiladas.
cajole [kə'dʒəʊl] *t* engatusar.
● to cajole sb. into doing sth., engatusar a algn. para que haga algo.
cajolery [kə'dʒəʊlərɪ] *n* engatusamiento, zalamería.
cake [keɪk] **1** *n* CULIN pastel *m*, tarta, torta. **2** (*of soap*) pas-tilla. – **3** *i* endurecerse.
● to be a piece of cake, estar tirado,-a, estar chu-pado,-a. ‖ to be caked with sth., estar cubierto,-a de algo, estar recubierto,-a de algo. ‖ to go like hot cakes

/ **sell like hot cakes,** venderse como rosquillas. ‖ **to have one's cake and eat it,** querer nadar y guardar la ropa, querer estar en misa y repicando. ‖ **to want a slice of the cake,** *fig* querer una tajada del pastel. ■ **cake shop,** pastelería. ‖ **cake tin,** molde *m.* ‖ **fruit cake,** plum cake *m.* ‖ **sponge cake,** bizcocho.

cal ['kælərɪ] *abbr* (*calorie*) caloría; (*abbreviation*) cal.

CAL [kæl] *abbr* (*computer-aided learning*) aprendizaje *m* con ayuda de ordenador.

calamine ['kæləmaɪn] *n* calamina.

calamitous [kə'læmɪtəs] *adj* calamitoso,-a.

calamity [kə'læmɪtɪ] *n* calamidad *f.*
▲ *pl* **calamities.**

calcification [kælsɪfɪ'keɪʃən] *n* calcificación *f.*

calcify ['kælsɪfaɪ] **1** *t* calcificar. – **2** *i* calcificarse.
▲ *pt* & *pp* **calcified,** *ger* **calcifying.**

calcium ['kælsɪəm] *n* calcio.

calculate ['kælkjəleɪt] **1** *t* calcular. – **2** *i* calcular.
◆ **to calculate on** *t insep* contar con.

calculated ['kælkjəleɪtɪd] *adj* (*risk*) calculado,-a; (*insult*) intencionado,-a; (*act*) premeditado,-a, deliberado,-a. ● **to be calculated to do sth.,** (*designed*) estar pensado,-a para hacer algo, estar planeado,-a para hacer algo, estar hecho,-a con la intención de hacer algo.

calculating ['kælkjəleɪtɪŋ] *adj* (*shrewd*) calculador,-ra.

calculation [kælkjə'leɪʃən] *n* cálculo.

calculator ['kælkjəleɪtəʳ] *n* calculador *m*, calculadora.

calculus ['kælkjələs] **1** *n* MATH cálculo matemático. – **2** **calculi,** *npl* MED cálculo.
▲ *pl* **calculi** o **calculuses.**

Calcutta [kæl'kʌtə] *n* Calcuta.

caldron ['kɔːldrən] *n* → **cauldron.**

calendar ['kælɪndəʳ] *n* (*gen*) calendario. ■ **calendar year,** año civil.

calf¹ [kɑːf] *n* ZOOL (*of cattle*) ternero,-a, becerro,-a; (*of whale*) ballenato; (*of other animals*) cría. ● **to be in calf / be with calf,** estar preñada.
▲ *pl* **calves.**

calf² [kɑːf] *n* ANAT pantorrilla.
▲ *pl* **calves.**

calfskin ['kɑːfskɪn] *n* piel *f* de becerro.

caliber ['kælɪbəʳ] *n* US → **calibre.**

calibrate ['kælɪbreɪt] *t* (*gun*) calibrar; (*thermometer*) graduar.

calibre ['kælɪbəʳ] *n* (*gen*) calibre *m.*

calico ['kælɪkəʊ] *n* calicó *m.*
▲ *pl* **calicoes** o **calicos.**

California [kælɪ'fɔːnɪə] *n* California.

Californian [kælɪ'fɔːnɪən] **1** *adj* californiano,-a. – **2** *n* californiano,-a.

calipers ['kælɪpəz] *npl* US → **callipers.**

calisthenics [kælɪs'θenɪks] *n* US → **callisthenics.**

call [kɔːl] **1** *n* (*shout, cry*) grito, llamada: *a call for help,* un grito de socorro. **2** (*by telephone*) llamada (telefónica): *there was a call for you,* te han llamado por teléfono; *she hasn't returned your call,* no te ha devuelto la llamada. **3** (*of bird*) reclamo. **4** (*demand*) demanda; (*need*) motivo: *there's not much call for typewriters nowadays,* hoy en día no hay mucha demanda de máquinas de escribir; *there's no call for that language,* no hay por qué utilizar ese lenguaje. **5** (*summons, vocation*) llamada; (*lure*) llamada, atracción *f*: *he felt the call of the priesthood,* sintió la llamada al sacerdocio; *the call of the wild,* el atractivo de la naturaleza. **6** (*request, demand*) llamamiento: *the community leader made a call for calm,* el líder de la comunidad hizo un llamamiento a la cal-

ma; *there have been calls for his resignation,* han pedido su dimisión. **7** (*short visit*) visita: *the doctor has several (house) calls to make,* el médico tiene que hacer varias visitas (a domicilio). – **8** *t* (*shout*) llamar: *I heard you call my name,* oí que me llamabas. **9** (*by telephone*) llamar: *I'll call you when we get home,* te llamaré cuando lleguemos a casa. **10** (*summon - meeting, strike, election*) convocar; (*announce - flight*) anunciar. **11** (*send for - police etc*) llamar: *she's been called to the manager's office,* la han llamado al despacho del director. **12** (*name, describe as*) llamar: *what have they called their baby?,* ¿qué nombre le han puesto al bebé?; *what's Peter's girlfriend called?,* ¿cómo se llama la novia de Peter?; *what's this called in Spanish?,* ¿cómo se llama esto en español? – **13** *i* (*shout*) llamar: *why didn't you come when I called?,* ¿por qué no viniste cuando te llamé? **14** (*by phone*) llamar: *I just called to say I love you,* sólo he llamado para decirte que te quiero; *who's calling please?,* ¿de parte de quién?. **15** (*visit*) pasar, hacer una visita: *I called round at Martin's this afternoon,* he pasado por casa de Martin esta tarde. **16** (*train*) parar (**at,** en).
◆ **to call away** *t sep* llamar: *he's been called away on business,* ha tenido que ausentarse por motivos de trabajo. ‖ **to call back 1** *t sep* (*by phone*) llamar, devolver la llamada. – **2** *i* (*by phone*) volver a llamar; (*visit*) volver a pasar. ‖ **to call for 1** *t insep* (*pick up*) pasar a buscar, pasar a recoger. **2** (*need, require*) exigir, requerir; (*demand*) pedir: *a statement calling for his release,* una declaración que pide su puesta en libertad; *this calls for a celebration,* esto hay que celebrarlo; *that kind of language isn't called for,* esta clase de lenguaje no es necesario. ‖ **to call in 1** *t sep* (*summon, send for*) llamar. **2** (*recall - books, banknotes*) retirar; (*loan*) exigir el pago de. ‖ **to call off 1** *t sep* (*suspend - gen*) suspender; (- *strike*) desconvocar. **2** (*dog*) llamar. ‖ **to call on 1** *t insep* (*visit*) visitar, ir a ver a. **2** *fml* (*invite*) invitar; (*request*) pedir; (*appeal to, urge*) apelar a, recurrir a: *I now call on Mr Smith to say a few words,* ahora invito al Señor Smith a que diga unas palabras. ‖ **to call out 1** *t sep* (*summon - fire brigade*) llamar; (*army, troops*) hacer intervenir; (*doctor*) hacer venir; (*workers*) llamar a la huelga. **2** (*shout*) gritar, llamar. ‖ **to call up 1** *t sep* MIL llamar a filas. **2** (*recall*) traer a la memoria.
● **let's call it a day,** démoslo por terminado, dejémoslo. ‖ **let's call it quits,** dejémoslo estar. ‖ **the call of duty,** la llamada del deber. ‖ **to answer a call of nature,** hacer sus necesidades. ‖ **to be on call,** estar de guardia. ‖ **to call a halt to sth.,** atajar algo, acabar con algo. ‖ **to call for sth./sb.,** pasar a recoger algo/a algn. ‖ **to call in on sb.,** ir a ver a algn. ‖ **to call os.,** considerarse: *he calls himself an anarchist,* se considera un anarquista. ‖ **to call sb. names,** poner verde a algn., insultar a algn. ‖ **to call sb. to account,** pedirle cuentas a algn. ‖ **to call sb.'s bluff,** devolver la pelota a algn. ‖ **to call sth. into question,** poner algo en duda. ‖ **to call sth. one's own,** tener algo de propiedad. ‖ **to call sth. to mind,** traer algo a la memoria. ‖ **to call the shots / call the tune,** llevar la batuta, llevar la voz cantante. ‖ **to give sb. a call,** llamar a algn. ‖ **to have first call on sth.,** tener prioridad sobre algo. ‖ **to have too many calls on one's time,** tener muchas obligaciones, estar muy ocupado,-a. ‖ **to pay a call on,** ir a ver a algn., hacer una visita a algn. ‖ **what time do you call this?,** ¿qué horas son éstas?. ■ **call box,** GB cabina telefónica. ‖ **call girl,** prostituta.

callboy ['kɔːlbɔɪ] *n* THEAT traspunte *m.*

caller ['kɔːləʳ] **1** *n* (*visitor*) visita, visitante *mf.* **2** (*by telephone*) persona que llama.

calligrapher [kə'lɪgrəfəʳ] *n* calígrafo,-a.
calligraphy [kə'lɪgrəfɪ] *n* caligrafía.
calling ['kɔːlɪŋ] *n* (*vocation*) vocación *f*, llamada; (*profession*) profesión *f*.
■ **calling card**, US tarjeta de visita.
callipers ['kælɪpəz] **1** *npl* TECH calibrador *m*. **2** MED aparato ortopédico (para la pierna).
callisthenics [kælɪs'θenɪks] *n* gimnasia sueca.
callous ['kæləs] *adj* duro,-a, insensible.
callousness ['kæləsnəs] *n* insensibilidad *f*, dureza.
call-up ['kɔːlʌp] *n* MIL llamamiento a filas.
callus ['kæləs] *n* callo.
▲ *pl* **calluses**.
calm [kɑːm] **1** *adj* (*sea*) en calma, tranquilo,-a, apacible; (*weather*) en calma, apacible. **2** (*person*) tranquilo,-a, sosegado,-a, calmado,-a: *keep calm!*, ¡tranquilo!, ¡calma! – **3** *n* (*of sea, weather*) calma: *the calm before the storm*, la calma que precede a la tormenta. **4** (*peace and quiet*) tranquilidad *f*, sosiego, serenidad *f*. – **5 to calm (down)**, *t* calmar, tranquilizar, sosegar.
◆ **to calm down** *i* tranquilizarse, calmarse.
● **to calm os.**, tranquilizarse, calmarse.
calmly ['kɑːmlɪ] *adv* con calma, tranquilamente.
calmness ['kɑːmnəs] *n* tranquilidad *f*, calma.
Calor Gas ['kælagæs] *n* (gas *m*) butano.
calorie ['kælərɪ] *n* caloría.
calorific [kælə'rɪfɪk] *adj* calorífico,-a.
calumny ['kæləmnɪ] *n* (*false statement*) calumnia; (*slander*) difamación *f*.
▲ *pl* **calumnies**.
calvary ['kælvərɪ] *n* calvario.
calve ['kɑːv] *i* parir (un becerro).
calves ['kɑːvz] *npl* → **calf**.
calypso [kə'lɪpsəʊ] *n* calipso.
▲ *pl* **calypsos**.
cam [kæm] *n* leva.
camaraderie [kæmə'rɑːdərɪ] *n* compañerismo, camaradería.
camber ['kæmbəʳ] **1** *n* (*curvature - of road*) peralte *m*. **2** ARCH combadura.
Cambodia [kæm'bəʊdɪə] *n* Camboya.
Cambodian [kæm'bəʊdɪən] **1** *adj* camboyano,-a. – **2** *n* (*person*) camboyano,-a. **3** (*language*) camboyano.
camcorder ['kæmkɔːdəʳ] *n* videocámara.
came [keɪm] *pt* → **come**.
camel ['kæməl] **1** *n* ZOOL camello,-a. **2** (*colour*) (color *m*) leonado. – **3** *adj* leonado,-a.
camelhair ['kæməlheəʳ] *n* pelo de camello.
camellia [kə'miːlɪə] *n* BOT camelia.
cameo ['kæmɪəʊ] *n* camafeo.
▲ *pl* **cameos**.
camera ['kæmərə] **1** *n* (*gen*) cámara (fotográfica), máquina fotográfica. **2** CINEM TV cámara.
● **in camera**, a puerta cerrada.
cameraman ['kæmərəmən] *n* cámara *mf*.
Cameroon [kæmə'ruːn] *n* Camerún *m*.
Cameroonian [kæmə'ruːnɪən] **1** *adj* camerunés,-esa. – **2** *n* camerunés,-esa.
camomile ['kæməmaɪl] *n* BOT manzanilla, camomila.
■ **camomile tea**, (infusión *f* de) manzanilla.
camouflage ['kæməflɑːʒ] **1** *n* camuflaje *m*. – **2** *t* camuflar.
camp¹ [kæmp] **1** *n* (*gen*) campamento. **2** (*group, faction*) bando. – **3 to camp (out)**, *i* acampar.
● **to pitch camp**, acampar. ‖ **to break camp / strike camp**, levantar el campamento.

■ **army camp**, campamento militar. ‖ **camp bed**, cama plegable. ‖ **camp site**, camping *m*, campamento. ‖ **holiday camp / summer camp**, (*gen*) colonia de verano, colonia de vacaciones; (*in tents*) campamento de verano.
camp² [kæmp] **1** *adj* (*affected, effeminate*) amanerado,-a, afeminado,-a; (*affectedly theatrical*) afectado,-a, exagerado,-a. – **2** *n* amaneramiento, afectación *f*.
campaign [kæm'peɪn] **1** *n* (*gen*) campaña. – **2** *i* hacer una campaña (**for**, en favor de).
campaigner [kæm'peɪnəʳ] *n* (*supporter*) defensor,-ra.
■ **old campaigner**, veterano,-a.
camper ['kæmpəʳ] **1** *n* (*person*) campista *mf*. **2 camper (van)**, (*vehicle*) caravana.
campfire ['kæmpfaɪəʳ] *n* fogata, hoguera.
camphor ['kæmfəʳ] *n* alcanfor *m*.
camping ['kæmpɪŋ] *n* camping *m*.
● "**no camping**", "prohibido acampar". ‖ **to go camping**, ir de camping.
■ **camping site**, camping *m*, campamento.
campus ['kæmpəs] *n* campus *m*, ciudad *f* universitaria.
▲ *pl* **campuses**.
camshaft ['kæmʃɑːft] *n* árbol *m* de levas.
can¹ [kæn] **1** *n* (*tin - for food, drinks*) lata, bote *m*. **2** (*container - for oil, petrol, etc*) bidón *m*. **3** US *sl* (*prison*) chirona, trullo. **4** US *sl* (*toilet*) trono. – **5** *t* (*put in cans*) enlatar.
● **can it!**, ¡basta ya! ‖ **to be in the can**, CINEM estar listo,-a. ‖ **to carry the can**, cargar con las culpas, pagar el pato. ‖ **to open up a can of worms**, destapar un escándalo.
■ **can opener**, abrelatas *m*. ‖ **trash can**, cubo de la basura.
▲ (*verbo*) *pt* & *pp* **canned**, *ger* **canning**.
can² [kæn] **1** *aux* (*be able to*) poder: *can you come tomorrow?*, ¿puedes venir mañana?; *can we afford it?*, ¿nos lo podemos permitir?; *they're doing all they can*, hacen todo lo que pueden. **2** (*know how to*) saber: *he can speak Chinese*, sabe hablar chino; *can you swim?*, ¿sabes nadar?; *I can't drive*, no sé conducir. **3** (*be allowed to*) poder, estar permitido,-a: *you can't smoke here*, no se puede fumar aquí; *you can go now*, ya te puedes ir; *female nurses couldn't wear trousers*, a las enfermeras no les estaba permitido llevar pantalones. **4** (*in requests*) poder: *can I borrow your car tonight?*, ¿me dejas el coche esta noche?; *can you get that box down for me?*, ¿me puedes bajar esa caja?; *can I have a cheese sandwich, please?*, (me pone) un bocadillo de queso, por favor. **5** (*with verbs of perception or mental activity*): *she couldn't see anything*, no veía nada; *I can smell burning*, huele a quemado; *can you hear me?*, ¿me oyes?; *I can't remember*, no me acuerdo. – **6** *t* (*possibility*) poder: *who can it be?*, ¿quién será?; *smoking can cause cancer*, fumar puede causar cáncer; *you can get tickets on the door*, se puede comprar las entradas en la taquilla. – **7** *aux* (*expressing bewilderment, incredulity*) poder: *he can't be here already!*, ¡no puede ser que ya haya llegado!; *you cannot be serious!*, ¡no hablarás en serio! **8** (*indicating typical behaviour*) poder: *he can be very annoying sometimes*, a veces es muy pesado; *it can be very cold in Madrid*, puede llegar a hacer mucho frío en Madrid.
▲ *pt* & *pp* **could**.
Canada ['kænədə] *n* Canadá, el Canadá.
Canadian [kə'neɪdɪən] **1** *adj* canadiense. – **2** *n* canadiense *mf*.
canal [kə'næl] *n* canal *m*.
canary [kə'neərɪ] *n* canario.
■ **canary yellow**, amarillo canario.

▲ *pl canaries.*

Canary Islands [kə'neərɪaɪləndz] *npl* Islas *fpl* Canarias.

cancel ['kænsəl] **1** *t* (*gen*) cancelar. **2** COMM anular. **3** (*revoke - permission*) retirar; (*order, decree*) revocar. **4** (*stamp*) matasellar. **5** (*delete*) tachar. **6** MATH eliminar.
◆ **to cancel out** *t sep* anular, compensar, contrarrestar.
▲ *pt & pp* **cancelled** (US **canceled**), *ger* **cancelling** (US **canceling**).

cancellation [kænsə'leɪʃən] **1** *n* (*gen*) cancelación *f*. **2** COMM anulación *f*. **3** (*of stamp*) matasellos *m*. **4** (*returned ticket*) devolución *f*.

cancer ['kænsəʳ] **1** *n* MED cáncer *m*. **2 Cancer,** ASTROL Cáncer *m*.
■ **breast cancer,** cáncer *m* de mama. ‖ **cancer research,** cancerología. ‖ **Tropic of Cancer,** trópico de Cáncer.

cancerous ['kænsərəs] *adj* canceroso,-a.

candelabra [kændə'lɑːbrə] *n* candelabro.

candid ['kændɪd] *adj* franco,-a, sincero,-a.
■ **candid camera,** cámara indiscreta.

candidacy ['kændɪdəsɪ] *n* candidatura.
▲ *pl candidacies.*

candidate ['kændɪdət] **1** *n* (*job, election*) candidato,-a. **2** (*in exam*) opositor,-ra.

candidature ['kændɪdətʃəʳ] *n* candidatura.

candidly ['kændɪdlɪ] *adv* con franqueza.

candied ['kændɪd] *adj* confitado,-a, escarchado,-a.

candle ['kændəl] *n* (*gen*) vela; (*in church*) cirio.
● **to burn the candle at both ends,** trabajar de sol a sol. ‖ **not to hold a candle to sb.,** no llegar a algn. a la suela del zapato.

candlelight ['kændəllaɪt] *n* luz *f* de vela.
● **by candlelight,** a la luz de una vela.

Candlemas ['kændəlməs] *n* REL candelaria.

candlestick ['kændəlstɪk] *n* (*gen*) candelero, palmatoria; (*in church*) cirial *m*.

candlewick ['kændəlwɪk] **1** *n* (*fabric*) tela afelpada. **2** (*wick*) pábilo, mecha.

candor ['kændəʳ] *n* US → **candour.**

candour ['kændəʳ] *n* franqueza, sinceridad *f.*

candy ['kændɪ] *n* US (*sweets*) caramelos *mpl*, golosinas *fpl*, dulces *mpl*; (*a sweet*) caramelo, dulce *m.*
▲ *pl candies.*

candyfloss ['kændɪflɒs] *n* GB algodón *m* de azúcar.

candy-striped ['kændɪstraɪpt] *adj* de rayas multicolores.

cane [keɪn] **1** *n* BOT (*of bamboo*) caña; (*of raspberry, blackberry, etc*) tallo leñoso. **2** (*stick*) bastón *m*; (*for punishment*) palmeta. **3** (*furniture*) mimbre *m*. **4** (*for plants*) rodrigón *m*. – **5** *t* castigar con la palmeta.
■ **cane chair,** silla de mimbre.

canine ['keɪnaɪn] *adj* ZOOL canino,-a.
■ **canine tooth,** (*diente m*) canino, colmillo.

caning ['keɪnɪŋ] *n* palmetazo.

canister ['kænɪstəʳ] *n* (*for tea, coffee, etc*) bote *m*, lata.

canker ['kæŋkəʳ] **1** *n* BOT cancro. **2** MED úlcera, llaga. **3** *fig* (*evil*) cáncer *m.*

cannabis ['kænəbɪs] *n* (*plant*) cáñamo indio; (*drug*) hachís *m.*

canned ['kænd] **1** *adj* enlatado,-a, envasado,-a, en lata. **2** (*music*) grabado,-a, enlatado,-a; (*laughter*) grabado,-a. **3** *sl* (*drunk*) mamado,-a.
■ **canned food,** conservas *fpl.*

cannery ['kænərɪ] *n* fábrica de conservas.
▲ *pl canneries.*

cannibal ['kænɪbəl] *n* caníbal *mf.*

cannibalism ['kænɪbəlɪzəm] *n* canibalismo.

cannibalize ['kænɪbəlaɪz] *t* reutilizar piezas sueltas de.

canning ['kænɪŋ] *n* enlatado.
■ **canning factory,** fábrica de conservas. ‖ **canning industry,** industria conservera.

cannon ['kænən] **1** *n* MIL cañón *m*. **2** (*in billiards*) carambola. – **3** *i* chocar (**against,** contra).
■ **cannon fodder,** carne *f* de cañón.
▲ *pl cannon o cannons.*

cannonball ['kænənbɔːl] *n* bala de cañón.

cannot ['kænɒt] *aux* → **can not.**

canny ['kænɪ] *adj* astuto,-a.
▲ *comp* **cannier,** *superl* **canniest.**

canoe [kə'nuː] **1** *n* canoa, piragua. – **2** *i* ir en canoa, ir en piragua.

canoeing [kə'nuːɪŋ] *n* piragüismo.

canoeist [kə'nuːɪst] *n* piragüista *mf.*

canon[1] ['kænən] **1** *n* (*rule, standard*) canon *m*. **2** REL (*decree*) canon *m.*
■ **cannon law,** derecho canónico.

canon[2] ['kænən] *n* (*priest*) canónigo.

canonize ['kænənaɪz] *t* canonizar.

canopy ['kænəpɪ] **1** *n* (*over throne, bed, altar*) dosel *m*, baldaquín *m*, baldaquino; (*ceremonial*) palio; (*of terrace, balcony*) toldo. **2** AV (*of cockpit*) cubierta transparente. **3** (*of sky*) bóveda.
▲ *pl canopies.*

cant [kænt] **1** *n* (*hypocrisy*) hipocresías *fpl*. **2** (*jargon*) jerga.

can't [kɑːnt] *aux* → **can.**

Cantab ['kæntæb] *abbr* (*Cantabrigiensis*) de la Universidad de Cambridge.

Cantabria [kæn'tæbrɪə] *n* Cantabria.

Cantabrian [kæn'tæbrɪən] **1** *adj* cántabro,-a. – **2** *n* cántabro,-a.

Cantabrigian [kæntə'brɪdʒɪən] **1** *adj* GB (*city*) de Cambridge. **2** (*university*) de la Universidad de Cambridge. **3** US (*city*) de Cambridge, Massachusetts. **4** (*university*) de la Universidad de Harvard. – **5** *n* habitante *mf* de Cambridge.

cantankerous [kən'tæŋkərəs] *adj* de mal genio, irascible, cascarrabias.

canteen [kæn'tiːn] **1** *n* (*restaurant*) cantina, comedor *m*. **2** (*set of cutlery*) juego de cubiertos. **3** (*flask*) cantimplora.

canter ['kæntəʳ] **1** *n* medio galope. – **2** *i* ir a medio galope.

cantilever ['kæntɪliːvəʳ] *n* ARCH voladizo.
■ **cantilever bridge,** puente *m* voladizo.

canvas ['kænvəs] **1** *n* (*cloth*) lona. **2** ART lienzo.
● **under canvas,** (*in a tent*) en una tienda (de campaña); (*of ship*) con velamen desplegado.

canvass ['kænvəs] **1** *i* POL hacer propaganda electoral (**for,** a favor de), hacer campaña (**for,** a favor de). – **2** *t* (*try to obtain - support, vote*) solicitar, tratar de conseguir, tratar de obtener. **3** POL (*ask - opinion*) sondear, hacer un sondeo de. **4** (*idea, plan*) proponer, presentar.

canvasser ['kænvəsəʳ] *n* POL persona que hace campaña a favor de un partido.

canvassing ['kænvəsɪŋ] *n* petición *f* de votos.
● **to go out canvassing,** hacer campaña de puerta en puerta.

canyon ['kænjən] *n* GEOG cañón *m.*
■ **the Great Canyon,** el Gran Cañón.

cap [kæp] **1** *n* (*type of hat - gen*) gorra; (*- soldier's, policeman's*) gorra de plato; (*- nurse's*) cofia; (*- academic, judge's*) bi-

rrete *m*; (- *cardinal's*) capelo, birrete *m*. 2 (*cover - of pen*) capuchón *m*; (- *of bottle*) tapón *m*, chapa; (- *of lens*) tapa. 3 GEOG casquete *m*. 4 (*for toy gun*) fulminante *m*. 5 (*upper limit*) tope *m*. 6 MED diafragma *m*. – 7 *t* (*mountains etc*) cubrir, coronar. 8 (*tooth*) poner una corona en. 9 (*joke, story*) superar. 10 GB SP seleccionar para el equipo nacional. 11 (*limit*) poner un tope a, limitar.
● **if the cap fits (wear it),** el que se pica, ajos come, a quien le pique, que se rasque. ‖ **to cap it all,** para colmo. ‖ **to go cap in hand,** ir a mendigar, pedir de rodillas.
■ **cloth cap / flat cap,** gorra. ‖ **Dutch cap,** diafragma *mf*. ‖ **swimming cap,** gorro de baño.
▲ (*verbo*) *pt* & *pp* **capped**.

capability [keɪpə'bɪlɪt] 1 *n* (*ability*) capacidad *f* (**to,** para/ de). 2 MIL capacidad *f*. – 3 **capabilities,** *npl* (*potential*) aptitudes *fpl*, posibilidades *fpl*.
▲ *pl* **capabilities**.

capable ['keɪpəbəl] 1 *adj* (*able*) capaz (**of,** de): *he's capable of breaking the world record,* es capaz de batir el récord mundial. 2 (*competent*) competente, capaz: *a very capable person,* una persona muy competente.

capacious [kə'peɪʃəs] *adj fml* espacioso,-a.

capacitor [kə'pæsɪtə'] *n* ELEC condensador *m*.

capacity [kə'pæsɪtɪ] 1 *n* (*maximum content - of container*) capacidad *f*, cabida; (- *of theatre*) aforo, capacidad *f*, cabida: *the cinema has a seating capacity of 300,* el cine tiene un aforo de 300 localidades. 2 (*ability*) capacidad *f* (**for,** de): *he has a great capacity for hard work,* tiene una gran capacidad de trabajo. 3 (*position, role*) calidad *f*: *speaking in my capacity as club secretary,* hablando en calidad de secretario del club.
● **in a personal capacity,** a título personal. ‖ **to be filled to capacity,** estar al completo. ‖ **to work at full capacity,** trabajar a pleno rendimiento.
■ **capacity crowd / capacity audience,** lleno completo, lleno total.
▲ *pl* **capacities**.

cape[1] [keɪp] *n* (*garment*) capa.

cape[2] [keɪp] *n* cabo.
■ **Cape Canaveral,** Cabo Cañaveral. ‖ **Cape Horn,** Cabo de Hornos. ‖ **Cape of Good Hope,** Cabo de Buena Esperanza. ‖ **Cape Province,** Provincia del Cabo. ‖ **Cape Town,** Ciudad *f* del Cabo. ‖ **Cape Verde,** Cabo Verde. ‖ **Cape Verdean,** caboverdiano,-a.

caper[1] ['keɪpə'] *n* CULIN alcaparra; BOT alcaparro.

caper[2] ['keɪpə'] 1 *n* (*jump*) brinco. 2 *fam* (*prank*) travesura, broma; (*scheme*) ardid *m*, estratagema, truco: *what's your little caper?,* ¿qué estás tramando?. – 3 *i* brincar, dar brincos.

capillary [kə'pɪlərɪ] *n* vaso capilar, capilar *m*.
▲ *pl* **capillaries**.

capital[1] ['kæpɪtəl] 1 *n* GEOG POL capital *f*: *what's the capital of Greece?,* ¿cuál es la capital de Grecia?. 2 FIN capital *m*: *starting capital,* capital inicial. 3 (*letter*) mayúscula: *write it in capitals,* escríbelo con mayúsculas. – 4 *adj* JUR (*offence*) capital. 5 (*letter*) mayúscula: *capital A,* A mayúscula. 6 (*very serious*) grave. 7 (*primary, chief, principal*) primordial, capital.
● **to make capital out of sth.,** sacar provecho de algo, sacar partido de algo.
■ **capital city,** capital *f*. ‖ **capital expenditure / capital investment,** inversión *f* de capital. ‖ **capital goods,** bienes *mpl* de equipo. ‖ **capital stock,** capital *m* social. ‖ **capital transfer tax,** impuesto sobre sucesiones.

capital[2] ['kæpɪtəl] *n* ARCH capitel *m*.

capitalism ['kæpɪtəlɪzəm] *n* capitalismo.

capitalist ['kæpɪtəlɪst] 1 *adj* capitalista. – 2 *n* capitalista *mf*.

capitalize ['kæpɪtəlaɪz] 1 *t* FIN capitalizar. 2 (*write in capital letters*) escribir con mayúsculas.
◆ **to capitalize on** *t insep* sacar provecho de, sacar partido de, sacar beneficio de.

capitulate [kə'pɪtjəleɪt] *i* capitular.

capitulation [kəpɪtjə'leɪʃən] *n* capitulación *f*.

capon ['keɪpən] *n* capón *m*.

caprice [kə'priːs] *n* capricho, antojo.

capricious [kə'prɪʃəs] *adj* caprichoso,-a, antojadizo,-a.

Capricorn ['kæprɪkɔːn] *n* ASTROL Capricornio.
■ **Tropic of Capricorn,** trópico de Capricornio.

capsicum ['kæpsɪkəm] *n* pimiento.

capsize [kæp'saɪz] 1 *i* zozobrar. – 2 *t* hacer zozobrar.

capstan ['kæpstən] *n* cabrestante *m*.

capsule ['kæpsjuːl] *n* cápsula.

Capt ['kæptn] *abbr* (*Captain*) Capitán *m*; (*abbreviation*) Cap.

captain ['kæptn] 1 *n* (*rank*) capitán *m*; (*leader*) capitán,-ana. – 2 *t* capitanear.

captaincy ['kæptnsɪ] *n* capitanía.

caption ['kæpʃən] 1 *n* (*under picture*) leyenda, pie *m* de foto; (*short title, headline*) título. 2 CINEM subtítulo.

captivate ['kæptɪveɪt] *t* cautivar, fascinar.

captivating ['kæptɪveɪtɪŋ] *adj* encantador,-ra, cautivador,-ra.

captive ['kæptɪv] 1 *adj* cautivo,-a. – 2 *n* cautivo,-a.
● **to have a captive audience,** tener un público obligado (a escuchar). ‖ **to hold sb. captive,** tener a algn. cautivo,-a, mantener a algn. cautivo,-a. ‖ **to take sb. captive,** hacer prisionero,-a a algn.

captivity [kæp'tɪvɪtɪ] *n* cautiverio, cautividad *f*.
● **in captivity,** en cautiverio.

captor ['kæptə'] *n* captor,-ra.

capture ['kæptʃə'] 1 *n* (*seizure - of person*) captura, apresamiento; (*of town*) toma, conquista. – 2 *t* (*seize - person*) capturar, apresar; (- *town*) tomar. 3 (*gain - share of market*) hacerse con; (- *votes*) conseguir, captar. 4 *fig* (*attract - attention, etc*) captar, atraer, acaparar; (*preserve - mood, etc*) captar, reproducir; (*on film, in painting, in words*) captar, plasmar.

car [kɑː'] 1 *n* AUTO coche *m*, automóvil *m*. 2 US (*railway carriage*) vagón *m*, coche *m*.
● **to go by car,** ir en coche.
■ **car bomb,** coche *m* bomba. ‖ **car park,** parking *m*, aparcamiento. ‖ **car wash,** túnel *m* de lavado. ‖ **dining car,** coche *m* restaurante.

carafe [kə'ræf] *n* garrafa.

caramel ['kærəmel] 1 *n* CULIN (*burnt sugar*) azúcar *m* quemado. 2 (*toffee*) caramelo.

carat ['kærət] *n* quilate *m*.

caravan ['kærə'væn] 1 *n* GB AUTO caravana, roulotte *f*. 2 GB (*covered cart*) carromato. 3 (*in desert*) caravana.
■ **caravan site,** camping *m* para caravanas.

caravel ['kærəvel] *n* carabela.

caraway ['kærəweɪ] *n* BOT alcaravea.
■ **caraway seed,** carví *m*.

carbohydrate [kɑːbəu'haɪdreɪt] *n* hidrato de carbono, carbohidrato.

carbolic acid [kɑː'bɒlɪk'æsɪd] *n* fenol *m*.

carbon ['kɑːbən] *n* CHEM carbono.
● **to be a carbon copy of sb./sth.,** ser un calco de algn./algo.

■ **carbon copy,** copia (hecha con papel carbón). ‖ **carbon dioxide,** dióxido de carbono. ‖ **carbon monoxide,** monóxido de carbono. ‖ **carbon paper,** papel *m* carbón.

carbonated [ˈkɑːbəneɪtɪd] *adj* (*fizzy*) gaseoso,-a, con gas.

carbonize [ˈkɑːbənaɪz] *t* carbonizar.

car-boot sale [kɑːˈbuːtseɪl] *n* GB *tipo de mercadillo donde se venden cosas desde el maletero de los coches.*

carboretor [ˈkɑːbjəretəʳ] *n* US → **carburettor.**

carboy [ˈkɑːbɔɪ] *n* garrafón *m.*

carbuncle [ˈkɑːbʌŋkəl] **1** *n* MED carbunco. **2** (*gem*) granate *m.*

carburettor [kɑːbjəˈretəʳ] *n* AUTO carburador *m.*

carcase [ˈkɑːkəs] *n* → **carcass.**

carcass [ˈkɑːkəs] **1** *n* (*dead animal*) res *f* muerta; (*at butcher's*) res *f* abierta en canal; (*of cooked bird*) huesos *mpl.* **2** (*frame, shell*) armazón *f.*

carcinogenic [kɑːsɪnəˈdʒenɪk] *adj* MED cancerígeno,-a, carcinógeno,-a.

card[1] [kɑːd] **1** *n* (*gen*) tarjeta: *my telephone number is on the card,* mi número de teléfono está en la tarjeta. **2** (*greetings card*) tarjeta de felicitación, felicitación *f.* **3** (*postcard*) tarjeta postal. **4** (*index card*) ficha. **5** (*of membership, identity*) carnet *m,* carné *m.* **6** (*stiff paper*) cartulina. **7** (*playing*) **card,** carta, naipe *m*: *shuffle the cards and deal them out,* baraja los naipes y repártelos. – **8 cards,** *npl* (*card-playing*) cartas *fpl*: *shall we play cards?,* ¿jugamos a cartas?

● **to be on the cards,** estar previsto,-a. ‖ **to get one's cards,** ser despedido,-a. ‖ **to lay one's cards on the table,** poner las cartas boca arriba, poner las cartas sobre la mesa. ‖ **to play one's cards right,** jugar bien las cartas.

■ **card index,** fichero. ‖ **debit card,** tarjeta de débito. ‖ **picture card,** cromo. ‖ **playing card,** carta, naipe *m.*

card[2] [kɑːd] **1** *n* (*for wool*) carda. – **2** *t* cardar.

Card [ˈkɑːdɪnəl] *abbr* (*Cardinal*) Cardenal *m*; (*abbreviation*) Card.

cardamom [ˈkɑːdəmən] *n* cardamomo.

cardboard [ˈkɑːdbɔːd] *n* cartón *m.*

■ **cardboard box,** caja de cartón.

cardiac [ˈkɑːdɪæk] *adj* cardíaco,-a.

■ **cardiac arrest,** paro cardíaco.

cardigan [ˈkɑːdɪgən] *n* rebeca, chaqueta de punto.

cardinal [ˈkɑːdɪnəl] **1** *adj* (*most important*) capital, fundamental, principal. – **2** *n* REL cardenal *m.*

■ **cardinal number,** número cardinal. ‖ **cardinal point,** punto cardinal. ‖ **cardinal sin,** pecado capital. ‖ **cardinal virtues,** virtudes *fpl* cardinales.

cardiologist [kɑːdɪˈɒlədʒɪst] *n* cardiólogo,-a.

cardiology [kɑːdɪˈɒlədʒɪ] *n* cardiología.

cardsharp [ˈkɑːdʃɑːp] *n* fullero,-a, tramposo,-a.

care [keəʳ] **1** *n* (*attention, carefulness*) cuidado, atención *f*: *she drew the picture with great care,* dibujó el cuadro con mucho cuidado; *he should take more care over his handwriting,* debería cuidar más su letra; *take care when driving at night,* (ten) cuidado al conducir de noche; *take care not to burn your fingers,* ten cuidado de no quemarte los dedos. **2** (*sympathetic concern, protection*) cuidado, atención *f*: *old people need a lot of care,* los ancianos necesitan mucha atención. **3** (*charge, protection, responsibility*) cuidado: *I left the baby in the care of my mother,* dejé al bebé al cuidado de mi madre; *under the doctor's care,* al cuidado del médico; *we are responsible for children in our care,* somos responsables

de los niños que están a nuestro cargo. **4** (*worry, grief*) preocupación *f,* inquietud *f*: *free of care,* sin preocupaciones; *she hasn't a care in the world,* no hay nada que le preocupe. – **5** *i* (*be worried, be concerned*) preocuparse (**about,** por), importar: *don't you care about the environment?,* ¿no te preocupa el medio ambiente?; *she only cares about her appearance,* lo único que le preocupa es su aspecto físico; *he doesn't care about me,* no le importo; *I don't care,* no me importa, me da igual; *see if I care!,* ¡me trae sin cuidado!, ¡me da igual!; *who cares!,* ¡y a mí qué!; *you can starve for all I care,* por mí puedes morirte de hambre. – **6** *t* (*feel concern, mind*) importar: *no-one cares if you're late,* a nadie le importa si llegas tarde; *I don't care what you do,* no me importa lo que hagas; *he doesn't care what people think,* no le importa lo que piense la gente. **7** *fml* (*like, want*) gustar: *would you care to dance?,* ¿te gustaría bailar?

◆ **to care for 1** *t insep* (*look after*) cuidar, atender. **2** (*like*) gustar; (*feel affection for*) querer, sentir cariño por. **3** (*in polite offers*) apetecer: *would you care for a drink?,* ¿le apetece una copa?

● **"care of ..."**, (*on envelopes*): *Judith Brown, care of Mrs M. Wells,* Sra. M. Wells (a la atención de Judith Brown). ‖ **"handle with care"**, "frágil". ‖ **take care!,** (*be careful*) ¡ten cuidado!; (*look after yourself*) ¡cuídate! ‖ **not to care less,** importarle a uno un bledo, traerle a uno sin cuidado. ‖ **to take care of os.,** cuidarse. ‖ **to take care of sb.,** (*child*) cuidar a/de algn., estar al cuidado de algn.; (*patient*) atender a, cuidar de. ‖ **to take care of sth.,** (*business, matters, etc*) ocuparse de algo, encargarse de algo; (*pet, plant, car, etc*) cuidar. ‖ **to take sb. into care,** internar a algn. en un centro de protección de menores.

■ **medical care,** asistencia médica.

career [kəˈrɪəʳ] **1** *n* (*profession*) carrera: *a career in politics,* una carrera en (la) política. **2** (*working life*) vida profesional. – **3** *adj* de carrera. – **4** *i* ir a toda velocidad: *the car careered off the road,* el coche salió disparado de la carretera.

■ **career ladder,** escalafón *m.* ‖ **careers advice,** orientación *f* profesional. ‖ **careers adviser / careers officer,** persona que orienta profesionalmente.

careerist [kəˈrɪərɪst] *n* ambicioso,-a, trepa *mf.*

carefree [ˈkeəfriː] *adj* despreocupado,-a, libre de preocupaciones.

careful [ˈkeəfʊl] **1** *adj* (*cautious*) prudente, cuidadoso,-a: *a careful driver,* un conductor prudente. **2** (*painstaking*) cuidadoso,-a, esmerado,-a: *a careful worker,* un,-a trabajador,-a cuidadoso,-a; *after careful consideration,* después de considerarlo detenidamente.

● **to be careful,** tener cuidado: *be careful crossing the street,* ten cuidado al cruzar la calle; *be careful with the plates,* ten cuidado con los platos; *be careful about what you say,* ten cuidado con lo que dices; *be careful not to wake the baby,* procura no despertar al bebé. ‖ **to be careful with one's money,** (*thrifty*) ser ahorrador,-ra; (*mean*) ser tacaño,-a, mirar mucho el dinero.

carefully [ˈkeəfʊlɪ] **1** *adv* (*cautiously*) con cuidado, con precaución: *drive carefully,* conduce con cuidado. **2** (*with great attention*) cuidadosamente, detenidamente; (*painstakingly*) con esmero: *think it over carefully,* piénsatelo bien; *listen carefully,* presta mucha atención.

careless [ˈkeələs] *adj* (*inattentive, thoughtless - person*) descuidado,-a, poco cuidadoso,-a; (*driving*) negligente; (*work*) dejado,-a, poco cuidado,-a: *he's careless with his money,* es muy descuidado con el dinero.

● **careless talk costs lives,** las indiscreciones cuestan vidas.
■ **careless mistake,** descuido.

carelessly ['keələslɪ] **1** adv (inattentively - gen) descuidadamente, a la ligera; (- drive) sin la debida atención, de forma imprudente. **2** (unconcernedly) despreocupadamente.

carelessness ['keələsnəs] **1** n (lack of attention) descuido, negligencia, falta de atención. **2** (lack of concern) despreocupación f.

carer ['keərəʳ] n persona encargada de cuidar a alguien.

caress [kə'res] **1** n caricia. – **2** t acariciar.

caretaker ['keəteɪkəʳ] n conserje m, portero,-a.
■ **caretaker government,** gobierno provisional.

cargo ['kɑːgəʊ] n (goods) carga; (load) cargamento.
■ **cargo ship,** buque m de carga, carguero.
▲ pl cargoes o cargos.

Caribbean [kærɪ'bɪən, ʃə kə'rɪbɪən] adj caribeño,-a.
■ **the Caribbean (Sea),** el (mar) Caribe.

caricature ['kærɪkətjʊəʳ] **1** n caricatura. – **2** t caricaturizar.

caricaturist ['kærɪkətjʊərɪst] n caricaturista mf.

caries ['keərɪz] n caries f.

caring ['keərɪŋ] adj (kind) bondadoso,-a, comprensivo,-a, atento,-a; (loving) cariñoso,-a, afectuoso,-a.
■ **caring professions,** profesiones fpl de vocación social.

carjacking ['kɑːdʒækɪŋ] n robo de coche.

carload ['kɑːləʊd] n coche m lleno: they came back from France with a carload of beer, volvieron de Francia con el coche lleno de cerveza.

carmine ['kɑːmaɪn] **1** n (color m) carmín m. – **2** adj (de color) carmín.

carnage ['kɑːnɪdʒ] n carnicería, matanza.

carnal ['kɑːnəl] adj carnal.

carnation [kɑː'neɪʃən] n clavel m.

carnival ['kɑːnɪvəl] n carnaval m.

carnivore ['kɑːnɪvɔː] n carnívoro,-a.

carnivorous [kɑː'nɪvərəs] adj carnívoro,-a.

carob ['kærəb] n BOT (bean) algarroba; (tree) algarrobo.

carol ['kærəl] n villancico.

Carolina [kærə'laɪnə] n Carolina.
■ **North Carolina,** Carolina del Norte. ‖ **South Carolina,** Carolina del Sur.

carousel [kærə'sel] **1** n US (roundabout) tiovivo, caballitos mpl, carrusel m. **2** (for baggage) cinta transportadora. **3** (for slides) carrete m de diapositivas.

carp[1] [kɑːp] n (fish) carpa.

carp[2] [kɑːp] i (complain) quejarse (**about/at,** de).

Carpathians [kɑː'peɪθɪənz] the Carpathians, n los (montes mpl) Cárpatos.

carpenter ['kɑːpɪntəʳ] n carpintero,-a.

carpentry ['kɑːpɪntrɪ] n carpintería.

carpet ['kɑːpɪt] **1** n (gen) alfombra; (fitted) moqueta. **2** fig alfombra. – **3** t alfombrar, enmoquetar. **4** fig cubrir, alfombrar. **5** fam (reprimand) echarle una bronca a.
● **to be on the carpet,** caerle a uno una buena. ‖ **sweep sth. under the carpet,** correr un velo sobre algo, echar tierra encima de algo.
■ **carpet slippers,** zapatillas fpl. ‖ **carpet sweeper,** cepillo mecánico (para alfombras).

carpeting ['kɑːpɪtɪŋ] n alfombrado.

carport ['kɑːpɔːt] n cobertizo para coches.

carriage ['kærɪdʒ] **1** n HIST (horse-drawn) carruaje m. **2** GB (railway vehicle) vagón m, coche m. **3** (of typewriter) carro;

(of gun) cureña. **4** (cost of transport) porte m, transporte m. **5** dated (bearing, deportment) porte m.
● **carriage forward,** cobro al destinatario. ‖ **carriage free,** franco de porte, sin porte. ‖ **carriage paid,** porte pagado.
■ **carriage clock,** reloj m de mesa.

carriageway ['kærɪdʒweɪ] n GB calzada: northbound carriageway, calzada en dirección norte.

carrier ['kærɪəʳ] **1** n (company, person) transportista mf. **2** AV compañía aérea, línea aérea. **3** MED (of disease) portador,-ra. **4** (on bicycle) cesta, canasta.
■ **aircraft carrier,** MAR portaaviones m. ‖ **carrier bag,** bolsa de papel, bolsa de plástico. ‖ **carrier pigeon,** paloma mensajera.

carrion ['kærɪən] n carroña.

carrot ['kærət] **1** n (vegetable) zanahoria. **2** fig incentivo, aliciente m, estímulo.

carroty ['kærətɪ] adj (hair) rojizo,-a.

carry ['kærɪ] **1** t (take, bear - gen) llevar; (- money, passport, gun, etc) llevar (encima). **2** (transport - goods, load, passengers) transportar, acarrear. **3** (conduct, convey - water, oil, blood) llevar; (- electricity) conducir. **4** (disease) ser portador,-ra de. **5** ARCH (support - weight) soportar, sostener. **6** (take - blame, responsibility) cargar con. **7** (entail, involve - responsibility) conllevar; (- penalty, consequences) implicar, conllevar. **8** (vote, bill, motion, etc) aprobar. **9** COMM (have for sale) tener, vender. **10** (news, story, report, etc) traer, publicar. **11** (be pregnant with) estar embarazada de. **12** MATH llevar(se). – **13** i (sound, voice) oírse, tener alcance.
◆ **to carry forward / carry over** t sep llevar a la columna siguiente, llevar a la página siguiente: carry this figure forward to the next page, lleva esta cifra a la página siguiente. ‖ **to carry off** t sep (part, action, duty) realizar con éxito, salir airoso,-a de: she carried the speech off well, salió airosa del discurso. **2** (prize) llevarse, hacerse con. ‖ **to carry on** t insep (continue) continuar con, seguir con; (conversation) mantener. – **2** i continuar, seguir. **3** fam (make a fuss) hacer una escena, montar un número. **4** fam (have an affair) tener un lío. ‖ **to carry on with** t insep (have affair with) estar liado,-a con. **2** (continue) seguir con. ‖ **to carry out** t sep (plan, work) llevar a cabo, realizar; (test) verificar; (fulfil - order, threat, promise) cumplir; (- duty) cumplir con. ‖ **to carry through** t sep (plan etc) llevar a cabo.
● **carried forward,** suma y sigue. ‖ **to carry the can for sth.,** pagar el pato. ‖ **to carry coals to Newcastle,** llevar leña al monte. ‖ **to carry weight (with sb.),** fig tener importancia: my opinion doesn't carry much weight, mi opinión no cuenta para mucho. ‖ **to get carried away,** exaltarse, desmadrarse.
▲ pt & pp carried, ger carrying.

carryall ['kærɪɔːl] n US bolsa de viaje.

carrycot ['kærɪkɒt] n capazo (de bebé).

carryings-on [kærɪɪŋz'ɒn] npl fam (affairs) enredos mpl, líos mpl; (noisy behaviour) escándalo.

carry-on [kærɪ'ɒn] n GB fam lío, jaleo, follón m.

carry-out ['kærɪaʊt] **1** n US (food) comida para llevar. **2** (drink) bebida para llevar.

carsick ['kɑːsɪk] adj mareado,-a (al ir en coche).
● **to get carsick,** marearse en coche.

cart [kɑːt] **1** n (horse-drawn) carro, carreta; (handcart) carretilla. – **2** t (carry in cart) carretear, transportar. **3** fam (carry in hands) llevar: I've been carting this umbrella around all day, he llevado el paraguas arriba y abajo todo el día; they carted him off to the police station, se lo llevaron a la comisaría.
● **to put the cart before the horse,** empezar la casa por el tejado.

■ **cart track,** camino de carros.
carte blanche [kɑːˈblɑːnʧ] *n* carta blanca.
cartel [kɑːˈtel] *n* cártel *m*.
Carthage [ˈkɑːθɪʤ] *n* Cartago.
Carthaginian [kɑːθəˈʤɪnɪən] **1** *adj* cartaginense. – **2** *n* cartaginense *mf*.
carthorse [ˈkɑːθɔːs] *n* caballo de tiro.
cartilage [ˈkɑːtɪlɪʤ] *n* cartílago.
cartload [ˈkɑːtləʊd] *n* carretada.
cartographer [kɑːˈtɒgrəfəʳ] *n* cartógrafo,-a.
cartography [kɑːˈtɒgrəfɪ] *n* cartografía.
carton [ˈkɑːtən] *n* (*of cream, yoghurt*) bote *m*; (*of milk, juice, cigarettes*) cartón *m*; (*of cereals etc*) caja.
cartoon [kɑːˈtuːn] **1** *n* (*drawing*) viñeta, chiste *m*; (*strip*) tira cómica, historieta. **2** CINEM TV dibujos *mpl* animados. **3** ART cartón *m*.
cartoonist [kɑːˈtuːnɪst] **1** *n* (*of drawings*) dibujante *mf*, humorista *mf* gráfico,-a. **2** CINEM TV dibujante *mf* de dibujos animados.
cartridge [ˈkɑːtrɪʤ] **1** *n* MIL cartucho. **2** (*for record-player*) portaagujas *m*; (*for pen*) recambio; (*for magnetic tape*) cartucho; (*for camera*) carrete *m*.
■ **cartridge belt,** canana, cartuchera. ‖ **cartridge paper,** papel *m* de dibujo.
cartwheel [ˈkɑːtwiːl] **1** *n* (*sideways somersault*) voltereta lateral, rueda. **2** (*wheel of cart*) rueda (de carreta). – **3** *i* hacer volteretas (laterales).
● **to do a cartwheel,** hacer la rueda, hacer una voltereta lateral.
carve [kɑːv] **1** *t* (*wood, stone*) tallar; (*statue etc*) esculpir; (*initials*) grabar: *this statue was carved from stone,* esta estatua está esculpida en piedra. **2** (*meat*) cortar, trinchar. – **3** *i* trinchar la carne, cortar la carne.
◆ **to carve out** *t sep fig* (*reputation*) forjarse; (*name*) hacerse. ‖ **to carve up** *t sep* (*divide*) dividir, repartir.
carver [ˈkɑːvəʳ] **1** *n* (*of wood*) tallista *mf*; (*of stone*) escultor,-ra. **2** (*knife*) trinchante *m*, cuchillo de trinchar.
carving [ˈkɑːvɪŋ] *n* (*of wood*) talla, tallado; (*of stone*) escultura.
■ **carving knife,** trinchante *m*.
cascade [kæsˈkeɪd] **1** *n* cascada. – **2** *i* caer en cascada.
case¹ [keɪs] **1** *n* (*instance, situation, circumstances*) caso: *it was a case of mistaken identity,* fue un caso de identificación equivocada; *that's not the case,* no es así; *in your case,* en tu caso. **2** (*problem*) caso: *an extreme case of food poisoning,* un caso extremo de intoxicación por alimentos; *a hopeless case,* un caso perdido; *a borderline case,* un caso límite. **3** JUR (*lawsuit*) causa, litigio, pleito; (*set of arguments*) argumentos *mpl*, razones *fpl*: *he won his case,* ganó el pleito; *you have a good case,* tus argumentos son buenos. **4** LING caso. **5** *fam* (*person*) caso.
● **a case in point,** un buen ejemplo. ‖ **as the case may be,** según (sea) el caso. ‖ **in any case,** en todo caso, en cualquier caso. ‖ **in case ...,** por si ..., en caso de que ...: *in case it rains,* por si llueve. ‖ **in case of sth.,** en caso de algo. ‖ **in no case,** bajo ninguna circunstancia, en ninguna circunstancia. ‖ **in that case,** en ese caso. ‖ **to make out a case for sth.,** exponer los argumentos en favor de algo. ‖ **the case for the defence / the case for the prosecution,** la defensa / la acusación *f*.
■ **case history,** MED historial *m* clínico. ‖ **case law,** JUR jurisprudencia. ‖ **case study,** estudio, trabajo.
case² [keɪs] **1** *n* (*suitcase*) maleta. **2** (*box*) caja, cajón *m*; (*small, hard container*) estuche *m*; (*soft container*) funda: *a*

case of wine, una caja de botellas de vino. **3** (*in printing*) caja: *lower case,* caja baja, minúscula; *upper case,* caja alta, mayúscula.
● **to case the joint,** *sl* reconocer el terreno (antes de cometer un robo).
caseload [ˈkeɪsləʊd] *n* número de casos.
casement window [ˈkeɪsməntwɪndəʊ] *n* ventana de bisagras.
casework [ˈkeɪswɜːk] *n* asistencia social que trata el estudio de casos individuales.
caseworker [ˈkeɪswɜːkəʳ] *n* asistente,-a social.
cash [kæʃ] **1** *n* (*notes and coins*) dinero (en) efectivo, metálico. **2** *fam* (*money*) dinero: *I'm a bit short of cash,* ando algo corto de dinero, ando escaso de dinero. – **3** *t* (*cheque*) cobrar, hacer efectivo.
◆ **to cash in** *i* sacar provecho (**on**, de). ‖ **to cash up** *i* hacer caja.
● **cash down,** a toca teja, al contado. ‖ **cash on delivery,** entrega contra reembolso. ‖ **to pay cash / pay in cash,** pagar al contado, pagar en efectivo.
■ **cash and carry,** (*shop*) almacén *m* de venta al por mayor. ‖ **cash crop,** cultivo industrial, cultivo comercial. ‖ **cash desk,** caja. ‖ **cash dispenser,** cajero automático. ‖ **cash flow,** movimiento de efectivo, flujo de efectivo. ‖ **cash register,** caja registradora. ‖ **cash sale,** venta al contado.
cash-and-carry [kæʃənˈkærɪ] **1** *adj* de venta al por mayor. – **2** *adv* de venta al por mayor.
cashew [kəˈʃuː] **cashew (nut),** *n* anacardo.
cashier¹ [kæˈʃɪəʳ] *n* cajero,-a.
cashier² [kæˈʃɪəʳ] *t* MIL dar de baja.
cashmere [kæʃˈmɪəʳ] **1** *n* cachemir *m*, cachemira. – **2** *adj* de cachemir, de cachemira.
casino [kəˈsiːnəʊ] *n* casino.
▲ *pl* **casinos**.
cask [kɑːsk] *n* tonel *m*, barril *m*.
casket [ˈkɑːskɪt] **1** *n* (*box*) cofre *m*. **2** (*coffin*) ataúd *m*.
Caspian Sea [ˈkæspɪənˈsiː] *n* mar *m* Caspio.
cassava [kəˈsɑːvə] *n* mandioca.
casserole [ˈkæsərəʊl] **1** *n* (*dish*) cazuela. **2** (*food*) guiso, guisado: *chicken casserole,* pollo a la cazuela. – **3** *t* guisar.
cassette [kəˈset] *n* casete *f*.
■ **cassette deck,** platina. ‖ **cassette player / cassette recorder,** casete *m*.
cassock [ˈkæsək] *n* sotana.
cast [kɑːst] **1** *n* (*throw*) lanzamiento. **2** THEAT reparto. **3** TECH (*mould*) molde *m*; (*product*) pieza. **4** ART (*product*) vaciado. – **5** *t* (*throw - gen*) lanzar, arrojar, tirar; (*- fishing line*) lanzar; (*- net*) echar; (*- dice*) tirar, echar. **6** (*shadow, light*) proyectar. **7** (*vote*) emitir. **8** THEAT (*play*) hacer el reparto de; (*part, role*) asignar el papel a, dar el papel de. **9** (*shed - snake's skin*) mudar, mudar de; (*horse's shoe*) perder. **10** TECH fundir. **11** ART vaciar.
◆ **to cast about for / cast around for** *t insep* buscar, andar buscando. ‖ **to cast aside** *t sep* (*person*) abandonar; (*inhibitions, doubts, etc*) desechar, descartar. ‖ **to cast off** *t sep* (*clothes*) desechar; (*person*) dejar, abandonar; (*stitch*) cerrar. – **2** *i* (*in knitting*) cerrar los puntos. **3** MAR soltar amarras. ‖ **to cast on** *i* (*in knitting*) montar los puntos. – **2** *t sep* (*stitch*) montar. ‖ **to cast out** *t sep fml* expulsar.
● **to be cast away,** naufragar. ‖ **to cast a shadow on sth.,** *fig* ensombrecer algo. ‖ **to cast a spell on sth./ sb.,** hechizar algo/a algn. ‖ **to cast doubts on sth.,** poner algo en duda. ‖ **to cast one's eye over sth.,**

echar un vistazo a algo, echar una ojeada a algo. ‖ **to cast one's mind back to sth.**, tratar de recordar algo. ‖ **to cast sb. in a different light**, mostrar a algn. de manera distinta. ‖ **to cast suspicion on sb.**, levantar sospechas sobre algn. ‖ **to have a cast in one's eye**, ser algo bizco,-a.

■ **cast iron**, hierro colado.

▲ (*verbo*) *pt* & *pp* **cast**.

castanets [kæstə'nets] *npl* castañuelas *fpl*.

castaway ['kɑːstəweɪ] *n* náufrago,-a.

caste [kɑːst] *n* casta.

caster ['kɑːstəʳ] *n* (*wheel*) ruedecilla.

■ **caster sugar**, azúcar *m* extrafino.

castigate ['kæstɪgeɪt] *t fml* castigar.

Castile [kæ'stiːl] *n* Castilla.

■ **New Castile**, Castilla la Nueva. ‖ **Old Castile**, Castilla la Vieja.

Castilian [kæ'stɪlɪən] 1 *adj* castellano,-a. – 2 *n* (*person*) castellano,-a. 3 (*language*) castellano.

casting ['kɑːstɪŋ] 1 *n* TECH (*process*) fundición *f*; (*object*) pieza fundida. 2 ART vaciado. 3 THEAT (*selection*) selección *f*, casting *m*, reparto de papeles.

■ **casting vote**, voto de calidad.

cast-iron ['kɑːstaɪən] 1 *adj* de hierro fundido, de hierro colado. 2 *fig* (*constitution, stomach*) de hierro; (*will*) férreo,-a; (*alibi*) a toda prueba; (*evidence*) irrefutable; (*guarantee, promise*) sólido,-a.

castle ['kɑːsəl] 1 *n* (*gen*) castillo. 2 (*chess*) torre *f*. – 3 *i* (*chess*) enrocar.

■ **castles in the air**, castillos *mpl* en el aire.

cast-off ['kɑːstɒf] *adj* desechado,-a.

castoffs ['kɑːstɒfs] *npl* (*clothes*) ropa desechada.

castor[1] ['kɑːstəʳ] *n* → **caster**.

castor[2] ['kɑːstəʳ] *n* ZOOL castor *m*.

■ **castor oil**, aceite *m* de ricino.

castrate [kæ'streɪt] *t* castrar, capar.

castration [kæ'streɪʃən] *n* castración *f*.

casual ['kæʒjuəl] 1 *adj* (*chance - visit, visitor*) ocasional; (- *meeting*) fortuito,-a, casual. 2 (*unconcerned*) despreocupado,-a; (*irresponsible*) descuidado,-a, informal: *a casual remark*, un comentario hecho de pasada. 3 (*superficial*) superficial; (*glance*) rápido,-a; (*reader*) ocasional: *a casual acquaintance*, un,-a conocido,-a. 4 (*informal*) informal; (*clothes*) (de) sport, informal, desenfadado,-a. 5 (*labour*) eventual, ocasional; (*worker*) eventual.

casually ['kæʒjuəlɪ] 1 *adv* (*dress*) de manera informal, informalmente. 2 (*unconcernedly*) despreocupadamente; (*indifferently*) con indiferencia. 3 (*employed*) de forma eventual.

casualty ['kæʒjuəltɪ] 1 *n* MIL baja. 2 (*of accident*) herido,-a. 3 *fig* víctima. – 4 **casualties**, *npl* pérdidas *fpl*.

■ **casualty department**, departamento de traumatología.

▲ *pl* **casualties**.

cat [kæt] *n* (*domestic*) gato,-a; (*lion, tiger*) felino,-a: *the cat family*, los felinos.

● **has the cat got your tongue?**, ¿te ha comido la lengua el gato? ‖ **there's not enough room to swing a cat in here**, no cabe ni un alfiler. ‖ **to be like a cat on hot bricks / be like a cat on a hot tin roof**, estar sobre ascuas. ‖ **to let the cat out of the bag**, descubrir el pastel. ‖ **to play cat and mouse with sb.**, jugar al gato y al ratón con algn. ‖ **to put the cat among the pigeons**, meter los perros en danza, provocar un revuelo. ‖ **to think one is the cat's whiskers**, creerse el

ombligo del mundo. ‖ **when the cat's away, the mice will play**, cuando el gato duerme, bailan los ratones.

■ **cat burglar**, ladrón,-ona que escala edificios.

cataclysm ['kætəklɪzəm] *n* cataclismo.

catacombs ['kætəkuːm] *n* catacumbas *fpl*.

Catalan ['kætələn] 1 *adj* catalán,-ana. – 2 *n* (*person*) catalán,-ana. 3 (*language*) catalán *m*.

catalog ['kætəlɒg] *n* US → **catalogue**.

catalogue ['kætəlɒg] 1 *n* catálogo. – 2 *t* catalogar.

Catalonia [kætə'ləʊnɪə] *n* Cataluña.

Catalonian [kætə'ləʊnɪən] *adj* → **Catalan**.

catalyst ['kætəlɪst] *n* catalizador *m*.

catamaran [kætəmə'ræn] *n* catamarán *m*.

catapult ['kætəpʌlt] 1 *n* (*for aircraft*) catapulta (de lanzamiento). 2 (*toy*) tirador *m*, tiragomas *m*, tirachinas *m*. – 3 *t* catapultar. – 4 *i* salir disparado,-a.

cataract ['kætərækt] 1 *n* (*waterfall*) catarata; (*in river*) rápido. 2 MED catarata.

● **to have a cataract operation**, operarse de cataratas.

catarrh [kə'tɑːʳ] *n* catarro.

catastrophe [kə'tæstrəfɪ] *n* catástrofe *f*.

catastrophic [kætə'strɒfɪk] *adj* catastrófico,-a.

catcall ['kætkɔːl] 1 *n* silbido. – 2 **catcalls**, *npl* silbas *fpl*, abucheos *mpl*.

catch [kætʃ] 1 *n* (*of ball*) parada. 2 (*of fish*) presa. 3 *fam* (*difficulty*) pega, trampa. 4 (*fastener on door*) pestillo. – 5 *t* (*grasp, take hold of*) coger, agarrar; (*capture, trap*) coger, atrapar; (*fish*) pescar: *the cat caught a mouse*, el gato atrapó un ratón; *bet you can't catch me!*, ¡a que no me coges! 6 (*surprise*) pillar, sorprender, coger, pescar; (*catch up with*) alcanzar, pillar: *they were caught trying to steal a car*, los pillaron intentando robar un coche; *I got caught in a traffic jam*, me cogió un atasco. 7 (*train, plane - take*) coger, tomar; (- *be in time for*) alcanzar: *I just caught the last train*, cogí el último tren con el tiempo justo. 8 *fam* (*manage to see, hear, attend*) pescar: *we caught the end of the news*, pescamos el final de las noticias; *I'll catch you later*, te veré luego. 9 (*hear, understand*) ofr, entender, captar: *sorry, I didn't quite catch that*, perdona, no lo he entendido bien. 10 (*entangle, get stuck - clothes, hair*) engancharse; (- *fingers*) pillarse. 11 (*become infected with*) contagiarse de, contraer. 12 (*hit*) dar con, darse con: *he caught his head on the ceiling*, se dio con la cabeza en el techo. 13 (*mood, likeness, etc*) captar, reflejar. – 14 *i* (*take hold of*) coger. 15 (*sleeve etc*) engancharse (on, en). 16 (*burn*) prender.

◆ **to catch on** 1 *i* (*understand*) entender, darse cuenta (**to**, de). 2 (*become popular*) ponerse de moda, imponerse. ‖ **to catch out** 1 *t sep* (*doing something wrong*) pillar, coger, pescar, sorprender; (*trick*) hacer que uno caiga. 2 SP (*in cricket*) eliminar. ‖ **to catch up** 1 *t sep* (*person*) alcanzar. – 2 *i* (*with news, studies, work*) ponerse al día; (*with person, country*) alcanzar: *he's staying late to catch up on some work*, se queda hasta tarde para ponerse al día con el trabajo; *she needs to catch up on some sleep*, necesita recuperar el sueño perdido.

● **to be a good catch**, (*boyfriend, girlfriend*) ser un buen partido. ‖ **to be caught out by sth.**, ser sorprendido,-a por algo. ‖ **to be caught up in sth.**, verse envuelto,-a en algo, estar envuelto,-a en algo. ‖ **to catch a cold**, resfriarse, coger un resfriado. ‖ **to catch hold of sth.**, agarrar algo, echar mano a algo. ‖ **to catch it**, ganarse una bronca. ‖ **to catch one's breath**, sostener la respiración. ‖ **to catch one's death (of cold)**, coger una pulmonía doble. ‖ **to catch sb. napping,** coger a algn. desprevenido,-a. ‖ **to catch sb. red-handed,** coger a algn. con las manos en la masa, coger a algn. in fraganti. ‖ **to catch sb. with their trousers down,** coger a algn. in fraganti. ‖ **to catch sb.'s attention/eye,** atraer la atención de algn., captar la atención de algn. ‖ **to catch sight of sth./sb. / catch a glimpse of sth./ sb.,** entrever algo/a algn. ‖ **to get caught up in sth.,** verse envuelto,-a en algo.

▲ (*verbo*) *pt* & *pp* **caught.**

catcher ['kætʃəʳ] *n* SP receptor,-ra, catcher *mf*.

catching ['kætʃɪŋ] *adj* (*contagious*) contagioso,-a.

catchment area ['kætʃməntɛərə] 1 *n* (*of school, hospital, etc*) zona de captación. 2 GEOG cuenca.

catchword ['kætʃwɔːd] *n* eslogan *m*.

catchy ['kætʃɪ] *adj* pegadizo,-a.

▲ *comp* **catchier,** *superl* **catchiest.**

catechism ['kætəkɪzəm] *n* catecismo.

categoric [kætə'gɒrɪk] *adj* categórico,-a.

categorical [kætə'gɒrɪkəl] *adj* categórico,-a.

categorize ['kætəgəraɪz] *t* clasificar.

category ['kætəgərɪ] *n* categoría.

▲ *pl* **categories.**

cater ['keɪtəʳ] *i* (*food*) proveer comida (**for,** para).

◆ **to cater for** *t insep* (*needs, interests, tastes*) atender a, satisfacer: *a magazine that caters for young people,* una revista dirigida a jóvenes. ‖ **to cater to** *t insep* (*desires, needs, demands, etc*) satisfacer.

caterer ['keɪtərəʳ] *n* proveedor,-ra.

catering ['keɪtərɪŋ] *n* (*business, course*) hostelería; (*service*) catering *m*.

● **to do the catering,** encargarse del catering, encargarse del servicio de comida y bebida.

caterpillar ['kætəpɪləʳ] *n* oruga.

catfish ['kætfɪʃ] *n* barbo.

catgut ['kætgʌt] *n* (*cord*) cuerda de tripa.

Cath ['kæθəlɪk] *abbr* (*Catholic*) católico,-a.

catharsis [kə'θɑːsɪs] *n* catarsis *f*.

▲ *pl* **catharses** [kə'θɑːsiːz].

cathartic [kə'θɑːtɪk] *adj* catártico,-a.

cathedral [kə'θiːdrəl] *n* catedral *f*: **cathedral city,** ciudad catedralicia.

Catherine wheel ['kæθrɪnwiːl] *n* rueda.

catheter ['kæθətəʳ] *n* catéter *m*.

cathode ['kæθəʊd] *n* cátodo.

■ **cathode ray,** rayo catódico.

catholic ['kæθəlɪk] *adj* (*views*) liberal; (*interests*) amplio,-a y variado,-a: *we have a catholic taste in music,* nos gusta todo tipo de música.

Catholic ['kæθəlɪk] 1 *adj* REL católico,-a. – 2 *n* REL católico,-a.

Catholicism [kə'θɒlɪsɪzəm] *n* REL catolicismo.

catkin ['kætkɪn] *n* BOT candelilla, amento.

catnap ['kætnæp] *n fam* siestecita, cabezada.

● **to have a catnap,** echar una siestecita, echar una cabezada.

Catseye ['kætsaɪ] *n* GB catafaro.

catsuit ['kætsuːt] *n* GB prenda ajustada que cubre todo el cuerpo.

cattery ['kætərɪ] *n* residencia para gatos.

▲ *pl* **catteries.**

cattle ['kætəl] *npl* ganado (vacuno): *fifty head of cattle,* cincuenta cabezas de ganado, cincuenta reses.

■ **cattle breeding,** ganadería. ‖ **cattle market,** feria de ganado. ‖ **cattle shed,** cobertizo para ganado.

cattle-grid ['kætəlgrɪd] *n* reja en la calzada para impedir que pase el ganado.

catty ['kætɪ] *adj* (*remark*) malicioso,-a, malintencionado,-a; (*person*) malicioso,-a, rencoroso,-a, malo,-a.

▲ *comp* **cattier,** *superl* **cattiest.**

catwalk ['kætwɔːk] *n* pasarela.

Caucasia [kɔː'keɪʒə] *n* el Cáucaso.

Caucasian [kɔː'keɪʒən] 1 *adj* (*race*) caucásico,-a. 2 GEOG caucáseo,-a, caucasiano,-a. – 3 *n* (*race*) caucásico,-a.

Caucasus ['kɔːkəsəs]. 1 **the Caucasus,** *n* (*region*) el Cáucaso. 2 (*mountains*) las montañas del Cáucaso.

caucus ['kɔːkəs] 1 *n* GB POL comité *m*. 2 US POL reunión *f* del comité central.

caught [kɔːt] *pt* & *pp* → **catch.**

cauldron ['kɔːldrən] *n* caldero.

cauliflower ['kɒlɪflaʊəʳ] *n* coliflor *f*.

■ **cauliflower cheese,** coliflor *f* con bechamel. ‖ **cauliflower ear,** oreja deformada.

causal ['kɔːzəl] *adj* causal.

causality [kɔː'zælɪtɪ] *n* causalidad *f*.

cause [kɔːz] 1 *n* (*origin*) causa: *we still do not know the cause of the accident,* todavía desconocemos la causa del accidente. 2 (*reason, grounds*) razón *f*, motivo: *you have cause for complaint,* tienes motivos para quejarte; *there's no cause for alarm,* no hay por qué asustarse; *without good cause,* sin motivo justificado. 3 (*principle, movement*) causa: *it's for a good cause,* es para una buena causa. 4 JUR causa, pleito. – 5 *t* causar.

● **to cause sb. to do sth.,** hacer que algn. haga algo.

causeway ['kɔːzweɪ] *n* (*road*) carretera elevada.

caustic ['kɔːstɪk] 1 *adj* CHEM cáustico,-a. 2 *fig* cáustico,-a, mordaz.

■ **caustic soda,** sosa cáustica.

cauterization [kɔːtəraɪ'zeɪʃən] *n* cauterización *f*.

cauterize ['kɔːtəraɪz] *t* cauterizar.

caution ['kɔːʃən] 1 *n* (*care, prudence*) cautela, precaución *f*, prudencia: *proceed with caution,* procedan con cautela. 2 (*warning*) aviso, advertencia. 3 GB JUR advertencia, reprensión *f*. – 4 *t* (*warn*) advertir: *they cautioned her against accepting lifts from strangers,* le advirtieron que no subiera a coches de desconocidos. 5 GB JUR amonestar.

● **to caution against sth.,** desaconsejar algo.

cautionary ['kɔːʃənərɪ] *adj* aleccionador,-ra: *a cautionary tale,* un cuento con moraleja.

cautious ['kɔːʃəs] *adj* cauteloso,-a, prudente, cauto,-a.

cautiously ['kɔːʃəslɪ] *adv* cautelosamente.

cautiousness ['kɔːʃəsnəs] *n* cautela, precaución *f*, prudencia.

cavalcade [kævəl'keɪd] *n* (*procession - gen*) desfile *m*; (*- on horseback*) cabalgata.

cavalier [kævə'lɪəʳ] 1 *n* caballero. – 2 *adj* arrogante, indiferente.

cavalry ['kævəlrɪ] *n* caballería.

▲ *pl* **cavalries.**

cavalryman ['kævəlrɪmən] *n* soldado de caballería.

cave [keɪv] *n* cueva.

◆ **to cave in** *i* (*roof etc*) hundirse, derrumbarse; (*opposition etc*) ceder.

■ **cave dweller,** cavernícola *mf*, troglodita *mf*. ‖ **cave painting,** pintura rupestre.

caveman ['keɪvmæn] *n* cavernícola *m*, troglodita *m*, hombre *m* de las cavernas.

cavern ['kævən] *n* caverna.

cavernous ['kævənəs] *adj* cavernoso,-a.

caviar ['kævɪɑːʳ] *n* caviar *m*.

caviare ['kævɪɑːʳ] n caviar m.
cavil ['kævɪl] i poner reparos (**about/at**, a).
▲ pt & pp **cavilled** (US **caviled**), ger **cavilling** (US **caviling**).
caving ['keɪvɪŋ] n espeleología.
● **to go caving**, hacer espeleología.
cavity ['kævɪtɪ] 1 n (hole) cavidad f. 2 (in tooth) caries f.
■ **cavity wall**, pared f de tabique doble, pared f con cámara de aire.
▲ pl **cavities**.
cavort [kə'vɔːt] i retozar.
caw [kɔː] 1 n graznido. – 2 i graznar.
cayenne [keɪ'en] **cayenne (pepper)**, n (pimienta de) cayena.
cayman ['keɪmən] n caimán m.
■ **Cayman Islands**, Islas fpl Cayman.
CBI ['siː'biː'aɪ] abbr GB (Confederation of British Industry) confederación británica de organizaciones empresariales.
CBS ['siː'biː'es] abbr US (Columbia Broadcasting System) sistema de radiodifusión Columbia.
cc¹ ['siː'siː] abr (cubic centimetre) centímetro cúbico; (abbreviation) cc.
cc² ['siː'siː] abbr (carbon copy) copia a papel carbón.
CD ['siː'diː] abbr (compact disc) disco compacto; (abbreviation) CD m.
Cdr [kə'mɑːndəʳ] abbr (Commander) Comandante m; (abbreviation) Cte.
Cdre ['kɒmədɔːʳ] abbr (Commodore) Comodoro.
CD-ROM ['siː'diː'rɒm] abbr (compact disc read-only memory) CD-ROM m.
CE ['siːəv'iː] abbr (Church of England) Iglesia Anglicana.
cease [siːs] 1 t (production etc) suspender. – 2 i cesar.
● **to cease fire**, MIL cesar el fuego. ‖ **to cease to do sth.**, dejar de hacer algo. ‖ **without cease**, sin cesar.
cease-fire [siːs'faɪəʳ] n alto el fuego.
ceaseless ['siːsləs] adj incesante.
cedar ['siːdəʳ] n BOT cedro.
cedarwood ['siːdəwʊd] n (madera de) cedro.
cede [siːd] t ceder.
cedilla [sə'dɪlə] n LING cedilla.
ceiling ['siːlɪŋ] 1 n (of room) techo. 2 (upper limit) tope m, límite m.
● **to hit the ceiling**, ponerse histérico,-a, poner el grito en el cielo.
celebrate ['selɪbreɪt] 1 t celebrar, festejar. 2 REL celebrar. – 3 i divertirse: let's celebrate!, ¡vamos a celebrarlo!
celebrated ['selɪbreɪtɪd] adj célebre, famoso,-a.
celebration [selɪ'breɪʃən] 1 n (event) fiesta, festejo; (activity) celebración f. – 2 **celebrations**, npl festividades fpl, festejos mpl.
celebrity [sə'lebrɪtɪ] n celebridad f, personaje m famoso.
▲ pl **celebrities**.
celery ['selərɪ] n apio.
celestial [sɪ'lestɪəl] 1 adj (heavenly) celestial. 2 ASTRON celeste.
celibacy ['selɪbəsɪ] n celibato.
celibate ['selɪbət] 1 adj célibe. – 2 n célibe mf.
cell [sel] 1 n (in prison, monastery) celda. 2 (of honeycomb) celdilla. 3 BIOL POL célula. 4 ELEC (in battery) pila.
cellar ['seləʳ] 1 n (basement) sótano. 2 (for wine) bodega.
cellist ['tʃelɪst] n violoncelista mf.
cello ['tʃeləʊ] n violoncelo.
▲ pl **cellos**.
cellophane ['seləfeɪn] n celofán m.

cellular ['seljələʳ] adj celular.
celluloid ['seljələɪd] n celuloide m.
cellulose ['seljələʊs] n celulosa.
Celsius ['selsɪəs] adj Celsio: 30 degrees Celsius, 30 grados Celsio.
Celt [kelt] n celta mf.
Celtiberian [kelti'bɪərɪən] 1 n (person) celtibérico,-a, celtíbero,-a, celtibero,-a. 2 (language) celtíbero, celtibero.
Celtic ['keltɪk] 1 adj celta. – 2 n (language) celta m.
cement [sɪ'ment] 1 n (in building) cemento. 2 (glue) adhesivo; (for filling teeth) empaste m. – 3 t (bind) unir con cemento; (cover) revestir de cemento. 4 fig cimentar.
■ **cement mixer**, hormigonera.
cemetery ['semətrɪ] n cementerio.
▲ pl **cemeteries**.
cenotaph ['senətɑːf] n cenotafio.
censer ['sensəʳ] n REL incensario.
censor ['sensəʳ] 1 n censor,-ra. – 2 t censurar.
censorship ['sensəʃɪp] n censura.
censure ['senʃəʳ] 1 n fml censura. – 2 t fml censurar.
census ['sensəs] n censo, padrón m.
● **to take a census**, realizar el censo.
cent [sent] n centavo, céntimo.
centaur ['sentɔːʳ] n centauro.
centenarian [sentə'neərɪən] n centenario,-a.
centenary [sen'tiːnərɪ] n centenario.
▲ pl **centenaries**.
centennial [sen'tenɪəl] 1 n US centenario. – 2 adj del centenario.
center ['sentəʳ] n US → **centre**.
centerfold ['sentəfəʊld] n US → **centrefold**.
centigrade ['sentɪɡreɪd] adj centígrado,-a.
centiliter ['sentɪliːtəʳ] n US → **centilitre**.
centilitre ['sentɪliːtəʳ] n centilitro.
centimeter ['sentɪmiːtəʳ] n US → **centimetre**.
centimetre ['sentɪmiːtəʳ] n centímetro.
centipede ['sentɪpiːd] n ciempiés m.
central ['sentrəl] 1 adj (government, bank, committee) central. 2 (of, at or near centre) céntrico,-a: her flat is very central, su piso es muy céntrico; she lives in central London, vive en el centro de Londres. 3 (main, principal) principal, fundamental: central character, personaje central, personaje principal.
● **to be central to sth.**, ser fundamental para algo.
■ **Central African Republic**, República Centroafricana. ‖ **central heating**, calefacción f central. ‖ **central locking**, cierre m centralizado. ‖ **central nervous system**, sistema m nervioso central. ‖ **central processing unit**, unidad f central de proceso. ‖ **central reservation**, GB mediana.
centralization [sentrəlaɪ'zeɪʃən] n centralización f.
centralize ['sentrəlaɪz] t centralizar.
centrally ['sentrəlɪ] adv: a centrally heated house, una casa con calefacción central; it's very centrally located, es muy céntrico.
centre ['sentəʳ] 1 n GB (gen) centro: I work in the city centre, trabajo en el centro de la ciudad. – 2 t (put in centre) centrar. – 3 i (focus on) centrarse (**on/upon**, en); (revolve round) girar (**around**, alrededor de/en torno a): our attention centres on the forthcoming elections, nuestra atención se centra en las próximas elecciones.
● **to be the centre of attention**, ser el centro de atención, ser el centro de todas las miradas.
■ **centre forward**, SP delantero centro. ‖ **centre half**, SP medio centro. ‖ **centre party**, POL partido centrista. ‖ **sports centre**, polideportivo.

centrefold ['sentəfəʊld] n página central.
centrepiece ['sentəpiːs] 1 n (decoration) centro de mesa.
2 (most important, noticeable, attractive part) plato fuerte.
centrifugal [sentrɪ'fjuːgəl] adj centrífugo,-a.
centripetal [sen'trɪpɪtəl] adj centrípeto,-a.
centrist ['sentrɪst] 1 adj centrista. – 2 n centrista mf.
centurion [sen'tjʊərɪən] n centurión m.
century ['sentʃərɪ] 1 n siglo: the twentieth century, el siglo veinte. 2 sp (in cricket) centena.
▲ pl centuries.
ceramic [sə'ræmɪk] 1 adj de cerámica. – 2 n cerámica.
ceramics [sə'ræmɪks] n (art) cerámica; (objects) objetos mpl de cerámica.
cereal ['sɪərɪəl] n (plant, grain) cereal m; (breakfast food) cereales mpl.
cerebral ['serɪbrəl] adj cerebral.
■ cerebral palsy, parálisis f cerebral.
ceremonial [serɪ'məʊnɪəl] 1 adj (gen) ceremonioso,-a; (dress) de gala; (occasion) solemne. – 2 n ceremonial m.
ceremonious [serɪ'məʊnɪəs] adj ceremonioso,-a.
ceremony ['serɪmənɪ] n ceremonia.
● to stand on ceremony, ser muy ceremonioso,-a.
▲ pl ceremonies.
cerise [sə'riːz] 1 adj de color cereza. – 2 n color m cereza.
cert [sɜːt] to be a cert, phr fam no caber duda: Induráin's a dead cert to win the Tour, no cabe duda que Induráin ganará el Tour.
certain ['sɜːtən] 1 adj (sure to happen, definite) seguro,-a: she's certain to pass, seguro que aprobará; prices are certain to rise, seguro que los precios suben; it's not certain that he's leaving, no es seguro que se vaya. 2 (completely sure, convinced, true) seguro,-a: I'm certain, estoy seguro,-a; are you certain they're coming?, ¿estás seguro (de) que vendrán?; we're not certain where she lives, no sabemos con certeza dónde vive. 3 (specific, particular) cierto,-a. 4 (named) tal: a certain Robert Smith, un tal Robert Smith. 5 (limited, some, slight) cierto,-a.
● for certain, con certeza, con toda seguridad: I can't say for certain, no lo puedo decir a ciencia cierta. ‖ to a certain extent, hasta cierto punto. ‖ to make certain of sth., asegurarse de algo.
certainly ['sɜːtənlɪ] 1 adv (definitely, surely) seguro: he'll certainly pass, seguro que aprobará; I'll certainly do my best, por supuesto que haré todo lo posible. 2 (when answering questions) desde luego, por supuesto: certainly not, por supuesto que no, de ninguna manera.
certainty ['sɜːtəntɪ] 1 n (state of being certain) certeza, seguridad f. 2 (certain thing) cosa segura.
● it's a certainty that ..., es seguro que ..., no cabe duda que ...
▲ pl certainties.
certifiable ['sɜːtɪfaɪəbəl] 1 adj certificable. 2 MED demente.
certificate [sə'tɪfɪkət] n (gen) certificado: birth certificate, partida de nacimiento; death certificate, certificado de defunción; marriage certificate, certificado de matrimonio.
certified ['sɜːtɪfaɪd] 1 adj (cheque) certificado,-a; (document) legalizado,-a. 2 MED declarado,-a demente.
certify ['sɜːtɪfaɪ] t certificar.
● to certify sb. insane, declarar demente a algn.
▲ pt & pp certified, ger certifying.
certitude ['sɜːtɪtjuːd] n certeza.
cervical ['sɜːvɪkəl] 1 adj (of neck) cervical. 2 (of uterus) del (cuello del) útero.
■ cervical cancer, cáncer m de útero. ‖ cervical smear, frotis m cervical, citología.

cervix ['sɜːvɪks] 1 n fml (neck) cerviz f, cuello. 2 (uterus) cuello del útero.
▲ pl cervixes o cervices.
Cesarian [sɪ'zeərɪən] n US → Caesarean.
cessation [se'seɪʃən] n fml cese m.
cesspit ['sespɪt] n pozo negro.
cesspool ['sespuːl] n pozo negro.
Ceylon [sɪ'lɒn] n Ceilán m.
Ceylonese [selə'niːz] 1 adj ceilanés,-esa. – 2 n ceilanés,-esa. – 3 the Ceylonese, npl los ceilaneses mpl.
cf. ['siː'ef] abbr (confer) compárese; (abbreviation) cfr.
CFC ['siː'ef'siː] abbr (chlorofluorocarbon) clorofluorocarbono; (abbreviation) CFC m.
CFE ['siː'ef'iː] abbr GB EDUC (College of Further Education) escuela de estudios superiores.
ch ['tʃæptə'] abbr (chapter) capítulo; (abbreviation) cap.
Chad [tʃæd] n Chad.
Chadian ['tʃædɪən] 1 adj chadiano,-a. – 2 n (persona) chadiano,-a.
chafe [tʃeɪf] 1 t (make sore) rozar, excoriar. 2 (make warm) frotar, friccionar. – 3 i (become sore) irritarse. 4 (become irritated) irritarse (at, por/con), enfadarse (at, por).
chaff [tʃæf] n (husks) barcia, granzas fpl; (fodder) paja.
chaffinch ['tʃæfɪntʃ] n ORN pinzón m vulgar.
chagrin ['ʃægrɪn] n disgusto, desilusión f.
chain [tʃeɪn] 1 n (metal rings) cadena. 2 (of shops, hotels, etc) cadena; (of events) cadena, serie f. – 3 to chain (up) t encadenar, atar: I don't want to be chained to a desk, no quiero estar atado a una mesa de trabajo.
● in chains, encadenado,-a. ‖ to pull the chain, tirar de la cadena.
■ chain gang, cadena de presos. ‖ chain letter, carta (de una cadena). ‖ chain mail, cota de malla. ‖ chain reaction, reacción f en cadena. ‖ chain saw, motosierra, sierra de cadena. ‖ chain stitch, punto de cadeneta. ‖ chain store, tienda (de una cadena). ‖ mountain chain, cordillera, cadena montañosa.
chain-smoke ['tʃeɪnsməʊk] i fumar un cigarrillo tras otro.
chair [tʃeə'] 1 n (gen) silla; (with arms) sillón m, butaca. – 2 t (meeting) presidir. – 3 the chair, n (in meeting) presidencia; (at university) cátedra.
● to address the chair, dirigirse al presidente, dirigirse a la presidencia.
■ chair lift, telesilla. ‖ folding chair, silla plegable.
chairman ['tʃeəmən] n presidente m.
chairmanship ['tʃeəmənʃɪp] n presidencia.
chairperson ['tʃeəpɜːsən] n presidente,-a.
chairwoman ['tʃeəwʊmən] n presidenta.
chaise longue [ʃeɪz'lɒŋ] n diván m.
Chaldean [kæl'diːən] 1 adj caldeo,-a. – 2 n caldeo,-a.
chalet ['ʃæleɪ] n (in mountains) chalet m, chalé m; (in holiday camp) bungaló m, bungalow m.
chalice ['tʃælɪs] n cáliz m.
chalk [tʃɔːk] 1 n (mineral) creta, roca caliza. 2 (for writing) tiza. – 3 t escribir con tiza. – 4 i escribir con tiza.
◆ to chalk out t sep marcar con tiza. ‖ to chalk up t insep fam (victory, success) apuntarse.
● not by a long chalk, ni mucho menos, con mucho. ‖ to be as different as chalk and cheese, ser la noche y el día, parecerse como un huevo a una castaña.
chalky ['tʃɔːkɪ] adj (soil) calcáreo,-a; (fingers) lleno,-a de tiza.
▲ comp chalkier, superl chalkiest.
challenge ['tʃælɪndʒ] 1 n (gen) reto, desafío: he rose to the challenge, aceptó el reto. 2 MIL alto, quién vive m.

3 JUR recusación *f*. – **4** *t* (*invite to compete*) retar, desafiar: *I challenge you to beat me*, te desafío a que me ganes; *he challenged me to a game of chess*, me retó a una partida de ajedrez. **5** (*question, dispute - person, authority*) poner a prueba, cuestionar; (*- statement*) poner en duda, cuestionar, poner en tela de juicio. **6** (*stimulate*) suponer un reto para, constituir un reto para. **7** MIL dar el alto a, dar el quién vive a. **8** JUR recusar.
● **to issue a challenge to sb.**, desafiar a algn., retar a algn.

challenger ['tʃælɪndʒəʳ] *n* (*for title, leadership*) aspirante *mf*; (*opponent, rival*) contrincante *mf*, rival *mf*.

challenging ['tʃælɪndʒɪŋ] *adj* (*task, job, problem*) que supone un reto, que supone un desafío; (*idea*) provocativo,-a, estimulante; (*look, tone*) provocativo,-a, desafiante.

chamber ['tʃeɪmbəʳ] **1** *n* arch (*room*) cámara. **2** (*hall*) sala; (*body*) cámara. **3** ANAT cámara. **4** (*of gun*) recámara. – **5** **chambers**, *npl* JUR (*barrister's office*) gabinete *m*, bufete *m*; (*judge's room*) despacho del juez.
● **in chambers**, a puerta cerrada.
■ **chamber music**, música de cámara. ‖ **chamber of commerce**, cámara de comercio. ‖ **Lower Chamber / Upper Chamber**, cámara baja / cámara alta.

chambermaid ['tʃeɪmbəmeɪd] *n* camarera (de hotel).

chamberpot ['tʃeɪmbəpɒt] *n* orinal *m*.

chameleon [kə'miːlɪən] *n* camaleón *m*.

chamois ['ʃæmwɑː] **1** *n* ZOOL gamuza. **2 chamois** (**leather**), gamuza.
▲ En **2** ['ʃæmɪ].

champ[1] [tʃæmp] *n fam* campeón,-ona.

champ[2] [tʃæmp] **1** *t* mascar, masticar. – **2** *i* mordisquear.
● **to be champing to do sth.**, estar impaciente por hacer algo. ‖ **to champ at the bit**, *fig* consumirle a uno la impaciencia.

champagne [ʃæm'peɪn] *n* (*French*) champán *m*, champaña; (*Catalan*) cava *m*.

champion ['tʃæmpɪən] **1** *n* campeón,-ona: *the world 100 metres champion*, el campeón mundial de los 100 metros lisos. **2** *fig* (*defender*) defensor,-ra, paladín,-ina. – **3** *adj* premiado,-a: *a champion boxer*, un campeón de boxeo. – **4** *t fig* defender, abogar por.

championship ['tʃæmpɪənʃɪp] **1** *n* SP campeonato. **2** *fig* defensa.

chance [tʃɑːns] **1** *n* (*fate, fortune*) azar *m*, casualidad *f*: *it was pure chance that I saw you*, te vi por pura casualidad; *we left nothing to chance*, no dejamos nada al azar. **2** (*opportunity*) oportunidad *f*, ocasión *f*: *I never miss a chance to travel*, nunca desperdicio una oportunidad de viajar; *the chance of a lifetime*, una oportunidad única en la vida; *you won't get another chance like this*, no se te presentará otra oportunidad como ésta. **3** (*possibility, likelihood*) posibilidad *f*: *any chance of a lift?*, no me podrías llevar, ¿verdad?; *what are our chances of winning?*, ¿qué posibilidades tenemos de ganar?; *he's got no chance*, lo tiene muy difícil. **4** (*risk, gamble*) riesgo: *that's a chance I'll have to take*, es un riesgo que tendré que correr. – **5** *adj* (*meeting, discovery, occurrence*) fortuito,-a, casual. – **6** *t* (*risk*) arriesgar: *let's chance it*, arriesguémonos.
● **as chance would have it**, da la casualidad. ‖ **by any chance**, por casualidad. ‖ **by chance**, por casualidad. ‖ **chance would be a fine thing!**, ¡ojalá! ‖ **no chance**, ¡ni en broma! ‖ **on the (off) chance**, por si acaso. ‖ **(the) chances are that ...**, lo más posible es que ... ‖ **to chance on sth.**, encontrar algo por casualidad. ‖ **to chance to do sth.**, hacer algo por casua-

lidad. ‖ **to have/stand a good chance of doing sth.**, tener muchas posibilidades de hacer algo. ‖ **to take chances**, arriesgarse, correr riesgos.
■ **game of chance**, juego de azar. ‖ **chance meeting**, encuentro casual.

chancel ['tʃɑːnsəl] *n* presbiterio.

chancellor ['tʃɑːnsələʳ] **1** *n* POL canciller *m*. **2** GB (*of university*) rector,-ra.
■ **Chancellor of the Exchequer**, GB ministro,-a de Hacienda.

chancy ['tʃɑːnsɪ] *adj fam* arriesgado,-a.
▲ *comp* **chancier**, *superl* **chanciest**.

chandelier [ʃændə'lɪəʳ] *n* araña (de luces).

change [tʃeɪndʒ] **1** *n* (*gen*) cambio: *there's going to be a change in the weather*, va a cambiar el tiempo; *a change of address*, un cambio de dirección; *this city has seen great changes*, esta ciudad ha vivido grandes cambios. **2** (*of clothes*) muda. **3** (*coins*) cambio, monedas *fpl*; (*money returned*) cambio, vuelta: *have you got any loose change?*, ¿tienes monedas sueltas?; *have you got change of a ten-pound note?*, ¿me puedes cambiar un billete de diez libras?; *you've given me the wrong change*, te has equivocado con el cambio. – **4** *t* cambiar (de): *he's changed his job*, ha cambiado de trabajo; *let's change the subject*, cambiemos de tema; *you should change gear now*, deberías cambiar de marcha ahora; *I've got to change some pounds into pesetas*, tengo que cambiar unas libras en pesetas. – **5** *i* cambiar, cambiarse: *she's changed a lot*, ha cambiado mucho; *you have to change at Mile End*, tienes que hacer transbordo en Mile End; *all change!*, ¡cambio de tren!; *have I got time to change?*, ¿tengo tiempo para cambiarme (de ropa)?; *he changed into a suit*, se cambió y se puso un traje.
◆ **to change down** *i* AUTO reducir (marcha). ‖ **to change over** *i* cambiar (**to**, a). ‖ **to change up** *i* AUTO cambiar (a una velocidad superior).
● **a change for the better/worst**, un cambio para mejor/peor. ‖ **a change of air**, una cambio de aire(s). ‖ **to have a change of heart**, cambiar de idea. ‖ **for a change**, para variar. ‖ **the change of life**, *euph* la menopausia. ‖ **to get changed**, cambiarse (de ropa). ‖ **to change into sth.**, convertirse en algo, transformarse en algo. ‖ **to change hands**, cambiar de dueño, cambiar de manos. ‖ **to change one's mind**, cambiar de opinión. ‖ **to change one's tune**, cambiar de parecer.

changeability [tʃeɪndʒə'bɪlɪtɪ] *n* variabilidad *f*.

changeable ['tʃeɪndʒəbəl] *adj* (*weather*) variable; (*person*) inconstante, voluble.

changed [tʃeɪndʒd] *adj* nuevo,-a: *he's a changed man*, es otro, es un hombre nuevo.

changeless ['tʃeɪndʒləs] *adj* inmutable.

changeover ['tʃeɪndʒəʊvəʳ] **1** *n* (*gen*) cambio, conversión *f*. **2** SP (*in relay*) relevo.

changing ['tʃeɪndʒɪŋ] **1** *adj* cambiante. – **2** *n* MIL cambio, relevo.
■ **changing room**, vestuario.

channel ['tʃænəl] **1** *n* GEOG (*sea passage*) canal *m*; (*passage for water, liquid*) canal *m*, acequia; (*bed of river etc*) cauce *m*, lecho. **2** *fig* (*course, way*) vía, conducto: *through the official channels*, por los conductos oficiales. **3** RAD TV canal *m*, cadena. – **4** *t* canalizar, encauzar, dirigir.
■ **the Channel Islands**, las Islas *fpl* Anglonormandas. ‖ **the Channel Tunnel**, el Eurotúnel *m*.
▲ (*verbo*) *pt & pp* **channelled** (US **channeled**), *ger* **channelling** (US **channeling**).

chant [tʃɑːnt] **1** *n* REL canto litúrgico, cántico. **2** (*of crowd*) eslogan *m*, consigna. – **3** *t* REL cantar. **4** (*crowd*) corear, gritar, repetir. – **5** *i* REL cantar. **6** (*crowd*) corear, gritar.

chaos ['keɪɒs] n caos m.
chaotic [keɪ'ɒtɪk] adj caótico,-a.
chap[1] [tʃæp] n fam tío, tipo.
chap[2] [tʃæp] 1 t agrietar, partir. – 2 i agrietarse, partirse.
■ chapped lips, labios mpl cortados.
▲ pt & pp chapped, ger chapping.
chap[3] ['tʃæptəʳ] abbr (chapter) capítulo; (abbreviation) cap.
chapel ['tʃæpəl] 1 n REL (building, room) capilla. 2 GB (branch of trade union) sección f sindical.
chaperon ['ʃæpərəʊn] n → chaperone.
chaperone ['ʃæpərəʊn] 1 n carabina, dama de compañía. – 2 t ir de carabina con, acompañar.
chaplain ['tʃæplɪn] n capellán m.
chapter ['tʃæptəʳ] 1 n (of book, of history) capítulo. 2 REL cabildo.
● a chapter of accidents, una serie de desgracias. ‖ to quote chapter and verse, citar textualmente.
chapterhouse ['tʃæptəhaʊs] n REL sala capitular.
char[1] [tʃaːʳ] 1 t chamuscar, carbonizar. – 2 i chamuscarse, carbonizarse.
▲ pt & pp charred, ger charring.
char[2] [tʃaːʳ] i trabajar de asistenta.
▲ pt & pp charred, ger charring.
character ['kærəktəʳ] 1 n (nature) carácter m: the British character, el carácter británico. 2 (reputation) reputación f; (integrity, moral strength) carácter m, personalidad f: a person of good character, una persona de buena reputación; a person of great character, una persona de gran carácter. 3 (in film, book, play) personaje m. 4 fam (person) tipo: an odd character, un tipo raro; a real character, todo un carácter. 5 (letter) carácter m.
● to be in/out of character, ser/no ser típico,-a.
■ character actor/actress, actor/actriz especializado,-a en personajes raros. ‖ character reference, referencias fpl.
characteristic [kærəktə'rɪstɪk] 1 adj característico,-a. – 2 n característica.
characterization [kærəktəraɪ'zeɪʃən] n caracterización f.
characterize ['kærəktəraɪz] t (be typical of) caracterizar; (describe character of) calificar (as, de); (in fiction) caracterizar, describir.
characterless ['kærəktələs] adj (person) de poco carácter, sin personalidad; (place) sin carácter.
charade [ʃə'rɑːd] 1 n (farce) farsa. – 2 charades, npl (game) charadas fpl.
charcoal ['tʃɑːkəʊl] 1 n carbón m (vegetal). 2 ART carboncillo.
■ charcoal drawing, dibujo al carboncillo. ‖ charcoal grey, gris m marengo.
chard [tʃaːd] n acelga.
charge [tʃaːdʒ] 1 n (price) precio; (fee(s)) honorarios mpl. 2 (responsibility) cargo: my husband has charge of the children at weekends, mi marido se hace cargo de los niños los fines de semana; who is in charge?, ¿quién es la persona encargada?; I'm leaving you in charge, dejo todo a tu cargo. 3 JUR cargo, acusación f: he was on a murder charge, fue acusado de asesinato. 4 MIL (attack) carga. 5 (explosive) carga explosiva. 6 ELEC carga. – 7 t (ask as a price - customer, amount) cobrar; (record as debit) cargar: they charged me £20 for a haircut, me cobraron £20 por un corte de pelo; how much do you charge?, ¿cuánto cobras?; charge it to my account, cárguelo en mi cuenta. 8 JUR acusar (with, de): she's been charged with stealing, la han acusado de robo. 9 ELEC cargar. 10 MIL cargar contra, atacar. – 11 i (ask in pay-

ment) cobrar: we don't charge for delivery, el reparto es gratis. 12 ELEC cargar. 13 (soldiers, police, etc) cargar (at, contra), arremeter (at, contra), atacar; (animal) arremeter (at, contra), embestir: charge!, ¡al ataque!, ¡a la carga! 14 (rush) irrumpir: he came charging into the office, irrumpió en la oficina; the children charged off, los niños salieron corriendo.
● to be in charge of, estar al cargo de. ‖ to bring a charge against sb., formular una acusación contra algn. ‖ to charge sb. to do sth., ordenar a algn. que haga algo. ‖ to drop charges, retirar la acusación, tirar los cargos. ‖ to take charge of sth., hacerse cargo de algo.
■ admission charge / entry charge, entrada. ‖ charge account, cuenta de crédito. ‖ charge card, tarjeta de pago. ‖ charge hand, encargado,-a. ‖ charge nurse, enfermero,-a jefe. ‖ charge sheet, atestado policial.
chargeable ['tʃaːdʒəbəl] 1 adj JUR (offence) perseguible, punible: if you steal, you are chargeable with theft, si robas, te pueden acusar de robo. 2 FIN (expenses, debt) a cargo (to, de).
charged [tʃaːdʒd] 1 adj ELEC cargado,-a. 2 fig (voice, atmosphere) cargado,-a (with, de). 3 fig (issue) emotivo,-a.
chargé d'affaires [ʃaːʒeɪdæ'feəʳ] n encargado,-a de negocios.
charger ['tʃaːdʒəʳ] 1 n ELEC cargador m. 2 (horse) corcel m.
chariot ['tʃærɪət] n carro (de guerra).
charisma [kə'rɪzmə] n carisma m.
charismatic [kærɪz'mætɪk] adj carismático,-a.
charitable ['tʃærɪtəbəl] 1 adj (person) caritativo,-a; (attitude) benévolo,-a, comprensivo,-a. 2 (organization) benéfico,-a.
charity ['tʃærɪtɪ] 1 n (generosity, kindness) caridad f. 2 (help given, alms) limosna, caridad f. 3 (organization) institución f benéfica, institución f de beneficencia; (relief projects) obras fpl de beneficencia.
● charity begins at home, la caridad (bien entendida) empieza por uno mismo. ‖ to raise money for charity, recaudar fondos para un fin benéfico.
■ charity performance, función f benéfica.
▲ pl charities.
charlady ['tʃaːleɪdɪ] n GB → charwoman.
▲ pl charladies.
charlatan ['ʃaːlətən] n (quack) curandero,-a.
charm [tʃaːm] 1 n (quality) encanto. 2 (object) amuleto. 3 (spell) hechizo. – 4 t (delight) encantar, cautivar, embelesar. 5 (influence or protect by magic) encantar, hechizar.
● to charm sb. into doing sth., utilizar sus encantos para que algn. haga algo. ‖ to have a charmed life, tener mucha suerte en la vida. ‖ to work like a charm, funcionar a las mil maravillas.
■ charm bracelet, pulsera de dijes.
charmer ['tʃaːməʳ] 1 n (charming person) persona encantadora. 2 (of snakes) encantador,-ra.
charming ['tʃaːmɪŋ] adj (delightful) encantador,-ra.
chart [tʃaːt] 1 n (table) tabla; (graph) gráfico; (map) carta, mapa m. 2 AV MAR carta de navegación. – 3 t (make a map of) trazar un mapa de; (plan, plot on map) trazar. 4 (record) registrar gráficamente; (follow) seguir; (show) mostrar, reflejar: this book charts her rise to fame, este libro describe su ascenso a la fama. – 5 the charts, npl MUS lista de éxitos, el hit parade m.
charter ['tʃaːtəʳ] 1 n (of town) fuero; (of company) escritura de constitución, estatutos mpl; (of university) estatutos

mpl: *by royal charter,* por cédula real. **2** (*constitution*) carta. **3** (*hiring of plane etc*) fletamento. – **4** *t* (*grant rights, priviledges to*) aprobar los estatutos de. **5** (*hire plane, boat, etc*) fletar, alquilar.
■ **charter flight,** vuelo chárter.

chartered ['tʃɑːtəd] *adj* (*qualified*) colegiado,-a.
■ **chartered accountant,** contable *mf* diplomado,-a.

charwoman ['tʃɑːwʊmən] *n* GB asistenta, mujer *f* de la limpieza.
▲ *pl* **charwomen** ['tʃɑːwɪmɪn].

chary ['tʃeərɪ] *adj fml* (*cautious*) cauteloso,-a, cauto,-a.
▲ *comp* **charier,** *superl* **chariest.**

chase¹ [tʃeɪs] **1** *n* (*gen*) persecución *f*; (*hunt*) caza. – **2** *t* (*gen*) perseguir, dar caza a; (*hunt*) cazar. **3** *fam* (*job, client, etc*) ir a la caza de; (*success*) ir en busca de, perseguir. – **4** *i* ir (**after,** tras), perseguir (**after,** -).
◆ **to chase about / chase around** *i* correr de un lado para otro. ‖ **to chase away / chase off / chase out** *t sep* ahuyentar. ‖ **to chase up** *t sep* (*person*) recordar; (*order etc*) averiguar qué pasa con: *I must chase him up about that money he owes me,* tengo que recordarle lo del dinero que me debe.
● **a wild goose chase,** una empresa descabellada, una empresa inútil. ‖ **to give chase,** salir en persecución de algn./algo.

chase² [tʃeɪs] *t* (*engrave, emboss*) cincelar, grabar.

chaser ['tʃeɪsə'] *n* GB copa de licor *que se toma típicamente después de una cerveza;* US bebida suave *que se toma después de otra fuerte.*

chasm ['kæzəm] **1** *n* GEOG sima. **2** *fig* abismo.

chassis ['ʃæsɪ] *n* chasis *m*.
▲ *pl* **chassis.**

chaste [tʃeɪst] **1** *adj* (*pure*) casto,-a, puro,-a. **2** (*not ornate*) sobrio,-a, sencillo,-a.

chasten ['tʃeɪsən] *t* (*discipline*) castigar, escarmentar.

chastise [tʃæs'taɪz] *t fml* castigar.

chastisement [tʃæs'taɪzmənt] *n* castigo, escarmiento.

chastity ['tʃæstɪtɪ] *n* castidad *f*.
■ **chastity belt,** cinturón *m* de castidad.

chat [tʃæt] **1** *n* charla. – **2** *i* charlar, hablar: *they were soon chatting away like old friends,* pronto estaban charlando como viejos amigos.
◆ **to chat up** *t sep fam* intentar ligar con.
● **to have a chat with sb.,** charlar con algn., hablar con algn.
■ **chat show,** programa *m* de entrevistas.
▲ (*verbo*) *pt & pp* **chatted,** *ger* **chatting.**

chattels ['tʃætəlz] *npl* JUR bienes *mpl* muebles.

chatter ['tʃætə'] **1** *n* (*rapid talk*) cháchara, parloteo. **2** (*noise - of teeth*) castañeteo; (*- of machine gun*) tableteo; (*- of birds*) gorjeo; (*- of monkeys*) chillidos *mpl*. – **3** *i* (*talk rapidly*) chacharear, parlotear, cotorrear. **4** (*teeth*) castañetear; (*birds*) piar, gorjear; (*monkeys*) chillar.

chatterbox ['tʃætəbɒks] *n fam* parlanchín,-ina, charlatán,-ana, tarabilla *mf*, cotorra *mf*.

chatty ['tʃætɪ] *adj* (*person*) hablador,-ra, parlanchín,-ina, conversador,-ra; (*style*) informal.
▲ *comp* **chattier,** *superl* **chattiest.**

chauffeur ['ʃəʊfə'] **1** *n* chófer *mf*, chofer *mf*. – **2** *t* hacer de chófer para.

chauvinism ['ʃəʊvɪnɪzəm] *n* chovinismo, chauvinismo, patriotería.
■ **male chauvinism,** machismo.

chauvinist ['ʃəʊvɪnɪst] **1** *n* chovinista *mf*, chauvinista *mf*, patriotero,-a. – **2** *adj* chovinista, chauvinista, patriotero,-a.

■ **male chauvinist,** machista *m*.

cheap [tʃiːp] **1** *adj* (*gen*) barato,-a; (*fare, ticket*) económico,-a: *it's cheaper by coach,* sale más barato en autocar. **2** (*of poor quality, shoddy*) ordinario,-a, de baratillo. **3** (*contemptible - trick, gibe, crook*) vil, bajo,-a; (*vulgar - joke, remark*) de mal gusto. **4** (*worthless, insincere*) fácil. – **5** *adv* barato.
● **to be cheap at half the price,** estar muy bien de precio. ‖ **to buy sth. on the cheap,** comprar algo barato. ‖ **to feel cheap,** avergonzarse, sentir vergüenza. ‖ **to go cheap,** venderse barato,-a.

cheapen ['tʃiːpən] **1** *t* (*in price*) abaratar, rebajar el precio de. **2** (*degrade*) degradar, rebajar.
● **to cheapen os.,** degradarse, rebajarse.

cheaply ['tʃiːplɪ] *adv* (*for a low price*) barato, a bajo precio; (*in a cheap manner*) económicamente, en plan barato.

cheapness ['tʃiːpnəs] **1** *n* (*low cost*) baratura, lo barato. **2** (*low quality*) baja calidad *f*. **3** (*vulgarity*) vulgaridad *f*, ordinariez *f*; (*bad taste*) mal gusto.

cheat [tʃiːt] **1** *n* (*person - at cards*) tramposo,-a, fullero,-a; (*in exam etc*) tramposo,-a; (*swindler*) estafador,-ra, timador,-ra. **2** (*trick*) trampa; (*swindle*) estafa, timo. – **3** *t* (*trick, deceive*) engañar; (*swindle*) estafar, timar. – **4** *i* (*gen*) hacer trampa(s); (*in exam*) hacer trampa, copiar.
● **to cheat death,** burlar la muerte. ‖ **to cheat on sb.,** engañar a algn., pegársela a algn., ponerle los cuernos a algn. ‖ **to cheat sb. out of sth.,** estafarle algo a algn.

cheating ['tʃiːtɪŋ] **1** *adj* tramposo,-a. – **2** *n* (*gen*) trampa; (*with money*) estafa, timo.

check [tʃek] **1** *n* (*examination - of documents, goods, people*) revisión *f*, control *m*; (*of work*) examen *m*, revisión *f*; (*of machine*) verificación *f*, inspección *f*; (*of results, facts, information*) comprobación *f*, verificación *f*. **2** (*stop, restraint*) control *m*, freno. **3** US → **cheque. 4** US (*bill*) cuenta, nota. **5** US (*receipt, ticket*) ticket *m*, resguardo. **6** (*chess*) jaque *m*. **7** (*pattern*) cuadro; (*cloth*) tela a cuadros, tela de cuadros: *a check shirt,* una camisa a cuadros. **8** US → **tick.** – **9** *interj* (*in chess*) ¡jaque! – **10** *t* (*examine - gen*) revisar, comprobar; (*exam, list*) repasar; (*machine, accounts*) revisar, verificar; (*result, facts*) comprobar, verificar: *have you checked the oil?,* ¿has comprobado el nivel del aceite?; *she checked the parcel to see if everything was there,* revisó el paquete para ver si estaba todo. **11** (*stop, restrain*) detener, frenar. **12** (*hold back*) contener, controlar. **13** (*chess*) dar jaque a. **14** US (*leave coat etc*) dejar en el guardarropa; (*leave luggage*) dejar en consigna. – **15** *i* (*make sure*) comprobar, verificar: *I'll just go and check,* iré a comprobarlo; *check that the gas is turned off,* mira bien que esté apagado el gas; *I'll check with Andrew first,* primero se lo preguntaré a Andrew.
◆ **to check in 1** *i* (*at airport*) facturar el equipaje; (*at hotel*) registrarse. – **2** *t sep* facturar. ‖ **to check off** *t sep* ir tachando (de una lista). ‖ **to check on** *t insep* (*baby etc*) ir a mirar; (*progress*) vigilar, controlar. ‖ **to check out 1** *i* pagar la cuenta e irse, dejar el hotel. – **2** *t sep* (*facts, information*) verificar, comprobar; (*place*) ir a ver; (*person*) hacer averiguaciones sobre. ‖ **to check over** *t sep* repasar. ‖ **to check up** *i* confirmar. ‖ **to check up on** *t insep* (*person - watch*) controlar, vigilar; (*- find out about*) hacer averiguaciones sobre; (*information, facts*) averiguar, confirmar.
● **to check sth. against sth.,** cotejar algo con algo. ‖ **to hold in check / keep in check,** (*emotions, disease*) contener, controlar; (*enemy*) mantener a raya. ‖ **to keep a check on,** vigilar, controlar, llevar el control de.

checkbook ['tʃekbʊk] *n* US → **chequebook.**

checked ['tʃekt] adj a cuadros.
checker ['tʃekə'] n us → **chequer**.
checkerboard ['tʃekəbɔːd] n us → **draughtboard**.
checkered ['tʃekəd] adj us → **chequered**.
checkers ['tʃekəz] npl us damas fpl.
check-in ['tʃekɪn] n (at airport) facturación f de equipaje; (in hotel) recepción f.
■ **check-in desk,** (at airport) mostrador m para la facturación de equipajes; (in hotel) recepción f.
checking account ['tʃekɪŋəkaʊnt] n us → **current account.**
checklist ['tʃeklɪst] n lista de control.
checkmate ['tʃekmeɪt] 1 n (jaque m) mate m. - 2 t dar (jaque) mate a.
checkout ['tʃekaʊt] n (in supermarket) caja.
■ **checkout boy/girl,** cajero,-a.
checkpoint ['tʃekpɔɪnt] n control m.
checkroom ['tʃekruːm] n us guardarropa.
checkup ['tʃekʌp] n (by doctor) chequeo, revisión f médica, reconocimiento médico; (by dentist) chequeo, revisión f.
● **to have a checkup,** hacerse un chequeo.
cheek [tʃiːk] 1 n ANAT (on face) mejilla; (buttock) nalga. 2 fam (nerve, impudence) descaro, frescura, cara: *what a cheek!,* ¡qué cara!; *she had the cheek to call me fat!,* ¡tuvo el descaro de decir que yo era gorda!; *that's enough of your cheek!,* ¡basta de impertinencias! - 3 t insolentarse con, replicar.
● **cheek by jowl (with sb.),** uno junto al otro. ‖ **to turn the other cheek,** poner la otra mejilla. ‖ **with tongue in cheek,** con la boca pequeña.
cheekbone ['tʃiːkbəʊn] n pómulo.
cheekily ['tʃiːkɪlɪ] adv con descaro.
cheekiness ['tʃiːkɪnəs] n descaro, frescura.
cheeky ['tʃiːkɪ] adj (person) descarado,-a, fresco,-a; (smile) pícaro,-a; (remark) impertinente.
■ **cheeky devil,** caradura mf.
▲ comp **cheekier,** superl **cheekiest.**
cheep ['tʃiːp] 1 n pío, piada, gorjeo. - 2 i piar, gorjear.
cheer [tʃɪə'] 1 n (shout of joy) viva m, vítor m, hurra m: *three cheers for Harry!,* ¡tres hurras para Harry!, ¡viva Harry! 2 (happiness) alegría. - 3 t (applaud with shouts) vitorear, aclamar. 4 (gladden) animar, alegrar. - 5 i aplaudir, aclamar.
◆ **to cheer on** t sep alentar, animar. ‖ **to cheer up** 1 t sep animar, alegrar. - 2 i animarse, alegrarse: *cheer up!,* ¡ánimo!, ¡alegra esa cara!
cheerful ['tʃɪəfʊl] 1 adj (happy - person) alegre, animado,-a, risueño,-a; (colour, room, disposition) alegre; (news) alentador,-ra. 2 (willing) contento,-a, entusiasta.
cheerfully ['tʃɪəfʊlɪ] adv (happily) alegremente; (willingly) con buena disposición, con entusiasmo.
cheerfulness ['tʃɪəfʊlnəs] n alegría, buen humor m.
cheering ['tʃɪərɪŋ] 1 n ovaciones fpl, aplausos mpl, vítores mpl. - 2 adj alentador,-ra.
cheerio [tʃɪərɪ'əʊ] interj GB fam ¡adiós!, ¡hasta luego!
cheerleader ['tʃɪəliːdə'] n animador,-ra (de un equipo deportivo).
cheerless ['tʃɪələs] adj (gen) triste; (news) poco alentador,-ra.
cheers [tʃɪəz] 1 interj fam (as toast) ¡salud! 2 fam (thanks) ¡gracias! 3 fam (goodbye) ¡adiós!, ¡hasta luego!
cheery ['tʃɪərɪ] adj (smile, mood, colour) alegre; (greeting) lleno,-a de alegría; (manner) optimista.
▲ comp **cheerier,** superl **cheeriest.**
cheese [tʃiːz] n queso: *a slice of cheese,* una loncha de queso; *a cheese sandwich,* un bocadillo de queso.

◆ **to cheese off** t sep fam fastidiar.
● **say cheese!,** (for photo) ¡patata!, ¡Luís! ‖ **to be cheesed off,** estar harto,-a. ‖ **to cut the cheese,** us sl tirarse un pedo.
cheeseboard ['tʃiːzbɔːd] n tabla para el queso.
cheeseburger ['tʃiːzbɜːgə'] n hamburguesa con queso.
cheesecake ['tʃiːzkeɪk] n tarta de queso.
cheesecloth ['tʃiːzklɒθ] n estopilla.
cheesed off [tʃiːzd'ɒf] adj GB fam harto,-a (**with,** de).
cheeseparing ['tʃiːzpeərɪŋ] 1 adj tacaño,-a. - 2 n tacañería.
cheesy ['tʃiːzɪ] adj (taste) con sabor a queso; (smell) con olor a queso.
▲ comp **cheesier,** superl **cheesiest.**
cheetah ['tʃiːtə] n guepardo.
chef [ʃef] n chef m, jefe,-a de cocina.
chemical ['kemɪkəl] 1 adj químico,-a. -- 2 n producto químico, sustancia química.
■ **chemical engineer,** ingeniero,-a químico,-a. ‖ **chemical engineering,** ingeniería química.
chemically ['kemɪkəlɪ] adv químicamente.
chemist ['kemɪst] 1 n CHEM químico,-a. 2 GB (pharmacist) farmacéutico,-a.
■ **chemist's (shop),** GB farmacia.
chemistry ['kemɪstrɪ] n química.
chemotherapy [kiːməʊ'θerəpɪ] n quimioterapia.
cheque [tʃek] n cheque m, talón m: *can I pay by cheque?,* ¿puedo pagar con talón?; *I'll write you a cheque for 30 pounds,* te extenderé un talón por valor de 30 libras; *a blank cheque,* un cheque en blanco.
● **to give sb. a blank cheque to do sth.,** darle a algn. carta blanca para hacer algo.
■ **cheque book,** talonario (de cheques). ‖ **cheque (guarantee) card,** tarjeta de identificación bancaria.
chequerboard ['tʃekəbɔːd] n tablero de damas.
chequered ['tʃekəd] 1 adj (cloth, pattern) a cuadros. 2 fig (past, history, career) con altibajos, accidentado,-a.
cherish ['tʃerɪʃ] 1 t (person) apreciar, querer, tenerle mucho cariño a. 2 (hope, memory, illusion) abrigar, albergar, acariciar.
cherry ['tʃerɪ] n (fruit) cereza, guinda; (wood) cerezo.
■ **cherry blossom,** flor f de cerezo. ‖ **cherry brandy,** aguardiente m de guindas, licor m de guindas. ‖ **cherry orchard,** cerezal m. ‖ **cherry red,** rojo cereza. ‖ **cherry tree,** cerezo.
▲ pl **cherries.**
cherub ['tʃerəb] n querubín m.
▲ pl **cherubs** o **cherubim.**
cheruboc [tʃə'ruːbɪk] adj de querubín, de ángel.
chervil ['tʃɜːvɪl] n cerafolio.
chess [tʃes] n ajedrez m: *a game of chess,* una partida de ajedrez.
chessboard ['tʃesbɔːd] n tablero de ajedrez.
chessmen ['tʃesmən] npl piezas fpl de ajedrez.
chesspiece ['tʃespiːs] n pieza de ajedrez.
chest [tʃest] 1 n (large) arca, arcón m; (small) cofre m; (tea chest, packing case) cajón m; (trunk) baúl m. 2 ANAT pecho: *chest pains,* dolores de pecho.
● **to get sth. off one's chest,** desahogarse.
■ **chest of drawers,** cómoda.
chestnut ['tʃesnʌt] 1 n BOT (tree, wood) castaño; (nut) castaña. 2 (colour) castaño. 3 (horse) alazán,-ana. 4 (story) historia vieja; (joke) chiste m viejo. - 5 adj (colour) castaño,-a; (horse) castaño,-a, zaino,-a, alazán,-ana.
chesty ['tʃestɪ] adj GB MED de pecho: *chesty cough,* tos de pecho.

● **to be chesty,** tener congestión de pecho.
▲ *comp* **chestier,** *superl* **chestiest**.
chevron ['ʃevrən] *n* galón *m*.
chew [tʃuː] **1** *t* (*food*) mascar, masticar; (*nails, pencil*) morder; (*gum, tobacco*) mascar. – **2** *n* (*of tobacco*) mascada; (*sweet*) caramelo.
● **to chew sth. over,** darle vueltas a algo. ‖ **to chew the cud,** rumiar.
chewing gum ['tʃuːɪŋɡʌm] *n* chicle *m*; goma de mascar.
chewy ['tʃuːɪ] *adj* (*difficult to chew*) correoso,-a, duro,-a; (*sweet, toffee*) masticable.
▲ *comp* **chewier,** *superl* **chewiest**.
chic [ʃiːk] **1** *adj* chic, elegante. – **2** *n* elegancia.
chick [tʃɪk] *n* (*young chicken*) pollito, polluelo; (*young bird*) polluelo.
chicken ['tʃɪkɪn] **1** *n* (*hen*) gallina; (*food*) pollo. **2** *fam* (*coward*) gallina *mf*. – **3** *adj fam* gallina.
◆ **to chicken out** *i fam* rajarse, no atreverse a: *he chickened out of jumping,* no se atrevió a saltar.
● **to be no (spring) chicken,** no ser ninguna niña.
■ **chicken feed,** una miseria. ‖ **chicken stock,** caldo de gallina. ‖ **chicken wire,** alambrera.
chickenpox ['tʃɪkɪnpɒks] *n* varicela.
chickpea ['tʃɪkpiː] *n* garbanzo.
chickweed ['tʃɪkwiːd] *n* pamplina.
chicory ['tʃɪkərɪ] *n* achicoria, chicoria.
chide [tʃaɪd] *t lit* regañar (**for,** por), reprender (**for,** por).
▲ *pt* **chided** o **chid,** *pp* **chid** o **chidden,** *ger* **chiding**.
chief [tʃiːf] **1** *n* (*gen*) jefe,-a; (*of party*) líder *mf*; (*of tribe*) cacique *m*. – **2** *adj* principal.
■ **Chief Constable,** jefe,-a de policía. ‖ **Chief of Staff,** MIL jefe *m* del estado mayor.
chiefly ['tʃiːflɪ] *adv* (*mainly*) principalmente; (*especially*) sobre todo.
chieftain ['tʃiːftən] *n* cacique *m*, jefe,-a.
chiffon ['ʃɪfɒn] *n* gasa.
chihuahua [tʃɪ'waːwə] *n* chihuahua *m*.
chilblain ['tʃɪlbleɪn] *n* sabañón *m*.
child [tʃaɪld] **1** *n* (*boy*) niño; (*girl*) niña: *some children,* unos niños; *he was very shy as a child,* de niño era muy tímido. **2** (*son*) hijo; (*daughter*) hija: *they've got three children,* tienen tres hijos.
● **child's play,** juego de niños.
■ **child abuse,** malos tratos *mpl*, abusos *mpl* a menores. ‖ **child benefit,** *subsidio que se recibe del Estado por cada hijo.* ‖ **child care,** puericultura. ‖ **child labour,** explotación *f* de menores. ‖ **child minder,** *persona que cuida a niños en su casa mientras los padres trabajan.* ‖ **children's home,** residencia de menores. ‖ **children's clothes,** ropa de niños. ‖ **children's games,** juegos *mpl* infantiles.
▲ *pl* **children**.
childbearing ['tʃaɪldbeərɪŋ] *n* maternidad *f*.
● **of childbearing age,** en edad fértil, en edad de tener hijos.
childbirth ['tʃaɪldbɜːθ] *n* parto, alumbramiento.
● **in childbirth,** de parto.
childhood ['tʃaɪldhʊd] *n* infancia, niñez *f*.
● **to be in one's second childhood,** estar en la segunda infancia.
childish ['tʃaɪldɪʃ] *adj* (*of a child*) infantil; (*immature*) pueril, infantil: *don't be childish!,* ¡no seas niño!
childishly ['tʃaɪldɪʃlɪ] *adv* de manera infantil, de manera pueril, como un niño.
childishness ['tʃaɪldɪʃnəs] *n* infantilismo, puerilidad *f*.

childless ['tʃaɪldləs] *adj* sin hijos.
childlike ['tʃaɪldlaɪk] *adj* infantil, ingenuo,-a.
childproof ['tʃaɪldpruːf] *adj* a prueba de niños.
children ['tʃɪldrən] *npl* → **child**.
Chile ['tʃɪlɪ] *n* Chile *m*.
Chilean ['tʃɪlɪən] **1** *adj* chileno,-a. – **2** *n* chileno,-a.
chili ['tʃɪlɪ] *n* US → **chilli**.
chill [tʃɪl] **1** *n* MED (*cold*) resfriado; (*shiver*) escalofrío. **2** (*coldness*) fresco, frío: *there was a chill in the air,* hacía un poco de fresco. – **3** *adj* (*wind etc*) frío,-a. – **4** *t* (*make cold*) enfriar. **5** (*wine, beer*) enfriar, poner a enfriar; (*meat*) refrigerar: *serve chilled,* sírvase frío. **6** *fig* hacer sentir escalofríos.
● **to be chilled to the bone,** estar helado,-a de frío. ‖ **to cast a chill over sth.,** *fig* (*sadden*) ensombrecer algo; (*make tense*) crispar el ambiente de algo. ‖ **to catch a chill,** resfriarse.
chilli ['tʃɪlɪ] *n* chile *m*.
chilling ['tʃɪlɪŋ] **1** *adj* glacial. **2** *fig* espeluznante, escalofriante.
chilly ['tʃɪlɪ] *adj* (*gen*) frío,-a: *it's chilly today,* hoy hace fresquito.
● **to feel chilly,** tener frío.
▲ *comp* **chillier,** *superl* **chilliest**.
chime [tʃaɪm] **1** *n* (*bells*) carillón *m*; (*sound of bells*) repique *m*; (*of clock*) campanada; (*of doorbell*) campanilla. – **2** *i* (*bells*) sonar, repicar; (*clock*) dar la hora, sonar. – **3** *t* (*bells*) tocar; (*clock*) dar.
◆ **to chime in** *i* (*interrupt*) intervenir, interrumpir.
chimney ['tʃɪmnɪ] *n* chimenea.
● **to smoke like a chimney,** fumar como un carretero.
■ **chimney stack,** fuste *m*. ‖ **chimney sweep,** deshollinador *m*.
chimneypot ['tʃɪmnɪpɒt] *n* cañón *m*.
chimp ['tʃɪmp] *n* chimpancé *m*.
chimpanzee [tʃɪmpæn'ziː] *n* chimpancé *m*.
chin [tʃɪn] *n* barbilla, mentón *m*.
● **to keep one's chin up,** no desanimarse.
china ['tʃaɪnə] **1** *n* (*white clay*) loza; (*fine*) porcelana. **2** (*crockery*) vajilla, objetos *mpl* de porcelana, loza.
China ['tʃaɪnə] *n* China.
■ **East China Sea,** Mar *m* de la China Oriental. ‖ **South China Sea,** Mar *m* de la China Meridional.
chinaware ['tʃaɪnəweə'] *n* objetos *mpl* de porcelana, vajilla de porcelana, loza.
Chinese [tʃaɪ'niːz] **1** *adj* chino,-a. – **2** *n* (*person*) chino,-a. **3** (*language*) chino. – **4 the Chinese,** *npl* los chinos *mpl*.
■ **Chinese lantern,** farolillo de papel.
chink[1] [tʃɪŋk] *n* (*crack - in wall, fence*) grieta, abertura; (*- in door*) rendija, resquicio.
● **a chink in sb.'s armour,** el punto débil de algn.
chink[2] [tʃɪŋk] **1** *n* (*noise*) tintineo. – **2** *t* hacer tintinear, hacer sonar. – **3** *i* tintinear, sonar.
chintz [tʃɪnts] *n* chintz *m*.
chinwag ['tʃɪnwæg] *n* GB *fam* charla, cháchara.
chip [tʃɪp] **1** *n* GB CULIN patata frita; US CULIN patata frita (de bolsa). **2** COMPUT chip *m*: *silicon chip,* chip de silicio. **3** (*of wood*) astilla; (*of stone*) lasca; (*of china*) pedacito, trocito. **4** (*flaw - in plate, glass*) desportilladura; (*- in picture*) astilladura: *this plate has a chip in it,* este plato está desportillado. **5** (*in gambling*) ficha. – **6** *t* GB CULIN cortar. **7** (*china, glass*) desportillar, resquebrar; (*paint*) desconchar; (*tooth*) romper un trocito de. **8** SP (*in football*) levantar el balón de manera que describa un arco y pase por encima de otro jugador: *he chipped the ball into the goal,*

metió un gol de vaselina; *he chipped the ball over the goalkeeper,* le hizo un sombrero al portero. – **9** *i (china, glass)* desportillarse (**off,** -); *(paint)* descascarrillarse, descoharse, saltarse. – **10 chip (shot),** *n* SP *(in football - gen)* sombrero; *(- scoring a goal)* vaselina; *(in golf)* chip *m.*

◆ **to chip away** *t sep* desconchar. ‖ **to chip away at** *t t insep (rock, marble, etc)* ir desconchando; *(authority)* ir minando, ir socavando. ‖ **to chip in** *i (in conversation)* meter cuchara; *(with money)* contribuir, poner algo.

● **a chip off the old block,** de tal palo tal astilla. ‖ **to have a chip on one's shoulder,** ser un,-a resentido,-a, estar amargado,-a. ‖ **when the chips are down,** a la hora de la verdad.

■ **chip shop,** pescadería *donde se venden patatas fritas.*

▲ *(verbo) pt & pp* **chipped,** *ger* **chipping.**

chipboard ['tʃɪpbɔːd] *n* aglomerado, madera aglomerada.

chipmunk ['tʃɪpmʌŋk] *n* ardilla listada.

chippings ['tʃɪpɪŋz] *npl (of stone)* gravilla, cascajo: *loose chippings,* gravilla suelta.

chiropodist [kɪˈrɒpədɪst] *n* podólogo,-a, pedicuro,-a, callista *mf.*

chiropody [kɪˈrɒpədɪ] *n* pedicura.

chirp [tʃɜːp] **1** *i (insect)* chirriar; *(bird)* gorjear. – **2** *n (of grasshopper)* chirrido; *(of bird)* gorjeo.

chirpy ['tʃɜːpɪ] *adj* GB *fam* alegre, animado,-a.

▲ *comp* **chirpier,** *superl* **chirpiest**

chirrup ['tʃɪrəp] *i* → **chirp.**

chisel ['tʃɪzəl] **1** *n (for stone)* cincel *m; (for wood)* formón *m,* escoplo. – **2** *t (stone)* cincelar; *(wood, metal)* labrar, tallar; *(hole etc)* grabar, cincelar: *a figure chiselled out of rock,* una figura esculpida en roca.

● **to chisel sth. out of sb.,** timarle algo a algn., estafarle algo a algn.

▲ *(verbo) pt & pp* **chiselled** (US **chiseled**), *ger* **chiselling** (US **chiseling**),

chit [tʃɪt] *n fam (note)* nota; *(memo)* memorándum *m; (receipt)* recibo, resguardo.

chitchat ['tʃɪtʃæt] *n fam* palique *m,* cháchara.

chivalrous ['ʃɪvəlrəs] *adj* caballeroso,-a.

chivalry ['ʃɪvəlrɪ] *n* caballerosidad *f.*

chives [tʃaɪvz] *npl* BOT cebollino, cebolleta.

chloride ['klɔːraɪd] *n* cloruro.

chlorinate ['klɔːrɪneɪt] *t* tratar con cloro.

chlorine ['klɔːriːn] *n* cloro.

chloroform ['klɒrəfɔːm] *n* cloroformo.

chlorophyll ['klɒrəfɪl] *n* clorofila.

choc-ice ['tʃɒkaɪs] *n* bombón *m* helado.

chock [tʃɒk] *n* calzo, cuña.

chock-a-block [tʃɒkəˈblɒk] *adj fam* hasta los topes, de bote en bote.

chock-full [tʃɒkˈfʊl] *adj fam* hasta los topes.

chocolate ['tʃɒkələt] **1** *n (substance)* chocolate *m: a bar of chocolate,* una chocolatina, una tableta de chocolate. **2** *(individual sweet)* bombón *m.* – **3** *adj* de chocolate: *the cake was decorated with chocolate flowers,* la tarta estaba adornada con flores de chocolate.

■ **milk chocolate,** chocolate *m* con leche. ‖ **dark chocolate,** chocolate *m* amargo. ‖ **drinking chocolate,** chocolate *m* a la taza. ‖ **plain chocolate,** chocolate *m* amargo.

choice [tʃɔɪs] **1** *n (act)* elección *f,* opción *f; (option)* opción *f,* alternativa: *if I had the choice,* si pudiera escoger; *you've got no choice,* no tienes opción, no tienes más remedio. **2** *(person, thing chosen)* elección *f: he's my*

choice for the post, es el candidato que recomiendo para el puesto; *the people's choice,* la elección del pueblo. **3** *(variety, range)* surtido, selección *f.* – **4** *adj (top quality)* selecto,-a, de primera calidad. **5** *iron (rude)* exquisito,-a.

● **by choice / from choice,** por decisión propia, por gusto. ‖ **of one's choice,** a elección. ‖ **to make a choice,** escoger, elegir.

choir ['kwaɪəʳ] *n (gen)* coro.

■ **choir practice,** ensayo de coro.

choirboy ['kwaɪəbɔɪ] *n* niño de coro.

choirmaster ['kweɪəmɑːstəʳ] *n (gen)* director *m* de coro; *(in church)* maestro de coro.

choke [tʃəʊk] **1** *t (person)* ahogar, asfixiar, estrangular. **2** *(block - pipe, drain, etc)* atascar, obstruir. – **3** *i* ahogarse, asfixiarse. – **4** *n* AUTO stárter *m.*

◆ **to choke back** *t sep* contener, tragarse.

● **to choke on sth.,** atragantarse con algo. ‖ **to choke to death,** morir asfixiado,-a.

choked [tʃəʊkt] *adj (upset)* disgustado,-a; *(disappointed)* decepcionado,-a; *(angry)* furioso,-a.

choker ['tʃəʊkəʳ] *n (necklace)* gargantilla.

cholera ['kɒlərə] *n* cólera *m.*

cholesterol [kəˈlestərɒl] *n* colesterol *m.*

choose [tʃuːz] **1** *t (select)* escoger, elegir; *(elect)* elegir: *I don't know which one to choose,* no sé cuál escoger. **2** *(decide)* decidir, optar por: *they chose to stay at home,* decidieron quedarse en casa. – **3** *i* escoger, elegir: *she had to choose between them,* tuvo que elegir entre ellos; *there are so many to choose from,* hay tantos para elegir. **4** *(prefer, like)* querer, preferir: *do as you choose,* haz lo que quieras.

● **there's not much to choose between them,** son muy parecidos,-as, no hay gran diferencia entre ellos.

▲ *pt* **chose,** *pp* **chosen,** *ger* **choosing.**

choosey ['tʃuːzɪ] *adj* → **choosy.**

choosy ['tʃuːzɪ] *adj fam* exigente, difícil de contentar: *he's very choosy about his food,* es muy maniático con la comida.

▲ *comp* **choosier,** *superl* **choosiest**

chop[1] [tʃɒp] **1** *n (blow)* tajo, golpe *m; (with axe)* hachazo. **2** CULIN chuleta. – **3** *t* cortar (**up,** -): *he's chopping firewood,* está cortando leña. **4** CULIN *(meat)* cortar en trozos (**up,** -); *(onions)* picar (**up,** -). **5** GB *fam (reduce)* recortar, reducir.

◆ **to chop down** **1** *t sep (tree etc)* cortar, talar. **2** SP *(player)* derribar. ‖ **to chop off** *t sep* cortar.

● **to get the chop,** *(person)* ser despedido,-a del trabajo; *(shop, factory, etc) (thing)* quitar, suprimir: *we all got the chop,* nos echaron a todos; *that programme's for the chop,* van a quitar ese programa.

■ **chop chop,** rápido.

▲ *(verbo) pt & pp* **chopped,** *ger* **chopping.**

chop[2] [tʃɒp] **to chop and change,** *i* cambiar continuamente.

▲ *(verbo) pt & pp* **chopped,** *ger* **chopping.**

chopper ['tʃɒpəʳ] **1** *n (short axe)* hacha pequeña; *(butcher's)* cuchilla de carnicero. **2** *fam (helicopter)* helicóptero.

chopping board ['tʃɒpɪŋbɔːd] *n* tabla de picar.

choppy ['tʃɒpɪ] *adj (sea)* picado,-a.

▲ *comp* **choppier,** *superl* **choppiest**

chops [tʃɒps] *npl fam* morro *m sing,* boca *f sing.*

● **to lick/smack one's chops,** relamerse.

chopsticks ['tʃɒpstɪks] *npl* palillos *mpl.*

choral ['kɔːrəl] *adj* coral.

■ **choral society,** coral *f,* orfeón *m.*

chorale [kə'rɑːl] n coral f.
chord¹ [kɔːd] 1 n MATH cuerda. 2 ANAT → **cord**.
● to strike/touch a chord with sb., afectar a algn., calar hondo en algn. ‖ to strike/touch a chord with sb., conmover a algn., tocarle la fibra sensible a algn.
chord² [kɔːd] n MUS acorde m.
chore [tʃɔːʳ] n (job) quehacer m, tarea; (boring job) lata.
● to do the chores, hacer los quehaceres domésticos, limpiar la casa.
choreograph ['kɒriəgrɑːf] t coreografiar, hacer la coreografía de.
choreographer [kɒri'ɒgrəfəʳ] n coreógrafo,-a.
choreography [kɒri'ɒgrəfi] n coreografía.
chorister ['kɒristəʳ] n corista mf.
chortle ['tʃɔːtəl] i reírse, reírse con ganas.
chorus ['kɔːrəs] 1 n MUS THEAT (choir) coro. 2 (of song) estribillo. 3 (outburst) coro.
● in chorus, a coro.
■ chorus girl, corista.
chose [tʃəuz] pt → **choose**.
chosen ['tʃəuzən] 1 pp → **choose**. – 2 adj elegido,-a, escogido,-a: the chosen few, los elegidos.
Christ [kraɪst] n Cristo, Jesucristo.
christen ['krɪsən] t bautizar.
christening ['krɪsənɪŋ] n (ritual) bautismo; (celebration) bautizo.
Christian ['krɪstɪən] 1 adj cristiano,-a. – 2 n cristiano,-a.
■ Christian name, nombre m de pila.
Christianity [krɪstɪ'ænɪtɪ] n cristianismo.
Christmas ['krɪsməs] n Navidad f, Navidades fpl: we usually spend Christmas with my parents, normalmente pasamos las Navidades con mis padres; did you see Emma at Christmas?, ¿viste a Emma en Navidad?
● "Merry Christmas!", "¡Felices Fiestas!", "¡Feliz Navidad!".
■ Christmas box, aguinaldo. ‖ Christmas card, tarjeta de Navidad, crismas m. ‖ Christmas carol, villancico. ‖ Christmas Eve, Nochebuena. ‖ Christmas Day, día m de Navidad. ‖ Christmas pudding, pastel m tradicional de Navidad hecho de frutas, pasas y cocido al vapor. ‖ Christmas tree, árbol m de Navidad.
chrome [krəum] n cromo.
chromium ['krəumɪəm] n cromo.
■ chromium plating, cromado.
chromosome ['krəuməsəum] n cromosoma m.
chronic ['krɒnɪk] 1 adj (disease, person, problem) crónico,-a. 2 GB fam (terrible) malísimo,-a, terrible.
chronicle ['krɒnɪkəl] 1 n crónica. – 2 t hacer la crónica de.
chronicler ['krɒnɪkləʳ] n HIST cronista mf.
chronological [krɒnə'lɒdʒɪkəl] adj cronológico,-a.
chronology [krə'nɒlədʒɪ] n cronología.
chronometer [krə'nɒmɪtəʳ] n cronómetro.
chrysalis ['krɪsəlɪs] n crisálida.
▲ pl chrysalises.
chrysanthemum [krɪ'sænθəməm] n crisantemo.
chubby ['tʃʌbɪ] adj (person) regordete, gordinflón,-ona, llenito,-a,; (part of body) regordete, llenito,-a: chubby cheeks, mofletes.
▲ comp chubbier, superl chubbiest.
chuck¹ [tʃʌk] n (of drill) portabrocas m.
chuck² [tʃʌk] 1 t fam (throw) tirar. 2 fam (give up) dejar, plantar.
◆ to chuck away t sep (rubbish) tirar; (money) derro-

char. ‖ to chuck in / chuck up t sep dejar. ‖ to chuck out t sep (person) echar; (rubbish) tirar. ‖ to chuck up i US sl (vomit) devolver.
● chuck it!, ¡basta ya!
chuckle ['tʃʌkəl] 1 i reírse (entre dientes). – 2 n risita.
chuffed [tʃʌft] adj GB fam contento,-a, satisfecho,-a.
● to be chuffed about/at sth., estar contento,-a por algo.
chug [tʃʌg] 1 n resoplido. – 2 i (engine) resoplar, dar resoplidos.
▲ (verbo) pt & pp chugged, ger chugging.
chum [tʃʌm] n fam compinche mf, compañero,-a, amigote m.
◆ to chum up with i hacerse amigo,-a de.
▲ (verbo) pt & pp chummed, ger chumming.
chummy ['tʃʌmɪ] adj amigo,-a.
● to be chummy with sb., ser amigo,-a de algn.
▲ comp chummier, superl chummiest.
chump [tʃʌmp] n fam imbécil mf.
● to be off one's chump, estar mal de la azotea.
■ chump chop, chuletón m.
chunk [tʃʌŋk] n fam (thick piece) cacho, pedazo; (large amount) buena parte f.
chunky ['tʃʌŋkɪ] adj (person, build) fornido,-a, macizo,-a, cuadrado,-a; (marmalade) con trozos grandes de fruta; (sweater etc) grueso,-a, gordo,-a; (jewellery) grueso,-a.
▲ comp chunkier, superl chunkiest.
church [tʃɜːtʃ] n iglesia.
● to enter the Church, hacerse sacerdote, hacerse monja, etc. ‖ to go to church, ir a misa. ‖ to have a church wedding, casarse por la iglesia.
■ church hall, sala parroquial. ‖ Church of England, Iglesia Anglicana. ‖ church service, oficio religioso.
churchgoer ['tʃɜːtʃgəuəʳ] n practicante mf.
churchwarden [tʃɜːtʃ'wɔːdən] n REL persona que ayuda al cura en asuntos seculares.
churchyard ['tʃɜːtʃjɑːd] n cementerio, camposanto.
churlish ['tʃɜːlɪʃ] adj grosero,-a, maleducado,-a.
churlishness ['tʃɜːlɪʃnəs] n grosería, mala educación f.
churn [tʃɜːn] 1 n GB (for milk) lechera. 2 (for butter) mantequera. – 3 t (butter) hacer; (milk, cream) batir. 4 (water, earth) agitar (up, -), revolver (up, -). – 5 i (liquid) arremolinarse. 6 (stomach) revolverse.
◆ to churn out t sep producir en serie, hacer como churros.
chute [ʃuːt] 1 n (slide) tobogán m. 2 (for waste, rubbish) conducto. 3 fam paracaídas m.
chutney ['tʃʌtnɪ] n conserva agridulce hecha a base de frutas, especias, vinagre y azúcar.
CIA ['siː'aɪ'eɪ] abbr (Central Intelligence Agency) agencia central de información; (abbreviation) CIA f.
cicada [sɪ'kɑːdə] n cigarra.
CID ['siː'aɪ'diː] abbr GB (Central Investigation Department) ≈ Brigada de Investigación Criminal; (abbreviation) BIC f.
cider ['saɪdəʳ] n sidra.
cig [sɪg] n fam (cigarette) pitillo.
cigar [sɪ'gɑːʳ] n puro, cigarro.
cigarette [sɪgə'ret] n cigarrillo.
■ cigarette butt / cigarette end, colilla. ‖ cigarette case, pitillera. ‖ cigarette holder, boquilla. ‖ cigarette lighter, encendedor m, mechero. ‖ cigarette paper, papel m de fumar.
C-in-C ['siːɪn'siː] abbr (Commander-in-Chief) Comandante m en jefe.
cinch [sɪntʃ] it's a cinch, phr fam está chupado,-a, está tirado,-a.

cinder ['sɪndə^r] 1 *n* ceniza, pavesa. – 2 **cinders,** *npl* ceniza *f sing,* carbonilla *f sing.*
● **to burn sth. to a cinder,** carbonizar algo.
Cinderella [sɪndə'relə] *n* (la) Cenicienta.
cine camera ['sɪnɪkæmərə] *n* cámara cinematográfica, tomavistas *m.*
cine film ['sɪnɪfɪlm] *n* película (cinematográfica).
cinema ['sɪnəmə] *n* cine *m: let's go to the cinema,* vamos al cine.
cinnamon ['sɪnəmən] *n* canela.
cipher ['saɪfə^r] 1 *n (code)* código, cifra, clave *f: written in cipher,* cifrado,-a, en clave. 2 *(zero)* cero; *(numeral)* cifra.
circa ['sɜːkə] *prep* hacia, alrededor de.
circle ['sɜːkəl] 1 *n (shape)* círculo; *(in geometry)* circunferencia. 2 *(ring)* círculo; *(of people)* corro. 3 *(group)* círculo: *in business circles,* en el mundo de los negocios. 4 THEAT piso. – 5 *t (encircle)* rodear, cercar; *(move in a circle)* dar vueltas alrededor de: *the lion circled its prey,* el león dio vueltas alrededor de su presa. 6 *(ring with pen, pencil)* trazar un círculo alrededor de, marcar con un círculo: *she circled his name in red,* marcó su nombre con un círculo rojo. – 7 *i (gen)* dar vueltas (**around,** alrededor de): *an eagle circled overhead,* una águila daba círculos en lo alto.
● **to come/go full circle,** volver al punto de partida. ‖ **to go round (and round) in circles,** *(person)* volver sobre lo mismo; *(discussion)* no ir a ninguna parte. ‖ **to run round in circles,** dar vueltas como loco,-a.
circuit ['sɜːkɪt] 1 *n (route, journey round)* recorrido; *(of running track)* vuelta. 2 ELEC circuito. 3 JUR *(regular journey made by judge)* recorrido; *(area covered)* distrito. 4 SP *(series of tournaments)* circuito. 5 *(motor racing track)* circuito.
■ **circuit breaker,** cortacircuitos *m.* ‖ **circuit judge,** juez *mf* de distrito. ‖ **circuit training,** tabla de ejercicios.
circuitous [sə'kjuːɪtəs] *adj fml* tortuoso,-a, indirecto,-a.
circular ['sɜːkjələ^r] 1 *adj (gen)* circular; *(bus, train route)* de circunvalación. 2 *fig (argument)* que no lleva a ninguna parte, que no conduce a nada. – 3 *n* circular *f.*
■ **circular tour,** circuito.
circulate ['sɜːkjəleɪt] 1 *i (gen)* circular; *(rumour, story)* circular, correr. – 2 *t (pass round)* hacer circular. 3 *(send circular to)* enviar una circular a.
circulation [sɜːkjə'leɪʃən] 1 *n (gen)* circulación *f.* 2 *(of newspaper, magazine)* tirada.
circumcise ['sɜːkəmsaɪz] *t* circuncidar.
circumcision [sɜːkəm'sɪʒən] *n* circuncisión *f.*
circumference [sə'kʌmfərəns] *n* circunferencia.
circumflex ['sɜːkəmfleks] *n* circunflejo.
circumlocution [sɜːkəmlə'kjuːʃən] *n* circunloquio.
circumnavigate [sɜːkəm'nævɪgeɪt] *t* circunnavegar.
circumscribe ['sɜːkəmskraɪb] 1 *t* MATH circunscribir. 2 *fml (restrict)* restringir, limitar.
circumspect ['sɜːkəmspekt] *adj* circunspecto,-a, prudente, cauto,-a, cauteloso,-a.
circumstance ['sɜːkəmstəns] 1 *n (condition, fact)* circunstancia: *in certain circumstances,* en algunas circunstancias; *force of circumstance,* razones de fuerza mayor. – 2 **circumstances,** *npl (financial position)* situación *f* económica.
● **in/under no circumstances,** en ningún caso, bajo ningún concepto. ‖ **in/under the circumstances,** dadas las circunstancias.
circumstantial [sɜːkəm'stænʃəl] *adj (evidence)* circunstancial; *(description)* detallado,-a, circunstanciado,-a.
circumvent [sɜːkəm'vent] *t fml (law, rule, regulation)* burlar; *(problem, difficulty, obstacle)* salvar, sortear.

circus ['sɜːkəs] 1 *n (entertainment)* circo. 2 GB *(in town)* glorieta, plaza redonda.
cirrhosis [sɪ'rəʊsɪs] *n* cirrosis *f.*
cirrus ['sɪrəs] *n* cirro.
▲ *pl cirri.*
cistern ['sɪstən] *n* cisterna.
citadel ['sɪtədəl] *n* ciudadela.
citation [saɪ'teɪʃən] 1 *n (quotation)* cita. 2 US MIL mención *f.* 3 JUR citación *f.*
cite [saɪt] 1 *t (quote)* citar. 2 US MIL mencionar. 3 JUR citar.
citizen ['sɪtɪzən] *n (of country)* ciudadano,-a, súbdito,-a; *(of town, city)* habitante *mf,* vecino,-a.
citizenship ['sɪtɪzənʃɪp] *n* ciudadanía.
citric ['sɪtrɪk] *adj* cítrico,-a.
■ **citric acid,** ácido cítrico.
citrous ['sɪtrəs] *adj* cítrico,-a.
citrus fruit ['sɪtrəsfruːt] *n* agrio, cítrico.
city ['sɪtɪ] *n* ciudad *f: city centre,* centro de la ciudad, centro urbano.
■ **city council,** GB ayuntamiento, municipio. ‖ **city desk,** GB sección *f* de economía; US sección *f* de noticias locales. ‖ **city editor,** GB redactor,-ra financiero,-a; US redactor,-ra de noticias locales. ‖ **city hall,** US ayuntamiento. ‖ **the City,** GB el centro financiero de Londres.
▲ *pl cities.*
civic ['sɪvɪk] *adj (duty, pride)* cívico,-a; *(leader, event)* municipal: *civic event,* acto municipal oficial.
■ **civic centre,** centro cívico.
civics ['sɪvɪks] *n* educación *f* cívica.
civil ['sɪvəl] 1 *adj (of citizens)* civil. 2 *(polite)* cortés,-esa, educado,-a.
■ **civil defence,** defensa civil. ‖ **civil disobedience,** resistencia pasiva, desobediencia civil. ‖ **civil engineer,** ingeniero,-a de caminos, canales y puertos. ‖ **civil engineering,** ingeniería civil. ‖ **civil law,** derecho civil. ‖ **civil liberties,** libertades *fpl* civiles. ‖ **civil rights,** derechos *mpl* civiles. ‖ **civil servant,** funcionario,-a. ‖ **the civil service,** *(government departments)* administración *f* pública; *(employees)* el funcionariado, los funcionarios *mpl.* ‖ **civil war,** guerra civil.
civilian [sɪ'vɪljən] 1 *adj (government, life)* civil. – 2 *n* civil *mf.* – 3 **civilians,** *npl* población *f sing* civil.
● **in civilian dress,** de paisano.
civility [sɪ'vɪlɪtɪ] *n* cortesía.
civilization [sɪvɪlaɪ'zeɪʃən] *n* civilización *f.*
civilize ['sɪvɪlaɪz] *t* civilizar.
civvies ['sɪvɪz] *npl* GB *fam* ropa *f sing* de paisano, traje *m sing* de paisano.
cl ['siː'el] *symb (centilitre)* centilitro; *(symbol)* cl.
clad [klæd] 1 *pt & pp →* **clothe.** – 2 *adj* vestido,-a.
claim [kleɪm] 1 *n (demand - for insurance)* reclamación *f; (for wages)* demanda, reivindicación *f; (for benefit, allowance)* solicitud *f.* 2 *(right - to title, right, property)* derecho. 3 *(assertion)* afirmación *f: everyone scoffed at his claim to be descended from the Royal Family,* todos se burlaron de él cuando afirmó que descendía de la familia real. 4 *(thing claimed - land)* concesión *f.* – 5 *t (right, property, title)* reclamar; *(land)* reclamar, reivindicar; *(compensation)* exigir, reclamar; *(immunity)* alegar. 6 *(apply for - benefit, allowance)* solicitar; *(- expenses)* pedir, solicitar; *(receive)* cobrar. 7 *(of disaster, accident, etc)* cobrar. 8 *(assert)* afirmar, sostener, decir. 9 *(attention)* reclamar; *(time)* exigir. – 10 *i* presentar un reclamación, reclamar.
● **sb.'s only claim to fame,** lo más cerca que algn. ha estado de la fama. ‖ **to claim for sth.,** reclamar

algo. ‖ **to claim on one's insurance,** reclamar el seguro. ‖ **to claim responsibility for,** reivindicar. ‖ **to have a claim on sth.,** tener derecho a algo. ‖ **to lay claim to sth.,** (*property etc*) reclamar el derecho a algo, reivindicar algo; (*to knowledge etc*) pretender algo. ‖ **to make a claim for damages,** presentar una demanda por daños, demandar por daños.

claimant ['kleɪmənt] **1** *n* (*of benefit, allowance*) solicitante *mf*; (*of insurance*) reclamante *mf*. **2** (*to throne*) pretendiente *mf*. **3** JUR demandante *mf*.

clairvoyance [kleə'vɔɪəns] *n* clarividencia.

clairvoyant [kleə'vɔɪənt] **1** *adj* clarividente. – **2** *n* clarividente *mf*.

clam [klæm] *n* almeja.
◆ **to clam up** *i fam* callarse, quedarse mudo,-a.
▲ (*verbo*) *pt & pp* **clammed,** *ger* **clamming.**

clamber ['klæmbə'] *i* trepar gateando (**over,** a).

clammy ['klæmɪ] *adj* (*weather*) bochornoso,-a; (*hands*) pegajoso,-a.
▲ *comp* **clammier,** *superl* **clammiest.**

clamor ['klæmə'] *n* US → **clamour.**

clamorous ['klæmərəs] *adj* (*demand*) clamoroso,-a; (*crowd*) vociferante, ruidoso,-a.

clamour ['klæmə'] **1** *n* (*shouting*) clamor *m*, griterío; (*loud protest*) clamor *m*. – **2** *i* clamar, gritar, dar voces, vociferar.
● **to clamour for justice,** pedir justicia, clamar por justicia. ‖ **to clamour for sth.,** pedir algo a gritos, exigir algo a gritos.

clamp [klæmp] **1** *n* (*gen*) abrazadera; (*in carpentry*) tornillo de banco. – **2** *t* (*gen*) sujetar con abrazaderas; (*wheel*) poner un cepo a.
◆ **to clamp down on** *t* poner freno a, tomar medidas drásticas contra.

clampdown ['klæmpdaʊn] *n* medidas *fpl* drásticas: *the police have announced that there is going to be a clampdown on drunken driving,* la policía ha anunciado que va a tomar medidas drásticas contra los conductores ebrios.

clan [klæn] *n* clan *m*.

clandestine [klæn'destɪn] *adj* clandestino,-a.

clang [klæŋ] **1** *n* sonido metálico (fuerte). – **2** *i* sonar. – **3** *t* hacer sonar.

clanger ['klæŋə'] *n fam* metedura *f* de pata.
● **to drop a clanger,** meter la pata.

clank [klæŋk] **1** *n* sonido seco y metálico. – **2** *i* hacer ruido, sonar. – **3** *t* hacer sonar.

clannish ['klænɪʃ] *adj* cerrado,-a, exclusivista.

clansman ['klænzmən] *n* miembro de un clan.
▲ *pl* **clansmen** ['klænzmən].

clap[1] [klæp] **1** *n* (*noise*) ruido seco. **2** (*applause*) aplauso. **3** (*slap*) palmada, golpecito con la mano. – **4** *t* (*applaud*) aplaudir. **5** (*slap*) dar una palmada a. – **6** *i* aplaudir.
◆ **to clap on** *t sep* (*add*) agregar.
● **to clap eyes on sth./sb.,** ver algo/a algn. ‖ **to clap hold of sth.,** coger algo. ‖ **to clap one's hands,** (*applaud*) aplaudir; (*to music*) dar palmadas. ‖ **to clap sb. on the back,** dar una palmada en la espalda a algn.
■ **clap of thunder,** trueno.

clap[2] [klæp] *n sl* (*disease*) gonorrea.

clapped-out [klæpt'aʊt] *adj* GB *fam* (*car, machine*) destartalado,-a; (*person*) rendido,-a, reventado,-a, hecho,-a polvo.

clapper ['klæpə'] *n* badajo.
● **to go like the clappers,** ir como un bólido.

clapperboard ['klæpəbɔːd] *n* claqueta.

clapping ['klæpɪŋ] *n* aplausos *mpl*.

claptrap ['klæptræp] *n fam* disparates *mpl*, tonterías *fpl*, paparruchas *fpl*.

claret ['klærət] *n* (*wine*) clarete *m*; (*colour*) granate *m*, color *m* burdeos.

clarification [klærɪfɪ'keɪʃən] *n* aclaración *f*.

clarify ['klærɪfaɪ] **1** *t* aclarar. – **2** *i* aclararse.
▲ (*verbo*) *pt & pp* **clarified,** *ger* **clarifying.**

clarinet [klærɪ'net] *n* clarinete *m*.

clarity ['klærɪtɪ] *n* claridad *f*.

clash [klæʃ] **1** *n* (*fight*) enfrentamiento, choque *m*; (*disagreement, argument*) desacuerdo. **2** (*conflict - of interests*) conflicto; (- *of personalities, cultures*) choque *m*; (- *of opinions*) disparidad *f*, choque *m*; (*coinciding - of times, dates, classes*) coincidencia; (*bad match - of colours*) falta de armonía. **3** (*loud noise*) sonido. – **4** *i* (*opposing forces - fight*) chocar; (- *disagree*) discutir, enfrentarse (**with,** a): *some angry demonstrators clashed with police,* hubo choques entre algunos manifestantes enfadados y la policía. **5** (*interests*) estar en conflicto. **6** (*dates, events*) coincidir: *the party clashes with my cousin's wedding,* la fiesta coincide con la boda de mi primo. **7** (*colours*) desentonar (**with,** con). **8** (*cymbals*) sonar.

clasp [klɑːsp] **1** *n* (*on necklace*) broche *m*; (*on belt*) cierre *m*, hebilla. **2** (*grasp*) apretón *m*; (*embrace*) abrazo. – **3** *t* (*object*) agarrar, sujetar; (*person*) abrazar. **4** (*necklace etc*) abrochar.
● **to clasp hands,** juntar las manos.

class [klɑːs] **1** *n* (*in society*) clase *f*: *working/middle/upper class,* clase obrera/media/alta. **2** EDUC clase *f*: *we're in the same class,* estamos en la misma clase; *I've got a history class,* tengo clase de historia; *the class of '88,* la promoción del 88. **3** (*kind*) clase *f*, tipo: *he's not in the same class as Pele,* no está a la altura de Pele. **4** BOT ZOOL clase *f*. **5** (*style*) clase *f*, estilo. – **6** *t* clasificar, catalogar.
● **to be in a class of its/one's own,** no tener igual, ser único,-a, ser inigualable.
■ **the class struggle,** la lucha de clases.

class-conscious [klɑːs'kɒnʃəs] *adj* con conciencia de clase, clasista.

classic ['klæsɪk] **1** *adj* (*high quality*) clásico,-a. **2** (*typical*) clásico,-a, típico,-a. – **3** *n* (*novel, film, play*) clásico. – **4** **classics,** *npl* (*literature*) clásicos *mpl*, obras *fpl* clásicas; (*languages*) clásicas *fpl*; (*clothes*) prendas *fpl* clásicas.

classical ['klæsɪkəl] *adj* (*gen*) clásico,-a.
■ **classical studies,** lenguas *fpl* clásicas.

classification [klæsɪfɪ'keɪʃən] *n* clasificación *f*.

classified ['klæsɪfaɪd] **1** *adj* (*categorized*) clasificado,-a. **2** (*secret*) secreto,-a, confidencial.
■ **classified advertisements,** anuncios *mpl* por palabras.

classify ['klæsɪfaɪ] **1** *t* (*categorize*) clasificar, catalogar. **2** (*declare secret*) clasificar como secreto,-a.
▲ *pt & pp* **classified,** *ger* **classifying.**

classless ['klɑːsləs] *adj* (*society*) sin clases.

classmate ['klɑːsmeɪt] *n* compañero,-a de clase.

classroom ['klɑːsruːm] *n* aula, clase *f*.

classy ['klɑːsɪ] *adj sl* con clase, con estilo.
▲ *comp* **classier,** *superl* **classiest.**

clatter ['klætə'] **1** *n* (*of pans, dishes, etc*) ruido; (*of something falling*) estrépito; (*of trains*) traqueteo; (*of hooves*) chacoloteo; (*of typewriter*) repiqueteo. – **2** *i* (*pans, dishes, etc*) hacer ruido; (*things falling*) hacer estrépito; (*trains*) traquetear; (*hooves*) chacolotear; (*typewriter*) repiquetear. – **3** *t* hacer ruido con.

clause [klɔːz] **1** n (in document) cláusula. **2** LING oración
f, cláusula.
claustrophobia [klɔːstrə'fəʊbɪə] n claustrofobia.
claustrophobic [klɔːstrə'fəʊbɪk] adj claustrofóbico,-a.
● **to get claustrophobic**, tener claustrofobia.
clavicle ['klævɪkəl] n clavícula.
claw [klɔː] **1** n (of lion, tiger, etc) garra, zarpa; (of cat) uña;
(of bird) garra; (of crab, lobster) pinza. **2** TECH garfio. – **3** t
arañar: the cat's clawed the sofa to pieces, el gato ha
destrozado el sofá con las uñas. – **4** i (scratch) arañar
(at, -); (grab) intentar agarrarse (at, a).
◆ **to claw back** t sep (logr025) recuperar.
● **to claw a hole in sth.**, desgarrar algo con las uñas.
‖ **to claw one's way through life/up**, fig abrirse paso
en la vida con uñas y dientes. ‖ **to get one's claws
into sb.**, caer en las garras de algn.
■ **claw hammer**, martillo de orejas.
clay [kleɪ] n arcilla.
■ **clay pigeon**, plato. ‖ **clay pigeon shooting**, tiro al
plato. ‖ **clay pipe**, pipa de cerámica, pipa de barro.
clean [kliːn] **1** adj (not dirty - gen) limpio,-a; (air) limpio,-
a, puro,-a; (sheet of paper) nuevo,-a, en blanco. **2** (not rude
- gen) decente; (joke) inocente; (life) sano,-a; (match, fight)
limpio,-a. **3** (well-formed) bien definido,-a, nítido,-a; (regular, even) limpio,-a: a clean cut, un corte limpio. – **4**
adv (fight, play) limpio, limpiamente. **5** fam (completely)
por completo. – **6** n limpieza. – **7** t (gen) limpiar; (teeth,
car) lavar: have you cleaned your teeth?, ¿te has lavado
los dientes?; will you clean these marks off the wall?,
¿quieres quitar estas marcas de la pared? – **8** i limpiarse.
◆ **to clean out** t sep (room etc) limpiar a fondo. **2** fam
(take all money) dejar limpio,-a, dejar sin blanca; (steal
everything) desplumar. ‖ **to clean up 1** t sep (room, mess,
etc) limpiar. **2** fam (money, fortune) hacer, sacar. – **3** i
(room etc) limpiar. **4** fam (make money) forrarse, barrer
con todo.
● **as clean as a new pin**, limpio,-a como una patena.
‖ **to come clean about sth.**, confesar algo. ‖ **to have
a clean (driving) licence**, no hacer cometido infrac-
ciones (de tráfico). ‖ **to have a clean record**, JUR no
tener antecedentes penales. ‖ **to have a clean slate**,
tener un historial sin mancha. ‖ **to have sth. cleaned**,
(dry-cleaned) llevar algo a la tintorería, hacer limpiar
algo en seco. ‖ **to give sb. a clean bill of health**, declarar a algn. en perfecto estado de salud. ‖ **to make
a clean break**, cortar por lo sano. ‖ **to make a clean
break with sth.**, cortar con algo, romper con algo. ‖
to make a clean breast of sth., confesar algo. ‖ **to
start with a clean sheet**, hacer borrón y cuenta nueva.
clean-cut [kliːn'kʌt] adj (outline, feature) bien definido,-
a, nítido,-a; (person, appearance) limpio,-a, muy cuidado,-a.
cleaner ['kliːnə'] **1** n (person) encargado,-a de la limpieza. **2** (product) limpiador m. **3** cleaner's, (place, shop) tintorería, tinte m.
● **to take sb. to the cleaners**, dejar limpio,-a a algn.,
dejar sin blanca a algn.
cleaning ['kliːnɪŋ] n limpieza.
● **to do the cleaning**, limpiar, hacer la limpieza.
■ **cleaning fluid**, líquido limpiador. ‖ **cleaning lady /
cleaning woman**, señora f de la limpieza, asistenta.
cleanliness ['klenlɪnəs] n limpieza: personal cleanliness, aseo personal.
cleanly ['klenlɪ] **1** adj limpio,-a. – **2** adv (gen) limpiamente. **3** SP con limpieza.

▲ (adverbio) ['kliːnlɪ].
cleanse [klenz] t limpiar (of, de).
cleanser ['klenzə'] n (detergent) producto de limpieza;
(lotion for skin) leche f limpiadora, crema limpiadora.
clean-shaven [kliːn'ʃeɪvən] adj (recently shaved) bien
afeitado,-a; (without beard or moustache) sin barba ni bigote.
cleansing ['klenzɪŋ] n limpieza.
■ **cleansing lotion**, loción f limpiadora. ‖ **cleansing
milk**, leche f limpiadora.
clear [klɪə'] **1** adj (glass, plastic, liquid) transparente; (sky,
day, etc) despejado,-a; (skin, complexion) bueno,-a: you
can see the Pyrenees on a clear day, cuando el día es
claro, se ven los Pirineos. **2** (not blocked - road, desk) despejado,-a; (free - time) libre: the roads are clear today,
las carreteras están despejadas hoy; we had a clear
view of the stage, pudimos ver muy bien el escenario.
3 (picture, outline) nítido,-a. **4** (voice, sound, speaker) claro,-
a: in a clear voice, con voz clara. **5** (understandable - explanation, instruction, ideas) claro,-a: is that clear?, ¿está
claro?, ¿queda claro?; she made it quite clear that we
were not to leave the house, dejó bien claro que no podíamos salir de la casa. **6** (not confused - thinking, mind)
lúcido,-a, claro,-a: I need to keep a clear head, necesito
estar despejado. **7** (obvious, evident) claro,-a, patente;
(certain) claro,-a: it's a clear case of bribery, es un caso
claro de soborno; it's quite clear what has happened,
está muy claro lo que ha pasado; she's not clear about
what she wants to do, no tiene muy claro lo que quiere
hacer. **8** (complete - day) entero,-a; (- profit) neto,-a;
(- majority) amplio,-a: he earns a clear £250 a week, saca
£250 netas por semana. – **9** adv (clearly - speak) claramente; (hear) perfectamente, bien. **10** (not touching) a
distancia: he jumped well clear of the bar, saltó muy por
encima de la barra; she parked clear of the kerb, aparcó
a bastante distancia del bordillo. – **11** t (table) quitar;
(floor, road) despejar; (pipe, drain) desatascar; (building,
room - of people) desalojar, despejar, desocupar; (house,
room - of furniture) vaciar: they cleared the pavement of
snow, limpiaron la acera de nieve; this will clear your
nose, esto te despejará la nariz; I like to clear my desk
before I leave, me gusta acabar todo el trabajo antes
de marcharme; the rain has really cleared the air, la lluvia ha limpiado el aire muchísimo; can you clear a
space for the salad?, ¿puedes hacer sitio para la ensalada? **12** (accused person) absolver, descargar, exculpar; (one's name) limpiar. **13** (approve - plans) aprobar;
(authorize) autorizar, dar el visto bueno a; (plane) dar autorización: you'd better clear it with Pat first, más vale
que se lo preguntes a Pat primero. **14** (debt) liquidar,
saldar; (earn - money) sacar; (- cheque) conformar, dar por
bueno. **15** (obstacle) salvar. **16** SP (ball) despejar. – **17** i
(sky, weather) despejarse; (fog) disiparse; (water) aclararse; (skin) mejorar. **18** (cheque) ser compensado,-a. **19**
COMPUT (screen) borrarse.
◆ **to clear away** t sep (dishes etc) recoger, quitar. ‖ **to
clear off 1** i fam largarse: clear off!, ¡largo!, ¡lárgate!,
¡fuera de aquí! – **2** t sep (debt) liquidar. ‖ **to clear out 1**
i fam largarse. – **2** t sep (cupboard, drawers, room) vaciar;
(old things) tirar. ‖ **to clear up 1** t sep (mystery, crime) resolver, esclarecer; (issue, misunderstanding) aclarar; (loose
ends) atar. **2** (tidy) recoger. – **3** i (tidy) ordenar. **4** (weather)
despejar, mejorar; (cold, illness) mejorarse, irse.
● **as clear as a bell**, muy claro. ‖ **as clear as day**, más
claro que el agua. ‖ **as clear as mud**, nada claro. ‖
"keep clear", "vado permanente". ‖ "reduced to
clear", "rebajado,-a por liquidación". ‖ "stand

clear", "apártense". ‖ **to be in the clear,** *fam (from danger)* estar fuera de peligro; *(from suspicion)* estar fuera de toda sospecha. ‖ **to clear customs,** pasar por la aduana. ‖ **to clear one's throat,** aclararse la garganta, carraspear. ‖ **to clear the air,** *(argument)* aclarar las cosas. ‖ **to clear the way,** abrir camino. ‖ **to have a clear conscience,** tener la conciencia tranquila. ‖ **to keep/ stay/steer clear of sth./sb.,** evitar algo/a algn., apartarse de algo/algn. ‖ **to make os. clear,** explicarse.
■ **clear soup,** consomé *m*.

clearance ['klɪərəns] **1** *n* SP despeje *m*. **2** *(of land, area)* despeje *m*. **3** *(space, distance)* espacio (libre): *a clearance of a few inches,* un espacio de unos pulgares. **4** *(permission)* autorización *f*. **5** *(of cheque)* compensación *f*.
■ **slum clearance,** erradicación *f* de chabolas.

clear-cut [klɪə'kʌt] *adj* claro,-a, bien definido,-a.

clear-headed [klɪə'hedɪd] *adj* lúcido,-a, despejado,-a.

clearing ['klɪərɪŋ] **1** *n (in wood)* claro. **2** *(of cheque)* compensación *f*.
■ **clearing bank,** GB FIN banco de compensación. ‖ **clearing house,** FIN cámara de compensación.

clearly ['klɪəlɪ] **1** *adv (speak, write, think)* claramente, con claridad; *(see)* claramente. **2** *(obviously)* evidentemente: *it was clearly very risky,* estaba claro que era muy arriesgado.

clearness ['klɪənəs] *n* claridad *f*.

clear-sighted [klɪə'saɪtɪd] *adj* perspicaz, lúcido,-a.

clearway ['klɪəweɪ] *n* GB AUTO *tramo de carretera donde está prohibido detenerse.*

cleavage ['kliːvɪdʒ] **1** *n fam (in dress)* escote *m*. **2** *(split, division)* división *f*; *(in rock)* hendidura, grieta.

cleave [kliːv] *t (split)* hender, partir.
▲ *pt* **cleft** o **cleaved** o **clove**, *pp* **cleft** o **cleaved** o **cloven**, *ger* **cleaving**.

cleaver ['kliːvə'] *n* cuchillo de carnicero.

clef [klef] *n* MUS clave *f*: *bass/treble clef,* clave de fa/de sol.

cleft [kleft] **1** *pt & pp →* **cleave**. – **2** *adj (chin, lip)* partido,-a. – **3** *n* hendidura, grieta.
■ **cleft palate,** paladar *m* hendido, fisura del paladar.

clematis ['klemətɪs] *n* clemátide *f*.

clemency ['klemənsɪ] **1** *n (mercy)* clemencia. **2** *(of weather)* benignidad *f*.

clement ['klemənt] *adj.(weather)* suave, benigno,-a.

clementine ['kleməntaɪn] *n* clementina.

clench [klentʃ] **1** *t (teeth, fist)* apretar. **2** *(grip)* apretar, agarrar.

clergy ['klɜːdʒɪ] *n* clero.

clergyman ['klɜːdʒɪmən] *n* clérigo.
▲ *pl* **clergymen** ['klɜːdʒɪmən].

clerical ['klerɪkəl] **1** *adj* REL clerical, eclesiástico,-a. **2** *(of a clerk)* de oficina, administrativo,-a: *clerical staff,* personal administrativo; *clerical error,* error administrativo.
■ **clerical collar,** alzacuello.

clerk [klɑːk, US klɜːrk] *n (office worker)* oficinista *mf*. administrativo,-a.
■ **bank clerk,** empleado,-a de banco. ‖ **clerk of the court,** secretario,-a de juzgado. ‖ **sales clerk,** US *(in shop)* dependiente,-a, vendedor,-ra.

clever ['klevə'] **1** *adj (person - intelligent)* listo,-a, inteligente, espabilado,-a; *(skillful)* hábil: *she's clever at maths,* es muy buena en mates; *he's clever with his hands,* es hábil con las manos; *clever boy/girl!,* ¡muy bien! **2** *(idea, plan, gadget)* ingenioso,-a; *(move)* hábil.
● **to be too clever by half,** pasarse de listo,-a.
■ **clever Dick / clever clogs,** sabelotodo *mf*, sabihondo,-a.

cleverly ['klevəlɪ] *adv (intelligently)* con inteligencia; *(skilfully)* hábilmente, ingeniosamente.

cleverness ['klevənəs] **1** *n (of person - intelligence)* inteligencia; *(- skill)* habilidad *f*. **2** *(of plan, gadget, etc)* ingenio.

cliché ['kliːʃeɪ] *n* cliché *m*, tópico.

click [klɪk] **1** *n (sound - gen)* clic *m*; *(of tongue, fingers)* chasquido. – **2** *t (tongue, fingers)* chasquear. – **3** *i (make noise)* hacer clic. **4** *(understand, relize)* caer en la cuenta, darse cuenta de: *I suddenly clicked,* de repente caí en la cuenta; *it finally clicked that she'd left him for good,* finalmente se dio cuenta de que lo había dejado para siempre. **5** *(become friendly)* congeniar; *(become popular)* tener éxito.
● **to click into place,** *fig* encajar. ‖ **to click one's heels,** taconear.

client ['klaɪənt] *n* cliente,-a.

clientele [kliːən'tel] *n* clientela.

cliff [klɪf] *n* acantilado, precipicio.

cliffhanger ['klɪfhæŋə'] *n* situación *f* de suspense: *the match was a cliffhanger,* fue un partido de nervios.

climactic [klaɪ'mæktɪk] *adj* culminante.

climate ['klaɪmət] **1** *n* GEOG clima *m*. **2** *fig* clima *m*, situación *f*: *the current economic climate,* la situación económica actual.

climatic [klaɪ'mætɪk] *adj* climático,-a.

climatology [klaɪmə'tɒlədʒɪ] *n* climatología.

climax ['klaɪmæks] **1** *n (peak)* clímax *m*, punto culminante. **2** *(orgasm)* orgasmo. – **3** *i (career, show, etc)* culminar (**in,** en), (**with,** con). **4** *(have orgasm)* tener un orgasmo.

climb [klaɪm] **1** *n (gen)* subida. **2** SP escalada. – **3** *t (ladder, stairs)* subir; *(tree)* trepar a, subirse a; *(mountain)* escalar, subir a. – **4** *i (move)* trepar: *can you climb up the ladder?,* ¿puedes subir la escalera?; *he climbed into the lorry,* se subió al camión; *she climbed into bed,* se metió en la cama. **5** *(socially)* escalar, ascender; *(of plants)* trepar. **6** *(of things)* subir, ascender.
◆ **to climb down 1** *i (descend)* bajar. **2** *fig (admit mistake, withdraw)* ceder, volverse atrás. – **3** *t insep* bajarse de.
● **to climb into one's clothes,** ponerse la ropa.

climb-down ['klaɪmdaʊn] *n fig* marcha atrás, vuelta atrás.

climber ['klaɪmə'] **1** *n* SP alpinista *mf*, escalador,-ra. **2** BOT enredadera, trepadora.

climbing ['klaɪmɪŋ] *n* SP alpinismo, montañismo.
● **to go climbing,** hacer alpinismo, hacer escalada.
■ **climbing frame,** barras *fpl*. ‖ **climbing plant,** planta trepadora.

clinch [klɪntʃ] **1** *n fam (embrace)* abrazo apasionado. **2** SP *(in boxing)* cuerpo a cuerpo. – **3** *t fam (deal)* cerrar; *(argument)* resolver; *(title)* hacerse con: *the offer of a company car clinched it for him and he took the job,* la oferta de un coche de la empresa lo decidió y aceptó el empleo. – **4** *i* SP *(in boxing)* abrazarse.

clincher ['klɪntʃə'] *n fam* factor *m* decisivo.

cling [klɪŋ] **1** *i (hold tightly)* agarrarse (**to,** a): *they clung together,* se agarraban el uno al otro. **2** *(stick - clothes)* pegarse, ceñirse; *(- smell)* pegarse: *the smell of smoke clings,* el olor a humo se pega. **3** *pej (stay too close to)* pegarse a. **4** *fig (retain - hope, belief)* aferrarse (**to,** a).
▲ *pt & pp* **clung**.

clingfilm ['klɪŋfɪlm] *n* film *m* transparente.

clinging ['klɪŋɪŋ] **1** *adj (clothes)* ceñido,-a, ajustado,-a. **2** *(child)* enmadrado,-a; *(person)* pegajoso,-a.

clingy ['klɪŋɪ] *adj fam (child)* enmadrado,-a; *(person)* pegajoso,-a.

▲ *comp* **clingier,** *superl* **clingiest.**

clinic [ˈklɪnɪk] 1 *n* (*private, specialized*) clínica. 2 (*in state hospital*) ambulatorio, dispensario. 3 MED (*of students*) clase *f* práctica.

clinical [ˈklɪnɪkəl] 1 *adj* MED clínico,-a. 2 (*manner, detachment*) frío,-a; (*room, building*) frío,-a, aséptico,-a.
■ **clinical thermometer,** termómetro (clínico). ‖ **clinical depression,** depresión *f* clínica.

clinically [ˈklɪnɪkəli] 1 *adv* MED clínicamente. 2 (*coldly*) fríamente.

clink¹ [klɪŋk] 1 *n* (*noise*) tintineo. – 2 *t* hacer tintinear. – 3 *i* tintinear.

clink² [klɪŋk] *n sl* (*prison*) chirona, trena, trullo.

clinker [ˈklɪŋkəʳ] *n* escoria de hulla.

clip¹ [klɪp] 1 *n* (*with scissors*) tijeretada. 2 (*of film*) fragmento. 3 *fam* (*blow*) cachete *m*. – 4 *t* (*cut - gen*) cortar; (*ticket*) picar; (*animals*) esquilar. 5 (*cut out*) recortar. 6 *fam* (*hit*) dar un cachete a.
● **at a fair clip / at a good clip,** a buen paso. ‖ **to clip sb.'s wings,** cortarle las alas a algn. ‖ **to give sb. a clip round the ear,** darle un tortazo a algn.
▲ (*verbo*) *pt* & *pp* **clipped,** *ger* **clipping.**

clip² [klɪp] 1 *n* (*for papers etc*) clip *m*, sujetapapeles *m*; (*for hair*) pasador *m*, clip *m*. 2 (*brooch*) broche *m*, alfiler *m* de pecho, prendedor *m*. – 3 *t* sujetar: *clip the papers together,* sujeta los papeles con un clip. – 4 *i* sujetarse mediante un clip: *do your earrings clip on?,* ¿tus pendientes son de clip? – 5 (**cartridge**) clip, *n* (*in rifle*) cargador *m*.
▲ (*verbo*) *pt* & *pp* **clipped,** *ger* **clipping.**

clipboard [ˈklɪpbɔːd] *n* tablilla con sujetapapeles.

clip-clop [ˈklɪpklɒp] *n* ruido de cascos.

clip-on [ˈklɪpɒn] *adj* de clip.

clipped [klɪpt] *adj* (*accent, tone, style*) entrecortado,-a.

clipper [ˈklɪpəʳ] *n* MAR clíper *m*.

clippers [ˈklɪpəz] *npl* (*for nails*) cortaúñas *m sing*; (*for hair*) maquinilla *f sing*; (*for hedge*) tijeras de podar.

clipping [ˈklɪpɪŋ] 1 *n* (*cutting*) recorte *m* de periódico, recorte *m* de prensa. – 2 **clippings,** *npl* (*of nails, sheep's wool*) recortes *mpl*; (*of grass*) hierba cortada.

clique [kliːk] *n pej* camarilla.

cliquey [ˈkliːki] *adj pej* exclusivista.
▲ *comp* **cliquier,** *superl* **cliquiest.**

cliquish [ˈkliːkɪʃ] *adj* → **cliquey.**

clitoris [ˈklɪtərɪs] *n* clítoris *m*.

Cllr [ˈkaʊnsələʳ] *abbr* GB (**councillor**) concejal,-la.

cloak [kləʊk] 1 *n* (*garment*) capa. 2 *fig* (*cover*) capa, manto. – 3 *t* encubrir.
● **to be cloaked in sth.,** estar envuelto,-a en algo. ‖ **under the cloak of darkness,** al amparo de la noche.

cloak-and-dagger [kləʊkənˈdægəʳ] 1 *adj* (*meeting*) secreto,-a. 2 LIT THEAT de capa y espada.

cloakroom [ˈkləʊkruːm] 1 *n* (*gen*) guardarropa. 2 GB *euph* (*toilet*) lavabo, servicios *mpl*.

clobber [ˈklɒbəʳ] 1 *n* GB *fam* trastos *mpl*, bártulos *mpl*. 2 GB *fam* dated (*clothes*) ropa. – 3 *t fam* (*hit, beat, defeat*) dar una paliza a, cascar. 4 *fam fig* (*harm, affect*) afectar gravemente a, ser un golpe para; (*criticize severely*) criticar duramente, atacar; (*punish*) castigar.

clock [klɒk] 1 *n* (*gen*) reloj *m* (de pared). 2 AUTO *fam* (*mileometer*) cuentakilómetros *m*; (*speedometer*) velocímetro; (*taximeter*) taxímetro: *this car's only got 8,000 miles on the clock,* este coche sólo ha hecho 8.000 millas. – 3 *t* (*time - athlete, race*) cronometrar. 4 (*register - speed, time*) registrar, hacer.
◆ **to clock in/on** *i* fichar (al llegar al trabajo). ‖ **to**

clock out/off *i* fichar (al salir del trabajo). ‖ **to clock up** *t insep* (*miles, hours*) hacer.
● **against the clock,** contra reloj. ‖ **around/round the clock,** día y noche. ‖ **to put the clock back/forward,** atrasar/adelantar el reloj. ‖ **to watch the clock,** tener ganas de acabar el trabajo.
■ **clock radio,** radiodespertador *f*.

clockface [ˈklɒkfeɪs] *n* esfera.

clockmaker [ˈklɒkmeɪkəʳ] *n* relojero,-a.

clocktower [ˈklɒktaʊəʳ] *n* torre *f* del reloj.

clock-watcher [ˈklɒkwɒtʃəʳ] *n fam* empleado,-a que sólo piensa en la hora de terminar.

clockwise [ˈklɒkwaɪz] 1 *adv* en el sentido de las agujas del reloj. – 2 *adj* en el sentido de las agujas del reloj.

clockwork [ˈklɒkwɜːk] *n* mecanismo de relojería.
● **to go like clockwork,** ir como una seda, ir sobre ruedas. ‖ **to run like/as regular as clockwork,** funcionar como un reloj.
■ **clockwork toy,** juguete *m* de cuerda.

clod [klɒd] *n* terrón *m*.

clodhopper [ˈklɒdhɒpəʳ] 1 *n* (*shoe*) zapatón *m*. 2 *fam* (*clumsy person*) patán *m*.

clog [klɒg] 1 *n* (*shoe*) zueco. – 2 **to clog (up),** *t* obstruir, atascar. – 3 *i* obstruirse, atascarse.
▲ (*verbo*) *pt* & *pp* **clogged,** *ger* **clogging.**

cloister [ˈklɔɪstəʳ] *n* claustro.

clone [kləʊn] 1 *n* clono. – 2 *t* clonar.

clonk [klɒŋk] 1 *n* ruido seco. – 2 *i* hacer un ruido seco.

close¹ [kləʊz] 1 *n* (*end*) fin *m*, final *m*: *the close of the day,* al caer el día; *at the close of the century,* a finales de siglo. 2 (*precincts*) recinto. – 3 *t* (*shut - gen*) cerrar: *close your eyes,* cierra los ojos; *I'd like to close my account,* quisiera cerrar mi cuenta. 4 (*end - deal*) cerrar; (*meeting*) cerrar, poner fin a; (*course, conference*) clausurar. – 5 *i* (*gen*) cerrar, cerrarse: *what time do you close?,* ¿a qué hora cierran?; *this drawer doesn't close properly,* este cajón no cierra bien. 6 (*end*) concluir, terminar: *the book closes with a murder,* el libro termina con un asesinato. 7 FIN cerrar (**at**, a).
◆ **to close down** 1 *t sep* cerrar (definitivamente). – 2 *i* (*shop, factory, etc*) cerrar (definitivamente). 3 RAD TV cerrar la emisión. ‖ **to close in** 1 *i* (*days*) acortarse. 2 (*get nearer*) acercarse, aproximarse. ‖ **to close up** 1 *i* (*of wound*) cicatrizar, cerrarse. 2 (*shop etc*) cerrar.
● **to bring sth. to a close,** concluir algo, poner fin a algo. ‖ **to close ranks,** cerrar filas. ‖ **to close in on sth./sb.,** rodear algo/a algn., cercar algo/a algn. ‖ **to close one's eyes to sth.,** cerrar los ojos a algo. ‖ **to close one's mind to sth.,** cerrarse a algo. ‖ **to come to a close / draw to a close,** tocar a su fin, llegar a su fin.
■ **close season,** veda, época de veda.

close² [kləʊs] 1 *adj* (*near*) cercano,-a (**to**, a), próximo,-a (**to**, a): *our flat is close to the park,* nuestro piso está cerca del parque; *the houses are in close proximity to each other,* las casas están muy próximas las unas de las otras. 2 (*friend*) íntimo,-a, allegado,-a; (*relation, family*) cercano,-a; (*link, tie, cooperation, collaboration*) estrecho,-a; (*contact*) directo,-a: *it's a close community,* una comunidad muy unida; *we're very close friends,* somos íntimos amigos; *he's very close to his father,* está muy unido a su padre. 3 (*haircut*) (cortado,-a) al rape; (*shave*) apurado,-a. 4 (*texture, weave*) tupido,-a, cerrado,-a, compacto,-a; (*print*) apretado,-a. 5 (*similar*) parecido,-a: *she bears a close resemblance to Madonna,* se parece mucho a Madonna. 6 MIL (*formation*) cerrado,-a. 7 (*weather*) bochornoso,-a, sofocante; (*room, air*) car-

gado,-a. **8** (*thorough, careful - study, examination, etc*) detallado,-a, detenido,-a; (*look*) de cerca; (*watch*) atento,-a; (*translation*) fiel: *pay close attention,* presta mucha atención; *on closer examination,* al mirarlo más de cerca. **9** (*game, contest, finish*) reñido,-a; (*result*) apretado,-a. **10** (*secretive*) reservado,-a. **11** LING (*vowel*) cerrado,-a. – **12** *adv* (*in position*) cerca: *their parents live close,* sus padres viven cerca; *don't get too close to me,* no te me acerques demasiado; *hold me close,* abrázame. **13** (*in time*) cerca: *the elections are getting close,* se acercan las elecciones.
● **at close quarters,** de cerca. ‖ **at close range,** a quemarropa. ‖ **close at/to hand,** al alcance de la mano, cerca. ‖ **close by,** cerca. ‖ **close on/to,** casi, cerca de: *she's close on fifty,* anda rondando los cincuenta. ‖ **close up,** de cerca. ‖ **to be/have a close shave/call/ thing,** salvarse por los pelos. ‖ **to be close to tears,** estar a punto de llorar. ‖ **to keep a close eye/watch on,** vigilar de cerca. ‖ **to keep sth. a close secret,** mantener algo en el más riguroso secreto.
closed [kləʊzd] *adj* (*gen*) cerrado,-a.
● **to be a closed book,** (*unknown*) ser desconocido,-a, ser chino; (*concluded*) estar zanjado,-a.
■ **closed circuit,** circuito cerrado. ‖ **closed shop,** *lugar de trabajo donde sólo se emplean a afiliados del sindicato.*
closed-circuit television [kləʊzdsɜːkɪtˈtelɪvɪʒən] *n* televisión *f* por circuito cerrado.
closedown [ˈkləʊzdaʊn] *n* cierre *m*.
close-fitting [kləʊsˈfɪtɪŋ] *adj* ceñido,-a, ajustado,-a.
close-knit [kləʊsˈnɪt] *adj* unido,-a.
closely [ˈkləʊslɪ] **1** *adv* (*connect*) estrechamente, muy: *we're closely related,* somos parientes próximos; *she worked closely with local artists,* trabajó en estrecha colaboración con artistas locales; *it was a closely contested match,* fue un partido muy reñido. **2** (*resemble*) mucho. **3** (*carefully - watch, listen*) atentamente; (*follow*) de cerca; (*question*) a fondo.
closeness [ˈkləʊsnəs] **1** *n* (*nearness*) proximidad *f*. **2** (*of relationship*) intimidad *f*. **3** (*of translation*) fidelidad *f*. **4** (*of weather*) falta de aire, bochorno.
close-set [kləʊsˈset] *adj* (*eyes*) junto,-a.
closet [ˈklɒzɪt] **1** *n* US armario. – **2** *adj fam* (*secret*) encubierto,-a.
● **to be closeted with sb.,** estar encerrado,-a con algn. ‖ **to closet os.,** encerrarse, recluirse.
close-up [ˈkləʊsʌp] *n* primer plano.
closing [ˈkləʊzɪŋ] *n* cierre *m*.
■ **closing ceremony,** acto de clausura. ‖ **closing day / closing date,** fecha límite. ‖ **closing price,** precio al cierre. ‖ **closing time,** hora de cierre.
closure [ˈkləʊʒəʳ] *n* (*gen*) cierre *m*; (*debate*) clausura.
clot [klɒt] **1** *n* (*of blood*) coágulo. **2** GB *fam* tonto,-a, bobo,-a. – **3** *t* coagular. – **4** *i* (*blood*) coagularse; (*cream*) cuajar.
● **to have a blood clot on the brain,** tener una embolia cerebral.
▲ (*verbo*) *pt* & *pp* **clotted,** *ger* **clotting.**
cloth [klɒθ] **1** *n* (*fabric*) tela; (*thick*) paño. **2** (*rag*) trapo; (*for dishes*) trapo de cocina, bayeta; (*tablecloth*) mantel *m*. **3 the cloth,** el clero: *a man of the cloth deserves respect,* un clérigo merece nuestro respeto.
■ **cloth cap,** gorra.
clothe [kləʊð] **1** *t* (*dress, provide clothes for*) vestir (**in/with,** de). **2** (*cover*) revestir (**in,** de), cubrir (**in,** de).
▲ *pt* & *pp* **clothed** *o* **clad.**
cloth-eared [ˈklɒθɪəd] *adj fam* sordo,-a.
clothes [kləʊðz] *npl* ropa *f sing*.
● **to put one's clothes on/take one's clothes off,**

ponerse/quitarse la ropa. ‖ **with one's clothes on / with no clothes on,** vestido,-a/desnudo,-a.
■ **clothes brush,** cepillo de la ropa. ‖ **clothes hanger,** percha, colgador *m*. ‖ **clothes peg,** pinza. ‖ **clothes shop,** tienda de moda, boutique *f*.
clotheshorse [ˈkləʊðhɔːs] *n* tendedero plegable.
clothesline [ˈkləʊðzlaɪn] *n* tendedero.
clothing [ˈkləʊðɪŋ] *n* ropa: *article/item of clothing,* prenda de vestir.
■ **clothing industry,** industria de la confección.
cloud [klaʊd] **1** *n* METEOR (*single*) nube *f*; (*mass*) nubes *fpl*, nubosidad *f*. **2** (*of insects, smoke, dust, etc*) nube *f*. – **3** *t* (*view, vision, eyes*) nublar; (*mirror*) empañar. **4** *fig* (*confuse, make difficult*) complicar; (*spoil, threaten*) obscurecer. – **5** *i* enturbiarse.
◆ **to cloud over** *i* (*sky*) nublarse; (*face, eyes*) empañarse.
● **every cloud has a silver lining,** no hay mal que por bien no venga. ‖ **to be on cloud nine,** estar en el séptimo cielo. ‖ **to cloud the issue,** complicar el tema, embrollar el asunto. ‖ **to cloud sb.'s judgement,** obnubilar a algn. ‖ **to be under a cloud,** estar bajo sospecha.
■ **cloud chamber,** PHYS cámara de Wilson.
cloudburst [ˈklaʊdbɜːst] *n* aguacero, chaparrón *m*.
cloud-cuckoo-land [klaʊdˈkukuːlænd] **to live in cloud-cuckoo-land,** *phr* vivir en las nubes.
cloudiness [ˈklaʊdɪnəs] **1** *n* (*of sky*) nubosidad *f*. **2** (*of liquid*) lo turbio.
cloudless [ˈklaʊdləs] *adj* (*sky*) sin una nube, totalmente despejado,-a, limpio,-a.
cloudy [ˈklaʊdɪ] **1** *adj* (*sky, weather, day*) nublado,-a. **2** (*liquid*) turbio,-a.
▲ *comp* **cloudier,** *superl* **cloudiest.**
clout [klaʊt] **1** *n fam* tortazo. **2** *fam* (*influence*) influencia, peso. – **3** *t fam* dar un tortazo a.
clove[1] [kləʊv] *n* (*spice*) clavo.
clove[2] [kləʊv] *n* (*of garlic*) diente *f*.
clove[3] [kləʊv] *pt* → **cleave.**
cloven [ˈkləʊvən] *pp* → **cleave.**
■ **cloven hoof,** pezuña partida, pezuña hendida.
clover [ˈkləʊvəʳ] *n* trébol *m*.
● **to be/live in clover,** vivir como un rey.
cloverleaf [ˈkləʊvəliːf] **1** *n* BOT hoja de trébol. **2** (*on motorway*) trébol *m*.
clown [klaʊn] *n* payaso, clown *m*.
◆ **to clown about / clown around** *i* hacer el payaso, hacer payasadas.
cloy [klɔɪ] *i* empalagar.
cloying [ˈklɔɪŋ] *adj* empalagoso,-a.
club [klʌb] **1** *n* (*group, society*) club *m*: *sports club,* club deportivo; *youth club,* club juvenil. **2** (*nightclub*) club *m* nocturno. **3** (*stick*) porra, garrote *m*. **4** SP (*in golf*) palo. **5** (*in cards - English pack*) trébol *m*; (*- Spanish pack*) basto. – **6** *t* aporrear, dar garrotazos a, pegar garrotazos a.
◆ **to club together** *i* pagar entre varios: *we clubbed together to buy the teacher a present,* le compramos un regalo al profesor entre todos.
● **to be in the club,** estar en estado, estar embarazada. ‖ **to club sb. to death,** aporrear a algn. hasta matarlo.
■ **club car,** US vagón *m* de primera. ‖ **club foot,** MED pie *m* zopo, pie *m* deforme. ‖ **club sandwich,** US sandwich *m* de dos pisos. ‖ **club soda,** US soda.
▲ (*verbo*) *pt* & *pp* **clubbed,** *ger* **clubbing.**
clubbing [ˈklʌbɪŋ] **to go clubbing,** *phr* ir de marcha, ir de juerga.

clubhouse ['klʌbhaʊs] *n* SP sede *f* de un club.
cluck [klʌk] 1 *n* cloqueo. – 2 *i* cloquear.
clue [kluː] *n* (*gen*) pista; (*in crossword*) clave *f*: *he hasn't got a clue*, no tiene (ni) idea.
◆ **to clue up** *t sep* informar, poner al tanto.
● **to be clued up** (**about/on sth.**), estar al tanto (de algo).
clueless ['kluːləs] *adj fam* despistado,-a, que no se entera de nada, que no tiene ni idea.
clump [klʌmp] 1 *n* (*of trees*) grupo; (*of plants*) mata, macizo. 2 (*of earth*) terrón *m*. 3 (*noise*) ruido de pisadas fuertes. – 4 *i* andar pesada y ruidosamente, caminar pisando fuerte.
● **to be clumped together**, estar amontonados,-as.
clumsily ['klʌmzɪlɪ] *adv* torpemente, con torpeza.
clumsiness ['klʌmzɪnəs] *n* torpeza.
clumsy ['klʌmzɪ] 1 *adj* (*person, movement*) torpe, patoso,-a. 2 (*tool, shape*) pesado,-a y difícil de manejar; (*furniture*) mal diseñado,-a. 3 (*apology, attempt, speech*) torpe, sin tacto; (*forgery, translation*) burdo,-a.
▲ *comp* **clumsier**, *superl* **clumsiest**.
clung [klʌŋ] *pt & pp* → **cling**.
clunk [klʌŋk] 1 *n* golpe *m* metálico. – 2 *i* golpetear.
cluster ['klʌstəʳ] 1 *n* (*of trees, stars, buildings, people*) grupo; (*of berries, grapes*) racimo; (*of plants*) macizo. – 2 *i* agruparse, apiñarse (**round**, alrededor de/en torno a).
● **to be clustered round sb./sth.**, estar agrupado,-a alrededor de algn./algo.
■ **cluster bomb**, bomba de dispersión. ‖ **consonant cluster**, LING grupo consonántico.
clutch[1] [klʌtʃ] 1 *n* AUTO embrague *m*. 2 (*grasp, grip*) agarrón *m*. – 3 *t* (*seize*) agarrar; (*hold tightly*) estrechar, apretar.
◆ **to clutch at** *t insep* tratar de agarrar.
● **to fall into sb.'s clutches**, caer en las garras de algn. ‖ **to clutch at straws**, aferrarse a cualquier cosa. ‖ **to let in the clutch**, AUTO embragar. ‖ **to let out the clutch**, AUTO desembragar.
■ **clutch bag**, cartera.
clutch[2] [klʌtʃ] *n* (*of eggs*) nidada.
clutter ['klʌtəʳ] 1 *n* (*things*) cosas *fpl*, trastos *mpl*; (*untidy state*) desorden *m*, revoltijo. – 2 **to clutter (up)**, *t* llenar, atestar, abarrotar.
● **to be in a clutter**, estar desordenado,-a.
cluttered ['klʌtəd] *adj* atestado,-a (**with**, de), abarrotado,-a (**with**, de).
cm ['siː'em] *symb* (*centimetre*) centímetro; (*symbol*) cm.
CND ['siː'en'diː] *abbr* GB (*Campaign for Nuclear Disarmament*) campaña para el desarme nuclear.
Co[1] [kəʊ] *abbr* (*Company*) Compañía; (*abbreviation*) Cía.
Co[2] ['kaʊntɪ] *abbr* (*County*) condado.
CO ['siː'əʊ] *abbr* (*Commanding Officer*) Comandante *m*; (*abbreviation*) Cte.
c/o ['keəɒv] *abbr* (*care of*) en casa de; (*abbreviation*) c/d.
coach [kəʊtʃ] 1 *n* GB (*bus*) autocar *m*. 2 (*carriage*) carruaje *m*, coche *m* de caballos. 3 (*on train*) coche *m*, vagón *m*. 4 EDUC (*tutor*) profesor,-ra particular. 5 SP (*trainer*) entrenador,-ra. – 6 *t* EDUC dar clases particulares a, preparar. 7 SP entrenar.
■ **coach station**, terminal *f* de autobuses. ‖ **coach trip**, excursión *f* en autocar.
coach-builder ['kəʊtʃbɪldəʳ] *n* carrocero,-a.
coaching ['kəʊtʃɪŋ] 1 *n* (*tutoring*) preparación *f*, clases *fpl* particulares. 2 (*training*) entrenamiento.
coachman ['kəʊtʃmən] *n* cochero.
coachwork ['kəʊtʃwɜːk] *n* carrocería.

coagluation [kəʊægjə'leɪʃən] *n* coagulación *f*.
coagulant [kəʊ'ægjələnt] *n* coagulante *m*.
coagulate [kəʊ'ægjəleɪt] 1 *t* coagular. – 2 *i* coagularse.
coal [kəʊl] *n* carbón *m*, hulla.
● **as black as coals**, negro,-a como el carbón. ‖ **to carry coals to Newcastle**, llevar leña al monte.
■ **coal bunker / coal cellar**, carbonera. ‖ **coal dust**, carbonilla. ‖ **coal gas**, gas *m* de hulla. ‖ **coal merchant**, carbonero. ‖ **coal mine**, mina de carbón. ‖ **coal mining**, explotación *f* hullera. ‖ **coal scuttle**, cubo para el carbón. ‖ **coal tar**, alquitrán *m* de hulla.
coalesce [kəʊə'les] *i* POL *fml* unirse; CHEM fundirse.
coalescence [kəʊə'lesəns] *n* POL unión *f*; CHEM fusión *f*.
coalface ['kəʊlfeɪs] *n* frente *m* de explotación de una mina de carbón.
coalfield ['kəʊlfiːld] *n* yacimiento de carbón.
coal-fired ['kəʊlfaɪd] *adj* de carbón.
coalition [kəʊə'lɪʃən] *n* coalición *f*.
■ **coalition government**, gobierno de coalición.
coarse [kɔːs] 1 *adj* (*fabric*) basto,-a, burdo,-a; (*skin*) áspero,-a; (*sand, salt*) grueso,-a. 2 (*language, joke*) grosero,-a, vulgar, ordinario,-a, basto,-a; (*manners, tastes*) ordinario,-a, basto,-a.
■ **coarse fish**, pez de agua dulce (*excepto el salmón y la trucha*). ‖ **coarse fishing**, pesca de agua dulce.
coarse-grained ['kɔːsgreɪnd] *adj* de grano grueso.
coarsely ['kɔːslɪ] 1 *adv* (*chop*) en trozos grandes. 2 (*speak*) de manera ordinaria.
coarseness ['kɔːsnəs] 1 *n* (*of manner*) ordinariez *f*, grosería. 2 (*of cloth*) tosquedad *f*.
coast [kəʊst] 1 *n* costa, litoral *m*: *a village on the coast*, un pueblo de la costa; *we spent the day by the coast*, pasamos el día en la costa; *it sank a few miles off the coast*, se hundió a unas millas de la costa. – 2 *i* (*in car*) ir en punto muerto; (*on bicycle*) deslizarse sin pedalear. 3 *fig* avanzar sin ningún esfuerzo: *she coasted through her exams*, aprobó sus exámenes sin ningún problema. 4 MAR costear, bordear la costa.
● **the coast is clear**, no hay moros en la costa.
coastal ['kəʊstəl] *adj* costero,-a.
coaster ['kəʊstəʳ] 1 *n* MAR barco de cabotaje. 2 (*small mat*) posavasos *m*.
coastguard ['kəʊstgɑːd] 1 *n* guardacostas *mf*. 2 **the coastguard**, (*organization*) los guardacostas *mpl*.
coastline ['kəʊstlaɪn] *n* costa, litoral *m*.
coat [kəʊt] 1 *n* (*overcoat*) abrigo; (*short*) chaquetón *m*: *fur coat*, abrigo de pieles. 2 (*of paint*) capa, mano *f*; (*of dust*) capa. 3 (*of animal*) pelo, pelaje *m*. – 4 *t* (*cover - gen*) cubrir (**in/with**, de). 5 CULIN (*with liquid*) cubrir (**in/with**, de), bañar (**in/with**, en); (*in breadcrumbs or batter*) rebozar.
● **to cut one's coat according to one's cloth**, vivir según sus posibilidades.
■ **coat of arms**, escudo de armas. ‖ **coat of mail**, cota de malla. ‖ **coat hanger**, percha. ‖ **white coat**, bata blanca.
coating ['kəʊtɪŋ] 1 *n* CULIN capa, baño. 2 (*of paint, dust, wax*) capa; (*of metal*) revestimiento.
coat-tails ['kəʊtteɪlz] *npl* faldones *mpl*.
coauthor [kəʊ'ɔːθəʳ] 1 *n* coautor,-ra. – 2 *t* escribir conjuntamente.
coax [kəʊks] *t* (*person*) engatusar.
● **to coax a machine to work**, lograr que una máquina funcione. ‖ **to coax sb. into doing sth.**, engatusar a algn. para que haga algo. ‖ **to coax sth. out of sb.**, sonsacar algo a algn.
coaxing ['kəʊksɪŋ] 1 *n* persuasión *f*, mano *f* izquierda. – 2 *adj* persuasivo,-a.

cob [kɒb] **1** *n* (*of corn*) mazorca (de maíz). **2** (*cobnut*) avellana. **3** (*horse*) jaca. **4** (*male swan*) cisne *m* macho.
cobalt ['kəʊbɔːlt] *n* cobalto.
■ **cobalt blue**, azul *m* cobalto.
cobble ['kɒbəl] **1** *n* adoquín *m*. – **2** *t* (*street*) adoquinar.
◆ **to cobble together** *t sep* (*meal*) improvisar; (*essay*) redactar a toda prisa.
cobbled ['kɒbəld] *t* adoquinado,-a.
cobbler ['kɒbələ'] *n dated* (*shoe repairer*) zapatero (remendón).
cobblers ['kɒbələz] *npl* GB *sl* (*nonsense*) chorradas *fpl*, gilipolleces *fpl*; (*rubbish*) birria, bodrio, asco: *his argument's a load of cobblers*, su argumento no son más que chorradas; *that programme's a load of cobblers*, ese programa es un bodrio.
cobblestone ['kɒbəlstəʊn] *n* adoquín *m*.
cobnut ['kɒbnʌt] *n* avellana.
cobra ['kəʊbrə] *n* cobra.
cobweb ['kɒbweb] *n* telaraña.
coca ['kəʊkə] *n* BOT coca.
Coca Cola ['kəʊkəkəʊlə] *n* Coca Cola.
▲ *Es marca registrada.*
cocaine [kə'keɪn] *n* cocaína.
coccyx ['kɒksɪks] *n* coxis *m*, cóccix *m*.
▲ *pl* coccyxes *o* coccyges.
cock [kɒk] **1** *n* (*rooster*) gallo; (*any male bird*) macho. **2** (*on firearm*) percutor *m*, percusor *m*. **3** GB *fam* (*mate*) macho. **4** *taboo* (*penis*) polla. – **5** *t* (*of firearm*) amartillar, montar. **6** (*head, hat*) ladear; (*ears, leg*) levantar.
◆ **to cock up** *t sep* GB *sl* fastidiar, joder, cagarla: *you've cocked it up*, la has cagado.
● **cock of the walk**, gallito.
cockade [kɒ'keɪd] *n* MIL escarapela.
cock-a-doodle-doo [kɒkəduːdəl'duː] *interj* quiquiriquí.
cock-a-hoop [kɒkə'huːp] *adj* como unas pascuas, más contento,-a que unas pascuas.
cock-and-bull story [kɒkən'bʊlstɔːrɪ] *n* cuento chino, camelo.
cockatoo [kɒkə'tuː] *n* cacatúa.
▲ *pl* cockatoos.
cockcrow ['kɒkkrəʊ] *n* amanecer *m*.
cocked hat [kɒkt'hæt] *n* sombrero de tres picos.
● **to knock sth. into a cocked hat**, dar mil vueltas a algo.
cockerel ['kɒkərəl] *n* gallito.
cocker spaniel [kɒkə'spænjəl] *n* cocker *m*.
cockeyed ['kɒkaɪd] **1** *adj fam* (*crooked*) torcido,-a; (*impractical, ridiculous*) disparatado,-a. **2** *fam* (*squinting, cross-eyed*) bizco,-a. **3** *fam* (*drunk*) borracho,-a, trompa.
cockfight ['kɒkfaɪt] *n* pelea de gallos.
cockfighting ['kɒkfaɪtɪŋ] *n* peleas *fpl* de gallos.
cockiness ['kɒkɪnəs] *n* engreimiento, petulancia, prepotencia.
cockle ['kɒkəl] *n* berberecho.
● **to warm the cockles of sb.'s heart**, enternecer a algn., llenar a algn. de alegría.
Cockney ['kɒknɪ] **1** *adj* del barrio obrero del este de Londres. – **2** *n* (*person*) persona del barrio obrero del este de Londres. **3** (*dialect*) dialecto que se habla en el barrio obrero del este de Londres.
cockpit ['kɒkpɪt] *n* (*in plane*) cabina del piloto, carlinga; (*in racing car*) cabina.
cockroach ['kɒkrəʊtʃ] *n* cucaracha.
cockscomb ['kɒkskəʊm] *n* (*on cock*) cresta.

cocksure [kɒk'ʃʊə'] *adj fam* creído,-a, petulante, presumido,-a, engreído,-a.
cocktail ['kɒkteɪl] *n* cóctel *m*.
■ **cocktail lounge**, bar *m*. ‖ **cocktail party**, cóctel *m*. ‖ **cocktail shaker**, coctelera. ‖ **cocktail stick**, palillo.
cockup ['kɒkʌp] *n* GB *sl* chapuza: *he made a complete cockup of it*, la cagó totalmente.
cocky ['kɒkɪ] *adj fam* creído,-a, chulo,-a.
● **to get cocky**, ponerse chulo,-a.
▲ *comp* cockier, *superl* cockiest.
cocoa ['kəʊkəʊ] *n* (*powder*) cacao; (*drink*) chocolate *m*.
■ **cocoa butter**, manteca de cacao.
coconut ['kəʊkənʌt] *n* coco.
■ **coconut ice**, dulce *m* de coco. ‖ **coconut matting**, estera de fibra de coco. ‖ **coconut palm**, cocotero. ‖ **coconut shy**, tiro al coco.
cocoon [kə'kuːn] **1** *n* capullo. – **2** *t fig* envolver, arropar.
cod [kɒd] *n* bacalao.
▲ *pl* cod.
COD ['siː'əʊ'diː] *abbr* GB (*cash on delivery*, US collect on delivery) contra reembolso.
coda ['kəʊdə] *n* coda.
coddle ['kɒdəl] *t* (*person*) mimar.
■ **coddled eggs**, huevos *mpl* escaldados.
code [kəʊd] **1** *n* (*set of laws, rules, principles*) código: *a code of conduct*, código de conducta; *a code of practice*, código de práctica; *moral code*, código de ética. **2** (*system of words, letters, signs, numbers*) clave *f*, código: *it's written in code*, está escrito en clave. **3** (*telephone*) prefijo; (*postal*) código (postal). – **4** *t* (*message etc*) poner en clave, cifrar. **5** (*mark*) codificar.
● **to break a code / crack a code / decipher a code**, descifrar una clave, descifrar un código.
■ **code name**, nombre *m* en clave. ‖ **highway code**, código de la circulación.
codeine ['kəʊdiːn] *n* codeína.
codfish ['kɒdfɪʃ] *n* bacalao.
codify ['kəʊdɪfaɪ] *t* codificar.
▲ (*verbo*) *pt* & *pp* codified, *ger* codifying.
cod-liver oil [kɒdlɪvər'ɔɪl] *n* aceite *m* de hígado de bacalao.
codswallop ['kɒdzwɒləp] *n fam* (*nonsense*) chorradas *fpl*, paparruchas *fpl*.
co-ed [kəʊ'ed] **1** *adj fam* (*coeducational*) mixto,-a. – **2** *n* GB EDUC *fam* (*school*) colegio mixto. **3** US EDUC *fam* (*female student*) alumna (de un colegio o universidad mixta).
coeducation [kəʊedjə'keɪʃən] *n* enseñanza mixta.
coeducational [kəʊedjə'keɪʃənəl] *adj* mixto,-a.
coefficient [kəʊɪ'fɪʃənt] *n* coeficiente *m*.
coerce [kəʊ'ɜːs] *t* coaccionar.
● **to coerce sb. into doing sth.**, coaccionar a algn. para que haga algo.
coercion [kəʊ'ɜːʃən] *n* coacción *f*.
coercive [kəʊ'ɜːsɪv] *adj* coercitivo,-a.
coexist [kəʊɪg'zɪst] *i* coexistir.
coexistence [kəʊɪg'zɪstəns] *n* coexistencia.
C of E ['siː'əv'iː] *abbr* (*Church of England*) Iglesia Anglicana.
coffee ['kɒfɪ] *n* café *m*: *would you like your coffee white or black?*, ¿quieres el café solo o con leche?
■ **black coffee**, café *m* solo. ‖ **coffee bar**, cafetería, café *m*. ‖ **coffee bean**, grano de café. ‖ **coffee beans**, café *m* en grano. ‖ **coffee break**, descanso (para tomar el café), pausa (para tomar el café). ‖ **coffee cup**, taza para café. ‖ **coffee filter**, filtro de café. ‖ **coffee grinder**, molinillo de café. ‖ **coffee mill**, molinillo de café.

‖ **coffee percolator,** cafetera de filtro. ‖ **coffee shop,** cafetería, café *m*. ‖ **coffee table,** mesita de café. ‖ **filter coffee,** café *m* (hecho con cafetera de filtro). ‖ **instant coffee,** café *m* instantáneo, café *m* soluble. ‖ **white coffee,** café *m* con leche.

coffeepot ['kɒfɪpɒt] *n* cafetera.

coffer ['kɒfəʳ] **1** *n* arca, cofre *m*. – **2 coffers,** *npl* fondos *mpl*, arcas *fpl*.

coffin ['kɒfɪn] *n* ataúd *m*, féretro.

cog [kɒg] **1** *n* (*teeth*) diente *m*. **2** *fig* pieza.

cogent ['kəʊdʒənt] *adj* convincente, contundente.

cognac ['kɒnjæk] *n* coñac *m*.

cognate ['kɒgneɪt] **1** *adj* afín (**with,** a), relacionado,-a (**with,** con). **2** LING cognado,-a (**with,** con). – **3** *n* LING palabra afín.

cogwheel ['kɒgwiːl] *n* rueda dentada.

cohabit [kəʊ'hæbɪt] *i* cohabitar.

cohabitation [kəʊhæbɪ'teɪʃən] *n* cohabitación *f*.

cohere [kəʊ'hɪəʳ] **1** *i* (*hold together*) adherirse. **2** (*be consistent*) ser coherente, ser congruente.

coherence [kəʊ'hɪərəns] **1** *n* (*connection*) coherencia, congruencia. **2** (*cohesion*) cohesión *f*.

coherent [kəʊ'hɪərənt] *adj* coherente, congruente.

cohesion [kəʊ'hiːʒən] *n* cohesión *f*.

cohesive [kəʊ'hiːsɪv] **1** *adj* PHYS cohesivo,-a. **2** (*group*) unido,-a.

coil [kɔɪl] **1** *n* (*of rope, wire*) rollo; (*of cable*) carrete *m*; (*of hair*) rizo, moño; (*of smoke*) espiral *m*, voluta. **2** (*single loop*) vuelta, lazada. **3** TECH bobina. – **4** *i* (*snake*) enroscarse (**round,** alrededor de). – **5** to coil (up), *t* enrollar. – **6** the coil, *n* MED (*contraceptive*) espiral *f*, dispositivo intrauterino, DIU *m*.

coin [kɔɪn] **1** *n* moneda. – **2** *t* (*money*) acuñar. **3** (*invent*) crear, acuñar.

● **to coin a phrase,** como se suele decir, por así decirlo. ‖ **to toss a coin,** echar a cara o cruz.

coinage ['kɔɪnɪdʒ] **1** *n* (*coins*) monedas *fpl*; (*making coins*) acuñación *f*. **2** (*system of coins*) sistema monetario. **3** (*inventing of new word*) acuñación *f*; (*new word*) palabra de nuevo cuño; (*new phrase*) frase *f* de nuevo cuño.

coincide [kəʊɪn'saɪd] *i* coincidir (**with,** con).

coincidence [kəʊ'ɪnsɪdəns] **1** *n* (*chance*) coincidencia, casualidad *f*. **2** (*coinciding*) coincidencia.

coincidental [kəʊɪnsɪ'dentəl] *adj* casual, fortuito,-a.

coincidentally [kəʊɪnsɪ'dentəlɪ] *adv* por casualidad, casualmente: *coincidentally, we went to the same restaurant,* dio la casualidad de que fuimos al mismo restaurante.

coitus ['kəʊɪtəs] *n* coito.

coke[1] [kəʊk] *n* (*coal*) coque *m*.

coke[2] [kəʊk] *n sl* (*cocaine*) coca.

Coke [kəʊk] *n* Coca Cola.

▲ Es marca registrada.

col [kɒl] **2** *abbr* (*column*) columna; (*abbreviation*) col.

Col ['kɜːnəl] *abbr* (*Colonel*) Coronel *m*; (*abbreviation*) Cnel.

colander ['kʌləndəʳ] *n* colador *m*.

cold [kəʊld] **1** *adj* (*gen*) frío,-a: *are you cold?,* ¿tienes frío?; *my hands are cold,* tengo las manos frías; *it's cold today, isn't it?,* hoy hace frío, ¿verdad?; *the coffee's cold,* el café está frío; *drink your tea or it'll get cold,* bébete el té o se te enfriará. **2** (*unenthusiastic, unfriendly*) frío,-a: *we got a cold reception,* nos recibieron con frialdad. – **3** *n* (*weather*) frío: *don't stand out there in the cold,* no te quedes allí fuera con el frío que hace. **4** MED resfriado, catarro, constipado: *I've got a cold,* estoy resfriado; *she's got a stinking cold,* tiene un catarro espantoso.

● **as cold as ice,** helado,-a. ‖ **to be cold comfort,** no servir de consuelo, ser poco consuelo. ‖ **to be left out in the cold,** quedarse al margen. ‖ **to catch a cold,** resfriarse, coger un resfriado, acatarrarse. ‖ **to catch cold,** coger frío. ‖ **to do sth. in cold blood,** hacer algo a sangre fría. ‖ **to feel the cold,** ser friolero,-a. ‖ **to get cold feet (about doing sth.),** entrarle miedo a algn. (de hacer algo). ‖ **to give sb. the cold shoulder,** tratar a algn. con frialdad. ‖ **to go cold turkey,** *sl* estar con el mono. ‖ **to have a cold,** estar resfriado,-a. ‖ **to knock sb. out cold,** dejar a algn. inconsciente (de un golpe). ‖ **to leave sb. cold,** dejar a algn. frío,-a, no darle a algn. ni frío no calor. ‖ **to pour cold water on sth.,** poner trabas a algo, poner pegas a algo, poner reparos a algo.

■ **cold cream,** crema limpiadora, crema hidratante, crema facial. ‖ **cold cuts,** US CULIN embutidos *mpl*, fiambres *mpl*. ‖ **cold fish,** persona fría, persona seca. ‖ **cold frame,** (*for plants*) cajonera. ‖ **cold front,** frente *m* frío. ‖ **cold meat,** embutido, fiambre *m*. ‖ **cold snap,** ola de frío. ‖ **cold sore,** herpes *m* labial. ‖ **cold storage,** almacenamiento en cámaras frigoríficas. ‖ **cold sweat,** sudor *m* frío. ‖ **cold truth,** verdad *f* (desagradable). ‖ **cold war,** guerra fría.

cold-blooded [kəʊld'blʌdɪd] **1** *adj* ZOOL de sangre fría. **2** *fig* (*person*) frío,-a, insensible; (*murderer*) despiadado,-a, desalmado,-a, cruel; (*crime*) a sangre fría.

cold-hearted [kəʊld'hɑːtɪd] *adj* frío,-a, insensible.

coldly ['kəʊldlɪ] *adv* con frialdad, fríamente.

coldness ['kəʊldnəs] *n* frialdad *f*.

cold-shoulder [kəʊld'ʃəʊldəʳ] *t* hacer el vacío a.

coleslaw ['kəʊlslɔː] *n* ensaladilla de col y zanahoria.

colic ['kɒlɪk] *n* cólico.

colitis [kɒ'laɪtɪs] *n* colitis *f*.

collaborate [kə'læbəreɪt] *i* colaborar (**with,** con).

collaboration [kəlæbə'reɪʃən] **1** *n* (*gen*) colaboración *f*. **2** (*with enemy*) colaboracionismo.

collaborator [kə'læbəreɪtəʳ] **1** *n* colaborador,-ra. **2** (*with enemy*) colaboracionista *mf*.

collage ['kɒlɑːʒ] *n* ART collage *m*.

collapse [kə'læps] **1** *n* (*falling down*) derrumbamiento; (*falling in*) hundimiento. **2** (*failure, breakdown*) fracaso. **3** COMM FIN (*prices, currency*) caída en picado; (*business, company*) quiebra. **4** MED colapso. – **5** *i* (*building, bridge, etc*) derrumbarse, desplomarse; (*roof*) hundirse, venirse abajo; (*tired person*) desplomarse: *she collapsed in an armchair,* se desplomó en un sillón. **6** MED (*person*) sufrir un colapso. **7** (*fail - project, talks, etc*) fracasar, venirse abajo; (*- hopes*) desvanecerse: *I felt as if my whole world had collapsed,* sentí como si el mundo entero se hundiera; *all opposition to the plan collapsed,* toda la oposición al plan fracasó. **8** COMM FIN (*prices, currency*) caer en picado; (*business, company*) quebrar, ir a la bancarrota. **9** (*chair, table*) plegarse. – **10** *t* (*table*) plegar.

● **to collapse with laughter,** desternillarse de risa.

■ **collapsed lung,** colapso pulmonar.

collapsible [kə'læpsəbəl] *adj* plegable.

collar ['kɒləʳ] **1** *n* (*of shirt etc*) cuello. **2** (*for dog*) collar *m*. **3** TECH collar *m*, abrazadera. – **4** *t fam* pescar, echar el guante a, pillar.

● **to get hot under the collar,** enfadarse. ‖ **to grab sb. by the collar,** agarrar a algn. por el cuello.

■ **detachable collar,** cuello falso.

collarbone ['kɒləbəʊn] *n* clavícula.

collate [kɒ'leɪt] **1** *t* (*compare*) cotejar, confrontar. **2** (*collect together*) reunir; (*order*) compaginar.

collateral [kə'lætərəl] **1** n FIN garantía subsidiaria. – **2** adj (relative) colateral. **3** (additional) circunstancial, colateral.

collation [kɒ'leɪʃən] **1** n (comparison) cotejo, comparación f. **2** (collecting together) reunión f, recopilación f; (putting in order) compaginación f.

colleague ['kɒliːg] n colega mf, compañero,-a.

collect [kə'lekt] **1** t (glasses, plates, belongings, etc) recoger; (information, data) reunir, recopilar: *can you collect (up) the empty cups?*, ¿puedes recoger las tazas vacías?; *that piano is just collecting dust,* aquel piano sólo está acumulando polvo. **2** (stamps, records, etc) coleccionar. **3** (taxes) recaudar; (rent) cobrar. **4** (for charity - money) recaudar, hacer una colecta de; (- old clothes, jumble) juntar. **5** (pick up, fetch) ir a buscar, recoger: *I'll collect you from the airport*, te vendré a buscar al aeropuerto; *they collect the rubbish on Fridays*, pasan a recoger la basura los viernes. – **6** i (dust, water) acumularse; (people) reunirse, congregarse. **7** (for charity) recaudar dinero, hacer una colecta.
● **to call collect,** us llamar a cobro revertido. ‖ **to collect one's thoughts,** ponerse en orden las ideas. ‖ **to collect os.,** serenarse, recobrar la calma.

collected [kə'lektɪd] **1** adj (composed) sereno,-a, sosegado,-a, tranquilo,-a. **2** LIT completo,-a: *the collected works,* las obras completas.

collection [kə'lekʃən] **1** n (of stamps, paintings, etc) colección f; (of poems, short stories) recopilación f; (of people) grupo. **2** (range of new clothes) colección f. **3** (for charity) colecta. **4** (of mail, of refuse) recogida: *it will be ready for collection tomorrow,* puede pasar a recogerlo mañana. **5** (of taxes) recaudación f; (of rent) cobro.
■ **collection box,** cepillo.

collective [kə'lektɪv] **1** adj colectivo,-a. – **2** n (enterprise) cooperativa; (people) colectivo, cooperativa.
■ **collective bargaining,** negociación f colectiva. ‖ **collective farm,** granja colectiva. ‖ **collective noun,** nombre m colectivo, sustantivo colectivo. ‖ **collective ownership,** propiedad f colectiva.

collectivize [kə'lektɪvaɪz] t colectivizar.

collector [kə'lektəʳ] **1** n (of stamps etc) coleccionista mf. **2** (of rent, debts, tickets) cobrador,-ra.
■ **collector's item / collector's piece,** pieza de coleccionista.

college ['kɒlɪdʒ] **1** n (for higher education or vocational training) escuela, instituto. **2** us (university) universidad f; (within university) facultad f, departamento. **3** GB (within university) colegio universitario. **4** (group of professional people) colegio.
■ **art college,** escuela de bellas artes.

collide [kə'laɪd] **1** i (crash) colisionar, chocar. **2** (of people, aims, opinions, etc) estar en conflicto, chocar.

collie ['kɒlɪ] n pastor m escocés, collie m.

collier ['kɒlɪəʳ] **1** n GB (miner) minero (de carbón). **2** (ship) barco carbonero.

colliery ['kɒljərɪ] n GB mina de carbón.
▲ pl collieries.

collision [kə'lɪʒən] n (between cars, trains, etc) colisión f, choque m; (between ships) abordaje m.

colloquial [kə'ləʊkwɪəl] adj familiar, coloquial.

colloquialism [kə'ləʊkwɪəlɪzəm] n (expression) expresión f coloquial; (word) palabra coloquial.

collude [kə'luːd] i coludir (with, con).

collusion [kə'luːʒən] n colusión f, connivencia.
● **to act in collusion with sb.,** actuar en connivencia con algn.

collywobbles ['kɒlɪwɒbəlz] npl fam molestar m de estómago.
● **to have the collywobbles,** estar muy nervioso,-a.

cologne [kə'ləʊn] n (agua de) colonia.

Cologne [kə'ləʊn] n Colonia.

Colombia [kə'lʌmbɪə] n Colombia.

Colombian [kə'lʌmbɪən] **1** adj colombiano,-a. – **2** n colombiano,-a.

colon¹ ['kəʊlən] n ANAT colon m.

colon² ['kəʊlən] n LING dos puntos mpl.

colonel ['kɜːnəl] n coronel m.

colonial [kə'ləʊnɪəl] **1** adj colonial. – **2** n colono,-a.

colonialism [kə'ləʊnɪəlɪzəm] n colonialismo.

colonialist [kə'ləʊnɪəlɪst] **1** n colonialista mf. – **2** adj colonialista.

colonist ['kɒlənɪst] n (inhabitant) colono; (colonizer) colono,-a, colonizador,-ra.

colonization [kɒlənaɪ'zeɪʃən] n colonización f.

colonize ['kɒlənaɪz] t colonizar.

colonnade [kɒlə'neɪd] n columnata.

colony ['kɒlənɪ] n (gen) colonia.
▲ pl colonies.

color ['kʌləʳ] n us → **colour**.

color-blind ['kʌləblaɪnd] adj us → **colour-blind**.

colored ['kʌləd] adj us → **coloured**.

colorful ['kʌləful] adj us → **colourful**.

coloring ['kʌlərɪŋ] n us → **colouring**.

colorless ['kʌlələs] adj us → **colourless**.

colossal [kə'lɒsəl] adj colosal, descomunal.

colour ['kʌləʳ] **1** n color m: *what colour is it?*, ¿de qué color es?; *what colour is her hair?*, ¿de qué color tiene el pelo?; *have you got it in any other colours?*, ¿lo tienen en otros colores?; *is the film in colour or in black and white?*, ¿la película es en color o en blanco y negro? **2** (skin - racial characteristic, complexion) color m: *he has a high colour*, tiene el color subido. – **3** adj (television, film, etc) en color. – **4** t (with pen, paint, crayon) pintar, colorear; (dye) teñir. **5** fig (affect negatively, influence) influir en: *don't let emotions colour your judgement*, no dejes que las emociones te ofusquen. – **6** i (blush) enrojecer, ruborizarse, sonrojarse, ponerse rojo,-a, ponerse colorado,-a. **7** (of leaves) ponerse amarillo,-a; (fruit) coger color. – **8 colours,** npl GB SP (worn by team, school) colores mpl. **9** MIL (flag) bandera, enseña.
◆ **to colour in** t sep pintar, colorear.
● **in full colour,** a todo color. ‖ **let's see the colour of your money!,** ¡a ver ese dinero!, ¡primero el dinero! ‖ **to be off colour,** no encontrarse bien. ‖ **to lend colour to sth.,** dar credibilidad a algo, hacer que algo parezca verdad. ‖ **to lose colour,** palidecer. ‖ **to nail one's colours to the mast,** tomar partido, definirse. ‖ **to show one's true colours,** mostrarse tal como se es, mostrarse como uno es en realidad.
■ **colour bar,** discriminación f racial. ‖ **colour blindness,** daltonismo. ‖ **colour code,** código de colores. ‖ **colour prejudice,** prejuicio racial. ‖ **colour printing,** cromolitografía. ‖ **colour scheme,** combinación f de colores. ‖ **colour supplement,** suplemento en color.

colour-blind ['kʌləblaɪnd] adj daltónico,-a.

coloured ['kʌləd] **1** adj (pencils, crayons) de color, de colores. **2** dated (person) de color. **3** (biased) parcial; (exaggerated) exagerado,-a. – **4** n dated persona de color. – **5 Coloured,** adj POL (in South Africa) de raza ni negra ni blanca. – **6** n POL (in South Africa) persona que es de raza ni negra ni blanca.

colourful ['kʌləful] **1** adj (full of colour, bright) lleno,-a de color, vistoso,-a; (brightly coloured) de colores vivos. **2**

(*interesting, exciting*) lleno,-a de color, lleno,-a de colorido; (*person*) pintoresco,-a: *a neighbour gave a very colourful account of the events,* una vecina dio una versión muy colorista de los hechos.

colouring ['kʌlərɪŋ] **1** *n* (*substance, dye*) colorante *m*. **2** (*person's skin, hair and eye colour*) color *m*. **3** (*of animal's skin, fur, plumage*) colorido, color *m*. **4** ART (*act*) coloración *f*; (*use of colour*) colorido.
■ **colouring book,** libro para colorear.

colourless ['kʌləlas] **1** *adj* (*without colour*) incoloro,-a, sin color; (*pale*) pálido,-a. **2** *fig* (*dull, uninteresting*) soso,-a, anodino,-a, gris.

colt [kəʊlt] *n* potro.

column ['kɒləm] *n* (*gen*) columna.

columnist ['kɒləmnɪst] *n* columnista *mf*.

coma ['kəʊmə] *n* MED coma *m*.
● **to go into a coma,** caer en coma, entrar en coma.

comatose ['kəʊmətəʊs] **1** *adj* MED en estado comatoso. **2** *fam* (*drowsy*) grogui.

comb [kəʊm] **1** *n* (*for hair*) peine *m*; (*ornamental*) peineta. **2** (*for wool, cotton*) carda. **3** (*of bird*) cresta. **4** (*of honeycomb*) panal *m*. – **5** *t* (*hair*) peinar. **6** (*wool, cotton*) cardar, peinar. **7** (*search - area*) rastrear, peinar; (*- files*) rebuscar: *the police combed the area for the missing child,* la policía peinó la zona en busca del niño desaparecido.
● **to comb one's hair,** peinarse. ‖ **to give one's hair a comb,** pasarse un peine, peinarse.

combat ['kɒmbæt] **1** *n* combate *m*. – **2** *adj* de combate. – **3** *t* combatir, luchar contra. – **4** *i* combatir (**against,** contra).
■ **armed combat,** combate *m* armado. ‖ **close combat,** combate *m* cuerpo a cuerpo. ‖ **combat dress,** uniforme *m* de campaña. ‖ **combat duty,** servicio de frente. ‖ **combat jacket,** guerrera.

combatant ['kɒmbətənt] *n* combatiente *mf*.

combative ['kɒmbətɪv] *adj* combativo,-a.

combination [kɒmbɪ'neɪʃən] **1** *n* (*gen*) combinación *f*. **2** GB (*motorbike with sidecar*) moto *f* con sidecar. – **3** **combinations,** *npl* (*undergarment*) combinación *f*.
● **to work in combination with sb.,** trabajar en asociación con algn., trabajar en colaboración con algn.
■ **combination lock,** cerradura de combinación.

combine [kəm'baɪn] **1** *t* (*gen*) combinar; (*efforts*) combinar, aunar; (*ingredients*) mezclar: *the awful weather, combined with the bad food, ruined the holiday for us,* el mal tiempo, junto con la mala comida, nos estropeó las vacaciones. **2** (*qualities, features*) reunir; (*activities*) combinar: *he combines intelligence with sensitivity,* reúne inteligencia y sensibilidad; *we can combine business with pleasure,* podemos combinar el trabajo con la diversión. – **3** *i* (*gen*) combinarse; (*teams, forces*) unirse; (*companies*) fusionarse: *hydrogen combines with oxygen,* el hidrógeno se combina con el oxígeno. – **4** *n* COMM grupo industrial, asociación *f*.
■ **combine harvester,** cosechadora.
▲ (*sustantivo*) ['kɒmbaɪn].

combined [kəm'baɪnd] *adj* combinado,-a, conjunto,-a: *a living room and dining room combined,* un comedor-living.
■ **combined efforts,** esfuerzos *mpl* combinados. ‖ **combined operations,** operaciones *fpl* conjuntas.

combustible [kəm'bʌstɪbəl] *adj* combustible, inflamable.

combustion [kəm'bʌstʃən] *n* combustión *f*.
■ **combustion chamber,** cámara de combustión. ‖ **combustion engine,** motor *m* de combustión.

come [kʌm] **1** *i* (*gen*) venir: *you must come and visit us!,* ¡tienes que venir a visitarnos!; *can you come to dinner on Saturday?,* ¿puedes venir a cenar el sábado?; *come here a minute,* ven un momento; *are you coming?,* ¿(te) vienes?; *we came by plane,* vinimos en avión; *I've come to read the meter,* vengo a mirar el contador; *can I come with you?,* ¿puedo ir contigo?; *coming!,* ¡ya voy! **2** (*arrive*) llegar: *they still haven't come,* aún no han llegado; *what time does he come home?,* ¿a qué hora llega a casa?; *winter came early,* el invierno llegó temprano; *Christmas is coming,* ya llega la Navidad; *the time has come to decide,* ha llegado el momento de decidir. **3** (*occupy place, position*) llegar: *my horse came first,* mi caballo llegó el primero; *my family comes first,* primero está mi familia. **4** (*reach*) llegar: *the water came up to our waist,* el agua nos llegaba a la cintura; *his hair comes down to his shoulders,* el pelo le llega a los hombros. **5** (*happen*) suceder: *it came to pass that...,* sucedió que ...; *how did you come to live here?,* ¿cómo es que vives aquí? **6** (*be available*) venir, suministrarse: *it comes in three sizes,* viene en tres tamaños. **7** (*become*) hacerse: *your laces have come undone,* se te han desatado los cordones; *the picture's come unstuck,* el cuadro se ha despegado; *the screw had come loose,* el tornillo se había aflojado; *it'll all come right in the end,* todo saldrá bien al final. **8** *fam* (*used with expressions of time*) para: *come next month,* para el mes que viene. **9** *sl* (*have orgasm*) correrse. – **10** *t* (*behave, play the part*) hacerse: *don't come the innocent with me,* no te hagas el inocente conmigo.
◆ **to come about** *i* (*happen*) ocurrir, suceder. ‖ **to come across 1** *t insep* (*thing*) encontrar, tropezar con; (*person*) encontrar, encontrarse con, tropezar con. – **2** *i* (*be understood*) ser comprendido,-a. **3** (*make an impression*) causar una impresión: *she came across very well,* causó muy buena impresión; *he came across as an idiot,* dio la impresión de ser un imbécil. ‖ **to come after** *t insep* seguir. ‖ **to come along 1** *i* (*progress*) ir, marchar. **2** (*hurry up*) darse prisa; (*give encouragement*) ir, venir: *come along!,* ¡date prisa!, ¡vamos!, ¡venga! **3** (*arrive*) venir, llegar; (*appear*) aparecer. ‖ **to come apart** *i* deshacerse. ‖ **to come at** *t insep* atacar. ‖ **to come away 1** *i* (*become detached*) despegarse, desprenderse, soltarse, separarse: *the plaster's coming away from the wall,* el yeso se desprende de la pared. **2** (*leave, depart*) salir (**from,** de), irse (**from,** de); (*move away*) apartarse (**from,** de): *when the fight started we came away,* cuando empezó la pelea nos fuimos; *come away from the edge!,* ¡apártate del borde! ‖ **to come back 1** *i* (*return*) volver (**from,** de): *he's coming back on Saturday,* volverá el sábado; *mini skirts are coming back,* vuelven las minifaldas. **2** (*remember*) volver a la memoria: *it's all coming back to me now,* estoy volviendo a recordarlo todo. **3** (*reply, question, idea*) volver (**to,** a); (*reply, retort*) replicar, contestar. ‖ **to come before 1** *t insep* JUR comparecer ante. **2** (*be more important than*) ser más importante que. ‖ **to come between** *t insep* interponerse entre, separar. ‖ **to come by** *t insep* (*obtain*) conseguir, obtener: *jobs are hard to come by,* los trabajos son difíciles de conseguir; *how did you come by that ring?,* ¿cómo te hiciste con ese anillo? ‖ **to come down 1** *i* (*gen*) bajar; (*collapse*) caerse, hundirse, venirse abajo; (*fall - rain, snow*) caer. **2** (*plane - land*) aterrizar; (*- fall*) caer. **3** (*price, temperature, etc*) bajar. **4** (*be passed down, inherited*) llegar (**to,** a). ‖ **to come down on** *t insep* (*rebuke*) pegar una bronca a; (*punish*) castigar: *they came down hard on him,* le pegaron una bronca. ‖ **to come down**

to *t insep* (*be a question of*) ser cuestión de, tratarse de, reducirse a. ‖ **to come down with** *t insep* (*illness*) caer enfermo,-a de, contraer, coger. ‖ **to come forward** *i* (*witness*) presentarse; (*volunteer*) ofrecerse, presentarse: *she came forward with some information,* facilitó alguna información. ‖ **to come from** *t insep* (*originate from - person*) ser de; (*- thing*) venir de; (*descend from*) descender de. ‖ **to come in** *i* (*enter*) entrar: *come in!,* ¡pase!, ¡adelante! **2** (*ship, train*) llegar; (*tide*) subir; (*person - to work*) venir; (*- in race*) llegar: *I came in fourth,* llegué en cuarta posición, llegué el cuarto. **3** (*be elected*) subir al poder. **4** (*become fashionable*) ponerse de moda; (*come into season*) empezar la temporada de. **5** (*be received - income*) entrar; (*- news, report*) llegar. **6** (*contribute to discussion*) intervenir. **7** (*have a part to play*) entrar: *where do I come in?,* ¿qué pinto yo? ‖ **to come in for** *t insep* (*receive*) ser objeto de. ‖ **to come in on** *t insep* participar en. ‖ **to come into** **1** *t insep* (*inherit*) heredar. **2** (*enter*) entrar en: *I said the first thing that came into my head,* dije la primera cosa que se me ocurrió. **3** (*be relevant*) ser cuestión de, tratar de. ‖ **to come of** *t insep* (*result*) resultar de: *no good will come of it,* de ahí no saldrá nada bueno. ‖ **to come off 1** *i* (*happen, take place*) tener lugar, suceder; (*turn out*) salir: *the play came off well,* la obra salió bien. **2** (*end up*) salir: *he came off worse than his rival,* salió peor parado que su rival. **3** (*fall - button*) caerse; (*- handle, wheel*) salirse, soltarse; (*- wallpaper, plaster*) caerse, soltarse, despegarse, desprenderse: *the handle came off in my hand,* me quedé con el asa en la mano. **– 4** *t insep* (*fall from*) caerse de. **5** (*stop taking*) dejar de tomar. ‖ **to come on 1** *i* (*make progress*) avanzar. **2** (*hurry up*) darse prisa; (*give encouragement*) ir, venir: *come on!,* ¡date prisa!, ¡vamos!, ¡venga! **3** (*follow on*) ir, venir. **4** (*of actor*) entrar en escena, salir a escena; (*of sports player*) entrar. **5** *fam* (*start - cold, winter*) empezar, comenzar; (*- rain, snow*) ponerse a: *it came on to rain,* se puso a llover. **6** (*lights, heating, etc*) encenderse. ‖ **to come out 1** *i* (*leave*) salir (**of,** de); (*tooth, hair*) caerse; (*stain*) salir, quitarse; (*colour, dye*) desteñirse. **2** (*sun, moon, stars*) salir; (*flowers*) aparecer, salir. **3** (*new book, record, magazine, figures*) salir, publicarse; (*film*) estrenarse. **4** (*news, truth, secret*) revelarse, salir a la luz. **5** (*of photographs*) resultar, salir; (*of person in photo*) salir. **6** (*be revealed, shown clearly*) mostrarse, revelarse; (*of words, speech*) salir: *it just came out,* se me escapó. **7** (*end, finish, have as outcome*) salir: *the figures have come out wrong,* han salido mal los números; *she came out top in the exam,* sacó la mejor nota en el examen. **8** GB (*stop work, strike*) declararse en huelga. **9** (*in society*) presentarse en sociedad. **10** (*declare openly that one is gay*) declararse homosexual. ‖ **to come out in** *t insep* (*spots, rash*) salirle a uno; (*cold sweat*) entrarle a uno. ‖ **to come out with** *t insep* (*say*) soltar, salir con. ‖ **to come over 1** *i* (*arrive*) venir, llegar: *I'll come over at about ten,* llegaré sobre las diez. **2** (*visit*) hacer una visita: *come over and see us,* ven a visitarnos. **3** (*project oneself*) dar la impresión: *he came over as very capable,* dio la impresión de ser muy capaz. **4** (*with adjective*) ponerse: *I came over faint,* me sentí mareado. **5** (*change sides, opinions*) pasarse (**to,** a). **– 6** *t insep* (*affect*) pasar, sobrevenir: *I don't know what came over me,* no sé qué me pasó. ‖ **to come round 1** *i* (*regain consciousness*) volver en sí. **2** (*be persuaded, change one's mind*) dejarse convencer, convencerse: *she eventually came round to our point of view,* finalmente aceptó nuestro punto de vista. **3** (*visit*) visitar, venir. **4** (*happen regularly, recur*) volver. **– 5** *t insep* (*corner*) doblar, dar la vuelta a; (*bend*) tomar. ‖ **to come through 1** *i* (*arrive*) llegar. **2**

(*survive*) sobrevivir. **3** (*into other room*) pasar. **– 4** *t insep* (*operation, accident*) sobrevivir, salir con vida de; (*illness*) recuperarse de; (*difficult period*) pasar por, atravesar. ‖ **to come to 1** *i* (*regain consciousness*) volver en sí. **– 2** *t insep* (*enter mind*) ocurrirse: *the answer suddenly came to her,* de repente se le ocurrió la respuesta. **3** (*reach a situation*) llegar a: *you'll come to love him,* llegarás a quererlo; *it has come to my notice that ...,* me he enterado de que ...; *hopefully, it won't come to that,* se espera que no sea necesario; *what is the world coming to?,* ¿a dónde vamos a ir a parar? **4** (*amount to, total*) subir a, ascender a, ser: *how much does it come to?,* ¿cuánto es? ‖ **to come under 1** *t insep* (*be controlled by*) estar bajo; (*be included within*) venir en, estar comprendido,-a en. **2** (*be target of*) ser objeto de, ser víctima de, ser blanco de. ‖ **to come up 1** *i* (*person - gen*) subir; (*- approach*) acercarse. **2** (*sun*) salir; (*flowers*) crecer, brotar; (*bruise, swelling*) hincharse. **3** (*occur, arise - problem, question*) presentarse, surgir; (*- vacancy*) producirse: *something's come up,* ha surgido algo. **4** (*be raised, be mentioned - point*) surgir; (*- name*) ser mencionado,-a, salir. **5** JUR (*case*) verse; (*person*) comparecer ante. **6** (*of food*) marchar. ‖ **to come up against** *t insep* topar con, encontrarse con, tropezar con. ‖ **to come up for** *t insep* (*promotion, parole*) considerar para. ‖ **to come up to 1** *t insep* (*equal*) alcanzar, llegar a, estar a la altura de. **2** (*approach - in space*) acercarse a; (*- in time*) ser casi. ‖ **to come up with** *t insep* (*idea*) tener, ocurrirse; (*solution*) encontrar; (*plan*) idear; (*proposal*) presentar, plantear. ‖ **to come upon** *t insep* encontrarse con, encontrar.

● **come again?,** ¿cómo?, ¿qué? ‖ **come off it!,** ¡venga ya!, ¡anda ya! ‖ **come what may,** pase lo que pase. ‖ **to be as ... as they come,** ser lo más ... que hay: *he's as silly as they come,* es lo más tonto que hay. ‖ **to come,** (*in the future*) venidero,-a: *in years to come,* en el futuro. ‖ **to come a long way,** (*progress*) progresar mucho. ‖ **to come and go,** ir y venir: *I don't know if I'm coming or going,* estoy hecho un lío; *fashions come and go,* las modas cambian. ‖ **to come as a shock/surprise to sb.,** ser un susto/sorpresa para algn.: *her death came as a shock to me to,* su muerte me sorprendió. ‖ **to come clean,** confesar, cantar. ‖ **to come down in the world,** venir a menos. ‖ **to come down on sb.'s side,** ponerse de parte de algn. ‖ **to come easily to sb.,** resultarle fácil a algn. ‖ **to come in handy / come in useful,** ser útil, resultar útil, venir bien. ‖ **to come into being,** nacer, ver la luz. ‖ **to come into fashion,** ponerse de moda. ‖ **to come into force,** entrar en vigor. ‖ **to come into the world,** nacer, ver la luz. ‖ **to come of age,** llegar a la mayoría de edad. ‖ **to come out in favour of sth. / come out against sth.,** declararse a favor de algo / declararse en contra de algo. ‖ **to come to an end,** acabar, terminar, tocar a su fin. ‖ **to come to nothing,** llegar a nada, quedar en nada, quedar en agua de borrajas. ‖ **to come to one's senses,** (*regain consciousness*) volver en sí; (*see sense*) recobrar la razón. ‖ **to come together,** (*people*) juntarse, reunirse; (*ideas*) cuajar. ‖ **to come true,** hacerse realidad. ‖ **to have it coming (to one),** tenérselo merecido. ‖ **to see sth. coming,** ver algo venir. ‖ **to take life as it comes,** aceptar la vida tal y como se presenta. ‖ **when it comes to ...,** en cuanto a ...

▲ *pt* **came** *pp* **come,** *ger* **coming.**

comeback ['kʌmbæk] **1** *n fam* (*of person*) reaparición *f,* vuelta, retorno. **2** (*way of obtaining compensation*) reclamación *f.* **3** (*reply*) réplica, respuesta.

comedian [kə'miːdɪən] *n* cómico, humorista *m.*

comedienne [kəmiːdɪ'en] *n* cómica, humorista.
comedown ['kʌmdaʊn] *n* degradación *f*, humillación *f*.
comedy ['kɒmədɪ] *n* comedia.
■ **comedy of manners,** comedia de costumbres.
▲ *pl* **comedies.**
comer ['kʌmə^r] *n* participante *mf*, asistente *mf*: *the race is open to all comers,* la carrera está abierta a todo el que se presente.
comet ['kɒmɪt] *n* cometa *m*.
comeuppance [kʌm'ʌpəns] *n* merecido, justo castigo.
● **to get one's comeuppance,** recibir su merecido.
comfort ['kʌmfət] **1** *n* (*well-being*) comodidad *f*, confort *m*, bienestar *m*. **2** (*thing, luxury*) comodidad *f*. **3** (*consolation*) consuelo: *if it's any comfort to you,* si te sirve de consuelo. – **4** *t* consolar.
● **to live in comfort,** vivir cómodamente. ‖ **to take comfort in/from sth.,** consolarse con algo.
■ **comfort station,** us servicios *mpl*, aseos *mpl*.
comfortable ['kʌmfətəbəl] **1** *adj* (*furniture, clothes, etc*) cómodo,-a. **2** (*patient*) tranquilo,-a. **3** (*job, income*) bueno,-a; (*life*) desahogado,-a, acomodado,-a: *they're comfortable,* viven bien, viven con desahogo. **4** (*lead, majority*) amplio,-a.
● **to feel comfortable,** estar a gusto. ‖ **to make os. comfortable,** ponerse cómodo,-a.
comfortably ['kʌmfətəblɪ] **1** *adv* (*sit, lie*) cómodamente. **2** (*live*) holgadamente. **3** (*win*) fácilmente.
● **to be comfortably off,** estar en una situación holgada, vivir cómodamente, vivir holgadamente.
comforter ['kʌmfətə^r] **1** *n* (*person*) consolador,-ra. **2** (*scarf*) bufanda. **3** (*dummy*) chupete *m*.
comforting ['kʌmfətɪŋ] *adj* reconfortante.
comfortless ['kʌmfətləs] *adj* incómodo,-a, sin comodidades.
comfy ['kʌmfɪ] *adj fam* cómodo,-a.
▲ *comp* **comfier,** *superl* **comfiest.**
comic ['kɒmɪk] **1** *adj* cómico,-a. – **2** *n* (*comedian*) cómico,-a, humorista *mf*. **3** (*magazine*) tebeo, comic *m*.
■ **comic opera,** ópera bufa. ‖ **comic strip,** tira cómica, historieta.
comical ['kɒmɪkəl] *adj* cómico,-a.
coming ['kʌmɪŋ] **1** *adj* (*gen*) próximo,-a; (*generation*) venidero,-a, futuro,-a: *this coming Sunday,* el domingo que viene, el próximo domingo. – **2** *n* (*arrival*) llegada. **3** REL advenimiento.
● **coming and going,** ir y venir, ajetreo, vaivén. ‖ **comings and goings,** idas y venidas.
coming-of-age ['kʌmɪŋəv'eɪdʒ] *n* mayoría de edad.
coming-out [kʌmɪŋ'aʊt] **1** *n* (*in society*) presentación *f* en sociedad. **2** (*of homosexual*) declaración *f* pública.
comma ['kɒmə] *n* coma.
■ **inverted comma,** comilla.
command [kə'mɑːnd] **1** *n* (*order*) orden *f*: *your wish is my command,* tus deseos son órdenes. **2** (*control, authority*) mando: *under the command of the king,* bajo el mando del rey; *who is in command?,* ¿quién está al mando? **3** MIL (*part of army, group of officers*) mando. **4** (*knowledge, mastery*) dominio: *he has a good command of Greek,* domina el griego. **5** COMPUT orden *f*. – **6** *t* (*order*) mandar, ordenar: *he commanded them to shoot,* les ordenó que disparasen. **7** MIL (*have authority over*) estar al mando de, tener el mando de, comandar. **8** (*have at one's disposal*) disponer de, contar con, tener: *the hotel commands a fantastic view of the city,* el hotel tiene una vista fantástica de la ciudad. **9** (*deserve - respect, admiration*) infundir, imponer, inspirar; (*- confidence*) inspirar;

(*- sympathy*) merecer: *it commanded a high price,* alcanzó un precio muy alto; *he can command a high salary,* puede exigir un sueldo alto. **10** (*of place, fort*) dominar. – **11** *i* mandar.
● **at sb.'s command,** por orden de algn. ‖ **to be at sb.'s command,** estar a las órdenes de algn. ‖ **to be in command of os.,** ser dueño,-a de sí mismo,-a. ‖ **to be in command of the situation,** dominar la situación. ‖ **to take command,** tomar el mando.
■ **command module,** módulo de maniobra y mando. ‖ **command performance,** *actuación a petición de un miembro de la familia real.* ‖ **command post,** puesto de mando.
commandant ['kɒməndænt] *n* MIL comandante *m*.
commandeer [kɒmən'dɪə^r] *t* MIL requisar.
commander [kə'mɑːndə^r] **1** *n* MIL comandante *m*. **2** MAR capitán *m* de fragata.
■ **commander in chief,** comandante *m* en jefe.
commanding [kə'mɑːndɪŋ] **1** *adj* (*voice, manner, appearance*) autoritario,-a, imperioso,-a. **2** (*position*) dominante, de superioridad.
■ **commanding officer,** oficial *m* al mando, comandante *m*.
commandment [kə'mɑːndmənt] *n* REL mandamiento.
commando [kə'mɑːndəʊ] *n* comando.
▲ *pl* **commandos** *o* **commandoes.**
commemorate [kə'meməreɪt] *t* conmemorar.
commemoration [kəmemə'reɪʃən] *n* conmemoración *f*.
commemorative [kə'memərətɪv] *adj* conmemorativo,-a.
commence [kə'mens] **1** *t* *fml* comenzar, iniciar, empezar. – **2** *i* *fml* comenzar, iniciarse, empezar.
commencement [kə'mensmənt] **1** *n* *fml* (*beginning*) comienzo, inicio. **2** us (*graduation*) (ceremonia de) graduación *f*.
commend [kə'mend] **1** *t* (*praise*) alabar (**for,** por), elogiar (**for,** por); (*recommend*) recomendar. **2** (*entrust*) encomendar (**to,** a).
commendable [kə'mendəbəl] *adj* encomiable, loable.
commendation [kɒmen'deɪʃən] **1** *n* (*praise*) elogio, elogios *mpl*. **2** (*award, prize*) mención *f* de honor, distinción *f*: *a commendation for bravery,* una distinción por su valor.
commensurate [kə'menʃərət] *adj fml* acorde.
● **commensurate with,** acorde con: *salary commensurate with experience,* sueldo según experiencia.
comment ['kɒment] **1** *n* comentario, observación *f*. – **2** *t* comentar, observar. – **3** *i* hacer comentarios (**on,** sobre).
● **no comment,** sin comentarios. ‖ **to be fair comment,** ser razonable. ‖ **to cause comment,** dar lugar a habladurías. ‖ **to make a comment about sb./sth.,** hacer un comentario sobre algn./algo, hacer una observación sobre algn./algo. ‖ **to refuse to comment,** negarse a hacer declaraciones.
commentary ['kɒməntərɪ] **1** *n* RAD TV (*spoken description*) comentario, comentarios *mpl*. **2** (*set of written remarks*) comentario, crítica.
■ **commentary box,** cabina de prensa.
▲ *pl* **commentaries.**
commentate ['kɒmənteɪt] *i* RAD TV comentar un partido, retransmitir un partido, hacer los comentarios (**on,** de): *he commentates on all the international matches,* él comenta todos los partidos internacionales.
commentator ['kɒmənteɪtə^r] *n* RAD TV comentarista *mf*.

commerce ['kɒmɜːs] *n* comercio.
commercial [kə'mɜːʃəl] **1** *adj* COMM comercial, mercantil. **2** (*intended to make money*) comercial. **– 3** *n* RAD TV (*advertisement*) anuncio, spot *m* publicitario.
■ **commercial art**, arte *m* publicitario. ‖ **commercial break**, pausa para la publicidad. ‖ **commercial law**, derecho mercantil. ‖ **commercial traveller**, viajante *mf* de comercio. ‖ **commercial vehicle**, vehículo para transporte de mercancías etc.
commercialism [kə'mɜːʃəlɪzəm] *n* comercialismo.
commercialization [kə'mɜːʃəlaɪzeɪʃən] *n* comercialización *f*.
commercialize [kə'mɜːʃəlaɪz] *t* comercializar.
commercially [kə'mɜːʃəlɪ] *adv* comercialmente.
● **to be commercially available**, estar a la venta.
commiserate [kə'mɪzəreɪt] *i* compadecerse (**with**, de): *I commiserated with her over the news,* le dije cuánto sentía la noticia.
commiseration [kəmɪzə'reɪʃən] **1** *n* (*sympathy*) conmiseración *f*. **– 2 commiserations**, *interj* ¡mala suerte!
● **to give/offer sb. one's commiserations**, decirle a algn. cuánto se siente algo.
commissar ['kɒmɪsɑːʳ] *n* comisario político.
commissariat [kɒmɪ'seərɪət] *n* comisariado.
commission [kə'mɪʃən] **1** *n* COMM comisión *f*: *he gets a 10% commisssion,* cobra el 10% de comisión. **2** (*piece of work*) encargo. **3** (*group of people*) comisión *f*. **4** MIL (*rank*) grado de oficial; (*document*) nombramiento. **5** *fml* (*act of committing a crime*) perpetración *f*. **– 6** *t* (*order*) encargar: *she's been commissioned to design a statue,* le han encargado el diseño de una estatua. **7** MIL nombrar. **8** MAR (*ship*) poner en servicio.
● **to be in commission**, estar en servicio. ‖ **to be out of commission**, estar fuera de servicio.
■ **commissioned officer**, oficial *m* (del ejército).
commissionaire [kəmɪʃə'neəʳ] *n* GB portero, conserje *m*.
commissioner [kə'mɪʃənəʳ] **1** *n* (*public official*) comisario. **2** (*member of a commission*) comisionado,-a, miembro de la comisión.
■ **Commissioner for Oaths**, GB JUR ≈ notario,-a.
commit [kə'mɪt] **1** *t* (*crime, error, sin*) cometer. **2** (*send to prison etc*) internar. **3** (*bind*) comprometer, obligar; (*pledge*) asignar, consignar, destinar.
● **to commit os. (to do/doing sth.)**, comprometerse (a hacer algo). ‖ **to commit suicide**, suicidarse. ‖ **to commit sth. to memory**, memorizar algo. ‖ **to commit sth. to paper**, poner algo por escrito. ‖ **to commit sb. to prison**, encarcelar a algn. ‖ **to commit sth. to sb.'s care**, confiar algo al cuidado de algn.
▲ *pt* & *pp* **committed**, *ger* **committing**.
commitment [kə'mɪtmənt] **1** *n* (*undertaking, obligation*) compromiso, obligación *f*; (*responsibility*) responsabilidad *f*. **2** (*dedication*) dedicación *f*, entrega.
committal [kə'mɪtəl] *n* (*to mental hospital*) reclusión *f*; (*to prison*) encarcelamiento.
● **committal for trial**, ≈ procesamiento.
■ **committal proceedings**, ≈ sumario.
committed [kə'mɪtɪd] *adj* (*to a cause*) comprometido,-a; (*dedicated*) dedicado,-a, entregado,-a.
● **to be committed to do/doing sth.**, estar comprometido,-a a hacer algo.
committee [kə'mɪtɪ] **1** *n* comité *m*, comisión *f*: *parliamentary committee*, comisión parlamentaria. **– 2** *adj* del comité, de la comisión: *committee room*, sala de reuniones.

● **to be on a committee / sit on a committee**, ser miembro de un comité, ser miembro de una comisión.
commode [kə'məud] **1** *n* (*chest of drawers*) cómoda. **2** (*chair*) silla con orinal.
commodious [kə'məudɪəs] *adj fml* espacioso,-a, amplio,-a.
commodity [kə'mɒdɪtɪ] **1** *n* COMM producto, artículo, mercancía. **2** FIN materia prima.
■ **commodities market**, mercado de materias primas.
▲ *pl* **commodities**.
commodore ['kɒmədɔːʳ] *n* GB MAR comodoro.
common ['kɒmən] **1** *adj* (*ordinary, average*) corriente: *the common people*, la gente corriente; *a common soldier*, un soldado raso. **2** (*usual, not scarce*) común, corriente: *the common cold*, el resfriado común; *it's quite common for mothers to suffer from postnatal depression*, es bastante común que las madres padezcan una depresión posparto. **3** (*shared, joint*) común: *common ground*, puntos en común; *for the common good*, por el bien común, por el bien de todos. **4** *pej* (*vulgar*) ordinario,-a. **– 5** *n* (*land*) campo comunal, terreno comunal, tierras *fpl* comunales.
● **as common as dirt / as common as muck**, muy ordinario,-a. ‖ **common or garden**, normal y corriente. ‖ **in common**, en común. ‖ **in common with**, (*like*) al igual que. ‖ **to be common knowledge**, ser de dominio público. ‖ **to have sth. in common with sb.**, tener algo en común con algn. ‖ **to make common cause with sb.**, hacer causa común con algn.
■ **common decency**, educación *f*. ‖ **common denominator**, denominador *m* común. ‖ **common factor**, factor *m* común. ‖ **common law**, derecho consuetudinario. ‖ **Common Market**, Mercado Común. ‖ **common noun**, nombre *m* común. ‖ **common room**, GB EDUC sala de reunión. ‖ **common sense**, sentido común. ‖ **common time**, MUS cuatro por cuatro. ‖ **the common touch**, el contacto con el pueblo.
commoner ['kɒmənəʳ] *n* plebeyo,-a.
common-law ['kɒmənlɔː] *adj* (*couple*) de hecho.
■ **common-law husband**, marido de hecho. ‖ **common-law wife**, mujer *f* de hecho.
commonly ['kɒmənlɪ] **1** *adv* (*usually*) comúnmente, vulgarmente. **2** *pej* (*vulgarly*) de manera ordinaria.
commonplace ['kɒmənpleɪs] **1** *adj* común, corriente. **– 2** *n* (*platitude*) lugar *m* común, tópico.
Commons ['kɒmənz] **the Commons**, *npl* GB POL los Comunes.
■ **the House of Commons**, la Cámara de los Comunes.
Commonwealth ['kɒmənwelθ] *n* GB Commonwealth *f*.
■ **the Commonwealth of Nations**, la Mancomunidad *f* Británica de Naciones.
commotion [kə'məuʃən] *n* (*scandal*) escándalo; (*noise, excitement*) alboroto, jaleo; (*confusion*) confusión *f*: *what a commotion!*, ¡qué jaleo!
● **to make a commotion**, (*scandal*) armar un escándalo; (*noise*) armar jaleo.
communal ['kɒmjənəl] *adj* (*shared*) comunal, común; (*of a community*) comunitario,-a.
commune[1] ['kɒmjuːn] *n* comuna.
commune[2] [kə'mjuːn] *i lit* estar en comunión (**with**, con).
communicable [kə'mjuːnɪkəbəl] **1** *adj* MED transmisible. **2** (*ideas etc*) comunicable.

communicant [kə'mjuːnɪkənt] *n* REL comulgante *mf*.

communicate [kə'mjuːnɪkeɪt] **1** *t* (*make known, convey*) comunicar. **2** MED transmitir, contagiar. – **3** *i* (*person*) comunicarse (**with,** con). **4** (*of rooms*) comunicarse.

communicating [kə'mjuːnɪkeɪtɪŋ] *adj* (*rooms*) que se comunican; (*door*) que comunica.

communication [kəmjuːnɪ'keɪʃən] **1** *n* (*gen*) comunicación *f*. **2** (*message*) comunicación *f*, comunicado. – **3** **communications,** *npl* comunicaciones *fpl*.
■ **communication cord,** GB ≈ timbre *m* de alarma.

communicative [kə'mjuːnɪkətɪv] *adj* comunicativo,-a.

communion [kə'mjuːnɪən] **1** *n fml* comunión *f*. **2** **Communion,** REL Comunión *f*.
● **to take Communion,** comulgar.
■ **Holy Communion,** Sagrada Comunión *f*, Santa Comunión *f*.

communiqué [kə'mjuːnɪkeɪ] *n* comunicado.

communism ['kɒmjənɪzəm] *n* comunismo.

communist ['kɒmjənɪst] **1** *adj* comunista. – **2** *n* comunista *mf*.

community [kə'mjuːnɪtɪ] **1** *n* (*people living in one place*) comunidad *f*: *all sections of the community,* todas las secciones de la comunidad. **2** (*group of people*) comunidad *f*, colectividad *f*: *the Muslim community,* la comunidad musulmana; *the business community,* la colectividad empresarial.
■ **community centre,** centro social. ‖ **community policing,** sistema *m* de policía de barrio. ‖ **community service,** trabajos *mpl* al servicio de la comunidad. ‖ **community spirit,** espíritu *m* comunitario. ‖ **the local community,** el vecindario.
▲ *pl* **communities.**

commute [kə'mjuːt] **1** *i* desplazarse diariamente al lugar de trabajo: *he commutes from Cambridge to London,* se desplaza cada día de Cambridge a Londres para trabajar. – **2** *t* (*sentence, punishment*) conmutar. **3** *fml* (*money payment, pension*) conmutar (**for/into,** por).

commuter [kə'mjuːtəʳ] *n* persona que se desplaza diariamente a su lugar de trabajo.
■ **the commuter belt,** los barrios *mpl* periféricos.

compact[1] [kəm'pækt] **1** *adj* (*gen*) compacto,-a; (*style*) conciso,-a. – **2** *n* (*for powder*) polvera de bolsillo. **3** US coche *m* utilitario. – **4** *t* compactar, comprimir.
■ **compact disc,** disco compacto, compact disc *m*. ‖ **compact disc player,** reproductor *m* de compact disc.
▲ (*sustantivo*) ['kɒmpækt].

compact[2] ['kɒmpækt] *n* (*agreement*) pacto, acuerdo, convenio.

companion [kəm'pænjən] **1** *n* (*partner, friend*) compañero,-a. **2** (*person employed*) persona de compañía. **3** (*either of pair or set*) compañero,-a, pareja. **4** (*guide*) guía, manual *m*.

companionable [kəm'pænjənəbəl] *adj* sociable, agradable.

companionship [kəm'pænjənʃɪp] *n* (*relationship*) compañerismo, camaradería; (*company*) compañía.

company ['kʌmpənɪ] **1** *n* (*companionship*) compañía: *I enjoy his company,* me gusta su compañía. **2** (*visitors*) visita: *we've got company,* tenemos visita. **3** COMM FIN (*business*) empresa, compañía, sociedad *f*: *public limited company,* sociedad anónima; *trading company,* sociedad mercantil. **4** THEAT compañía. **5** MIL compañía.
● **in company,** en público. ‖ **in company with,** (*together with*) junto,-a con. ‖ **to be good company,** ser muy sociable, ser muy agradable. ‖ **to be in good company,** no ser el/la único,-a. ‖ **to keep bad com-**

pany, andar con malas compañías. ‖ **to keep sb. company,** hacerle (mucha) compañía a algn. ‖ **to part company,** (*separate*) separarse (**with,** de); (*disagree*) diferir (**on,** sobre). ‖ **two's a company, three's a crowd,** dos son compañía, tres multitud. ‖ **you know a man by the company he keeps,** dime con quién andas y te diré quién eres.
■ **company car,** coche *m* de la compañía, coche *m* de la empresa. ‖ **ship's company,** MAR tripulación *f*.
▲ *pl* **companies.**

comparable ['kɒmpərəbəl] *adj* comparable (**to,** a) (**with,** con), equiparable (**to,** a) (**with,** con): *the two players are not comparable,* los dos jugadores no se pueden comparar.

comparative [kəm'pærətɪv] **1** *adj* (*relative*) relativo,-a: *he's a comparative stranger,* es prácticamente un desconocido. **2** (*making a comparison*) comparado,-a: *a comparative study,* un estudio comparativo. **3** LING comparativo,-a. – **4** *n* LING comparativo.

comparatively [kəm'pærətɪvlɪ] *adv* relativamente.

compare [kəm'peəʳ] **1** *t* comparar (**to/with,** con): *I'm going to compare prices in some other shops,* voy a comparar los precios en otras tiendas; *she's always being compared to Marilyn Monroe,* siempre la comparan con Marilyn Monroe; *you can't compare them,* no los puedes comparar. – **2** *i* compararse (**with,** con): *cheap red wine just doesn't compare with Rioja,* el vino tinto barato no se puede comparar con el Rioja; *how does his new film compare with his previous ones?,* ¿qué tal su nueva película comparada con las anteriores?; *it compares favourably with the others,* es mejor que los otros.
● **beyond compare,** sin comparación, incomparable.
‖ **compared with,** comparado,-a con, en comparación con.

comparison [kəm'pærɪsən] *n* comparación *f*.
● **by comparison / in comparison,** en comparación. ‖ **there's no comparison,** no hay punto de comparación. ‖ **not to bear comparison with / not stand comparison with,** no admitir comparación con.

compartment [kəm'pɑːtmənt] *n* (*in wallet, fridge, desk*) compartimento, compartimiento; (*in train*) departamento, compartimento, compartimiento.

compartmentalize [kɒmpɑːt'mentəlaɪz] *t* compartimentar.

compass ['kʌmpəs] **1** *n* (*magnetic*) brújula, compás *m*: *the points of the compass,* los puntos cardinales. **2** (*for drawing*) compás *m*: *a pair of compasses,* un compás. **3** *fig* (*range, scope*) alcance *m*.
■ **compass rose,** rosa de los vientos.
▲ En **2** también se usa en *pl* con el mismo significado.

compassion [kəm'pæʃən] *n* compasión *f*.

compassionate [kəm'pæʃənət] *adj* compasivo,-a.
■ **compassionate leave,** GB permiso por asuntos familiares.

compatibility [kəmpætə'bɪlɪtɪ] *n* compatibilidad *f*.

compatible [kəm'pætɪbəl] *adj* compatible (**with,** con).

compatriot [kəm'pætrɪət] *n* compatriota *mf*.

compel [kəm'pel] *t* (*force*) obligar, forzar, compeler. **2** *fig* (*inspire - respect*) imponer, infundir, inspirar; (*- admiration*) despertar, inspirar, infundir.
● **to compel sb. to do sth.,** obligar a algn. a hacer algo, forzar a algn. a hacer algo. ‖ **to be compelled to do sth.,** verse obligado,-a a hacer algo.
▲ *pt & pp* **compelled,** *ger* **compelling.**

compelling [kəm'pelɪŋ] *adj* (*novel, account, story*) irresistible; (*reason, argument*) convincente, persuasivo,-a, de peso.

compendium [kəm'pendɪəm] **1** n (book, account, summary) compendio. **2** GB (set of games) juegos mpl reunidos.
▲ pl compendiums o compendia.

compensate ['kɒmpənseɪt] **1** t (recompense, indemnify) indemnizar (**for,** por), compensar (**for,** por): he was compensated for the injury, lo indemnizaron por la lesión. **2** (counterbalance) compensar. – **3** i compensar (**for,** -): her enthusiasm compensates for her lack of experience, su entusiasmo compensa su falta de experiencia.

compensation [kɒmpən'seɪʃən] **1** n (money, damages) indemnización f (**for,** por): you are entitled to compensation, tienes derecho a una indemnización; he received $10,000 in compensation, le dieron $10.000 de indemnización. **2** (way of compensating) compensación f (**for,** por).

compensatory [kɒmpen'seɪtərɪ] adj compensador,-ra.
■ compensatory payment, indemnización f.

compere ['kɒmpeə'] **1** n GB presentador,-ra. – **2** t GB presentar.

compete [kəm'piːt] i (try to win) disputarse; (take part in) competir, participar: some children compete for their parents' attention, algunos hijos se disputan la atención de sus padres; he has competed in three Olympic Games, ha participado en tres Juegos Olímpicos.
● to compete against sb./sth., competir contra algn./algo. ‖ to compete with sb./sth., competir con algn./algo.

competence ['kɒmpɪtəns] **1** n (ability) competencia, capacidad f, aptitud f: a fair level of competence in German, un buen nivel de alemán. **2** JUR (legal authority) competencia.

competent ['kɒmpɪtənt] **1** adj (person) competente; (work, novel, etc) aceptable, bastante bien: he is very competent at his job, es muy competente en su trabajo. **2** JUR competente.
● to be competent to do sth., estar capacitado,-a para hacer algo.

competition [kɒmpə'tɪʃən] **1** n (gen) concurso; (race, sporting event) competición f; (literary) certamen m. **2** (rivalry) competencia.
● to be in competition with sb./sth., competir con algn./algo.

competitive [kəm'petɪtɪv] **1** adj (gen) competitivo,-a; (person) competitivo,-a, que tiene espíritu competitivo. **2** COMM (price, goods, etc) competitivo,-a.
■ competitive examination, oposición f.

competitiveness [kəm'petɪtɪvnəs] **1** n (of person) espíritu m competitivo. **2** COMM competitividad f.

competitor [kəm'petɪtə'] **1** n COMM (rival) competidor,-ra, rival mf. **2** SP (in race etc) participante mf; (opponent) contrincante mf. **3** (in quiz etc) concursante mf, participante mf; (in competitive examination) opositor,-ra.

compilation [kɒmpɪ'leɪʃən] **1** n (act) compilación f, recopilación f. **2** (record etc) recopilación f.

compile [kəm'paɪl] **1** t (produce book, list, etc) compilar; (collect information) recopilar. **2** COMPUT compilar.

complacency [kəm'pleɪsənsɪ] n autocomplacencia, suficiencia.

complacent [kəm'pleɪsənt] adj (person) satisfecho,-a de sí mismo,-a, suficiente; (manner, attitude) de complacencia.

complacently [kəm'pleɪsəntlɪ] adv con suficiencia.

complain [kəm'pleɪn] **1** i quejarse (**about/of,** de): I can't complain, no me puedo quejar; he complained about the noise, se quejó del ruido; she complained of chest pains, se quejó de dolores en el pecho. – **2** t quejarse, protestar.

complaint [kəm'pleɪnt] **1** n (gen) queja (**about,** de); (formal) reclamación f: we have had complaints about your appearance, hemos recibido quejas de tu aspecto; he wrote a letter of complaint, escribió una carta quejándose. **2** MED enfermedad f (leve), achaque m, dolencia.
● to have cause for complaint, tener motivo de queja. ‖ to lodge a complaint, presentar una queja, hacer una reclamación. ‖ to make a complaint, quejarse.

complaisance [kəm'pleɪzəns] n fml sumisión f.

complaisant [kəm'pleɪzənt] adj fml sumiso,-a.

complement ['kɒmplɪmənt] **1** n (gen) complemento (**to,** de). – **2** t complementar.
● a full complement of sth., la totalidad de algo.

complementary [kɒmplɪ'mentərɪ] adj (gen) complementario,-a.

complete [kəm'pliːt] **1** adj (entire) completo,-a: the complete works of Lorca, las obras completas de Lorca. **2** (finished) acabado,-a, terminado,-a. **3** (thorough, absolute, total) total, completo,-a: he's a complete stranger, es un completo desconocido; you're a complete idiot, eres tonto de remate; a complete surprise, una verdadera sorpresa. – **4** t (make whole) completar. **5** (finish) acabar, terminar. **6** (fill in - form) rellenar.
● complete with sth., con algo incluido,-a: a large house complete with swimming pool, una casa enorme con piscina incluida.

completely [kəm'pliːtlɪ] adv completamente, totalmente, por completo: he's completely mad, está completamente loco.

completion [kəm'pliːʃən] n (act, state) finalización f, terminación f: the hotel is nearing completion, falta poco para acabar el hotel.
● on completion, en cuanto se termine. ‖ to bring sth. to completion, terminar algo.

complex ['kɒmpleks] **1** adj (gen) complejo,-a. – **2** n (group, system) complejo: sports complex, complejo deportivo. **3** (in psychology) complejo: inferiority complex, complejo de inferioridad.
● to have a complex about sth., tener complejo de algo.

complexion [kəm'plekʃən] **1** n (quality of skin) cutis m; (colour or tone of skin) tez f. **2** (aspect, character) aspecto, cariz m, naturaleza, carácter m: that puts a different complexion on things, eso le da otro cariz a las cosas.

complexity [kəm'pleksɪtɪ] n complejidad f.
▲ pl complexities.

compliance [kəm'plaɪəns] **1** n (obedience) conformidad f. **2** (tendency to agree, willingness) buena voluntad, buena disposición f.
● in compliance with, de acuerdo con, conforme con, en conformidad con.

compliant [kəm'plaɪənt] adj sumiso,-a, dócil.

complicate ['kɒmplɪkeɪt] t complicar.

complicated ['kɒmplɪkeɪtɪd] adj complicado,-a.

complication [kɒmplɪ'keɪʃən] **1** n (gen) complicación f. – **2** complications, npl MED complicaciones fpl.

complicity [kəm'plɪsɪtɪ] n complicidad f (**in,** en).

compliment ['kɒmplɪmənt] **1** t felicitar (**on,** por): he complimented her on her speech, la felicitó por su discurso. – **2** n (praise) cumplido, halago. – **3** compliments, npl saludos mpl: my compliments to the chef, felicite al cocinero de mi parte, felicitaciones al cocinero.

● **compliments of the season,** Felices Fiestas. ‖ **to pay sb. a compliment,** hacerle un cumplido a algn., halagar a algn. ‖ **with the compliments of,** obsequio de, gentileza de, cortesía de.
■ **compliments slip,** tarjeta comercial.
complimentary [kɒmplɪ'mentərɪ] **1** *adj* (*expressing praise*) elogioso,-a, halagüeno,-a. **2** (*free*) gratuito,-a, de regalo.
■ **complimentary ticket,** invitación *f.*
comply [kəm'plaɪ] *i* (*order*) obedecer (**with,** -), cumplir (**with,** con), acatar (**with,** -); (*request*) acceder (**with,** a); (*law*) acatar (**with,** -); (*standards*) cumplir (**with,** con): *it complies with European standards,* cumple con la normativa europea.
▲ (*verbo*) *pt* & *pp* **complied,** *ger* **complying.**
component [kəm'pəʊnənt] **1** *adj* componente. – **2** *n* (*gen*) componente *m.* **3** AUTO pieza.
■ **component part,** componente *m,* parte *f* componente.
compose [kəm'pəʊz] **1** *t* (*music, poem*) componer; (*letter*) redactar. **2** (*constitute*) componer. **3** (*one's thoughts*) poner en orden. – **4** *i* MUS componer.
● **to be composed of,** componerse de, estar compuesto,-a de. ‖ **to compose os.,** calmarse, serenarse, recobrar la compostura.
composed [kəm'pəʊzd] *adj* (*calm*) sereno,-a, sosegado,-a, tranquilo,-a.
composer [kəm'pəʊzə'] *n* compositor,-ra.
composite ['kɒmpəzɪt] **1** *adj* compuesto,-a. – **2** *n* combinación *f,* conjunto.
■ **composite picture,** US retrato robot.
composition [kɒmpə'zɪʃən] **1** *n* (*gen*) composición *f.* **2** (*essay*) redacción *f.* **3** (*substance*) mezcla. – **4** *adj* sintético,-a.
compositor [kəm'pɒzɪtə'] *n* cajista *mf.*
compost ['kɒmpɒst] *n* abono orgánico, abono vegetal.
composure [kəm'pəʊʒə'] *n* calma, serenidad *f,* compostura.
compound¹ ['kɒmpaʊnd] **1** *adj* compuesto,-a. – **2** *n* CHEM compuesto. **3** (*substance*) mezcla. **4** LING palabra compuesta. – **5** *t* (*mix*) componer, combinar, mezclar. **6** (*worsen, exacerbate - problem*) agravar, exacerbar; (*- difficulty*) acrecentar, aumentar. – **7** COMM (*reach agreement*) transigir (**for,** en).
● **to be compounded of,** estar compuesto,-a de.
■ **compound fracture,** fractura complicada. ‖ **compound interest,** interés *m* compuesto. ‖ **compound sentence,** frase *f* compuesta.
▲ (*verbo*) [kəm'paʊnd].
compound² ['kɒmpaʊnd] *n* (*enclosed area*) recinto.
comprehend [kɒmprɪ'hend] **1** *t* (*understand*) comprender. **2** *fml* (*include*) comprender, abarcar.
comprehensible [kɒmprɪ'hensəbəl] *adj* comprensible.
comprehension [kɒmprɪ'henʃən] *n* comprensión *f: it's beyond my comprehension,* me resulta incomprensible.
comprehensive [kɒmprɪ'hensɪv] **1** *adj* (*thorough*) detallado,-a, global, completo,-a; (*broad*) amplio,-a, extenso,-a. – **2** **comprehensive (school),** *n* GB EDUC ≈ instituto de enseñanza secundaria.
■ **comprehensive insurance,** seguro a todo riesgo.
comprehensively [kɒmprɪ'hensɪvlɪ] *adv* exhaustivamente.
compress ['kɒmpres] **1** *n* compresa. – **2** *t* (*air, straw*) comprimir. **3** (*text, argument, speech*) condensar.
▲ (*verbo*) [kəm'pres].
compression [kəm'preʃən] *n* compresión *f.*

compressor [kəm'presə'] *n* compresor *m.*
comprise [kəm'praɪz] *t* (*consist of, be made up of*) comprender, constar de; (*constitute, form*) componer, constituir: *the committee comprises 20 members,* el comité consta de 20 miembros; *pensioners comprise 30% of the total population,* los jubilados componen un 30% de la población total.
compromise ['kɒmprəmaɪz] **1** *n* acuerdo mutuo, término medio, compromiso, solución *f* de compromiso. – **2** *i* llegar a un acuerdo, transigir: *we compromised on a price,* llegamos a un acuerdo en el precio. – **3** *t* (*endanger, weaken*) comprometer.
● **to compromise os.,** comprometerse. ‖ **to reach a compromise,** llegar a un acuerdo, llegar a un compromiso.
compromising ['kɒmprəmaɪzɪŋ] *adj* (*situation*) comprometido,-a, comprometedor,-ra; (*evidence, details, document*) comprometedor,-ra.
compulsion [kəm'pʌlʃən] **1** *n* (*force*) obligación *f,* coacción *f: there's no compulsion to buy,* no hay obligación de comprar; *he acted under compulsion,* actuó bajo coacción. **2** (*urge*) compulsión *f.*
compulsive [kəm'pʌlsɪv] **1** *adj* (*compelling, fascinating*) fascinante, irresistible, absorbente: *it's compulsive viewing,* no se lo puede perder, hay que verlo. **2** (*obsessive*) obsesivo,-a: *she's a compulsive eater,* come por obsesión; *he's a compulsive gambler,* es adicto al juego.
compulsory [kəm'pʌlsərɪ] *adj* (*subject, military service*) obligatorio,-a; (*retirement, redundancy*) forzoso,-a.
■ **compulsory purchase,** expropiación *f.* ‖ **compulsory purchase order,** orden *f* de expropiación.
compunction [kəm'pʌŋkʃən] *n fml* remordimiento.
● **without compunction,** sin escrúpulos.
computation [kɒmpjʊ'teɪʃən] *n* cálculo, cómputo.
compute [kəm'pjuːt] *t* computar, calcular.
computer [kəm'pjuːtə'] *n* ordenador *m,* computadora.
■ **computer game,** juego de ordenador. ‖ **computer programmer,** programador,-ra de ordenadores. ‖ **computer science,** informática.
computerization [kəmpjuːtəraɪ'zeɪʃən] *n* (*of data*) computerización *f,* computadorización *f;* (*of system, business*) informatización *f.*
computerize [kəm'pjuːtəraɪz] *t* (*data*) computarizar, computerizar; (*system, business*) informatizar.
computing [kəm'pjuːtɪŋ] *n* informática.
comrade ['kɒmreɪd] **1** *n* POL camarada *mf,* compañero,-a. **2** *dated* compañero,-a.
comrade-in-arms [kɒmreɪdɪn'ɑːmz] *n* compañero,-a de armas.
comradeship ['kɒmreɪdʃɪp] *n* camaradería.
con¹ [kɒn] **1** *n fam* estafa, timo. – **2** *t fam* (*money*) estafar, timar; (*person*) embaucar, engañar: *I was conned out of £20,* me estafaron £20; *we were conned into thinking we'd won a prize,* nos engañaron haciéndonos creer que habíamos ganado un premio.
■ **con man / con artist / con merchant,** *fam* estafador *m.* ‖ **con trick,** *fam* estafa, timo.
▲ (*verbo*) *pt* & *pp* **conned,** *ger* **conning.**
con² [kɒn] *n sl* → **convict.**
con³ [kɒn] *n* (*disadvantage*) contra *m.*
▲ *Véase también* **pro.**
Con [kɒn] *abbr* GB POL (*Conservative*) conservador,-ra.
concave ['kɒnkeɪv] *adj* cóncavo,-a.
conceal [kən'siːl] *t* (*gen*) ocultar; (*facts*) encubrir; (*feelings*) disimular.
● **to conceal sth. from sb.,** ocultar algo a algn.

concealed [kən'siːld] *adj* (*gen*) oculto,-a; (*lighting*) indirecto,-a.
■ "concealed entrance", "entrada de vehículos". ‖ "concealed exit", "salida de vehículos".
concealment [kən'siːlmənt] *n* ocultación *f*.
● in concealment, oculto,-a.
concede [kən'siːd] **1** *t* (*admit*) reconocer, admitir. **2** (*allow, give away*) conceder. – **3** *i* ceder, rendirse.
● to concede defeat, admitir la derrota.
conceit [kən'siːt] *n* (*pride*) vanidad *f*, presunción *f*, engreimiento.
conceited [kən'siːtɪd] *adj* engreído,-a, presuntuoso,-a, vanidoso,-a.
conceivable [kən'siːvəbəl] *adj* concebible, imaginable: *there's no conceivable reason*, no hay ninguna razón; *it's conceivable that ...,* cabe la posibilidad de que ..., existe la posibilidad de que ...
conceivably [kən'siːvəblɪ] *adv* posiblemente: *she can't conceivably be serious*, no puede ser que lo diga en serio.
conceive [kən'siːv] **1** *t* (*child*) concebir. **2** (*devise, think up*) concebir. **3** (*understand*) entender: *I cannot conceive how you could do such a thing*, no entiendo cómo pudiste hacer tal cosa. – **4** *i* concebir.
◆ to conceive of *t insep* imaginar, concebir.
concentrate ['kɒnsəntreɪt] **1** *n* concentrado. – **2** *t* (*gen*) concentrar (**on**, en). – **3** *i* (*person*) concentrarse (**on**, en); (*talks, book, government*) centrarse (**on**, en): *please be quiet, I can't concentrate*, cállate por favor, no puedo concentrarme. **4** (*gather together*) concentrarse.
● to concentrate the mind, concentrarse.
concentrated ['kɒnsəntreɪtɪd] *adj* (*solution etc*) concentrado,-a; (*study, effort, fire*) intenso,-a.
concentration [kɒnsən'treɪʃən] *n* (*gen*) concentración *f* (**on**, en).
■ concentration camp, campo de concentración.
concentric [kən'sentrɪk] *adj* concéntrico,-a.
concept ['kɒnsept] *n* concepto.
conception [kən'sepʃən] **1** *n* (*of child, idea, plan*) concepción *f*. **2** (*idea*) concepto, idea, noción *f*.
conceptual [kən'septʃʊəl] *adj* conceptual.
concern [kən'sɜːn] **1** *n* (*worry*) preocupación *f*, inquietud *f*: *there's no cause for concern*, no hay motivo de preocupación, no hay motivo para preocuparse; *a matter of some concern*, un tema que preocupa. **2** (*interest*) interés *m*; (*affair*) asunto: *it's no concern of mine*, no es asunto mío; *what concern is it of yours?*, ¿y a ti qué te importa? **3** COMM (*company, business*) negocio: *a going concern*, un negocio en marcha. – **4** *t* (*affect, involve*) afectar, concernir, importar; (*interest*) interesar: *that doesn't concern you*, eso no te importa; *this concerns all of us*, esto nos afecta a todos. **5** (*worry*) preocupar. **6** (*book, film, article, etc*) tratar de.
● to concern os. (about sth.), preocuparse (por algo). ‖ to whom it may concern, a quien corresponda.
concerned [kən'sɜːnd] **1** *adj* (*affected*) afectado,-a; (*involved*) involucrado,-a: *the people concerned*, los interesados. **2** (*worried*) preocupado,-a (**about/for**, por): *I'm concerned for her well-being*, me preocupa su bienestar; *they're concerned about you*, están preocupados por ti.
● as far as I'm concerned, por lo que a mí se refiere, por lo que a mí respecta. ‖ where sth. is concerned, en cuanto a algo. ‖ to be concerned in sth., estar involucrado,-a en algo. ‖ to be concerned with sth., interesarle a uno algo.

concerning [kən'sɜːnɪŋ] *prep* referente a, con respecto a, en cuanto a, respecto a.
concert ['kɒnsət] *n* concierto.
● at concert pitch, (*prepared, ready*) completamente preparado,-a. ‖ in concert, (*live*) en concierto, en directo. ‖ in concert with sb., (*together*) conjuntamente con algn., de común acuerdo con algn.
■ concert grand, piano de cola, piano de concierto. ‖ concert hall, sala de conciertos.
concerted [kən'sɜːtɪd] *adj* concertado,-a, coordinado,-a.
concertgoer ['kɒnsɜːtgəʊəʳ] *n* persona que asiste a conciertos a menudo.
concertina [kɒnsə'tiːnə] *n* concertina.
concerto [kən'tʃeətəʊ] *n* concierto: *a piano concerto*, un concierto para piano.
▲ *pl concertos o concerti* [kən'tʃeətɪ].
concession [kən'seʃən] **1** *n* (*act or thing granted*) concesión *f* (**to**, a): *they refused to make any concessions*, se negaron a hacer concesiones. **2** COMM concesión *f*.
● "concessions", (*reduced entrance price*) tarifa reducida *para estudiantes, jubilados, parados*.
concessionaire [kənseʃə'neəʳ] *n* concesionario,-a.
concessionary [kən'seʃənərɪ] *adj* (*rates etc*) reducido,-a.
conciliate [kən'sɪlɪeɪt] **1** *t* conciliar. – **2** *i* conciliar.
conciliation [kənsɪlɪ'eɪʃən] *n* conciliación *f*.
conciliatory [kən'sɪlɪətərɪ] *adj* conciliatorio,-a, conciliador,-ra.
concise [kən'saɪs] *adj* conciso,-a.
■ concise dictionary, diccionario abreviado.
concisely [kən'saɪslɪ] *adv* con concisión.
conciseness [kən'saɪsnəs] *n* concisión *f*.
concision [kən'sɪʒən] *n* concisión *f*.
conclave ['kɒŋkleɪv] *n* REL cónclave *m*.
conclude [kən'kluːd] **1** *t* (*end*) concluir, finalizar. **2** (*settle - deal*) cerrar; (*- agreement*) llegar a; (*- treaty*) firmar. **3** (*deduce*) concluir, llegar a la conclusión de. – **4** *i* concluir, terminar.
concluding [kən'kluːdɪŋ] *adj* final.
conclusion [kən'kluːʒən] **1** *n* (*decision*) conclusión *f*: *I've come to the conclusion that ...*, he llegado a la conclusión de que ...; *everybody can draw their own conclusions*, todos pueden sacar sus propias conclusiones. **2** (*end*) final *m*, conclusión *f*: *a foregone conclusion*, un desenlace esperado. **3** (*settling - of deal*) cierre *m*; (*- of treaty*) firma.
● in conclusion, para concluir, como conclusión, en conclusión. ‖ to jump to conclusions, precipitarse (a sacar conclusiones), sacar conclusiones precipitadas.
conclusive [kən'kluːsɪv] *adj* (*evidence, proof*) concluyente, definitivo,-a; (*argument*) concluyente, decisivo,-a.
conclusively [kən'kluːsɪvlɪ] *adv* definitivamente.
concoct [kən'kɒkt] **1** *t* (*dish, sauce, drink*) confeccionar, preparar. **2** (*story, excuse, explanation*) inventar, inventarse.
concoction [kən'kɒkʃən] *n* pej (*food*) mejunje *m*, mezcolanza; (*drink*) brebaje *m*.
concomitant [kən'kɒmɪtənt] *adj fml* concomitante.
concord ['kɒŋkɔːd] **1** *n fml* (*harmony*) concordia. **2** LING concordancia.
concordance [kən'kɔːdəns] **1** *n* (*similarity, concord*) concordancia. **2** (*index*) concordancias *fpl*.
concordant [kən'kɔːdənt] *adj fml* concordante.
concourse ['kɒŋkɔːs] **1** *n* (*hall*) vestíbulo; (*in station*) explanada. **2** *fml* (*gathering*) concurrencia, concurso.
concrete ['kɒŋkriːt] **1** *adj* (*definite, not abstract*) concreto,-a. **2** (*made of concrete*) de hormigón. – **3** *n* hormigón *m*.

– 4 t (wall) revestir de hormigón; (ground) pavimentar con hormigón.
■ **concrete mixer,** hormigonera.
concretely [kɒn'kriːtlɪ] adv concretamente.
concubine ['kɒŋkjəbaɪn] n concubina.
concur [kən'kɜːʳ] **1** i (agree) estar de acuerdo, coincidir. **2** (coincide) coincidir, concurrir.
▲ pt & pp concurred, ger concurring.
concurrence [kən'kʌrəns] **1** n (agreement) acuerdo, coincidencia. **2** (of events etc) concurrencia, coincidencia.
concurrent [kən'kʌrənt] adj (in time) simultáneo,-a, concurrente.
concurrently [kən'kʌrəntlɪ] adv simultáneamente.
concussion [kən'kʌʃən] n MED conmoción f cerebral.
condemn [kən'dem] **1** t (criticize, denounce) condenar, censurar: the terrorist attack was condemned by all the political parties, todos los partidos políticos condenaron el atentado. **2** (sentence) condenar: they were condemned to death, los condenaron a muerte. **3** (building) declarar en ruina.
condemnation [kɒndem'neɪʃən] **1** n (strong disapproval) condena, repulsa; (criticism) crítica. **2** JUR condena.
condemned [kən'demd] **1** adj (person) condenado,-a. **2** (building) que ha sido declarado,-a en ruina.
■ **condemned cell,** celda de los condenados a muerte.
condensation [kɒnden'seɪʃən] **1** n CHEM (process) condensación f; (on glass) vaho. **2** (of report, history, etc) condensación f.
condense [kən'dens] **1** t CHEM condensar. **2** (shorten) condensar, abreviar, resumir. **– 3** i CHEM condensarse.
condensed [kən'denst] adj condensado,-a.
condensor [kən'densəʳ] n condensador m.
condescend [kɒndɪ'send] **1** i (deign) condescender, dignarse: she condescended to eat with us, se dignó a comer con nosotros. **2** (patronize) tratar con condescendencia.
condescending [kɒndɪ'sendɪŋ] adj (attitude, answer) condescendiente: he's condescending to his employees, es condescendiente con sus empleados.
condescension [kɒndɪ'senʃən] n condescendencia.
condiment ['kɒndɪmənt] n condimento.
condition [kən'dɪʃən] **1** n (state) condición f, estado: it's in good/bad condition, está en buen/mal estado; you're in no condition to play, no estás en condiciones de jugar. **2** (requirement, provision) condición f: the conditions of the lease, las condiciones del contrato de arrendamiento; I'll lend you the money on one condition, te dejaré el dinero con una condición. **3** MED afección f, enfermedad f: he has a heart condition, tiene una afección cardíaca. **– 4** t (determine, accustom) condicionar. **5** (treat - hair) acondicionar, suavizar. **– 6 conditions,** npl (circumstances) condiciones fpl: working conditions, condiciones de trabajo.
● **on condition that,** a condición de que. ‖ **on no condition,** de ningún modo. ‖ **to be out of condition,** (unfit) no estar en forma.
■ **conditioned reflex,** reflejo condicionado.
conditional [kən'dɪʃənəl] **1** adj condicional. **– 2 the conditional,** n LING el condicional m.
● **to be conditional upon sth.,** estar condicionado,-a a algo.
conditioner [kən'dɪʃənəʳ] n (for hair) acondicionador m, suavizante m.
condolence [kən'dəʊləns] **1** n condolencia, pésame m: a letter of condolence, una carta de pésame. **– 2 condolences,** npl pésame m sing.

● **please accept my condolences,** le acompaño en el sentimiento. ‖ **to send one's condolences,** dar el pésame.
condom ['kɒndəm] n condón m, preservativo.
condominium [kɒndə'mɪnɪəm] **1** n POL condominio. **2** US (apartment block) bloque m de pisos; (apartment) apartamento, piso.
condone [kən'dəʊn] t (person) aprobar, consentir; (action, behaviour) consentir: we cannot be seen to condone violence, es necesario que la gente vea que no consentimos la violencia.
condor ['kɒndɔːʳ] n cóndor m.
conducive [kən'djuːsɪv] adj propicio,-a (to, para): this atmosphere is not conducive to study, este ambiente no favorece el estudio.
conduct ['kɒndʌkt] **1** n (behaviour) conducta, comportamiento. **2** (management) dirección f, gestión f, administración f: the UN's conduct of the negotiations, la manera en que las Naciones Unidas han llevado las negociaciones. **– 3** t (direct - survey, campaign) llevar a cabo, realizar; (- business) administrar. **4** (lead, guide) conducir, guiar. **5** (transmit - heat etc) conducir. **6** MUS dirigir. **– 7** i MUS dirigir.
● **to conduct os.,** comportarse, conducirse.
■ **conducted tour,** visita acompañada.
▲ (verbo) [kən'dʌkt].
conduction [kən'dʌkʃən] n PHYS conducción f.
conductive [kən'dʌktɪv] adj PHYS conductivo,-a.
conductor [kən'dʌktəʳ] **1** n ELEC PHYS conductor m. **2** MUS director,-ra de orquesta. **3** (on bus) cobrador,-ra. **4** US (on train) revisor,-ra.
conductress [kən'dʌktrəs] n (on bus) cobradora.
conduit ['kɒndjuɪt] n conducto.
cone [kəʊn] **1** n (shape, for traffic) cono. **2** (for ice cream) cucurucho. **3** BOT (fruit of pine etc) piña.
confab ['kɒnfæb] n fam charla, plática.
confectioner [kən'fekʃənəʳ] n confitero,-a, pastelero,-a.
■ **confectioner's (shop),** confitería, pastelería. ‖ **confectioner's sugar,** US azúcar m glas.
confectionery [kən'fekʃənərɪ] n dulces mpl.
confederacy [kən'fedərəsɪ] n confederación f.
▲ pl confederacies.
confederate [kən'fedərət] **1** adj confederado,-a. **– 2** n confederado,-a. **3** JUR (accomplice) cómplice mf. **– 4** i confederarse.
■ **Confederate States,** Estados mpl Confederados.
▲ (verbo) [kən'fedəreɪt].
confederation [kənfedə'reɪʃən] n confederación f.
confer [kən'fɜːʳ] **1** t (award, grant, bestow) conferir, conceder. **– 2** i (consult, discuss) consultar (**with,** con) (**about/on,** sobre).
▲ pt & pp conferred, ger conferring.
conference ['kɒnfərəns] **1** n (large event, convention) congreso, conferencia. **2** (meeting) reunión f, conferencia, junta.
● **to be in conference,** estar reunido,-a.
■ **conference room,** sala de reuniones.
confess [kən'fes] **1** t confesar. **– 2** i (admit) confesar: he confessed to a weakness for chocolate, confesó que tenía debilidad por el chocolate; she confessed to the murder, confesó el asesinato. **3** REL confesarse.
confessed [kən'fest] adj declarado,-a.
confession [kən'feʃən] n confesión f.
● **to go to confession,** ir a confesarse. ‖ **to hear sb.'s confession,** confesar a algn. ‖ **to make a confession,** confesar, hacer una confesión.

confessional [kənˈfeʃənəl] *n* confesionario.
confessor [kənˈfesəʳ] *n* REL confesor *m*.
confetti [kənˈfetɪ] *n* confeti *m*.
confidant [ˈkɒnfɪdænt] *n* confidente *m*.
confidante [ˈkɒnfɪdænt] *n* confidenta.
confide [kənˈfaɪd] **1** *t* (*tell*) confiar: *she confided to me that she was in love*, me confió que estaba enamorada; *I have never confided my secret to anyone but you*, nunca he confiado mi secreto a nadie más que a ti. **2** *fml* (*entrust*) confiar (**to**, a).
◆ **to confide in** *i* confiar en: *can I confide in you?*, ¿puedo confiar en ti?
confidence [ˈkɒnfɪdəns] **1** *n* (*trust, faith*) confianza (**in**, en), fe *f* (**in**, en): *I have every confidence in you*, tengo absoluta confianza en ti. **2** (*self-confidence*) confianza, seguridad *f*: *he lacks confidence*, le falta seguridad. **3** (*secrecy*) confianza: *I told you in confidence*, te lo dije en confianza. **4** (*secret*) confidencia.
● **to take sb. in to one's confidence**, depositar su confianza en algn.
■ **confidence trick**, estafa, timo.
confident [ˈkɒnfɪdənt] **1** *adj* (*certain*) seguro,-a: *we are confident that the record will be a hit*, estamos seguros de que el disco será un éxito. **2** (*self-confident*) seguro,- a de sí mismo,-a.
● **to be confident of sth.**, confiar en algo.
confidential [kɒnfɪˈdenʃəl] *adj* confidencial.
confidentiality [kɒnfɪdenʃɪˈælɪtɪ] *n* confidencialidad *f*, reserva.
confidentially [kɒnfɪˈdenʃəlɪ] *adv* confidencialmente, en confianza.
confidently [ˈkɒnfɪdəntlɪ] *adv* con seguridad.
confiding [kənˈfaɪdɪŋ] *adj* confiado,-a.
confine [kənˈfaɪn] **1** *t* (*person*) confinar, recluir; (*animal*) encerrar: *he was confined to barracks*, estaba retenido en el cuartel. **2** (*limit, restrict*) limitar: *kindly confine yourself to the subject*, por favor, limítese al tema.
● **to be confined to bed**, tener que guardar cama.
confined [kənˈfaɪnd] *adj* (*space*) reducido,-a, limitado,-a.
confinement [kənˈfaɪnmənt] **1** *n* (*imprisonment*) reclusión *f*. **2** MED (*in childbirth*) parto.
● **to be in solitary confinement**, estar incomunicado,-a.
confines [ˈkɒnfaɪnz] *npl* límites *mpl*, confines *mpl*.
confirm [kənˈfɜːm] **1** *t* (*prove true, verify*) confirmar: *this only confirms my suspicions*, esto no hace más que confirmar mis sospechas; *I'd like to confirm a booking*, quisiera confirmar una reserva. **2** (*ratify*) ratificar. **3** REL confirmar.
confirmation [kɒnfəˈmeɪʃən] **1** *n* (*proof, verification*) confirmación *f*. **2** (*ratification*) ratificación *f*. **3** REL confirmación *f*.
confirmed [kənˈfɜːmd] *adj* (*inveterate*) empedernido,-a.
confiscate [ˈkɒnfɪskeɪt] *t* confiscar.
confiscation [kɒnfɪsˈkeɪʃən] *n* confiscación *f*.
conflagration [kɒnfləˈɡreɪʃən] *n* conflagración *f*.
conflict [ˈkɒnflɪkt] **1** *n* conflicto. **- 2** *i* chocar (**with**, con), estar en conflicto (**with**, con), entrar en desacuerdo (**with**, con).
● **to come into conflict with sb./sth.**, entrar en conflicto con algn./algo.
▲ (*verbo*) [kənˈflɪkt].
conflicting [kənˈflɪktɪŋ] *adj* (*evidence, accounts*) contradictorio,-a; (*opinions, interests*) contrario,-a, opuesto,-a.
confluence [ˈkɒnfluəns] *n* confluencia.
conform [kənˈfɔːm] **1** *i* (*comply with rules, standards, regulations*) ajustarse (**to/with**, a), someterse (**to/with**, a),

cumplir (**to/with**, con): *all models conform to official safety standards*, todos los modelos cumplen con las normas de seguridad oficiales; *you must conform to the rules*, hay que someterse a las reglas. **2** (*agree, be consistent with*) avenirse (**to**, a), conformarse (**to/with**, con), concordar (**with**, con): *your ideas do not conform with mine*, tus ideas no concuerdan con las mías; *that proposal would not conform with most people's wishes*, esa propuesta no se avendría a los deseos de la mayoría de la gente. **3** (*fit in, behave like other people*) ser conformista.
conformist [kənˈfɔːmɪst] **1** *adj* conformista, convencional. **- 2** *n* conformista *mf*.
conformity [kənˈfɔːmɪtɪ] *n* conformidad *f*.
● **in conformity with**, conforme a, en conformidad con.
confound [kənˈfaʊnd] **1** *t* (*puzzle, perplex*) confundir, desconcertar. **2** *dated* (*defeat*) frustrar.
● **confound it!**, ¡maldita sea! ‖ **to confound sth. with sth.**, confundir algo con algo.
confounded [kənˈfaʊndɪd] *adj fam* maldito,-a, condenado,-a.
confront [kənˈfrʌnt] **1** *t* (*person, enemy, opponent*) hacer frente a, plantar cara a, enfrentarse a: *you're going to have to confront him about it*, tendrás que planteárselo cara a cara; *the actress had to confront a crowd of reporters*, la actriz tuvo que enfrentarse a un grupo de periodistas. **2** (*task, difficulty, reality, question*) enfrentar, enfrentarse a, afrontar, hacer frente a: *I had to confront many dangers*, tuve que enfrentarme a muchos peligros; *the government has refused to confront the problem*, el gobierno se ha negado a hacer frente al problema; *it's a problem that confronts all of us*, éste es un problema que se nos plantea a todos.
● **to confront sb. with sb./sth.**, poner a algn. cara a cara con algn./algo: *she broke down when the police confronted her with the evidence*, perdió el control cuando la policía le mostró las pruebas. ‖ **to be confronted by/with sth.**, verse frente a algo: *his mind went blank when confronted by the TV cameras*, se quedó en blanco al verse frente a las cámaras de televisión.
confrontation [kɒnfrʌnˈteɪʃən] **1** *n* (*dispute, conflict, opposition*) confrontación *f*, enfrentamiento. **2** JUR (*of witnesses*) careo.
confuse [kənˈfjuːz] **1** *t* (*make unclear, muddle*) confundir, complicar, enredar: *don't confuse the issue*, no compliques el asunto. **2** (*bewilder*) desconcertar, confundir, desorientar: *you've completely confused me*, me has desconcertado por completo. **3** (*mix up, mistake*) confundir: *he always confuses Sweden with Switzerland*, siempre confunde Suecia con Suiza; *I think you're confusing me with someone else*, creo que me has confundido con otra persona.
confused [kənˈfjuːzd] **1** *adj* (*person*) confundido,-a, desconcertado,-a, turbado,-a. **2** (*mind, ideas, account*) confuso,-a.
● **to get confused**, confundirse.
confusing [kənˈfjuːzɪŋ] *adj* confuso,-a.
confusion [kənˈfjuːʒən] *n* confusión *f*.
congeal [kənˈdʒiːl] *i* (*blood*) coagularse; (*fat*) solidificarse.
congenial [kənˈdʒiːnɪəl] *adj* (*person*) simpático,-a, agradable; (*climate, environment, hobby*) agradable.
congenital [kənˈdʒenɪtəl] **1** *adj* MED congénito,-a. **2** *fig* instintivo,-a, natural: *a congenital liar*, un mentiroso por naturaleza.

conger ['kɒŋɡəʳ] conger (eel), *n* congrio.
congested [kənˈdʒestɪd] 1 *adj (with traffic)* colapsado,-a, congestionado,-a; *(with people)* abarrotado,-a de gente, repleto,-a de gente. 2 MED congestionado,-a.
congestion [kənˈdʒestʃən] 1 *n (with traffic)* congestión *f*; *(with people)* aglomeración *f*. 2 MED congestión *f*.
conglomerate [kənˈɡlɒmərət] 1 *n* COMM conglomerado (de empresas). 2 GEOL conglomerado. – 3 *i* conglomerarse.
▲ *(verbo)* [kənˈɡlɒməreɪt].
conglomeration [kənɡlɒməˈreɪʃən] *n* conglomerado.
Congo ['kɒŋɡəʊ] *n* Congo.
Congolese [kɒŋɡəˈliːz] 1 *adj* congoleño,-a. – 2 *n* congoleño,-a. – 3 the Congolese, *npl* los congoleños *mpl*.
congratulate [kənˈɡrætjəleɪt] *t* felicitar (on, por), dar la enhorabuena a (on, por).
● to congratulate os., felicitarse, congratularse.
congratulation [kənˈɡrætjəleɪʃənz] 1 *n* felicitación *f*. – 2 congratulations, *npl* felicitaciones *fpl*, enhorabuena. – 3 congratulations!, *interj* ¡felicidades! *fpl*, ¡enhorabuena!
● to offer sb. one's congratulations on sth., dar a algn. la enhorabuena por algo.
congratulatory [kənɡrætjəˈleɪtərɪ] *adj* de felicitación, de enhorabuena.
congregate ['kɒŋɡrɪɡeɪt] *i* congregarse.
congregation [kɒŋɡrɪˈɡeɪʃən] *n* REL *(people gathered)* fieles *mpl*; *(parishioners)* feligreses *mpl*.
congress ['kɒŋɡres] 1 *n* congreso. 2 Congress, US el Congreso.
congressional [kənˈɡreʃənəl] *adj* US del Congreso.
■ Congressional district, distrito electoral.
Congressman ['kɒŋɡresmən] *n* miembro del Congreso, congresista *m*.
Congresswoman ['kɒŋɡreswʊmən] *n* miembro *f* del Congreso, congresista.
▲ *pl* Congresswomen ['kɒŋɡreswɪmɪn].
congruent ['kɒŋɡrʊənt] *adj* MATH congruente.
congruous ['kɒŋrʊəs] *adj fml* congruente (with, con).
conic ['kɒnɪk] *adj* cónico,-a.
conical ['kɒnɪkəl] *adj* cónico,-a.
conifer ['kɒnɪfəʳ] *n* conífera.
coniferous [kəˈnɪfərəs] *adj* conífero,-a.
conjectural [kənˈdʒektʃərəl] *adj* conjetural, basado,-a en conjeturas.
conjecture [kənˈdʒektʃəʳ] 1 *n* conjetura, suposición *f*: *it's pure conjecture*, no son más que conjeturas. – 2 *t* conjeturar. – 3 *i* hacer conjeturas.
conjugal ['kɒndʒəɡəl] *adj* conyugal.
conjugate ['kɒndʒəɡeɪt] 1 *t* conjugar. – 2 *i* conjugarse.
conjugation [kɒndʒəˈɡeɪʃən] *n* conjugación *f*.
conjunction [kənˈdʒʌŋkʃən] *n* conjunción *f*.
● in conjunction with, conjuntamente con.
conjunctivitis [kəndʒʌŋktɪˈvaɪtɪs] *n* conjuntivitis *f*.
conjure ['kʌndʒəʳ] 1 *i* hacer magia, hacer juegos de manos. – 2 to conjure (up), *t (by magic)* hacer aparecer como por arte de magia; *(meal etc)* preparar, improvisar.
◆ to conjure up *t sep (evoke - memories)* evocar, traer a la memoria; *(summon - spirits)* invocar.
■ a name to conjure with, *(influential)* un nombre todopoderoso, un nombre que abre puertas; *(difficult)* un nombre difícil de pronunciar.
conjurer ['kʌndʒərəʳ] *n* mago,-a, prestidigitador,-ra.
conjuring ['kʌndʒərɪŋ] *n* magia, prestidigitación *f*.
■ conjuring trick, truco de magia, juego de manos.

conjuror ['kʌndʒərəʳ] *n* → conjurer.
conk [kɒŋk] 1 *t* GB *fam (nose)* napia, napias *fpl*. 2 *fam* pegarle una piña a.
◆ to conk out 1 *i fam (machine, car)* averiarse. 2 *fam (person)* quedarse como un tronco, quedarse roque.
conker ['kɒŋkəʳ] *n fam* castaña (de Indias).
connect [kəˈnekt] 1 *t (join, attach - gen)* unir, enlazar, conectar; *(- wires, cables, pipes)* empalmar, conectar; *(- rooms, buildings)* comunicar, unir; *(- cities)* unir, conectar: *the new road connects our village with the capital*, la nueva carretera conecta nuestro pueblo con la capital; *I connected my computer to her printer*, conecté mi ordenador a su impresora. 2 *(join to power supply)* conectar, enchufar: *the phone hasn't been connected yet*, todavía no han conectado el teléfono; *make sure it's connected to the mains*, asegúrate de que esté conectado a la red. 3 *(associate)* relacionar, asociar. 4 *(on telephone)* poner (with, con): *I'm just connecting you*, en seguida le pongo. – 5 *i (join, link - gen)* unirse; *(- rooms)* comunicarse; *(- wires, cables, pipes)* empalmar, conectarse. 6 *(be fitted)* estar conectado,-a (to, a). 7 *(train, flight)* enlazar (with, con), empalmar (with, con). 8 *fam (blow, punch)* arrear.
connected [kəˈnektɪd] 1 *adj (related, joined)* relacionado,-a, conectado,-a. 2 *(to power supply)* conectado,-a, enchufado,-a. 3 *(related by birth)* emparentado,-a.
● to be well connected, tener buenos contactos, tener enchufe.
connecting [kəˈnektɪŋ] *adj (rooms)* que se comunican; *(door)* que comunica; *(flight, train)* de enlace.
connection [kəˈnekʃən] 1 *n (link)* unión *f*, enlace *m*. 2 ELEC TECH conexión *f*, empalme *m*: *there's a faulty connection*, hay una mala conexión. 3 *(relation)* relación *f*, conexión *f*. 4 *(train, plane)* conexión *f*, enlace *m*: *they missed their connection*, perdieron la conexión. – 5 connections, *npl (professional)* contactos *mpl*; *(relatives)* familia, parientes *mpl*.
● in connection with, en relación con, con relación a. ‖ in that connection, a este respecto, con respecto a esto. ‖ to have connections, *fam* tener enchufe.
connective [kəˈnektɪv] *n* conector *m*.
■ connective tissue, tejido conjuntivo.
connexion [kəˈnekʃən] *n* GB → connection.
connivance [kəˈnaɪvəns] *n* complicidad *f*, connivencia.
connive [kəˈnaɪv] *i (conspire)* conspirar, confabularse.
● to connive at sth., *(disregard)* hacer la vista gorda con algo.
conniving [kəˈnaɪvɪŋ] *adj* intrigante, maquinador,-ra.
connoisseur [kɒnəˈsɜːʳ] *n* entendido,-a, conocedor,-ra.
connotation [kɒnəˈteɪʃən] *n* connotación *f*.
conquer ['kɒŋkəʳ] *t (country, mountain, heart)* conquistar; *(enemy, disease, fear)* vencer.
conquering ['kɒŋkərɪŋ] *adj* conquistador,-ra.
conqueror ['kɒŋkərəʳ] *n* conquistador,-ra, vencedor,-ra.
conquest ['kɒŋkwest] *n* conquista.
consanguinity [kɒnsæŋˈɡwɪnɪtɪ] *n* consanguinidad *f*.
conscience ['kɒnʃəns] *n* conciencia.
● in all conscience, en conciencia. ‖ to have a clear conscience, tener la conciencia limpia, tener la conciencia tranquila. ‖ to have a guilty conscience, sentirse culpable, remorderle a uno la conciencia. ‖ to have sth. on one's conscience, remorderle a uno la conciencia.
■ conscience money, *dinero pagado para sentirse menos culpable*.
conscience-stricken ['kɒnʃənsstrɪkən] *adj* lleno,-a de remordimientos.

conscientious [kɒnʃɪ'enʃəs] *adj* (*work*) concienzudo,-a; (*person*) aplicado,-a, serio,-a.
■ **conscientious objector**, objetor,-ra de conciencia.
conscientiously [kɒnʃɪ'enʃəslɪ] *adv* a conciencia, concienzudamente.
conscientiousness [kɒnʃɪ'enʃəsnəs] *n* escrupulosidad *f.*
conscious ['kɒnʃəs] **1** *adj* MED consciente. **2** (*aware*) consciente: *I was conscious of being watched,* era consciente de que me vigilaban; *workers are becoming less politically conscious,* los trabajadores tienen cada vez menos conciencia política. **3** (*intentional, deliberate*) deliberado,-a: *we made a conscious effort to be friendly,* nos esforzamos por ser simpáticos.
● **to be conscious of sth.**, ser consciente de algo, tener conciencia de algo. ‖ **to become conscious of sth.**, darse cuenta de algo.
consciousness ['kɒnʃəsnəs] **1** *n* MED conocimiento. **2** (*awareness*) conciencia.
● **to lose consciousness**, perder el conocimiento.
conscript ['kɒnskrɪpt] **1** *n* recluta. – **2** *t* reclutar.
▲ (*verbo*) [kən'skrɪpt].
conscription [kən'skrɪpʃən] *n* servicio militar obligatorio.
consecrate ['kɒnsɪkreɪt] *t* consagrar.
consecration [kɒnsɪ'kreɪʃən] *n* consagración *f.*
consecutive [kən'sekjətɪv] *adj* consecutivo,-a: *on three consecutive days,* tres días seguidos.
consecutively [kən'sekjətɪvlɪ] *adv* consecutivamente.
consensus [kən'sensəs] *n* consenso: *the consensus of opinion,* la opinión general.
consent [kən'sent] **1** *n* consentimiento. – **2** *i* consentir (**to**, en), acceder (**to**, en).
● **by common consent**, de común acuerdo.
■ **consenting adults**, adultos que actúan libremente.
consequence ['kɒnsɪkwəns] **1** *n* (*result*) consecuencia: *this policy could have disastrous consequences,* esta política podría tener consecuencias desastrosas. **2** (*importance*) importancia, trascendencia: *it is of no consequence,* no tiene importancia; *a person of consequence,* una persona importante, una persona de peso.
● **in consequence**, por consiguiente. ‖ **in consequence (of sth.)**, a consecuencia (de algo). ‖ **to take the consequences**, aceptar las consecuencias, atenerse a las consecuencias.
consequent ['kɒnsɪkwənt] *adj* consiguiente.
● **to be consequent on**, ser debido a, ser resultado de, resultar de.
consequential [kɒnsɪ'kwenʃəl] **1** *adj* (*resultant*) consiguiente, resultante. **2** *fml* (*important*) importante, trascendente.
consequently ['kɒnsɪkwəntlɪ] *adv* por consiguiente.
conservation [kɒnsə'veɪʃən] *n* conservación *f.*
■ **conservation area**, zona protegida.
conservationist [kɒnsə'veɪʃənɪst] *n* ecologista *mf.*
conservatism [kən'sɜːvətɪzəm] *n* POL conservadurismo.
conservative [kən'sɜːvətɪv] **1** *adj* (*traditional*) conservador,-ra. **2** (*cautious*) cauteloso,-a, prudente. – **3** *n* (*traditionalist*) conservador,-ra. – **4 Conservative**, *adj* POL conservador,-ra. – **5** *n* POL conservador,-ra.
● **at a conservative estimate**, calculando por lo bajo.
conservatoire [kən'sɜːvətwɑːʳ] *n* conservatorio.
conservatory [kən'sɜːvətrɪ] **1** *n* MUS conservatorio. **2** (*greenhouse*) invernadero.

▲ *pl* **conservatories.**
conserve [kən'sɜːv] **1** *t* (*nature, wildlife, etc*) conservar, proteger; (*save*) conservar, ahorrar; (*resources*) conservar, preservar. – **2** *n* CULIN (*jam*) confitura.
● **to conserve one's strength**, reservar las fuerzas, ahorrar energías.
consider [kən'sɪdəʳ] **1** *t* (*think about, examine, contemplate*) considerar: *I'm considering buying a flat,* estoy pensando en comprar un piso; *we had considered that possibility,* habíamos considerado esa posibilidad. **2** (*regard as*) considerar: *do you consider it likely?,* ¿crees que es posible?; *she is considered to be the finest soprano in the world,* está considerada la mejor soprano del mundo; *consider yourself lucky,* puedes considerarte afortunado; *consider it done!,* ¡dalo por hecho! **3** (*take into account*) tener en cuenta, considerar: *if you consider that ...,* teniendo en cuenta que ...
● **all things considered**, pensándolo bien, bien mirado. ‖ **it is my considered opinion that ...**, después de pensarlo mucho, opino que ...
considerable [kən'sɪdərəbəl] *adj* considerable.
considerably [kən'sɪdərəblɪ] *adv* bastante, considerablemente.
considerate [kən'sɪdərət] *adj* considerado,-a, atento,-a.
consideration [kənsɪdə'reɪʃən] **1** *n* (*thoughtfulness*) consideración *f*: *out of consideration for his family,* en consideración a su familia; *try to show some consideration for others,* intenta tratar a los demás con más consideración. **2** (*factor to consider*) factor *m* a tener en cuenta, factor *m* que se tiene en cuenta: *time is an important consideration,* el tiempo es un factor que hay que tener muy en cuenta. **3** (*attention, thought*) consideración *f*, atención *f*: *I'll give it my careful consideration,* lo estudiaré detenidamente; *the proposal is under consideration,* se está estudiando la propuesta.
● **in consideration of**, en consideración a. ‖ **to take sth. into consideration**, tomar algo en consideración.
considering [kən'sɪdərɪŋ] **1** *prep* teniendo en cuenta. – **2** *conj* teniendo en cuenta que, dado que. – **3** *adv* después de todo.
consign [kən'saɪn] **1** *t* COMM (*send - goods*) consignar. **2** *fml* (*entrust, hand over, give up*) confiar, encomendar.
● **to be consigned to oblivion**, ser relegado,-a al olvido.
consignment [kən'saɪnmənt] *n* COMM remesa, envío.
● **on consignment**, en consignación.
■ **consignment note**, talón *m* de expedición.
consist [kən'sɪst] **1** *i fml* (*have as chief element*) consistir (**in**, en). **2** (*comprise, be composed of*) constar (**of**, de), estar compuesto,-a (**of**, de).
consistency [kən'sɪstənsɪ] **1** *n* (*of actions, behaviour, policy*) consecuencia, coherencia, lógica. **2** (*of mixture*) consistencia.
consistent [kən'sɪstənt] *adj* (*of person, behaviour, beliefs*) coherente (**with**, con), consecuente (**with**, con); (*denial, improvement*) constante: *the government has always been consistent on this matter,* el gobierno siempre ha mantenido una actitud coherente al respecto.
● **to be consistent with sth.**, ser consecuente con algo.
consistently [kən'sɪstəntlɪ] *adv* (*unchangingly*) consecuentemente, coherentemente; (*constantly*) constantemente.
consolation [kɒnsə'leɪʃən] *n* consuelo: *you were a great consolation to me,* fuiste un gran consuelo para mí.
■ **consolation prize**, premio de consolación.

console¹ ['kɒnsəʊl] *n* MUS TECH consola.
console² [kən'səʊl] *t* consolar.
consolidate [kən'sɒlɪdeɪt] 1 *t* (*gen*) consolidar. 2 COMM (*merge*) fusionar. – 3 *i* (*gen*) consolidarse. 4 COMM (*merge*) fusionarse.
consolidation [kənsɒlɪ'deɪʃən] 1 *n* (*gen*) consolidación *f*. 2 COMM fusión *f*.
consoling [kən'səʊlɪŋ] *adj* de consuelo, consolador,-ra.
consommé ['kɒnsɒmeɪ] *n* consomé *m*.
consonant ['kɒnsənənt] *n* consonante *f*.
consort ['kɒnsɔːt] 1 *n* consorte *mf*. – 2 *i* asociarse (**with,** con).
■ prince consort, príncipe *m* consorte.
▲ (*verbo*) [kən'sɔːt].
consortium [kən'sɔːtɪəm] *n* consorcio.
▲ *pl* consortia.
conspicuous [kəns'pɪkjʊəs] *adj* (*clothes*) llamativo,-a; (*mistake, difference, lack*) evidente, obvio,-a: *wear something a little less conspicuous next time,* ponte algo menos llamativo la próxima vez; *in a conspicuous position,* en un lugar visible, a la vista.
● to be conspicuous by one's absence, brillar por su ausencia. ‖ to be conspicuous for sth., destacar por algo. ‖ to make os. conspicuous, llamar la atención.
■ conspicuous consumption, consumo ostentoso.
conspicuously [kəns'pɪkjʊəslɪ] *adv* (*loudly*) de forma llamativa; (*markedly*) notoriamente.
conspiracy [kən'spɪrəsɪ] *n* conspiración *f*: *a conspiracy to murder,* una conspiración de asesinato.
■ conspiracy theory, teoría de la conspiración.
▲ *pl* conspiracies.
conspirator [kən'spɪrətə'] *n* conspirador,-ra.
conspiratorial [kənspɪrə'tɔːrɪəl] *adj* conspirador,-ra.
conspire [kən'spaɪə'] *i* (*people*) conspirar (**against,** contra); (*events*) conspirar, confabularse: *they conspired to blackmail the King,* conspiraron para chantajear al Rey.
constable ['kʌnstəbəl] *n* policía *mf*, guardia *mf*, agente *mf* (de policía).
constabulary [kən'stæbjələrɪ] *n* GB policía *f*.
▲ *pl* constabularies.
constancy ['kɒnstənsɪ] 1 *n* (*freedom from change*) constancia. 2 (*faithfulness, loyalty*) fidelidad *f*, lealtad *f*.
constant ['kɒnstənt] 1 *adj* (*continual*) continuo,-a, constante. 2 (*unchanging*) constante. 3 (*loyal*) leal, fiel. – 4 *n* constante *f*.
Constantinople [kɒnstænti'nəʊpəl] *n* Constantinopla.
constantly ['kɒnstəntlɪ] *adv* constantemente, continuamente.
constellation [kɒnstə'leɪʃən] *n* constelación *f*.
consternation [kɒnstə'neɪʃən] *n* consternación *f*.
constipated ['kɒnstɪpeɪtɪd] *adj* estreñido,-a.
constipation [kɒnstɪ'peɪʃən] *n* estreñimiento.
constituency [kən'stɪtjʊənsɪ] *n* circunscripción *f*, distrito electoral.
▲ *pl* constituencies.
constituent [kəns'tɪtjʊənt] 1 *adj* (*part etc*) constitutivo,-a, constituyente. 2 POL constituyente. – 3 *n* (*component*) componente *m*. 4 POL elector,-ra.
constitute ['kɒnstɪtjuːt] *t* constituir.
constitution [kɒnstɪ'tjuːʃən] 1 *n* (*gen*) constitución *f*. 2 (*of person*) constitución *f*, complexión *f*.
constitutional [kɒnstɪ'tjuːʃənəl] 1 *adj* constitucional. – 2 *n* dated paseo.
constrain [kəns'treɪn] 1 *t* (*oblige, force*) constreñir, obligar, forzar. 2 (*restrict, hold back*) contener.

constrained [kən'streɪnd] 1 *adj* (*voice, manner*) forzado,-a, poco natural. 2 (*forced*) forzado,-a, obligado,-a: *I felt constrained to attend,* me vi obligado a asistir.
constraint [kən'streɪnt] 1 *n* (*compulsion, coercion*) constreñimiento, coacción *f*, obligación *f*. 2 (*restriction*) restricción *f*, limitación *f*. 3 *fml* (*uneasiness, unnatural manner*) inquietud *f*, confusión *f*: *he showed constraint in her presence,* se sintió coartado ante ella.
constrict [kən'strɪkt] 1 *t* (*blood vessels*) estrangular; (*breathing, movement*) dificultar; (*neck*) apretar, oprimir. 2 *fig* (*action, behaviour*) limitar, coartar.
constriction [kən'strɪkʃən] 1 *n* MED (*narrow part*) estrangulamiento; (*tightness*) opresión *f*. 2 *fig* (*limitation*) restricción *f*, limitación *f*, constricción *f*.
construct [kəns'trʌkt] *t* (*gen*) construir; (*model*) armar, montar.
construction [kəns'trʌkʃən] 1 *n* (*gen*) construcción *f*. 2 *fig* (*meaning*) interpretación *f*.
● to be under construction, estar en construcción. ‖ to put a wrong construction on sth., malinterpretar algo.
■ construction industry, industria de la construcción. ‖ construction site, obra.
constructive [kən'strʌktɪv] *adj* constructivo,-a.
constructively [kən'strʌktɪvlɪ] *adv* constructivamente, de manera constructiva.
constructor [kən'strʌktə'] *n* constructor,-ra.
construe [kən'struː] *t* interpretar.
consul ['kɒnsəl] *n* cónsul *mf*.
consular ['kɒnsjələ'] *adj* consular.
consulate ['kɒnsjələt] *n* consulado.
consult [kən'sʌlt] 1 *t* consultar. – 2 *i* consultar.
consultant [kən'sʌltənt] 1 *n* (*expert, advisor*) asesor,-ra, consultor,-ra. 2 GB MED especialista *mf*.
consultation [kɒnsəl'teɪʃən] 1 *n* (*act, process*) consulta. 2 MED consulta. 3 (*discussion*) discusión *f*, conversación *f*; (*meeting*) reunión *f*: *after consultations with my lawyer,* después de consultar con mi abogado.
● in consultation with sb., con la aprobación de algn.
consultative [kən'sʌltətɪv] *adj* consultivo,-a.
consulting [kən'sʌltɪŋ] *adj* (*architect, engineer*) asesor,-ra, consultor,-ra.
■ consulting room, MED consulta.
consume [kən'sjuːm] *t* (*gen*) consumir; (*fire*) consumir, reducir a cenizas.
● to be consumed with sth., *fig* estar muerto,-a de algo: *she was consumed with jealousy,* estaba muerta de celos, los celos la consumían.
consumer [kən'sjuːmə'] *n* consumidor,-ra.
■ consumer advice, orientación *f* al consumidor. ‖ consumer durables, bienes *mpl* de consumo duraderos. ‖ consumer goods, artículos *mpl* de consumo, bienes *mpl* de consumo. ‖ consumer rights, derechos *mpl* del consumidor.
consuming [kən'sjuːmɪŋ] *adj* (*interest*) arrollador,-ra; (*passion*) devorador,-ra.
consummate ['kɒnsəmət] 1 *adj fml* consumado,-a. – 2 *t fml* consumar.
▲ (*verbo*) ['kɒnsəmeɪt].
consummation [kɒnsə'meɪʃən] *n* consumación *f*.
consumption [kən'sʌmpʃən] 1 *n* (*of food, energy, resources*) consumo: *water consumption must be reduced,* hay que reducir el consumo de agua; *it's not fit for human consumption,* no es apto para el consumo humano. 2 MED dated tisis *f*.

cont[1] ['kɒntents] *abbr* (*contents*) contenido.
cont[2] [kɒn'tɪnjuːd] *abbr* (*continued*) sigue.
contact ['kɒntækt] **1** *n* (*gen*) contacto: *have you been in contact with Susie?*, ¿has estado en contacto con Susie?; *I lost contact with her years ago*, perdí el contacto con ella hace años; *her father's got contacts*, su padre tiene contactos; *I've got a contact in the ministry*, tengo un contacto en el ministerio. – **2** *t* ponerse en contacto con, contactar con.
● **to avoid eye contact with sb.**, evitar mirar a algn. a los ojos. ‖ **to break contact**, ELEC interrumpir el contacto. ‖ **to come into contact with sth.**, (*touch*) hacer contacto con algo. ‖ **to get in contact with sb.**, ponerse en contacto con algn. ‖ **to make contact**, ELEC hacer contacto. ‖ **to make contact with**, (*touch*) tocar; (*get in touch*) establecer contacto con, entrar en contacto con.
■ **contact lenses**, lentillas *fpl*, lentes *fpl* de contacto. ‖ **contact number**, teléfono de contacto. ‖ **contact print**, contacto. ‖ **contact sport**, deporte *m* en el que hay contacto físico.
contagion [kən'teɪdʒən] *n* contagio.
contagious [kən'teɪdʒəs] *adj* contagioso,-a.
contain [kən'teɪn] **1** *t* (*hold*) contener. **2** (*hold back, restrain, control*) contener.
● **to contain os.**, contenerse.
container [kən'teɪnə'] **1** *n* (*receptacle*) recipiente *m*; (*packaging*) envase *m*. **2** (*for transporting goods*) contenedor *m*, container *m*.
■ **container ship**, portacontenedores *m*.
containment [kən'teɪnmənt] *n* contención *f*.
contaminate [kən'tæmɪneɪt] *t* contaminar.
contamination [kəntæmɪ'neɪʃən] *n* contaminación *f*.
contd [kɒn'tɪnjuːd] *abbr* (*continued*) sigue.
contemplate ['kɒntempleɪt] **1** *t* (*look at*) contemplar; (*consider thoughtfully*) considerar, contemplar. **2** (*consider possibility of*) considerar, pensar (en); (*expect*) prever: *she's contemplating early retirement*, está pensando en la jubilación anticipada; *I'm not contemplating having children yet*, aún no pienso tener hijos. **3** (*meditate*) meditar sobre. – **4** *i* pensar: *it's too awful to contemplate*, me horroriza pensarlo. **5** (*meditate*) meditar.
contemplation [kɒntem'pleɪʃən] **1** *n* (*act of looking at*) contemplación *f*; (*deep thought, meditation*) reflexión *f*, meditación *f*. **2** (*consideration, intention*) intención *f*.
● **to be deep in contemplation**, estar absorto,-a, estar ensimismado,-a.
contemplative ['kɒntempleɪtɪv] **1** *adj* (*thoughtful*) pensativo,-a, meditabundo,-a. **2** REL contemplativo,-a.
contemporaneous [kɒntempə'reɪnɪəs] *adj fml* contemporáneo,-a, coetáneo,-a.
contemporary [kən'tempərərɪ] **1** *adj* (*of the same period*) contemporáneo,-a, coetáneo,-a. **2** (*modern*) contemporáneo,-a, actual. – **3** *n* contemporáneo,-a.
▲ (*sustantivo*) *pl* **contemporaries**.
contempt [kən'tempt] *n* desprecio, desdén *m*, menosprecio: *she felt contempt for her boss*, sentía desprecio por su jefe.
● **to be beneath contempt**, ser despreciable. ‖ **contempt of court**, JUR desacato al tribunal. ‖ **to hold sth./sb. in contempt**, despreciar algo/a algn.
contemptible [kən'temptəbəl] *adj* despreciable.
contemptuous [kən'temptjʊəs] *adj* (*attitude*) despreciativo,-a, despectivo,-a; (*person*) desdeñoso,-a.
● **to be contemptuous of sth./sb.**, despreciar algo/a algn., desdeñar algo/a algn.

contend [kən'tend] **1** *i* (*compete*) contender, competir: *22 teams are contending for the championship*, 22 equipos compiten por el campeonato. **2** (*deal with, struggle against*) enfrentarse a, lidiar con: *he had a lot of problems to contend with*, tuvo que lidiar con muchos problemas. – **3** *t* (*claim, state*) sostener, afirmar.
contender [kən'tendə'] *n* contendiente *mf* (**for**, por).
content[1] ['kɒntent] *n* contenido: *cheese has a very high fat content*, el queso contiene mucha grasa. – **2** contents, *npl* contenido *m sing*: *she emptied out the contents of her handbag*, vació su bolso; *have you read the contents of the letter?*, ¿has leído la carta?
■ **table of contents**, índice *m* de materias.
content[2] [kən'tent] **1** *adj* contento,-a, satisfecho,-a: *he's content to watch the match at home*, se conforma con mirar el partido en casa. – **2** *n* contento. – **3** *t* contentar, satisfacer.
● **not content with ...**, no contento,-a con ... ‖ **to be content with**, contentarse con, conformarse con. ‖ **to content os. with**, contentarse con, conformarse con. ‖ **to one's heart content**, todo lo que uno,-a quiera, hasta quedar satisfecho,-a.
contented [kən'tentɪd] *adj* contento,-a, satisfecho,-a: *a contented smile*, una sonrisa de satisfacción.
contention [kən'tenʃən] **1** *n* (*opinion, assertion*) opinión *f*: *it is my contention that ...*, sostengo que ..., mi opinión es que ... **2** (*dispute, disagreement*) discusión *f*, controversia: *there's been a lot of contention about the results*, se ha discutido mucho sobre los resultados; *that matter is not in contention*, ese asunto no se discute. **3** (*competition*) competición *f*: *they are in contention for the title*, compiten por el título.
● **bone of contention**, manzana de la discordia.
contentious [kən'tenʃəs] *adj* (*issue, decision, view*) contencioso,-a, polémico,-a, muy discutido,-a; (*person*) discutidor,-ra.
contentment [kən'tentmənt] *n* contento, satisfacción *f*.
contest ['kɒntest] **1** *n* (*competition - gen*) concurso; (*-sports*) competición *f*; (*-boxing*) combate *m*. **2** (*struggle, attempt*) contienda, lucha. – **3** *t* (*championship, seat*) competir por, luchar por, disputarse; (*election*) presentarse como candidato,-a a: *a keenly contested game*, un partido muy reñido. **4** (*dispute*) refutar, rebatir. **5** JUR (*appeal against*) impugnar.
● **no contest!**, ¡ni comparación!
▲ (*verbo*) [kən'test].
contestant [kən'testənt] *n* (*in competition, quiz, game*) concursante *mf*; (*for post, position*) candidato,-a, aspirante *mf*.
context ['kɒntekst] *n* contexto: *the newspaper took my words out of context*, el periódico me citó fuera de contexto.
contiguous [kən'tɪgjʊəs] *adj* contiguo,-a.
continent ['kɒntɪnənt] **1** *n* continente *m*. **2 the Continent**, GB Europa (continental).
continental [kɒntɪ'nentəl] **1** *adj* continental. **2 Continental**, GB europeo,-a.
■ **continental breakfast**, desayuno continental (*café con croissants o bollos, mantequilla y mermelada*). ‖ **continental drift**, deriva de los continentes. ‖ **continental quilt**, edredón *m* nórdico.
contingency [kən'tɪndʒənsɪ] *n* contingencia, eventualidad *f*.
■ **contingency plan**, plan *m* de emergencia.
contingent [kən'tɪndʒənt] **1** *adj* contingente. – **2** *n* contingente *m*.

● **to be contingent on sth.,** depender de algo.
continual [kən'tɪnjʊəl] *adj* continuo,-a, constante.
continually [kən'tɪnjʊəlɪ] *adv* continuamente, constantemente.
continuance [kən'tɪnjʊəns] *n fml* continuación *f*.
continuation [kəntɪnjʊ'eɪʃən] **1** *n* (*resumption*) continuación *f*; (*prolongation*) prolongación *f*. **2** (*extension*) prolongación *f*, continuación *f*. **3** US JUR aplazamiento.
continue [kən'tɪnjuː] **1** *t* continuar, seguir con: *they voted to continue the strike*, votaron para continuar con la huelga. – **2** *i* continuar, seguir: *the article continues on page 12*, el artículo continúa en la página 12; *please continue*, siga, por favor; *I continued on my way*, reanudé el camino.
● **to be continued,** continuará. ‖ **to continue doing sth.,** **continue to do sth.,** continuar haciendo algo, seguir haciendo algo.
continued [kən'tɪnjuːd] *adj* continuo,-a, ininterrumpido,-a.
continuing [kən'tɪnjʊɪŋ] *adj* continuado,-a.
■ **continuing education,** educación *f* para adultos.
continuity [kɒntɪ'njuːɪtɪ] *n* continuidad *f*.
■ **continuity announcer,** locutor,-ra de continuidad. ‖ **continuity girl,** CINEM secretaria de rodaje. ‖ **continuity man,** CINEM secretario de rodaje.
continuous [kən'tɪnjʊəs] *adj* continuo,-a.
■ **continuous performance,** CINEM sesión *f* continua. ‖ **past continuous,** LING pasado continuo. ‖ **present continuous,** LING presente *m* continuo.
continuously [kən'tɪnjʊəslɪ] *adv* continuamente, sin interrupción.
contort [kən'tɔːt] **1** *t* (*face*) contraer. – **2** *i* contraerse.
● **to contort one's body,** contorsionarse.
contorted [kən'tɔːtɪd] *adj* (*face*) contraído,-a; (*limb*) contorsionado,-a, deformado,-a; (*branches*) torcido,-a.
contortion [kən'tɔːʃən] *n* contorsión *f*.
contortionist [kən'tɔːʃənɪst] *n* contorsionista *mf*.
contour ['kɒntʊə'] *n* contorno.
■ **contour line,** línea de nivel. ‖ **contour map,** mapa topográfico.
contraband ['kɒntrəbænd] *n* contrabando.
contraception [kɒntrə'sepʃən] *n* anticoncepción *f*.
contraceptive [kɒntrə'septɪv] **1** *adj* anticonceptivo,-a. – **2** *n* anticonceptivo.
contract ['kɒntrækt] **1** *n* (*gen*) contrato; (*for public work, services*) contrata. – **2** *t* (*place under contract*) contratar. **3** (*make smaller*) contraer. **4** *fml* (*debt, habit, illness*) contraer. – **5** *i* (*enter into agreement*) hacer un contrato, firmar un contrato. **6** (*become smaller*) contraerse.
◆ **to contract out** *t sep* (*job, work*) subcontratar.
● **breach of contract,** incumplimiento de contrato. ‖ **to be under contract (to sb.),** tener un contrato (con algn.). ‖ **to contract to do sth.,** comprometerse por contrato a hacer algo. ‖ **to enter into a contract (with sb.),** hacer un contrato (con algn.). ‖ **to put a contract out on sb.,** ponerle un precio a la cabeza de algn. ‖ **to put sth. out to contract,** sacar algo a concurso (público).
■ **contract bridge,** contrato.
▲ (*verbo*) [kən'trækt].
contraction [kən'trækʃən] *n* contracción *f*.
contractor [kən'træktə'] *n* contratista *mf*.
contractual [kən'træktʊəl] *adj* contractual.
contradict [kɒntrə'dɪkt] **1** *t* (*gen*) contradecir: *don't contradict the teacher*, no contradigas al profesor; *their stories contradict each other*, sus versiones se contradicen. – **2** *i* contradecir.

● **to contradict os.,** contradecirse.
contradiction [kɒntrə'dɪkʃən] *n* contradicción *f*.
● **to be a contradiction in terms,** ser contradictorio,-a, no tener lógica.
contradictory [kɒntrə'dɪktərɪ] *adj* contradictorio,-a.
contraflow ['kɒntrəfləʊ] *n* GB *sistema por el que los vehículos circulan en dos sentidos por un lado de la carretera mientras que otro está en obras.*
contralto [kən'træltəʊ] **1** *n* (*voice*) contralto *m*; (*woman singer*) contralto *f*. – **2** *adj* de contralto.
▲ *pl* **contraltos** *o* **contralti** [kɒn'trɑːltiː].
contraption [kən'træpʃən] *n fam* cacharro, artefacto, aparato, artilugio.
contrariness [kɒn'treərɪnəs] *n* terquedad *f*, obstinación *f*.
contrary ['kɒntrərɪ] **1** *adj* (*opposite*) contrario,-a. **2** (*stubborn*) terco,-a, obstinado,-a, tozudo,-a. – **3** the **contrary,** *n* lo contrario.
● **contrary to,** en contra de, al contrario de, contrariamente a. ‖ **on the contrary,** (*however*) por el contrario; (*quite the reverse*) todo lo contrario, al contrario. ‖ **to the contrary,** en contra: *if I don't hear anything to the contrary*, si no me dices lo contrario; *there is no evidence to the contrary*, no hay pruebas en contra.
▲ (*adjetivo*) [kɒn'treərɪ].
contrast ['kɒntræst] **1** *n* contraste *m*. – **2** *t* contrastar, comparar. – **3** *i* contrastar.
● **by contrast / in contrast,** por contraste. ‖ **in contrast to/with,** en contraste con, a diferencia de. ‖ **to be a contrast to sb./sth.,** contrastar con algn./algo. ‖ **to contrast sb./sth. with sb./sth.,** comparar algn./ algo con algn./algo.
▲ (*verbo*) [kən'træst].
contrasting [kən'trɑːstɪŋ] *adj* opuesto,-a.
contravene [kɒntrə'viːn] *t* JUR contravenir, infringir, violar.
contravention [kɒntrə'venʃən] *n* JUR contravención *f*, infracción *f*.
contribute [kən'trɪbjuːt] **1** *t* (*money*) contribuir (**to,** a), (**towards,** para); (*ideas, information*) aportar. **2** (*article, poem, etc*) escribir. – **3** *i* (*gen*) contribuir (**to,** a), (**towards,** para); (*in discussion*) participar (**to,** en): *we all contributed towards his present*, todos contribuimos con dinero para su regalo. **4** (*to newspaper, magazine, etc*) colaborar (**to,** en), escribir (**to,** para).
contribution [kɒntrɪ'bjuːʃən] **1** *n* (*of money*) contribución *f*; (*of ideas, experience, etc*) aportación *f*: *Heaney's contribution to Irish literature*, la aportación de Heaney a la literatura irlandesa. **2** (*to newspaper etc*) colaboración *f*. **3** (*participation*) participación *f*, intervención *f*.
contributor [kən'trɪbjətə'] **1** *n* (*to charity, appeal, etc*) donante *mf*. **2** (*to newspaper, magazine, etc*) colaborador,-ra.
contributory [kən'trɪbjətərɪ] *adj* (*factor, cause*) contribuyente, que contribuye.
■ **contributory negligence,** JUR negligencia de la parte actora. ‖ **contributory pension scheme,** plan *m* de pensiones.
contrite ['kɒntraɪt] *adj fml* contrito,-a.
contrition [kən'trɪʃən] *n* contrición *f*.
contrivance [kən'traɪvəns] **1** *n* (*device, tool*) artefacto, invento, cacharro, artilugio, aparato. **2** (*plan*) estratagema, artimaña, treta.
contrive [kən'traɪv] **1** *t* (*way, device*) idear, inventar; (*meeting*) arreglar; (*meal, dress, etc*) improvisar. **2** (*manage*) conseguir, lograr: *he somehow contrived an interview with the singer*, se las arregló para entrevistarse con el cantante.

contrived [kən'traɪvd] *adj* artificial, forzado,-a, afectado,-a.

control [kən'trəʊl] **1** *t* (*govern, rule*) controlar: *he controlled the country for 36 years,* controló el país durante 36 años; *a state-controlled industry,* una industria bajo control estatal. **2** (*have control over - person, animal, vehicle*) controlar; (*- emotions*) controlar, dominar: *a good teacher can control his class,* un buen profesor sabe controlar su clase; *you must try to control your temper,* debes intentar dominar tu mal genio. **3** (*regulate - temperature, volume, pressure, rate, flow*) controlar, regular; (*- traffic*) dirigir; (*- prices, inflation, spending*) controlar. **4** (*verify, check*) controlar. – **5** *n* (*power, command*) poder *m*, dominio, mando; (*authority*) autoridad *f*: *the military have gained control,* los militares se han hecho con el poder; *his son took control of the business,* su hijo se hizo con el control de la empresa; *more parental control should be exercised,* los padres deberían imponer su autoridad. **6** (*restriction, means of regulating*) control *m*. **7** (*place, people in control*) control *m*. **8** TECH (*standard of comparison*) patrón *m* de comparación. **9** (*switch, button*) botón *m*, mando: *the volume control doesn't work,* el mando del volumen no funciona. – **10** controls, *npl* (*of vehicle*) mandos *mpl*.
● **out of control,** fuera de control. ‖ **under control,** bajo control. ‖ **to be at the controls,** AUTO estar al volante; AV estar al mando. ‖ **to be beyond sb.'s control,** estar fuera del control de algn. ‖ **to be in control,** estar al mando, mandar. ‖ **to bring sth. under control,** conseguir controlar algo, llegar a controlar algo. ‖ **to control os.,** controlarse. ‖ **to gain control of sth.,** hacerse con el control de algo. ‖ **to go out of control,** descontrolarse. ‖ **to lose control of os.,** perder el control de sí mismo,-a, perder los estribos. ‖ **to lose control of sth.,** perder el control de algo.
■ **control panel,** tablero de instrumentos. ‖ **control room,** MIL MAR centro de operaciones; RAD TV sala de control. ‖ **control tower,** torre *f* de control. ‖ **import control,** control *m* de importaciones. ‖ **passport control,** control *m* de pasaportes. ‖ **price controls,** control *m* de precios. ‖ **traffic control,** control *m* de tráfico. ‖ **wage controls,** regulación *f sing* salarial.

controllable [kən'trəʊləbəl] *adj* controlable.

controller [kən'trəʊlə^r] **1** *n* FIN interventor,-ra. **2** RAD TV director,-ra de programación.
■ **air traffic controller,** controlador,-ra aéreo,-a.

controlling [kən'trəʊlɪŋ] *adj* controlador,-ra.
■ **controlling interest,** participación *f* mayoritaria.

controversial [kɒntrə'vɜːʃəl] *adj* controvertido,-a, polémico,-a.

controversy [kən'trɒvəsɪ] *n* controversia, polémica.
▲ *pl* controversies.

controvert [kɒntrə'vɜːt] *t* controvertir, contradecir.

contusion [kən'tjuːʒən] *n* contusión *f*.

conundrum [kə'nʌndrəm] *n* enigma *m*, problema *m*, adivinanza, acertijo.

conurbation [kɒnɜː'beɪʃən] *n* conurbación *f*.

convalesce [kɒnvə'les] *i* convalecer, recuperarse.

convalescence [kɒnvə'lesəns] *n* convalecencia.

convalescent [kɒnvə'lesənt] **1** *adj* convaleciente. – **2** *n* convaleciente *mf*.
■ **convalescent home,** clínica de reposo.

convection [kən'vekʃən] *n* convección *f*.
■ **convection heater,** estufa de convección.

convector [kən'vektə^r] *n* estufa de convección.

convene [kən'viːn] **1** *t* convocar. – **2** *i* reunirse.

convenience [kən'viːnɪəns] *n* conveniencia, comodidad *f*: *marriage of convenience,* matrimonio de conveniencia.
● **all modern conveniences,** totalmente equipado,-a. ‖ **at your convenience,** cuando le convenga, cuando le sea posible. ‖ **at your earliest convenience,** a la mayor brevedad posible.
■ **convenience food,** comida precocinada. ‖ **public conveniences,** GB servicios *mpl* públicos.

convenient [kən'viːnɪənt] *adj* (*time, arrangement*) conveniente, oportuno,-a; (*thing*) práctico,-a, cómodo,-a; (*place - near, easy to reach*) bien situado,-a: *is 11 o'clock convenient for you?,* ¿las once le va bien?; *our flat is very convenient for the station,* nuestro piso queda muy cerca de la estación.

conveniently [kən'viːnɪəntlɪ] **1** *adv* (*handily*) convenientemente. **2** (*expediently*) oportunamente.

convent ['kɒnvənt] *n* convento.

convention [kən'venʃən] **1** *n* (*conference*) convención *f*, congreso. **2** (*tacit agreement, custom*) convención *f*. **3** (*treaty*) convención *f*.

conventional [kən'venʃənəl] *adj* (*gen*) convencional; (*style*) tradicional, clásico,-a.

converge [kən'vɜːdʒ] *i* (*lines, roads*) convergir (**on**, en), converger (**on**, en); (*people*) reunirse.

convergence [kən'vɜːdʒəns] *n* convergencia.

convergent [kən'vɜːdʒənt] *adj* convergente.

conversant [kən'vɜːsənt] *adj* familiarizado,-a (**with,** con), versado,-a (**with,** en).
● **to become conversant with sth.,** familiarizarse con algo.

conversation [kɒnvə'seɪʃən] *n* conversación *f*.
● **to get into conversation with sb.,** entablar conversación con algn. ‖ **to have a conversation about sth.,** hablar de algo, conversar sobre algo. ‖ **to hold a conversation,** mantener una conversación.
■ **conversation piece,** tema *m* de conversación.

conversationalist [kɒnvə'seɪʃənəlɪst] *n* conversador,-ra.

conversational [kɒnvə'seɪʃənəl] *adj* coloquial, familiar.

converse¹ ['kɒnvɜːs] **1** *adj* opuesto,-a, contrario,-a. – **2** the converse, *n* lo opuesto, lo contrario.

converse² [kən'vɜːs] *i* conversar, hablar.

conversely [kən'vɜːslɪ] *adv* a la inversa.

conversion [kən'vɜːʃən] **1** *n* (*gen*) conversión *f* (**to,** a), (**into,** en); (*of buildings*) transformación *f*: *a company that carries out house conversions,* una empresa que transforma casas. **2** REL conversión *f*. **3** SP (*in rugby*) transformación *f*, conversión *f*.
■ **conversion table,** tabla de conversión.

convert [kən'vɜːt] **1** *t* (*gen*) convertir (**into,** en) (**to,** a); (*building*) convertir, transformar: *can you convert pounds into pesetas?,* ¿sabes convertir libras en pesetas?; *I've been converted to classical music,* me han convertido a la música clásica; *the warehouse has been converted into a nightclub,* han transformado el almacén en un club nocturno. **2** SP (*in rugby*) transformar, convertir. – **3** *i* convertirse (**into/to,** en): *this sofa converts into a bed,* este sofá se convierte en cama; *many people have converted to Catholicism,* mucha gente ha convertido al catolicismo. – **4** *n* REL converso,-a.
▲ (*sustantivo*) ['kɒnvɜːt].

converted [kən'vɜːtɪd] *adj* (*building*) transformado,-a en vivienda; (*flat*) reformado,-a.

converter [kən'vɜːtə^r] *n* convertidor *m*.

convertible [kən'vɜːtəbəl] **1** *adj* (*gen*) convertible; (*car*) descapotable. – **2** *n* AUTO descapotable *m*.

convex ['kɒnveks] *adj* convexo,-a.

convey [kən'veɪ] 1 *t* (*goods, people, electricity*) transportar, conducir; (*sound*) transmitir, llevar. 2 (*opinion, feeling, idea*) comunicar, expresar, transmitir; (*thanks*) hacer llegar, transmitir. 3 JUR (*property, land*) preparar escrituras de traspaso, transferir.

conveyance [kən'veɪəns] 1 *n* (*transport*) transporte *m*. 2 *fml* (*vehicle*) vehículo. 3 JUR traspaso, transferencia.

conveyancing [kən'veɪənsɪŋ] *n* JUR preparación *f* de escrituras de traspaso.

conveyor [kən'veɪəʳ] *n* transportista *mf*.
■ **conveyor belt,** cinta transportadora.

convict ['kɒnvɪkt] 1 *n* presidiario,-a, recluso,-a. – 2 *t* JUR declarar culpable, condenar: *a convicted murderer,* un asesino convicto.
● **to be convicted of sth.,** ser condenado,-a por algo.
▲ (*verbo*) [kən'vɪkt].

conviction [kən'vɪkʃən] 1 *n* (*belief*) convicción *f*, creencia. 2 JUR condena (**for,** por): *he had no previous convictions,* no tenía antecedentes penales.

convince [kən'vɪns] *t* convencer: *he convinced me of his innocence,* me convenció de su inocencia; *I convinced her that I was serious,* la convencí de que hablaba en serio.
● **to convince sb. to do sth.,** convencer a algn. para que haga algo.

convinced [kən'vɪnst] *adj* convencido,-a.

convincing [kən'vɪnsɪŋ] *adj* convincente.

convivial [kən'vɪvɪəl] *adj* (*party, atmosphere*) alegre, jovial, festivo,-a, cordial; (*person*) sociable.

conviviality [kɒnvɪvɪ'ælɪtɪ] *n* alegría, jovialidad *f*.

convocation [kɒnvə'keɪʃən] 1 *n* (*summoning*) convocatoria. 2 GB EDUC asamblea. 3 REL sínodo, asamblea.

convoke [kən'vəʊk] *t* convocar.

convoluted ['kɒnvəluːtɪd] 1 *adj* (*complicated*) complicado,-a, enredado,-a, intrincado,-a, enrevesado,-a. 2 BIOL (*twisted, curved, coiled*) convoluto,-a, enrollado,-a.

convoy ['kɒnvɔɪ] 1 *n* convoy *m*. – 2 *t* escoltar, convoyar.
● **in convoy,** en convoy.

convulse [kən'vʌls] 1 *t* MED convulsionar. 2 *fig* convulsionar, sacudir. – 3 *i* MED tener convulsiones.
● **to be convulsed with laughter,** troncharse de risa. ‖ **to convulse with pain,** retorcerse de dolor.

convulsion [kən'vʌlʃən] *n* convulsión *f*.
● **to be in convulsions,** partirse de risa. ‖ **to have convulsions,** tener convulsiones.

convulsive [kən'vʌlsɪv] *adj* convulsivo,-a.

coo [kuː] 1 *i* (*dove, pigeon*) arrullar; (*baby*) hacer gorgoritos. – 2 *t* susurrar.
● **to coo over sb./sth.,** babear por algn./algo.

cooing ['kuːɪŋ] *n* (*of dove, pigeon*) arrullo; (*of baby*) gorjeos *mpl*.

cook [kʊk] 1 *n* cocinero,-a: *you're a good cook,* guisas bien. – 2 *t* (*food*) guisar, cocinar; (*meals*) preparar, hacer. – 3 *i* (*person*) cocinar, guisar, cocer; (*food*) hacerse, cocerse. 4 *fam* (*be planned*) cocerse, tramarse: *what's cooking?,* ¿qué se está cocinando?
◆ **to cook up** *t sep* (*excuse*) inventarse; (*scheme*) tramar.
● **to cook sb.'s goose,** estropearle los planes a algn. ‖ **to cook the books,** amañar la cuentas, falsificar las cuentas. ‖ **too many cooks spoil the broth,** muchas manos en un plato hacen mucho garabato.

cookbook ['kʊkbʊk] *n* US libro de cocina.

cooked [kʊkt] *adj* (*gen*) cocido,-a; (*meal, breakfast*) caliente: *I don't think the chicken is cooked,* creo que el pollo no está hecho.

cooker ['kʊkəʳ] 1 *n* (*stove*) cocina. 2 (*apple*) manzana ácida para cocinar.

cookery ['kʊkərɪ] *n* cocina.
■ **cookery book,** libro de cocina.

cookie ['kʊkɪ] *n* US galleta.

cooking ['kʊkɪŋ] 1 *n* cocina: *home cooking,* cocina casera. – 2 *adj* (*apple, sherry*) para cocinar; (*oil*) comestible.
● **to do the cooking,** cocinar.

cookout ['kʊkaʊt] *n* US comida al aire libre, barbacoa.

cool [kuːl] 1 *adj* (*weather, breeze, clothes*) fresco,-a; (*drink*) fresco,-a, frío,-a: *the weather's turning cool,* está refrescando. 2 (*unfriendly, reserved*) frío,-a. 3 (*calm*) tranquilo,-a, sereno,-a: *keep cool!,* ¡tranquilo! 4 *fam* (*great*) guay: *he looked so cool,* estaba super guay; *cool, man!,* ¡guay, tío! 5 (*self-confident*) impasible. 6 *fam* (*with numbers*): *a cool million dollars,* la friolera de un millón de dólares. – 7 *n* (*of weather etc*) fresco, frescor *m*. 8 (*calmness*) calma. – 9 *t* (*air, room*) refrescar, refrigerar; (*drink, food, engine*) enfriar. – 10 *i* (*air, room*) refrigerarse; (*drink, food, engine*) enfriarse.
◆ **to cool down** 1 *t sep* (*food*) enfriar; (*person*) refrescar. 2 (*person*) calmar. – 3 *i* (*food, feelings*) enfriarse; (*person*) calmarse. ‖ **to cool off** *i* (*person*) calmarse; (*feelings*) enfriarse.
● **a cool customer,** un,-a fresco,-a. ‖ **as cool as a cucumber,** fresco,-a como una lechuga. ‖ **cool it!,** ¡calma!, ¡tranquilo,-a! ‖ **to keep one's cool,** mantener la calma. ‖ **to lose one's cool,** perder la calma. ‖ **to play it cool,** tomarse las cosas con calma.
■ **cool bag / cool box,** nevera portátil.

coolant ['kuːlənt] *n* líquido refrigerante.

cooler ['kuːləʳ] 1 *n* refrigerador *m*, nevera. 2 *sl* (*prison*) chirona.
● **to be in the cooler,** (*in prison*) estar a la sombra.

cooling ['kuːlɪŋ] *n* (*of engine*) refrigeración *f*.
■ **cooling system,** circuito de refrigeración. ‖ **cooling tower,** torre *f* de refrigeración.

cooling-off [kuːlɪŋ'ɒf] *n* (*of love, enthusiasm, relations*) enfriamiento.
■ **cooling-off period,** período de reflexión.

coolly ['kuːlɪ] 1 *adv* (*unenthusiastically*) fríamente, con frialdad. 2 (*calmy*) con serenidad, con calma. 3 (*boldly*) descaradamente.

coolness ['kuːlnəs] 1 *n* (*of air etc*) frescura, frescor *m*. 2 (*unfriendliness*) frialdad *f*. 3 (*calm*) serenidad *f*, sangre *f* fría. 4 (*boldness*) frescura, descaro.

coop [kuːp] *n* gallinero.
◆ **to coop up** *t sep* encerrar.

co-op ['kəʊɒp] *n* cooperativa.

co-operate [kəʊ'ɒpəreɪt] *i* cooperar, colaborar.

co-operation [kəʊɒpə'reɪʃən] *n* cooperación *f*, colaboración *f*.

co-operative [kəʊ'ɒpərətɪv] 1 *adj* (*helpful*) cooperador,-ra, dispuesto,-a a cooperar. 2 (*joint*) conjunto,-a. 3 COMM cooperativo,-a. – 4 *n* cooperativa.
■ **cooperative society,** cooperativa.

co-opt [kəʊ'ɒpt] *t* nombrar como nuevo miembro (**onto,** de).

co-ordinate [kəʊ'ɔːdɪneɪt] 1 *t* coordinar. – 2 *n* MATH coordenada. – 3 **co-ordinates,** *npl* prendas de mujer que pueden formar conjunto con otras, pero que se venden sueltas.
■ **co-ordinate clause,** LING cláusula coordinada.
▲ (*sustantivo*) [kəʊ'ɔːdɪnət].

co-ordinating [kəʊ'ɔːdɪneɪtɪŋ] *adj* a juego.

co-ordination [kəʊɒdɪ'neɪʃən] *n* coordinación *f*.

co-ordinator [kəʊ'ɔːdɪneɪtəʳ] *n* coordinador,-ra.

coot [kuːt] *n* focha común.

cop¹ [kɒp] **1** *n sl* (*policeman*) poli *mf.* – **2** *t sl* (*arrest*) pillar, pescar. **3** *sl* (*take*) llevarse. – **4 the cops,** *npl sl* la pasma *f sing.*
◆ **to cop out** *i sl* rajarse.
● **it's a fair cop,** me han pillado. ‖ **to cop hold of sth.,** coger algo. ‖ **to cop it,** ganarse una buena, llevarse una buena.
■ **cop shop,** *sl* comisaría.
▲ (*verbo*) *pt* & *pp* **copped,** *ger* **copping.**

cop² [kɒp] **not to be much cop,** *phr* GB *sl* no ser nada del otro jueves, no ser gran cosa, no matar.

cope [kəʊp] *i* arreglárselas, poder: *I don't know how you cope,* no sé cómo te las arreglas; *he couldn't cope with the extra work,* no podía con el trabajo adicional; *I just can't cope!,* ¡es que no doy abasto!

Copenhagen [kəʊpən'heɪgən] *n* Copenhague.

copier ['kɒpɪə'] *n* copiadora.

copilot ['kəʊpaɪlət] *n* copiloto.

coping ['kəʊpɪn] *n* albardilla, remate *m.*

copious ['kəʊpɪəs] *adj* copioso,-a, abundante.

cop-out ['kɒpaʊt] *n sl* escaqueo: *what a cop-out!,* ¡vaya escaqueo!

copper ['kɒpə'] **1** *n* (*metal*) cobre *m.* **2** GB *fam* (*coin*) penique *m,* pela, perra. **3** *sl* (*policeman*) poli *mf.*

copperplate ['kɒpəpleɪt] *n* (*writing*) letra inglesa.

coppice ['kɒpɪs] *n* → **copse.**

copse [kɒps] *n* arboleda, bosquecillo.

copulate ['kɒpjəleɪt] *i* copular.

copulation [kɒpjə'leɪʃən] *n* cópula.

copy ['kɒpɪ] **1** *n* (*reproduction*) copia. **2** (*of book, magazine, etc*) ejemplar *m.* **3** TECH (*written text to be printed*) manuscrito, texto; (*text*) artículo, texto. – **4** *t* (*make a copy of*) copiar; (*photocopy*) fotocopiar. **5** (*imitate, cheat*) copiar: *he copied the answers from his friend,* le copió las respuestas a su amigo. – **6** *i* copiar.
● **to make good copy,** ser de interés: *disasters make good copy,* los desastres venden bien. ‖ **to write good copy,** redactar bien.
■ **back copy,** número retrasado. ‖ **rough copy,** borrador *m.* ‖ **top copy,** original *m.*
▲ (*sustantivo*) *pl* **copies;** (*verbo*) *pt* & *pp* **copied,** *ger* **copying.**

copybook ['kɒpɪbʊk] **1** *n* cuaderno. – **2** *adj* clásico,-a, modélico,-a.
● **to blot one's copybook,** manchar su reputación.

copycat ['kɒpɪkæt] **1** *n fam* copión,-ona. – **2** *adj* (*crime*) inspirado,-a.

copyright ['kɒpɪraɪt] **1** *n* copyright *m,* derechos *mpl* de autor. – **2** *adj* protegido,-a por el copyright. – **3** *t* obtener el copyright de, registrar los derechos de autor.
● **to hold the copyright on sth.,** tener el copyright de algo, tener los derechos de algo.

copywriter ['kɒpɪraɪtə'] *n* redactor,-ra publicitario,-a.

cor [kɔː'] *interj fam* ¡guau!, ¡ostras!

coral ['kɒrəl] **1** *n* coral *m.* – **2** *adj* (*made of coral*) de coral, coralino,-a. **3** (*pink, reddish orange*) de color coral.
■ **coral island,** isla coralina, isla de coral. ‖ **coral reef,** arrecife *m* de coral.

corbel ['kɔːbəl] *n* ménsula.

cord [kɔːd] **1** *n* (*string, rope*) cuerda. **2** ELEC cable *m.* **3** (*corduroy*) pana. – **4 cords,** *npl fam* pantalones *mpl* de pana.

cordial ['kɔːdɪəl] **1** *adj* cordial. – **2** *n* (*soft drink*) refresco; (*liqueur*) licor *m.*

cordless ['kɔːdləs] *adj* inalámbrico,-a.

cordon ['kɔːdən] *n* cordón *m.*
◆ **to cordon off** *t sep* acordonar.

corduroy ['kɔːdərɔɪ] *n* pana.

core [kɔː'] **1** *n* (*of earth*) núcleo, centro; (*of magnet, nuclear reactor*) núcleo; (*of computer*) núcleo magnético. **2** (*of apple, pear, etc*) corazón *m.* **3** (*most important part*) núcleo, meollo: *the core of the problem,* el meollo del problema. – **4** *t* quitarle el corazón a.
● **to the core,** *fig* hasta la médula: *he's rotten to the core,* está totalmente corrompido, está corrompido hasta la médula.
■ **core curriculum,** programa *m* de estudios obligatorios.

co-respondent [kəʊrɪ'spɒndənt] *n* JUR un juicio de divorcio, persona con quien el cónyuge demandado ha cometido supuestamente adulterio.

Corfu [kɔː'fuː] *n* Corfú.

corgi ['kɔːgɪ] *n* corgi *mf.*

coriander [kɒrɪ'ændə'] *n* cilantro, culantro.

cork [kɔːk] **1** *n* (*material*) corcho. **2** (*stopper*) tapón *m,* corcho. – **3** *adj* de corcho. – **4** *t* poner el corcho a, encorchar.
◆ **to cork up** *t sep* (*feelings*) reprimir.
■ **cork oak,** alcornoque *m.*

corked [kɔːkt] *adj* (*wine*) que sabe a corcho.

corkscrew ['kɔːkskruː] *n* sacacorchos *m,* tirabuzón *m.*
■ **corkscrew curl,** tirabuzón *m.*

corm [kɔːm] *n* bulbo.

cormorant ['kɔːmərənt] *n* cormorán *m* grande.

corn¹ [kɔːn] *n* (*gen*) cereales *mpl;* (*wheat*) trigo; (*oats*) avena; (*maize*) maíz *m.*
■ **corn oil,** aceite *m* de maíz. ‖ **corn on the cob,** mazorca de maíz.

corn² [kɔːn] *n* MED callo.

corncob ['kɔːnkɒb] *n* mazorca de maíz.

cornea ['kɔːnɪə] *n* córnea.

corned beef [kɔːnd'biːf] *n* carne *f* en conserva.

corner ['kɔːnə'] **1** *n* (*of street*) esquina; (*bend in road*) curva, recodo; (*of table etc*) esquina, punta: *let's meet on the corner,* quedemos en la esquina; *it's just round the corner,* está a la vuelta de la esquina. **2** (*of room, cupboard, etc*) rincón *m;* (*of mouth*) comisura; (*of eye*) rabillo; (*of page, envelope*) ángulo: *write the address in the top right-hand corner,* escribe la dirección en el ángulo superior derecho. **3 corner (kick),** SP (*in football*) córner *m,* saque *m* de esquina. **4** SP (*in boxing*) esquina. **5** COMM monopolio. – **6** *t* (*enemy, animal*) arrinconar, acorralar; (*person*) arrinconar. **7** COMM acaparar, monopolizar.
● **from all corners of the world,** de todas partes del mundo. ‖ **to be in a tight corner,** estar en un aprieto. ‖ **to cut corners,** tomar atajos. ‖ **to see sth. out of the corner of one's eye,** ver algo con el rabillo del ojo. ‖ **to turn the corner,** *fig* empezar a levantarse, empezar a repuntar.
■ **corner piece,** (*of book*) cantonera. ‖ **corner shop,** tienda de la esquina. ‖ **corner table,** mesa rinconera. ‖ **corner unit,** rinconera.

cornerstone ['kɔːnəstəʊn] **1** *n* ARCH piedra angular. **2** *fig* base *f,* pilar *m.*

cornet ['kɔːnɪt] **1** *n* MUS corneta. **2** GB (*for ice-cream*) cucurucho.

cornfield ['kɔːnfiːld] **1** *n* GB (*of wheat*) trigal *m;* (*of oats*) avenal *m;* (*of barley*) cebadal *m.* **2** US campo de maíz, maizal *m.*

cornflakes ['kɔːnfleɪks] *npl* copos *mpl* de maíz.

cornflour ['kɔːnflaʊə'] *n* harina de maíz, maicena.

cornflower ['kɔːnflaʊə'] *n* aciano, azulina.

cornice ['kɔːnɪs] *n* cornisa.

Cornish ['kɔːnɪʃ] *adj* de Cornualles.
■ **Cornish pasty,** empanadilla de carne y verduras.
cornstarch ['kɔːnstɑːtʃ] *n* US harina de maíz, maicena.
Cornwall ['kɔːnwəl] *n* Cornualles.
corny ['kɔːnɪ] *adj fam* (*joke, story*) gastado,-a, sobado,-a, malo,-a; (*film*) cursi, hortera.
▲ *comp* **cornier,** *superl* **corniest.**
corolla [kə'rɒlə] *n* corola.
corollary [kə'rɒlərɪ] *n* corolario.
▲ *pl* **corollaries.**
coronary ['kɒrənərɪ] **1** *adj* MED coronario,-a. – **2** coronary (thrombosis), *n* MED trombosis *f* coronaria.
▲ (*sustantivo*) *pl* **coronaries.**
coronation [kɒrə'neɪʃən] *n* coronación *f.*
coroner ['kɒrənəʳ] *n* juez *mf* de instrucción.
Corp¹ ['kɔːpərəl] *abbr* (*corporal*) cabo.
Corp² [kɔːpe'reɪʃən] *abbr* (*Corporation*) sociedad *f* anónima; (*abbreviation*) S.A.
corporal¹ ['kɔːpərəl] *adj* corporal.
corporal² ['kɔːpərəl] *n* MIL cabo.
corporate ['kɔːpərət] **1** *adj* (*collective*) colectivo,-a. **2** (*of a corporation*) de la empresa, de la compañía.
■ **corporate body,** corporación *f.* ‖ **corporate image,** imagen *f* corporativa, imagen *f* de empresa.
corporation [kɔːpə'reɪʃən] **1** *n* COMM corporación *f,* sociedad *f* anónima. **2** GB (*council*) ayuntamiento, corporación *f* municipal. – **3** *adj* GB municipal.
■ **corporation tax,** impuesto de sociedades.
corporeal [kɔː'pɔːrɪəl] *adj fml* corpóreo,-a.
corps [kɔːʳ] *n* cuerpo.
▲ *pl* **corps** [kɔːz].
corpse [kɔːps] *n* cadáver *m.*
corpulence ['kɔːpjələns] *n* corpulencia.
corpulent ['kɔːpjələnt] *adj* corpulento,-a.
corpuscle ['kɔːpʌsəl] *n* corpúsculo, glóbulo.
corral [kə'rɑːl] *n* US corral *m.*
correct [kə'rekt] **1** *adj* (*true, right, accurate*) correcto,-a, exacto,-a: *would I be correct in thinking that ...,* ¿estaría en lo cierto si pensara que ...,* sería correcto si pensara que ...; *that's correct,* eso es, correcto. **2** (*of behaviour, manners, dress*) correcto,-a, formal. – **3** *t* (*person, mistake, defect*) corregir, rectificar; (*exams etc*) corregir: *correct me if I'm wrong but ...,* puede que me equivoque, pero creo que ...; *I stand corrected,* reconozco mi error.
correction [kə'rekʃən] *n* corrección *f.*
■ **correction fluid,** líquido corrector.
corrective [kə'rektɪv] *adj* correctivo,-a.
correctly [kə'rektlɪ] *adv* correctamente.
correctness [kə'rektnəs] **1** *n* (*accuracy*) exactitud *f.* **2** (*behaviour, dress*) corrección *f.*
correlate ['kɒrəleɪt] **1** *t* correlacionar. – **2** *i* guardar correlación (**with,** con). – **3** *n* correlato.
correlation [kɒrə'leɪʃən] *n* correlación *f.*
correspond [kɒrɪs'pɒnd] **1** *i* (*match, be consistent*) corresponderse (**with,** con), concordar (**with,** con); (*be equivalent, be similar*) corresponder (**to,** a), equivaler (**to,** a): *the two stories don't correspond,* las dos versiones no concuerdan. **2** (*write*) escribirse (**with,** con), mantener correspondencia (**with,** con).
correspondence [kɒrɪs'pɒndəns] **1** *n* (*agreement, similarity*) correspondencia. **2** (*letters*) correo, correspondencia.
■ **correspondence course,** curso por correspondencia.
correspondent [kɒrɪs'pɒndənt] *n* corresponsal *mf: war correspondent,* corresponsal de guerra.

■ **special correspondent,** enviado,-a especial.
corresponding [kɒrɪs'pɒndɪŋ] *adj* (*related*) correspondiente (**to,** a); (*equivalent*) equivalente (**to,** a).
correspondingly [kɒrɪ'spɒndɪŋlɪ] *adv* (*proportionately*) proporcionalmente, en proporción; (*as a result*) por consiguiente, en consecuencia; (*used as linker*) de la misma manera.
corridor ['kɒrɪdɔːʳ] *n* pasillo, corredor *m.*
● **the corridors of power,** las altas esferas.
corroborate [kə'rɒbəreɪt] *t* corroborar.
corroboration [kərɒbə'reɪʃən] *n* corroboración *f.*
corroborative [kə'rɒbərətɪv] *adj* corroborante.
corrode [kə'rəʊd] **1** *t* corroer. – **2** *i* corroerse.
corrosion [kə'rəʊʒən] **1** *n* (*process*) corrosión *f.* **2** (*substance*) herrumbre *f,* orín *m.* **3** *fig* ruina, destrucción *f.*
corrosive [kə'rəʊsɪv] **1** *adj* CHEM corrosivo,-a. **2** *fig* (*fierce*) cáustico,-a, mordaz; (*destructive*) destructivo,-a, negativo,-a.
corrugated ['kɒrəgeɪtɪd] *t* (*iron, paper*) ondulado,-a.
corrupt [kə'rʌpt] **1** *adj* (*person, government, system, etc*) corrompido,-a, corrupto,-a; (*actions, morals, behaviour*) deshonesto,-a. **2** (*language, text, manuscript*) viciado,-a. – **3** *t* (*gen*) corromper; (*bribe*) sobornar. **4** (*language etc*) viciar. – **5** *i* corromper.
● **to become corrupted,** corromperse.
■ **corrupt practices,** corrupción *f.*
corruption [kə'rʌpʃən] **1** *n* (*gen*) corrupción *f.* **2** (*of language*) deformación *f.*
corruptness [kə'rʌptnəs] *n* corrupción *f.*
corset ['kɔːsɪt] *n* corsé *m.*
Corsica ['kɔːsɪkə] *n* Córcega.
Corsican ['kɔːsɪkən] **1** *adj* corso,-a. – **2** *n* corso,-a.
cortège [kɔː'teɪʒ] *n* cortejo.
cortex ['kɔːteks] *n* corteza.
cortisone ['kɔːtɪzəʊn] *n* cortisona.
Corunna [kə'rʌnə] *n* La Coruña.
cos¹ [kɒs] *n* (*lettuce*) lechuga romana.
cos² ['kəʊsaɪn] *abbr* (*cosine*) coseno; (*abbreviation*) cos.
cosh [kɒʃ] **1** *n* GB porra. – **2** *t* GB dar un porrazo a, aporrear.
cosine ['kəʊsaɪn] *n* MATH cosino.
cosmetic [kɒz'metɪk] **1** *adj* (*for skin, hair, etc*) cosmético,-a. **2** (*superficial*) superficial. – **3** cosmetics, *npl* cosméticos *mpl,* productos *mpl* de belleza.
■ **cosmetic surgery,** cirugía estética.
cosmic ['kɒzmɪk] *adj* cósmico,-a.
cosmonaut ['kɒzmənɔːt] *n* cosmonauta *mf.*
cosmopolitan [kɒzmə'pɒlɪtən] *adj* cosmopolita.
cosmos ['kɒzmɒs] *n* cosmos *m.*
cosset ['kɒsɪt] *t* mimar.
cost [kɒst] **1** *t* (*have as a price*) costar, valer: *how much does this book cost?,* ¿cuánto cuesta este libro?; *it cost me ten pounds to send a telegram,* me costó diez libras enviar un telegrama; *but it'll cost you,* pero te va a salir caro. **2** (*result in the loss of*) costar: *it cost him his job,* le costó el trabajo; *reckless driving costs lives,* conducir con imprudencia cuesta muchas vidas; *her decision cost her dear,* pagó cara su decisión. **3** (*calculate cost of*) calcular el coste de. – **4** *i* costar, valer. – **5** *n* (*price*) coste *m,* costo, precio; (*expense*) gasto: *the cost of running a car,* los gastos de mantenimiento de un coche. – **6** costs, *npl* JUR costas *fpl.*
● **at all costs,** a toda costa, a cualquier precio. ‖ **at cost price,** a precio de coste. ‖ **at no extra cost,** sin cargo adicional. ‖ **at the cost of sth.,** a costa de algo:

at the cost of his own life, a costa de su propia vida. ‖ **to cost an arm and a leg / cost the earth / cost a packet,** costar un ojo de la cara, costar un riñón, costar una fortuna. ‖ **to cover one's costs,** cubrir los gastos. ‖ **to cut costs,** reducir (los) gastos. ‖ **to learn sth. to one's cost,** aprender algo por experiencia propia. ‖ **to pay costs,** JUR pagar las costas. ‖ **whatever the cost,** cueste lo que cueste.

■ **cost of living,** coste *m* de la vida.

▲ *pt & pp cost.*

co-star ['kəʊstɑːʳ] **1** *n* coprotagonista *mf.* – **2** *t* coprotagonizar.

▲ *(verbo) pt & pp* **co-starred,** *ger* **co-starring.**

Costa Rica [kɒstə'riːkə] *n* Costa Rica.

Costa Rican [kɒstə'riːkən] **1** *adj* costarricense. – **2** *n* costarricense *mf.*

cost-effective [kɒstɪ'fektɪv] *adj* rentable.

costing ['kɒstɪŋ] *n* cálculo de costes.

costliness ['kɒstlɪnəs] *n* alto precio.

costly ['kɒstlɪ] *adj* costoso,-a.

▲ *comp* **costlier,** *superl* **costliest.**

cost-of-living index [kɒstəv'lɪvɪŋɪndeks] *n* índice *m* del coste de la vida.

costume ['kɒstjuːm] **1** *n* traje *m.* – **2** **costumes,** *npl* THEAT vestuario.

● **in full costume,** con el traje de salir a escena.

■ **bathing costume,** bañador *m,* traje *m* de baño. ‖ **costume drama,** drama *m* de época. ‖ **costume jewellery,** bisutería. ‖ **costume party,** US fiesta de disfraces. ‖ **fancy-dress costume,** disfraz *m.* ‖ **swimming costume,** bañador *m,* traje *m* de baño.

cosy ['kəʊzɪ] **1** *adj (room, house, atmosphere)* acogedor,-ra: *it's nice and cosy in here,* aquí se está muy bien. **2** *(chat)* íntimo,-a y agradable. **3** *pej (arrangement, deal)* de lo más conveniente. – **4** *n (for teapot)* cubreteteras *m; (for boiled egg)* cubrehuevos *m.*

▲ *comp* **cosier,** *superl* **cosiest.**

cot [kɒt] **1** *n (for baby)* cuna. **2** US *(camp bed)* cama de campaña.

■ **cot death,** muerte *f* súbita de un bebé.

cottage ['kɒtɪdʒ] *n* casita, casa de campo.

■ **cottage cheese,** requesón *m.* ‖ **cottage hospital,** GB hospital *m* rural. ‖ **cottage industry,** industria casera. ‖ **cottage pie,** → **shepherd's pie.**

cotton ['kɒtən] **1** *n (cloth, plant)* algodón *m.* **2** *(thread)* hilo (de coser). – **3** *adj (shirt etc)* de algodón.

◆ **to cotton on** *i* caer en la cuenta (**to,** de), darse cuenta (**to,** de).

■ **cotton bud,** bastoncillo. ‖ **cotton candy,** US algodón *m* de azúcar. ‖ **cotton gin,** almarrá *m.* ‖ **cotton industry,** industria algodonera. ‖ **cotton plant,** algodonero. ‖ **cotton wool,** algodón *m* hidrófilo.

couch [kaʊtʃ] **1** *n (sofa)* canapé *m,* sofá *m; (bed-like seat)* diván *m.* – **2** *t* expresar, formular.

■ **couch potato,** teleadicto,-a.

couchette [kuː'ʃet] *n* litera.

cougar ['kuːgəʳ] *n* puma *m.*

cough [kɒf] **1** *n* tos *f.* – **2** *i* toser.

◆ **to cough up 1** *t sep fam (money)* soltar, aflojar. **2** MED escupir. – **3** *i fam (pay)* soltar la pasta, aflojar la pasta. **4** *sl (confess)* cantar.

● **to have a (bad) cough,** tener (mucha) tos.

■ **cough medicine / cough mixture,** jarabe *m* para la tos. ‖ **cough sweet / cough drop,** pastilla para la tos.

could [kʊd] **1** *pt* → **can.** – **2** *aux (asking permission)* poder: *could I ask you a question?,* ¿podría hacerte una pre-

gunta?; *could I use your 'phone?,* ¿me dejas llamar por teléfono? **3** *(requests)* poder: *could I see the manager?,* ¿podría ver al director?; *could you close the door, please?,* ¿te importa cerrar la puerta? **4** *(possibility)* poder: *I could fit you in on Monday,* te podría hacer un hueco el lunes; *it could rain,* podría llover; *that could be why ...,* quizá sea por eso que ...; *they could have missed the train,* puede que hayan perdido el tren; *it could have dropped out of your bag,* a lo mejor se te ha caído del bolso; *it couldn't have been Glen, he's on holiday,* no pudo ser Glen, está de vacaciones. **5** *(suggestions)* poder: *you could always try next door,* podrías probar en la casa de al lado. **6** *(conditional use): I'm so hungry I could eat a horse,* tengo tanta hambre que me comería un buey; *honestly, I could have hit her,* de verdad, le hubiera pegado; *you could have told me!,* ¡podías habérmelo dicho!

● **could do with sth.,** necesitar algo: *I could do with a coffee,* necesito un café; *this towel could do with a wash,* hay que lavar esta toalla.

council ['kaʊnsəl] **1** *n (elected group)* consejo. **2** GB *(of town, city)* ayuntamiento: *he's on the council,* es concejal del ayuntamiento. **3** REL concilio.

■ **council chamber,** sala consistorial. ‖ **council estate,** *conjunto de viviendas propiedad del ayuntamiento alquiladas a bajo precio.* ‖ **council flat / council house,** *vivienda propiedad del ayuntamiento alquilada a bajo precio.* ‖ **council of war,** consejo de guerra.

councillor ['kaʊnsələʳ] *n* concejal,-la.

councilor ['kaʊnsələʳ] *n* US → **councillor.**

counsel ['kaʊnsəl] **1** *n (advice)* consejo. **2** JUR abogado,-a. – **3** *t (advise)* aconsejar. **4** *(give professional advice)* orientar, aconsejar.

● **to keep one's own counsel,** guardar silencio, reservarse la opinión. ‖ **to take counsel with sb.,** consultar con algn.

■ **counsel for the defence,** abogado,-a defensor,-ra. ‖ **counsel for the prosecution,** fiscal *mf.*

counselling ['kaʊnsəlɪŋ] *n* orientación *f.*

counsellor ['kaʊnsələʳ] **1** *n (adviser)* consejero,-a, asesor,-ra. **2** US JUR abogado,-a.

count[1] [kaʊnt] **1** *n (act of counting)* recuento, cómputo; *(of votes)* escrutinio; *(total)* total *m,* suma: *at the final count the liberals had won 98 seats,* en el recuento final los liberales habían ganado 98 escaños. **2** JUR *(crime)* cargo. **3** *(point in discussion, argument)* punto; *(way, reason)* motivo, razón *f: I agree with you on both counts,* estoy de acuerdo contigo en los dos puntos. – **4** *t (gen)* contar: *I'm going to count the money,* voy a contar el dinero; *have you tried counting sheep?,* ¿has intentado contar ovejas? **5** *(include)* contar: *there are five in our family, counting me,* somos cinco en nuestra familia, contándome a mí; *there'll be 100 people, not counting the children,* seremos 100 personas, sin contar a los niños. **6** *(consider)* considerar: *I count you among my best friends,* te cuento entre mis amigos íntimos. – **7** *i (enumerate)* contar: *she can count up to 20,* sabe contar hasta 20. **8** *(be valid)* contar, valer, importar: *that doesn't count,* eso no cuenta, eso no vale; *it's the thought that counts,* lo que importa es el detalle; *you're the only one who counts,* eres el único que me importa.

◆ **to count against** *t insep* perjudicar. – **2** *t sep* tomar en cuenta, tener en cuenta. ‖ **to count down** *i* contar atrás. ‖ **to count in** *t sep fam* incluir, contar con: *count me in!,* ¡yo me apunto! ‖ **to count on** *t insep (rely on)* contar con; *(depend on)* confiar en. ‖ **to count out 1** *t sep (money, objects)* contar (uno por uno). **2** *(boxer)* declarar fuera de combate. – **3** *t insep fam* no incluir, no contar con.

● **don't count your chickens before they're hatched,** no hay que vender la piel de oso (antes de cazarlo). ‖ **on the count of three!,** ¡a la de tres! ‖ **to be out for the count,** (*in boxing*) estar fuera de combate; (*be asleep*) estar frito,-a. ‖ **to count os. lucky,** considerarse afortunado,-a. ‖ **to count the cost of sth.,** (*consider all likely effects*) considerar todos los posibles riesgos de algo; (*suffer consequences*) sufrir las consecuencias de algo. ‖ **to keep count of sth.,** llevar la cuenta de algo. ‖ **to lose count of sth.,** perder la cuenta de algo.

■ **blood count,** recuento de hemoglobina. ‖ **count noun,** nombre *m* contable. ‖ **sperm count,** cuenta espermática.

count² [kaʊnt] *n* (*nobleman*) conde *m*.

countable [ˈkaʊntəbəl] *adj* contable.

countdown [ˈkaʊntdaʊn] *n* cuenta atrás: *the countdown to the election,* la cuenta atrás para las elecciones.

countenance [ˈkaʊntənəns] **1** *n fml* (*face*) rostro, semblante *m*. **2** *fml* (*support, approval*) aprobación *f*. – **3** *t fml* aprobar, dar aprobación a.

● **to give countenance to sth.,** aprobar algo, dar aprobación a algo. ‖ **to keep one's countenance,** no perder la compostura, guardar la calma.

counter¹ [ˈkaʊntəʳ] **1** *n* (*in shop*) mostrador *m*; (*individual*) ventanilla. **2** (*in board games*) ficha.

● **to be available over the counter,** (*medicines*) poderse comprar sin receta médica. ‖ **under the counter,** bajo mano, clandestinamente.

counter² [ˈkaʊntəʳ] *n* (*apparatus*) contador *m*.

counter³ [ˈkaʊntəʳ] **1** *n* SP contraataque *m*, contragolpe *m*. – **2** *adv* en contra (**to,** de). – **3** *t* (*claim, accusation*) rebatir, refutar; (*tendency, threat*) contrarrestar: *we must counter the rise in violence,* hay que contrarrestar el aumento de violencia. – **4** *i* contestar, replicar: *she countered that ...,* replicó que ...

● **to act as a counter to sth.,** contrarrestar algo. ‖ **to run counter to sth.,** ser contrario,-a a algo.

counteract [kaʊntəˈrækt] *t* contrarrestar.

counterattack [ˈkaʊntərətæk] **1** *n* contraataque *m*. – **2** *t* contraatacar. – **3** *i* contraatacar.

counterbalance [ˈkaʊntəbæləns] **1** *n* contrapeso (**to,** a). – **2** *t* contrapesar.

counterclockwise [kaʊntəˈklɒkwaɪz] **1** *adj* US en sentido contrario a las agujas del reloj. – **2** *adv* US en sentido contrario a las agujas del reloj.

counterespionage [kaʊntərˈespɪənɑːʒ] *n* contraespionaje *m*.

counterfeit [ˈkaʊntəfɪt] **1** *adj* falso,-a, falsificado,-a. – **2** *n* falsificación *f*. – **3** *t* falsificar.

counterfoil [ˈkaʊntəfɔɪl] *n* matriz *f*.

counterintelligence [kaʊntərɪnˈtelɪdʒəns] *n* contraespionaje *m*.

countermand [kaʊntəˈmɑːnd] **1** *t* contramandar. – **2** *n* contraorden *f*.

countermeasure [ˈkaʊntəmeʒəʳ] *n* contramedida *f*.

counteroffensive [ˈkaʊntərəfensɪv] *n* contraofensiva *f*.

counterpane [ˈkaʊntəpeɪn] *n* GB cubrecama *m*.

counterpart [ˈkaʊntəpɑːt] *n* homólogo,-a: *the President met his French counterpart,* el Presidente se reunió con su homólogo francés.

counterpoint [ˈkaʊntəpɔɪnt] *n* MUS contrapunto *m*.

counterproductive [kaʊntəprəˈdʌktɪv] *adj* contraproducente *m*.

counter-revolution [kaʊntərevəˈluːʃən] *n* contrarrevolución *f*.

counter-revolutionary [kaʊntərevəˈluːʃənərɪ] **1** *adj* contrarrevolucionario,-a. – **2** *n* contrarrevolucionario,-a.

▲ (*sustantivo*) *pl counter-revolutionaries.*

countersign [ˈkaʊntəsaɪn] **1** *t* refrendar. – **2** *n* contraseña.

countess [ˈkaʊntəs] *n* condesa.

countless [ˈkaʊntləs] *adj* incontable, innumerable: *on countless occasions,* en infinidad de ocasiones.

countrified [ˈkʌntrɪfaɪd] *adj* rústico,-a, rural.

country [ˈkʌntrɪ] **1** *n* (*state, nation*) país *m*; (*people*) pueblo; (*native land*) país *m*, patria, tierra. **2** (*rural area*) campo: *she lives in a very big house in the country,* vive en una casa muy grande en el campo. **3** (*region, area of land*) región *f*, zona, territorio: *this is lion country, be careful,* esta es zona de leones, ten cuidado; *the wooded country in the north is cooler,* la zona boscosa del norte es más fresca. **4** **country (music),** MUS música country, country *m*. – **5** *adj* (*rural - life, lane*) rural; (*- house*) de campo.

● **to fight for one's country,** luchar por la patria. ‖ **to go to the country,** celebrar elecciones generales.

■ **country dance,** baile *m* regional. ‖ **country dancing,** los bailes *mpl* regionales. ‖ **country seat,** casa solariega.

▲ *pl countries.*

countryfolk [ˈkʌntrɪfəʊk] *n* gente *f* del campo.

countryman [ˈkʌntrɪmən] **1** *n* (*man from country*) campesino. **2** (*compatriot*) compatriota *m*.

countryside [ˈkʌntrɪsaɪd] *n* (*area*) campo, campiña; (*scenery*) paisaje *m*.

countrywoman [ˈkʌntrɪwʊmən] **1** *n* (*woman from country*) campesina. **2** (*compatriot*) compatriota.

county [ˈkaʊntɪ] *n* condado.

■ **county council,** GB ≈ municipio. ‖ **county court,** ≈ audiencia provincial. ‖ **county town,** capital *f* del condado.

▲ *pl counties.*

coup [kuː] *n* golpe *m*.

■ **coup d'état,** golpe *m* de estado. ‖ **coup de grace,** golpe *m* de gracia.

coupé [ˈkuːpeɪ] *n* cupé *m*.

couple [ˈkʌpəl] **1** *n* (*two things*) par *m*; (*a few*) unos,-as: *a couple of days,* un par de días; *a couple of minutes,* unos minutos, un par de minutos. **2** (*two people*) pareja. – **3** *t* (*gen*) conectar, acoplar; (*railway carriage*) enganchar, acoplar; (*names, people, events*) asociar. – **4** *i arch* (*mate*) aparearse.

● **coupled with,** junto con, unido a: *no rainfall coupled with high temperatures has led to forest fires,* la falta de lluvia junto con las altas temperaturas ha provocado incendios forestales. ‖ **to have had a couple,** *fam* haber bebido más de la cuenta.

■ **a married couple,** un matrimonio.

couplet [ˈkʌplɪt] *n* pareado.

coupling [ˈkʌplɪŋ] **1** *n* (*for railway carriages*) enganche *m*, acoplamiento. **2** *arch* (*mating*) apareamiento.

coupon [ˈkuːpɒn] **1** *n* COMM (*for discount, free gift, etc*) cupón *m*, vale *m*. **2** (*form to send off for information*) cupón *m*. **3** GB SP (*for competition, football pools*) boleto.

courage [ˈkʌrɪdʒ] *n* coraje *m*, valor *m*, valentía *f*.

● **to have the courage of one's convictions,** ser fiel a sus convicciones, tener el valor de atenerse a sus principios. ‖ **to lack the courage of one's convic-**

tions, no ser consecuente con sus principios. ‖ **to pluck up courage to do sth.**, armarse de valor para hacer algo. ‖ **to take one's courage in both hands**, hacer de tripas corazón.

courageous [kə'reɪdʒəs] *adj* (*person*) valiente, corajudo,-a; (*act, decision*) valeroso,-a, de valor, de valentía; (*words*) valiente.

courgette [kʊə'ʒet] *n* calabacín *m*.

courier ['kʊərɪəʳ] **1** *n* (*messenger*) mensajero,-a. **2** (*guide*) guía *mf* turístico,-a.

course [kɔːs] **1** *n* (*direction - gen*) curso, dirección *f*; (*of ship*) rumbo; (*of river*) curso: *they were sailing a southerly course*, navegaban con rumbo sur. **2** *fig* (*direction - of person's life*) rumbo. **3** (*way of acting, plan of action*) plan *m* de acción, línea de acción: *we may have to adopt a similiar course*, puede que tengamos que adoptar una línea parecida; *what courses are open to us?*, ¿qué opciones tenemos?; *your best course of action is to forget about it*, lo mejor que puedes hacer es olvidarlo; *it's the only course of action open to us*, es lo único que podemos hacer. **4** (*development, progress*) curso, marcha: *in the course of time*, con el tiempo; *the course of events*, la marcha de los acontecimientos; *the course of history*, el curso de la historia; *in the course of the meeting*, en el curso de la reunión. **5** EDUC (*year-long*) curso; (*short*) cursillo; (*series*) ciclo; (*at university*) carrera; (*individual subject*) asignatura: *the sociology course lasts three years*, la carrera de sociología es de tres cursos. **6** MED serie *f*, tanda: *a course of injections*, una tanda de inyecciones. **7** (*of meal*) plato: *a three-course meal*, una comida de dos platos y postre. **8** SP (*for golf*) campo; (*racecourse*) hipódromo; (*stretch, distance*) curso, recorrido: *obstacle course*, pista de obstáculos. **9** (*of bricks*) hilada. – **10** *i* correr, fluir.

● **in due course**, a su debido tiempo. ‖ **of course**, claro, desde luego, por supuesto, naturalmente: *yes, of course!*, ¡claro que sí!; *of course not!*, ¡claro que no! ‖ **to be on course**, (*ship, plane*) seguir el rumbo; (*plan, company, etc*) ir encaminado,-a, llevar camino (**for**, de): *the government is on course for trouble with the unions*, el gobierno lleva camino de tener problemas con los sindicatos. ‖ **to be off course**, perder el rumbo, desviarse del rumbo. ‖ **to change course**, cambiar de rumbo. ‖ **to set course for**, poner rumbo a. ‖ **to take its course / run its course**, seguir su curso.

■ **course of treatment**, MED tratamiento. ‖ **first course**, primer plato, entrante *m*. ‖ **refresher course**, EDUC cursillo de reciclaje. ‖ **second course**, segundo plato. ‖ **sweet course**, postre *m*.

court [kɔːt] **1** *n* JUR (*place, people*) tribunal *m*; (*building*) juzgado: *he had to appear in court*, tuvo que comparecer ante el tribunal; *the court adjourned*, el tribunal levantó la sesión; *silence in court!*, ¡silencio! **2** (*royal*) corte *f*: *at court*, en la corte. **3** SP (*tennis, squash, etc*) pista, cancha. **4** (*courtyard*) patio. – **5** *t* (*woman*) cortejar, hacer la corte a; (*influential person*) tratar de ganarse el favor de, tratar de ganarse la aceptación de. **6** (*support, approval, popularity*) tratar de ganarse, buscar; (*favour, publicity*) buscar. **7** (*failure, disaster, death, danger*) exponerse a, buscarse. – **8** *i* tener novio, tener novia: *are you courting yet?*, ¿ya tienes novio,-a?

● **to go to court**, acudir a los tribunales. ‖ **to hold court**, (*entertain admirers*) estar rodeado,-a de admiradores. ‖ **to settle out of court**, llegar a un acuerdo antes de ir a juicio. ‖ **to take sb. to court**, llevar a algn. a juicio, llevar a algn. a los tribunales.

■ **court card**, figura. ‖ **court case**, causa, juicio. ‖

court jester, bufón *m*. ‖ **court martial**, consejo de guerra. ‖ **court of inquiry**, comisión *f* de investigación. ‖ **court order**, orden *f* judicial. ‖ **court shoe**, zapato salón. ‖ **court usher**, ujier *mf*. ‖ **high court**, tribunal *m* supremo.

courteous ['kɜːtɪəs] *adj* (*person, behaviour*) cortés,-esa, fino,-a, educado,-a; (*thing*) cortés,-esa.

courtesy ['kɜːtəsɪ] **1** *n* (*good manners*) cortesía, educación *f*: *he didn't even have the courtesy to say thank you*, ni siquiera tuvo la cortesía dar las gracias. **2** (*polite act or remark*) favor *m*, atención *f*.

● **(by) courtesy of**, (*favour*) por gentileza de; (*permission*) con permiso de.

■ **courtesy call**, visita de cortesía. ‖ **courtesy light**, AUTO luz *f* interior. ‖ **courtesy title**, tratamiento de cortesía. ‖ **courtesy visit**, visita de cortesía.

▲ *pl* **courtesies**.

courthouse ['kɔːthaʊs] *n* juzgado.

courtier ['kɔːtɪəʳ] *n* cortesano,-a.

courtly ['kɔːtlɪ] *adj* fino,-a, distinguido,-a.

court-martial [kɔːt'mɑːʃəl] *t* someter a consejo de guerra.

courtroom ['kɔːtruːm] *n* sala de justicia, tribunal *m*.

courtship ['kɔːtʃɪp] **1** *n* (*of people*) noviazgo. **2** (*of animals*) cortejo.

courtyard ['kɔːtjɑːd] *n* patio.

cousin ['kʌzən] *n* primo,-a.

■ **first cousin**, primo,-a hermano,-a. ‖ **second cousin**, primo,-a segundo,-a.

couture [kuː'tʊəʳ] **haute couture**, *n* alta costura.

cove [kəʊv] *n* cala, caleta, ensenada.

coven ['kʌvn] *n* aquelarre *m*.

covenant ['kʌvənənt] *n* JUR (*formal agreement*) convenio, pacto; (*clause*) cláusula, provisión *f*.

Coventry ['kɒvəntrɪ] **to send sb. to Coventry**, *phr* hacer el vacío a algn.

cover ['kʌvəʳ] **1** *n* (*lid*) tapa, cubierta. **2** (*thing that covers - gen*) funda; (*- book*) forro, cubierta. **3** (*outside pages - of book*) cubierta, tapa; (*- of magazine*) portada: *look who's on the front cover!*, ¡mira quién sale en la portada! **4** (*insurance*) cobertura. **5** (*shelter, protection*) abrigo, protección *f*. **6** MIL cobertura. **7** (*front*) tapadera, pantalla; (*false identity*) identidad *f* falsa. **8** (*substitution, reserve duty*) suplencia, sustitución *f*. **9** (*envelope*) sobre *m*: *under plain cover*, en sobre sin membrete. – **10** *t* (*place over - gen*) cubrir (**with**, de); (*- floor, wall*) revestir (**with**, de); (*- sofa*) tapizar; (*- cushion*) ponerle una funda a; (*- book*) forrar. **11** (*with lid, hands*) tapar. **12** (*hide*) tapar; (*mask*) disimular, ocultar, tapar. **13** (*extend over surface*) cubrir. **14** (*protect by shooting*) cubrir; (*aim gun at*) apuntar a. **15** (*financially*) cubrir: *do you think 50 pounds will cover it?*, ¿crees que alcanzará con 50 libras? **16** (*insurance*) asegurar, cubrir: *are you covered against theft?*, ¿estás asegurado contra robo? **17** (*deal with - book*) abarcar; (*- syllabus*) cubrir; (*- topic*) tratar; (*include*) incluir, comprender; (*provide for, take into account*) contemplar, tener en cuenta: *this book covers the period 1931-1936*, este libro abarca el período de 1931-1936; *the regulations don't cover this case*, las reglas no contemplan este caso. **18** (*of journalist*) cubrir, hacer un reportaje sobre. **19** (*travel - distance*) recorrer. **20** SP (*opponent*) marcar. **21** MUS versionar, hacer una versión de. – **22** *i* (*substitute for*) sustituir (**for**, a), suplir (**for**, a). **23** (*conceal truth*) encubrir (**for**, a). – **24** **the covers**, *npl* (*bedclothes*) las mantas *fpl*.

◆ **to cover up 1** *t sep* (*cover - gen*) cubrir; (*hide - facts*,

truth, scandal) ocultar, tapar; (- *feeling, mistake, flaw*) disimular. – 2 *i* (*body*) abrigarse, taparse. ‖ **to cover up for** *t insep* (*person*) encubrir a.
● **to cover os. (up)**, cubrirse. ‖ **to cover one's tracks**, no dejar rastro. ‖ **to read sth. from cover to cover**, leer algo de cabo a rabo. ‖ **to take cover**, abrigarse, refugiarse, guarecerse, ponerse a cubierto. ‖ **under cover**, bajo cubierto. ‖ **under cover of darkness**, al abrigo de la oscuridad. ‖ **under separate cover**, por separado.
■ **cover charge**, precio del cubierto. ‖ **cover girl**, chica de portada. ‖ **cover note**, GB seguro provisional. ‖ **cover story**, tema *m* de portada. ‖ **cover version**, MUS versión *f*.

coverage ['kʌvərɪdʒ] 1 *n* (*in press*) cobertura: *television coverage of the elections*, cobertura televisiva de las elecciones; *the death of the Prime Minister got blanket coverage*, la muerte del primer ministro recibió una cobertura exhaustiva. 2 (*insurance*) cobertura.

coveralls ['kʌvərɔːlz] *npl* US → **overalls**.

covered ['kʌvəd] *adj* (*gen*) cubierto,-a (**in/with**, de); (*roofed*) cubierto,-a, techado,-a.
■ **covered market**, mercado cubierto. ‖ **covered wagon**, carromato.

covering ['kʌvərɪŋ] *n* (*protective*) cubierta, envoltura; (*layer*) capa.
■ **covering letter**, carta adjunta.

coverlet ['kʌvələt] *n* cubrecama *m*, colcha, cobertor *m*.

covert ['kʌvət] *adj* secreto,-a, disimulado,-a, encubierto,-a.

covertly [kəʊ'vɜːtlɪ] *adv* secretamente, encubiertamente.

cover-up ['kʌvərʌp] *n* encubrimiento: *accusations of a cover-up have been denied*, se han desmentido las acusaciones de encubrimiento.

covet ['kʌvət] *t* codiciar.

covetous ['kʌvətəs] *adj* codicioso,-a.

covetousness ['kʌvətəsnəs] *n* codicia.

cow¹ [kaʊ] 1 *n* (*female adult of ox family*) vaca. 2 (*female adult elephant, rhinoceros, whale, etc*) hembra. 3 GB *fam pej* arpía, bruja: *silly cow!*, ¡tonta!, ¡bruja!
● **until the cows come home**, hasta el día del juicio final.

cow² [kaʊ] *t* intimidar, acobardar.

coward ['kaʊəd] *n* cobarde *mf*.

cowardice ['kaʊədɪs] *n* cobardía.

cowardliness ['kaʊədlɪnəs] *n* cobardía.

cowardly ['kaʊədlɪ] *adj* cobarde.

cowbell ['kaʊbel] *n* cencerro.

cowboy ['kaʊbɔɪ] 1 *n* (*gen*) vaquero. 2 GB *fam pej* (*dishonest person*) estafador,-ra, timador,-ra.
■ **cowboy boots**, botas *fpl* camperas, camperas *fpl*.

cower ['kaʊəʳ] *i* (*cringe*) agacharse; (*in fear*) encogerse de miedo.

cowgirl ['kaʊgɜːl] *n* vaquera.

cowhide ['kaʊhaɪd] *n* piel *f* de vaca.

cowl [kaʊl] 1 *n* (*hood*) capucha. 2 (*of chimney etc*) sombrerete *m*.

co-worker ['kəʊwɜːkəʳ] *n* (*workmate*) compañero,-a de trabajo, colega *mf*; (*collaborator*) colaborador,-ra.

cowpat ['kaʊpæt] *n* boñiga.

cowshed ['kaʊʃed] *n* establo.

cowslip ['kaʊslɪp] *n* primavera, prímula.

cox [kɒks] 1 *n* timonel *mf*. – 2 *t* timonear. – 3 *i* timonear.

coy [kɔɪ] *adj* (*shy*) tímido,-a; (*affectedly demure*) recatado,-a, remilgado,-a; (*secretive*) evasivo,-a.

coyote [kaɪ'əʊtɪ] *n* coyote *m*.

cozy ['kəʊzɪ] *adj* US → **cosy**.
▲ *comp* **cozier**, *superl* **coziest**.

CP ['siː'piː] *abbr* (*Communist Party*) Partido Comunista; (*abbreviation*) PC *m*.

Cpl¹ ['kɔːpərəl] *abbr* (*corporal*) cabo.

cpu ['siː'piː'juː] *abbr* (*central processing unit*) unidad *f* central de procesamiento; (*abbreviation*) cpu *f*.

crab [kræb] *n* (*shellfish*) cangrejo.
■ **crab stick**, palito de cangrejo.

crab apple ['kræbæpəl] *n* manzana silvestre.

crabbed ['kræbɪd] 1 *adj* (*of writing*) apretado,-a. 2 → **crabby**.

crabby ['kræbɪ] *adj* (*irritable, bad-tempered*) rezongón,-ona, refunfuñón,-ona, irritable, malhumorado,-a.
▲ *comp* **crabbier**, *superl* **crabbiest**.

crack [kræk] 1 *t* (*break - cup, glass, etc*) rajar; (- *bone*) fracturar, romper: *she's cracked a bone in her foot*, se ha fracturado un hueso del pie. 2 (*break open - safe*) forzar; (- *egg*) cascar, romper; (- *nut*) cascar, partir; (- *bottle*) destapar, abrir, descorchar. 3 (*hit*) pegar, golpear: *he cracked his head on the pavement*, se golpeó la cabeza contra el suelo. 4 (*whip*) hacer restallar, hacer chasquear; (*knuckles*) hacer crujir. 5 *fig* (*solve - problem*) solucionar, resolver, dar con la solución de; (- *code*) descifrar, dar con. 6 (*tell - joke*) contar. – 7 *i* (*break - cup, glass*) rajarse, resquebrarse; (- *rock, plaster, paint, wall*) agrietarse; (- *lips*) partirse, agrietarse. 8 (*whip*) restallar, chasquear; (*bone*) crujir. 9 (*voice*) cascarse, quebrarse. 10 (*relationship, system*) venirse abajo; (*person*) sufrir una crisis nerviosa; (*witness, suspect, spy*) no poder contenerse más, perder el control. – 11 *n* (*in cup, glass*) raja; (*in ice, wall, ground, pavement, etc*) grieta. 12 (*slit, narrow opening*) rendija. 13 (*of whip*) restallido, chasquido; (*of shot*) estallido; (*of thunder*) estruendo; (*of bone*) crujido. 14 (*blow*) golpetazo. 15 (*wisecrack*) réplica aguda, comentario socarrón. 16 (*attempt*) intento. 17 *fig* (*defect*) defecto. 18 (*drug*) crack *m*. – 19 *adj* (*troops, regiment, shot*) de primera.
◆ **to crack down** *i* tomar medidas enérgicas (**on**, contra), actuar con severidad (**on**, contra). ‖ **to crack up** 1 *i* (*person*) desquiciarse, venirse abajo, sufrir una crisis nerviosa. 2 (*burst out laughing*) partirse (de risa). – 3 *t sep* (*make laugh*) matar de risa.
● **at the crack of dawn**, al amanecer. ‖ **not to be all sth. is cracked up to be**, no ser tan bueno,-a como se dice. ‖ **to crack a smile**, sonreír. ‖ **to crack the whip**, *fig* apretar las clavijas, apretar las tuercas. ‖ **to get cracking**, (*start working*) poner manos a la obra; (*hurry*) moverse. ‖ **to give sb. a fair crack of the whip**, darle una oportunidad a algn. ‖ **to have a crack at sth.**, intentar algo.

crackbrained ['krækbreɪnd] *adj fam* (*idea, scheme*) descabellado,-a; (*person*) chalado,-a, chiflado,-a.

crackdown ['krækdaʊn] *n* medidas *fpl* enérgicas (**on**, contra).

cracked [krækt] *adj fam* (*mad, crazy*) chiflado,-a, chalado,-a, loco,-a.

cracker ['krækəʳ] 1 *n* (*biscuit*) galleta seca. 2 (*firework*) petardo, buscapiés *m*. 3 *fam* (*attractive person*) pimpollo; (*woman*) bombón *m*; (*man*) guaperas *m*; (*thing*) chulada, maravilla: *that's a cracker of a bike!*, ¡qué chulada de bici!; *her latest novel is a cracker*, su última novela es buenísima.
■ **Christmas cracker**, sorpresa detonante.

crackers ['krækəz] *adj fam* chiflado,-a, chalado,-a, loco,-a.

cracking ['krækɪŋ] *adj fam* (*shot, goal*) de primera, sensacional; (*pace*) muy rápido,-a.

crackle ['krækəl] **1** *n* (*of twigs etc*) crujido, chasquido; (*of fire*) chisporroteo; (*of radio, telephone*) ruido, interferencia; (*of gunfire*) traqueteo. – **2** *i* (*twigs etc*) chasquear; (*fire*) chisporrotear, crepitar; (*radio, telephone*) hacer ruido.

crackling ['krækəlɪŋ] **1** *n* (*skin of pork*) chicharrones *mpl*, cortezas *fpl* de cerdo. **2** (*sound of fire*) chisporroteo.

crackpot ['krækpɒt] **1** *n fam* chiflado,-a, chalado,-a. – **2** *adj fam* (*idea etc*) excéntrico,-a, descabellado,-a.

cradle ['kreɪdəl] **1** *n* (*for baby*) cuna. **2** (*for telephone*) soporte *m*. **3** (*scaffold*) andamio volante; (*for ship*) basada. – **4** *t* (*baby*) acunar (en los brazos), mecer.
● from the cradle to the grave, (durante) toda la vida. ‖ the cradle of sth., *lit* la cuna de algo.
■ cradle snatcher, infanticida *mf*.

craft [krɑːft] **1** *n* (*occupation*) oficio. **2** (*art*) arte *m*; (*skill*) habilidad *f*, destreza. **3** MAR embarcación *f*; AV nave *f*. – **4** *t* trabajar.
■ craft fair, feria artesanal, feria de artesanía.

craftily ['krɑːftɪlɪ] *adv* astutamente, con astucia.

craftiness [krɑːftɪnəs] *n* astucia, picardía.

craftsman ['krɑːftsmən] *n* artesano.

craftsmanship ['krɑːftsmənʃɪp] *n* (*skill*) arte *m*, habilidad *f*, destreza; (*signs of skill*) artesanía.

crafty ['krɑːftɪ] *adj* (*person*) astuto,-a, taimado,-a, mañoso,-a; (*child*) pícaro,-a, pillo,-a; (*method, idea, etc*) hábil, artero,-a.
▲ *comp* craftier, *superl* craftiest.

crag [kræg] *n* peña, risco, peñasco.

craggy ['krægɪ] **1** *adj* GEOG (*hills etc*) peñascoso,-a, escarpado,-a. **2** *fig* (*feature*) (bien) marcado,-a; (*face*) de facciones (bien) marcadas.
▲ *comp* craggier, *superl* craggiest.

cram [kræm] **1** *t* (*stuff, fill*) henchir (**with**, de), atestar (**with**, de), atiborrar (**with**, de): *she crammed the sandwich into her mouth,* se embutió el bocadillo en la boca; *they crammed six people into the car,* metieron a seis personas en el coche; *the drawer was crammed with papers,* el cajón estaba atestado de papeles. – **2** *i fam* (*learn for exam*) empollar.
▲ *pt & pp* crammed, *ger* cramming.

cram-full [kræm'fʊl] *adj fam* atiborrado,-a, atestado,-a.

cramp[1] [kræmp] **1** *n* MED calambre *m*, rampa: *I got (a) cramp,* me dio (una) rampa. – **2** cramps, *npl* (*gen*) retortijones *mpl*; (*period pains*) molestias *fpl* menstruales.

cramp[2] [kræmp] *t* obstaculizar.
● to cramp sb.'s style, cortarle las alas a algn.

cramp[3] [kræmp] cramp (iron), *n* grapa.

cramped [kræmpt] **1** *adj* (*closed in, restricted*) apretujado,-a, apretado,-a, estrecho,-a; (*schedule*) apretado,-a: *it's very cramped in here,* hay muy poco espacio aquí; *the cramped conditions in the office meant that they had to work shifts,* por la falta de espacio en la oficina tuvieron que trabajar por turnos. **2** (*writing*) apretado,-a.
● to be cramped for space, tener muy poco sitio.

crampon ['kræmpɒn] *n* crampón *m*.

cranberry ['krænbərɪ] *n* arándano.
▲ *pl* cranberries.

crane [kreɪn] **1** *n* ZOOL grulla común. **2** (*machine*) grúa. – **3** *t* (*neck*) estirar. – **4** *i* estirarse.
■ crane fly, típula.

cranium ['kreɪnɪəm] *n* cráneo.
▲ *pl* craniums o crania ['kreɪnɪə].

crank [kræŋk] **1** *n* (*crankshaft*) cigüeñal *m*. **2** (*starting handle*) manivela. **3** *fam* (*person*) maniático,-a, bicho

raro. **4** US (*grouch*) gruñón,-ona, cascarrabias *mf*. – **5** to crank (up), *t* (*car*) arrancar con la manivela.

crankshaft ['kræŋkʃɑːft] *n* (árbol *m* del) cigüeñal *m*.

cranky ['kræŋkɪ] **1** *adj fam* (*person - eccentric*) chiflado,-a, excéntrico,-a, maniático,-a, raro,-a. **2** US (*bad-tempered*) malhumorado,-a. **3** (*machine, apparatus, etc*) poco fiable.
▲ *comp* crankier, *superl* crankiest.

cranny ['krænɪ] *n* grieta, ranura.
● in every nook and cranny, en todos los rincones.
▲ *pl* crannies.

crap [kræp] **1** *n fam* (*excrement*) mierda; (*act*) cagada. **2** *fam* (*nonsense*) estupideces *fpl*, gilipolleces *fpl*; (*rubbish*) porquerías *fpl*, basura, mierda: *the film was a load of crap,* la película era una mierda. – **3** *adj fam* malísimo,-a, de mierda: *it's a crap job,* es una mierda de trabajo. – **4** *i fam* (*vague*).
● to have a crap, cagar.
▲ (*verbo*) *pt & pp* crapped, *ger* crapping.

crappy ['kræpɪ] *adj fam* malísimo,-a, de mierda.
▲ *comp* crappier, *superl* crappiest.

crash [kræʃ] **1** *n* (*noise*) estrépito. **2** (*of thunder*) trueno, estallido. **2** (*collision*) choque *m*, colisión *f*, accidente *m*: *I had a slight crash,* tuve un pequeño accidente. **3** COMM (*collapse*) quiebra. – **4** *i* (*make loud noise*) retumbar. **5** (*fall noisily*) chocar: *the waves crashed against the rocks,* las olas chocaban contra las rocas; *the building came crashing down,* el edificio se derrumbó estrepitosamente. **6** (*collide*) chocar (**into**, con/contra); (*car, plane*) estrellarse (**into**, contra): *two cars crashed into each other,* dos coches chocaron. **7** COMM quebrar. **8** COMPUT fallar. **9** *fam* (*stay the night*) quedarse a dormir. – **10** *t* (*smash - car*) estrellar (**into**, contra): *she crashed the car,* tuvo un accidente con el coche. **11** (*make noise*) hacer ruido con; (*drop noisily*) dejar caer estrepitosamente. **12** *fam* (*party*) colarse en.
◆ to crash out *i fam* quedarse frito,-a, quedarse roque.
● crash!, ¡cataplún!, ¡pataplún!
■ car crash, accidente *m* de coche. ‖ crash barrier, barrera de protección. ‖ crash course, curso intensivo. ‖ crash diet, régimen *m* muy estricto. ‖ crash helmet, casco, casco protector.

crashing bore ['kræʃɪŋ] *n* pelma *mf*, pelmazo, plomo *mf*, pesado,-a.

crash-land [kræʃ'lænd] *i* hacer un aterrizaje forzoso.

crash-landing [kræʃ'lændɪŋ] *n* aterrizaje *m* forzoso.

crass [kræs] *adj* (*remark, person*) grosero,-a, (*error*) craso,-a, garrafal; (*stupidity*) extremo,-a; (*ignorance*) supino,-a.

crate [kreɪt] **1** *n* caja, cajón *m* (para embalar). – **2** *t* embalar.

crater ['kreɪtə'] *n* cráter *m*.

cravat [krə'væt] *n* pañuelo *de hombre para el cuello*.

crave [kreɪv] *t* (*admiration, attention*) ansiar, tener ansias de.
● to crave for sth., (*gen*) morirse de ganas de algo; (*in pregnancy*) tener antojo de algo.

craving ['kreɪvɪŋ] *n* (*gen*) ansia (**for**, de), ansias *fpl* (**for**, de); (*in pregnancy*) antojo (**for**, de).

crawfish ['krɔːfɪʃ] *n* → **crayfish**.

crawl [krɔːl] **1** *i* (*move slowly - person, snake*) arrastrarse; (*baby*) gatear, andar a gatas; (*insect*) andar: *she felt an insect crawling along her arm,* notó cómo un insecto le subía por el brazo. **2** (*car, traffic*) avanzar lentamente, ir a paso de tortuga. **3** (*be covered with, be full of*) estar lleno,-a de, estar plagado,-a de: *the town was crawling with tourists,* la ciudad estaba llena de turistas. **4** *fam*

crawler

pej (try to gain favour) arrastrarse (**to**, ante), rebajarse (**to**, ante), humillarse (**to**, ante). **– 5** *n* SP *(in swimming)* crol *m.*
● **to do the crawl**, nadar a crol. ‖ **to make sb.'s flesh crawl**, ponerle los pelos de punta a algn. ‖ **to move at a crawl**, avanzar muy lentamente, ir a paso de tortuga.

crawler ['krɔːləʳ] *n fam pej (sycophant)* pelota *mf*, cobista *mf*, adulador,-ra.

crayfish ['kreɪfɪʃ] *n* cangrejo de río.
▲ *pl* **crayfish**.

crayon ['kreɪɒn] *n (charcoal)* carboncillo; *(chalk)* pastel *m*, lápiz *m* pastel; *(wax)* lápiz *m* de cera.

craze [kreɪz] *n (fashion)* moda; *(game, sport, hobby, etc)* manía: *the piercing craze*, la moda de hacerse agujeros en el cuerpo; *tattoos are the latest craze*, los tatuajes son el último grito.

crazed [kreɪzd] *adj (look, expression)* de loco,-a; *(person)* enloquecido,-a.
● **to be crazed with sth.**, estar enloquecido,-a por algo. ‖ **to become crazed**, enloquecer.

crazily ['kreɪzɪlɪ] *adv* como (un) loco.

craziness ['kreɪzɪnəs] *n* locura.

crazy ['kreɪzɪ] *adj fam* loco,-a: *you must be crazy*, estás loco.
● **like crazy**, como (un) loco. ‖ **to be crazy about sb./sth.**, estar loco,-a por algn./algo. ‖ **to drive sb. crazy**, volver loco,-a a algn. ‖ **to go crazy**, volverse loco,-a, enloquecer.
■ **crazy paving**, GB enlosado *(de diseño irregular).*
▲ *comp* **crazier**, *superl* **craziest.**

creak [kriːk] **1** *i (floorboard, stairs, joints)* crujir, hacer un crujido; *(door, hinge)* chirriar. **– 2** *n (of floorboards, boots, joints)* crujido; *(of door, hinge)* chirrido.

creaky ['kriːkɪ] *adj (floorboard, bed, stairs)* que cruje; *(door, hinge)* que chirría, chirriante.
▲ *comp* **creakier**, *superl* **creakiest.**

cream [kriːm] **1** *n (of milk)* nata, crema (de leche). **2** *(cosmetic)* crema; *(medical)* pomada, crema. **3** *(colour)* color *m* crema. **– 4** *adj* crema, (de) color crema. **– 5** *t* CULIN *(beat)* batir. **– 6 the cream**, *n fig* la crema, la flor y nata.
◆ **to cream off** *t sep fig* seleccionar.
■ **cream cake**, *(individual)* pastelito de nata; *(large)* tarta de nata, pastel *m* de nata. ‖ **cream cheese**, queso cremoso, queso para untar. ‖ **cream cracker**, galleta salada. ‖ **cream of ... soup**, crema de ...: *cream of mushroom soup*, crema de champiñones. ‖ **creamed potatoes**, puré *m* de patatas. ‖ **cream soda**, *refresco con sabor a vainilla.* ‖ **cream tea**, GB merienda *(consistente en té con bollos, pastelitos, mermelada y nada montada).* ‖ **hand cream**, crema para las manos. ‖ **suntan cream**, bronceador *m.* ‖ **whipped cream**, nata montada.

creamer ['kriːməʳ] **1** *n (powdered milk)* leche *f* en polvo. **2** US *(container)* jarrito.

creamery ['kriːmərɪ] *n (shop)* lechería, mantequería; *(factory)* fábrica de productos lácteos.
▲ *pl* **creameries.**

creamy ['kriːmɪ] *adj (like cream)* cremoso,-a; *(containing cream)* con nata.
▲ *comp* **creamier**, *superl* **creamiest.**

crease [kriːs] **1** *n (wrinkle)* arruga; *(fold)* pliegue *m*; *(ironed)* raya. **2** SP *(in cricket)* línea. **– 3** *t (make wrinkled)* arrugar; *(fold)* doblar, plegar; *(with iron)* hacer la raya. **– 4** *i* arrugarse.
◆ **to crease up 1** *i* GB *fam* partirse (de risa). **– 2** *t sep* GB *fam* matar de risa.

create [kriː'eɪt] **1** *t (make - gen)* crear. **2** *(cause - sensation, impression)* producir, causar; *(- difficulty, problem)* crear, causar; *(- fuss, scandal)* armar. **3** *(invest)* nombrar. **– 4** *i* GB *fam* armar (un) jaleo.
● **to create a diversion**, distraer la atención.

creation [kriː'eɪʃən] *n* creación *f.*

creative [kriː'eɪtɪv] *adj* creativo,-a: *creative writing*, creación literaria.
■ **creative accounting**, manipulación *f* de las cuentas.

creativity [kriːeɪ'tɪvətɪ] *n* creatividad *f.*

creator [kriː'eɪtəʳ] *n* creador,-ra.

creature ['kriːtʃəʳ] **1** *n (animal)* criatura. **2** *(human being)* ser *m.*
● **to be a creature of habit**, ser un animal de costumbres.
■ **creature comforts**, comodidades *fpl.*

crèche [kreɪʃ] *n* GB guardería.

credence ['kriːdəns] *n* crédito.
● **to add/lend credence to sth.**, dar crédito a algo. ‖ **to give credence to sth.**, creer algo.

credentials [krɪ'denʃəlz] *npl (qualifications)* credenciales *fpl.* **2** *(documents)* cartas *fpl* credenciales.

credibility [kredɪ'bɪlətɪ] *n* credibilidad *f.*
■ **credibility gap**, falta de credibilidad.

credible ['kredɪbəl] *adj* creíble.

credit ['kredɪt] **1** *n (praise, approval)* mérito, reconocimiento: *I can't claim all the credit*, el mérito no es sólo mío. **2** *(cause of honour)* honor *m*: *our nurses do the hospital credit*, nuestras enfermeras hacen honor al hospital. **3** *(belief, trust, confidence)* crédito. **4** COMM FIN *(gen)* crédito; *(in accountancy)* haber *m*; *(on statement)* saldo acreedor. **5** EDUC crédito. **– 6** *t (believe)* creer, dar crédito a. **7** COMM FIN abonar, acreditar. **– 8 credits**, *npl* CIN TV ficha técnica.
◆ **to credit with** *t sep* atribuir.
● **credit where credit's due**, reconocimiento al mérito. ‖ *"no credit given"*, "no se fía". ‖ **on credit**, a crédito. ‖ **to be a credit to sb./sth.**, hacer honor a algn./algo: *your son is a credit to you*, puede estar orgulloso de su hijo, su hijo le hace honor. ‖ **to be in credit**, tener saldo positivo. ‖ **to buy sth. on credit**, comprar algo a crédito. ‖ **to give sb. credit for sth.**, reconocer a algn. el mérito por algo: *he was given no credit for the work he did*, no le reconocieron el trabajo que hizo. ‖ **to have sth. to one's credit**, tener algo a sus espaldas. ‖ **to sb.'s credit**, dicho sea en honor de algn. ‖ **to take credit for sth.**, atribuirse el mérito de algo: *his boss took all the credit for the slogan*, su jefe se atribuyó el mérito de haber ideado el eslogan.
■ **credit account**, cuenta a crédito. ‖ **credit and debit**, debe y haber *m.* ‖ **credit balance**, saldo positivo. ‖ **credit card**, tarjeta de crédito. ‖ **credit note**, vale *m* de devolución. ‖ **credit squeeze**, restricciones *fpl* al crédito. ‖ **credit terms**, facilidades *fpl* de pago. ‖ **interest-free credit**, crédito sin intereses.

creditable ['kredɪtəbəl] *adj* loable, digno,-a de crédito, encomiable, meritorio,-a.

creditor ['kredɪtəʳ] *n* acreedor,-ra.

creditworthy ['kredɪtwɜːðɪ] *adj* solvente.

credo ['kriːdəʊ] *n* credo.
▲ *pl* **credos.**

credulity [krɪ'djuːlətɪ] *n* credulidad *f.*

credulous ['kredjələs] *adj* crédulo,-a.

creed [kriːd] *n* credo.

creek [kriːk] **1** *n* GB cala. **2** US riachuelo, arroyo.
● **to be up the creek**, estar en un apuro. ‖ **to be up shit creek without a paddle**, *sl* estar jodido,-a.

creel [kriːl] *n* nasa.
creep [kriːp] **1** *i* (*move quietly*) moverse sigilosamente, deslizarse. **2** (*move with the body close to the ground*) arrastrarse, reptar. **3** (*move slowly*) moverse poco a poco, ir muy despacio: *the traffic crept along*, el tráfico iba a paso de tortuga. **4** (*plants, vine*) trepar. **5** *fig* (*slip in*) introducirse, deslizarse: *new words creep into the language all the time*, nuevas palabras se introducen en el idioma continuamente; *mistakes creep in when you're tired*, se deslizan errores cuando estás cansado. – **6** *n fam pej* (*crawler*) pelota *mf*, pelotillero,-a; (*unpleasant person*) ser *m* repulsivo.
  ● to creep in / creep out, entrar sigilosamente / salir sigilosamente. ‖ to creep down / creep up, bajar sigilosamente / subir sigilosamente: *they crept downstairs*, bajaron la escalera sigilosamente; *inflation has crept up to 15%*, la inflación ha alcanzado un 15%. ‖ to creep up on sb./sth., sorprender a algn.: *he crept up behind me*, me sorprendió por detrás; *old age creeps up on us*, envejecemos sin darnos cuenta. ‖ to give sb. the creeps, dar asco a algn., ponerle la piel de gallina a algn.
  ▲ (*verbo*) *pt & pp* crept.
creeper ['kriːpəʳ] *n* (planta) trepadora.
creeping ['kriːpɪŋ] *adj* progesivo,-a.
  ■ creeping paralysis, parálisis *f* progresiva.
creepy ['kriːpi] *adj* escalofriante, espeluznante.
  ▲ *comp* creepier, *superl* creepiest.
creepy-crawly [kriːpiˈkrɔːli] *n fam* bicho.
cremate [krɪˈmeɪt] *t* incinerar.
cremation [krɪˈmeɪʃən] *n* incineración *f*.
crematorium [kreməˈtɔːriəm] *n* (horno) crematorio.
  ▲ *pl* crematoriums *o* crematoria.
crème [krem] *n* crema.
  ■ crème caramel, flan *m*. ‖ crème de la crème, la flor y nata. ‖ crème de menthe, crema de menta.
creole ['kriːəʊl] **1** *n* (*language*) criollo. **2** Creole, (*person*) criollo,-a. – **3** *adj* criollo,-a.
creosote ['krɪəsəʊt] *n* creosota.
crepe [kreɪp] **1** *n* (*fabric*) crepé *m*, crespón *m*. **2** (*rubber*) crepé *m*. **3** (*pancake*) crepe *m*.
  ■ crepe rubber, crepé *m*. ‖ crepe paper, papel *m* crespón.
crept [krept] *pt & pp* → creep.
crescendo [krɪˈʃendəʊ] **1** *n* MUS crescendo. **2** *fig* punto culminante.
  ▲ *pl* crescendos *o* crescendi [krɪˈʃendi].
crescent ['kresənt] **1** *n* (*shape*) medialuna. **2** (*street*) calle *f* en forma de medialuna. – **3** *adj* creciente.
  ■ crescent moon, luna creciente.
cress [kres] *n* berro.
crest [krest] **1** *n* (*of cock*) cresta; (*of helmet*) penacho, cimera. **2** (*of hill*) cima, cumbre *f*; (*of wave*) cresta. **3** (*insignia*) blasón *m*.
  ● on the crest of a wave, en la cresta de la ola.
crested ['krestɪd] **1** *adj* (*notepaper*) con timbre. **2** (*of bird*) con cresta.
crestfallen ['krestfɔːlən] *adj* abatido,-a, desanimado,-a, alicaído,-a.
Cretan ['kriːtən] *adj* cretense.
Crete [kriːt] *n* Creta.
cretin ['kretɪn] **1** *n* (*stupid person*) cretino,-a, imbécil *mf*. **2** MED cretino,-a.
cretinous ['kretɪnəs] *adj* cretino,-a.
crevasse [krəˈvæs] *n* grieta, fisura.
crevice ['krevɪs] *n* grieta, raja, hendedura.

crew¹ [kruː] **1** *n* AV MAR tripulación *f*. **2** (*working team*) equipo. **3** SP (*rowing team*) equipo de remo. **4** *fam* (*gang*) banda, pandilla: *a motley crew*, una banda variopinta; *ground crew*, personal *m* de tierra.
  ■ camera crew, equipo de filmación. ‖ film crew, equipo de rodaje. ‖ crew cut, (*hair style*) corte *m* al rape. ‖ crew member, AV MAR miembro de la tripulación, tripulante *mf*. ‖ crew neck, (*on sweater*) cuello redondo.
crew² [kruː] *pt* → crow.
crib [krɪb] **1** *n* (*manger*) pesebre *m*; (*Nativity scene*) belén *m*, pesebre *m*. **2** (*for baby*) cuna. **3** (*for cheating*) chuleta; (*copied answer*) copia. – **4** *t* plagiar, copiar. – **5** *i* copiar.
  ■ crib note, chuleta.
  ▲ (*verbo*) *pt & pp* cribbed, *ger* cribbing.
crick [krɪk] **1** *n* (*in neck*) torticolis *f*. – **2** *t* hacer un mal gesto con.
cricket¹ ['krɪkɪt] *n* (*insect*) grillo.
cricket² ['krɪkɪt] **1** *n* SP cricket *m*. – **2** *adj* de cricket.
  ● that's not cricket, eso no se hace.
cricketer ['krɪkɪtəʳ] *n* SP jugador,-ra de cricket.
cried [kraɪd] *pp* → cry.
crikey ['kraɪki] *interj* ¡caramba!, ¡ostras!
crime [kraɪm] **1** *n* (*act, offence*) delito, crimen *m*; (*law-breaking, criminal activity*) delincuencia: *a life of crime*, una vida de delincuencia. **2** *fam* (*sin*) crimen *m*, pecado.
  ● crime doesn't pay, no hay crimen sin castigo. ‖ to commit a crime, cometer un delito. ‖ to prevent crime, prevenir la criminalidad.
  ■ crime fiction, novelas *fpl* policíacas. ‖ crime rate, índice *m* de criminalidad. ‖ crime wave, ola delictiva.
criminal ['krɪmɪnəl] **1** *adj* (*case, organization*) criminal; (*act, behaviour*) delictivo,-a. **2** (*law*) penal. **3** (*disgraceful*) vergonzoso,-a, criminal. – **4** *n* delincuente *mf*, criminal *mf*.
  ■ criminal court, juzgado de lo penal. ‖ criminal damage, delito(s) contra la propiedad. ‖ Criminal Investigation Department, Brigada de Investigación Criminal. ‖ criminal law, derecho penal. ‖ criminal lawyer, abogado,-a criminalista, abogado,-a penalista. ‖ criminal negligence, negligencia criminal. ‖ criminal offender, infractor,-ra. ‖ criminal offence, delito. ‖ criminal record, antecedentes *mpl* penales, penales *mpl*.
criminologist [krɪmɪˈnɒlədʒɪst] *n* criminólogo,-a.
criminology [krɪmɪˈnɒlədʒi] *n* criminología.
crimp [krɪmp] *t* (*hair*) rizar, ondular; (*cloth, paper*) plisar.
crimson ['krɪmzən] **1** *adj* carmesí. – **2** *n* carmesí *m*.
cringe [krɪndʒ] **1** *i* (*cower*) encogerse, agacharse; (*in fear*) encogerse de miedo. **2** *pej* (*without self-respect*) rebajarse (**before/to**, ante). **3** (*with embarrassment*) morirse de vergüenza: *I cringed at the thought of meeting his parents*, me moría de vergüenza sólo de pensar en conocer a sus padres.
crinkle ['krɪŋkəl] **1** *n* arruga. – **2** *t* arrugar. – **3** *i* arrugarse.
crinkle-cut ['krɪŋkəlkʌt] *adj* ondulado,-a.
crinkly ['krɪŋkəli] *adj* (*cloth, paper*) arrugado,-a; (*hair*) rizado,-a.
  ▲ *comp* crinklier, *superl* crinkliest.
crinoline ['krɪnəlɪn] *n* crinolina.
cripple ['krɪpəl] **1** *n* lisiado,-a, tullido,-a. – **2** *t* (*person*) dejar cojo,-a, lisiar: *she was crippled for life*, quedó lisiada de por vida. **3** *fig* (*industry, country*) paralizar.
crippled ['krɪpəld] *adj* lisiado,-a, tullido,-a.
crippling ['krɪpəlɪŋ] **1** *adj* (*pain*) atroz; (*attack, disease*) que deja lisiado,-a. **2** *fig* (*debts, costs, prices*) agobiante.
crisis ['kraɪsɪs] *n* crisis *f*: *economic crisis*, crisis económica; *housing crisis*, crisis de la vivienda; *cabinet crisis*, crisis ministerial.

● **to reach crisis point,** hacer crisis.
▲ *pl* **crises** [ˈkraɪsiːz].

crisp [krɪsp] **1** *adj* (*pastry, biscuits, etc*) crujiente; (*lettuce*) fresco,-a; (*paper, banknote*) nuevo,-a; (*clothes etc*) recién planchado,-a. **2** (*weather, air*) frío,-a y seco,-a; (*snow*) crujiente. **3** (*of curls*) apretado,-a; (*of hair*) muy rizado,-a. **4** (*style, manner, reply, answer, speech*) directo,-a, escueto,-a, resuelto,-a; (*picture*) nítido,-a. – **5** *n* GB patata frita (*de bolsa o churrería*).

crispbread [ˈkrɪspbred] *n* biscote *m* delgado y crujiente.

crisply [ˈkrɪsplɪ] *adv* (*say*) resueltamente, decididamente.

crispy [ˈkrɪspɪ] *adj* crujiente.
▲ *comp* **crispier,** *superl* **crispiest.**

crisscross [ˈkrɪskrɒs] **1** *t* entrecruzar. – **2** *i* entrecruzarse. – **3** *adj* entrecruzado,-a. – **4** *adv* de forma entrecruzada.

criterion [kraɪˈtɪərɪən] *n* criterio.
▲ *pl* **criteria.**

critic [ˈkrɪtɪk] **1** *n* (*reviewer*) crítico,-a. **2** (*negative person*) criticón,-ona.

critical [ˈkrɪtɪkəl] **1** *adj* (*anaylsis, essay, work, etc*) crítico,-a. **2** (*negative, finding fault*) criticón,-ona, quisquilloso,-a. **3** (*decisive, crucial, very serious*) crítico,-a: *he's in a critical condition,* se encuentra en estado crítico.
● **to be critical of sth./sb.,** criticar algo/a algn. ‖ **to be very critical,** ser dado,-a a las críticas. ‖ **to go critical,** (*of nuclear reactor*) iniciar una reacción en cadena. ‖ **to receive critical acclaim,** recibir buenas críticas.
■ **critical temperature,** temperatura crítica.

critically [ˈkrɪtɪklɪ] **1** *adv* (*look*) con ojo crítico; (*speak*) en tono de crítica; (*analyse*) desde un punto de vista crítico. **2** (*ill*) gravemente; (*important*) fundamentalmente.

criticism [ˈkrɪtɪsɪzəm] *n* crítica: *she can't take criticism,* no soporta que la critiquen.
■ **literary criticism,** crítica literaria.

criticize [ˈkrɪtɪsaɪz] **1** *t* (*express disapproval*) criticar. **2** (*film, play, etc*) criticar, hacer la crítica de.

critique [krɪˈtiːk] *n* crítica.

croak [krəʊk] **1** *n* (*of raven*) graznido; (*of frog*) canto. **2** (*of person*) voz *f* ronca. – **3** *i* (*raven*) graznar; (*frog*) croar. **4** (*person*) hablar con voz ronca. **5** *sl* (*die*) estirar la pata, diñarla. – **6** *t* (*person*) decir con voz ronca.

Croat [ˈkrəʊæt] **1** *adj* croata. – **2** *n* (*person*) croata *mf.* **3** (*language*) croata *m.*

Croatia [krəʊˈeɪʃə] *n* Croacia.

Croatian [krəʊˈeɪʃən] **1** *adj* croata. – **2** *n* (*person*) croata *mf.* **3** (*language*) croata *m.*

crochet [ˈkrəʊʃeɪ] **1** *n* ganchillo. – **2** *i* hacer ganchillo. – **3** *t* hacer a ganchillo.
■ **crochet hook,** aguja de ganchillo.

crock¹ [krɒk] **1** *n* (*earthenware pot*) cántaro, vasija de barro. – **2** **crocks,** *npl* (*crockery*) vajilla *f sing.*

crock² [krɒk] *n* GB *fam* (*old car*) trasto, cacharro; (*old person*) carca *mf,* carroza *mf.*

crockery [ˈkrɒkərɪ] *n* loza, vajilla.

crocodile [ˈkrɒkədaɪl] **1** *n* ZOOL cocodrilo. **2** GB *fam* (*line*) fila (de dos en dos).
● **crocodile tears,** lágrimas de cocodrilo.

crocus [ˈkrəʊkəs] *n* azafrán *m.*

croissant [ˈkrwɑːsɒŋ] *n* croissant *m,* cruasán *m.*

crone [krəʊn] *n pej* vieja, bruja.

crony [ˈkrəʊnɪ] *n fam* compinche *mf,* amigote *mf.*
▲ *pl* **cronies.**

crook [krʊk] **1** *n* (*of shepherd*) cayado, gancho; (*of bishop*) báculo. **2** *fam* (*criminal*) sinvergüenza *mf,* caco, delin-

cuente *mf;* (*cheat, dishonest person*) estafador,-ra, timador,-ra. **3** (*bend, curve - in river, path*) curva; (- *in arm*) parte *f* interior del codo. – **4** *t* (*finger, arm*) doblar.

crooked [ˈkrʊkɪd] **1** *adj* (*not straight - stick, picture*) torcido,-a; (- *path, road*) tortuoso,-a, sinuoso,-a. **2** *fam* (*person, deal, etc*) deshonesto,-a, corrupto,-a.

croon [kruːn] **1** *t* canturrear. – **2** *i* canturrear.

crooner [ˈkruːnə^r] *n* cantante *mf* melódico,-a, cantante *mf* de música ligera.

crop [krɒp] **1** *n* (*plant*) cultivo; (*harvest*) cosecha: *their main crops are corn and wheat,* sus cultivos principales son el maíz y el trigo; *a bumper crop,* una cosecha récord. **2** (*group, batch*) tanda. **3** (*hairstyle*) corte *m* al rape; (*haircut*) pelo al rape. **4** (*of bird*) buche *m.* **5** (*whip*) fusta. – **6** *t* (*grass, plants*) pacer, pastar; (*hair*) cortar al rape, rapar; (*horse's tail, ears*) cortar. – **7** *i* (*of plants, fields*) darse.
◆ **to crop up** *i* (*happen, appear*) surgir.
■ **crop rotation,** rotación *f* de cultivos. ‖ **crop spraying,** fumigación *f* de cultivos.
▲ (*verbo*) *pt & pp* **cropped,** *ger* **cropping.**

cropper [ˈkrɒpə^r] *n* (*plant*) planta.
● **to come a cropper,** (*fall over*) darse un porrazo, pegarse un porrazo; (*fail*) fracasar.

croquet [ˈkrəʊkeɪ] *n* croquet *m.*

croquette [krəʊˈket] *n* croqueta.

crosier [ˈkrəʊzɪə^r] *n* báculo.

cross [krɒs] **1** *n* (*gen*) cruz *f.* **2** BIOL (*hybrid*) cruce *m.* **3** *fig* (*mixture*) mezcla, cruce *m: it's a cross between heavy rock and rap,* es una mezcla de rock duro y rap. **4** SP (*in football*) pase *m* cruzado. **5** SEW sesgo *m: cut on the cross,* cortado al sesgo. **6** (*source of worry etc*) cruz *f: we all have our cross to bear,* todos llevamos nuestra cruz. – **7** *t* (*street, river, bridge, etc*) cruzar, atravesar; (*arms, legs*) cruzar. **8** (*cheque*) cruzar. **9** BIOL (*animal, plant*) cruzar. **10** (*thwart - person*) contrariar; (- *plans, wishes*) frustrar. **11** SP (*pass - ball*) cruzar. – **12** *i* (*walk across*) cruzar (**over,** -); (*intersect, pass each another*) cruzarse: *they crossed into Spain,* pasaron la frontera a España. – **13** *adj* (*angry*) enojado,-a, enfadado,-a, furioso,-a: *he makes me so cross,* me da tanta rabia. **14** (*transverse*) cruzado,-a, transversal; (*winds*) lateral.
◆ **to cross off / cross out** *t sep* tachar.
● **cross my heart (and hope to die),** te lo juro. ‖ **fingers crossed,** con los dedos cruzados. ‖ **to cross one's mind,** ocurrírsele a uno: *it has crossed my mind that ...,* se me ha ocurrido que ... ‖ **to cross os.,** santiguarse, persignarse, hacer la señal de la cruz. ‖ **to cross swords with sb.,** pelearse con algn., reñir con algn. ‖ **to get cross about sth.,** enfadarse por algo. ‖ **to have/get a crossed line,** (*on phone*) haberse cruzado las líneas. ‖ **to have/get one's lines/wires crossed,** no hablar de lo mismo.

crossbar [ˈkrɒsbɑː^r] *n* (*of goal*) travesaño, larguero; (*of bicycle*) barra.

crossbeam [ˈkrɒsbiːm] *n* viga transversal.

crossbow [ˈkrɒsbəʊ] *n* ballesta.

crossbred [ˈkrɒsbred] *adj* híbrido,-a.

crossbreed [ˈkrɒsbriːd] **1** *t* cruzar. – **2** *n* cruce *m.*
▲ (*verbo*) *pt & pp* **crossbred.**

crosscheck [ˈkrɒstʃek] **1** *t* comprobar por otro sistema, verificar por otro sistema. – **2** *n* comprobación *f* (**on,** de), verificación *f* (**on,** de).

cross-country [krɒsˈkʌntrɪ] **1** *adj* (*running, drive, route*) campo (a) través, a campo traviesa; (*skiing*) de fondo. – **2** *adv* campo (a) través, a campo traviesa.
■ **cross-country race,** cross *m.*

▲ (sustantivo) pl *cross-countries*.
cross-dressing [krɒs'dresɪŋ] n travestismo.
cross-examination [krɒsɪgzæmɪ'neɪʃən] n interrogatorio.
cross-examine [krɒsɪg'zæmɪn] t interrogar.
cross-eyed ['krɒsaɪd] adj bizco,-a.
crossfire ['krɒsfaɪəʳ] n MIL fuego cruzado.
● **to be caught in the crossfire,** *fig* estar entre dos fuegos.
crossing ['krɒsɪŋ] 1 n MAR travesía. 2 (*intersection, crossroads*) cruce m.
■ border crossing, paso fronterizo.
cross-legged [krɒs'legɪd] adj con las piernas cruzadas.
crossly ['krɒslɪ] adv de mal humor, enojado,-a, enfadado,-a.
cross-purposes [krɒs'pɜ:pəsɪz] to be at cross-purposes, *phr* hablar de cosas distintas.
cross-reference [krɒs'refərəns] 1 n remisión f. – 2 t remitir.
crossroads ['krɒsrəʊdz] n encrucijada, cruce m.
cross-section ['krɒssekʃən] 1 n (*drawing*) sección f, corte m transversal. 2 (*representative part, group*) muestra representativa.
crosswind ['krɒswɪnd] n viento lateral.
crosswise ['krɒswaɪz] adv de través, transversal.
crossword ['krɒswɜ:d] crossword (puzzle), n crucigrama m.
crotch [krɒtʃ] n entrepierna.
crotchet ['krɒtʃɪt] n MUS negra.
crotchety ['krɒtʃɪtɪ] adj fam cascarrabias, malhumorado,-a, gruñón,-ona.
crouch [kraʊtʃ] to crouch (down), i (*person*) agacharse, ponerse en cuclillas; (*cat*) agazaparse.
croup [kru:p] n MED crup m.
croupier ['kru:pɪəʳ] n crupier mf, crupié mf.
crouton ['kru:tɒn] n picatoste m.
crow¹ [krəʊ] n ORN cuervo.
● **as the crow flies,** en línea recta. ‖ to eat crow, US humillarse.
■ crow's-feet, patas fpl de gallo. ‖ crow's nest, vigía, cofa.
crow² [krəʊ] i (*cock*) cantar, cacarear; (*baby*) gorjear; (*person*) alardear, pavonearse.
● **to crow about/over sth.,** alardear de algo, jactarse de algo.
▲ pt *crowed* o *crew*.
crowbar ['krəʊbɑ:ʳ] n palanca.
crowd [kraʊd] 1 n (*large number of people*) multitud f, muchedumbre f, gentío; (*at match, concert, etc*) público: *a crowd gathered,* se formó una muchedumbre; *the local derby drew a large crowd,* el derby atrajo mucho público; *there were crowds of people,* había muchísima gente. 2 (*particular group*) gente f; (*clique*) pandilla, grupo. – 3 t (*fill*) llenar, atestar, abarrotar; (*cram*) meter, apiñar. 4 fam (*push, put pressure on*) acosar, hostigar. – 5 i apiñarse, aglomerarse, agolparse: *people crowded round her,* la gente se aglomeraba a su alrededor.
◆ **to crowd out** t sep (*keep out*) desplazar, hacer salir.
● **to follow the crowd / move with the crowd,** seguir a la mayoría, dejarse llevar por la corriente.
■ crowd control, control m de multitudes. ‖ crowd scene, CINEM escena de masas.
crowded ['kraʊdɪd] adj atestado,-a de gente, abarrotado,-a de gente, concurrido,-a: *the shops are crowded today,* hoy las tiendas están abarrotadas de gente.
● **to get crowded,** llenarse de gente.

crown [kraʊn] 1 n (*of king, queen*) corona. 2 ANAT (*of head*) coronilla; (*of tooth*) corona. 3 (*top - of hat, tree*) copa; (- *of hill*) cima; (- *of road*) parte f central. 4 GB (*coin*) corona. – 5 t (*monarch*) coronar. 6 (*form top of, be on the top of*) coronar, rematar. 7 (*complete, conclude*) coronar. 8 (*tooth*) poner una corona en. 9 fam (*hit on head*) dar un golpe en la cabeza a, dar un coscorrón a. – 10 the Crown, n la corona.
● **to crown it all,** y para colmo.
■ crown court, tribunal m superior. ‖ crown jewels, joyas fpl de la corona. ‖ crown prince, príncipe m heredero. ‖ crown princess, princesa heredera. ‖ crown prosecutor, JUR fiscal mf. ‖ crowned head, testa coronada.
crowning ['kraʊnɪŋ] adj (*achievement, success*) supremo,-a, final, mayor; (*moment*) culminante; (*touch*) último,-a.
● **to be sb.'s crowning glory,** coronar la belleza de algn.
crucial ['kru:ʃəl] 1 adj (*critical*) crucial, decisivo,-a, crítico,-a. 2 GB sl (*excellent*) guay.
crucible ['kru:sɪbəl] n crisol m.
crucifix ['kru:sɪfɪks] n crucifijo.
crucifixion [kru:sɪ'fɪkʃən] n crucifixión f.
crucify ['kru:sɪfaɪ] 1 t (*kill*) crucificar. 2 fig (*criticize severely*) destrozar; (*punish severely*) matar; (*beat easily*) dar una paliza a.
▲ pt & pp *crucified*, ger *crucifying*.
crude [kru:d] 1 n (*manners, style*) tosco,-a, grosero,-a; (*joke*) grosero,-a, ordinario,-a. 2 (*oil*) crudo,-a. – 3 adj (*tool, device*) primitivo,-a, rudimentario,-a; (*figure, amount*) aproximado,-a. – 4 n (*oil*) crudo.
crudely ['kru:dlɪ] 1 adv (*speak etc*) groseramente. 2 (*make etc*) de manera rudimentaria.
crudeness ['kru:dnəs] 1 n (*of method, drawing, etc*) crudeza, tosquedad f. 2 (*rude remark, act, etc*) grosería, ordinariez f.
crudités ['kru:dɪteɪ] npl verduras fpl crudas.
crudity ['kru:dɪtɪ] n → **crudeness**.
cruel [kru:əl] adj (*gen*) cruel; (*winter*) crudo,-a; (*blow*) duro,-a; (*luck*) malo,-a.
● **to be cruel to sb.,** ser cruel con algn. ‖ you've got to be cruel to be kind, quien bien te quiere te hará llorar.
▲ comp *crueller*, superl *cruellest*.
cruelly ['kru:əlɪ] adv cruelmente.
cruelty ['kru:əltɪ] n crueldad f (to, hacia).
▲ pl *cruelties*.
cruet ['kru:ɪt] n (*for vinegar*) vinagrera; (*for oil*) aceitera.
■ cruet stand, vinagreras fpl.
cruise [kru:z] 1 i MAR (*for pleasure*) hacer un crucero; (*in wartime*) navegar, patrullar. 2 AUTO (*travel at steady speed*) ir, circular (*a una velocidad constante y sin forzar el motor*); AV volar, desplazarse: *we shall be cruising at a speed of 500 miles per hour,* nuestra velocidad de crucero será de 500 millas por hora. 3 sl (*look for sexual partner*) buscar plan, ir de ligue. – 4 n MAR crucero.
● **to cruise to victory,** lograr cómodamente la victoria. ‖ to go on a cruise, hacer un crucero.
■ cruise missile, misil m de crucero.
cruiser ['kru:zəʳ] 1 n (*warship*) crucero. 2 (*pleasure boat*) yate m.
cruising speed ['kru:zɪŋspi:d] adj velocidad f de crucero.
crumb [krʌm] 1 n (*of bread etc*) miga, migaja. 2 (*of information, comfort, hope*) pizca. – 3 crumbs, interj GB fam ¡recórcholis!

crumble ['krʌmbəl] **1** t (gen) desmenuzar, deshacer; (bread) desmigar, desmigajar. – **2** i (food) desmenuzarse, deshacerse; (cliff, building) desmoronarse. **3** fig (empire, support, marriage) derrumbarse; (hopes) desvanecerse, derrumbarse, venirse abajo. – **4** n CULIN compota de fruta cubierta de una masa de harina, mantequilla y azúcar.

crumbly ['krʌmbəlɪ] adj (gen) que se deshace fácilmente; (bread) que se desmigaja.
▲ comp **crumblier**, superl **crumbliest**.

crummy ['krʌmɪ] adj chungo,-a, malo,-a, horrible.
▲ comp **crummier**, superl **crummiest**.

crumpet ['krʌmpɪt] **1** n GB CULIN bollo de forma aplastada y de cierto grosor que se come tostado. **2** GB sl pej (attractive women) tías fpl buenas.

crumple ['krʌmpəl] **1** t (clothes) arrugar; (paper) estrujar: he crumpled the letter up into a ball, hizo una bola estrujando la carta. – **2** i (clothes, material, face) arrugarse; (car) abollarse.

crunch [krʌntʃ] **1** t (food) mascar, ronzar. **2** (with feet, tyres) hacer crujir. – **3** i (eat noisily) mascar, ronzar (**on**, -); (of snow etc) crujir. – **4** n crujido.
● when it comes to the crunch, a la hora de la verdad.

crunchy ['krʌntʃɪ] adj crujiente.
▲ comp **crunchier**, superl **crunchiest**.

crusade [kru:'seɪd] **1** n cruzada. – **2** i hacer una cruzada (**against**, en contra) (**for**, a favor de), hacer una campaña (**against**, en contra), (**for**, a favor de).

crusader [kru:'seɪdəʳ] **1** n HIST cruzado. **2** (campaigner) defensor,-ra, paladín,-ina.

crush [krʌʃ] **1** t (squash - gen) aplastar; (squeeze) estrujar, apretujar; (- garlic) machacar; (- grapes) prensar; (- clothes) arrugar: we crushed everyone into the car, los apretujamos a todos en el coche. **2** (smash, pound - gen) triturar; (- ice) picar. **3** (defeat) aplastar; (shock badly) abatir: her hopes were crushed, sus esperanzas se vieron destruidas. – **4** i (material) arrugarse. – **5** n (of people) aglomeración f: there was a terrible crush at the front, había una aglomeración horrible delante. **6** GB (soft drink) refresco.
● to have a crush on sb., estar chiflado,-a por algn.
■ crush barrier, valla de protección.

crushing ['krʌʃɪŋ] adj (defeat, blow) aplastante, abrumador,-ra; (reply, remark, look) demoledor,-ra, apabullante.

crust [krʌst] **1** n (of bread) corteza, cuscurro, costra; (of pie) pasta. **2** (of earth, snow) corteza.

crustacean [krʌˈsteɪʃən] n crustáceo.

crusty ['krʌstɪ] **1** adj (bread, roll, pastry) crujiente. **2** fam (person) brusco,-a, malhumorado,-a.
▲ comp **crustier**, superl **crustiest**.

crutch [krʌtʃ] **1** n (for walking) muleta: he's on crutches, anda con muletas. **2** fig apoyo. **3** GB → **crotch**.

crux [krʌks] n quid m, meollo: the crux of the matter, el quid de la cuestión.

cry [kraɪ] **1** t (shout, call) gritar. **2** (weep) llorar. – **3** i (shout, call) gritar; (of bird) chillar. **4** (weep) llorar (**about/ at/over**, por): she was crying with pain, lloraba de dolor; he made me cry, me hizo llorar; I feel like crying, me entran ganas de llorar. – **5** n (shout, call) grito; (of bird) chillido. **6** (weep) llanto.
◆ to cry down t sep despreciar. ‖ to cry off i echarse atrás. ‖ to cry out i gritar. ‖ to cry out for t insep pedir a gritos.
● a cry for help, un grito/una llamada de socorro. ‖
● for crying out loud!, ¡por el amor de Dios! ‖ it's no use/good crying over spilt milk, a lo hecho, pecho.

‖ to be in full cry, pedir a gritos. ‖ to cry one's eyes/ heart out, llorar a lágrima viva, deshacerse en lágrimas. ‖ to cry os. to sleep, llorar hasta quedarse dormido,-a. ‖ to cry wolf, llamar "al lobo", dar una falsa alarma. ‖ to have a (good) cry, desahogarse llorando.
▲ (sustantivo) pl cries; (verbo) pt & pp cried, ger crying.

crybaby ['kraɪbeɪbɪ] n fam llorón,-ona, llorica mf.
▲ pl **crybabies**.

crying ['kraɪɪŋ] **1** n (weeping) llanto, llorera. – **2** adj fig (need) urgente, apremiante; (injustice) que clama al cielo: it's a crying shame, es una vergüenza.

crypt [krɪpt] n cripta.

cryptic ['krɪptɪk] adj enigmático,-a, críptico,-a.

crystal ['krɪstəl] **1** n cristal m. – **2** adj (vase, ball) de cristal; (water) cristalino,-a.
■ crystal gazing, predicciones fpl del futuro mirando una bola de cristal.

crystal-clear [krɪstəl'klɪəʳ] adj (water) cristalino,-a; (meaning, evidence) claro,-a, transparente, obvio,-a: she made it crystal-clear, lo dejó muy claro.

crystalline ['krɪstəlaɪn] adj cristalino,-a.

crystallize ['krɪstəlaɪz] **1** t CHEM GEOL cristalizar; CULIN confitar, escarchar. **2** fig (ideas, plans, etc) materializar. – **3** i (gen) cristalizarse.

ct[1] ['kærət] abbr (**carat**) quilate m; (abbreviation) quil.

ct[2] [sent] abbr (**cent**) céntimo, centavo.

cu ['kju:bɪk] abbr (**cubic**) cúbico,-a.

cub [kʌb] **1** n ZOOL cachorro,-a. **2** Cub (Scout), (niño) explorador m.

Cuba ['kju:bə] n Cuba.

Cuban ['kju:bən] **1** adj cubano,-a. – **2** n cubano,-a.

cubbyhole ['kʌbɪhəʊl] n chiribitil m.

cube [kju:b] **1** n (shape) cubo; (of sugar) terrón m; (of ice) cubito; (of cheese, meat, etc) dado. **2** MATH cubo. – **3** t CULIN (cut into cubes) cortar en dados. **4** MATH elevar al cubo.
■ cube root, raíz f cúbica.

cubic ['kju:bɪk] adj cúbico,-a.
■ cubic capacity, AUTO cubicaje m.

cubicle ['kju:bɪkəl] n (compartment) cubículo; (changing-room in shop) probador m.

cubism ['kju:bɪzəm] n cubismo.

cubist ['kju:bɪst] **1** n cubista mf. – **2** adj cubista.

cuckoo ['kuku:] **1** n ORN (bird) cuco (común), cuclillo; (call) cucú m. – **2** adj fam (foolish) majareta.
■ cuckoo clock, reloj m de cuco.
▲ pl **cuckoos**.

cucumber ['kju:kʌmbəʳ] n pepino.

cud [kʌd] to chew the cud, phr (cow) rumiar; (person) rumiar el asunto.

cuddle ['kʌdəl] **1** t abrazar, acariciar. – **2** i abrazarse. – **3** n abrazo.
● to cuddle up to sb., acurrucarse contra algn. ‖ to have a cuddle, hacerse arrumacos.

cuddly ['kʌdlɪ] adj (loveable) adorable, encantador,-ra; (nice to cuddle) mimoso,-a.
■ cuddly toy, muñeco de peluche.
▲ comp **cuddlier**, superl **cuddliest**.

cudgel ['kʌdʒəl] **1** n porra, garrote m. – **2** t aporrear.
● to cudgel one's brains, devanarse los sesos. ‖ to take up the cudgels for/on behalf of sb./sth., salir en defensa de algn./algo, romper una lanza por algn./ algo.
▲ (verbo) pt & pp **cudgelled** (US **cudgeled**), ger **cudgelling** (US **cudgeling**).

cue[1] [kju:] **1** n THEAT pie m; MUS entrada. **2** (signal) señal f. **3** (example) ejemplo.

◆ **to cue in** t sep dar entrada a.
● **right on cue,** en el momento justo, justo en aquel instante. ‖ **to miss one's cue,** salir a destiempo a escena. ‖ **to take one's cue from,** seguir el ejemplo de.
cue² [kjuː] n (in billiards etc) taco.
■ **cue ball,** bola blanca.
cuff¹ [kʌf] **1** n (of sleeve) puño. **2** US (of trousers) dobladillo.
– **3 cuffs,** npl sl esposas fpl.
● **off the cuff,** improvisando.
cuff² [kʌf] **1** t abofetear, dar un bofetada a. – **2** n bofetada, cachete m, bofetón m.
cufflinks ['kʌflɪŋks] npl gemelos mpl.
cuisine [kwɪ'ziːn] n cocina.
cul-de-sac ['kʌldɪsæk] n calle f sin salida.
culinary ['kʌlɪnərɪ] adj culinario,-a.
cull [kʌl] **1** t (kill) eliminar. **2** (select) seleccionar, escoger.
– **3** n reducción f controlada de la población de un animal.
culminate ['kʌlmɪneɪt] i culminar (**in,** en).
culmination [kʌlmɪ'neɪʃən] n culminación f, punto culminante, apogeo.
culottes [kjuː'lɒts] npl falda pantalón f sing.
culpability [kʌlpə'bɪlətɪ] n culpabilidad f.
culpable ['kʌlpəbəl] adj culpable.
culprit ['kʌlprɪt] n culpable mf.
cult [kʌlt] **1** n (gen) culto; (sect) secta: *personality cult,* culto a la personalidad.
■ **cult figure,** ídolo. ‖ **cult film,** película de culto. ‖ **cult following,** seguidores mpl fanáticos.
cultivate ['kʌltɪveɪt] t cultivar.
cultivated ['kʌltɪveɪtɪd] **1** adj (person) culto,-a, cultivado,-a. **2** (land etc) cultivado,-a.
cultivation [kʌltɪ'veɪʃən] n cultivo.
● **to be under cultivation,** estar en cultivo.
cultivator ['kʌltɪveɪtə'] **1** n (person) cultivador,-ra. **2** (machine) cultivadora.
cultural ['kʌltʃərəl] adj cultural.
culture ['kʌltʃə'] **1** n (gen) cultura: *a person of culture,* una persona culta. **2** AGR BIOL cultivo.
■ **culture gap,** diferencia cultural. ‖ **culture shock,** choque m cultural. ‖ **culture vulture,** devorador,-ra de cultura.
cultured ['kʌltʃəd] adj (person) culto,-a.
■ **cultured pearl,** perla cultivada.
cumbersome ['kʌmbəsəm] **1** adj (thing2) incómodo,-a, voluminoso,-a, pesado,-a. **2** (procedure) torpe, engorroso,-a.
cumin ['kʌmɪn] n comino.
cumulative ['kjuːmjələtɪv] adj acumulativo,-a.
cumulus ['kjuːmjələs] n cúmulo.
cunning ['kʌnɪŋ] **1** adj (person) astuto,-a; (thing) ingenioso,-a. – **2** n astucia.
cunt [kʌnt] **1** n taboo (vagina) coño. **2** taboo pej (person) hijo,-a de puta.
cup [kʌp] **1** n (for drinking) taza. **2** SP (trophy) copa. **3** (chalice) cáliz m. **4** (drink) ponche m. **5** (of bra) copa.
● **to cup one's hands,** (to drink etc) ahuecar las manos; (to shout) hacer bocina con las manos. ‖ **to be sb.'s cup of tea,** ser del gusto de algn., ser santo de la devoción de algn.
■ **Cup Final,** final f de la copa. ‖ **cup holder,** campeón,-ona de la copa. ‖ **cup tie,** partido de copa. ‖ **paper cup,** vaso de papel. ‖ **plastic cup,** vaso de plástico.
▲ (verbo) pt & pp cupped, ger cupping.
cupboard ['kʌbəd] n (for clothes etc) armario; (for food) alacena; (for crockery) aparador m: *there's loads of cupboard space,* hay mucho sitio en los armarios.

■ **cupboard love,** amor m interesado.
cupful ['kʌpfʊl] n taza.
Cupid ['kjuːpɪd] n Cupido.
cupidity [kjuː'pɪdɪtɪ] n codicia.
cupola ['kjuːpələ] n cúpula.
cuppa ['kʌpə] n fam taza de té.
cur [kɜː'] **1** n dated (dog) chucho, perro callejero. **2** fig (person) canalla mf.
curable ['kjʊərəbəl] adj curable,' que tiene cura.
curate ['kjʊərət] n coadjutor m.
● **to be a curate's egg / be like the curate's egg,** tener cosas buenas y malas.
curative ['kjʊərətɪv] adj curativo,-a.
curator [kjʊ'reɪtə'] n (of museum) conservador,-ra.
curb [kɜːb] **1** n (for horse) barbada. **2** (control) freno. **3** US → **kerb.** – **4** t (horse) refrenar. **5** (excess, abuse) poner freno a, frenar; (feelings) dominar, refrenar, contener.
● **to put a curb on sth.,** poner freno a algo, poner coto a algo.
curd [kɜːd] n (from milk) cuajada; (from eggs, butter, sugar) crema: *lemon curd,* crema de limón.
■ **curd cheese,** requesón m. ‖ **curds and whey,** cuajada y suero (de la leche).
curdle ['kɜːdəl] **1** t (cause to form curds) cuajar; (cause to go bad) cortar. – **2** i (form curds) cuajarse; (go bad) cortarse.
● **to make one's blood curdle,** helarle la sangre a uno.
cure [kjʊə'] **1** t (illness) curar (of, de); (habit) quitar. **2** fig (problem, inflation, etc) remediar, poner remedio a. **3** (meat, fish, tobacco, etc) curar. – **4** n (for disease, illness) cura; (for problem) remedio; (return to health) curación f, restablecimiento; (course of treatment) cura: *there's still no cure for Aids,* el SIDA aún no tiene cura.
cure-all ['kjʊərɔːl] n panacea.
curfew ['kɜːfjuː] n toque m de queda.
curiosity [kjʊərɪ'ɒsətɪ] n curiosidad f.
● **curiosity killed the cat,** por querer saber, la zorra perdió la cola.
▲ pl curiosities.
curious ['kjʊərɪəs] **1** adj (inquisitive) curioso,-a. **2** (strange, odd) curioso,-a, extraño,-a; (interesting) interesante: *the curious thing is that ...,* lo curioso es que ...
● **to be curious to know sth.,** tener curiosidad por saber algo.
curiously ['kjʊərɪəslɪ] **1** adv (inquisitively) con curiosidad. **2** (strangely) curiosamente.
● **curiously enough,** aunque parezca mentira.
curl [kɜːl] **1** t (hair) rizar; (leaves, paper) enrollar. – **2** i (hair) rizarse; (smoke) formar volutas, hacer volutas; (leaves, paper) enrollarse, ondularse, rizarse; (plants, tendrils) enrollarse; (river, path) serpentear. – **3** n (of hair) rizo; (ringlet) bucle m, tirabuzón m; (of smoke) espiral f, voluta.
◆ **to curl up 1** i (person) acurrucarse; (cat) hacerse un ovillo: *I feel like curling up on the sofa with a good book,* me apetece acurrucarme en el sofá con un buen libro. **2** (laugh) partirse (de risa).
● **to curl one's lip,** hacer una mueca. ‖ **with a curl of the lip,** con una mueca.
curler ['kɜːlə'] n rulo.
curlew ['kɜːljuː] n zarapito real.
curling ['kɜːlɪŋ] n SP curling m.
■ **curling tongs,** tenacillas fpl para rizar el pelo.
curly ['kɜːlɪ] adj (hair) rizado,-a; (tail, leaves) enroscado,-a; (pattern) con volutas.
▲ comp curlier, superl curliest.
currant ['kʌrənt] **1** n (dried grape) pasa (de Corinto). **2** (fruit) grosella.

■ **currant bun,** bollo con pasas. ‖ **currant bush,** grosellero.

currency ['kʌrənsɪ] **1** *n* FIN moneda. **2** (*acceptance*) aceptación *f*.
● **to gain currency,** ganar fuerza, extenderse.
■ **hard currency,** divisa fuerte.
▲ *pl* **currencies**.

current ['kʌrənt] **1** *adj* (*present, existing - gen*) actual; (*- month, year*) en curso; (*most recent - issue*) último,-a; (*- legislation, licence*) vigente. **2** (*generally accepted*) corriente, común, habitual, general. **– 3** *n* (*gen*) corriente *f*.
■ **current account,** cuenta corriente.

currently ['kʌrəntlɪ] **1** *adv* (*at present*) actualmente, en la actualidad. **2** (*commonly*) comúnmente.

curriculum [kə'rɪkjələm] *n* EDUC plan *m* de estudios.
■ **curriculum vitae,** currículum *m,* historial *m*.

curry[1] ['kʌrɪ] **1** *n* CULIN curry *m*: *we had a very hot chicken curry,* comimos un pollo al curry muy picante. **– 2** *t* preparar al curry.
■ **curry powder,** curry *m*.
▲ (*sustantivo*) *pl* **curries**; (*verbo*) *pt & pp* **curried**, *ger* **currying**.

curry[2] ['kʌrɪ] *t* (*leather*) curtir; (*horse*) almohazar.
● **to curry favour with sb.,** congraciarse con algn.
▲ (*verbo*) *pt & pp* **curried**, *ger* **currying**.

currycomb ['kʌrɪkəʊm] *n* almohaza.

curse [kɜːs] **1** *n* (*evil spell*) maldición *f*. **2** (*oath*) palabrota. **3** *fig* (*cause of trouble*) azote *m,* plaga, lacra; (*burden*) cruz *f,* carga. **– 4** *t* (*put evil spell on*) maldecir. **5** (*utter curses*) maldecir; (*swear at*) insultar: *I cursed him for making me late,* le maldije por hacerme llegar tarde. **– 6** *i* maldecir, decir palabrotas, blasfemar. **– 7 the curse,** *n* (*period*) la regla.

cursed [kɜːst] *adj* (*damned*) maldito,-a.
● **to be cursed with sth.,** padecer de algo.

cursive ['kɜːsɪv] *adj* cursivo,-a.

cursor ['kɜːsə'] *n* cursor *m*.

cursorily ['kɜːsərəlɪ] *adv* someramente, por encima, superficialmente.

cursory ['kɜːsərɪ] *adj* (*glance, look*) rápido,-a; (*study, reading*) superficial, por encima.

curt [kɜːt] *adj* seco,-a, brusco,-a, cortante.

curtail [kɜː'teɪl] *t* (*spending*) reducir; (*rights, freedom*) restringir; (*speech, holiday, text*) abreviar, acortar.

curtain ['kɜːtən] **1** *n* (*gen*) cortina. **2** THEAT telón *m*. **3** *fig* (*of rain, mist, smoke*) cortina, velo; (*of fog*) manto; (*of secrecy*) halo, velo.
◆ **to curtain off** *t sep* separar con una cortina.
● **"curtain up at ..."**, THEAT "la obra empieza a ...". ‖ **to be curtains for sb./sth.,** ser el fin de algn./algo: *it's curtains for you,* estás acabado. ‖ **to draw the curtains,** correr las cortinas.
■ **curtain call,** llamada a escena, salida a escena. ‖ **curtain rail,** riel *m*. ‖ **curtain raiser,** (*in theatre*) entremés *m,* sainete *m*; (*foretaste*) aperitivo. ‖ **curtain rod,** varilla de la cortina. ‖ **net curtain,** visillo. ‖ **the Iron Curtain,** el telón de acero.

curtsey ['kɜːtsɪ] **1** *n* reverencia. **– 2** *i* hacer una reverencia.

curtsy ['kɜːtsɪ] *n* → **curtsey**.
▲ *pl* **curtsies**.

curvaceous [kɜː'veɪʃəs] *adj* curvilíneo,-a.

curvature ['kɜːvətʃə'] **1** *n* (*of surface*) curvatura. **2** MED encorvamiento.

curve [kɜːv] **1** *n* (*gen*) curva. **– 2** *t* encorvar. **– 3** *i* (*of road, river, ball*) describir una curva, torcer; (*surface*) estar curvado,-a, combarse, encorvarse.

curved [kɜːvd] *adj* (*line*) curvo,-a; (*surface*) curvado,-a.

curvy ['kɜːvɪ] *adj* (*line*) curvo,-a; (*road*) con muchas curvas; (*figure*) curvilíneo,-a.
▲ *comp* **curvier**, *superl* **curviest**.

cushion ['kʊʃən] **1** *n* (*gen*) cojín *m*; (*large*) almohadón *m*. **2** (*on billiard table*) banda. **3** *fig* (*protection*) amortiguador *m*. **– 4** *t fig* (*blow, fall*) suavizar, amortiguar; (*person*) proteger.
■ **air cushion,** colchón *m* de aire.

cushy ['kʊʃɪ] *adj* fácil, cómodo,-a.
■ **cushy number,** chollo.
▲ *comp* **cushier**, *superl* **cushiest**.

cusp [kʌsp] **1** *n* ASTROL cúspide *f*. **2** (*of curves*) vértice *m*; (*of moon*) cuerno.

cussed ['kʌsɪd] *adj fam* terco,-a, tozudo,-a, difícil.

custard ['kʌstəd] *n* (*cold, set*) natillas *fpl*; (*hot, liquid*) crema.
■ **custard apple,** chirimoya.

custodian [kʌs'təʊdɪən] *n* (*of museum*) conservador,-ra; (*of morals*) guardián,-ana.

custody ['kʌstədɪ] **1** *n* (*care*) custodia, guarda. **2** (*imprisonment*) encarcelamiento.
● **to award/grant custody of sb. to sb.,** otorgar la custodia de algn. a algn. ‖ **to be in (police) custody,** estar detenido,-a en prisión preventiva. ‖ **to remand in custody,** decretar la prisión preventiva: *he was remanded in custody,* se decretó su prisión preventiva. ‖ **to leave sth. in safe custody,** dejar algo en un lugar seguro. ‖ **to take sb. into custody,** detener a algn.

custom ['kʌstəm] **1** *n* (*tradition, habit*) costumbre *f*: *it is his custom retire to bed early,* tiene por costumbre acostarse pronto. **2** COMM (*patronage*) clientela.
● **to lose custom,** perder clientes, perder clientela. ‖ **to withdraw one's custom / take one's custom elsewhere,** dejar de ser cliente de una tienda.

customary ['kʌstəmərɪ] *adj* (*habitual*) acostumbrado,-a, habitual, de costumbre; (*traditional*) tradicional.

custom-built [kʌstəm'bɪlt] *adj* hecho,-a por encargo.

customer ['kʌstəmə'] **1** *n* (*client*) cliente *mf*. **2** *fam* (*person*) tipo,-a.
■ **customer services,** servicio al cliente.

customize ['kʌstəmaɪz] *t* hacer por encargo, hacer a la medida.

custom-made [kʌstəm'meɪd] *adj* (*clothes etc*) hecho,-a a medida; (*furniture*) hecho,-a de encargo, hecho,-a a medida.

customs ['kʌstəmz] *n* aduana.
● **to go through customs,** pasar por la aduana.
■ **customs duty,** derechos de aduana. ‖ **customs house,** aduana. ‖ **customs officer,** agente *mf* de aduana.
▲ *Puede ser tanto singular como plural.*

cut [kʌt] **1** *t* (*gen*) cortar; (*stone, glass*) tallar; (*record*) grabar; (*key, hole*) hacer: *I've cut my hand,* me he cortado la mano; *you've had your hair cut,* te has cortado el pelo. **2** (*divide*) cortar, partir, dividir: *cut it in two,* córtalo por la mitad; *he cut the cake into eight pieces,* cortó el pastel en ocho trozos. **3** (*reduce - level, number*) reducir; (*budget, spending*) recortar; (*- price*) rebajar, reducir: *the firm cut the workforce by 50%,* la empresa redujo la plantilla en un 50%. **4** (*shorten*) acortar; (*remove*) cortar; (*edit*) editar; (*censor*) hacer cortes en, censurar: *a scene has been cut from the film,* han cortado una escena de la película. **5** (*hurt feelings of, cause pain*) herir. **6** (*adulterate*) mezclar, cortar. **– 7** *i* (*knife, scissors*) cortar. **8** (*of food*) cortarse. **9** CINEM cortar: *cut!,* ¡corten! **– 10** *n* (*wound,*

incision) corte *m*; (*deep cut*) tajo; (*knife wound*) cuchillada. 11 (*of meat - joint*) corte *m*; (*- piece cut off*) trozo. 12 (*share*) parte *f*, tajada. 13 (*reduction - in budget, services, wages*) recorte *m*; (*- in level, number, price*) reducción *f*: **tax cuts,** reducción de impuestos; *fight the cuts!,* ¡luchad contra los recortes! 14 (*deletion, removal*) corte *m*; (*part deleted*) trozo omitido. 15 ELEC corte *m*, apagón *m*: *there's been a power cut,* han cortado la luz. 16 (*of hair, garment*) corte *m*. 17 (*insult*) desaire *m*, corte *m*. − 18 *adj* (*flowers*) cortado,-a; (*glass*) tallado,-a.
◆ **to cut across** 1 *t insep* (*go across limits of*) trascender. 2 (*take short cut*) cortar por, tomar un atajo a través de. ‖ **to cut back** 1 *t sep* (*prune*) podar, recortar. 2 (*reduce - budget, spending*) recortar, reducir. − 3 *i* reducir gastos. ‖ **to cut back on** *t insep* (*reduce*) reducir, recortar: *the government plans to cut back on non-essential services,* el gobierno piensa hacer recortes en los servicios no esenciales. ‖ **to cut down** *t sep* (*tree*) talar, cortar; (*kill*) matar. ‖ **to cut down on** *t insep* (*reduce*) reducir el consumo de, consumir menos: *you must cut down on cigarettes,* tienes que fumar menos. ‖ **to cut in** 1 *i* (*interrupt*) interrumpir. 2 AUTO *meterse delante de otro coche cerrándole el paso: that car just cut in in front of me!,* ¡ese coche acaba de meterse delante mío!, ¡ese coche me acaba de cerrar! ‖ **to cut off** 1 *t sep* (*sever*) cortar; (*limb*) amputar, cortar. 2 (*disconnect, discontinue*) cortar: *our phone's been cut off,* nos han cortado el teléfono; *we were cut off,* se cortó la comunicación. 3 (*isolate, separate*) aislar: *she felt cut off,* se sentía aislada. 4 *fig* (*disinherit*) desheredar. ‖ **to cut out** 1 *t sep* (*from newspaper*) recortar; (*in sewing*) cortar. 2 (*exclude*) suprimir, eliminar: *cut it out!,* ¡basta ya!, ¡corta el rollo! − 3 *i* (*of machine, engine*) pararse. ‖ **to cut up** 1 *t sep* (*in small pieces*) cortar en pedazos. 2 *fam* (*upset*) disgustar.
● **cut the crap!,** ¡corta el rollo! ‖ **to be a cut above sb./sth.,** ser superior a algn./algo. ‖ **to be cut out for sth.,** estar hecho,-a para algo. ‖ **to be cut up about sth.,** estar disgustado por algo, estar afectado,-a por algo. ‖ **to cut a long story short,** en resumidas cuentas. ‖ **to cut a tooth,** salirle un diente a uno. ‖ **to cut both/two ways,** ser de doble filo. ‖ **to cut classes/school/lessons,** hacer novillos. ‖ **to cut one's hair,** cortarse el pelo (uno,-a mismo,-a). ‖ **to cut it fine,** llegar con el tiempo justo, dejar poco margen. ‖ **to cut no ice (with sb.),** no convencer (a algn.). ‖ **to cut off one's nose to spite one's face,** tirar piedras sobre su tejado. ‖ **to cut one's losses,** reducir las pérdidas. ‖ **to cut sb. dead,** desairar a algn., volverle la cara a algn. ‖ **to cut sb. down in their prime,** segar la juventud de algn. ‖ **to cut sb. down to size,** bajarle los humos a algn. ‖ **to cut sb. loose/free,** soltar a algn. ‖ **to cut sth./sb. short,** interrumpir algo/a algn., cortar algo/a algn. en seco. ‖ **to cut the ground from under sb.'s feet,** echar por tierra los planes de algn. ‖ **to have one's work cut out,** costarle a uno, tener que trabajar mucho.
■ **the cut and thrust (of sth.),** el toma y daca (de algo).
▲ (*verbo*) *pt & pp* **cut,** *ger* **cutting.**
cutaneous [kjuːˈteɪnɪəs] *adj* cutáneo,-a.
cutback [ˈkʌtbæk] *n* reducción *f*, recorte *m*.
cute [kjuːt] 1 *adj* (*sweet*) mono,-a, rico,-a; (*good-looking*) guapo,-a, lindo,-a. 2 US (*clever*) listo,-a.
cuticle [ˈkjuːtɪkəl] *n* cutícula.
cutlass [ˈkʌtləs] *n* alfanje *m*.
cutlery [ˈkʌtlərɪ] *n* cubiertos *mpl*, cubertería.

cutlet [ˈkʌtlət] 1 *n* CULIN (*meat chop*) chuleta. 2 (*croquette*) croqueta (*de forma aplastada*).
cutoff [ˈkʌtɒf] 1 *n* (*level, point*) límite *m*, tope *m*. 2 (*stopping*) corte *m*, cese *m*. − 3 **cutoffs,** *npl* (*shorts*) bermudas *fpl* vaqueras.
■ **cutoff date,** fecha límite, fecha tope.
cutout [ˈkʌtaʊt] 1 *n* (*shape*) recortable *m*, figura para recortar. 2 (*device, switch*) cortacircuitos *m*.
cut-price [kʌtˈpraɪs] *adj* (*goods*) a precio rebajado; (*shop*) de ocasión.
cutter [ˈkʌtəʳ] 1 *n* (*person*) cortador,-ra. 2 (*tool*) cúter *m*; (*machine, knife*) cortadora: *cigar cutter,* cortapuros. 3 MAR (*ship's boat*) bote *m*; (*sailing boat*) cúter *m*; (*government ship*) patrullero, guardacostas *m*. − 4 **cutters,** *npl* (*for wire*) cizalla, cortaalambres *m*.
cutthroat [ˈkʌtθrəʊt] *adj* feroz, salvaje.
■ **cutthroat razor,** navaja.
cutting [ˈkʌtɪŋ] 1 *n* (*from newspaper*) recorte *m*. 2 BOT esqueje *m*. 3 (*for road, railway*) tajo. − 4 *adj* (*tool, blade*) cortante; (*wind*) penetrante, cortante; (*remark*) mordaz, hiriente: *the cutting edge,* el filo.
■ **cutting room,** sala de montaje.
cuttlefish [ˈkʌtəlfɪʃ] *n* jibia, sepia.
cv [ˈsiːˈviː] *abbr* (*curriculum vitae*) currículum *m* vitae.
cwt [ˈhʌndrədweɪt] *abbr* (*hundredweight*) quintal *m*.
cyanide [ˈsaɪənaɪd] *n* cianuro.
cybernetics [saɪbəˈnetɪks] *n* cibernética.
cyclamen [ˈsɪkləmən] *n* ciclamen *m*.
cycle [ˈsaɪkəl] 1 *n* (*series of events, of songs etc*) ciclo; (*of washing machine*) programa *m*. 2 (*bicycle*) bicicleta; (*motorcycle*) moto *f*. − 3 *i* ir en bicicleta.
■ **cycle lane/path/way,** carril *m* para bicicletas. ‖ **cycle track,** velódromo.
cyclic [ˈsɪklɪk, ˈsaɪklɪk] *adj* cíclico,-a.
cyclical [ˈsɪklɪkəl, ˈsaɪklɪkəl] *adj* cíclico,-a.
cycling [ˈsaɪklɪŋ] *n* ciclismo.
● **to go cycling,** ir en bicicleta.
cyclist [ˈsaɪklɪst] *n* ciclista *mf*.
cyclone [ˈsaɪkləʊn] *n* METEOR (*windstorm*) ciclón *m*; (*low pressure area*) ciclón *m*, borrasca.
cygnet [ˈsɪgnət] *n* pollo de cisne.
cylinder [ˈsɪlɪndəʳ] 1 *n* (*shape*) cilindro. 2 (*in engine*) cilindro. 3 (*for gas*) bombona. 4 (*of gun*) tambor *m*.
cylindrical [sɪˈlɪndrɪkəl] *adj* cilíndrico,-a.
cymbal [ˈsɪmbəl] *n* címbalo, platillo.
cynic [ˈsɪnɪk] *n* cínico,-a.
cynical [ˈsɪnɪkəl] *adj* cínico,-a.
cynicism [ˈsɪnɪsɪzəm] *n* cinismo.
cypress [ˈsaɪprəs] *n* ciprés *m*.
Cypriot [ˈsɪprɪət] 1 *adj* chipriota,-a. − 2 *n* (*person*) chipriota *mf*. 3 (*language*) chipriota *m*.
Cyprus [ˈsaɪprəs] *n* Chipre *m*.
cyst [sɪst] *n* quiste *m*.
cystic fibrosis [sɪstɪkfaɪˈbrəʊsɪs] *n* fibrosis *f* quística.
cystitis [sɪˈstaɪtɪs] *n* cistitis *f*.
czar [zɑːʳ] *n* zar *m*.
Czech [tʃek] 1 *adj* checo,-a. − 2 *n* (*person*) checo,-a. 3 (*language*) checo.
■ **Czech Republic,** República Checa.
Czechoslovak [tʃekəˈsləʊvæk] 1 *adj* checoslovaco,-a. − 2 *n* checoslovaco,-a.
Czechoslovakia [tʃekəsləˈvækɪə] *n* Checoslovaquia.
Czechoslovakian [tʃekəsləˈvækɪən] 1 *adj* checoslovaco,-a. − 2 *n* checoslovaco,-a

D

D, d [diː] **1** n (the letter) D, d f. **2** MUS re m.
'd [əd] **1** aux → **would**: I'd go, iría. **2** → **had**: he'd seen, había visto. **3** fam → **did**: what'd you do?, ¿qué hiciste?
D.A. [ˈdiːˈeɪ] abbr US (District Attorney) fiscal mf.
dab¹ [dæb] **1** n (of paint) toque m; (of perfume) gota; (of butter) poquito. **– 2** t (touch gently) tocar ligeramente, dar ligeros toques en: she dabbed the sweat from his brow, le secó suavemente el sudor de la frente. **3** (apply with light strokes) dar unos toques de, aplicar un poquito de: she dabbed some perfume behind her ears, se puso unas gotas de perfume detrás de las orejas; he dabbed the wound with antiseptic, aplicó un poquito de antiséptico en la herida. **– 4** i dar ligeros toques (**at**, en): the nurse dabbed at the cut with cotton wool, le enfermera limpió suavemente la herida con algodón. **– 5** dabs, npl GB sl (fingerprints) huellas fpl dactilares.
▲ (verbo) pt & pp dabbed, ger dabbing.
dab² [dæb] n (fish) ≈ acedía.
dab³ [dæb] to be a dab hand at sth., n tener buena mano para algo, ser un manitas para algo.
dabble [ˈdæbəl] **1** i (in activity) aficionarse (**in**, a), tener escarceos (**in**, con): he dabbled in politics when he was young, tuvo sus escarceos con la política cuando era joven. **– 2** t (in water) chapotear.
dabbler [ˈdæbləʳ] n aficionado,-a, amateur mf, diletante mf.
dachshund [ˈdækshʊnd] n perro salchicha.
dad [dæd] n fam papá m.
daddy [ˈdædɪ] n fam papá m, papi m.
▲ pl daddies.
daddy-longlegs [dædɪˈlɒŋlegz] n GB fam típula.
▲ pl daddy-longlegs.
daffodil [ˈdæfədɪl] n narciso.
daft [dɑːft] adj GB fam (person) chalado,-a, chiflado,-a; (idea, action) tonto,-a.
dagger [ˈdægəʳ] **1** n (weapon) daga, puñal m. **2** (obelisk) cruz f.
● to be at daggers drawn with sb., estar a matar con algn. ‖ to look daggers at sb., fulminar a algn. con la mirada, asesinar a algn. con la vista.
dahlia [ˈdeɪljə] n dalia.
daily [ˈdeɪlɪ] **1** adj (newspaper, prayers) diario,-a; (routine) diario,-a, cotidiano,-a: our daily bread, el pan nuestro de cada día; he is paid on a daily basis, le pagan por días. **– 2** adv diariamente, a diario: twice daily, dos veces al día. **– 3** n (newspaper) diario. **4** daily (help), GB fam (cleaning woman) asistenta, mujer f de la limpieza.
● to earn one's daily bread, ganarse la vida, ganarse el pan.
▲ (sustantivo) pl dailies.
daintily [ˈdeɪntɪlɪ] adv delicadamente, finamente.
dainty [ˈdeɪntɪ] **1** adj (delicate - thing) delicado,-a, fino,-a; (- person) precioso,-a, delicado,-a, refinado,-a. **2** (refined) refinado,-a; (fastidious) remilgado,-a, melindroso,-a. **– 3** dainties, npl (small cakes) pastelitos mpl.

▲ comp daintier, superl daintiest.
dairy [ˈdeərɪ] **1** n (on farm) vaquería. **2** (shop) lechería; (company) central f lechera.
■ dairy cattle, ganado lechero. ‖ dairy farm, granja lechera. ‖ dairy farming, industria lechera. ‖ dairy produce, productos mpl lácteos.
▲ pl dairies.
dais [ˈdeɪɪs] n (raised platform) tarima; (stage) estrado, tribuna.
▲ pl daises.
daisy [ˈdeɪzɪ] n margarita.
● to be pushing up (the) daisies, estar criando malvas.
■ daisy chain, guirnalda de margaritas.
▲ pl daisies.
daisywheel [ˈdeɪzɪwiːl] n margarita.
■ daisywheel printer, impresora de margarita.
Dakota [dəˈkəʊtə] n Dakota.
■ North Dakota, Dakota del Norte. ‖ South Dakota, Dakota del Sur.
dale [deɪl] n valle m.
dally [ˈdælɪ] i (waste time) perder el tiempo; (linger) entretenerse (**about**, -): he dallied over the work, tardó mucho en hacer el trabajo.
◆ to dally with t insep (person) jugar con; (idea) acariciar.
▲ pt & pp dallied, ger dallying.
Dalmatian [dælˈmeɪʃən] n perro dálmata, dálmata m.
dam¹ [dæm] **1** n (barrier) dique m. **2** (reservoir) embalse m, presa. **– 3** to dam (up), t represar, embalsar.
◆ to dam up t sep fig reprimir, contener.
▲ (verbo) pt & pp dammed, ger damming.
dam² [dæm] n ZOOL madre f.
damage [ˈdæmɪdʒ] **1** n (gen) daño; (to reputation, cause, health) perjuicio, daños mpl; (destruction) destrozos mpl, daños mpl, estragos mpl: the scandal did a great deal of damage to his reputation, el escándalo causó grave perjuicio a su reputación; the storm caused serious damage to several buildings, la tormenta produjo daños importantes en varios edificios. **– 2** t (gen) dañar, hacer daño a; (health, reputation, cause) dañar, perjudicar: smoking damages your health, el tabaco perjudica la salud; the theatre was severely damaged by the fire, el teatro sufrió grandes daños en el incendio; it has damaged her self-confidence, su autoestima se ha visto mermada. **– 3** damages, npl JUR daños mpl y perjuicios.
● to be damaged / get damaged, dañarse. ‖ what's the damage?, (asking for bill) tráeme la dolorosa, ¿cuánto se debe?
■ brain damage, lesión f cerebral.
damaging [ˈdæmɪdʒɪŋ] adj perjudicial (**to**, para).
Damascus [dəˈmæskəs] n Damasco.
damask [ˈdæməsk] n damasco.
dame [deɪm] **1** n US fam mujer f, tía, tipa. **2** (in pantomime) vieja (representada por un hombre). **3** Dame, GB (title) título honorífico concedido a una mujer.

dammit ['dæmɪt] *interj* ¡mecachis!
● **as near as dammit,** poco más o menos.
damn [dæm] **1** *interj fam* ¡mecachis!, ¡caray! – **2** *adj fam* maldito,-a, condenado,-a, puñetero,-a: *damn fool!,* ¡maldito imbécil! – **3** *adv fam* muy, sumamente: *you know damn well what I'm talking about,* sabes muy bien de qué estoy hablando; *you were damn lucky,* tuviste mucha suerte. – **4** *t* REL condenar. **5** (*curse*) maldecir: *damn it!,* ¡maldita sea! **6** (*criticize, condemn*) condenar.
● **damn all,** nada de nada, absolutamente nada. ‖ **not to care a damn / not give a damn,** no importarle a uno un bledo/pito/comino/rábano: *I don't give a damn,* me importa un bledo. ‖ **not to be worth a damn,** no valer nada.
damnation [dæm'neɪʃən] **1** *n* condenación *f.* – **2** *interj* ¡maldición!
damned [dæmd] **1** *adj fam* maldito,-a, condenado,-a, puñetero,-a: *you've got a damned cheek!,* ¡qué cara tienes! **2** REL condenado,-a. – **3 the damned,** *n* los condenados *mpl.*
● **well, I'm damned / I'll be damned!,** ¡mecachis!, ¡vaya por Dios!: *I'm damned if I'm going to pay for it!,* ¡yo no pienso pagarlo de ninguna manera!
damnedest ['dæmdɪst] **to do one's damnedest,** *phr* hacer todo lo posible (**to,** para).
damning ['dæmɪŋ] *adj* (*evidence, facts*) irrefutable, condenatorio,-a; (*criticism, indictment*) adverso,-a, mordaz, feroz, duro,-a; (*remark*) crítico,-a, mordaz.
damp [dæmp] **1** *adj* (*gen*) húmedo,-a; (*wet*) mojado,-a. – **2** *n* humedad *f.* – **3** *t* (*dampen*) humedecer. **4** to damp (**down**), (*fire*) sofocar. **5** (*reduce - noise*) amortiguar; (-*instrument*) poner una sordina a. **6** (*enthusiasm, energy, ardour*) apagar, enfriar, hacer perder: *it really damped our spirits,* nos desanimó.
sanimar.
■ **a damp squib,** un fiasco.
dampcourse ['dæmpkɔːs] *n* aislante *m* hidrófugo.
dampen ['dæmpən] **1** *t* (*make damp*) humedecer. **2** *fig* (*enthusiasm, ardour, etc*) hacer perder, apagar, enfriar; (*person's spirits*) desanimar: *the accident dampened his enthusiasm for adventure sports,* el accidente le hizo perder el entusiasmo por los deportes de aventura; *the incident with the police really dampened everyone's spirits,* el incidente con la policía nos desanimó a todos.
damper ['dæmpəʳ] **1** *n* (*of chimney*) regulador *m* de tiro. **2** MUS sordina.
● **to put the damper on sth.,** estropear, amargar, aguar: *the bad weather put the damper on our holiday,* el mal tiempo nos estropeó las vacaciones.
dampness ['dæmpnəs] *n* humedad *f.*
damp-proof course ['dæmppruːf kɔːs] *n* → **damp-course.**
damsel ['dæmzəl] *n* doncella.
■ **a damsel in distress,** una chica en apuros.
damson ['dæmzən] *n* (*fruit*) ciruela damascena; (*tree*) ciruelo damasceno.
dance [dɑːns] **1** *n* (*gen*) baile *m*; (*classical, tribal*) danza: *may I have the pleasure of this dance?,* ¿me concede este baile? – **2** *i* (*gen*) bailar: *we danced the whole night long,* bailamos toda la noche; *why don't you ask her to dance,* ¿por qué no la sacas a bailar? **3** *fig* (*trees, leaves, flowers, etc*) agitarse, mecerse, moverse; (*waves*) agitarse, moverse. – **4** *t* (*kind of dance*) bailar: *can you dance the waltz?,* ¿sabes bailar el vals? **5** (*child etc*) hacer bailar.
● **to dance attendance on sb.,** desvivirse por complacer a algn. ‖ **to dance to sb.'s tune,** obedecer a

algn. ‖ **to lead sb. a merry dance,** traer a algn. al retortero.
■ **dance band,** orquesta de baile. ‖ **dance floor,** pista de baile. ‖ **dance hall,** salón *m* de baile. ‖ **dance music,** música de baile.
dancer ['dɑːnsəʳ] **1** *n* (*person dancing*) bailador,-ra. **2** (*professional*) bailarín,-ina; (*flamenco*) bailador,-ra.
dancing ['dɑːnsɪŋ] **1** *n* baile *m*: *she loves going dancing,* le encanta ir a bailar. – **2** *adj* de baile.
dandelion ['dændɪlaɪən] *n* diente *m* de león.
dandruff ['dændrəf] *n* caspa.
dandy ['dændɪ] **1** *n* dandy *m*, petimetre *m.* – **2** *adj* US *fam* estupendo,-a.
● **fine and dandy,** perfecto,-a, de perlas.
▲ *pl* **dandies.**
Dane [deɪn] *n* danés,-esa.
danger ['deɪndʒəʳ] *n* (*peril, hazard*) peligro; (*risk*) riesgo: *are you aware of the dangers of smoking,* ¿eres consciente de los riesgos de fumar?; *there's no danger of him working too hard,* no hay peligro de que trabaje demasiado.
● **"Danger", "Peligro".** ‖ **to be in danger,** estar en peligro. ‖ **to be in danger of doing sth.,** correr peligro de hacer algo. ‖ **to be on the danger list,** estar en estado crítico. ‖ **to be out of danger,** estar fuera de peligro.
■ **danger money,** plus *m* de peligrosidad, prima de peligrosidad. ‖ **danger sign,** señal *f* de peligro.
dangerous ['deɪndʒərəs] *adj* (*gen*) peligroso,-a; (*risky*) arriesgado,-a; (*illness*) grave.
■ **dangerous driving,** JUR conducción *f* temeraria.
dangerously ['deɪndʒərəslɪ] *adv* (*gen*) peligrosamente; (*ill*) gravemente; (*drive*) con temeridad.
● **to live dangerously,** llevar una vida arriesgada.
dangle ['dæŋgəl] **1** *t* (*hang*) colgar; (*swing*) balancear: *the children dangled their legs over the wall,* los niños colgaban las piernas del muro. – **2** *i* colgar, pender: *she had long earrings dangling from her ears,* llevaba unos pendientes largos que le colgaban de las orejas.
● **to dangle sth. in front of sb.,** ofrecerle algo a algn. (como incentivo).
Danish ['deɪnɪʃ] **1** *adj* danés,-esa. – **2** *n* (*language*) danés *m.* – **3 the Danish,** *npl* los daneses *mpl.*
■ **Danish blue,** tipo de queso azul. ‖ **Danish pastry,** bollo relleno cubierto de azúcar glas, almendras, *etc.*
dank [dæŋk] *adj* húmedo,-a y frío,-a.
Danube ['dænjuːb] *n* el Danubio *m.*
dapper ['dæpəʳ] *adj* (*smart*) atildado,-a, pulcro,-a.
dappled ['dæpəld] *adj* (*mottled - colour, shade, sunlight*) moteado,-a; (*horse*) rodado,-a, moteado,-a.
dapple-grey [dæpəl'greɪ] **1** *adj* tordo,-a. – **2** *n* caballo tordo.
dare [deəʳ] **1** *i* atreverse (**to,** a), osar (**to,** -): *how dare you speak to me like that!,* ¡cómo te atreves a hablarme así!; *I didn't dare tell him the price,* no me atreví a decirle el precio; *I daren't say anything,* no me atrevo a decir nada; *just you dare!,* ¡atrévete y verás!; *don't you dare!,* ¡ni se te ocurra! – **2** *t* (*challenge*) desafiar: *they dared him to steal an apple,* lo desafiaron a que robara una manzana; *go on, I dare you!,* ¡venga, a que no te atreves! – **3** *n* desafío, reto.
● **I dare say,** (*perhaps*) quizá, posiblemente; (*I suppose*) supongo, me imagino; (*I bet*) ya lo creo: *I dare say you're right,* supongo que tienes razón.
daredevil ['deədevəl] *n* atrevido,-a, temerario,-a.
daresay [deə'seɪ] *t* → **dare say.**

daring ['deərɪŋ] 1 *adj* (*bold, brave*) audaz, osado,-a, atrevido,-a; (*provocative*) atrevido,-a. – 2 *n* osadía, arrojo, atrevimiento, audacia.

dark [dɑːk] 1 *adj* (*without light*) oscuro,-a. 2 (*colour*) oscuro,-a. 3 (*hair, skin*) moreno,-a; (*eyes*) negro,-a; (*glasses*) oscuro,-a. 4 (*gloomy*) triste, sombrío,-a; (*future*) negro,-a, tenebroso,-a. 5 (*sinister*) siniestro,-a, oscuro,-a, tenebroso-a. 6 (*secret*) misterioso,-a, secreto,-a, oscuro,-a. – 7 *n* (*darkness*) oscuridad *f*: *she's afraid of the dark*, le da miedo la oscuridad. 8 (*nightfall*) anochecer *m*.
● **after dark**, después del anochecer. ‖ **before dark**, antes del anochecer, antes de que anochezca. ‖ **to be in the dark**, *fig* no saber nada. ‖ **to get dark**, oscurecer, hacerse de noche. ‖ **to keep sb. in the dark**, *fig* ocultarle algo a algn. ‖ **to keep sth. dark**, mantener algo en secreto.
■ **a dark horse**, (*secretive person*) un enigma, una incógnita; (*surprise winner*) un,-a ganador,-ra sorpresa. ‖ **the Dark Ages**, la Alta Edad *f* Media, la Edad *f* de las tinieblas. ‖ **dark meat**, carne *f* más oscura.

darken ['dɑːkən] 1 *t* oscurecer, hacer más oscuro,-a. 2 *fig* entristecer, ensombrecer. – 3 *i* (*sky*) oscurecerse, ponerse más oscuro,-a. 4 *fig* (*face*) ensombrecerse.
● **to darken sb.'s door**, poner los pies en casa de algn.: *never darken my door again!*, ¡no vuelvas a poner los pies en mi casa!

darkish ['dɑːkɪʃ] *adj* (*colour*) tirando a oscuro,-a, bastante oscuro,-a; (*hair, skin*) tirando a moreno,-a, bastante moreno,-a.

darkness ['dɑːknəs] *n* oscuridad *f*.
● **in darkness**, a oscuras.

darkroom ['dɑːkruːm] *n* cuarto oscuro.

darling ['dɑːlɪŋ] 1 *n* (*lover*) querido,-a, amor *m*, cariño; (*popular person*) niño,-a mimado,-a. – 2 *adj* (*loved*) querido,-a. 3 *fam* (*charming*) precioso,-a, encantador,-ra, mono,-a.

darn[1] [dɑːn] 1 *n* zurcido *m*. – 2 *t* (*sock etc*) zurcir.

darn[2] [dɑːn] *interj fam euph* → **damn**.

darning ['dɑːnɪŋ] 1 *n* (*act*) zurcido. 2 (*clothes*) ropa para zurcir.
■ **darning needle**, aguja de zurcir.

dart [dɑːt] 1 *n* (*object*) dardo, flechilla, rehilete *m*. 2 (*rush*) movimiento rápido. 3 SEW (*fold*) pinza. – 4 *t* (*look, glance*) lanzar; (*tongue*) disparar. – 5 *i* (*move quickly - person*) lanzarse, precipitarse; (*- butterfly etc*) revolotear: *he darted across the road*, cruzó la calle corriendo; *she darted out the door*, salió por la puerta como una flecha. – 6 **darts**, *npl* (*game*) dardos *mpl*.
● **to make a dart for sth.**, abalanzarse sobre algo, precipitarse hacia algo. ‖ **to play darts**, jugar a los dardos.

dartboard ['dɑːtbɔːd] *n* diana, blanco de tiro.

dash[1] [dæʃ] 1 *n* (*sudden run*) carrera. 2 SP carrera, sprint *m*. 3 (*small amount*) poco, poquito; (*of salt, spice, etc*) pizca; (*of liquid*) chorrito, chorrillo, gota. 4 (*horizontal mark*) raya; (*hyphen*) guión *m*; (*in Morse code*) raya. 5 (*style, panache*) elegancia, garbo, salero; (*energy, vitality*) brío, dinamismo. 6 US AUTO (*dashboard*) salpicadero. – 7 *t* (*hit*) lanzar, arrojar; (*smash*) romper, estrellar: *he dashed the vase to pieces*, hizo el florero añicos. 8 (*hopes*) truncar: *our hopes of peace were dashed*, nuestras esperanzas de conseguir la paz se truncaron. – 9 *i* (*rush*) correr: *everyone dashed to the window*, todo el mundo corrió hacia la ventana; *I've been dashing around all day*, llevo todo el día corriendo de un lado a otro; *I must dash*, me voy pitando. 10 (*waves*) romper.
◆ **to dash off** 1 *t sep* (*essay etc*) escribir deprisa y corriendo, escribir en un momento. – 2 *i* irse corriendo.

● **to cut a dash**, causar sensación, llamar la atención. ‖ **to make a dash for sth.**, precipitarse hacia algo.

dash[2] [dæʃ] **dash (it)!**, *interj* ¡mecachis!

dashboard ['dæʃbɔːd] *n* salpicadero.

dashing ['dæʃɪŋ] *adj* (*person*) gallardo,-a, garboso,-a; (*clothes*) elegante.

data ['deɪtə] *npl* datos *mpl*, información *f*.
■ **data bank**, COMPUT banco de datos. ‖ **data capture**, recolección *f* de datos. ‖ **data processing**, procesamiento de datos.

database ['deɪtəbeɪs] *n* COMPUT base *f* de datos.

date[1] [deɪt] 1 *n* (*in time*) fecha: *what's the date today?*, ¿a qué fecha estamos? 2 (*appointment*) cita, compromiso: *we've made a date to go to the cinema*, hemos quedado para ir al cine; *she's got a date with David tonight*, tiene una cita con David esta noche; *he's out on a date*, ha salido con una chica; *right, it's a date!*, ¡vale, quedamos fijo! 3 US (*person*) ligue *m*, amigo,-a, pareja: *have you got a date for the dance?*, ¿tienes pareja para el baile? 4 (*performance, booking*) actuación *f*. – 5 *t* (*write a date on*) fechar. 6 (*determine the date of*) datar. 7 (*show the age of*) demostrar la edad de. 8 US *fam* (*go out with*) salir con. – 9 *i* (*have existed since*) datar (**from**, de), remontarse (**back to**, a). 10 (*go out of fashion*) pasar de moda. 11 US (*go out together*) salir juntos, ser novios.
● **at a later date**, más tarde, en una fecha posterior. ‖ **out of date**, (*ideas*) anticuado,-a; (*clothes*) pasado,-a de moda; (*technology*) desfasado,-a, obsoleto,-a; (*ticket, food*) caducado,-a. ‖ **to date**, hasta la fecha. ‖ **up to date**, actualizado,-a, al día. ‖ **to be up to date (on sth.)**, estar al tanto (de algo), estar al corriente de algo). ‖ **to set a date for sth.**, fijar la fecha para algo.
■ **closing date**, fecha tope, fecha límite. ‖ **date of birth**, fecha de nacimiento. ‖ **date rape**, violación *f* en una cita. ‖ **date stamp**, (*date*) fecha; (*instrument*) matasellos *m inv*. ‖ **sell-by date**, fecha de caducidad.

date[2] [deɪt] *n* (*fruit*) dátil *m*.

dated ['deɪtɪd] *adj* (*ideas*) anticuado,-a; (*clothes*) pasado,-a de moda; (*expression*) anticuado,-a desusado,-a.

dateline ['deɪtlaɪn] *n* (*in newspaper*) fecha.
■ **International Dateline**, línea internacional del cambio de fecha.

dative ['deɪtɪv] *n* LING dativo.
■ **dative case**, dativo.

daub [dɔːb] 1 *n* (*small bit, smear*) mancha. 2 (*bad painting*) pintarrajo. – 3 *t* (*cover - with mud, paint, ink*) embadurnar (**with**, con/de); (*with oil, grease*) untar (**with**, con): *the library had been daubed with graffiti*, habían cubierto la biblioteca de grafitis. – 4 *i fam* (*paint badly*) pintarrajear.

daughter ['dɔːtə'] *n* hija.

daughter-in-law ['dɔːtərɪnlɔː] *n* nuera.

daunt [dɔːnt] *t* (*frighten*) intimidar; (*dishearten*) desanimar, desalentar.
● **nothing daunted**, impertérrito,-a, sin inmutarse. ‖ **to be daunted by sth.**, amilanarse ante algo.

daunting ['dɔːntɪŋ] *adj* desalentador,-ra.

dauntless ['dɔːntləs] *adj* impávido,-a, intrépido,-a.

dawdle ['dɔːdəl] *i* (*walk slowly*) andar despacio; (*waste time*) perder el tiempo, entretenerse.
● **to dawdle over sth.**, eternizarse haciendo algo.

dawn [dɔːn] 1 *n* alba, aurora, amanecer *m*: *we got up as dawn was breaking*, nos levantamos al romper el alba; *from dawn till dusk*, de sol a sol. 2 *fig* (*beginning*) amanecer *m*, albores *mpl*, aurora. – 3 *i* (*day*) amanecer, alborear, clarear: *the day dawned bright and sunny*, el día amaneció muy soleado. 4 (*new age, year*) alborear, na-

cer. **5** (*become known, obvious*) brillar: *the truth dawned,* la verdad brilló.
◆ **to dawn on** *t insep* caer en la cuenta: *it dawned on me that ...,* caí en la cuenta de que ...
■ **the dawn chorus,** el canto de los pájaros al amanecer. ‖ **dawn raid,** MIL ataque *m* militar de madrugada.
day [deɪ] **1** *n* (*24 hours*) día *m*: *in a few day's time,* dentro de unos días. **2** (*time between sunrise and sunset*) día *m*: *it's been raining all day,* lleva lloviendo todo el día; *how was your day?,* ¿qué tal tu día? **3** (*period of work*) jornada, día *m*: *we work an eight-hour day,* trabajamos una jornada de ocho horas. **4** (*period of success*) día *m*: *he was very famous in his day,* fue muy famoso en su día. **5** (*period of time*) época, tiempo: *in my day ...,* en mis tiempos ... – **6 days,** *npl* (*period*) época, tiempos *mpl*: *in the old days,* antiguamente; *the good old days,* los viejos tiempos.
● a nine days' wonder, un prodigio efímero. ‖ any day now, cualquier día de éstos. ‖ by day, de día, durante el día. ‖ day after day, día tras día. ‖ day and night, día y noche. ‖ day by day, día a día, de día en día. ‖ day in, day out, todos los días. ‖ every day, todos los días. ‖ every other day, un día sí un día no, cada dos días. ‖ from one day to the next, de un día para (el) otro. ‖ have a nice day!, ¡que tengas un buen día! ‖ in this day and age, hoy (en) día. ‖ in those days, en aquellos tiempos, en aquella época. ‖ it's all in a day's work, todo forma parte del trabajo. ‖ that'll be the day, cuando las ranas críen pelos. ‖ the day after tomorrow, pasado mañana. ‖ the day before yesterday, anteayer, antes de ayer. ‖ the following day, al día siguiente. ‖ these days, hoy en día. ‖ ... to the day, hoy hace exactamente ... ‖ to this day, hasta el día de hoy. ‖ not to be my (your, his, etc) day, no ser mi (tu, su, etc) día. ‖ sb.'s/sth.'s days are numbered, tener algn./algo los días contados. ‖ to be ... if one's a day, tener como mínimo ... años: *she's 50 if she's a day,* tiene como mínimo 50 años, no puede tener menos de 50 años. ‖ to call it a day, dar algo por terminado. ‖ to carry the day / win the day, prevalecer. ‖ to have had one's day, haber pasado a la historia, haber pasado de moda. ‖ to be one of those days, ser un día de aquéllos. ‖ to have one of those days, tener un día de aquéllos. ‖ to make a day of it, quedarse todo el día. ‖ to make sb.'s day, alegrarle la vida a algn.
■ day labourer, jornalero,-a. ‖ day nursery, guardería (infantil). ‖ day off, día libre. ‖ day of reckoning, día *m* del juicio final. ‖ day release, *sistema que permite a un,-a empleado,-a asistir a un curso un día de la semana.* ‖ day return, billete *m* de ida y vuelta para el mismo día. ‖ day room, sala comunal en hospitales etc. ‖ day school, colegio sin internado. ‖ day shift, turno de día. ‖ day trip, excursión *f* (de un día).
daybreak ['deɪbreɪk] *n* amanecer *m*, alba.
daydream ['deɪdriːm] **1** *n* ensueño, ensoñación *f*. – **2** *i* soñar despierto,-a, fantasear.
daylight ['deɪlaɪt] *n* luz *f* de día: *let's go while it's still daylight,* vamos mientras aún sea de día.
● to beat/knock the living daylights out of sb., pegarle una soberana paliza a algn. ‖ to scare/frighten the living daylights out of sb., darle un susto de muerte a algn. ‖ it's daylight robbery!, ¡es un (auténtico) robo!, ¡es un timo! ‖ in broad daylight, en pleno día, a plena luz del día.
daytime ['deɪtaɪm] **1** *n* día *m*. – **2** *adj* (*flight*) diurno,-a.
● in the daytime, de día, durante el día.

day-to-day ['deɪtədeɪ] **1** *adj* (*daily*) cotidiano,-a, diario,-a; (*ordinary*) de cada día. **2** (*existence*) rutinario,-a.
● to do sth. on a day-to-day basis, hacer algo de día en día.
daze [deɪz] **1** *n* aturdimiento. – **2** *t* aturdir: *we were dazed by the terrible news,* las terribles noticias nos aturdieron.
● to be in a daze, estar aturdido,-a.
dazed [deɪzd] *adj* aturdido,-a.
dazzle ['dæzəl] **1** *n* (*brilliance*) resplandor *m*, brillo. – **2** *t* deslumbrar.
dazzling ['dæzlɪŋ] *adj* (*light, sky, jewels*) deslumbrante, resplandeciente; (*success, intellect*) deslumbrante, deslumbrador,-ra.
dB ['diːˈbiː] *abbr* (*decibel*) decibelio; (*abbreviation*) dB.
D-day ['diːdeɪ] **1** *n* (*in war*) día *m* D. **2** (*important date*) el día *m* señalado.
DDT ['diːˈdiːˈtiː] *abbr* (*dichlorodiphenyltrichloroethane*) diclorodietiltricloroetano; (*abbreviation*) DDT *m*.
DEA ['diːˈiːˈeɪ] *abbr* US (*Drug Enforcement Administration*) agencia norteamericana contra el narcotráfico; (*abbreviation*) DEA.
deacon ['diːkən] *n* diácono.
deaconess ['diːkənɪs] *n* diaconisa.
deactivate [diːˈæktɪveɪt] *t* desactivar.
dead [ded] **1** *adj* (*not alive*) muerto,-a: *she's dead,* está muerta; *he was shot dead,* lo mataron de un tiro, lo mataron a tiros; *he was dead on arrival at the hospital,* ingresó cadáver en el hospital. **2** (*obsolete - language*) muerto,-a; (- *custom*) desusado,-a, en desuso; (*finished with - topic, issue, debate*) agotado,-a, pasado,-a; (- *glass, bottle*) terminado,-a, acabado,-a: *is this glass dead?,* ¿has terminado con el vaso? **3** (*numb*) entumecido,-a, dormido,-a: *my feet have gone dead,* se me han dormido los pies. **4** (*not functioning - telephone*) desconectado,-a, cortado,-a; (- *machine*) averiado,-a; (- *battery*) descargado,-a, gastado,-a; (- *match*) gastado,-a: *the line's dead,* no hay línea. **5** *fam* (*very tired*) muerto,-a. **6** (*dull, quiet, not busy*) muerto,-a: *the town's dead at night,* la ciudad está muerta por la noche. **7** (*sounds*) sordo,-a; (*colours*) apagado,-a. **8** SP (*ball*) muerto,-a. **9** (*total*) total, completo,-a, absoluto,-a: *there was dead silence,* se hizo un silencio sepulcral. – **10** *adv* (*completely, absolutely*) completamente, sumamente; (*as intensifier*) muy: *I'm dead sure,* estoy segurísimo; *he was dead drunk,* estaba completamente borracho; *it's dead easy,* está tirado. **11** (*exactly*) justo: *we arrived dead on time,* llegamos puntualísimos. – **12 the dead,** *n* los,-las muertos,-as.
● a dead duck, un fracaso total. ‖ in the dead of winter, en pleno invierno, en lo más crudo del invierno. ‖ over my dead body!, ¡sobre mi cadáver! ‖ to be a dead cert, ser algo seguro,-a: *this horse is a dead cert,* segurísimo que gana este caballo. ‖ to be a dead loss, no servir para nada, ser un desastre. ‖ to be a dead ringer for sb., ser idéntico,-a a algn. ‖ to be dead beat, estar hecho,-a polvo. ‖ to be dead on one's feet, estar hecho,-a polvo. ‖ to be dead (set) against sth., oponerse totalmente a algo. ‖ to be dead set on doing sth., estar empeñado,-a en hacer algo, estar decidido,-a a hacer algo. ‖ to be dead to the world, estar dormido,-a como un tronco. ‖ to be the dead spit of sb., ser el vivo retrato de algn. ‖ to come to a dead end, llegar a un callejón sin salida. ‖ to come to a dead stop, detenerse en seco. ‖ to drop dead, caer muerto,-a: *drop dead!,* ¡vete al cuerno! ‖ to stop dead, parar(se) en seco. ‖ not to be seen dead doing

sth., no hacer algo por nada del mundo: *I wouldn't be seen dead with him!*, ¡no saldría con él por nada del mundo!, ¡no saldría con él ni muerta!
■ dead body, cadáver *m*. ‖ dead calm, calma chicha. ‖ dead end, callejón *m* sin salida. ‖ dead heat, empate *m*. ‖ dead letter, JUR letra muerta. ‖ dead weight, peso muerto. ‖ dead wood, (*trees etc*) ramas *fpl* secas; (*useless people*) personal *m* inútil; (*useless things*) trastos *mpl*. ‖ the Dead Sea, el Mar Muerto.

deadbeat ['dedbiːt] *n* US *fam* (*idler*) vago,-a, flojo,-a; (*dropout*) marginado,-a.

deaden ['dedən] *t* (*pain*) calmar, aliviar; (*noise, blow*) amortiguar.

dead-end job [dedend'dʒɒb] *n* trabajo sin porvenir, trabajo sin futuro.

deadline ['dedlaɪn] *n* (*date*) fecha límite, fecha tope, plazo de entrega; (*time*) hora límite, hora tope.
● to meet a deadline, acabar un trabajo dentro del plazo previsto. ‖ to work to a deadline, trabajar con miras a un plazo determinado.

deadlock ['dedlɒk] *n* punto muerto, impasse *m*.
● to break the deadlock, salir del impasse. ‖ to end in deadlock, acabar en un punto muerto.

deadly ['dedlɪ] 1 *adj* (*disease*) mortal; (*weapon, gas*) mortífero,-a; (*enemy*) a muerte, mortal; (*aim*) certero,-a. 2 (*as intensifier*) enorme, total: *in deadly silence*, en absoluto silencio. 3 *fam* (*dull*) aburridísimo,-a. – 4 *adv* (*as intensifier*) terriblemente: *he was deadly serious*, lo decía muy en serio.
■ deadly nightshade, belladona. ‖ deadly sin, pecado capital.
▲ *comp* deadlier, *superl* deadliest.

deadpan ['dedpæn] 1 *adj* (*face, look*) de póquer, de palo, sin expresión; (*tone*) inexpresivo,-a. – 2 *adv* de manera inexpresiva.
■ deadpan humour, humor *m* socarrón.

deaf [def] 1 *adj* sordo,-a. – 2 the deaf, *n* los sordos *mpl*.
● to be be as deaf as a post, estar más sordo,-a que una tapia. ‖ to be deaf in one ear, ser sordo,-a de un oído. ‖ to be deaf to sth., hacer oídos sordos a algo. ‖ to be stone deaf, estar más sordo,-a que una tapia. ‖ to fall on deaf ears, caer en oídos sordos. ‖ to go deaf, quedarse sordo,-a. ‖ to turn a deaf ear, hacerse el sordo.

deaf-aid ['defeɪd] *n* audífono.

deaf-and-dumb [defən'dʌm] *adj* sordomudo,-a.

deafen ['defən] *t* ensordecer.

deafening ['defənɪŋ] *adj* ensordecedor,-ra.

deaf-mute [def'mjuːt] *n* sordomudo,-a.

deafness ['defnəs] *n* sordera.

deal [diːl] 1 *n* (*agreement*) trato, acuerdo, pacto; (*financial*) acuerdo: *it's a deal!*, ¡trato hecho!; *the deal's off!*, ¡no hay trato!; *management and unions have reached a pay deal*, la patronal y los sindicatos han llegado a un acuerdo salarial. 2 (*treatment*) trato: *she's had a bit of a rough deal*, lo ha pasado bastante mal. 3 (*amount*) cantidad *f*: *a great deal of money*, mucho dinero; *she's a great deal better*, está mucho mejor; *he learnt a great deal from his father*, aprendió mucho de su padre. 4 (*in card games*) reparto: *it's your deal*, te toca a ti repartir. – 5 *t* (*cards*) repartir, dar. 6 (*drugs*) traficar. – 7 *i* (*cards*) repartir, dar. 8 (*drugs*) traficar.
◆ to deal in *t insep* (*trade in*) comerciar en, tratar en. ‖ to deal out *t sep* (*money, presents, etc*) repartir, distribuir; (*sentence*) dictar. ‖ to deal with 1 *t insep* COMM (*trade with*) tratar con, tener relaciones comerciales con. 2 (*tackle -*

problem etc) abordar, ocuparse de, atacar; (*- task*) encargarse de, ocuparse de; (*- person*) tratar (con), lidiar con. 3 (*be about, have as subject*) tratar de; (*discuss*) tratar.
● big deal!, ¡vaya cosa!, ¡qué horror! ‖ it's no big deal, no es nada de otro mundo. ‖ to deal sb. a blow/ deal a blow to sb., asestarle un golpe a algn. ‖ to do a deal with sb. / make a deal with sb., llegar a un acuerdo con algn., tener un trato con algn. ‖ to make a big deal out of sth., hacer un problema de algo.
■ fair deal / square deal, trato justo.
▲ *pt & pp dealt*.

dealer ['diːlə'] 1 *n* COMM comerciante *mf*, negociante *mf*: *used-car dealer*, vendedor,-ra de coches de ocasión; *antiques dealer*, anticuario,-a. 2 (*illegal - in drugs*) traficante *mf*; (*- in stolen goods*) perista *mf*. 3 FIN corredor,-ra de bolsa, corredor,-ra de valores. 4 (*cards*) repartidor,-ra.

dealing ['diːlɪŋ] 1 *n* COMM (*way of behaving*) negocios *mpl*. 2 FIN transacciones *fpl*. – 3 dealings, *npl* (*relations*) trato, relaciones *fpl*.
● to have dealings with sb., tener trato con algn.

dealt [delt] *pt & pp* → deal.

dean [diːn] 1 *n* REL deán *m*. 2 EDUC decano,-a.

dear [dɪə'] 1 *adj* (*loved - person*) querido,-a; (*- thing*) preciado,-a: *she's a dear friend*, es una amiga muy querida; *what a dear little cat!*, ¡qué gatito más mono! 2 (*as form of address*) querido,-a: *my dear Charles!*, ¡mi querido Charles!; *Diana my dear*, Diana, querida; *my dear Mrs Spencer*, mi buena señora Spencer. 3 *fam* (*in letter*) querido,-a; *fml* apreciado,-a, estimado,-a: *Dear John*, Querido John; *Dear Sir*, Muy señor mío; *Dear Mrs Smith*, Estimada Sra. Smith. 4 (*expensive*) caro,-a. – 5 *n* (*as form of address - to loved one*) querido,-a, cariño, cielo; (*- to anyone*) chato,-a, rey,-reina, guapo,-a. 6 (*nice person*) cielo, sol *m*: *be a dear and put the kettle on*, sé bueno y pon el agua a hervir; *she's such a dear*, es un cielo. – 7 *interj* ¡Dios mío!: *oh dear!*, ¡ay!, ¡uy!; *dear me!*, ¡vaya por Dios! – 8 *adv* caro.
● to be dear to sb., significar mucho para algn. ‖ hold sb. dear, tener mucha estima a algn., apreciar mucho a algn.

dearly ['dɪəlɪ] 1 *adv* (*very much*) mucho. 2 (*at a cost*) caro.
● dearly beloved, REL (amados) hermanos.

dearth [dɜːθ] *n* escasez *f*.

death [deθ] 1 *n* (*gen*) muerte *f*; (*decease, demise*) fallecimiento, defunción *f*: *he died a natural death*, murió de muerte natural. 2 (*end - of custom, institution*) fin *m*.
● at death's door, a las puertas de la muerte. ‖ on pain of death, bajo pena de muerte. ‖ to be bored to death, aburrirse como una ostra. ‖ to be scared to death, estar muerto,-a de miedo. ‖ to be sick to death of sb./sth., estar hasta la coronilla de algn./algo. ‖ to be the death of sb., acabar con algn. ‖ to be worried to death, estar preocupadísimo,-a. ‖ to beat/kick/ stab sb. to death, matar a algn. a golpes/patadas/puñaladas. ‖ to bleed to death, morir desangrado,-a. ‖ to do sth. to death, repetir algo hasta la saciedad. ‖ to drink os. to death, matarle a alguien la bebida. ‖ to fight to the death, luchar hasta la muerte. ‖ to freeze to death, morir(se) de frío. ‖ to look like death warmed up, parecer un muerto viviente, parecer un cadáver. ‖ to put sb. to death, ejecutar a algn. ‖ to sentence sb. to death, condenar a algn. a muerte.
■ death certificate, certificado de defunción. ‖ death knell, toque de difuntos, doble *m*: *video clubs spell the death knell of many cinemas*, los videoclubs suponen la muerte de muchos cines. ‖ death bell, toque de di-

funtos, doble *m*. ‖ **death mask,** mascarilla. ‖ **death penalty,** pena de muerte. ‖ **death rate,** índice *m* de mortalidad. ‖ **death rattle,** estertor *m* de la muerte. ‖ **death row,** corredor *m* de la muerte. ‖ **death squad,** escuadrón *m* de la muerte. ‖ **death throes,** agonía. ‖ **death toll,** número de víctimas (mortales). ‖ **death warrant,** sentencia de muerte. ‖ **death wish,** ganas *fpl* de morir.

deathbed ['deθbed] *n* lecho de muerte.

deathblow ['deθbləʊ] *n* golpe *m* mortal.

deathly ['deθlɪ] *adj* (*silence*) sepulcral, de muerte, mortal; (*pallor*) cadavérico,-a, de muerte.
● **to be deathly pale,** estar blanco,-a como el papel.
▲ *comp* **deathlier,** *superl* **deathliest.**

deathtrap ['deθtræp] *n fam* lugar peligroso.

deathwatch beetle ['deθwɒtʃbiːtəl] *n* escarabajo del reloj de la muerte.

debacle [deɪ'baːkəl] *n* debacle *m*, desastre *m*, fiasco.

debar [dɪ'baːʳ] *t* (*from place*) excluir (**from**, de); (*of right*) privar; (*from profession*) incapacitar, inhabilitar: *he has been debarred from holding public office,* ha sido inhabilitado para ocupar cargos públicos; *I was debarred from the club,* me prohibieron entrar en el club.
▲ *pt & pp* **debarred,** *ger* **debarring.**

debase [dɪ'beɪs] **1** *t* (*degrade, devalue - idea, principle*) desvalorizar, envilecer; (- *language*) corromper, viciar; (*word, phrase*) quitar el sentido de. **2** (*coinage*) alterar. **3** (*demean, humiliate - person*) degradar.
● **to debase os.,** rebajarse, degradarse.

debasement [dɪ'beɪsmənt] *n* degradación *f.*

debatable [dɪ'beɪtəbəl] *adj* discutible.

debate [dɪ'beɪt] **1** *n* (*public meeting, in Parliament*) debate *m*; (*discussion*) debate *m*, discusión *f*: *that's a matter for debate,* eso es un asunto discutible; *the nuclear power debate,* el debate de la energía nuclear. – **2** *t* (*discuss*) debatir, discutir. **3** (*consider, think over*) considerar, dar vueltas a. – **4** *i* (*discuss*) discutir (**about/on**, sobre).

debater [dɪ'beɪtəʳ] *n* persona que participa en un debate.

debating [dɪ'beɪtɪŋ] *n* discusión *f.*
■ **debating society,** grupo de debate y discusión.

debauch [dɪ'bɔːtʃ] **1** *t* corromper, pervertir. – **2** *n* orgía.

debauched [dɪ'bɔːtʃt] *adj* vicioso,-a, libertino,-a.

debauchery [dɪ'bɔːtʃərɪ] *n* libertinaje *m*, disipación *f.*

debenture [dɪ'bentʃəʳ] *n* FIN (*bond*) obligación *f*, bono.

debilitate [dɪ'bɪlɪteɪt] *t* (*weaken*) debilitar; (*exhaust*) extenuar.

debilitating [dɪ'bɪlɪteɪtɪŋ] *adj* (*disease*) debilitante; (*heat, climate*) extenuante.

debility [dɪ'bɪlɪtɪ] *n* debilidad *f*, decaimiento *m.*
▲ *pl* **debilities.**

debit ['debɪt] **1** *n* FIN débito. – **2** *t* cargar en cuenta: *they debited his account with the amount,* cargaron la suma en su cuenta.
■ **debit balance,** saldo deudor. ‖ **debit side,** debe *m.*

debonair [debə'neəʳ] *adj* apuesto,-a, gallardo,-a, garboso,-a.

debrief [diː'briːf] *t* interrogar, pedir un informe a: *the soldiers are debriefed after every mission,* los soldados son interrogados después de cada misión.

debriefing [diː'briːfɪŋ] *n* interrogatorio.
■ **debriefing session,** *sesión en que se informa sobre una misión terminada.*

debris ['deɪbriː] *n* (*ruins*) escombros *mpl*; (*wreckage*) restos *mpl.*

debt [det] *n* (*something owed*) deuda; (*indebtedness*) endeudamiento.

● **to be in of debt,** tener deudas, estar endeudado,-a. ‖ **to be in sb.'s debt,** estar en deuda con algn. ‖ **to get into debt,** contraer deudas, endeudarse. ‖ **to pay off a debt,** saldar una deuda. ‖ **to run up debts,** contraer deudas, endeudarse.
■ **debt collector,** cobrador,-ra de deudas.

debtor ['detəʳ] *n* deudor,-ra.

debug [dɪ'bʌg] **1** *t* (*computer programme, system*) depurar. **2** (*room, building, etc*) quitar los micrófonos ocultos de.
▲ *pt & pp* **debugged,** *ger* **debugging.**

debunk [diː'bʌŋk] *t fam* (*person*) desmitificar, desenmascarar; (*idea, belief*) desacreditar, desprestigiar.

debut ['deɪbjuː] *n* debut *m.*
● **to make one's debut,** debutar, hacer su debut.

debutante ['debjʊtaːnt] *n* debutante *f.*

Dec [dɪ'sembəʳ] *abbr* (*December*) diciembre.

decade ['dekeɪd] *n* década, decenio.

decadence ['dekədəns] *n* decadencia.

decadent ['dekədənt] *adj* decadente.

decaffeinated [dɪ'kæfɪneɪtɪd] *adj* (*coffee, tea*) descafeinado,-a; (*cola*) sin cafeína.

decamp [dɪ'kæmp] **1** *i fam* (*leave suddenly*) esfumarse, largarse. **2** MIL (*leave camp*) levantar campamento.

decant [dɪ'kænt] **1** *t* (*wine*) decantar. – **2** *i* CHEM transvasar.

decanter [dɪ'kæntəʳ] *n* licorera.

decapitate [dɪ'kæpɪteɪt] *t* decapitar.

decapitation [dɪkæpɪ'teɪʃən] *n* decapitación *f.*

decathlete [dɪ'kæθliːt] *n* decatleta *m*, decatlonista *m.*

decathlon [dɪ'kæθlɒn] *n* decatlón *m.*

decay [dɪ'keɪ] **1** *n* (*of organic matter*) descomposición *f*; (*of teeth*) caries *f.* **2** (*of building*) deterioro, desmoronamiento. **3** *fig* (*of culture, values*) decadencia. – **4** *i* (*gen*) descomponerse, pudrirse; (*wood*) pudrirse; (*teeth*) cariarse. **5** (*buildings*) deteriorarse, desmoronarse. **6** *fig* decaer, declinar, estar en decadencia. – **7** *t* (*gen*) descomponer; (*wood*) pudrir; (*teeth*) cariar.
● **to fall into decay,** (*building*) estar en un estado ruinoso.

decease [dɪ'siːs] *n* fallecimiento, defunción *f.*

deceased [dɪ'siːst] **1** *adj* difunto,-a, fallecido,-a. – **2 the deceased,** *n* (*man*) el difunto; (*woman*) la difunta. – **3** *npl* (*gen*) los difuntos; (*women*) las difuntas.

deceit [dɪ'siːt] *n* (*trick*) engaño; (*deceiving*) falsedad *f*: *by deceit,* mediante engaños.

deceitful [dɪ'siːtfʊl] *adj* (*person*) falso,-a, embustero,-a, mentiroso,-a; (*action*) engañoso,-a.

deceitfulness [dɪ'siːtfʊlnəs] *n* falsedad *f*, engaño.

deceive [dɪ'siːv] *t* engañar.
● **to deceive os.,** engañarse. ‖ **to deceive sb. into doing sth.,** engañar a algn. para que haga algo: *they deceived her into believing that,* le hicieron creer que.

deceiver [dɪ'siːvəʳ] *n* impostor,-ra.

decelerate [diː'seləreɪt] **1** *i* reducir la velocidad, desacelerar. – **2** *t* reducir la velocidad de, desacelerar.

deceleration [diːselə'reɪʃən] *n* desaceleración *f.*

December [dɪ'sembəʳ] *n* diciembre *m.*
▲ *Véase también* **May.**

decency ['diːsənsɪ] **1** *n* (*seemliness*) decencia, decoro. **2** (*politeness*) buena educación *f*, cortesía, consideración *f*: *she didn't even have the decency to apologize,* ni siquiera tuvo la educación de disculparse. – **3 decencies,** *npl* convenciones *fpl* sociales.
▲ *pl* **decencies.**

decent ['diːsənt] **1** *adj* (*socially acceptable - dress, behaviour, language*) decente, decoroso,-a; (*person*) decente, hon-

rado,-a: *are you decent?*, ¿estás presentable? **2** *(adequate - meal, wage, housing)* decente, adecuado,-a: *I haven't had a decent night's sleep for ages,* hace mucho que no duermo una noche entera. **3** *fam (nice, kind)* bueno,-a, amable: *that's jolly decent of you, old chap!,* ¡muy amable de tu parte, querido amigo!
● **to do the decent thing**, hacer lo que es correcto, hacer lo que se debe.

decently ['diːsəntlɪ] **1** *adv (respectably)* decentemente, con decencia. **2** *(acceptably)* bastante bien. **3** *(kindly)* amablemente.

decentralization [diːsentrəlaɪ'zeɪʃən] *n* descentralización *f*.

decentralize [diː'sentrəlaɪz] **1** *t* descentralizar. – **2** *i* descentralizarse.
● **to become decentralized**, descentralizarse.

deception [dɪ'sepʃən] *n (trick)* engaño; *(deceiving)* falsedad *f*.

deceptive [dɪ'septɪv] *adj* engañoso,-a: *appearances can be deceptive,* las apariencias engañan.

deceptively [dɪ'septɪvlɪ] *adv* engañosamente, aparentemente: *it looks deceptively easy,* no es tan fácil como parece.

decibel ['desɪbel] *n* decibelio, decibel *m*.

decide [dɪ'saɪd] **1** *t (person)* decidir: *have you decided what to do?,* ¿has decidido qué hacer?; *they decided to go to Greece,* decidieron ir a Grecia. **2** *(cause to reach a decision)* decidir: *what decided you to study philosophy?,* ¿qué es lo que te decidió a estudiar filosofía? **3** *(settle, determine - of event, action)* decidir, determinar: *the penalty decided the game,* el penalty decidió el partido. – **4** *i* decidirse, tomar una decisión: *I don't mind - you decide,* me da igual - decide tú; *they decided against buying the house,* decidieron no comprar la casa; *the judge decided in favour of the defendant,* el juez resolvió a favor del demandado.
◆ **to decide on** *t insep (date, place)* decidir; *(candidate)* decidirse por.

decided [dɪ'saɪdɪd] **1** *adj (resolute, determined - person)* decidido,-a, resuelto,-a. **2** *(clear - change, improvement, opinion, etc)* marcado,-a, claro,-a.

decidedly [dɪ'saɪdɪdlɪ] **1** *adv (in a very decided manner)* decididamente, con decisión. **2** *(clearly, definitely)* sin duda, decididamente.

deciding [dɪ'saɪdɪŋ] *adj (factor, influence, vote, point)* decisivo,-a; *(match)* de desempate.

deciduous [dɪ'sɪdjʊəs] *adj* de hoja caduca.

decimal ['desɪməl] **1** *adj* decimal: *accurate to four decimal places,* exacto hasta la cuarta cifra (decimal). – **2** *n* decimal *m*.
■ **decimal point**, coma decimal.

decimalization [desɪməlaɪ'zeɪʃən] *n* conversión *f* al sistema decimal.

decimalize ['desɪməlaɪz] *t* convertir al sistema decimal.

decimate ['desɪmeɪt] *t* diezmar.

decimation [desɪ'meɪʃən] *n* reducción *f* catastrófica, acción de diezmar.

decipher [dɪ'saɪfə'] *t* descifrar.

decision [dɪ'sɪʒən] **1** *n (choice, verdict)* decisión *f*. **2** *(resolution, ability to decide, decisiveness)* resolución *f*, decisión *f*, determinación *f*.
● **to come to a decision / reach a decision**, llegar a una decisión. ‖ **to make a decision / take a decision**, tomar una decisión.

decisive [dɪ'saɪsɪv] **1** *adj (conclusive - gen)* decisivo,-a; *(- victory)* contundente. **2** *(firm, resolute - person)* decidido,-a, resuelto,-a; *(- reply, action)* firme.

decisively [dɪ'saɪsɪvlɪ] **1** *adv (win)* contundentemente. **2** *(act, say)* con decisión.

decisiveness [dɪ'saɪsɪvnəs] **1** *n (of victory)* contundencia. **2** *(of person)* decisión *f*, firmeza.

deck [dek] **1** *n (of ship)* cubierta: *below deck,* bajo cubierta; *on deck,* en cubierta; *which deck is the restaurant on?,* ¿en qué cubierta está el restaurante? **2** *(of bus, coach)* piso: *top deck,* piso de arriba. **3** US *(of cards)* baraja. **4** *(of record player)* plato. **5** US *(raised roofless area)* terraza. – **6** *t* US *fam (knock down)* tumbar. **7 to deck (out)**, *(decorate)* adornar **(with,** con), engalanar **(in/with,** con).
● **to be decked out in all one's finery**, ir de punta en blanco. ‖ **to clear the decks**, prepararse para algo. ‖ **to hit the deck**, caerse al suelo.
■ **deck chair**, tumbona, silla de playa.

deckhand ['dekhænd] *n* marinero.

declaim [dɪ'kleɪm] **1** *t* declamar. – **2** *i* declamar.

declamation [deklə'meɪʃən] *n* declamación *f*.

declamatory [dɪ'klæmətərɪ] *adj* declamatorio,-a.

declaration [deklə'reɪʃən] *n* declaración *f*.

declare [dɪ'kleə'] **1** *t (gen)* declarar; *(opinion)* manifestar: *he declared himself bankrupt,* se declaró en bancarrota; *Thompson was declared the winner,* Thompson fue declarado ganador; *they declared their support for the campaign,* manifestaron su apoyo a la campaña. **2** *(at customs)* declarar. – **3** *i* SP *(in cricket)* dejar de batear un equipo creyendo que ya tiene suficientes puntos. **4** pronunciar **(against,** en contra), **(for,** a favor de).
● **I (do) declare!,** ¡vaya por Dios! ‖ **to declare war on,** declarar la guerra a.

declared [dɪ'kleəd] *adj* declarado,-a.

declassify [dɪ'klæsɪfaɪ] *t* levantar el secreto oficial de.
▲ *pt & pp* **declassified,** *ger* **declassifying.**

declension [dɪ'klenʃən] *n* LING declinación *f*.

decline [dɪ'klaɪn] **1** *n (decrease)* disminución *f*, descenso. **2** *(deterioration - gen)* deterioro, declive *m*, decadencia; *(in health)* deterioro, empeoramiento: *the decline of the empire,* la decadencia del imperio. – **3** *i (decrease - gen)* disminuir, decrecer; *(interest)* disminuir, decaer: *the party's popularity has declined,* la popularidad del partido ha disminuido. **4** *(deteriorate - gen)* deteriorarse; *(health)* deteriorarse, empeorarse; *(standard, quality)* decaer, disminuir. **5** *(refuse)* rehusar una invitación, declinar una invitación. **6** LING declinarse. – **7** *t (refuse)* rehusar, declinar. **8** LING declinar.
● **to be in decline**, estar en declive, estar en decadencia. ‖ **to be on the decline**, *(fall, decrease)* ir disminuyendo, estar descendiendo; *(become less important)* ir a menos; *(worsen)* empezar a empeorar. ‖ **to fall into decline**, entrar en decadencia.

declining [dɪ'klaɪnɪŋ] *adj (decreasing)* decreciente, en declive; *(deteriorating)* en decadencia.
● **in one's declining years**, en sus últimos años.

declutch [dɪ'klʌtʃ] *i* desembragar.

decode [diː'kəʊd] *t* descifrar.

decolonize [diː'kɒlənaɪz] *t* descolonizar.

decompose [diːkəm'pəʊz] **1** *t* descomponer. – **2** *i* descomponerse, pudrirse. **3** CHEM descomponerse.

decomposition [diːkɒmpə'zɪʃən] *n* descomposición *f*.

decompress [diːkəm'pres] *t* someter a descompresión.

decompression [diːkəm'preʃən] *n* descompresión *f*.
■ **decompression chamber**, cámara de descompresión. ‖ **decompression sickness**, aeroembolismo.

decongestant [diːkən'dʒestənt] **1** *n* descongestionante *m*. – **2** *adj* descongestionante.

decontaminate [diːkən'tæmɪneɪt] *t* descontaminar.

decontamination [diːkəntæmɪ'neɪʃən] *n* descontaminación *f*.

decor ['deɪkɔːʳ] **1** *n (furnishings)* decoración *f*. **2** THEAT decorado.

décor ['deɪkɔːʳ] *n* → **decor**.

decorate ['dekəreɪt] **1** *t (adorn, make beautiful)* decorar (**with**, con), adornar (**with**, con). **2** *(paint)* pintar; *(wallpaper)* empapelar. **3** *(honour)* condecorar (**for**, por). – **4** *i (paint)* pintar; *(wallpaper)* empapelar.

decorating ['dekəreɪtɪŋ] *n (painting)* pintura; *(wallpapering)* empapelado.
● **to do the decorating,** decorar, pintar, empapelar *(la casa, habitación, etc)*.

decoration [dekə'reɪʃən] **1** *n (act, art)* decoración *f*. **2** *(ornament)* adorno: *have you put up the Christmas decorations yet?,* ¿ya has puesto los adornos navideños? **3** *(medal)* condecoración *f*.

decorative ['dekərətɪv] *adj* decorativo,-a, ornamental.

decorator ['dekəreɪtəʳ] *n (designer)* decorador,-ra, interiorista *mf*; *(painter)* pintor,-ra; *(wallpaperer)* empapelador,-ra.

decorous ['dekərəs] *adj fml* decoroso,-a.

decorum [dɪ'kɔːrəm] *n fml* decoro.

decoy ['diːkɔɪ] **1** *n (bird)* cimbel *m*; *(in hunting)* señuelo, reclamo. **2** *fig (lure)* señuelo, carnada, gancho. – **3** *t* atraer con señuelo.

decrease [dɪ'kriːs] **1** *n* disminución *f*, descenso. – **2** *t* disminuir, reducir. – **3** *i (amount, numbers, power, etc)* disminuir, decrecer; *(quality)* disminuir, bajar; *(interest)* disminuir, decaer; *(prices)* bajar; *(in knitting)* menguar: *the speed at which he was travelling decreased suddenly,* la velocidad a la que iba disminuyó de repente.

decreasing [dɪ'kriːsɪŋ] *adj* decreciente.

decreasingly [dɪ'kriːsɪŋlɪ] *adv* cada vez menos.

decree [dɪ'kriː] **1** *n* MIL POL decreto. **2** US JUR sentencia. – **3** *t* decretar.
● **to issue a decree,** promulgar un decreto.
■ **decree absolute,** sentencia definitiva de divorcio. ‖ **decree nisi,** sentencia provisional de divorcio.

decrepit [dɪ'krepɪt] *adj (person)* decrépito,-a; *(furniture)* destartalado,-a; *(house)* deteriorado,-a, desvencijado,-a.

decrepitude [dɪ'krepɪtjuːd] *n (of person)* decrepitud *f*; *(of house etc)* deterioro.

decry [dɪ'kraɪ] *t (condemn, criticize)* censurar, criticar, condenar; *(disparage)* menospreciar, despreciar.
▲ *pt & pp* **decried,** *ger* **decrying.**

dedicate ['dedɪkeɪt] **1** *t (devote - oneself, time, effort)* dedicar, consagrar: *she dedicated her life to helping the poor,* consagró su vida a ayudar a los pobres. **2** *(book, poem, performance, etc)* dedicar. **3** REL *(consecrate)* dedicar.

dedicated ['dedɪkeɪtɪd] **1** *adj (devoted, committed)* dedicado,-a (**to**, -a), entregado,-a (**to**, a): *they are dedicated to getting rid of nuclear weapons,* están dedicados a eliminar las armas nucleares; *he's a dedicated father,* es un padre entregado; *she's a dedicated teacher,* es una maestra dedicada a su trabajo. **2** COMPUT dedicado,-a.

dedication [dedɪ'keɪʃən] **1** *n (devotion)* dedicación *f*, entrega. **2** *(act of dedicating)* dedicación *f*. **3** *(written message in book etc)* dedicatoria.

deduce [dɪ'djuːs] *t* deducir (**from**, de), inferir (**from**, de).

deduct [dɪ'dʌkt] *t (gen)* descontar, deducir; *(from taxes)* desgravar.

deductible [dɪ'dʌktəbəl] *adj* deducible: *tax deductible,* desgravable.

deduction [dɪ'dʌkʃən] **1** *n (subtraction)* deducción *f*, descuento; *(from taxes)* desgravación *f*. **2** *(reasoning)* deducción *f*.

deductive [dɪ'dʌktɪv] *adj* deductivo,-a.

deed [diːd] **1** *n lit (act)* acto, acción *f*, obra; *(feat)* hazaña, proeza. **2** JUR escritura.
● **to do one's good deed for the day,** hacer la buena acción del día.
■ **deed box,** caja de caudales, caja fuerte. ‖ **deed poll,** escritura unilateral: *she changed her name by deed poll,* se cambió el nombre por escritura oficial.

deejay ['diːdʒeɪ] *n* pinchadiscos *mf*, disc jockey *mf*.

deem [diːm] *t fml* juzgar, considerar.

deep [diːp] **1** *adj (river, hole, well, etc)* hondo,-a, profundo,-a; *(wound, cut)* profundo,-a; *(dish)* hondo,-a: *it's ten metres deep,* tiene diez metros de profundidad; *the deep end of the swimming pool,* la parte honda de la piscina. **2** *(shelf, wardrobe)* de fondo; *(hem, border)* ancho,-a: *it's 50 cms deep,* tiene 50 cms de fondo. **3** *(sound, voice)* grave, bajo,-a, profundo,-a; *(note)* grave; *(breath)* hondo,-a; *(sigh)* profundo,-a, hondo,-a. **4** *(colour)* intenso,-a, subido,-a. **5** *(intense - sleep, love, impression)* profundo,-a; *(- interest)* vivo,-a, profundo,-a; *(- outrage, shame)* grande; *(- mourning)* riguroso,-a: *she had a deep distrust of policemen,* desconfiaba mucho de los policías; *he felt a deep sense of pride,* se sintió profundamente orgulloso; *you have my deepest sympathies,* mi más sentido pésame. **6** *(profound - thought, mind, mystery, secret)* profundo,-a; *(person)* profundo,-a, serio,-a. – **7** *adv (to a great depth)* profundamente: *the knife cut deep into his flesh,* el cuchillo le hizo un corte profundo en la carne. **8** *(far from the outside)* lejos: *he kicked the ball deep into the other half,* lanzó el balón lejos al campo contrario; *deep in the forest,* en lo profundo del bosque. **9** *(far in time, late)* tarde: *we talked deep into the night,* hablamos hasta bien entrada la noche. – **10** **the deep,** *n* las profundidades *fpl*, el piélago.
● **deep down,** en el fondo (de su corazón). ‖ **to be deep in debt,** estar muy endeudado,-a. ‖ **to be deep in thought,** estar absorto,-a, estar ensimismado,-a. ‖ **to be in deep trouble,** estar en un serio apuro, estar en un buen lío. ‖ **to be in deep water(s),** estar con el agua al cuello. ‖ **to dig deep,** cavar hondo. ‖ **to go deep into sth.,** profundizar en algo. ‖ **to go off at the deep end,** salirse de sus casillas, perder los estribos, ponerse como una fiera. ‖ **to look deep into sb.'s eyes,** penetrar en algn. con la mirada, mirar a algn. fijamente a los ojos. ‖ **to park two/three deep,** aparcar en doble/triple fila. ‖ **to be thrown in at the deep end,** tener que empezar por lo más difcil.

deepen ['diːpən] **1** *t (well, channel, river)* profundizar, hacer más profundo,-a, hacer más hondo,-a. **2** *(knowledge)* profundizar, ahondar; *(sympathy)* aumentar; *(colour, emotion)* intensificar; *(sound, voice)* hacer más grave. – **3** *i (river, water, sea)* hacerse más profundo,-a, volverse más profundo,-a. **4** *(love)* crecer, hacerse más profundo,-a; *(mystery, understanding, knowledge, concern)* crecer, aumentar; *(crisis, despair)* acentuarse; *(colour)* intensificarse; *(voice)* hacerse más grave.

deep-freeze ['diːp'friːz] **1** *n* congelador *m*. – **2** *t (at home)* congelar; *(commercially)* ultracongelar.
▲ *pt* **deep-froze** *pp* **deep-frozen.**

deep-fry [diːp'fraɪ] *t* freír en abundante aceite.
▲ *pt & pp* **deep-fried,** *ger* **deep-frying.**

deeply ['diːplɪ] **1** *adv (cut, bite)* profundamente. **2** *(sigh)* profundamente, hondo; *(breathe)* hondo; *(look)* fijamente. **3** *(intensely - grateful, concerned, love)* profundamente; *(- interested)* sumamente; *(profoundly - think, consider)* a fondo: *he's deeply religious,* es profundamente religioso; *she was deeply hurt,* la hirió en lo más vivo.

deep-rooted [diːpˈruːtɪd] *adj* profundamente arraigado,-a.

deep-sea [ˈdiːpsiː] *n* (*fishing, diving*) de altura.

deep-seated [diːpˈsiːtɪd] *adj* profundamente arraigado,-a.

deep-set [diːpˈset] *adj* (*eyes*) hundido,-a.

deer [dɪəʳ] *n* ciervo, venado.
▲ *pl* **deer**.

deface [dɪˈfeɪs] *t* (*damage, spoil*) desfigurar; (*scrawl on*) pintarrajear.

de facto [deɪˈfæktəʊ] **1** *adj* de hecho. – **2** *adv* de hecho.

defamation [defəˈmeɪʃən] *n fml* difamación *f*.

defamatory [dɪˈfæmətəri] *adj fml* difamatorio,-a.

defame [dɪˈfeɪm] *t fml* difamar.

default [dɪˈfɔːlt] **1** *n* (*failure to act*) omisión *f*, negligencia. **2** (*failure to pay*) incumplimiento de pago, mora, demora. **3** JUR rebeldía. **4** SP incomparecencia. – **5** *i* (*fail to act*) faltar a sus compromisos, incumplir un acuerdo. **6** (*fail to pay*) no pagar (**on,** -), demorarse (**on,** en). **7** JUR declararse en rebeldía. **8** SP no comparecer, no presentarse.
● **in default of,** a falta de. ‖ **to be in default on sth.,** demorarse en el pago de algo. ‖ **to win by default,** SP ganar por incomparecencia del rival.
■ **default setting,** COMPUT valor *m* por defecto.

defaulter [dɪˈfɔːltəʳ] **1** *n* FIN (*on loan, rent, mortgage*) moroso,-a. **2** JUR MIL rebelde *mf*.

defeat [dɪˈfiːt] **1** *n* (*of army, team*) derrota; (*of motion, bill*) rechazo. **2** *fig* (*of hopes, plans*) fracaso. – **3** *t* (*opponent*) derrotar, vencer; (*opposition, government*) derrotar; (*bill, motion*) rechazar. **4** *fig* (*hopes, plans*) frustrar.
● **to defeat the object / defeat the purpose,** ir en contra del propósito.

defeatism [dɪˈfiːtɪzəm] *n* derrotismo.

defeatist [dɪˈfiːtɪst] *n* derrotista *mf*.

defecate [ˈdefəkeɪt] *i fml* defecar.

defecation [defəˈkeɪʃən] *n fml* defecación *f*.

defect [ˈdiːfekt] **1** *n* (*gen*) defecto; (*flaw*) desperfecto, tara: *she has a speech defect,* tiene un defecto en el habla; *it's a defect in his character,* es un defecto de su carácter; *there's a defect in this glass,* esta copa tiene una tara. – **2** *i* (*party, team*) desertar, pasarse al bando contrario; (*country*) huir.
▲ (*verbo*) [dɪˈfekt].

defection [dɪˈfekʃən] *n* (*from party, team*) deserción *f*, defección *f*; (*from country*) fuga, huida.

defective [dɪˈfektɪv] **1** *adj* (*faulty*) defectuoso,-a; (*flawed*) con desperfectos; (*incomplete, lacking*) deficiente. **2** LING defectivo,-a.

defector [dɪˈfektəʳ] *n* POL tránsfuga *mf*, trásfuga *mf*.

defence [dɪˈfens] **1** *n* (*gen*) defensa; (*protection*) defensa, protección *f*: *she carried a gun for defence,* llevaba una pistola para defenderse; *government spending on defence,* los gastos de defensa del gobierno; *the body's defences,* las defensas del organismo. **2** JUR defensa: *counsel for the defence,* abogado,-a defensor,-ra; *witness for the defence,* testigo de la defensa. **3** SP defensa: *he plays in defence,* juega de defensa.
● **to come to sb.'s defence,** salir en defensa de algn.
■ **defence lawyer,** abogado,-a defensor,-ra. ‖ **defence mechanism,** mecanismo de defensa. ‖ **Ministry of Defence,** Ministerio de Defensa.

defenceless [dɪˈfensləs] *adj* indefenso,-a.

defend [dɪˈfend] **1** *t* (*gen*) defender; (*protect*) defender, proteger: *the militia defended the town,* la milicia defendió la ciudad; *he was defending his title,* defendía su título. – **2** *i* SP jugar de defensa.

● **to defend os.,** defenderse.

defendant [dɪˈfendənt] *n* JUR (*in civil case*) demandado,-a; (*in criminal case*) acusado,-a.

defender [dɪˈfendəʳ] **1** *n* (*gen*) defensor,-ra. **2** SP defensa *mf*.

defending [dɪˈfendɪŋ] *adj que defiende*.
■ **defending champion,** SP campeón,-ona actual. ‖ **defending counsel,** abogado,-a defensor,-ra.

defense [dɪˈfens] *n* US → **defence**.

defenseless [dɪˈfensləs] *adj* US → **defence**.

defensible [dɪˈfensəbəl] *adj* (*town, position*) defendible; (*idea, opinion, system*) defendible, justificable.

defensive [dɪˈfensɪv] *adj* defensivo,-a.
● **to be defensive / get defensive,** ponerse a la defensiva. ‖ **to be on the defensive,** estar a la defensiva.

defer[1] [dɪˈfɜːʳ] *t* (*postpone*) aplazar, posponer, retrasar: *we deferred our departure,* aplazamos nuestra partida; *the judge deferred sentence,* el juez aplazó la sentencia.
▲ *pt & pp* **deferred**.

defer[2] [dɪˈfɜːʳ] *t* **to defer to,** *i* (*submit to*) deferir a: *I defer to your judgement,* defiero a tu juicio.
▲ *pt & pp* **deferred,** *ger* **deferring**.

deference [ˈdefərəns] *n* deferencia.
● **in deference to,** por deferencia a.

deferential [defəˈrenʃəl] *adj* deferente.

deferment [dɪˈfɜːmənt] *n* aplazamiento.

deferral [dɪˈfɜːrəl] *n* aplazamiento.

deferred [dɪˈfɜːd] **1** *adj* FIN diferido,-a. **2** JUR aplazado,-a.

defiance [dɪˈfaɪəns] *n* desafío.
● **in defiance of,** a despecho de.

defiant [dɪˈfaɪənt] *adj* (*attitude, behaviour*) desafiante, de desafío; (*person*) rebelde.

deficiency [dɪˈfɪʃənsɪ] **1** *n* (*lack*) deficiencia; (*shortage*) escasez *f*, falta, déficit *m*. **2** (*fault, shortcoming*) defecto, deficiencia.
▲ *pl* **deficiencies**.

deficient [dɪˈfɪʃənt] *adj* deficiente, insuficiente.
● **to be deficient in sth.,** carecer de algo, estar falto,-a de algo.

deficit [ˈdefɪsɪt] *n* déficit *m*.

defile[1] [dɪˈfaɪl] **1** *t* (*make dirty, pollute - countryside*) dañar; (*- water, river*) contaminar; (*corrupt - mind*) corromper, envilecer; (*spoil - reputation, honour*) mancillar, manchar; (*- memory*) profanar. **2** REL (*desecrate*) profanar.

defile[2] [dɪˈfaɪl] *n* desfiladero.

definable [dɪˈfaɪnəbəl] *adj* definible.

define [dɪˈfaɪn] **1** *t* (*word, expression, concept*) definir. **2** (*duties, role, rights, etc*) delimitar. **3** (*outline*) definir, perfilar.

definite [ˈdefɪnət] **1** *adj* (*final, fixed - gen*) definitivo,-a; (*- opinions*) fijo,-a: *the date is now definite,* la fecha ya es definitiva. **2** (*clear, distinct*) claro,-a; (*clear, appreciable*) notable, sensible; (*exact, specific*) específico,-a, preciso,-a: *there's a definite smell of burning,* huele claramente a quemado. **3** (*sure, certain*) seguro,-a, confirmado,-a: *is it definite?,* ¿es seguro?; *she was very definite about it,* estaba muy segura.

definitely [ˈdefɪnətlɪ] **1** *adv* (*without doubt*) sin duda, indudablemente, seguramente: *she definitely said that she'd be here at 4.00pm,* seguro que dijo que estaría aquí a las cuatro; *it was definitely him,* sin duda era él; *I'm definitely going!,* ¡yo voy, seguro! **2** (*definitively*) definitivamente. – **3** *interj* ¡desde luego!, ¡claro que sí!, ¡por supuesto!: *definitely not!,* ¡claro que no!, ¡de ninguna manera!

definition [defɪˈnɪʃən] **1** *n* (*explanation*) definición *f*: *what's the definition of irony?,* ¿cómo se define la ironía?; *what's your definition of a night on the town?*, ¿tú qué entiendes por una noche de marcha?; *by definition*, por definición. **2** (*description of features*) definición *f*; (*delimitation*) delimitación *f*. **3** (*clarity of shape, colour*) nitidez *f*, definición *f*; (*of sound*) nitidez *f*, claridad *f*.

definitive [dɪ'fɪnɪtɪv] **1** *adj* (*final, conclusive*) definitivo,-a. **2** (*ultimate - study etc*) de mayor autoridad; (*- performance*) inmejorable, insuperable.

definitively [dɪ'fɪnɪtɪvlɪ] *adv* definitivamente.

deflate [dɪ'fleɪt] **1** *t* (*balloon, tyre*) desinflar, deshinchar. **2** *fig* (*humble*) rebajar, humillar, bajar los humos a; (*discourage*) desanimar, desalentar. **3** ECON provocar la deflación de. – **4** *i* desinflarse, deshincharse.
● **to feel deflated**, sentirse desilusionado,-a, sentirse por los suelos.

deflation [dɪ'fleɪʃən] **1** *n* (*of ballon, tyre*) desinflamiento. **2** ECON deflación *f*.

deflationary [dɪ'fleɪʃənərɪ] *adj* ECON deflacionario,-a, deflacionista.

deflect [dɪ'flekt] **1** *t* desviar. – **2** *i* desviarse.

deflection [dɪ'flekʃən] *n* desviación *f*.

deflower [dɪ'flauəʳ] *t* desflorar, desvirgar.

defoliant [dɪ'fəʊlɪənt] *n* defoliante *m*.

defoliate [dɪ'fəʊlɪeɪt] *t* defoliar.

deforestation [dɪfɒrɪs'teɪʃən] *n* deforestación *f*, despoblación *f* forestal.

deform [dɪ'fɔːm] *t* deformar.

deformation [dɪ'fɔːmeɪʃən] *n* deformación *f*.

deformed [dɪ'fɔːmd] *adj* deforme.

deformity [dɪ'fɔːmɪtɪ] *n* deformidad *f*.
▲ *pl* **deformities**.

defraud [dɪ'frɔːd] *t* estafar.
● **to defraud sb. of sth.**, estafarle algo a algn.

defrost [diː'frɒst] **1** *t* (*freezer, food*) descongelar. **2** US (*windscreen*) desempañar. – **3** *i* descongelarse.

deft [deft] *adj* diestro,-a, hábil.
● **to be deft at doing sth.**, ser hábil haciendo algo.

defunct [dɪ'fʌŋkt] *adj* (*person*) difunto,-a; (*practice, law*) (que ha caído,-a) en desuso, caduco,-a; (*organization, scheme*) desaparecido,-a, extinto,-a.

defuse [dɪ'fjuːz] **1** *t* (*bomb*) desactivar. **2** (*situation*) distender, reducir la tensión de; (*anger, crisis*) calmar.

defy [dɪ'faɪ] **1** *t* (*ignore, refuse to give in to*) desafiar; (*disobey - law, order, authority*) desobedecer, desacatar: *the members defied their union leader*, los miembros desobedecieron a su líder sindical; *it seems to defy the law of gravity*, parece desafiar la ley de la gravedad. **2** (*make impossible*) ser imposible: *the mess in your room defies description*, el desorden en tu habitación es indescriptible; *the problem defied solution*, no hubo manera de resolver el problema; *it defies reason*, se escapa a la razón. **3** (*challenge*) retar, desafiar: *I defy you to disprove my theory*, te desafío a que refutes mi teoría.
● **to defy all logic**, ir en contra de la lógica.
▲ *pt & pp* **defied**, *ger* **defying**.

degeneracy [dɪ'dʒenərəsɪ] *n* degeneración *f*.

degenerate [dɪ'dʒenərət] **1** *adj* degenerado,-a. – **2** *n* degenerado,-a. – **3** *i* (*gen*) degenerar (**into**, en); (*health*) deteriorarse.
▲ (*verbo*) [dɪ'dʒenəreɪt].

degeneration [dɪdʒenə'reɪʃən] *n* degeneración *f*.

degenerative [dɪ'dʒenərətɪv] *adj* degenerativo,-a.

degrade [dɪ'greɪd] **1** *t* (*debase*) degradar, envilecer. **2** BIOL CHEM degradar. – **3** *i* BIOL CHEM degradarse.
● **to degrade os.**, degradarse, rebajarse.

degrading [dɪ'greɪdɪŋ] *adj* degradante.

degree [dɪ'griː] **1** *n* (*unit of measurement*) grado: *an angle of 45 degrees*, un ángulo de 45 grados; *it's 25 degrees today*, hoy estamos a 25 grados; *the city lies at a latitude of 20 degrees North*, la ciudad se encuentra a 20 grados latitud norte. **2** (*extent, level, point*) grado, nivel *m*, punto; (*amount*) algo: *I agree with you to some degree*, estoy de acuerdo contigo hasta cierto punto; *to a lesser degree*, en menor grado; *a degree of danger*, algo de peligro; *a certain degree of optimism*, un cierto optimismo; *some degree of truth*, algo de verdad; *a high degree of skill*, un alto nivel de habilidad; *I'm not in the slightest degree worried*, no estoy preocupada en absoluto; *there isn't the slightest degree of doubt*, no hay la más mínima duda. **3** (*stage, grade, step*) grado, etapa: *third-degree burns*, quemaduras de tercer grado; *first-degree murder*, homicidio en primer grado. **4** EDUC título: *she has a degree in physics*, es licenciada en física.
● **by degrees**, poco a poco, gradualmente, paulatinamente. ‖ **to take a degree**, licenciarse (**in**, en).
■ **first degree**, licenciatura. ‖ **honourary degree**, título honoris causa.

dehumanize [diː'hjuːmənaɪz] *t* deshumanizar.

dehydrate [diːhaɪ'dreɪt] **1** *t* deshidratar. – **2** *i* deshidratarse.

dehydrated [diːhaɪ'dreɪtɪd] *adj* (*person, vegetables*) deshidratado,-a; (*milk*) en polvo.

dehydration [diːhaɪ'dreɪʃən] *n* deshidratación *f*.

de-ice [diː'aɪs] *t* quitar el hielo a, deshelar.

de-icer [diː'aɪsəʳ] *n* descongelante *m*.

deify ['deɪfaɪ] *t* deificar.
▲ *pt & pp* **deified**, *ger* **deifying**.

deign [deɪn] *i* dignarse (**to**, a).

deity ['deɪtɪ] **1** *n* deidad *f*. **2 the Deity**, Dios *m*.
▲ *pl* **deities**.

dejected [dɪ'dʒektɪd] *adj* abatido,-a, desalentado,-a, desanimado,-a.

dejection [dɪ'dʒekʃən] *n* abatimiento, desaliento, desánimo.

dekko ['dekəʊ] **to have a dekko at sth.**, *n* echar un vistazo a algo.
▲ *pl* **dekkos**.

delay [dɪ'leɪ] **1** *n* (*act, state*) demora, tardanza, dilación *f*; (*amount of time*) retraso, demora; (*traffic hold-up*) embotellamiento, atasco: *without delay*, sin demora, sin dilación; *a delay of two hours*, dos horas de retraso; *trains are subject to delay*, los trenes pueden retrasarse; *heavy traffic is causing delays on the M15*, el denso tráfico está provocando retrasos en la M15. – **2** *t* (*defer, postpone - game*) aplazar, retrasar; (*payment*) aplazar, diferir. **3** (*make late - flight, train*) retrasar, demorar; (*person*) entretener: *our plane was delayed*, nuestro avión se retrasó; *I've been delayed*, me han entretenido. – **4** *i* (*be late*) tardar; (*act slowly*) entretenerse: *don't delay!*, ¡no tardes!

delayed [dɪ'leɪd] *adj* retardado,-a.
■ **delayed action**, acción *f* retardada.

delaying [dɪ'leɪŋ] *adj* dilatorio,-a.

delectable [dɪ'lektəbəl] *adj* delicioso,-a.

delegate ['delɪgət] **1** *n* delegado,-a. – **2** *t* (*duties, responsibility, etc*) delegar (**to**, en). – **3** *i* delegar.
● **to delegate sb. to do sth.**, delegar en algn. para que haga algo.
▲ (*verbo*) ['delɪgeɪt].

delegation [delɪ'geɪʃən] *n* delegación *f*.

delete [dɪ'liːt] *t* (*remove*) eliminar, suprimir; (*cross out*) tachar: *delete as appropriate*, táchese lo que no proceda.

deleterious [delɪ'tɪərɪəs] *adj fml* nocivo,-a, perjudicial.
deletion [dɪ'liːʃən] 1 *n* (*act*) eliminación *f* supresión *f*. 2 (*word, letter crossed out*) tachadura.
deliberate [dɪ'lɪbərət] 1 *adj* (*intentional*) deliberado,-a, intencionado,-a; (*studied*) premeditado,-a: *a deliberate lie,* una mentira descarada; *I think it was deliberate,* creo que lo hizo adrede. 2 (*slow, unhurried*) pausado,-a, lento,-a; (*careful*) reflexivo,-a. – 3 *t* deliberar, considerar. – 4 *i* deliberar (**on,** sobre).
▲ (*verbo*) [dɪ'lɪbəreɪt].
deliberately [dɪ'lɪbərətlɪ] 1 *adv* (*intentionally*) a propósito, adrede, aposta, deliberadamente. 2 (*slowly*) pausadamente.
deliberation [dɪlɪbə'reɪʃən] 1 *n* (*consideration*) deliberación *f*. 2 (*slowness, carefulness*) calma, parsimonia.
delicacy ['delɪkəsɪ] 1 *n* (*softness, tenderness*) delicadeza. 2 (*fragility*) fragilidad *f*. 3 (*skill, careful treatment*) lo delicado. 4 (*tact, restraint, sensitivity*) delicadeza. 5 (*of colours, food, smells*) lo delicado. 6 (*food*) manjar *m* (exquisito), esquisitez *f*.
▲ *pl* **delicacies**.
delicate ['delɪkət] 1 *adj* (*finely made, fine, exquisite - gen*) delicado,-a; (*- embroidery, handiwork*) fino,-a, esmerado,-a, delicado,-a. 2 (*fragile, easily damaged*) frágil; (*easily made ill*) delicado,-a. 3 (*requiring careful treatment, requiring tact*) delicado,-a. 4 (*subtle - colour*) suave, delicado,-a; (*flavour, taste*) delicado,-a, fino,-a; (*perfume*) delicado,-a. 5 (*sensitive - instrument*) sensible; (*sense of smell, taste*) fino,-a.
delicately ['delɪkətlɪ] 1 *adv* (*make, carve, paint, etc*) delicadamente, con finura. 2 (*act, behave, treat, handle, word, etc*) con delicadeza, con consideración. 3 (*balance*) con sensibilidad. 4 (*patterned, perfumed, flavoured*) delicadamente.
delicatessen [delɪkə'tesən] *n* charcutería selecta.
delicious [dɪ'lɪʃəs] 1 *adj* (*food*) delicioso,-a, riquísimo,-a; (*taste, smell*) exquisito,-a. 2 (*delightful, attractive, pleasant*) delicioso,-a, agradable.
delight [dɪ'laɪt] 1 *n* (*great pleasure, joy*) placer *m*, gusto, alegría, deleite *m*. 2 (*source of pleasure*) encanto, delicia, placer *m*. – 3 *t* (*give pleasure to*) deleitar, encantar, dar gusto; (*make very happy*) llenar de alegría. – 4 *i* deleitarse (**in,** en/con).
delighted [dɪ'laɪtɪd] *adj* (*person*) encantado,-a, contentísimo,-a; (*smile, shout, look*) de alegría: *I'd be delighted!,* ¡estaría encantado!; *delighted to meet you,* encantado,-a (de conocerle), mucho gusto (en conocerle); *we'd be delighted to help out,* ayudaríamos encantados; *I'm delighted that you can make it to the party,* me alegro mucho de que puedas venir a la fiesta; *I'd be delighted to come to dinner on Saturday,* me encantaría ir a cenar el sábado; *the children were delighted with their toys,* los niños estaban encantados con sus juguetes; *we were delighted by your news,* tu noticia nos causó una enorme alegría.
delightful [dɪ'laɪtfʊl] *adj* (*person, place*) encantador,-ra; (*evening, weather, time*) muy agradable; (*meal*) delicioso,-a; (*dress etc*) precioso,-a.
delightfully [dɪ'laɪtfʊlɪ] *adv* de maravilla, deliciosamente.
delimit [dɪ'lɪmɪt] *t* delimitar.
delineate [dɪ'lɪnɪeɪt] 1 *t* (*by drawing*) delinear, esbozar, perfilar. 2 (*by describing*) trazar, describir.
delinquency [dɪ'lɪŋkwənsɪ] 1 *n* (*behaviour*) delincuencia. 2 (*act*) delito.
delinquent [dɪ'lɪŋkwənt] 1 *adj* (*youth*) delincuente; (*activity*) delictivo,-a. 2 FIN (*person*) moroso,-a. – 3 *n* delincuente *mf*.

delirious [dɪ'lɪrɪəs] 1 *adj* MED delirante. 2 *fig* (*happy*) loco,-a de alegría.
● **to be delirious,** MED delirar, desvariar.
deliriously [dɪ'lɪrɪəslɪ] 1 *adv* MED delirantemente. 2 *fig* locamente.
● **to be deliriously happy,** estar loco,-a de alegría.
delirium [dɪ'lɪrɪəm] 1 *n* MED delirio, desvarío. 2 (*excited happiness*) delirio.
● **to go into delirium,** *fig* enloquecer.
■ **delirium tremens,** delírium tremens *m*.
deliver [dɪ'lɪvər] 1 *t* (*take, give, hand over - goods etc*) entregar; (*- message*) dar, entregar; (*distribute*) repartir (a domicilio). 2 (*hit, kick, push*) dar; (*blow, punch*) propinar, atestar; (*shot, fast ball*) lanzar. 3 (*say - speech, sermon, verdict*) pronunciar; (*lecture, sermon, ultimatum*) dar; (*warning*) hacer; (*judgement*) dictar, pronunciar, emitir. 4 (*produce, provide, fulfil*) cumplir. 5 MED (*baby*) asistir en el parto de, atender en el parto de. 6 *fml* (*free, save*) liberar. – 7 *i* (*goods, groceries, etc*) hacer repartos a domicilio. 8 (*fulfil promise etc*) cumplir.
deliverance [dɪ'lɪvərəns] *n fml* liberación *f*.
delivery [dɪ'lɪvərɪ] 1 *n* (*act - gen*) entrega, reparto; (*- of mail*) reparto: *we get two postal deliveries a day,* recibimos dos repartos diarios; *this order is ready for delivery,* este pedido está preparado para entregar; *delivery is free when you spend over 20 pounds,* el reparto es gratuito si gasta más de 20 libras. 2 (*consignment*) partida, remesa. 3 (*manner of speaking*) modo de hablar. 4 (*of baby*) parto, alumbramiento. 5 (*throwing, launching - of ball, missile*) lanzamiento.
● **to pay on delivery,** pagar a la entrega de la mercancía. ‖ **to take delivery of sth.,** recibir algo.
■ **delivery charges,** gastos *mpl* de envío, gastos *mpl* de transporte. ‖ **delivery man,** repartidor *m*. ‖ **delivery note,** albarán *m* de entrega. ‖ **delivery period,** plazo de entrega. ‖ **delivery room,** sala de partos. ‖ **delivery service,** servicio de reparto a domicilio. ‖ **delivery van,** GB camioneta de reparto, furgoneta de reparto.
▲ *pl* **deliveries**.
dell [del] *n lit* valle *m* pequeño, hondonada.
delphinium [del'fɪnɪəm] *n* espuela de caballero.
delta ['deltə] 1 *n* GEOG delta *m*. 2 (*Greek letter*) delta.
delude [dɪ'luːd] *t* engañar: *he was deluded into thinking that everything was going smoothly,* le hicieron creer que todo iba sobre ruedas.
● **to delude os.,** dejarse engañar, engañarse, hacerse ilusiones.
deluge ['deljuːdʒ] 1 *n* (*rain*) diluvio; (*flood*) inundación *f*. 2 *fig* avalancha, alud *m*, aluvión *m*. – 3 *t* (*flood*) inundar (**with,** de). 4 *fig* inundar (**with,** de), abrumar (**with,** con): *we've been deluged with applications,* hemos recibido un aluvión de solicitudes.
delusion [dɪ'luːʒən] 1 *n* (*false belief*) falsa ilusión *f*; (*mistaken idea*) error *m*: *she's under the delusion that he loves her,* piensa equivocadamente que él la quiere. 2 (*act, state*) engaño.
● **to have delusions of grandeur,** tener delirios de grandeza.
delusive [dɪ'luːsɪv] 1 *adj* (*misleading*) engañoso,-a. 2 (*illusory*) ilusorio,-a.
de luxe [də'lʌks] *adj* de lujo.
delve [delv] 1 *i* (*rummage, search*) hurgar (**into,** en). 2 (*study - gen*) ahondar (**into,** en); (*the past*) hurgar (**into,** en), escarbar (**into,** en).
demagogue ['deməgɒg] *n* demagogo,-a.

demand [dɪ'mɑːnd] **1** *n* (*request*) solicitud *f*, petición *f*; (*claim*) exigencia; (*for pay rise, rights, etc*) reclamación *f*: *by popular demand,* a petición del público; *they refuse to agree to the highjackers' demands,* se niegan a aceptar las exigencias de los secuestradores; *the committee makes great demands on my time,* el comité me absorbe gran parte del tiempo. **2** ECON demanda: *there's a big demand for computers,* hay una gran demanda de ordenadores; *Spanish products are in great demand,* los productos españoles están muy solicitados. **3** (*note, warning*) aviso. – **4** *t* (*call for, insist on*) exigir; (*rights, conditions, etc*) reclamar: *I demand to see the manager,* exijo ver al director; *the union is demanding a 6% increase,* el sindicato exige un aumento del 6%; *he demanded to see their identity cards,* exigió que le enseñaran sus carnets de identidad. **5** (*need, require*) exigir, requerir: *this work demands a high degree of concentration,* este trabajo requiere un alto grado de concentración.
● **on demand,** a petición: *they want abortion on demand,* quieren que el aborto sea libre. ‖ **to make demands of/on sb.,** pedir mucho de algn.

demanding [dɪ'mɑːndɪŋ] **1** *adj* (*person - gen*) exigente; (*awkward*) difícil. **2** (*tiring - job etc*) agotador,-ra.

demarara [demə'reərə] demarara (*sugar*), *n* azúcar *mf* moreno,-a.

demarcation [diːmɑː'keɪʃən] *n* demarcación *f*.
■ **demarcation dispute,** conflicto de competencias. ‖ **demarcation line,** línea de demarcación.

demean [dɪ'miːn] *i fml* degradar, rebajar.
● **to demean os.,** rebajarse, degradarse.

demeaning [dɪ'miːnɪŋ] *adj* humillante, vergonzoso,-a, degradante.

demeanour [dɪ'miːnəʳ] **1** *n fml* (*behaviour*) comportamiento, conducta. **2** (*bearing*) porte *m*.

demented [dɪ'mentɪd] **1** *adj* MED demente. **2** *fig* (*agitated*) histérico,-a.

dementia [dɪ'menʃɪə] *n* demencia.

demerit [dɪ'merɪt] *n* demérito.

demigod ['demɪgɒd] *n* semidiós *m*.

demise [dɪ'maɪz] **1** *n* (*death*) fallecimiento, defunción *f*. **2** *fig* (*end*) desaparición *f*; (*failure*) fracaso.

demist [diː'mɪst] *t* desempañar.

demo ['deməʊ] **1** *n* (*recording, tape*) maqueta. **2** *fam* (*demonstration*) mani *f*, manifestación *f*.
▲ *pl* demos.

demob [dɪ'mɒb] *t* desmovilizar.
▲ *pt & pp* demobbed, *ger* demobbing.

demobilize [dɪ'məʊbɪlaɪz] *t* desmovilizar.

democracy [dɪ'mɒkrəsɪ] *n* democracia.
▲ *pl* democracies.

democrat ['deməkræt] *n* demócrata *mf*.
■ **Christian Democrat,** democratacristiano,-a.

democratic [demə'krætɪk] *adj* democrático,-a.
■ **Democratic party,** US partido demócrata.

democratically [demə'krætɪklɪ] *adv* democráticamente.

demography [dɪ'mɒgrəfɪ] *n* demografía.

demolish [dɪ'mɒlɪʃ] **1** *t* (*building*) derribar, demoler, echar abajo. **2** *fig* (*theory, proposal*) destruir, echar por tierra. **3** *fam* (*eat*) zamparse.

demolition [demə'lɪʃən] **1** *n* (*of building*) demolición *f*, derribo. **2** *fig* (*of argument, idea, belief*) demolición *f*, destrucción *f*.

demon ['diːmən] **1** *n* (*evil spirit*) demonio, diablo. **2** *fam* (*naughty child*) diablillo. **3** (*energetic person*) fiera, bestia; (*talented person*) fiera, hacha: *he's a demon for work,* es

una bestia trabajando; *she's a demon at tennis,* es una fiera jugando al tenis.
■ **the demon drink,** el demonio de la bebida.

demoniac [dɪ'məʊnɪæk] *adj* (*person*) endemoniado,-a, demoniaco,-a; (*laughter*) diabólico,-a, demoniaco,-a; (*activity*) desenfrenado,-a.

demoniacal [diːmə'naɪəkəl] *adj* → **demoniac**.

demonic [dɪ'mɒnɪk] *adj* demoniaco,-a.

demonstrable [dɪ'mɒnstrəbəl] *adj* demostrable.

demonstrate ['demənstreɪt] **1** *t* (*show, prove*) demostrar: *these figures clearly demonstrate the enormity of the problem,* estas cifras demuestran claramente la magnitud del problema. **2** (*express, display*) demostrar, dar prueba de: *his reply demonstrated a complete lack of sensitivity,* su respuesta demostró una falta total de sensibilidad. **3** (*in shop etc*) hacer una demostración de. – **4** *i* (*protest*) manifestarse.

demonstration [demən'streɪʃən] **1** *n* (*act of showing*) demostración *f*, muestra. **2** (*in shop etc*) demostración *f*. **3** (*march*) manifestación *f*.

demonstrative [dɪ'mɒnstrətɪv] **1** *adj* (*person - showing feelings*) abierto,-a, franco,-a, efusivo,-a, expresivo,-a. **2** *fml* (*proving something*) concluyente: *the results are demonstrative of the need for more training,* los resultados demuestran la necesidad de mayor preparación. **3** LING demostrativo,-a.

demonstrator ['demənstreɪtəʳ] **1** *n* POL manifestante *mf*. **2** (*in shop etc*) demostrador,-ra.

demoralize [dɪ'mɒrəlaɪz] *t* desmoralizar.
● **to become demoralized,** desmoralizarse.

demoralizing [dɪ'mɒrəlaɪzɪŋ] *adj* desmoralizante, desmoralizador,-ra, desalentador,-ra.

demote [dɪ'məʊt] **1** *t* (*gen*) bajar de categoría. **2** MIL degradar.

demotion [dɪ'məʊʃən] **1** *n* (*gen*) descenso de categoría. **2** MIL degradación *f*.

demur [dɪ'mɜːʳ] *i fml* (*object*) oponerse, objetar.
● **to demur at sth./doing sth.,** poner reparos a algo/hacer algo. ‖ **without demur,** sin poner reparos, sin poner objeciones.
▲ *pt & pp* demurred, *ger* demurring.

demure [dɪ'mjʊəʳ] *adj* (*person*) recatado,-a; (*behaviour*) tímido,-a, discreto,-a.

demystify [dɪ'mɪstɪfaɪ] *t* desmitificar.
▲ *pt & pp* demystified, *ger* demystifying.

den [den] **1** *n* (*of animals*) guarida. **2** (*secret meeting-place*) antro; (*of thieves*) guarida: *a den of iniquity,* un antro de perdición. **3** *fam* (*room*) cuarto; (*for study*) estudio.

denial [dɪ'naɪəl] **1** *n* (*of accusation*) mentís *m*, desmentido, refutación *f*: *the minister's denial changes nothing,* el desmentido del ministro no cambia nada; *the politician issued a denial of the rumours,* el político desmintió los rumores; *she made a denial of all the charges,* negó todos los cargos. **2** (*of principle*) negación *f*: *a denial of the principle of equality,* una negación del principio de igualdad. **3** (*of rights, justice*) denegación *f*. **4** (*of request*) negativa, rechazo.

denier ['denɪəʳ] *n* denier *m*.

denigrate ['denɪgreɪt] *t* (*person, character*) denigrar; (*achievements, efforts*) menospreciar.

denim ['denɪm] **1** *n* tela vaquera, tela tejana. – **2** *adj* tejano,-a, vaquero,-a. – **3 denims,** *npl* vaqueros *mpl*, tejanos *mpl*.

denizen ['denɪzən] *n lit* habitante *mf*, morador,-ra.

Denmark ['denmɑːk] *n* Dinamarca.

denomination [dɪnɒmɪ'neɪʃən] **1** *n* REL confesión *f*. **2** (*standard of value*) valor *m*.

denominational [dɪnɒmɪ'neɪʃənəl] *adj* REL confesional.
denominator [dɪ'nɒmɪneɪtəʳ] *n* MATH denominador *m*.
denote [dɪ'nəʊt] **1** *t fml* (*indicate, represent*) denotar, indicar. **2** LING (*mean*) denotar, significar.
denouement [deɪ'nuːmənt] *n* desenlace *m*.
denounce [dɪ'naʊns] *t* denunciar: *they denounced the execution of the writer,* denunciaron la ejecución del escritor.
dense [dens] **1** *adj* (*closely packed - population, traffic*) denso,-a; (*- forest, jungle, vegetation*) denso,-a, espeso,-a; (*- crowd*) compacto,-a, apretado,-a. **2** (*thick - fog, smoke*) espeso,-a, denso,-a. **3** PHYS (*heavy - substance, rock, star*) denso,-a. **4** *fam* (*stupid - person*) corto,-a (de luces), torpe, estúpido,-a, burro,-a, duro,-a de entendederas.
densely ['denslɪ] *adv* (*populated, forested, etc*) densamente; (*packed*) apretadamente.
denseness ['densnəs] **1** *n* (*stupidity*) falta de luces. **2** → **density**.
density ['densɪtɪ] *n* (*gen*) densidad *f*: *the density of the fog,* la densidad de la niebla.
■ **population density,** densidad *f* de población.
▲ *pl* **densities**.
dent [dent] **1** *n* (*in car, metal*) abolladura. – **2** *t* (*car, metal*) abollar. **3** (*pride, reputation*) hacer mella en; (*confidence*) hacer perder. – **4** *i* (*metal*) abollarse.
● **to make a dent in,** (*car etc*) abollar; (*savings etc*) comerse una parte de, menguar, mermar.
dental[1] ['dentəl] *adj* (*gen*) dental: *I've got a dental appointment,* tengo hora con el dentista.
■ **dental floss,** hilo dental, seda dental. ‖ **dental hygienist,** ayudante *mf* de dentista, asistente *mf* de dentista. ‖ **dental surgeon,** odontólogo,-a. ‖ **dental surgery,** consultorio odontológico, clínica dental.
dental[2] ['dentəl] **1** *adj* LING dental. – **2** *n* LING dental *f*.
dentist ['dentɪst] *n* dentista *mf*, odontólogo,-a.
dentistry ['dentɪstrɪ] *n* odontología.
denture ['dentʃəʳ] **1** *n* (*plate*) prótesis *f* dental. – **2** **dentures,** *npl* dentadura *f sing* postiza.
denude [dɪ'njuːd] **1** *t* GEOG desnudar, denudar. **2** (*strip*) despojar (**of,** de).
denunciation [dɪnʌnsɪ'eɪʃən] *n* denuncia.
deny [dɪ'naɪ] **1** *t* (*repudiate - accusation, fact*) negar; (*rumour, report*) desmentir; (*charge*) rechazar: *the minister denied the allegations,* el ministro negó las acusaciones; *she denies all involvement,* niega toda participación. **2** (*refuse - request*) denegar; (*- rights, equality*) privar de; (*- access*) negar: *I was denied access to the information,* me negaron el acceso a la información; *she was denied opportunity,* le privaron de la oportunidad. **3** *fml* (*disown - person*) desconocer, negar a; (*- faith, country*) renegar de; (*not admit, disclaim*) negar: *he denied all knowledge of the affair,* negó tener conocimiento del asunto; *she denied all responsibility,* negó toda responsabilidad.
● **there's no denying that ...,** es innegable que ... ‖ **to deny os.,** sacrificarse. ‖ **to deny os. of sth.,** privarse de algo.
▲ *pt & pp* **denied,** *ger* **denying**.
deodorant [diː'əʊdərənt] *n* desodorante *m*.
deodorize [diː'əʊdəraɪz] *t* desodorizar.
dep [dɪ'paːtəʳ] *abbr* (*departure*) salida.
depart [dɪ'paːt] *i fml* (*leave*) partir, salir.
◆ **to depart from** *t insep* (*truth*) apartarse de, alejarse de; (*subject*) desviarse de; (*tradition*) apartarse de; (*routine*) salirse de.
● **to depart this life,** dejar de existir.
departed [dɪ'paːtɪd] **1** *adj euph* difunto,-a. **2** *fml* (*youth*) perdido,-a; (*glories*) pasado,-a. – **3 the departed,** *n*

(*man*) el difunto; (*woman*) la difunta. – **4** *npl* (*gen*) los difuntos; (*women*) las difuntas.
department [dɪ'paːtmənt] **1** *n* (*in shop*) sección *f*; (*in company, organization*) departamento, sección *f*; (*in university, school, hospital*) departamento; (*in government*) ministerio: *Mrs Scott is the new head of the English Department,* la Señora Scott es la nueva jefa del departamento de inglés; *I'm just going up to the toy department,* subo un momento a la sección de juguetes. **2** *fam* (*responsibility*) campo, esfera, terreno: *the cleaning is Andy's department,* la limpieza es cosa de Andy.
■ **department store,** grandes almacenes *mpl*.
departmental [diːpaːt'mentəl] *adj* departamental: *departmental manager,* jefe,-a de departamento.
departure [dɪ'paːtʃəʳ] **1** *n* (*of person*) partida, marcha; (*of plane, train, etc*) salida: *their departure was delayed,* su salida fue retrasada; *we were shocked by her sudden departure,* su marcha repentina nos conmocionó. **2** *fig* (*divergence*) desviación *f*; (*venture, type of activity*) innovación *f*: *this represents a departure from our usual practice,* esto supone una desviación con respecto a nuestra práctica habitual.
● **to take one's departure,** retirarse.
■ **departure lounge,** sala de embarque. ‖ **departure time,** hora de salida. ‖ **point of departure,** punto de partida.
depend [dɪ'pend] *i* depender: *it depends,* depende; *it depends what time I finish work,* depende de la hora en que termine de trabajar.
◆ **to depend on 1** *t insep* (*trust*) confiar en/con, fiarse de; (*count on*) contar con: *I'm depending on you to keep it a secret,* confío en que lo mantengas en secreto; *I knew I could depend on you,* sabía que podía contar contigo; *you can depend on it,* cuenta con ello. **2** (*be dependent on*) depender de: *we depend on them for money,* dependemos de su dinero; *she depends too much on her mother,* depende demasiado de su madre. **3** (*be decided by*) depender de: *it depends on the price,* depende del precio; *it depends on where you live,* depende de dónde vivas.
● **that depends,** según, eso depende.
dependability [dɪpendə'bɪlɪtɪ] *n* (*of people*) formalidad *f*, seriedad *f*; (*of things, cars, machines*) fiabilidad *f*.
dependable [dɪ'pendəbəl] *adj* (*person*) responsable, formal, digno,-a de confianza; (*source of income*) seguro,-a; (*thing, car, machine*) fiable.
dependant [dɪ'pendənt] *n* dependiente *mf*, persona a su cargo.
dependence [dɪ'pendəns] *n* dependencia (**on,** de).
■ **drug dependence,** drogodependencia.
dependency [dɪ'pendənsɪ] *n* dependencia.
▲ *pl* **dependencies**.
dependent [dɪ'pendənt] *adj* dependiente.
● **to be dependent on sb./sth.,** depender de algn./algo. ‖ **to be dependent on drugs,** ser drogodependiente.
■ **dependent clause,** LING oración *f* subordinada.
depict [dɪ'pɪkt] **1** *t* (*portray visually, in music*) pintar, representar, retratar. **2** (*describe in writing*) describir, pintar, retratar.
depilatory [dɪ'pɪlətərɪ] **1** *adj* depilatorio,-a. – **2** *n* depilatorio.
deplete [dɪ'pliːt] *t fml* reducir, agotar: *we are depleting the Earth's natural resources,* estamos agotando los recursos naturales de la Tierra.
depleted [dɪ'pliːtɪd] *adj* (*weakened, exhausted*) debilitado,-a, agotado,-a.

depletion [dɪ'pliːʃən] *n fml* (*reduction*) reducción *f*, disminución *f*; (*exhaustion*) agotamiento.

deplorable [dɪ'plɔːrəbəl] *adj* (*appalling, disgraceful*) deplorable, vergonzoso,-a; (*regrettable*) lamentable.

deplore [dɪ'plɔːʳ] *t* (*condemn, criticize*) deplorar, condenar; (*regret*) lamentar, deplorar.

deploy [dɪ'plɔɪ] **1** *t* MIL desplegar. **2** (*use effectively*) utilizar, hacer uso de. – **3** *i* MIL desplegarse.

deployment [dɪ'plɔɪmənt] **1** *n* MIL despliegue *m*. **2** (*use*) utilización *f*.

depopulate [diː'pɒpjəleɪt] *t* despoblar.

deport [dɪ'pɔːt] *t* deportar.

deportation [diːpɔː'teɪʃən] *n* deportación *f*.

deportment [dɪ'pɔːtmənt] **1** *n* GB *fml* porte *m*. **2** US comportamiento, conducta.

depose [dɪ'pəʊz] **1** *t* (*remove from power - leader, president*) deponer, destituir; (*- king*) destronar. **2** JUR declarar, deponer.

deposit [dɪ'pɒzɪt] **1** *n* (*sediment*) sedimento, depósito; (*in wine bottle*) poso, heces *mpl*; (*layer*) capa. **2** (*mining - of gold, copper, tin, etc*) yacimiento; (*of gas*) depósito. **3** FIN (*payment into account*) depósito, ingreso. **4** COMM (*returnable payment*) depósito, fianza; (*on smaller purchase*) paga y señal *f*; (*first payment*) entrada: *we put a deposit of £1,000 on the house,* dimos una entrada de 1.000 libras para la casa; *if you leave a deposit, we can keep it for you,* si dejas una paga y señal, te lo podemos guardar. – **5** *t* (*leave - gen*) depositar, dejar; (*put down, set down, drop*) depositar, poner; (*of silt, sediment*) depositar: *she deposited her suitcase in the left luggage office,* depositó su maleta en la consigna; *the bus deposited me right outside their house,* el autobús me dejó justo delante de su casa. **6** (*pay money into account*) ingresar. **7** (*pay as a deposit*) entregar como depósito, pagar un depósito de.

■ **deposit account,** cuenta de ahorros.

deposition [depə'zɪʃən] **1** *n* (*from power - of leader, president*) deposición *f*, destitución *f*; (*- of king*) destronamiento. **2** JUR declaración *f*.

depositor [dɪ'pɒzɪtəʳ] *n* depositante *mf*.

depot ['depəʊ] **1** *n* (*storehouse*) almacén *m*. **2** MIL depósito. **3** US (*railway station*) estación *f* de ferrocarriles; (*bus station*) estación *f* de autobuses, terminal *f* de autobuses. **4** GB (*bus garage*) cochera de autobuses; (*train*) depósito de locomotoras.

deprave [dɪ'preɪv] *t* depravar.

depraved [dɪ'preɪvd] *adj* depravado,-a.

depravity [dɪ'prævɪtɪ] **1** *n* (*state*) depravación *f*. **2** (*act*) acto depravado.

▲ *pl* **depravities**.

deprecate ['deprɪkeɪt] **1** *t fml* (*deplore*) censurar, condenar, criticar, reprobar. **2** *fml* (*belittle*) menospreciar, despreciar.

deprecatory ['deprɪkətərɪ] **1** *adj* (*disapproving - remark, view*) desaprobatorio,-a, reprobatorio,-a. **2** (*smile, laugh*) de desprecio.

depreciate [dɪ'priːʃɪeɪt] **1** *i* FIN depreciarse. – **2** *t* FIN depreciar, amortizar. **3** *fml* (*denigrate*) menospreciar.

depreciation [dɪpriːʃɪ'eɪʃən] *n* FIN (*loss of value*) depreciación *f*; (*of currency*) desvalorización *f*, depreciación *f*; (*on balance sheet*) depreciación *f*.

depreciatory [dɪ'priːʃətərɪ] *adj* de desaprobación, desaprobatorio,-a.

depress [dɪ'pres] **1** *t* (*make sad*) deprimir, desanimar, abatir. **2** ECON (*reduce - prices, sales, wages*) reducir, hacer bajar, disminuir; (*- market*) deprimir. **3** *fml* (*press down*) pulsar, apretar.

depressant [dɪ'presənt] **1** *n* depresivo. – **2** *adj* depresivo,-a.

depressed [dɪ'prest] **1** *adj* (*person*) deprimido,-a, desanimado,-a, abatido,-a. **2** ECON (*area*) deprimido,-a; (*market*) paralizado,-a. **3** (*flattened*) hundido,-a, deprimido,-a.

● **to become/get depressed,** deprimirse.

depressing [dɪ'presɪŋ] *adj* deprimente.

depression [dɪ'preʃən] **1** *n* (*sadness*) depresión *f*, abatimiento. **2** ECON depresión *f*, crisis *f*. **3** (*hollow place*) depresión *f*. **4** METEOR depresión *f* (atmosférica).

depressive [dɪ'presɪv] **1** *adj* depresivo,-a. – **2** *n* (*person*) depresivo,-a.

deprivation [deprɪ'veɪʃən] **1** *n* (*lack*) privación *f*; (*loss*) pérdida. **2** (*hardship, poverty*) privación *f*, penuria.

deprive [dɪ'praɪv] **to deprive of,** *t* (*take away*) privar de; (*prevent from having or using*) despojar de, privar de: *he had been deprived of his civil rights,* lo privaron de sus derechos civiles; *you're not depriving us of your company!,* ¡no nos prives de tu compañía!

● **to deprive os. of sth.,** privarse de algo.

deprived [dɪ'praɪvd] *adj* (*child*) necesitado,-a; (*background, area*) pobre, necesitado,-a.

Dept [dɪ'pɑːtmənt] *abbr* (*Department*) departamento; (*abbreviation*) dpt, dpto.

depth [depθ] **1** *n* (*of hole, swimming pool, mine, etc*) profundidad *f*; (*of cupboard, shelf*) fondo; (*of hem, border*) ancho. **2** (*of sound, voice*) profundidad *f*. **3** (*of emotion, colour*) intensidad *f*; (*of shame, silence, mystery*) profundidad *f*. **4** (*of ideas, knowledge, understanding*) profundidad *f*. – **5** **depths,** *npl* (*lowest part*) profundidades *fpl*: *the depths of the sea,* las profundidades del mar.

● **in depth,** a fondo, en profundidad. ‖ **in the depth(s) of sth.,** en las profundidades de algo: *in the depth(s) of the forest,* en la espesura del bosque; *in the depth(s) of night,* en lo más profundo de la noche; *in the depth(s) of winter,* en lo más crudo del invierno, en pleno invierno; *in the depth(s) of despair,* hundido,-a en la desesperación, completamente desesperado,-a. ‖ **to be out of one's depth / be beyond one's depth,** (*in subject, topic, conversation*) perderse, no entender nada. ‖ **to go/get out of one's depth,** (*in water*) perder pie. ‖ **to sink to such depths/a depth,** caer tan bajo.

■ **depth charge,** carga de profundidad.

deputation [depjʊ'teɪʃən] *n* delegación *f*.

depute [dɪ'pjuːt] *t fml* (*work, authority*) delegar (**to,** en), encomendar (**to,** a); (*person*) diputar (**to,** para), comisionar (**to,** para).

deputize ['depjətaɪz] *i* reemplazar (**for,** a), sustituir (**for,** a).

deputy ['depjətɪ] **1** *n* (*substitute*) sustituto,-a, suplente *mf*. **2** POL diputado,-a. **3** US ayudante *mf* del shérif.

■ **deputy chairman,** vicepresidente,-a. ‖ **deputy director,** subdirector,-ra, director,-ra adjunto,-a. ‖ **deputy head,** EDUC subdirector,-ra. ‖ **deputy manager,** subdirector,-ra.

▲ *pl* **deputies**.

derail [dɪ'reɪl] *t* (*train*) hacer descarrilar.

derailment [dɪ'reɪlmənt] *n* descarrilamiento.

deranged [dɪ'reɪndʒd] *adj* trastornado,-a, desquiciado,-a, loco,-a.

derby ['dɑːbɪ] **1** *n* SP (*between two local teams*) derby *m*. **2** US SP (*horse race*) carrera (de caballos). **3** US (*bowler hat*) bombín *m*, hongo, sombrero (de) hongo. **4** **the Derby,** GB SP (*horse race*) el Derby *m*.

▲ *pl* **derbies**.

deregulate [diː'regjəleɪt] *t* desregular, liberalizar.
deregulation [diː'regjəleɪʃən] *n* desregularización *f*, liberalización *f*.
derelict ['derɪlɪkt] *adj* (*building*) abandonado,-a, en ruinas.
dereliction [derɪ'lɪkʃən] *n* (*ruin*) abandono.
● dereliction of duty, incumplimiento del deber.
deride [dɪ'raɪd] *t* burlarse de, ridiculizar, reírse de, mofarse de.
de rigueur [də riː'gɜːʳ] *adj* de rigor.
derision [dɪ'rɪʒən] *n* escarnio, mofa, burla, irrisión *f*: *they treated his proposal with derision,* se burlaron de su propuesta.
● to be an object of derision, ser el hazmerreír de todos, ser objeto de escarnio.
derisive [dɪ'raɪsɪv] *adj* burlón,-ona, irónico,-a.
derisory [dɪ'raɪzərɪ] *adj* (*offer etc*) irrisorio,-a, ridículo,-a.
derivation [derɪ'veɪʃən] *n* (*process*) derivación *f*; (*origin*) origen *m*.
derivative [dɪ'rɪvətɪv] **1** *adj* (*art, writing, music*) carente de originalidad, poco original; (*plot, theme*) manido,-a, trillado,-a. – **2** *n* (*word*) derivado; (*language*) lengua derivada. **3** (*substance*) derivado.
derive [dɪ'raɪv] **1** *t* (*get, obtain*) sacar, recibir: *she derives great pleasure from painting,* pintar le proporciona mucho placer; *we can derive comfort from the fact that he is still in good health,* es un consuelo para nosotros que aún esté bien de salud. – **2** *i* LING (*word*) derivar, derivarse (**from**, de). **3** (*stem from - problem, attitude*) provenir (**from**, de); (*- idea*) tener su origen (**from**, en).
● to be derived from, (*language, word*) derivarse de; (*substance*) obtenerse (a partir) de.
dermatitis [dɜːmə'taɪtɪs] *n* dermatitis *f*.
dermatology [dɜːmə'tɒlədʒɪ] *n* dermatología.
derogatory [dɪ'rɒgətərɪ] *adj* (*remark, attitude, article*) despectivo,-a; (*meaning, sense*) peyorativo,-a.
derrick ['derɪk] **1** *n* (*crane*) grúa. **2** (*tower over oil well*) torre *f* de perforación.
DES ['diː'iː'es] *abbr* GB (*Department of Education and Science*) ≈ Ministerio de Educación y Ciencia; (*abbreviation*) MEC.
descale [diː'skeɪl] *t* quitar el sarro a.
descant ['deskænt] *n* MUS contrapunto.
descend [dɪ'send] **1** *i* (*road, sun, plane, etc*) descender, bajar. **2** (*in importance*) descender. **3** (*night, darkness*) caer; (*mist*) descender; (*rain*) caer; (*silence, gloom*) abatirse (**on/ upon**, sobre). **4** (*of properties, qualities, rights, etc*) provenir: *the title descended to him from his father,* heredó el título de su padre. – **5** *t* descender, bajar.
◆ to descend on **1** *t insep* (*attack*) atacar, caer sobre, lanzarse sobre. **2** (*visit*) visitar, invadir: *they descended on us around midnight,* se dejaron caer por casa alrededor de medianoche. ‖ to descend to *t insep* rebajarse a: *I never thought he would descend to stealing,* nunca me hubiera imaginado que se rebajaría a robar.
● to be descended from sb., ser descendiente de algn., descender de algn.
descendant [dɪ'sendənt] *n* descendiente *mf*.
descending [dɪ'sendɪŋ] *adj* descendiente, descendente.
● in descending order, en orden decreciente.
descent [dɪ'sent] **1** *n* (*by plane, climbers, etc*) descenso, bajada; (*slope*) pendiente *f*, declive *m*, bajada. **2** *fig* (*decline*) caída. **3** (*family origins*) ascendencia: *she is of Irish descent,* es de ascendencia irlandesa. **4** *fig* (*attack*) incursión *f*, asalto.

describe [dɪ'skraɪb] **1** *t* (*depict in words*) describir: *can you describe the man to me?,* ¿me puedes describir al hombre?; *he described how he had escaped,* describió cómo se había escapado. **2** (*call, characterize*) calificar, definir: *I would hardly describe her as generous,* no la calificaría precisamente de generosa; *the estate agent described it as perfect,* el agente inmobiliario lo calificó de perfecto; *he describes himself as normal,* se define como alguien normal. **3** (*move in shape of arc, circle, curve, etc*) describir; (*draw*) trazar.
description [dɪ'skrɪpʃən] **1** *n* (*portrayal, account*) descripción *f*: *the book gives a detailed description of their journey,* el libro da una descripción detallada de su viaje; *they have issued a description of the man,* han hecho pública una descripción del hombre. **2** (*type, sort*) clase *f*, tipo: *of all descriptions,* de toda clase, de todo tipo; *things of that description,* cosas de ese tipo, cosas con esas características; *a flat of some description,* alguna clase de piso.
● to answer a description, responder a una descripción. ‖ to be beyond/past description, ser indescriptible.
descriptive [dɪ'skrɪptɪv] *adj* descriptivo,-a.
desecrate ['desɪkreɪt] *t* profanar.
desecration [desɪ'kreɪʃən] *n* profanación *f*.
desegregate [diː'segrɪgeɪt] *t* suprimir la segregación racial de.
desert¹ ['dezət] *n* desierto: *the Sahara Desert,* el desierto del Sáhara.
■ desert island, isla desierta.
desert² [dɪ'zɜːt] **1** *t* (*family, person, place*) abandonar; (*political party, idea*) desertar (**from**, de). **2** (*quality, attribute*) abandonar. – **3** *i* MIL desertar.
deserted [dɪ'zɜːtɪd] *adj* (*place*) desierto,-a.
deserter [dɪ'zɜːtəʳ] *n* desertor,-ra.
desertion [dɪ'zɜːʃən] **1** *n* (*of family, partner*) abandono. **2** MIL deserción *f*. **3** POL defección *f*.
deserts [dɪ'zɜːts] *npl* merecido.
● to get one's just deserts, llevarse su merecido, recibir su merecido.
deserve [dɪ'zɜːv] *t* (*gen*) merecer, merecerse; (*attention*) merecer, ser digno,-a de: *you deserve a break,* te mereces un descanso; *he deserved to win,* merecía ganar; *she deserves it,* lo tiene merecido, se lo merece.
● to deserve well/ill of sb., merecer el reconocimiento/la condena de algn. ‖ to get what one deserves, llevarse su merecido.
deservedly [dɪ'zɜːvədlɪ] *adv* merecidamente.
deserving [dɪ'zɜːvɪŋ] **1** *adj* (*person*) que vale, de valía. **2** (*action, cause*) meritorio,-a.
● to be deserving of sth., ser digno,-a de.
desiccated ['desɪkeɪtɪd] *adj* deshidratado,-a: *desiccated coconut,* coco rallado.
design [dɪ'zaɪn] **1** *n* ART (*gen*) diseño, dibujo; (*of fashion*) diseño de modas, creación *f*. **2** (*arrangement, planning*) diseño: *the design of the car,* el diseño del coche. **3** (*plan, drawing*) plano, proyecto; (*sketch*) boceto; (*of dress*) patrón *m*; (*of product, model*) modelo. **4** (*decorative pattern*) diseño, dibujo, motivo. **5** *fig* (*purpose, intention*) plan *m*, intención, propósito: *was it by accident or by design?,* ¿ocurrió por casualidad o bien a propósito? – **6** *t* (*make drawing, plan, model*) diseñar, proyectar; (*fashion, set, product*) diseñar; (*course, programme*) planear, estructurar: *Jean-Paul designed the costumes,* Jean-Paul diseñó el vestuario. **7** (*develop for a purpose*) diseñar, concebir, idear; (*intend, mean*) pensar, destinar: *the programme is*

designed for use in schools, el programa está pensado para ser utilizado en institutos; *the prison was originally designed to hold 500 inmates,* la cárcel fue concebida al principio para 500 presos. – **8** *i* diseñar.
● **to have designs on sb./sth.**, tener las miradas puestas en algn., tener los ojos puestos en algn./algo.
designate ['deziɡneɪt] **1** *t fml (indicate, mark, show)* indicar, señalar. **2** *(appoint)* designar, nombrar. – **3** *adj fml* designado,-a, nombrado,-a.
▲ *(adjetivo)* ['dezɪɡnət].
designation [dezɪɡ'neɪʃən] **1** *n fml (appointment)* designación *f*, nombramiento. **2** *fml (title, name)* denominación *f*.
designer [dɪ'zaɪnəʳ] **1** *n* diseñador,-ra: *she wants to be a dress designer,* quiere ser diseñadora de modas. – **2** *adj (clothes etc)* de marca.
■ **designer drug,** droga de diseño. ‖ **set designer / stage designer,** escenógrafo,-a.
designing [dɪ'zaɪnɪŋ] *adj pej* intrigante, maquinador,-ra.
desirable [dɪ'zaɪərəbəl] **1** *adj (location, asset, job)* atractivo,-a; *(residence)* de alto standing. **2** *(person)* deseable, seductor,-ra; *(habit)* atractivo,-a. **3** *(necessary, useful)* conveniente, deseable; *(advisable)* aconsejable: *it is desirable that you should speak English,* sería deseable que hablaras inglés.
desire [dɪ'zaɪəʳ] **1** *n (wish, urge, longing)* deseo, anhelo, ansia; *(sexual)* deseo: *I've got a burning desire to visit India,* mi mayor deseo es visitar la India; *his desire for fame and fortune,* sus deseos de ser famoso y rico; *several listeners have expressed a desire to participate,* varios oyentes han manifestado su deseo de participar. – **2** *t (gen)* desear, anhelar, ansiar; *(sexually)* desear: *he desired nothing other than to continue writing,* no deseaba nada más que seguir escribiendo. **3** *fml (request)* rogar, solicitar.
● **one's heart's desire,** su mayor deseo, su deseo ferviente. ‖ **to leave a lot to be desired,** dejar mucho que desear.
desired [dɪ'saɪəd] *adj* deseado,-a: *it had the desired effect,* tuvo el efecto deseado.
desirous [dɪ'zaɪərəs] *adj fml* deseoso,-a.
desist [dɪ'zɪst] *i fml* desistir (**from,** de).
desk [desk] **1** *n (in school)* pupitre *m*; *(in office)* escritorio. **2** *(service area)* mostrador *m*. **3** *(newspaper office)* sección *f*.
■ **desk clerk,** recepcionista *mf*. ‖ **desk job / desk work,** trabajo de oficina.
desktop publishing ['desktɒp'pʌblɪʃɪŋ] *n* autoedición *f*.
desolate ['desələt] **1** *adj (place)* deshabitado,-a, desierto,-a, despoblado,-a, solitario,-a. **2** *(person - sad)* triste, desconsolado,-a, afligido,-a; *(lonely)* solitario,-a. – **3** *t* desolar.
desolation [desə'leɪʃən] **1** *n (of place)* desolación *f*. **2** *(of person)* desconsuelo, aflicción *f*.
despair [dɪs'peəʳ] **1** *n* desesperación *f*, desesperanza: *he was in despair,* estaba desesperado. – **2** *i* desesperar **(of,** de), desesperarse **(of,** por), perder la esperanza **(of,** de): *he began to despair of ever being released,* empezó a perder las esperanzas de ser liberado algún día; *don't despair!,* ¡no te desanimes!, ¡no te desesperes!
● **to be the despair of sb.,** ser una cruz para algn. ‖ **to drive sb. to despair,** sacar de quicio a algn., volver loco,-a a algn.: *her behaviour drove them to despair,* su conducta les sacaba de quicio.
despairing [dɪ'speərɪŋ] *adj (look, cry, voice)* de desesperación; *(attempt)* desesperado,-a.

despairingly [dɪ'speərɪŋlɪ] *adv* con desesperación, desesperadamente.
despatch [dɪs'pætʃ] *n* → **dispatch**.
desperate ['despərət] **1** *adj (reckless, risky)* desesperado,-a: *he made one last desperate attempt,* hizo un último intento desesperado; *desperate measures,* medidas tomadas en la desesperación. **2** *fam (in urgent need)* desesperado,-a **(for,** por). **3** *(critical, grave - situation, state)* grave, desesperado,-a; *(- need)* apremiante, urgente: *a desperate shortage of water,* una grave escasez de agua.
● **to be desperate for sth.,** necesitar urgentemente algo, necesitar desesperadamente algo: *they're desperate for money,* necesitan dinero desesperadamente. ‖ **to be desperate to do sth.,** estar que uno se muere por hacer algo: *he's desperate to get out of the army,* está que se muere por salir del ejército; *I'm desperate to go to the toilet!,* ¡estoy que no aguanto más! ‖ **to do sth. desperate,** cometer un acto de desesperación, hacer alguna locura. ‖ **to get desperate,** empezar a desesperarse.
desperately ['desprətlɪ] *adv (struggle, fight, try)* desesperadamente; *(need)* urgentemente, con urgencia; *(ill)* gravemente, de gravedad; *(as intensifier - difficult, serious, urgent)* sumamente, extremadamente; *(in love)* locamente: *she desperately wants a baby,* está que se muere por tener un niño; *they're desperately busy before Christmas,* están ocupadísimos antes de Navidad.
desperation [despə'reɪʃən] *n* desesperación *f*.
● **in desperation,** a la desesperada. ‖ **out of desperation,** de desesperación.
despicable [dɪ'spɪkəbəl] *adj (person, act)* despreciable, vil, infame, bajo,-a; *(behaviour)* indigno,-a.
despicably [dɪ'spɪkəblɪ] *adv* vilmente, de manera despreciable, de manera infame.
despise [dɪ'spaɪz] *t* despreciar, menospreciar.
despite [dɪ'spaɪt] *prep* a pesar de: *she went to work despite having a bad cold,* se fue a trabajar a pesar de estar muy resfriada; *demand for cars is still high despite the recession,* aún hay mucha demanda de coches a pesar de la crisis económica; *despite what people say, she still loves him,* a pesar de lo que dice la gente, todavía lo quiere.
despondency [dɪ'spɒndənsɪ] *n* desaliento, abatimiento.
despondent [dɪ'spɒndənt] *adj* desalentado,-a, desanimado,-a, abatido,-a, descorazonado,-a.
despondently [dɪ'spɒndəntlɪ] *adv* con desánimo.
despot ['despɒt] *n* déspota *mf*.
despotism ['despətɪzəm] *n* despotismo.
dessert [dɪ'zɜːt] *n* postre *m*: *what would you like for dessert?,* ¿qué quiere de postre?
■ **dessert wine,** vino dulce.
dessertspoon [dɪ'zɜːtspuːn] **1** *n (spoon)* cuchara de postre. **2** *(measure)* cucharada de postre.
destabilize [diː'steɪbəlaɪz] *t* desestabilizar.
destination [destɪ'neɪʃən] *n* destino.
destined ['destɪnd] *adj (intended, meant)* destinado,-a: *the money was destined for a local charity,* el dinero iba destinado a una organización benéfica del barrio; *a building destined for demolition,* un edificio destinado a ser derribado. **2** *(fated)* destinado,-a, destinado,-a: *we were destined to meet,* estábamos destinados a conocernos; *the project was destined to fail,* el proyecto estaba condenado al fracaso. **3** *(bound)* con destino **(for,** a): *a train destined for Liverpool,* un tren con destino a Liverpool.

destiny ['destɪnɪ] *n* destino, sino.
▲ *pl destinies.*
destitute ['destɪtjuːt] **1** *adj* indigente, mísero,-a. – **2 the destitute**, *npl* los desposeídos *mpl*.
● **to be left destitute**, quedarse en la miseria. ‖ **to be destitute of sth.**, carecer de algo.
destitution [destɪ'tjuːʃən] *n* indigencia, miseria.
destroy [dɪ'strɔɪ] **1** *t* (*gen*) destruir; (*vehicle, old furniture*) destrozar. **2** (*plans, hopes, chances*) destruir, destrozar; (*life*) arruinar, destrozar; (*reputation, confidence, friendship*) acabar con; (*health, career, reputation*) destruir, arruinar. **3** (*animal*) matar, abatir.
destroyer [dɪ'strɔɪəʳ] **1** *n* (*warship*) destructor *m*. **2** (*person, thing*) destructor,-ra.
destructible [dɪ'strʌktəbəl] *adj* destructible.
destruction [dɪ'strʌkʃən] **1** *n* (*of city, books, documents, forest*) destrucción *f*; (*of reputation, civilization*) destrucción *f*, ruina. **2** (*cause of downfall*) ruina, perdición *f*. **3** (*damage*) daños *mpl*, estragos *mpl*, destrozos *mpl*.
destructive [dɪ'strʌktɪv] *adj* (*storm, fire, weapon*) destructor,-ra; (*tendency, power*) destructivo,-a; (*child*) destrozón,-ona; (*criticism*) destructivo,-a, negativo,-a.
destructively [dɪ'strʌktɪvlɪ] *adv* destructivamente, de manera destructiva.
destructiveness [dɪ'strʌktɪvnəs] *n* (*physical*) capacidad *f* destructora; (*of criticism*) carácter *m* destructivo, carácter *m* negativo.
desultorily ['desəltərɪlɪ] **1** *adv fml* (*randomly*) vagamente. **2** *fml* (*half-heartedly*) sin entusiasmo, sin ganas, con poco entusiasmo, con desgana.
desultory ['desəltərɪ] **1** *adj fml* (*without clear plan, purpose*) poco sistemático,-a, poco metódico,-a, irregular. **2** *fml* (*showing little interest*) desganado,-a, poco entusiasta.
detach [dɪ'tætʃ] **1** *t* (*separate, remove*) separar, quitar; (*unstick*) despegar: *you can detach the collar from the coat*, se puede quitar el cuello del abrigo. **2** MIL destacar.
● **to detach os. from sth.**, distanciarse de algo.
detachable [dɪ'tætʃəbəl] *adj* (*handle*) separable; (*cover*) de quita y pon; (*lining*) desmontable: *detachable collar*, cuello postizo, cuello de quita y pon.
detached [dɪ'tætʃt] **1** *adj* (*separated - gen*) separado,-a, suelto,-a. **2** (*house*) independiente. **3** (*person, manner - impartial*) objetivo,-a, imparcial; (*- aloof*) distante, indiferente: *a detached observer*, un observador desinteresado.
● **to become detached**, (*separated*) separarse; (*unstuck*) despegarse.
■ **detached retina**, MED desprendimiento de retina.
detachment [dɪ'tætʃmənt] **1** *n* (*act*) separación *f*. **2** (*impartiality*) objetividad *f*, imparcialidad *f*; (*aloofness*) distancia, indiferencia, desapego. **3** MIL destacamento.
detail ['diːteɪl] **1** *n* (*point, fact, item*) detalle *m*, pormenor *m*: *she described her operation in great detail*, me describió su operación con todo detalle; *spare me all the gory details*, ahórrate los detalles morbosos. **2** ART (*of picture, pattern*) detalle *m*. **3** MIL destacamento, cuadrilla. – **4** *t* (*describe*) detallar, exponer en detalle. **5** MIL destacar. – **6 details**, *npl* (*information*) información *f*; (*particulars*) datos *mpl*: *I'll send you full details*, le enviaré información detallada; *may I have your details please?*, ¿puede darme sus datos por favor?
● **to describe/explain sth. in detail**, describir/explicar algo detalladamente. ‖ **to go into detail**, entrar en detalles, pormenorizar. ‖ **to have an eye for detail**, fijarse en los detalles, ser muy detallista.
detailed ['diːteɪld] *adj* (*description, account*) detallado,-a, minucioso,-a, pormenorizado,-a; (*explanation*) minucioso,-a, detenido,-a.

detain [dɪ'teɪn] **1** *t* (*hold - in custody*) detener. **2** (*delay*) entretener, demorar, retener.
detainee [diːteɪ'niː] *n* JUR detenido,-a; POL preso,-a.
detect [dɪ'tekt] **1** *t* (*notice, sense - gen*) detectar, advertir; (*sarcasm, difference*) notar; (*sound, small*) percibir: *I detected a note of irritation in her voice*, noté un cierto tono de irritación en su voz; *dogs can detect very high-pitched sounds*, los perros perciben sonidos muy agudos. **2** (*find - object, substance*) detectar, encontrar: *small quantities of morphine were detected in his blood*, detectaron pequeñas cantidades de morfina en su sangre. **3** (*discover - crime, criminal, fraud*) descubrir.
detectable [dɪ'tektəbəl] *adj* detectable, perceptible.
detection [dɪ'tekʃən] **1** *n* (*of error*) descubrimiento; (*of substance*) detección *f*; (*of small, sound*) percepción *f*. **2** (*discovery of crime, criminal, fraud*) descubrimiento.
■ **detection work**, investigaciones *fpl*.
detective [dɪ'tektɪv] *n* (*private*) detective *mf*; (*in police force*) agente *mf*, oficial *mf*.
■ **detective agency**, agencia de detectives. ‖ **detective novel/story**, novela policíaca. ‖ **detective work**, investigaciones *fpl*.
detector [dɪ'tektəʳ] *n* detector *m*: *metal detector*, detector *m* de metales.
detente ['deɪtɒnt] *n* distensión *f*.
detention [dɪ'tenʃən] **1** *n* JUR (*of suspect*) detención *f*, arresto. **2** EDUC (*of pupil*) castigo.
● **to be in detention**, EDUC estar castigado,-a. ‖ **to get detention**, EDUC quedar castigado,-a.
■ **detention home/centre**, JUR (*gen*) centro de detención; (*for young offenders*) correccional *m*.
deter [dɪ'tɜːʳ] **1** *t* (*person - dissuade*) disuadir (**from**, de): *they tried deter him from smoking*, trataron de disuadirlo de fumar; *high prices deter people from buying new houses*, los altos precios hacen que la gente desista de comprar casas nuevas; *he was not deterred*, no desistió (de su propósito). **2** (*prevent, stop*) impedir.
▲ *pt & pp* **deterred**, *ger* **deterring**.
detergent [dɪ'tɜːdʒənt] *n* detergente *m*.
deteriorate [dɪ'tɪərɪəreɪt] *i* (*economy, health, situation, relations, material*) deteriorarse; (*weather, work*) empeorar.
● **to deteriorate into sth.**, degenerar en algo.
deterioration [dɪtɪərɪə'reɪʃən] *n* (*gen*) empeoramiento; (*of material*) deterioro.
determination [dɪtɜːmɪ'neɪʃən] **1** *n* (*resolution*) determinación *f*, resolución *f*, decisión *f*: *with an air of determination*, con (un) aire decidido. **2** *fml* (*setting, deciding*) determinación *f*.
determine [dɪ'tɜːmɪn] **1** *t* (*find out, ascertain - cause, position, meaning*) determinar, establecer, averiguar: *they still haven't determined the cause of death*, aún no han determinado la causa de la muerte. **2** (*influence*) determinar, condicionar: *your character is determined in part by heredity*, el carácter viene en parte determinado por la herencia. **3** (*settle, fix - date, price*) decidir, fijar; (*mark - boundary, limit*) determinar, definir, demarcar: *they determined a date for the wedding*, fijaron una fecha para la boda. **4** *fml* (*resolve, decide*) decidir, resolver, tomar la determinación de: *the jury determined that the man was innocent*, el jurado decidió que el hombre era inocente.
determined [dɪ'tɜːmɪnd] *adj* (*person*) decidido,-a, resuelto,-a; (*attempt, effort*) enérgico,-a, persistente: *she was determined to succeed*, estaba decidida a triunfar; *he was determined that his children would not go without*, estaba resuelto a que sus hijos no pasaran privaciones.

determiner [dɪ'tɜːmɪnəʳ] n LING determinante m.

deterrent [dɪ'terənt] 1 adj disuasivo,-a, disuasorio,-a. – 2 n fuerza disuasoria, fuerza disuasiva, fuerza de disuasión: *the death penalty is supposed to act as a deterrent,* se supone que la pena de muerte sirve como fuerza disuasoria.
■ nuclear deterrent, arma m nuclear disuasoria.

detest [dɪ'test] t detestar, odiar, aborrecer: *I detest cooking,* odio cocinar.

detestable [dɪ'testəbəl] adj detestable, odioso,-a, aborrecible.

detestation [diːtes'teɪʃən] n aversión f, odio.

dethrone [dɪ'θrəʊn] t destronar.

detonate ['detəneɪt] 1 i estallar, detonar, explotar. – 2 t hacer estallar, hacer explotar.

detonation [detə'neɪʃən] n detonación f.

detonator ['detəneɪtəʳ] n detonador m.

detour ['diːtʊəʳ] n (in traffic) desvío.
● to make a detour, dar un rodeo.

detract [dɪ'trækt] to detract from, t (achievement) quitar mérito(s) a, restar valor a; (beauty) deslucir.

detractor [dɪ'træktəʳ] n detractor,-ra.

detriment ['detrɪmənt] n fml detrimento (to, para), perjuicio (to, para).

detrimental [detrɪ'mentəl] adj fml perjudicial (to, para).

detritus [dɪ'traɪtəs] 1 n GEOL detrito, detritus m. 2 (debris) deshechos mpl.

deuce [djuːs] 1 n (in tennis) cuarenta mpl iguales. 2 (in games) dos m.

devaluation [diːvæljuːˈeɪʃən] n FIN devaluación f, desvaloración f.

devalue [diːˈvæljuː] 1 t FIN (currency) devaluar, desvalorizar. 2 (person, achievement) subvalorar.

devastate ['devəsteɪt] 1 t (city, area, country) devastar. 2 fam fig (person) anonadar, apabullar: *we were devastated,* (nos) quedamos anonadados.

devastating ['devəsteɪtɪŋ] 1 adj (destructive) devastador,-ra, asolador,-ra, desastroso,-a; (causing severe shock) espeluznante: *this could have devastating effects on the economy,* esto podría tener efectos desastrosos para la economía. 2 (criticism, argument) demoledor,-ra, apabullante, aplastante; (wit) tremendo,-a. 3 fam (beauty, charm) irrestistible; (insight) brillante: *she looked devasting!,* ¡estaba guapísima!

devastatingly ['devəsteɪtɪŋlɪ] adv (witty) tremendamente; (beautiful) irresistiblemente.

devastation [devə'steɪʃən] n devastación f, asolación f, asolamiento.

develop [dɪ'veləp] 1 t (cultivate, cause to grow - gen) desarrollar; (foster - trade, arts) fomentar, promover; (expand - business, industry) ampliar; (build up, improve - skill, ability, talent) perfeccionar. 2 (elaborate, expand - idea, argument, story) desarrollar; (- theory, plan) desarrollar, elaborar. 3 (start - roots) echar; (devise, invent - policy, method, strategy) idear, desarrollar; (- drug, product, technology) crear. 4 (acquire - habit, quality, feature) contraer, adquirir; (- talent, interest) mostrar; (- tendency) revelar, manifestar; (get - illness, disease) contraer; (- immunity, resistance) desarrollar: *he's developed a sudden interest in tennis,* muestra un repentino interés por el tenis; *the machine has developed a fault,* ha surgido un problema con la máquina. 5 (exploit - resources) explotar; (- site, land) urbanizar. 6 (film, photograph) revelar. – 7 i (grow - person, body, nation, region, etc) desarrollarse; (- system) perfeccionarse; (feeling, interest) aumentar, crecer. 8 (evolve - emotion) convertirse (**into,** en), transformarse (**into,** en),

evolucionar; (plot, novel) desarrollarse. 9 (appear - problem, complication, symptom) aparecer, surgir; (situation, crisis) producirse. 10 (of film, photograph) salir.
● to develop a taste for sth., cogerle gusto a algo: *she developed a taste for cocktails,* le cogió el gusto a los cócteles.

developer [dɪ'veləpəʳ] 1 n (of land, property - company) promotora inmobiliaria, empresa constructora; (- person) constructor,-ra. 2 (for photographs) revelador m. 3 (child): *a slow/late developer,* un niño de desarrollo lento/tardío.

developing [dɪ'veləpɪŋ] adj (country) en vías de desarrollo.

development [dɪ'veləpmənt] 1 n (growth, formation - gen) desarrollo; (- of skill, system) perfección f; (fostering) fomento, promoción f; (growth, expansion - of firm, industry, country) desarrollo; (evolution) evolución f. 2 (elaboration - of idea, argument, play) desarrollo, elaboración f; (evolution - of situation, events) desarrollo, evolución f. 3 (invention - of product) creación f. 4 (event, incident) acontecimiento, suceso; (advance) avance m, conquista: *let me know if there are any developments,* hazme saber si hay novedades. 5 (of resources) explotación f; (of site, land, etc) urbanización f.
■ development area, zona de reindustrialización. ‖ housing development, urbanización f, conjunto residencial.

developmental [dɪveləp'mentəl] adj del desarrollo.

deviance ['diːvɪəns] n desviación f.

deviant ['diːvɪənt] 1 adj anormal. – 2 n pervertido,-a.

deviate ['diːvɪeɪt] i (from course) desviarse (**from,** de); (from norm) apartarse (**from de)).**

deviation [diːvɪ'eɪʃən] n desviación f.

device [dɪ'vaɪs] 1 n (object, equipment) aparato, artefacto; (mechanism) mecanismo, dispositivo: *electronic device,* dispositivo electrónico; *explosive device,* artefacto explosivo; *nuclear device,* arma nuclear. 2 (scheme, trick) ardid m, estratagema f. 3 lit (method) recurso. 4 (on shield) emblema m.
● to leave sb. to his own devices, dejar que algn. que se las arregle solo, abandonar a algn. a sus propios recursos.

devil¹ ['devəl] 1 n (Satan, evil spirit) diablo, demonio. 2 fam (person) diablo: *he's a little devil,* es un diablillo; *poor devil,* pobre diablo; *you lucky devil!,* ¡qué suerte tienes! 3 fam (for emphasis): *what the devil are you doing?,* ¿qué diablos estás haciendo?; *I had a devil of a job changing the wheel,* las pasé negras cambiando la rueda; *it's a devil of a problem,* es un problema de mil demonios.
● better the devil you know (than the devil you don't), más vale malo conocido (que bueno por conocer). ‖ between the devil and the deep blue sea, entre la espada y la pared. ‖ talk/speak of the devil!, ¡hablando del rey de Roma! ‖ to be a devil, atreverse: *go on, be a devil!,* ¡anda, atrévete! ‖ to play devil's advocate, hacer de abogado,-a del diablo.

devil² ['devəl] 1 t GB CULIN cocer en una salsa picante: *devilled eggs,* huevos duros con salsa picante.
▲ pt & pp devilled (us deviled), ger devilling (us deviling).

devilish ['devəlɪʃ] 1 adj (wicked, cruel) diabólico,-a, malvado,-a. 2 (very difficult) diabólico,-a. – 3 adv endemoniadamente.

devilishly ['devəlɪʃlɪ] adv muy, sumamente.

devilment ['devəlmənt] n diablura.

devilry ['devəlrɪ] n diablura.
● to be full of devilry, ser un diablillo, ser de la piel del diablo.

devious ['diːvɪəs] **1** *adj* (*of route, path, etc*) tortuoso,-a, si-nuoso,-a. **2** *pej* (*cunning, dishonest - person*) taimado,-a, artero,-a, zorro,-a; (*- plan, method, scheme*) astuto,-a.
● **by devious means,** con artimañas.
deviousness ['diːvɪəsnəs] *n* artería, astucia, maña.
devise [dɪ'vaɪz] **1** *t* (*plan, scheme, system*) idear, concebir, crear; (*object, tool, machine*) inventar.
● **to devise and bequeath,** JUR legar.
devoid [dɪ'vɔɪd] *adj* carente (**of,** de), desprovisto,-a (**of,** de).
● **to be devoid of sth.,** carecer de algo.
devolution [diːvə'luːʃən] **1** *n* GB POL *traspaso de competencias del gobierno central a un gobierno regional.* **2** (*delegation*) delegación *f*, transferencia.
devolve [dɪ'vɒlv] **1** *i* (*work, duties*) recaer (**on/upon,** sobre); (*power, responsibility*) pasar (**to,** a). **2** (*land, goods, property*) pasar (**to,** a). **- 3** *t* (*power, responsibility*) delegar, transferir (**to,** a).
● **to devolve government on/to the regions,** dar autonomía a las regiones.
devote [dɪ'vəʊt] *t* (*time, effort*) dedicar, consagrar: *he dedicated his life to looking after his mother,* consagró su vida a cuidar a su madre; *she decided to devote more time to her family,* decidió dedicar más tiempo a su familia; *four whole pages are devoted to yesterday's tragic shooting,* cuatro páginas enteras están dedicadas al tiroteo trágico de ayer.
● **to devote os. to sth.,** dedicarse a algo.
devoted [dɪ'vəʊtɪd] *adj* (*loyal - friend*) fiel (**to,** a), leal (**to,** a); (*- couple*) unido,-a; (*- follower, supporter*) ferviente; (*selfless*) abnegado,-a: *your devoted daughter,* tu hija que te quiere; *he's devoted to her,* la quiere mucho.
devotee [devə'tiː] **1** *n* REL devoto,-a. **2** (*enthusiast*) adepto,-a, aficionado,-a, partidario,-a.
devotion [dɪ'vəʊʃən] **1** *n* (*loyalty*) lealtad *f*, fidelidad *f*; (*love*) cariño, afecto, amor *m*. **2** (*to work, research, cause*) dedicación *f*, entrega. **3** REL (*devoutness*) devoción *f*; (*prayer*) oración *f*, rezo.
● **to be at one's devotions,** estar rezando.
devour [dɪ'vaʊəʳ] **1** *t* (*food*) devorar, zampar. **2** (*book etc*) devorar. **3** (*destroy - of fire*) devorar, destruir.
● **to be devoured by sth.,** devorarle a uno algo, consumirle a uno algo: *I was devoured by jealousy,* me consumían los celos.
devouring [dɪ'vaʊərɪŋ] *adj* devorador,-ra.
devout [dɪ'vaʊt] **1** *adj* REL devoto,-a, piadoso,-a. **2** (*hope, prayer, wish*) sincero,-a.
devoutly [dɪ'vaʊtlɪ] **1** *adv* REL muy. **2** (*sincerely*) sinceramente, con todo corazón, fervientemente.
dew [djuː] *n* rocío.
dewy [djuːɪ] *adj* cubierto,-a de rocío.
▲ *comp* **dewier,** *superl* **dewiest.**
dewy-eyed [djuːɪ'aɪd] **1** *adj* (*naive, trusting*) ingenuo,-a. **2** (*with tears*) con los ojos húmedos.
dexterity [dek'sterɪtɪ] *n* (*manual*) destreza, habilidad *f*, maña; (*intellectual*) habilidad *f*.
dexterous ['dekstrəs] *adj* (*skillful with hands*) diestro,-a, hábil; (*with mind*) hábil.
dextrose ['dekstrəʊz] *n* dextrosa.
dextrous ['dekstrəs] *adj* → **dexterous.**
diabetes [daɪə'biːtiːz] *n* diabetes *f*.
▲ *pl* **diabetes.**
diabetic [daɪə'betɪk] **1** *adj* (*gen*) diabético,-a; (*food*) para diabéticos. **- 2** *n* diabético,-a.
diabolical [daɪə'bɒlɪkəl] **1** *adj* (*evil*) diabólico,-a, satánico,-a. **2** GB *fam* (*extremely bad*) espantoso,-a, atroz.

diagnose ['daɪəgnəʊz] **1** *t* MED diagnosticar: *it was diagnosed as cancer,* le diagnosticaron cáncer. **2** (*fault*) descubrir. **- 3** *i* MED diagnosticar.
diagnosis [daɪəg'nəʊsɪs] *n* MED diagnóstico: *to make/give a diagnosis,* hacer un diagnóstico.
▲ *pl* **diagnoses** [daɪəg'nəʊsiːz].
diagnostic [daɪəg'nɒstɪk] *adj* diagnóstico,-a.
diagonal [daɪ'ægənəl] **1** *adj* (*line*) diagonal; (*path*) en diagonal. **- 2** *n* diagonal *f*.
diagonally [daɪ'ægənəlɪ] *adv* (*cut*) en diagonal; (*go across*) diagonalmente.
diagram ['daɪəgræm] *n* (*gen*) diagrama *m*; (*graph*) gráfico, gráfica; (*of process, system*) esquema *m*.
dial ['daɪəl] **1** *n* (*of clock, watch, barometer*) esfera; (*on radio*) dial *m*; (*of telephone*) disco; (*of measuring instrument*) cuadrante *m*. **- 2** *t* (*number*) marcar; (*make call*) llamar. **- 3** *i* (*dialling number*) marcar (el número); (*make call*) llamar: *you can dial direct,* hay línea directa.
▲ (*verbo*) *pt & pp* **dialled** (US **dialed**), *ger* **dialling** (US **dialing**).
dialect ['daɪəlekt] *n* dialecto.
dialectic [daɪə'lektɪk] *n* dialéctica.
dialectics [daɪə'lektɪks] *n* dialéctica.
dialling ['daɪəlɪŋ]. **1** dialling code, *n* prefijo. **2 dialling tone,** señal *f* de marcar.
dialog ['daɪəlɒg] *n* US → **dialogue.**
dialogue ['daɪəlɒg] **1** *n* (*conversation*) diálogo. **2** (*communication, talks*) diálogo, negociaciones *fpl*. **3** (*discussion*) discusión *f*, debate *m*.
dialysis [daɪ'ælɪsɪs] *n* diálisis *f*.
■ **dialysis machine,** dializador *m*.
diameter [daɪ'æmɪtəʳ] *n* diámetro.
diametrically [daɪə'metrɪkəlɪ] *adv* diametralmente.
diamond ['daɪəmənd] **1** *n* (*stone*) diamante *m*, brillante *m*. **2** (*shape*) rombo. **3** (*in cards*) diamante *m*.
● **to be a rough diamond,** ser un diamante (en) bruto.
■ **diamond ring,** anillo de diamantes, anillo de brillantes. ‖ **diamond wedding (anniversary),** bodas *fpl* de diamante.
diaper ['daɪəpəʳ] *n* US pañal *m*.
diaphanous [daɪ'æfənəs] *adj* diáfano,-a, transparente.
diaphragm ['daɪəfræm] *n* (*gen*) diafragma *m*.
diarrhea [daɪə'rɪə] *n* → **diarrhoea.**
diarrhoea [daɪə'rɪə] *n* diarrea.
diary ['daɪərɪ] **1** *n* (*of thoughts, events, etc*) diario. **2** (*for appointments*) agenda: *desk diary,* agenda de sobremesa, agenda de escritorio.
● **to keep a diary,** llevar un diario, escribir un diario.
▲ *pl* **diaries.**
diatribe ['daɪətraɪb] *n* diatriba, invectiva.
dice [daɪs] **1** *n* dado. **- 2** *t* cortar en dados.
● **to dice with death,** jugar con la muerte. ‖ **to play dice,** jugar a los dados.
▲ (*sustantivo*) *pl* **dice.**
dicey ['daɪsɪ] *adj* (*risky*) arriesgado,-a; (*dangerous*) peligroso,-a; (*uncertain*) dudoso,-a, incierto,-a.
▲ *comp* **dicier,** *superl* **diciest.**
dichotomy [daɪ'kɒtəmɪ] *n* dicotomía.
▲ *pl* **dichotomies.**
dick[1] [dɪk] **1** *n sl* (*penis*) polla. **2** *sl* (*stupid man*) imbécil *m*, gilipollas *m*.
dick[2] [dɪk] *n* US *sl* sabueso.
dickhead ['dɪkhed] *n sl* imbécil *m*, gilipollas *m*.
dictate [dɪk'teɪt] **1** *t* (*letter etc*) dictar. **2** (*state, lay down - law, demands, trends*) ordenar; (*terms, conditions*) imponer:

the government wants to dictate what is taught in schools, el gobierno quiere ordenar lo que se enseña en las escuelas. **3** (*determine, influence*) determinar, condicionar: *the money we had dictated the kind of house we could buy,* el dinero de que disponíamos determinó el tipo de casa que compramos. – **4** *i* (*read out*) dictar. – **5** *n* mandato.

◆ **to dictate to** *t insep* mandar, dar órdenes a: *I won't be dictated to!,* ¡a mí no me manda nadie!

▲ (*sustantivo*) ['dɪkteɪt].

dictation [dɪk'teɪʃən] **1** *n* (*of letter, passage, etc*) dictado. **2** (*giving orders*) mandato.

● **to take dictation,** escribir al dictado.

dictator [dɪk'teɪtəʳ] *n* dictador,-ra.

dictatorial [dɪktə'tɔːrɪəl] *adj* dictatorial.

dictatorship [dɪk'teɪtəʃɪp] *n* dictadura.

diction ['dɪkʃən] *n* dicción *f*.

dictionary ['dɪkʃənərɪ] *n* diccionario.

▲ *pl* dictionaries.

dictum ['dɪktəm] **1** *n* (*saying, maxim*) máxima, dicho; (*statement of opinion*) sentencia, afirmación *f*. **2** JUR dictamen *m*.

did [dɪd] *pt* → **do.**

didactic [dɪ'dæktɪk] *adj* didáctico,-a.

diddle ['dɪdəl] *t fam* estafar, timar.

● **to diddle sb. out of sth.,** estafar algo a algn.

didn't ['dɪdənt] *contr* → **did not.**

die[1] [daɪ] **1** *i* (*person, animal, plant*) morir, morirse: *he died of AIDS,* murió de sida; *she died in her sleep,* murió mientras dormía. **2** *fam fig* (*be overcome*) morirse: *I nearly died!,* ¡casi me muero! **3** *fig* (*love, tradition, custom*) morir; (*flame*) extinguirse, apagarse; (*engine*) apagarse, dejar de funcionar: *her secret died with her,* se llevó el secreto a la tumba. **4** (*engine, motor*) apagarse, dejar de funcionar. – **5** *t* morir: *he died a natural death,* murió de muerte natural.

◆ **to die away** *i* (*noise*) desvanecerse, irse apagando; (*breeze*) amainar. ‖ **to die down** *i* (*fire, flames, noise*) extinguirse, apagarse, irse apagando; (*storm, wind*) amainar; (*anger, excitement*) calmarse; (*rumours*) disminuir. ‖ **to die off** *i* morir uno por uno, ir muriendo. ‖ **to die out** *i* (*race, species*) perderse, extinguirse; (*custom, tradition*) morir, caer en desuso.

● **to be dying for sth. / be dying to do sth.,** morirse por algo, morirse de ganas de hacer algo. ‖ **to die a death,** quedar en nada. ‖ **to die hard,** tardar en desaparecer: *old habits die hard,* las viejas costumbres no se pierden fácilmente. ‖ **to die laughing,** morirse de risa. ‖ **to die with one's boots on,** morirse con las botas puestas. ‖ **to do or die,** vencer o morir.

die[2] [daɪ] **1** *n* (*for coins*) cuño, troquel *m*. **2** *arch* dado.

● **the die is cast,** la suerte está echada.

▲ *1 pl* dies, *2 pl* dice.

die-hard ['daɪhɑːd] *n* intransigente *mf*.

diesel ['diːzəl] **1** *n* (*fuel*) gasóleo, gasoil *m*. **2** (*car*) coche *m* diesel; (*lorry*) camión *m* diesel.

■ **diesel engine,** motor *m* diesel.

diet ['daɪət] **1** *n* (*food*) dieta (alimenticia), alimentación *f*: *the Mediterranean diet,* la dieta mediterránea. **2** (*restricted food*) régimen *m*, dieta: *a low-calorie diet,* un régimen bajo en calorías. – **3** *adj* (*food*) de régimen, bajo,-a en calorías; (*drinks*) bajo,-a en calorías, light. – **4** *i* estar a régimen, estar a dieta, hacer régimen, hacer dieta.

● **to be on a diet / go on a diet,** estar a régimen / ponerse a régimen.

dietary ['daɪətərɪ] *adj* alimenticio,-a.

■ **dietary fibre,** fibra dietética.

dietician [daɪə'tɪʃən] *n* dietista *mf*, experto,-a en dietética.

differ ['dɪfəʳ] **1** *i* (*be unlike*) ser distinto,-a (**from,** de), ser diferente (**from,** de), diferir (**from,** de): *my taste in music differs from hers,* mis gustos musicales son distintos de los suyos; *people's interpretations differ greatly,* las interpretaciones de la gente son muy diferentes; *they differ in that this one has pockets,* se diferencian en que éste tiene bolsillos. **2** (*disagree*) discrepar (**about/on,** en): *they differ about many things,* discrepan en muchas cosas; *I beg to differ,* lamento discrepar.

difference ['dɪfərəns] **1** *n* (*dissimilarity*) diferencia: *what's the difference in price?,* ¿qué diferencia de precio hay?; *can you tell the difference?,* ¿notas la diferencia?; *a hotel with a difference,* un hotel diferente? **2** (*disagreement*) desacuerdo, diferencia: *we have our differences,* tenemos nuestras diferencias.

● **to have a difference of opinion,** discrepar. ‖ **to make a difference,** (*have effect on*) afectar, cambiar; (*be important, matter*) importar: *what difference does it make?,* ¿qué importa?; *it makes a big difference,* importa mucho; *it would've made all the difference,* eso lo hubiera cambiado todo; *it makes no difference,* da lo mismo, lo mismo da, da igual. ‖ **to split the difference,** dividirse la diferencia (a partes iguales).

different ['dɪfərənt] **1** *adj* (*unlike, not the same*) diferente (**from,** de), distinto,-a (**from,** de): *the two brothers are quite different,* los dos hermanos son muy diferentes; *you look completely different,* estás muy cambiado,-a, pareces otro,-a; *this sweater comes in ten different colours,* este jersey viene en diez colores distintos. **2** (*various, several*) distinto,-a, vario,-a: *different people have mentioned it to me,* varias personas me lo han mencionado. **3** *fam* (*unusual, original*) diferente, original: *well, it's different,* bueno, es original.

differential [dɪfə'renʃəl] **1** *adj* diferencial. – **2** *n* COMM FIN diferencial *m*. **3** (*gear*), AUTO diferencial *m*.

■ **differential calculus,** cálculo diferencial.

differentiate [dɪfə'renʃɪeɪt] **1** *t* diferenciar (**from de**)), distinguir (**from,** de). – **2** *i* distinguir (**between,** entre).

differently ['dɪfərəntlɪ] *adv* de otra manera, de otra forma, de manera diferente.

difficult ['dɪfɪkəlt] *adj* (*gen*) difícil: *she's difficult to please,* es difícil de complacer; *it was difficult for him to find a job,* le fue difícil encontrar un empleo; *the difficult part is ...,* lo difícil es ..., la dificultad está en ...; *she's at that difficult age,* está en esa edad difícil.

● **to find sth. difficult,** costarle (trabajo) a uno hacer algo: *I find it difficult to believe,* me cuesta creerlo; *he finds English very difficult,* le cuesta mucho el inglés. ‖ **to make life difficult for sb.,** hacerle la vida imposible a algn. ‖ **to make sth. difficult for sb.,** dificultar algo a algn.: *not knowing French makes my job difficult,* desconocer el francés me dificulta el trabajo.

difficulty ['dɪfɪkəltɪ] **1** *n* (*trouble*) dificultad *f*: *he has difficulty breathing,* respira con dificultad; *I had great difficulty (in) getting hold of him,* tuve dificultad para localizarlo, me costó mucho localizarlo; *she did it, but with some difficulty,* consiguió hacerlo, pero con dificultad. **2** (*problem*) dificultad *f*, problema *m*: *financial difficulties,* problemas económicos; *learning difficulties,* dificultades de aprendizaje.

● **to be in difficulties,** tener problemas, estar en un apuro, pasar dificultades. ‖ **to get into difficulties,** meterse en dificultades. ‖ **to make difficulties,** crear problemas, poner pegas.

▲ *pl* **difficulties.**
diffidence ['dɪfɪdəns] *n* falta de seguridad en sí mismo,-a, confianza en sí mismo,-a.
diffident ['dɪfɪdənt] *adj* poco seguro,-a de sí mismo,-a.
diffuse [dɪ'fjuːs] **1** *adj* (*light, gas*) difuso,-a. **2** *pej* (*speech, style, writer*) prolijo,-a. – **3** *t* (*light, heat, news*) difundir. – **4** *i* difundirse.
▲ (*verbo*) [dɪ'fjuːz].
diffusion [dɪ'fjuːʒən] *n* difusión *f*.
dig [dɪg] **1** *n* (*poke, prod*) codazo. **2** *fam* (*gibe*) pulla; (*hint*) indirecta. **3** (*by archaeologists*) excavación *f*. – **4** *t* (*ground, garden*) cavar (en); (*by machine - tunnel, trench*) excavar; (*by hand - hole*) hacer, cavar; (*potatoes etc*) sacar; (*site*) excavar. **5** (*thrust, jab, press*) clavar, hincar. **6** *fam dated* (*like, enjoy*) gustar, molar; (*understand*) entender. – **7** *i* (*person - by hand*) cavar; (*- by machine*) excavar; (*animal*) escarbar; (*on site*) hacer excavaciones, excavar. **8** (*cut*) clavarse. **9** (*mine - for oil*) hacer prospecciones de; (*- for minerals*) extraer. **10** (*search*) buscar (**for,** -). **11** *fam dated* (*understand*) entender. – **12** digs, *npl* GB (*lodgings*) alojamiento *m sing*, pensión *f sing*; (*room*) habitación *f sing* alquilada.
◆ **to dig in 1** *i* MIL atrincherarse. **2** *fam* (*start eating*) atacar. ‖ **to dig into 1** *t insep* (*investigate, examine*) investigar. **2** (*resources, savings, reserves*) echar mano de. ‖ **to dig out** *t sep* (*trapped person, car*) sacar, desenterrar; (*information, truth*) encontrar, descubrir, sacar; (*old photo, clothes, etc*) sacar, desempolvar, desenterrar. ‖ **to dig up** *t sep* (*weeds, bulbs*) arrancar; (*buried object, treasure*) desenterrar; (*land, earth, lawn, pavement, road*) levantar; (*facts, information, scandal*) sacar a la luz.
● **to be dug in,** (*settled*) estar instalado,-a. ‖ **to dig deep into one's pockets,** (*willingly*) contribuir generosamente; (*reluctantly*) rascarse el bolsillo. ‖ **to dig os. in,** MIL atrincherarse. ‖ **to dig os. into a hole,** meterse en un apuro. ‖ **to dig one's heels in,** mantenerse en sus trece. ‖ **to dig one's own grave,** cavarse su propia tumba. ‖ **to dig sb. in the ribs,** darle un codazo a algn. ‖ **to dig (up) (the) dirt on sb.,** sacarle los trapos sucios a relucir a algn. ‖ **to have/take/make a dig at sb.,** meterse con algn.
▲ (*verbo*) *pt* & *pp* dug, *ger* digging.
digest ['daɪdʒest] **1** *n* (*summary*) resumen *m*, compendio. – **2** *t* (*food*) digerir; (*facts, information*) asimilar, digerir.
▲ (*verbo*) [dɪ'dʒest].
digestible [dɪ'dʒestəbəl] *adj* digerible.
digestion [dɪ'dʒestʃən] *n* digestión *f*.
digestive [dɪ'dʒestɪv] *adj* digestivo,-a.
■ digestive biscuit, galleta integral. ‖ digestive system, aparato digestivo.
digger ['dɪgəʳ] **1** *n* (*machine*) excavadora. **2** (*person*) excavador,-ra.
digit ['dɪdʒɪt] **1** *n* MATH dígito. **2** ANAT (*finger*) dedo; (*thumb*) pulgar *m*.
digital ['dɪdʒɪtəl] **1** *adj* (*watch, display, recording*) digital. **2** ANAT dactilar, digital.
digitally ['dɪdʒɪtəli] *adv* digitalmente.
dignified ['dɪgnɪfaɪd] *adj* (*showing dignity - manner*) solemne, serio,-a; (*- person*) digno,-a, circunspecto,-a; (*- speech*) solemne; (*stately*) majestuoso,-a.
dignify ['dɪgnɪfaɪ] **1** *t* (*ennoble*) dignificar, ennoblecer; (*make respectable*) dar categoría a. **2** (*give important name to*) dar un nombre importante a.
▲ *pt* & *pp* dignified, *ger* dignifying.
dignitary ['dɪgnɪtəri] *n* dignatario,-a.
▲ *pl* dignitaries.

dignity ['dɪgnɪti] **1** *n* (*seriousness, calmness - of person*) dignidad *f*; (*of occasion*) solemnidad *f*: *she behaved with great dignity,* se comportó con gran dignidad. **2** (*self-respect*) dignidad *f*, amor *m* propio: *have you no dignity?,* ¡qué poca dignidad la tuya!; *work gives a person dignity,* el trabajo dignifica a la persona. **3** *fml* (*high rank, title*) dignidad *f*.
● **to be beneath one's dignity,** ser una degradación. ‖ **to stand on one's dignity,** hacerse respetar, mantener las distancias.
digress [daɪ'gres] *i* divagar, desviarse del tema, hacer digresiones: *but I digress,* pero estoy divagando.
digression [daɪ'greʃən] *n* digresión *f*.
dike [daɪk] *n* US → **dyke.**
dilapidated [dɪ'læpɪdeɪtɪd] *adj* (*furniture*) desvencijado,-a, en mal estado; (*building*) ruinoso,-a; (*car*) desvencijado,-a, destartalado,-a.
dilapidation [dɪlæpɪ'deɪʃən] *n* deterioro, mal estado.
dilate [daɪ'leɪt] **1** *t* dilatar. – **2** *i* dilatarse.
◆ **to dilate on** *t insep* extenderse sobre.
dilatory ['dɪlətəri] *adj* (*causing delay*) dilatorio,-a; (*slow in acting*) tardío,-a.
● **to be dilatory in doing sth.,** tardar en hacer algo.
dilemma [dɪ'lemə] *n* dilema *m*.
dilettante [dɪlɪ'tɑːnt] *n* diletante *mf*.
▲ *pl* dilettantes o dilettanti [dɪle'tænti].
diligence ['dɪlɪdʒəns] *n* diligencia.
diligent ['dɪlɪdʒənt] *adj* (*worker, student*) diligente, aplicado,-a; (*work, study, etc*) esmerado,-a, concienzudo,-a, hecho,-a a conciencia; (*search*) minucioso,-a, cuidadoso,-a.
dill [dɪl] *n* eneldo.
dilute [daɪ'luːt] **1** *t* (*liquid, concentrate*) diluir. **2** *fig* (*criticism, effect, influence*) atenuar, suavizar. – **3** *i* diluirse. – **4** *adj* diluido,-a.
dilution [daɪ'luːʃən] **1** *n* dilución *f*. **2** *fig* atenuación *f*.
dim [dɪm] **1** *adj* (*light*) débil, tenue; (*room, corridor, corner*) oscuro,-a, poco iluminado,-a; (*shape, outline, memory, recollection, etc*) borroso,-a; (*idea, awareness*) vago,-a; (*eyesight*) defectuoso,-a: *her eyes are growing dim,* le falla la vista. **2** *fam* (*person*) tonto,-a, corto,-a (de luces). **3** (*prospects, prospectives*) nada halagüeño,-a, nada prometedor,-ra, sombrío,-a. – **4** *t* (*light*) atenuar, bajar; (*eyes*) nublar, empañar; (*memory*) borrar, ir borrando, eliminar. – **5** *i* (*light*) bajarse, irse atenuando; (*eyesight*) nublarse, empañarse; (*memory*) borrarse, difuminarse, irse borrando; (*hopes*) apagarse.
● **to take a dim view of sth.,** ver algo con malos ojos.
▲ (*adjetivo*) *comp* dimmer, *superl* dimmest; (*verbo*) *pt* & *pp* dimmed, *ger* dimming.
dime [daɪm] *n* US moneda de diez centavos.
● **to be a dime a dozen,** (*common*) haber a porrillo/a montones/a patadas/a punta de pala; (*cheap*) ser baratísimo,-a.
dimension [dɪ'menʃən] **1** *n* dimensión *f*. – **2** dimensions, *npl* dimensiones *fpl*.
dimensional [daɪ'menʃənəl] *adj* dimensional.
diminish [dɪ'mɪnɪʃ] **1** *t* (*reduce - size, cost*) disminuir, reducir; (*- enthusiasm*) disminuir, apagar; (*- resolve*) disminuir; (*- horror*) hacer perder: *nothing could ever diminish the horror of that place,* nada podría hacer olvidar los horrores de aquel sitio. **2** (*belittle - person*) denigrar, rebajar; (*- achievements, work*) menospreciar. – **3** *i* (*cost, number, amount*) disminuir, reducirse; (*enthusiasm*) disminuir, apagarse: *the value of property has diminished greatly,* el valor de las propiedades ha disminuido mucho.

■ **diminished responsibility,** JUR responsabilidad *f* disminuida. ‖ **diminishing returns,** ECON rendimientos *mpl* decrecientes.

diminution [dɪmɪ'njuːʃən] *n* disminución *f*, reducción *f*.

diminutive [dɪ'mɪnjətɪv] **1** *adj* diminuto,-a. **2** LING diminutivo,-a. **– 3** *n* LING diminutivo.

dimmer ['dɪmə'] **dimmer (switch)**, *n* regulador *m* de intensidad (de la luz).

dimness ['dɪmnəs] **1** *n* (*of light*) palidez *f*; (*of room*) penumbra; (*of shape, outline*) lo borroso; (*of memory*) imprecisión *f*; (*of eyesight*) debilidad *f*. **2** (*of prospects, future*) lo sombrío. **3** *fam* (*of person*) torpeza, cortedad *f*.

dimple ['dɪmpəl] *n* hoyuelo.

dimwit ['dɪmwɪt] *n fam* tonto,-a, mentecato,-a, imbécil *mf*.

din [dɪn] *n* (*of voices*) barullo, bulla, alboroto; (*of traffic*) estruendo, ruido.

dine [daɪn] *i fml* (*gen*) comer (**on**, -); (*in evening*) cenar (**on**, -): *we dined on salmon,* comimos salmón.

◆ **to dine out** *i* cenar fuera.

diner ['daɪnə'] **1** *n* (*person*) comensal *mf*. **2** US restaurante *m* barato.

dinghy ['dɪŋgɪ] *n* bote *m*.

■ **rubber dinghy,** bote *m* neumático. ‖ **sailing dinghy,** bote *m* con vela.

▲ *pl* **dinghies.**

dingo ['dɪŋgəʊ] *n* dingo.

▲ *pl* **dingoes.**

dingy ['dɪndʒɪ] *adj* (*dark, depressing - room, house, street*) lúgubre, sombrío,-a, deprimente, oscuro,-a, sórdido,-a; (*drab - colour, wall, curtains*) deslucido,-a; (*dirty*) sucio,-a.

▲ *comp* **dingier,** *superl* **dingiest.**

dining car ['daɪnɪŋ kɑː'] *n* vagón *m* restaurante.

dining room ['daɪnɪŋruːm] *n* comedor *m*.

dining table ['daɪnɪŋ teɪbəl] *n* mesa de comedor.

dinner ['dɪnə'] *n* (*at midday*) comida; (*in evening*) cena: *we're having a few friends round for dinner,* hemos invitado a unos amigos a cenar a casa.

● **to have dinner,** (*midday*) comer; (*evening*) cenar. ‖ **to have done sth. more than you've had hot dinners,** haber hecho algo muchas veces: *I've had more jobs than you've had hot dinners,* he tenido más trabajos que tú pelos en la cabeza.

■ **dinner dance,** cena con baile. ‖ **dinner jacket,** esmoquin *m*, smoking *m*. ‖ **dinner party,** cena. ‖ **dinner service/set,** vajilla. ‖ **dinner table,** mesa: *don't read at the dinner table,* no leas en la mesa.

dinosaur ['daɪnəsɔː'] *n* dinosaurio.

dint [dɪnt] **by dint of,** *n* a fuerza de.

diocese ['daɪəsɪs] *n* diócesis *f*.

dioxide [daɪ'ɒksaɪd] *n* dióxido, bióxido: *carbon dioxide,* dióxido de carbono, anhídrido carbónico.

dip [dɪp] **1** *n* (*downward slope*) declive *m*, pendiente *f*; (*in ground*) depresión *f*, hondonada; (*drop - in prices, temperature, sales, production, profits*) caída, descenso. **2** *fam* (*quick swim*) chapuzón *m*. **3** (*for sheep*) baño desinfectante; (*for cleaning silver*) baño. **4** CULIN (*sauce*) salsa. **– 5** *t* (*put into liquid - pen, brush, bread*) mojar; (*- hand, spoon*) meter. **6** (*sheep*) desinfectar. **7** (*lower - head*) agachar, bajar. **– 8** *i* (*slope down*) descender, bajar; (*move down - bird, plane*) bajar en picado; (*- sun*) desaparecer; (*drop - sales, prices, etc*) bajar.

◆ **to dip into** **1** *t insep* (*book, magazine, report*) hojear, leer por encima; (*subject*) estudiar superficialmente. **2** (*savings, reserves, etc*) echar mano de.

● **to dip the headlights,** AUTO poner las luces de cruce, poner las cortas.

▲ (*verbo*) *pt* & *pp* **dipped,** *ger* **dipping.**

Dip Ed [dɪp'ed] *abbr* GB (*Diploma in Education*) ≈ certificado de aptitud pedagógica.

diphtheria [dɪp'θɪərɪə] *n* difteria.

diphthong ['dɪfθɒŋ] *n* LING diptongo.

diploma [dɪ'pləʊmə] *n* diploma *m*.

diplomacy [dɪ'pləʊməsɪ] *n* diplomacia.

diplomat ['dɪpləmæt] **1** *n* (*ambassador etc*) diplomático,-a. **2** (*tactful person*) persona diplomática.

diplomatic [dɪplə'mætɪk] *adj* diplomático,-a.

■ **diplomatic bag,** valija diplomática. ‖ **diplomatic corps / diplomatic body,** cuerpo diplomático. ‖ **diplomatic immunity,** inmunidad *f* diplomática.

dipper ['dɪpə'] **1** *n* (*for sherry*) venencia; (*for soup*) cazo, cacillo, cucharón *m*. **2** ORN mirlo acuático.

■ **big dipper,** (*at fairground*) montaña rusa. ‖ **the Big Dipper,** ASTRON la Osa Mayor.

dipsomania [dɪpsəʊ'meɪnɪə] *n* dipsomanía.

dipsomaniac [dɪpsəʊ'meɪnɪæk] *n* dipsómano,-a, dipsomaníaco,-a.

dipstick ['dɪpstɪk] *n* AUTO varilla del aceite.

Dir [daɪ'rektə'] *abbr* (*Director*) Director,-ra; (*abbreviation*) Dir.

dire ['daɪə'] **1** *adj* (*desperate, extreme*) extremo,-a, urgente: *they live in dire poverty,* viven en la más extrema pobreza. **2** (*serious, ominous*) serio,-a, grave: *he issued a dire warning,* hizo una grave advertencia; *this will have dire consequences,* esto tendrá graves consecuencias. **3** (*terrible, dreadful*) terrible, espantoso,-a, atroz: *that play was absolutely dire!,* ¡vaya película más espantosa!

● **to be in dire straits,** estar en una situación desesperada.

direct [dɪ'rekt, 'daɪrekt] **1** *adj* (*route, flight, train*) directo,-a. **2** (*contact, cause, consequence*) directo,-a: *this is a direct result of your carelessness,* esto es consecuencia directa de tu falta de atención; *there is a direct link between new technology and unemployment,* hay una relación directa entre las nuevas tecnologías y el desempleo; *keep the plant out of direct sunlight,* no expongas la planta directamente al sol. **3** (*exact, complete*) exacto,-a: *he's very sweet – the direct opposite of his wife,* es encantador – la antítesis de su mujer. **4** (*frank, straightforward - person, manner*) franco,-a, sincero,-a; (*- question*) directo,-a; (*- answer*) claro,-a. **– 5** *adv* (*go, write, phone*) directamente; (*broadcast*) en directo: *does this train go direct to Bristol?,* ¿este tren va directo a Bristol? **– 6** *t* (*tell, show the way*) indicar el camino a. **7** (*address - letter, parcel*) mandar, dirigir. **8** (*aim - attention, remark, criticism*) dirigir. **9** (*control, be in charge of - traffic, organization, inquiry*) dirigir. **10** CINEM THEAT dirigir. **11** *fml* (*order, command*) ordenar. **– 12** *i* CINEM THEAT dirigir.

● **to be a direct descendent of sb.,** ser descendiente directo,-a de algn., descender de algn. por línea directa. ‖ **to make/score a direct hit,** dar en el blanco.

■ **direct current,** corriente *f* continua. ‖ **direct debit,** domiciliación *f* de pagos. ‖ **direct object,** complemento directo. ‖ **direct speech,** estilo directo.

direction [dɪ'rekʃən, daɪ'rekʃən] **1** *n* (*way, course*) dirección *f*: *in all directions,* en todas direcciones; *in the direction of ...,* en dirección a ...; *sense of direction,* sentido de la orientación; *it's a step in the right direction,* es un paso hacia adelante. **2** (*control, management*) dirección *f*: *under the direction of ...,* bajo la dirección de ... **– 3 directions,** *npl* (*to place*) señas *fpl*, indicaciones *fpl*; (*for use, assembly*) instrucciones *fpl*, indicaciones *fpl*: *we had to ask someone for directions,* tuvimos que preguntar el camino.

● **"directions for use"**, "modo de empleo", "instrucciones de uso".
directional [dɪˈrekʃənəl] *adj* direccional.
directive [dɪˈrektɪv] *adj* directiva, directriz *f*.
directly [dɪˈrektlɪ, daɪˈrektlɪ] **1** *adv* (*go, fly, drive*) directamente, directo. **2** (*without intermediaries*) directamente: *you are directly responsible to the manager*, eres el responsable directo ante el gerente; *we buy directly from the manufacturers*, compramos directamente del fabricante. **3** (*exactly - opposite, above*) justo: *he sat directly in front of me*, se sentó justo delante de mí; *the sun was directly overhead*, el sol caía de pleno. **4** (*descend*) directamente, por línea directa. **5** (*speak*) francamente, claro; (*ask*) directamente. **6** (*very soon, shortly*) en seguida, dentro de poco; (*immediately, at once*) inmediatamente: *he'll be with you directly*, en seguida está contigo; *she went directly to bed*, se fue inmediatamente a la cama. – **7** *conj* GB (*as soon as*) en cuanto, tan pronto como: *I came directly I heard*, vine en cuanto me enteré.
directness [dɪˈrektnəs, daɪˈrektnəs] *n* (*of manner, character, comment, etc*) franqueza, sinceridad *f*.
director [dɪˈrektəʳ, daɪˈrektəʳ] *n* (*gen*) director,-ra; (*of company*) director,-ra, directivo,-a.
■ **board of directors**, consejo de administración, junta directiva. ‖ **director general**, director,-ra general. ‖ **Director of Public Prosecutions**, Fiscal *mf* General de Estado.
directorate [dɪˈrektərət] *n* dirección *f*, consejo de administración, junta directiva.
directorship [dɪˈrektəʃɪp] *n* (*position*) dirección *f*, cargo de director; (*time*) dirección *f*.
directory [dɪˈrektərɪ, daɪˈrektərɪ] **1** *n* (*telephone*) guía telefónica, listín *m* (de teléfonos); (*book, lost, index*) directorio, guía. **2** (**street**) **directory**, callejero.
■ **directory enquiries**, información *f* telefónica.
▲ *pl* **directories**.
dirge [dɜːdʒ] *n* canto fúnebre.
dirt [dɜːt] **1** *n* (*dirtiness*) suciedad *f*; (*filth, grime*) mugre *f*, roña, porquería; (*mud*) barro; (*dust*) polvo: *the carpet's covered in dirt*, la alfombra está toda sucia; *this coat shows the dirt*, en este abrigo se nota la suciedad. **2** (*earth*) tierra. **3** *fam* (*excrement*) porquería, mierda, caca. **4** *fam* (*scandal, gossip*) chismes *mpl*, trapos *mpl* sucios: *the press managed to get all the dirt on the actor*, la prensa consiguió sacar a relucir todos los trapos sucios del actor. **5** *fam* (*obscene thought, talk*) porquerías *fpl*, guarradas *fpl*.
● **to be as common as dirt**, ser muy ordinario,-a. ‖ **to fling/throw dirt at sb.**, manchar la reputación de algn. ‖ **to treat sb. like dirt**, tratar a algn. como a un perro, tratar a algn. como una zapatilla.
■ **dirt track**, camino de tierra.
dirt-cheap [ˈdɜːtˈtʃiːp] *adj* baratísimo,-a, tirado,-a, regalado,-a.
● **to sell sth. dirt cheap**, vender algo regalado.
▲ *Se escribe* **dirt cheap** *cuando no se antepone a un sustantivo.*
dirtiness [ˈdɜːtɪnəs] *n* suciedad *f*.
dirty [ˈdɜːtɪ] **1** *adj* (*not clean, soiled*) sucio,-a; (*stained*) manchado,-a: *a dirty mark*, una mancha; *your bedroom is filthy dirty*, tu habitación está hecha un asco; *cleaning the oven is dirty work*, limpiar el horno es trabajo sucio. **2** (*obscene - magazine, film*) porno; (*story, book*) indecente, cochino,-a, guarro,-a; (*- joke*) verde; (*- mind, sense of humour*) pervertido,-a: *you've got a dirty mind!*, ¡tienes una mente pervertida! **3** (*night, weather*) asqueroso,-a, de perros. **4** *fam* (*unfair, dishonest - gen*) sucio,-a, deshones-

to,-a; (*- player, fighter*) sucio,-a, tramposo,-a; (*- thief, cheat*) vil, despreciable; (*- lie*) descarado,-a; (*- deed*) malo,-a: *you dirty rat!*, ¡canalla! – **5** *adv fam* (*very*) muy: *a dirty great hole*, un agujero enorme. **6** (*play*) sucio. – **7** *t* ensuciar. – **8** *i* ensuciarse.
● **a dirty old man**, un viejo verde. ‖ **to do sb.'s dirty work**, hacerle el trabajo sucio a algn. ‖ **to do the dirty on sb.**, jugarle una mala pasada a algn. ‖ **to get dirty**, ensuciarse. ‖ **to give sb. a dirty look**, fulminar a algn. con la mirada, lanzar a algn. una mirada asesina. ‖ **to talk dirty**, decir guarradas.
■ **dirty language**, palabrotas *fpl*. ‖ **dirty trick**, cochinada, guarrada. ‖ **dirty weekend**, aventura de fin de semana. ‖ **dirty word**, (*swear word*) palabrota, taco; (*disapproved word*) palabra tabú.
▲ *comp* **dirtier**, *superl* **dirtiest**.
disability [dɪsəˈbɪlɪtɪ] *n* (*state*) invalidez *f*, discapacidad *f*, incapacidad *f*, minusvalía; (*handicap*) desventaja, hándicap *m*: *she doesn't let her disability stop her from going out*, no deja que su minusvalía le impida de salir.
■ **disability allowance / disability pension**, subsidio por invalidez / pensión *f* por invalidez.
▲ *pl* **disabilities**.
disabled [dɪsˈeɪbəld] **1** *adj* minusválido,-a: *mentally disabled people*, los disminuidos psíquicos. – **2 the disabled**, *npl* los minusválidos.
■ **disabled access**, acceso para minusválidos.
disabuse [dɪsəˈbjuːz] *t fml* desengañar.
● **to disabuse sb. of sth.**, quitarle algo a algn. de la cabeza.
disadvantage [dɪsədˈvɑːntɪdʒ] *n* (*drawback*) desventaja; (*obstacle*) inconveniente *m*.
● **to be at a disadvantage**, estar en desventaja. ‖ **to place/put sb. at a disadvantage**, poner a algn. en (una) situación de desventaja. ‖ **to sb.'s disadvantage**, en perjuicio de algn.
disadvantaged [dɪsədˈvɑːntɪdʒd] **1** *adj* desfavorecido,-a, desheredado,-a, discriminado,-a. – **2 the disadvantaged**, *npl* los desfavorecidos *mpl*.
disadvantageous [dɪsædvɑːnˈteɪdʒəs] *adj* desventajoso,-a (**to**, para), desfavorable (**to**, para).
disaffected [dɪsəˈfektɪd] *adj* desafecto,-a.
disaffection [dɪsəˈfekʃən] *n* desafección *f*.
disagree [dɪsəˈgriː] **1** *i* (*not agree*) no estar de acuerdo (**on**, en), (**with**, con), disentir (**with**, de), discrepar (**with**, de), (**on**, en): *we disagreed on/over what film to see*, no estuvimos de acuerdo en qué película ir a ver; *I disagree with you*, discrepo contigo, no estoy de acuerdo contigo. **2** (*differ, not match - statements, reports, figures*) no coincidir (**with**, con), no corresponder (**with**, a), discrepar (**with**, de). **3** (*food*) sentar mal (**with**, a); (*weather*) no convenir (**with**, a): *spicy food disagrees with me*, la comida picante me sienta mal.
disagreeable [dɪsəˈgrɪəbəl] *adj* desagradable.
disagreement [dɪsəˈgriːmənt] **1** *n* (*difference of opinion*) desacuerdo, disconformidad *f*; (*argument*) discusión *f*, riña, altercado: *we've never had a serious disagreement*, nunca hemos discutido en serio. **2** (*lack of similarity*) discrepancia.
● **to be in disagreement with sb./sth.**, estar en desacuerdo con algn./algo, no estar de acuerdo con algn./algo.
disallow [dɪsəˈlaʊ] *t* (*objection, claim, evidence*) denegar, rechazar, desestimar; (*goal*) anular.
disappear [dɪsəˈpɪəʳ] *i* (*gen*) desaparecer; (*worries, fears*) desvanecerse.
● **to disappear from sight/view**, perderse de vista. ‖

to **disappear without trace,** desaparecer sin dejar rastro, esfumarse. ‖ **to do a disappearing act,** esfumarse como por arte de magia.

disappearance [dɪsəˈpɪərəns] *n* desaparición *f*.

disappoint [dɪsəˈpɔɪnt] *t* (*person*) decepcionar, defraudar, desilusionar; (*hope, desire, plan, ambition*) defraudar, frustrar: *the hotel disappointed my expectations,* el hotel me decepcionó.

disappointed [dɪsəˈpɔɪntɪd] *adj* (*person*) decepcionado,-a, desilusionado,-a; (*hope, plan*) frustrado,-a: *she was disappointed at/about her exam results,* los resultados de los exámenes la decepcionaron; *his parents are disappointed in/with him,* sus padres están decepcionados con él; *I felt really disappointed,* me llevé un buen chasco.

disappointing [dɪsəˈpɔɪntɪŋ] *adj* decepcionante: *the response was very disappointing,* la reacción fue muy decepcionante.

disappointment [dɪsəˈpɔɪntmənt] *n* (*state, emotion*) desilusión *f*, decepción *f*; (*person, thing*) decepción *f*, chasco: *book early to avoid disappointment,* haga su reserva ahora para no llevarse una decepción.

● **to express/voice one's disapproval of sb./sth.,** expresar su desaprobación respecto a algn./algo.

disapprove [dɪsəˈpruːv] **1** *t* desaprobar (**of,** -): *I disapprove,* estoy en contra, no me parece bien; *her parents disapproved of her boyfriend,* sus padres desaprobaron a su novio. **2** US POL (*legislation, plan, etc*) rechazar, no aprobar.

disapproving [dɪsəˈpruːvɪŋ] *n* de desaprobación.

disarm [dɪsˈɑːm] **1** *t* (*person, group, etc*) desarmar; (*bomb*) desactivar. **2** *fig* (*criticism*) desbaratar. **3** (*charm, win over*) desarmar. – **4** *i* (*nation*) desarmarse.

disarmament [dɪsˈɑːməmənt] *n* desarme *m*: *nuclear disarmament,* desarme nuclear; *disarmament conference,* conferencia de desarme.

disarming [dɪsˈɑːmɪŋ] *adj* (*smile*) que desarma; (*person*) encantador,-ra.

disarray [dɪsəˈreɪ] *n* (*organization, group, etc*) desorganización *f*; (*of appearance*) desaliño; (*of room, papers, affairs, etc*) desorden *m*, caos *m*; (*of thoughts*) confusión *f*: *her hair was in complete disarray,* su pelo estaba todo revuelto.

● **to throw sth. into disarray,** desbaratar algo, trastornar algo.

disaster [dɪˈzɑːstəʳ] **1** *n* (*flood, earthquake*) desastre *m*, catástrofe *f*; (*crash, sinking, fire*) desastre *m*, siniestro: *the worst air disaster since 1990,* el peor desastre aéreo desde 1990; *it was then that disaster struck,* fue entonces cuando se produjo la catástrofe. **2** *fam* (*failure*) desastre *m*.

● **to be a recipe for disaster,** buscarse problemas. ‖ **to spell disaster for sb./sth.,** resultar desastroso,-a para algn./algo.

■ **disaster area,** (*site of disaster*) zona siniestrada; (*mess*) desastre *m*. ‖ **disaster fund,** fondo para los damnificados.

disastrous [dɪˈzɑːstərəs] *adj* desastroso,-a, catastrófico,-a.

disavow [dɪsəˈvaʊ] *t fml* negar tener: *he disavows any part in the robbery,* niega tener nada que ver con el robo.

disband [dɪsˈbænd] **1** *t* (*group, organization*) disolver, deshacer; (*army*) licenciar. – **2** *i* (*group, organization*) disolverse, deshacerse; (*army*) licenciarse.

disbelief [dɪsbɪˈliːf] *n* incredulidad *f*: *she stared at me in desbelief,* me miró incrédula, me miro con incredulidad.

disbelieve [dɪsbɪˈliːv] **1** *t* no creer. – **2** *i* no creer (**in,** en), no dar crédito (**in,** a).

disburse [dɪsˈbɜːs] *t* desembolsar.

disbursement [dɪsˈbɜːsmənt] *n* desembolso.

disc [dɪsk] *n* (*gen*) disco.

■ **disc brake,** freno de disco. ‖ **disc jockey,** disc-jockey *m*, pinchadiscos *mf*.

discard [dɪsˈkɑːd] **1** *t* (*old things, unwanted things*) desechar, deshacerse de; (*theory, idea, belief*) desechar, descartar, rechazar; (*playing card*) descartarse de. – **2** *i* (*in card games*) descartarse.

discern [dɪˈsɜːn] *t* (*see*) percibir, distinguir; (*tell difference*) distinguir, discernir; (*realize*) percibir, darse cuenta: *he discerned that she was lying,* se dio cuenta de que mentía.

discernible [dɪˈsɜːnəbəl] *adj* (*shape*) visible; (*fault, drawback, merit, influence*) perceptible; (*likeness, difference, change, improvement*) apreciable: *there is no discernible reason,* no está claro.

discerning [dɪˈsɜːnɪŋ] *adj* (*person*) exigente, con criterio, entendido,-a; (*palate, taste*) exigente, fino,-a, refinado,-a; (*eye, ear*) educado,-a.

discernment [dɪˈsɜːnmənt] *n* (buen) criterio, discernimiento.

discharge [ˈdɪstʃɑːdʒ] **1** *n* (*of electric current*) descarga; (*of smoke, fumes, gases*) emisión *f*; (*of sewage, waste*) vertido. **2** MED (*of wound*) supuración *f*; (*secretion*) secreción *f*. **3** (*of cargo*) descarga. **4** (*of weapon*) descarga. **5** (*of prisoner*) liberación *f*, puesta en libertad; (*of patient*) alta; (*of soldier*) licencia (absoluta); (*of injured soldier*) baja. **6** (*of worker*) despido. **7** (*of debt*) liquidación *f*, pago; (*of duties*) cumplimiento, ejercicio. – **8** *t* (*give, send out - sewage, waste, oil*) verter; (*smoke, fumes*) despedir; (*- electric current*) descargar. **9** (*unload - cargo*) descargar; (*- passengers*) desembarcar. **10** (*fire - arrow*) arrojar, lanzar; (*- shot*) descargar. **11** (*allow to go - prisoner*) liberar, soltar, poner en libertad; (*patient*) dar de alta; (*juror*) dispensar; (*soldier*) licenciar; (*injured soldier*) dar de baja. **12** (*dismiss*) despedir. **13** *fml* (*pay - debt*) saldar, liquidar; (*perform - duty, responsibility, obligation*) cumplir con. – **14** *i* (*river*) desembocar; (*sewer*) verter. **15** (*wound*) supurar. **16** ELEC (*battery*) descargarse.

■ **absolute discharge,** JUR libertad *f* absoluta. ‖ **conditional discharge,** JUR libertad *f* condicional. ‖ **unconditional discharge,** JUR libertad *f* incondicional. ‖ **vaginal discharge,** flujo vaginal.

▲ (*verbo*) [dɪsˈtʃɑːdʒ].

disciple [dɪˈsaɪpəl] **1** *n* REL discípulo,-a. **2** (*follower*) seguidor,-ra, discípulo,-a.

disciplinary [ˈdɪsɪplɪnərɪ] *adj* disciplinario,-a.

discipline [ˈdɪsɪplɪn] **1** *n* (*training, behaviour*) disciplina. **2** (*punishment*) castigo. **3** (*subject*) disciplina. – **4** *t* (*train, control*) disciplinar. **5** (*punish - child, pupil*) castigar; (*- worker*) sancionar; (*- official*) expedientar.

● **to discipline os. to do sth.,** imponerse la disciplina de hacer algo, obligarse a hacer algo.

disclaim [dɪsˈkleɪm] *t* (*knowledge, responsibility*) negar: *he disclaimed ownership of the weapon,* negó que el arma fuera suya.

disclaimer [dɪsˈkleɪməʳ] *t* (*denial*) mentís *m*, desmentido.

● **to issue a disclaimer,** publicar un desmentido.

disclose [dɪsˈkləʊz] **1** *t* (*make known*) revelar, dar a conocer. **2** (*show*) mostrar, dejar ver.

disclosure [dɪs'kləʊʒəʳ] n revelación f.
disco ['dɪskəʊ] n fam disco f, discoteca.
▲ pl discos.
discolor [dɪs'kʌləʳ] t US → **discolour**.
discoloration [dɪskʌlə'reɪʃən] n (process, fading) decoloración f, descoloración f; (stain) mancha.
discolour [dɪs'kʌləʳ] 1 t (fade, bleach) decolorar, descolorar; (stain) manchar: smoking discolours your teeth, fumar mancha los dientes. – 2 i (lose colour) decolorarse, descolorarse; (become stained) volverse amarillento,-a, mancharse.
discomfiture [dɪs'kʌmfɪtʃəʳ] n fml desconcierto, turbación f.
discomfort [dɪs'kʌmfət] 1 n (lack of comfort) incomodidad f. 2 (pain) malestar m, molestia. 3 (unease, embarrassment) inquietud f, desasosiego, preocupación f.
disconcert [dɪskən'sɜːt] t desconcertar.
disconcerting [dɪskən'sɜːtɪŋ] adj desconcertante.
disconnect [dɪskə'nekt] t (from mains) desconectar; (gas, electricity, phone, etc) cortar: operator, we were disconnected, operadora, se cortó la comunicación.
disconnected [dɪskə'nektɪd] 1 adj (from power supply) desconectado,-a; (gas, electricity, phone, etc) cortado,-a. 2 (from reality) desconectado,-a. 3 fig (of speech, writing) deshilvanado,-a; (thoughts, remarks) inconexo,-a.
disconsolate [dɪs'kɒnsələt] adj desconsolado,-a.
discontent [dɪskən'tent] n descontento.
discontented [dɪskən'tentɪd] adj descontento,-a (with, con).
discontentment [dɪskən'tentmənt] n descontento.
discontinuance [dɪʃkən'tɪnjʊəns] n suspensión f.
discontinue [dɪskən'tɪnjuː] t (service) suspender, interrumpir; (model) dejar de fabricar: discontinued lines, restos de serie.
discontinuity [dɪskɒntɪ'njuːɪtɪ] 1 n (lack of continuity) discontinuidad f. 2 (gap, break) interrupción f.
discontinuous [dɪskən'tɪnjʊəs] adj (line, pattern) discontinuo,-a; (process) con interrupciones, interrumpido,-a.
discord ['dɪskɔːd] 1 n (disagreement) discordia. 2 MUS disonancia, discordancia.
discordant [dɪs'kɔːdənt] n (gen) discordante; (atmosphere) de discordia.
● **to strike a discordant note,** dar la nota discordante.
discotheque ['dɪskətek] n fml discoteca.
discount ['dɪskaʊnt] 1 n descuento: staff get a 15% discount, los empleados tienen un descuento del 15%; they gave me a discount on the coat because it was shop-soiled, me hicieron un descuento en el precio del abrigo por estar deteriorado. – 2 t (goods) rebajar; (price) reducir; (amount, bill of exchange) descontar. 3 (disregard - possibility) descartar; (ignore) no tener en cuenta.
● **to be at a discount,** (goods etc) tener descuento, estar rebajado,-a; (qualities) no contar.
■ **discount shop / discount store,** tienda de saldos.
▲ (verbo) [dɪs'kaʊnt].
discourage [dɪs'kʌrɪdʒ] 1 t (dishearten) desanimar, desalentar. 2 (prevent - action) poner freno a; (investment, initiative) no fomentar, no estimular, desanimar; (advances) rechazar, resistirse a: this government's policies discourage investors, la política de este gobierno no estimula a los inversores. 3 (dissuade) disuadir (from, de), hacer desistir (from, de): his parents discouraged him from getting a motorbike, sus padres lo disuadieron de comprarse una moto; we discourage smoking in this school, en esta escuela se quiere evitar que la gente fume.

● **to be discouraged,** desanimarse.
discouragement [dɪs'kʌrɪdʒmənt] 1 n (dejection) desaliento, desánimo. 2 (dissuasion) disuasión f, desaprobación f. 3 (deterrent) freno; (obstacle) obstáculo, contrariedad f.
discouraging [dɪs'kʌrɪdʒɪŋ] adj desalentador,-ra, descorazonador,-ra, desmoralizador,-ra.
discourse ['dɪskɔːs] 1 n fml (spoken - speech) discurso; (-discussion) discusión f, debate m; (written) disertación f. 2 LING discurso. – 3 t disertar (on/upon, sobre).
discourteous [dɪs'kɜːtɪəs] adj descortés.
discourtesy [dɪs'kɜːtəsɪ] n descortesía.
discover [dɪ'skʌvəʳ] 1 t (find - gen) descubrir; (mistake, loss, fact) descubrir, darse cuenta de; (missing object, person) encontrar, hallar: Columbus discovered America, Colón descubrió América; he discovered that his flat had been broken into, descubrió que le habían entrado en el piso. 2 (find out) descubrir, enterarse de: when man discovered how to cultivate the fields, cuando el hombre descubrió el cultivo del campo; did you discover what happened at the end?, ¿descubriste qué pasó al final?
discoverer [dɪ'skʌvərəʳ] n descubridor,-ra.
discovery [dɪ'skʌvərɪ] n descubrimiento.
▲ pl discoveries.
discredit [dɪs'kredɪt] 1 n (dishonour, disgrace) descrédito: the English hooligans brought discredit on their team, los hinchas ingleses trajeron el descrédito a su equipo. 2 (person, thing) vergüenza (to, para). 3 (disbelief, doubt) duda. – 4 t (theory, claim) desacreditar; (person, government) desacreditar, desprestigiar. 5 (refuse to believe) poner en duda, poner en tela de juicio.
● **to be to sb.'s discredit,** ir en descrédito de algn.
discreditable [dɪs'kredɪtəbəl] adj vergonzoso,-a, deshonroso,-a.
discreet [dɪ'skriːt] adj (person, enquiries, silence) discreto,-a; (distance) prudencial; (perfume, colour) discreto,-a.
discrepancy [dɪ'skrepənsɪ] n discrepancia.
▲ pl discrepancies.
discrete [dɪs'kriːt] adj diferenciado,-a, distinto,-a.
discretion [dɪ'skreʃən] 1 n (quality of being discreet) discreción f; (prudence) prudencia: she's the soul of discretion, es la discreción personificada. 2 (judgement) criterio, juicio: use your own discretion, usa tu propio criterio.
● **at the discretion of,** a juicio de, a criterio de, a discreción de. ‖ discretion is the better part of valour, la prudencia es la madre de la ciencia.
discretionary [dɪs'kreʃənərɪ] adj discrecional.
discriminate [dɪ'skrɪmɪneɪt] 1 i (treat differently) discriminar (**against**, a) (**between**, entre): he was sure he had been discriminated against because of his race, estaba seguro de que lo habían discriminado a causa de su raza; some companies discriminate in favour of women, algunas empresas favorecen a las mujeres. – 2 t (see a difference) distinguir (**from**, de), discriminar.
discriminating [dɪ'skrɪmɪneɪtɪŋ] adj (person) entendido,-a, exigente; (judgement) sagaz; (taste) refinado,-a, educado,-a, fino,-a; (palate) exigente; (eye) educado,-a.
discrimination [dɪskrɪmɪ'neɪʃən] 1 n (bias) discriminación f. 2 (distinction) diferenciación f, distinción f. 3 (judgement) discernimiento, criterio.
discriminatory [dɪ'skrɪmɪnətərɪ] adj discriminatorio,-a.
discursive [dɪ'skɜːsɪv] 1 adj pej (speaker, writer) que se va por las ramas, divagador,-ra, que diverga; (account, writing, essay) prolijo,-a, extenso,-a, repleto,-a de digresiones. 2 (in philosophy) discursivo,-a.

discus ['dɪskəs] 1 n (object) disco. 2 the discus, (event, sport) el lanzamiento de disco.
▲ pl discuses o disci ['dɪskaɪ].

discuss [dɪ'skʌs] 1 t (talk about - person) hablar de; (- subject, topic) hablar de, tratar; (- plan, problem) discutir: have you discussed this with your parents?, ¿has hablado de eso con tus padres?; he refused to discuss the matter any further, se negó a discutir más el asunto. 2 (examine) analizar, examinar. 3 (in writing) tratar de: this chapter discusses the problems facing single-parent families, este capítulo trata de los problemas con que se enfrentan las familias monoparentales.

discussion [dɪ'skʌʃən] n (gen) discusión f, debate m: after much discussion, después de mucho discutirlo; management are holding discussions with the unions, la patronal mantiene negociaciones con los sindicatos; the subject is still under discussion, el tema aún se está discutiendo.
■ discussion group, grupo de debate.

disdain [dɪs'deɪn] 1 n desdén m, desprecio, menosprecio. – 2 t desdeñar, despreciar, menospreciar.
● to disdain to do sth., no dignarse a hacer algo.

disdainful [dɪs'deɪnful] adj desdeñoso,-a, despectivo,-a.
● to be disdainful of, (thing) despreciar, desdeñar; (person) mostrarse desdeñoso,-a con, tratar con desdén.

disease [dɪ'ziːz] 1 n (illness) enfermedad f. 2 fig mal m, enfermedad f.

diseased [dɪ'ziːzd] 1 adj MED (part of body) afectado,-a; (plant, animal) enfermo,-a. 2 fig (imagination, mind) enfermizo,-a, morboso,-a; (society) enfermo,-a.

disembark [dɪsɪm'baːk] 1 t desembarcar. – 2 i desembarcar (from, de).

disembarkation [dɪsɪmbaː'keɪʃən] n (of people) desembarco; (of goods) desembarque m.

disembodied [dɪsɪm'bɒdɪd] adj incorpóreo,-a.

disembowel [dɪsɪm'bauəl] t destripar.
▲ pt & pp disembowelled (us disemboweled), ger disembowelling (us disemboweling).

disenchanted [dɪsɪn'tʃaːntɪd] adj desencantado,-a, desilusionado,-a.

disenchantment [dɪsɪn'tʃaːntmənt] n desencanto, desilusión f.

disenfranchise [dɪsɪn'fræntʃaɪz] t privar del derecho al voto.

disengage [dɪsɪn'geɪdʒ] 1 t (free - gen) soltar (from, de); (gears, mechanism) desconectar. 2 MIL (troops) retirar (from, de). – 3 i MIL retirarse.
● to disengage os. from sth., conseguir soltarse de algo. ‖ to disengage the clutch, desembragar, soltar el embrague.

disentangle [dɪsɪn'tæŋgəl] 1 t (unravel) desenredar, desenmarañar. 2 fig (separate - truth, facts) separar.
● to disentangle os. from sth., lograr salir de algo, lograr soltarse de algo.

disfavor [dɪs'feɪvəʳ] n us → **disfavour**.

disfavour [dɪs'feɪvəʳ] n desaprobación f: he regarded the proposal with disfavour, desaprobaba la propuesta.
● to be in disfavour, haber caído en desgracia. ‖ to fall into disfavour, caer en desgracia.

disfigure [dɪs'fɪgəʳ] t (face, person) desfigurar; (building, town, landscape) afear, estropear.

disfigurement [dɪs'fɪgəmənt] n (of face, person) desfiguración f; (of building, town, landscape) afeamiento.

disgorge [dɪs'gɔːdʒ] 1 t (liquid, waste) verter; (smoke, fumes) emitir; (people) echar. 2 (vomit) devolver, arrojar.

3 fam (give up, hand over) entregar. – 4 i (of river) desembocar. 5 fig (crowds) salir.

disgrace [dɪs'greɪs] 1 n (loss of favour) desgracia; (loss of honour) deshonra, deshonor m; (public dishonour) ignominia. 2 (shame) escándalo, vergüenza. – 3 t (bring shame on) deshonrar. 4 (discredit) desacreditar.
● to be a disgrace (to sb./sth.), ser una vergüenza (para algn./algo). ‖ to be in disgrace, (adult) estar desacreditado,-a, haber caído en desgracia; (child) estar castigado,-a. ‖ to bring disgrace on sb., traer la deshonra a algn. ‖ to disgrace os., hacer el ridículo. ‖ to fall into disgrace, caer en desgracia.

disgraceful [dɪs'greɪsful] adj vergonzoso,-a: it's disgraceful, es vergonzoso, es una vergüenza.

disgruntled [dɪs'grʌntəld] adj (upset) contrariado,-a, disgustado,-a; (dissatisfied) descontento,-a; (annoyed) fastidiado,-a, contrariado,-a; (resentful) resentido,-a, ofendido,-a.

disguise [dɪs'gaɪz] 1 n disfraz m. – 2 t (person) disfrazar (as, de); (voice, handwriting) cambiar. 3 (feelings, opinions) disfrazar, disimular; (mistake) ocultar: there's no disguising the fact that ..., no se puede ocultar el hecho de que ...
● in disguise, disfrazado,-a. ‖ to diguise os., disfrazarse.

disgust [dɪs'gʌst] 1 n (revulsion) asco, repugnancia; (strong disapproval) indignación f: she left the room in disgust, salió indignada de la habitación; the demostrators wanted to show their disgust at the killings, los manifestantes querían mostrar su indignación por los asesinatos. – 2 t (revolt) repugnar, dar asco a; (disapprove) indignar: he disgusts me, me da asco.
● to fill sb. with disgust, dar asco a algn., repugnar a algn.

disgusted [dɪs'gʌstɪd] adj (revolted) asqueado,-a; (indignant) indignado,-a.
● to be disgusted at/by sth., indignarle a uno algo: I'm disgusted at the way he treats his wife, me indigna la manera en que trata a su mujer. ‖ to be disgusted with sb., estar furioso,-a con algn., estar indignado,-a con algn.: I'm disgusted with myself, estoy indignado conmigo mismo.

disgusting [dɪs'gʌstɪŋ] 1 adj (loathsome) asqueroso,-a, repugnante; (unpleasant) desagradable; (awful) horroroso,-a; (weather) asqueroso,-a, horrible: how disgusting!, ¡qué asco! 2 (intolerable, unacceptable) intolerable; (causing outrage) vergonzoso,-a.

dish [dɪʃ] 1 n (plate) plato; (for serving) fuente f. 2 CULIN (food) plato. 3 TV antena parabólica. 4 fam (attractive man) guaperas m; (attractive woman) bombón m. – 5 dishes, npl (crockery) platos mpl, vajilla f sing.
◆ to dish out t sep (distribute - insults, abuse, awards, money, leaflets, etc) repartir; (advice, compliments) dar; (food) servir. ‖ to dish up t sep (food) servir; (arguments) ofrecer.
● to dish it out, (verbally) criticar; (physically) dar una buena paliza. ‖ to do the dishes, lavar los platos.
■ dish rack, escurreplatos m.

dishcloth ['dɪʃklɒθ] n trapo, bayeta.

dishearten [dɪs'haːtən] t descorazonar, desanimar, desalentar.

disheartening [dɪs'haːtənɪŋ] adj desalentador,-ra, descorazonador,-ra.

disheveled [dɪ'ʃevəld] adj us → **dishevelled**.

dishevelled [dɪ'ʃevəld] adj (referring to hair) despeinado,-a, desmelenado,-a; (referring to appearance, clothes) desaliñado,-a, desarreglado,-a.

dishonest [dɪs'ɒnɪst] adj (person, answer) deshonesto,-a, poco honrado,-a; (means etc) fraudulento,-a, deshonesto,-a.

dishonesty [dɪs'ɒnɪstɪ] *n* (*gen*) deshonestidad *f*, falta de honradez; (*of statement*) falsedad *f*; (*of means*) fraudulencia.

dishonor [dɪs'ɒnə^r] *n* US → **dishonour**.

dishonorable [dɪs'ɒnərəbəl] *adj* US → **dishonourable**.

dishonour [dɪs'ɒnə^r] **1** *n* deshonra, deshonor *m*. – **2** *t* (*family, country, team, etc*) deshonrar. **3** (*renege on - agreement*) no respetar; (*- promise*) no cumplir, faltar a; (*- cheque, debt*) no pagar.

dishonourable [dɪs'ɒnərəbəl] *adj* deshonroso,-a.

dishtowel ['dɪʃtaʊəl] *n* US paño de cocina.

dishwasher ['dɪʃwɒʃə^r] *n* (*machine*) lavaplatos *m*, lavavajillas *m*; (*person*) lavaplatos *mf*.

dishy ['dɪʃɪ] *adj* GB *fam* guapo,-a: *he's really dishy*, está muy bueno, está como un tren.
▲ *comp* **dishier**, *superl* **dishiest**.

disillusion [dɪsɪ'luːʒən] *t* desilusionar.
● **to become disillusioned**, desilusionarse.

disillusionment [dɪsɪ'luːzənmənt] *n* desilusión *f*.

disincentive [dɪsɪn'sentɪv] *n* freno.
● **to be a disincentive to sth.**, ser un freno para algo.

disinclination [dɪsɪnklɪ'neɪʃən] *n* aversión *f*, desgana.
● **to have a disinclination for sth.**, ser reacio,-a a algo. ‖ **to have a disinclination to do sth.**, no estar dispuesto,-a a hacer algo.

disinfect [dɪsɪn'fekt] *t* desinfectar.

disinfectant [dɪsɪn'fektənt] **1** *adj* desinfectante. – **2** *n* desinfectante *m*.

disingenuous [dɪsɪn'dʒenjʊəs] *adj* falso,-a, insincero,-a.

disinherit [dɪsɪn'herɪt] *t* desheredar.

disintegrate [dɪs'ɪntɪgreɪt] **1** *t* desintegrar. – **2** *i* desintegrarse.

disintegration [dɪsɪntɪ'greɪʃən] *n* desintegración *f*.

disinter [dɪsɪn'tɜː^r] *t* fml desenterrar.
▲ *pt & pp* **disinterred**, *ger* **disinterring**.

disinterested [dɪs'ɪntrəstɪd] *adj* (*action*) desinteresado,-a; (*decision, advice*) imparcial.

disjointed [dɪs'dʒɔɪntɪd] *adj* (*speech, writing*) inconexo,-a, deshilvanado,-a.

disk [dɪsk] *n* (*gen*) disco.
■ **disk drive**, COMPUT disquetera.

diskette [dɪs'ket] *n* COMPUT disquete *m*.

dislike [dɪs'laɪk] **1** *n* aversión *f*, antipatía: *my mother took an immediate dislike to him*, mi madre le cogió antipatía inmediatamente; *he has an extreme dislike of cats*, no le gustan nada los gatos, tiene aversión a los gatos; *we all have our likes and dislikes*, todos tenemos cosas que nos gustan y que no nos gustan. – **2** *t* (*thing*) no gustarle a; (*person*) tener antipatía a, caerle mal a: *I dislike wearing a skirt*, no me gusta llevar falda; *she dislikes him*, le cae mal.

dislocate ['dɪsləkeɪt] **1** *t* MED dislocar: *she dislocated her hip*, se dislocó la cadera. **2** *fig* (*system, plan, traffic*) trastornar.

dislocation [dɪslə'keɪʃən] **1** *n* MED dislocación *f*. **2** *fig* trastorno.

dislodge [dɪs'lɒdʒ] **1** *t* (*object*) sacar. **2** (*person*) desalojar (**from** , de), desplazar (**from**, de).

disloyal [dɪs'lɔɪəl] *adj* desleal (**to**, a/con).

disloyalty [dɪs'lɔɪəltɪ] *n* deslealtad *f* (**to**, a/con).

dismal ['dɪzməl] **1** *adj* (*gloomy - place*) sombrío,-a, deprimente, lúgubre; (*person*) triste; (*tone, look, manner*) sombrío,-a, deprimente; (*prospect, outlook, news*) sombrío,-a; (*future*) negro,-a. **2** *fam* (*very bad - weather*) malísimo,-a, pésimo,-a; (*performance, music, result, etc*) pésimo,-a, lamentable: *a dismal failure*, un fracaso estrepitoso.

dismantle [dɪs'mæntəl] **1** *t* (*take apart - machinery*) desmontar; (*- furniture*) desarmar. **2** (*strip - building, ship*) desmantelar. **3** *fig* (*system, organization, legislation*) desmantelar. – **4** *i* desmontarse, desarmarse.

dismay [dɪs'meɪ] **1** *n* consternación *f*: *to our dismay*, para nuestra consternación; *they watched in/with dismay*, miraron consternados. – **2** *t* consternar.
● **to be dismayed**, consternarse, quedarse consternado,-a. ‖ **to be filled with dismay**, dejarle a uno consternado,-a, consternarle a uno.

dismember [dɪs'membə^r] **1** *t* (*person's body*) desmembrar; (*animal*) descuartizar. **2** (*country, empire*) desmembrar, dividir.

dismiss [dɪs'mɪs] **1** *t* (*reject - idea, possibility, suggestion*) descartar, desechar; (*- subject*) despachar; (*- thoughts, feelings*) apartar, desterrar; (*- theory, request*) rechazar: *he was dismissed as a no-hoper*, quedó descartado como un caso perdido. **2** (*sack - employee*) despedir; (*- official, executive, minister*) destituir. **3** (*send away, allow to go*) dar permiso para retirarse: *the teacher dismissed the class early*, el maestro dejó salir a su clase antes de la hora; *troops dismissed!*, ¡rompan filas! **4** JUR (*case*) desestimar; (*charge, appeal*) desestimar, denegar.

dismissal [dɪs'mɪsəl] **1** *n* (*of idea, suggestion*) descarte *m*, abandono; (*of theory, request, plan*) rechazo. **2** (*sacking - of employee*) despido; (*- of official, executive, minister*) destitución *f*. **3** (*sending away*) autorización *f* para retirarse. **4** JUR (*of claim*) desestimación *f*.
■ **unfair dismissal**, despido improcedente.

dismissive [dɪs'mɪsɪv] *adj* (*attitude, smile*) desdeñoso,-a: *he was dismissive of her*, se mostró desdeñoso con ella.

dismount [dɪs'maʊnt] *i* desmontarse (**from**, de), apearse (**from**, de), bajarse (**from**, de).

disobedience [dɪsə'biːdɪəns] *n* desobediencia.

disobedient [dɪsə'biːdɪənt] *adj* desobediente.
● **to be disobedient to sb.**, desobedecer a algn.

disobey [dɪsə'beɪ] **1** *t* desobedecer. – **2** *i* desobedecer.

disobliging [dɪsə'blaɪdʒɪŋ] *adj* fml (*unhelpful*) poco complaciente, desatento,-a, poco servicial.

disorder [dɪs'ɔːdə^r] **1** *n* (*untidiness*) desorden *m*. **2** (*confusion*) desorden *m*, confusión *f*, caos *m*. **3** (*disturbance of public order*) alteración *f*; (*riot*) disturbios *mpl*, desórdenes *mpl*: *civil disorder*, desórdenes públicos. **4** MED (*illness*) indisposición *f*, afección *f*, problema *m*; (*of mind*) trastorno.
● **to retreat in great disorder**, retirarse a la desbandada.

disordered [dɪs'ɔːdəd] **1** *adj* (*untidy*) desordenado,-a, desarreglado,-a. **2** (*disorganized*) desordenado,-a, caótico,-a. **3** (*ill*) indispuesto,-a; (*mind*) trastornado,-a, enfermo,-a, enfermizo,-a.

disorderly [dɪs'ɔːdəlɪ] **1** *adj* (*untidy*) desordenado,-a. **2** (*unruly - crowd*) alborotado,-a, escandaloso,-a; (*- person*) revoltoso,-a.
● **to be drunk and disorderly**, estar en estado de embriaguez y alterando el orden público.
■ **disorderly house**, (*brothel*) casa de lenocinio, prostíbulo; (*gaming house*) casa de juegos.

disorganization [dɪsɔːgənaɪ'zeɪʃən] *n* desorganización *f*.

disorganize [dɪs'ɔːgənaɪz] *t* desorganizar.

disorganized [dɪs'ɔːgənaɪzd] *t* desorganizado,-a.

disorient [dɪs'ɔːrɪent] *t* desorientar.

disorientate [dɪs'ɔːrɪənteɪt] *t* desorientar.
● **to get disorientated**, desorientarse.

disown [dɪs'əʊn] *t* (*child, person, country*) renegar de, repudiar; (*signature, comment, opinion*) no reconocer como 2propio,-a.

disparage [dɪ'spærɪdʒ] t menospreciar, despreciar.

disparaging [dɪ'spærɪdʒɪŋ] adj despectivo,-a, despreciativo,-a, desdeñoso,-a.

disparagingly [dɪs'pærədʒɪŋlɪ] adv en tono despectivo, despectivamente, en tono despreciativo, en tono desdeñoso.

disparate ['dɪspərɪt] adj fml dispar, distinto,-a, diferente.

disparity [dɪ'spærɪtɪ] n fml (inequality) disparidad f; (difference) discrepancia.
▲ pl disparities.

dispassionate [dɪs'pæʃənət] adj (account, analysis) desapasionado,-a, objetivo,-a; (observer) imparcial.

dispatch [dɪ'spætʃ] 1 n (message) mensaje m; (official message) despacho. 2 MIL parte m. 3 (journalist's report) noticia, reportaje m. 4 (sending) despacho, envío, expedición f. 5 fml (speed) prontitud f, rapidez f. – 6 t (send) enviar, despachar, expedir. 7 (finish quickly - task, duty, job) despachar; (- food) despacharse, zampar. 8 euph (kill) despachar, matar.
■ dispatch box, valija ministerial. ‖ dispatch case, portafolios m. ‖ dispatch note, aviso de envío. ‖ dispatch rider, mensajero,-a.

dispel [dɪ'spel] t disipar.
▲ pt & pp dispelled, ger dispelling.

dispensable [dɪ'spensəbəl] adj prescindible, innecesario,-a.

dispensary [dɪ'spensərɪ] n (in hospital) dispensario; (in school) enfermería.
▲ pl dispensaries.

dispensation [dɪspen'seɪʃən] 1 n fml (act of handing out) administración f. 2 fml (arrangement of events, fate) bendición f. 3 (exemption, permission) exención f, dispensa. 4 REL (exemption, permission) dispensa. 5 POL (system) administración f, régimen m.

dispense [dɪ'spens] 1 t (give out, distribute - supplies, funds) distribuir, repartir; (- money, grants, alms) dar; (- advice, wisdom) ofrecer; (- favours) conceder; (of machine) expender. 2 JUR (justice) administrar. 3 fml (system, public service) suministrar, administrar. 4 (medicines) preparar y despachar.
◆ to dispense with t insep (manage without) prescindir de, pasar sin; (get rid of) desechar, deshacerse de; (make unnecessary) eliminar.

dispenser [dɪ'spensəʳ] 1 n (machine) máquina expendedora. 2 (pharmacist) farmacéutico,-a.
■ soap dispenser, dosificador m de jabón.

dispensing chemist [dɪspensɪŋ'kemɪst] adj GB farmacéutico,-a.

dispersal [dɪ'spɜːsəl] n dispersión f.

disperse [dɪ'spɜːs] 1 t dispersar. – 2 i dispersarse.

dispersed [dɪs'pɜːst] adj disperso,-a.

dispirited [dɪ'spɪrɪtɪd] adj abatido,-a, desanimado,-a.

displace [dɪs'pleɪs] 1 t (gen) desplazar; (bone) dislocar. 2 (replace) sustituir, reemplazar; (official) destituir.
■ displaced person, expatriado,-a, refugiado,-a, desplazado,-a.

displacement [dɪs'pleɪsmənt] 1 n (removal) desplazamiento. 2 (supplanting, replacement) sustitución f, reemplazo. 3 PHYS desplazamiento.

display [dɪ'spleɪ] 1 n (of goods, paintings, etc) exposición f, muestra; (arrangement) arreglo. 2 (of strength, force) exhibición f, despliegue m; (of feelings, skills) demostración f, exteriorización f. 3 COMPUT visualización f. – 4 t (put on show - china, medals) exhibir; (goods, paintings) exponer; (notice, advertisement, permit) colocar. 5 (flaunt) hacer alar-

de de, hacer gala de, hacer despliegue de. 6 (show - feelings, emotions) demostrar, exteriorizar; (- anger, interest, concern) demostrar, manifestar; (skill, tact, courage) - demostrar, dar prueba de; (- qualities, talent) lucir, mostrar. 7 (headlines) hacer resaltar. 8 COMPUT visualizar.
● to be on display, estar expuesto,-a.
■ display cabinet, vitrina. ‖ display window, escaparate m. ‖ firework display, fuegos mpl artificiales.

displease [dɪs'pliːz] t fml disgustar, contrariar.
● to be displeased at sth., molestarle a uno algo. ‖ to be displeased with sb., estar disgustado,-a con algn.

displeasure [dɪs'pleʒəʳ] n disgusto, desagrado.

disport [dɪ'spɔːθ] to disport os., t entretenerse, divertirse.

disposable [dɪ'spəuzəbəl] 1 adj (throwaway) desechable, de usar y tirar. 2 (available - income) disponible.

disposal [dɪ'spəuzəl] 1 n (removal of waste etc) eliminación f. 2 (of possessions) enajenación f; (of property) traspaso. 3 fml (arrangement - gen) disposición f; (of troops) despliegue m. 4 (availability) disponibilidad f.
● at sb.'s disposal, a disposición de algn.: I had a car at my disposal, tenía un coche a mi disposición.
■ waste disposal unit, triturador m de basuras.

dispose [dɪ'spəuz] 1 t (arrange) disponer, colocar. 2 fml (incline) predisponer (to/towards, hacia).
◆ to dispose of 1 t insep (get rid of - rubbish) tirar; (- unwanted object) deshacerse de; (- rival, opponent) deshacerse de, liquidar; (kill) liquidar, despachar; (sell) vender. 2 (deal with - argument, problem, task, question) despachar. 3 fml (have available) disponer de.

disposed [dɪ'spəuzd] 1 adj (willing) dispuesto,-a (to, a): I didn't feel disposed to help them, no me sentía dispuesta a ayudarlos. 2 (prone, liable) propenso,-a (to, a).
● to be favourably/well disposed towards sb./sth., estar bien dispuesto,-a hacia algn./algo. ‖ to be ill disposed towards sb./sth., estar mal dispuesto,-a hacia algn./algo.

disposition [dɪspə'zɪʃən] 1 n fml (nature, temperament) carácter m, genio, naturaleza, manera de ser, temperamento: she is of a cheerful/nervous disposition, es de temperamento alegre/nervioso. 2 fml (inclination, tendency) predisposición f (to, a), intención f (to, de). 3 (arrangement, placing) disposición f.

dispossess [dɪspə'zes] 1 t desposeer, despojar. – 2 the dispossessed, npl los desposeídos mpl.

dispossession [dɪspə'zeʃən] n desposeimiento.

disproportion [dɪsprə'pɔːʃən] n desproporción f, desmesura.

disproportionate [dɪsprə'pɔːʃənət] adj desproporcionado,-a (to, a): there are a disproportionate number of men in the government, hay un número desproporcionado de hombres en el gobierno; we spend a disproportionate amount of money on rent, lo que gastamos en el alquiler es desproporcionado.
● to be disproportionate to sth., ser desproporcionado,-a respecto a algo.

disprove [dɪs'pruːv] t (theory) refutar, rebatir, impugnar; (allegation, claim, charge) desmentir.

disputable [dɪ'spjuːtəbəl] adj discutible.

dispute ['dɪspjuːt] 1 n (disagreement) discusión f; (controversy) controversia, polémica, disputa; (quarrel) disputa, discusión f: there's been a lot of dispute over the name of the coin, ha habido mucha polémica respecto al nombre de la moneda; the land has been the object of a long-running dispute, el terreno ha sido objeto de

una larga disputa; *a border dispute,* un conflicto fronterizo. **2** (*industrial action*) conflicto (laboral): *a pay dispute,* un conflicto salarial. **– 3** *t* (*question - claim, right*) refutar; (*- statement, fact, theory*) discutir, cuestionar; (*- result*) poner en duda; (*will, decision*) impugnar. **4** (*argue about - matter, question, point*) discutir, debatir: *a hotly disputed affair,* un asunto muy controvertido. **5** (*fight for - territory, possession*) disputar(se). **– 6** *i* (*argue*) discutir (**about/over,** de/sobre), (**with,** con).
● beyond/past/without dispute, indiscutiblemente.
‖ to be in/under dispute, estar en litigio: *the territory in dispute,* el territorio en litigio. ‖ to be open to dispute, ser discutible.
▲ (*verbo*) [dɪ'spjuːt].

disqualification [dɪskwɒlɪfɪ'keɪʃən] *n* (*from exam, competition, championship*) descalificación *f;* (*from office, service, driving*) inhabilitación *f.*

disqualify [dɪs'kwɒlɪfaɪ] *t* (*bar - from exam, competition, championship*) descalificar; (*- from office, service, driving*) inhabilitar, incapacitar; (*prevent*) impedir: *he was disqualified from holding public office,* fue inhabilitado para ocupar cargos públicos; *she was disqualified from driving for a year,* le retiraron el carnet por un año.
▲ *pt & pp* disqualified, *ger* disqualifying.

disquiet [dɪs'kwaɪət] **1** *n* inquietud *f,* preocupación *f,* desasosiego, intranquilidad *f.* **– 2** *t fml* inquietar.

disquieting [dɪs'kwaɪətɪŋ] *adj* preocupante, inquietante.

disquisition [dɪskwɪ'zɪʃən] *n fml* disquisición *f* (**on,** sobre/acerca de).

disregard [dɪsrɪ'gɑːd] **1** *n* (*gen*) indiferencia (**for,** hacia); (*for risk, safety*) despreocupación *f:* *with a complete disregard for my feelings,* sin tener en cuenta mis sentimientos; *with a total disregard of the law,* con una indiferencia total hacia la ley. **– 2** *t* (*danger, difficulty*) ignorar, despreciar; (*advice, wishes, warning*) hacer caso omiso de, no presta atención a; (*feelings, behaviour*) no tener en cuenta: *they completely disregarded our objections,* hicieron caso omiso de nuestras objeciones.

disrepair [dɪsrɪ'peəʳ] *n* mal estado.
● to fall into disrepair, deteriorarse.

disreputable [dɪs'repjətəbəl] *adj* (*person, place*) de mala fama; (*firm, company*) de dudosa reputación; (*behaviour, action*) vergonzoso,-a.

disrepute [dɪsrɪ'pjuːt] *n* mala reputación *f,* oprobio, descrédito, desprestigio.
● to bring sth. into disrepute, desacreditar algo. ‖ to fall into disrepute, caer en descrédito.

disrespect [dɪsrɪ'spekt] *n* falta de respeto (**for,** hacia), desacato (**for,** a): *no disrespect (to you),* sin ánimo de ofender; *I didn't mean any disrespect,* no quise ofenderle, no fue mi intención ofenderle.

disrespectful [dɪsrɪ'spektful] *adj* (*person*) irrespetuoso,-a (**to/towards,** para con); (*attitude*) irreverente.

disrobe [dɪs'rəub] *i* desnudarse, desvestirse.

disrupt [dɪs'rʌpt] *t* (*meeting, class*) interrumpir, perturbar el desarrollo de; (*traffic, communications*) crear problemas de, afectar a; (*schedule, plans, order*) desbaratar, trastocar, trastornar: *I will not have you disrupting my class!,* ¡no permitiré que interrumpas mi clase!

disruption [dɪs'rʌpʃən] *n* (*of meeting*) interrupción *f;* (*of traffic*) problemas *mpl;* (*of schedule, plans, order*) trastorno, desbaratamiento: *the mass strikes are causing serious disruption,* las huelgas masivas están provocando serios trastornos.

disruptive [dɪs'rʌptɪv] *adj* (*influence, behaviour*) perjudicial, nocivo,-a; (*child, student, etc*) perturbador,-ra, que

trastorna todo: *your son is a disruptive influence on the other pupils,* su hijo ejerce una influencia nociva sobre los otros alumnos.

dissatisfaction [dɪssætɪs'fækʃən] *n* insatisfacción *f,* descontento.

dissatisfied [dɪs'sætɪsfaɪd] *adj* insatisfecho,-a, descontento,-a.

dissect [dɪ'sekt, daɪ'sekt] **1** *t* (*cut open*) disecar, diseccionar. **2** (*analyse*) examinar minuciosamente, analizar minuciosamente, diseccionar.

dissemble [dɪ'sembəl] **1** *t fml* (*feelings, emotions*) disimular; (*intentions, motives, truth*) ocultar. **– 2** *i fml* fingir.

disseminate [dɪ'semɪneɪt] *t fml* (*information, knowledge, ideas*) divulgar, difundir, diseminar.

dissemination [dɪsemɪ'neɪʃən] *n fml* diseminación *f,* difusión *f.*

dissension [dɪ'senʃən] *n* disensión *f,* desacuerdo.

dissent [dɪ'sent] **1** *n* desacuerdo, disconformidad *f,* disensión *f:* *there is some dissent within the party,* hay disensión dentro del partido. **– 2** *i* disentir, discrepar.

dissenter [dɪ'sentəʳ] *n* disidente *mf.*

dissenting [dɪ'sentɪŋ] *adj* discrepante.

dissertation [dɪsə'teɪʃən] **1** *n* (*formal discourse*) disertación *f.* **2** EDUC (*for lower degree, master's*) tesina; (*for PhD*) tesis *f* (*doctoral*).

disservice [dɪs'sɜːvɪs] *n* perjuicio.
● to do sb./sth. a disservice, (*person*) perjudicar; (*cause*) perjudicar: *you've done a disservice to the cause,* has perjudicado la causa por la que luchamos.

dissident ['dɪsɪdənt] **1** *adj* disidente. **– 2** *n* disidente *mf.*

dissimilar [dɪ'sɪmɪləʳ] *adj* diferente (**to,** de), distinto,-a (**to,** de/a).

dissimilarity [dɪsɪmɪ'lærɪtɪ] *n* diferencia, disimilitud *f.*

dissimulate [dɪ'sɪmjəleɪt] **1** *t fml* (*feelings*) disimular; (*truth, fact*) ocultar, encubrir. **– 2** *i fml* disimular.

dissimulation [dɪsɪmjə'leɪʃən] *n fml* disimulo, disimulación *f.*

dissipate ['dɪsɪpeɪt] **1** *t* (*crowd*) dispersar; (*heat*) difundir. **2** (*dispel - fears, anxiety*) disipar, (hacer) desvanecer. **3** (*squander, waste - fortune, wealth*) derrochar, disipar, dilapidar; (*energies, efforts*) desperdiciar. **– 4** *i* (*mist, fog*) disiparse; (*crowd*) dispersarse; (*enthusiasm, anger, doubts, fears*) disiparse, desvanecerse.

dissipated ['dɪsɪpeɪtɪd] *adj* disoluto,-a, disipado,-a.

dissipation [dɪsɪ'peɪʃən] **1** *n* (*of fear, hope, anxiety*) disipación *f.* **2** (*of fortune*) dilapidación *f,* derroche *m;* (*of energy*) derroche *m.* **3** (*dissipated living, debauchery*) disolución *f,* libertinaje *m.*

dissociate [dɪ'səuʃɪeɪt] *t* (*separate*) disociar (**from,** de), separar (**from,** de).
● to dissociate os. from sb./sth., desvincularse de algn./algo.

dissoluble [dɪ'sɒljəbəl] *adj* disoluble.

dissolute ['dɪsəluːt] *adj* disoluto,-a.

dissolution [dɪsə'luːʃən] *n* (*gen*) disolución *f;* (*of empire*) desintegración *f.*

dissolve [dɪ'zɒlv] **1** *t* (*in liquid*) disolver. **2** (*end - partnership, marriage, parliament, etc*) disolver. **– 3** *i* (*in liquid*) disolverse. **4** (*come to end, break up*) disolverse. **5** (*disappear*) desvanecerse, esfumarse.
● to dissolve into tears/laughter, deshacerse en lágrimas/risas.

dissuade [dɪ'sweɪd] *t* disuadir (**from,** de): *we couldn't dissuade him from buying the car,* no pudimos disuadirlo de que se comprara el coche.

dissuasion [dɪ'sweɪʒən] *n* disuasión *f.*

dissuasive [dɪ'sweɪsɪv] *adj* disuasorio,-a, disuasivo,-a.

distance ['dɪstəns] **1** *n* (*gen*) distancia: *what's the distance between London and Bristol?*, ¿qué distancia hay entre Londres y Bristol?; *it's no distance to the station,* la estación queda muy cerquita, la estación está a dos pasos; *she lives within walking distance of the school,* puede ir andando desde casa a la escuela. **2** *fig* (*coldness, aloofness*) distancia, distanciamiento. – **3** *t* distanciar.
● **at/from a distance,** de lejos. ‖ **in the distance,** a lo lejos, en la distancia. ‖ **to distance os. from sb./sth.,** (*emotionally*) distanciarse de algn./algo; (*dissociate os.*) desvincularse de algn./algo. ‖ **to go the distance,** (*race*) acabar la carrera; (*boxing match*) llegar al último round; (*course, project, etc*) acabar la prueba, aguantar hasta el final. ‖ **to keep one's distance,** mantenerse alejado,-a, guardar las distancias. ‖ **to keep sb. at a distance,** guardar las distancias con algn., tratar a algn. con frialdad.
■ **distance learning,** enseñanza a distancia.

distant ['dɪstənt] **1** *adj* (*place*) lejano,-a, distante, remoto,-a, apartado,-a; (*time, past*) lejano,-a, remoto,-a; (*look*) distraído,-a, ausente; (*cousin, relative*) lejano,-a: *a distant journey,* un viaje muy largo; *he could hear the distant sound of the sea,* oía el mar a los lejos. **2** (*cold, aloof*) distante, frío,-a.

distantly ['dɪstəntlɪ] **1** *adv* (*see, hear*) a lo lejos, de lejos. **2** (*coldly*) con frialdad; (*absent-mindedly*) distraídamente; (*remember*) vagamente. **3** (*connected*) vagamente: *we are distantly related,* somos parientes lejanos.

distaste [dɪs'teɪst] *n* aversión *f*, desagrado.

distasteful [dɪs'teɪstʊl] *adj* (*idea, task*) desagradable; (*joke, remark*) de mal gusto.

distemper[1] [dɪs'tempəʳ] **1** *n* ART (*paint*) temple *m*; (*method*) pintura al temple. – **2** *t* pintar al temple.

distemper[2] [dɪs'tempəʳ] *n* (*disease*) moquillo.

distend [dɪ'stend] **1** *t* dilatar, hinchar. – **2** *i* dilatarse, hincharse.

distil [dɪs'tɪl] **1** *t* (*liquid, spirits*) destilar. **2** (*draw, derive - information, ideas, advice*) extraer; (*reduce*) sintetizar.
■ **distilled water,** agua destilada.
▲ *pt* & *pp* *distilled, ger distilling.*

distill [dɪs'tɪl] *t* US → **distil**.

distillation [dɪstɪ'leɪʃən] **1** *n* (*process*) destilación *f*. **2** (*substance*) destilado. **3** (*reduction, essence*) síntesis *f*.

distiller [dɪs'tɪləʳ] *n* destilador,-ra.

distillery [dɪs'stɪlərɪ] *n* destilería.
▲ *pl* *distilleries.*

distinct [dɪ'stɪŋkt] **1** *adj* (*different, separate*) distinto,-a (**from,** a), diferente (**from,** de): *there are two distinct trends,* hay dos tendencias distintas; *this problem is quite distinct from the other one,* este problema es totalmente distinto al otro. **2** (*noticeable - likeness, change*) marcado,-a; (- *smell*) inconfundible, fuerte; (*idea, sign, intention, thought*) claro,-a, evidente; (*tendency*) bien determinado,-a; (*improvement*) decidido,-a, marcado,-a: *there's a distinct smell of gas,* hay un fuerte olor a gas; *I had the distinct impression that she didn't like me,* tenía el convencimiento de que no le caía bien. **3** (*possibility, advantage*) innegable: *there's a distinct possibility of a strike,* es muy probable que haya huelga.
● **as distinct from,** a diferencia de.

distinction [dɪ'stɪŋkʃən] **1** *n* (*difference, contrast*) diferencia, distinción *f*: *there's a clear distinction between the dialects,* hay una diferencia muy clara entre los dialectos. **2** (*worth, excellence*) distinción *f*; (*honour*) honor *m*: *a poet of distinction,* un poeta distinguido. **3** GB EDUC ≈ matrícula de honor.
● **to draw/make a distinction between sth.,** distinguir entre algo.

distinctive [dɪ'stɪŋktɪv] *adj* (*smell, taste, marking, etc*) distintivo,-a, característico,-a; (*laugh, walk, gesture*) personal, inconfundible; (*dress, decor*) particular.

distinctly [dɪ'stɪŋktlɪ] *adv* (*clearly - speak*) con claridad; (- *remember, hear*) perfectamente, claramente; (*decidedly*) decididamente: *I distinctly remember putting it here,* recuerdo perfectamente que lo puse aquí; *she looked distinctly nervous,* se veía claramente que estaba nerviosa.

distinguish [dɪ'stɪŋgwɪʃ] **1** *t* (*differentiate*) distinguir (**from,** de), diferenciar (**from,** de): *can children distinguish right from wrong?,* ¿los niños saben distinguir el bien del mal? **2** (*manage to see, make out*) distinguir. – **3** *i* distinguir (**between,** entre).
● **to distinguish os.,** distinguirse, destacarse.

distinguishable [dɪ'stɪŋgwɪʃəbəl] *adj* distinguible.
● **to be distinguishable (from sb./sth.),** distinguirse (de algn./algo).

distinguished [dɪ'stɪŋgwɪʃt] *adj* (*appearance*) distinguido,-a; (*career, position, person*) distinguido,-a, eminente.

distinguishing [dɪ'stɪŋgwɪʃɪŋ] *adj* distintivo,-a, característico,-a.

distort [dɪ'stɔːt] **1** *t* (*deform - shape, object*) deformar; (*face*) distorsionar; (*image*) distorsionar, deformar; (*sound*) distorsionar. **2** (*misrepresent - words, statement*) distorsionar, tergiversar; (*truth*) desfigurar, distorsionar.

distortion [dɪ'stɔːʃən] **1** *n* (*of shape, object*) deformación *f*; (*of features*) distorsión *f*, alteración *f*; (*of image*) distorsión *f*, deformación *f*; (*of sound*) distorsión *f*. **2** (*of case, motive, truth*) deformación *f*, distorsión *f*; (*of words, facts, news*) distorsión *f*, tergiversación *f*.

distract [dɪ'strækt] *t* (*person*) distraer (**from,** de).
● **to distract sb.'s attention,** distraer a algn., distraer la atención de algn. ‖ **to distract sb. from sth.,** distraer a algn. de algo.

distracted [dɪ'stræktɪd] *adj* (*not concentrating*) distraído,-a; (*nervous, anxious, confused*) trastornado,-a (**with,** por).

distracting [dɪ'stræktɪŋ] *adj* (*noise*) molesto,-a; (*presence*) que distrae.

distraction [dɪ'strækʃən] **1** *n* (*interruption*) distracción *f*, interrupción *f*. **2** (*amusement, entertainment*) distracción *f*, entretenimiento, diversión *f*. **3** (*mental distress*) desconsuelo, aflicción *f*.
● **to bore sb. to distraction,** aburrir a algn. como una ostra. ‖ **to drive sb. to distraction,** sacar a algn. de quicio. ‖ **to love sb. to distraction,** estar loco,-a por algn., estar perdidamente enamorado,-a de algn.

distraught [dɪ'strɔːt] *adj* afligido,-a, consternado,-a, angustiado,-a: *we were distraught with worry,* estábamos consternados por la preocupación.

distress [dɪ'stres] **1** *n* (*mental*) aflicción *f*, angustia; (*physical*) dolor *m*; (*exhaustion*) agotamiento. **2** (*poverty*) penuria, miseria. **3** (*danger*) peligro. – **4** *t* (*upset*) afligir, dar pena a; (*grieve*) consternar.
● **to distress os.,** afligirse.
■ **distress call / distress signal,** señal *f* de socorro.

distressed [dɪ'strest] *adj* afligido,-a, consternado,-a: *I was most distressed to hear of your loss,* la noticia de tu pérdida me afligió mucho.
■ **distressed area,** zona deprimida, zona empobrecida.

distressing [dɪ'stresɪŋ] *adj* penoso,-a, angustioso,-a.

distribute [dɪˈstrɪbjuːt] **1** *t* (*hand out*) distribuir, repartir; (*share out*) repartir. **2** COMM (*supply for sale*) distribuir. **3** (*spread out*) distribuir.
distribution [dɪstrɪˈbjuːʃən] **1** *n* (*gen*) distribución *f*, reparto; (*of dividends*) reparto. **2** COMM distribución *f*. **3** (*spread*) distribución *f*.
■ **distribution network / distribution system,** red *f* de distribución / sistema *m* de distribución.
distributor [dɪˈstrɪbjətər] **1** *n* COMM distribuidor,-ra; CINEM distribuidora. **2** AUTO delco.
district [ˈdɪstrɪkt] *n* (*of town, city*) distrito, barrio; (*of country*) región *f*, zona.
■ **district attorney,** US JUR fiscal *mf* (del distrito). ‖ **district council,** municipio. ‖ **district nurse,** *enfermero,-a que realiza visitas a domicilio en una zona*. ‖ **Federal District,** distrito federal. ‖ **postal district,** distrito postal.
distrust [dɪsˈtrʌst] **1** *n* desconfianza, recelo: *her deep distrust of politicians,* su desconfianza en los políticos. **– 2** *t* desconfiar de, no fiarse de.
distrustful [dɪsˈtrʌstful] *adj* desconfiado,-a, receloso,-a.
● **to be distrustful of sb.,** desconfiar de algn., recelar de algn.
disturb [dɪsˈtɜːb] **1** *t* (*interrupt - concentration*) interrumpir, distraer, hacer perder; (*sleep*) despertar; (*silence*) romper; (*calm*) perturbar: *if he's asleep, don't disturb him,* si está durmiendo, no lo despiertes. **2** (*inconvenience*) molestar, estorbar; (*burst in on*) sorprender: *I'm sorry to disturb you,* siento molestarte. **3** (*disarrange - papers etc*) desordenar, tocar; (*- lake, grass*) agitar, mover. **4** (*worry, trouble*) perturbar, inquietar, preocupar.
● **"do not disturb",** "se ruega no molestar". ‖ **to disturb the peace,** alterar el orden público.
disturbance [dɪsˈtɜːbəns] **1** *n* (*noisy disruption*) alboroto, tumulto; (*nuisance*) molestia; (*noise*) ruido; (*interruption*) interrupción *f*. **2** (*riot, unrest*) disturbio. **3** (*of routine*) alteración *f*. **4** (*mental illness*) trastorno.
disturbed [dɪsˈtɜːbd] **1** *adj* (*person, mind*) trastornado,-a, con trastornos emocionales: *mentally disturbed,* con trastornos mentales. **2** (*worried, anxious*) perturbado,-a, preocupado,-a.
disturbing [dɪsˈtɜːbɪŋ] *adj* (*worrying*) inquietante, perturbador,-ra; (*alarming*) alarmante: *she found the film very disturbing,* encontró la película muy inquietante.
disunite [dɪsjuːˈnaɪt] *t* desunir.
disunity [dɪsˈjuːnɪtɪ] *n* desunión *f*.
disuse [dɪsˈjuːs] *n* desuso.
● **to fall into disuse,** (*words, customs, laws*) caer en desuso.
disused [dɪsˈjuːzd] *adj* (*factory, warehouse, mine*) abandonado,-a; (*machinery, railway line*) en desuso.
ditch [dɪtʃ] **1** *n* (*gen*) zanja, foso, cuneta; (*at roadside*) cuneta; (*for irrigation*) acequia. **– 2** *t fam* (*get rid of - object*) deshacerse de, tirar; (*boyfriend, girlfriend*) plantar, abandonar. **3** *fam* (*plan*) abandonar, desechar. **– 4** *i* AV hacer un amerizaje forzoso.
● **to ditch a plane,** hacer un amerizaje forzoso. ‖ **to the last ditch,** hasta el final.
dither [ˈdɪðər] *i* vacilar, titubear: *stop dithering!,* ¡decídete ya!
● **to be all of a dither,** estar neura, estar nervioso,-a. ‖ **to have the dithers,** vacilar, titubear.
ditto [ˈdɪtəʊ] **1** *n* (*in list*) ídem *m*. **– 2** *adv fam* lo mismo, ídem.
■ **ditto marks,** comillas *fpl*.
ditty [ˈdɪtɪ] *n* cantinela, cancioncilla.
▲ *pl* **ditties**.

diuretic [daɪjəˈretɪk] **1** *adj* diurético,-a. **– 2** *n* diurético: *coffee acts as a diuretic,* el café tiene efectos diuréticos.
diurnal [daɪˈɜːnəl] *adj* diurno,-a.
divan [dɪˈvæn] **1** *n* (*couch*) diván *m*, canapé *m*. **2 divan (bed),** cama turca.
dive [daɪv] **1** *n* (*into water*) zambullida, salto (de cabeza); (*in competition*) salto de trampolín; (*underwater*) buceo; (*of submarine, whale*) inmersión *f*. **2** (*of plane*) picado; (*of bird*) descenso (en picado). **3** (*sudden movement, lunge*) embestida, arremetida. **4** SP (*of goalkeeper*) estirada. **5** *fam* (*seedy bar, club*) antro. **– 6** *i* (*into water*) zambullirse, tirarse (de cabeza); (*in competition*) saltar; (*underwater*) bucear; (*submarine, whale*) sumergirse. **7** (*birds, planes*) bajar en picado. **8** (*move suddenly*) precipitarse hacia, abalanzarse hacia; (*put hand into*) meter la mano en, echar mano a: *he dived under the bed,* se precipitó debajo de la cama; *she dived for the phone,* se abalanzó hacia el teléfono. **9** SP (*goalkeeper*) lanzarse; (*player looking for penalty*) tirarse. **10** (*drop suddenly - currency, sales, prices*) caer en picado.
◆ **to dive in 1** *i* (*into water*) zambullirse, tirarse de cabeza, tirarse al agua. **2** *fam* (*eat*) atacar: *dive in!,* ¡al ataque! **3** (*involve oneself completely*) meterse de lleno en la tarea.
● **to go diving,** ir a hacer submarinismo, ir a bucear. ‖ **to take a dive,** (*in boxing*) hacer tongo, dejarse ganar.
▲ US *pt* **dove**.
diver [ˈdaɪvər] **1** *n* (*person*) buceador,-ra; (*professional*) buzo, submarinista *mf*; (*in competition*) saltador,-ra. **2** ORN colimbo.
diverge [daɪˈvɜːdʒ] **1** *i* (*lines*) divergir; (*roads*) bifurcarse. **2** (*opinion, views*) divergir.
● **to diverge from sth.,** discrepar de algo.
divergence [daɪˈvɜːdʒəns] *n* divergencia.
divergent [daɪˈvɜːdʒənt] *adj* divergente.
diverse [daɪˈvɜːs] *adj* (*varied*) diverso,-a, variado,-a; (*unlike, different*) distinto,-a, diferente.
diversification [daɪvɜːsɪfɪˈkeɪʃən] **1** *n* (*variety*) variedad *f*. **2** COMM diversificación *f*.
diversify [daɪˈvɜːsɪfaɪ] **1** *t* diversificar. **– 2** *i* diversificarse.
▲ *pt & pp* **diversified,** *ger* **diversifying**.
diversion [daɪˈvɜːʃən] **1** *n* (*of water*) desviación *f*; (*of flights, railway line*) desvío. **2** GB (*detour*) desvío. **3** (*distraction*) distracción *f*. **4** (*entertainment*) diversión *f*, entretenimiento.
diversity [daɪˈvɜːsɪtɪ] *n* diversidad *f*.
divert [daɪˈvɜːt] **1** *t* (*redirect*) desviar. **2** (*distract - attention*) distraer. **3** (*amuse*) divertir, entretener.
divest [daɪˈvest] *t* (*take away*) despojar (**of,** de), privar (**of,** de): *they divested him of all his powers,* lo despojaron de todos sus poderes.
● **to divest os. of sth.,** despojarse de algo, quitarse algo.
divide [dɪˈvaɪd] **1** *t* (*split*) dividir (**into,** en), (**up,** -); (*separate*) separar (**from,** de): *divide it in half,* divídelo en dos; *a fence divides our garden from next door's,* una cerca separa nuestro jardín del de los vecinos. **2** (*share*) repartir (**among/between,** entre), dividir: *they divided the sweets among all the children,* repartieron los caramelos entre todos los niños; *I divide my time between home and the hospital,* me reparto el tiempo entre casa y el hospital. **3** (*cause to disagree*) dividir: *the issue of abortion divided the coalition,* el tema del aborto dividió la coalición. **4** MATH dividir: *divide 20 by 4,* dividir 20 entre 4, dividir 20 por 4; *35 divided by 5 is 7,* 35 dividido

entre 5 son 7, 35 dividido por 5 son 7. **– 5** *i (fork - road, stream)* dividirse, bifurcarse; *(split - particles, group, people)* dividirse (**up**, -): *I want you to divide up into small groups,* quiero que os dividáis en pequeños grupos. **6** GB POL *(vote)* proceder a la votación. **7** MATH dividir. **– 8** *n fml (difference, split)* división *f*, diferencia. **9** US GEOG *(watershed)* (línea) divisoria de (las) aguas.
● **divide and rule,** divide y vencerás. ‖ **to cross the great divide,** emprender el último viaje.
divided [dɪˈvaɪdɪd] *adj (opinion)* dividido,-a.
■ **divided highway,** US autovía.
dividend [ˈdɪvɪdend] **1** *n* COMM FIN dividendo. **2** MATH dividendo.
● **to pay dividends,** dar dividendos, reportar beneficios.
divider [dɪˈvaɪdəʳ] *n (in file)* separador *m*; *(in room)* mampara.
dividers [dɪˈvaɪdəz] *npl* compás *m* de punta (fija).
dividing line [dɪˈvaɪdɪŋ laɪn] *n* línea divisoria.
divination [dɪvɪˈneɪʃən] *n* adivinación *f*.
divine[1] [dɪˈvaɪn] **1** *adj* REL divino,-a: *divine retribution,* castigo divino. **2** *dated (wonderful)* divino,-a, precioso,-a: *you look divine!,* ¡estás divina!
■ **divine service** / **divine worship,** oficio religioso.
divine[2] [dɪˈvaɪn] **1** *t fml (guess - truth)* adivinar; *(- future)* adivinar. **2** *(dowse)* descubrir *con una varilla de zahorí*. **– 3** *i* buscar agua con una varilla de zahorí.
divinely [dɪˈvaɪnlɪ] **1** *adv* REL por Dios. **2** *fam* divinamente.
diviner [dɪˈvaɪnəʳ] *n* zahorí *m*.
diving [ˈdaɪvɪŋ] **1** *n (underwater)* buceo, submarinismo. **2** *(n competition)* saltos *mpl* (de trampolín).
■ **diving bell,** campana de inmersión, campana de buzo. ‖ **diving board,** trampolín *m*. ‖ **diving suit,** escafandra, traje *m* de buzo.
divining-rod [dɪˈvaɪnɪŋrɒd] *n* varilla de zahorí.
divinity [dɪˈvɪnɪtɪ] **1** *n (quality, state)* divinidad *f*. **2** *(subject)* teología.
▲ *pl divinities.*
divisible [dɪˈvɪzəbəl] *adj* divisible.
division [dɪˈvɪʒən] **1** *n (separation)* división *f*; *(sharing)* reparto: *the division of Bosnia,* la división de Bosnia; *the division of the chores,* el reparto de las tareas. **2** *(section, part, group)* sección *f*: *she works in the export division,* trabaja en la sección de exportación. **3** MIL división *f*. **4** SP *(in football)* división *f*. **5** *(dividing line, boundary)* división *f*: *class divisions,* divisiones de clase. **6** *(difference, split)* división *f*; *(disagreement)* desacuerdo, diferencia: *the divisions in society,* las divisiones en la sociedad; *there are divisions in the party,* hay diferencias en el seno del partido. **7** MATH división *f*. **8** GB POL votación *f*.
■ **the division of labour,** la distribución *f* del trabajo. ‖ **division sign,** signo de división, signo de dividir.
divisional [dɪˈvɪʒənəl] *adj* MIL de división.
divisive [dɪˈvaɪsɪv] *adj* divisivo,-a.
divisor [dɪˈvaɪzəʳ] *n* divisor *m*.
divorce [dɪˈvɔːs] **1** *n* JUR divorcio. **2** *(separation)* divorcio. **– 3** *t* JUR divorciarse de: *he divorced her,* se divorció de ella. **4** *(separate)* divorciar (**from**, de). **– 5** *i* divorciarse.
divorcé [dɪˈvɔːseɪ] *n* divorciado.
divorced [dɪˈvɔːst] *adj* divorciado,-a.
● **to get divorced,** divorciarse.
divorcée [dɪvɔːˈsiː] *n* divorciada.
divulge [daɪˈvʌldʒ] *t* divulgar, revelar.
DIY [ˈdiːˈaɪˈwaɪ] *abbr* GB *(do-it-yourself)* bricolaje *m*.
dizziness [ˈdɪzɪnəs] *n (giddiness)* mareo; *(of heights)* vértigo.

dizzy [ˈdɪzɪ] **1** *adj (person)* mareado,-a. **2** *(speed, pace)* vertiginoso,-a; *(height)* de vértigo.
● **to feel dizzy,** *(giddy)* estar mareado,-a; *(because of heights)* sentir vértigo. ‖ **to have a dizzy spell,** darle a uno,-a un mareo, darle a uno,-a un vahído. ‖ **to get dizzy,** marearse.
▲ *comp dizzier, superl dizziest.*
DJ[1] [ˈdiːˈdʒeɪ] *abbr* GB FAM *(dinner jacket)* esmoquin *m*, smoking *m*.
DJ[2] [ˈdiːˈdʒeɪ] **2** *abbr (disc jockey)* pinchadiscos *m*, discjockey *m*.
Djakarta [dʒəˈkɑːtə] *n* Yakarta.
Djibouti [dʒɪˈbuːtɪ] *n* Djibuti.
D Litt [ˈdiːˈlɪt] *abbr (Doctor of Letters)* doctor,-ra en literatura.
DNA [ˈdiːˈenˈeɪ] *abbr (deoxyribonucleic acid)* ácido desoxirribonucleico; *(abbreviation)* ADN *m*.
do [duː] **1** *aux (used in questions) no se traduce: do you smoke?,* ¿fumas?; *do you know Susan?,* ¿conoces a Susan?; *what do they want?,* ¿qué quieren?; *where does Neil live?,* ¿dónde vive Neil?; *what film did you see?,* ¿qué película viste?; *when did they leave?,* ¿cuándo se fueron? **2** *(used in negatives) no se traduce: I don't want to go,* no quiero ir; *I don't play tennis,* no juego al tenis; *they don't like meat,* no les gusta la carne; *she doesn't live in London,* no vive en Londres; *he didn't watch the match,* no vio el partido; *we didn't go out yesterday,* no salimos ayer. **3** *(emphatic): do come with us!,* ¡ánimo, vente con nosotros!; *I do like your dress,* me encanta tu vestido; *I did post it, I swear!,* ¡sí que lo mandé, te lo juro! **4** *(substituting main verb): do you like basketball? - yes, I do,* ¿te gusta el baloncesto? - sí, me gusta; *did you see the film? - no, I didn't,* ¿viste la película? - no, no la vi; *he plays chess and so do I,* él juega al ajedrez y yo también; *I don't feel well - neither do I,* no me encuentro bien - yo tampoco; *she likes jazz and so does he,* a ella le gusta el jazz y a él también; *they went to the concert and so did we,* ellos fueron al concierto y nosotros también; *who wears glasses? - Brian does,* ¿quién lleva gafas? - Brian; *who broke the vase? - I did,* ¿quién rompió el florero? - yo. **5** *(in question tags): you don't smoke, do you?,* no fumas, ¿verdad?; *you like fish, don't you?,* a ti te gusta el pescado, ¿verdad?; *she lives in Madrid, doesn't she?,* vive en Madrid, ¿verdad?; *you went to their wedding, didn't you?,* tú fuiste a su boda, ¿verdad?; *they didn't believe you, did they?,* no te creyeron, ¿verdad? **– 6** *t (gen)* hacer: *what are you doing here?,* ¿qué haces aquí?; *what are you doing this weekend?,* ¿qué vas a hacer este fin de semana?; *we'll have to do something about that door,* tendremos que hacer algo con esa puerta; *do the right thing,* haz lo que debas; *there's nothing to do in this town,* no hay nada que hacer en este pueblo; *you do nothing but complain,* no haces más que quejarte; *whatever you do, don't drink alcohol,* hagas lo que hagas, no bebas alcohol; *what can I do about it?,* ¿qué quieres que haga yo? **7** *(as job)* hacer, dedicarse: *what do you do (for a living)?,* ¿a qué te dedicas?; *what does he want to do when he leaves university?,* ¿a qué quiere dedicarse cuando deje la universidad? **8** *(carry out - job, task)* hacer, realizar, llevar a cabo; *(- duty)* cumplir con: *I've got to do the cooking/cleaning,* tengo que cocinar/limpiar; *have you done your homework?,* ¿has hecho los deberes?; *we do the shopping on Saturdays,* hacemos la compra los sábados. **9** *(study)* estudiar: *do you do biology at school?,* ¿estudias biología en el instituto?; *we're doing Shakespeare this year,* estamos estudiando a Shakespeare

este curso; *she's doing French at university,* estudia filología francesa en la Universidad; *he did Politics at Oxford,* estudió Ciencias Políticas en Oxford. **10** (*solve - puzzle*) solucionar; (*- crossword, sum*) hacer. **11** (*produce, make - meal*) preparar, hacer; (*drawing, painting, translation, etc*) hacer; (*offer - service*) servir, tener, hacer; (*- discount*) hacer: *does this pub do food?,* ¿sirven comidas en este pub? **12** (*attend to*) atender, servir: *what can I do for you?,* ¿en qué le puedo servir? **13** (*put on, produce - play, opera, etc*) presentar, dar, poner en escena; (*play the part of*) hacer el papel de. **14** (*finish, complete*) terminar: *have you done moaning?,* ¿has terminado de protestar? **15** (*achieve*) lograr, conseguir: *he's done it!,* ¡lo ha conseguido! **16** (*travel over - distance*) recorrer, hacer; (*complete - journey*) hacer, ir; (*travel at - speed*) ir a: *that car was doing at least 150kph,* aquel coche iba como mínimo a 150 kilómetros por hora; *we did London to Nottingham in two and a half hours,* fuimos de Londres a Nottingham en dos horas y media. **17** (*be sufficient for*) ser suficiente; (*be satisfactory for, acceptable to*) ir bien a: *will 6 glasses do you?,* ¿será suficiente con seis vasos?; *yes, that will do me nicely,* sí, eso me irá perfectamente. **18** *fam* (*cheat, swindle*) estafar, timar; (*rob*) robar; (*arrest, convict*) coger; (*fine*) encajar una multa; (*serve time in prison*) cumplir: *you've been done!,* ¡te han timado! – **19** *i* (*act, behave*) hacer: *you'll do as you're told,* harás lo que te digan; *do as I do,* haz lo que yo hago; *do as you would be done by,* trata a los demás como tú quisieras ser tratado. **20** (*progress*) ir: *how are you doing?,* ¿qué tal vas?, ¿cómo te van las cosas?; *she did badly in the exams,* le fueron mal los exámenes; *both mother and baby are doing well,* madre e hija se encuentran bien; *how are we doing for time?,* ¿cómo andamos de tiempo?; *he's done really well for himself,* ha prosperado mucho; *we did quite well out of that,* hemos salido bastante bien parados de eso. **21** (*complete, finish*) terminar: *have you done with the hairdryer?,* ¿has terminado con el secador? **22** (*be sufficient*) bastar, ser suficiente, alcanzar: *will one slice do for you?,* ¿tendrás suficiente con una rebanada?; *that'll do!,* ¡basta! **23** (*be satisfactory, suitable*) servir, estar bien: *well, I suppose it'll have to do,* bueno, supongo que tendrá que servir; *it doesn't do to be late,* no hay que llegar tarde; *it (just/simply) won't do,* no puede ser; *this cushion will do as/for a pillow,* este cojín servirá de almohada. – **24** *n fam* (*party*) fiesta, guateque *m*.

◆ **to do away with 1** *t insep* (*abolish - tax*) abolir, suprimir; (*- need*) eliminar, acabar con. **2** *fam* (*kill*) eliminar, matar. ‖ **to do down** *t sep* hablar mal de, ser crítico,-a con. ‖ **to do for 1** *t insep* (*manage*) arreglárselas para conseguir: *what do you do for money?,* ¿de dónde sacas el dinero? **2** *fam* (*ruin, destroy*) acabar con, destrozar; (*kill*) matar: *if I don't finish this today, I'm done for,* si no acabo esto hoy, estoy perdido. **3** GB (*do cleaning for*) venir a limpiar. ‖ **to do in** *t sep fam* (*kill*) matar, cargarse, liquidar; (*tire*) agotar, reventar; (*injure*) hacerse daño en; (*ruin*) estropear, cargarse: *I'm done in,* estoy hecho,-a polvo. ‖ **to do out** *t sep* GB (*clean*) hacer una limpieza a fondo de; (*decorate*) decorar. ‖ **to do out of** *t sep fam* quitar, birlar. ‖ **to do over** *t sep fam* dar una paliza a. ‖ **to do up 1** *t sep fam* (*fasten, belt*) abrochar(se); (*zip*) subir; (*laces*) atar. **2** (*wrap*) envolver. **3** (*dress up*) arreglar; (*decorate*) renovar, arreglar. ‖ **to do with** *t insep* (*need*) venir bien a: *I could do with a rest,* un descanso me vendría muy bien; *this room could do with a good clean,* no le vendría mal una limpieza a fondo a esta habitación. ‖ **to do without** *t* *t insep* pasar sin, prescindir de, arreglárselas sin: *do you think you could do without cigarettes?,* ¿crees que podrías pasar sin tabaco?; *I could do without this!,* ¡esto no me hacía ninguna falta! – **2** *i* arreglárselas sin.

● **how do you do?,** (*greeting*) ¿cómo está usted?; (*answer*) mucho gusto, encantado,-a. ‖ **that does it!,** ¡esto ya es la gota que colma el vaso!, ¡ya está bien! ‖ **to be/have to do with sb./sth.,** tener que ver con algn./algo: *it has nothing to do with you,* no tiene nada que ver contigo; *his job has something to do with computers,* su trabajo está relacionado con los ordenadores. ‖ **to do business with sb.,** negociar con algn. ‖ **to do drugs,** drogarse, consumir drogas. ‖ **to do one's best,** hacer lo mejor posible. ‖ **to do one's hair,** peinarse. ‖ **to do one's military service,** hacer el servicio militar. ‖ **to do one's nails,** arreglarse las uñas. ‖ **to do sth. again,** volver a hacer algo. ‖ **to do sth. for sb.,** (*help*) hacer algo por algn.; (*flatter, suit*) favorecer a algn., quedarle bien a algn.; (*please*) atraer a algn., decirle algo a algn. ‖ **what's done is done,** a lo hecho, pecho. ‖ **you've done it now,** ahora sí que la has hecho buena.

■ **do's and don'ts,** reglas *fpl* de conducta, normas *fpl*. ▲ (*verbo*) 3rd *pers sing pres* **does,** *pt* **did,** *pp* **done,** *ger* **doing**.

doc [dɒk] *n fam* doctor,-ra.

docile ['dəʊsaɪl] *adj* (*person*) dócil, sumiso,-a; (*animal*) manso,-a.

dock[1] [dɒk] **1** *n* MAR (*gen*) muelle *m*; (*for cargo*) dársena. **2** JUR banquillo (de los acusados). – **3** *t* (*ship*) atracar (*at,* a); (*spaceship*) acoplar. – **4** *i* (*ship*) atracar, fondear; (*spaceship*) acoplarse. – **5 docks,** *npl* puerto.
● **to be in dock,** (*ship*) estar en puerto; (*car*) estar en reparaciones.
■ **dock worker,** trabajador,-ra portuario,-a.

dock[2] [dɒk] **1** *t* (*animal's tail*) cortar. **2** (*wages*) descontar dinero de.

dock[3] [dɒk] *n* BOT acedera.

docker ['dɒkə'] *n* estibador,-ra, cargador,-ra.

docket ['dɒkɪt] **1** *n* GB COMM (*label*) rótulo, etiqueta; (*contents list*) lista de contenido; (*delivery note*) resguardo de entrega. **2** US JUR (*list of cases*) lista de casos. – **3** *t* rotular, etiquetar.
■ **customs docket,** certificado de aduanas.

dockland ['dɒklænd] *n* zona del puerto, zona portuaria.
▲ *Su uso en plural es muy frecuente.*

dockside ['dɒksaɪd] *n* dársena.

dockyard ['dɒkjɑːd] *n* astillero.

doctor ['dɒktə'] **1** *n* MED médico,-a, doctor,-ra: *family doctor,* médico,-a de cabecera; *you should go to the doctor's,* deberías ir al médico. **2** EDUC doctor,-ra (*of,* en). – **3** *pej* (*change - results, evidence*) falsificar, amañar; (*text, document*) arreglar, amañar; (*food, drink*) adulterar. **4** *euph* (*animal*) castrar.
● **to be under the doctor,** ser atendido,-a por un,-a médico,-a.

doctoral ['dɒktərəl] *adj* doctoral.

doctorate ['dɒktərət] *n* doctorado.
● **to get a doctorate,** doctorarse.

doctrinal [dɒk'traɪnəl] *adj* doctrinal.

doctrine ['dɒktrɪn] *n* doctrina.

document ['dɒkjəmənt] **1** *n* (*gen*) documento. **2** JUR escritura. – **3** *t* documentar.

documentary [dɒkjə'mentərɪ] **1** *adj* (*gen*) documental. – **2** *n* documental *m*.
▲ (*sustantivo*) *pl* **documentaries**.

documentation [dɒkjəmen'teɪʃən] *n* documentación *f*.

dodder ['dɒdə'] i *fam* andar tambaleándose, andar con paso inseguro.

doddering ['dɒdərɪŋ] *adj fam* chocho,-a.

doddery ['dɒdərɪ] *adj fam* chocho,-a.

doddle ['dɒdəl] it's a doddle, *n fam* es pan comido, está chupado,-a está tirado,-a.

dodge [dɒdʒ] **1** *n* (*quick movement*) regate *m*. **2** *fam* (*trick*) truco, astucia, treta, artimaña. – **3** *t* (*avoid - blow etc*) esquivar; (*pursuer*) despistar, dar esquinazo a, sacudirse. **4** (*question*) esquivar, soslayar; (*problem, issue*) soslayar, eludir; (*work, duty, responsibility*) eludir, rehuir; (*tax*) evadir. – **5** *i* (*move quickly*) echarse a un lado, apartarse: *he dodged into a betting shop*, se metió en una tienda de apuestas.
● **to be up to all the dodges**, sabérselas todas.
■ **tax dodge**, evasión *f* fiscal.

dodgems ['dɒdʒəmz] *npl* coches *mpl* de choque, autos *mpl* de choque.

dodger ['dɒdʒə'] *n* persona que intenta eludir algo: *tax dodger*, evasor,-ra de impuestos.

dodgy ['dɒdʒɪ] **1** *adj fam* (*risky*) arriesgado,-a, inseguro,-a; (*tricky*) peliagudo,-a, difícil, problemático,-a; (*dangerous*) peligroso,-a; (*bad*) chungo,-a. **2** *fam* (*dishonest - person*) que no es de fiar, poco fiable, de poca confianza, sospechoso,-a; (- *business*) sospechoso,-a, poco fiable.
▲ *comp* **dodgier**, *superl* **dodgiest**.

dodo ['dəudəu] *n* ORN dodo.
● **as dead as a dodo**, muerto,-a y bien muerto,-a, requetemuerto,-a.
▲ *pl* **dodos** o **dodoes**.

doe [dəu] *n* (*of deer*) gama; (*of hare*) liebre *f*; (*of rabbit*) coneja.

DOE ['diː'əu'iː] *abbr* GB (*Department of the Environment*) departamento del medio ambiente.

doer ['duːə'] *n* persona emprendedora, persona dinámica.

does [dʌz] *3rd pers sing pres* → **do**.

doesn't ['dʌzənt] *contr* → **does not**.

doff [dɒf] *t* quitar.
● **to doff one's hat to sb.**, quitarse el sombrero ante algn., descubrirse ante algn.

dog [dɒg] **1** *n* (*gen*) perro,-a: *a guard dog*, un perro guardián; *a pedigree dog*, un perro de raza; *a police dog*, un perro policía. **2** (*male canine*) macho: *dog fox*, zorro; *dog wolf*, lobo. **3** *fam* (*person*) tipo,-a: *dirty dog*, canalla, sinvergüenza. – **4** *t* (*pursue*) perseguir. – **5** **the dogs**, *npl* las carreras *fpl* de galgos.
● **a dog's life**, una vida de perros. ‖ **it's dog eat dog**, hay una competencia despiadada. ‖ **every dog has his/its day**, a todos les llega su momento de gloria. ‖ **let sleeping dogs lie**, peor es meneallo, deja las cosas como están. ‖ **to be dressed up like a dog's dinner**, estar hecho,-a un mamarracho. ‖ **not to have a dog's chance**, no tener ni la más remota posibilidad. ‖ **to go to the dogs**, venirse abajo. ‖ **to put on the dog**, darse pisto.
■ **dog biscuit**, galleta para perros. ‖ **dog collar**, (*dog's*) collar *m* de perro; (*priest's*) alzacuello. ‖ **dog tag**, placa de identificación. ‖ **dog paddle**, estilo perro. ‖ **dog sled / dog sledge**, trineo. ‖ **the dog days**, la canícula. ‖ **the Dog Star**, Sirio.
▲ (*verbo*) *pp & pt* **dogged**, *ger* **dogging**.

dogcart ['dɒgkaːt] *n* carro de dos ruedas tirado por un caballo.

dog-eared ['dɒgɪəd] *adj* (*book*) sobado,-a y con las esquinas dobladas.

dog-end ['dɒgend] *n* colilla.

dogfight ['dɒgfaɪt] **1** *n* (*between dogs*) pelea de perros; (*between people*) refriega, reyerta. **2** AV combate *m* aéreo.

dogfish ['dɒgfɪʃ] *n* (*fish*) cazón *m*, perro marino.

dogged ['dɒgɪd] *adj* (*determined, tenacious*) terco,-a, obstinado,-a.

doggie ['dɒgɪ] *n* → **doggy**.

doggy ['dɒgɪ] *n* perrito,-a.
■ **doggy bag**, bolsita para el perro. ‖ **doggy paddle**, estilo perrito.
▲ *pl* **doggies**.

doghouse ['dɒghaus] *n* perrera, casita del perro.
● **to be in the doghouse**, haber caído en desgracia.

dogma ['dɒgmə] *n* dogma *m*.

dogmatic [dɒg'mætɪk] *adj* dogmático,-a.

do-gooder [duː'gudə'] *n* bienhechor,-ra, persona bien intencionada.

dogsbody ['dɒgzbɒdɪ] *n* GB *fam* burro de carga.
▲ *pl* **dogsbodies**.

dog-tired ['dɒgtaɪəd] *adj* rendido,-a, hecho,-a polvo, muerto,-a de cansancio.

doh [dəu] *n* MUS do.

doily ['dɔɪlɪ] *n* tapete *m* (decorativo).
▲ *pl* **doilies**.

doing ['duːɪŋ] **1** *n* (*action*) obra: *is this your doing?*, ¿lo has hecho tú? **2** (*hard work*) trabajo: *it'll take some doing*, costará trabajo hacerlo, va a dar trabajo. – **3** **doings**, *npl* (*activities*) actividades *fpl*.

do-it-yourself [duːɪtjɔː'self] *n* bricolaje *m*.
■ **do-it-yourself shop**, tienda de bricolaje.

doldrums ['dɒldrəmz] **the doldrums**, *npl* la zona de las calmas ecuatoriales.
● **to be in the doldrums**, (*person*) estar abatido,-a, estar deprimido,-a; (*business, trade*) estar estancado,-a.

dole [dəul] **the dole**, *n* GB *fam* el subsidio de desempleo, el paro.
◆ **to dole out** *t sep* repartir, dar.
● **to be on the dole**, estar en el paro. ‖ **to go on the dole**, apuntarse para cobrar el paro.
■ **dole money**, dinero del paro, subsidio del paro. ‖ **dole queue**, número de parados.

doleful ['dəulful] *adj* triste, compungido,-a, afligido,-a.

doll [dɒl] *n* muñeca.
◆ **to doll up** *t sep fam* poner guapo,-a.
● **to doll os. up**, ponerse guapo,-a, emperifollarse. ‖ **to get dolled up**, ponerse guapo,-a, emperifollarse.
■ **doll's house**, casa de muñecas.

dollar ['dɒlə'] *n* dólar *m*.
● **to feel like a million dollars**, sentirse en el séptimo cielo, sentirse en las nubes. ‖ **to look like a million dollars**, tener un aspecto maravilloso, estar despampanante.
■ **dollar bill**, billete *m* de un dólar. ‖ **the sixty-four thousand dollar question**, la pregunta del millón.

dollop ['dɒləp] *n fam* (*spoonful*) cucharada; (*serving, measure*) ración *f*.

dolly ['dɒlɪ] **1** *n* (*doll*) muñeca, muñequita. **2** CINEM (*moveable support*) dolly *m*, plataforma móvil.
▲ *pl* **dollies**.

dolmen ['dɒlmən] *n* dolmen *m*.

Dolomites ['dɒlə'maɪts] **the Dolomites**, *n* los Dolomitas *mpl*.

dolphin ['dɒlfɪn] *n* delfín *m*.

domain [də'meɪn] **1** *n* (*lands*) dominios *mpl*. **2** (*sphere of knowledge*) campo, esfera; (*area of activity*) ámbito: *that's outside my domain*, eso está fuera de mi campo; *in the public domain*, de(l) dominio público.

dome [dəʊm] *n* ARCH (*roof*) cúpula; (*ceiling*) bóveda.

domestic [də'mestɪk] **1** *adj* (*of the home*) doméstico,-a: *domestic animal,* animal doméstico; *domestic bliss,* felicidad conyugal. **2** (*home-loving*) hogareño,-a, casero,-a. **3** (*news, flight*) nacional; (*trade, policy*) interior; (*affairs, policy, market*) interno,-a. – **4** *n* empleado,-a doméstico,-a.
■ **domestic science,** economía doméstica, hogar *m*. ‖ **domestic service,** servicio doméstico. ‖ **domestic violence,** violencia en el hogar.

domesticate [də'mestɪkeɪt] **1** *t* (*animal*) domesticar. **2** (*person*) volver hogareño,-a a, volver casero,-a a.
● **to become domesticated,** volverse hogareño,-a, volverse casero,-a.

domesticity [dəʊme'stɪsɪtɪ] *n* (*of person*) vida de hogar, vida casera; (*of animal*) domesticidad *f*.

domicile ['dɒmɪsaɪl] *n* JUR domicilio.

dominance ['dɒmɪnəns] **1** *n* (*power, control*) dominio, control *m*: *their dominance of the market,* su control del mercado. **2** (*importance, predominance*) predominio, preponderancia.

dominant ['dɒmɪnənt] **1** *adj* (*more powerful, stronger*) dominante: *brown eyes are dominant,* los ojos marrones son dominantes. **2** (*predominant, most important*) predominante, preponderante, dominante. – **3** *n* BIOL MUS dominante *f*.

dominate ['dɒmɪneɪt] **1** *t* dominar: *he dominates the meetings,* domina las reuniones; *the huge cathedral dominates the city,* la enorme catedral domina la ciudad. – **2** *i* (*have control*) dominar; (*predominate*) predominar.

dominating ['dɒmɪneɪtɪŋ] *adj* dominante.

domination [dɒmɪ'neɪʃən] *n* dominación *f*.

domineer [dɒmɪ'nɪəʳ] *i* avasallar.
● **to dominate over sb.,** ser muy dominante con algn.

domineering [dɒmɪ'nɪərɪŋ] *adj* dominante.

Dominica [dɒmɪ'niːkə] *n* Dominica.

Dominican [də'mɪnɪkən] **1** *adj* dominicano,-a. – **2** *n* dominicano,-a.
■ **Dominican Republic,** República Dominicana.

dominion [də'mɪnjən] *n* dominio.

domino ['dɒmɪnəʊ] **1** *n* ficha de dominó. – **2** dominoes, *npl* (*game*) dominó *m*.
■ **domino effect,** efecto dominó.
▲ *pl* dominoes.

don[1] [dɒn] *n* profesor,-ra universitario,-a.

don[2] [dɒn] **1** *t* (*put on*) ponerse. **2** *fig* asumir.
▲ *pt & pp* donned, *ger* donning.

donate [dəʊ'neɪt] *t* (*blood, organ*) donar; (*money*) donar, hacer un donativo de; (*services*) prestar desinteresadamente.

donation [dəʊ'neɪʃən] **1** *n* (*act*) donación *f*. **2** (*gift*) donativo.

done [dʌn] **1** *pp* → do. – **2** *adj* (*finished*) terminado,-a, acabado,-a, hecho,-a: *are you done in there yet?,* ¿ya has acabado allí dentro?; *it's nearly done,* casi está (acabado); *this has got to be done by tomorrow,* esto tiene que estar terminado para mañana. **3** *fam* (*tired*) agotado,-a. **4** (*cooked - vegetables*) cocido,-a; (- *meat*) hecho,-a: *the turkey's done to a turn,* el pavo está en su punto. **5** (*socially acceptable*) bien visto,-a: *it isn't done to ...,* es de mal gusto ..., no está bien visto ... – **6** *interj fam* ¡trato hecho!, ¡vale!
● **it's over and done with,** se acabó. ‖ **to be the done thing,** ser de rigor, ser lo que se hace. ‖ **to be/have**

done with sth., acabar con algo. ‖ **to have sth. done,** hacerse hacer algo: *have you had you hair done?,* ¿te has arreglado el pelo?

donkey ['dɒŋkɪ] **1** *n* (*animal*) burro,-a, asno. **2** (*stupid person*) burro,-a.
● **donkey's years,** siglos, mucho tiempo: *we've known each other for donkey's years,* nos conocemos desde hace siglos.
■ **donkey jacket,** chaquetón *m* de obrero, chaqueta gruesa de obrero. ‖ **donkey work,** trabajo pesado.

donor ['dəʊnəʳ] *n* donante *m*.

don't [dəʊnt] *aux* (*do + not*) → do.

donut ['dəʊnʌt] *n* → doughnut.

doodle ['duːdəl] **1** *i* garabatear. – **2** *n* garabato.

doom [duːm] **1** *n* (*fate*) destino, sino; (*ruin*) perdición *f*, fatalidad *f*; (*death*) muerte *f*. – **2** *t* (*destine*) destinar; (*condemn*) condenar.
● **doom and gloom,** pesimismo. ‖ **to meet one's doom,** encontrar la muerte.

doomed [duːmd] *adj* condenado,-a.
● **to be doomed to failure,** estar condenado,-a al fracaso.

doomsday ['duːmzdeɪ] *n* día *m* del juicio final.

door [dɔːʳ] **1** *n* (*gen*) puerta: *front/back door,* puerta principal/trasera; *will you answer the door?,* ¿quieres abrir la puerta?; *there's someone at the door,* hay alguien en la puerta. **2** (*entrance*) puerta, entrada.
● **behind closed doors,** a puerta cerrada. ‖ (**from**) **door to door,** de puerta en puerta. ‖ **next door,** al lado: *who lives next door?,* ¿quién vive en la casa de al lado?; *we live next door to a supermarket,* vivimos al lado de un supermercado. ‖ **by the back door,** *fig* de forma ilegal, ilegalmente. ‖ **out of doors,** al aire libre. ‖ **to be on the door,** hacer de portero,-a. ‖ **to lay sth. at sb.'s door,** echar la culpa de algo a algn. ‖ **to show sb. the door,** echar a algn., enseñarle la puerta a algn. ‖ **to show sb. to the door,** acompañar a algn. hasta la puerta. ‖ **to shut/slam the door in sb.'s face,** dar a algn. con la puerta en las narices.
■ **door handle,** manilla de la puerta. ‖ **door key,** llave de la puerta.

doorbell ['dɔːbel] *n* timbre *m*.

doorknob ['dɔːnɒb] *n* pomo.

doorman ['dɔːmən] *n* portero.

doormat ['dɔːmæt] **1** *n* felpudo, esterilla. **2** *fig* (*person*) trapo.
● **to treat sb. like a doormat,** tratar a algn. como un trapo.

doornail ['dɔːneɪl] **as dead as a doornail,** *n* muerto,-a y bien muerto,-a, requetemuerto,-a.

doorstep ['dɔːstep] **1** *n* peldaño, umbral *m*. **2** GB *fam* (*thick slice of bread*) rebanada gruesa de pan.
● **on the/one's doorstep,** al lado de casa, a la vuelta de la esquina.

doorstop ['dɔːstɒp] *n* (*wedge*) cuña; (*on floor, wall*) tope *m* (de la puerta).

door-to-door [dɔːtə'dɔː] *adj* de puerta en puerta, a domicilio.
■ **door-to-door salesman,** vendedor *m* a domicilio.

doorway ['dɔːweɪ] *n* entrada, portal *m*.

dope [dəʊp] **1** *n* sl (*drug - gen*) droga; (*marijuana*) hachís *m*, chocolate *m*. **2** *fam* (*person*) imbécil *mf*, tarugo,-a, pelmazo *mf*. – **3** *t* *fam* (*food, drink*) adulterar con drogas, poner droga en. **4** SP (*athlete, horse*) dopar, drogar.

dopey ['dəʊpɪ] **1** *adj* *sl* (*with drugs, sleep*) grogui, atontado,-a. **2** (*stupid*) estúpido,-a, tonto,-a, lelo,-a, bobo,-a.

▲ *comp dopier, superl* **dopiest.**
dopy [ˈdəʊpɪ] *adj* → **dopey.**
▲ *comp dopier, superl* **dopiest.**
Dordogne [dɔːˈdɔɪn] *n* el Dordoña *m.*
dormant [ˈdɔːmənt] **1** *adj* (*volcano*) inactivo,-a; (*animal, plant*) aletargado,-a. **2** *fig* (*idea, emotion, rivalry*) latente.
dormer [ˈdɔːmə^r] **dormer (window),** *n* buhardilla.
dormitory [ˈdɔːmɪtərɪ] **1** *n* (*in boarding school, hostel*) dormitorio. **2** us residencia de estudiantes, colegio mayor.
■ **dormitory town,** cuidad *f* dormitorio.
▲ *pl* **dormitories.**
dormouse [ˈdɔːmaʊs] *n* lirón *m.*
dorsal [ˈdɔːsəl] *adj* dorsal.
dosage [ˈdəʊsɪdʒ] *n* (*amount*) dosis *f;* (*on medicine bottle*) posología.
● **do not exceed the stated dosage,** no exceder la dosis recomendada.
dose [dəʊs] **1** *n* MED dosis *f.* **2** *fig* (*amount*) cantidad *f: a nasty dose of flu,* una gripe muy fuerte. **– 3** *t* medicar (**up,** -).
● **to dose os. up,** automedicarse.
doss [dɒs] **1** *n fam* (*short sleep*) cabezada. **– 2** *i fam* (*sleep*) dormir. **3** *fam* (*be lazy*) haraganear, holgazanear, gandulear.
◆ **to doss down** *i* GB *fam* echarse a dormir, dormir.
● **to be a doss,** ser pan comido, estar tirado,-a.
dosser [ˈdɒsə^r] **1** *n fam* (*tramp*) vagabundo,-a, indigente *mf.* **2** *fam* (*lazy person*) vago,-a, gandul,-la, manta *m.*
dosshouse [ˈdɒshaʊs] *n* pensión *f* barata, pensión *f* de mala muerte.
dossier [ˈdɒsɪeɪ] *n* expediente *m,* dossier *m.*
● **to keep a dossier on sb.,** llevar un expediente sobre algn.
dot [dɒt] **1** *n* (*spot*) punto. **– 2** *t* (*letter*) poner el punto a. **3** (*scatter*) esparcir, salpicar.
● **on the dot,** en punto. ‖ **since the year dot,** desde el año de la pera, desde el año de María Castaña.
▲ (*verbo*) *pt & pp* **dotted,** *ger* **dotting.**
dotage [ˈdəʊtɪdʒ] *n* chochez *f.*
● **to be in one's dotage,** estar chocho,-a.
dote [dəʊt] **to dote on,** *i* adorar.
dotted [ˈdɒtɪd] *adj* (*line*) de puntos.
● **to be dotted with sth.,** estar salpicado,-a de algo.
dotty [ˈdɒtɪ] *adj* GB *fam* chiflado,-a.
▲ *comp* **dottier,** *superl* **dottiest.**
double [ˈdʌbəl] **1** *adj* (*gen*) doble: *double doors,* puertas dobles; *double whisky,* whisky doble; *double four three five two six (44 35 26),* cuarenta y cuatro treinta y cinco veintiséis. **– 2** *adv* doble: *I thought I was seeing double,* pensaba que veía doble; *she folded the sheet double,* dobló la sábana por la mitad. **– 3** *n* (*amount*) doble *m.* **4** (*person - lookalike*) viva imagen *f,* vivo retrato; (*- substitute*) doble *mf.* **5** SP (*in games*) doble *m.* **– 6** *t* (*increase twofold*) doblar, duplicar: *we need to double our profits,* hay que doblar los beneficios. **7** (*fold in half*) doblar por la mitad. **– 8** *i* (*increase twofold*) doblarse, duplicarse: *sales have doubled,* las ventas se han doblado. **9** (*have dual function - thing*) hacer las veces de, usarse de; (*- person*) doblar (**for,** -): *the sofa doubles as a bed,* el sofá también se usa como cama. **10** (*in bridge*) doblar. **– 11 doubles,** *npl* (*tennis*) partido *m* de dobles.
◆ **to double back** *i* volver sobre sus pasos. ‖ **to double up 1** *t sep* doblar. **– 2** *i* (*with pain, laughter*) doblarse; (*with laughter*) partirse, mondarse. **3** (*share*) compartir la habitación.
● **double or quits,** (el) doble o nada. ‖ **at/on the dou-**

ble, enseguida. ‖ **to be bent double,** estar encorvado,-a. ‖ **to be doubled up with laughter,** morirse de risa, desternillarse de risa. ‖ **to be doubled up with pain,** retorcerse de dolor. ‖ **to do the double,** SP hacer el doblete. ‖ **to have double standards,** tener una doble moral. ‖ **to run a double check on sth.,** verificar algo dos veces. ‖ **to do a double take,** reaccionar (tardíamente).
■ **double act,** pareja de humoristas, pareja de cómicos. ‖ **double agent,** agente *mf* doble. ‖ **double bass,** contrabajo. ‖ **double bill,** programa *m* doble. ‖ **double booking,** doble reserva. ‖ **double chin,** papada. ‖ **double cream,** nata para montar. ‖ **double Dutch,** (*gibberish*) chino. ‖ **double entendre,** doble sentido. ‖ **double entry,** entrada doble. ‖ **double fault,** SP doble falta. ‖ **double glazing,** doble vidrio. ‖ **double room,** habitación *f* doble. ‖ **double talk,** palabras *fpl* ambiguas, ambigüedades *fpl.* ‖ **double time,** (*wage rate*) paga doble; (*slow run*) paso ligero. ‖ **double vision,** doble visión *f.*
double-barrelled [ˈdʌbəlbærəld] **1** *adj* (*gun*) de dos cañones. **2** (*surname*) compuesto,-a.
double-breasted [ˈdʌbəlbrestɪd] *adj* cruzado,-a.
double-check [dʌbəlˈtʃek] *t* volver a revisar.
double-cross [dʌbəlˈkrɒs] *t fam* engañar, traicionar.
double-dealing [dʌbəlˈdiːlɪŋ] *n* doble juego.
double-decker [dʌbəlˈdekə^r] **1 double-decker (bus),** *n* GB autobús *m* de dos pisos. **2 double-decker (sandwich),** sandwich *m* doble, sandwich *m* de dos pisos.
double-edged [dʌbəlˈedʒd] **1** *adj* (*knife, blade*) de doble filo. **2** (*law*) de doble filo. **3** *fig* (*of remark, argument*) con doble sentido, con segundas.
double-jointed [dʌbəlˈdʒɔɪntɪd] *adj* con articulaciones dobles.
double-park [dʌbəlˈpɑːk] *t* aparcar en doble fila.
double-quick [ˈdʌbəlkwɪk] **1** *adj* muy rápido,-a. **– 2** *adv* volando.
doubly [ˈdʌblɪ] *adv* doblemente: *you must be doubly careful,* hay que tener el doble de cuidado; *you're doubly wrong,* te equivocas doblemente, te equivocas en dos puntos.
● **to make doubly sure of sth.,** asegurarse bien de algo.
doubt [daʊt] **1** *n* (*gen*) duda; (*uncertainty*) incertidumbre *f: I have my doubts about him,* tengo mis dudas acerca de él; *there's no doubt about it/that,* de eso no cabe duda, de eso no hay duda; *there's still some doubt about his fitness,* aún existen ciertas dudas acerca de su forma física. **– 2** *t* (*be uncertain about, not trust*) dudar de: *I'm sorry I doubted your word,* siento haber dudado de tu palabra. **3** (*consider unlikely*) dudar: *I doubt whether he'll come,* dudo que venga, no creo que venga; *I very much doubt it,* lo dudo mucho. **– 4** *i* dudar.
● **beyond (a/any) doubt,** sin duda alguna, fuera de (toda) duda. ‖ **beyond all reasonable doubt,** JUR más allá de toda duda fundada. ‖ **if/when in doubt,** en caso de duda. ‖ **no doubt,** sin duda, seguramente. ‖ **to be in doubt,** (*fact, integrity*) estar en duda, estar en tela de juicio, ser dudoso,-a; (*outcome, result*) ser incierto,-a. ‖ **to be in doubt about sth.,** dudar algo. ‖ **to cast doubt on sth.,** poner algo en duda, poner algo en tela de juicio. ‖ **to give sb. the benefit of the doubt,** conceder a algn. el beneficio de la duda. ‖ **without (a) doubt,** sin duda alguna, sin la menor duda, indudablemente.
doubter [ˈdaʊtə^r] *n* escéptico,-a.
doubtful [ˈdaʊtfʊl] **1** *adj* (*uncertain - outcome, result, future*) dudoso,-a, incierto,-a; (*unlikely*) poco probable; (*look,*

feeling, expression, etc) de duda, dubitativo,-a: *I'm doubtful if they'll come,* dudo que vengan; *it is doubtful that they know,* no es seguro que lo sepan. **2** (*questionable, dubious*) dudoso,-a, sospechoso,-a.
● **to be doubtful about sth.,** tener dudas acerca de algo.
doubtless ['daʊtləs] *adv* sin duda, seguramente, indudablemente.
dough [daʊ] **1** *n* CULIN masa. **2** *sl* (*money*) pasta.
doughnut ['dəʊnʌt] *n* rosquilla, donut *m*.
dour [daʊə'] *adj* hosco,-a, adusto,-a.
Douro ['dʊərəʊ] *n* el Duero *m*.
douse [daʊs] **1** *t* (*extinguish - light, candle*) apagar. **2** (*soak*) mojar, empapar.
dove[1] [dʌv] **1** *n* ORN paloma (blanca). **2** POL *fig* (*person*) paloma.
■ **turtle dove,** tórtola común.
dove[2] [dəʊv] *pp* US → **dive**.
dovecote ['dʌvkəʊt] *n* palomar *m*.
dovetail ['dʌvteɪl] **1** *t* (*wood*) ensamblar a cola de milano. **2** *fig* (*plans, schedules, etc*) sincronizar, encajar. – **3** *i* encajar (**into**, en) (**with**, con). – **4 dovetail** (**joint**), *n* cola de milano.
dowager ['daʊədʒə'] **1** *n* (*widow*) viuda (de un noble): *dowager countess/duchess,* condesa/duquesa viuda. **2** (*rich old lady*) vieja dama.
dowdy ['daʊdɪ] *adj pej* (*clothes*) sin gracia, poco elegante, poco atractivo,-a; (*person*) sin gracia, sin estilo.
▲ *comp* **dowdier,** *superl* **dowdiest.**
dowel ['daʊəl] *n* clavija.
down[1] [daʊn] **1** *prep* (*to a lower level*) (hacia) abajo: *the car rolled down the hill,* el coche se fue rodando cuesta abajo; *tears streamed down her face,* las lágrimas le corrían por la cara; *he ran down the stairs,* corrió escaleras abajo; *she ran her finger down the list,* recorrió la lista con el dedo. **2** (*at a lower level*) abajo: *can you see that cottage down below in the valley?,* ¿ves aquella casita allá abajo en el valle? **3** (*along*) por: *cut it down the middle,* córtalo por la mitad; *we drove down the coast,* condujimos por la costa; *she walked down the street,* iba por la calle. **4** GB *fam* (*to, in*) a, en: *we went down the pub,* fuimos al pub. **5** (*in time*) a través de: *down the ages,* a través de los tiempos. – **6** *adv* (*to lower level*) (hacia) abajo; (*to the floor*) al suelo; (*to the ground*) a tierra: *he looked down at his feet,* miró a sus pies; *why don't you go and lie down?,* ¿por qué no te echas?; *the boy fell down,* el chico se cayó (al suelo); *she bent down to pick up the coin,* se agachó para recoger la moneda; *the girl was knocked down,* la chica fue atropellada; *the river flows down to the sea,* el río fluye hasta el mar; *let's walk down instead of getting the lift,* bajemos a pie en vez de coger el ascensor. **7** (*at lower level*) abajo: *down here/there,* aquí/allí abajo; *it's in the third drawer down,* está en el tercer cajón; *she'll be down in a minute,* enseguida baja. **8** (*in or towards the south*) a: *we're moving down to Southampton,* nos mudamos a Southampton. **9** (*less - of price, quantity, volume, etc*): *sales are down by 10%,* las ventas han bajado un diez por ciento; *profits are down on last year's,* las ganancias han bajado desde el año pasado; *they were two goals down after 10 minutes,* iban perdiendo por dos goles después de 10 minutos; *turn the volume down,* baja el volumen. **10** (*on paper, in writing*): *she wrote his phone number down,* apuntó su teléfono; *put me down for the lottery,* apúntame para la lotería. **11** (*of money - to be paid at once in cash*) al contado; (*- out of pocket*) menos: *you have to pay 100 pounds down,* hay que pagar un depósito de cien libras; *at the end I was*

a fiver down, al final había perdido cinco libras. – **12** *adj* (*to a lower level- escalator*) de bajada; (*- train*) que va hacia las afueras. **13** *fam* (*finished, dealt with*) acabado,-a, hecho,-a: *seven down, three to go!,* ¡he hecho siete, faltan tres! **14** (*not in operation*) no operativo,-a: *the lines are down,* las líneas están cortadas; *the system's down,* el sistema no funciona. **15** *fam* (*depressed*) deprimido,-a: *she's feeling a bit down,* anda un poco deprimida. – **16** *t* (*knock over, force to ground*) derribar, tumbar. **17** *fam* (*drink*) tragarse rápidamente, beberse rápidamente: *he downed the glass in one,* se bebió la copa de un trago. – **18** *interj* (*to dog*) ¡quieto!
● **down to,** (*as far as*) hasta. ‖ **down under,** (en) Australia. ‖ **down with ...!,** ¡abajo ...! ‖ **to be down on sb.,** tenerle ojeriza a algn. ‖ **to be down to sth.,** quedar sólo algo: *I'm down to my last pound,* no me queda más que una sola libra. ‖ **to be down to sb.,** (*responsibility*) ser responsabilidad de; (*fault*) ser culpa de: *it's all down to me now,* ya todo depende de mí. ‖ **to be/come/go down with sth.,** MED estar con algo. ‖ **to down tools,** dejar de trabajar. ‖ **to have a down on sb.,** tenerle ojeriza a algn., tenerle manía a algn. ‖ **to keep food down,** retener comida: *he can't keep any food down,* no puede retener nada de comida. ‖ **to put sth. down,** dejar algo: *can you put that book down for a second?,* ¿puedes dejar ese libro un momento? ‖ **to put the phone down,** colgar: *she put the phone down on me,* me colgó.
down[2] [daʊn] *n* (*on bird*) plumón *m*; (*on peach*) pelusa; (*on body, face*) vello, pelusilla; (*on upper lip*) bozo, pelusilla.
down-and-out ['daʊnənaʊt] *n* vagabundo,-a, indigente *mf*.
● **to be down-and-out,** estar en la miseria.
down-at-heel [daʊnət'hiːl] *adj* (*person*) desastrado,-a, desaliñado,-a.
downbeat ['daʊnbiːt] **1** *adj fam* (*depressed, gloomy*) deprimente; (*low-key, relaxed, unemphatic*) relajado,-a. – **2** *n* MUS compás *m* acentuado.
downcast ['daʊnkɑːst] *adj* (*dejected*) abatido,-a, alicaído,-a.
● **with downcast eyes,** con la mirada baja, mirando al suelo.
downer ['daʊnə'] **1** *n* (*drug*) calmante *m*, sedante *m*. **2** (*blow, depressing experience*) palo.
● **to be on a downer,** estar depre.
downfall ['daʊnfɔːl] **1** *n fig* (*of person*) perdición *f*, ruina. **2** (*of regime, dictator, etc*) caída.
downgrade ['daʊngreɪd] **1** *t* (*demote*) bajar de categoría. **2** (*make seem unimportant*) restar importancia a.
downhearted [daʊn'hɑːtɪd] *adj* desanimado,-a, desmoralizado,-a, descorazonado,-a.
downhill [daʊn'hɪl] **1** *adv* cuesta abajo. – **2** *adj* (*path etc*) cuesta abajo, en pendiente; (*in skiing*) de descenso. **3** *fam* (*easy*) fácil: *it's all downhill from now on,* de aquí en adelante todo va a marchar sobre ruedas. – **4** *n* (*in skiing*) descenso contra-reloj.
● **to go downhill,** (*get worse, deteriorate*) empeorar, ir de mal en peor.
down-market [daʊn'mɑːkɪt] *adj* (*newspaper, book*) popular; (*products, services*) barato,-a.
● **to go/move downmarket,** perder categoría.
downpour ['daʊnpɔː'] *n* chaparrón *m*, aguacero.
downright ['daʊnraɪt] **1** *adj fam* (*lie, insolence*) descarado,-a; (*liar, thief, etc*) redomado,-a, de tomo y lomo; (*madness, stupidity*) total y absoluto,-a: *it's a downright disgrace!,* ¡es una verdadera vergüenza! – **2** *adv fam* muy, absolutamente: *she was downright rude,* estuvo de lo más grosera.

downs [daʊnz] *npl* GB GEOG colinas *fpl*.

Down's syndrome ['daʊnz sɪndrəʊm] *n* MED síndrome *m* de Down.

downstairs [daʊn'steəz] **1** *adv* (*down the stairs*) abajo; (*on or to lower floor*) a la planta baja: *he's downstairs,* está abajo; *can you come downstairs?,* ¿puedes bajar? – **2** *adj* (*room*) (del piso) de abajo. – **3** *n* planta baja.

downstream [daʊn'striːm] *adv* río abajo.

down-to-earth [daʊntʊ'ɜːθ] *adj* práctico,-a, realista.

downtown [daʊn'taʊn] **1** *adv* US (*movement*) al centro de la ciudad; (*situation*) en el centro de la ciudad. – **2** *adj* US céntrico,-a. – **3** *n* US centro de la ciudad.

downtrodden ['daʊntrɒdən] *adj* oprimido,-a.

downturn ['daʊntɜːn] *n* ECON bajón *m*, bache *m* económico.

downward ['daʊnwəd] **1** *adj* (*movement*) descendente; (*direction, pressure*) hacia abajo. **2** FIN a la baja. – **3** *adv* → **downwards**.
■ **downward mobility**, movilidad *f* social descendente.

downwards ['daʊnwədz] *adv* hacia abajo.
● **face downwards**, boca abajo.

downy ['daʊnɪ] *adj* aterciopelado,-a.
▲ *comp* **downier**, superl **downiest**.

dowry ['daʊərɪ] *n* dote *f*.
▲ *pl* **dowries**.

dowse¹ [daʊs] *t* → **douse**.

dowse² [daʊz] to **dowse for water**, *i* buscar agua con una varilla de zahorí.

doyley ['dɔɪlɪ] *n* → **doily**.

doz ['dʌzən] *abbr* (*dozen*) docena; (*abbreviation*) doc.

doze [dəʊz] **1** *n* cabezada. – **2** *i* dormitar, echar una cabezada.
◆ to **doze off** *i* quedarse dormido,-a, dormirse.
● to **have a doze**, echar una cabezada.

dozen ['dʌzən] *n* (*set of twelve*) docena: *a dozen eggs,* una docena de huevos; *half a dozen,* media docena.
● **a baker's dozen**, una docena del fraile. ‖ **by the dozen**, (*in sets of twelve*) por docena(s); (*like hot cakes*) como rosquillas, como pan caliente. ‖ **dozens of**, (*things*) montones de; (*times*) miles de. ‖ **to talk nineteen to the dozen**, hablar por los codos.

dozy ['dəʊzɪ] **1** *adj* (*sleepy*) adormilado,-a. **2** GB *fam* (*stupid*) tonto,-a.
▲ *comp* **dozier**, superl **dozier**.

D Ph ['diː'piː'eɪtʃ] *abbr* (*Doctor of Philosophy*) Doctor,-ra en Filosofía.

D Phil ['diː'fɪl] *abbr* (*Doctor of Philosophy*) Doctor,-ra en Filosofía.

DPP ['diː'piː'piː] *abbr* GB JUR (*Director of Public Prosecutions*) ≈ Fiscal General del Estado.

Dr ['dɒktə'] *abbr* (*Doctor*) Doctor,-ra; (*abbreviation*) Dr., Dra.

drab [dræb] **1** *adj* (*colour*) apagado,-a; (*building, clothes, appearance*) soso,-a, sin gracia. **2** (*dreary - life, existence*) monótono,-a, gris.

drachma ['drækmə] *n* dracma.
▲ *pl* **drachmas** o **drachmae** ['drækmiː].

Draconian [dræ'kəʊnɪən] *adj* draconiano,-a.

draft [drɑːft] **1** *n* (*rough copy - of letter, speech, etc*) borrador *m*; (*of plot*) bosquejo, esbozo; (*of plan, project*) anteproyecto. **2** FIN (*bill of exchange*) letra de cambio, giro. **3** US MIL (*conscription*) (reclutamiento para el) servicio militar obligatorio. **4** US → **draught**. – **5** *t* (*letter, document, contract*) hacer un borrador de, redactar (el borrador de); (*speech*) preparar; (*plan, plot*) esbozar, bosquejar. **6** (*po-*

lice) hacer intervenir (**in**, -); (*new staff*) contratar (in, -)). **7** US MIL (*conscript*) reclutar, llamar a filas. – **8** *adj* (*version, copy*) preliminar.
■ **draft bill**, JUR anteproyecto de ley. ‖ **draft dodger**, prófugo,-a.

draftsman ['drɑːftsmən] *n* US → **draughtsman**.

draftsmanship ['drɑːftsmənʃɪp] *n* US → **draughtmanship**.

drafty ['drɑːftɪ] *adj* US → **draughty**.

drag [dræg] **1** *n* (*hindrance*) estorbo (**on**, para), carga (**on**, para). **2** *fam* (*boring thing*) lata, rollo, plomo, coñazo; (*boring person*) plomo, pelmazo. **3** *fam* (*on cigarette*) calada, chupada. **4** TECH (*resistance*) resistencia (aerodinámica). **5** (*dragnet*) rastra, red *f* barredera. **6** US *sl* (*road, street*) calle *f*. – **7** *t* (*pull, cause to trail*) arrastrar, llevar a rastras: *he was dragging a sledge along behind him,* arrastraba un trineo. **8** (*persuade to go unwillingly*) sacar, llevar a rastras: *if I can drag you away from the TV,* si consigo sacarte de enfrente del televisor; *he dragged me out to the pub,* me llevó a rastras al pub. **9** (*trawl, dredge*) rastrear, dragar. – **10** *i* (*trail - coat, dress, etc*) arrastrar; (*anchor*) garrar: *her skirt dragged in the mud,* arrastraba la falda por el lodo. **11** (*go slowly - person*) rezagarse; (- *play, film, etc*) hacerse largo,-a; (- *work*) hacerse pesado,-a: *today's really dragged!,* ¡hoy se ha hecho eterno!
◆ to **drag down** *t sep* arrastrar. ‖ to **drag in** *t sep* (*subject*) traer por los pelos; (*person*) meter. ‖ to **drag on** *i* alargarse, prolongarse, hacerse interminable. ‖ to **drag out** *t sep* alargar, prolongar. ‖ to **drag up** **1** *t sep* (*revive, recall*) sacar a relucir. **2** GB (*raise*) criar (a la buena de Dios).
● **not to be able to drag os. away**, no tener ninguna gana de irse, serle imposible a uno marcharse. ‖ to **be in drag**, estar vestido de mujer. ‖ to **drag one's feet/ heels**, *fig* dar largas al asunto. ‖ to **drag sth. out of sb.**, sacarle algo a algn. con sacacorchos.
■ **drag artist**, transformista *mf*. ‖ **drag queen**, reinona. ‖ **drag race**, carrera de coches trucados. ‖ **drag show**, espectáculo de transformistas.
▲ (*verbo*) *pt* & *pp* **dragged**, *ger* **dragging**.

dragnet ['drægnet] **1** *n* (*net*) red barredera, rastra. **2** (*system*) operación *f* policial de captura.

dragon ['drægən] **1** *n* (*mythology*) dragón *m*. **2** *fam* (*woman*) bruja.

dragonfly ['drægənflaɪ] *n* libélula.
▲ *pl* **dragonflies**.

dragoon [drə'guːn] **1** *n* MIL dragón *m*. – **2** *t* presionar, obligar.
● to **dragoon sb. into doing sth.**, presionar a algn. para que haga algo.

dragster ['drægstə'] *n* coche *m* de carreras trucado.

drain [dreɪn] **1** *n* (*pipe - for water*) (tubería de) desagüe *m*, desaguadero; (*underground pipe - for sewage*) alcantarilla; (*grating*) alcantarilla, sumidero. **2** US (*plughole*) desagüe. **3** *fig* (*thing, person*) desgaste *m*, agotamiento, sangría: *the boys are a drain on her energy,* los niños la dejan agotada; *defence spending is a drain on our country,* los gastos de defensa son una sangría para nuestro país; *the mortgage is a real drain on your income,* la hipoteca es una sangría para los ingresos. – **4** *t* (*empty - radiator, engine, tank, etc*) vaciar; (- *wound, bladder, blood*) drenar. **5** (*rice, pasta, vegetables, etc*) escurrir. **6** (*dry out - swamp, marshes*) drenar, avenar; (*pond, river, channel, reservoir, region*) desecar, desaguar. **7** (*drink up - glass, etc*) apurar, vaciar. **8** *fig* (*exhaust - strength, energy, resources*) agotar, consumir; (*weaken - person*) agotar: *looking after her*

grandchildren drains all her energy, cuidar a los niños la agota. **– 9** *i (discharge - pipes, rivers)* desaguar; *(flow away)* irse: *the sewage drains off into the sea,* las aguas residuales desaguan en el mar; *the blood drained from her face,* perdió el color de la cara. **10** *(dry out)* escurrir **(off,** -), escurrirse **(off,** -): *leave the glasses to drain,* deja que los vasos se escurran. **11** *fig (strength, energy, etc)* irse agotando. **– 12 the drains,** *npl (of town)* el acantarillado *m sing; (of building)* las tuberías *fpl* del desagüe.
◆ **to drain away 1** *i (liquid - empty)* vaciarse; *(- dry up)* irse: *the bathwater gradually drained away,* la bañera se fue vaciando poco a poco. **2** *fig (strength, energy, etc)* irse agotando, agotarse, desaparecer: *she felt the tension slowly draining away,* notó cómo la tensión desaparecía lentamente; *his strength is draining away,* se está quedando sin fuerzas.
● **to go down the drain,** *(business etc)* venirse abajo. ‖ *that's money down the drain,* eso es tirar el dinero.
drainage [ˈdreɪnɪdʒ] **1** *n (drying out - of marshes, fields)* avenamiento, drenaje *m; (- of pond, river, channel, region, reservoir)* desagüe *m; (- of land)* desecación *f.* **2** *(drains - of town)* alcantarillado; *(of building)* desagüe *m.*
■ **drainage basin,** cuenca hidrográfica. ‖ **drainage channel,** canal *m* de drenaje.
drained [dreɪnd] *adj* agotado,-a.
draining board [ˈdreɪnɪŋ bɔːd] *n* escurridero.
drainpipe [ˈdreɪnpaɪp] **1** *n (pipe)* tubo de desagüe. **– 2 drainpipes,** *npl (trousers)* pantalones *mpl* pitillo.
drake [dreɪk] *n* pato (macho).
dram [dræm] *n fam* trago, traguito, copita, chupito.
drama [ˈdrɑːmə] **1** *n* THEAT *(play)* obra de teatro, drama *m,* obra dramática; *(plays, literature)* teatro, drama *m.* **2** *(as school subject)* expresión *f* corporal; *(at drama school)* arte *m* dramático. **3** *fig (exciting situation)* drama *m; (excitement)* dramatismo: *don't make a drama out of a crisis,* no hagas un drama de una crisis.
■ **drama critic,** crítico *mf* teatral.
dramatic [drəˈmætɪk] **1** *adj* THEAT dramático,-a, teatral. **2** *(moment, escape, development, event, announcement)* emocionante, dramático,-a; *(change, reduction, recovery)* impresionante, espectacular, drástico,-a. **3** *(entrance, pause)* teatral, dramático,-a, histriónico,-a.
dramatics [drəˈmætɪks] **1** *n* THEAT teatro: *amateur dramatics,* teatro amateur, teatro de aficionados. **2** *(histrionics)* afectación *f,* teatro.
dramatist [ˈdræmətɪst] *n* dramaturgo,-a.
dramatization [dræmətaɪˈzeɪʃən] *n* adaptación *f* teatral, dramatización *f.*
dramatize [ˈdræmətaɪz] **1** *t* THEAT hacer una adaptación teatral de. **2** *(exaggerate)* dramatizar, exagerar. **– 3** *i* dramatizar, exagerar.
drank [dræŋk] *pt* → **drink.**
drape [dreɪp] **1** *t (decorate)* drapear, colocar formando pliegues; *(cover)* cubrir **(in/with,** con): *the coffin was draped in/with a flag,* el ataúd estaba cubierto con una bandera. **2** *(part of body)* descansar, acomodar: *he draped his feet over the seat in front,* acomodó los pies sobre el asiento de delante. **– 3** *n (of cloth)* caída. **– 4 drapes,** *npl* US *(curtains)* cortinas *fpl.*
draper [ˈdreɪpəʳ] *n* GB pañero,-a.
■ **draper's (shop),** pañería.
drapery [ˈdreɪpərɪ] **1** *n* GB *(trade, goods)* pañería. **2** *(cloth)* tela; *(hanging)* colgadura. **– 3 draperies,** *npl* US cortinas *fpl.*
▲ *pl* **draperies.**
drastic [ˈdræstɪk] **1** *adj (extreme, radical)* drástico,-a, severo,-a, radical. **2** *(dramatic, striking)* radical, drástico,-a, espectacular.

drastically [ˈdræstɪklɪ] *adv* drásticamente.
draught [drɑːft] **1** *n (of cold air)* corriente *f* (de aire). **2** *(swallow of beer etc)* trago. **3** *(medicine)* pócima. **4** MAR *(depth)* calado. **5** *(haulage)* tiro. **6** *(piece in game)* dama, pieza. **– 7** *adj (animal)* de tiro. **– 8 draughts,** *npl* GB damas *fpl.*
● **on draught,** a presión, de barril. ‖ **to make a draught,** hacer aire.
■ **draught beer,** cerveza de barril.
draughtboard [ˈdrɑːftbɔːd] *n* damero, tablero de damas.
draughtmanship [ˈdrɑːftsmənʃɪp] *n (drawing)* dibujo lineal; *(skill)* ejecución *f* gráfica.
draughtsman [ˈdrɑːftsmən] *n* ARCH delineante *mf,* dibujante *mf;* ART dibujante *mf.*
draughty [ˈdrɑːftɪ] *adj* con corrientes de aire: *it's draughty,* hay corriente.
▲ *comp* **draughtier,** *superl* **draughtiest.**
draw [drɔː] **1** *n (raffle, lottery)* sorteo. **2** SP *(tie - gen)* empate *m; (- in chess)* tablas *fpl.* **3** *(attraction)* atracción *f,* gancho. **4** *(on cigarette, pipe, etc)* calada, chupada. **– 5** *t (sketch - picture)* dibujar; *(- line, circle, plans)* trazar; *(- map)* hacer; *(describe)* pintar. **6** *(move)* llevar: *she drew me aside,* me llevó a un lado. **7** *(pull along - cart, sledge, plough)* tirar de; *(- train, carriage)* arrastrar. **8** *(curtains - open)* descorrer; *(- close)* correr; *(blinds)* bajar. **9** *(pull out, take out - gen)* sacar, extraer; *(gun)* desenfundar, sacar; *(sword, dagger)* desenvainar, sacar; *(bow)* tensar. **10** FIN *(receive - salary, wage, pension)* cobrar; *(write out - cheque)* librar, extender, girar; *(withdraw - money)* sacar, retirar: *I need to draw 100 pounds from my account,* necesito sacar cien libras de mi cuenta. **11** SP *(tie)* empatar. **12** *(attract - crowd, customers, audience)* atraer; *(- attention)* llamar: *I must draw your attention to paragraph three,* les ruego se fijen en el tercer apartado. **13** *(produce, elicit - response, reaction)* provocar, obtener; *(- praise)* conseguir; *(criticism, protest)* provocar, suscitar; *(applause, laughter)* arrancar: *I won't be drawn into your argument,* no quiero que me enredéis en vuestra discusión. **14** *(derive, gain, obtain - support)* obtener; *(- strength)* sacar: *he drew comfort from his family,* se consoló con su familia; *I drew courage from their example,* su ejemplo me dio ánimo; *she draws inspiration from her journeys abroad,* se inspira en sus viajes al extranjero. **15** *(make sb. say more)* sacar información a. **16** *(choose - gen)* escoger; *(playing card)* sacar; *(in contest, tournament)* tocar en el sorteo: *the little girl drew the winning number,* la niña sacó el número ganador; *Spain have been drawn against Yugoslavia,* a España le ha tocado Yugoslavia en el sorteo. **17** *(formulate, establish - comparison)* hacer; *(- conclusion)* sacar, llegar a; *(parallel, distinction, analogy)* establecer: *we drew a valuable lesson from the experience,* sacamos una lección valiosa de la experiencia. **18** MAR *(of ship)* tener un calado de. **– 19** *i (sketch)* dibujar. **20** *(move)* moverse, desplazarse: *the sports car drew ahead of the others,* el coche deportivo se adelantó a los otros; *we drew alongside a Mercedes,* alcanzamos un Mercedes. **21** SP *(tie - gen)* empatar; *(- in chess)* hacer tablas: *they drew two all,* empataron a dos. **22** *(choose)* tirar a suertes: *we drew to see who would go first,* tiramos a suertes a ver quién iba primero. **23** *(take in air - chimney, fireplace)* tirar; *(cigar, pipe)* tirar **(at/on,** -).
◆ **to draw back 1** *i (move away)* retirarse, retroceder. **2** *(pull out)* echarse atrás, volverse atrás. ‖ **to draw in 1** *i (of days)* acortarse, hacerse más corto,-a. **2** *(train)* llegar. ‖ **to draw off** *t sep (liquid)* sacar, extraer. ‖ **to draw on 1** *t insep (make use of - experience etc)* recurrir a.

hacer uso de, inspirarse en, aprovecharse de; (- *money, savings*) utilizar, recurrir a, hacer uso de. – **2** *i* (*approach - winter, night, etc*) acercarse. ‖ **to draw out 1** *t sep* (*prolong*) alargar, estirar. **2** (*make talk, bring out*) hacer hablar, desatar la lengua. – **3** *t insep* (*withdraw - money*) sacar; (*information*) sacar, sonsacar; (*confession*) arrancar. – **4** *i* (*of days*) hacerse más largo,-a. **5** (*train*) salir. ‖ **to draw up 1** *t sep* (*draft - contract, treaty, etc*) preparar, redactar; (- *list*) hacer; (- *plan*) esbozar. – **2** *i* (*of vehicle*) detenerse, pararse.

● the luck of the draw, toca a quien toca, es cuestión de suerte. ‖ **to be drawn (on sth.),** decir algo (sobre algo). ‖ **to be drawn to/towards sb./sth.,** sentirse atraído,-a por/hacia algn./algo. ‖ **to be quick on the draw,** (*with gun*) ser rápido,-a en desenfundar; (*with reply*) pescarlas al vuelo. ‖ **to draw a blank,** seguir sin saber algo. ‖ **to draw apart,** separarse (**from,** de), alejarse (**from,** de), distanciarse (**from,** de). ‖ **to draw blood,** hacer sangrar, sacar sangre. ‖ **to draw breath,** respirar. ‖ **to draw close/near,** acercarse. ‖ **to draw lots (for sth.),** echar (algo) a suerte. ‖ **to draw os. up to one's full height,** enderezarse totalmente. ‖ **to draw the line (at sth.),** decir basta (a algo). ‖ **to draw to an end/close,** terminar, finalizar.

▲ (*verbo*) *pt drew, pp drawn.*

drawback ['drɔːbæk] *n* inconveniente *m*, desventaja.

drawbridge ['drɔːbrɪdʒ] *n* puente *m* levadizo.

drawer ['drɔːəʳ] **1** *n* (*in furniture*) cajón *m*. **2** (*draughtsperson*) dibujante *mf.*

drawers [drɔːz] *npl dated* (*pants - men's*) calzoncillos *mpl*; (- *women's*) bragas *fpl.*

drawing ['drɔːɪŋ] *n* dibujo: *she's good at drawing,* dibuja muy bien.

● to go back to the drawing board, volver a empezar, empezar de nuevo.

■ drawing board, tablero de dibujo. ‖ drawing pin, GB chincheta. ‖ drawing room, sala de estar, salón *m.*

drawl [drɔːl] **1** *n* manera de hablar lenta en que se arrastran las palabras: *a southern/Texan drawl,* un acento sureño/tejano. – **2** *i* hablar arrastrando las palabras. – **3** *t* decir arrastrando las palabras.

drawn [drɔːn] **1** *pp* → **draw**. – **2** *adj* (*face - tired, haggard*) ojeroso,-a, cansado,-a, demacrado,-a; (- *worried*) preocupado,-a: *a face drawn with grief,* una cara transida de dolor. **3** SP (*match etc*) empatado,-a.

drawstring ['drɔːstrɪŋ] *n* cordón *m.*

■ drawstring waist, talle *m* fruncido con un cordón.

dread [dred] **1** *n* terror *m*, pavor *m*: *her dread of growing old,* su terror a hacerse vieja. – **2** *t* temer, tener pavor a, tener terror a: *he's dreading the exam,* el examen le da terror; *she's dreading his parents' visit,* espera la visita de sus padres con aprensión; *I dread to think what would happen,* no quiero ni pensar en lo que pasaría.

dreadful ['dredful] **1** *adj* (*shocking*) terrible, espantoso,-a, atroz. **2** *fam* (*awful*) fatal, horrible, malísimo,-a: *how dreadful!,* ¡qué horror!

dreadfully ['dredfulɪ] *adv fam* (*horribly*) terriblemente, fatal; (*very*) muy, sumamente: *I'm dreadfully sorry,* lo siento muchísimo.

dream [driːm] **1** *n* (*while asleep*) sueño: *I had a bad dream,* tuve una pesadilla; *sweet dreams!,* ¡felices sueños!; ¡que duermas bien!, ¡que sueñes con los angelitos! **2** (*daydream*) ensueño, sueño: *he lives in a dream,* vive en las nubes. **3** (*hope, fantasy*) sueño (dorado), deseo, ilusión *f*: *she was happy beyond her wildest dreams,* era más feliz de lo que jamás había soñado; *it's like a dream come true!,* ¡es como un sueño hecho realidad!;

the house of your dreams, la casa de tus sueños. **4** *fam* (*wonderful thing, person*) sueño, encanto, maravilla: *it all went like a dream,* todo salió a las mil maravillas. – **5** *adj* (*imaginary*) imaginario,-a; (*ideal*) ideal, de ensueño: *your dream holiday,* las vacaciones de tus sueños. – **6** *t* (*while asleep*) soñar: *I dreamt that I was flying,* soñé que volaba. **7** (*imagine*) imaginarse: *I never dreamt you'd actually do it,* nunca me imaginé que lo harías de verdad. – **8** *i* (*while asleep*) soñar (**about/of,** con); (*daydream*) soñar (despierto,-a): *I dreamt about you last night,* soñé contigo anoche; *dream on,* sigue soñando. **9** (*imagine*) soñar (**of,** con); (*contemplate*) soñar, ocurrírsele a uno: *I often dream of having my own business,* sueño a menudo con tener mi propia empresa; *I wouldn't dream of asking him,* no se lo pediría ni en sueños.

◆ to dream away *t insep* pasarse soñando. ‖ to dream up *t sep fam pej* (*excuse*) inventarse; (*plan*) idear.

● to have a dream (about sb./sth.), soñar (con algn./algo). ‖ to live in a dream world, vivir en las nubes.

■ dream team, SP equipo de ensueño. ‖ dream ticket, POL lista de ensueño.

▲ (*verbo*) *pt & pp dreamed o dreamt.*

dreamer ['driːməʳ] *n* soñador,-ra.

dreamlike ['driːmlaɪk] *adj* de ensueño, irreal.

dreamt [dremt] *pt & pp* → **dream**.

dreamy ['driːmɪ] **1** *adj* (*person*) soñador,-ra, fantasioso,-a. **2** (*dreamlike - gen*) de ensueño, irreal; (*music*) etéreo,-a, sutil. **3** *fam* (*wonderful, desirable*) maravilloso,-a.

▲ *comp* dreamier, *superl* dreamiest.

dreary ['drɪərɪ] **1** *adj* (*gloomy - weather, day*) triste, deprimente; (- *room, landscape*) deprimente, lóbrego,-a, sombrío,-a. **2** *fam* (*dull, uninteresting*) pesado,-a, monótono,-a, aburrido,-a.

▲ *comp* drearier, *superl* dreariest.

dredge[1] [dredʒ] **1** *t* (*river, lake, etc*) dragar, rastrear. – **2** *i* (*in river, lake, etc*) dragar, rastrear.

◆ to dredge up **1** *t sep* (*body*) sacar del agua. **2** *fig* (*scandal etc*) desenterrar, sacar a la luz.

dredge[2] [dredʒ] *t* CULIN (*with sugar*) espolvorear; (*with flour*) enharinar, rebozar.

dredger ['dredʒəʳ] **1** *n* (*machine*) draga (*ship*) dragador *m.* **2** CULIN espolvoreador *m.*

dregs [dregz] **1** *npl* (*in liquid*) heces *fpl*, sedimento, poso. **2** *fig* (*scum*) escoria, hez *f.*

drench [drentʃ] *t* empapar.

● to be/get drenched, empaparse. ‖ to be drenched to the skin, estar calado,-a hasta los huesos.

Dresden ['drezdən] *n* Dresde.

dress [dres] **1** *n* (*for women*) vestido. **2** (*clothing*) ropa, vestimenta. – **3** *adj* (*shirt, suit*) de etiqueta. – **4** *t* (*person*) vestir. **5** MED (*wound*) vendar. **6** CULIN (*poultry, crab*) aderezar, preparar; (*salad*) aliñar. **7** (*shop window*) arreglar, decorar; (*Christmas tree*) decorar, adornar; (*hair*) arreglar. – **8** *i* (*gen*) vestir; (*formally*) vestirse de etiqueta.

◆ to dress down **1** *t sep* (*scold*) regañar; (*rebuke*) echar una bronca, echar una regañina a. – **2** *i* (*dress informally*) vestirse informalmente. ‖ to dress up **1** *i* (*in fancy dress*) disfrazarse (**as,** de); (*dress formally*) ponerse de tiros largos, ir de tiros largos, ponerse elegante. – **2** *t sep fig* (*truth, facts, etc*) disfrazar.

● all dressed up and nowhere to go, compuesta y sin novio. ‖ to be dressed, estar vestido,-a. ‖ to be dressed in red, black, etc, ir vestido,-a de rojo, negro, etc. ‖ to be dressed to kill, ir de punta en blanco, ir de tiros largos. ‖ to be dressed up to the nines, vestirse de tiros largos, ponerse de punta en blanco. ‖ to be well/badly dressed, ir bien/mal vestido,-a. ‖

to get dressed, vestirse. ‖ to have good dress sense, tener buen gusto para vestirse.
■ dress circle, THEAT primer piso, piso principal. ‖ dress rehearsal, THEAT ensayo general. ‖ fancy dress, disfraz m. ‖ period dress, traje m de época. ‖ sun dress, vestido sin mangas.

dresser ['dresəʳ] 1 n GB (in kitchen) aparador m. 2 US (chest of drawers) tocador m. 3 THEAT ayudante mf de camerino.
● to be a snappy/fashionable dresser, vestir(se) con estilo/a la moda.

dressing ['dresɪŋ] 1 n (gen) apósito; (bandage) vendaje m. 2 (act of getting dressed) el vestir(se) m. 3 CULIN (for salad) aliño. 4 US CULIN (stuffing) relleno.
■ dressing gown, bata. ‖ dressing room, THEAT camerino. ‖ dressing table, tocador m.

dressing-down ['dresɪŋdaʊn] n reprimenda, rapapolvo, bronca.
● to give sb. a dressing-down, echarle un rapapolvo a algn.

dressmaker ['dresmeɪkəʳ] n modista mf.

dressmaking ['dresmeɪkɪŋ] n costura.

dressy [dresɪ] adj (clothes) elegante, de vestir; (person) arreglado,-a, elegante.
▲ comp dressier, superl dressiest.

drew [druː] pt → draw.

dribble ['drɪbəl] 1 n (saliva) saliva, baba. 2 (of water, blood) gotas fpl, hilo, chorrito. 3 SP dribling m. – 4 i (baby) babear. 5 (liquid) gotear. – 6 t (liquid) chorrear, dejar caer: he's dribbling saliva, babea; she's dribbling milk, la leche le chorreaba por la boca. 7 SP (ball) driblar.

dribs [drɪbz] in dribs and drabs, phr poco a poco.

dried [draɪd] 1 pp → dry. – 2 adj (fruit) seco,-a; (milk) en polvo.

drier ['draɪəʳ] n → dryer.

drift [drɪft] 1 n (of snow) ventisquero; (of sand) montón m. 2 MAR (flow of water) deriva; (deviation - of ship) desviación f. 3 (movement) movimiento, desplazamiento; (tendency) tendencia; (shift) cambio: the drift of people from the country to cities, el desplazamiento de la gente del campo a las ciudades; the drift towards war, la marcha hacia la guerra. 4 (meaning, gist) significado, sentido, idea: do you get my drift?, ¿me entiendes?, ¿entiendes lo que quiero decir? 5 GEOL (deposits of earth, gravel, rock, etc) terreno de acarreo. – 6 i (float on water) dejarse llevar por la corriente; (be or go adrift) ir a la deriva, derivar; (float in air) moverse empujado,-a por el viento: we drifted out to sea, íbamos a la deriva hacia alta mar. 7 (pile up - of snow, sand, leaves, etc) amontonarse. 8 fig (person) ir sin rumbo, vivir sin rumbo, vagar; (government) ir a la deriva: he drifts in and out of jobs, cambia de trabajo continuamente; the conversation drifted from one subject to another, la conversación iba derivando de un tema a otro; the crowds began to drift away, poco a poco la gente empezó a marcharse; she just drifts in when she feels like it, se deja caer por aquí cuando le apetece; I drifted into teaching, por aquello que pasa acabé dando clases. – 9 t (snow, sand, etc) amontonar.
● to drift apart, distanciarse. ‖ to drift off to sleep, quedarse dormido,-a.

drifter ['drɪftəʳ] 1 n (person - wanderer) trotamundos mf, vagabundo,-a; (- without fixed job) persona sin ocupación fija. 2 MAR trainera, (barco) pesquero.

driftwood ['drɪftwʊd] n madera flotante.

drill¹ [drɪl] 1 n (handtool) taladro, taladradora; (large machine) barreno, perforadora; (dentist's) fresa; (drill head, bit) broca: pneumatic drill, taladradora. 2 MIL instrucción f. 3 EDUC (ex-

ercise) ejercicio. 4 (rehearsal, practice) simulacro; (procedures to be followed) procedimiento: fire drill, simulacro de incendio; safety drill, instrucciones de seguridad. 5 GB fam (procedure) procedimiento, trámite m: what's the drill for getting paid?, ¿qué hay que hacer para cobrar? – 6 t (wood, metal, etc) taladrar, perforar, barrenar; (hole) hacer, perforar. 7 MIL instruir. 8 (teach) hacer ejercicios (in, de), hacer practicar. – 9 i (for oil, coal) perforar, hacer perforaciones, sondar: drilling for, perforar en busca de. 10 MIL entrenarse.
● to drill sth. into sb., inculcarle algo a algn.

drill² [drɪl] n (material) dril m.

drill³ [drɪl] n AGR (machine) sembradora; (furrow) hilera, surco.

drily ['draɪlɪ] adj → dryly.

drink [drɪŋk] 1 n (gen, alcohol) bebida; (alcoholic drink) copa, trago; (soft drink) refresco: let's go for a drink!, ¡vamos a tomar algo!, ¡vamos a tomar una copa!; would you like a drink?, ¿quieres tomar algo?; we just had one drink, sólo tomamos una (copa); I want a drink of water, quiero (beber) agua; she has a drink problem, tiene problemas con la bebida. – 2 t (gen) beber, tomar: you haven't drunk your tea, no te has bebido el té; what do you want to drink?, ¿qué quieres beber?, ¿qué quieres tomar? – 3 i beber: she doesn't drink (alcohol), no bebe (alcohol); don't drink and drive, si bebes, no conduzcas. – 4 the drink, n fam (the sea) el mar, la mar.
◆ to drink in t sep (scene, sights, sounds etc) absorber, empaparse de; (success) saborear. ‖ to drink up 1 i bebérselo todo,-a, terminar la copa. – 2 t sep beberse.
● to drink a toast to sb., brindar por algn. ‖ to drink like a fish, beber como un cosaco, beber como una esponja. ‖ to drink os. into a stupor, ponerse como una cuba, beber hasta perder el conocimiento. ‖ to drink os. to death, matar a uno la bebida. ‖ to drive sb. to drink, empujar a algn. a la bebida. ‖ to drink sb. under the table, aguantar más bebiendo que algn. ‖ to drink to sth./sb., brindar por algo/algn. ‖ to have sth. to drink, tomar(se) algo.
▲ (verbo) pt drank; pp drunk.

drinkable ['drɪŋkəbəl] adj (water) potable; (wine, beer, etc) aceptable.

drink-driving [drɪŋk'draɪvɪŋ] n JUR conducción f bajo la influencia del alcohol, conducción f en estado de embriaguez.

drinker ['drɪŋkəʳ] n bebedor,-ra: he's a social drinker, bebe sólo en compañía; she's a heavy drinker, es una gran bebedora, es una bebedora empedernida.

drinking ['drɪŋkɪŋ] n (alcohol) bebida; (action) beber m: we did a lot of drinking, bebimos mucho.
● to give up drinking, dejar la bebida.
■ drinking and driving, → drink-driving. ‖ drinking companion, compañero,-a de copas. ‖ drinking fountain, fuente f de agua potable. ‖ drinking water, agua potable.

drip [drɪp] 1 n (drop of liquid) goteo; (sound) gotear m. 2 MED gota a gota m: they put him on a drip, le pusieron el gota a gota. 3 fam (person) soso,-a. – 4 i (fall in drops) gotear, caer; (fall heavily) chorrear: water is dripping from the ceiling, caen gotas del techo, el techo gotea; the tap drips, el grifo gotea; she was dripping with sweat, estaba chorreando de sudor. – 5 t dejar caer gota a gota: he dripped blood everywhere, chorreaba sangre por todas partes.
● to drip with flattery, rezumar halagos. ‖ to drip with jewels, ir cargado,-a de joyas.
▲ (verbo) pt & pp dripped, ger dripping.

drip-dry ['drɪpdraɪ] *adj* de lavar y poner, que se seca rápidamente y no necesita plancha.

dripping ['drɪpɪŋ] 1 *n* GB CULIN pringue *mf*, grasa de carne asada. – **2** *adj* empapado,-a. – **3** *adv* chorreando.
● **to be dripping wet,** estar chorreando.

drive [draɪv] 1 *n* (*trip*) paseo en coche, vuelta en coche; (*journey*) viaje *m*: *we went for a drive*, dimos una vuelta en coche; *it's only a 20-minute's drive (away),* sólo está a 20 minutos en coche; *it's a two-hour drive,* es un viaje de dos horas. **2** (*road*) calle *f*; (*driveway*) camino de entrada. **3** SP (*golf*) golpe *m* inicial, tiro de salida; (*tennis*) golpe *m* fuerte, drive *m*. **4** (*campaign*) campaña: *sales drive,* promoción; *membership drive,* campaña para atraer socios; *a no-smoking drive,* una campaña antitabaco. **5** MIL ofensiva, avanzada. **6** (*energy, initiative*) energía, ímpetu *m*, empuje *m*, dinamismo. **7** (*need, compulsion*) necesidad *f*, impulso, instinto: *sex drive,* instinto sexual. **8** (*propulsion system*) transmisión *f*, propulsión *f*; AUTO tracción *f*: *front-wheel drive,* tracción delantera; *four-wheel drive,* tracción en las cuatro ruedas; *right/left-hand drive,* con el volante a la derecha/izquierda. **9** GB (*competition, tournament*) torneo: *whist drive,* torneo de whist. – **10** *t* (*operate - vehicle*) conducir: *she can drive a lorry,* sabe conducir un camión; *what car do you drive?,* ¿qué coche tienes?; *he drives a bus,* es conductor de autobús. **11** (*take - person*) llevar (en coche): *I'll drive you home,* te llevaré a casa; *could you drive me to the airport?,* ¿podrías llevarme al aeropuerto? **12** (*cause to move - person*) hacer, obligar a; (*- animal*) arrear: *he was driven back by the flames,* las llamas le hicieron retroceder; *the war is driving prices up,* la guerra está haciendo subir los precios. **13** (*of wind - blow*) llevar; (*of water*) llevarse: *the wind drove the boat off course,* el viento alejó al barco de su rumbo. **14** (*provide power for, keep going*) hacer funcionar, mover: *the river drives the waterwheel,* el río mueve el molino. **15** (*strike in - stake*) hincar; (*- nail*) clavar; (*hit - ball*) mandar. **16** (*construct - tunnel*) perforar, abrir; (*- motorway*) construir. **17** (*force, compel to act*) forzar, obligar; (*cause to be in state*) llevar, empujar: *you're driving me crazy,* me estás volviendo loco; *the pain was driving her mad,* el dolor la enloquecía; *he is driven by greed,* lo impulsa la codicia. **18** (*make work hard, overwork*) hacer trabajar: *you've been driving yourself to hard,* te has estado exigiendo demasiado. – **19** *i* (*vehicle*) conducir: *can you drive?,* ¿sabes conducir?; *he's learning to drive,* está aprendiendo a conducir; *I drove here,* vine en coche; *don't drive so fast,* no vayas tan rápido, no corras; *in England, people drive on the left,* en Inglaterra, la gente conduce por la izquierda. **20** (*of rain, hail, snow*) azotar, barrer.
◆ **to drive at** *t insep* insinuar, querer decir. ‖ **to drive away** *t sep* (*fend off - attacker, animal*) ahuyentar; (*throw out*) alejar. ‖ **to drive off** 1 *t sep* ahuyentar. – **2** *i* (*car, driver*) irse. ‖ **to drive on** 1 *i* seguir (adelante). – **2** *t sep* empujar, llevar a. ‖ **to drive out** *t sep* expulsar.
● **to drive a coach and horses through sth.,** saltarse algo a la torera. ‖ **to drive a hard bargain,** saber cómo conseguir lo que uno,-a quiere, ser buen,-na negociador,-ra. ‖ **to drive sth. home,** hacer entender algo.
▲ *pt* **drove,** *pp* **driven.**

drive-in ['draɪvɪn] *n* US (*cinema*) autocine *m*; (*restaurant*) restaurante *m* donde se atiende a los clientes desde el coche.
■ **drive-in bank,** autobanco.

drivel ['drɪvəl] 1 *n* tonterías *fpl*, bobadas *fpl*, memeces *fpl*. – **2 to drivel (on),** *i* decir tonterías, decir bobadas, decir memeces.

▲ (*verbo*) *pt* & *pp* **drivelled** (US **driveled**), *ger* **drivelling** (US **driveling**).

driven ['drɪvən] *pp* → **drive**.

driver ['draɪvəʳ] 1 *n* (*of bus, car*) conductor,-ra; (*of taxi*) taxista *mf*; (*of lorry*) camionero,-a; (*of racing car*) piloto *mf*; (*of train*) maquinista *mf*: *he's a very good driver,* conduce muy bien. **2** SP (*golf club*) madera número 1.
● **to be in the driver's seat,** estar al frente, llevar las riendas.
■ **driver's licence,** US carnet *m* de conducir, permiso de conducir.

driveway ['draɪvweɪ] *n* camino de entrada.

driving ['draɪvɪŋ] 1 *n* AUTO conducción *f*: *what do you think of Mum's driving?,* ¿te gusta como conduce mamá?, ¿qué te parece la manera de conducir de mamá?; *we shared the driving,* nos turnamos para conducir; *he was found guilty of dangerous driving,* lo declararon culpable de conducción temeraria. – **2** *adj* (*dynamic - personality*) dinámico,-a; (*force*) motriz: *she was the driving force behind the company,* ella era la impulsora de la empresa. **3** (*rain*) torrencial; (*snow, wind*) que azota.
■ **driving licence,** carnet *m* de conducir, permiso de conducir. ‖ **driving range,** (*in golf*) campo de prácticas. ‖ **driving school,** autoescuela. ‖ **driving test,** examen *m* de conducir.

drizzle ['drɪzəl] 1 *n* llovizna, chirimiri *m*. – **2** *i* lloviznar.

droll [drəʊl] *adj* (*amusing*) gracioso,-a, chistoso,-a; (*odd, quaint*) curioso,-a.

dromedary ['drɒmədəri] *n* dromedario.
▲ *pl* **dromedaries.**

drone[1] [drəʊn] 1 *n* (*bee*) zángano. **2** GB *pej* (*parasite*) zángano,-a, parásito,-a.

drone[2] [drəʊn] 1 *n* (*noise - of bee, engine*) zumbido; (*- of traffic, plane*) ruido, zumbido. **2** (*monotonous talk*) cantinela, sonsonete *m*. – **3** *i* (*bee, plane, engine*) zumbar.
◆ **to drone on** *i* hablar con monotonía, hablar en tono monótono.

drool [druːl] 1 *n* (*of baby*) baba, babas *fpl*. **2** (*drivel*) tonterías *fpl*, bobadas *fpl*, memeces *fpl*. – **3** *i* (*of baby, dog*) babear. **4** (*of person*) babear (**over,** por), caérsele la baba a (**over,** por): *the boys were drooling over the pin-up,* a los chicos se les caía la baba mirando la foto.

droop [druːp] 1 *n* (*of shoulders*) caída, inclinación *f*, encorvamiento. – **2** *i* (*head*) inclinarse, caerse; (*shoulders*) encorvarse; (*eyelids*) cerrar. **3** (*flower*) marchitarse, ponerse mustio,-a; (*branches*) inclinarse. **4** (*spirits*) flaquear, decaer.

droopy ['druːpɪ] *adj* caído,-a.
▲ *comp* **droopier,** *superl* **droopiest.**

drop [drɒp] 1 *n* (*of liquid*) gota: *she carried the cup without spilling a drop,* llevó la taza sin derramar ni una gota; *we could do with a drop of rain,* nos iría bien un poco de lluvia; *I never touch a drop,* no pruebo ni gota (de alcohol); *a tear drop,* una lágrima. **2** (*sweet*) pastilla, caramelo. **3** (*descent, distance down*) desnivel *m*, caída: *a sheer drop,* una caída a plomo. **4** (*fall - gen*) caída; (*in price*) bajada, caída; (*in sales*) disminución *f*, descenso; (*in temperature*) descenso. **5** (*collection point*) lugar *m* de recogida: *mail drop,* dirección postal. **6** US (*delivery - from plane*) lanzamiento; (*- from van*) entrega, reparto. – **7** *t* (*let fall - accidentally*) caérsele a uno: *he dropped the glass,* se le cayó el vaso; *don't drop it!,* ¡que no se te caiga!; *I must have dropped it,* se me debe haber caído; *the goalkeeper dropped the ball,* al portero se le escapó el balón. **8** (*let fall - deliberately*) dejar caer, tirar; (*let go of*) soltar; (*launch - bomb, supplies*) lanzar: *she dropped her*

handkerchief by his chair, dejó caer su pañuelo al lado de su silla; *drop it!,* ¡suéltalo! **9** (*lower - voice*) bajar; (*- speed*) reducir; (*- prices*) bajar, reducir. **10** *fam* (*set down - passenger*) dejar (**off,** -); (*- delivery*) dejar, pasar a dejar (**off,** -): *where shall I drop you?,* ¿dónde quieres que te deje? **11** (*give up, abandon - school subject, course, etc*) dejar, abandonar; (*- idea, plan*) abandonar, renunciar a; (*- case*) abandonar; (*- charge*) retirar; (*- boyfriend, girlfriend*) plantar: *let's drop the subject,* cambiemos de tema; *drop everything,* dejarlo todo plantado; *drop it!,* ¡déjalo ya!, ¡basta ya!, ¡ya está bien! **12** (*omit, leave out - in speaking*) no pronunciar, comerse; (*in writing*) omitir: *don't drop your "h's",* no te comas las "haches"; *the gerund drops the final "e",* el gerundio pierde la "e" final. **13** SP (*player from team*) echar, sacar; (*- player from team*) no seleccionar; (*lose*) perder. **14** (*in knitting*) soltar, dejar escapar. **15** *sl* (*take drug*) tomarse. – **16** *i* (*fall - object*) caer, caerse; (*- person*) dejarse caer, tirarse: *an orange dropped out of her bag,* se le cayó una naranja de la bolsa; *he dropped to his knees,* cayó de rodillas. **17** (*collapse*) desplomarse, caer rendido,-a: *dance till you drop,* baila hasta que no puedas más; *she dropped into an armchair,* se desplomó en un sillón. **18** (*prices*) bajar, caer, descender; (*wind*) amainar; (*temperature*) bajar, descender; (*speed*) reducirse, disminuir; (*voice*) bajar. **19** (*land, ground*) caer. **20** (*lapse*) dejar: *let it drop!,* ¡déjalo ya!, ¡basta ya! – **21 drops,** *npl* MED gotas *fpl*: *I'll give you some eye drops,* te daré un colirio.
◆ to drop away **1** *i* (*support, interest*) disminuir. **2** (*ground*) caer. ‖ to drop back / drop behind *i* rezagarse, quedarse atrás. ‖ to drop by **1** *i* pasar. – **2** *t insep* pasar por. ‖ to drop in **1** *i* (*visit*) pasar. – **2** *t sep* (*deliver*) dejar en casa (de algn.), pasar a dejar. ‖ to drop in on *t insep* pasar a ver a, dejarse caer por casa de. ‖ to drop off **1** *i fam* (*fall asleep*) quedarse dormido,-a, dormirse. **2** (*sales, interest, etc*) disminuir. ‖ to drop out *i* (*of school, etc*) dejar los estudios, abandonar los estudios, colgar los libros; (*of group*) dejar el grupo; (*of race, competition*) abandonar; (*of society*) marginarse. ‖ to drop round **1** *i* pasar. – **2** *t sep* pasar a dejar.
● a drop in the ocean, una gota de agua en el mar, un grano de arena en el desierto. ‖ to do sth. at the drop of a hat, hacer algo en cualquier momento, hacer algo sin más ni más. ‖ to drop a brick / drop a clanger, hacer una plancha, meter la pata. ‖ to drop a hint, soltar una indirecta. ‖ to drop dead, caerse muerto,-a: *drop dead!,* ¡vete a la porra!, ¡vete al demonio! ‖ to drop names, mencionar a gente importante. ‖ to drop sb. a line / drop sb. a note, escribir cuatro/unas líneas a algn. ‖ to have a drop too much, beber más de la cuenta. ‖ to let drop that ..., dejar caer/escapar que ...
■ drop curtain, THEAT telón *m.* ‖ drop kick, (*in rugby*) botepronto. ‖ drop shot, dejada.
▲ (*verbo*) *pt & pp* dropped, *ger* dropping.

droplet ['drɒplət] *n* gotita.

dropout ['drɒpaʊt] *n* (*from school*) alumno,-a que no termina el curso, alumno,-a que no completa los estudios; (*from university*) estudiante *mf* que deja los estudios; (*from society*) marginado,-a.

dropper ['drɒpə'] *n* cuentagotas *m.*

droppings ['drɒpɪŋz] *npl* (*of birds*) excremento, caca, cagadas *fpl*; (*of sheep, goats, rabbits*) cagarrutas *fpl*, caca, cacas *fpl*.

dropsy ['drɒpsɪ] *n* hidropesía.

dross [drɒs] *n* **1** (*of metal*) escoria. **2** (*rubbish*) basura.

drought [draʊt] *n* sequía.

drove [drəʊv] **1** *pt* → drive. – **2** *n* (*of cattle*) manada. **3** (*of people*) multitud *f*: *they came in droves,* vinieron a montones.

drown [draʊn] **1** *t* (*person, animal*) ahogar. **2** (*submerge - place*) inundar, anegar. **3** (*smother - food*) ahogar; (*drink*) aguar. **4** (*sound, noise, voice, etc*) ahogar (**out,** -). – **5** *i* ahogarse, morir ahogado,-a.
● to be drowned, ahogarse, morir ahogado,-a. ‖ to drown one's sorrows, ahogar las penas.

drowning ['draʊnɪŋ] *adj* que se ahoga.

drowse [draʊz] *i* dormitar.

drowsiness ['draʊzɪnəs] *n* somnolencia, sopor *m*, modorra.

drowsy ['draʊzɪ] **1** *adj* (*person, look*) somnoliento,-a, soñoliento,-a, adormilado,-a: *these tablets make me drowsy,* estas pastillas me dan sueño. **2** (*atmosphere, day*) somnoliento,-a, soñoliento,-a; (*village, scene*) aletargado,-a, amodorrado,-a, somnoliento,-a, soñoliento,-a.
● to feel drowsy, tener ganas de dormir, tener sueño.
▲ *comp* drowsier, *superl* drowsiest.

drudge [drʌdʒ] **1** *n* (*person*) esclavo,-a, machaca *mf*, burro de carga. – **2** *i* trabajar como un,-a esclavo,-a.

drudgery ['drʌdʒərɪ] *n* trabajo duro y pesado.

drug [drʌg] **1** *n* (*medicine*) medicamento, medicina, fármaco. **2** (*narcotic*) droga, estupefaciente *m*, narcótico: *hard/soft drugs,* drogas duras/blandas. – **3** *t* (*person, animal*) drogar. **4** (*food, drink*) adulterar con drogas.
● to be on/do/take drugs, drogarse.
■ drug abuse, consumo de drogas. ‖ drug addict, drogadicto,-a, toxicómano,-a. ‖ drug addiction, drogadicción *f*, toxicomanía. ‖ drug dealer, traficante *mf* de drogas. ‖ drug pusher, camello *mf*. ‖ drug squad, brigada de estupefacientes.
▲ (*verbo*) *pt & pp* drugged, *ger* drugging.

druggist ['drʌgɪst] *n* US farmacéutico,-a.

drugstore ['drʌgstɔːʳ] *n* US *establecimiento donde se puede comprar medicamentos, cosméticos, periódicos y otras cosas.*

druid ['druːɪd] *n* druida *m.*

drum [drʌm] **1** *n* (*instrument*) tambor *m.* **2** (*container*) bidón *m.* **3** TECH tambor *m.* – **4** *i* (*play a drum*) tocar el tambor, tamborilear. **5** (*rain, hooves*) repiquetear; (*person*) tamborilear, tabalear. – **6 drums,** *npl* (*set*) batería.
◆ to drum out *t sep* expulsar (**of,** de). ‖ to drum up *t insep* (*support, votes*) conseguir, obtener; (*enthusiasm*) despertar; (*business*) fomentar, atraer.
● to drum one's fingers, tamborilear con los dedos. ‖ to drum sth. into sb., hacerle aprender algo a algn. a fuerza de repetírselo, hacerle aprender algo a algn. a fuerza de machacárselo. ‖ to play the drums, tocar la batería.
■ drum major, tambor *m* mayor. ‖ drum majorette, bastonera.
▲ (*verbo*) *pt & pp* drummed, *ger* drumming.

drumbeat ['drʌmbiːt] *n* son *m* del tambor.

drummer ['drʌmə'] *n* (*in marching band*) tambor *mf*; (*in pop group, jazz band*) batería *mf.*

drumstick ['drʌmstɪk] **1** *n* MUS baqueta, palillo (de tambor). **2** CULIN muslo (de ave).

drunk [drʌŋk] **1** *pp* → drink. – **2** *adj* (*gen*) borracho,-a. **3** *fig* (*elated*) ebrio,-a, borracho,-a (**with,** de). – **4** *n* (*person*) borracho,-a.
● to be blind drunk / dead drunk, estar borracho,-a perdido,-a, estar como una cuba. ‖ to be drunk and disorderly, JUR estar en estado de embriaguez y alterando el orden público. ‖ to get drunk, emborracharse.

drunkard ['drʌŋkəd] *n* borracho,-a.

drunken ['drʌŋkən] *adj* (*person*) borracho,-a; (*party*) de borrachos: *drunken driver,* conductor,-ra en estado de embriaguez.

● **in a drunken stupor,** atontado,-a por la bebida.
drunkenness ['drʌŋkənnəs] *n* embriaguez *f.*
dry [draɪ] **1** *adj* (*gen*) seco,-a; (*bread - stale*) duro,-a; (- *without butter*) sin mantequilla: *tomorrow will be hot and dry,* mañana hará un tiempo cálido y seco; *dry white wine,* vino blanco seco. **2** (*cow*) sin leche, que no da leche. **3** (*dull, uninteresting*) aburrido,-a, árido,-a. **4** (*amusing, ironic*) agudo,-a, mordaz, cáustico,-a. **– 5** *t* (*gen*) secar: *dry your hands on this towel,* sécate las manos en esta toalla. **– 6** *i* (*become dry*) secarse (**off**, -): *just leave the glasses to dry,* deja que los vasos se sequen. **7 to dry (up),** (*dry the dishes*) secar (los platos).
◆ **to dry out 1** *i* (*gen*) secarse. **2** (*alcoholic*) curarse. ‖ **to dry up 1** *i* (*reservoir, river, etc*) secarse; (*funds, supply, resources, etc*) agotarse. **2** (*actor etc*) quedarse en blanco: *dry up!,* ¡cállate!, ¡cierra el pico!
● **there wasn't a dry eye in the house,** no hubo quien no llorara. ‖ **as dry as a bone,** completamente seco,-a. ‖ **as dry as dust,** muy árido,-a. ‖ **to be dry / feel dry,** (*thirsty*) tener la garganta seca, tener sed. ‖ **to dry one's eyes,** enjugarse las lágrimas. ‖ **to dry os. (off),** secarse. ‖ **to run dry,** (*river, well*) secarse. ‖ **to wipe sth. dry,** secar algo.
■ **dry dock,** dique *m* seco. ‖ **dry goods,** GB comestibles *mpl* no perecederos; US artículos *mpl* de mercería. ‖ **dry ice,** hielo seco. ‖ **dry land,** tierra firme. ‖ **dry law,** US ley *f* seca. ‖ **dry rot,** putrefacción *f* de la madera. ‖ **dry run,** simulacro.
▲ (*verbo*) *pp & pt* **dried**, *ger* **drying**; (*adjetivo*) *comp* **drier**, *superl* **driest**.
dry-clean [draɪ'kliːn] *t* limpiar en seco.
dry-cleaner's [draɪ'kliːnəz] *n* tintorería, tinte *m.*
dryer ['draɪəʳ] *n* (*for clothes*) secadora; (*for hair*) secador *m.*
dry-eyed [draɪ'aɪd] *adj* sin una lágrima.
dryly ['draɪlɪ] *adv* (*coldly*) secamente, con sequedad; (*ironically*) con guasa, irónicamente.
dryness ['draɪnəs] **1** *n* (*gen*) sequedad *f.* **2** (*coldness*) sequedad *f;* (*irony*) ironía, guasa. **3** (*dullness*) aridez *f.*
D Sc ['diːes'siː] *abbr* (*Doctor of Science*) doctor,-ra en ciencias.
DSS ['diːes'es] *abbr* GB (*Department of Social Services*) departamento de servicios sociales.
DTI ['diːtiː'aɪ] *abbr* GB (*Department of Trade and Industry*) departamento de comercio e industria.
DTs ['diː'tiːz] *abbr* (*delirium tremens*) delírium *m* trémens.
dual ['djuːəl] *adj* (*gen*) doble.
■ **dual carriageway,** GB carretera de doble calzada.
dual-control [djuːəlkən'trəʊl] *adj* de doble mando, de doble control.
dual-purpose [djuːəl'pɜːpəs] *adj* (*utensil*) de doble uso; (*furniture*) de doble función.
dub¹ [dʌb] *t* CINEM TV (*subtitle*) doblar (**into**, a).
▲ *pt & pp* **dubbed**, *ger* **dubbing**.
dub² [dʌb] **1** *t* (*give nickname*) apodar. **2** (*knight*) armar.
▲ *pt & pp* **dubbed**, *ger* **dubbing**.
dub³ [dʌb] *n* MUS dub *m.*
dubbing ['dʌbɪŋ] *n* CINEM TV doblaje *m.*
dubious ['djuːbɪəs] **1** *adj* (*questionable, suspect - morals, activities, origin*) dudoso,-a, sospechoso,-a; (*past, record*) turbio,-a; (*compliment*) ambiguo,-a, equívoco,-a; (*character*) sospechoso,-a. **2** (*unsure*) dudoso,-a, indeciso,-a.
● **to be dubious about sth.,** tener dudas sobre algo, tener reservas sobre algo.
Dublin ['dʌblɪn] *n* Dublín.
Dubliner ['dʌblɪnəʳ] *n* (*person*) dublinés,-esa.

ducal ['djuːkəl] *adj* ducal.
duchess ['dʌtʃəs] *n* duquesa.
duchy ['dʌtʃɪ] *n* ducado.
▲ *pl* **duchies**.
duck¹ [dʌk] **1** *n* ORN pato,-a. **2** CULIN pato. **3** GB *fam* (*as term of address*) majo,-a, guapo,-a. **4** SP (*in cricket*) cero.
● **to be like water off a duck's back,** serle indiferente a uno. ‖ **to take to sth. like a duck to water,** adaptarse bien a algo.
duck² [dʌk] **1** *i* (*bend down*) agacharse; (*hide*) esconderse: *she ducked behind the sofa,* se escondió detrás del sofá. **– 2** *t* (*head*) agachar, bajar. **3** (*in water*) hundir, sumergir, zambullir. **4** (*dodge - duty, responsibility*) evadir, eludir; (- *question*) eludir, esquivar.
● **to duck out of sth.,** escabullirse de algo.
ducking ['dʌkɪŋ] *n* chapuzón *m.*
duckling ['dʌklɪŋ] *n* patito.
duct [dʌkt] *n* (*gen*) conducto.
ductile ['dʌktaɪl] **1** *adj* (*metal*) dúctil. **2** *fig* (*person*) dúctil, dócil.
dud [dʌd] **1** *n* *fam* (*object*) trasto inútil, engañifa; (*person*) desastre *m,* inútil *mf.* **2** (*grenade, bomb, firework, etc*) granada, bomba, fuego artificial, etc que no estalla. **– 3** *adj* (*defective*) defectuoso,-a; (*worthless, useless*) inútil, que no sirve; (*valueless - note, coin*) falso,-a; (*grenade, bomb, firework*) que no estalla.
■ **dud cheque,** cheque *m* sin fondos.
dude [djuːd] **1** *n* US (*city man*) ciudadano. **2** (*guy, man*) tío, tipo.
■ **dude ranch,** rancho para turistas.
due [djuː] **1** *adj* (*expected, supposed to happen*) esperado,-a: *her new book is due out in December,* su nuevo libro saldrá en diciembre; *the train is due (in) at five o'clock,* el tren debe llegar a las cinco; *he's due back any minute,* volverá en cualquier momento; *when is the baby due?,* ¿para cuándo espera el bebé?; *we were due there at nine o'clock,* teníamos que estar allí a las nueve. **2** *fml* (*proper, correct*) debido,-a: *he was driving without due care and attention,* conducía de forma imprudente y sin prestar la debida atención; *after due consideration,* con las debidas consideraciones. **3** (*payable, requiring immediate payment*) pagadero,-a, que vence: *a bill due today,* una factura que vence hoy; *the rent isn't due till next week,* no hay que pagar el alquiler hasta la semana que viene. **4** (*owed as right*) merecido,-a; (*owed as debt*) debido,-a: *thanks are due to all the staff at London Hospital,* gracias a todo el personal del Hospital de Londres; *credit where credit's due,* hay que reconocer su mérito; *I'm due for a rise,* me corresponde un aumento de sueldo; *how much are you due?,* ¿cuánto te deben?; *I'm still due 5 days' holiday,* aún me deben cinco días de vacaciones. **– 5** *n* merecido. **– 6** *adv* derecho hacia: *due north,* derecho hacia el norte. **– 7 dues,** *npl* (*charges, payments, fees*) cuota: *have you paid your dues?,* ¿has pagado la cuota?
● **due to,** debido a. ‖ **to become due,** FIN vencer, hacerse efectivo,-a. ‖ **to be due to,** deberse a, ser causado,-a por. ‖ **to give sb. his/her due,** dar a algn. su merecido, ser justo,-a con algn., hacer justicia a algn. ‖ **with all due respect,** con el debido respeto, con todo el respeto que se merece, sin ganas de ofender.
■ **due date,** (fecha de) vencimiento.
duel ['djuːəl] **1** *n* duelo. **– 2** *i* batirse en duelo (**with**, con).
▲ (*verbo*) *pt & pp* **duelled** (US **dueled**), *ger* **duelling** (US **dueling**).
duet [djuː'et] *n* dúo.
● **to play/sing a duet,** tocar/cantar a dúo.

duff [dʌf] *adj* GB *fam* (*useless*) inútil, que no sirve; (*defective*) defectuoso,-a.
◆ **to duff up** *t sep* dar una paliza a.
duffel ['dʌfəl] *n* tela gruesa de lana, muletón *m*.
■ **duffel bag**, talego, petate *m*. ‖ **duffel coat**, trenca.
duffle ['dʌfəl] *n* → **duffel**.
dug [dʌg] *pt & pp* → **dig**.
dugout ['dʌgaʊt] **1** *n* MIL (*shelter*) refugio subterráneo. **2** SP (*in sportsground*) banquillo (*a un nivel inferior al del campo*). **3** dugout (canoe), (*boat*) piragua.
duke [djuːk] *n* duque *m*.
dukedom ['djuːkdəm] *n* ducado.
dull [dʌl] **1** *adj* (*boring - job*) monótono,-a, pesado,-a; (*- person, life, film*) pesado,-a, aburrido,-a, soso,-a; (*- place, town*) aburrido,-a, sin interés. **2** (*not bright - colours*) apagado,-a; (*light*) pálido,-a; (*overcast - weather, day*) gris, triste, feo,-a; (*- sky*) cubierto,-a, nublado,-a; (*not shiny - hair, complexion, eyes*) sin brillo. **3** (*muffled - sound*) sordo,-a, amortiguado,-a; (*- pain, ache*) sordo,-a; (*blunt- edge, blade*) romo,-a, embotado,-a. **4** (*slow-witted*) torpe, lerdo,-a. **5** COMM (*sluggish - trade*) flojo,-a. **– 6** *t* (*pain*) aliviar, calmar; (*sound*) amortiguar; (*hearing*) embotar.
duly ['djuːlɪ] **1** *adv fml* (*properly*) debidamente. **2** (*as expected*) como era de esperar.
dumb [dʌm] **1** *adj* (*unable to speak*) mudo,-a. **2** (*silent*) callado,-a. **3** US *fam* (*stupid*) tonto,-a, estúpido,-a, bobo,-a. **– 4** the dumb, *npl* los mudos *mpl*.
● **to act dumb**, hacerse el tonto. ‖ **to be struck dumb**, quedarse mudo,-a, enmudecer.
dumbbell ['dʌmbel] **1** *n* SP pesa. **2** US (*stupid person*) tonto,-a, imbécil *mf*, estúpido,-a.
dumbfound [dʌm'faʊnd] *t* pasmar, dejar sin habla.
dumbfounded [dʌm'faʊndɪd] *adj* pasmado,-a, atónito,-a.
dumbly ['dʌmlɪ] *adv* sin decir nada.
dumbstruck ['dʌmstrʌk] *adj* estupefacto,-a.
dummy ['dʌmɪ] **1** *n* (*in shop window, dressmaker's*) maniquí *m*; (*ventriloquist's, for tests*) muñeco. **2** (*fake*) imitación *f*. **3** (*in printing*) maqueta. **4** GB (*for baby*) chupete *m*. **5** *fam* imbécil *mf*. **6** SP (*in football, rugby*) regateo, finta. **7** (*in bridge - cards*) mano *f* de muerto; (*player*) muerto. **– 8** *adj* falso,-a, de imitación.
■ **dummy run**, ensayo, prueba, simulacro.
▲ *pl* **dummies**.
dump [dʌmp] **1** *n* (*tip - for rubbish*) vertedero, basurero; (*- for cars*) cementerio (de coches). **2** MIL depósito. **3** *fam pej* (*place*) lugar *m* de mala muerte; (*town*) poblacho; (*dwelling*) tugurio. **4** COMPUT volcado de memoria. **– 5** *t* (*drop, unload - rubbish*) verter, descargar; (*leave*) dejar, poner: *he dumped his dirty washing on the floor,* dejó su ropa sucia en el suelo. **6** (*get rid of, abandon - gen*) deshacerse de, tirar, abandonar; (*- boyfriend, girlfriend*) plantar, dejar. **7** COMM *pej* inundar el mercado con algo barato: *they dump these medicines in the Third World,* inundan el mercado del Tercer Mundo con estos medicamentos baratos. **8** COMPUT volcar.
● **to dump os. on sb.**, plantarse en casa de algn.
dumper-truck ['dʌmpətrʌk] *n* volquete *m*.
dumping ['dʌmpɪŋ] *n* vertido.
● *"no dumping"*, "prohibido arrojar basuras".
■ **dumping ground**, vertedero, basurero.
dumpling ['dʌmplɪŋ] *n* CULIN (*in stew*) bola de masa hervida para acompañar carnes etc; (*as dessert*) (tipo de) budín *m* relleno.
dumps [dʌmps] **to be down in the dumps**, *phr* estar depre.

dumpy ['dʌmpɪ] *adj fam* rechoncho,-a, regordete.
▲ *comp* **dumpier**, *superl* **dumpiest**.
dunce [dʌns] *n* tonto,-a, burro,-a.
dune [djuːn] **(sand) dune**, *n* duna.
dung [dʌŋ] *n* (*manure*) estiércol *m*; (*excrement*) excremento, boñiga.
dungarees [dʌŋgə'riːz] *n* (*garment*) pantalones *mpl* de peto, peto; (*overalls*) mono.
dungeon ['dʌndʒən] *n* calabozo, mazmorra.
dunk [dʌŋk] *t* (*bread, biscuit, etc*) mojar.
duo ['djuːəʊ] *n* dúo.
▲ *pl* **duos**.
duodena [djuːə'diːnə] *npl* → **duodenum**.
duodenal [djuːə'diːnəl] *adj* duodenal.
duodenum [djuːə'diːnəm] *n* duodeno.
▲ *pl* **duodenums** *o* **duodena**.
dupe [djuːp] **1** *n* ingenuo,-a, inocentón,-ona, primo,-a. **– 2** *t* engañar, embaucar.
● **to dupe sb. into doing sth.**, embaucar a algn. para que haga algo.
duplex ['djuːpleks] *n* US (*house*) casa adosada; (*flat, apartment*) dúplex *m*.
duplicate ['djuːplɪkət] **1** *adj* duplicado,-a: *a duplicate key*, una copia de una llave. **– 2** *n* copia, duplicado. **– 3** *t* (*copy*) duplicar, hacer copias de. **4** (*repeat*) repetir.
● **in duplicate**, por duplicado.
▲ (*verbo*) [ˈdjuːplɪkeɪt].
duplication [djuːplɪ'keɪʃən] **1** *n* (*of document*) copia, duplicación *f*. **2** (*repetition*) repetición *f*.
duplicator ['djuːplɪkeɪtə'] *n* multicopista.
duplicity [djuː'plɪsɪtɪ] *n fml* duplicidad *f*.
durability [djʊərə'bɪlɪtɪ] *n* durabilidad *f*.
durable ['djʊərəbəl] **1** *adj* duradero,-a. **– 2 durables**, *npl* bienes *mpl* (de consumo) duraderos.
duration [djʊə'reɪʃən] *n* duración *f*.
● **for the duration**, MIL mientras dure la guerra.
duress [djʊ'res] **under duress**, *n fml* bajo coacción.
during ['djʊərɪŋ] *prep* durante: *I lived in France during the war*, viví en Francia durante la guerra; *she's out at work during the day*, trabaja fuera de casa durante el día.
dusk [dʌsk] *n* anochecer *m*.
● **at dusk**, al anochecer.
dust [dʌst] **1** *n* (*gen*) polvo: *a cloud of dust*, una polvareda. **– 2** *t* (*room, furniture, ornaments, etc*) quitar el polvo a, limpiar el polvo a. **3** (*cake, plant*) espolvorear. **– 4** *i* (*clean*) quitar el polvo.
● **to bite the dust**, (*person*) morder el polvo; (*plan etc*) irse a pique. ‖ **to dust os. down**, sacudirse el polvo. ‖ **to gather dust**, llenarse de polvo. ‖ **to give sth. a dust**, quitar el polvo a algo, limpiar el polvo a algo. ‖ **not to see sb. for dust**, poner los pies en polvorosa. ‖ **when the dust has settled**, cuando se calme la borrasca, cuando haya pasado la tormenta.
■ **dust bowl**, GEOG región *f* de sequía, zona semi-árida, zona semidesértica. ‖ **dust cover**, (*for furniture*) funda; (*for book*) sobrecubierta. ‖ **dust jacket**, sobrecubierta. ‖ **dust storm**, tormenta de polvo.
dustbin ['dʌstbɪn] *n* GB cubo de la basura.
■ **dustbin man**, basurero.
dustcart ['dʌstkɑːt] *n* camión *m* de la basura.
duster ['dʌstə'] *n* (*for dusting*) paño, trapo (del polvo); (*for blackboard*) borrador *m*.
dustman ['dʌstmən] *n* GB basurero.
dustpan ['dʌstpæn] *n* recogedor *m*, pala.
dust-up ['dʌstʌp] *n* GB *fam* (*fight*) pelea.
dusty ['dʌstɪ] **1** *adj* (*track, town*) polvoriento,-a; (*room*) lleno,-a de polvo; (*furniture*) cubierto,-a de polvo. **2** (*of colour*) grisáceo,-a, ceniciento,-a.

● **to get a dusty answer,** recibir una evasiva.
▲ *comp dustier, superl dustiest.*
Dutch [dʌtʃ] 1 *adj* holandés,-esa, neerlandés,-esa. – 2 *n* (*language*) holandés *m.* – 3 **the Dutch,** *npl* los holandeses *mpl.*
● **to go Dutch (with sb.),** pagar cada uno lo suyo, pagar a escote, pagar a la catalana.
■ **Dutch courage,** valor *m* que da la bebida. ‖ **Dutch elm,** olmo. ‖ **Dutch elm disease,** grafiosis *f* del olmo.
Dutchman ['dʌtʃmən] *n* holandés *m,* neerlandés *m.*
● **I'm a Dutchman,** yo soy el Papa de Roma.
▲ *pl Dutchmen* ['dʌtʃmən].
Dutchwoman ['dʌtʃwumən] *n* holandesa.
▲ *pl Dutchwomen* ['dʌtʃwimin].
dutiable ['djuːtiəbəl] *adj* sujeto,-a a derechos arancelarios.
dutiful ['djuːtiful] *adj* consciente de sus deberes, obediente y respetuoso,-a.
duty ['djuːti] 1 *n* (*obligation*) deber *m,* obligación *f: I feel it's my duty to go,* creo que es mi obligación ir; *he went to the funeral out of a sense of duty,* asistió al funeral porque le parecía que era su deber. 2 (*task*) función *f,* cometido: *her duties include dealing with public,* sus funciones incluyen atender al público. 3 (*service*) guardia, servicio. 4 (*tax*) impuesto: *there's duty to pay on that,* hay que pagar un impuesto por eso.
● **to be off duty,** (*doctor, nurse, etc*) no estar de guardia; (*police, firefighter, etc*) no estar de servicio. ‖ **to be on duty,** (*doctor, nurse, etc*) estar de guardia; (*police, firefighter*) estar de servicio: *she's on night duty,* tiene guardia nocturna. ‖ **to do duty as sth.,** servir de algo, hacer las veces de algo. ‖ **to do one's duty,** cumplir con su deber. ‖ **to make it one's duty to do sth.,** encargarse de hacer algo. ‖ **to neglect one's duties,** descuidar sus responsabilidades. ‖ **to take up one's duties,** entrar en funciones.
■ **customs duties,** derechos *mpl* de aduana, aranceles *mpl.* ‖ **duty roster,** lista de guardias.
▲ *pl duties.*
duty-bound ['djuːtibaund] *adj* moralmente obligado,-a.
duty-free ['djuːtifriː] 1 *adj* libre de impuestos. – 2 *adv* libre de impuestos, sin pagar impuestos. – 3 *n* (*object*) artículo libre de impuestos.
■ **duty-free shop,** duty-free *m,* tienda libre de impuestos.
duvet ['duːveɪ] *n* GB edredón *m.*
■ **duvet cover,** funda de edredón.
DV ['diː'viː] *abbr* (**Deo volente**) Dios mediante; (*abbreviation*) Dm.
dwarf [dwɔːf] 1 *n* (*gen*) enano,-a. – 2 *adj* enano,-a. – 3 *t* hacer parecer pequeño,-a.

▲ *pl dwarfs o dwarves* [dwɔːvz].
dwell [dwel] *i fml* morar, habitar, vivir.
◆ **to dwell on** *t insep* (*think about*) pensar demasiado en; (*talk about*) hablar extensamente de, detenerse demasiado en: *let's not dwell on it,* olvidémoslo.
▲ *pt & pp dwelt.*
dweller ['dwelə'] *n* morador,-ra, habitante *mf: cave dweller,* cavernícola; *city dweller,* persona que vive en la ciudad.
dwelling ['dwelɪŋ] *n fml* morada, vivienda.
dwelt [dwelt] *pt & pp →* **dwell.**
dwindle ['dwɪndəl] *i* menguar, disminuir, reducirse.
● **to dwindle away to nothing,** quedar reducido,-a a nada.
dwindling ['dwɪndlɪŋ] *adj* (*numbers, population*) cada vez más reducido,-a; (*resources*) cada vez más limitado,-a.
dye [daɪ] 1 *n* tinte *m,* tintura, colorante *m.* – 2 *t* teñir: *dyed her hair green,* se tiñó el pelo de verde. – 3 *i* teñirse.
dyed-in-the-wool [daɪdɪnðə'wul] *adj pej* acérrimo,-a, inflexible, intransigente.
dying ['daɪɪŋ] 1 *adj* (*person, animal*) moribundo,-a, agonizante; (*race, breed, art, industry*) en vías de extinción; (*custom*) en vías de desaparición; (*flame, embers*) mortecino,-a; (*words, breath*) último,-a, postrero,-a. – 2 *n* muerte *f.* – 3 **the dying,** *npl* los moribundos *mpl.*
● **to be sb.'s dying wish,** ser el último deseo de algn.
‖ **to one's dying day,** hasta el fin de sus días, hasta que se muera.
dyke [daɪk] 1 *n* (*bank*) dique *m,* barrera; (*causeway*) terraplén *m.* 2 *sl pej* (*lesbian*) tortillera.
dynamic [daɪ'næmɪk] 1 *adj* (*gen*) dinámico,-a. – 2 *n* TECH dinámica.
dynamics [daɪ'næmɪks] *n* PHYS dinámica.
dynamism ['daɪnəmɪzəm] *n* dinamismo.
dynamite ['daɪnəmaɪt] 1 *n* (*explosive*) dinamita. 2 *fam* (*shocking thing*) una bomba; (*wonderful thing, person*) sensación *f: if the press got hold of this, it could be dynamite,* si se enterara la prensa de esto, podría ser una bomba; *their new singer is dynamite!,* ¡su nuevo cantante es sensacional! – 3 *t* dinamitar, volar con dinamita.
dynamo ['daɪnəməu] *n* dinamo *f,* dínamo *f.*
▲ *pl dynamos.*
dynasty ['dɪnəsti] *n* dinastía.
▲ *pl dynasties.*
dysentery ['dɪsəntri] *n* disentería.
dyslexia [dɪs'leksiə] *n* dislexia.
dystrophy ['dɪstrəfi] *n* distrofia

E

E, e [iː] **1** *n* (*the letter*) E, e *f.* **2** MUS mi *m*.

E [iːst] *abbr* (*east*) este *m*; (*abbreviation*) E.

each [iːtʃ] **1** *adj* cada: *each day,* cada día, todos los días; *each year,* cada año, todos los años; *each person brought something different,* cada persona trajo algo diferente. **– 2** *pron* cada uno,-a: *they each have their own car,* cada uno tiene su coche; *each with his wife,* cada uno con su esposa. **– 3** *adv* cada uno,-a: *apples cost 15p each,* las manzanas cuestan 15 peniques la pieza; *the girls bought two each,* las niñas se compraron dos cada una.
● **each and every one (of them),** todos,-as y cada uno,-a (de ellos): *I love each and every one of them,* los quiero a todos y a cada uno de ellos. ‖ **each other,** el uno al otro, la una a la otra, mutuamente: *they back each other up,* se respaldan mutuamente; *we saw each other yesterday,* nos vimos ayer; *they've known each other for years,* se conocen desde hace años. ‖ **each to his own,** cada uno,-a a lo suyo.

eager [ˈiːgəʳ] **1** *adj* (*anxious*) ávido,-a (**to**, de), ansioso,-a (**to**, de); (*desirous*) deseoso,-a (**to**, de); (*impatient*) impaciente (**to**, por): *he's eager to please,* se muestra deseoso por complacer; *she was eager to see him go,* ansiaba que se marchara; *they are eager for success,* tienen muchas ansias de éxito. **2** (*excited, full of interest*) ilusionado,-a, entusiasta: *it was nice to see their eager faces,* daba gusto ver sus caras ilusionadas.
● **to be eager to do sth.,** ansiar hacer algo, desear hacer algo.
■ **eager beaver,** *fam* trabajador,-ra incansable.

eagerly [ˈiːgəli] *adv* (*enthusiastically*) con afán, con entusiasmo; (*anxiously*) con impaciencia.

eagerness [ˈiːgənəs] *n* (*enthusiasm*) afán *m*, ilusión *f*; (*anxiety*) impaciencia, ansia.

eagle [ˈiːgəl] **1** *n* (*bird*) águila. **2** (*in golf*) eagle *m*.
■ **golden eagle,** águila real.

eagle-eyed [iːgəlˈaɪd] *adj* con ojos de lince.

eaglet [ˈiːglət] *n* aguilucho.

ear[1] [ɪəʳ] **1** *n* ANAT oreja. **2** (*sense*) oído.
● **by ear,** de oído. ‖ **to be all ears,** ser todo,-a oídos. ‖ **to be out on one's ear,** encontrarse de patitas en la calle. ‖ **to be up to one's ears in sth.,** estar hasta el cuello de algo. ‖ **to have a good ear for sth.,** tener oído para algo: *he's got a good ear for music,* tiene oído para la música. ‖ **to have the ear of sb.,** hacerse escuchar por algn. ‖ **to go in at one ear and out the other,** entrarle por un oído y salirle por el otro. ‖ **to keep one's ear to the ground,** estar al corriente. ‖ **to play sth. by ear,** tocar algo de oído. ‖ **to play it by ear,** *fig* improvisar. ‖ **to turn a deaf ear,** hacer oídos sordos. ‖ **sb.'s ears are burning,** le silban los oídos a algn.
■ **ear lobe,** lóbulo. ‖ **ear, nose and throat specialist,** otorrinolaringólogo,-a. ‖ **ear trumpet,** trompetilla. ‖ **thick ear,** bofetada.

ear[2] [ɪəʳ] *n* (*of cereal*) espiga.

earache [ˈɪəreɪk] *n* dolor *m* de oídos.

eardrops [ˈɪədrɒps] *npl* gotas *fpl* para el oído.

eardrum [ˈɪədrʌm] *n* tímpano.

earful [ˈɪəfʊl] **to give sb. an earful,** *phr fam* (*bore*) pegarle un rollo a algn.; (*tell off*) cantarle las cuarenta a algn., decirle a algn. cuatro verdades.

earl [ɜːl] *n* conde *m*.

earldom [ˈɜːldəm] *n* condado.

early [ˈɜːli] **1** *adj* (*before expected*) temprano,-a, pronto: *we were early,* llegamos temprano; *the baby was a fortnight early,* el bebé se adelantó quince días; *early daffodils,* narcisos tempranos; *an early reply,* una respuesta pronta. **2** (*initial*) primero,-a: *take the early train,* coge el primer tren de la mañana; *what are your earliest memories?,* ¿cuáles son tus primeros recuerdos?; *in the early stages,* en los comienzos. **3** (*near beginning*): *she's in her early forties,* tiene poco más de cuarenta años; *in early January,* a principios de enero; *in the early 1960's,* a principios de los sesenta; *he started working at an early age,* se puso a trabajar siendo muy joven. **4** *adv* (*before expected*) temprano, pronto; (*soon*) pronto: *the train left ten minutes early,* el tren salió con diez minutos de adelanto; *she got up early,* se levantó temprano; *they left early,* se fueron pronto; *I'll be there as early as possible,* llegaré tan pronto como sea posible. **5** (*near beginning*) temprano: *early in the morning,* a primera hora de la mañana, por la mañana temprano; *early in the season,* al principio de la temporada; *earlier that day,* antes ese mismo día; *as early as 1920,* ya en 1920. **6** (*in good time*) con tiempo, con anticipación: *book early to avoid disappointment,* reserve con tiempo para evitarse una desilusión; *we got there early to get a good seat,* llegamos con tiempo para coger buen sitio.
● **at the earliest,** como muy pronto. ‖ **earlier on,** antes. ‖ **it's still early days,** aún es pronto. ‖ **at your earliest convenience,** con la mayor brevedad. ‖ **the early bird catches the worm,** a quien madruga Dios le ayuda. ‖ **to have an early night,** acostarse pronto. ‖ **to make an early start,** salir temprano.
■ **early bird / early riser,** madrugador,-ra. ‖ **early man,** el hombre *m* primitivo. ‖ **early closing day,** GB día en que los comercios abren sólo por la mañana: *Wednesday is early closing day here,* aquí los miércoles por la tarde todo cierra. ‖ **early retirement,** jubilación *f* anticipada. ‖ **early warning system,** sistema de alerta roja. ‖ **the early hours / the early morning,** la madrugada.
▲ *comp* **earlier,** *superl* **earliest**.

earmark [ˈɪəmɑːk] *t* destinar (**for**, a), reservar (**for**, para).

earmuff [ˈɪəmʌf] *n* orejera.

earn [ɜːn] **1** *t* (*money, wages*) ganar: *how much do you earn a month?,* ¿cuánto ganas al mes? **2** (*interest*) devengar. **3** (*respect, approval, gratitude, etc*) ganarse, valer; (*deserve*)

merecer, merecerse: *it earned her the praise of all the faculty,* le valió el elogio de todo el cuerpo docente; *a well-earned holiday,* unas vacaciones bien merecidas.
● **to earn one's living,** ganarse la vida.
earner ['ɜːnəʳ] **1** *n* (*person*) persona que gana dinero: *I'm the only earner in the family,* soy el único de la familia que gana un sueldo. **2** (*thing*) cosa rentable.
earnest ['ɜːnɪst] *adj* serio,-a, formal.
● **in earnest,** en serio, de veras. ‖ **to be in earnest,** ir en serio.
earnestly ['ɜːnɪstlɪ] *adv* seriamente.
earnestness ['ɜːnɪstnəs] *n* seriedad *f*.
● **in all earnestness,** con toda seriedad.
earnings ['ɜːnɪŋz] **1** *npl* (*personal*) ingresos *mpl*. **2** (*of company*) ganancias *fpl*.
■ **take-home earnings,** ingresos *mpl* netos. ‖ **earnings-related pension scheme,** plan de jubilación de acuerdo con los ingresos.
earphones ['ɪəfəʊnz] *npl* auriculares *mpl*.
earpiece ['ɪəpiːs] *n* (*of telephone*) auricular *m*.
earplug ['ɪəplʌg] *n* tapón *m para los oídos*.
earring ['ɪərɪŋ] *n* pendiente *m*.
earshot ['ɪəʃɒt]. **1** out of earshot, *phr* fuera del alcance del oído. **2** within earshot, al alcance del oído.
earth [ɜːθ] **1** *n* (*gen*) tierra: *the rocket returned to Earth,* el cohete volvió a la Tierra; *the highest mountain on earth,* la montaña más alta de la tierra; *plant the seeds in damp earth,* siembra las semillas en tierra húmeda. **2** GB toma de tierra, tierra. **3** GB (*of fox, badger*) madriguera. – **4** *t* GB conectar a tierra.
● **to come back/down to earth,** *fig* volver a la realidad. ‖ **to cost the earth,** costar un ojo de la cara, costar un riñón. ‖ **to feel/look like nothing on earth,** *fam* estar fatal. ‖ **to promise sb. the earth,** prometer a algn. el oro y el moro. ‖ **to run to earth,** acorralar. ‖ **to run sb./sth. to earth,** dar con algn./algo. ‖ **what/ where/who** (*etc*) **on earth ...?,** *fam* ¿qué/dónde/quién (*etc*) demonios ...?
▲ A menudo se escribe con mayúscula cuando se refiere al planeta Tierra.
earthbound ['ɜːθbaʊnd] **1** *adj* (*confined to Earth*) que no puede despegar; (*heading for Earth*) que se dirige hacia la Tierra. **2** *fig* (*dull*) corriente, poco imaginativo,-a, prosaico,-a.
earthen ['ɜːðən] **1** *adj* (*of earth*) de tierra. **2** (*of baked clay*) de barro, de arcilla.
earthenware ['ɜːðənweəʳ] **1** *n* loza. – **2** *adj* de arcilla, de barro.
earthiness ['ɜːθɪnəs] *n* desinhibición *f*.
earthling ['ɜːθlɪŋ] *n* terrícola *mf*.
earthly ['ɜːθlɪ] **1** *adj* (*on earth*) terrenal. **2** *fam* posible.
● **not to have an earthly,** *fam* no tener ninguna posibilidad, tenerlo muy negro. ‖ **to be/see no earthly reason to,** no haber/ver razón alguna para. ‖ **to be no earthly use,** no servir para nada.
earthquake ['ɜːθkweɪk] *n* terremoto.
earthshattering ['ɜːθʃætərɪŋ] *adj* trascendental.
earthward ['ɜːθwəd] *adj* hacia la tierra.
earthworm ['ɜːθwɜːm] *n* lombriz *f*.
earthy ['ɜːθɪ] **1** *adj* (*colour*) terroso,-a; (*smell*) a tierra. **2** (*frank, straightforward*) desinhibido,-a: *an earthy sense of humour,* un sentido del humor desenfadado.
▲ *comp* **earthier,** *superl* **earthiest**.
earwig ['ɪəwɪg] *n* tijereta.
ease [iːz] **1** *n* (*lack of difficulty*) facilidad *f*: *she jumped over the fence with ease,* saltó la valla con facilidad; *for ease*

of access, para facilitar el acceso. **2** (*natural manner*) soltura, naturalidad *f*, desenvoltura: *he handled the situation with ease,* manejó la situación con soltura. **3** (*freedom from pain*) alivio: *the medicine will bring immediate ease,* la medicina te aliviará de inmediato. **4** (*leisure, affluence*) comodidad *f*, desahogo: *a life of ease,* una vida cómoda, una vida desahogada. – **5** *t* (*relieve, alleviate*) aliviar (**of,** de), calmar: *the drug eased the pain,* la droga alivió el dolor. **6** (*improve*) mejorar, facilitar; (*make easier*) facilitar. **7** (*move gently*) mover con cuidado: *we eased the old lady into the car,* metimos a la anciana en el coche con cuidado; *she eased the bandage off as gently as possible,* quitó la venda con el mayor cuidado. **8** (*loosen*) aflojar. – **9** *i* (*pain*) aliviarse, calmarse, disminuir; (*tension etc*) disminuir. **10** (*become easier*) mejorar.
◆ **to ease off / ease up 1** (*pain*) aliviarse, calmarse, disminuir; (*tension etc*) disminuir; (*rain*) amainar: *the amount of work has eased off,* el volumen de trabajo ha disminuido; *the rain began to ease up,* la lluvia empezó a amainar. **2** (*slow down*) ir más despacio. ‖ **to ease up on** *t insep fam* (*go easy, be more moderate*) aflojar, no pasarse con: *ease up on the work!,* ¡deja de trabajar tanto!; *ease up on the children!,* ¡no riñas tanto a los niños!
● **at ease!,** MIL ¡descansen! ‖ **to stand at ease,** MIL quedarse en posición de descanso. ‖ **to be ill at ease,** sentirse incómodo,-a, sentirse molesto,-a. ‖ **to be at (one's) ease / feel at (one's) ease,** estar cómodo,-a, sentirse a gusto, sentirse a sus anchas. ‖ **to ease sb.'s mind,** tranquilizar a algn. ‖ **to put sb. at their ease,** lograr que algn. se sienta cómodo,-a. ‖ **to put/set sb.'s mind at ease,** tranquilizar a algn. ‖ **to take one's ease,** *fml* tomarse un respiro.
■ **ease of mind,** tranquilidad *f*.
easel ['iːzəl] *n* caballete *m*.
easily ['iːzɪlɪ] **1** *adv* (*without difficulty*) fácilmente, con facilidad. **2** (*by far*) con mucho; (*without doubt*) sin duda: *this is easily the best flat we've seen,* es con mucho el mejor piso que hemos visto. **3** (*possibly*) fácilmente, perfectamente.
easiness ['iːzɪnəs] **1** *n* (*of task*) facilidad *f*. **2** (*of manner*) soltura, naturalidad *f*.
east [iːst] **1** *adj* (*gen*) este, oriental; (*wind*) del este: *I'm from the East Coast,* soy de la costa este; *a cold east wind,* un viento frío del este. – **2** *adv* hacia el este, en dirección este: *they headed east,* se dirigieron al este; *the room faces east,* la habitación da al este; *Liverpool is east of Manchester,* Liverpool está al este de Manchester. – **3** *n* (*gen*) este *m*. **4 the East,** (*Asia*) Oriente *m*; (*Eastern Europe*) el Este *m*.
■ **East End,** *zona popular del este de Londres*. ‖ **East Ender,** *persona del este de Londres*. ‖ **the Far East,** el Lejano Oriente. ‖ **the Middle East,** Oriente Medio.
eastbound ['iːstbaʊnd] *adj* (*train*) que va en dirección este; (*carriageway*) en dirección este.
Easter ['iːstəʳ] **1** *n* REL Pascua, Pascua de Resurrección. **2** (*holiday*) Semana Santa.
■ **Easter egg,** huevo de Pascua. ‖ **Easter Sunday,** Domingo de Pascua, Domingo de Resurrección.
easterly ['iːstəlɪ] **1** *adj* (*to the east*) al este, hacia el este. **2** (*from the east*) del este. – **3** *n* viento del este.
▲ (*sustantivo*) *pl* **easterlies**.
eastern ['iːstən] *adj* oriental, del este.
■ **Eastern Bloc,** POL el Este *m*, bloque *m* de los países del Este.
Easterner ['iːstənəʳ] *n* US nativo,-a *del Este de los Estados Unidos*.

eastward ['iːstwəd] *adj* hacia el este.
eastwards ['iːstwədz] *adv* hacia el este.
easy ['iːzɪ] **1** *adj* (*not difficult*) fácil, sencillo: *it's an easy dish to make*, es un plato fácil de hacer; *is it easy to get a bank loan?*, ¿es fácil conseguir un crédito del banco?; *getting here was no easy matter*, llegar aquí no ha sido nada fácil; *she's really easy to talk to*, resulta fácil hablar con ella. **2** (*comfortable*) cómodo,-a, holgado,-a: *she leads a very easy life*, tiene una vida muy cómoda. **3** (*unworried, relaxed*) tranquilo,-a: *an easy temperament*, un temperamento tranquilo; *at an easy pace*, tranquilamente; *with an easy mind*, con la mente tranquila. **4** (*readily exploited, cheated*) fácil: *an easy victim*, una víctima fácil. **– 5** *adv* con cuidado, con calma: *go easy with that vase, it's valuable*, ten cuidado con aquel jarrón - es valioso; *easy on the whisky!*, ¡no te pases con el whisky!
● **easy on the ear**, agradable al oído. ‖ **easy on the eye**, agradable a la vista. ‖ **easy to please**, poco exigente. ‖ **easy come, easy go**, así como viene se va. ‖ **easy does it**, poco a poco, con cuidado. ‖ **I'm easy**, *fam* me da igual. ‖ **it's easier said than done**, del dicho al hecho hay mucho trecho. ‖ **stand easy**, MIL descansen. ‖ **take it easy!**, ¡tranquilo,-a! ‖ **to be easy as pie**, *fam* estar chupado,-a. ‖ **to go easy on sb.**, no reñir tanto a algn. ‖ **to go easy on sth.**, no pasarse con algo. ‖ **to take it easy / take things easy**, tomar(se) las cosas con calma.
■ **easy chair**, sillón *m*, butaca. ‖ **easy game / easy prey**, presa fácil. ‖ **easy listening**, música ligera. ‖ **easy money**, dinero fácil. ‖ **easy terms**, facilidades *fpl* de pago.
▲ *comp* **easier**, *superl* **easiest**.
easy-going [iːzɪg'əʊɪŋ] *adj* (*relaxed*) tranquilo,-a; (*easy to please*) fácil de complacer, poco exigente.
eat [iːt] **1** *t* comer: *I don't eat fish*, no como pescado; *he's eating an ice-cream*, está comiendo un helado; *she eats cereals for breakfast*, desayuna cereales. **– 2** *i* comer: *don't eat so quickly*, no comas tan deprisa; *we always eat at 7.00*, siempre cenamos a las 7.00; *have you eaten?*, ¿has comido? **– 3** *eats*, *npl fam* comida *sing*.
◆ **to eat away** *t sep* (*mice*) roer; (*termites*) carcomer; (*acid*) corroer; (*sea*) desgastar. ‖ **to eat into** *t insep* (*acid, rust*) corroer. **2** *fig* (*cost*) comerse: *the holiday has eaten into our savings*, las vacaciones se nos han comido parte de los ahorros. ‖ **to eat out** *i* (*lunch*) comer fuera; (*dinner*) cenar fuera. ‖ **to eat up** *t sep* (*finish food*) comerse: *eat it all up!*, ¡cómetelo todo! **2** (*consume*) consumir, tragar, devorar: *this heater eats up electricity*, esta estufa devora electricidad.
● **to be eaten up with jealousy/envy**, consumirle a uno los celos/la envidia. ‖ **to eat crow**, US *fam* humillarse. ‖ **to eat one's heart out**, morirse de envidia. ‖ **to eat humble pie**, humillarse. ‖ **to eat like a horse**, comer como una vaca. ‖ **to eat like a bird**, comer como un pajarito. ‖ **to eat one's words**, tragarse lo dicho. ‖ **to eat sb. alive**, comerse a algn. vivo,-a. ‖ **to eat sb. out of house and home**, más vale hacerle un traje a algn. ‖ **to have sb. eating out of one's hand**, tener a algn. en el bolsillo. ‖ **I'll eat my hat!**, ¡que me maten! ‖ **what's eating you?**, ¿qué mosca te ha picado?
▲ *pt* **ate**, *pp* **eaten**.
eatable ['iːtəbəl] *adj* comestible.
eaten ['iːtən] *pp* → **eat**.
eater ['iːtəʳ] *n* comedor,-ra.
● **to be a big eater**, ser un,-a comilón,-ona. ‖ **to be a fussy eater**, ser maniático,-a para la comida. ‖ **to be a slow eater**, comer lento, ser lento,-a comiendo.

eating ['iːtɪŋ] *n* el comer *m*.
■ **eating apple**, manzana de mesa. ‖ **eating disorder**, problema *m* alimentario. ‖ **eating place**, restaurante *m*.
eau de Cologne [əʊdəkə'ləʊn] *n* colonia.
eaves [iːvz] *npl* alero *m sing*.
eavesdrop ['iːvzdrɒp] *i* escuchar a escondidas (**on**, -).
▲ *pt* & *pp* **eavesdropped**, *ger* **eavesdropping**.
eavesdropper ['iːvzdrɒpəʳ] *n* fisgón,-ona.
ebb [eb] **1** *n* reflujo. **– 2** *i* (*water*) bajar. **3** *fig* disminuir, decaer.
◆ **to ebb away** *i fig* ir disminuyendo: *his strength ebbed away*, fue perdiendo las fuerzas.
● **to be at a low ebb**, *fig* estar en un punto bajo. ‖ **to be on the ebb**, estar bajando.
■ **the ebb and flow**, el flujo y reflujo. ‖ **the ebb and flow of sth.**, *fig* los cambios continuos de algo. ‖ **ebb tide**, marea menguante.
ebony ['ebənɪ] **1** *n* ébano. **– 2** *adj* de ébano.
ebullience [ɪ'bʌljəns] *n* exaltación *f*, euforia.
ebullient [ɪ'bʌljənt] *adj* exaltado,-a, eufórico,-a.
eccentric [ɪk'sentrɪk] **1** *adj* (*unusual*) excéntrico,-a, estrafalario,-a. **2** (*of circles*) excéntrico,-a. **– 3** *n* (*person*) excéntrico,-a.
eccentricity [eksen'trɪsɪtɪ] *n* excentricidad *f*.
▲ *pl* **eccentricities**.
ecclesiastic [ɪkliːzɪ'æstɪk] **1** *adj* eclesiástico,-a. **– 2** *n* eclesiástico, clérigo.
ecclesiastical [ɪkliːzɪ'æstɪkəl] *adj* eclesiástico,-a.
ECG [iːsiː'dʒiː] **1** *n* (*abbr of electrocardiograph*) electrocardiógrafo. **2** (*abbr of electrocardiogram*) electrocardiograma *m*.
echelon ['eʃəlɒn] **1** *n* MIL escalón *m*. **– 2 echelons**, *npl* (*levels*) niveles *mpl*, esferas *fpl*, estratos *mpl*, capas *fpl*.
● **in echelon**, MIL en escalafón.
echo ['ekəʊ] **1** *n* eco. **2** *fig* resonancia. **– 3** *t* repetir (**back**, -). **4** *fig* (*words*) repetir, imitar; (*opinions*) hacerse eco de. **– 5** *i* hacer eco, resonar: *the valley echoed with laughter*, la risa resonaba en el valle; *her shout echoed around the cave*, su grito resonó en la cueva.
▲ *pl* **echoes**.
éclair [ɪ'kleəʳ] *n* petisú *m* de nata.
■ **chocolate éclair**, petisú *m* con chocolate.
eclectic [ɪ'klektɪk] **1** *adj fml* ecléctico,-a. **– 2** *n* ecléctico,-a.
eclecticism [ɪ'klektɪsɪzəm] *n fml* eclecticismo.
eclipse [ɪ'klɪps] **1** *n* eclipse *m*. **– 3** *t* eclipsar. **4** *fig* eclipsar, brillar más que, hacer sombra a.
● **to be in eclipse**, *fig* estar en declive: *in the late seventies, her career was in eclipse*, al final de los años setenta, su carrera estaba en declive.
■ **lunar eclipse**, eclipse *m* lunar. ‖ **solar eclipse**, eclipse *m* solar.
ecliptic [ɪ'klɪptɪk] *n* eclíptica.
ecofriendly [ekəʊ'frendlɪ] *adj* no perjudicial para el medio ambiente, que no perjudica el medio ambiente.
ecological [iːkə'lɒdʒɪkəl] *adj* ecológico,-a.
ecologically [iːkə'lɒdʒɪklɪ] *adv* ecológicamente.
ecologist [ɪ'kɒlədʒɪst] *n* ecologista *mf*.
ecology [ɪ'kɒlədʒɪ] *n* ecología.
economic [ekə'nɒmɪk, iːkə'nɒmɪk] **1** *adj* (*gen*) económico,-a. **2** (*profitable*) rentable.
economical [ekə'nɒmɪkəl, iːkə'nɒmɪkəl] **1** *adj* (*gen*) económico,-a; (*cheap*) barato,-a. **2** (*frugal, careful, not wasteful*) económico,-a, ahorrador,-ra.
● **to be economical with sth.**, economizar en algo.

economically [ekə'nɒmɪklɪ, i:kə'nɒmɪklɪ] *adv* económicamente: *economically speaking,* en términos económicos.

economics [ekə'nɒmɪks, i:kə'nɒmɪks] **1** *n* (*science*) economía. **2** EDUC económicas *fpl*, ciencias *fpl* económicas. **- 3** *npl* (*financial aspect*) aspecto económico.

economise [ɪ'kɒnəmaɪz] *i* → **economize**.

economist [ɪ'kɒnəmɪst] *n* economista *mf*.

economize [ɪ'kɒnəmaɪz] *i* economizar (**on**, en), ahorrar (**on**, en).

economy [ɪ'kɒnəmɪ] **1** *n* (*saving*) economía, ahorro: *buying cheap batteries is a false economy,* comprarse pilas baratas sale más caro. **2** (*science*) economía; (*system*) sistema *m* económico, economía: *Spain's economy relies heavily on tourism,* la economía española depende de mucho del turismo; *experts say that the economy is recovering,* los expertos dicen que la economía se está recuperando.
■ **economy class,** AER clase *f* turista. ‖ **economy drive,** ajuste *m* económica. ‖ **economy size,** tamaño familiar.
▲ *pl economies.*

ecosystem ['i:kəʊsɪstəm] *n* ecosistema *m*.

ecstasy ['ekstəsɪ] *n* éxtasis *m*.
● **to be in ecstasies,** estar extasiado,-a. ‖ **to go into ecstasies,** extasiarse (**over**, ante), quedarse extasiado,-a (**over**, ante).
▲ *pl ecstasies.*

ecstatic [ek'stætɪk] *adj* extasiado,-a.

ECT [i:si:'ti:] *n* MED (*abbr of electro-convulsive therapy*) terapia electroconvulsiva.

ectoplasm ['ektəplæzəm] *n* ectoplasma *m*.

ECU ['eɪkju:] *abbr* (*European Currency Unit*) unidad de cuenta europea, ECU.

Ecuador ['ekwədɔ:ʳ] *n* Ecuador *m*.

Ecuadorian [ekwə'dɔ:rɪən] **1** *adj* ecuatoriano,-a. **- 2** ecuatoriano,-a.

ecumenical [i:kju'menɪkəl] *adj* ecuménico,-a.

eczema ['eksɪmə] *n* eccema *m*.

Edam ['i:dæm] *n* queso de bola.

eddy ['edɪ] **1** *n* remolino. **- 2** *i* arremolinarse.
▲ (*sustantivo*) *pl eddies*; (*verbo*) *pt & pp eddied, ger eddying.*

edelweiss ['eɪdəlvaɪs] *n* BOT edelweiss *m*.

Eden ['i:dən] (the garden of) Eden, *n* el Edén *m*.

edge [edʒ] **1** *n* (*of cliff, wood, etc*) borde *m*. **2** (*of coin, step, etc*) canto. **3** (*of knife*) filo. **4** (*of water*) orilla. **5** (*of town*) afueras *fpl: he lives on the edge of town,* vive en las afueras (del pueblo). **6** (*of paper*) margen *m*. **7** (*brink*) borde *m*. **8** (*to voice*) tono. **- 9** *t* (*supply with border*) bordear: *a garden edged with flowers,* un jardín bordeado de flores. **10** SEW ribetear. **- 11** *i* (*move in small stages*) moverse con cautela, moverse poco a poco.
◆ **to edge away** *i* alejarse poco a poco. ‖ **to edge forward** *i* avanzar lentamente, avanzar poco a poco. ‖ **to edge out** *t sep* (*displace*) eliminar, apartar, quitar: *I've been edged out of my job,* me han apartado del trabajo.
● **to be on edge,** estar nervioso,-a, tener los nervios de punta. ‖ **to be on the edge of sth.,** estar a punto de algo. ‖ **to have the edge on/over sb.,** llevar ventaja a algn. ‖ **to take the edge off sth.,** suavizar algo: *that'll take the edge off your hunger,* eso te engañará el estómago.

edgeways ['edʒweɪz] *adv* de lado.
● **to (not) get a word in edgeways,** (no) poder meter baza.

edgewise ['edʒwaɪz] *adv* → **edgeways.**

edging ['edʒɪŋ] *n* ribete *m*, orla.
■ **edging shears,** tijeras *fpl* de podar.

edgy ['edʒɪ] *adj* nervioso,-a.
▲ *comp edgier, superl edgiest.*

edible ['edɪbəl] *adj* comestible.

edict ['i:dɪkt] **1** *n* edicto. **2** JUR decreto.

edification [edɪfɪ'keɪʃən] *n fml* (*improvement of mind*) edificación *f*.

edifice ['edɪfɪs] **1** *n fml* (*building*) edificio, gran edificio. **2** *fig* estructura.

edify ['edɪfaɪ] *t fml* edificar.
▲ *pt & pp edified, ger edifying.*

edifying ['edɪfaɪɪŋ] *adj fml* edificante.

Edinburgh ['edɪnbərə] *n* Edimburgo.

edit ['edɪt] **1** *t* (*prepare for printing*) preparar para la imprenta. **2** (*correct*) corregir; (*put together*) editar. **3** (*run newspaper etc*) dirigir: *edited by,* bajo la dirección de. **4** CINEM TV montar, editar.
◆ **to edit out** *t sep* cortar.

edition [ɪ'dɪʃən] *n* edición *f*.
■ **first edition,** primera edición *f*. ‖ **limited edition,** edición *f* limitada. ‖ **revised edition,** edición *f* revisada.

editor ['edɪtəʳ] **1** *n* (*of book*) editor,-ra; (*writer*) redactor,-ra; (*proofreader*) corrector,-ra. **2** (*of newspaper etc*) director,-ra. **3** CINEM TV montador,-ra.
■ **editor in chief,** redactor,-ra jefe. ‖ **editor's note,** nota de la redacción.

editorial [edɪ'tɔ:rɪəl] **1** *adj* editorial. **- 2** *n* editorial *m*.
■ **editorial staff,** redacción *f*.

educate ['edjʊkeɪt] *t* educar, formar: *she was educated at a private school,* se educó en una escuela privada; *we must educate people about the environment,* tenemos que educar a la gente en el medio ambiente.

educated ['edjʊkeɪtɪd] *adj* culto,-a, cultivado,-a.
● **an educated guess,** una conjetura fundamentada.

education [edjʊ'keɪʃən] **1** *n* (*system of teaching*) educación *f*, enseñanza: *education is not compulsory after the age of 16,* la enseñanza no es obligatoria a partir de los 16 años. **2** (*training*) formación *f*, preparación *f*, instrucción *f*. **3** (*acquisition of knowledge*) estudios *mpl*, formación *f* académica. **4** (*theory of teaching*) pedagogía. **5** (*knowledge, culture*) cultura.
■ **university education,** estudios *mpl* universitarios. ‖ **Minister of Education,** Ministro,-a de Educación. ‖ **Ministry of Education and Science,** Ministerio de Educación y Ciencia.

educational [edjʊ'keɪʃənəl] *adj* educativo,-a.

educationalist [edʒʊ'keɪʃənəlɪst] *n* pedagogo,-a.

educationist [edʒʊ'keɪʃənɪst] *n* pedagogo,-a.

educator ['edʒʊkeɪtəʳ] *n* educador,-ra.

eel [i:l] *n* anguila.

eerie ['ɪərɪ] *adj* misterioso,-a, siniestro,-a.

efface [ɪ'feɪs] *t fml* borrar.
● **to efface os.,** pasar desapercibido,-a.

effect [ɪ'fekt] **1** *n* (*gen*) efecto: *he was acting under the effects of alcohol,* actuaba bajo los efectos del alcohol; *the effects of smoking,* los efectos del tabaco; *we tried to put out the fire, but with little effect,* tratamos de apagar el fuego, pero sin éxito. **2** (*impression*) impresión *f*, efecto: *the background gives the effect of being in the jungle,* el fondo da la impresión de estar en la selva; *don't move, or you'll spoil the effect,* no te muevas, estropearás el efecto. **- 3** *t fml* efectuar, provocar. **- 4** effects, *npl* (*property*) efectos *mpl*.
● **for effect,** para impresionar. ‖ **in effect,** (*in fact*) de

hecho; (*in use*) en vigor. ‖ **to no effect,** sin resultado alguno. ‖ **to come into effect,** entrar en vigor. ‖ **to have an effect on,** afectar, producir un efecto en: *the violence in the film had no effect on her,* la violencia de la película no la afectó. ‖ **to put sth. into effect,** aplicar algo. ‖ **to take effect,** (*drug etc*) surtir efecto, hacer efecto; (*law*) entrar en vigor. ‖ **to good effect,** con buenos resultados. ‖ **to the effect that ...,** en el sentido de que ... ‖ **or words to that effect,** o algo por el estilo. ‖ **with effect from ...,** con efecto a partir de ... ■ **side effect,** efecto secundario.

effective [ɪ'fektɪv] **1** *adj* (*successful*) eficaz: *effective ways of bringing down inflation,* métodos eficaces para reducir la inflación. **2** (*real, actual*) efectivo,-a: *effective income after taxes,* ingresos efectivos deducidos los impuestos. **3** (*operative*) vigente: *the law became effective from midnight,* la ley entró en vigor a medianoche. **4** (*impressive*) impresionante; (*striking*) llamativo,-a.

effectively [ɪ'fektɪvlɪ] **1** *adv* (*efficiently*) eficazmente. **2** (*in effect*) de hecho, en efecto.

effectiveness [ɪ'fektɪvnəs] *n* eficacia.

effectual [ɪ'fektʊəl] *adj fml* eficaz.

effectuate [ɪ'fektjʊeɪt] *t* efectuar, realizar.

effeminacy [ɪ'femɪnəsɪ] *n* afeminación *f*.

effeminate [ɪ'femɪnət] *adj* afeminado,-a.

effervesce [efə'ves] **1** *i* (*of liquids*) entrar en efervescencia. **2** *fig* (*of people*) ser efervescente, ser muy vivo,-a.

effervescence [efə'vesəns] *n* efervescencia.

effervescent [efə'vesənt] *adj* efervescente.

effete [e'fiːt] *adj* (*weak*) débil, impotente; (*feeble*) agotado,-a.

efficacious [efɪ'keɪʃəs] *adj* eficaz.

efficacy ['efɪkəsɪ] *n* eficacia.

efficiency [ɪ'fɪʃənsɪ] **1** *n* (*of person*) eficiencia, competencia. **2** (*of system, product*) eficacia. **3** (*of machine*) rendimiento.

efficient [ɪ'fɪʃənt] **1** *adj* (*person*) eficiente, competente. **2** (*system, product*) eficaz. **3** (*machine*) de buen rendimiento.

efficiently [ɪ'fɪʃəntlɪ] **1** *adv* (*of person*) eficientemente, competentemente. **2** (*of system, product*) eficazmente. **3** (*of machine*) con buen rendimiento.

effigy ['efɪdʒɪ] *n* efigie *f*.
▲ *pl* **effigies**.

efflorescence [eflɔː'resəns] *n lit* florecimiento.

effluent ['efluənt] **1** *n* (*waste matter*) aguas *fpl* residuales, residuos *mpl*. **2** (*stream*) corriente *f*.

effort ['efət] **1** *n* (*exertion*) esfuerzo: *put a bit more effort into it!,* ¡haz un poco más de esfuerzo!; *what a waste of time and effort!,* ¡vaya pérdida de tiempo y esfuerzo! **2** (*attempt, struggle*) intento, tentativa: *in an effort to combat unemployment,* en un intento de combatir el desempleo. **3** (*achievement*) obra.
● **an effort of will,** una fuerza de voluntad. ‖ **to be worth the effort,** valer la pena. ‖ **to make an effort,** hacer un esfuerzo, esforzarse: *we'll make an effort to go,* haremos un esfuerzo para ir; *she made no effort to enjoy herself,* no intentó siquiera divertirse. ‖ **to make every effort to do sth.,** no regatear medios para hacer algo, hacer todo lo posible para hacer algo.

effortless ['efətləs] *adj* fácil, sin esfuerzo.

effortlessly ['efətləslɪ] *adv* fácilmente, sin esfuerzo.

effrontery [ɪ'frʌntərɪ] *n* descaro, desfachatez *f*, frescura.

effusion [ɪ'fjuːʒən] *n* efusión *f*.

effusive [ɪ'fjuːsɪv] *adj* efusivo,-a.

effusively [ɪ'fjuːsɪvlɪ] *adv* efusivamente, con efusividad.

EFL ['iː'ef'el] *abbr* (*English as a foreign language*) inglés como idioma extranjero.

egalitarian [ɪgælɪ'teərɪən] *adj* igualitario,-a.

egalitarianism [ɪgælɪ'teərɪənɪzəm] *n* igualitarismo.

egg[1] [eg] **1** *n* (*laid by birds etc*) huevo. **2** BIOL (*ovum*) óvulo.
● **to be a bad egg,** ser una mala persona, ser un sinvergüenza. ‖ **to have egg on one's face,** quedar en ridículo. ‖ **to put all one's eggs in one basket,** jugárselo todo a una carta.
■ **boiled egg,** huevo pasado por agua. ‖ **egg cup,** huevera. ‖ **egg custard,** natillas *fpl*. ‖ **egg timer,** reloj *m* de arena. ‖ **egg white,** clara de huevo. ‖ **egg whisk,** batidor *m*. ‖ **egg yolk,** yema de huevo. ‖ **fried egg,** huevo frito. ‖ **hard-boiled egg,** huevo duro. ‖ **poached egg,** huevo escalfado. ‖ **scrambled eggs,** huevos *mpl* revueltos.

egg[2] [eg] **to egg on,** *t* animar, incitar: *everyone was egging me on to ask her out,* todos me animaban a pedirle una cita.

egghead [eghed] *n pej* intelectual *mf*.

eggnog [eg'nɒg] *n* ponche *m* de huevo.

eggplant ['egplɑːnt] *n* berenjena.

eggshell ['egʃel] *n* cáscara de huevo.
■ **eggshell china / eggshell porcelain,** porcelana fina.

ego ['iːgəʊ] **1** *n* (*in psychology*) ego. **2** *fam* amor *m* propio: *it was a blow to my ego,* fue un golpe para mi amor propio.
● **to boost sb.'s ego,** levantar la moral a algn. ‖ **to deflate sb.'s ego,** bajar los humos a algn.
■ **alter ego,** alter ego *m*. ‖ **ego trip,** autobombo.
▲ *pl* **egos**.

egocentric [iːgəʊ'sentrɪk] *adj* egocéntrico,-a.

egocentrical [iːgəʊ'sentrɪkəl] *adj* egocéntrico,-a.

egoism ['iːgəʊɪzəm] *n* egoísmo.

egoist ['iːgəʊɪst] *n* egoísta *mf*.

egoistic [egəʊ'ɪstɪk] *adj* egoísta.

egoistical [egəʊ'ɪstɪkəl] *adj* egoísta.

egotism ['iːgətɪzəm] *n* egotismo.

egotist ['iːgətɪst] *n* egoísta *mf*.

egotistic [iːgə'tɪstɪk] *adj* egoísta.

egotistical [iːgə'tɪstɪkəl] *adj* egoísta.

Egypt ['iːdʒɪpt] *n* Egipto.

Egyptian [ɪ'dʒɪpʃən] **1** *adj* egipcio,-a. – **2** *n* (*person*) egipcio,-a. **3** (*language*) egipcio.

eiderdown ['aɪdədaʊn] *n* edredón *m*.

eight [eɪt] **1** *adj* ocho. – **2** *n* ocho. **3** SP (*oarsmen*) ocho.
● **to have one over the eight,** llevar una copa de más.
▲ *Véase también* **six**.

eighteen [eɪ'tiːn] **1** *adj* dieciocho. – **2** *n* dieciocho.
▲ *Véase también* **six**.

eighteenth [eɪ'tiːnθ] **1** *adj* decimoctavo,-a. – **2** *adv* en decimoctavo lugar. – **3** *n* (*in series*) decimoctavo,-a. **4** (*fraction*) decimoctavo; (*one part*) decimoctava parte *f*.
▲ *Véase también* **sixth**.

eighth [eɪtθ] **1** *adj* octavo,-a. – **2** *adv* octavo, en octavo lugar. – **3** *n* (*in series*) octavo,-a. **4** (*fraction*) octavo; (*one part*) octava parte *f*.
▲ *Véase también* **sixth**.

eighties ['eɪtɪz] **the eighties,** *npl* los años *mpl* ochenta, los ochenta *mpl*.
● **to be in one's eighties,** tener entre ochenta y noventa años, tener ochenta y tantos años, estar en los ochenta.
▲ *Véase también* **sixties**.

eightieth ['eɪtɪɪθ] 1 *adj* octogésimo,-a. – 2 *adv* en octogésimo lugar. – 3 *n* (*in series*) octogésimo,-a. 4 (*fraction*) octogésimo; (*one part*) octogésima parte *f*.
▲ *Véase también* sixtieth.

eighty ['eɪtɪ] 1 *adj* ochenta. – 2 *n* ochenta.
▲ *Véase también* sixty.

Eire ['eərə] *n* Eire *m*.

either ['aɪðəʳ, 'iːðəʳ] 1 *pron* (*affirmative*) cualquiera: *either of them,* cualquiera de los dos; *either is fine,* cualquiera está bien. 2 (*negative*) ni el uno ni el otro, ni la una ni la otra, ninguno de los dos, ninguna de las dos: *she doesn't like either of them,* no le gusta ninguno de los dos; *I can't stand either,* no aguanto ni el uno ni el otro. – 3 *adj* cualquier: *either way, I think you should go,* de cualquier manera, creo que deberías ir; *in either case,* en cualquiera de los dos casos. 4 (*both*) cada, los dos, las dos, ambos,-as: *with a gun in either hand,* con una pistola en cada mano; *there were candelabras at either end of the table,* había candelabros en los dos extremos de la mesa. 5 (*neither*) ninguno de los dos, ninguna de las dos: *he didn't agree with either statement,* no estaba de acuerdo con ninguna de las dos afirmaciones. – 6 *conj* (*affirmative*) o: *either fruit or ice-cream,* o fruta o helado; *he'll arrive either today or tomorrow,* llegará u hoy o mañana. 7 (*negative*) ni: *I didn't go to either the wedding or the party,* no fui ni a la boda ni a la fiesta. – 8 *adv* (*after negative*) tampoco: *Ann didn't come either,* tampoco vino Ann; *I can't ski either,* yo tampoco sé esquiar; *he's not ugly, but he's not exactly good-looking either,* no es que sea feo, pero tampoco es muy guapo.

ejaculate [ɪ'dʒækjʊleɪt] 1 *i* (*eject fluid*) eyacular. 2 (*exclaim*) exclamar.

ejaculation [ɪdʒækjʊ'leɪʃən] 1 *n* (*ejection*) eyaculación *f*. 2 (*exclamation*) exclamación *f*.

eject [ɪ'dʒekt] 1 *t* (*person*) expulsar, echar: *the landlord ejected the boys from the pub,* el dueño expulsó a los chicos del pub. 2 (*thing*) expulsar. – 3 *i* AV eyectar(se).

ejection [ɪ'dʒekʃən] 1 *n* expulsión *f*. 2 AER eyección *f*.

ejector [ɪ'dʒektəʳ] *n* eyector *m*.
■ ejector seat, asiento eyectable.

eke [iːk] to eke out, 1 (*make last*) hacer alcanzar, estirar, racionar: *we had to eke out the last bit of food,* tuvimos que racionar lo que quedaba de comida; *try to eke your money out,* procura estirar el dinero.
● to eke out a living / eke out an existence, ganar lo justo para vivir.

EKG [iːkeɪ'dʒiː] *n* US → ECG.

elaborate [ɪ'læbərət] 1 *adj* (*detailed, extensive*) detallado,-a. 2 (*ornate, intricate*) muy trabajado,-a, esmerado,-a. 3 (*complex, intricate*) complicado,-a. – 4 *t* (*work out in detail, refine*) elaborar, desarrollar. – 5 *i* (*discuss in detail*) explicarse, explicar detalladamente; (*expand*) ampliar, dar más detalles, explicar con más detalles: *there's no need to elaborate,* no hace falta dar más detalles.
▲ (*verbo*) [ɪ'læbəreɪt]

elaborately [ɪ'læbərətlɪ] 1 *adv* (*in detail, extensively*) detalladamente, con todo detalle. 2 (*ornately, richly*) esmeradamente. 3 (*complexly, intricately*) de manera complicada.

elaboration [ɪlæbə'reɪʃən] 1 *n* (*working out in detail*) elaboración *f*, desarrollo. 2 (*additional detail*) complicación *f*, detalle *m*.

elapse [ɪ'læps] *i* transcurrir.

elastic [ɪ'læstɪk] 1 *adj* elástico,-a. 2 *fig* flexible. – 3 *n* elástico.
■ elastic band, goma elástica.

elasticity [ɪlæ'stɪsətɪ] 1 *n* elasticidad *f*. 2 *fig* flexibilidad *f*.

Elastoplast [ɪ'læstəplɑːst] *n* tirita.

elated [ɪ'leɪtɪd] *adj* eufórico,-a, jubiloso,-a: *the students were elated at the news,* los estudiantes se regocijaron con la noticia.

elation [ɪ'leɪʃən] *n* euforia, júbilo.

elbow ['elbəʊ] 1 *n* ANAT codo. 2 (*bend*) recodo. – 3 *t* (*jostle*) dar un codazo a, empujar con el codo.
◆ to elbow aside *t sep* apartar a codazos.
● at one's elbow, a mano. ‖ out at the elbows, raído,-a. ‖ to elbow one's way through, abrirse paso a codazos (por). ‖ to give sb. the elbow, (*dismiss*) echar a algn.; (*break up with*) romper con algn.
■ elbow grease, sudor *m*.

elbowroom ['elbəʊruːm] *n* espacio, sitio.

elder[1] ['eldəʳ] 1 *adj* mayor: *my elder brother,* mi hermano mayor; *she is the elder of my two daughters,* es la mayor de mis dos hijas. – 2 *n* mayor *m*: *he is my elder by three years,* es tres años mayor que yo. 3 REL anciano,-a. – 4 elders, *npl* ancianos,-as, mayores *mpl*: *the elders of the tribe,* los ancianos de la tribu; *we should respect our elders,* deberíamos respetar a nuestros mayores. – 5 the elder, *adj fml* el viejo: *William the elder,* William viejo.
■ elder statesman, viejo estadista *m*.

elder[2] ['eldəʳ] *n* BOT saúco.

elderberry ['eldəbærɪ] *n* baya del saúco.
▲ *pl* elderberries.

elderly ['eldəlɪ] 1 *adj* mayor, anciano,-a. – 2 the elderly, *n* los ancianos *mpl*.

eldest ['eldɪst] 1 *adj* mayor: *David is my eldest son,* David es mi hijo mayor. – 2 *n* el mayor, la mayor: *my eldest has just had a baby,* mi hija mayor acaba de dar a luz.

elect [ɪ'lekt] 1 *adj* electo,-a: *the president elect,* el presidente electo. – 2 *t* (*vote for*) elegir: *Jack's been elected* (*as*) *treasurer,* Jack ha sido elegido tesorero; *they elected her* (*to be*) *Mayoress,* la eligieron alcaldesa. 3 (*choose, decide*) decidir: *she elected to take early retirement,* decidió acogerse a la jubilación anticipada. – 4 the elect, *n* los elegidos *mpl*.

election [ɪ'lekʃən] 1 *n* elección *f*: *who did you vote for at the last election?,* ¿a quién votaste en las últimas elecciones? – 2 *adj* electoral.
● to hold an election / hold elections, convocar elecciones. ‖ to stand for election, presentarse a las elecciones.
■ general election, elecciones *fpl* generales.

electioneering [ɪlekʃə'nɪərɪŋ] 1 *n* electoralismo, maniobras *fpl* electorales. – 2 *adj* electoralista.

elector [ɪ'lektəʳ] *n* elector,-ra.

electoral [ɪ'lektərəl] *adj* electoral.
■ electoral college, colegio electoral. ‖ electoral roll / electoral register, censo electoral.

electorate [ɪ'lektərət] *n* electorado.

electric [ɪ'lektrɪk] 1 *adj* eléctrico,-a. 2 *fig* electrizante.
■ electric blanket, manta eléctrica. ‖ electric blue, azul *m* eléctrico. ‖ electric chair, silla eléctrica. ‖ electric field, campo eléctrico. ‖ electric fire, estufa eléctrica. ‖ electric guitar, guitarra eléctrica. ‖ electric shock, (*treatment*) electrochoque *m*; (*accident*) descarga eléctrica. ‖ electric storm, tormenta eléctrica.

electrical [ɪ'lektrɪkəl] *adj* eléctrico,-a.
■ electrical appliance, electrodoméstico. ‖ electric engineer, ingeniero electrotécnico. ‖ electrical engineering, ingeniería electrotécnica. ‖ electrical fault, fallo eléctrico.

electrically [ɪ'lektrɪkəlɪ] *adv* por electricidad: *it's electrically operated,* funciona con electricidad.
electrician [ɪlek'trɪʃən] *n* electricista *mf.*
electricity [ɪlek'trɪsɪtɪ] *n* electricidad *f.*
■ **electricity bill,** factura de la luz. ‖ **electricity supply,** suministro eléctrico.
electrification [ɪlektrɪfɪ'keɪʃən] *n* electrificación *f.*
electrify [ɪ'lektrɪfaɪ] **1** *t* electrificar. **2** *fig* electrizar.
▲ *pt & pp* **electrified,** *ger* **electrifying.**
electrifying [ɪ'lektrɪfaɪɪŋ] *adj fig* electrizante.
electrocardiograph [ɪlektrəʊ'kɑːdɪəʊɡrɑːf] *n* MED electrocardiógrafo.
electrocardiogram [ɪlektrəʊ'kɑːdɪəʊɡræm] *n* MED electrocardiograma *m.*
electrocute [ɪ'lektrəkjuːt] *t* electrocutar: *he was electrocuted on the railway line,* se electrocutó en la vía del tren; *the prisoner is going to be electrocuted,* el preso será electrocutado.
electrode [ɪ'lektrəʊd] *n* electrodo.
electroencephalogram [ɪlektrəʊen'sefələɡræm] *n* MED electroencefalograma *m.*
electroencephalograph [ɪlektrəʊen'sefələɡrɑːf] *n* MED electroencefalógrafo.
electrolysis [ɪlek'trɒləsɪs] *n* electrólisis *f.*
electrolyte [ɪ'lektrəlaɪt] *n* electrolito, electrólito.
electromagnet [ɪlektrəʊ'mæɡnɪt] *n* electroimán *m.*
electromagnetism [ɪlektrəʊ'mæɡnɪtɪzəm] *n* electromagnetismo.
electromagnetic [ɪlektrəʊmæɡ'metɪk] *adj* electromagnético,-a.
electron [ɪ'lektrɒn] *n* electrón *m.*
■ **electron gun,** cañón *m* de electrones. ‖ **electron microscope,** microscopio electrónico.
electronic [ɪlek'trɒnɪk] *adj* electrónico,-a.
■ **electronic mail,** correo electrónico. ‖ **electronic mailbox,** buzón *m* electrónico.
electronics [ɪlek'trɒnɪks] **1** *n* (*science, technology*) electrónica. – **2** *npl* (*circuits and devices*) componentes *mpl* electrónicos.
■ **electronics industry,** industria electrónica.
elegance ['elɪɡəns] *n* elegancia.
elegant ['elɪɡənt] *adj* elegante.
elegantly ['elɪɡəntlɪ] *adv* con elegancia.
elegy ['elədʒɪ] *n* elegía.
▲ *pl* **elegies..**
element ['elɪmənt] **1** *n* CHEM elemento. **2** (*necessary part of a whole*) parte *f,* componente *m.* **3** (*important feature or quality*) factor *m.* **4** (*small amount, hint*) parte *f,* algo: *there's an element of truth in it,* hay algo de verdad en ello. **5** ELEC resistencia. **6** (*group, section*) fracción *f.* **7** (*earth, air, fire, water*) elemento. – **8 elements,** *npl* (*weather*) los elementos *mpl.* **9** (*basics*) rudimentos *mpl.*
● **to be in one's element,** estar en su elemento, estar muy a gusto. ‖ **to be out of one's element,** estar como pez fuera del agua.
elemental [elɪ'mentəl] *adj* elemental, básico,-a.
elementary [elɪ'mentərɪ] **1** *adj* (*basic*) elemental, básico,-a. **2** (*easy*) fácil, sencillo,-a.
■ **elementary education,** enseñanza primaria. ‖ **elementary mathematics,** matemáticas *fpl* elementales. ‖ **elementary particle,** partícula elemental. ‖ **elementary school,** escuela primaria.
elephant ['elɪfənt] *n* elefante *m.*
● **white elephant,** (*building etc*) elefante *m* blanco; (*unwanted object*) objeto superfluo.
elephantine [elɪ'fæntaɪn] **1** *adj* (*huge*) mastodóntico,-a, descomunal. **2** (*clumsy*) torpe, patoso,-a.

elevate ['elɪveɪt] **1** *t fml* (*raise*) elevar; (*promote*) ascender, promover. **2** *fig* (*improve in quality*) elevar.
elevated ['elɪveɪtɪd] *adj fml* (*fine, noble*) elevado,-a, noble.
■ **elevated railway / elevated railroad,** ferrocarril *m* elevado.
elevating ['elɪveɪtɪŋ] *adj* (*uplifting*) elevador,-ra, edificante.
elevation [elɪ'veɪʃən] **1** *n fml* (*nobility*) elevación *f.* **2** (*angle*) elevación *f.* **3** *fml* (*in rank*) ascenso. **4** (*height*) altitud *f,* altura. **5** *fml* (*hill, high place*) elevación *f.* **6** ARCH alzado.
elevator ['elɪveɪtə'] **1** *n* US ascensor *m.* **2** (*machine*) montacargas *m.* **3** AV timón *m* de profundidad.
eleven [ɪ'levən] **1** *adj* once. – **2** *n* once *m.* **4** SP equipo, once *m.*
▲ *Véase también* **six.**
elevenses [ɪ'levnzɪz] *npl* GB *fam* desayuno, almuerzo.
eleventh [ɪ'levənθ] **1** *adj* undécimo,-a. – **2** *adv* en undécimo lugar. – **3** *n* (*in series*) undécimo,-a, onceno,-a. **4** (*fraction*) onceavo, undécimo; (*one part*) onceava parte *f,* undécima parte *f.*
● **at the eleventh hour,** en el último momento.
▲ *Véase también* **sixth.**
elf [elf] *n* duende *m,* elfo.
▲ *pl* **elves** [elvz].
elfin ['elfɪn] *adj fig* delicado,-a.
elfish ['elfɪʃ] *adj* travieso,-a.
elicit [ɪ'lɪsɪt] **1** *t fml* (*facts, information*) sonsacar, obtener: *we managed to elicit the truth from her,* logramos sonsacarle la verdad. **2** (*reaction, response*) provocar.
eligibility [elɪdʒə'bɪlɪtɪ] *n* elegibilidad *f,* idoneidad *f.*
eligible ['elɪdʒəbəl] **1** *adj* (*qualified, suitable*) idóneo,-a, apto,-a. **2** (*desirable*) deseable: *an eligible young man,* un buen partido.
● **to be eligible for sth.,** tener derecho a algo, cumplir los requisitos para algo: *you might be eligible for a grant,* puede que tengas derecho a una beca.
eliminate [ɪ'lɪmɪneɪt] **1** *t* (*remove, get rid of*) eliminar, erradicar; (*expel*) expulsar: *you must eliminate fat from your diet,* tienes que eliminar la grasa de tu dieta. **2** (*rule out*) descartar, excluir, eliminar: *that man has been eliminated from our enquiries,* hemos eliminado a aquel hombre de la investigación. **3** *fam* (*kill*) eliminar, suprimir. **4** (*knock out*) eliminar, derrotar: *they were eliminated in the first round,* fueron eliminados en la primera vuelta.
elimination [ɪlɪmɪ'neɪʃən] *n* eliminación *f: a process of elimination,* un proceso de eliminación.
élite [eɪ'liːt] **1** *n* elite *f.* – **2** *adj* exclusivo,-a, selecto,-a.
élitism [eɪ'liːtɪzəm] *n* elitismo.
élitist [eɪ'liːtɪst] *adj* elitista.
elixir [ɪ'lɪksə'] *n* elixir *m.*
Elizabethan [ɪlɪzə'biːθən] **1** *adj* isabelino,-a. – **2** *n* isabelino,-a.
elk [elk] *n* GB alce *m.*
ellipsis [ɪ'lɪpsɪs] *n* elipsis *f.*
▲ *pl* **ellipses** [ɪ'lɪpsiːz].
elliptical [ɪ'lɪptɪkəl] *adj* elíptico,-a.
elm [elm] *n* olmo.
elocution [elə'kjuːʃən] *n* elocución *f: elocution lessons,* clases de elocución.
elongate ['iːlɒŋɡeɪt] *t* alargar, extender.
elongated ['iːlɒŋɡeɪtɪd] *adj* alargado,-a.
elongation [iːlɒŋ'ɡeɪʃən] *n* alargamiento, elongación *f.*
elope [ɪ'ləʊp] *i* fugarse (para casarse).
elopement [ɪ'ləʊpmənt] *n* fuga (para casarse).

eloquence ['eləkwəns] *n* elocuencia.

eloquent ['eləkwənt] *adj* elocuente.

eloquently ['eləkwəntlɪ] *adv* con elocuencia, elocuentemente.

El Salvador [el'sælvədɔːʳ] *n* El Salvador.

else [els] *adv* más, otro,-a: *anything else?,* ¿algo más?; *nothing else, thank you,* nada más, gracias; *does anyone else want to go?,* ¿alguien más quiere ir?; *nobody else cares,* a nadie más le importa; *is there someone else?,* ¿hay alguien más?; *let's go somewhere else,* vamos a otro sitio; *there's nothing else to eat,* no hay nada más para comer; *what else do you expect?,* ¿qué más esperas?; *where else have you been?,* ¿en qué otro(s) sitio(s) has estado?; *don't say anything else,* no digas nada más; *everyone else is going,* todos los demás van; *who else knows?,* ¿quién más lo sabe?; *everything else was all right,* todo lo demás estaba bien.
● **or else,** (*otherwise, if not*) si no, o; (*used as threat*) si no: *behave yourself or else ...,* pórtate bien, si no (ya verás); *hurry up or else we'll be late!,* ¡date prisa, si no llegaremos tarde!; *either you come today, or else don't bother coming,* o vienes hoy, o no te molestes en venir; *he must be drunk, or else he's gone mad,* debe de estar borracho, si no es que se ha vuelto loco. ‖ **if nothing else,** como mínimo.

elsewhere [els'weəʳ] *adv* en otro sitio, en otra parte.

elucidate [ɪ'luːsɪdeɪt] *t fml* aclarar, dilucidar, poner en claro.

elucidation [ɪluːsɪ'deɪʃən] *n* aclaración *f*, dilucidación *f*.

elude [ɪ'luːd] **1** *t* (*escape from*) escaparse de: *to elude the police, he crossed the border,* para escaparse de la policía, cruzó la frontera. **2** (*avoid*) eludir: *you can't elude your responsibilities,* no puedes eludir tus responsabilidades. **3** (*not remember*) no recordar, no acordarse; (*not understand*) no entenderse: *the title eludes me,* no me acuerdo del título; *his reasons for leaving elude me,* no entiendo por qué se fue.

elusive [ɪ'luːsɪv] **1** *adj* (*difficult to capture*) huidizo,-a, esquivo,-a, escurridizo,-a. **2** (*difficult to remember*) difícil de recordar; (*difficult to understand*) difícil de entender.

emaciated [ɪ'meɪsɪeɪtɪd] *adj* (*body*) enflaquecido,-a; (*face*) demacrado,-a.
● **to become emaciated,** (*get thin*) enflaquecer; (*waste away*) demacrarse.

emaciation [ɪmeɪsɪ'eɪʃən] *n* (*of body*) enflaquecimiento; (*of face*) demacración *f*.

emanate ['emaneɪt] *i fml* emanar (**from,** de), provenir (**from,** de), proceder (**from,** de).

emanation [emə'neɪʃən] *n* emanación *f*.

emancipate [ɪ'mænsɪpeɪt] *t* emancipar.

emancipation [ɪmænsɪ'peɪʃən] *n* emancipación *f*.

emasculate [ɪ'mæskjuleɪt] **1** *t fml* (*weaken*) debilitar. **2** (*castrate*) capar, castrar, emascular.

emasculation [ɪmæskju'leɪʃən] *n* castración *f*, emasculación *f*.

embalm [ɪm'baːm] *t* embalsamar.

embankment [ɪm'bæŋkmənt] **1** *n* (*wall, earth, etc*) terraplén *m*. **2** (*river bank*) dique *m*.

embargo [em'baːgəʊ] **1** *n* embargo, prohibición *f*: *there's an embargo on arms,* está prohibido comerciar con armas. – **2** *t* (*prohibit*) prohibir, imponer un embargo sobre. **3** (*seize*) embargar.
● **to impose/put/lay an embargo on sth.,** (*forbid trade*) imponer un embargo sobre algo; (*prohibit*) prohibir algo. ‖ **to lift/raise/remove an embargo on sth.,** levantar un embargo sobre algo.

■ **trade embargo,** embargo comercial.
▲ (*sustantivo*) *pl* **embargoes**; (*verbo*) *pt* & *pp* **embargoed,** *ger* **embargoing.**

embark [ɪm'baːk] **1** *t* (*take on board*) embarcar. – **2** *i* (*board*) embarcar (**for,** con rumbo a), embarcarse (**for,** con rumbo a): *we embarked at Bilbao,* nos embarcamos en Bilbao; *they embarked for Dover,* se embarcaron con rumbo a Dover.
◆ **to embark on** *t insep* emprender: *he decided to embark on a new career,* decidió emprender una nueva carrera.

embarkation [ɪmbaː'keɪʃən] *n* embarque *m*, embarco.

embarrass [ɪm'bærəs] *t* (*make ashamed*) avergonzar, azorar, abochornar, hacer pasar vergüenza a; (*make awkward*) desconcertar: *don't embarrass me in public!,* ¡no me hagas pasar vergüenza en público!; *it embarrasses me to talk about such things,* me da vergüenza hablar de tales cosas; *the demonstration clearly embarrassed the minister,* la manifestación desconcertó al ministro.

embarrassed [ɪm'bærəst] *adj* (*behaviour, action*) embarazoso,-a; (*person*) avergonzado,-a, violento,-a, molesto,-a: *an embarrassed laugh,* una risa nerviosa; *an embarrassed silence,* un silencio embarazoso.
● **to feel embarrassed,** tener vergüenza, pasar vergüenza, sentirse avergonzado,-a: *she felt embarrassed about what had happened,* se sintió avergonzada por lo (que había) ocurrido; *I was so embarrassed when he asked me out,* me sentí muy violenta cuando me pidió que saliera con él; *come on, don't be embarrassed!,* ¡venga, no tengas vergüenza! ‖ **to get embarrassed,** avergonzarse, azorarse, abochornarse.

embarrassing [ɪm'bærəsɪŋ] *adj* embarazoso,-a, violento,-a, desconcertante: *you've put me in a very embarrassing position,* me has puesto en una situación muy violenta; *what an embarrassing question!,* ¡vaya pregunta más embarazosa!; *how embarrassing!,* ¡qué vergüenza!; *I hate being late - it's embarrassing,* odio llegar tarde - me resulta violento.

embarrassingly [ɪm'bærəsɪŋlɪ] *adv* con vergüenza, con embarazo.

embarrassment [ɪm'bærəsmənt] **1** *n* (*state*) turbación *f*, vergüenza, desconcierto: *his large nose was the cause of much embarrassment,* su narizote le hacía pasar mucha vergüenza; *I couldn't hide my obvious embarrassment,* no pude disimular mi desconcierto; *much to her embarrassment,* para gran vergüenza suya. **2** (*person, object*) vergüenza, estorbo: *you're an embarrassment to your parents,* eres una vergüenza para tus padres. **3** (*event, situation*) disgusto, vergüenza.
● **an embarrassment of riches,** un exceso de riquezas.

embassy ['embəsɪ] *n* embajada.
▲ *pl* **embassies.**

embed [ɪm'bed] **1** *t* (*jewels, stones*) incrustar; (*weapon, nails*) clavar (**in,** en). **2** *fig* fijar, grabar: *that day was embedded in my mind,* aquel día lo tengo grabado en la mente.
▲ *pt* & *pp* **embedded,** *ger* **embedding.**

embellish [ɪm'belɪʃ] **1** *t* (*adorn*) adornar, embellecer. **2** *fig* (*add details*) adornar.

embellishment [ɪm'belɪʃmənt] *n* adorno.

ember ['embəʳ] **1** *n* brasa, ascua, rescoldo. **2** *fig* vestigio.

embezzle [ɪm'bezəl] *t* desfalcar, malversar: *he'd been embezzling money from the bank where he worked for years,* llevaba años malversando dinero del banco donde trabajaba.

embezzlement [ɪm'bezəlmənt] *n* desfalco, malversación *f*.

embezzler [ɪm'bezələ^r] *n* desfalcador,-ra, malversador,-ra.

embitter [ɪm'bɪtə^r] *t* amargar, acibarar.

embittered [ɪm'bɪtəd] *adj* amargado,-a, resentido,-a.

emblem ['embləm] *n* emblema *m*.

emblematic [emblə'mætɪk] *adj* emblemático,-a, simbólico,-a.

embodiment [ɪm'bɒdɪmənt] *n* encarnación *f*, personificación *f*.

embody [ɪm'bɒdɪ] **1** *t* (*give visible form to*) encarnar, personificar. **2** (*express*) expresar, manifestar. **3** (*include*) incorporar, incluir, abarcar, comprender.
▲ *pt & pp embodied, ger embodying.*

embolden [ɪm'bəʊldən] *t fml* envalentonar, dar confianza a, encorajar.

embolism ['embəlɪzəm] *n* embolia.

emboss [ɪm'bɒs] *t* (*leather, metal*) repujar; (*initials*) grabar en relieve.

embrace [ɪm'breɪs] **1** *n* abrazo. − **2** *t* (*hug*) abrazar, dar un abrazo a: *she embraced him lovingly*, lo abrazó tiernamente. **3** (*include*) abarcar, incluir. **4** *fml* (*accept - opportunity etc*) aprovechar; (*- offer*) aceptar. **5** *fml* (*adopt - religion etc*) convertirse a; (*- political doctrine*) adherirse a; (*- new idea*) abrazar. − **6** *i* abrazarse: *the two friends embraced*, los dos amigos se abrazaron.

embroider [ɪm'brɔɪdə^r] **1** *t* SEW bordar. − **2** *fig* adornar. − **3** *i* SEW bordar.

embroidery [ɪm'brɔɪdərɪ] **1** *n* SEW bordado. **2** *fig* adorno.

embroil [ɪm'brɔɪl] *t* enredar, liar: *they embroiled him in the argument*, lo enredaron en la discusión.
● **to be embroiled in sth.**, estar enredado,-a en algo, estar liado,-a en algo. ‖ **to become embroiled in sth.**, enredarse en algo, liarse en algo.

embryo ['embrɪəʊ] **1** *n* embrión *m*. **2** *fig* germen *m*. − **3** *adj* embrionario,-a.
● **in embryo**, en embrión.
▲ *pl embryos.*

embryonic [embrɪ'ɒnɪk] *adj* embrionario,-a.

emend [ɪ'mend] *t* corregir, enmendar.

emendation [iːmen'deɪʃən] *n* corrección *f*, enmienda.

emerald ['emərəld] **1** *n* (*stone*) esmeralda *f*. **2** (*colour*) esmeralda *m*. − **3** *adj* (de color) esmeralda.
■ **the Emerald Isle**, Irlanda.

emerge [ɪ'mɜːdʒ] **1** *i* (*come out*) emerger, aparecer, salir, surgir: *the monster emerged from the water*, el monstruo emergió del agua; *she emerged from behind a tree*, apareció de detrás de un árbol; *the Greens emerged as the only real political force*, los Verdes surgieron como la única fuerza política; *he emerged from the accident unharmed*, salió ileso del accidente. **2** (*become known*) resultar: *it emerged that ...*, resultó que ...; *no new evidence of any significance has emerged*, no se ha descubierto ninguna prueba nueva.

emergence [ɪ'mɜːdʒəns] *n* aparición *f*, surgimiento.

emergency [ɪ'mɜːdʒənsɪ] **1** *n* emergencia, crisis *f*. **2** MED caso de urgencia, caso urgente, urgencia. − **3** *adj* de emergencia, de urgencia.
● **in an emergency / in case of emergency**, en caso de emergencia.
■ **emergency exit**, salida de emergencia. ‖ **emergency landing**, aterrizaje *m* forzoso. ‖ **emergency measures**, medidas *fpl* de urgencia. ‖ **emergency room**, US urgencias *fpl*. ‖ **emergency services**, servicios *mpl* de urgencia. ‖ **emergency stop**, AUTO parada en seco. ‖ **emergency supplies**, provisiones *mpl* (para imprevistos). ‖ **emergency talks**, negociaciones *fpl* de emer-

gencia. ‖ **emergency ward**, sala de urgencias. ‖ **state of emergency**, estado de excepción.
▲ *pl emergencies.*

emergent [ɪ'mɜːdʒənt] **1** *adj* (*emerging*) emergente. **2** (*of countries, nations*) en vías de desarrollo.

emery ['emərɪ] *n* esmeril *m*.
■ **emery board**, lima de uñas. ‖ **emery paper**, papel *m* de lija, papel *m* esmerilado.

emigrant ['emɪgrənt] *n* emigrante *mf*.

emigrate ['emɪgreɪt] *i* emigrar.

emigration [emɪ'greɪʃən] *n* emigración *f*.

émigré ['emɪgreɪ] *n* emigrado,-a.

eminence ['emɪnəns] *n* eminencia.
■ **Your Eminence**, Su Eminencia.

eminent ['emɪnənt] **1** *adj* (*of person*) eminente. **2** (*of qualities*) destacado,-a.

eminently ['emɪnəntlɪ] *adv* sumamente, eminentemente.

emir [e'mɪə^r] *n* emir *m*.

emirate ['emɪrət] *n* emirato.
■ **United Arab Emirates**, Emiratos *mpl* Arabes Unidos.

emissary ['emɪsərɪ] *n* emisario,-a.
▲ *pl emissaries.*

emission [ɪ'mɪʃən] *n* emisión *f*.

emit [ɪ'mɪt] *t* (*signal, heat, light, smoke*) emitir, producir; (*sound, noise*) producir; (*smell*) despedir; (*cry*) dar.
▲ *pt & pp emitted, ger emitting.*

emotion [ɪ'məʊʃən] **1** *n* (*feeling*) sentimiento. **2** (*strong feeling*) emoción *f*: *she trembled with emotion*, temblaba de emoción.

emotional [ɪ'məʊʃənəl] **1** *adj* (*connected with feelings*) emocional, afectivo,-a: *she's got emotional problems*, tiene problemas emocionales. **2** (*moving*) conmovedor,-ra, emotivo,-a: *it's a very emotional scene*, es una escena muy conmovedora. **3** (*sensitive*) emotivo,-a, sentimental, muy sensible. **4** (*upset*) emocionado,-a, exaltado,-a.
● **to get emotional**, emocionarse, exaltarse.

emotionalism [ɪ'məʊʃənəlɪzəm] *n* emotividad *f*, sentimentalismo.

emotionally [ɪ'məʊʃənəlɪ] **1** *adv* (*psychologically*) emocionalmente: *he's emotionally disturbed*, tiene problemas emocionales. **2** (*emotively*) emotivamente, con emoción. **3** (*sentimentally*) sentimentalmente.

emotionless [ɪ'məʊʃənləs] *adj* impasible.

emotive [ɪ'məʊtɪv] *adj* emotivo,-a.

empathy ['empəθɪ] *n* empatía.

emperor ['empərə^r] *n* emperador *m*.

emphasis ['emfəsɪs] **1** *n* (*importance*) énfasis *m*, importancia: *there is more emphasis on coursework than exams*, se le concede más importancia al trabajo de curso que a los exámenes. **2** LING acento, énfasis *m*.
● **to lay/place/put emphasis on sth.**, hacer hincapié en algo, poner énfasis en algo.
▲ *pl emphases* ['emfəsiːz].

emphasize ['emfəsaɪz] **1** *t* (*of words*) enfatizar, poner énfasis en: *he emphasized the word "not"*, puso énfasis en la palabra "no". **2** (*stress importance*) hacer hincapié en, enfatizar, subrayar, destacar, recalcar, insistir en: *she emphasized the importance of punctuality*, hizo hincapié en la importancia de la puntualidad; *I really must emphasize this point*, debo insistir en este punto. **3** (*highlight*) poner de relieve; (*bring out*) resaltar: *the report emphasizes the need for safety measures*, el informe pone de relieve la necesidad de medidas de seguridad;

that colour emphasizes your eyes, ese color te resalta los ojos.

emphatic [em'fætɪk] **1** *adj* (*forceful - tone, gesture*) enfático,-a, enérgico,-a. **2** (*insistent - refusal, rejection, assertion*) categórico,-a, rotundo,-a: *an emphatic reply,* una respuesta rotunda; *she was most emphatic that she should speak to you,* insistió en que tenía que hablar con usted. **3** (*definite, clear*) rotundo,-a: *an emphatic victory,* una victoria rotunda.

emphatically [ɪm'fætɪklɪ] **1** *adv* (*forcefully*) enérgicamente, en tono enfático. **2** (*definitely*) categóricamente, rotundamente.

empire ['empaɪə'] *n* imperio: *the British Empire,* el Imperio Británico.

empirical [em'pɪrɪkəl] *adj* empírico,-a.

empiricism [em'pɪrɪsɪzəm] *n* empirismo.

empiricist [em'pɪrɪsɪst] *n* empírico,-a.

emplacement [ɪm'pleɪsmənt] *n* emplazamiento.

employ [ɪm'plɔɪ] **1** *n fml* empleo. **– 2** *t* (*give work to*) emplear; (*appoint*) contratar: *the firm employs 50 workers,* la empresa emplea a 50 trabajadores; *we've just employed someone,* acabamos de contratar a alguien; *she was employed to enrol students,* la contrataron para matricular a los estudiantes; *he was employed as a waiter,* trabajaba de camarero; *you're employed to clean the house,* te pagamos para limpiar la casa. **3** *fml* (*make use of, use*) emplear, usar: *he had to employ drastic measures,* tuvo que emplear medidas drásticas. **4** (*occupy*) ocupar: *looking after his birds employs a lot of his time,* cuidar los pájaros le ocupa mucho tiempo.
● **to be in sb.'s employ,** ser empleado de algn., trabajar para algn.

employable [ɪm'plɔɪəbl] *adj que reúne las condiciones para ser contratado: when you're over 50 you're no longer employable,* a partir de los cincuenta ya no te quieren contratar.

employed [em'plɔɪd] **1** *adj* (*in work*) empleado,-a. **2** (*busy*) ocupado,-a.

employee [em'plɔɪiː, emplɔɪ'iː] *n* empleado,-a.

employer [em'plɔɪə'] **1** *n* (*manager, boss*) empresario,-a; (*of domestic worker*) patrón,-ona. **2** (*company, organization*) empresa, organismo.

employment [em'plɔɪmənt] **1** *n* (*work*) trabajo; (*availability of work*) empleo: *the new factory will provide employment for local people,* la nueva fábrica dará trabajo a la gente del pueblo; *are you in regular employment?,* ¿tienes un trabajo fijo? **2** (*use*) empleo, uso.
■ **employment agency,** agencia de trabajo, agencia de colocaciones. ‖ **employment exchange,** bolsa de trabajo. ‖ **full employment,** pleno empleo.

emporium [ɪm'pɔːrɪəm] *n fml* emporio (comercial), gran almacén *m*.

empower [ɪm'paʊə'] *t fml* autorizar, facultar, habilitar: *the new law empowered police to detain suspects for 7 days,* la nueva ley autorizó a la policía a detener a los sospechosos durante 7 días.

empress ['emprəs] *n* emperatriz *f*.

emptiness ['emptɪnəs] **1** *n* (*nothingness*) vacío. **2** (*meaninglessness*) vaciedad *f*, vacuidad *f*.

empty ['emptɪ] **1** *adj* (*gen*) vacío,-a; (*place*) desierto,-a; (*house*) desocupado,-a, deshabitado,-a; (*seat, table, palce*) libre, desocupado: *the roads were empty,* las carreteras estaban desiertas; *the pub is almost empty,* el pub está casi vacío; *see if you can find an empty seat,* a ver si encuentras un asiento libre. **2** *fam* (*hungry*) hambriento,-a: *ten minutes after a Chinese meal I feel empty again,*

diez minutos después de una comida china vuelvo a tener hambre. **3** (*purposeless*) vano,-a, inútil; (*meaningless*) carente de sentido; (*words, threats, promises*) vano,-a: *empty threats,* amenazas vanas; *her life was empty,* su vida carecía de sentido. **– 4** *t* vaciar: *empty your pockets,* vacía tus bolsillos; *he emptied the bottle in one go,* vació la botella de un trago; *his speech emptied the hall,* su discurso dejó la sala vacía; *he emptied the box into the dustbin,* vació la caja en el cubo de la basura. **– 5** *i* vaciarse: *the cinema slowy began to empty,* el cine se fue vaciando poco a poco. **6** (*of rivers*) desembocar (**into,** en). **– 7** empties, *npl* envases *mpl*, cascos *mpl*.
▲ *comp* **emptier,** *superl* **emptiest.**

empty-handed ['emptɪ'hændɪd] *adj* con las manos vacías.

empty-headed ['emptɪ'hedɪd] *adj* (*foolish*) tonto,-a; (*frivolous*) frívolo,-a: *an empty-headed boy,* un cabeza hueca.

emu ['iːmjuː] *n* emú *m*.

emulate ['emjəleɪt] *t fml* emular: *she's always trying to emulate her peers,* siempre intenta emular a sus coetáneos.

emulsifier [ɪ'mʌlsɪfaɪə'] *n* emulsionante *m*, emulsivo.

emulsify [ɪ'mʌlsɪfaɪ] *t* emulsionar.
▲ *pt & pp* **emulsified,** *ger* **emulsifying.**

emulsion [ɪ'mʌlʃən] *n* (*gen*) emulsión *f*.
■ **emulsion paint,** pintura para techos y paredes.

enable [ɪ'neɪbəl] *t* permitir: *this will enable us to cut costs,* esto nos permitirá reducir gastos.

enabling [ɪ'neɪblɪŋ] *adj* habilitante.
■ **enabling legislation,** legislación *f que permite hacer algo: the enabling legislation has not yet been passed,* la legislación que lo permitiría aún no ha sido aprobada.

enact [ɪ'nækt] **1** *t* (*law*) promulgar. **2** (*play*) representar.

enamel [ɪ'næməl] **1** *n* esmalte *m*. **– 2** *t* esmaltar.

enamoured [ɪ'næməd] *adj* enamorado,-a.
● **to be enamoured of/with sth.,** estar entusiasmado,-a con algo, encantarle algo a uno,-a.

encamp [ɪn'kæmp] *i* acampar.

encampment [ɪn'kæmpmənt] *n* campamento.

encapsulate [ɪn'kæpsjʊleɪt] *t* encapsular.

enchant [ɪn'tʃɑːnt] **1** *t* (*delight*) encantar, cautivar: *the little girl's voice enchanted the audience,* la voz de la niña cautivó al público. **2** (*cast spell on*) hechizar.

enchanted [ɪn'tʃɑːntɪd] *adj* encantado,-a.
● **to be enchanted by/with sth.,** estar encantado,-a con algo.

enchanter [ɪn'tʃɑːntə'] *n* hechicero, mago.

enchanting [ɪn'tʃɑːntɪŋ] *adj* encantador,-ra.

enchantment [ɪn'tʃɑːntmənt] **1** *n* (*delight*) encanto. **2** (*spell*) hechizo.

enchantress [ɪn'tʃɑːntrəs] *n* hechicera.

encircle [ɪn'sɜːkəl] *t* rodear, cercar.

enclave ['enkleɪv] *n* enclave *m*.

enclose [ɪn'kləʊz] **1** *t* (*surround*) encerrar; (*with wall or fence*) cercar, rodear. **2** (*include in letter*) adjuntar: *please find cheque enclosed,* le envío talón adjunto; *enclosed herewith,* adjunto a la presente.

enclosed [ɪn'kləʊzd] *adj* cerrado.
■ **enclosed order,** REL orden *f* de clausura.

enclosure [ɪn'kləʊʒə'] **1** *n* (*land*) cercado; (*area*) recinto. **2** (*act*) cercamiento, encierro. **3** (*with letter*) anexo, documento adjunto.

encompass [ɪn'kʌmpəs] *t* (*include*) abarcar.

encore ['ɒŋkɔː'] **1** *interj* ¡otra! **– 2** *n* repetición *f*, bis *m*.

encounter [ɪn'kaʊntə'] **1** *n* encuentro. **– 2** *t* (*meet*) encontrar, encontrarse con; (*be faced with*) tropezar con.

encourage [ɪnˈkʌrɪdʒ] **1** *t* (*cheer, inspire*) animar, alentar: *my parents encouraged me to learn to drive,* mis padres me animaron a aprender a conducir; *when he saw his friends, it encouraged him to finish the race,* ver a sus amigos le animó a terminar la carrera; *don't encourage him!,* ¡no le des cuerda! **2** (*develop, stimulate*) fomentar, favorecer, estimular: *we need to encourage attendance,* hay que fomentar la asistencia; *the management encourages rivalry,* la dirección estimula la rivalidad.

encouragement [ɪnˈkʌrɪdʒmənt] **1** *n* (*act*) aliento, ánimo. **2** (*development*) fomento, estímulo.

encouraging [ɪnˈkʌrɪdʒɪŋ] *adj* (*hopeful*) alentador,-ra; (*promising*) prometedor,-ra.

encouragingly [ɪnˈkʌrɪdʒɪŋlɪ] *adv* de un modo alentador.

encroach [ɪnˈkrəʊtʃ] **to encroach on**, *i* (*territory, property*) pasar los límites de, invadir; (*rights*) cercenar, usurpar, abusar; (*time, freedom*) quitar, robar.

encroachment [ɪnˈkrəʊtʃmənt] *n* (*of land*) invasión *f*; (*of rights etc*) cercenamiento, usurpación *f*, abuso; (*of time*) abuso.

encrust [ɪnˈkrʌst] *t* incrustar.

encrusted [ɪnˈkrʌstɪd] *adj* incrustado,-a (**with,** de).

encumber [ɪnˈkʌmbəʳ] **1** *t* (*physically*) estorbar. **2** (*financially*) gravar.

encumbrance [ɪnˈkʌmbrəns] **1** *n* estorbo. **2** gravamen *m*.

encyclopaedia [ensaɪkləˈpiːdɪə] *n* enciclopedia.

encyclopaedic [ensaɪkləˈpiːdɪk] *adj* enciclopédico,-a.

encyclopedia [ensaɪkləˈpiːdɪə] *n* enciclopedia.

encyclopedic [ensaɪkləˈpiːdɪk] *adj* enciclopédico,-a.

end [end] **1** *n* (*extremity - of rope*) cabo; (- *of street, room, queue*) final *m*; (- *of table, sofa, bed, line*) extremo; (- *of stick, tail, hair*) punta; (- *of box*) lado: *we sat at opposite ends of the table,* estábamos sentados en los extremos opuestos de la mesa; *let's meet at the end of the road,* quedamos al final de la calle. **2** (*final part, finish*) fin *m*, final *m*, conclusión *f*: *have you got enough money to last until the end of the month?,* ¿tienes suficiente dinero para llegar hasta final del mes?; *what did you think of the end of the film?,* ¿qué te pareció el final de la película? **3** (*aim*) objeto, objetivo, fin *m*: *for political ends,* para fines políticos. **4** (*remnant*) resto, cabo; (*of cigarette*) colilla. **5** *euph* muerte *f*. **6** (*on telephone*) lado (de la línea). **7** (*half of sports pitch*) lado. – **8** *adj* final, último,-a: *they live in the end house,* viven en la última casa. – **9** *t* (*conclude*) acabar, terminar. **10** (*stop*) terminar, poner fin a, acabar con: *they decided to end the strike,* decidieron terminar la huelga. – **11** *i* acabar, terminar: *when does term end?,* ¿cuándo acaba el trimestre?; *our journey ends here,* nuestro viaje acaba aquí.

◆ **to end in** *i* acabar en, terminar con: *the word ends in "-ing",* la palabra acaba en "-ing"; *the holiday ended in disaster,* las vacaciones acabaron mal. ‖ **to end off** **1** *t sep* acabar: *they ended the meal off with coffee and liqueurs,* acabaron la comida con café y licores. – **2** *i* acabar: *he ends off by saying that he misses us all,* acaba diciendo que nos echa de menos a todos. ‖ **to end up** *i* acabar, terminar, ir a parar: *if you carry on like that, you'll end up out of a job,* si continúas así, acabarás sin trabajo; *she ended up marrying him,* terminó casándose con él; *we ended up in Bournemouth,* acabamos en Bournemouth.

● **(not) to be the end of the world,** (no) ser el fin del mundo. ‖ **at the end of,** al final de. ‖ **at the end of one's tether,** hasta la coronilla. ‖ **at the end of the**

day, al fin y al cabo, al final. ‖ **end to end,** juntando los dos extremos. ‖ **in the end,** al fin. ‖ **no end,** muchísimo: *it annoys me no end,* me molesta muchísimo. ‖ **no end of,** la mar de, la tira de, cantidad de: *no end of problems,* cantidad de problemas. ‖ **on end,** (*upright*) sobre el extremo; (*continuously*) enteros,-as: *for hours on end,* durante horas y horas. ‖ **till the end of time,** para siempre más. ‖ **to be an end in itself,** ser un fin en sí mismo. ‖ **to be at a loose end,** no tener nada que hacer. ‖ **to be at an end,** estar acabado,-a. ‖ **to be the end,** ser el colmo. ‖ **to come/ draw to an end,** acabarse. ‖ **to end it all,** suicidarse. ‖ **to go to the ends of the earth,** ir hasta el fin del mundo, ir hasta los confines de la tierra. ‖ **to keep one's end up,** seguir animado,-a. ‖ **to make ends meet,** llegar a final de mes. ‖ **to put an end to sth.,** poner fin a algo, acabar con algo.

■ **end product,** producto final. ‖ **loose ends,** cabos *mpl* sueltos.

endanger [ɪnˈdeɪndʒəʳ] *t* poner en peligro.

endangered [ɪnˈdeɪndʒəd] *adj* en peligro.

■ **endangered species,** especie *f* en peligro (de extinción).

endear [ɪnˈdɪəʳ] *t* ganar las simpatías de, hacerse querer.

● **to endear os. to sb.,** granjearse el cariño de algn.

endearing [ɪnˈdɪərɪŋ] *adj* simpático,-a, atractivo,-a.

endearingly [ɪnˈdɪərɪŋlɪ] *adv* con simpatía.

endearment [ɪnˈdɪəmənt] *n* expresión *f* cariñosa, palabra *f* cariñosa.

endeavour [ɪnˈdevəʳ] **1** *n fml* esfuerzo, empeño. – **2** esforzarse, intentar, procurar.

endemic [enˈdemɪk] *adj* endémico,-a.

ending [ˈendɪŋ] **1** *n* final *m*, conclusión *f*, desenlace *m*. **2** LING terminación *f*.

endive [ˈendaɪv] *n* endibia.

■ **curly endive,** escarola.

endless [ˈendləs] **1** *adj* (*wait, questions, etc*) sin fin, interminable, eterno,-a; (*resources, patience, etc*) inacabable, inagotable: *the wait seemed endless,* la espera se hizo interminable; *I've had endless interviews,* he tenido un sinfín de entrevistas. **2** (*with ends joined*) continuo,-a.

endlessly [ˈendləslɪ] *adv* interminablemente, eternamente.

endocrine [ˈendəʊkrɪn] *adj* endocrino,-a.

■ **endocrine gland,** glándula endocrina.

endorse [ɪnˈdɔːs] **1** *t* (*of cheque etc*) endosar. **2** (*approve*) aprobar, apoyar, respaldar. **3** GB (*driving license*) escribir la sanción en.

endorsement [ɪnˈdɔːsmənt] **1** *n* (*of cheque etc*) endoso. **2** (*approval*) aprobación *f*, apoyo, respaldo. **3** AUTO nota de sanción.

endow [ɪnˈdaʊ] **1** *t* (*bless*) dotar. **2** (*give money*) dotar (de fondos).

● **to be endowed with sth.,** estar dotado,-a de algo.

endowment [ɪnˈdaʊmənt] **1** *n* (*attribute*) atributo, dote *m & f*. – **2 endowments,** *npl* (*money*) donaciones *fpl*.

■ **endowment mortgage,** hipoteca de inversión. ‖ **endowment policy,** póliza diferida.

endpaper [ˈendpeɪpəʳ] *n* guarda.

endurable [ɪnˈdjʊərəbəl] *adj* soportable, tolerable.

endurance [ɪnˈdjʊərəns] **1** *n* resistencia, aguante *m*. – **2** *adj* de resistencia.

● **beyond endurance / past endurance,** intolerable, insoportable.

■ **endurance test,** prueba de resistencia.

endure [ɪn'djʊəʳ] **1** *t* (*suffer patiently*) soportar, resistir. **2** (*bear, tolerate*) soportar, aguantar. **– 3** *i* (*continue to exist, survive*) durar, perdurar.

enduring [ɪn'djʊərɪŋ] *adj* duradero,-a, perdurable.

endways ['endweɪz] *adv* de lado, de canto.

endwise ['endwaɪz] *adv* → **endways**.

enema ['enɪmə] *n* enema *m*, lavativa.

enemy ['enəmɪ] **1** *n* enemigo,-a. **– 2** *adj* enemigo,-a.
● **to make enemies,** hacerse enemigos.
■ **enemy forces,** fuerzas *fpl* enemigas.
▲ *pl* **enemies.**

energetic [enə'dʒetɪk] *adj* enérgico,-a, activo,-a.

energetically [enə'dʒetɪklɪ] *adv* enérgicamente, con energía.

energize ['enədʒaɪz] *t* activar, dar energía a.

energy ['enədʒɪ] **1** *n* (*gen*) energía. **– 2 energies,** *npl* (*efforts*) energías *fpl*, fuerzas *fpl*.
■ **energy crisis,** crisis *f* energética.
▲ *pl* **energies.**

enervate ['enəveɪt] *t* enervar, debilitar.

enervating ['enəveɪtɪŋ] *adj* enervador,-ra, enervante.

enfeeble [ɪn'fiːbəl] *t* debilitar.

enfold [ɪn'fəʊld] **1** *t* (*embrace*) estrechar. **2** (*enclose*) envolver.

enforce [ɪn'fɔːs] **1** *t* (*force to obey*) hacer cumplir, hacer respetar: *the role of the police is to enforce the law,* el papel de la policía es hacer cumplir la ley. **2** (*impose, make happen*) imponer: *you can't enforce loyalty on your staff,* no se puede imponer la lealtad al personal.

enforceable [ɪn'fɔːsəbəl] *adj* que se puede hacer cumplir.

enforced [ɪn'fɔːst] *adj* forzado,-a, impuesto,-a.

enforcement [ɪn'fɔːsmənt] *n* imposición *f*: *the police are responsible for the enforcement of the law,* la policía es responsable de hacer cumplir la ley.

enfranchise [ɪn'fræntʃaɪz] **1** *t* POL conceder el derecho de votar. **2** (*set free*) liberar.

enfranchisement [ɪn'fræntʃɪzmənt] **1** *n* POL concesión *f* del derecho a voto. **2** liberación *f*.

engage [ɪn'geɪdʒ] **1** *t* (*hire*) contratar: *he engaged a new chauffeur,* contrató a un nuevo chófer. **2** (*take up, occupy*) ocupar, entretener: *the game engaged his attention for hours,* el juego lo ocupó durante horas. **3** (*attract*) llamar, atraer, captar. **4** *fml* (*attack*) entablar combate con. **5** AUTO (*gear*) engranar, meter; (*clutch*) apretar. **6** TECH engranar con. **– 7** *i* TECH engranar. **8** *fml* (*attack*) entablar combate.
◆ **to engage in** *i* (*take part, participate*) ocuparse en, dedicarse a: *I have no wish to engage in politics,* no deseo dedicarme a la política.
● **to engage sb. in conversation,** entablar conversación con algn. ‖ **to engage the clutch,** embragar.

engaged [ɪn'geɪdʒd] **1** *adj* (*to be married*) prometido,-a: *we're engaged,* estamos prometidos. **2** (*busy*) ocupado,-a: *sorry, I'm otherwise engaged,* lo siento, tengo un compromiso. **3** (*of toilet*) ocupado,-a.
● **to be engaged,** (*of telephone*) estar comunicando. ‖ **to get engaged,** prometerse.
■ **engaged tone,** (*telephone*) señal *f* de estar comunicando.

engagement [ɪn'geɪdʒmənt] **1** *n* (*to be married*) petición *f* de mano; (*period*) noviazgo: *they announced their engagement at the party,* anunciaron su compromiso en la fiesta. **2** (*appointment*) compromiso, cita: *I have a prior engagement,* tengo una cita previa. **3** MIL combate *m*. **4** (*employment*) contrato, empleo.

■ **engagement ring,** anillo de compromiso.

engaging [ɪn'geɪdʒɪŋ] *adj* atractivo,-a, simpático,-a, encantador,-ra.

engagingly [ɪn'geɪdʒɪŋlɪ] *adv* atractivamente, simpáticamente.

engender [ɪn'dʒendəʳ] *t fml* engendrar.

engine ['endʒɪn] **1** *n* motor *m*. **2** (*of train*) máquina, locomotora.
■ **engine driver,** maquinista *mf*. ‖ **engine room,** sala de máquinas.

engineer [endʒɪ'nɪəʳ] **1** *n* (*graduate*) ingeniero,-a; (*technician*) técnico,-a. **2** US maquinista *mf*. **– 3** *t* (*contrive*) maquinar, tramar, urdir: *you engineered the whole thing,* tú lo maquinaste todo. **4** (*plan as engineer*) crear por ingeniería.
■ **Royal Engineers,** Cuerpo de Ingenieros.

engineering [endʒɪ'nɪərɪŋ] *n* ingeniería.

England ['ɪŋglənd] *n* Inglaterra.

English ['ɪŋglɪʃ] **1** *adj* inglés,-esa. **– 2** *n* (*language*) inglés *m*. **– 3 the English,** *npl* los ingleses *mpl*.
■ **English breakfast,** desayuno inglés. ‖ **the English Channel,** el Canal *m* de la Mancha.

Englishman ['ɪŋglɪʃmən] *n* inglés *m*.
▲ *pl* **Englishmen.**

English-speaking ['ɪŋglɪʃspiːkɪŋ] *adj* de habla inglesa.

Englishwoman ['ɪŋglɪʃwʊmən] *n* inglesa.
▲ *pl* **Englishwomen.**

engrave [ɪn'greɪv] *t* (*gen*) grabar.

engraver [ɪn'greɪvəʳ] *n* grabador,-ra.

engraving [ɪn'greɪvɪŋ] **1** *n* (*picture*) grabado. **2** (*art*) grabación *f*.

engross [ɪn'grəʊs] **1** *t* (*occupy completely*) absorber.

engrossed [ɪn'grəʊst] *adj* absorto,-a (**in,** en): *she was engrossed in her work,* estaba absorta en su trabajo.
● **to become engrossed in sth.,** enfrascarse en algo.

engrossing [ɪn'grəʊsɪŋ] *adj* fascinante, apasionante.

engulf [ɪn'gʌlf] *t* envolver.

enhance [ɪn'hɑːns] *t* (*beauty, taste*) realzar; (*quality, performance, chances*) mejorar; (*power, reputation, value*) aumentar. **2** COMPUT procesar.

enhancement [ɪn'hɑːnsmənt] *n* (*of beauty, taste*) realce *m*; (*of quality, performance*) mejora; (*of value*) aumento.

enigma [ɪ'nɪgmə] *n* enigma *m*.

enigmatic [enɪg'mætɪk] *adj* enigmático,-a.

enjoy [ɪn'dʒɔɪ] **1** *t* (*get pleasure from*) disfrutar de; (*like*) gustarle a uno: *he enjoys life to the full,* disfruta de la vida al máximo; *did you enjoy the show?,* ¿te gustó el espectáculo?; *I enjoy swimming,* me gusta nadar; *I hope you enjoy your stay,* (espero) que tengas una buena estancia. **2** (*benefit from*) gozar de, tener: *they enjoy a high standard of living,* gozan de un alto nivel de vida.
● **enjoy your meal,** que aproveche. ‖ **to enjoy os.,** divertirse, pasarlo bien: *enjoy yourself!,* ¡pásalo bien!, ¡que te diviertas!; *the children thoroughly enjoyed themselves,* los niños se lo pasaron la mar de bien.

enjoyable [ɪn'dʒɔɪəbəl] *adj* agradable, divertido,-a.

enjoyably [ɪn'dʒɔɪəblɪ] *adv* de manera agradable.

enjoyment [ɪn'dʒɔɪmənt] *n* placer *m*, goce *m*, disfrute *m*, gusto: *the enjoyment on their faces,* el placer en sus caras.
● **to spoil sb.'s enjoyment,** quitarle el gusto a algn.

enlarge [ɪn'lɑːdʒ] **1** *t* (*gen*) extender, aumentar, ampliar; (*photograph*) ampliar. **– 2** *i* extenderse, aumentar, ampliarse.
◆ **to enlarge on** *t insep* extenderse sobre, explicar con más detalles.

enlargement [ɪnˈlɑːdʒmənt] **1** n (photograph) ampliación f. **2** extensión f, aumento, ampliación f.
enlarger [ɪnˈlɑːdʒəʳ] n (photo) ampliadora.
enlighten [ɪnˈlaɪtən] **1** t (free from ignorance) iluminar, ilustrar. **2** (inform) informar, instruir.
● **to enlighten sb. about/on sth.**, aclararle algo a algn.
enlightened [ɪnˈlaɪtənd] **1** adj (factually well-informed) bien informado,-a; (learned) culto,-a, ilustrado,-a. **2** (tolerant) liberal, tolerante.
enlightening [ɪnˈlaɪtənɪŋ] adj instructivo,-a, informativo,-a.
enlightenment [ɪnˈlaɪtənmənt] **1** n fml (act) aclaración f, explicación f. **2** (liberalism) tolerancia. **3** the Enlightenment, la Ilustración f.
■ **the Age of Enlightenment**, el Siglo de las Luces, el Siglo de la Ilustración f.
enlist [ɪnˈlɪst] **1** t MIL alistar, reclutar. **2** (help, support, etc) conseguir, lograr: we enlisted their help, conseguimos su ayuda. – **3** i MIL alistarse.
enlisted [ɪnˈlɪstɪd] adj MIL alistado,-a.
■ **enlisted man**, US soldado raso, soldado de tropa.
enliven [ɪnˈlaɪvən] t avivar, animar.
enmity [ˈenmɪtɪ] n enemistad f, hostilidad f.
▲ pl enmities.
enormity [ɪˈnɔːmɪtɪ] **1** n fam (enormousness) enormidad f, inmensidad f, magnitud f. **2** (extreme wickedness) atrocidad f. **3** fml (crime) atrocidad f, barbaridad f.
▲ pl enormities.
enormous [ɪˈnɔːməs] adj enorme, inmenso,-a, descomunal: they live in an enormous house, viven en una casa enorme; we made an enormous paella, hicimos una paella enorme.
enormously [ɪˈnɔːməslɪ] adv enormemente: The Beatles are still enormously popular, los Beatles aún son enormemente populares; you've changed enormously, has cambiado muchísimo.
enormousness [ɪˈnɔːməsnəs] n enormidad f, inmensidad f, magnitud f.
enough [ɪˈnʌf] **1** adj bastante, suficiente: I think there are enough chairs for everyone, creo que hay bastantes sillas para todos; have you got enough money?, ¿tienes suficiente dinero?; I didn't have enough time to finish, no tuve tiempo suficiente para acabar; she had enough photocopies, tenía bastantes fotocopias. – **2** adv bastante, suficientemente: is it big enough?, ¿es bastante grande?; you aren't old enough, no eres bastante mayor; he's not good enough for the first team, no es lo suficientemente bueno para el primer equipo; she seemed honest enough, parecía bastante honesta. – **3** pron lo bastante, lo suficiente: do you have enough to live on?, ¿tienes lo suficiente para vivir?; that'll be enough, con eso ya hay bastante; I've got enough to be getting on with, tengo bastante para ir haciendo; you've drunk more than enough, has bebido más que suficiente; it was enough to drive you round the bend, era para volverse loco.
● **enough is enough!**, ¡ya está!, ¡basta! ‖ enough said, no digas más, no hace falta que digas más. ‖ oddly enough / curiously enough / strangely enough, por extraño que parezca, curiosamente. ‖ to have had enough (of sth./sb.), estar harto,-a (de algo/algn.).
enquire [ɪŋˈkwaɪəʳ] **1** t preguntar. – **2** i preguntar, informarse. **3** JUR investigar (into, -).
enquiry [ɪŋˈkwaɪərɪ] **1** n pregunta. **2** JUR investigación f.
● **to make enquiries**, preguntar, informarse. ‖ "enquiries", "información".

■ **enquiry desk**, información f.
▲ pl enquiries.
enrage [ɪnˈreɪdʒ] t enfurecer.
enrich [ɪnˈrɪtʃ] t enriquecer.
enrol [ɪnˈrəʊl] **1** t matricular, inscribir. – **2** i matricularse, inscribirse, apuntarse.
▲ pt & pp enrolled, ger enrolling.
enroll [ɪnˈrəʊl] t US → enrol.
enrollment [ɪnˈrəʊlmənt] n US → enrolment.
enrolment [ɪnˈrəʊlmənt] n matrícula, inscripción f.
ensemble [ɒnˈsɒmbəl] n conjunto.
ensign [ˈensaɪn] **1** n (flag) bandera, pabellón m. **2** US (naval officer) alférez m.
enslave [ɪnˈsleɪv] t esclavizar.
ensue [ɪnˈsjuː] **1** i (follow) seguir. **2** (result) resultar (from, de).
ensuing [ɪnˈsjuːɪŋ] adj consiguiente, subsiguiente.
ensure [ɪnˈʃʊəʳ] **1** t (make sure) asegurarse: please ensure that no-one enters this room, asegúrate de que nadie entre en esta habitación. **2** (assure) asegurar: the publicity campaign assured commercial success, la campaña publicitaria aseguraba el éxito comercial.
entail [ɪnˈteɪl] **1** t (involve, mean) suponer, implicar; (make necessary, bring about) ocasionar, acarrear: moving house entails great expense, cambiar de casa acarrea muchos gastos. **2** JUR vincular. – **3** n JUR vínculo.
entangle [ɪnˈtæŋgəl] **1** t enredar, enmarañar. **2** fig enredar, involucrar.
● **to get/become entangled in sth.**, enredarse en algo; fig enredarse en algo, verse involucrado,-a en algo.
entanglement [ɪnˈtæŋgəlmənt] **1** n (gen) enredo. **2** (in barbed wire) alambrada.
enter [ˈentəʳ] **1** t (gen) entrar en: she entered the room, entró en la habitación; he entered my life, entró en mi vida. **2** (join) ingresar en; (school etc) matricularse en; (army etc) alistarse en. **3** (participate) participar en, tomar parte en; (register) inscribirse en: how many people have entered the race?, ¿cuántos se han inscrito en la carrera? **4** (write down, record) anotar, apuntar: have you entered it in the account?, ¿lo has anotado en la cuenta? **5** fml (present for consideration, submit) formular, presentar. – **6** i (gen) entrar: he entered without knocking, entró sin llamar. **7** (theatre) entrar en escena.
◆ **to enter for 1** t sep inscribir en. – **2** i (race) inscribirse en; (exam) presentarse a: I'm going to enter for the competition, me voy a presentar al concurso. ‖ to enter into **1** t insep (negotiations) iniciar; (contract) firmar; (agreement) llegar a, concertar; (relations) establecer (with, con); (conversation) entablar (with, con). **2** (figure in) entrar en; (matter) importar, contar: money didn't enter into the conversation, el dinero no entró en la conversación; what you think doesn't enter into it, no importa nada lo que tú puedas pensar. ‖ to enter on / enter upon t insep fml (career) emprender; (term of office) empezar.
● **to enter into the spirit of sth.**, entrar en el ambiente de algo. ‖ to enter sb.'s head / enter sb.'s mind, pasarse por la cabeza de algn., ocurrírsele a algn.
enterprise [ˈentəpraɪz] **1** n (venture) empresa, proyecto. **2** (initiative) energía, iniciativa, espíritu m emprendedor. **3** (firm) empresa.
■ **enterprise zone**, zona de urgente reindustrialización. ‖ private enterprise, el sector privado, la iniciativa privada. ‖ public enterprise, el sector público.
enterprising [ˈentəpraɪzɪŋ] adj emprendedor,-ra.

entertain [entəˈteɪn] 1 *t* (*amuse*) entretener, divertir: *Peter never fails to entertain us with his jokes,* Peter nunca deja de divertirnos con sus chistes. **2** *fml* (*suggestion etc*) considerar, tener en cuenta; (*doubts etc*) abrigar. **3** (*invite*) recibir, invitar: *they're always entertaining somebody,* siempre tienen algún invitado. **– 4** *i* (*act as host*) tener invitados: *they used to entertain a lot,* solían tener muchos invitados.

entertainer [entəˈteɪnə'] *n* (*presenter*) animador,-ra; (*on stage*) artista *mf*.

entertaining [entəˈteɪnɪŋ] *adj* divertido,-a, entretenido,-a.

entertainment [entəˈteɪnmənt] 1 *n* (*amusement*) entretenimiento, diversión *f*. **2** THEAT espectáculo, función *f*. ■ **entertainment business,** negocio del espectáculo. ‖ **local entertainments,** (*in newspaper*) guía de espectáculos.

enthral [ɪnˈθrɔːl] *t* cautivar.
▲ *pt & pp* **enthralled,** *ger* **enthralling.**

enthrall [ɪnˈθrɔːl] *t* US → **enthral**.

enthralling [ɪnˈθrɔːlɪŋ] *adj* cautivador,-ra, fascinante.

enthrone [ɪnˈθrəʊn] *t* entronizar.

enthronement [ɪnˈθrəʊnmənt] *n* entronización *f*.

enthuse [ɪnˈθjuːz] 1 *i fam* (*be enthusiastic*) entusiasmarse (**over,** por), (**about,** con): *he was enthusing about his new car,* se entusiasmaba con su nuevo coche. **– 2** *t* entusiasmar, animar.

enthusiasm [ɪnˈθjuːzɪæzəm] *n* entusiasmo (**about/for,** por).

enthusiast [ɪnˈθjuːzɪæst] *n* entusiasta *mf*: *she's a gardening enthusiast,* es una entusiasta de la jardinería.

enthusiastic [ɪnθjuːzɪˈæstɪk] 1 *adj* (*reaction*) entusiástico,-a, caluroso,-a. **2** (*person*) entusiasta. ● **to be enthusiastic about/over sth.,** entusiasmarse por algo.

enthusiastically [ɪnθjuːzɪˈæstɪklɪ] *adv* con entusiasmo, entusiasmado,-a.

entice [ɪnˈtaɪs] *t* persuadir, tentar, engatusar: *he enticed her away from her studies,* la persuadió para que dejara sus estudios. ● **to entice sb. into doing sth.,** lograr persuadir a algn. para que haga algo.

enticing [ɪnˈtaɪsɪŋ] *adj* tentador,-ra, atractivo,-a, seductor,-ra.

entire [ɪnˈtaɪə'] *adj* entero,-a, completo,-a, íntegro,-a, todo,-a: *it wiped out the entire population,* exterminó a toda la población; *an entire day,* un día entero; *in my entire life,* en toda mi vida; *his entire support,* su apoyo total.

entirely [ɪnˈtaɪəlɪ] 1 *adv* (*totally*) enteramente, totalmente, completamente: *I entirely agree,* estoy totalmente de acuerdo; *they're entirely different,* son completamente distintos. **– 2** *adj* (*exclusively*) únicamente, exclusivamente: *it's made entirely of recycled paper,* está hecho exclusivamente con papel reciclado.

entirety [ɪnˈtaɪrətɪ] *n* totalidad *f*: *in its entirety,* en su totalidad.

entitle [ɪnˈtaɪtəl] 1 *t* (*give right to*) dar derecho (**to,** a): *this ticket entitles you to a free drink,* este tíquet te da derecho a una consumición. **2** (*book etc*) titular. ● **to be entitled,** (*book etc*) titularse; (*person*) tener derecho (**to,** a): *you're not entitled to benefit,* no tienes derecho a un subsidio; *I feel entitled to an explanation,* creo que se me debe una explicación.

entitlement [ɪnˈtaɪtəlmənt] *n* derecho (**to,** a).

entity [ˈentɪtɪ] *n* entidad *f*.
▲ *pl* **entities.**

entomology [entəˈmɒlədʒɪ] *n* entomología *f*.

entourage [ɒntuˈrɑːʒ] *n* séquito.

entrails [ˈentreɪlz] *npl* entrañas *fpl,* tripas *fpl,* vísceras *fpl.*

entrance¹ [ˈentrəns] 1 *n* (*way in*) entrada; (*door, gate*) puerta, entrada; (*hall*) vestíbulo, hall *m,* entrada: *where's the entrance?,* ¿dónde está la entrada?; *we went in the back entrance,* entramos por la puerta trasera. **2** (*act of entering*) entrada; (*on stage*) entrada en escena, aparición *f.* **3** (*admission*) entrada, admisión *f;* (*to school, university*) ingreso: *we were refused entrance,* no nos dejaron entrar. ■ **entrance examination,** examen *m* de ingreso. ‖ **entrance fee,** (*of museum etc*) entrada; (*of club, society, etc*) cuota, inscripción *f.* ‖ **entrance hall,** vestíbulo. ‖ **main entrance,** puerta principal.

entrance² [ɪnˈtrɑːns] *t* arrebatar, extasiar, encantar.

entrancing [ɪnˈtrɑːnsɪŋ] *adj* fascinante, encantador,-ra.

entrant [ˈentrənt] *n* (*competitor*) participante *mf*; (*applicant*) aspirante *mf*.

entreat [ɪnˈtriːt] *t fml* suplicar, rogar.

entrench [ɪnˈtrentʃ] 1 *t* (*with trench*) atrincherar. **2** *fig* (*establish firmly*) reafirmar, consolidar.

entrenched [ɪnˈtrentʃt] *adj* firmemente enraizado,-a: *entrenched ideas,* ideas muy enraizadas. ● **to be entrenched in sth.,** atrincherarse en algo.

entrepreneur [ɒntrəprəˈnɜː'] *n* (*business person*) empresario,-a.

entrepreneurial [ɒntrəprəˈnɜːrɪəl] *adj* empresarial.

entrust [ɪnˈtrʌst] *t* confiar, encargar, encomendar: *the boss entrusted her with the task of locking up,* el jefe le confió la tarea de cerrar; *he entrusted me with the key,* me confió la llave; *I entrust the children to your care,* dejo a los niños a tu cuidado, te confío el cuidado de los niños.

entry [ˈentrɪ] 1 *n* (*entrance*) entrada; (*joining*) ingreso: *she made a grand entry,* hizo una entrada triunfal; *Spain's entry into the EC,* el ingreso de España en la CE. **2** (*right to enter*) admisión *f,* acceso: *he was refused entry to the club,* le negaron el acceso al club. **3** US (*door, gate*) puerta, entrada. **4** (*item in accounts*) entrada, asiento; (*in diary*) anotación *f,* entrada; (*in dictionary*) entrada: *I need to check all yesterday's entries,* tengo que revisar todas las entradas de ayer. **5** (*in competition - participant*) participante *mf*; (- *total number of participants*) participación *f,* número de participantes; (- *thing entered*) ejemplar *m*: *how many entries are there for the race?,* ¿cuántos participantes hay en la carrera?; *this is the winning entry,* éste es el ejemplar ganador; *Madge's entry was a chocolate cake,* Madge presentó un pastel de chocolate. ● *"no entry",* (*traffic*) "dirección prohibida"; (*people*) "prohibido el paso"; (*on door*) "prohibida la entrada" ‖ **to force an entry,** allanar la morada. ■ **entry fee,** inscripción *f,* cuota. ‖ **entry form,** formulario de inscripción.
▲ *pl* **entries.**

enunciate [ɪˈnʌnsɪeɪt] 1 *t* (*pronounce*) pronunciar, articular. **2** (*express*) expresar, enunciar.

envelop [ɪnˈveləp] *t* envolver.

envelope [ˈenvələʊp] *n* (*of letter*) sobre *m*; (*covering*) envoltura.

enviable [ˈenvɪəbəl] *adj* envidiable.

envious [ˈenvɪəs] *adj* (*person*) envidioso,-a; (*look etc*) de envidia. ● **to be envidious of sb./sth.,** tener envidia de algn./algo.

enviously [ˈenvɪəslɪ] *adv* con envidia, envidiosamente.

environment [ɪn'vaɪrənmənt] **1** *n* (*ecology*) medio ambiente *m*: *we need to protect the environment,* hemos de proteger el medio ambiente. **2** (*surroundings*) ambiente *m*, entorno; (*habitat*) hábitat *m*: *a happy home environment is essential,* un ambiente familiar feliz es esencial.
● **environment friendly,** no perjudial para el medio ambiente.
■ **Department of the Environment,** Departamento de Medio Ambiente.

environmental [ɪnvaɪrən'mentəl] **1** *adj* (*ecological*) del medio ambiente, ambiental: *environmental pollution,* contaminación del medio ambiente. **2** (*of surroundings*) ambiental.
■ **Environmental Health Officer,** Inspector-ra de Sanidad. ‖ **Environmental Health Service,** Departamento de Sanidad.

environmentalist [ɪnvaɪrən'mentəlɪst] **1** *n* ecologista *mf*. – **2** *adj* ecologista.

environmentally [ɪnvaɪrən'mentəlɪ] *adv en lo que se refiere al medio ambiente: this detergent is environmentally friendly,* este detergente no es perjudicial para el medio ambiente; *people are becoming more environmentally aware,* la gente está cada vez más sensibilizada con los problemas del medio ambiente.

environs [ɪn'vaɪrənz] *npl* alrededores *mpl*.

envisage [ɪn'vɪzɪdʒ] **1** *t* (*foresee*) prever. **2** (*imagine*) imaginarse.

envoy ['envɔɪ] *n* enviado,-a.
■ **special envoy,** enviado,-a especial.

envy ['envɪ] **1** *n* envidia (**at/of,** de). – **2** *t* envidiar, tener envidia de: *I don't envy you,* no te envidio.
● **to be green with envy,** estar corroído,-a por la envidia, morirse de envidia. ‖ **to be the envy of sb.,** ser la envidia de algn.
▲ (*sustantivo*) *pl* **envies**; (*verbo*) *pt & pp* **envied,** *ger* **envying.**

enzyme ['enzaɪm] *n* enzima *m & f*.

epaulet [epə'let] *n* US → **epaulette.**

epaulette [epə'let] *n* charretera.

épée ['epeɪ] *n* florete *m*.

ephemeral [ɪ'femərəl] *adj* efímero,-a.

epic ['epɪk] **1** *adj* (*poem, film, novel*) épico,-a; (*achievement*) colosal. – **2** *n* (*poem*) epopeya, poema *m* épico; (*film*) película épica; (*novel*) epopeya.

epicentre ['epɪsentə'] *n* epicentro.

epicure ['epɪkjʊə'] *n* sibarita *mf*.

epidemic [epɪ'demɪk] **1** *n* epidemia. – **2** *adj* epidémico,-a.

epidermis [epɪ'dɜːmɪs] *n* epidermis *f*.

epigram ['epɪɡræm] *n* epigrama *m*.

epilepsy ['epɪlepsɪ] *n* epilepsia.

epileptic [epɪ'leptɪk] **1** *adj* epiléptico,-a. – **2** *n* epiléptico,-a.
■ **epileptic fit,** ataque *m* epiléptico, ataque *m* de epilepsia.

epilog ['epɪlɒɡ] *n* US → **epilogue.**

epilogue ['epɪlɒɡ] *n* epílogo.

episcopal [ɪ'pɪskəpəl] *adj* episcopal.

episode ['epɪsəʊd] **1** *n* episodio. **2** TV RAD capítulo.

episodic [epɪ'sɒdɪk] *adj* episódico,-a.

epistle [ɪ'pɪsəl] *n* epístola.

Epistle [ɪ'pɪsəl] *n* REL Epístola.

epitaph ['epɪtɑːf] *n* epitafio.

epithet ['epɪθet] *n* epíteto.

epitome [ɪ'pɪtəmɪ] *n* (*model, perfect example*) personificación *f*: *he's the epitome of laziness,* es la pereza en persona, es la personificación de la pereza.

epitomize [ɪ'pɪtəmaɪz] *t* personificar, ejemplificar, ser la personificación de.

epoch ['iːpɒk] *n* época.

epoch-making ['iːpɒkmeɪkɪŋ] *adj* histórico,-a, transcendental, que hace historia.

eponymous [ɪ'pɒnɪməs] *adj* epónimo,-a.

equable ['ekwebəl] **1** *adj* (*climate*) uniforme, regular. **2** (*person*) ecuánime.

equal ['iːkwəl] **1** *adj* (*identical*) igual; (*same*) mismo,-a: *divide it into equal parts,* divídelo en partes iguales; *they are equal in size,* son de igual tamaño; *with equal enthusiasm,* con el mismo entusiasmo; *now we're equal!,* ¡ya estamos iguales! **2** (*capable*) capaz. – **3** *n* igual *mf*: *she is your equal,* es igual que tú; *he has no intellectual equal,* intelectualmente no tiene igual. – **4** *t* MATH ser igual a, equivaler a: *10 + 10 equals 20,* 10 + 10 son 20; *x equals y,* x es igual a y. **5** (*match*) igualar: *no-one can equal him,* nadie lo iguala; *he's equalled the world record,* ha igualado el récord mundial.
● **all (other) things being equal,** si todo sigue igual. ‖ **to be equal to,** (*situation, task*) estar a la altura de; (*effort*) sentirse con fuerzas para: *she's equal to the occasion,* está a la altura de las circunstancias; *are you equal to climbing these stairs?,* ¿te sientes con fuerzas para subir esta escalera? ‖ **to be on equal terms (with sb.),** estar en igualdad de condiciones con algn. ‖ **to treat sb. as an equal,** tratar a algn. de igual a igual.
■ **equal opportunities,** igualdad *f* de oportunidades. ‖ **equal opportunity,** la misma oportunidad. ‖ **equal pay,** igualdad *f* de salario. ‖ **equals sign,** signo de igualdad. ‖ **equal rights,** igualdad *f* de derechos.

equality [iː'kwɒlɪtɪ] *n* igualdad *f*.
▲ *pl* **equalities.**

equalize ['iːkwəlaɪz] **1** *i* SP empatar, igualar el marcador, lograr el empate: *they've equalized!,* ¡han empatado! – **2** *t* igualar.

equalizer ['iːkwəlaɪzə'] *n* SP gol *m* del empate.

equally ['iːkwəlɪ] **1** *adv* igualmente, igual de: *my children are equally bright,* mis hijos son igual de listos; *we are both equally responsible,* somos igualmente responsables. **2** en partes iguales, equitativamente: *divide the money equally,* divide el dinero en partes iguales. **3** (*similarly*) del mismo modo, asimismo.

equanimity [ekwə'nɪmɪtɪ] *n* ecuanimidad *f*.

equate [ɪ'kweɪt] *t* equiparar (**with,** con), comparar (**with,** con).

equation [ɪ'kweɪʒən] **1** *n* MATH ecuación *f*. **2** *fml* (*relationship*) relación *f*.
■ **simple equation,** ecuación *f* de primer grado.

equator [ɪ'kweɪtə'] *n* ecuador *m*.

equatorial [ekwə'tɔːrɪəl] *adj* ecuatorial.

equestrian [ɪ'kwestrɪən] **1** *adj* ecuestre. – **2** *n* (*man*) jinete *m*; (*woman*) amazona.

equidistant [iːkwɪ'dɪstənt] *adj* equidistante.

equilateral [iːkwɪ'lætərəl] *adj* equilátero,-a.
■ **equilateral triangle,** triángulo equilátero.

equilibrium [iːkwɪ'lɪbrɪəm] *n* equilibrio.

equine ['ekwaɪn] *adj* equino,-a.

equinox ['iːkwɪnɒks] *n* equinoccio.
■ **autumnal equinox,** equinoccio de otoño. ‖ **spring equinox / vernal equinox,** equinoccio de primavera.

equip [ɪ'kwɪp] *t* (*fit out, supply*) equipar (**with,** con), proveer (**with,** de): *they equipped us with torches,* nos equiparon con linternas; *it'll cost millions to equip the hospital,* equipar el hospital costará millones. **2** (*pre-*

pare) preparar (**for/to,** para): *a good education equips you for the real world,* una buena educación te prepara para el mundo real.
● **to equip os. with sth.,** proveerse de algo.
▲ *pt & pp* **equipped,** *ger* **equipping.**

equipment [ɪˈkwɪpmənt] **1** *n* (*materials*) equipo, material *m*. **2** (*act of equipping*) equipamiento.
■ **office equipment,** material *m* de oficina. ‖ **sports equipment,** material deportivo.

equipped [ɪˈkwɪpt] **1** *adj* (*supplied*) equipado,-a, provisto,-a: *a well-equipped school,* un colegio bien equipado; *I'm not equipped to go diving,* no tengo el equipo necesario para hacer submarinismo. **2** (*prepared*) preparado,-a (**for,** para).

equitable [ˈekwɪtəbəl] *adj fml* equitativo,-a.

equity [ˈekwəti] **1** *n* equidad *f*. **2 Equity,** GB sindicato de actores. – **3 equities,** *npl* acciones *fpl* ordinarias.
▲ *pl* **equities.**

equivalence [ɪˈkwɪvələns] *n* equivalencia.

equivalent [ɪˈkwɪvələnt] **1** *adj* equivalente. – **2** *n* equivalente *m*.
● **to be equivalent to sth.,** equivaler a algo.

equivocal [ɪˈkwɪvəkəl] **1** *adj* (*ambiguous*) equívoco,-a. **2** (*questionable, dubious*) dudoso,-a.

era [ˈɪərə] *n* era, época.

eradicate [ɪˈrædɪkeɪt] *t* (*eliminate*) erradicar, extirpar; (*uproot*) desarraigar.

eradication [ɪrædɪˈkeɪʃən] *n* erradicación *f*, extirpación *f*.

erase [ɪˈreɪz] *t* borrar.

eraser [ɪˈreɪzəʳ] *n* goma de borrar.

erasure [ɪˈreɪʒəʳ] *n fml* borradura.

erect [ɪˈrekt] **1** *adj* (*upright*) derecho,-a, erguido,-a. **2** ANAT erecto,-a. – **3** *t* (*build*) erigir, levantar; (*put up - tent*) armar; (*- flagstaff*) izar.

erection [ɪˈrekʃən] **1** *n* ANAT erección *f*. **2** (*building*) construcción *f*.

ermine [ˈɜːmɪn] **1** *n* armiño. – **2** *adj* de armiño.

erode [ɪˈrəʊd] **1** *t* (*rock, soil*) erosionar. **2** (*metal*) corroer, desgastar. **3** *fig* (*power, confidence, rights, etc*) minar.
◆ **to erode away 1** *i* (*rock, soil*) erosionarse. **2** (*metal*) corroerse, desgastarse. **3** *fig* ir se minando.

erogenous [ˈɪrɒdʒənəs] *adj* erógeno,-a.
■ **erogenous zones,** zonas *fpl* erógenas.

erosion [ɪˈrəʊʒən] **1** *n* (*of rock, soil*) erosión *f*. **2** (*of metal*) corrosión *f*, desgaste *m*. **3** *fig* desgaste *m*.

erosive [ɪˈrəʊsɪv] *adj* erosivo,-a, corrosivo,-a.

erotic [ɪˈrɒtɪk] *adj* erótico,-a.

err [ɜːʳ] *i fml* errar, equivocarse.
● **to err on the side of sth.,** pecar por exceso de algo, pecar de algo. ‖ **to err is human (to forgive divine),** errar es humano (perdonar, divino).

errand [ˈerənd] *n* encargo, recado.
● **an errand of mercy,** una misión de socorro. ‖ **to run an errand,** hacer un recado.
■ **errand boy,** recadero.

errant [ˈerənt] **1** *adj fig* errante. **2** (*of knight*) andante.

errata [ɪˈrɑːtə] *npl fe f sing* de erratas.

erratic [ɪˈrætɪk] *adj* (*behaviour, performance*) irregular, inconstante; (*weather*) muy variable.

erratically [ɪˈrætɪklɪ] *adv* de manera irregular.

erratum [ɪˈrɑːtəm] *n* errata.
▲ *pl* **errata** [eˈrɑːtə].

erroneous [ɪˈrəʊnɪəs] *adj* erróneo,-a, equivocado,-a.

erroneously [ɪˈrəʊnɪəslɪ] *adv* erróneamente, equivocadamente.

error [ˈerəʳ] *n* error *m*, equivocación *f*: *a typing error,* un error de máquina.
● **in error,** por error, por equivocación. ‖ **to be in error,** estar equivocado,-a, estar en un error. ‖ **an error of judgement,** un error. ‖ **to make an error,** cometer un error. ‖ **to see the error of one's ways,** reconocer sus errores.

error-free [ˈerəfriː] *adj* sin errores.

erudite [ˈerʊdaɪt] *adj* erudito,-a.

erudition [erʊˈdɪʃən] *n* erudición *f*.

erupt [ɪˈrʌpt] **1** *i* (*volcano*) entrar en erupción. **2** *fig* (*war, violence, fire*) estallar; (*sudden movement*) irrumpir: *when the police moved in, violence erupted,* al intervenir la policía, la violencia estalló; *in the late seventies punk erupted on the scene,* al final de los setenta el movimiento punk irrumpió en la escena. **3** *fam* (*people - in anger*) estallar en cólera; (*- in laughter*) estallar de risa; (*- in enthusiasm*) volverse loco,-a, exaltarse: *he erupted when I told him,* estalló en cólera cuando se lo dije; *when Elvis came out, the crowd erupted,* cuando salió Elvis, el público se volvió loco. **4** MED (*rash, spots, etc*) brotar, salir; (*tooth*) salir.

eruption [ɪˈrʌpʃən] **1** *n* (*volcano*) erupción *f*. **2** *fig* (*war*) estallido, comienzo; (*violence*) estallido, brote *m*; (*anger*) estallido, explosión *f*; (*new force etc*) irrupción *f*. **3** (*disease*) brote *m*, epidemia; (*rash, spots, etc*) erupción *f*.

escalate [ˈeskəleɪt] **1** *t* (*war*) intensificar, agravar. – **2** *i* (*war, violence, etc*) intensificarse, agravarse. **3** (*prices etc*) aumentar, subir.
● **to escalate in/into,** terminar en, degenerar en.

escalation [eskəˈleɪʃən] **1** *n* (*war*) intensificación *f*, agravación *f*, escalada. **2** (*prices*) subida, aumento.

escalator [ˈeskəleɪtəʳ] *n* escalera mecánica.

escalope [ˈeskəlɒp] *n* escalope.

escapade [ˈeskəpeɪd, eskəˈpeɪd] *n* aventura.

escape [ɪsˈkeɪp] **1** *n* (*flight*) fuga, huida (**from,** de): *it was a spectacular escape,* fue una fuga espectacular. **2** (*of gas*) fuga, escape *m*. **3** (*escapism*) evasión *f*: *television is an escape from reality,* la televisión es una evasión de la realidad. – **4** *i* (*get free, get away*) escaparse, fugarse, huir: *three prisoners have escaped from jail,* tres presos se han escapado de la cárcel; *the thief received a tip-off and escaped,* el ladrón recibió un aviso y huyó; *we managed to escape unharmed,* conseguimos huir ilesos; *they escaped to South America,* huyeron a Sudamérica. **5** (*gas etc*) escapar. – **6** *t* (*avoid*) escapar a, salvarse de, librarse de: *he was lucky and escaped punishment,* tuvo suerte y se libró del castigo; *he escaped death by inches,* se salvó de la muerte por muy poco. **7** (*be forgotten or unnoticed*) escaparse, no recordar: *the exact figure escapes me,* ahora mismo no recuerdo la cifra exacta; *his name escaped me,* no recordaba su nombre; *nothing escapes you,* no se te escapa nada.
● **to escape one's notice,** pasarle a uno desapercibido. ‖ **to have a narrow escape,** salvarse por los pelos. ‖ **to make (good) one's escape,** escaparse.
■ **escape clause,** cláusula de excepción. ‖ **escape hatch,** escotilla de salvamento. ‖ **escape route,** vía de escape. ‖ **escape valve,** válvula de escape. ‖ **escape vehicle,** vehículo de la fuga.

escapee [ɪsˈkeɪpiː] *n* fugitivo,-a.

escapism [ɪsˈkeɪpɪzəm] *n* evasión *f*.

eschew [ɪsˈtʃuː] *t fml* evitar, abstenerse de.

escort [esˈkɔːt] **1** *n* acompañante *mf*. **2** MIL escolta. – **3** *t* acompañar: *I'll escort you home,* te acompañaré a casa. **4** MIL escoltar.

● **under police escort,** escoltado,-a por la policía, con escolta policial.
▲ *(verbo)* [ɪˈskɔːt].
Eskimo [ˈeskɪməʊ] **1** *n (person)* esquimal *mf.* **2** *(language)* esquimal *m.* – **3** *adj* esquimal.
▲ *(sustantivo) pl* Eskimos *o* Eskimo.
ESL [ˈiːˈesˈel] *abbr (English as a second language)* inglés como segundo idioma.
esoteric [esəʊˈterɪk] *adj* esotérico,-a.
ESP[1] [ˈiːˈesˈpiː] *abbr (extrasensory perception)* percepción *f* extrasensorial.
ESP[2] [ˈiːˈesˈpiː] *abbr (English for Specific Purposes)* cursos de inglés especializados.
especial [ɪsˈpeʃəl] *adj* especial, particular.
especially [esˈpeʃəlɪ] *adv* especialmente, sobre todo.
Esperanto [espəˈræntəʊ] *n* esperanto.
espionage [ˈespɪənɑːʒ] *n* espionaje *m.*
esplanade [espləˈneɪd] *n* paseo marítimo.
espousal [ɪˈspaʊzəl] *n fml (taking up)* adhesión *f* (**of,** a), adopción *f* (**of,** de); *(support)* apoyo (**of,** de).
espouse [ɪˈspaʊz] *t fml (take up)* abrazar, adoptar, adherirse a; *(support)* apoyar, propugnar.
esquire [ɪsˈkwaɪəʳ] *n* GB *fml* señor *m* don: *Mr Richard Broddle Esquire,* Sr. Don Richard Broddle.
essay [ˈeseɪ] **1** *n (school)* redacción *f,* composición *f; (university)* trabajo. **2** *(literary)* ensayo. **3** *fml (attempt)* intento. – **4** *t fml* intentar.
essence [ˈesəns] **1** *n (central quality)* esencia; *(perfect model)* personificación *f:* *the essence of his philosophy,* la esencia de su filosofía; *she is the essence of gentleness,* es la ternura personificada, es la ternura en persona. **2** *(extract)* esencia, perfume *m.*
● **in essence,** esencialmente, fundamentalmente. ‖ **to be of the essence,** ser esencial: *time is of the essence,* el tiempo es esencial.
essential [ɪˈsenʃəl] **1** *adj (necessary)* esencial, imprescindible: *experience is essential for this job,* la experiencia es imprescindible en este trabajo; *it is essential that you are punctual,* es imprescindible que llegues puntual. **2** *(most important, basic)* fundamental, central, básico,-a: *the essential difference,* la diferencia fundamental. – **3** *n (necessary thing)* necesidad *f* básica: *a knowledge of English is an essential,* el conocimiento del inglés es imprescindible; *do you consider a dishwasher an essential?,* ¿crees que un lavaplatos es una necesidad?; *just take the bare essentials,* lleva sólo lo imprescindible. – **4** **essentials,** *npl* lo esencial *m sing,* lo fundamental *m sing: the essentials of Spanish,* lo fundamental del español.
■ **essential oil,** aceite *m* esencial.
essentially [ɪˈsenʃəlɪ] *adv* esencialmente, fundamentalmente.
EST [ˈiːˈesˈtiː] *abbr* US *(Eastern Standard Time)* hora del meridiano 75 al oeste de Greenwich.
establish [ɪˈstæblɪʃ] **1** *t (set up)* establecer, fundar, crear: *this company was established in 1895,* esta empresa fue fundada en 1895. **2** *(find out, determine)* determinar, averiguar; *(prove correct, show to be true)* probar, demostrar, verificar: *we must establish the cause of death,* hay que averiguar la causa de la muerte; *he set out to establish the truth of the matter,* se propuso demostrar la verdad del caso; *can we just establish the facts?,* ¿podemos verificar los hechos?; *they established the prisoner's innocence,* probaron la inocencia del preso. **3** *(cause to be accepted - precedent, theory)* sentar; *(- fame, reputation)* consolidar, consagrar; *(- habit, belief, custom)* establecer: *his*

second film established his fame as a director, su segunda película consagró su fama como director; *we've established a precedent,* hemos sentado un precedente; *they established the custom of eating strawberries and cream at Wimbledon,* establecieron la costumbre de comer fresas con nata en Wimbledon. **4** *(set up - contact, communication, etc)* establecer, entablar: *we've established a close working relationship,* hemos establecido una estrecha relación laboral.
● **to establish os.,** establecerse (como algo): *she established herself as a photographer,* se estableció como fotógrafa. ‖ **to establish sb.,** ayudar a algn. a establecerse.
established [ɪˈstæblɪʃt] **1** *adj (practice, custom)* consolidado,-a, arraigado,-a. **2** *(person - set up)* establecido,-a; *(- well known)* reconocido,-a: *he's well established as a lawyer,* es un abogado conocido, tiene buena reputación como abogado; *he's an established author,* es un autor reconocido. **3** *(business)* establecido,-a, sólido,-a; *(clientele)* fijo,-a. **4** *(order, authority)* establecido,-a; *(theory)* sentado,-a. **5** *(fact)* comprobado,-a.
■ **Established Church,** iglesia oficial del estado.
establishment [ɪˈstæblɪʃmənt] **1** *n (setting up)* establecimiento, fundación *f.* **2** *(premises)* establecimiento; *(business)* negocio. **3** *(staff)* plantilla, personal *m.* **4 the Establishment,** GB el sistema, el poder.
■ **educational establishment,** centro de estudios. ‖ **reserach establishment,** centro de investigación.
estate [ɪˈsteɪt] **1** *n (land)* finca. **2** GB *(with houses)* urbanización *f.* **3** *(money and property)* propiedad *f,* bienes *mpl; (inheritance)* herencia.
■ **estate agent,** agente *mf* inmobiliario,-a. ‖ **estate agent's,** agencia inmobiliaria. ‖ **estate car,** GB coche *m* familiar.
esteem [ɪˈstiːm] **1** *t (respect)* apreciar, estimar. **2** *(regard)* considerar, estimar. – **3** *n* aprecio, estima, estimación *f.*
● **to hold sb. in great/high esteem,** tener a algn. en gran estima, apreciar mucho a algn., estimar (en) mucho a algn.
estimate [ˈestɪmət] **1** *n (calculation - of amount, size)* cálculo, estimación *f; (- of value, cost)* valoración *f,* estimación *f; (- for work)* presupuesto. **2** *(judgement)* evaluación *f,* juicio, opinión *f.* – **3** *t (calculate)* calcular. **4** *(judge, form opinion about)* pensar, creer, estimar. – **5** *i (for work)* hacer un presupuesto (**for,** de).
● **at a rough estimate,** según un cálculo aproximado.
▲ *(verbo)* [ˈestɪmeɪt].
estimated [ˈestɪmeɪtɪd] *adj* aproximado,-a: *its estimated cost is £1M,* su coste aproximado es de un millón de libras; *there are an estimated five thousand deer in the park,* se calcula que hay cinco mil ciervos en el parque; *the estimated time of arrival,* la hora de llegada prevista.
estimation [estɪˈmeɪʃən] **1** *n* opinión *f,* juicio: *in my estimation,* a mi juicio. **2** *(esteem)* estima, estimación *f,* aprecio.
● **to go down in sb.'s estimation,** perder la estima de algn. ‖ **to go up in one's estimation,** ganarse la estima de algn.
Estonia [eˈstəʊnɪə] *n* Estonia.
Estonian [eˈstəʊnɪən] **1** *adj* estonio,-a. – **2** *n (person)* estonio,-a. **3** *(language)* estonio.
estrange [ɪˈstreɪndʒ] *t* alejar (**from,** de).
estranged [ɪˈstreɪndʒd] *adj* alejado,-a, separado,-a: *his estranged wife,* su mujer, de quien está separado.
● **to be estranged from sb.,** estar separado,-a de algn.

estrangement [ɪ'streɪndʒmənt] *n* alejamiento, separación *f*.

Estremadura [estrəmə'duərə] *n* Extremadura.

Estremaduran [estrəmə'duərən] 1 *adj* extremeño,-a. – 2 *n* extremeño,-a.

estuary ['estjuərɪ] *n* estuario.
▲ *pl* **estuaries.**

ETA ['iː'tiː'eɪ] *abbr* (*estimated time of arrival*) hora prevista de llegada.

etch [etʃ] 1 *t* grabar al agua fuerte. 2 *fig* grabar. – 3 *i* grabar al agua fuerte.

etching ['etʃɪŋ] *n* aguafuerte *m & f*.

eternal [ɪ'tɜːnəl] 1 *adj* (*everlasting*) eterno,-a: *eternal love*, amor eterno. 2 *fam* (*unceasing*) incesante: *stop your eternal arguing!*, ¡basta de vuestras incesantes riñas! 3 (*immutable*) inmutable: *eternal truths*, verdades inmutables. – 4 **the Eternal**, *n* Dios.
● **the eternal triangle**, el triángulo amoroso.

eternally [ɪ'tɜːnəlɪ] 1 *adv* eternamente. 2 *fam* (*always*) siempre.

eternity [ɪ'tɜːnətɪ] *n* eternidad *f*: *it seemed like an eternity*, parecía una eternidad.
■ **eternity ring**, anillo de brillantes.

ether ['iːθəʳ] *n* éter *m*.

ethereal [ɪ'θɪərɪəl] *adj* etéreo,-a.

ethic ['eθɪk] *n* ética.

ethical ['eθɪkəl] *adj* ético,-a, moral.

ethically ['eθɪkəlɪ] *adv* éticamente, moralmente.

ethics ['eθɪks] 1 *n* (*science*) ética. – 2 *npl* (*moral correctness*) moralidad *f*.
■ **medical ethics**, ética profesional médica.

Ethiopia [iːθɪ'əupɪə] *n* Etiopía.

Ethiopian [iːθɪ'əupɪən] 1 *adj* etíope,-a. – 2 *n* (*person*) etíope *mf*, etiope *mf*. 3 (*language*) etíope *m*.

ethnic ['eθnɪk] *adj* étnico,-a.
■ **ethnic minority**, minoría étnica.

ethnically ['eθnɪklɪ] *adv* étnicamente.

ethnographer [eθ'nɒɡrəfəʳ] *n* etnógrafo,-a.

ethnography [eθ'nɒɡrəfɪ] *n* etnografía.

ethnologist [eθ'nɒlədʒɪst] *n* etnólogo,-a.

ethnology [eθ'nɒlədʒɪ] *n* etnología.

ethos ['iːθɒs] *n* carácter *m* distintivo, espíritu *m*.

ethyl ['iːθaɪl, 'eθɪl] *n* CHEM etilo.
■ **ethyl alcohol**, alcohol *m* etílico.

etiquette ['etɪket] *n* protocolo, etiqueta.
■ **professional etiquette**, ética profesional.

Etruscan [ɪ'trʌskən] 1 *adj* etrusco,-a. – 2 *n* (*person*) etrusco,-a. 3 (*language*) etrusco.

etymological [etɪmə'lɒdʒɪkəl] *adj* etimológico,-a.

etymologist [etɪ'mɒlədʒɪst] *n* etimólogo,-a.

etymology [etɪ'mɒlədʒɪ] *n* etimología.
▲ *pl* **etymologies.**

eucalyptus [juːkə'lɪptəs] *n* eucalipto.
■ **eucalyptus oil**, aceite *m* de eucalipto. ‖ **eucalyptus tree**, eucalipto.

Eucharist ['juːkərɪst] *n* Eucaristía.

eulogize ['juːlədʒaɪz] *t* elogiar.

eulogy ['juːlədʒɪ] *n* elogio.
▲ *pl* **eulogies.**

eunuch ['juːnək] *n* eunuco.

euphemism ['juːfəmɪzəm] *n* eufemismo.

euphemistic [juːfɪ'mɪstɪk] *adj* eufemístico,-a.

euphemistically [juːfə'mɪstɪklɪ] *adv* de manera eufemística.

euphony ['juːfənɪ] *n* eufonía.

euphoria [juː'fɔːrɪə] *n* euforia.

euphoric [juː'fɒrɪk] *adj* eufórico,-a.

Euphrates [juː'freɪtiːz] *n* el Eufrates *m*.

Eurasian [juə'reɪʒən] 1 *n* euroasiático,-a. – 2 *adj* euroasiático,-a.

eureka [juə'riːkə] *interj* ¡eureka!

eurhythmics [juə'rɪðmɪks] *n* gimnasia rítmica.

Eurocheque ['juərəutʃek] *n* eurocheque *m*.

Eurocommunism [juərəu'kɒmjənɪzəm] *n* POL eurocomunismo.

Eurocommunist [juərəu'kɒmjənɪst] 1 *n* POL eurocomunista *mf*. – 2 *adj* POL eurocomunista.

Eurocrat ['juərəkræt] *n* eurócrata *mf*.

Eurocurrency ['juərəukʌrənsɪ] *n* FIN eurodivisa *f*.

Eurodollar ['juərəudɒləʳ] *n* FIN eurodólar *m*.

Europe ['juərəp] *n* Europa.

European [juərə'pɪən] 1 *adj* europeo,-a. – 2 *n* (*person*) europeo,-a.
■ **European Economic Community**, Comunidad *f* Económica Europea. ‖ **European Parliament**, Parlamento Europeo. ‖ **European Union**, Unión *f* Europea.

euthanasia [juːθə'neɪzɪə] *n* eutanasia.

evacuate [ɪ'vækjueɪt] 1 *t* (*people*) evacuar. 2 (*place*) desalojar; (*mil*) desocupar.

evacuation [ɪvækju'eɪʃən] 1 *n* (*of people*) evacuación *f*. 2 (*of place*) desalojamiento, desalojo.

evacuee [ɪvækju'iː] *n* evacuado,-a.

evade [ɪ'veɪd] 1 *t* (*gen*) evadir, eludir, esquivar: *they successfully evaded the police*, consiguieron esquivar a la policía; *he spent years evading military service*, pasó años eludiendo el servicio militar. 2 (*question*) eludir. 3 (*tax*) evadir.

evaluate [ɪ'væljueɪt] 1 *t* (*assess*) evaluar, juzgar; (*estimate value*) valorar, calcular (el valor de), tasar: *the teachers evaluated their students' abilities*, los profesores evaluaron la capacidad de sus alumnos; *he evaluated the property*, tasó la propiedad. 2 MATH hallar el valor numérico de.

evaluation [ɪvælju'eɪʃən] *n* evaluación *f*.

evanescent [iːvə'nesənt] *adj* evanescente.

evangelical [iːvæn'dʒelɪkəl] *adj* evangélico,-a.

evangelism [ɪ'vændʒəlɪzəm] *n* evangelismo.

evangelist [ɪ'vændʒəlɪst] *n* evangelista *mf*.

evangelize [ɪ'vændʒəlaɪz] *t* evangelizar.

evaporate [ɪ'væpəreɪt] 1 *t* evaporar. – 2 *i* evaporarse. 3 *fig* desvanecerse, esfumarse: *all our hopes evaporated*, todas nuestras esperanzas se desvanecieron.

evaporated milk [ɪ'væpəreɪtɪd'mɪlk] *n* leche *f* evaporada.

evaporation [ɪvæpə'reɪʃən] *n* evaporación *f*.

evasion [ɪ'veɪʒən] 1 *n* (*gen*) evasión *f*. 2 (*excuse etc*) evasiva.

evasive [ɪ'veɪsɪv] *adj* evasivo,-a: *she became very evasive*, se comportó de forma muy evasiva; *the minister gave an evasive answer*, el ministro respondió con evasivas.
● **to take evasive action**, MIL realizar maniobras para eludir un ataque.

evasively [ɪ'veɪsɪvlɪ] *adv* de manera evasiva.

evasiveness [ɪ'veɪsɪvnəs] *n* condición *f* de evasivo.

eve [iːv] *n* víspera, vigilia.
● **on the eve of sth.**, en vísperas de algo.

even ['iːvən] 1 *adj* (*level, flat*) llano,-a, plano,-a; (*smooth*) liso,-a: *this surface isn't even*, esta superficie no es plana. 2 (*regular, steady*) uniforme, regular, constante: *an*

even temperature, una temperatura constante; *an even pace,* un ritmo regular. **3** (*evenly balanced*) igual, igualado,-a: *it was an even match,* fue un partido igualado; *the scales are even,* la balanza está igualada. **4** (*equal in measure, quantity, number*) igual: *add even amounts of milk and water,* añadir igual cantidad de leche y agua, añadir leche y agua a partes iguales; *the distribution of income is fairly even,* la distribución de la renta es bastante igual; *the scores were even,* iban iguales. **5** (*number*) par. **6** (*placid - character*) apacible, tranquilo,-a: (*-voice*) imperturbable. **7** (*on the same level as*) a nivel (**with,** de). – **8** *adv* hasta, incluso, aun: *even the Queen was there,* hasta la reina estaba allí; *it's always sunny, even in winter,* siempre hace sol, incluso en invierno; *it's open every day, even on Sundays,* abren cada día, incluso los domingos; *even a child knows that,* hasta un niño lo sabe. **9** (*with negative*) siquiera, ni siquiera: *he didn't even ask me the score,* ni siquiera me preguntó el resultado; *without even opening the present,* sin abrir el regalo siquiera; *even you wouldn't understand,* ni siquiera tú lo entenderías; *she never even said hello,* ni siquiera me saludó. **10** (*before comparative*) aun, todavía: *she's even more beautiful than I remembered,* es aun más guapa de lo que recordaba; *I'm even angrier now,* ahora estoy todavía más enfadada. – **11** *t* (*level*) nivelar, allanar. **12** (*score*) igualar; (*situation*) equilibrar.
◆ **to even out 1** *t sep* (*make level*) nivelar; (*make equal*) igualar; (*spread equally*) repartir equitativamente. – **2** *i* (*become level*) nivelarse; (*become equal*) igualarse; (*balance out*) estabilizarse: *prices have evened out quite a bit,* los precios se han estabilizado bastante. ‖ **to even up 1** *t sep* (*balance*) equilibrar; (*make equal*) igualar: *if I pay for the next round that'll even things up,* si yo pago la próxima ronda quedamos en paz. – **2** *i* igualarse.
● **even as,** mientras, justo cuando: *even as we speak,* en este mismo momento. ‖ **even if,** aun si, aunque. ‖ **even so,** incluso ahora, aun ahora. ‖ **even so,** incluso así, aun así, a pesar de eso. ‖ **even then,** incluso entonces, aun entonces. ‖ **even though,** aunque, aun cuando. ‖ **to be even with sb.,** estar en paz con algn. ‖ **to break even,** cubrir gastos. ‖ **to get even with sb.,** desquitarse con algn.: *I'll get even with you!,* ¡me las pagarás! ‖ **even chances,** cincuenta por ciento de posibilidades.
even-handed [ˈiːvənhændɪd] *adj* imparcial.
evening [ˈiːvənɪŋ] *n* (*early*) tarde *f*; (*late*) noche *f*: *we went out in the evening,* salimos por la noche; *are you coming round this evening?,* ¿vendrás a casa esta tarde?; *tomorrow evening,* mañana por la noche; *yesterday evening,* ayer por la tarde.
● **good evening!,** ¡buenas tardes!, ¡buenas noches!
■ **evening class,** clase *f* nocturna. ‖ **evening dress,** (*woman*) vestido de noche; (*man*) traje *m* de etiqueta. ‖ **evening paper,** periódico de la tarde. ‖ **evening performance,** función *f* de noche. ‖ **evening service,** misa vespertina. ‖ **evening star,** estrella vespertina.
evenly [ˈiːvənlɪ] **1** *adv* (*uniformly*) uniformemente, de modo uniforme, regularmente. **2** (*fairly, equally*) equitativamente, igualmente. – **3** *adj* (*of voice*) en el mismo tono, con calma.
evenness [ˈiːvənnəs] **1** *n* (*uniformity*) uniformidad *f*. – **2** *adj* (*equality, fairness*) igualdad *f*, ecuanimidad *f*, imparcialidad *f*.
evensong [ˈiːvənsɒŋ] *n* vísperas *fpl*.
event [ɪˈvent] **1** *n* (*happening*) suceso, acontecimiento: *the main events of 1995,* los principales sucesos de 1995; *the most important social event of the year,* el

acontecimiento social más importante del año; *the events leading up to his resignation,* los sucesos que llevaron a su dimisión. **2** SP prueba.
● **at all events,** en todo caso. ‖ **in any event,** pase lo que pase. ‖ **in the event,** tal como resultó después. ‖ **in the event of,** en caso de: *in the event of fire,* en caso de incendio. ‖ **in the event that sth. happens,** en caso de que pase algo: *in the event of his arriving late,* en el caso de que llegue tarde. ‖ **in either event,** en cualquiera de los dos casos. ‖ **in that event,** en ese caso. ‖ **in the normal course of events,** si todo sigue su curso normal.
even-tempered [ˈiːvəntempərd] *adj* plácido,-a, ecuánime, apacible.
eventful [ɪˈventfʊl] *adj* (*memorable*) lleno,-a (de acontecimientos), memorable; (*busy*) ajetreado,-a, agitado,-a; (*troubled*) accidentado,-a: *an eventful year,* un año memorable; *an eventful day,* un día ajetreado; *an eventful journey,* un viaje accidentado.
eventual [ɪˈventʃʊəl] **1** *adj* (*final, ultimate*) final. **2** (*resulting*) consiguiente. **3** (*possible*) posible.
eventuality [ɪventʃʊˈælɪtɪ] *n* eventualidad *f*: *we must be prepared for all eventualities,* hemos de estar preparados para cualquier eventualidad.
▲ *pl* eventualities.
eventually [ɪˈventʃʊəlɪ] *adv* finalmente, con el tiempo.
ever [ˈevəʳ] **1** *adv* (*in negative sentences*) nunca, jamás: *nobody ever comes,* no viene nunca nadie; *nothing this has ever happened before,* nunca ha pasado nada semejante; *don't ever do that again,* no vuelves a hacer esto jamás. **2** (*in questions*) alguna vez: *have you ever seen "Dracula"?,* ¿has visto "Drácula" alguna vez?; *have you ever been to London?,* ¿has estado en Londres alguna vez?; *do you ever think about life after death?,* ¿piensas alguna vez en la vida después de la muerte?; *if you ever go to England, come and visit me,* si vas alguna vez a Inglaterra, ven a visitarme; *did you ever meet my ex-husband?,* ¿llegaste a conocer a mi ex-marido? **3** (*always*) siempre: *and they lived happily ever after,* y vivieron felices para siempre; *I'll love you for ever,* te amaré para siempre. **4** (*after comparative and superlative*) nunca: *this is the best meal I've ever tasted,* ésta es la mejor comida que he probado nunca; *I'm feeling better than ever,* estoy mejor que nunca; *it's hurting more than ever,* me duele más que nunca. **5** (*emphatic use*): *what ever shall I do?,* ¿qué demonios hago?; *how ever did you lose your coat?,* ¿cómo demonios has perdido el abrigo?; *why ever not?,* ¿y por qué no?
● **all sb. ever does is ...,** lo único que algn. hace es ... ‖ **as ever,** como siempre. ‖ **as (adjective) as ever,** tan (adjetivo) como siempre: *he's still as boring as ever,* aún es tan aburrido como siempre. ‖ **ever since,** desde, desde entonces: *ever since the war,* desde la guerra; *I've been here ever since,* estoy aquí desde entonces. ‖ **ever so,** muy ...: *I'm ever so pleased,* estoy muy contenta; *thanks ever so (much),* muchas gracias. ‖ **ever such ...,** muy ...: *she's ever such a nice person,* es muy simpática. ‖ **for ever (and ever),** para siempre (jamás). ‖ **ever more,** más y más, cada vez más. ‖ **did you ever ...!,** ¡hábráse visto! ‖ **ever yours, ... / yours ever, ...,** (*in letters*) recibe un abrazo de ...
evergreen [ˈevəgriːn] **1** *adj* BOT de hoja perenne. – **2** *n* (*tree*) árbol *m* de hoja perenne; (*bush*) arbusto de hoja perenne.
■ **evergreen oak,** encina.
everlasting [evəˈlɑːstɪŋ] **1** *adj* (*eternal, lasting for ever*) eterno,-a, perpetuo,-a. **2** (*lasting for long time*) duradero,-a, perdurable. **3** *pej* (*incessant*) continuo,-a, incesante.

■ **the Everlasting,** Dios.

everlastingly [evə'lɑːstɪŋlɪ] **1** adv eternamente. **2** pej continuamente, incesantemente.

evermore [evə'mɔːʳ] adv eternamente.
● **for evermore,** para siempre.

every ['evrɪ] **1** adj (each) cada; (all) todos,-as: every day, cada día, todos los días; every weekend, cada fin de semana, todos los fines de semana; she cries every time, llora cada vez; I re-read every letter, volví a leer cada carta; every student passed, todos los estudiantes aprobaron; we enjoyed every minute of the film, nos gustó la película de principio a fin; he drank every last drop, bebió hasta la última gota. **2** (once in each) cada: there are elections every five years, hay elecciones cada cinco años; she has a check-up once every six months, le hacen un chequeo cada seis meses; one in every twelve women suffer from cancer, una de cada doce mujeres padece de cáncer. **3** (all possible): you have every chance of passing, tienes grandes posibilidades de aprobar; we encourage people to help in every way, animamos a la gente a que ayude de cualquier manera; I have every confidence in them, tengo plena confianza en ellos; you had every right to be pleased, tenías todo el derecho a estar contento.
● every other day, un día sí un día no, cada dos días. || every other week, cada dos semanas. || every now and then, de vez en cuando. || every so often, de cuando en cuando. || to be every bit as ... as ..., ser igual de ... que ...: it's every bit as good as the other one, es igual de bueno que el otro; I'm every bit as clever as him, yo soy tan inteligente como él.

everybody ['evrɪbɒdɪ] pron todos,-as, todo el mundo: have you met everybody?, ¿conoces a todos?; everybody has a car, todo el mundo tiene coche.

everyday ['evrɪdeɪ] adj (day-to-day) diario,-a, de todos los días; (ordinary) corriente, cotidiano,-a: for everyday use, para uso diario; our everyday routine, nuestra rutina diaria; they wanted to get back to their normal everyday life, querían volver a su vida de cada día; an everyday ocurrence, un suceso cotidiano.

everyone ['evrɪwʌn] pron → **everybody**.

everyplace ['evrɪpleɪs] adv US → **everywhere**.

everything ['evrɪθɪŋ] pron todo: is everything all right?, ¿todo (va) bien?; everything's ready, todo está preparado; I'll see to everything, yo me ocuparé de todo; she remembered to bring everything, se acordó de traer todo; you're everything to me, tú lo eres todo para mí; we've tried everything, lo hemos intentado todo.

everywhere ['evrɪweəʳ] **1** adv (place) en todas partes, por todas partes: he's been everywhere, ha estado en todas partes; she looked everywhere, buscó por todas partes; it's the same everywhere, en todas partes pasa lo mismo; children everywhere love Mickey Mouse, los niños de todo el mundo quieren a Mickey Mouse. **2** (movement) a todas partes: she took her baby everywhere, llevó a su bebé a todas partes; he follows me everywhere, me sigue a todas partes.

evict [ɪ'vɪkt] t desahuciar, desalojar.

eviction [ɪ'vɪkʃən] n desahucio, desalojo.
■ **eviction order,** orden f de desahucio.

evidence ['evɪdəns] **1** n (proof) prueba, pruebas fpl: we don't have enough evidence against him, no tenemos suficientes pruebas en contra suya; anything you say may be used in evidence against you, cualquier cosa que digas puede ser utilizado en contra tuyo; the video was part of the prosecution's evidence, el vídeo formaba parte de las pruebas del fiscal; you haven't got a shred of evidence, no tenéis ni la más mínima prueba. **2** (sign, indication) indicio, indicios mpl, señal f: there is no evidence to suggest that ..., no hay indicios que sugieran que ...; she showed no evidence of being upset, no daba muestras de estar disgustada. **3** JUR (testimony) testimonio, declaración f. – **4** t (prove) demostrar, probar. **5** (give proof of) justificar.
● to give evidence, prestar declaración, declarar como testigo. || to turn King's/Queen's evidence, delatar a un cómplice. || to turn state's evidence, US delatar a un cómplice. || in evidence, visible. || to be in evidence, estar a la vista, hacerse notar. || on the evidence of sth., basándose en algo.

evident ['evɪdənt] adj evidente, patente, manifiesto,-a: it was evident that he had been lying to us, era evidente que nos había mentido; his motives were not evident, sus motivos no eran evidentes.

evidently ['evɪdəntlɪ] **1** adv (obviously, clearly) evidentemente. **2** (apparently) por lo visto, al parecer.

evil ['iːvəl] **1** adj (wicked) malo,-a, malvado,-a. **2** (harmful) malo,-a, pernicioso,-a, nocivo,-a. **3** (foul - smell) horrible, fétido,-a, repugnante; (- temper) geniudo,-a, terrible, de perros; (- weather) malo,-a, de perros. **4** (unlucky) aciago,-a, de mal agüero. – **5** n (wickedness) mal m, maldad f: good and evil, el bien y el mal; the evils of drink, los males de la bebida.
● to give sb. the evil eye, echar mal de ojo a algn. || to have an evil tongue, tener una lengua viperina. || to speak evil of sb., hablar mal de algn.

evildoer ['iːvəlduːəʳ] n malhechor,-ra.

evilly ['iːvəlɪ] adv con maldad.

evil-minded ['iːvəlmaɪndɪd] adj malvado,-a, malpensado,-a.

evocation [evə'keɪʃən] n evocación f.

evocative [ɪ'vɒkətɪv] adj evocador,-ra.

evoke [ɪ'vəʊk] **1** t (bring to mind) evocar. **2** fml (produce, cause) provocar.

evolution [iːvə'luːʃən] **1** n (biol) evolución f: Darwin's theory of evolution, la teoría de la evolución de Darwin. **2** (gradual development) desarrollo.

evolutionary [iːvə'luːʃənərɪ] adj evolutivo,-a.

evolve [ɪ'vɒlv] **1** t (develop) desarrollar. **2** (give off) desprender. – **3** i (develop) desarrollarse. **4** (biol) evolucionar.

ewe [juː] n oveja.

ex[1] [eks] n fam (husband) ex marido; (wife) ex mujer f.

ex[2] [eks] prep FIN sin: ex dividend, sin dividendo, sin cupón; ex interest, sin interés.
■ ex factory price, precio de fábrica. || ex warehouse price, precio de almacén.

ex- [eks] pref ex, ex-.

exacerbate [ɪg'zæsəbeɪt] t exacerbar, agravar.

exact [ɪg'zækt] **1** adj (precise) exacto,-a: an exact copy, una copia exacta; the exact sum, la cantidad exacta; my exact words, mis palabras exactas. **2** (meticulous) meticuloso,-a: an exact student, un estudiante meticuloso. **3** (accurate) preciso,-a: an exact definition, una definición precisa; an exact science, una ciencia exacta. **4** (specific, particular) justo: this is the exact spot where ..., fue en este mismo lugar donde ..., fue justo en este lugar donde ...; that's the exact type of material I need, ese es justamente el tipo de tela que necesito. – **5** t (demand, insist on) exigir (from, a): they exacted a sum of £1000, exigieron una cantidad de £1000; he exacts obedience from his children, exige obediencia a sus hijos. **6** (require) exigir, requerir: this job exacts great patience, este trabajo requiere mucha paciencia.

● **to be exact,** para ser preciso, para ser exacto, concretamente.

exacting [ɪg'zæktɪŋ] *adj* exigente.

exactitude [ɪg'zæktɪtjuːd] *n* exactitud *f*.

exactly [ɪg'zæktlɪ] **1** *adv* (*in precise detail, correctly, accurately*) exactamente, precisamente: *you have exactly two hours from now,* tenéis exactamente dos horas a partir de ahora; *where exactly in London do you live?,* ¿exactamente dónde vives en Londres?; *she arrived at exactly 9.00am,* llegó a las 9.00 en punto; *what exactly are you trying to do?,* ¿exactamente qué intentas hacer?; *your baby's exactly like you,* tu bebé es igual que tú. **2** (*precisely*) justo, exactamente: *that's exactly what I wanted,* eso es justo lo que quería; *that's exactly what she said,* eso es exactamente lo que dijo. – **3** *interj* ¡exacto!, ¡exactamente!

● **not exactly,** *iron* precisamente: *it wasn't exactly what I had in mind,* no era precisamente lo que tenía pensado; *she wasn't exactly thrilled with the present,* no es que le gustara mucho el regalo.

exactness [ɪg'zæktnəs] *n* exactitud *f*, precisión *f*.

exaggerate [ɪg'zædʒəreɪt] **1** *t* exagerar: *I think you're exaggerating the problem somewhat,* creo que estás exagerando un tanto el problema. – **2** *i* exagerar: *come on! don't exaggerate!,* ¡venga ya! ¡no exageres!

exaggerated [ɪg'zædʒəreɪtɪd] *adj* exagerado,-a: *exaggerated figures,* cifras exageradas; *an exaggerated movement,* un movimiento exagerado.

exaggeratedly [ɪg'zædʒəreɪtlɪ] *adv* exageradamente.

exaggeration [ɪgzædʒə'reɪʃən] *n* exageración *f*.

exalt [ɪg'zɔːlt] **1** *t fml* (*elevate*) exaltar, elevar. **2** (*praise, extol*) ensalzar.

exaltation [egzɔːl'teɪʃən] *n* exaltación *f*.

exam [ɪg'zæm] *n fam* examen *m*.

examination [ɪgzæmɪ'neɪʃən] **1** *n* EDUC examen *m*: *I've got an English examination tomorrow,* tengo un examen de inglés mañana. **2** (*inspection*) inspección *f*, examen *m*; (*of house, room*) registro: *detailed examination of the gun revealed new fingerprints,* en un examen detallado del arma se descubrieron nuevas huellas dactilares. **3** MED reconocimiento: *the doctor gave him a full examination,* el doctor le hizo un reconocimiento completo. **4** JUR interrogatorio: *the prosecution subjected the witness to yet another examination,* el fiscal sometió al testigo a otro interrogatorio.

● **to be under examination,** (*questioned*) estar sometido,-a a un interrogatorio; (*looked at, investigated*) estar sometido,-a a examen. ‖ **to sit an examination / take an examination,** examinarse.

■ **examination paper,** examen *m*.

examine [ɪg'zæmɪn] **1** *t* (*inspect*) inspeccionar, examinar; (*check*) comprobar; (*consider*) examinar, estudiar: *experts are still examining the plane's black box,* los expertos aún están examinando la caja negra del avión; *have you examined all the facts?,* ¿has comprobado todos los hechos?; *we have examined your proposal very carefully,* hemos estudiado su propuesta muy detalladamente. **2** (*customs*) registrar: *they examined my things,* me registraron el equipaje. **3** EDUC examinar (**in/on**, de). **4** MED hacer un reconocimiento a. **5** JUR interrogar.

examinee [ɪgzæmɪ'niː] *n* examinado,-a.

examiner [ɪg'zæmɪnəʳ] *n* examinador,-ra.

example [ɪg'zɑːmpəl] **1** *n* (*gen*) ejemplo: *give me an example of a verb,* dame un ejemplo de un verbo; *his courage should be an example to us all,* su coraje debería servirnos de ejemplo a todos; *that was an ex-* *ample of what not to do,* eso ha sido un ejemplo de lo que no hay que hacer. **2** (*specimen*) ejemplo: *this building is a perfect example of modernist architecture,* este edificio es un ejemplo perfecto de la arquitectura modernista.

● **for example,** por ejemplo. ‖ **let this be an example to you,** que esto te sirva de ejemplo. ‖ **to make an example of sb.,** dar un castigo ejemplar a algn. ‖ **to set a good example,** dar buen ejemplo. ‖ **to set a bad example,** dar mal ejemplo.

exasperate [ɪg'zɑːspəreɪt] *t* exasperar, irritar.

● **to get exasperated,** exasperarse, irritarse.

exasperating [ɪg'zæspəreɪtɪŋ] *adj* exasperante, irritante.

exasperation [ɪg'zæspəreɪʃən] *n* exasperación *f*, irritación *f*.

● **in exasperation,** exasperado,-a, irritado,-a.

excavate ['ekskəveɪt] *t* excavar.

excavation [ekskə'veɪʃən] *n* excavación *f*.

excavator ['ekskəveɪtəʳ] **1** *n* (*person*) excavador,-ra. **2** (*machine*) excavadora.

exceed [ɪk'siːd] *t* (*be greater than*) exceder, sobrepasar; (*go beyond*) exceder, sobrepasar: *the price must not exceed £100,* el precio no debe exceder las 100 libras; *do not exceed the speed limit,* no sobrepasar el límite de velocidad.

exceedingly [ɪk'siːdɪŋlɪ] *adv* extremadamente, sumamente.

excel [ɪk'sel] **1** *t* (*surpass*) aventajar, superar. – **2** *i* (*be very good at*) destacar (**at/in**, en), sobresalir (**at/in**, en), descollar (**at/in**, en): *he excels at swimming,* destaca en natación; *he excels as a doctor,* es un gran médico.

● **to excel os.,** superarse.

▲ *pt* & *pp* **excelled,** *ger* **excelling.**

excellence ['eksələns] *n* excelencia.

Excellency ['eksələnsɪ] *n* Excelencia.

▲ *pl* **Excellencies.**

excellent ['eksələnt] **1** *adj* excelente, sobresaliente. – **2** *interj fam* ¡estupendo!, ¡fantástico!

excellently ['eksələntlɪ] *adv* excelentemente, estupendamente.

except [ɪk'sept] **1** *prep* excepto, salvo, a excepción de, menos: *everyone went to the pub except Jim,* todos se fueron al pub menos Jim; *she knew all the answers except one,* sabía todas las respuestas excepto una; *everything was fine except for the weather,* todo estuvo bien menos el tiempo; *I remember very little about him, except that he was bald,* me acuerdo muy poco de él, salvo que era calvo. – **2** *t fml* excluir, exceptuar.

exception [ɪk'sepʃən] *n* excepción *f*.

● **the exception proves the rule,** la excepción confirma la regla. ‖ **to make an exception of,** hacer una excepción de. ‖ **to take exception to sth.,** ofenderse por algo. ‖ **with the exception of,** a excepción de.

exceptionable [ɪk'sepʃənəbəl] *adj* censurable.

exceptional [ɪk'sepʃənəl] *adj* excepcional, extraordinario,-a.

exceptionally [ɪk'sepʃənəlɪ] *adv* excepcionalmente, extraordinariamente.

excerpt ['eksɜːpt] *n* extracto.

excess [ɪk'ses] **1** *n* exceso: *an excess of fat,* un exceso de grasa. **2** COMM excedente *m*. – **3** *adj* excedente, sobrante. – **4 excesses,** *npl* excesos *mpl*.

● **in excess,** en exceso. ‖ **in excess of,** superior a. ‖ **to excess,** con exceso, en exceso. ‖ **to do sth. to excess,** hacer algo con/en exceso.

■ **excess demand,** exceso de demanda. ‖ **excess fare,** suplemento. ‖ **excess baggage,** exceso de equipaje. ‖ **excess supply,** exceso de oferta.
excessive [ɪkˈsesɪv] *adj* excesivo,-a.
excessively [ɪkˈsesɪvlɪ] *adv* excesivamente, en exceso.
exchange [ɪksˈtʃeɪndʒ] **1** *n* (*gen*) cambio. **2** (*of ideas, information, etc*) intercambio. **3** (*of prisoners*) canje *m*. **4** FIN cambio. **5** (*dialogue*) intercambio de palabras; (*argument*) enfrentamiento. **6** (*building*) lonja. **7** (*telephone*) central *f* telefónica. **8** EDUC (*reciprocal visit*) intercambio. **9** (*of gunfire*) tiroteo. – **10** *t* (*gen*) cambiar: *can I exchange this shirt for a bigger one?,* ¿puedo cambiar esta camisa por una más grande? **11** (*ideas, information, etc*) intercambiar. **12** (*prisoners*) canjear.
● **in exchange,** a cambio. ‖ **in exchange for,** a cambio de. ‖ **to exchange blows,** golpearse. ‖ **to exchange glances,** mirarse. ‖ **to exchange greetings,** saludarse. ‖ **to exchange words,** cruzar unas palabras.
■ **bill of exchange,** letra de cambio. ‖ **Corn Exchange,** lonja de granos. ‖ **exchange rate,** tipo de cambio. ‖ **rate of exchange,** tipo de cambio. ‖ **Stock Exchange,** Bolsa.
exchangeable [ɪksˈtʃeɪndʒəbəl] *adj* cambiable, canjeable.
exchequer [ɪksˈtʃekəʳ] **1** *n* (*treasury*) tesoro público. **2** **the Exchequer,** Hacienda.
excise¹ [ɪkˈsaɪz] *t fml* extirpar.
excise² [ˈeksaɪz] *n* impuesto sobre el consumo.
■ **excise duty,** impuesto sobre el consumo.
excision [ɪkˈsɪʒən] *n fml* extirpación *f*, excisión *f*.
excitability [ɪksaɪtəˈbɪlətɪ] *n* excitabilidad *f*.
excitable [ɪkˈsaɪtəbəl] *adj* excitable, nervioso,-a.
excite [ɪkˈsaɪt] **1** *t* (*enthuse, thrill*) emocionar, entusiasmar, apasionar: *the idea of travelling abroad excited her,* la idea de viajar al extranjero le entusiasmaba. **2** *fml* (*bring about*) provocar: *troublemakers excited a riot,* unos alborotadores provocaron un motín. **3** (*cause, arouse*) provocar, despertar: *the case has excited great public interest,* el juicio ha provocado un gran interés público. **4** (*arouse sexually*) excitar. **5** MED (*stimulate*) excitar.
excited [ɪkˈsaɪtɪd] **1** *adj* emocionado,-a, entusiasmado,-a, ilusionado,-a: *I'm really excited about Christmas this year,* este año estoy muy ilusionado con las Navidades; *the children are so excited!,* ¡los niños están tan ilusionados! **2** (*sexually*) excitado,-a, caliente.
● **to get excited,** (*enthusiastically*) emocionarse, entusiasmarse, apasionarse; (*sexually*) excitarse, ponerse caliente.
excitedly [ɪkˈsaɪtɪdlɪ] *adv* con emoción, con entusiasmo, con ilusión.
excitement [ɪkˈsaɪtmənt] **1** *n* (*strong feeling*) emoción *f*, entusiasmo, ilusión *f*: *we couldn't hide our excitement,* no podíamos ocultar nuestra emoción. **2** (*commotion*) agitación *f*, conmoción *f*, revuelo: *the discovery caused great excitement,* el descubrimiento causó gran revuelo.
exciting [ɪkˈsaɪtɪŋ] *adj* emocionante, apasionante: *how exciting!,* ¡qué ilusión!
exclaim [ɪksˈkleɪm] **1** *t* exclamar, gritar. – **2** *i* exclamar.
exclamation [ekskləˈmeɪʃən] *n* exclamación *f*.
■ **exclamation mark,** signo de admiración. ‖ **exclamation point,** US signo de admiración.
exclamatory [ɪksˈklæmətrɪ] *adj* exclamatorio,-a.
exclude [ɪksˈkluːd] **1** *t* (*leave out, not include*) excluir, no incluir. **2** (*debar, prevent from entering*) no admitir. **3** (*reject*) excluir, descartar.

excluding [ɪksˈkluːdɪŋ] *prep* (*excepting*) excepto, con excepción de.
exclusion [ɪksˈkluːʒən] *n* exclusión *f*.
● **to the exclusion of,** excluyendo.
exclusive [ɪksˈkluːsɪv] **1** *adj* (*not shared, sole*) exclusivo,-a. **2** (*select*) selecto,-a, exclusivo,-a. **3** (*press*) en exclusiva. – **4** *n* (*press*) exclusiva.
● **exclusive of,** excluyendo, sin incluir. ‖ **to be exclusive to,** ser exclusivo,-a de.
exclusively [ɪksˈkluːsɪvlɪ] *adv* exclusivamente.
exclusiveness [ekˈskluːsɪvnəs] *n* exclusividad *f*.
excommunicate [ekskəˈmjuːnɪkeɪt] *t* excomulgar.
excommunication [ekskəmjuːnɪˈkeɪʃən] *n* excomunión *f*.
excrement [ˈekskrɪmənt] *n* excremento.
excrete [ɪkˈskriːt] *t* excretar.
excretion [ɪkˈskriːʃən] *n* excreción *f*.
excruciating [ɪkˈskruːʃɪeɪtɪŋ] **1** *adj* insoportable, atroz, agudísimo,-a. **2** *euph* fatal, horrible.
excruciatingly [ɪkˈskruːʃɪeɪtɪŋlɪ] *adv* atrozmente, horriblemente.
excursion [ɪkˈskɜːʒən] *n* (*outing*) excursión *f*, viaje *m*: *we went on an excursion round the island,* hicimos una excursión por la isla.
■ **shopping excursion,** excursión *f* para hacer compras.
excusable [ɪkˈskjuːzəbəl] *adj* perdonable, disculpable.
excuse [ɪkˈskjuːs] **1** *n* (*apology*) disculpa: *there's simply no excuse for this,* esto no admite ninguna disculpa. **2** (*pretext*) excusa: *his excuse for being late was that he had missed the train,* su excusa por llegar tarde fue que había perdido el tren. – **3** *t* perdonar, disculpar: *please excuse my handwriting,* perdone mi letra; *excuse me for being late,* siento llegar tarde. **4** (*justify*) justificar: *nothing can excuse such violent conduct,* no hay nada que justifique una conducta tan violenta. **5** (*exempt*) dispensar, eximir; (*military*) rebajar: *you may be excused gym today,* hoy te dispensamos (de) la clase de gimnasia.
● **excuse me,** (*when interrupting*) perdone; (*when leaving*) disculpe, con permiso; (*to get sb.'s attention*) oiga, por favor; (*to apologize*) perdón, perdone; (*asking for repetition*) ¿cómo?, ¿perdón? ‖ **to make one's excuses,** pedir disculpas. ‖ **may I be excused?,** ¿puedo salir un momento?
▲ (*verbo*) [ɪkˈskjuːz].
ex-directory [eksdaɪˈrektərɪ] *adj* (*tel*) que no figura en la guía telefónica.
execute [ˈeksɪkjuːt] **1** *t* (*put to death*) ejecutar, ajusticiar. **2** (*carry out*) ejecutar; (*orders*) cumplir; (*tasks*) realizar, llevar a cabo. **3** (*music etc*) interpretar. **4** JUR (*will*) cumplir.
execution [eksɪˈkjuːʃən] **1** *n* (*carrying out*) ejecución *f*; (*of task*) realización *f*. **2** (*putting to death*) ejecución *f*. **3** JUR (*of will*) cumplimiento. **4** (*of music etc*) interpretación *f*.
executioner [eksɪˈkjuːʃənəʳ] *n* verdugo.
executive [ɪgˈzekjʊtɪv] **1** *adj* ejecutivo,-a. – **2** *n* (*person*) ejecutivo,-a; (*committee*) ejecutiva. **3** **the executive,** (*government*) el poder ejecutivo, el ejecutivo.
executor [ɪgˈzekjʊtəʳ] *n* JUR albacea.
exemplary [ɪgˈzemplərɪ] *adj* ejemplar.
exemplification [ɪgzemplɪfɪˈkeɪʃən] *n* ejemplificación *f*, ejemplo.
exemplify [ɪgˈzemplɪfaɪ] *t* ejemplificar, servir de ejemplo para.

exempt 208

▲ *pt & pp* exemplified, *ger* exemplifying.
exempt [ɪgˈzempt] **1** *adj* exento,-a, libre (**from**, de). – **2** *t* eximir, dispensar (**from**, de).
exemption [ɪgˈzempʃən] *n* exención *f* (**from**, de).
exercise [ˈeksəsaɪz] **1** *n* (*gen*) ejercicio: *you should take more exercise,* deberías hacer más ejercicio; *have you finished this exercise?,* ¿has acabado este ejercicio? **2** (*use, application*) ejercicio, uso: *the exercise of one's rights,* el ejercicio de sus derechos. – **3** *t* (*employ, make use of*) ejercer, emplear: *he had to exercise extreme re-straint,* tuvo que emplear mucha moderación; *you must exercise great care,* hay que tener mucho cuidado. **4** (*give exercise to - dog*) sacar de paseo; (*- horse*) entrenar. – **5** *i* hacer ejercicio, entrenarse: *how often do you ex-ercise?,* ¿con qué frecuencia haces ejercicio? – **6** *t fml* (*trouble*) inquietar. – **7 exercises,** *npl* US (*ceremonies*) ceremonia.
■ **exercise book,** cuaderno.
exert [ɪgˈzɜːt] *t* ejercer: *he exerted pressure on his players,* ejerció presión sobre sus jugadores.
● **to exert os.,** esforzarse.
exertion [ɪgˈzɜːʃən] **1** *n* (*great effort*) esfuerzo. **2** (*use, application*) ejercicio, uso.
ex gratia [eksˈɡreɪʃə] **ex gratia payment,** *n* pago discrecional.
exhalation [ekshəˈleɪʃən] *n* exhalación *f*.
exhale [eksˈheɪl] **1** *t* (*breathe out*) exhalar. – **2** *i* (*give off*) despedir.
exhaust [ɪgˈzɔːst] **1** *n* (*pipe*) (tubo de) escape *m*. **2** (*fumes*) gases *mpl* de combustión. – **3** *t* (*gen*) agotar: *the long walk exhausted me,* la caminata me agotó; *they ex-hausted the food supplies,* agotaron las provisiones de comida; *you've exhausted my patience,* has agotado mi paciencia; *we've exhausted that subject,* hemos agota-do aquel tema. **4** (*empty*) vaciar.
● **to exhaust os.,** agotarse.
exhausted [ɪgˈzɔːstɪd] *adj* agotado,-a.
exhausting [ɪgˈzɔːstɪŋ] *adj* agotador,-ra.
exhaustion [ɪgˈzɔːstʃən] *n* agotamiento.
exhaustive [ɪgˈzɔːstɪv] *adj* exhaustivo,-a, completo,-a: *an exhaustive enquiry,* una investigación exhaustiva.
exhaustively [ɪgˈzɔːstɪvlɪ] *adv* de modo exhaustivo, ex-haustivamente.
exhibit [ɪgˈzɪbɪt] **1** *n* ART objeto expuesto. **2** JUR prueba instrumental. – **3** *t* (*display, show*) exponer, presentar: *she has exhibited her work in several countries,* ha ex-puesto su obra en varios países. **4** *fml* (*manifest*) ma-nifestar, mostrar, presentar, dar muestras de: *the patient exhibits signs of stress,* el paciente presenta sín-tomas de estrés. – **5** *i* (*of artist*) exponer.
exhibition [eksɪˈbɪʃən] **1** *n* (*art etc*) exposición *f*. **2** (*dis-play*) demostración *f*, muestra. **3** GB EDUC premio, beca.
● **to be on exhibition,** estar expuesto,-a. ‖ **to make an exhibition of os.,** ponerse en ridículo, hacer el ri-dículo.
exhibitionism [eksɪˈbɪʃənɪzəm] *n* exhibicionismo.
exhibitionist [eksɪˈbɪʃənɪst] *n* exhibicionista *mf*.
exhibitor [ɪgˈzɪbɪtəʳ] *n* expositor,-ra.
exhilarate [ɪgˈzɪləreɪt] *t* (*make cheerful*) animar, alegrar; (*enliven, stimulate*) avivar, estimular.
exhilarating [ɪgˈzɪləreɪtɪŋ] *adj* (*invigorating*) estimulante; (*exciting*) emocionante.
exhilaration [ɪgzɪləˈreɪʃən] *n* (*state*) alegría, regocijo; (*act*) estímulo.
exhort [ɪgˈzɔːt] *t fml* exhortar.
exhume [eksˈhjuːm] *t* exhumar, desenterrar.

exigency [ˈeksɪdʒənsɪ, ɪgˈzɪdʒənsɪ] **1** *n fml* (*need*) exigen-cia. **2** *fml* (*emergency*) caso de emergencia.
▲ *pl* exigencies.
exigent [ˈeksɪdʒənt] **1** *adj fml* (*demanding*) exigente. **2** *fml* (*urgent*) urgente.
exiguous [ekˈsɪgjʊəs] *adj fml* exiguo,-a.
exile [ˈeksaɪl] **1** *n* (*action*) destierro, exilio. **2** (*person*) des-terrado,-a, exiliado,-a. – **3** *t* desterrar, exiliar.
exist [ɪgˈzɪst] **1** *i* (*gen*) existir. **2** (*subsist*) subsistir (**on**, a base de).
existence [ɪgˈzɪstəns] *n* existencia.
● **to be in existence,** existir. ‖ **to come into exist-ence,** nacer.
existent [ɪgˈzɪstənt] *adj* existente.
existential [egzɪˈstenʃəl] *adj* existencial.
existentialism [egzɪˈstenʃəlɪzəm] *n* existencialismo.
existentialist [egzɪˈstenʃəlɪst] *n* existencialista *mf*.
existing [egzɪˈstɪŋ] *adj* existente, actual.
exit [ˈeksɪt] **1** *n* (*gen*) salida. **2** THEAT mutis *m*. – **3** *i* THEAT hacer mutis, salir de escena.
■ **exit sign,** indicador *m* de salida.
exodus [ˈeksədəs] *n* éxodo.
ex officio [eks əˈfɪʃɪəʊ] **1** *adj* de oficio. – **2** *adv* de oficio.
exonerate [ɪgˈzɒnəreɪt] *t* exonerar, exculpar.
exoneration [ɪgzɒnəˈreɪʃən] *n* exoneración *f*, exculpa-ción *f*.
exorbitance [ɪgˈzɔːbɪtəns] *n* exorbitancia.
exorbitant [ɪgˈzɔːbɪtənt] *adj* exorbitante, desorbitado,-a, excesivo,-a: *the rent is exorbitant,* el alquiler es ex-cesivo.
exorbitantly [ɪgˈzɔːbɪtəntlɪ] *adv* excesivamente.
exorcise [ˈeksɔːsaɪz] **1** *t* exorcizar. **2** *fig* (*memory*) borrar; (*feeling*) quitar, librar.
exorcism [ˈeksɔːsɪzəm] *n* exorcismo.
exorcist [ˈeksɔːsɪst] *n* exorcista *mf*.
exorcize [ˈeksɔːsaɪz] *t* → **exorcise**.
exotic [egˈzɒtɪk] *adj* exótico,-a.
expand [ɪkˈspænd] **1** *t* (*enlarge - business*) ampliar; (*- num-ber*) aumentar, incrementar. **2** (*gas, metal*) dilatar, ex-pandir. – **3** *i* (*grow larger*) crecer, aumentar: *the business has expanded greatly,* el negocio ha crecido mucho; *the population expanded rapidly,* la población creció rápi-damente. **4** (*metal*) dilatarse; (*gas*) expandirse, expan-sionarse. **5** (*spread out*) extenderse. **6** (*become friendlier*) abrirse, volverse expansivo,-a.
◆ **to expand on** *t insep* ampliar, desarrollar.
expanse [ɪkˈspæns] *n* extensión *f*.
expansion [ɪkˈspænʃən] **1** *n* crecimiento, aumento. **2** (*gas, metal*) dilatación *f*, expansión *f*. **3** (*trade*) desarrollo.
expansionism [ɪkˈspænʃənɪzəm] *n* expansionismo.
expansionist [ɪkˈspænʃənɪst] *n* expansionista *mf*.
expansive [ɪkˈspænsɪv] **1** *adj* (*friendly, talkative*) expan-sivo,-a, hablador,-ra, comunicativo,-a. **2** (*able to expand*) expansivo,-a.
expatiate [ɪkˈspeɪʃɪeɪt] *i fml* extenderse.
expatriate [ekˈspætrɪət] **1** *adj* expatriado,-a. – **2** *n* ex-patriado,-a. – **3** *t* desterrar, expatriar.
▲ (*verbo*) [eksˈpætrɪeɪt].
expect [ɪkˈspekt] **1** *t* (*anticipate*) esperar: *I never expected to win,* no esperaba ganar; *she expected him to pass,* esperaba que él aprobara; *the hotel wasn't as good as we expected,* el hotel no era tan bueno como esperá-bamos; *I was expecting you two hours ago,* te esperaba hace dos horas; *were you expecting a parcel?,* ¿espe-rabas un paquete?; *she's expecting a baby,* está espe-

rando un niño. **2** (*demand*) esperar, contar con: *I don't expect you to pay,* no espero que pagues; *what did you expect me to do?,* ¿qué esperabas que hiciera?; *you are expected to help out in the house,* se cuenta con que ayudes en la casa; *he expects you to be punctual,* cuenta con que seas puntual. **3** GB *fam* (*suppose*) suponer, imaginar: *I expect he's at lunch,* me imagino que habrá salido a comer; *I expect it was Susan,* supongo que era Susan.
● **I expect so,** supongo que sí. ‖ **to be expecting,** *fam* estar embarazada. ‖ **to expect too much (of sb.),** esperar demasiado (de algn.). ‖ **(only) to be expected,** ser de esperar, ser natural.
expectancy [ɪk'spektənsɪ] *n* (*anticipation*) expectación *f*, expectativa; (*hope*) ilusión *f*.
expectant [ɪk'spektənt] *adj* (*expecting*) expectante; (*hopeful*) ilusionado,-a.
■ **expectant mother,** futura madre *f*, mujer *f* embarazada.
expectation [ekspek'teɪʃən] **1** *n* (*hope, firm belief*) esperanza: *we watched in expectation,* observamos esperanzados. – **2 expectations,** *npl* (*confident feelings*) expectativas *fpl*: *I had great expectations for the future,* tenía grandes expectativas de futuro.
● **contrary to expectations,** contrariamente a lo que se esperaba. ‖ **in expectation of,** con la esperanza de. ‖ **to be beyond sb.'s expectations,** ser mejor de lo esperado. ‖ **to fall short of sb.'s expectations,** no alcanzar las expectativas de algn. ‖ **not to come up to sb.'s expectations,** no alcanzar las expectativas de algn.
expectorant [ɪk'spektərənt] *n* expectorante *m*.
expectorate [ɪk'spektəreɪt] *t* MED expectorar.
expedience [ɪk'spiːdɪəns] *n* → **expediency**.
expediency [ɪk'spiːdɪənsɪ] *n* conveniencia, oportunidad *f*.
expedient [ɪk'spiːdɪənt] **1** *adj* conveniente, oportuno,-a. – **2** *n* expediente *m*, recurso.
expediently [ɪk'spiːdɪəntlɪ] *adv* oportunamente, convenientemente.
expedite ['ekspədaɪt] *t fml* (*hasten, speed up*) acelerar.
expedition [ekspɪ'dɪʃən] **1** *n* (*gen*) expedición *f*. **2** *fml* (*speed*) aceleración *f*, prontitud *f*.
■ **shopping expedition,** excursión *f* para hacer compras.
expeditionary [ekspɪ'dɪʃənərɪ] *adj* expedicionario,-a.
■ **expeditionary force,** cuerpo expedicionario.
expeditious [ekspɪ'dɪʃəs] *adj fml* expeditivo,-a, expedito,-a.
expeditiously [ekspɪ'dɪʃəslɪ] *adv fml* expeditivamente.
expel [ɪk'spel] **1** *t* (*dismiss officially*) expulsar: *the boys were expelled for fighting,* los chicos fueron expulsados por pelearse. **2** (*force out*) expulsar.
▲ *pt* & *pp* **expelled,** *ger* **expelling.**
expend [ɪk'spend] **1** *t fml* (*spend, use*) gastar, emplear. **2** *fml* (*use up, exhaust*) agotar.
expendable [ɪk'spendəbəl] *adj fml* prescindible.
expenditure [ɪk'spendɪtʃəʳ] *n* gasto, desembolso.
expense [ɪk'spens] **1** *n* gasto, desembolso. – **2 expenses,** *npl* gastos *mpl*.
● **at great expense to sb.,** costándole caro a algn., pagándolo caro algn. ‖ **at little expense to sb.,** costándole poco a algn. ‖ **at no expense to sb.,** sin costarle nada a algn. ‖ **at sb.'s expense,** (*with sb. paying*) corriendo algn. con los gastos; (*to make seem foolish*) a costa de algn. ‖ **at the expense of sth.,** *fig* a expensas

de algo, a costa de algo. ‖ **no expense spared,** sin escatimar gastos, sin parar en gastos. ‖ **to go to the expense of sth./doing sth.,** gastar mucho dinero en algo. ‖ **to put sb. to the expense of sth./doing sth.,** hacer que algn. gaste dinero en algo. ‖ **to spare no expense,** no escatimar gastos. ‖ **with all expenses paid,** con todos los gastos pagados.
■ **expense account,** cuenta de gastos de representación, dietas *fpl*.
expensive [ɪk'spensɪv] *adj* caro,-a, costoso,-a.
expensively [ɪk'spensɪvlɪ] *adv*: *she was expensively dressed,* llevaba ropa cara; *expensively priced goods,* artículos caros.
experience [ɪk'spɪərɪəns] **1** *n* experiencia: *he's got three years' experience,* tiene tres años de experiencia; *I know from experience,* sé por experiencia. – **2** *t* (*sensation, situation, etc*) experimentar; (*difficulty*) tener; (*loss*) sufrir.
experienced [ɪk'spɪərɪənst] *adj* experimentado,-a, con experiencia.
experiment [ɪk'sperɪmənt] **1** *n* experimento. – **2** *i* experimentar, hacer experimentos.
experimental [ɪksperɪ'mentəl] *adj* experimental.
experimentally [ɪksperɪ'mentəlɪ] *adv* de forma experimental.
experimentation [ɪksperɪmen'teɪʃən] *n fml* experimentación *f*.
expert ['ekspɜːt] **1** *n* experto,-a (**at/in/on,** en). – **2** *adj* experto,-a: *you should seek expert advice,* deberías solicitar el consejo de un experto; *visible only to the expert eye,* visible solo para un ojo experto.
expertise [ekspɜː'tiːz] *n* (*skill*) pericia, habilidad *f*; (*knowledge*) conocimiento (práctico).
expertly ['ekspɜːtlɪ] *adv* expertamente.
expertness ['ekspɜːtnəs] *n* pericia.
expiate ['ekspɪeɪt] *t fml* expiar.
expiation [ekspɪ'eɪʃən] *n fml* expiación *f*.
expiration [ekspɪ'reɪʃən] **1** *n fml* vencimiento, caducidad *f*. **2** MED espiración *f*.
expire [ɪk'spaɪəʳ] **1** *i* (*come to end*) terminar, acabarse; (*die*) expirar, morir. **2** (*run out - contract*) vencer; (*- passport, ticket*) caducar. **3** MED (*breathe out*) espirar.
expiry [ɪk'spaɪərɪ] **1** *n* (*ending*) expiración *f*, terminación *f*. **2** (*of contract, bill of exchange*) vencimiento; (*of passport, driving licence, etc*) caducidad *f*.
■ **expiry date,** fecha de caducidad.
explain [ɪk'spleɪn] **1** *t* (*gen*) explicar; (*clarify*) aclarar: *could you explain this word to me?,* ¿me puedes explicar esta palabra?; *she explained what had happened,* explicó lo que había pasado; *that would explain why he hasn't phoned,* eso explicaría por qué no ha llamado; *he tried to explain the situation,* intentó aclarar la situación. – **2** *i* explicar(se): *let me explain,* deja que me explique.
◆ **to explain away** *t sep* dar razones por, justificar.
● **to explain os.,** (*clarify*) explicarse; (*justify*) justificarse.
explanation [eksplə'neɪʃən] **1** *n* (*gen*) explicación *f*: *there must be some explanation,* tiene que haber alguna explicación. **2** (*clarification*) aclaración *f*.
explanatory [ɪk'splænətərɪ] *adj* explicativo,-a.
expletive [ɪk'spliːtɪv] *n fml* taco, palabrota.
explicable [ɪk'splɪkəbəl] *adj fml* explicable.
explicate ['eksplɪkeɪt] *t fml* aclarar, explicar.
explicit [ɪk'splɪsɪt] *adj* explícito,-a.
explicitly [ɪk'splɪsɪtlɪ] *adv* explícitamente.

explicitness [ɪk'splɪsɪtnəs] *n* lo explícito.
explode [ɪk'spləʊd] **1** *t* (*blow up - bomb etc*) hacer estallar, hacer explotar; (*- mine*) hacer volar. **2** (*refute - theory*) refutar; (*- rumour*) desmentir. **– 3** *i* (*blow up*) estallar, explotar, hacer explosión. **4** (*react violently*) reventar, explotar, estallar: *he exploded with anger*, reventó de rabia; *they exploded with laughter*, estallaron en risas. **5** (*increase rapidly*) aumentar rápidamente, crecer rápidamente.
exploit ['eksplɔɪt] **1** *n* hazaña, proeza. **– 2** *t* (*work, develop fully*) explotar. **3** (*use unfairly*) aprovecharse de, explotar.
▲ (*verbo*) [ɪk'splɔɪt].
exploitable [ɪk'splɔɪtəbəl] *adj* explotable.
exploitation [eksplɔɪ'teɪʃən] *n* explotación *f.*
exploration [eksplə'reɪʃən] *n* exploración *f.*
exploratory [ɪk'splɒrətərɪ] *adj* exploratorio,-a.
explore [ɪk'splɔːʳ] **1** *t* (*gen*) explorar. **2** (*examine*) examinar. **– 3** *i* explorar.
explorer [ɪk'splɔːrəʳ] *n* explorador,-ra.
explosion [ɪk'spləʊʒən] **1** *n* (*gen*) explosión *f*, estallido. **2** (*violent outburst*) ataque *m*, arrebato: *an explosion of rage*, un ataque de rabia. **3** (*increase*) aumento rápido, crecimiento rápido: *population explosion*, explosión demográfica.
explosive [ɪk'spləʊsɪv] **1** *adj* (*gen*) explosivo,-a: *an explosive situation*, una situación explosiva. **– 2** *n* explosivo.
explosively [ɪk'spləʊsɪvlɪ] *adv* explosivamente.
exponent [ɪk'spəʊnənt] **1** *n* (*gen*) exponente *m*; (*supporter*) defensor,-ra (**of**, de), partidario,-a (**of**, de). **2** (*performer*) intérprete *mf*; (*expert*) experto,-a. **3** MATH exponente *m.*
exponential [ekspə'nenʃəl] *adj* MATH exponencial.
export ['ekspɔːt] **1** *n* (*trade*) exportación *f.* **2** (*article*) artículo de exportación. **– 3** *t* exportar.
■ **export duties**, aranceles *mpl* de exportación. ‖ **export licence**, licencia de exportación. ‖ **export subsidy**, ayudas *fpl* a la exportación.
▲ (*verbo*) [ɪk'spɔːt].
exportation [ekspɔː'teɪʃən] *n* exportación *f.*
exporter [ek'spɔːtəʳ] *n* exportador,-ra.
expose [ɪk'spəʊz] **1** *t* (*uncover, make visible*) exponer: *we shouldn't expose our skin to the sun*, no deberíamos exponer la piel al sol. **2** (*make known - secret etc*) revelar, descubrir, desvelar, destapar; (*- person*) desenmascarar: *her secret has been exposed*, su secreto se ha desvelado; *they exposed the scandal to the press*, revelaron el secreto a la prensa; *she exposed him as a fraud*, descubrió que era un impostor. **3** *fig* (*lay open*) exponerse: *he exposed himself to criticism*, se expuso a ser criticado. **4** (*introduce, acquaint with*) exponer (**to**, a), verse expuesto,-a: *he has never been exposed to these problems so he doesn't know what to do*, como nunca se ha visto expuesto a estos problemas, no sabe qué hacer. **5** (*photo*) exponer.
● **to expose os.**, exhibirse desnudo,-a.
exposé [ek'spəʊzeɪ] *n* (*disclosure*) revelación *f*; (*statement*) exposición *f.*
exposed [ɪk'spəʊzd] *adj* (*not sheltered*) desabrigado,-a, al descubierto; (*not protected*) expuesto,-a (**to**, a).
exposition [ekspə'zɪʃən] **1** *n* (*exhibition*) exposición *f.* **2** (*account*) explicación *f.*
expostulate [ɪk'spɒstjʊleɪt] *i fml* protestar (**about/on**, por), discutir (**about/on**, por), reconvenir (**about/on**, por).

● **to expostulate with sb. about sth.**, reconvenir a algn. por algo.
expostulation [ɪkspɒstjʊ'leɪʃən] *n* protesta, reconvención *f.*
exposure [ɪk'spəʊʒəʳ] **1** *n* (*being exposed*) exposición *f.* **2** (*revelation, disclosure*) revelación *f*, descubrimiento; (*exposé*) desenmascaramiento: *he was threatened with public exposure if he didn't cooperate*, lo amenazaron con desenmascararlo públicamente si no cooperaba. **3** (*in photography - picture*) fotografía *f*; (*- time*) exposición *f.* **4** (*position of house etc*) situación *f*, orientación *f.* **5** (*publicity*) publicidad *f*; (*coverage*) cobertura.
● **to die of exposure**, morir de frío.
■ **exposure meter**, fotómetro.
expound [ɪk'spaʊnd] *t fml* exponer.
express [ɪk'spres] **1** *adj* (*explicit*) expreso,-a, claro,-a. **2** (*fast - mail*) urgente; (*- train, coach*) expreso: *she sent it by express delivery*, lo envió por correo urgente. **– 3** *adv* urgente. **– 4** *n* (*rail*) (tren *m*) expreso. **– 5** *t* expresar: *you should express your views*, deberías expresar tus opiniones; *he couldn't express his sadness*, no pudo expresar su tristeza. **6** *fml* (*juice*) exprimir.
● **to express os.**, expresarse: *she expresses herself well*, se expresa bien; *I can express myself better in English*, me expreso mejor en inglés.
expression [ɪk'spreʃən] **1** *n* (*gen*) expresión *f*; (*manifestation*) manifestación *f*: *freedom of expression*, libertad de expresión; *it's a slang expression*, es una expresión coloquial; *did you see the expression on her face?*, ¿has visto la expresión de su cara?; *this painting is an expression of the artist's pain*, este cuadro expresa el dolor del artista; *she plays with real expression*, toca con mucho sentimiento. **2** MATH expresión *f.*
expressionism [ɪk'spreʃənɪzəm] *n* expresionismo.
expressionist [ɪk'spreʃənɪst] *n* expresionista *mf.*
expressionless [ɪk'spreʃənləs] *adj* (*of face*) sin expresión; (*of voice, music, etc*) sin emoción.
expressive [ɪk'spresɪv] *adj* expresivo,-a.
● **expressive of sth.**, que expresa algo.
expressively [ɪk'spresɪvlɪ] *adv* expresivamente.
expressiveness [ɪk'spresɪvnəs] *n* expresividad *f.*
expressly [ɪk'spreslɪ] *adv* expresamente, claramente.
expressway [ɪk'spresweɪ] *n* US autopista *f.*
expropriate [ɪk'sprəʊprɪeɪt] *t* expropiar.
expropriation [ɪksprəʊprɪ'eɪʃən] *n* expropiación *f.*
expulsion [ɪk'spʌlʃən] *n* expulsión *f.*
expurgate ['ekspəɡeɪt] *t* expurgar.
expurgation [ekspə'ɡeɪʃən] *n* expurgación *f.*
exquisite [ek'skwɪzɪt, 'ekskwɪzɪt] **1** *adj* (*delicate etc*) exquisito,-a, perfecto,-a. **2** *fml* (*of emotion*) intenso,-a; (*of power to feel*) delicado,-a.
exquisitely [ek'skwɪzɪtlɪ, 'ekskwɪzɪtlɪ] *adv* exquisitamente.
exquisiteness [ek'skwɪzɪtnəs] *n* exquisitez *f.*
ex-serviceman [eks'sɜːvɪsmən] *n* ex-combatiente *m.*
▲ *pl* **ex-servicemen** [eks'sɜːvɪsmən].
ex-servicewoman [eks'sɜːvɪswʊmən] *n* ex-combatiente *f.*
▲ *pl* **ex-servicewomen** [eks'sɜːvɪswɪmɪn].
extant [ek'stænt] *adj* existente.
extemporaneous [ekstempə'reɪnɪəs] *adj fml* improvisado,-a.
extemporaneously [ekstempə'reɪnɪəslɪ] *adv* de manera improvisada, de forma improvisada.
extempore [ɪk'stempərɪ] **1** *adj* improvisado,-a. **– 2** *adv* de improviso, improvisadamente.

extemporize [ɪkˈstempəraɪz] *i* improvisar.

extend [ɪkˈstend] **1** *t* (*enlarge*) ampliar; (*lengthen - line, road*) prolongar, alargar: *we'd like to extend our house,* nos gustaría ampliar la casa; *they've extended the railway,* han prolongado el ferrocarril. **2** (*over time*) prolongar, alargar; (*deadline*) prorrogar: *they agreed to extend his visa,* han consentido en prorrogar su visado; *you can extend a car's life if you look after it,* se puede alargar la vida de un coche si se cuida; *can't you extend your visit?,* ¿no puedes prolongar tu visita? **3** (*stretch out - arm, hand*) alargar, tender; (*- leg*) estirar; (*- wing*) desplegar, extender; (*- rope, ladder, etc*) extender: *he extended his hand to the President,* tendió su mano al Presidente; *extend the ladder as far as it will go,* extiende la escalera al máximo. **4** (*offer, give*) dar, ofrecer, rendir. **5** () . **6** (*enlarge - scope, range, influence*) ampliar, extender: *the military have extended controls to the city centre,* los militares han extendido los controles al centro de la ciudad; *pub opening hours have been extended,* han ampliado el horario de los bares. **7** (*stretch mentally*) exigir el máximo esfuerzo, apretar: *the course doesn't extend the students enough,* el curso no exige suficiente esfuerzo a los estudiantes; *she has never been extended,* nunca le han apretado. – **8** *i* (*in space*) continuar, extenderse, llegar hasta: *the road extends far beyond the village,* la carretera continúa más allá del pueblo; *his land extends as far as the river,* su tierra se extiende hasta el río. **9** (*in time*) prolongarse, alargarse, durar: *the winter extended into March,* el invierno se alargó hasta marzo; *my working day often extends well into the night,* mi jornada laboral se alarga muchas veces hasta bien entrada la noche. **10** (*become extended - ladder etc*) extenderse. **11** (*include, affect*) incluir, abarcar, extenderse a: *the consequences of the recession extend beyond pure economics,* las consecuencias de la crisis se extienden más allá de la pura economía.
● **to extend a warm welcome to sb.,** darle una calurosa bienvenida a algn. ‖ **to extend an invitation to sb.,** invitar a algn. ‖ **to extend os.,** trabajar al máximo, esforzarse: *all athletes should extend themselves more,* todos los atletas deberían esforzarse más.

extended [ɪkˈstendɪd] *adj* (*time*) prolongado,-a; (*wide, broad*) amplio,-a, extenso,-a; (*stretched out*) extendido,-a: *extended leave,* permiso prolongado; *the story received extended news coverage,* la historia recibió una amplia cobertura.
■ **extended family,** *familia en el sentido más amplio.*

extended-play [ɪkstendɪdˈpleɪ] *adj* EP.

extension [ɪkˈstenʃən] **1** *n* (*widening*) ampliación *f*, extensión *f*. **2** (*of line, road, etc*) prolongación *f*. **3** (*of time*) prórroga, prolongación *f*: *I asked for an extension to my visa,* solicité una prórroga de mi visado; *he asked for an extension on his essay,* pidió una prórroga del plazo de entrega de la composición. **4** (*of school, hospital, etc*) anexo *m*; (*of house*) ampliación *f*: *the house is too small, we need an extension,* la casa es demasiado pequeña, nos hace falta un anexo; *we had an extension built,* hicimos ampliaciones. **5** (*telephone line*) extensión *f*; (*telephone*) supletorio: *extension 241, please,* con la extensión 241 por favor.
● **by extension,** por extensión.
■ **extension ladder,** escalera extensible. ‖ **extension lead,** alargador *m*, alargadera, extensión *f*.

extensive [ɪkˈstensɪv] **1** *adj* (*area*) extenso,-a, amplio,-a: *the manor has extensive grounds,* la casa solariega tiene una gran extensión de terreno. **2** (*wide-ranging*) vasto,-a, amplio,-a, extenso,-a; (*thorough*) exhaustivo, minu-

cioso,-a: *extensive knowledge of a subject,* conocimientos extensos de un tema; *extensive coverage in the press,* amplia cobertura en la prensa. **3** (*very great in effect, widespread*) importante, múltiple: *extensive damage,* daños importantes; *extensive alterations,* reformas importantes.
● **to make extensive use of sth.,** hacer abundante uso de algo.
■ **extensive agriculture,** agricultura extensiva.

extensively [ɪkˈstensɪvlɪ] **1** *adv* (*widely*) extensamente, ampliamente: *she has travelled extensively,* ha viajado mucho. **2** (*thoroughly, at length*) exhaustivamente, en detalle, a fondo: *the drug is being extensively researched,* se está investigando la droga exhaustivamente.

extent [ɪkˈstent] **1** *n* (*expanse*) extensión *f*. **2** (*range, scale, scope*) amplitud *f*, vastedad *f*, alcance *m*: *the full extent of the damage is not known,* no se conoce el alcance total de los daños; *the extent of her knowledge,* la amplitud de sus conocimientos. **3** (*point*) punto.
● **to a certain extent,** hasta cierto punto. ‖ **to a large extent,** en gran parte, en gran medida. ‖ **to some extent,** hasta cierto punto. ‖ **to such an extent that ...,** hasta tal punto que ... ‖ **to that extent,** hasta tal punto. ‖ **to the extent that ...,** hasta el punto de que ... ‖ **to what extent?,** ¿hasta qué punto?

extenuate [ɪkˈstenjʊeɪt] *t fml* atenuar.

extenuating [ɪkˈstenjʊeɪtɪŋ] *adj* JUR atenuante.
■ **extenuating circumstances,** circunstancias *fpl* atenuantes.

exterior [ɪkˈstɪərɪəʳ] **1** *adj* exterior, externo,-a: *exterior walls,* paredes exteriores. – **2** *n* exterior *m*. **3** (*of person*) aspecto externo, apariencia.

exterminate [ɪkˈstɜːmɪneɪt] *t* exterminar.

extermination [ɪsktɜːmɪˈneɪʃən] *n* exterminación *f*, exterminio.

external [ekˈstɜːnəl] **1** *adj* externo,-a, exterior: *for external use only,* de uso externo; *external pressures,* presiones externas. – **2 externals,** *npl fml* aspecto *m sing* externo.
■ **external ear,** oído externo. ‖ **external examiner,** examinador,-ra de otra institución académica.

externally [ekˈstɜːnəlɪ] *adv* externamente.

extinct [ɪkˈstɪŋkt] **1** *adj* (*of animal*) extinguido,-a. **2** (*of volcano*) extinguido,-a, apagado,-a.

extinction [ɪkˈstɪŋkʃən] *n* extinción *f*.

extinguish [ɪkˈstɪŋgwɪʃ] *t* extinguir, apagar.

extinguisher [ɪkˈstɪŋgwɪʃəʳ] *n* extintor *m*.

extirpate [ˈekstəpeɪt] *t fml* extirpar.

extol [ɪksˈtəʊl] *t fml* ensalzar, alabar.
▲ *pt & pp* **extolled,** *ger* **extolling.**

extoll [ɪksˈtəʊl] *t US* → **extol.**

extort [ɪksˈtɔːt] *t* (*money*) sacar, conseguir a la fuerza, conseguir con amenazas; (*promise, confession*) arrancar, obtener: *he's extorted money from us,* nos ha extorsionado, nos ha sacado dinero.

extortion [ɪksˈtɔːʃən] *n* extorsión *f*.

extortionate [ɪksˈtɔːʃənət] *adj* exorbitante, desorbitado,-a, excesivo,-a: *extortionate prices,* precios desorbitados.

extra [ˈekstrə] **1** *adj* (*additional*) extra, más, otro,-a; (*spare*) de sobra; (*on top*) aparte: *we need some extra books,* necesitamos algunos libros más; *take an extra jumper in case it's cold,* llévate otro jersey por si hace frío; *get an extra pint of milk,* compra otra botella de leche; *can you make an extra copy?,* ¿puedes hacer una copia más?; *they put on extra trains,* pusieron más trenes; *they took*

on 10 extra people, contrataron a diez personas más; *you'll be paid an extra ten pounds,* cobrarás diez libras más; *I've got an extra ticket,* me sobra una entrada; *breakfast is extra,* el desayuno se cobra aparte; *there are no extra costs,* no hay gastos extras. **– 2** *adv (more than usually)* extra, muy; *(additional)* aparte: *I promise to work extra hard,* prometo trabajar muy duro; *be extra nice to the customer,* sé muy amable con el cliente; *this beer is extra strong,* esta cerveza es muy fuerte; *delivery is extra,* el reparto va aparte; *postage and packing extra,* gastos de envío aparte. **– 3** *n (additional thing)* extra *m,* complemento; *(additional charge)* suplemento; *(luxury)* lujo: *the new car had many extras,* el nuevo coche tenía muchos extras; *there are no hidden extras,* no hay suplementos. **4** CINEM extra *mf.* **5** *(press)* edición *f* especial.
■ **extra time,** SP prórroga.

extract ['ekstrækt] **1** *n (product)* extracto: *beef extract,* extracto de carne. **2** *(excerpt)* extracto, fragmento, trozo: *an extract from her new book,* un fragmento de su nuevo libro. **– 3** *t (pull out)* extraer, sacar: *he's had a tooth extracted,* le han extraído un diente. **4** *(obtain - confession, promise, etc)* arrancar, obtener; *(- information, passage, quotation)* extraer, sacar: *they extracted a confession from him,* le arrancaron una confesión. **5** *(produce)* extraer, sacar: *they extract gold from the rocks,* de las rocas extraen oro; *oil is extracted from olives,* el aceite se extrae de las aceitunas.
▲ *(verbo)* [ɪk'strækt].

extraction [ɪk'strækʃən] **1** *n (gen)* extracción *f.* **2** *(of tooth)* extracción *f: you need two extractions,* hay que extraerte dos muelas. **3** *(descent)* origen *m: to be of Irish extraction,* ser de origen irlandés.

extractor [ɪk'stræktə'] *n* extractor *m.*
■ **extractor fan,** extractor *m* de humos.

extracurricular [ekstrəkə'rɪkjulə'] *adj* extracurricular.

extradite ['ekstrədaɪt] *t* extraditar, extradir.

extradition [ekstrə'dɪʃən] *n* extradición *f.*

extramarital [ekstrə'mærɪtəl] *adj* extramatrimonial.

extraneous [ɪk'steɪnɪəs] *adj* ajeno,-a, extraño,-a.

extraordinarily [ɪk'strɔːdnərəlɪ] *adv* extraordinariamente.

extraordinary [ɪk'strɔːdnərɪ] **1** *adj (exceptional)* extraordinario,-a, fuera de lo común; *(very strange, unusual)* raro,-a: *it's a truly extraordinary film,* es una película realmente extraordinaria. **2** *fml (special, additional)* extraordinario,-a, especial.

extrapolate [ɪk'stræpəleɪt] **1** *t fml (maths)* extrapolar. **2** *fml (estimate)* extrapolar.

extrasensory [ekstrə'sensərɪ] *adj* extrasensorial.
■ **extrasensory perception,** percepción *f* extrasensorial.

extraterritorial [ekstrəterɪ'tɔːrɪəl] *adj* extraterritorial.

extravagance [ɪk'strævəgəns] *n (spending)* derroche *m,* despilfarro, lujo; *(behaviour)* extravagancia.

extravagant [ɪk'strævəgənt] **1** *adj (wasteful - person)* derrochador,-ra, despilfarrador,-ra; *(- thing)* ineficaz, ineficiente. **2** *(extreme)* extravagante, exagerado,-a, estrafalario,-a. **3** *(luxurious)* lujoso,-a, suntuoso,-a.

extravagantly [ɪk'strævəgəntlɪ] **1** *adv (luxuriously)* lujosamente; *(wastefully)* de manera excesiva. **2** *(extremely)* excesivamente; *(unusually)* de manera estrafalaria, de manera exagerada.

extravaganza [ɪkstrævə'gænzə] *n* espectáculo fantástico, fantasía.

extreme [ɪk'striːm] **1** *adj (furthest, very great)* extremo,-a: *in the extreme north,* en el extremo norte; *in extreme old age,* en la vejez extrema; *extreme heat,* calor intensísimo; *extreme pain,* dolor agudo; *extreme poverty,* pobreza extrema; *take extreme care,* ten extremo cuidado. **2** *(not moderate)* extremo,-a, radical: *extreme views,* opiniones radicales. **3** *(severe, unusual)* excepcional: *they had to use extreme methods,* tuvieron que emplear métodos excepcionales; *an extreme case,* un caso excepcional; *extreme weather conditions,* condiciones atmosféricas extremas. **– 4** *n* extremo: *extremes of temperature,* temperaturas extremas.
● **in the extreme,** en sumo grado, en extremo: *he is tightfisted in the extreme,* es extremadamente tacaño. ‖ **to go to extremes,** llegar a extremos. ‖ **to go from one extreme to the other,** pasar de un extremo a otro. ‖ **to take sth. to extremes,** ser extremado,-a en algo.

extremely [ɪk'striːmlɪ] *adv* extremadamente, sumamente: *I'm extremely sorry,* lo siento de veras; *this is extremely important,* esto es de suma importancia; *she's extremely tired,* está cansadísima.

extremism [ɪk'striːmɪzəm] *n* extremismo, radicalismo.

extremist [ɪk'striːmɪst] *n* extremista *mf.*

extremity [ɪk'stremɪtɪ] **1** *n fml (furthest point)* extremo. **2** *fml (extreme degree, situation)* extremo, situación *f* extrema, situación *f* límite. **– 3 extremites,** *npl* ANAT extremidades *fpl.*
▲ *pl* **extremities.**

extricate ['ekstrɪkeɪt] *t fml* librar, sacar.
● **to extricate os.,** lograr salir **(from,** de).

extrovert ['ekstrəvɜːt] **1** *adj* extrovertido,-a. **– 2** *n* extrovertido,-a.

extrude [ɪk'struːd] *t* extrudir.

extrusion [ɪk'struːzən] *n* extrusión *f.*

exuberance [ɪg'zjuːbərəns] *n (vigour)* exuberancia; *(high spirits)* euforia.

exuberant [ɪg'zjuːbərənt] **1** *adj (of person)* eufórico,-a. **2** *(of plants)* exuberante. **3** *fig* vivo,-a.

exude [ɪg'zjuːd] **1** *t fml (of sweat etc)* exudar, rezumar. **2** *fig (of feeling)* rebosar: *she exudes confidence,* rebosa de confianza. **– 3** *i (of sweat etc)* exudar, rezumar.

exult [ɪg'zʌlt] *i fml* regocijarse **(in,** con).

exultant [ɪg'zʌltənt] *adj* jubiloso,-a, regocijado,-a, triunfante.

exultation [ɪgzʌl'teɪʃən] *n* exultación *f,* júbilo.

eye [aɪ] **1** *n* ANAT ojo: *open your eyes,* abre los ojos. **2** *(sense)* vista. **3** *(of needle, potato, storm)* ojo. **– 4** *t (observe)* mirar, observar; *(look at longingly)* echar el ojo a.
● **all eyes were on ...,** todas las miradas estaban puestas en ... ‖ **an eye for an eye,** ojo por ojo. ‖ **as far as the eye can see,** hasta donde alcanza la vista. ‖ **before sb.'s very eyes,** delante de los propios ojos de algn. ‖ **eyes right/left/front,** vista a la derecha/izquierda/al frente. ‖ **for sb.'s eyes only,** sólo para los ojos de algn. ‖ **if you had half an eye,** si tuvieras dos dedos de frente. ‖ **in the eyes of the law,** según la Ley. ‖ **in the eyes of sb. / in sb.'s eyes,** a ojos de algn., para algn. ‖ **my eye!,** ¡y un pepino! ‖ **not to be able to believe one's eyes,** no poder dar crédito a sus ojos, no poder creer lo que uno está viendo. ‖ **not to take one's eyes off sth./sb.,** no quitar la vista de encima de algo/a algn., no perder de vista algo/a algn. ‖ **sb.'s eyes are bigger than their stomach,** comer con los ojos. ‖ **to be all eyes,** ser todo,-a ojos. ‖ **to be one in the eye for sb.,** suponer un chasco para algn. ‖ **to be unable to look sb. in the eye,** no poder mirar a algn. a la cara. ‖ **to be unable to take one's eyes**

off sb./sth., no poder quitar la vista de encima de algn./algo. ‖ to be up to one's eyes in sth., estar hasta el cuello de algo. ‖ to cast one's eyes over sth. / run one's eyes over sth., ojear algo, echar una ojeada a algo. ‖ to catch sb.'s eye, llamar la atención de algn. ‖ to clap/lay/set eyes on sb./sth., ver a algn./algo, poner los ojos en algn./algo. ‖ to close one's eyes to sth., hacer la vista gorda a algo. ‖ to eye sb. up and down, comerse a algn. con los ojos. ‖ to give sb. the eye, lanzar miraditas a algn. ‖ to have an eye for sth., tener buen ojo para algo. ‖ to have eyes in the back of one's head, darse cuenta de todo, tener cien ojos. ‖ to have one's eyes on, (watch) observar, vigilar; fig echar el ojo: I've got my eye on you, te estoy vigilando; I've had my eye on that house for some time, hace tiempo que le tengo el ojo echado a esa casa. ‖ to keep an eye on, (watch) vigilar; (not let out of sight) no perder de vista. ‖ to keep an eye open/out for sb./ sth., mantener los ojos bien abiertos por si se ve a algn./algo. ‖ to keep one's eyes peeled, estar ojo avizor. ‖ to look sb. in the eye, mirar a algn. a los ojos. ‖ to make eyes at sb. / make sheep's eyes at sb., dirigir miraditas a algn. ‖ to only have eyes for sb. / have eyes only for sb., sólo tener ojos para algn. ‖ to open sb.'s eyes, abrirle los ojos a algn. ‖ to see eye to eye with sb., estar de acuerdo con algn. ‖ to turn a blind eye to sth., hacer la vista gorda a algo. ‖ with an eye to doing sth., con la intención de hacer algo, con miras a hacer algo. ‖ with one's eyes open, con los ojos abiertos. ‖ with one's eyes shut, con los ojos cerrados. ‖ with the naked eye, a simple vista.

■ eye contact, contacto ocular. ‖ eye shadow, sombra de ojos. ‖ eye socket, cuenca del ojo, órbita. ‖ private eye, detective mf privado,-a.

eyeball ['aɪbɔːl] n globo ocular.

eyebrow ['aɪbraʊ] n ceja.

eye-catching ['aɪkætʃɪŋ] adj llamativo,-a.

eyeful ['aɪful] **1** n (of dust, sand, etc): I fell on the beach and got an eyeful of sand, me caí en la playa y se me llenó el ojo de arena. **2** (attractive sight) cosa atractiva: the new secretary's an eyeful, la nueva secretaria está como un tren.

● to get an eyeful of sth., echar un vistazo a algo.

eyeglass ['aɪglɑːs] n monóculo.

eyelash ['aɪlæʃ] n pestaña.

eyelet ['aɪlət] n ojete m.

eyelid ['aɪlɪd] n párpado.

eyeliner ['aɪlaɪnəʳ] n lápiz m de ojos.

eye-opener ['aɪəʊpənəʳ] n revelación f, gran sorpresa.

eyepiece ['aɪpiːs] n ocular m.

eyeshade ['aɪʃeɪd] n visera.

eyesight ['aɪsaɪt] n vista.

eyesore ['aɪsɔːʳ] n monstruosidad f.

eyestrain ['aɪstreɪn] n vista cansada.

eyetooth [aɪˈtuːθ] n colmillo.

eyewash ['aɪwɒʃ] **1** n MED colirio. **2** fam (nonsense) tonterías fpl: it's all eyewash!, ¡eso son disparates!

eyewitness ['aɪwɪtnəs] n testigo presencial, testigo ocular.

eyrie ['ɪərɪ] n aguilera

F

F, f [ef] **1** *n* (*the letter*) F, f *f*. **2** MUS fa *m*.

f ['femɪnɪn] *abbr* LING (*feminine*) femenino; (*abbreviation*) f.

F ['færənhaɪt] *abbr* (*Fahrenheit*) Fahrenheit; (*abbreviation*) F.

FA ['ef'eɪ] *abbr* GB SPORT (*Football Association*) Federación *f* de fútbol.

fab [fæb] *adj fam dated* (*abbr of fabulous*) fabuloso,-a, bestial, bárbaro,-a.
  ▲ *comp* **fabber**, *superl* **fabbest**.

fable ['feɪbəl] *n* fábula.

fabled ['feɪbəld] *adj* legendario,-a.

fabric ['fæbrɪk] **1** *n* (*material*) tela, tejido. **2** (*structure*) fábrica, estructura. **3** *fig* estructura.

fabricate ['fæbrɪkeɪt] **1** *t* (*story*) inventar; (*document*) falsificar. **2** (*build*) fabricar.

fabrication [fæbrɪ'keɪʃən] *n* invención *f*: *it was a complete fabrication,* eran puras invenciones.

fabulous ['fæbjələs] *adj* fabuloso,-a.

facade [fə'sɑːd] *n* fachada.

façade [fə'sɑːd] *n* fachada.

face [feɪs] **1** *n* (*of person*) cara, rostro: *she's got a lovely face,* tiene una cara muy bonita. **2** (*surface*) superficie *f*. **3** (*side*) cara. **4** (*of card, coin*) cara. **5** (*of dial*) cuadrante *m*. **6** (*of watch*) esfera. **7** *fig* (*of earth*) faz *f*: *he disappeared off the face of the earth,* desapareció de la faz de la tierra. **8** (*look*) cara, expresión *f*: *he looked at me with a worried face,* me miró con cara de preocupación. **– 9** *t* (*look towards*) mirar hacia: *she turned to face me,* se volvió hacia mí, se volvió para mirarme; *everybody face the blackboard!,* ¡todo el mundo mira cara a la pizarra! **10** (*look onto*) mirar hacia, estar orientado,-a hacia, dar a: *our house faces south,* nuestra casa está orientada hacia el sur. **11** (*be opposite to*) estar enfrente de: *the two children sat facing each other,* los dos niños estaban sentados cara a cara. **12** (*confront*) presentarse, plantearse; (*deal with*) enfrentarse a: *many difficulties faced him,* se le presentaron muchas dificultades; *the problems facing this government seem insurmountable,* los problemas a los que se enfrenta este gobierno parecen insuperables; *we must face facts,* tenemos que aceptar la realidad; *he faces three charges of robbery,* se le acusa de tres delitos de robo. **13** (*tolerate*) soportar: *I can't face another day in this hotel,* no puedo soportar otro día en este hotel; *she couldn't face the thought of seeing him again,* no soportaba la idea de volver a verlo. **14** (*cover - building*) revestir (**with,** de), recubrir (**with,** de); (*- material*) forrar (**with,** de).
  ◆ **to face up to** *t insep* afrontar, enfrentar, enfrentarse a: *you must face up to your responsibilities,* tienes que enfrentarte a tus responsabilidades.
  ● **face down,** (*person, card*) boca abajo. ‖ **face to face,** cara a cara. ‖ **face up,** (*person, card*) boca arriba. ‖ **in the face of,** ante. ‖ **let's face it,** seamos realistas, reconozcámoslo. ‖ **on the face of it,** a primera vista. ‖ **shut your face!,** ¡cierra el pico! ‖ **to face the music,** dar la cara. ‖ **to have a long face,** andar con cara larga. ‖

to have the face to do sth., tener la cara de hacer algo. ‖ **to keep a straight face,** mantenerse serio,-a, contener la risa. ‖ **to look sb. in the face,** poder mirar a algn. en la cara. ‖ **to lose face,** quedar mal. ‖ **to make faces,** hacer muecas. ‖ **to pull faces,** hacer muecas. ‖ **to put on a brave face,** poner al mal tiempo buena cara. ‖ **to save face,** salvar las apariencias. ‖ **to say sth. to sb.'s face,** decirle algo a algn. a la cara. ‖ **to show one's face,** aparecer: *he'll never show his face round here again,* no volverá a aparecer por aquí jamás.
  ■ **face cloth,** toallita. ‖ **face cream,** crema facial. ‖ **face flannel,** toallita. ‖ **face pack,** mascarilla facial. ‖ **face value,** valor *m* nominal.

faceless ['feɪsləs] *adj* anónimo,-a.

facelift ['feɪslɪft] **1** *n* lifting *m*, estiramiento facial. **2** *fig* (*building*) lavado de cara.

face-saver ['feɪsseɪvə'] *n* acto o situación que permite salvar las apariencias.

face-saving ['feɪsseɪvɪŋ] *adj* para salvar las apariencias.

facet ['fæsɪt] *n* faceta.

facetious [fə'siːʃəs] *adj* burlón,-ona.

facial ['feɪʃəl] **1** *adj* facial. **– 2** *n* masaje *m* facial, tratamiento facial.

facile ['fæsaɪl] **1** *adj pej* (*meaningless*) superficial. **2** (*easy*) fácil.

facilitate [fə'sɪlɪteɪt] *t* facilitar.

facility [fə'sɪlɪtɪ] **1** *n* facilidad *f*. **– 2 facilities,** *npl* (*equipment*) instalaciones *fpl*, servicios *mpl*. **3** (*means*) facilidades *fpl*.
  ▲ *pl* **facilities**.

facing ['feɪsɪŋ] **1** *n* (*of garment*) forro, entretela. **2** (*of building*) revestimiento. **– 3 facings,** *npl* (*of garment*) vueltas *fpl*.

facsimile [fæk'sɪmɪlɪ] *n* facsímil *m*, facsímile *m*.
  ■ **facsimile edition,** edición *f* facsímil.

fact [fækt] **1** *n* (*event, happening*) hecho: *and these are the facts,* y éstos son los hechos; *it's the fact that he lied that worries me,* lo que me preocupa es el hecho de que mintiera. **2** (*the truth*) realidad *f*: *fact or fiction?,* ¿realidad o ficción?; *a story based on fact,* una historia basada en hechos reales.
  ● **as a matter of fact,** en realidad. ‖ **for a fact,** a ciencia cierta. ‖ **in fact,** de hecho, en realidad. ‖ **it's a fact of life,** es la realidad. ‖ **the fact of the matter is that ...,** el hecho es que ..., lo cierto es que ... ‖ **the fact remains that ...,** a pesar de eso ..., no obstante ... ‖ **the facts speak for themselves,** los hechos hablan por sí mismos.
  ■ **fact sheet,** hoja informativa. ‖ **the facts of life,** *euph* (*sex*) los misterios de la vida.

fact-finding ['fæktfaɪndɪŋ] *adj* investigador,-ra: *fact-finding commission,* comisión *f* investigadora.

faction ['fækʃən] *n* (*group*) facción *f*.

factitious [fæk'tɪʃəs] adj facticio,-a.
factor ['fæktə'] n factor m.
factorize ['fæktəraɪz] t descomponer en factores.
factory ['fæktərɪ] n fábrica.
■ **factory farm**, granja donde se practica la cría intensiva. ‖ **factory farming**, cría intensiva de animales. ‖ **factory floor**, (workplace) taller m; (workers) obreros mpl, trabajadores mpl: the decision was badly received on the factory floor, la decisión no fue bien recibida por los trabajadores. ‖ **factory prices**, precios mpl de fábrica. ‖ **factory ship**, buque m factoría. ‖ **factory worker**, obrero,-a.
▲ pl factories.
factotum [fæk'təʊtəm] n factótum m.
factual ['fæktʃʊəl] adj factual.
faculty ['fækəltɪ] 1 n (power, ability) facultad f. 2 (univ) facultad f. 3 US (at university) profesorado.
▲ pl faculties.
fad [fæd] 1 n (fashion) moda pasajera. 2 (personal) manía.
faddy ['fædɪ] adj maniático,-a.
▲ comp faddier, superl faddiest.
fade [feɪd] 1 t (colour) descolorar, descolorir, desteñir: the sun has faded the curtains, el sol ha descolorido las cortinas. – 2 i (colour) desteñirse, descolorarse, descolorirse: my jeans have faded, mis tejanos se han desteñido. 3 (light) irse apagando, perder intensidad: it was six o'clock and the light was fading, eran las seis y oscurecía. 4 (sound) desvanecerse, apagarse. 5 (hopes, memory, etc) acabarse, esfumarse, desvanecerse: hopes for an early settlement faded, se esfumaron las esperanzas de llegar rápidamente a un acuerdo; his interest in her soon faded, su interés por ella pronto se esfumó. 6 (looks, smile) desaparecer. 7 (flower) marchitarse.
◆ to **fade away** 1 i (become less intense, strong, etc) desvanecerse, esfumarse: time fades away, el tiempo se esfuma. 2 (die) morirse: she's very ill and fading fast, está muy enferma y su vida se apaga. ‖ to **fade in** t sep TV CINEM fundir. ‖ to **fade out** 1 t sep TV CINEM fundir. – 2 i (sound) desvanecerse.
faded ['feɪdɪd] 1 adj (colour) desteñido,-a. 2 (flower) marchito,-a.
faeces ['fiːsiːz] npl heces fpl.
faff [fæf] to **faff (about)** / **faff around**, i perder el tiempo: stop faffing about with that and come here, deja de perder el tiempo con eso y ven aquí.
fag [fæg] 1 n GB fam (cigarette) pitillo. 2 sl (drag) lata, rollo. 3 US fam (gay) marica m. 4 GB (public school) fámulo. – 5 i fam (work hard) trabajar mucho. 6 GB (work as a fag) hacer de fámulo.
◆ to **fag out** t sep fam dejar hecho,-a polvo: I'm fagged out, estoy hecho polvo.
■ **fag end**, fam colilla.
▲ (verbo) pt & pp fagged, ger fagging.
fagged [fægd] adj hecho,-a polvo, molido,-a.
faggot[1] ['fægət] 1 n (sticks) haz m de leña. 2 (meat) especie de albóndiga.
faggot[2] ['fægət] n US pej (homosexual) marica m, maricón m.
Fahrenheit ['færənhaɪt] adj Fahrenheit: 32 degrees Fahrenheit, 32 grados Fahrenheit.
fail [feɪl] 1 n EDUC suspenso. – 2 t (let down) fallar, decepcionar; (desert) fallar, faltar: he won't fail us, no nos fallará; his strength failed him, le abandonaron las fuerzas; words fail me, no encuentro las palabras, me faltan palabras. 3 EDUC suspender: I failed my driving test, suspendí el examen de conducir; she failed En-

glish, la suspendieron en inglés; the teacher failed him on the oral, el profesor lo suspendió en el examen oral. – 4 i (neglect) dejar de: she never fails to phone every Sunday, nunca deja de llamar cada domingo. 5 (not succeed) fracasar, no hacer algo: the plan failed, el plan fracasó; he failed to finish the race, no acabó la carrera; the team failed to reach the final, el equipo no consiguió llegar a la final. 6 (crops) fallar, echarse a perder. 7 (stop working) fallar: the brakes failed, los frenos fallaron. 8 (light) acabarse, irse apagando: the light was failing fast and they had to abandon the search, oscurecía por momentos y tuvieron que abandonar la búsqueda. 9 (become weak) debilitarse, fallar: his sight is failing, le falla la vista. 10 COMM (become bankrupt) quebrar, fracasar.
● **without fail**, sin falta. ‖ I **fail to see ...**, no veo ..., no comprendo ...
failed [feɪld] adj fracasado,-a.
failing ['feɪlɪŋ] 1 n (fault) defecto, fallo; (weakness) punto débil. – 2 prep a falta de: failing that ..., si eso no es posible ...
fail-safe ['feɪlseɪf] adj (device, mechanism) de seguridad; (plan) infalible.
failure ['feɪljə'] 1 n (lack of success) fracaso. 2 COMM quiebra. 3 EDUC suspenso. 4 (person) fracasado,-a. 5 (breakdown) fallo, avería: the delay is due to engine failure, el retraso se debe a un fallo mecánico. 6 (of crops) pérdida. 7 (inability) incapacidad f; (neglect) falta: her failure to answer, el hecho de que no pudiera contestar; failure to attend, falta de asistencia; failure to pay, falta de pago.
■ **heart failure**, paro cardíaco.
faint [feɪnt] 1 adj (sound, voice) débil, tenue. 2 (colour) pálido,-a; (outline) borroso,-a. 3 (slight - memory etc) vago,-a; (- hope) poco,-a; (- resemblance) ligero,-a: I haven't the faintest idea, no tengo ni la más mínima idea. 4 (halfhearted) débil, poco entusiasta. 5 (unsteady, giddy) mareado,-a. – 6 n mareo. – 7 i desmayarse (from, de).
faint-hearted ['feɪnt'hɑːtɪd] adj (person) timorato,-a, medroso,-a; (attempt) tímido,-a.
faintness ['feɪntnəs] 1 n debilidad f, lo débil: the faintness of his voice made it hard to distinguish what he said, su voz era tan débil que era difícil distinguir lo que decía. 2 MED mareos mpl: this drug can cause faintness, esta droga puede causar mareos.
fair[1] [feə'] 1 adj (just) justo,-a, equitativo,-a; (impartial) imparcial; (reasonable) razonable: it's not fair, no es justo, no hay derecho; that's a fair question, es una pregunta razonable; they gave him a fair trial, tuvo un juicio justo. 2 (considerable) considerable: there were a fair number of people, había bastante gente. 3 (idea, guess, etc) bastante bueno,-a, más o menos acertado,-a: I had a fair idea of what was going on, tenía bastante idea de lo que sucedía. 4 (average) regular. 6 (hair) rubio,-a; (skin) blanco,-a. 7 fml bello,-a: the fair sex, el bello sexo.
● **a fair crack of the whip**, una buena oportunidad. ‖ **by fair means or foul**, por las buenas o por las malas. ‖ **by one's own fair hand**, con las propias manos. ‖ **fair and square**, (sincerely) sinceramente, francamente; (directly) directamente, claramente; (correctly) honradamente. ‖ **fair enough**, (okay) de acuerdo, vale; (true) muy bien. ‖ **fair to middling**, regular. ‖ **fair's fair!**, ¡por favor!, ¡ya está bien! ‖ **to have (more than) one's fair share of sth.**, tener (más de) lo que le corresponde a uno,-a. ‖ **to play fair**, jugar limpio.
■ **fair copy**, copia en limpio. ‖ **fair game**, presa fácil, blanco de burlas. ‖ **fair play**, juego limpio. ‖ **fair rent**, alquiler m razonable.

fair² [feəʳ] **1** *n* (*market*) mercado, feria. **2** (*show*) feria; (*funfair*) parque *m* de atracciones.
■ **trade fair,** feria (de muestras). ‖ **world fair,** exposición *f* internacional.

fairground ['feəgaʊnd] *n* (*site*) recinto ferial; (*show*) feria; (*funfair*) parque *m* de atracciones.

fair-haired ['feəheəd] *adj* rubio,-a.

fairly ['feəlɪ] **1** *adv* (*justly*) justamente. **2** (*moderately*) bastante. **3** (*completely*) completamente.

fair-minded [feə'maɪndɪd] *adj* justo,-a.

fairness ['feənəs] **1** *n* justicia, imparcialidad *f.* **2** (*of hair*) color *m* rubio; (*of skin*) palidez *f,* blancura.
● **in all fairness,** para ser justo,-a.

fair-sized ['feəsaɪzd] *adj* bastante grande, de buen tamaño.

fair-skinned ['feəskɪnd] *adj* de piel blanca.

fairway ['feəweɪ] **1** *n* (*golf*) calle *f.* **2** (*sea*) canal *m* navegable.

fair-weather friend ['feəweðəʳfrend] *n* amigo,-a de conveniencia.

fairy ['feərɪ] **1** *n* hada. **2** *fam* marica *m.*
■ **fairy godmother,** hada madrina. ‖ **fairy lights,** bombillas *fpl* de colores. ‖ **fairy story,** cuento de hadas. ‖ **fairy tale,** cuento de hadas.
▲ *pl* **fairies**.

fairyland ['feərɪlænd] *n* el país *m* de las hadas.

fait accompli [feɪtə'kɒmpliː] *n* hecho consumado.

faith [feɪθ] **1** *n* fe *f.* **2** (*trust, confidence*) confianza (**in,** en), fe *f* (**in,** en). **3** REL fe *f.*
● **in good faith / in bad faith,** de buena fe / de mala fe. ‖ **to break faith with sb.,** traicionar a algn., ser infiel a algn. ‖ **to keep faith with sb.,** ser fiel a algn.

faithful ['feɪθfʊl] **1** *adj* (*loyal*) fiel (**to,** a), leal (**to,** a/con): *have you been faithful to me?,* ¿me has sido fiel?; *my faithful dog,* mi perro fiel. **2** (*accurate*) fiel, exacto,-a. – **3** the **faithful,** *npl* REL los fieles *mpl.*

faithfully ['feɪθfʊlɪ] *adv* fielmente.
● **yours faithfully,** (*in letter*) le saluda atentamente, atentamente.

faithfulness ['feɪθfʊlnəs] *n* fidelidad *f.*

faith-healer ['feɪθhiːləʳ] *n* curandero,-a.

faith-healing ['feɪθhiːlɪŋ] *n* curación *f* por fe.

fake [feɪk] **1** *n* falsificación *f.* **2** (*person*) impostor,-ra, farsante *mf.* – **3** *adj* falso,-a, falsificado,-a. – **4** *t* (*falsify*) falsificar. **5** (*pretend*) fingir: *she faked illness,* fingió estar enferma.

falcon ['fɔːlkən] *n* halcón *m.*

Falklander ['fɔːlkləndəʳ] *n* malvinero,-a, malvinense *mf.*

Falkland Islands ['fɔːlkləndaɪləndz] *npl* Islas *fpl* Malvinas.

fall [fɔːl] **1** *n* (*act of falling*) caída: *she had a nasty fall,* sufrió una mala caída. **2** (*of rock*) desprendimiento; (*of snow*) nevada. **3** (*decrease*) baja, descenso, disminución *f: a fall in output,* una disminución de la producción; *a fall in temperature,* un descenso de temperaturas, una bajada de temperaturas. **4** (*defeat*) caída: *the fall of the government,* la caída del gobierno. **5** US (*autumn*) otoño. – **6** *i* (*gen*) caer, caerse: *he fell 20 metres,* cayó 20 metros; *she listened to the rain falling,* escuchó como caía la lluvia; *the cat fell off the balcony,* el gato se cayó del balcón; *the boy has fallen into the river,* el niño ha caído al río. **7** (*hang loosely*) caer: *her hair falls over her shoulders,* el pelo le cae sobre los hombros. **8** (*decrease*) bajar, descender: *the price of shares has fallen,* el precio de las acciones ha descendido. **9** (*slope downwards*) bajar, descender: *the land fell away to the left,* el terreno descen-

día hacia la izquierda. **10** (*be defeated*) caer; (*be killed*) caer, perecer: *the regime fell,* el régimen cayó; *the city fell to the enemy,* la ciudad cayó en manos del enemigo. **11** (*happen*) caer: *this year Christmas Day falls on a Sunday,* este año el día de Navidad cae en domingo. **12** (*figurative uses*): *night fell,* cayó la noche, anocheció, se hizo de noche; *a silence fell on the guests,* el silencio se apoderó de los invitados; *my eyes fell on a ring on the table,* mis ojos se fijaron en un anillo que había sobre la mesa; *his face fell when he heard the news,* puso cara larga cuando oyó la noticia. **13** (*wind*) amainar. **14** *fig* (*at cricket*) caerse: *two wickets fell in half an hour,* se eliminaron dos jugadores en media hora. – **15** the **Fall,** *n* REL la Caída. – **16** **falls,** *npl* (*waterfall*) cascada *f sing,* cataratas *fpl.*
◆ **to fall about** *i* troncharse, partirse (de risa): *they fell about laughing,* se troncharon de risa. ‖ **to fall apart** *i* romperse, deshacerse, caerse a pedazos: *this jacket is falling apart,* esta chaqueta se está cayendo a trozos; *our relationship has fallen apart,* nuestra relación se ha ido a pique. ‖ **to fall away 1** *i* (*desert, leave*) disminuir: *attendance has fallen away,* la asistencia ha disminuido. **2** (*disappear*) desaparecer: *many old customs have fallen away,* muchas costumbres antiguas han desaparecido. **3** (*break off*) desprenderse. ‖ **to fall back** *i* (*retreat*) retroceder, retirarse. ‖ **to fall back on** *t insep* (*resort to*) recurrir a, echar mano de, apoyarse en: *she had no money to fall back on,* no tenía dinero al que echar mano. ‖ **to fall behind** *i* (*be overtaken*) retrasarse, quedarse atrás, rezagarse. ‖ **to fall behind with** *i* retrasarse: *we've fallen behind with the repayments,* nos hemos retrasado en los pagos. ‖ **to fall down 1** *i* (*person*) caer, caerse; (*building*) derrumbarse, venirse abajo. **2** (*fail*) fallar: *his plan fell down,* su proyecto falló. ‖ **to fall for 1** *t insep* (*be tricked*) dejarse engañar por, picar: *it was obviously a trick, but I fell for it,* estaba claro que era un timo, pero piqué. **2** *fam* (*fall in love*) enamorarse de: *he fell for her in a big way,* se enamoró locamente de ella. ‖ **to fall in 1** *i* (*collapse*) desplomarse, venirse abajo. **2** MIL alinearse, formar filas, ponerse en filas. ‖ **to fall in with** *t insep* (*meet, become involved with*) encontrarse con, juntarse con: *he's fallen in with a bad crowd,* se ha juntado con mala gente. **2** (*agree with, support*) convenir en, aprobar, aceptar: *we fell in with the general consensus,* aceptamos la opinión general. ‖ **to fall into** *t insep* (*be divided into*) dividirse en, clasificarse en: *they fall into four types,* se dividen en cuarto tipos. **2** (*develop, acquire*) adquirir: *I've fallen into bad habits,* he adquirido malos hábitos. ‖ **to fall off 1** *i* (*decrease in quantity*) bajar, disminuir; (*in quality*) empeorar: *numbers have fallen off this term,* el número de estudiantes ha bajado este trimestre. **2** (*become detached*) desprenderse, caerse. ‖ **to fall on** *t insep* (*be borne by*) incidir en, recaer en, tocar a: *it fell upon me to decide where to go,* me tocó a mí decidir dónde ir. **2** (*attack*) atacar, caer sobre. ‖ **to fall out 1** *i* (*quarrel*) reñir (**with,** con), pelearse (**with,** con): *let's not fall out over this,* no nos vayamos a pelear por eso. – **2** *t sep* MIL romper filas. – **3** *i* (*drop*) caerse. ‖ **to fall over 1** *t insep* caer, tropezar con: *she fell over the children's toys,* tropezó con los juguetes de los niños. – **2** *i* caerse: *I slipped and fell over,* resbalé y me caí. ‖ **to fall through** *i* (*come to nothing*) fracasar, quedar en nada: *the deal fell through,* el acuerdo quedó en nada. ‖ **to fall to 1** *t insep* (*begin*) empezar a, ponerse a: *she fell to thinking about the past,* se puso a pensar en el pasado. **2** (*become duty of*) corresponder a, incumbir a, tocar a: *it fell to Andrew to break the news,*

le tocó a Andrew comunicar la noticia. ‖ **to fall under** *t insep* clasificarse en, estar incluido,-a en: *which category does this fall under?*, ¿en qué categoría se clasifica esto?
● **to fall asleep**, dormirse. ‖ **to fall flat**, *fig* salir mal, no tener el éxito deseado: *her joke fell flat*, su chiste no hizo gracia. ‖ **to fall foul of**, tener problemas con, tener líos con. ‖ **to fall ill**, caer enfermo,-a, enfermar. ‖ **to fall from one's lips**, salir de la boca de uno. ‖ **to fall in love**, enamorarse. ‖ **to fall into conversation with sb.**, entablar una conversación con algn. ‖ **to fall into the clutches of**, caer en las garras de. ‖ **to fall into the hands of**, caer en manos de. ‖ **to fall on one's feet**, tener mucha suerte. ‖ **to fall over backwards to do sth.**, hacer todo lo posible para hacer algo, desvivirse por hacer algo. ‖ **to fall over os. to do sth.**, desvivirse por hacer algo. ‖ **to fall short**, no alcanzar (**of**, -). ‖ **to fall silent**, callarse. ‖ **to fall to one's knees**, caerse de rodillas.
■ **fall from grace**, caída en desgracia. ‖ **fall guy**, cabeza de turco, chivo expiatorio.
▲ (*verbo*) *pt* **fell**, *pp* **fallen**.
fallacious [fə'leɪʃəs] *adj* erróneo,-a, engañoso,-a.
fallacy ['fæləsɪ] *n* falacia.
▲ *pl* **fallacies**.
fallen ['fɔːlən] **1** *pp* → **fall**. – **2** *adj* (*not virtuous*) perdido,-a. – **3 the fallen**, *npl* los caídos *mpl*.
■ **fallen arches**, pies *mpl* planos.
fallible ['fælɪbəl] *adj* falible.
falliblility [fælɪ'bɪlətɪ] *n* falibilidad *f*.
falling-off ['fɔːlɪŋɒf] *n* (*in quantity*) disminución *f*; (*in price, quality*) descenso.
Fallopian tube [fəlaupɪən'tjuːb] *n* trompa de Falopio.
fall-out ['fɔːlaut] (**radioactive**) **fall-out**, *n* lluvia radioactiva.
■ **fall-out shelter**, refugio atómico.
fallow ['fæləu] *adj* en barbecho.
■ **fallow deer**, gamo.
false [fɔːls] *adj* (*untrue*) falso,-a. **2** (*artificial*) postizo,-a.
● **to play sb. false**, traicionar a algn., engañar a algn. ‖ **under false pretences**, por medio de engaños.
■ **false alarm**, falsa alarma. ‖ **false bottom**, doble fondo. ‖ **false friend**, LING falso amigo. ‖ **false move / false step**, paso en falso. ‖ **false start**, salida nula. ‖ **false teeth**, dentadura postiza.
falsehood ['fɔːlshud] **1** *n* (*lying*) falsedad *f*. **2** (*lie*) mentira.
falsely ['fɔːlslɪ] *adv* falsamente.
falseness ['fɔːlsnəs] *n* falsedad *f*.
falsetto [fɔːl'setəu] *n* falsete.
▲ *pl* **falsettos**.
falsies ['fɔːlsɪz] *npl fam* rellenos *mpl*.
falsification [fɔːlsɪfɪ'keɪʃən] *n* falsificación *f*.
falsify ['fɔːlsɪfaɪ] **1** *t* (*alter falsely*) falsificar. **2** (*misrepresent*) falsear.
▲ *pt & pp* **falsified**, *ger* **falsifying**.
falter ['fɔːltə'] *i* (*person*) vacilar, titubear; (*voice*) fallar.
fame [feɪm] *n* fama.
famed [feɪmd] *adj* famoso,-a (**for**, por).
familiar [fə'mɪlɪə'] **1** *adj* (*well-known*) familiar, conocido,-a (**to**, a): *I was glad to see a familiar face*, me alegré de ver una cara familiar; *your voice sounds familiar*, me suena tu voz. **2** (*aware*) al corriente (**with**, de), familiarizado,-a (**with**, con): *I am familiar with your work*, estoy familiarizado con sus obras. **3** (*intimate*) íntimo,-a; (*too informal*) fresco,-a.

● **to be on familiar terms with sb.**, tener confianza con algn. ‖ **to become familiar with sth.**, familiarizarse con algo. ‖ **to get too familiar with sb.**, tomarse demasiadas libertades con algn.
familiarity [fəmɪlɪ'ærɪtɪ] **1** *n* familiaridad *f*. **2** (*knowledge*) conocimiento (**with**, de).
● **familiarity breeds contempt**, la confianza da asco.
familiarize [fə'mɪlɪəraɪz] **1** *t* (*become acquainted*) familiarizarse (**with**, con): *I need time to familiarize myself with the surroundings*, necesito tiempo para familiarizarme con el entorno. **2** (*divulge*) popularizar.
family ['fæmɪlɪ] **1** *n* familia. – **2** *adj* familiar.
● **to be in the family way**, estar embarazada. ‖ **to be one of the family**, ser de la familia. ‖ **to run in the family**, venir de familia.
■ **family business**, negocio familiar. ‖ **family car**, coche *m* familiar. ‖ **family circle**, familia, familiares *mpl*. ‖ **family doctor**, médico de cabecera. ‖ **family film**, película apta para todos los públicos, película tolerada. ‖ **family life**, vida familiar, vida en familia. ‖ **family likeness**, parecido de familia. ‖ **family man**, hombre *m* casado con familia, hombre *m* hogareño. ‖ **family name**, US apellido. ‖ **family planning**, planificación *f* familiar. ‖ **family ties**, lazos *mpl* familiares. ‖ **family tree**, árbol *m* genealógico.
▲ *pl* **families**.
famine ['fæmɪn] *n* hambruna, hambre *f*.
famished ['fæmɪʃt] *adj fam* muerto,-a de hambre.
famous ['feɪməs] *adj* famoso,-a (**for**, por), célebre (**for**, por).
● **famous last words!**, ¡habrá que verlo!, ¡ya lo veremos!
famously ['feɪməslɪ] *adv fam* estupendamente.
fan [fæn] **1** *n* (*object*) abanico. **2** ELEC ventilador *m*. **3** (*follower*) aficionado,-a; (*of pop star etc*) admirador,-ra, fan *mf*. **4** (*of football*) hincha *mf*. – **5** *t* (*face*) abanicar; (*elec*) ventilar; (*fire*) avivar. **6** *fig* avivar, atizar. – **7** *i* abanicarse.
◆ **to fan out 1** *i* desplegarse en abanico. – **2** *t sep* desplegar.
● **to fan the flames**, *fig* echar leña al fuego.
■ **fan belt**, correa del ventilador. ‖ **fan club**, club *m* de fans. ‖ **fan heater**, calefactor *m*. ‖ **fan mail**, cartas *fpl* de los fans.
▲ *pt & pp* **fanned**, *ger* **fanning**.
fanatic [fə'nætɪk] **1** *n* fanático,-a: *they are religious fanatics*, son fanáticos religiosos; *my brother's a sports fanatic*, mi hermano es un fanático de los deportes. – **2** *adj* fanático,-a (**about**, de).
fanatical [fə'nætɪkəl] *adj* fanático,-a.
fanaticism [fə'nætɪsɪzəm] *n* fanatismo.
fancier ['fænsɪə'] *n* aficionado,-a.
fanciful ['fænsɪful] **1** *adj* (*idea*) imaginario,-a, fantástico,-a. **2** (*extravagant*) caprichoso,-a, rebuscado,-a, estrafalario,-a.
fancy ['fænsɪ] **1** *n* (*imagination*) fantasía, imaginación *f*. **2** (*whim*) capricho, antojo. – **3** *adj* (*jewels, goods etc*) de fantasía. **4** (*unusual*) estrafalario,-a. **5** (*high-class, posh*) elegante, de lujo. **6** (*prices*) exagerado,-a, excesivo,-a, exorbitante. – **7** *t* (*want*) apetecer, querer: *do you fancy a drink?*, ¿te apetece una copa?; *I don't fancy going there*, no me apetece ir allí. **8** (*find attractive*) encontrar atractivo,-a: *my friend fancies you*, a mi amigo le gustas mucho. **9** (*think*) creer, suponer: *I'm not sure, but I fancy she was wearing blue*, no estoy seguro, pero creo que iba vestida de azul. **10** (*think likely to do well*) creer, parecer: *who do you fancy for the 400 metres hurdles?*, ¿quién crees que ganará los 400 metros vallas?

● **fancy that!**, ¡fíjate!, ¡pues vaya! ‖ **fancy!**, ¿quién lo habría dicho?, ¡vaya!, ¡qué casualidad!: *fancy Nigel losing his job!*, ¿quién habría dicho que Nigel perdiera su trabajo? ‖ **to take a fancy to sb./sth.**, encapricharse con algn./algo. ‖ **to catch sb.'s fancy / take sb.'s fancy**, hacerle gracia a algn., encantarle a algn. ‖ **to fancy os.**, ser creído,-a, ser presumido,-a. ‖ **to fancy os. as sth.**, dárselas de algo, creerse algo.
■ **fancy cake**, pastelito fino. ‖ **fancy dress**, disfraz *m*. ‖ **fancy dress ball**, baile *m* de disfraces. ‖ **fancy man**, amante *m*. ‖ **fancy woman**, amante *f*. ‖ **flights of fancy**, ilusiones *fpl*.
▲ (*verbo*) *pt* & *pp* **fancied**, *ger* **fancying**; (*sustantivo*) *pl* **fancies**.
fancy-free [ˈfænsɪˈfriː] *adj* sin compromiso.
fanfare [ˈfænfeəʳ] *n* fanfarria.
fang [fæŋ] *n* colmillo.
fanlight [ˈfænlaɪt] *n* montante *m*.
fanny [ˈfænɪ] **1** *n* GB *sl* (*vulva*) chocho, coño. **2** US *sl* (*bottom*) culo, trasero.
▲ *pl* **fannies**.
fantasize [ˈfæntəsaɪz] *i* fantasear (**about**, sobre).
fantastic [fænˈtæstɪk] *adj* fantástico,-a.
fantasy [ˈfæntəsɪ] *n* fantasía.
▲ *pl* **fantasies**.
FAO [ˈefˈeɪˈəʊ] *abbr* (*Food and Agriculture Organization*) Organización para la Agricultura y la Alimentación; (*abbreviation*) FAO *f*.
far [fɑːʳ] **1** *adj* (*distant*) lejano,-a, remoto,-a: *a far country*, un país lejano. **2** (*more distant*) opuesto,-a, extremo,-a: *the far end of the hall*, el otro extremo de la sala. – **3** *adv* (*a long way*) lejos: *is it far from here?*, ¿está lejos de aquí?; *how far is?*, ¿a qué distancia está?; *how far is it to Rome?*, ¿cuánto hay de aquí a Roma?; *how far have we travelled?*, ¿cuántos kilómetros hemos hecho?; *it isn't as far as it looks*, no está tan lejos como parece. **4** (*a long time*) lejos: *they existed as far back as the 12th century*, existían ya en el siglo doce; *the day when we'll be able to shop by computer is not so far off*, el día en que se pueda comprar por ordenador no está tan lejos; *they talked far into the night*, estuvieron hablando hasta muy entrada la noche. **5** (*much*) mucho: *it's far better than the other*, está mucho mejor que el otro; *far bigger*, mucho más grande.
● **as far as ... is concerned**, en cuanto a ..., por lo que a ... se refiere: *as far as I am concerned*, por lo que a mí se refiere. ‖ **as far as I know**, que yo sepa. ‖ **as far as the eye can see**, hasta donde alcanza la vista. ‖ **by far**, mucho, con mucho: *it's cheaper by far to go by coach*, es mucho más barato ir en autocar; *it's by far the tallest building*, es con mucho el edificio más alto. ‖ **far and away**, con mucho, con diferencia: *she's far and away the best*, es con mucho la mejor. ‖ **far and wide / far and near**, por todas partes. ‖ **far away**, lejos. ‖ **far be it from me to ...**, no es que yo quiera ... ‖ **far from ...**, lejos de ...: *far from causing problems, he was very helpful*, lejos de causar problemas, fue muy amable. ‖ **far from it**, de eso nada, nada de eso, qué va: *was the film bad? –far from it, it was excellent!*, ¿era mala la película? –¡de eso nada, era buenísima! ‖ **far off**, a lo lejos. ‖ **not to be not far out / not to be far wrong / not to be far off**, no ir desencaminado,-a. ‖ **so far**, (*until now*) hasta ahora; (*to a point*) hasta cierto punto. ‖ **so far, so good**, hasta aquí bien, hasta ahora bien. ‖ **to be a far cry from**, no tener nada que ver con. ‖ **to go far**, (*money*) comprar mucho; (*food, supplies etc*) cundir; (*person*) llegar lejos. ‖ **to go too far**, pasarse

de la raya. ‖ **to take sth. too far**, llevar las cosas demasiado lejos.
■ **the far left / the far right**, la extrema izquierda / la extrema derecha.
▲ *comp* **farther** o **further**, *superl* **farthest** o **furthest**.
faraway [ˈfɑːrəweɪ] *adj* lejano,-a, remoto,-a; (*look*) distraído,-a, en las nubes.
farce [fɑːs] *n* farsa.
farcical [ˈfɑːsɪkəl] *adj* absurdo,-a, ridículo,-a.
fare [feəʳ] **1** *n* (*price*) tarifa, precio del billete, precio del viaje; (*boat*) pasaje *m*. **2** (*passenger*) viajero,-a, pasajero,-a. **3** (*food*) comida. – **4** *i* (*progress, get on*) desenvolverse: *he fared well in the exam*, le fue bien en el examen.
farewell [feəˈwel] **1** *interj* ¡adiós! – **2** *n* despedida.
far-fetched [fɑːˈfetʃt] **1** *adj* (*strained*) rebuscado,-a, forzado,-a. **2** (*incredible*) inverosímil.
far-flung [ˈfɑːflʌŋ] **1** *adj* (*distant*) lejano,-a. **2** (*vast*) vasto,-a.
far-gone [ˈfɑːgɒn] *adj* (*very ill*) en las últimas; (*very drunk*) borracho,-a.
farm [fɑːm] **1** *n* granja. – **2** *adj* agrícola, de granja: *fresh farm eggs*, huevos frescos de granja. – **3** *t* (*use land*) cultivar, labrar. **4** (*breed animals*) criar. – **5** *i* (*grow crops*) cultivar la tierra.
◆ **to farm out** *t sep* (*work*) encargar a terceros, encargar fuera; (*children*) dejar con alguien.
farmer [ˈfɑːməʳ] *n* granjero,-a, agricultor,-ra.
farm-hand [ˈfɑːmhænd] *n* peón *m* agrícola.
farmhouse [ˈfɑːmhaʊs] *n* granja.
farming [ˈfɑːmɪŋ] *n* agricultura.
■ **farming industry**, industria agropecuaria.
farmyard [ˈfɑːmjɑːd] *n* corral *m*.
far-off [ˈfɑːrɒf] *adj* lejano,-a, remoto,-a.
far-out [ˈfɑːraʊt] *adj* extravagante, atrevido,-a.
far-reaching [fɑːˈriːtʃɪŋ] *adj* de gran alcance.
farrier [ˈfærɪəʳ] *n* herrero.
farrow [ˈfærəʊ] **1** *i* parir. – **2** *t* parir.
far-sighted [fɑːˈsaɪtɪd] *adj* previsor,-ra.
far-sightedness [fɑːˈsaɪtɪdnəs] *n* previsión *f*.
fart [fɑːt] **1** *n fam* pedo. **2** (*fool*) carcamal *m*, carroza *m*. – **3** *i* tirarse un pedo.
◆ **to fart about / fart around** *i* hacer el indio, hacer el gilipollas.
■ **old fart**, muermo.
farther [ˈfɑːðəʳ] **1** *adj comp* → **far**: *Bilbao is farther than Valencia*, Bilbao está más lejos que Valencia. – **2** *adv comp* → **far**: *I can't walk any farther*, no puedo andar más.
farthest [ˈfɑːðɪst] **1** *adj superl* → **far**: *Pluto is the farthest planet from the Sun*, Plutón es el planeta más alejado del Sol. – **2** *adv superl* → **far**: *who lives farthest from the school?*, ¿quién vive más lejos de la escuela?
farthing [ˈfɑːðɪŋ] *n* cuarto de penique.
● **it's not worth a brass farthing**, no vale un real.
fascinate [ˈfæsɪneɪt] *t* fascinar.
fascinating [ˈfæsɪneɪtɪŋ] *adj* fascinante.
fascination [fæsɪˈneɪʃən] *n* fascinación *f*.
fascism [ˈfæʃɪzəm] *n* fascismo.
fascist [ˈfæʃɪst] **1** *n* fascista *mf*. – **2** *adj* fascista.
fashion [ˈfæʃən] **1** *n* (*style*) moda. **2** (*way*) modo. – **3** *t* (*clay*) formar; (*metal*) labrar.
● **to be all the fashion**, estar muy de moda. ‖ **after a fashion**, en cierto modo. ‖ **after the fashion of / in the fashion of**, a la manera de. ‖ **to be in fashion**, estar de moda. ‖ **to be out of fashion**, estar pasado,-

a de moda. ‖ **to come into fashion,** ponerse de moda. ‖ **to go out of fashion,** pasar de moda.

fashionable [ˈfæʃənəbəl] *adj* de moda.

fashionably [ˈfæʃənəblɪ] *adv* a la moda.

fast¹ [fɑːst] **1** *adj* (*gen*) rápido,-a: *he drives a fast car,* conduce un coche rápido; *I paid her a fast visit,* le hice una visita rápida. **2** (*tight, secure*) firme, seguro,-a: *the boat was fast,* el barco estaba bien amarrado. **3** (*clock*) adelantado,-a: *my watch is fast,* llevo el reloj adelantado. **4** (*colours*) sólido,-a. **5** (*active*) muy activo,-a, ajetreado,-a. – **6** *adv* rápidamente, deprisa: *how fast was he going?,* ¿a qué velocidad iba?; *news travels fast,* las noticias vuelan; *don't drive so fast,* no corras tanto; *he can run faster than me,* él corre más rápido que yo. **7** (*securely*) firmemente; (*thoroughly*) profundamente: *they're fast asleep,* duermen profundamente.

● **fast and furious,** a un ritmo vertiginoso. ‖ **to be stuck fast,** estar bien encajado,-a, estar atrancado,-a. ‖ **to hold fast to sth.,** agarrarse bien a algo. ‖ **to live in the fast lane,** vivir deprisa, vivir a tope. ‖ **to play fast and loose with sb.,** jugar con algn. ‖ **to pull a fast one on sb.,** jugar una mala pasada a algn. ‖ **to stand fast,** mantenerse firme. ‖ **not so fast!,** *fam* ¡un momento!

■ **fast food,** comida rápida. ‖ **fast lane,** carril *m* rápido.

fast² [fɑːst] **1** *n* ayuno. – **2** *i* ayunar.

fasten [ˈfɑːsən] **1** *t* (*attach*) fijar, sujetar. **2** (*tie*) atar. **3** (*box, door, window*) cerrar; (*belt, dress*) abrochar: *please fasten your seatbelts,* abróchense los cinturones por favor. – **4** *i* (*box, door etc*) cerrarse; (*dress etc*) abrocharse.

◆ **to fasten on/onto** *t insep* agarrarse a, aferrarse a.

● **to fasten one's eyes on,** fijar los ojos en. ‖ **to fasten the blame on sb.,** echar la culpa a algn.

fastener [ˈfɑːsənəʳ] *n* cierre *m*.

fastidious [fæˈstɪdɪəs] *adj* quisquilloso,-a, melindroso,-a.

fastidiousness [fæˈstɪdɪəsnəs] *n* melindres *mpl*.

fat [fæt] **1** *adj* (*person*) gordo,-a. **2** (*thick*) grueso,-a, gordo,-a. **3** (*meat*) que tiene mucha grasa. **4** (*profit, cheque, etc*) sustancioso,-a. **5** (*rich, fertile*) fértil. **6** *fam iron* (*very little*) poco,-a: *fat chance you stand of passing your test!,* ¡muchas posibilidades tienes tú de sacarte el carnet!; *fat lot of good it'll do her!,* ¡no le servirá de nada! – **7** *n* (*of meat*) grasa; (*of person*) carnes *fpl*. **8** (*for cooking*) manteca; (*lard*) lardo.

● **the fat is in the fire,** se va a armar la de Dios, se va a armar una buena. ‖ **to get fat,** engordar, engordarse. ‖ **to live off the fat of the land,** vivir como un rey. ‖ **to run to fat,** echar carnes.

■ **fat cat,** pez *m* gordo.

▲ (*adjetivo*) *comp* **fatter,** *superl* **fattest**.

fatal [ˈfeɪtəl] **1** *adj* (*causing disaster*) fatal, funesto,-a; (*serious*) grave. **2** (*causing death*) mortal. **3** (*fateful*) fatídico,-a.

fatalism [ˈfeɪtəlɪzəm] *n* fatalismo.

fatalist [ˈfeɪtəlɪst] *n* fatalista *mf*.

fatalistic [feɪtəˈlɪstɪk] *adj* fatalista.

fatality [fəˈtælɪtɪ] *n* víctima mortal.

▲ *pl* **fatalities**.

fatally [ˈfeɪtəlɪ] *adv* mortalmente.

fate [feɪt] **1** *n* (*destiny*) destino: *fate was against me,* el destino iba en contra mía. **2** (*person's lot*) suerte *f*: *the jury would decide my fate,* el jurado decidiría mi suerte. – **3 The Fates,** *npl* las Parcas *fpl*.

● **a fate worse than death,** lo peor que pudiera pasar. ‖ **to tempt fate,** tentar a la suerte.

fated [ˈfeɪtɪd] *adj* predestinado,-a, condenado,-a: *we were fated to meet,* estábamos predestinados a conocernos; *it was fated that we would lose,* estábamos condenados a perder.

fateful [ˈfeɪtfʊl] *adj* fatídico,-a, aciago,-a.

fathead [ˈfæthed] *n fam* imbécil *mf*.

father [ˈfɑːðəʳ] **1** *n* (*male parent*) padre *m*. **2** (*priest*) padre *m*. – **3** *t* (*beget*) engendrar. **4** *fig* (*create, originate*) inventar, crear. – **5** **fathers,** *npl* (*ancestors*) antepasados *mpl*.

● **from father to son,** de padre a hijo. ‖ **like father like son,** de tal palo, tal astilla. ‖ **to be a father to sb.,** ser un padre para algn. ‖ **to father sth. on sb.,** atribuir algo a algn.

■ **father figure,** figura paterna. ‖ **Father's Day,** el día del padre. ‖ **Father Christmas,** Papá *m* Noel. ‖ **Father Time,** el Tiempo.

fatherhood [ˈfɑːðəhʊd] *n* paternidad *f*.

father-in-law [ˈfɑːðərɪnlɔː] *n* suegro.

fatherland [ˈfɑːðəlænd] *n* patria.

fatherly [ˈfɑːðəlɪ] *adj* paternal.

fathom [ˈfæðəm] **1** *n* (*measurement*) brazo. – **2** *t* (*measure*) sondear. **3** *fig* penetrar en, comprender.

◆ **to fathom out** *t sep* comprender, entender: *I can't fathom it out,* no lo entiendo.

fatigue [fəˈtiːg] **1** *n* fatiga, cansancio. **2** TECH fatiga. **3** MIL faena. – **4** *t fml* fatigar, cansar. – **5 fatigues,** *npl* US MIL traje *m* de faena.

■ **metal fatigue,** fatiga del metal.

fatso [ˈfætsəʊ] *n fam* gordo,-a, gordinflón,-ona.

▲ *pl* **fatsos** o **fatsoes**.

fatten [ˈfætən] **1** *t* (*animal*) cebar (**up,** -). **2** (*person*) engordar (**up,**-).

fattening [ˈfætənɪŋ] *adj* que engorda: *biscuits are fattening,* las galletas engordan.

fatty [ˈfætɪ] **1** *adj* (*greasy*) graso,-a. – **2** *n fam pej* gordinflón,-ona.

▲ (*adjetivo*) *comp* **fattier,** *superl* **fattiest**; (*sustantivo*) *pl* **fatties**.

fatuous [ˈfætjʊəs] *adj* fatuo,-a, necio,-a.

faucet [ˈfɔːsɪt] *n* US grifo.

fault [fɔːlt] **1** *n* (*in character, system etc*) defecto. **2** (*in merchandise*) defecto, desperfecto, tara. **3** (*blame*) culpa: *it's his fault,* es culpa suya. **4** (*mistake*) error *m*, falta. **5** (*in earth*) falla. **6** (*in tennis etc*) falta. – **7** *t* criticar, encontrar defectos a: *he cannot be faulted on reasoning,* su razonamiento es intachable.

● **to a fault,** en exceso. ‖ **to be at fault,** tener la culpa. ‖ **to find fault with sb./sth.,** poner reparos a algn./algo.

fault-finding [ˈfɔːltfaɪndɪŋ] *adj* criticón,-ona.

faultless [ˈfɔːltləs] *adj* perfecto,-a, intachable, impecable.

faulty [ˈfɔːltɪ] *adj* defectuoso,-a.

▲ *comp* **faultier,** *superl* **faultiest**.

fauna [ˈfɔːnə] *n* fauna.

faux pas [fəʊˈpɑː] *n* metedura de pata.

▲ *pl* **faux pas** [fəʊˈpɑː].

favour [ˈfeɪvəʳ] **1** *n* (*kindness*) favor *m*: *can you do me a favour?,* ¿puedes hacerme un favor?; *I need to ask you a favour,* necesito pedirte un favor. **2** (*approval*) aprobación *f*, favor *m*: *your parents will look with favour on your decision,* tus padres aprobarán tu decisión. **3** (*favouritism*) parcialidad *f*, favoritismo: *the youngest was treated with favour,* se trató al más joven con favoritismo. – **4** *t* (*prefer*) preferir, inclinarse por: *I*

favour the second option, me inclino por la segunda opción. **5** (*benefit, aid*) favorecer; (*treat with partiality*) dar un trato de favor: *the wind favoured the server,* el viento favoreció al saque; *a teacher should never favour any one pupil,* un profesor nunca debería dar un trato de favor a ningún alumno. – **6 favours,** *npl* (*sexual pleasure*) favores *mpl.*
● **do me a favour!,** ¡venga ya! ‖ **in favour of,** a favor de: *the judge found in our favour,* el juez dictó a nuestro favor. ‖ **to be in favour of,** ser partidario,-a de, estar a favor de. ‖ **to be in favour,** estar en auge, estar de moda. ‖ **to be in favour with sb.,** tener la aceptación de algn., contar con el apoyo de algn. ‖ **to be out of favour,** no estar de moda. ‖ **to be out of favour with sb.,** no contar con el apoyo de algn., perder el apoyo de algn. ‖ **to find favour with sb.,** caer en gracia a algn., ganar el apoyo de algn. ‖ **to fall out of favour with sb.,** perder el favor de algn.

favourable ['feɪvərəbəl] **1** *adj* favorable (**to/towards,** a). **2** (*suitable*) propicio,-a (**for,** para).

favourably ['feɪvərəblɪ] *adv* favorablemente.

favourite ['feɪvərɪt] **1** *n* preferido,-a, favorito,-a. – **2** *adj* preferido,-a, predilecto,-a, favorito,-a.

favouritism ['feɪvərɪtɪzəm] *n* favoritismo.

fawn [fɔːn] *n* ZOOL cervato. **2** (*colour*) beige *m*, color *m* café claro. – **3** *adj* beige, de color café claro.
◆ **to fawn on** *t insep* adular, lisonjear.

faze [feɪz] *t fam* desconcertar, perturbar: *nothing fazes him,* nada le desconcierta.

FBI ['efbiː'aɪ] *abbr* (*Federal Bureau of Investigation*) oficina federal de investigación; (*abbreviation*) FBI *f.*

FC ['ef'siː] *abbr* GB SPORT (*Football Club*) Club *m* de Fútbol; (*abbreviation*) CF.

fealty ['fɪəltɪ] *n* lealtad *f.*

fear [fɪər] **1** *n* miedo, temor *m*: *fear of flying,* miedo a volar; *he showed no fear,* no mostraba ningún miedo; *it confirmed our fears,* confirmó nuestros temores. – **2** *t* temer, tener miedo a: *she fears death,* teme a la muerte; *she feared he was dead,* temía que hubiera muerto. – **3** *i* temer, tener miedo: *fear not!,* ¡no temas!, ¡no tengas miedo!
◆ **to fear for** *t insep* temer por: *I fear for the children's safety,* temo por la seguridad de los niños.
● **for fear of ...,** por miedo de ..., por temor a ... ‖ **for fear that,** por miedo de que. ‖ **I fear that ...,** me temo que ... ‖ **never fear,** no hay cuidado, no temas. ‖ **no fear!,** ¡ni hablar!, ¡ni loco,-a!, ¡ni muerto,-a! ‖ **there's no fear of ...,** no hay peligro de que ... ‖ **to be in fear of one's life,** temer por su vida. ‖ **to fear the worst,** temer lo peor. ‖ **to hold no fears for sb.,** no dar miedo a algn. ‖ **to put the fear of God into sb.,** dar un susto mortal a algn.

fearful ['fɪəfʊl] **1** *adj* (*frightened*) temeroso,-a (**of,** de). **2** (*terrible*) terrible, espantoso,-a, tremendo,-a.

fearless ['fɪələs] *adj* intrépido,-a, audaz.
● **fearless of ...,** sin temor a ...

fearlessly ['fɪələslɪ] *adv* sin temor.

fearlessness ['fɪələsnəs] *n* intrepidez *f,* audacia.

fearsome ['fɪəsəm] *adj* temible.

feasibility ['fiːzəbɪlɪtɪ] *n* viabilidad *f.*
■ **feasibility study,** estudio de viabilidad.

feasible ['fiːzəbəl] **1** *adj* (*viable*) factible, viable. **2** (*plausible*) verosímil.

feast [fiːst] **1** *n* festín *m,* banquete *m.* **2** *fam* comilona. **3** REL fiesta de guardar, día *m* de fiesta. – **4** *i* banquetear, festejar.

● **to feast on sth.,** *fig* regalarse con algo. ‖ **to feast one's eyes on sth.,** regalarse la vista con algo.

feat [fiːt] *n* proeza, hazaña.

feather ['feðər] **1** *n* pluma. – **2** *t* emplumar. **3** (*oar*) alzar.
● **to be a feather in sb.'s cap,** ser un triunfo para algn. ‖ **to feather one's own nest,** *pej* barrer para casa. ‖ **to be birds of a feather,** ser de la misma calaña. ‖ **birds of a feather, flock together,** Dios los cría y ellos se juntan. ‖ **you could've knocked me down with a feather,** me quedé patidifuso,-a.
■ **feather bed,** colchón *m* de plumas. ‖ **feather boa,** boa *mf.* ‖ **feather duster,** plumero.

feather-brained ['feðəbreɪnd] *adj fam* cabeza hueca, despistado,-a.

featherweight ['feðəweɪt] *n* (*boxing*) peso pluma.

feature ['fiːtʃər] **1** *n* (*of face*) rasgo, facción *f.* **2** (*characteristic*) rasgo, característica, aspecto. **3** (*press*) artículo especial, especial *m.* – **4** *t* (*have*) tener; (*film*) tener como protagonista: *this car features the latest safety devices,* este coche incorpora los últimos dispositivos de seguridad; *a film featuring Kenneth Williams,* una película con Kenneth Williams como protagonista. – **5** *i* (*appear*) figurar (**in,** en): *his name featured in the police report,* su nombre figuró en el informe policial.
■ **feature (film),** largometraje *m.*

featureless ['fiːtʃələs] *adj* monótono,-a.

Feb [feb] *abbr* (*February*) febrero.

February ['februərɪ] *n* febrero.
▲ *Véase también* May.

feckless ['fekləs] *adj* incompetente, inútil.

fecund ['fiːkənd] *adj* fecundo,-a, fértil.

fecundity [fe'kʌndɪtɪ] *n* fecundidad *f.*

fed [fed] *pt & pp* → **feed.**
● **to be fed up with,** *fam* estar harto,-a de.

federal ['fedərəl] *adj* federal.

federation [fedə'reɪʃən] *n* federación *f.*

fee [fiː] **1** *n* (*doctor's etc*) honorarios *mpl;* (*for tuition*) derechos *mpl* (de matrícula). **2** (*membership*) cuota, cuota de socio.
■ **registration fee,** matrícula.

feeble ['fiːbəl] **1** *adj* (*person*) débil. **2** (*light, sound*) tenue, débil. **3** (*argument, excuse*) de poco peso.

feeble-minded [fiːbəl'maɪndɪd] *adj* imbécil.

feebleness ['fiːbəlnəs] *n* debilidad *f.*

feed [fiːd] **1** *n* comida. **2** *fam* comilona. **3** (*for cattle*) pienso. **4** TECH alimentación *f.* – **5** *t* alimentar, dar de comer a: *could you feed our cat while we're away?,* ¿podrías dar de comer a nuestro gato mientras estamos fuera?; *I'll be glad when the baby can feed himself,* me alegraré cuando el bebé pueda comer por sí solo. **6** (*breastfeed*) amamantar a, dar de mamar a; (*bottle-feed*) dar el biberón a. **7** *fig* (*fire, passion*) alimentar. **8** TECH alimentar, suministrar. **9** (*insert*) introducir; (*coins*) meter. – **10** *i* (*people*) comer, alimentarse (**on,** de); (*animals*) pacer.
◆ **to feed up** *t sep* (*animal*) cebar; (*person*) engordar.
■ **feed pipe,** tubo de alimentación.
▲ *pt & pp* fed.

feedback ['fiːdbæk] **1** *n* TECH realimentación *f.* **2** *fig* reacción *f,* respuesta, impresión *f.*

feeder ['fiːdər] **1** *n* TECH alimentador *m.* **2** (*road*) ramal *m,* carretera.

feeding ['fiːdɪŋ] **1** **feeding bottle,** *n* biberón *m.* **2** **feeding time,** hora de la comida, hora de dar de comer.

feel [fiːl] **1** *n* (*sense, texture*) tacto: *I like the feel of it,* me gusta el tacto que tiene; *it has a rough feel,* tiene un tacto áspero; *have a feel of this material,* toca esta tela.

2 (*atmosphere*) aire *m*, ambiente *m*: *you'll love the feel of the place,* te encantará el ambiente que hay. – **3** *t* (*touch*) tocar, palpar: *the doctor felt my back,* el médico me palpó la espalda; *feel how soft this is,* toca y verás qué suave. **4** (*search with fingers*) buscar. **5** (*sense, experience*) sentir, experimentar, tener la impresión: *she felt something crawling up her leg,* sentía cómo algo se le subía por la pierna; *I love to feel the wind on my face,* me encanta sentir el viento en la cara; *he felt a sudden pain in his arm,* sintió un dolor súbito en el brazo. **6** (*notice*) notar, apreciar: *everyone will feel the knock-on effects of this investment,* todo el mundo notará las consecuencias de esta inversión. **7** (*suffer*) sentir, afectar: *she feels the cold,* es muy friolera; *he felt the death of his father very much,* le afectó mucho la muerte de su padre. **8** (*believe*) creer: *I feel you are making a mistake,* creo que te equivocas; *she felt sure that he would pass,* estaba segura de que aprobaría. – **9** *i* (*be*) sentir(se), encontrarse, experimentar: *how are you feeling? –I feel terrible,* ¿cómo te encuentras? –me encuentro fatal; *she felt happy,* se sentía feliz; *we were feeling cold, tired and hungry,* teníamos frío, sueño y hambre; *you'll feel much better after a nice bath,* te sentirás mucho mejor después de un buen baño; *he doesn't feel quite himself,* no se encuentra del todo bien; *how does it feel to be famous?,* ¿qué se siente cuando se es famoso?; *I felt a right idiot,* me sentí una idiota. **10** (*seem*) parecer: *it feels like leather,* parece piel; *it feels like summer,* parece verano; *it feels like rain,* me parece que va a llover; *your feet feel cold,* tienes los pies fríos. **11** (*perceive, sense*) sentir: *as I walked in, I felt the tension in the room,* al entrar, sentí la tensión en la sala; *he felt a sudden urge to scream,* sintió un deseo apremiante de gritar; *she could feel all eyes upon her,* sentía que todos la miraban. **12** (*believe*) opinar, pensar: *how do you feel about exams?,* ¿qué opinas de los exámenes?
◆ **to feel for** *t insep* (*have sympathy for*) compadecer a, compadecerse de. ‖ **to feel up to** *t insep* sentirse con ánimos para, sentirse con fuerzas para: *are you sure you feel up to it?,* ¿seguro que te sientes con fuerzas?
● **feel free,** como quieras. ‖ **to feel as if / feel as though,** sentir como si, tener la impresión de. ‖ **to feel bad about,** sentir, saber mal. ‖ **to feel like doing sth.,** tener ganas de hacer algo. ‖ **to feel like sth.,** apetecerle algo, tener ganas de algo: *I feel like an ice cream,* me apetece un helado. ‖ **to feel one's age,** sentirse mayor. ‖ **to feel one's way,** (*walk carefully*) andar a tientas; (*proceed cautiously*) tantear el terreno. ‖ **to feel strongly about sth.,** parecer importante algo. ‖ **to get the feel of sth.,** acostumbrarse a algo. ‖ **to have a feel for sth.,** tener facilidad para algo.
▲ *pt & pp* **felt**.
feeler ['fiːlə'] *n* antena.
● **to put out feelers,** hacer un sondeo, tantear el terreno.
■ **feeler gauge,** galga de espesores.
feeling ['fiːlɪŋ] **1** *n* (*emotion*) sentimiento, emoción *f*: *she suffered from a feeling of guilt,* padecía un sentimiento de culpabilidad; *the feeling's mutual,* el sentimiento es mutuo; *she spoke with feeling about the war,* habló con pasión sobre la guerra. **2** (*sensation*) sensación *f*: *he had a feeling of nausea,* tenía una sensación de náusea. **3** (*sense*) sensibilidad: *I've lost all feeling in my legs,* he perdido la sensibilidad en las piernas. **4** (*concern*) compasión *f*, ternura: *you have no feeling!,* ¡qué insensible eres! **5** (*impression*) impresión *f*, sensación *f*, presentimiento: *I have the feeling that ...,* tengo la impresión de

que ... **6** (*artistic*) sensibilidad *f*, talento: *she plays with great feeling,* toca con una gran sensibilidad. **7** (*opinion*) sentir *m*, opinión *f*, actitud *f*, parecer *m*: *my own feeling is that ...,* en mi opinión ...; *the general feeling was ...,* la opinión general era ... **8** (*atmosphere*) ambiente *m*. – **9** *adj* sensible, compasivo,-a: *he's a very feeling person,* es una persona muy sensible. – **10 feelings,** *npl* sentimientos *mpl*: *you hurt my feelings,* me has herido los sentimientos, me has ofendido; *don't try to hide your feelings,* no intentes ocultar tus sentimientos; *feelings were running high,* los ánimos estaban muy exaltados.
● **I know the feeling,** te entiendo perfectamente. ‖ **no hard feelings,** *fam* no nos guardemos rencor. ‖ **to have a feeling for sth.,** tener sensibilidad por algo. ‖ **to have mixed feelings,** tener sentimientos enfrentados.
■ **bad feeling / ill feeling,** resentimiento, rencor *m*.
fee-paying ['fiːpeɪɪŋ] **1** *adj* (*pupil*) que paga. **2** (*school*) de pago.
feet [fiːt] *npl* → **foot**.
feign [feɪn] *t* fingir, aparentar: *she feigned illness to get off school,* fingió estar enferma para no ir a la escuela.
feint [feɪnt] **1** *n fml* (*fencing*) finta; (*boxing*) treta, estratagema. – **2** *adj* (*paper*) rayado,-a.
feisty ['faɪstɪ] *adj* (*forceful*) batallador,-ra; (*irritable*) irritable.
▲ *comp* **feistier,** *superl* **feistiest.**
feline ['fiːlaɪn] **1** *adj* felino,-a. – **2** *n* felino,-a.
fell[1] [fel] *adj* feroz, cruel.
● **at one fell swoop,** de un solo golpe.
fell[2] [fel] **1** *t* (*tree*) talar. **2** (*enemy*) derribar.
fell[3] [fel] *n* GEOG (*moorland*) páramo alto; (*hilly land*) monte *m*, colina.
fell[4] [fel] *pt* → **fall**.
fellatio [fə'leɪʃɪəʊ] *n* felación *f*.
felling ['felɪŋ] *n* tala.
fellow ['feləʊ] **1** *n fam* (*chap*) tipo, tío: *my dear fellow!,* ¡hombre!; *old fellow,* viejo amigo; *poor fellow!,* ¡pobrecito! **2** (*companion, comrade*) compañero,-a, camarada *mf*. **3** (*member*) socio,-a. **4** (*univ*) miembro (del claustro de profesores). **5** US (*graduate*) graduado,-a. **6** *fml* (*one of a pair*) pareja.
■ **fellow citizen,** conciudadano,-a. ‖ **fellow countryman / fellow countrywoman,** compatriota *mf*. ‖ **fellow student,** compañero,-a de estudios. ‖ **fellow traveller,** compañero,-a de viaje. ‖ **fellow worker,** compañero,-a de trabajo.
fellowship ['feləʊʃɪp] **1** *n* (*group*) asociación *f*, sociedad *f*. **2** (*companionship*) compañerismo, camaradería. **3** EDUC (*scholarship*) beca.
felon ['felən] *n* criminal *mf*.
felony ['felənɪ] *n* crimen *m*, delito mayor.
▲ *pl* **felonies.**
felt[1] [felt] *pt & pp* → **feel**.
felt[2] [felt] **1** *n* fieltro. – **2** *adj* de fieltro.
felt-tip ['felttɪp] felt-tip (pen), *n* rotulador *m*.
fem ['femɪn] *abbr* (*feminine*) femenino; (*abbreviation*) f.
female ['fiːmeɪl] **1** *n* hembra. **2** (*woman*) mujer *f*; (*girl*) chica. – **3** *adj* femenino,-a. **4** ZOOL hembra.
feminine ['femɪnɪn] **1** *adj* femenino,-a. – **2** *n* femenino,-a.
femininity [femə'nɪnətɪ] *n* feminidad *f*.
feminism ['femɪnɪzəm] *n* feminismo.
feminist ['femɪnɪst] *n* feminista *mf*.
femur ['fiːmə'] *n* fémur *m*.
fen [fen] **1** *n* GEOG terreno pantanoso. – **2** **the Fens,** *npl* zona llana y pantanosa del este de Inglaterra.

fence [fens] **1** *n* (*structure*) valla, cerca. **2** *sl* (*buyer and seller of stolen goods*) perista *mf*. – **3** *i* SP practicar la esgrima. **4** (*land*) cercar.
◆ **to fence in** *t sep* (*animals*) encerrar en un cercado, meter en un cercado; (*land*) cercar. ‖ **to fence off** *t sep* separar mediante cercas.
● **to sit on the fence,** ver los toros desde la barrera.
fencer ['fensə'] *n* SP esgrimidor,-ra.
fencing ['fensɪŋ] **1** *n* SP esgrima. **2** (*structure*) cercado. **3** (*material*) material *m* para cercas.
■ **fencing foil,** florete *m*.
fend [fend] **to fend for os.,** *i* valerse por sí mismo,-a, apañárselas por su cuenta.
◆ **to fend off** *t sep* (*blow*) parar, desviar; (*question*) esquivar; (*attack*) rechazar, defenderse de.
fender ['fendə'] **1** *n* (*for fire*) pantalla. **2** US AUTO parachoques *m*. **3** (*on boat*) defensa.
fennel ['fenəl] *n* hinojo.
ferment ['fɜːmənt] **1** *n* (*substance*) fermento. **2** (*unrest*) agitación *f*. – **3** *t* fermentar. – **4** *i* fermentar.
▲ (*verbo*) [fə'ment].
fermentation [fɜːmen'teɪʃən] *n* fermentación *f*.
fern [fɜːn] *n* helecho.
ferocious [fə'rəʊʃəs] *adj* feroz.
ferociously [fə'rəʊʃəslɪ] *adv* ferozmente.
ferocity [fə'rɒsɪtɪ] *n* ferocidad *f*.
ferret ['ferɪt] **1** *n* hurón *m*. – **2** *i* huronear.
◆ **to ferret about** *i* buscar (**for,** -), husmear (**for,** -). ‖ **to ferret out** *t sep* descubrir.
ferric ['ferɪk] *adj* férrico,-a.
ferrous ['ferəs] *adj* ferroso,-a.
ferry ['ferɪ] **1** *n* (*small*) barca de pasaje; (*large*) transbordador *m*, ferry *m*. – **2** *t* transportar.
▲ (*sustantivo*) *pl* **ferries**; (*verbo*) *pt* & *pp* **ferried,** *ger* **ferrying**.
ferryboat ['ferɪbəʊt] *n* → **ferry**.
ferryman ['ferɪmæn] *n* barquero.
▲ *pl* **ferrymen** ['ferɪmən].
fertile ['fɜːtaɪl] *adj* fértil, fecundo,-a.
fertility [fə'tɪlɪtɪ] *n* fertilidad *f*.
fertilization [fɜːtɪlaɪ'zeɪʃən] **1** *n* (*soil*) fertilización *f*. **2** (*egg*) fecundación *f*.
fertilize ['fɜːtɪlaɪz] **1** *t* (*soil*) fertilizar, abonar. **2** (*egg*) fecundar.
fertilizer ['fɜːtɪlaɪzə'] *n* fertilizante *m*, abono.
fervent ['fɜːvənt] *adj* fervoroso,-a.
fervour ['fɜːvə'] *n* fervor *m*.
fester ['festə'] **1** *i* MED supurar, enconarse. **2** *fig* amargarse.
festival ['festɪvəl] **1** *n* (*event*) festival *m*. **2** (*celebration*) fiesta.
festive ['festɪv] *adj* festivo,-a.
■ **the festive season,** las Navidades *fpl*, las fiestas *pl* de Navidad.
festivity [fe'stɪvɪtɪ] **1** *n* (*celebration*) fiesta, festividad *f*. – **2 festivities,** *npl* fiestas *fpl*, festejos *mpl*.
▲ *pl* **festivities**.
festoon [fe'stuːn] **1** *n* (*decoration*) adorno, guirnalda. **2** (*in sewing*) festón *m*. – **3** *t* (*decorate*) adornar, decorar (**with,** de). **4** (*in sewing*) festonear.
fetch [fetʃ] **1** *t* (*go and get*) ir por, ir a buscar, buscar; (*bring*) traer: *she's gone to fetch the children from school,* ha ido a buscar a los niños de la escuela; *do you want me to fetch you anything?,* ¿quieres que te traiga algo? **2** *fam* (*sell for*) venderse por, alcanzar: *this should fetch a good price,* esto se debería vender por un buen precio.

◆ **to fetch up** *i* ir a parar.
● **to fetch and carry,** trajinar. ‖ **to fetch and carry for sb.,** ser el machaca de algn.
fetching ['fetʃɪŋ] *adj* atractivo,-a.
fête [feɪt] **1** *n* (*party*) fiesta; (*fair*) feria. – **2** *t* festejar.
fetid ['fetɪd] *adj* fétido,-a.
fetish ['fetɪʃ] *n* fetiche *m*.
fetishism ['fetɪʃɪzəm] *n* fetichismo.
fetishist ['fetɪʃɪst] *n* fetichista *mf*.
fetlock ['fetlɒk] *n* espolón *m*.
fetter ['fetə'] **1** *t* encadenar. **2** *fig* estorbar, poner trabas a. – **3 fetters,** *npl* grillo *m sing*, grilletes *mpl*, cadenas *fpl*: *they were in fetters,* estaban encadenados. **4** *fig* trabas *fpl*.
fettle ['fetəl] *n* estado, condiciones *fpl*.
● **to be in fine fettle,** (*thing*) estar en buenas condiciones; (*person*) estar en buena forma.
fetus ['fiːtəs] *n* US → **foetus**.
feud [fjuːd] **1** *n* enemistad *f* (*duradera*): *there's been a feud between the two families for years,* hace años que existe una enemistad entre ambas familias. – **2** *i* disentir, reñir, pelear.
feudal ['fjuːdəl] *adj* feudal.
feudalism ['fjuːdəlɪzəm] *n* feudalismo.
fever ['fiːvə'] **1** *n* (*temperature*) fiebre *f*: *he's got a fever,* tiene fiebre. **2** (*nervous excitement*) fiebre *f*, excitación *f*.
● **at fever pitch,** al rojo vivo.
■ **hay fever,** fiebre *f* del heno.
feverish ['fiːvərɪʃ] **1** *adj* (*having a fever*) febril. **2** (*excited*) nervioso,-a, excitado,-a, febril.
feverishly ['fiːvərɪʃlɪ] *adv* febrilmente.
few [fjuː] **1** *adj* (*not many*) poco,-a, pocos,-as: *very few cars,* muy pocos coches. **2** (*some*) uno,-a cuantos,-as, algunos,-as: *a few days ago,* hace unos días; *a few friends,* algunos amigos; *in the next few days,* dentro de unos días. – **3** *pron* (*not many*) pocos,-as: *many try but few succeed,* muchos lo intentan pero pocos lo consiguen; *the few who were there enjoyed themselves,* los pocos que asistieron lo pasaron bien. **4** (*some*) unos,-as cuantos,-as, algunos,-as: *a few of them,* algunos de ellos; *there are a few left,* quedan unos cuantos.
● **a good few,** un buen número. ‖ **as few as,** solamente. ‖ **few and far between,** poquísimos,-as, contadísimos,-as, muy escasos,-as. ‖ **no fewer than,** no menos de. ‖ **quite a few,** un buen número, bastantes: *there were quite a few people there,* había bastante gente. ‖ **to have had a few too many,** haber tomado una copa de más.
■ **the chosen few,** los elegidos *mpl*.
fey [feɪ] *adj* (*whimsical*) fantasioso,-a; (*clairvoyant*) clarividente.
fez [fez] *n* fez *m*.
▲ *pl* **fezzes**.
fiancé [fɪ'ænseɪ] *n* prometido, novio.
fiancée [fɪ'ænseɪ] *n* prometida, novia.
fiasco [fɪ'æskəʊ] *n* fiasco, fracaso.
▲ *pl* **fiascos,** US **fiascoes**.
fib [fɪb] **1** *n* *fam* bola, trola. – **2** *i* *fam* contar bolas, contar trolas.
▲ (*verbo*) *pt* & *pp* **fibbed,** *ger* **fibbing**.
fibber ['fɪbə'] *n* *fam* trolero,-a, mentiroso,-a.
fiber ['faɪbə'] *n* US → **fibre**.
fibre ['faɪbə'] **1** *n* fibra. **2** *fig* (*moral*) nervio, carácter *m*.
■ **fibre optics,** fibra óptica. ‖ **man-made fibre,** fibra artificial.

fibreglass ['faɪbəglɑːs] n fibra de vidrio.
fibrositis [faɪbrə'saɪtɪs] n fibrositis f.
fibrous ['faɪbrəs] adj fibroso,-a.
fickle ['fɪkəl] adj inconstante, voluble.
fickleness ['fɪkəlnəs] n inconstancia, volubilidad f.
fiction ['fɪkʃən] 1 n (novels) novela, narrativa. 2 (invention) ficción f.
fictional ['fɪkʃənəl] adj ficticio,-a.
fictitious [fɪk'tɪʃəs] adj ficticio,-a.
fiddle ['fɪdəl] 1 n fam violín m. 2 fam (fraud) estafa, trampa. – 3 i tocar el violín. 4 fam (play) juguetear (**with**, con). – 5 t fam (cheat) amañar, falsificar.
◆to **fiddle about / fiddle around** i fam perder el tiempo.
● to **be on the fiddle**, hacer trampas, estar metido,-a en chanchullos. ‖ to **play second fiddle**, desempeñar un papel secundario, ser el segundón.
■ **tax fiddle**, evasión f fiscal.
fiddler ['fɪdlə'] 1 n fam (violinist) violinista mf. 2 fam (cheat) tramposo,-a.
fiddlesticks ['fɪdlstɪks] interj tonterías fpl, bobadas fpl.
fiddly ['fɪdlɪ] adj fam difícil, complicado,-a.
▲ comp fiddlier, superl fiddliest.
fidelity [fɪ'delɪtɪ] n fidelidad f.
fidget ['fɪdʒɪt] 1 n persona inquieta. – 2 i (move about) moverse, no poder estar(se) quieto,-a; (play about) jugar (**with**, con): stop fidgeting!, ¡estáte quieto!
● to **be a fidget**, ser culo de mal asiento.
fidgety ['fɪdʒɪtɪ] adj inquieto,-a.
field [fiːld] 1 n (gen) campo: a corn field, un campo de maíz; they work in the fields, trabajan en los campos; our school has a sports field, nuestra escuela tiene un campo de deportes. 2 (for mining) yacimiento. 3 MIL campo: the field of battle, el campo de batalla. 4 (subject, area) campo, terreno: he's famous in the field of politics, es famoso en el campo de la política; what's your field?, ¿cuál es tu especialidad?; that's outside my field, eso no es de mi competencia. 5 SP (competitors) competidores mpl; (horses) participantes mpl. 6 TECH campo: a magnetic field, un campo magnético; the earth's gravitational field, el campo gravitacional de la tierra; our field of vision, nuestro campo visual. – 7 t SP parar y devolver. – 8 i SP parar y devolver la pelota. – 9 t SP (select to play) presentar.
● to **have a field day**, fam (enjoyment) divertirse mucho, estar encantado,-a; (financially) hacer su agosto. ‖ to **play the field**, salir con mucha gente. ‖ to **take the field**, salir al campo.
■ **field day**, MIL día m de maniobras. ‖ **field event**, SP prueba de atletismo. ‖ **field glasses**, gemelos mpl, prismáticos mpl. ‖ **field gun**, cañón m de campaña. ‖ **field hockey**, hockey m sobre hierba. ‖ **field marshall**, mariscal m de campo. ‖ **field officer**, oficial mf superior. ‖ **field sports**, caza y pesca. ‖ **field trip**, viaje m de estudios. ‖ **field work**, trabajo de campo. ‖ **field worker**, trabajador,-ra de campo.
fielder ['fiːldə'] n SP jugador,-ra del equipo que no batea.
fieldfare ['fiːldfeə'] n zorzal m real.
fieldmouse [fiːldmaʊs] n ratón m de campo.
▲ pl fieldmice.
field-test ['fiːldtest] 1 n prueba sobre el terreno. – 2 t testar sobre el terreno.
fiend [fiːnd] 1 n demonio, diablo. 2 fam fanático,-a.
fiendish ['fiːndɪʃ] adj diabólico,-a.
fierce [fɪəs] 1 adj (gen) feroz. 2 fig (heat, competition, etc) fuerte, intenso,-a; (argument) acalorado,-a.

fiercely ['fɪəslɪ] 1 adv (gen) con ferocidad. 2 (fight) con fiereza. 3 fig (burn) con virulencia. 4 (argue) acaloradamente.
fierceness ['fɪəsnəs] 1 n ferocidad f. 2 (of heat, competition, etc) intensidad f, fuerza.
fiery ['faɪərɪ] 1 adj (colour) encendido,-a, rojo,-a. 2 (burning) ardiente. 3 (food) muy picante; (drink) muy fuerte. 4 fig (person) acalorado,-a, fogoso,-a; (words) vehemente, apasionado,-a.
▲ comp fierier, superl fieriest.
fife [faɪf] n pífano.
fifteen [fɪf'tiːn] 1 adj quince. – 2 n quince m.
▲ Véase también six.
fifteenth [fɪf'tiːnθ] 1 adj decimoquinto,-a. – 2 adv en decimoquinto lugar. – 3 n (in series) decimoquinto,-a. 4 (fraction) decimoquinto; (one part) decimoquinta parte f.
▲ Véase también sixth.
fifth [fɪfθ] 1 adj quinto,-a. – 2 adv quinto, en quinto lugar. – 3 n (in series) quinto,-a. 4 (fraction) quinto; (one part) quinta parte f.
▲ Véase también sixth.
fifth-former ['fɪfθfɔːmə'] n GB alumno,-a de quinto curso.
fifties ['fɪftɪz] the fifties, npl los años mpl cincuenta, los cincuenta mpl.
● to **be in one's fifties**, estar en la cincuentena, tener entre cincuenta y sesenta años.
▲ Véase también sixties.
fiftieth ['fɪftɪəθ] 1 adj quincuagésimo,-a. – 2 adv en quincuagésimo lugar. – 3 n (in series) quincuagésimo,-a. 4 (fraction) quincuagésimo; (one part) quincuagésima parte f.
▲ Véase también sixtieth.
fifty ['fɪftɪ] 1 adj cincuenta. – 2 n cincuenta m.
▲ Véase también sixty.
fifty-fifty ['fɪftɪ'fɪftɪ] 1 adv fam mitad y mitad, a medias. – 2 adj fam del cincuenta por ciento: we've got a fifty-fifty chance of winning, tenemos un cincuenta por ciento de posibilidades de ganar.
● to **go fifty-fifty on sth.**, pagar algo a medias.
fig[1] ['fɪgə'] abbr (figure) dibujo, figura; (abbreviation) fig.
fig[2] [fɪg] 1 n higo. 2 (tree) higuera.
● not to **care a fig / not give a fig**, no importarle un rábano a uno, no importarle un pimiento a uno.
fight [faɪt] 1 n (struggle) lucha: the fight for Barcelona, la lucha por Barcelona; the fight against poverty, la lucha contra la pobreza. 2 (physical violence) pelea; (quarrel) riña; (argument) disputa: the police broke up the fight, la policía disolvió la pelea. 3 (boxing) combate m. 4 (resistance) combatividad f, ánimo: he had plenty of fight left in him, aún le quedaba mucho ánimo. – 5 i (quarrel) pelear(se) (**about/over**, por), discutir (**about/over**, por): they're always fighting about money, siempre discuten por dinero; it's not worth fighting over, no vale la pena discutir por eso. 6 (in boxing) pelear (**against**, contra). 7 (with physical violence) pelearse (**with**, con) (**against**, contra), luchar (**with**, con) (**against**, contra): he's always fighting with the other children, siempre se está peleando con los otros niños. 8 fig luchar (**for**, por) (**against**, contra), combatir: fight for human rights, luchar por los derechos humanos. – 9 t (bull) lidiar. 10 (engage in - battle) librar; (- war) hacer; (- election) presentarse a. 11 (with physical violence) pelearse, luchar: fight the enemy, luchar contra el enemigo; they were fighting some kids from another school, se peleaban con unos

chicos de otro colegio. **12** *fig* (*strive to overcome, prevent*) luchar, combatir: *fight racism,* combatir el racismo; *fight drug trafficking,* luchar contra el narcotráfico. **13** JUR recurrir contra. **14** (*fire*) apagar, combatir.

◆ **to fight back 1** *i* defenderse, resistir. – **2** *t sep* (*tears*) contener. ‖ **to fight off 1** *t sep* vencer, rechazar. **2** *fig* (*illness*) librarse de, combatir; (*sleep*) sacudirse.

● **to fight a case,** JUR defenderse contra un cargo. ‖ **to fight it out,** decidirlo, resolverlo. ‖ **to fight one's way through,** lograr abrirse paso. ‖ **to fight for one's life,** luchar por la vida. ‖ **to fight like a tiger,** luchar como un jabato. ‖ **to fight a losing battle,** luchar por una causa perdida. ‖ **to fight shy of sth./sb.,** evitar algo/a algn. ‖ **to fight to the finish,** luchar hasta el final. ‖ **to pick a fight with sb.,** meterse con algn. ‖ **to put up a fight,** oponer resistencia.

▲ *pt & pp* **fought.**

fighter ['faɪtəʳ] **1** *n* (*war*) combatiente *mf.* **2** (*boxing*) boxeador,-ra, púgil *mf.* **3** *fig* luchador,-ra.

■ **fighter plane,** AV (avión *m* de) caza *m.* ‖ **fighter pilot,** piloto de caza.

fighting ['faɪtɪŋ] **1** *n* peleas *fpl: I don't want any fighting in this pub,* no quiero peleas en este bar; *there's been a lot of street fighting,* ha habido muchas peleas callejeras. – **2** *adj* de combate, militar.

● **to be in with a fighting chance / have a fighting chance,** tener posibilidades de ganar.

■ **fighting spirit,** combatividad *f.*

fig-leaf ['fɪgliːf] *n* hoja de parra.

figment ['fɪgmənt] *n cosa imaginada: it's a figment of your imagination,* es producto de tu imaginación.

figurative ['fɪgərətɪv] *adj* figurado,-a.

figuratively ['fɪgərətɪvlɪ] *adv* metafóricamente, en sentido figurado.

figure ['fɪgəʳ, *E* 'fɪgjəʳ] **1** *n* (*number, sign*) cifra, número. **2** (*money, price*) cantidad *f*, precio, suma. **3** (*in art*) figura. **4** (*human form*) figura, tipo, línea: *she's got a good figure,* tiene buen tipo; *I'm trying to keep my figure,* intento guardar la línea; *he's a fine figure of a man,* es un hombre bien plantado. **5** (*personality*) figura, personaje *m.* **6** (*diagram*) diagrama *m*, dibujo, grabado, ilustración *f.* **7** (*shape*) forma, figura. **8** (*pattern*) figura. – **9** *i* (*appear*) figurar, constar: *does you name figure in the list?,* ¿tu nombre figura en la lista?; *he figured among the prizewinners,* figuraba entre los ganadores. – **10** *t* US (*think*) suponer, imaginar: *I figured you'd be late,* ya me imaginaba que llegarías tarde. – **11** **figures,** *npl* (*arithmetic*) matemáticas *fpl.*

◆ **to figure on** *t insep* contar con, esperar: *he figures on being back by Tuesday,* espera estar de vuelta el martes. ‖ **to figure out** *t sep fam* (*gen*) comprender, explicarse; (*problem*) resolver, calcular: *I can't figure him out!,* ¡no lo comprendo!; *have you figured out what happened?,* ¿has podido saber lo que pasó?

● **that figures!,** ¡ya me parecía a mí!, ¡eso tiene sentido!

■ **figure of speech,** figura retórica. ‖ **figure skating,** patinaje *m* artístico.

figurehead ['fɪgəhed] **1** *n* MAR mascarón *m* de proa. **2** *fig* figura decorativa.

Fiji ['fiːdʒiː] *n* Fidji.

Fijian [fiː'dʒiːən] **1** *adj* fidjiano,-a. – **2** *n* (*person*) fidjiano,-a. **3** (*language*) fidjiano.

filament ['fɪləmənt] *n* filamento.

filch [fɪltʃ] *t fam* (*steal*) birlar, afanar, chorizar.

file [faɪl] **1** *n* (*tool*) lima. **2** (*folder*) carpeta. **3** (*archive*) archivo, expediente *m.* **4** COMPUT archivo. **5** (*line*) fila. – **6**

t (*smooth*) limar. **7** (*put away*) archivar; (*in card index*) fichar. **8** JUR presentar. – **9** *i* (*walk in line*) desfilar.

● **to be on file,** estar archivado,-a. ‖ **to have a file on sb.,** tener a algn. fichado,-a.

■ **single file,** fila india.

filial ['fɪlɪəl] *adj* filial.

filibuster ['fɪlɪbʌstəʳ] **1** *n* POL (*person*) obstruccionista *mf.* **2** (*speech*) intervención parlamentaria hecha para impedir que una moción se vote. – **3** *t* obstaculizar. – **4** *i* practicar una política obstruccionista.

filigree ['fɪlɪgriː] *n* filigrana.

filing ['faɪlɪŋ] **1** *n* clasificación *f.* – **2** **filings,** *npl* limaduras *fpl.*

■ **filing cabinet,** archivador *m.* ‖ **filing clerk,** archivero,-a.

Filipino [fɪlɪ'piːnəʊ] **1** *adj* filipino,-a. – **2** *n* (*person*) filipino,-a. **3** (*language*) filipino.

▲ (*sustantivo*) *pl* **Filipinos.**

fill [fɪl] **1** *t* (*make full*) llenar (**with,** de). **2** (*time*) ocupar. **3** (*cover*) cubrir. **4** CULIN rellenar. **5** (*tooth*) empastar. **6** (*hold a position*) ocupar; (*appoint*) cubrir. **7** (*fulfill*) satisfacer. – **8** *i* llenarse (**with,** de).

◆ **to fill in 1** *t sep* (*space, form*) rellenar. **2** (*inform*) poner al corriente (**on,** de). ‖ **to fill in for** *t insep* sustituir a. ‖ **to fill out 1** *i* engordar. – **2** *t sep* rellenar. ‖ **to fill up 1** *t sep* llenar. – **2** *i* llenarse.

● **to drink one's fill,** beber hasta saciarse. ‖ **to eat one's fill,** comer hasta saciarse. ‖ **to fill sb.'s shoes,** ocupar el puesto de algn. ‖ **to have had one's fill of sth./sb.,** *fam* estar harto,-a de algo/algn.

filler ['fɪləʳ] **1** *n* (*for cracks*) masilla. **2** (*for bulk*) relleno.

fillet ['fɪlɪt] **1** *n* filete *m.* – **2** *t* cortar en filetes, filetear.

filleted ['fɪlɪtɪd] *adj* en filetes, fileteado,-a.

filling ['fɪlɪŋ] **1** *n* (*in tooth*) empaste *m.* **2** CULIN relleno.

■ **filling station,** gasolinera.

filly ['fɪlɪ] *n* potra.

▲ *pl* **fillies.**

film [fɪlm] **1** *n* CINEM película, filme *m*, film *m.* **2** (*coating of dust etc*) capa, película. **3** (*of photos*) carrete *m*, rollo. – **4** *t* CINEM rodar, filmar; TV grabar. **5** (*event*) filmar. – **6** *i* CINEM rodar.

■ **film industry,** industria cinematográfica. ‖ **film library,** cinemateca. ‖ **film set,** plató *m.* ‖ **film star,** estrella de cine. ‖ **film strip,** película. ‖ **film studio,** estudio de cine. ‖ **film test,** prueba (cinematográfica).

filter ['fɪltəʳ] **1** *n* filtro. – **2** *t* filtrar. – **3** *i* filtrarse. **4** (*move gradually*) moverse poco a poco: *people filtered into the church,* la gente iba entrando poco a poco en la iglesia. **5** GB AUTO girar a la derecha o a la izquierda (*mientras el semáforo principal está cerrado*).

◆ **to filter out 1** *t sep* (*remove*) eliminar. – **2** *i fig* (*news etc*) llegar a saberse, trascender. ‖ **to filter through 1** *i fig* (*news etc*) llegar. **2** (*sunlight etc*) filtrarse.

■ **filter paper,** papel *m* de filtro. ‖ **filter tip,** (*tip*) boquilla filtro; (*cigarette*) cigarrillo emboquillado. ‖ **traffic filter,** semáforo para girar.

filth [fɪlθ] **1** *n* (*dirt*) suciedad *f*, porquería. **2** *fig* (*obscenity*) obscenidades *fpl*, porquerías *fpl.* **3** *sl* (*police*) pasma, bofia.

filthy ['fɪlθɪ] **1** *adj* (*dirty*) sucio,-a, asqueroso,-a. **2** (*obscene*) obsceno,-a, grosero,-a, asqueroso,-a. **3** *fam* (*very bad*) malo,-a. – **4** *adv* asquerosamente: *filthy dirty,* asquerosamente sucio. **5** *fam* (*very*) muy: *she's filthy rich,* está podrida de dinero.

▲ *comp* **filthier,** *superl* **filthiest.**

fin [fɪn] *n* aleta.

final ['faɪnəl] **1** *adj* (*last*) final, último,-a. **2** (*definitive*) definitivo,-a. **– 3** *n* SP final *f*. **– 4 finals**, *npl* (*at university*) exámenes *mpl* finales.
● **and that's final!**, ¡y no hay nada más que decir!

finale [fɪ'nɑːlɪ] *n* final *m*.

finalist ['faɪnəlɪst] *n* finalista *mf*.

finality [faɪ'næləti] *n* carácter *m* definitivo.
● **to say with finality**, decir de modo definitivo.

finalize ['faɪnəlaɪz] *t* (*plans, arrangements*) ultimar; (*date*) fijar.

finally ['faɪnəlɪ] **1** *adv* (*at last*) por fin, al final. **2** (*lastly*) por último, finalmente. **3** (*definitively*) definitivamente, de forma definitiva.

finance ['faɪnæns] **1** *n* (*management of money*) finanzas *fpl*. **– 2** *t* financiar. **– 3 finances**, *npl* (*money available*) fondos *mpl*.
■ **finance company**, sociedad *f* financiera. ‖ **Minister of Finance**, Ministro,-a de Hacienda.

financial [faɪ'nænʃəl] *adj* financiero,-a.
■ **financial year**, año fiscal.

financier [faɪ'nænsɪə'] *n* financiero,-a.

finch [fɪntʃ] *n* ORN pinzón *m*.

find [faɪnd] **1** *n* (*act, thing found*) hallazgo: *this shop is a real find*, esta tienda es un hallazgo. **– 2** *t* (*locate*) encontrar, hallar: *she found a note on her door*, encontró una nota en la puerta; *did you find your keys?*, ¿encontraste tus llaves? **3** (*discover*) descubrir, encontrar: *they still haven't found a cure for the common cold*, aún no han descubierto un remedio para el resfriado; *oil's been found nearby*, se ha descubierto petróleo cerca. **4** (*exist*) hallarse, encontrarse, existir: *this species is found all over England*, esta especie se encuentra por toda Inglaterra. **5** (*obtain, get*) encontrar: *she can never find the time to do her homework*, nunca tiene tiempo para hacer sus deberes; *could you find me a job?*, ¿podrías encontrarme un trabajo?; *we managed to find the money to pay for the trip*, conseguimos reunir el dinero para pagar el viaje; *he found the strength to tell her the truth*, encontró el valor para decirle la verdad. **6** (*think, consider*) encontrar, parecer: *she did not find him at all funny*, no lo encontró nada gracioso; *she found the exam quite easy*, encontró muy fácil el examen; *I find the rice a little salty*, el arroz está un poco salado. **7** (*become aware, realize*) encontrar, darse cuenta: *I'm finding him much nicer than I thought*, lo encuentro mucho más simpático de lo que pensaba; *he found it impossible to make himself understood*, le fue imposible hacerse entender. **8** (*end up, arrive at, reach*) ir a parar a, llegar a: *I doubt whether the supplies actually find their way to Bosnia*, dudo que las provisiones lleguen a Bosnia. **9** JUR declarar: *he was found guilty*, lo declararon culpable.
◆ **to find out 1** *t sep* (*enquire*) preguntar, averiguar; (*discover*) descubrir, enterarse de: *shall I find out the price?*, ¿pregunto el precio?; *find out her telephone number*, averigua su teléfono; *I'll find out what happened*, me enteraré de lo que pasó; *we found out that he had been lying to us*, descubrimos que nos había mentido. **2** (*rumble*) calar, pillar, descubrir el juego: *the boss found him out*, el jefe lo caló, el jefe le descubrió el juego. **– 3** *i* (*enquire*) informarse (**about**, sobre), averiguar: *I've got to find out about the times of flights*, tengo que informarme sobre las horas de los vuelos. **4** (*discover*) enterarse (**about**, de), (llegar a) saber: *oh God!, if Mary ever finds out ...*, Dios mío!, si llega a enterarse Mary ...; *his parents found out about the party*, sus padres se enteraron de la fiesta.
● **all found**, todo incluido. ‖ **to be nowhere to be found**, no estar en ninguna parte. ‖ **to find fault with**, criticar. ‖ **to find for sb. / find against sb.**, JUR fallar a favor de algn. / fallar en contra de algn. ‖ **to find it in one's heart to do sth.**, tener el valor de hacer algo. ‖ **to find one's tongue**, soltarse a hablar. ‖ **to find one's way about/around**, (*town etc*) orientarse; (*office etc*) familiarizarse. ‖ **to find os.**, (*gen*) encontrarse, verse; (*true self*) encontrarse a sí mismo,-a. ‖ **to find out for os.**, averiguarlo por sus propios medios. ‖ **to take sb. as one finds them**, no prejuzgar a algn., aceptar a algn. tal como es.
▲ *pt & pp* **found**.

finder ['faɪndə'] *n* descubridor,-ra.
● **finders keepers**, quien lo encuentra se lo queda.

finding ['faɪndɪŋ] **1** *n* (*of inquiry*) conclusión *f*, resultado: *the report's main findings are ...*, las principales conclusiones del informe son ... **2** JUR fallo,, veredicto.
▲ *Often used in plural with same meaning.*

fine¹ [faɪn] **1** *adj* (*thin – hair, thread, sand, rain*) fino,-a: *she's got very fine hair*, tiene el pelo muy fino; *a pen with a fine nib*, una estilográfica con el plumín fino. **2** (*delicate*) fino,-a, delicado,-a: *fine workmanship*, artesanía fina; *fine china*, porcelana fina. **3** (*subtle*) sutil, delicado,-a: *a fine distinction*, una diferencia sutil. **4** (*high-quality*) excelente: *a fine performance*, una actuación excelente; *we use only the finest ingredients*, sólo utilizamos los mejores ingredientes. **5** (*metals*) puro,-a, refinado,-a: *fine gold*, oro puro. **6** (*weather*) bueno,-a: *if it's fine we'll go for a walk*, si hace bueno saldremos a pasear. **7** (*healthy*) bien: *I'm fine, thanks*, estoy bien, gracias. **8** *fam* (*all right*) bien: *yeah, that'll be fine for me*, sí, ya me está bien. **9** *iron* (*terrible*) menudo,-a: *that's another fine mess you've got me into!*, ¡en menudo lío me has metido!; *you're a fine one to talk!*, ¡mira quién habla! **– 10** *adv* (*in small bits*) fino, finamente: *chop the parsley fine*, pica el perejil muy fino. **11** *fam* (*very well*) muy bien, a la perfección: *that suits me fine*, me va muy bien; *it was working fine before*, funcionaba muy bien antes.
● **not to put too fine a point on it**, hablando en plata. ‖ **to cut it fine**, dejar algo para muy tarde: *you're cutting it a bit fine, the train leaves in half an hour!*, ¡has dejado muy poco tiempo, el tren sale en media hora! ‖ **to get sth. down to a fine art**, hacer algo a la perfección.
■ **fine arts**, bellas artes *fpl*. ‖ **fine print**, letra menuda.

fine² [faɪn] **1** *n* (*punishment*) multa. **– 2** *t* multar, poner una multa: *he was fined 50 pounds*, le pusieron una multa de 50 libras.

finely ['faɪnlɪ] **1** *adv* (*very thin, in small bits*) fino, finamente. **2** (*well, spendidly*) elegantemente: *finely dressed*, elegantemente vestido. **3** (*with precision, subtly*) delicadamente, minuciosamente: *a finely tuned guitar*, una guitarra bien afinada; *a finely tuned engine*, un motor ajustado con mucha precisión.

finery ['faɪnərɪ] *n* galas *fpl*.
● **in all one's finery**, con sus mejores galas.

finesse [fɪ'nes] *n* delicadeza, diplomacia, sutileza.

fine-tooth comb ['faɪntuːθ'kəʊm] *n* peine *m* de púas finas.
● **to go through sth. with a fine-tooth comb**, mirar algo con lupa.

finger ['fɪŋgə'] **1** *n* dedo: *index finger*, dedo índice; *middle finger*, dedo del corazón; *ring finger*, dedo anular; *little finger*, dedo meñique. **– 2** *t* tocar; *pej* manosear.
● **to be all fingers and thumbs**, ser torpe. ‖ **to burn one's fingers / get one's fingers burnt**, pillarse los dedos. ‖ **to get one's finger out**, espabilarse. ‖ **to have a finger in every pie**, estar metido,-a en todo.

‖ to have green fingers, tener buena mano para las plantas. ‖ to have light fingers, tener las manos largas. ‖ to have one's finger on the pulse, estar al corriente de lo que sucede. ‖ to have one's fingers in the till, robar (de la empresa), meter mano en la caja. ‖ to lay a finger on sb./sth., tocar a algn./algo. ‖ to lift a finger / raise a finger, mover un dedo. ‖ to point the finger at sb., señalar a algn. con el dedo. ‖ to put one's finger on sth., dar en el clavo, poner el dedo en la llaga. ‖ to work one's fingers to the bone, dejarse los codos trabajando.
■ finger bowl, lavadedos m.

finger-mark ['fɪŋgəʳmɑːk] n huella (del dedo).
fingernail ['fɪŋgəneɪl] n uña.
fingerprint ['fɪŋgəprɪnt] n huella digital, huella dactilar.
fingertip ['fɪŋgətɪp] n punta del dedo, yema del dedo.
● to have sth. at one's fingertips, fig saberse algo al dedillo.
finicky ['fɪnɪkɪ] 1 adj (person) remilgado,-a, quisquilloso,-a, melindroso,-a. 2 (job) engorroso,-a.
finish ['fɪnɪʃ] 1 n fin m, final m, conclusión f. 2 sp llegada. 3 (for surface) acabado: matt/gloss finish, acabado mate/brillo. – 4 t (end) acabar, terminar: I must finish this book, tengo que acabar este libro; what time do you finish work?, ¿a qué hora sales del trabajo?; we finished the meal and left, acabamos la comida y nos fuimos. 5 (consume the remainder of) acabar (off/up, -), terminar (off/up, -): finish (up) your potatoes, cómete todas las patatas, termínate las patatas; who finished (off) the wine?, ¿quién ha acabado el vino? 6 (complete) acabar (off, -), terminar (off, -): he finished the essay as quickly as possible, acabó la redacción lo más rápido posible; when will this building be finished?, ¿cuándo acabarán este edificio? 7 fam (exhaust) agotar (off, -), acabar con: that last lap just about finished me off, esta última vuelta me ha dejado hecho polvo. – 8 i (end) acabar, terminar: when does term finish?, ¿cuándo acaba el trimestre?; the film finishes at 10.00pm, la película termina a las 10.00; I haven't finished reading that yet!, ¡aún no he terminado de leerlo!; she finished by saying that ..., terminó diciendo ... 9 sp llegar: he finished second, llegó en segundo lugar, llegó el segundo.
◆ to finish off t sep fam (kill) rematar, despachar, acabar con. ‖ to finish up i (end up) ir a parar a/en: we caught the wrong train and finished up in Madrid, nos equivocamos de tren y fuimos a parar a Madrid; he finished up working in the Ritz, acabó trabajando en el Ritz. ‖ to finish with 1 t insep acabar con: put that book back when you've finished with it, devuelve el libro a su sitio cuando hayas acabado con él; hold on - I haven't finished with you yet, espera - aún no he acabado contigo. 2 (person) romper con: I've finished with Jim, he roto con Jim.
● to the finish, hasta el final.
■ close finish, sp final m muy reñido.
finished ['fɪnɪʃt] 1 adj (ended) acabado,-a: I'm finished with men, he acabado con los hombres; if the press find out, he's finished, si se entera la prensa, está acabado. 2 (properly made, completed) acabado,-a.
finishing ['fɪnɪʃɪŋ] adj final.
■ finishing line, (línea de) meta. ‖ finishing school, escuela privada de modales para señoritas.
finite ['faɪnaɪt] adj finito,-a.
Finland ['fɪnlənd] n Finlandia.
Finn [fɪn] n (person) finlandés,-esa.
Finnish ['fɪnɪʃ] 1 adj finlandés,-esa. – 2 n (language) finlandés m. 3 the Finnish, – npl los finlandeses mpl.

fiord [fɪ'ɔːd] n fiordo.
fir [fɜːʳ] n abeto.
fire ['faɪəʳ] 1 n (gen) fuego. 2 (blaze) incendio, fuego. 3 (heater) estufa. 4 MIL fuego. 5 (strong emotion) ardor m, pasión f, entusiasmo. – 6 t (weapon) disparar; (rocket) lanzar. 7 (questions etc) disparar, bombardear. 8 (pottery) cocer. 9 fig (stimulate) inflamar, enardecer, excitar, exaltar. 10 fam (dismiss) despedir. – 11 i (shoot) disparar (at, sobre), hacer fuego. 12 AUTO encenderse. – 13 interj ¡fuego!
● fire away!, ¡va! ¡adelante! ‖ to be on fire, estar ardiendo, estar en llamas. ‖ to be under fire, ser atacado,-a. ‖ to come under fire, fig ser criticado,-a. ‖ to catch fire, incendiarse, encenderse. ‖ to open fire, abrir fuego. ‖ to play with fire, jugar con fuego. ‖ to set fire to sth. / set sth. on fire, prender fuego a algo, incendiar algo.
■ fire alarm, alarma de incendios. ‖ fire brigade, cuerpo de bomberos, los bomberos mpl. ‖ fire drill, simulacro de incendio. ‖ fire engine, camión m de bomberos. ‖ fire escape, escalera de incendios. ‖ fire exit, salida de emergencia. ‖ fire extinguisher, extintor m. ‖ fire fighter, bombero mf. ‖ fire hydrant, boca de incendio. ‖ fire raiser, incendiario,-a. ‖ fire station, parque m de bomberos.
firearm ['faɪərɑːm] n arma de fuego.
firebomb ['faɪəbɒm] n bomba incendiaria.
firecracker ['faɪəkrækəʳ] n petardo.
firefighter ['faɪəfaɪtəʳ] n bombero mf.
fire-fighting ['faɪəfaɪtɪŋ] n tareas fpl de extinción.
firefly ['faɪəflaɪ] n luciérnaga.
▲ pl fireflies.
fireguard ['faɪəgɑːd] n pantalla.
fireman ['faɪəmən] n bombero.
▲ pl firemen ['faɪəmən].
fireplace ['faɪəpleɪs] 1 n (structure) chimenea. 2 (hearth) hogar m.
fireproof ['faɪəpruːf] adj incombustible.
fireside ['faɪəsaɪd] n hogar m.
● by the fireside, al calor de la lumbre.
■ fireside chair, sillón m.
firewoman ['faɪəwumən] n mujer bombero.
▲ pl firewomen ['faɪəwɪmɪn].
firewood ['faɪəwud] n leña.
fireworks ['faɪəwɜːks] 1 npl fuegos mpl artificiales, fuegos mpl de artificio. 2 fig escándalo m sing.
firing ['faɪərɪŋ] n tiroteo.
● to be in the firing line, estar en la línea de fuego.
■ firing line, línea de fuego. ‖ firing squad, pelotón m de fusilamiento.
firm[1] [fɜːm] n (business) empresa.
firm[2] [fɜːm] 1 adj (strong, solid, steady) firme, sólido,-a: firm soil, tierra firme; firm foundations, fundamentos sólidos. 2 (definite, not changing) firme, en firme: firm offer, oferta en firme; firm decision, decisión firme; firm date, fecha definitiva. 3 (strict, strong) duro,-a: firm discipline, disciplina dura; you must be firm with them, tienes que tratarlos con firmeza. 4 FIN (steady) firme, estable: the pound remained firm against the dollar, la libra se mantuvo firme al dólar.
◆ to firm up t sep (deal etc) concretar, confirmar.
● to be on firm ground, estar seguro,-a.
■ firm hand, mano f dura.
firmly ['fɜːmlɪ] adv firmemente, con firmeza.
firmness ['fɜːmnəs] n firmeza.
first [fɜːst] 1 adj primero,-a: what was your first job?, ¿cuál fue tu primer trabajo?; who was the first man on the

moon?, ¿quién fue el primer hombre que pisó la luna?; *she was his first wife,* fue su primera esposa; *for the first time in my life ...,* por primera vez en mi vida ...; *my first reaction was to ...,* mi reacción inicial fue ... **– 2** *adv (before anything else)* primero: *Jane spoke first,* Jane habló primero; *when you get up, what do you do first?,* al levantarte, ¿qué es lo primero que haces?; *first, I have to go to the bank,* primero, tengo que ir al banco. **3** *(for the first time)* por primera vez: *when we first met, he hated me,* cuando nos conocimos, me odiaba; *the book was first published in 1990,* el libro fue editado por primera vez en 1990. **4** *(in first place)* primero, en primer lugar: *there are several reasons: first, ...,* hay varias razones: en primer lugar, ... **5** *(in preference to)* antes: *he said he'd die first,* dijo que antes, preferiría morir. **– 6** *n* la primera vez: *it's a first for me too!,* ¡es la primera vez para mí también! **– 7** *pron* el primero, la primera, lo primero: *Jack was the first to arrive,* Jack fue el primero en llegar; *the first I knew about it,* lo primero que supe; *that's the first I've heard about it,* primera noticia; *Elizabeth I (the First),* Isabel I (primera). **– 8** *n (first-class degree)* ≈ sobresaliente *m (título universitario que corresponde a la nota más alta).* **9** *(gear)* primera: *I can't put it into first,* no puedo meter primera.
● **at first,** al principio. ‖ **at first sight,** a primera vista. ‖ **to come first,** *(in race)* llegar el primero; *(in order)* estar primero. ‖ **first come, first served,** el que llega primero tiene prioridad. ‖ **first of all,** en primer lugar. ‖ **first thing,** a primera hora (de la mañana). ‖ **first things first,** lo primero es lo primero. ‖ **from the first,** desde el principio. ‖ **from first to last,** de principio a fin, desde el principio hasta el final.
■ **first aid,** primeros auxilios *mpl.* ‖ **first class,** primera clase *f.* ‖ **First Communion,** primera comunión *f.* ‖ **first floor,** GB primer piso; US planta baja. ‖ **First Lady,** Primera Dama. ‖ **first lieutenant,** teniente *m* de navío. ‖ **first mate,** primer oficial *m.* ‖ **first name,** nombre *m* de pila. ‖ **first night,** estreno. ‖ **first offender,** delincuente *m* sin antecedentes. ‖ **first person,** LING primera persona. ‖ **First World War,** Primera Guerra Mundial.
first-aid [fɜːst'eɪd] *adj* de primeros auxilios.
■ **first-aid kit,** botiquín *m.*
first-born ['fɜːstbɔːn] **1** *adj* primogénito,-a. **– 2** *n* primogénito,-a.
first-class ['fɜːstklɑːs] **1** *adj* de primera clase: *a first-class ticket is more expensive,* un billete de primera clase es más caro. **2** *fig* de primera, excelente: *your work really is first-class,* tu trabajo es realmente excelente. **– 3** *adv* en primera: *to travel first-class,* viajar en primera, viajar en preferente.
■ **first-class mail,** GB *servicio de correo en que las cartas se reparten al día siguiente.* ‖ **first-class (hounours) degree,** ≈ sobresaliente *m (título universitario que corresponde a la nota más alta).*
first-former ['fɜːstfɔːməʳ] *n* GB alumno,-a del primer curso.
first-hand [fɜːst'hænd] **1** *adj* de primera mano. **– 2** *adv* de primera mano, directamente: *she got the information first-hand,* consiguió la información de primera mano; *he experienced it first-hand,* lo experimentó él mismo.
firstly ['fɜːstlɪ] *adv* en primer lugar, ante todo.
first-rate ['fɜːstreɪt] **1** *adj* de primera, excelente: *that was a first-rate meal,* ha sido una comida de primera. **– 2** *adv* de primera: *I feel first-rate,* me encuentro de primera.
fiscal ['fɪskəl] *adj* fiscal.

fish [fɪʃ] **1** *n* pez *m*: *did you catch any fish?,* ¿pescaste algo? **2** CULIN pescado: *she prefers fish to meat,* prefiere el pescado a la carne. **– 3** *t* pescar en. **– 4** *i* pescar (**for,** -).
◆ **to fish for** *t insep* buscar. ‖ **to fish out** *t sep* sacar.
● **like a fish out of water,** como pez fuera del agua, como gallo en corral ajeno. ‖ **to drink like a fish,** beber como una esponja. ‖ **to have other fish to fry,** tener cosas más importantes que hacer. ‖ **there are plenty of other fish in the sea,** hay mucho más donde elegir.
■ **fish and chips,** pescado con patatas. ‖ **fish cake,** ≈ croqueta de pescado y patatas. ‖ **fish farm,** piscifactoría. ‖ **fish shop,** pescadería. ‖ **fish slice,** pala de cocina. ‖ **fish tank,** pecera. ‖ **odd fish / queer fish,** tipo raro.
▲ *pl* fish o fishes.
fisherman ['fɪʃəmən] *n* pescador *m.*
▲ *pl* fishermen ['fɪʃəmən].
fishery ['fɪʃərɪ] **1** *n (industry)* industria pesquera. **2** *(place)* pesquería.
▲ *pl* fisheries.
fishfinger [fɪʃ'fɪŋgəʳ] *n* palito de pescado rebozado.
fish-hook ['fɪʃhʊk] *n* anzuelo.
fishing ['fɪʃɪŋ] *n* pesca.
● **to go fishing,** ir de pesca.
■ **fishing line,** sedal *m.* ‖ **fishing net,** red *f* de pesca. ‖ **fishing rod,** caña de pescar. ‖ **fishing tackle,** aparejo de pescar.
fishmonger ['fɪʃmʌŋgəʳ] *n* GB pescadero,-a.
■ **fishmonger's (shop),** pescadería.
fishnet ['fɪʃnet] **1** *n* US red *f* de pesca. **2** *(mesh fabric)* red *f.*
■ **fishnet stockings,** medias *fpl* de malla de red.
fishwife ['fɪʃwaɪf] **1** *n* pescadera. **2** *pej* verdulera.
▲ *pl* fishwives.
fishy ['fɪʃɪ] **1** *adj (taste, smell)* a pescado: *it smells fishy in here,* aquí huele a pescado. **2** *(suspicious)* sospechoso,-a: *it sounds a bit fishy to me,* a mí me da que hay gato encerrado.
▲ *comp* fishier, *superl* fishiest.
fission ['fɪʃən] *n* fisión *f.*
fissure ['fɪʃəʳ] *n* fisura, grieta.
fist [fɪst] *n* puño.
fistful ['fɪstfʊl] *n* puñado.
fisticuffs ['fɪstɪkʌfs] *npl dated* puñetazos *mpl.*
fit¹ [fɪt] **1** *n* MED ataque *m,* acceso. **2** *(of laughter)* arrebato, ataque *m*; *(of rage, panic)* arranque *m* arrebato.
● **to be in fits (of laughter),** desternillarse de risa, troncharse de risa. ‖ **by fits and starts / in fits and starts,** a trompicones. ‖ **to give sb. a fit,** darle un susto a algn. ‖ **to have a fit / throw a fit,** darle un ataque a uno: *she'd have a fit if she knew,* si lo supiera le daría un ataque.
fit² [fɪt] **1** *adj (suitable, appropriate)* adecuado,-a, apto,-a, apropiado,-a; *(qualified for)* capacitado,-a hábil, capaz; *(worthy, deserving)* digno,-a: *it's not fit for human consumption,* no es apto para el consumo humano; *a meal fit for a king,* una comida digna de un rey. **2** *(in good health)* sano,-a, bien de salud, en (plena) forma; *(physically)* en forma: *are you sure you're fit enough to go back to work?,* ¿seguro que estás bien para volver al trabajo?; *he keeps fit by jogging every day,* se mantiene en forma haciendo footing cada día. **3** *fam (ready)* a punto de: *they looked fit to drop,* parecían a punto de caerse. **– 4** *t (be right size for)* sentar bien, quedar bien, ir bien a: *this dress fits me perfectly,* este vestido me queda

perfectamente; *he was wearing a coat which didn't fit him,* llevaba un abrigo que no le sentaba bien. **5** (*try* (*clothing*) *on sb.*) probar: *he's being fitted for a suit,* le están probando un traje. **6** (*key*) abrir: *does this key fit the lock?,* ¿esta llave abre la cerradura? **7** (*install*) instalar, poner, colocar: *we're having a carpet fitted,* nos van a colocar moqueta; *they had a new lock fitted,* pusieron una nueva cerradura. **8** *fig* (*be appropriate*) cuadrar con, corresponder a, responder a: *the facts fit the theory,* los hechos cuadran con la teoría; *make the punishment fit the crime,* hacer que el castigo corresponda al crimen; *he doesn't fit the description,* no responde a la descripción. **9** (*adapt*) ajustar, adaptar, adecuar; (*make suitable*) capacitar: *you have to fit the ideas to the philosophy,* hay que adaptar las ideas a la filosofía; *her experience fits her for the job,* su experiencia la capacita para el puesto. **– 10** *i* (*be right size/shape*) sentar bien, ir bien: *does this piece fit here?,* ¿esta pieza va bien aquí?; *these shoes don't fit,* estos zapatos no me van bien. **11** (*be of right size in space*) caber, encajar, ajustar: *do all your clothes fit in that drawer?,* ¿toda tu ropa cabe en ese cajón?; *the new sofa wouldn't fit through the door,* el nuevo sofá no cabía por la puerta; *if it doesn't fit, don't force it,* si no cabe, no lo fuerces; *only four people can fit in,* sólo caben cuatro personas. **12** (*be right*) cuadrar, corresponder, encajar: *something doesn't quite fit,* hay algo que no cuadra; *his face didn't fit,* no encajó. **– 13** *n* (*of clothes*): *it's a perfect fit,* me va perfectamente. **14** (*in space*): *it'll be a tight fit,* vamos a estar muy apretados.
◆ **to fit in 1** *i* (*get on*) llevarse bien, integrarse: *he doesn't fit in with the other children,* no se lleva bien con los otros niños. **2** (*suit*) encajar; (*harmonize*) pegar, quedar bien; (*tally*) cuadrar: *it doesn't fit in with our ideas,* no encaja con nuestras ideas; *it doesn't fit in with the room's colour scheme,* no pega con los colores de la habitación; *that does not fit in with what I've been told,* eso no cuadra con lo que me han dicho. **– 3** *t sep* (*physically*) hacer sitio para, meter: *I think we can fit one more in,* creo que hay sitio para una persona más, *she fitted everything in the box,* consiguió meter todo en la caja. **4** (*in timetable*) hacer un hueco para, tener tiempo para: *the doctor can fit you in on Friday,* el doctor te podrá ver el viernes, el doctor puede hacerte un hueco el viernes; *how do you fit in so many activities in one day?,* ¿cómo puedes hacer tantas cosas en un solo día? **5** (*harmonize*) encajar, cuadrar. ‖ **to fit out** *t sep* (*ship*) equipar, pertrechar; (*person*) equipar: *they fitted us out with uniforms,* nos equiparon con uniformes. ‖ **to fit up 1** *t sep* (*building*) acondicionar. **2** GB *sl* (*frame*) incriminar.
● **to fit sb. like a glove,** irle a algn. como un guante. ‖ **to be as fit as a fiddle,** estar fuerte como un roble. ‖ **to be fit to do sth.,** estar en condiciones de hacer algo. ‖ **to see fit / think fit,** estimar conveniente, parecer conveniente: *do as you think fit,* haga lo que mejor le parezca.
▲ (adjetivo) *comp* **fitter,** *superl* **fittest;** (*verbo*) *pt* & *pp* **fitted,** *ger* **fitting.**

fitful [ˈfɪtfʊl] *adj* irregular, discontinuo,-a, intermitente.
fitfully [ˈfɪtfəlɪ] *adv* a rachas, por intervalos, de manera irregular.
fitment [ˈfɪtmənt] *n* mueble *m.*
fitness [ˈfɪtnəs] **1** *n* (*health*) buena forma física, buen estado físico. **2** (*suitability*) capacidad *f* (**for,** para).
fitted [ˈfɪtɪd] *adj* (*cupboard*) empotrado,-a; (*room*) amueblado,-a; (*clothes*) entallado,-a.
■ **fitted carpet,** moqueta. ‖ **fitted sheet,** sábana ajustable.

fitter [ˈfɪtəʳ] **1** *n* TECH montador,-ra. **2** SEW probador,-ra.
fitting [ˈfɪtɪŋ] **1** *adj* (*appropriate, proper*) apropiado,-a, adecuado,-a: *it was fitting that he should get the prize,* fue justo que él ganara el premio. **– 2** *n* SEW prueba. **– 3** **fittings,** *npl* (*accessories*) accesorios *mpl.* **4** (*furnishings*) muebles, cortinas y alfombras.
five [faɪv] **1** *n* cinco. **– 2** *adj* cinco.
■ **five o'clock shadow,** sombra de barba.
▲ *Véase también* **six.**
five-a-side [ˈfaɪvəˈsaɪd] **five-a-side (football),** *n* fútbol sala *m,* futbito.
fiver [ˈfaɪvəʳ] *n* GB *fam* billete *m* de cinco libras.
fix [fɪks] **1** *n fam* (*difficult situation*) apuro, aprieto: *I'm in a real fix,* estoy en un apuro. **2** (*position of ship, aircraft*) posición *f.* **3** (*dishonest arrangement*) tongo: *it's a fix!,* ¡hay tongo! **4** *sl* (*of drugs*) dosis *f,* chute *m,* pico. **– 5** *t* (*fasten*) fijar, sujetar: *could you fix this sign on the door?,* ¿podrías sujetar este letrero en la puerta? **6** *fig* (*stick*) fijar, grabar: *I fixed the name in my mind,* me grabé el nombre en la cabeza. **7** (*direct - eyes, attention*) fijar, clavar, poner: *his eyes were fixed on the scoreboard,* tenía los ojos clavados en el marcador. **8** (*decide*) decidir; (*date, meeting, etc*) fijar: *we just need to fix the time of the next meeting,* sólo nos falta fijar la hora de la próxima reunión; *let's fix a price,* fijemos un precio. **9** (*organize*) arreglar, organizar: *do you want me to fix you a date?,* ¿quieres que te arregle una cita?; *I'll fix it,* ya lo arreglaré. **10** (*dishonestly*) amañar: *the game was fixed,* el partido estaba amañado. **11** (*repair*) arreglar: *can you fix this tap?,* ¿puedes arreglar este grifo? **12** US (*prepare*) preparar: *let me fix you a sandwich,* te preparo un bocadillo. **13** (*tidy*) arreglar: *I'll just fix my hair,* me arreglaré el pelo. **14** (*photo*) fijar.
◆ **to fix on** *t insep* (*decide, select - person*) decidir, optar por, escoger; (*- date*) fijar. ‖ **to fix up 1** *t sep* (*accommodate, provide with*) proveer (**with,** de); conseguir: *they fixed me up with somewhere to stay for the night,* me consiguieron un sitio donde dormir. **2** (*organize*) arreglar, organizar: *I've fixed up an outing to the seaside,* he organizado una excursión a la costa. **3** (*repair, redecorate*) arreglar; (*install*) poner: *we spend our weekends fixing up the flat,* pasamos los fines de semana arreglando el piso.
● **to fix the blame on sb.,** echarle la culpa a algn.
fixation [fɪkˈseɪʃən] *n* obsesión *f,* idea fija.
fixed [fɪkst] **1** *adj* (*set*) fijo,-a: *a fixed rate,* un precio fijo; *fixed ideas,* ideas fijas. **2** (*dishonestly*) amañado,-a.
● **to be fixed for sth.,** andar de algo: *how are you fixed for money?,* ¿cómo andas de dinero? ‖ *of no fixed address,* sin domicilio fijo.
■ **fixed costs,** gastos *mpl* generales.
fixedly [ˈfɪksədlɪ] *adv* fijamente.
fixture [ˈfɪkstʃəʳ] **1** *n* SP encuentro. **– 2 fixtures,** *npl* (*furniture*) muebles *mpl* empotrados.
fizz [fɪz] **1** *n* burbujeo, efervescencia. **– 2** *i* burbujear.
fizzle [ˈfɪzəl] *i* burbujear.
◆ **to fizzle out** *i* esfumarse, perder fuerza, quedar en nada.
fizzy [ˈfɪzɪ] *adj* (*gen*) gaseoso,-a, con gas; (*wine*) espumoso,-a.
▲ *comp* **fizzier,** *superl* **fizziest.**
flab [flæb] *n fam pej* michelines *mpl.*
flabbergasted [ˈflæbəgɑːstɪd] *adj* pasmado,-a, atónito,-a.
flabby [ˈflæbɪ] **1** *adj* (*part of body*) fofo,-a. **2** *fig* (*weak*) débil, soso,-a.

▲ comp *flabbier,* superl *flabbiest.*
flaccid ['flæksɪd] *adj* fláccido,-a.
flag[1] [flæg] *n* (*rock*) → **flagstone.**
flag[2] [flæg] **1** *n* (*gen*) bandera. **2** MAR pabellón *m.* **3** (*for charity*) banderita. – **4** *t* (*put up flags*) decorar con banderas. **5** (*mark*) señalar.
◆ **to flag down** *t sep* hacer señales para que un coche se detenga.
● **to fly the flag / show the flag / wave the flag,** hacer acto de presencia. ‖ **to keep the flag flying,** mantener el pabellón alto.
■ **flag day,** día *m* de la banderita. ‖ **flag of convenience,** bandera de conveniencia.
▲ *verbo* pt & pp **flagged,** ger **flagging.**
flag[3] [flæg] *n* BOT lirio.
flag[4] [flæg] *i* (*lose strength*) decaer, flaquear, languidecer: *her spirits flagged,* sus ánimos decayeron; *the conversation was flagging,* la conversación decaía. **2** (*plants*) marchitarse.
▲ (*verbo*) pt & pp **flagged,** ger **flagging.**
flagellate ['flædʒəleɪt] *t* flagelar.
flagon ['flægən] *n* jarro, jarra.
flagpole ['flægpəʊl] *n* asta de bandera.
flagrant ['fleɪgrənt] *adj* flagrante, escandaloso,-a, descarado,-a.
flagship ['flægʃɪp] *n* buque *m* insignia.
flagstone ['flægstəʊn] *n* (*large*) losa; (*small*) loseta.
flail [fleɪl] **1** *n* mayal *m.* – **2** *t* golpear, azotar. – **3** **to flail about** *i* agitarse, debatirse.
flair [fleəʳ] *n* talento, don *m,* facilidad *f.*
flak [flæk] **1** *n* MIL fuego antiaéreo. **2** (*criticism*) críticas *fpl* (negativas): *the minister came in for a lot of flak,* el ministro recibió muchas críticas.
■ **flak jacket,** chaleco antibalas.
flake [fleɪk] **1** *n* (*of snow, oats*) copo. **2** (*of skin, soap*) escama. **3** (*of paint*) desconchón *m,* trozo desprendido. – **4 to flake away/off** *i* (*gen*) descamarse; (*paint*) desconcharse.
◆ **to flake out** *i* (*collapse*) caer rendido,-a.
flaky ['fleɪkɪ] *adj* (*paint*) desconchado,-a; (*skin*) escamoso,-a.
■ **flaky pastry,** hojaldre *m.*
▲ comp **flakier,** superl **flakiest.**
flambé ['flɒmbeɪ] *adj* CULIN flameado,-a.
flamboyance [flæm'bɔɪəns] *n* extravagancia.
flamboyant [flæm'bɔɪənt] *adj* llamativo,-a, extravagante.
flame [fleɪm] **1** *n* llama: *the building was in flames,* el edificio estaba en llamas; *the car burst into flames,* el coche estalló en llamas; *everything went up in flames,* todo se incendió. **2** *fig* (*intense feeling*) llama. – **3** *i* (*burn*) arder. **4** (*glow, shine*) brillar, encenderse. **5** (*become angry*) montar en cólera.
■ **old flame,** antiguo amor.
flameproof ['fleɪmpruːf] *adj* ignífugo,-a.
flaming ['fleɪmɪŋ] **1** *adj* (*burning*) en llamas; (*glowing*) ardiente. **2** (*colour*) encendido,-a. **3** (*passionate, violent*) apasionado,-a, violento,-a, ardiente: *he's got a flaming temper,* tiene muy mal genio. **4** *fam* (*damn*) maldito,-a, condenado,-a.
flamingo [flə'mɪŋgəʊ] *n* flamenco.
▲ *pl* **flamingos** o **flamingoes.**
flammable ['flæməbəl] *adj* inflamable.
flan [flæn] *n* CULIN tarta rellena.
Flanders ['flɑːndəz] *n* Flandes *m.*
flange [flændʒ] *n* (*on wheel*) pestaña; (*on pipe*) reborde *m.*

flank [flæŋk] **1** *n* (*of animal*) ijada, ijar *m.* **2** MIL flanco. **3** (*of building, mountain etc*) lado, falda. – **4** *t* flanquear, bordear.
flannel ['flænəl] **1** *n* (*material*) franela. **2** (*for face*) toallita. **3** *fam* (*words*) palabrería: *he gave me a lot of old flannel,* me dio mucha coba. – **4 flannels,** *npl* pantalón *m sing* de franela.
flannelette [flænə'let] *n* muletón *m,* franela de algodón.
flap [flæp] **1** *n* (*of envelope, pocket*) solapa. **2** (*of tent*) faldón *m.* **3** (*of plane*) alerón *m.* **4** (*of table*) hoja (abatible). **5** (*action, sound*) aleteo. **6** *fam* pánico. – **7** *t* (*wings*) batir; (*arms*) agitar. – **8** *i* (*wings*) aletear. **9** (*flag, sails*) ondear. **10** *fam* inquietarse.
● **to get into a flap,** ponerse nervioso,-a.
■ **cat flap,** gatera.
▲ (*verbo*) pt & pp **flapped,** ger **flapping.**
flapjack ['flæpdʒæk] *n* US CULIN hojuela, tortita; GB *galleta hecha de copos de avena, mantequilla y miel.*
flare [fleəʳ] **1** *n* (*flame*) llamarada. **2** (*signal*) bengala. – **3** *i* llamear. **4** *fig* estallar, encenderse: *tempers flared,* los ánimos se encendieron.
◆ **to flare up** *i* (*blow up, erupt*) estallar, encenderse; (*get angry*) enfadarse, montar en cólera: *trouble flared up outside the ground,* estalló la violencia fuera del estadio.
■ **flare path,** pista iluminada para aterrizar.
flared [fleəd] *adj* acampanado,-a.
flare-up ['fleərʌp] *n* (*of flame*) llamarada. **2** (*of violence*) estallido.
flash [flæʃ] **1** *n* (*of light*) destello, centelleo; (*of lightning*) relámpago. **2** (*from firearm*) fogonazo. **3** *fig* destello, rayo: *a flash of inspiration,* una inspiración. **4** (*photography*) flash *m.* **5** MIL (*patch*) distintivo. – **6** *adj fam pej* (*showy*) ostentoso,-a, chulo,-a. – **7** *i* relampaguear, destellar. **8** *fig* (*eyes*) brillar. **9** (*dash*) pasar como un rayo. **10** (*expose os.*) exhibirse. – **11** *t* (*shine - light*) dirigir, lanzar; (*- torch*) encender, dirigir. **12** (*communicate with light*) hacer señales con: *that driver's flashing his lights at you,* aquel conductor te está haciendo señales con las luces. **13** RAD TV (*send message*) transmitir. **14** *fig* (*look, smile*) lanzar. **15** (*show quickly*) enseñar rápidamente.
◆ **to flash about / flash around** *t sep* hacer ostentación de. ‖ **to flash back** *i* CINEM retroceder.
● **in a flash / like a flash,** en un instante, como un relámpago, como un rayo.
■ **flash card,** tarjeta. ‖ **flash in the pan,** triunfo fugaz, éxito pasajero. ‖ **news flash,** flash *m,* noticia de última hora. ‖ **flash point,** punto álgido.
flashback ['flæʃbæk] *n* escena retrospectiva, flashback *m.*
flasher ['flæʃəʳ] *n* exhibicionista *m.*
flashlight ['flæʃlaɪt] **1** *n* (*torch*) linterna. **2** (*photo*) flash *m.*
flashy ['flæʃɪ] *adj* llamativo,-a, ostentoso,-a.
▲ comp **flashier,** superl **flashiest.**
flask [flɑːsk] **1** *n* frasco. **2** CHEM matraz *m.*
■ **(thermos) flask,** termo.
flat[1] [flæt] *n* (*apartment*) piso.
flat[2] [flæt] **1** *adj* (*level, even*) llano,-a, plano,-a; (*smooth*) liso,-a: *people thought the earth was flat,* la gente creía que la tierra era plana; *he's got flat feet,* tiene los pies planos; *put it on a flat surface,* ponlo en una superficie plana. **2** (*shallow*) llano,-a: *a flat dish,* un plato llano. **3** (*shoes*) sin tacón. **4** (*tyre, ball etc*) desinflado,-a. **5** (*battery*) descargado,-a. **6** (*drink*) sin gas: *this beer's flat,* esta cerveza no tiene gas. **7** *fig* (*dull*) monótono,-a, soso,-a: *he spoke in a flat voice,* habló en voz monótona; *it was a*

very flat performance, fue una actuación muy insulsa. **8** (*having single price*) fijo,-a: *there's a flat fare,* hay un precio fijo. **9** (*firm, absolute, categorical*) rotundo,-a: *he gave us a flat denial,* se negó categóricamente. **10** (*exact*) justo,-a: *a flat thirty minutes,* unos treinta minutos justos. **11** MUS (*key*) bemol; (*voice, instrument*) desafinado,-a. – **12** *n* (*plain*) llano, llanura. **13** (*of hand*) palma. **14** MUS bemol *m*. **15** US (*tyre*) pinchazo. – **16** *adv* (*completely*) categóricamente: *he told me flat,* me lo dijo categóricamente; *she turned me down flat,* me rechazó de plano. **17** MUS desafinadamente. **18** (*exactly*) exactamente: *in ten seconds flat,* en diez segundos justos. – **19** flats, *npl* (*low level plain*) llano *sing.*
● **and that's flat,** no hay más que decir. ‖ **as flat as a pancake,** liso,-a como la palma de la mano. ‖ **flat broke,** sin blanca. ‖ **to be in a flat spin,** (*person*) estar hecho,-a un lío. ‖ **to fall flat,** (*joke etc*) caer mal, no hacer gracia. ‖ **to fall flat on one's face,** caer de bruces. ‖ **to go flat out,** ir a toda pastilla, ir a todo gas. ‖ **to lay flat,** estirar, extender. ‖ **to play flat / sing flat,** desafinar.
■ **flat cap,** gorra. ‖ **flat racing,** carreras *fpl* de caballos sin vallas. ‖ **flat spin,** AV barrena. ‖ **mud flats,** marismas *fpl.*
▲ *comp* **flatter,** *superl* **flattest.**

flat-bottomed [ˈflæt'bɒtəmd] *adj* (*boat*) de poco calado.

flatfish [ˈflætfɪʃ] *n* pez *m* de cuerpo plano.

flat-footed [ˈflæt'fʊtɪd] **1** *adj* (*having flat feet*) que tiene los pies planos. **2** (*clumsy*) torpe, patoso,-a.

flatly [ˈflætlɪ] **1** *adv* (*categorically*) categóricamente, rotundamente. **2** (*voice*) con voz monótona.

flatmate [ˈflætmaɪt] *n* compañero,-a de piso.

flatten [ˈflætən] **1** *t* (*make flat*) allanar, aplanar (**out,** -); (*smooth*) alisar: *she tried to flatten her hair,* intentó alisarse el pelo; *he flattened himself against the wall,* se arrimó contra la pared. **2** (*crush*) aplastar; (*knock down*) derribar, tumbar; (*knock over*) atropellar. **3** *fig* (*defeat*) desconcertar. – **4** *i* allanarse, aplanarse (**out,** -): *the land flattens out here,* la tierra se aplana aquí.

flatter [ˈflætə'] **1** *t* (*praise*) halagar, adular. **2** (*give pleasure*) halagar: *I was extremely flattered that he remembered my name,* me sentí muy halagada al ver que recordaba mi nombre. **3** (*suit*) favorecer: *that new hairstyle really flatters you,* ese nuevo peinado te favorece de verdad. **4** (*believe*) felicitarse, preciarse de; (*delude os.*) hacerse ilusiones: *he flatters himself on his objectivity,* se felicita por su objetividad.

flatterer [ˈflætərə'] *n* adulador,-ra.

flattering [ˈflætərɪŋ] **1** *adj* (*words*) lisonjero,-a, halagüeño,-a. **2** (*clothes etc*) favorecedor,-ra.

flattery [ˈflætərɪ] *n* adulación *f,* halagos *mpl: flattery will get you nowhere,* la adulación no te va a conseguir nada.

flatulence [ˈflætjələns] *n fml* flatulencia.

flaunt [flɔːnt] *t* hacer alarde de, hacer ostentación de.

flautist [ˈflɔːtɪst] *n* flautista *mf.*

flavour [ˈfleɪvə'] **1** *n* sabor *m,* gusto. **2** *fig* atmósfera. – **3** *t* sazonar, condimentar (**with,** con).

flavouring [ˈfleɪvərɪŋ] *n* condimento.
■ **artificial flavouring,** aromatizante *m* artificial.

flaw [flɔː] **1** *n* (*fault - in material, product, etc*) defecto, desperfecto, tara, fallo. **2** (*failing - in character*) defecto; (- *in argument*) error *m.*

flawed [flɔːd] **1** *adj* (*product etc*) defectuoso,-a. **2** (*argument*) erróneo,-a.

flawless [ˈflɔːləs] *adj* sin defecto, impecable, perfecto,-a: *a flawless complexion,* una cara perfecta; *a flawless performance,* una actuación impecable.

flax [flæks] *n* lino.

flaxen [ˈflæksən] *adj* muy rubio,-a.

flay [fleɪ] **1** *t* (*remove skin*) desollar, despellejar; (*whip*) azotar. **2** *fig* (*criticize*) despellejar.

flea [fliː] *n* pulga.
● **with a flea in one's ear,** con cajas destempladas.
■ **flea collar,** collar *m* antipulgas. ‖ **flea market,** rastro, mercadillo.

fleck [flek] **1** *n* mota, punto. – **2** *t* salpicar (**with,** de), motear (**with,** de).

fledged [fledʒd] *adj* plumado,-a.

fledgeling [ˈfledʒlɪŋ] **1** *n* ORN pajarito. **2** (*inexperienced person*) novato,-a.

flee [fliː] **1** *t* (*run away*) huir de: *hundreds fled the country,* cientos de personas huyeron del país. – **2** *i* (*run away, escape*) huir: *the people fled in fear,* la gente huyó espantada; *she had to flee to America,* tuvo que huir a América. **3** (*vanish*) desaparecer.
▲ *pt & pp* **fled** [fled].

fleece [fliːs] **1** *n* (*sheep's coat, fabric*) lana. **2** (*sheared*) vellón *m.* – **3** *t* (*shear*) esquilar. **4** *fam* (*swindle*) desplumar, robar, timar.

fleecy [ˈfliːsɪ] **1** *adj* (*material*) lanoso,-a. **2** (*cloud*) aborregado,-a.
▲ *comp* **fleecier,** *superl* **fleeciest.**

fleet [fliːt] **1** *n* MIL armada; MAR flota. **2** (*of vehicles*) escuadra.
■ **fleet admiral,** almirante *m* de la flota.

fleeting [ˈfliːtɪŋ] *adj* fugaz, breve, efímero,-a.

Fleming [ˈflemɪŋ] *n* (*person*) flamenco,-a.

Flemish [ˈflemɪʃ] **1** *adj* flamenco,-a. – **2** *n* (*language*) flamenco. – **3 the Flemish,** *npl* los flamencos *mpl.*

flesh [fleʃ] **1** *n* (*of animals*) carne *f.* **2** (*of fruit*) carne *f,* pulpa. **3 the flesh,** *fig* la carne *f.*
● **to flesh out** *t sep* (*add more details*) desarrollar.
● **in the flesh,** en persona, en carne y hueso. ‖ **to be one's own flesh and blood,** ser de la propia sangre de uno. ‖ **to make sb.'s flesh creep,** ponerle a algn. la piel de gallina.
■ **flesh wound,** herida superficial. ‖ **flesh and blood,** carne *f* y hueso.

fleshy [ˈfleʃɪ] *adj* (*plump*) gordo,-a, metido,-a en carnes; (*pulpy*) carnoso,-a.
▲ *comp* **fleshier,** *superl* **fleshiest.**

flew [fluː] *pt* → **fly.**

flex [fleks] **1** *n* GB cable *m.* – **2** *t* (*body, joints*) doblar; (*muscles*) flexionar.

flexible [ˈfleksəbəl] *adj* flexible.

flexitime [ˈfleksɪtaɪm] *n* horario flexible.

flick [flɪk] **1** *n* (*jerk*) movimiento rápido, movimiento brusco: *with a flick of the wrist,* con un golpe de muñeca; *at the flick of a switch,* con sólo apretar un botón. **2** (*of fingers*) capirotazo; (*of whip*) latigazo, chasquido; (*of tail*) coletazo. **3** (*of pages*) hojeada. – **4** *t* (*with finger*) dar un capirotazo a: *he flicked a pea at me,* me dio un capirotazo con un guisante. **5** (*switch*) dar al interruptor: *she flicked the light on/off,* encendió/apagó la luz. **6** (*whip*) chasquear, dar con el látigo; (*tail*) dar un coletazo: *the horse flicked it's tail,* el caballo dio un coletazo. **7** (*remove*) sacudirse: *she flicked the ash from her sleeve,* se sacudió la ceniza de la manga. – **8 the flicks,** *npl dated* el cine *m sing.*
◆ **to flick away** *t sep* quitar, sacudirse. ‖ **to flick**

231

flood

through *t insep* hojear: *she flicked through the magazine,* hojeó la revista.
● **to flick channels,** cambiar de canal, hacer zapping.
■ **flick knife,** navaja automática.
flicker ['flɪkə'] **1** *n (of flame, eyelids)* parpadeo; *(of light)* titileo, parpadeo. **2** *fig (slight sign)* señal *f*, muestra; *(faint emotion)* chispa, pizca: *a flicker of hope,* una chispa de esperanza. – **3** *i (flame)* vacilar, parpadear; *(light)* titilar, parpadear; *(shadow)* bailar. **4** *(eyelids)* parpadear. **5** *(smile)* esbozarse: *a smile flickered across her face,* en su rostro se esbozó una sonrisa.
flier [flaɪə'] **1** *n (pilot)* aviador,-ra. **2** *(bird, insect etc)* volador,-ra. **3** *(leaflet)* folleto.
flight [flaɪt] **1** *n (journey by air)* vuelo: *he caught the next flight to London,* cogió el siguiente vuelo a Londres; *our flight has been delayed,* nuestro vuelo se ha retrasado. **2** *(path)* trayectoria. **3** *(flock of birds)* bandada. **4** *(of stairs)* tramo. **5** *(escape)* huida, fuga.
● **to be in full flight,** *(escaping)* huir; *(speaking)* estar en pleno discurso. ‖ **to take flight,** *(escape)* darse a la fuga; *(fly)* emprender el vuelo.
■ **flight attendant,** auxiliar *mf* de vuelo. ‖ **flight deck,** cubierta de vuelo. ‖ **flight lieutenant,** capitán *m* (de la Fuerza Aérea). ‖ **flight of fancy,** fantasía, sueño, ilusión *f*. ‖ **flight path,** ruta. ‖ **flight recorder,** caja negra. ‖ **flight simulator,** simulador *m* de vuelo. ‖ **in-flight service,** servicio a bordo.
flightless ['flaɪtləs] *adj* no volador,-ra.
flighty ['flaɪtɪ] *adj (not serious)* frívolo,-a, poco serio,-a, casquivano,-a.
▲ *comp* **flightier,** *superl* **flightiest.**
flimsy ['flɪmzɪ] **1** *adj (thin)* fino,-a, ligero,-a. **2** *(structure)* poco sólido,-a. **3** *fig (unconvincing)* flojo,-a, pobre, poco convincente. – **4** *n* papel *m* cebolla.
▲ *comp* **flimsier,** *superl* **flimsiest.**
flinch [flɪntʃ] **1** *i (wince)* estremecerse. **2** *(shun)* retroceder **(from,** ante).
fling [flɪŋ] **1** *n (throw)* lanzamiento. **2** *(wild time)* juerga. **3** *(affair)* aventura (amorosa), romance *m*: *we had a brief fling,* tuvimos una aventura. – **4** *t (throw)* arrojar, tirar, lanzar: *he flung the ball away,* lanzó la pelota con violencia; *the teacher flung the door open,* el profesor abrió la puerta de golpe; *she flung her coat on the chair,* echó su abrigo a la silla. **5** *(move)* echar, lanzar: *she flung her arms around me,* me echó los brazos encima; *he flung himself in front of a car,* se arrojó a un coche. **6** *(say)* lanzar: *don't fling accusations at me,* no me lances acusaciones.
◆ **to fling off** *t sep (clothes)* quitarse de prisa. ‖ **to fling on** *t sep (clothes)* ponerse de prisa. ‖ **to fling out** *t sep (thing) tirar; (person)* echar, expulsar.
● **to fling os. at sb.,** arrojarse sobre algn. ‖ **to fling os. into sth.,** entregarse a algo. ‖ **to fling up one's hands in horror,** horrorizarse. ‖ **to have a fling,** echar una cana al aire, correrla.
▲ *pt & pp* **flung.**
flint [flɪnt] **1** *n (stone)* sílex *m*; *(piece)* pedernal *m*. **2** *(tool)* sílex *m*. **3** *(of lighter)* piedra, piedra de mechero.
■ **flint axe,** hacha de sílex.
flintlock ['flɪntlɒk] *n* escopeta de chispa, fusil *m* de chispa.
flinty ['flɪntɪ] **1** *adj (material)* silíceo,-a, de pedernal. **2** *(person)* insensible, cruel.
▲ *comp* **flintier,** *superl* **flintiest.**
flip [flɪp] **1** *n (light blow)* golpecito: *by the flip of a coin,* echándolo a cara o cruz. **2** *(somersault)* voltereta (en el aire). – **3** *adj fam (flippant)* frívolo,-a, poco serio,-a. – **4**

interj fam ¡ostras! – **5** *t (toss - gen)* echar, tirar al aire; *(-coin)* echar a cara o cruz. **6** *(switch)* dar a: *he flipped a switch and the light came on,* le dio al interruptor y se encendió la luz. **7** *(turn over)* dar la vuelta a. – **8** *i fam (get angry)* perder los estribos; *(go mad)* volverse loco,-a.
◆ **to flip through** *t insep* echar un vistazo a.
● **to flip one's lid,** *(go crazy)* volverse loco,-a; *(get angry)* explotar, reventar. ‖ **to flip open,** abrir de golpe.
■ **flip side,** cara B.
▲ *(verbo) pt & pp* **flipped,** *ger* **flipping.**
flip-flop ['flɪpflɒp] *n* chancla.
flippancy ['flɪpənsɪ] *n* falta de seriedad.
flippant ['flɪpənt] *adj* frívolo,-a, poco serio,-a.
flipper ['flɪpə'] *n* aleta.
flipping ['flɪpɪŋ] *adj* GB fam maldito,-a.
flirt [flɜːt] **1** *n* coqueto,-a, ligón,-ona. – **2** *i (coquette)* flirtear **(with,** con), coquetear **(with,** con).
● **to flirt with an idea,** acariciar una idea. ‖ **to flirt with death,** jugar con la muerte.
flirtation [flɜːˈteɪʃən] *n* coqueteo, flirteo.
flirtatious [flɜːˈteɪʃəs] *adj* coqueto,-a, ligón,-ona.
flit [flɪt] **1** *n (escape)* escapada. – **2** *i (birds, insects)* revolotear, volar; *(people)* mover: *the bird flitted from one tree to another,* el pájaro revoloteaba de árbol en árbol; *she flits from one subject to another,* salta de un tema a otro.
● **to do a moonlight flit,** irse a la chita callando.
▲ *pt & pp* **flitted,** *ger* **flitting.**
float [fləʊt] **1** *n (for fishing)* boya, flotador *m*. **2** *(for swimming)* flotador *m*. **3** *(of aircraft)* pontón *m*, flotador *m*. **4** *(vehicle - in procession)* carroza; *(- for delivery)* furgoneta. **5** *(money)* cambio. – **6** *i (gen)* flotar: *wood floats,* la madera flota; *a bottle floated to the surface,* una botella salió a la superficie; *the parasol floated out to sea,* la sombrilla se hizo a la mar. – **7** *t* poner a flote, hacer flotar: *they floated some paper boats down the river,* hicieron flotar algunos barquitos de papel en el río. **8** FIN *(company)* lanzar a bolsa; *(shares)* emitir; *(currency)* dejar flotar. **9** *(suggest, present)* sugerir: *several ideas have been floated,* se han sugerido varias ideas.
◆ **to float about / float around 1** *i (rumour)* circular; *(object)* estar: *there's a rumour floating around that ...,* circula el rumor de que ...; *is my pencil floating around here?,* ¿está por aquí mi lápiz? **2** *(do nothing)* holgazanear: *I floated about all summer,* pasé el verano holgazaneando.
flock¹ [flɒk] **1** *n (of sheep, goats)* rebaño; *(of birds)* bandada. **2** *fam (crowd)* multitud *f*, tropel *m*: *people came in flocks,* la gente acudió en tropel. **3** REL grey *f* rebaño.
● **to flock together,** congregarse, reunirse.
flock² [flɒk] **1** *n (material)* borra. **2** *(stuffing)* relleno.
flog [flɒg] **1** *t (beat)* azotar. **2** GB fam *(sell)* vender.
● **to flog a dead horse,** perder el tiempo, machacar en hierro frío.
▲ *pt & pp* **flogged,** *ger* **flogging.**
flogging ['flɒgɪŋ] *n* azotaina, flagelación *f*.
● **to give sb. a flogging,** azotar a algn.
flood [flʌd] **1** *n (overflow of water)* inundación *f*. **2** *(of river)* riada. **3** *fig (great quantity)* torrente *m*, avalancha, diluvio: *a flood of refugees,* una avalancha de refugiados. – **4** *t (gen)* inundar, anegar; *(engine)* ahogar: *the washing machine flooded the kitchen,* la lavadora inundó la cocina. **5** *fig (with calls, applications, etc)* llover, inundar **(with,** de): *we've been flooded with offers,* nos han llovido las ofertas. – **6** *i (river)* desbordarse. **7** *fig (cover, fill)* invadir, inundar: *relief flooded over her,* sintió un gran alivio.

◆ **to flood in** i (things) llegar a montones, llover; (people) entrar a raudales, entrar en tropel: *donations have been flooding in,* ha habido una avalancha de donativos; *peasants flooded in from the surrounding area,* los campesinos llegaron en tropel de las afueras; *daylight flooded in,* la luz entraba a raudales. ‖ **to flood out** t *sep* inundar: *we're flooded out,* estamos inundados.

● **to flood the market,** inundar el mercado, saturar el mercado. ‖ **to be in floods of tears,** llorar a mares.

floodgate ['flʌdgaɪt] n compuerta.

● **to open the floodgates,** abrir las compuertas.

flooding ['flʌdɪŋ] n inundación f.

floodlight ['flʌdlaɪt] 1 n foco. – 2 t iluminar con focos.

floor [flɔːʳ] 1 n (surface) suelo. 2 GEOG fondo. 3 (storey) piso, planta. 4 (dance) pista. – 5 t (provide with floor) solar, entarimar (**with**, de). 6 (knock down) derribar, tumbar. 7 fig (confuse, defeat) apabullar, desconcertar, dejar perplejo,-a. – 8 **the floor,** n POL la sala, el hemiciclo.

● **to have the floor,** tener la palabra. ‖ **to hold the floor,** tener la palabra durante mucho rato. ‖ **to take the floor,** (get up to speak) tomar la palabra, hacer uso de la palabra; (get up to dance) salir a bailar. ‖ **to wipe the floor with sb.,** hacer morder polvo a algn.

■ **floor show,** espectáculo de cabaret.

floorboard ['flɔːbɔːd] n tabla (del suelo).

flooring ['flɔːrɪŋ] n suelo, pavimento.

flop [flɒp] 1 n fam fracaso. – 2 i (fall clumsily) abalanzarse, arrojarse (**into**, en); (sit or lie clumsily) tumbarse, dejarse caer: *I was so tired I flopped down on the sofa,* estaba tan cansado que me dejé caer en el sofá; *she flopped into bed,* se tumbó en la cama. 3 fam (fail) fracasar.

▲ (verbo) pt & pp **flopped,** ger **flopping.**

floppy ['flɒpɪ] adj blando,-a, flexible.

■ **floppy disk,** COMPUT disco flexible, disquete m.

▲ comp **floppier,** superl **floppiest.**

flora ['flɔːrə] n flora.

floral ['flɔːrəl] adj floral.

■ **floral tribute,** ofrenda floral.

Florence ['flɒrəns] n Florencia.

Florentine ['flɒrəntaɪn] 1 adj florentino,-a. – 2 n florentino,-a.

florid ['flɒrɪd] 1 adj (style) florido,-a, recargado,-a. 2 (ruddy) rojizo,-a, colorado,-a.

florist ['flɒrɪst] n florista mf.

■ **florist's (shop),** floristería.

floss [flɒs] n cardazo, seda floja.

flotation [fləʊ'teɪʃən] n FIN (of shares) emisión f.

flotsam ['flɒtsəm] n MAR desechos mpl en el mar.

■ **flotsam and jetsam,** (people) gente f sin oficio ni beneficio; (things) restos mpl, trastos mpl.

flounce [flaʊns] 1 n SEW volante m. 2 (jerk) gesto exagerado, gesto de enfado. – 3 i moverse exageradamente.

◆ **to flounce in / flounce out** i entrar airadamente / salir airadamente.

flounder ['flaʊndəʳ] 1 n (fish) platija. – 2 i (struggle, move with difficulty) forcejear. 3 fig (hesitate, dither) vacilar: *the candidate floundered for a moment,* el candidato vaciló un momento.

flour ['flaʊəʳ] 1 n harina. – 2 t enharinar.

flourish ['flʌrɪʃ] 1 n (gesture) ademán m, gesto teatral, gesto exagerado. 2 (signature) rúbrica; (of pen) plumada. 3 MUS (guitar) floreo; (fanfare) toque m de trompeta; (singing) floritura. – 4 t (wave about) agitar, blandir. – 5 i (be successful) florecer, prosperar: *business is flourishing,* el negocio está prosperando. 6 (plant) crecer bien.

flourishing ['flʌrɪʃɪŋ] adj floreciente, próspero,-a.

floury ['flaʊərɪ] adj harinoso,-a.

▲ comp **flourier,** superl **flouriest.**

flout [flaʊt] t (rule) mofarse de, burlarse de; (convention, tradition) ignorar, no hacer caso de; (law) desacatar: *she flouted the school rules,* se mofaba de las reglas del colegio.

flow [fləʊ] 1 n (gen) flujo. 2 (of river) corriente f. 3 (of traffic) circulación f. 4 (of words) torrente m. 5 (of people, goods) afluencia. 6 (of capital) movimiento. 7 (of tide) flujo. – 8 i (move freely - liquid, river, blood) fluir, discurrir, correr: *blood flows through our veins,* la sangre fluye por las venas. 9 (pour out - blood) manar; (- tears) correr: *blood flowed from the wound,* la sangre manaba de la herida. 10 (tide) subir. 11 (traffic) circular; (electricity) fluir. 12 (speech, writing, thoughts) fluir. 13 (hair, clothes) ondear. 14 (be available, abound) abundar (**with**, -): *the drink was really flowing,* abundaba la bebida.

◆ **to flow in** i entrar a raudales. ‖ **to flow into** i (river) desembocar en: *the Ebro flows into the sea at Amposta,* el Ebro desemboca en el mar en Amposta. ‖ **to flow out** i salir a raudales.

● **to be in full flow,** estar en pleno discurso.

■ **flow chart,** organigrama m, diagrama m de flujo.

flower ['flaʊəʳ] 1 n flor f. – 2 i florecer.

● **to be in flower,** estar en flor, estar florido,-a. ‖ **to come into flower,** florecer. ‖ **say it with flowers,** dígaselo con flores.

■ **flower bed,** parterre m, macizo. ‖ **flower show,** exposición f de flores. ‖ **the flower of youth,** la flor de la juventud.

flowered ['flaʊəd] adj (patterned) floreado,-a.

flowering ['flaʊərɪŋ] n floración f, florecimiento.

flowerpot ['flaʊəpɒt] n maceta, tiesto.

flowery ['flaʊərɪ] 1 adj (pattern) de flores, floreado,-a. 2 (style) florido,-a.

▲ comp **flowerier,** superl **floweriest.**

flowing ['fləʊɪŋ] 1 adj (liquid) que fluye. 2 (style) fluido,-a, suelto,-a. 3 (dress) de mucho vuelo.

flown [fləʊn] pp → **fly.**

flu [fluː] n gripe f: *he's got (the) flu,* tiene la gripe.

fluctuate ['flʌktjʊeɪt] i fluctuar, variar.

fluctuation [flʌktjʊ'eɪʃən] n fluctuación f, variación f.

flue [fluː] 1 n (of chimney) cañón m. 2 (of stove, boiler) conducto de humos.

fluency ['fluːənsɪ] 1 n fluidez f. 2 (of language) dominio (**in**, de).

fluent ['fluːənt] 1 adj (gen) fluido,-a. 2 (language) fluido,-a: *he speaks fluent English,* habla inglés con soltura.

● **to be fluent,** dominar: *he is fluent in English,* domina el inglés.

fluently ['fluːəntlɪ] adv con soltura.

fluff [flʌf] 1 n (down, material) pelusa, lanilla. 2 fam (mistake, blunder) pifia, fallo. – 3 t fam (do badly, fail) hacer mal: *the actor fluffed his lines,* el actor se equivocó en su papel; *she fluffed her exam,* suspendió el examen, cateó el examen.

◆ **to fluff out / fluff up** t sep (pillow, cushion) ahuecar, mullir.

fluffy ['flʌfɪ] 1 adj (feathery) mullido,-a. 2 (toys) de peluche. 3 (light, airy) esponjoso,-a.

▲ comp **fluffier,** superl **fluffiest.**

fluid ['fluːɪd] 1 adj (not solid) fluido,-a, líquido,-a. 2 (smooth, graceful) natural, con soltura. 3 (not fixed) flexible. – 4 n fluido, líquido.

fluke [fluːk] n fam chiripa.

flummox ['flʌməks] *t* desconcertar, confundir.

flung [flʌŋ] *pt & pp* → **fling**.

flunk [flʌŋk] *t* suspender, catear: *he flunked maths,* suspendió las mates.

◆ **to flunk out** *i* suspender, catear.

fluorescent [fluə'resənt] *adj* fluorescente.

■ **fluorescent light/lamp,** fluorescente *m*.

fluoride ['fluəraɪd] **1** *n* CHEM fluoruro. **2** (*in toothpaste*) flúor *m*.

flurry ['flʌrɪ] **1** *n* (*of wind*) ráfaga; (*of snow*) nevisca. **2** *fig* (*burst*) nerviosismo, agitación *f*, frenesí *m*.

● **to be in a flurry,** estar nervioso,-a. ‖ **to get in a flurry,** ponerse nervioso,-a, aturullarse.

▲ *pl* **flurries**.

flush[1] [flʌʃ] *n* (*in cards*) color *m*.

flush[2] [flʌʃ] **flush with,** *adj* (*level*) al mismo nivel que, alineado,-a con.

● **to be flush,** (*have money*) andar bien de dinero, ir desahogado,-a.

flush[3] [flʌʃ] **1** *n* (*blush*) rubor *m*. **2** (*of emotion*) acceso, arrebato. **3** *t* (*toilet*) cisterna. – **4** *t* (*cause to blush*) ruborizar, sonrojar. **5** (*clean*) limpiar con agua. **6** (*toilet*) tirar (de) la cadena: *flush the toilet after use,* tira la cadena después de utilizar el wáter; *flush it down the toilet,* tíralo al wáter. – **7** *i* (*blush*) ruborizarse. **8** (*toilet*) funcionar: *the toilet won't flush,* la cisterna del wáter no funciona.

◆ **to flush out** *t sep* (*enemy*) hacer salir.

● **in the full flush of youth,** en la primera juventud.

■ **hot flush,** sofoco.

flushed [flʌʃt] **1** *adj* (*excited*) emocionado,-a (**with,** por). **2** (*blushing*) sonrojado,-a.

fluster ['flʌstə'] **1** *t* poner nervioso,-a. – **2** *n* confusión *f*, agitación *f*.

● **to get in a fluster,** ponerse nervioso,-a, aturullarse.

flute [fluːt] **1** *n* flauta. – **2** *t* ARCH acanalar: *fluted columns,* columnas acanaladas.

fluting ['fluːtɪŋ] *n* acanaladuras *fpl*, estrías *fpl*.

flutter ['flʌtə'] **1** *n* (*excitement*) agitación *f*, emoción *f*. **2** (*of wings*) aleteo. **3** (*of eyelashes*) pestañeo. **4** *fam* (*bet*) apuesta. **5** (*of aircraft*) vibración *f*. – **6** *t* (*eyelashes*) parpadear. **7** (*wings*) aletear. – **8** *i* (*flag*) ondear. **9** (*wings*) aletear. **10** (*flit*) revolotear. **11** (*heart*) palpitar.

● **to be in a flutter,** *fig* estar nervioso,-a.

fluvial ['fluːvɪəl] *adj* fluvial.

flux [flʌks] **1** *n* (*flow*) flujo. **2** (*instability*) inestabilidad *f*.

● **to be in a state of flux,** estar cambiando constantemente.

fly[1] [flaɪ] **1** *i* volar: *birds fly south in winter,* los pájaros vuelan hacia el sur en invierno; *we will be flying at an altitude of 9,000 metres,* volaremos a una altitud de 9.000 metros. **2** (*go by plane*) ir en avión: *you can fly to Madrid in an hour,* se puede ir a Madrid en avión en una hora. **3** (*flag, hair*) ondear. **4** (*sparks*) saltar. **5** (*rush, move quickly*) irse volando, irse a toda prisa: *I really must fly,* me tengo que ir volando; *the express train flew past,* el expreso pasó volando; *she came flying through the door,* entró a toda prisa por la puerta. **6** (*time*) volar, pasar volando: *time flies when you're having fun,* el tiempo pasa volando cuando te diviertes; *the holiday has flown by,* las vacaciones han pasado volando. **7** (*flee*) huir: *when the police arrived, the thieves had flown,* cuando llegó la policía los ladrones habían huido. – **8** *t* (*plane*) pilotar: *can you fly a plane?,* ¿sabes pilotar un avión? **9** (*send by plane*) transportar. **10** (*travel over*) sobrevolar: *planes fly the Atlantic in a few hours,* los aviones sobrevuelan el Atlántico en pocas horas. **11** (*kite*)

hacer volar. **12** (*flag*) enarbolar, izar. **13** (*flee*) huir (**from,** de), salir de, abandonar. – **14** *n* (*of tent*) doble techo. – **15 flies,** *npl* (*on trousers*) bragueta *f sing.* **16** (*theatre*) telar *m sing.*

◆ **to fly at** *i* lanzarse sobre. ‖ **to fly away** *i* irse volando. ‖ **to fly off** *i* (*bird etc*) irse volando; (*object*) volar.

● **to fly in the face of sth.,** burlarse de algo. ‖ **to fly into a rage / fly into a temper,** ponerse furioso,-a, montar en cólera, subirse por las paredes. ‖ **to fly off the handle,** perder los estribos. ‖ **to let fly at sb.,** arremeter contra algn.: *she let fly at him with a paperweight,* le tiró un pisapapeles. ‖ **to go flying,** caerse: *her glasses went flying,* le cayeron las gafas. ‖ **to send sb. flying,** mandar a algn. por los aires.

■ **fly sheet,** doble techo.

▲ *pt* **flew,** *pp* **flown,** *ger* **flying**.

fly[2] [flaɪ] *adj* GB *fam* (*smart*) astuto,-a.

▲ *comp* **flier,** *superl* **fliest**.

fly[3] [flaɪ] *n* mosca.

● **not to hurt a fly,** ser incapaz de matar una mosca. ‖ **there are no flies on ...,** ... no se chupa el dedo. ‖ **to drop/fall like flies,** caer como moscas. ‖

■ **fly spray,** spray *m* matamoscas, matamoscas *m*, insecticida *m*. ‖ **fly in the ointment,** dificultad *f*, problema *m*.

▲ *pl* **flies**.

flyaway ['flaɪəweɪ] **1** *adj* (*hair*) suelto,-a. **2** *fig* (*frivolous*) frívolo,-a.

fly-by-night ['flaɪbaɪnaɪt] **1** *n* persona de poco fiar. – **2** *adj* de poca confianza, sospechoso,-a.

flycatcher ['flaɪkætʃə'] *n* papamoscas *m*.

■ **pied flycatcher,** papamoscas *m* cerrojillo. ‖ **spotted flycatcher,** papamoscas *m* gris.

fly-fish ['flaɪfɪʃ] *i* pescar con moscas.

flying ['flaɪɪŋ] **1** *n* AV aviación *f*. **2** (*action*) vuelo: *she's scared of flying,* tiene miedo a volar. – **3** *adj* (*soaring*) volante; (*animal, machine*) volador,-ra, que vuela: *it's some kind of flying insect,* es un tipo de insecto volador. **4** (*quick*) rápido,-a.

● **to do sth. with flying colours,** salir airoso,-a de algo. ‖ **to get off to a flying start,** empezar con buen pie. ‖ **to take a flying jump,** tomar impulso y saltar.

■ **flying buttress,** arbotante *m*. ‖ **flying doctor,** médico,-a *que viaja en avión*. ‖ **flying fish,** pez *m* volador. ‖ **flying picket,** piquete *m* informativo. ‖ **flying saucer,** platillo volante. ‖ **flying squad,** patrulla volante. ‖ **flying tackle,** placaje *m* en el aire. ‖ **flying visit,** visita relámpago.

flyleaf ['flaɪliːf] *n* guarda.

flyover ['flaɪəʊvə'] *n* GB paso elevado.

fly-past ['flaɪpɑːst] *n* desfile *m* aéreo, desfile *m* de aviones.

flyposting ['flaɪpəʊstɪŋ] *n* pegar carteles ilegalmente.

flyswatter ['flaɪswɒtə'] *n* matamoscas *m*.

flytrap ['flaɪtræp] *n* BOT atrapamoscas *f*.

flyweight ['flaɪweɪt] *n* SP peso mosca.

flywheel ['flaɪwiːl] *n* volante *m*.

FM ['ef'em] *abbr* (*Frequency Modulation*) modulación *f* de frecuencia; (*abbreviation*) FM *f*.

FO ['ef'əʊ] *abbr* GB (*Foreign Office*) ≈ Ministerio de Asuntos Exteriores.

foal [fəʊl] **1** *n* potro,-a. – **2** *i* parir.

foam [fəʊm] **1** *n* espuma. – **2** *i* (*liquid*) hacer espuma. **3** (*person*) echar espumarajos, espumajear.

● **to foam at the mouth,** estar que rabia.

■ **foam rubber,** gomaespuma.

foamy ['fəʊmɪ] *adj* espumoso,-a.
▲ *comp* **foamier**, *superl* **foamiest**.
fob[1] [fɒb] *n* cadenilla de reloj.
■ **fob watch**, reloj *m* de bolsillo.
fob[2] [fɒb] *t* engañar, engatusar.
● **to fob sb. off with excuses**, darle largas a algn. ‖ **to fob sth. off on sb.**, endilgar algo a algn., colocar algo a algn.
▲ *pt* & *pp* **fobbed**, *ger* **fobbing**.
focal ['fəʊkəl] *adj* focal.
■ **focal distance**, distancia focal. ‖ **focal point**, centro, foco.
focus ['fəʊkəs] **1** *n* foco. **2** (*centre*) centro: *she's always the focus of attention*, ella es siempre el centro de atención. − **3** *t* (*camera etc*) enfocar (**on**, -). **4** *fig* (*concentrate*) fijar (**on**, en), centrar (**on**, en): *all eyes were focused on her*, todas las miradas se fijaron en ella. − **5** *i* (*camera, eyes, etc*) enfocar (**on**, -), fijar (**on**, en). **6** (*concentrate*) centrarse, concentrarse (**on**, en).
● **in focus**, enfocado,-a. ‖ **out of focus**, desenfocado,-a.
▲ (*verbo*) *pt* & *pp* **focused** *o* **focussed**, *ger* **focussing** *o* **focusing**; (*sustantivo*) *pl* **focuses** *o* **foci** ['fəʊsaɪ].
fodder ['fɒdə'] *n* pienso, forraje *m*.
foe [fəʊ] *n* enemigo.
foetal ['fiːtəl] *adj* fetal.
foetus ['fiːtəs] *n* feto.
fog [fɒg] **1** *n* niebla. − **2** *t* (*mirror etc*) empañar. **3** (*photo*) velar. **4** *fig* complicar. − **5** *i* empañarse (**up/over**, -).
■ **fog bank**, banco de niebla.
▲ (*verbo*) *pt* & *pp* **fogged**, *ger* **fogging**.
fogbound ['fɒgbaʊnd] *adj* inmovilizado,-a a causa de la niebla, paralizado,-a a causa de la niebla.
fogey ['fəʊgɪ] *n* carca *mf*, persona chapada a la antigua.
● **old fogey**, carroza *mf*.
foggy ['fɒgɪ] **1** *adj* de niebla: *it's foggy*, hay niebla. **2** (*confused*) confuso,-a.
● **not to have the foggiest idea**, no tener la más mínima idea.
▲ *comp* **foggier**, *superl* **foggiest**.
foghorn ['fɒghɔːn] *n* sirena de niebla.
foglamp ['fɒglæmp] *n* faro antiniebla.
fogy ['fəʊgɪ] *n* → **fogey**.
▲ *pl* **fogies**.
foible ['fɔɪbəl] *n* (*peculiarity*) manía; (*weakness*) punto flaco, debilidad *f*.
foil[1] [fɔɪl] *n* (*fencing*) florete *m*.
foil[2] [fɔɪl] *t* (*prevent, frustrate*) frustrar: *he was foiled in his attempt to steal the ring*, frustraron su tentativa de robar el anillo.
foil[3] [fɔɪl] **1** *n* (*metal paper*) hoja de metal, papel *m* de plata. **2** (*contrast*) contraste *m*.
● **to act as a foil to**, realzar, hacer resaltar.
■ **tin foil**, papel *m* de estaño.
foist [fɔɪst] **to foist sth. on sb.**, *phr* endilgar algo a algn., encajar algo a algn.
fold[1] [fəʊld] **1** *n* (*for sheep*) redil *m*, aprisco. **2 the fold**, REL el redil *m*.
fold[2] [fəʊld] **1** *n* (*crease*) pliegue *m*, doblez *m*. **2** GEOG pliegue *m*. − **3** *t* doblar, plegar (**up**, -): *will you help me fold the sheet?*, ¿me ayudas a doblar la sábana? **4** (*wrap*) envolver. − **5** *i* doblarse, plegarse. **6** (*go bankrupt*) quebrar.
◆ **to fold away** *i* plegarse: *this bed folds away*, esta cama se pliega. ‖ **to fold in** *t sep* CULIN incorporar sin batir: *fold the flour into the egg whites*, incorpora la ha-

rina a las claras sin batir. ‖ **to fold up** *i* (*collapse - person*) doblarse; (- *business*) fracasar, quebrar.
● **to fold one's arms**, cruzar los brazos.
foldaway ['fəʊldəweɪ] *adj* plegable.
folder ['fəʊldə'] *n* carpeta.
folding ['fəʊldɪŋ] *adj* plegable.
■ **folding door**, puerta plegable.
foliage ['fəʊlɪdʒ] *n fml* follaje *m*.
folio ['fəʊlɪəʊ] **1** *n* (*sheet*) folio. **2** (*book*) libro en folio.
▲ *pl* **folios**.
folk [fəʊk] **1** *npl* gente *f sing*. − **2** *adj* popular. − **3 folks**, *npl* **fam** (*family*) familia *f sing*; (*friends*) amigos *mpl*.
■ **folk dance**, baile *m* popular, baile *m* tradicional. ‖ **folk music**, música folk. ‖ **folk singer**, cantante *mf* de música folk. ‖ **folk song**, canción *f* tradicional, canción *f* folk.
folklore ['fəʊklɔː'] *n* folklor(e) *m*.
follow ['fɒləʊ] **1** *t* (*gen*) seguir: *follow me!*, ¡sígueme!; *follow that car*, sigue aquel coche; *spring follows winter*, la primavera sigue al invierno; *the road follows the coast*, la carretera va por la costa. **2** (*understand*) entender, seguir: *I don't follow you*, no te entiendo; *he couldn't follow what the teacher was saying*, no entendía lo que decía el profesor. **3** (*pursue*) perseguir: *the police were following them*, la policía los perseguían. **4** (*advice, example, etc*) seguir: *follow the instructions*, sigue las instrucciones. **5** (*take interest in*) seguir, estar al corriente de: *we followed the World Cup closely*, seguimos muy de cerca los mundiales. − **6** *i* (*gen*) seguir: *you go on ahead and I'll follow*, tú pasa delante y yo te seguiré; *in the days that followed*, durante los días siguientes. **7** (*understand*) entender: *I don't follow*, no entiendo. **8** (*be logical*) resultar, derivarse: *it follows that ...*, resulta que ...
◆ **to follow through 1** *t sep* (*complete*) llevar a cabo. − **2** *i* SP acompañar el golpe. ‖ **to follow up 1** *t sep* (*develop*) profundizar en. **2** (*investigate*) investigar.
● **as follows**, como sigue, así. ‖ **to follow in sb.'s footsteps**, seguir los pasos a algn. ‖ **to follow one's nose**, seguir todo recto. ‖ **to follow suit**, (*at cards*) jugar del mismo palo; (*figuratively*) hacer lo mismo.
follower ['fɒləʊə'] *n* seguidor,-ra.
following ['fɒləʊɪŋ] **1** *adj* siguiente: *the following day*, el día siguiente; *you will need to bring the following items*, tendrás que traer las siguientes cosas. **2** (*winds, currents*) de cola. − **3** *prep* después de: *she never went out following her husband's death*, no volvió a salir después de la muerte de su marido. − **4** *n* (*supporters*) seguidores *mpl*: *this group has a large following*, este grupo tiene muchos seguidores. **5 the following**, lo siguiente *m sing*, los siguientes *mpl*: *will the following please remain behind?*, ¿las siguientes personas podrán quedarse, por favor?; *the following appeared in a national newspaper*, lo siguiente apareció en un periódico nacional:.
follow-through ['fɒləʊθruː] *n* SP acompañamiento del golpe.
follow-up ['fɒləʊʌp] *n* (*sequel*) continuación *f*; (*further treatment*) seguimiento.
■ **follow-up interview**, segunda entrevista. ‖ **follow-up letter**, segunda carta. ‖ **follow-up visit**, visita de seguimiento.
folly ['fɒlɪ] *n fml* locura, desatino: *it would be folly to get involved*, sería una locura enredarse.
▲ *pl* **follies**.
foment [fəʊ'ment] *t* instigar, provocar.
fond [fɒnd] **1** *adj* (*loving*) cariñoso,-a. **2** (*indulgent*) indulgente. **3** (*hope, belief*) vano,-a.

● **to be fond of sb.**, tenerle cariño a algn. ‖ **to be fond of sth.**, ser aficionado,-a a algo, gustarle mucho algo a uno.

fondle ['fɒndəl] t acariciar.

fondly ['fɒndlɪ] **1** adv (lovingly) cariñosamente. **2** (naively) ingenuamente.

fondness ['fɒndnəs] **1** n cariño (**for**, a). **2** (liking) afición f (**for**, a/por).

fondue ['fɒndjuː] n CULIN fondue f.

font [fɒnt] n pila (bautismal).

food [fuːd] n comida, alimento: what's your favourite food?, ¿cuál es tu comida preferida?; we haven't got any food in the house, no tenemos nada de comida en casa; do you like Chinese food?, ¿te gusta la comida china?; health food, comida sana.
● **to be off one's food**, no tener apetito.
■ **food additive**, aditivo (alimenticio). ‖ **food chain**, cadena alimentaria, cadena trófica. ‖ **food for thought**, algo en qué pensar. ‖ **food mixer**, batidora. ‖ **food poisoning**, intoxicación f alimenticia. ‖ **food processor**, robot m de cocina. ‖ **food supplies**, víveres mpl, provisiones fpl.

foodstuffs ['fuːdstʌfs] npl alimentos mpl, productos mpl alimenticios.

fool[1] [fuːl] n mousse f de fruta.

fool[2] [fuːl] **1** n tonto,-a, imbécil mf: don't be a fool, no seas tonto. **2** (jester) bufón,-ona. – **3** t engañar. – **4** i bromear: I was only fooling, lo decía en broma.
◆ **to fool about / fool around 1** i (be stupid) hacer el tonto, hacer el payaso. **2** (waste time) perder el tiempo neciamente.
● **a fool and his money are soon parted**, a los tontos no les dura el dinero. ‖ **to be nobody's fool**, no dejarse engañar por nadie, no chuparse el dedo. ‖ **to make a fool of sb.**, poner en ridículo a algn., dejar a algn. en ridículo. ‖ **to act the fool / play the fool**, hacer el tonto. ‖ **more fool sb.**, peor para algn.: my car's been stolen. –more fool you, you should have locked it, me han robado el coche. –peor para ti, debiste cerrarlo con llave. ‖ **there is no fool like an old fool**, no hay peor tonto que un viejo tonto.

foolhardy ['fuːlhɑːdɪ] **1** adj (risky) temerario,-a. **2** (person) intrépido,-a.

foolish ['fuːlɪʃ] **1** adj (silly) tonto,-a: he did something foolish, hizo una tontería. **2** (stupid) estúpido,-a; (unwise) imprudente. **3** (ridiculous) ridículo,-a.

foolishly ['fuːlɪʃlɪ] adv tontamente.

foolishness ['fuːlɪʃnəs] n tontería, estupidez f.

foolproof ['fuːlpruːf] **1** adj (plan, method, idea) infalible. **2** (machine) seguro,-a.

foolscap ['fuːlskæp] n papel m tamaño folio, folio.

foot [fʊt] **1** n ANAT pie m: my left foot hurts, me duele el pie izquierda. **2** (measurement) pie m: the mountain is 1,000 feet high, la montaña tiene 1.000 pies de altura; he's six foot tall, ≈ mide dos metros. – **3** m (bottom) pie m: she sat at the foot of the stairs, estaba sentada al pie de la escalera; the answer is at the foot of the page, la respuesta está al pie de la página. – **4** n (of animal) pata.
● **in bare feet**, descalzo,-a. ‖ **on foot**, a pie. ‖ **to foot the bill**, pagar, pagar la cuenta, correr con los gastos. ‖ **to foot it**, ir a pie, ir andando. ‖ **to be on one's feet**, estar de pie. ‖ **on foot**, a pie. ‖ **to be on one's feet again**, estar recuperado,-a. ‖ **to drag one's feet**, querer echarse atrás, hacerse el remolón,-ona. ‖ **to fall on one's feet / land on one's feet**, caer de pie, tener buena suerte. ‖ **to find one's feet**, acostumbrarse, ha-

bituarse. ‖ **to get off on the wrong foot**, fam empezar con mal pie. ‖ **to get to one's feet**, levantarse, ponerse de pie, ponerse en pie. ‖ **to get a foot in the door**, abrirse una brecha. ‖ **to get cold feet**, entrarle miedo a uno, dar marcha atrás. ‖ **to have feet of clay**, tener pies de barro. ‖ **to have both feet on the ground**, ser realista. ‖ **to have one foot in the grave**, estar con un pie en la tumba. ‖ **to keep one's feet**, mantenerse en pie. ‖ **to put a foot wrong**, equivocarse. ‖ **to put one's feet up**, descansar. ‖ **to put one's foot in it**, meter la pata. ‖ **to put one's foot down**, fam imponerse, ponerse firme. ‖ **to rush sb. off his feet**, hacer ir de culo a algn. ‖ **to set foot, pisar**: when man first set foot on the moon, cuando el hombre pisó por primera vez la luna; I've never set foot in that club, nunca he pisado ese club. ‖ **to stand on one's own two feet**, ser independiente, valerse por sí mismo. ‖ **my foot!**, ¡qué va!, ¡ni hablar!
■ **foot fault**, falta de pie. ‖ **foot pump**, bomba de pie. ‖ **foot soldier**, soldado de infantería.
▲ pl **feet**.

footage ['fʊtɪdʒ] n metraje m.

foot-and-mouth disease [fʊtən'maʊθdɪziːz] n fiebre f aftosa.

football ['fʊtbɔːl] **1** n (game) fútbol m. **2** (ball) balón m. ■ **football ground**, campo de fútbol. ‖ **football match**, partido de fútbol. ‖ **football player**, futbolista mf, jugador,-ra de fútbol. ‖ **football pools**, quinielas fpl.

footballer ['fʊtbɔːləʳ] n futbolista mf, jugador,-ra de fútbol.

footbridge ['fʊtbrɪdʒ] n puente m para peatones.

foothill ['fʊthɪl] n estribaciones fpl.

foothold ['fʊthəʊld] **1** n hueco para apoyar el pie. **2** (in job) posición f segura.
● **to get a foothold / gain a foothold**, afianzarse, introducirse.

footing ['fʊtɪŋ] **1** n equilibrio. **2** (basis) base f, nivel m. **3** (relationship) relación f.
● **to be on an equal footing with sb.**, estar en igualdad de condiciones con algn.

footle ['fuːtl] i perder el tiempo, hacer el tonto.

footlights ['fʊtlaɪts] npl candilejas fpl.

footling ['fuːtlɪŋ] adj trivial.

footloose ['fʊtluːs] adj libre.
● **footloose and fancy-free**, libre y sin compromiso.

footman ['fʊtmən] n lacayo, criado.
▲ pl **footmen** ['fʊtmən].

footmark ['fʊtmɑːk] n huella, pisada.

footnote ['fʊtnəʊt] n nota a pie de página.

footpath ['fʊtpɑːθ] n sendero, camino.

footplate ['fʊtpleɪt] n plataforma.

footprint ['fʊtprɪnt] n huella, pisada.

footslog ['fʊtslɒg] i andar.
▲ pt & pp **footslogged**, ger **footslogging**.

footsore ['fʊtsɔːʳ] adj con los pies doloridos.

footstep ['fʊtstep] n paso, pisada.

footstool ['fʊtstuːl] n taburete m para los pies, banqueta para los pies.

footway ['fʊtweɪ] n acera.

footwear ['fʊtweəʳ] n calzado.

footwork ['fʊtwɜːk] n SP juego de pies, juego de piernas.

foppish ['fɒpɪʃ] adj dated (vain) presumido,-a.

for [fɔːʳ] **1** prep (intended) para: it's a present for you, es un regalo para ti; save some cake for me, guarda un poco de pastel para mí; *there's a phone call for Mr. Smith,* hay una llamada para el Sr. Smith. **2** (*purpose*) para: *what's this for?,* ¿para qué sirve esto?; *I need something for a cough,* necesito algo para la tos; *shall we meet for lunch?,* ¿quedamos para comer? **3** (*destination*) para: *he's left for work,* ha salido para el trabajo; *where do I catch the train for Newcastle?,* ¿dónde se coge el tren para Newcastle?; *passengers for London now boarding,* pasajeros con destino a Londres pueden embarcar; *it's a novel for teenagers,* es una novela para quinceañeros; *flat for rent,* piso para alquilar. **4** (*in order to help, on behalf of*) por: *do it for me,* hazlo por mí; *I'll get that for you if you can't reach,* yo te lo cogeré si no llegas; *I think I speak for everyone,* creo que hablo en nombre de todos; *it's for your own good,* es por tu propio bien. **5** (*because of, on account of*) a causa de: *York is famous for its cathedral,* York es famoso por su catedral; *he dare not speak for fear of waking the baby,* no se atreve a hablar por miedo a despertar al bebé; *I couldn't sleep for the noise,* no pude dormir por el ruido; *if it weren't for him,* si no fuera por él. **6** (*past time*) durante; (*future time*) por; (*specific point in time*) para: *we went for two weeks,* fuimos por dos semanas; *we talked for a while,* hablamos durante un rato; *we're going for a fortnight,* vamos por quince días; *I'd like to go away for a few days,* me gustaría ir fuera unos días; *I'll love you for ever,* te amaré para siempre; *I've booked a table for tomorrow,* he reservado una mesa para mañana; *a meeting has been called for 10.00,* se ha convocado una reunión para las 10.00; *that's all for today,* es todo por hoy; *I've lived here for 5 years,* hace 5 años que vivo aquí, vivo aquí desde hace 5 años; *she hadn't seen him for a year,* hacía un año que no le veía; *it's the first accident here for a long time,* es el primer accidente que ocurre aquí desde hace mucho tiempo. **7** (*distance*): *I walked for five miles,* caminé cinco millas. **8** (*in exchange, as replacement of*) por: *I got it for £500,* lo conseguí por 500 libras; *the record went for $50,* el disco se vendió por 50 dólares; *he exchanged his old car for a new one,* cambió su viejo coche por uno nuevo; *you shouldn't translate word for word,* no deberías traducir palabra por palabra; *the manager substituted Jones for Lee,* el entrenador sustituyó a Jones por Lee. **9** (*in favour of, in support of*) por, a favor de: *this is a campaign for peace,* es una campaña a favor de la paz; *who did you vote for?,* ¿a quién votaste?; *he'd give his life for him,* daría su vida por él; *he fought for his country,* luchó por la patria; *he's played for his country,* ha jugado en la selección nacional; *are you for or against the new laws?,* ¿estás a favor o en contra de las nuevas leyes?; *I'm all for a state lottery,* soy partidario de una lotería estatal. **10** (*despite*) a pesar de, para; (*considering, contrast*) para: *she's very tall for her age,* es muy alta para su edad; *he does it really well for a child,* lo hace muy bien por ser un niño; *he's quite nice for a policeman,* es bastante simpático para ser policía; *I still love him, for all his faults,* lo quiero, a pesar de todos sus defectos. **11** (*as*) de, como, por: *what do they use for fuel?,* ¿qué utilizan de combustible?; *he was left for dead,* lo dieron por muerto. **12** (*in order to obtain*) para: *for further details ...,* para más información ....; *she went to her mother for advice,* acudió a su madre para que le aconsejara; *100 people applied for the job,* 100 personas solicitaron el puesto; *we ran for our lives,* tuvimos que correr para salvarnos; *I only did it for the money,* lo hice solamente por el dinero; *she sent for the doctor,* llamó al médico. **13** (*representing*) por; (*meaning*) de: *she's the MP for Southampton,* es la

diputada por Southampton; *I can't go to the meeting - will you go for me?,* no puedo asistir a la reunión - ¿quieres ir en mi lugar?; *a cheque for 20 pounds,* un talón (por valor) de 20 libras; *B for Barcelona,* B de Barcelona; *what's the Spanish for "pool"?,* ¿cómo se dice "pool" en castellano?; *red for danger,* rojo de peligro. **14** (*as regards, concerning*) por, en cuanto a: *for my part, he can do as he likes,* por mí, que haga lo que quiera; *as for him, who cares?,* en cuanto a él, ¿a quién le importa?; *luckily for us, it didn't rain,* afortunadamente para nosotros, no llovió. **15** (*as part of, as being*) por, para: *I took him for the manager,* lo tomé por el director; *do you know that for a fact?,* ¿lo sabes a ciencia cierta?; *what do you want for dinner?,* ¿qué quieres para comer? **– 16** *conj fml* lit ya que, puesto que. **– 17** *prep* para: *it's easy for you to say that,* para ti es fácil decir eso; *it's impossible for me to come to the wedding,* me es imposible asistir a la boda; *there's no need for you to do that,* no hace falta que hagas eso; *it's time for you to go,* es hora de que te marches; *I bought it for you to wear tonight,* lo compré para que te lo pusieras esta noche; *it's for you to use at work,* es para que lo uses en el trabajo; *that's no reason for you to get so upset,* no es motivo para que te preocupes tanto.

● *as for me,* por mi parte, en cuanto a mí. ‖ *for all I know,* que yo sepa. ‖ *for all that,* a pesar de todo, con todo. ‖ *for good,* para siempre. ‖ *for the first time,* por primera vez. ‖ *for the last time,* por última vez. ‖ *oh for ...!,* ¡ojalá tuviera ...!: *oh for a star to guide my way!,* ¡ojalá tuviera una estrella que me guiara los pasos!‖ *there's nothing for it but ...,* no hay más remedio que ... ‖ *to be for it,* cargársela: *he'll be for it if they find out,* se la va a cargar si se enteran.

forage ['fɒrɪdʒ] **1** *n* (*food*) forraje *m.* **– 2** *i* (*search, hunt*) buscar (*for, -*). **– 3** *t* (*rummage*) hurgar, revolver.

foray ['fɒreɪ] **1** *n* (*attack, raid*) incursión *f,* correría. **2** (*involvement in activity*) incursión *f.* **– 3** *i* asaltar.

forbade [fɔː'beɪd] *pt* → **forbid**.

forbear [fɔː'beə'] *i fml* abstenerse (**from,** de).
▲ *pt* forbore, *pp* forborne.

forbearance [fɔː'beərəns] *n* paciencia, tolerancia.

forbearing [fɔː'beərɪŋ] *adj* paciente, tolerante.

forbid [fɔː'bɪd] **1** *t* (*prohibit*) prohibir: *I forbid you to see my daughter again,* te prohíbo que vuelvas a ver a mi hija; *smoking is forbidden,* (está) prohibido fumar. **2** (*make impossible*) impedir: *decency forbids me to give more details,* la decencia me impide dar más detalles.

● *God forbid / Heaven forbid,* Dios no lo quiera: *Heaven forbid that Mother should find out,* Dios no quiera que se entere mamá.

■ *forbidden fruit,* fruta prohibida. ‖ *forbidden ground,* (*place*) lugar *m* prohibido; (*subject*) tema *m* tabú.

▲ *pt* forbade, *pp* forbidden [fə'bɪdən], *ger* forbidding.

forbidding [fə'bɪdɪŋ] *adj* (*stern*) severo,-a; (*unfriendly*) formidable; (*dangerous*) peligroso,-a.

forbore [fɔː'bɔː'] *pt* → **forbear**.

forborne [fɔː'bɔːn] *pp* → **forbear**.

force [fɔːs] **1** *n* (*strength, power, violence*) fuerza. **2** PHYS fuerza. **3** MIL cuerpo. **– 4** *t* (*oblige*) forzar, obligar: *he was forced to resign,* lo obligaron a dimitir; *they forced me to tell them,* me obligaron a decírselo. **5** (*break open*) forzar. **6** (*produce unnaturally*) forzar. **7** (*plants*) hacer madurar temprano.

◆ *to force back* **1** *t sep* hacer retroceder. **2** (*emotion*) contener. ‖ *to force down* **1** *t sep* (*food*) tragar por fuerza. **2** (*aircraft*) hacer aterrizar. ‖ *to force on* *t sep* imponer.

● **by force,** por la fuerza, a la fuerza. ‖ **to come into force,** entrar en vigor. ‖ **from force of habit / by force of habit,** por la fuerza de costumbre. ‖ **in force,** (*people*) en gran número; (*law, rule*) en vigor, vigente: *the police arrived in force,* llegó un gran contingente de policías; *this law is still in force,* esta ley sigue vigente. ‖ **to force sb.'s hand,** forzar la mano de algn. ‖ **to force the pace,** apretar el paso. ‖ **to force os. to do sth.,** hacer un esfuerzo por hacer algo, obligarse a hacer algo. ‖ **to force sb. into doing sth.,** obligar a algn. a hacer algo.

forced [fɔːst] **1** *adj* (*smile, laugh*) forzado,-a. **2** (*landing*) forzoso,-a.

■ **forced labour,** trabajos *mpl* forzados. ‖ **forced march,** marcha forzada.

force-feed ['fɔːsfiːd] *t* alimentar a la fuerza.
▲ *pt & pp force-fed.*

forceful ['fɔːsfʊl] *adj* (*person, manner*) enérgico,-a; (*speech*) contundente; (*argument*) convincente.

forcefully ['fɔːsfʊlɪ] *adv* (*act*) enérgicamente; (*speak*) convincentemente.

forceps ['fɔːseps] *npl* fórceps *m inv.*

forcible ['fɔːsəbəl] **1** *adj* (*violent*) forzoso,-a. **2** (*convincing*) convincente.

■ **forcible entry,** JUR allanamiento de morada.

forcibly ['fɔːsəblɪ] **1** *adv* (*violently*) a la fuerza. **2** convincentemente.

ford [fɔːd] **1** *n* vado. – **2** *t* vadear.

fore¹ [fɔːˈ] *adj* (*on plane*) anterior, delantero,-a; (*on ship*) de proa.

● **to come to the fore,** saltar a primera plana, empezar a destacar. ‖ **fore and aft,** de popa a proa.

fore² [fɔːˈ] *interj* (*golf*) ¡atención!

forearm ['fɔːrɑːm] *n* antebrazo.

forebear [fɔːˈbeəˈ] *n* antepasado,-a.

forebode [fɔːˈbəʊd] *t* presagiar, anunciar.

foreboding [fɔːˈbəʊdɪŋ] *n* presentimiento.

forecast ['fɔːkɑːst] **1** *n* pronóstico, previsión *f*. – **2** *t* pronosticar.
▲ *pt & pp forecast o forecasted* ['fɔːkɑːstɪd].

forecourt ['fɔːkɔːt] *n* (*of garage*) área de servicio.

forefathers ['fɔːfɑːðəz] *npl* antepasados *mpl*.

forefinger ['fɔːfɪŋɡəˈ] *n* (dedo) índice *m*.

forefront ['fɔːfrʌnt] *n* vanguardia.

forego¹ [fɔːˈɡəʊ] *t* (*precede*) preceder.
▲ *pt forewent, pp foregone, ger foregoing.*

forego² [fɔːˈɡəʊ] *t* → **forgo.**

foregoing [fɔːˈɡəʊɪŋ] *adj* precedente.

foregone ['fɔːɡɒn] **1** *pp* → **forego.** – **2** *adj* inevitable.

■ **foregone conclusion,** resultado inevitable.

foreground ['fɔːɡraʊnd] *n* primer plano, primer término.

forehand ['fɔːhænd] *n* SP golpe *m* de derecho.

forehead ['fɒrɪd, 'fɔːhed] *n* frente *f*.

foreign ['fɒrɪn] **1** *adj* (*from abroad*) extranjero,-a. **2** (*dealing with other countries*) exterior. **3** (*strange*) ajeno,-a, extraño,-a.

■ **foreign affairs,** asuntos *mpl* exteriores. ‖ **foreign aid,** ayuda exterior. ‖ **foreign body,** cuerpo extraño. ‖ **foreign currency,** divisas *fpl*. ‖ **foreign correspondent,** corresponsal *mf* extranjero,-a. ‖ **foreign exchange,** divisas *fpl*. ‖ **foreign language,** lengua extranjera, idioma *m* extranjero. ‖ **foreign legion,** legión *f* extranjera. ‖ **Foreign Minister,** Ministro,-a de Asuntos Exteriores. ‖ **Foreign Ministry,** Ministerio de Asuntos Exteriores. ‖ **Foreign Office,** GB Ministerio de Asuntos Exteriores. ‖ **foreign policy,** política exterior.

‖ **Foreign Secretary,** GB Ministro,-a de Asuntos Exteriores. ‖ **foreign trade,** comercio exterior.

foreigner ['fɒrɪnəˈ] *n* extranjero,-a.

foreleg ['fɔːleg] *n* pata delantera.

foreman ['fɔːmən] **1** *n* (*of workers*) capataz *m*. **2** (*of jury*) presidente *m* del jurado.
▲ *pl foremen* ['fɔːmən].

foremost ['fɔːməʊst] *adj* principal.

● **first and foremost,** ante todo.

forename ['fɔːneɪm] *n* nombre *m* (de pila).

forensic [fəˈrensɪk] *adj* forense.

forerunner ['fɔːrʌnəˈ] *n* precursor,-ra.

foresee [fɔːˈsiː] *t* prever.
▲ *pt foresaw* [fɔːˈsɔː], pp *foreseen* [fɔːˈsiːn], ger *foreseeing.*

foreseeable [fɔːˈsiːəbəl] *adj* previsible.

● **in the foreseeable future,** en un futuro inmediato.

foresight ['fɔːsaɪt] *n* previsión *f.*

foreskin ['fɔːskɪn] *n* prepucio.

forest ['fɒrɪst] **1** *n* (*gen*) bosque *m*. **2** (*jungle*) selva. – **3** *adj* forestal.

■ **forest fire,** incendio forestal.

forestall [fɔːˈstɔːl] **1** *t* (*preempt*) anticiparse a. **2** (*prevent*) prevenir.

forestry ['fɒrɪstrɪ] *n* silvicultura, selvicultura.

foretaste ['fɔːteɪst] *n* anticipo, muestra.

foretell [fɔːˈtel] *t* predecir, pronosticar.
▲ *pt & pp foretold.*

forethought ['fɔːθɔːt] **1** *n* previsión *f*. **2** JUR premeditación *f.*

foretold [fɔːˈtəʊld] *pt & pp* → **foretell.**

forever [fəˈrevəˈ] **1** *adv* (*all the time*) siempre. **2** (*for good*) para siempre.

forewarn [fɔːˈwɔːn] *t* prevenir.

● **forewarned is forearmed,** hombre prevenido vale por dos.

forewent [fɔːˈwent] *pp* → **forego.**

foreword ['fɔːwɜːd] *n* prólogo.

forfeit ['fɔːfɪt] **1** *n* (*penalty*) pena, multa. **2** (*in games*) prenda. – **3** *t* perder, perder (el derecho de): *you've forfeited your deposit,* has perdido tu depósito.

● **to pay a forfeit,** pagar una prenda.

forgave [fəˈɡeɪv] *pt* → **forgive.**

forge¹ [fɔːdʒ] *i* avanzar, adelantar(se).

◆ **to forge ahead** *i* (*go ahead*) seguir adelante; (*make good progress*) hacer grandes progresos.

forge² [fɔːdʒ] **1** *n* (*apparatus*) fragua. **2** (*smithy*) forja. – **3** *t* (*counterfeit*) falsificar. **4** (*metal*) forjar, fraguar. **5** *fig* (*links etc*) forjar, formar.

forgery ['fɔːdʒərɪ] *n* falsificación *f.*
▲ *pl forgeries.*

forget [fəˈɡet] **1** *t* (*gen*) olvidar, olvidarse de: *I'm sorry but I've forgotten your name,* lo siento pero he olvidado tu nombre; *I'll never forget the day we met,* nunca olvidaré el día en que nos conocimos. **2** (*leave behind*) dejar: *I forgot my bag,* he dejado el bolso. – **3** *i* olvidarse de, no recordar, descuidar: *don't forget to water the plants,* no te olvides de regar las plantas; *he forgot to give her the key,* se olvidó de darle la llave; *I forget,* no me acuerdo; *I'd forgotten,* se me había olvidado; *I forgot all about it,* se me olvidó por completo.

● **forget it!,** ¡olvídalo!, ¡déjalo! ‖ **and don't you forget it!,** ¡y que no se te olvide! ‖ **not forgetting ...,** sin olvidar ... ‖ **to forget os.,** *fig* perder el control.
▲ *pt forgot, pp forgotten, ger forgetting.*

forgetful [fəˈɡetfʊl] *adj* despistado,-a, olvidadizo,-a.

forgetfulness [fə'getfəlnəs] *n* (*lack of memory*) falta de memoria; (*absentmindedness*) despiste *m*.

forget-me-not [fə'getmɪnɒt] *n* BOT nomeolvides *f*.

forgivable [fə'gɪvəbəl] *adj* perdonable.

forgive [fə'gɪv] **1** *t* (*pardon*) perdonar: *I'll never forgive you*, no te perdonaré nunca; *she forgave him for forgetting her birthday*, lo perdonó por haberse olvidado de su cumpleaños; *he can't forgive himself for what he did*, no se puede perdonar por lo que hizo; *one could be forgiven for thinking that ...*, se le puede perdonar pensar que ... **2** (*let off debt*) perdonar: *he forgave me the debt*, me perdonó la deuda.
● **to forgive and forget**, perdonar y olvidar.
▲ *pt* **forgave**, *pp* **forgiven** [fə'gɪvən].

forgiveness [fə'gɪvnəs] *n* perdón *m*.

forgo [fɔː'gəʊ] *t* renunciar a, sacrificar.
▲ *pt* **forwent**, *pp* **forgone**, *ger* **forgoing**.

forgone [fɔː'gɒn] *pp* → **forgo**.

forgot [fə'gɒt] *pt* → **forget**.

forgotten [fə'gɒtən] *pp* → **forget**.

fork [fɔːk] **1** *n* (*for eating*) tenedor *m*. **2** AGR horca, horquilla. **3** (*in road, river etc*) bifurcación *f*. – **4** *i* (*road, river etc*) bifurcarse. **5** (*person, car*) torcer, girar: *fork right at the junction*, tuerce a la derecha en el próximo cruce. – **6 forks**, *npl* (*on bike*) horquilla.
◆ **to fork out 1** *t sep fam* (*money*) soltar, aflojar. – **2** *i fam* desembolsar, soltar dinero: *I had to fork out for her driving lessons*, tuve que soltar dinero para sus clases de conducir.
■ **tuning fork**, diapasón *m*.

forked [fɔːkt] **1** *adj* (*road*) bifurcado,-a. **2** (*tongue*) bífido,-a.
■ **forked lightning**, relámpago en zigzag.

fork-lift truck [fɔːklɪft'trʌk] *n* carretilla elevadora.

forlorn [fə'lɔːn] **1** *adj* (*forsaken*) abandonado,-a. **2** (*desolate*) triste. **3** (*hopeless*) desesperado,-a.
■ **forlorn hope**, esperanza inútil, esperanza vana.

form [fɔːm] **1** *n* (*shape, mode etc*) forma *f*: *it's a cake in the form of a train*, es un pastel en forma de tren. **2** (*kind*) clase *f*, tipo: *she hates exercise in any form*, odia cualquier tipo de ejercicio. **3** (*formality*) formas *fpl*; (*behaviour*) educación *f*: *what is the form?*, ¿qué hay que hacer? **4** (*physical condition*) forma: *she's in excellent form*, está en muy buena forma. **5** (*mood, spirit*) humor *m*: *your father is in fine form tonight*, tu padre está de muy buen humor esta noche. **6** (*document*) formulario, impreso, hoja: *sign this form, please*, firme esta hoja, por favor. **7** EDUC (*age group*) curso; (*class*) clase *f*. **8** (*bench*) banco. **9** GB *sl* (*criminal record*) antecedentes *mpl* penales. – **10** *t* (*mould*) moldear, modelar; (*make*) hacer, formar; (*character*) formar: *the child formed the clay into a bowl*, el niño moldeó el barro en un bol; *try to form complete sentences*, intenta hacer frases completas; *the children formed themselves into groups*, los niños formaron grupos; *early experiences form a person's character*, las primeras experiencias forman el carácter de una persona. **11** (*set up*) formar: *the committee was formed in 1980*, el comité se formó en 1980; *he was asked to form a government*, le pidieron que formara un gobierno. **12** (*be, constitute*) formar, constituir: *socialists formed the bulk of the group*, los socialistas formaban la mayor parte del grupo; *interviews and letters form the bulk of the book*, la mayor parte del libro la forman entrevistas y cartas. **13** *fig* (*idea*) hacerse; (*impression, opinion*) formarse; (*relationship*) hacer; (*habit*) adquirir; (*plan*) concebir: *I formed the wrong impression of you*, me formé una mala impresión de ti. – **14** *i* formarse: *a long queue*

had formed, una larga cola se había formado; *a crowd formed*, se formó una multitud.
● **as a matter of form**, por educación, por cortesía. ‖ **in any shape or form**, de cualquier forma. ‖ **to be bad form**, ser de mala educación. ‖ **to be on form**, estar en forma. ‖ **to be off form**, estar en baja forma. ‖ **to take form**, tomar forma.

formal ['fɔːməl] **1** *adj* (*official*) formal, oficial: *there will have to be a formal inquiry*, tendrá que realizarse una investigación oficial; *the minister made a formal denial*, el ministro hizo una renuncia oficial; *he has had no formal education as such*, no ha recibido una educación convencional. **2** (*correct*) formal; (*traditional*) tradicional: *a formal letter*, una carta formal; *the wedding was extremely formal*, la boda fue muy tradicional. **3** (*dress, dinner*) de etiqueta. **4** (*visit*) de cumplido. **5** (*person, language*) ceremonioso,-a, formalista: *she has a very formal manner*, es muy ceremoniosa. **6** (*ordered*) formal, ordenado,-a.

formality [fɔː'mælɪtɪ] *n* (*correctness*) formalidad *f*; (*convention*) ceremonia: *it was just a formality*, fue una mera formalidad.
▲ *pl* **formalities**.

formalize ['fɔːməlaɪz] **1** *t* (*make offical*) formalizar. **2** (*make formal*) dar carácter formal a. **3** (*give form to*) dar forma a.

formally ['fɔːməlɪ] **1** *adv* (*correctly*) formalmente. **2** (*officially*) oficialmente.

format ['fɔːmæt] **1** *n* formato. – **2** *t* COMPUT formatear.
▲ (*verbo*) *pt* & *pp* **formatted**, *ger* **formatting**.

formation [fɔː'meɪʃən] **1** *n* (*gen*) formación *f*. **2** (*establishment*) creación *f*.

formative ['fɔːmətɪv] *adj* formativo,-a.

former ['fɔːmə'] **1** *adj* (*earlier*) antiguo,-a; (*person*) ex: *this museum was a former palace*, este museo es un antiguo palacio; *the former champion*, el ex campeón; *the former president*, el ex presidente. **2** (*of two*) primero,-a: *the former suggestion seems better*, la primera sugerencia parece mejor. – **3** **the former**, *pron* aquél, aquélla.
● **in former times**, en otros tiempos, antiguamente.

formerly ['fɔːməlɪ] *adv* (*previously*) antiguamente, antes.

Formica [fɔː'maɪkə] *n* formica.
▲ Es marca registrada.

formidable ['fɔːmɪdəbəl] **1** *adj* (*impressive*) formidable. **2** (*daunting*) temible, imponente. **3** (*difficult to overcome*) enorme.

Formosa [fɔː'məʊzə] *n* Formosa.

formula ['fɔːmjələ] *n* fórmula.
■ **formula one**, fórmula uno.
▲ *pl* **formulas** *o* **formulae** ['fɔːmjuliː].

formulate ['fɔːmjəleɪt] *t* formular.

formulation [fɔːmjə'leɪʃən] *n* formulación *f*.

fornicate ['fɔːnɪkeɪt] *i fml* fornicar.

fornication [fɔːnɪ'keɪʃən] *n fml* fornicación *f*.

forsake [fə'seɪk] **1** *t fml* (*abandon*) abandonar. **2** (*give up*) renunciar a.
▲ *pt* **forsook** [fə'sʊk], *pp* **forsaken** [fə'seɪkən].

forswear [fɔː'sweə'] *t fml* renunciar a, abjurar de.
▲ *pt* **forswore** [fɔː'swɔː'], *pp* **forsworn** [fɔː'swɔːn].

fort [fɔːt] *n* fuerte *m*.
● **to hold the fort**, quedarse vigilando, hacerse cargo.

forte[1] ['fɔːteɪ] *n* fuerte *m*: *English was never my forte*, el inglés no ha sido nunca mi fuerte.

forte[2] ['fɔːteɪ] **1** *adj* MUS forte. – **2** *adv* forte.

forth [fɔːθ] *adv* (*onwards*) en adelante: *from that day forth*, de ese día en adelante, a partir de aquel día.

● **and so forth,** y cosas así. ‖ **and so on and so forth,** y así sucesivamente. ‖ **to go back and forth,** ir de acá para allá.

forthcoming [fɔːθ'kʌmɪŋ] **1** *adj fml* (*happening in near future*) próximo,-a: *the forthcoming elections,* las próximas elecciones; *his forthcoming book,* su próximo libro. **2** (*available*) disponible. **3** (*communicative*) comunicativo,-a, dispuesto,-a a hablar.

forthright ['fɔːθraɪt] **1** *adj* (*person*) franco,-a. **2** (*speech, action etc*) directo,-a.

forthwith [fɔːθ'wɪθ] *adv fml* inmediatamente.

forties ['fɔːtɪz] the forties, *npl* los años *mpl* cuarenta, los cuarenta *mpl*.

● **to be in one's forties,** tener entre cuarenta y cincuenta años, tener cuarenta y tantos años.

▲ *Véase también* **sixties**.

fortieth ['fɔːtɪəθ] **1** *adj* cuadragésimo,-a. – **2** *adv* en cuadragésimo lugar. – **3** *n* (*fraction*) cuadragésimo; (*one part*) cuadragésima parte *f*.

▲ *Véase también* **sixtieth**.

fortification [fɔːtɪfɪ'keɪʃən] *n* fortificación *f*.

fortify ['fɔːtɪfaɪ] **1** *t* MIL fortificar. **2** (*strengthen*) fortalecer. **3** (*wine*) fortificar, encabezar; (*food*) enriquecer.

▲ *pt & pp* **fortified,** *ger* **fortifying**.

fortitude ['fɔːtɪtjuːd] *n* fortaleza, fuerza.

fortnight ['fɔːtnaɪt] *n* GB quincena, quince días *mpl*: *we're going for a fortnight,* nos vamos por quince días; *he comes for dinner once a fortnight,* viene a comer cada quince días; *a fortnight today,* de hoy en quince.

fortnightly ['fɔːtnaɪtlɪ] **1** *adj* quincenal: *a fortnightly visit,* una visita quincenal. – **2** *adv* cada quince días: *I go home fortnightly,* voy a casa cada quince días.

fortress ['fɔːtrəs] *n* fortaleza.

fortuitous [fɔː'tjuːɪtəs] **1** *adj* (*lucky*) fortuito,-a, casual. **2** (*accidental*) accidental.

fortunate ['fɔːtʃənət] *adj* afortunado,-a: *I was fortunate to ...,* tuve la suerte de ...; *it was fortunate for him that ... ...,* afortunadamente para él ...; *those less fortunate than ourselves,* aquellos menos afortunados que nosotros.

fortunately ['fɔːtʃənətlɪ] *adv* afortunadamente, por suerte.

fortune ['fɔːtʃən] **1** *n* (*fate*) fortuna; (*luck*) suerte *f*: *I had the good fortune to find a friend,* tuve la suerte de encontrar un amigo; *have you ever had your fortune told?,* ¿te han dicho la buenaventura alguna vez? **2** (*money*) fortuna: *he inherited a fortune,* heredó una fortuna; *that painting's worth a fortune,* aquel cuadro vale un dineral. – **3** fortunes, *npl* (*luck*) suerte *f*; (*ups and downs*) vicisitudes *fpl*: *Richard's fortunes were looking up,* la suerte de Richard iba mejorando; *we follow the hero's fortunes through a series of adventures,* seguimos las vicisitudes del protagonista a través de una serie de aventuras.

■ **fortune cookie,** galleta de la buenaventura. ‖ **fortunes of war,** peripecias *fpl* de la guerra.

fortune-hunter ['fɔːtʃənhʌntəʳ] *n* (*gen*) aventurero,-a; (*through marriage*) cazadotes *mf*.

fortune-teller ['fɔːtʃəntələʳ] *n* adivino,-a.

forty ['fɔːtɪ] **1** *adj* cuarenta. – **2** *n* cuarenta *m*.

▲ *Véase también* **sixty**.

forum ['fɔːrəm] *n* foro.

forward ['fɔːwəd] **1** *adv* (*gen*) hacia adelante: *to go forward,* ir hacia adelante; *it's a step forward,* es un paso (hacia) adelante. **2** (*time*) en adelante: *from this day forward,* de hoy en adelante. – **3** *adj* (*position*) delantero,-a, frontal; (*movement*) hacia delante: *a forward step,* un paso hacia delante. **4** (*future*) a largo plazo: *forward*

planning, planificación a largo plazo. **5** (*advanced*) adelantado,-a, precoz: *a forward child,* un niño precoz. **6** (*too bold, too eager*) atrevido,-a, descarado,-a, fresco,-a. – **7** *n* SP delantero,-a. – **8** *t* (*send on to new address*) remitir; (*send goods*) enviar, expedir. **9** *fml* (*further, advance*) adelantar, fomentar.

● **to bring sth. forward,** (*in time*) adelantar algo. ‖ **to put the clock forward,** adelantar el reloj.

■ **forward roll,** SP voltereta (hacia delante).

▲ En acepción 1 también **forwards**.

forwarding ['fɔːwədɪŋ] *n* transporte *m* de mercancías.

■ **forwarding address,** nueva dirección *f*. ‖ **forwarding agent,** agente *mf* transporte.

forward-looking ['fɔːwədlʊkɪŋ] *adj* previsor,-ra.

forwards ['fɔːwədz] *adv* → **forward**.

forwent [fɔː'went] *pt* → **forgo**.

fossil ['fɒsəl] **1** *n* fósil *m*. – **2** *adj* fósil.

■ **fossil fuel,** combustible *m* fósil.

fossilize ['fɒsəlaɪz] **1** *t* fosilizar. – **2** *i* fosilizarse.

foster ['fɒstəʳ] **1** *t* (*child*) acoger temporalmente. **2** (*encourage*) fomentar, promover. – **3** *adj* adoptivo,-a.

■ **foster child,** hijo,-a adoptivo,-a. ‖ **foster father,** padre *m* adoptivo. ‖ **foster home,** hogar *m* adoptivo. ‖ **foster mother,** madre *f* adoptiva.

fought [fɔːt] *pt & pp* → **fight**.

foul [faʊl] **1** *adj* (*dirty, disgusting*) asqueroso,-a; (*smell*) fétido,-a. **2** (*unpleasant, very bad*) horrible; (*weather*) feo,-a, horrible, de perros; (*temper*) mal, de perros. **3** (*language*) grosero,-a, obsceno,-a. **4** SP (*unfair*) sucio,-a, tramposo,-a. **5** *fml* (*evil*) vil, atroz. **6** (*chimney, pipe etc*) atascado,-a. – **7** *n* SP falta (**on,** contra). – **8** *t* (*dirty*) ensuciar; (*pollute*) contaminar. **9** (*snag*) enredar. **10** SP cometer una falta contra. – **11** *i* enredarse en.

◆ **to foul up** *t sep fam* estropear, fastidiar.

● **to fall foul of,** (*gen*) tener problemas con; (*person*) ganarse la enemistad de. ‖ **to foul one's own nest,** tirar piedras contra su propio tejado.

■ **foul play,** SP juego sucio; JUR hecho delictivo.

foul-mouthed [faʊl'maʊðd] *adj* malhablado,-a.

foul-up ['faʊlʌp] *n* metedura de pata, cagada.

found[1] [faʊnd] *t* (*metals*) fundir.

found[2] [faʊnd] **1** *t* (*establish*) fundar: *this company was founded in 1894,* esta empresa fue fundada en 1894. **2** (*base*) basar (**on,** en): *a film founded on fact,* una película basada en un hecho real.

found[3] [faʊnd] *pt & pp* → **find**.

foundation [faʊn'deɪʃən] **1** *n* (*act, organization*) fundación *f*. **2** (*basis*) fundamento, base *f*. **3** (*make-up*) base *f*. – **4** foundations, *npl* cimientos *mpl*.

■ **foundation course,** curso de introducción. ‖ **foundation stone,** primera piedra.

founder[1] ['faʊndəʳ] **1** *i* (*plan etc*) irse a pique, fracasar, malograrse. **2** (*ship*) hundirse. **3** (*horse*) dar un traspié.

founder[2] ['faʊndəʳ] *n* (*person*) fundador,-ra.

■ **founder member,** miembro fundador,-ra.

founding father ['faʊndɪŋ'faːðəʳ] *n* fundador *m*.

■ **the Founding Fathers,** los Padres *mpl* de la Constitución Americana.

foundry ['faʊndrɪ] *n* fundición *f*.

▲ *pl* **foundries**.

fountain ['faʊntən] **1** *n* fuente *f*. **2** (*jet*) surtidor *m*, chorro. **3** (*source, origin*) fuente *f*.

■ **fountain pen,** pluma estilográfica.

four [fɔːʳ] **1** *adj* cuatro. – **2** *n* cuatro *m*.

● **on all fours,** a gatas.

▲ *Véase también* **six**.

four-eyes ['fɔːraɪz] n cuatrojos mf inv.
fourfold ['fɔːfəʊld] 1 adj cuádruple. – 2 adv cuatro veces.
four-legged [fɔːr'legɪd] adj de cuatro patas.
four-letter word ['fɔːletə'wɜːd] n euph taco.
four-poster bed ['fɔːpəʊstə'bed] n cama con dosel.
foursome ['fɔːsəm] n grupo de cuatro personas.
four-square ['fɔːskweəʳ] adj cuadrado,-a.
fourteen [fɔː'tiːn] 1 adj catorce. – 2 n catorce m.
▲ Véase también six.
fourteenth [fɔː'tiːnθ] 1 adj decimocuarto,-a. – 2 adv en decimocuarto lugar. – 3 n (in series) decimocuarto,-a. 4 (fraction) decimocuarto; (one part) decimocuarta parte f.
▲ Véase también sixth.
fourth [fɔːθ] 1 adj cuarto,-a. – 2 adv cuarto, en cuarto lugar. – 3 n (in series) cuarto,-a. 4 (fraction) cuarto; (one part) cuarta parte f.
▲ Véase también sixth.
fourth-former ['fɔːθfɔːməʳ] n GB alumno,-a del cuarto curso.
four-wheel drive [fɔːwiːl'draɪv] n tracción f integral.
fowl [faʊl] n ave f de corral.
▲ pl fowl.
fox [fɒks] 1 n (animal) zorro,-a. 2 (person) zorro,-a. – 3 t fam (trick) engañar. 4 (confuse) dejar perplejo,-a, confundir, despistar.
■ fox hunt, caza de zorras. ‖ fox terrier, fox m terrier.
foxglove ['fɒksglʌv] n dedalera, digital f.
foxhound ['fɒkʃaʊnd] n perro raposero.
fox-hunting ['fɒkshʌntɪŋ] n caza del zorro.
foxtrot ['fɒkstrɒt] n foxtrot m.
foxy ['fɒksɪ] 1 adj fam astuto,-a. 2 US sl (sexy) sexy.
▲ comp foxier, superl foxiest.
foyer ['fɔɪeɪ, 'fɔɪəʳ] n vestíbulo.
Fr¹ ['fɑːðəʳ] abbr REL (Father) Padre m; (abbreviation) P., Pe.
Fr² [frentʃ] abbr (French) francés,-esa; (abbreviation) fr.
fracas ['fræka:] n reyerta.
fraction ['frækʃən] 1 n (division) fracción f. 2 (small part, bit) poquito.
fractional ['frækʃənəl] 1 adj (in fractions) fraccionario,-a. 2 (very small) muy pequeño,-a, ínfimo,-a.
fractionally ['frækʃənəlɪ] adv mínimamente, ligeramente.
fractious ['frækʃəs] adj irritable, malhumorado,-a.
fracture ['fræktʃəʳ] 1 n fractura. – 2 t fracturar: she fractured her hip, se fracturó la cadera. – 3 i fracturarse.
fragile ['frædʒaɪl] 1 adj frágil. 2 fig (health) delicado,-a.
fragility [frə'dʒɪlɪtɪ] n fragilidad f.
fragment ['frægmənt] 1 n fragmento. – 2 i fragmentarse.
▲ (verbo) [fræg'ment].
fragmentary ['frægməntərɪ, fræg'mentərɪ] adj fragmentario,-a.
fragmentation [frægmən'teɪʃən] n fragmentación f.
fragrance ['freɪgrəns] n fragancia.
fragrant ['freɪgrənt] adj fragante.
frail [freɪl] 1 adj frágil, delicado,-a. 2 (morally weak) débil.
frailty ['freɪltɪ] n fragilidad f, debilidad f, delicadeza.
■ human frailties, flaquezas fpl humanas.
▲ pl frailties.
frame [freɪm] 1 n (of building, machine, tent) armazón f. 2 (of bed) armadura. 3 (of bicycle) cuadro. 4 (of spectacles) montura. 5 (of human, animal - body) cuerpo; (- build) constitución f. 6 (of window, door, picture etc) marco. 7 (order, system) estructura, sistema m, marco. 8 CINEM fotograma m. 9 (of comic) viñeta. 10 (in billiards - triangle)

triángulo; (- round) jugada. – 11 t (picture) enmarcar. 12 (door) encuadrar. 13 (face, scene) enmarcar, encuadrar. 14 fam (set up) incriminar, culpar. 15 fml (question, proposal) formular; (plan) elaborar.
■ frame of mind, estado de ánimo. ‖ frame of reference, marco de referencia.
frame-up ['freɪmʌp] n fam trampa.
framework ['freɪmwɜːk] 1 n armazón f. 2 fig estructura, sistema m, marco.
franc [fræŋk] n franco.
France [frɑːns] n Francia.
franchise ['fræntʃaɪz] 1 n COMM concesión f, franquicia. 2 (vote) derecho de voto.
frank [fræŋk] 1 adj franco,-a. – 2 t franquear.
Frank [fræŋk] n (person) franco,-a.
Frankfurt ['fræŋkfɜːt] n Francfort.
frankfurter ['fræŋkfɜːtəʳ] n salchicha de Frankfurt.
frankincense ['fræŋkɪnsens] n incienso.
frankly ['fræŋklɪ] adv francamente.
frankness ['fræŋknəs] n franqueza.
frantic ['fræntɪk] 1 adj (hectic) frenético,-a: it's been a frantic week, ha sido una semana de locos. 2 (anxious) desesperado,-a.
● to be frantic with worry, estar preocupadísimo,-a.
frantically ['fræntɪklɪ] adv desesperadamente, como un,-a loco,-a: he rushed around frantically, corría de lado a otro como un loco.
fraternal [frə'tɜːnəl] adj fraternal.
fraternity [frə'tɜːnɪtɪ] 1 n (brotherhood) fraternidad f. 2 (society) asociación f. 3 REL hermandad f, cofradía. 4 US (university) club m de estudiantes.
▲ pl fraternities.
fraternize ['frætənaɪz] i fraternizar.
fratricide ['frætrɪsaɪd] 1 n (crime) fratricidio. 2 (person) fratricida mf.
fraud [frɔːd] 1 n (act) fraude m. 2 (person) impostor,-ra, farsante mf.
fraudulent ['frɔːdjələnt] adj fraudulento,-a.
fraught [frɔːt] 1 adj (filled, charged) lleno,-a (with, de), cargado,-a (with, de): a situation fraught with danger, una situación llena de peligro. 2 fam (worried) nervioso,-a, alterado,-a, tenso,-a.
fray¹ [freɪ] 1 i (cloth) deshilacharse, raerse. 2 (tempers, nerves, etc) crisparse.
fray² [freɪ] n contienda, lucha.
● to enter the fray, entrar en liza. ‖ to return to the fray, volver al ataque.
frazzle ['fræzəl] n agotamiento.
● to be worn to a frazzle, quedarse reventado,-a, quedarse hecho,-a polvo. ‖ to be burnt to a frazzle, quedar carbonizado,-a, quedar achicharrado,-a.
FRCS ['ef'ɑː'siː'es] abbr GB (Fellow of the Royal College of Surgeons) miembro del colegio oficial de cirujanos.
freak [friːk] 1 n (monster) monstruo; (strange person) bicho raro. 2 (strange event) anomalía. 3 fam (fan) fanático,-a: he's a Rolling Stones freak, es un fanático de los Rolling Stones. 4 (eccentric) estrafalario,-a. – 5 adj (unusual) insólito,-a, extraño,-a, anormal; (unexpected) inesperado,-a, imprevisto,-a.
◆ to freak out 1 t sep flipar, alucinar. – 2 i fliparse, alucinar.
freakish ['friːkɪʃ] adj insólito,-a, extraño,-a, anormal.
freckle ['frekəl] n peca.
freckled ['frekəld] adj pecoso,-a.
free [friː] 1 adj (gen) libre: it's a free country, isn't it?, un país libre, ¿verdad?; you're free to do what you like,

eres libre de hacer lo que quieras. **2** (*without cost*) gratuito,-a, gratis; (*exempt*) libre (**from**, de): *help yourself to tea and coffee - it's free,* sírvete té o café - es gratis. **3** (*not occupied*) libre: *is that seat free?,* ¿está libre esa silla?; *do you know when the hall is free?,* ¿sabes cuando la sala está libre? **4** (*not busy*) libre: *she'll be free after 4.00pm,* estará libre después de las 4.00; *I don't have much free time,* no tengo mucho tiempo libre; *are you free for dinner?,* ¿estás libre para comer? **5** (*translations*) libre. **6** (*in chemistry*) libre. **– 7** *adv* (*gratis*) gratis: *children travel free,* los niños viajan gratis. **8** (*loose*) suelto,-a: *the screws have worked themselves free,* los tornillos se han aflojado. **9** (*in free manner*) libremente, con toda libertad: *animals in the wild can roam free,* los animales salvajes pueden vagar libremente. **– 10** *t* (*liberate, release - person*) poner en libertad, liberar; (*- animal*) soltar: *the prisoner was freed,* el prisionero fue puesto en libertad. **11** (*rid*) deshacerse (**of/from**, de), librarse (**of/from**, de). **12** (*loosen, untie*) soltar, desatar. **13** (*exempt*) eximir (**from**, de).
● **feel free!,** ¡tú mismo,-a! ‖ **for free,** gratis. ‖ **free and easy,** despreocupado,-a. ‖ **free of charge,** gratuito,-a, gratis. ‖ **free of tax,** libre de impuestos. ‖ **free on board,** franco a bordo. ‖ **to be free from / be free of,** estar libre de, quedar libre de: *I was free from all my responsibilities,* quedé libre de todas mis responsabilidades. ‖ **to be free with,** repartir generosamente, ser generoso,-a con: *he's very free with his money,* es muy generoso con su dinero. ‖ **to have a free hand in sth.,** tener carta blanca en algo. ‖ **to run free,** andar suelto,-a. ‖ **to set sb. free,** liberar a algn., poner en libertad a algn.
■ **free admission,** entrada libre. ‖ **free agent,** persona libre de hacer lo que quiera. ‖ **free enterprise,** libre empresa. ‖ **free fall,** caída libre. ‖ **free gift,** regalo. ‖ **free house,** *pub independiente que sirve varias marcas diferentes de cerveza.* ‖ **free kick,** saque *m* de falta. ‖ **free love,** amor *m* libre. ‖ **free market economy,** economía libre de mercado. ‖ **free port,** puerto franco. ‖ **free speech,** libertad *f* de expresión. ‖ **free ticket,** invitación *f.* ‖ **free trade,** libre cambio. ‖ **free verse,** verso libre. ‖ **free vote,** voto libre. ‖ **free will,** libre albedrío. ‖ **Free World,** Mundo Libre.
freebie ['friːbɪ] *n fam* regalo.
freedom ['friːdəm] *n* libertad *f.*
■ **freedom fighter,** luchador,-ra por la libertad.
free-for-all ['friːfərɔːl] *n fam* pelea, batalla campal.
freehand ['friːhænd] *adj* a mano alzada.
free-handed ['friːhændɪd] *adj* (*generous*) generoso,-a, liberal.
freehold ['friːhəʊld] *n* JUR derecho de dominio absoluto.
freeholder ['friːhəʊldə'] *n* propietario,-a absoluto,-a.
▲ *Véase también* leaseholder.
freelance ['friːlɑːns] **1** *adj* independiente, autónomo,-a. **– 2** *n* persona que trabaja por cuenta propia. **– 3** *i* trabajar por cuenta propia.
freeload ['friːləʊd] *i fam* gorrear.
freeloader ['friːləʊdə'] *n fam* gorrón,-ona, buitre *m.*
freely ['friːlɪ] **1** *adv* (*without obstruction*) libremente, con libertad; (*easily*) con facilidad. **2** (*willingly, readily*) voluntariamente. **3** (*openly, honestly*) abiertamente, francamente. **4** (*generously*) liberalmente; (*abundantly*) abundantemente.
freemason ['friːmeɪsən] *n* masón,-ona, francmasón,-ona.
freemasonry ['friːmeɪsənrɪ] *n* masonería, francmasonería.

free-range ['friːreɪndʒ] *adj* de granja.
■ **free-range eggs,** huevos de granja.
freesia ['friːʒə] *n* fresia.
freestanding [friː'stændɪŋ] *adj* independiente.
free-style ['friːstaɪl] *n* (*swimming*) estilo libre.
freethinker [friː'θɪŋkə'] *n* librepensador,-ra.
freethinking [friː'θɪŋkɪŋ] *adj* librepensador,-ra.
freeway ['friːweɪ] *n* US autopista.
freewheel [friː'wiːl] *i* (*cycle*) ir a rueda libre; (*car*) ir en punto muerto.
freewheeling [friː'wiːlɪŋ] *adj fam* despreocupado,-a.
freeze [friːz] **1** *n* METEOR helada. **2** COMM congelación *f:* *price freeze,* congelación de precios. **– 3** *t* (*gen*) congelar: *can you freeze fish?,* ¿se puede congelar el pescado?; *the government has frozen wages,* el gobierno ha congelado los salarios. **– 4** *i* (*liquid*) helarse; (*food*) congelarse: *water freezes at zero degrees,* el agua se hiela a cero grados; *fruit doesn't freeze very well,* la fruta no se congela bien; *the earth is frozen,* la tierra está helada. **5** METEOR helar. **6** *fig* (*stop suddenly*) quedarse inmóvil, quedarse paralizado,-a.
◆ **to freeze out** *t sep fam* (*exclude*) excluir de un negocio. ‖ **to freeze over** *i* helarse: *the lake froze over,* el lago se heló. ‖ **to freeze up** *i* helarse: *the waterpipes have frozen up,* las cañerías se han helado.
● **to freeze sb.'s blood / make sb.'s blood freeze,** hacer que se le hiela la sangre a algn.: *when I saw them it made my blood freeze,* cuando los vi se me heló la sangre. ‖ **to freeze to death,** morirse de frío.
▲ *pt* froze, *pp* frozen, *ger* freezing.
freeze-dry ['friːzdraɪ] *t* liofilizar.
▲ *pt & pp* freeze-dried, *ger* freeze-drying.
freeze-frame ['friːzfreɪm] *n* imagen *f* congelada.
freezer ['friːzə'] *n* congelador *m.*
freeze-up ['friːzʌp] *n* helada.
freezing ['friːzɪŋ] **1** *adj* glacial. **2** *fam* (*very cold*) helado,-a: *I'm freezing,* estoy helado,-a. **– 3** *n* congelación *f.*
■ **freezing point,** punto de congelación.
freight [freɪt] **1** *n* (*transport*) transporte *m.* **2** (*goods*) carga, flete *m.* **3** (*price*) flete *m.* **– 4** *t* transportar.
■ **freight car,** US wagon *m* de mercancías. ‖ **freight train,** US tren *m* de mercancías.
freighter ['freɪtə'] *n* AV avión *m* de carga; MAR buque *m* de carga.
French [frentʃ] **1** *adj* francés,-esa. **– 2** *n* (*language*) francés *m.* **– 3** the French, *npl* los franceses *mpl.*
● **to take French leave,** despedirse a la francesa.
■ **French bread,** pan *m* francés. ‖ **French dressing,** vinagreta. ‖ **French fries,** patatas *fpl* fritas. ‖ **French horn,** trompa de pistones. ‖ **French letter,** *fam* condón *m.* ‖ **French loaf / French stick,** barra de pan (francés). ‖ **French toast,** torrija. ‖ **French window,** puerta vidriera.
Frenchman ['frentʃmən] *n* francés *m.*
▲ *pl* Frenchmen ['frentʃmən].
Frenchwoman ['frentʃwʊmən] *n* francesa.
▲ *pl* Frenchwomen ['frentʃwɪmɪn].
frenetic [frə'netɪk] *adj* frenético,-a.
frenetically [frə'netɪklɪ] *adv* frenéticamente.
frenzied ['frenzɪd] *adj* frenético,-a.
frenzy ['frenzɪ] *n* frenesí *m.*
● **to be in a frenzy,** estar frenético,-a.
▲ *pl* frenzies.
frequency ['friːkwənsɪ] *n* frecuencia.
▲ *pl* frequencies.
frequent ['friːkwənt] **1** *adj* frecuente. **– 2** *t* frecuentar.
▲ (*verbo*) [frɪ'kwent].

frequently [ˈfriːkwəntlɪ] *adv* frecuentemente, con frecuencia.

fresco [ˈfreskəʊ] *n* fresco.
▲ *pl* **frescos** o **frescoes**.

fresh [freʃ] **1** *adj* (*food*) fresco,-a: *fresh bread*, pan del día; *fresh fruit*, fruta fresca. **2** (*water*) dulce. **3** (*air*) puro,-a. **4** (*weather*) fresco,-a; (*wind*) recio,-a. **5** (*complexion*) sano,-a. **6** (*clothes*) limpio,-a. **7** *fig* (*new*) nuevo,-a: *open a fresh packet*, abre otro paquete; *I'll make a fresh pot of tea*, haré otra tetera; *there's some fresh evidence*, hay nuevas pruebas. **8** (*made recently*) reciente, fresco,-a: *fresh tracks*, huellas recientes; *fresh paint*, recién pintado. **9** (*original*) nuevo,-a: *a fresh approach*, un nuevo énfasis. **10** (*refreshed, alert*) fresco,-a, lleno,-a de vigor. **11** (*bold, forward, cheeky*) fresco,-a, carota: *don't get fresh with me!*, ¡basta de familiaridades!
● **as fresh as a daisy**, fresco,-a como una rosa. ‖ **in the fresh air**, al aire libre. ‖ **fresh from / fresh out of**, recién salido,-a de, recién llegado,-a de: *she's fresh out of college*, acaba de salir de la universidad. ‖ **to be fresh out of sth.**, habérsele acabado algo a uno: *we're fresh out of coffee*, se nos ha acabado el café. ‖ **to make a fresh start**, volver a empezar, empezar de nuevo.

freshen [ˈfreʃən] **1** *t* refrescar. – **2** *i* refrescarse.
◆ **to freshen up 1** *t sep* refrescar: *that shower has really freshened me up*, aquella ducha me ha refrescado mucho. – **2** *i* asearse, refrescarse: *I think I'll go and freshen up before dinner*, me parece que me refrescaré un poco antes de cenar.

freshener [ˈfreʃənəʳ] *n* ambientador *m*.

fresher [ˈfreʃəʳ] *n* GB estudiante *mf* de primer curso (de universidad), novato,-a.

freshly [ˈfreʃlɪ] *adv* recién: *freshly cut flowers*, flores recién cortadas; *freshly made tea*, té recién hecho; *freshly squeezed orange juice*, zumo de naranja recién exprimido.

freshman [ˈfreʃmən] *n* US estudiante *mf* de primer curso (de universidad), novato,-a.
▲ *pl* **freshmen**.

freshness [ˈfreʃnəs] **1** *n* (*brightness*) frescura. **2** (*cool*) frescor *m*. **3** (*newness*) novedad *f*. **4** *fam* (*cheek*) descaro.

freshwater [ˈfreʃwɔːtəʳ] *adj* de agua dulce: *freshwater fish*, pez de agua dulce.

fret[1] [fret] **1** *i* preocuparse (**about/at/over**, por): *don't fret*, no te preocupes; *she was fretting about her sick cat*, estaba preocupada por su gato enfermo. – **2** *t* (*wear away*) raer, desgastar. – **3** *t* (*worry*) preocupación *f*.
● **to be in a fret**, estar preocupado,-a.
▲ (*verbo*) *pt* & *pp* **fretted**, *ger* **fretting**.

fret[2] [fret] *n* (*on guitar*) traste *m*.

fret[3] [fret] *n* (*fretwork*) calado.
■ **fret saw**, sierra de calados.
▲ *pt* & *pp* **fretted**, *ger* **fretting**.

fretful [ˈfretfʊl] **1** *adj* (*worried*) preocupado,-a. **2** (*irritable*) irritable, malhumorado,-a.

fretwork [ˈfretwɜːk] *n* calado.

Freudian [ˈfrɔɪdɪən] *adj* freudiano,-a.
■ **Freudian slip**, lapsus *m*.

FRG [ˈefˈɑːˈdʒiː] *abbr* (*Federal Republic of Germany*) República Federal de Alemania; (*abbreviation*) RFA.

Fri [ˈfraɪdɪ] *abbr* (*Friday*) viernes *m*; (*abbreviation*) viern.

friable [ˈfraɪəbəl] *adj* friable.

friar [ˈfraɪəʳ] *n* fraile *m*.

friary [ˈfraɪərɪ] *n* monasterio.
▲ *pl* **friaries**.

fricassee [ˈfrɪkəsiː] *n* estofado.

fricative [ˈfrɪkətɪv] **1** *adj* fricativo,-a. – **2** *n* fricativa.

friction [ˈfrɪkʃən] **1** *n* (*conflict*) fricción *f*, roces *mpl*. **2** (*rubbing*) rozamiento, roce *m*.

Friday [ˈfraɪdɪ] *n* viernes *m*.
▲ *Véase también* **Thursday**.

fridge [frɪdʒ] *n* nevera, frigorífico.

fried [fraɪd] *adj* frito,-a.

friend [frend] **1** *n* amigo,-a, compañero,-a: *I'd like to introduce you to a friend of mine*, me gustaría presentarte a un amigo mío; *Maria and I have been best friends for years*, Maria y yo somos amigas íntimas desde hace años; *they say that they're just good friends*, dicen que sólo son buenos amigos. **2** (*helper, supporter*) amigo,-a (**of/to**, de): *friends of the arts*, amigos de las artes. **3** (*Quaker*) cuáquero,-a.
● **a friend in need (is a friend indeed)**, en la necesidad se conoce a los amigos. ‖ **my honorable friend**, POL mi respetable colega. ‖ **my learned friend**, JUR mi eminente colega. ‖ **to be friends with sb.**, ser amigo,-a de algn. ‖ **to have friends in high places**, tener enchufe. ‖ **to make friends with sb.**, trabar amistad con algn., hacerse amigo,-a de algn.
■ **Friends of the Earth**, Los Amigos de la Tierra.

friendless [ˈfrendləs] *adj* sin amigos.

friendly [ˈfrendlɪ] **1** *adj* (*person*) simpático,-a, amable. **2** (*atmosphere*) acogedor,-ra. **3** (*smile, manner etc*) amable. **4** (*relationship*) amistoso,-a.
● **to become friendly**, hacerse amigos,-as. ‖ **to be on friendly terms with sb.**, estar en buenos términos con algn.
■ **friendly game / friendly match**, SP partido amistoso. ‖ **Friendly Society**, mutua.
▲ *comp* **friendlier**, *superl* **friendliest**.

friendship [ˈfrendʃɪp] *n* amistad *f*.

Friesian [ˈfriːʒən] **1** *adj* frisón,-ona, frisio,-a. – **2** *n* (*person*) frisón,-ona, frisio,-a,. **3** (*language*) frisón *m*, frisio.

Friesland [ˈfriːzlənd] *n* Frisia.

frieze [friːz] *n* friso.

frigate [ˈfrɪgət] *n* fragata.

fright [fraɪt] **1** *n* (*shock*) susto: *I got quite a fright*, me pegué un buen susto. **2** (*fear*) miedo.
● **to take fright**, asustarse (**at**, de). ‖ **to look a fright**, *fam* estar hecho,-a un adefesio, estar hecho,-a una facha.

frighten [ˈfraɪtən] *t* asustar, espantar: *you frightened me!*, ¡me has asustado!
◆ **to frighten away / frighten off** *t* ahuyentar, espantar: *be quiet, or you'll frighten the birds away*, cállate, o espantarás a los pájaros.
● **to frighten sb. into doing sth.**, hacer que algn. haga algo con amenazas. ‖ **to frighten sb. to death**, dar un susto de muerte a algn. ‖ **to frighten the life out of sb.**, dar un susto de muerte a algn.

frightened [ˈfraɪtənd] *adj* asustado,-a.
● **to be frightened**, tener miedo (**of**, de).

frightening [ˈfraɪtənɪŋ] *adj* espantoso,-a.

frightful [ˈfraɪtfʊl] *adj* espantoso,-a, horroroso,-a.

frightfully [ˈfraɪtfʊlɪ] *adv fam* muchísimo.

frigid [ˈfrɪdʒɪd] **1** *adj* (*sexually*) frígido,-a. **2** (*icy*) glacial, muy frío,-a. **3** (*unfriendly*) glacial.

frill [frɪl] **1** *n* (*on dress*) volante *m*. – **2 frills**, *npl* (*decorations*) adornos *mpl*.
● **with no frills**, sencillo,-a, sin adornos.

frilly [ˈfrɪlɪ] *adj* con volantes.
▲ *comp* **frillier**, *superl* **frilliest**.

fringe [frɪndʒ] **1** *n* (*decorative*) fleco. **2** (*of hair*) flequillo. **3** (*edge*) borde *m*. – **4** *t* poner un fleco.

● **to be fringed by/with sth.**, estar rodeado,-a de algo. ‖ **to live on the fringe of society**, vivir al margen de la sociedad.
■ **fringe benefits**, extras *mpl*. ‖ **fringe group**, grupo marginal. ‖ **fringe theatre**, teatro experimental, teatro alternativo.

Frisbee ['frɪzbiː] *n* frisbi *m*.
▲ *Es marca registrada.*

frisk [frɪsk] **1** *t* (*search*) registrar, cachear. – **2** *i* (*frolic*) brincar, retozar.

frisky ['frɪskɪ] *adj* (*child, animal*) retozón,-ona, juguetón,-ona; (*adult*) vivo,-a, vital.
▲ *comp* **friskier**, *superl* **friskiest**.

fritter ['frɪtəʳ] *n* CULIN buñuelo.
◆ **to fritter away** *i pej* (*money*) malgastar; (*time*) desperdiciar.

frivolity [frɪ'vɒlətɪ] *n* frivolidad *f*.
▲ *pl* **frivolities**.

frivolous ['frɪvələs] *adj* frívolo,-a.

frizzle ['frɪzl] *i* achicharrarse.

frizzy ['frɪzɪ] *adj* crespo,-a, rizado,-a.
▲ *comp* **frizzier**, *superl* **frizziest**.

fro [frəʊ] **to and fro**, *adv* de un lado para otro.

frock [frɒk] *n* vestido.

frock-coat ['frɒkkəʊt] *n* levita.

frog [frɒg] *n* rana.
● **to have a frog in one's throat**, tener carraspera.

frogman ['frɒgmən] *n* hombre *m* rana.
▲ *pl* **frogmen** ['frɒgmen].

frogmarch ['frɒgmɑːtʃ] *t* llevar a alguien a la fuerza sujetándole los brazos.

frogspawn ['frɒgspɔːn] *n* huevas *fpl* de rana.

frolic ['frɒlɪk] **1** *i* juguetear, retozar. – **2** *n* aventura.

frolicsome ['frɒlɪksəm] *adj* juguetón,-ona.

from [frɒm] **1** *prep* (*starting at*) de; (*train, plane*) procedente de: *what time does he get home from work?*, ¿a qué hora llega del trabajo?; *we're travelling from London to Rome*, viajamos desde Londres hasta Roma; *the train from Madrid*, el tren procedente de Madrid. **2** (*origin, source*) de, desde: *where are you from?*, ¿de dónde eres?; *this water comes from a spring*, esta agua es de manantial; *it's a quote from Burns*, es una cita de Burns; *I bought it from Jack*, se lo compré a Jack. **3** (*number, price, etc*) de, desde, a partir de: *prices start from $10*, precios a partir de 10 dólares; *it's reduced from £25 to £20*, está rebajado de 25 a 20 libras. **4** (*time*) de, desde: *we work from 9.00 until 5.00*, trabajamos de 9.00 a 5.00; *from next Monday onwards*, a partir del próximo lunes; *she's been blind from birth*, es ciega de nacimiento. **5** (*sent or given by*) de: *I've got a letter from my mum*, tengo una carta de mi madre; *say hello to him from me*, dale recuerdos de mi parte; *this is Mr Singh from the Council*, es el Sr. Singh del Ayuntamiento. **6** (*using, out of*) de, con: *beer is made from hops*, la cerveza se hace con cebada; *cheese is made from milk*, de la leche se hace el queso. **7** (*distance*) de: *the hotel is 500 yards from the beach*, el hotel está a 500 metros de la playa. **8** (*indicating separation, removal, etc*) de; (*subtraction*) a: *she is sparated from her husband*, está separada de su marido; *I've borrowed some books from the library*, he cogido prestado unos libros de la biblioteca; *take five from ten*, réstale cinco a diez. **9** (*because of*) por, a causa de: *the boys died from exposure*, los chicos murieron de frío. **10** (*considering, according to*) según, por: *from what I can gather*, por lo que yo entiendo; *from the look of him, I'd say he's a tramp*, por su aspecto, diría que es indigente; *I know*

from experience, lo sé por experiencia. **11** (*indicating difference*) de; (*when distinguishing*) entre: *how different is Catalan from Spanish?*, ¿en qué se diferencia el catalán del español? **12** (*indicating position*) desde: *from above, you can see the whole stadium*, desde encima, se puede ver todo el estadio; *from my point of view*, desde mi punto de vista.

frond [frɒnd] *n* fronda.

front [frʌnt] **1** *n* (*forward part*) parte *f* delantera, frente *m*: *she prefers to sit at the front of the class*, prefiere sentarse en las primeras filas de la clase; *there are trees at the front of the house*, hay árboles en la parte de delante de la casa; *he wants to sit in the front of the car*, quiere sentarse en la parte delantera del coche; *I want you to turn to the front of your books*, quiero que vayáis al principio del libro. **2** (*of shirt etc*) pechera. **3** METEOR frente *m*. **4** (*facade*) fachada: *the front of the building is neo-Gothic*, la fachada del edificio es neogótica. **5** MIL frente *m*: *he was sent to the front*, lo mandaron al frente. **6** (*promenade*) paseo marítimo: *let's go for a walk along the front*, vamos al dar una vuelta por el paseo marítimo. **7** *fig* (*illegal business etc*) tapadera: *the bar was a front for drug deals*, el bar servía de tapadera para el tráfico de drogas. **8** *fig* (*outward appearance*) apariencia; (*pretence*) fachada: *his offhandedness is just a front*, su brusquedad es pura fachada. **9** (*specific field of activity*) asunto, terreno: *what's happening on the domestic front?*, ¿qué pasa en el terreno nacional? – **10** *adj* delantero,-a, de delante: *front seat*, asiento delantero; *we sat in the front row*, nos sentamos en la primera fila. – **11** *i* (*face*) dar (**on/onto**, a): *the hotel fronts onto the lake*, el hotel da al lago. – **12** *t* (*lead, head*) encabezar: *the organization is fronted by an ex-policeman*, la organización está encabezada por un ex-policía. **13** (*present*) presentar: *Tom Jenkins is going to front "News Today"*, Tom Jenkins presentará "News Today".
● **at the front**, delante, por delante: *this dress does up at the front*, este vestido se abrocha por delante. ‖ **in front (of)**, delante (de). ‖ **out front**, (*in theatre*) entre el público. ‖ **to put on a bold front**, hacer de tripas corazón. ‖ **up front**, (*in advance*) por adelantado.
■ **front door**, puerta principal. ‖ **front garden**, jardín *m* pequeño en la parte de delante. ‖ **front line**, (*of fighting*) frente *m*; (*vanguard*) vanguardia. ‖ **front man**, hombre *m* al frente. ‖ **front page**, primera plana, portada. ‖ **front room**, saleta. ‖ **front tooth**, incisivo. ‖ **front wheel**, rueda delantera, rueda de delante. ‖ **the front bench**, GB POL *las dos primeras filas de escaños ocupadas por miembros del gobierno y de la oposición*.

frontal ['frʌntəl] *adj* frontal.
■ **full frontal**, desnudo total.

front-bench ['frʌntbentʃ] *adj* GB POL *de las dos primeras filas de escaños*.

frontier ['frʌntɪəʳ] **1** *n* frontera. – **2** *adj* fronterizo,-a: *a frontier zone*, una zona fronteriza. – **3 the frontiers**, *npl* fronteras *fpl*, límites *mpl*: *the frontiers of science*, las fronteras de la ciencia.
■ **frontier post**, puesto fronterizo.

frontispiece ['frʌntɪspiːs] *n* portada.

front-line ['frʌntlaɪn] *adj* de la primera línea: *front-line troops*, tropas de primera línea de combate.

front-page ['frʌntpeɪdʒ] *adj* de portada, de primera plana: *front-page news*, noticias de primera plana.

frontrunner ['frʌnt'rʌnəʳ] *n* favorito,-a.

frost [frɒst] **1** *n* (*covering*) escarcha: *the windscreen is covered with frost*, el parabrisas está cubierto de escarcha. **2** (*freezing*) helada: *there was a heavy frost last night*, la

noche pasada heló. – **3** t helar, cubrir de escarcha: *the cold has frosted the pavement,* el frío ha helado la acera. **4** (*plants*) quemar. **5** (*glass*) esmerilar. **6** (*cake etc*) recubrir con azúcar glas, escarchar.
◆ **to frost over / frost up** i cubrirse de escarcha, helar.

frostbite ['frɒstbaɪt] n congelación f.

frostbitten ['frɒstbɪtən] adj congelado,-a.

frosted ['frɒstɪd] **1** adj (*glass*) esmerilado,-a. **2** CULIN recubierto,-a de azúcar glas, escarchado,-a.

frostily ['frɒstɪlɪ] adv fríamente.

frostiness ['frɒstɪnəs] n frialdad f.

frosty ['frɒstɪ] **1** adj METEOR (*cold with frost*) de helada; (*very cold*) helado,-a, muy frío,-a: *it's frosty today,* hoy es día de helada; *the air is frosty,* el aire está helado. **2** METEOR (*covered with frost*) escarchado,-a, cubierto,-a de escarcha: *frosty grass,* hierba cubierta de escarcha. **3** fig (*unfriendly*) glacial: *she gave me a frosty welcome,* me dio una bienvenida glacial.
▲ *comp* **frostier,** *superl* **frostiest.**

froth [frɒθ] **1** n (*gen*) espuma. **2** (*from mouth*) espumarajos *mpl.* **3** fig (*worthless ideas etc*) banalidades *fpl.* – **4** i (*liquid*) hacer espuma. **5** (*from mouth*) espumajear, echar espumarajos por la boca.
● **to be frothing at the mouth,** fig (*angry*) echar humo.

frothy ['frɒθɪ] **1** adj espumoso,-a. **2** fig superficial, vacío,-a.
▲ *comp* **frothier,** *superl* **frothiest.**

frown [fraʊn] **1** n ceño. – **2** i fruncir el ceño.
◆ **to frown on** t insep fig desaprobar, censurar: *promiscuity is frowned upon,* la promiscuidad se desaprueba.
● **to frown at sb.,** mirar a algn. con el ceño fruncido, mirar a algn. frunciendo el ceño.

froze [frəʊz] pt → **freeze.**

frozen ['frəʊzən] **1** pp → **freeze.** – **2** adj (*water, ground*) helado,-a. **3** (*food*) congelado,-a.

FRS ['ef'ɑːr'es] abbr GB (*Fellow of the Royal Society*) miembro de la *Royal Society.*

fructify ['frʌktɪfaɪ] i fructificar, dar fruto.
▲ *pt & pp* **fructified,** *ger* **fructifying.**

fructose ['frʌktəʊz] n fructosa.

frugal ['fruːgəl] adj frugal.

frugality [fruː'gælɪtɪ] n frugalidad f.

frugally ['fruːgəlɪ] adv frugalmente.

fruit [fruːt] **1** n (*food*) fruta: *a piece of fruit,* una fruta. **2** BOT fruto. **3** (*result, reward*) fruto. – **4** adj de fruta. – **5** i dar fruto.
● **to bear fruit,** (*tree*) dar fruto; (*plan, idea*) dar fruto, dar resultados.
■ **fruit bowl / fruit dish,** frutero. ‖ **fruit cocktail,** macedonia (de frutas). ‖ **fruit cup,** (*drink*) ≈ sangría. ‖ **fruit fly,** mosca de la fruta. ‖ **fruit juice,** zumo de fruta. ‖ **fruit knife,** cuchillo de fruta. ‖ **fruit machine,** máquina tragaperras. ‖ **fruit salad,** macedonia (de frutas). ‖ **fruit tree,** árbol m frutal.

fruitcake ['fruːtkeɪk] **1** n (*cake*) plumcake m, pastel m con frutos secos. **2** fam (*eccentric person*) excéntrico,-a.

fruiterer ['fruːtərəʳ] n frutero,-a.

fruitful ['fruːtfʊl] adj fructífero,-a, provechoso,-a.

fruition [fruː'ɪʃən] n realización f.
● **to bring sth. to fruition,** llevar algo a buen término, realizar algo. ‖ **to come to fruition,** llevarse a cabo, realizarse.

fruitless ['fruːtləs] adj infructuoso,-a.

fruity ['fruːtɪ] **1** adj (*taste*) a fruta, afrutado,-a. **2** (*jokes etc*) picante. **3** (*voice*) pastoso,-a.
▲ *comp* **fruitier,** *superl* **fruitiest.**

frump [frʌmp] n fam pej adefesio, espantajo.

frumpish ['frʌmpɪʃ] adj anticuado,-a.

frustrate [frʌ'streɪt] **1** t (*thwart*) frustrar. **2** (*upset*) frustrar: *not having any money frustrated him,* no tener dinero le frustraba.

frustrated [frʌ'streɪtɪd] adj (*dissatisfied*) frustrado,-a, insatisfecho,-a, descontento,-a; (*unfulfilled*) frustrado,-a: *she felt frustrated in her job,* se sentía frustrada en su trabajo; *he's a frustrated actor,* es un actor frustrado.

frustrating [frʌ'streɪtɪŋ] adj (*irritating*) frustrante.

frustration [frʌ'streɪʃən] n frustración f.

fry[1] [fraɪ] **1** t freír. – **2** i freírse. **3** fig (*in sun*) asarse, achicharrarse.
▲ *pt & pp* **fried,** *ger* **frying.**

fry[2] [fraɪ] *npl* (*fish*) alevines *mpl.*
▲ *pl* **fry.**

fryer ['fraɪəʳ] **1** n (*frying pan*) sartén f. **2** US pollo tomatero.
■ **deep fat fryer,** freidora.

frying ['fraɪɪŋ] frying pan, n sartén f.
● **to jump out of the frying pan into the fire,** salir del fuego y meterse en las brasas, ir de Guatemala a Guatepeor.

fry-up ['fraɪʌp] n GB fam (*mixed fried food*) fritada.

ft ['fʊt, 'fiːt] abbr (*foot, feet*) pie m, pies *mpl.*

fuchsia ['fjuːʃə] n fucsia.

fuck [fʌk] **1** t taboo joder, follar. – **2** i taboo joder, follar. – **3** n taboo (*act*) polvo. – **4** the fuck, phr taboo (*used as intensifier*) coño, hostias: *where the fuck have you been?,* ¿dónde hostias has estado?; *what the fuck's going on?,* ¿qué coño pasa?
◆ **to fuck about / fuck around 1** i taboo (*behave stupidly*) joder. – **2** t sep taboo (*treat badly*) joder: *they've fucked me around,* me han jodido. ‖ **to fuck off** i taboo largarse, pirarse, darse el piro. ‖ **to fuck up** taboo t sep joder, cagar, jorobar: *you've really fucked it up this time!,* ¡ahora sí que las has cagado de verdad!
● **fuck it!,** taboo ¡joder! ‖ **fuck off!,** taboo ¡vete a la mierda!, ¡vete a tomar por culo! ‖ **fuck this for a game of soldiers!,** taboo ¡a joderse!, ¡a tomar por culo! ‖ **fuck you!,** taboo ¡vete a tomar por culo! ‖ **not to give a fuck / not care a fuck,** taboo importarle a uno una mierda, importarle a uno una hostia: *I don't give a fuck about politics!,* me importa una mierda la política!

fuck-all ['fʌkɔːl] **1** n taboo (*nothing at all*) ni hostia, ni folla: *we've done fuck-all this weekend,* no hemos hecho ni folla en todo el fin de semana; *you know fuck-all!,* ¡no tienes ni puta idea! – **2** adj taboo puto,-a: *this car's fuck-all use now!,* ¡este coche no vale una puta mierda!

fucked [fʊkt] adj taboo jodido,-a.

fucker ['fʌkəʳ] n taboo hijo de puta, gilipollas m, cabrón m.

fucking ['fʌkɪŋ] **1** adj taboo jodido,-a, puto,-a, de mierda: *where's my fucking dinner?,* ¿dónde está la jodida comida? – **2** adv taboo (*intensifier*): *a fucking good goal!,* ¡un golazo de puta madre!; *I'm fucking pissed off with you,* estoy hasta los cojones de ti.

fuck-up ['fʌkʌp] n taboo (*mess*) chapuza, cagada.

fuddle ['fʌdəl] **1** t (*confuse*) confundir; (*intoxicate*) emborrachar. – **2** n confusión f.

fuddled ['fʊdəld] adj confuso,-a.

fuddy-duddy ['fʌdɪdʌdɪ] n fam persona chapada a la antigua.
▲ *pl* **fuddy-duddies.**

fudge¹ [fʌdʒ] *n dulce hecho con azúcar, leche y mantequilla.*

fudge² [fʌdʒ] **1** *t (do clumsily)* pifiar, fallar. **2** *(falsify)* amañar. **3** *(evade)* eludir: *the minister completely fudged the issue,* el ministro eludió por completo el problema.

fuel [fjʊəl] **1** *n (gen)* combustible *m.* **2** *(for motors)* carburante *m.* **3** *fig* pábulo. – **4** *t (plane)* abastecer de combustible; *(car)* echar gasolina. **5** *fig (make worse)* empeorar; *(encourage)* alimentar: *the rumours of riots were fuelled by the press,* la prensa alimentó los rumores de disturbios. – **6** *i* abastecerse de combustible, repostar: *planes must fuel before departure,* los aviones deben abastecerse de combustible antes de despegar.
● **to add fuel to the flames,** echar leña al fuego.

fug [fʌg] *n fam* aire *m* cargado, aire *m* viciado.

fuggy [ˈfʌgɪ] *adj* cargado,-a.
▲ *comp* **fuggier,** *superl* **fuggiest.**

fugitive [ˈfjuːdʒətɪv] **1** *n (from danger, war, etc)* fugitivo,-a; *(from justice)* prófugo,-a. – **2** *adj* fugitivo,-a. **3** *lit (fleeting)* fugaz, efímero,-a.

fulcrum [ˈfʊlkrəm] *n* fulcro.

fulfil [fʊlˈfɪl] **1** *t (promise, duty)* cumplir. **2** *(task, plan, ambition)* realizar. **3** *(role, function, order)* efectuar, desempeñar. **4** *(need, desire, wish)* satisfacer.
● **to fulfil os.,** realizarse, sentirse realizado,-a.
▲ *pt & pp* **fulfilled,** *ger* **fulfilling.**

fulfill [fʊlˈfɪl] *t us →* **fulfil.**

fulfilled [fʊlˈfɪld] **1** *pt & pp →* **fulfill.** – **2** *adj* realizado,-a, satisfecho,-a.

fulfilment [fʊlˈfɪlmənt] **1** *n (of plan, ambition, etc)* realización *f.* **2** *(of duty, promise, etc)* cumplimiento. **3** *(of order etc)* ejecución *f.* **4** *(of need, wish, etc)* satisfacción *f.* **5** *(feeling of satisfaction)* satisfacción *f.*

full [fʊl] **1** *adj (gen)* lleno,-a: *my suitcase is already full,* mi maleta ya está llena; *the cupboard is full of old toys,* el armario está lleno de juguetes viejos; *the trains are always full at this time,* los trenes siempre van llenos a esta hora; *hey! this glass is only half full!,* ¡ey! ¡este vaso sólo está medio lleno!; *the room's full of smoke,* la habitación está llena de humo. **2** *(week, day)* cargado,-a, movido,-a: *we've had a very full week,* hemos tenido una semana muy movida. **3** *(entire, complete)* completo,-a: *I need your full name,* necesito su nombre completo; *full instructions are included,* instrucciones completas incluidas; *the hotel is full,* el hotel está completo; *I'd like a full English breakfast,* quisiera un desayuno inglés completo; *she swam the full length of the pool,* nadó toda la piscina; *I wanted them to get the full meaning of what I was saying,* quería que me entendieran perfectamente; *we've been waiting a full hour,* llevamos esperando una hora entera. **4** *(highest or greatest possible)* máximo,-a: *the radio was on at full volume,* la radio estaba al máximo. **5** *(plump - figure)* llenito,-a, relleno,-a; *(- face)* redondo,-a, lleno,-a; *(- lips)* grueso,-a. **6** *(clothing - loose fitting)* holgado,-a, amplio,-a; *(skirt)* de mucho vuelo; *(sleeve)* ancho,-a. – **7** *adv (directly)* justo, de lleno: *he hit me full in the face,* me pegó de lleno en la cara.
● **at full blast,** a toda potencia, al máximo. ‖ **at full pelt / at full speed / at full tilt,** a toda velocidad, a toda pastilla. ‖ **at full stretch,** al máximo de capacidad. ‖ **full of beans / full of life,** rebosante de salud, lleno,-a de vigor. ‖ **full of the joys of spring,** lleno,-a de alegría. ‖ **full speed ahead / full steam ahead,** adelante a toda máquina. ‖ **full to the brim,** lleno,-a hasta los topes. ‖ **full up,** completamente lleno,-a. ‖ **full well,** muy bien, perfectamente, de sobra: *you know full well you shouldn't do that,* sabes perfectamente que no debes hacer eso. ‖ **in full,** completo,-a, en su to-

talidad. ‖ **in full sail,** a toda vela, con todas las velas desplegadas. ‖ **in full swing,** *fam* en pleno auge. ‖ **in full view of ...,** delante mismo de ... ‖ **to be full of sth.,** no hablar más que de algo, no parar de hablar de algo: *she was full of her holiday,* no paraba de hablar de sus vacaciones; *the whole school is full of the news,* toda la escuela habla de la noticia. ‖ **to be full of os.,** ser engreído,-a, creérselo. ‖ **to be full of one's own importance,** ser prepotente. ‖ **to come full circle,** volver al punto de partida. ‖ **to come to a full stop,** pararse por completo. ‖ **to fall full length,** caer de bruces. ‖ **to the full,** al máximo.
■ **full board,** pensión *f* completa. ‖ **full dress,** traje *m* de etiqueta. ‖ **full house,** *(in theatre)* lleno, llenazo; *(in bingo)* bingo; *(in poker)* full *m.* ‖ **full marks,** *(in exam)* sobresaliente; *(when praising sb.)* buena nota. ‖ **full moon,** luna llena. ‖ **full score,** partitura de orquesta. ‖ **full stop,** *(punctuation mark)* punto: *full stop, new paragraph,* punto y aparte; *full stop, new sentence,* punto y seguido. ‖ **full time,** final *m* de partido.

fullback [ˈfʊlbæk] *n* SP defensa *mf* central.

full-blooded [ˈfʊlblʌdɪd] *adj (thoroughbred)* de pura sangre. **2** *(vigorous, hearty)* vigoroso,-a.

full-blown [ˈfʊlbləʊn] **1** *adj (having all characteristics)* auténtico,-a, verdadero,-a. **2** *(in full bloom)* en flor.

full-bodied [ˈfʊlbɒdɪd] *adj (wine)* con cuerpo.

fuller [ˈfʊləʳ] *n* abatanador *m.*
■ **fuller's earth,** tierra de batán.

full-grown [ˈfʊlɡrəʊn] **1** *adj (plant)* crecido,-a. **2** *(person, animal)* adulto,-a.

full-length [ˈfʊlˈlenθ] **1** *adj (mirror, portrait)* de cuerpo entero. **2** *(garment)* largo,-a. **3** *(film)* de largo metraje.
■ **full-length feature film,** largometraje *m.*

fullness [ˈfʊlnəs] **1** *n (being full)* plenitud *f,* abundancia. **2** *(width)* amplitud *f.*
● **in the fullness of time,** con el tiempo.

full-page [ˈfʊlpeɪdʒ] *adj* de una página.
■ **full-page advertisement,** anuncio de una página entera.

full-scale [ˈfʊlˈskeɪl] **1** *adj (actual size)* de tamaño natural. **2** *(complete, total - gen)* completo,-a, total; *(- investigation, search)* a fondo: *full-scale war,* guerra total, guerra generalizada.

full-time [ˈfʊlˈtaɪm] **1** *adj* a tiempo completo, de jornada completa: *it's a full-time job,* es un trabajo de jornada completa. – **2** *adv* a tiempo completo.
● **to work full-time,** trabajar a tiempo completo, hacer una jornada completa.

fully [ˈfʊlɪ] **1** *adv (completely)* completamente, enteramente, plenamente: *I am fully aware of the consequences,* soy plenamente consciente de las consecuencias; *she was fully dressed,* estaba completamente vestida. **2** *(at least, quite)* por lo menos: *it was fully an hour before the bus arrived,* el autobús tardó por lo menos una hora en llegar.
● **to be fully qualified,** ser titulado,-a, ser diplomado,-a.

fully-fledged [ˈfʊlɪfledʒd] *adj* hecho,-a y derecho,-a, de verdad, con todas las de la ley.

fulminate [ˈfʌlmɪneɪt] *i* tronar (**against,** contra).

fulmination [fʌlmɪˈneɪʃən] *n* fulminación *f.*

fulsome [ˈfʊlsəm] *adj* exagerado,-a, excesivo,-a.

fumble [ˈfʌmbəl] **1** *t* dejar caer: *the goalkeeper fumbled the ball,* el portero dejó caer el balón. – **2** **to fumble for,** *i* buscar a tientas: *she fumbled in her purse for some coins,* buscó a tientas unas monedas en su monedero.

3 to fumble with, hacer torpemente: *he fumbled with his keys,* intentó torpemente meter la llave.
◆ **to fumble about / fumble around** *i* andar a tientas.
fume [fjuːm] **1** *i* (*produce smoke etc*) echar humo. **2** *fig* (*show anger*) echar humo, subirse por las paredes: *when I got home my father was fuming,* cuando llegué a casa mi padre estaba que se subía por las paredes. – **3 fumes,** *npl* humos *mpl*.
fumigate [ˈfjuːmɪgeɪt] *t* fumigar.
fun [fʌn] **1** *n* (*enjoyment, pleasure*) diversión *f*: *she gets a lot of fun out of painting,* lo pasa muy bien pintando; *it'll be good fun when we go camping,* lo pasaremos muy bien cuando nos vayamos de camping; *skiing is great fun!,* ¡esquiar es divertidísimo! **2** (*amusement*) gracia: *it's no fun staying in alone on Saturday night,* no tiene gracia quedarse solo en casa el sábado por la noche; *well it's not much fun for me,* pues yo no le veo la gracia. – **3** *adj* (*humorous, amusing*) divertido,-a: *she's great fun to be with,* es una persona muy divertida; *swimming is a fun sport,* nadar es un deporte divertido; *the outing was fun,* la excursión fue divertida.
● **in fun,** en broma: *he didn't mean what he said, it was just in fun,* no lo decía en serio, sólo era en broma. ‖ **for fun / for the fun of it,** (*for pleasure*) para divertirse; (*for a joke*) para hacer la gracia: *I'm learning Russian just for fun,* aprendo ruso porque me gusta. ‖ **to have fun,** divertirse, pasarlo bien: *we had great fun at the party,* nos divertimos mucho en la fiesta. ‖ **to make fun of,** reírse de, mofarse de, burlarse de. ‖ **to poke fun at,** burlarse de, mofarse de. ‖ **to spoil the fun,** aguar la fiesta: *don't spoil all the fun!,* ¡no seas un aguafiestas! ‖ **what fun!,** ¡qué divertido!
funcionalism [ˈfʌŋkʃənəlɪzəm] *n* funcionalismo.
funcionalist [ˈfʌŋkʃənəlɪst] *n* funcionalista *mf*.
function [ˈfʌŋkʃən] **1** *n* (*purpose, use, duty*) función *f*: *that is not the function of a mere assistant,* eso no corresponde a un simple ayudante; *in my function as chairperson,* en mi calidad de presidente. **2** (*ceremony*) acto, ceremonia; (*reception*) recepción *f*. **3** MATH función *f*. – **4** *i* (*work*) funcionar: *do you know how this machine functions?,* ¿sabes cómo funciona esta máquina? **5** (*act*) funcionar: *the human brain functions as a computer,* el cerebro humano funciona como un ordenador.
● **to fulfil a function,** desempeñar una función.
■ **function key,** tecla.
functional [ˈfʌŋkʃənəl] **1** *adj* (*operational*) funcional. **2** (*practical, useful*) práctico,-a.
functionary [ˈfʌŋkʃənərɪ] *n* funcionario,-a.
▲ *pl* **functionaries.**
fund [fʌnd] **1** *n* (*sum of money*) fondo. **2** (*supply*) fuente *f*. – **3** *t* (*finance*) patrocinar. **4** (*debt*) consolidar. – **5 funds,** *npl* (*financial resources*) fondos *mpl*.
● **to be short of funds,** andar corto,-a de dinero.
fundalmentalism [fʌndəˈmentəlɪzəm] *n* REL fundamentalismo.
fundamental [fʌndəˈmentəl] **1** *adj* (*central, basic*) fundamental, básico,-a. **2** (*necessary, essential*) esencial (**to,** para). – **3 fundamentals,** *npl* (*essential part, basic rule*) fundamentos *mpl,* reglas *fpl* básicas.
fundamentalist [fʌndəˈmentəlɪst] *n* REL fundamentalista *mf*.
fundamentally [fʌndəˈmentəlɪ] **1** *adv* (*basically*) básicamente. **2** (*radically*) fundamentalmente.
funeral [ˈfjuːnərəl] **1** *n* entierro, funeral *m*. – **2** *adj* fúnebre.
● **it's your** (*his, her, etc*) **funeral!,** ¡es tu (*su etc*) problema!, ¡allá tú (*él, ella, etc*)!

■ **funeral director,** director de funeraria. ‖ **funeral procession,** cortejo fúnebre. ‖ **funeral parlor,** US funeraria. ‖ **funeral pyre,** pira funeraria.
funereal [fjuːˈnɪərɪəl] *adj* fúnebre.
funfair [ˈfʌnfeəʳ] *n* GB feria, parque *m* de atracciones.
fungicide [ˈfʌndʒɪsaɪd] *n* fungicida *m*.
fungus [ˈfʌŋgəs] *n* hongo.
▲ *pl* **funguses** o **fungi** [ˈfʌndʒaɪ].
funicular [fjuːˈnɪkjələʳ] *n* funicular *m*.
funk[1] [fʌŋk] **1** *n* fam (*fear, anxiety*) canguelo, acojone *m*. **2** (*coward*) cagado,-a, gallina. – **3** *t* (*avoid through fear*) rajarse ante, cagarse.
● **to be in a funk,** estar cagado,-a de miedo, estar acojonado,-a.
funk[2] [fʌŋk] *n* MUS funky *m*.
funky [ˈfʌŋkɪ] **1** *adj* MUS funky. **2** fam (*fashionable*) guai, chulo,-a.
▲ *comp* **funkier,** *superl* **funkiest.**
funnel [ˈfʌnəl] **1** *n* (*for liquid*) embudo. **2** (*chimney*) chimenea. – **3** *t* verter por un embudo. – **4** *i* verterse. – **5** *t* fig (*channel*) encauzar.
▲ (*verbo*) *pt & pp* **funnelled** (US **funneled**), *ger* **funnelling** (US **funneling**).
funnily [ˈfʌnɪlɪ] *adv* (*strangely*) de manera extraña, de modo raro.
● **funnily enough,** curiosamente, aunque parezca extraño.
funny [ˈfʌnɪ] **1** *adj* (*amusing*) gracioso,-a, divertido,-a: *it's a very funny film,* es una película muy divertida; *my little niece is so funny,* mi sobrinita es tan graciosa; *I don't find your remarks at all funny,* tus comentarios no son nada graciosos. **2** (*strange*) raro,-a, extraño,-a, curioso,-a: *that's funny - it was here a minute ago,* qué raro - estaba aquí hace un momento; *what's that funny noise?,* ¿qué es aquel ruido extraño?; *I think there's something funny going on,* creo que pasa algo raro; *the funny thing is that ...,* lo curioso es que ... **3** fam (*slightly ill*) rarillo,-a, malito,-a; (*slightly mad*) chiflado,-a: *I feel funny,* no me encuentro bien.
■ **funny bone,** hueso de la alegría. ‖ **funny business,** negocios *mpl* sucios, chanchullos *mpl*, tejemanejes *mpl*. ‖ **funny farm,** fam manicomio.
▲ *comp* **funnier,** *superl* **funniest.**
fur [fɜːʳ] **1** *n* (*of living animal*) pelo, pelaje *m*. **2** (*of dead animal*) piel *f*. **3** (*garment*) abrigo de piel. **4** (*on appliance*) sarro; (*on tongue*) sarro, saburra. – **5** *adj* de piel. – **6** *i* calcificarse.
■ **fur coat,** abrigo de pieles.
furbish [ˈfɜːbɪʃ] *t* pulir.
◆ **to furbish up** *t sep* renovar, restaurar.
furious [ˈfjʊərɪəs] **1** *adj* (*very angry*) furioso,-a: *she'll be furious if we break anything,* se pondrá furiosa si rompemos algo; *he's got a furious temper,* tiene muy mal genio. **2** (*violent, wild, uncontrolled*) furioso,-a, violento,-a; (*vigorous*) vertiginoso,-a, frenético,-a: *he drove at a furious speed,* conducía a una velocidad vertiginosa; *they're going at a furious pace,* van a toda velocidad.
furiously [ˈfjʊərɪəslɪ] **1** *adv* (*angrily*) con furia, furiosamente. **2** (*vigorously*) frenéticamente.
furl [fɜːl] **1** *t* arrollar, enrollar. – **2** *i* arrollarse, enrollarse.
furlong [ˈfɜːlɒŋ] *n* ≈ 201 metros.
furnace [ˈfɜːnɪs] *n* horno.
furnish [ˈfɜːnɪʃ] **1** *t* (*house etc*) amueblar (**with,** de): *I'd like to rent a furnished flat,* quisiera alquilar un piso amueblado. **2** fml (*supply - material*) suministrar, proveer; (- *information etc*) facilitar, proporcionar.

furnishings ['fɜːnɪʃɪŋz] npl muebles, cortinas y alfombras.

furniture ['fɜːnɪtʃəʳ] n mobiliario, muebles mpl: I need some new furniture, necesito unos muebles nuevos. ● to be a part of the furniture, formar parte del decorado. ■ a piece of furniture, un mueble. ‖ furniture polish, cera para muebles. ‖ furniture shop, tienda de muebles. ‖ furniture van, camión m de mudanzas.

furor ['fjuːrɔːʳ] n US → furore.

furore [fjuˈrɔːrɪ] n (uproar - anger) ola de protestas; (- enthusiasm) ola de entusiasmo.

furrier ['fʌrɪəʳ] n peletero,-a.

furrow ['fʌrəʊ] 1 n AGR surco. 2 (wrinkle) arruga. – 3 t AGR surcar. 4 (forehead) arrugar.

furry ['fɜːrɪ] 1 adj (hairy) peludo,-a. 2 (scaly) sarroso,-a. ▲ comp furrier, superl furriest.

further ['fɜːðəʳ] 1 adj (farther) más lejos: she lives further down the road, vive más abajo de la calle. 2 (more, additional) más, adicional; (new) nuevo,-a: I have just one further question, tengo una pregunta más; this office will remain closed until further notice, esta oficina permanecerá cerrada hasta nuevo aviso; for further information, please contact ..., para más información, póngase en contacto con ...; he had nothing further to say on the matter, no tuvo nada más que decir sobre el asunto; we had to wait a further 3 hours, tuvimos que esperar otras tres horas más. – 3 adv (farther) más lejos: is it much further?, ¿queda mucho más?; don't go any further, no vayas más lejos; it's further to the East, está más al este; nothing could be further from my mind, nada más lejos de mi intención; looking further ahead, mirando más adelante. 4 (more, to a greater degree) más: the police want to take the matter further, la policía quiere investigar más el asunto; I'd like to go further into this subject, me gustaría estudiar el tema más a fondo; and she hasn't heard anything further, y no ha vuelto a saber nada más; the situation is still further complicated than we thought, la situación es aún más complicada de lo que pensábamos; I don't want to detain you any further, no quiero entretenerte más. 5 fml (besides) además: further, I'd like to complain about the lack of parking spaces, además, quisiera quejarme de la falta de aparcamientos. – 6 t (advance, promote) fomentar, promover: he would have gone to any lengths to further his career, hubiera hecho cualquier cosa para promover su propia carrera.
● this must not go any further, esto tiene que quedar entre nosotros, esto no tiene que salir de aquí. ‖ further to, con referencia a, referente a: further to your letter of the 6th inst, con referencia a su carta del día 6 del corriente. ■ further education, estudios mpl superiores. ▲ En 1 and 3 véase también far.

furtherance ['fɜːðərəns] n promoción f, fomento, avance m.

furthermore [fɜːðəˈmɔːʳ] adv fml además.

furthermost ['fɜːðərməʊst] adj → far, further.

furthest ['fɜːðɪst] 1 adj → far, further. – 2 adv → far, further.

furtive ['fɜːtɪv] adj furtivo,-a.

furtively ['fɜːtɪvlɪ] adv furtivamente.

furtiveness ['fɜːtɪvnəs] n sigilo.

fury ['fjʊərɪ] 1 n (rage) furia, rabia, ira: there was fury in her eyes, tenía los ojos llenos de furia; he was speechless with fury, estaba mudo de ira. 2 (wild force) furor m, violencia, frenesí m: the fury of the storm, el furor de la tormenta. – 3 The Furies, npl las Furias fpl.

● to do sth. like fury, hacer algo con furia, hacer algo como un,-a loco,-a. ‖ to be in a fury, estar furioso,-a. ‖ to fly into a fury, ponerse hecho,-a una furia. ▲ pl furies.

fuse [fjuːz] 1 n ELEC fusible m, plomo: I've blown a fuse, he hecho saltar el fusible; the fuses blew, saltaron los fusibles, se fundieron los plomos. 2 (wick) mecha; (detonator) espoleta. – 3 t (cause to stop working, melt) fundir: you could fuse the light, podrías fundir los plomos; the heat has fused all the metal, el calor ha fundido todo el metal. 4 fig (merge) fusionar. – 5 i (stop working, melt) fundirse: the lights have fused, se han fundido los plomos. 6 fig (merge) fusionarse: the two companies fused, las dos empresas se fusionaron.
● to blow a fuse, (appliance) saltar el fusible de, fundirse el plomo de; (person) estallar, explotar. ■ fuse box, caja de fusibles. ‖ fuse wire, alambre m de fusible.

fuselage ['fjuːzəlɑːʒ] n AER fuselaje m.

fusilier [fjuːzəˈlɪəʳ] n fusilero.

fusillade [fjuːzəˈleɪd] 1 n tiroteo, descarga cerrada, cortina de fuego. 2 fig lluvia, torrente m.

fusion ['fjuːʒən] 1 n fusión f, fundición f. 2 fig fusión f.

fuss [fʌs] 1 n (commotion, nervous excitement) alboroto, jaleo, bulla, ruido: what's all the fuss about?, ¿por qué tanto jaleo?; don't get in(to) such a fuss, no te pongas así, no hay para tanto; a lot of fuss about nothing, mucho ruido y pocas nueces. 2 (angry scene, dispute) escándalo, problemas mpl; (complaints) quejas fpl: there'll be a right fuss if Dad finds out, habrá un escándalo si se entera papá; there was a fuss about the bill, hubo quejas por la cuenta. – 3 t (pester, annoy, bother) molestar: stop fussing me, no me molestes. – 4 i (worry, fret) preocuparse, inquietarse: don't fuss, we'll get there on time, no te preocupes, llegaremos a tiempo; she's always fussing about her hair, siempre se preocupa por su pelo. 5 (pay excessive attention to) mimar (con exceso), preocuparse excesivamente (over, por): she loves to fuss over her grand-daughter, le encanta mimar a su nieta; I think they fuss over him too much, creo que le miman demasiado.
● to make a fuss / kick up a fuss, (complain strongly) armar un escándalo, armar un lío, montar una escena: he kicked up a fuss about his hotel room, armó un escándalo por su habitación; please don't make a fuss, no montes una escena por favor. ‖ to make a fuss of sb., hacer mimos a algn., deshacerse por algn.: everyone made a fuss of the new baby, todos hicieron mimos al nuevo bebé. ‖ not to be fussed, darle igual a uno: what do you want to do? –I'm not fussed, ¿qué quieres hacer? –me da igual.

fusspot ['fʌspɒt] n quisquilloso,-a, tiquismiquis mf.

fussy ['fʌsɪ] 1 adj (concerned with details) quisquilloso,-a, exigente, especial, particular: he's very fussy about his food, es muy exigente con la comida; she's very fussy about punctuality, es muy quisquillosa con la puntualidad. 2 (nervous about small things) nervioso,-a. 3 (too elaborate) recargado,-a. ▲ comp fussier, superl fussiest.

fusty ['fʌstɪ] 1 adj (musty) mohoso,-a, rancio,-a; (stale) que huele a cerrado. 2 (old-fashioned) chapado,-a a la antigua. ▲ comp fustier, superl fustiest.

futile ['fjuːtaɪl] 1 adj (pointless) vano,-a, inútil: a futile attempt to save him, un intento inútil de salvarlo. 2 (inane) necio,-a, fatuo,-a, inútil.

futility [fjuːˈtɪlətɪ] n inutilidad f, lo inútil.

futon [fuːˈtɒn] *n* futón *m*.
future [ˈfjuːtʃəʳ] **1** *adj* futuro,-a: *my future husband,* mi futuro marido; *we arranged to meet at some future time,* quedamos para vernos en un futuro. – **2** *n* futuro, porvenir *m*: *the future is bleak,* el futuro no es nada prometedor; *who knows what the future holds?,* ¿quién sabe lo que tiene reservado el futuro?; *your future with this company is uncertain,* tu futuro en esta empresa es inseguro; *it's a good idea to save for the future,* es buena idea ahorrar para el futuro; *my job has no future,* mi trabajo no tiene porvenir. **3** LING futuro.
● **in future,** en el futuro, de aquí en adelante. ‖ **in the future,** en el futuro. ‖ **in the distant future,** en un fu-

turo lejano. ‖ **in the near future,** en un futuro próximo. ‖ **in the not too distant future,** en un futuro no muy lejano.
futurism [ˈfjuːtʃərɪzəm] *n* futurismo.
futurist [ˈfjuːtʃərɪst] *adj* futurista.
futuristic [fjuːtʃəˈrɪstɪk] *adj* futurístico,-a.
fuzz [fʌz] *n* (*fluff*) pelusa; (*fine hair*) vello.
■ **the fuzz,** SL la bofia.
fuzzy [ˈfʌzɪ] **1** *adj* (*frizzy*) rizado,-a, crespo,-a; (*fluffy*) con pelusilla. **2** (*blurred*) borroso,-a, movido,-a.
▲ *comp* **fuzzier,** *superl* **fuzziest.**
fwd [ˈfɔːwəd] *abbr* (*forward*) adelante.

G

G, g [giː] 1 *n* (*the letter*) G, g *f*. 2 MUS sol *m*.
g [græm] *symb* (*gram, gramme*) gramo; (*abbreviation*) g.
gab [gæb] 1 *n* labia, palique *m*. – 2 *i* charlar, parlotear.
● **to have the gift of the gab**, tener un pico de oro, tener mucha labia.
▲ *pt* & *pp* **gabbed**, *ger* **gabbing**.
gabardine ['gæbədiːn] *n* gabardina, impermeable *m*.
gabble ['gæbəl] 1 *n* chapurreo, charloteo, farfulla. – 2 *t* farfullar, charlotear, hablar atropelladamente.
gaberdine ['gæbədiːn] *n* → **gabardine**.
gable ['geɪbəl] *n* ARCH aguilón *m*.
■ **gable roof**, tejado de dos aguas.
Gabon [gə'bɒn] *n* Gabón.
Gabonese [gæbə'niːz] 1 *adj* gabonés,-esa. – 2 *n* gabonés,-esa. – 3 **the Gabonese**, *npl* los gaboneses *mpl*.
gad [gæd] **to gad about / gad around**, *i fam* callejear.
▲ *pt* & *pp* **gadded**, *ger* **gadding**.
gadabout ['gædəbaut] *n fam* callejero,-a, azotacalles *mf*.
gadfly ['gædflaɪ] *n* ZOOL tábano.
▲ *pl* **gadflies**.
gadget ['gædʒɪt] *n fam* aparato, artilugio, dispositivo, chisme *m*.
gadgetry ['gædʒɪtrɪ] *n fam* artilugios *mpl*, chismes *mpl*.
gadwall ['gædwɔːl] *n* ORN ánade *m* friso.
Gaelic ['geɪlɪk] 1 *adj* gaélico,-a. – 2 *n* (*language*) gaélico.
gaff [gæf] *n* (*fishing*) garfio, harpón *m*.
● **to blow the gaff**, *fam* descubrir el pastel.
gaffe [gæf] *n* metedura de pata, plancha.
● **to make a gaffe**, meter la pata.
gaffer ['gæfə'] 1 *n* (*in film-making*) jefe *m* de eléctricos. 2 GB *fam* (*foreman*) jefe *m*, encargado. 3 GB *fam* (*old man*) vejete *m*.
gag [gæg] 1 *n* (*cover for the mouth*) mordaza. 2 (*joke*) chiste *m*, gag *m*, broma. 3 THEAT *fam* morcilla. – 4 *t* amordazar. – 5 *i* tener náuseas.
▲ *pt* & *pp* **gagged**, *ger* **gagging**.
gaga ['gɑːgɑː] *adj fam* chocho,-a.
● **to be gaga**, chochear. ‖ **to go gaga**, empezar a chochear.
gage [geɪdʒ] *n* US → **gauge**.
gaggle ['gægəl] *n* (*geese*) manada: *a gaggle of geese*, una manada de ocas; *a gaggle of schoolgirls*, un corro de colegialas.
gaiety ['geɪətɪ] *n* alegría, diversión *f*, regocijo.
▲ *pl* **gaieties**.
gaily ['geɪlɪ] *adv* alegremente.
gain [geɪn] 1 *n* (*achievement*) logro. 2 (*profit*) ganancia, beneficio: *the sale of the company brought him considerable gains*, la venta de la empresa le supuso unas ganancias considerables. 3 (*increase*) aumento. – 4 *t* (*achieve*) lograr, conseguir. 5 (*obtain*) ganar. 6 (*increase*) aumentar. 7 (*clock*) adelantar. – 8 *i* (*clock*) adelantar. 9 (*shares*) subir.
● **to gain ground**, ganar terreno. ‖ **to gain weight**,

aumentar de peso, engordar. ‖ **to stand to gain**, tener probabilidad de ganar.
■ **capital gain**, plusvalía. ‖ **capital gains tax**, impuesto sobre plusvalías. ‖ **windfall gain**, ganancia inesperada.
gainful ['geɪnfʊl] *adj fml* lucrativo,-a, remunerado,-a, retribuido,-a.
■ **gainful activity**, actividad *f* lucrativa.
gainsay [geɪn'seɪ] *t fml* (*generally negative*) negar: *there's no gainsaying his talent*, su talento es innegable.
▲ *pt* & *pp* **gainsaid** [geɪn'sed].
gait [geɪt] *n* andares *mpl*, forma de andar.
gaiter ['geɪtə'] *n* polaina.
gal[1] [gæl] *n fam dated* chica, muchacha, tía.
gal[2] [gæl] *abbr* (*gallon*) galón *m*.
gala ['gɑːlə] 1 *n* gala, fiesta. 2 SP competición *f*, festival *m*, certamen *m*.
■ **gala dress**, traje *m* de etiqueta. ‖ **gala night**, noche *f* de gala.
galactic [gə'læktɪk] *adj* galáctico,-a.
Galapagos [gə'læpəgəs] **the Galapagos Islands**, *npl* las Islas Galápagos.
galaxy ['gæləksɪ] *n* galaxia.
▲ *pl* **galaxies**.
gale [geɪl] *n* (*wind*) vendaval *m*; (*storm*) tempestad *f*.
■ **gales of laughter**, carcajadas *fpl*: *we could hear gales of laughter from next door*, oímos carcajadas que venían de al lado.
Galicia [gə'lɪʃə] *n* Galicia.
Galician [gə'lɪʃən] 1 *adj* gallego,-a. – 2 *n* (*person*) gallego,-a. 3 (*language*) gallego.
Galilean [gælɪ'liːən] 1 *adj* galileo,-a. – 2 *n* galileo,-a.
Galilee ['gælɪliː] *n* Galilea.
■ **Sea of Galilee**, Mar *m* de Galilea.
gall[1] [gæl, 'gælən] *abbr* (*gallon*) galón *m*.
gall[2] [gɔːl] 1 *n fig* descaro, caradura.
■ **gall bladder**, vesícula biliar.
gall[3] [gɔːl] *t* irritar, molestar.
gallant ['gælənt] 1 *adj* (*brave*) valiente. 2 (*chivalrous*) galante.
gallantry ['gæləntrɪ] 1 *n* (*bravery*) valentía. 2 (*chivalry*) galantería.
galleon ['gælɪən] *n* galeón *m*.
gallery ['gælərɪ] 1 *n* (*gen*) galería. 2 (*in theatre*) gallinero. 3 (*for spectators*) tribuna.
● **to play to the gallery**, actuar de cara a la galería.
▲ *pl* **galleries**.
galley ['gælɪ] 1 *n* (*ship*) galera. 2 (*kitchen on ships*) cocina.
■ **galley proof**, galerada. ‖ **galley slave**, galeote *m*.
Gallic ['gælɪk] *adj* gálico,-a, galo,-a.
Gallicism ['gælɪsɪzəm] *n* galicismo.
galling ['gɔːlɪŋ] *adj* irritante.
gallivant [gælɪ'vænt] *i fam* callejear, corretear.
gallon ['gælən] *n* galón *m*.
▲ *Equivale en* GB *a 4,55 litros y en* US *3,78 litros*.

gallop ['gæləp] 1 n galope m. - 2 i galopar.
galloping ['gæləpɪŋ] adj galopante.
■ galloping leucaemia, leucemia galopante.
gallows ['gæləʊz] npl horca sing, patíbulo sing, cadalso sing.
gallstone ['gɔːlstəʊn] n cálculo biliar.
Gallup poll ['gæləppəʊl] n encuesta, sondeo.
▲ Es marca registrada.
galore [gə'lɔːʳ] adj en abundancia, en gran cantidad: there was food galore at the party, había un montón de comida en la fiesta.
galosh [gə'lɒʃ] n chanclo.
galvanization [gælvənaɪ'zeɪʃən] n galvanización f.
galvanize ['gælvənaɪz] t galvanizar.
● to galvanize sb. into action, galvanizar a algn.
galvanized ['gælvənaɪzd] adj galvanizado,-a.
Gambia ['gæmbɪə] n Gambia.
Gambian ['gæmbɪən] 1 adj gambiano,-a. - 2 n gambiano,-a.
gambit ['gæmbɪt] 1 n (in chess) gambito. 2 fig táctica, estratagema, truco.
gamble ['gæmbəl] 1 n (risky undertaking) empresa arriesgada: he took a big gamble when he decided to change jobs, se arriesgó mucho cuando decidió cambiar de trabajo. 2 (risk) riesgo. 3 (bet) jugada, apuesta. - 4 t jugar(se): he gambled away the entire family fortune, se jugó toda la fortuna familiar. - 5 i (bet) apostar, jugar: she loves gambling on anything, le encanta apostar a cualquier cosa. 6 (take a risk) arriesgarse, confiar: he gambled on the idea that he wouldn't be found out, confió en que no lo descubrirían.
gambler ['gæmbləʳ] n jugador,-ra.
■ pathological gambler, ludópata mf.
gambling ['gæmblɪŋ] n juego: gambling was his ruin, el juego le perdió.
■ gambling den, garito. ‖ gambling game, juego de envite. ‖ gambling house, casa de juego.
gambol ['gæmbəl] i brincar, saltar.
▲ pt & pp gambolled (US gamboled), ger gambolling (US gamboling).
game [geɪm] 1 n juego: game of chance, juego de azar. 2 (match) partido. 3 (of cards, chess, etc) partida. 4 (hunting) caza. 5 fig presa: she was easy game, era una presa fácil. - 6 adj dispuesto,-a, listo,-a. - 7 games, npl GB EDUC educación f sing física.
● to be game for, estar listo,-a para, estar preparado,-a para. ‖ to be game for anything, estar dispuesto,-a a todo. ‖ to be on the game, GB sl ejercer la prostitución. ‖ the game is up, fig se acabó el juego. ‖ to give the game away, fig enseñar las cartas. ‖ to play the game, fig jugar limpio. ‖ two can play at that game, fig donde las dan las toman. ‖ what's her game?, ¿a qué juega?, ¿qué pretende?
■ board games, juegos mpl de mesa. ‖ game bird, ave f de caza. ‖ game reserve, coto de caza. ‖ the Olympic Games, los Juegos mpl Olímpicos.
gamekeeper ['geɪmkiːpəʳ] n guardabosque mf.
gamma ['gæmə] n gamma.
■ gamma globulin, gammaglobulina. ‖ gamma rays, rayos mpl gamma.
gammon ['gæmən] n GB jamón m (ahumado o curado a la sal).
gammy ['gæmɪ] adj GB fam lisiado,-a, tullido,-a.
▲ comp gammier, superl gammiest.
gamut ['gæmət] n gama, serie f.
● to run the (whole) gamut of ....,, pasar por toda la gama de .....

gander ['gændəʳ] n ganso.
gang [gæŋ] 1 n (criminals) banda. 2 (youths) pandilla. 3 (workers) cuadrilla, brigada. 4 (friends) pandilla, grupo.
◆ to gang up on t insep (join forces) unirse contra; (plot against) confabularse contra, conspirar contra. ‖ to gang up with i unirse a.
gang-bang ['gæŋbæŋ] n GB sl violación f múltiple (cometida por un grupo de violadores).
ganger ['gæŋəʳ] n GB fam capataz m.
Ganges ['gændʒiːz] n el Ganges m.
gangland ['gæŋlænd] n fam hampa, submundo, bajos fondos mpl.
gangling ['gæŋglɪŋ] adj (esp of boys) desgarbado,-a, larguirucho,-a.
ganglion ['gæŋglɪən] n ganglio.
gangplank ['gæŋplæŋk] n (on ship) plancha.
gangrene ['gæŋgriːn] n gangrena.
gangrenous ['gæŋgrɪnəs] adj gangrenoso,-a.
gangster ['gæŋstəʳ] n gángster m.
gangway ['gæŋweɪ] 1 n GB (aisle, passage) pasillo. 2 (on ship) pasarela.
● gangway!, GB ¡paso!
gannet ['gænɪt] 1 n (bird) alcatraz m. 2 fam (person) tragón,-ona, zampón,-ona, comilón,-ona.
gantry ['gæntrɪ] n (for barrels) caballete m, poíno m; (for rocket) torre f de lanzamiento; (for railway signals) puente m de señales.
■ gantry crane, grúa de pórtico.
▲ pl gantries.
gaol [dʒeɪl] n GB cárcel f.
▲ Véase también jail.
gap [gæp] 1 n (hole) abertura, hueco. 2 (crack) brecha. 3 (empty space) espacio. 4 (blank) blanco. 5 (time) intervalo. 6 (deficiency) laguna: there are certain gaps in his education, su formación presenta algunas lagunas. 7 (emptiness) vacío; (gulf) diferencia.
● to bridge a gap / fill a gap, llenar un hueco.
■ age gap, diferencia de edades.
gape [geɪp] 1 i abrirse. 2 (stare) mirar boquiabierto,-a.
gaping ['geɪpɪŋ] 1 adj (mouth) abierto,-a; (hole) enorme. 2 (person) boquiabierto,-a. 3 fig profundo,-a, hondo,-a.
■ a gaping wound, una herida profunda.
garage ['gæraːʒ, 'gærɪdʒ] 1 n garaje m. 2 (for repairs) taller m mecánico. 3 (for petrol etc) gasolinera.
garb [gaːb] 1 n fml atavío, atuendo, traje m, vestido. - 2 t fml ataviar, vestir: the prince was garbed in blue, el príncipe vestía de azul.
garbage ['gaːbɪdʒ] 1 n US basura. 2 GB desperdicios mpl. 3 fig tonterías fpl, majaderías fpl, sandeces fpl.
■ garbage can, US cubo de la basura. ‖ garbage collector, US basurero. ‖ garbage truck, US camión m de la basura.
garbled ['gaːbəld] adj confuso,-a, incomprensible.
garden ['gaːdən] 1 n jardín m. - 2 i cuidar el jardín. - 3 gardens, npl (public park) jardines mpl.
● to lead sb. up the garden path, enredar a algn., embaucar a algn.
■ garden city, ciudad f jardín. ‖ garden party, recepción f al aire libre.
gardener ['gaːdənəʳ] n gen jardinero,-a; (of vegetables) hortelano,-a.
■ landscape gardener, jardinista mf, arquitecto,-a paisajista.
gardenia [gaː'diːnɪə] n gardenia.
gardening ['gaːdənɪŋ] n jardinería.
● to do the gardening, cuidar el jardín.

garfish ['gɑːfɪʃ] *n* (*fish*) aguja *f*.
gargle ['gɑːgəl] **1** *i* hacer gárgaras, gargarizar. – **2** *n* (*act*) gárgaras *fpl*. **3** (*liquid*) gargarismo.
gargoyle ['gɑːgɔɪl] *n* gárgola.
garish ['geərɪʃ] *adj* (*colour*) chillón,-ona, llamativo,-a; (*light*) cegador,-ra, deslumbrante.
garland ['gɑːlənd] **1** *n* guirnalda. – **2** *t* adornar con guirnaldas.
garlic ['gɑːlɪk] *n* ajo: *a clove of garlic*, un diente de ajo.
■ **garlic bread**, pan *m* de ajo.
garment ['gɑːmənt] *n* (*clothes*) prenda.
garnet ['gɑːnɪt] *n* granate *m*.
garnish ['gɑːnɪʃ] **1** *n* guarnición *f*. – **2** *t* guarnecer.
Garonne [gæ'rɒn] *n* el Garona *m*.
garotte [gə'rɒt] **1** *n* garrote *m*. – **2** *t* agarrotar, ejecutar con garrote.
garret ['gærət] *n* (*room*) buhardilla; (*attic, loft*) desván *m*.
garrison ['gærɪsən] **1** *n* guarnición *f*. – **2** *t* guarnecer.
■ **garrison town**, ciudad *f* de guarnición.
garrulous ['gærələs] *adj fml* gárrulo,-a, locuaz, parlanchín,-ina.
garter ['gɑːtəʳ] *n* liga.
■ **garter belt**, liguero, portaligas *m*. ‖ **the Order of the Garter**, la Orden de la Jarretera.
gas [gæs] **1** *n* (*substance*) gas *m*. **2** US gasolina. **3** (*anaesthetic*) anestesia: *he had gas*, lo anestesiaron. **4** US *fig* algo divertido: *the party was a real gas*, la fiesta fue muy divertida; *we had a real gas*, lo pasamos bomba, lo pasamos pipa. – **5** *t* asfixiar con gas. – **6** *i fam* charlotear.
● **to step on the gas**, *fam* pisar el acelerador a fondo.
■ **Calor gas**, gas *m* butano. ‖ **gas chamber**, cámara de gas. ‖ **gas cooker**, cocina de gas. ‖ **gas fire**, estufa de gas. ‖ **gas mask**, careta antigás, máscara antigás. ‖ **gas meter**, contador *m* de gas. ‖ **gas ring**, fogón *m*. ‖ **gas pipeline**, gasoducto. ‖ **gas station**, US gasolinera.
▲ *pl* gases *o* gasses.
gasbag ['gæsbæg] *n fam* cotorra, parlanchín,-ina.
Gascon ['gæskən] **1** *adj* gascón,-ona. – **2** *n* gascón,-ona.
Gascony ['gæskənɪ] *n* Gascuña.
gaseous ['gæsɪəs] *adj* gaseoso,-a.
gash [gæʃ] **1** *n* cuchillada, herida profunda, raja. – **2** *t* acuchillar, rajar.
gasket ['gæskɪt] *n* junta.
gaslight ['gæslaɪt] *n* luz *f* de gas, alumbrado de gas.
gasoline ['gæsəliːn] *n* US gasolina.
gasometer [gæ'sɒmɪtəʳ] *n* gasómetro.
gasp [gɑːsp] **1** *i* (*in astonishment*) quedar boquiabierto,-a. **2** (*to pant*) jadear. – **3** *n* (*cry of surprise etc*) grito; (*last breath*) boqueada.
● **to be at one's last gasp**, *fig* estar en las últimas. ‖ **to gasp for air**, hacer esfuerzos por respirar.
gassy ['gæsɪ] *adj* gaseoso,-a.
▲ *comp* gassier, *superl* gassiest.
gastric ['gæstrɪk] *adj* gástrico,-a.
■ **gastric juice**, jugo gástrico. ‖ **gastric ulcer**, úlcera gástrica.
gastritis [gæs'traɪtəs] *n* gastritis *f*.
gastroenteritis [gæstrəʊentə'raɪtəs] *n* gastroenteritis *f*.
gastronome ['gæstrənəʊm] *n* gastrónomo,-a *mf*.
gastronomic [gæstrə'nɒmɪk] *n* gastronómico,-a.
gastronomy [gæs'trɒnəmɪ] *n* gastronomía.
gasworks ['gæswɜːks] *n* fábrica de gas.
gate [geɪt] **1** *n* (*door*) puerta, verja. **2** (*at airport*) puerta; (*at stadium*) entrada. **3** GB (*attendance*) asistencia: *we're*

expecting a big gate next Saturday, esperamos una gran asistencia el sábado que viene.
■ **gate money**, recaudación *f*, taquilla.
gateau ['gætəʊ] *n* pastel *m*, tarta.
▲ *pl gateaux* ['gætəʊz].
gatecrash ['geɪtkræʃ] **1** *t fam* colarse en. – **2** *i fam* colarse.
gatecrasher ['geɪtkræʃəʳ] *n fam* persona que se cuela.
gatepost ['geɪtpəʊst] *n* poste *m*.
● **between you, me, and the gatepost**, *fam* entre nosotros, en confianza.
gateway ['geɪtweɪ] **1** *n* entrada, puerta. **2** *fig* camino, pasaporte *m*, puerta: *the gateway to happiness*, el camino hacia la felicidad.
gather ['gæðəʳ] **1** *t* (*collect*) juntar. **2** (*call together*) reunir. **3** (*pick up*) recoger. **4** (*fruit, flowers*) coger. **5** (*taxes*) recaudar. **6** (*gain*) ganar, cobrar. **7** (*in sewing*) fruncir. **8** (*deduce*) deducir, inferir, suponer. – **9** *i* (*come together*) reunirse, juntarse. **10** (*build up*) acumularse. **11** (*form*) formarse: *a large crowd gathered*, se formó una gran muchedumbre; *a big storm was gathering on the horizon*, una gran tormenta se formaba en el horizonte.
◆ **to gather round** *i* acercarse, agruparse. ‖ **to gather up** *t sep* recoger.
● **to gather speed**, ganar velocidad. ‖ **to gather strength**, cobrar fuerzas.
gathering ['gæðərɪŋ] **1** *n* reunión *f*, asamblea: *a family gathering*, una reunión familiar. **2** (*in sewing*) pliegue *m*, frunce *m*. – **3** *adj* creciente: *gathering uncertainty*, una incertidumbre creciente.
GATT [gæt] *abbr* (*General Agreement on Tariffs and Trade*) Acuerdo General sobre Aranceles Aduaneros y Comercio; (*abbreviation*) GATT *m*.
gauche [gəʊʃ] *adj* (*awkward*) torpe, desmañado,-a; (*tactless*) sin tacto, torpe.
gaucheness ['gəʊʃnəs] *n* (*awkwardness*) torpeza; (*tactlessness*) falta de tacto, falta de delicadeza, insensibilidad *f*.
gaudily ['gɔːdɪlɪ] *adv* llamativamente: *gaudily dressed*, vestido,-a llamativamente.
gaudy ['gɔːdɪ] *adj* chillón,-ona, llamativo,-a.
▲ *comp gaudier, superl gaudiest*.
gauge [geɪdʒ] **1** *n* (*device*) indicador *m*, calibrador *m*. **2** (*measure*) medida estándar. **3** (*railways*) ancho de vía. **4** *fig* (*indication*) indicación *f*, muestra. – **5** *t* (*measure*) medir, calibrar. **6** *fig* apreciar, calcular, determinar, estimar, juzgar.
■ **narrow gauge**, (*railways*) de vía estrecha. ‖ **tyre gauge**, manómetro para neumáticos.
Gaul [gɔːl] **1** *n* (*place*) Galia. **2** (*person*) galo,-a.
Gaulish ['gɔːlɪʃ] **1** *adj* galo,-a. – **2** *n* (*language*) galo.
gaunt [gɔːnt] *adj* (*lean*) demacrado,-a. **2** *fig* (*desolate*) lúgubre; (*grim*) siniestro,-a.
gauntlet ['gɔːntlət] *n* (*armour*) guantelete *m*; (*glove*) guante *m*.
● **to run the gauntlet of**, *fig* sufrir, experimentar, estar sometido,-a a. ‖ **to take up the gauntlet**, *fig* recoger el guante. ‖ **to throw down the gauntlet**, *fig* arrojar el guante.
gauze [gɔːz] *n* gasa.
gave [geɪv] *pt* → **give**.
gavel ['gævəl] *n* (*for judges and auctioneers*) martillo.
gawky ['gɔːkɪ] *adj* desgarbado,-a.
▲ *comp gawkier, superl gawkiest*.
gawp [gɔːp] *to gawp at*, *i* GB mirar boquiabierto,-a.
gay [geɪ] **1** *adj fam* (*homosexual*) gay, homosexual. **2** (*happy, lively*) alegre. **3** (*bright*) vistoso,-a. – **4** *n fam* (*man*) gay *m*, homosexual *m*. **5** *fam* (*woman*) lesbiana.

gayness ['geɪnəs] *n* homosexualidad *f*.
gaze [geɪz] **1** *n* mirada fija. – **2** *i* mirar fijamente.
gazebo [gə'ziːbəʊ] *n* belvedere *m*.
▲ *pl gazebos o gazeboes.*
gazelle [gə'zel] *n* gacela.
gazette [gə'zet] **1** *n* gaceta. **2** US periódico.
gazetteer [gæzə'tɪəʳ] *n* diccionario geográfico.
gazump [gə'zʌmp] *t* GB *fam romper un compromiso de venta para vender a otro comprador a un precio más alto.*
GB ['dʒiː'biː] *abbr* GB (*Great Britain*) Gran Bretaña.
GCE ['dʒiː'siː'iː] *abbr* GB (*General Certificate of Education*) ≈ Curso de Orientación Universitaria; (*abbreviation*) COU *m*.
GCSE ['dʒiː'siː'es'iː] *abbr* GB (*General Certificate of Secondary Education*) ≈ Enseñanza Secundaria Ordinaria; (*abbreviation*) ESO *f*.
Gdns ['gɑːdənz] *abbr* (*Gardens*) ≈ calle; (*abbreviation*) c/.
GDP ['dʒiː'diːpiː] *abbr* ECON (*gross domestic product*) producto interior bruto; (*abbreviation*) PIB *m*.
GDR ['dʒiː'diː'ɑːʳ] *abbr* (*German Democratic Republic*) República Democrática Alemana; (*abbreviation*) RDA.
gear [gɪəʳ] **1** *n* TECH engranaje *m*. **2** AUTO marcha, velocidad *f*. **3** (*equipment*) equipo. **4** *fam* (*belongings*) efectos *mpl* personales, cosas *fpl*, pertenencias *fpl*; (*clothes*) ropa.
◆ **to gear to** *t insep* adaptar, ajustar: *public spending should be geared to people's needs*, el gasto público debe ajustarse a las necesidades de la gente. ‖ **to gear up** *t sep fam* preparar: *I was all geared up to start*, estaba preparado para empezar.
● **to gear sb. up with sth.**, suministrar algo a algn., dar algo a algn.: *they geared me up with boots, skis and sticks*, me dieron botas, esquis y bastones.
■ **gear lever**, palanca de cambio.
gearbox ['gɪəbɒks] *n* caja de cambios.
gearshift ['gɪəʃɪft] *n* US cambio de marchas.
gearstick ['gɪəstɪk] *n* AUTO palanca de cambio.
gee¹ [dʒiː] *interj* US *fam* ¡caramba!
gee² [dʒiː] **to gee up**, *t* arrear.
● **gee up!**, ¡arre!
gee-gee ['dʒiːdʒiː] *n* GB *fam* caballo.
geese [giːs] *npl* → **goose**.
geezer ['giːzəʳ] *n fam* tío.
■ **an old geezer**, un viejo.
gel [dʒel] **1** *n* gel *m*. **2** (*for hair*) gomina, fijador *m*. – **3** *i* CHEM gelificarse. **4** *fig* (*ideas etc*) cuajar. – **5** *t* (*hairdressing*) engominar.
▲ *pt & pp gelled, ger gelling*.
gelatine ['dʒelətiːn] *n* gelatina.
gelatinous [dʒə'lætɪnəs] *adj* gelatinoso,-a.
geld [geld] *t* castrar, capar.
gelding ['geldɪŋ] *n* caballo castrado.
gelignite ['dʒelɪgnaɪt] *n* gelignita.
gem [dʒem] **1** *n* (*jewel*) gema, piedra preciosa. **2** *fig* (*person, thing*) joya, alhaja.
Gemini ['dʒemɪnaɪ] *n* ASTRON Géminis *m*.
gen [dʒen] *n* GB *fam dated* información *f*, datos *mpl*: *she gave me all the gen I asked for*, me proporcionó todos los datos que necesitaba.
Gen¹ ['dʒenərəl] *abbr* (*General*) General *m*; (*abbreviation*) Gral., Genl.
Gen² [dʒen] *abbr* (*Genesis*) Génesis.
gender ['dʒendəʳ] *n* LING género. **2** (*sex*) sexo.
gene [dʒiːn] *n* gene *m*, gen *m*.
genealogical [dʒiːnɪə'lɒdʒɪkəl] *adj* genealógico,-a.
genealogist [dʒiːnɪ'ælədʒɪst] *n* genealogista *mf*.

genealogy [dʒiːnɪ'ælədʒɪ] *n* genealogía.
genera ['dʒenərə] *npl* → **genus**.
general ['dʒenərəl] **1** *adj* general: *could you give me a general idea?*, ¿me podrías dar una idea general?; *it's in the general interest*, es en beneficio de todos. – **2** *n* MIL general *m*.
● **as a general rule**, por regla general, como norma. ‖ **in general**, por lo general.
■ **general knowledge**, conocimientos *mpl* generales. ‖ **general practice**, medicina general. ‖ **general practitioner**, médico,-a de cabecera.
generality [dʒenə'rælɪtɪ] *n* generalidad *f*.
▲ *pl generalities.*
generalization [dʒenərəlaɪ'zeɪʃən] *n* generalización *f*.
generalize ['dʒenərəlaɪz] **1** *t* generalizar. – **2** *i* generalizar.
generally ['dʒenərəlɪ] *adv* generalmente, por lo general, en general.
● **generally speaking ...**, hablando en términos generales ...
general-purpose [dʒenərəl'pɜːpəs] *adj* de uso general.
generate ['dʒenəreɪt] *t* (*gen*) generar; *fig* producir, generar.
generating ['dʒenəreɪtɪŋ] *adj* generador,-ra.
■ **generating plant**, instalación *f* productora de energía eléctrica, grupo electrógeno. ‖ **generating station**, central *f* generadora, central *f* eléctrica.
generation [dʒenə'reɪʃən] *n* generación *f*: *from generation to generation*, de generación en generación.
● **the younger generation**, los jóvenes *mpl*, la juventud *f*, la nueva generación *f*.
generator ['dʒenəreɪtəʳ] *n* generador *m*.
generic [dʒə'nerɪk] *adj* genérico,-a.
generosity [dʒenə'rɒsətɪ] *n* generosidad *f*.
generous ['dʒenərəs] **1** *adj* generoso,-a. **2** (*abundant*) abundante, copioso,-a.
generously ['dʒenərəslɪ] *adv* generosamente.
genesis ['dʒenəsɪs] *n* génesis *f*, origen *m*.
▲ *pl geneses* ['dʒenɪsiːz]
Genesis ['dʒenəsɪs] *n* REL Génesis *m*.
genetic [dʒə'netɪk] *adj* genético,-a.
■ **genetic code**, código genético. ‖ **genetic engineering**, ingeniería genética.
geneticist [dʒə'netɪsɪst] *n* genetista *mf*.
genetics [dʒə'netɪks] *n* genética.
Geneva ['dʒəviːvə] *n* Ginebra.
Genevan [dʒə'niːvən] **1** *n* ginebrino,-a. – **2** *adj* ginebrino,-a.
genial ['dʒiːnɪəl] *adj* afable, amable, cordial, simpático,-a.
geniality [dʒiːnɪ'ælɪtɪ] *n* afabilidad *f*, amabilidad *f*, cordialidad *f*, simpatía.
genie ['dʒiːnɪ] *n* genio, duende *m*.
genital ['dʒenɪtəl] **1** *adj* genital. – **2 genitals**, *npl* órganos *mpl* genitales, genitales *mpl*.
genitive ['dʒenɪtɪv] **1** *adj* genitivo,-a. – **2** *n* genitivo.
genius ['dʒiːnɪəs] **1** *n* (*person*) genio. **2** (*gift*) don *m*.
● **to have a genius for sth.**, tener un don para algo.
▲ *pl geniuses*.
Genoa ['dʒenəʊə] *n* Génova.
genocide ['dʒenəsaɪd] *n* genocidio.
Genoese [dʒenəʊ'iːz] **1** *adj* genovés,-esa. – **2** *n* genovés,-esa. – **3 the Genoese**, *npl* los genoveses *mpl*.
Genovese [dʒenə'viːz] *adj* → **genoese**.
genre ['ʒɑːnrə] *n* género.

gent [dʒent] *n fam* caballero, señor *m*.
■ **the gents,** GB el servicio de caballeros. ‖ **gents'** underwear, ropa interior de hombre.
genteel [dʒen'tiːl] 1 *adj dated (refined)* fino,-a, distinguido,-a. 2 *pej* afectado,-a, cursi.
gentile ['dʒentail] 1 *adj (not Jewish)* no judío,-a; *(pagan)* pagano,-a. – 2 *n (not Jew)* no judío,-a; *(pagan)* gentil *mf*, pagano,-a.
gentle ['dʒentəl] 1 *adj (person)* bondadoso,-a, dulce, tierno,-a. 2 *(breeze, movement, touch, etc)* suave. 3 *(hint)* discreto,-a. 4 *(noble)* noble: *of gentle birth,* de buena familia, de buena cuna, bien nacido,-a.
■ **the gentle sex,** *dated* el sexo débil.
gentleman ['dʒentəlmən] *n* caballero, señor *m*.
■ **gentleman's agreement,** acuerdo entre caballeros.
gentleness ['dzentəlnəs] 1 *n (kindness)* amabilidad *f*; *(goodness)* bondad *f*, ternura. 2 *(mildness)* suavidad *f*.
gently ['dʒentlɪ] 1 *adv (smoothly)* suavemente. 2 *(slowly)* despacio, poco a poco. 3 *(kindly)* amablemente.
● **gently does it!,** ¡con cuidado!
gentry ['dʒentrɪ] *n (of high birth)* pequeña nobleza; *(of high standing)* alta sociedad *f*.
genuflect ['dʒenjʊflekt] *i* REL *fml* hacer una genuflexión.
genuflection [dʒenju'flekʃən] *n* genuflexión *f*.
genuflexion [dʒenju'flekʃən] *n →* **genuflection**.
genuine ['dʒenjuɪn] 1 *adj (authentic, true)* genuino,-a, auténtico,-a, verdadero,-a: *he has several genuine Picassos in his house,* tiene varios originales de Picasso en su casa, tiene varios picassos auténticos en su casa. 2 *(sincere)* sincero,-a: *her devotion to her father was genuine,* su devoción hacia su padre era sincera.
genuinely ['dʒenjuɪnlɪ] *adv* auténticamente, verdaderamente, realmente, sinceramente: *he was genuinely pleased with the gift,* estaba realmente contento con el regalo.
genus ['dʒiːnəs] *n* género.
▲ *pl* **genera**.
geocentric [dʒiːəʊ'sentrɪk] *adj* geocéntrico,-a.
geodesic [dʒiːəʊ'desɪk] *adj* geodésico,-a.
geographer [dʒɪ'ɒgrəfə'] *n* geógrafo,-a.
geographic [dʒɪə'græfɪk] *adj* geográfico,-a.
geographical [dʒɪə'græfɪkəl] *adj* geográfico,-a.
geography [dʒɪ'ɒgrəfɪ] *n* geografía.
geologic [dʒɪə'lɒdʒɪk] *adj* geológico,-a.
geological [dʒɪə'lɒdʒɪkəl] *adj* geológico,-a.
geologist [dʒɪ'ɒlədʒɪst] *n* geólogo,-a.
geology [dʒɪ'ɒlədʒɪ] *n* geología.
geomagnetic [dʒiːəməg'netɪk] *adj* geomagnético,-a.
geometric [dʒɪə'metrɪk] *adj* geométrico,-a.
geometrical [dʒɪə'metrɪkəl] *adj* geométrico,-a.
geometrician [dʒɪəmɪ'trɪʃən] *n* geómetra *mf*.
geometry [dʒɪ'ɒmətrɪ] *n* geometría.
geomorphic [dʒɪə'mɔːfɪk] *adj* geomórfico,-a.
geophysical [dʒɪə'fɪzɪkəl] *adj* geofísico,-a.
geophysics [dʒiːə'fɪzɪks] *n* geofísica.
geopolitical [dʒiːəʊpə'lɪtɪkəl] *adj* geopolítico,-a.
geopolitics [dʒiːəʊ'pɒlɪtɪks] *n* geopolítica.
Georgia ['dʒɔːdʒə] *n* Georgia.
■ **South Georgia,** Georgia del Sur.
Georgian ['dʒɔːdʒən] 1 *adj* georgiano,-a. – 2 *n (person)* georgiano,-a. 3 *(language)* georgiano.
georgic ['dʒɔːdʒɪk] 1 *adj* geórgico,-a. – 2 **georgics,** *npl* geórgicas *fpl*.
geranium [dʒə'reɪnɪəm] *n* geranio.

gerbil ['dʒɜːbəl] *n* gerbo, jerbo.
geriatric [dʒerɪ'ætrɪk] 1 *adj* geriátrico,-a. 2 *pej* caduco,-a, viejo,-a.
geriatrician [dʒerɪə'trɪʃən] *n* geriatra *mf*.
geriatrics [dʒerɪ'ætrɪks] *n* geriatría.
germ [dʒɜːm] 1 *n (gen)* germen *m*. 2 *(of a disease)* bacilo, microbio; *(bacteria)* bacteria. 3 *fig* germen *m*, principio.
German ['dʒɜːmən] 1 *adj* alemán,-ana. – 2 *n (person)* alemán,-ana. 3 *(language)* alemán *m*.
■ **East German,** alemán,-ana del este. ‖ **German shepherd,** US pastor *m* alemán. ‖ **West German,** alemán,-ana occidental.
Germanic [dʒɜː'mænɪk] *adj* germánico,-a, germano,-a.
Germany ['dʒɜːmənɪ] *n* Alemania.
■ **East Germany,** Alemania oriental. ‖ **West Germany,** Alemania occidental.
germ-free ['dʒɜːmfriː] *adj* esterilizado,-a.
germicidal [dʒɜːmɪ'saɪdəl] *adj* germicida, bactericida.
germicide ['dʒɜːmɪsaɪd] *n* germicida *m*.
germinate ['dʒɜːmɪneɪt] 1 *i* germinar. – 2 *t* hacer germinar.
germination [dʒɜːmɪ'neɪʃən] *n* germinación *f*.
gerontocracy [dʒerɒn'tɒkrəsɪ] *n* gerontocracia.
▲ *pl* **gerontocracies**.
gerontologist [dʒerɒn'tɒlədʒɪst] *n* gerontólogo,-a.
gerontology [dʒerɒn'tɒlədʒɪ] *n* gerontología.
gerrymandering [dʒerɪ'mændərɪŋ] *n pej* división de los distritos electorales *para perjudicar a algún partido*.
gerund ['dʒerənd] *n* gerundio.
gestate ['dʒesteɪt] 1 *t* BIOL gestar. 2 *fig (idea etc)* meditar, idear.
gestation [dʒes'teɪʃən] 1 *n* BIOL gestación *f*. 2 *fig (of idea etc)* gestación *f*.
gestatorial [dʒestə'tɔːrɪəl] *adj* gestatorio,-a.
gesticulate [dʒes'tɪkjəleɪt] *i* gesticular.
gesticulation [dʒestɪkjə'leɪʃən] *n* gesticulación *f*.
gesture ['dʒestʃə'] 1 *n* ademán *m*, gesto. 2 *fig (token)* detalle *m*, gesto, muestra. – 3 *i* hacer gestos, hacer ademanes.
● **as a gesture of,** en señal de.
get [get] 1 *t (obtain)* obtener, conseguir: *I want to get a job,* quiero conseguir un trabajo; *she got £1,000 for her car,* le dieron mil libras por su coche; *he got a bank loan,* le concedieron un crédito bancario; *what did you get in maths?,* ¿qué sacaste en mates? 2 *(receive)* recibir: *I got your letter yesterday,* recibí tu carta ayer; *I got a bike for my birthday,* me regalaron una bici para mi cumpleaños; *I got the sack,* me despidieron; *I got a life sentence for murder,* le echaron cadena perpetua por asesinato; *how did you get that cut?,* ¿cómo te hiciste ese corte? 3 *(buy)* comprar: *where did you get your jeans?,* ¿dónde compraste tus vaqueros?; *I've got him a CD,* le he comprado un compact; *she got herself a new dress,* se compró un vestido nuevo. 4 *(fetch)* traer: *get the car,* traiga el coche; *get the fire brigade,* llama a los bomberos; *I've got to go and get Liam,* tengo que ir a buscar a Liam. 5 *(catch illnesses, means of transport)* coger: *she got the flu,* cogió la gripe; *he always gets a taxi when it rains,* siempre coge un taxi cuando llueve. 6 RAD TV *(receive)* captar, recibir, coger. 7 *(ask)* pedir, decir; *(persuade)* persuadir, convencer: *get your brother to help you,* pídele a tu hermano que te ayude; *get him to phone me,* dile que me llame; *can you get her to lend us the money?,* ¿puedes convencerla para que nos deje el dinero? 8 *(meals, drinks)* preparar: *can I get you something to eat?,* ¿te preparo algo para comer? 9 *fam*

(*jokes etc*) entender, captar, coger: *I don't get it,* no lo entiendo. **10** *fam* (*annoy*) poner nervioso,-a, fastidiar: *what really gets me is his laziness,* lo que me fastidia es su pereza; *this bad weather gets on my nerves,* este mal tiempo me pone de mal humor. **11** (*earn*) ganar, cobrar: *he gets a good salary,* gana un buen sueldo. **12** (*telephone - contact*) poner con; (- *answer*) contestar, atender, coger; (*door*) abrir: *can you get me the Embassy Hotel?,* ¿me puede poner con el Hotel Embassy? **13** (*make do sth.*) conseguir, lograr: *I can't get the car to start,* no consigo arrancar el coche. **14** (*have sth. done*) hacer algo a uno: *she loves getting her hair done,* le encanta que le arreglen el pelo; *he got his car repaired in no time,* le repararon el coche en un santiamén. **15** (*wound, injure*) dar, alcanzar: *she got hit by a stray bullet,* le alcanzó una bala perdida. – **16** *i* (*become*) ponerse, volverse: *she gets very angry if we're late,* se pone furiosa si llegamos tarde. **17** (*go*) ir: *how do you get there?,* ¿cómo se va hasta allí?; *can you get there by bus?,* ¿se puede ir en autobús? – **18** *i fig* ir, llevar: *this isn't getting us anywhere,* esto no nos lleva a ninguna parte; *where do you think she's got to?,* ¿dónde crees que se ha metido? – **19** *i* (*arrive*) llegar: *we'll get there soon,* pronto llegaremos; *how did you get home?,* ¿cómo llegaste a casa? **20** (*come to*) llegar a: *you'll get to like it in the end,* acabará gustándote; *I got to know him very well,* llegué a conocerlo muy bien. **21** (*manage*) llegar a: *we never got to visiting the museum,* no llegamos a visitar el museo; *I get to travel quite a bit in my job,* tengo la oportunidad de viajar bastante en mi trabajo. **22** (*start*) empezar a: *we got talking,* empezamos a hablar, nos pusimos a hablar.
◆ **to get about 1** *i* (*person*) moverse, desplazarse, salir; (*travel*) viajar. **2** (*news etc*) difundirse. ‖ **to get across 1** *t insep* (*cross - street, road*) cruzar; (- *bridge*) atravesar. – **2** *t sep* (*idea etc*) hacer comprender, hacer entender. – **3** *i* hacerse entender. ‖ **to get ahead** *i* adelantar, progresar. ‖ **to get along 1** *i* (*manage*) arreglárselas, apañárselas. **2** (*leave*) marcharse, irse: *we'll have to be getting along soon,* tenemos que marcharnos pronto. ‖ **to get along with 1** *t insep* (*person*) llevarse (bien) con. **2** (*progress*) marchar, ir con: *how are you getting along with your project?,* ¿qué tal te va con el proyecto? ‖ **to get around 1** *i* (*person*) moverse, desplazarse; (*travel*) viajar. **2** (*news*) difundirse. – **3** *t insep* (*avoid*) evitar, sortear. ‖ **to get around to** *i* encontrar tiempo para: *we didn't get around to seeing the Tower,* no encontramos tiempo para ver la Torre. ‖ **to get at 1** *t insep* (*reach*) alcanzar, llegar a: *he couldn't get at it,* no lo pudo coger; *he wanted to get at the heart of the matter,* quería llegar al fondo de la cuestión. **2** (*insinuate*) insinuar: *what is she trying to get at?,* ¿qué insinúa?, ¿adónde quiere llegar? **3** (*criticize*) criticar; (*tease*) meterse con: *stop getting at me!,* ¡deja de meterte conmigo! ‖ **to get away 1** *i* escaparse, irse: *she likes to get away now and again,* le gusta hacer una escapada de vez en cuando; *he got away from us,* se nos escapó. – **2** *t sep* alejar, quitar, sacar: *get him away from the fire!,* ¡aléjalo del fuego! ‖ **to get away with** *t insep* salir impune de: *you won't get away with this!,* ¡no saldrás impune de ésta! ‖ **to get back 1** *i* (*return*) volver, regresar: *he didn't get back home until yesterday,* no volvió a casa hasta ayer. **2** (*move backwards*) moverse hacia atrás, retroceder: *everyone get back!,* ¡todos atrás! – **3** *t sep* (*recover*) recuperar: *did you get your money back?,* ¿te devolvieron el dinero? ‖ **to get behind** *i* atrasarse. ‖ **to get by 1** *i* (*manage*) arreglárselas: *he can get by with very little money,* se las arregla con muy poco dinero. **2** (*pass*) pasar:

could you let me get by, please?, ¿por favor, me deja pasar? ‖ **to get down 1** *t sep* (*depress*) deprimir, desanimar: *it's getting him down,* se está desanimando. **2** (*gen*) bajar: *can you get that case down for me?,* ¿me puedes bajar esa maleta?; *they've got inflation down to 4%,* han conseguido reducir la inflación a 4%. **3** (*write down*) apuntar, anotar. **4** (*swallow*) tragar. – **5** *i* (*descend*) bajarse: *she got down quickly,* se bajó rápidamente. ‖ **to get down to** *i* ponerse a: *he's finally got down to studying,* por fin se ha puesto a estudiar; *let's get down to details,* vayamos a los detalles. ‖ **to get in 1** *i* (*arrive*) llegar: *the coach gets in at eight,* el autocar llega a las ocho. **2** (*enter*) entrar; (*car*) subir; (*be elected*) ser elegido,-a: *get in the car,* sube al coche; *the Conservatives got in by a narrow margin,* los conservadores ganaron por un margen muy estrecho. – **3** *t sep* (*insert*) meter. **4** (*harvest*) recoger, cosechar; (*washing*) recoger; (*supplies*) comprar. **5** (*summon*) llamar. ‖ **to get into 1** *t insep* (*arrive*) llegar a. **2** (*enter*) entrar en; (*car*) subir a: *he opened the door and got into the car,* abrió la puerta y subió al coche; *I can't get into these jeans,* estos vaqueros ya no me entran; *she's getting into bad habits,* está adquiriendo malas costumbres. ‖ **to get off 1** *t sep* (*remove*) quitarse: *he couldn't get the dirt off his hands,* no pudo quitarse la suciedad de las manos. – **2** *t insep* (*vehicle, horse, etc*) bajarse de. – **3** *i* bajarse: *he got on the roundabout, but he couldn't get off,* subió al tiovivo, pero no pudo bajarse; *I told him where to get off,* lo mandé a hacer puñetas. **4** (*leave*) salir: *we must be getting off now,* tenemos que irnos ya; *I get off at 6.00 pm,* salgo (de trabajar) a las seis. **5** (*begin*) comenzar: *they got off to a flying start,* empezaron con viento en popa; *he couldn't get off to sleep,* no pudo conciliar el sueño. **6** (*escape*) escaparse: *he got off lightly,* salió bien librado; *he got off with a small fine,* se libró con una multa pequeña. ‖ **to get off with** *t insep fam* ligar: *John got off with Mary,* John ligó con Mary. ‖ **to get on 1** *t insep* (*vehicle*) subir a, subirse a; (*bicycle, horse, etc*) montar a. – **2** *i* (*make progress*) progresar, avanzar, ir: *how is she getting on?,* ¿cómo le van las cosas? **3** (*succeed*) tener éxito. **4** (*be friendly*) llevarse bien, avenirse, entenderse: *they get on very well,* se llevan muy bien. **5** (*continue*) seguir, continuar: *get on with what you are doing!,* ¡seguid con lo que estáis haciendo! **6** (*grow old*) hacerse mayor, envejecerse. ‖ **to get on for** *t insep* ser casi: *it's getting on for 5 o'clock,* son casi las cinco; *she's getting on for forty,* le falta poco para los cuarenta; *there were getting on for 600 people,* había casi seiscientas personas. ‖ **to get on to 1** *t insep* (*person*) ponerse en contacto con, localizar: *try to get on to him as soon as possible,* intenta localizarlo lo antes posible. **2** (*subject*) empezar a hablar de, pasar a: *let's get on to the matter in hand,* pasemos al tema en cuestión. ‖ **to get out 1** *t sep* (*thing*) sacar; (*stain*) quitar: *she got her purse out,* sacó su monedero. – **2** *i* (*leave*) salir: *the lift broke down and he couldn't get out,* el ascensor se averió y no pudo salir. **3** (*of car etc*) bajar de, bajarse de: *the taxi stopped and a man got out,* se paró el taxi y bajó un hombre. **4** (*escape*) escapar(se): *the prisoner tried to dig a tunnel to get out,* el prisionero intentó cavar un túnel para escaparse. **5** (*news, rumours etc*) llegar a saberse, hacerse público,-a. ‖ **to get out of 1** *t insep* (*avoid*) librarse de: *he tried to get out of doing the dishes,* intentó librarse de lavar los platos. – **2** *i* (*stop*) dejar, perder la costumbre: *he got out of the habit of going to sleep in class,* perdió la costumbre de dormirse en clase. ‖ **to get over 1** *t insep* (*illness*) recuperarse de. **2** (*recover from*) sobreponerse a; (*forget*) olvidar: *she can't get over*

it, no lo puede olvidar; *he'll get over it in the long run,* se le pasará con el tiempo. **3** (*obstacle*) salvar; (*difficulty*) vencer. **– 4** *t sep* (*idea etc*) comunicar, hacer comprender. ‖ **to get over with** *t sep* acabar con: *let's get the speeches over with and then the party can start,* acabemos con los discursos y luego puede empezar la fiesta. ‖ **to get round 1** *t insep* (*obstacle*) salvar. **2** (*law, regulation*) evitar, soslayar. **3** (*person*) convencer, persuadir. **– 4** *i* (*news*) difundirse, hacerse público,-a, llegar a saber: *if this gets round, we'll be in trouble,* si ésto sale a la luz pública, tendremos problemas. ‖ **to get round to** *t insep* encontrar tiempo para: *he got round to doing it in the end,* finalmente encontró tiempo para hacerlo. ‖ **to get through 1** *i* (*gen*) llegar: *he got through to the semifinals,* llegó a las semifinales; *the general sent reinforcements, but they never got through,* el general mandó refuerzos, pero nunca llegaron. **2** (*on 'phone*) conseguir hablar (**to**, con). **3** (*communicate*) hacerse comprender (**to**, a): *I've tried talking to her, but I just can't get through,* he intentado hablar con ella, pero no consigo hacer que me comprenda. **– 4** *t insep* (*finish*) acabar, terminar: *he got through the book in a day,* terminó el libro en un día. **5** (*consume*) consumir; (*money*) gastar; (*drink*) beber. **6** (*exam*) aprobar: *he studied hard, but he didn't get through the exam,* estudió mucho, pero no aprobó el examen. ‖ **to get together 1** *i* (*people*) reunirse, juntarse. **– 2** *t sep* (*people*) juntar, reunir. **3** (*assemble*) montar; (*money*) recoger, reunir: *they got enough money together to buy him a present,* reunieron suficiente dinero para comprarle un regalo. ‖ **to get up 1** *i* (*rise*) levantarse; (*climb up*) subir: *what time do you get up?,* ¿a qué hora te levantas? **2** (*become stronger - wind, storm*) levantarse. **– 3** *t sep* (*wake up*) despertar; (*get out of bed*) levantar: *get me up early tomorrow,* despiértame temprano mañana. **4** (*disguise os.*) disfrazarse. ‖ **to get up to 1** *t insep* hacer: *what have you been getting up to?,* ¿qué has estado haciendo? **2** (*reach*) llegar a.
● **get along with you!,** ¡déjate de bobadas!, ¡no seas bobo,-a! ‖ **to get along without sth.,** pasar sin algo: *we can get along without a dishwasher,* nos podemos pasar sin un lavaplatos. ‖ **to get better,** mejorar(se). ‖ **to get dark,** oscurecer. ‖ **to get dirty,** ensuciarse. ‖ **to get divorced,** divorciarse. ‖ **to get down on one's knees,** arrodillarse. ‖ **to get dressed,** vestirse. ‖ **to get drunk,** emborracharse. ‖ **to get into trouble,** meterse en un lío. ‖ **to get late,** hacerse tarde. ‖ **to get lost,** perderse. ‖ **to get married,** casarse. ‖ **to get old,** hacerse mayor, envejecer. ‖ **to get on sb.'s nerves,** irritar a algn., poner nervioso,-a a algn. ‖ **to get one's own way,** salirse con la suya. ‖ **to get paid,** cobrar. ‖ **to get ready,** preparar, prepararse. ‖ **to get rid of,** deshacerse de. ‖ **to get tired,** cansarse. ‖ **to get wet,** mojarse. ‖ **to get worse,** empeorar(se).
▲ *pt* **got,** *pp* **got** (US **gotten**), *ger* **getting.**
get-at-able [get'ætəbəl] *adj fam* accesible.
getaway ['getəweɪ] *n fam* fuga, huida.
● **to make one's getaway,** fugarse.
■ **getaway car,** coche *m* usado en una fuga.
get-together ['gettəgeðəʳ] *n fam* (*meeting*) reunión *f*; (*party*) fiesta.
getup ['getʌp] *n fam* atavío, atuendo.
get-well card [get'welkɑːd] *n* tarjeta (*deseando la pronta recuperación de algn.*).
geyser ['giːzəʳ, US 'gaɪzər] **1** *n* (*natural spring*) géiser *m*. **2** (*water heater*) calentador *m* de agua.
Ghana ['gɑːnə] *n* Ghana.
Ghanaian [gɑː'neɪən] **1** *adj* ghanés,-esa. **– 2** *n* ghanés,-esa.

ghastly ['gɑːstlɪ] **1** *adj* espantoso,-a, horrible, horroroso,-a. **2** (*pale*) pálido,-a, mortecino,-a.
▲ *comp* **ghastlier,** *superl* **ghastliest.**
Ghent [gent] *n* Gante.
gherkin ['gɜːkɪn] *n* pepinillo.
ghetto ['getəʊ] *n* ghetto, gueto.
▲ *pl* **ghettos** o **ghettoes.**
ghost [gəʊst] **1** *n* fantasma *m,* espectro. **2** (*duplicate image on a TV screen*) sombra. **– 3** *t* (*literature*) escribir: *the journalist ghosted the politician's memoirs,* el periodista escribió las memorias del político.
● **to give up the ghost,** *fam* entregar el alma. ‖ **the ghost of a chance,** *fam* la más remota posibilidad.
■ **ghost town,** pueblo fantasma. ‖ **the Holy Ghost,** REL el Espíritu Santo.
ghostly ['gəʊstlɪ] *adj* espectral, fantasmal.
▲ *comp* **ghostlier,** *superl* **ghostliest.**
ghostwrite ['gəʊstraɪt] *t* (*literature*) hacer de negro, escribir para otro.
ghostwriter ['gəʊstraɪtəʳ] *n* (*literature*) negro,-a *mf.*
ghoul [guːl] **1** *n fam* persona de gustos macabros. **2** (*evil spirit*) espíritu *m* maligno.
ghoulish ['guːlɪʃ] *adj* macabro,-a.
GHQ ['dʒiː'eɪtʃ'kjuː] *abbr* (**General Headquarters**) Cuartel *m* General.
giant ['dʒaɪənt] **1** *n* gigante,-a. **– 2** *adj* gigante, gigantesco,-a.
gibber ['dʒɪbəʳ] *i* farfullar, mascullar, hablar atropelladamente.
gibberish ['dʒɪbərɪʃ] *n* galimatías *m,* guirigay *m.*
gibbet ['dʒɪbɪt] *n* horca, patíbulo.
gibbon ['gɪbən] *n* ZOOL gibón *m.*
gibe [dʒaɪb] **1** *n* mofa, sarcasmo, pulla. **– 2** *i* mofarse (**about/at,** de).
giblets ['dʒɪblɪts] *npl* menudillos *mpl.*
Gibraltar [dʒɪ'brɔːltəʳ] *n* Gibraltar *m.*
Gibraltarian [dʒɪbrɔːl'teərɪən] **1** *adj* gibraltareño,-a. **– 2** *n* gibraltareño,-a.
giddiness ['gɪdɪnəs] *n* mareo, vértigo.
giddy ['gɪdɪ] *adj* (*dizzy*) mareado,-a: *heights make me giddy,* me dan vértigo las alturas.
● **to feel giddy,** sentirse mareado,-a.
▲ *comp* **giddier,** *superl* **giddiest.**
gift [gɪft] **1** *n* (*present*) regalo, obsequio. **2** (*talent*) don *m.* **3** REL ofrenda. **4** JUR donación *f.* **5** GB *fam* (*bargain*) ganga.
● **to have the gift of the gab,** tener un pico de oro.
■ **gift shop,** tienda de artículos de regalo. ‖ **gift token,** vale *m.*
gifted ['gɪftɪd] *adj* dotado,-a, talentoso,-a.
gift-wrapped ['gɪftræpt] *adj* envuelto,-a para regalo.
gig[1] [gɪg] **1** *n* (*carriage*) calesa, calesín *m.*
gig[2] [gɪg] *n fam* (*booking*) bolo; (*performance*) actuación *f.*
gigantic [dʒaɪ'gæntɪk] *adj* gigantesco,-a.
giggle ['gɪgəl] **1** *n* risita, risa tonta: *she got the giggles,* le dio por reírse, le dio la risa tonta. **2** GB *fam* broma, diversión *f*: *we did it for a giggle,* lo hicimos en broma, lo hicimos para divertirnos. **– 3** *i* reírse tontamente.
gigolo ['dʒɪgələʊ] *n* gigolo.
▲ *pl* **gigolos.**
gild [gɪld] **1** *t* dorar.
● **to gild the lily,** GB sobrecargar.
gill[1] [gɪl] *n* (*of fish*) agalla, branquia.
● **to look pale about the gills / look green about the gills,** tener mala cara.
gill[2] [dʒɪl] *n* (*measurement*) cuarto de pinta (*equivale a* 0,142 *litros*).

gilt [gɪlt] **1** adj dorado,-a. – **2** n dorado.

gilt-edged ['gɪltedʒd] adj FIN de máxima garantía: *gilt-edged securities,* títulos de crédito de máxima garantía.

gimlet ['gɪmlət] n TECH barrena de mano.

gimmick ['gɪmɪk] n fam (*device*) reclamo, truco; (*gadget*) artilugio.
■ **sales gimmick,** truco para aumentar ventas.

gimmicky ['gɪmɪkɪ] adj fam truculento,-a.

gin [dʒɪn] n ginebra.

ginger ['dʒɪndʒəʳ] **1** n (*spice*) jengibre m. – **2** adj (*hair*) rojo,-a; (*person*) pelirrojo,-a.
◆ **to ginger up** t sep animar, estimular.
■ **ginger ale,** ginger ale m.

gingerbread ['dʒɪndʒəbred] n pan m de jengibre.

gingerly ['dʒɪndʒəlɪ] **1** adv cautelosamente. – **2** adj cauteloso,-a.

gingernut ['dʒɪndʒənʌt] n galleta de jengibre.

gingersnap ['dʒɪndʒəsnæp] n US galleta de jengibre.

gingham ['gɪŋəm] n (*kind of cotton*) guinga f, guingán m.

gingivitis [dʒɪndʒɪ'vaɪtəs] n MED gingivitis f.

gipsy ['dʒɪpsɪ] n gitano,-a.
▲ pl *gipsies.*

giraffe [dʒɪ'rɑːf] n jirafa.

gird [gɜːd] **1** t lit (*fasten*) ceñir. **2** (*surround*) rodear (**de,** with).
● **to gird (up) one's loins,** fig prepararse para la lucha. ‖ **to gird os. for sth.,** prepararse para algo.
▲ pt & pp girt [gɜːt] o *girded.*

girder ['gɜːdəʳ] n (*construction*) viga.

girdle ['gɜːdəl] **1** n (*clothes*) faja. **2** fig cinturón m. – **3** t fig rodear.

girl [gɜːl] **1** n chica, muchacha, joven f; (*small*) niña. **2** (*daughter*) hija.
■ **girl guide,** GB exploradora. ‖ **girl scout,** US exploradora. ‖ **girl Friday,** (*in office*) chica para todo.

girlfriend ['gɜːlfrend] **1** n (*partner*) novia. **2** (*friend*) amiga, compañera. **3** (*lover*) amante f.

girlhood ['gɜːlhʊd] n (*childhood*) niñez f; (*youth*) juventud f.

girlie magazine ['gɜːlɪmægəziːn] n fam revista de destape.

girlish ['gɜːlɪʃ] adj (*of girl*) de niña; (*effeminate*) afeminado,-a.

giro ['dʒaɪrəʊ] n GB giro.
■ **bank giro,** giro bancario, transferencia bancaria.
▲ pl *giros.*

girt [gɜːt] pt & pp → **gird**.

girth [gɜːθ] **1** n TECH (*measure*) contorno, circunferencia, perímetro. **2** fig gordura, obesidad f. **3** (*of saddle*) cincha.

gismo ['gɪzməʊ] n fam chisme m.
▲ pl *gismos.*

gist [dʒɪst] n (*general idea*) idea general, sentido general; (*fundamental idea*) lo esencial: *I got the gist of things,* me enteré de lo esencial; *the gist of what he said is that we must work harder,* la esencia de lo que dijo es que debemos trabajar más.

give [gɪv] **1** n (*flexibility*) elasticidad f, flexibilidad f. – **2** t (*gen*) dar: *you've given me a great ideal,* ¡me has dado una idea estupenda!; *his training gave him a good start in life,* su formación le proporcionó un buen comienzo en la vida. **3** (*deliver, convey*) dar, entregar: *could you give him a message?,* ¿me podrías dar un mensaje? **4** (*as a gift*) dar, regalar: *he gave her a pretty dress,* le regaló un vestido bonito. **5** (*provide*) dar, suministrar: *she gave him a meal,* le dio de comer; *to give one's word,* dar su

palabra. **6** (*pay*) pagar, dar: *how much did you give for it?,* ¿cuánto pagó por ello?; *many people would give anything for a decent job,* mucha gente daría cualquier cosa por tener un buen empleo. **7** (*perform a concert etc*) dar; (*speech*) pronunciar. **8** (*dedicate*) dedicar, consagrar: *he gave a lot of thought to the project,* reflexionó largo y tendido sobre el proyecto. **9** (*cause*) causar, ocasionar: *she gave him to understand that she wasn't interested,* le dio a entender que no le interesaba. **10** (*yield*) ceder, conceder: *I'll give you that it isn't easy,* te concedo que no es fácil, te doy la razón en que no es fácil. – **11** i (*yield*) ceder; (*cloth, elastic*) dar de sí.
◆ **to give away 1** t sep (*gen*) distribuir, repartir; (*present*) regalar; (*prize*) entregar. **2** (*betray*) delatar, traicionar; (*disclose*) revelar, descubrir: *his voice gave him away,* lo delató su voz. ‖ **to give back** t sep (*return*) devolver. ‖ **to give in 1** i (*admit defeat*) darse por vencido,-a, rendirse; (*yield*) ceder. – **2** t sep (*hand in*) entregar. ‖ **to give in to** i ceder ante. ‖ **to give off** t sep (*smell, heat, etc*) despedir, desprender, emitir. ‖ **to give onto** i dar a: *her flat gives onto a park,* su piso da a un parque. ‖ **to give out 1** t sep (*distribute*) distribuir, repartir. **2** (*announce*) anunciar. – **3** i (*supplies*) acabarse, agotarse; (*break down*) averiarse, sufrir una avería. ‖ **to give over 1** t sep (*hand over*) entregar; (*allocate*) dedicar, asignar: *houses given over to the down-and-out,* casas asignadas a los deshuciados. – **2** i fam (*stop*) dejar de: *give over!,* ¡basta ya!, ¡para ya! ‖ **to give up 1** t sep (*renounce*) dejar; (*idea*) abandonar, renunciar a: *to give up smoking,* dejar de fumar. **2** (*relinquish, hand over*) ceder, renunciar a: *he gave up his life to save her,* dio su vida para salvarla. **3** (*devote*) dedicar: *he gave up every spare minute of his time to aiding the sick,* dedicó cada minuto de su tiempo libre a ayudar a los enfermos. **4** (*surrender*) entregarse: *he gave himself up to the police,* se entregó a la policía. – **5** i (*admit defeat*) darse por vencido,-a, rendirse: *he never gave up,* nunca se dio por vencido; *I give up!,* ¡me rindo! ‖ **to give up on** t insep abandonar, desistir: *she gave up on the idea of ever finishing the book,* abandonó la idea de acabar el libro algún día.
● **not to give a damn,** importarle a uno un bledo. ‖ **to give evidence,** prestar declaración. ‖ **to give it all one's got,** dar lo mejor de sí. ‖ **to give the game away,** descubrir el pastel. ‖ **"give way",** AUTO "ceda el paso". ‖ **to give way,** (*gen*) ceder, conceder; (*ground*) hundirse; (*ladder*) romperse; (*legs*) doblarse. ‖ **don't give me that!,** fam ¡no me vengas con esas! ‖ **give me ... every time!,** fam ¡para mí no hay nada como ...! ‖ **to give sb. one's support,** prestarle apoyo a algn. ‖ **to give sb. up for dead,** dar por muerto,-a a algn.: *the climbers were given up for dead,* dieron por muertos a los montañeros. ‖ **what gives?,** fam ¿qué pasa?
▲ pt gave [geɪv], pp given ['gɪvən].

giveaway ['gɪvəweɪ] **1** n fam (*unintentional disclosure*) revelación f involuntaria. **2** (*gift*) regalo.
■ **giveaway price,** precio de saldo.

given ['gɪvən] **1** pp → **give**. – **2** adj (*fixed*) dado,-a, determinado,-a, previsto,-a: *the march began at the given time,* la marcha empezó a la hora prevista; *at any given moment,* en cualquier momento. **3** (*prone*) dado,-a, propenso,-a: *he is given to fits of anger,* es propenso a arrebatos de ira. – **4** prep (*considering*) dado,-a, teniendo en cuenta: *given his age, he's pretty fit,* dada su edad está bastante en forma. **5** (*if*) si: *given half a chance, he would do something else,* si tuviera la oportunidad, haría otra cosa.
● **given that,** dado que.

■ given name, US nombre *m* de pila.

gizmo ['gɪzməʊ] *n fam* → **gismo**.
▲ *pl gizmos.*

gizzard ['gɪzəd] *n* (*of bird*) molleja.
● it sticks in my gizzard, no lo puedo tragar.

Gk [griːk] *abbr* (*Greek*) griego,-a.

glacé ['glæseɪ] *adj* CULIN escarchado,-a, glaseado,-a.
■ glacé cherry, cereza escarchada.

glacial ['gleɪʃəl] **1** *adj* GEOL glaciar. **2** (*icy*) glacial: *glacial winds swept the plains,* vientos glaciales barrieron las llanuras. **3** *fam fig* glacial: *she gave him a glacial look,* le lanzó una mirada glacial.
■ glacial periods, períodos *mpl* glaciares.

glacier ['glæsɪər, 'gleɪʃər] *n* GEOL glaciar *m.*

glad [glæd] *adj* (*pleased*) contento,-a, alegre; (*happy*) feliz.
● to be glad, alegrarse. ‖ to be glad of, agradecer.
■ glad rags, ropa *f sing* de fiesta.

gladden ['glædən] *t* alegrar.

glade ['gleɪd] *n* (*clearing*) claro.

gladiator ['glædɪeɪtər] *n* HIST gladiador *m.*

gladiolus [glædɪ'əʊləs] *n* BOT gladiolo.
▲ *pl gladioli* [glædɪ'əʊlaɪ].

gladly ['glædlɪ] *adv* de buena gana, con mucho gusto.

gladness ['glædnəs] *n* (*pleasure*) satisfacción *f;* (*happiness*) alegría.

glamorize ['glæməraɪz] *t* GB adornar, embellecer, hacer más atractivo,-a.

glamorous ['glæmərəs] **1** *adj* atractivo,-a. **2** (*charming*) encantador,-ra.

glamour ['glæmər] **1** *n* atractivo. **2** (*charm*) encanto.

glance [glɑːns] **1** *n* mirada, vistazo, ojeada. – **2** *i* dar una mirada, echar un vistazo (**at,** a).
◆ to glance off *t insep* (*ball, bullet etc*) rebotar en.
● at a glance, de un vistazo. ‖ at first glance, a primera vista. ‖ to glance through, ojear.

glancing ['glɑːnsɪŋ] *adj* (*blow*) oblicuo,-a.

gland [glænd] *n* ANAT glándula.

glandular ['glændjʊlər] *adj* glandular.
■ glandular fever, MED mononucleosis *f* infecciosa.

glare [gleər] **1** *n* (*light*) luz *f* deslumbrante. **2** AUTO deslumbramiento. **3** (*look*) mirada furiosa, mirada hostil. – **4** *i* (*dazzle*) deslumbrar. **5** (*look*) lanzar una mirada furiosa: *she glared at me,* me miró furiosa.

glaring ['gleərɪŋ] **1** *adj* (*dazzling*) deslumbrador,-ra, deslumbrante; (*colour*) chillón,-ona; (*bright*) brillante, resplandeciente. **2** (*blatant*) patente, evidente.

glass [glɑːs] **1** *n* (*material*) vidrio, cristal *m.* **2** (*for drinking*) vaso; (*with stem*) copa: *a glass of milk,* un vaso de leche. **3** GB barómetro. – **4** glasses, *npl* gafas *fpl.*
● wine glass, copa (de vino).

glassblower ['glɑːsbləʊər] *n* soplador,-ra de vidrio.

glassblowing ['glɑːsbləʊɪŋ] *n* soplado del vidrio.

glasshouse ['glɑːshaʊs] **1** *n* (*gardening*) invernadero. **2** GB *sl* (*military*) prisión *f* militar.

glassware ['glɑːsweər] *n* cristalería.

glassy ['glɑːsɪ] **1** *adj fig* (*eyes*) vidrioso,-a. **2** (*like glass*) vítreo,-a; (*smooth*) liso,-a; (*water*) cristalino,-a, transparente.
▲ *comp glassier, superl glassiest.*

glaucoma [glɔːˈkəʊmə] *n* MED glaucoma *m.*

glaze [gleɪz] **1** *n* (*for pottery*) vidriado; (*lustre*) brillo, lustre *m*; (*varnish*) barniz *m*, esmalte *m.* – **2** *t* (*pottery*) vidriar, esmaltar. **3** (*windows*) poner cristales a. **4** CULIN glasear.
■ glaze kiln, (*pottery*) horno de esmaltar, horno de vidriar.

glazed ['gleɪzd] **1** *adj* (*of eyes, look etc*) vidrioso,-a, ausente; (*of surface*) vidriado,-a. **2** (*of paper*) satinado,-a; (*of leather*) barnizado,-a.

glazier ['gleɪzɪər] *n* vidriero,-a, cristalero,-a.

glazing ['gleɪzɪŋ] *n* (*windows*) colocación *f* de cristales; (*windowpanes*) cristales *mpl*, vidriería.

gleam [gliːm] **1** *n* destello, rayo. **2** *fig* rayo, resquicio, vislumbre *m.* – **3** *i* brillar, destellar, relucir.
● a gleam of hope, un rayo de esperanza.

gleaming ['gliːmɪŋ] *adj* brillante, reluciente.

glean [gliːn] **1** *t* AGR espigar. **2** *fig* recoger, cosechar: *he wasn't able to glean much information on his trip,* no pudo recoger mucha información en su viaje.

glee [gliː] *n* alegría, júbilo, regocijo.

gleeful ['gliːfʊl] *adj* alegre, jubiloso,-a, recocijado,-a.

gleefully ['gliːfʊlɪ] *adv* con alegría, con júbilo, con regocijo.

glen [glen] *n* cañada.

glib [glɪb] *adj* (*person*) de mucha labia, charlatán,-ana; (*reply etc*) superficial, fácil.
▲ *comp glibber, superl glibbest.*

glibness ['glɪbnəs] *n* (*of person*) labia; (*shallowness*) falta de sinceridad *f*, superficialidad *f.*

glide [glaɪd] **1** *n* deslizamiento. **2** AV planeo, vuelo sin motor. **3** LING semivocal *f.* – **4** *i* deslizarse. **5** AV planear.

glider ['glaɪdər] *n* AV planeador *m.*

gliding ['glaɪdɪŋ] **1** *n* AV planeo. **2** SP vuelo sin motor.

glimmer ['glɪmər] **1** *n* (*light*) luz *f* tenue. – **2** *i* brillar con luz tenue.
● a glimmer of hope, un rayo de esperanza.

glimpse [glɪmps] **1** *n* vislumbre *f*, visión *f* fugaz. – **2** *t* vislumbrar, entrever.
● to catch a glimpse of, vislumbrar.

glint [glɪnt] **1** *n* destello, centelleo. – **2** *i* destellar, centellear.

glisten ['glɪsən] *i* brillar, relucir.

glitter ['glɪtər] **1** *n* brillo. – **2** *i* brillar, relucir.

glittering ['glɪtərɪŋ] *adj* brillante, reluciente.

gloat [gləʊt] *i* regodearse (**over,** con), regocijarse (**over,** con), recrearse (**over,** con).

global ['gləʊbəl] **1** *adj* mundial. **2** (*total*) global.

globe [gləʊb] **1** *n* globo, esfera. **2** (*map*) globo terrestre.

globe-trotter ['gləʊbtrɒtər] *n fam* trotamundos *mf.*

globular ['glɒbjʊlər] *adj* globular.

globule ['glɒbjuːl] *n* glóbulo.

gloom [gluːm] **1** *n* (*darkness*) penumbra, tenebrosidad *f.* **2** (*sadness*) tristeza, melancolía. **3** (*hopelessness*) desolación *f*, pesimismo.

gloomy ['gluːmɪ] **1** *adj* (*dark*) lóbrego,-a, oscuro,-a, tenebroso,-a. **2** (*sad*) melancólico,-a, triste; (*depressing*) deprimente, desalentador,-ra. **3** (*pessimistic*) pesimista: *the country's prospects are gloomy,* las perspectivas del país son pesimistas. **4** (*weather*) gris, encapotado,-a.
▲ *comp gloomier, superl gloomiest.*

glorified ['glɔːrɪfaɪd] *adj pej* pretencioso,-a.

glorify ['glɔːrɪfaɪ] *t* (*God*) glorificar; (*praise*) alabar.
▲ (*verbo*) *pt & pp glorified, ger glorifying.*

glorious ['glɔːrɪəs] **1** *adj* glorioso,-a. **2** (*wonderful*) espléndido,-a, magnífico,-a.

glory ['glɔːrɪ] **1** *n* (*gen*) gloria. **2** *fig* esplendor *m.* – **3** *i* gloriarse (**in,** de).
▲ (*sustantivo*) *pl glories;* (*verbo*) *pt & pp gloried, ger glorying.*

gloss [glɒs] **1** *n* lustre *m*, brillo. **2** (*explanation*) glosa. **3** *fig* oropel *m.* – **4** *t* (*text*) glosar, comentar.
◆ to gloss over *t insep* (*play down*) paliar, suavizar; (*hide*) encubrir; (*ignore*) pasar por alto.
■ gloss paint, esmalte *m*, pintura brillante.

glossary ['glɒsərɪ] n glosario.
▲ pl **glossaries**.
glossy ['glɒsɪ] adj brillante, lustroso,-a.
■ **glossy magazine**, revista de lujo. ‖ **glossy paper**, papel m glaseado, papel m satinado.
▲ comp **glossier**, superl **glossiest**.
glottis ['glɒtɪs] n ANAT glotis f.
glove [glʌv] n guante m.
● **to fit like a glove**, sentar como anillo al dedo, sentar como un guante.
■ **glove compartment**, AUTO guantera.
glow [gləʊ] 1 n (of lamp) luz f; (of jewel) brillo. 2 (of fire) calor m vivo; (of sky) arrebol m; (of fire, metal etc) incandescencia. 3 (of face) rubor m. 4 fig sensación f de bienestar, satisfacción f. – 5 i (jewel, sun etc) brillar; (of metal) estar al rojo vivo; (fire) arder. 6 fig rebosar de.
● **to glow with health**, rebosar de salud.
glower ['glaʊəʳ] i mirar con el ceño fruncido.
glowing ['gləʊɪŋ] 1 adj fig (report etc) entusiasta; (style) cálido,-a. 2 (fire) incandescente; (metal) al rojo vivo. 3 (fire, colour) vivo,-a; (light) brillante. 4 (complexion) rojo,-a; (cheeks) encendido,-a.
glow-worm ['gləʊwɜːm] n ZOOL luciérnaga, gusano de luz.
glucose ['gluːkəʊz] n CHEM glucosa.
glue [gluː] 1 n cola, pegamento. – 2 t encolar, pegar.
● **to be glued to**, fam fig estar pegado,-a a: she had her eyes glued to the road, tenía los ojos pegados a la carretera.
glue-sniffing ['gluːsnɪfɪŋ] n inhalación f de cola.
gluey ['gluːɪ] adj pegajoso,-a, viscoso,-a.
▲ comp **gluier**, superl **gluiest**.
glum [glʌm] adj (mood) abatido,-a, desanimado,-a, triste; (by nature) taciturno,-a, melancólico,-a.
▲ comp **glummer**, superl **glummest**.
glumly ['glʌmlɪ] adv con desánimo, con abatimiento.
glut [glʌt] 1 n (of the market) superabundancia, exceso; (of food) saciedad f, hartazgo m. – 2 t (market) inundar, saturar.
● **to glut os.**, hartarse, saciarse.
▲ (verbo) pt & pp **glutted**, ger **glutting**.
glutinous ['gluːtɪnəs] adj fml pegajoso,-a, glutinoso,-a.
glutton ['glʌtən] n glotón,-ona: he's a glutton for work, es un trabajador incansable; she's a glutton for punishment, es masoquista.
gluttonous ['glʌtənəs] adj glotón,-ona, goloso,-a.
gluttony ['glʌtənɪ] n glotonería, gula.
glycerin ['glɪsərɪn] n → **glycerine**.
glycerine ['glɪsəˈrɪn] n glicerina.
GMT ['dʒiː'em'diː] abbr (Greenwich Mean Time) hora media de Greenwich; (abbreviation) GMT.
gnarled [nɑːld] adj nudoso,-a, retorcido,-a.
gnash [næʃ] t (teeth) hacer rechinar.
gnat [næt] n ZOOL mosquito.
gnaw [nɔː] 1 t (bite) roer. 2 fig (worry) corroer: his hatred kept gnawing away inside, su odio lo corroía por dentro.
gnawing ['nɔːɪŋ] adj (anxiety, fear) constante, permanente; (pain) insistente.
gnome [nəʊm] n gnomo.
GNP ['dʒiː'en'piː] abbr (gross national product) producto nacional bruto; (abbreviation) PNB m.
go [gəʊ] 1 n (energy) energía, empuje m: they're always on the go, no paran nunca. 2 (turn) turno: it's my go, me toca a mí. 3 (try) intento: I'd like to have a go at hang gliding, me gustaría intentar vuelo con ala delta. 4 (start) principio: we knew from the word go, lo sabíamos desde el principio. – 5 i (gen) ir: you can come and go as you please, puedes ir y venir a tu antojo; to go by underground, ir en metro; to go for a walk, dar un paseo; to go on holiday, irse de vacaciones. 6 (leave) marcharse, irse; (bus, train, etc) salir: let's go!, ¡vámonos!; we'd better be going now, más vale que nos vayamos ya. 7 (vanish) desaparecer: my car has gone, mi coche ha desaparecido. 8 (function) funcionar, marchar: his business is going very well, su negocio marcha muy bien; he can't get the engine to go, no le arranca el motor. 9 (become) volverse, ponerse, quedarse: to go deaf, volverse sordo,-a. 10 (fit) entrar, caber: the bed won't go into the room, la cama no cabrá en la habitación. 11 (break) romperse, estropearse; (yield) ceder; (blow) fundirse. 12 (be kept) guardarse: the knives and forks go here, los cuchillos y los tenedores se guardan aquí. 13 (sell) venderse: clothes are going cheap at the moment, la ropa se está vendiendo barata actualmente. 14 (progress) ir, marchar, andar: the party went well, la fiesta fue un éxito; things aren't going too well for him, no le van muy bien las cosas. 15 (be spent on) irse, gastarse: all his money goes on records, se gasta todo el dinero en discos. 16 (be available) quedar, haber: there are very few good jobs going, hay muy pocos empleos buenos; is there any more meat going?, ¿queda algo de carne? 17 (be acceptable) valer: almost anything goes to win, para ganar, casi todo vale. 18 (make a noise, gesture, etc) hacer: go like this with your head, haz así con la cabeza. 19 (time - pass) pasar; (- be remaining) faltar: the years went by slowly, los años pasaron lentamente; only two weeks to go, sólo faltan dos semanas; it's just gone ten, acaban de dar las diez. 20 (say) decir: as the saying goes, según el dicho; there she goes again, otra vez con el mismo rollo, otra vez con la misma canción. – 21 t (make a noise) hacer: it goes tick-tock, hace tic-tac. 22 (travel) hacer, recorrer: they had only gone a mile when the car stopped, sólo habían recorrido una milla cuando se les paró el coche. – 23 go!, interj (starting races) ¡ya!: ready, steady, go!, ¡preparados, listos, ya!
◆ **to go about** 1 t insep (task) emprender, hacer: how do you go about finding a job?, ¿qué hay que hacer para encontrar trabajo? 2 (everyday activities) continuar: she went about her business as though nothing had happened, continuó con su cometido, como si nada hubiera ocurrido. ‖ **to go after** t insep (pursue) perseguir, andar tras: she went after him until he said yes, anduvo tras él hasta que dijo que sí. ‖ **to go against** t insep (oppose) ir en contra de; (sentence) ser desfavorable a. ‖ **to go ahead** i (proceed) proceder: go ahead!, ¡adelante! ‖ **to go ahead with** i (proceed) proceder: she went ahead with her idea, llevó adelante su idea. ‖ **to go along** t insep (street etc) pasar por; (progress) progresar, ir. – 2 i (accompany) ir. ‖ **to go along with** t insep estar de acuerdo con. ‖ **to go around** 1 i (be enough) bastar, ser suficiente, haber: is there enough cake to go round?, ¿hay suficiente pastel para todos? 2 (rumour, illness) correr, circular. 3 (travel round) ir, andar. 4 (spend time) salir (**with**, con), andar (**with**, con). 5 (revolve) girar, dar vueltas. – 6 t insep recorrer. ‖ **to go away** i marcharse. ‖ **to go back** i (return) volver, regresar; (date from) datar de, remontarse a: his family goes back to the last century, el origen de su familia se remonta al siglo pasado. ‖ **to go back on** t insep (break) romper, no cumplir: he's always going back on his word, siempre falta a su palabra. ‖ **to go by** 1 i (time) pasar. – 2 t insep (rules) atenerse a, seguir; (instinct) dejarse llevar por; (appearances)

juzgar por. ‖ **to go down 1** *i (gen)* bajar; *(tyre)* deshincharse; *(sun)* ponerse; *(ship)* hundirse. **2** *(be received)* ser acogido,-a. ‖ **to go down with** *i (catch)* coger, pillar: *he went down with a serious bout of flu,* cogió una gripe de campeonato. ‖ **to go for 1** *t insep (attack)* atacar. **2** *(fetch)* ir a buscar. **3** *fam (like)* gustar. **4** *fam (be valid)* valer para. ‖ **to go in** *i* entrar. ‖ **to go in for** *t insep (enter - race, competition)* participar en, tomar parte en; *(- exam)* presentarse a; *(- career)* dedicarse a; *(like, agree with)* ser partidario,-a de: *I don't go in for that,* eso no me va. ‖ **to go into 1** *t insep (gen)* entrar en. **2** *(investigate)* investigar. **3** *(crash)* chocar contra. ‖ **to go off 1** *i (leave)* marcharse. **2** *(bomb)* estallar; *(alarm)* sonar; *(gun)* dispararse. **3** *(food)* estropearse, pasarse; *(milk)* cortarse. **4** *(stop operating)* apagarse. – **5** *t insep (stop liking)* perder el gusto por, perder el interés por. ‖ **to go off with** *i fam (elope)* escaparse con. ‖ **to go on 1** *i (continue)* seguir, continuar. **2** *(happen)* pasar, ocurrir: *what's going on?,* ¿qué pasa? **3** *(complain)* quejarse **(about,** de); *(talk at length)* hablar sin parar. **4** *(light etc)* encenderse. **5** *(age)* estar a punto de cumplir: *she's ten going on eleven,* está a punto de cumplir los once años. ‖ **to go out 1** *i (leave)* salir: *he goes out a lot,* sale mucho; *they've been going out for some time now,* llevan saliendo juntos algún tiempo ya. **2** *(fire, light)* apagarse. ‖ **to go over** *t insep (check, revise)* revisar, repasar. ‖ **to go over to 1** *t insep (betray)* pasarse a: *he went over to the opposition,* se pasó a la oposición. **2** *(change to)* cambiar a, pasar a: *they went over to gas central heating,* cambiaron a calefacción de gas. ‖ **to go round 1** *i (gyrate)* dar vueltas, girar. **2** *(visit)* pasar por casa de, visitar. ‖ **to go through 1** *t insep (undergo)* pasar por, sufrir, padecer. **2** *(examine)* examinar; *(search)* registrar; *(spend)* gastar; *(explain)* explicar. – **3** *i (act, law)* ser aprobado,-a. ‖ **to go through with** *t insep* llevar a cabo. ‖ **to go towards** *i (reserve for)* destinar a, reservar para. ‖ **to go under** *i (ship)* hundirse; *fig* fracasar. ‖ **to go up 1** *i (gen)* subir; *(approach)* acercarse: *he went up to her and kissed her,* se acercó a ella y la besó. **2** *(curtain in theatre)* levantarse. **3** *(explode)* estallar; *(burst into flames)* prenderse fuego: *to go up in flames,* incendiarse. ‖ **to go with 1** *t insep (accompany)* acompañar; *(be part of)* ir con, estar incluido,-a: *the house goes with the post,* la casa va con el puesto. **2** *(match)* hacer juego con: *that outfit goes with your hat,* ese conjunto hace juego con tu sombrero. ‖ **to go without** *t insep* pasar sin, prescindir de: *he can't go without his daily game of tennis,* no puede pasar sin su partido diario de tenis.
● **go on!,** *(incredulity)* ¡no me digas!, ¡vaya!, ¡anda ya!; *(coaxing)* ¡venga!, ¡adelante! ‖ **it's no go,** es inútil, no hay nada que hacer. ‖ **to be all the go,** estar muy de moda. ‖ **to go about one's business,** ocuparse de sus asuntos. ‖ **to be going to,** estar a punto de: *they were just going to start, when it started to rain,* estaban a punto de empezar, cuando la lluvia hizo acto de presencia. ‖ **to go one better than sb.,** superar a algn. ‖ **to go too far,** ir demasiado lejos, pasarse de la raya, pasarse. ‖ **to go to sleep,** dormirse. ‖ **to have a go at sb.,** criticar a algn., meterse con algn. ‖ **to make a go of sth.,** tener éxito en algo.
▲ *(verbo)* *pt* **went,** *pp* **gone,** *ger* **going.**

goad [gəʊd] **1** *n (stick)* aguijada. – **2** *t* aguijonear.

go-ahead ['gəʊəhed] **1** *n* visto bueno. – **2** *adj* emprendedor,-ra.
● **to give sb./sth. the go-ahead,** dar el visto bueno a algn./algo.

goal [gəʊl] **1** *n* sp *(area)*meta, portería. **2** sp *(point)* gol *m,* tanto. **3** *(aim)* fin *m,* objetivo, meta.

● **to score a gol,** marcar un gol, marcar un tanto.
■ **goal area,** área del gol. ‖ **goal average,** promedio de goles. ‖ **goal kick,** saque *m* de puerta. ‖ **goal line,** línea de gol.

goalie ['gəʊlɪ] *n* sp *fam* → **goalkeeper.**

goalkeeper ['gəʊlkiːpə'] *n* portero,-a, guardameta *mf.*

goalpost ['gəʊlpəʊst] *n* sp poste *m.*

goat [gəʊt] *n (female)* cabra; *(male)* macho cabrío.
● **to get on sb.'s goat,** *fig* fastidiar a algn.

goatee ['gəʊtiː] *n (beard)* perilla.

goatherd ['gəʊthɜːd] *n* guardacabras *mf,* cabrero,-a.

goatskin ['gəʊtskɪn] *n* piel *f* de cabra.

gob[1] [gɒb] *n* GB *sl (mouth)* pico: *shut your gob!,* ¡cierra el pico!

gob[2] [gɒb] **1** *n* GB *sl (spit)* escupitajo, gargajo. – **2** *i* GB *sl (spit)* escupir.

gobble[1] ['gɒbəl] **to gobble (up),** *t* engullir, zamparse: *he gobbled up all the sandwiches,* se zampó todos los bocadillos.

gobble[2] ['gɒbəl] **1** *n (turkey)* gluglú *m.* – **2** *i (turkey)* glutear.

gobbledegook[2] ['gɒbəldɪguːk] *n fam* → **gobbledygook.**

gobbledygook[2] ['gɒbəldɪguːk] *n fam* jerga burocrática: *it's complete gobbledygook,* esto me suena a chino.

go-between ['gəʊbɪtwiːn] **1** *n* intermediario,-a. **2** *(between lovers)* alcahuete,-ta.

Gobi ['gəʊbɪ] **Gobi Desert,** *n* GEOG desierto de Gobi.

goblet ['gɒblət] *n* copa.

goblin ['gɒblɪn] *n* duende *m,* trasgo.

gobstopper ['gɒbstɒpə'] *n* bola de caramelo.

goby ['gəʊbɪ] *n* ZOOL gobio.
▲ *pl* **gobies** ['gəʊbɪz].

go-by ['gəʊaɪt] **to give sth./sb. the go-by,** *phr* prescindir de algo/algn.

go-cart ['gəʊkɑːt] *n* sp kart *m.*

go-carting ['gəʊkɑːtɪŋ] *n* sp karting *m,* carrera de karts.

god [gɒd] **1** *n (deity, idol)* dios *m: a Greek god,* un dios griego. **2 God,** Dios *m.* – **3 the gods,** *npl* THEAT el gallinero.
● **to give thanks to God,** dar gracias a Dios. ‖ **act of God,** obra de Dios. ‖ **God be praised!,** ¡alabado sea Dios! ‖ **God bless you!,** ¡que Dios le bendiga! ‖ **God help us!,** ¡que Dios nos coja confesados! ‖ **God only knows,** sólo Dios sabe. ‖ **God willing,** si Dios quiere. ‖ **may God be with you!,** ¡vaya con Dios! ‖ **may God repay you!,** ¡que Dios se lo pague! ‖ **my God!,** ¡Dios mío! ‖ **thank God!,** ¡gracias a Dios! ‖ **God bless!,** ¡un abrazo! ‖ **he thinks he's God's gift,** cree que es el rey del mambo.
■ **Almighty God,** Dios *m* Todopoderoso. ‖ **God's Acre,** el cementerio. ‖ **God's truth,** la verdad pura y simple.

god-awful ['gɒdɔːfəl] *adj* US *sl (film, book, etc)* espantoso,-a, horroroso,-a; *(place, town)* de mala muerte.

godchild ['gɒdtʃaɪld] *n* ahijado,-a.
▲ *pl* **godchildren** ['gɒdtʃɪldrən].

goddamn ['gɒdæm] **1** *interj* US *sl* ¡maldito sea! – **2** *adj* US *sl* maldito,-a: *this goddamn radio won't work,* esta maldita radio no funciona.
● **goddam you!,** US *sl* ¡maldito seas!

goddamned ['gɒdæm] *adj* US *sl* maldito,-a.

goddaughter ['gɒddɔːtə'] *n* ahijada.

goddess ['gɒdəs] *n* diosa.

godfather ['gɒdfɑːðə'] *n* padrino.

godfearing ['gɒdfɪərɪŋ] *adj* timorato,-a.

godforsaken ['gɒdfəseɪkən] *adj* de mala muerte, dejado,-a de la mano de Dios.
godhead ['gɒdhed] *n* divinidad *f*.
godless ['gɒdləs] *n* ateo,-a.
godmother ['gɒdmʌðəʳ] *n* madrina.
godparents ['gɒdpeərənts] *npl* padrinos *mpl*.
godsend ['gɒdsend] *n* regalo llovido del cielo.
godson ['gɒdsʌn] *n* ahijado.
godwit ['gɒdwɪt] *n* ORN aguja.
go-getter ['gəʊgetəʳ] *n* buscavidas *mf*, trepa *mf*.
goggle ['gɒgəl] *i* quedarse atónito,-a.
● **to goggle at sth./sb.**, mirar algo/a algn. con asombro.
goggle-box ['gɒgəlbɒks] *n* GB *fam* (*television*) caja tonta.
goggle-eyed ['gɒgəlaɪd] *adj* asombrado,-a.
goggles ['gɒgəlz] *npl* gafas *fpl* protectoras.
going ['gəʊɪŋ] **1** *n* (*departure*) ida, salida. **2** (*pace*) paso,
ritmo. **3** (*path, road*) estado del camino. – **4** *adj* (*price,
rate*) actual, corriente. **5** (*business*) que marcha bien.
● **he's** (*she's, etc*) **got a lot going for him** (*her, etc*),
tiene muchos puntos a su favor. ‖ **to be hard going**,
(*path, road*) ser accidentado,-a, ser difícil de atravesar.
‖ **to be heavy going**, (*book, film, person*) ser pesado,-a.
‖ **that was good going**, (*on journey*) hemos llegado rápido. ‖ **to be going on with**, de momento: *that's
enough to be going on with*, con esto tenemos bastante
de momento. ‖ **while the going is good**, mientras podamos, mientras tengamos la oportunidad. ‖ **when
the going gets tough ...**, cuando las cosas se pongan
difíciles ...
■ **going concern**, COMM empresa que funciona bien.
going-over [gəʊɪŋ 'əʊvəʳ] **1** *n fam* (*inspection*) repaso, inspección *f*. **2** (*thrashing*) paliza.
goings-on [gəʊɪŋz'ɒn] *npl fam* tejemanejes *mpl*, chanchullos *mpl*.
goiter ['gɔɪtəʳ] *n* US → **goitre**.
goitre ['gɔɪtəʳ] *n* MED bocio *m*.
go-kart ['gəʊkɑːt] *n* SP kart *m*.
go-karting ['gəʊkɑːtɪŋ] *n* SP karting *m*, carrera de karts.
Golan ['gəʊlæn] **the Golan Heights**, *n* GEOG los altos
de Golán.
gold [gəʊld] **1** *n* (*metal*) oro. – **2** *adj* (*colour*) dorado,-a. **3**
(*made of gold*) de oro: *a gold bracelet*, una pulsera de oro.
● **all that glitters is not gold**, no es oro todo lo que
reluce. ‖ **to be worth its weight in gold**, valer su peso
en oro.
■ **gold disc**, disco de oro. ‖ **gold leaf**, pan *m* de oro.
‖ **gold medal**, medalla de oro. ‖ **gold mine**, mina de
oro. ‖ **gold rush**, fiebre *f* del oro. ‖ **black gold**, (*oil*) oro
negro. ‖ **white gold**, oro blanco.
goldcrest ['gəʊldkrest] *n* ORN reyezuelo.
gold-digger ['gəʊlddɪgəʳ] **1** *n* (*miner*) buscador,-ra de
oro. **2** *fig* (*woman*) aventurera.
golden ['gəʊldən] **1** *adj* de oro. **2** (*colour*) dorado,-a. **3**
(*hair*) rubio,-a.
■ **golden age**, época dorada. ‖ **Golden Age**, (*in Spain*)
Siglo de Oro. ‖ **golden boy**, niño bonito. ‖ **golden
girl**, niña bonita. ‖ **golden calf**, becerro de oro. ‖
golden delicious, (*apple*) manzana golden. ‖ **Golden
Fleece**, (*mythology*) el Vellocino de Oro. ‖ **golden
goose**, la gallina de los huevos de oro. ‖ **golden
handshake**, gratificación *f* extraordinaria *que uno recibe
al dejar el trabajo en reconocimiento de su largo servicio*. ‖ **gold-
en oldie**, (*record*) viejo éxito. ‖ **golden opportunity**,
ocasión *f* de oro. ‖ **golden rule**, regla de oro. ‖ **Golden
State**, California. ‖ **golden wedding**, bodas *fpl* de oro.

goldfinch ['gəʊldfɪntʃ] *n* ORN jilguero.
goldfish ['gəʊldfɪʃ] *n* pez *m* de colores.
▲ *pl goldfish* ['gəʊldfɪʃ].
gold-plated ['gəʊldpleɪtɪd] *adj* chapado,-a en oro.
goldsmith ['gəʊldsmɪθ] *n* orfebre *mf*.
golf [gɒlf] **1** *n* golf *m*. – **2** *i* jugar al golf.
■ **golf ball**, bola de golf. ‖ **golf cart**, carro de golf. ‖
golf club, (*stick*) palo de golf; (*place*) club *m* de golf. ‖
golf course, campo de golf.
golfer ['gɒlfəʳ] *n* jugador,-ra de golf.
golfing ['gɒlfɪŋ] *n* el golf.
● **to go golfing**, jugar al golf.
■ **golfing tournament**, torneo de golf.
golly ['gɒlɪ] *interj* GB ¡caramba!
gonad ['gəʊnæd] *n* ANAT gónada.
gondola ['gɒndələ] *n* góndola.
gondolier [gɒndə'lɪə] *n* gondolero *m*.
gone [gɒn] **1** *pp* → **go**. – **2** *adj* (*time*) pasado,-a: *he won't
arrive until gone six*, no llegará hasta pasadas las seis.
3 (*dead*) muerto,-a. **4** *fam* (*pregnant*): *she's three months
gone*, está de tres meses. **5** *fam* (*entranced*) entusiasmado,-a, flipado,-a.
● **to be gone**, estar fuera: *he'll be gone for a week*, estará una semana fuera. ‖ **to be gone on sth./sb.**, *fam*
estar loco,-a por algo/algn. ‖ **to be too far gone**, ser
un caso perdido.
goner ['gɒnəʳ] *n fam* (*dead*) muerto,-a: *he's a goner*, está
muerto.
gong [gɒŋ] **1** *n* gong *m*, batintín *m*. **2** *fam fig* (*award, prize*)
galardón *m*.
gonorrhea ['gɒnərɪə] *n* US → **gonorrhoea**.
gonorrhoea ['gɒnərɪə] *n* MED gonorrea.
good [gʊd] **1** *adj* bueno,-a; (*before m sing noun*) buen: *she's
a good daughter*, es una buena hija; *he's a good son*, es
un buen hijo. **2** (*healthy*) sano,-a: *olive oil is good for you*,
el aceite de oliva es muy sano. **3** (*beneficial*) bueno,-a:
taking exercise is good for your health, hacer ejercicio
es bueno para la salud. **4** (*kind*) amable: *they've been
very good to him*, han sido muy amables con él; *he was
so good as to help us*, tuvo la amabilidad de ayudarnos.
5 (*well-behaved*) bueno,-a: *be good!*, ¡sé bueno! **6** (*useful*)
servible: *the only good plate in the cupboard*, el único
plato servible en el armario. – **7** *adj* muy: *a pair of good
strong boots*, un par de botas muy resistentes. – **8** *interj*
¡bien! – **9** *n* bien *m*: *good and evil*, el bien y el mal; *its
for your own good*, es por tu propio bien. – **10 goods**,
npl (*property*) bienes *mpl*. **11** COMM (*in shop*) género *m sing*,
artículos *mpl*. **12** COMM (*merchandise*) mercancías *fpl*.
● **a good deal**, bastante: *a good deal of money*, bastante dinero; *he worked a good deal harder than she did*,
él trabajó bastante más que ella. ‖ **all in good time**,
todo a su debido tiempo. ‖ **as good as**, como si, prácticamente, casi: *it's as good as finished*, está casi acabado. ‖ **for good**, para siempre. ‖ **for the good of**, en
bien de: *for the good of the people*, en bien del pueblo.
‖ **good afternoon**, buenas tardes. ‖ **good evening**,
buenas tardes. ‖ **Good Friday**, Viernes Santo. ‖ **good
heavens!, good grief!**, ¡cielo santo! ‖ **good morning**, buenos días. ‖ **good night**, buenas noches. ‖ **it's
a good job**, menos mal: *it's a good job that we brought
an umbrella*, menos mal que trajimos un paraguas. ‖
that's a good one!, (*joke*) ¡ésta sí que es buena! ‖ **to
be as good as new**, estar como nuevo,-a: *the clock
is as good as new*, el reloj está como nuevo. ‖ **to be as
good as gold**, ser un ángel. ‖ **to be good at**, tener
aptitudes para: *she's good at maths*, tiene aptitudes

para las matemáticas. ‖ **to be good for a laugh,** *fam* ser muy divertido,-a, ser muy cachondo,-a. ‖ **to be good for,** (*last*) durar; (*be useful for*) servir: *it'll be good for another couple of years,* durará un par de años más; *he'll be good for a long time yet,* tiene mucha vida por delante; *it's good for getting rid of stains,* sirve para quitar las manchas; *he's good for nothing,* no sirve para nada, es un inútil. ‖ **to be up to no good,** estar tramando algo. ‖ **to deliver the goods,** (*literally*) repartir las mercancías; (*fig*) cumplir sus compromisos. ‖ **to do good,** hacer bien. ‖ **to feel good,** sentirse bien. ‖ **to have a good time,** pasarlo bien. ‖ **to look good,** (*person*) tener buen aspecto; (*food*) tener buena pinta. ‖ **to make good,** (*be successful*) tener éxito, salir bien; (*reform*) reformarse; (*compensate*) indemnizar. ‖ **what's the good of** + *ger?,* ¿de qué sirve + *inf?: what's the good of denying it?,* ¿de qué sirve negarlo?
■ **goods train,** tren *m* de mercancías. ‖ **goods wagon,** furgón *m*, vagón *m* de mercancías. ‖ **goods yard,** estación *f* de mercancías. ‖ **stolen goods,** objetos *mpl* robados.
▲ *comp* **better,** *superl* **best.**

goodbye [gʊd'baɪ] **1** *n* adiós *m*. **– 2** *interj* ¡adiós!
● **to say goodbye to,** despedirse de.
▲ *También se escribe* **good-bye.**

good-for-nothing ['gʊdfənʌθɪŋ] **1** *n* inútil *mf*. **– 2** *adj* inútil.

good-hearted [gʊd'hɑːtɪd] *adj* de buen corazón.

good-humoured [gʊd'hjuːməd] *adj* de buen humor, campechano,-a.

good-looking [gʊd'lʊkɪŋ] *adj* guapo,-a, bien parecido,-a.

good-natured [gʊd'neɪtʃəd] *adj* bondadoso,-a.

goodness ['gʊdnəs] **1** *n* (*virtue*) bondad *f*. **2** (*in food*) lo nutritivo.
● **for goodness sake!,** ¡por Dios! ‖ **my goodness!,** ¡Dios mío!

goods [gʊdz] *npl* → **good.**

good-tempered [gʊd'tempəd] *adj* de buen carácter.

goodwill [gʊd'wɪl] *n* buena voluntad *f*: *a goodwill mission,* una visita de buena voluntad.

goody ['gʊdɪ] **1** *n fam* (*in film, story*) el bueno: *the goody and the baddy,* el bueno y el malo. **– 2 goodies,** *npl fam* (*sweets*) golosinas *fpl*, chucherías *fpl*.
▲ *pl* **goodies.**

goody-goody ['gʊdɪgʊdɪ] **1** *n fam* santurrón,-ona, gazmoño,-a. **– 2** *interj fam* ¡qué guay!, ¡estupendo!
▲ *pl* **goody-goodies.**

gooey ['guːɪ] **1** *adj fam* (*sticky*) pegajoso,-a, viscoso,-a; (*of food*) empalagoso,-a. **2** *fam* (*sentimental*) sensiblero,-a, empalagoso,-a,.
▲ *comp* **gooier,** *superl* **gooiest.**

goof [guːf] **1** *n us fam* (*mistake*) pifia, plancha. **2** (*person*) zoquete *m*. **– 3** *t us fam* (*botch*) chapucear, chafallar. **– 4** *i* pifiarla.
● **to make a goof,** hacer una plancha.

goof-ball ['guːfbɔːl] *n us fam* (*person*) zoquete *m*.
■ **goof-ball comedy,** comedia alocada.

goofy ['guːfɪ] **1** *adj fam* (*stupid*) necio,-a, bobo,-a. **2** (*teeth*) salido,-a; (*person*) dentón,-ona: *he's got goofy teeth,* tiene los dientes salidos.
▲ *comp* **goofier,** *superl* **goofiest.**

goolies ['guːlɪ] *npl* GB *sl* cojones *mpl*.

goon ['guːn] **1** *adj fam* (*idiot*) zoquete *m*, imbécil *mf*. **2** *us* matón *m* contratado para atemorizar a políticos y empresarios.

goosander ['guːsændə'] *n* ORN serreta.

goose [guːs] **1** *n* ORN ganso, oca.
● **to cook sb.'s goose,** hacerle la pascua a algn. ‖ **to kill the goose that lays the golden eggs,** matar la gallina de los huevos de oro.
■ **goose barnacle,** ZOOL percebe *m*. ‖ **goose pimples,** piel *f* de gallina: *he came out in goose pimples,* se le puso la piel de gallina.
▲ *pl* **geese.**

gooseberry ['gʊzbərɪ] **1** *n* BOT grosella espinosa. **2** GB *fam fig* (*person*) carabina.
● **to play gooseberry,** GB *fam fig* ir de carabina, hacer de carabina, llevar la cesta. ‖ **they found him (her) under a gooseberry bush,** lo (la) trajo la cigüeña.
■ **gooseberry bush,** grosellero espinoso.
▲ *pl* **gooseberries.**

gooseflesh ['guːsfleʃ] *n* piel *f* de gallina.

goose-step ['guːsstep] **1** *n* paso de la oca. **– 2** *i* marchar a paso de la oca.
▲ (*verbo*) *pt & pp* **goose-stepped,** *ger* **goose-stepping.**

gopher ['gəʊfə'] *n* ZOOL ardilla terrera.

Gordian ['gɔːdɪən] **Gordian knot,** *n* nudo gordiano.

gore[1] [gɔː'] *n* sangre *f* derramada.

gore[2] [gɔː'] *t* cornear, dar una cornada a.
● **to be gored,** recibir una cornada.

gorge [gɔːdʒ] *n* (*mountain pass*) desfiladero; (*ravine*) barranco.
● **to gorge os. on,** atiborrarse de, atracarse de: *he gorged himself on cakes and biscuits,* se atiborró de pasteles y galletas.

gorgeous ['gɔːdʒəs] **1** *adj* magnífico,-a, espléndido,-a. **2** (*person*) guapísimo,-a. **– 3** *n fam* guapo,-a: *hello gorgeous!,* ¡hola guapa!

gorgon ['gɔːgən] **1** *n* (*mythology*) Gorgona. **2** *fig* (*woman*) arpía.

gorilla [gə'rɪlə] *n* ZOOL gorila *m*.

gormless ['gɔːmləs] *adj* GB *fam* lerdo,-a.

gorse [gɔːs] *n* BOT tojo, aulaga.

gory ['gɔːrɪ] *adj* sangriento,-a.
▲ *comp* **gorier,** *superl* **goriest.**

gosh [gɒʃ] *interj fam* ¡cielos!

goshawk ['gɒshɔːk] *n* ORN azor *m*.

gosling ['gɒzlɪŋ] *n* ORN ansarón *m*.

go-slow [gəʊ'sləʊ] *n* huelga de celo.

gospel ['gɒspəl] **1** *n* REL evangelio: *the Gospel according to Saint Mark,* el Evangelio según San Marcos. **2** MUS música gospel.
● **to speak the gospel truth,** decir como el evangelio. ‖ **and that's gospel truth,** y eso va a misa, y eso es la pura verdad.

gossamer ['gɒsəmə'] **1** *n* (*spiders' webs*) hilos *mpl* de telaraña. **2** (*cloth*) gasa fina. **– 3** *adj* muy fino,-a.

gossip ['gɒsɪp] **1** *n* (*talk*) cotilleo, chismorreo. **2** (*person*) cotilla *mf*, chismoso,-a. **– 3** *i* cotillear, chismorrear.
● **to gossip about sth./sb.,** cotillear sobre algo/algn., chismorrear sobre algo/algn.
■ **a piece of gossip,** un chisme. ‖ **gossip column,** crónica de sociedad. ‖ **gossip columnist,** cronista *mf* de sociedad.

gossipy ['gɒsɪpɪ] **1** *adj fam* (*person*) chismoso,-a. **2** *fam* (*style*) informal.

got [gɒt] *pt & pp* → **get.**

Goth [gɒθ] **1** *n* (*person*) godo,-a. **2** (*music*) música siniestra; (*person*) siniestro,-a.

Gothic ['gɒθɪk] **1** *adj* godo,-a. **2** (*language, architecture, type*) gótico,-a. **– 3** *n* (*language*) gótico.

gotten ['gɒtən] *pp* US → **get**.

gouache [gʊ'æs] *n* ART aguada, guache *m*.

gouge [gaʊdʒ] 1 *n* (*hollow chisel*) gubia. – 2 *t* escoplear con gubia.

● **to gouge sb.'s eyes out,** arrancar los ojos a algn.

gourd [gʊəd] *n* calabaza.

gourmand ['gʊəmənd] *n* goloso,-a.

gourmet ['gʊəmeɪ] *n* gastrónomo,-a, gurmet *mf*.

gout [gaʊt] *n* MED gota.

Gov[1] ['gʌvənə'] *abbr* (*Governor*) Gobernador,-ra; (*abbreviation*) Gobr.

Gov[2] ['gʌvənmənt] *abbr* (*Government*) Gobierno; (*abbreviation*) Gob, Gobno.

govern ['gʌvən] 1 *t* gobernar, dirigir. 2 LING regir. 3 (*determine*) dictar. – 4 *i* gobernar. 5 (*predominate*) predominar, prevalecer.

governable ['gʌvənəbəl] *adj* gobernable.

governess ['gʌvənəs] *n* institutriz *f*.

governing ['gʌvənɪŋ] *adj* gobernante, dirigente.

■ **governing body,** consejo de administración. ‖ **the governing classes,** las clases *fpl* dirigentes.

government ['gʌvənmənt] 1 *n* gobierno. – 2 *adj* (*of government*) del gobierno, gubernamental: *government affairs,* asuntos gubernamentales; *government policy,* política del gobierno. 3 (*of a governor*) del gobernador.

■ **government department,** ministerio.

governmental [gʌvən'mentəl] *adj* gubernamental.

governor ['gʌvənə'] 1 *n* (*town, state, bank*) gobernador,-ra. 2 (*prison*) director,-ra. 3 (*school*) administrador,-ra. 4 GB *fam* (*employer*) jefe *m*.

Governor-General ['gʌvənə'dʒenərəl] *n* GB gobernador,-ra general.

▲ *pl Governors-General* o *Governor-Generals*.

Govt ['gʌvənmənt] *abbr* (*Government*) Gobierno; (*abbreviation*) Gob, Gobno.

gown [gaʊn] 1 *n* vestido largo. 2 (*judge's, academic's*) toga. 3 (*surgeon's*) bata. 4 (*at hairdresser's*) peinador *m*.

GP ['dʒiː'piː] *abbr* (*general practioner*) médico,-a de cabecera.

▲ *pl GPs*.

GPO ['dʒiː'piː'əʊ] *abbr* GB (*General Post Office*) Oficina Central de Correos.

grab [græb] 1 *t* (*seize, snatch*) coger, agarrar, asir: *she grabbed him by the hair,* lo agarró por los cabellos; *he grabbed her handbag,* le cogió el bolso. 2 (*capture, arrest*) pillar, coger: *they grabbed the thieves,* pillaron a los ladrones. 3 *fam* entusiasmar: *the idea doesn't grab me,* no me entusiasma la idea; *how does that grab you?,* qué te parece eso? – 4 *n* asimiento, agarrón *m*. 5 TECH cuchara.

◆ **to grab at** *t insep* intentar coger.

● **to be up for grabs,** estar disponible.

▲ *pt & pp grabbed, grabbing*.

grace [greɪs] 1 *n* gracia, elegancia. 2 (*deportment*) garbo. 3 (*courtesy*) delicadeza, cortesía: *he had the grace to apologize,* tuvo la delicadeza de disculparse. 4 (*blessing*) bendición *f*. 5 REL gracia: *by the grace of God,* por la gracia de Dios; *in a state of grace,* en estado de gracia. 6 (*delay*) plazo: *he gave them two weeks grace to pay,* les dio un plazo de dos semanas para pagar, les dio dos semanas de plazo para pagar. – 7 *t* (*adorn*) adornar: *a candelabra graced the table,* un candelabro adornaba la mesa. 8 (*honour*) honrar: *he graced us with his presence,* nos honró con su presencia.

● **with good grace,** de buena gana. ‖ **with bad grace,** a regañadientes, de mala gana. ‖ **to fall from grace,**

caer en desgracia. ‖ **to say grace,** REL bendecir la comida, bendecir la mesa.

■ **Your Grace,** (*bishop*) Su Ilustrísima; (*duke, duchess*) Su Excelencia. ‖ **the Three Graces,** (*mythology*) las tres Gracias.

graceful ['greɪsfʊl] *adj* elegante, garboso,-a.

gracefulness ['greɪsfʊlnəs] *n* garbo, elegancia.

graceless ['greɪsləs] *adj* desgarbado,-a, sin gracia.

gracious ['greɪʃəs] 1 *adj* gracioso,-a: *Her Gracious Majesty,* Su Graciosa Majestad. 2 (*polite*) cortés. 3 (*kind*) amable. 4 (*benevolent*) benévolo,-a. – 5 *interj* ¡Dios mío!

graciousness ['greɪʃəsnəs] 1 *n* gracia. 2 (*kindness*) amabilidad *f*, bondad *f*. 3 (*benevolence*) benevolencia.

gradation [grə'deɪʃən] *n* gradación *f*.

grade [greɪd] 1 *n* (*degree, level*) grado. 2 (*quality*) calidad *f*. 3 (*class, category*) clase *f*, categoría. 4 (*rank*) rango, grado. 5 (*mark*) nota. 6 US (*gradient*) pendiente *f*. 7 US (*form*) clase *f*. – 8 *t* (*sort, classify*) clasificar. 9 (*road*) nivelar. 10 (*student*) calificar, poner una nota. 11 (*colours*) degradar.

◆ **to grade up** *t sep* subir de categoría. ‖ **to grade down** *t sep* bajar de categoría.

● **to make the grade,** (*reach desired standard*) alcanzar el nivel necesario; (*succeed*) tener éxito.

■ **grade crossing,** US paso a nivel. ‖ **grade school,** US escuela primaria.

gradient ['greɪdɪənt] 1 *n* declive *m*, pendiente *f*: *a gradient of one in ten,* una pendiente del diez por ciento. 2 PHYS gradiente *m*.

gradual ['grædjʊəl] *adj* gradual, paulatino,-a.

gradually ['grædjʊəlɪ] *adv* poco a poco, gradualmente, paulatinamente.

graduate ['grædjʊət] 1 *n* EDUC (*after 3 year course*) diplomado,-a; (*after 5 year course*) licenciado,-a: *a graduate in Spanish,* un licenciado en filología española. – 2 *t* (*grade, classify*) graduar. – 3 *i* (*after 3 year course*) diplomarse (**in**, en); (*after 5 year course*) licenciarse (**in**, en): *he's just graduated in physics,* acaba de licenciarse en física.

■ **graduate school,** US escuela para graduados.

▲ En *acepciones* 2 y 3 ['grædjʊeɪt].

graduation [grædjʊ'eɪʃən] 1 *n* EDUC graduación *f*, ceremonia de entrega de un título universitario. 2 TECH graduación *f*.

graffiti [grə'fiːtɪ] 1 *npl* grafitis *mpl*, pintadas *fpl*. – 2 *t* hacer grafitis.

graft[1] [grɑːft] 1 *n* AGR MED injerto. 2 *t* AGR MED injertar (**onto**, en). – 3 *i* AGR MED injertarse. 4 AGR MED (*make a graft*) hacer un injerto.

graft[2] [grɑːft] 1 *n* US (*bribery*) soborno. 2 US(*corruption*) corrupción *f*. 3 US (*illicit dealings*) tejemanejes *mpl*, chanchullos *mpl*. 4 GB *fam* trabajo. – 5 *t* US (*bribe*) sobornar. 6 US(*swindle*) timar, estafar. 7 GB *fam* trabajar duro, currar, pringar.

grafter ['grɑːftə'] 1 *n* US (*swindler*) timador,-ra, estafador,-ra. 2 (*worker*) persona trabajadora.

Grail [greɪl] *n* REL grial *m*.

■ **the Holy Grail,** el Santo Grial.

grain [greɪn] 1 *n* (*gen*) grano: *a grain of rice,* un grano de arroz. 2 (*cereals*) cereales *mpl*. 3 (*in wood*) veta, fibra; (*in stone*) filón *m*, veta; (*of leather*) flor *f*. – 4 *t* (*give granular texture*) granular. – 5 *i* (*become granular*) granularse.

● **to saw against the grain,** (*wood*) serrar contra veta. ‖ **to saw with the grain,** (*wood*) serrar en el sentido de la veta. ‖ **to go against the grain,** ir en contra de los principios de algn.: *it goes against the grain,* va en contra de mis principios. ‖ **there's not a grain of truth in it,** no tiene ni pizca de verdad.

gram [græm] n gramo.

grammar ['græmə^r] n gramática.
■ **grammar school,** GB instituto de enseñanza secundaria (*para alumnos de cierto nivel académico*).

grammarian [grə'meəriən] n gramático,-a.

grammatical [grə'mætɪkəl] 1 adj gramatical. 2 (*correct*) correcto,-a: *he doesn't speak grammatical Spanish,* no habla un español correcto.

gramme [græm] n gramo.

gramophone ['græməfəʊn] 1 n gramófono. 2 dated (*record-player*) tocadiscos m.

Grampians ['græmpɪənz] the Grampians, npl los montes Grampianos.

gran [græn] n fam abuela.

Granada [grə'nɑːdə] n Granada.

granary ['grænərɪ] 1 n granero. 2 Granary, adj que contiene granos de trigo malteado.
▲ (*sustantivo*) pl *granaries; en* 2 *es marca registrada.*

grand [grænd] 1 adj (*splendid*) grandioso,-a, espléndido,-a, magnífico,-a. 2 (*impressive*) impresionante. 3 (*important - person*) distinguido,-a, importante. 4 fam (*great*) fenomenal.
● **on a grand scale,** a gran escala.
■ **the Grand Canyon,** GEOG el Gran Cañón. ‖ **grand duke,** gran duque m. ‖ **grand duchess,** gran duquesa. ‖ **a grand,** sl (*pounds*) mil libras; (*dollars*) mil dólares: *a couple of grand,* dos mil libras, dos mil dólares. ‖ **grand jury,** US JUR jurado de acusación. ‖ **grand piano,** piano de cola. ‖ **Grand Prix,** gran premio. ‖ **grand staircase,** escalera principal. ‖ **grand total,** total m.

grandchild ['græntʃaɪld] n nieto,-a.

granddad ['grændæd] n fam abuelo.

granddaughter ['grændɔːtə^r] n nieta.

grandee [græn'diː] n (*nobleman*) grande m: *a Spanish grandee,* un grande de España.

grandeur ['grændʒə^r] 1 n (*nobility*) grandeza, nobleza. 2 (*splendour*) grandiosidad f, magnificencia.

grandfather ['grændfɑːðə^r] n abuelo.
■ **grandfather clock,** reloj m de caja.

grandiose ['grændɪəʊs] adj grandioso,-a.

grandma ['grænmɑː] n fam abuela.

grandmaster [grænd'mɑːstə^r] n (*chess*) gran maestro.

grandmother ['grænmʌðə^r] n abuela.

grandpa ['grænpɑː] n fam abuelo.

grandparents ['grændpeərənts] npl abuelos mpl.

grandson ['grændsʌn] n nieto.

grandstand ['grændstænd] n tribuna.

grange ['greɪndʒ] n cortijo.

granite ['grænɪt] 1 n granito. – 2 adj de granito.

granite-like ['grænɪtlaɪk] n granítico,-a.

granny ['grænɪ] n fam abuela.
■ **granny flat / granny annexe,** parte de la casa familiar transformada en vivienda para la abuela o el abuelo. ‖ **Granny Smith,** manzana Granny Smith, manzana ácida.
▲ pl *grannies.*

grant [grɑːnt] 1 n EDUC beca. 2 (*subsidy*) subvención f. 3 JUR (*rights, property*) cesión f. – 4 t conceder, otorgar: *they granted him the scholarship,* le concedieron la beca. 5 JUR ceder, transferir: *they granted him the house,* le cedieron la casa.
● **I grant you that ...,** reconozco que: *I grant you that I didn't agree at first,* reconozco que al principio no estuve de acuerdo. ‖ **granted,** de acuerdo: *granted, I didn't believe you when you told me,* de acuerdo, no te creí cuando me lo dijiste. ‖ **to take sb. for granted,** no apreciar a algn. como es debido. ‖ **to take sth. for granted,** dar algo por sentado,-a.

grant-aided [grɑːnt'eɪdɪd] adj subvencionado,-a.

granting ['grɑːntɪŋ] 1 n (*awarding - grant, money*) concesión f, otorgamiento. 2 JUR (*rights, property*) concesión f.

granular ['grænjʊlə^r] 1 adj (*with grains*) granular. 2 (*texture*) granulado,-a.

granulated ['grænjʊleɪtɪd] adj granulado,-a.

granulation [grænjʊ'leɪʃən] n granulación f.

granule ['grænjuːl] n gránulo m.

grape [greɪp] n uva: *a bunch of grapes,* un racimo de uvas.
■ **the grape harvest,** la vendimia. ‖ **grape juice,** zumo de uva, mosto.

grapefruit ['greɪpfruːt] n pomelo.
▲ pl *grapefruits* o *grapefruit.*

grapevine ['greɪpvaɪn] n (*gen*) parra; (*vine*) vid f.
● **to hear it on the grapevine,** enterarse por radio macuto, escucharlo en radio macuto.

graph [grɑːf] n gráfica, gráfico.
■ **graph paper,** papel m milimetrado.

graphic ['græfɪk] 1 adj (*gen*) gráfico,-a. 2 (*vivid*) muy gráfico,-a, vívido,-a: *a graphic description,* una descripción muy gráfica.
■ **graphic arts,** artes fpl gráficas. ‖ **graphic design,** diseño gráfico. ‖ **graphic equalizer,** ecualizador m gráfico.

graphics ['græfɪks] 1 n (*graphic design*) diseño gráfico, grafismo. – 2 npl COMPUT gráficos mpl.

graphite ['græfaɪt] n grafito.

graphologist [grə'fɒlədʒɪst] n grafólogo,-a.

graphology [grə'fɒlədʒɪ] n grafología.

grapple ['græpəl] 1 i (*person*) luchar (**with,** con), forcejear (**with,** con). 2 (*problem etc*) lidiar (**with,** con).

grappling iron ['græplɪŋaɪən] n garfio.

grasp [grɑːsp] 1 n (*grip, hold*) asimiento, apretón m: *he's got a strong grasp,* agarra muy fuerte; *he lost his grasp on the rope,* se le escapó la cuerda. 2 fig (*control, power*) control m, dominio: *he had her in his grasp,* la tenía en sus garras. 3 (*reach*) alcance m: *success is within our grasp,* el éxito está a nuestro alcance; *victory was beyond their grasp,* la victoria estaba fuera de su alcance. 4 (*understanding*) comprensión f; (*knowledge*) conocimientos mpl: *she has a sound grasp of economics,* tiene sólidos conocimientos de economía; *you have a good grasp of the problem,* comprendes bien el problema. – 5 t (*seize - with hands*) agarrar, asir; (*opportunity, offer*) aprovechar: *he grasped me by the arm,* me agarró del brazo. 6 (*understand*) comprender, captar: *he failed to grasp the significance of the problem,* no comprendió la importancia del problema. –
◆ **to grasp at** 1 t insep tratar de agarrar. 2 fig (*opportunity*) aprovechar.
● **to lose one's grasp on reality,** perder contacto con la realidad.

grasping ['grɑːspɪŋ] adj avaricioso,-a, avaro,-a, codicioso,-a.

grass [grɑːs] 1 n (*plant*) hierba, yerba; (*lawn*) césped m; (*pasture*) pasto; (*dried*) paja: *a blade of grass,* una brizna de hierba. 2 sl (*marijuana*) hierba, maría. 3 GB sl (*informer*) soplón,-ona. – 4 t (*turf*) plantar césped en (**over,** -). – 5 i sl (*inform*) chivarse (**on,** a), soplar (**on,** a).
● **keep off the grass,** prohibido pisar el césped. ‖ **the grass is always greener on the other side (of the fence),** nadie está contento con su suerte. ‖ **not to let the grass to grow under one's feet,** no perder el tiempo, no quedarse dormido,-a. ‖ **to put sb. out to grass,** jubilar a algn.

■ **grass court,** pista de hierba. ‖ **grass roots,** POL las bases *fpl.* ‖ **grass snake,** culebra. ‖ **grass widow,** *(separated)* mujer *f* separada; *(divorced)* mujer divorciada; *(husband away) mujer que está sola porque su marido está fuera.* ‖ **grass widower,** *(separated)* hombre separado; *(divorced)* hombre divorciado; *(wife away)* Rodríguez *m.*

grasshopper [ˈɡrɑːʃɒpəʳ] *n* saltamontes *m.*

grassland [ˈɡrɑːslænd] *n (land covered with grass)* prado; *(for grazing)* pasto, pastizal *m.*
▲ *Se usa frecuentemente el plural* **grasslands** *con el mismo significado.*

grass-roots [ˈɡrɑːsruːts] *adj* POL de las bases: *at grass-roots level,* a nivel de las bases.

grassy [ˈɡrɑːsɪ] *adj* cubierto,-a de hierba.
▲ *comp* **grassier,** *superl* **grassies.**

grate[1] [ɡreɪt] **1** *t* CULIN rallar. **2** *(scrape - gen)* rascar; *(- teeth)* hacer rechinar. **– 3** *i (screech)* chirriar, rechinar. **4** *fig (annoy)* ser crispante: *her voice really grates on me,* me crispa su voz.
● **to grate on one's nerves,** crisparle a uno los nervios.

grate[2] [ɡreɪt] *n (metal frame)* rejilla; *(fireplace)* chimenea.

grateful [ˈɡreɪtful] *adj (person)* agradecido,-a; *(letter, smile)* de agradecimiento.
● **to be grateful,** agradecer: *I'd be grateful if you could send me a brochure,* le agradecería que me enviara un folleto; *I'm grateful for all your help,* te agradezco toda tu ayuda; *I'd be grateful if you could finish it today,* te agradecería que lo acabaras hoy.

gratefully [ˈɡreɪtfulɪ] *adv (accept, take)* con gratitud; *(smile)* agradecido,-a: *all suggestions will be gratefully received,* agradecemos cualquier sugerencia.

grater [ˈɡreɪtəʳ] *n* rallador *m.*

gratification [ɡrætɪfɪˈkeɪʃən] *n* gratificación *f,* satisfacción *f,* placer *m.*

gratified [ˈɡrætɪfaɪd] *adj* satisfecho,-a, complacido,-a.

gratify [ˈɡrætɪfaɪ] **1** *t (satisfy - desire etc)* satisfacer. **2** *(give pleasure to)* complacer, gratificar.
▲ *pt & pp* **gratified,** *ger* **gratifying.**

gratifying [ˈɡrætɪfaɪɪŋ] *adj (gen)* grato,-a; *(task)* gratificante.

grating[1] [ˈɡreɪtɪŋ] *n* rejilla, reja.

grating[2] [ˈɡreɪtɪŋ] *adj (irritating)* crispante; *(harsh)* chirriante, rechinante.

gratis [ˈɡrætɪs, ˈɡrɑːtɪs] *adv* gratis.

gratitude [ˈɡrætɪtjuːd] *n* gratitud *f,* agradecimiento: *please accept this as a token of my gratitude,* por favor acepta esto como muestra de mi agradecimiento; *we wanted to show our gratitude for the help you've given us,* queríamos demostrar nuestra gratitud por la ayuda que nos has prestado.

gratuitous [ɡrəˈtjuːɪtəs] *adj* gratuito,-a.

gratuitously [ɡrəˈtjuːɪtəslɪ] *adv* gratuitamente.

gratuitousness [ɡrəˈtruːɪtəsnəs] *n* gratuidad *f.*

gratuity [ɡrəˈtjuːɪtɪ] **1** *n (tip)* propina. **2** GB *(gift of money)* gratificación *f.*
▲ *pl* **gratuities.**

grave[1] [ɡreɪv] **1** *n (tomb)* tumba, sepultura. **2** *lit (death)* tumba.
● **as silent as the grave,** como una tumba. ‖ **from the cradle to the grave,** (durante) toda la vida. ‖ **to have one foot in the grave,** estar con un pie en la sepultura, tener un pie en la tumba. ‖ **to turn in one's grave,** revolverse en su tumba.

grave[2] [ɡreɪv] **1** *adj (solemn - voice, look, etc)* grave. **2** *(serious - situation, consequences, error, etc)* grave, serio,-a. **3** LING *(accent)* grave.

▲ *En acepción 3* [ɡrɑːv].

gravedigger [ˈɡreɪvdɪɡəʳ] *n* sepulturero,-a, enterrador,-ra.

gravel [ˈɡrævəl] **1** *n* grava, gravilla, guijo. **– 2** *t* cubrir de grava, cubrir de gravilla.
■ **gravel pit,** gravera.
▲ *(verbo) pt & pp* **gravelled** (US **graveled**), *ger* **gravelling** (US **graveling**).

gravestone [ˈɡreɪvstəʊn] *n* lápida.

graveyard [ˈɡreɪvjɑːd] *n* cementerio.
■ **graveyard shift,** turno de noche.

gravitate [ˈɡrævɪteɪt] *i* PHYS gravitar (**towards,** hacia).
◆ **to gravitate to / gravitate towards** *t insep (be drawn to)* sentirse atraído,-a por; *(move towards)* desplazarse hacia: *people gravitated to the cities,* la gente se desplazaba hacia las ciudades.

gravitation [ɡrævɪˈteɪʃən] *n* PHYS gravitación *f.*

gravitational [ɡrævɪˈteɪsənəl] *adj* gravitacional.

gravity [ˈɡrævɪtɪ] **1** *n* PHYS gravedad *f: the law of gravity,* la ley de la gravedad. **2** *(importance, seriousness - of situation)* gravedad *f; (of person, manner)* gravedad *f,* circunspección *f.*

gravy [ˈɡreɪvɪ] *n* CULIN salsa de carne, jugo de la carne.
■ **gravy boat,** salsera. ‖ **gravy train,** US *sl* chollo.

gray [ɡreɪ] *adj* US → **grey.**

graze[1] [ɡreɪz] **1** *n* rasguño, roce *m.* **– 2** *t (scrape)* rascar, rasguñar: *he grazed his knee,* se rasguñó la rodilla. **3** *(touch lightly)* rozar.

graze[2] [ɡreɪz] **1** *i* pacer, pastar. **– 2** *t (sheep, cattle)* pastar, pastorear, apacentar.

grazing [ˈɡreɪzɪŋ] **grazing (land),** *n* (tierra de) pasto, tierra de pastoreo.

grease [ɡriːs] **1** *n (gen)* grasa. **– 2** *t (part of car, machine, device)* engrasar. **3** CULIN untar con mantequilla, untar con manteca.
■ **grease gun,** pistola engrasadora. ‖ **grease monkey,** ayudante *mf* de mecánico.

greasepaint [ˈɡriːspeɪnt] *n* THEAT maquillaje *m.*

greaseproof paper [ˈɡriːspruːfˈpeɪpəʳ] *n* papel *m* de cera, papel *m* encerado, papel *m* parafinado.

greasy [ˈɡriːsɪ] **1** *adj (oily - hands)* grasiento,-a; *(hair, skin, food)* graso,-a. **2** *(slippery)* resbaladizo,-a. **3** *fam pej (smarmy)* adulador,-ra, pelota.
▲ *comp* **greasier,** *superl* **greasiest.**

great [ɡreɪt] **1** *adj (large)* grande; *(before sing noun)* gran: *a great deal of money,* muchísimo dinero; *a great many people,* muchísima gente; *the great majority,* la gran mayoría; *in a great number of cases,* en un gran número de casos. **2** *(considerable, profound, intense)* grande; *(before sing noun)* gran: *it gives me great pleasure to ...,* tengo el gran placer de ...; *he felt great sorrow,* sintió un gran dolor. **3** *(famous, important, outstanding)* grande, importante; *(before sing noun)* gran, importante: *he was a great politician,* fue un gran político; *Ireland's greatest living poet,* el poeta vivo más importante de Irlanda. **4** *fam (excellent, wonderful)* estupendo,-a, fantástico,-a, sensacional, fabuloso,-a: *I had a great time last night,* lo pasé fenomenal anoche; *it's great to see you!,* ¡me alegro mucho de verte!; *this stuff is great for cleaning pots and pans,* esto es fantástico para limpiar cacharros; *she's great at maths,* es muy buena en mates; *how was the film? - great!,* ¿qué tal la película? - ¡fenomenal!; *what a great idea,* ¡qué idea más buena! **5** *(for emphasis)* grande; *(before sing noun)* gran: *we're great friends,* somos grandes amigos; *he's a great player,* es un gran jugador; *a great big cockroach,* una cucaracha enorme;

you great brute!, ¡pedazo de animal! – **6** *adv fam* muy bien, estupendamente, fenomenal: *they're doing just great*, están muy bien; *she's not feeling too great*, no se encuentra muy bien. – **7** *n* (*person*) grande *mf*. – **8 the great**, *npl* (*people*) los grandes *mpl*, la gente *f* importante.
● **to be no great shakes**, no ser gran cosa. ‖ **to go great guns**, ir a las mil maravillas, ir viento en popa.
■ **the Great Barrier Reef**, la Gran Barrera de Coral. ‖ **the Great Bear**, la Osa Mayor. ‖ **great circle**, círculo máximo. ‖ **Great Dane**, gran danés *m*. ‖ **the Great War**, la Gran Guerra, la primera Guerra Mundial.

great-aunt [greɪt'ɑːnt] *n* tía abuela.

greatcoat ['greɪtkəʊt] *n* abrigo, sobretodo, gabán *m*.

great-grandchild [greɪt'græntʃaɪld] *n* bisnieto,-a, biznieto,-a.

great-granddaughter [greɪt'grænddɔːtəʳ] *n* bisnieta, biznieta.

great-grandfather [greɪt'grændfɑːðəʳ] *n* bisabuelo.

great-grandmother [greɪt'grænmʌðəʳ] *n* bisabuela.

great-grandson [greɪt'grændsʌn] *n* bisnieto, biznieto.

great-great-grandmother [greɪtgreɪt'grænmʌðəʳ] *n* tatarabuela.

great-great-grandfather [greɪtgreɪt'grændfɑːðəʳ] *n* tatarabuelo.

greatly ['greɪtlɪ] *adv* mucho, enormemente: *he greatly admires his father*, admira mucho a su padre; *I greatly regret giving up the piano*, me arrepiento mucho de haber dejado de tocar el piano.

greatness ['greɪtnəs] *n* (*importance*) grandeza; (*size*) enormidad *f*, magnitud *f*.

great-uncle [greɪt'ʌŋkəl] *n* tío abuelo.

grebe [griːb] *n* ORN somormujo, somorgujón *m*.

Greece [griːs] *n* Grecia.

greed [griːd] **1** *n* (*for money, power*) codicia, avaricia. **2** (*for food*) gula, glotonería.

greedily ['griːdɪlɪ] **1** *adv* (*avariciously*) con avaricia, avariciosamente. **2** (*eat, look*) con gula, con glotonería.

greediness ['griːdɪnəs] **1** *n* (*for money, power*) codicia, avaricia. **2** (*for food*) gula, glotonería.

greedy ['griːdɪ] **1** *adj* (*for money, possessions*) codicioso,-a (**for**, de); (*for power, knowledge*) ávido,-a (**for**, de). **2** (*for food*) glotón,-ona.
▲ *comp* **greedier**, *superl* **greediest**.

Greek [griːk] **1** *adj* griego,-a. – **2** *n* (*person*) griego,-a. **3** (*language*) griego.
● **it's all Greek to me**, me suena a chino.

green [griːn] **1** *adj* (*colour*) verde. **2** (*unripe, not dried*) verde. **3** (*environment friendly*) verde, ecológico,-a. **4** (*pale*) pálido,-a. **5** (*inexperienced*) novato,-a, verde; (*gullible*) ingenuo,-a, crédulo,-a. **6** (*jealous*) envidioso,-a. – **7** *n* (*colour*) verde *m*. **7** (*stretch of grass*) césped *m*; (*in golf*) green *m*; (*in village*) césped público ubicado en medio de un pueblo. – **8 greens**, *npl* (*vegetables*) verduras *fpl*. **9 the Greens**, POL los verdes *mpl*.
● **to be green with envy**, morirse de envidia: *she was green with envy*, se moría de envidia, se la comía la envidia. ‖ **to give sth. the green light**, dar luz verde a algo. ‖ **to have green fingers**, GB tener buena mano para las plantas. ‖ **to have green thumbs**, US tener buena mano para las plantas.
■ **green belt**, zona verde. ‖ **green card**, US permiso de residencia y trabajo. ‖ **green paper**, GB libro verde. ‖ **green pepper**, pimiento verde. ‖ **green salad**, ensalada verde.

greenback ['griːnbæk] *n* US *fam* dólar *m*, verde *m*, lechuga *f*.

greenery ['griːnərɪ] *n* follaje *m*, vegetación *f*.

green-eyed ['griːnaɪd] *adj* de ojos verdes.

greenfinch ['griːnfɪntʃ] *n* verderón *m* común.

greenfly ['griːnflaɪ] *n* pulgón *m*.
▲ *pl* **greenflies**.

greengage ['griːngeɪdʒ] *n* ciruela claudia.

greengrocer ['griːngrəʊsəʳ] *n* verdulero,-a.
■ **greengrocer's (shop)**, verdulería.

greenhorn ['griːnhɔːn] *n fam* novato,-a.

greenhouse ['griːnhaʊs] *n* invernadero.
■ **greenhouse effect**, efecto invernadero.

greenish ['griːnɪʃ] *adj* verdoso,-a.

Greenland ['griːnlənd] *n* Groenlandia.

Greenlander ['griːnləndəʳ] *n* groenlandés,-esa.

Greenlandic [griːˈlændɪk] **1** *adj* groenlandés,-esa. – **2** *n* (*language*) groenlandés *m*.

greenness ['griːnnəs] *n* verdor *m*.

greenroom ['griːnruːm] *n* THEAT *dated* camerino.

greenstuff ['griːnstʌf] *n* verdura.

greet [griːt] **1** *t* (*wave at, say hello to*) saludar; (*welcome*) dar la bienvenida a; (*receive*) recibir. **2** (*react*) acoger, recibir. **3** *fig* (*meet*) llegar, presentarse: *I was greeted by a strong smell of burning*, me llegó un fuerte olor a quemado.

greeting ['griːtɪŋ] **1** *n* saludo. – **2 greetings**, *npl* saludos *mpl*, recuerdos *mpl*.
● **birthday greetings**, feliz cumpleaños.
■ **greetings card**, tarjeta de felicitación.

gregarious [greˈgeərɪəs] *adj* gregario,-a, sociable.

Gregorian [grɪˈgɔːrɪən] *adj* gregoriano,-a.
■ **gregorian chant**, canto gregoriano.

gremlin ['gremlɪn] *n* duende *m*, duendecillo.

Grenada [grəˈneɪdə] *n* Granada.

grenade [grəˈneɪd] *n* MIL granada.

Grenadian [grəˈneɪdɪən] **1** *adj* granadino,-a. – **2** *n* granadino,-a.

grenadier [grenəˈdɪəʳ] *n* MIL granadero.

grenadine ['grenədiːn] *n* (*syrup*) granadina.

grew [gruː] *pt* → **grow**.

grey [greɪ] **1** *adj* (*colour*) gris; (*hair*) cano,-a; (*sky*) nublado,-a, gris. **2** (*gloomy*) triste, gris. – **3** *n* (*colour*) gris *m*. **4** (*horse*) caballo tordo.
● **to go grey**, (*hair, person*) encanecer, volverse cano,-a; (*sky*) nublarse.
■ **grey area**, zona gris. ‖ **grey matter**, materia gris.

grey-haired ['greɪheəd] *adj* de pelo cano, canoso,-a.

greyhound ['greɪhaʊnd] *n* galgo.

greying ['greɪɪŋ] *adj* canoso,-a.

greyish ['greɪɪʃ] *adj* (*gen*) grisáceo,-a; (*hair*) entrecano,-a.

grid [grɪd] **1** *n* (*grating*) reja, parrilla, rejilla. **2** ELEC (*network*) red *f* nacional de tendido eléctrico. **3** (*on map*) cuadrícula.
■ **grid reference**, coordenadas *fpl* cartográficas.

griddle ['grɪdəl] *n* CULIN plancha.

gridiron ['grɪdaɪən] **1** *n* CULIN plancha. **2** US SP (*football*) campo.

grief [griːf] *n* dolor *m*, pena.
● **to come to grief**, (*vehicle*) sufrir un accidente; (*plans*) irse al traste, fracasar. ‖ **good grief!**, *fam* ¡Dios mío!, ¡por Dios!

grief-stricken ['griːfstrɪkən] *adj* (*person*) desconsolado,-a, consternado,-a.

grievance ['griːvəns] *n* (*ground for complaint*) motivo de queja; (*complaint*) queja: *she had a grievance against society*, estaba resentida con la sociedad.
● **to air one's grievances**, quejarse. ‖ **to harbour a grievance / nurse a grievance**, guardar rencor.

grieve [griːv] 1 t afligir, apenar, dar pena a, entristecer.
– 2 i apenarse, afligirse.
● to grieve for sb., llorar a algn., llorar la muerte de algn. ‖ to grieve over sth., lamentar algo.
grievous ['griːvəs] 1 adj (causing grief - loss, news, wrongs) penoso,-a, doloroso,-a. 2 (severe, serious - injury, wound) de extrema gravedad; (- error, fault, crime, sin) grave.
● grievous bodily harm, JUR lesiones fpl corporales graves.
griffin ['grifin] n grifo.
grill [gril] 1 n CULIN (over cooker) grill m; (on charcoal) parrilla. 2 CULIN (dish) parrillada. 3 (grillroom) parrilla, asador m, grill m. 4 → **grille**. – 5 t CULIN (in grill over cooker) hacer al grill; (over charcoal) asar a la parrilla. 6 fam (interrogate) interrogar.
grille [gril] 1 n (partition) reja, verja, enrejado; (protective covering) rejilla. 2 (radiator) grill, AUTO calandra, parrilla.
grilling ['grilɪŋ] n interrogatorio.
● to give sb. a good grilling, acribillar a algn. a preguntas.
grillroom ['grilruːm] n parrilla, asador m, grill m.
grim [grim] 1 adj (serious - person, manner) austero,-a, adusto,-a, severo,-a; (expression, look) ceñudo,-a. 2 (unpleasant, depressing - news, picture) horroroso,-a, pesimista; (- prospect, outlook) nefasto,-a, desalentador,-ra; (- reality) crudo,-a, duro,-a. 3 (gloomy - landscape, place) lúgubre, sombrío,-a. 4 (resolute, unyielding) inflexible, inexorable: with a grim determination, con una voluntad de hierro; with a grim smile, con una sonrisa sardónica. 5 (sinister - joke) macabro,-a. 6 fam (very bad) malísimo,-a, penoso,-a, desastroso,-a; (ill) fatal.
● to hang on like grim death / hold on like grim death, aferrarse con todas sus fuerzas, agarrarse con todas sus fuerzas.
■ Grim Reaper, la Parca, la muerte.
▲ comp grimmer, superl grimmest.
grimace ['griməs] 1 n mueca. – 2 i hacer una mueca.
grime [graim] n mugre f, suciedad f.
grimly ['grimli] 1 adv (severely - speak) con gravedad, en tono grave. – 2 adj (resolutely) inexorablemente.
grimy ['graimi] adj mugriento,-a, sucio,-a.
▲ comp grimier, superl grimiest.
grin [grin] 1 n (genuine) sonrisa (abierta); (mocking) sonrisa burlona. – 2 i sonreír (abiertamente).
● to grin and bear it, aguantarse, poner al mal tiempo buena cara.
▲ (verbo) pt & pp grinned, ger grinning.
grind [graind] 1 t (mill) moler; (crush) machacar, triturar; (crystals, ore) pulverizar; (lens, mirror) pulir; (knife, blade) afilar. 2 US (mince - beef) picar. 3 (teeth) hacer rechinar: she grinds her teeth, le rechinan los dientes. 4 (press down hard on) incrustar, aplastar; (press in) meter: the dirt had been ground into the carpet, la suciedad estaba bien metida en la alfombra. – 5 i (crush) triturarse. 6 (make harsh noise) rechinar, chirriar. 7 US (swot) empollar, machacar. – 8 n fam (work) trabajo pesado; (effort) paliza: the daily grind, la rutina diaria. 9 US fam (swot) empollón,-ona.
◆ to grind down t sep (oppress) oprimir. ‖ to grind out t sep (music) tocar.
● to grind the faces of the poor into the dust, oprimir a los pobres. ‖ to grind to a halt / grind to a standstill, (vehicle) detenerse ruidosamente, pararse ruidosamente; (production) irse parando poco a poco; (negotiations) estancarse, llegar a un punto muerto. ‖ to have an axe to grind, tener un interés personal.

▲ pt & pp ground.
grinder ['graində'] n (machine - for coffee) molinillo; (person - for knives etc) afilador,-ra.
grinding ['graindɪŋ] adj (screeching) chirriante.
● grinding poverty, miseria absoluta. ‖ to bring sth. to a grinding halt, (strike etc) paralizar algo. ‖ to come to a grinding halt, → to grind to a halt.
grindstone ['graindstəʊn] n muela, piedra de afilar.
● to keep one's nose to the grindstone, trabajar sin levantar cabeza.
gringo ['grɪŋgəʊ] n pej gringo,-a.
▲ pl gringos.
grip [grip] 1 n (tight hold) asimiento: he released his grip on her, la soltó; I had a firm grip on the rail, tenía la barra bien agarrada; she tightened her grip on my arm, me agarró el brazo más fuerte. 2 (of tyre) adherencia, agarre m. 3 fig (control, force) control m, dominio: he took a firm grip on the company, se hizo con el control de la empresa; the country was in the grip of a depression, una crisis económica asolaba el país. 4 SP (way of holding) la forma en que uno coge la raqueta etc; (part of handle) asidero, empuñadura. 5 (hairgrip) horquilla. 6 US (large bag) bolsa de viaje. 7 CINEM TV ayudante mf de cámara. – 8 t (hold tightly - pen) agarrar, asir, sujetar: he gripped my arm, me agarró del brazo. 9 (adhere to) tener agarre, agarrarse, adherirse. 10 fig (film, story, play) captar el interés de, captar la atención de. – 11 i adherirse.
● to be gripped by sth., ser presa de algo. ‖ to come to grips with / get to grips with, (problem, challenge) abordar, atacar; (subject, system) entender; (situation) aceptar, asumir. ‖ to get a grip on os. / take a grip on os., controlarse. ‖ to lose one's grip, perder el control.
▲ (verbo) pt & pp gripped, ger gripping.
gripe [graip] 1 i fam (complain) quejarse, refunfuñar. – 2 n fam (complaint) queja. – 3 the gripes, npl (stomach pains) retortijones mpl.
■ gripe water, calmante m para el cólico infantil.
gripping ['grɪpɪŋ] adj (film, story, etc) apasionante.
grisly ['grɪzlɪ] adj espeluznante, horripilante, truculento,-a.
▲ comp grislier, superl grisliest.
grist [grist] it's all grist to the mill, phr todo ayuda, todo es útil.
gristle ['grɪsəl] n cartílago, ternilla.
gristly ['grɪsəlɪ] adv con mucho cartílago, cartilaginoso,-a, ternilloso,-a.
▲ comp gristlier, superl gristliest.
grit [grit] 1 n (fine) arena; (coarse) gravilla; (dirt) polvo. 2 fam (determination) valor m, agallas fpl. – 3 t (road) echar arenilla en.
● to grit one's teeth, apretar los dientes.
▲ (verbo) pt & pp gritted, ger gritting.
gritty ['grɪtɪ] 1 adj (flour) arenoso,-a; (mussels, cockles) lleno,-a de arena. 2 (determination etc) enérgico,-a.
▲ comp grittier, superl grittiest.
grizzle ['grɪzəl] i GB fam (whine) lloriquear; (complain) refunfuñar.
grizzly ['grɪzlɪ] grizzly (bear), n oso pardo.
groan [grəʊn] 1 n (of pain) gemido, quejido. 2 fam (of disapproval) gruñido. 3 (creak) crujido. – 4 i (in pain) gemir, quejarse; (with disapproval) gruñir. 5 (creak) crujir. 6 fam (complain) quejarse (about, de), refunfuñar (about, por), rezongar (about, de).
grocer ['grəʊsə'] n tendero,-a.
■ grocer's (shop), tienda de ultramarinos, tienda de comestibles, colmado.

groceries [ˈgrəʊsərɪz] *npl* comestibles *mpl.*

grocery [ˈgrəʊsərɪ] *n* US tienda de ultramarinos, tienda de comestibles, colmado.
▲ *pl groceries.*

groggy [ˈgrɒgɪ] *adj fam* grogui.
▲ *comp groggier, superl groggiest.*

groin [grɔɪn] 1 *n* ANAT ingle *f.* 2 US → **groyne.**

groom [gruːm] 1 *n* (*bridegroom*) novio. 2 (*for horses*) mozo de cuadra. – 3 *t* (*horse*) almohazar; (*dog*) cepillar. 4 (*person*) arreglar.
● **to groom sb. for sth.**, preparar a algn. para algo.

groomed [gruːmd] *adj* arreglado,-a.

groove [gruːv] 1 *n* (*gen*) ranura; (*for door*) guía; (*in column*) acanaladura. 2 (*on record*) surco.
● **to be (stuck) in a groove**, anquilosarse, estancarse en la rutina.

groovy [ˈgruːvɪ] *adj fam* guay, genial.
▲ *comp groovier, superl grooviest.*

grope [grəʊp] 1 *i* (*fumble*) andar a tientas. – 2 *t fam* (*touch up*) meter mano a, magrear, sobar. – 3 *n* magreo.
● **to grope for sth.**, buscar algo a tientas. ‖ **to grope one's way towards sth.**, avanzar a tientas hacia algo.

gross [grəʊs] 1 *adj* (*flagrant - injustice*) flagrante; (- *ignorance*) craso,-a; (- *error*) grave. 2 (*fat*) muy gordo,-a, obeso,-a. 3 (*coarse, crude, vulgar - person, behaviour, manners*) grosero,-a, tosco,-a, basto,-a; (- *language*) soez; (*disgusting*) asqueroso,-a: *oh gross!,* ¡qué asco! 4 COMM ECON (*total - profit, weight, income*) bruto,-a. – 5 *n* COMM gruesa, doce docenas *fpl.* – 6 *t* (*person*) ganar en bruto, obtener unos ingresos brutos de; (*film etc*) recaudar, obtener unos ingresos de: *the film grossed over $200 million,* la película recaudó más de 200 millones de dólares.
◆ **to gross out** *t sep* US dar asquear, dar asco a.
■ **gross indecency,** ultraje *m* contra la moral pública. ‖ **gross national product,** producto nacional bruto. ‖ **gross negligence,** negligencia temeraria.
▲ *pl gross.*

grossly [ˈgrəʊslɪ] 1 *adv* (*extremely*) terriblemente, extremadamente, enormemente. 2 (*bluntly, crudely*) groseramente.

grotesque [grəʊˈtesk] 1 *adj* grotesco,-a: *a grotesque distortion of the truth,* una distorsión grotesca de la verdad. 2 ART grotesco,-a. – 3 *n* personaje *m* grotesco. 4 **the grotesque,** ART el grotesco.

grotto [ˈgrɒtəʊ] *n* gruta.
▲ *pl grottoes o grottos.*

grotty [ˈgrɒtɪ] *adj* GB *fam* asqueroso,-a, de mala muerte.
● **to feel grotty,** encontrarse fatal.
▲ *comp grottier, superl grottiest.*

grouch [graʊtʃ] 1 *n fam* (*person*) gruñón,-ona, cascarrabias *mf.* 2 *fam* (*complaint*) queja, protesta. – 3 *i fam* refunfuñar, quejarse, rezongar.

grouchy [ˈgraʊtʃɪ] *adj fam* refunfuñón,-ona, quejica, protestón,-ona, rezongón,-ona, cascarrabias.
▲ *comp grouchier, superl grouchiest.*

ground¹ [graʊnd] 1 *n* (*surface of earth*) suelo; (*soil, earth*) tierra; (*terrain, land*) terreno: *at ground level,* a nivel del suelo; *the glass fell to the ground,* la copa cayó al suelo. 2 (*land used for particular purpose*) campo, terreno: *football ground,* campo de fútbol; *waste ground,* terreno baldío. 3 US ELEC tierra. 4 ART (*background*) fondo. 5 (*area of knowledge, experience*) terreno: *you're on dangerous ground,* estás pisando terreno peligroso; *you have to find some common ground,* hay que encontrar puntos en común. 6 (*position of advantage*) terreno. 7 (*matter, subject*) aspec-

to, punto: *the first lecture covered a lot of ground,* la primera conferencia trató muchos aspectos del tema. – 8 *t* AV obligar a quedarse en tierra; MAR varar, hacer encallar: *all planes were grounded by fog,* no pudo despegar ningún avión a causa de la niebla. 9 US *fam* (*child, teenager*) castigar, no dejar salir. 10 (*base*) fundar. – 11 *i* (*instruct*) dar buenos conocimientos (**in,** de), enseñar los conocimientos básicos. – 12 *t* US ELEC conectar a tierra. – 13 *i* MAR encallar. – 14 **grounds,** *npl* (*reason, justification*) razón *f,* motivo: *you have no grounds for complaint,* no tienes motivo de queja; *he sued them on grounds of unfair dismissal,* les demandó por motivos de despido improcedente; *grounds for divorce,* motivo de divorcio; *on grounds of ill health,* por motivos de mala salud. 15 (*of coffee*) poso, posos *mpl.* 16 (*gardens*) jardines *mpl;* (*area of land*) terreno.
● **above ground,** vivo,-a. ‖ **below ground,** muerto,-a. ‖ **on the ground,** sobre el terreno. ‖ **to be on one's own ground,** estar en su elemento. ‖ **to break new ground,** abrir nuevos caminos, abrir nuevos horizontes. ‖ **to burn sth. to the ground,** reducir algo a cenizas: *the house was burnt to the ground,* la casa quedó reducida a cenizas. ‖ **to cut the ground from under sb.'s feet,** tomarle la delantera a algn. ‖ **to drive/run/work os. into the ground,** dejarse el pellejo en el trabajo. ‖ **to gain ground,** ganar terreno. ‖ **to get off the ground,** (*plan, project, scheme*) llevarse a cabo, realizarse. ‖ **to go to ground,** esconderse. ‖ **to hold/keep/stand one's ground,** mantenerse firme. ‖ **to lose ground,** perder terreno. ‖ **to prepare the ground (for sth.),** preparar el terreno (para algo). ‖ **to shift/change one's ground,** cambiar de postura. ‖ **to suit sb. down to the ground,** (*situation*) venirle a algn. de perlas; (*clothes*) quedarle a algn. que ni pintado. ‖ **to touch ground,** MAR tocar fondo.
■ **ground control,** control *m* de tierra. ‖ **ground floor,** planta baja. ‖ **ground glass,** vidrio molido, cristal *m* molido. ‖ **ground rule,** directriz *f.* ‖ **ground staff,** AV personal *m* de tierra; SP personal *m* de mantenimiento. ‖ **ground swell,** mar *m* & *f* de fondo.

ground² [graʊnd] 1 *pp* → **grind.** – 2 *adj* (*coffee*) molido,-a. 3 US (*beef*) picado,-a.

groundhog [ˈgraʊndhɒg] *n* marmota.
■ **Groundhog Day,** día *m* dos de febrero.

grounding [ˈgraʊndɪŋ] *n* base *f,* conocimientos *mpl.*
● **to have a good grounding in sth.,** tener una sólida base en algo, tener buenos conocimientos de algo.

groundless [ˈgraʊndləs] *adj* infundado,-a.

groundnut [ˈgraʊndnʌt] *n* GB cacahuete *m,* maní *m.*

groundsheet [ˈgraʊndʃiːt] *n* GB tela impermeable.

groundsman [ˈgraʊndzmən] *n* encargado (del mantenimiento del campo).

groundwork [ˈgraʊndwɜːk] *n* trabajo preliminar, trabajo preparatorio.

group [gruːp] 1 *n* (*gen*) grupo. 2 MUS grupo, conjunto. 3 POL agrupación *f,* asociación *f,* colectivo, grupo: *pressure group,* grupo de presión. – 4 *t* agrupar. – 5 *i* agruparse, formar un grupo.
■ **group practice,** MED gabinete *m* médico (*donde trabajan varios médicos*). ‖ **group therapy,** terapia de grupo.

groupie [ˈgruːpɪ] *n fam* grupi *mf.*

grouping [ˈgruːpɪŋ] *n* agrupación *f.*

grouse¹ [graʊs] *n* ORN urogallo.

grouse² [graʊs] 1 *n fam* (*complaint*) queja. – 2 *i fam* quejarse (**about,** de), refunfuñar (**about,** por).

grout [graʊt] 1 *n* lechada. – 2 *t* enlechar.

grove [grəʊv] *n* arboleda, bosquecillo: *an olive grove,* un olivar; *an orange grove,* un naranjal.

grovel ['grɒvəl] **1** *i* (*behave humbly*) humillarse, rebajarse, arrastrarse: *he made me grovel for forgiveness,* hizo que me humillara a pedirle perdón; *stop grovelling to the teacher!,* ¡deja de humillarte ante el profesor! **2** (*lie, crawl*) arrastrarse, postrarse, prosternarse.
● **to grovel at sb.'s feet,** postrarse a los pies de algn.
▲ (*verbo*) *pt & pp* **grovelled** (US **groveled**), *ger* **grovelling** (US **groveling**).

groveller ['grɒvələ'] *n* adulador,-ra, pelota *mf.*

grovelling ['grɒvəlɪŋ] *adj* servil, rastrero,-a.

grow [grəʊ] **1** *i* (*gen*) crecer: *hasn't your hair grown!,* ¡cómo te ha crecido el pelo! **2** (*increase, expand - quantity, population*) aumentar; (*city, company, money*) crecer: *the club's popularity continues to grow,* la popularidad del club sigue creciendo. **3** (*become*) hacerse, volverse: *she grew impatient,* se impacientó; *he grew old,* envejeció; *it grew dark,* oscureció, anocheció, se hizo de noche; *I grew tired of waiting,* me cansé de esperar. **4** (*begin gradually*) llegar a: *I grew to hate him,* llegué a odiarlo; *she grew to like cabbage,* llegó a gustarle la col. – **5** *t* (*crop, plant, flower*) cultivar. **6** (*beard etc*) dejarse (crecer); (*hair, nails*) dejarse crecer.
◆ **to grow apart** *i* distanciarse. ‖ **to grow away from** *t insep* distanciarse de. ‖ **to grow into 1** *t insep* (*become*) convertirse en, hacerse: *tadpoles grow into frogs,* los renacuajos se convierten en ranas. **2** (*clothes etc*): *she'll grow into it,* le quedará bien al crecer un poco. ‖ **to grow on** *t insep* llegar a gustar. ‖ **to grow out of** *t insep* (*habit*) perder, quitarse; (*clothes*) quedarle pequeño,-a a. ‖ **to grow up 1** *i* (*become adult*) hacerse mayor; (*spend childhood*) criarse, crecer: *what do you want to be when you grow up?,* ¿qué quieres ser cuando seas mayor?; *oh grow up!,* ¡no seas infantil! **2** (*spring up*) surgir, nacer, desarrollarse.
● **money doesn't grow on trees,** el dinero no cae del cielo.
▲ *pt* **grew,** *pp* **grown.**

grower ['grəʊə'] *n* (*farmer*) cultivador,-ra: *a wine grower,* vinicultor,-ra, viticultor,-ra.

growing ['grəʊɪŋ] *adj* creciente, que crece.
■ **growing pains,** (*pains*) dolores *mpl* de crecimiento; (*problems*) dificultades *fpl* iniciales, problemas *mpl* iniciales.

growl [graʊl] **1** *n* gruñido. – **2** *i* gruñir. – **3** *t* decir refunfuñando.

grown [grəʊn] **1** *pp* → **grow.** – **2** *adj* adulto,-a.

grown-up ['grəʊnʌp] **1** *adj* mayor, adulto,-a. – **2** *n* persona mayor, adulto.

growth [grəʊθ] **1** *n* (*gen*) crecimiento; (*increase*) aumento; (*development*) desarrollo: *population growth,* aumento de población; *smoking stunts your growth,* fumar atrofia el crecimiento; *personal growth,* crecimiento personal. **2** MED (*tumour*) bulto, tumor *m.* **3** (*of beard*) barba.
■ **growth area,** IND sector *m* en expansión. ‖ **growth industry,** industria en crecimiento, industria en expansión.

groyne [grɔɪn] *n* espigón *m.*

grub [grʌb] **1** *n* (*larva*) larva, gusano. **2** *fam* (*food*) manduca, papeo. – **3** *i* (*by digging*) escarbar, hurgar. **4** *fig* rebuscar.
◆ **to grub out** *t sep* arrancar. ‖ **to grub up** *t sep* sacar (de la tierra), desenterrar.
▲ (*verbo*) *pt & pp* **grubbed,** *ger* **grubbing.**

grubby ['grʌbɪ] **1** *adj* (*rather dirty*) mugriento,-a, sucio,-a. **2** *fig* (*seamy, sordid*) asqueroso,-a.

▲ *comp* **grubbier,** *superl* **grubbiest.**

grudge [grʌdʒ] **1** *n* resentimiento, rencor *m.* – **2** *t* (*begrudge, resent*) dar a regañadientes, dar de mala gana: *she grudged having to pay so much,* le daba rabia tener que pagar tanto. **3** (*envy*) envidiar: *I don't grudge you your house,* no te envidio la casa.
● **to bear a grudge,** guardar rencor. ‖ **to hold/bear a grudge against sb.,** guardarle rencor a algn.

grudging ['grʌdʒɪŋ] *adj* hecho,-a a regañadientes, hecho,-a de mala gana: *I don't like him, but I have a grudging respect for him,* no me gusta, pero lo respeto; *she was grudging in her thanks,* le costó mucho dar las gracias.

grudgingly ['grʌdʒɪŋlɪ] *adv* de mala gana, a regañadientes.

gruel ['gruːəl] *n* gachas *fpl.*

gruelling ['gruːəlɪŋ] *adj* (*race, journey*) agotador,-ra; (*ordeal, experience*) duro,-a, penoso,-a.

gruesome ['gruːsəm] *adj* espantoso,-a, horrible, horripilante.

gruff [grʌf] *adj* (*manner*) brusco,-a; (*voice*) áspero,-a, bronco,-a.

gruffly ['grʌflɪ] *adv* en un tono brusco, bruscamente, ásperamente.

gruffness ['grʌfnəs] *n* (*of manner*) brusquedad *f*; (*of voice*) aspereza.

grumble ['grʌmbəl] **1** *n* (*complaint*) queja. **2** (*of thunder*) estruendo. – **3** *i* (*moan, complain*) refunfuñar, rezongar, quejarse (**about,** de): *he's always grumbling about something,* siempre se está quejando de algo; *mustn't grumble,* no puedo quejarme. **4** (*rumble - thunder*) retumbar; (- *stomach*) hacer ruido.

grumbler ['grʌmbələ'] *n* refunfuñón,-ona, rezongón,-ona.

grumbling ['grʌmbəlɪŋ] **1** *adj* (*person*) gruñón,-ona, refunfuñón,-ona. – **2** *n* (*complaints*) quejas *fpl.* **3** (*of thunder*) estruendo.

grumpily ['grʌmpɪlɪ] *adv* de mal humor, malhumoradamente.

grumpy ['grʌmpɪ] *adj* gruñón,-ona, malhumorado,-a, de mal humor.
▲ *comp* **grumpier,** *superl* **grumpiest.**

grunge [grʌndʒ] *n* MUS grunge *m.*

grunt [grʌnt] **1** *n* gruñido. – **2** *i* gruñir. – **3** *t* decir gruñiendo.

Guadaloupe [gwɑːdəˈluːp] *n* Guadalupe.

guarantee [gærənˈtiː] **1** *n* (*gen*) garantía; (*certificate*) certificado de garantía: *manufacturer's guarantee,* garantía de fábrica; *we want a guarantee that something will be done,* queremos que nos garanticen que se hará algo; *there's no guarantee that it'll be sunny tomorrow,* no hay ninguna garantía de que haga sol mañana. – **2** *t* (*gen*) garantizar; (*assure, promise*) asegurar, garantizar: *I guarantee that you'll enjoy it,* te aseguro que lo pasarás bien; *they guarantee to deliver within 30 minutes,* garantizan entregarlo dentro de 30 minutos. **3** (*debt*) avalar, garantizar.
● **to be under guarantee,** estar bajo garantía.

guaranteed [gærənˈtiːd] **1** *adj* COMM garantizado,-a. **2** (*certain*) asegurado,-a, garantizado,-a.

guarantor [gærənˈtɔː'] *n* garante *mf*, fiador,-ra.

guard [gɑːd] **1** *n* (*sentry, soldier*) guardia *mf*; (*security guard*) guarda *mf*, guarda jurado,-a, guarda de seguridad; (*prison officer*) carcelero,-a. **2** (*group of sentries*) guardia. **3** (*duty*) guardia. **4** GB (*on train*) jefe,-a de tren. **5** (*on machine*) dispositivo de seguridad; (*on gun*) seguro. **6** (*posi-*

tion) guardia. – **7** *t* (*watch over - building, prisioner*) vigilar, custodiar; (*protect - person, reputation*) proteger; (*keep - secret*) guardar: *a dog guarded the house*, un perro vigilaba la casa. **8** (*control - tongue*) cuidar, controlar.
◆ **to guard against** *t insep* (*injury*) evitar; (*risks*) protegerse contra; (*infection, disease*) prevenir.
● **to be off one's guard,** estar desprevenido,-a. ‖ **to be on guard,** estar de guardia. ‖ **to be on one's guard,** estar en guardia, estar en alerta. ‖ **the changing of the guard,** el relevo de la guardia. ‖ **to keep guard over sth. / stand guard over sth.,** montar (la) guardia ante algo, vigliar algo.
■ **guard dog,** perro guardián. ‖ **guard duty,** guardia. ‖ **guard's van,** furgón *m* de cola.
guarded ['gɑːdɪd] *adj* (*person, remark*) cauteloso,-a.
guardhouse ['gɑːdhaʊs] *n* MIL (*quarters*) cuartel *m*; (*prison*) prisión *f* militar, cárcel *f* militar.
guardian ['gɑːdɪən] **1** *n* (*defender*) guardián,-ana, defensor,-ra. **2** JUR (*of child*) tutor,-ra.
■ **guardian angel,** ángel *m* de la guarda.
guardrail ['gɑːdreɪl] *n* barandilla.
guardsman ['gɑːdzmən] *n* guardia *m*.
Guatemala [gwəʊtə'mɑːlə] *n* Guatemala.
Guatemalan [gwætə'mɑːlən] **1** *adj* guatemalteco,-a. – **2** *n* guatemalteco,-a.
guava ['gwɑːvə] *n* (*fruit*) guayaba.
■ **guava tree,** guayabo.
gudgeon[1] ['gʌdʒən] *n* (*fish*) gobio.
gudgeon[2] ['gʌdʒən] *n* TECH gorrón *m*.
guerilla [gə'rɪlə] *n* → **guerrilla**.
Guernsey ['gɜːnzɪ] *n* Guernesey.
guerrilla [gə'rɪlə] **1** *n* guerrillero,-a. – **2** *adj* guerrillero,-a: *guerrilla warfare*, guerrilla.
guess [ges] **1** *n* (*conjecture*) conjetura; (*estimate*) cálculo: *have a guess!*, ¡a ver si adivinas!; *he made a wild guess*, hizo una conjetura al azar; *I'll give you three guesses*, te doy tres oportunidades para adivinarlo; *my guess is that they'll arrive around 8.00pm*, calculo que llegarán a eso de las ocho. – **2** *t* (*gen*) adivinar: *guess who I saw today!*, ¡adivina a quién he visto hoy!; *guess what!*, ¿sabes qué?; *I bet you can't guess how old I am*, ¿a que no adivinas cuántos años tengo?; *you'll never guess what happened*, no te puedes imaginar lo que pasó. **3** US *fam* (*suppose*) suponer, pensar, creer: *I guess so*, supongo que sí; *I guess not*, supongo que no; *I guess I'd better be going*, supongo que debería irme. – **4** *i* adivinar: *when did you guess?*, ¿cuándo lo adivinaste?; *we can only guess at the number of victims*, sólo podemos hacer conjeturas sobre el número de víctimas.
● **at a guess,** a primera vista, al ojo. ‖ **at a rough guess,** a ojo de buen cubero. ‖ **... is anybody's guess,** vete tú a saber ... ‖ **to guess right,** acertar, adivinar. ‖ **to guess wrong,** equivocarse. ‖ **to keep sb. guessing,** tener a algn. en suspenso, tener a algn. en la incertidumbre. ‖ **your guess is as good as mine,** ¿quién sabe?, vete tú a saber.
guesstimate ['gestɪmət] *n fam* cálculo aproximado.
guesswork ['geswɜːk] *n* conjeturas *fpl*, suposiciones *fpl*.
guest [gest] **1** *n* (*at home, to theatre, restaurant, etc*) invitado,-a; (*in hotel*) cliente,-a, huésped,-da: *guest of honor*, invitado,-a de honor; *paying guest*, huésped,-da de pago. **2** RAD TV invitado,-a.
● **be my guest!,** ¡por supuesto!, ¡faltaría más!
■ **guest appearance,** aparición *f* especial. ‖ **guest speaker,** orador,-ra invitado,-a. ‖ **guest star,** estrella invitada.

guesthouse ['gesthaʊs] *n* casa de huéspedes, pensión *f*.
guestroom ['gestruːm] *n* cuarto de (los) invitados.
guffaw [gʌ'fɔː] **1** *n* carcajada, risotada. – **2** *i* reírse a carcajadas.
Guiana [gaɪ'ænə, gɪ'ɑːnə] *n* Guayana.
■ **French Guiana,** Guayana francesa.
Guianan [gaɪ'ɑːnən] *adj-n* → **Guianese**.
Guianese [gaɪə'niːz] **1** *adj* guayanés,-esa. – **2** *n* guayanés,-esa. – **3** the Guianese, *npl* los guayaneses *mpl*.
guidance ['gaɪdəns] *n* (*help, advice*) orientación *f*, consejos *mpl*: *vocational guidance*, orientación profesional.
■ **guidance system,** (*of missile*) sistema *m* de teledirección.
guide [gaɪd] **1** *n* (*person*) guía *mf*. **2** (*book*) guía: *a guide to Portugal*, una guía de Portugal. **3** (*indicator*) guía, modelo: *use this pattern as a guide*, utiliza este patrón como modelo; *I used the recipe as a rough guide*, la receta me sirvió de guía. – **4** *t* (*show the way*) guiar; (*lead*) conducir: *the woman guided us round the museum*, la mujer nos hizo de guía en el museo. **5** (*advise, influence*) guiar, orientar, aconsejar.
■ **guide dog,** perro lazarillo.
guidebook ['gaɪdbʊk] *n* guía.
guided ['gaɪdɪd] *adj* dirigido,-a.
● **to give sb. a guided tour of sth.,** enseñar algo a algn. de arriba a abajo.
■ **guided missile,** misil *m* teledirigido. ‖ **guided tour,** visita guiada, visita con guía.
guideline ['gaɪdlaɪn] *n* pauta, directriz *f*.
guiding ['gaɪdɪŋ] *adj* que guía, que sirve de guía.
■ **guiding principle,** principio rector. ‖ **guiding light,** norte *m*.
guild [gɪld] *n* (*of workers*) gremio; (*association*) asociación *f*, agrupación *f*.
guile [gaɪl] *n* (*craftiness*) astucia; (*trickery*) mañas *fpl*, engaño.
guileless ['gaɪlləs] *adj* ingenuo,-a, cándido,-a.
guillemot ['gɪlɪmɒt] *n* ORN arao común.
guillotine ['gɪlətiːn] **1** *n* guillotina. – **2** *t* (*person, paper*) guillotinar.
guilt [gɪlt] **1** *n* JUR culpabilidad *f*. **2** (*blame*) culpa; (*remorse*) remordimiento: *I felt a terrible sense of guilt*, me sentí muy culpable, tuve un gran sentimiento de culpabilidad; *guilt feelings*, sentimiento de culpa, sentimiento de culpabilidad.
■ **guilt complex,** complejo de culpa.
guilty ['gɪltɪ] *adj* culpable (*of*, de).
● **to feel guilty,** sentirse culpable. ‖ **to have a guilty conscience,** tener remordimientos de conciencia, tener la conciencia sucia. ‖ **to plead guilty/not guilty,** declararse culpable/no culpable.
▲ *comp* **guiltier,** *superl* **guiltiest**.
guinea ['gɪnɪ] *n* (*coin*) guinea.
■ **guinea fowl,** gallina de Guinea, pintada. ‖ **guinea pig,** conejillo de Indias, cobayo,-a.
Guinea ['gɪnɪ] *n* Guinea.
■ **Equatorial Guinea,** Guinea Ecuatorial. ‖ **Gulf of Guinea,** golfo de Guinea. ‖ **New Guinea,** Nueva Guinea.
Guinea-Bissau [gɪnɪbɪ'saʊ] *n* Guinea Bissau.
Guinean ['gɪnɪən] **1** *adj* guineano,-a. – **2** *n* guineano,-a.
guise [gaɪz] *n* apariencia, forma, aspecto: *in various guises*, de varias formas.
● **in the guise of,** disfrazado,-a de: *in the guise of a doctor*, disfrazado de médico. ‖ **under the guise of,** so

pretexto de: *under the guise of philosophy,* bajo capa de filosofía.
guitar [gɪˈtɑːʳ] *n* guitarra.
guitarist [gɪˈtɑːrɪst] *n* guitarrista *mf.*
gulf [gʌlf] **1** *n* GEOG golfo. **2** *fig* abismo.
■ **Gulf of Mexico,** Golfo de Méjico. ‖ **Persian Gulf,** Golfo Pérsico. ‖ **the Gulf States,** (*in Middle East*) los países del Golfo Pérsico; (*in United States*) *los estados que lindan con el golfo de Méjico.* ‖ **Gulf Stream,** Corriente *f* del Golfo. ‖ **the Gulf War,** la guerra del Golfo.
gull [gʌl] *n* ORN gaviota.
gullet [ˈgʌlɪt] *n* garganta, gaznate *m.*
gulley [ˈgʌlɪ] *n* → **gully.**
gullible [ˈgʌlɪbəl] *adj* crédulo,-a.
gully [ˈgʌlɪ] **1** *n* GEOG (*small valley, ravine*) barranco, torrentera. **2** (*deep ditch, waterway, channel*) surco, cauce *m.*
▲ *pl* **gullies2.**
gulp [gʌlp] **1** *n* (*of drink*) trago; (*of air*) bocanada: *he drank his glass in one gulp,* se bebió la copa de un trago. – **2** *t* (*drink*) beberse de un trago (**down,** -), tomarse de un trago (**down,** -); (*food*) engullir (**down,** -). – **3** *i* (*swallow air*) tragar aire; (*with fear*) tragar saliva.
◆ **to gulp back** *t insep* tragarse.
gum[1] [gʌm] *n* ANAT encía.
gum[2] [gʌm] **1** *n* (*natural substance*) goma, resina. **2** (*chewing gum*) goma de mascar, chicle *m.* **3** (*glue*) goma (de pegar), pegamento. **4** (*gumdrop*) pastilla de goma. **5** (*gumtree*) gomero, árbol *m* del caucho. – **6** *t* pegar (con goma).
◆ **to gum up** *t sep* pegar: *her eyes were all gummed up,* tenía los ojos llenos de legañas.
● **by gum!,** ¡caramba! ‖ **to gum up the works,** fastidiarlo todo.
▲ *pp* & *pt* **gummed,** *ger* **gumming.**
gumboil [ˈgʌmbɔɪl] *n* flemón *m.*
gumboot [ˈgʌmbuːt] *n* bota de agua.
gummed [gʌmd] *adj* engomado,-a.
gummy [ˈgʌmɪ] **1** *adj* (*sticky*) pegajoso,-a. **2** (*smile*) muy amplio,-a.
▲ *comp* **gummier,** *superl* **gummiest.**
gumption [ˈgʌmpʃən] *n fam* (*good sense*) sentido común, juicio, seso; (*courage*) agallas *fpl.*
gumtree [ˈgʌmtriː] *n* gomero, árbol *m* del caucho.
● **to be up a gumtree,** estar en un aprieto, estar metido,-a en un lío.
gun [gʌn] **1** *n* (*gen*) arma de fuego; (*handgun*) pistola, revólver *m;* (*rifle*) rifle *m,* fusil *m;* (*shotgun*) escopeta; (*cannon*) cañón *m.* **2** SP pistola.
◆ **to gun down** *t sep* matar a tiros. ‖ **to gun for** *t insep* andar a la caza de.
● **to carry a gun,** ir armado,-a. ‖ **to jump the gun,** (*gen*) adelantarse (a los acontecimientos), precipitarse; (*in race*) salir en falso, salir antes de tiempo, tomar la salida en falso. ‖ **to pull a gun on sb.,** apuntar a algn. con una pistola. ‖ **to stick to one's guns,** mantenerse en sus trece.
■ **gun carriage,** cureña. ‖ **gun dog,** perro de caza. ‖ **gun licence,** licencia de armas.
gunboat [ˈgʌnbəʊt] *n* (*lancha*) cañonera.
■ **gunboat diplomacy,** diplomacia de cañón.
gunfight [ˈgʌnfaɪt] *n* tiroteo.
gunfire [ˈgʌnfaɪəʳ] *n* (*gen*) fuego, disparos *mpl;* (*shooting*) tiroteo; (*shellfire*) cañoneo, cañonazos *mpl.*
gunge [gʌndʒ] *n* GB *fam* porquería.
gunk [gʌŋk] *n* US *fam* porquería.
gunman [ˈgʌnmən] *n* pistolero.

gunner [ˈgʌnəʳ] *n* artillero.
gunnery [ˈgʌnərɪ] *n* artillería.
gunpoint [ˈgʌnpɔɪnt] **at gunpoint,** *phr* a punta de pistola.
gunpowder [ˈgʌnpaʊdəʳ] *n* pólvora.
gunrunner [ˈgʌnrʌnəʳ] *n* traficante *mf* de armas.
gunrunning [ˈgʌnrʌnɪŋ] *n* tráfico de armas.
gunshot [ˈgʌnʃɒt] *n* disparo, tiro.
■ **gunshot wound,** herida de bala.
gunsmith [ˈgʌnsmɪθ] *n* armero,-ra.
gunwale [ˈgʌnəl] *n* MAR borda.
gurgle [ˈgɜːgəl] **1** *n* (*of water*) gorgoteo, borboteo; (*of baby*) gorjeo. – **2** *i* (*water, brook*) gorgotear, borbotar; (*baby*) gorjear.
guru [ˈguːruː] *n* gurú *m.*
gush [gʌʃ] **1** *n* (*of liquid*) chorro, borbotón *m;* (*of words*) torrente *m;* (*of emotion*) efusión *f.* – **2** *i* (*liquid*) salir a borbotones, brotar a chorros, salir a chorros. **3** (*person*) ser efusivo,-a: *everyone was gushing over her new baby,* todos se deshacían en elogios con su nuevo bebé. – **4** *t* chorrear, derramar.
gushing [ˈgʌʃɪŋ] *adj* (*person*) efusivo,-a.
gusset [ˈgʌsɪt] *n* (*gen*) escudete *m;* (*in briefs*) cuadradillo.
gust [gʌst] **1** *n* (*of wind*) ráfaga, racha; (*of rain*) chaparrón *m.* **2** *fig* (*of anger*) arrebato: *gust of laughter,* carcajada. – **3** *i* soplar.
gusto [ˈgʌstəʊ] *n* entusiasmo.
gusty [ˈgʌstɪ] *adj* (*wind*) racheado,-a; (*day*) ventoso,-a.
▲ *comp* **gustier,** *superl* **gustiest.**
gut [gʌt] **1** *n* ANAT intestino, tripa. **2** *fam* (*belly*) panza, barriga, tripa. **3** (*catgut*) cuerda de tripa. – **4** *t* (*fish*) destripar, limpiar; (*rabbit*) destripar. **5** (*building*) destruir el interior de. – **6** *adj* visceral: *gut reaction,* reacción visceral. – **7 guts,** *npl* (*entrails*) entrañas *fpl,* tripas *fpl,* vísceras *fpl.* **8** *fam* (*courage*) agallas *fpl: it takes guts to do what you did,* hay que tener agallas para hacer lo que hiciste.
● **to cough one's guts up,** reventar tosiendo. ‖ **to hate sb.'s guts,** odiar a algn. a muerte, no poder ni ver a algn. ‖ **to have sb.'s guts for garters,** sacarle las tripas a algn. ‖ **to work/slog one's guts out,** echar los bofes.
▲ (*verbo*) *pt* & *pp* **gutted,** *ger* **gutting.**
gutsy [ˈgʌtsɪ] *adj fam* (*person*) con agallas.
▲ *comp* **gutsier,** *superl* **gutsiest.**
gutter [ˈgʌtəʳ] **1** *n* (*in street*) arroyo, cuneta; (*on roof*) canal *m,* canalón *m.* **2 the gutter,** (*in society*) los bajos fondos *mpl,* el arroyo, la cloaca.
■ **gutter press,** prensa amarilla, prensa sensacionalista.
guttural [ˈgʌtərəl] *adj* gutural.
guy[1] [gaɪ] **1** *n fam* (*man*) tipo, tío: *he's a great guy,* es un tío estupendo; *a tough guy,* un tipo duro. **2** US *fam* (*person*) tío,-a: *come on you guys,* venga tíos. **3** GB (*effigy*) efigie *m* de Guy Fawkes.
guy[2] [gaɪ] **guy (rope),** *n* viento, cuerda (tensora).
Guyana [gaɪˈænə] *n* Guyana, Guayana.
Guyanan [gaɪˈænən] *adj-n* → **Guyanese.**
Guyanese [gaɪəˈniːz] **1** *adj* guayanés,-esa, guyanés,-esa. – **2** *n* guayanés,-esa, guyanés,-esa. – **3 the Guyanese,** *npl* los guayaneses *mpl,* los guyaneses *mpl.*
guzzle [ˈgʌzəl] **1** *t fam* (*eat*) zamparse, engullirse; (*drink*) chupar, tragar. – **2** *i fam* (*eat*) engullir; (*drink*) chupar, tragar.
guzzler [ˈgʌzələʳ] *n fam* (*person - big eater*) comilón-ona, glotón-ona; (- *drinker*) tragón,-ona; (*car*) que traga mucho.

gym [dʒɪm] 1 *n fam* (*gymnasium*) gimnasio. 2 (*gymnastics*) gimnasia.
- **gym shoes,** zapatillas *fpl* de deporte.
gymkhana [dʒɪmˈkɑːnə] *n* gymkhana.
gymnasium [dʒɪmˈneɪzɪəm] *n* gimnasio.
▲ *pl gymnasiums o gymnasia*.
gymnast [ˈdʒɪmnæst] *n* gimnasta *mf*.
gymnastics [dʒɪmˈnæstɪks] *n* gimnasia.
gynaecological [gaɪnəkəˈlɒdʒɪkəl] *adj* ginecológico,-a.
gynaecologist [gaɪnɪˈkɒlədʒɪst] *n* ginecólogo,-a.
gynaecology [gaɪnɪˈkɒlədʒɪ] *n* ginecología.
gyp¹ [dʒɪp] *n* GB *fam* (*pain*, *trouble*) dolor *m*; (*punishment*) bronca: *my leg's been giving me gyp,* la pierna me ha estado fastidiando.

gyp² [dʒɪp] 1 *n fam* (*swindle*) estafa, timo. – 2 *t* estafar, timar.
gypsum [ˈdʒɪpsəm] *n* yeso.
gypsy [ˈdʒɪpsɪ] 1 *n* gitano,-a. – 2 *adj* gitano,-a.
▲ *pl gypsies.*
gyrate [dʒaɪˈreɪt] *i* girar.
gyration [dʒaɪˈreɪʃən] *n* giro, rotación *f*.
gyratory [ˈdʒaɪrətərɪ] *adj* giratorio,-a.
gyrocompass [ˈdʒaɪrəʊkʌmpəs] *n* girocompás *m*, brújula giroscópica.
gyroscope [ˈdʒaɪrəskəʊp] *n* giroscopio, giróscopo.
gyroscopic [dʒaɪrəˈskɒpɪk] *adj* giroscópico,-a

H

H, h [eɪtʃ] *n* (*the letter*) H, h *f*.
ha [ˈhektɑːʳ] *abbr* (*hectare*) hectárea; (*abbreviation*) ha.
haberdasher [ˈhæbədæʃəʳ] **1** *n* GB (*shopkeeper*) mercero,- a. **2** US (*person*) camisero.
haberdashery [hæbəˈdæʃərɪ] **1** *n* GB (*shop*) mercería; (*materials*) artículos *mpl* de mercería. **2** US (*shop*) tienda de ropa para caballero; (*clothes*) ropa para caballero.
habit [ˈhæbɪt] **1** *n* (*custom*) hábito, costumbre *f*. **2** REL (*garment*) hábito.
● **to be in the habit of,** tener la costumbre de. ‖ **to get into the habit of,** coger la costumbre de, acostumbrarse a. ‖ **to get out of the habit of,** perder la costumbre de.
■ **bad habit,** vicio, mala costumbre *f*.
habitable [ˈhæbɪtəbəl] *adj fml* habitable.
habitat [ˈhæbɪtæt] *n* hábitat *m*.
habitation [hæbɪˈteɪʃən] *n fml* (*the act of living in a place*) habitación *f*; (*dwelling*) morada: *this flat is unfit for human habitation,* este piso no es apto para ser habitado, este piso es inhabitable.
habit-forming [ˈhæbɪtfɔːmɪŋ] *adj* que crea hábito, que crea dependencia.
habitual [həˈbɪtʃʊəl] **1** *adj* (*usual*) habitual, acostumbrado,-a. **2** (*liar etc*) empedernido,-a, inveterado,-a.
habitually [həˈbɪtʃʊəlɪ] *adv* habitualmente, por costumbre.
habituate [həˈbɪtʃʊeɪt] *t fml* acostumbrarse (**to,** a), habituarse (**to,** a): *many animals have become habituated to living in zoos,* muchos animales se han acostumbrado a vivir en zoos.
habitué [həˈbɪtʃʊeɪ] *n* asiduo,-a, cliente,-a habitual.
hack¹ [hæk] **1** *n* (*cut*) corte *m*, tajo; (*with axe*) hachazo; (*with machete*) machetazo. – **2** *t* (*cut*) cortar, acuchillar, rajar: *they hacked their way through the undergrowth,* se abrieron paso a hachazos entre la maleza. **3** (*notch*) mellar.
◆ **to hack about** *t sep* (*in writing*) cortar, mutilar.
hack² [hæk] **1** *n* (*horse - worn-out*) penco, jamelgo, rocín *m*; (*- hired*) caballo de alquiler. **2** *fam* (*writer*) escritorzuelo,-a; (*journalist*) gacetillero,-a, periodista de pacotilla; (*politician*) politicastro,-a. – **3** *i* GB *fam* montar a caballo.
hacker [ˈhækəʳ] *n fam* (*in computers*) pirata *mf*.
hacking¹ [ˈhækɪŋ] *adj* (*horseriding*) de montar.
■ **hacking jacket,** chaqueta de montar.
hacking² [ˈhækɪŋ] *adj* (*cough*) áspero,-a, seco,-a.
hackles [ˈhækəlz] *n* ZOOL (*feathers*) collar *m*, plumas *fpl* del cuello; (*fur*) pelo del cuello.
● **to make sb.'s hackles rise / put sb.'s hackles up,** poner furioso,-a a algn., enfurecer a algn.
hackneyed [ˈhæknɪd] *adj* gastado,-a, trillado,-a.
hacksaw [ˈhæksɔː] *n* sierra de arco para metales.
had [hæd] *pt & pp* → **have**.
haddock [ˈhædək] *n* (*fish*) eglefino.

haemoglobin [hiːməʊˈgləʊbɪn] *n* MED hemoglobina.
haemophilia [hiːməʊˈfiːlɪə] *n* MED hemofilia.
haemophiliac [hiːməʊˈfiːlɪæk] **1** *adj* MED hemofílico,-a. – **2** *n* MED hemofílico,-a.
haemorrhage [ˈhemərɪdʒ] *n* MED hemorragia.
haemorrhoids [ˈhemərɔɪdz] *npl* MED hemorroides *fpl*, almorranas *fpl*.
haft [hɑːft, hæft] *n* TECH (*of knife*) mango; (*of sword*) puño, empuñadura.
hag [hæg] *n pej* (*ugly and evil old woman*) bruja, arpía.
haggard [ˈhægəd] *adj* (*look exhausted*) ojeroso,-a, trasnochado,-a; (*look drawn and pale*) macilento,-a.
haggis [ˈhægɪs] *n* CULIN *plato típico escocés hecho con las asaduras del cordero*.
haggish [ˈhægɪʃ] *adj* de bruja.
haggle [ˈhægəl] *i* regatear (**over,** -).
● **to haggle over the price of sth.,** regatear el precio de algo.
haggling [ˈhægəlɪŋ] *n* regateo.
hagiography [hægɪˈɒgrəfɪ] *n* hagiografía.
▲ *pl hagiographies.*
Hague [heɪg] **The Hague,** *n* La Haya.
hah [hɑː] *interj* ¡a!
ha-ha [hɑːˈhɑː] *interj* ¡¡ja ja!
hail¹ [heɪl] **1** *n* (*greeting*) saludo; (*shout*) grito. – **2** *i* (*call a taxi*) llamar. **3** (*acclaim*) aclamar.
● **hail Caesar!,** ¡Salve César! ‖ **to hail from,** ser de.
■ **Hail Mary,** avemaría.
hail² [heɪl] **1** *n* METEOR granizo, pedrisco. **2** *fig* lluvia: *the soldiers were met by a hail of bullets,* los soldados se encontraron con una lluvia de balas. – **3** *i* METEOR granizar.
hailstone [ˈheɪlstəʊn] *n* granizo, piedra.
hailstorm [ˈheɪlstɔːm] *n* granizada.
hair [heəʳ] **1** *n* (*on head*) cabello, pelo, cabellera. **2** (*on body*) vello. **3** (*horse's mane*) crin *f*.
● **keep your hair on!,** *fam* ¡tranquilo,-a! ¡cálmate! ‖ **not to turn a hair,** no inmutarse. ‖ **to have long hair,** tener el pelo largo, tener melena. ‖ **to have one's hair cut,** cortarse el pelo. ‖ **to have white hair / have grey hair,** tener canas. ‖ **to let one's hair down,** *fig* desmadrarse. ‖ **to make sb.'s hair stand on end,** *fig* ponerle a algn. los pelos de punta. ‖ **to split hairs,** *fig* hilar muy fino, buscar tres pies al gato. ‖ **to tear one's hair out,** *fig* desesperarse, volverse loco,-a.
■ **hair lacquer,** laca.
hairband [ˈheəbænd] *n* (*for hair*) cinta.
hairbrush [ˈheəbrʌʃ] *n* cepillo para el pelo.
haircut [ˈheəkʌt] *n* corte *m* de pelo.
● **to have a haircut,** cortarse el pelo.
hairdo [ˈheəduː] *n fam* peinado.
▲ *pl hairdos.*
hairdresser [ˈheədresəʳ] *n* peluquero,-a.
■ **hairdresser's (shop),** peluquería.

hairdressing ['heədresɪŋ] *n* (*profession*) peluquería.
hairdryer ['heədraɪəʳ] *n* secador *m* (de pelo).
hair-grip ['heəgrɪp] *n* horquilla, pasador *m*.
hairless ['heələs] *adj* sin pelo, calvo,-a.
hairline ['heəlaɪn] **1** *n* nacimiento del pelo. **2** TECH grieta fina. – **3** *adj* fino,-a, preciso,-a, exacto,-a.
■ **hairline crack,** (*gen*) grieta imperceptible; (*in metals*) grieta capilar interna. ‖ **receding hairline,** entradas *fpl.*
hairnet ['heənet] *n* redecilla.
hairpiece ['heəpiːs] *n* peluquín *m*, postizo.
hairpin ['heəpɪn] *n* horquilla.
■ **hairpin bend,** AUTO curva muy cerrada.
hair-raising ['heəreɪzɪŋ] *adj* espeluznante, que pone los pelos de punta.
hair-remover ['heərɪmuːvəʳ] *n* depilatorio.
hairslide ['heəslaɪd] *n* pasador *m*.
hair-splitting ['heəsplɪtɪŋ] **1** *n* sutilezas *fpl*, sofismos *mpl*. – **2** *adj pej* sutil, nimio,-a.
hairspray ['heəspreɪ] *n* laca para el pelo.
hairstyle ['heəstaɪl] *n* peinado.
hairy ['heərɪ] **1** *adj* peludo,-a. **2** *fig* (*scary*) espeluznante, espantoso,-a.
▲ *comp* **hairier,** *superl* **hairiest.**
Haiti ['heɪtɪ] *n* Haití *m*.
Haitian ['heɪʃən] **1** *adj* haitiano,-a. – **2** *n* (*person*) haitiano,-a. **3** (*language*) haitiano.
hake [heɪk] *n* (*fish*) merluza; (*young*) pescadilla.
halcyon ['hælsɪən] **1** *n* (*in mythology*) alción *m*. – **2** *adj lit* (*weather*) sereno,-a, tranquilo,-a; (*times*) próspero,-a, rico,-a. **3** *lit* (*days*) feliz, despreocupado,-a: *halcyon days of childhood,* los días dorados de la infancia.
hale [heɪl] *adj* sano,-a, fuerte, robusto,-a.
● **hale and hearty,** fuerte y sano.
half [haːf] **1** *n* mitad *f*: *she gave me half,* me dio la mitad, *a kilo and a half,* un kilo y medio. **2** SP (*period*) parte *f*, mitad *f*, tiempo. **3** (*beer*) media pinta. – **4** *adj* medio,-a: *children usually pay half fare on public transport,* normalmente los niños pagan media tarifa en los transportes públicos; *he's been gone for half an hour,* lleva fuera media hora. – **5** *adv* medio, a medias: *they left him half dead,* lo dejaron medio muerto; *she's half Spanish,* es medio española.
● **and a half,** *fam* muy bueno,-a: *that was a meal and a half,* ¡vaya comida que nos hemos pegado! ‖ **in half,** por la mitad. ‖ **not half,** *fam* (*very*) muy; (*emphatic reply*) ¡y tanto!, ¡ya lo creo!, ¡ni que lo digas!: *it isn't half cold today!,* ¡vaya frío que hace hoy!; *she isn't half ugly,* es feísima; *do you fancy a beer? –not half!,* ¿te apetece una cerveza? –¡y tanto!; *it doesn't half use some petrol,* gasta muchísima gasolina; *she can't half sing,* canta fenomenal. ‖ **to do things by halves,** hacer las cosas a medias. ‖ **to go halves on,** pagar a medias.
■ **first half,** primer tiempo. ‖ **half measures,** medias tintas *fpl.*
▲ *pl* **halves.**
half-baked [haːf'beɪkt] **1** *adj* CULIN medio cocido,-a. **2** *fam fig* (*idea, plan etc*) disparatado,-a, mal concebido,-a.
half-breed ['haːfbriːd] **1** *n* mestizo,-a. – **2** *adj* mestizo,-a.
half-brother ['haːfbrʌðəʳ] *n* hermanastro.
half-caste ['haːfkaːst] **1** *n* mestizo,-a. – **2** *adj* mestizo,-a.
half-closed [haːf'kləʊzd] *adj* entreabierto,-a.
half-cock [haːf'kɒk] *n* (*guns*) seguro.
● **at half-cock,** con el seguro echado. ‖ **to go off at half-cock,** *fig* (*ideas, plans*) salir mal, fracasar.

half-day [haːf'deɪ] *n* media jornada.
half-empty [haːf'emptɪ] *adj* medio vacío,-a.
half-hearted [haːf'haːtɪd] *adj* poco entusiasta.
half-heartedly [haːf'haːtɪdlɪ] *adv* sin entusiasmo, sin ganas.
half-hour [haːf'aʊəʳ] **1** *n* media hora. – **2** *adj* de media hora: *half-hour trip,* viaje de media hora.
half-hourly [haːf'aʊəlɪ] *adv* cada media hora.
half-life ['haːflaɪf] *n* CHEM media vida, período.
half-light ['haːflaɪt] *n* media luz *f*, luz *f* crepuscular, penumbra.
half-mast [haːf'maːst] **at half-mast,** *phr* a media asta.
half-note ['haːfnəʊt] *n* US MUS blanca.
halfpenny ['heɪpnɪ] *n* (*coin*) medio penique *m*.
● **not to have two halfpennies to rub together,** *fam* no tener ni cinco.
▲ *pl* **halfpennies.**
half-price [haːf'praɪs] *adv* a mitad de precio.
half-sister ['haːfsɪstəʳ] *n* hermanastra.
half-time [haːf'taɪm] *n* SP descanso, media parte *f*.
half-tone ['haːftəʊn] **1** *n* (*in printing*) medio tono, media tinta. **2** MUS semitono.
halfway [haːf'weɪ] **1** *adj* medio,-a, intermedio,-a: *the runners got to the halfway mark within record time,* los corredores pasaron por el ecuador de la carrera con un crono récord. – **2** *adv* a medio camino, a mitad de camino.
● **to meet sb. halfway,** *fig* llegar a un acuerdo mutuo.
■ **halfway point,** punto medio. ‖ **halfway stage,** etapa intermedia.
half-wit ['haːfwɪt] *n pej* imbécil *mf*, tonto,-a.
half-witted ['haːfwɪtɪd] *adj pej* imbécil, tonto,-a.
half-yearly [haːf'jɪəlɪ] **1** *adj* semestral. – **2** *adv* semestralmente.
halibut ['hælɪbət] *n* (*fish*) halibut *m*.
hall [hɔːl] **1** *n* (*entrance*) vestíbulo, entrada. **2** (*for concerts etc*) sala. **3** (*mansion*) casa solariega, mansión *f*. **4** US (*corridor*) pasillo, corredor *m*.
■ **hall of residence,** colegio mayor, residencia universitaria.
hallmark ['hɔːlmaːk] **1** *n* (*on gold etc*) contraste *m*. **2** *fig* sello.
hallo [hə'ləʊ] *interj* → **hello**.
hallowed ['hæləʊd] *adj fml dated* santo,-a, santificado,-a, bendito,-a: *some centuries ago, suicides weren't buried in hallowed ground,* siglos atrás, los suicidas no recibían sepultura en campo santo.
● **hallowed be Thy Name,** santificado sea Tu Nombre.
Halloween [hæləʊ'iːn] *n* víspera de Todos los Santos.
Hallowe'en [hæləʊ'iːn] *n* → **Halloween**.
hallstand ['hɔːlstænd] *n* perchero.
hallucinate [hə'luːsɪneɪt] *i* alucinar.
hallucination [həluːsɪ'neɪʃən] *n* alucinación *f*.
hallucinatory [hə'luːsɪnətərɪ] *adj* (*drug*) alucinógeno,-a; (*state*) de alucinación.
hallucinogenic [həluːsɪnə'dʒenɪk] *adj* alucinógeno,-a.
hallway ['hɔːlweɪ] *n* US vestíbulo.
halo ['heɪləʊ] **1** *n* ASTRON halo. **2** REL aureola.
▲ *pl* **haloes** o **halos.**
halt [hɔːlt] **1** *n* alto, parada. **2** (*railway*) apeadero. – **3** *t* parar, detener, interrumpir. – **4** *i* hacer alto, pararse, interrumpirse.
● **to come to a halt,** pararse. ‖ **to call a halt to sth.,** poner fin a algo.

halter [ˈhɔːltəʳ] *n* cabestro, ronzal *m*.
halterneck [ˈhɔːltənek] *adj* sin espalda.
halting [ˈhɔːltɪŋ] *adj* vacilante, titubeante.
halve [haːv] **1** *t* (*cut in two*) partir en dos. **2** (*reduce*) reducir a la mitad. **3** (*share*) compartir. **4** (*golf*) empatar.
halves [haːvz] *npl* → **half**.
ham[1] [hæm] *n* (*food*) jamón *m*.
■ **boiled ham**, jamón *m* cocido, jamón *m* de York, jamón *m* en dulce. ‖ **cured ham**, jamón *m* serrano. ‖ **Parma ham**, jamón *m* serrano.
ham[2] [hæm] **1** *n* RAD radioaficionado,-a. **2** (*actor*) comicastro,-a, histrión *m*. **3** (*acting*) histrionismo. – **4** *i* sobreactuar. – **5** *t* sobreactuar.
● **to ham it up**, exagerar.
▲ (*verbo*) *pt* & *pp* **hammed**, *ger* **hamming**.
Hamburg [ˈhæmbɜːg] *n* Hamburgo.
hamburger [ˈhæmbɜːgəʳ] *n* (*food*) hamburguesa.
ham-fisted [hæmˈfɪstɪd] **1** *adj fam* torpe, desmañado,-a. **2** *fig* torpe, poco delicado,-a, manazas.
ham-handed [hæmˈhændɪd] *adj* → **ham-fisted**.
hamlet [ˈhæmlət] *n* aldea, pueblecito.
hammer [ˈhæməʳ] **1** *n* (*tool*) martillo; (*piano*) macillo. **2** (*gun*) percursor *m*; (*sport*) martillo. – **3** *t* (*gen*) martillar, martillear; (*nail*) clavar. **4** *fam* (*beat*) dar una paliza, machacar. – **5** *i* (*gen*) martillar, martillear, golpear.
◆ **to hammer away** *i* trabajar con ahínco. ‖ **to hammer out** *t sep* (*metal, dent*) trabajar con el martillo, desabollar; (*deal, plan, etc*) lograr, alcanzar, llegar a.
● **the hammer and the sickle**, POL la hoz y el martillo. ‖ **to come under the hammer**, *fig* salir a subasta. ‖ **to go at it hammer and tongs**, *fig* luchar a brazo partido. ‖ **to hammer at the door**, aporrear la puerta. ‖ **to hammer sth. home**, *fig* insistir en algo. ‖ **to hammer sth. into sb.**, hacer entender a algn. a fuerza de repetirlo.
hammerhead [ˈhæməhed] *n* ZOOL pez *m* martillo.
hammering [ˈhæmərɪŋ] **1** *n* (*knocking noise*) martilleo, golpeteo. **2** *fig* paliza.
hammock [ˈhæmək] **1** *n* hamaca. **2** MAR coy *m*.
hamper[1] [ˈhæmpəʳ] **1** *n* cesta, canasta.
■ **Christmas hamper**, cesta de Navidad.
hamper[2] [ˈhæmpəʳ] *t* estorbar, obstaculizar.
hamster [ˈhæmstəʳ] *n* ZOOL hámster *m*.
hamstring [ˈhæmstrɪŋ] **1** *n* ANAT tendón *m* de la corva. – **2** *t* desjarretar. **3** *fig* paralizar, limitar, incapacitar.
▲ *pt* & *pp* (*hamstrung*) [ˈhæmstrʌŋ].
hand [hænd] **1** *n* mano *f*. **2** (*worker*) trabajador,-ra, operario,-a; (*sailor*) tripulante *mf*, marinero,-a. **3** (*of clock*) manecilla, aguja. **4** (*handwriting*) letra. **5** (*of cards*) mano *f*, cartas *fpl*. **6** (*applause*) aplauso. – **7** *t* dar, entregar.
◆ **to hand around** *t sep* repartir, ofrecer, pasar. ‖ **to hand back** *t sep* devolver. ‖ **to hand down** *t sep* (*songs etc*) transmitir; (*clothes*) pasar; (*possessions*) dejar en herencia. ‖ **to hand in** *t sep* (*work etc*) entregar; (*resignation etc*) presentar, notificar. ‖ **to hand on** *t sep* (*traditions etc*) transmitir, heredar; (*give*) pasar, dar. ‖ **to hand out** *t sep* (*distribute*) repartir, distribuir; (*give - gen*) dar; (- *punishment*) aplicar. ‖ **to hand over** *t sep* (*give*) entregar; (*one's possessions etc*) ceder. ‖ **to hand round** *t sep* (*sweets etc*) → **hand around**.
● **all hands on deck!**, ¡todos a cubierta! ‖ **at first hand**, de primera mano. ‖ **at hand**, a mano. ‖ **by hand**, a mano. ‖ **hands off!**, ¡no toques!, ¡quita las manos! ‖ **hands up!**, ¡manos arriba! ‖ **I have to hand it to you**, *fam fig* me quito el sombrero ante Vd, tengo que felicitarlo. ‖ **on hand**, disponible. ‖ **on the one**

hand ... on the other hand, por una parte ... por otra parte. ‖ **the job in hand**, *fig* lo que nos ocupa. ‖ **to ask for sb.'s hand**, *fig* pedir la mano de algn. ‖ **to force sb.'s hand**, *fig* forzarle la mano a algn. ‖ **to get out of hand**, *fig* descontrolarse, desmadrarse. ‖ **to give sb. a big hand**, dedicar a algn. una gran ovación. ‖ **to have a hand in**, *fig* intervenir en, participar en. ‖ **to have one's hands full**, *fam fig* estar muy ocupado,-a. ‖ **to have the upper hand**, llevar ventaja. ‖ **to have time in hand**, *fig* sobrarle tiempo. ‖ **to hold hands**, estar cogidos,-as de la mano. ‖ **to keep one's hand in**, *fig* no perder la práctica. ‖ **to know sth. like the back of one's hand**, *fig* conocer algo como la palma de la mano. ‖ **to lend a hand**, echar una mano. ‖ **to shake hands**, estrecharse la mano, darse la mano. ‖ **to show one's hand**, *fig* poner las cartas sobre la mesa, poner las cartas boca arriba. ‖ **to turn one's hand to**, *fig* dedicarse a, meterse en. ‖ **to wash one's hands**, *fig* lavarse las manos.
■ **farm hand**, AGR peón *m*. ‖ **a free hand**, carta blanca.
handbag [ˈhændbæg] *n* bolso.
handball [ˈhændbɔːl] *n* SP balonmano.
handbook [ˈhændbʊk] *n* (*guidebook*) guía; (*reference book*) manual *m*.
handbrake [ˈhændbreɪk] *n* freno de mano.
handclap [ˈhændklæp] *n* aplauso.
handcuff [ˈhændkʌf] **1** *t* esposar. – **2 handcuffs**, *npl* esposas *fpl*.
handful [ˈhændfʊl] *n* puñado.
● **to be quite a handful**, ser difícil de controlar, dar mucha guerra.
hand-grenade [ˈhændgrəneɪd] *n* granada de mano.
handgun [ˈhændgʌn] *n* pistola.
handicap [ˈhændɪkæp] **1** *n* MED (*physical or mental*) incapacitación *f*, invalidez *f*, deficiencia, disminución *f*. **2** SP hándicap *m*, desventaja. **3** *fig* obstáculo. – **4** *t* obstaculizar, impedir, perjudicar. **5** SP handicapar, conceder un hándicap a.
▲ (*verbo*) *pt* & *pp* **handicapped**, *ger* **handicapping**.
handicapped [ˈhændɪkæpt] **1** *adj* (*physically*) minusválido,-a, discapacitado,-a; (*mentally*) retrasado,-a. **2** *fig* desfavorecido,-a.
■ **the handicapped**, los minusválidos *mpl*, los discapacitados *mpl*.
handicraft [ˈhændɪkrɑːft] **1** *n* (*job, art*) artesanía; (*objects*) objetos *mpl* de artesanía. **2** (*manual skill*) habilidad *f* manual, destreza manual.
■ **handicraft teacher**, profesor,-ra de manualidades.
handiwork [ˈhændɪwɜːrk] *n* (*work*) trabajo, obra; (*craft*) artesanía.
handkerchief [ˈhæŋkətʃiːf] *n* pañuelo.
handle [ˈhændəl] **1** *n* (*of door*) pomo, manilla. **2** (*of drawer*) tirador *m*. **3** (*of cup*) asa. **4** (*of knife*) mango. **5** (*lever*) palanca. **6** (*crank*) manivela. **7** *fig* pretexto. – **8** *t* (*gen*) manejar, manipular. **9** (*people*) tratar. **10** (*tolerate*) aguantar. **11** (*control*) controlar, dominar. **12** (*deal with*) ocuparse de. **13** (*manage*) poder con, tener la capacidad para. **14** (*responsibility*) encargarse de. **15** *fam* soportar, aguantar. – **16** *i* (*car*) comportarse, manejarse.
● **"handle with care"**, "frágil". ‖ **to fly off the handle**, salirse de sus casillas.
handlebar [ˈhændəlbɑːʳ] *n* manillar *m*.
handler [ˈhændləʳ] *n* cuidador,-ra.
■ **baggage handler**, mozo de equipajes. ‖ **dog handler**, cuidador,-ra de perros.
handmade [hændˈmeɪd] *adj* hecho,-a a mano.

handmaiden [ˈhændmeɪdən] *n dated* criada.
hand-me-down [ˈhændmɪdaʊn] **1** *adj* usado,-a, heredado,-a. – **2 hand-me-downs,** *npl fam* ropa usada, ropa heredada.
handout [ˈhændaʊt] **1** *n* (*leaflet*) folleto, prospecto; (*political*) octavilla. **2** EDUC material *m*. **3** (*press*) comunicado de prensa, nota de prensa. **4** (*charity*) limosna, dádiva, caridad *f*.
handover [ˈhændəʊvəʳ] *n* (*power, responsibility etc*) traspaso, transferencia.
hand-picked [hænd'pɪkt] *adj* escogido,-a a mano.
handrail [ˈhændreɪl] *n* pasamano, barandilla.
handset [ˈhændset] *n* microteléfono.
handshake [ˈhændʃeɪk] *n* apretón *m* de manos.
handsome [ˈhænsəm] **1** *adj* (*man*) apuesto, guapo, de buen ver; (*woman*) bella, hermosa, guapa. **2** (*elegant*) elegante. **3** (*generous*) considerable, generoso,-a.
handsomely [ˈhænsəmlɪ] **1** *adv* (*elegantly*) con elegancia, elegantemente. **2** (*generously*) generosamente.
hands-on [ˈhændzɒn] *adj* (*for computers*) práctico,-a: *the computer course included lots of hands-on training,* el curso de informática ofrecía mucha formación práctica.
handspring [ˈhændsprɪŋ] *n* SP voltereta sobre las manos, salto mortal.
handstand [ˈhændstænd] *n* SP pino, vertical.
hand-to-hand [ˈhændtəhænd] **1** *adj* cuerpo a cuerpo. – **2** *adv* cuerpo a cuerpo.
■ **hand-to-hand combat,** combate *m* cuerpo a cuerpo.
handwriting [ˈhændraɪtɪŋ] *n* letra, escritura.
handwritten [ˈhændˈrɪtən] *adj* escrito,-a a mano, manuscrito,-a.
handy [ˈhændɪ] **1** *adj* (*person*) hábil. **2** (*close at hand*) a mano, cercano,-a. **3** (*useful*) práctico,-a, cómodo,-a, útil: *mopeds are very handy for getting around cities,* los ciclomotores son muy prácticos para desplazarse por la ciudad.
● to come in handy, venir bien. ‖ to keep sth. handy, tener algo a mano.
▲ *comp* handier, *superl* handiest.
hang [hæŋ] **1** *t* (*gen*) colgar. **2** (*wallpaper*) colocar. **3** JUR ahorcar. – **4** *i* colgar, pender; (*float*) flotar. **5** JUR ser ahorcado,-a. **6** (*dress etc*) caer. – **7** *n* (*of dress etc*) caída.
◆ to hang about / hang around **1** *i* esperar. **2** (*waste time*) perder el tiempo. – **3** *t insep* frecuentar. ‖ to hang back **1** *i* quedarse atrás. **2** *fig* vacilar. ‖ to hang down *i* colgar, caer. ‖ to hang on **1** *i* (*hold tight*) agarrarse. **2** (*wait*) esperar. ‖ to hang out **1** *t sep* (*washing*) tender. – **2** *i fam* soler estar: *this is where the local rockers hang out,* aquí es donde suelen estar los roqueros de la zona. ‖ to hang up **1** *t sep* colgar. – **2** *i* colgar.
● hang loose!, *fam* ¡tranqui! ‖ to get the hang of sth., cogerle el truquillo a algo. ‖ to hang in the air, flotar en el aire. ‖ to hang up one's boots, colgar las botas.
▲ *pt* & *pp* hung, excepto en *3* y *5* que son regulares.
hangar [ˈhæŋəʳ] *n* AER hangar *m*.
hangdog [ˈhændɒg] *adj* (*expression on face*) avergonzado,-a, triste.
hanger [ˈhæŋəʳ] *n* percha.
hanger-on [hæŋərˈɒn] *n fam pej* (*person*) lapa, parásito.
▲ *pl* hangers-on.
hang-glider [ˈhæŋglaɪdəʳ] *n* ala delta.
hang-gliding [ˈhæŋglaɪdɪŋ] *n* vuelo con ala delta.
hanging [ˈhæŋɪŋ] **1** *adj* colgante. – **2** *n* ejecución *f* en la horca, ahorcamiento. – **3 hangings,** *npl* (*on wall*) colgaduras *fpl*.

■ **hanging bridge,** puente *m* colgante.
hangman [ˈhæŋmən] **1** *n* verdugo. **2** (*game*) el ahorcado.
▲ *pl* (*hangmen*) [ˈhæŋmən].
hangnail [ˈhæŋneɪl] *n* padrastro.
hangout [ˈhæŋaʊt] *n fam* guarida, lugar *m* de reunión habitual.
hangover [ˈhæŋəʊvəʳ] **1** *n* (*after too much drinking*) resaca. **2** (*remains*) resto, vestigio.
hang-up [ˈhæŋʌp] **1** *n fam* (*problem*) problema *m*. **2** (*complex*) complejo.
hanker [ˈhæŋkəʳ] to hanker after / hanker for, *i* ansiar, anhelar.
hankering [ˈhæŋkərɪŋ] *n* anhelo, ansia.
hankie [ˈhæŋkɪ] *n fam* → **handkerchief.**
hanky-panky [hæŋkɪˈpæŋkɪ] *n fam* tejemanejes *mpl*.
haphazard [hæpˈhæzəd] **1** *adj* desordenado,-a. **2** (*plans etc*) improvisado,-a.
haphazardly [hæpˈhæzədlɪ] *adv* sin orden ni concierto.
hapless [ˈhæpləs] *adj* desdichado,-a.
happen [ˈhæpən] *i* (*occur*) ocurrir, pasar, suceder: *what's happening?*, ¿qué pasa?; *what happened to Jim?*, ¿qué le pasó a Jim? **2** (*by chance*) dar la casualidad de: *she happened to go to the same school,* dio la casualidad de que iba al mismo colegio.
● as it happens, ..., da la casualidad de que ...
happening [ˈhæpənɪŋ] *n* acontecimiento.
happily [ˈhæpɪlɪ] **1** *adv* (*in a happy way*) felizmente, con alegría. **2** (*luckily*) afortunadamente.
● and they lived happily ever after, y vivieron felices para siempre más, vivieron felices y comieron perdices.
happiness [ˈhæpɪnəs] *n* felicidad *f*, alegría.
happy [ˈhæpɪ] **1** *adj* (*cheerful*) feliz, alegre, dichoso,-a, afortunado,-a: *we were happy to hear of your success,* nos alegramos mucho al enterarnos de tu éxito. **2** (*glad*) contento,-a, satisfecho,-a: *he was very happy with his performance,* estuvo muy satisfecho con su actuación.
● happy birthday!, ¡feliz cumpleaños! ‖ to be as happy as a lark, estar más feliz que unas pascuas.
■ happy ending, final *m* feliz, desenlace *m* feliz. ‖ happy medium, término medio.
▲ *comp* happier, *superl* happiest.
happy-go-lucky [hæpɪgəʊlˈʌkɪ] *adj* despreocupado,-a.
● a happy-go-lucky type, un viva la virgen.
hara-kiri [hærəˈkɪrɪ] *n* harakiri *m*.
harangue [həˈræŋ] **1** *t* arengar. – **2** *n* arenga.
harass [ˈhærəs] **1** *t* acosar, hostigar. **2** (*military*) hostilizar, hostigar: *the soldiers harassed the enemy,* los soldados hostigaron al enemigo. **3** (*worries, problems*) atormentar, agobiar.
harassment [ˈhærəsmənt] *n* acoso, hostigamiento.
harbinger [ˈhɑːbɪndʒəʳ] *n lit* (*person*) heraldo, nuncio, precursor,-ra; (*thing*) presagio.
harbor [ˈhɑːbəʳ] *n-t* US → **harbour.**
harbour [ˈhɑːbəʳ] **1** *n* puerto. – **2** *t* (*criminal*) encubrir. **3** (*doubts*) abrigar. **4** (*suspicions*) tener; (*contain, hide*) contener, esconder: *harbouring criminals is a punishable offence,* esconder a criminales es castigable por la ley.
● to harbour a grudge, guardar rencor.
■ harbour master, capitán *m* de puerto.
hard [hɑːd] **1** *adj* (*gen*) duro,-a; (*solid*) sólido,-a. **2** (*difficult*) difícil. **3** (*harsh*) severo,-a. **4** (*work*) arduo,-a, penoso,-a, agotador,-ra. **5** *fig* cruel, rudo,-a. **6** (*fight, match*) reñido,-a, disputado,-a; (*decision*) injusto,-a. **7** (*fact*) innegable:

(*luck*) malo,-a. **8** (*final decision*) definitivo,-a, irrevocable; (*person*) severo,-a, inflexible. **9** LING fuerte. – **10** *adv* (*forcibly*) fuerte; (*diligently*) mucho, de firme, concienzudamente, con ahínco.

● **hard of hearing,** duro,-a de oído. ‖ **to be hard done by,** sentirse mal tratado,-a, ser tratado,-a injustamente. ‖ **to be hard hit by,** *fig* quedar muy afectado,- a por. ‖ **to be hard on sb.,** *fig* tratar a algn. con severidad, tratar a algn. con dureza. ‖ **to be hard on sb.'s heels,** *fig* pisar los talones a algn. ‖ **to be hard pushed to do sth.,** *fig* verse apurado,-a para realizar algo. ‖ **to be hard up,** *fam* estar sin blanca. ‖ **to drive a hard bargain,** *fig* negociar con dureza. ‖ **to have a hard time,** *fam* pasarlo canutas, pasarlo mal. ‖ **to take sth. very hard,** tomar algo muy a pecho, encajar algo muy mal. ‖ **to work hard,** trabajar mucho.

■ **hard core,** (*group*) núcleo; (*material*) lecho de grava. ‖ **hard drinker,** bebedor,-ra empedernido,-a. ‖ **hard evidence,** pruebas *fpl* definitivas. ‖ **hard labour,** trabajos *mpl* forzados. ‖ **hard luck,** mala suerte. ‖ **hard shoulder,** arcén *m.*

hard-and-fast [hɑːdən'fɑːst] *adj* fijo,-a, rígido,-a, inflexible.

hardback ['hɑːdbæk] *n* (*in printing*) edición *f* en tela, edición *f* de tapas duras.

hard-bitten [hɑːd'bɪtən] *adj* tenaz, duro,-a.

hardboard ['hɑːdbɔːd] *n* chapa de madera dura, contrachapado.

hard-boiled ['hɑːdbɔɪld] *adj* (*egg*) duro,-a; (*person*) duro,-a, insensible.

hard-core ['hɑːdkɔːʳ] *adj* irreductible, incondicional.
■ **hard-core supporter,** partidario,-a a ultranza, partidario,-a acérrimo,-a.

hardcourt ['hɑːdkɔːt] *n* SP (*tennis*) pista dura, cancha dura.

harden ['hɑːdən] **1** *t* endurecer. **2** *fig* insensibilizar. – **3** *i* endurecerse.

hardened ['hɑːdənd] *adj* (*gen*) endurecido,-a; (*criminal*) habitual.

hard-headed ['hɑːd'hedɪd] *adj* frío,-a, cerebral, práctico,-a.

hard-hearted ['hɑːd'hɑːtɪd] *adj* cruel, duro,-a, insensible.

hardliner [hɑːd'laɪnəʳ] *n* (*ideas, especially in politics*) duro,- a, partidario,-a de la línea dura.

hardly ['hɑːdlɪ] *adv* (*scarcely*) apenas, casi; (*not easily*) difícilmente, duramente, con dificultad: *he can hardly see anymore,* ya casi no ve nada; *she had hardly opened the door when the phone rang,* apenas había abierto la puerta cuando sonó el teléfono; *he could hardly believe his ears,* apenas pudo dar crédito a lo que oía.
● **hardly anyone,** casi nadie. ‖ **hardly ever,** casi nunca. ‖ **hardly!,** ¡ni hablar!, ¡qué va!

hardness ['hɑːdnəs] **1** *n* (*gen*) dureza. **2** (*difficulty*) dificultad *f.* **3** (*severity*) severidad *f*; (*of winter*) rigor *m.* **4** (*of heart*) insensibilidad *f.*

hard-nosed ['hɑːd'nəʊzd] *adj fam* realista, práctico,-a, nada sentimental.

hard-on ['hɑːdɒn] *n taboo* erección *f.*

hard-pressed ['hɑːd'prest] *adj* en aprietos, en apuros, apurado,-a: *she is always hard-pressed to make ends meet,* siempre está en apuros para llegar a un final de mes.

hardship ['hɑːdʃɪp] *n* (*usually economic*) privación *f*, apuro, dificultad *f.*

hardware ['hɑːdweəʳ] **1** *n* (*goods*) ferretería, quincallería. **2** COMPUT hardware *m*, soporte *m* físico. **3** MIL armamento. **4** TECH equipos *mpl*, maquinaria.

■ **hardware dealer,** ferretero,-a. ‖ **hardware shop,** ferretería.

hardwearing [hɑːd'weərɪŋ] *adj* (*especially articles of clothing*) duradero,-a, resistente.

hardworking ['hɑːdwɜːkɪŋ] *adj* trabajador,-ra.

hardy ['hɑːdɪ] **1** *adj* fuerte, robusto,-a. **2** (*plant*) resistente.
▲ *comp* **hardier,** *superl* **hardiest.**

hare [heəʳ] **1** *n* ZOOL liebre *f.* – **2** *i* correr muy deprisa, ir muy deprisa: *he went haring past me,* me pasó a toda pastilla.
● **as mad as a March hare,** loco,-a como una cabra.

harebrained ['heəbreɪnd] *adj* irreflexivo,-a, atolondrado,-a, absurdo,-a.

harelip ['heəlɪp] *n* MED labio leporino.

harem [hɑː'riːm, 'heərəm] *n* harén *m.*

haricot bean [hærɪkəʊ'biːn] *n* alubia, judía.

hark [hɑːk] *i arch* escuchar.
◆ **to hark at** *t insep fam* escuchar a, oír: *hark at her talking!,* ¡mira quién habla!, ¡mira cómo habla aquélla! ‖ **to hark back** *i fam* volver a, recordar: *he's always harking back to his childhood,* siempre está recordando su infancia.

harlequin ['hɑːlɪkwɪn] *n* arlequín *m.*

harlot ['hɑːlət] *n arch* ramera.

harm [hɑːm] **1** *n* mal *m*, daño, perjuicio: *the frost caused a lot of harm to the crops,* las heladas causaron mucho daño en los cultivos; *there's no harm in trying,* no hay nada malo en intentarlo; *the little girl came to no harm,* no le pasó nada a la pequeña. – **2** *t* dañar, perjudicar.
● **to be out of harm's way,** estar a salvo. ‖ **he/she wouldn't harm a fly,** es inofensivo,-a.

harmful ['hɑːmful] *adj* dañino,-a, nocivo,-a, perjudicial.

harmless ['hɑːmləs] *adj* inocuo,-a, inofensivo,-a.

harmonic [hɑː'mɒnɪk] *adj* armónico,-a.

harmonica [hɑː'mɒnɪkə] *n* MUS armónica.

harmonics [hɑː'mɒnɪks] *n* MUS armonía.

harmonious [hɑː'məʊnɪəs] *adj* armonioso,-a.

harmonize ['hɑːmənaɪz] **1** *t* armonizar. – **2** *i* armonizar.

harmony ['hɑːmənɪ] *n* armonía.
▲ *pl* **harmonies.**

harness ['hɑːnəs] **1** *n* (*for animals*) arreos *mpl*, guarniciones *fpl*, arneses *mpl.* **2** (*for children*) andadores *mpl.* – **3** *t* (*horse*) enjaezar, poner los arreos a. **4** (*hitch*) enganchar. **5** *fig* (*resources*) aprovechar, utilizar.
● **to die in harness,** *fig* morir con las botas puestas, morir al pie del cañón. ‖ **to get back in harness,** *fam* volver al trabajo. ‖ **to work in harness with,** colaborar con.

harp [hɑːp] *n* MUS arpa.
● **to harp on about sth.,** insistir en algo, machacar algo.

harpist ['hɑːpɪst] *n* MUS arpista *mf.*

harpoon [hɑː'puːn] **1** *n* arpón *m.* – **2** *t* arponear.
■ **harpoon gun,** cañón *m* lanzaarpones.

harpsichord ['hɑːpsɪkɔːd] *n* MUS clavicordio, clavicémbalo.

harpy ['hɑːpɪ] **1** *n lit* arpía *f.* **2** *fig* arpía.
▲ *pl* **harpies.**

harrier¹ ['hærɪəʳ] *n* ORN aguilucho.

harrier² ['hærɪəʳ] **1** *n* (*dog*) perro de caza. **2** (*runner*) corredor,-ra de cros.

harrow ['hærəʊ] **1** *n* AGR grada, rastrillo. – **2** *t* rastrillar.

harrowing ['hærəʊɪŋ] *adj* angustioso,-a, desgarrador,- ra, terrible.

harry ['hærɪ] *t fml fig* (*to harass*) acosar, hostigar; (*devastate*) arrasar, asolar, hostilizar.

▲ *pt & pp* **harried,** *ger* **harrying.**

harsh [hɑːʃ] **1** *adj* (*cruel*) cruel, duro,-a, severo,-a. **2** (*sound*) discordante. **3** (*rough*) áspero,-a.

harshly ['hɑːʃlɪ] *adv* (*gen*) ásperamente, duramente, severamente.

harshness ['hɑːʃnəs] **1** *n* (*gen*) severidad *f*, dureza; (*of touch, taste*) aspereza. **2** (*of sound*) discordancia.

hart [hɑːt] *n* ZOOL ciervo.

harvest ['hɑːvɪst] **1** *n* (*gen*) cosecha, siega; (*vegetables*) recolección *f*, cosecha. **2** (*grapes*) vendimia. **3** *fig* cosecha. – **4** *t* cosechar, recoger. **5** (*grapes*) vendimiar.
■ **harvest festival,** fiesta de la cosecha. ‖ **harvest time,** siega.

harvester ['hɑːvɪstə'] **1** *n* (*person*) segador,-ra. **2** (*machine*) segadora, cosechadora.

has [hæz] *3rd pers sing pres* → **have.**

has-been ['hæzbiːn] *n fam* vieja gloria.

hash[1] [hæʃ] **1** *n* CULIN *sofrito de carne picada.* **2** *fam* (*mess*) embrollo, lío.
◆ **to hash up** *t sep fam* hacer mal, estropear, pifiar.
● **to make a hash of sth.,** estropear algo.

hash[2] [hæʃ] *n fam* (*drug*) hachís *m*.

hashish ['hæʃiːʃ] *n* hachís *m*.

hasp [hɑːsp] **1** *n* (*of window*) falleba; (*of door*) picaporte *m*, cierre *m*. **2** (*of padlock*) aldaba, cerrojo, pestillo; (*of album etc*) broche *m*, cierre *m*.

hassle ['hæsəl] **1** *n fam* (*nuisance*) rollo, follón *m*, jaleo; (*problem*) problema *m*, lío. **2** (*argument*) bronca, discusión *f*, pelea, riña. – **3** *t* molestar, fastidiar: *stop hassling me!,* ¡deja de fastidiarme!

hassock ['hæsək] *n* REL cojín *m*, almohadilla.

haste [heɪst] *n* prisa, precipitación *f*.
● **to make haste,** apresurarse, darse prisa. ‖ **more haste, less speed,** vísteme despacio que tengo prisa.

hasten ['heɪsən] **1** *t fml* apresurar, acelerar el paso de, dar prisa a. – **2** *i* darse prisa, apresurarse: *he hastened home,* volvió a casa de prisa.

hastily ['heɪstɪlɪ] *adv* (*quickly*) de prisa, apresuradamente; (*rashly*) sin reflexionar, a la ligera, precipitadamente.

hastiness ['heɪstɪnəs] *n* prisa, rapidez *f*, precipitación *f*.

hasty ['heɪstɪ] **1** *adj* (*hurried*) apresurado,-a, precipitado,-a. **2** (*rash*) apresurado,-a, imprudente, irreflexivo,-a. **3** (*hot-headed*) impaciente, con genio; (*superficial*) ligero,-a.
▲ *comp* **hastier,** *superl* **hastiest.**

hat [hæt] *n* sombrero.
● **I'll eat my hat if ...,** *fig* que me ahorquen si ..., que me maten si ... ‖ **to be old hat,** *fam* ser historia. ‖ **to keep sth. under one's hat,** *fml* guardar un secreto. ‖ **to take one's hat off to,** *fig* descubrirse ante. ‖ **to talk through one's hat,** decir tonterías.

hatband ['hætbænd] *n* cinta de sombrero.

hatbox ['hætbɒks] *n* sombrerera.

hatch [hætʃ] **1** *n* (*on ship*) escotilla. **2** (*of chickens, brood*) pollada. – **3** *t* (*eggs*) empollar, incubar. **4** *fig* (*plot, plan*) idear, tramar. – **5** *i* salir del cascarón, salir del huevo.
● **down the hatch!,** *fam* ¡salud!
■ **serving hatch,** ventanilla.

hatchback ['hætʃbæk] *n* AUTO *coche con portón trasero.*

hatchery ['hætʃərɪ] *n* criadero, piscifactoría.
▲ *pl* **hatcheries.**

hatchet ['hætʃɪt] *n* hacha.
● **to bury the hatchet,** enterrar el hacha de la guerra, hacer las paces.
■ **hatchet job,** *fam* diatriba. ‖ **hatchet man,** *fam* matón *m*.

hate [heɪt] **1** *n* odio. – **2** *t fam* (*detest*) odiar, detestar, aborrecer: *she hates school dinners,* no soporta las comidas del colegio. **3** *fam* (*regret*) lamentar, sentir: *I hate to trouble you, but ...,* lamento molestarle, pero ...
■ **pet hate,** bestia negra.

hateful ['heɪtfʊl] *adj* odioso,-a, repugnante.

hatpin ['hætpɪn] *n* alfiler *m* de sombrero.

hatred ['heɪtrəd] *n* odio.

hatstand ['hætstænd] *n* percha (para sombreros).

haughtiness ['hɔːtɪnəs] *n* altanería, arrogancia, altivez *f*.

haughty ['hɔːtɪ] *adj* altanero,-a, arrogante, altivo,-a, engreído,-a.
▲ *comp* **haughtier,** *superl* **haughtiest.**

haul [hɔːl] **1** *n* (*pull*) tirón *m*, estirón *m*. **2** (*distance*) recorrido, trayecto, trecho, camino: *it's a long haul yet,* aún falta mucho camino. **3** (*fish*) redada. **4** (*loot*) botín *m*. – **5** *t* (*drag*) tirar de, arrastrar. **6** (*boat*) halar; (*car, caravan etc*) remolcar.
◆ **to haul up** *t sep fam* llevar ante el tribunal, llevar a juicio, llevar ante el juez: *he was hauled up for drunken driving,* lo llevaron ante el juez por conducir en estado de embriaguez.
● **to haul sb. over the coals,** echarle un rapapolvo a algn.

haulage ['hɔːlɪdʒ] **1** *n* (*activity*) transporte *m*, acarreo. **2** (*cost*) (gastos *mpl* de) transporte *m*.
■ **haulage contractor,** transportista *mf*.

haulier ['hɔːljə'] *n* transportista *mf*.

haunch [hɔːntʃ] **1** *n* ANAT cadera y muslo, anca. **2** CULIN pierna, pernil *m*.
● **to sit on one's haunches,** ponerse en cuclillas.

haunt [hɔːnt] **1** *n* (*of people*) sitio preferido, lugar *m* predilecto; (*of criminals, animals*) guarida. – **2** *t* (*frequent - gen*) frecuentar; (*- ghost*) aparecer en, rondar por: *the house is haunted by ghosts,* aparecen fantasmas en la casa. **3** (*memory, thought*) obsesionar, perseguir: *she is haunted by the memories of her childhood,* le obsesionan los recuerdos de su infancia.

haunted ['hɔːntɪd] *adj* encantado,-a, embrujado,-a.
■ **haunted castle,** castillo encantado.

haunting ['hɔːntɪŋ] *adj* obsesionante.

Havana [hə'vænə] *n* La Habana.
■ **Havana cigar,** puro, puro habano, habano: *he enjoys a Havana now and again,* le encanta fumarse un puro habano de vez en cuando.

have [hæv] **1** *t* (*possess*) tener, poseer: *she has a house in Whitby,* tiene una casa en Whitby; *he had blue eyes,* tenía los ojos azules. **2** (*food*) comer, tomar; (*drink*) beber, tomar: *I think I'll have the turbot,* creo que tomaré el rodaballo; *will you have a brandy?,* ¿quieres tomar un coñac?; *to have breakfast/lunch/tea/dinner,* desayunar/comer/merendar/cenar. **3** (*cigarette*) fumar: *how many cigarettes have you had today?,* ¿cuántos cigarros has fumado hoy? **4** (*shower, bath, etc*) tomar: *when she got home she had a shower,* cuando llegó a casa se dio una ducha, cuando llegó a casa se duchó; *in Finland I had a sauna,* en Finlandia hice una sauna; *have you had a wash and a shave?,* ¿te has lavado y afeitado?; *I'll have a swim before lunch,* me bañaré antes de comer. **5** (*treatment*) recibir: *I had an injection,* me dieron una inyección; *she had a heart operation,* la operaron del corazón; *I have a massage every Thursday,* cada jueves voy al masajista; *she's having physiotherapy,* acude a fisioterapia. **6** (*illness*) tener: *he didn't come because he had flu,* no vino porque tenía la gripe; *I have a head-*

ache, tengo dolor de cabeza. **7** (*experience*) tener: *I had a scare,* tuve un susto, me asusté; *have a good time!,* ¡diviértos!, ¡pasadlo bien!; *I had quite a surprise,* me llevé una gran sorpresa. **8** (*receive, invite*) recibir, invitar: *we had John and Mary for dinner last night,* invitamos a John y Mary a cenar anoche. **9** (*borrow*) pedir prestado, dejar: *can I have your book for a second, please?,* ¿me dejas tu libro un segundo, por favor? **10** (*party*) celebrar, tener, dar; (*meeting*) celebrar, tener: *they're always having parties,* no paran de dar fiestas; *are you going to have a party for your birthday?,* ¿vas a hacer una fiesta para tu cumpleaños?; *they had their annual meeting last week,* celebraron su reunión anual la semana pasada. **11** (*according to*) según: *rumour has it that ...,* corre el rumor de que ... **12** (*baby*) tener, dar a luz. **13** (*cause to happen*) hacer, mandar: *he had the house painted,* hizo pintar la casa; *she had her hair cut,* se cortó el cabello; *they had him killed,* lo mandaron matar. **14** (*allow*) permitir, consentir: *I can't have you walking about naked,* no puedo permitir que vayas por ahí desnudo. **15** *fam* (*cheat*) timar: *if you paid £200 pounds for that you were had,* si has pagado doscientas libras por eso te han timado. – **16** *aux* haber: *I have seen her,* la he visto; *I hadn't seen the film so I went to the cinema,* no había visto la película así que fui al cine.

◆ **to have on 1** *t sep* (*wear*) llevar puesto,-a. **2** (*tease*) tomar el pelo a: *you're having me on,* me estás tomando el pelo, estás bromeando. ‖ **to have out** *t sep* (*tooth*) sacarse; (*appendix*) operarse de.

● **had better,** más vale que: *you'd better come alone,* más vale que vengas solo; *we'd better not tell her about it,* sería mejor no decírselo. ‖ **have got,** GB tener: *Sue's got a new car,* Sue tiene un coche nuevo; *you've got a stain on your shirt,* tienes una mancha en la camisa; *he said he'd got a hangover,* dijo que tenía resaca. ‖ **to have done with,** acabar con. ‖ **to have had it,** (*broken*) estar hecho,-a polvo, estar fastidiado,-a; (*in trouble*) haberlo,-a cagado,-a; (*finished*) estar acabado,-a: *this radio's had it,* I'll have to get a new one,* esta radio está en las últimas, tendré que comprar una nueva; *your dad's seen you, you've had it now!,* te ha visto tu padre, ¡la has cagado!; *if this scandal gets out he's had it as an MP,* si la gente se entera de este escándalo, se han acabado sus días de diputado. ‖ **to have it away / have it off,** *taboo* echar un polvo. ‖ **to have it in for sb.,** tenerla tomada con algn. ‖ **to have it out with sb.,** ajustar las cuentas con algn. ‖ **to have it over and done with,** acabar algo de una vez y para siempre. ‖ **to have just,** acabar de: *she's just finished the letter,* acaba de terminar la carta. ‖ **to have sb. over to one's house / have sb. round to one's house,** invitar a algn. a casa. ‖ **to have sb. up for sth.,** JUR llevar a algn. ante los tribunales por algo, procesar a algn. por algo. ‖ **to have sth. on,** tener algo planeado, tener algo que hacer. ‖ **to have sth. on sb.,** tener información comprometedora sobre algn., saber algo comprometedor acerca de algn. ‖ **to have to,** tener que, haber de: *I have to see you,* tengo que verte. ‖ **to have to do with,** tener que ver con: *that has nothing to do with you,* eso no tiene nada que ver contigo.

▲ *3rd pers pres sing* **has,** *pt & pp* **had,** *ger* **having.**

haven ['heɪvən] **1** *n fig* refugio, asilo. **2** (*harbour*) puerto.

have-nots ['hævnɒts] *npl* desposeídos *mpl,* pobres *mpl,* desvalidos *mpl.*

haversack ['hævəsæk] *n* mochila.

havoc ['hævək] *n* estragos *mpl.*

● **to play havoc with,** hacer estragos en.

Hawaian [hə'waɪən] **1** *adj* hawaiano,-a. – **2** *n* hawaiano,-a.

Hawaii [hə'waɪ] *n* Hawai.

Hawaiian [hə'waɪən] *adj* → **Hawaian.**

hawfinch ['hɔːfɪntʃ] *n* ORN picogordo.

hawk¹ [hɔːk] *n* halcón *m.*

● **to have eyes like a hawk,** tener ojo de lince.

■ **hawks and doves,** halcones *mpl* y palomas.

hawk² [hɔːk] **1** *t* (*in the street*) vender en la calle; (*door to door*) vender de puerta en puerta. **2** (*gossip, news*) divulgar, pregonar, difundir. – **3** *i* carraspear.

hawker ['hɔːkə'] *n* vendedor,-ra ambulante.

hawk-eyed ['hɔːkaɪd] *adj fig* con ojos de lince.

hawser ['hɔːzə'] *n* guindaleza.

hawthorn ['hɔːθɔːn] *n* BOT espino.

hay [heɪ] *n* BOT heno.

● **to hit the hay,** *fam* acostarse. ‖ **to make hay while the sun shines,** *fam* la ocasión la pintan calva.

hay-fever ['heɪfiːvə'] *n* MED fiebre *f* del heno.

hayfork ['heɪfɔːk] *n* AGR bieldo.

haymaker ['heɪmeɪkə'] *n* heneador,-ra, labrador,-ra, segador,-ra.

haymaking ['heɪmeɪkɪŋ] *n* AGR henificación *f,* siega del heno.

haystack ['heɪstæk] *n* almiar *m.*

haywire ['heɪwaɪə'] *adj fam* (*confused*) en desorden, confuso,-a; (*mad*) chalado,-a, loco,-a.

● **to go haywire,** *fam* (*person*) volverse loco,-a, volverse majara; (*machine*) estropearse; (*plan, scheme*) embrollarse, liarse.

hazard ['hæzəd] **1** *n* (*risk*) riesgo, peligro. **2** (*in sports in general*) obstáculo. – **3** *t fml* arriesgar, poner en peligro. **4** *fml* (*guess, remark*) aventurar, atreverse a hacer.

hazardous ['hæzədəs] *adj* arriesgado,-a, peligroso,-a, aventurado,-a.

haze [heɪz] **1** *n* neblina. **2** *fig* confusión *f,* vaguedad *f.* – **3** *t us* hacer una novatada a.

hazel ['heɪzəl] **1** *n* BOT avellano. – **2** *adj* (de color de) avellana.

hazelnut ['heɪzəlnʌt] *n* BOT avellana.

hazily ['heɪzɪlɪ] *adv fig* vagamente.

haziness ['heɪzɪnəs] **1** *n* nebulosidad *f,* calina. **2** *fig* nebulosidad *f,* vaguedad *f.*

hazy ['heɪzɪ] **1** *adj* brumoso,-a, calinoso,-a, nebuloso,-a. **2** *fig* vago,-a, nebuloso,-a, vago,-a.

▲ *comp* **hazier,** *superl* **haziest.**

H-bomb ['eɪtʃbɒm] *n* MIL bomba H.

he [hiː] **1** *pron* él: *he came yesterday,* (él) vino ayer. **2** (*gen*) el que, quien: *he who wants to come, raise his hand,* el que quiera venir, que levante la mano. – **3** *n* (*male animals*) macho: *is it a he or a she?,* ¿es macho o hembra? **4** (*man*) hombre *m,* varón *m.* – **5** *adj* macho.

■ **he-goat,** macho cabrío.

HE [hɪz'eksələnsɪ, hər'eksələnsɪ] *abbr* (*His Excellency, Her Excellency*) Su Excelencia; (*abbreviation*) S.E.

head [hed] **1** *n* (*gen*) cabeza; (*mind*) mente *f: my head was spinning,* la cabeza me daba vueltas. **2** (*on tape recorder, video*) cabezal *m.* **3** (*of bed, table*) cabecera. **4** (*of page*) principio. **5** (*on beer*) espuma. **6** (*cape*) cabo, punta. **7** (*of school, company*) director,-ra. **8** (*cattle*) res *f: four hundred head of cattle,* cuatrocientas reses, cuatrocientas cabezas de ganado. **9** (*coin*) cara. **10** (*of cabbage, lettuce*) cogollo; (*of cauliflower*) pella. – **11** *adj* principal, jefe: *he's the head gardener,* es el jardinero jefe. – **12** *t* (*company, list etc*) encabezar: *she heads the list of winners,* ella encabeza la lista de ganadores. **13** (*ball*) rematar de cabeza, dar un cabezazo a, cabecear: *he headed the ball into the net,* metió un gol de un cabezazo.

◆ **to head for** *t insep* dirigirse hacia: *where are you heading for?,* ¿adónde te diriges?; *the company is heading for big trouble,* la compañía se enfrenta a graves problemas, la compañía va a tener problemas. ‖ **to head off** 1 *i* marcharse, irse: *it's time I was heading off,* es hora de que me marche. – 2 *t sep (divert)* interceptar; *(avoid)* evitar: *if we take this short cut we can head them off at the river,* si tomamos este atajo le interceptaremos en el río; *can we head off disaster?,* ¿podemos evitar el desastre?

● **from head to toe / from head to foot,** de pies a cabeza. ‖ **heads or tails?,** ¿cara o cruz? ‖ **off the top of one's head,** sin pensárselo, así de entrada. ‖ **on your own head be it!,** ¡allá te las compongas! ‖ **per head,** por barba, por cabeza: *it cost us £12 per head,* nos costó doce libras por barba. ‖ **to be head over heels in love with sb.,** estar locamente enamorado,-a de algn. ‖ **to be off one's head,** estar chiflado,-a. ‖ **to bite sb.'s head off,** *fam* echar una bronca a algn. ‖ **to do sth. standing on one's head,** hacer algo con los ojos vendados. ‖ **to have a good head for figures,** tener facilidad para los números. ‖ **to have a head for hights,** no padecer vértigo. ‖ **to keep one's head above water,** mantenerse a flote. ‖ **to keep one's head,** mantener la calma. ‖ **to laugh one's head off,** reírse a carcajadas. ‖ **two heads are better than one,** cuatro ojos ven más que dos.

■ **head teacher,** director,-ra. ‖ **head start,** ventaja. ‖ **head office,** oficina central.

headache ['hedeɪk] 1 *n* dolor *m* de cabeza. 2 *fig* quebradero de cabeza.

headband ['hedbænd] *n* cinta (para la cabeza).

headboard ['hedbɔːd] *n* cabecera.

headdress ['heddres] *n* tocado.

headed ['hedɪd] *adj (paper)* con membrete.

header ['hedəʳ] *n (football)* cabezazo; *(dive)* salto de cabeza.

head-first [hed'fɜːst] *adv* de cabeza.

headgear ['hedgɪəʳ] *n (hat)* sombrero; *(for women)* tocado.

head-hunter [hed'hʌntəʳ] 1 *n* cazador,-ra de cabezas, jíbaro,-a. 2 *fam fig* cazatalentos *mf.*

heading ['hedɪŋ] 1 *n (of chapter)* encabezamiento, título. 2 *(letterhead)* membrete *m.*

headlamp ['hedlæmp] *n* AUTO faro.

headland ['hedlənd] *n* cabo, punta, promontorio.

headlight ['hedlaɪt] *n* AUTO faro.

headline ['hedlaɪn] 1 *n* titular *m.* – 2 *t (newspaper)* poner en los titulares. 3 *(emphasize)* remarcar, subrayar. 4 US encabezar la lista de artistas de: *Bruce Springsteen headlines tomorrow's Charity Performance,* Bruce Springsteen encabecerá el Concierto Benéfico de mañana.

● **to hit the headlines,** ser noticia de actualidad, ser noticia de primera plana.

■ **news headlines,** resumen *m* de las noticias más destacadas.

headlong ['hedlɒŋ] 1 *adj (headfirst)* de cabeza; *(hasty)* precipitado,-a, impetuoso,-a. – 2 *adv (hastily)* precipitadamente, impetuosamente: *they rushed headlong into setting up the new venture,* se volcaron precipitadamente en el montaje de la nueva empresa. 3 *(headfirst)* de cabeza.

headmaster [hed'mɑːstəʳ] *n* director *m.*

headmistress [hed'mɪstrəs] *n* directora.

head-on [hed'ɒn] 1 *adj* frontal: *the car was involved in a head-on collision,* el coche se vio involucrado en un choque frontal. 2 *fig* frontal: *management and unions are set for a head-on confrontation,* la patronal y los sindicatos están encaminados hacia una confrontación frontal. – 3 *adv* de frente.

headphones ['hedfəʊnz] *npl* auriculares *mpl,* cascos *mpl.*

headquarters ['hedkwɔːtəz] 1 *n (of an organization)* sede *f;* *(main office)* oficina central. 2 *(of a firm)* razón *f* social, domicilio social. 3 MIL cuartel *m* general. 4 *fig* centro de operaciones, cuartel *m* general.

▲ *Puede usarse indistintamente con verbo en singular o en plural.*

headrest ['hedrest] *n* cabecero, cabezal *m.*

headroom ['hedruːm] 1 *n* altura libre sobre la cabeza, espacio libre sobre la cabeza. 2 *(bridges etc)* altura libre de paso, luz *f.*

headscarf ['hedskɑːf] *n* pañuelo.

▲ *pl* **headscarves** ['hedskɑːvz].

headset ['hedset] *n* auriculares *mpl.*

headship ['hedʃɪp] *n (gen)* dirección *f.*

headstand ['hedstænd] *n* posición *f* de cabeza.

headstone ['hedstəʊn] 1 *n (tombstone)* lápida mortuoria. 2 ARCH piedra angular.

headstrong ['hedstrɒŋ] *adj* cabezota, obstinado,-a, testarudo,-a.

headway ['hedweɪ] *n (progress - gen)* progreso; *(of - ship)* salida.

● **to make headway,** *fig* avanzar, progresar, hacer progresos.

headwind ['hedwɪnd] *n* viento de proa, viento contrario.

headword ['hedwɜːd] *n* entrada, lema.

heady ['hedɪ] *adj (intoxicating)* embriagador,-ra, fuerte.

▲ *comp* **headier,** *superl* **headiest.**

heal [hiːl] 1 *t (disease, patient)* curar; *(wound)* cicatrizar, curar. 2 *fig* curar, remediar. – 3 *i (wounds)* cicatrizar, cicatrizarse; *(people)* curarse, sanar. 4 *fig* remediarse.

◆ **to heal up** *i* curarse, cicatrizarse.

healer ['hiːləʳ] *n* curador,-ra, sanador,-ra.

healing ['hiːlɪŋ] 1 *n (of disease)* curación *f,* cura; *(of wound)* cicatrización *f.* – 2 *adj (ointment)* cicatrizante; *(remedy)* curativo,-a; *(soothing)* apaciguador,-ra, conciliador,-ra.

health [helθ] 1 *n* salud *f.* 2 *(service)* sanidad *f.* 3 *fig* prosperidad *f.*

● **to be in good/bad health,** estar bien/mal de salud. ‖ **to drink to sb.'s health,** beber a la salud de algn. ‖ **to your health!,** ¡a tu salud!

■ **health authorities,** autoridades *fpl* sanitarias. ‖ **health centre,** ambulatorio, centro médico. ‖ **health certificate,** certificado médico. ‖ **health foods,** alimentos *mpl* naturales. ‖ **health service,** Dirección *f* General de Sanidad. ‖ **health visitor,** A.T.S., enfermero,-a visitante.

healthful ['helθful] *adj fml dated* saludable, sano,-a.

healthy ['helθɪ] 1 *adj (gen)* sano,-a. 2 *(good for health)* saludable. 3 *(appetite)* bueno,-a: *he has a healthy appetite,* tiene buen apetito. 4 *(prosperous)* próspero,-a; *(disposition)* sensato,-a. 5 *fig* sano,-a: *she has a very healthy outlook on life,* su actitud de cara a la vida es muy sana.

▲ *comp* **healthier,** *superl* **healthiest.**

heap [hiːp] 1 *n* montón *m.* – 2 *t (pile)* amontonar, apilar. 3 *(spoons)* colmar; *(plate)* llenar. 4 *(praise, presents)* colmar: *the president heaped praises on him,* el presidente lo colmó de elogios.

● **to be at the bottom of the heap,** *fam* ser el último mono. ‖ **heaps of,** *fam* montones de, cantidad de, muchísimo,-a: *she's got heaps of money,* tiene montones de dinero.

hear [hɪəʳ] **1** *t* (*gen*) oír: *do you hear me?,* ¿me oyes? **2** (*perceive*) sentir; (*listen to*) escuchar. **3** (*lecture*) asistir a; (*a news item*) saber. **4** JUR (*case*) ver; (*witness, defendant*) oír. **5** (*refuse*) negarse a: *she wouldn't hear of moving house,* se negó rotundamente a trasladarse; *I won't hear of it!,* ¡ni hablar! **6** (*find out*) enterarse: *I've heard she's leaving,* me he enterado que se marcha.

◆ **to hear out** *t sep* escuchar hasta el final.

● **have you heard the one about ...,** (*humour*) sabes el chiste de ... ‖ **hear, hear!,** ¡muy bien! ‖ **I can't hear myself think,** *fam* no puedo pensar con tanto ruido. ‖ **to hear from,** tener noticias de. ‖ **to hear of,** oír hablar de.

▲ *pt & pp heard* [hɜːd].

hearer ['hɪərəʳ] *n* oyente *mf*.

hearing ['hɪərɪŋ] **1** *n* (*sense*) oído. **2** (*act of hearing*) audición *f.* **3** JUR audiencia, vista.

● **to be hard of hearing,** ser duro,-a de oído, ser sordo,-a. ‖ **to give sb. a fair hearing,** *fig* escuchar a algn. con imparcialidad, dejar hablar a algn. ‖ **within hearing distance,** al alcance del oído.

■ **hearing aid,** audífono.

hearsay ['hɪəseɪ] *n* rumores *mpl*: *it's just hearsay,* son sólo rumores.

● **by hearsay,** de oídas.

hearse [hɜːs] *n* coche *m* fúnebre.

heart [hɑːt] **1** *n* ANAT corazón *m*: *he has serious heart trouble,* padece gravemente del corazón. **2** (*centre of feeling*) corazón *m*: *she broke his heart,* le rompió el corazón; *he has a kind heart,* tiene buen corazón. **3** (*courage*) valor *m*, corazón *m*. **4** (*of lettuce etc*) cogollo; (*of place*) corazón *m*, centro; (*of question*) fondo, quid *m*, meollo: *we soon got to the heart of the matter,* pronto llegamos al fondo de la cuestión. – **5** hearts, *npl* (*cards*) corazones *mpl*; (*Spanish cards*) copas *fpl*.

● **a change of heart,** un cambio de opinión. ‖ **after my own heart,** de los/las que me gustan: *he's a man after my own heart,* es un hombre de los que me gustan. ‖ **at heart,** en el fondo. ‖ **by heart,** de memoria. ‖ **have a heart!,** ¡ten piedad! ‖ **his (her etc) heart sank,** se le cayó el alma a los pies. ‖ **to get to the heart of sth.,** llegar al fondo de algo. ‖ **to have one's heart in one's mouth,** tener el alma en un hilo. ‖ **to have one's heart in sth.,** volcarse en cuerpo y alma en algo. ‖ **to have one's heart in the right place,** ser buena persona. ‖ **to lose heart,** descorazonarse, desanimarse. ‖ **to pour one's heart out,** abrir el corazón. ‖ **to take sth. to heart,** tomarse algo muy a pecho. ‖ **to wear one's heart on one's sleeve,** ir con el corazón en la mano.

■ **heart attack,** infarto de miocardio. ‖ **heart transplant,** trasplante *m* de corazón.

heartbeat ['hɑːtbiːt] *n* latido del corazón.

heartbreak ['hɑːtbreɪk] *n* angustia, congoja.

heartbreaking ['hɑːtbreɪkɪŋ] *adj* angustioso,-a, desgarrador,-ra, penoso,-a: *it was heartbreaking to see them like this,* daba pena verlos así.

heartbroken ['hɑːtbrəʊkən] *adj* hundido,-a, angustiado,-a.

● **to be heartbroken,** tener el corazón destrozado.

heartburn ['hɑːtbɜːn] *n* ardor *m* de estómago, acedía, ardores *mpl*.

hearten ['hɑːtən] *t* animar, alentar.

heartening ['hɑːtənɪŋ] *adj* alentador,-ra.

heartfelt ['hɑːtfelt] *adj* sincero,-a, cordial, sentido,-a: *my heartfelt thanks,* mi más efusivo agradecimiento; *my most heartfelt sympathy,* mi más sentido pésame.

hearth [hɑːθ] **1** *n* (*of fireplace*) hogar *m*, chimenea. **2** *fig* hogar *m*.

● **without hearth or home,** sin casa ni hogar.

hearthache ['hɑːteɪk] **1** *n* angustia, pena, pesar *m*. **2** (*deep feeling of sorrow*) congoja.

heartily ['hɑːtɪlɪ] **1** *adv* (*warmly*) cordialmente; (*sincerely*) sinceramente. **2** (*strongly*) enérgicamente, fuertemente; (*hungrily*) con ganas. **3** (*effusively*) efusivamente; (*enthusiastically*) con entusiasmo.

heartiness ['hɑːtɪnəs] **1** *n* (*warmth*) cordialidad *f*; (*sincerity*) sinceridad *f*. **2** (*enthusiasm*) entusiasmo; (*friendliness*) campechanía, afabilidad *f*.

heartless ['hɑːtləs] *adj* cruel, insensible, despiadado,-a, inhumano,-a.

heartlessly ['hɑːtləslɪ] *adv* cruelmente, despiadadamente.

heartlessness ['hɑːtləsnəs] *n* crueldad *f*, inhumanidad *f*.

heart-rending ['hɑːtrendɪŋ] *adj* angustioso,-a, desgarrador,-ra, conmovedor,-ra.

heartstrings ['hɑːtstrɪŋz] *npl* corazón *m*, fibras *fpl* del corazón.

● **it tugs at your heartstrings,** cala muy hondo, toca la fibra sensible.

heartthrob ['hɑːtθrɒb] *n fam* ídolo.

heart-to-heart [hɑːttə'hɑːt] **1** *n* charla íntima y franca: *we must get together and have a good heart-to-heart,* tenemos que quedar y sincerarnos el uno con el otro. – **2** *adj* franco,-a, sincero,-a, íntimo,-a.

hearty ['hɑːtɪ] **1** *adj* (*person*) campechano,-a. **2** (*welcome*) cordial. **3** (*meal*) abundante.

▲ *comp heartier, superl heartiest.*

heat [hiːt] **1** *n* (*warmth*) calor *m*. **2** *fig* calor *m*, pasión *f*, ardor *m*, vehemencia: *in the heat of the moment she said things she later regretted,* en un arrebato de furia dijo cosas de las que luego se arrepintió; *in the heat of the moment I left the keys inside,* con las prisas olvidé las llaves dentro de casa. **3** (*heating*) calefacción *f.* **4** SP eliminatoria, serie *f.* **5** ZOOL celo. – **6** *t* calentar. **7** *fig* acalorar.

◆ **to heat up 1** *i* (*warm up*) calentarse; (*to raise excitement etc*) acalorarse. – **2** *t sep* calentar. **3** *fig* acalorar.

● **on heat / in heat,** en celo. ‖ **to turn on the heat,** presionar, ejercer presiones.

■ **heat rash,** sarpullido.

heated ['hiːtɪd] **1** *adj fig* (*argument*) acalorado,-a. **2** (*room*) con calefacción *f.*

● **to get heated about sth.,** acalorarse por algo.

heater ['hiːtəʳ] *n* calentador *m.*

heath [hiːθ] **1** *n* (*land*) brezal *m.* **2** (*plant*) brezo.

heathen ['hiːðən] **1** *n* (*non Christian*) pagano,-a. **2** *fig* bárbaro, salvaje *m.* – **3** *adj* (*not Christian*) pagano,-a. **4** *fig* bárbaro,-a, salvaje.

■ **the heathen,** los paganos *mpl.*

heather ['heðəʳ] *n* BOT brezo.

heating ['hiːtɪŋ] *n* calefacción *f.*

heatstroke ['hiːtstrəʊk] *n* MED insolación *f.*

heatwave ['hiːtweɪv] *n* ola de calor.

heave [hiːv] **1** *n* (*pull*) tirón *m*; (*push*) empujón *m*. – **2** *t* (*pull*) tirar; (*lift*) levantar. **3** (*push*) empujar. **4** *fam* (*throw*) lanzar, arrojar. – **5** *i* (*rise and fall*) subir y bajar; (*pant*) jadear. **6** (*retch*) tener náuseas; (*chest*) jadear. **7** MAR cabecear.

◆ **to heave to** *i* MAR ponerse al pairo.
● **to heave a sigh of relief,** *fig* suspirar con alivio.
▲ En **7** y *heave to* *pt* & *pp* *hove* [həʊv].
heaven ['hevən] **1** *n* cielo. **2** *fam* gloria, paraíso. – **3** heavens, *npl* cielo.
● **to be in seventh heaven,** estar en el séptimo cielo.
‖ **to stink to high heaven,** *fam* apestar. ‖ **this is heaven!,** *fam* ¡ésto es la gloria! ‖ **heavens!,** ¡cielos! ‖ **good heavens!,** *fam* ¡santo cielo!, ¡por Dios!, ¡madre mía!
‖ **thank heavens!,** ¡gracias a Dios! ‖ **for heaven's sake!,** *fam* ¡por el amor de Dios! ‖ **heaven knows!,** *fam* ¡ni idea! ‖ **heaven forbid!,** ¡no lo quiera Dios! ‖ **to move heaven and earth,** mover cielo y tierra.
heavenly ['hevənlɪ] **1** *adj* celestial. **2** *fig* divino,-a. **3** ASTRON celeste.
■ **heavenly body,** cuerpo celeste.
heaven-sent ['hevən'sent] *adj fig* llovido,-a del cielo, milagroso,-a.
heavenward ['hevənwəd] *adv* hacia el cielo.
heavenwards ['hevənwədz] *adv* → **heavenward**.
heavily ['hevɪlɪ] **1** *adv* (*fall, move, step, etc*) pesadamente; (*rain*) fuertemente, mucho. **2** (*sleep etc*) profundamente; (*drink*) con exceso, mucho; (*breathe*) con dificultad *f*.
● **to lose heavily,** SP sufrir una fuerte derrota; (*in gambling*) perder muchísimo dinero.
heaviness ['hevɪnəs] *n* (*of body*) pesadez *f*; (*of weight*) peso.
■ **heaviness of heart,** tristeza.
heavy ['hevɪ] **1** *adj* (*gen*) pesado,-a. **2** (*rain, blow*) fuerte, pesado,-a. **3** (*traffic*) denso,-a. **4** (*sleep*) profundo,-a: *he's a very heavy sleeper,* tiene el sueño muy profundo. **5** (*crop*) abundante. **6** (*atmosphere*) cargado,-a. **7** (*loss, expenditure*) grande, considerable, cuantioso,-a: *he got a heavy fine for speeding,* le pusieron una multa elevada por exceso de velocidad.
● **to be a heavy drinker/smoker,** beber/fumar mucho.
▲ *comp* **heavier,** *superl* **heaviest**.
heavy-duty ['hevɪ'djuːtɪ] *adj* (*clothes, shoes etc*) de faena, resistente; (*equipment, machinery etc*) reforzado,-a, robusto,-a, para grandes cargas.
heavy-handed ['hevɪ'hændɪd] *adj* (*harsh, unkind*) severo,-a, poco amable, autoritario,-a; (*clumsy*) torpe; (*tactless*) poco considerado,-a, poco delicado,-a.
heavyweight ['hevɪweɪt] **1** *n* SP peso pesado. **2** *fig* peso pesado.
Hebrew ['hiːbruː] **1** *adj* hebreo,-a. – **2** *n* (*person*) hebreo,-a. **3** (*language*) hebreo.
Hebrides ['hebrɪdiːz] *n* Islas Hébridas, Hébridas.
heck [hek] *interj fam* ¡jolín!
● **a heck of a lot,** *fam* ¡cantidad! ¡un montón! ‖ **what the heck!,** *fam* ¡qué más da!, ¡qué demonios!
heckle ['hekəl] *t* interrumpir, provocar.
heckler ['heklə'] *n* altercador,-ra, follonero,-a.
heckling ['heklɪŋ] *n* altercado, interrupción *f* con gritos e insultos.
hectare ['hektɑː'] *n* hectárea.
hectic ['hektɪk] *adj* agitado,-a, ajetreado,-a, movido,-a: *it's been a hectic week,* ha sido una semana muy movida.
hectogram ['hektəgræm] *n* hectogramo.
hector ['hektə'] *t* intimidar, tiranizar.
hectoring ['hektərɪŋ] *adj* tiránico,-a, intimidador,-ra.
he'd [hiːz] **1** *contr* he had. **2** he would.
hedge [hedʒ] **1** *n* seto vivo. **2** *fig* protección *f*, barrera. – **3** *i* contestar con evasivas. – **4** *t* cercar, separar con un

seto. **5** *fig* (*protect*) proteger, guardar; (*protect os. against*) protegerse.
◆ **to hedge in** *t sep* cercar, rodear.
● **to be hedged about with / be hedged around with,** estar rodeado,-a de. ‖ **to hedge one's bets,** cubrir las apuestas, hacer apuestas compensatorias.
hedgehog ['hedʒhɒg] *n* ZOOL erizo.
hedgerow ['hedʒrəʊ] *n* seto vivo.
heed [hiːd] **1** *n* atención *f*: *he paid no heed to his father's advice,* hizo caso omiso a los consejos de su padre. – **2** *t* prestar atención a, hacer caso de.
heedless ['hiːdləs] *adj* desatento,-a, descuidado,-a, despreocupado,-a.
● **to be heedless of,** no hacer caso de.
heedlessly ['hiːdləslɪ] *adv* a la ligera, despreocupadamente.
hee-haw ['hiːhɔː] *n* rebuzno.
heel[1] [hiːl] **1** *n* ANAT talón *m*. **2** (*on shoe*) tacón *m*; (*of sock*) talón *m*. – **3** *t* poner tacón a. **4** SP talonar. **5** MAR inclinar. – **6** *i* MAR escorar.
● **to bring sb. to heel,** controlar a algn., meter a algn. en cintura. ‖ **to dig one's heels in,** ser tozudo,-a. ‖ **to be down at heel,** ir mal vestido,-a, estar desaseado,-a. ‖ **to be head over heels in love,** estar locamente enamorado,-a. ‖ **to take to one's heels,** darse a la fuga, salir pitando. ‖ **to be on sb's heels,** pisarle a algn. los talones. ‖ **to kick one's heels,** matar el tiempo. ‖ **under the heel of,** bajo el control férreo de.
■ **high heels,** zapatos *mpl* de tacón alto.
heel[2] [hiːl] **1** *t* MAR inclinar. – **2** *i* MAR escorar.
◆ **to heel over** *i* (*gen*) inclinarse; (*ship*) escorar.
heeled ['hiːld] *adj* (*shoe*) de tacón.
hefty ['heftɪ] *adj* (*person*) fuerte, fornido,-a, robusto,-a; (*object*) pesado,-a; (*large quantity*) grande, importante, considerable: *he won a hefty amount of money,* ganó una suma importante de dinero; *he received a hefty blow on the chin,* encajó un golpe fuerte en la barbilla.
▲ *comp* **heftier,** *superl* **heftiest**.
heifer ['hefə'] *n* novilla, vaquilla.
height [haɪt] **1** *n* (*gen*) altura. **2** (*altitude*) altitud *f*. **3** (*of person*) estatura: *what height is he?,* ¿cuánto mide?, ¿qué estatura tiene? **4** GEOG cumbre *f*, cima. **5** *fig* (*highest point*) colmo, cumbre *f*, cima: *the height of stupidity,* el colmo de la tontería.
● **to be afraid of heights,** tener vértigo. ‖ **to gain height,** subir. ‖ **to lose height,** bajar.
■ **the Golan Heights,** Los Altos de Golán. ‖ **average height,** estatura media, estatura normal.
heighten ['haɪtən] **1** *t fig* (*enhance*) intensificar, realzar. **2** *fig* (*enjoyment*) aumentar. **3** elevar, levantar, hacer más alto. – **4** *i* (*to increase*) aumentar; (*intensify*) intensificarse.
heinous ['heɪnəs] *adj fml lit* atroz.
heir [eə'] *n* heredero.
■ **heir apparent,** JUR heredero forzoso. ‖ **heir presumptive,** JUR presunto heredero.
heiress ['eəres] *n* heredera.
heirloom ['eəluːm] **1** *n* reliquia, joya de familia. **2** *fig* herencia.
held [held] *pt* & *pp* → **hold**.
helicopter ['helɪkɒptə'] *n* helicóptero.
heliport ['helɪpɔːt] *n* helipuerto.
helium ['hiːlɪəm] *n* CHEM helio.
hell [hel] *n* infierno.
● **a hell of a,** *fam* (*good*) estupendo,-a, fantástico,-a, genial; (*bad*) fatal, horrible. ‖ **go to hell!,** ¡vete al diablo! ‖ **like hell!,** *fam* ¡ni hablar! ‖ **to give sb. hell,** hacerle

pasar un mal rato a algn. ‖ **to have a hell of a time,** (*good*) pasarlo a lo grande, pasarlo pipa, pasarlo bomba; (*bad*) pasarlo fatal, pasarlas canutas. ‖ **to knock the hell out of,** dejar hecho,-a polvo. ‖ **to play hell with,** hacer estragos en. ‖ **... the hell?,** ¿ ... demonios?: *what the hell do you think you're doing?,* ¿qué demonios crees que estás haciendo?; *who the hell does she think she is?,* ¿quién demonios se cree que es?; *where the hell is he?,* ¿dónde demonios está?

he'll [hiːl] *contr* he will, he shall.

hell-bent [hel'bent] *adj fam* empeñado,-a, totalmente convencido,-a: *she's hell-bent on making it to the top,* está empeñada en llegar a la cima.

hellish ['helɪʃ] *adj fam* infernal.

hellishly ['helɪʃlɪ] *adv fam* muy: *it's hellishly cold there in winter,* hace un frío de mil demonios allí en invierno.

hello [he'ləʊ] **1** *interj* ¡hola! **2** (*on telephone - answering*) ¡diga!; (*- calling*) ¡oiga! **3** (*to get sb.'s attention*) ¡oiga!, ¡oye! **4** (*expressing surprise*) ¡vaya!: *hello, hello, hello! What's going on here?,* ¡vaya, vaya, vaya! ¿Qué pasa aquí?
▲ *pl* **hellos**.

helm [helm] *n* MAR timón *m*.
● **to be at the helm,** *fig* llevar el timón, gobernar.

helmet ['helmɪt] *n* casco.

helmsman ['helmzmən] *n* timonel *m*.
▲ *pl* **helmsmen** ['helmzmən].

help [help] **1** *n* (*gen*) ayuda: *I asked him for help,* le pedí ayuda; *there's no help for it,* no hay más remedio. **2** (*servant*) asistenta, criada. – **3** *interj* ¡socorro! – **4** *t* (*gen*) ayudar: *can you help us?,* ¿nos puedes ayudar?; *can I help you?,* ¿qué desea?, ¿le puedo servir en algo? **5** (*be of use*) ayudar, servir: *his ideas didn't help us at all,* sus ideas no nos sirvieron de nada. **6** (*to relieve*) aliviar: *this ointment will help the pain,* esta pomada aliviará el dolor. **7** (*avoid*) evitar.
◆ **to help out** *t sep* ayudar, echar una mano a.
● **I** (*he etc*) **can't help it,** (*I can't stop myself*) no puedo (*puede etc*) evitarlo; (*not my fault*) no es culpa mía (*suya etc*). ‖ **I couldn't help** + ger, no pude por menos que + inf: *I couldn't help wondering,* no pude por menos que preguntarme. ‖ **it can't be helped,** no hay nada que hacer. ‖ **to help os.,** servirse a sí mismo,-a: *help yourself,* ¡sírvete tú mismo!

helper ['helpə'] **1** *n* ayudante,-a *mf*, auxiliar *mf*. **2** (*collaborator*) colaborador,-ra.

helpful ['helpfʊl] **1** *adj* (*thing*) útil, práctico,-a,. **2** (*person*) amable.

helpfully ['helpfʊlɪ] *adv* amablemente.

helpfulness ['helpfʊlnəs] *n* (*usefulness*) utilidad *f*; (*kindness*) amabilidad *f*.

helping ['helpɪŋ] **1** *n* ración *f*, porción *f*: *would you like a second helping?,* ¿quiere repetir? – **2** *adj* ayuda.
● **to give sb. a helping hand,** echarle una mano a algn.

helpless ['helpləs] **1** *adj* (*unprotected*) desamparado,-a, indefenso,-a, desvalido,-a. **2** (*powerless*) impotente, incapaz, inútil: *to feel helpless,* sentirse inútil.

helplessly ['helpləslɪ] *adv* en vano, inútilmente.

helplessness ['helpləsnəs] *n* (*powerlessness*) impotencia, desamparo; (*incapability*) incapacidad *f*, inutilidad *f*.

Helsinki [hel'sɪŋkɪ] *n* Helsinki.

helter-skelter [heltə'skeltə'] **1** *adv* atropelladamente, en desbandada. – **2** *adj* ajetreado,-a. – **3** *n* (*at fair*) tobogán *m*; (*confusion*) desbandada.

Helvetia [hel'viːʃə] *n* Helvecia.

Helvetian [hel'viːʃən] **1** *adj* helvético,-a. – **2** *n* helvético,-a.

hem [hem] **1** *n* SEW dobladillo. – **2** *t* hacer un dobladillo en.
◆ **to hem in** *t sep fig* cercar, rodear.
▲ (*verbo*) *pt* & *pp* **hemmed**, *ger* **hemming**.

he-man ['hiːmæn] *n* machote *m*.
▲ *pl* **he-men** ['hiːmen].

hemisphere ['hemɪsfɪə'] *n* hemisferio.

hemispherical [hemɪs'ferɪkəl] *adj* hemisférico,-a.

hemline ['hemlaɪn] *n* (*of garment*) bajo.

hemlock ['hemlɒk] *n* BOT (*plant*) cicuta; (*tree*) tsuga.

hemoglobin [hiːmə'gləʊbɪn] *n* US → **haemoglobin**.

hemophilia [hiːmə'fiːlɪə] *n* US → **haemophilia**.

hemophiliac [hiːmə'fɪlɪæk] *adj-n* US → **haemophiliac**.

hemorrhage ['hemərɪdʒ] *n* US → **haemorrhage**.

hemorrhoids ['hemərɔɪdz] *npl* US → **haemorrhoids**.

hemp [hemp] **1** *n* BOT cáñamo. **2** (*drug*) hachís *m*, marihuana.

hemstitch ['hemstɪtʃ] *n* SEW vainica.

hen [hen] *n* (*chicken*) gallina; (*female bird*) hembra.
■ **hen party,** *fam* reunión *f* de mujeres, despedida de soltera.

hence [hens] **1** *adv fml* (*so*) por eso, por lo tanto, de ahí: *he lost his house, hence his worry,* perdió su casa, de ahí su preocupación. **2** (*from now*) de aquí a, dentro de: *five years hence,* de aquí a cinco años.

henceforth [hens'fɔːθ] *adv* de ahora en adelante.

henchman ['hentʃmən] **1** *n pej* secuaz *m*, partidario. **2** (*bodyguard*) guardaespaldas *m*.
▲ *pl* **henchmen**.

henhouse ['henhaʊs] *n* gallinero.

henna ['henə] *n* BOT alheña.

henpecked ['henpekt] *adj* dominado por la mujer: *a henpecked husband,* un calzonazos.

hepatic [hɪ'pætɪk] *adj* MED hepático,-a.

hepatitis [hepə'taɪtəs] *n* MED hepatitis *f*.

heptagon ['heptəgən] *n* heptágono.

heptagonal [hep'tægənəl] *adj* heptagonal.

her [hɜː', *unstressed* hə] **1** *pron* (*direct object*) la: *I love her,* la quiero. **2** (*indirect object*) le; (*with other third person pronouns*) se: *give her the money,* dale el dinero; *give it to her,* dáselo. **3** (*after preposition*) ella: *go with her,* vete con ella. **4** *fam* (*as subject*) ella: *listen, that's her!,* ¡escucha, es ella! – **5** *adj* su, sus; (*emphatic*) de ella: *she lent me her car,* me dejó su coche; *she took her children to school,* acompañó a sus hijos al colegio.

herald ['herəld] **1** *n* heraldo. **2** *fig* precursor *m*, anunciador *m*. – **3** *t fml lit* anunciar, proclamar.

heraldic [he'rældɪk] *adj* heráldico,-a.

heraldry ['herəldrɪ] *n* heráldica.

herb [hɜːb] *n* hierba.
■ **herb tea,** infusión de hierbas.

herbaceous [hɜː'beɪʃəs] *adj* herbáceo,-a.

herbal ['hɜːbəl] *adj* herbario,-a.

herbalist ['hɜːbəlɪst] *n* herbolario,-a.

herbicide ['hɜːbɪsaɪd] *n* herbicida *m*.

herbivore ['hɜːbɪvɔː'] *n* ZOOL herbívoro,-a.

herbivorous [hɜː'bɪvərəs] *adj* ZOOL herbívoro,-a.

herd [hɜːd] **1** *n* (*cattle*) manada; (*goats*) rebaño; (*pigs*) piara. **2** *fam* (*people*) montón *m*, multitud *f*. – **3** *t* (*animals - group*) juntar en manada; (*- drive*) conducir en manada; (*people*) llevar. – **4** *i* juntarse en manada, juntarse en rebaño.
● **to go with the herd,** ir con las masas.

■ **herd instinct,** instinto gregario.

herdsman ['hɜːdzmən] *n* (*of cattle*) vaquero; (*of sheep*) pastor *m*; (*of goats*) cabrero.
▲ *pl* **herdsmen** ['hɜːdzmən].

here [hɪəʳ] *adv* aquí: *here's the bus!*, ¡aquí viene el autobús!; *here are the envelopes you asked for,* aquí tienes los sobres que pediste; *there are lots around here,* hay muchos por aquí.
● **here and there,** aquí y allá. ‖ **here's to ...!**, ¡brindemos por ...!: *here's to the future!*, ¡brindemos por el futuro! ‖ **look here!**, ¡oye!, ¡oiga! ‖ **to be neither here nor there,** no venir al caso.

hereafter [hɪər'ɑːftəʳ] **1** *adv* de ahora en adelante. – **2 the hereafter,** *n* el más allá *m*.

hereby [hɪə'baɪ] *adv* por la presente.

hereditary [hɪ'redɪtərɪ] *adj* hereditario,-a.

heredity [hɪ'redɪtɪ] *n* herencia.

herein [hɪə'rɪn] *adv* (*inside*) aquí; (*in letter etc*) aquí mencionado,-a.

heresy ['herəsɪ] *n* herejía.
▲ *pl* **heresies.**

heretic ['herətɪk] *n* hereje *mf.*

heretical [he'retɪkəl] *adj* herético,-a.

herewith [hɪə'wɪð] *adv* adjunto,-a.

heritage ['herɪtɪdʒ] *n* herencia, patrimonio.

hermaphrodite [hɜː'mæfrədaɪt] **1** *adj* hermafrodita. – **2** *n* hermafrodita *mf.*

hermetic [hɜː'metɪk] *adj* hermético,-a.

hermetically [hɜː'metɪklɪ] *adv* herméticamente.

hermit ['hɜːmɪt] *n* ermitaño,-a, eremita *mf.*
■ **hermit crab,** ermitaño, paguro.

hermitage ['hɜːmɪtɪdʒ] *n* ermita.

hernia ['hɜːnɪə] *n* hernia.

hero ['hɪərəʊ] **1** *n* (*gen*) héroe *m.* **2** (*in novel*) protagonista *m*, personaje *m* principal.
■ **hero worship,** idolatría.
▲ *pl* **heroes.**

heroic [hɪ'rəʊɪk] **1** *adj* heroico,-a. – **2 heroics,** *npl* (*words*) grandilocuencia *f sing*; (*deeds*) actos heroicos *mpl.*

heroically [he'rəʊɪkəlɪ] *adv* heroicamente.

heroin ['herəʊɪn] *n* (*drug*) heroína.
■ **heroin addict,** heroinómano,-a.

heroine ['herəʊɪn] **1** *n* heroína. **2** (*in novel*) protagonista *f*, personaje *m* principal.

heroism ['herəʊɪzəm] *n* heroísmo.

heron ['herən] *n* garza.
■ **night heron,** martinete *m.* ‖ **purple heron,** garza imperial.

herpes ['hɜːpiːz] *n* herpe *m*, herpes *m.*

herring ['herɪŋ] *n* arenque *m.*
▲ *pl* **herring** *o* **herrings.**

herringbone ['herɪŋbəʊn] *n* (*pattern*) espinapez *m*; (*in cloth*) espiga, espiguilla.

hers [hɜːz] *pron* (*sing*) (el) suyo, (la) suya; (*pl*) (los) suyos, (las) suyas; (*emphatic*) de ella: *this pencil is hers,* este lápiz es suyo; *this pen is hers, not his,* esta pluma es de ella, no de él; *he's a friend of hers,* es amigo suyo; *hers are the nicest flowers in the street,* las suyas son las flores más bonitas de la calle.

herself [hɜː'self] **1** *pron* (*reflexive use*) se: *she poisoned herself,* se envenenó. **2** (*emphatic*) ella misma: *she made it all herself,* lo hizo todo ella misma.

hertz [hɜːts] *n* hertz *m*, hercio *m.*

he's [hiːz] **1** *contr* he is. **2** he has.

hesitant ['hezɪtənt] *adj* indeciso,-a.

hesitantly ['hezɪtəntlɪ] *adv* indecisamente, con indecisión.

hesitate ['hezɪteɪt] *i* vacilar, dudar: *please don't hesitate to call me,* no dudes en llamarme.

hesitation [hezɪ'teɪʃən] *n* duda, indecisión.
● **without hesitation,** sin dudar.

hessian ['hesɪən] *n* arpillera.

heterogeneous [hetərəʊ'dʒiːnɪəs] *adj* heterogéneo,-a.

heterosexual [hetərəʊ'seksjuəl] **1** *adj* heterosexual. – **2** *n* heterosexual *mf.*

het up [het'ʌp] *adj fam* nervioso,-a.

heuristic [hjʊ'rɪstɪk] **1** *adj* heurístico,-a. – **2 heuristics,** *n* heurística.

hew [hjuː] *t* talar.
▲ *pt* **hewed,** *pp* **hewed** *o* **hewn.**

hexagon ['heksəgən] *n* hexágono.

hexagonal [hek'sægənəl] *adj* hexagonal.

hey [heɪ] *interj* ¡eh!, ¡oye!, ¡oiga!

heyday ['heɪdeɪ] **1** *n* auge *m*, apogeo. **2** *fig* flor *f*, los mejores años: *she was in the heyday of youth when an accident ended it all,* estaba en la flor de la juventud cuando un accidente lo truncó todo.

HGV ['eɪtʃ'dʒiː'viː] *abbr* GB (*heavy goods vehicle*) vehículo de carga pesada.

HH [hɪz'haɪnəs, hɜː'haɪnəs] *abbr* (*His Highness, Her Highness*) Su Alteza; (*abbreviation*) SA.

hi [haɪ] *interj fam* ¡hola!

hiatus [haɪ'eɪtəs] **1** *n* LING hiato. **2** *fml fig* (*gap*) laguna, interrupción *f*, vacío.
▲ *pl* **hiatuses** *o* **hiatus.**

hibernate ['haɪbəneɪt] *i* hibernar.

hibernation [haɪbə'neɪʃən] *n* hibernación *f.*

hibiscus [haɪ'bɪskəs] *n* BOT hibisco *m.*

hiccough ['hɪkʌp] *n-i* → **hiccup.**

hiccup ['hɪkʌp] **1** *n* hipo: *to have hiccups,* tener hipo. – **2** *i* tener hipo, hipar.
▲ (*verbo*) *pt & pp* **hiccupped,** *ger* **hiccupping.**

hick [hɪk] **1** *n* US *fam* (*yokel*) cateto,-a, paleto,-a, palurdo,-a. – **2** *adj* cateto,-a, paleto,-a, palurdo,-a.

hickory ['hɪkərɪ] *n* BOT nogal *m* americano.
▲ *pl* **hickories.**

hid [hɪd] *pt & pp* → **hide.**

hidden ['hɪdən] **1** *pp* → **hide.** – **2** *adj* escondido,-a. **3** *fig* oculto,-a.

hide¹ [haɪd] **1** *n* (*concealed place*) puesto de observación, escondrijo, escondite *m.* – **2** *t* (*conceal*) esconder; (*obscure*) ocultar, tapar: *he's good at hiding his feelings,* sabe muy bien cómo ocultar sus sentimientos; *the clouds hid the sun all day,* las nubes taparon el sol todo el día. – **3** *i* esconderse, ocultarse.
▲ *pt* **hid,** *pp* **hid** *o* **hidden.**

hide² [haɪd] **1** *n* piel *f*, cuero. **2** *fig* (*of a person*) pellejo.
● **to see neither hide nor hair of sb.,** *fig* no haberle visto el pelo a algn. ‖ **to have a hide like an elephant,** *fig* tener la sensibilidad de un paquidermo.

hide-and-seek [haɪdən'siːk] *n* escondite *m.*
● **to play hide-and-seek,** jugar al escondite.

hidebound ['haɪdbaʊnd] *adj* chapado,-a a la antigua, conservador,-ra, rígido,-a.

hideous ['hɪdɪəs] **1** *adj* (*terrible*) horroroso,-a, atroz. **2** (*ugly*) horrendo,-a, espantoso.

hideously ['hɪdɪəslɪ] *adv* horrorosamente, horriblemente, terriblemente: *he was hideously deformed,* era terriblemente deforme.

hide-out ['haɪdaʊt] *n* escondrijo, escondite *m*, guarida.

hiding¹ [ˈhaɪdɪŋ] *n* (*beating*) paliza.
● **to give sb. a good hiding,** propinarle a algn. una buena paliza.
hiding² [ˈhaɪdɪŋ] *n* ocultación *f.*
● **to go into hiding,** esconderse.
hierarchic [haɪəˈrɑːkɪk] *adj* jerárquico,-a.
hierarchical [haɪˈrɑːkɪkəl] *adj* jerárquico,-a.
hierarchy [ˈhaɪərɑːkɪ] *n* jerarquía.
▲ *pl* **hierarchies.**
hieroglyph [ˈhaɪərəglɪf] *n* jeroglífico.
hieroglyphics [haɪərəˈglɪfɪks] *npl* jeroglíficos *mpl.*
hi-fi [ˈhaɪfaɪ] *n* hifi *m,* alta fidelidad *f.*
● **hi-fi equipment,** equipo de alta fidelidad.
higgledy-piggledy [hɪgəldɪˈpɪgəldɪ] **1** *adj* desordenado,-a, revuelto,-a. – **2** *adv* a la buena de Dios, en desorden.
high [haɪ] **1** *adj* alto,-a: *there are many high buildings in New York,* Nueva York tiene muchos edificios altos; *how high is that mountain?,* ¿qué altura tiene aquella montaña? **2** (*elevated, intense*) alto,-a, elevado,-a: *he's always had high blood pressure,* siempre ha tenido la presión sanguínea alta; *consumer prices are high,* los precios al consumo son elevados. **3** (*important*) alto,-a, importante; (*strong*) fuerte: *she has a high position in life,* ostenta una posición elevada en la vida; *high winds swept in from the north,* soplaron vientos fuertes del norte; *he has a very high opinion of his wife,* habla muy bien de su esposa. **4** MUS alto,-a. **5** (*very good*) bueno,-a,: *she has a very high standard,* ella tiene un nivel muy alto; *to have high principles,* tener buenos principios. **6** (*going rotten - food*) pasado,-a; (*- game*) manido,-a. **7** (*of time*) pleno,-a. **8** *sl* (*on drugs*) flipado,-a, colocado,-a. – **9** *adv* alto: *feelings often run high at football games,* a menudo los ánimos se exaltan en los partidos de fútbol. – **10** *n* punto máximo, récord *m*: *the stock market reached an all-time high,* la Bolsa marcó un récord absoluto. **11** METEOR zona de alta presión, anticiclón *m.*
● **to be in for the high jump,** *fam* tener los días contados. ‖ **to be in high spirits,** estar de buen humor. ‖ **to be on a high,** sentirse muy bien. ‖ **to fly high,** (*bird, plane*) volar alto, volar a gran altura; (*person*) picar alto. ‖ **to have friends in high places,** estar muy bien relacionado,-a. ‖ **to leave sb. high and dry,** dejar plantado,-a a algn. ‖ **to search high and low for sth.,** buscar algo por todas partes.
■ **high chair,** trona. ‖ **High Commissioner,** Alto Comisario, Alto Comisionado. ‖ **High Court,** Tribunal *m* Supremo. ‖ **high fidelity,** alta fidelidad *f.* ‖ **high jump,** SP salto de altura. ‖ **high noon,** mediodía *m.* ‖ **high priest,** sumo sacerdote *m.* ‖ **high road,** carretera principal. ‖ **high season,** temporada alta. ‖ **high school,** GB instituto de enseñanza secundaria (*para alumnos de entre 11 y 18 años*); US instituto de enseñanza secundaria (*para alumnos de entre 15 y 18 años*). ‖ **high tea,** merienda-cena. ‖ **the high life,** la buena vida. ‖ **the High Street,** la Calle Mayor.
high-and-mighty [haɪənˈmaɪtɪ] *adj* (*arrogant*) engreído,-a.
highball [ˈhaɪbɔːl] *n* (*us*) whisky *m* con sifón y hielo.
highborn [ˈhaɪbɔːn] *adj* linajudo,-a, de alta alcurnia.
highbrow [ˈhaɪbraʊ] **1** *adj* intelectual. – **2** *n* intelectual *mf.*
high-class [haɪˈklɑːs] *adj* (*classy*) de categoría; (*superior*) de calidad *f,* de categoría superior.
higher [ˈhaɪəʳ] **1** *comp* → **high.** – **2** *adj* superior. **3** (*bigger*) más alto,-a; (*number, velocity etc*) mayor.

■ **higher education,** enseñanza superior.
highfalutin [haɪfəˈluːtɪn] *adj fam pej* pomposo,-a, presumido,-a, presuntuoso,-a.
highfaluting [haɪfəˈluːtɪŋ] *adj* → **highfalutin.**
high-flown [ˈhaɪˈfləʊn] *adj* altisonante, rimbombante.
high-flyer [haɪˈflaɪəʳ] *n fig* persona muy ambiciosa.
high-flying [ˈhaɪˈflaɪɪŋ] *adj* (*aircraft*) de vuelo alto; (*person*) ambicioso,-a.
high-frecuency [haɪˈfriːkwensɪ] *adj* RAD de alta frecuencia.
high-grade [ˈhaɪˈgreɪd] *adj* de calidad superior.
high-handed [ˈhaɪˈhændɪd] *adj* (*arbitrary*) arbitrario,-a; (*authoritarian*) autoritario,-a, despótico,-a, tiránico,-a.
high-heeled [ˈhaɪˈhiːld] *adj* de tacón alto.
highland [ˈhaɪlənd] *adj* montañoso,-a.
highlander [ˈhaɪləndəʳ] *n* montañés,-esa.
highlands [ˈhaɪləndz] *npl* GEOG tierras *fpl* altas.
highlight [ˈhaɪlaɪt] **1** *t* destacar, hacer resaltar: *her words highlighted the importance of the event,* sus palabras pusieron de relieve la importancia del acontecimiento. **2** (*with pen*) marcar (*con un rotulador fosforescente*). – **3** *n* ART toque *m* de luz. **4** (*hairdressing*) reflejo. **5** *fig* (*especially in showbusiness*) atracción *f* principal; (*most outstanding*) punto culminante, momento culminante; (*aspect or feature*) característica notable, aspecto notable: *the highlights of the game will be shown again tonight,* las jugadas más interesantes serán transmitidas de nuevo esta noche.
■ **highlight bar,** barra seleccionadora.
highly [ˈhaɪlɪ] *adv* (*very*) muy; (*favourably*) muy bien: *he thinks very highly of you,* le tiene en mucho a Vd; *she was highly pleased,* estuvo muy contenta.
highly-strung [haɪlɪˈstrʌŋ] *adj* tenso,-a, hipertenso,-a, muy nervioso,-a.
high-minded [haɪˈmaɪndɪd] *adj* noble, magnánimo,-a.
Highness [ˈhaɪnəs] *n* Alteza *mf.*
● **Your Highness,** Su Alteza *mf.*
high-pitched [ˈhaɪˈpɪtʃt] *adj* (*sound, voice*) agudo,-a, estridente; (*roof*) empinado,-a.
high-powered [ˈhaɪˈpaʊəd] **1** *adj* (*engine*) de gran potencia. **2** (*person*) dinámico,-a.
high-ranking [haɪˈræŋkɪŋ] *adj* de alta graduación, superior, de categoría.
■ **high-ranking official,** alto funcionario.
high-rise [ˈhaɪraɪz] **1** *adj* (*buildings*) alto,-a. – **2** *n* rascacielos *m,* bloque *m* de pisos: *lots of people live in high-rises,* mucha gente vive en bloques de pisos.
high-speed [ˈhaɪspiːd] **1** *adj* rápido,-a, de gran velocidad. – **2** *adv* rápido,-a, de gran velocidad.
■ **high-speed lens,** objetivo ultrarrápido. ‖ **high-speed train,** tren *m* de alta velocidad.
high-spirited [haɪˈspɪrɪtɪd] *adj* (*person*) muy animado,-a, alegre; (*horse*) fogoso,-a.
highway [ˈhaɪweɪ] **1** *n* US autovía. **2** JUR vía pública.
■ **Highway Code,** GB código de la circulación.
highwayman [ˈhaɪweɪmən] *n* salteador *m* de caminos, bandido.
hijack [ˈhaɪdʒæk] **1** *n* secuestro. – **2** *t* secuestrar.
hijacker [ˈhaɪdʒækəʳ] *n* (*gen*) secuestrador,-ra; (*of plane*) secuestrador,-ra, pirata *m* del aire.
hijacking [ˈhaɪdʒækɪŋ] *n* secuestro.
hike [haɪk] **1** *n* (*walk*) excursión *f* a pie. **2** US *fam* aumento de precio. – **3** *i* ir de excursión, hacer una excursión. – **4** *t fam* aumentar los precios: *many stores hiked up their prices after the summer,* muchas tiendas aumentaron sus precios después del verano.

● **to go on a hike / go for a hike,** ir de excursión, hacer una excursión a pie.
hiker ['haɪkəʳ] *n* excursionista *mf.*
hiking ['haɪkɪŋ] *n* excursionismo a pie.
● **to go hiking,** ir de excursión, hacer una excursión.
hilarious [hɪ'leərɪəs] *adj* graciosísimo,-a, hilarante, divertidísimo,-a.
hilariously [hɪ'leərɪəslɪ] hilariously funny, *adj* graciosísimo,-a, divertidísimo,-a, para partirse de risa.
hilarity [hɪ'lærɪtɪ] *n* hilaridad *f.*
hill [hɪl] **1** *n* colina, cerro. **2** *(slope)* cuesta.
● **to be as old as the hills,** ser más viejo,-a que Matusalén. ‖ **to be over the hill,** *fam* ser viejo,-a ya. ‖ **to take to the hills,** echarse al monte.
■ **hill climb,** subida en cuesta.
hillbilly ['hɪlbɪlɪ] *n us pej* palurdo,-a, paleto,-a, cateto,-a.
▲ *pl hillbillies.*
hillock ['hɪlək] *n (small hill)* altozano, collado; *(mound)* montículo.
hillside ['hɪlsaɪd] *n* ladera.
hilltop ['hɪltɒp] *n* cumbre *f,* cima.
hilly ['hɪlɪ] *adj* montañoso,-a, accidentado,-a: *it's very hilly country,* es una zona muy montañosa.
▲ *comp hillier, superl hilliest.*
hilt [hɪlt] *n* puño, empuñadura.
● **up to the hilt,** al máximo, totalmente: *he's up to the hilt in debts,* está endeudado hasta el cuello.
him [hɪm] **1** *pron (direct object)* lo: *I love him,* lo quiero. **2** *(indirect object)* le; *(with other pronouns)* se: *give him the money,* dale el dinero; *give it to him,* dáselo. **3** *(after preposition)* él: *we went with him,* fuimos con él. **4** *fam (as subject)* él: *it's him!,* ¡es él!
Himalayan [hɪmə'leɪən] *adj* himalayo,-a.
Himalayas [hɪmə'leɪəz] the Himalayas, *npl* el Himalaya *m sing.*
himself [hɪm'self] **1** *pron (reflexive)* se; *(alone)* solo, por sí mismo: *he cut himself,* se cortó; *he did it by himself,* lo hizo solo. **2** *(emphatic)* él mismo, sí mismo, en persona: *he told me so himself,* me lo dijo en persona, me lo dijo él mismo.
hind[1] [haɪnd] *adj* trasero,-a.
● **to talk the hind legs off a donkey,** hablar por los codos.
hind[2] [haɪnd] *n (deer)* cierva.
hinder ['hɪndəʳ] **1** *t* dificultar, entorpecer, estorbar, impedir: *to hinder sb. from doing sth.,* impedir a algn. hacer algo. – **2** *i* ser un estorbo.
hindquarters ['haɪndkwɔːtəz] *npl* cuartos *mpl* traseros.
hindrance ['hɪndrəns] *n* estorbo, obstáculo.
hindsight ['haɪndsaɪt] *n* retrospectiva.
Hindu [hɪn'duː, 'hɪnduː] **1** *n* hindú *mf.* – **2** *adj* hindú.
Hinduism ['hɪnduɪzəm] *n* hinduismo.
hinge [hɪndʒ] **1** *n* TECH gozne *m,* bisagra. **2** *(for stamps)* fijasellos *m.* **3** *fig* eje *m.* – **4** *t* engoznar. – **5** *i* girar sobre goznes.
◆ **to hinge on** *t insep* depender de: *the result of the test hinges on many factors,* el resultado de la prueba depende de muchos factores.
hinged [hɪndʒd] *adj* de bisagra, con goznes *mpl.*
hint [hɪnt] **1** *n* insinuación *f,* indirecta: *to drop a hint,* lanzar una indirecta. **2** *(advice)* consejo, sugerencia: *hints for tourists,* consejos para turistas. **3** *(clue)* pista: *he gave me lots of useful hints,* me dio muchas pistas útiles. **4** *(trace)* pizca: *the sauce had a hint of curry,* la salsa tenía una pizca de curry. **5** *(sign)* sombra: *there isn't a hint of truth in her story,* no hay una sombra de verdad

en su historia. – **6** *t (imply)* insinuar, aludir a: *she hinted at the need for change,* aludió a la necesidad de efectuar cambios. – **7** *i (suggest indirectly)* lanzar indirectas: *she hinted at going out with him,* ella le lanzó indirectas para salir con él.
● **to take a hint,** darse por aludido,-a.
hinterland ['hɪntəlænd] *n* GEOG interior *m.*
hip[1] [hɪp] *n* ANAT cadera.
■ **hip bath,** baño de asiento. ‖ **hip flask,** petaca.
hip[2] [hɪp] *n* BOT escaramujo.
hip[3] [hɪp] **hip hip hooray!,** *phr* ¡hurra!
hip[4] [hɪp] *adj sl* marchoso,-a, en la onda: *he's a hip guy,* es un tío marchoso.
hipbone ['hɪpbəʊn] *n* ANAT hueso de la cadera.
hippie ['hɪpɪ] **1** *n fam* hippie *mf.* – **2** *adj* hippie.
hippo ['hɪpəʊ] *n* ZOOL *fam* hipopótamo.
▲ *pl hippos.*
hippopotamus [hɪpə'pɒtəməs] *n* ZOOL hipopótamo.
hippy ['hɪpɪ] **1** *n fam* hippie *(mf).* – **2** *adj* hippie.
▲ *pl hippies.*
hire ['haɪəʳ] **1** *n* alquiler *m*: *in-line skates for hire,* se alquilan patines en línea; *taxi for hire,* taxi libre. – **2** *t (rent)* alquilar: *we hired a sailing boat,* alquilamos un velero. **3** *(employ)* contratar: *he hired five workers,* contrató cinco trabajadores.
◆ **to hire out** *t sep (equipment, vehicles etc)* alquilar; *(people)* contratar.
■ **car hire,** alquiler *m* de coches. ‖ **hire purchase,** compra a plazos.
hired ['haɪəd] *adj* alquilado,-a, de alquiler.
■ **hired assassin,** asesino,-a a sueldo.
hireling ['haɪəlɪŋ] *n pej* mercenario,-a.
hirsute ['hɜːsjuːt] *adj fml* hirsuto,-a.
his [hɪz] **1** *adj* su, sus: *his dog,* su perro. **2** *(emphatic)* de él. – **3** *pron* (el) suyo, (la) suya, (los) suyos, (las) suyas.
Hispanic [hɪs'pænɪk] **1** *adj* hispánico,-a. – **2** *n us* hispano,-a, latino,-a.
Hispanicist [hɪ'spænɪsɪst] *n* hispanista *mf.*
Hispanicize [hɪ'spænɪsaɪz] *t* españolizar.
Hispaniola [hɪspæn'jəʊlə] *n* la Española.
hispanist ['hɪspənɪst] *n* hispanista *mf.*
hiss [hɪs] **1** *n (gen)* siseo. **2** *(air, snake, steam etc)* silbido. **3** *(protest)* silbido. – **4** *t* sisear, silbar. **5** *(in protest)* silbar, pitar, abuchear. – **6** *i* silbar.
hissing ['hɪsɪŋ] *n (gen)* siseo; *(of snake, steam etc)* silbido.
histamine ['hɪstəmiːn] *n* BIOL histamina.
histology [hɪ'stɒlədʒɪ] *n* MED histología.
historian [hɪ'stɔːrɪən] *n* historiador,-ra.
historic [hɪ'stɒrɪk] *adj* histórico,-a.
historical [hɪ'stɒrɪkəl] *adj* histórico,-a.
■ **historical novel,** novela histórica.
historically [hɪ'stɒrɪkəlɪ] *adj* históricamente.
history ['hɪstərɪ] *n* historia.
● **that's past history / that's ancient history,** eso es cosa vieja. ‖ **to go down in history,** pasar a la historia.
■ **medical history,** *(of patient)* historial *m* médico, historial *m* clínico.
▲ *pl histories.*
hit [hɪt] **1** *n (blow)* golpe *m.* **2** *(success)* éxito, acierto: *she was a hit with children's audiences,* tuvo mucho éxito con el público infantil. **3** *(shot)* impacto. **4** *fig (damaging remark)* pulla. **5** *us sl* asesinato. – **6** *t (strike)* golpear, pegar: *he hit his head on the door,* dio con la cabeza contra la puerta; *the idea suddenly hit me,* de pronto me vino la idea. **7** *(crash into)* chocar contra: *the car hit the*

tree, el coche chocó contra el árbol. **8** *(affect)* afectar: *farmers were hit badly by the drought,* la sequía afectó adversamente a los agricultores. **9** *(reach)* alcanzar.

◆ **to hit back** *i (strike in return)* devolver golpe por golpe; *(reply to criticism)* defenderse. ‖ **to hit on** *t insep* dar con: *he hit on a great idea,* se le ocurrió una idea brillante. ‖ **to hit out at / hit out against** *t insep (condemn verbally)* condenar a, atacar a; *(try to attack)* atacar a: *she hit out at him to protect herself,* ella lo atacó para protegerse; *the Trade Unions hit out at what they consider unfair measures,* los sindicatos atacaron lo que ellos consideran medidas injustas.

● **it hits you in the eye,** *fam* salta a la vista. ‖ **it suddenly hit him,** *fig* de pronto se dio cuenta. ‖ **to hit below the belt,** *fam* dar un golpe bajo. ‖ **to hit it off with,** llevarse bien con, caer bien a algn. ‖ **to hit the bottle,** *fam* darse a la bebida. ‖ **to hit the headlines,** ser noticia. ‖ **to hit the nail on the head,** *fig* dar en el clavo. ‖ **to hit the road,** *fam* ponerse en camino. ‖ **to hit the roof,** *fam* explotar, subirse por las paredes. ‖ **to hit the sack,** *fam* irse al catre. ‖ **to make a hit with,** caer simpático,-a a algn. ‖ **to score a direct hit,** dar en el blanco.

■ **direct hit,** impacto directo. ‖ **hit man,** *sl* asesino a sueldo. ‖ **hit parade,** hit-parade *m,* lista de éxitos. ‖ **hit record,** disco de éxito.

▲ *(verbo)* pt & pp *hit,* ger *hitting.*

hit-and-miss [hɪtən'mɪs] *adj* al azar, casual, a la buena de Dios.

hit-and-run [hɪtən'rʌn] *adj* AUTO que atropella a algn. y se da a la fuga.

hitch [hɪtʃ] **1** *n* obstáculo, tropiezo, dificultad *f.* – **2** *t (tie)* enganchar, atar. – **3** *i fam* hacer autoestop, ir a dedo, hacer dedo.

◆ **to hitch up** *t sep* arremangarse, remangarse.

● **without a hitch,** sin problema alguno.

hitched [hɪtʃt] **to get hitched,** *phr fam* casarse.

hitch-hike ['hɪtʃhaɪk] *i* hacer autoestop.

hitch-hiker ['hɪtʃhaɪkəʳ] *n* autoestopista *mf.*

hitherto [hɪðə'tuː] *adv fml* hasta ahora, hasta la fecha.

hit-or-miss [hɪtɔː'mɪs] *adj →* **hit-and-miss.**

Hittite ['hɪtaɪt] **1** *adj* hitita. – **2** *n (person)* hitita *mf.* **3** *(language)* hitita *m.*

HIV ['eɪtʃ'aɪ'viː] *abbr (human immunodeficiency virus)* virus *m* de inmunodeficiencia humana; *(abbreviation)* VIH *m.*

● **to be diagnosed HIV negative,** dar negativo,-a en la prueba del sida. ‖ **to be HIV positive,** ser seropositivo,-a, ser portador,-ra del virus del sida.

■ **HIV carrier,** seropositivo,-a, portador,-ra del virus del sida.

hive [haɪv] **1** *n* colmena. **2** *fig* lugar *m* muy activo.

◆ **to hive off 1** *t sep* separar. – **2** *i* GB *fam* largarse, pirarse: *John's hived off again,* John se ha largado otra vez.

hives ['haɪvz] *npl* MED urticaria *f sing.*

HM ['eɪtʃ'em] *abbr (His Majesty, Her Majesty)* Su Majestad; *(abbreviation)* SM.

HMS ['eɪtʃ'em'es] *abbr* GB *(His/Her Majesty's Ship)* barco de su majestad.

HNC ['eɪtʃ'en'siː] *abbr* GB *(Higher National Certificate)* título de formación profesional.

HND ['eɪtʃ'en'diː] *abbr* GB *(Higher National Diploma)* título de formación profesional.

hoard [hɔːd] **1** *n (provisions)* reserva. **2** *(money)* tesoro escondido: *the pirate's hoard has never been found,* nunca

se ha encontrado el tesoro escondido del pirata. – **3** *t (objects)* acumular, amontonar. **4** *(money)* atesorar.

hoarder ['hɔːdəʳ] *n* acaparador,-ra *m,* acumulador,-ra *m.*

hoarding ['hɔːdɪŋ] *n (billboard)* valla publicitaria; *(construction)* valla.

hoarfrost ['hɔːfrɒst] *n* escarcha.

hoarse [hɔːs] *adj* ronco,-a, áspero,-a: *we were all hoarse after the concert,* todos teníamos la voz ronca después del concierto.

hoarseness ['hɔːsnəs] **1** *n* MED ronquera. **2** *(quality of voice)* ronquedad *f.*

hoary ['hɔːrɪ] *adj lit* cano,-a, canoso,-a; *(very old person)* viejo,-a; *(joke)* viejo,-a, pasado,-a.

▲ *comp* hoarier, *superl* hoariest.

hoax [həʊks] **1** *n (trick)* trampa, engaño; *(joke)* broma pesada. – **2** *t* engañar a, gastar una broma a.

● **to play a hoax on sb.,** gastarle una broma a algn.

hob [hɒb] *n (of cooker)* encimera; *(next to fireplace)* repisa.

hobble ['hɒbəl] **1** *i (limp)* cojear, andar con dificultad *f.* – **2** *t (tie)* trabar, manear. **3** *fig* poner trabas a, obstaculizar.

hobby[1] ['hɒbɪ] *n* afición *f,* hobby *m,* pasatiempo favorito.

hobby[2] ['hɒbɪ] *n* ORN alcotán *m.*

▲ *pl* hobbies.

hobbyhorse ['hɒbɪhɔːs] **1** *n (toy)* caballito de juguete. **2** *fig (fixed idea)* caballo de batalla.

hobgoblin [hɒb'gɒblɪn] *n* duende *m.*

hobnailed ['hɒbneɪld] *adj* con clavos, con tachuelas.

■ **hobnailed boots,** botas *fpl* con clavos.

hobnob ['hɒbnɒb] *i fam* codearse: *she hobnobs a lot with the managers of the company,* se codea mucho con los jefes de su compañía.

▲ *pt & pp* hobnobbed, *ger* hobnobbing.

hobo ['həʊbəʊ] *n* US vagabundo,-a.

▲ *pl* hoboes o hobos.

hockey ['hɒkɪ] *n* SP hockey *m.*

■ **roller skate hockey,** hockey *m* sobre patines.

hocus-pocus [həʊkəs'pəʊkəs] *n (trickery)* trampa. **2** *(magic word)* abracadabra *m.*

hod [hɒd] *n (trough)* artesa; *(for bricks)* capacho de albañil.

hoe [həʊ] **1** *n* azada, azadón *m.* – **2** *t (earth)* azadonar, cavar; *(weeds)* sachar.

hog [hɒg] **1** *n* cerdo, puerco, marrano. **2** *fam pej (not a nice person)* indeseable *mf.* – **3** *t* acaparar.

● **to go the whole hog,** llegar hasta el final, liarse la manta a la cabeza.

▲ *(verbo)* pt & pp *hogged,* ger *hogging.*

Hogmanay ['hɒgməneɪ] *n (Scotland)* Nochevieja.

hogwash ['hɒgwɒʃ] *n* US *fam pej* disparates *mpl,* tonterías *fpl,* pamplinas *fpl.*

hoi polloi [hɔɪpə'lɔɪ] **the hoi polloi,** *n fam pej* el vulgo, la plebe.

hoist [hɔɪst] **1** *n (crane)* grúa. **2** *(lift)* montacargas *m.* – **3** *t* levantar, subir. **4** *(flag)* izar.

hoity-toity [hɔɪtɪ'tɔɪtɪ] *adj fam pej (haughty)* arrogante, presumido,-a.

hold [həʊld] **1** *n (grip)* asimiento. **2** *(place to grip)* asidero. **3** *(in ship, plane)* bodega. **4** *(control)* autoridad *f,* control *m; (influence)* influencia: *governments should exert a strong hold on public expenditure,* los gobiernos deben aplicar un control riguroso sobre el gasto público; *she has a strong hold over him,* ella ejerce una influencia poderosa sobre él. **5** *(in wrestling)* llave *f.* – **6** *t (keep in one's hand)* aguantar, sostener; *(grip tightly)* agarrar; *(support)* soportar, aguantar: *hold my bag,* aguántame el

bolso. **7** (*maintain - opinion*) sostener. **8** (*contain*) dar cabida a, tener capacidad para: *the stadium holds a lot of people,* el estadio tiene capacidad para mucha gente. **9** *fig* deparar: *I don't know what the future holds for me,* no sé lo que el futuro me deparará, no sé lo que me espera en el futuro. **10** (*meeting*) celebrar; (*conversation*) mantener: *political parties often hold meetings in parks,* los partidos políticos celebran a menudo sus mítines en los parques; *she loves holding long chats with her best friend,* le encanta mantener largas charlas con su mejor amiga. **11** (*think*) creer, considerar. **12** (*keep*) guardar. – **13** *i* resistir; *fig* seguir siendo válido,-a.
◆ to hold back **1** *t sep* (*suspect*) retener. **2** (*information*) ocultar; (*restrain*) contener; (*feelings*) reprimir; (*keep*) guardar. – **3** *i* (*hesitate*) vacilar, no atreverse; (*abstain*) abstenerse. ‖ to hold down *t sep* (*control*) dominar; (*job*) desempeñar; *he can't hold down a job,* es incapaz de mantener un empleo. ‖ to hold forth *i* hablar largo y tendido (**on/about,** sobre). ‖ to hold off **1** *t sep* (*maintain separate*) mantener alejado,-a. – **2** *i* (*refrain*) refrenarse: *he held off from joining the club,* aplazó la decisión de hacerse socio del club; *I hope the snow holds off,* espero que no nieve. ‖ to hold on **1** *i* (*grip tightly*) agarrarse fuerte, agarrarse bien: *hold on tight!,* ¡agárrate bien! **2** (*wait*) esperar; (*on 'phone*) no colgar. ‖ to hold on to **1** *t insep* (*grasp*) cogerse a, agarrarse a. **2** (*keep*) guardar: *I think I'll hold onto this, it might be valuable,* creo que guardaré esto, podría tener algún valor. ‖ to hold out **1** *t sep* (*hand*) tender, ofrecer. – **2** *i* (*last - things*) durar; (*- person*) resistir: *he held out till the rescue team arrived,* resistió hasta que llegó el equipo de rescate. ‖ to hold over *t sep* (*meeting etc*) aplazar. ‖ to hold up **1** *t sep* (*rob*) atracar, asaltar. **2** (*delay*) retrasar: *we were held up by bad weather,* el mal tiempo nos retrasó. **3** (*raise*) levantar: *he held up his hand to answer the question,* levantó la mano para contestar la pregunta. **4** (*support*) aguantar, sostener: *the roof is held up by four pillars,* cuatro columnas sostienen el techo. – **5** *i* aguantar, resistir. ‖ to hold with *t insep* estar de acuerdo con.
● to catch hold of, agarrar, asir, coger. ‖ to get hold of, (*grab*) agarrar, asir, coger; (*obtain*) hacerse con, encontrar, localizar: *wait till I get hold of you!,* ¡espera a que te coja!; *I can't get hold of that book anywhere,* no encuentro ese libro en ninguna parte; *she couldn't get hold of him all afternoon,* no lo pudo localizar en toda la tarde. ‖ to hold one's head high, llevar bien alta la cabeza. ‖ to hold one's own, *fig* defenderse: *he can hold his own in Spanish,* se defiende en español. ‖ to hold sb., abrazar a algn. ‖ to hold sb.'s hand, cogerle la mano a algn. ‖ to hold the road, AUTO agarrarse a la carretera.
▲ *pt & pp* held.
holdall ['həʊldɔːl] *n* GB bolsa de viaje.
holdback ['həʊldbæk] *n fig* estorbo, inconveniente *m,* obstáculo.
holder ['həʊldəʳ] **1** *n* (*owner*) poseedor,-ra; (*of passport*) titular *mf.* **2** (*container*) recipiente *m,* receptáculo. **3** (*bearer - gen*) portador,-ra; (*- of bonds*) tenedor,-ra. **4** (*handle*) asidero. **5** (*tenant - on land*) arrendatario,-a; (*- of a flat*) inquilino,-a.
holding ['həʊldɪŋ] **1** *n* (*possession*) posesión *f;* (*piece of land*) propiedad *f,* terreno. **2** (*of an event*) celebración *f.* **3** (*stocks, shares, bonds*) valor *m* en cartera.
■ holding company, holding *m,* sociedad *f* de cartera de valores.
hold-up ['həʊldʌp] **1** *n* (*robbery*) atraco; (*of train etc*) asalto. **2** (*delay*) retraso. **3** AUTO atasco.

hole [həʊl] **1** *n* (*gen*) agujero; (*in ground*) hoyo. **2** (*golf*) hoyo: *hole in two,* hoyo en dos. **3** (*in road*) bache *m.* **4** (*of rabbits*) madriguera; (*cavity*) cavidad *f.* **5** *fam* (*town*) poblacho. **6** *fam* (*place to live*) cuchitril *m;* (*unsavoury place*) antro. **7** (*a tight spot*) aprieto, apuro. – **8** *t* (*make holes - small*) agujerear; (*large*) hacer un boquete en. **9** (*at golf*) meter en el hoyo. – **10** *i* (*at golf*) meter la pelota en el hoyo.
◆ to hole up *i* (*animal*) hibernar; (*to go into hiding*) esconderse.
● to make a hole in, (*literally*) agujerear; (*figuratively*) comerse gran parte, agotar gran parte: *the rent for this month will make a hole in my salary,* el alquiler de este mes se comerá gran parte de mi sueldo. ‖ to be in a hole, estar en apuros. ‖ to pick holes in sth., encontrar defectos en algo, criticar algo.
holiday ['hɒlɪdeɪ] **1** *n* (*one day*) fiesta, día *m* de fiesta, día *m* festivo: *Friday is a holiday,* el viernes es fiesta. **2** (*period*) vacaciones *fpl: they spend their summer holidays in Spain,* suelen veranear en España. – **3** *i* GB (*gen*) pasar las vacaciones; (*in summer*) veranear.
● to be on holiday, estar de vacaciones. ‖ to go on holiday, ir de vacaciones. ‖ to take a holiday, coger unas vacaciones.
■ holiday atmosphere, ambiente *m* festivo. ‖ holiday pay, paga extra (de vacaciones). ‖ holiday resort, lugar *m* turístico.
holiday-maker ['hɒlɪdeɪmeɪkəʳ] *n* GB (*gen*) turista *mf;* (*in summer*) veraneante *mf.*
holier-than-thou [həʊlɪəðən'ðaʊ] *adj pej* gazmoño,-a, mojigato,-a, santurrón,-ona.
holiness ['həʊlɪnəs] *n* REL santidad *f: His Holiness Pope John XXIII,* Su Santidad el Papa Juan XXIII.
holistic [həʊ'lɪstɪk] *adj* holístico,-a.
■ holistic learning, aprendizaje *m* holístico.
Holland ['hɒlənd] *n* Holanda.
hollandaise sauce [hɒləndeɪz'sɔːs] *n* salsa holandesa.
hollow ['hɒləʊ] **1** *adj* (*sound, thing*) hueco,-a. **2** (*cheeks etc*) hundido,-a. **3** *fig* (*laugh*) falso,-a; (*promise*) vacío,-a. – **4** *n* hueco. **5** GEOG hondonada. – **6** to hollow out, *t* vaciar.
holly ['hɒlɪ] *n* acebo.
▲ *pl* hollies.
hollyhock ['hɒlɪhɒk] *n* malvarrosa.
holocaust ['hɒləkɔːst] *n* holocausto.
holograph ['hɒləgrɑːf] *n* hológrafo.
holographic [hɒlə'græfɪk] *adj* holográfico,-a.
holster ['həʊlstəʳ] *n* pistolera.
holy ['həʊlɪ] **1** *adj* REL (*sacred*) santo,-a, sagrado,-a. **2** (*blessed*) bendito,-a.
■ Holy Ghost, Espíritu Santo. ‖ Holy Land, Tierra Santa. ‖ holy orders, órdenes *fpl* sagradas. ‖ Holy See, Santa Sede *f.* ‖ Holy Week, Semana Santa.
▲ *comp* holier, *superl* holiest.
homage ['hɒmɪdʒ] *n* homenaje *m.*
● to pay homage to / do homage to, rendir homenaje a
home [həʊm] **1** *n* (*house*) hogar *m,* casa. **2** *fml* domicilio. **3** (*institution*) asilo: *she lives in an old people's home,* vive en un asilo de ancianos. **4** (*country, village etc*) patria, tierra: *she's a long way from home,* ella está lejos de su tierra. **5** ZOOL hábitat *m.* **6** SP casa: *to play at home,* jugar en casa. – **7** *adj* casero,-a. **8** POL (del) interior. **9** (*native*) natal. **10** SP de casa, en casa. – **11** *adv* en casa, de casa: *she's (at) home,* está en casa; *he went home,* se fue a casa; *I want to leave home,* quiero irme de casa.

● **at home,** en casa. ‖ **home sweet home,** hogar dulce hogar. ‖ **to be nothing to write home about,** no ser nada del otro mundo, no ser nada del otro jueves. ‖ **to come home to sb.**, darse cuenta: *it suddenly came home to me that I was all alone,* de repente me di cuenta de que estaba totalmente solo. ‖ **to feel at home,** *fig* estar a gusto, sentirse en casa. ‖ **to make os. at home,** ponerse cómodo,-a.

■ **Home Office,** GB Ministerio del Interior. ‖ **home rule,** autonomía. ‖ **Home Secretary,** GB Ministro *mf* del Interior. ‖ **home help,** asistenta. ‖ **home base,** (*in baseball*) base *f* del bateador. ‖ **home run,** (*in baseball*) carrera completa. ‖ **home team,** equipo local, equipo de casa. ‖ **home town,** pueblo natal, patria chica.

homecoming ['həʊmkʌmɪŋ] *n* regreso (a casa).

home-grown ['həʊm'grəʊn] *adj* (*produced locally*) del país; (*cultivated in one's own garden*) de cosecha propia, casero,-a.

homeland ['həʊmlænd] *n* (*gen*) patria; (*birthplace*) tierra natal.

homeless ['həʊmləs] *adj* sin hogar, sin techo.
■ **the homeless,** los sin techo, los desvalidos, los desamparados.

home-loving ['həʊmlʌɪŋ] *adj* casero,-a, hogareño,-a.

homely ['həʊmlɪ] **1** *adj* GB (*attractive, cosy, domesticated*) sencillo,-a, casero,-a, familiar. **2** US (*unattractive*) feo,-a, sin atractivo.

home-made ['həʊm'meɪd] *adj* casero,-a, de fabricación casera, hecho,-a en casa.

homeopath ['həʊmɪəpæθ] *n* MED homeópata *mf*.

homeopathy [həʊmɪ'ɒpəθɪ] *n* MED homeopatía.

homesick ['həʊmsɪk] *adj* nostálgico,-a.
● **to be homesick,** tener morriña.

homesickness ['həʊmsɪknəs] *n* añoranza, morriña, nostalgia.

homestead ['həʊmsted] *n* US granja.

homeward ['həʊmwəd] *adv* hacia casa.

homewards ['həʊmwədz] *adv* → **homeward**.

homework ['həʊmwɜːk] *n* deberes *mpl*: *to do one's homework,* hacer los deberes.

homicidal [hɒmɪ'saɪdəl] *adj* homicida.

homicide ['hɒmɪsaɪd] **1** *n* (*crime*) homicidio. **2** (*criminal*) homicida *mf*.

homily ['hɒmɪlɪ] *n* homilía.
▲ *pl* **homilies**.

homing ['həʊmɪŋ] *adj* TECH buscador,-ra.
■ **homing device,** (*gen*) indicador *m* automático de ruta; (*in missile*) cabeza buscadora. ‖ **homing pigeon,** paloma mensajera.

homoeopath ['həʊmɪəpæθ] *n* → **homeopath**.

homoeopathy [həʊmɪ'ɒpəθɪ] *n* → **homeopathy**.

homogeneous [hɒmə'dʒiːnɪəs] *adj* homogéneo,-a.

homogenization [hɒmɒdzənaɪ'zeɪʃən] *n* homogeneización *f*.

homogenize [hɒ'mɒdzənaɪz] *t* homogeneizar.

homogenous [hə'mɒdzənəs] *adj* → **homogeneous**.

homologate [hɒ'mɒləgeɪt] *t* homologar.

homological [həʊmə'lɒdzɪkəl] *adj* homológico,-a.

homologous [həʊ'mɒləgəs] *adj* → **homological**.

homology [həʊ'mɒlədzɪ] *n* homología.

homonym ['hɒmənɪm] *n* homónimo.

homophone ['hɒməfəʊn] *n* homófono.

homosexual [həʊməʊ'seksjʊəl] **1** *adj* homosexual. **– 2** *n* homosexual *mf*.

homosexuality [həʊməʊseksjʊ'ælɪtɪ] *n* homosexualidad *f*.

Hon ['ɒnərərɪ, 'ɒnərəbəl] **1** *abbr* (*Honorary* - *member*) honorario,-a; (- *secretary etc*) no remunerado,-a. **2** (*Honourable*) ilustre.

Honduran [hɒn'djʊərən] **1** *adj* hondureño,-a. **– 2** *n* hondureño,-a.

Honduras [hɒn'djʊərəs] *n* Honduras *m*.

honest ['ɒnɪst] **1** *adj* (*trustworthy*) honrado,-a, honesto,-a: *she has an honest face,* ella tiene cara de honrada; *to do an honest day's work,* ganarse la jornada honradamente. **2** (*frank*) sincero,-a, franco,-a: *I'll be honest with you,* seré sincero contigo. **3** (*fair*) justo,-a, equitativo,-a, decente. **– 4** *adv fam* de verdad: *I didn't take it, honest!,* te juro que no lo cogí yo.
● **the honest truth,** la pura verdad.

honestly ['ɒnɪstlɪ] **1** *adv* (*fairly*) honradamente. **2** (*frankly*) sinceramente, francamente, con franqueza: *quite honestly, I don't think you should do it,* con toda franqueza, no creo que debieras hacerlo. **3** (*truthfully*) de verdad, a decir verdad. **– 4** *interj* (*question*) ¿de verdad?; (*exclamation*) ¡hay que ver!

honesty ['ɒnɪstɪ] *n* honradez *f*, rectitud *f*.

honey ['hʌnɪ] **1** *n* miel *f*. **2** US *fam* (*dear*) cariño, cielo.

honeycomb ['hʌnɪkəʊm] *n* panal *m*.

honeyed ['hʌnɪd] *adj* dulzón,-ona, meloso,-a, melifluo,-a: *honeyed words,* palabras melosas.

honeymoon ['hʌnɪmuːn] **1** *n* luna de miel, viaje *m* de novios. **– 2** *i* pasar la luna de miel, hacer el viaje de novios.

honeymooner ['hʌnɪmuːnə'] *n* recién casado,-a.

honeysuckle ['hʌnɪsʌkəl] *n* BOT madreselva.

honied ['hʌnɪd] *adj* → **honeyed**.

honk [hɒŋk] **1** *n* (*goose*) graznido. **2** (*car horn*) bocinazo *m*. **– 3** *i* (*goose*) graznar. **4** (*car*) tocar la bocina.

honky ['hɒŋkɪ] *n* US *sl pej* blanco,-a.
▲ *pl* **honkies**.

honor ['ɒnə'] *n-t* US → **honour**.

honorable ['ɒnərəbəl] *adj* US → **honourable**.

honorarium [ɒnə'reərɪəm] *n* honorarios *mpl*.
▲ *pl* **honorariums** o **honoraria** [ɒnə'reərɪə].

honorary ['ɒnərərɪ] *adj* (*member*) honorario,-a; (*duties*) honorífico,-a.
● **to receive an honorary degree,** ser nombrado,-a doctor,-ra honoris causa.

honour ['ɒnə'] **1** *n* (*virtue*) honor *m*, honra: *in honour of,* en honor de; *to defend one's honour,* defender su honra; *to have the honour of doing sth.,* tener el honor de hacer algo. **2** (*title*) Su Señoría: *Her Honour, His Honour, Your Honour,* Su Señoría. **– 3** *t* (*respect*) honrar. **4** (*cheque*) pagar, aceptar; (*promise, word, agreement*) cumplir. **– 5** **honours,** *npl* MIL honores *mpl*: *he was buried with full military honours,* lo enterraron con honores militares.
● **to do honour to,** rendir honores a. ‖ **to do the honours,** hacer los honores.
■ **Honours degree,** licenciatura.

honourable ['ɒnərəbəl] **1** *adj* (*person*) honrado,-a; (*title*) honorable. **2** (*actions*) honorífico,-a, honroso,-a.
■ **the honourable member,** POL el/la ilustre diputado,-a, el/la ilustre representante. ‖ **honourable mention,** mención *f* honorífica.

Hons ['ɒnəz] *abbr* GB EDUC (*Honours*) licenciado,-a.

hooch [huːtʃ] *n* US *sl* → **hootch**.

hood [hʊd] **1** *n* (*of clothes*) capucha. **2** (*on pram etc*) capota. **3** US (*car bonnet*) capó *m*. **4** (*of hawk*) capirote *m*, capillo *m*.

hooded ['hʊdɪd] **1** *adj* (*person*) con capucha, encapuchado,-a; (*clothes*) con capucha. **2** (*hawk*) encapirotado,-a.

hoodlum ['huːdləm] *n sl* matón *m*, gorila *m*.

hoodwink ['hʊdwɪŋk] *t* engañar, tomar el pelo.

hoof [huːf] **1** *n* (*of sheep, cow, goat, etc*) pezuña; (*of horse*) casco. – **2** *t sl* caminar.
● **to hoof it**, ir a pie, ir a pata.
▲ *pl* **hoofs** *o* **hooves**.

hoofed ['huːft] *adj* ungulado,-a.

hoofer ['huːfəʳ] *n us sl* bailarín,-ina de claqué.

hoo-ha ['huːhaː] *n fam* follón *m*, jaleo.

hook [hʊk] **1** *n* (*gen*) gancho. **2** (*for fishing*) anzuelo. **3** (*boxing*) gancho. – **4** *t* (*catch*) enganchar: *his shirt got hooked on the fence*, se le enganchó la camisa en la valla. **5** (*fishing*) pescar, coger. **6** (*boxing*) pegar un gancho.
◆ **to hook up** *t sep* (*connect*) conectar: *his computer is hooked up to international networks*, su ordenador está conectado a redes internacionales.
● **to take the phone off the hook**, descolgar el teléfono. ‖ **by hook or by crook**, *fig* por las buenas o por las malas. ‖ **to be off the hook**, *sl* haberse librado. ‖ **to get one's hooks into sb.**, tener a algn. en las garras. ‖ **to let sb. off the hook**, dejar salir a algn. del atolladero.
■ **hooks and eyes**, (*sewing*) corchetes *mpl*.

hookah ['hʊkə] *n* narguile *m*.

hooked [hʊkt] **1** *adj* (*nose*) aquilino,-a; (*hook-shaped*) ganchudo,-a. **2** (*on drug etc*) enganchado,-a; (*attracted*) prendado,-a, encariñado,-a.
● **to get hooked (on)**, engancharse.

hooker ['hʊkəʳ] **1** *n* (*rugby*) talonador,-ra *mf*. **2** *sl* (*us*) puta.

hookey ['hʊkɪ] **to play hookey**, *phr us fam* hacer novillos.

hook-up ['hʊkʌp] **1** *n* (*in electronics, computers etc*) conexión *f*. **2** RAD TV emisión *f* transmitida a distintos países.

hooky ['hʊkɪ] *n →* **hookey**.

hooligan ['huːlɪgən] *n* gamberro,-a.

hooliganism ['huːlɪgənɪzəm] *n* gamberrismo.

hoop [huːp] **1** *n* (*gen*) aro; (*of barrel*) fleje *m*; (*of wheel*) llanta. – **2** *t* (*a cask*) enarcar.
● **to put sb. through the hoop(s)**, hacérselas pasar canutas a algn.

hoopoe ['huːpuː] *n* ORN abubilla.

hoorah [hʊ'raː] *interj* ¡hurra!

hooray [hʊ'reɪ] *interj* ¡hurra!

hoot [huːt] **1** *n* (*of owl*) ululato, grito. **2** (*of car*) bocinazo. **3** *fam* (*funny thing*) cosa divertida; (*funny person*) persona divertida: *the show was a hoot*, el espectáculo era divertidísimo. – **4** *i* (*owl*) t ular, gritar. **5** (*car*) dar un bocinazo; (*driver*) tocar la bocina; (*train*) silbar; (*siren*) pitar.
● **not to give a hoot** / **not to give two hoots**, importar a algn. un carajo, importar a algn. un pepino.
■ **hoots of laughter**, carcajadas *fpl*, risotadas *fpl*.

hootch [huːtʃ] *n sl* aguardiente *m*.

hooter ['huːtəʳ] **1** *n* (*siren*) sirena. **2** (*on car*) bocina, claxon *m*. **3** GB (*nose*) narizota, napia.

Hoover ['huːvəʳ] **1** *n* GB aspiradora. – **2** *t* pasar la aspiradora.
▲ Es marca registrada.

hop¹ [hɒp] **1** *n* salto, brinco: *he crossed the puddle in one hop*, atravesó el charco de un salto. **2** *fam* (*dance*) baile *m*. **3** AV *fam* vuelo corto. – **4** *i* saltar, dar brincos, dar saltos. – **5** *t* US *fam* (*train etc*) coger. **6** AV cruzar.
● **hop it!**, GB *sl* ¡lárgate! ¡esfúmate! ‖ **to be on the hop**, *fam* estar muy atareado,-a. ‖ **to catch sb. on the hop**, GB *fam* coger desprevenido,-a a algn. ‖ **to hop on**

one leg, andar a la pata coja. ‖ **hop in!**, *fam* (*into car*) ¡sube! ‖ **to hop on the bus/train**, *fam* subirse al autobús/tren.
▲ (*verbo*) *pt & pp* **hopped**, *ger* **hopping**.

hop² [hɒp] *n* (*plant*) lúpulo.

hope [həʊp] **1** *n* (*gen*) esperanza; (*false*) ilusión *f*: *don't get your hopes up too soon*, no te hagas ilusiones antes de tiempo; *she had high hopes for her son*, tenía grandes esperanzas puestas en su hijo. – **2** *t* esperar: *I hope you're well*, espero que estés bien. – **3** *i* esperar.
● **I hope not**, espero que no. ‖ **I hope so**, espero que sí. ‖ **not a hope!**, *fam* ¡ni hablar! ‖ **some hope!**, *fam* ¡qué va! ‖ **to have little hope of doing sth.**, tener pocas posibilidades de hacer algo.
■ **hope chest**, US ajuar *m*.

hopeful ['həʊpfʊl] **1** *adj* (*promising*) esperanzador,-ra, prometedor,-ra, alentador,-ra. **2** (*confident*) optimista. – **3** *n* persona que promete.
■ **young hopeful**, joven *mf* promesa.

hopefully ['həʊpfʊlɪ] **1** *adv* (*confidently*) con esperanza, con ilusión, con optimismo. **2** *fam* (*all being well*) se espera que: *hopefully it won't rain*, espero que no llueva.

hopeless ['həʊpləs] **1** *adj* desesperado,-a. **2** *fam* (*useless*) inútil: *he's hopeless at sports*, es negado para los deportes.
● **it's hopeless**, es imposible.
■ **a hopeless case**, un caso perdido.

hopelessly ['həʊpləslɪ] *adv* sin esperanza, con desesperación, desesperadamente.
● **hopelessly in love**, locamente enamorado,-a. ‖ **hopelessly lost**, totalmente perdido,-a.

hopper ['hɒpəʳ] *n* TECH tolva.

hop-picker ['hɒppɪkəʳ] *n* recogedor,-ra de lúpulo.

hop-picking ['hɒppɪkɪŋ] *n* cosecha de lúpulo.

hopping ['hɒpɪŋ] *n* brincos *mpl*, saltos *mpl*.
● **to be hopping mad**, estar que se sube por las paredes, estar que trina, estar que bota.

hopscotch ['hɒpskɒtʃ] *n* (*game*) infernáculo, rayuela.

horde [hɔːd] **1** *n* horda. **2** *fig* multitud *f*, muchedumbre *f*.

horizon [hə'raɪzən] *n* horizonte *m*.

horizontal [hɒrɪ'zɒntəl] *adj* horizontal.

hormonal [hɔː'məʊnəl] *adj* hormonal.

hormone ['hɔːməʊn] *n* hormona.

horn [hɔːn] **1** *n* ZOOL asta, cuerno. **2** AUTO bocina, claxon *m*. **3** MUS cuerno, trompa.
● **to be on the horns of a dilemma**, estar entre la espada y la pared. ‖ **to sound the horn**, dar un bocinazo. ‖ **to take the bull by the horns**, coger el toro por los cuernos.

hornbeam ['hɔːnbiːm] *n* BOT carpe *m*.

horned [hɔːnd] *adj* con cuernos.

hornet ['hɔːnɪt] *n* ZOOL avispón *m*.
● **to stir up a hornet's nest**, *fig* meterse en un avispero.

hornpipe ['hɔːnpaɪp] **1** *n* (*instrument*) chirimía. **2** (*dance*) baile de marineros.

horn-rimmed ['hɔːnrɪmd] *adj* (*glasses*) de concha, con montura de concha.

horny ['hɔːnɪ] **1** *adj* (*skin, hands*) calloso,-a. **2** *fam* (*sexually*) cachondo,-a, caliente.
▲ *comp* **hornier**, *superl* **horniest**.

horology [hɒ'rɒlədʒɪ] *n* relojería.

horoscope ['hɒrəskəʊp] *n* horóscopo.

horrendous [hə'rendəs] *adj* horrendo,-a.

horrible ['hɒrɪbəl] *adj* (*gen*) horrible, horroroso,-a; (*person*) antipático,-a: *what a horrible person!*, ¡qué persona más antipática!

horribly ['hɒrɪblɪ] *adv* horriblemente: *it was horribly cold,* hacía un frío horroroso.

horrid ['hɒrɪd] *adj* (*horrible*) horroroso,-a, horrible; (*unkind*) antipático,-a, odioso,-a; (*child*) inaguantable, insoportable.

horrific [hə'rɪfɪk] *adj* horrendo,-a, horroroso,-a.

horrify ['hɒrɪfaɪ] *t* horrorizar, espantar: *I was horrified at the thought,* me horrorizaba sólo de pensarlo.
▲ *pt* & *pp* **horrified,** *ger* **horrifying.**

horror ['hɒrəʳ] **1** *n* horror *m,* terror *m.* – **2 horrors** *interj* ¡qué horror!
● **to have a horror of sth.,** tener horror a algo.
■ **horror film,** película de terror, película de miedo. || **little horror,** diablillo, monstruito,-a.

horror-stricken ['hɒrəstrɪkən] *adj* horrorizado,-a.

horror-struck ['hɒrəstrʌk] *adj* → **horror-stricken.**

hors d'oeuvre [ɔː'dɜːvʳ] *n* CULIN entremés *m.*
▲ *pl* **hors d'oeuvre** o **hors d'oeuvres.**

horse [hɔːs] **1** *n* ZOOL caballo. **2** (*in gym*) potro. **3** TECH caballete *m.* **4** *sl* (*heroin*) caballo.
◆ **to horse about / horse around** *i* hacer el indio, hacer el payaso.
● **hold your horses!,** *fig* ¡para el carro! || **to eat like a horse,** comer como una lima, tener buen saque. || **to get on one's high horse,** *fig* darse ínfulas, tener muchos humos. || **to get sth. straight from the horse's mouth,** *fig* saber algo de buena tinta. || **wild horses wouldn't ...,** nada en el mundo ...: *wild horses wouldn't make me go back to him,* no volvería con él por nada en el mundo.
■ **horse chestnut,** BOT (*tree*) castaño de Indias; (*fruit*) castaña de Indias. || **horse doctor,** veterinario,-a. || **horse racing,** carreras *fpl* de caballos. || **horse race,** carrera de caballos. || **horse rider,** (*man*) jinete; (*woman*) amazona. || **horse riding,** equitación *f.* || **horse sense,** sentido común.

horseback ['hɔːsbæk] *n* a caballo.
● **on horseback,** a caballo.
■ **horseback riding,** equitación *f.*

horsebox ['hɔːsbɒks] *n* furgón *m* remolque para caballos.

horseflesh ['hɔːsfleʃ] *n* carne *f* de caballo.

horsefly ['hɔːsflaɪ] *n* ZOOL (*insect*) tábano.
▲ *pl* **horseflies.**

horsehair ['hɔːsheəʳ] *n* crin *m* de caballo.
■ **horsehair mattress,** colchón *m* de crin de caballo.

horseman ['hɔːsmən] *n* jinete *m,* caballista *m.*
▲ *pl* **horsemen** ['hɔːsmən].

horsemanship ['hɔːsmənʃɪp] *n* equitación *f.*

horseplay ['hɔːspleɪ] *n* payasadas *fpl.*
● **to indulge in horseplay,** hacer el payaso.

horsepower ['hɔːspaʊəʳ] **1** *n* AUTO caballo de vapor, caballo. **2** potencia.

horseradish ['hɔːsrædɪʃ] *n* BOT rábano picante.

horseshoe ['hɔːsʃuː] *n* herradura.

horsewoman ['hɔːswʊmən] *n* amazona, caballista.
▲ *pl* **horsewomen** ['hɔːswɪmɪn].

horsey ['hɔːsɪ] **1** *adj pej* (*horse-like*) caballuno,-a. **2** (*keen on horses*) aficionado,-a a los caballos.
■ **horsey features,** rasgos caballunos.
▲ *comp* **horsier,** *superl* **horsiest.**

horsy ['hɔːsɪ] *adj* → **horsey.**
▲ *comp* **horsier,** *superl* **horsiest.**

horticultural [hɔːtɪ'kʌltʃərəl] *adj* hortícola.

horticulture ['hɔːtɪkʌltʃəʳ] *n* horticultura.

hose¹ [həʊz] **1** *n* (*pipe*) manguera. – **2** *t* regar, lavar.
● **to hose down,** (*grass, lawn, etc with water*) regar con una manguera; (*wash*) lavar con una manguera.

hose² [həʊz] *npl* (*socks*) calcetines *mpl;* (*stockings*) medias *fpl.*
▲ *pl* **hose.**

hosiery ['həʊzɪərɪ] *n* calcetería.

hospice ['hɒspɪs] **1** *n* (*hostel*) hospicio. **2** (*hospital*) residencia para enfermos terminales.

hospitable [hʊ'spɪtəbəl] *adj* hospitalario,-a, acogedor,-ra.

hospitably [hʊ'spɪtəblɪ] *adv* con hospitalidad.

hospital ['hɒspɪtəl] *n* hospital *m.*

hospitality [hɒspɪ'tælɪtɪ] *n* hospitalidad *f.*

hospitalize ['hɒspɪtəlaɪz] *t* hospitalizar, ingresar.

host¹ [həʊst] **1** *n* (*person*) anfitrión,-ona; (*place*) sede *f.* **2** (TV *presenter*) presentador,-ra. **3** BIOL ZOOL huésped *m.* – **4** *t* TV presentar. **5** celebrar, albergar: *Atlanta hosted the 1996 Olympic Games,* Atlanta albergó los Juegos Olímpicos de 1996.
■ **host country,** país *m* organizador, país *m* anfitrión.

host² [həʊst] *n* (*large number*) multitud *f,* montón *m,* la tira *f: he gave her a host of things,* le regaló un montón de cosas.

Host [həʊst] *n* REL hostia.

hostage ['hɒstɪdʒ] *n* rehén *mf.*
● **to hold sb. hostage,** tener a algn. como rehén. || **to take sb. hostage,** tomar a algn. como rehén.

hostel ['hɒstəl] *n* residencia, hostal *m.*

hostess ['həʊstəs] **1** *n* (*at home*) anfitriona. **2** (*on plane etc*) azafata. **3** (*in club*) camarera. **4** TV presentadora.

hostile ['hɒstaɪl] *adj* hostil, enemigo,-a.

hostility [hʊ'stɪlɪtɪ] *n* hostilidad *f: the peace conference put an end to two years' hostilities,* la conferencia de paz puso fin a dos años de hostilidades.
▲ *pl* **hostilities.**

hot [hɒt] **1** *adj* (*gen*) caliente. **2** METEOR caluroso,-a, cálido,-a. **3** (*food - spicy*) picante; (*- not cold*) caliente: *Mexican food is hot,* la comida mexicana es picante; *people prefer hot meals in winter,* en invierno la gente prefiere comer caliente. **4** (*news*) de última hora. **5** (*temper*) fuerte; (*anger*) rabioso,-a, colérico,-a. **6** (*good*) bueno,-a, enterado,-a: *he's not as hot as I thought,* no es tan bueno como pensaba; *that film isn't so hot,* esa película no mata. **7** (*dangerous*) peligroso,-a. **8** *sl* (*stolen*) robado,-a.
◆ **to hot up** *i fam* animarse, ponerse interesante: *things are really hotting up,* se está animando el asunto.
● **to be hot,** (*person*) tener calor; (*weather*) hacer calor: *it's very hot today,* hoy hace mucho calor. || **to be hot on sth.,** saber mucho de algo. || **to be hot stuff,** *sl* estar bueno,-a, estar como un tren. || **to be in the hot seat,** *fam* estar en la línea de fuego. || **to blow hot and cold,** *fig* ser veleta. || **to get hot under the collar,** *fam* ponerse nervioso,-a, acalorarse. || **to get into hot water,** *fig* meterse en líos. || **to make things hot for sb.,** *fig* hacerle la vida difícil a algn.
■ **hot air,** *fig* palabrería. || **hot dog,** perrito caliente. || **hot line,** *fig* (*telephone*) teléfono rojo. || **hot potato,** *fam* patata caliente, asunto delicado. || **hot rod,** US *sl* bólido. || **hot sauce,** salsa picante. || **hot spot,** (*nightclub*) club *m* nocturno.
▲ *comp* **hotter,** *superl* **hottest.**

hotbed ['hɒtbed] *n fig* hervidero, semillero.

hot-blooded [hɒt'blʌdɪd] *adj* de sangre caliente.
● **to be hot-blooded,** tener la sangre caliente.

hotch-potch ['hɒtʃpɒtʃ] **1** *n fam fig* revoltijo, mezcolanza, batiburrillo. **2** CULIN (*stew*) estofado de carne.

hotel [həʊ'tel] *n* hotel *m.*
■ **hotel business / hotel trade,** hostelería.

hotelier [həʊ'teliɛɪ] *n* hotelero,-a.
hotelkeeper [həʊtel'kiːpəʳ] *n* → **hotelier**.
hotfoot ['hɒtfʊt] *adv fam* a toda prisa. – **2** *i* ir corriendo.
hothead ['hɒthed] *n fam* exaltado,-a, fanático,-a, cabeza *mf* loca.
hot-headed ['hɒthedɪd] *adj* impetuoso,-a, impulsivo,-a.
hothouse ['hɒthaʊs] *n* invernadero.
hotplate ['hɒtpleɪt] *n* (*cooker*) placa de cocina; (*to keep food warm*) calientaplatos *m*.
hotpot ['hɒtpɒt] *n* GB CULIN estofado.
hotshot ['hɒtʃɒt] **1** *n* US *sl* hacha *m*, lince *m*. – **2** *adj* US *sl* excelente, de primera.
hot-tempered [hɒt'tempəd] *adj* de genio violento, de genio vivo.
hot-water [hɒt'wɔːtəʳ] *adj* de agua caliente.
■ hot-water bottle, bolsa de agua caliente.
hound [haʊnd] **1** *n* perro de caza. – **2** *t* (*harass*) acosar, perseguir: *he was hounded by the mass media,* los medios de comunicación lo acosaron; *they were hounded out of their homes,* los obligaron a abandonar sus casas.
hour [aʊəʳ] *n* hora: *an hour and a half,* una hora y media; *a quarter of an hour,* un cuarto de hora; *every hour,* cada hora; *half an hour,* media hora; *her hour had come,* le había llegado su hora; *in an hour / in an hour's time,* dentro de una hora; *on the hour,* a la hora en punto; *50 miles an hour,* 50 millas por hora; *the clock struck the hour,* el reloj dio la hora; *she gets paid by the hour,* cobra por horas.
■ hour hand, aguja horaria, manecilla. ‖ office hours / business hours, horas *fpl* de oficina. ‖ small hours, la madrugada.
hourly ['aʊəlɪ] **1** *adj* cada hora: *there's an hourly bus service,* pasa el autobús cada hora. – **2** *adv* a cada hora, por horas: *many people get paid hourly,* mucha gente cobra por horas.
house [haʊs] **1** *n* (*gen*) casa; (*official use*) domicilio: *at our house,* en nuestra casa. **2** POL cámara. **3** THEAT sala. **4** (*company*) empresa, casa. – **5** *t* (*gen*) alojar, albergar; (*supply housing*) proveer de vivienda. **6** (*store*) guardar, almacenar; (*fit*) dar cabida a.
● "house full", "agotadas las localidades". ‖ on the house, *fig* invita la casa. ‖ to bring the house down, ser un exitazo. ‖ to get on with sb. like a house on fire, *fam* llevarse de maravilla con algn. ‖ to keep house for sb., llevar la casa a algn. ‖ to move house, mudarse de casa, trasladarse.
■ house arrest, JUR arresto domiciliario. ‖ house of cards, castillo de naipes. ‖ House of Commons, Cámara de los Comunes. ‖ House of Lords, Cámara de los Lores. ‖ House of Representatives, US Cámara de Representantes. ‖ house plant, planta de interior. ‖ house rules, normas *fpl* de la casa. ‖ Houses of Parliament, Parlamento. ‖ publishing house, editorial *f*.
▲ (*verbo*) [haʊz].
houseboat ['haʊsbəʊt] *n* casa flotante.
housebreaker ['haʊsbreɪkəʳ] *n* ladrón,-ona *mf*.
housebreaking ['haʊsbreɪkɪŋ] *n* JUR allanamiento de morada.
housecoat ['haʊskəʊt] *n* bata.
houseful ['haʊsfʊl] *n* casa llena: *we have a houseful of guests,* tenemos la casa llena de invitados.
household ['haʊshəʊld] **1** *n* casa, familia, hogar *m*: *the whole household joined in the celebration,* toda la familia participó en la celebración. – **2** *adj* de la casa,

doméstico,-a: *household chores,* las tareas de la casa; *household expenses,* los gastos domésticos.
● to become a household name, *fig* ser archiconocido,-a, ser muy popular.
householder ['haʊshəʊldəʳ] *n* dueño,-a de la casa.
househusband ['haʊshʌzbənd] *n fam* hombre *m* que hace de ama de casa.
housekeeper ['haʊskiːpəʳ] *n* ama de llaves.
housekeeping ['haʊskiːpɪŋ] **1** *n* administración *f* de la casa. **2** housekeeping (money), dinero para los gastos de la casa.
housemaid ['haʊsmeɪd] *n* criada.
■ housemaid's knee, MED bursitis *f* de rodilla.
houseman ['haʊsmən] *n* MED interno.
housemaster ['haʊsmɑːstəʳ] *n* EDUC tutor *m*.
housemistress ['haʊsmɪstrəs] *n* EDUC tutora.
houseroom ['haʊsruːm] *n fam* sitio en casa: *I wouldn't give it houseroom,* no lo tendría en casa.
house-to-house ['haʊstə'haʊs] *adj* de casa en casa, de puerta en puerta.
■ a house-to-house salesman, vendedor a domicilio.
house-train ['haʊstreɪn] *t* (*pet*) educar, enseñar.
house-trained ['haʊstreɪnd] *adj* (*pet*) adiestrado,-a, limpio,-a.
house-warming ['haʊswɔːmɪŋ] *n* inauguración *f* de una casa.
■ house-warming party, fiesta para estrenar una casa.
housewife ['haʊswaɪf] *n* ama *f* de casa.
housework ['haʊswɜːk] *n* quehaceres *mpl* domésticos, faenas *fpl* de la casa.
housing ['haʊzɪŋ] **1** *n* vivienda. **2** TECH bastidor *m*, caja.
■ housing estate, urbanización *f*. ‖ Ministry of Housing, Ministerio de la Vivienda.
hovel ['hɒvəl] *n* casucha, cuchitril *m*.
hover ['hɒvəʳ] **1** *i* (*aircraft*) permanecer inmóvil (*en el aire*). **2** (*bird*) cernerse, revolotear: *the hawk hovered over its prey,* el halcón se cernía sobre su presa. **3** (*move around*) rondar. **4** (*hesitate*) dudar, vacilar: *he's hovering between one job and another,* está dudando entre uno u otro trabajo.
hovercraft ['hɒvəkrɑːft] *n* aerodeslizador *m*, hovercraft *m*.
how [haʊ] **1** *adv* (*in questions - direct*) ¿cómo?; (*- indirect*) cómo: *how are you?,* ¿cómo estás?; *how can I help you?,* ¿cómo la puedo ayudar?; *how old are you?,* ¿cuántos años tienes?; *how long is it?,* ¿cuánto mide de largo?; *how often do you go to the cinema?,* ¿con qué frecuencia vas al cine?; ¿cada cuánto vas al cine?; *I don't know how to thank you,* no sé cómo agradecérselo; *tell me how to do it,* dime cómo se hace. **2** (*in exclamations*) qué: *how odd!,* ¡qué extraño!, ¡qué raro!; *how kind of you!,* ¿qué amable de tu parte!; *how well she dances!,* ¡qué bien baila!
● and how!, *fam* ¡y tanto! ‖ how about ..., ¿y si.?, ¿qué te parece si ...?: *how about a drink?,* ¿y si nos tomáramos una copa?; *how about going for a drive?,* ¿qué te parece si damos una vuelta con el coche? ‖ how about that!, ¡vaya! ‖ how come ...?, *fam* ¿por qué ...?, ¿cómo es que ...?: *how come this door's not locked?,* ¿cómo es que esta puerta no está cerrada? ‖ how come?, *fam* ¿y eso?, ¿por qué? ‖ how many?, (*number*) cuántos,-as. ‖ how much?, (*quantity*) cuánto,-a.
howdy ['haʊdɪ] *interj* US *fam* ¿qué hay? ¿qué tal?, ¡hola!
however [haʊ'evəʳ] **1** *adv* (*nevertheless*) sin embargo, no obstante: *there are, however, other facts to consider,* sin

embargo, hay otros hechos que considerar. **2** (*with adj*) por: *however hard it may be,* por difícil que sea; *however much,* por más que, por mucho que. **3** (*how*) ¿cómo?: *however did she do it?,* ¿cómo diablos lo hizo?

howl [haʊl] **1** *n* (*cry*) aullido. – **2** *i* aullar.
◆ **to howl down** *t sep* abuchear.
● **to be a howl,** *sl* (*funny person, thing etc*) ser la monda. ‖ **to howl with laughter,** *fam* reír a carcajadas.

howler [ˈhaʊləʳ] *n fam* despiste *m*, pifia, plancha.
● **to make a howler,** cometer un error garrafal.

howling [ˈhaʊlɪŋ] **1** *adj* (*that howls*) aullador,-ra; (*wind*) rugiente. – **2** *n* (*of dog, wolf etc*) aullido; (*of pain*) alaridos *mpl*. **3** (*of wind*) rugido, rumor *m*.

HP¹ [ˈeɪtʃˈpiː] *abbr* GB (*hire-purchase*) compra a plazos.

HP² [ˈeɪtʃˈpiː] *abbr* (*horsepower*) caballos *mpl* de vapor; (*abbreviation*) cv *mpl*.

HQ [ˈeɪtʃˈkjuː] *abbr* (*headquarters*) cuartel *m* general; *fig* centro de operaciones.

hr [aʊəʳ] *abbr* (*hour*) hora; (*abbreviation*) h.
▲ *pl* **hrs**.

HRH [ˈeɪtʃˈɑːrˈeɪts] *abbr* (*His/Her Royal Highness*) Su Alteza Real; (*abbreviation*) S.A.R.

hub [hʌb] **1** *n* AUTO cubo. **2** *fig* centro, eje *m*.

hubbub [ˈhʌbʌb] *n* (*tumult*) alboroto, bullicio, jaleo; (*voices*) vocerío, griterío.

hubby [ˈhʌbɪ] *n fam* marido.
▲ *pl* **hubbies**.

hubcap [ˈhʌbkæp] *n* AUTO tapacubos *m*.

huckleberry [ˈhʌkəlberɪ] *n* BOT arándano.
▲ *pl* **huckleberries**.

huddle [ˈhʌdəl] **1** *n* grupo. – **2** *i* (*crouch*) acurrucarse, apiñarse, amontonarse. **3** (*cluster*) apiñarse.
● **to go into a huddle,** conferenciar, discutir en conferencia.

Hudson [ˈhʌdsən] *n* el río Hudson.
■ **Hudson Bay,** la Bahía de Hudson.

hue [hjuː] *n* (*colour*) tinte *m*; (*shade*) matiz *m*.

hue and cry [hjuːənˈkraɪ] *n* protesta clamorosa, revuelo.

huff [hʌf] *n* enfado, enojo.
● **to be in a huff,** estar enojado,-a, estar indignado,-a. ‖ **to go into a huff,** enfadarse, enfurruñarse. ‖ **to huff and puff,** resoplar.

huffy [ˈhʌfɪ] *adj* enojadizo,-a, enfadadizo,-a, malhumorado,-a.
▲ *comp* **huffier,** *superl* **huffiest**.

hug [hʌg] **1** *n* abrazo. – **2** *t* abrazar. **3** *fig* (*kerb, coast*) pegarse a, ceñirse a.
● **to hug oneself,** *fig* congratularse, sentirse satisfecho,-a.
▲ *pt & pp* **hugged,** *ger* **hugging**.

huge [hjuːdʒ] *adj* enorme, inmenso,-a: *a huge undertaking,* una empresa gigantesca.
■ **a huge success,** un exitazo, un éxito rotundo.

hugely [ˈhjuːdʒlɪ] *adv* enormemente.

huh [hʌ] *interj fam* (*expressing surprise or disapproval*) ¡vaya!, ¡caramba!; (*inquiry*) ¿eh?, ¿qué?

hulk [hʌlk] **1** *n* (*ship*) buque *m* viejo, casco. **2** (*thing, person*) armatoste *m*, mole *f*, masa.

hulking [ˈhʌlkɪŋ] *adj* grueso,-a, pesado,-a.

hull [hʌl] **1** *n* (*of ship*) casco. **2** BOT (*shell*) cáscara; (*pod*) vaina. – **3** *t* (*peas, beans, etc*) desvainar.

hullabaloo [hʌləbəˈluː] *adj* griterío, follón *m*, escándalo, lío.

hullo [hʌˈləʊ] *interj* → **hello**.
▲ *pl* **hullos**.

hum [hʌm] **1** *n* (*of bees, engine*) zumbido. – **2** *i* (*bees, engine etc*) zumbar. **3** (*sing*) tararear, canturrear. **4** (*bustling with activity*) hervir. – **5** *t* (*tune*) tararear, canturrear. – **6** *i fam* (*smell*) apestar.
● **to hum and haw,** vacilar.
▲ (*verbo*) *pt & pp* **hummed,** *ger* **humming**.

human [ˈhjuːmən] **1** *adj* humano,-a. – **2** **human / human being,** *n* ser *m* humano, humano.
■ **human interest,** interés *m* humano. ‖ **human nature,** naturaleza humana. ‖ **human race,** raza humana. ‖ **human rights,** derechos *mpl* humanos.

humane [hjuːˈmeɪn] *adj* humano,-a.

humanely [hjuːˈmeɪnlɪ] *adv* de forma humanitaria.

humanism [ˈhjuːmənɪzəm] *n* humanismo.

humanist [ˈhjuːmənɪst] **1** *n* humanista *mf*. – **2** *adj* humanista.

humanitarian [hjuːmænɪˈteərɪən] **1** *adj* humanitario,-a, filantrópico,-a. – **2** *n* filántropo,-a.

humanity [hjuːˈmænɪtɪ] **1** *n* (*virtue*) humanidad *f*. **2** (*mankind*) género humano, raza humana.
■ **the humanities,** las humanidades.
▲ *pl* **humanities**.

humanly [ˈhjuːmənlɪ] *adv* humanamente: *it's not humanly possible,* no es humanamente posible.

humanoid [ˈhjuːmənɔɪd] *n* humanoide *mf*.

humble [ˈhʌmbəl] **1** *adj* humilde. – **2** *t* humillar.
● **to eat humble pie,** admitir estar equivocado,-a.

humbleness [ˈhʌmbəlnəs] *n* humildad *f*.

humbly [ˈhʌmblɪ] *adv* humildemente.

humbug [ˈhʌmbʌg] **1** *n fam* (*lie*) bola, embuste *m*. **2** (*person*) farsante *mf*, embaucador,-ra. **3** (*nonsense*) tonterías *fpl*, disparates *mpl*. **4** GB (*sweet*) caramelo de menta.

humdrum [ˈhʌmdrʌm] *adj* monótono,-a, aburrido,-a.

humerus [ˈhjuːmərəs] *n* ANAT (*bone*) húmero.
▲ *pl* **humeri** [ˈhjuːmərai].

humid [ˈhjuːmɪd] *adj* húmedo,-a.

humidifier [hjuːˈmɪdɪfaɪəʳ] *n* humidificador *m*.

humidity [hjuːˈmɪdɪtɪ] *n* humedad *f*.

humiliate [hjuːˈmɪlɪeɪt] *t* humillar.

humiliation [hjuːmɪlɪˈeɪʃən] *n* humillación *f*.

humility [hjuːˈmɪlɪtɪ] *n* humildad *f*.

hummingbird [ˈhʌmɪŋbɜːd] *n* ORN colibrí *m*.

humor [ˈhjuːməʳ] *n* US → **humour**.

humorist [ˈhjuːmərɪst] **1** *n* (*writer or teller of funny stories*) humorista *mf*. **2** (*joker*) bromista *mf*.

humorous [ˈhjuːmərəs] **1** *adj* (*funny*) gracioso,-a, divertido,-a. **2** (*writer*) humorístico,-a, humorista.

humour [ˈhjuːməʳ] **1** *n* humor *m*. **2** (*of a joke*) gracia. **3** (*whim*) capricho. – **4** *t* complacer, seguir el humor a.
● **to be out of humour,** estar de mal humor.
■ **sense of humour,** sentido del humor.

hump [hʌmp] **1** *n* (*on back*) giba, joroba. **2** (*hillock*) montículo. – **3** *t* GB *fam* (*carry*) cargar. **4** *taboo* joder, follar. – **5** *i taboo* joder, follar.
● **to be over the hump,** haber hecho lo más difícil. ‖ **to have the hump,** GB *fam* estar de mal humor.

humpback [ˈhʌmpbæk] *n* jorobado,-a.

humpbacked [ˈhʌmpbækt] *adj* jorobado,-a, corcovado,-a.
■ **humpbacked bridge,** puente *m* peraltado.

humus [ˈhjuːməs] *n* AGR mantillo, humus *m*.

Hun [hʌn] **1** *n* HIST huno,-a. **2** *fam pej* alemán,-ana.

hunch [hʌntʃ] **1** *n* presentimiento, intuición *f*: *he acts on his hunches,* actúa por intuición. – **2** *t* encorvar.
● **to have a hunch,** tener una corazonada.

hunchback ['hʌntʃbæk] *n* (*person*) jorobado,-a.

hundred ['hʌndrəd] **1** *n* cien: *a hundred volunteers,* cien voluntarios; *a hundred and ten kilos,* ciento diez kilos; *five hundred years ago,* hace quinientos años; *it costs two hundred pesetas,* cuesta doscientas pesetas; *a hundred and fifty cars,* ciento cincuenta coches; *in the eighteen hundreds,* en el siglo diecinueve; *he lived to be a hundred,* llegó a los cien años. – **2 hundreds,** *npl* (*many*) centenares *mpl,* cientos *mpl: there were hundreds of cyclists,* había centenares de ciclistas; *there are hundreds of ways to save money,* hay cientos de maneras de ahorrar dinero.
● **a hundred per cent,** (*literally*) ciento por ciento; (*figuratively*) totalmente: *a hundred per cent of the votes have been counted,* el ciento por ciento de los votos han sido escrutados; *I agree with you a hundred per cent,* estoy totalmente de acuerdo contigo.

hundredth ['hʌndrədθ] **1** *adj* centésimo,-a. – **2** *adv* en centésimo lugar. – **3** *n* (*in series*) centésimo,-a. **4** *n* (*fraction*) centésimo; (*one part*) centésima parte *f.* **5** (*of time*) centésima.

hundredweight ['hʌndrədweit] *n* quintal *m.*
▲ *pl* **hundredweight** *o* **hundredweights;** *en Gran Bretaña equivale a 50,8 kg; en Estados Unidos equivale a 45,4 kg.*

hung [hʌŋ] *pt & pp →* **hang.**
● **to be hung over,** tener resaca, estar con resaca. ‖ **to be hung up,** estar acomplejado,-a. ‖ **to be hung up on,** estar obsesionado,-a con. ‖ **to be well hung,** estar bien dotado.
■ **hung jury,** *jurado cuyos miembros no se ponen de acuerdo.* ‖ **hung parliament,** *parlamento en el que ningún partido cuenta con una mayoría suficiente para formar gobierno.*

Hungarian [hʌŋ'geərɪən] **1** *adj* húngaro,-a. – **2** *n* (*person*) húngaro,-a. **3** (*language*) húngaro.

Hungary ['hʌŋgərɪ] *n* Hungría.

hunger ['hʌŋgəʳ] **1** *n* hambre *f: to die of hunger,* morirse de hambre *f.* **2** *fig* sed *f: hunger for revenge,* sed de venganza.
◆ **to hunger after / hunger for** *t insep* ansiar, anhelar, tener hambre de.
■ **hunger strike,** huelga de hambre.

hungry ['hʌŋgrɪ] **1** *adj* hambriento,-a. **2** *fig* ávido,-a, sediento,-a: *we're hungry for news from him,* estamos ávidos de recibir noticias suyas.
● **to be hungry,** tener hambre. ‖ **to go hungry,** pasar hambre. ‖ **to make sb. hungry,** abrir el apetito a algn., dar hambre a algn.
▲ *comp* **hungrier,** *superl* **hungriest.**

hunk [hʌŋk] **1** *n fam* (*piece*) pedazo (grande), buen trozo. **2** *fam* (*man*) cachas *m,* machote *m.*

Hunnish ['hʌnɪʃ] *adj* huno,-a.

hunt [hʌnt] **1** *n* (*gen*) caza, cacería. **2** (*search*) búsqueda. – **3** *t* caza. – **4** *i* (*for game*) cazar; (*search*) buscar.
◆ **to hunt down** *t sep* (*corner*) acorralar, perseguir; (*to find*) dar con, encontrar. ‖ **to hunt out / hunt up** *t sep* (*to find*) encontrar; (*to look for*) buscar.
● **to be on the hunt for,** ir en busca de, ir a la búsqueda de. ‖ **to hunt for,** buscar. ‖ **to hunt high and low for,** buscar por todas partes.

hunter ['hʌntəʳ] **1** *n* cazador,-ra *mf.* **2** zool caballo de caza. **3** (*watch*) saboneta.

hunting ['hʌntɪŋ] *n* (*gen*) caza; (*expedition*) cacería, montería.
● **a happy hunting ground for,** *fig* un terreno propicio para. ‖ **to go hunting,** ir de caza.
■ **hunting ground,** terreno de caza, coto de caza. ‖ **hunting horn,** cuerno de caza. ‖ **hunting knife,** cuchillo de caza, navaja de caza, navaja de monte.

huntress ['hʌntrəs] *n* cazadora.

huntsman ['hʌntsmən] *n* (*gen*) cazador *m;* (*of big game*) montero.
▲ *pl* **huntsmen** ['hʌntsmən].

hurdle ['hɜːdəl] **1** *n* sp valla. **2** *fig* obstáculo. – **3** *t* sp (*barrier*) saltar.

hurdler ['hɜːdləʳ] *n* sp corredor,-ra de vallas.

hurdling ['hɜːdlɪŋ] *n* sp carrera de vallas.

hurdy-gurdy ['hɜːdɪgɜːdɪ] *n* mus organillo.
▲ *pl* **hurdy-gurdies.**

hurl [hɜːl] **1** *t* lanzar, arrojar, tirar: *he hurled himself from the top of the building,* se arrojó de lo alto del edificio. **2** (*insults*) soltar.
● **to hurl abuse at sb.,** soltar una retahíla de insultos a algn.

hurling ['hɜːlɪŋ] *n* sp *juego irlandés parecido al rugby con quince jugadores en cada equipo.*

hurly-burly ['hɜːlɪbɜːlɪ] *n* alboroto, ajetreo, bullicio.

hurrah [hʊ'rɑː] **1** *interj* ¡hurra!: *hurrah for Peter!,* ¡viva Peter! – **2** *t* vitorear, aclamar. – **3** *i* dar vítores.

hurray [hʊ'reɪ] *interj* ¡hurra!

hurricane ['hʌrɪkən, 'hʌrɪkeɪn] *n* huracán *m.*
■ **hurricane lamp,** lámpara protegida contra el viento.

hurried ['hʌrɪd] *adj* apresurado,-a, hecho,-a de prisa.

hurriedly ['hʌrɪdlɪ] *adv* apresuradamente, deprisa.

hurry ['hʌrɪ] **1** *n* prisa: *what's the hurry!,* ¿a qué viene tanta prisa?; *are you in a hurry for the report?,* ¿le corre prisa el informe?; *I won't do that again in a hurry,* me lo pensaré dos veces la próxima vez. – **2** *i* apresurarse, darse prisa: *he hurried through his meal,* comió a toda prisa; *hurry!,* ¡date prisa! – **3** *t* dar prisa, meter prisa: *he's always hurrying me,* siempre me mete prisa; *they hurried her to hospital,* la llevaron a toda prisa al hospital.
◆ **to hurry up 1** *i* darse prisa. – **2** *t sep* dar prisa a, apresurar.
● **in a hurry,** de prisa. ‖ **to be in a hurry,** tener prisa.
▲ (*verbo*) *pt & pp* **hurried,** *ger* **hurrying.**

hurt [hɜːt] **1** *n* (*harm*) daño, dolor *m,* mal *m.* **2** (*wound*) herida. **3** *fig* daño, perjuicio. – **4** *adj* (*physically*) herido,-a. **5** (*offended*) dolido,-a. – **6** *t* (*cause injury*) lastimar, hacer daño; (*to wound*) herir: *he has hurt his arm,* se ha hecho daño en el brazo. **7** sp lesionar. **8** (*offend*) herir, ofender: *you hurt her feelings,* la has ofendido, le has herido los sentimientos. – **9** *i* doler: *my eyes hurt,* me duelen los ojos. **10** *fam* venir mal, ir mal: *it doesn't hurt to have a drink now and again,* no viene mal tomarse un trago de vez en cuando; *it wouldn't hurt for him to work a little harder,* no le iría nada mal trabajar un poco más.
● **not to hurt a fly,** ser incapaz de matar una mosca. ‖ **to hurt os.,** hacerse daño, lastimarse.
▲ *pt & pp* **hurt.**

hurtful ['hɜːtfʊl] *adj* (*remark*) hiriente; (*experience*) doloroso,-a.

hurtle ['hɜːtəl] **1** *i* lanzarse, precipitarse: *they hurtled down the road,* se lanzaron a toda velocidad por la carretera. – **2** *t* lanzar.

husband ['hʌzbənd] *n* marido, esposo.

husbandry ['hʌzbəndrɪ] *n* AGR *fml* agricultura.
■ **animal husbandry,** cría de ganado.

hush [hʌʃ] **1** *n* quietud *f,* silencio. – **2** *t* callar, silenciar. – **3** *interj* ¡silencio! ¡cállate! ¡cállese! ¡chito!
◆ **to hush up** *t sep* (*affair*) echar tierra a; (*person*) hacer callar.

■ **hush money,** *fam* soborno (*que se paga para que alguien no hable*).

hush-hush [ˈhʌʃˈhʌʃ] *adj fam* confidencial, secreto,-a.

husk [hʌsk] **1** *n* (*of cereals etc*) cáscara; (*of beans etc*) vaina. **– 2** *t* (*nuts, cereals*) descascarar, descascarillar; (*beans, peas*) pelar, desvainar.

huskiness [ˈhʌskɪnəs] *n* ronquera.

husky¹ [ˈhʌskɪ] *adj* ronco,-a: *he has a husky voice,* tiene la voz ronca.
▲ *comp* **huskier,** *superl* **huskiest.**

husky² [ˈhʌskɪ] *n* (*dog*) perro esquimal.
▲ *pl* **huskies.**

hussar [huˈzaːʳ] *n* MIL húsar *m.*

hussy [ˈhʌzɪ] *n dated* (*woman*) fresca, descarada.
▲ *pl* **hussies.**

hustings [ˈhʌstɪŋz] *npl* GB POL (*platform*) tribuna *f sing* electoral; (*election*) elecciones *fpl*: *there have been heated debates at the hustings this year,* ha habido debates acalorados durante la campaña electoral este año.

hustle [ˈhʌsəl] **1** *n* bullicio. **– 2** *t* (*hurry*) dar prisa a. **3** (*jostle*) empujar, dar empujones a. **4** US *fam* hacerse con. **– 5** *i* apresurarse.
■ **hustle and bustle,** ajetreo.

hustler [ˈhʌsləʳ] **1** *n* (*cheat*) estafador,-ra, buscavidas *mf*. **2** US *sl* (*prostitute - man*) puto, chapero; (*- woman*) puta.

hut [hʌt] **1** *n* cabaña. **2** (*in garden*) cobertizo. **3** MIL barraca.

hutch [hʌtʃ] *n* jaula.

hyacinth [ˈhaɪəsɪnθ] *n* BOT jacinto.

hyaena [haɪˈiːnə] *n* hiena.

hybrid [ˈhaɪbrɪd] **1** *adj* híbrido,-a. **– 2** *n* híbrido.

hydrangea [haɪˈdreɪndʒə] *n* BOT hortensia.

hydrant [ˈhaɪdrənt] *n* boca de riego.

hydraulic [haɪˈdrɔːlɪk] *adj* hidráulico,-a.
■ **hydraulic brake,** freno hidráulico.

hydraulics [haɪˈdrɔːlɪks] *n* (*science*) hidráulica.

hydric [ˈhaɪdrɪk] *adj* hídrico,-a.

hydro [ˈhaɪdrəʊ] *n* GB (*spa*) balneario, estación *f* termal.
▲ *pl* **hydros.**

hydrocarbon [haɪdrəʊˈkaːbən] *n* CHEM hidrocarburo.

hydrochloric [haɪdrəˈklɒrɪk] *adj* clorhídrico,-a.
■ **hydrochloric acid,** ácido clorhídrico.

hydroelectric [haɪdrəʊɪˈlektrɪk] *adj* hidroeléctrico,-a.
■ **hydroelectric power station,** central *f* hidroeléctrica.

hydroelectricity [haɪdrəʊɪlekˈtrɪsɪtɪ] *n* hidroelectricidad *f.*

hydrofoil [ˈhaɪdrəfɔɪl] *n* hidroala *m.*

hydrogen [ˈhaɪdrədʒən] *n* CHEM hidrógeno.
■ **hydrogen bomb,** bomba de hidrógeno. ‖ **hydrogen peroxide,** TECH agua oxigenada.

hydrographer [haɪˈdrɒgrəfəʳ] *n* hidrógrafo,-a.

hydrography [haɪˈdrɒgrəfɪ] *n* hidrografía.

hydrolysis [haɪˈdrɒlɪsɪs] *n* CHEM hidrólisis *f.*

hydrophobia [haɪdrəˈfəʊbɪə] *n* MED hidrofobia.

hydroplane [ˈhaɪdrəpleɪn] *n* hidroavión *m,* hidroplano.

hydroponics [haɪdrəˈpɒnɪks] *n* hidroponía.

hydrotherapy [haɪdrəʊˈθerəpɪ] *n* MED hidroterapia.

hyena [haɪˈiːnə] *n* ZOOL hiena.

hygiene [ˈhaɪdʒiːn] *n* higiene *f.*

hygienic [haɪˈdʒiːnɪk] *adj* higiénico,-a.

hygrometer [haɪˈgrɒmɪtəʳ] *n* higrómetro.

hymen [ˈhaɪmən] *n* ANAT himen *m.*

hymn [hɪm] *n* himno.
■ **hymn book,** cantoral *m.*

hymnal [ˈhɪmnəl] *n* cantoral *m.*

hynotize [ˈhɪpnətaɪz] *t* hipnotizar.

hype [haɪp] **1** *t fam* exagerar, dar mucho bombo a. **– 2** *n fam* campaña publicitaria, bombo.
● **to be hyped up,** *fig* estar excitado,-a.

hyper- [ˈhaɪpəʳ] *pref* hiper-.

hyperactive [haɪpəˈæktɪv] *adj* hiperactivo,-a.

hyperbola [haɪˈpɜːbələ] *n* hipérbola.
▲ *pl* **hyperbole** [haɪˈpɜːbəlɪ] o **hyperbolas.**

hyperbole [haɪˈpɜːbəlɪ] *n* hipérbole *f.*

hypercritical [haɪpəˈkrɪtɪkəl] *adj* hipercrítico,-a.

hypermarket [ˈhaɪpəmaːkɪt] *n* GB hipermercado.

hypersensitive [haɪpəˈsensɪtɪv] *adj* hipersensible.

hypertension [haɪpəˈtenʃən] *n* MED hipertensión *f.*

hyphen [ˈhaɪfən] *n* guión *m.*

hyphenate [ˈhaɪfəneɪt] *t* escribir con guión, unir con guión.

hypnosis [hɪpˈnəʊsɪs] *n* MED hipnosis *f.*

hypnotic [hɪpˈnɒtɪk] *adj* hipnótico,-a.

hypnotism [ˈhɪpnətɪzəm] *n* hipnotismo.

hypnotist [ˈhɪpnətɪst] *n* hipnotizador,-ra.

hypnotize [ˈhɪpnətaɪz] *t* hipnotizar.

hypo [ˈhaɪpəʊ] **1** *n* (*photography*) fijador *m.* **2** *fam* jeringa.
▲ En **2** *pl* **hypos.**

hypo- [ˈhaɪpəʊ] *pref* hipo-.

hypoallergenic [haɪpəæləˈdzenɪk] *adj* (*cosmetics etc*) hipoalérgico,-a.

hypochondria [haɪpəˈkɒndrɪə] *n* hipocondría.

hypochondriac [haɪpəˈkɒndrɪæk] **1** *n* hipocondríaco,-a. **– 2** *adj* hipocondríaco,-a.

hypocrisy [hɪˈpɒkrɪsɪ] *n* hipocresía.

hypocrite [ˈhɪpəkrɪt] *n* hipócrita *mf.*

hypocritical [hɪpəˈkrɪtɪkəl] *adj* hipócrita.

hypodermic [haɪpəˈdɜːmɪk] *adj* hipodérmico,-a.

hypotension [haɪpəʊˈtenʃən] *n* MED hipotensión *f.*

hypotenuse [haɪˈpɒtənjuːz] *n* (*geometry*) hipotenusa.

hypothermia [haɪpəʊθɜːmɪə] *n* MED hipotermia.

hypothesis [haɪˈpɒθəsɪs] *n* hipótesis *f.*
▲ *pl* **hypotheses** [haɪˈpɒθɪsiːz].

hypothetic [haɪpəˈθetɪk] *adj* hipotético,-a.

hypothetical [haɪpəˈθetɪkəl] *adj* hipotético,-a.

hysterectomy [hɪstəˈrektəmɪ] *n* MED histerectomía.
▲ *pl* **hysterectomies.**

hysteria [hɪˈstɪərɪə] *n* histeria.

hysterical [hɪˈsterɪkəl] *adj* histérico,-a.
■ **hysterical laughter,** risa incontrolable.

hysterically [hɪˈsterɪkəlɪ] *adv* histéricamente.

hysterics [hɪˈsterɪks] **1** *n* (*attack*) ataque *m* de histeria. **2** *fam* ataque *m* de risa.
● **to have hysterics,** mondarse de risa.

HZ [ˈeɪtʃˈzed] *abbr* (*hertz*) hercio, hercios; (*abbreviation*) Hz

I

I, i [aɪ] *n* (*the letter*) I, i *f*.

I [aɪ] *pron* yo: *my name's Paul, I'm English,* me llamo Paul, soy inglés; *I'm going home,* me voy a casa; *my husband and I,* mi marido y yo.
● **I, for one,** personalmente.

IATA [iːˈɑːtə] *abbr* (*International Air Transport Association*) Asociación *f* del Transporte Aéreo Internacional; (*abbreviation*) IATA *f*.

IBA [ˈaɪˈbiːˈeɪ] *abbr* GB (*Independent Broadcasting Authority*) ente que regulaba las televisiones privadas.
▲ Véase también **ITC**.

Iberia [aɪˈbɪərɪə] *n* Iberia.

Iberian [aɪˈbɪərɪən] **1** *adj* (*modern*) ibérico,-a; (*historically*) ibero,-a, íbero,-a, ibérico,-a. – **2** *n* (*person - now*) ibérico,-a; (*- historically*) ibero,-a, íbero,-a. **3** (*language*) ibero, íbero.
■ **Iberian Peninsula,** Península Ibérica.

ibex [ˈaɪbeks] *n* íbice *m*.
▲ *pl* **ibex** [ˈaɪbeks] o **ibexes** [ˈaɪbeksɪz].

ibis [ˈaɪbɪs] *n* ibis *f*.
▲ *pl* **ibis** [ˈaɪbɪs] o **ibises** [ˈaɪbɪsɪz].

Ibiza [ɪˈbiːθə] *n* Ibiza.

Ibizan [ɪˈbiːθən] **1** *adj* ibicenco,-a. – **2** *n* ibicenco,-a.

ICBM [ˈaɪˈsiːˈbiːˈem] *abbr* (*intercontinental ballistic missile*) proyectil *m* balístico intercontinental; (*abbreviation*) PBI *m*.

ice [aɪs] **1** *n* (*frozen water*) hielo: *there was ice on the road,* la carretera estaba helada. **2** (*ice-cream*) helado. – **3** *t* (*cake*) glasear.
◆ **to ice over** *i* (*lake etc*) helarse; (*windscreen etc*) cubrirse de hielo. ‖ **to ice up** *i* → **ice over**.
● **to break the ice,** romper el hielo. ‖ **to cut no ice (with sb.),** dejar frío,-a (a algn.). ‖ **to keep on ice,** (*wine*) mantener en frío; (*project, plan, etc*) congelar. ‖ **to put sth. on ice,** (*wine*) poner a enfriar; (*project, plan, etc*) congelar. ‖ **to skate on thin ice / tread on thin ice,** pisar un terreno resbaladizo, estar en la cuerda floja.
■ **ice age,** período glacial. ‖ **ice axe,** piolet *m*, piqueta de alpinista. ‖ **ice cube,** cubito de hielo, cubito. ‖ **ice field,** banquisa. ‖ **ice floe2,** témpano. ‖ **ice hockey,** hockey *m* sobre hielo. ‖ **ice man,** US vendedor *m* de hielo, repartidor *m* de hielo. ‖ **ice pack,** bolsa de hielo. ‖ **ice pick,** picahielos *m*. ‖ **ice show,** espectáculo sobre hielo. ‖ **ice skate,** patín *m* de hielo. ‖ **ice water,** US agua *m* helada.

iceberg [ˈaɪsbɜːɡ] **1** *n* iceberg *m*. **2** *fig* persona fría.
■ **iceberg lettuce,** lechuga iceberg.

icebound [ˈaɪsbaʊnd] *adj* (*harbour etc*) bloqueado,-a por el hielo; (*ship*) atrapado,-a por el hielo.

icebox [ˈaɪsbɒks] **1** *n* US nevera. **2** (*freezing compartment*) congelador *m*.

icebreaker [ˈaɪsbreɪkə^r] *n* rompehielos *m inv*.

icecap [ˈaɪskæp] *n* casquete *m* polar.

ice-cold [ˈaɪskəʊld] *adj* helado,-a.

ice-cream [ˈaɪskriːm] *n* helado.
■ **ice-cream cone,** cucurucho de helado. ‖ **ice-cream cornet,** cucurucho de helado. ‖ **ice-cream parlour,** heladería. ‖ **ice-cream van,** *furgoneta ambulante para la venta de helados.*

iced [aɪst] *n* (*drink*) con hielo; (*cake*) glaseado,-a.

Iceland [ˈaɪslənd] *n* Islandia.

Icelander [ˈaɪsləndə^r] *n* (*person*) islandés,-esa.

Icelandic [aɪsˈlændɪk] **1** *adj* islandés,-esa. – **2** *n* (*language*) islandés *m*.

ice-skate [ˈaɪsskeɪt] *i* patinar sobre hielo.

ice-skater [ˈaɪsskeɪtə^r] *n* patinador,-ra sobre hielo.

ice-skating [ˈaɪsskeɪtɪŋ] *n* patinaje *m* sobre hielo.

icicle [ˈaɪsɪkəl] *n* carámbano.

icing [ˈaɪsɪŋ] *n* cobertura.
● **the icing on the cake,** remate *m*, guinda. ‖ **icing sugar,** azúcar *m* & *f* glas, azúcar *m* & *f* lustre.

icon [ˈaɪkɒn] *n* icono.

iconoclast [aɪˈkɒnəklæst] *n* iconoclasta *mf*.

iconoclastic [aɪkɒnəˈklæstɪk] *adj* iconoclasta.

icy [ˈaɪsɪ] **1** *adj* (*very cold - hand etc*) helado,-a; (*- wind*) glacial. **2** (*covered with ice*) cubierto,-a de hielo. **3** *fig* glacial: *an icy look,* una mirada glacial.
▲ *comp* **icier**, *superl* **iciest**.

ID [ˈaɪˈdiː] *abbr* (*identification*) identificación *f*.
■ **ID card,** documento nacional de identidad, DNI *m*.

I'd [aɪd] *contr* I would, I had.

idea [aɪˈdɪə] **1** *n* (*gen*) idea; (*opinion*) idea, opinión *f*: *that's a good idea!,* ¡es una buena idea!; *I've got an idea!,* ¡tengo una idea!, ¡se me ocurre una idea!; *whose idea was this anyway?,* ¿de quién era la idea?, ¿a quién se le ocurrió esto?; *people have some very odd ideas,* la gente tiene ideas muy raras; *you've got no idea what I'm talking about,* no tienes ni idea de lo que estoy hablando; *this sketch will give you a rough idea,* este dibujo te dará una idea aproximada; *he didn't have the faintest idea what time it was,* no tenía ni la menor idea de la hora que era; *we're toying with the idea of moving,* estamos acariciando la idea de mudarnos; *whatever gave you that idea?,* ¿cómo se te ha ocurrido (pensar) eso?, ¿de dónde has sacado esta idea?; *do you know where he is? -no, but I've got a very good idea!,* ¿sabes dónde está? –no, pero tengo una ligera sospecha; *well, you might as well get used to the idea,* bueno, ya puedes irte haciendo a la idea. **2** (*intuition*) impresión *f*, sensación *f*: *she had the idea that something was wrong,* tenía la impresión de que pasaba algo; *I've an idea you threw it away,* creo que lo tiraste, tengo la impresión de que lo tiraste. **3** (*concept*) concepto: *what's your idea of happiness?,* ¿cuál es tu concepto de la felicidad?; *this is not my idea of having fun,* esto no es lo que yo entiendo por diversión. **4** the idea, (*aim, purpose*) idea, intención *f*, objetivo: *the idea was to lose weight,* la idea era perder peso; *the idea of the game is to get the ball*

ideal

in the goal, el objetivo del juego es meter la pelota en la portería.
● **the (very) idea of it!,** ¡vaya ocurrencia!, ¡qué ocurrencia!, ¡a quién se le ocurre!, ¡ni hablar! ‖ **to get the idea,** *(understand)* comprender, entender, captar; *(learn)* aprender. ‖ **to get ideas,** hacerse ilusiones. ‖ **to give sb. ideas,** dar ilusiones a algn. ‖ **to have no idea,** no tener idea, no tener ni idea: *I've no idea!,* ¡ni idea! ‖ **not to have the first idea about sth.,** no tener ni la más mínima idea de algo. ‖ **to hit on the idea of sth.,** ocurrírsele la idea a algn.: *then we hit on the idea of using silicon,* entonces se nos ocurrió la idea de usar silicona. ‖ **to put ideas into sb.'s head,** meter ideas en la cabeza a algn. ‖ **that's the idea!,** ¡eso es!, ¡así se hace! ‖ **what's the big idea?,** ¿qué pasa aquí?, ¿qué es esto?, ¿qué te has creído?

ideal [aɪˈdiːl] **1** *adj* ideal, perfecto,-a: *the ideal relationship,* la relación ideal; *the ideal person for the job,* la persona idónea para el trabajo; *in an ideal world,* en un mundo perfecto. – **2** *n (perfect example)* ideal *m*: *she's many men's ideal of what a woman should look like,* ella representa el ideal femenino para muchos hombres. **3** *(principle)* principio *m*, ideal *m*: *we are committed to our socialist ideals,* estamos comprometidos con nuestros principios socialistas; *I used to have high ideals,* yo tuve grandes ideales.

idealise [aɪˈdɪəlaɪz] *n →* **idealize**.

idealism [aɪˈdɪəlɪzəm] *n* idealismo: *youthful idealism,* idealismo juvenil.

idealist [aɪˈdɪəlɪst] *n* idealista *mf.*

idealistic [aɪdɪəˈlɪstɪk] *adj* idealista.

idealistically [aɪdɪəˈlɪstɪklɪ] *adv* de forma idealista.

idealize [aɪˈdɪəlaɪz] *t* idealizar: *they tend to idealize the past,* tienden a idealizar el pasado.

ideally [aɪˈdɪəlɪ] **1** *adv (perfectly)* idealmente, perfectamente: *he's ideally suited to the job,* está hecho para este puesto; *the house is ideally situated,* la casa está situada en el lugar perfecto. **2** *(preferably)* a ser posible: *ideally, everyone would have a job,* lo ideal sería que todo el mundo tuviera trabajo; *you can either ... or ... or, ideally, both,* o puedes ... o ... a ser posible, las dos cosas.

identical [aɪˈdentɪkəl] **1** *adj (exactly alike)* idéntico,-a **(to/ with,** a): *they were wearing identical dresses,* llevaban vestidos idénticos. **2 the identical,** *(the same)* el mismo, la misma: *he is the identical man who was here last week,* es el mismo hombre que estuvo aquí la semana pasada.
■ **identical twins,** gemelos,-as.

identification [aɪdentɪfɪˈkeɪʃən] **1** *n (gen)* identificación *f.* **2** *(papers)* documentación *f: have you got any means of identification?,* ¿tiene alguna documentación?
■ **identification parade,** rueda de reconocimiento.

identify [aɪˈdentɪfaɪ] **1** *t (prove or show identity of, recognize)* identificar: *she identified him as the man who had attacked her,* lo identificó como el hombre que la había atacado; *he has been identified as The Fox,* se le ha identificado como El Zorro; *I had to identify the body,* tuve que identificar el cadáver; *she can identify a bird by its call,* sabe identificar un pájaro por su canto. **2** *(discover)* descubrir, averiguar, identificar: *they've identified the cause of the epidemic,* han identificado la causa de la epidemia. **3** *(associate)* asociar **(with,** con), relacionar **(with,** con): *do you identify money with happiness?,* ¿relacionas el dinero con la felicidad?
◆ **to identify with 1** *t sep (associate)* relacionar con, asociar con: *people tend to identify him with the far left,*

suelen relacionarlo con la extrema izquierda. – **2** *i (sympathize)* identificarse con: *I couldn't identify with the protagonist of the film,* no podía identificarme con el protagonista de la película.
● **to identify os.,** identificarse.
▲ *pt & pp identified, ger identifying.*

Identikit [aɪˈdentɪkɪt] **Identikit picture,** *n* retrato robot.

identity [aɪˈdentɪtɪ] *n* identidad *f: you must give proof of identity,* tiene que acreditar su identidad; *it was a case of mistaken identity,* fue un error de identificación.
■ **identity card,** carnet *m* de identidad.
▲ *pl identities.*

ideological [aɪdɪəˈlɒdʒɪkəl] *adj* ideológico,-a.

ideology [aɪdɪˈɒlədʒɪ] *n* ideología: *according to Marxist ideology,* según la ideología marxista.
▲ *pl ideologies.*

idiocy [ˈɪdɪəsɪ] **1** *n (stupidity)* idiotez *f.* **2** *(stupid act etc)* estupidez *f.*
▲ *pl idiocies.*

idiom [ˈɪdɪəm] **1** *n (phrase)* locución *f,* modismo, frase *f* hecha. **2** *(language)* lenguaje *m,* idioma *m; (style)* estilo.

idiomatic [ɪdɪəˈmætɪk] *adj* idiomático,-a.
■ **idiomatic expression,** locución *f,* modismo, frase *f* hecha.

idiosyncrasy [ɪdɪəˈsɪŋkrəsɪ] *n* idiosincrasia, rareza, manía.
▲ *pl idiosincrasies.*

idiosyncratic [ɪdɪəsɪŋˈkrætɪk] *adj* idiosincrásico,-a.

idiot [ˈɪdɪət] **1** *n fam* idiota *mf,* imbécil *mf,* tonto,-a. **2** MED idiota *mf.*

idiotic [ɪdɪˈɒtɪk] *adj* idiota, imbécil, tonto,-a.

idiotically [ɪdɪˈɒtɪklɪ] *adv* como un idiota.

idle [ˈaɪdəl] **1** *adj (lazy)* perezoso,-a, holgazán,-ana, vago,-a: *my brother's so idle,* mi hermano es tan vago. **2** *(not working - person)* parado,-a, desempleado,-a, sin trabajo, inactivo,-a; *(- machinery)* parado,-a; *(- money)* improductivo,-a. **3** *(time)* libre, de ocio. **4** *(groundless - threat, hope, promise)* fútil, vano,-a, inútil; *(- fear, suspicion)* infundado,-a: *it's idle to speculate,* es inútil especular. **5** *(frivolous, trivial)* frívolo, trivial, banal, sin importancia, insignificante: *idle curiosity,* pura curiosidad; *idle pleasures,* placeres frívolos, frivolidades; *it's only idle gossip,* no son más que habladurías. – **6** *i (waste time)* gandulear, holgazanear, perder el tiempo. **7** *(engine)* funcionar en vacío.
◆ **to idle away** *t sep* desperdiciar, perder.
● **to be bone idle,** no dar ni golpe, ser gandul,-la.

idleness [ˈaɪdəlnəs] **1** *n (laziness)* holgazanería. **2** *(unemployment)* paro, desempleo. **3** *(inactivity)* inactividad *f; (leisure)* holganza, ociosidad *f.*

idler [ˈaɪdələ] *n* holgazán,-ana, vago,-a, gandul,-la.

idly [ˈaɪdlɪ] **1** *adv (abstractedly)* distraídamente. **2** *(lazily)* perezosamente. **3** *(groundlessly)* vanamente, inútilmente.

idol [ˈaɪdəl] *n* ídolo.

idolatry [aɪˈdɒlətrɪ] *n* idolatría.
▲ *pl idolatries.*

idolise [ˈaɪdəlaɪz] *t →* **idolize**.

idolize [ˈaɪdəlaɪz] *t* idolatrar.

idyll [ˈɪdɪl] *n* idilio.

idyllic [ɪˈdɪlɪk] *adj* idílico,-a.

idyllically [ɪˈdɪlɪklɪ] *adv* idílicamente.

ie [ˈaɪˈiː] *abbr (id est)* esto es, a saber; *(abbreviation)* i.e.

if [ɪf] **1** *conj (supposing)* si: *if it rains, we'll stay at home,* si llueve, nos quedaremos en casa; *if anyone phones, I'm out,* si llama alguien, no estoy; *if she should arrive ...,* si llegase ...; *you can come if you want,* puedes venir si quieres; *if my mother were here, she'd know what to do,* si estuviera mi madre, sabría qué hacer; *what would you do if you won the lottery?,* ¿qué harías si ganaras la lotería?; *if you hadn't gone to bed so late, you wouldn't be so tired,* si no te hubieras acostado tan tarde, no estarías tan cansado; *if you'd studied harder, you would have passed the exam,* si hubieras estudiado más, habrías aprobado el examen; *if you heat water to 100 degrees, it boils,* te calientas el agua a 100 grados, hierve; *if you're not sure about anything, don't hesitate to ask,* si no estás seguro de algo, no dudes en preguntar. **2** (*whether*) si: *do you know if she got the job?,* ¿sabes si consiguió el trabajo?; *I'll ask him if he's going to the concert,* le preguntaré si va al concierto; *find out if she's free tonight,* entérate de si está libre esta noche. **3** (*used after verbs expressing feelings*) que: *I'd appreciate it if you didn't tell anyone,* te agradecería que no se lo dijeras a nadie; *I'm sorry if I woke you,* siento haberte despertado, perdona que te haya despertado; *do you mind if I open the window?,* ¿te importa que abra la ventana? **4** (*but*) aunque, pero: *a clever if rather talkative child,* un niño inteligente aunque demasiado hablador; *it's good, if a little slow at times,* es bueno pero algo lento a veces. **5** (*in exclamations*): *well, if it isn't Jimmy Jazz!,* vaya, ¡pero si es Jimmy Jazz! **6** *n fam* (*uncertainty*) expresa duda: *if she passes - and it's a big if ...,* suponiendo que apruebe - y ya es suponer ...

● *if any,* en caso de que ..., si es que ...: *there were very few mistakes, if any,* había muy pocos errores, si es que había alguno. ‖ *if anything,* más bien, en todo caso: *she's no better, if anything, she's worse,* no está mejor, en todo caso está peor. ‖ *if ever,* si alguna vez. ‖ *if I were you,* yo que tú, yo en tu lugar. ‖ *if not,* si no. ‖ *if only,* (*present or future time*) ¡ojalá!, ¡si al menos!; (*past events*) si: *if only we were rich,* ojalá fuéramos ricos; *if only I'd known,* si lo hubiera sabido, de haberlo sabido; *if only you'd told me!,* ¡si me lo hubieras dicho!, ¡habérmelo dicho!; *if only it were Friday,* ¡ojalá fuese viernes!; *come to the wedding, if only to please your mother,* ven a la boda, aunque sólo sea para complacer a tu madre. ‖ *if so,* de ser así, si así fuese. ‖ *ifs and buts,* pegas *fpl,* dudas *fpl,* peros *mpl,* reservas *fpl.* ‖ *it's not as if ... / it isn't as if ...,* no es que ...

iffy ['ɪfɪ] *adj fam* dudoso,-a.
▲ *comp* **iffier,** *superl* **iffiest.**

igloo ['ɪgluː] *n* iglú *m.*
▲ *pl* **igloos.**

ignite [ɪg'naɪt] **1** *t* encender, prender fuego. – **2** *i* encenderse, prender.

ignition [ɪg'nɪʃən] **1** *n* ignición *f.* **2** AUTO encendido, arranque *m.*
■ **ignition key,** llave *f* de contacto.

ignoble [ɪg'nəʊbəl] *adj* innoble, vil, infame.

ignobly [ɪg'nəʊbəlɪ] *adv* innoblemente, vilmente.

ignominious [ɪgnə'mɪnɪəs] *n* ignominioso,-a, vergonzoso,-a.

ignominiously [ɪgnə'mɪnɪəslɪ] *adv* ignominiosamente, vergonzosamente.

ignominy ['ɪgnəmɪnɪ] *n* ignominia, oprobio.
▲ *pl* **ignominies.**

ignoramus [ɪgnə'reɪməs] *n* ignorante *mf.*

ignorance ['ɪgnərəns] *n* ignorancia.
● *to be in ignorance of,* ignorar, desconocer, no saber. ‖ *ignorance is bliss,* bendita ignorancia.

ignorant ['ɪgnərənt] **1** *adj* (*unaware*) ignorante (**of,** de). **2** *fam* (*rude*) descortés, maleducado,-a.

● *to be ignorant of,* desconocer, ignorar, no saber.

ignore [ɪg'nɔːʳ] **1** *t* (*order, warning*) no hacer caso de, hacer caso omiso de; (*behaviour, fact*) pasar por alto: *he chose to ignore my question,* decidió no hacer caso de mi pregunta; *they ignored my advice and went ahead,* no hicieron caso de mi consejo y siguieron adelante; *he ignored the speed limit,* no respetó el límite de velocidad; *we can ignore that point for the moment,* de momento podemos pasar por alto este punto; *this report ignores the fact that ...,* este informe no tiene en cuenta el hecho de que ... **2** (*person*) hacer como si no existiese: *she completely ignored me,* hizo como si no existiera, hizo como si no me viera; *just ignore him,* no le hagas caso.

iguana [ɪ'gwɑːnə] *n* iguana.

ilk [ɪlk] *of that ilk, phr* de esa clase, de ese jaez.

ill [ɪl] **1** *adj* (*sick*) enfermo,-a: *she's been very ill,* ha estado muy enferma; *he was taken ill last night,* se puso enfermo anoche; *I feel ill,* me encuentro mal; *she looked quite ill,* hacía muy mala cara. **2** (*harmful, unpropitious*) malo,-a: *he suffers from ill health,* está mal de salud; *he suffered no ill effects,* no experimentamos efectos desfavorables; *ill repute,* mala fama; *ill luck,* mala suerte. – **3** *n fml* (*harm, evil*) mal *m.* – **4** *adv* (*badly*) mal: *the proposal was ill received,* la propuesta fue mal recibida. **5** (*unfavourably*) mal: *I won't speak ill of her,* no hablaré mal de ella. **6** (*with difficulty, hardly*) mal, a duras penas: *I can ill afford it,* difícilmente me lo puedo permitir, a duras penas puedo permitírmelo. – **7** *ills, npl* (*problems, misfortunes*) desgracias *fpl.*
● *to be ill at ease,* estar incómodo,-a. ‖ *to bear sb. no ill will,* no guardarle a algn. ningún rencor. ‖ *to fall ill,* caer enfermo,-a. ‖ *it's an ill wind that blows nobody any good,* no hay mal que por bien no venga. ‖ *bird of ill omen,* pájaro agorero, pájaro de mal agüero.
■ **ill feeling,** resentimiento. ‖ **ill humour,** mal humor *m.* ‖ **ill temper,** mal humor *m.* ‖ **ill will,** rencor *m.*

I'll [aɪl] *contr* I will, I shall.

ill-advised [ɪləd'vaɪzd] *adj* desaconsejable, poco aconsejable, desacertado,-a: *you would be ill-advised to leave your job now,* no sería aconsejable que dejaras tu trabajo ahora; *an ill-advised project,* un proyecto descabellado.

ill-behaved [ɪlbɪ'heɪvd] *adj* maleducado,-a.

ill-bred [ɪl'bred] *adj* maleducado,-a, malcriado,-a.

ill-considered [ɪlkən'sɪdəd] *adj* poco meditado,-a, poco pensado,-a, imprudente.

ill-defined [ɪldɪ'faɪnd] *adj* indefinido,-a.

ill-disposed [ɪldɪ'spəʊzd] *adj fml* (*unfriendly*) mal dispuesto,-a, poco dispuesto,-a; (*unsympathetic*) indiferente, impasible.
● *to be ill-disposed towards sb.,* estar predispuesto,-a en contra de algn., tener una actitud poco favorable hacia algn.

illegal [ɪ'liːgəl] *adj* ilegal.

illegality [ɪlɪ'gælɪtɪ] *n* ilegalidad *f.*
▲ *pl* **illegalities.**

illegally [ɪ'liːgəlɪ] *adv* ilegalmente.

illegible [ɪ'ledʒɪbəl] *adj* ilegible.

illegitimacy [ɪlɪ'dʒɪtɪməsɪ] *n* ilegitimidad *f.*

illegitimate [ɪlɪ'dʒɪtɪmət] *adj* ilegítimo,-a.

ill-equipped [ɪlɪ'kwɪpt] *adj* (*equipment*) mal equipado,-a; (*ability*) mal preparado,-a.

ill-fated [ɪl'feɪtɪd] *adj* (*doomed*) funesto,-a, malhadado,-a, desafortunado,-a.

ill-founded [ɪl'faʊndɪd] *adj* (*fear, suspicion, accusation, rumour, etc*) infundado,-a; (*confidence, hope*) vano,-a.

ill-gotten ['ɪlgɒtən] *adj* mal adquirido,-a, adquirido,-a ilegalmente: *ill-gotten gains,* bienes adquiridos de forma ilícita.

illicit [ɪ'lɪsɪt] *adj* ilícito,-a.

illicitly [ɪ'lɪsɪtlɪ] *adv* ilícitamente.

illiteracy [ɪ'lɪtərəsɪ] *n* analfabetismo.

illiterate [ɪ'lɪtərət] **1** *adj* (*unlettered*) analfabeto,-a. **2** (*uneducated*) ignorante, inculto,-a. **3** (*poor style*) inculto,-a, pobre. – **4** *n* (*unlettered person*) analfabeto,-a.

ill-mannered [ɪl'mænəd] *adj* maleducado,-a, descortés.

illness ['ɪlnəs] *n* enfermedad *f.*
▲ *pl illnesses.*

illogical [ɪ'lɒdʒɪkəl] *adj* ilógico,-a.

illogically [ɪ'lɒdʒɪklɪ] *adv* ilógicamente.

ill-omened [ɪl'əʊmənd] *adj* de mal agüero, nefasto,-a.

ill-starred [ɪl'stɑːd] *adj* desdichado,-a, malhadado,-a.

ill-tempered [ɪl'tempəd] *adj* (*person*) de mal genio; (*remark etc*) malhumorado,-a.

ill-timed [ɪl'taɪmd] *adj* inoportuno,-a.

ill-treat [ɪl'triːt] *t* maltratar.

ill-treatment [ɪl'triːtmənt] *n* malos tratos *mpl.*

illuminate [ɪ'luːmɪneɪt] *t* iluminar.

illuminating [ɪ'luːmɪneɪtɪŋ] *adj* (*revealing*) revelador,-ra; (*instructive*) instructivo,-a.

illumination [ɪluːmɪ'neɪʃən] **1** *n* (*light*) iluminación *f.* **2** (*clarification*) aclaración. – **3 illuminations,** *npl* iluminación *f sing,* luces *fpl,* iluminaciones *fpl,* alumbrado decorativo.

illusion [ɪ'luːʒən] *n* ilusión *f,* falsa impresión *f: it's not real, it's just an illusion,* no es real, no es más que un engaño.
● **to be under the illusion that ...,** creer equivocadamente que ..., engañarse pensando que ... ‖ **to have no illusions about sth.,** no hacerse ilusiones respecto a algo.

illusive [ɪ'luːsɪv] *adj* ilusorio,-a.

illusory [ɪ'luːsərɪ] *adj* ilusorio,-a.

illustrate ['ɪləstreɪt] *t* ilustrar.

illustration [ɪləs'treɪʃən] **1** *n* (*gen*) ilustración *f.* **2** (*example*) ejemplo.

illustrative ['ɪləstrətɪv] **1** *adj* (*gen*) ilustrativo,-a, ilustrador,-ra. **2** (*example*) aclaratorio,-a.

illustrator ['ɪləstreɪtəʳ] *n* ilustrador,-ra.

illustrious [ɪ'lʌstrɪəs] *adj* ilustre.

ILO ['aɪ'el'əʊ] *abbr* (*International Labour Organization*) Organización *f* Internacional del Trabajo; (*abbreviation*) OIT *f.*

I'm [aɪm] *contr* I am.

image ['ɪmɪdʒ] **1** *n* (*gen*) imagen *f.* **2** (*reputation*) imagen *f,* fama, reputación *f: we need to improve our public image,* tenemos que mejorar nuestra imagen.
● **to be the spitting image of ...,** ser la viva imagen de ...

imagery ['ɪmɪdʒərɪ] *n lit* imágenes *fpl.*

imaginable [ɪ'mædʒɪnəbəl] *adj* imaginable, concebible.

imaginary [ɪ'mædʒɪnərɪ] *adj* imaginario,-a, inventado,-a.

imagination [ɪmædʒɪ'neɪʃən] *n* (*gen*) imaginación *f;* (*inventiveness*) inventiva: *it's your imagination,* son imaginaciones tuyas; *her drawings reveal a vivid imagination,* sus dibujos revelan una imaginación viva.
● **to let one's imagination run away with one,** dejarse llevar por la imaginación.

imaginative [ɪ'mædʒɪnətɪv] *adj* (*person*) imaginativo,-a, de gran inventiva; (*creation*) lleno,-a de imaginación, lleno,-a de fantasía.

imagine [ɪ'mædʒɪn] **1** *t* (*visualize*) imaginar: *try to imagine you're lying on the beach,* intenta imaginar que estás tumbado en la playa; *I can't imagine her at a disco,* no la puedo imaginar en una discoteca; *he often imagined what it would be like to be rich,* solía imaginar cómo sería ser rico; *she couldn't imagine life without George,* no podía imaginar la vida sin George; *you're imagining things,* son imaginaciones tuyas. **2** (*suppose*) suponer, imaginar(se), figurarse: *I imagine Dave'll be going,* me imagino que Dave irá; *she was far nicer than I imagined,* era mucho más simpática de lo que me imaginaba; *you can just imagine how I felt,* ya te puedes imaginar cómo me sentía.
● **just imagine!,** ¡imagínate!, ¡fíjate!

imbalance [ɪm'bæləns] *n* desequilibrio, falta de equilibrio.

imbecile ['ɪmbəsiːl] *n* imbécil *mf.*

imbibe [ɪm'baɪb] **1** *t fml* (*liquids*) beber. **2** (*knowledge*) asimilar, absorber, imbuirse de. – **3** *i* beber.

imbue [ɪm'bjuː] *t fml* imbuir (**with,** de), infundir.
● **to be imbued with sth.,** estar lleno,-a de algo, estar empapado,-a de algo. ‖ **to become imbued with sth.,** imbuirse de algo.

IMF ['aɪ'em'ef] *abbr* (*International Monetary Fund*) Fondo Monetario Internacional; (*abbreviation*) FMI *m.*

imitate ['ɪmɪteɪt] *t* (*gen*) imitar, copiar; (*for fun*) imitar: *he can imitate Elvis really well,* sabe imitar muy bien a Elvis.

imitation [ɪmɪ'teɪʃən] **1** *n* (*gen*) imitación *f,* copia; (*for fun*) imitación *f: she does a good imitation of Margaret Thatcher,* hace una buena imitación de Margaret Thatcher. **2** (*reproduction*) reproducción *f.* – **3** *adj* de imitación: *imitation leather,* piel de imitación.
● **beware of cheap imitations,** desconfíe de las imitaciones.

imitative ['ɪmɪtətɪv] *adj* imitativo,-a.

immaculate [ɪ'mækjʊlət] **1** *adj* (*perfectly clean, spotless*) inmaculado,-a; (*perfectly tidy*) perfectamente ordenado,-a; (*clothes, appearance*) impecable. **2** (*perfect, flawless*) perfecto,-a.
■ **the Immaculate Conception,** la Inmaculada Concepción.

immaculately [ɪ'mækjʊlətlɪ] **1** *adv* (*spotlessly*) inmaculadamente; (*clothes, appearance*) impecablemente: *immaculately dressed,* impecablemente vestido,-a. **2** (*perfectly, flawlessly*) perfectamente.

immaterial [ɪmə'tɪərɪəl] **1** *adj* (*unimportant*) irrelevante: *the price is immaterial,* da igual el precio, el precio no importa; *it's immaterial to me what you do,* me trae sin cuidado lo que hagas, me es indiferente lo que hagas. **2** (*incorporeal*) inmaterial, incorpóreo,-a.

immature [ɪmə'tjʊəʳ] **1** *adj* (*gen*) inmaduro,-a; (- *plant*) joven. **2** (*childish*) inmaduro,-a, pueril: *adolescent boys are so immature,* los chicos adolescentes son tan inmaduros.

immaturity [ɪmə'tjʊərətɪ] *n* inmadurez *f,* falta de madurez.

immeasurable [ɪ'meʒərəbəl] *adj* inconmensurable, incalculable.

immediacy [ɪ'miːdɪəsɪ] **1** *n* (*urgency*) urgencia, carácter *m* urgente. **2** (*nearness*) proximidad *f,* inmediación *f.*

immediate [ɪ'miːdɪət] **1** *adj* (*instant*) inmediato,-a; (*urgent*) urgente: *his immediate reaction was to phone the* *police,* su reacción inmediata fue llamar a la policía; *we must take immediate action,* hay que actuar inmediatamente; *a more immediate matter,* un asunto más urgente. **2** *(nearest)* inmediato,-a, más próximo,-a: *the immediate future,* el futuro inmediato; *in the immediate vicinity,* en las inmediaciones; *my immediate family,* mi familia directa; *there is no immediate danger of fire,* no existe peligro inminente de incendio. **3** *(direct)* primero,-a, principal: *immediate cause,* causa inmediata. ■ immediate heir, heredero,-a en línea directa.

immediately [ɪˈmiːdɪətlɪ] **1** *adv (instantly, at once)* inmediatamente, de inmediato, en seguida, en el acto: *I have to leave immediately,* me tengo que ir de inmediato; *he responded immediately,* respondió en seguida; *phone home immediately,* llama a casa inmediatamente; *the connection may not be immediately obvious,* puede que la relación no sea obvia a primera vista. **2** *(nearest in time or space)* directamente, inmediatamente; *(directly, very closely)* directamente, muy de cerca: *this information immediately concerns us,* esta información nos afecta directamente; *the years immediately following the war,* los años inmediatamente posteriores a la guerra; *he sat down immediately behind me,* se sentó inmediatamente detrás de mí. **3** *conj (as soon as)* en cuanto, tan pronto como: *I came immediately I knew,* vine en cuanto lo supe.

immemorial [ɪməˈmɔːrɪəl] *adj fml* inmemorial. ● from time immemorial, desde tiempos inmemoriales.

immense [ɪˈmens] *adj* inmenso,-a, enorme.

immensely [ɪˈmenslɪ] *adv (extremely)* enormemente, sumamente: *he's immensely pleased,* está sumamente agradecido; *I enjoyed myself immensely,* me lo pasé en grande.

immensity [ɪˈmensɪtɪ] *n* inmensidad *f.*

immerse [ɪˈmɜːs] *t* sumergir (**in,** en), hundir (**in,** en). ● to be immersed in sth., *fig* estar absorto,-a en algo. ‖ to immerse os. in sth., *fig* sumergirse en algo.

immersion [ɪˈmɜːʃən] **1** *n* inmersión *f,* submersión *f.* **2** *fig* absorción *f.* ■ immersion heater, calentador *m* de agua eléctrico.

immigrant [ˈɪmɪɡrənt] **1** *adj* inmigrante. **– 2** *n* inmigrante *mf.*

immigrate [ˈɪmɪɡreɪt] *i* inmigrar.

immigration [ɪmɪˈɡreɪʃən] *n* inmigración *f.* ■ immigration control, control *m* de inmigración.

imminence [ˈɪmɪnəns] *n* inminencia.

imminent [ˈɪmɪnənt] *adj* inminente.

immobile [ɪˈməʊbaɪl] *adj* inmóvil.

immobility [ɪməˈbɪlɪtɪ] *n* inmovilidad *f.*

immobilize [ɪˈməʊbɪlaɪz] *t* inmovilizar.

immoderate [ɪˈmɒdərət] *adj (gen)* excesivo,-a, desmesurado,-a, descomedido,-a; *(language)* soez.

immoderately [ɪˈmɒdərətlɪ] *adv* excesivamente, desmedidamente.

immodest [ɪˈmɒdɪst] **1** *adj (conceited)* presumido,-a, engreído,-a, creído,-a. **2** *(indecent)* indecente, impúdico,-a, deshonesto,-a.

immodesty [ɪˈmɒdɪstɪ] **1** *n (conceitedness)* presunción *f,* engreimiento. **2** *(indecency)* indecencia, falta de pudor.

immoral [ɪˈmɒrəl] *adj* inmoral. ■ immoral earnings, ganancias ilícitas.

immorality [ɪməˈrælətɪ] *n* inmoralidad *f.* ▲ *pl* immoralities.

immortal [ɪˈmɔːtəl] **1** *adj (god, soul, etc)* inmortal. **2** *fig (fame, memory, etc)* imperecedero,-a, perdurable. **– 3** *n* inmortal *mf.*

immortality [ɪmɔːˈtælɪtɪ] *n* inmortalidad *f.*

immortalize [ɪˈmɔːtəlaɪz] *t* inmortalizar.

immovable [ɪˈmuːvəbəl] **1** *adj (object)* inamovible. **2** *(person)* inconmovible, inflexible; *(opinion)* inflexible, inamovible.

immune [ɪˈmjuːn] **1** *adj (gen)* inmune (**to,** a): *she's immune to measles,* es inmune al sarampión; *he's immune to criticism,* es inmune a la crítica, no le afecta la crítica. **2** *(exempt)* exento,-a: *immune from taxes,* exento de impuestos.

immunity [ɪˈmjuːnɪtɪ] **1** *n (gen)* inmunidad *f.* **2** *(exemption)* exención *f.*

immunization [ɪmjənaɪˈzeɪʃən] *n* inmunización *f.*

immunize [ˈɪmjənaɪz] *t* inmunizar (**against,** contra).

immutable [ɪˈmjuːtəbəl] *adj fml* inmutable, inalterable.

imp [ɪmp] **1** *n (small devil)* diablillo, duendecillo. **2** *fig (naughty child)* pillo,-a, diablillo.

impact [ˈɪmpækt] **1** *n (gen)* impacto; *(crash)* choque *m*: *the bomb exploded on impact,* la bomba hizo explosión al chocar. **2** *(impression, effect)* efecto, impresión *f,* impacto: *the impact of confidence on the housing market,* el impacto de la confianza en el mercado de la vivienda. **– 3** *t US (have impact on)* impresionar. ● to make an impact on sb., producir un impacto a algn., impresionar a algn. ▲ *(verbo)* [ɪmˈpækt].

impacted [ɪmˈpæktɪd] *adj* impactado,-a.

impair [ɪmˈpeəʳ] **1** *t (damage - gen)* afectar, perjudicar; *(- health)* afectar, perjudicar. **2** *(weaken)* debilitar: *he suffers from impaired hearing,* tiene problemas de oído.

impale [ɪmˈpeɪl] *t (gen)* empalar; *(with sword etc)* atravesar.

impalpable [ɪmˈpælpəbəl] **1** *adj fml* impalpable, intangible. **2** *(difficult to understand)* abstruso,-a.

impart [ɪmˈpɑːt] **1** *t fml (inform)* comunicar, hacer saber; *(teach)* impartir, transmitir. **2** *fml (give - flavour)* dar; *(- quality)* otorgar, conferir.

impartial [ɪmˈpɑːʃəl] *adj* imparcial.

impartiality [ɪmpɑːʃɪˈælɪtɪ] *n* imparcialidad *f.*

impassable [ɪmˈpɑːsəbəl] *adj (road etc)* intransitable, impracticable; *(barrier)* infranqueable.

impasse [æmˈpɑːs] *n* punto muerto, impasse *m.*

impassioned [ɪmˈpæʃənd] *adj (gen)* apasionado,-a.

impassive [ɪmˈpæsɪv] *adj (expressionless)* impasible, imperturbable; *(indifferent)* indiferente.

impatience [ɪmˈpeɪʃəns] **1** *n (eagerness)* impaciencia, ansiedad *f.* **2** *(irritation)* impaciencia, irritación *f.*

impatient [ɪmˈpeɪʃənt] **1** *adj (eager)* impaciente, ansioso,-a: *she was impatient to arrive,* estaba impaciente por llegar; *the children are impatient for Christmas,* los niños están ansiosos de que llegue Navidad. **2** *(irritable)* irritable: *I get impatient with other drivers,* los demás conductores me hacen perder la paciencia. **3** *fml (intolerant)* intolerante. ● to become impatient with sb., perder la paciencia con algn. ‖ to grow impatient at sth., impacientarse por algo.

impatiently [ɪmˈpeɪʃəntlɪ] *adv* con impaciencia, impacientemente.

impeach [ɪmˈpiːtʃ] **1** *t JUR (accuse)* acusar; *(try)* procesar. **2** *fml (question)* poner en tela de juicio.

impeachment [ɪmˈpiːtʃmənt] *n JUR (accusation)* acusación *f,* denuncia; *(trial)* proceso.

impeccable [ɪmˈpekəbəl] *adj (gen)* impecable, perfecto,-a: *impeccable behaviour,* conducta intachable.

impeccably [ɪmˈpekəblɪ] *adv* impecablemente.

impecunious [ɪmpɪˈkjuːnɪəs] *adj fml* indigente, necesitado,-a.

impede [ɪm'piːd] *t* (*hinder*) estorbar, dificultar, impedir; (*obstruct*) poner obstáculos a, poner trabas a, obstaculizar: *the search was seriously impeded by bad weather,* la búsqueda se vió seriamente obstaculizada por el mal tiempo.

impediment [ɪm'pedɪmənt] **1** *n* (*gen*) impedimento, estorbo, obstáculo (**to,** para). **2** MED defecto.

impel [ɪm'pel] *t* impeler, impulsar: *she felt impelled to speak out against the plan,* se veía impelida a hablar en contra del proyecto.

▲ *pt & pp* **impelled,** *ger* **impelling.**

impending [ɪm'pendɪŋ] *adj* inminente.

impenetrable [ɪm'penɪtrəbəl] **1** *adj* (*gen*) impenetrable. **2** (*mystery, problem, etc*) insondable, inescrutable, impenetrable.

impenitent [ɪm'penɪtənt] *adj fml* impenitente.

imperative [ɪm'perətɪv] **1** *adj* (*indispensable*) imprescindible: *it's imperative that you come immediately,* es imprescindible que vengas de inmediato. **2** (*authoritative*) imperativo,-a, imperioso,-a: *an imperative tone of voice,* un tono de voz imperativo. **3** LING imperativo,-a. – **4** *n* LING imperativo.

imperceptible [ɪmpə'septəbəl] *adj* imperceptible.

imperceptibly [ɪmpə'septəblɪ] *adv* imperceptiblemente.

imperfect [ɪm'pɜːfekt] **1** *adj* (*gen*) imperfecto,-a; (*goods, sight*) defectuoso,-a. **2** LING imperfecto,-a. – **3** the imperfect, *n* LING el imperfecto.

imperfection [ɪmpə'fekʃən] *n* (*gen*) imperfección *f*; (*defect*) defecto, tara, tacha; (*blemish*) mancha.

imperial [ɪm'pɪərɪəl] **1** *adj* (*gen*) imperial. **2** (*weight, measure*) del sistema métrico británico: *an imperial gallon is equivalent to about four and a half litres,* un galón británico equivale a unos cuatro litros y medio.

imperialism [ɪm'pɪərɪəlɪzəm] *n* imperialismo.

imperialist [ɪm'pɪərɪəlɪst] **1** *n* imperialista *mf.* – **2** *adj* imperialista.

imperil [ɪm'perəl] *t fml* poner en peligro, arriesgar.

imperious [ɪm'pɪərɪəs] *adj* imperioso,-a, autoritario,-a.

imperishable [ɪm'perɪʃəbəl] *adj* imperecedero,-a.

impermanent [ɪm'pɜːmənənt] *adj* impermanente, caduco,-a.

impermeable [ɪm'pɜːmɪəbəl] *adj* impermeable.

impermissable [ɪmpə'mɪsəbəl] *adj fml* prohibido,-a.

impersonal [ɪm'pɜːsənəl] *adj* impersonal.

impersonate [ɪm'pɜːsəneɪt] *t* (*imitate to deceive*) hacerse pasar por. **2** (*imitate to entertain*) imitar.

impersonation [ɪmpɜːsə'neɪʃən] *n* imitación *f*.

impersonator [ɪm'pɜːsəneɪtər] *n* imitador,-ra.

impertinence [ɪm'pɜːtɪnəns] *n* impertinencia, descaro.

impertinent [ɪm'pɜːtɪnənt] *adj* impertinente, descarado,-a: *impertinent remark,* impertinencia.

impertinently [ɪm'pɜːtɪnəntlɪ] *adv* impertinentemente.

imperturbable [ɪmpə'tɜːbəbəl] *adj* imperturbable.

impervious [ɪm'pɜːvɪəs] **1** *adj* (*rock etc*) impermeable. **2** (*person*) insensible (**to,** a).

impetuosity [ɪmpetjʊ'ɒsətɪ] *n* impetuosidad *f*, irreflexión *f*.

impetuous [ɪm'petjʊəs] *adj* impetuoso,-a, irreflexivo,-a, impulsivo,-a.

impetuously [ɪm'petjʊəslɪ] *adv* impetuosamente, irreflexivamente.

impetus ['ɪmpətəs] **1** *n* (*drive*) ímpetu *m*, impulso, estímulo. **2** (*force*) ímpetu *m*.

impiety [ɪm'paɪətɪ] *n fml* impiedad *f*.

impinge [ɪm'pɪndʒ] **1** *i* (*affect*) afectar (**on,** a), repercutir (**on,** en), incidir (**on,** en). **2** (*encroach on*) vulnerar (**on,** -).

implacable [ɪm'plækəbəl] *adj* implacable.

implant ['ɪmplɑːnt] **1** *t* MED implantar, injertar. **2** (*ideas etc*) inculcar (**in,** en). – **3** *n* MED implantación *f*, injerto.

▲ En **3** (*sustantivo*) ['ɪmplɑːnt].

implausible [ɪm'plɔːzəbəl] *adj* inverosímil, poco probable, poco convincente.

implement ['ɪmpləmənt] **1** *n* (*instrument*) instrumento, utensilio; (*tool*) herramienta: *farm instruments,* aperos *mpl* de labranza. – **2** *t* (*plan, suggestion, etc*) llevar a cabo, poner en práctica; (*law, policy*) aplicar.

▲ En **2** (*verbo*) ['ɪmplɪment].

implementation [ɪmpləmen'teɪʃən] *n* (*of plan etc*) puesta en práctica, desarrollo; (*of law etc*) aplicación *f*.

implicate ['ɪmplɪkeɪt] *t* implicar, (**in,** en).

● **to be implicated in sth.,** estar implicado,-a en algo.

implication [ɪmplɪ'keɪʃən] **1** *n* (*in crime etc*) implicación *f*. **2** (*inference, suggestion*) implicación *f*, inferencia. **3** (*consequence*) consecuencia, repercusión *f*.

● **by implication,** por inferencia.

implicit [ɪm'plɪsɪt] **1** *adj* (*implied*) implícito,-a, tácito,-a. **2** (*absolute*) absoluto,-a, incondicional.

implicitly [ɪm'plɪsɪtlɪ] **1** *adv* (*not directly*) implícitamente. **2** (*absolutely*) absolutamente, incondicionalmente.

implied [ɪm'plaɪd] *adj* implícito,-a, tácito,-a: *implied criticism,* crítica implícita.

implore [ɪm'plɔːr] *t* implorar, suplicar.

imploring [ɪm'plɔːrɪŋ] *adj* suplicante, de súplica.

imploringly [ɪm'plɔːrɪŋlɪ] *adv* (*look*) de modo suplicante; (*beg*) en tono suplicante.

imply [ɪm'plaɪ] **1** *t* (*involve, entail*) implicar, suponer, presuponer: *the fact that you came implies you're interested,* el hecho de que hayas venido implica que estás interesado. **2** (*mean*) significar, querer decir; (*hint*) insinuar, dar a entender: *what are you implying?,* ¿qué insinúas?; *she didn't mean to imply that Fred was stupid,* no quería dar a entender que Fred fuera un estúpido.

▲ *pt & pp* **implied** [ɪm'plaɪd].

impolite [ɪmpə'laɪt] *adj* maleducado,-a, descortés.

impolitely [ɪmpə'laɪtlɪ] *adv* descortésmente.

impoliteness [ɪmpə'laɪtnəs] *n* descortesía, mala educación *f*.

imponderable [ɪm'pɒndərəbəl] **1** *adj* imponderable. – **2** imponderables, *npl* imponderables *mpl*.

import[1] ['ɪmpɔːt] **1** *n* (*article*) artículo de importación: *foreign imports,* importaciones extranjeras. **2** (*activity*) importación *f*: *you can only get this record on import,* sólo puedes obtener este disco de importación. – **3** *t* importar: *we import this cheese from Holland,* importamos este queso de Holanda; *this meat is imported,* esta carne es de importación.

■ **import controls,** controles *mpl* de importación. ‖ **import trade,** comercio de importación.

import[2] [ɪm'pɔːt] **1** *n fml* (*meaning*) significado. **2** *fml* (*importance*) importancia. – **3** *t fml* (*mean*) significar.

importance [ɪm'pɔːtəns] *n* (*gen*) importancia: *it is of the utmost importance,* es de suma importancia; *we attach great importance to experience,* concedemos mucha importancia a la experiencia.

● **to be full of one's own importance,** ser muy engreído,-a.

important [ɪm'pɔːtənt] **1** *adj* (*gen*) importante: *it is important that you understand,* es importante que entiendas; *your health is the most important thing,* tu salud es lo más importante; *this is a very important decision,* esta

es una decisión muy importante; *I hope you realize how important this is to me,* espero que sepas cuánto significa esto para mí; *it's not important,* no importa, no tiene importancia. **2** (*influential*) de categoría: *he's a very important person,* es un hombre de mucha categoría; *he tries to look important,* intenta darse aires de importancia.
importantly [ɪm'pɔːtəntlɪ] *adv* (*speak, say, etc*) dándose aires: *"put it on my account",* *she said importantly,* "añádalo a mi cuenta," dijo dándose aires.
● **and more importantly,** y lo que es más importante.
importation [ɪmpɔː'teɪʃən] *n* importación *f.*
importer [ɪm'pɔːtəʳ] *n* importador,-ra.
impose [ɪm'pəʊz] *t* (*gen*) imponer (**on,** a): *the judge imposed a twelve-year sentence,* el juez impuso una condena de doce años; *he's always imposing his opinions on us,* siempre nos impone sus opiniones.
◆ **to impose on** *t insep* (*take advantage of*) abusar de, aprovecharse de: *don't let her impose on you,* no dejes que se aproveche de ti.
● **to impose os. on sb.,** aprovecharse de algn.
imposing [ɪm'pəʊzɪŋ] *adj* imponente, impresionante.
imposition [ɪmpə'zɪʃən] **1** *n* (*gen*) imposición *f:* *the imposition of a fine,* la imposición de una multa. **2** (*unfair demand*) imposición *f,* abuso, molestia: *I hope it's not going to be an imposition,* espero que no sea demasiada molestia; *if it's not too much of an imposition,* si no es pedir demasiado.
impossibility [ɪmpɒsə'bɪlɪtɪ] *n* imposibilidad *f.*
impossible [ɪm'pɒsɪbəl] **1** *adj* (*gen*) imposible: *it's impossible for me to finish this today,* me es imposible acabar esto hoy; *it's impossible to predict the future,* es imposible predecir el futuro; *it's an impossible situation,* es una situación imposible. **2** (*intolerable*) insoportable, inaguantable: *you're impossible!,* ¡eres insoportable! – **3 the impossible,** *n* lo imposible *m.*
● **to ask for the impossible,** pedir lo imposible. || **to make life impossible for sb.,** hacerle la vida imposible a algn.
impossibly [ɪm'pɒsɪblɪ] *adv* (*intolerably*) insoportablemente; (*inconceivably*) increíblemente; (*hopelessly*) desesperadamente: *life became impossibly difficult,* la vida se hizo desesperadamente difícil; *she is getting impossibly thin,* se está quedando increíblemente delgada; *he was impossibly misbehaved,* se comportó de una manera insoportable.
impostor [ɪm'pɒstəʳ] *n* impostor,-ra.
imposture [ɪm'pɒstʃəʳ] *n fml* impostura.
impotence ['ɪmpətəns] *n* impotencia.
impotent ['ɪmpətənt] *adj* impotente.
impotently ['ɪmpətəntlɪ] *adv* con impotencia.
impound [ɪm'paʊnd] *t* JUR confiscar, incautarse de, embargar.
impoverish [ɪm'pɒvərɪʃ] **1** *t* (*person*) empobrecer. **2** (*land*) agotar.
impoverished [ɪm'pɒvərɪst] **1** *adj* (*person, country*) empobrecido,-a, necesitado,-a. **2** (*land, resources*) agotado,-a.
● **to become impoverished,** empobrecerse.
impoverishment [ɪmˌpɒvərɪsmənt] *n* empobrecimiento.
impracticability [ɪmpræktɪkə'bɪlɪtɪ] *n* impracticabilidad *f.*
impracticable [ɪm'præktɪkəbəl] *adj* irrealizable, impracticable, no factible.

impractical [ɪm'præktɪkəl] **1** *adj* (*person*) poco práctico,-a, nada práctico,-a. **2** (*project etc*) poco viable, poco factible.
impracticality [ɪmpræktɪ'kælətɪ] *n* impracticabilidad *f.*
imprecise [ɪmprə'saɪs] *adj* impreciso,-a, inexacto,-a.
imprecisely [ɪmprə'saɪslɪ] *adv* de forma imprecisa.
imprecision [ɪmprə'sɪʒən] *n* imprecisión *f,* falta de precisión.
impregnable [ɪm'pregnəbəl] **1** *adj* (*structure*) inexpugnable. **2** *fig* inexpugnable, invulnerable.
impregnate ['ɪmpregneɪt] **1** *t* (*saturate*) impregnar (**with,** de), empapar (**with,** de); (*pervade*) penetrar en. **2** *fig* (*influence*) extenderse por. **3** *fml* (*fertilize*) fecundar.
● **to become impregnated with sth.,** impregnarse de algo.
impresario [ɪmprə'saːrɪəʊ] *n* empresario,-a.
▲ *pl* impresarios.
impress [ɪm'pres] **1** *t* (*cause respect*) impresionar: *she impressed her boss,* impresionó a su jefe, causó buena impresión a su jefe; *I'm impressed!,* ¡estoy impresionada!; *he was not at all impressed,* le causó mala impresión, no le causó buena impresión; *his charm never fails to impress,* su encanto no deja nunca de impresionar; *she's easily impressed,* se deja impresionar con facilidad. **2** (*emphasize, stress*) subrayar, convencer, recalcar; *fig* grabar: *he impressed on them the danger of going near the edge,* les recalcó el peligro de acercarse al borde; *she impressed the importance of punctuality on him,* le subrayó la importancia de la puntualidad; *her words remained impressed on my mind,* sus palabras quedaron grabadas en mi mente.
impression [ɪm'preʃən] **1** *n* (*gen*) impresión *f:* *first impressions,* primeras impresiones; *what's your impression of the new teacher?,* ¿qué te parece el nuevo profesor?; *he had the impression that the boss didn't like him,* tenía la sensación de que no le gustaba al jefe; *I don't want you to get the wrong impression,* no quiero que me interpretes mal. **2** (*imitation*) imitación *f:* *he does a good impression of Julio Iglesias,* hace una buena imitación de Julio Iglesias. **3** (*imprint, mark*) marca, señal *f,* impresión *f;* (*in wax, plaster*) molde *m;* (*of foot etc*) huella. **4** (*reprint*) impresión *f,* edición *f.*
● **to be under the impression that ...,** tener la impresión de que ... || **to create a good/bad impression,** causar buena/mala impresión. || **to make an impression on sb.,** impresionar a algn.
impressionability [ɪmpreʃənə'bɪlətɪ] *n* impresionabilidad *f.*
impressionable [ɪm'preʃənəbəl] *adj* impresionable, influenciable.
impressionism [ɪm'preʃənɪzəm] *n* ART impresionismo.
impressionist [ɪm'preʃənɪst] **1** *adj* ART impresionista. – **2** *n* ART impresionista. **3** (*mimic*) imitador,-ra.
impressionistic [ɪmpreʃən'ɪstɪk] *adj* impresionista.
impressive [ɪm'presɪv] *adj* impresionante.
impressively [ɪm'presɪvlɪ] *adv* de modo impresionante.
impressiveness [ɪm'presɪvnəs] *n* grandiosidad *f,* solemnidad *f.*
imprint [ɪm'prɪnt] **1** *t* (*mark*) dejar huella (**on,** en), marcar (**on,** en); (*stamp*) imprimir (**on,** en), estampar (**on,** en): *the footprints imprinted on the sand,* las huellas marcadas en la arena. **2** *fig* grabar: *his face was imprinted on my mind,* su cara quedó grabada en mi mente. – **3** *n* (*physical mark*) marca, huella, señal *f,* sello, impresión *f;* (*stamp*) marca, sello; (*of hand etc*) huella. **4** *fig* huella, marca: *he left an imprint on all of us,* dejó huella en todos nosotros. **5** pie *m* de imprenta.

imprison 302

▲ *(sustantivo)* [ˈɪmprɪnt].
imprison [ɪmˈprɪzən] *t* encarcelar, meter en la cárcel.
imprisonment [ɪmˈprɪzənmənt] *n* encarcelamiento.
improbability [ɪmprɒbəˈbɪlɪtɪ] **1** *n* (*of event*) improbabilidad *f*. **2** (*of story, explanation*) inverosimilitud *f*.
▲ *pl* **improbabilities**.
improbable [ɪmˈprɒbəbəl] **1** *adj* (*event*) improbable. **2** (*story, explanation*) inverosímil.
impromptu [ɪmˈprɒmptjuː] **1** *adj* (*improvised*) improvisado,-a, no preparado,-a; (*unexpected*) imprevisto,-a. – **2** *adv* (*spontaneously*) improvisadamente; (*unexpectedly*) de improviso. – **3** *n* MUS impromptu *m*, improvisación *f*.
improper [ɪmˈprɒpə˞] **1** *adj* (*behaviour*) impropio,-a; (*method, conditions*) inadecuado,-a; (*remark*) inoportuno,-a; (*dress*) incorrecto,-a. **2** (*use*) incorrecto,-a, indebido,-a. **3** (*language*) indecente. **4** (*proposal*) deshonesto,-a.
improperly [ɪmˈprɒpəlɪ] **1** *adv* (*incorrectly*) incorrectamente. **2** (*indecently*) indecentemente. **3** (*dishonestly*) deshonestamente.
impropriety [ɪmprəˈpraɪətɪ] *n fml* (*indecent behaviour*) impropiedad *f*, falta de decoro; (*dishonest practice*) deshonestidad *f*, indecencia.
▲ *pl* **improprieties**.
improve [ɪmˈpruːv] **1** *t* (*quality etc*) mejorar: *we have improved the quality*, hemos mejorado la calidad; *the council intends to improve public transport*, el ayuntamiento se propone mejorar el transporte público. **2** (*skill, knowledge*) perfeccionar: *I'd like to improve my French*, quisiera perfeccionar mi francés. **3** (*mind*) cultivar: *he reads to improve his mind*, lee para cultivarse. **4** (*property*) hacer mejoras en. **5** (*increase*) aumentar: *start practising if you want to improve your chances*, empieza a practicar si quieres aumentar tus posibilidades. – **6** *i* (*get better*) mejorar, mejorarse: *her health has improved quite a lot*, su salud ha mejorado bastante; *if the weather doesn't improve, we'll go home*, si el tiempo no mejora, volveremos a casa; *his work has improved during the last year*, su trabajo ha mejorado durante el último año; *Michael's German is improving*, Michael está haciendo progresos en alemán.
◆ *to improve on t insep* (*better*) superar: *can he improve on his last jump?*, ¿puede superar su último salto?; *I think we've improved on our last effort*, creo que nos hemos superado en nuestro último intento; *it cannot be improved on*, es inmejorable, es insuperable.
● *to improve os.*, (*in mind*) cultivarse, educarse; (*in wealth*) mejorar. ‖ *to improve with age*, mejorar con el tiempo.
improvement [ɪmˈpruːvmənt] **1** *n* (*gen*) mejora, mejoramiento; (*in health*) mejoría: *we demand an improvement in working conditions*, exigimos una mejora en las condiciones laborales; *there's still room for improvement*, aún se puede mejorar; *this patient is showing signs of improvement*, este paciente muestra señales de mejoría. **2** (*in knowledge*) perfeccionamiento. **3** (*increase*) aumento.
● *to be an improvement on sth.*, ser mejor que algo: *it's certainly an improvement on the old one*, ciertamente, es un una mejoría respecto al antiguo.
■ *home improvements*, reformas *fpl* domésticas.
improvidence [ɪmˈprɒvɪdəns] *n* prodigalidad *f*.
improvident [ɪmˈprɒvɪdənt] *adj fml* (*wasteful*) pródigo,-a, gastador,-ra, despilfarrador,-ra; (*shortsighted*) imprevisor,-ra, incauto,-a.
improvidently [ɪmˈprɒvɪdntlɪ] **1** *adv* (*wastefully*) con prodigalidad. **2** (*shortsightedly*) sin previsión.

improvisation [ɪmprəvaɪˈzeɪʃən] *n* improvisación *f*.
improvise [ˈɪmprəvaɪz] **1** *t* improvisar. – **2** *i* improvisar.
improvised [ˈɪmprəvaɪzd] *adj* improvisado,-a.
imprudence [ɪmˈpruːdəns] *n* (*unwise behaviour*) imprudencia; (*rashness*) precipitación *f*.
imprudent [ɪmˈpruːdənt] *adj fml* (*unwise*) imprudente; (*rash*) precipitado,-a.
imprudently [ɪmˈpruːdəntlɪ] *adv* (*unwisely*) imprudentemente, con imprudencia; (*rashly*) precipitadamente.
impudence [ˈɪmpjʊdəns] *n* insolencia, frescura, descaro.
impudent [ˈɪmpjʊdənt] *adj* insolente, fresco,-a, descarado,-a.
impudently [ˈɪmpjʊdəntlɪ] *adv* insolentemente, descaradamente.
impugn [ɪmˈpjuːn] *t fml* impugnar.
impulse [ˈɪmpʌls] **1** *n* (*sudden urge*) impulso, capricho; (*stimulus, drive*) impulso, estímulo, ímpetu *m*: *she felt a sudden impulse to hit him*, de repente le entraron ganas de pegarle; *I bought it on impulse*, lo compré por capricho. **2** TECH impulso.
● *to act on impulse*, dejarse llevar por un impulso. ‖ *to do sth. on impulse*, hacer algo por capricho, hacer algo por impulso. ‖ *to check an impulse*, controlar un impulso. ‖ *to yield to an impulse*, ceder a un impulso.
■ *impulse buying*, compra por impulso.
impulsion [ɪmˈpʌlʃən] *n fml* impulsión *f*.
impulsive [ɪmˈpʌlsɪv] *adj* impulsivo,-a, irreflexivo,-a.
impulsively [ɪmˈpʌlsɪvlɪ] *adv* por impulso, sin reflexión.
impulsiveness [ɪmˈpʌlsɪvnəs] *n* irreflexión *f*.
impunity [ɪmˈpjuːnɪtɪ] *n* impunidad *f*.
● *with impunity*, con impunidad, impunemente.
impure [ɪmˈpjʊə˞] **1** *adj* (*contaminated*) contaminado,-a; (*adulterated*) adulterado,-a. **2** (*morally - act*) impuro,-a; (*- thought*) impúdico,-a, deshonesto,-a.
impurity [ɪmˈpjʊərɪtɪ] **1** *n* (*substance*) impureza. **2** (*moral*) deshonestidad *f*, falta de pudor.
▲ *pl* **impurities**.
impute [ɪmˈpjuːt] *t fml* imputar, atribuir.
● *to impute sth. to sb./sth.*, (*crime, blame*) imputar algo a algn./algo; (*cause, false motive*) atribuir algo a algn./algo.
in¹ [ɪn] **1** *prep* (*place*) en, dentro de: *it's in the box*, está en la caja; *we live in Spain*, vivimos en España; *the children are in bed*, los niños están en la cama; *she's in hospital*, está en el hospital; *wait in the car*, espera en el coche; *who's in the film?*, ¿quién sale en la película? **2** (*motion*) en, a: *put it in your pocket*, métalo en el bolsillo; *we arrived in Bonn*, llegamos a Bonn; *he went in the shop*, entró en la tienda; *she dived in the water*, se tiró al agua; *you're going in the wrong direction*, vas mal encaminado, vas en dirección equivocada. **3** (*time - during*) en, durante: *in May*, en mayo; *in the morning*, por la mañana; *in 1980*, en 1980; *in summer*, en verano; *she learnt to ski in a week*, aprendió a esquiar en una semana; *we haven't heard from them for months*, hace meses que no sabemos nada de ellos. **4** (*time - within*) en, dentro de: *we'll be back in 20 minutes*, volveremos dentro de 20 minutos; *ring me back in half an hour*, vuelve a llamarme en media hora. **5** (*wearing*) en, vestido,-a de: *the woman in black*, la mujer vestida de negro; *he's in uniform*, está de uniforme; *the one in the hat*, el del sombrero; *you look good in red*, el rojo te sienta bien. **6** (*manner*) en: *in public*, en público; *in writing*, por escrito; *written in pencil*, escrito en lápiz; *in French*, en

francés; *pay in cash,* paga en metálico, paga en efectivo; *in Swiss francs,* en francos suizos; *in a loud voice,* en voz alta; *this title is no longer in print,* este título ya no se edita; *chicken in wine,* pollo al vino. **7** *(state, condition)* en: *everything's in order,* todo está en orden; *they're in love,* están enamorados; *in shock,* en estado de shock; *in danger,* en peligro; *I'm in pain,* sufro; *she's in a good/bad mood,* está de buen/mal humor; *I'm in a hurry,* tengo prisa. **8** *(ratio, measurement, number)* varias traducciones: *in twos,* de dos en dos; *cut it in two,* córtalo por la mitad; *one in ten people,* una de cada diez personas; *you have a one in twenty chance,* tienes una posibilidad entre veinte; *they arrived in hundreds,* llegaron por cientos; *she's in her thirties,* tiene treinta y tantos años. **9** *(form, shape)* varias traducciones: *in rows,* en filas; *in a queue,* en una cola; *wear one's hair in a bun,* llevar el pelo recogido en un moño; *they were sitting in a circle,* estaban sentados en círculo. **10** *(profession)* en: *she's in television,* trabaja en la televisión; *he's in business,* se dedica a los negocios; *they're in the army,* son militares. **11** *(weather, light)* varias traducciones: *walking in the rain,* caminando bajo la lluvia; *sit in the sun/shade,* siéntate al sol/a la sombra; *in the dark,* en la oscuridad; *I can't work in this heat,* no puedo trabajar con este calor. **12** *(regarding)* varias traducciones: *low in calories,* bajo,-a en calorías; *deaf in one ear,* sordo,-a de un oído; *a change in direction,* un cambio de dirección; *it measures six feet in length,* mide dos metros de largo. **13** *(after superlative)* de: *the best player in the world,* el mejor jugador del mundo; *the tallest in the class,* el más alto de la clase. **14** *(with pres part)* al, cuando: *I made a mistake in doing that,* al hacer eso cometí un error. **– 15** *adv (motion)* dentro: *throw it in there,* tíralo allí dentro; *come in!,* ¡adelante!. ¡pase!; *let me in!,* ¡déjame entrar! **16** *(transport)*: *the train's in,* el tren ha llegado; *what time does the plane get in?,* ¿a qué hora aterriza el avión? **17** SP *(ball, shuttlecock)*: *the ball was in!,* ¡la pelota entró!, ¡la pelota fue buena! **18** *(tide)* alto,-a. **19** *(fashionable)* de moda: *hats are in,* los sombreros están de moda. **20** *(in power)* en el poder: *the Tories got in,* los conservadores ganaron las elecciones. **21** *(letters etc)*: *applications must be in by Friday,* las solicitudes deben recibirse antes del viernes. **22** *(on sale, obtainable)* disponible: *have you got that book in?,* ¿tienes aquel libro?, ¿ha llegado aquel libro?; *it hasn't come in yet,* aún no me ha llegado. **23** *(crops)* recogido,-a. **– 24** *adj (fashionable)* de moda: *it's the in bar,* es el bar de moda; *platform shoes are the in thing,* los zapatos con plataforma están de moda; *the in crowd,* la gente de moda. **25** *(private)* particular: *an in joke,* un chiste particular. **– 26 ins and outs,** *npl (details)* detalles *mpl,* pormenores *mpl.* **– 27 to be in,** *phr (at home)* estar en casa; *(at work)* estar: *you're never in,* nunca estás en casa; *is Jack in?,* ¿está Jack?; *the manager won't be in until this afternoon,* el jefe no estará hasta este tarde; *she's not in yet,* aún no ha llegado.
● **to be all in,** estar agotado,-a, estar rendido,-a. ‖ **to be in for sth.,** *(be about to experience)* estar a punto de recibir algo, estar a punto de tener algo: *she's in for a surprise,* le espera una sorpresa; *we're in for some rain,* vamos a tener lluvia; *you're in for it!,* ¡la que te espera!; *are you in for this game?,* ¿vas a jugar? ‖ **to be in on sth.,** estar enterado,-a de algo, estar al tanto de algo: *were you in on it too?,* ¿también estabas enterado? ‖ **to be (well) in with sb.,** llevarse (muy) bien con algn., tener (mucha) confianza con algn. ‖ **to have it in for sb.,** tenerla tomada con algn. ‖ **what's in it for me?,** ¿y yo qué saco?, ¿y yo qué gano?

in² [ɪntʃ] *abbr (inch)* pulgada.
inability [ɪnə'bɪlɪtɪ] *n* incapacidad *f*: *my inability to escape,* mi incapacidad para escapar.
inaccessibility [ɪnæksesə'bɪlətɪ] *n* inaccesibilidad *f*.
inaccessible [ɪnæk'sesəbəl] *adj* inaccesible.
inaccessibly [ɪnæk'sesəblɪ] *adv* inaccesiblemente.
inaccuracy [ɪn'ækjərəsɪ] **1** *n (gen)* inexactitud *f*. **2** *(error)* error *m*, incorrección *f*.
▲ *pl* **inaccuracies.**
inaccurate [ɪn'ækjərət] *adj (gen)* inexacto,-a; *(incorrect)* incorrecto,-a, erróneo,-a.
inaction [ɪn'ækʃən] *n* inacción *f*.
inactive [ɪn'æktɪv] *adj* inactivo,-a.
inactivity [ɪnæk'tɪvətɪ] *n* inactividad *f*.
inadequacy [ɪn'ædɪkwəsɪ] **1** *n (lack)* insuficiencia. **2** *(of person)* incapacidad *f*, incompetencia. **3** *(defect)* defecto, imperfección *f*.
▲ *pl* **inadequacies.**
inadequate [ɪn'ædɪkwət] **1** *adj (not sufficient)* insuficiente; *(not appropriate)* inadecuado,-a. **2** *(person)* incapaz, incompetente: *he makes her feel inadequate,* le hace sentir incapaz; *he's socially inadequate,* es un inadaptado. **3** *(defective)* defectuoso,-a, imperfecto,-a.
inadequately [ɪn'ædɪkwətlɪ] *adv (insufficiently)* insuficientemente, inadecuadamente.
inadmissibility [ɪnədmɪsə'bɪlətɪ] **1** *n* inadmisibilidad *f*. **2** JUR improcedencia.
inadmissible [ɪnəd'mɪsəbəl] **1** *adj* inadmisible, intolerable. **2** JUR improcedente.
inadmissibly [ɪnəd'mɪsəblɪ] *adv* inadmisiblemente.
inadvertence [ɪnəd'vɜːtəns] *n (oversight)* descuido, error *m*, distracción *f*; *(lack of attention)* falta de atención.
inadvertent [ɪnəd'vɜːtənt] *adj (unintentional)* involuntario,-a; *(inattentive)* desatento,-a, distraído,-a.
inadvertently [ɪnæd'vɜːtntlɪ] *adv (unintentionally)* involuntariamente, sin querer, por descuido; *(unconsciously)* inconscientemente; *(inattentively)* sin prestar atención.
inadvisability [ɪnədvaɪzə'bɪlətɪ] *n* inconveniencia, imprudencia.
inadvisable [ɪnəd'vaɪzəbəl] *adj* poco aconsejable, imprudente, inconveniente.
inane [ɪ'neɪn] *adj* fatuo,-a, necio,-a, tonto,-a, estúpido,-a.
inanely [ɪ'neɪnlɪ] *adv* neciamente, tontamente.
inanimate [ɪn'ænɪmət] *adj* inanimado,-a.
inanity [ɪ'nænətɪ] *n* necedad *f*, fatuidad *f*, tontería, estupidez *f*.
▲ *pl* **inanities.**
inapplicability [ɪnæplɪkə'bɪlətɪ] *n* inaplicabilidad *f*.
inapplicable [ɪn'æplɪkəbəl] *adj* inaplicable **(to,** a).
inappropriate [ɪnə'prəʊprɪət] *adj (unsuitable - clothes, behaviour)* poco apropiado,-a, no apropiado,-a; *(- time, remark)* inoportuno,-a, inconveniente: *it would be inappropriate for you to come,* no sería oportuno que vinieras.
inappropriately [ɪnə'prəʊprɪətlɪ] *adv (dress, behave)* inapropiadamente, inadecuadamente; *(arrive, speak)* inoportunamente.
inappropriateness [ɪnə'prəʊprɪətnəs] *n (of clothes, behaviour)* lo inapropiado; *(of timing)* lo inoportuno.
inapt [ɪn'æpt] *adj* poco apto,-a.
inarticulate [ɪnɑː'tɪkjʊlət] **1** *adj (person)* incapaz de expresarse. **2** *(speech, words, writing)* mal expresado,-a, incoherente. **3** *(cry, sound)* inarticulado,-a. **4** *(joints)* inarticulado,-a.

inarticulately [ɪnɑːˈtɪkjʊlətlɪ] *adv* incoherentemente.
inasmuch as [ɪnəzˈmʌtʃəz] **1** *conj fml* (*since*) puesto que, ya que. **2** *fml* (*to the extent that*) en la medida en que, en tanto que.
inattention [ɪnəˈtenʃən] *n* falta de atención.
inattentive [ɪnəˈtentɪv] *adj* (*not paying attention*) poco atento,-a, distraído,-a; (*not attentive*) poco atento,-a.
inattentively [ɪnəˈtentɪvlɪ] *adv* distraídamente.
inattentiveness [ɪnəˈtentɪvnəs] *n* falta de atención.
inaudibility [ɪnɔːdəˈbɪlətɪ] *n* inaudibilidad *f*.
inaudible [ɪnˈɔːdəbəl] *adj* inaudible, imperceptible.
inaudibly [ɪnˈɔːdəblɪ] *adv* de modo inaudible.
inaugural [ɪˈnɔːgjʊrəl] *adj* inaugural, de inauguración, de apertura: *she made the inaugural speech,* hizo el discurso de apertura.
inaugurate [ɪˈnɔːgjʊreɪt] **1** *t* (*building, exhibition, etc*) inaugurar. **2** (*president etc*) investir.
inauguration [ɪnɔːgjʊˈreɪʃən] **1** *n* (*of building etc*) inauguración *f*. **2** (*of president etc*) investidura, toma de posesión.
inaugurator [ɪnɔːgjʊˈreɪtəʳ] *n* inaugurador,-ra.
inauspicious [ɪnɔːˈspɪʃəs] *adj* (*start, moment*) poco propicio,-a; (*circumstance*) desfavorable, adverso,-a.
inauspiciously [ɪnɔːˈspɪʃəslɪ] *adv* de modo poco propicio.
inborn [ˈɪnbɔːn] *adj* innato,-a.
inbred [ˈɪnbred] **1** *adj* (*innate*) innato,-a. **2** (*produced by inbreeding*) endogámico,-a.
inbreeding [ˈɪnbriːdɪŋ] *n* endogamia.
Inc [ɪnˈkɔːpəreɪtɪd] *abbr* us (*Incorporated*) ≈ sociedad *f* anónima; (*abbreviation*) S.A.
Inca [ˈɪŋkə] **1** *n* (*person*) inca *mf*. **2** (*language*) inca *m*.
incalculable [ɪnˈkælkjʊləbəl] **1** *adj* (*beyond calculation*) incalculable. **2** (*uncertain, unpredictable*) imprevisible.
incalculably [ɪnˈkælkjʊləblɪ] *adv* incalculablemente.
incandescence [ɪnkænˈdesəns] *n* incandescencia.
incandescent [ɪnkænˈdesənt] *adj* incandescente.
■ **incandescent lamp,** lámpara incandescente.
incantation [ɪnkænˈteɪʃən] *n* conjuro, ensalmo.
incapability [ɪnkeɪpəˈbɪlətɪ] *n* incapacidad *f*.
incapable [ɪnˈkeɪpəbəl] **1** *adj* (*unable*) incapaz: *he's incapable of lying,* es incapaz de mentir; *I'm incapable of murder,* soy incapaz de matar. **2** (*incompetent*) incompetente: *he's incapable as a doctor,* como médico, es incompetente. **3** (*helpless*) impotente, imposibilitado,-a.
incapacitate [ɪnkəˈpæsɪteɪt] **1** *t* (*gen*) incapacitar, inhabilitar, imposibilitar; (*disable*) imposibilitar: *the accident incapacited him for work,* el accidente lo incapacitó para trabajar. **2** (*disqualify*) inhabilitar.
incapacity [ɪnkəˈpæsɪtɪ] *n* incapacidad *f*.
incarcerate [ɪnˈkɑːsəreɪt] *t fml* encarcelar.
incarceration [ɪnkɑːsəˈreɪʃən] *n fml* encarcelamiento, encarcelación *f*.
incarnate [ɪnˈkɑːnət] **1** *adj* (*embodied*) encarnado,-a. **2** (*personified*) personificado,-a. **– 3** *t fml* (*give bodily form to*) encarnar. **4** (*personify*) personificar.
■ **the Devil incarnate,** el mismísimo diablo.
incarnation [ɪnkɑːˈneɪʃən] **1** *n* (*embodiment*) encarnación *f*. **2** (*personification*) personificación *f*.
■ **the Incarnation,** la Encarnación.
incautious [ɪnˈkɔːʃəs] *adj* incauto,-a, imprudente.
incautiously [ɪnˈkɔːʃəslɪ] *adv* incautamente, imprudentemente.
incendiary [ɪnˈsendɪərɪ] **1** *adj* incendiario,-a,: *an incendiary speech,* un discurso incendiario. **– 2** *n* (*bomb*)

bomba incendiaria. **3** (*person - arsonist*) incendiario,-a, pirómano,-a; (*- agitator*) agitador,-ra.
■ **incendiary device,** artefacto incendiario.
incense¹ [ˈɪnsens] *n* incienso.
incense² [ɪnˈsens] *t* (*make angry*) enfurecer, poner furioso,-a, sacar de quicio.
● **to be incensed at/by sth.,** enfurecerse por algo.
incentive [ɪnˈsentɪv] **1** *n* (*stimulus*) incentivo, estímulo, aliciente *m*: *there's no incentive to study,* no hay estímulos para estudiar. **2** (*payment*) incentivo económico.
● **to give sb. an incentive,** incentivar a algn.
■ **incentive scheme,** plan *m* de incentivos.
inception [ɪnˈsepʃən] *n fml* principio, comienzo.
incessant [ɪnˈsesənt] *adj* (*continuous*) incesante, ininterrumpido,-a; (*continual*) constante, continuo,-a.
incessantly [ɪnˈsesətlɪ] *adv* sin cesar, sin parar, incesantemente.
incest [ˈɪnsest] *n* incesto.
incestuous [ɪnˈsestjʊəs] **1** *adj* (*gen*) incestuoso,-a. **2** *pej* (*group*) endogámico,-a, cerrado,-a.
incestuously [ɪnˈsestjʊəslɪ] *adv* incestuosamente.
inch [ɪntʃ] **1** *n* (*measurement*) pulgada. **2** (*small amount*) poco, pelo, ápice *m*.
◆ **to inch along / inch forward** *i* avanzar poco a poco.
● **by inches / by an inch,** por poco: *the bullet missed me by inches,* por poco me toca la bala. || **every inch,** todo,-a: *he's every inch a champion,* es todo un campeón. || **every inch of,** (*all of*) todo,-a, cada rincón de, cada centímetro de: *we searched every inch of the house,* registramos cada centímetro de la casa. || **inch by inch,** poco a poco. || **give him** (*her etc*) **an inch and he'll** (*she'll etc*) **take a mile,** le das la mano y te coge el brazo. || **not to budge an inch,** no ceder ni un ápice. || **within an inch of sth.,** a dos dedos de algo: *she came within an inch of death,* estuvo a dos dedos de la muerte.
▲ Equivale a 2,54 *cm*.
incidence [ˈɪnsɪdəns] **1** *n* (*occurrence*) frecuencia, extensión *f*: *there is a high incidence of crime in this area,* hay un alto índice de delincuencia en esta zona. **2** PHYS incidencia.
incident [ˈɪnsɪdənt] *n* (*event*) incidente *m*; (*violent episode*) altercado: *an international incident,* un incidente internacional.
● **to go off without incident,** pasar sin incidentes.
■ **incident room,** centro de operaciones.
incidental [ɪnsɪˈdentəl] **1** *adj* (*unimportant*) secundario,-a, incidental, de poca importancia. **2** (*inherent*) inherente. **3** (*fortuitous*) fortuito,-a, casual. **– 4 incidentals,** *npl* imprevistos *mpl*.
■ **incidental music,** música de fondo.
incidentally [ɪnsɪˈdentəlɪ] **1** *adv* (*by the way*) a propósito, por cierto, dicho sea de paso. **2** (*by chance*) por casualidad.
incinerate [ɪnˈsɪnəreɪt] *t* incinerar, quemar.
incineration [ɪnsɪnəˈreɪʃən] *n* incineración *f*, quema.
incinerator [ɪnˈsɪnəreɪtəʳ] *n* incinerador *m*.
incipient [ɪnˈsɪpɪənt] *adj fml* incipiente.
incise [ɪnˈsaɪz] *t* (*cut*) cortar; (*carve, engrave*) grabar, tallar.
incision [ɪnˈsɪʒən] *n* incisión *f*.
incisive [ɪnˈsaɪsɪv] **1** *adj* (*comment, wit*) incisivo,-a, mordaz. **2** (*mind*) penetrante.
incisively [ɪnˈsaɪsɪvlɪ] *adv* (*comment*) con agudeza, incisivamente; (*attack*) mordazmente.
incisiveness [ɪnˈsaɪsɪvnəs] *n* (*of comment*) agudeza; (*of attack*) mordacidad *f*.

incisor [ɪn'saɪzəʳ] *n* (diente *m*) incisivo.

incite [ɪn'saɪt] **1** *t* (*urge*, *encourage*) incitar, provocar: *they incited the crowd to violence,* incitaron a la multitud a la violencia. **2** (*cause*, *lead to*) instigar (**to,** a): *incite a riot,* instigar a un disturbio.

incitement [ɪn'saɪtmənt] *n* incitación *f,* provocación *f,* instigación *f.*

incivility [ɪnsɪ'vɪlətɪ] *n fml* descortesía, falta de cortesía.
  ▲ *pl* **incivilities.**

inclemency [ɪn'klemənsɪ] *n* inclemencia.

inclement [ɪn'klemənt] *adj fml* inclemente.

inclination [ɪnklɪ'neɪʃən] **1** *n* (*tendency*) inclinación *f,* tendencia; (*disposition*) disposición *f,* propensión *f: I have no inclination to marry,* no tengo intención de casarme; *people tend to follow their inclinations,* la gente tiende a seguir sus inclinaciones. **2** (*slope*) inclinación *f,* pendiente *f.* **3** (*bow*) inclinación *f.*

incline ['ɪnklaɪn] **1** *n* pendiente *f,* inclinación *f,* cuesta. – **2** *t* (*bend forward*) inclinar. **3** *fml* (*persuade*, *influence*) inclinar, predisponer: *something about him inclines me to believe his story,* hay algo en él que me inclina a creer su historia; *her speech inclined me towards the ecologists,* su discurso hizo que me inclinara hacia los ecologistas. – **4** *i* (*slope*) inclinarse, estar inclinado,-a. **5** (*tend*) tender a, tener tendencia a: *she inclines towards frivolity,* tiende a ser frívola; *he inclines to meanness,* tiende a ser tacaño.
  ▲ (*verbo*) [ɪn'klaɪn].

inclined [ɪn'klaɪnd] **1** *adj* (*disposed*, *encouraged*) dispuesto,-a (**to,** a): *I'm inclined to believe him,* estoy dispuesto a creerle; *I'm inclined to agree with you,* estoy bastante de acuerdo contigo; *she only cleans the house when she feels inclined,* sólo limpia la casa cuando le apetece. **2** (*tending to*) propenso,-a: *she's inclined to be lazy,* tiene tendencia a ser perezosa. **3** (*having natural ability*) dotado,-a: *he's musically inclined,* tiene aptitud para la música, se le da muy bien la música. **4** (*sloping*) inclinado,-a.
  ● **to be that way inclined,** ser así. ‖ **if you feel so inclined,** si quieres, si Vd quiere.

inclose [ɪn'kləʊz] *t* → **enclose.**

inclosure [ɪn'kləʊʒəʳ] *n* → **enclosure.**

include [ɪn'kluːd] *t* incluir: *the crew includes two women,* la tripulación incluye dos mujeres; *government proposals include lowering taxes,* entre las propuestas gubernamentales se incluye la reducción de impuestos; *the price includes post and packaging,* el precio incluye gastos de envío y embalaje; *they're going to include my article,* van a publicar mi artículo; *all of us, myself included, decided to complain,* todos nosotros, incluso yo, decidimos quejarnos; *batteries are not included,* las pilas no van incluidas.

including [ɪn'kluːdɪŋ] *prep* incluyendo, inclusive, con inclusión de: *£200 including VAT,* 200 libras con IVA incluido; *£15.00 per night including breakfast,* 15 libras la noche con desayuno incluido; *there are ten of us including me,* somos diez contándome a mí; *up to and including last week,* hasta la semana pasada inclusive.

inclusion [ɪn'kluːʒən] *n* inclusión *f.*

inclusive [ɪn'kluːsɪv] *adj* inclusivo,-a: *closed from 14th until 29th inclusive,* cerrado desde el 14 hasta el 29 ambos inclusive; *read pages 10 to 20 inclusive,* lee de la página 10 a la 20 ambas inclusive.
  ● **to be inclusive of,** incluir: *the price is inclusive of tax,* el precio incluye impuestos.

inclusively [ɪn'kluːsɪvlɪ] *adv* inclusivamente, incluso.

incognito [ɪnkɒg'niːtəʊ] **1** *adv* de incógnito. – **2** *adj* incógnito,-a. – **3** *n* incógnito.

incoherence [ɪnkəʊ'hɪərəns] **1** *n* (*lack of cohesion*) incoherencia. **2** (*inarticulateness*) ininteligibilidad *f.*

incoherent [ɪnkəʊ'hɪərənt] **1** *adj* (*unclear*) incoherente, inconexo,-a. **2** (*unintelligible*) ininteligible, incoherente.

incoherently [ɪnkəʊ'hɪərəntlɪ] *adv* incoherentemente, de manera incoherente.

incombustible [ɪnkəm'bʌstəbəl] *adj fml* incombustible.

income ['ɪnkʌm] *n* (*from work*) ingresos *mpl,* renta; (*from investment*) réditos *mpl: do you have any other income apart from your salary?,* ¿tienes otros ingresos aparte del salario?; *she has a very small income,* tiene unos ingresos muy bajos; *his monthly income is about 1,000 pounds,* sus ingresos mensuales son de unas mil libras.
  ■ **earned income,** ingresos gananciales. ‖ **income tax,** impuesto sobre la renta. ‖ **income tax return,** declaración *f* de renta.

incoming ['ɪnkʌmɪŋ] **1** *adj* (*tide*) ascendente; (*plane*) de llegada; (*passenger*) que llega; (*missile*, *fire*) enemigo,-a; (*message, mail, etc*) recibido,-a. **2** (*to post, job*) entrante.

incommensurable [ɪnkə'menʃərəbəl] *adj fml* inconmensurable.
  ● **to be incommensurable with sth.,** no guardar relación con algo.

incommensurate [ɪnkə'menʃərət] *adj fml* desproporcionado,-a.
  ● **to be incommensurate with sth.,** no guardar relación con algo.

incommode [ɪnkə'məʊd] *t fml* incomodar, molestar.

incommunicable [ɪnkə'mjuːnɪkəbəl] *adj* incomunicable.

incommunicado [ɪnkəmjuːnɪ'kɑːdəʊ] **1** *adj* incomunicado,-a. – **2** *adv* sin comunicación.

incomparable [ɪn'kɒmpərəbəl] *adj* incomparable, inigualable, sin par.

incomparably [ɪn'kɒmpərəblɪ] *adv* sin comparación: *incomparably better,* muchísimo mejor.

incompatibility [ɪnkəmpætə'bɪlɪtɪ] *n* incompatibilidad *f.*
  ▲ *pl* **incompatibilities.**

incompatible [ɪnkəm'pætəbəl] *adj* incompatible (**with,** con).

incompetence [ɪn'kɒmpətəns] *n* incompetencia, ineptitud *f,* incapacidad *f.*

incompetent [ɪn'kɒmpətənt] **1** *adj* incompetente, inepto,-a, incapaz. – **2** *n* incompetente *mf,* inepto,-a.

incompetently [ɪn'kɒmpətəntlɪ] *adv* incompetentemente, de manera inepta.

incomplete [ɪnkəm'pliːt] **1** *adj* (*not whole*) incompleto,-a; (*not finished*) inacabado,-a, sin terminar. **2** (*partial*) parcial.

incompletely [ɪnkəm'pliːtlɪ] *adv* de manera incompleta.

incompleteness [ɪnkəm'pliːtnəs] *n* lo incompleto.

incomprehensible [ɪnkɒmprɪ'hensəbəl] *adj* incomprensible.

incomprehension [ɪnkɒmprɪ'henʃən] *n* incomprensión *f.*

inconceivable [ɪnkən'siːvəbəl] **1** *adj* inconcebible. **2** *fam* imposible, increíble.

inconceivably [ɪnkən'siːvəblɪ] *adv* increíblemente.

inconclusive [ɪnkən'kluːsɪv] **1** *adj* (*debate, vote, etc*) no decisivo,-a. **2** (*evidence, result, etc*) no concluyente.

incongruity [ɪnkɒn'gruːɪtɪ] *n* incongruencia.
  ▲ *pl* **incongruities.**

incongruous [ɪn'kɒŋgrʊəs] *adj* incongruente, incongruo,-a, fuera de lugar.

incongruously [ɪn'kɒŋgrʊəslɪ] *adv* incongruentemente.

inconsequent [ɪn'kɒnsɪkwənt] **1** *adj* (*not following logically*) inconsecuente. **2** (*inconsequential*) de poca importancia, sin trascendencia.

inconsequential [ɪnkɒnsɪ'kwenʃəl] *adj* de poca importancia, sin trascendencia.

inconsiderable [ɪnkən'sɪdərəbəl] *adj* insignificante: *it's not an inconsiderable amount of money,* no es una cantidad insignificante.

inconsiderate [ɪnkən'sɪdərət] *adj* desconsiderado,-a, inconsiderado,-a, poco atento,-a: *you're so inconsiderate!,* ¡eres tan desconsiderado!

inconsiderately [ɪnkən'sɪdərətlɪ] *adv* con poca consideración.

inconsiderateness [ɪnkən'sɪdərətnəs] *n* falta de consideración.

inconsistency [ɪnkən'sɪstənsɪ] **1** *n* (*gen*) inconsecuencia. **2** (*contradiction*) contradicción *f*, discrepancia.
▲ *pl* **inconsistencies**.

inconsistent [ɪnkən'sɪstənt] **1** *adj* (*not agreeing with, at variance with*) inconsecuente; (*contradictory*) contradictorio,-a: *it's inconsistent with the facts,* no concuerda con los hechos; *behaviour inconsistent with that of a monarch,* comportamiento inconsecuente con el de un monarca. **2** (*changeable - weather*) variable; (*- person*) inconstante, voluble, irregular; (*- behaviour*) imprevisible, irregular.

inconsistently [ɪnkən'sɪstəntlɪ] **1** *adv* (*contradictorily*) de manera contradictoria. **2** (*irregularly*) de manera irregular.

inconsolable [ɪnkən'səʊləbəl] *adj* inconsolable, desconsolado,-a.

inconsolably [ɪnkən'səʊləblɪ] *adv* desconsoladamente.

inconspicuous [ɪnkən'spɪkjʊəs] *adj* (*not noticeable*) que pasa desapercibido,-a, que no llama la atención; (*unobtrusive*) discreto,-a.
● **to be os. inconspicuous,** pasar desapercibido,-a, no llamar la atención.

inconspicuously [ɪnkən'spɪkjʊəslɪ] *adv* sin llamar la atención.

inconstancy [ɪn'kɒnstənsɪ] *n* inconstancia.
▲ *pl* **inconstancies**.

inconstant [ɪn'kɒnstənt] **1** *adj* (*person*) inconstante, veleidoso,-a, mudable. **2** (*not fixed*) variable.

incontinence [ɪn'kɒntɪnəns] *n* incontinencia.

incontinent [ɪn'kɒntɪnənt] *adj* incontinente.

incontrovertible [ɪnkɒntrə'vɜːtəbəl] *adj* incontrovertible.

incontrovertibly [ɪnkɒntrə'vɜːtəblɪ] *adv* incontrovertiblemente.

inconvenience [ɪnkən'viːnɪəns] **1** *n* (*gen*) inconveniente *m*; (*trouble, difficulty*) molestia, dificultad *f*; (*hindrance*) estorbo, obstáculo; (*discomfort*) incomodidad *f*: *I'm sorry to cause you so much inconvenience,* siento causarle tanta molestia; *it's no inconvenience,* no es ninguna molestia. **2** *t* (*annoy*) causar molestia a, molestar; (*cause difficulty*) incomodar: *the neighbours were inconvenienced by the noise,* el ruido molestaba a los vecinos.
● **to go to great inconvenience to do sth.,** sufrir muchos inconvenientes para hacer algo. ‖ **to put sb. to great inconvenience,** molestar a algn., incomodar a algn.

inconvenient [ɪnkən'viːnɪənt] **1** *adj* (*gen*) inconveniente, molesto,-a, incómodo,-a; (*place*) mal situado,-a; (*time*) mal, inoportuno,-a; (*arrangement*) poco práctico,-a: *it's very inconvenient living so far from the station,* es muy incómodo vivir tan lejos de la estación; *it's rather an inconvenient time,* esta hora me viene un poco mal; *it's a bit inconvenient at the moment,* no es muy conveniente ahora. **2** (*fact*) incómodo,-a.

inconveniently [ɪnkən'viːnɪəntlɪ] *adv* (*gen*) de forma inconveniente; (*time*) a deshora, inoportunamente.

incorporate [ɪn'kɔːpəreɪt] **1** *t* (*make part of, include in*) incorporar (**in/into,** a), incluir (**in/into,** en); (*include, contain*) incluir, contener: *they incorporated some of her ideas,* incorporaron algunas de sus ideas; *the design incorporates the company's logo,* el diseño incluye el logotipo de la empresa. **2** US COMM constituir, constituir en sociedad. **– 3** *adj* US COMM (*incorporated*) constituido,-a, constituido,-a en sociedad.

incorporated [ɪn'kɔːpəreɪtɪd] *adj* US COMM constituido,-a en sociedad.
■ **incorporated company,** ≈ sociedad *f* anónima.

incorporation [ɪnkɔːpə'reɪʃən] **1** *n* incorporación *f*, inclusión *f*. **2** US COMM constitución *f*, constitución *f* en sociedad.

incorporeal [ɪnkɔː'pɔːrɪəl] *adj fml* incorpóreo,-a.

incorrect [ɪnkə'rekt] **1** *adj* (*wrong, untrue*) incorrecto,-a, erróneo,-a, equivocado,-a: *incorrect English,* inglés incorrecto; *he gave an incorrect answer,* su respuesta fue incorrecta; *the information was incorrect,* la información fue errónea. **2** (*improper - behaviour*) incorrecto,-a; (*- dress*) impropio,-a, inadecuado,-a.

incorrectly [ɪnkə'rektlɪ] **1** *adv* (*wrongly*) incorrectamente, erróneamente, equivocadamente: *it's incorrectly spelt,* está mal escrito. **2** (*improperly*) incorrectamente.

incorrectness [ɪnkə'rektnəs] *n* incorrección *f*.

incorrigible [ɪn'kɒrɪdʒəbəl] *adj* incorregible.

incorruptible [ɪnkə'rʌptəbəl] *adj* incorruptible.

increase ['ɪnkriːs] **1** *n* (*gen*) aumento, incremento; (*in price, temperature*) subida, alza: *they want a wage increase,* quieren un aumento de sueldo; *an increase in the numbers of old-age pensioners,* un incremento en el número de pensionistas; *an increase of 10% on last year,* un aumento del 10% respecto al año pasado; *new techniques have led to an increase in output,* nuevas técnicas han resultado en un aumento de producción. **– 2** *t* (*gen*) aumentar; (*temperature*) subir: *he increased his speed,* aumentó la velocidad; *they have increased the number of police in the neighbourhood,* han aumentado el número de policías en el barrio. **– 3** *i* (*gen*) aumentar, incrementar; (*price*) aumentar, subir; (*temperature*) subir: *the population has increased,* la población ha crecido; *unemployment is increasing,* el paro está aumentando; *prices have increased,* los precios han subido.
● **to be on the increase,** ir en aumento, ir en alza.
▲ (*verbo*) [ɪn'kriːs].

increasing [ɪn'kriːsɪŋ] *adj* creciente: *there is increasing interest in the subject,* hay un interés creciente en el tema, cada vez hay más interés en el tema.

increasingly [ɪn'kriːsɪŋlɪ] *adv* cada vez más: *it is becoming increasingly difficult,* se está haciendo cada vez más difícil.

incredible [ɪn'kredɪbəl] *adj* (*unbelievable*) increíble, inverosímil; (*amazing, fantastic*) increíble, fantástico,-a: *he made up some incredible excuse,* inventó una excusa increíble; *she's got an incredible voice,* tiene una voz increíble; *it's incredible that she's got four children,* parece mentira que tenga cuatro hijos.

incredibly [ɪn'kredəblɪ] *adv* (*extremely*) increíblemente; (*amazingly*) sorprendentemente, aunque parece mentira: *it's incredibly cold,* hace un frío increíble; *incredibly, no-one had ever been there before,* sorprendentemente nadie había estado allí antes.

incredulity [ɪnkrɪ'djuːlətɪ] *n* incredulidad *f*.

incredulous [ɪn'kredjələs] *adj* incrédulo,-a: *she sounded incredulous,* parecía incrédula; *an incredulous look,* una mirada de incredulidad.

incredulously [ɪn'kredjələslɪ] *adv* con incredulidad.

increment ['ɪnkrɪmənt] *n* aumento, incremento: *salary increment,* aumento de salario.

incriminate [ɪn'krɪmɪneɪt] *t* incriminar: *he incriminated his brother,* incriminó a su hermano.
● **to incriminate os.,** autoincriminarse.

incriminating [ɪn'krɪmɪneɪtɪŋ] *adj* JUR incriminatorio,-a: *incriminating evidence,* pruebas incriminatorias.

incriminatory [ɪn'krɪmɪnətərɪ] *adj* JUR incriminatorio,-a.

incrustation [ɪnkrʌ'steɪʃən] *n* incrustación *f*.

incubate ['ɪnkjubeɪt] **1** *t* incubar. – **2** *i* (*of eggs*) incubar; (*of bird*) empollar.

incubation [ɪnkju'beɪʃən] *n* incubación *f*.
■ **incubation period,** período de incubación.

incubator ['ɪnkjubeɪtə'] *n* incubadora.

inculcate ['ɪnkʌlkeɪt] *t fml* inculcar (**in/into,** a) (**with,** en): *they inculcated the idea of honesty in their children,* inculcaron a sus hijos la idea de honestidad.

incumbency [ɪn'kʌmbənsɪ] **1** *n* (*office, duty, tenure*) titularidad *f*, mandato. **2** REL beneficio.

incumbent [ɪn'kʌmbənt] **1** *n* (*holder of office*) titular *mf*; (*clergyman*) beneficiado. – **2** *adj* (*holding office*) actual, titular, en ejercicio: *the incumbent president,* el presidente actual.
● **to be incumbent on/upon sb. to do sth.,** incumbir a algn. hacer algo, corresponder a algn. hacer algo.

incur [ɪn'kɜː'] **1** *t* (*blame, anger*) incurrir en, provocar: *incur the wrath of God,* incurrir en la ira de Dios. **2** (*debt, expense*) contraer, incurrir en. **3** (*injury, loss*) sufrir. **4** (*risk*) correr.
▲ *pt* & *pp* **incurred,** *ger* **incurring**.

incurable [ɪn'kjʊərəbəl] **1** *adj* (*disease*) incurable. **2** *fig* (*loss*) irremediable; (*habit, optimist*) incorregible. – **3** *n* enfermo,-a incurable.

incurably [ɪn'kjʊrəblɪ] **1** *adv* (*ill*) incurablemente. – **2** *adj fig* irremediablemente.

incursion [ɪn'kɜːʃən] **1** *n fml* incursión *f*, invasión *f* (**in/into,** en). **2** *fig* invasión *f*.

incurved [ɪn'kɜːvd] *adj* curvado,-a.

Ind [ɪndɪ'pendənt] *abbr* GB POL (*Independent*) independiente *mf*.

indebted [ɪn'detɪd] **1** *adj* (*in debt*) endeudado,-a. **2** *fig* (*grateful*) agradecido,-a: *I am deeply indebted to you for your help,* le agradezco muchísimo su ayuda.
● **to be indebted to sb. for sth.,** estar en deuda con algn. por algo, agradecer algo a algn.

indebtedness [ɪn'detɪdnəs] **1** *n* (*money*) deuda, endeudamiento. **2** (*gratitude*) agradecimiento.

indecency [ɪn'diːsənsɪ] *n* indecencia, obscenidad *f*.

indecent [ɪn'diːsənt] **1** *adj* (*obscene*) indecente, indecoroso,-a, obsceno,-a. **2** (*improper*) impropio,-a, indebido,-a, injustificado,-a: (*undue*) excesivo,-a: *in indecent haste,* con premura excesiva.
■ **indecent exposure,** exhibicionismo.

indecently [ɪn'diːsəntlɪ] **1** *adv* (*obscenely*) indecentemente. **2** (*excessively*) excesivamente, demasiado.

indecipherable [ɪndɪ'saɪfərəbəl] *adj* indescifrable.

indecision [ɪndɪ'sɪʒən] *n* indecisión *f*, irresolución *f*.

indecisive [ɪndɪ'saɪsɪv] **1** *adj* (*hesitant*) indeciso,-a, irresoluto,-a. **2** (*inconclusive*) poco concluyente, no concluyente, no decisivo,-a.

indecisively [ɪndɪ'saɪsɪvlɪ] **1** *adv* (*hesitantly*) de manera indecisa. **2** (*inconclusively*) sin resultados definitivos.

indecisiveness [ɪndɪ'saɪsɪvnɪs] *n* indecisión *f*, falta de decisión.

indecorous [ɪn'dekərəs] *adj fml* indecoroso,-a.

indecorum [ɪndɪ'kɔːrəm] *n fml* indecoro, falta de decoro.

indeed [ɪn'diːd] **1** *adv* (*yes, certainly*) efectivamente, en efecto: *are you Mr Fox? yes, indeed,* ¿es el Sr Fox? sí, efectivamente; *do you like chocolates? yes, indeed I do,* ¿te gustan los bombones? sí, mucho; *did you hear that bang? indeed I did!,* ¿has oído esa explosión? ¡ya lo creo!; *may I? indeed you may,* ¿puedo? claro que puedes. **2** (*intensifier*) realmente, de veras, de verdad: *that is praise indeed,* eso sí que es un elogio; *thank you very much indeed,* muchísimas gracias; *it's very hot indeed,* hace muchísimo calor; *very expensive indeed,* verdaderamente caro. **3** *fml* (*in fact*) realmente, en realidad, de hecho; (*what is more*) es más: *I was happy, indeed delighted, that you won,* me alegré, en realidad me encantó, tu victoria. – **4** *interj* (*showing surprise, disbelief, etc*) ¿de verdad?, ¿de veras?, ¡no me digas!: *he said you gave it to him - did he indeed?,* dijo que se lo habías regalado - ¿de veras?; *a new car indeed! whatever next!,* ¡un coche nuevo dices! ¡vaya, vaya!

indefatigable [ɪndɪ'fætɪgəbəl] *adj fml* incansable, infatigable.

indefensible [ɪndɪ'fensəbəl] **1** *adj* (*idea, statement, view, etc*) insostenible; (*behaviour*) injustificable, inexcusable. **2** (*place, building, position*) indefendible, indefensible, indefensable.

indefensibly [ɪndɪ'fensəblɪ] *adv* (*behaviour*) injustificablemente, inexcusablemente.

indefinable [ɪndɪ'faɪnəbəl] *adj* indefinible.

indefinite [ɪn'defɪnət] **1** *adj* (*vague, not precise*) indefinido,-a, vago,-a, impreciso,-a: *an indefinite answer,* una respuesta imprecisa. **2** (*not fixed - period of time, amount, number*) indefinido,-a, indeterminado,-a: *they called an indefinite strike,* declararon una huelga indefinida.

indefinitely [ɪn'defɪnətlɪ] *adv* indefinidamente: *it's been closed indefinitely,* lo han cerrado por tiempo indefinido; *we can't carry on like this indefinitely,* no podemos seguir así indefinidamente.

indelible [ɪn'delɪbəl] **1** *adj* (*ink etc*) indeleble, imborrable. **2** *fig* (*memory etc*) inolvidable, imborrable.

indelibly [ɪn'delɪblɪ] *adv* indeleblemente, imborrablemente.

indelicacy [ɪn'delɪkəsɪ] *n* (*act*) indelicadeza, falta de delicadeza; (*remark*) indiscreción *f*.
▲ *pl* **indelicacies**.

indelicate [ɪn'delɪkət] **1** *adj* (*rude, embarrassing*) poco delicado,-a, indelicado,-a. **2** (*tactless*) indiscreto,-a.

indemnification [ɪndemnɪfɪ'keɪʃən] **1** *n* (*act*) indemnización *f*. **2** (*compensation, repayment*) indemnización *f*, reparación *f*, compensación *f*.

indemnify [ɪn'demnɪfaɪ] **1** *t fml* (*insure*) asegurar (**against,** contra). **2** *fml* (*compensate*) indemnizar (**for,** por/de).
▲ *pt* & *pp* **indemnified,** *ger* **indemnifying**.

indemnity [ɪn'demnɪtɪ] **1** *n* (*insurance, guarantee*) indemnidad *f* (**against,** contra). **2** (*compensation*) indemnización *f* (**for,** por), reparación *f*, compensación *f*.

indent 308

▲ *pl* **indemnities.**
indent [ɪn'dent] **1** *t* (*in text*) sangrar. – **2** *i* GB COMM hacer un pedido (**for**, de), encargar (**for**, -). – **3** *n* GB COMM pedido.
▲ En *3* (*sustantivo*) ['ɪndent].
indentation [ɪnden'teɪʃən] **1** *n* (*in text*) sangría. **2** (*notch in edge, mark*) mella, muesca.
indented [ɪn'dentɪd] **1** *adj* (*text*) sangrado,-a. **2** (*edge*) mellado,-a, marcado,-a.
indenture [ɪn'dentʃə] **1** *t* contratar como aprendiz,-za. – **2 indentures,** *npl* contrato *m sing* de aprendizaje.
independence [ɪndɪ'pendəns] *n* independencia (**from**, de).
● **to obtain independence,** obtener la independencia.
■ **Independence Day,** día *m* de la Independencia.
independent [ɪndɪ'pendənt] **1** *adj* (*gen*) independiente: *they called for an independent inquiry,* pidieron una investigación independiente; *she's financially independent,* es económicamente independiente; *young people are fairly independent of their parents,* los jóvenes son bastante independientes de sus padres. – **2** *n* POL (candidato,-a) independiente *mf.*
● **to become independent,** independizarse. ‖ **to be of independent means,** disponer de rentas.
■ **independent school,** GB colegio no subvencionado. ‖ **independent television,** televisión *f* privada.
independently [ɪndɪ'pendəntlɪ] *adv* (*gen*) independientemente; (*separately*) por separado, cada uno por un lado.
in-depth [ɪn'depθ] *adj* minucioso,-a, exhaustivo,-a, a fondo: *an in-depth study,* un estudio minucioso.
indescribable [ɪndɪ'skraɪbəbəl] **1** *adj* (*gen*) indescriptible. **2** (*too good*) inefable. **3** *pej* (*too bad*) indecible, incalificable.
indescribably [ɪndɪ'skraɪbeblɪ] **1** *adv* (*gen*) indescriptiblemente. **2** (*too good*) inefablemente. **3** *pej* (*too bad*) inefablemente, indeciblemente: *indescribably awful,* tan malo que no se puede explicar.
indestructible [ɪndɪ'strʌktəbəl] *adj* indestructible.
indeterminable [ɪndɪ'tɜːmɪnəbəl] *adj fml* indeterminable.
indeterminate [ɪndɪ'tɜːmɪnət] *adj* indeterminado,-a.
index ['ɪndeks] **1** *n* (*in book*) índice *m*; (*list*) lista; (*in library*) índice *m*, catálogo. **2** ECON índice *m*: *cost-of-living index,* índice del coste de la vida. **3** *fig* indicación *f*, señal *f*: *the sale of new cars is an index of economic prosperity,* la venta de coches nuevos es una indicación de la prosperidad económica. **4** (*math*) índice *m*. – **5** *t* (*book*) poner un índice a; (*collection*) catalogar, clasificar. **6** ECON (*wages, pensions, etc*) vincular: *the indexing of wages to inflation,* el vínculo de los salarios a la inflación.
■ **card index,** ficha. ‖ **index finger,** dedo índice.
▲ *pl* **indices** ['ɪndɪsiːz].
index-linked ['ɪndekslɪŋkt] *adj* ECON vinculado,-a al índice de precios al consumo.
India ['ɪndɪə] *n* (la) India.
■ **India rubber,** caucho.
Indian ['ɪndɪən] **1** *adj* indio,-a, hindú *mf.* – **2** *n* indio,-a, hindú.
● **Indian file,** fila india. ‖ **Indian summer,** veranillo de San Martín.
■ **Indian corn,** US maíz *m.* ‖ **Indian hemp,** (*hemp*) cannabis *m*, cáñamo índico; (*drug*) cannabis *m*, hachís *m.* ‖ **the Indian Ocean,** el océano Índico.
indicate ['ɪndɪkeɪt] **1** *t* (*point to, draw attention to*) indicar, señalar: *I sat down on the chair she indicated,* me senté

en la silla que me indicó. **2** (*show, make clear*) indicar, ser indicio de, ser señal de: *this front indicates a change in the weather,* este frente indica un cambio en el tiempo; *all the evidence indicates that he is guilty,* todas las pruebas indican su culpabilidad. **3** (*mark*) señalar; (*register*) indicar, marcar: *the thermometer indicated 39°,* el termómetro marcaba 39°. **4** (*require, call for*) necesitarse: *given all the problems, a new approach is indicated,* dados los problemas, se necesita un nuevo enfoque. **5** AUTO indicar, señalizar. – **6** *i* AUTO poner el intermitente.
indication [ɪndɪ'keɪʃən] *n* (*gen*) indicio, señal *f*, indicación *f*: *there's every indication that the economy is on the upturn,* todo indica que la economía está mejorando; *he gave no indication to the contrary,* no dio ninguna indicación en contra.
indicative [ɪn'dɪkətɪv] **1** *adj fml* indicativo,-a (**of**, de): *this attitude is indicative of her apathy,* esta actitud indica su apatía. **2** LING indicativo,-a. – **3** *n* LING indicativo *m.*
indicator ['ɪndɪkeɪtə'] **1** *n* (*gen*) indicador *m.* **2** AUTO intermitente *m.*
indict [ɪn'daɪt] *t* JUR acusar (**for**, de): *he was indicted for murder,* fue acusado de asesinato.
indictable [ɪn'daɪtəbəl] *adj* JUR encausable, procesable.
indictment [ɪn'daɪtmənt] **1** *n* JUR acusación *f*, sumario. **2** *fig* (*criticism*) crítica.
● **to be under indictment for sth.,** ser acusado,-a de algo. ‖ **to bring in an indictment against sb.,** presentar cargos contra algn., formular cargos contra algn.
indifference [ɪn'dɪfərəns] *n* indiferencia (**to**, ante): *he treats her with complete indifference,* la trata con absoluta indiferencia.
indifferent [ɪn'dɪfərənt] **1** *adj* (*gen*) indiferente (**to**, a): *he was indifferent to my plea,* fue indiferente a mi súplica; *the divers seemed indifferent to the cold,* a los submarinistas parecía no importarles el frío. **2** (*mediocre, average*) mediocre, regular, pobre.
indifferently [ɪn'dɪfərəntlɪ] **1** *adv* (*uninterestedly*) con indiferencia. **2** (*averagely*) regular, de forma mediocre, sin pena ni gloria.
indigenous [ɪn'dɪdʒənəs] *adj fml* indígena, autóctono,-a (**to**, de).
indigent ['ɪndɪdʒənt] *adj fml* indigente.
indigestible [ɪndɪ'dʒestəbəl] *adj* (*food*) indigesto,-a, no digerible; (*facts*) difícil de digerir.
indigestion [ɪndɪ'dʒestʃən] *n* indigestión *f*, empacho: *rich food gives me indigestion,* la comida fuerte me sienta mal; *you'll get indigestion!,* ¡te vas a indigestar!
● **to suffer from indigestion,** tener una indigestión, tener un empacho.
■ **indigestion pills/tablets,** pastillas para la indigestión.
indignant [ɪn'dɪgnənt] *adj* (*person*) indignado,-a; (*look etc*) de indignación: *I was most indignant at having to wait so long,* me indigné en tener que esperar tanto; *he got very indignant with me,* se indignó conmigo.
● **to become/get indignant about/at/over sth.,** indignarse por algo.
indignantly [ɪn'dɪgnəntlɪ] *adv* con indignación, indignado,-a.
indignation [ɪndɪg'neɪʃən] *n* indignación *f* (**about/over**, por) (**at**, ante/por): *public indignation at the terrorist attack,* indignación pública por el ataque terrorista.
indignity [ɪn'dɪgnətɪ] *n* indignidad *f*, humillación *f.*
▲ *pl* **indignities.**

indigo ['ɪndɪgəʊ] 1 *n* añil *m*. – 2 *adj* (de color) añil.

indirect [ɪndɪ'rekt] *adj* indirecto,-a: *indirect lighting,* alumbrado indirecto; *an indirect route,* una ruta indirecta; *she gave an indirect answer,* dio una respuesta evasiva.
■ **indirect object,** LING objeto indirecto, complemento indirecto. ‖ **indirect question,** LING pregunta indirecta. ‖ **indirect speech,** LING estilo indirecto. ‖ **indirect tax,** impuesto indirecto.

indirectly [ɪndɪ'rektlɪ] *adv* indirectamente.

indiscernible [ɪndɪ'sɜːnəbəl] *adj* imperceptible, indiscernible.

indiscipline [ɪn'dɪsəplɪn] *n* indisciplina.

indiscreet [ɪndɪ'skriːt] *adj* (*person*) indiscreto,-a, poco discreto,-a, poco diplomático,-a, falto de tacto; (*question, remark*) indiscreto,-a.

indiscreetly [ɪndɪ'skriːtlɪ] *adv* indiscretamente, con indiscreción.

indiscretion [ɪndɪ'skreʃən] *n* indiscreción *f*.

indiscriminately [ɪndɪ'skrɪmɪnətlɪ] *adv* (*randomly*) indiscriminadamente; (*without careful choice*) sin criterio, sin discernimiento.

indiscriminate [ɪndɪ'skrɪmɪnət] *adj* (*violence, attack, etc*) indiscriminado,-a; (*praise, reading, viewing, etc*) sin criterio, sin discernimiento.

indispensable [ɪndɪ'spensəbəl] *adj* indispensable, imprescindible (**to,** para).

indisposed [ɪndɪ'spəʊzd] 1 *adj* (*ill*) indispuesto,-a. 2 *fml* (*not willing*) poco dispuesto,-a (**to,** a): *indisposed to help,* con pocas ganas de ayudar.

indisposition [ɪndɪspə'zɪʃən] *n* (*illness*) indisposición *f*.

indisputable [ɪndɪ'spjuːtəbəl] *adj* (*gen*) indiscutible, indisputable, incuestionable; (*winner, leader, etc*) indiscutible; (*fact*) irrefutable.

indisputably [ɪndɪ'spjuːtəblɪ] *adv* indiscutiblemente.

indissolubility [ɪndɪsɒljə'bɪlətɪ] *n* indisolubilidad *f*.

indissoluble [ɪndɪ'sɒljəbəl] *adj fml* (*cannot be dissolved*) indisoluble; (*cannot be broken*) inseparable.

indistinct [ɪndɪ'stɪŋkt] *adj* (*gen*) indistinto,-a, impreciso,-a; (*memory*) confuso,-a, vago,-a; (*shape, area, etc*) borroso,-a; (*sound, speech*) confuso,-a, poco claro,-a: *I have a very indistinct memory of my grandmother,* tengo unos recuerdos muy vagos de mi abuela; *his voice was so indistinct that I couldn't understand a word,* su voz era tan confusa que no pude entender ni una palabra.

indistinctly [ɪndɪ'stɪŋktlɪ] *adv* (*gen*) indistintamente, imprecisamente; (*remember*) vagamente; (*see*) con poca claridad; (*speak*) confusamente.

indistinguishable [ɪndɪ'stɪŋgwɪʃəbəl] *adj* indistinguible (**from,** de).

individual [ɪndɪ'vɪdjʊəl] 1 *adj* (*single, separate*) por separado: *each individual student,* cada uno de los estudiantes, cada estudiante por separado. 2 (*for one person*) individual: *individual portions,* raciones individuales; *individual tuition,* clases particulares; *individual attention,* atención individual. 3 (*particular, personal*) personal, propio,-a. 4 (*different, unique*) personal, original. – 5 *n* (*person*) individuo, persona: *rights of the individual,* derechos del individuo; *you should treat people as individuals,* deberías tratar a la gente como personas. 6 *fam* individuo, tipo, tío,-a.

individualism [ɪndɪ'vɪdjʊəlɪzəm] *n* individualismo.

individualist [ɪndɪ'vɪdjʊəlɪst] *n* individualista *mf*.

individualistic [ɪndɪvɪdjʊə'lɪstɪk] *adj* individualista.

individuality [ɪndɪvɪdjʊ'ælətɪ] *n* individualidad *f*, personalidad *f*.

individualize [ɪndɪ'vɪdjʊəlaɪz] *t* individualizar, personalizar.

individually [ɪndɪ'vɪdjʊəlɪ] *adv* (*separately*) individualmente, por separado; (*one by one*) uno por uno: *I want you to work individually,* quiero que trabajéis por separado; *each chocolate comes individually wrapped,* cada bombón viene individualmente envuelto.

indivisible [ɪndɪ'vɪzəbəl] *adj* indivisible.

indoctrinate [ɪn'dɒktrɪneɪt] *t* adoctrinar.

indoctrination [ɪndɒktrɪ'neɪʃən] *n* adoctrinamiento.

indolence ['ɪndələns] *n fml* indolencia, pereza.

indolent ['ɪndələnt] *adj fml* indolente, perezoso,-a.

indolently ['ɪndələntlɪ] *adv fml* perezosamente, con pereza.

indomitable [ɪn'dɒmɪtəbəl] *adj fml* indomable, indómito,-a.

indomitably [ɪn'dɒmɪtəblɪ] *adv fml* de forma indomable.

Indonesia [ɪndə'niːzɪə] *n* Indonesia.

Indonesian [ɪndə'niːzɪən] 1 *adj* indonesio,-a. – 2 *n* indonesio,-a.

indoor ['ɪndɔːr] 1 *adj* (*aerial, plant, photography, etc*) interior; (*clothes etc*) de estar por casa. 2 DEP (*swimming pool, running track*) cubierto,-a.
■ **indoor football,** fútbol *m* sala. ‖ **indoor games,** juegos *mpl* de salón. ‖ **indoor record,** récord *m* en pista cubierta.

indoors [ɪn'dɔːz] *adv* (*inside house*) dentro (de casa); (*at home*) en casa; (*inside building*) a cubierto, dentro: *if it rains, the concert will be held indoors,* si llueve, el concierto se celebrará a cubierto.
● **to go indoors,** ir adentro, entrar en (la) casa. ‖ **to stay indoors,** quedarse en casa.

indorse [ɪn'dɔːs] *t* → **endorse**.

indubitable [ɪn'djuːbɪtəbəl] *adj fml* indudable.

indubitably [ɪn'djuːbɪtəblɪ] *adv* indudablemente, sin duda.

induce [ɪn'djuːs] 1 *t* (*persuade*) inducir, persuadir, llevar: *what induced you to go there?,* ¿qué te indujo a ir allí? 2 (*cause*) causar, producir, provocar: *lunchtime drinking induces drowsiness,* beber a mediodía produce somnolencia. 3 MED (*childbirth*) provocar, inducir.
● **to induce sb. to do sth.,** inducir a algn. a hacer algo.

inducement [ɪn'djuːsmənt] 1 *n* incentivo, estímulo, aliciente *m*: *an inducement to invest,* un incentivo para invertir. 2 MED inducción *f*. 3 *euph* soborno.

induct [ɪn'dʌkt] 1 *t* (*introduce to organization*) admitir, instalar. 2 US MIL reclutar.

induction [ɪn'dʌkʃən] 1 *n* (*initiation - gen*) admisión *f*, ingreso; (*- of priest*) instalación *f*. 2 MED (*of childbirth*) provocación *f*, inducción *f*. 3 US MIL reclutamiento. 4 (*logic*) inducción *f*. 5 PHYS ELEC inducción *f*. 6 (*in engine*) admisión *f*.
■ **induction coil,** bobina de inducción. ‖ **induction course,** curso de iniciación *f*. ‖ **induction motor,** motor *m* de inducción.

inductive [ɪn'dʌktɪv] *adj* inductivo,-a.

indulge [ɪn'dʌldʒ] 1 *t* (*satisfy - desire, whim*) satisfacer, ceder a, consentir; (*- passion*) dar rienda suelta a: *it pleases me to indulge your wishes,* me gusta satisfacer tus deseos; *he indulges her every whim,* le consiente todos los caprichos; *he spent a week indulging his passion for skiing,* pasó una semana dando rienda suelta a su pasión por el esquí. 2 (*pamper - person*) complacer; (*- child*) mimar, consentir: *they indulge their children too much,*

miman demasiado a sus hijos; *she indulged him in/with presents*, ella lo mimaba con regalos. **– 3** *i* (*gen*) permitirse; (*eat*) comer (lo que uno quiera); (*drink*) beber (lo que uno quiera): *she sometimes indulges in the luxury of a beauty treatment*, a veces se permite el lujo de un tratamiento de belleza; *he always indulges at Christmas*, siempre bebe (demasiado) en Navidad.
● **to indulge os.**, permitirse un lujo, darse algún gusto.

indulgence [ɪn'dʌldʒəns] **1** *n* (*luxury*) (pequeño) lujo; (*bad habit*) vicio: *smoking is my only indulgence*, fumar es mi único vicio; *you have to allow youself small indulgences*, hay que permitirse pequeños lujos. **2** (*of desire, whim*) satisfacción *f*, complacencia; (*partaking - of food, drink*) abuso; (*of person*) consentimiento; (*of child*) mimo: *indulgence in rich food can lead to obesity*, abusar de la comida puede provocar la obesidad. **3** REL indulgencia.
indulgent [ɪn'dʌldʒənt] *adj* indulgente (**towards**, con).
Indus ['ɪndʌs] *n* el Indo *m*.
industrial [ɪn'dʌstrɪəl] *adj* industrial.
■ **industrial accident**, accidente *m* laboral, accidente de trabajo. ‖ **industrial action**, huelga: *they took industrial action*, se declararon en huelga. ‖ **industrial dispute**, conflicto laboral. ‖ **industrial estate**, polígono industrial, zona industrial. ‖ **industrial relations**, relaciones *fpl* laborales. ‖ **Industrial Revolution**, Revolución *f* Industrial. ‖ **industrial unrest**, conflictividad *f* laboral. ‖ **industrial tribunal**, tribunal *m* laboral. ‖ **industrial waste**, residuos *mpl* industriales.
industrialise [ɪn'dʌstrɪəlaɪz] *t* → **industrialize**.
industrialism [ɪn'dʌstrɪəlɪzəm] *n* industrialismo.
industrialist [ɪn'dʌstrɪəlɪst] *n* industrial *mf*, empresario,-a.
industrialization [ɪndʌstrɪəlaɪ'zeɪʃən] *n* industrialización *f*.
industrialize [ɪn'dʌstrɪəlaɪz] **1** *t* industrializar. **– 2** *i* industrializarse.
● **to become industrialized**, industrializarse.
industrially [ɪn'dʌstrɪəlɪ] *adv* industrialmente.
industrious [ɪn'dʌstrɪəs] *adj* (*hard-working*) trabajador,-ra, laborioso,-a; (*diligent*) diligente, aplicado,-a.
industriously [ɪn'dʌstrɪəslɪ] *adv* con diligencia.
industriousness [ɪn'dʌstrɪəsnəs] *n* diligencia.
industry ['ɪndʌstrɪ] **1** *n* (*gen*) industria. **2** *fml* (*hard work*) diligencia.
■ **heavy industry**, industria pesada. ‖ **light industry**, industria ligera. ‖ **clothing industry**, industria textil. ‖ **film industry**, industria cinematográfica. ‖ **coal industry**, industria minera. ‖ **tourist industry**, turismo. ▲ *pl* **industries**.
inebriate [ɪ'niːbrɪət] **1** *adj fml* ebrio,-a. **– 2** *n fml* ebrio,-a. **– 3** *t fml* embriagar.
inebriated [ɪn'iːbrɪeɪtɪd] *adj fml* ebrio,-a, embriagado,-a.
inebriation [ɪniːbrɪ'eɪʃən] *n* embriaguez *f*.
inedible [ɪn'edəbəl] *adj* incomible, incomestible.
ineffable [ɪn'efəbəl] *adj fml* inefable.
ineffably [ɪn'efəblɪ] *adv fml* inefablemente.
ineffective [ɪnɪ'fektɪv] **1** *adj* (*method, cure*) ineficaz, inútil; (*attempt*) infructuoso,-a: *the treatment proved ineffective*, el tratamiento no surtió efecto. **2** (*person*) incapaz, incompetente, ineficiente: *he's completely ineffective as a lawyer*, es un abogado totalmente incompetente.
ineffectively [ɪnɪ'fektɪvlɪ] *adv* ineficazmente, inútilmente.
ineffectiveness [ɪnɪ'fektɪvnəs] **1** *n* (*of method, cure*) ineficacia, inutilidad *f*. **2** (*of person*) incapacidad *f*, incompetencia.

ineffectual [ɪnɪ'fektʃʊəl] **1** *adj* (*policy, protest, attempt, etc*) ineficaz, inútil. **2** (*person*) incapaz, incompetente.
ineffectually [ɪnɪ'fektʃʊəlɪ] *adv* ineficazmente, inútilmente.
inefficiency [ɪnɪ'fɪʃənsɪ] **1** *n* (*gen*) ineficacia. **2** (*of person*) incompetencia, ineficiencia, ineptitud *f*.
inefficient [ɪnɪ'fɪʃənt] **1** *adj* (*gen*) ineficaz. **2** (*person*) incompetente, ineficiente, poco eficiente.
inefficiently [ɪnɪ'fɪʃəntlɪ] **1** *adv* (*gen*) ineficazmente. **2** (*person*) incompetentemente.
inelastic [ɪnɪ'læstɪk] **1** *adj* PHYS no elástico,-a. **2** *fig* (*rigid*) rígido,-a, poco flexible.
inelegant [ɪn'elɪgənt] *adj* poco elegante.
ineligibility [ɪnelɪdʒə'bɪlətɪ] *n* falta de cualificación.
ineligible [ɪn'elɪdʒəbəl] *adj* inelegible; (*not suitable*) inadecuado,-a: *he is ineligible for a pension*, no tiene derecho a una pensión; *she's ineligible for benefit*, no tiene derecho al subsidio.
inept [ɪ'nept] *adj* (*person*) inepto,-a, incapaz; (*remark*) torpe.
ineptitude [ɪ'neptɪtjuːd] *n* (*incompetence*) ineptitud *f*, incapacidad *f*; (*of remark*) torpeza.
inequality [ɪnɪ'kwɒlətɪ] *n* desigualdad *f*.
▲ *pl* **inequalities**.
inequitable [ɪn'ekwɪtəbəl] *adj fml* injusto,-a.
inequitably [ɪn'ekwɪtəblɪ] *adv* injustamente.
inequity [ɪn'ekwətɪ] *n* injusticia.
▲ *pl* **inequities**.
ineradicable [ɪnɪ'rædɪkəbəl] *adj* inextirpable.
inert [ɪ'nɜːt] **1** *adj* (*gas, matter, etc*) inerte. **2** (*immobile*) inerte, inmóvil: *he lay inert*, yacía inerte. **3** *pej* (*sluggish, without vigour*) poco enérgico,-a, sin vigor.
inertia [ɪ'nɜːʃə] **1** *n* PHYS inercia. **2** (*lethargy*) inercia, letargia, apatía: *he lay on the sofa all day through sheer inertia*, se quedó tumbado en el sofá todo el día por pura apatía.
inescapable [ɪnɪ'skeɪpəbəl] *adj* ineludible, inevitable.
inescapably [ɪnɪ'skeɪpəblɪ] *adv* ineludiblemente, inevitablemente.
inessential [ɪnɪ'senʃəl] **1** *adj* no esencial, innecesario,-a. **– 2 inessentials**, *npl* cosas *fpl* sin importancia.
inestimable [ɪn'estɪməbəl] *adj fml* (*gen*) inestimable, inapreciable; (*damage*) incalculable.
inevitability [ɪnevɪtə'bɪlətɪ] *n* inevitabilidad *f*.
inevitable [ɪn'evɪtəbəl] **1** *adj* (*unavoidable*) inevitable: *the break up of their marriage was inevitable*, el fracaso de su matrimonio era inevitable. **2** *fam* (*usual*) sempiterno,-a, consabido,-a, de siempre: *with the inevitable cigarette in his hand*, con el cigarrillo de siempre en la mano. **– 3 the inevitable**, *n* lo inevitable *m sing*.
inevitably [ɪn'evɪtəblɪ] *adv* inevitablemente.
inexact [ɪnɪg'zækt] *adj* inexacto,-a.
inexactitude [ɪnɪg'zæktɪtjuːd] *n* inexactitud *f*.
inexcusable [ɪnɪk'skjuːzəbəl] *adj* inexcusable, imperdonable, injustificable.
inexhaustible [ɪnɪg'zɔːstəbəl] *adj* inagotable.
inexorable [ɪn'eksərəbəl] *adj fml* inexorable, implacable.
inexpensive [ɪnɪk'spensɪv] *adj* barato,-a, económico,-a.
inexperience [ɪnɪk'spɪərɪəns] *n* inexperiencia, falta de experiencia.
inexperienced [ɪnɪk'spɪərɪənst] *adj* inexperto,-a, sin experiencia: *he's inexperienced in marketing*, no tiene mucha experiencia en mercadotecnia.
inexpert [ɪn'ekspɜːt] *adj* (*person*) inexperto,-a, inhábil (**at**, en); (*advice etc*) inexperto,-a.

inexpertly [ɪn'ekspɜːtlɪ] *adv* sin habilidad.
inexplicable [ɪnɪk'splɪkəbəl] *adj* inexplicable.
inexplicably [ɪnɪk'splɪkəblɪ] *adv* inexplicablemente.
inexpressible [ɪnɪk'spresəbəl] *adj* inexpresable, inefable.
inexpressive [ɪnɪk'spresɪv] *adj* inexpresivo,-a.
inextinguishable [ɪnɪk'stɪŋgwɪʃəbəl] *adj fml* inextinguible, inapagable.
inextricable [ɪn'ekstrɪkəbəl] *adj* inextricable.
inextricably [ɪnɪk'strɪkəblɪ] *adv* inextricablemente: *a series of factors which are inextricably linked,* una serie de factores inextricablemente relacionados.
infallibility [ɪnfælə'bɪlətɪ] *n* infalibilidad *f.*
infallible [ɪn'fæləbəl] *adj* infalible, indefectible.
infamous ['ɪnfəməs] **1** *adj* (*notorious*) infame. **2** *fml* (*wicked*) infame, ruin.
infamy ['ɪnfəmɪ] **1** *n fml* (*wickedness*) infamia, maldad *f.* **2** *fml* (*disgrace*) infamia, desgracia.
　▲ *pl infamies.*
infancy ['ɪnfənsɪ] **1** *n* (*childhood*) infancia, niñez *f.* **2** GB JUR minoría de edad.
　● to be in its infancy, *fig* estar en mantillas.
infant ['ɪnfənt] **1** *n* (*baby*) bebé *m*, niño,-a; (*at infant school*) niño,-a, párvulo,-a. **2** GB JUR menor *mf* de edad.
　■ infant mortality, mortalidad *f* infantil. ‖ infant prodigy, niño,-a prodigio,-a. ‖ infant school, parvulario. ‖ infant teacher, maestro,-a, de párvulos.
infanticide [ɪn'fæntɪsaɪd] **1** *n* (*crime*) infanticidio. **2** (*person*) infanticida *mf.*
infantile ['ɪnfəntaɪl] **1** *adj* infantil. **2** *pej* infantil, pueril.
　■ infantile paralysis, parálisis *f* infantil.
infantry ['ɪnfəntrɪ] *n* infantería *f.*
infantryman ['ɪnfəntrɪmən] *n* soldado de infantería.
　▲ *pl infantrymen* ['ɪnfəntrɪmən].
infatuated [ɪn'fætjʊeɪtɪd] *adj* encaprichado,-a (**with/by,** con), locamente enamorado,-a (**with/by,** de).
infatuation [ɪnfætjʊ'eɪʃən] *n* encaprichamiento (**with/by,** con), enamoramiento (**with/by,** de).
infect [ɪn'fekt] **1** *t* (*wound, cut, etc*) infectar; (*food, water, etc*) contaminar; (*person*) contagiar: *this wound is infected,* esta herida está infectada; *he became infected with malaria,* contrajo paludismo. **2** *fig* (*emotions*) contagiar: *her laughter infected everyone,* su risa contagió a todos. **3** (*poison*) envenenar: *minds infected by hatred,* mentes envenenadas por el odio.
infection [ɪn'fekʃən] **1** *n* (*of wound, cut, etc*) infección *f*; (*of food, water, etc*) contaminación *f*; (*with illness*) infección *f*, contagio. **2** (*disease*) infección *f.*
infectious [ɪn'fekʃəs] **1** *adj* (*disease*) infeccioso,-a, contagioso,-a. **2** *fig* contagioso,-a: *she's got an infectious laugh,* tiene una risa contagiosa.
infer [ɪn'fɜːʳ] *t* inferir (**from,** de), deducir (**from,** de).
　▲ *pt & pp inferred, ger inferring.*
inference ['ɪnfərəns] *n* inferencia, deducción *f.*
　● to draw inferences from sth., sacar conclusiones de algo.
inferential [ɪnfə'renʃəl] *adj* ilativo,-a, deductivo,-a.
inferior [ɪn'fɪərɪəʳ] **1** *adj* inferior (**to,** a). **–2** *n* inferior *mf.*
　● to make sb. feel inferior, hacer que algn. se sienta inferior.
inferiority [ɪnfɪərɪ'ɒrətɪ] *n* inferioridad *f.*
　■ inferiority complex, complejo de inferioridad.
infernal [ɪn'fɜːnəl] **1** *adj* infernal. **2** *fam* (*tiresome*) maldito,-a.
inferno [ɪn'fɜːnəʊ] **1** *n* (*like hell*) infierno. **2** (*fire*) llamas *fpl*: *the building was a blazing inferno,* el edificio ardía en llamas.

　▲ *pl infernos.*
infertile [ɪn'fɜːtaɪl] *adj* estéril.
infertility [ɪnfə'tɪlətɪ] *n* esterilidad *f.*
infest [ɪn'fest] *t* infestar (**with,** de), plagar (**with,** de).
infestation [ɪnfe'steɪʃən] *n* plaga, infestación *f.*
infidel ['ɪnfɪdəl] *n* infiel *mf.*
infidelity [ɪnfɪ'delətɪ] *n* infidelidad *f.*
　▲ *pl infidelities.*
infighting ['ɪnfaɪtɪŋ] **1** *n fam fig* luchas *fpl* internas. **2** SP (*boxing*) lucha cerrada.
infill ['ɪnfɪl] *n* relleno.
infiltrate ['ɪnfɪltreɪt] **1** *t* infiltrarse (**into,** en): *there were fears of police having infiltrated the party,* temían que la policía se hubiese infiltrado en el partido. **– 2** *i* infiltrarse.
infiltration [ɪnfɪl'treɪʃən] *n* infiltración *f.*
infiltrator [ɪnfɪl'treɪtəʳ] *n* infiltrado,-a.
infinite ['ɪnfɪnət] **1** *adj* (*endless*) infinito,-a; (*very great*) sin límites: *infinite wisdom,* sabiduría infinita; *an infinite number of demeaning jobs,* una infinidad de trabajos humillantes. **– 2 the Infinite,** *n* Dios *m.*
infinitely ['ɪnfɪnətlɪ] *adv* infinitamente: *this is infinitely preferable to working,* esto es infinitamente mejor que trabajar.
infinitesimal [ɪnfɪnɪ'tesɪməl] *adj* infinitesimal, infinitésimo,-a.
infinitive [ɪn'fɪnɪtɪv] *n* LING infinitivo.
infinitude [ɪn'fɪnɪtjuːd] *n fml* infinidad *f.*
infinity [ɪn'fɪnɪtɪ] **1** *n* (*gen*) infinidad *f.* **2** MATH infinito.
infirm [ɪn'fɜːm] **1** *adj* débil, endeble, enfermizo,-a, achacoso,-a. **– 2 the infirm,** *npl* los enfermos, los que necesitan atención médica.
　● infirm of purpose, indeciso,-a.
infirmary [ɪn'fɜːmərɪ] **1** *n* (*hospital*) hospital *m.* **2** (*in school etc*) enfermería *f.*
　▲ *pl infirmaries.*
infirmity [ɪn'fɜːmɪtɪ] *n* (*weakness*) debilidad *f*; (*illness*) enfermedad *f*: *the infirmities of old age,* los achaques de la vejez.
　▲ *pl infirmities.*
inflame [ɪn'fleɪm] *t* (*anger*) encender; (*passion*) inflamar: *his gesture inflamed the crowd,* su gesto inflamó al público.
inflamed [ɪn'fleɪmd] **1** *adj* MED inflamado,-a. **2** *fig* (*passion*) inflamado,-a, encendido,-a; (*anger*) encendido,-a.
　● to become inflamed, inflamarse.
inflammable [ɪn'flæməbəl] **1** *adj* inflamable. **2** *fam fig* explosivo,-a.
inflammation [ɪnflə'meɪʃən] *n* inflamación *f.*
inflammatory [ɪn'flæmətərɪ] **1** *adj* MED inflamatorio,-a. **2** *fig* incendiario,-a.
inflatable [ɪn'fleɪtəbəl] *adj* inflable.
inflate [ɪn'fleɪt] **1** *t* inflar, hinchar. **2** *fig* inflar, hinchar, exagerar. **3** ECON inflar. **– 4** *i* inflarse, hincharse.
inflated [ɪn'fleɪtɪd] **1** *adj* (*blown up*) inflado,-a, hinchado,-a. **2** (*prices*) inflacionista, inflacionario,-a. **3** *fig* exagerado,-a.
　● to have an inflated opinion of os., ser muy engreído,-a.
inflation [ɪn'fleɪʃən] *n* inflación *f.*
inflationary [ɪn'fleɪʃənərɪ] *adj* inflacionista, inflacionario,-a.
inflect [ɪn'flekt] **1** *t* LING (*verb*) conjugar; (*noun*) declinar. **2** (*voice*) modular. **– 3** *i* LING (*verb*) conjugarse; (*noun*) declinarse. **4** (*voice*) modularse.

inflected [ɪn'flektɪd] *adj* LING flexional.
inflection [ɪn'flekʃən] **1** *n* LING inflexión *f*, flexión *f*. **2** *(of voice)* inflexión *f*.
inflexibility [ɪnfleksə'bɪlɪtɪ] *n* inflexibilidad *f*.
inflexible [ɪn'fleksɪbəl] *adj* inflexible, rígido,-a.
inflict [ɪn'flɪkt]. **1 to inflict on**, *t (grief, suffering, pain)* causar a; *(blow)* dar a, asestar a, propinar a; *(defeat, punishment)* infligir a, imponer a; *(grief, suffering, pain)* causar a. **2** *fig (view etc)* imponer a.
● **to inflict os. on sb.**, imponer su presencia a algn.
infliction [ɪn'flɪkʃən] **1** *n (act)* imposición *f*. **2** *(thing inflicted)* castigo.
in-flight [ɪn'flaɪt] *adj* durante el vuelo.
inflorescence [ɪnflə'resəns] *n* BOT florescencia.
inflow ['ɪnfləʊ] *n* afluencia.
influence ['ɪnfluəns] **1** *n (gen)* influencia: *he used his influence to get his son a job,* se valió de su influencia para conseguir un trabajo para su hijo; *television has had a great influence on our lives,* la televisión ha tenido mucha influencia en nuestras vidas; *you're a bad influence on me,* ejerces una mala influencia sobre mí; *it's easy to see his musical influences,* sus influencias musicales son evidentes. **– 2** *t (decision etc)* influir en/sobre; *(person)* influenciar: *I don't want to influence your decision,* no quiero influir en tu decisión; *she's been influenced by her parents,* sus padres la han influenciado.
● **to be easily influenced**, ser influenciable. ‖ **to be under the influence (of alcohol)**, estar bajo la influencia del alcohol, estar bajo los efectos del alcohol.
influential [ɪnflu'enʃəl] *adj* influyente.
● **to be influential**, tener influencias, ser influyente.
influenza [ɪnflu'enzə] *n* gripe *f*.
influx ['ɪnflʌks] *n* afluencia, oleada.
info ['ɪnfəʊ] *n fam* información *f*.
inform [ɪn'fɔːm] **1** *t* informar, notificar, avisar: *please inform your teacher if you're going to be away,* por favor informa a tu profesor si vas a faltar; *kindly keep me informed,* por favor manténganme al corriente; *why was I not informed?,* ¿por qué no me avisaron? **– 2 to inform against/on**, *i* denunciar a, delatar a: *he informed on his mates,* denunció a sus colegas.
● **to inform os.**, informarse.
informal [ɪn'fɔːməl] **1** *adj (speech)* informal, familiar; *(discussion)* informal. **2** *(manner, tone, atmosphere, person)* informal, relajado,-a, familiar; *(gathering, meeting, occasion, visit)* informal, sin etiqueta, sin ceremonia; *(dress)* sin etiqueta. **3** *(unofficial)* informal.
informality [ɪnfɔː'mælɪtɪ] *n (of person)* sencillez *f*; *(of occasion)* falta de ceremonia; *(treatment)* familiaridad *f*.
informally [ɪn'fɔːməlɪ] **1** *adv (talk, discuss)* de manera informal, sin ceremonias; *(dress)* de manera informal. **2** *(unofficially)* informalmente.
informant [ɪn'fɔːmənt] *n* informante *mf*.
information [ɪnfə'meɪʃən] *n (gen)* información *f*; *(facts)* datos *mpl*: *for your information,* para su información; *according to my information,* según mis datos; *I'd like some information about summer courses,* quisiera informarme sobre cursos de verano; *for further information ...,* para más información ...; *a useful piece/bit of information,* una información útil, un dato útil.
■ **classified information**, información *f* secreta. ‖ **information bureau**, centro de información. ‖ **information desk**, información *f*. ‖ **information science / information technology**, informática. ‖ **information superhighway**, superautopista de la información.
informative [ɪn'fɔːmətɪv] *adj* informativo,-a.

informed [ɪn'fɔːmd] *adj (gen)* informado,-a; *(well-informed)* enterado,-a, al corriente, al tanto.
● **an informed guess**, una suposición bien fundada.
informer [ɪn'fɔːmə'] **1** *n (gen)* delator,-ra. **2** *(to police)* informador,-ra, chivato,-a, soplón,-ona.
infraction [ɪn'frækʃən] *n fml* infracción *f*.
infra dig [ɪnfrə'dɪg] *adj* degradante.
infrared [ɪnfrə'red] *adj* infrarrojo,-a.
infrastructure ['ɪnfrəstrʌktʃə'] *n* infraestructura.
infrequency [ɪn'friːkwənsɪ] *n* infrecuencia.
infrequent [ɪn'friːkwənt] *adj* infrecuente, poco frecuente, raro,-a.
infrequently [ɪn'friːkwəntlɪ] *adv* rara vez, con poca frecuencia.
infringe [ɪn'frɪndʒ] **1** *t (law, rule, etc)* infringir, transgredir, violar; *(copyright, agreement, etc)* no respetar; *(liberty, rights)* violar, usurpar. **– 2 to infringe on/upon**, *i (rights)* usurpar, abusar; *(privacy, territory)* invadir.
infringement [ɪn'frɪndʒmənt] *n (of law, rule, etc)* infracción *f*, transgresión *f*, violación *f*; *(of copyright, agreement)* violación *f*; *(of rights, liberty)* violación *f*, usurpación *f*, abuso; *(of privacy)* invasión *f*.
infuriate [ɪn'fjʊərɪeɪt] *t* enfurecer, poner furioso,-a, sacar de quicio: *you really infuriate me,* me sacas de quicio.
● **to be infuriated**, estar furioso,-a.
infuriating [ɪn'fjʊərɪeɪtɪŋ] *adj* exasperante: *you can be infuriating at times,* a veces eres exasperante.
infuriatingly [ɪn'fjʊərɪeɪtɪŋlɪ] *adv* con exasperación.
infuse [ɪn'fjuːz] **1** *t (life, energy, etc)* infundir *(into*, a*)*. **2** *(tea, herbs)* hacer una infusión. **– 3** *i (tea, herbs)* reposar.
infusion [ɪn'fjuːʒən] **1** *n (of tea, herbs)* infusión *f*, tisana. **2** *(of capital, resources, etc)* inversión *f*; *(of life, energy, etc)* inyección *f*.
ingenious [ɪn'dʒiːnɪəs] *adj (person, thing)* ingenioso,-a; *(idea)* genial.
ingenuity [ɪndʒɪ'njuːɪtɪ] *n* ingenio, ingeniosidad *f*, inventiva.
ingenuous [ɪn'dʒenjuəs] *adj fml* ingenuo,-a.
ingest [ɪn'dʒest] *t fml* ingerir.
inglorious [ɪn'glɔːrɪəs] *adj* vergonzoso,-a, ignominioso,-a.
ingot ['ɪŋgət] *n* lingote *m*.
ingrained [ɪn'greɪnd] **1** *adj (dirt, stains, etc)* incrustado,-a. **2** *(habit, tendency, etc)* arraigado,-a.
ingratiate [ɪn'greɪʃɪeɪt] **to ingratiate os. with sb.**, *t fml pej* congraciarse con algn.
ingratitude [ɪn'grætɪtjuːd] *n* ingratitud *f*.
ingredient [ɪn'griːdɪənt] **1** *n* CULIN ingrediente *m*. **2** *fig* componente *m*, elemento.
ingrowing ['ɪngrəʊɪŋ] *adj* que crece hacia dentro.
■ **ingrowing toenail**, uña encarnada, uñero.
inhabit [ɪn'hæbɪt] *t* habitar, vivir en, ocupar, poblar.
inhabitable [ɪn'hæbɪtəbəl] *adj* habitable.
inhabitant [ɪn'hæbɪtənt] *n* habitante *mf*.
inhale [ɪn'heɪl] **1** *t (air)* aspirar, respirar; *(gas, vapour)* inhalar; *(cigarette smoke)* tragar. **– 2** *i (cigarette smoke)* tragar(se) el humo; *(air)* aspirar, respirar.
inherent [ɪn'hɪərənt] *adj* inherente **(in**, a), intrínseco,-a **(in**, as), propio,-a **(in**, de): *the dangers inherent in sport,* los peligros propios del deporte.
inherently [ɪn'hɪərəntlɪ] *adv* intrínsecamente.
inherit [ɪn'herɪt] *t* heredar **(from**, de): *he inherited a large sum of money,* heredó una gran cantidad de dinero.
inheritance [ɪn'herɪtəns] *n (money, property, etc)* herencia **(from**, de); *(succession)* sucesión *f*.

● **to come into an inheritance,** heredar.
inheritor [ɪn'herɪtəʳ] *n* heredero,-a.
inhibit [ɪn'hɪbɪt] **1** *t* (*person*) inhibir, cohibir. **2** (*hold back - attempt*) inhibir: *this drug will inhibit the spread of the disease,* este fármaco inhibirá la propagación de la enfermedad. **3** (*prevent*) impedir, restringir.
inhibited [ɪn'hɪbɪtɪd] *adj* inhibido,-a, cohibido,-a.
● **to be/feel inhibited,** sentirse cohibido,-a.
inhibition [ɪnhɪ'bɪʃən] *n* inhibición *f*, cohibición *f*.
inhospitable [ɪn'hɒspɪtəbəl] **1** *adj* (*people*) inhospitalario,-a. **2** (*place*) inhóspito,-a.
inhuman [ɪn'hjuːmən] *adj* inhumano,-a.
inhumane [ɪnhju'meɪn] *adj* inhumano,-a.
inhumanity [ɪnhju'mænətɪ] *n* inhumanidad *f*.
▲ *pl* inhumanities.
inimical [ɪ'nɪmɪkəl] **1** *adj fml* (*hostile*) hostil (**to,** a). **2** (*harmful, unfavourable*) desfavorable (**to,** a), perjudicial (**to,** para), contrario,-a (**to,** a).
inimitable [ɪ'nɪmɪtəbəl] *adj* inimitable.
iniquitous [ɪ'nɪkwɪtəs] *adj fml* (*wicked*) inicuo,-a; (*unjust*) injusto,-a.
iniquity [ɪ'nɪkwətɪ] *n* (*wickedness*) iniquidad *f*; (*unjustness*) injusticia.
▲ *pl* iniquities.
initial [ɪ'nɪʃəl] **1** *adj* inicial, primero,-a: *my initial reaction,* mi primera reacción; *after the initial shock,* después del susto inicial; *at the initial stage,* al principio. **– 2** *n* inicial *f*, letra inicial. **– 3** *t* firmar con las iniciales. **– 4** **initials,** *npl* (*of name*) iniciales *fpl*; (*of abbreviation*) siglas *fpl*.
initially [ɪ'nɪʃəlɪ] *adv* al principio, en primer lugar.
initiate ['ɪnɪʃɪeɪt] **1** *t* (*gen*) iniciar; (*reform, plan, etc*) promover: *our school has initiated a scheme to save energy,* nuestra escuela ha iniciado un proyecto para ahorrar energía. **2** JUR entablar. **3** (*admit, introduce*) admitir (**into,** en); (*give instruction or knowledge*) iniciar (**into,** en). **– 4** *n* iniciado,-a.
▲ En **4** (*sustantivo*) [ɪ'nɪʃɪət].
initiated [ɪ'nɪʃɪetɪd] **the initiated,** *npl* los iniciados *mpl*.
initiation [ɪnɪʃɪ'eɪʃən] **1** *n* (*start*) iniciación *f* (**of,** de), principio (**of,** de). **2** (*admission*) admisión *f* (**into,** en), iniciación *f* (**into,** en).
■ **initiation ceremony,** ceremonia de iniciación.
initiative [ɪ'nɪʃɪətɪv] *n* iniciativa: *we welcome the initiative,* aplaudimos la iniciativa; *it's clear who has the initiative,* está claro quien tiene la iniciativa; *he showed great initiative,* demostró una gran iniciativa.
● **on one's own initiative,** por iniciativa propia. ‖ **to take the initiative,** tomar la iniciativa.
inject [ɪn'dʒekt] **1** *t* (*drug etc*) inyectar; (*person*) poner una inyección a, pinchar. **2** *fig* (*new ideas, enthusiasm, etc*) infundir, inyectar; (*money, resources, etc*) invertir.
injection [ɪn'dʒekʃən] **1** *n* MED inyección *f*: *I had an injection,* me pusieron una inyección. **2** *fig* (*of new ideas, interest, etc*) inyección *f*; (*of money, resources, etc*) inversión *f*.
● **to give sb. an injection,** ponerle una inyección a algn.
injudicious [ɪndʒuː'dɪʃəs] *adj fml* (*gen*) poco discreto,-a, imprudente; (*time, moment*) inoportuno,-a.
injunction [ɪn'dʒʌŋkʃən] *n* JUR mandamiento judicial, requerimiento judicial.
● **to seek/obtain out an injunction against sb.,** solicitar/obtener un mandamiento judicial contra algn.
injure ['ɪndʒəʳ] **1** *t* herir, lesionar, lastimar. **2** *fig* (*feelings*) herir; (*health, reputation, etc*) perjudicar.

● **to injure os.,** hacerse daño, lesionarse.
injured ['ɪndʒəd] **1** *adj* (*hurt*) herido,-a, lesionado,-a, lastimado,-a: *two of the best players are injured,* dos de los mejores jugadores están lesionados. **2** *fig* (*offended - feeling*) herido,-a; (*- look, tone, etc*) ofendido,-a. **3** (*wronged*) ofendido,-a. **– 4 the injured,** *npl* los heridos.
● **to be/get injured,** lesionarse.
injurious [ɪn'dʒʊərɪəs] **1** *adj fml* (*harmful*) perjudicial. **2** *fml* (*insulting*) injurioso,-a, ofensivo,-a.
injury ['ɪndʒərɪ] **1** *n* herida, lesión *f*: *a head injury,* una lesión en la cabeza; *she suffered severe injuries,* sufrió heridas graves; *he won't be playing due to injury,* no jugará a causa de una lesión. **2** *fig* (*to feelings etc*) daño; (*to reputation*) agravio.
● **to do os. an injury,** hacerse daño, lastimarse.
■ **injury time,** SP tiempo de descuento.
▲ *pl* injuries.
injustice [ɪn'dʒʌstɪs] *n* injusticia.
● **to do sb. an injustice,** (*judge unfairly*) ser injusto,-a con algn., juzgar mal a algn.; (*fail to show true merits*) hacerle una injusticia a algn.
ink [ɪŋk] **1** *n* tinta. **– 2** *t* entintar.
◆ **to ink in** *t sep* repasar con tinta.
● **to write in ink,** escribir con tinta.
■ Indian ink, tinta china.
inkblot ['ɪŋkblɒt] *n* borrón *m*.
inkling ['ɪŋklɪŋ] *n* (*vague idea*) noción *f*, idea; (*suspicion*) sospecha; (*hint*) señal *m*, indicio, atisbo: *I had no inkling whatsoever of what was going on,* no tenía ni la menor idea de lo que pasaba.
● **to have an inkling of sth.,** presentir algo.
inkpad ['ɪŋkpæd] *n* tampón *m* de entintar, almohadilla.
inkstand ['ɪŋkstænd] *n* escribanía.
inkwell ['ɪŋkwel] *n* tintero.
inky ['ɪŋkɪ] **1** *adj* (*dirty*) manchado,-a de tinta. **2** (*black*) negro,-a.
▲ *comp* inkier, *superl* inkiest.
inlaid [ɪn'leɪd] **1** *adj* (*embedded - with wood*) taraceado,-a; (*- gems, ivory*) incrustado,-a; (*- iron, gold*) damasquinado,-a. **2** (*decorated*) adornado,-a (con marquetería). **– 3** *pp* → **inlay**.
inland ['ɪnlənd] **1** *adj* (del) interior. **2** GB COMM interior. **– 3** *adv* (*travel*) tierra adentro, hacia el interior; (*live*) en el interior.
■ **Inland Revenue,** GB Hacienda.
▲ En **2** (*adverbio*) [ɪn'lænd].
in-laws ['ɪnlɔːz] *npl fam* familia *f sing* política.
inlay ['ɪnleɪ] **1** *n* (*in wood*) taracea; (*of gems*) incrustación *f*; (*in metal*) damasquinado *f*; (*of marquetry*) marquetería. **2** (*in tooth*) empaste *m*. **– 3** *t* (*wood*) taracear; (*gems, ivory*) incrustar; (*iron, gold*) damasquinar. **4** (*decorate*) adornar (con marquetería).
▲ En **3** y **4** (*verbo*) [ɪn'leɪ], *pt* & *pp* inlaid, *ger* inlaying.
inlet ['ɪnlet] **1** *n* (*from sea or lake*) cala, ensenada; (*between islands*) brazo de mar. **2** TECH entrada, admisión *f*.
inmate ['ɪnmeɪt] **1** *n* (*gen*) residente *mf*. **2** (*of prison*) preso,-a, interno,-a. **3** (*of hospital*) enfermo,-a. **4** (*of asylum, camp*) internado,-a.
inmost ['ɪnməʊst] *adj* → **innermost**.
inn [ɪn] *n* (*with lodgings*) posada, fonda, mesón *m*; (*in country*) venta; (*pub*) taberna.
■ **Inns of Court,** Colegio de Abogados.
innards ['ɪnədz] *npl fam* entrañas *fpl*, tripas *fpl*.
innate [ɪ'neɪt] *adj* innato,-a.
inner ['ɪnəʳ] **1** *adj* (*room, region etc*) interior; (*organization*) interno,-a: *an inner courtyard,* un patio interior. **2** (*feelings etc*) interior, íntimo,-a.

■ **inner circle,** círculo íntimo. ‖ **inner ear,** oído interno. ‖ **inner tube,** cámara de aire. ‖ **the inner man** *(o woman),* *(soul)* alma; *(appetite)* hambre *f,* estómago.

inner-city [ɪnə'sɪtɪ] *adj* del centro de la ciudad: *depressed inner-city areas,* zonas deprimidas del centro de las ciudades.

innermost ['ɪnəməʊst] **1** *adj (most inward)* más interior. **2** *fig (most private)* más íntimo,-a, más secreto,-a.

innings ['ɪnɪŋz] *npl* SP entrada, turno.
● **to have had a good innings,** *fig* haber disfrutado de una vida larga y feliz.

innkeeper ['ɪnkiːpə'] *n (of lodgings)* posadero,-a, mesonero,-a; *(in country)* ventero,-a; *(of pub)* tabernero,-a.

innocence ['ɪnəsəns] *n* inocencia: *he protested his innocence,* protestó de su inocencia; *I did it in all innocence,* lo hice con toda inocencia.

innocent ['ɪnəsənt] **1** *adj (gen)* inocente; *(harmless)* inocuo,-a, inofensivo,-a; *(naive)* ingenuo,-a: *she was so young and innocent,* era tan joven e inocente; *innocent until proved guilty,* inocente hasta que se pruebe lo contrario; *innocent passers-by were injured,* transeúntes inocentes resultaron heridos; *an innocent question,* una pregunta ingenua. – **2** *n* inocente *mf,* ingenuo,-a.

innocently ['ɪnəsəntlɪ] *adv* inocentemente.

innocuous [ɪ'nɒkjʊəs] *adj* inocuo,-a, inofensivo,-a.

innovate ['ɪnəveɪt] *i* innovar.

innovation [ɪnə'veɪʃən] *n* innovación *f.*

innovative ['ɪnəvətɪv] *adj* innovador,-ra.

innovator ['ɪnəveɪtə'] *n* innovador,-ra.

innovatory ['ɪnəveɪtərɪ] *adj* innovador,-ra.

innuendo [ɪnjʊ'endəʊ] *n* indirecta, insinuación *f.*
▲ *pl* **innuendoes.**

innumerable [ɪ'njuːmərəbəl] *adj* innumerable.

innumeracy [ɪ'njuːmərəsɪ] *n* incapacidad para realizar operaciones aritméticas.

innumerate [ɪ'njuːmərət] *adj* incapaz de realizar operaciones aritméticas.

inoculate [ɪ'nɒkjʊleɪt] *t* inocular, vacunar.

inoculation [ɪnɒkjʊ'leɪʃən] *n* inoculación *f.*

inoffensive [ɪnə'fensɪv] *adj* inofensivo,-a.

inoperable [ɪn'ɒpərəbəl] *adj* inoperable.

inoperative [ɪn'ɒpərətɪv] *adj* inoperante.

inopportune [ɪn'ɒpətjuːn] *adj* inoportuno,-a.

inopportunely [ɪn'ɒpətjuːnlɪ] *adv* inoportunamente, a deshora.

inordinate [ɪn'ɔːdɪnət] *adj fml (beyond normal limits)* desmesurado,-a; *(excessive)* excesivo,-a.

inordinately [ɪn'ɔːdɪnətlɪ] *adv* desmesuradamente, excesivamente.

inorganic [ɪnɔː'gænɪk] *adj* inorgánico,-a.
■ **inorganic chemistry,** química inorgánica.

inpatient ['ɪnpeɪʃənt] *n* (paciente) interno,-a.

input ['ɪnpʊt] **1** *n (of power)* entrada; *(of money, resources)* inversión *f; (of data)* input *m.* – **2** *t* COMPUT entrar, introducir.
▲ *pt & pp* **input** ['ɪnpʊt] o **imputted** ['ɪnpʊtɪd].

inquest ['ɪnkwest] **1** *n* investigación *f* judicial, encuesta judicial. **2** *fam* investigación *f.*

inquire [ɪn'kwaɪə'] **1** *t fml (ask)* preguntar: *he inquired my name,* me preguntó el nombre; *I inquired the way to the station,* pregunté el camino hasta la estación. – **2** *i (ask for information)* preguntar **(about,** por); *(find out)* averiguar **(about,** -), informarse **(about,** de): *I'll inquire,* preguntaré, me informaré; *she inquired about train times,* preguntó por el horario de los trenes; *there was a man*

inquiring after you, vino un hombre que preguntaba por ti.
◆ **to inquire into** *t insep* investigar.
● **to inquire sth. of sb.,** preguntar algo a algn. ‖ *"inquire within",* "razón aquí".

inquirer [ɪn'kwaɪərə'] *n persona que pregunta.*

inquiring [ɪn'kwaɪərɪŋ] *adj (mind)* curioso,-a; *(look etc)* inquisidor,-ra.

inquiry [ɪn'kwaɪərɪ] **1** *n fml (question)* pregunta: *in answer to your inquiry,* en respuesta a su pregunta; *we've had quite a few inquiries,* ha habido bastante gente interesada. **2** *(investigation)* investigación *f: there will be a public inquiry,* se hará una investigación pública.
● *"inquiries",* "información" *f.* ‖ *"all inquiries to ...",* "dirigirse a ...". ‖ **to call for an inquiry,** exigir una investigación. ‖ **to make inquiries about sth.,** investigar algo, pedir informes sobre algo. ‖ **to hold an inquiry into sth.,** investigar algo, examinar algo. ‖ **to set up an inquiry,** abrir una investigación.
■ **inquiry desk / inquiry office,** información *f.* ‖ **directory inquiries,** *(tel)* información *f.*
▲ *pl* **inquiries.**

inquisition [ɪnkwɪ'zɪʃən] **1** *n* investigación *f,* inquisición *f.* **2** **the Inquisition,** HIST la Inquisición *f.*

inquisitive [ɪn'kwɪzɪtɪv] *adj (curious)* curioso,-a, inquisidor,-ra; *(nosy)* preguntón,-ona.

inquisitively [ɪn'kwɪzətɪvlɪ] *adv* con curiosidad *f.*

inquisitiveness [ɪn'kwɪzətɪvnəs] *n* curiosidad *f.*

inroads ['ɪnrəʊdz] **1** *npl (raid)* incursión *f sing.* – **2** *n fig (encroachment)* intrusión *f.*
● **to make inroads into/on sth.,** *(have effect on)* hacer avances en algo; *(use up)* mermar algo; *(reduce)* reducir algo: *the company is making inroads into the computer market,* la empresa está haciendo avances en el mercado de la informática; *training makes great inroads into my free time,* entrenar me quita mucho tiempo libre; *the repairs on the car made deep inroads into my savings,* las reparaciones del coche se comieron buena parte de mis ahorros.

insalubrious [ɪnsə'luːbrɪəs] *adj fml* insalubre.

insane [ɪn'seɪn] **1** *adj (person)* loco,-a, demente; *(act)* insensato,-a. **2** *fam (idea etc)* loco,-a. – **3** **the insane,** *npl* los enfermos *mpl* mentales.
● **to go insane,** enloquecer, volverse loco,-a. ‖ **to drive sb. insane,** volver loco,-a a algn.

insanitary [ɪn'sænɪtərɪ] *adj* insalubre, antihigiénico,-a.

insanity [ɪn'sænɪtɪ] *n (of person)* locura, demencia; *(of act)* insensatez *f.*
● **to enter a plea of insanity,** declararse demente.

insatiable [ɪn'seɪʃəbəl] *adj* insaciable **(for,** de).

inscribe [ɪn'skraɪb] *t (tombstone, ring, etc)* inscribir, grabar; *(book)* dedicar.

inscription [ɪn'skrɪpʃən] *n (gen)* inscripción *f; (in book)* dedicatoria.

inscrutable [ɪn'skruːtəbəl] *adj* inescrutable, insondable, impenetrable.

insect ['ɪnsekt] *n* insecto.
■ **insect bite,** picadura.

insecticide [ɪn'sektɪsaɪd] *n* insecticida *m.*

insecure [ɪnsɪ'kjʊə'] *adj* inseguro,-a: *she feels very insecure,* se siente muy insegura.

insecurely [ɪnsɪ'kjʊəlɪ] *adv* de manera insegura: *the window was insecurely closed,* la ventana estaba mal cerrada.

insecurity [ɪnsɪ'kjʊərɪtɪ] *n* inseguridad *f: job insecurity,* inseguridad laboral.

inseminate [ɪn'semɪneɪt] *t* inseminar.
insemination [ɪnsemɪ'neɪʃən] *n* inseminación *f*.
insensibility [ɪnsensə'bɪlətɪ] 1 *n fml* (*unconsciousness*) inconsciencia, pérdida de conciencia. 2 *fml* (*lack of feeling*) insensibilidad *f* (**to**, hacia); (*indifference*) indiferencia (**to**, ante).
insensible [ɪn'sensəbəl] 1 *adj fml* (*unconscious*) inconsciente, sin conocimiento. 2 *fml* (*unaware*) inconsciente; (*not able to feel*) insensible.
insensitive [ɪn'sensətɪv] *adj* insensible.
insensitively [ɪn'sensətɪvlɪ] *adv* insensiblemente.
insensitivity [ɪnsensɪ'tɪvɪtɪ] *n* insensibilidad *f*.
inseparable [ɪn'sepərəbəl] *adj* inseparable (**from**, de): *they are inseparable friends,* son amigos inseparables.
inseparably [ɪn'sepərəblɪ] *adv* inseparablemente, estrechamente: *we're inseparably close,* estamos estrechamente unidos.
insert [ɪn'sɜːt]. 1 to insert in/into, *t* (*gen*) introducir en, meter en; (*comment, clause, paragraph, etc*) incluir en, insertar en; (*advertisement*) poner en. – 2 *n* (*in book, newspaper*) encarte *m*; (*in clothing*) añadido.
insertion [ɪn'sɜːʃən] 1 *n* (*gen*) introducción *f*; (*of comment, clause, paragraph, etc*) inclusión *f*, inserción *f*. 2 (*advertisement*) anuncio.
in-service training [ˈɪnsɜːvɪs'treɪnɪŋ] *n* formación *f* profesional en el trabajo.
inset [ˈɪnset] 1 *n* (*diagram etc*) recuadro. – 2 *t* insertar (**into**, en).
▲ (*verbo*) [ɪn'set], *pt* & *pp* **inset**, *ger* **insetting**.
inshore [ɪnˈʃɔːʳ] 1 *adj* (*fishing, navigation*) costero,-a; (*wind*) de mar. – 2 *adv* (*fish, sail*) cerca de la costa; (*blow, flow*) hacia la costa.
inside [ɪn'saɪd] 1 *n* interior *m*, parte *f* interior: *she locked the door from the inside,* cerró la puerta con llave por dentro; *the inside of this pan is dirty,* el interior de esta olla está sucio. 2 (*driving on left*) la izquierda; (*driving on right*) la derecha; (*on running track*) interior: *he was fined for overtaking on the inside,* lo multaron por adelantar por la izquierda; *the American is coming up on the inside,* el americano avanza por el interior. – 3 *adj* interior, interno,-a: *the article is one of the inside pages,* el artículo está en una de las páginas interiores. – 4 *adv* (*position*) dentro; (*movement*) adentro: *come inside,* entra, pasa adentro; *let's look inside,* miremos dentro. 5 *sl* (*in prison*) en la cárcel, en chirona. – 6 *prep* dentro de: *put it inside the box,* métclo dentro de la caja; *they're inside the house,* están dentro de la casa; *get some food inside you,* cómete algo, mete algo de comida en el estómago; *I always travel inside the speed limit,* siempre circulo dentro del límite de velocidad. 7 (*time*) en menos de, dentro de: *it'll be finished inside a week,* estará acabado dentro de una semana. – 8 **insides**, *npl fam* entrañas *fpl*, tripas *fpl*.
● **inside out,** al revés: *you've got your socks on inside out,* llevas los calcetines al revés; *turn the jeans inside out,* vuelve los vaqueros del revés; *she turned the cupboard inside out,* revolvió todo el armario. ‖ **to know sth. inside out,** conocer algo al dedillo. ‖ **on the inside,** dentro: *we need someone on the inside,* necesitamos a alguien de dentro.
■ **inside information,** información *f* privilegiada: *the robbery was an inside job,* el robo fue organizado por alguien de dentro. ‖ **inside lane,** AUTO carril *m* interior; SP calle *f* interior. ‖ **inside left,** SP interior *mf* izquierda. ‖ **inside leg measurement,** entrepierna. ‖ **inside pocket,** bolsillo interior. ‖ **inside right,** SP interior *mf* derecha. ‖ **inside toilet,** lavabo interior.

insider [ɪn'saɪdəʳ] *n* persona enterada.
■ **insider dealing / insider trading,** *uso indebido de información privilegiada y confidencial para operaciones bursátiles.*
insidious [ɪn'sɪdɪəs] *adj* insidioso,-a.
insidiously [ɪn'sɪdɪəslɪ] *adv* insidiosamente.
insight [ˈɪnsaɪt] 1 *n* (*deep understanding, perception*) perspicacia, penetración *f*. 2 (*sudden understanding*) idea.
● **to gain/get an insight into sth.,** llegar a comprender algo, hacerse una idea de algo: *I got an insight into what it would be like to win the lottery,* me hice una idea de lo que debía ser ganar la lotería.
insignia [ɪn'sɪgnɪə] *n* insignia, insignias *fpl*.
▲ *pl* **insignia** [ɪn'sɪgnɪə].
insignificance [ɪnsɪg'nɪfɪkəns] *n* insignificancia.
● **to pale into insignificance,** perder toda su importancia.
insignificant [ɪnsɪg'nɪfɪkənt] *adj* insignificante.
insincere [ɪnsɪn'sɪəʳ] *adj* poco sincero,-a, insincero,-a, falso,-a.
insincerely [ɪnsɪn'sɪəlɪ] *adv* con poca sinceridad, insinceramente.
insincerity [ɪnsɪn'serətɪ] *n* falta de sinceridad, insinceridad *f*, falsedad *f*.
insinuate [ɪn'sɪnjʊeɪt] 1 *t* (*hint, suggest*) insinuar, dar a entender: *she insinuated that my husband had been cheating on me,* insinuó que mi marido me había engañado. 2 (*worm, install*) insinuarse (**into**, en).
● **to insinuate os. into sb.'s favour,** insinuarse en favor de algn.
insinuation [ɪnsɪnjʊ'eɪʃən] *n* insinuación *f*, indirecta.
insipid [ɪn'sɪpɪd] *adj* (*food, drink*) insípido,-a, soso,-a; (*person, activity*) insulso,-a, soso,-a.
insipidity [ɪnsɪ'pɪdətɪ] *n* insipidez *f*, sosería, insulsez *f*.
insist [ɪn'sɪst] 1 *t* (*declare firmly*) insistir en: *he insisted that he was right,* insistió en que tenía razón. 2 (*demand forcefully*) insistir en, exigir: *I insist that you leave immediately,* insisto en que te vayas inmediatamente; *he insisted that I should apply for the job,* insistió en que solicitara el puesto. – 3 *i* (*declare firmly*) insistir (**on**, en): *she insisted on his innocence,* insistió en su inocencia. 4 (*demand forcefully*) insistir (**on**, en), exigir; (*persist*) empeñarse (**on**, en), obstinarse (**on**, en): *if you insist,* si insistes; *he insisted on paying,* se empeñó en pagar; *I insisted on a contract,* exigí un contrato; *he will insist on wearing the most awful ties,* se obstina en llevar las corbatas más horribles.
insistence [ɪn'sɪstəns] *n* insistencia (**on**, en), empeño (**on**, en).
● **at sb.'s insistence,** ante la insistencia de algn.
insistent [ɪn'sɪstənt] 1 *adj* (*person*) insistente: *she was insistent that we (should) talk,* insistió en que habláramos; *he was most insistent about that,* se empeñó mucho en ello. 2 (*urgent, compelling*) apremiante, urgente; (*repeated*) persistente: *insistent demands,* peticiones urgentes; *insistent ringing,* sonido persistente.
insistently [ɪn'sɪstəntlɪ] *adv* con insistencia.
insofar as [ɪnsəʊ'fɑːrəz] *adv* en la medida en que, en tanto que.
insolence [ˈɪnsələns] *n* insolencia, descaro, frescura.
insolent [ˈɪnsələnt] *adj* insolente, descarado,-a, fresco,-a.
insoluble [ɪn'sɒljəbəl] 1 *adj* (*of substances*) insoluble, indisoluble. 2 *fig* sin solución, insoluble.
insolvency [ɪn'sɒlvənsɪ] *n* insolvencia.
insolvent [ɪn'sɒlvənt] *adj* insolvente.
insomnia [ɪn'sɒmnɪə] *n* insomnio.

insomniac [ɪnˈsɒmnɪæk] *n* insomne *mf*.
insomuch [ɪnsəʊˈmʌtʃ]. **1 insomuch as,** *adv phr* puesto que, visto que, ya que. **2 insomuch that,** hasta tal punto que.
insouciance [ɪnˈsuːsɪəns] *n fml* despreocupación *f*, indiferencia.
Insp [ɪnˈspektəʳ] *abbr* (*Inspector*) Inspector,-ra; (*abbreviation*) Inspec.
inspect [ɪnˈspekt] **1** *t* (*gen*) inspeccionar, examinar, revisar: *he inspected the gun for fingerprints,* examinó la pistola en busca de huellas; *she inspected the work for errors,* revisó el trabajo en busca de errores. **2** (*factory etc*) inspeccionar. **3** (*luggage*) registrar. **4** (*troops*) pasar revista a.
inspection [ɪnˈspekʃən] **1** *n* (*gen*) inspección *f*, examen, revisión *f*: *the policeman made a detailed inspection of the room,* el policía examinó la habitación minuciosamente; *on inspection, the gun turned out to be a toy,* al inspeccionar la pistola, resultó que era de juguete; *closer inspection revealed signs of malnutrition,* un examen más minucioso reveló síntomas de malnutrición. **2** (*of factory, school, etc*) inspección *f*: *the Fire Brigade carry out frequent inspections,* los bomberos hacen inspecciones con frecuencia; *a tour of inspection,* una visita de inspección. **3** (*of luggage*) registro. **4** (*of troops*) revista.
inspector [ɪnˈspektəʳ] *n* (*gen*) inspector,-ra; (*on train*) revisor,-ra; (*in police*) inspector,-ra de policía.
■ **customs inspector,** aduanero,-a. ‖ **inspector of taxes / tax inspector,** inspector,-ra de hacienda.
inspectorate [ɪnˈspektərət] *n* cuerpo de inspectores.
inspiration [ɪnspɪˈreɪʃən] **1** *n* (*gen*) inspiración *f*: *your work shows true inspiration,* tu trabajo demuestra verdadera inspiración; *she should be an inspiration to us all,* ella debería inspirarnos a todos. **2** *fam* (*good idea*) genialidad *f*.
● **to draw/find/get inspiration from sb./sth.,** inspirarse en algn./algo.
inspire [ɪnˈspaɪəʳ] **1** *t* (*gen*) inspirar: *his example inspired us all,* su ejemplo nos inspiró a todos; *the beauty of the English countryside inspired Constable,* la belleza del paisaje inglés inspiró a Constable. **2** (*encourage*) estimular, animar, mover: *she was inspired to work harder,* la animó a esforzarse más. **3** (*fill with - fear*) infundir; (- *confidence, respect*) inspirar.
● **to be inspired by sb./sth.,** inspirarse en algn./algo: *Dalí was inspired by Gala,* Dalí se inspiraba en Gala.
inspired [ɪnˈspaɪəd] **1** *adj* (*filled with creative power*) inspirado,-a: *an inspired writer,* un escritor inspirado. **2** (*based on intuition*) genial: *an inspired guess,* una inspiración.
inspiring [ɪnˈspaɪərɪŋ] *adj* inspirador,-ra.
Inst [ˈɪnstɪtjuːt] *abbr* (*Institute*) Instituto; (*abbreviation*) Inst.
instability [ɪnstəˈbɪlɪti] *n* inestabilidad *f*.
install [ɪnˈstɔːl] **1** *t* (*equipment etc*) instalar: *they've installed a new air conditioning system,* han instalado un nuevo sistema de aire acondicionado; *we're going to have central heating installed,* vamos a instalar calefacción central. **2** (*person*) instalar, colocar.
● **to install os.,** instalarse: *she installed herself in the armchair,* se instaló en el sillón. ‖ **to be installed,** estar instalado,-a.
installation [ɪnstəˈleɪʃən] **1** *n* (*of equipment etc*) instalación *f*. **2** MIL instalación *f* militar. **3** *adj* de instalación: *installation costs,* gastos de instalación.
installment [ɪnˈstɔːlmənt] *n* → **instalment**.

instalment [ɪnˈstɔːlmənt] **1** *n* (*of payment*) plazo. **2** (*of book, story, etc*) entrega; (*of collection*) fascículo.
● **to pay for sth. by/in instalments,** pagar algo a plazos.
■ **instalment plan,** US compraventa a plazos. ‖ **annual instalment,** anualidad *f*. ‖ **monthly instalment,** mensualidad *f*.
instance [ˈɪnstəns] **1** *n* ejemplo, caso. – **2** *t* poner por caso, citar como ejemplo.
● **at the instance of sb.,** a instancia de algn., a petición de algn. ‖ **for instance,** por ejemplo. ‖ **in the first instance,** en primer lugar. ‖ **in this instance,** en este caso.
instant [ˈɪnstənt] **1** *n* instante *m*, momento: *come back this instant!,* ¡vuelve ahora mismo!; *I recognized him the instant I saw him,* lo reconocí en cuanto lo vi; *I'll be back in an instant,* vuelvo en un instante; *he hesitated for an instant,* vaciló por un segundo; *not an instant too soon,* justo a tiempo. – **2** *adj* (*at once*) inmediato,-a: *an instant success,* un éxito inmediato; *instant relief,* alivio inmediato; *I took an instant dislike to her,* me cayó mal enseguida. **3** (*coffee etc*) instantáneo,-a. **4** *fml* (*urgent*) urgente: *we're in instant need of help,* necesitamos urgentemente ayuda. **5** COMM (*of the present month*) del corriente.
instantaneous [ɪnstənˈteɪnɪəs] *adj* instantáneo,-a.
instantaneously [ɪnstənˈteɪnɪslɪ] *adv* instantáneamente.
instantly [ˈɪnstəntlɪ] **1** *adv* al instante, inmediatamente: *he died instantly,* se murió al instante, su muerte fue instantánea; *she instantly regretted having said that,* inmediatamente se arrepintió de haberlo dicho. – **2** *conj* en cuanto: *tell me instantly they arrive,* avísame en cuanto lleguen.
instead [ɪnˈsted] **1** *adv* en cambio, en su lugar: *I haven't got any tea. Would you like coffee instead?,* no tengo té. ¿Quieres café en lugar de té?; *Mrs Jones couldn't do the class so I did it instead,* la Señora Jones no pudo dar la clase así que yo la di en su lugar; *the theatre was full so we went to the cinema instead,* el teatro estaba lleno así que fuimos al cine; *Suzie doesn't like sport. Instead she prefers to sunbathe,* a Suzie no le gusta el deporte. Prefiere tomar el sol. – **2 instead of,** *prep* en vez de, en lugar de: *let's go out instead of staying in every night,* salgamos en vez de quedarnos en casa cada noche; *we should eat more fish instead of meat,* deberíamos comer más pescado en lugar de carne.
instep [ˈɪnstep] *n* empeine *m*.
instigate [ˈɪnstɪgeɪt] *t* instigar.
instigation [ɪnstɪˈgeɪʃən] *n* instigación *f*: *we did so at his instigation,* lo hicimos a instigación suya.
instigator [ˈɪnstɪgeɪtəʳ] *n* instigador,-ra.
instil [ɪnˈstɪl] *t* (*idea*) inculcar (**in,** a/en); (*respect etc*) infundir (**in,** a): *she instilled a sense of pride in her children,* inculcó en sus hijos un sentimiento de orgullo.
▲ *pt & pp instilled, ger instilling.*
instill [ɪnˈstɪl] *t* → **instil**.
instinct [ˈɪnstɪŋkt] *n* instinto: *by instinct,* por instinto; *trust your instincts,* fíate de tus instintos.
● **to act on instinct,** reaccionar instintivamente. ‖ **to have an instinct for sth.,** tener un don para algo.
■ **maternal instinct,** instinto maternal.
instinctive [ɪnˈstɪŋktɪv] *adj* instintivo,-a, intuitivo,-a.
instinctively [ɪnˈstɪŋktɪvlɪ] *adv* instintivamente, por instinto.
institute [ˈɪnstɪtjuːt] **1** *n* (*gen*) instituto, centro. **2** (*professional body*) colegio, asociación *f*; (*educational*) escuela. –

3 t fml (organize, establish) instituir, establecer, fundar; (initiate - enquiry) iniciar, empezar; (- proceedings) iniciar, entablar: *we've instituted a new system,* hemos instituido un nuevo sistema; *the Pope instituted the Holy Year of Compostela,* el papa instituyó el Año Santo Compostelano; *they're going to institute legal proceedings against him,* van a entablar un proceso contra él.

institution [ɪnstɪˈtjuːʃən] **1** n (act - gen) institución f, establecimiento, introducción f; (- of inquiry, proceedings) iniciación f. **2** (organization) institución f, organismo, asociación f. **3** (home) asilo; (asylum) hospital m psiquiátrico, manicomio; (orphanage) orfanato. **4** (custom, practice) institución f, tradición f, costumbre f: *the institution of marriage,* la institución del matrimonio. **5** fam institución f.

institutional [ɪnstɪˈtjuːʃənəl] adj institucional.

institutionalize [ɪnstɪˈtjuːsənəlaɪz] t institucionalizar.

instruct [ɪnˈstrʌkt] **1** t (teach) instruir, enseñar; (inform) informar: *he instructs them in physics,* les enseña física. **2** MIL instruir. **3** (order) ordenar, mandar, dar instrucciones: *we've been instructed to wait here,* nos han ordenado esperar aquí; *I've instructed them to take you home,* les he mandado llevarte a casa. **4** JUR (solicitor, barrister) dar instrucciones a; (jury) instruir.

instruction [ɪnˈstrʌkʃən] **1** n (teaching) instrucción f, enseñanza. **2** (order) orden f, mandato, instrucción f: *I'm just going on the boss's instructions,* sólo cumplo órdenes del jefe. – **3 instructions,** npl (information) instrucciones fpl: *have you read the instructions?,* ¿has leído las instrucciones?
  ● "instructions for use", "modo de empleo", "instrucciones de uso". ‖ "operating instructions", "instrucciones de funcionamiento".

instructive [ɪnˈstrʌktɪv] adj instructivo,-a, formativo,-a.

instructor [ɪnˈstrʌktəʳ] n (gen) instructor,-ra; (of driving) profesor,-ra; (of sport) monitor,-ra.

instrument [ˈɪnstrəmənt] n instrumento: *musical instrument,* instrumento musical; *surgical instrument,* instrumento quirúrgico; *(set of) instruments,* instrumental m.
  ■ instrument panel, tablero de mandos.

instrumental [ɪnstrəˈmentəl] **1** adj MUS instrumental. **2** (helpful, significant) decisivo,-a.
  ● to be instrumental in sth., contribuir decisivamente a algo, jugar un papel decisivo en algo: *he was instrumental in bringing about the minister's downfall,* jugó un papel decisivo en la caída del ministro.

instrumentalist [ɪnstruˈmentəlɪst] n instrumentista mf.

instrumentation [ɪnstrumenˈteɪʃən] **1** n MUS instrumentación f. **2** (in car etc) instrumentos mpl.

insubordinate [ɪnsəˈbɔːdɪnət] adj insubordinado,-a, indisciplinado,-a, desobediente, rebelde.

insubordination [ɪnsəbɔːdɪˈneɪʃən] n insubordinación f, indisciplina, desobediencia, rebeldía.

insubstantial [ɪnsəbˈstænʃəl] **1** adj (gen) insustancial; (meal) poco nutritivo,-a; (structure) poco sólido,-a, poco seguro,-a, frágil. **2** fig (tenuous) poco convincente, flojo,-a. **3** (imaginary, unreal) imaginario,-a.

insufferable [ɪnˈsʌfərəbəl] adj insoportable, inaguantable, insufrible.

insufferably [ɪnˈsʌfərəblɪ] adv de manera insoportable: *he was insufferably rude,* fue extremadamente grosero.

insufficiency [ɪnsəˈfɪʃənsɪ] n insuficiencia, carencia, falta.
  ▲ pl insufficiencies.

insufficient [ɪnsəˈfɪʃənt] adj insuficiente: *we have insufficient funds,* no tenemos suficientes fondos; *insufficient evidence,* falta de pruebas.

insufficiently [ɪnsəˈfɪʃəntlɪ] adv insuficientemente.

insular [ˈɪnsjʊləʳ] **1** adj (of island) insular. **2** pej (narrowminded) estrecho,-a de miras.

insularity [ɪnsjʊˈlærətɪ] n pej estrechez f de miras.

insulate [ˈɪnsjəleɪt] **1** t TECH aislar (against/from, de). **2** fig (protect) proteger (against, contra), (from, de).

insulated [ˈɪnsjəleɪtɪd] adj TECH aislado,-a.

insulating [ˈɪnsjəleɪtɪŋ] adj TECH aislante.
  ■ insulating tape, cinta aislante.

insulation [ɪnsjəˈleɪʃən] n TECH aislamiento.

insulator [ˈɪnsjəleɪtəʳ] n TECH aislante m, aislador m.

insulin [ˈɪnsjəlɪn] n insulina.

insult [ˈɪnsʌlt] **1** n (words) insulto. **2** (action) afrenta, ofensa, ultraje m: *don't take it as an insult,* no te ofendas. – **3** t insultar, ofender, injuriar: *he just insulted me,* me acaba de insultar; *she felt deeply insulted,* se sintió muy ofendida.
  ● an insult to sb.'s intelligence, una ofensa a la inteligencia de algn. ‖ to add insult to injury, para colmo de males, por si fuera poco.
  ▲ En 3 (verbo) [ɪnˈsʌlt].

insulting [ɪnˈsʌltɪŋ] adj insultante, ofensivo,-a, injurioso,-a: *insulting language,* lenguaje ofensivo.

insuperable [ɪnˈsuːpərəbəl] adj fml (problems etc) insuperable; (barrier etc) infranqueable.

insupportable [ɪnsəˈpɔːtəbəl] adj fml insoportable.

insurance [ɪnˈʃʊərəns] **1** n seguro: *insurance against theft/fire,* seguro contra robo/incendios; *he works in insurance,* trabaja en una compañía de seguros. **2** fig (safeguard) salvaguarda, protección f, garantía.
  ● to take out insurance, hacerse un seguro, contratar un seguro.
  ■ fully comprehensive insurance, seguro a todo riesgo. ‖ insurance broker, agente mf de seguros. ‖ insurance company, compañía de seguros. ‖ insurance policy, póliza (de seguro). ‖ insurance premium, prima (de seguro). ‖ car insurance, seguro de coche. ‖ national insurance, seguridad f social. ‖ private health insurance, seguro médico privado. ‖ third-party insurance, seguro a terceros.

insure [ɪnˈʃʊəʳ] **1** t asegurar (against, contra): *we've insured the house,* hemos asegurado la casa. **2** US (ensure) asegurar. – **3** i asegurarse (against, contra): *they planted extra to insure against crop failure,* plantaron de más para asegurarse contra una mala cosecha.
  ● to insure os./one's life, hacerse un seguro de vida.

insured [ɪnˈʃʊəd] **1** adj asegurado,-a: *are you insured?,* ¿estás asegurado?; *the car's insured against theft,* el coche está asegurado contra robo. – **2 the insured,** n el/la asegurado,-a.

insurer [ɪnˈʃʊərəʳ] n asegurador,-ra.

insurgent [ɪnˈsɜːdʒənt] **1** adj insurgente, insurrecto,-a. – **2** n insurgente mf, insurrecto,-a.

insurmountable [ɪnsəˈmaʊntəbəl] adj fml insuperable.

insurrection [ɪnsəˈrekʃən] n insurrección f.

insurrectionist [ɪnsəˈrekʃənɪst] adj insurrecto,-a.

intact [ɪnˈtækt] adj intacto,-a: *the parcel arrived intact,* el paquete llegó intacto; *he survived with his reputation intact,* su reputación quedó intacta.

intake [ˈɪnteɪk] **1** n (of food etc) consumo; (of breath) inhalación f. **2** TECH (of air, water) entrada; (of electricity, gas, water) toma. **3** (number of people) número de personas inscritas: *the yearly intake of students,* el número de alumnos matriculados anualmente; *this year's intake of soldiers,* la leva de este año.

intangible [ɪnˈtændʒɪbəl] adj intangible.

integer ['ɪntɪdʒəʳ] *n* MATH entero, número entero.
integral ['ɪntɪgrəl] 1 *adj* (*intrinsic, essential*) integral, esencial, fundamental: *elections are an integral part of democracy,* las elecciones son parte integral de la democracia. 2 (*built-in*) incorporado,-a. 3 MATH integral. − 4 *n* MATH integral *f*.
■ **integral calculus,** cálculo integral.
integrate ['ɪntɪgreɪt] 1 *t* integrar (**into/with,** en), incorporar (**into/with,** a): *they've integrated computer technology into the school curriculum,* han incorporado informática al plan de estudios del centro; *we should integrate all ethnic minorities into society,* deberíamos integrar a todas las minorías étnicas en la sociedad. 2 MATH integrar. − 3 *i* integrarse (**into/with,** en), incorporarse (**into/with,** a): *some immigrants integrate very quickly into the community,* algunos inmigrantes se integran con gran rapidez en la comunidad.
integrated ['ɪntɪgreɪtɪd] 1 *adj* (*gen*) integrado,-a. 2 (*psychologically*) equilibrado,-a.
■ **integrated circuit,** circuito integrado. ‖ **integrated school,** *escuela a la que acuden alumnos sin ningún tipo de segregación.*
integration [ɪntɪ'greɪʃən] *n* integración *f* (**into,** en).
integrity [ɪn'tegrɪtɪ] 1 *n* (*honesty*) integridad *f*, honradez *f*: *a man of integrity,* un hombre de integridad. 2 (*completeness*) totalidad *f*: *the integrity of the nation,* la totalidad de la nación.
intellect ['ɪntəlekt] 1 *n* (*intelligence*) intelecto, inteligencia. 2 (*person*) intelectual *mf*.
intellectual [ɪntə'lektjʊəl] 1 *adj* intelectual. − 2 *n* intelectual *mf*.
intellectually [ɪntə'lektʃʊəlɪ] *adv* intelectualmente.
intelligence [ɪn'telɪdʒəns] 1 *n* (*gen*) inteligencia: *a person of average intelligence,* una persona de inteligencia media. 2 (*information*) información *f*, espionaje *m*: *military intelligence,* servicio de información.
■ **intelligence officer,** oficial del servicio de información. ‖ **intelligence test,** prueba de inteligencia.
intelligent [ɪn'telɪdʒənt] *adj* inteligente: *an intelligent question,* una pregunta inteligente; *is there intelligent life on other planets?,* ¿hay vida inteligente en otros planetas?
intelligently [ɪn'telɪdʒəntlɪ] *adv* inteligentemente, con inteligencia: *you deal with problems very intelligently,* te enfrentas a los problemas de manera muy inteligente.
intelligentsia [ɪntelɪ'dʒentsɪə] **the intelligentsia,** *n* la intelectualidad *f*.
intelligible [ɪn'telɪdʒəbəl] *adj* inteligible, comprensible: *intelligible speech,* pronunciación inteligible.
intelligibly [ɪn'telɪdʒəblɪ] *adv* de manera inteligible.
intemperate [ɪn'tempərət] 1 *adj fml* (*behaviour, emotion*) inmoderado,-a, desaforado,-a, excesivo,-a; (*speech*) violento,-a, ultrajante; (*drinker*) dado,-a a la bebida. 2 (*climate*) riguroso,-a.
intend [ɪn'tend] 1 *t* (*plan, mean, have in mind*) tener la intención de, tener el propósito de, proponerse, pensar, querer: *I didn't intend staying so long,* no tenía la intención de quedarme tanto tiempo; *they intend to marry,* tienen la intención de casarse; *it didn't quite turn out as they intended,* no salió tal y como lo habían pensado; *I don't intend to put up with this any longer,* no pienso soportar esto ni un momento más; *what do you intend to do/doing about it?,* ¿qué piensas hacer al respecto?; *I intend you to inherit everything,* quiero que heredes todo; *what did she intend by that?,* ¿qué ha querido decir con eso?; *it was intended as a joke,* sólo era una bro-

ma; *no offence was intended,* no quería ofenderte. 2 (*destine for*) ir dirigido,-a a: *that comment was intended for you,* aquel comentario iba dirigido a ti, eso lo ha dicho por ti; *that shot was intended for the President,* ese disparo iba dirigido al Presidente; *the course is intended for writers,* el curso va dirigido a escritores.
intended [ɪn'tendɪd] 1 *adj* (*meant, desired*) intencionado,-a, deseado,-a: *intended effect,* efecto deseado. 2 (*planned for future*) previsto,-a, proyectado,-a: *our intended visit,* la visita que tenemos prevista. 3 (*planned for, designed for*) para, dirigido,-a a: *a book intended for beginners,* un libro para principiantes. − 4 *n dated* (*fiancé,-e*) prometido,-a.
intense [ɪn'tens] 1 *adj* (*gen*) intenso,-a, fuerte; (*stare*) penetrante: *intense heat,* calor intenso; *intense activity,* actividad intensa; *an intense discussion,* una fuerte discusión. 2 (*emotions*) profundo,-a, grande, vivo,-a: *intense grief,* pena grande; *intense bitterness,* profunda amargura. 3 (*person*) muy serio,-a: *she is so intense,* es muy seria.
intensely [ɪn'tenslɪ] *adv* extremadamente, sumamente: *he's intensely jealous,* es extremadamente celoso; *I dislike her intensely,* me cae muy mal.
intensification [ɪntensɪfɪ'keɪʃən] *n* intensificación *f*.
intensifier [ɪn'tensɪfaɪəʳ] *n* LING partícula enfática.
intensify [ɪn'tensɪfaɪ] 1 *t* (*search, campaign*) intensificar; (*effort*) redoblar; (*production, pollution, pain*) aumentar: *we've intensified our sales campaign,* hemos intensificado nuestra campaña de ventas; *the police intensified their search,* la policía intensificó su búsqueda. − 2 *i* intensificarse, aumentar.
▲ *pt & pp intensified, ger intensifying.*
intensity [ɪn'tensɪtɪ] 1 *n* intensidad *f*: *intensity of feeling,* intensidad de sentimiento; *with renewed intensity,* con nuevas fuerzas. 2 (*of person*) seriedad *f*.
▲ *pl intensities.*
intensive [ɪn'tensɪv] 1 *adj* (*course, training, etc*) intensivo,-a: *intensive farming,* cultivo intensivo. 2 (*search*) minucioso,-a; (*study*) profundo,-a.
■ **intensive care,** cuidados *mpl* intensivos. ‖ **intensive care unit,** unidad *f* de vigilancia intensiva, unidad *f* de cuidados intensivos.
intensively [ɪn'tensɪvlɪ] *adv* (*gen*) intensivamente; (*study*) profundamente.
intent [ɪn'tent] 1 *adj* (*look etc*) atento,-a. 2 (*determined*) decidido,-a, resuelto,-a, empeñado,-a: *she's intent on winning the race,* está decidida a ganar la carrera; *he's intent on becoming President,* tiene el firme propósito de llegar a ser presidente. 3 (*absorbed*) absorto,-a, concentrado,-a: *I was intent on my work,* estaba concentrado en mi trabajo. − 4 *n* intención *f*, propósito: *a declaration of intent,* una declaración de intenciones; *with intent to kill,* con la intención de matar.
● **to all intents (and purposes),** a todos los efectos.
‖ **to loiter with intent,** merodear con fines delictivos.
intention [ɪn'tenʃən] *n* (*purpose, aim, plan, determination*) intención *f*, propósito: *I have no intention of staying in this place another day,* no pienso quedarme aquí otro día más, no tengo intención de quedarme aquí otro día más; *she had every intention of going,* tenía la firme intención de asistir; *he's full of good intentions,* está lleno de buenas intenciones; *his intentions are strictly honourable,* sus intenciones son totalmente honradas.
● **to do sth. with the best of intentions,** hacer algo con buena voluntad.
intentional [ɪn'tenʃənəl] *adj* intencional, deliberado,-a: *it wasn't intentional,* fue sin querer, no lo hice (*hizo etc*) a propósito.

intentionally [ɪn'tenʃənəlɪ] *adv* adrede, a propósito, expresamente.

intently [ɪn'tentlɪ] *adv* atentamente.

inter [ɪn'tɜːʳ] *t fml* enterrar, sepultar.
▲ *pt & pp* **interred**, *ger* **interring**.

interact [ɪntər'ækt] 1 *i (people)* relacionarse, interactuar. 2 CHEM reaccionar.

interaction [ɪntər'ækʃən] *n* interacción *f*: *social interaction*, interacción social.

interactive [ɪntər'æktɪv] *adj* interactivo,-a: *interactive programme*, programa interactivo.

intercede [ɪntə'siːd] *i fml* interceder: *he interceded on my behalf*, intercedió por mí.

intercept [ɪntə'sept] *t* interceptar: *he discovered that someone had been intercepting his mail*, descubrió que alguien había estado interceptando su correspondencia.

interception [ɪntə'sepʃən] *n* interceptación *f*.

interceptor [ɪntə'septəʳ] *n* AV avión *m* interceptor.

intercession [ɪntə'seʃən] *n* intercesión *f*, mediación *f*.

interchange ['ɪntətʃeɪndʒ] 1 *n (exchange)* intercambio. 2 *(on motorway)* enlace *m*. – 3 *t* intercambiar **(with**, con): *they interchanged presents*, intercambiaron regalos.

interchangeable [ɪntə'tʃeɪndʒəbəl] *adj* intercambiable.

inter-city [ɪntə'sɪtɪ] 1 *adj* interurbano,-a, de largo recorrido. – 2 *n* tren *m* interurbano, tren *m* de largo recorrido.

intercom ['ɪntəkɒm] *n* interfono.

interconnect [ɪntəkə'nekt] *i* interconectar.

interconnecting [ɪntəkə'nektɪŋ] *adj* que comunica.

intercontinental [ɪntəkɒntɪ'nentəl] *adj* intercontinental.
■ **intercontinental ballistic missile**, misil *m* balístico intercontinental.

intercourse ['ɪntəkɔːs] 1 *n (dealings)* trato. 2 *(sexual)* coito, relaciones *fpl* sexuales.

interdependence [ɪntədɪ'pendəns] *n* interdependencia.

interdependent [ɪntədɪ'pendənt] *adj* interdependiente.

interdict [ɪntə'dɪkt] 1 *n* JUR interdicto; REL interdicto, entredicho. – 2 *t* JUR REL prohibir.

interdisciplinary [ɪntədɪsɪ'plɪnərɪ] *adj* interdisciplinario,-a.

interest ['ɪntrest] 1 *n (gen)* interés *m*: *only three students showed any interest in the subject*, sólo tres estudiantes mostraron interés en el tema; *I haven't the slightest interest in cars*, los coches no me interesan en lo más mínimo; *there's never anything of any interest on TV*, nunca hacen nada interesante por la televisión; *football is of no interest for her*, el fútbol no le interesa en absoluto; *this article might be of interest to you*, este artículo te podría interesar. 2 *(hobby)* afición *f*, interés *m*: *what are your interests?*, ¿cuáles son tus aficiones?; *he has a variety of interests*, le interesan muchas cosas. 3 *(advantage, benefit)* provecho, beneficio: *it's in your own interest*, es por tu propio bien, es en tu propio beneficio; *unions look after the interests of their members*, los sindicatos se ocupan de los intereses de sus afiliados; *in the interests of national security*, por razones de seguridad nacional. 4 COMM *(share, stake)* participación *f*, interés *m*: *he has business interests in Spain*, tiene negocios en España; *I've got financial interests in that company*, tengo acciones en esa empresa. 5 FIN *(money)* interés *m*, rédito: *they pay interest at 10% on their mortgage*, pagan un interés del 10% sobre su hipoteca. – 6

t interesar: *politics doesn't interest me*, no me interesa la política; *it may interest you to know*, puede que te interese saber; *can I interest you in this catalogue?*, ¿le interesaría este catálogo?
● **to bear/earn/pay interest**, dar interés, devengar interés. ‖ **to lose interest in sth.**, perder interés en algo. ‖ **to take an interest in sth.**, interesarse por algo. ‖ **to repay sth. with interest**, devolver algo con creces.
■ **interest group**, grupo de intereses. ‖ **vested interest**, *(personal)* interés *m* (personal); *(legal)* derecho adquirido.

interested ['ɪntrestɪd] *adj* interesado,-a (**in**, en): *she simply isn't interested in literature*, sencillamente no le interesa la literatura; *I'm interested to know what will happen now*, me interesa saber qué pasará ahora; *Lorca was interested in popular Andalusian song*, Lorca se interesó por la canción popular andaluza; *an interested look*, una mirada de interés; *the interested party*, la parte interesada.

interest-free ['ɪntrestfriː] *adj* sin intereses.
■ **interest-free loan**, préstamo sin intereses.

interesting ['ɪntrestɪŋ] *adj* interesante: *an interesting question*, una pregunta interesante; *he's a really interesting person*, es una persona muy interesante; *the interesting thing is that ...*, lo curioso (del caso) es que ...

interestingly ['ɪntrestɪŋlɪ] *adv* de manera interesante.
● **interestingly enough**, curiosamente, por raro que parezca.

interface ['ɪntəfeɪs] 1 *n* COMPUT interface *f*. 2 *fig* terreno común.

interfacing ['ɪntəfeɪsɪŋ] *n* entretela.

interfere [ɪntə'fɪəʳ] *i (meddle)* entrometerse (**in**, en), meterse (**in**, en), inmiscuirse (**in**, en): *stop interfering!*, ¡deja de entrometerte!; *don't interfere in my affairs!*, ¡no te metas en mis asuntos! 2 **to interfere with**, *(prevent advancement)* afectar, dificultar, estorbar, impedir, interferir: *having children will not interfere with my career*, tener hijos no dificultará mi carrera; *that noise is interfering with my work*, aquel ruido me impide trabajar. 3 *(fiddle with, mess about with)* tocar, manosear: *who's been interfering with my papers?*, ¿quién ha tocado mis papeles? 4 RAD TV interferir. 5 **to interfere with**, GB *euph (sexually assault)* abusar de.

interference [ɪntə'fɪərəns] 1 *n (meddling)* intromisión *f*, entrometimiento, injerencia: *state interference in people's lives*, la injerencia del estado en la vida de las personas. 2 RAD TV interferencia.

interfering [ɪntə'fɪərɪŋ] *adj* entrometido,-a.

interim ['ɪntərɪm] 1 *adj* interino,-a, provisional: *an interim arrangement*, un arreglo provisional. – 2 *n* ínterin *m*.
● **in the interim**, en el ínterin, mientras tanto.

interior [ɪn'tɪərɪəʳ] 1 *adj* interior. – 2 *n* interior *m*, parte *f* interior: *the car has a luxurious interior*, el coche tiene un interior lujoso. 3 **the interior**, *(inland)* el interior.
■ **Department of the Interior**, US Ministerio del Interior. ‖ **interior decorator**, decorador *mf*. ‖ **interior design**, interiorismo. ‖ **interior designer**, interiorista *mf*. ‖ **Minister of the Interior**, US Ministro del Interior.

interject [ɪntə'dʒekt] *t* interponer.

interjection [ɪntə'dʒekʃən] 1 *n* GRAM interjección *f*. 2 *(comment)* interposición *f*.

interlace [ɪntə'leɪs] 1 *t* entrelazar. – 2 *i* entrelazarse.

interlink [ɪntə'lɪŋk] 1 *t* entrelazar, unir. – 2 *i* entrelazarse, unirse.

interlock [ɪntə'lɒk] 1 *t (fingers)* entrelazar; *(cogs)* engranar, endentar; *(parts, pieces, units)* enganchar, trabar. –

2 *i (fingers)* entrelazarse; *(cogs)* engranarse, endentarse; *(units)* engancharse, trabarse.
interlocutor [ɪntə'lɒkjʊtəʳ] *n fml* interlocutor,-ra.
interloper ['ɪntələʊpəʳ] *n* intruso,-a.
interlude ['ɪntəluːd] **1** *n (break)* intervalo, pausa; *(respite)* respiro, tregua. **2** *(music)* interludio; *(play etc)* intermedio, descanso.
intermarriage [ɪntə'mærɪdʒ] **1** *n (between different groups, races, etc)* matrimonio mixto. **2** *(within family)* matrimonio entre consanguíneos.
intermediary [ɪntə'miːdɪərɪ] **1** *n* intermediario,-a. – **2** *adj* intermediario,-a.
▲ En **1** *(sustantivo) pl* **intermediaries**.
intermediate [ɪntə'miːdɪət] *adj* intermedio,-a.
■ **intermediate range (ballistic) missile,** misil *m* de medio alcance.
interment [ɪn'tɜːmənt] *n fml* entierro.
interminable [ɪn'tɜːmɪnəbəl] *adj* interminable, inacabable, sin fin: *the wait seemed interminable,* la espera se hacía interminable.
interminably [ɪn'tɜːmɪnəblɪ] *adv* interminablemente: *I waited interminably,* esperé una eternidad.
intermingle [ɪntə'mɪŋgəl] **1** *i* entremezclarse. – **2** *t* entremezclar.
intermission [ɪntə'mɪʃən] *n* US *(interval)* intermedio, descanso.
intermittent [ɪntə'mɪtənt] *adj* intermitente: *intermittent showers,* chubascos ocasionales.
intern ['ɪntɜːn] **1** *n* US interno,-a. – **2** *t* internar, recluir.
▲ En **2** *(verbo)* [ɪn'tɜːn].
internal [ɪn'tɜːnəl] **1** *adj (inside place)* interior; *(within organization)* interno,-a: *internal audit,* auditoría interna; *internal inquiry,* investigación interna. **2** POL ECON *(domestic)* interior.
■ **internal combustion,** combustión *f* interna. ‖ **internal examiner,** examinador,-ra interno,-a. ‖ **internal medicine,** medicina interna. ‖ **internal organ,** órgano interno. ‖ **Internal Revenue,** US Hacienda.
internalize [ɪn'tɜːnəlaɪz] *t (feelings)* interiorizar.
internally [ɪn'tɜːnəlɪ] *adv* interiormente, internamente.
international [ɪntə'næʃənəl] **1** *adj* internacional: *international relations,* relaciones internacionales. – **2** *n* SP *(player)* internacional *mf*; *(match)* partido internacional. **3 the International,** POL la Internacional *f*.
■ **International Brigade(s),** Brigada(s) Internacional(es). ‖ **International Date Line,** línea internacional de cambio de fecha. ‖ **international law,** derecho internacional. ‖ **International Monetary Fund,** Fondo Monetario Internacional.
Internationale [ɪntənæʃə'nɑːl] **the Internationale,** *n* la Internacional *f*.
internationalism [ɪntə'næʃənəlɪzəm] *n* internacionalismo.
internationalist [ɪntə'næʃənəlɪst] *n* internacionalista *mf*.
internationally [ɪntə'næʃənəlɪ] *adv* internacionalmente.
internecine [ɪntə'niːsaɪn] *adj* de destrucción recíproca.
internee [ɪntɜː'niː] *n* interno,-a, preso,-a.
internment [ɪn'tɜːnmənt] *n* internamiento.
interpersonal [ɪntə'pɜːsənəl] *adj* interpersonal.
interplay ['ɪntəpleɪ] *n* interacción *f*.
Interpol ['ɪntəpɒl] *abbr (International Criminal Police Organization)* Interpol *f*.
interpolate [ɪn'tɜːpəleɪt] *t fml* interpolar, intercalar.
interpose [ɪntə'pəʊz] **1** *t (place between)* interponer. **2** *(interrupt)* interrumpir. – **3** *i* interrumpir.

● **to interpose os.,** interponerse.
interposition [ɪntəpə'zɪʃən] *n fml* interposición *f*.
interpret [ɪn'tɜːprət] **1** *t (gen)* interpretar; *(understand)* interpretar, entender: *she interpreted the song in her own way,* interpretó la canción a su manera; *she can interpret dreams,* sabe interpretar los sueños; *I interpreted his silence as a no,* interpreté su silencio como un no; *it all depends on how you interpret the law,* todo depende de cómo se interprete la ley. – **2** *i* actuar de intérprete, hacer de intérprete: *could you interpret for us?,* ¿podrías hacernos de intérprete?
interpretation [ɪntɜːprə'teɪʃən] *n* interpretación *f*: *this text is open to interpretation,* este texto está abierto a interpretaciones; *what is your interpretation of González's statement?,* ¿cómo interpretas la declaración de González?; *he gave a brilliant interpretation of Hamlet,* hizo una interpretación brillante de Hamlet.
interpretative [ɪn'tɜːprətətɪv] *adj* interpretativo,-a.
interpreter [ɪn'tɜːprətəʳ] *n* intérprete *mf*.
interpreting [ɪn'tɜːprətɪŋ] *n* interpretación *f*.
interracial [ɪntə'reɪʃəl] *adj* interracial.
interregnum [ɪntə'regnəm] *n* interregno.
interrelate [ɪntərɪ'leɪt] **1** *t* interrelacionar. – **2** *i* interrelacionarse.
interrelated [ɪntərɪ'leɪtɪd] *adj* estrechamente relacionado,-a.
interrogate [ɪn'terəgeɪt] *t* interrogar.
interrogation [ɪnterə'geɪʃən] *n* interrogatorio.
interrogative [ɪntə'rɒgətɪv] **1** *adj fml* interrogativo,-a. – **2** *n* LING *(word)* palabra interrogativa; *(phrase)* oración *f* interrogativa.
interrogator [ɪn'terəgeɪtəʳ] *n* interrogador,-ra.
interrupt [ɪntə'rʌpt] **1** *t* interrumpir: *we interrupt this programme with a news flash,* interrumpimos este programa con una noticia de última hora; *work on the building was interrupted by the war,* la construcción del edificio fue interrumpida por la guerra; *the speaker was constantly interrupted,* el orador fue interrumpido constantemente; *a flat landscape interrupted only by a few trees,* un paisaje llano interrumpido solamente por unos árboles. – **2** *i* interrumpir: *don't interrupt when I'm talking,* no interrumpas cuando estoy hablando; *sorry to interrupt,* perdona (por) la interrupción.
interruption [ɪntə'rʌpʃən] *n* interrupción *f*.
intersect [ɪntə'sekt] **1** *t (road etc)* cruzar, atravesar. **2** *(in geometry)* cruzar, intersecar. – **3** *i (road etc)* cruzarse, juntarse. **4** *(in geometry)* intersecarse.
intersection [ɪntə'sekʃən] **1** *n (of roads)* cruce *m*. **2** *(in geometry)* intersección *f*.
intersperse [ɪntə'spɜːs] **1** *t (scatter)* esparcir, entremezclar: *intersperse flowers among shrubs,* entremezclar arbustos y flores; *mainly sunshine interspersed with the odd shower,* predominio del sol con alguna posibilidad de chubascos dispersos. **2** *(diversify)* salpicar: *he interspersed his speech with anecdotes,* salpicó el discurso de anécdotas.
interstate ['ɪntəsteɪt] *adj (esp us)* interestatal, entre estados.
interstice [ɪn'tɜːstɪs] *n fml* intersticio.
intertwine [ɪntə'twaɪn] **1** *t* entrelazar (**with,** con). – **2** *i* entrelazarse (**with,** con).
interval ['ɪntəvəl] **1** *n (in time, space)* intervalo (**between,** entre): *he returned after an interval of three hours,* volvió pasado un intervalo de tres horas; *the interval between his escape and recapture,* el intervalo entre su huida y su captura. **2** *(in play, film, etc)* intermedio, descanso;

(in play) entreacto. **3** *(pause, break)* pausa; *(silence)* silencio; *(rest)* descanso. **4** MUS intervalo. – **5 intervals,** *npl* METEOR intervalos *mpl: sunny intervals,* intervalos de sol.
● **at intervals,** *(in time)* a intervalos, a ratos, de vez en cuando; *(in space)* a intervalos: *at 10-minute intervals,* cada 10 minutos, a intervalos de 10 minutos; *at weekly intervals,* cada semana; *at 6 ft intervals,* cada 2 metros. || **at regular intervals,** con regularidad.

intervene [ɪntə'viːn] **1** *i* *(person)* intervenir **(in,** en): *he was forced to intervene,* se vio obligado a intervenir; *I intervened on her behalf,* intervine por (parte de) ella; *she intervened in their quarrel,* intervino en la riña. **2** *(event etc)* sobrevenir, ocurrir: *the war intervened,* la guerra sobrevino. **3** *fml (time)* transcurrir, mediar.

intervening [ɪntə'viːnɪŋ] *adj* intermedio,-a: *in the intervening period,* en el ínterin; *in the intervening years,* en los años que transcurrieron.

intervention [ɪntə'venʃən] *n* intervención *f: armed intervention,* intervención armada; *divine intervention,* intervención divina.

interventionist [ɪntə'venʃənɪst] **1** *n* intervencionista *mf.* – **2** *adj* intervencionista.

interview ['ɪntəvjuː] **1** *n* *(gen)* entrevista; *(press)* entrevista: *I've got an interview for a job,* tengo una entrevista para un trabajo. – **2** *t* entrevistar, hacer una entrevista a, entrevistarse con: *she interviewed several candidates,* entrevistó a varias candidatas; *he's going to interview the President,* va a hacerle una entrevista al presidente. – **3** *i* entrevistarse: *I'm interviewing all day,* tengo entrevistas todo el día.
● **to give an interview,** conceder una entrevista. || **to have an interview with sb.,** entrevistarse con algn.

interviewee [ɪntəvjuː'iː] *n* entrevistado,-a.

interviewer ['ɪntəvjuːəʳ] *n* entrevistador,-ra.

interweave [ɪntə'wiːv] **1** *t* entretejer. **2** *fig* entrelazar, cruzar. – **3** *i* entretejer.
▲ *pt* **interwove** [ɪntə'wəʊv], *pp* **interwoven** [ɪntə'wəʊvən].

intestate [ɪn'testeɪt] *adj* JUR intestado,-a.

intestinal [ɪn'testɪnəl] *adj* intestinal.

intestine [ɪn'testɪn] *n* intestino.
■ **large intestine,** intestino grueso. || **small intestine,** intestino delgado.

intimacy ['ɪntɪməsɪ] **1** *n* *(closeness)* intimidad *f.* **2** *euph* *(sexual activity)* relaciones *fpl* íntimas. – **3 intimacies,** *npl* *(actions)* intimidades *fpl.*

intimate¹ ['ɪntɪmət] **1** *adj* *(gen)* íntimo,-a; *(link etc)* estrecho,-a: *intimate friend,* amigo,-a íntimo,-a; *intimate details,* detalles íntimos; *intimate restaurant,* restaurante íntimo. **2** *(knowledge)* profundo,-a. – **3** *n* *(friend)* amigo,-a íntimo,-a, íntimo,-a.
● **to be intimate with sb.,** *(friendly)* ser muy amigos,-as con algn.; *(having sexual relations)* tener relaciones (íntimas) con algn. || **to be/get on intimate terms with sb.,** intimar con algn.

intimate² ['ɪntɪmeɪt] *i* *fml* insinuar, dar a entender: *she intimated (to me) that we should leave,* me insinuó que deberíamos marcharnos.

intimately ['ɪntɪmətlɪ] **1** *adv* *(familiarly)* íntimamente. **2** *(closely)* estrechamente. **3** *(in detail)* profundamente, a fondo.

intimation [ɪntɪ'meɪʃən] **1** *n* *fml* *(sign)* indicio; *(hint)* sugerencia, indirecta. **2** *fml* *(feeling)* presentimiento.
● **to have an intimation of sth.,** presentir algo.

intimidate [ɪn'tɪmɪdeɪt] *t* intimidar: *they tried to intimidate him into confessing,* intentaron intimidarlo para que confesara.

intimidating [ɪn'tɪmɪdeɪtɪŋ] **1** *adj* intimidante, amenazador,-ra. **2** *fig* que infunde temor.

intimidation [ɪntɪmɪ'deɪʃən] *n* intimidación *f.*

intimidatory [ɪntɪmɪ'deɪtərɪ] *adj* amenazador,-ra.

into ['ɪntʊ] **1** *prep* *(indicating movement)* en, dentro de, a; *(in direction of)* a, hacia; *(against)* contra, con: *I'm going into town,* voy al centro; *they went into the house,* entraron en la casa; *she's got to go into hospital,* tienen que ingresarla en el hospital; *he jumped into the water,* saltó al agua; *they climbed into bed,* se metieron en la cama; *I bit into the apple,* mordí la manzana, di un mordisco a la manzana; *the cheque must be paid into a bank account,* hay que ingresar el cheque en una cuenta bancaria; *look into my eyes,* mira a mis ojos; *speak into the receiver,* habla al auricular; *I bumped into him,* me topé con él; *he crashed into a tree,* chocó contra un árbol; *I walked into a door,* me topé con una puerta. **2** *(time, age)* hasta: *she worked long into the night,* trabajó hasta muy avanzada la noche; *he remained a bachelor until well into middle age,* permaneció soltero hasta bien entrada la mediana edad; *I can see into the future,* puedo ver el futuro; *three days into our holiday ...,* a los tres días de empezar las vacaciones ... **3** *(indicating change)* en, a: *he turned water into wine,* transformó el agua en vino; *he changed into a monster,* se convirtió en un monstruo; *translate this into Spanish,* traduce esto al español; *she wants to change some pounds into pesetas,* quiere cambiar libras en pesetas; *cut it into small pieces,* cortadlo en trozos pequeños; *a house divided into flats,* una casa dividida en pisos; *I'll change into a dress,* me pondré un vestido; *they came into power,* llegaron al poder; *she went into journalism,* se dedicó al periodismo; *an inquiry into the disaster,* una investigación sobre la catástrofe. **4** MATH entre: *what's four into twenty?,* ¿cuánto son veinte entre cuatro?; *four into eight goes two,* ocho entre cuatro son dos.
● **to be into sth.,** *fam* *(keen on)* gustarle a uno algo; *(interested in)* ser aficionado,-a a algo: *she's into skating,* le gusta patinar; *he's into heavy rock,* le gusta el rock duro.

intolerable [ɪn'tɒlərəbəl] *adj* intolerable, inaceptable, inadmisible, inaguantable.

intolerance [ɪn'tɒlərəns] *n* intolerancia, intransigencia.

intolerant [ɪn'tɒlərənt] *adj* intolerante, intransigente.

intonation [ɪntə'neɪʃən] *n* entonación *f.*

intoxicate [ɪn'tɒksɪkeɪt] **1** *t* *fml* embriagar, emborrachar. **2** *fig* embriagar.

intoxicated [ɪn'tɒksɪkeɪtɪd] *adj* ebrio,-a, borracho,-a.

intoxicating [ɪn'tɒksɪkeɪtɪŋ] *adj* embriagador,-ra.
■ **intoxicating liquor,** bebida alchólica.

intoxication [ɪntɒksɪ'keɪʃən] *n* embriaguez *f.*

intractable [ɪn'træktəbəl] *adj* *fml* intratable.

intramuscular [ɪntrə'mʌskjʊəʳ] *adj* intramuscular.

intransigence [ɪn'trænsɪdʒəns] *n* intransigencia, intolerancia.

intransigent [ɪn'trænsɪdʒent] *adj* intransigente, intolerante.

intransitive [ɪn'trænsɪtɪv] *adj* LING intransitivo,-a.

intrauterine [ɪntrə'juːtəraɪn] *adj* MED intrauterino,-a.
■ **intraurine device,** dispositivo intrauterino.

intravenous [ɪntrə'viːnəs] *adj* MED intravenoso,-a.

intrepid [ɪn'trepɪd] *adj* intrépido,-a, audaz.

intrepidity [ɪntrə'pɪdətɪ] *n* intrepidez *f.*

intricacy ['ɪntrɪkəsɪ] **1** *n* complejidad *f.* – **2 intricacies,** *npl* complicaciones *fpl,* detalles *mpl,* pormenores *mpl.*
▲ *pl* **intricacies.**

intricate ['ɪntrɪkət] *adj* (*plot etc*) complejo,-a, complicado,-a; (*pattern*) intrincado,-a.
intricately ['ɪntrɪkətlɪ] *adv* intrincadamente.
intrigue [ɪn'triːg] **1** *n* (*gen*) intriga; (*conspiracy*) conspiración *f.* **2** (*love affair*) amorío, aventura. – **3** *t* (*fascinate*) intrigar, fascinar, interesar: *you intrigue me,* me fascinas; *I'm intrigued by this story,* me intriga esta historia. – **4** *i* (*scheme, plot*) intrigar.
intriguer [ɪn'triːgəʳ] *n* intrigante *mf.*
intriguing [ɪn'triːgɪŋ] *adj* intrigante, fascinante, interesante: *what an intriguing idea,* qué idea más interesante; *that sounds intriguing,* eso parece fascinante.
intrinsic [ɪn'trɪnsɪk] *adj* intrínseco,-a, inherente.
intrinsically [ɪn'trɪnsɪklɪ] *adv* intrínsecamente.
intro ['ɪntrəʊ] **1** *n fam* (*of person*) presentación *f.* **2** MUS introducción *f.*
   ▲ *pl* intros.
introduce [ɪntrə'djuːs] **1** *t* (*person, programme*) presentar: *allow me to introduce Dr. Kelly,* déjeme presentarle al doctor Kelly; *I don't think we've been introduced,* me parece que no nos han presentado; *I'd like to introduce you to a few people,* me gustaría presentarte a algunas personas. **2** (*bring in - gen*) introducir; (*- new product etc*) presentar, lanzar; (*law, procedure, etc*) introducir, instituir: *we're going to introduce some innovations,* vamos a introducir algunas innovaciones; *potatoes were introduced into Europe 400 years ago,* las patatas fueron introducidas en Europa hace 400 años; *when was decimal currency introduced?,* ¿cuándo se introdujo el sistema decimal?; *the government has introduced a ban on smoking in public places,* el gobierno ha prohibido fumar en lugares públicos. **3** (*to hobby, habit*) iniciar (**to,** en): *they introduced him to alcohol,* le iniciaron en el alcohol. **4** (*bring up*) proponer, sugerir, plantear, introducir: *he tactfully introduced the subject of money into the conversation,* sacó a colación con mucho tacto el tema del dinero; *her comment introduced a note of sadness into our conversation,* su comentario dio un tono de tristeza a nuestra conversación. **5** POL (*propose*) presentar: *he introduced a bill to Parliament,* presentó un proyecto de ley ante el parlamento. **6** *fml* (*insert*) introducir, meter, insertar: *introduce a needle into the vein,* introduce una aguja en la vena.
introduction [ɪntrə'dʌkʃən] **1** *n* (*of person, programme*) presentación *f: she's a person who needs no introduction,* es una persona que no necesita presentación; *a letter of introduction,* una carta de recomendación. **2** (*to book, speech, etc*) introducción *f: the plot is explained in the short introduction,* se explica el argumento en la introducción; *an introduction to Spanish Literature,* una introducción a la literatura española. **3** (*bringing in - gen*) introducción *f;* (*- of new product etc*) presentación *f,* lanzamiento; (*- of law, procedure, etc*) introducción *f,* institución *f: the possible introduction of identity cards,* la posible introducción de carnets de identidad; *the introduction of new technology,* la introducción de la nueva tecnología. **4** (*first experience*) iniciación *f: my introduction into the world of drugs,* mi iniciación en el mundo de las drogas. **5** MUS introducción *f.*
introductory [ɪntrə'dʌktərɪ] *adj* (*gen*) introductorio,-a; (*words, remarks, etc*) preliminar; (*offer, price*) de lanzamiento.
introspect [ɪntrə'spekt] *i* practicar la introspección.
introspection [ɪntrə'spekʃən] *n* introspección *f.*
introspective [ɪntrə'spektɪv] *adj* introspectivo,-a.
introversion [ɪntrə'vɜːʃən] *n* introversión *f.*

introvert ['ɪntrəvɜːt] *n* introvertido,-a.
introverted ['ɪntrəvɜːtɪd] *adj* introvertido,-a.
intrude [ɪn'truːd] **1** *i* (*disturb*) importunar, molestar: *I don't want to intrude,* no quiero molestar; *she didn't want to intrude on their grief,* no quería importunarles en su dolor. **2** (*interfere*) entrometerse, inmiscuirse, meterse. – **3** *t fml* importunar, introducir.
intruder [ɪn'truːdəʳ] *n* intruso,-a.
intrusion [ɪn'truːʒən] **1** *n* (*into place*) intrusión *f.* **2** (*on privacy, mood, etc*) invasión *f: I consider that to be an intrusion into my private life,* eso lo considero una invasión de mi vida privada.
intrusive [ɪn'truːsɪv] *adj* (*intruding*) intruso,-a; (*nosy*) entrometido,-a; (*annoying, unwelcome*) que molesta, que estorba, molesto,-a.
intuit [ɪn'tjuːɪt] **1** *t fml* intuir. – **2** *i fml* intuir.
intuition [ɪntjuː'ɪʃən] *n* intuición *f: intuition told me something was wrong,* mi intuición me dijo que pasaba algo; *female intuition,* intuición femenina.
intuitive [ɪn'tjuːɪtɪv] *adj* intuitivo,-a.
intuitively [ɪn'tjuːɪtɪvlɪ] *adv* intuitivamente.
inundate ['ɪnʌndeɪt] **1** *t* inundar (**with,** de). **2** *fig* inundar (**with,** de): *I was inundated with letters,* recibí un montón de cartas.
inundation [ɪnʌn'deɪʃən] *n* inundación *f.*
inure [ɪ'njuəʳ] *t fml* acostumbrar (**to,** a), habituar (**to,** a).
invade [ɪn'veɪd] **1** *t* (*gen*) invadir: *the Germans invaded France,* los alemanes invadieron Francia; *a small village invaded by tourists,* un pueblo invadido por turistas; *she felt that the questions invaded her privacy,* creía que las preguntas invadían su intimidad. – **2** *i* invadir.
invader [ɪn'veɪdəʳ] *n* invasor,-ra.
invalid[1] ['ɪnvəlɪd] **1** *n* (*disabled person*) inválido,-a, minusválido,-a; (*sick person*) enfermo,-a. – **2** *adj* (*disabled*) inválido,-a, minusválido,-a; (*sick*) enfermo,-a.
   ◆ **to invalid out** *t sep* MIL licenciar por invalidez.
   ■ **invalid chair,** silla de ruedas.
invalid[2] [ɪn'vælɪd] *adj* (*gen*) inválido,-a, no válido,-a, nulo,-a; (*out of date*) caducado,-a.
invalidate [ɪn'vælɪdeɪt] *t* (*result, rule, etc*) invalidar, anular; (*argument*) refutar, demostrar el error de.
invalidation [ɪnvælɪ'deɪʃən] *n* invalidación *f,* anulación *f.*
invalidity[1] [ɪnvə'lɪdətɪ] *n* (*of invalid*) invalidez *f.*
   ■ **invalidity pension,** pensión *f* de invalidez.
invalidity[2] [ɪnvə'lɪdətɪ] *n* (*not valid*) invalidez *f,* nulidad *f.*
invaluable [ɪn'væljuəbəl] *adj* inestimable, inapreciable.
invariability [ɪnveərɪə'bɪlətɪ] *n* invariabilidad *f,* constancia.
invariable [ɪn'veərɪəbəl] *adj* invariable, constante.
invariably [ɪn'veərɪəblɪ] *adv* invariablemente, siempre: *he invariably wins,* siempre gana.
invasion [ɪn'veɪʒən] *n* (*gen*) invasión *f: an invasion of privacy,* una invasión de la intimidad.
invective [ɪn'vektɪv] *n fml* invectiva, improperio.
inveigle [ɪn'veɪgəl] *t* engatusar, embaucar.
   ● **to inveigle sb. into doing sth.,** embaucar a algn. para que haga algo.
invent [ɪn'vent] *t* inventar, inventarse: *who invented the telephone?,* ¿quién inventó el teléfono?; *she invented the whole story,* se lo inventó todo.
invention [ɪn'venʃən] **1** *n* (*gen*) invento, invención *f;* (*lying*) invención *f,* mentira: *the answerphone is a fantastic invention,* el contestador es un invento fantástico; *the article is a complete invention,* el artículo es pura invención. **2** (*capacity for inventing*) inventiva.

inventive [ɪn'ventɪv] *adj* inventivo,-a.
inventiveness [ɪn'ventɪvnəs] *n* inventiva.
inventor [ɪn'ventə'] *n* inventor,-ra.
inventory ['ɪnventrɪ] **1** *n* inventario. – **2** *t* inventariar.
▲ *(sustantivo) pl inventories; (verbo) pt & pp inventoried, ger inventorying.*
inverse [ɪn'vɜːs] **1** *adj* inverso,-a. – **2 the inverse,** *n* lo inverso, lo contrario.
● **in inverse ratio/proportion,** en proporción inversa.
inversely [ɪn'vɜːslɪ] *adv* inversamente.
inversion [ɪn'vɜːʃən] *n* inversión *f.*
invert [ɪn'vɜːt] *t* invertir.
invertebrate [ɪn'vɜːtɪbrət] **1** *adj* invertebrado,-a. – **2** *n* invertebrado,-a.
inverted [ɪn'vɜːtɪd] *adj* invertido,-a.
■ **inverted commas,** comillas *fpl.*
invest [ɪn'vest] **1** *t (money)* invertir **(in,** en): *we invested all our money in the business,* invertimos todo nuestro dinero en el negocio. **2** *(time, effort, etc)* emplear **(in,** en), invertir **(in,** en): *I invested a year in that project,* invertí un año en ese proyecto. **3** *fml (right, rank, power, etc)* investir **(with,** con), conferir **(with,** -), otorgar **(with,** -): *he was invested with full authority,* le confirieron plena autoridad. **4** *fml (quality, characteristic, etc)* revestir **(with,** con), envolver **(with,** de). **5** MIL *dated* sitiar, cercar. – **6** *i* hacer una inversión **(in,** en), invertir dinero **(in,** en): *it's not a good time to invest,* no es un buen momento para invertir. **7** *fam (buy)* comprar **(in,** -): *I'm thinking of investing in a gold watch,* estoy pensando en comprarme un reloj de oro.
investigate [ɪn'vestɪgeɪt] **1** *t (crime)* investigar; *(cause, possibility)* examinar, estudiar. – **2** *i fam (check)* mirar.
investigation [ɪnvestɪ'geɪʃən] *n (of crime)* investigación *f* **(into,** sobre); *(of cause, possibility)* examen *m* **(into,** de), estudio **(into,** de): *police investigations into the crime,* investigaciones policiales sobre el crimen.
investigative [ɪn'vestɪgətɪv] *adj* investigador,-ra: *investigative journalism,* periodismo de investigación.
investigator [ɪn'vestɪgeɪtə'] *n* investigador,-ra.
investiture [ɪn'vestɪtʃə'] *n* investidura.
investment [ɪn'vestmənt] **1** *n (of money)* inversión *f.* **2** *(investiture)* investidura.
investor [ɪn'vestə'] *n* inversor,-ra, inversionista *mf.*
inveterate [ɪn'vetərət] *adj (person)* empedernido,-a; *(habit, feeling, etc)* arraigado,-a, consolidado,-a.
invidious [ɪn'vɪdɪəs] **1** *adj (task, job, etc)* odioso,-a, ingrato,-a. **2** *(comparison, choice, etc)* injusto,-a.
invigilate [ɪn'vɪdʒɪleɪt] **1** *t* GB vigilar. – **2** *i* GB vigilar.
invigilator [ɪn'vɪdʒɪleɪtə'] *n* GB vigilante *mf.*
invigorate [ɪn'vɪgəreɪt] *t* tonificar, vigorizar.
invigorating [ɪn'vɪgəreɪtɪŋ] *adj* tonificante, vigorizante, estimulante.
invincible [ɪn'vɪnsəbəl] *adj* invencible.
inviolable [ɪn'vaɪələbəl] *adj* inviolable.
inviolate [ɪn'vaɪələt] *adj fml* inviolado,-a.
● **to remain inviolate,** permanecer intacto,-a.
invisibility [ɪnvɪzə'bɪlətɪ] *n* invisibilidad *f.*
invisible [ɪn'vɪzəbəl] *adj* invisible.
■ **invisible ink,** tinta simpática. ‖ **invisible mending,** zurcido invisible.
invisibly [ɪn'vɪzəblɪ] *adv* invisiblemente.
invitation [ɪnvɪ'teɪʃən] *n* invitación *f:* *they sent out the invitations,* enviaron las invitaciones; *we have a standing invitation to visit her,* podemos visitarla cuando queramos; *leaving the door unlocked is an open invitation to*

thieves, dejar la puerta sin cerrar es tentar a los ladrones.
● **by invitation only,** entrada por invitación.
invite [ɪn'vaɪt] **1** *t (guest etc)* invitar, convidar; *(candidate, participant)* pedir, invitar: *have they invited you to their wedding?,* ¿te han invitado a su boda?; *we've been invited for/to dinner,* nos han invitado a cenar; *she was invited to speak at a conference,* le pidieron que hablara en una conferencia; *let's invite a few friends round,* invitemos a algunos amigos a casa. **2** *(comment, suggestion, etc)* solicitar: *questions will be invited at the end,* las preguntas se solicitarán al final. **3** *(criticism, disaster, etc)* provocar, incitar: *if you leave the window open, you're just inviting trouble,* si dejas la ventana abierta, te estás buscando problemas. – **4** *n fam* invitación *f.*
▲ En **3** *(sustantivo)* ['ɪnvaɪt].
inviting [ɪn'vaɪtɪŋ] *adj (tempting)* tentador,-ra; *(attractive)* atractivo,-a, atrayente; *(tasty)* apetitoso,-a.
in vitro [ɪn'viːtrəʊ] *phr* in vitro.
■ **in vitro fertilization,** fertilización *f* in vitro.
invoice ['ɪnvɔɪs] **1** *n* COMM factura. – **2** *t* COMM facturar, pasar factura.
● **as per invoice,** según factura. ‖ **to draw up/make out an invoice,** extender una factura.
■ **pro forma invoice,** factura pro forma.
invoke [ɪn'vəʊk] *t* invocar.
involuntarily [ɪn'vɒləntrəl] *adv* sin querer.
involuntary [ɪn'vɒləntərɪ] *adj* involuntario,-a, sin querer.
involve [ɪn'vɒlv] **1** *t (entail)* suponer, implicar, conllevar; *(give rise to)* acarrear, ocasionar: *organizing a party involves a lot of work,* organizar una fiesta supone mucho trabajo; *what does the job involve?,* ¿en qué consiste el trabajo?; *this course involves studying abroad,* esta carrera comprende un período de estudio en el extranjero. **2** *(include, affect, concern)* tener que ver con, afectar a: *a police operation involving officers from different countries,* una operación policial que incluía a oficiales de diferentes países; *listen carefully because this involves you,* escucha bien porque esto te afecta a ti; *an accident involving three cars,* un accidente en el que se vieron implicados tres coches. **3** *(implicar)* implicar, involucrar, meter: *don't involve me in your argument,* no me metas en vuestra discusión; *she didn't want to involve the children,* no quería involucrar a los niños.
● **to involve os. in sth.,** tomar parte en algo.
involved [ɪn'vɒlvd] **1** *adj (complicated)* complicado,-a, enrevesado,-a. **2** *(implicated, associated)* implicado,-a, involucrado,-a; *(mixed up in)* metido,-a, envuelto,-a, mezclado,-a: *several politicians are involved,* hay varios políticos implicados; *the people allegedly involved,* las personas presuntamente implicadas; *are you involved in some kind of trouble?,* ¿estás metido en algún lío?; *you should get more involved in the club's social activities,* deberías participar más en las actividades sociales del club; *don't get involved in anything illegal,* no te metas en nada ilegal. **3** *(engrossed)* absorto,-a, enfrascado,-a; *(busy)* ocupado,-a: *you're too involved in your work,* estás demasiado ocupado con tu trabajo. **4** *(included, entailed)*: *I don't think you understand what's involved,* creo que no entiendes lo que esto implica; *he had no idea of the work involved,* no tenía ni idea del trabajo que suponía; *there's too much money involved,* hay demasiado dinero en juego. **5** *(emotionally)* enredado,-a, liado,-a, enrollado,-a: *she's involved with a married man,* tiene relaciones con un hombre casado; *I don't want to get involved with anyone right now,* no quiero una relación seria con alguien ahora mismo.

● **to be involved in an accident,** sufrir un accidente.
involvement [ɪn'vɒlvmənt] **1** *n* (*participation*) participación *f: the active involvement of hundreds of children,* la participación activa de cientos de niños. **2** (*in crime*) complicidad *f,* implicación *f: his involvement in the swindle,* su implicación en la estafa. **3** (*affair*) enredo, lío, relación *f.*
■ **military involvement,** intervención *f* militar.
invulnerability [ɪnvʌlnərə'bɪlətɪ] *n* invulnerabilidad *f.*
invulnerable [ɪn'vʌlnərəbəl] *adj* invulnerable.
inward ['ɪnwəd] **1** *adj* interior. **- 2** *adv* hacia dentro.
inwardly ['ɪnwədlɪ] *adv* interiormente, por dentro.
inwardness ['ɪnwədnəs] *n* espiritualidad *f.*
inwards ['ɪnwədz] *adv* hacia dentro.
iodine ['aɪədiːn] *n* yodo.
iodise ['aɪədaɪz] *t →* **iodize.**
iodize ['aɪədaɪz] *t* yodar.
ion ['aɪən] *n* ion *m.*
Ionian [aɪ'əʊnɪən] *adj* jónico,-a.
Ionic [aɪ'ɒnɪk] *adj* jónico,-a.
ionise ['aɪənaɪz] *t →* **ionize.**
ionization [aɪənaɪ'zeɪʃən] *n* ionización *f.*
ionize ['aɪənaɪz] *t* ionizar.
iota [aɪ'əʊtə] *n* pizca, ápice *m.*
● **not an iota,** ni jota.
IOU ['aɪ'əʊ'juː] *abbr* (*I owe you*) pagaré *m.*
IPA ['aɪ'piː'eɪ] *abbr* (*International Phonetic Alphabet*) Alfabeto Fonético Internacional; (*abbreviation*) AFI *m.*
IQ ['aɪ'kjuː] *abbr* (*intelligence quotient*) coeficiente *m* de inteligencia; (*abbreviation*) CI *m.*
IRA ['aɪ'ɑːr'eɪ] *abbr* (*Irish Republican Army*) Ejército Republicano irlandés; (*abbreviation*) IRA *m.*
Iran [ɪ'rɑːn] *n* Irán.
Iranian [ɪ'reɪnɪən] **1** *adj* iranio,-a, iraní. **- 2** *n* (*person*) iranio,-a, iraní. **3** (*language*) iranio.
Iraq [ɪ'rɑːk] *n* Irak.
Iraqi [ɪ'rɑːkɪ] **1** *adj* iraquí. **- 2** *n* iraquí *mf.*
irascible [ɪ'ræsɪbəl] *adj fml* irascible, colérico,-a, iracundo,-a.
irate [aɪ'reɪt] *adj fml* airado,-a, iracundo,-a, furioso,-a.
irately [aɪ'reɪtlɪ] *adv* airadamente.
IRBM ['aɪ'ɑː'biː'em] *abbr* (*intermediate-range ballistic missile*) proyectil *m* balístico de alcance intermedio; (*abbreviation*) PBAI *m.*
ire ['aɪər] *n fml* ira, cólera, enojo, enfado.
Ireland ['aɪələnd] *n* Irlanda.
■ **Northern Ireland,** Irlanda del norte.
iridescence [ɪrɪ'desəns] *n fml* iridiscencia.
iridescent [ɪrɪ'desənt] *adj fml* iridiscente.
iris ['aɪrɪs] **1** *n* (*of eye*) iris *m inv.* **2** BOT lirio.
Irish ['aɪrɪʃ] **1** *adj* irlandés,-esa. **- 2** *n* (*language*) irlandés *m.* **- 3 the Irish,** *npl* los irlandeses *mpl.*
■ **Irish coffee,** café *m* irlandés. ‖ **Irish Sea,** Mar *m* de Irlanda. ‖ **Irish setter,** setter *m* irlandés. ‖ **Irish stew,** estofado irlandés. ‖ **Northern Irish,** norirlandés,-esa. ‖ **Northern Irishman,** norirlandés *m.* ‖ **Northern Irishwoman,** norirlandesa.
Irishman ['aɪrɪʃmən] *n* irlandés *m.*
▲ *pl* **Irishmen** ['aɪrɪʃmən].
Irishwoman ['aɪrɪʃwʊmən] *n* irlandesa.
▲ *pl* **Irishwomen** ['aɪrɪʃwɪmɪn].
irk [ɜːk] *t* fastidiar, molestar: *it irks me to see people drop rubbish on the pavement,* me fastidia ver gente que tira la basura en la acera.
irksome ['ɜːksəm] *adj* fastidioso,-a, molesto,-a, pesado,-a: *an irksome journey,* un viaje molesto; *how irksome!,* ¡qué fastidio!

iron ['aɪən] **1** *n* (*metal*) hierro: *cast iron,* hierro colado; *scrap iron,* chatarra; *wrought iron,* hierro forjado. **2** (*appliance*) plancha. **3** (*for golf*) hierro, palo de hierro. **- 4** *adj* de hierro. **- 5** *t* (*clothes*) planchar. **- 6** *i* planchar. **- 7 irons,** *npl* (*fetters*) grillos *mpl,* grilletes *mpl.*
◆ **to iron out 1** *t sep* (*clothes*) planchar. **2** *fig* (*problem, difficulty, etc*) resolver, solucionar.
● **to have an iron constitution,** ser de hierro, tener una salud de hierro. ‖ **to have a will of iron / have an iron will,** tener una voluntad de hierro. ‖ **to have many irons in the fire,** tener muchas cosas entre manos. ‖ **to put/clap sb. in irons,** encadenar a algn. ‖ **to strike while the iron is hot,** lo mejor es actuar de inmediato.
■ **Iron Age,** Edad de Hierro. ‖ **Iron Cross,** cruz *f* de hierro. ‖ **Iron Curtain,** telón *m* de acero. ‖ **iron foundry,** fundición *f* (de hierro). ‖ **iron grey,** gris oscuro. ‖ **iron lung,** pulmón *m* de acero. ‖ **iron maiden,** dama de hierro. ‖ **iron ore,** mineral *m* de hierro.
ironic [aɪ'rɒnɪk] *adj* irónico,-a.
ironical [aɪ'rɒnɪkəl] *adj* irónico,-a.
ironically [aɪ'rɒnɪklɪ] **1** *adv* (*sarcastically*) irónicamente, con ironía. **2** (*strangely*) curiosamente.
ironing ['aɪənɪŋ] *n* (*clothes to be ironed*) ropa por planchar, plancha; (*clothes ironed*) ropa planchada, plancha.
● **to do the ironing,** planchar (la ropa).
■ **ironing board,** tabla de planchar.
ironmonger ['aɪənmʌŋgər] *n* GB ferretero,-a.
■ **ironmonger's (shop),** ferretería.
ironmongery ['aɪənmʌŋgərɪ] *n* GB ferretería.
ironstone ['aɪənstəʊn] *n* mineral *m* de hierro.
ironware ['aɪənweər] *n* objetos *mpl* de hierro, ferretería.
ironwork ['aɪənwɜːk] *n* herraje *m.*
ironworks ['aɪənwɜːks] *npl* GB fundición *f* (de hierro).
irony ['aɪrənɪ] *n* ironía: *the irony (of it) is that ...,* lo irónico (del caso) es que ...; *one of life's little ironies,* una de las pequeñas ironías de la vida.
▲ *pl* **ironies.**
irradiate [ɪ'reɪdɪeɪt] *t fml* irradiar.
irrational [ɪ'ræʃənəl] *adj* irracional.
irreconcilable [ɪ'rekənsaɪləbəl] *adj fml* irreconciliable, inconciliable.
irrecoverable [ɪrɪ'kʌvərəbəl] *adj fml* irrecuperable.
irredeemable [ɪrɪ'diːməbəl] **1** *adj fml* irremediable. **2** FIN no amortizable.
irreducible [ɪrɪ'djuːsəbəl] *adj fml* irreducible, irreductible.
irrefutable [ɪrɪ'fjuːtəbəl] *adj fml* irrefutable.
irrefutably [ɪrɪ'fjuːtəblɪ] *adv* irrefutablemente.
irregular [ɪ'regjələr] **1** *adj* (*gen*) irregular; (*uneven*) desigual: *irregular hours,* horario irregular; *irregular coastline,* costa recortada. **2** (*unusual, abnormal*) raro,-a, anormal; (*against the rules*) inadmisible. **3** (*troops*) irregular. **- 4 irregulars,** *npl* (*troops*) tropas *fpl* irregulares.
■ **irregular verb,** verbo irregular.
irregularity [ɪregjə'lærɪtɪ] **1** *n* (*gen*) irregularidad *f;* (*unevenness*) desigualdad *f.* **2** (*abnormality*) anormalidad *f,* anomalía.
▲ *pl* **irregularities.**
irregularly [ɪ'regjələlɪ] *adv* irregularmente, con irregularidad, sin regularidad.
irrelevance [ɪ'reləvəns] *n* falta de pertinencia.
irrelevancy [ɪ'reləvənsɪ] **1** *n* (*state*) falta de pertinencia. **2** (*remark*) observación *f* que no viene al caso. **3** (*matter*) cosa que no viene al caso.
irrelevant [ɪ'reləvənt] **1** *adj* (*unimportant - fact, detail, etc*) irrelevante. **2** (*out of place*) que no viene al caso: *that's*

irrelevant, eso no tiene nada que ver, eso no viene al caso.

irrelevantly [ɪ'reləvəntlɪ] *adv* sin venir al caso: *she said irrelevantly,* dijo, sin que eso viniera al caso.

irreligious [ɪrɪ'lɪdʒəs] *adj* irreligioso,-a.

irremediable [ɪrɪ'miːdɪəbəl] *adj* irremediable.

irremediably [ɪrɪ'miːdɪəblɪ] *adv* irremediablemente.

irremovable [ɪrɪ'muːvəbəl] *adj* inamovible.

irreparable [ɪ'repərəbəl] *adj* irreparable.

irreplaceable [ɪrɪ'pleɪsəbəl] *adj* irremplazable, insustituible.

irrepressible [ɪrɪ'presəbəl] *adj* incontenible, incontrolable.

irreproachable [ɪrɪ'prəʊtʃəbəl] *adj* irreprochable, intachable.

irresistible [ɪrɪ'zɪstəbəl] 1 *adj* (*temptation, impulse, etc*) irresistible: *an irresistible urge,* un impulso irrefrenable. 2 (*person, thing*) irresistible.

irresistibly [ɪrɪ'zɪstəblɪ] *adv* irresistiblemente.

irresolute [ɪ'rezəluːt] *adj fml* indeciso,-a, vacilante, irresoluto,-a.

irrespective [ɪrɪ'spektɪv] **irrespective of,** *prep* sin tener en cuenta, sin tomar en consideración, independientemente de.

irresponsibility [ɪrɪspɒnsə'bɪlətɪ] *n* irresponsabilidad *f,* falta de seriedad.

irresponsible [ɪrɪ'spɒnsəbəl] *adj* irresponsable, poco serio,-a.

irresponsibly [ɪrɪ'spɒnsəblɪ] *adv* irresponsablemente.

irretrievable [ɪrɪ'triːvəbəl] *adj fml* (*object*) irrecuperable; (*mistake, damage, harm, etc*) irreparable; (*loss, situation, breakdown, etc*) irremediable.

irreverance [ɪ'revərəns] *n* irreverencia, falta de respeto.

irreverent [ɪ'revərənt] *adj* irreverente, irrespetuoso,-a.

irreverently [ɪ'revərəntlɪ] *adv* irreverentemente.

irreversible [ɪrɪ'vɜːsəbəl] *adj* (*process, damage*) irreversible; (*judgement, decision*) irrevocable.

irrevocable [ɪ'revəkəbəl] *adj fml* irrevocable, inalterable.

irrigable ['ɪrɪgəbəl] *adj* irrigable, regadío,-a.

irrigate ['ɪrɪgeɪt] 1 *t* AGR regar, irrigar. 2 MED irrigar.

irrigation [ɪrɪ'geɪʃən] *n* AGR riego, irrigación *f.*
■ **irrigation channel,** acequia, canal *m* de riego. ‖ **irrigation farming,** cultivo de regadío. ‖ **irrigation system,** sistema *m* de regadío.

irritability [ɪrɪtə'bɪlətɪ] *n* irritabilidad *f,* mal humor *m.*

irritable ['ɪrɪtəbəl] *adj* irritable, de mal humor.

irritably ['ɪrɪtəblɪ] *adv* con tono malhumorado, de mal humor.

irritant ['ɪrɪtənt] 1 *adj* irritante. – 2 *n* agente *m* irritante. 3 *fig* molestia, motivo de irritación.

irritate ['ɪrɪteɪt] 1 *t* (*annoy*) irritar, molestar, fastidiar. 2 MED (*cause discomfort*) irritar; (*make inflamed*) inflamar.
● **to get irritate,** (*angry*) irritarse, enfadarse.

irritating ['ɪrɪteɪtɪŋ] 1 *adj* (*annoying*) irritante, molesto,-a, fastidioso,-a, pesado,-a. 2 MED irritante.

irritation [ɪrɪ'teɪʃən] 1 *n* MED irritación *f.* 2 (*cause of annoyance*) molestia, fastidio. 3 (*anger*) mal humor *m,* enfado, irritación *f.*

irruption [ɪ'rʌpʃən] *n fml* irrupción *f.*

is [ɪz] *3rd pers sing pres* → **be.**

Islam ['ɪzlɑːm] *n* islam *m.*

Islamic [ɪz'læmɪk] *adj* islámico,-a.

island ['aɪlənd] 1 *n* isla. – 2 *adj* isleño,-a.
■ **safety island,** US isla de peatones, isleta, refugio. ‖ **traffic island,** isla de peatones, isleta, refugio.

islander ['aɪləndəʳ] *n* isleño,-a.

isle [aɪl] *n* isla.
■ **the British Isles,** las Islas Británicas.

islet ['aɪlət] *n* islote *m.*

isobar ['aɪsəbɑːʳ] *n* isobara.

isolate ['aɪsəleɪt] *t* aislar (**from,** de): *the boy has been isolated from the others,* el niño ha sido aislado de los otros; *scientists have isolated the germ,* los científicos han aislado el microbio.

isolated ['aɪsəleɪtɪd] 1 *adj* (*solitary*) aislado,-a, apartado,-a: *an isolated house,* una casa aislada; *I live a very isolated life,* llevo una vida muy solitaria. 2 (*single*) aislado,-a, único,-a, excepcional: *an isolated case,* un caso aislado.

isolation [aɪsə'leɪʃən] *n* aislamiento (**from,** de): *a feeling of isolation from the real world,* una sensación de aislamiento del mundo real; *she prefers to work in complete isolation,* prefiere trabajar completamente aislada; *the gradual isolation of the radicals,* el aislamiento gradual de los extremistas.
● **in isolation,** (*separately*) por separado: *each problem must be looked at in isolation,* hay que examinar cada problema por separado.
■ **isolation hospital,** hospital de aislamiento. ‖ **isolation ward,** sala de aislamiento.

isolationism [aɪsə'leɪʃənɪzəm] *n* aislacionismo.

isolationist [aɪsə'leɪʃənɪst] 1 *adj* aislacionista. – 2 *n* aislacionista *mf.*

isometric [aɪsə'metrɪk] *adj* isométrico,-a.

isosceles [aɪ'sɒsəliːz] *adj* isósceles.
■ **isosceles triangle,** triángulo isósceles.

isotherm ['aɪsəθɜːm] *n* isotermo.

isotope ['aɪsətəʊp] *n* isótopo.

Israel ['ɪzreɪl] *n* Israel.

Israeli [ɪz'reɪlɪ] 1 *adj* israelí. – 2 *n* israelí *mf.*

Israelite ['ɪzrɪlaɪt] 1 *adj* israelita. – 2 *n* israelita *mf.*

issue ['ɪʃuː] 1 *n* (*subject, topic*) tema *m,* cuestión *f,* asunto: *where do you stand on this issue?,* ¿cuál es tu postura respecto a esta cuestión?; *she raised the issue of the sackings,* planteó el tema de los despidos; *the issue is whether we're going to support them or not,* la cuestión es si vamos a apoyarlos o no; *we must settle this issue once and for all,* hay que zanjar este asunto de una vez por todas. 2 (*of newspaper, magazine, etc*) número: *have you got this month's issue of Vax?,* ¿tienes el Vax de este mes?; *do you sell back issues?,* ¿vendéis números atrasados? 3 (*of stamps, shares, back notes, etc*) emisión *f;* (*of book*) publicación *f.* 4 (*of passport, licence*) expedición *f.* 5 (*of equipment, supplies, etc*) distribución *f,* reparto, suministro: *the issue of firearms to soldiers,* el suministro de armas de fuego a los soldados; *where's the point of issue?,* ¿dónde está el punto de reparto? 6 *fml* (*emergence - of water, blood*) flujo. 7 *fml* (*children*) descendencia. 8 *fml* (*result, outcome*) resultado, consecuencia, desenlace *m.* – 9 *t* (*book, article*) publicar. 10 (*stamps, shares, banknotes, etc*) emitir. 11 (*passport, visa*) expedir. 12 (*equipment, supplies, etc*) distribuir, repartir, suministrar, proporcionar: *each soldier will be issued with a gun,* a cada soldado se le suministrará un arma; *the homeless were issued with blankets,* distribuyeron mantas entre los sin techo. 13 (*order, instruction*) dar; (*statement, warning*) dar, hacer público; (*writ, summons*) dictar, expedir; (*decree*) promulgar; (*warrant*) expedir. – 14 *i fml* (*liquid, blood*) fluir, manar; (*smell etc*) salir. 15 *fml* (*result*) resultar (**from,** de), provenir (**from,** de), derivar(se) (**from,** de).
● **at issue,** en cuestión, en discusión: *his ability is not*

at issue, su capacidad está en tela de juicio; *our children's future is at issue here,* aquí estamos hablando del futuro de nuestros hijos. ‖ **to address an issue,** tratar una cuestión. ‖ **to cloud/confuse the issue,** complicar el asunto. ‖ **to die without issue,** morir sin dejar descendencia. ‖ **to evade/duck the issue,** eludir el problema, evitar el tema. ‖ **to force the issue,** forzar una decisión. ‖ **to make an issue (out) of sth.,** dar demasiada importancia a algo, insistir demasiado sobre algo. ‖ **to take issue with sb.,** manifestar su desacuerdo con algn., discrepar con algn.: *she took issue with him about his ideas,* discrepó con él por sus ideas.
■ **side issue,** cuestión *f* secundaria.

Istanbul [ɪstænˈbʊl] *n* Estambul.

isthmus [ˈɪsməs] *n* istmo.

it [ɪt] **1** *pron (subject)* él, ella, ello: *where's my supper? it's in the oven!,* ¿dónde está mi cena? ¡está en el horno!; *whose is this coat? it's mine!,* ¿de quién es este abrigo? ¡es mío!; *is it a boy or a girl?,* ¿es niño o niña?; *who's that? who is it? it's me!,* ¿quién eres? ¿quién es? ¡soy yo! **2** *(object - direct)* lo, la; *(- indirect)* le: *I doubt it,* lo dudo; *I've just got this letter. Can you read it for me?,* acabo de recibir esta carta. ¿Me la puedes leer?; *do you like skiing? yes, I love it,* ¿te gusta esquiar? sí, me encanta; *she went up to the horse and patted it,* se acercó al caballo y lo acarició; *can you manage that bag? Give it to me,* ¿puedes con esa bolsa? Dámela. **3** *(after prep)* él, ella, ello: *a vase with flowers in it,* un florero con flores dentro; *the train was still there so I ran for it,* el tren aún estaba allí así que corrí para cogerlo; *you're not frightened of it, are you?,* no le tienes miedo, ¿verdad?; *tell me about it,* explícamelo, cuéntamelo. **4** *(abstract)* ello: *let's get on with it,* vamos a por ello. **5** *(impersonal) no se traduce: it's cold,* hace frío; *it's too early,* es demasiado temprano; *it's six o'clock,* son las seis; *it's Wednesday,* es miércoles; *it's cloudy,* está nublado; *it's not far,* no está lejos; *it's impossible,* es imposible; *it's importante,* es importante; *it's worth it,* vale la pena; *it doesn't matter,* no importa; *what's it like?,* ¿cómo es?; *it cost a fiver,* costó cinco libras; *it's true,* es verdad; *it seems (that) she failed,* parece que suspendió.
● **if it weren't for/if it hadn't been for,** si no fuera por/si no hubiera sido por. ‖ **that's it,** *(that is the end)* ya está, se acabó; *(agreeing)* eso es, eso mismo; *(disapproving)* basta ya. ‖ **this is it,** ha llegado el momento, ha llegado la hora. ‖ **how's it going?,** ¿qué tal?, ¿cómo va todo?

IT [ˈaɪˈtiː] *abbr (information technology)* informática.

Italian [ɪˈtæljən] **1** *adj* italiano,-a. – **2** *n (person)* italiano,-a. **3** *(language)* italiano.

italic [ɪˈtælɪks] *adj* (letra) cursiva.
● **in italics,** en cursiva. ‖ **my italics,** la cursiva es mía.

Italy [ˈɪtəlɪ] *n* Italia.

ITC [ˈaɪˈtiːˈsiː] *abbr* GB *(Independent Television Commission) ente que regula las televisiones privadas.*
▲ *Véase también IBA.*

itch [ɪtʃ] **1** *n* MED picazón *f,* picor *m.* **2** *fam fig (strong desire)* deseo, anhelo, ansia: *an itch to travel,* un deseo de via-

jar. – **3** *i* picar: *my feet itch,* me pican los pies; *I'm itching all over,* me pica todo; *this blanket itches,* esta manta pica.
● **to be itching for sth./to do sth.,** estar impaciente por hacer algo, morirse de ganas de hacer algo: *I'm itching to go,* me muero por ir; *he was itching to tell her,* se moría de ganas de decírselo.

itchiness [ˈɪtʃɪnəs] *n* picor *m,* picazón *m.*

itchy [ˈɪtʃɪ] *adj* que pica: *this jumper's itchy,* este jersey me pica.
● **to feel itchy,** picar, tener picor. ‖ **to get/have itchy feet,** tener ganas de viajar.
▲ *comp itchier, superl itchiest.*

it'd [ˈɪtəd] **1** *contr* it had. **2** it would.

item [ˈaɪtəm] **1** *n (on list)* artículo, cosa; *(in collection)* pieza. **2** *(on agenda)* asunto, punto. **3** *(on bill)* partida, asiento. **4** *(in show)* número. – **5** *adv* también.
■ **item of clothing,** prenda de vestir.

itemize [ˈaɪtəmaɪz] **1** *t (contents)* hacer una lista de. **2** *(bill)* detallar.

iterate [ˈɪtəreɪt] *t fml* iterar.

itinerant [ɪˈtɪnərənt] *adj* itinerante, ambulante.

itinerary [aɪˈtɪnərərɪ] *n* itinerario, ruta.
▲ *pl itineraries.*

it'll [ˈɪtəl] *contr* it will.

its [ɪts] *adj (one thing)* su; *(more than one thing)* sus: *the cat washed its paws,* el gato se lavó las patas; *the baby's in its pram,* el bebé está en su cochecito; *the film has its good points,* la película tiene sus puntos buenos.

it's [ɪts] **1** *contr* → **it is.** **2** → **it has.**

itself [ɪtˈself] **1** *pron (reflexive)* se: *the bird preened itself,* el pájaro se arregló las plumas; *Barcelona has opened itself up to the sea,* Barcelona se ha abierto al mar. **2** *(emphatic)* en sí: *the house itself is quite old,* la casa en sí es bastante vieja; *the job itself isn't that difficult,* el trabajo en sí no es muy difícil; *she is politeness itself,* es la cortesía personificada. **3** *(after prep)* sí: *the committee wants to keep all the profits for itself,* el comité quiere guardar todos los beneficios para sí; *each dog has a kennel to itself,* cada perro tiene su propia casita; *the idea in itself isn't bad,* la idea en sí no está mal; *the first course was a meal in itself,* el primer plato ya era una comida de por sí.
● **by itself,** solo,-a: *it switches off by itself,* se apaga solo, se apaga automáticamente; *the baby did it all by itself,* el niño lo hizo él solo.

ITV [ˈaɪˈtiːˈviː] *abbr* GB *(Independent Television) conjunto de televisiones privadas.*

I've [aɪv] *contr* I have.

ivory [ˈaɪvərɪ] **1** *n (substance)* marfil *m; (colour)* color *m* marfil. – **2** *adj* de marfil. – **3** **ivories,** *npl (objects)* objetos *mpl* de marfil; *(teeth)* dientes *mpl; (piano keys)* teclas *fpl.*
● **an ivory tower,** una torre de marfil.
■ **Ivory Coast,** Costa de Marfil.

ivy [ˈaɪvɪ] *n* hiedra, yedra.
■ **Ivy League,** *ocho prestigiosas universidades privadas del nordeste de los Estados Unidos*

J

J, J [dʒeɪ] *n (the letter)* J, j *f.*

jab [dʒæb] **1** *n* pinchazo; *(with elbow)* codazo. **2** *fam* inyección *f: a flu jab,* una inyección contra la gripe. **3** *(in boxing)* gancho. – **4** *t* pinchar; *(with elbow)* dar un codazo a: *someone jabbed me in the back with their elbow,* me dieron un codazo en la espalda; *she jabbed a knife into the tyre,* clavó un cuchillo en el neumático.
▲ *(verbo)* pt & pp **jabbed,** ger **jabbing.**

jabber ['dʒæbə'] **1** *n* parloteo. – **2** *t* farfullar, decir atropellada e ininteligiblemente: *she jabbered out a confused explanation,* farfulló una explicación confusa e ininteligible. – **3** *i* hablar atropellada e ininteligiblemente: *loads of people jabbering away in foreign languages,* un montón de gente parloteando en lenguas extranjeras.

jabbering ['dʒæbərɪŋ] *n* parloteo.

jacaranda [dʒækə'rændə] *n* jacarandá.

jack [dʒæk] **1** *n* AUTO gato. **2** *(in cards)* jota; *(Spanish pack)* sota. **3** *(in bowls)* boliche *m.* **4** *(flag)* banderín *m* de popa. **5** ELEC enchufe *m.*
◆ **to jack in** *t sep* GB *sl* dejar, colgar: *he jacked in his job and joined the navy,* dejó su trabajo y se alistó en la armada. ‖ **to jack off 1** *i* US *taboo* meneársela. – **2** *t sep* US *taboo* masturbar. ‖ **to jack up 1** *t sep (car)* levantar con gato. **2** *(prices)* subir.
■ **jack plug,** ELEC jack *m,* clavija.

Jack [dʒæk] *prn (John)* Juanito.
● **before you can say Jack Robinson,** en un periquete, en un santiamén. ‖ **every man Jack (of them),** hasta el último. ‖ **I'm all right Jack!,** ¡aquí me las den todas! ‖ **Jack of all trades, master of none,** quien mucho abarca poco aprieta.
■ **Jack Frost,** *personificación del hielo.* ‖ **Jack the Ripper,** Jack el Destripador.

jackal ['dʒækɔːl] *n* chacal *m.*

jackass ['dʒækæs] *n fam* burro, mastuerzo.

jackboot ['dʒækbuːt] **1** *n* bota militar. **2** *fig* represión *f.*

jackdaw ['dʒækdɔː] *n* grajilla.

jacket ['dʒækɪt] **1** *n (in general)* chaqueta; *(of suit)* americana; *(leather etc)* cazadora. **2** *(of book)* sobrecubierta. **3** US *(of record)* funda.
■ **jacket potato,** patata asada *(con su piel).*

jackhammer ['dʒækhæmə'] *n* martillo neumático.

jack-knife ['dʒæknaɪf] **1** *n* navaja. – **2** *i (lorry)* dar un coletazo.

jack-of-all-trades ['dʒækəvɔːltreɪdz] **1** *n (handyman)* manitas *m.* **2** *pej* persona de muchos oficios.

jackpot ['dʒækpɒt] *n (premio)* gordo.
● **to hit the jackpot,** tocarle a algn. el gordo.

Jacobean [dʒækə'bɪən] **1** *adj* de la época de Jacobo I de Inglaterra (1603-1625). – **2** *n* persona que vivió durante el reinado de Jacobo I.

Jacobin ['dʒækəbɪn] **1** *adj* jacobino,-a. – **2** *n* jacobino,-a.

Jacobinism ['dʒækəbɪnɪzəm] *n* jacobinismo.

Jacobite ['dʒækəbaɪt] **1** *adj* jacobita. – **2** *n* jacobita *mf.*

jacuzzi [dʒ'kuːzɪ] *n* jacuzzi *m,* bañera de hidromasaje.
▲ Es marca registrada.

jade¹ [dʒeɪd] *n* jade *m.*

jade² [dʒeɪd] **1** *n (horse)* rocín *m.* **2** *(whore)* mujerzuela.

jaded ['dʒeɪdɪd] *adj* agotado,-a, cansado,-a.

jaffa ['dʒæfə] **jaffa (orange),** *n* naranja grande *(procedente de Israel).*

jag [dʒæg] *n* GB *fam* juerga, borrachera.

jagged ['dʒægɪd] *adj* irregular, dentado,-a.

jaguar ['dʒægjuə'] *n* jaguar *m.*

jaguarondi [dʒægwə'rɒndɪ] *n* yaguarundi *m.*

jail [dʒeɪl] **1** *n* cárcel *f,* prisión *f.* – **2** *t* encarcelar: *he was jailed for life,* lo condenaron a cadena perpetua.

jailbird ['dʒeɪlbɜːd] *n* preso,-a reincidente.

jailbreak ['dʒeɪlbreɪk] *n* fuga de la cárcel.

jailer ['dʒeɪlə'] *n* carcelero,-a.

jailhouse ['dʒeɪlhaus] *n* US cárcel *f.*

Jainism ['dʒaɪnɪzəm] *n* jainismo.

Jakarta ['dʒəkɑːtə] *n* Yakarta.

jalopy [dʒə'lɒpɪ] *n fam (car)* cacharro.
▲ *pl* **jalopies.**

jam¹ [dʒæm] **1** *n* mermelada, confitura. **2** *fam (luck)* churra.
■ **jam jar,** bote *m* de mermelada.

jam² [dʒæm] **1** *n (tight spot)* aprieto, apuro. – **2** *t (fill)* abarrotar, atestar: *thousands of people jammed the streets,* miles de personas abarrotaban las calles. **3** *(cram)* embutir, meter a la fuerza: *she jammed all her things into the bag,* embutió todas sus cosas en la bolsa. **4** RAD interferir: *the rebels jammed government radio broadcasts,* los rebeldes interfirieron las emisiones de radio del gobierno. **5** *(block)* bloquear: *the switchboard was jammed with calls of complaint,* las llamadas de protesta bloquearon la centralita. – **6** *i (stick)* atrancarse: *the door is jammed, I can't open it,* la puerta se ha atrancado, no puedo abrirla. **7** *(machine parts)* atascarse, agarrotarse: *the lock has jammed, it won't open,* se ha atascado la cerradura, no abre. **8** MUS tocar en una sesión improvisada de jazz o rock.
● **to get into a jam,** meterse en un apuro. ‖ **to jam the brakes on,** pegar un frenazo, frenar de golpe.
■ **jam session,** sesión improvisada de jazz o rock.

Jamaica [dʒə'meɪkə] *n* Jamaica.

Jamaican [dʒə'meɪkən] **1** *adj* jamaicano,-a. – **2** *n* jamaicano,-a.

jamb [dʒæm] *n* jamba.

jamboree [dʒæmbə'riː] **1** *n* juerga. **2** *(scout meeting)* reunión *f* de boy-scouts.

jamming ['dʒæmɪŋ] *n (of radio)* interferencia.

jammy ['dʒæmɪ] **1** *adj* lleno,-a de mermelada: *don't touch that book with your jammy fingers!,* ¡no toques el libro con los dedos llenos de mermelada! **2** *fam* suer-

tudo,-a: *what a jammy so-and-so he is!,* ¡vaya suerte que tiene el tío!
▲ *comp* **jammier**, *superl* **jammiest**.
jam-packed [dʒæm'pækt] *adj fam* de bote en bote.
Jan ['dʒænjuərɪ] *abbr* (*January*) enero.
jangle ['dʒæŋɡəl] **1** *i* sonar de un modo discordante. – **2** *t* hacer sonar de un modo discordante. – **3** *n* sonido discordante.
janitor ['dʒænɪtə'] *n* conserje *m*, portero.
January ['dʒænjuərɪ] *n* enero.
▲ *Véase también* **March**.
japan [dʒə'pæn] **1** *n* laca de China. – **2** *t* barnizar con laca de China.
Japan [dʒə'pæn] *n* (el) Japón *m*.
■ **Sea of Japan**, Mar *m* del Japón.
Japanese [dʒæpə'niːz] **1** *adj* japonés,-esa. – **2** *n* (*person*) japonés,-esa. **3** (*language*) japonés *m*. – **4 the Japanese**, *npl* los japoneses *mpl*.
jape [dʒeɪp] **1** *n dated* chanza. – **2** *i dated* chancearse.
jar [dʒɑː'] **1** *n* (*glass*) tarro, bote *m*: *a jar of strawberry jam,* un tarro de mermelada de fresa. **2** (*earthenware*) vasija, tinaja. **3** (*shake, shock*) sacudida: *it gave me a bit of a jar,* me chocó bastante. **4** *fam* (*drink*) copa: *let's go and have a few jars!,* ¡vamos a tomar unas copas! – **5** *t* (*shake*) golpear, dar un golpe a: *the bus braked sharply and jarred me against the window,* el autobús frenó en seco y me dió un golpe contra la ventana; *he fell and jarred his knee,* se cayó y le crujió la rodilla. – **6** *i* (*sounds*) chirriar, discordar: *this kind of music jars on my nerves,* este tipo de música me pone los nervios de punta. **7** (*colours*) no pegar, desentonar.
▲ (*verbo*) *pt & pp* **jarred**, *ger* **jarring**.
jargon ['dʒɑːɡən] *n* jerga, jerigonza.
jarring ['dʒɑːrɪŋ] *adj* discordante.
jasmine ['dʒæzmɪn] *n* jazmín *m*.
jasper ['dʒæspə'] *n* jaspe *m*.
jaundice ['dʒɔːndɪs] *n* ictericia.
jaundiced ['dʒɔːndɪst] *adj fig* cínico,-a.
jaunt [dʒɔːnt] **1** *n* excursión *f*. – **2** *i* ir de excursión.
jaunty ['dʒɔːntɪ] *adj* garboso,-a.
▲ *comp* **jauntier**, *superl* **jauntiest**.
Java ['dʒɑːvə] *n* Java.
■ **Java man**, Hombre *m* de Java. ‖ **Java Sea**, Mar *m* de Java.
Javan ['dʒɑːvən] **1** *adj* javanés,-esa. – **2** *n* javanés,-esa.
Javanese [dʒɑːvə'niːz] **1** *adj* javanés,-esa. – **2** *n* (*person*) javanés,-esa. **3** (*language*) javanés *m*. – **4 the Javanese**, *npl* los javaneses *mpl*.
javelin ['dʒævəlɪn] *n* jabalina.
● **to throw the javelin**, lanzar la jabalina.
■ **javelin competition**, lanzamiento de jabalina.
jaw [dʒɔː] **1** *n* ANAT mandíbula. **2** ZOOL mandíbula, quijada, carrillera. **3** *fam* (*talk*) charla: *we had a really good jaw,* tuvimos una buena charla. – **4** *i fam* (*talk*) charlar, darle a la sinhueso.
■ **upper jaw**, maxilar *m* superior. ‖ **lower jaw**, maxilar *m* inferior.
jawbone ['dʒɔːbəun] **1** *n* (*of person*) mandíbula, maxilar *m*. **2** (*of animal*) quijada.
jawbreaker ['dʒɔːbreɪkə'] *n sl* trabalenguas *m*.
jay [dʒeɪ] *n* arrendajo común.
jaywalk ['dʒeɪwɔːk] *t* cruzar la calle de manera imprudente: *he was fined for jaywalking,* lo multaron por cruzar la calle de manera imprudente.
jaywalker ['dʒeɪwɔːlkə'] *n* peatón *m* imprudente.
jazz [dʒæz] **1** *n* jazz *m*. – **2** *adj* de jazz, jazzístico,-a.
◆ **to jazz up** *t sep* (*in general*) hacer más alegre, dar vida a; (*party*) animar.

● **and all that jazz,** y demás, y toda la pesca, y todo el rollo. ‖ **don't give me that jazz!,** ¡no me vengas con cuentos!
■ **jazz band**, conjunto de jazz.
jazzy ['dʒæzɪ] **1** *adj fam fig* llamativo,-a. **2** MUS jazzístico,-a.
▲ *comp* **jazzier**, *superl* **jazziest**.
jealous ['dʒeləs] **1** *adj* celoso,-a. **2** (*envious*) envidioso,-a.
● **to be jealous of sb.,** tener celos de algn., estar celoso,-a de algn. ‖ **to make sb. jealous,** poner celoso,-a a a algn.
jealously ['dʒeləslɪ] **1** *adv* celosamente. **2** (*enviously*) con envidia.
jealousy ['dʒeləsɪ] **1** *n* celos *mpl*. **2** (*envy*) envidia.
▲ *pl* **jealousies**.
jeans [dʒiːnz] *npl* vaqueros *mpl*, tejanos *mpl*.
Jedda ['dʒedə] *n* Yeda.
jeep [dʒiːp] *n* jeep *m*, todoterreno.
jeer [dʒɪə'] **1** *i* (*mock*) burlarse (**at**, de), mofarse (**at**, de). – **2** *t* (*boo*) abuchear. – **3** *i* (*boo*) abuchear. – **4 jeers**, *npl* (*booing*) abucheos *mpl*; (*mocking*) burlas *fpl*, mofas *fpl*, befas *fpl*.
jeering ['dʒɪərɪŋ] **1** *n* (*booing*) abucheos *mpl*; (*mocking*) burlas *fpl*, mofas *fpl*, befas *fpl*. – **2** *adj* burlón,-ona.
Jehovah [dʒɪ'həuvə] *n* REL Jehová *m*.
■ **Jehova's Witness**, testigo *mf* de Jehová.
jejune [dʒə'dʒuːn] **1** *adj fml* (*dull*) insulso,-a, insípido,-a. **2** (*childish*) inmaduro,-a.
jell [dʒel] *i* cuajar.
jellied ['dʒelɪd] *adj* CULIN en gelatina.
jello ['dʒeləu] *n* US gelatina, jalea.
jelly ['dʒelɪ] **1** *n* (*in general*) jalea. **2** (*fruit*) gelatina.
■ **jelly baby**, gominola en forma de niño. ‖ **jelly bean**, gominola en forma de judía. ‖ **jelly roll**, US ≈ brazo de gitano.
▲ *pl* **jellies**.
jellyfish ['dʒelɪfɪʃ] *n* medusa.
jemmy ['dʒemɪ] *n* GB palanqueta.
▲ *pl* **jemmies**.
je ne sais quoi [ʒənəseɪ'kwɑː] *n* algo, no sé qué: *it has a certain je ne sais quoi,* tiene un algo, tiene un no sé qué.
jeopardize ['dʒepədaɪz] *t* poner en peligro, hacer peligrar.
jeopardy ['dʒepədɪ] *n* peligro.
● **to be in jeopardy,** estar en peligro, peligrar. ‖ **to put in jeopardy,** poner en peligro, hacer peligrar.
jerboa [dʒɜː'bəuə] *n* jerbo, gerbo.
Jeremiah [dʒerɪ'maɪæd] *n fml* jeremiada.
jerk [dʒɜːk] **1** *n* (*pull*) tirón *m*; (*jolt*) sacudida. **2** *fam* imbécil *mf*, subnormal *mf*. – **3** *t* dar una sacudida a, tirar de. – **4** *i* dar una sacudida.
◆ **to jerk off 1** *i taboo* hacerse una paja. – **2** *t sep* hacer una paja a.
● **with a jerk,** bruscamente.
jerkily ['dʒɜːkɪlɪ] *adv* bruscamente, a tirones, a sacudidas.
jerkin ['dʒɜːkɪn] **1** *n* chaleco. **2** (*historically*) jubón *m*.
jerky ['dʒɜːkɪ] *adj* espasmódico,-a.
▲ *comp* **jerkier**, *superl* **jerkiest**.
Jerry ['dʒerɪ] *n fam pej* alemán,-ana.
▲ *pl* **Jerries**.
jerry-build ['dʒerɪbɪld] *t* construir mal.
▲ *pt & pp* **jerry-built**.
jerry-builder ['dʒerɪbɪldə'] *n* chapucero,-a.

jerry-built ['dʒerɪbɪlt] *adj* mal construido,-a.
jerrycan ['dʒerɪkæn] *n* bidón *m*.
jersey ['dʒɜːzɪ] *n* jersey *m*, suéter *m*.
Jersey ['dʒɜːzɪ] **1** *n* Jersey. **2** (*cow*) vaca jersey.
Jerusalem [dʒə'ruːsələm] *n* Jerusalén.
jest [dʒest] **1** *n* broma. – **2** *i* bromear.
● in jest, en broma.
jester ['dʒestə'] *n* HIST bufón *m*.
Jesuit ['dʒezjʊɪt] *n* jesuita *m*.
Jesuitical [dʒezjʊ'ɪtɪkəl] *adj* jesuítico,-a.
Jesus ['dʒiːzəs] **1** *n* Jesús *m*, Jesucristo. – **2** Jesus!, *interj fam* ¡joder!
■ Jesus Christ, Jesucristo.
jet¹ [dʒet] **1** *n* (*aircraft*) reactor *m*. **2** (*stream*) chorro. **3** (*outlet*) boquilla, mechero. – **4** *i* salir a chorro. **5** *fam* viajar en avión.
■ jet engine, reactor *m*. ‖ jet foil, deslizador *m*. ‖ jet lag, jet lag *m*, desarreglo horario. ‖ jet set, la jet set *f*, la jet *f*. ‖ jet propulsion, propulsión *f* a chorro. ‖ jet ski, moto *f* acuática. ‖ jet stream, corriente *f* en chorro.
jet² [dʒet] *n* (*mineral*) azabache *m*.
jet-black ['dʒet'blæk] *adj* negro,-a como el azabache.
jet-lagged ['dʒetlægd] *adj* que tiene jet lag: *he was jet-lagged after the flight from Sydney*, tenía jet lag después del vuelo desde Sydney.
jet-propelled [dʒetprə'peld] *adj* de propulsión a chorro.
jetsam ['dʒetsəm] *n* MAR echazón *m*.
jet-setter ['dʒetsetə'] *n* miembro *mf* de la jet set.
jettison ['dʒetɪsən] **1** *t* MAR echar por la borda. **2** *fig* deshacerse de, echar por la borda. **3** (*idea*) olvidarse de.
jetty ['dʒetɪ] *n* (*stone*) malecón *m*; (*wooden*) embarcadero.
▲ *pl* jetties.
Jew [dʒuː] *n* REL judío,-a.
■ Jew's harp, birimbao.
jewel ['dʒuːəl] **1** *n* joya, alhaja. **2** (*stone*) piedra preciosa. **3** (*in watch*) rubí *m*.
■ jewel box, joyero. ‖ jewel case, joyero.
jewelled ['dʒuːəld] *adj* adornado,-a con piedras preciosas.
jeweller ['dʒuːələ'] *n* joyero,-a.
■ jeweller's (shop), joyería.
jewellery ['dʒuːəlrɪ] *n* joyas *fpl*.
Jewess ['dʒuːes] *n* judía.
Jewish ['dʒuːɪʃ] *adj* judío,-a.
Jewry ['dʒʊərɪ] *n* los judíos *mpl*, el pueblo judío.
Jezebel ['dʒezəbel] *n* Jezabel.
jib¹ [dʒɪb] *n* MAR (*sail*) foque *m*.
■ jib boom, botalón *m* de foque.
jib² [dʒɪb] *n* (*beam*) aguilón *m*, brazo.
jib³ [dʒɪb] *i* (*animal*) plantarse; (*person*) resistirse, negarse: *she jibbed at wearing the new uniform*, se resistió a llevar el nuevo uniforme.
jibe [dʒaɪb] *n-i* → **gibe**.
Jibouti [dʒɪ'buːtɪ] *n* Djibouti.
Jiddah ['dʒɪdə] *n* Yeda.
jiffy ['dʒɪfɪ] *n fam* instante *m*.
● in a jiffy, en un santiamén.
▲ *pl* jiffies.
jig [dʒɪg] **1** *n* giga. **2** TECH plantilla. – **3** *i* bailar la giga.
▲ (*verbo*) *pt* & *pp* jigged, *ger* jigging.
jigger ['dʒɪgə'] **1** *n* US medida de licores. **2** US chisme *m*.
jiggered ['dʒɪgəd] *adj* (*tired*) cansado,-a, rendido,-a.
● well, I'm jiggered!, ¡vaya por dios!, ¡caramba!
jiggery-pokery [dʒɪgərɪ'pəʊkərɪ] *n* trampas *fpl*.

jiggle ['dʒɪgəl] *t* menear, zangolotear.
◆ to jiggle about *i* menearse.
jigsaw ['dʒɪgsɔː] **1** *n* (*saw*) sierra de vaivén. **2** (*puzzle*) rompecabezas *m*, puzzle *m*.
jihad [dʒɪ'hɑːd] *n* guerra santa, yihad *f*.
jilt [dʒɪlt] *i* abandonar, dejar plantado,-a a.
jimjams ['dʒɪmdʒæmz] **1** *npl sl* delírium trémens *m*. **2** *sl* (*jitters*) canguelo, nervios *mpl*: *it gives me the jimjams*, me da canguelo.
jimmy ['dʒɪmɪ] *n* US → **jemmy**.
▲ *pl* jimmies.
jingle ['dʒɪngəl] **1** *n* tintineo. **2** TV tonadilla *f* publicitaria. – **3** *i* tintinear. – **4** *t* hacer sonar.
jingoism ['dʒɪngəʊɪzəm] *n* patriotería, jingoísmo.
jingoistic [dʒɪngəʊ'ɪstɪk] *adj* patriotero,-a, jingoísta *mf*.
jinks [dʒɪŋks] high jinks, *npl* jolgorio, juerga.
● to get up to high jinks, organizar una juerga.
jinn [dʒɪn] *n* → **genie**.
jinx [dʒɪŋks] **1** *n* (*person*) gafe *mf*. **2** (*bad luck*) mala suerte *f*: *there's a jinx on this computer*, este ordenador está gafado. – **3** *t* gafar.
jinxed [dʒɪŋkst] *adj* gafado,-a.
jitters ['dʒɪtəz] *npl fam* nervios *mpl*.
● to get the jitters, ponerse nervioso,-a.
jittery ['dʒɪtərɪ] *adj* nervioso,-a.
jiujitsu [dʒuː'dʒɪtsuː] *n* SP yiu-yitsu *m*.
jive [dʒaɪv] **1** *n* (*dance*) swing *m*. **2** US *sl* (*drug*) hierba, chocolate *m*. **3** (*back talk*) rollo. **4** US *sl* (*lies*) embustes *mpl*. – **5** *i* bailar el swing.
■ jive talk, US *sl* argot *m*, jerga.
Jnr ['dʒuːnɪə'] *abbr* (*junior*) hijo.
job [dʒɒb] **1** *n* (*employment*) empleo, (puesto de) trabajo: *what's your job?*, ¿en qué trabajas?; *he lost his job*, perdió su empleo; *I can't find a job*, no encuentro trabajo. **2** (*piece of work*) trabajo; (*task*) tarea: *he did a good job (of work)*, hizo un buen trabajo; *the bricklayer made a good job of the wall*, el albañil dejó muy bien la pared. **3** (*difficult thing*) trabajo: *it snowed so much that we had a job to get home*, nevó tanto que nos costó trabajo llegar a casa; *you'll have a job to persuade him*, te va a costar trabajo convencerlo. **4** (*duty*) deber *m*, responsabilidad *f*, misión *f*: *it's your job to lock all the doors*, es responsabilidad tuya cerrar todas las puertas. **5** *fam* (*robbery*) robo; (*holdup*) atraco: *he did four bank jobs before he got caught*, atracó cuatro bancos antes de que lo cogieran. **6** *fam* (*plastic surgery*) cirugía estética: *she's had a nose job*, se ha operado la nariz. **7** *fam* (*example*) espécimen *m*, ejemplar *m*: *this car's a lovely job*, este coche es una maravilla.
● it's a good job that ..., menos mal que ... ‖ just the job!, ¡perfecto!, ¡estupendo!: *this is just the job!*, ¡esto es justo lo que hacía falta! ‖ on the job, trabajando. ‖ out of a job, parado,-a. ‖ to give sth. up as a bad job, dejar algo por inútil. ‖ to make the best of a bad job, poner a mal tiempo buena cara.
■ job centre, oficina de empleo. ‖ job creation, creación *f* de empleo. ‖ job description, descripción *f* del trabajo. ‖ job hunting, búsqueda de trabajo. ‖ job losses, pérdida de puestos de trabajo. ‖ job lot, lote *m* mixto a precio de saldo. ‖ job satisfaction, satisfacción *f* profesional. ‖ job security, seguridad *f* en el trabajo. ‖ job sharing, empleo compartido. ‖ jobs for the boys, amiguismo, enchufismo.
Job [dʒəʊb] *n* Job.
jobber ['dʒɒbə'] *n* GB corredor,-ra de bolsa.
jobbing ['dʒɒbɪŋ] *adj* GB que trabaja a destajo: *a jobbing plumber*, un fontanero que trabaja a destajo.

jobless ['dʒɒbləs] *adj* parado,-a.
■ **the jobless**, los parados *mpl*.
joblessness ['dʒɒbləsnəs] *n* desempleo.
Jo' burg ['dʒəʊbɜːg] *n fam* Johanesburgo.
jock [dʒɒk] *n us fam pej* deportista *mf* (*universitario,-a*).
jockey ['dʒɒkɪ] **1** *n* jockey *m.* – **2** *t* persuadir: *we finally managed to jockey them into signing the contract*, por fin pudimos convencerles para que firmaran el contrato.
● **to jockey for position**, maniobrar para colocarse en buena posición.
jockstrap ['dʒɒkstræp] *n* suspensorio.
jocose [dʒə'kəʊs] *adj* jocoso,-a.
jocosely [dʒə'kəʊslɪ] *adv* jocosamente.
jocoseness [dʒə'kəʊsnəs] *n* jocosidad *f.*
jocosity [dʒə'kɒsɪtɪ] *n* jocosidad *f.*
jocular ['dʒɒkjələʳ] *adj* (*person*) gracioso,-a; (*comment*) humorístico,-a.
jocularity [dʒɒkjə'lærɪtɪ] *n* gracia.
jocularly ['dʒɒkjələlɪ] *adv* jocosamente.
jocund ['dʒɒkənd] *adj* LIT jocundo.
jocundity [dʒəʊ'kʌndɪtɪ] *n* LIT jocundidad *f.*
jodhpurs ['dʒɒdpəz] *npl* pantalones *mpl* de montar.
Joe [dʒəʊ] *n* (*diminutive of Joseph*) Pepe.
■ **Joe Bloggs / Joe Public**, GB *fam* el hombre de la calle.
jog [dʒɒg] **1** *n* (*push*) empujoncito, sacudida. **2** (*pace*) trote *m.* – **3** *t* empujar, sacudir. – **4** *i* hacer footing.
◆ **to jog along 1** *i* andar a trote corto. **2** *fig* ir tirando: *we just jog along from day to day*, vamos tirando día a día.
● **at a jog trot**, a trote corto. ‖ **to go for a jog**, (ir a) hacer footing. ‖ **to jog sb.'s memory**, refrescarle la memoria a algn.
jogger ['dʒɒgəʳ] *n* persona que hace footing.
jogging ['dʒɒgɪŋ] *n* footing *m.*
● **to go jogging**, hacer footing.
joggle ['dʒɒgəl] *t* menear.
Johannesburg [dʒəʊ'hænəzbɜːg] *n* Johanesburgo.
john [dʒɒn] *n us* wáter *m.*
John [dʒɒn] *n* Juan.
■ **John Doe**, us el hombre de la calle. ‖ **John Dory**, (*fish*) gallo, pez *m* de San Pedro. ‖ **John Hancock**, us firma, autógrafo. ‖ **John the Baptist**, San Juan Bautista.
johnny ['dʒɒnɪ] (*rubber*) johnny, *n* GB *sl* condón *m*, goma.
▲ *pl* **johnnies**.
joie de vivre [ʒwɑːdə'vɪvrə] *n* alegría de vivir.
join [dʒɔɪn] **1** *t* (*bring together*) juntar, unir. **2** (*connect*) unir, conectar: *the two cities are joined by a bridge*, las dos ciudades están unidas por un puente. **3** (*company etc*) incorporarse a: *Mr Osuna joined the company last year*, el Sr Osuna se incorporó a la empresa el año pasado. **4** (*armed forces*) alistarse en; (*police*) ingresar en. **5** (*club*) hacerse socio,-a de. **6** (*party*) afiliarse a, ingresar en. **7** (*be with sb.*) reunirse con, unirse a: *would you like to join us for the evening?*, ¿les gustaría pasar la tarde con nosotros?; *will you join me in a whisky?*, ¿quiere tomar un whisky conmigo? – **8** *i* juntarse, unirse. **9** (*rivers*) confluir; (*roads*) juntarse, empalmar. – **10** *n* juntura: *you can't see the join*, no se ve la juntura.
◆ **to join in 1** *i* participar. – **2** *t insep* (*debate*) intervenir en. ‖ **to join up** *i* alistarse.
● **join the club!**, ¡ya somos dos *etc*! ‖ **to join battle with**, trabar batalla con. ‖ **to join forces**, aunar esfuerzos. ‖ **to join forces with sb.**, unirse a algn. ‖ **to join hands**, cogerse de las manos.

joiner ['dʒɔɪnəʳ] *n* carpintero *que se dedica a puertas, ventanas etc.*
joinery ['dʒɔɪnərɪ] *n* carpintería.
joint [dʒɔɪnt] **1** *n* junta, juntura, unión *f*; (*wood*) ensambladura. **2** ANAT articulación *f.* **3** CULIN (*raw*) corte *m* de carne *para asar*; (*when cooked*) asado. **4** *sl* (*drugs*) porro. **5** *sl* (*place*) antro, tugurio. – **6** *adj* colectivo,-a, mutuo,-a. – **7** *t* CULIN descuartizar.
● **to put out of joint**, (*elbow, shoulder etc*) dislocar: *she put her shoulder out of joint*, se dislocó el hombro. ‖ **to put sb.'s nose out of joint**, disgustar a algn., molestar a algn.
■ **joint account**, cuenta conjunta, cuenta indistinta. ‖ **joint owner**, copropietario,-a. ‖ **joint ownership**, copropiedad *f.* ‖ **joint resolution**, resolución *f* conjunta.
jointed ['dʒɔɪntɪd] **1** *adj* articulado,-a. **2** (*chicken etc*) cortado,-a a piezas.
jointly ['dʒɔɪntlɪ] *adv* conjuntamente.
joint-stock ['dʒɔɪnt'stɒk] **joint-stock company**, *n* FIN sociedad *f* anónima.
joist [dʒɔɪst] *n* vigueta.
joke [dʒəʊk] **1** *n* chiste *m*: *shall I tell you a joke?*, ¿te cuento un chiste? **2** (*practical*) broma: *John can't take a joke*, John no aguanta una broma. **3** (*person*) payaso. – **4** *i* bromear.
● **it's no joke**, (*not funny*) no tiene gracia; (*difficult, serious*) no es ningún chiste, no es para reírse. ‖ **to be beyond a joke**, pasar de castaño oscuro. ‖ **to be joking**, estar de broma. ‖ **to crack a joke**, contar un chiste. ‖ **to joke about sth.**, reírse de algo. ‖ **to make a joke of sth.**, reírse de algo. ‖ **to play a joke on sb.**, gastar una broma a algn. ‖ **to tell a joke**, contar un chiste. ‖ **you must be joking!**, ¡venga ya!
joker ['dʒəʊkəʳ] **1** *n* bromista *mf*: *some joker put salt in the sugar*, algún gracioso ha puesto sal en el azúcar. **2** (*card*) comodín *m.* **3** *fam* idiota *mf.*
■ **the joker in the pack**, un elemento desconocido.
jokey ['dʒəʊkɪ] *adj* gracioso,-a.
joking ['dʒəʊkɪŋ] *n* bromas *fpl.*
● **joking apart**, bromas aparte.
jokingly ['dʒəʊkɪŋlɪ] *adv* en broma, de broma.
jollification [dʒɒlɪfɪ'keɪʃən] *n* jolgorio, festividades *fpl.*
jollily ['dʒɒlɪlɪ] *adv* alegremente.
jollity ['dʒɒlɪtɪ] *n* alegría.
jolly ['dʒɒlɪ] **1** *adj* (*cheerful*) alegre, animado,-a: *she was a very jolly person*, era una persona muy animada. **2** *dated* (*amusing*) divertido,-a: *we had a terribly jolly time*, nos divertimos muchísimo. – **3** *adv* GB *fam* muy: *it's jolly difficult*, es la mar de difícil. **4** **jolly well**, decididamente: *if you don't leave right now, I'll jolly well call the police*, si no te vas ya, te juro que llamaré a la policía; *don't answer me back, you'll jolly well do as I say!*, ¡no me repliques, harás lo que yo te diga!
◆ **to jolly along** *t sep* dar ánimos a, animar. ‖ **to jolly up** *t sep* alegrar, animar.
■ **Jolly Roger**, bandera pirata, bandera negra.
▲ (*adjetivo*) *comp* **jollier**, *superl* **jolliest**; (*verbo*) *pt & pp* **jollied**, *ger* **jollying**.
jolt [dʒəʊlt] **1** *n* sacudida. **2** (*fright*) susto. – **3** *t* sacudir. – **4** *i* dar tumbos. – **5** *t fig* dar un choque a: *I was jolted out of my daydreams by a loud noise*, un fuerte ruido me sacó de mis ensoñaciones; *he was jolted into action by the terrible news*, la terrible noticia hizo que se pusiera en acción.
Joneses ['dʒəʊnzɪz] **to keep up with the Joneses**, *phr* no ser menos que el vecino.

Jordan [ˈdʒɔːdən] **1** n (country) Jordania. **2** (river) el Jordán m.

Jordanian [dʒɔːˈdeɪnɪən] **1** adj jordano,-a. – **2** n jordano,-a.

joss stick [ˈdʒɒsstɪk] n varita de incienso.

jostle [ˈdʒɒsəl] **1** t empujar. – **2** i dar empujones: *the crowds jostled to get into the stadium*, el gentío daba empujones para entrar en el estadio. **3** fig competir.

jot [dʒɒt] **1** n pizca: *there isn't a jot of truth in it*, no hay pizca de verdad en esto; *I don't care a jot*, me importa un bledo. – **2** t apuntar, anotar.
 ◆ **to jot down** t sep apuntar.
 ▲ (verbo) pt & pp jotted, ger jotting.

jotter [ˈdʒɒtəʳ] n GB bloc m.

jottings [ˈdʒɒtɪŋz] npl apuntes mpl.

joule [dʒuːl] n julio.

journal [ˈdʒɜːnəl] **1** n (magazine) revista. **2** (diary) diario.

journalese [dʒɜːnəˈliːz] n lenguaje m periodístico.

journalism [ˈdʒɜːnəlɪzəm] n periodismo.

journalist [ˈdʒɜːnəlɪst] n periodista mf.

journalistic [dʒɜːnəˈlɪstɪk] adj periodístico,-a.

journey [ˈdʒɜːnɪ] **1** n viaje m: *it's a 100 mile journey*, es un viaje de 100 millas. – **2** i viajar.
 ● **to break a journey in** ..., hacer escala en ... ‖ **to go on a journey**, hacer un viaje.

journeyman [ˈdʒɜːnɪmən] n jornalero.
 ▲ pl journeymen [ˈdʒɜːnɪmən].

joust [dʒaʊst] i HIST justar, justear.

Jove [dʒəʊv] n Jove, Júpiter.
 ● **by Jove!**, ¡por Dios!

jovial [ˈdʒəʊvɪəl] adj jovial, alegre.

joviality [dʒəʊvɪˈælətɪ] n jovialidad f.

jovially [ˈdʒəʊvɪəlɪ] adv jovialmente, con jovialidad.

jowl [dʒaʊl] n (cheek) carrillo.

joy [dʒɔɪ] **1** n alegría, júbilo: *her face was a picture of joy*, estaba radiante de alegría; *he's a joy to work with*, da gusto trabajar con él. **2** fam (satisfaction) satisfacción f; (luck) suerte f; (success) éxito: *you can complain all you like, but you'll get no joy*, quéjate todo lo que quieras, pero no te servirá de nada.

joyful [ˈdʒɔɪfʊl] adj jubiloso,-a, alegre.

joyfully [ˈdʒɔɪfʊlɪ] adv con júbilo, alegremente.

joyfulness [ˈdʒɔɪfʊlnəs] n alegría.

joyless [ˈdʒɔɪləs] adj triste.

joylessly [ˈdʒɔɪləslɪ] adv tristemente, sin alegría.

joylessness [ˈdʒɔɪləsnəs] n tristeza.

joyous [ˈdʒɔɪəs] adj lit alegre.

joyously [ˈdʒɔɪəslɪ] adv lit con alegría, alegremente.

joyride [ˈdʒɔɪraɪd] n fam paseo en un coche robado.

joyrider [ˈdʒɔɪraɪdəʳ] n fam persona que se da un paseo en un coche robado.

joyriding [ˈdʒɔɪraɪdɪŋ] n fam darse un paseo en un coche robado.

joystick [ˈdʒɔɪstɪk] **1** n AV palanca de mando. **2** COMPUT joystick m.

JP [ˈdʒeɪˈpiː] abbr (Justice of the Peace) juez mf de paz.

jubilant [ˈdʒuːbɪlənt] adj radiante de alegría.

jubilantly [ˈdʒuːbɪləntlɪ] adv con júbilo, jubilosamente.

jubilation [dʒuːbɪˈleɪʃən] n júbilo.

jubilee [ˈdʒuːbɪliː] **1** n festejos mpl. **2** (anniversary) aniversario.
 ■ **diamond jubilee**, sesenta aniversario. ‖ **golden jubilee**, cincuenta aniversario. ‖ **silver jubilee**, veinticinco aniversario.

Judaea [dʒuːˈdɪə] n Judea.

Judaean [dʒuːˈdɪən] **1** adj judío,-a. – **2** n judío,-a.

Judah [ˈdʒuːdə] n Judá m.

Judaic [dʒuːˈdeɪk] adj judaico,-a.

Judaism [ˈdʒuːdeɪɪzəm] n judaísmo.

Judas [ˈdʒuːdəs] n Judas.
 ■ **Judas tree**, árbol m del amor, árbol m de Judas, ciclamor m.

judder [ˈdʒʌdəʳ] **1** i vibrar (violentamente). – **2** n vibración f (violenta).

judge [dʒʌdʒ] **1** n (man) juez m; (woman) juez f, jueza. **2** (in competition) jurado, miembro del jurado: *the judges' decision is final*, la decisión del jurado es inapelable. – **3** t (court case) juzgar. **4** (calculate) calcular: *it's hard to judge how much we need*, es difícil calcular cuánto necesitamos. **5** (consider) considerar: *the meat was judged unfit for human consumption*, la carne se consideró no apta para el consumo humano. **6** (competition) hacer de jurado en: *the competition was judged by my mother*, mi madre hizo de jurado en el concurso.
 ● **judging from** ..., a juzgar por ... ‖ **to be a good judge of** ..., ser buen,-a conocedor,-ra de ..., entender mucho de ... ‖ **to be a good judge of character**, saber juzgar a la gente. ‖ **to judge by** ..., a juzgar por ...

judgement [ˈdʒʌdʒmənt] **1** n (ability) (buen) juicio, (buen) criterio. **2** (opinion) juicio, opinión f: *my personal judgement is that* ..., mi opinión es que ...; *in my judgement* ..., a mi juicio ... **3** (decision) fallo. **4** (criticism) crítica.
 ● **against my (his etc) better judgement**, a pesar de mis (sus etc) reservas. ‖ **to reserve judgement**, reservarse la opinión. ‖ **to pass judgement on** ..., (in court) pronunciar sentencia sobre ...; (give opinion) pronunciarse sobre ..., opinar sobre ... ‖ **to sit in judgement on** ..., erigirse en juez de ..., juzgar a ...
 ■ **error of judgement**, error m de cálculo. ‖ **judgement day**, día m del juicio. ‖ **Last Judgement**, juicio final.
 ▲ También se escribe judgment.

judgemental [dʒʌdʒˈmentəl] adj crítico,-a.

judicature [ˈdʒuːdɪkətʃəʳ] n judicatura.

judicial [dʒuːˈdɪʃəl] adj judicial.
 ■ **judicial inquiry**, investigación f judicial.

judicially [dʒuːˈdɪʃəlɪ] adv judicialmente.

judiciary [dʒuːˈdɪʃərɪ] n judicatura.

judicious [dʒuːˈdɪʃəs] adj juicioso,-a, sensato,-a, prudente.

judiciously [dʒuːˈdɪʃəslɪ] adv prudentemente.

judiciousness [dʒuːˈdɪʃəsnəs] n (buen) juicio, prudencia.

judo [ˈdʒuːdəʊ] n yudo, judo.

jug [dʒʌg] **1** n jarra, jarro. **2** sl (prison) chirona. – **3** t CULIN estofar. – **4** jugs, npl sl (breasts) cántaros mpl, tetas fpl.

jugful [ˈdʒʌgfʊl] n jarra: *I drank a jugful of milk*, me bebí una jarra (entera) de leche.

juggernaut [ˈdʒʌgənɔːt] n GB camión m pesado.

juggle [ˈdʒʌgəl] **1** i hacer juegos malabares (**with**, con). **2** fig (figures etc) jugar (**with**, con).

juggler [ˈdʒʌgələʳ] n malabarista mf.

jugular [ˈdʒʌgjələʳ] **1** adj yugular. – **2** n yugular f.
 ● **to go for the jugular**, saltarle a algn. a la yugular.
 ■ **jugular vein**, vena yugular.

juice [dʒuːs] **1** n (gen) zumo. **2** (of fruit) zumo, AM jugo. **3** fam (petrol) gasolina; (electricity) fuerza, luz f.

juiciness [ˈdʒuːsɪnəs] n jugosidad f.

juicy [ˈdʒuːsɪ] **1** adj jugoso,-a. **2** fam (gossip etc) picante, escabroso,-a.
 ▲ comp juicier, superl juiciest.

jujitsu [dʒuːˈdʒɪtsuː] *n* yiu-yitsu *m*, jiu-jitsu *m*.
juju [ˈdʒuːdʒuː] **1** *n* (*charm*) talismán *m*. **2** (*magic*) magia.
jujube [ˈdʒuːdʒuːb] **1** *n* (*tree*) azufaifo. **2** (*pastille*) pastilla de goma.
jukebox [ˈdʒuːkbɒks] *n* máquina de discos.
Jul [dʒuːˈlaɪ] *abbr* (*July*) julio.
julep [ˈdʒuːlɪp] *n* julepe *m*.
July [dʒuːˈlaɪ] *n* julio.
  ▲ *Véase también* **May**.
jumble [ˈdʒʌmbəl] **1** *n* revoltijo, mezcolanza. – **2** *t* desordenar.
  ■ **jumble sale**, rastrillo benéfico.
jumbo [ˈdʒʌmbəʊ] **1** *adj* gigante. – **2 jumbo (jet)**, *n* AV jumbo *m*.
jumbo-sized [ˈdʒʌmbəʊsaɪzd] *adj* gigante.
jump [dʒʌmp] **1** *n* salto: *a parachute jump*, un salto en paracaídas. **2** (*in prices etc*) salto, aumento importante, disparo: *there's been a tremendous jump in profits*, ha habido un aumento importante de los beneficios. **3** (*fence*) valla, obstáculo: *the horse refused at the first jump*, el caballo se plantó en el primer obstáculo. – **4** *i* saltar: *she jumped out of the window*, saltó por la ventana. **5** (*rise sharply*) dar un salto: *inflation jumped 2% last month*, la inflación dio un salto de un 2% el mes pasado. – **6** *t* saltar: *he tried to jump the wall, but it was too high*, intentó saltar el muro, pero era demasiado alto.
  ◆ **to jump at** *t insep* aceptar sin pensarlo: *when they offered him the job, he jumped at it*, cuando le ofrecieron el trabajo lo aceptó sin pensar.
  ● **to give sb. a jump**, pegar un susto a algn. ‖ **to jump down sb.'s throat**, saltar a algn., echársele encima a algn. ‖ **to jump for joy**, saltar de alegría. ‖ **to jump out of one's skin**, pegarse un susto de muerte. ‖ **to jump rope**, US saltar a la comba. ‖ **to jump the gun**, precipitarse, adelantarse. ‖ **to jump the lights**, saltarse el semáforo en rojo. ‖ **to jump the queue**, colarse. ‖ **to jump the rails**, descarrilar. ‖ **to jump to conclusions**, llegar a conclusiones precipitadas. ‖ **to keep one jump ahead of sb.**, ir un paso por delante de algn. ‖ **to make sb. jump**, dar un susto a algn.
  ■ **jump leads**, cables *mpl* de emergencia. ‖ **jump seat**, asiento plegable. ‖ **jump suit**, mono.
jumped-up [ˈdʒʌmptʌp] *adj* presuntuoso,-a.
jumper[1] [ˈdʒʌmpə'] **1** *n* GB jersey *m*. **2** US (*skirt*) pichi *m*.
jumper[2] [ˈdʒʌmpə'] *n* SP saltador,-ra.
jumpiness [ˈdʒʌmpinəs] *n* nerviosismo.
jumping-off [dʒʌmpɪŋˈɒf] **jumping-off place / jumping-off point**, *n* punto de partida.
jumpy [ˈdʒʌmpi] *adj* nervioso,-a.
  ▲ *comp* **jumpier**, *superl* **jumpiest**.
Jun[1] [dʒuːn] *abbr* (*June*) junio.
Jun[2] [ˈdʒuːnɪə'] *abbr* (*junior*) hijo.
junction [ˈdʒʌŋkʃən] **1** *n* (*railways*) empalme *m*. **2** (*roads*) cruce *m*.
  ■ **junction box**, caja de empalmes.
juncture [ˈdʒʌŋktʃə'] *n* coyuntura.
  ● **at this juncture**, en esta coyuntura.
June [dʒuːn] *n* junio.
  ▲ *Véase también* **May**.
jungle [ˈdʒʌŋgəl] *n* selva, jungla.
junior [ˈdʒuːnɪə'] **1** *adj* (*in rank*) subalterno,-a. **2** (*in age*) menor, más joven. **3** US (*after name*) hijo: *Cyrus P. Doberman, Jr.*, Cyrus P. Doberman, hijo. – **4** *n* (*in rank*) subalterno,-a. **5** (*in age*) menor *mf*: *she is three years my junior*, tiene tres años menos que yo. **6** GB alumno,-a

de EGB. **7** US hijo: *where's your mom, Junior?*, ¿dónde está tu mamá, hijo?
  ■ **junior college**, US *colegio universitario para los dos primeros cursos*. ‖ **junior high school**, US instituto de enseñanza secundaria. ‖ **junior minister**, GB subsecretario,-a. ‖ **junior school**, GB escuela primaria.
juniper [ˈdʒuːnɪpə'] *n* enebro.
  ■ **juniper berry**, nebrina.
junk[1] [dʒʌŋk] *n* trastos *mpl*.
  ■ **junk food**, comida basura. ‖ **junk mail**, propaganda (*que se echa en el buzón*). ‖ **junk shop**, chamarilería.
junk[2] [dʒʌŋk] **2** *n* (*boat*) junco.
junket [ˈdʒʌŋkɪt] **1** *n* (*dessert*) postre *m* de leche cuajada. **2** *fam* (*trip*) viaje de lujo pagado con dinero público. – **3** *i* ir de juerga.
junketing [ˈdʒʌŋkɪtɪŋ] *n fam* juergas *fpl*.
junkie [ˈdʒʌŋkɪ] *n sl* yonqui *mf*.
junkyard [ˈdʒʌŋkjɑːd] *n* chatarrería.
junta [ˈdʒʌntə] *n* POL junta (militar).
Jupiter [ˈdʒuːpɪtə'] *n* Júpiter *m*.
juridical [dʒuːˈrɪdɪkəl] *adj* jurídico,-a.
jurisdiction [dʒʊərɪsˈdɪkʃən] *n* jurisdicción *f*.
jurisprudence [dʒʊərɪsˈpruːdəns] *n* jurisprudencia.
jurist [ˈdʒʊərɪst] *n* jurista *mf*.
juror [ˈdʒʊərə'] *n* jurado.
jury [ˈdʒʊərɪ] *n* jurado.
  ● **to sit on a jury**, ser miembro de un jurado. ‖ **to do jury service**, formar parte de un jurado popular.
  ■ **jury box**, tribuna del jurado.
  ▲ *pl* **juries**.
juryman [ˈdʒʊərɪmən] *n* jurado, miembro del jurado.
  ▲ *pl* **jurymen** [ˈdʒʊərɪmən].
jurywoman [ˈdʒʊərɪwʊmən] *n* jurado.
  ▲ *pl* **jurywomen** [ˈdʒʊərɪwɪmɪn].
just[1] [dʒʌst] **1** *adj* (*fair*) justo,-a: *a just man*, un hombre justo. **2** (*justifiable*) fundado,-a, justificado,-a: *just criticism*, una crítica justificada. **3** (*deserved*) merecido,-a.
  ● **to get one's just desserts**, llevar su merecido.
just[2] [dʒʌst] **1** *adv* (*exactly*) exactamente, precisamente, justo: *just as I expected*, tal como esperaba; *just as you like*, como quieras; *just over there*, allí mismo; *this is just what I needed*, esto es justo lo que necesitaba. **2** (*only*) solamente, sólo: *just a moment, please*, un momento, por favor; *no sugar for me, please, just milk*, no quiero azúcar, gracias, sólo leche; *don't worry, it's just a scratch!*, ¡no te preocupes, no es más que un rasguño! **3** (*barely*) apenas, por poco: *I ran all the way and (only) just caught the bus*, fui corriendo y cogí el autobús por poco. **4** (*right now*) en este momento: *I'm just finishing it*, lo acabo ahora mismo. **5** (*simply*) sencillamente: *we could just stay here and wait for her*, pues, sencillamente podríamos quedarnos aquí y esperarla. **6** (*for emphasis*): *I just don't know*, es que no lo sé; *he's just as clever as you are*, él es tan inteligente como tú. **7** (*used to interrupt*): *just shut up, will you?*, ¡cállese, por favor! **8** *fam* (*really*) realmente, verdaderamente: *the weather's just marvellous*, hace un tiempo realmente maravilloso. – **9 to have just** + *pres. part.*, *phr* acabar de + *infin*: *he has just telephoned*, acaba de telefonear.
  ● **just about**, prácticamente. ‖ **just as well**, menos mal. ‖ **just in case**, por si acaso. ‖ **just like that!**, ¡sin más! ‖ **just so**, (*tidy*) ordenado,-a, arreglado,-a; (*as a reply*) sí, exactamente. ‖ **just then**, en ese momento. ‖ **just the same**, (*not different*) exactamente igual; (*nevertheless*) sin embargo, no obstante. ‖ **just the thing**, justo lo que hacía falta.

justice ['dʒʌstɪs] 1 *n* justicia. 2 (*judge - man*) juez *m*; (-*woman*) juez *f*, jueza.
● **to bring to justice,** llevar ante los tribunales. ‖ **to do justice to sb.,** hacer justicia a algn.
■ **Justice of the Peace,** juez *mf* de paz.
justifiable [dʒʌstɪ'faɪəbəl] *adj* justificable.
justifiably [dʒʌstɪ'faɪəblɪ] *adv* con razón.
justification [dʒʌstɪfɪ'keɪʃən] *n* justificación *f*.
justified ['dʒʌstɪfaɪd] *adj* justificado,-a.
justify ['dʒʌstɪfaɪ] *t* justificar.
▲ *pt & pp justified, ger justifying.*
justly ['dʒʌstlɪ] *adv* justamente, con razón, con justicia.

justness ['dʒʌstnəs] *n* justicia.
jut [dʒʌt] to jut (out), *i* sobresalir.
▲ *pt & pp jutted, ger jutting.*
jute [dʒuːt] *n* yute *m*.
Jute [dʒuːt] *n* (*person*) yuto,-a.
juvenile ['dʒuːvənaɪl] 1 *adj* juvenil. 2 (*childish*) infantil. – 3 *n* menor *mf*.
■ **juvenile court,** tribunal *m* (tutelar) de menores. ‖ **juvenile delinquency,** delincuencia juvenil. ‖ **juvenile delinquent,** delincuente *mf* juvenil.
juxtapose ['dʒʌkstəpəuz] *t* yuxtaponer.
juxtaposition [dʒʌkstəpə'zɪʃən] *n* yuxtaposición *f*

K

K, k [keɪ] *n (the letter)* K, k *f.*
kaftan [ˈkæftæn] *n* caftán *m.*
Kaiser [ˈkaɪzəʳ] *n* káiser *m.*
kale [keɪl] *n* col *f* rizada.
kaleidoscope [kəˈlaɪdəskəʊp] *n* calidoscopio.
kaleidoscopic [kəlaɪdəˈskɒpɪk] *adj* calidoscópico,-a.
kamikaze [kæmɪˈkɑːzɪ] **1** *n* kamikaze *m.* − **2** *adj* kamikaze.
Kampuchea [kæmpʊˈtʃɪə] *n* Kampuchea.
Kampuchean [kæmpʊˈtʃɪən] **1** *adj* kampucheo,-a. − **2** *n* kampucheo,-a.
kangaroo [kæŋɡəˈruː] *n* canguro.
■ **kangaroo court,** tribunal *m* desautorizado.
▲ *pl* **kangaroos.**
kaolin [ˈkeɪəlɪn] *n* caolín *m.*
kapok [ˈkeɪpɒk] *n* kapok *m.*
kaput [kəˈpʊt] *adj fam* roto,-a, estropeado,-a.
karaoke [kærɪˈəʊkɪ] *n* karaoke *m.*
■ **karaoke bar,** karaoke *m.* ‖ **karaoke machine,** karaoke *m.*
karat [ˈkærət] *n* US → **carat.**
karate [kəˈrɑːtɪ] *n* kárate *m.*
karma [ˈkɑːmə] *n* karma *m.*
kart [kɑːt] *n* kart *m.*
karting [ˈkɑːtɪŋ] *n* kárting *m.*
kasbah [ˈkæzbɑː] *n* casba, casbah *f.*
Kashmir [kæʃˈmɪəʳ] *n* Cachemira.
Kashmiri [kæʃˈmɪərɪ] **1** *adj* cachemir. − **2** *n* cachemir *mf.*
Kathmandu [kætmænˈduː] *n* → **Katmandu.**
Katmandu [kætmænˈduː] *n* Katmandú.
kayak [ˈkaɪæk] *n* kayac *m.*
kazoo [kəˈzuː] *n* mirlitón *m.*
▲ *pl* **kazoos.**
KC [ˈkeɪˈsiː] *abbr* GB JUR *(King's Counsel)* abogado,-a del estado.
kebab [kɪˈbæb] *n* pincho moruno, broqueta.
kedgeree [ˈkedʒəriː] *n plato de pescado, arroz y huevo duro.*
keel [kiːl] *n* quilla.
● **to keel over** *i (ship)* zozobrar; *(person)* desplomarse.
● **on an even keel,** en equilibrio.
keen[1] [kiːn] **1** *adj (eager)* entusiasta, aficionado,-a: *he's a very keen pupil,* es un alumno muy entusiasta; *she's a keen tennis player,* es muy aficionada al tenis; *the children are keen to go to the circus,* los niños tienen muchas ganas de ir al circo. **2** *(sharp - mind, senses etc)* agudo,-a, vivo,-a; *(- look)* penetrante; *(- wind)* cortante; *(- edge, point)* afilado,-a. **3** *(feeling)* profundo,-a, intenso,-a. **4** *(competition)* fuerte, reñido,-a. **5** *(price)* competitivo,-a.
● **to be as keen as mustard,** ser muy entusiasta. ‖ **to be keen on sth.,** ser aficionado,-a a algo, gustarle algo a algn.: *she's very keen on the idea,* le entusiasma la idea. ‖ **to be keen on sb.,** gustarle alguien a algn.:

he's very keen on your sister, le gusta mucho tu hermana. ‖ **to take a keen interest in,** mostrar un gran interés por.
keen[2] [kiːn] **1** *n* canción fúnebre acompañada de lamentaciones. − **2** *i* llorar la pérdida de una persona de esta manera.
keenly [ˈkiːnlɪ] *adv (feeling)* profundamente, intensamente; *(look)* atentamente; *(competition)* intensamente, reñidamente; *(interest, work)* con entusiasmo.
keenness [ˈkiːnnəs] **1** *n (eagerness)* entusiasmo, interés *m,* afición *f.* **2** *(sharpness)* agudeza; *(competition)* fuerza.
keep [kiːp] **1** *n (board)* sustento, mantenimiento: *to earn one's keep,* ganarse el pan. **2** *(of castle)* torreón *m,* torre *f* del homenaje. − **3** *t (not throw away)* guardar: *I kept all your letters,* guardé todas tus cartas. **4** *(not give back)* quedarse con: *you can keep that book I lent you,* quédate con aquel libro que te dejé; *keep the change,* quédese con el cambio. **5** *(have)* tener; *(carry)* llevar: *you should always keep paper and pencil handy,* siempre hay que tener a mano lápiz y papel; *I keep a spare pair of glasses in the car,* llevo unas gafas de recambio en el coche. **6** *(look after, save)* guardar: *can you keep me a loaf of bread for Friday?,* ¿me guarda una barra de pan para el viernes?; *John kept my place while I made a phone call,* John me guardó el sitio mientras hacía una llamada. **7** *(put away, store)* guardar: *where do you keep the glasses?,* ¿dónde guardas los vasos?; *I always keep a little brandy for emergencies,* siempre guardo un poco de coñac para una emergencia. **8** *(reserve)* reservar: *I keep this whisky for special occasions,* reservo este whisky para las ocasiones especiales. **9** *(detain)* retener, hacer esperar; *(hold up)* entretener: *they kept her in hospital overnight,* la retuvieron en el hospital toda la noche; *she kept me talking for hours,* me entretuvo hablando durante horas; *what kept you?,* ¿cómo es que llegas tan tarde?; *sorry to keep you waiting,* discúlpeme por hacerle esperar. **10** *(shop, hotel etc)* tener, llevar: *they keep a small hotel on the coast,* tienen un pequeño hotel en la costa. **11** *(have in stock)* tener, vender: *I'm afraid we don't keep cigars,* lo siento, pero no vendemos puros. **12** *(support)* mantener: *I don't know how they manage to keep a family on their wage,* no sé cómo pueden mantener una familia con lo que ganan. **13** *(animals)* tener: *children love keeping pets,* a los niños les encanta tener animales de compañía; *our eggs are really fresh, we keep our own hens,* nuestros huevos son fresquísimos, tenemos gallinas. **14** *(promise)* cumplir: *promises are made to be kept,* las promesas se deben cumplir. **15** *(secret)* guardar: *can you keep a secret?,* ¿sabes guardar un secreto? **16** *(appointment)* acudir a, no faltar a: *please 'phone if you are unable to keep your appointment,* por favor, llame si no puede acudir a la visita. **17** *(order)* mantener: *teachers must keep order in their classes,* los profesores deben mantener el orden en sus clases. **18** *(tradition)* observar: *many old traditions are not kept nowadays,* muchas tradiciones antiguas ya

no se observan. **19** (*with adj, verb, etc*) mantener: *these doors must be kept locked,* estas puertas deben mantenerse cerradas; *the stove keeps the whole house warm,* la estufa mantiene caliente toda la casa; *this game will keep the children amused,* este juego entretendrá a los niños; *this yoghurt must be kept cold,* este yogur debe conservarse en frío. – **20** *i* (*do repeatedly*) no dejar de; (*do continuously*) seguir, continuar: *I keep thinking about her,* no dejo de pensar en ella; *don't keep interrupting me!,* ¡deja de interrumpirme!; *she was exhausted but kept swimming,* estaba agotada pero siguió nadando; *keep trying until you succeed,* sigue intentándolo hasta que lo consigas. **21** (*stay fresh*) conservarse: *this food will keep for five days in the fridge,* esta comida se conserva durante cinco días en la nevera; *I've got some news for you, but it'll keep till tomorrow,* tengo algo que decirte, pero puede esperar hasta mañana. **22** (*continue in direction*) continuar, seguir: *keep left/right,* circula por la izquierda/derecha; *keep to the path,* no abandonar el sendero. **23** (*with adj, verb etc*) quedarse, permanecer: *please keep quiet,* cállese por favor; *keep still!,* ¡estáte quieto!; *we must keep calm,* debemos mantener la calma.

◆ **to keep at** *t insep* (*work, study etc*) perseverar en algo; (*person*) no dejar a paz, machacar: *keep at it!,* ¡persevera!; *she kept at him until he gave her back her money,* lo estuvo machacando hasta que le devolvió el dinero. ‖ **to keep away 1** *t sep* mantener a distancia (**from,** de), no dejar a uno acercarse (**from,** a): *keep plastic bags away from children,* mantenga las bolsas de plástico fuera del alcance de los niños. – **2** *i* mantenerse a distancia, evitar contacto con: *keep away from the fire,* manténganse alejados del fuego. ‖ **to keep back 1** *t sep* (*money etc*) retener, guardar; (*information*) ocultar, no revelar; (*emotions*) contener: *the press kept back the identity of the victim,* la prensa no reveló el nombre de la víctima. **2** (*enemy*) tener a raya; (*work, progress etc*) estorbar, impedir: *I don't want to keep you back from your work,* no quiero impedir que trabajes. **3** mantener atrás, contener: *the police could not keep the crowd back,* la policía no podía contener la multitud. – **4** *i* mantenerse atrás, alejarse: *children! keep back from the edge!,* ¡niños! ¡alejaos del borde! ‖ **to keep down 1** *t sep* (*oppress*) oprimir, sujetar; (*price, voice*) mantener bajo; (*growth, spending*) limitar, controlar; (*food*) mantener en el estómago: *the government has failed to keep down inflation,* el gobierno no ha podido controlar la inflación. – **2** *i* (*lie low*) agacharse, no levantar la cabeza. ‖ **to keep from 1** *t insep* (*refrain from*) abstenerse de, guardarse de: *I couldn't keep from laughing,* no pude contener la risa. ‖ **to keep in 1** *t sep* (*gen*) no dejar salir; (*in school*) hacer quedar. **2** (*feelings*) contener. **3** (*pay for*) costear, pagar: *he doesn't earn enough to keep his wife in hats,* no gana para pagar los sombreros de su mujer. ‖ **to keep in with** *i* mantener buenas relaciones con. ‖ **to keep off 1** *i* (*stay away*) mantenerse a distancia; (*of rain*) no llover: *if the rain keeps off, we'll be able to play tennis,* si no llueve, podremos jugar a tenis. – **2** *t sep* (*make stay away*) no dejar entrar, no dejar acercarse; (*avoid*) no tocar, no hablar de: *keep that dog off!,* ¡no dejes que se acerque el perro!; *"keep off the grass",* "no pisar la hierba"; *try to keep him off that subject,* procura que no hable de aquel tema. ‖ **to keep on 1** *i* seguir, continuar. – **2** *t sep* (*clothes*) no quitarse. ‖ **to keep on about** *i* insistir en, no parar de hablar de. ‖ **to keep on at** *t insep* no dejar en paz, machacar: *keep on at him until he pays you,* no lo dejes en paz hasta que te pa-

gue. ‖ **to keep out 1** *t sep* no dejar entrar, no dejar pasar. – **2** *i* no entrar. ‖ **to keep out of** *i* (*place*) no entrar en; (*affair*) no meterse en. ‖ **to keep to** *t insep* (*rules*) atenerse a, cumplir; (*path*) no dejar, no salir de. ‖ **to keep together** *i* mantenerse juntos,-as, no separarse. ‖ **to keep under** *t sep* tener subyugado. ‖ **to keep up 1** *t sep* (*gen*) mantener, seguir. **2** (*from sleeping*) mantener despierto,-a, tener en vela. – **3** *i* (*not fall behind*) aguantar el ritmo. **4** (*stay in touch*) mantenerse al día. ‖ **to keep up with 1** *t insep* (*not fall behind*) seguir: *I can't keep up with you, you run too fast,* no te puedo seguir, corres demasiado. **2** (*be aware of*) mantenerse al corriente de: *there are so many changes I can't keep up with them,* hay tantos cambios que no puedo mantenerme al día. **3** (*stay in touch*) mantener el contacto con: *we still keep up with each other,* aún estamos en contacto.

● **for keeps,** para siempre. ‖ **how are you keeping?,** ¿cómo estás? ‖ **keep it up!,** ¡ánimo! ‖ **keep the change,** quédese con la vuelta. ‖ **to keep going,** seguir (adelante). ‖ **to keep one's head,** no perder la cabeza. ‖ **to keep quiet,** callarse, no hacer ruido. ‖ **keep sb. company,** hacerle compañía a algn. ‖ **to keep sb. from doing sth.,** impedir que algn. haga algo. ‖ **to keep sth. from sb.,** ocultar algo a algn. ‖ **to keep sth. clean,** conservar algo limpio,-a. ‖ **to keep sth. to os.,** no decir algo, guardar algo para sí. ‖ **to keep os. to os.,** ser discreto,-a. ‖ **you can't keep a good man down,** los buenos siempre salen adelante. ▲ *pt* & *pp* **kept** [kept].

keeper ['kiːpəʳ] **1** *n* (*in zoo*) guardián,-ana. **2** (*in park*) guarda *mf*. **3** (*in museum*) conservador,-ra; (*in archives*) archivador,-ra.

● **I am not my brother's keeper,** no soy guardián de mi hermano.

keep-fit [kiːpˈfɪt] *n* SP ejercicios *mpl* de mantenimiento, mantenimiento.

keeping ['kiːpɪŋ] **1** *n* cuidado, custodia: *he left his keys in his mother's keeping,* le dejó las llaves a su madre; *I entrusted the money to John for safe keeping,* confié el dinero a John para mayor seguridad.

● **in keeping with,** conforme a, en armonía con. ‖ **out of keeping with,** en desacuerdo con.

keepsake ['kiːpseɪk] *n* recuerdo.

keg [keg] *n* barrilete *m*, cuñete *m*.

■ **keg beer,** cerveza de barril.

kelp [kelp] *n* alga (*especialmente del género Laminaria*).

ken [ken] **1** *n* conocimiento. – **2** *t* (*Scot*) saber, conocer.

● **beyond one's ken,** incomprensible para uno.

kendo ['kendəʊ] *n* kendo.

kennel ['kenəl] **1** *n* perrera, caseta para perros. – **2** **kennels,** *npl* (*boarding*) residencia *f sing* canina.

Kenya ['kenjə] *n* Kenia.

Kenyan ['kenjən] **1** *adj* keniano,-a. – **2** *n* keniano,-a.

kept [kept] *pt* & *pp* → **keep**.

■ **kept woman,** mantenida.

kerb [kɜːb] *n* bordillo.

kerb-crawler ['kɜːbkrɔːləʳ] *n* persona que busca una prostituta desde su coche.

kerb-crawling ['kɜːbkrɔːlɪŋ] *n* acción de circular despacio junto al bordillo en busca de una prostituta.

kerchief ['kɜːtʃɪf] *n* pañuelo.

kerfuffle [kəˈfʌfəl] *n fam* bulla, lío, jaleo.

kernel ['kɜːnəl] **1** *n* (*of nut, fruit*) semilla. **2** *fig* núcleo, grano.

kerosene ['kerəsiːn] *n* US queroseno.

■ **kerosene lamp,** lámpara de petróleo.

kestrel ['kestrəl] *n* cernícalo vulgar.

ketchup ['ketʃəp] *n* ketchup *m*, catsup *m*.

kettle ['ketəl] *n* tetera (*para hervir agua*), hervidor *m*: *will you put the kettle on to make some tea?*, ¿quieres poner el agua a hervir para hacer té?

● *that's a different kettle of fish*, eso es harina de otro costal.

kettledrum ['ketəldrʌm] *n* timbal *m*.

key[1] [kiː] **1** *n* (*of door, car etc*) llave *f*. **2** (*of clock, mechanical*) llave *f*. **3** *fig* (*to problem, map, code*) clave *f*; (*to exercises*) respuestas *fpl*. **4** (*on computer, piano etc*) tecla. **5** MUS (*on wind instrument*) llave *f*, pistón *m*; (*set of notes*) clave *f*; (*tone, style*) tono. – **6** *adj* clave, principal: *the key word is ...*, la palabra clave es ...; *tourism is the country's key industry*, el turismo es la industria principal del país. – **7** *t* introducir, teclear: *she keyed in the data*, introdujo los datos.

◆ *to key to t sep* adaptar: *the course is keyed to the needs of the students*, el curso se adapta a las necesidades de los estudiantes.

■ **key money**, entrada. ‖ **key ring**, llavero. ‖ **key signature**, armadura.

key[2] [kiː] *n* GEOG cayo, isleta.

keyboard ['kiːbɔːd] **1** *n* teclado. – **2 keyboards**, *npl* teclados *mpl*.

■ **keyboard player**, teclista *mf*.

keyed up [kiːd'ʌp] *adj* nervioso,-a, excitado,-a.

keyhole ['kiːhəʊl] *n* ojo de la cerradura.

keynote ['kiːnəʊt] **1** *n* tónica, clave *f*. **2** (*mus*) tónica.

■ **keynote speech**, discurso que da la tónica de un congreso etc.

keystone ['kiːstəʊn] **1** *n* ARCH clave *f*. **2** *fig* piedra angular.

kg ['kɪləgræm] *symb* (*kilogram, kilogramme*) kilo, kilogramo; (*symbol*) kg.

khaki ['kɑːkɪ] **1** *n* caqui *m*. – **2** *adj* caqui.

Khartoum [kɑː'tuːm] *n* Khartum.

kHz ['kɪləhɜːts] *symb* (*kilohertz*) kilohercio, kilohercios; (*symbol*) kHz.

kibbutz [kɪ'bʊts] *n* kibutz *m*.

kick [kɪk] **1** *n* (*by person*) puntapié *m*, patada: *if the door won't open, give it a kick*, si no se abre la puerta, dale una patada; *I gave him a kick up the backside*, le di una patada en el culo. **2** (*sp*) golpe *m*, tiro. **3** (*by animal*) coz *f*. **4** *fam* (*pleasure*) diversión *f*, emoción *f*: *he gets a kick out of driving fast*, se divierte conduciendo rápido; *she does it just for kicks*, lo hace sólo para divertirse. **5** (*new interest*) moda, manía: *my mother's on a health-food kick*, a mi madre le ha dado por comer sano. **6** (*of drink*) fuerza: *this cocktail's got a real kick to it*, este cóctel es muy fuerte. **7** (*of gun*) culatazo. – **8** *t* (*hit ball*) dar un puntapié a, golpear, golpear con el pie; (*score*) marcar: *he kicked the ball so hard it broke the net*, golpeó la pelota tan fuerte que rompió la red. **9** (*hit person*) dar una patada a; (*move legs*) patalear: *the boy kicked his sister*, el niño dio una patada a su hermana. **10** (*by animal*) dar coces a, cocear. – **11** *i* (*gun*) dar un culatazo.

◆ *to kick against sth. t insep* protestar contra, reaccionar contra. ‖ *to kick around* **1** *i* (*exist, be there*) andar por ahí. – **2** *t sep* (*discuss ideas etc*) dar vueltas a. ‖ *to kick in t sep* romper a patadas. ‖ *to kick off* **1** *i* (*sp*) sacar, hacer el saque inicial; (*begin*) empezar, comenzar: *they kicked off by talking about the fires*, empezaron hablando de los incendios. – **2** *t sep* (*begin*) empezar, comenzar, iniciar. **3** (*remove - shoes*) quitarse. ‖ *to kick out t sep* echar a uno: *they were kicked out of the pub*, los echaron del pub.

● *a kick in the teeth*, una patada en el estómago. ‖ *to kick a habit*, quitarse un vicio. ‖ *to kick one's heels*, rascarse la barriga. ‖ *to kick os.*, darse contra la pared. ‖ *to kick sb. when they are down*, ensañarse con algn. ‖ *to kick the bucket*, *fam* estirar la pata. ‖ *to kick up a fuss / kick up a stink*, *fam* armar un lío, armar un jaleo.

kickback ['kɪkbæk] **1** *n* (*gun*) culatazo. **2** (*bribe*) soborno.

kickboxing ['kɪkbɒksɪŋ] *n* kickboxing *m*, boxeo tailandés.

kick-off ['kɪkɒf] *n* SP saque *m* inicial.

kickstand ['kɪkstænd] *n* caballete *m*.

kick-start ['kɪkstɑːt] **1** *n* arranque *m*. – **2** *t* (*start engine*) arrancar, poner en marcha; (*begin, launch*) dar un impulso a.

kick-starter ['kɪkstɑːtəʳ] *n* pedal *m* de arranque.

kid[1] [kɪd] **1** *n fam* crío,-a, niño,-a, chico,-a, chaval,-la. **2** (*animal*) cabrito. **3** (*leather*) cabritilla. – **4** *adj* (*brother, sister*) menor.

● *to treat sb. with kid gloves*, tratar a algn. con guantes de seda. ‖ *kids' stuff*, cosas de niños.

kid[2] [kɪd] **1** *t* (*deceive, tease*) tomar el pelo a, engañar. **2** (*fool os.*) engañarse a sí mismo, hacerse ilusiones. – **3** *i* estar de broma: *you're kidding!*, ¡estás de broma!, ¡no me digas!; *no kidding!*, ¡en serio!

kiddie ['kɪdɪ] *n* → **kiddy**.

kiddy ['kɪdɪ] *n* niño,-a.

▲ *pl* **kiddies**.

kidnap ['kɪdnæp] *t* secuestrar, raptar.

▲ *pt* & *pp* **kidnapped**, *ger* **kidnapping**.

kidnapper ['kɪdnæpəʳ] *n* secuestrador,-ra.

kidnapping ['kɪdnæpɪŋ] *n* secuestro.

kidney ['kɪdnɪ] *n* riñón *m*.

■ **kidney disease**, enfermedad *f* renal. ‖ **kidney failure**, fallo renal. ‖ **kidney machine**, riñón *m* artificial. ‖ **kidney transplant**, transplante *m* de riñón.

kill [kɪl] **1** *n* (*act*) matanza; (*animal*) pieza. – **2** *t* matar, asesinar. **3** *fig* (*hope, conversation etc*) destruir, acabar con; (*pain*) aliviar. **4** (*hurt*) doler mucho: *my back's killing me*, me duele mucho la espalda.

◆ *to kill off t sep* exterminar, matar.

● *I'll do it if it kills me*, lo haré pase lo que pase. ‖ *to be in at the kill*, estar presente en el momento de la verdad. ‖ *to kill os.*, matarse, suicidarse. ‖ *to kill os. laughing*, morirse de risa. ‖ *to kill time*, pasar el rato, matar el tiempo. ‖ *to kill two birds with one stone*, matar dos pájaros de un tiro. ‖ *to move in for the kill*, entrar a matar.

killer ['kɪləʳ] *n* (*person*) asesino,-a; (*thing*) mortal, que mata.

■ **killer bee**, abeja asesina. ‖ **killer instinct**, instinto asesino. ‖ **killer whale**, orca.

killing ['kɪlɪŋ] **1** *n* (*act*) matanza; (*of person*) asesinato. – **2** *adj fig* agotador,-ra, duro,-a.

● *to make a killing*, ganar una fortuna, hacer el negocio del siglo.

killjoy ['kɪldʒɔɪ] *n* aguafiestas *mf*.

kiln [kɪln] *n* horno.

kilo ['kiːləʊ] *n* kilo.

▲ *pl* **kilos**.

kilogram ['kɪləgræm] *n* kilogramo.

kilohertz ['kɪləhɜːts] *n* kilohercio.

kilometre [kɪ'lɒmɪtəʳ] *n* kilómetro.

kilowatt ['kɪləwɒt] *n* kilowatt *m*, kilovatio.

kilt [kɪlt] *n* falda escocesa.

kimono [kɪ'məʊnəʊ] *n* quimono.

▲ *pl* **kimonos**.

kin [kɪn] *n* parientes *mpl*, familia.
■ **next of kin,** pariente *m* más próximo.
kind [kaɪnd] **1** *adj* (*person*) amable: *she is the sweetest, kindest person I know,* es la persona más dulce y amable que conozco; *that's very kind of you,* eres muy amable. – **2** *n* (*sort*) tipo, género, clase *f*: *what kind of ...?,* ¿qué clase de ...?; *he's the kind who'll look after you,* es de ese tipo de personas que te protegerán; *she met all kinds of people,* conoció a todo tipo de personas; *it's a kind of fruit,* es una clase de fruta. – **3** kind of, *adv* bastante, algo, un poco: *it's kind of difficult,* es un poco difícil; *have you finished? –Kind of ...,* ¿has acabado? –Más o menos; *... and that kind of thing,* ... y cosas por el estilo.
● **nothing of the kind,** nada por el estilo. ‖ **to be one of a kind,** ser único,-a. ‖ **to be so kind as to ...,** tener la bondad de ..., hacer el favor de ..., tener la amabilidad de ... ‖ **to be two of a kind,** ser tal para cual. ‖ **to pay in kind,** pagar en especie; (*treatment*) pagar con la misma moneda.
kindergarten ['kɪndəgɑːtən] *n* parvulario, guardería.
kind-hearted [kaɪnd'hɑːtɪd] *adj* bondadoso,-a.
kindle ['kɪndəl] *t* encender.
kindliness ['kaɪndlɪnəs] *n* bondad *f*, amabilidad *f*.
kindling ['kɪndlɪŋ] *n* leña, astilla.
kindly ['kaɪndlɪ] **1** *adj* bondadoso,-a, amable. – **2** *adv* con amabilidad: *she very kindly lent me £5,* tuvo la amabilidad de prestarme cinco libras. **3** (*please*) por favor: *kindly shut up!,* ¡haz el favor de callarte!
● **not to take kindly to sb./sth.,** no gustar de algo/algn.: *she doesn't take kindly to being told what to do,* no le gusta nada que le digan lo que tiene que hacer. ‖ **to look kindly on,** mirar con buenos ojos.
▲ (*adjetivo*) *comp* **kindlier,** *superl* **kindliest.**
kindness ['kaɪndnəs] **1** *n* bondad *f*, amabilidad *f*. **2** (*favour*) favor *m*.
kindred ['kɪndrəd] **1** *n* familiares *mpl*. – **2** *adj* (*related*) emparentado,-a; (*similar*) semejante, afín.
● **kindred spirits,** almas gemelas.
kinetic [kɪ'netɪk] *adj* cinético,-a.
kinetics [kɪ'netɪks] *n* cinética.
king [kɪŋ] **1** *n* rey *m*. **2** GB JUR departamento del Tribunal Supremo (*cuando reina un rey*).
■ **the king and queen,** los reyes *mpl*. ‖ **the Three Kings,** los Reyes *mpl* Magos.
kingdom ['kɪŋdəm] *n* reino.
kingfisher ['kɪŋfɪʃə'] *n* martín pescador *m*.
kingpin ['kɪŋpɪn] *n* (*bolt*) clavija maestra; (*essential person*) persona clave.
king-size ['kɪŋsaɪz] *adj* extragrande, extralargo,-a.
kink [kɪŋk] **1** *n* (*in rope, wire etc*) coca, enroscadura; (*in hair*) rizo. **2** (*peculiarity*) peculiaridad *f*, manía; (*sexual*) perversión *f*.
kinky ['kɪŋkɪ] *adj fam* peculiar; (*sexual*) pervertido, -a.
▲ *comp* **kinkier,** *superl* **kinkiest.**
kinship ['kɪnʃɪp] *n* parentesco.
kiosk ['kiːɒsk] **1** *n* quiosco. **2** (*telephone*) cabina telefónica.
kip [kɪp] **1** *i fam* dormir. – **2** *n* cabezada.
● **to have a kip,** dormir, echar una cabezada.
▲ (*verbo*) *pt & pp* **kipped,** *ger* **kipping.**
kipper ['kɪpə'] *n* arenque *m* ahumado.
Kiribati [kɪrɪ'bætɪ] *n* Kiribati.
kirk [kɜːk] *n* (*in Scotland*) iglesia.
kiss [kɪs] **1** *n* beso. – **2** *t* besar, dar un beso a: *he kissed her on the cheek,* le dio un beso en la mejilla. – **3** *i* besarse, darse un beso.

● **to give sb. a kiss,** dar un beso a algn. ‖ **to kiss sb. goodbye,** despedirse de algn. con un beso. ‖ **to kiss sth. goodbye,** despedirse de algo.
■ **kiss of death,** beso de la muerte. ‖ **kiss of life,** (*resuscitation*) respiración *f* artificial; (*new life*) beso de la vida.
kit [kɪt] **1** *n* (*equipment, gear*) equipo, equipaje *m*. **2** (*clothes*) ropa. **3** MIL avíos *mpl*. **4** (*model*) maqueta, kit *m*.
◆ **to kit out** *t sep* equipar.
kitbag ['kɪtbæg] *n* mochila.
kitchen ['kɪtʃɪn] *n* cocina.
● **to take everything but the kitchen sink,** ir con la casa a cuestas.
■ **kitchen garden,** huerto. ‖ **kitchen unit,** módulo de cocina.
kitchenette [kɪtʃɪ'net] *n* cocina pequeña.
kite [kaɪt] **1** *n* ORN milano. **2** (*toy*) cometa: *to fly a kite,* hacer volar una cometa.
● **go fly a kite!,** ¡vete por ahí! ‖ **to fly a kite,** *lanzar una idea para sondear la opinión.* ‖ **to be as high as a kite,** (*on drugs, alcohol*) estar totalmente colocado,-a; (*excited*) estar entusiasmado,-a. ‖ **to kite a check,** US extender un cheque sin fondos.
Kitemark ['kaɪtmɑːk] *n marchamo oficial de calidad.*
kith [kɪθ] **kith and kin,** *n* parientes *mpl* y amigos.
kitsch [kɪtʃ] **1** *n* kitsch *m*, cursilería. – **2** *adj* kitsch, cursi.
kitten ['kɪtən] *n* gatito,-a.
● **to have kittens,** tener un ataque: *I nearly had kittens!,* ¡por poco me da un ataque!
kittenish ['kɪtənɪʃ] *adj* (*playful*) juguetón,-a,; (*flirtatious*) coqueta.
kittiwake ['kɪtɪweɪk] *n* gaviota tridáctila.
kitty ['kɪtɪ] **1** *n fam* (*cat*) minino,-a. **2** (*in card games*) bote *m*; (*for bills, drinks*) fondo común.
▲ *pl* **kitties.**
kiwi ['kiːwiː] **1** *n* ORN kiwi *m*. **2** (*fruit*) kiwi *m*. **3** (*New Zealander*) neozelandés,-a.
■ **kiwi fruit,** kiwi *m*.
klaxon ['klæksən] *n* claxon *m*.
Kleenex ['kliːneks] *n* kleenex *m*.
▲ *Es marca registrada.*
kleptomania [kleptə'meɪnɪə] *n* cleptomanía.
kleptomaniac [kleptə'meɪnɪæk] *n* cleptómano,-a.
km [kɪ'lɒmɪtə', 'kɪləmɪtə'] *abbr* (*kilometre*) kilómetro; (*abbreviation*) km.
▲ *pl* **km** o **kms.**
knack [næk] *n* (*skillful method*) maña, truco, tino, tranquillo; (*talent*) don *m*: *he has a knack of turning up at the right time,* tiene el don de aparecer en el momento justo; *it's easy to do once you've got the knack of it,* es fácil hacerlo cuando le coges el tranquillo.
knacker ['nækə'] **1** *n* matarife *m* de caballos. – **2** *t fam* agotar, reventar. – **3** knackers, *npl taboo* cojones *mpl*, huevos *mpl*.
■ **knacker's yard,** matadero.
knackered ['nækəd] *adj fam* reventado,-a, agotado,-a, hecho,-a polvo.
knapsack ['næpsæk] *n* mochila.
knave [neɪv] **1** *n* (*cards*) jota; (*Spanish pack*) sota. **2** *arch* (*dishonest man*) pícaro, bribón *m*.
knavery ['neɪvərɪ] *n arch* picardía.
knavish ['neɪvɪʃ] *adj arch* pícaro,-a.
knead [niːd] *t* amasar.
knee [niː] **1** *n* ANAT rodilla. **2** (*of trousers*) rodillera: *on one's knees,* de rodillas. – **3** *t* dar un rodillazo a.
● **to go down on one's knees,** arrodillarse. ‖ **to**

bring sb. to their knees, humillar a algn. ‖ to bring the country to its knees, llevar el país al borde de la ruina.

knee-breeches ['niːbrɪtʃɪz] *n arch* calzones *mpl.*

kneecap ['niːkæp] **1** *n* rótula. – **2** *t* disparar a las rótulas a.

knee-deep ['niːdiːp] *adj* que cubre hasta las rodillas.
● to be knee-deep in work, estar muy ocupado,-a. ‖ to be knee-deep in trouble, estar metido,-a en problemas.

knee-high ['niːhaɪ] *adj* que llega hasta las rodillas.
● knee-high to a grasshopper, muy pequeño,-a: *when I was knee-high to a grasshopper,* cuando era apenas un renacuajo.

knee-jerk ['niːdʒɜːk] **1** *n* reflejo rotular. – **2** *adj fig* instintivo,-a, automático,-a.

kneel [niːl] *i* arrodillarse.
▲ *pt & pp* knelt.

knee-length ['niːleŋθ] *adj* hasta las rodillas.

kneeling ['niːlɪŋ] *adj* de rodillas, arrodillado,-a.

kneepad ['niːpæd] *n* rodillera.

knees-up ['niːzʌp] *n fam* guateque *m*, fiesta.

knell [nel] *n* toque *m* de difuntos.

knelt [nelt] *pt & pp* → **kneel**.

knew [njuː] *pt* → **know**.

knickerbocker ['nɪkəbɒkə] knickerbockers, *npl arch* pantalones *mpl* cortos.
■ knickerbocker glory, copa de helado con fruta, nueces etc.

knickers ['nɪkəz] *npl* bragas *fpl*: *she bought three pairs of knickers,* compró tres bragas.
● to get one's knickers in a twist, ponerse nervioso,-a.

knick-knack ['nɪknæk] *n* chuchería.

knife [naɪf] **1** *n (gen)* cuchillo; *(folding)* navaja. – **2** *t* apuñalar, acuchillar.
● to get one's knife into sb., ensañarse con algn. ‖ to go under the knife, someterse a cirugía. ‖ to twist the knife in the wound, hurgar en las heridas. ‖ you could cut the atmosphere with a knife, el ambiente se podía cortar con un cuchillo.
■ knife and fork, cubierto.
▲ *pl* knives.

knife-edge ['naɪfedʒ] *n* filo de cuchillo, filo.
● to be on a knife-edge, estar nervioso,-a, estar preocupado,-a. ‖ to be balanced on a knife-edge, pender de un hilo.

knight [naɪt] **1** *n arch* caballero. **2** *(chess)* caballo. **3** caballero, *(hombre que lleva el título de Sir)*. – **4** *t arch* armar caballero. **5** nombrar caballero a.
● knight in shining armour, príncipe *m* azul.

knight-errant ['naɪt'erənt] *n* caballero andante.

knighthood ['naɪthʊd] *n* título de caballero.

knit [nɪt] **1** *t* tejer. – **2** *i* hacer punto, hacer media. **3** MED soldarse. **4** *fig* unirse.
● to knit one's brow, fruncir.
▲ *pt & pp* knit o knitted, ger knitting.

knitted ['nɪtɪd] *adj* de punto.

knitter ['nɪtə'] *n* persona que hace punto: *she's a real knitter,* le encanta hacer punto.

knitting ['nɪtɪŋ] *n (material)* punto; *(activity)* labor *f* de punto.
■ knitting machine, tricotosa, máquina de tejer. ‖ knitting needle, aguja de tejer, aguja de hacer punto. ‖ plain knitting, punto de media, punto del derecho. ‖ purl knitting, punto del revés.

knitwear ['nɪtweə'] *n* género de punto.

knob [nɒb] **1** *n (on door - large)* pomo; *(- small)* tirador *m*. **2** *(on stick)* puño. **3** *(natural)* bulto, protuberancia. **4** *(on radio etc)* botón *m*. **5** *taboo* polla.

knobbly ['nɒblɪ] *adj* nudoso,-a.

knock [nɒk] **1** *n (blow)* golpe *m*: *the boy got a knock on his leg,* el niño recibió un golpe en la pierna. **2** *(on door)* llamada: *was that a knock at the door?,* ¿han llamado a la puerta?; *knock, knock!,* ¡toc, toc! **3** *fig (bad luck)* revés *m*: *you have to learn to take a few knocks in this business,* hay que aprender a aguantar muchos reveses en esta profesión. – **4** *t (to hit)* golpear, darse un golpe en: *he knocked his head on the ceiling,* se golpeó la cabeza contra el techo; *the mugger knocked her to the ground,* el atracador la tiró al suelo. **5** *fam (criticize)* criticar, hablar mal de: *the newspapers are forever knocking the England manager,* los periódicos siempre critican al entrenador de la selección inglesa. – **6** *i (at door)* llamar: *please knock before entering,* por favor, llamen antes de entrar. **7** *(of car engine)* golpear, martillear.
◆ to knock about **1** *n (travel)* rodar, recorrer; *(spend time)* andar con: *he's knocked about the world a bit,* ha rodado mucho mundo; *she's knocking about with that new boy,* anda con aquel chico nuevo. – **2** *t sep (beat up)* pegar, maltratar: *they say he knocks his wife around,* dicen que pega a su mujer. ‖ to knock around *t-i* →
knock about. ‖ to knock back **1** *t sep (drink)* beberse de un trago, rápidamente o en grandes cantidades: *he knocked back a double whisky,* se bebió un whisky doble de un trago; *you were knocking it back last night, mate!,* ¡cómo trincabas anoche, macho! **2** *(cost)* soplar, costar: *how much did that car knock you back?,* ¿cuánto te soplaron por aquel coche? ‖ to knock down **1** *t sep (building)* derribar. **2** *(person - with a car)* atropellar; *(- with a blow)* derribar. **3** *(price)* rebajar: *the stallholder knocked the price down to a pound,* el vendedor rebajó el precio a una libra. **4** *(sell at auction)* adjudicar (to, a): *the painting was knocked down to an anonymous bidder,* el cuadro se adjudicó a un pujador anónimo. ‖ to knock off **1** *t sep (make fall)* tirar, hacer caer: *he accidentally knocked the glass off the table,* tiró el vaso de la mesa sin querer. – **2** *t insep fam (steal)* birlar, mangar, chorizar, afanar: *they knocked off a load of videos,* mangaron cantidad de vídeos. – **3** *t sep sl (kill)* cargarse, liquidar. **4** *(deduct - money)* descontar; *(reduce - time)* quitar: *I'll knock five pounds off the price,* te descuento cinco libras del precio, te rebajo el precio en cinco libras; *she knocked two seconds off the record,* rebajó el récord en dos segundos. – **5** *i (stop work)* acabar, salir del trabajo: *what time do you knock off work?,* ¿a qué hora sales del trabajo? ‖ to knock out **1** *t sep (make unconscious)* dejar sin conocimiento; *(put to sleep)* dejar dormido,-a; *(boxing)* poner fuera de combate, dejar K.O. **2** *(from competition)* eliminar: *Spain were knocked out in the semifinal,* la selección española fue eliminada en la semifinal. **3** *(make or do quickly)* hacer rápidamente, producir rápidamente: *they knocked out 100 models in an hour,* produjeron 100 modelos en una hora. **4** *(astonish)* dejar pasmado,-a, dejar boquiabierto,-a: *the news simply knocked me out,* la noticia me dejó completamente pasmado. ‖ to knock over **1** *t sep (overturn)* volcar, tirar: *as she reached for the salt, she knocked over the bottle of wine,* mientras alargaba la mano para coger la sal, volcó la botella de vino. **2** *(run over)* atropellar. ‖ to knock together **1** *t sep (do quickly)* hacer de prisa, hacer rápidamente. – **2** *i (knees)* entrechocarse. ‖ to knock up **1** *t sep* GB *fam* despertar, llamar. **2** *(prepare quickly)* hacer deprisa, preparar preparar: *I'll knock us up something to*

eat, prepararé algo rápido para comer. **3** US *sl* dejar embarazada. **– 4** *i* (*tennis etc*) pelotear: *we always knock up for half an hour before starting a match,* siempre peloteamos durante media hora antes de empezar un partido.
● **he's knocking on 70,** va para los 70 años. ‖ **to knock on the head,** (*project*) matar; (*plans*) echar por tierra. ‖ **to knock some sense into sb.,** hacer entrar en vereda a algn. ‖ **to knock spots off,** dar mil vueltas a. ‖ **to knock the bottom out of the market,** reventar los precios. ‖ **knock it off!,** ¡basta ya!

knockabout ['nɒkəbaʊt] **1** *adj* bullicioso,-a. **– 2** *n* SP peloteo.
■ **knockabout comedy,** payasadas *fpl.*

knock-back ['nɒkbæk] *n* rechazo.

knockdown ['nɒkdaʊn] *adj* rebajado.
■ **knockdown price,** precio de saldo.

knocker ['nɒkəʳ] **1** *n* aldaba. **2** (*critic*) detractor,-ra. **– 3** knockers, *npl sl* tetas *fpl,* melones *mpl.*

knocking ['nɒkɪŋ] **1** *n* golpeo. **2** (*at door*) llamada. **3** (*car*) golpeteo.

knock-kneed [nɒk'niːd] *adj* patizambo,-a.

knock-on ['nɒk'ɒn] *n* SP autopase *m.*
■ **knock-on effect,** repercusiones *fpl,* consecuencias *fpl.*

knockout ['nɒkaʊt] **1** *n* SP knock-out *m,* fuera de combate *m.* **2** *fam* maravilla: *it's a knockout!,* ¡es alucinante! **– 3** *adj* SP que deja K.O. **4** (*competition*) eliminatorio,-a. **5** *fam* maravilloso,-a, estupendo,-a.
■ **knockout drops,** somnífero *m sing.*

knock-up ['nɒkʌp] *n* peloteo.

knoll [nəʊl] *n* otero.

knot [nɒt] **1** *n* (*gen*) nudo. **2** (*people*) corrillo, grupo. **– 3** *t* anudar.
● **get knotted!,** ¡vete a la porra! ¡fastídiate! ‖ **to get tied up in knots,** liarse, embrollarse, hacerse un lío. ‖ **to tie the knot,** casarse.
▲ (*verbo*) *pt & pp* **knotted,** *ger* **knotting.**

knotty ['nɒtɪ] **1** *adj* nudoso,-a. **2** (*problem*) difícil, espinoso,-a.
▲ *comp* **knottier,** *superl* **knottiest.**

know [nəʊ] **1** *t* (*be acquainted with*) conocer: *do you know Colin?,* conoces a Colin?; *we've known each other for years,* nos conocemos desde hace años; *this building is known as "La Pedrera",* este edificio se conoce como "La Pedrera"; *their terrorist activities were known to the police,* la policía tenía conocimiento de sus actividades terroristas. **2** (*recognize*) reconocer: *I'd know him if I saw him again,* lo reconocería si lo volviera a ver. **3** (*have knowledge of*) saber: *I don't know the answer,* no sé la respuesta; *do you know English?,* ¿sabes inglés?; *do you know where the station is?,* ¿sabe dónde está la estación?
◆ **to know about 1** *t insep* saber de, entender de: *ask Patrick, he knows about cars,* pregúntaselo a Patrick, él entiende de coches. **2** (*have heard about*) saber de: *do you know about the meeting on Friday?,* ¿sabes lo de la reunión del viernes? ‖ **to know of** *t insep* saber de, haber oído hablar de: *do you know of any good restaurants near here?,* ¿sabes de algún restaurante por aquí que esté bien?; *I know of him, but I've never met him,* he oído hablar de él, pero no lo conozco.
● **I know!,** ¡lo sé!, ¡ya lo sé! ‖ **who knows?,** ¿quién sabe? ‖ **as far as I know,** que yo sepa. ‖ **for all I know,** ¡vete a saber!: *he could be dead for all I know,* podría estar muerto, ¡vete a saber! ‖ **don't I know it!,** ¿y me lo dices a mí?, ¡ni que lo digas! ‖ **how should I**

know?, ¿yo qué sé? ‖ **if only I'd known!,** ¡haberlo sabido! ‖ **not that I know of,** que yo sepa, no. ‖ **to know apart,** saber distinguir: *they're so similar that I never know them apart,* se parecen tanto que no los sé distinguir. ‖ **to know ... from ...,** distinguir entre ... y ... ‖ **you know what?,** ¿sabes qué? ‖ **you never know,** nunca se sabe. ‖ **I know what!,** ¡ya lo tengo! ‖ **I might've known,** debí imaginármelo. ‖ **to be in the know,** estar enterado,-a. ‖ **to get to know sb.,** (llegar a) conocer a algn. ‖ **you know best,** tú sabes mejor que yo, sabes lo que más te conviene. ‖ **to know better,** tener más juicio: *you ought to know better at your age!,* ¡a tu edad deberías saber comportarte mejor! ‖ **to know by sight,** conocer de vista. ‖ **to know how to do sth.,** saber hacer algo. ‖ **to know what one's talking about,** hablar con conocimiento de causa. ‖ **to make os. known,** presentarse, darse a conocer.
■ **"don't know",** persona que no sabe, no contesta.
▲ *pt* **knew,** *pp* **known.**

know-all ['nəʊɔːl] *n* sabelotodo *mf.*

know-how ['nəʊhaʊ] *n* saber hacer *m,* conocimiento práctico.

knowing ['nəʊɪŋ] **1** *adj* (*smile, look*) de complicidad; (*person*) sagaz, astuto,-a. **– 2** *n* manera de saber.
● **there's no knowing,** no hay manera de saberlo, es imposible saberlo. ‖ **to be worth knowing,** valer la pena saberse.

knowingly ['nəʊɪŋlɪ] *adv* (*intentionally*) a sabiendas, adrede; (*look etc*) con complicidad.

know-it-all ['nəʊɪtɔːl] *n* US sabelotodo *mf.*

knowledge ['nɒlɪdʒ] **1** *n* (*learning, information*) conocimientos *mpl: his knowledge of football is amazing,* sus conocimientos de fútbol son increíbles. **2** (*awareness*) conocimiento: *at that time I had no knowledge of what was happening,* entonces no tenía conocimiento de lo que estaba pasando.
● **to my knowledge,** que yo sepa. ‖ **not to my knowledge,** que yo sepa, no. ‖ **to the best of my knowledge,** según mi leal entender y saber. ‖ **to be common knowledge that ...,** ser notorio que ..., todo el mundo sabe que ... ‖ **it has come to my knowledge that ...,** he llegado a saber que ... ‖ **to have a good knowledge of sth.,** conocer algo bien. ‖ **to have a working knowledge of sth.,** dominar los fundamentos de algo.

knowledgeable ['nɒlɪdʒəbəl] *adj* entendido,-a: *he's very knowledgeable about music,* es muy entendido en música.

knowledgeably ['nɒlɪdʒəblɪ] *adv* de forma entendida, entendidamente.

known [nəʊn] **1** *pp* → **know.** **– 2** *adj* conocido,-a: *he's a known criminal,* es un conocido delincuente; *there is no known cure for AIDS,* el sida no tiene cura conocida; *the deadliest poison known to man,* el veneno más mortífero que se conoce.
● **the known facts,** los hechos establecidos.

knuckle ['nʌkəl] *n* nudillo.
◆ **to knuckle down** *i fam* ponerse a trabajar en serio. ‖ **to knuckle under** *i* pasar por el aro.
● **to be near the knuckle,** rayar en la indecencia.

knuckleduster ['nʌkldʌstəʳ] *n* puño de hierro.

KO ['keɪ'əʊ] *abbr* (*knockout*) fuera de combate *m;* (*abbreviation*) KO *m.*

koala [kəʊ'ɑːlə] *n* koala *m.*

kohlrabi [kəʊl'rɑːbɪ] *n* colinabo.

kook [kuːk] *n* US *sl* chiflado,-a, majara *mf,* majareta *mf.*

kookaburra ['kʊkəbʌrə] *n* ORN cucaburra *m*.
kooky ['kuːkɪ] *adj* US *sl* chiflado,-a, majara, majareta.
▲ *comp* **kookier,** *superl* **kookiest.**
Koran [kɔː'rɑːn] *n* Alcorán *m*, Corán *m*.
Koranic [kɔː'rænɪk] *adj* alcoránico,-a, coránico,-a.
Korea [kə'rɪə] *n* Corea.
■ **North Korea,** Corea del Norte. ‖ **South Korea,** Corea del Sur.
Korean [kə'rɪən] **1** *adj* coreano,-a. – **2** *n* (*person*) coreano,-a. **3** (*language*) coreano.
■ **North Korean,** norcoreano,-a. ‖ **South Korean,** surcoreano,-a.
kosher ['kəʊʃəʳ] **1** *adj* (*meat*) cosher (*permitido por la ley dietética judía*). **2** *fam* (*genuine*) legal, auténtico,-a.
kowtow [kaʊ'taʊ] *i* humillarse (**to,** ante), rebajarse (**to,** ante).

kph ['keɪ'piː'eɪtʃ] *abbr* (*kilometres per hour*) kilómetros *mpl* por hora; (*abbreviation*) km/h.
kraut [kraʊt] **1** *n pej* alemán,-ana. – **2** *adj pej* alemán,-ana.
krypton ['krɪptən] *n* criptón *m*.
kudos ['kjuːdɒs] *n* prestigio, gloria.
kumquat ['kʌmkwɒt] *n* tipo de naranja china.
kung fu [kʊŋ'fuː] *n* kung-fu *m*.
Kurd [kɜːd] **1** *adj* kurdo,-a. – **2** *n* (*person*) kurdo,-a.
Kurdish ['kɜːdɪʃ] **1** *adj* kurdo,-a. – **2** *n* (*language*) kurdo.
Kuwait [kʊ'weɪt] *n* Kuwait.
Kuwaiti [kʊ'weɪtɪ] **1** *adj* kuwaití. – **2** *n* kuwaití *mf*.
kW ['kɪləwɒt] *symb* (*kilowatt*) kilovatio, kilowatt; (*symbol*) kW.
kWh [kɪləwɒt'aʊəʳ] *abbr* (*kilowatt-hour*) kilovatio, kilowatt-hora *m*; (*abbreviation*) kw/h

L

L, l [el] *n* (*the letter*) L, l *f*.
L¹ [el] *abbr* (*Learner driver*) conductor en prácticas.
L² [laːdʒ] *abbr* (*large size*) talla grande; (*abbreviation*) G.
l ['liːtəʳ] *symb* (*litre* US *liter*) litro; (*symbol*) l.
lab¹ [læb] *n fam* (*abbr of laboratory*) laboratorio.
lab² ['leɪbəʳ] *abbr* (*Labour*) laborista.
label ['leɪbəl] **1** *n* etiqueta. **2** (*record company*) casa discográfica. – **3** *t* etiquetar, poner etiqueta a. **4** *fig* calificar (**as**, de): *most people unjustly labelled him (as) a fool*, la mayoría le calificaba injustamente de imbécil.
▲ (*verbo*) *pt & pp* **labelled** (US **labeled**), *ger* **labelling** (US **labeling**).
labial ['leɪbɪəl] *adj* labial.
labiodental [leɪbɪəʊ'dentəl] **1** *adj* labiodental. – **2** *n* labiodental *f*.
labor ['leɪbəʳ] *n* US → **labour**.
■ **Labor Day**, Día *m* del Trabajador (*primer lunes de septiembre*). ‖ **labor union**, sindicato.
laboratory [lə'bɒrətərɪ, US 'læbrətɔːrɪ] *n* laboratorio.
■ **laboratory assistant**, ayudante *mf* de laboratorio.
▲ *pl* **laboratories**.
laborious [lə'bɔːrɪəs] *adj* laborioso,-a, penoso,-a.
laboriously [lə'bɔːrɪəslɪ] *adv* con gran dificultad, penosamente.
labour ['leɪbəʳ] **1** *n* (*work*) trabajo. **2** (*task*) labor *f*, tarea, faena; (*involving manual work*) mano *f* de obra. **3** (*workforce*) mano *f* de obra. **4** (*childbirth*) parto. **5** (*effort*) esfuerzo: *you must be quite exhausted after your labours!*, ¡debes estar muy agotado después de tanto esfuerzo! – **6** *i* (*work hard*) trabajar duro. **7** (*move slowly*) avanzar penosamente; (*engine*) funcionar con dificultad: *she laboured up the stairs*, subió penosamente las escaleras. – **8** *t* machacar. – **9 Labour**, *n* GB los laboristas *mpl*, el Partido Laborista.
◆ **to labour under** *t insep* dejarse llevar por: *it became apparent that he was labouring under a delusion*, se hizo patente que sólo se dejaba llevar por las ilusiones.
● **to be in labour**, estar de parto. ‖ **to labour the point**, insistir en el tema.
■ **labour camp**, campo de trabajos forzados. ‖ **labour costs**, coste *m* de la mano de obra. ‖ **labour exchange**, GB oficina de empleo. ‖ **labour force**, mano *f* de obra. ‖ **labour market**, mercado laboral. ‖ **labour of love**, trabajo *m* placentero.
laboured ['leɪbəd] **1** *adj* (*breathing*) fatigoso,-a. **2** (*style*) forzado,-a.
labourer ['leɪbərəʳ] *n* peón *m*, jornalero,-a, bracero.
■ **farm labourer**, peón *m* agrícola.
labour-intensive [leɪbərɪn'tensɪv] *adj* con mucha mano de obra.
labour-saving ['leɪbəseɪvɪŋ] *adj* que ahorra trabajo.
■ **labour-saving device**, electrodoméstico.
laburnum [lə'bɜːnəm] *n* laburno, codeso.
labyrinth ['læbərɪnθ] *n* laberinto.

lace [leɪs] **1** *n* (*material*) encaje *m*. **2** (*shoestring*) cordón *m*. – **3** *t* (*pull string through*) poner los cordones a. **4** (*drink*) añadir alcohol a: *he laced the coffee with a bit of brandy*, añadió un poco de coñac al café.
◆ **to lace into** *t insep fam* meterse con, atacar. ‖ **to lace up** *t sep* acordonar, atar los cordones de: *he forgot to lace up his shoes*, se olvidó de atarse los cordones (de los zapatos).
lacerate ['læsəreɪt] *t* lacerar.
lachrimal ['lækrɪməl] *adj* lagrimal, lacrimal.
lachrimose ['lækrɪməʊs] **1** *adj* (*tearful*) llorón,-ona, lacrimoso,-a. **2** *pej* lacrimógeno,-a.
lack [læk] **1** *n* falta, carencia, escasez *f*: *she has no lack of self-confidence*, no le falta confianza en sí misma. – **2** *t* carecer de.
● **for lack of**, por falta de. ‖ **to lack for nothing**, no hacerle falta nada a uno. ‖ **through lack of**, por falta de.
lackadaisical [lækə'deɪzɪkəl] *adj pej* indiferente, apático,-a.
lackey ['lækɪ] *n pej* lacayo.
lacking ['lækɪŋ] *adj* carente de: *there was something lacking in the room*, en la habitación faltaba algo; *he's somewhat lacking in enthusiasm*, carece de algo de entusiasmo.
lackluster ['læklʌstəʳ] *adj* US → **lacklustre**.
lacklustre ['læklʌstəʳ] *adj* sin interés, insulso,-a.
laconic [lə'kɒnɪk] *adj* lacónico,-a.
laconically [lə'kɒnɪklɪ] *adv* lacónicamente.
lacquer ['lækəʳ] **1** *n* laca. – **2** *t* (*metal, wood*) lacar, pintar con laca; (*hair*) poner laca a.
lacrosse [lə'krɒs] *n* lacrosse *m*.
lactation [læk'teɪʃən] *n* lactancia.
lactic ['læktɪk] *adj* láctico,-a.
■ **lactic acid**, ácido láctico.
lactose ['læktəʊs] *n* lactosa.
lacuna [lə'kjuːnə] *n* laguna, hueco.
▲ *pl* **lacunas** o **lacunae** [lə'kjuːniː].
lacy ['leɪsɪ] **1** *adj* (*of lace*) de encaje. **2** (*like lace*) parecido,-a al encaje.
▲ *comp* **lacier**, *superl* **laciest**.
lad [læd] **1** *n* GB *fam* muchacho, chaval *m*, chico: *he's just a lad*, no es más que un chaval; *he's out with the lads*, ha salido con los muchachos. **2** GB *fam* diablillo, pillo: *John's a bit of a lad, don't you think?*, John es un poco pillo, ¿no te parece? **3** (*stable boy*) mozo de cuadra.
ladder ['lædəʳ] **1** *n* escalera (de mano). **2** GB (*in stocking*) carrera. **3** *fig* escala. – **4** *i* GB hacerse una carrera. – **5** *t* GB hacerse una carrera en.
■ **rope ladder**, escalera de cuerda.
laddie ['lædɪ] *n fam* (*in Scotland*) chaval *m*, muchacho.
laden ['leɪdən] *adj* cargado,-a (**with**, de).
● **to be fully laden**, estar lleno,-a hasta el tope, estar hasta los topes.

la-di-da [lɑːdɪ'dɑː] *adj fam pej* pijo,-a.
ladies ['leɪdɪz] *n* GB (*toilet*) lavabo (de señoras).
■ **ladies room,** US lavabo (de señoras).
lading ['leɪdɪŋ] *n* embarque *m*.
■ **bill of lading,** conocimiento de embarque.
ladle ['leɪdəl] **1** *n* cucharón *m*. – **2** *t* servir con cucharón.
◆ **to ladle out** *t sep* repartir.
lady ['leɪdɪ] *n* señora; (*of high social position*) dama.
● **ladies and gentlemen,** señoras y señores. ‖ **my old lady,** *fam* mi vieja.
■ **ladies' man,** mujeriego. ‖ **lady friend,** *fam* amiguita. ‖ **ladies' fingers,** quingombó.
Lady ['leɪdɪ] *n* (*title*) lady *f*: *Lady Elizabeth Hastings,* lady Elizabeth Hastings.
▲ *pl* **ladies.**
ladybird ['leɪdɪbɜːd] *n* mariquita.
ladybug ['leɪdɪbʌg] *n* US mariquita.
lady-in-waiting [leɪdɪn'weɪtɪŋ] *n* dama de honor.
▲ *pl* **ladies-in-waiting.**
lady-killer ['leɪdɪkɪlə'] *n* donjuán *m*.
ladylike ['leɪdɪlaɪk] *adj* delicado,-a, elegante.
ladyship ['leɪdɪʃɪp] *n* señoría: *Her Ladyship has arrived,* ha llegado su señoría.
lag [læg] **1** *n* retraso. **2** GB *sl* preso. – **3** *t* TECH revestir.
● **to lag behind,** rezagarse, quedarse atrás.
■ **old lag,** *fam* reincidente *m*. ‖ **time lag,** retraso, demora.
▲ (*verbo*) *pt & pp* **lagged,** *ger* **lagging.**
lager ['lɑːgə'] *n* cerveza rubia.
lagging ['lægɪŋ] *n* TECH revestimiento (calorífugo).
lagoon [lə'guːn] *n* laguna.
laid [leɪd] **1** *pt & pp* → **lay**². – **2 to be laid up,** *i fam* guardar cama.
● **to get laid,** *taboo* echar un polvo: *so she meets this guy and gets laid and ...,* así que conoce a un tío y echan un polvo y ...
laid-back [leɪd'bæk] *adj fam* (*relaxed*) tranquilo,-a; (*easy-going*) flexible.
lain [leɪn] *pp* → **lie**².
lair [leə'] *n* guarida.
laird [leəd] *n* terrateniente *m* (*escocés*).
laissez-faire [leɪseɪ'feə'] *adj* (*policy etc*) liberal.
lake [leɪk] *n* lago.
lam [læm] **to lam into,** *t sl* meterse con.
▲ *pt & pp* **lammed,** *ger* **lamming.**
lama ['lɑːmə] *n* lama *m*.
lamb [læm] **1** *n* cordero,-a. **2** (*meat*) carne *f* de cordero. **3** *fam* (*person*) cordero,-a: *poor lamb!,* ¡pobrecito,-a! – **4** *i* parir.
■ **lamb chop,** chuleta de cordero. ‖ **lamb's wool,** lambswool *m*.
lambast ['læmbæst] *t fam* → **lambaste.**
lambaste ['læmbeɪst] *t fam* fustigar.
lambskin ['læmskɪn] *n* piel *f* de cordero.
lamb's-wool ['læmswʊl] *adj* de lambswool.
lame [leɪm] **1** *adj* cojo,-a: *lame in one leg,* cojo,-a de una pierna. **2** *fig* débil; (*excuse*) poco convincente; (*business*) fallido,-a.
■ **lame duck,** inútil *mf*; US *persona u organismo todavía en funciones.*
lamely ['leɪmlɪ] *adv fig* sin convicción.
lameness ['leɪmnəs] **1** *n* cojera. **2** *fig* debilidad *f*, poca convicción *f*.
lament [lə'ment] **1** *n* lamento. **2** MUS endecha. – **3** *t* lamentar, llorar. – **4** *i* lamentarse (**over,** de).

■ **the late lamented,** el/la recientemente fallecido,-a.
lamentable ['læməntəbəl] *adj* lamentable.
lamentation [læmən'teɪʃən] *n* lamentación *f*.
laminate ['læmɪneɪt] **1** *t* laminar. – **2** *n* laminado.
▲ (*substantivo*) ['læmɪnət].
laminated ['læmɪneɪtɪd] **1** *adj* (*metal*) laminado,-a; (*glass*) inastillable. **2** (*paper*) plastificado,-a.
lamp [læmp] **1** *n* lámpara. **2** (*on car, train*) faro.
lamplight ['læmplaɪt] *n* luz *f* de lámpara.
lamplit ['læmplɪt] *adj* iluminado,-a con luz de lámpara.
lampoon [læm'puːn] **1** *n* pasquín *m*, sátira. – **2** *t* satirizar.
lamp-post ['læmppəʊst] *n* (poste *m* de) farol *m*.
lamprey ['læmprɪ] *n* (*fish*) lamprea.
lampshade ['læmpʃeɪd] *n* pantalla (de lámpara).
lance [lɑːns] **1** *n* (*spear*) lanza. **2** MED lanceta. – **3** *t* MED abrir con lanceta.
■ **lance corporal,** GB MIL cabo interino.
lancet ['lɑːnsɪt] *n* lanceta.
land [lænd] **1** *n* (*gen*) tierra: *by land and sea,* por tierra y por mar; *on dry land,* en tierra firme. **2** (*soil*) suelo, tierra. **3** (*country, region*) tierra: *in foreign lands,* en tierras extranjeras. **4** (*property*) terreno, tierras *fpl*: *a piece of land,* un terreno; *a plot of land,* una parcela. – **5** *i* (*plane etc*) aterrizar, tomar tierra; (*bird*) posarse. **6** (*disembark*) desembarcar. **7** (*fall*) caer. – **8** *t* (*plane etc*) hacer aterrizar. **9** (*disembark*) desembarcar; (*unload*) descargar. **10** (*fish*) sacar del agua. **11** *fam* (*get*) conseguir: *she's landed a good job in a bank,* ha conseguido un buen puesto en un banco. **12** *fam* (*hit*) asestar: *he landed me a punch in the face,* me asestó un puñetazo en la cara.
◆ **to land in** *t sep* causar, traer: *he's bound to land you in trouble,* seguro que te traerá problemas. ‖ **to land up** *i* acabar: *his business landed up deeply in debt,* su negocio acabó cargado de deudas.
● **land ahoy!,** ¡tierra a la vista! ‖ **the land of milk and honey,** la tierra de la leche y la miel. ‖ **to be in the land of the living,** estar entre los vivos. ‖ **to get landed with sth.,** *fam* (tener que) cargar con algo. ‖ **to land on one's feet,** caer de pies. ‖ **to land on the moon,** alunizar. ‖ **to make a living from the land,** vivir de la tierra. ‖ **to make land,** llegar a tierra. ‖ **to see how the land lies,** tantear el terreno.
■ **farm land,** tierras *fpl* de cultivo. ‖ **land agent,** GB encargado,-a de una granja, cortijero,-a. ‖ **land forces,** MIL ejército *m* de tierra. ‖ **land mass,** masa continental. ‖ **land reform,** reforma agraria. ‖ **land register,** registro de la propiedad. ‖ **native land,** tierra natal, patria.
landed ['lændɪd] *adj* hacendado,-a.
■ **the landed gentry,** los terratenientes *mpl*. ‖ **landed property,** bienes *mpl* raíces.
landfall ['lændfɔːl] *n* MAR recalada.
landing ['lændɪŋ] **1** *n* (*plane*) aterrizaje *m*. **2** (*on stairs*) descansillo, rellano. **3** (*of people*) desembarco.
■ **crash landing,** aterrizaje *m* de emergencia. ‖ **forced landing,** aterrizaje *m* forzoso. ‖ **landing card,** tarjeta de inmigración. ‖ **landing craft,** lancha de desembarco. ‖ **landing field,** pista de aterrizaje. ‖ **landing gear,** tren *m* de aterrizaje. ‖ **landing net,** salabre *m*. ‖ **landing stage,** desembarcadero. ‖ **landing strip,** pista de aterrizaje.
landlady ['lændleɪdɪ] **1** *n* (*of flat*) propietaria, dueña; (*house*) casera. **2** (*of boarding house*) patrona. **3** (*of pub*) dueña.
▲ *pl* **landladies.**

landlocked [ˈlændlɒkt] *adj* sin salida al mar.

landlord [ˈlændlɔːd] **1** *n* (*of flat*) propietario, dueño; (*of house*) casero. **2** (*of boarding house*) patrón *m*. – **3** *m* (*of pub*) patrón *m*, dueño.

landmark [ˈlændmɑːk] **1** *n fig* (*building, place*) monumento *o edificio muy conocido*: *the Statue of Liberty is New York's most famous landmark,* la Estatua de la Libertad es el monumento más famoso de Nueva York. **2** (*reference point*) punto de referencia: *in the desert there are no landmarks to orient yourself by,* en el desierto no hay puntos de referencia para orientarse. **3** *fig* (*milestone*) hito.

landmine [ˈlændmaɪn] *n* mina (de tierra).

landowner [ˈlændəʊnəʳ] *n* propietario,-a, terrateniente *mf*, hacendado,-a.

landscape [ˈlændskeɪp] **1** *n* paisaje *m*. – **2** *t* ajardinar.
■ **landscape gardening,** jardinería paisajista. ‖ **landscape painter,** paisajista *mf*. ‖ **landscape painting,** paisaje *m*.

landslide [ˈlændslaɪd] *n* desprendimiento de tierras.
■ **landslide victory,** triunfo arrollador, triunfo aplastante.

landward [ˈlændwəd] *adj* hacia la tierra.

lane [leɪn] **1** *n* (*in country*) camino, sendero, vereda; (*in town*) callejuela, callejón *m*. **2** AUTO carril *m*. **3** SP calle *f*. **4** AV MAR ruta.
● **to live in the fast lane,** vivir deprisa.

language [ˈlæŋgwɪdʒ] **1** *n* (*faculty, way of speaking*) lenguaje *m*: *watch your language!,* ¡no digas palabrotas! **2** (*tongue*) idioma *m*, lengua: *the French language,* el (idioma) francés. **3** (*school subject*) lengua.
● **to use bad language,** ser mal hablado,-a.
■ **bad language,** palabrotas *fpl*, tacos *mpl*. ‖ **language laboratory,** laboratorio de idiomas.

languid [ˈlæŋgwɪd] *adj* lánguido,-a.

languish [ˈlæŋgwɪʃ] *i* languidecer; (*in prison*) pudrirse.

languor [ˈlæŋgəʳ] *n* languidez *f*.

lank [læŋk] *adj* lacio,-a.

lanky [ˈlæŋkɪ] *adj* larguirucho,-a.
▲ *comp* lankier, *superl* lankiest.

lanolin [ˈlænəlɪn] *n* lanolina.

lantern [ˈlæntən] *n* linterna, farol *m*.

lantern-jawed [ˈlæntəndʒɔːd] *adj* de cara larga.

Lao [laʊ] *n* (*language*) laosiano.

Laos [laʊz, laʊs] *n* Laos.

Laotian [ˈlaʊʃən] **1** *adj* laosiano,-a. – **2** *n* laosiano,-a.

lap[1] [læp] *n* regazo; (*knees*) rodillas *fpl*; (*skirt*) falda.
● **it's in the lap of the gods,** el destino lo dirá, está en manos de Dios. ‖ **to live in the lap of luxury,** *fam* vivir como un pachá.

lap[2] [læp] **1** *n* SP vuelta. **2** *fig* (*stage*) etapa. – **3** *t* SP (*overtake*) doblar. – **4** *i* (*go round*) dar la vuelta.
▲ (*verbo*) *pt & ger lapped, ger lapping*.

lap[3] [læp] **1** *t* (*animal*) beber a lengüetadas. **2** (*waves*) lamer, besar. – **3** *i* (*waves*) chapalear.
◆ **to lap up 1** *t sep* beber a lengüetadas. **2** *fig* (*wallow in*) disfrutar con. **3** *fig* (*believe*) tragar, tragarse.
▲ (*verbo*) *pt & pp lapped, ger lapping*.

laparoscopy [læpəˈrɒskəpɪ] *n* laparoscopia.
▲ *pl laparoscopies*.

lapdog [ˈlæpdɒg] *n* perrito faldero.

lapel [ləˈpel] *n* solapa.

lapse [læps] **1** *n* (*in time*) intervalo, lapso. **2** (*slip*) desliz *m*. **3** (*when speaking*) lapsus *m*; (*of memory*) fallo. – **4** *i* (*time*) transcurrir. **5** (*err*) cometer un desliz. **6** (*contract etc*) caducar. **7** (*fall back*) volver a caer (**into**, en): *after only one hit record he lapsed into obscurity,* después de su único gran éxito, volvió a caer en la oscuridad; *everyone lapsed into silence,* todos se quedaron callados.

lapsed [læpst] **1** *adj* REL no practicante. **2** JUR caducado,-a.

laptop [ˈlæptɒp] **laptop (computer),** *n* ordenador *m* portátil.

lapwing [ˈlæpwɪŋ] *n* avefría.

larceny [ˈlɑːsənɪ] *n* latrocinio.
■ **grand larceny,** robo importante. ‖ **petty larceny,** robo de menor cuantía.
▲ *pl larcenies*.

larch [lɑːtʃ] *n* alerce *m*.

lard [lɑːd] **1** *n* manteca de cerdo. – **2** *t* mechar. **3** *fig* cargar, recargar (**with**, de).

larder [ˈlɑːdəʳ] *n* despensa.

large [lɑːdʒ] **1** *adj* grande; (*before sing noun*) gran; (*sum, amount*) importante; (*meal*) abundante. **2** (*family*) numeroso,-a. **3** (*extensive*) amplio,-a, extenso,-a.
● **(as) large as life,** *fam* en persona. ‖ **at large,** (*as a whole*) en general. ‖ **by and large,** por lo general. ‖ **on a large scale,** a gran escala. ‖ **to be at large,** andar suelto,-a, estar en libertad. ‖ **to be larger than life,** ser exagerado,-a.
■ **large employers,** grandes empresas *fpl*.

largely [ˈlɑːdʒlɪ] *adv* (*mainly*) en gran parte; (*chiefly*) principalmente.

largeness [ˈlɑːdʒnəs] **1** *n* (*size*) magnitud *f*, amplitud *f*. **2** (*importance*) importancia.

large-scale [ˈlɑːdʒskeɪl] **1** *adj* de gran escala. **2** (*map*) a gran escala.

largesse [lɑːˈdʒes] *n fml* generosidad *f*.

lark[1] [lɑːk] *n* (*bird*) alondra.

lark[2] [lɑːk] *n fam* (*bit of fun*) broma: *what a lark!,* ¡qué risa!
◆ **to lark about / lark around** *i fam* hacer el indio.

larva [ˈlɑːvə] *n* larva.
▲ *pl larvae* [ˈlɑːviː].

larynges [ləˈrɪndʒiːz] *npl* → **larynx**.

laryngitis [lærɪnˈdʒaɪtəs] *n* laringitis *f*.

larynx [ˈlærɪŋks] *n* laringe *f*.
▲ *pl larynxes o larynges* [ləˈrɪndʒiːz].

lasagna [ləˈzɑːnjə] *n* lasaña.

lascivious [ləˈsɪvɪəs] *adj* lascivo,-a.

lasciviousness [ləˈsɪvɪəsnəs] *n* lascivia, lujuria.

laser [ˈleɪzəʳ] *n* láser *m*.

lash [læʃ] **1** *n* (*blow with whip*) latigazo, azote *m*; (*with tail*) coletazo. **2** (*whip*) látigo; (*thong*) tralla. **3** (*eyelash*) pestaña. – **4** *t* (*in general*) azotar. **5** (*fasten*) sujetar. – **6** *i* (*fall hard*) caer con fuerza (**against**, contra).
◆ **to lash out 1** *i* arremeter (**against/at**, contra). **2** (*splurge*) gastarse un montón (de dinero) (**on**, en).

lashing [ˈlæʃɪŋ] *n* (*beating*) azotes *mpl*.
● **lashings of,** GB *fam* un montón enorme de.

lash-up [ˈlæʃʌp] *n fam* chapuza.

lass [læs] *n fam* chica, chavala.

lassitude [ˈlæsɪtjuːd] *n* lasitud *f*.

lasso [læˈsuː] **1** *n* lazo. – **2** *t* lazar, coger con el lazo.
▲ (*sustantivo*) *pl lassos o lassoes*; (*verbo*) *pt & pp lassoed, ger lassoing*.

last[1] [lɑːst] **1** *adj* (*final*) último,-a. **2** (*most recent*) último,-a: *the last time,* la última vez. **3** (*past*) pasado,-a; (*previous*) anterior: *last Monday,* el lunes pasado; *last night,* anoche; *last week,* la semana pasada; *the night before last,* anteanoche; *the month/year before last,* hace dos meses/años; *she's been studying hard for the last week,* hace una semana que estudia mucho; *Spielberg's new*

film is much better than his last one, la nueva película de Spielberg es mucho mejor que la anterior. **– 4** *adv* por última vez: *that's when he last came to see me,* eso es cuando me vino a ver por última vez. **5** (*at the end*) en último lugar; (*in race*) en última posición: *who came last in the 1000 metres?,* ¿quién acabó último en la carrera de los 1000 metros? **– 6** *n* (*person*) el/la último,-a; (*thing*) lo último: *are you the last?,* ¿eres tú el último?; *the first shall be last and the last shall be first,* los primeros serán los últimos y los últimos serán los primeros; *he drank the last of the wine,* se bebió lo que quedaba del vino; *the last I heard he was back in Ireland,* lo último que sé es que volvió a Irlanda; *I'm sure we haven't heard the last of it,* estoy seguro de que aquí no se ha acabado la historia. **– 7** *i* (*continue*) durar; (*hold out*) aguantar, resistir. **– 8** *t* durar.
◆ **to last out** *i* resistir, aguantar.
● **at last,** al fin, por fin. ‖ **at long last,** por fin. ‖ **if it's the last thing I do,** cueste lo que cueste, aunque sea lo último que haga. ‖ **last but not least,** por último lugar, pero no por eso menos importante. ‖ **last but one,** penúltimo,-a. ‖ **to be the last straw,** *fam* ser el colmo. ‖ **to be the last word,** *fam* ser el último grito. ‖ **to breathe one's last,** dar el último suspiro. ‖ **to have seen the last of sb.,** haber visto a algn. por última vez. ‖ **to have the last word,** decir la última palabra. ‖ **to the last,** hasta el final.
■ **the Last Judgment,** el Juicio Final. ‖ **the last rites,** la extremaunción *f*.
last² [lɑːst] *n* (*shoemaker's*) horma.
last-ditch [lɑːst'dɪtʃ] *adj* último,-a, desesperado,-a.
lasting [ˈlɑːstɪŋ] *adj* duradero,-a, perdurable.
lastly [ˈlɑːstlɪ] *adv* por último, finalmente.
last-minute [lɑːst'mɪnɪt] *adj* de última hora.
latch [lætʃ] *n* pestillo: *come in, the door's on the latch,* entra, el pestillo no está echado.
◆ **to latch on** *i fam* caer en la cuenta. ‖ **to latch onto 1** *t insep fam* (*understand*) captar. **2** *fam* (*cling to*) pegarse a. **3** (*take an interest in*) poner interés en, interesarse por.
latchkey [ˈlætʃkiː] *n* llavín *m*.
■ **latchkey child,** *niño que pasa mucho tiempo solo en casa porque los padres trabajan.*
late [leɪt] **1** *adj* (*not on time*) tardío,-a: *you're ten minutes late,* llegas diez minutos tarde; *it was late,* llegó con retraso. **2** (*far on in time*) tarde: *in late May,* a finales de mayo; *it's getting late,* se hace tarde; *he's in his late thirties,* tiene cerca de cuarenta años. **3** *euph* (*dead*) difunto,-a, fallecido,-a: *the late minister,* el ministro fallecido. **4** (*former*) anterior. **5** (*last-minute*) de última hora. **– 6** *adv* tarde: *I stayed up late last night,* anoche me acosté muy tarde; *late in life,* a una edad avanzada; *late at night,* a altas horas de la noche. **7** (*recently*) recientemente: *as late as yesterday,* ayer mismo.
● **of late,** últimamente. ‖ **to be late in doing sth.,** tardar en hacer algo. ‖ **to keep late hours,** acostarse tarde.
latecomer [ˈleɪtkʌmə^r] *n* tardón,-ona, persona que llega tarde.
lately [ˈleɪtlɪ] *adv* últimamente, recientemente: *until lately,* hasta hace poco.
latency [ˈleɪtənsɪ] *n* latencia.
lateness [ˈleɪtnəs] **1** *n* (*of arrival*) retraso; (*of delivery*) atraso. **2** (*of hour*) lo avanzado.
late-night [ˈleɪtnaɪt] *adj* de noche, de madrugada: *the late-night film,* la película de medianoche.
latent [ˈleɪtənt] **1** *adj* latente. **2** (*hidden*) oculto,-a.
■ **latent heat,** calor *m* latente.

later [ˈleɪtə^r] **1** *adj* más tardío,-a: *we'll discuss that at a later date,* hablaremos de eso más adelante. **2** (*more recent*) más reciente. **3** (*in series*) posterior. **– 4** *adv* más tarde: *five minutes later,* cinco minutos más tarde; *see you later!,* ¡hasta luego!; *I'll tell you later,* ya te lo diré; *no later than tomorrow,* mañana a más tardar. **5** (*afterwards*) después, luego.
● **later on,** más adelante, más tarde.
lateral [ˈlætərəl] *adj* lateral.
■ **lateral thinking,** pensamiento lateral.
latest [ˈleɪtɪst] **1** *adj* último,-a, más reciente. **– 2** *n* lo último: *it's the latest in computers,* es el último grito en informática, es lo último en informática.
● **at the latest,** a más tardar, como máximo.
latex [ˈleɪteks] *n* látex *m*.
lath [læθ, lɑːθ] *n* listón *m*.
lathe [leɪð] *n* torno.
■ **lathe operator,** tornero,-a.
lather [ˈlɑːðə^r] **1** *n* (*of soap*) espuma. **2** (*sweat*) sudor *m*. **– 3** *t* enjabonar. **– 4** *i* hacer espuma: *this soap lathers easily,* este jabón hace mucha espuma.
● **in a lather,** *fam* agobiado,-a y sudando. ‖ **to work os. into a lather,** *fam* agobiarse.
Latin [ˈlætɪn] **1** *adj* latino,-a: *the Latin Quarter,* el barrio latino. **– 2** *n* (*person*) latino,-a. **3** (*language*) latín *m*.
■ **Latin American,** latinoamericano,-a.
latitude [ˈlætɪtjuːd] *n* latitud *f*.
latrine [ləˈtriːn] *n* retrete *m*.
latter [ˈlætə^r] **1** *adj* (*last*) último,-a: *the latter days of his life were very happy,* los últimos días de su vida fueron muy felices. **2** (*second*) segundo,-a: *in the latter half of September,* durante la segunda quincena de septiembre. **– 3 the latter,** *pron* éste,-a, este,-a último,-a.
latter-day [ˈlætədeɪ] *adj* actual, de hoy.
lattice [ˈlætɪs] *n* celosía, enrejado.
■ **lattice window,** ventana de celosía.
lattice-work [ˈlætɪswɜːk] *n* enrejado.
laud [lɔːd] *t arch* alabar, elogiar.
● **to laud sth. to the skies,** poner algo por las nubes.
laudable [ˈlɔːdəbəl] *adj* laudable, loable.
laudanum [ˈlɔːdənəm] *n* láudano.
laugh [lɑːf] **1** *i refr* reírse: *it makes me laugh,* me da risa; *don't laugh,* no te rías; *he'll laugh in your face,* se te reirá en la cara; *you've got to laugh, haven't you?,* es mejor tomárselo a risa; *don't make me laugh!,* ¡no me hagas reír! **– 2** *n* risa: *we had a really good laugh,* nos reímos muchísimo; *we did it for a laugh,* lo hicimos para divertirnos; *what a laugh!,* ¡qué risa!; *she's a good laugh,* es muy divertida, tiene mucha gracia.
◆ **to laugh at 1** *t insep* reírse de: *she laughs at all his jokes,* le ríe todos sus chistes. **2** (*scoff at*) mofarse de. ‖ **to laugh off** *t sep* tomar a risa.
● **he who laughs last laughs longest,** quien ríe último ríe mejor. ‖ **to burst out laughing,** echarse a reír. ‖ **to have the last laugh,** reír el/la último,-a. ‖ **to laugh like a drain,** *fam* reírse a carcajada limpia. ‖ **to laugh one's head off,** *fam* partirse de risa, troncharse de risa, desternillarse de risa. ‖ **to laugh on the other side of one's face,** llevarse un chasco. ‖ **to laugh up one's sleeve,** reír disimuladamente.
laughable [ˈlɑːfəbəl] *adj* ridículo,-a, irrisible; (*sum*) irrisorio,-a.
laughing [ˈlɑːfɪŋ] **1** *adj* risueño,-a. **– 2** *n* risas *fpl*; (*loud*) carcajadas *fpl*.
● **not to be a laughing matter,** no ser (cosa) de risa.
■ **laughing gas,** gas *m* hilarante.

laughingly ['lɑːfɪŋlɪ] 1 adv (with laughter) con risas. 2 (absurdly) risiblemente.

laughing-stock ['lɑːfɪŋstɒk] n hazmerreír m.

laughter ['lɑːftəʳ] n risas fpl: *a fit of laughter,* un ataque de risa.
● to die of laughter, fam morirse de risa.

launch [lɔːntʃ] 1 t lanzar: *it will be launched on the market next year,* se lanzará al mercado el año que viene. 2 (ship) botar; (lifeboat) echar al mar. 3 (film etc) estrenar; (book) presentar. 4 (company) fundar. 5 (scheme, attack) iniciar. – 6 n (boat) lancha. 7 → **launching**.

launcher ['lɔːntʃəʳ] n lanzador m.
■ grenade launcher, lanzagranadas m.

launching ['lɔːntʃɪŋ] 1 n lanzamiento. 2 (of ship) botadura. 3 (of film) estreno; (of book) presentación f.

launchpad ['lɔːntʃpæd] n plataforma de lanzamiento.

launder ['lɔːndəʳ] 1 t (clothes) lavar (y planchar). 2 fig (money) blanquear.

launderette [lɔːn'dæret] n lavandería automática.

laundromat ['lɔːdrəmæt] n us → **launderette**.

laundry ['lɔːndrɪ] 1 n (place) lavandería. 2 (dirty) ropa sucia, colada; (clean) ropa limpia, ropa lavada.
● to do the laundry, lavar la ropa.
■ laundry basket, cesto de la ropa sucia.
▲ pl laundries.

laureate ['lɔːrɪət] n ganador,-ra: *he was a Nobel laureate in literature,* fue (ganador del) premio Nobel de literatura.

laurel ['lɒrəl] n laurel m.
● to look to one's laurels, no dormirse en los laureles. || to rest on one's laurels, dormirse en los laureles.
■ laurel wreath, corona de laureles.

Lausanne [ləʊ'zæn] n Lausana.

lava ['lɑːvə] n lava.

lavatory ['lævətərɪ] 1 n váter m. 2 (room) lavabo, baño. 3 (public) servicios mpl, aseos mpl.
▲ pl lavatories.

lavender ['lævɪndəʳ] 1 n espliego, lavanda. – 2 adj (colour) de color lavanda.
■ lavender water, agua de lavanda.

lavish ['lævɪʃ] 1 adj (generous) pródigo,-a, generoso,-a. 2 (abundant) abundante. 3 (luxurious) lujoso,-a. – 4 t prodigar (on, a).

law [lɔː] 1 n ley f. 2 EDUC derecho. 3 the law, fam la poli f, la pasma.
● against the law, contra la ley. || by law, por ley. || in law, por ley. || laws are made to be broken, hecha la ley, hecha la trampa. || the law of the jungle, la ley del más fuerte. || to be a law unto os., dictar sus propias leyes. || to be outside the law, estar fuera de la ley. || to go to law, recurrir a la ley. || to keep within the law, obrar según la ley. || to take the law into one's own hands, tomarse la justicia por su mano.
■ law and order, orden m público. || law court, tribunal m de justicia. || law firm, bufete m de abogados. || law school, us facultad f de derecho.

law-abiding ['lɔːəbaɪdɪŋ] adj observante de la ley.

law-breaker ['lɔːbreɪkəʳ] n infractor,-ra de la ley.

lawful ['lɔːfʊl] 1 adj legal. 2 (allowed by law) lícito,-a.

lawless ['lɔːləs] 1 adj sin ley; (ungovernable) ingobernable. 2 (person) anárquico,-a.

lawlessness ['lɔːləsnəs] n anarquía, desorden m.

lawmaker ['lɔːmeɪkəʳ] n legislador,-ra.

lawn [lɔːn] n césped m.
■ lawn party, us fiesta (en el jardín). || lawn tennis, tenis m sobre hierba.

lawnmower ['lɔːnməʊəʳ] n cortacésped m & f.

lawsuit ['lɔːsjuːt] n pleito, juicio.

lawyer ['lɔːjəʳ] n abogado,-a.
■ labour lawyer, abogado,-a laboralista.

lax [læks] 1 adj (unstrict) poco disciplinario,-a, flojo,-a; (relaxed) relajado,-a. 2 (negligent) negligente. 3 (of intestine) suelto,-a.

laxative ['læksətɪv] 1 adj laxante. – 2 n laxante m.

laxity ['læksɪtɪ] 1 n (lacking strictness) poca disciplina, flojedad f; (relaxation) relajamiento, relajación f. 2 (negligence) negligencia.

lay¹ [leɪ] 1 adj REL laico,-a, seglar. 2 (non-professional) lego,-a, no profesional.
■ lay brother, hermano lego. || lay figure, maniquí. || lay preacher, predicador,-ra seglar. || lay sister, hermana lega.

lay² [leɪ] 1 t (gen) poner, colocar; (spread out) extender. 2 (bricks, carpet) poner; (cable, pipe) tender; (foundations, basis) echar; (bomb) colocar. 3 (prepare) preparar; (curse) lanzar. 4 (eggs) poner. 5 (bet) apostar. 6 (charge) formular. 7 taboo follar. – 8 i (hen) poner huevos.
◆ to lay about t insep agredir. || to lay aside t sep dejar a un lado; fig dejar de lado. || to lay before t insep presentar. || to lay by t sep guardar; (money) ahorrar. || to lay down 1 t sep (let go) dejar, soltar: *they were forced to lay down their arms,* se les obligó a deponer las armas. 2 (give up) entregar: *he would lay down his life for his best friend,* daría la vida por su mejor amigo. 3 (establish) imponer, fijar; (principles etc) sentar. 4 (wine) guardar (en bodega). || to lay in t insep proveerse de. || to lay into t insep atacar. || to lay off 1 t sep (worker) despedir. – 2 t insep fam (stop) dejar en paz, dejar de molestar: *lay off my brother!,* ¡deja ya de molestar a mi hermano! – 3 i fam parar: *lay off kicking me!,* ¡deja ya de darme patadas!; *lay off!,* ¡ya está bien!, ¡para ya! || to lay on 1 t sep (provide) facilitar, suministrar. – 2 t insep (burden) cargar: *that's a hard job to lay on one person alone,* es un trabajo demasiado duro para que se lo cargue a una sola persona. || to lay out 1 t sep (spread out) tender, extender. 2 (arrange) disponer, colocar. 3 (present) presentar, exponer. 4 (town etc) hacer el trazado de; (garden) diseñar. 5 fam (knock down) dejar fuera de combate. 6 fam (spend) desembolsar. || to lay over i us (gen) hacer una parada (at/in, en); (plane) hacer escala (at/in, en). || to lay up t sep (store) almacenar.
● to lay a great lay, taboo ser muy bueno,-a en la cama. || to be laid low, estar enfermo,-a (with, de). || to be laid up, tener que guardar cama. || to lay claim to sth., hacer valer su derecho a algo. || to lay down the law, dictar la ley. || to lay emphasis on sth., hacer hincapié en algo. || to lay it on / lay it on a bit thick, fam cargar la mano, cargar las tintas; (praise) hacer la pelota. || to lay one on sb., GB fam hacerle una jugarreta a algn. || to lay one's hands on sb., pillar a algn. || to lay open to ..., exponer a ...: *this would lay us open to criticism,* esto nos expondría a las críticas. || to lay sth. flat, derribar algo. || to lay sth. on the line, (make clear) dejar algo bien claro; (risk) arriesgar: *she laid her life on the line for her children,* se jugó la vida por sus hijos. || to lay the table, poner la mesa. || to lay the blame on sb., echar la culpa a algn. || to lay up trouble for os., crearse problemas. || to lay waste to, arrasar, asolar.
■ the lay of the land, us la topografía.
▲ (verbo) pt & pp laid.

lay³ [leɪ] pt → **lie²**.

lay⁴ [leɪ] n LIT (ballad) romance m.

layabout [ˈleɪəbaʊt] *n* GB *fam* gandul,-la, holgazán,-ana.

lay-by [ˈleɪbaɪ] *n* área de descanso.
▲ *pl* **lay-bys.**

layer [ˈleɪəʳ] **1** *n* capa. **2** (*of rock*) estrato. **3** (*installer*) colocador,-ra: *he's a carpet layer,* es colocador de moquetas, coloca moquetas. **4** (*hen*) gallina ponedora. – **5** *t* (*cake, dish*) dividir en capas. **6** (*hair*) hacer un corte escalonado a.

layette [leɪˈet] *n* canastilla.

layman [ˈleɪmən] **1** *n* REL laico. **2** (*not expert*) profano.
● **in layman's language,** en lenguaje llano.
▲ *pl* **laymen** [ˈleɪmən].

lay-off [ˈleɪɒf] *n* despido.

layout [ˈleɪaʊt] **1** *n* (*arrangement*) disposición *f*; (*presentation*) presentación *f*. **2** (*printing*) composición *f*, formato. **3** (*plan*) trazado.

layover [ˈleɪəʊvəʳ] *n* US parada; AV escala.

layperson [ˈleɪpɜːsən] *n* REL laico,-a.
▲ *pl* **laypeople** [ˈleɪpiːpəl].

laywoman [ˈleɪwʊmən] *n* REL laica.
▲ *pl* **laywomen** [ˈleɪwɪmɪn].

laze [leɪz] **1** *i* gandulear, holgazanear. – **2** *n* siesta.
◆ **to laze about / laze around** *i* hacer el vago. ‖ **to laze away** *t sep* pasar canduleando: *she lazed the afternoon away in her hammock,* se pasó la tarde ganduleando en su hamaca.

lazily [ˈleɪzɪlɪ] *adv* perezosamente.

laziness [ˈleɪzɪnəs] *n* pereza.

lazy [ˈleɪzɪ] **1** *adj* gandul,-la, vago,-a, perezoso,-a. **2** (*river*) perezoso,-a.
● **lazy eye,** ojo gandul.
▲ *comp* **lazier,** *superl* **laziest.**

lazybones [ˈleɪzɪbəʊnz] *n* perezoso,-a, gandul,-la.
▲ *pl* **lazybones.**

lb [paʊnd] *abbr* (*pound*) libra.
▲ *pl* **lb** o **lbs.**

LCD [elsiːˈdiː] *abbr* (*of liquid crystal display*) pantalla de cristal líquido.

LCM [elsiːˈem] *abbr* (*of lowest common multiple*) mínimo común múltiplo.

L-driver [ˈeldraɪvəʳ] *n* GB conductor,-ra novato,-a.

leach [liːtʃ] *t* TECH lixiviar.

lead¹ [led] **1** *n* (*metal*) plomo. **2** (*in pencil*) mina. **3** *sl* (*bullets*) plomo.
● **to swing the lead,** *fam* hacer el vago.
■ **lead poisoning,** saturnismo.

lead² [liːd] **1** *t* (*guide*) llevar, conducir: *our tour guide led the way to the cathedral,* la guía nos llevó a la catedral. **2** (*be leader of*) liderar, dirigir. **3** (*be first in*) ocupar el primer puesto en. **4** (*influence*) llevar: *he is easily led,* se deja llevar fácilmente. **5** (*life*) llevar: *I lead a very busy life,* llevo una vida muy ajetreada. **6** MUS (*orchestra*) ser el primer violín de. **7** (*us mus*) dirigir. **8** (*cards*) salir con. – **9** *i* (*road*) conducir, llevar (**to,** a): *this path leads to the beach,* este sendero lleva a la playa; *this could lead to the president's resignation,* esto podría llevar a la dimisión del presidente. **10** (*command*) tener el mando. **11** (*go first*) ir primero,-a; (*in race*) llevar la delantera. **12** (*cards*) salir. – **13** *n* (*front position*) delantera. **14** SP liderato; (*difference*) ventaja. **15** THEAT primer papel *m*. **16** GB (*for dog*) correa. **17** ELEC cable *m*. **18** (*clue*) pista. **19** (*cards*) mano *f*: *it's my lead,* es mi turno.
◆ **to lead off 1** *i* (*begin*) empezar. – **2** *t insep* (*room, door*) dar a. ‖ **to lead on 1** *t sep* (*deceive*) engañar, tomar el pelo a. **2** (*coerce*) coaccionar. – **3** *i* ir adelante: *lead on!,* ¡adelante! ‖ **to lead up to** *t insep* llevar a, conducir a.

● **to be in the lead,** ir en cabeza. ‖ **to follow sb.'s lead,** seguir el ejemplo de algn. ‖ **to lead a dog's life,** llevar una vida de perros. ‖ **to lead sb. to believe sth.,** llevar a algn. a creer algo. ‖ **to lead the way,** enseñar el camino. ‖ **to take the lead,** (*in race*) tomar la delantera; (*in score*) adelantarse en el marcador.
■ **lead time,** tiempo de planificación y producción.
▲ (*verbo*) *pt* & *pp* **lead** [led].

leaded [ˈledɪd] *adj* (*window*) emplomado,-a.

leaden [ˈledən] **1** *adj* (*colour*) plomizo,-a. **2** *fig* de plomo, pesado,-a.

leader [ˈliːdəʳ] **1** *n* POL líder *mf*, dirigente *mf*: *he's a born leader,* es un líder nato. **2** (*in race*) líder *mf* (**of/in,** de). **3** GB MUS primer violín *m*. **4** US MUS director,-ra. **5** GB (*in newspaper*) editorial *m*.

leadership [ˈliːdəʃɪp] **1** *n* (*position*) liderato, liderazgo. **2** (*qualities*) dotes *mpl* de mando. **3** (*leaders*) dirección *f*.

lead-free [ˈledfriː] *adj* sin plomo.

lead-in [ˈliːdɪn] *n* introducción *f*, presentación *f*.

leading [ˈliːdɪŋ] *adj* destacado,-a, principal.
■ **leading lady,** actriz *f* principal. ‖ **leading light,** *fam* cerebro. ‖ **leading man,** actor *m* principal. ‖ **leading question,** pregunta tendenciosa.

leaf [liːf] **1** *n* (*of plant*) hoja. **2** (*of book*) hoja, página. **3** (*of table*) hoja abatible.
◆ **to leaf through** *t insep* hojear.
● **to be in leaf,** tener hojas. ‖ **to come into leaf,** echar hojas. ‖ **to take a leaf out of sb.'s book,** seguir el ejemplo de algn. ‖ **to turn over a new leaf,** hacer borrón y cuenta nueva, volver la página.
■ **leaf mould,** mantillo.
▲ *pl* **leaves** [liːvz].

leaflet [ˈliːflət] **1** *n* (*folded*) folleto; (*single sheet*) octavilla, hoja suelta. – **2** *i* GB repartir folletos, repartir octavillas.

leafy [ˈliːfɪ] *adj* frondoso,-a.
▲ *comp* **leafier,** *superl* **leafiest.**

league [liːg] **1** *n* liga. **2** *fam* (*level*) altura: *they're not in the same league as French bakeries,* no están a la altura de las panaderías francesas. **3** (*measure*) legua.
● **to be in league with sb.,** estar conchabado,-a con algn. ‖ **to be out of one's league,** no estar a la altura.
■ **league championship,** campeonato de liga. ‖ **league match,** partido de liga. ‖ **League of Nations,** Sociedad *f* de Naciones.

leak [liːk] **1** *i* (*container*) tener un agujero; (*pipe*) tener un escape. **2** (*roof*) gotear. **3** (*boat*) hacer agua; (*shoes*) dejar entrar agua. **4** (*gas, fluid*) escaparse. – **5** *t* (*let out*) dejar salir, dejar escapar; (*spill out*) derramar. **6** *fig* (*information etc*) pasar (**to,** a): *he was sacked for leaking information to the press,* fue despedido por pasar información a la prensa. – **7** *n* (*hole*) agujero. **8** (*in roof*) gotera. **9** (*of gas*) fuga, escape *m*; (*of liquid*) escape *m*. **10** (*spill*) derrame *m*. **11** *fig* (*of information etc*) filtración *f*.
◆ **to leak out 12** *i* (*gas, fluid*) escaparse. **13** *fig* filtrarse.
● **to have a leak / take a leak,** *sl* mear, echar una meada.

leakage [ˈliːkɪdʒ] **1** *n* (*of gas*) fuga, escape *m*; (*of liquid*) escape *m*. **2** (*spill*) derrame *m*.

leaky [ˈliːkɪ] **1** *adj* (*container*) agujereado,-a; (*pipe*) con un escape. **2** (*roof*) que tiene goteras. **3** (*pipe*) que tiene escapes. **4** (*boat*) que hace agua; (*shoe*) que deja entrar agua.
▲ *comp* **leakier,** *superl* **leakiest.**

lean¹ [liːn] **1** *adj* (*person*) delgado,-a, flaco,-a. **2** (*meat*) magro,-a. **3** (*harvest*) malo,-a, escaso,-a; (*year*) malo,-a, pobre: *it was a lean year for car sales,* fue un mal año para la venta de coches. – **4** *n* (*meat*) carne *f* magra.

lean² [liːn] **1** *i* inclinarse. **2** (*for support*) apoyarse (**on,** en) (**against,** contra). **– 3** *t* apoyar. **– 4** *n* inclinación *f.*
◆ **to lean on 1** *t insep* (*depend on*) depender de. **2** (*pressure*) presionar a. ‖ **to lean towards** *t insep* estar a favor de, tirar hacia.
● **to lean back,** reclinarse, recostarse. ‖ **to lean down,** agacharse. ‖ **to lean forward,** inclinarse hacia delante. ‖ **to lean out,** asomarse (-, por). ‖ **to lean over,** inclinarse. ‖ **to lean over backwards (to help sb.),** desvivirse (por ayudar a algn.).
▲ (*verbo*) *pt* & *pp* **leaned** *o* **leant** [lent].
leaning [ˈliːnɪŋ] **1** *adj* inclinado,-a. **– 2** *n* inclinación *f,* tendencia.
leant [lent] *pt* & *pp* → **lean².**
lean-to [ˈliːntʊ] *n* cobertizo.
▲ *pl* **lean-tos.**
leap [liːp] **1** *i* saltar, brincar: *the children leapt for joy,* los niños dieron saltos de alegría; *the dog can't leap over the fence,* el perro no puede saltar la valla; *everyone leapt to their feet,* todos se levantaron de un salto; *my heart leapt,* mi corazón dio un vuelco; *those gaudy illustrations leap off the page at you,* esas ilustraciones chillonas saltan de la página. **– 2** *n* salto, brinco. **3** *fig* salto: *these reforms are a leap forward for the country,* estas reformas significan un paso hacia adelante para el país.
◆ **to leap at** *t insep* no dejar escapar, aprovechar.
● **a leap in the dark,** un salto en el vacío. ‖ **by leaps and bounds,** a pasos agigantados. ‖ **to leap up,** (*person*) levantarse de un salto; (*flame*) brotar, saltar.
■ **leap year,** año bisiesto.
▲ (*verbo*) *pt* & *pp* **leaped** *o* **leapt** [lept].
leapfrog [ˈliːpfrɒg] **1** *n* pídola. **– 2** *t fig* (*skip*) saltarse.
▲ (*verbo*) *pt* & *pp* **leapfrogged,** *ger* **leapfrogging.**
leapt [lept] *pt* & *pp* → **leap.**
learn [lɜːn] **1** *t* aprender: *I'd love to learn (how) to ice-skate,* me encantaría aprender a patinar sobre hielo; *he's learning how to play the flute,* estudia flauta; *you must learn this poem by heart,* debes aprenderte este poema de memoria. **2** (*find out about*) enterarse de, saber. **– 3** *i* aprender. **4** (*find out*) enterarse (**about/of,** de).
● **to learn from one's mistakes,** aprender de sus errores. ‖ **to learn from experience,** aprender por experiencia. ‖ **to learn one's lesson / learn the hard way,** aprender de sus errores.
▲ *pt* & *pp* **learned** *o* **learnt** [lɜːnt].
learned [ˈlɜːnəd] *adj* erudito,-a.
learner [ˈlɜːnəʳ] *n* estudiante *mf:* *he's a slow learner,* tiene dificultades para aprender.
■ **learner driver,** aprendiz,-za de conductor.
learning [ˈlɜːnɪŋ] *n* saber *m:* *she was a woman of great learning,* fue una gran erudita.
learnt [lɜːnt] *pt* & *pp* → **learn.**
lease [liːs] **1** *n* contrato de arrendamiento *que transfiere la propiedad al arrendatario por un cierto período de tiempo:* *they've taken a lease on the office,* han arrendado la oficina; *they bought the house on a 99-year lease,* firmaron un contrato que les concede la propiedad de la casa durante 99 años. **– 2** *t* arrendar.
● **to give sb. a new lease on life,** dar nueva vida a algn.
leasehold [ˈliːshəʊld] **1** *adj* arrendado,-a. **– 2** *adv* en arriendo.
▲ *Véase también* **lease.**
leaseholder [ˈliːshəʊldəʳ] *n* arrendatario *cuya titularidad se especifica mediante un lease.*

leash [liːʃ] *n* correa.
leasing [ˈliːsɪŋ] **1** *n* arrendamiento, arriendo. **2** FIN leasing *m.*
least [liːst] **1** *adj* menor, menos: *he makes the least money,* es el que gana menos dinero. **– 2** *adv* menos: *when you least expect it,* cuando menos lo esperas; *nobody was interested, least of all him,* no le interesó a nadie, y a él menos; *tourism is on the rise, not least because of the new exchange rate,* el turismo está en alza, debido en gran parte al nuevo tipo de cambio. **– 3** *n* lo menos: *it's the least I can do,* es lo menos que puedo hacer; *the least you could have done was phone in a while,* ¿qué menos que llamar de vez en cuando?; *that's the least of my problems,* eso es lo de menos.
● **at (the) least,** por lo menos, al menos, cuando menos. ‖ **not in the least!,** ¡en absoluto!, ¡qué va!: *he's not in the least tired,* no está cansado en lo más mínimo. ‖ **not least,** en gran parte. ‖ **to say the least,** por no decir más.
leather [ˈleðəʳ] **1** *n* piel *f,* cuero. **– 2** *adj* de piel, de cuero.
leatherette [leðəˈret] *n* imitación *f* de piel, polipiel *f.*
leathery [ˈleðərɪ] **1** *adj* (*skin*) curtido,-a. **2** (*meat*) correoso,-a.
leave¹ [liːv] **1** *t* (*go away from*) dejar, abandonar; (*go out of*) salir de: *she left home when she was 16,* se marchó de casa a los 16 años. **2** (*stop being with*) marcharse de: *when I left New York,* cuando me fui de Nueva York. **3** (*forget*) dejarse, olvidar, olvidarse: *yesterday I left my handbag on the train,* ayer me dejé el bolso en el tren. **4** (*allow to remain*) dejar: *let's leave that until tomorrow,* dejemos eso para mañana; *please leave the door open,* por favor, deja la puerta abierta; *shall I leave him a message?,* ¿quiere que le dé algún recado?; *leave the washing up to me,* deja que yo lave los platos; *let's leave it at that!,* ¡dejémoslo así! **5** (*cause to remain*) dejar: *the glass left a ring on the table,* el vaso dejó un cerco en la mesa. **6** (*be survived by*) dejar. **7** (*bequeath*) dejar, legar. **8** MATH dar: *two from six leaves four,* seis menos dos dan cuatro. **– 9** *i* marcharse, irse, partir: *I'm leaving in five minutes,* me voy dentro de cinco minutos; *he left for Rome this morning,* esta mañana salió hacia Roma.
◆ **to leave off 1** *t insep* dejar de: *there was so much noise that I had to leave off studying,* había tanto ruido que tuve que dejar de estudiar. **– 2** *i* acabar, terminar: *we'll start where we left off yesterday,* empezaremos donde acabamos ayer. ‖ **to leave out 1** *t sep* (*omit*) omitir, excluir. **2** (*not make welcome*) excluir: *you shouldn't feel left out,* no deberías sentirte excluido.
● **leave it out!,** GB *sl* ¡venga ya!, ¡déjalo ya! ‖ **to leave behind,** dejar atrás. ‖ **to leave go of sth. / hold of sth.,** soltar algo. ‖ **to leave sb. alone / leave sb. be,** dejar a algn. en paz. ‖ **to leave sb. cold,** dejar frío,-a a algn., dejar indiferente a algn. ‖ **to leave sb. to themself / leave sb. to their own devices,** dejar que algn. se las apañe solo,-a. ‖ **to leave sth. about,** dejar algo tirado. ‖ **to leave standing,** (*in race*) dejar clavado,-a. ‖ **to leave well enough alone,** dejar las cosas tal como están.
▲ (*verbo*) *pt* & *pp* **left,** *ger* **leaving.**
leave² [liːv] **1** *n* (*time off*) baja; MIL permiso. **2** (*permission*) permiso.
● **to be on leave,** MIL estar de permiso. ‖ **to go on sick leave,** tener la baja por enfermedad. ‖ **to take French leave,** despedirse a la francesa. ‖ **to take leave of one's senses,** perder la razón. ‖ **to take one's leave of sb.,** despedirse de algn.
■ **leave of absence,** excedencia.

leaven ['levən] *n* levadura.
leavening ['levənɪŋ] **1** *n* → **leaven**. **2** *fig* (*dash*) toque *m*, nota.
leaves [liːvz] *npl* → **leaf**.
leave-taking ['liːvteɪkɪŋ] *n* despedida.
leaving ['liːvɪŋ] **1** *n* (*departure*) salida. – **2 leavings,** *npl* (*remains*) restos *mpl*; (*of food*) sobras *fpl*.
Lebanese [lebə'niːz] **1** *adj* libanés,-esa. – **2** *n* libanés,- esa. – **3 the Lebanese,** *npl* los libaneses *mpl*.
Lebanon ['lebənən] *n* Líbano.
lecherous ['letʃərəs] *adj* lujurioso,-a, lascivo,-a.
lechery ['letʃəri] *n* lujuria, lascivia.
lectern ['lektən] *n* atril *m*; (*in church*) facistol *m*.
lecture ['lektʃəʳ] **1** *n* conferencia. **2** (*in university*) clase *f*. **3** (*telling-off*) reprimenda, sermón *m*. – **4** *i* dar una conferencia (**on,** sobre). **5** (*in university*) dar clase. – **6** *t* (*scold*) sermonear, echar una reprimenda a.
lecturer ['lektʃərəʳ] **1** *n* conferenciante *mf*. **2** (*in university*) profesor,-ra.
lectureship ['lektʃəʃɪp] *n* cargo de profesor,-ra.
led [led] *pt & pp* → **lead²**.
ledge [ledʒ] **1** *n* (*shelf*) repisa; (*of window*) antepecho, alféizar *m*. **2** (*of rock*) saliente *m*.
ledger ['ledʒəʳ] *n* COMM libro mayor.
■ **ledger line,** MUS línea postiza.
lee [liː] **1** *n* MAR sotavento, socaire *m*. **2** (*shelter*) abrigo.
● **in the lee of,** al abrigo de.
● **lee tide,** marea de sotavento.
leech [liːtʃ] *n* sanguijuela.
● **to cling to sb. like a leech,** pegarse a algn. como una lapa.
leek [liːk] *n* puerro.
leer [lɪəʳ] **1** *i* mirar con lascivia (**at,** -). – **2** *n* mirada lasciva.
leeringly ['lɪərɪŋlɪ] *adv* con lascivia.
leery ['lɪrɪ] *adj fam* receloso,-a.
● **to be leery of,** recelar de, desconfiar de, no fiarse de: *I'm a bit leery of that new porter,* no me fío de ese nuevo portero.
▲ *comp* **leerier,** *superl* **leeriest.**
lees [liːz] *npl* poso *m sing*.
leeward ['liːwəd] **1** *adj* de sotavento. – **2** *adv* a sotavento. – **3** *n* sotavento.
■ **Leeward Islands,** Islas *fpl* de Sotavento.
leeway ['liːweɪ] **1** *n* (*freedom*) libertad *f*: *from now on I'll have a certain amount of leeway,* a partir de ahora tendré cierto margen de libertad. **2** GB (*backlog*) tiempo perdido: *he's got a lot of leeway to make up,* tiene que recuperar mucho tiempo perdido. **3** MAR deriva.
left¹ [left] **1** *adj* izquierdo,-a. **2** POL de izquierdas: *the left wing of the party,* el ala izquierda del partido. – **3** *adv* a la izquierda, hacia la izquierda. – **4** *n* izquierda: *keep to the left,* manténgase a la izquierda. **5** (*punch*) golpe *m* de la izquierda.
● **on the left,** a mano izquierda. ‖ **to be on the Left,** ser de izquierdas.
■ **the far Left,** la extrema izquierda.
left² [left] *pt & pp* → **leave¹**.
● **to be left,** quedar: *is there any milk left?,* ¿queda leche? ‖ **to be left over,** sobrar, quedar. ‖ **to have sth. left,** quedar algo a uno: *we have no tickets left,* no nos quedan entradas.
left-hand ['lefthænd] *adj* izquierdo,-a: *the shop is on the left-hand side,* la tienda está a mano izquierda.
● **left-hand drive,** con el volante a la izquierda.
left-handed [left'hændɪd] **1** *adj* (*person*) zurdo,-a. **2** (*object*) para zurdos. **3** (*action*) con la mano izquierda.

left-hander [left'hændəʳ] **1** *n* (*blow*) golpe *m* con la izquierda. **2** (*person*) zurdo,-a.
leftist ['leftɪst] **1** *adj* izquierdista. – **2** *n* izquierdista *mf*.
left-luggage [left'lʌgɪdʒ] **left-luggage office,** *n* consigna.
leftover ['leftəuvəʳ] **1** *adj* sobrante, restante. – **2 leftovers,** *npl* sobras *fpl*, restos *mpl*.
leftward ['leftwəd] **1** *adj* a la izquierda, hacia la izquierda. – **2** *adv* US → **leftwards**.
leftwards ['leftwədz] *adj* a la izquierda, hacia la izquierda.
left-wing ['leftwɪŋ] *adj* de izquierdas.
lefty ['leftɪ] **1** *n* GB POL *fam* izquierdista *mf*, izquierdoso,- a. **2** US FAM zurdo,-a.
▲ *pl* **lefties.**
leg [leg] **1** *n* ANAT pierna; (*of animal*) pata. **2** CULIN (*lamb etc*) pierna; (*chicken etc*) muslo. **3** (*of furniture*) pata, pie *m*. **4** (*of trousers*) pernera. **5** (*stage*) etapa.
● **not to have a leg to stand on,** no tener en qué basarse. ‖ **to be on one's last legs,** estar en las últimas. ‖ **to give sb. a leg up,** *fam* ayudar a algn. a subir (aguantándole un pie). ‖ **to leg it,** *fam* (*run away*) irse corriendo, poner pies en polvorosa; (*walk*) ir andando. ‖ **to pull sb.'s leg,** *fam* tomarle el pelo a algn. ‖ **to shake a leg,** *fam* (*hurry*) espabilarse; (*dance*) bailotear. ‖ **to show a leg,** *fam* levantarse de la cama.
legacy ['legəsɪ] *n* legado, herencia.
▲ *pl* **legacies.**
legal ['liːgəl] **1** *adj* legal, lícito,-a. **2** (*relating to the law*) jurídico,-a, legal: *the legal profession,* la abogacía.
● **to take legal action,** entablar un pleito (**against,** contra).
■ **legal adviser,** asesor,-ra jurídico,-a; (*office*) asesoría jurídica. ‖ **legal aid,** *ayuda económica para afrontar gastos de representación legal.* ‖ **legal costs,** costas *fpl*. ‖ **legal holiday,** US fiesta nacional. ‖ **legal tender,** moneda de curso legal.
legalistic [liːgə'lɪstɪk] *adj* legalista.
legality [lɪ'gælɪtɪ] *n* legalidad *f*.
▲ *pl* **legalities.**
legalize ['liːgəlaɪz] *t* legalizar.
legate ['legət] *n* legado.
legation [lɪ'geɪʃən] *n* legación *f*.
legend ['ledʒənd] *n* leyenda.
● **a legend in one's own lifetime,** una leyenda viva.
legendary ['ledʒəndərɪ] *adj* legendario,-a: *this bar is legendary for its cocktails,* este bar es legendario por sus cócteles.
leger ['ledʒəʳ] **leger (line),** *n* MUS línea postiza.
legerdemain [ledʒədə'meɪn] *n dated* juegos *mpl* de manos.
leggings ['legɪŋz] *npl* polainas *fpl*.
leggy ['legɪ] *adj* zanquilargo,-a, patilargo,-a; (*woman*) de piernas esculturales.
▲ *comp* **leggier,** *superl* **leggiest.**
legibility [ledʒə'bɪlɪtɪ] *n* legibilidad *f*.
legible ['ledʒəbəl] *adj* legible.
legibly ['ledʒəblɪ] *adv* legiblemente, con claridad.
legion ['liːdʒən] *n* legión *f*.
■ **Foreign Legion,** Legión *f* Extranjera.
legionnaire [liːdʒə'neəʳ] *n* legionario.
■ **legionnaire's disease,** enfermedad *f* del legionario.
legislate ['ledʒɪsleɪt] *i* legislar.
legislation [ledʒɪs'leɪʃən] *n* legislación *f*.
legislative ['ledʒɪslətɪv] *adj* legislativo,-a.
legislator ['ledʒɪsleɪtəʳ] *n* legislador,-ra.

legislature [ˈledʒɪsleɪtʃəˈ] n cuerpo legislativo.
legit [lɪˈdʒɪt] adj sl legal, legítimo,-a.
legitimacy [lɪˈdʒɪtɪməsɪ] n legitimidad f.
legitimate [lɪˈdʒɪtɪmət] adj legítimo,-a.
legitimatize [lɪˈdʒɪtɪmətaɪz] t → **legitimize**.
legitimize [lɪˈdʒɪtɪmaɪz] t legitimar.
legless [ˈleɡləs] adj fam ciego,-a, trompa.
leg-pull [ˈleɡpʊl] n fam tomadura de pelo.
legroom [ˈleɡruːm] n sitio para las piernas, espacio para las piernas.
legume [ˈleɡjuːm] n legumbre f.
leg-warmers [ˈleɡwɔːməz] npl calentadores mpl, calientapiernas mpl.
legwork [ˈleɡwɜːk] to do the legwork, i fam hacer el trabajo duro.
lei [leɪ] n collar de flores hawaiano.
leisure [ˈleʒəˈ, us ˈliːʒəˈ] n ocio, tiempo libre.
● **at leisure**, (with free time) en su tiempo libre; (calmly) tranquilamente. ‖ **to do sth. at one's leisure**, hacer algo cuando uno pueda. ‖ **to live a life of leisure**, vivir a cuerpo de rey.
■ **leisure activities**, pasatiempos mpl. ‖ **leisure centre**, (sports) club m deportivo; (cultural) centro cultural.
leisured [ˈleʒəd, us ˈliːʒərd] adj ocioso,-a.
leisurely [ˈleʒəlɪ, us ˈliːʒərlɪ] adj sin prisa.
leitmotif [ˈlaɪtməʊtiːf] n leimotiv m.
leitmotiv [ˈlaɪtməʊtiːf] n leimotiv m.
lemon [ˈlemən] **1** n limón m. **2** GB sl (fool) primo,-a. **3** sl (car) cacharro. – **4** adj (colour) de color limón.
■ **lemon curd**, GB crema de limón. ‖ **lemon ice**, granizado de limón. ‖ **lemon sole**, mendo limón. ‖ **lemon squash**, limonada. ‖ **lemon squeezer**, exprimelimones m, exprimidor m, exprimidera.‖ **lemon tea**, té m con limón. ‖ **lemon tree**, limonero.
lemonade [leməˈneɪd] **1** n (fizzy - plain) gaseosa; (- lemony) limonada. **2** (still) limonada.
lend [lend] **1** t dejar, prestar: could you lend me some money?, ¿me dejas un poco de dinero? **2** fig (add) dotar de, prestar.
● **to lend an ear (to sb.)**, escuchar (a algn.). ‖ **to lend os. to sth.**, prestarse a algo, prestarse para algo. ‖ **to lend (sb.) a hand**, echar una mano (a algn.).
▲ pt & pp lent [lent].
lending [ˈlendɪŋ] lending library, n biblioteca pública.
lenghtwise [ˈlenθwaɪz] adv → **lengthways**.
length [lenθ] **1** n longitud f: it's 4 metres in length, tiene una longitud de 4 metros; what length is the skirt?, ¿qué largo tiene la falda? **2** (of time) duración f. **3** (piece) trozo; (of cloth) largo. **4** (of road) tramo; (of swimming pool) largo: Tom won by a length, Tom ganó por un largo; we walked the length of the river, anduvimos a lo largo del río.
● **at length**, (finally) a la larga; (in depth) en detalle, a fondo: they talked at length, hablaron largo y tendido. ‖ **the length and breadth of sth.**, a lo largo y ancho de algo. ‖ **to go to any lengths to do sth.**, hacer lo que sea para hacer algo. ‖ **to go to great lengths to do sth.**, hacer lo imposible por hacer algo. ‖ **to keep sb. at arm's length**, mantener las distancias con algn. ‖ **to measure one's length**, fig medir el suelo.
lengthen [ˈlenθən] **1** t (skirt etc) alargar. **2** (lifetime) prolongar. – **3** i (skirt etc) alargarse. **4** (lifetime) prolongarse; (days) crecer.
lengthways [ˈlenθweɪz] adv a lo largo, longitudinalmente.
lengthy [ˈlenθɪ] **1** adj (in general) largo,-a. **2** (film, illness) de larga duración. **3** (speech, discussion) prolongado,-a.

▲ comp **lengthier**, superl **lengthiest**.
lenience [ˈliːnɪəns] n indulgencia, lenidad f.
leniency [ˈliːnɪənsɪ] n → **lenience**.
lenient [ˈliːnɪənt] adj (person) indulgente; (punishment) poco severo,-a.
Leningrad [ˈlenɪŋɡræd] n Leningrado.
Leninist [ˈlenɪnɪst] **1** adj leninista. – **2** n leninista mf.
lens [lenz] **1** n (of glasses) lente m & f. **2** (of camera) objetivo. **3** ANAT cristalino.
lent [lent] pt & pp → **lend**.
Lent [lent] n REL Cuaresma.
lentil [ˈlentəl] n lenteja: lentil soup, sopa de lentejas.
Leo [ˈliːəʊ] n Leo, León m.
▲ pl **Leos**.
leonine [ˈliːənaɪn] adj fml leonino,-a.
leopard [ˈlepəd] n leopardo.
leopardess [ˈlepədes] n leopardo hembra.
leotard [ˈliːətɑːd] n malla.
leper [ˈlepəˈ] n leproso,-a.
leprechaun [ˈleprəkɔːn] n duende m.
leprosy [ˈleprəsɪ] n lepra.
leprous [ˈleprəs] adj leproso,-a.
lesbian [ˈlezbɪən] **1** adj lesbiano,-a. – **2** n lesbiana.
Lesotho [lɪˈsuːtuː] n Lesotho.
less [les] **1** adj menos. – **2** pron menos: we see less of each other these days, últimamente nos vemos menos; no less than two hundred people attended, asistieron nada menos que doscientas personas; the less you eat, the less you'll spend, cuánto menos comas, menos gastarás; it was no less a person than the Prince, fue nada menos que el príncipe. – **3** adv menos: less and less, cada vez menos; he was being less than sincere, no fue nada sincero. – **4** prep menos.
● **any the less**, menos: he made a mistake, but I don't think any the less of him for it, cometió un error, pero no por eso le respeto menos. ‖ **much less**, menos aún: he can't drive, much less fly a plane, no sabe conducir, ni mucho menos pilotar un avión. ‖ **in less than no time**, dentro de un momento, en seguida. ‖ **no less**, nada menos. ‖ **nothing less than**, nada menos que. ‖ **still less**, menos aún. ‖ **to think (all) the less of sb.**, tener a algn. en menos consideración.
lessee [leˈsiː] n arrendatario,-a.
lessen [ˈlesən] **1** t disminuir, reducir. – **2** i disminuir, reducirse.
lessening [ˈlesənɪŋ] n disminución f, reducción f.
lesser [ˈlesəˈ] adj menor.
● **the lesser of two evils**, el mal menor. ‖ **to a lesser extent**, en menor grado.
lesson [ˈlesən] **1** n (class) clase f: I'm taking lessons in Spanish, voy a clases de español. **2** (warning) lección f.
● **let that be a lesson to you!**, ¡que te sirva de lección! ‖ **to teach sb. a lesson**, dar una lección a algn.
lessor [leˈsɔːˈ] n arrendador,-ra.
lest [lest] **1** conj arch (in order not to) a fin de que no: let me clarify this matter lest there (should) be any misunderstanding, permítanme aclarar este asunto a fin de que no haya malentendidos. **2** (for fear that) por miedo a que: he tiptoed up the stairs lest he (should) be heard, subió las escaleras de puntillas por miedo a que lo oyesen.
let¹ [let] **1** t (allow) dejar: he lets the children watch cartoon videos, a los niños les deja mirar vídeos de dibujos animados; you should let your beard grow, deberías dejarte barba; let me drive you home, déjame acompañarte a casa (en coche). – **2** aux que (+ subj): let him

come, que venga; *let this be a warning,* que esto sirva de advertencia; *let us pray,* oremos; *let's go!,* ¡vamos!, ¡vámonos!; *let's not argue about it,* no discutamos. – **3** *t* GB (*rent*) alquilar: *"house to let",* "se alquila casa". – **4** *n* GB (*renting*) alquiler *m: a short let,* un alquiler a corto plazo.
◆ **to let down 1** *t sep* (*lower*) bajar. **2** (*lengthen*) alargar. **3** (*deflate*) desinflar. **4** (*disappoint*) fallar, defraudar: *he promised he would come, but he let me down,* me prometió que vendría, pero me falló. ‖ **to let in** *t sep* dejar entrar: *her father let me in,* me abrió su padre; *let yourself in!,* ¡abre la puerta tú mismo!; *the roof lets in water,* entra agua por el tejado. ‖ **to let into 1** *t sep* dejar entrar a: *they refused to let him into the country,* no le dejaron entrar en el país; *this key will let you into the garage,* con esta llave podrás entrar en el garaje. **2** (*inlay into*) incrustar en. **3** (*reveal*) revelar. ‖ **to let off 1** *t sep* (*leave off*) dejar. **2** (*bomb*) hacer explotar; (*fireworks*) hacer estallar. **3** (*person - forgive*) perdonar; (*- let leave*) dejar marcharse; (*- free*) dejar en libertad: *I think she was let off lightly,* yo creo que se merecía un castigo más fuerte. ‖ **to let on 1** *i fam* (*tell*) decir, descubrir: *you won't let on, will you?,* no lo dirás, ¿verdad? – **2** *t insep fam* (*pretend*) hacer ver: *she let on (that) she was going out shopping,* hizo ver que se iba de compras. ‖ **to let out 1** *t sep* (*in general*) dejar salir; (*release*) soltar (**from,** de): *he was let out of prison yesterday,* ayer salió de la prisión; *you should let air out of those tyres,* deberías desinflar un poco los neumáticos. **2** (*utter*) soltar: *he let out a shriek of pain,* soltó un grito de dolor. **3** (*widen*) ensanchar. **4** (*make public*) divulgar, hacer público,-a. **5** GB (*rent*) alquilar. ‖ **to let through** *t sep* dejar pasar. ‖ **to let up** *i* parar: *the rain didn't let up until evening,* no dejó de llover hasta el atardecer. ‖ **to let up on** *t insep fam* dejar en paz.
● **let alone ...,** y mucho menos ... ‖ **let me see / let's see,** a ver. ‖ **to feel let down,** sentirse defraudado,-a. ‖ **to let by,** dejar pasar. ‖ **to let go of,** soltar. ‖ **to let loose,** soltar, desatar. ‖ **to let off steam,** desfogarse. ‖ **to let os. in for trouble,** meterse en un lío. ‖ **to let sb. alone,** dejar a algn. en paz, no molestar a algn. ‖ **to let sth. alone,** no tocar algo. ‖ **to let sb. down lightly,** decírselo a algn. con tacto. ‖ **to let sb. in on sth.,** revelar algo a algn. ‖ **to let sb. know,** hacer saber a algn., avisar a algn.: *I'll let you know,* ya te lo diré.
▲ *pt & pp* **let,** *ger* **letting.**
let² [let] *n* (*tennis*) let *m.*
letdown ['letdaʊn] *n fam* disgusto, chasco, desilusión *f.*
lethal ['liːθəl] *adj* letal, mortal.
lethargic [lə'θɑːdʒɪk] *adj* aletargado,-a.
lethargy ['leθədʒɪ] *n* letargo.
let's [lets] *contr →* **let us.**
letter ['letəʳ] **1** *n* (*of alphabet*) letra. **2** (*message*) carta. – **3** **letters,** *npl* letras *fpl: a man of letters,* un hombre de letras.
● **to the letter,** al pie de la letra.
■ **capital letter,** mayúscula. ‖ **letter bomb,** cartabomba. ‖ **letter box,** GB buzón *m.* ‖ **letter of attorney,** poderes *mpl.* ‖ **letter of credit,** carta de crédito. ‖ **letter of introduction,** carta de presentación, carta de recomendación. ‖ **small letter,** minúscula.
lettered ['letəd] *adj arch* de letras.
letterhead ['letəhed] *n* membrete *m.*
letterheading ['letəhedɪŋ] *n* membrete *m.*
lettering ['letərɪŋ] *n* rotulación *f.*
letter-opener ['letərəʊpənəʳ] *n* US abrecartas *m.*
letterpress ['letəpres] *n* impresión *f* tipográfica.

letting ['letɪŋ] *n* GB piso de alquiler, casa de alquiler.
lettuce ['letɪs] *n* lechuga.
let-up ['letʌp] *n fam* respiro, tregua.
leucocyte ['luːkəsaɪt] *n* leucocito.
leucotomy [luː'kɒtəmɪ] *n* GB lobotomía.
▲ *pl* **leucotomies.**
leukaemia [luː'kiːmɪə] *n* GB leucemia.
leukemia [luː'kiːmɪə] *n* leucemia.
leukocyte ['luːkəsaɪt] *n* leucocito.
levee ['levɪ] *n* US dique *m.*
level ['levəl] **1** *adj* (*horizontal*) llano,-a, plano,-a. **2** (*even*) a nivel, nivelado,-a; (*spoonful etc*) raso,-a: *the table's not level,* la mesa no está nivelada; *his head is level with the door frame,* su cabeza está a la misma altura que el marco de la puerta. **3** (*equal*) igual, igualado,-a. **4** (*steady*) estable; (*voice*) llano,-a. – **5** *n* nivel *m: above sea level,* sobre el nivel del mar; *at ground level,* a ras de tierra. **6** (*flat ground*) llano, llanura. – **7** *t* (*make level, survey*) nivelar. **8** (*raze*) arrasar, rasar. **9** (*aim*) apuntar: *he levelled a blow at his brother,* le asestó un golpe a su hermano. – **10** *adv* a ras (**with,** de).
◆ **to level off 1** *i* (*plane*) enderezarse; (*prices etc*) estabilizarse. **2** (*ground*) nivelarse. – **3** *t sep* nivelar. ‖ **to level out** *i →* **to level off.**
● **on the level,** *fam* de fiar, honrado,-a. ‖ **to be on a level with,** estar al mismo nivel que. ‖ **to do one's level best,** hacer todo lo posible. ‖ **to draw level,** igualar (**with,** con). ‖ **to find one's (own) level,** estar con los suyos. ‖ **to keep a level head,** no perder la cabeza. ‖ **to level accusations against sb.,** dirigir acusaciones a algn. ‖ **to level with sb.,** *fam* hablar claro con algn.
■ **level crossing,** paso a nivel.
level-headed [levəl'hedɪd] *adj* sensato,-a.
lever ['liːvəʳ] **1** *n* palanca. – **2** *t* apalancar: *the new engine was levered into position,* se colocó el motor nuevo con palanca.
leverage ['liːvərɪdʒ] **1** *n* acción *f* de palanca. **2** *fig* (*influence*) influencias *fpl,* enchufe *m.*
leveret ['levərət] *n* lebrato, lebratón *m.*
leviathan [lɪ'vaɪəθən] *n* leviatán *m.*
levitate ['levɪteɪt] **1** *i* levitar. – **2** *t* hacer levitar.
levitation [levɪ'teɪʃən] *n* levitación *f.*
levity ['levɪtɪ] *n fml* ligereza, frivolidad *f.*
levy ['levɪ] **1** *t* recaudar; (*fine*) imponer. – **2** *n* recaudación *f;* (*of fine*) imposición *f.*
▲ (*verbo*) *pt & pp* **levied,** *ger* **levying;** (*sustantivo*) *pl* **levies.**
lewd [luːd] **1** *adj* lascivo,-a. **2** (*obscene*) obsceno,-a.
lewdness ['luːdnəs] **1** *n* lascivia. **2** (*obscenity*) obscenidad *f.*
lexical ['leksɪkəl] *adj* léxico,-a.
lexicographer [leksɪ'kɒɡrəfəʳ] *n* lexicógrafo,-a.
lexicography [leksɪ'kɒɡrəfɪ] *n* lexicografía.
lexicology [leksɪ'kɒlədʒɪ] *n* lexicología.
lexicon ['leksɪkən] **1** *n* (*dictionary*) léxico, lexicón *m;* (*list*) lista de vocabulario. **2** TECH léxico.
lexis ['leksɪs] *n* TECH léxico.
lhd ['lefthænd'draɪv] *abbr* (*left hand drive*) (*coche*) con volante a la izquierda.
liability [laɪə'bɪlətɪ] **1** *n* JUR responsabilidad *f.* **2** *fam* desastre *m: my cousin is a real liability,* mi primo es un desastre total. – **3** **liabilities,** *npl* COMM pasivo *m sing.*
▲ *pl* **liabilities.**
liable ['laɪəbəl] **1** *adj* (*likely, susceptible*) propenso,-a (**to,** a): *the car is liable to stall,* el coche tiende a calarse; *she's liable to be late,* suele llegar tarde; *it's liable to happen,*

es muy probable que así suceda. **2** (*susceptible*) susceptible (**to**, a). **3** JUR (*responsible*) responsable (**for**, de). **4** (*to fine*) expuesto,-a; (*to duties*) sujeto,-a: *I'm liable for military service,* pueden llamarme para hacer el servicio militar.

liaise [lɪˈeɪz] *i* comunicarse, tener contacto (**with**, con).
liaison [lɪˈeɪzən] **1** *n* enlace *m*. **2** (*sexual*) amorío.
■ **liaison committee**, comité *m* de enlace. ‖ **liaison officer**, oficial *mf* de enlace.
liar [ˈlaɪəʳ] *n* mentiroso,-a, embustero,-a: *he's such a liar!,* ¡menudo embustero está hecho!
lib [lɪb] *n fam* (*abbr of liberation*) → **liberation**.
Lib [lɪb] *n* (*abbr of Liberal Party*) (el) Partido Liberal.
libber [ˈlɪbəʳ]. **1 women's libber**, *n fam* militante *f* feminista. **2 gay libber**, *fam* militante *mf* gay.
libel [ˈlaɪbəl] **1** *n* calumnia, difamación *f*; (*written*) libelo. – **2** *t* difamar.
▲ (*verbo*) *pt & pp* **libelled** (*us* **libeled**), *ger* **libelling** (*us* **libeling**).
libellous [ˈlaɪbələs] *adj* calumnioso,-a, difamatorio,-a.
liberal [ˈlɪbərəl] **1** *adj* (*in general*) liberal. **2** (*abundant*) abundante.
■ **liberal arts**, artes *fpl* liberales; US letras *fpl*.
Liberal [ˈlɪbərəl] **1** *adj* POL liberal. – **2** *n* POL liberal *mf*.
■ **Liberal Party**, (el) Partido Liberal.
liberalism [ˈlɪbərəlɪzəm] *n* liberalismo.
liberalize [ˈlɪbərəlaɪz] *t* liberalizar.
liberate [ˈlɪbəreɪt] *t* (*in general*) liberar; (*prisoner etc*) poner en libertad, libertar, emancipar: *a liberated woman,* una mujer liberada.
● **to become liberated**, liberarse, emanciparse.
liberation [lɪbəˈreɪʃən] *n* liberación *f*.
■ **liberation theology**, teología de la liberación. ‖ **women's liberation**, liberación *f* de la mujer.
liberator [ˈlɪbəreɪtəʳ] *n* libertador,-ra.
Liberia [laɪˈbɪərɪə] *n* Liberia.
Liberian [laɪˈbɪərɪən] **1** *adj* liberiano,-a. – **2** *n* liberiano,-a.
libertarian [lɪbəˈteərɪən] **1** *n* libertario,-a. – **2** *adj* libertario,-a.
libertine [ˈlɪbətiːn] **1** *n* libertino,-a. – **2** *adj* libertino,-a.
libertinism [ˈlɪbətiːnɪzəm] *n* libertinaje *m*.
liberty [ˈlɪbətɪ] *n* libertad *f*.
● **at liberty**, en libertad, libre (**to**, de). ‖ **to take liberties with sb./sth.**, tomarse libertades con algn./algo. ‖ **to take the liberty of doing sth.**, tomarse la libertad de hacer algo. ‖ **what a liberty!**, *fam* ¡qué cara más dura!
▲ *pl* **liberties**.
libidinous [lɪˈbɪdɪnəs] *adj* libidinoso,-a.
libido [lɪˈbiːdəʊ] *n* libido *f*.
▲ *pl* **libidos**.
Libra [ˈliːbrə] *n* Libra *m*.
librarian [laɪˈbreərɪən] *n* bibliotecario,-a.
library [ˈlaɪbrərɪ] **1** *n* biblioteca. **2** (*collection*) colección *f*.
■ **library ticket**, carnet *m* de biblioteca. ‖ **newspaper library**, hemeroteca.
▲ *pl* **libraries**.
librettist [lɪˈbretəst] *n* libretista *mf*.
libretto [lɪˈbretəʊ] *n* libreto.
▲ *pl* **librettos** o **libretti** [lɪˈbretiː].
Libya [ˈlɪbɪə] *n* Libia.
Libyan [ˈlɪbɪən] **1** *adj* libio,-a. – **2** *n* libio,-a.
lice [laɪs] *npl* → **louse**.
licence [ˈlaɪsəns] **1** *n* (*permit*) licencia, permiso. **2** (*freedom*) libertad *f*; (*excessive freedom*) licencia.

● **under licence from**, bajo licencia de.
■ **licence number**, matrícula. ‖ **licence plate**, US (placa de) matrícula. ‖ **poetic licence**, licencia poética.
license [ˈlaɪsəns] **1** *t* autorizar, dar licencia a. – **2** *n* US → **licence**.
licensed [ˈlaɪsənst] *adj* autorizado,-a.
■ **licensed practical nurse**, US enfermero,-a. ‖ **licensed premises**, local *m sing* autorizado para la venta de bebidas alcohólicas. ‖ **licensed victualler**, (*shop*) vendedor,-ra autorizado,-a de bebidas alcohólicas; (*pub*) dueño,-a de un bar.
licensee [laɪsənˈsiː] **1** *n* (*in general*) concesionario,-a. **2** (*of pub*) dueño,-a.
licentious [laɪˈsenʃəs] *adj* licencioso,-a.
lichen [ˈlaɪkən, ˈlɪtʃən] *n* liquen *m*.
lick [lɪk] **1** *t* lamer. **2** *fam* (*defeat - team*) vencer a, derrotar; (- *problem*) superar, solucionar. – **3** *n* lamedura, lengüetada. **4** *fam* (*of paint*) mano *f*. – **5 to lick against**, *t* lamer.
● **at full lick / at quite a lick**, *fam* a toda pastilla. ‖ **to give os. a lick and a promise**, *fam dated* lavarse rápidamente. ‖ **to lick one's lips**, relamerse. ‖ **to lick one's wounds**, lamerse las heridas. ‖ **to lick sb.'s boots**, dar coba a algn. ‖ **to lick sth. into shape**, *fam* poner algo a punto.
licking [ˈlɪkɪŋ] *n fam* paliza.
licorice [ˈlɪkərɪs, ˈlɪkərɪʃ] *n* regaliz *m*.
lid [lɪd] **1** *n* (*cover*) tapa. **2** (*of eye*) párpado.
● **to put the (tin) lid on sth.**, ser el colmo de los colmos. ‖ **to put the lid on it**, *sl* cerrar el pico. ‖ **to take the lid off sth.**, *fig* destapar algo.
lie[1] [laɪ] **1** *i* mentir. – **2** *n* mentira.
● **to be a pack of lies / be a tissue of lies**, ser pura mentira. ‖ **to give the lie to**, desmentir. ‖ **to lie through one's teeth**, *fam* mentir uno más que habla. ‖ **to tell lies**, mentir.
■ **lie detector**, detector *m* de mentiras.
▲ (*verbo*) *pt & pp* **lied**, *ger* **lying**.
lie[2] [laɪ] **1** *i* (*adopt a flat position*) acostarse, tumbarse; (*be in a flat position*) estar acostado,-a, estar tumbado,-a. **2** (*decision*) depender (**with**, de); (*responsibility*) ser (**with**, de), corresponder (**with**, a): *the final decision lies only with the president,* la decisión final sólo depende del presidente; *we must determine where the responsibility lies,* hemos de determinar de quién es la responsabilidad. **3** (*be situated*) estar (situado,-a), encontrarse: *the monastery lies north of the city,* el monasterio está al norte de la ciudad; *the problem lies mainly in his stubbornness,* el problema radica principalmente en su intransigencia; *what lies behind his offer of help?,* ¿qué esconde tras su oferta de ayuda? **4** (*be buried*) yacer. **5** (*remain*) quedarse, permanecer: *he lay still watching the deer,* permaneció inmóvil mirando el ciervo. – **6** *n* (*position*) posición *f*, situación *f*; (*direction*) orientación *f*.
◆ **to lie about / lie around** *i* (*person*) estar tumbado,-a; (*things*) estar tirado,-a. ‖ **to lie back** *i* recostarse. ‖ **to lie down 2** *i* acostarse, tumbarse, echarse. ‖ **to lie in** *i* GB levantarse tarde. ‖ **to lie up** *i* guardar cama.
● **the lie of the land**, la topografía (del terreno); *fig* el estado de las cosas. ‖ **to lie down on the job**, columpiarse, dormirse. ‖ **to lie low**, estar escondido,-a. ‖ **take sth. lying down**, aceptar algo sin chistar.
▲ (*verbo*) *pt* **lay**, *pp* **lain**, *ger* **lying**.
Liechtenstein [ˈlɪktənstaɪn] *n* Liechtenstein.
lie-down [ˈlaɪdaʊn] *n* siesta *f*.
● **to have a lie-down**, echarse una siesta.
lie-in [ˈlaɪɪn] **to have a lie-in**, *phr fam* levantarse tarde.

lien [lɪən] *n* JUR derecho de retención.
lieu [luː] in lieu of, *phr* en lugar de.
Lieut [lefˈtenənt, US luːˈtenənt] *abbr* (*Lieutenant*) Teniente *m*; (*abbreviation*) Tente., Tte.
lieutenant [lefˈtenənt, US luːˈtenənt] **1** *n* MIL teniente *m*. **2** (*non-military*) lugarteniente *m*.
■ **lieutenant general**, teniente *m* general.
life [laɪf] **1** *n* vida: *she can't play tennis for her life,* es una negada para el tenis; *never in my life have I heard such nonsense!,* ¡jamás en la vida había oído tales estupideces! **2** (*of battery*) duración *f*.
● **for dear life**, con toda su fuerza. ‖ **it's a matter of life and death**, es cuestión de vida o muerte. ‖ **not on your life!**, *fam* ¡ni hablar! ‖ **run for your life** *(lives)!*, ¡sálvese quien pueda! ‖ **to be the life and soul of the party**, ser el alma de la fiesta. ‖ **to bring sb. back to life**, resucitar a algn. ‖ **to come to life**, cobrar vida. ‖ **to have the time of one's life**, pasárselo como nunca. ‖ **to live the life of Riley**, *fam* pegarse la gran vida. ‖ **to lose one's life**, perder la vida. ‖ **to take one's life in one's hands**, (*risk*) arriesgar la vida; (*control*) controlar su propia vida. ‖ **to take one's own life**, suicidarse, quitarse la vida. ‖ **to take sb.'s life**, matar a algn.
■ **life belt / life buoy**, salvavidas *m*. ‖ **life cycle**, ciclo vital. ‖ **life expectancy**, esperanza de vida. ‖ **life insurance**, seguro de vida. ‖ **life imprisonment**, cadena perpetua. ‖ **life jacket**, chaleco salvavidas. ‖ **life preserver**, US salvavidas *m*. ‖ **life sentence**, cadena perpetua. ‖ **life story**, biografía. ‖ **life style**, estilo de vida.
▲ *pl* **lives** [laɪvz].
life-and-death [ˈlaɪfəndeθ] *adj* a vida o muerte.
lifeblood [ˈlaɪfblʌd] *n fig* alma, impulso vital.
lifeboat [ˈlaɪfbəʊt] **1** *n* (*on shore*) lancha de socorro. **2** (*on ship*) bote *m* salvavidas.
lifeguard [ˈlaɪfɡɑːd] *n* socorrista *mf*.
lifeless [ˈlaɪfləs] **1** *adj* exánime, inánime. **2** *fig* sin vida, soso,-a.
lifelike [ˈlaɪflaɪk] *adj* fiel.
lifeline [ˈlaɪflaɪn] **1** *n* (*rope*) cuerda de salvamento. **2** *fig* cordón *m* umbilical.
lifelong [ˈlaɪflɒŋ] *adj* de toda la vida.
life-sized [ˈlaɪfsaɪzd] *adj* (de) tamaño natural.
lifespan [ˈlaɪfspæn] *n* vida: *men are said to have a shorter lifespan than women,* se dice que los hombres viven menos que las mujeres.
lifetime [ˈlaɪftaɪm] **1** *n* vida: *in her lifetime,* en su vida. **2** *fam* eternidad *f*.
● **it's the chance of a lifetime**, es la oportunidad de tu vida.
lift [lɪft] **1** *t* (*in general*) levantar; (*head etc*) levantar, alzar; (*baby*) levantar en brazos; (*pick up*) coger: *he never lifts a finger to help,* no mueve (ni) un dedo para ayudar. **2** AER transportar. **3** *fam* (*steal*) afanar, birlar; (*copy*) copiar, copiarse. – **4** *i* (*of movable parts*) levantarse: *the car bonnet won't lift,* el capó no se levanta. – **5** *n* (*boost*) estímulo: *it gave him a real lift to hear the good news,* la buena noticia lo animó mucho. **6** GB ascensor *m*.
● **to give sb. a lift**, (*in car*) llevar a algn. en coche; (*cheer up*) animar. ‖ **to hitch a lift**, hacer autostop.
lift-off [ˈlɪftɒf] *n* despegue *m*.
ligament [ˈlɪɡəmənt] *n* ligamento.
light¹ [laɪt] **1** *n* (*gen*) luz *f*: *by the light of a table lamp,* a la luz de una lámpara de mesa; *bring it into the light,* tráelo aquí a la luz. **2** (*lamp*) luz *f*, lámpara; (*traffic light*) se-

máforo: *the lights were (at) red,* el semáforo estaba (en) rojo. **3** (*for cigarette, fire*) fuego: *could you give me a light, please?,* ¿tiene fuego, por favor?; *the boy set light to the branch,* el niño prendió fuego a la rama. – **4** *t* (*ignite*) encender. **5** (*illuminate*) iluminar, alumbrar. – **6** *i* encenderse. – **7** *adj* (*colour*) claro,-a; (*complexion*) blanco,-a: *light blue,* azul claro. **8** (*bright*) con mucha claridad: *it was getting light when we got home,* cuando llegamos a casa ya se hacía de día.
◆ **to light up 1** *t sep* iluminar. **2** *fam* (*cigarette etc*) encender. – **3** *i* iluminarse. **4** *fam* encender un cigarrillo.
● **according to one's own lights**, *fml* según su propio criterio. ‖ **in (the) light of**, GB en vista de, teniendo en cuenta. ‖ **to bring sth. to light**, sacar algo a la luz. ‖ **to come to light**, salir a luz. ‖ **to go out like a light**, *fam* quedarse roque. ‖ **to see the light at the end of the tunnel**, ver la luz al final del túnel. ‖ **to see things in a new light**, ver las cosas bajo otro aspecto. ‖ **to shed light on sth.**, aclarar algo, arrojar luz sobre algo. ‖ **to show sb. in a bad light**, hacer quedar mal a algn. ‖ **to throw light on sth.**, aclarar algo, arrojar luz sobre algo.
■ **light bulb**, bombilla. ‖ **light meter**, fotómetro. ‖ **light pen**, COMPUT lápiz *m* óptico. ‖ **light year**, año luz.
▲ (*verbo*) *pt* & *pp* **lighted** *o* **lit**.
light² [laɪt] **1** *adj* (*not heavy*) ligero,-a; (*rain*) fino,-a; (*breeze*) suave: *as light as a feather,* ligero,-a como una pluma; *give it a light tap with the hammer,* dale un golpe suave con el martillo; *I'm a light smoker,* fumo poco. **2** (*sentence, wound*) leve. **3** (*head*) mareado,-a.
● **to be light on sth.**, *fam* andar mal de algo. ‖ **to be light on one's feet**, ser ligero,-a de pies. ‖ **to have light fingers**, tener los dedos largos, tener los dedos rápidos. ‖ **to make light of sth.**, dar poca importancia a algo. ‖ **to travel light**, viajar con poco equipaje. ‖ **with a light heart**, con el corazón alegre.
■ **light aircraft**, avioneta. ‖ **light ale**, cerveza clara. ‖ **light opera**, opereta. ‖ **light reading**, lectura fácil.
light³ [laɪt] *i fml arch* (*alight*) posarse. (**on**, en).
◆ **to light out** *i* US escabullirse (**for**, hacia). ‖ **to light on / light upon** *i lit* descubrir, dar con.
▲ (*verbo*) *pt* & *pp* **lighted** *o* **lit**.
lighten¹ [ˈlaɪtən] **1** *t* (*colour*) aclarar. **2** (*room*) iluminar. **3** *i* (*colour*) aclararse.
lighten² [ˈlaɪtən] **1** *t* (*make less heavy*) aligerar. – **2** *i* (*mood etc*) alegrarse.
● **to lighten sb.'s load**, hacerle la vida más fácil a algn.
lighter¹ [ˈlaɪtəʳ] (*cigarette*) **lighter**, *n* encendedor *m*, mechero.
lighter² [ˈlaɪtəʳ] *n* MAR barcaza, gabarra.
light-fingered [ˈlaɪtfɪŋɡəd] *adj* largo,-a de dedos.
light-haired [ˈlaɪtheəd] *adj* de pelo claro, de pelo rubio.
light-headed [laɪtˈhedɪd] **1** *adj* (*dizzy*) mareado,-a. **2** (*frivolous*) liviano,-a, ligero,-a.
light-hearted [laɪtˈhɑːtɪd] **1** *adj* (*cheerful*) alegre, despreocupado,-a. **2** (*not serious*) desenfadado,-a.
lighthouse [ˈlaɪthaʊs] *n* faro.
■ **lighthouse keeper**, farero,-a.
lighting [ˈlaɪtɪŋ] **1** *n* (*in general*) iluminación *f*. **2** (*system*) alumbrado.
lightly [ˈlaɪtlɪ] **1** *adv* (*not heavily*) ligeramente. **2** (*not seriously*) a la ligera: *don't take it lightly,* no te lo tomes a la ligera.
● **to get off lightly**, salir casi indemne.
lightness¹ [ˈlaɪtnəs] **1** *n* (*of colour*) claridad *f*. **2** (*brightness*) luminosidad *f*, claridad *f*.

lightness² [ˈlaɪtnəs] *n* (*of weight*) ligereza.
lightning [ˈlaɪtnɪŋ] *n* rayo; (*flash only*) relámpago: *as quick as lightning,* veloz como un rayo.
■ **lightning conductor,** pararrayos *m.* ‖ **lightning rod,** us pararrayos *m.* ‖ **lightning strike,** huelga relámpago. ‖ **lightning visit,** visita *f* relámpago.
lights-out [ˈlaɪtsaʊt] *n* la hora de apagar las luces: *there's no talking after lights-out,* después de apagar la luces no se puede hablar.
lightweight [ˈlaɪtweɪt] **1** *n* (*boxing*) peso ligero. **2** *pej* don nadie *m,* peso ligero: *he's an intellectual lightweight,* intelectualmente, es un don nadie. – **3** *adj* (*clothing*) ligero,-a. **4** (*boxing*) de peso ligero. **5** *pej* flojo,-a, poco convincente.
Liguria [lɪˈgjʊərɪə] *n* Liguria.
Ligurian [lɪˈgjʊərɪən] **1** *adj* ligur, ligurino,-a. – **2** *n* ligur, ligurino,-a.
■ **Ligurian Sea,** Mar *m* Ligur.
like¹ [laɪk] **1** *prep* (*the same as*) como: *the flat looks like new,* el piso está como nuevo; *what's the new boss like?,* ¿cómo es el nuevo jefe?; *do it like this,* hazlo así; *that'll cost something like a thousand pesetas,* eso costará unas mil pesetas. **2** (*typical of*) propio,-a de: *it isn't like her to make a scene,* no es propio de ella armar un escándalo. **3** *fam* como: *we had to run like hell,* tuvimos que correr como locos. – **4** *adj* (*such as*) como. **5** *fml* semejante, parecido,-a. – **6** *adv fam* (*as it were*) pues: *so I thought, like, what'll happen next?,* y yo pensé, pues, ¿qué pasará ahora? – **7** *conj fam* como. – **8** *n* algo parecido: *I've never seen the like of it,* nunca he vista cosa igual.
● **and the like,** y cosas así. ‖ **(as) like as not,** *fam* seguramente. ‖ **to be as like as two peas in a pod,** ser como dos gotas de agua. ‖ **like enough,** *fam* seguramente. ‖ **like father, like son,** de tal palo tal astilla. ‖ **that's more like it!,** *fam* ¡eso está mejor!, ¡así me gusta! ‖ **to look like sb.,** parecerse a algn. ‖ **to look like sth.,** parecer algo: *it looks like rain,* parece que va a llover. ‖ **something like that,** algo así, algo por el estilo. ‖ **to be of like mind,** *fml* ser del mismo parecer. ‖ **to feel like,** tener ganas de: *I don't feel like going,* no me apetece ir.
■ **like poles,** ELEC polos *mpl* iguales.
like² [laɪk] **1** *t* (*enjoy*) gustar: *I like wine,* me gusta el vino; *he likes skiing,* le gusta esquiar; *how do you like Barcelona?,* ¿te gusta Barcelona? **2** (*want*) querer, gustar: *I'd like a cup of coffee,* me gustaría tomar un café; *would you like me to leave?,* ¿quieres que me vaya?; *how would you like your egg, boiled or fried?,* ¿cómo quieres el huevo, pasado por agua o frito? – **3** *i* querer: *if you like,* si quieres. – **4** **likes,** *npl* gustos *mpl.*
● **I like that!,** *fam iron* ¡pues mira qué bien! ‖ **to like sth. better,** preferir algo. ‖ **whether you like it or not,** quieras o no (quieras), a la fuerza.
likeable [ˈlaɪkəbəl] *adj* simpático,-a.
likelihood [ˈlaɪklɪhʊd] *n* probabilidad *f.*
● **in all likelihood,** con toda seguridad.
likeliness [ˈlaɪklɪnəs] *n* → **likelihood.**
likely [ˈlaɪklɪ] **1** *adj* probable: *he's likely to leave late,* es probable que salga tarde. – **2** *adv* probablemente: *I'll most likely come by bus,* lo más probable es que venga en autobús.
● **as likely as not,** *fam* lo más seguro. ‖ **not bloody likely!,** *fam* ¡ni hablar!, ¡y un jamón! ‖ **that's a likely story!,** *fam iron* ¡anda ya!
like-minded [laɪkˈmaɪndɪd] *adj* del mismo parecer.
liken [ˈlaɪkən] *t* comparar (**to,** con).
● **to be likened to,** compararse con.

likeness [ˈlaɪknəs] **1** *n* (*similarity*) semejanza, parecido. **2** (*portrait*) retrato.
● **in one's likeness,** a su semejanza.
likewise [ˈlaɪkwaɪz] **1** *adv* (*the same*) lo mismo, igualmente: *to do likewise,* hacer lo mismo. **2** (*also*) asimismo, además.
liking [ˈlaɪkɪŋ] *n* (*for thing*) gusto, afición *f*; (*for person*) simpatía; (*for friend*) cariño.
● **to be to sb.'s liking,** *fml* gustarle a algn. ‖ **to have a liking for sth.,** (*thing*) gustarle algo; (*activity*) tener afición por algo. ‖ **to take a liking to sb.,** tomar cariño a algn.
lilac [ˈlaɪlək] **1** *n* BOT lila. **2** (*colour*) lila *m.* – **3** *adj* (de color) lila.
Lilo [ˈlaɪləʊ] *n* GB colchoneta.
▲ *Es marca registrada; pl* Lilos.
lilt [lɪlt] *n* (*in voice*) melodía; (*in song*) ritmo alegre.
lilting [ˈlɪltɪŋ] *adj* (*voice*) melodioso,-a, cantarín,-ina; (*tune*) ondulante.
lily [ˈlɪlɪ] *n* lirio, azucena.
■ **lily of the valley,** muguete *m.*
▲ *pl* lilies.
lily-livered [ˈlɪlɪlɪvəd] *adj fam* miedoso,-a: *he's too lily-livered to do it,* es demasiado miedoso para hacerlo.
lily-white [lɪlɪˈwaɪt] *adj lit* níveo,-a; *fig* impecable.
lima bean [ˈlaɪməbiːn] *n* frijol *m.*
limb [lɪm] **1** *n* ANAT miembro. **2** (*branch*) rama.
● **out on a limb,** (*in danger*) en peligro; (*isolated*) aislado,-a.
limber [ˈlɪmbə] *adj* (*person*) ágil; (*thing*) flexible.
◆ **to limber up 1** *i* SP entrar en calor. – **2** *t sep* calentar.
limbo [ˈlɪmbəʊ] **1** *n* REL limbo. – **2** *adj fig* incertidumbre *f.*
● **to be in limbo,** estar en el limbo.
lime¹ [laɪm] **1** *n* CHEM cal *f.* – **2** *t* (*fields*) abonar con cal.
lime² [laɪm] **1** *n* (*citrus fruit*) lima. **2** (*citrus tree*) limero.
■ **lime juice,** zumo de lima.
lime³ [laɪm] *n* BOT (*linden*) tilo.
■ **broad-leaved lime,** tilo de hoja grande. ‖ **European lime,** tilo común. ‖ **silver lime,** tilo plateado. ‖ **weeping silver lime,** tilo péndulo.
limeade [laɪmˈeɪd] *n* zumo de lima (con azúcar).
lime-green [laɪmˈgriːn] *adj* (de color) verde lima.
limelight [ˈlaɪmlaɪt] *n* luz *f* de calcio.
● **to be in the limelight,** estar en el candelero.
limerick [ˈlɪmərɪk] *n* quintilla humorística.
limestone [ˈlaɪmstəʊn] *n* piedra caliza.
limey [ˈlaɪmɪ] *n* us *fam pej* inglés,-esa.
limit [ˈlɪmɪt] **1** *n* límite *m*: *there's a limit to everything,* todo tiene un límite; *the driver was found to be over the limit,* el conductor dio positivo en la prueba de alcoholemia. – **2** *t* limitar, restringir (**to,** a): *you should limit yourself to three cigarettes a day,* no deberías fumar más de tres cigarrillos al día.
● **that's the limit!,** *fam* ¡eso es el colmo! ‖ **to be off limits,** estar en zona prohibida (**to,** para). ‖ **to know no limits,** no conocer límites. ‖ **within limits,** dentro de ciertos límites.
limitation [lɪmɪˈteɪʃən] *n* limitación *f.*
limited [ˈlɪmɪtɪd] *adj* limitado,-a, restringido,-a: *tickets are limited to 200,* sólo hay 200 entradas.
■ **limited company,** sociedad *f* anónima.
limiting [ˈlɪmɪtɪŋ] *adj* restrictivo,-a.
limitless [ˈlɪmɪtləs] *adj* ilimitado,-a, sin límites.
limo [ˈlɪməʊ] **1** *n fam* (*abbr of* **limousine**) limusina. **2** *fam* (*big car*) cochazo de lujo.

▲ *pl limos.*
limousine [lɪməˈziːn] *n* limusina.
limp¹ [lɪmp] 1 *i* cojear. – 2 *n* cojera.
limp² [lɪmp] 1 *adj* (*floppy*) flojo,-a, fláccido,-a; (*lettuce*) mustio,-a. 2 (*weak*) débil.
limpet [ˈlɪmpɪt] *n* lapa.
limpid [ˈlɪmpɪd] *adj lit* límpido,-a.
limply [ˈlɪmplɪ] *adv* lánguidamente, débilmente.
limp-wristed [lɪmpˈrɪstɪd] *adj pej* (*weak*) débil; (*effeminate*) afeminado,-a.
limy [ˈlaɪmɪ] *adj* calizo,-a.
▲ *comp* limier, *superl* limiest.
linchpin [ˈlɪntʃpɪn] 1 *n* TECH pezonera. 2 *fig* pieza clave.
linctus [ˈlɪŋktəs] *n* GB jarabe *m* para la tos.
linden [ˈlɪndən] *n* tilo.
line¹ [laɪn] 1 *n* (*in general*) línea: *in a straight line,* en línea recta; *draw a line under the correct answer,* subraye la respuesta correcta; *along the usual lines,* en la línea habitual; *he said something along those lines,* dijo algo por el estilo; *hold the line, please,* un momento, por favor, no cuelgue. 2 (*drawn on paper*) raya. 3 (*of text*) línea, renglón *m*; (*of poetry*) verso: *new line,* punto y aparte. 4 (*row*) fila, hilera: *a line of trees,* una hilera de árboles. 5 US (*queue*) cola. 6 (*wrinkle*) arruga. 7 (*cord*) cuerda, cordel *m*; (*fishing*) sedal *m*; (*wire*) cable *m*. 8 (*route*) vía. 9 *fam* (*speciality*) especialidad *f*: *that's not my line!,* ¡eso no es especialidad mía!; *what's your line?,* ¿qué haces?, ¿de qué trabajas? 10 *fam* (*story*) rollo: *so then he gave me the usual line,* y entonces me vino con el rollo de siempre. 11 *sl* (*of cocaine*) raya. – 12 *t* (*draw lines on*) dibujar rayas en. 13 (*mark with wrinkles*) arrugar. 14 (*form rows along*) bordear: *trees lined the country road,* la carretera rural estaba bordeada de árboles; *the crowds lined the streets to greet the local hero,* la multitud se alineaba a lo largo de las calles para aclamar al héroe local.
◆ **to line up** 1 *i* ponerse en fila; (*in queue*) hacer cola. – 2 *t sep* poner en fila. 3 *fam* preparar, organizar: *have you got anything lined up for tomorrow?,* ¿tienes algo organizado para mañana?
● **all along the line,** (*from the beginning*) desde el principio; (*in detail*) con todo detalle. ‖ **hard lines!,** *fam* ¡qué mala suerte! ‖ **in line with,** *fig* conforme a. ‖ **to be in line for,** estar a punto de recibir: *he's in line for a rise soon,* pronto le subirán el sueldo. ‖ **to be on the right lines,** ir por buen camino. ‖ **to be out of line,** *fig* no coincidir (**with,** con). ‖ **to bring sb. into line,** *fam* pararle los pies a algn. ‖ **to come to the end of the line,** llegar al final. ‖ **to draw the line at sth.,** decir basta a algo. ‖ **to drop sb. a line,** *fam* mandar cuatro líneas a algn. ‖ **to fall into line,** cerrar filas. ‖ **to know where to draw the line,** saber decir basta. ‖ **to learn one's lines,** THEAT aprenderse el papel. ‖ **to read between the lines,** leer entre líneas. ‖ **to stand in line,** US hacer cola. ‖ **to step out of line,** salirse de la fila; *fig* saltarse las reglas. ‖ **to take a tough line with sb.,** tener mano dura con algn.
■ **dotted line,** línea de puntos. ‖ **line drawing,** dibujo lineal. ‖ **line of fire,** línea de fuego. ‖ **line of vision,** campo visual. ‖ **line printer,** impresora de líneas. ‖ **line spacer,** interlineador *m*.
line² [laɪn] 1 *t* (*with material*) forrar; (*pipes*) revestir. 2 (*walls*) llenar.
● **to line one's pockets,** *fam* forrarse.
lineage [ˈlɪnɪdʒ] *n fml* linaje *m*.
linear [ˈlɪnɪəʳ] *adj* lineal.
lined¹ [laɪnd] 1 *pt & pp* → **line**¹. – 2 *adj* (*paper*) rayado,-a. 3 (*face*) arrugado,-a. 4 (*garment*) forrado,-a.

lined² [laɪnd] 1 *pt & pp* → **line**². – 2 *adj* (*garment*) forrado,-a, con forro.
lineman [ˈlaɪnmən] 1 *n* (*railway*) encargado del mantenimiento de las vías. 2 (*telephone*) encargado del mantenimiento del tendido telefónico.
▲ *pl* linemen [ˈlaɪnmən].
linen [ˈlɪnɪn] 1 *n* (*material*) lino, hilo. 2 (*sheets etc*) ropa blanca, lencería.
● **to wash one's dirty linen in public,** sacar a relucir los trapos sucios.
■ **bed linen,** ropa de cama. ‖ **linen basket,** cesto para la ropa sucia. ‖ **linen room,** lencería. ‖ **table linen,** mantelería.
liner¹ [ˈlaɪnəʳ] *n* (*mar*) transatlántico.
liner² [ˈlaɪnəʳ] *n* (*lining*) forro.
■ **bin liner,** bolsa de basura. ‖ **nappy liner,** metedor *m*.
linesman [ˈlaɪnzmən] *n* juez *mf* de línea, linier *m*.
▲ *pl* linesmen [ˈlaɪnzmən].
line-up [ˈlaɪnʌp] 1 *n* (*of people*) alineación *f*, formación *f*. 2 US (*of criminals*) rueda de reconocimiento.
linger [ˈlɪŋgəʳ] 1 *i* (*stay*) quedarse. 2 (*persist*) persistir, perdurar.
● **to linger over doing sth.,** tardar en hacer algo. ‖ **to linger over sth.,** tardar con algo.
lingerie [ˈlɒnʒəriː] *n fml* lencería.
lingering [ˈlɪŋgərɪŋ] 1 *adj* (*slow*) lento,-a. 2 (*persistent*) persistente.
lingo [ˈlɪŋgəʊ] *n sl* idioma *m*.
▲ *pl* lingoes.
lingua franca [lɪŋgwəˈfræŋkə] *n* lingua franca.
lingual [ˈlɪŋgwəl] *adj* lingual.
linguist [ˈlɪŋgwɪst] 1 *n* lingüista *mf*. 2 (*fam*) políglota *mf*.
linguistic [lɪŋˈgwɪstɪk] *adj* lingüístico,-a.
linguistically [lɪŋˈgwɪstɪklɪ] *adv* lingüísticamente.
linguistics [lɪŋˈgwɪstɪks] *n* lingüística.
liniment [ˈlɪnɪmənt] *n* linimento.
lining [ˈlaɪnɪŋ] 1 *n* TECH revestimiento. 2 forro.
link [lɪŋk] 1 *n* (*in chain*) eslabón *m*: *the missing link,* el eslabón perdido; (*connection*) enlace *m*: *a rail link,* un enlace ferroviario. 3 *fig* vínculo, lazo: *cultural links,* lazos culturales. – 4 *t* unir, conectar. 5 *fig* vincular, relacionar: *these phenomena may actually be linked,* estos fenómenos podrían estar relacionados. – 6 **links,** *npl* campo *m sing* de golf.
◆ **to link up** 1 *i* (*be related*) estar relacionado,-a (**with,** con). 2 (*meet*) encontrarse (**with,** con). 3 RAD TV conectar (**with,** con). 4 (*spaceships*) acoplarse.
● **to link arms,** tomarse del brazo.
■ **weak link,** *fig* punto débil.
linkage [ˈlɪŋkɪdʒ] *n* conexión *f*.
linkman [ˈlɪŋkmən] *n* presentador,-ra.
▲ *pl* linkmen [ˈlɪŋkmən].
link-up [ˈlɪŋkʌp] 1 *n* (*in general*) conexión *f*. 2 (*meeting*) encuentro. 3 (*of spaceships*) acoplamiento.
linnet [ˈlɪnɪt] *n* pardillo.
lino [ˈlaɪnəʊ] *n* GB (*abbr of linoleum*) linóleo.
linocut [ˈlaɪnəʊkʌt] *n* linóleo, huecorrelieve *m*.
linoleum [lɪˈnəʊlɪəm] *n* (*suelo de*) linóleo.
linseed [ˈlɪnsiːd] *n* linaza.
■ **linseed oil,** aceite *m* de linaza.
lint [lɪnt] 1 *n* hilas *fpl*. 2 US (*fluff*) pelusa.
lintel [ˈlɪntəl] *n* dintel *m*.
lion [ˈlaɪən] *n* león *m*.
● **a lion in the path,** un obstáculo. ‖ **the lion's share,**

la parte del león. ‖ **to put one's head into the lion's mouth**, meterse en la boca del lobo.

lioness [ˈlaɪənəs] n leona.

lion-hearted [laɪənˈhɑːtɪd] adj lit valentísimo,-a.

lionize [ˈlaɪənaɪz] t venerar.

lion-like [ˈlaɪənlaɪk] adj leonino,-a.

Lions [laɪənz] Gulf of Lions, n golfo de León.

lip [lɪp] 1 n labio: upper lip, labio superior. 2 (of cup etc) borde m. 3 sl (rude talk) groserías fpl: I'll have less of your lip!, ¡basta de groserías!
● my lips are sealed, fig soy una tumba. ‖ to be on everybody's lips, ser la comidilla de todos. ‖ to bite one's lip, morderse la lengua. ‖ to keep a stiff upper lip, poner al mal tiempo buena cara. ‖ to lick one's lips, relamerse.

lip-read [ˈlɪpriːd] 1 t leer en los labios. – 2 i leer en los labios.
▲ pt & pp lip-read [ˈlɪpred].

lip-reading [ˈlɪpriːdɪŋ] n lectura en los labios.

lip-service [ˈlɪpsɜːvɪs] n jarabe m de pico, palabrería: she merely pays lip-service to socialism, hace ver que tiene ideas socialistas, pero no es más que palabrería.

lipstick [ˈlɪpstɪk] n (stick) barra de labios, lápiz m de labios; (substance) pintura de labios.

liquefy [ˈlɪkwɪfaɪ] 1 t licuar. – 2 i licuarse.
▲ pt & pp liquefied, ger liquefying.

liqueur [lɪˈkjʊəʳ, US lɪˈkɜːʳ] n licor m.

liquid [ˈlɪkwɪd] 1 n líquido. 2 LING líquida. – 3 adj líquido,-a. 4 lit transparente.

liquidate [ˈlɪkwɪdeɪt] 1 t (assets etc) liquidar. 2 fam (person) eliminar, liquidar.

liquidation [lɪkwɪˈdeɪʃən] n liquidación f.
● to go into liquidation, entrar en liquidación.

liquidator [ˈlɪkwɪdeɪtəʳ] n liquidador,-ra.

liquidity [lɪˈkwɪdɪtɪ] n liquidez f.

liquidize [ˈlɪkwɪdaɪz] t licuar.

liquidizer [ˈlɪkwɪdaɪzəʳ] n licuadora.

liquor [ˈlɪkəʳ] n US licor m: we don't sell liquor here, aquí no vendemos bebidas alcohólicas.
■ liquor store, tienda de bebidas alcohólicas.

liquorice [ˈlɪkərɪs, ˈlɪkərɪʃ] n regaliz m.

lira [ˈlɪərə] n lira.
▲ pl liras o lire [ˈlɪərə].

Lisbon [ˈlɪzbən] n Lisboa.

lisp [lɪsp] 1 n ceceo. – 2 i cecear. – 3 t decir ceceando.

lispingly [ˈlɪspɪŋlɪ] adv ceceando.

lissom [ˈlɪsəm] adj lit grácil.

list¹ [lɪst] 1 n lista. – 2 t hacer una lista de: your name is not listed, su nombre no aparece en la lista.
● to be on the danger list, MED estar grave. ‖ to enter the lists, entrar en acción.
■ listed building, edificio de interés histórico. ‖ list price, precio de catálogo.

list² [lɪst] 1 n MAR escora. – 2 i MAR escorar.

listen [ˈlɪsən] i escuchar (to, -): I tried to convince him, but he wouldn't listen, traté de convencerle, pero no me quiso escuchar; listen, I've got an idea!, ¡oye, tengo una idea!
◆ to listen in 1 i (radio) escuchar (to, -). 2 (secretly) escuchar (a escondidas) (on, -). ‖ to listen out i fam estar a la escucha, estar en escucha (for, de).
● to have a listen to sth., fam escuchar algo.

listenable [ˈlɪsənəbəl] adj fam que se puede escuchar.

listener [ˈlɪsənəʳ] 1 n (in general) oyente mf: she's a good listener, sabe escuchar. 2 RAD radioyente mf.

listing [ˈlɪstɪŋ] n listado.

listless [ˈlɪstləs] adj lánguido,-a, apático,-a.

listlessness [ˈlɪstləsnəs] n languidez f, apatía.

lit [lɪt] pt & pp → **light¹** & **light³**.

litany [ˈlɪtənɪ] n letanía.
▲ pl litanies.

liter [ˈliːtəʳ] n us litro.

literacy [ˈlɪtərəsɪ] 1 n (ability to read) alfabetización f. 2 (knowledge) conocimientos mpl, nociones fpl: computer literacy is required, se requieren conocimientos de informática.

literal [ˈlɪtərəl] adj literal.

literally [ˈlɪtərəlɪ] adv literalmente; (really) realmente, verdaderamente: literally hundreds of people pushed their way in, centenares de personas, literalmente, entraron a empujones.

literary [ˈlɪtərərɪ] adj literario,-a.

literate [ˈlɪtərət] 1 adj (able to read) alfabetizado,-a. 2 (learned) letrado,-a. 3 (with knowledge) con conocimientos de, con nociones de: if you aren't computer-literate, you won't find a job, si no tienes nociones de informática, no encontrarás trabajo.

literati [lɪtəˈrɑːtɪ] the literati, npl fml los literatos mpl.

literature [ˈlɪtərətʃə] 1 n literatura. 2 (bibliography) bibliografía. 3 fam (leaflet etc) folleto: my letter box is stuffed with promotional literature, tengo el buzón repleto de correo comercial.

lithe [laɪð] adj ágil.

lithely [ˈlaɪðlɪ] adj ágilmente.

lithograph [ˈlɪθəgrɑːf] 1 n litografía. – 2 t litografiar. – 3 i litografiar.

lithographer [lɪˈθɒgrəfəʳ] n litógrafo,-a.

lithography [lɪˈθɒgrəfɪ] n litografía.

litigant [ˈlɪtɪgənt] n litigante mf.

litigate [ˈlɪtɪgeɪt] i litigar.

litigation [lɪtɪˈgeɪʃən] n litigio.

litmus [ˈlɪtməs] n tornasol m.
■ litmus paper, papel m de tornasol. ‖ litmus test, fig prueba definitiva.

litre [ˈliːtəʳ] n GB litro.

litter [ˈlɪtəʳ] 1 n (rubbish) basura, desperdicios mpl; (paper) papeles mpl. 2 (of kittens etc) camada. 3 (for animal's bed) pajaza; (for animal's waste) arena, tierra. – 4 t (dirty) ensuciar (with, con); (cover) cubrir; (fill) llenar (with, de): littered with books, lleno,-a de libros, cubierto,-a de libros.
■ litter bin, GB papelera. ‖ litter tray, cubeta de arena, cubeta de tierra.

litterbug [ˈlɪtəbʌg] n → **litterlout**.

litter-free [ˈlɪtəfriː] adj limpio,-a.

litterlout [ˈlɪtəlaut] n GB persona que ensucia los lugares públicos; fam marrano,-a.

little [ˈlɪtəl] 1 adj (small) pequeño,-a: it's a very little flat, es un piso muy pequeño; a little cup, una tacita; let's take a little break, vamos a descansar un ratito; you poor little thing!, ¡pobrecillo! 2 (not much) poco,-a: a little milk, un poco de leche; I have little time to relax, tengo poco tiempo para relajarme. – 3 pron poco: more tea? –just a little, please, ¿quieres más té? –un poco, por favor; she gives very little of herself to her work, se dedica muy poco al trabajo. – 4 adv poco: I'm a little (bit) tired, estoy un poco cansada; it takes little over an hour to get there, se tarda poco más de una hora en llegar; as little as possible, lo menos posible; little did I know that ..., yo no tenía la menor idea de que ...
● little by little, poco a poco. ‖ little or nothing, casi

nada. ‖ **not a little**, *iron* muy: *he was not a little impressed*, se quedó muy impresionado. ‖ **to make little of**, *(play down)* quitar importancia a; *(not understand)* no captar: *I could make very little of what he was saying*, entendí muy poco de lo que decía.
■ **little finger**, dedo meñique. ‖ **little woman**, *pej (wife)* mujer *f*.

littoral ['lɪtərəl] **1** *n* litoral *m*. – **2** *adj* litoral.

liturgical [lɪ'tɜːdʒɪkəl] *adj* litúrgico,-a.

liturgy ['lɪtədʒɪ] *n* liturgia.
▲ *pl* **liturgies**.

livable ['lɪvəbəl] **1** *adj (habitable)* habitable: *the flat isn't livable (in) yet*, el piso aún no es habitable. **2** *(bearable)* soportable.

live¹ [lɪv] **1** *i* vivir: *he lived to a great age*, vivió una larga vida; *cows live on grass*, las vacas viven de la hierba; *for years they had nothing to live on*, durante años no tenían de qué vivir; *they live by fishing*, viven de la pesca. – **2** *t* vivir: *the old woman had lived a life of luxury*, la vieja había llevado una vida llena de lujos.
◆ **to live by** *t insep* seguir, adherirse a. ‖ **to live down** *t sep* lograr que se olvide. ‖ **to live for** *t insep* vivir por: *painting has given him something to live for*, la pintura le ha dado algo por lo que vivir. ‖ **to live in** *i (student)* estar internado,-a; *(servant)* vivir con la familia. ‖ **to live off** *t insep* vivir de: *they've been living off the state for years now*, viven del cuento desde hace años. ‖ **to live on** *i* sobrevivir; *(memory)* seguir vivo,-a. ‖ **to live out 1** *t sep (finish)* acabar. **2** *(fulfil)* realizar, hacer realidad. – **3** *i (student)* ser externo,-a; *(servant)* no vivir con la familia. ‖ **to live through** *t insep* sobrevivir. ‖ **to live together** *i* vivir juntos,-as. ‖ **to live up to** *t insep* cumplir con: *the show didn't live up to my expectations*, el espectáculo no era lo que yo me esperaba. ‖ **to live with 1** *t insep* vivir con. **2** *(tolerate)* tolerar, soportar.
● **to live and learn**, vivir para ver. ‖ **to live and let live**, vivir y dejar vivir. ‖ **to live by one's wits**, vivir del ingenio. ‖ **to live from day to day**, vivir al día. ‖ **to live in sin**, vivir en el pecado. ‖ **to live in style**, *fam* vivir a lo grande. ‖ **to live it up**, *fam* pasárselo bomba. ‖ **to live on fresh air**, *fig* vivir del aire. ‖ **to live out of a suitcase**, *fam* ir de hotel en hotel. ‖ **to live out of cans**, *fam* vivir (a base) de latas.

live² [laɪv] **1** *adj (not dead)* vivo,-a: *it's a real live snake*, es una serpiente de verdad. **2** *(still burning)* vivo,-a, candente; *(issue)* candente. **3** *(ammunition)* real; *(bomb)* sin explotar. **4** ELEC con corriente. **5** TV RAD en directo: *a live broadcast*, una transmisión en directo. – **6** *adv* en directo, en vivo: *I saw the Beatles perform live in 1969*, yo vi actuar a los Beatles en vivo en 1969.
■ **live wire**, cable *m* vivo; *(person)* nervio, torbellino.

live-in ['lɪvɪn] **1** *adj* que convive con uno: *a live-in housekeeper*, una criada; *she has a live-in boyfriend*, vive con su novio. – **2** *n fam* pareja.

livelihood ['laɪvlɪhʊd] *n* sustento: *that's how I earn my livelihood*, así es como me gano la vida.

liveliness ['laɪvlɪnəs] **1** *n* vivacidad *f*, animación *f*. **2** *(of colour)* viveza.

lively ['laɪvlɪ] **1** *adj* vivo,-a, animado,-a; *(interest)* entusiasmado,-a. **2** *(colour)* vivo,-a. **3** *fam (difficult)* difícil, interesante: *things were getting lively*, las cosas se ponían interesantes.
● **at a lively pace**, con un ritmo acelerado.

liven ['laɪvən]. **1 to liven up**, *t* animar. – **2 liven up**, *i* animarse.

liver ['lɪvə] *n* ANAT hígado.
■ **liver sausage**, GB embutido de paté de hígado.

liverish ['lɪvərɪʃ] *adj fam* malo,-a: *he's feeling a bit liverish*, se encuentra mal.

Liverpudlian [lɪvə'pʌdlɪən] **1** *adj* de Liverpool. – **2** *n* nativo o habitante de Liverpool.

liverwurst ['lɪvəwɜːst] *n* US embutido de paté de hígado.

livery ['lɪvərɪ] *n* librea.
■ **livery stable**, picadero, hípica.
▲ *pl* **liveries**.

lives [laɪvz] *npl* → **life**.

livestock ['laɪvstɒk] *n* ganado.
● **livestock farming**, ganadería.

livid ['lɪvɪd] **1** *adj fam* furioso,-a: *your father will be livid if he finds out*, si se entera tu padre, se pondrá furioso. **2** *(bluish)* lívido,-a.

living ['lɪvɪŋ] **1** *adj* vivo,-a: *one of the greatest living writers*, uno de los mejores escritores contemporáneos; *every living creature*, todo bicho viviente; *a living language*, una lengua viva; *it was a living death*, fue como estar enterrado vivo. – **2** *n* vida: *living conditions*, condiciones de vida; *one needs a bit of living space*, se necesita un poco de espacio vital; *what do you do for a living?*, ¿cómo te ganas la vida? – **3** **the living**, *npl* los vivos *mpl*.
● **to be the living image of sb.**, ser la viva imagen de algn. ‖ **to earn a living / make a living**, ganarse la vida: *she makes a good living selling pottery*, se gana bien la vida vendiendo cerámica.
■ **living expenses**, dietas *fpl*. ‖ **living room**, salón *m*, sala de estar. ‖ **living standards**, nivel *m sing* de vida. ‖ **living wage**, sueldo mínimo.

lizard ['lɪzəd] *n* lagarto; *(small)* lagartija.

llama ['lɑːmə] *n* ZOOL llama.

lo [ləʊ] lo and behold, *interj fam* ¡madre mía!, ¡mira por donde!

load [ləʊd] **1** *n (in general)* carga: *a lorry shed its load on the motorway yesterday*, ayer un camión perdió su carga en la autopista. **2** *(weight)* peso: *that took a load off my mind*, eso me quitó un peso de encima. – **3** *t* cargar **(with**, de): *they loaded up the van with furniture*, cargaron la furgoneta de muebles. – **4** *i* cargar.
◆ **to load down** *t sep* cargar **(with**, de); *(with worries etc)* agobiar **(with**, de/por): *he's loaded down with responsibilities*, está agobiado por las responsabilidades.
● **a load of ... / loads of ...**, *fam* montones de ..., un montón de ...: *she's given me loads of things*, me ha dado un montón de cosas; *that magazine is a load of old rubbish*, esa revista es una birria. ‖ **get a load of this!**, *fam* ¡fíjate en esto!, ¡mira esto!

loaded ['ləʊdɪd] **1** *pt & pp* → **load**. – **2** *adj (dice)* trucado,-a; *(question)* tendencioso,-a. **3** *sl (rich)* forrado,-a. **4** *fam (drunk)* mamado,-a, trompa.

loading ['ləʊdɪŋ] **1** *n (act)* carga. **2** *(insurance)* plus *m* de riesgo.
■ **loading bay**, cargadero.

loaf¹ [ləʊf] **1** *n* pan *m*; *(French)* barra; *(sliced)* pan *m* de molde. **2** *fam (head)* mollera: *use your loaf!*, ¡usa la mollera!
▲ *pl* **loaves** [ləʊvz].

loaf² [ləʊf] **to loaf about / loaf around**, *i fam* holgazanear.

loafer ['ləʊfə] **1** *n fam (person)* holgazán,-ana, vago,-a. **2** US mocasín *m*.

loan [ləʊn] **1** *n* préstamo; FIN empréstito. – **2** *t* US prestar: *could you loan me your car?*, ¿me prestas el coche?
● **on loan**, prestado,-a; *(footballer)* cedido,-a: *I got this*

book on loan from the library, este libro lo he sacado prestado de la biblioteca. ‖ **to raise a loan,** FIN hacer un empréstito.

loanword ['ləʊnwɜːd] *n* préstamo.

loath [ləʊθ] *adj* reacio,-a: *he was loath to give her back the keys,* era reacio a devolverle las llaves.

loathe [ləʊð] *t* odiar, aborrecer.

loathing ['ləʊðɪŋ] *n* odio, aborrecimiento.

loathsome ['ləʊðsəm] *adj* odioso,-a, repelente.

loaves [ləʊvz] *npl* → **loaf**.

lob [lɒb] **1** *n* (*tennis*) lob *m*, globo. – **2** *i* hacer un lob, hacer un globo. – **3** *t* fam lanzar.
▲ (*verbo*) *pt* & *pp* **lobbed,** *ger* **lobbing**.

lobby ['lɒbɪ] **1** *n* (*hall*) vestíbulo. **2** POL grupo de presión. – **3** *i* presionar (**for,** para) (**against,** en contra de): *we must continue to lobby for a better health system,* debemos seguir presionando para que mejore el sistema sanitario. – **4** *t* POL presionar, ejercer presión sobre.
▲ *pl* **lobbies**.

lobbyist ['lɒbɪɪst] *n* POL activista *mf* de un grupo de presión.

lobe [ləʊb] *n* lóbulo.

lobotomy [la'bɒtəmɪ] *n* lobotomía.
▲ *pl* **lobotomies**.

lobster ['lɒbstə'] *n* bogavante *m*.
■ Norway lobster, cigala. ‖ lobster pot, nasa. ‖ spiny lobster, langosta.

local ['ləʊkəl] **1** *adj* (*in general*) local. **2** (*person*) del barrio, de la zona. **3** (*government*) municipal, regional. – **4** *n fam* (*person*) vecino,-a: *one of the locals,* uno de los vecinos. **5** GB fam bar *m*, pub *m* (*del barrio*). **6** US (*train*) tren *m* de cercanías; (*bus*) autobús *m*.
■ local area network, COMPUT red *f* de área local. ‖ local authority, ayuntamiento. ‖ local call, llamada urbana. ‖ local time, hora local.

locale [ləʊ'kɑːl] *n fml* (*place*) lugar *m*; (*scene*) escenario.

locality [ləʊ'kælɪtɪ] *n fml* localidad *f*.
▲ *pl* **localities**.

localize ['ləʊkəlaɪz] *t fml* localizar.

locally ['ləʊkəlɪ] **1** *adv* (*in the area*) en la localidad, en el lugar. **2** (*in particular areas*) localmente: *there may be showers locally,* podrían producirse algunos chubascos locales.

locate [ləʊ'keɪt] **1** *t fml* (*find*) localizar. **2** *fml* (*situate*) situar, ubicar.

location [ləʊ'keɪʃən] **1** *n* (*place*) lugar *m*. **2** (*act of placing*) ubicación *f*. **3** (*finding*) localización *f* exacta. **4** CINEM exteriores *mpl*: *it was filmed on location in Turkey,* se rodó en Turquía.

loc cit ['lɒk'sɪt] *abbr* (*loco citato*) en el lugar citado; (*abbreviation*) loc. cit.

loch [lɒk] *n* (*in Scotland*) lago.

loci ['ləʊsaɪ] *npl* → **locus**.

lock[1] [lɒk] **1** *n* (*on door etc*) cerradura; (*padlock*) candado; (*on steering wheel*) retén *m*. **2** (*in canal*) esclusa. **3** (*wrestling*) llave *f*. **4** GB AUT ángulo de giro. – **5** *t* (*with key*) cerrar con llave; (*with padlock*) cerrar con candado. **6** *fig* enzarzar: *the two men were locked in a dispute,* los dos hombres estaban enzarzados en una discusión; *they were locked in an embrace,* se fundieron en un abrazo. – **7** *i* (*door etc*) cerrarse (con llave). **8** (*wheel*) trabarse.
◆ **to lock away 1** *t sep* (*valuables*) guardar bajo llave. **2** *fam* (*person*) encerrar. ‖ **to lock in** *t sep* encerrar: *I got locked in the bathroom this morning,* esta mañana me quedé encerrada en el baño. ‖ **to lock onto** *t insep* (*missile*) seguir el rastro de. ‖ **to lock out 1** *t sep* cerrar la

puerta a; (*leave outside*) dejar fuera a. **2** IND cerrar el paso a. ‖ **to lock up 1** *t sep* → **to lock away**. **2** (*building*) cerrar con llave. **3** (*money*) invertir. – **4** *i* cerrar las puertas con llave.
■ lock keeper, esclusero,-a.

lock[2] [lɒk] *n* (*of hair*) mecha, mechón *m*.

locker ['lɒkə'] *n* armario, taquilla.
■ Davy Jones's locker, *fam* el fondo del mar. ‖ locker room, SP vestuarios *mpl*.

locket ['lɒkɪt] *n* (*with picture*) medallón *m*; (*with hair*) guardapelo.

lockout ['lɒkaʊt] *n* locáut *m*, cierre *m* patronal.

locksmith ['lɒksmɪθ] *n* cerrajero.

lockup ['lɒkʌp] *n* (*local prison*) cárcel *f* (*pequeña*).

locomotion [ləʊkə'məʊʃən] *n* locomoción *f*.

locomotive [ləʊkə'məʊtɪv] **1** *n* locomotora. – **2** *adj* locomotor,-ra.

locum ['ləʊkəm] *n* suplente *mf*.

locus ['ləʊkəs] *n* TECH lugar *m*.
▲ *pl* **loci** ['ləʊsaɪ].

locust ['ləʊkəst] *n* langosta.

locution [lə'kjuːʃən] *n* locución *f*.

lode [ləʊd] *n* TECH mena.

lodge [lɒdʒ] **1** *n* (*in general*) casita; (*hunter's*) refugio. **2** (*porter's*) portería. **3** (*masonic*) logia. **4** (*beaver's*) madriguera. – **5** *i* (*as guest*) alojarse, hospedarse. **6** (*become fixed*) quedarse atrapado,-a: *a fishbone lodged in my throat,* se me quedó clavada en la garganta una espina de pescado. **7** (*accomodate*) alojar, hospedar. – **8** *t* (*complaint*) presentar.

lodger ['lɒdʒə'] *n* huésped,-da.

lodging ['lɒdʒɪŋ] **1** *n* alojamiento. – **2** lodgings, *npl* realquiler *m*: *he's staying in lodgings,* está de realquiler.
■ lodging house, casa de huéspedes.

loft [lɒft] **1** *n* desván *m*, buhardilla. **2** US (*apartment*) ático grande. – **3** *t* SP lanzar al aire.

lofty ['lɒftɪ] **1** *adj* (*high*) alto,-a. **2** *pej* (*haughty*) altivo,-a.
▲ *comp* **loftier**, *superl* **loftiest**.

log [lɒg] **1** *n* tronco; (*for fire*) leño. **2** (*on ship*) cuaderno de bitácora, diario de a bordo; (*on plane*) diario de vuelo. **3** MATH *fam* (*abbr of logarithm*) logaritmo. – **4** *t* registrar, anotar. **5** (*cover*) recorrer.
◆ **to log in** *i* COMPUT entrar (en el sistema). ‖ **to log off** *i* COMPUT salir (del sistema). ‖ **to log on** *i* COMPUT entrar (en el sistema). ‖ **to log out** *i* COMPUT salir (del sistema).
■ log cabin, cabaña (de troncos).
▲ (*verbo*) *pt* & *pp* **logged,** *ger* **logging**.

loganberry ['ləʊgənbərɪ] *n* frambuesa/zarza de Logan.
■ loganberry bush, frambueso de Logan.
▲ *pl* **loganberries**.

logarithm ['lɒgərɪðəm] *n* logaritmo.

logbook ['lɒgbʊk] *n* GB (*of vehicle*) documentación *f*, cédula.

logger ['lɒgə'] *n* leñador,-ra.

loggerheads ['lɒgəhedz] to be at loggerheads, *phr* estar enfrentados,-as.

logic ['lɒdʒɪk] *n* lógica: *there's no logic in her behaviour,* su comportamiento no tiene lógica.

logical ['lɒdʒɪkəl] *adj* lógico,-a: *the logical thing would be to say yes,* lo lógico sería decir que sí.

logically ['lɒdʒɪklɪ] *adv* lógicamente.

logician [lə'dʒɪʃən] *n* lógico,-a.

logistics [lə'dʒɪstɪks] *n* logística.

logjam ['lɒgdʒæm] **1** *n* (*on river*) acumulación *f* de troncos. **2** US punto muerto.

logo ['ləʊgəʊ] *n* logotipo.
▲ *pl* **logos**.

logy [ˈlɒgɪ] *adj* US *fam* pesado,-a, lento,-a.
▲ *comp* **logier**, *superl* **logiest**.
loin [lɔɪn] **1** *n* (*of animal*) ijada, ijar *m*. **2** CULIN (*of pork*) lomo; (*of beef*) solomillo. – **3** **loins**, *npl euph* ingle *f sing*.
● **to gird up one's loins**, prepararse para la lucha.
loincloth [ˈlɔɪnklɒθ] *n* taparrabo, taparrabos *m sing*.
Loire [lwɑːʳ] *n* el Loira *m*.
loiter [ˈlɔɪtəʳ] **1** *i* holgazanear; *pej* merodear: *"no loitering"*, "no merodear", "prohibido merodear". **2** (*lag behind*) rezagarse.
● **to loiter with intent to commit a felony**, merodear con intención de delinquir.
loiterer [ˈlɔɪtərəʳ] *n* holgazán,-ana; *pej* merodeador,-ra.
loll [lɒl] **1** *i* (*sit*) repantigarse. **2** (*droop*) colgar.
lollipop [ˈlɒlɪpɒp] **1** *n* pirulí *m*, piruleta. **2** GB (*iced*) polo.
■ **lollipop lady / lollipop man**, guardia *mf* (que para el tráfico para que puedan cruzar la calle los colegiales).
lollop [ˈlɒləp] *i fam* moverse torpe y lentamente.
lolly [ˈlɒlɪ] **1** *n* GB *fam* pirulí *m*, piruleta. **2** GB *fam* (*iced*) polo. **3** GB *sl* (*money*) pasta.
■ **ice lolly**, polo.
▲ *pl* **lollies**.
London [ˈlʌndən] *n* Londres.
Londoner [ˈlʌndənəʳ] *n* londinense *mf*.
lone [ləʊn] **1** *adj lit* (*single*) solo,-a. **2** *lit* (*solitary*) solitario,-a.
■ **lone wolf**, *fig* persona solitaria.
loneliness [ˈləʊnlɪnəs] *n* soledad *f*.
lonely [ˈləʊnlɪ] **1** *adj* (*person*) solo,-a. **2** (*place*) solitario,-a, aislado,-a.
■ **lonely hearts club**, club para personas que quieren entablar nuevas amistades. ‖ **lonely hearts column**, sección *f* de contactos.
▲ *comp* **lonelier**, *superl* **loneliest**.
loner [ˈləʊnəʳ] *n* persona solitaria.
lonesome [ˈləʊnsəm] *adj* US → **lonely**.
long¹ [lɒŋ] **1** *adj* largo,-a: *how long was the film?*, ¿cuánto duró la película?; *the garden is 30 metres long*, el jardín hace 30 metros de largo; *we were a long way from the beach*, estábamos lejos de la playa; *it took him a long time to finish*, tardó mucho en acabar. – **2** *adv* mucho tiempo: *how long have you been waiting?*, ¿cuánto hace que esperas?; *it wasn't long before they returned*, no tardaron en volver. – **3** *n* lo largo; (*if*) con tal que.
● **(for) a long time**, **for long**, mucho tiempo. ‖ **in the long run**, a la larga. ‖ **long ago**, hace mucho tiempo. ‖ **no longer / not any longer**, ya no: *he doesn't live here any longer*, ya no vive aquí. ‖ **not by a long chalk / not by a long shot**, *fam* ni por mucho, ni de lejos. ‖ **so long**, US *fam* (*goodbye*) hasta la vista. ‖ **so long as**, → **as long as**. ‖ **the long and the short of it is ...**, en resumidas cuentas ... ‖ **to be a bit long in the tooth**, *fam* tener años. ‖ **to pull a long face**, poner cara larga.
■ **long jump**, salto de longitud. ‖ **long johns**, calzones *mpl* largos. ‖ **long ton**, tonelada (*equivale a 2240 libras o 1016,047 kilogramos*). ‖ **long vacation**, GB vacaciones *fpl* de verano. ‖ **long wave**, onda larga.
long² [lɒŋ] **to long to do sth.**, *phr* tener muchos deseos de hacer algo: *he's longing to see you*, tiene muchas ganas de verte.
◆ **to long for** *t insep* (*yearn*) anhelar; (*nostalgically*) añorar.
long³ [ˈlɒŋgɪtjuːd] *abbr* (*longitude*) longitud *f*; (*abbreviation*) long.

longboat [ˈlɒŋbəʊt] *n* chalupa, lancha.
longbow [ˈlɒŋbəʊ] *n* arco.
long-distance [lɒŋˈdɪstəns] **1** *adj* de larga distancia. **2** (*phone call*) interurbano,-a: *she phoned him long-distance from Miami*, le puso una conferencia desde Miami.
■ **long-distance call**, conferencia. ‖ **long-distance race**, carrera de fondo. ‖ **long-distance runner**, corredor,-ra de fondo.
long-drawn-out [lɒŋdrɔːnˈaʊt] *adj* largo,-a, interminable.
longevity [lɒnˈdʒevɪtɪ] *n* longevidad *f*.
longhaired [lɒŋˈheəd] **1** *adj* (*animal*) de pelo largo. **2** *pej* (*person*) melenudo,-a.
longhand [ˈlɒŋhænd] *n* escritura a mano: *I wrote out the letter in longhand first*, primero escribí la carta a mano.
longing [ˈlɒŋɪŋ] *n* (*yearning*) ansia, anhelo; (*nostalgia*) nostalgia.
longingly [ˈlɒŋɪŋlɪ] *adv* (*with yearning*) ansiosamente; (*nostalgically*) con nostalgia.
longish [ˈlɒŋɪʃ] *adj fam* más bien largo,-a, bastante largo,-a.
longitude [ˈlɒndʒɪtjuːd] *n* longitud *f*.
longitudinal [lɒndʒɪˈtjuːdɪnəl] *adj* longitudinal.
long-life [ˈlɒŋlaɪf] **long-life milk**, *n* leche *f* UHT, leche *f* uperizada.
long-lived [lɒŋˈlɪvd] *adj* de larga vida; (*for a long time*) de toda la vida.
long-playing [lɒŋˈpleɪɪŋ] *adj* de larga duración.
■ **long-playing record**, elepé *m*.
long-range [ˈlɒŋreɪndʒ] **1** *adj* (*distance*) de largo alcance. **2** (*plans*, *forecast*) a largo plazo.
long-sighted [lɒŋˈsaɪtɪd] **1** *adj* GB présbita. **2** GB *fig* perspicaz.
long-sightedness [lɒŋˈsaɪtɪdnəs] **1** *n* GB presbicia. **2** GB *fig* perspicacia.
long-standing [lɒŋˈstændɪŋ] *adj* antiguo,-a.
long-suffering [lɒŋˈsʌfərɪŋ] *adj* sufrido,-a.
long-term [lɒŋˈtɜːm] *adj* a largo plazo, de largo plazo: *long-term effects*, efectos a largo plazo.
longways [ˈlɒŋweɪz] *adv* GB a lo largo.
long-wearing [lɒŋˈweərɪŋ] *adj* US duradero,-a, resistente.
long-winded [lɒŋˈwɪndɪd] *adj* (*person*) prolijo,-a; (*speech etc*) interminable.
loo [luː] *n* GB *fam* váter *m*.
▲ *pl* **loos**.
loofah [ˈluːfə] *n* esponja vegetal.
look [lʊk] **1** *i* mirar (**at**, -): *look at her running*, mira cómo corre; *what are they looking at?*, ¿qué miran? **2** (*seem*) parecer: *that doesn't look difficult*, eso no parece difícil; *you're looking well*, tienes buen aspecto; *how do I look?*, ¿qué tal estoy?; *he looks tired*, parece cansado; *it looks that way*, eso parece. – **3** *t* mirar: *they looked him up and down*, lo miraron de arriba abajo; *I can't look him in the face*, no puedo mirarle a la cara. **4** (*seem*) parecer: *he doesn't look his age*, no aparenta la edad que tiene; *she always looks her best*, siempre cuida su apariencia. **5** *fam* (*plan*) pensar, tener pensado,-a: *she's looking to buy a flat*, piensa comprarse un piso. – **6** *n* (*glance*) mirada: *have a look at this*, mira esto; *she took one look at him and laughed*, nada más mirarlo se puso a reír. **7** (*appearance*) aspecto, apariencia: *her haircut gives her a new look*, el corte de pelo le da un nuevo aire; *I didn't like the look of it*, me dio mala espina. **8** (*expression*) expresión *f*: *I could tell by the look of him that he wasn't at all interested*, a juzgar por su expresión no le intere-

saba lo más mínimo. **9** (*fashion*) moda: *I'm not into the punk look,* no me va la moda punk. **– 10** *interj* ¡mira! **– 11 looks,** *npl* belleza *f sing:* *she's kept her looks throughout the years,* a pesar de los años sigue siendo guapa.
◆ **to look after** *t insep* (*deal with*) ocuparse de, atender a; (*take care of*) cuidar (de): *I can look after myself,* me las arreglo yo sola; *goodbye, look after yourself!,* ¡adiós, y cuídate!; *she only looks after her own interests,* sólo mira por su interés. ‖ **to look ahead** *i* mirar hacia adelante; *fig* mirar el futuro. ‖ **to look at 1** *t insep* (*consider*) mirar, considerar. **2** (*examine*) mirar: *you should have that knee looked at,* deberías ir a que te miren esa rodilla. ‖ **to look back** *i* mirar atrás: *I now look back on those years with a different view,* ahora miro esos años desde otra perspectiva. ‖ **to look down on** *t insep* despreciar. ‖ **to look for** *t insep* buscar: *what are you looking for?,* ¿qué buscas?; *he's looking for trouble if he continues to misbehave,* si sigue portándose mal, se buscará problemas. ‖ **to look forward to** *t insep* esperar (con ansia): *he's looking forward to going home,* espera con ilusión volver a casa; *I look forward to your reply,* espero noticias suyas. ‖ **to look in on** *t insep fam* pasar (un momento) por. ‖ **to look into** *t insep* investigar. ‖ **to look on 1** *t insep* considerar: *I look on him as a close friend,* lo considero un amigo íntimo. **– 2** *i* observar. ‖ **to look like** *t insep* parecerse a: *he looks like his father,* se parece a su padre; *it looks like snow,* parece que va a nevar. ‖ **to look onto** *t insep* dar a. ‖ **to look out 1** *i* (*be careful*) ir con cuidado: *look out - a car's coming!,* ¡cuidado, que viene un coche! **– 2** *t sep* GB (*search for*) buscarse. ‖ **to look out for** *t insep* esperar: *look out for that play,* estáte al tanto de cuándo hacen esa obra de teatro. ‖ **to look over** *t sep* (*study quickly*) mirar por encima. ‖ **to look round 1** *i* (*turn one's head*) volver la cabeza. **2** (*in shop etc*) mirar: *I'm just looking round,* sólo estoy mirando. **– 3** *t insep* (*shop*) mirar. **4** (*sightseeing*) visitar. ‖ **to look through** *t insep* (*check*) revisar (bien); (*quickly*) ojear. ‖ **to look to 1** *t insep* (*depend on*) contar con: *he looked to his father for help,* contó con la ayuda de su padre. **2** (*concentrate on*) centrarse en: *look to it that you leave on time,* asegúrate de salir puntual. ‖ **to look up 1** *i fam* (*improve*) mejorar: *things are finally looking up!,* ¡por fin mejoran las cosas! **– 2** *t sep* (*in dictionary etc*) consultar, buscar: *look it up in the dictionary,* consúltalo en el diccionario. **3** (*visit*) ir a ver. ‖ **to look up to** *t insep* respetar.
● **by the look(s) of it,** por lo visto. ‖ **look alive! / look lively!,** *fam* ¡espabílate! ‖ **look before you leap,** antes de que te cases mira lo que haces. ‖ **not to be much to look at,** *fam* no ser demasiado guapo,-a, no ser ninguna belleza. ‖ **to have a look for sth.,** buscar algo. ‖ **to look around for sth.,** andar buscando algo. ‖ **to look down one's nose at sb.,** mirar a algn. mal. ‖ **to look on the bright side (of things),** mirar el lado bueno de las cosas. ‖ **to look sharp,** GB *fam* (*hurry*) darse prisa; (*be careful*) tener cuidado. ‖ **to look well on sb.,** sentar bien a algn.
lookalike ['lʊkəlaɪk] *n fam* doble *mf,* sosia *m.*
looker ['lʊkə*] *n fam* (*woman*) preciosidad *f.*
look-in ['lʊkɪn] *n fam* oportunidad *f,* ocasión *f.*
looking glass ['lʊkɪŋglæs] *n arch* espejo.
lookout ['lʊkaʊt] **1** *n* (*person*) vigía *mf.* **2** (*place*) atalaya *f.* **3** *fam* (*outlook*) futuro: *if you aren't done on time, it's your (own) lookout!,* si no terminas a tiempo, ¡allá tú!
● **to be on the lookout for,** estar al acecho de.
loom[1] [luːm] *n* telar *m.*
loom[2] [luːm] **1** *i* vislumbrarse; (*causing fear*) amenazar.
◆ **to loom up** *i* surgir.

● **to loom large,** causar mucha preocupación.
loony ['luːnɪ] *adj fam* chiflado,-a, chalado,-a.
■ **loony bin,** *fam* manicomio.
▲ *comp* **loonier,** *superl* **looniest.**
loop [luːp] **1** *n* (*in string etc*) lazo. **2** (*contraceptive*) esterilete *m,* diu *m.* **3** (*made by aircraft*) rizo. **4** COMPUT bucle *m.* **– 5** *t pasar:* *loop the rope round the post,* pasa la cuerda alrededor del poste. **– 6** *i* formar un lazo.
● **to loop the loop,** rizar el rizo.
loophole ['luːphəʊl] *n fig* escapatoria.
■ **tax loophole,** laguna impositiva.
loopy ['luːpɪ] *adj fam* tocado,-a, chiflado,-a.
▲ *comp* **loopier,** *superl* **loopiest.**
loose [luːs] **1** *adj* (*in general*) suelto,-a. **2** (*not tight*) flojo,-a; (*clothes*) holgado,-a. **3** (*not tied*) suelto,-a, desatado,-a. **4** (*not packaged*) suelto,-a, a granel: *he buys coffee loose,* compra el café a granel. **5** (*not connected*) desconectado,-a. **6** (*inexact*) inexacto,-a; (*translation*) libre. **7** *pej* (*lax*) relajado,-a: *a loose woman,* una mujer fácil; *loose living,* la vida alegre. **– 8** *t* soltar.
● **to be at a loose end,** GB *fam* no tener nada que hacer. ‖ **to be at loose ends,** US *fam* no tener nada que hacer. ‖ **to be on the loose,** andar suelto,-a. ‖ **to break loose,** escaparse. ‖ **to come loose / work loose,** desprenderse; (*shoelace*) desatarse. ‖ **to cut loose,** *fam* largarse. ‖ **to let sb. loose,** soltar a algn.: *don't let her loose in your kitchen,* no la sueltes en tu cocina. ‖ **to set loose / turn loose,** soltar. ‖ **to stay loose / hang loose,** US *fam* relajarse. ‖ **to tie up loose ends,** *fig* no dejar cabo suelto.
■ **loose change,** cambio suelto, suelto. ‖ **loose cover,** funda. ‖ **loose end,** cabo suelto. ‖ **loose talk,** chismorreo. ‖ **loose tobacco,** tabaco en hebras.
loose-fitting [luːs'fɪtɪŋ] *adj* holgado,-a, amplio,-a.
loose-leaf [luːs'liːf] *adj* de hojas sueltas.
loosely ['luːslɪ] **1** *adv* (*not tightly*) suelto,-a. **2** (*approximately*) aproximadamente; (*translate*) libremente.
loosen ['luːsən] **1** *t* (*gen*) soltar, aflojar; (*belt*) desabrochar: *can you loosen this knot?,* ¿puedes aflojar este nudo?; *loosen this screw,* afloja este tornillo; *the champagne loosened up her tongue,* el champán le soltó la lengua. **– 2** *i* soltarse, aflojarse. **3** (*become untied*) desatarse.
◆ **to loosen up 1** *i* SP desentumecerse. **2** (*relax*) relajarse. **– 3** *t sep* desentumecer, relajar.
looseness ['luːsnəs] **1** *n* (*in general*) soltura. **2** (*of clothes*) holgura. **3** (*of morals etc*) relajamiento. **4** (*imprecision*) falta de precisión; (*of translation*) libertad *f.*
loot [luːt] **1** *n* botín *m.* **– 2** *t* saquear. **– 3** *i* saquear.
looting ['luːtɪŋ] *n* saqueo.
lop [lɒp] **1** *t* podar: *he's lopped a few branches off the pine tree,* ha podado un poco el pino. **2** *fig* recortar.
▲ *pt & pp* **lopped,** *ger* **lopping.**
lope [ləʊp] **1** *i* andar a zancadas: *the giraffe loped off,* la jirafa se fue a zancadas.
● **at a lope,** *adv phr* a zancadas.
lop-eared ['lɒpɪəd] *adj* de orejas gachas, de orejas caídas.
lopsided [lɒp'saɪdɪd] **1** *adj* (*walk, table*) cojo,-a; (*unbalanced*) desigual. **2** *fig* injusto,-a.
loquacious [lə'kweɪʃəs] *adj fml* locuaz.
loquacity [lə'kwæsɪtɪ] *n fml* locuacidad *f.*
lord [lɔːd] **1** *n* señor *m.* **2** GB (*title*) lord *m.* **3** (*judge*) señoría *mf:* *no, my Lord,* no, señoría. **4** (*powerful man*) barón *m.*
● **good Lord!,** ¡ay Dios!, ¡Dios mío! ‖ **Lord (only) knows ...,** quién sabe ... ‖ **to live like a lord,** vivir a

cuerpo de rey. ‖ **to lord it over sb.**, *fam* comportarse como si uno fuera dueño,-a y señor,-ra de algn.
■ **Lord Mayor,** *(man)* alcalde *m*; *(woman)* alcaldesa. ‖ **lord and master,** amo y señor. ‖ **the House of Lords,** la Cámara de los Lores. ‖ **the Lord,** REL el Señor. ‖ **the Lord's Prayer,** el padrenuestro.

lordly ['lɔːdlɪ] **1** *adj pej* despótico,-a. **2** *(grand)* grandioso,-a.
▲ *comp* **lordlier,** *superl* **lordliest.**

lordship ['lɔːdʃɪp] *n* *(title)* señoría: *Your Lordship,* su señoría.

lore [lɔːʳ] *n* saber *m* popular.

lorry ['lɒrɪ] *n* GB camión *m*.
■ **lorry park,** aparcamiento para camiones.
▲ *pl* **lorries.**

lose [luːz] **1** *t* *(in general)* perder: *he's lost his car keys,* ha perdido las llaves del coche; *he lost himself in the middle of his explanation,* se perdió a mitad de la explicación. **2** *(immerse)* sumergir **(in,** en): *she lost herself in the novel,* estaba absorta en la novela. **3** *(clock)* atrasar: *this watch loses 5 minutes a day,* este reloj atrasa 5 minutos por día. – **4** *i* *(in general)* perder: *Liverpool lost to United,* el Liverpool perdió ante el United. **5** *(clock)* atrasarse.
◆ **to lose out** *i* salir perdiendo **(to,** ante).
● **to have nothing to lose,** *fam* no tener nada que perder. ‖ **to lose one's head,** perder la cabeza. ‖ **to lose one's heart (to sb.),** enamorarse (de algn.). ‖ **to lose one's life,** perder la vida, perecer. ‖ **to lose one's way,** perderse. ‖ **to lose sight of sth.,** perder algo de vista. ‖ **to lose weight,** adelgazar, perder peso.
▲ *pt & pp* **lost** [lɒst], *ger* **losing.**

loser ['luːzəʳ] *n* perdedor,-ra: *the real loser is the consumer,* el que sale perdiendo es el consumidor.
● **to be a born loser,** *pej* ser un fracaso. ‖ **to be a good/bad loser,** saber/no saber perder. ‖ **to be on a loser,** *fam* llevar las de perder.

loss [lɒs] **1** *n* *(in general)* pérdida: *loss of appetite,* pérdida del apetito; *the factory has made huge losses so far this year,* la fábrica ha sufrido enormes pérdidas en lo que va de año. **2** MIL *(death)* baja: *the army suffered heavy losses,* el ejército sufrió muchas bajas.
● **to be a dead loss,** *fam* ser un desastre. ‖ **to be at a loss,** quedarse confuso,-a. ‖ **to be at a loss for words,** quedarse de una pieza. ‖ **to make a loss,** perder. ‖ **to sell sth. at a loss,** vender algo con pérdida.

lost [lɒst] **1** *pt & pp* → **lose.** – **2** *adj* perdido,-a: *a lost chance,* una oportunidad perdida; *I'd say your wallet is as good as lost,* creo que la cartera la puedes dar por perdida. **2** *(wasted)* inútil: *any advice is lost on her,* es inútil darle consejos.
● **get lost!,** *sl* ¡vete a la porra! ‖ **to be lost for words,** quedarse de una pieza. ‖ **to be lost in thought,** estar perdido,-a en sus pensamientos. ‖ **to get lost,** perderse.
■ **lost cause,** causa perdida. ‖ **lost property,** objetos *mpl* perdidos. ‖ **lost property office,** oficina de objetos perdidos.

lost-and-found [lɒstən'faʊnd] **lost-and-found** (department), *n* US oficina de objetos perdidos.

lot [lɒt] **1** *n* *(large number)* cantidad *f*: *he talks a lot,* habla mucho; *a lot of books,* muchos libros; *a lot of people,* mucha gente; *she's got a lot (of work) to do,* tiene mucho (trabajo) que hacer; *what a lot of space there is!,* ¡cuánto espacio hay! **2** *(group)* grupo: *the next lot of passengers,* el próximo grupo de pasajeros; *you can wait here,* vosotros podéis esperaros aquí. **3** *(in auction)* lote *m*. **4** *(fate)* suerte *f*: *the common lot,* la suerte de

todos. **5** US *(land)* solar *m*. **6** **the lot,** todo,-a, todos,-as: *she liked the books and bought the lot,* le gustaron los libros y se los compró todos. – **7** **lots of,** *phr* mucho,-a, muchos,-as, cantidad de: *she's got lots (of work) to do,* tiene mucho (trabajo) que hacer.
● **thanks a lot!,** ¡muchísimas gracias! ‖ **to cast lots for sth.** / **draw lots for sth.,** echar algo a suertes.

loth [ləʊθ] *adj* → **loath.**

lotion ['ləʊʃən] *n* loción *f*.

lottery ['lɒtərɪ] *n* lotería.
▲ *pl* **lotteries.**

lotus ['ləʊtəs] *n* loto.

lotus-eater ['ləʊtəsiːtəʳ] *n* soñador,-ra.

loud [laʊd] **1** *adj* *(sound)* fuerte. **2** *(voice)* alto,-a. **3** *(colour)* chillón,-ona. **4** *(behaviour)* vulgar, ordinario,-a. – **5** *adv* fuerte, alto.
● **out loud,** en voz alta: *I was thinking out loud,* pensaba en voz alta.

loud-hailer [laʊd'heɪləʳ] *n* GB megáfono.

loudmouth ['laʊdmaʊθ] *n* *fam pej* vocearas *mf*, bocazas *mf*.
▲ *pl* **loudmouths** ['laʊdmaʊðz].

loudness ['laʊdnəs] *n* *(of sound)* fuerza, intensidad *f*; *(noisiness)* bullicio.

loudspeaker [laʊd'spiːkəʳ] *n* altavoz *m*.

Louisiana [luːɪzɪ'ænə] *n* Luisiana.

lounge [laʊndʒ] **1** *n* salón *m*. – **2** *i* *(on sofa etc)* repantigarse. **3** *(idle)* holgazanear: *he lounges about all afternoon,* se pasa la tarde holgazaneando.
■ **lounge suit,** *fam* traje *m*.

lounger ['laʊndʒəʳ] *n* *pej* holgazán,-ana, vago,-a.

louse [laʊs] **1** *n* piojo. **2** *fam* canalla *mf*.
◆ **to louse up** *t sep* US *sl* fastidiar.
▲ *(substantivo)* *pl* **lice.**

lousy ['laʊzɪ] **1** *adj fam* fatal, malísimo,-a: *the weather was lousy,* hizo un tiempo de perros; *he felt lousy,* se encontraba fatal; *what a lousy trick!,* ¡vaya cochinada! **2** *(with lice)* piojoso,-a.
● **to be lousy with,** *sl* apestar de.
▲ *comp* **lousier,** *superl* **lousiest.**

lout [laʊt] *n pej* patán *m*, animal *m*.

loutish ['laʊtɪʃ] *adj pej* animal.

louver ['luːvəʳ] *n* US persiana.

louvre ['luːvəʳ] *n* persiana.

lovable ['lʌvəbəl] *adj* adorable.

love [lʌv] **1** *n* *(in general)* amor *m*; *(affection)* cariño; *(liking)* afición *f* **(for,** a). **2** GB *fam (person)* guapo,-a, chato,-a. **3** *(regards)* recuerdos *mpl*: *(give my) love to your parents,* muchos recuerdos a tus padres. **4** *(tennis)* cero. – **5** *t* amar, querer: *do you love him?,* ¿lo quieres? **6** *(like a lot)* encantarle a uno, gustarle a uno mucho: *I love playing tennis,* me encanta jugar a tenis; *we'd love to see you,* nos encantaría verte; *I love to watch her dancing,* me gusta mucho verla bailar.
● **for the love of it,** por amor al arte. ‖ **love at first sight,** amor a primera vista. ‖ **not for love or money,** por nada del mundo. ‖ **to be in love with,** estar enamorado,-a de. ‖ **to fall in love,** enamorarse. ‖ **to make love,** hacer el amor **(to,** a).
■ **love affair,** aventura amorosa, lío. ‖ **love child,** hijo,-a natural. ‖ **love life,** vida sentimental; *(sexual)* vida sexual.

lovebirds ['lʌvbɜːzd] *npl* tortolitos.

loveless ['lʌvləs] *adj* sin amor.

loveliness ['lʌvlɪnəs] *n* encanto, hermosura.

lovely ['lʌvlɪ] **1** *adj* *(wonderful)* estupendo,-a, maravilloso,-a. **2** *(beautiful)* hermoso,-a, precioso,-a; *(charming)* encantador,-ra.

▲ *comp* lovelier, *superl* loveliest.

love-making ['lʌvmeɪkɪŋ] *n* (*courtship*) galanteo; (*sexual*) relaciones *fpl* sexuales.

lover ['lʌvəʳ] *n* amante *mf*: *for music lovers,* para los amantes de la (buena) música.

lovesick ['lʌvsɪk] *adj* enfermo,-a de amor.

lovey ['lʌvɪ] *n* GB *fam* guapo,-a, encanto.

lovey-dovey [lʌvɪ'dʌvɪ] *adj iron* empalagoso,-a, zalamero,-a.

loving ['lʌvɪŋ] *adj* cariñoso,-a: *your loving son, Paul,* tu hijo que te quiere, Paul; *in loving memory of,* a la memoria de.

lovingly ['lʌvɪŋlɪ] *adv* con cariño.

low¹ [ləʊ] **1** *adj* (*in general*) bajo,-a; (*neckline*) escotado,-a: *low clouds,* nubes bajas; *a low income,* pocos ingresos; *I'm getting low on paper,* se me está acabando el papel; *cook on a low heat,* cocinar a fuego lento. **2** (*battery*) gastado,-a. **3** (*depressed*) deprimido,-a, abatido,-a. **4** MUS grave. – **5** *adv* bajo: *we're running low in petrol,* se nos acaba la gasolina. – **6** *n* (*low level*) punto bajo: *sales have fallen to an all-time low this month,* las ventas han tocado fondo este mes. **7** METEOR área de baja presión.

● to keep a low profile, ser discreto,-a.

■ low comedy, farsa. ‖ low life, bajos fondos *mpl.* ‖ the Low Countries, los Países Bajos.

low² [ləʊ] *i* (*moo*) mugir.

lowbrow ['ləʊbraʊ] *n pej* inculto,-a.

lowdown ['ləʊdaʊn] **1** *n fam* detalles *mpl,* información *f.* – **2** *adj fam* despreciable.

lower ['ləʊəʳ] **1** *adj* inferior. – **2** *t* (*in general*) bajar; (*price*) rebajar. **3** (*flag*) arriar.

● to lower os., rebajarse.

■ lower case, caja baja, minúscula. ‖ lower class, clase *f* baja. ‖ Lower House, Cámara Baja.

lower-class [ləʊə'klɑːs] *adj* de clase baja.

lowermost ['ləʊəməʊst] *adj fml* más bajo,-a.

lowest ['ləʊɪst] **1** *adj* más bajo,-a; (*price, speed*) mínimo,-a. – **2** *n* mínimo: *at the lowest,* como mínimo.

■ lowest common denominator, mínimo común denominador *m.* ‖ lowest common multiple, mínimo común múltiplo.

low-key [ləʊ'kiː] **1** *adj* (*controlled*) discreto,-a. **2** (*informal*) informal.

lowlands ['ləʊləndz] *npl* tierras *fpl* bajas.

■ the Lowlands, las tierras bajas de Escocia.

low-level ['ləʊlevəl] *adj* bajo, de bajo nivel.

lowly ['ləʊlɪ] *adj* humilde, modesto,-a.

▲ *comp* lowlier, *superl* lowliest.

low-lying [ləʊ'laɪɪŋ] *adj* bajo,-a.

low-necked [ləʊ'nekt] *adj* escotado,-a.

low-pitched [ləʊ'pɪtʃt] **1** *adj* (*note*) grave. **2** (*roof*) de poca pendiente.

low-profile [ləʊ'prəʊfaɪl] *adj* discreto,-a.

low-spirited [ləʊ'spɪrɪtɪd] *adj* abatido,-a.

loyal ['lɔɪəl] *adj* leal, fiel.

loyalist ['lɔɪəlɪst] **1** *n* leal *mf.* **2** HIST legitimista *mf.*

loyalty ['lɔɪəltɪ] *n* lealtad *f,* fidelidad *f.*

▲ *pl* loyalties.

lozenge ['lɒzɪndʒ] **1** *n* pastilla. **2** (*geometry*) rombo.

LP ['el'piː] *abbr* (*long-player*) disco de larga duración, elepé *m;* (*abbreviation*) LP.

L-plate ['elpleɪt] *n* GB placa de la ele.

LSD ['el'es'diː] *abbr* (*lysergic acid diethylamide*) dietilamida del ácido lisérgico; (*abbreviation*) LSD.

Lt [lef'tenənt, US luː'tenənt] *abbr* (*Lieutenant*) Teniente *m;* (*abbreviation*) Tente., Tte.

Ltd ['lɪmɪtɪd] *abbr* GB COMM (*Limited*) Limitada; (*abbreviation*) Ltda.

lubricant ['luːbrɪkənt] *n* lubricante *m,* lubrificante *m.*

lubricate ['luːbrɪkeɪt] *t* lubricar, engrasar.

lubrication [luːbrɪ'keɪʃən] *n* lubricación *f,* engrase *m.*

lucerne [luː'sɜːn] *n* GB alfalfa.

lucid ['luːsɪd] *adj* lúcido,-a.

lucidity [luː'sɪdɪtɪ] *n* lucidez *f.*

luck [lʌk] *n* suerte *f:* *with any luck, he'll be here on time,* con un poco de suerte llegará puntual.

● any luck?, *fam* ¿qué?, ¿cómo ha ido? ‖ as luck would have it, por suerte. ‖ bad luck! / hard luck! / tough luck!, ¡mala suerte! ‖ better luck next time!, ¡otra vez será! ‖ good luck! / best of luck!, ¡suerte! ‖ just my luck!, *iron* ¡qué mala suerte he tenido! ‖ no such luck!, ¡ojalá! ‖ to be down on one's luck, tener muy mala suerte. ‖ to be in luck, estar de suerte. ‖ to be out of luck, estar de malas, tener mala suerte. ‖ to push one's luck, tentar la suerte. ‖ to try one's luck, probar fortuna.

luckily ['lʌkɪlɪ] *adv* afortunadamente.

luckless ['lʌkləs] *adj fml* desafortunado,-a.

lucky ['lʌkɪ] *adj* (*in general*) afortunado,-a; (*timely*) oportuno,-a: *how lucky you were!,* ¡qué suerte tuviste!; *this could be your lucky day,* hoy podrías estar de suerte; *he'll be lucky to pass the exam,* tendrá suerte si aprueba el examen; *lucky you came when you did,* menos mal que llegaste en ese momento.

● you'll be lucky!, *fam iron* ¡lo tienes negro!

■ lucky break, golpe *m* de suerte. ‖ lucky charm, amuleto. ‖ lucky dip, GB caja de las sorpresas.

▲ *comp* luckier, *superl* luckiest.

lucrative ['luːkrətɪv] *adj* lucrativo,-a.

ludicrous ['luːdɪkrəs] *adj* ridículo,-a.

ludo ['luːdəʊ] *n* GB parchís *m.*

lug¹ [lʌg] *t fam* arrastrar.

▲ *pt & pp* lugged, *ger* lugging.

lug² [lʌg] *n fam* (*ear*) oreja.

luggage ['lʌgɪdʒ] *n* GB equipaje *m.*

■ luggage van, furgón *m* de equipaje.

lughole ['lʌghəʊl] *n* GB *fam* oreja.

lugubrious [ləˈguːbrɪəs] *adj* lúgubre.

lukewarm ['luːkwɔːm] *adj* tibio,-a, templado,-a.

lull [lʌl] **1** *n* (*in storm*) momento de calma, recalmón *m;* (*in activity*) respiro. – **2** *t* adormecer.

● a lull before the storm, la calma antes de la tempestad. ‖ to lull sb. into a false sense of security, infundir a algn. una falsa seguridad.

lullaby ['lʌləbaɪ] *n* canción *f* de cuna, nana.

▲ *pl* lullabies.

lumbago [lʌm'beɪgəʊ] *n* lumbago.

lumbar ['lʌmbəʳ] *adj* lumbar.

lumber ['lʌmbəʳ] **1** *n* US (*timber*) leña. **2** GB (*junk*) trastos *mpl* viejos. – **3** *i* US cortar leña. – **4** *t* GB *fam* cargar (**with,** con): *I got lumbered with the bill,* me tocó pagar la cuenta a mí.

lumberjack ['lʌmbədʒæk] *n* leñador *m.*

lumberyard ['lʌmbəjɑːd] *n* almacén *m* de madera, almacén *m* de leña.

luminary ['luːmɪnərɪ] *n lit* luminario,-a.

▲ *pl* luminaries.

luminous ['luːmɪnəs] *adj* luminoso,-a.

lump [lʌmp] **1** *n* (*chunk*) pedazo, trozo; (*in sauce*) grumo. **2** (*swelling*) bulto, protuberancia; (*in throat*) nudo. **3** (*of sugar*) terrón *m.* **4** *fam* (*idiot*) burro,-a. – **5** to lump it, *phr* GB *fam* aguantarse, apechugar: *if you don't like it,*

you'll have to lump it, si no te gusta, tendrás que aguantarte.
◆ **to lump together** *t sep* juntar.
● **to bring a lump to sb.'s throat,** hacérsele a algn. un nudo en la garganta: *that scene brought a lump to my throat,* en esa escena se me hizo un nudo en la garganta.
■ **lump sum,** suma global.
lumpy ['lʌmpɪ] *adj* lleno,-a de bultos; (*sauce*) grumoso,-a.
▲ *comp* **lumpier,** *superl* **lumpiest**
lunacy ['luːnəsɪ] *n* locura.
● **to be sheer lunacy,** ser una locura.
lunar ['luːnəʳ] *adj* lunar.
■ **lunar landing,** alunizaje *m.* ‖ **lunar month,** mes *m* lunar.
lunatic ['luːnətɪk] **1** *adj* loco,-a. – **2** *n* loco,-a, lunático,-a.
■ **lunatic asylum,** manicomio. ‖ **the lunatic fringe,** los fanáticos *mpl.*
lunch [lʌntʃ] **1** *n* comida, almuerzo: *we'll have lunch at one,* comeremos a la una; *I take a packed lunch to the office,* traigo la comida hecha al despacho. – **2** *i fml* comer, almorzar.
■ **business lunch,** almuerzo de trabajo. ‖ **lunch hour,** hora de comer. ‖ **pub lunch,** GB comida de pub.
luncheon ['lʌntʃən] *n fml* almuerzo.
luncheonette [lʌntʃə'net] *n* US cafetería, restaurante *m* pequeño.
lunchtime ['lʌntʃtaɪm] *n* hora de comer, hora de almorzar.
lung [lʌŋ] *n* pulmón *m*: *her little girl has a good pair of lungs!,* ¡su hijita tiene buenos pulmones!
■ **lung cancer,** cáncer *m* de pulmón.
lunge [lʌndʒ] **1** *i* arremeter, embestir (**at/towards,** contra). – **2** *n* arremetida, embestida: *she made a lunge at him with a stick,* arremetió contra él con un palo.
lurch [lɜːtʃ] **1** *i* (*vehicle*) dar tumbos, dar bandazos; (*person*) tambalearse. – **2** *n* (*vehicle*) tumbo, bandazo; (*of person*) tambaleo.
● **to leave sb. in the lurch,** dejar a algn. en la estacada.
lure [lʊəʳ] **1** *n* (*decoy*) señuelo. **2** *fig* aliciente *m.* – **3** *t* seducir, atraer: *the stranger lured him into a room,* el extraño le incitó a entrar en una habitación.
lurid ['lʊərɪd] **1** *adj* (*colour etc*) chillón,-ona. **2** (*details*) horripilante, espeluznante.
lurk [lɜːk] *i* (*wait*) estar al acecho. **2** (*hide*) esconderse: *a doubt that lurked in my mind,* una duda que aún me atormentaba.
luscious ['lʌʃəs] **1** *adj* delicioso,-a, exquisito,-a. **2** *fam* (*sexy*) apetitoso,-a.
lush¹ [lʌʃ] **1** *adj* (*vegetation*) exuberante. **2** (*plush*) lujoso,-a.

lush² [lʌʃ] *n sl* bebedor,-ra.
lust [lʌst] **1** *n* (*sexual*) lujuria. **2** (*greed*) codicia; (*strong desire*) ansia.
◆ **to lust after 3** *t insep* codiciar; (*sexually*) desear, lujuriar.
lustful ['lʌstfʊl] **1** *adj* lujurioso,-a. **2** (*greedy*) codicioso,-a.
lustre ['lʌstəʳ] *n* lustre *m*, brillo.
lustrous ['lʌstrəs] *adj lit* lustroso,-a.
lusty ['lʌstɪ] *adj* fuerte, robusto,-a.
▲ *comp* **lustier,** *superl* **lustiest**
lutanist ['luːtənɪst] *n* tañedor,-ra de laúd.
lute [luːt] *n* laúd *m.*
Lutheran ['luːθərən] **1** *adj* luterano,-a. – **2** *n* (*person*) luterano,-a.
Lutheranism ['luːθərənɪzəm] *n* luteranismo.
luv [lʌv] *n* GB *fam* guapo,-a, chato,-a.
Luxembourg ['lʌksəmbɜːg] *n* Luxemburgo.
Luxembourger ['lʌksəmbɜːgəʳ] *n* luxemburgués,-esa.
luxuriance [lʌg'zjʊərɪəns] **1** *n* (*of vegetation*) exuberancia; (*of hair*) abundancia. **2** (*of prose*) estilo recargado.
luxuriant [lʌg'zjʊərɪənt] **1** *adj* (*vegetation*) exuberante; (*hair*) abundante. **2** (*prose*) recargado,-a.
luxuriate [lʌg'zjʊərɪeɪt] **to luxuriate in,** *phr* gozar de, deleitarse con.
luxurious [lʌg'zjʊərɪəs] *adj* lujoso,-a.
luxury ['lʌkʃərɪ] *n* lujo: *it's a luxury to get off work early,* es un lujo salir temprano de trabajar.
■ **luxury goods,** artículos *mpl* de lujo. ‖ **luxury hotel,** hotel *m* de lujo.
▲ *pl* **luxuries**
LW ['lɒŋweɪv] *abbr* (**long wave**) onda larga; (*abbreviation*) OL.
lychee ['laɪtʃiː] *n* lichi *m.*
lying ['laɪɪŋ] **1** *ger* → **lie¹** & **lie².** – **2** *adj* (*deceitful*) mentiroso,-a. – **3** *n* (*lies*) mentiras *fpl.*
lymph [lɪmf] *n* linfa.
■ **lymph gland,** glándula linfática.
lymphatic [lɪm'fætɪk] *adj* linfático,-a.
lynch [lɪntʃ] *t* linchar.
■ **lynch law,** los linchamientos *mpl.*
lynching ['lɪntʃɪŋ] *n* linchamiento.
lynx [lɪŋks] *n* lince *m.*
lyre [laɪəʳ] *n* MUS lira.
lyric ['lɪrɪk] **1** *adj* lírico,-a. – **2** *n* poema *m* lírico. – **3** **lyrics,** *npl* (*of song*) letra *f sing.*
lyrical ['lɪrɪkəl] *adj* lírico,-a.
● **to wax lyrical about sth.,** poner algo por las nubes.
lyricism ['lɪrɪsɪzəm] *n* lirismo.
lyricist ['lɪrɪsɪst] *n* letrista *mf*

M

M, m [em] *n (the letter)* M, m *f.*

M[1] ['mɪlɪən] *abbr (million)* millón: *£24M,* veinticuatro millones de libras.

M[2] ['miːdɪəm] *abbr (medium size)* talla mediana; *(abbreviation)* M.

M[3] [em] *abbr* GB *(motorway)* autopista: *there are roadworks on the M18,* hay obras en la autopista M18.

ma [mɑː] *n fam (mother)* mamá.

MA ['em'eɪ] *abbr (Master of Arts)* master en letras.

ma'am [mæm, mɑːm] *n fml* señora.

mac [mæk] *n* GB *fam (mackintosh)* impermeable *m.*

macabre [mə'kɑːbrə] *adj* macabro,-a.

macaroni [mækə'rəʊnɪ] *n* macarrones *mpl.*
■ **macaroni cheese,** macarrones *mpl* al gratén.

macaroon [mækə'ruːn] *n* mostachón *m.*

macaw [mə'kɔː] *n* guacamayo, ara *m.*

mace[1] [meɪs] *n (spice)* macis *f inv.*

mace[2] [meɪs] *n (club, staff)* maza.

macebearer ['meɪsbeərəʳ] *n* macero,-a.

Macedonia [mæsə'dəʊnɪə] *n* Macedonia.

Macedonian [mæsə'dəʊnɪən] **1** *adj* macedonio,-a. – **2** *n (person)* macedonio,-a. **3** *(language)* macedonio.

macerate ['mæsəreɪt] **1** *t* macerar. – **2** *i* macerarse.

maceration [mæsə'reɪʃən] *n* maceración *f.*

Mach [mæk, mɑːk] *adj* Mach.
■ **Mach number,** número de Mach.

machete [mə'ʃetɪ] *n* machete *m.*

Machiavellian [mækɪə'velɪən] *adj* maquiavélico,-a.

machinations [mækɪ'neɪʃənz] *npl* intrigas *fpl,* maquinaciones *fpl.*

machine [mə'ʃiːn] **1** *n (gen)* máquina, aparato. **2** *(organization, system)* organización *f,* sistema *m,* aparato. – **3** *t* TECH trabajar a máquina. **4** SEW coser a máquina. – **5** **machines,** *npl (machinery)* maquinaria *f sing.*
■ **machine gun,** ametralladora. || **machine language,** COMPUT lenguaje *m* máquina. || **machine operator,** operario,-a. || **machine shop,** taller *m* de máquinas. || **machine tool,** máquina herramienta.

machine-gun [mə'ʃiːngʌn] *t* ametrallar.
▲ *pt & pp* machine-gunned, *ger* machine-gunning.

machinery [mə'ʃiːnərɪ] **1** *n (machines)* maquinaria. **2** *(workings)* mecanismo. **3** *(organization)* organización *f,* sistema *m.*

machinist [mə'ʃiːnɪst] **1** *n (gen)* operario,-a. **2** *(of sewing machine)* maquinista *mf.*

machismo [mə'tʃɪzməʊ] *n* machismo.

macho ['mætʃəʊ] **1** *adj fam pej* macho, machista. – **2** *n* macho, machista *m.*
▲ *pl* machos.

mack [mæk] *n →* mackintosh.

mackerel ['mækərəl] *n* caballa.

mackintosh ['mækɪntɒʃ] *n* impermeable *m.*

macramé [mə'krɑːmɪ] *n* macramé *m.*

macrobiotic [mækrəʊbaɪ'ɒtɪk] *adj* macrobiótico,-a.

macrocosm ['mækrəʊkɒzəm] **1** *n* macrocosmo. **2 the macrocosm,** el universo.

macroeconomics [mækrəʊiːkə'nɒmɪks] *n* macroeconomía.

mad [mæd] **1** *adj (insane)* loco,-a, demente: *she's quite mad,* está completamente loca. **2** *fam (person)* loco,-a; *(crazy - idea, plan)* disparatado,-a, descabellado,-a: *you must be mad!,* ¡estás loco! **3** *fam (enthusiastic)* loco,-a (**about,** por), chiflado,-a: *he's mad about her,* está loco por ella; *he's football mad,* está loco por el fútbol. **4** *fam (wild, frantic)* desenfrenado,-a, frenético,-a: *they made a mad rush for the exit,* corrieron como locos hacia la salida; *I was in a mad panic,* estaba frenética. **5** *fam (angry)* enfadado,-a, furioso,-a (**at/with,** con): *he was mad at me for losing the key,* estaba enfadado conmigo por haber perdido la llave. **6** *(dog)* rabioso,-a.
● **as mad as a March hare / as mad as a hatter,** más loco que una cabra, loco,-a de remate. || **hopping mad,** furioso,-a. || **like mad,** como un,-a loco,-a. || **to be in a mad rush,** ir como un,-a loco,-a, ir a toda prisa. || **to be mad keen on sb./sth.,** estar loco,-a por algn./algo. || **to be mad keen to do sth.,** tener muchas ganas de hacer algo. || **to drive sb. mad / send sb. mad,** volver a algn. loco,-a, traer loco,-a a algn. || **to get mad,** enfadarse. || **to go mad,** volverse loco,-a, enloquecer.
▲ *comp* madder, *superl* maddest.

Madagascan [mædə'gæskən] **1** *adj* malgache. – **2** *n (person)* malgache *mf.*

Madagascar [mædə'gæskəʳ] *n* Madagascar.

madam ['mædəm] **1** *n fml* señora. **2** *fam pej (spoilt girl)* niña marimandona, niña repipi. **3** *(of brothel)* patrona, ama.
● **Dear Madam,** *(in letter)* Muy señora mía, Estimada señora.

madcap ['mædkæp] *adj* disparatado,-a, descabellado,-a.

madden ['mædən] *t (annoy)* enfurecer, enloquecer.

maddening ['mædənɪŋ] *adj (annoying)* exasperante, enloquecedor,-ra.

made [meɪd] **1** *pt & pp →* make. – **2** *adj (produced)* hecho,-a, fabricado,-a: *made in England,* hecho,-a en Inglaterra.
● **to be made for each other,** estar hechos,-as el/la uno,-a para el/la otro,-a. || **to be made from sth.,** estar hecho,-a de algo: *wine is made from grapes,* de la uva sale el vino. || **to be made of sth.,** ser de algo, estar hecho,-a de algo, estar compuesto,-a de algo: *it's made of copper,* está hecho de cobre, es de cobre. || **to have it made,** tener el éxito asegurado.

Madeira [mə'dɪərə] **1** *n (island)* Madeira. **2** *(wine)* madeira, madera.
■ **Madeira cake,** bizcocho.

made-to-measure [meɪdtə'meʒəʳ] *adj* hecho,-a a medida.

made-up ['meɪdʌp] **1** *adj* (*face, person*) maquillado,-a; (*eyes, lips*) pintado,-a. **2** (*story, excuse*) inventado,-a.

madhouse ['mædhaʊs] **1** *n fam dated* (*mental hospital*) manicomio. **2** *fam* (*uproar, confusion*) casa de locos.

madly ['mædlɪ] **1** *adv* (*frantically*) como un,-a loco,-a. **2** *fam* (*intensely - gen*) terriblemente; (*- love*) locamente.
● **to be madly in love with sb.**, estar locamente enamorado,-a de algn.

madman ['mædmæn] *n* loco.
▲ *pl* **madmen** ['mædmen].

madness ['mædnəs] **1** *n* (*insanity*) locura, demencia. **2** (*foolishness*) locura: *it's sheer madness!,* ¡es una locura!, ¡es de locos!; *it is madness to drive in this weather,* es una locura conducir con el tiempo que hace.

madonna [mə'dɒnə] **1** *n* (*in art*) madona. **2 the Madonna,** la Virgen *f*.

Madrid [mə'drɪd] *n* Madrid.

madrigal ['mædrɪɡəl] *n* madrigal *m*.

madwoman ['mædwʊmən] *n* loca.
▲ *pl* **madwomen** ['mædwɪmɪn].

maelstrom ['meɪlstrəʊm] *n* remolino, torbellino.

maestro ['maɪstrəʊ] *n* maestro.
▲ *pl* **maestros**.

Mafia ['mæfɪə] *n* mafia.

magazine [mæɡə'ziːn] **1** *n* (*periodical*) revista. **2** (*in rifle*) recámara. **3** MIL (*store - for arms etc*) almacén *m*; (*- for explosives*) polvorín *m*. **4** RAD TV magacín *m*, magazine *m*. **5** (*for slides - box*) bandeja; (*- circular*) carrusel *m*.

magenta [mə'dʒentə] **1** *n* magenta. **–2** *adj* (de color) magenta.

maggot ['mæɡət] *n* larva, cresa, gusano.

maggoty ['mæɡətɪ] *adj* agusanado,-a.

Magi ['meɪdʒaɪ] *npl* Reyes *mpl* Magos.

magic ['mædʒɪk] **1** *n* magia. **–2** *adj* mágico,-a: *he did some magic tricks for us,* nos hizo unos trucos de magia; *he has a magic touch,* tiene un toque mágico. **– 3** *interj fam* (*great*) guay, fetén, chachi.
● **as if by/like magic,** como por arte de magia, como por ensalmo.
■ **magic spell,** hechizo, encanto, ensalmo. ‖ **white magic,** magia blanca.

magical ['mædʒɪkəl] *adj* mágico,-a.

magician [mə'dʒɪʃən] **1** *n* (*conjurer*) prestidigitador,-ra, ilusionista *mf*. **2** (*wizard*) mago,-a.

magisterial [mædʒɪ'stɪərɪəl] *adj fml* (*showing authority*) magistral.

magistracy ['mædʒɪstrəsɪ] *n* JUR (*gen*) magistratura.

magistrate ['mædʒɪstreɪt] *n* JUR magistrado,-a, juez *mf*.
■ **Magistrate's Court,** juzgado de primera instancia.

magnanimity [mæɡnə'nɪmɪtɪ] *n* magnanimidad *f*.

magnanimous [mæɡ'nænɪməs] *adj* magnánimo,-a.

magnate ['mæɡneɪt] *n* magnate *m*.

magnesia [mæɡ'niːʃə] *n* magnesia.

magnesium [mæɡ'niːzɪəm] *n* magnesio.

magnet ['mæɡnət] *n* imán *m*.

magnetic [mæɡ'netɪk] **1** *adj* (*force etc*) magnético,-a. **2** *fig* (*personality, charm*) carismático,-a, magnético,-a.
● **to have a magnetic personality,** tener imán.
■ **magnetic compass,** brújula. ‖ **magnetic field,** campo magnético. ‖ **magnetic north,** norte *m* magnético. ‖ **magnetic tape,** cinta magnetofónica.

magnetism ['mæɡnɪtɪzəm] **1** *n* (*force*) magnetismo. **2** *fig* (*personal charm*) carisma *m*, magnetismo.

magnetize ['mæɡnɪtaɪz] **1** *t* (*object*) magnetizar, imanar, imantar. **2** *fig* (*person*) magnetizar, cautivar, fascinar.

magnification [mæɡnɪfɪ'keɪʃən] **1** *n* (*increase*) aumento, ampliación *f*. **2** (*power of lens etc*) aumento.

magnificence [mæɡ'nɪfɪsəns] *n* magnificencia, esplendor *m*.

magnificent [mæɡ'nɪfɪsənt] *adj* (*splendid*) magnífico,-a, espléndido,-a; (*sumptuous*) suntuoso,-a.

magnify ['mæɡnɪfaɪ] **1** *t* (*enlarge*) aumentar, ampliar. **2** *fig* (*exaggerate*) exagerar, agrandar.
▲ *pt & pp* **magnified,** *ger* **magnifying.**

magnifying glass ['mæɡnɪfaɪɪŋɡlɑːs] *n* lupa.

magnitude ['mæɡnɪtjuːd] *n* (*size*) magnitud *f*; (*importance*) magnitud *f*, envergadura, alcance *m*.

magnolia [mæɡ'nəʊlɪə] **1** *n* (*tree*) magnolio, magnolia. **2** (*flower*) magnolia. **3** (*colour*) color *m* magnolia.

magnum ['mæɡnəm] *n botella de 1.5 litros de capacidad.*

magpie ['mæɡpaɪ] *n* ORN urraca.

mahogany [mə'hɒɡənɪ] **1** *n* (*wood, tree*) caoba; (*colour*) color *m* caoba. **– 2** *adj* (*furniture*) de caoba; (*colour*) caoba.

maid [meɪd] **1** *n* (*servant*) criada, sirvienta, muchacha, chacha; (*in hotel*) camarera. **2** *arch* (*unmarried woman, girl*) doncella.
● **old maid,** *pej* solterona.
■ **maid of honour,** (*chief bridesmaid*) dama de honor; (*queen's maid*) doncella.

maiden ['meɪdən] **1** *n* (*unmarried woman, girl*) doncella. **– 2** *adj* (*first of its kind - speech, voyage*) inaugural.
■ **maiden aunt,** tía soltera. ‖ **maiden name,** apellido de soltera.

mail¹ [meɪl] *n* (*body armour*) malla.

mail² [meɪl] **1** *n* (*system*) correo: *send it by mail,* envíalo por correo. **2** (*letters etc*) correo, cartas *mpl*, correspondencia: *the mail hasn't arrived yet,* el correo aún no ha llegado. **– 3** *t* US (*post*) echar al buzón, echar al correo. **4** (*send*) enviar por correo, mandar por correo.
■ **mail order,** venta por correo. ‖ **mail train,** tren *m* correo.

mailbag ['meɪlbæɡ] *n* valija, saca de correo.

mailbox ['meɪlbɒks] *n* US buzón *m*.

mailing list ['meɪlɪŋlɪst] *n* lista de direcciones.

mailman ['meɪlmæn] *n* US cartero.

mailshot ['meɪlʃɒt] *n* mailing *m*, envío postal.

maim [meɪm] *t* mutilar, lisiar.

main [meɪn] **1** *adj* (*most important*) principal: *be careful when you cross the main road,* ten cuidado al cruzar la carretera principal; *we have our main meal at 7.00pm,* tomamos la comida principal a las 7.00 de la tarde; *the main points of a speech,* los puntos más importantes de un discurso; *the main thing is that ...,* lo principal es que ..., lo más importante es que ... **– 2** *n* (*pipe*) conducto principal, cañería principal, tubería principal; (*wire, cable*) cable *m* principal. **– 3 mains,** *adj* que se enchufa a la red, que funciona con corriente. **– 4 the mains,** *npl* ELEC la red eléctrica: *it works off the mains,* se enchufa a la red; *switch the electricity off at the mains,* desconecta el interruptor general. **5** (*water system, gas system*) la cañería principal, la tubería principal: *turn the water off at the mains,* cierra la llave de paso del agua. **6** (*sewer*) colector *m*.
● **in the main,** (*in general*) en general, por regla general; (*for the most part*) en su mayoría.
■ **main beam,** ARCH viga maestra. ‖ **main clause,** LING oración *f* principal. ‖ **main course,** plato principal, segundo plato. ‖ **main deck,** cubierta principal. ‖ **main door,** puerta principal. ‖ **main drag,** US calle *f* principal. ‖ **main line,** (*railway*) vía principal, línea principal.

‖ **main mast,** palo mayor. ‖ **main office,** oficina central. ‖ **main sail,** vela mayor. ‖ **main square,** plaza mayor. ‖ **main street,** US calle *f* mayor.

mainframe ['meɪnfreɪm] **mainframe computer,** *n* unidad *f* central, ordenador *m* central.

mainland ['meɪnlənd] *n continente o isla grande en contraposición a una isla cercana más pequeña: a ferry links Islay to the mainland of Scotland,* un transbordador une Islay a Escocia; *he lives on a little island and seldom goes to the mainland,* vive en una isla pequeña y raras veces va al continente; *there is now a tunnel between Great Britain and mainland Europe,* ahora un túnel conecta Gran Bretaña con el continente europeo.

mainline ['meɪnlaɪn] **1** *adj* (*train, station, etc*) interurbano,-a. – **2** *t sl* picarse, chutarse, pincharse. – **3** *i sl* picarse, chutarse, pincharse.

mainly ['meɪnlɪ] *adv* (*chiefly*) principalmente, sobre todo; (*mostly*) en su mayoría.

mainstay ['meɪnsteɪ] **1** *n* MAR estay *m* mayor. **2** *fig* (*support*) pilar *m*, sostén *m*, puntal *m*.

mainstream ['meɪnstriːm] **1** *n* corriente *f* principal, corriente *f* dominante. – **2** *adj* convencional, dominante: *mainstream politics,* la política dominante; *mainstream cinema,* cine para el gran público.

maintain [meɪn'teɪn] **1** *t* (*preserve, keep up - gen*) mantener; (*- silence, appearances*) guardar. **2** (*support financially*) mantener, sostener. **3** (*keep in good condition*) conservar en buen estado. **4** (*assert as true*) mantener, sostener.

maintenance ['meɪntənəns] **1** *n* (*preservation*) mantenimiento, conservación *f*. **2** (*running, upkeep*) mantenimiento: *these machines need very little maintenance,* estas máquinas necesitan muy poco mantenimiento. **3** (*upkeep of family*) manutención *f*. **4** JUR (*divorce allowance*) pensión *f* alimenticia.
■ **maintenance costs,** gastos *mpl* de mantenimiento. ‖ **maintenance grant,** beca de manutención. ‖ **maintenance man,** encargado de mantenimiento. ‖ **maintenance order,** JUR orden *f* de pagar una pensión alimenticia.

maisonette [meɪzə'net] **1** *n* dúplex *m*. **2** *dated* casita.

maize [meɪz] *n* maíz *m*.

majestic [mə'dʒestɪk] *adj* majestuoso,-a.

majesty ['mædʒəstɪ] **1** *n* majestad *f*. **2 Majesty,** Majestad *f*: *Her Majesty the Queen,* Su Majestad la Reina; *Their Majesties,* Sus Majestades.
▲ *pl* majesties.

major ['meɪdʒəʳ] **1** *adj* (*more important, greater*) mayor, principal: *tourism is the major industry,* el turismo es la industria principal; *she's got a major role in the film,* tiene un papel principal en la película. **2** (*important - gen*) importante; (*- issue*) de gran envergadura; (*- illness*) grave: *they've encountered major problems,* han tropezado con problemas importantes. **3** MUS (*key, scale*) mayor: *a sonata in D major,* una sonata en re mayor. – **4** *n* MIL comandante *m*. **5** US EDUC (*main subject*) asignatura principal, especialidad *f*; (*student*) estudiante *mf* que se especializa en una asignatura: *she's a history major,* estudia historia como asignatura principal. **6** MUS (*major key*) clave *f* mayor.
◆ **to major in** *t insep* US EDUC especializarse en.
■ **major general,** MIL general *m* de división. ‖ **major league,** liga nacional. ‖ **major premise,** premisa mayor.

Majorca [mə'dʒɔːkə] *n* Mallorca.

Majorcan [mə'dʒɔːkən] **1** *adj* mallorquín,-ina. – **2** *n* (*person*) mallorquín,-ina. **3** (*dialecto*) mallorquín.

majorette [meɪdʒər'et] *n* batonista.

majority [mə'dʒɒrɪtɪ] **1** *n* mayoría: *the great majority of students,* la gran mayoría de los estudiantes; *they won by a huge majority,* ganaron por una mayoría enorme; *they voted by a vast majority to reject the offer,* votaron por mayoría en contra de la oferta. **2** JUR (*adulthood*) mayoría de edad. – **3** *adj* mayoritario,-a.
● **to be in a/the majority,** ser mayoría.
■ **majority leader,** US POL líder *mf* de la mayoría. ‖ **majority rule,** gobierno mayoritario. ‖ **majority verdict,** veredicto por mayoría. ‖ **silent majority,** mayoría silenciosa.
▲ *pl* majorities.

make [meɪk] **1** *n* (*brand*) marca: *what make of car did you buy?,* ¿de qué marca es el coche que compraste? – **2** *t* (*produce - gen*) hacer; (*construct*) construir; (*manufacture*) fabricar; (*create*) crear; (*prepare*) preparar: *we've already made plans for the weekend,* ya hemos hecho planes para el fin de semana; *have you made a list?,* ¿has hecho una lista?; *he made a fortune,* hizo una fortuna; *I'll make some tea,* haré un poco de té; *she made some sandwiches,* hizo unos bocadillos, preparó unos bocadillos; *he's making a film about the civil war,* está haciendo una película sobre la guerra civil; *they're going to make a record,* van a grabar un disco; *Parliament makes laws,* el Parlamento hace las leyes; *she makes all her own clothes,* ella misma se hace toda su ropa; *stop making all that noise!,* ¡dejad de hacer tanto ruido!; *these cakes have been made using the finest ingredients,* estos pastelitos han sido elaborados con ingredientes de primera calidad. **3** (*carry out, perform*) hacer: *we made a long journey,* hicimos un largo viaje; *may I make a suggestion?,* ¿puedo hacer una sugerencia?; *the cat's made a hole in the armchair,* el gato ha hecho un agujero en el sillón; *I must make a phone call,* tengo que hacer una llamada; *she made an important decision,* tomó una decisión importante; *he has to make a speech,* tiene que pronunciar un discurso; *I made a terrible mistake,* cometí un gran error; *we've made arrangements for you to be met at the airport,* hemos dispuesto que alguien vaya a buscarte al aeropuerto. **4** (*cause to be*) hacer, poner, volver: *the fish made her ill,* el pescado le sentó mal; *the gift made him happy,* el regalo lo hizo feliz; *you make me so angry,* me sacas de quicio; *the decision made me unpopular,* le decisión me hizo impopular; *that dress makes you look slim,* aquel vestido te hace delgada; *the news has been made public,* la noticia se ha hecho pública; *she couldn't make herself understood,* no se hacía entender. **5** (*force, compel*) hacer, obligar; (*cause to do*) hacer: *they make me go to bed early,* me obligan a acostarme temprano; *they made him wait,* le hicieron esperar; *peeling onions makes her cry,* pelar cebollas le hace llorar; *he makes me laugh,* me hace reír; *what makes you say that?,* ¿por qué dices eso? **6** (*be, become*) ser, hacer; (*cause to be*) hacer, convertir en: *she'll make a good singer,* será buena cantante, tiene madera de cantante; *he'll make somebody a good husband,* será un buen marido para alguien; *we'll make a champion of you,* te convertiremos en campeón; *it'll make a change,* será un cambio; *this book makes great reading,* este libro es estupendo; *don't make a habit of it,* que no se convierta en una costumbre; *you'll make a mess of it,* lo vas a estropear. **7** (*earn*) ganar, hacer: *she made 1,000 pounds last week,* ganó 1.000 libras la semana pasada; *he makes a living selling imitation jewellery,* se gana la vida vendiendo bisutería. **8** (*achieve*) conseguir, alcanzar; (*arrive at, reach*) alcanzar, llegar a; (*manage to attend*) poder (ir): *we made it!,* ¡lo conseguimos!; *he made it to the airport just in time,* llegó al aeropuerto con el tiempo justo; *their record made number one,* su disco alcanzó el número uno; *I can't make it to your party,* no puedo ir a tu fiesta; *I can't make it Friday,* el viernes no puedo. **9** (*appoint*) nombrar; (*elect*) elegir: *the king made him a duke,* el rey lo nombró duque; *they made her treasurer,* la eligieron tesorera. **10** (*calculate, estimate, reckon*) calcular: *I make it ten pounds altogether,* calculo que son diez libras en total; *how much do you make it?,* ¿a ti cuánto te da?; *what time do you make it?,* ¿qué hora tienes? **11** (*total, equal*) ser, equivaler a: *three and four make seven,* tres más cuatro son siete; *with the baby that makes eight of us,* con el bebé somos ocho; *that makes the third time you've asked me!,* ¡es la tercera vez que me lo preguntas! **12** (*complete, finish off*) dar el toque final a, completar; (*assure success of*) consagrar: *the new curtains really make the room,* las nuevas cortinas dan el toque final a la habitación; *this book will make her as a novelist,* este libro la consagrará como novelista. – **13** *i* (*to be about to*) hacer como, hacer además de, simular: *he made as if to kiss her,* hizo como si la besara.

◆ **to make after** *t insep* (*chase, pursue*) seguir a, perseguir a. ‖ **to make for 1** *t insep* (*move towards*) dirigirse hacia. **2** (*prepare to attack*) abalanzarse sobre. **3** (*result in, make possible*) contribuir a, crear, conducir a. ‖ **to make into** *t sep* (*change, convert, turn into*) convertir en, transformar en: *wood is made into paper,* la madera se convierte en papel; *I'll make this material into a cushion cover,* con esta tela haré una funda de cojín. ‖ **to make of** *t insep* (*think of*) pensar, opinar, parecer; (*understand*) entender: *what do you make of President Clinton?,* ¿qué te parece el presidente Clinton?; *I don't know what to make of it,* no lo acabo de entender. **2** (*give importance to*) dar importancia a: *I think you're making too much of it,* creo que le estás dando demasiado importancia. ‖ **to make off** *i* (*escape*) escaparse, largarse, huir. ‖ **to make off with / make away with** *t insep* (*steal*) llevarse, escaparse con. ‖ **to make out 1** *t sep* (*write - list, receipt*) hacer; (*- cheque*) extender, hacer; (*- report*) redactar. **2** (*see*) distinguir, divisar; (*writing*) descifrar. **3** (*understand*) entender, comprender. – **4** *t insep fam* (*pretend, claim*) pretender, hacerse pasar por. – **5** *i* (*manage*) arreglárselas, apañárselas; (*get on*) ir: *how did you make out?,* ¿qué tal te fue? **6** US (*sexually*) hacer el lote, pegarse el lote. ‖ **to make over 1** *t sep* JUR (*assign*) ceder, transferir, traspasar. **2** US (*convert*) convertir, transformar. ‖ **to make up 1** *t sep* (*invent*) inventar. **2** (*put together*) hacer; (*assemble*) montar; (*bed, prescription*) preparar; (*page*) componer; (*clothes, curtains*) confeccionar, hacer. **3** (*complete*) completar. **4** (*constitute*) componer, formar, integrar; (*represent*) representar. **5** (*cosmetics*) maquillar. **6** (*compensate for - loss*) compensar; (*- deficit*) cubrir; (*- lack*) suplir; (*- lost time, ground*) recuperar. – **7** *i* maquillarse, pintarse. **8** (*become friends again*) hacer las paces, reconciliarse: *we kissed and made up,* nos besamos e hicimos las paces; *I've made it up with my sister,* he hecho las paces con mi hermana. ‖ **to make up for** *t insep* (*compensate for*) compensar. ‖ **to make up to 1** *t insep* (*flatter*) halagar a; (*try to gain favour with*) congraciarse con. – **2** *t sep* (*pay back*) recompensar, pagar: *how can I make it up to you?,* ¿cómo te puedo pagar lo que has hecho? ‖ **to make with** *t insep* US *fam* (*give, bring*) dar, traer.

● **to be on the make,** (*for profit*) andar tras el dinero, andar intentando sacar tajada; (*for power*) barrer para dentro, barrer para casa; (*for sex*) estar de ligue, andar buscando aventuras. ‖ **to make a fresh start,** volver a empezar. ‖ **to make a go of sth.,** sacar algo adelante. ‖ **to make a loss,** perder dinero. ‖ **to make a name for os.,** hacerse un nombre. ‖ **to make a note of sth.,** apuntar algo. ‖ **to make a profit,** ganar dinero. ‖ **to make a will,** hacer su testamento. ‖ **to make believe,** hacer ver, imaginarse: *the children made believe they were on a desert island,* los niños hacían ver que estaban en una isla desierta. ‖ **to make do (with sth.),** arreglárselas (con algo). ‖ **to make friends,** hacer amigos. ‖ **to make fun of,** burlarse de. ‖ **to make it a rule to do sth.,** tener como norma hacer algo. ‖ **to make good,** triunfar. ‖ **to make sth. good,** (*pay for, replace*) pagar; (*carry out, fulfil*) cumplir con; (*repair*) arreglar. ‖ **to make it,** (*be successful*) tener éxito, llegar hasta arriba. ‖ **to make like,** hacer ver, fingir: *make like you haven't seen him,* haz ver que no lo has visto. ‖ **to make nothing of sth.,** (*achieve easily*) hacer algo sin ningún problema; (*treat as trifling*) quitar importancia a algo. ‖ **to make or break sb./sth.,** significar la consagración o la ruina de algn./algo. ‖ **to make sense,** tener sentido. ‖ **to make sb.'s day,** alegrarle el día a algn. ‖ **to make sth. clear,** aclarar algo, dejar algo claro. ‖ **to make sth. known,** dar a conocer algo. ‖ **to make sure (of sth.),** asegurarse (de algo). ‖ **to make the best/most of sth.,** sacar partido de algo. ‖ **to make the bed,** hacer la cama.

▲ (*verbo*) *pt & pp* **made,** *ger* **making.**

make-believe [ˈmeɪkbɪliːv] **1** *n* (*fantasy*) fantasía, imaginación *f;* (*pretence*) simulación *f,* fingimiento: *it's only make-believe,* es pura fantasía. – **2** *adj* (*world*) imaginario,-a, falso,-a; (*game, toy*) juguete, de mentira.

● **to live in a world of make-believe,** vivir en un mundo de fantasía.

maker [ˈmeɪkəʳ] **1** *n* (*of product*) fabricante *mf;* (*of film etc*) creador,-ra. **2 the/our Maker,** el Creador *m.* – **3 the makers,** *npl* los fabricantes *mpl.*

● **to meet one's Maker,** morirse.

makeshift [ˈmeɪkʃɪft] *adj* (*temporary*) provisional, temporal; (*improvised*) improvisado,-a.

make-up [ˈmeɪkʌp] **1** *n* (*cosmetics*) maquillaje *m: she never wears make-up,* nunca se maquilla, nunca se pone maquillaje. **2** (*composition, combination*) composición *f: the make-up of the committee,* la composición del comité. **3** (*of person*) carácter *m: it's part of her make-up,* forma parte de su carácter. **4** (*arrangement of book, page*) compaginación *f.*

■ **make-up artist,** maquillador,-ra. ‖ **make-up bag,** neceser *m.* ‖ **make-up remover,** desmaquillador *m.*

making [ˈmeɪkɪŋ] *n* (*manufacture*) fabricación *f;* (*construction*) construcción *f;* (*creation*) creación *f;* (*preparation*) preparación *f,* elaboración *f.*

● **in the making,** (*person*) potencial, en potencia, futuro,-a: *he's a novelist in the making,* es un novelista en potencia; *the film was three years in the making,* la película tardó tres años en hacerse. ‖ **this is history in the making,** esto pasará a la historia. ‖ **to be of sb.'s own making,** ser culpa de uno,-a mismo,-a: *his problems are of his own making,* los problemas se los ha buscado él mismo. ‖ **to be the making of sb.,** significar el éxito de algn. ‖ **to have the makings of sth.,** (*person*) tener madera de algo; (*thing*) tener todo lo necesario para ser algo, tener potencial para convertirse en algo: *he has the makings of a footballer,* tiene madera de futbolista, es un futbolista en ciernes.

maladjusted [mæləˈdʒʌstɪd] *adj* inadaptado,-a.

maladjustment [mælə'dʒʌstmənt] *n* inadaptación *f*.
maladroit [mælə'drɔɪt] *adj fml* torpe.
malady ['mælədɪ] *n fml* mal *m*, enfermedad *f*.
▲ *pl maladies*.
Malagasy ['mæləgæsɪ] **1** *adj* malgache. – **2** *n* (*person*) malgache *mf*. **3** (*language*) malgache *m*.
■ **Malagasy Republic**, República Malgache.
malaise [mæ'leɪz] *n fml* malestar *m*.
malaria [mə'leərɪə] *n* malaria, paludismo.
Malawi [mə'lɑːwɪ] *n* Malawi.
Malawian [mə'lɑːwɪən] **1** *adj* malawiano,-a. – **2** *n* malawiano,-a.
Malay [mə'leɪ] **1** *adj* malayo,-a. – **2** *n* (*person*) malayo,-a. **3** (*language*) malayo.
Malaya [mə'leɪə] *n* Malaya.
Malaysia [mə'leɪzɪə] *n* Malaysia, Malasia.
Malaysian [mə'leɪzɪən] **1** *adj* malasio,-a. – **2** *n* malasio,-a.
Maldives ['mɔːldaɪvz] *n* Maldivas.
Maldivian [mɔːl'dɪvɪən] **1** *adj* maldivo,-a. – **2** *n* maldivo,-a.
male [meɪl] **1** *adj* (*animal, plant*) macho; (*person, child*) varón; (*sex, hormone, character, organ*) masculino,-a. **2** (*manly*) varonil, viril. **3** TECH (*screw, plug*) macho. – **4** *n* (*man, boy*) varón *m*; (*animal, plant*) macho.
■ **male chauvinist pig**, falócrata *m*. ‖ **male nurse**, enfermero. ‖ **male voice choir**, coro masculino.
malevolence [mə'levələns] *n* malevolencia.
malevolent [mə'levələnt] *adj* malévolo,-a.
malformation [mælfɔː'meɪʃən] *n* malformación *f*.
malformed [mæl'fɔːmd] *adj* malformado,-a, deformado,-a.
malfunction [mæl'fʌŋkʃən] **1** *n* mal funcionamiento, funcionamiento defectuoso. – **2** *i* funcionar mal.
Mali ['mɑːlɪ] *n* Mali.
Malian ['mɑːlɪən] **1** *adj* maliense. – **2** *n* maliense *mf*.
malice ['mælɪs] *n* malicia.
● **to bear sb. malice**, guardar rencor a algn. ‖ **with malice aforethought**, JUR con premeditación.
malicious [mə'lɪʃəs] *adj* (*wicked*) malévolo,-a; (*bitter*) rencoroso,-a: *malicious gossip*, malas lenguas.
malign [mə'laɪn] **1** *adj fml* (*gen*) maligno,-a, malévolo,-a; (*influence*) perjudicial. – **2** *t* (*slander*) calumniar, difamar.
malignant [mə'lɪgnənt] **1** *adj* (*person*) malévolo,-a, malvado,-a, malo,-a; (*action, behaviour, influence, etc*) maligno,-a, perjudicial. **2** MED maligno,-a.
malinger [mə'lɪŋgə'] *i pej* fingirse enfermo,-a.
malingerer [mə'lɪŋgərə'] *n pej* enfermo,-a fingido,-a.
mall [mæl, mɔːl] *n* US (*covered*) centro comercial; (*street*) zona comercial.
mallard ['mælɑːd] *n* ánade *m* real.
malleable ['mælɪəbəl] **1** *adj* (*metal*) maleable. **2** *fig* (*person*) dócil.
mallet ['mælət] *n* mazo.
mallow ['mæləʊ] *n* malva.
malnourished [mæl'nʌrɪʃt] *adj* desnutrido,-a.
malnutrition [mælnjuː'trɪʃən] *n* desnutrición *f*.
malpractice [mæl'præktɪs] **1** *n* MED negligencia. **2** JUR procedimiento ilegal.
malt [mɔːlt] **1** *n* (*grain*) malta. – **2** *t* hacer germinar.
■ **malt whisky**, whisky *m* de malta.
Malta ['mɔːltə] *n* Malta.
malted ['mɔːltɪd] *adj* malteado,-a, preparado,-a con malta: *malted milk*, leche malteada.
Maltese [mɔːl'tiːz] **1** *adj* maltés,-esa. – **2** *n* (*person*) maltés,-esa. **3** (*language*) maltés *m*. – **4** **the Maltese**, *npl* los malteses *mpl*.

maltreat [mæl'triːt] *t fml* maltratar, tratar mal.
maltreatment [mæl'triːtmənt] *n* malos tratos *mpl* maltrato.
mammal ['mæməl] *n* mamífero.
mammary ['mæmərɪ] *adj* mamario,-a.
■ **mammary gland**, mama.
mammography [mæ'mɒgrəfɪ] *n* mamografía.
▲ *pl mammographies*.
mammoth ['mæməθ] **1** *n* ZOOL mamut *m*. – **2** *adj* (*huge*) gigantesco,-a, descomunal, inmenso,-a: *it's a mammoth task*, es una tarea enorme.
mammy ['mæmɪ] *n fam* mamá.
▲ *pl mammies*.
man [mæn] **1** *n* (*adult male*) hombre *m*, señor *m*: *an old man*, un hombre mayor, un señor mayor, un viejo; *a young man*, un hombre joven, un joven. **2** (*human being, person*) ser *m* humano, el hombre *m*: *all men are born equal*, todos los hombres nacen iguales; *chimpanzees are not very different from men*, los chimpancés no son muy diferentes de los seres humanos; *a two-man tent*, una tienda para dos personas. **3** (*the human race*) el hombre *m*: *the most precious metal known to man*, el metal más precioso conocido por el hombre. **4** (*type*) tipo: *I'm a whisky man myself*, prefiero el whisky; *I'm not a rugby man*, no me gusta el rugby. **5** (*manservant, valet*) criado, sirviente *m*. **6** (*husband*) marido, hombre *m*; (*boyfriend*) novio; (*partner*) pareja: *man and wife*, marido y mujer. **7** (*representative*) representante *m*; (*correspondent*) corresponsal *m*. **8** (*chess piece*) pieza; (*draughts*) ficha. – **9** *interj fam* hombre, tío, macho. – **10** *t* (*operate - post, phones*) servir, atender; (*boat, plane*) tripular; (*barricades*) defender: *can you man the desk while I'm at lunch*, ¿puedes atender la recepción mientras voy a comer?
● **as one man**, como un solo hombre, todos a la vez. ‖ **every man for himself**, sálvese quien pueda, que cada cual se las apañe como pueda. ‖ **man to man**, de hombre a hombre. ‖ **to a man**, todos sin excepción. ‖ **to be a family man**, (*with children*) ser padre de familia; (*home-loving*) ser muy casero. ‖ **to be man enough to do sth.**, ser lo bastante hombre como para hacer algo. ‖ **to be one's own man**, ir por libre. ‖ **to make a man of sb.**, hacer hombre a algn. ‖ **to sort out the men from the boys**, separar los que valen de los que no.
■ **man about town**, hombre *m* de mundo. ‖ **man Friday**, factótum *m*. ‖ **man of letters**, hombre *m* de letras. ‖ **man of the match**, mejor jugador *m*. ‖ **man of the world**, hombre *m* de mundo. ‖ **the man in the street**, el hombre de la calle.
▲ *pl men*.
Man [mæn] **Isle of Man**, *n* Isla de Man.
manacle ['mænəkəl] **1** *t* esposar. – **2** **manacles**, *npl* esposas *fpl*, grillos *mpl*.
manage ['mænɪdʒ] **1** *t* (*run - business, company*) dirigir, llevar, administrar; (*- property*) administrar; (*- household*) llevar; (*handle - money, affairs*) manejar, administrar: *she manages a shop*, es la encargada de una tienda, lleva una tienda. **2** (*handle, cope with - child, person*) llevar, manejar; (*- animal*) domar; (*- work, luggage, etc*) poder con: *can you manage that suitcase?*, ¿puedes con esa maleta? **3** (*succeed*) conseguir, lograr: *we managed it!*, ¡lo conseguimos!; *she managed a smile*, logró esbozar una sonrisa; *they managed to finish everything in time*, lograron acabarlo todo a tiempo; *did you manage to find a present for Neil?*, ¿conseguiste encontrar un regalo para Neil? **4** (*have room for, have time for*) poder: *I think I could just manage another small piece*, creo que podría

comer otro trocito más; *can you manage lunch on Sunday?*, ¿puedes venir a comer el domingo? – **5** *i poder: can you manage?*, ¿puedes?; *I can manage, thanks,* ya puedo, gracias. **6** (*financially*) arreglárselas, apañarse: *they manage on 100 pounds a week,* se las arreglan con 100 libras a la semana; *we'll just have to manage without her,* tendremos que arreglárnoslas sin ella; *I'm managing,* voy tirando.

manageable ['mænɪdʒəbəl] *adj* manejable.

management ['mænɪdʒmənt] **1** *n* (*running of business etc*) dirección *f*, administración *f*, gestión *f*. **2** (*people in charge*) dirección *f*, gerencia, patronal *f*. **3** (*board of directors*) junta directiva, consejo de administración.
● "*under new management*", "nueva dirección".
■ **management studies course,** curso de administración *f* de empresas.

manager ['mænɪdʒəʳ] **1** *n* (*of company, bank*) director,-ra, gerente *mf*; (*of estate*) administrador,-ra. **2** (*of shop, restaurant*) encargado,-a; (*of department*) jefe,-a; (*of cinema, theatre*) gerente *mf*. **3** (*of actor, group, etc*) representante *mf*, manager *mf*. **4** SP (*of football team*) entrenador *m*, míster *m*.

manageress [mænɪdʒə'res] **1** *n* (*of company, bank*) directora, gerente *f*; (*of estate*) administradora. **2** (*of shop, restaurant, etc*) encargada, jefa; (*of department*) jefa; (*of cinema, theatre*) gerente *f*. **3** (*of actor, group*) representante *f*, manager *f*.

managerial [mænɪ'dʒɪərɪəl] *adj* directivo,-a, administrador,-ra.

managing ['mænɪdʒɪŋ] *adj* directivo,-a.
■ **managing director,** director,-ra.

Manchu [mæn'tʃuː] **1** *adj* manchú. – **2** *n* (*person*) manchú *mf*. **3** (*language*) manchú *m*.

Manchuria [mæn'tʃʊərɪə] *n* Manchuria.

Mancunian [mæn'kjuːnɪən] **1** *adj* de Manchester. – **2** *n* (*person*) persona de Manchester, habitante *mf* de Manchester.

mandarin ['mændərɪn] **1** *n* mandarina. **2** GB POL *pej* (*government official*) mandarín *m*. **3 Mandarin,** (*language*) mandarín *m*.
■ **mandarin duck,** pato mandarín. ‖ **mandarin orange,** mandarina.

mandate ['mændeɪt] **1** *n* mandato. – **2** *t* (*authorize*) autorizar.
● **to be mandated to do sth.,** tener instrucciones de hacer algo.

mandatory ['mændətərɪ] **1** *adj* (*compulsory*) obligatorio,-a. **2** JUR mandatario,-a.

mandible ['mændɪbəl] *n* mandíbula.

mandolin ['mændəlɪn] *n* mandolina.

mane [meɪn] *n* (*of horse*) crin *f*; (*of lion*) melena.

maneuver [mə'nuːvəʳ] *n* US → **manoeuvre**.

maneuverable [mə'nuːvərəbəl] *adj* manejable.

maneuvrability [mənuːvrə'bɪlətɪ] *n* maniobrabilidad *f*.

manful ['mænfʊl] *adj* valiente.

manfully ['mænfʊlɪ] *adv* valientemente.

manger ['meɪndʒəʳ] *n* pesebre *m*.

mangetout [mɒnʒ'tuː] *n* guisante *m* mollar.
■ **mangetout pea,** guisante *m* mollar.

mangle¹ ['mæŋgəl] **1** *n* (*wringer*) escurridor *m*. – **2** *t* pasar por el escurridor.

mangle² ['mæŋgəl] **1** *t* (*cut to pieces*) destrozar, despedazar; (*crush*) aplastar. **2** *fig* mutilar.

mango ['mæŋgəʊ] *n* mango.
▲ *pl* **mangoes** o **mangos**.

mangy ['meɪndʒɪ] **1** *adj* (*dog*) sarnoso,-a. **2** *fig* (*carpet etc*) raído,-a.

▲ *comp* **mangier,** *superl* **mangiest**.

manhandle ['mænhændəl] **1** *t* (*person*) maltratar. **2** (*object*) manipular.

manhole ['mænhəʊl] *n* boca de acceso.
■ **manhole cover,** tapa de registro, tapa de alcantarilla.

manhood ['mænhʊd] **1** *n* (*state*) madurez *f*. **2** (*qualities*) virilidad *f*, hombría. **3** (*men collectively*) hombres *mpl*.
● **to reach manhood,** llegar a la edad viril.

manhunt ['mænhʌnt] *n* persecución *f*, búsqueda (*a gran escala*).

mania ['meɪnɪə] *n* manía.

maniac ['meɪnɪæk] **1** *n* MED maníaco,-a. **2** *fam* (*wild person*) loco,-a. **3** *fam* (*fan*) entusiasta *mf*, fanático,-a, loco,-a.

maniacal [mə'naɪəkəl] *adj* MED maníaco,-a, maniaco,-a.

manic ['mænɪk] *adj* maníaco,-a, maniaco,-a.

manic-depressive [mænɪkdɪ'presɪv] *n* MED maníaco,-a depresivo,-a.

manicure ['mænɪkjʊəʳ] **1** *n* manicura. – **2** *t* hacer la manicura.
● **to give sb. a manicure,** hacer la manicura a algn. ‖ **to have a manicure,** hacerse la manicura.
■ **manicure set,** estuche *m* de manicura.

manicurist ['mænɪkjʊərɪst] *n* manicuro,-a.

manifest ['mænɪfest] **1** *adj fml* manifiesto,-a, patente. – **2** *t fml* manifestar.
● **to manifest itself/themselves,** manifestarse.

manifestation [mænɪfe'steɪʃən] *n fml* manifestación *f*.

manifesto [mænɪ'festəʊ] *n* manifiesto.
▲ *pl* **manifestos** o **manifestoes**.

manifold ['mænɪfəʊld] **1** *adj fml* (*many*) múltiples; (*varied*) varios,-as, diversos,-as. – **2** *n* AUTO colector *m* de escape.

manila [mə'nɪlə] *n* papel *m* de estraza.
■ **manila hemp,** cáñamo.

manipulate [mə'nɪpjəleɪt] **1** *t* (*work - machine*) manipular, manejar; (*- knob, lever*) accionar. **2** MED dar masajes a. **3** (*control, influence*) manipular.

manipulation [mənɪpjə'leɪʃən] **1** *n* (*handling*) manipulación *f*, manejo. **2** MED masaje *m*. **3** (*control, influence*) manipulación *f*.

manipulative [mə'nɪpjələtɪv] *adj* manipulador,-ra.

manipulator [mə'nɪpjəleɪtəʳ] *n* manipulador,-ra.

mankind [mæn'kaɪnd] *n* la humanidad *f*, el género humano, los hombres *mpl*.

manliness ['mænlɪnəs] *n* virilidad *f*, hombría.

manly ['mænlɪ] *adj* varonil, viril, macho.
▲ *comp* **manlier,** *superl* **manliest**.

man-made [mæn'meɪd] **1** *adj* (*lake etc*) artificial. **2** (*fabric etc*) sintético,-a.

mannequin ['mænɪkɪn] **1** *n* (*dummy*) maniquí *m*. **2** *dated* (*model*) modelo *f*.

manner ['mænəʳ] **1** *n* (*way, method*) manera, modo: *they did it in a very businesslike manner,* lo hicieron con mucha eficiencia. **2** (*way of behaving*) forma de ser, comportamiento, aire *m*: *she has a pleasant manner,* tiene una forma de ser agradable. **3** *fml* (*sort, kind*) clase *f*, índole *f*. – **4 manners,** *npl* (*social behaviour*) maneras *fpl*, modales *mpl*; (*customs*) costumbres *fpl*.
● **all manner of ...,** toda clase de ... ‖ **in a manner of speaking,** por decirlo así, hasta cierto punto. ‖ **in the manner of sb.,** al estilo de algn. ‖ **in this manner,** de esta manera, así. ‖ **not by any manner of means,** de ninguna manera. ‖ **(as/as if) to the manner born,** como si lo hubiera hecho toda la vida.

■ **bad manners,** falta de educación. ‖ **good manners,** buenos modales *mpl.*

mannered ['mænəd] *adj (affected)* amanerado,-a, afectado,-a.

mannerism ['mænərɪzəm] **1** *n (quirk)* manía, rareza, gesto, peculiaridad *f; (way of speaking)* deje *m.* **2** *pej (affectation)* amaneramiento.

mannish ['mænɪʃ] *adj* hombruno,-a.

manoeuvre [mə'nuːvə'] **1** *n (gen)* maniobra. **2** *fig* maniobra, estratagema. – **3** *t (gen)* maniobrar. **4** *(person)* manipular, manejar. – **5** *i* maniobrar.

● **to be on manoeuvres,** estar de maniobras. ‖ **to have room for manoeuvre,** tener un amplio margen de maniobra.

manometer [mə'nɒmɪtə'] *n* manómetro.

manor ['mænə'] **1** *n (estate)* señorío. **2** *sl (area)* territorio.

■ **manor house,** casa solariega.

manpower ['mænpaʊə'] *n* mano *f* de obra.

manservant ['mænsɜːvənt] *n* criado, sirviente *m.*

mansion ['mænʃən] *n (gen)* casa grande; *(country)* casa solariega.

man-size ['mænsaɪz] *adj fam* extra-grande, muy grande.

manslaughter ['mænslɔːtə'] *n* JUR homicidio involuntario.

mantelpiece ['mæntəlpiːs] *n* repisa de chimenea.

mantis ['mæntɪs] *n* mantis *f.*

mantle ['mæntəl] **1** *n (cloak)* capa, manto. **2** *fig (layer)* manto, capa. **3** *lit (responsibilities, duties)* cargas *fpl,* responsabilidades *fpl:* **he had to assume the mantle of president,** tuvo que hacerse cargo de las responsabilidades de presidente. **4** GEOL manto. – **5** *t fig (cover)* cubrir, envolver.

man-to-man [mæntə'mæn] *adj* de hombre a hombre.

manual ['mænjʊəl] **1** *adj* manual. – **2** *n* manual *m.*

manually ['mænjʊəlɪ] *adv* a mano, manualmente.

manufacture [mænjə'fæktʃə'] **1** *n (gen)* fabricación *f; (of clothing)* confección *f; (of foodstuffs)* elaboración *f.* – **2** *t (gen)* fabricar; *(clothing)* confeccionar; *(foodstuffs)* elaborar. **3** *fig (excuse etc)* inventar.

manufacturer [mænjə'fæktʃərə'] *n* fabricante *mf.*

manufacturing [mænjə'fæktʃərɪŋ] *n* fabricación *f.*

■ **manufacturing industry,** industria fabril, industria manufacturera.

manure [mə'njʊə'] **1** *n* abono, estiércol *m.* – **2** *t* abonar, estercolar.

manuscript ['mænjəskrɪpt] **1** *n (historic handwritten book)* manuscrito. **2** *(original copy of text)* original *m,* texto original. – **3** *adj* manuscrito,-a.

Manx [mæŋks] *adj* de la Isla de Man.

■ **Manx cat,** *gato sin cola de la isla de Man.*

Manxman ['mæŋksmən] *n* hombre *m* de la Isla de Man.

Manxwoman ['mæŋkswʊmən] *n* mujer *f* de la Isla de Man.

▲ *pl* Manxwomen |'mæŋkswɪmɪn|.

many ['menɪ] **1** *adj* mucho,-a, muchos,-as: *many people never go abroad,* mucha gente nunca va al extranjero; *he hasn't got many friends,* no tiene muchos amigos; *many years ago,* hace muchos años; *there are twice as many people tonight,* hay el doble de gente esta noche; *there are too many cars,* hay demasiados coches; *he took four exams in as many days,* hizo cuatro exámenes en otros tantos días; *I have one ticket too many,* tengo una entrada de más. – **2** *pron* muchos,-as: *I don't want many,* no quiero muchos. – **3** **the many,** *n* la mayoría.

● **a good/great many,** muchísimos,-as. ‖ **as many ... as,** tantos,-as ... como. ‖ **how many?,** ¿cuántos,-as? ‖

many a ..., muchos,-as ... ‖ **many's the ...,** son muchos,-as ... ‖ **not many,** pocos,-as, no muchos,-as. ‖ **to have had one too many,** haber tomado una copa de más. ‖ **too many,** demasiados,-as.

▲ *comp* **more,** *superl* **most.**

many-sided ['menɪsaɪdɪd] **1** *adj* multilateral, de muchos lados. **2** *fig (personality, talent)* polifacético,-a; *(question etc)* complejo,-a.

Maori ['maʊrɪ] **1** *adj* maorí. – **2** *n (person)* maorí *mf.* **3** *(language)* maorí *m.*

map [mæp] **1** *n (of country, region)* mapa *m; (of town, bus, tube)* plano. – **2** *t (area)* trazar un mapa de.

◆ **to map out** *t sep (future, career, etc)* proyectar, planear, organizar; *(route)* trazar un mapa.

● **to put sb./sth. on the map,** dar a conocer a algn./algo.

■ **map of the world,** mapamundi *m.* ‖ **weather map,** carta meteorológica.

▲ *(verbo)* *pt & pp* **mapped,** *ger* **mapping.**

maple ['meɪpəl] *n (tree, wood)* arce *m.*

■ **maple syrup,** jarabe *m* de arce.

mapmaker ['mæpmeɪkə'] *n* cartógrafo,-a.

mapmaking ['mæpmeɪkɪŋ] *n* cartografía.

mar [maː'] *t (spoil - gen)* estropear, echar a perder; *(- happiness)* afectar; *(- enjoyment)* aguar.

▲ *pt & pp* **marred,** *ger* **marring.**

Mar [maːtʃ] *abbr (March)* marzo.

marathon ['mærəθən] **1** *n* maratón *m.* – **2** *adj fig* maratoniano,-a, larguísimo,-a.

marauder [mə'rɔːdə'] *n* merodeador,-ra.

marauding [mə'rɔːdɪŋ] *adj* merodeador,-ra.

marble ['maːbəl] **1** *n (stone, statue)* mármol *m.* **2** *(glass ball)* canica. – **3** *adj (floor, statue)* de mármol, marmóreo,-a; *(industry)* del mármol. **4** *fig (like marble)* marmóreo,-a. – **5** **marbles,** *npl (game)* canicas *fpl.* **6** ART mármoles *mpl.*

● **to have lost one's marbles,** estar chiflado,-a.

march [maːtʃ] **1** *n* MIL marcha. **2** *(walk)* caminata. **3** *(demonstration)* manifestación *f.* **4** *fig (of time, events)* marcha, paso. **5** MUS marcha. – **6** *i* MIL marchar, hacer una marcha: *forward march!,* ¡de frente!; *quick march!,* ¡paso ligero! **7** *(walk)* caminar, marchar. **8** *(walk purposefully and determinedly)* ir resueltamente, ir decididamente: *he came marching in,* entró muy decidido; *I marched up to him,* lo abordé muy decidido; *she marched angrily out of the room,* salió enfadada de la habitación. **9** *(demonstrate)* manifestarse, hacer una manifestación. **10** *fig (time etc)* pasar. – **11** *t* hacer marchar: *they marched him off to the police station,* se lo llevaron a la comisaría.

◆ **to march past** *i* MIL desfilar.

● **a day's march,** un día de marcha. ‖ **on the march,** en marcha.

■ **march past,** desfile *m.*

March [maːtʃ] *n* marzo.

▲ *Véase también* May.

marcher ['maːtʃə'] *n (demonstrator)* manifestante *mf.*

marching ['maːtʃɪŋ] *adj* que marcha: *marching troops,* tropas en marcha, tropas marchando.

● **to get one's marching orders,** ser despedido,-a. ‖ **to give sb. his/her marching orders,** despedir a algn.

■ **marching band,** banda de marcha.

marchioness ['maːʃənəs] *n* marquesa.

mare [meə'] *n* yegua.

margarine [maːdʒə'riːn] *n* margarina.

marge [maːdʒ] *n* GB *fam* margarina.

margin ['maːdʒɪn] **1** *n (on page)* margen *m: there were comments written in the margin,* había comentarios escritos en el margen. **2** (*difference, leeway*) margen *m*: *the Tories won by a narrow margin,* los conservadores ganaron por un reducido margen de votos; *there is no margin for error,* no hay margen de error. **3** (*edge, border*) margen *m & f*; (*of river*) margen *m & f*.

marginal [ˈmɑːdʒɪnəl] **1** *adj* (*small, minor*) menor, pequeño,-a, mínimo,-a: *a marginal improvement,* una mejora mínima; *it's of marginal interest,* es de escaso interés. **2** (*artist*) marginal. **3** (*land*) de poco valor agrícola, poco productivo,-a. **4** GB POL (*won by small majority*) obtenido,-a por escasa mayoría. – **5** *n* GB POL (*seat*) escaño ganado por muy pocos votos.

marginally [ˈmɑːdʒɪnəlɪ] *adv* ligeramente, un poco.

marigold [ˈmærɪɡəʊld] *n* BOT maravilla, caléndula.

marihuana [mærɪˈhwɑːnə] *n* → **marijuana**.

marijuana [mærɪˈhwɑːnə] *n* marihuana, marijuana.

marina [məˈriːnə] *n* puerto deportivo.

marinade [mærɪˈneɪd] **1** *n* adobo. – **2** *t* adobar.

marinate [ˈmærɪneɪt] *t* adobar.

marine [məˈriːn] **1** *n* (*life, flora, etc*) marino,-a, marítimo,-a. – **2** *adj* (*law, stores, etc*) marítimo,-a. – **3** *n* soldado de infantería de marina. – **4 the Marines,** *npl* GB la infantería de marina.

■ **marine engineer,** ingeniero,-a marítimo,-a. ‖ **marine insurance,** seguro marítimo. ‖ **the Marine Corps,** US la infantería de marina.

mariner [ˈmærɪnəʳ] *n* marinero.

marionette [mærɪəˈnet] *n* marioneta, títere *m*.

marital [ˈmærɪtəl] *adj* (*realtions, problems*) matrimonial, marital; (*bliss*) conyugal.

■ **marital status,** estado civil.

maritime [ˈmærɪtaɪm] *adj* marítimo,-a.

marjoram [ˈmɑːdʒərəm] *n* mejorana.

mark[1] [mɑːk] *n* FIN (*currency*) marco.

mark[2] [mɑːk] **1** *n* (*imprint, trace*) huella; (*from blow*) señal *f*; (*stain*) mancha: *there's a mark on this blouse,* esta blusa tiene una mancha; *she has a small mark on her forehead,* tiene una pequeña señal en la frente. **2** (*sign, symbol*) marca, señal *f*: *I've put a mark by the things I'm interested in,* he señalado las cosas que me interesan. **3** (*instead of signature*) cruz *f*. **4** (*characteristic feature*) impronta, señal *f*, sello: *this work bears the mark of genius,* esta obra tiene la impronta de un genio. **5** (*token, proof*) señal *f*: *as a mark of respect,* en señal de respeto. **6** EDUC nota, calificación *f*, puntuación *f*: *he got a good mark in maths,* sacó una buena nota en mates. **7** SP (*starting line - of race*) línea de salida; (*- of jump*) línea de batida. **8** (*level*) punto, nivel; (*number*) cifra: *unemployment has passed the three million mark,* la tasa de desempleo ha superado la cifra de tres millones; *we're at the halfway mark,* estamos a mitad de camino. **9** (*target*) blanco. **10** TECH (*type, model*) serie *f*, modelo: *a Mark III Cortina,* un Cortina de la tercera serie. **11** (*oven setting*) número: *preheat the oven at gas mark 6,* precalentar el horno al (número) 6. – **12** *t* (*make mark on*) marcar, señalar, poner una señal en: *he marked the winning numbers with a cross,* señaló los números premiados con una cruz; *the price is marked on the bottom,* el precio está marcado en el fondo; *the file was marked "secret",* en la carpeta ponía "secreto". **13** (*scar*) señalar, desfigurar, marcar; (*stain*) manchar: *his face has been marked by acne,* su cara ha quedado marcada por el acné; *the cup has marked the table,* la taza ha manchado la mesa. **14** (*denote, show position of*) señalar, indicar; (*show*) mostrar: *a floral tribute marked the spot where the accident occurred,* un tributo floral señala el sitio donde ocurrió

el accidente; *the refuge is not marked on the map,* el refugio no está indicado en el mapa; *the route is marked,* la ruta está señalizada. **15** (*be a sign of*) significar; (*commemorate*) conmemorar: *his death marks the end of an era,* su muerte significa el final de una época; *a celebration to mark their wedding anniversary,* una celebración para conmemorar su aniversario de bodas. **16** EDUC (*correct*) corregir; (*grade - student*) poner nota a; (*- exam, essay, etc*) puntuar, calificar. **17** SP (*opponent*) marcar. **18** (*be typical of, characterize*) caracterizar. **19** (*listen carefully, heed*) fijarse en, prestar atención a: *you mark my words!,* ¡fíjate en lo que te digo! – **20** *i* (*stain*) mancharse.

◆ **to mark down 1** *t sep* (*reduce price of*) rebajar el precio de: *it's marked down to £3,* el precio está rebajado a tres libras. **2** (*reduce marks of*) bajar la nota de. **3** (*note in writing*) apuntar. ‖ **to mark off 1** *t sep* (*separate*) separar, dividir, distinguir; (*area*) delimitar; (*boundary*) trazar. **2** (*put line through*) tachar. ‖ **to mark out 1** *t sep* (*area*) marcar, delimitar; (*boundary*) marcar, trazar. **2** (*choose*) señalar, seleccionar. ‖ **to mark up 1** *t sep* (*increase price of*) subir (el precio de), aumentar (el precio de). **2** (*increase marks of*) subir la nota de.

● **mark you,** de todas formas. ‖ **on your marks!,** SP ¡preparados! ‖ **to be quick off the mark,** ser muy rápido,-a. ‖ **to be slow off the mark,** ser muy lento,-a. ‖ **to be up to the mark,** estar a la altura, dar la talla. ‖ **to be/fall wide of the mark,** no dar en el blanco. ‖ **to hit the mark,** dar en el blanco, acertar. ‖ **to make one's mark on sth.,** dejar su huella en algo, dejar su impronta en algo. ‖ **to leave its mark on sb.,** marcar a algn. ‖ **to mark time,** (*soldiers*) marcar el paso; (*wait*) hacer tiempo.

markdown [ˈmɑːkdaʊn] *n* (*of price*) rebaja.

marked [mɑːkt] *adj* (*noticeable - gen*) marcado,-a, notable; (*- improvement*) sensible, apreciable; (*- accent*) acusado,-a, fuerte.

● **to be a marked man,** ser un hombre fichado.

markedly [ˈmɑːkɪdlɪ] *adv* (*different*) marcadamente, notablemente, acusadamente; (*better*) sensiblemente.

marker [ˈmɑːkəʳ] **1** *n* (*stake, pole*) jalón *m*. **2** (*bookmark*) punto de libro. **3** EDUC (*person*) examinador,-ra. **4** SP (*person*) marcador,-ra.

■ **marker buoy,** boya, baliza. ‖ **marker pen,** rotulador *m*.

market [ˈmɑːkɪt] **1** *n* (*selling fruit, vegetables, etc*) mercado; (*selling clothes etc*) mercadillo; (*marketplace*) plaza: *I always go to the market on Saturdays,* siempre voy al mercado los sábados. **2** (*trade*) mercado: *the property market,* el mercado inmobiliario. **3** (*demand, desire to buy*) demanda, salida, mercado: *there isn't a market for fur coats in summer,* no hay demanda de abrigos de pieles en verano; *we need to look for new markets,* tenemos que buscar nuevos mercados. – **4** *t* (*sell*) vender, poner en venta; (*offer for sale*) lanzar al mercado, promocionar, comercializar.

● **to be in the market for sth.,** interesarse en comprar algo. ‖ **to be on the market,** estar en venta. ‖ **to come onto the market,** salir al mercado, ponerse en venta, ponerse a la venta. ‖ **to play the market,** jugar a la bolsa.

■ **market day,** día *m* de mercado. ‖ **market economy,** economía de mercado. ‖ **market forces,** tendencias del mercado. ‖ **market garden,** GB huerta. ‖ **market leader,** líder *m* del mercado. ‖ **market price,** precio de mercado. ‖ **market research,** estudio de mercado. ‖ **market researcher,** investigador,-ra de mercado. ‖

market square, plaza del mercado. ‖ **market stall**, puesto. ‖ **market town**, población *f* con mercado. ‖ **market trader**, vendedor,-ra de mercado. ‖ **market value**, valor *m* en el mercado. ‖ **the Common Market**, el Mercado Común.

marketable [ˈmɑːkɪtəbəl] *adj* vendible, comerciable.

marketing [ˈmɑːkɪtɪŋ] *n* marketing *m*, mercadotecnia.

marketplace [ˈmɑːkɪtpleɪs] *n* (*gen*) mercado; (*square*) plaza.

marking [ˈmɑːkɪŋ] **1** *n* (*on bird, animal*) mancha. **2** (*drawn, written*) marca. **3** EDUC correcciones *fpl*: *I've got a pile of marking to do*, tengo un montón de correcciones. **4** SP marcaje *m*.
■ **marking ink**, tinta indeleble.

marksman [ˈmɑːksmən] *n* tirador *m*.

marksmanship [ˈmɑːksmənʃɪp] *n* puntería.

mark-up [ˈmɑːkʌp] **1** *n* (*percentage added*) margen *m* de beneficio. **2** (*increase in price*) subida, aumento.

marmalade [ˈmɑːməleɪd] *n* mermelada (de cítricos).

Marmara [ˈmɑːmərə] **Sea of Marmara**, *n* Mar *m* de Mármara.

maroon[1] [meˈruːn] *t* (*abandon*) aislar, abandonar.

maroon[2] [məˈruːn] **1** *adj* granate. – **2** *n* (*color m*) granate *m*.

marooned [məˈruːnd] *adj* (*abandoned*) abandonado,-a, aislado,-a; (*trapped*) atrapado,-a.

marquee [mɑːˈkiː] **1** *n* (*large tent*) carpa, entoldado. **2** US (*canopy, awning*) marquesina.

marquess [ˈmɑːkwɪs] *n* marqués *m*.

marquetry [ˈmɑːkɪtrɪ] *n* marquetería, taracea.

marquis [ˈmɑːkwɪs] *n* marqués *m*.

marriage [ˈmærɪdʒ] **1** *n* (*state, institution*) matrimonio. **2** (*act, wedding*) boda, casamiento, enlace *m* matrimonial.
● **to be related by marriage**, ser parientes políticos. ‖ **to give sb. in marriage**, dar a algn. en matrimonio. ‖ **to take sb. in marriage**, casarse con algn., contraer matrimonio con algn.
■ **marriage bureau**, agencia matrimonial. ‖ **marriage certificate**, certificado de matrimonio. ‖ **marriage guidance**, terapia de pareja. ‖ **marriage licence**, licencia matrimonial. ‖ **marriage of convenience**, matrimonio de conveniencia.

marriageable [ˈmærɪdʒəbəl] *adj* casadero,-a, en edad de casarse, en edad casadera.

married [ˈmærɪd] **1** *adj* (*person, status*) casado,-a (**to**, con): *a married couple*, un matrimonio. **2** (*life, bliss*) matrimonial, conyugal.
● **to get married**, casarse (**to**, con).
■ **married name**, apellido de casada. ‖ **married quarters**, residencias *fpl* para familias.

marrow [ˈmærəʊ] **1** (*bone*) **marrow**, *n* ANAT (*of bone*) tuétano, médula. **2** *fig* (*inner meaning*) meollo. **3** (*vegetable*) **marrow**, GB BOT calabacín *m* grande.
● **to the marrow**, hasta la médula.

marrowbone [ˈmærəʊbəʊn] *n* CULIN hueso con tuétano, hueso de caña de vaca.
■ **marrowbone jelly**, tuétano.

marry [ˈmærɪ] **1** *t* (*take in marriage*) casarse con, contraer matrimonio con. **2** (*unite in marriage*) casar. **3** *fig* unir. – **4** *i* casarse. **5** *fig* unirse.
◆ **to marry into** *t insep* emparentar con: *she married into the royal family*, emparentó con la familia real; *he married into money*, se casó con una mujer rica. ‖ **to marry off** *t sep* casar a. ‖ **to marry up** *i* corresponder, cuadrar.
● **marry in haste, repent at leisure**, a la hora de ca-

sarse, no precipitarse. ‖ **to get married**, casarse (**to**, with). ‖ **to marry again**, volver a casarse.
▲ *pt* & *pp* **married**, *ger* **marrying**.

Mars [mɑːz] *n* Marte *m*.

Marseilles [mɑːˈseɪ] *n* Marsella.

marsh [mɑːʃ] **1** *n* (*bog*) pantano. **2** (*area*) zona con pantanos, pantanal *m*.
■ **marsh gas**, gas *m* metano.

marshal [ˈmɑːʃəl] **1** *n* MIL mariscal *m*. **2** (*at sports event, demonstration*) oficial *mf*, organizador,-ra. **3** US (*like sheriff*) shérif *m*, alguacil *m*. **4** US (*head of police*) jefe,-a de policía; (*head of fire department*) jefe,-a de bomberos. – **5** *t* (*crowds, troops etc*) reunir. **6** *fig* (*facts, thoughts, etc*) ordenar, poner en orden.
▲ (*verbo*) *pt* & *pp* **marshalled** (US **marshaled**), *ger* **marshalling** (US **marshaling**).

marshland [ˈmɑːʃlænd] *n* tierra pantanosa, pantanal *m*.

marshmallow [mɑːʃˈmæləʊ] **1** *n* (*sweet*) golosina de merengue blando. **2** BOT malvavisco.

marshy [ˈmɑːʃɪ] *adj* pantanoso,-a.
▲ *comp* **marshier**, *superl* **marshiest**.

marsupial [mɑːˈsuːpɪəl] **1** *n* marsupial *m*. – **2** *adj* marsupial.

martial [ˈmɑːʃəl] *adj* marcial.
■ **martial arts**, artes *fpl* marciales. ‖ **martial law**, ley *f* marcial.

Martian [ˈmɑːʃən] **1** *n* marciano,-a. – **2** *adj* marciano,-a.

martin [ˈmɑːtɪn] *n* ORN avión *m*.

Martinique [mɑːtɪnˈiːk] *n* La Martinica.

martyr [ˈmɑːtə] **1** *n* mártir *mf*. **2** *fam* víctima (**to**, de). – **3** *t* martirizar.
● **to make a martyr of os.**, hacerse el/la mártir.

martyrdom [ˈmɑːtədəm] *n* martirio.

marvel [ˈmɑːvəl] **1** *n* (*wonder*) maravilla: *don't expect marvels*, no esperes maravillas; *it's a marvel no-one was hurt*, es un milagro que no hubiera heridos. **2** (*person*) maravilla: *he's a marvel*, es una maravilla, es maravilloso. – **3** *i* maravillarse (**at**, con), asombrarse (**at**, de). **4** *fml* maravillarse, sorprenderse: *we marvelled that she could run so far*, nos maravillamos de que pudiera correr tanto.
● **to do marvels / work marvels**, hacer maravillas.
▲ (*verbo*) *pt* & *pp* **marvelled** (US **marveled**), *ger* **marvelling** (US **marveling**).

marvellous [ˈmɑːvələs] *adj* maravilloso,-a, magnífico,-a, estupendo,-a: *what a marvellous view!*, ¡qué vista más maravillosa!; *how marvellous!*, ¡qué fantástico!

marvellously [ˈmɑːvələslɪ] *adv* maravillosamente, estupendamente.

marvelous [ˈmɑːvələs] *adj* US → **marvellous**.

Marxism [ˈmɑːksɪzəm] *n* marxismo.

Marxist [ˈmɑːksɪst] **1** *n* marxista *mf*. – **2** *adj* marxista.

marzipan [ˈmɑːzɪpæn] *n* mazapán *m*, pasta de almendras.

mascara [mæˈskɑːrə] *n* rímel *m*.

mascot [ˈmæskɒt] *n* mascota.

masculine [ˈmɑːskjəlɪn] **1** *adj* masculino,-a. – **2** *n* LING masculino.

masculinity [mæskjəˈlɪnɪtɪ] *n* masculinidad *f*.

mash [mæʃ] **1** *n* CULIN *fam* (*potatoes*) puré *m* de patatas. **2** (*for animals*) afrecho. – **3** *t* (*beat, crush*) triturar (**up**, -), machacar (**up**, -). **4** CULIN (*potatoes*) hacer un puré de.
■ **mashed potatoes**, puré *m* de patatas.

masher [ˈmæʃə] *n* (*for potatoes*) utensilio para hacer puré de patatas.

mask [mɑːsk] **1** n (gen) máscara; (disguise) careta, carátula; (around eyes) antifaz m. **2** MED mascarilla. **– 3** t (gen) enmascarar.
● to put on a mask, enmascararse.
■ diving mask, gafas fpl de bucear. ‖ face mask, (american football) casco con protector; (motorcyclist) gafas fpl de motorista; (diver's) gafas fpl de bucear. ‖ fencing mask, careta. ‖ stocking mask, media usada para taparse la cara.
masked [mɑːskt] adj enmascarado,-a.
■ masked ball, baile m de disfraces, baile m de máscaras.
masking tape ['mɑːskɪŋteɪp] n cinta adhesiva.
masochism ['mæsəkɪzəm] n masoquismo.
masochist ['mæsəkɪst] **1** n masoquista. **– 2** adj masoquista.
masochistic [mæsə'kɪstɪk] adj masoquista.
mason ['meɪsən] n (builder) albañil m.
Mason ['meɪsən] n (Freemason) masón m, francmasón m.
masonic [mə'sɒnɪk] adj masónico,-a.
masonry ['meɪsənrɪ] n (stonework) albañilería; (building) construcción f.
Masonry ['meɪsənrɪ] n (Freemasonry) masonería, francmasonería.
masquerade [mæskə'reɪd] **1** n (pretence) farsa, mascarada. **2** (dance) mascarada. **– 3** i disfrazarse (**as**, de), hacerse pasar (**as**, por).
mass[1] [mæs] **1** n (large quantity) montón m, masa; (of people) masa, multitud f, muchedumbre f: a mass of rubble, un montón de escombros; the garden is a mass of colour, el jardín está lleno de colores. **2** (majority) mayoría. **3** (large solid lump) masa. **4** PHYS (amount of matter) masa. **– 5** i (crowd) congregarse, reunirse en gran número; (troops) concentrarse; (clouds) amontonarse. **– 6** t reunir. **– 7** adj masivo,-a, multitudinario,-a, de masas: there was a mass meeting, se celebró un mitin multitudinario; mass unemployment, desempleo masivo. **– 8** masses, npl fam (lots) cantidad f, montones mpl, mogollón m. **9** the masses, POL las masas fpl.
■ mass grave, fosa común. ‖ mass hysteria, histeria colectiva. ‖ mass media, medios mpl de comunicación (de masas). ‖ mass murderer, asesino,-a múltiple. ‖ mass production, fabricación f en serie.
mass[2] [mæs] n REL misa.
● to hear mass, oír misa. ‖ to say mass, decir misa.
■ high mass, misa mayor. ‖ low mass, misa rezada. ‖ requiem mass, misa de difuntos.
massacre ['mæsəkər] **1** n masacre f, carnicería, matanza. **2** fam (defeat) machaque m, paliza. **– 3** t masacrar, asesinar en masa. **4** fam (defeat) machacar, dar una paliza a.
massage ['mæsɑːʒ] **1** n masaje m. **– 2** t (person, body) dar un masaje a; (part of body) dar un masaje en. **3** fig (ego) inflar. **4** fig (facts, figures) manipular, falsificar.
■ massage parlour, salón m de masajes.
masseur [mæ'sɜːr] n masajista m.
masseuse [mæ'sɜːz] n masajista.
Massif Central [mæ'siːf sen'trɑːl] n Macizo Central.
massive ['mæsɪv] **1** adj (huge) enorme, gigantesco: the temple is built of massive granite blocks, el templo está construido con enormes bloques de granito; he suffered a massive heart attack, sufrió un infarto muy grave. **2** (extensive) masivo,-a, extenso,-a: there was massive coverage of the event, el acontecimiento recibió extensa cobertura. **3** (solid, weighty) sólido,-a, macizo,-a: massive walls, paredes macizas.

massively ['mæsɪvlɪ] adv enormemente.
mass-produce [mæsprə'djuːs] n fabricar en serie.
mast [mɑːst] **1** n MAR mástil m, palo. **2** (flagpole) asta (de bandera), mástil m. **3** RAD TV torre f, poste m.
mastectomy [mæ'stektəmɪ] n MED mastectomía.
▲ pl mastectomies.
master ['mɑːstər] **1** n (of slave, servant, dog) amo; (of household) señor m; (owner) dueño. **2** MAR (of ship) capitán m; (of fishing boat) patrón m. **3** GB (teacher - infant school) maestro, profesor m; (- secondary) profesor m. **4** (expert, artist, musician, etc) maestro. **5** (original copy of film, tape, etc) original m. **6** Master, EDUC (second level degree) máster m; (holder of master's degree) máster mf; (head of certain university colleges) director,-ra. **– 7** adj (expert, skilled) maestro,-a, experto,-a. **8** (original) original. **9** (overall, complete) total, general, global. **10** (main, principal) principal, maestro,-a. **– 11** t (control) dominar; (overcome) superar, vencer. **12** (learn - subject, skill) llegar a dominar; (- craft) llegar a ser experto,-a en.
● to be master of a situation, ser dueño de una situación. ‖ to be master of one's own fate, decidir su propio destino. ‖ to meet one's master, ser vencido,-a.
■ master bedroom, dormitorio principal. ‖ master builder, (skilled workman) maestro de obras; (self-employed builder) contratista mf. ‖ master copy, original m. ‖ master key, llave f maestra. ‖ master of ceremonies, maestro de ceremonias. ‖ master plan, proyecto maestro. ‖ master race, (nazi) raza superior. ‖ master's degree, licenciatura con tesina, master m. ‖ master switch, interruptor m central.
masterful ['mɑːstəful] **1** adj (dominating, authoritative) autoritario,-a, dominante. **2** (showing great skill) magistral.
masterly ['mɑːstəlɪ] adj magistral, genial.
mastermind ['mɑːstəmaɪnd] **1** n (person) cerebro, genio. **– 2** t (plan cleverly) dirigir, ser el cerebro de.
masterpiece ['mɑːstəpiːs] n obra maestra.
masterstroke ['mɑːstəstrəʊk] n golpe m maestro.
mastery ['mɑːstərɪ] **1** n (power, control) dominio (**of/over**, de), autoridad f; (supremacy) supremacía, superioridad f. **2** (skill, expertise) maestría, dominio (**of**, de).
masticate ['mæstɪkeɪt] **1** t masticar. **– 2** i masticar.
masturbate ['mæstəbeɪt] **1** t masturbar. **– 2** i masturbarse.
masturbation [mæstə'beɪʃən] n masturbación f.
mat [mæt] **1** n (rug) alfombrilla; (doormat) felpudo. **2** (rush mat) estera; (beach mat) esterilla. **3** (tablemat) salvamanteles m inv; (beer mat) posavasos m inv; (under vase etc) tapete m. **4** SP colchoneta. **5** (hair) mata; (threads) maraña. **– 6** adj (not shiny) mate. **– 7** t enmarañar. **– 8** i (hair etc) enmarañarse.
▲ (verbo) pt & pp matted, ger matting.
matador ['mætədɔːr] n matador,-ra.
match[1] [mætʃ] n (light) cerilla, fósforo.
match[2] [mætʃ] **1** n SP (football, hockey, etc) partido, encuentro; (boxing, wrestling) combate m; (tennis) partido, match m. **2** (equal) igual mf: when it comes to chess, she's no match for you, ella no puede competir contigo al ajedrez. **3** (marriage) casamiento, matrimonio: they are a good match, hacen buena pareja; he's a good match, es un buen partido. **4** (clothes, colour, etc) juego, combinación f: they're a perfect match, combinan perfectamente; this hat is a good match for my coat, este sombrero hace juego con mi abrigo. **– 5** t (equal) igualar: we have to match their prices, tenemos que igualar sus precios; no-one can match him at poker, no tiene

igual en póker; *this restaurant can't be matched for quality,* en cuanto a calidad este restaurante no tiene par. **6** *(go well with)* hacer juego (con), combinar (con): *the curtains match the carpet,* las cortinas hacen juego con la alfombra; *her shoes match her dress,* los zapatos hacen juego con el vestido. **7** *(be like, correspond to)* corresponder a, ajustarse a: *his feelings matched yours,* sus sentimientos correspondían a los tuyos. – **8** *i (go together)* hacer juego, combinar: *do these colours match?,* ¿estos colores combinan?; *a scarf and gloves to match,* una bufanda y unos guantes que hacen juego. **9** *(tally)* coincidir, concordar. **10** *(people)* llevarse bien, avenirse.
◆ **to match up 1** *i (tally)* coincidir. – **2** *t sep (connect together)* emparejar, aparejar. || **to match up to** *t insep (be as good as)* estar a la altura de.
● **to be well-matched,** *(couple)* hacer buena pareja; *(opponents, teams)* ser del mismo nivel. || **to match sb. against sb.,** enfrentar algn. a algn. || **to meet one's match,** encontrar la horma de su zapato.
■ **match point,** *(in tennis)* pelota de partido.
matchbox ['mætʃbɒks] *n* caja de cerillas.
matching ['mætʃɪŋ] *adj* que hace juego, a juego.
matchless ['mætʃləs] *adj* sin par, sin igual.
matchmaker ['mætʃmeɪkəʳ] *n* casamentero,-a.
matchstick ['mætʃstɪk] **1** *n (match)* cerilla, fósforo. **2** *(stick)* palillo.
■ **matchstick man,** hombre *m* de palotes.
mate[1] [meɪt] **1** *n (chess)* mate *m*. – **2** *t* dar jaque mate a.
mate[2] [meɪt] **1** *n (schoolfriend, fellow worker, etc)* compañero,-a, colega *mf; (friend)* amigo,-a, colega *mf,* compinche *mf.* **2** *(assistant)* ayudante *mf,* aprendiz,-za. **3** MAR *(ship's officer)* oficial *m* (de cubierta). **4** ZOOL pareja; *(male)* macho; *(female)* hembra. – **5** *t* ZOOL aparear, acoplar. – **6** *i* ZOOL aparearse, acoplarse.
material [mə'tɪərɪəl] **1** *n (physical substance)* materia, material *m:* *raw material,* materia prima; *building materials,* materiales de construcción. **2** *(cloth)* tela, tejido: *how much material do you need?,* ¿cuánta tela necesitas? **3** *(information, ideas, etc)* material *m,* datos *mpl,* documentación *f.* **4** *(equipment)* material *m.* **5** *fig (quality)* madera: *she's executive material,* tiene madera de ejecutiva. – **6** *adj (physical)* material. **7** *(important)* importante, substancial; *(relevant)* pertinente.
■ **material damage,** daños *mpl* materiales. || **material evidence,** pruebas *fpl* substanciales.
materialism [mə'tɪərɪəlɪzəm] *n* materialismo.
materialist [mə'tɪərɪəlɪst] **1** *n* materialista *mf.* – **2** *adj* materialista.
materialistic [mətɪərɪə'lɪstɪk] *adj* materialista.
materialize [mə'tɪərɪəlaɪz] **1** *i (hopes, plan, project, idea)* materializarse, realizarse, hacerse realidad; *(strike, protest)* producirse, llegar a producirse. **2** *(person)* aparecer, presentarse.
materially [mə'tɪərɪəlɪ] **1** *adv (physically)* materialmente. **2** *(essentially)* esencialmente, en esencia. **3** *(noticeably)* sensiblemente; *(significantly)* considerablemente.
maternal [mə'tɜːnəl] **1** *adj (motherly)* maternal. **2** *(related to mother)* materno,-a.
maternity [mə'tɜːnɪtɪ] *n* maternidad *f.*
■ **maternity allowance/benefit,** subsidio por maternidad. || **maternity dress,** vestido premamá. || **maternity hospital,** maternidad *f.* || **maternity leave,** baja por maternidad.
math [mæθ] *n* US → **maths**.
mathematical [mæθə'mætɪkəl] *adj* matemático,-a.
● **to have a mathematical mind,** estar dotado,-a para las matemáticas.

mathematically [mæθə'mætɪkəlɪ] *adv* matemáticamente.
● **to be mathematically inclined,** tener disposición para las matemáticas.
mathematician [mæθəmə'tɪʃən] *n* matemático,-a.
mathematics [mæθə'mætɪks] *n* matemáticas *fpl.*
maths [mæθs] *n fam* mates *fpl.*
matinée ['mætɪneɪ] *n (cinema)* primera sesión *f* de tarde; *(theatre)* función *f* de tarde.
mating ['meɪtɪŋ] *n* ZOOL acoplamiento, apareamiento.
■ **mating call,** ORN reclamo. || **mating season,** época de apareamiento, época de celo.
matins ['mætɪnz] *npl* REL *(Catholic)* maitines *mpl.*
matriarch ['meɪtrɪɑːk] *n* matriarca.
matriarchal ['meɪtrɪɑːkəl] *adj* matriarcal.
matriarchy ['meɪtrɪɑːkɪ] *n* matriarcado.
matrices ['meɪtrɪsiːz] *npl* → **matrix**.
matricide ['mætrɪsaɪd] **1** *n (act)* matricidio. **2** *(person)* matricida *mf.*
matriculate [mə'trɪkjəleɪt] **1** *t* matricular. – **2** *i* matricularse.
matriculation [mətrɪkjə'leɪʃən] *n* matrícula, matriculación *f.*
matrimonial [mætrɪ'məʊnɪəl] *adj* matrimonial.
matrimony ['mætrɪmənɪ] *n fml* matrimonio.
matrix ['meɪtrɪks] *n* matriz *f.*
▲ *pl* **matrixes** *o* **matrices** ['meɪtrɪsiːz].
matron ['meɪtrən] **1** *n* GB *dated (in hospital)* enfermera jefe. **2** GB *(in school)* ama de llaves. **3** *(middle-aged married woman)* matrona.
■ **matron of honour,** dama de honor.
matronly ['meɪtrənlɪ] *adj* madura y recia.
matt [mæt] *adj* mate.
matted ['mætɪd] *adj* enmarañado,-a.
matter ['mætəʳ] **1** *n (affair, subject)* asunto, cuestión *f: it's a personal matter,* es un asunto personal; *we must get to the root of the matter,* hay que ir al quid de la cuestión; *we have several matters to discuss,* tenemos varias cuestiones que discutir; *this is a matter of utmost importance,* es una cuestión de suma importancia; *it's only a matter of time,* sólo es cuestión de tiempo. **2** *(trouble, problem)* problema *m: what's the matter?,* ¿qué pasa?; *what's the matter with Susan?,* ¿qué le pasa a Susan?; *is anything the matter?,* ¿pasa algo?; *nothing's the matter,* no pasa nada. **3** PHYS *(physical substance)* materia, sustancia. **4** *(type of substance, things of particular kind)* materia. **5** MED *(pus)* pus *m.* – **6** *i (be important)* importar **(to,** a): *it doesn't matter,* no importa, es igual, da igual; *you're the only thing that matters to me,* tú eres lo único que me importa; *it doesn't matter which way you go,* no importa por donde vayas; *does it matter if you're late?,* ¿pasa algo si llegas tarde?; *it doesn't matter what you wear,* da igual lo que lleves, no importa lo que lleves; *getting that article published mattered a lot to her,* publicar aquel artículo le importaba mucho; *what matters most is that you're home,* lo importante es que estás en casa. – **7** **matters,** *npl (the situation)* la situación *f,* las cosas *fpl: his financial matters,* su situación económica; *his attitude doesn't exactly help matters,* su actitud no facilita las cosas, precisamente.
● **(as) a matter of course,** por norma. || **as a matter of fact,** en realidad, de hecho. || **as matters stand,** tal y como están las cosas. || **for that matter,** en realidad. || **no matter,** no importa: *no matter what,* pase lo que pase; *no matter what I say,* diga lo que diga; *no matter who it is,* sea quién sea, quienquiera que sea; *no matter*

how busy I am, por muy ocupado que esté; *no matter how much you insist,* por mucho que insistas; *no matter how much it costs,* cueste lo que cueste; *no matter where he goes,* dondequiera que vaya. ‖ **to be a matter of life or death,** ser cuestión de vida o muerte. ‖ **to be a matter of opinion,** ser discutible. ‖ **to be no laughing matter,** no ser cosa de risa, no ser motivo de risa, no ser para reírse. ‖ **to be another matter,** ser otra cosa. ‖ **to let the matter drop/rest,** dejarlo correr. ‖ **to make matters worse,** para colmo (de desgracias). ‖ **to take matters into one's own hands,** tomarse la justicia por su mano.

■ **matters arising,** asuntos *mpl* varios. ‖ **printed matter,** impresos *mpl.* ‖ **the matter in hand,** el asunto de que se trata. ‖ **vegetable matter,** materia vegetal. ‖ **waste matter,** residuos *mpl.*

matter-of-fact [mætərəv'fækt] *adj (person)* práctico,-a, realista; *(account)* realista; *(style)* prosaico,-a; *(voice)* impersonal.

matting ['mætɪŋ] *n* estera.

mattock ['mætək] *n* azadón *m.*

mattress ['mætrəs] *n* colchón *m.*

mature [mə'tʃʊəʳ] **1** *adj (gen)* maduro,-a. **2** FIN vencido,-a. – **3** *t* madurar. – **4** *i* madurar. **5** FIN vencer.

■ **mature student,** estudiante *mf* mayor de 25 años.

maturely [mə'tjʊəlɪ] *adv* maduramente.

maturity [mə'tʃʊərətɪ] *n* madurez *f.*

maudlin ['mɔːdlɪn] *adj (tearful)* llorón,-ona; *(sentimental)* sensiblero,-a.

maul [mɔːl] **1** *t (wound)* herir, agredir. **2** *(handle roughly)* maltratar. **3** *fig (criticize)* vapulear.

Maundy ['mɔːndɪ] **Maundy Thursday,** *n* Jueves *m* Santo.

■ **Maundy money,** *dinero que reparte el soberano el día de Jueves Santo.*

Mauritania [mɒrɪ'teɪnɪə] *n* Mauritania.

Mauritanian [mɒrɪ'teɪnɪən] **1** *adj* mauritano,-a. – **2** *n* mauritano,-a.

Mauritian [mə'rɪʃən] **1** *adj* de Mauricio. – **2** *n* nativo o habitante *mf* de Mauricio.

Mauritius [mə'rɪʃəs] *n* Mauricio.

mausoleum [mɔːsə'lɪəm] *n* mausoleo.

mauve [məʊv] **1** *adj* malva. – **2** *n* malva *m.*

maverick ['mævərɪk] **1** *n* inconformista *mf,* independiente *mf.* **2** POL disidente *mf.* **3** US *(calf)* res *f* sin marcar. – **4** *adj* inconformista, independiente. **5** POL disidente.

mawkish ['mɔːkɪʃ] *adj* sensiblero,-a, empalagoso,-a.

max [mæks, 'mæksɪməm] *abbr (maximum)* máximo; *(abbreviation)* max.

maxim ['mæksɪm] *n* máxima.

maximize ['mæksɪmaɪz] **1** *t (increase as much as possible)* maximizar, llevar al máximo, aumentar al máximo. **2** *(make the best use of)* aprovechar al máximo.

maximum ['mæksɪməm] **1** *adj* máximo,-a. – **2** *n* máximo, máximum *m.*

● **as a maximum,** como máximo. ‖ **to the maximum,** al máximo.

may[1] [meɪ] **1** *aux (possibility, probability)* poder, ser posible: *he may come,* es posible que venga, puede que venga; *these pills may cause drowsiness,* estas pastillas pueden causar somnolencia; *she may have got lost,* puede que se haya perdido; *that may or may not be true,* puede que eso sea o no sea verdad; *you may laugh, but I think it's serious,* tú bien puedes reír, pero yo creo que es grave; *I'll go so that you may be alone,* me iré para que podáis estar solos. **2** *(permission)* poder: *may I help*

you?, ¿en qué puedo servirle?; *may I go?,* ¿puedo irme?; *may I?,* ¿me permite? **3** *(wish)* ojalá: *may it be so,* ojalá sea así.

● **be that as it may,** sea como sea. ‖ **sb. may well ...,** bien puede ser que algn. ...: *he may well be angry,* bien puede ser que esté enfadado; *you may well not feel like eating,* es posible que no te apetezca comer. ‖ **may (just) as well ...,** más vale que ...: *I may as well stay now,* más vale que me quede ahora; *she may just as well finish off the whole cake,* más vale que acabe el pastel entero.

▲ *pt* **might.**

may[2] [meɪ] **1** *n* BOT *(flower)* flor *f* de espina. **2** *(tree)* espino.

May [meɪ] *n* mayo: *she was born in May,* nació en mayo; *his birthday is on the twentieth of May,* su cumpleaños es el veinte de mayo; *at the beginning/end of May,* a principios/finales de mayo; *in the middle of May,* a mediados de mayo; *last May,* en mayo del año pasado; *next May,* en mayo del año que viene.

■ **May Day,** el primero de mayo, el uno de mayo, el día *m* de los trabajadores.

Maya ['maɪə] **1** *n (person)* maya *mf.* **2** *(language)* maya *m.*

Mayan ['maɪən] **1** *adj* maya. – **2** *n (language)* maya *m.*

maybe ['meɪbiː] *adv* quizá, quizás, tal vez: *maybe it'll rain,* tal vez llueva; *maybe you're right,* quizás tengas razón, a lo mejor tienes razón; *maybe we could have lunch sometime,* quizá podríamos comer juntos algún día.

mayday ['meɪdeɪ] *n* señal *f* de socorro, S.O.S. *m.*

mayfly ['meɪflaɪ] *n* ZOOL cachipolla, efímera.

▲ *pl* **mayflies.**

mayhem ['meɪhem] *n* caos *m,* jaleo.

mayonnaise [meɪə'neɪz] *n* mayonesa, mahonesa.

mayor [meəʳ] *n (man)* alcalde *m;* *(woman)* alcaldesa.

■ **lady mayor,** alcaldesa.

mayoress ['meəres] *n* alcaldesa.

maypole ['meɪpəʊl] *n* mayo.

maze [meɪz] *n* laberinto.

MB[1] ['em'biː] *abbr (Bachelor of Medicine)* Licenciado,-a en Medicina; *(abbreviation)* Lic. en Med.

MB[2] ['megəbaɪt] *abbr (megabyte)* megabyte *m;* *(abbreviation)* Mb.

MC[1] ['em'siː] *abbr (Master of Ceremonies)* maestro de ceremonias.

MC[2] ['mjuːzɪkəset] *abbr (musicassette)* casete *f.*

MD ['em'diː] *abbr (Doctor of Medicine)* doctor,-a en Medicina; *(abbreviation)* Dr.,-ra. en Medicina.

me[1] [miː] *n* MUS mi *m.*

me[2] [miː] **1** *pron (as object of verb)* me: *follow me,* sígueme; *give it to me,* dámelo; *he looked at me,* me miró. **2** *(after prep)* mí: *it's for me,* es para mí; *are you talking to me?,* ¿me lo dices a mí?; *come with me,* ven conmigo. **3** *(emphatic)* yo: *it's me!,* ¡soy yo!; *it's me, David,* soy David.

meadow ['medəʊ] *n* prado, pradera.

meagre ['miːgəʳ] **1** *adj (very small quantity)* escaso,-a, exiguo,-a. **2** *(thin)* magro,-a.

meal[1] [miːl] *n (flour)* harina.

meal[2] [miːl] *n (gen)* comida: *three meals a day,* tres comidas al día; *that was a delicious meal,* ha sido una comida deliciosa; *we went out for a meal last night,* salimos a cenar ayer.

● **to have a meal,** *(lunch)* comer; *(supper)* cenar. ‖ **to make a meal of sth.,** *(do too much)* pasarse con algo; *(blow up)* explotar algo al máximo.

■ **meal ticket,** US *(luncheon voucher)* ticket *m* restaurante; *(person etc providing income)* sustento.

mealtime ['miːltaɪm] *n* hora de comer.
mealy ['miːlɪ] *adj* harinoso,-a.
▲ *comp* **mealier**, *superl* **mealiest**.
mealy-mouthed [miːlɪ'maʊðd] *adj pej* evasivo,-a, embustero,-a.
mean¹ [miːn] **1** *adj* (*miserly, selfish - person*) mezquino,-a, tacaño,-a, agarrado,-a; (*portion etc*) mezquino,-a, miserable. **2** (*unkind*) malo,-a, antipático,-a; (*petty*) mezquino,-a; (*ashamed*) avergonzado,-a: *that was a mean thing to do,* vaya cosa más mezquina; *she felt mean about not letting the children go to the circus,* le sabía mal no haber dejado a los niños ir al circo. **3** *us fam* (*person - nasty*) malo,-a; (*- bad-tempered*) malhumorado,-a; (*animal*) feroz. **4** *dated* (*low, poor*) humilde, pobre. **5** *fam* (*skilful, great*) excelente, de primera, genial: *he makes a mean paella,* hace una paella buenísima; *she plays a mean guitar,* toca la guitarra de miedo.
● **to be no mean,** ser todo,-a un,-a: *that was no mean feat,* fue toda una hazaña; *she's no mean singer,* es una cantante genial.
mean² [miːn] **1** *t* (*signify, represent*) significar, querer decir; (*to be a sign of, indicate*) ser señal de, significar: *what does "mug" mean?,* ¿qué significa "mug"?, ¿qué quiere decir "mug"?; *that sign means that no smoking is allowed,* esa señal significa que está prohibido fumar; *when he whistles it means he's in a good mood,* cuando silba significa que está de buen humor; *does the name "Curtis" mean anything to you?,* ¿el nombre "Curtis" te dice algo? **2** (*have in mind*) pensar, tener pensado,-a, tener la intención de; (*intend, wish*) querer, pretender: *I never meant to hurt you,* nunca quise hacerte daño, nunca fue mi intención hacerte daño; *she didn't mean to do it,* lo hizo sin querer; *I meant to post it yesterday,* tenía la intención de enviarlo ayer, quería enviarlo ayer; *I've been meaning to write to you for ages,* hace tiempo que quiero escribirte; *I didn't mean you to read that,* no quería que leyeras eso; *his parents meant him to be a doctor,* sus padres querían que fuera médico. **3** (*involve, entail*) suponer, implicar; (*have as result*) significar: *but that would mean moving flat,* pero eso implicaría cambiar de piso; *that would mean spending a lot of money,* eso supondría gastar mucho dinero; *that means we can't go on holiday,* eso significa que no podemos irnos de vacaciones. **4** (*refer to, intend to say*) referirse a, querer decir; (*be serious about*) decir en serio: *I know who you mean,* sé a quién te refieres; *I know what you mean,* te entiendo; *do you mean me?,* ¿te refieres a mí?; *what do you mean by that?,* ¿qué quieres decir con eso?; *what do you mean you forgot?,* ¿cómo que se te olvidó?; *she said thirty, but she meant thirsty,* dijo treinta, pero quería decir sedienta; *I meant what I said,* te lo he dicho en serio. **5** (*be important*) significar: *you mean a lot to me,* significas mucho para mí, eres muy importante para mí; *her job means everything to her,* su trabajo es todo para ella; *five pounds means a lot to a child,* cinco libras es mucho dinero para un niño.
● **to be meant for,** (*be intended for*) ser para; (*be destined for*) estar dirigido,-a a, ir dirigido,-a a: *these shoes are meant for light walking,* estos zapatos son para pasear; *the letter bomb was meant for the Prime Minister,* la carta bomba iba dirigida al primer ministro; *that remark was meant for you,* ese comentario iba por ti; *they were meant for each other,* están hechos el uno para el otro.
‖ **to be meant to,** (*to be supposed to*) suponerse, deber, tener que; (*to be fated*) estar destinado,-a: *you're meant to wait until you're called,* se supone que debes esperar hasta que te llamen; *they were meant to arrive yester-*

day, tenían que llegar ayer; *you weren't meant to be a star,* no naciste para ser una estrella; *this was meant to be a good restaurant,* se suponía que era un buen restaurante; *it was meant to be a surprise,* tenía que ser una sorpresa; *it was meant to happen,* tenía que pasar, el destino así lo quiso. ‖ **to mean well,** tener buenas intenciones.
▲ *pt & pp* **meant**.
mean³ [miːn] **1** *adj* (*average*) medio,-a: *mean temperature,* temperatura media. **– 2** *n* (*average*) promedio. **3** MATH media. **4** (*middle term*) término medio.
meander [mɪ'ændəʳ] **1** *i* (*river etc*) serpentear. **2** (*person*) vagar, deambular, andar sin rumbo fijo. **3** *fig* (*conversation*) divagar. **– 4** *n* (*of river etc*) meandro.
meandering [mɪ'ændərɪŋ] **1** *adj* (*river etc*) que serpentea. **2** *fig* (*speech etc*) inconexo,-a, confuso,-a, incoherente. **– 3 meanderings,** *npl* (*of river etc*) ondulaciones *fpl*. **4** (*wandering*) vagabundeo *m sing*; (*talk*) divagaciones *fpl*.
meaning ['miːnɪŋ] **1** *n* (*sense - of word*) sentido, significado; (*- in dictionary*) acepción *f*; (*- of symbol, act*) significado: *what's the meaning of "draft"?,* ¿qué significa "draft"?, ¿qué quiere decir "draft"?; *do you get my meaning?,* ¿entiendes lo que te quiero decir? **2** (*significance, importance*) sentido; (*purpose, intention*) intención *f*: *my life has no meaning,* mi vida carece de sentido; *a glance full of meaning,* una mirada llena de intención. **– 3** *adj* (*significant*) significativo,-a.
meaningful ['miːnɪŋfʊl] *adj* (*significant*) significativo,-a, importante; (*worthwhile*) útil, que vale la pena: *a meaningful look,* una mirada significativa.
meaningless ['miːnɪŋləs] **1** *adj* (*word, phrase, etc*) sin sentido. **2** (*futile*) sin sentido, inútil, vano,-a.
meanness ['miːnnəs] **1** *n* (*miserliness*) tacañería, mezquindad *f*, avaricia. **2** (*nastiness*) maldad *f*.
means [miːnz] **1** *n* (*way, method*) medio, manera: *there's no means of escape,* no hay escapatoria, no hay manera de escapar; *a means of transport,* un medio de transporte. **– 2** *npl* (*resources*) medios *mpl* de vida, recursos *mpl* económicos, ingresos *mpl*; (*income*) renta *f sing*: *a person of means,* una persona acaudalada, una persona de buena posición económica; *they have private means,* viven de renta.
● **a means to an end,** un medio de conseguir un objetivo, un medio para lograr un fin. ‖ **by all means,** naturalmente, por supuesto. ‖ **by means of,** por medio de, mediante. ‖ **by no means / not by any means,** de ninguna manera, de ningún modo. ‖ **to be beyond sb.'s means,** no estar al alcance de algn. ‖ **to live beyond one's means,** vivir por encima de sus posibilidades. ‖ **to live within one's means,** vivir dentro de sus posibilidades.
■ **means of identification,** identificación *f*. ‖ **means test,** *investigación de la situación económica de una persona*.
▲ *pl* **means**.
meant [ment] *pt & pp* → **mean**.
meantime ['miːntaɪm] *adv* mientras tanto, entretanto.
● **in the meantime,** mientras tanto.
meanwhile ['miːnwaɪl] *adv* mientras tanto, entretanto.
measles ['miːzəlz] *n* MED sarampión *m*.
■ **German measles,** rubéola.
measly ['miːzlɪ] *adj fam pej* miserable, mezquino,-a.
▲ *comp* **measlier**, *superl* **measliest**.
measurable ['meʒərəbəl] *adj* mensurable, medible.
measure ['meʒəʳ] **1** *n* (*system*) medida: *liquid measure,* medida para líquidos; *measure of weight,* medida de peso. **2** (*indicator*) indicador *m*: *it's a measure of her pop-*

ularity, es un indicador de su popularidad. **3** (*ruler*) regla: *tape measure,* cinta métrica. **4** (*measured amount, unit*) medida. **5** (*amount, degree, extent*) grado, cantidad *f: some measure of happiness,* cierta felicidad. **6** (*method, step, remedy*) medida, disposición *f: safety measures,* medidas de seguridad. **7** US MUS (*bar*) compás *m,* ritmo. **– 8** *t* (*area, object, etc*) medir. **9** (*person*) tomar las medidas de. **10** *fig* (*assess*) evaluar; (*consider carefully*) sopesar, pensar bien. **– 11** *i* (*be*) medir: *it measures 3 feet by 6 feet,* mide 1 metro por 2 metros.

◆ **to measure against** 1 *t sep* (*for size*) medir con, comparar con. **2** (*judge*) juzgar, calibrar. ‖ **to measure off** *t sep* medir. ‖ **to measure out** *t sep* (*length*) medir; (*weight*) pesar. ‖ **to measure up** 1 *i* (*be up to*) dar la talla, estar a la altura (**to,** de). **– 2** *t sep* (*person*) tomar las medidas de.

● **beyond measure,** inconmensurable, inconmensurablemente: *rich beyond measure,* inconmensurablemente rico. ‖ **for good measure,** para que no falte. ‖ **half measures,** medias tintas. ‖ **in large measure,** en gran parte, en gran medida. ‖ **in some measure,** hasta cierto punto, en cierta medida. ‖ **to give sb. full measure,** dar la medida exacta a algn. ‖ **to give sb. short measure,** dar de menos a algn. ‖ **to have the measure of sb.,** tener calado,-a a algn. ‖ **to make sth. to measure,** hacer algo a (la) medida. ‖ **to take measures,** tomar medidas, adoptar medidas.

measured ['meʒəd] **1** *adj* (*action*) estudiado,-a; (*tone*) mesurado,-a: (*statement*) prudente, circunspecto,-a; (*language*) moderado,-a, comedido,-a. **2** (*step etc*) acompasado,-a, regular, rítmico,-a.

measurement ['meʒəmənt] **1** *n* (*act*) medición *f.* **2** (*length etc*) medida.
● **to take sb.'s measurements,** tomarle las medidas a algn.
■ **chest measurement,** contorno de pecho. ‖ **leg measurement,** largo de pierna.

measuring ['meʒərɪŋ] *n* (*act*) medición *f.*
■ **measuring jug,** vaso medidor. ‖ **measuring spoon,** cuchara medidora. ‖ **measuring tape,** cinta métrica, metro.

meat [miːt] **1** *n* carne *f: I prefer meat to fish,* me gusta más la carne que el pescado. **2** *fig* (*main part*) meollo, enjundia.
● **one man's meat is another man's poison,** lo que a uno cura a otro mata. ‖ **to be meat and drink to sb.,** ser lo que más le gusta a algn., ser la pasión de algn.
■ **cold meat / cooked meat,** fiambre *m.* ‖ **meat pie,** empanada de carne. ‖ **meat product,** producto cárnico.

meatball ['miːtbɔːl] *n* albóndiga.

meatloaf ['miːtləʊf] *n* pastel *m* de carne.

meaty ['miːtɪ] **1** *adj* (*pie, chop, bone, etc*) con mucha carne; (*smell, taste*) a carne. **2** *fig* (*book, discussion, etc*) sustancioso,-a, jugoso,-a, enjundioso,-a.
▲ *comp* **meatier,** *superl* **meatiest.**

Mecca ['mekə] **1** *n* (*in Saudi Arabia*) la Meca. **2** *mecca,* (*famous place*) meca.

mechanic [mə'kænɪk] *n* (*person*) mecánico,-a.

mechanical [mə'kænɪkəl] *adj* mecánico,-a.
■ **mechanical engineer,** ingeniero,-a mecánico,-a. ‖ **mechanical engineering,** ingeniería mecánica.

mechanically [mə'kænɪklɪ] *adv* mecánicamente.

mechanics [mə'kænɪks] **1** *n* (*science*) mecánica. **– 2** *the mechanics,* *npl* (*working parts*) el mecanismo *m sing.* **– 3** *n* (*processes*) el funcionamiento.

mechanism ['mekənɪzəm] *n* mecanismo.

mechanization [mekənaɪ'zeɪʃən] *n* mecanización *f.*

mechanize ['mekənaɪz] **1** *t* mecanizar. **– 2** *i* mecanizarse.

M Ed ['em'ed] *abbr* (*Master of Education*) ≈ master en pedagogía.

medal ['medəl] *n* medalla: *gold/silver/bronze medal,* medalla de oro/plata/bronce.

medallion [mə'dælɪən] *n* medallón *m.*

medallist ['medəlɪst] *n* medalla *mf,* campeón,-ona: *he was the gold medallist,* fue medalla de oro.

meddle ['medəl] **1** *i* (*interfere*) entrometerse (**in,** en). **2** (*handle*) manosear (**with,** -).

meddler ['medələ'] *n* entrometido,-a, entremetido,-a.

meddlesome ['medəlsəm] *adj fml* entrometido,-a, entremetido,-a.

meddling ['medəlɪŋ] *adj* entrometido,-a, entremetido,-a.

Mede [miːd] *n* medo,-a.

media ['miːdɪə] *the media,* *npl* los medios *mpl* de comunicación.
■ **media coverage,** cobertura periodística.
▲ *Véase también* **medium.**

mediaeval [medɪ'iːvəl] *adj* medieval.

medial ['miːdɪəl] *adj fml* medial.

median ['miːdɪən] **1** *adj* MATH mediano,-a. **– 2** *n* MATH (*line*) mediana; (*quantity*) valor *m* mediano.

Median ['miːdɪən] **1** *adj* medo,-a, médico,-a. **– 2** *n* (*person*) medo,-a. **3** (*language*) medo.

mediate ['miːdɪeɪt] **1** *i* (*arbitrate*) mediar (**between,** entre), (**in,** en). **– 2** *t* (*bring about*) lograr, conseguir.

mediation [miːdɪ'eɪʃən] *n* mediación *f.*

mediator ['miːdɪeɪtə'] *n* mediador,-ra.

medic ['medɪk] *n fam* (*doctor*) médico,-a; (*medical student*) estudiante *mf* de medicina.

medical ['medɪkəl] **1** *adj* (*treatment, care, examination*) médico,-a; (*book, student*) de medicina. **– 2** *n fam* (*check-up*) chequeo, reconocimiento médico, revisión *f* médica.
■ **medical practitioner,** médico,-a. ‖ **medical school,** (*univ*) facultad *f* de medicina. ‖ **the medical profession,** la profesión *f* médica, los médicos *mpl.*

medically ['medɪkəlɪ] *adv* desde el punto de vista médico: *he was pronounced medically fit,* lo declararon sano.
● **to be medically examined,** ser reconocido,-a por un médico.

medicated ['medɪkeɪtɪd] *adj* medicinal.

medication [medɪ'keɪʃən] *n* medicación *f.*

medicinal [mə'dɪsɪnəl] *adj* medicinal.

medicine ['medsən] **1** *n* (*science*) medicina. **2** (*drugs etc*) medicina, medicamento.
● **to give sb. a taste/dose of their own medicine,** pagar a algn. con la misma moneda.
■ **medicine chest / medicine cabinet,** botiquín *m.*

medieval [medɪ'iːvəl] *adj* medieval.

mediocre [miːdɪ'əʊkə'] *adj* mediocre.

mediocrity [miːdɪ'ɒkrətɪ] *n* mediocridad *f.*

meditate ['medɪteɪt] **1** *i* meditar, reflexionar (**on/upon,** sobre). **– 2** *t* meditar.

meditation [medɪ'teɪʃən] *n* meditación *f.*

meditative ['medɪtətɪv] *adj* meditabundo,-a, meditativo,-a.

Mediterranean [medɪtə'reɪnɪən] **1** *adj* mediterráneo,-a. **– 2** *n* mediterráneo,-a.
■ **The Mediterranean,** el (mar) Mediterráneo.

medium ['miːdɪəm] 1 adj (average) mediano,-a, regular, normal: *a man of medium height,* un hombre de estatura media; *a medium steak,* un filete al punto. – 2 n (means) medio. 3 (environment) medio (ambiente). 4 (middle position) punto medio, término medio. 5 (spiritualist) médium mf.
● to strike a happy medium, hallar un término medio.
■ medium dry, (wine) semiseco,-a, abocado,-a. ‖ medium wave, onda media.
▲ En 2 y 3 pl media.

medium-range ['miːdɪəm'reɪndʒ] adj (weapon etc) de alcance medio.

medium-sized ['miːdɪəm'saɪzd] adj (thing) de tamaño mediano.

medlar ['medlə'] n BOT níspero.

medley ['medlɪ] 1 n MUS popurrí m. 2 (mixture) mezcla; (variety, assortment) variedad f. 3 SP (swimming race) estilos mpl.

meek [miːk] adj manso,-a, dócil, sumiso,-a.
● to be as meek as a lamb, ser un cordero, ser un corderito.

meekness ['miːknəs] n mansedumbre f, docilidad f.

meet [miːt] 1 t (by chance) encontrar, encontrarse con; (in street) cruzar con, topar con: *she met an old friend,* se encontró con un viejo amigo; *guess who I met today!,* ¡a que no sabes con quién he topado hoy! 2 (by arrangement) encontrar, reunirse con, citarse, quedar con; (formally) entrevistarse con; (informally) ver: *meet me in the park,* encontrémonos en el parque; *I'll meet you tomorrow,* te veré mañana; *I'm meeting Rob tomorrow,* he quedado con Rob para mañana; *I've arranged to meet them in the pub,* he quedado con ellos en el pub. 3 (meet for first time) conocer: *I met him at a party,* lo conocí en una fiesta; *have you met my wife?,* ¿conoces a mi mujer?; *I'd like you to meet a friend,* quiero presentarle a un amigo; *I'm pleased to meet you,* estoy encantado de conocerte. 4 (collect) ir a buscar, pasar a buscar; (await arrival of) esperar; (receive) ir a recibir: *he'll meet me at the station,* me vendrá a buscar a la estación; *all the family were there to meet her at the airport,* toda la familia fue a recibirla al aeropuerto; *there's a coach that meets the train,* hay un autocar que enlaza con el tren. 5 (face - danger, difficulty) encontrar; (- problem) hacer frente a. 6 SP (opponent) enfrentarse con. 7 (touch) tocar. 8 (fulfil - standards, demands, wishes) satisfacer; (- obligations, deadline) cumplir con; (- requirements) reunir, cumplir. 9 (bill, debt) pagar; (deficit) cubrir; (cost, expenses) hacerse cargo de. – 10 i (by chance) encontrarse: *we'll meet again,* nos volveremos a encontrar. 11 (by arrangement) reunirse, verse, quedar, encontrarse; (formally) entrevistarse: *we arranged to meet on Saturday,* quedamos para el sábado; *we must meet for lunch one day,* tenemos que quedar para comer un día; *where shall we meet?,* ¿dónde quedamos?; *the women's group meets on Fridays,* el grupo de mujeres se reúne los viernes. 12 (get acquainted) conocerse: *where did you meet?,* ¿dónde os conocisteis?; *I think we've already met,* creo que ya nos conocemos. 13 SP enfrentarse. 14 (join) unirse; (touch) tocarse; (rivers) confluir; (roads) empalmar; (eyes) cruzarse. – 15 n SP encuentro. 16 GB (hunting) partida de caza.
◆ to meet up i fam (by arrangement) quedar, reunirse (with, con); (by chance) encontrar, encontrarse con. ‖ to meet with 1 t insep (difficulty, problem) encontrar, tropezar con; (loss, accident) sufrir; (success) tener. 2 US (person) reunirse con, entrevistarse con.

● to be more to sth. than meets the eye, ser más complicado,-a de lo que parece. ‖ to make ends meet, fam llegar a fin de mes. ‖ to meet one's death, encontrar la muerte, morir. ‖ to meet one's Maker, morirse. ‖ to meet sb.'s eye, mirar a algn. a la cara. ‖ to meet sb. halfway, llegar a un acuerdo con algn.
▲ (verbo) pt & pp met.

meeting ['miːtɪŋ] 1 n (gen - prearranged) reunión f; (- formal) entrevista; (- date) cita. 2 (chance encounter) encuentro. 3 (people gathered) reunión f. 4 (of club, committee, etc) reunión f; (of assembly) sesión f; (of shareholders, creditors) junta. 5 POL (rally) mitin m. 6 SP encuentro. 7 (of rivers) confluencia.
● to be in a meeting, estar reunido,-a. ‖ to call a meeting, convocar una reunión. ‖ to hold a meeting, celebrar una reunión, celebrar una sesión. ‖ to open/close a meeting, abrir/levantar la sesión.
■ annual general meeting, junta general anual. ‖ meeting place, lugar m de encuentro, lugar m de reunión.

megabyte ['megəbaɪt] n COMPUT megabyte m, megaocteto.

megahertz ['megəhɜːts] n megahercio.

megalith ['megəlɪθ] n megalito.

megalomaniac [megələ'meɪnɪæk] 1 n megalómano,-a. – 2 adj megalómano,-a.

megaphone ['megəfəʊn] n megáfono, altavoz m.

melamine ['meləmiːn] n melamina.

melancholic [melən'kɒlɪk] adj melancólico,-a.

melancholy ['melənkəlɪ] 1 n melancolía. – 2 adj melancólico,-a.

melanin ['melənɪn] n melanina.

melée ['meleɪ] n (crowd) tumulto, gentío; (struggle) pelea confusa.

mellifluous [mə'lɪflʊəs] adj melifluo,-a.

mellow ['meləʊ] 1 adj (fruit) maduro,-a; (wine) añejo,-a. 2 (colour, voice) suave. 3 (person - mature, calm) sosegado,-a, sereno,-a; (genial, cheerful) relajado,-a, apacible. – 4 t (person) serenar, suavizar el carácter de. – 5 i (colour, voice) suavizar(se); (fruit) madurar; (wine) añejarse. 6 (person) serenarse; (views) moderarse.

melodic [mə'lɒdɪk] adj melódico,-a.

melodious [mə'ləʊdɪəs] adj melodioso,-a.

melodrama ['melədrɑːmə] 1 n melodrama m. 2 fam fig dramón m.

melodramatic [melədrə'mætɪk] adj melodramático,-a.

melody ['melədɪ] n melodía.
▲ pl melodies.

melon ['melən] n (honeydew etc) melón m; (watermelon) sandía.

melt [melt] 1 t (ice, snow, butter, etc) derretir. 2 (metal) fundir (down, -). 3 (sugar, chemical) disolver. 4 fig (anger etc) atenuar, disipar; (sb.'s heart) ablandar. – 5 i (ice, snow) derretirse (away, -). 6 (metal) fundirse. 7 (sugar, chemical) disolverse. 8 fig (food) derretirse, deshacerse: *it melts in the mouth,* se deshace en la boca. 9 fig (sb.'s heart) ablandarse, derretirse. 10 (colour, sound, etc) desvanecer.
◆ to melt away 1 i (money, crowd, person) desaparecer. 2 fig (confidence etc) desvanecerse, esfumarse; (anger) disiparse, desaparecer.
● to melt into tears, deshacerse en lágrimas. ‖ to melt into the crowd, perderse entre la multitud.

melting ['meltɪŋ] 1 adj fig (voice, look) tierno,-a, dulce. – 2 n (of metal) fundición f; (of snow) derretimiento.
● to be in the melting pot, estar por decidir.

■ **melting point,** punto de fusión. ‖ **melting pot,** crisol *m.*

member ['membə^r] **1** *n* (*gen*) miembro *mf*; (*of club*) socio,-a; (*of union, party*) afiliado,-a: *the youngest member of the family,* el miembro más joven de la familia; *an active member of the Labour Party,* un militante del partido laborista; *are you a member of any clubs?,* ¿eres socio de algún club? **2** POL (*of Parliament*) diputado,-a; (*of European Parliament*) eurodiputado,-a. **3** ANAT miembro. **4** ARCH viga. – **5** *adj* (*country, state*) miembro,-a.
● **members only,** sólo para socios,-as.
■ **member of staff,** (*gen*) empleado,-a; (*teacher*) profesor,-ra. ‖ **member of the public,** cuidadano,-a: *the gardens are closed to members of the public,* los jardines están cerrados al público.

membership ['membəʃip] **1** *n* (*of club - state*) calidad *f* de socio,-a, pertenencia; (*- entry*) ingreso: *I applied for membership of the club,* solicité el ingreso en el club; *membership is only open to people over 30,* sólo los mayores de 30 años pueden hacerse socios. **2** (*of political party, union - state*) afiliación *f*; (*- entry*) ingreso. **3** (*members - of club*) miembros *mpl*, socios *mpl*; (*- of political party*) afiliados *mpl*: *membership of our club is on the increase,* nuestro club cada vez tiene más socios.
■ **membership card,** (*of club*) carnet *m* de socio; (*of party*) carnet *m* de afiliado. ‖ **membership fee,** cuota.

membrane ['membrein] *n* membrana.

memento [mə'mentəʊ] *n* recuerdo, recordatorio.
▲ *pl* **mementos** o **mementoes**.

memo ['meməʊ] **1** *n* (*official*) memorándum *m.* **2** (*personal note*) nota, apunte *m.*
■ **memo pad,** bloc *m* de notas.
▲ *pl* **memos**.

memoir ['memwɑː^r] **1** *n* (*essay*) memoria. – **2 memoirs,** *npl* (*autobiography*) memorias *fpl*, autobiografía.

memorabilia [memərə'biliə] *npl* (*souvenirs*) recuerdos *mpl*.

memorable ['memərəbəl] *adj* memorable.

memorandum [memə'rændəm] **1** *n* (*official note*) memorándum *m*, memorando. **2** (*personal note*) nota, apunte *m.*
▲ *pl* **memorandums** o **memoranda** [memə'rændə].

memorial [mə'mɔːriəl] **1** *adj* (*plaque etc*) conmemorativo,-a. – **2** *n* (*monument*) monumento conmemorativo; (*ceremony*) homenaje *m.*
■ **Memorial Day,** Día *m* de Conmemoración de los Caídos.

memorize ['meməraiz] *t* memorizar, aprender de memoria.

memory ['meməri] **1** *n* (*ability, computers*) memoria: *she's got a good memory for names,* tiene buena memoria para los nombres; *I'm quoting from memory,* cito de memoria. **2** (*recollection*) recuerdo.
● *if my memory serves me well,* si no recuerdo mal. ‖ *in memory of,* (*person*) en memoria de, a la memoria de; (*thing*) en conmemoración de. ‖ *to commit sth. to memory,* memorizar algo, aprender algo de memoria. ‖ *to have a memory like a sieve,* tener muy mala memoria. ‖ *to lose one's memory,* perder la memoria. ‖ *within sb.'s memory,* que algn. recuerde. ‖ *within living memory,* que se recuerde.
▲ *pl* **memories**.

men [men] *npl* → **man**.

menace ['menəs] **1** *n* (*threat*) amenaza (**to,** para); (*danger*) peligro (**to,** para). **2** *fam* (*nuisance - person*) pesado,-a; (*- thing*) lata, molestia. – **3** *t* amenazar (**with,** de).

menacing ['menəsiŋ] *adj* amenazador,-ra, amenazante.

menacingly ['menəsiŋli] *adv* de manera amenazadora.

menagerie [mə'nædʒəri] *n* (*collection*) colección *f* de animales salvajes; (*zoo*) zoo.

mend [mend] **1** *t* (*repair - gen*) reparar, arreglar; (*sew*) coser; (*patch*) remendar; (*darn*) zurcir: *can you mend my watch?,* ¿me puedes arreglar el reloj? **2** (*improve*) mejorar. – **3** *i* (*health*) mejorarse, reponerse; (*part of body, injury, wound*) curarse; (*fracture, bone*) soldarse. – **4** *n* (*patch*) remiendo; (*darn*) zurcido.
● *to be on the mend,* ir mejorando. ‖ *to mend one's ways,* enmendarse, reformarse.

mender ['mendə^r] *n* (*of shoes*) zapatero,-a, zapatero,-a remendón,-ona; (*of watches*) relojero,-a.
■ **mender's shop,** (*shoes*) zapatero; (*watches*) relojería.

mending ['mendiŋ] **1** *n* (*repairing - gen*) reparación *f*, arreglo. **2** (*clothes to be mended*) ropa para remendar.
● *to do the mending,* (*sew*) coser; (*patch*) remendar; (*darn*) zurcir.

menfolk ['menfəʊk] *npl* los hombres *mpl.*

menial ['miːniəl] **1** *adj* (*task etc*) servil, bajo,-a. – **2** *n fml pej* (*servant*) criado,-a.

meningitis [menin'dʒaitəs] *n* MED meningitis *f.*

menopausal [menə'pɔːzəl] *adj* menopáusico,-a.

menopause ['menəpɔːz] *n* menopausia.

menstrual ['menstrʊəl] *adj* menstrual.
■ **menstrual cycle,** ciclo menstrual. ‖ **menstrual period,** regla, período.

menstruate ['menstrʊeit] *i* menstruar.

menstruation [menstrʊ'eiʃən] *n* menstruación *f*, regla.

menswear ['menzweə^r] *n* ropa de caballero, ropa de hombres.

mental ['mentəl] **1** *adj* (*of the mind*) mental: *mental effort,* esfuerzo mental; *mental health,* salud mental. **2** (*in the mind*) mental: *mental arithmetic,* cálculo mental; *mental block,* bloqueo mental; *mental note,* nota mental. **3** *fam pej* (*mad*) chalado,-a, tocado,-a.
■ **mental age,** edad *f* mental. ‖ **mental defective,** *pej* (*person*) subnormal *mf.* ‖ **mental deficiency,** deficiencia mental. ‖ **mental handicap,** disminución *f* psíquica. ‖ **mental home / mental hospital,** (hospital *m*) psiquiátrico. ‖ **mental patient,** enfermo,-a mental.

mentality [men'tæləti] *n* mentalidad *f.*
▲ *pl* **mentalities**.

mentally ['mentəli] *adv* mentalmente.
● *to be mentally deranged,* ser demente. ‖ *to be mentally handicapped,* ser un,-a disminuido,-a psíquico,-a. ‖ *to be mentally ill,* padecer una enfermedad mental.

menthol ['menθɒl] **1** *n* mentol *m.* – **2** *adj* (*cigarette*) mentolado,-a.

mention ['menʃən] **1** *n* mención *f*: *she made no mention of your visit,* no mencionó tu visita; *I see you got a brief mention in the newspaper,* veo que sale tu nombre en el periódico. – **2** *t* mencionar, hacer mención de, aludir a: *he never mentioned the money,* no mencionó el dinero; *she mentioned in passing that she'd seen James,* mencionó de pasada que había visto a James.
● *don't mention it!,* ¡de nada!, ¡no hay de qué! ‖ *not to mention ...,* además de ...

mentor ['mentɔː^r] *n* mentor *m.*

menu ['menjuː] **1** *n* (*list of dishes*) carta; (*fixed meal*) menú *m.* **2** COMPUT menú *m.*

meow [mi'aʊ] **1** *n* maullido, miau *m.* – **2** *i* maullar.

MEP ['em'iː'piː] *abbr* (*Member of the European Parliament*) miembro del Parlamento Europeo.

mercantile ['mɜːkəntail] *adj* mercantil, comercial.

mercenary ['mɜːsənərɪ] 1 *adj* mercenario,-a. – 2 *n* mercenario,-a.
▲ *pl* **mercenaries**.
merchandise ['mɜːtʃəndaɪz] 1 *n* mercancías *fpl*, géneros *mpl*. – 2 *t* (*sell*) vender, poner en venta; (*promote*) promocionar.
merchant ['mɜːtʃənt] 1 *n* COMM FIN (*trader*) comerciante *mf*; (*dealer, businessperson*) negociante *mf*; (*retailer*) detallista *mf*, minorista; (*shopkeeper*) tendero,-a. 2 *arch* mercader *m*.
■ **merchant bank**, banco comercial. ‖ **merchant navy**, marina mercante. ‖ **merchant seaman**, marinero mercante. ‖ **merchant ship**, barco mercante, buque *m* mercante. ‖ **merchant shipping**, navegación *f* comercial.
merciful ['mɜːsɪfʊl] 1 *adj* (*forgiving*) misericordioso,-a (**to/towards**, con) clemente (**to/towards**, con), compasivo,-a (**to/towards**, con). 2 (*fortunate*) bienaventurado,-a.
mercifully ['mɜːsɪfʊlɪ] 1 *adv* (*showing mercy*) con compasión. 2 (*fortunately*) afortunadamente.
merciless ['mɜːsɪləs] *adj* despiadado,-a, sin piedad.
mercurial [mɜː'kjʊərɪəl] 1 *adj* (*people, mood*) voluble, volátil. 2 *fml* (*of mercury, like mercury*) mercurial.
mercury ['mɜːkjərɪ] *n* mercurio.
Mercury ['mɜːkjərɪ] *n* ASTRON Mercurio.
mercy ['mɜːsɪ] 1 *n* (*compassion*) misericordia, clemencia, piedad *f*: *have mercy upon me!*, ¡tenga piedad de mí!; *they showed him no mercy*, no fueron clementes con él. 2 *fam* (*good fortune*) suerte *f*, milagro; (*blessing*) bendición *f*: *it was a mercy no-one was hurt*, fue una suerte que no hubiera heridos. – 3 *adj* de ayuda, de socorro.
● **to be at the mercy of sb./sth.**, estar a la merced de algn./algo. ‖ **to be thankful for small mercies**, darse con un canto en los dientes. ‖ **to beg for mercy / plead for mercy**, pedir clemencia. ‖ **to throw os. on sb.'s mercy**, abandonarse a la merced de algn.
■ **mercy killing**, eutanasia.
▲ *pl* **mercies**.
mere¹ [mɪəʳ] *n* (*lake*) lago, laguna.
mere² [mɪəʳ] 1 *adj* mero,-a, simple, puro,-a. 2 **merest**, (*slightest*) el/la más mínimo,-a: *the merest suggestion that she was fat made her furious*, la más mínima insinuación de que estaba gorda le hacía perder los estribos.
merely ['mɪəlɪ] *adv* solamente, simplemente.
merge [mɜːdʒ] 1 *t* (*combine - gen*) unir (**with**, a), combinar (**with**, con); (*- road*) empalmar (**into**, con); (*- river*) desembocar (**into**, en); (*- firms, businesses*) fusionar. – 2 *i* (*combine - gen*) unirse, combinarse; (*- firms, businesses*) fusionarse; (*- roads, rivers*) juntarse; (*- rivers*) confluir. 3 (*blend, fade*) ir convirtiéndose (**into**, en).
● **to merge into the background**, perderse de vista. ‖ **to merge into the darkness**, desaparecer en la oscuridad.
merger ['mɜːdʒəʳ] *n* COMM fusión *f*.
meridian [məˈrɪdɪən] *n* meridiano.
meridional [məˈrɪdɪənəl] *adj* meridional.
meringue [məˈræŋ] *n* merengue *m*.
merit ['merɪt] 1 *n* (*worth*) mérito, valía: *a person of merit*, una persona de valía; *there's some merit in what he did*, lo que hizo tiene algo de mérito. 2 (*advantage, good point*) ventaja, mérito: *it has the merit of being short*, tiene la ventaja de ser corto; *what are the merits of this project?*, ¿cuáles son las ventajas de este proyecto? – 3 *t* (*deserve*) merecer, ser digno,-a de.

● **to judge sth. on its own merits**, juzgar algo por sus méritos.
mermaid ['mɜːmeɪd] *n* sirena.
merrily ['merɪlɪ] *adv* alegremente.
merriment ['merɪmənt] *n* alegría, regocijo.
merry ['merɪ] 1 *adj* (*cheerful*) alegre; (*amusing*) divertido,-a, gracioso,-a. 2 *fam* (*slightly drunk*) alegre, achispado,-a.
● **merry Christmas!**, ¡felices Navidades! ‖ **the more, the merrier**, cuántos más mejor. ‖ **to make merry**, divertirse.
▲ *comp* **merrier**, *superl* **merriest**.
merry-go-round ['merɪɡəʊraʊnd] *n* tiovivo, caballitos *mpl*.
merry-making ['merɪmeɪkɪŋ] *n dated* juerga, fiesta.
mesh [meʃ] 1 *n* (*of thread*) malla; (*of wire*) malla metálica, tela metálica; (*net*) red *f*. 2 TECH engranaje *m*. 3 (*holes, spaces*) malla: *a net with a fine mesh*, una red de malla fina. – 4 *i* TECH engranar. 5 (*fit in, harmonize*) encajar, combinar (**with**, con).
● **in mesh**, engranado,-a.
mesmerize ['mezməraɪz] 1 *t* (*hypnotize*) hipnotizar. 2 (*fascinate*) fascinar, cautivar.
Mesopotamia [mesəpəˈteɪmɪə] *n* Mesopotamia.
Mesopotamian [mesəpəˈteɪmɪən] 1 *adj* mesopotamio,-a. – 2 *n* mesopotamio,-a.
mess [mes] 1 *n* (*untidy state*) desorden *m*, revoltijo: *everything's a mess*, todo está desordenado, todo está patas arriba; *your room is a complete mess!*, ¡tu habitación está toda desordenada!; *don't make a mess!*, ¡no lo desordenes todo! 2 (*confusion, mix-up*) confusión *f*, lío, follón *m*; (*person, thing*) desastre *m*: *what a mess!*, ¡vaya lío!; *my life is a mess*, mi vida es un desastre; *you've got yourself into a right mess*, te has metido en un buen lío. 3 *fam euph* (*animal excrement*) caca. 4 MIL (*room*) comedor *m*; (*group of people who eat in mess*) oficiales *mpl*. – 5 *t* (*untidy*) desordenar; (*dirty*) ensuciar. – 6 *i* MIL (*eat in mess*) comer el rancho.
◆ **to mess about / mess around** 1 *i* (*idle*) gandulear; (*kill time*) pasar el tiempo; (*potter about*) entretenerse. 2 (*act the fool*) hacer el primo, tontear: *stop messing about!*, ¡déjate de tonterías!, ¡basta de tonterías! – 3 *t sep* (*treat badly*) fastidiar, tomar el pelo a. ‖ **to mess about / mess around with** 1 *t insep* (*fiddle with*) tocar, manosear; (*play with*) jugar con. – 2 *t sep* (*get involved with*) meterse con. – 3 *t insep* (*have affair with*) tener un lío con, estar liado,-a con. 4 (*sexually interfere with*) abusar de. ‖ **to mess up** 1 *t sep fam* (*untidy*) desordenar; (*dirty*) ensuciar. 2 (*spoil*) estropear, echar a perder. – 3 *i US sl* (*make a mistake*) hacerla buena, pifiarla. ‖ **to mess with** 1 *t insep* (*get involved with*) meterse con. 2 (*play with*) jugar con.
● **no messing**, (*directly*) y nada de tonterías; (*seriously*) no es broma, va en serio. ‖ **to look a mess**, estar horroroso,-a. ‖ **to make a mess of sth.**, (*dirty*) ensuciar algo; (*untidy*) desordenar algo; (*mess up*) estropear algo.
message ['mesɪdʒ] 1 *n* (*communication*) recado, mensaje *m*: *could you give her a message?*, ¿podrías darle un recado?; *can I leave a message?*, ¿puedo dejar un recado?; *make sure that he gets the message*, asegúrate de que reciba el recado. 2 (*of story, film, etc*) mensaje *m*.
● **to get the message**, (*understand*) entender, darse cuenta.
messenger ['mesɪndʒəʳ] *n* mensajero,-a.
■ **messenger boy**, recadero.
Messiah [məˈsaɪə] *n* REL Mesías *m*.
messily ['mesɪlɪ] *adv* (*gen*) con poco esmero; (*untidily*) descuidadamente.

Messrs ['mesəz] *abbr* COMM (*messieurs*) Señores; (*abbreviation*) Sres.

mess-up ['mesʌp] 1 *n fam* (*confusion*) lío, follón *m*, enredo; (*misunderstanding*) malentendido. 2 *fam* (*botch*, *cock-up*) chapuza.

messy ['mesɪ] 1 *adj* (*untidy*) desordenado,-a, en desorden; (- *dirty*) sucio,-a: *cleaning the oven is a messy job*, limpiar el horno es un trabajo sucio; *do you have to be so messy?*, ¿tienes que desordenarlo todo? 2 (*confused*) confuso,-a, complicado,-a, lioso,-a, enredado,-a; (*awkward*) difícil; (*unpleasant*) desagradable: *a messy divorce*, un divorcio reñido.
▲ *comp* **messier**, *superl* **messiest**.

met [met] *pt & pp* → **meet**.

metabolic [metə'bɒlɪk] *adj* metabólico,-a.

metabolism [mə'tæbəlɪzəm] *n* metabolismo.

metabolize [mə'tæbəlaɪz] *t* metabolizar.

metal ['metəl] 1 *n* metal *m*. – 2 *adj* metálico,-a, de metal.
■ metal detector, detector *m* de metales.

metallic [mə'tælɪk] *adj* metálico,-a.
■ metallic blue, azul *m* metalizado.

metallurgist [mə'tælədʒɪst] *n* metalúrgico,-a.

metallurgy [mə'tælədʒɪ] *n* metalurgia.

metalwork ['metəlwɜːk] 1 *n* (*craft*) metalistería. 2 (*objects*) objetos *mpl* de metal.

metalworker ['metəlwɜːkəʳ] *n* metalista *mf*.

metamorphose [metə'mɔːfəʊz] 1 *t* metamorfosear. – 2 *i* metamorfosearse.

metamorphosis [metə'mɔːfəsɪs] *n* metamorfosis *f*.
▲ *pl* **metamorphoses** [metə'mɔːfəsiːz].

metaphor ['metəfɔːʳ] *n* metáfora.

metaphorical [metə'fɒrɪkəl] *adj* metafórico,-a.

metaphysical [metə'fɪzɪkəl] *adj* metaffsico,-a.

metaphysics [metə'fɪzɪks] *n* metafísica.

mete [miːt] to mete out, *t fml* (*punishment*, *fine*, *etc*) imponer; (*justice*) repartir.

meteor ['miːtɪəʳ] *n* meteorito.

meteoric [miːtɪ'ɒrɪk] *adj* (*gen*) meteórico,-a.

meteorite ['miːtɪəraɪt] *n* meteorito.

meteorological [miːtɪərə'lɒdʒɪkəl] *adj* meteorológico,-a.

meteorologist [miːtɪə'rɒlədʒɪst] *n* meteorólogo,-a.

meteorology [miːtɪə'rɒlədʒɪ] *n* meteorología.

meter¹ ['miːtəʳ] *n* US → **metre**.

meter² ['miːtəʳ] 1 *n* contador *m*: *I've come to read the gas meter*, vengo a hacer la lectura del contador del gas. – 2 *t* medir.

methadone ['meθədəʊn] *n* metadona.

methane ['miːθeɪn] *n* metano.

method ['meθəd] 1 *n* (*manner*, *way*) método, forma. 2 (*system*, *order*) sistema *m*, orden *m*, lógica. 3 (*technique*) técnica.
● there's method in his/her madness, no es tan loco,-a como parece.

methodical [mə'θɒdɪkəl] *adj* metódico,-a, ordenado,-a.

methodically [mɪ'θɒdɪkəlɪ] *adv* metódicamente, de manera metódica.

Methodism ['meθədɪzəm] *n* REL metodismo.

Methodist ['meθədɪst] *n* metodista *mf*.

methodology [meθə'dɒlədʒɪ] *n* metodología.
▲ *pl* **methodologies**.

meths [meθs] *n fam* → **methylated spirits**.

Methuselah [mə'θjuːzələ] *n* Matusalén *m*.
● as old as Methuselah, más viejo,-a que Matusalén.

methylated spirits [meθəleɪtɪd'spɪrɪts] *n* alcohol *m* de quemar, alcohol *m* desnaturalizado.

meticulous [mə'tɪkjələs] *adj* meticuloso,-a, minucioso,-a.

meticulously [mə'tɪkjələslɪ] *adv* con meticulosidad, minuciosamente.

meticulousness [mə'tɪkjələsnəs] *n* meticulosidad *f*, minuciosidad *f*.

metre¹ ['miːtəʳ] *n* (*in poetry*) metro.

metre² ['miːtəʳ] *n* (*measure*) metro.
■ cubic metre, metro cúbico.

metric ['metrɪk] *adj* métrico,-a.
■ metric system, sistema métrico. ‖ metric ton, tonelada métrica.

metrication [metrɪ'keɪʃən] *n* adopción *f* del sistema métrico, conversión *f* al sistema métrico.

metronome ['metrənəʊm] *n* metrónomo.

metropolis [mə'trɒpəlɪs] *n* metrópoli *f*, metrópolis *f*.
▲ *pl* **metropolises**.

metropolitan [metrə'pɒlɪtən] *adj* metropolitano,-a.
■ the Metropolitan Police, la policía de Londres.

mettle ['metəl] *n fml* (*courage*, *spirit*) valor *m*, valentía, temple *m*, entereza; (*character*) carácter *m*.
● to be on one's mettle, tener que hacerlo lo mejor posible, tener que dar lo mejor de sí. ‖ to put sb. on their mettle, poner a prueba el valor de algn. ‖ to show one's mettle / prove one's mettle, demostrar lo que se vale, mostrar su valor.

Meuse [mɜːz] *n* el Mosa *m*.

mew [mjuː] 1 *i* maullar. – 2 *n* maullido.

mews [mjuːz] *n* GB *callejuela con antiguas caballerizas reconvertidas en viviendas.*

Mexican ['meksɪkən] 1 *adj* mejicano,-a. – 2 *n* mejicano,-a.

Mexico ['meksɪləʊ] *n* Méjico.
■ New Mexico, Nuevo Méjico.

mezzanine ['mezəniːn] 1 *n* entresuelo. 2 US (*in theatre*) piso principal.

mezzo ['metsəʊ] 1 *n fam* → **mezzo-soprano**. – 2 *adv* medio.
▲ (*sustantivo*) *pl* **mezzos**.

mezzo-soprano ['metsəʊsə'prɑːnəʊ] *n* mezzosoprano *f*.

mg ['em'dʒiː, 'mɪlɪgræm] *symb* (*milligram*, *milligramme*) miligramo; (*symbol*) mg.

Mgr [mɒn'siːnjəʳ] *abbr* (*Monsignor*) Monseñor *m*; (*abbreviation*) Mons.

MHz ['megəhɜːts] *abbr* (*megahertz*) megaherz *m*; (*abbreviation*) MHz.

mi [miː] *n* MUS mi *m*.

miaow [miː'aʊ] 1 *n* maullido. – 2 *i* maullar.

mice [maɪs] *npl* → **mouse**.

mickey ['mɪkɪ] to take the mickey (out of sb.), *n fam* tomarle el pelo (a algn.).

micro ['maɪkrəʊ] *n fam* microordenador *m*, microcomputador *m*.
▲ *pl* **micros**.

microbe ['maɪkrəʊb] *n* microbio.

microbiologist [maɪkrəʊbaɪ'ɒlədʒɪst] *n* microbiólogo,-a.

microbiology [maɪkrəʊbaɪ'ɒlədʒɪ] *n* microbiología.

microchip ['maɪkəʊtʃɪp] *n* microchip *m*, microplaqueta.

microcomputer [maɪkrəʊkəm'pjuːtəʳ] *n* microordenador *m*, microcomputador *m*.

microcosm ['maɪkrəʊkɒzəm] *n* microcosmos *m inv*.

microdot ['maɪkrəʊdɒt] *n* micropunto.
microeconomics [maɪkrəʊekə'nɒmɪks] *n* microeconomía.
microelectronics [maɪkrəʊɪlek'trɒnɪks] *n* microelectrónica.
microfiche ['maɪkrəʊfiːʃ] *n* microficha.
microfilm ['maɪkrəʊfɪlm] **1** *n* microfilme *m*. – **2** *t* microfilmar.
■ **microfilm reader**, lector de microfilmes.
microphone ['maɪkrəfəʊn] *n* micrófono.
microprocessor [maɪkrəʊ'prəʊsesəʳ] *n* microprocesador *m*.
microscope ['maɪkrəskəʊp] *n* microscopio.
microscopic [maɪkrə'skɒpɪk] *adj* microscópico,-a.
microsurgery [maɪkrəʊ'sɜːdʒərɪ] *n* microcirugía.
microwave ['maɪkrəweɪv] **1** *n* microonda. – **2** *t* cocinar en el microondas.
■ **microwave oven**, horno de microondas, microondas *m inv*.
mid- [mɪd] *adj* medio,-a: *in mid-afternoon*, a media tarde; *in mid-May*, a mediados de mayo; *in the mid-1970's*, a mediados de los setenta; *she's in her mid-thirties*, tiene unos treinta y cinco años.
midair [mɪd'eəʳ] *adj* en el aire: *a midair collision*, una colisión en el aire.
● **in midair**, en el aire: *the planes crashed in midair*, los aviones chocaron en el aire.
midday [mɪd'deɪ] **1** *n* mediodía *m*. – **2** *adj* de mediodía.
● **at midday**, al mediodía.
middle ['mɪdəl] **1** *adj* (*central*) de en medio, central; (*medium*) mediano,-a, medio,-a: *our house is the middle one*, nuestra casa es la de en medio; *he's the middle son*, él es el hijo mediano; *the middle fortnight of August*, la quincena central de agosto; *a flat of middle size*, un piso de tamaño mediano. – **2** *n* (*centre*) medio, centro: *there's a pond in the middle of the garden*, hay un estanque en medio del jardín; *stand in the middle of the room*, ponte en el centro de la habitación; *I'm the one in the middle*, soy el de en medio; *he was cycling down the middle of the road*, iba en bici por el centro de la calle; *we sat in the middle of the row*, nos sentamos en medio de la fila; *this doughnut's got jam in the middle*, este donut está relleno de mermelada. **3** (*halfway point of period, activity*) mitad *f*: *in the middle of a storm*, en medio de una tormenta; *in the middle of the night*, en plena noche; *in the middle of winter*, en pleno invierno; *we were right in the middle of lunch*, estábamos en plena comida; *I can't help you now, I'm in the middle of something else*, no puedo ayudarte ahora, estoy haciendo otra cosa; *I'm in the middle of writing this article*, estoy ocupado con este artículo. **4** *fam* (*waist*) cintura.
● **in the middle of nowhere**, en el quinto pino. ‖ **to be in one's middle twenties** (*thirties etc*), tener unos veinticinco (*treinta y cinco etc*) años. ‖ **to be sb.'s middle name**, (*characteristic*) ser algo mismo,-a, ser algo personificado,-a: *kindness is her middle name*, es la bondad misma, es la bondad personificada. ‖ **to split sth. down the middle**, partir algo por la mitad. ‖ **to take a middle course**, tomar una opción intermedia.
■ **middle age**, mediana edad *f*. ‖ **middle America**, (*class*) clase *f* media tradicional estadounidense; (*geographical area*) América Central con Méjico y la Antillas. ‖ **middle C**, do medio. ‖ **middle class**, clase *f* media. ‖ **middle distance**, ART PHOTO segundo plano. ‖ **middle ear**, oído medio. ‖ **Middle East**, Oriente *m* Medio. ‖

Middle English, lengua inglesa entre 1100 y 1450 aproximadamente. ‖ **middle finger**, dedo corazón. ‖ **middle ground**, término medio, acuerdo. ‖ **middle management**, mandos *mpl* intermedios. ‖ **middle name**, segundo nombre *m*. ‖ **middle school**, GB colegio para niños de entre 8 y 13 años. ‖ **the Middle Ages**, la Edad Media.
middle-aged [mɪdəl'eɪdʒd] *adj* de mediana edad.
■ **middle-aged spread**, la curva de la felicidad.
middlebrow ['mɪdəlbraʊ] **1** *n persona de gustos culturales medios*. – **2** *adj* de nivel cultural medio.
middle-class [mɪdəl'klɑːs] *adj* de la clase media.
middle-distance [mɪdəl'dɪstəns] *adj* SP de medio fondo.
■ **middle-distance runner**, mediofondista *mf*.
middleman ['mɪdəlmən] *n* intermediario.
▲ *pl* **middlemen** ['mɪdəlmen].
middle-of-the-road [mɪdələvðə'rəʊd] *adj* (*views, candidate, etc*) moderado,-a; (*music*) para todos los públicos.
middle-sized ['mɪdəlsaɪzd] *adj* de tamaño mediano, mediano,-a.
middleweight ['mɪdəlweɪt] *n* (*boxing*) peso medio.
middling ['mɪdəlɪn] *adj* mediano,-a, regular.
midfield [mɪd'fiːld] **1** *n* SP (*of pitch*) centrocampo. **2** SP (*players*) los centrocampistas *mpl*. – **3** *adj* SP centrocampista.
midfielder [mɪd'fiːldəʳ] *n* SP centrocampista *mf*.
midge [mɪdʒ] *n* mosquito.
midget ['mɪdʒɪt] **1** *n* enano,-a. – **2** *adj* (*very small*) diminuto,-a, pequeñísimo,-a; (*miniature*) en miniatura.
Midlands ['mɪdləndz] *npl* la región central de Inglaterra.
midlife crisis [mɪdlaɪf'kraɪsɪs] *n* crisis *f* de los cuarenta.
midnight ['mɪdnaɪt] *n* medianoche *f*: *we got home at midnight*, llegamos a casa a medianoche; *around midnight*, alrededor de la medianoche.
● **to burn the midnight oil**, quemarse las pestañas.
■ **Midnight Mass**, Misa del gallo. ‖ **midnight sun**, sol *m* de medianoche.
midriff ['mɪdrɪf] **1** *n* (*belly*) estómago. **2** ANAT diafragma *m*.
midshipman ['mɪdʃɪpmən] *n* MAR guardia *m* marina, guardiamarina *m*.
midst¹ [mɪdst] *prep* lit en medio de, entre.
midst² [mɪdst] *n* **in the midst of**, *n* en medio de, entre.
● **in our/your/their midst**, entre nosotros/vosotros/ellos.
midstream [mɪd'striːm] **in midstream**, *n* (*river*) en medio de la corriente.
● **to stop in midstream**, parar en plena parrafada.
midsummer [mɪd'sʌməʳ] **1** *n* pleno verano. – **2** *adj* de pleno verano.
● **midsummer madness**, locura de verano.
■ **Midsummer's Day**, día *m* de San Juan, día *m* 24 de junio.
midway ['mɪdweɪ] **1** *adv* a medio camino, a mitad del camino. – **2** *adj* (*point etc*) intermedio,-a.
midweek ['mɪdwiːk] **1** *adj* de entre semana. – **2** *adv* entre semana.
midwife ['mɪdwaɪf] *n* comadrona, partera, matrona.
midwifery ['mɪdwɪfərɪ] *n* obstetricia.
midwinter [mɪd'wɪntəʳ] **1** *n* pleno invierno. – **2** *adj* de pleno invierno.
miff [mɪf] *t fam* ofender, molestar.
miffed [mɪft] *adj fam* molesto,-a, picado,-a.
miffy ['mɪfɪ] *adj* susceptible.
▲ *comp* **miffier**, *superl* **miffiest**.

might¹ [maɪt] *n* poder *m*, fuerza.
● **might is right,** el poder tiene la razón. ‖ **with all one's might,** con todas sus fuerzas. ‖ **with might and main,** a más no poder, hasta más no poder.

might² [maɪt] **1** *aux* (*possibility*) poder: *we might never see each other again,* es posible que no nos volvamos a ver; *why don't you go out? –I might,* ¿por qué no sales? –puede que lo haga; *don't touch it! it might be a bomb!,* ¡no lo toques! ¡podría ser una bomba!; *that might be them now,* quizás sean ellos ahora, a lo mejor son ellos ahora; *I thought this might happen,* yo me temía que esto podría pasar; *you might have been killed,* podrías haberte matado; *you might think you know everything,* puede que creas saberlo todo; *they might have forgotten about the dinner,* es posible que se hayan olvidado de lo de la cena. **2** (*in suggestions or requests*) poder: *you might try the hardware shop,* podrías probar en la ferretería; *I thought we might go out for lunch,* pensaba que podríamos ir a comer; *you might at least say thank you,* como mínimo podrías darme las gracias; *you might have told me!,* ¡podrías habérmelo dicho!; *you might have waited!,* ¡podrías haber esperado! **3** (*permission*) poder: *might I suggest make a suggestion?,* ¿podría hacer una sugerencia?; *if I might just interrupt,* si pudiera interrumpir; *he asked if he might come in,* pidió permiso para entrar; *who are you, if I might ask?,* ¿quién eres tú? si se puede saber. **4** (*sarcastic use*) *and where might that be?,* ¿y dónde se supone que está eso?; *and who might you be?,* ¿y tú quién demonios eres? **5** (*subjunctive use*) poder: *he died that others might live,* murió para que otros pudieran vivir, murió para que otros vivieran.
● **I might have known!,** ¡debí imaginármelo!, ¡típico! ‖ **might (just) as well,** más vale que: *you might as well give it away,* más vale que lo regales.
▲ *Véase también* **may**.

mightily [ˈmaɪtɪlɪ] **1** *adv* (*with great effort*) vigorosamente, con todas sus fuerzas. **2** *fam* (*very*) muy, enormemente, sumamente.

mighty [ˈmaɪtɪ] **1** *adj* (*very strong*) muy fuerte; (*powerful*) poderoso,-a, potente. **2** (*great, imposing*) enorme, imponente. **– 3** *adv* us *fam* (*very*) muy. **– 4** **the mighty,** *npl* los poderosos *mpl*.
▲ *comp* **mightier,** *superl* **mightiest.**

migraine [ˈmaɪgreɪn] *n* jaqueca, migraña.

migrant [ˈmaɪgrənt] **1** *adj* migratorio,-a. **– 2** *n* (*person*) emigrante *mf*; (*bird*) ave *f* migratoria.
■ **migrant worker,** trabajador,-ra emigrante.

migrate [maɪˈgreɪt] *i* migrar.

migration [maɪˈgreɪʃən] *n* migración *f*.

migratory [ˈmaɪgrətərɪ] *adj* migratorio,-a.

mike [maɪk] *n fam* micro *m*.

mild [maɪld] **1** *adj* (*person, character*) apacible, afable, dulce. **2** (*climate, weather*) benigno,-a, templado,-a, suave, blando,-a; (*soap, detergent*) suave: *it's been a mild winter,* ha hecho un invierno suave. **3** (*food, tobacco*) suave. **4** (*protest, attempt*) ligero,-a; (*punishment, fever*) leve; (*illness, attack*) ligero,-a, leve; (*criticism, rebuke*) suave, leve. **– 5** **mild (ale),** *n* GB (*beer*) cerveza de sabor suave.
■ **mild steel,** acero bajo en carbono.

mildew [ˈmɪldjuː] **1** *n* (*on fabric, wall*) moho. **2** (*on plants*) mildiu *m*, mildeu *m*.

mildly [ˈmaɪldlɪ] **1** *adv* (*softly, gently*) suavemente. **2** (*slightly*) ligeramente.
● **to put it mildly,** por no decir algo peor.

mildness [ˈmaɪldnəs] **1** *n* (*of person, character*) apacibilidad *f*, afabilidad. **2** (*of climate, weather*) suavidad *f*, lo templado; (*of soap, detergent*) suavidad *f*. **3** (*of food, tobacco*) suavidad *f*. **4** (*of punishment, illness*) levedad *f*.

mile [maɪl] **1** *n* milla (1,6 kms): *the beach is a mile from the hotel,* la playa está a una milla del hotel; *he was driving at 80 miles an hour,* conducía a 80 millas por hora. **– 2** **miles,** *npl* (*much*) mucho, muchísimo: *I'm miles better,* estoy mucho mejor; *it's miles away,* está muy lejos; *you're miles out,* vas muy mal encaminado, estás muy equivocado; *he's the best player by miles,* es el mejor jugador con diferencia.
● **to be miles from anywhere,** estar en el quinto pino. ‖ **to run a mile (from sth./sb.),** salir corriendo (para evitar algo/a algn.). ‖ **to see sth. a mile off,** ver algo a la legua. ‖ **to stick out a mile,** verse a la legua, notarse a la legua, saltar a la vista.

mileage [ˈmaɪlɪdʒ] **1** *n* AUTO (*miles travelled by a car*) ≈ kilómetros *mpl*, kilometraje *m*: *a car with a low mileage,* un coche con pocos kilómetros; *what mileage does this car do to the gallon?,* ¿cuánto gasta este coche a los cien kilómetros? **2** *fam fig* (*benefit, advantage, use*) jugo, partido: *the press can get a lot of mileage out of this,* la prensa puede sacarle mucho partido a esto, la prensa puede explotar esto al máximo.
■ **mileage allowance,** ≈ kilometraje *m*.

mileometer [maɪˈlɒmɪtəʳ] *n* AUTO = cuentakilómetros *m*.

milestone [ˈmaɪlstəʊn] **1** *n* hito, mojón *m*. **2** *fig* hito.

milieu [ˈmiːljɜː] *n* entorno, medio ambiente.
▲ *pl* **milieux** [ˈmiːljəː] o **milieus** [ˈmiːljəːz].

militant [ˈmɪlɪtənt] **1** *adj* POL militante. **– 2** *n* POL militante *mf*.

militarism [ˈmɪlɪtərɪzəm] *n* militarismo.

militarist [ˈmɪlɪtərɪst] *n* militarista *mf*.

militaristic [mɪlɪtəˈrɪstɪk] *adj* militarista.

military [ˈmɪlɪtərɪ] **1** *adj* militar. **– 2** **the military,** *n* los militares, las fuerzas armadas.
● **to do one's military service,** hacer el servicio militar.
■ **military service,** servicio militar.

militate [ˈmɪlɪteɪt] **to militate against,** *phr fml* ir en contra de, incidir negativamente en.

militia [mɪˈlɪʃə] *n* milicia.

militiaman [mɪˈlɪʃəmən] *n* miliciano.
▲ *pl* **militiamen.**

milk [mɪlk] **1** *n* (*gen*) leche *f*. **– 2** *adj* (*bottle, production*) de leche; (*product*) lácteo,-a. **– 3** *t* (*from cow, goat*) ordeñar. **4** (*from plant, tree*) sacar, extraer; (*from snake*) extraer el veneno de. **5** *fig* (*exploit*) chupar, sacar jugo a: *they milked what they could out of the system,* chuparon lo que pudieron del sistema. **– 6** *i* (*of cow, goat*) dar leche.
● **it's no use crying over spilt milk,** a lo hecho, pecho. ‖ **to milk sth. for all its worth / milk sth. dry,** chupar la sangre a algo, sacar todo el jugo a algo.
■ **condensed milk,** leche *f* condensada. ‖ **dried milk,** leche *f* en polvo. ‖ **powdered milk,** leche *f* en polvo. ‖ **evaporated milk,** leche *f* evaporada. ‖ **milk churn,** lechera. ‖ **milk float,** furgoneta (*del reparto de la leche*). ‖ **milk of magnesia,** leche *f* de magnesia. ‖ **milk pudding,** arroz *m* etc con leche. ‖ **milk round,** (*milkman's route*) recorrido del repartidor de la leche; (*univ*) visitas que hacen las grandes empresas a universidades para buscar personal. ‖ **milk shake,** batido. ‖ **milk tooth,** diente *m* de leche. ‖ **pasteurized milk,** leche *f* pasterizada. ‖ **semi-skimmed milk,** leche semi-desnatada. ‖ **skimmed milk,** leche desnatada, leche descremada. ‖ **the milk of human kindness,** la humanidad *f*, la bondad humana *f*. ‖ **whole milk,** leche *f* entera.

milking [ˈmɪlkɪn] *n* ordeño.
● **to do the milking,** ordeñar.

■ **milking machine,** ordeñadora (mecánica).

milkmaid ['mɪlkmeɪd] *n* lechera.

milkman ['mɪlkmən] *n* lechero, repartidor *m* de la leche.
▲ *pl milkmen* ['mɪlkmen].

milky ['mɪlkɪ] **1** *adj* (*liquid, jewel*) turbio,-a. **2** (*coffee, tea*) con mucha leche; (*substance*) lechoso,-a. **3** (*colour*) pálido,-a.
■ **Milky Way,** Vía Láctea.
▲ *comp milkier, superl milkiest.*

mill [mɪl] **1** *n* (*machinery*) molino. **2** (*for coffee, pepper, etc*) molinillo. **3** (*factory*) fábrica: *cotton mill,* hilandería; *paper mill,* fábrica de papel. **4** (*for metals*) fresadora. – **5** *t* (*crush, grind*) moler. **6** (*shape metal*) fresar.
◆ **to mill about/around** *i* arremolinarse, apiñarse.
● **to go through the mill,** pasarlas moradas. ‖ **to put sb. through the mill,** hacérselas pasar moradas a algn., hacerle sudar la gota gorda a algn.

millennium [mɪ'lenɪəm] *n* milenio, milenario.

miller ['mɪlə'] *n* molinero,-a.

millet ['mɪlɪt] *n* mijo.

millibar ['mɪlɪbɑː'] *n* milibar *m.*

milligram ['mɪlɪgræm] *n* miligramo.

millilitre ['mɪlɪliːtə'] *n* mililitro.

millimetre ['mɪlɪmiːtə'] *n* milímetro.

milliner ['mɪlɪnə'] *n* sombrerero,-a.

millinery ['mɪlɪnərɪ] **1** *n* (*hats*) sombreros *mpl* de señora. **2** (*shop*) sombrerería.

milling ['mɪlɪŋ] **1** *n* AGR molienda. **2** (*of steel*) laminado.
■ **milling machine,** fresadora.

million ['mɪljən] **1** *n* millón *m: one million dollars,* un millón de dólares; *three million people,* tres millones de personas. – **2 millions,** *npl fam* (*lots*) millones *mpl.*
● **like a million dollars,** maravilloso,-a, fantástico,-a. ‖ **to be one in a million,** (*person*) ser una joya, ser uno entre un millón. ‖ **to have a chance in a million,** tener una remotísima posibilidad.

millionaire [mɪljə'neə'] *n* millonario,-a.

millionairess [mɪljə'eəres] *n* millonaria.

millionth ['mɪljənθ] **1** *adj* millonésimo,-a. – **2** *n* millonésimo, millonésima parte *f.*

millipede ['mɪlɪpiːd] *n* milpiés *m inv.*

millisecond ['mɪlɪsekənd] *n* milésima de segundo.

millstone ['mɪlstəʊn] *n* muela, rueda de molino.
● **to be a millstone round sb.'s neck,** ser una cruz para algn.

mime [maɪm] **1** *n* (*art*) mimo. **2** (*performance*) pantomima, representación *f* de mimo. **3** (*person*) mimo *mf.* – **4** *t* (*express by mime*) expresar haciendo mímica: *she mimed the answer to me,* me explicó la respuesta haciendo mímica; *he mimed someone eating spaghetti,* hizo mímica simulando que comía espaguettis. – **5** *i* (*pretend to sing*) hacer playback.

mimic ['mɪmɪk] **1** *n* imitador,-ra, remedador,-ra. – **2** *t* (*copy*) imitar, remedar. **3** BIOL (*sound*) imitar; (*appearance*) imitar la apariencia de.
▲ *pt & pp mimicked, ger mimicking.*

mimicry ['mɪmɪkrɪ] **1** *n* (*art*) mímica; (*imitation*) imitación *f*, remedo. **2** BIOL mimetismo.

mimosa [mɪ'məʊzə] *n* mimosa.

minaret ['mɪnəret] *n* alminar *m*, minarete *m.*

mince [mɪns] **1** *n* GB CULIN (*meat*) carne *f* picada. – **2** *t* (*chop, cut*) picar. – **3** *i* (*walk*) andar de manera amanerada; (*speak*) hablar con afectación.
● **not to mince one's words,** no tener pelos en la lengua.

■ **mince pie,** CULIN pastelito de picadillo de fruta.

mincemeat ['mɪnsmiːt] **1** *n* (*sweet*) conserva de picadillo de fruta. **2** US CULIN (*meat*) carne *f* picada.
● **to make mincemeat of sb.,** hacer picadillo a algn.: *he'll make mincemeat of you,* te hará picadillo.

mincer ['mɪnsə'] *n* máquina de picar carne, picadora de carne.

mincing ['mɪnsɪŋ] *adj* afectado,-a, amanerado,-a.

mind [maɪnd] **1** *n* (*intellect*) mente *f: she's got a brilliant mind,* tiene una mente brillante. **2** (*mentality*) mentalidad *f: you've got a dirty mind!,* ¡qué guarro eres! **3** (*brain, thoughts*) cabeza, cerebro: *her mind was very confused,* estaba confusa; *my mind went blank,* me quedé en blanco. **4** (*person*) cerebro. – **5** *t* (*heed, pay attention to*) hacer caso de; (*care about*) importar, preocupar: *don't mind me!,* ¡no me hagas caso!; *I mind what people say,* me importa lo que dice la gente. **6** (*be careful with*) tener cuidado con: *mind the step!,* ¡cuidado con el escalón!; *mind your head!,* ¡ojo con la cabeza! **7** (*look after - child*) cuidar, cuidar de; (- *house*) vigilar; (- *shop*; - *seat, place*) guardar: *could you mind the baby for a minute?,* ¿me puedes cuidar el bebé un momento? **8** (*object to, be troubled by*) tener inconveniente en, importar, molestar: *I don't mind staying,* no tengo inconveniente en quedarme, no me importa quedarme; *are you sure you don't mind going?,* ¿seguro que no te importa ir?; *do you mind the noise?,* ¿te molesta el ruido?; *would you mind waiting?,* ¿le importaría esperar? **9** (*fancy, quite like*) venir bien: *I wouldn't mind a coffee,* me vendría bien un café. – **10** *i* (*be careful*) tener cuidado: *mind (out)!,* ¡cuidado!, ¡ojo! **11** (*object to*) importar, molestar, tener inconveniente: *do you mind if I open the window?,* ¿le importa que abra la ventana?; *would you mind if I used your phone?,* ¿podría utilizar su teléfono?; *I hope you don't mind,* espero que no te importe; *do you want a biscuit? –I don't mind if I do!,* ¿quieres una galleta? –¡pues sí!; *she won't mind,* no le importará; *if you don't mind,* si no tienes inconveniente.
● **mind you ...,** ten en cuenta que ..., la verdad es que ... ‖ **mind your own business,** no te metas en lo que no te importa. ‖ **never mind,** (*it doesn't matter*) no importa, da igual; (*don't worry*) no te preocupes; (*let alone*) ni hablar de. ‖ **never you mind!,** ¿a ti qué te importa? ‖ **to be all in the mind,** no ser más que imaginaciones. ‖ **to be in one's right mind,** estar en su sano juicio. ‖ **to be in two minds about sth.,** estar indeciso,-a respecto a algo. ‖ **to be of one mind / be of the same mind,** ser del mismo parecer, tener la misma opinión. ‖ **to be of sound mind,** estar en pleno uso de sus facultades (mentales). ‖ **to be on one's mind,** preocupar a uno. ‖ **to be out of one's mind,** estar loco,-a. ‖ **to bear sth. in mind,** tener algo en cuenta, tener algo presente. ‖ **to blow sb.'s mind,** alucinar a algn. ‖ **to bring sth. to mind / call sth. to mind,** recordar algo, traer algo a la memoria. ‖ **to change one's mind,** cambiar de opinión, cambiar de parecer. ‖ **to come to mind,** ocurrírsele a uno, venir a la mente. ‖ **to cross sb.'s mind,** ocurrírsele a algn., pasar por la cabeza de algn. ‖ **to get sth./sb. out of one's mind,** quitarse algo/a algn. de la cabeza. ‖ **to give one's mind to sth.,** aplicarse en algo. ‖ **to give sb. a piece of one's mind,** decir cuatro verdades a algn. ‖ **to go out of one's mind,** volverse loco,-a. ‖ **to have a mind of one's own,** saber decidirse por sí mismo,-a. ‖ **to have a good mind to do sth.,** estar por hacer algo, estar casi decidido,-a a hacer algo. ‖ **to have half a mind to do sth.,** estar por hacer algo, estar casi de-

cidido,-a a hacer algo. ‖ to have it in mind to do sth., pensar hacer algo. ‖ to have sb./sth. in mind, estar pensando en algn./algo. ‖ to have sth. on one's mind, estar preocupado,-a por algo. ‖ to keep an open mind, tener una mente abierta. ‖ to keep one's mind on sth., estar atento,-a a algo, prestar atención a algo, concentrarse en algo. ‖ to lose one's mind, perder el juicio. ‖ to make up one's mind, decidirse. ‖ to put sb. in mind of sth., recordarle a algn. algo. ‖ to put sth. out of one's mind, no pensar más en algo. ‖ to put/set sb.'s mind at ease/rest, tranquilizar a algn. ‖ to put/set/turn one's mind to sth., proponerse algo. ‖ to slip sb.'s mind, olvidársele a uno: *it slipped my mind*, se me olvidó. ‖ to sb.'s mind, en la opinión de algn.: *to my mind*, en mi opinión, a mi parecer. ‖ to speak one's mind, hablar sin rodeos, decir lo que uno piensa. ‖ to take a load/weight off sb.'s mind, quitarle a algn. un peso de encima. ‖ to take sb.'s mind off sth., distraer a algn. ‖ to turn sth. over in one's mind, darle vueltas a algo.

mind-blowing ['maɪndbləʊɪŋ] *adj* alucinante.

mind-boggling ['maɪndbɒgəlɪŋ] *adj fam* alucinante, inconcebible.

minded ['maɪndɪd] *adj fml* inclinado,-a.

minder ['maɪndər] 1 *n fam* (*bodyguard*) guardaespaldas *m inv*, gorila *m*. 2 (*attendant*) persona encargada de cuidar algo: *she works as a child minder*, trabaja de niñera; *machine minder*, vigilante de una máquina.

mindful ['maɪndfʊl] *adj fml* consciente (of, de).

mindless ['maɪndləs] 1 *adj* (*tedious*) monótono,-a, mecánico,-a. 2 *pej* (*senseless - behaviour*) absurdo,-a, estúpido,-a, carente de sentido; (*person*) - salvaje.
■ mindless violence, violencia gratuita.

mind-reader ['maɪndriːdər] *n* adivino,-a.

mind-reading ['maɪndriːdɪŋ] *n* adivinación *f* de pensamientos.

mine[1] [maɪn] 1 *n* (*gen*) mina. – 2 *t* (*coal, gold, etc*) extraer; (*area*) explotar. 3 *MIL* sembrar minas en, minar. – 4 *i* explotar una mina: *they're mining for coal*, están explotando una mina de carbón, están buscando carbón.
● to be a mine of information, ser una mina de información, ser un pozo de información. ‖ to go down the mine, trabajar en las minas. ‖ to work a mine, explotar una mina.

mine[2] [maɪn] *pron* (el) mío, (la) mía, (los) míos, (las) mías, lo mío: *hey! that's mine!*, ¡ey! ¡eso es mío!; *here are your gloves but where are mine?*, aquí están tus guantes, ¿pero dónde están los míos?; *a friend of mine*, un/una amigo,-a mío,-a; *this money is mine*, este dinero es mío.

minefield ['maɪnfiːld] *n* campo de minas.

minelayer ['maɪnleɪər] *n* minador *m*.

miner ['maɪnər] *n* minero,-a.

mineral ['mɪnərəl] 1 *adj* mineral. – 2 *n* mineral *m*.
■ mineral oil, GB petróleo; US parafina líquida, aceite *m* de parafina. ‖ mineral water, agua mineral.

mineralogy [mɪnəˈrælədʒɪ] *n* mineralogía.

minestrone [mɪnɪˈstrəʊnɪ] *n* (sopa) minestrone *f*.

minesweeper ['maɪnswiːpər] *n* dragaminas *m inv*.

mineworker ['maɪnwɜːkər] *n* minero,-a.

mingle ['mɪŋgəl] 1 *t* mezclar. – 2 *i* (*liquids*) mezclarse; (*sounds, smells, etc*) confundirse. 3 (*people*) circular, mezclarse con la gente.

mingy ['mɪndʒɪ] *adj* GB *fam* (*person*) tacaño,-a, roñoso,-a, rácano,-a; (*amount, portion*) miserable, mezquino,-a.
▲ *comp* mingier, *superl* mingiest.

mini ['mɪnɪ] 1 *n* (*car*) mini *m*. 2 (*skirt*) minifalda, mini *f*.

miniature ['mɪnɪtʃər] 1 *n* miniatura. – 2 *adj* (en) miniatura.
● in miniature, en miniatura.
■ miniature artist, miniaturista *mf*. ‖ miniature golf, minigolf *m*.

minibus ['mɪnɪbʌs] *n* microbús *m*.

minicab ['mɪnɪkæb] *n* GB taxi *m*.

minicomputer [mɪnɪkəmˈpjuːtər] *n* microordenador *m*.

minim ['mɪnɪm] *n* GB MUS blanca.

minimal ['mɪnɪməl] *adj* mínimo,-a.

minimise ['mɪnɪmaɪz] *t* → minimize.

minimize ['mɪnɪmaɪz] 1 *t* (*reduce*) minimizar, reducir al mínimo. 2 (*play down*) minimizar, quitar importancia a.

minimum ['mɪnɪməm] 1 *adj* mínimo,-a. – 2 *n* mínimo: *try to walk for a minimum of thirty minutes*, intenta caminar durante un mínimo de treinta minutos; *we must reduce costs to a minimum*, hay que reducir los gastos al mínimo; *it'll cost a minimum of £200*, costará como mínimo £200.
■ minimum lending rate, tipo de interés mínimo. ‖ minimum wage, salario mínimo.

mining ['maɪnɪŋ] 1 *n* minería, explotación *f* de minas: *coal mining*, extracción de carbón. – 2 *adj* (*area, town, industry*) minero,-a.
■ mining engineer, ingeniero,-a de minas.

minion ['mɪnjən] *n pej* adlátere *mf*.

mini-roundabout [mɪnɪˈraʊndəbaʊt] *n* AUTO rotonda pequeña.

miniseries [mɪnɪˈsɪəriːz] *n* TV miniserie *f*.

miniskirt ['mɪnɪskɜːt] *n* minifalda.

minister ['mɪnɪstər] 1 *n* GB POL ministro,-a (for, de): *Minister of Defence*, Ministro,-a de Defensa. 2 (*diplomat*) ministro,-a plenipotenciario,-a. 3 GB REL pastor,-ra. – 4 *i* atender (to, a), cuidar (to, a).
■ minister without portfolio, ministro,-a sin cartera.

ministerial [mɪnɪˈstɪərɪəl] *adj* ministerial: *ministerial crisis*, crisis de gobierno; *ministerial office*, cargo de ministro.

ministry ['mɪnɪstrɪ] 1 *n* GB POL ministerio. 2 the ministry, GB REL el clero, la clerecía, el sacerdocio.
● to enter the ministry, (*catholic*) hacerse sacerdote; (*protestant*) hacerse pastor, hacerse clérigo.
▲ *pl* ministries.

mink [mɪŋk] *n* visón *m*.
■ mink coat, abrigo de visón.

minnow ['mɪnəʊ] *n* piscardo.

minor ['maɪnər] 1 *adj* (*unimportant*) menor; (*secondary*) secundario,-a: *it caused minor damage*, ocasionó daños menores; *he got a minor part in a film*, consiguió un papel secundario en una película; *a minor operation*, una operación de poca importancia. 2 MUS menor: *in a minor key*, en tono menor; *in F minor*, en fa menor. – 3 *n* JUR menor *mf*: *he's a minor*, es menor de edad.
■ minor offence, JUR delito de menor cuantía. ‖ minor planet, asteroide *m*.

Minorca [mɪˈnɔːkə] *n* Menorca.

Minorcan [mɪˈnɔːkən] 1 *adj* menorquín,-ina. – 2 *n* (*person*) menorquín,-ina.

minority [maɪˈnɒrɪtɪ] 1 *n* minoría: *a small minority spoilt the party*, una pequeña minoría estropeó la fiesta; *only a minority of people don't have a TV*, sólo una minoría de personas no tiene televisor. 2 JUR minoría de edad. – 3 *adj* minoritario,-a.
● to be in a minority, estar en minoría.
■ religious minority, minoría religiosa.

▲ *pl* minorities.

minster ['mɪnstə'] *n* iglesia importante, catedral *f*.

minstrel ['mɪnstrəl] *n* trovador *m*, juglar *m*.

mint[1] [mɪnt] **1** *n* FIN (*place*) casa de la moneda. **2** *fam* (*large amount of money*) dineral *m*, fortuna. – **3** *t* (*coins, words*) acuñar.
● in mint condition, en perfecto estado.

mint[2] [mɪnt] **1** *n* BOT menta. **2** (*sweet*) caramelo de menta; (*chocolate*) bombón *m* de menta.
■ mint sauce, salsa de menta.

minuet [mɪnjʊ'et] *n* minué *m*.

minus ['maɪnəs] **1** *prep* MATH menos: *four minus three equals one*, cuatro menos tres es igual a uno. **2** METEOR bajo cero: *minus five degrees*, cinco grados bajo cero. **3** *fam* (*without*) sin. – **4** *adj* negativo,-a. – **5** *n* MATH menos *m*. **6** (*disadvantage*) desventaja, contra *m*.
■ minus sign, signo de menos, menos *m*.

minuscule ['mɪnəskjuːl] *adj* minúsculo.

minute[1] [maɪ'njuːt] **1** *adj* (*tiny*) diminuto,-a, minúsculo,-a. **2** (*precise, exact*) minucioso,-a, detallado,-a.

minute[2] ['mɪnɪt] **1** *n* (*of time*) minuto: *the train leaves at seven minutes past four*, el tren sale a las cuatro y siete minutos; *it's a five minute walk*, es un paseo de cinco minutos. **2** *fam* (*moment*) momento; (*instant*) instante *m*: *I'll be back in a minute*, ahora vuelvo, vuelvo en un momento; *hang on a minute*, espera un momento; *this very minute*, ahora mismo, este mismo instante. **3** (*of angle*) minuto. – **4** *t* (*make note, record*) hacer constar en el acta. – **5** minutes, *npl* (*notes*) acta *f sing*, actas *fpl*.
● (at) any minute now, en cualquier momento, de un momento a otro. ‖ at the last minute, en el último momento, a última hora. ‖ the minute (that), en el momento en que. ‖ to leave sth. till the last minute, dejar algo para el último momento.
■ minute book, libro de actas. ‖ minute hand, minutero.

minutiae [mɪ'njuːʃiː] *npl* pequeños detalles *mpl*.

miracle ['mɪrəkəl] **1** *n* (*gen*) milagro: *it was a miracle she didn't fall*, fue un milagro que no se cayera; *an economic miracle*, un milagro económico. – **2** *adj* milagroso,-a: *miracle drug*, remedio milagroso.
● to do/work miracles, hacer milagros.
■ miracle play, auto.

miraculous [mɪ'rækjələs] *adj* milagroso,-a: *he made a miraculous recovery*, su recuperación fue milagrosa; *we had a miraculous escape*, nos salvamos de milagro.

miraculously [mɪ'rækjələslɪ] *adv* de milagro, milagrosamente.

mirage [mɪ'rɑːʒ] *n* espejismo.

mire ['maɪə'] **1** *n* (*mud*) fango, lodo; (*muddy area*) lodazal *m*. **2** *fig* (*unpleasant situation*) atolladero, lío, embrollo.
● to drag sb.'s name through the mire, manchar la reputación de algn.

mirror ['mɪrə'] **1** *n* (*gen*) espejo: *stop looking at yourself in the mirror*, deja de mirarte en el espejo. **2** *fig* espejo, reflejo. – **3** *t* reflejar.
■ driving mirror, espejo (retrovisor). ‖ mirror image, imagen *f* especular.

mirth [mɜːθ] *n* (*happiness*) alegría, regocijo; (*laughter*) risas *fpl*.

misadventure [mɪsəd'ventʃə'] *n* desventura, desgracia.
● death by misadventure, GB JUR muerte *f* accidental.

misanthrope ['mɪzənθrəʊp] *n* misántropo,-a.

misanthropist [mɪ'zænθrəpɪst] *n* misántropo,-a.

misapprehend [mɪsæprɪ'hend] *t fml* entender mal, malinterpretar.

misapprehension [mɪsæprɪ'henʃən] *n* malentendido, equivocación *f*.
● to labour under a misapprehension, estar equivocado,-a, creer equivocadamente.

misappropriate [mɪsə'prəʊprɪeɪt] *t* malversar.

misappropriation [mɪsəpəʊprɪ'eɪʃən] *n* malversación *f*.

misbehave [mɪsbɪ'heɪv] *i* portarse mal, comportarse mal.

misbehaviour [mɪsbɪ'heɪvjə'] *n* mala conducta, mal comportamiento.

miscalculate [mɪs'kælkjəleɪt] **1** *t* calcular mal. – **2** *i* calcular mal.

miscalculation [mɪskælkjə'leɪʃən] *n* error *m* de cálculo.

miscarriage [mɪs'kærɪdʒ] *n* MED aborto (espontáneo).
■ miscarriage of justice, JUR error *m* judicial.

miscarry [mɪs'kærɪ] **1** *i* MED abortar (espontáneamente), tener un aborto. **2** (*plans etc*) fracasar, frustrarse, malograrse. **3** (*letters etc*) extraviarse.
▲ *pt & pp* miscarried, *ger* miscarrying.

miscast [mɪs'kɑːst] *t* dar un papel poco apropiado a.
● to be miscast, tener un papel poco apropiado.
▲ *pt & pp* miscast.

miscellaneous [mɪsɪ'leɪnɪəs] *adj* (*mixed, varied*) variado,-a, vario,-a, diverso,-a, misceláneo,-a: *miscellaneous goods*, artículos diversos; *look in the box marked "miscellaneous"*, mira en la caja que pone "varios".

miscellany [mɪ'selənɪ] **1** *n* (*mixture*) miscelánea. **2** (*book*) antología.
▲ *pl* miscellanies.

mischance [mɪs'tʃɑːns] *n fml* desgracia, mala suerte *f*.

mischief ['mɪstʃɪf] **1** *n* (*naughtiness*) travesura, diablura: *he's always getting into mischief*, siempre anda metido en travesuras; *I know you're up to some mischief*, sé que estás haciendo alguna travesura. **2** *fml* daño, mal *m*.
● to do os. a mischief, hacerse daño. ‖ to make mischief, crear problemas.

mischievous ['mɪstʃɪvəs] **1** *adj* (*naughty - person*) travieso,-a; (*- look, grin, etc*) pícaro,-a. **2** (*causing harm*) malicioso,-a.

misconceived [mɪskən'siːvd] *adj* (*badly planned*) desacertado,-a, equivocado,-a, mal pensado,-a.

misconception [mɪskən'sepʃən] *n* idea equivocada, idea falsa, concepto erróneo, concepto falso.

misconduct [mɪs'kɒndʌkt] **1** *n* (*improper behaviour*) mala conducta. **2** (*bad management*) mala administración *f*. – **3** *t* administrar mal.
■ professional misconduct, falta de ética profesional.

misconstruction [mɪskən'strʌkʃən] *n* mala interpretación *f*.
● to be open to misconstruction, poder interpretarse mal, poder malinterpretarse.

misconstrue [mɪskən'struː] *t* interpretar mal, malinterpretar.

miscount [mɪs'kaʊnt] **1** *t* contar mal. – **2** *n* cómputo erróneo.

misdeed [mɪs'diːd] *n fml* delito, fechoría.

misdemeanour [mɪsdɪ'miːnə'] **1** *n fam* (*misdeed*) fechoría. **2** JUR delito menor.

misdirect [mɪsdɪ'rekt] **1** *t* (*letter*) poner mal las señas en. **2** (*person*) orientar mal a, informar mal a. **3** (*energy, talent, qualities, etc*) encaminar mal, encauzar mal; (*money*) emplear mal; (*funds*) malversar. **4** JUR (*inform incorrectly*) instruir mal.

miser ['maɪzə'] *n* avaro,-a.

miserable ['mɪzərəbəl] **1** *adj* (*person - unhappy*) abatido,- a, triste, deprimido,-a, infeliz; (- *bad-tempered*) antipático,-a. **2** (*place etc*) deprimente, triste; (*weather*) horrible, malísimo,-a. **3** (*paltry*) miserable, mezquino,-a, despreciable; (*pathetic*) lamentable: *a miserable wage,* un sueldo mezquino.

miserably ['mɪzərəblɪ] **1** *adv* (*unhappily*) tristemente. **2** (*poorly*) miserablemente. **3** (*pathetically*) lamentablemente, de manera lamentable; (*badly*) pésimamente.

miserly ['maɪzəlɪ] *adj* avaro,-a, tacaño,-a, mezquino,-a.

misery ['mɪzərɪ] **1** *n* (*wretchedness, unhappiness*) desgracia, desdicha, tristeza. **2** (*suffering*) sufrimiento, dolor *m*, suplicio. **3** (*poverty*) pobreza, miseria. **4** *fam* (*person*) amargado,-a.
● to make sb.'s life a misery, amargarle la vida a algn. ‖ to put sb. out of their misery, no hacer esperar más a algn.: *put me out of my misery and tell me what happened,* no me tengas más tiempo en ascuas y cuéntame lo que pasó. ‖ to put an animal out of its misery, sacrificar un animal.
▲ *pl* miseries.

misfire [mɪs'faɪəʳ] *i* fallar.

misfit ['mɪsfɪt] *n* (*person*) inadaptado,-a.

misfortune [mɪs'fɔːtʃən] *n* infortunio, desgracia, mala fortuna.

misgiving [mɪs'gɪvɪŋ] *n* (*doubt*) duda, recelo; (*fear*) temor *m*; (*worry*) preocupación *f*: *I had misgivings about lending him the money,* le presté el dinero con recelo, le presté el dinero pero no sin recelo.

misguided [mɪs'gaɪdɪd] *adj* desacertado,-a, equivocado,-a.

mishandle [mɪs'hændəl] *t* (*deal with badly*) llevar mal, manejar mal; (*treat roughly*) maltratar.

mishap ['mɪshæp] *n* percance *m*, contratiempo.
● without mishap, sin contratiempo.

mishear [mɪs'hɪəʳ] **1** *t* oír mal, entender mal: *I think I misheard you,* creo que te he oído bien. – **2** *i* oír mal.
▲ *pt & pp* misheard [mɪs'hɜːd].

mishit [mɪs'hɪt] *t* golpear mal, dar mal a.

mishmash ['mɪʃmæʃ] *n fam* batiburrillo, mezcolanza.

misinform [mɪsɪn'fɔːm] *t* informar mal.

misinformation [mɪsɪnfə'meɪʃən] *n* información *f* errónea, información *f* falsa.

misinterpret [mɪsɪn'tɜːprət] *t* (*accidentally*) interpretar mal; (*deliberatelt*) tergiversar.

misinterpretation [mɪsɪntɜːprɪ'teɪʃən] *n* (*accidental*) mala interpretación *f*; (*deliberate*) tergiversación *f*.

misjudge [mɪs'dʒʌdʒ] **1** *t* (*person, situation*) juzgar mal. **2** (*distance, speed, etc*) calcular mal.

mislay [mɪs'leɪ] *t* extraviar, perder.
▲ *pt & pp* mislaid [mɪs'leɪd], ger *mislaying.*

mislead [mɪs'liːd] **1** *t* (*muddle*) despistar; (*deceive*) engañar: *we were misled into believing that the house was new,* nos engañaron haciéndonos creer que la casa era nueva. **2** (*lead in wrong direction*) llevar en dirección equivocada, enseñar el mal camino a. **3** *fig* (*lead astray*) llevar por mal camino. **4** JUR inducir a error.
● to be misled, dejarse engañar. ‖ to mislead sb. into doing sth., engañar a algn. para que haga algo.
▲ *pt & pp* misled [mɪs'led], ger *misleading.*

misleading [mɪs'liːdɪŋ] *adj* engañoso,-a, falso,-a.

mismanage [mɪs'mænɪdʒ] *t* dirigir mal, administrar mal.

mismanagement [mɪs'mænɪdʒmənt] *n* mala administración *f*.

misogynist [mɪ'sɒdʒənɪst] *n* misógino,-a.

misogyny [mɪ'sɒdʒənɪ] *n* misoginia.

misplace [mɪs'pleɪs] **1** *t* (*mislay*) perder, extraviar. **2** (*trust etc*) encauzar mal: *your confidence in me is misplaced,* no merezco tu confianza. **3** (*put in wrong job*) colocar mal.

misplaced [mɪs'pleɪst] **1** *adj* (*mislaid*) extraviado,-a, perdido,-a. **2** (*trust etc*) inapropiado,-a, equivocado,-a. **3** (*word, remark*) fuera de lugar; (*accent*) mal puesto,-a. **4** (*in wrong job*) mal colocado,-a.

misprint ['mɪsprɪnt] **1** *n* errata, error *m* de imprenta. – **2** *t* imprimir mal.

mispronounce [mɪsprə'naʊns] *t* pronunciar mal.

mispronounciation [mɪsprənʌnsɪ'eɪʃən] *n* pronunciación *f* incorrecta.

misquotation [mɪskwəʊ'teɪʃən] *n* cita incorrecta.

misquote [mɪs'kwəʊt] *t* (*accidentally*) citar incorrectamente; (*deliberately*) distorsionar las palabras de.

misread [mɪs'riːd] **1** *t* (*read wrongly*) leer mal. **2** (*interpret wrongly*) interpretar mal, malinterpretar.
▲ *pt & pp* misread [mɪs'red], ger *misreading.*

misrepresent [mɪsreprɪ'zent] *t* (*person*) tergiversar la palabras de; (*words*) tergiversar, distorsionar; (*actions, facts*) deformar, falsear.

misrepresentation [mɪsreprɪzen'teɪʃən] *n* (*of truth etc*) falsificación *f*, deformación *f*; (*of words etc*) tergiversación *f*, distorsión *f*.

miss¹ [mɪs] **1** *n* señorita: *Miss Brown,* la señorita Brown. **2** (*beauty contestant*) miss *f*: *Miss World,* Miss Mundo.

miss² [mɪs] **1** *n* (*catch, hit, etc*) fallo; (*shot*) tiro errado. – **2** *t* (*not to hit, score, etc*) fallar; (*shot*) errar: *he missed a penalty,* falló un penalti; *she missed the target,* no dio en el blanco. **3** (*not catch*) perder: *I missed the bus,* perdí el autobús; *we've missed the train!,* ¡se nos ha escapado el tren! **4** (*not experience*) perderse: *don't miss this concert!,* ¡no te pierdas este concierto!; *he never misses a game,* nunca se pierde un partido; *I wouldn't have missed this for the world!,* ¡no me hubiera perdido esto por nada del mundo!; *you don't know what you're missing!,* ¡no sabes lo que te pierdes! **5** (*not see*) perderse: *we missed each other in the crowd,* nos perdimos entre la muchedumbre; *go straight ahead, you can't miss it,* sigue todo recto, no tiene pérdida; *she doesn't miss anything,* no se le escapa nada. **6** (*avoid, escape*) evitar: *we'll try to miss the rush hour,* intentaremos evitar la hora punta; *that car just missed me!,* ¡por poco me atropella aquel coche!; *that just missed your head!,* ¡por poco te da en la cabeza! **7** (*not attend - meeting etc*) no asistir a; (- *class, work*) faltar a. **8** (*omit, skip*) saltarse; (*disregard*) pasar por alto; (*overlook, fail to notice*) dejarse, dejar pasar: *she missed a line,* se saltó una línea; *look! you've missed a bit over there!,* ¡mira! ¡te has dejado un trozo allí! **9** (*not understand*) no entender, no captar; (*not hear*) no oír: *you've missed the point,* no has entendido la idea; *I missed the punchline,* no oí la última frase. **10** (*opportunity, chance, bargain, etc*) perder, dejar pasar. **11** (*long for - person*) echar de menos; (- *place*) añorar: *she misses her family,* echa de menos a su familia; *I miss playing with my nephews,* echo de menos jugar con mis sobrinos. **12** (*discover loss of*) echar en falta. – **13** *i* (*catch, kick, etc*) fallar; (*shot*) errar el tiro. **14** (*engine*) fallar. **15** (*fail*) fallar.
◆ to miss out **1** *t sep* (*omit, fail to include*) saltarse, omitir; (*overlook, disregard*) pasar por alto, dejarse: *hey! you've missed me out!,* ¡ey! ¡me has saltado a mí!; *I think you've missed out a paragraph here,* creo que te has dejado un párrafo aquí. – **2** *i* (*lose opportunity*) dejar pasar, perderse: *you missed out on a wonderful concert,*

te has perdido un concierto maravilloso; *he feels he's
missing out,* cree que se pierde algo.
● **a miss is as good as a mile,** lo importante es que
no pasó nada. ‖ **to have a near miss,** escapar por los
pelos, salvarse por los pelos. ‖ **to not miss a trick,** no
perderse ni una, no escapársele a algn. ni una. ‖ **to be
too good to miss,** ser demasiado bueno,-a como
para perdérselo. ‖ **to miss the boat,** *fig* perder el tren,
perder la ocasión. ‖ **to give sth. a miss,** (*not do sth.*)
pasar de hacer algo: *I think I'll give the pub a miss tonight,* creo que voy a pasar de ir al pub esta noche.

misshapen [mɪsˈʃeɪpən] *adj* (*badly formed*) deforme; (*out
of shape*) deformado,-a.

missile [ˈmɪsaɪl] **1** *n* (*explosive weapon*) misil *m*. **2** (*object
thrown*) proyectil *m*.
▪ **missile launcher,** lanzamisiles *m inv*.

missing [ˈmɪsɪŋ] **1** *adj* (*object - lost*) perdido,-a, extraviado,-a: *has the missing money turned up yet?,* ¿ya ha aparecido el dinero que faltaba? **2** (*person - disappeared*)
desaparecido,-a; (*- absent*) ausente: *she's been missing
for a week,* hace una semana que desapareció.
● **missing in action,** desaparecido,-a en combate. ‖
to be missing, faltar: *is anything missing?,* ¿falta algo?;
there's a page missing, falta una página. ‖ **to go missing,** desaparecer. ‖ **to report sb. missing,** dar parte
de la desaparición de algn.
▪ **missing link,** eslabón *m* perdido. ‖ **missing person,** desaparecido,-a.

mission [ˈmɪʃən] **1** *n* (*task*) misión *f*: *her mission in life
was to help the poor,* su misión en la vida era ayudar a
los pobres; *he was sent on a peace mission,* fue enviado
en misión de paz. **2** REL misión *f*. **3** (*group of people*) delegación *f*, misión *f*: *a trade mission,* una delegación comercial.
● **mission accomplished,** misión cumplida.
▪ **mission control,** centro de control.

missionary [ˈmɪʃənərɪ] **1** *n* misionero,-a. **– 2** *adj* misionero,-a.
▲ *pl* *missionaries*.

Mississippi [mɪsɪˈsɪpɪ] **1** *n* (*river*) el Misisipí *m*. **2** (*state*)
Misisipí *m*.

missive [ˈmɪsɪv] *n* misiva.

misspell [mɪsˈspel] *t* (*write*) escribir mal; (*say out loud*) deletrear mal.
▲ *pt & pp* *misspelled* o *misspelt* [mɪsˈspelt], ger *misspell-
ing*.

misspend [mɪsˈspend] *t* (*money*) malgastar; (*time*) desperdiciar, desaprovechar.
▲ *pt & pp* *misspent*.

misspent [mɪsˈspent] **1** *pp* → **misspend**. **– 2** *adj* (*money*) malgastado,-a; (*time*) perdido,-a; (*youth*) disipado,-a.

missus [ˈmɪsɪz] *n fam* (*wife*) parienta.

mist [mɪst] **1** *n* (*gen*) neblina; (*sea*) bruma; (*haze*) calima.
2 (*on window, mirror, etc*) vaho. **3** (*fine spray of liquid*) vaporización *f*. **4** *fig* velo: *she could hardly see through the
mist of tears,* apenas veía a través del velo de lágrimas.
– 5 *t* (*plants*) pulverizar.
◆ **to mist over / mist up 1** *i* (*windows, glasses, etc*) empañarse. **2** (*countryside*) cubrirse de neblina. **3** *fig* (*eyes*)
llenarse de lágrimas, empañarse.
● **in the mists of time,** en la noche de los tiempos.

mistake [mɪsˈteɪk] **1** *n* (*error*) equivocación *f*, error *m*; (*in
test*) falta; (*oversight*) descuido: *there must be some mistake,* debe haber algún error; *it was a mistake to take
so many clothes,* fue un error llevar tanta ropa; *you're
making a big mistake,* cometes un gran error. **– 2** *t* (*mis-*

understand) entender mal; (*misinterpret*) interpretar mal.
3 (*confuse*) confundir (**for,** con), equivocarse: *he mistook
me for my cousin,* me confundió con mi prima; *there's
no mistaking that laugh!,* ¡esta risa es inconfundible!
● **and no mistake!,** ¡y de eso no hay duda! ‖ **by mistake,** (*in error*) por error, por equivocación; (*unintentionally*) sin querer. ‖ **make no mistake about it!,** ¡que
quede bien claro! ‖ **to make a mistake,** equivocarse,
cometer un error.
▲ *pt* *mistook,* *pp* *mistaken* [mɪsˈteɪkən].

mistaken [mɪsˈteɪkən] **1** *pp* → **mistake**. **– 2** *adj* (*wrong,
incorrect*) equivocado,-a, erróneo,-a, falso,-a.
● **to be mistaken,** equivocarse: *you're mistaken if you
think you're going to get away with this,* te equivocas si
crees que vas a salir impune de esto; *if/unless I'm not
mistaken,* si no me equivoco.
▪ **a case of mistaken identity,** un error de identificación.

mister [ˈmɪstə'] *n* señor *m*.

mistime [mɪsˈtaɪm] *t* (*do at wrong time*) calcular mal: *he
mistimed his stroke and the ball went out,* calculó mal el
golpe y la pelota no entró.

mistimed [mɪsˈtaɪmd] *adj* inoportuno,-a.

mistletoe [ˈmɪsəltəʊ] *n* muérdago.

mistook [mɪsˈtʊk] *pt* → **mistake**.

mistreat [mɪsˈtriːt] *t* maltratar, tratar mal.

mistress [ˈmɪstrəs] **1** *n* (*owner - gen*) dueña, ama, señora;
(*of dog*) ama, dueña. **2** (*lover*) amante *f*; (*sweetheart*) querida. **3** GB EDUC (*teacher - primary*) maestra; (*- secondary*)
profesora.
● **to be mistress of the situation,** dominar la situación. ‖ **to be one's own mistress,** ser dueña de sí
misma.

mistrust [mɪsˈtrʌst] **1** *n* desconfianza, recelo. **– 2** *t* desconfiar de, dudar de, recelar de.

mistrustful [mɪsˈtrʌstfʊl] *adj* desconfiado,-a, receloso,-a.
● **to be mistrustful of,** desconfiar de, recelar de.

misty [ˈmɪstɪ] **1** *adj* METEOR neblinoso,-a: *it's misty,* hay
neblina. **2** (*window, glasses, etc*) empañado,-a. **3** (*eyes*)
empañado,-a, lloroso,-a. **4** (*photograph*) movido,-a, borroso,-a; (*outline*) borroso,-a, difuso,-a. **5** *fig* (*memory*)
borroso,-a.
▲ *comp* *mistier,* *superl* *mistiest*.

misunderstand [mɪsʌndəˈstænd] *t* (*gen*) entender mal,
comprender mal; (*misinterpret*) malinterpretar.
▲ *pt & pp* *misunderstood*.

misunderstanding [mɪsʌndəˈstændɪŋ] *n* malentendido (**about,** sobre).

misunderstood [mɪsʌndəˈstʊd] **1** *pp* → **misunderstand**. **– 2** *adj* (*person*) incomprendido,-a.

misuse [mɪsˈjuːs] **1** *n* (*of tool, resources, word, etc*) mal uso,
uso incorrecto; (*of funds*) malversación *f*; (*of power, authority*) abuso. **– 2** *t* (*tool, resources, word, etc*) utilizar mal,
emplear mal; (*funds*) malversar; (*power, authority*) abusar
de.
▲ (*verbo*) [mɪsˈjuːz].

mite¹ [maɪt] *n* (*insect*) ácaro, acárido.

mite² [maɪt] **1** *n* (*small amount*) pizca, pelín *m*. **2** (*small
child*) chiquillo,-a, criatura. **– 3 a mite,** *adv* un poquito,
un poquitín.

mitigate [ˈmɪtɪɡeɪt] *t* mitigar.

mitigating [ˈmɪtɪɡeɪtɪŋ] *adj* mitigador,-ra.
▪ **mitigating circumstances,** JUR circunstancias *fpl*
atenuantes.

mitigation [mɪtɪˈɡeɪʃən] *n* (*alleviation*) mitigación *f*; (*extenuation*) atenuante *m*.

● **to plead sth. in mitigation,** JUR alegar algo como atenuante.
mitre ['maɪtəʳ] **1** *n* REL mitra. **2** TECH inglete *m*. − **3** *t* TECH ingletear.
■ **metre joint,** inglete *m*.
mitt [mɪt] **1** *n* → **mitten.** **2** *fam (hand)* manaza, manota.
■ **baseball mitt,** guante *m* de béisbol. ‖ **oven mitt,** manopla de cocina.
mitten ['mɪtən] *n (fingers covered)* manopla; *(fingers exposed)* mitón *m*.
mix [mɪks] **1** *n (mixture - gen)* mezcla. **2** CULIN preparado. **3** MUS mezcla. − **4** *t (combine)* mezclar, combinar: *mix the sugar with the butter,* mezclar el azúcar con la mantequilla; *you shouldn't mix your drinks,* no deberías mezclar las bebidas; *gradually mix in the milk,* poco a poco vaya añadiendo la leche; *one can mix business with pleasure,* se puede compaginar los negocios con la diversión. **5** *(make, prepare - plaster, cement)* amasar; *(- cocktail, salad, medicine)* preparar. − **6** *i (substances)* mezclarse. **7** *(clothes, colours, food)* combinar bien, ir bien juntos,-as. **8** *(people - come together)* mezclarse con la gente; *(- get on)* llevarse bien **(with,** con): *she made no attempt to mix at the party,* no hizo ningún intento de mezclarse con la gente en la fiesta.
◆ **to mix up 1** *t sep (ingredients)* mezclar bien. **2** *(prepare)* preparar. **3** *(confuse)* confundir: *people often mix him up with his brother,* la gente suele confundirlo con su hermano. **4** *(mess up, put in disorder)* desordenar, revolver, mezclar: *don't mix my papers up,* no revuelvas mis papeles.
mixed [mɪkst] **1** *adj (of different kinds)* variado,-a: *mixed weather,* tiempo variable; *mixed biscuits,* galletas surtidas; *mixed salad,* ensalada mixta, ensalada variada. **2** *(ambivalent)* desigual: *I have mixed feelings about it,* me provoca sentimientos contradictorios; *the film received mixed reviews,* la película tuvo críticas muy diversas. **3** *(for both sexes)* mixto,-a.
● **to be mixed up in sth.,** estar metido,-a en algo, estar involucrado,-a en algo. ‖ **to be/get mixed up with sb.,** liarse con algn., estar liado,-a con algn. ‖ **to be/get all mixed up,** hacerse un lío, confundirse. ‖ **to get mixed up in sth.,** meterse en algo.
■ **mixed bag,** batiburrillo, mezcolanza, popurrí *m*. ‖ **mixed doubles,** dobles *mpl* mixtos. ‖ **mixed economy,** economía mixta. ‖ **mixed grill,** parrillada. ‖ **mixed marriage,** *(different races)* matrimonio interracial; *(different religions)* matrimonio interconfesional.
mixed-up [mɪkst'ʌp] **1** *adj (objects, papers, etc)* revuelto,-a. **2** *(person)* desconcertado,-a, desorientado,-a, hecho,-a un lío.
mixer ['mɪksəʳ] **1** *n* CULIN batidora, robot *m* de cocina. **2** *(drink)* refresco. **3** TV CIN *(machine)* mezclador; *(person)* mezclador,-ra, sonido.
● **to be a good mixer,** *(person)* ser sociable, llevarse bien con la gente.
mixing bowl ['mɪksɪŋbəʊl] *n (gen)* bol *m*, tazón *m*; *(earthenware)* cuenco.
Mixtec ['miːstek] **1** *n (person)* mixteca *mf*, mixteco,-a. **2** *(language)* mixteca *m*, mixteco.
mixture ['mɪkstʃəʳ] **1** *n (gen)* mezcla. **2** MED preparado.
■ **cough mixture,** jarabe *m* para la tos.
mix-up ['mɪksʌp] *n fam (confusion)* lío, confusión *f*, enredo; *(misunderstanding)* malentendido.
ml¹ [maɪl] *abbr (mile)* milla.
ml² [mɪlɪliːtə] *abbr (millilitre)* mililitro; *(abbreviation)* ml.
M Litt ['em'lɪt] *abbr (Master of Letters)* ≈ master en literatura.

mm ['mɪlɪmiːtəʳ] *symb (millimetre)* milímetro; *(abbreviation)* mm.
mnemonic [nə'mɒnɪk] **1** *adj* nemotécnico,-a, mnemotécnico,-a. − **2** *n* frase *f* mnemotécnica. − **3** mnemonics, *npl* mnemotecnia *f sing*.
mo [məʊ] *n* GB *fam* momentito.
▲ *pl* mos.
MO ['em'əʊ] *abbr (Medical Officer)* médico,-a militar.
moan [məʊn] **1** *n (groan)* gemido, quejido. **2** *(complaint)* queja, protesta. − **3** *i (groan)* gemir. **4** *(complain)* quejarse **(about,** de), protestar **(about,** por). **5** *fig (wind)* gemir. − **6** *t* gemir, decir gimiendo.
moaner ['məʊnəʳ] *n* quejica *mf*.
moaning ['məʊnɪŋ] **1** *n (groaning)* gemidos *mpl*. **2** *(complaining)* quejas *fpl*.
moat [məʊt] *n* foso.
mob [mɒb] **1** *n (large crowd)* muchedumbre *f*, turba, multitud *f*. **2** *(group of friends)* pandilla, grupo, peña. **3** *pej (gang)* banda, pandilla. − **4** *t (crowd round)* acosar, rodear; *(attack)* asaltar, atacar: *the singer was mobbed by hysterical girls,* el cantante fue rodeado por chicas histéricas. − **5 the mob,** *n (common people)* el populacho. **6 the Mob,** US *(mafia)* la mafia.
■ **mob law / mob rule,** ley *f* de la calle. ‖ **mob violence,** violencia callejera.
▲ *pt & pp* **mobbed,** *ger* **mobbing.**
mobile ['məʊbaɪl] **1** *adj (object, troops, etc)* móvil, movible. **2** *(face)* expresivo,-a. **3** *(person)* varias traducciones: *she'll soon be fully mobile,* pronto podrá caminar con normalidad; *workers who are geografically mobile,* trabajadores dispuestos a desplazarse; *now we're mobile!,* ¡ya estamos motorizados! − **4** *n (hanging ornament)* móvil *m*.
■ **mobile home,** caravana, remolque *m*. ‖ **mobile library,** biblioteca ambulante. ‖ **mobile phone,** teléfono móvil.
mobility [mə'bɪlɪtɪ] *n* movilidad *f*.
■ **mobility allowance,** subsidio por minusvalía *para ayudar a las personas minusválidas a desplazarse.*
mobilization [məʊbɪlaɪ'zeɪʃən] *n* movilización *f*.
mobilize ['məʊbɪlaɪz] **1** *t* movilizar. − **2** *i* movilizarse.
mobster ['mɒbstəʳ] *n* gángster *m*, mafioso,-a.
moccasin ['mɒkəsɪn] *n* mocasín *m*.
mocha ['mɒkə] *n* moca.
mock [mɒk] **1** *adj (object)* de imitación. **2** *(event)* de prueba: *a mock exam,* examen de prueba; *a mock battle,* un simulacro de batalla. **3** *(feeling)* fingido,-a, simulado,-a; *(modesty)* falso,-a. − **4** *n (exam)* examen *m* de prueba. − **5** *t (laugh at, make fun of)* burlarse de, mofarse de. **6** *(imitate)* imitar, remedar. **7** *fml (defy contemptuously)* desafiar, burlar; *(frustrate)* frustrar. − **8** *i* burlarse **(at,** de).
● **to make a mock of sb./sth.,** poner a algn./algo en ridículo.
mockers ['mɒkəʳz] **to put the mockers on sth.,** *phr* echar algo a perder, estropear algo.
mockery ['mɒkərɪ] **1** *n (ridicule)* burla, mofa. **2** *(farce)* farsa; *(travesty)* parodia.
● **to make a mockery of sth.,** poner algo en ridículo.
mocking ['mɒkɪŋ] *adj* burlón,-ona.
mockingbird ['mɒkɪŋbɜːd] *n* sinsonte *m*.
mock-up ['mɒkʌp] *n (model)* maqueta, modelo a escala.
mod [mɒd] *n* mod *mf*.
MOD ['em'əʊ'diː] *abbr* GB *(Ministry of Defence)* Ministerio de Defensa.
modal ['məʊdəl] *adj* modal.
■ **modal auxiliary,** auxiliar *m* modal. ‖ **modal auxil-**

iary verb, verbo auxiliar modal. ‖ **modal verb,** verbo modal.

mod cons [mɒd'kɒnz] *npl* GB *fam* → **cons.**

mode [məud] **1** *n fml* (*means*) medio; (*manner, way*) modo: *mode of transport,* medio de transporte. **2** (*fashion*) moda. **3** MUS modo. **4** MATH modo.

model ['mɒdəl] **1** *n* (*small representation*) modelo, maqueta: *he made a model of the Eiffel Tower,* hizo una maqueta de la Torre Eiffel. **2** (*design*) modelo, patrón *m*. **3** (*type of car etc*) modelo: *the latest model,* el último modelo. **4** (*perfect example*) modelo, pauta: *I'll use yours as a model,* utilizaré el tuyo como modelo; *based on the American model of democracy,* basado en el modelo democrático americano; *a role model,* un modelo de comportamiento. **5** (*fashion model*) modelo *mf*, maniquí *mf*; (*artist's model*) modelo *mf*. – **6** *adj* (*miniature*) en miniatura, a escala; (*toy*) de juguete: *model aeroplane,* aeromodelo. **7** (*exemplary*) ejemplar; (*ideal*) modelo: *model student,* estudiante ejemplar; *model husband,* marido modelo; *a model prison,* una cárcel modelo. – **8** *t* (*clay etc*) modelar. **9** (*clothes*) presentar, vestir, modelar. – **10** *i* (*clay etc*) modelar. **11** (*work as fashion model*) trabajar de modelo.
◆ **to model on** *t insep* (*form as copy of*) inspirarse en.
● **to model os. on/upon sb.,** seguir el ejemplo de algn.
▲ *pt & pp* **modelled** (US **modeled**), *ger* **modelling** (US **modeling**).

modeller ['mɒdələ'] *n* (*of small representations*) maquetista *mf*; (*of clay*) modelador,-ra.

modelling ['mɒdəlɪŋ] **1** *n* (*of clay*) modelado; (*of small representations*) modelismo. **2** (*of fashion*) profesión *f* de modelo: *I did some modelling,* trabajé de modelo.

modem ['məudem] *n* COMPUT modem *m*.

moderate ['mɒdərət] **1** *adj* (*average*) mediano,-a, regular: *moderate size,* tamaño mediano; *moderate speed,* velocidad regular. **2** (*not extreme*) moderado,-a; (*reasonable*) razonable: *moderate views,* opiniones moderadas; *moderate behaviour,* comportamiento razonable. **3** (*price*) módico,-a. **4** (*weather*) templado,-a; (*sea*) rizado,-a; (*wind*) moderado,-a. **5** (*talent, ability, performance*) mediocre, regular. – **6** *n* POL moderado,-a. – **7** *t* moderar. – **8** *i* (*pain*) aliviarse, calmarse. **9** (*wind, storm*) amainar, calmarse. **10** (*act as moderator*) hacer de moderador,-ra.
● **to be a moderate drinker,** beber con moderación.

moderately ['mɒdərətlɪ] **1** *adv* (*not very*) medianamente, bastante. **2** (*to a moderate degree*) con moderación.

moderation [mɒdə'reɪʃən] *n* moderación *f*.
● **in moderation,** con moderación.

moderator ['mɒdəreɪtə'] *n* (*in debate*) moderador,-ra.

modern ['mɒdən] **1** *adj* (*up-to-date*) moderno,-a. **2** (*history, literature, etc*) contemporáneo,-a.
■ **modern language,** lengua moderna.

modern-day ['mɒdəndeɪ] *adj* moderno,-a, actual, de hoy en día.

modernism ['mɒdənɪzəm] *n* modernismo.

modernist ['mɒdənɪst] **1** *adj* modernista. – **2** *n* modernista *mf*.

modernity [mə'dɜːnɪtɪ] *n* modernidad *f*.

modernization [mɒdənaɪ'zeɪʃən] *n* modernización *f*.

modernize ['mɒdənaɪz] **1** *t* modernizar. – **2** *i* modernizarse.

modest ['mɒdɪst] **1** *adj* (*person - unassuming*) modesto,-a, humilde; (*- shy*) tímido,-a. **2** (*not large - house, income, etc*) modesto,-a; (*- improvement, increase*) - modesto,-a; (*- price*) módico,-a; (*- demand, ambition*) moderado,-a; (*-*

rise, success) discreto,-a, moderado,-a. **3** *dated* (*chaste*) púdico,-a, recatado,-a.

modesty ['mɒdɪstɪ] **1** *n* (*humility*) modestia, humildad *f*. **2** (*chastity*) pudor *m*, recato.

modicum ['mɒdɪkəm] *n* (*small amount*) atisbo, mínimo (**of,** de): *a modicum of sense,* un mínimo de sentido común.

modification [mɒdɪfɪ'keɪʃən] *n* modificación *f*.

modify ['mɒdɪfaɪ] **1** *t* (*change*) modificar. **2** (*moderate*) moderar. **3** LING modificar.
▲ *pt & pp* **modified**, *ger* **modifying**.

modulate ['mɒdjəleɪt] *t* modular.

modulation [mɒdjə'leɪʃən] *n* modulación *f*.

module ['mɒdjuːl] *n* módulo.

Mogadiscio [mɒgə'dɪʃɪəu] *n* Mogadiscio.

Mogadishu [mɒgə'dɪʃuː] *n* Mogadiscio.

mogul ['məugʌl] *n* magnate *m*.

mohair ['məuheə'] *n* mohair *m*.

Mohican [məu'hiːkən] *n* mohicano,-a.

moist [mɔɪst] *adj* (*damp*) húmedo,-a; (*slightly wet*) ligeramente mojado,-a: *the soil must be kept moist,* la tierra debe mantenerse húmeda; *a moist sponge cake,* un bizcocho tierno.

moisten ['mɔɪsən] **1** *t* (*dampen*) humedecer; (*wet*) mojar ligeramente. – **2** *i* (*eyes*) llenarse de lágrimas.

moisture ['mɔɪstʃə'] **1** *n* (*dampness*) humedad *f*. **2** (*on glass*) vaho.

moisturize ['mɔɪstʃəraɪz] *t* hidratar.

moisturizer ['mɔɪstʃəraɪzə'] *n* hidratante *m*.

moisturizing ['mɔɪstʃəraɪzɪŋ] *adj* hidratante.
■ **moisturizing cream,** crema hidratante.

molar ['məulə'] *n* muela.

molasses [mə'læsɪz] *n* melaza.

mold [məuld] *n* US → **mould.**

Moldavia [mɒl'deɪvɪə] *n* Moldavia.

Moldavian [mɒl'deɪvɪən] **1** *adj* moldavo,-a. – **2** *n* moldavo,-a.

molder ['məuldə'] *i* US → **moulder.**

molding ['məuldɪŋ] *n* US → **moulding.**

Moldova [mɒl'dəuvə] *n* Moldova.

moldy ['məuldɪ] *adj* US → **mouldy.**
▲ *comp* **moldier**, *superl* **moldiest.**

mole¹ [məul] *n* (*on skin*) lunar *m*.

mole² [məul] **1** *n* ZOOL topo. **2** *fam* (*spy*) topo *mf*, espía *mf*.

molecular [mə'lekjələ'] *adj* molecular.

molecule ['mɒlɪkjuːl] *n* molécula.

molehill ['məulhɪl] *n* topera.
● **to make a mountain out of a molehill,** hacer una montaña de un grano de arena.

molest [mə'lest] **1** *t* (*trouble, annoy*) importunar, molestar; (*pester*) hostigar, acosar. **2** (*attack - person*) atacar, asaltar; (*- dog*) perseguir, atacar. **3** (*sexually*) abusar sexualmente.

mollify ['mɒlɪfaɪ] *t* aplacar, apaciguar, calmar.
▲ *pt & pp* **mollified**, *ger* **mollifying.**

mollusc ['mɒləsk] *n* molusco.

mollycoddle ['mɒlɪkɒdəl] *t fam* mimar, consentir.

Molotov cocktail [mɒlətɒf'kɒkteɪl] *n* cóctel *m* Molotov.

molt [məult] *i* US → **moult.**

molten ['məultən] *adj* fundido,-a, derretido,-a: *molten lava,* lava líquida.

mom [mɒm] *n* US *fam* mamá *f*.

moment ['məumənt] *n* (*instant*) momento, instante *m*: *it won't take a moment,* sólo será un momento; *just a* *moment,* un momentito; *I didn't believe that story for a moment,* no me creí ese cuento ni por un momento; *just at that moment the phone rang,* justo en aquel instante sonó el teléfono; *he's just this moment come in,* acaba de entrar ahora mismo; *you have to pick the right moment,* tienes que escoger el momento oportuno. ● **at any moment,** de un momento a otro, en cualquier momento. ‖ **at the moment,** en este momento. ‖ **at the last moment,** a última hora. ‖ **for the moment,** de momento, por el momento. ‖ **in a moment,** dentro de un momento. ‖ **on the spur of the moment,** sin pensarlo, a bote pronto. ‖ **the moment (that)** ..., en cuanto ... ‖ **to have its moments,** tener momentos buenos. ■ **the moment of truth,** la hora de la verdad.

momentarily [məʊmən'terəlɪ] **1** *adv (for a short time)* momentáneamente. **2** US *(very soon)* dentro de un momento.

momentary ['məʊməntərɪ] *adj* momentáneo,-a, breve.

momentous [mə'mentəs] *adj* trascendental, de suma importancia.

momentum [mə'mentəm] **1** *n* PHYS momento. **2** *(impetus)* ímpetu *m,* impulso. ● **to gather momentum,** cobrar velocidad.

mommy ['mɒmɪ] *n* US *fam* mamá. ▲ *pl* **mommies.**

Mon ['mʌndɪ] *abbr (Monday)* lunes *m; (abbreviation)* lun.

Monaco ['mɒnəkəʊ] *n* Mónaco.

monarch ['mɒnək] *n* monarca *m.*

monarchical [mə'nɑːkɪkəl] *adj* monárquico,-a.

monarchism ['mɒnəkɪzəm] *n* monarquismo.

monarchist ['mɒnəkɪst] *n* monárquico,-a.

monarchy ['mɒnəkɪ] *n* monarquía. ▲ *pl* **monarchies.**

monastery ['mɒnəstərɪ] *n* monasterio. ▲ *pl* **monasteries.**

monastic [mə'næstɪk] *adj* monástico,-a.

Monday ['mʌndɪ] *n* lunes *m inv.* ▲ *Véase también* **Saturday.**

Monegasque ['mɒnəgæsk] **1** *n* monegasco,-a. **2** monegasco,-a.

monetarism ['mʌnɪtərɪzəm] *n* monetarismo.

monetarist ['mʌnɪtərɪst] **1** *adj* monetarista. – **2** *n* monetarista *mf.*

monetary ['mʌnɪtərɪ] *adj* monetario,-a.

money ['mʌnɪ] **1** *n (gen)* dinero: *how much money have you got?,* ¿cuánto dinero tienes?; *I want my money back,* quiero que me devuelvan el dinero; *careful! that's worth a lot of money,* ¡cuidado! eso vale mucho dinero; *I paid good money for that,* eso me ha costado mucho dinero. **2** *(currency)* moneda: *I've only got Spanish money,* solo tengo moneda española. – **3 moneys / monies,** *npl* JUR *arch* dinero. ● **for my money** ..., en mi opinión ..., para mí ...: *for my money, this is the best car on the road,* para mí, este es el mejor coche que hay. ‖ *it's money for old rope,* es dinero regalado. ‖ **money is the root of all evil,** el dinero es el origen de todos los males. ‖ **money makes the world go round,** el dinero mueve el mundo. ‖ **money talks,** poderoso caballero es don Dinero. ‖ **there's money in sth.,** algo es un buen negocio, dar algo mucho dinero: *there's money in scrap metal,* la chatarra da mucho dinero; *there's no money in teaching,* nunca te harás rico dando clase. ‖ **to be in the money,** ser rico,-a. ‖ **to be made of money,** estar forrado,-a de dinero. ‖ **to be rolling in money,** estar fo-

rrado,-a de dinero. ‖ **to come into money,** heredar una suma de dinero. ‖ **to get one's money's worth,** sacar partido del dinero. ‖ **to have money to burn,** tener dinero de sobra. ‖ **to make money,** *(person)* ganar dinero, hacer dinero; *(business)* dar dinero. ‖ **to put money into sth.,** invertir en algo. ‖ **to put money on sth.,** apostar por algo. ‖ **to put one's money where one's mouth is,** obrar de acuerdo con lo que uno dice. ‖ **your money or your life!,** ¡la bolsa o la vida! ■ **money market,** mercado financiero. ‖ **money order,** giro postal. ‖ **money supply,** masa monetaria.

moneybags ['mʌnɪbægz] *n fam* ricachón,-ona.

moneybox ['mʌnɪbɒks] *n* hucha.

moneyed ['mʌnɪd] *adj* adinerado,-a, rico,-a.

moneylender ['mʌnɪlendə'] *n* prestamista *mf.*

moneylending ['mʌnɪlendɪŋ] *n* préstamo.

moneymaker ['mʌnɪmeɪkə'] *n (gen)* cosa lucrativa, cosa que da mucho dinero; *(product)* producto rentable; *(business)* negocio rentable.

moneymaking ['mʌnɪmeɪkɪŋ] *adj* rentable, lucrativo,-a.

money-spinner ['mʌnɪspɪnə'] *n* GB *fam* negocio rentable.

Mongol ['mɒŋgɒl] *n* mongol,-la, mogol,-la.

Mongolia [mɒŋ'gəʊlɪə] *n* Mongolia.

Mongolian [mɒŋ'gəʊlɪən] **1** *adj* mongol,-la, mogol,-la. – **2** *n (person)* mongol,-la, mogol,-la. **3** *(language)* mongol *m,* mogol *m.*

mongolism ['mɒŋgəlɪzəm] *n taboo* mongolismo.

mongoose ['mɒŋguːs] *n* mangosta.

mongrel ['mʌŋgrəl] *n (dog)* perro callejero.

monied ['mʌnɪd] *adj dated* rico,-a, adinerado,-a.

monitor ['mɒnɪtə'] **1** *n (screen)* monitor *m.* **2** RAD *(person)* escucha *mf.* **3** *(school pupil)* responsable *mf,* encargado,-a. **4** *(lizard)* varano. – **5** *t* RAD *(listen to)* escuchar. **6** *(check)* controlar; *(follow)* seguir de cerca; *(watch)* observar.

monitoring ['mɒnɪtərɪŋ] **1** *n (of radio broadcast)* escucha. **2** *(checking)* control *m,* seguimiento.

monk [mʌŋk] *n* monje *m.*

monkey ['mʌŋkɪ] **1** *n (gen)* mono,-a; *(long-tailed)* mico,-a. **2** *fam (child)* diablillo, pillo,-a. ◆ **to monkey about / monkey around** *i* hacer tonterías, hacer el tonto. ‖ **to monkey about with** *t insep* juguetear con. ● **not to give a monkey's,** importarle a uno un rábano, importarle a uno un pepino. ‖ **to make a monkey (out) of sb.,** poner a algn. en ridículo. ■ **monkey business,** *(mischief)* travesuras *fpl; (swindle)* trampas *fpl.* ‖ **monkey tricks,** travesuras *fpl.* ‖ **monkey nut,** cacahuete *m.* ‖ **monkey puzzle (tree),** araucaria. ‖ **monkey wrench,** llave *f* inglesa.

monkish ['mʌŋkɪʃ] *adj* monacal.

mono ['mɒnəʊ] **1** *n fam* mono, monofonía. – **2** *adj fam* mono, monofónico,-a.

monochrome ['mɒnəkrəʊm] **1** *adj (one colour)* monocromo,-a. **2** *(black and white)* en blanco y negro. – **3** *n* monocromía.

monocle ['mɒnəkəl] *n* monóculo.

monogamous [mə'nɒgəməs] *adj* monógamo,-a.

monogamy [mə'nɒgəmɪ] *n* monogamia.

monogram ['mɒnəgræm] *n* monograma *m.*

monograph ['mɒnəgrɑːf] *n* monografía.

monolingual [mɒnə'lɪŋgwəl] *adj* monolingüe.

monolith ['mɒnəlɪθ] *n* monolito.

monologue ['mɒnəlɒg] *n* monólogo.

monoplane ['mɒnəpleɪn] *n* monoplano.

monopolize [mə'nɒpəlaɪz] **1** *t* COMM FIN monopolizar. **2** *fig* (*attention etc*) acaparar, monopolizar.
monopoly [mə'nɒpəlɪ] *n* monopolio.
▲ *pl* **monopolies**.
monorail ['mɒnəʊreɪl] *n* monorraíl *m*, monocarril *m*.
monosyllabic [mɒnəsɪ'læbɪk] **1** *adj* (*word*) monosílabo,-a. **– 2** *n* (*answer etc*) monosilábico,-a.
monosyllable ['mɒnəsɪləbəl] *n* monosílabo.
monotone ['mɒnətəʊn] **1** *n* tono monocorde. **– 2** *adj* monótono,-a.
● **to speak in a monotone**, hablar con voz monótona.
monotonous [mə'nɒtənəs] *adj* monótono,-a.
monotony [mə'nɒtənɪ] *n* monotonía.
monoxide [mə'nɒksaɪd] *n* monóxido.
monsoon [mɒn'suːn] **1** *n* (*wind*) monzón *m*. **2** (*rainy season*) estación *f* lluviosa, estación *f* de las lluvias.
■ **monsoon rains**, lluvias *fpl* monzónicas.
monster ['mɒnstə'] **1** *n* (*gen*) monstruo. **– 2** *adj fam* (*huge*) enorme, gigantesco,-a.
monstrosity [mɒn'strɒsətɪ] *n* monstruosidad *f*.
▲ *pl* **monstrosities**.
monstrous ['mɒnstrəs] **1** *adj* (*huge*) enorme, gigantesco,-a. **2** (*hideous*) monstruoso,-a. **3** (*shocking*) escandaloso,-a, atroz, monstruoso,-a.
montage ['mɒntɑːʒ] *n* montaje *m*.
Monte Carlo [mɒntɪ'kɑːləʊ] *n* Montecarlo.
Montenegrin [mɒntɪ'niːgrɪn] **1** *adj* montenegrino,-a. **– 2** *n* montenegrino,-a.
Montenegro [mɒntɪ'niːgrəʊ] *n* Montenegro.
month [mʌnθ] **1** *n* mes *m*: *I'm going on holiday at the end of the month,* me voy de vacaciones a final de mes; *the baby's 18 months old,* el bebé tiene 18 meses; *she earns £800 a month,* gana £800 al mes; *he got six months for theft,* lo condenaron a seis meses de cárcel por robo. **– 2 months,** *npl* (*ages*) siglos *mpl*: *it took months before I found a flat,* tardé siglos en encontrar un piso.
● **in a month of Sundays,** desde hace mucho tiempo: *I haven't been out in a month of Sundays,* hace mucho que no salgo de casa. ‖ **month in, month out,** mes tras mes.
■ **calendar month,** mes *m* civil.
monthly ['mʌnθlɪ] **1** *adj* mensual. **– 2** *adv* mensualmente, cada mes. **– 3** *n* (*magazine*) revista mensual.
■ **monthly instalment/payment,** mensualidad *f*. ‖ **monthly season ticket,** (*rail*) abono mensual.
monument ['mɒnjəmənt] *n* monumento (**to,** a).
monumental [mɒnjə'mentəl] **1** *adj* (*gen*) monumental. **2** *fam* (*lie, blunder, etc*) garrafal, monumental.
■ **monumental mason,** marmolista *mf*.
moo [muː] **1** *n* (*of cow*) mugido. **– 2** *i* mugir.
▲ *pt & pp* **mooed,** *ger* **mooing.**
mooch [muːtʃ] *t* US *fam* (*cadge*) gorrear (**off/from,** a).
◆ **to mooch about / mooch around** *i* dar vueltas, deambular: *she just mooches round the house all day,* no hace más que dar vueltas por la casa todo el día.
mood¹ [muːd] *n* LING modo.
mood² [muːd] **1** *n* (*humour*) humor *m*: *her moods change very quickly,* cambia de humor de repente. **2** (*bad temper*) mal humor *m*: *he's in a mood,* está de malas. **3** (*atmosphere*) atmósfera, ambiente *m*: *amid a mood of rising tension,* en medio de una atmósfera de crispación creciente.
● **to be in a good/bad mood,** estar de buen/mal humor. ‖ **to be in no mood for sth.,** no estar para algo. ‖ **to be in the mood for sth.,** tener ganas de algo, estar de humor para algo.

moodiness ['muːdɪnəs] *n* (*changeable moods*) cambios *mpl* de humor; (*bad mood*) mal humor *m*; (*depression*) depresión *f*.
moody ['muːdɪ] **1** *adj* (*bad-tempered*) malhumorado,-a, de mal humor; (*sad, gloomy*) deprimido,-a, triste. **2** (*changeable*) de humor cambiadizo, lunático,-a, temperamental.
▲ *comp* **moodier,** *superl* **moodiest.**
moon [muːn] **1** *n* luna: *full moon,* luna llena. **– 2** *adj* lunar.
◆ **to moon about / moon around** *i* dar vueltas, deambular. ‖ **to moon over** *t insep* soñar con, fantasear sobre.
● **many moons ago,** años ha. ‖ **to be over the moon,** estar en el séptimo cielo, no caber en sí. ‖ **to ask for the moon / want the moon,** pedir peras al olmo, pedir la luna.
■ **moon boot,** moon boot *m*. ‖ **moon landing,** alunizaje *m*.
moonbeam ['muːnbiːm] *n* rayo de luna.
moonless ['muːnləs] *adj* sin luna.
moonlight ['muːnlaɪt] **1** *n* claro de luna, luz *f* de luna: *by/in the moonlight,* a la luz de la luna. **– 2** *adj* (*night*) de luna. **– 3** *i fam* estar pluriempleado,-a.
● **to do a moonlight flit,** largarse a la chita callando.
▲ *pt & pp* **moonlighted.**
moonlighter ['muːnlaɪtə'] *n fam* pluriempleado,-a.
moonlighting ['muːnlaɪtɪŋ] *n fam* pluriempleo.
moonlit ['muːnlɪt] *adj* (*landscape etc*) iluminado,-a por la luna; (*night*) de luna.
moonshine ['muːnʃaɪn] **1** *n* (*nonsense*) bobadas *fpl*, pamplinas *fpl*. **2** US (*alcohol*) licor *m* ilegalmente destilado.
moonstruck ['muːnstrʌk] *adj* tocado,-a, trastornado,-a, lunático,-a.
moor¹ [mʊə'] **1** *n* (*heath*) brezal *m*. **– 2 moors,** *npl* páramo *m sing*.
moor² [mʊə'] **1** *t* (*with rope*) amarrar; (*with anchor*) anclar. **– 2** *i* (*with anchor*) anclar; (*with rope*) echar amarras.
Moor [mʊə'] *n* moro,-a.
moorhen ['mʊəhen] *n* polla de agua.
mooring ['mʊərɪŋ] **1** *n* (*place*) amarradero. **– 2 moorings,** *npl* (*ropes etc*) amarras *fpl*.
Moorish ['mʊərɪʃ] *adj* moro,-a.
moorland ['mʊərlənd] *n* páramo.
moose [muːs] *n* alce *m*.
moot [muːt] *t fml* (*raise, propose, suggest*) plantear, proponer, sugerir: *the idea of moving had been mooted before,* ya se había planteado la idea de mudarnos.
● **to be a moot point/question,** ser discutible.
mop [mɒp] **1** *n* (*for floor*) fregona. **2** *fam* (*of hair*) mata de pelo. **– 3** *t* (*floor*) fregar, limpiar. **4** (*brow, tears*) enjugarse (**with,** con), secarse.
◆ **to mop up** **1** *t sep* (*spilt liquid*) enjugar, limpiar. **2** GB (*sauce, gravy*) mojar. **3** (*complete, deal with*) acabar con. **4** (*funds, profits*) absorber, llevarse. **5** MIL (*eliminate remaining forces*) acabar con.
● **to give sth. a mop,** pasar la fregona por algún lugar.
▲ (*verbo*) *pt & pp* **mopped,** *ger* **mopping.**
mope [məʊp] *i* estar abatido,-a, estar deprimido,-a.
◆ **to mope about / mope around** *i* andar abatido,-a, andar deprimido,-a.
moped ['məʊped] *n* ciclomotor *m*.
mopping-up [mɒpɪŋ'ʌp] *n* MIL limpieza.
■ **mopping-up operation,** operación *f* de limpieza.

moral ['mɒrəl] **1** *adj* moral: *on moral grounds,* por motivos morales. **2** (*person*) virtuoso,-a, moral. – **3** *n* (*of story*) moraleja. – **4 morals,** *npl* moral *f* sing, moralidad *f* sing.
■ **moral fibre,** nervio, carácter *m.* ∥ **moral support,** apoyo moral. ∥ **moral victory,** victoria moral. ∥ **the Moral Majority,** us POL grupo que defiende los valores tradicionales cristianos.

morale [mə'rɑːl] *n* moral *f,* estado de ánimo: *the victory has boosted the teams's morale,* la victoria ha levantado la moral del equipo.

moralist ['mɒrəlɪst] *n* moralista *mf.*

moralistic [mɒrə'lɪstɪk] *adj* moralizador,-ra.

morality [mə'rælɪtɪ] *n* moralidad *f,* moral *f.*

moralize ['mɒrəlaɪz] *i* moralizar.

morally ['mɒrəlɪ] *adv* moralmente: *morally right/wrong,* moral/inmoral.

morass [mə'ræs] **1** *n* (*marsh*) cenagal *m,* ciénaga. **2** *fig* cenagal *m,* lío, maraña: *we got bogged down in a morass of paperwork,* nos atascamos en un lío de papeles.

moratorium [mɒrə'tɔːrɪəm] *n* moratoria.
▲ *pl moratoria* [mɒrə'tɔːrɪə].

morbid ['mɔːbɪd] **1** *adj* (*mind, ideas*) morboso,-a, enfermizo,-a; (*curiosity*) malsano,-a: *don't be so morbid,* no seas tan morboso. **2** MED mórbido,-a.

morbidity [mɔː'bɪdətɪ] *n* (*gen*) morbosidad *f;* (*sick interest*) morbo.

mordant ['mɔːdənt] *adj fml* mordaz.

more [mɔːʳ] **1** *adj* más: *more than half an hour,* más de media hora; *do you want some more wine?,* ¿quieres más vino?; *there were no more than twenty people,* no había más de veinte personas; *no more tears!,* ¡basta de llorar! – **2** *pron* más: *we need some more,* necesitamos más; *I can't eat any more,* no puedo (comer) más; *it's more than enough,* sobra y basta; *we've got no more coffee,* no nos queda más café; *there's more to life than work,* hay cosas más importantes en la vida que el trabajo. – **3** *adv* más: *it's more expensive,* es más caro; *I don't live there any more,* ya no vivo allí; *I won't do it any more,* no lo volveré a hacer; *I couldn't agree more,* estoy totalmente de acuerdo.
● **more and more,** cada vez más. ∥ **more or less,** (*approximately*) más o menos; (*almost*) casi. ∥ **to be more than happy to do sth.,** hacer algo con mucho gusto. ∥ **the more ..., the more ...,** cuanto más ..., más ... ∥ **the more ..., the less ...,** cuanto más ..., menos ... ∥ **to see more of sb.,** ver a algn. más a menudo. ∥ **what is more,** además, lo que es más.
▲ *Véanse también many y much.*

moreish ['mɔːrɪʃ] *adj* GB *fam* (*very tasty*) vicioso,-a: *this wine's rather moreish,* es difícil tomarse sólo una copa de este vino.

moreover [mɔː'rəʊvəʳ] *adv fml* además, por otra parte.

mores ['mɔːreɪz] *npl fml* costumbres *fpl,* tradiciones *fpl.*

morgue [mɔːg] *n* depósito de cadáveres.

moribund ['mɒrɪbʌnd] *adj* moribundo,-a.

morning ['mɔːnɪŋ] **1** *n* (*gen*) mañana; (*early*) madrugada: *what are you doing this morning?,* ¿qué vas a hacer esta mañana?; *I usually go shopping in the morning,* suelo ir a comprar por la mañana; *he came home at three in the morning,* llegó a casa a las tres de la madrugada; *tomorrow/yesterday morning,* mañana/ayer por la mañana; *the following morning,* a la mañana siguiente. – **2** *adj* matutino,-a, de la mañana. – **3 mornings,** *adv* por la mañana, por las mañanas.
● **from morning till night,** desde la mañana hasta la noche, todo el día. ∥ **good morning!,** ¡buenos días! ∥ **in the morning,** (*tomorrow before noon*) mañana por la mañana. ∥ **morning, noon and night,** a todas horas.
■ **morning coat,** chaqué *m.* ∥ **morning dress,** chaqué *m* y sombrero de copa. ∥ **morning glory,** BOT dondiego de día. ∥ **morning paper,** periódico de la mañana, matutino. ∥ **morning sickness,** náuseas *fpl* del embarazo. ∥ **morning suit,** chaqué *m* y pantalón. ∥ **the morning after,** la mañana después. ∥ **the morning star,** el lucero del alba, la estrella matutina.

morning-after [mɔːnɪŋ'ɑːftəʳ] *adj.*
● **to have that morning-after feeling,** tener resaca.
■ **morning-after pill,** píldora abortiva.

Moroccan [mə'rɒkən] **1** *adj* marroquí,-ina. – **2** *n* marroquí,-ina.

Morocco [mə'rɒkəʊ] *n* Marruecos.

moron ['mɔːrɒn] **1** *n fam pej* imbécil *mf,* idiota *mf.* **2** MED retrasado,-a mental.

morose [mə'rəʊs] *adj* malhumorado,-a, hosco,-a, taciturno,-a.

morpheme ['mɔːfiːm] *n* LING morfema *m.*

morphine ['mɔːfiːn] *n* morfina.

morphology [mɔː'fɒlədʒɪ] *n* (*gen*) morfología.

Morse [mɔːs] *n* Morse *m.*
■ **Morse code,** alfabeto Morse.

morsel ['mɔːsəl] **1** *n* (*of food*) bocado. **2** *fig* trozo, fragmento, pizca.

mortal ['mɔːtəl] **1** *adj* (*gen*) mortal: *a mortal wound,* una herida mortal. – **2** *n* mortal *mf.*

mortality [mɔː'tælətɪ] **1** *n* (*condition, number of deaths*) mortalidad *f.* **2** (*number of victims*) mortandad *f.*
■ **mortality rate,** tasa de mortalidad.

mortally ['mɔːtəlɪ] *adv* mortalmente: *mortally wounded,* herido de muerte.

mortar ['mɔːtəʳ] **1** *n* (*cement*) mortero, argamasa. **2** MIL (*gun*) mortero. **3** CULIN (*bowl*) mortero, almirez *m.* – **4** *t* (*join*) unir con mortero, unir con argamasa. **5** MIL bombardear con morteros.
● **to put one's money into bricks and mortar,** invertir dinero en asuntos inmobiliarios.

mortarboard ['mɔːtəbɔːd] *n* (*academic cap*) birrete *m.*

mortgage ['mɔːgɪdʒ] **1** *n* hipoteca. – **2** *adj* hipotecario,-a. – **3** *t* hipotecar.
● **to pay off a mortgage,** redimir una hipoteca, acabar de pagar una hipoteca. ∥ **to take out a mortgage on sth.,** constituir una hipoteca sobre algo, hipotecar algo.
■ **mortgage payment,** pago hipotecario.

mortgagee [mɔːgɪ'dʒiː] *n* acreedor,-ra hipotecario,-a.

mortgager ['mɔːgɪdʒəʳ] *n* deudor,-ra hipotecario,-a.

mortice ['mɔːtɪs] *n* → **mortise.**

mortician [mɔː'tɪʃən] *n* us empresario,-a de pompas fúnebres.

mortification [mɔːtɪfɪ'keɪʃən] **1** *n* REL *fml* mortificación *f.* **2** (*chagrin*) vergüenza.

mortify ['mɔːtɪfaɪ] **1** *t* REL *fml* mortificar. **2** (*embarrass*) avergonzar, dar vergüenza a, humillar: *she was mortified,* se sintió avergonzada, le dio mucha vergüenza.
▲ *pt & pp mortified, ger mortifying.*

mortise ['mɔːtɪs] *n* muesca, mortaja.
■ **mortise lock,** cerradura embutida.

mortuary ['mɔːtʃʊərɪ] **1** *n* depósito de cadáveres. – **2** *adj* mortuorio,-a.
▲ *pl mortuaries.*

mosaic [mə'zeɪɪk] *adj* mosaico: *a mosaic floor,* un suelo de mosaico.

Moscow ['mɒskəʊ, ʲə 'mɒskaʊ] n Moscú.
Moses ['məʊzɪz] n Moisés m.
■ Moses basket, moisés m.
Moslem ['mɒzləm] n → **Muslim**.
mosque [mɒsk] n mezquita.
mosquito [məs'kiːtəʊ] n mosquito.
■ mosquito bite, picadura de mosquito. ‖ mosquito net, mosquitero, mosquitera.
▲ pl mosquitoes o mosquitos.
moss [mɒs] n BOT musgo.
■ moss stitch, (knitting) punto de arroz.
mossy ['mɒsɪ] adj musgoso,-a, cubierto,-a de musgo.
▲ comp mossier, superl mossiest.
most [məʊst] 1 adj (greatest in quantity) más: Simon's got the most points, Simon tiene más puntos; who's got the most money?, ¿quién tiene más dinero? 2 (majority) la mayoría de, la mayor parte de: most people live in flats, la mayoría de la gente vive en pisos; we spent most time on the beach, pasamos la mayor parte del tiempo en la playa; he likes most music, le gusta casi toda la música. – 3 adv más: the most difficult question, la pregunta más difcil. – 4 pron (greatest part) la mayor parte: most of it is finished, la mayor parte está terminada, casi todo está acabado; it rained most of the time, llovió durante la mayor parte del tiempo. 5 (greatest number or amount) lo máximo: the most I can do is loan you the money, lo máximo que puedo hacer es prestarte el dinero; he lied the most, mintió más que nadie. 6 (the majority of people) la mayoría: as most of you already know, como ya sabe la mayoría de vosotros. – 7 adv (superlative) más: the most beautiful girl, la chica más guapa; the most expensive restaurant, el restaurante más caro; the most exciting holiday, las vacaciones más emocionantes. 8 (to the greatest degree) más: I enjoyed the music most, lo que más me gustó fue la música; what angered me most was the way she spoke, lo que más me enojó fue su manera de hablar. 9 (very) muy, de lo más: it was most kind of you, ha sido muy amable de su parte; a most delightful evening, una tarde muy agradable. 10 US (almost) casi: he goes out most every night, sale casi todas las noches.
● at (the) (very) most, como máximo. ‖ for the most part, por lo general. ‖ most likely, muy probablemente. ‖ most of all, sobre todo. ‖ to do the most one can, hacer todo lo que se pueda, hacer lo máximo que se pueda. ‖ to make the most of sth., aprovechar algo al máximo.
▲ Véanse también many y much.
mostly ['məʊstlɪ] 1 adv (mainly) principalmente, en su mayor parte. 2 (generally) generalmente; (usually) normalmente.
MOT ['em'əʊ'tiː] abbr GB (Ministry of Transport) Ministerio de Trasporte: MOT test, inspección f técnica de vehículos, ITV f.
motel [məʊ'tel] n motel m.
moth [mɒθ] n mariposa nocturna.
■ clothes moth, polilla.
mothball ['mɒθbɔːl] n bola de naftalina.
moth-eaten ['mɒθiːtən] 1 adj (clothes) apolillado,-a. 2 fam (worn out) gastado,-a, raído,-a.
mother ['mʌðəʳ] 1 n madre f: a single mother, una madre soltera. – 2 t (care for) cuidar como una madre; (rear) criar. 3 (spoil) mimar.
■ mother country, patria, madre patria. ‖ mother figure, figura maternal. ‖ Mother Nature, la Madre f Naturaleza. ‖ mother's boy, niño de mamá. ‖ Moth-

er's Day, Día de la Madre. ‖ mother's help, niñera. ‖ mother ship, buque m nodriza. ‖ mother's ruin, fam ginebra. ‖ mother superior, madre f superior. ‖ mother tongue, lengua materna.
motherhood ['mʌðəhʊd] n maternidad f.
mothering ['mʌðərɪŋ] Mothering Sunday, n Día m de la Madre.
mother-in-law ['mʌðərɪnlɔː] n suegra.
▲ pl mothers-in-law.
motherland ['mʌðəlænd] n patria, madre f patria.
motherless ['mʌðələs] adj huérfano,-a de madre.
motherly ['mʌðəlɪ] adj maternal.
mother-of-pearl [mʌðərəv'pɜːl] n madreperla, nácar m.
mother-to-be [mʌðətə'biː] n futura madre f.
▲ pl mothers-to-be.
mothproof ['mɒθpruːf] adj a prueba de polillas.
motif [məʊ'tiːf] 1 n (pattern, design) motivo. 2 (decoration) adorno. 3 LIT MUS (theme) tema m.
motion ['məʊʃən] 1 n (movement) movimiento. 2 (gesture) gesto, ademán m. 3 POL (proposal) moción f. 4 fml (of bowels) evacuación f del vientre, deposición f. – 5 t hacer señas. – 6 i hacer señas, hacer una señal.
● in motion, en movimiento. ‖ in slow motion, CINEM a cámara lenta. ‖ to go through the motions (of doing sth.), hacer algo como es debido pero sin convicción. ‖ to motion to sb. to do sth., hacer señas a algn. para que haga algo. ‖ to put/set sth. in motion, poner algo en movimiento.
■ motion picture, película. ‖ motion pictures, el cine m. ‖ motion sickness, mareo.
motionless ['məʊʃənləs] adj inmóvil.
motivate ['məʊtɪveɪt] t motivar.
motivation [məʊtɪ'veɪʃən] n motivación f.
motive ['məʊtɪv] 1 n (reason) motivo. 2 JUR móvil m. – 3 adj motor,-ra, motriz.
■ motive force / motive power, fuerza motriz. ‖ profit motive, afán m de lucro. ‖ ulterior motive, motivo oculto.
motiveless ['məʊtɪvləs] adj sin motivo.
motley ['mɒtlɪ] 1 adj (multicoloured) abigarrado,-a, multicolor. 2 pej (of different kinds) variopinto,-a: a motley crew, un grupo variopinto.
motocross ['məʊtəkrɒs] n SP motocross m, motocrós m.
motor ['məʊtəʳ] 1 n (engine) motor m. 2 GB fam (car) coche m, automóvil m. – 3 adj TECH motor,-ra. 4 BIOL motor,-ra, motriz. – 5 i GB dated (travel by car) ir en coche.
■ motor industry, industria del automóvil. ‖ motor mechanic, mecánico,-a de coches. ‖ motor racing, carreras fpl de coches. ‖ motor show, salón m del automóvil. ‖ motor trade, sector m del automóvil. ‖ motor vehicle, vehículo a motor.
motorbike ['məʊtəbaɪk] n fam motocicleta, moto f.
motorboat ['məʊtəbəʊt] n lancha motora, motora.
motorcade ['məʊtəkeɪd] n desfile m de coches.
motorcar ['məʊtəkɑːʳ] n coche m, automóvil m.
motorcycle ['məʊtəsaɪkəl] n motocicleta, moto f.
motorcyclist ['məʊtəsaɪklɪst] n motociclista mf, motorista mf.
motoring ['məʊtərɪŋ] 1 adj automovilístico,-a, del automóvil: motoring offence, infracción de tráfico; motoring holiday, vacaciones fpl en coche. – 2 n automovilismo.
motorist ['məʊtərɪst] n automovilista mf, conductor,-ra (de coche).

motorize ['məʊtəraɪz] *t* motorizar.
motorized ['məʊtəraɪzd] *adj* motorizado,-a.
motorman ['məʊtəmən] *n* (*train driver*) maquinista *m*.
motorway ['məʊtəweɪ] *n* GB autopista.
mottled ['mɒtəld] *adj* (*skin, animal*) con manchas, moteado,-a.
motto ['mɒtəʊ] *n* lema *m*.
▲ *pl* **mottos** *o* **mottoes**.
mould[1] [məʊld] *n* (*growth*) moho.
mould[2] [məʊld] **1** *n* (*cast*) molde *m*. **2** *fig* (*type*) carácter *m*, temple *m*. – **3** *t* (*figure*) moldear; (*clay*) modelar. **4** *fig* (*shape character*) formar; (*influence*) influir en.
● **to be cast in the same mould,** ser cortado,-a por el mismo patrón. ‖ **to break the mould,** romper moldes.
mould[3] [məʊld] *n* (*loose soil*) mantillo.
moulder ['məʊldə'] **1** *i* (*go mouldy*) enmohecerse; (*rot*) pudrirse, descomponerse. **2** *fig* (*plan etc*) acumular polvo.
moulding ['məʊldɪŋ] **1** *n* (*on wall, ceiling, frame*) moldura. **2** (*object produced from mould*) molde *m*. **3** (*shaping*) modelado. **4** *fig* formación *f*.
mouldy ['məʊldɪ] *adj* (*food etc*) mohoso,-a; (*smell*) a humedad, a moho.
● **to go mouldy,** enmohecerse.
▲ *comp* **mouldier,** *superl* **moldiest**.
moult [məʊlt] **1** *i* ZOOL mudar. – **2** ZOOL muda.
mound [maʊnd] **1** *n* (*small hill*) montículo: *a burial mound,* un túmulo funerario. **2** (*pile, heap*) montón *m*.
mount[1] [maʊnt] *n* (*mountain*) monte *m*.
mount[2] [maʊnt] **1** *n* (*horse etc*) montura. **2** (*for machine, gun, trophy*) soporte *m*, base *f*; (*for photo, picture*) fondo; (*for jewel*) engaste *m*, engarce *m*; (*for slide*) marquito; (*for specimen*) platina, portaobjetos *m inv*. – **3** *t* (*horse*) montar, montarse en; (*bicycle*) montar en, subir a; (*stage, platform*) subir a; (*stairs*) subir. **4** (*fix - photo, picture*) montar; (- *stamp*) fijar; (- *jewel*) montar, engastar, engarzar; (- *specimen*) colocar en el portaobjetos. **5** (*organize - attack*) montar, preparar; (- *campaign*) montar, organizar. **6** ZOOL montar, cubrir. – **7** *i* (*go up*) subir, ascender. **8** (*get on horse*) montar. **9** (*increase*) subir, aumentar, crecer.
◆ **to mount up** *i* (*accumulate*) amontonarse, acumularse.
● **to mount guard,** montar la guardia. ‖ **to mount the throne,** subir al trono.
mountain ['maʊntən] **1** *n* GEOG montaña. **2** *fig* (*large amount*) montaña, montón *m*. – **3** *adj* de montaña: *the fresh mountain air,* el aire fresco de la montaña.
■ **mountain ash,** BOT serbal *m*. ‖ **mountain bike,** bicicleta de montaña. ‖ **mountain lion,** puma *m*. ‖ **mountain range,** cordillera, sierra. ‖ **mountain sickness,** mal *m* de montaña.
mountaineer [maʊntə'nɪə'] *n* SP alpinista *mf*; US andinista *mf*.
mountaineering [maʊntə'nɪərɪŋ] *n* SP alpinismo; US andinismo.
● **to go mountaineering,** SP hacer alpinismo; US hacer andinismo.
mountainous ['maʊntənəs] **1** *adj* (*region*) montañoso,-a. **2** (*huge*) enorme, gigantesco,-a.
mountainside ['maʊntənsaɪd] *n* ladera de montaña.
mountaintop ['maʊntəntɒp] *n* cima (de la montaña), cumbre *f* (de la montaña).
mounted ['maʊntɪd] **1** *adj* (*on horse*) montado,-a. **2** (*photo etc*) montado,-a.

■ **the mounted police,** la policía montada.
Mountie ['maʊntɪ] *n* policía *mf* montado,-a canadiense.
mounting ['maʊntɪŋ] *adj* (*increasing*) creciente.
mourn [mɔːn] *t* (*person*) llorar la muerte de; (*thing*) llorar, añorar.
◆ **to mourn for / mourn over** *t insep* (*person*) llorar a, llorar la muerte de; (*thing*) llorar.
mourner ['mɔːnə'] *n* persona que asiste a los funerales de alguien.
mournful ['mɔːnfʊl] *adj* (*person*) triste, afligido,-a, apenado,-a; (*voice, tone, look*) triste, melancólico,-a; (*cry*) lastimero,-a; (*occasion, music*) fúnebre, lúgubre.
mourning ['mɔːnɪŋ] *n* luto, duelo.
● **to be in mourning for sb.,** estar de luto por algn. ‖ **to be dressed in mourning,** ir vestido,-a de luto. ‖ **to go into mourning,** ponerse de luto.
mouse [maʊs] *n* (*gen*) ratón *m*.
▲ *pl* **mice**.
mouser ['maʊsə'] *n* (*cat*) cazador,-ra de ratones.
mousetrap ['maʊstræp] *n* ratonera.
mousse [muːs] **1** *n* CULIN mousse *f*. **2** (*for hair*) espuma (moldeadora).
moustache [məs'tɑːʃ] *n* bigote *m*.
mousy ['maʊsɪ] **1** *adj* (*colour*) pardusco,-a; (*hair*) castaño claro,-a; (*person - shy*) tímido,-a; (- *plain*) poco agraciado,-a; (- *drab*) soso,-a.
▲ *comp* **mousier,** *superl* **mousiest**.
mouth [maʊθ] **1** *n* ANAT boca. **2** (*of river*) desembocadura; (*of bottle*) boca; (*of tunnel, cave*) boca, entrada. **3** (*person to feed*) boca. – **4** *t pej* (*say - without sincerity*) decir; (- *without understanding*) recitar, repetir: *he mouthed a few platitudes about charity,* nos dijo algunos lugares comunes sobre la caridad. **5** (*say without making sound*) decir con los labios: *he just mouthed the words, he didn't sing,* simplemente movía los labios, no cantaba. – **6** *i* (*speak without making sound*) mover los labios.
◆ **to mouth off** *i* (*express opinions*) fanfarronear, fardar, jactarse (**about**, de); (*complain*) protestar (**about**, por).
● **by word of mouth,** de palabra. ‖ **down in the mouth,** deprimido,-a. ‖ **not to open one's mouth,** no abrir la boca, no decir ni pío, no decir esta boca es mía. ‖ **shut your mouth!,** ¡cierra el pico! ‖ **to be all mouth,** ser un fantasma. ‖ **to have a big mouth,** ser un bocazas. ‖ **to keep one's mouth shut,** mantener la boca cerrada, no decir nada. ‖ **to make sb.'s mouth water,** hacerse a algn. la boca agua.
■ **mouth organ,** armónica.
▲ (*verbo*) [maʊð].
mouthful ['maʊθfʊl] **1** *n* (*of food*) bocado; (*of drink*) trago; (*of air*) bocanada. **2** *fam* (*long word, phrase*) trabalenguas *m*, palabreja: *your name's a bit of a mouthful,* ¡vaya nombre más difícil de pronunciar!
mouthpiece ['maʊθpiːs] **1** *n* (*of instrument, pipe*) boquilla. **2** (*of phone*) micrófono. **3** *pej* (*newspaper, person*) voz *f*.
mouth-to-mouth [maʊθtə'maʊθ] **mouth-to-mouth (resuscitation)**, *n* boca a boca *m*.
mouthwash ['maʊθwɒʃ] *n* enjuague *m* bucal.
mouthwatering ['maʊθwɔːtərɪŋ] *adj* muy apetitoso,-a, delicioso,-a.
movable ['muːvəbəl] **1** *adj* movible, móvil. – **2 movables,** *npl* JUR bienes *mpl* muebles.
■ **movable feast,** fiesta móvil.
move [muːv] **1** *n* (*act of moving, movement*) movimiento: *he watched my every move,* observó todos mis movimientos; *one move and you're dead!,* ¡cómo te muevas, te mato! **2** (*to new home*) mudanza; (*to new job*) traslado.

3 (*in game*) jugada; (*turn*) turno: *whose move is it?,* ¿a quién le toca jugar?; *that was a bad move,* esa jugada fue mala. **4** (*action, step*) paso, acción *f,* medida; (*decision*) decisión *f;* (*attempt*) intento: *the latest moves to end the dispute have failed,* los últimos intentos de terminar con el conflicto han fracasado; *buying those shares was a good move,* la decisión de comprar esas acciones fue muy acertada. – **5** *t* (*gen*) mover; (*furniture etc*) cambiar de sitio, trasladar; (*transfer*) trasladar; (*out of the way*) apartar: *I can't move my legs,* no puedo mover las piernas; *you've moved the furniture!,* ¡habéis cambiado los muebles de sitio!; *the prisoner has been moved to Brixton,* el preso ha sido trasladado a Brixton; *can we move the date of the meeting?,* ¿podemos cambiar la fecha de la reunión?; *the car's badly parked, so I have to move it,* el coche está mal aparcado, así que tengo que cambiarlo de sitio; *move your trolley, I can't get past,* aparta tu carrito, que no paso. **6** (*affect emotionally*) conmover. **7** (*in games*) mover, jugar. **8** (*prompt*) inducir, mover; (*persuade*) convencer, persuadir; (*change mind*) hacer cambiar de opinión: *what moved you to leave your job?,* ¿qué te convenció para dejar el trabajo?; *when the spirit moves him,* cuando se le antoje, cuando le dé la gana, cuando esté de humor. **9** (*resolution, motion, etc*) proponer. **10** MED (*bowels*) evacuar. – **11** *i* (*gen*) moverse; (*change - position*) trasladarse, desplazarse; (*- house*) mudarse; (*- post, department*) trasladarse: *don't move,* no te muevas; *she was so scared she couldn't move,* tenía tanto miedo que no podía moverse; *I can't move in this dress,* no me puedo mover con este vestido; *they move in very select circles,* se mueven en círculos muy selectos; *voters are moving to the right,* los votantes se inclinan hacia la derecha. **12** (*travel, go*) ir: *that car was really moving,* ese coche iba muy rápido. **13** (*be moving*) estar en marcha, estar en movimiento: *don't distract the driver when the bus is moving,* no distraer al conductor cuando el autobús está en marcha. **14** (*leave*) irse, marcharse: *it's time we were moving,* es hora de que nos vayamos. **15** (*in game - player*) jugar; (*- pieces*) moverse: *have you moved?,* ¿has jugado? **16** (*take action*) tomar medidas, actuar: *when is the government going to move?,* ¿cuándo piensa el gobierno tomar medidas?; *we must move fast,* hemos de actuar deprisa. **17** (*advance*) progresar, avanzar: *work on the tunnel is moving very quickly,* las obras del túnel avanzan rápidamente; *things are finally moving,* por fin las cosas empiezan a moverse. **18** (*change mind*) cambiar de opinión; (*yield*) ceder: *I've tried to persuade her, but she won't move,* he intentado persuadirla, pero no cede.

◆ **to move about / move around 1** *t sep* (*object*) cambiar de sitio, cambiar de lugar, trasladar. – **2** *i* (*fidget, be restless*) moverse (mucho), ir y venir; (*travel*) viajar de un lugar a otro: *I could hear someone moving about in the flat upstairs,* oía a alguien moverse en el piso de arriba. ‖ **to move along** *i* circular: *move along now, please!,* ¡circulen, por favor! ‖ **to move away 1** *i* (*move aside etc*) alejarse, apartarse. **2** (*change house*) mudarse de casa. ‖ **to move back 1** *t sep* (*object*) mover hacia atrás; (*crowd etc*) hacer retroceder. **2** (*to original place*) volver. – **3** *i* (*return*) volver. ‖ **to move down** *i* bajar. ‖ **to move for** *t insep* US JUR proponer. ‖ **to move forward 1** *t sep* (*gen*) avanzar, adelantar; (*clock*) adelantar. – **2** *i* (*advance*) avanzar, adelantarse. ‖ **to move in 1** *i* (*into new home*) instalarse. **2** (*prepare to take control, attack, etc*) acercarse. **3** (*go into action*) intervenir. ‖ **to move in on** *t insep* (*people, enemies*) avanzar sobre; (*area, territory*) invadir. ‖ **to move off** *i* (*set off - person*) marcharse, ponerse en ca-

mino; (*- train*) salir; (*- car*) arrancar. ‖ **to move on 1** *i* (*continue journey*) seguir, seguir el viaje. **2** (*police officer's order*) circular. **3** (*go on, change to*) pasar a: *let's move on to the next item on the list,* pasemos al próximo punto de la lista. **4** (*develop, progress*) avanzar, evolucionar: *things have moved on a lot since then,* las cosas han avanzado mucho desde entonces. **5** (*time*) pasar, transcurrir. – **6** *t sep* (*police officer's order*) hacer circular. ‖ **to move out 1** *i* (*leave house*) mudarse. **2** (*leave*) irse, marcharse. ‖ **to move over 1** *t sep* (*step aside*) apartarse: *he decided to move over and make way for someone younger,* decidió apartarse y dejarle sitio a una persona más joven. – **2** *i* (*make room*) correrse, moverse. ‖ **to move up 1** *t sep* (*promote*) promover, ascender. – **2** *i* (*rise in grade*) ascender. **3** (*make room*) correrse.

● **to be on the move,** (*travel - gen*) viajar, desplazarse; (*- army etc*) estar en marcha; (*be busy*) no parar. ‖ **to get a move on,** darse prisa, moverse. ‖ **to get moving,** (*leave*) irse, marcharse. ‖ **to get sth. moving,** poner algo en marcha. ‖ **to make a move,** (*leave*) irse, marcharse; (*act*) dar un paso, actuar. ‖ **to make the first move,** dar el primer paso. ‖ **to move house,** mudarse de casa, trasladarse. ‖ **to move heaven and earth,** remover cielo y tierra. ‖ **to move with the times,** mantenerse al día. ‖ **not to move a muscle,** no inmutarse.

moveable ['muːvəbəl] *adj* → **movable**.

movement ['muːvmənt] **1** *n* (*act, motion*) movimiento; (*gesture*) gesto, ademán *m.* **2** (*of goods*) traslado; (*of troops*) desplazamiento; (*of population*) movimiento. **3** POL LIT (*trend*) tendencia, corriente *f.* **5** COMM (*of stock market*) actividad *f;* (*of prices*) variación *f.* **6** TECH (*moving parts in mechanism*) mecanismo. **7** MUS movimiento. **8** MED evacuación *f.* – **9 movements,** *npl* (*activities*) movimientos *mpl,* actividades *fpl.*

mover ['muːvəʳ] **1** *n* (*proposer*) proponedor,-ra. **2** US (*removal man*) mozo de mudanzas.

● **to be a lovely mover,** (*dancing*) bailar muy bien; (*walking*) andar con mucho garbo.

movie ['muːvɪ] **1** *n* US película. – **2 the movies,** *npl* cine *m sing.*

● **to go to the movies,** ir al cine.

■ **movie house/theater,** cine *m.* ‖ **movie star,** estrella de cine.

moviegoer ['muːvɪgəʊəʳ] *n* aficionado,-a al cine, asiduo,-a al cine.

moving ['muːvɪŋ] **1** *adj* (*that moves*) móvil; (*in motion*) en movimiento, en marcha: *it has no moving parts,* no tiene piezas móviles. **2** (*causing motion*) motor,-ra, motriz. **3** (*causing action, motivating*) instigador,-ra, promotor,-ra. **4** (*emotional*) conmovedor,-ra.

■ **moving staircase,** escalera mecánica.

mow [məʊ] *t* (*lawn*) cortar, segar; (*corn, wheat*) segar.

◆ **to mow down** *t sep* matar, acribillar, segar.

▲ *pt* **mowed,** *pp* **mowed** o **mown** [məʊn].

mower ['məʊəʳ] *n* (*for lawn*) cortacésped *m & f,* segadora de césped; (*for fields*) segadora.

mown [məʊn] *pp* → **mow**.

Mozambique [məʊzæmˈbiːk] *n* Mozambique.

Mozambiquean [məʊzæmˈbiːkən] **1** *adj* mozambiqueño,-a. – **2** *n* mozambiqueño,-a.

Mozarab [məʊˈzærəb] **1** *adj* mozárabe. – **2** *n* mozárabe *mf.*

MP¹ ['emˈpiː] *abbr* (*Member of Parliament*) miembro de la Cámara de los Comunes.

MP² ['emˈpiː] *abbr* (*Military Police*) policía militar.

mpg ['emˈpiːˈdʒiː] *abbr* (*miles per gallon*) ≈ litros/100 km.

mph ['em'piː'eɪtʃ] *abbr* (*miles per hour*) millas por hora.

MPhil ['em'fɪl] *abbr* (*Master of Philosophy*) *master en cualquier asignatura de letras.*

MRBM ['em'ɑː'biː'em] *abbr* MIL (*medium-range balistic missile*) proyectil *m* balístico de alcance intermedio; (*abbreviation*) PBAI.

MRP ['em'ɑː'piː] *abbr* (*maker's recommended price*) precio recomendado por el fabricante.

MS. ['mænjʊskrɪpt] *abbr* (*manuscript*) manuscrito; (*abbreviation*) ms.
▲ *pl* MSS..

MSc ['em'es'siː] *abbr* (*Master of Science*) master en ciencias.

Mt [maʊnt] *abbr* (*Mount, Mountain*) monte *m*, montaña.

much [mʌtʃ] **1** *adj* mucho,-a: *we haven't got much bread,* no tenemos mucho pan; *he didn't have much time,* no tenía mucho tiempo; *we've made too much jam,* hemos hecho demasiada mermelada; *why is there so much traffic?,* ¿por qué hay tanto tráfico?; *take as much time as you need,* tómate tanto tiempo como necesites; *how much money have you got?,* ¿cuánto dinero tienes? – **2** *pron* mucho: *there's not much to do round here,* no hay mucho que hacer por aquí; *much has been learned from this experience,* se ha aprendido mucho de esta experiencia; *much remains to be seen,* queda mucho por ver; *how much is it?,* ¿cuánto vale?; *we don't see much of each other,* nos vemos poco, no nos vemos muy a menudo; *I slept much of the time,* dormí durante la mayor parte del tiempo. – **3** *adv* mucho: *he felt much better,* se encontraba mucho mejor; *it's much more expensive,* es mucho más caro; *she didn't say very much,* no dijo gran cosa; *thank you ever so much,* muchísimas gracias; *I'm very much looking forward to meeting you,* tengo muchísimas ganas de conocerte; *much to her chagrin,* para gran disgusto suyo.
● **a bit much,** un poco demasiado, un poco excesivo,-a. ‖ **as much,** (*equal*) equivalente a; (*the same*) lo mismo: *that's as much as saying I'm a thief,* eso equivale a decir que soy un ladrón; *I thought as much,* ya lo suponía. ‖ **it is as much as sb. can do to ...,** apenas ..., a duras penas ...: *it was as much as I could do to restrain myself,* apenas pude contenerme. ‖ **much as,** (*although*) por mucho que + *subj*: *much as I'd like to,* por mucho que quisiera. ‖ **to be much the same,** ser más o menos igual, ser más o menos iguales. ‖ **not to be much of a ...,** no ser muy buen,-na ...: *he's not much of a singer,* no es muy buen cantante, no canta muy bien. ‖ **not to be much good at sth.,** no ser muy bueno,-a en algo. ‖ **that's not saying much,** eso no significa gran cosa, eso no es mucho decir. ‖ **to make much of sth.,** dar mucha importancia a algo. ‖ **to not be up to much,** no valer gran cosa. ‖ **without so much as,** sin siquiera.
▲ *comp* **more,** *superl* **most.**

muchness ['mʌtʃnəs] *to be much of a muchness,* *phr* ser más o menos iguales.

muck [mʌk] **1** *n* (*dirt*) suciedad *f,* porquería; (*mud*) lodo: *you've got muck all over the carpet!,* ¡has llenado la alfombra de lodo! **2** (*manure*) estiércol *m.* **3** *fig* (*filth, rubbish*) porquería.
◆ **to muck about / muck around 1** *i* (*idle*) gandulear, perder el tiempo; (*play the fool*) hacer el tonto. **2** (*fiddle*) manosear (**with,** con), juguetear (**with,** con). – **3** *t sep* (*irritate*) fastidiar, jorobar. ‖ **to muck in** *i fam* (*help*) echar una mano. ‖ **to muck out** *t sep* (*stable*) limpiar. ‖ **to muck up 1** *t sep* (*clothes*) ensuciar; (*hair*) despeinar. **2** (*spoil*) estropear, echar a perder, arruinar.

● **in a muck,** en desorden. ‖ **to make a muck of sth.,** (*spoil*) echar algo a perder; (*do badly*) meter la pata en algo.

muckraker ['mʌkreɪkə'] **1** *n* (*gossip*) chismoso,-a, cotilla *mf.* **2** (*journalist*) periodista *mf* sensacionalista.

muckraking ['mʌkreɪkɪŋ] **1** *n* (*gossiping*) cotilleo, chismorreo, chismografía. **2** (*by newspapers*) publicación *f* de escándalos.

muck-up ['mʌkʌp] *n fam* (*bungle*) chapuza, cagada, pifia; (*mess*) follón *m,* lío.
● **to make a muck-up of sth.,** hacerse un lío con algo.

mucky ['mʌkɪ] **1** *adj* (*dirty*) sucio,-a; (*muddy*) lodoso,-a. **2** (*obscene, dirty*) obsceno,-a, verde. **3** (*of weather*) asqueroso,-a.
▲ *comp* **muckier,** *superl* **muckiest.**

mucous ['mjuːkəs] *adj* mucoso,-a.
■ **mucous membrane,** membrana mucosa.

mucus ['mjuːkəs] *n* mucosidad *f.*

mud [mʌd] *n* (*gen*) barro, lodo; (*thick*) fango.
● **here's mud in your eye!,** (*cheers*) ¡salud! ‖ **mud sticks,** es difícil quitarse la mala fama de encima. ‖ **his (her etc) name is mud,** tiene muy mala fama. ‖ **to sling mud at sb. / throw mud at sb.,** lanzar acusaciones a algn., insultar a algn.
■ **mud bath,** (*medicinal*) baño de lodo; (*state*) barrizal *m.* ‖ **mud flat,** marisma.

muddle ['mʌdəl] **1** *n* (*mess*) desorden *m*: *everything's in a muddle,* todo está en desorden. **2** (*confusion, mix-up*) confusión *f,* embrollo, lío: *I'm in a muddle,* estoy hecho un lío. – **3** **to muddle (up),** *t* (*untidy*) revolver, desordenar: *who's muddled up my papers?,* ¿quién ha desordenado mis papeles? **4** (*confuse mentally*) liar, confundir, embarullar: *don't muddle me!,* ¡no me lies! **5** (*confuse, mix up*) confundir: *people always muddle me up with my cousin,* la gente siempre me confunde con mi primo.
◆ **to muddle along** *i* actuar a la buena de Dios, actuar al buen tuntún. ‖ **to muddle through** *i* arreglárselas.
● **to get in a muddle,** hacerse un lío, embarullarse: *she got in a muddle with the order,* se hizo un lío con el pedido. ‖ **to get muddled,** liarse, enredarse, embarullarse.

muddleheaded ['mʌdəlhedɪd] *adj* (*person*) despistado,-a; (*idea, argument, etc*) confuso,-a.

muddy ['mʌdɪ] **1** *adj* (*path, road, etc*) fangoso,-a, barroso,-a, lodoso,-a. **2** (*person, hands, shoes*) cubierto,-a de barro, lleno,-a de barro. **3** (*water*) turbio,-a; (*river etc*) cenagoso,-a. **4** (*colour*) sucio,-a. **5** (*thinking, idea, etc*) confuso,-a, turbio,-a. – **6** *t* (*dirty - floor etc*) ensuciar de barro, llenar de barro; (*- water*) turbiar. **7** *fig* enredar.
● **to muddy the waters,** enredar las cosas.
▲ *comp* **muddier,** *superl* **muddiest.**

mudflap ['mʌdflæp] *n* faldón *m.*

mudguard ['mʌdgɑːd] *n* guardabarros *m inv.*

mudpack ['mʌdpæk] *n* mascarilla facial de lodo.

muesli ['mjuːzlɪ] *n* muesli *m.*

muff[1] [mʌf] *n* (*for hands*) manguito.
■ **ear muffs,** orejeras *fpl.*

muff[2] [mʌf] **1** *t* (*catch*) fallar; (*shot*) errar; (*lines, words*) salirle mal a, equivocarse con. – **2** *n* fallo, pifia.
● **to muff it,** pifiarla.

muffin ['mʌfɪn] *n* GB *panecillo redondo que se come tostado y con mantequilla.*

muffle ['mʌfəl] **1** *t* (*sound*) amortiguar, ensordecer. **2** (*keep warm - person*) abrigar; (*face*) embozar.

● **to muffle os. up,** abrigarse.
muffled ['mʌfəld] 1 adj (sound, voice) sordo,-a, apagado,-a. 2 (wrapped up - person) abrigado,-a; (- face) embozado,-a.
muffler ['mʌfələʳ] 1 n dated (scarf) bufanda. 2 US AUTO silenciador m.
mufti ['mʌftɪ] in mufti, n MIL vestido,-a de paisano.
mug¹ [mʌg] n (large cup) taza alta, tazón m.
mug² [mʌg] 1 n GB fam (fool) tonto,-a, ingenuo,-a, idiota mf. 2 sl (face) jeta, careto. – 3 t (rob violently) atracar, asaltar.
◆ **to mug up** 1 t sep fam empollar. – 2 i fam empollar (on, -).
● **to be a mug's game,** ser cosa de tontos.
■ **mug shot,** foto f (de la cara de una persona detenida).
▲ (verbo) pt & pp **mugged,** ger **mugging.**
mugger ['mʌgəʳ] n atracador,-ra, asaltante mf.
mugging ['mʌgɪŋ] n atraco, asalto.
muggy ['mʌgɪ] adj (weather) bochornoso,-a.
▲ comp **muggier,** superl **muggiest.**
mulatto [mjuːˈlætəʊ] n mulato,-a.
▲ pl **mulattos** o **mulattoes.**
mulberry ['mʌlbərɪ] 1 n (fruit) mora. 2 (tree) morera, moral m. 3 (colour) morado.
▲ pl **mulberries.**
mulch [mʌltʃ] 1 n abono orgánico. – 2 t cubrir con abono orgánico.
mule¹ [mjuːl] n ZOOL mulo,-a.
● **as stubborn/obstinate as a mule,** terco,-a como una mula.
mule² [mjuːl] n (slipper) chinela.
mulish ['mjuːlɪʃ] adj terco,-a, testarudo,-a, tozudo,-a.
mull¹ [mʌl] t (wine, beer) calentar con especias.
mull² [mʌl] **to mull over,** t (ponder) reflexionar sobre, meditar sobre: I've been mulling it over, he estado reflexionando.
mullet ['mʌlɪθ]. 1 grey mullet, n mújol m. 2 red mullet, salmonete m.
mullion ['mʌlɪən] n ARCH (of window) parteluz m.
multiaccess [mʌltɪˈækses] n COMPUT acceso múltiple.
■ **multiaccess system,** sistema m multiacceso, sistema m de acceso múltiple.
multicoloured [mʌltɪˈkʌləd] adj multicolor.
multicultural [mʌltɪˈkʌltʃərəl] adj multicultural.
multifaceted [mʌltɪˈfæsɪtɪd] adj multifacético,-a.
multifarious [mʌltɪˈfeərɪəs] adj múltiple, muy diverso,-a.
multilateral [mʌltɪˈlætərəl] adj multilateral.
multilingual [mʌltɪˈlɪŋgwəl] adj plurilingüe.
multimillionaire [mʌltɪmɪljəˈneəʳ] n multimillonario,-a.
multinational [mʌltɪˈnæʃənəl] 1 adj multinacional. – 2 n multinacional f.
multiple ['mʌltɪpəl] 1 adj múltiple. – 2 n MATH múltiplo.
■ **multiple choice,** examen m tipo test. ‖ **multiple pile-up,** AUTO colisión f múltiple. ‖ **multiple sclerosis,** MED esclerosis f en placas, esclerosis f múltiple.
multiple-choice [mʌltɪpəlˈtʃɔɪs] adj tipo test.
multiplex ['mʌltɪpleks] 1 adj (cinema) multicine m. 2 TECH múltiple.
multiplication [mʌltɪplɪˈkeɪʃən] n multiplicación f.
■ **multiplication sign,** signo de multiplicar. ‖ **multiplication table,** tabla de multiplicar.
multiplicity [mʌltɪˈplɪsətɪ] n multiplicidad f, diversidad f.

multiply ['mʌltɪplaɪ] 1 t MATH multiplicar (by, por). – 2 i multiplicarse.
▲ pt & pp **multiplied,** ger **multiplying.**
multipurpose [mʌltɪˈpɜːpəs] adj multiuso inv.
multiracial [mʌltɪˈreɪʃəl] adj multirracial.
multistorey [mʌltɪˈstɔːrɪ] adj (building) de varios pisos, de varias plantas.
■ **multistorey car park,** aparcamiento de varias plantas (no subterráneo).
multitude ['mʌltɪtjuːd] 1 n (crowd) multitud f, muchedumbre f. 2 a multitude of, múltiples: a multitude of reasons, múltiples razones. 3 the multitude, las masas fpl, la masa f sing.
multitudinous [mʌltɪˈtjuːdɪnəs] adj multitudinario,-a.
mum¹ [mʌm] n GB fam mamá f.
mum² [mʌm] adj (silent) callado,-a.
● **mum's the word!,** ¡chitón! ‖ **to keep mum,** no decir ni pío, guardar silencio.
mumble ['mʌmbəl] 1 t (gen) decir entre dientes, mascullar; (prayer) musitar. – 2 i hablar entre dientes, farfullar.
mummify ['mʌmɪfaɪ] t momificar.
▲ pt & pp **mummified,** ger **mummifying.**
mummy¹ ['mʌmɪ] n (dead body) momia.
▲ pl **mummies.**
mummy² ['mʌmɪ] n GB fam (mother) mamá f.
▲ pl **mummies.**
mumps [mʌmps] n MED paperas fpl.
munch [mʌntʃ] 1 t mascar ruidosamente, masticar ruidosamente. – 2 i mascar ruidosamente, masticar ruidosamente.
munchies ['mʌntʃɪz] npl (snacks) cosas fpl para picar.
● **to have the munchies,** tener hambre.
mundane [mʌnˈdeɪn] 1 adj (wordly) mundano,-a. 2 pej (banal) rutinario,-a, monótono,-a, banal.
municipal [mjuːˈnɪsɪpəl] adj municipal.
municipality [mjuːnɪsɪˈpælɪtɪ] n municipio.
▲ pl **municipalities.**
munitions [mjuːˈnɪʃənz] 1 npl municiones fpl. – 2 adj de municiones.
mural ['mjʊərəl] n pintura mural, mural m.
murder ['mɜːdəʳ] 1 n asesinato, homicidio: he's been accused of murder, lo han acusado de asesinato; who committed the murder?, ¿quién cometió el asesinato? 2 fam fig (difficult experience) pesadilla: it was sheer murder!, ¡vaya pesadilla!; it's murder driving in the city centre, es imposible conducir por el centro de la ciudad. – 3 t (kill) asesinar, matar. 4 fam fig (be angry with) matar: if you do that again, I'll murder you!, ¡cómo vuelves a hacer esto, te mato! 5 fam fig (spoil, destroy) destrozar, arruinar.
● **to get away with murder,** hacer lo que a uno le da la gana. ‖ **to scream blue murder,** poner el grito en el cielo.
■ **murder story,** novela negra, novela policíaca. ‖ **murder weapon,** arma m homicida.
murderer ['mɜːdərəʳ] n asesino,-a, homicida mf.
murderess ['mɜːdərəs] n asesina, homicida.
murderous ['mɜːdərəs] adj asesino,-a, homicida.
murky ['mɜːkɪ] 1 adj (night) oscuro,-a, tenebroso,-a; (weather, day) gris, nublado,-a; (place) lóbrego,-a, sombrío,-a. 2 (water) turbio,-a. 3 (colour) sucio,-a. 4 fig (business, past) turbio,-a.
▲ comp **murkier,** superl **murkiest.**
murmur ['mɜːməʳ] 1 n (of voice) murmullo, susurro. 2 (of traffic) rumor m; (of insects) zumbido; (of wind) murmullo; (of water) susurro. 3 MED soplo. – 4 t murmurar: they

murmured their approval, hubo un murmullo de aprobación. – **5** _i_ murmurar, susurrar. **6** (_complain_) quejarse (**against/at,** de).
● **without a murmur,** sin rechistar.
Musak [ˈmjuːzæk] _n_ hilo _m_ musical.
Muscat [ˈmʌskæt] _n_ Mascate.
muscle [ˈmʌsəl] **1** _n_ ANAT músculo. **2** (_muscle power_) fuerza. **3** _fig_ (_strength, power_) poder _m,_ fuerza.
◆ **to muscle in** _i_ (_situation_) entrometerse (**on,** en), inmiscuirse (**on,** en); (_place_) introducirse por la fuerza.
● **to flex one's muscles,** flexionar los músculos. ‖ **to not move a muscle,** no inmutarse. ‖ **to pull a muscle,** sufrir un tirón en un músculo.
Muscovite [ˈmʌskəvaɪt] **1** _adj_ moscovita. – **2** _n_ moscovita _mf._
muscular [ˈmʌskjələ^r] **1** _adj_ (_pain, tissue_) muscular. **2** (_person_) musculoso,-a.
■ **muscular dystrophy,** distrofia muscular.
muse¹ [mjuːz] **1** _i_ meditar (**on/over,** -), reflexionar (**on/over,** sobre). – **2** _t_ pensar.
muse² [mjuːz] **1** _n_ musa. – **2 the Muses,** _npl_ las Musas _fpl._
museum [mjuːˈzɪəm] _n_ museo.
■ **museum piece,** (_fine_) pieza de museo; (_old-fashioned_) antigualla.
mush [mʌʃ] **1** _n_ (_food_) papilla, pasta. **2** US CULIN gachas _fpl._ **3** _fam_ (_writing, speech, film_) sentimentalismo.
mushroom [ˈmʌʃruːm] **1** _n_ BOT seta, hongo. **2** CULIN (_button mushroom_) champiñón _m;_ (_wild_) seta. – **3** _i_ (_gather mushrooms_) recoger setas, ir a buscar setas. **4** (_spring up_) crecer de la noche a la mañana, aparecer como hongos; (_spread_) multiplicarse. **5** (_smoke_) subir en forma de hongo.
● **to mushroom into sth.,** convertirse rápidamente en algo.
■ **mushroom cloud,** hongo nuclear.
mushy [ˈmʌʃɪ] **1** _adj_ (_food_) blando,-a, como una papilla. **2** _fam_ (_words, film, etc_) sentimentaloide, sensiblero,-a.
■ **mushy peas,** _guisantes secos cocidos en puré._
music [ˈmjuːzɪk] _n_ música.
● **to be music to one's ears,** ser música para los oídos. ‖ **to put/set sth. to music,** poner música a algo. ‖ **to read music,** leer música.
■ **music box,** caja de música. ‖ **music centre,** equipo de música. ‖ **music hall,** teatro de variedades. ‖ **music lover,** melómano,-a. ‖ **music score,** partitura. ‖ **music stand,** atril _m._
musical [ˈmjuːzɪkəl] **1** _adj_ (_gen_) musical. **2** (_person - gifted_) dotado,-a para la música; (- _fond of music_) aficionado,- a a la música, melómano,-a. – **3** _n_ musical _m._
■ **musical box,** caja de música. ‖ **musical comedy,** comedia musical. ‖ **musical instrument,** instrumento musical.
musician [mjuːˈzɪʃən] _n_ músico,-a.
musk [mʌsk] _n_ (_substance_) almizcle _m._
■ **musk deer,** almizclero.
musket [ˈmʌskɪt] _n_ mosquete _m._
musketeer [mʌskəˈtɪə^r] _n_ mosquetero.
muskrat [ˈmʌskræt] _n_ almizclera.
musky [ˈmʌskɪ] _adj_ almizcleño,-a.
▲ _comp_ **muskier,** superl **muskiest.**
Muslim [ˈmʌzlɪm] **1** _adj_ musulmán,-ana. – **2** _n_ musulmán,-ana.
muslin [ˈmʌzlɪn] _n_ muselina.
musquash [ˈmʌzkwɒʃ] **1** _n_ US ZOOL almizclera. **2** (_fur_) piel de almizclera.

mussel [ˈmʌsəl] _n_ mejillón _m._
■ **mussel bed,** criadero de mejillones.
must¹ [mʌst] **1** _aux_ (_necessity, obligation_) deber, tener que: _I must leave now,_ tengo que marcharme ahora; _you must work harder,_ debes trabajar más; _you really must go and see this film,_ tienes que ir a ver esta película. _It must be said that she's very efficient,_ hay que reconocer que es muy eficiente; _you mustn't breathe a word about this,_ no digas ni una palabra a nadie; _must you play your music so loud?,_ ¿es necesario poner la música tan fuerte?; _I'd rather you didn't, but if you must ...,_ preferiría que no lo hicieras, pero si te empeñas ... **2** (_probability_) deber de: _she must be tired,_ debe de estar cansada; _he must be Australian,_ debe de ser australiano; _you must be Mr. Black,_ debe de ser el Sr. Black; _it must be about ten o'clock,_ deben de ser las diez; _it must have been awful,_ debió de ser terrible; _but someone must have seen her,_ pero alguien debe de haberla visto; _you must have known all along,_ debías de saberlo desde el principio; _it must have been about two o'clock,_ deberían de ser sobre las dos. – **3** _n_ (_need_) necesidad _f: it's an absolute must for all film buffs,_ es imprescindible para todos los cinéfilos.
● **if I must,** si no hay más remedio. ‖ **if you must know, ...,** si te empeñas en saberlo, ...
must² [mʌst] _n_ (_of grapes_) mosto.
must³ [mʌst] _n_ (_mould_) moho.
mustache [ˈmʌstɑːʃ] _n_ US → **moustache.**
mustard [ˈmʌstəd] _n_ (_gen_) mostaza.
■ **mustard gas,** gas _m_ mostaza. ‖ **mustard pot,** mostacera.
muster [ˈmʌstə^r] **1** _t_ (_supporters, troops_) reunir; (_army_) lograr formar. **2** (_courage, strength_) cobrar, armarse de (**up,** -); (_support_) conseguir, lograr; (_votes_) obtener. – **3** _i_ (_supporters_) reunirse, juntarse; (_troops, soldiers_) congregarse. – **4** _n_ MIL (_gathering_) asamblea; (_inspection_) revista.
● **to pass muster,** ser aceptable.
mustiness [ˈmʌstɪnəs] _n_ olor _m_ a humedad.
musty [ˈmʌstɪ] _adj_ que huele a moho, que huele a humedad.
▲ _comp_ **mustier,** superl **mustiest.**
mutant [ˈmjuːtənt] **1** _n_ mutante _mf._ – **2** _adj_ mutante.
mutation [mjuːˈteɪʃən] _n_ BIOL LING mutación _f._
mute [mjuːt] **1** _adj_ (_dumb, silent_) mudo,-a. – **2** _n_ LING mudo,-a. **3** (_dumb person_) mudo,-a. **4** MUS sordina. – **5** _t_ MUS poner sordina a.
■ **deaf mute,** sordomudo,-a. ‖ **mute swan,** cisne _m._
muted [ˈmjuːtɪd] **1** _adj_ (_sound_) apagado,-a, sordo,-a. **2** (_colour_) suave, apagado,-a. **3** (_emotion, feeling_) contenido,-a. **4** MUS con sordina.
mutilate [ˈmjuːtɪleɪt] _t_ mutilar.
mutilation [mjuːtɪˈleɪʃən] _n_ mutilación _f._
mutineer [mjuːtɪˈnɪə^r] _n_ amotinado,-a.
mutinous [ˈmjuːtɪnəs] **1** _adj_ (_guilty of mutiny_) amotinado,-a. **2** (_rebellious_) rebelde, desobediente.
mutiny [ˈmjuːtɪnɪ] **1** _n_ motín _m,_ amotinamiento, sublevación _f,_ rebelión _f._ – **2** _i_ amotinarse.
▲ (_sustantivo_) pl **mutinies;** (_verbo_) pt & pp **mutinied,** ger **mutinying.**
mutt [mʌt] **1** _n_ _fam_ (_dog_) perro callejero. **2** _fam_ (_fool_) tonto,-a, estúpido,-a.
mutter [ˈmʌtə^r] **1** _n_ murmullo, refunfuño. – **2** _t_ (_mumble_) murmurar, mascullar, decir entre dientes, refunfuñar: _he muttered something about feeling ill,_ murmuró algo acerca de que no se encontraba bien. – **3** _i_ (_mumble_) murmurar, hablar entre dientes: _stop muttering!,_ ¡deja

de murmurar! **4** (*complain*) refunfuñar, rezongar, quejarse: *the guests are beginning to mutter about the food,* los clientes empiezan a quejarse de la comida.
muttering ['mʌtərɪŋ] *n* quejas *fpl*, rezongos *mpl*, refunfuños *mpl*.
mutton ['mʌtən] *n* (*sheep meat*) carne *f* de oveja, carne *f* ovina; (*lamb*) carne *f* de cordero.
● mutton dressed up as lamb, una vieja vestida de jovencita.
■ mutton chop, chuleta de cordero.
mutual ['mjuːtʃʊəl] **1** *adj* (*help, love, etc*) mutuo,-a, recíproco,-a. **2** (*friend, interest, etc*) común.
● by mutual consent, de común acuerdo. ‖ the feeling is mutual, es un sentimiento compartido.
■ mutual benefit society, mutualidad *f*. ‖ mutual fund, US fondo común de inversión. ‖ mutual insurance, seguro mutuo. ‖ mutual insurance company, mutua aseguradora.
mutually ['mjuːtʃʊəlɪ] *adv* mutuamente.
● mutually exclusive, mutuamente excluyentes.
muzzle ['mʌzəl] **1** *n* (*snout*) hocico. **2** (*guard*) bozal *m*. **3** (*of gun*) boca. – **4** *t* (*dog*) poner un bozal a. **5** *fig* (*person, press, etc*) amordazar.
muzzy ['mʌzɪ] **1** *adj* (*blurred*) borroso,-a. **2** (*groggy*) atontado,-a, espeso,-a, embotado,-a.
▲ *comp muzzier, superl muzziest.*
MW ['miːdɪəmweɪv] *abbr* (*medium wave*) onda media; (*abbreviation*) OM.
my [maɪ] **1** *adj* mi, mis: *my book,* mi libro; *my records,* mis discos; *one of my friends,* un amigo mío; *I broke my arm,* me rompí el brazo; *I'm going to wash my hair,* voy a lavarme el pelo. – **2** *interj* ¡caramba!, ¡caray!
myopia [maɪ'əʊpɪə] *n* miopía.
myopic [maɪ'ɒpɪk] *adj* miope.
myriad ['mɪrɪəd] *n* miríada.

myrrh [mɜːʳ] *n* mirra.
myrtle ['mɜːtəl] *n* BOT arrayán *m*, mirto.
myself [maɪ'self] **1** *pron* (*reflexive*) me: *I cut myself,* me corté; *I helped myself,* me serví. **2** (*after preposition*) mí (mismo,-a): *I kept it for myself,* lo guardé para mí; *I said to myself,* me dije a mí mismo. **3** (*emphatic*) yo mismo,-a: *I did it by myself,* lo hice yo mismo,-a; *I said so myself,* yo mismo,-a lo dije; *I'm a stranger here myself,* yo soy forastero aquí también.
● all by myself, (*alone*) solo,-a; (*without help*) yo solo,-a. ‖ to myself, (*private*) para mí solo,-a.
mysterious [mɪ'stɪərɪəs] *adj* misterioso,-a.
mysteriously [mɪ'stɪərɪəslɪ] *adv* misteriosamente.
mystery ['mɪstərɪ] **1** *n* misterio: *it's a mystery to me why he ever married her,* no entiendo por qué se casó con ella. – **2** *mysteries, npl* misterios *mpl*.
■ mystery play, auto sacramental *m*, misterio.
▲ *pl mysteries.*
mystic ['mɪstɪk] **1** *adj* místico,-a. – **2** *n* místico,-a.
mystical ['mɪstɪkəl] *adj* místico,-a.
mysticism ['mɪstɪsɪzəm] **1** *n* REL misticismo. **2** LIT mística.
mystify ['mɪstɪfaɪ] *t* dejar perplejo,-a, desconcertar: *she was completely mystified,* se quedó pasmada.
▲ *pt & pp mystified, ger mystifying.*
mystique [mɪs'tiːk] *n* halo de misterio.
myth [mɪθ] **1** *n* (*ancient story*) mito. **2** (*fallacy*) falacia.
● to explode the myth, refutar el mito.
mythical ['mɪθɪkəl] **1** *adj* (*of a myth*) mítico,-a. **2** (*not real, imagined*) imaginario,-a, fantástico,-a.
mythological [mɪθə'lɒdʒɪkəl] *adj* mitológico,-a.
mythology [mɪ'θɒlədʒɪ] *n* mitología.
myxomatosis [mɪksəmə'təʊsɪs] *n* mixomatosis *f*

N

N, n [en] *n (the letter)* N, n *f.*

N [nɔːθ] *abbr (north)* norte *m;* (*abbreviation*) N.

n [ˈnjuːtəʳ] *abbr (neuter)* neutro; (*abbreviation*) n.

Naafi [ˈnæfɪ] *n* GB *tienda de comestibles o cantina para las fuerzas armadas.*

naan [nɑːn] *n* → **nan²**.

nab [næb] *t fam* pillar.
▲ *pt & pp* **nabbed**, *ger* **nabbing**.

nabob [ˈneɪbɒb] *n* nabab *m.*

nacelle [næˈsel] *n* AV góndola.

nacre [ˈneɪkəʳ] *n* nácar *m.*

nadir [ˈneɪdɪəʳ] **1** ASTRON nadir *m.* **2** *fig (lowest point)* punto más bajo.

naff¹ [næf] **1** *adj sl (bad)* chungo,-a. **2** *sl (defective)* defectuoso,-a. **3** *sl (in bad taste)* hortera.

naff² [næf] **naff off!**, *interj sl* ¡vete al carajo!
◆ **to naff about** *i sl* hacer el tonto.

nag¹ [næg] *n (horse)* jamelgo, penco.

nag² [næg] **1** *t (annoy)* molestar, fastidiar. **2** *(complain)* dar la tabarra a. – **3** *i* quejarse. – **4** *n* regañón,-ona, gruñón,-ona.
▲ *pt & pp* **nagged**, *ger* **nagging**.

nagger [ˈnægəʳ] *n* regañón,-ona, gruñón,-ona.

naiad [ˈnaɪæd] *n* náyade *f.*

nail [neɪl] **1** *n* ANAT uña: **to bite/cut/trim one's nails**, morderse/cortarse/arreglarse las uñas. **2** *(metal)* clavo. – **3** *t* clavar, fijar con clavos. **4** *fam* pillar, coger.
◆ **to nail down 1** *t sep (thing)* clavar, sujetar con clavos. **2** *fig (person)* conseguir que algn. se comprometa: *I couldn't nail him down to a price*, no pude conseguir que me concretara un precio. ‖ **to nail up 1** *t sep (to wall etc)* clavar. **2** *(completely)* cerrar con clavos.
● **as hard as nails**, más duro,-a que una piedra. ‖ **to pay on the nail**, pagar a tocateja. ‖ **to hit the nail on the head**, dar en el clavo.
■ **nail clippers**, cortaúñas *m.* ‖ **nail enamel**, US esmalte *m* para las uñas. ‖ **nail polish**, esmalte *m* para las uñas. ‖ **nail scissors**, tijeras *fpl* para las uñas. ‖ **nail varnish**, esmalte *m* para las uñas. ‖ **nail varnish remover**, quitaesmaltes *m.*

nail-biting [ˈneɪlbaɪtɪŋ] *adj* emocionantísimo,-a.

nailbrush [ˈneɪlbrʌʃ] *n* cepillo de uñas.

nailfile [ˈneɪlfaɪl] *n* lima de uñas.

naive [naɪˈiːv] *adj* ingenuo,-a.

naïveté [naɪˈiːvteɪ] *n* ingenuidad *f.*

naivety [naɪˈiːvtɪ] *n* ingenuidad *f.*

naked [ˈneɪkɪd] **1** *adj (body)* desnudo,-a; *(flame)* sin protección; *(light)* sin pantalla. **2** *(unhidden)* abierto,-a: *naked agression*, agresión patente.
● **with the naked eye**, a simple vista.
■ **the naked truth**, la pura verdad.

nakedly [ˈneɪkɪdlɪ] *adv* abiertamente.

nakedness [ˈneɪkɪdnəs] *n* desnudez *f.*

namby-pamby [næmbɪˈpæmbɪ] **1** *adj* ñoño,-a. – **2** *n* ñoño,-a.

▲ *pl* **namby-pambies**.

name [neɪm] **1** *n (first name)* nombre *m;* (*surname*) apellido: *his name's Richard*, se llama Richard; *what's your name?*, ¿cómo te llamas?; *a girl by the name of Alice*, una chica llamada Alice; *he knows them all by name*, los conoce a todos por su nombre; *it's in my wife's name*, está a nombre de mi mujer. **2** *(fame)* fama, reputación *f:* *she made her name in the theatre*, se hizo famosa en el teatro; *they've got a good name*, tienen buena reputación. – **3** *t* llamar: *they named the child Dominic after his uncle*, al niño le pusieron Dominic por su tío. **4** *(appoint)* nombrar: *he was named Minister of Transport*, lo nombraron Ministro de Transportes.
● **in name only**, sólo de nombre. ‖ **in the name of ...**, en nombre de ... ‖ **to call sb. names**, insultar a algn. ‖ **to go by the name of ...**, conocerse por el nombre de ... ‖ **to make a name for os.**, hacerse un nombre. ‖ **to name names**, citar nombres, dar nombres. ‖ **to put one's name down for sth.**, apuntarse para algo. ‖ **to take sb.'s name in vain**, faltar al respeto a algn.
■ **big name**, pez *m* gordo. ‖ **name day**, santo.

name-drop [ˈneɪmdrɒp] *i* dárselas de conocer a gente famosa.
▲ *pt & pp* **name-dropped**, *ger* **name-dropping**.

name-dropper [ˈneɪmdrɒpəʳ] *n persona que se las da de conocer a gente famosa.*

name-dropping [ˈneɪmdrɒpɪŋ] *n hecho de dárselas de conocer a gente famosa.*

nameless [ˈneɪmləs] **1** *adj (unnamed)* anónimo,-a. **2** *(indescribable)* indescriptible.
● **to remain nameless**, permanecer en el anonimato.

namely [ˈneɪmlɪ] *adv* a saber.

nameplate [ˈneɪmpleɪt] *n* placa con el nombre.

namesake [ˈneɪmseɪk] *n* tocayo,-a.

nametape [ˈneɪmteɪp] *n* cinta con el nombre.

Namibia [nəˈmɪbɪə] *n* Namibia.

Namibian [nəˈmɪbɪən] **1** *adj* namibio,-a. – **2** *n* namibio,-a.

nan¹ [næn] *n* GB *fam* yaya, abuela.

nan² [næn] *n* nan bread, *n* pan plano indio con poca levadura.

nancy [ˈnænsɪ] *n* GB marica *m.*
■ **nancy boy**, marica *m.*
▲ *pl* **nancies**.

nanna [ˈnænə] *n* GB *fam* yaya, abuela.

nanny¹ [ˈnænɪ] *n (carer)* niñera. **2** GB *fam* ((*grandmother*) yaya, abuela.
▲ *pl* **nannies**.

nanny² [ˈnænɪ] nanny goat, *n* cabra.
▲ *pl* **nannies**.

nap¹ [næp] **1** *n* siesta. – **2** *i* dormir la siesta.
● **to catch sb. napping**, coger a algn. desprevenido,-a. ‖ **to have a nap / take a nap**, echar la siesta.
▲ *pt & pp* **napped**, *ger* **napping**.

nap² [næp] *n (on cloth)* lanilla.

napalm ['neɪpɑːm] 1 n napalm m. – 2 t atacar con napalm.
nape [neɪp] n nuca, cogote m.
naphtha ['næfθə] n nafta.
naphthalene ['næfθəliːn] n naftalina.
napkin ['næpkɪn] n servilleta.
■ **napkin ring,** servilletera.
Naples ['neɪpəlz] n Nápoles.
Napoleon [nə'pəʊlɪən] n Napoleón.
Napoleonic [nəpəʊlɪ'ɒnɪk] adj napoleónico,-a.
napper ['næpə'] n GB fam coco.
nappy ['næpɪ] n GB pañal m.
▲ pl nappies.
narcissi [nɑː'sɪsaɪ] npl → **narcissus**.
narcissism ['nɑːsɪsɪzəm] n narcisismo.
narcissist ['nɑːsɪsɪst] n narcisista mf.
narcissistic [nɑːsɪ'sɪstɪk] adj narcisista.
narcissus [nɑː'sɪsəs] n narciso.
▲ pl narcissi or narcissuses.
narcotic [nɑː'kɒtɪk] 1 adj narcótico,-a. – 2 n narcótico.
nark [nɑːk] 1 n fam soplón,-ona. – 2 t fam cabrear.
narky ['nɑːkɪ] adj fam malhumorado,-a.
▲ comp narkier, superl narkiest.
narrate [nə'reɪt] t narrar.
narration [nə'reɪʃən] n narración f.
narrative ['nærətɪv] 1 adj narrativo,-a. – 2 n narración f.
3 (genre) narrativa.
narrator [nə'reɪtə'] n narrador,-ra.
narrow ['nærəʊ] 1 adj estrecho,-a: a narrow road, una carretera estrecha. 2 (restricted) reducido,-a, restringido,-a: a narrow circle of friends, un círculo reducido de amigos. 3 (by very little) escaso,-a: by a narrow majority, por una escasa mayoría; to have a narrow escape, escaparse por los pelos; to have a narrow lead over sb., aventajar a algn. por un escaso margen. 4 (strict) estricto,-a, exacto,-a: in the narrowest sense of the term, en el sentido más estricto del término. 5 (limited in outlook) estrecho,-a de miras. 6 (careful) minucioso,-a. – 7 t (make narrower) estrechar. 8 (reduce) reducir, acortar: Leeds narrowed Hull's lead to only 1 point, el Leeds redujo la ventaja del Hull a 1 solo punto. 9 (eyes) entornar: she narrowed her eyes threateningly, entornó los ojos de manera amenazadora. – 10 i (become narrower) estrecharse: the road narrows after the bridge, la carretera se estrecha después del puente. 11 (eyes) entornarse. – 12 narrows, npl estrecho m sing.
◆ to narrow down t sep reducir, limitar.
■ narrow boat, barcaza.
narrow-gauge ['nærəʊgeɪdʒ] adj (railway) de vía estrecha.
narrowly ['nærəʊlɪ] 1 adv (by very little) por poco, por un escaso margen. 2 (carefully) minuciosamente.
narrow-minded [nærəʊ'maɪndɪd] adj estrecho,-a de miras.
narrowness ['nærəʊnəs] n estrechez f.
narwhal ['nɑːwəl] n narval m.
NASA ['næsə] abbr US (National Aeronautics and Space Administration) Administración f Nacional de Aeronáutica y del Espacio; (abbreviation) NASA f.
nasal ['neɪzəl] 1 adj nasal. 2 (way of speaking) gangoso,-a.
nasality [neɪ'zælɪtɪ] n nasalidad f.
nasalization [neɪzəlaɪ'zeɪʃən] n nasalización f.
nasalize ['neɪzəlaɪz] t nasalizar.
nasally ['neɪzəlɪ] adv nasalmente.

nascent ['næsənt] adj naciente.
nastily ['nɑːstɪlɪ] adv de manera desagradable.
nastiness ['nɑːstɪnəs] n lo desagradable, cosas fpl desagradables.
nasturtium [nəs'tɜːʃəm] n capuchina.
nasty ['nɑːstɪ] 1 adj (unpleasant) desagradable, repugnante, horrible: what a nasty smell!, ¡qué olor más desagradable! 2 (malicious) malintencionado,-a; (unkind) antipático,-a: she was really nasty to everyone, se mostró muy antipática con todos. 3 (dangerous) peligroso,-a: this bend is really nasty, esta curva es muy peligrosa. 4 (tricky) peliagudo,-a: it's quite a nasty little problem, es un problema bastante peliagudo. 5 (serious) grave: a nasty cold, un resfriado de cuidado.
● to have a nasty mind, ser mal pensado,-a. ‖ to turn nasty, ponerse feo,-a.
▲ comp nastier, superl nastiest.
natal ['neɪtəl] adj natal.
nation ['neɪʃən] 1 n (country) nación f, país m. 2 (ethnic group) pueblo, nación f.
national ['næʃənəl] 1 adj nacional. – 2 n súbdito,-a, ciudadano,-a.
■ national anthem, himno nacional. ‖ national costume, traje m típico nacional. ‖ national curriculum, GB programa m de estudios nacional. ‖ national debt, deuda pública. ‖ national dress, traje m típico nacional. ‖ National Front, GB partido minoritario de la extrema derecha británica. ‖ national government, gobierno nacional de coalición. ‖ national grid, GB red f nacional de tendido eléctrico. ‖ National Guard, US Guardia Nacional. ‖ National Health Service, GB ≈ Insalud m. ‖ National Insurance, ≈ Seguridad f Social. ‖ national park, parque m nacional. ‖ national service, GB servicio militar. ‖ National Trust, GB organización que vela por la conservación del patrimonio nacional, tanto natural como arquitectónico.
nationalism ['næʃənəlɪzəm] n nacionalismo.
nationalist ['næʃənəlɪst] 1 adj nacionalista. – 2 n nacionalista mf.
nationalistic ['næʃənəlɪstɪk] adj nacionalista.
nationality [næʃə'nælɪtɪ] n nacionalidad f.
▲ pl nationalities.
nationalization [næʃənəlaɪ'zeɪʃən] n nacionalización f.
nationalize [næʃənə'laɪz] t nacionalizar.
nation-state [neɪʃən'steɪt] n país independiente cuyos límites coinciden con los de una etnia.
nationwide ['neɪʃənwaɪd] 1 adj de ámbito nacional, a escala nacional: a nationwide broadcast, una emisión a todo el país. – 2 adv por todo el país.
▲ (adverbio) [neɪʃən'waɪd].
native ['neɪtɪv] 1 adj (place) natal; (language) materno,-a: her native country, su país natal; his native tongue is Danish, su lengua materna es el danés; we need a native speaker of English, necesitamos un hablante de inglés que sea nativo. 2 (plant, animal) originario,-a: it's native to Australia, es originario de Australia; native varieties of grape, variedades autóctonas de vid. 3 (relating to natives) de los indígenas: native customs, costumbres de los indígenas. – 4 n natural mf, nativo,-a: she's a native of Orense, es natural de Orense. 5 (original inhabitant) indígena mf: the natives turned out to be hostile, los nativos resultaron ser hostiles.
■ Native American, indio,-a americano,-a.
nativity [nə'tɪvɪtɪ] n fml natividad f.
■ nativity play, representación (infantil) de la Natividad.
Nativity [nə'tɪvɪtɪ] n Natividad f.

NATO ['neɪtəʊ] *abbr* (*North Atlantic Treaty Organization*) Organización *f* del Tratado del Atlántico Norte; (*abbreviation*) OTAN *f*.
▲ *También se escribe* Nato.
natter ['nætə'] **1** *i* GB *fam* charlar. – **2** *n* GB *fam* charla.
nattily ['nætɪlɪ] *adv* (*smartly*) elegantemente: *he was nattily dressed,* iba bien vestido.
natty ['nætɪ] **1** *adj* (*smart*) elegante, chulo,-a. **2** (*clever*) ingenioso,-a.
▲ *comp* nattier, *superl* nattiest.
natural ['nætʃərəl] **1** *adj* natural: *the natural world,* el mundo natural. **2** (*born*) nato,-a: *he's a natural footballer,* es un futbolista nato. **3** (*usual*) natural, normal: *it's only natural to feel afraid,* es normal tener miedo. – **4** *n* MUS (*note*) nota natural; (*sign*) becuadro.
● **to die of natural causes,** morir por causas naturales, fallecer de muerte natural.
■ **natural childbirth,** parto natural. ‖ **natural gas,** gas *m* natural. ‖ **natural history,** historia natural. ‖ **natural resources,** recursos *mpl* naturales. ‖ **natural science,** ciencias *fpl* naturales. ‖ **natural selection,** selección *f* natural. ‖ **natural wastage,** *reducción de plantilla consistente en no substituir a los que se jubilen o se marchen.*
naturalism ['nætʃərəlɪzəm] *n* naturalismo.
naturalist ['nætʃərəlɪst] *n* naturalista *mf*.
naturalistic ['nætʃərəlɪstɪk] *adj* naturalista.
naturalization [nætʃərəlaɪ'zeɪʃən] *n* naturalización *f*.
naturalize ['nætʃərəlaɪz] *t* naturalizar.
naturally ['nætʃərəlɪ] **1** *adv* (*by nature*) por naturaleza. **2** (*unaffectedly*) con naturalidad. **3** (*not artificially*) de manera natural. **4** (*of course*) naturalmente, por supuesto.
● **to come naturally to sb.,** hacerse sin esfuerzo: *it comes naturally to him,* lo hace sin esfuerzo.
nature ['neɪtʃə'] **1** *n* (*gen*) naturaleza. **2** (*character*) carácter *m*, forma de ser: *it's in her nature to be like that,* es así por naturaleza. **3** (*type*) índole *f*.
● **by nature,** por naturaleza. ‖ **to let nature take it's course,** dejar que la naturaleza siga su curso.
■ **nature conservation,** conservación *f* de la naturaleza. ‖ **nature lover,** amante *mf* de la naturaleza. ‖ **nature reserve,** reserva natural. ‖ **nature study,** ciencias *fpl* naturales. ‖ **nature trail,** *itinerario señalizado que permite observar diferentes entornos naturales.* ‖ **second nature,** (*habit*) costumbre *f* muy arraigada, hábito; (*reflex action*) acto reflejo.
naturism ['neɪtʃərɪzəm] *n* naturismo.
naturist ['neɪtʃərɪst] **1** *adj* naturista. – **2** *n* naturista *mf*.
naturopath ['neɪtʃərəpæθ] *n* naturópata *mf*.
naturopathic [neɪtʃərə'pæθɪk] *n* naturopático,-a.
naturopathy [neɪtʃə'rɒpəθɪ] *n* naturopatía.
naught [nɔːt] *n* nada.
● **to come to naught,** fracasar. ‖ **to set at naught,** despreciar.
naughtily ['nɔːtɪlɪ] *adv* mal.
naughtiness ['nɔːtɪnəs] *n* travesuras *fpl*, mala conducta.
naughty ['nɔːtɪ] **1** *adj* travieso,-a, malo,-a. **2** (*risqué*) atrevido,-a.
▲ *comp* naughtier, *superl* naughtiest.
Nauru ['naʊru:, naʊ'ru:] *n* Nauru.
Nauruan [naʊ'ru:ən] **1** *adj* nauruano,-a. – **2** *n* nauruano,-a.
nausea ['nɔːzɪə] **1** *n* (*physical*) náusea. **2** (*disgust*) asco, repugnancia.
nauseate ['nɔːzɪeɪt] **1** *t* (*physically*) dar náuseas a. **2** (*disgust*) dar asco a, repugnar.

nauseating ['nɔːzɪeɪtɪŋ] **1** *adj* (*physically*) nauseabundo,-a. **2** (*disgusting*) asqueroso,-a, repugnante.
nauseous ['nɔːzɪəs] **1** *adj* (*disgusting*) repugnante. **2** (*physically*) nauseabundo,-a.
nautical ['nɔːtɪkəl] *adj* náutico,-a.
■ **nautical mile,** milla náutica.
nautilus ['nɔːtɪləs] *n* nautilo.
Navaho ['nævəhəʊ] **1** *adj* navajo,-a. – **2** *n* (*person*) navajo,-a. **3** (*language*) navajo.
▲ *pl* Navaho, Navahos *o* Navahoes.
Navajo ['nævəhəʊ] *adj-n* → **Navaho.**
naval ['neɪvəl] *adj* naval.
■ **naval battle,** batalla naval. ‖ **naval officer,** oficial *mf* de marina. ‖ **naval power,** potencia naval.
Navarre [nə'vɑː'] *n* Navarra.
Navarrese [nævə'ri:z] **1** *adj* navarro,-a. – **2** *n* navarro,-a. **3** the Navarrese, *npl* los navarros *mpl*.
nave [neɪv] *n* nave *f*.
navel ['neɪvəl] *n* ombligo.
■ **navel orange,** naranja navel.
navigability [nævɪgə'bɪlɪtɪ] *n* navegabilidad *f*.
navigable ['nævɪgəbəl] *adj* navegable.
navigate ['nævɪgeɪt] **1** *t* (*river, sea*) navegar por. **2** (*steer-ship*) gobernar; (*- plane*) pilotar. – **3** *i* (*when sailing, flying*) dirigir; (*when driving*) guiar: *you drive, I'll navigate,* tu conduce, yo te guiaré.
navigation [nævɪ'geɪʃən] *n* navegación *f*.
navigator ['nævɪgeɪtə'] *n* MAR navegante *mf*.
navvy ['nævɪ] *n* GB peón *m*.
▲ *pl* navvies.
navy ['neɪvɪ] *n* marina de guerra, armada.
■ **navy blue,** azul marino.
▲ *pl* navies.
nay [neɪ] **1** *adv arch* (*more than that*) más aun. **2** (*in votes*) no. – **3** *n* voto negativo, no: *the nays have it,* ganan los noes.
Nazi ['nɑːtsɪ] **1** *adj* nazi. – **2** *n* nazi *mf*.
Nazism ['nɑːtsɪzəm] *n* nazismo.
NB ['en'bi:] *abbr* (*nota bene*) observa bien; (*abbreviation*) N.B.
▲ *También se escribe* nb, N.B. *y* n.b..
NBA ['en'bi:'eɪ] *abbr* US (*National Basketball Association*) asociación nacional de baloncesto; (*abbreviation*) NBA *f*.
NBC ['en'bi:'si:] *abbr* US (*National Broadcasting Company*) sociedad nacional de radiodifusión; (*abbreviation*) NBC *f*.
NCO ['en'si:'əʊ] *abbr* GB (*non-commissioned officer*) suboficial *m*.
NE [nɔː'θ'i:st] *abbr* (*northeast*) nordeste *m*; (*abbreviation*) NE.
Neanderthal [nɪ'ændətɑːl] *adj* de Neanderthal.
■ **Neanderthal man,** hombre *m* de Neanderthal.
neap [niːp] *n* neap (tide), *n* marea muerta.
Neapolitan [nɪə'pɒlɪtən] **1** *adj* napolitano,-a. – **2** *n* napolitano,-a.
near [nɪə'] **1** *adj* cercano,-a: *where is the nearest bank?,* ¿dónde está el banco más cercano?; *Barclays is quite near,* Barclays queda bastante cerca. **2** (*relations*) cercano,-a: *a near relative,* un pariente cercano; *one's nearest and dearest,* los más queridos. **3** (*time*) próximo,-a: *in the near future,* en un futuro próximo. **4** (*similar*) parecido,-a: *this is the nearest we have, I'm afraid,* lo siento, pero esto es lo más parecido que tenemos. – **5** *adv* cerca: *I live quite near (by),* vivo bastante cerca. – **6** *prep* cerca de: *it's near the market,* está cerca del

mercado; *near the end of the book,* hacia el final del libro. **7 near (to),** a punto de: *she was near to crying,* estuvo a punto de llorar. **– 8** *t* acercarse a: *we are nearing the day when ...,* nos acercamos al día en que ...
● **to come near,** acercarse. ‖ **to come near to doing sth.,** estar en un tris de hacer algo. ‖ **to draw near,** acercarse.
■ **near miss,** (*shot*) *tiro que no da en el blanco por poco*; (*situation*) *situación que no se produce por poco*: *it was a near miss,* falló por poco; *the lorry almost hit us, it was a near miss,* por poco nos da el camión, nos escapamos por los pelos.

nearby [ˈnɪəbaɪ] **1** *adj* cercano,-a: *a nearby hotel,* un hotel cercano. **– 2** *adv* cerca: *is there one nearby?,* ¿hay alguno cerca?
▲ (*adverbio*) [nɪəˈbaɪ].

nearly [ˈnɪəlɪ] *adv* casi.
● **not nearly,** ni mucho menos, ni con mucho: *there's not nearly enough time to finish,* el tiempo para acabar es del todo insuficiente.

nearness [ˈnɪənəs] *n* proximidad *f.*

nearside [ˈnɪəsaɪd] **1** *n* AUTO (*right-hand drive*) lado izquierdo; (*left-hand drive*) lado derecho. **– 2** *adj* AUTO (*right-hand drive*) del lado izquierdo; (*left-hand drive*) del lado derecho.

near-sighted [nɪəˈsaɪtɪd] *adj* miope, corto,-a de vista.

near-sightedness [nɪəˈsaɪtdnəs] *adj* miopía.

neat [niːt] **1** *adj* (*room*) ordenado,-a; (*garden*) bien arreglado,-a. **2** (*person*) pulcro,-a; (*in habits*) ordenado,-a. **3** (*writing*) claro,-a. **4** (*clever*) ingenioso,-a, apañado,-a. **5** (*drinks*) solo,-a. **6** US fantástico,-a, estupendo,-a, chulo,-a, guay.

neaten [ˈniːtən] *t* arreglar, ordenar.

neatly [ˈniːtlɪ] **1** *adv* cuidadosamente, con esmero. **2** (*cleverly*) con ingenio, con habilidad.

neatness [ˈniːtnəs] *n* esmero.

nebula [ˈnebjʊlə] *n* nebulosa.
▲ *pl* **nebulae** [ˈnebjʊliː] o **nebulas**.

nebular [ˈnebjʊləʳ] *adj* nebular.

nebulous [ˈnebjʊləs] *adj* nebuloso,-a.

nebulously [ˈnebjʊləslɪ] *adv* nebulosamente.

necessaries [ˈnesəsərɪz] *npl* → **necessary**.

necessarily [nesəˈserɪlɪ] **1** *adv* necesariamente. **2** (*inevitably*) inevitablemente, forzosamente.

necessary [ˈnesɪsərɪ] **1** *adj* necesario,-a. **2** (*inevitable*) inevitable, forzoso,-a. **– 3 necessaries,** *npl* lo necesario, cosas *fpl* necesarias.
● **to do the necessary,** hacer lo necesario.

necessitate [nɪˈsesɪteɪt] *t* requerir, exigir, hacer necesario,-a.

necessitous [nəˈsesɪtəs] *adj* necesitado,-a.

necessity [nɪˈsesɪtɪ] **1** *n* necesidad *f: it's a necessity,* es indispensable. **2** (*item*) requisito indispensable.
● **necessity is the mother of invention,** la necesidad aviva el ingenio. ‖ **of necessity,** inevitablemente. ‖ **to make a virtue out of necessity,** hacer de la necesidad una virtud.
▲ *pl* **necessities**.

neck [nek] **1** *n* cuello. **– 2** *i fam* (*kiss*) morrearse; (*caress*) pegarse el lote.
● **in this neck of the woods,** por aquí. ‖ **to be neck and neck,** ir parejos,-as. ‖ **to be up to one's neck in sth.,** estar hasta el cuello de algo. ‖ **to be in sth. up to one's neck,** estar metido,-a en algo hasta el cuello. ‖ **to break one's neck,** desnucarse. ‖ **to break one's neck doing sth.,** matarse haciendo algo. ‖ **to break**

sb.'s neck, romper el pescuezo a algn. ‖ **to get it in the neck,** *fam* cargárselas. ‖ **to risk one's neck,** jugarse el tipo. ‖ **to stick one's neck out,** arriesgarse. ‖ **to win by a neck,** ganar por una cabeza.

neckband [ˈnekbænd] *n* tirilla.

neckerchief [ˈnekətʃiːf] *n* pañuelo.

necklace [ˈnekləs] *n* collar *m.*

necklet [ˈneklət] *n* gargantilla.

neckline [ˈneklaɪn] *n* escote *m.*
● **with a low neckline,** muy escotado,-a.

necktie [ˈnektaɪ] *n* corbata.

necromancer [ˈnekrənænsəʳ] *n* nigromante *mf.*

necromancy [ˈnekrəmænsɪ] *n* nigromancia, necromancia.

necrophilia [nekrəˈfɪlɪə] *n* necrofilia.

necrophiliac [nekrəˈfɪlɪæk] **1** *adj* necrófilo,-a. **– 2** *n* necrófilo,-a.

necropolis [nəˈkrɒpəlɪs] *n* necrópolis *f.*

nectar [ˈnektəʳ] *n* néctar *m.*

nectarine [ˈnektəriːn] *n* nectarina.

née [neɪ] *adj* de soltera: *Mrs Hastings, née Lawley,* la Sra. Hastings, de soltera Lawley.

need [niːd] **1** *n* necesidad *f: there's no need for all of you to come with me,* no hace falta que me acompañéis todos; *I have enough to satisfy my needs,* tengo suficiente para satisfacer mis necesidades; *his need is greater than ours,* le hace más falta a él que a nosotros. **2** (*poverty*) necesidad *f,* infortunio: *to help sb. in time of need,* ayudar a algn. en tiempos de necesidad. **– 3** *t* necesitar: *you'll need a pencil,* necesitarás un lápiz; *we didn't need to show our passes,* no nos hizo falta enseñar los pases; *I need to see you,* tengo que verte; *your hair needs washing,* tendrías que lavarte el pelo. **– 4** *aux* hacer falta: *need we all go?,* ¿hace falta que vayamos todos?; *need you drive so fast?,* ¿tienes que conducir tan deprisa?; *you needn't come in tomorrow,* no hace falta que vengas mañana; *you needn't have bought me a present,* no hacía falta que me compraras ningún regalo.
● **if need be,** si hace falta. ‖ **if the need arises,** si surge la necesidad, si hace falta. ‖ **to be in need of,** necesitar. ‖ **to have need of,** necesitar, tener necesidad de.

needful [ˈniːdfʊl] *adj* necesario,-a.

needle [ˈniːdəl] **1** *n* (*gen*) aguja. **2** US *fam* (*friction*) pique *m.* **3** US *fam* (*injection*) inyección *f.* **4** (*leaf*) hoja: *pine needles,* hojas de pino. **– 5** *t fam* pinchar.
● **it's like looking for a needle in a haystack,** es como buscar una aguja en un pajar. ‖ **to get the needle,** GB *fam* picarse.

needlecord [ˈniːdəlkɔːd] *n* pana fina.

needlecraft [ˈniːdəlkrɑːft] *n* arte *f* de la costura.

needless [ˈniːdləs] *adj* innecesario,-a.

needlewoman [ˈniːdəlwʊmən] *n* costurera.
▲ *pl* **needlewomen** [ˈniːdəlwɪmɪn].

needlework [ˈniːdəlwɜːk] **1** *n* (*sewing*) costura. **2** (*embroidery*) bordado *m.*

needn't [ˈniːdənt] *aux* → **need**.

needs [niːdz] *adv arch* forzosamente.
● **if needs must,** si falta hace.

needy [ˈniːdɪ] **1** *adj* necesitado,-a. **– 2 the needy,** *npl* los necesitados *mpl.*
▲ *comp* **needier,** *superl* **neediest**.

ne'er [neəʳ] *adv arch* nunca.

ne'er-do-well [ˈneəduːwel] *n* vago,-a, inútil *mf.*

nefarious [nɪˈfeərɪəs] *adj* infame, nefario,-a.

neg [ˈnegətɪv] *abbr* (*negative*) negativo,-a; (*abbreviation*) negat.

negate [nɪ'geɪt] **1** *t* (*invalidate*) anular, invalidar. **2** (*deny*) negar.

negation [nɪ'geɪʃən] **1** *n* (*denial*) negación *f*. **2** (*invalidation*) anulación *f*, invalidación *f*.

negative ['negətɪv] **1** *adj* negativo,-a. – **2** *n* LING negación *f*. **3** (*answer*) negativa. **4** (*photograph*) negativo.
● **to answer in the negative,** dar una respuesta negativa.

negatively ['negətɪvlɪ] *adv* negativamente.

neglect [nɪ'glekt] **1** *n* (*of thing*) descuido, desatención *f*, abandono: *the house was in a state of neglect,* la casa estaba totalmente descuidada, la casa se encontraba en un estado de abandono. **2** (*of duty*) incumplimiento. – **3** *t* (*not take care of*) tener abandonado,-a, desatender: *I've been neglecting my friends recently,* tengo abandonados a mis amigos. **4** (*fail to attend to*) descuidar: *with so much sport you've been neglecting your academic work,* con tanto deporte tienes los estudios muy descuidados. **5** (*forget to do*) olvidar: *she neglected to lock the safe,* olvidó cerrar la caja con llave.

neglectful [nɪ'glektful] *adj* negligente, descuidado,-a.
● **to be neglectful of,** desatender, descuidar.

negligée ['neglɪʒeɪ] *n* salto de cama.

negligence ['neglɪdʒəns] *n* negligencia.

negligent ['neglɪdʒənt] *adj* negligente.

negligently ['neglɪdʒəntlɪ] *adv* con negligencia, negligentemente.

negligible ['neglɪdʒəbəl] *adj* insignificante.

negotiable [nɪ'gəʊʃɪəbəl] *adj* negociable.

negotiate [nɪ'gəʊʃɪeɪt] **1** *t* negociar. **2** (*obstacle*) salvar. – **3** *i* negociar.

negotiating [nɪ'gəʊʃɪeɪtɪŋ] **negotiating table,** *n* la mesa de las negociaciones.

negotiation [nɪgəʊʃɪ'eɪʃən] *n* negociación *f*: *the agreement is under negotiation,* el acuerdo se está negociando.

negotiator [nɪ'gəʊʃɪeɪtəʳ] *n* negociador,-ra.

Negress ['niːgrəs] *n* negra.

Negro ['niːgrəʊ] **1** *adj* negro,-a. – **2** *n* negro.
▲ *pl* **Negroes**.

Negroid ['niːgrɔɪd] **1** *adj* negroide. – **2** *n* negroide *mf*.

neigh [neɪ] **1** *n* relincho. – **2** *i* relinchar.

neighbor ['neɪbəʳ] *n* US → **neighbour**.

neighborhood ['neɪbəhʊd] *n* US → **neighbourhood**.

neighboring ['neɪbərɪŋ] *adj* US → **neighbouring**.

neighborliness ['neɪbəlɪnəs] *n* US → **neighbourliness**.

neighborly ['neɪbəlɪ] *adj* US → **neighbourly**.

neighbour ['neɪbəʳ] **1** *n* vecino,-a. **2** (*fellow man*) prójimo,-a.

neighbourhood ['neɪbəhʊd] **1** *n* vecindad *f*, barrio. **2** (*people*) vecindario.
■ **neighbourhood watch,** grupo de vigilancia vecinal.

neighbouring ['neɪbərɪŋ] *adj* vecino,-a.

neighbourliness ['neɪbəlɪnəs] *n* amabilidad *f*.

neighbourly ['neɪbəlɪ] *adj* de buen vecino, amable.

neither ['naɪðəʳ, 'niːðəʳ] **1** *adj* ninguno de los dos, ninguna de las dos: *neither boy knew the answer,* ninguno de los dos chicos sabía la respuesta. – **2** *pron* ninguno de los dos, ninguna de las dos: *neither is here,* ninguno de los dos está aquí. – **3** *adv* ni: *he's neither fat nor thin,* no es ni gordo ni delgado. **4** tampoco: *I don't like it and neither does my wife,* no me gusta a mí, y a mi mujer tampoco.

● **neither ... nor ...,** ni ... ni ...: *she neither smokes nor drinks,* ni fuma ni bebe.

nelly ['nelɪ] not on your nelly!, *phr* GB *fam* ¡ni hablar!

nem con ['nem'kɒn] *adv* JUR sin oposición.

nemesis ['nemǝsɪs] *n* némesis *f*, castigo.

neoclassical [niːəʊ'klæsɪkəl] *adj* neoclásico,-a.

neoclassicism [niːəʊ'klæsɪsɪzəm] *n* neoclasicismo.

neocolonialism [niːəʊkə'ləʊnɪəlɪzəm] *n* neocolonialismo.

neolithic [niːəʊ'lɪθɪk] *adj* neolítico,-a.

neologism [niː'ɒlədʒɪzəm] *n* neologismo.

neon ['niːɒn] *n* neón *m*.
■ **neon light,** luz *f* de neón. ‖ **neon sign,** rótulo con tubos de neón.

neonazi [niːəʊ'nɑːtsɪ] **1** *adj* neonazi. – **2** *n* neonazi *mf*.

neophyte ['niːəfaɪt] *n* neófito,-a.

Nepal [nǝ'pɔːl] *n* Nepal.

Nepalese [nepǝ'liːz] **1** *adj* nepalés,-esa, nepalí. – **2** *n* (*person*) nepalés,-esa, nepalí *mf*. **3** (*language*) nepalés *m*, nepalí *m*. – **4 the Nepalese,** *npl* los nepaleses *mpl*, los nepalíes *mpl*.

Nepali [nǝ'pɔːlɪ] *adj* → **Nepalese**.

nephew ['nevjuː] *n* sobrino.

nephritic [nɪ'frɪtɪk] *adj* nefrítico,-a.

nephritis [nɪ'fraɪtǝs] *n* nefritis *f*.

Neptune ['neptjuːn] *n* Neptuno.

nerd [nɜːd] *n sl* gilipollas *mf*.

nereid ['nɪərɪd] *n* nereida.

nerve [nɜːv] **1** *n* nervio. **2** (*daring*) valor *m*. **3** (*cheek*) descaro, jeta, cara: *what a nerve!,* ¡qué cara!
● **to be a bundle of nerves,** estar hecho,-a un manojo de nervios. ‖ **to get on sb.'s nerves,** crispar los nervios a algn. ‖ **to lose one's nerve,** rajarse.
■ **nerve cell,** neurona. ‖ **nerve centre,** centro neurálgico. ‖ **nerve gas,** gas *m* nervioso.

nerveless ['nɜːvlǝs] **1** *adj* (*weak*) débil. **2** (*brave*) valiente.

nerve-racking ['nɜːvrækɪŋ] *adj* angustioso,-a.

nervous ['nɜːvǝs] **1** *adj* nervioso,-a. **2** (*afraid*) miedoso,-a; (*timid*) tímido,-a. **3** (*apprehensive*) aprensivo,-a.
■ **nervous breakdown,** crisis *f* nerviosa. ‖ **nervous system,** sistema *m* nervioso. ‖ **nervous wreck,** manojo de nervios.

nervousness ['nɜːvǝsnǝs] **1** *n* nerviosismo, nerviosidad *f*. **2** (*fear*) miedo.

nervy ['nɜːvɪ] **1** *adj* GB *fam* nervioso,-a. **2** US *fam* descarado,-a.
▲ *comp* **nervier**, *superl* **nerviest**.

nest [nest] **1** *n* nido; (*hen's*) nidal *m*. **2** (*wasp's*) avispero; (*animal's*) madriguera. **3** *fig* nido, refugio. – **4** *i* anidar, nidificar. – **5** *t* COMPUT anidar.
■ **nest egg,** ahorrillos *mpl*. ‖ **nest of tables,** mesas *fpl* nido.

nestle ['nesǝl] **1** *i* ponerse cómodo,-a, acomodarse, arrellanarse, repantigarse: *she nestled down in the armchair to read,* se arrellanó en el sillón para leer. **2** (*lie hidden*) esconderse: *the village nestled beneath the mountain,* el pueblo yacía escondido al pie de la montaña. – **3** *t* recostar: *she nestled her head against my shoulder,* recostó su cabeza contra mi hombro.

nestling ['neslɪŋ] *n* pajarito.

net[1] [net] **1** *n* red *f*. – **2** *t* coger con red.
■ **net cord,** (*in tennis, etc*) cinta de la red. ‖ **net curtains,** visillos.
▲ *pt & pp* **netted**, *ger* **netting**.

net[2] [net] **1** *adj* FIN neto,-a: *they made a net profit of £1.5M,* tuvieron beneficios netos de un millón y medio de li-

bras. – **2** *t* (*earn*) ganar neto,-a: *he netted £8,000,* ganó ocho mil libras netas. **3** (*produce*) reportar un beneficio neto de: *this deal will net me £20,000,* este negocio me reportará un beneficio neto de veinte mil libras.
■ **net result,** resultado final. ‖ **net weight,** peso neto.
▲ *pt & pp* **netted,** *ger* **netting.**
netball ['netbɔːl] *n* ≈ baloncesto (femenino).
nether ['neðəʳ] *adj lit* inferior, de abajo.
Netherlander ['neðəlændəʳ] *n* neerlandés,-esa.
Netherlands ['neðələndʒ] **the Netherlands,** *n* los Países *mpl* Bajos.
nethermost ['neðəməʊst] *adj lit* más bajo,-a, más profundo,-a.
nett [net] *adj* → **net²**.
netting ['netɪŋ] *n* malla, red *f.*
nettle ['netəl] **1** *n* ortiga. – **2** *t* irritar.
● **to grasp the nettle,** coger el toro por los cuernos.
■ **nettle rash,** urticaria.
network ['netwɜːk] **1** *n* red *f.* – **2** *t* COMPUT conectar en red.
neuralgia [njʊ'rældʒɪə] *n* neuralgia.
neuralgic [njʊ'rældʒɪk] *adj* neurálgico,-a.
neurasthenia [njʊərəs'θiːnɪə] *n* neurastenia.
neurasthenic [njʊərəs'θiːnɪk] *adj* neurasténico,-a.
neuritis [njʊ'raɪtəs] *n* neuritis *f.*
neurological [njʊərə'lɒdʒɪkəl] *adj* neurológico,-a.
neurologist [njʊ'rɒlədʒɪst] *n* neurólogo,-a.
neurology [njʊ'rɒlədʒɪ] *n* neurología.
neuron ['njʊərɒn] *n* neurona.
neurone ['njʊərəʊn] *n* → **neuron**.
neurosis [njʊ'rəʊsɪs] *n* neurosis *f.*
▲ *pl* **neuroses** [njʊ'rəʊsiːz].
neurotic [njʊ'rɒtɪk] **1** *adj* neurótico,-a. – **2** *n* neurótico,-a.
neuter ['njuːtəʳ] **1** *adj* neutro,-a. – **2** *n* LING neutro. – **3** *t* (*castrate*) castrar.
neutral ['njuːtrəl] **1** *adj* (*in general*) neutro,-a: *a neutral colour/shampoo,* un color/champú neutro. **2** POL neutral: *a neutral country,* un país neutral. **3** (*impartial*) neutral, imparcial: *a neutral judgment,* un juicio imparcial. – **4** *n* AUTO punto muerto: *leave the car in neutral,* deja el coche en punto muerto.
neutrality [njuː'trælətɪ] *n* neutralidad *f.*
neutralization [njuːtrəlaɪ'zeɪʃən] *n* neutralización *f.*
neutralize ['njuːtrəlaɪz] *t* neutralizar.
neutron ['njuːtrɒn] *n* neutrón *m.*
■ **neutron bomb,** bomba de neutrones.
never ['nevəʳ] *adv* nunca, jamás: *I have never been there,* jamás he estado allí; *we never go there any more,* ya no vamos allí nunca; *never have I heard such rubbish,* en mi vida he oído tales tonterías; *he never so much as thanked me,* ni siquiera me dio las gracias.
● **never again,** nunca más. ‖ **never mind!,** ¡no importa! ‖ **well, I never (did)!,** ¡no me digas!
never-ending [nevə'rendɪŋ] *adj* interminable.
nevermore [nevə'mɔːʳ] *adv* LIT nunca más.
never-never [nevə'nevəʳ] **on the never-never,** *phr* GB *fam* a plazos: *they buy everything on the never-never,* lo compran todo a plazos.
■ **never-never land,** la tierra del nunca jamás.
nevertheless [nevəðə'les] *adv* sin embargo.
new [njuː] **1** *adj* nuevo,-a: *a new car,* un coche nuevo; *new bread,* pan recién hecho. **2** (*baby*) recién nacido,-a: *she's got a new baby,* acaba de tener un hijo.
● **as good as new,** como nuevo,-a. ‖ **to be new to**

sth., ser nuevo,-a en algo. ‖ **what's new?,** ¿qué hay de nuevo?
■ **new blood,** sangre *f* nueva. ‖ **new deal,** programa *m* de reformas. ‖ **New Delhi,** Nueva Delhi. ‖ **New England,** Nueva Inglaterra. ‖ **New Englander,** nativo *o* habitante de Nueva Inglaterra. ‖ **New Hampshire,** Nueva Hampshire. ‖ **New Jersey,** Nueva Jersey. ‖ **new moon,** luna nueva. ‖ **New Orleans,** Nueva Orleans. ‖ **New South Wales,** Nueva Gales del Sur. ‖ **New Testament,** Nuevo Testamento. ‖ **new town,** GB *ciudad nueva de promoción pública.* ‖ **new wave,** nueva ola. ‖ **New World,** Nuevo Mundo. ‖ **New Year,** Año Nuevo. ‖ **New Year's Day,** día *m* de Año Nuevo. ‖ **New Year's Eve,** Nochevieja. ‖ **New York,** Nueva York. ‖ **New Yorker,** neoyorquino,-a. ‖ **New Zealand,** Nueva Zelanda. ‖ **New Zealander,** neocelandés,-esa.
newborn ['njuːbɔːn] *adj* recién nacido,-a.
newcomer ['njuːkʌməʳ] *n* recién llegado,-a.
newfangled [njuː'fæŋɡld] *adj pej* novedoso,-a.
Newfoundland ['njuːfəndlənd] *n* Terranova.
newly ['njuːlɪ] *adv* recién: *newly baked bread,* pan recién hecho.
newlywed ['njuːlɪwed] *n* recién casado,-a.
news [njuːz] *n* noticias *fpl.*
● **bad news travels fast,** las malas noticias corren deprisa. ‖ **it's news to me,** *fam* ahora me entero. ‖ **no news is good news,** la falta de noticias son buenas noticias. ‖ **to break the news to sb.,** dar la noticia a algn.
■ **a piece of news,** una noticia. ‖ **news agency,** agencia de noticias. ‖ **news bulletin,** boletín *m* de noticias. ‖ **news conference,** conferencia de prensa. ‖ **news dealer,** US vendedor,-ra de periódicos. ‖ **news item,** noticia.
newsagent ['njuːzeɪdʒənt] *n* vendedor,-ra de periódicos.
■ **newsagent's (shop),** quiosco, puesto de periódicos.
newscast ['njuːzkɑːst] *n* (*gen*) informativo, noticias *fpl;* (*on television*) telediario.
newscaster ['njuːzkɑːstəʳ] *n* presentador,-ra del informativo.
newsflash ['njuːzflæʃ] *n* noticia de última hora.
newshound ['njuːzhaʊnd] *n* reportero,-a.
newsletter ['njuːzletəʳ] *n* hoja informativa, boletín *m.*
newsman ['njuːzmæn] *n* periodista *m.*
▲ *pl* **newsmen** ['njuːzmen].
newspaper ['njuːspeɪpəʳ] *n* diario, periódico.
newsprint ['njuːzprɪnt] *n* papel *m* de periódico.
newsreader ['njuːzriːdəʳ] *n* RAD TV presentador,-ra del informativo.
newsreel ['njuːzriːl] *n* noticiario *en el cine.*
newsroom ['njuːzruːm] *n* sala de redacción.
newssheet ['njuːzʃiːt] *n* hoja informativa.
newsstand ['njuːzstænd] *n* quiosco, puesto de periódicos.
newsvendor ['njuːzvendəʳ] *n* vendedor,-ra de periódicos.
newsworthy ['njuːzwɜːðɪ] *adj* de interés periodístico.
newsy ['njuːzɪ] *adj fam* lleno,-a de noticias.
▲ *comp* **newsier,** *superl* **newsiest.**
newt [njuːt] *n* tritón *m.*
next [nekst] **1** *adj* (*following – in order*) próximo,-a, siguiente; (*– in time*) próximo,-a, que viene: *the next street on the left,* la próxima calle a la izquierda; *it's on the next page,* está en la página siguiente; *not this stop, the next,*

esta parada no, la siguiente; *what time is the next bus to Leeds?*, ¿a qué hora pasa el próximo autobús para Leeds?; *next Thursday (Friday etc)*, el próximo jueves (*viernes etc*); el jueves (*viernes etc*) que viene; *next week/month/year*, la semana/el mes/el año que viene. **2** (*room, house, etc*) de al lado: *they live in the next house*, viven en la casa de al lado. – **3** *adv* luego, después, a continuación: *what did you say next?*, ¿qué dijiste luego?; *what do you want to de next?*, ¿qué quieres hacer ahora? – **4 next to**, *prep* al lado de: *it's next to the cinema*, está al lado del cine.
● **next to nothing**, casi nada.
■ **next door**, al lado, la casa de al lado: *they live next door*, viven (en la casa de) al lado. ‖ **the next world**, el más allá *m*, el otro mundo.
next-door ['neksdɔːᵊ] *adj* de al lado, de la casa de al lado: *my next-door neighbours*, los vecinos de al lado.
nexus ['neksəs] *n* nexo.
▲ *pl* **nexus**.
NHS ['en'eɪtʃ'es] *abbr* GB (*National Health Service*) ≈ Insalud *m*.
niacin ['naɪəsɪn] *n* niacina.
nib [nɪb] *n* plumilla.
nibble ['nɪbəl] **1** *n* (*action*) mordisco, mordisquito: *I felt a nibble at my bait*, sentí como mordía el cebo. **2** (*piece*) bocadito: *just a little nibble of cheese*, solo un bocadito de queso. – **3** *i* picar: *I've been nibbling all morning so I'm not hungry*, no tengo hambre porque he estado picando toda la mañana; *someone's been nibbling at this cheese*, alguien ha estado picando de este queso.
nibs [nɪbz] *his nibs*, *phr fam iron* su señoría.
Nicaragua [nɪkə'ræɡjʊə] *n* Nicaragua.
Nicaraguan [nɪkə'ræɡjʊən] **1** *adj* nicaragüeño,-a. – **2** *n* nicaragüeño,-a.
nice [naɪs] **1** *adj* (*person*) amable, simpático,-a, majo,-a: *he's such a nice boy!*, ¡es un chico tan simpático! **2** (*thing*) bueno,-a, agradable: *nice day today, isn't it?*, hace buen día, ¿verdad? **3** (*food*) delicioso,-a, bueno,-a. **4** (*pretty*) bonito,-a, mono,-a, guapo,-a. **5** (*subtle*) sutil: *a nice distinction*, una distinción sutil. **6** *iron* menudo,-a, bonito,-a: *a nice mess you made of that, didn't you?*, menuda la hiciste, ¿eh?; *a nice way to speak to your mother that is!*, ¡bonita manera de hablar a tu madre!
● **nice and ...**, bien ...: *nice and cool/warm*, bien fresquito/calentito.
Nice [niːs] *n* Niza.
nicely ['naɪslɪ] **1** *adv* (*well*) bien: *she was very nicely dressed*, iba muy bien vestida. **2** (*properly*) bien: *behave nicely, dear*, compórtate bien, cariño. **3** *fam* (*very well*) perfecto, estupendo: *Friday would suit me nicely*, el viernes me iría perfecto.
nicety ['naɪsətɪ] *n* detalle *m*: *there isn't time for all these niceties, let's get to the point*, no hay tiempo para tantos detalles, vayamos al grano.
● **to a nicety**, con suma precisión, a la perfección.
▲ *pl* **niceties**.
niche [niːʃ] *n* nicho, hornacina.
nick [nɪk] **1** *n* mella, muesca. **2** GB *fam* condiciones *fpl*: *in good/bad nick*, en buenas/malas condiciones. **3** GB *sl* (*gaol*) chirona, gayola, trena. – **4** *t* (*notch*) mellar; (*cut*) cortar: *I nicked myself when I was shaving*, me corté mientras me afeitaba. **5** *sl* (*steal*) birlar, mangar, chorizar: *somebody's nicked my wallet*, me han mangado la cartera. **6** GB *sl* (*arrest*) trincar, pillar: *he was nicked for speeding*, lo trincaron por exceso de velocidad.

● **in the nick of time**, en el momento crítico, justo a tiempo.
Nick [nɪk] *n* (*diminutive of Nicholas*) Nicolás.
■ **Old Nick**, el diablo.
nickel ['nɪkəl] **1** *n* níquel *m*. **2** US moneda de cinco centavos. – **3** *t* niquelar.
■ **nickel silver**, metal *m* blanco.
nickel-plate [nɪkəl'pleɪt] *t* niquelar.
nicker ['nɪkəᵊ] *n* GB *sl* libra.
nicknack ['nɪknæk] *n* → **knick-knack**.
nickname ['nɪkneɪm] **1** *n* apodo. – **2** *t* apodar: *he was nicknamed "Lanky"*, lo apodaron "Lanky".
nicotine ['nɪkətiːn] *n* nicotina.
niece [niːs] *n* sobrina.
niff [nɪf] **1** *n* GB *fam* tufo, tufillo. – **2** *i* GB *fam* atufar.
niffy ['nɪfɪ] *adj* GB *fam* apestoso,-a.
▲ *comp* **niffier**, *superl* **niffiest**.
nifty ['nɪftɪ] **1** *adj fam* (*smart*) chulo,-a. **2** *fam* (*clever*) ingenioso,-a, apañado,-a; (*deft*) hábil. **3** *fam* (*quick*) rápido,-a.
▲ *comp* **niftier**, *superl* **niftiest**.
Niger [niː'ʒeəᵊ] *n* Níger.
Nigeria [naɪ'dʒɪərɪə] *n* Nigeria.
Nigerian [naɪ'dʒɪərɪən] **1** *adj* nigeriano,-a. – **2** *n* nigeriano,-a.
niggard ['nɪɡəd] *n* avaro,-a, tacaño,-a.
niggardliness ['nɪɡədlɪnəs] *n* tacañería, mezquindad *f*.
niggardly ['nɪɡədlɪ] **1** *adj* (*person*) avaro,-a, tacaño,-a. **2** (*sum*) miserable, mezquino,-a.
nigger ['nɪɡəᵊ] *n taboo* negro,-a.
■ **nigger in the woodpile**, obstáculo, dificultad *f*.
niggle ['nɪɡəl] **1** *n* (*doubt*) duda. **2** (*worry*) preocupación *f*. – **3** *i* (*worry*) preocupar. – **4** *t* (*annoy*) molestar. – **5** *i* (*fuss*) reparar en nimiedades; (*complain*) quejarse.
niggling ['nɪɡəlɪŋ] **1** *adj* (*trifling*) insignificante, baladí, nimio,-a. **2** (*persistent*) persistente. **3** (*worrying*) preocupante.
nigh [naɪ] *adv lit* cerca: *the end of the world is nigh*, el fin del mundo está cerca.
● **nigh on**, casi: *it's nigh on four o'clock*, son casi las cuatro. ‖ **well nigh**, prácticamente.
night [naɪt] **1** *n* noche *f*. – **2** **nights**, *adv fam* de noche, por la noche: *I can't sleep nights*, no puedo dormir por la noche.
● **all night long**, toda la santa noche. ‖ **at dead of night**, en mitad de la noche. ‖ **at night**, de noche. ‖ **by night**, de noche. ‖ **last night**, anoche. ‖ **late at night**, a altas horas de la noche. ‖ **night and day**, noche y día. ‖ **to have a bad night**, pasar una mala noche. ‖ **to have a good night**, (*sleep well*) dormir bien; (*have fun*) pasárselo bien. ‖ **to have a late night**, acostarse tarde. ‖ **to have a night out**, salir de juerga por la noche. ‖ **to have an early night**, acostarse temprano. ‖ **to make a night of it**, salir de juerga hasta tarde.
■ **night blindness**, nictalopía. ‖ **night court**, juzgado de guardia. ‖ **night owl**, ave *f* nocturna, trasnochador,-ra. ‖ **night porter**, portero,-a de noche. ‖ **night safe**, caja permanente, depósito nocturno. ‖ **night school**, escuela nocturna. ‖ **night shift**, turno de noche. ‖ **night stick**, US porra. ‖ **night watchman**, vigilante *m* nocturno.
night-bird ['naɪtbɜːd] *n* ave nocturna, trasnochador,-ra.
nightcap ['naɪtkæp] **1** *n* (*hat*) gorro de dormir. **2** (*drink*) bebida que se toma antes de acostarse.
nightclub ['naɪtklʌb] *n* club *m* nocturno.

nightdress ['naɪtdres] *n* camisón *m.*
nightfall ['naɪtfɔːl] *n* anochecer *m.*
nightgown ['naɪtgaʊn] *n* camisón *m.*
nightie ['naɪtɪ] *n fam* camisón *m.*
nightingale ['naɪtɪŋgeɪl] *n* ruiseñor *m.*
nightjar ['naɪtdʒɑːʳ] *n* chotacabras *m.*
nightlife ['naɪtlaɪf] *n* ambiente *m* nocturno.
nightlight ['naɪtlaɪt] *n* (*candle*) velita; (*electric*) lucecita.
nightlong ['naɪtlɒŋ] **1** *adj* que dura toda la noche. – **2** *adv* toda la noche.
nightly ['naɪtlɪ] **1** *adv* cada noche: *she prayed nightly for a child,* rezaba cada noche por tener un hijo. – **2** *adj* cada noche: *his nightly medicine,* su medicina de cada noche.
nightmare ['naɪtmeəʳ] *n* pesadilla.
nightmarish ['naɪtmeərɪʃ] *adj* de pesadilla.
nights [naɪts] *adv fam* → **night**.
nightshade ['naɪtʃeɪd]. **1 deadly nightshade,** *n* belladona. **2 woody nightshade,** dulcamara, dulzamara, hierba mora.
nightshirt ['naɪtʃɜːt] *n* camisón *m.*
nighttime ['naɪttaɪm] *n* noche *f.*
nihilism ['nɪhɪlɪzəm] *n* nihilismo.
nihilist ['nɪhɪlɪst] *n* nihilista *mf.*
nihilistic [nɪhɪ'lɪstɪk] *adj* nihilista.
nil [nɪl] **1** *n* cero, nada: *costs have been reduced to practically nil,* los costes se han reducido prácticamente a cero. **2** sp cero: *Lincoln beat Grantham two goals to nil,* Lincoln ganó a Grantham por dos goles a cero.
Nile [naɪl] *n* el Nilo *m.*
Nilotic [naɪ'lɒtɪk] *adj* nilótico,-a.
nimble ['nɪmbəl] *adj* ágil.
nimbleness ['nɪmbəlnəs] *n* agilidad *f.*
nimbly ['nɪmblɪ] *adv* con agilidad.
nimbus ['nɪmbəs] *n* nimbo.
nincompoop ['nɪŋkəmpuːp] *n* memo,-a, mentecato,-a, tonto,-a.
nine [naɪn] **1** *adj* nueve. – **2** *n* nueve *m.*
● **nine times out of ten,** en el noventa por ciento de los casos.
■ **nine day's wonder,** fenómeno efímero.
▲ *Véase también* **six**.
ninepin ['naɪnpɪn] **1** *n* bolo. – **2 ninepins,** *npl* juego de bolos.
● **to go down like ninepins,** caer como moscas.
nineteen [naɪn'tiːn] **1** *adj* diecinueve. – **2** *n* diecinueve *m.*
● **to talk nineteen to the dozen,** hablar por los codos.
▲ *Véase también* **six**.
nineteenth [naɪn'tiːnθ] **1** *adj* decimonono,-a. – **2** *adv* en decimonono lugar. – **3** *n* (*in series*) decimonono,-a. **4** (*fraction*) decimonono; (*one part*) decimonona parte *f.*
▲ *Véase también* **sixth**.
nineties ['naɪntɪz] the nineties, *npl* los años *mpl* noventa, los noventa *mpl.*
● **to be in one's nineties,** tener entre noventa y cien años, tener noventa y tantos años.
▲ *Véase también* **sixties**.
ninetieth ['naɪntɪəθ] **1** *adj* nonagésimo,-a. – **2** *adv* en nonagésimo lugar. – **3** *n* (*in series*) nonagésimo,-a. **4** (*fraction*) nonagésimo; (*one part*) nonagésima parte *f.*
▲ *Véase también* **sixtieth**.
ninety ['naɪntɪ] **1** *adj* noventa. – **2** *n* noventa *m.*
▲ *Véase también* **sixty**.

ninny ['nɪnɪ] *n fam* bobo,-a.
▲ *pl* ninnies.
ninth [naɪnθ] **1** *adj* nono,-a, noveno,-a. – **2** *adv* en nono lugar, en noveno lugar. – **3** *n* (*in series*) nono,-a, noveno,-a. **4** (*fraction*) noveno; (*one part*) novena parte *f.*
▲ *Véase también* **sixth**.
nip [nɪp] **1** *n* (*pinch*) pellizco: *she gave him a nip,* le pegó un pellizco. **2** (*bite*) mordisco, mordedura: *the dog gave me a nip on the ankle,* el perro me pegó un mordisco en el tobillo. **3** (*drink*) trago: *a nip of whisky,* un trago de whisky. – **4** *t* (*pinch*) pellizcar: *a crab nipped my finger,* un cangrejo me pellizcó el dedo. **5** (*bite*) morder (*con poca fuerza*): *the dog nipped me,* el perro me mordió. – **6** *i* (*pinch*) pellizcar: *crabs nip,* los cangrejos pellizcan. **7** (*bite*) morder: *some dogs nip,* algunos perros muerden. **8** (*go quickly*) ir (en un momento): *she's nipped out to the shop,* ha salido un momentín a la tienda.
● **to nip in the bud,** cortar de raíz. ‖ **there's a nip in the air,** hace fresquillo.
▲ *pt & pp* nipped, *ger* nipping.
nipper ['nɪpəʳ] **1** *n* GB *fam* crío,-a, chiquillo,-a. **2** (*of crab*) pinza.
nippiness ['nɪpɪnəs] **1** *n fam* rapidez *f.* **2** *fam* (*cold*) frescor *m.*
nipple ['nɪpəl] **1** *n* (*female*) pezón *m.* **2** (*male*) tetilla. **3** (*teat*) tetilla. **4** TECH pezón *m.*
Nipponese [nɪpə'niːz] **1** *adj* nipón,-ona. – **2** *n* nipón,-ona.
nippy ['nɪpɪ] **1** *adj fam* (*quick*) rápido,-a. **2** *fam* (*cold*) fresquillo,-a: *it's a bit nippy,* hace fresquillo.
▲ *comp* nippier, *superl* nippiest.
nirvana [nɪə'vɑːnə] *n* nirvana.
nisi ['naɪsaɪ] **decree nisi,** *n* JUR sentencia provisional de divorcio.
Nissen hut ['nɪsənhʌt] *n* GB *cobertizo metálico en forma de tubo y con suelo de hormigón.*
nit [nɪt] **1** *n* liendre *f.* **2** GB *fam* imbécil *mf.*
niter ['naɪtəʳ] *n* US salitre *m.*
nitpicker ['nɪtpɪkəʳ] *n fam* quisquilloso,-a: *he's a nitpicker,* siempre busca tres pies al gato.
nitpicking ['nɪtpɪkɪŋ] **1** *adj fam* quisquilloso,-a, puñetero,-a. – **2** *n fam*: *I hate all this nitpicking,* odio que la gente sea tan quisquillosa.
nitrate ['naɪtreɪt] *n* nitrato.
nitre ['naɪtəʳ] *n* salitre *m.*
nitric ['naɪtrɪk] *adj* nítrico,-a.
■ **nitric acid,** ácido nítrico, agua fuerte.
nitrite ['naɪtraɪt] *n* nitrito.
nitrogen ['naɪtrədʒən] *n* nitrógeno.
nitroglycerine [naɪtrəʊ'glɪsəriːn] *n* nitroglicerina.
nitrous ['naɪtrəs] *adj* nitroso,-a.
■ **nitrous oxide,** óxido nitroso.
nitty-gritty [nɪtɪ'grɪtɪ] **to get down to the nitty-gritty,** *phr fam* ir al grano.
nitwit ['nɪtwɪt] *n fam* imbécil *mf.*
nix [nɪks] **1** *n* US nada. – **2** *t* US rechazar.
No ['nʌmbəʳ] *abbr* (*number*) número; (*abbreviation*) nº, núm.
▲ *También se escribe* no; *pl* Nos, nos.
no [nəʊ] **1** *adv* no: *have you seen it? –no!,* ¿lo has visto? –¡no!; *he's no better than a thief,* no es más que un ladrón. – **2** *adj* ninguno,-a; (*before masc sing*) ningún: *no doctors were available,* no había ningún médico disponible; *I have no time,* no tengo tiempo; *this is no use to me,* esto no me sirve; *"no smoking/parking/bathing",* "prohibido fumar/aparcar/bañarse"; *"no motorcycles/*

dogs", "motos/perros no". **- 3** *n* no: *there were two noes, nine yeses and one abstention,* hubo dos noes, nueve síes y una abstención.
● **no end of ...**, *fam* un mogollón de ... ‖ **no way** (José)!, ¡ni hablar! ‖ **there's no knowing / there's no telling ...**, no se puede saber ..., es imposible saber ...: *there's no telling what will happen now,* no se puede saber lo que pasará ahora.
no-account ['nəʊəkaunt] *n* US inútil *mf*, cero a la izquierda.
Noah [nəʊə] *n* Noé.
■ **Noah's ark,** el arca *f* de Noé.
nob [nɒb] *n* GB *fam dated* pez *m* gordo.
nobble ['nɒbəl] **1** *t* GB *fam* (*drug*) drogar. **2** GB *fam* (*bribe*) sobornar; (*blackmail*) chantajear. **3** (*corner*) abordar, atrapar: *he nobbled me at the party and wouldn't let me go,* me abordó en la fiesta y no me soltaba. **4** GB *fam* (*steal*) mangar.
nobility [nəʊ'bɪlɪtɪ] *n* nobleza.
noble ['nəʊbəl] **1** *adj* noble. **- 2** *n* noble *mf*.
nobleman ['nəʊbəlmən] *n* noble *m*.
▲ *pl* **noblemen** ['nəʊbəlmən].
nobleness ['nəʊbəlnəs] *n* nobleza.
noblewoman ['nəʊbəlwʊmən] *n* noble *f*.
▲ *pl* **noblewomen** ['nəʊbəlwɪmɪn].
nobly ['nəʊblɪ] **1** *adv* noblemente, con nobleza. **2** *fig* con generosidad.
nobody ['nəʊbədɪ] **1** *pron* nadie: *nobody went to the party,* no fue nadie a la fiesta. **- 2** *n* don nadie *m*.
● **like nobody's business,** *fam* como nadie.
no-claims bonus [nəʊ'kleɪmzbəʊnəs] *n* (*car insurance*) bonificación *f* de no-siniestralidad.
nocturnal [nɒk'tɜːnəl] *adj* nocturno,-a.
nocturnally [nɒk'tɜːnəlɪ] *adv* por la noche.
nocturne ['nɒktɜːn] *n* MUS nocturno.
nod [nɒd] **1** *n* saludo *con la cabeza.* **2** (*in agreement*) señal *f* de asentimiento. **- 3** *i* saludar *con la cabeza.* **4** (*agree*) asentir (*con la cabeza*).
◆ **to nod off** *i* dormirse, dar cabezadas.
● **a nod's as good as a wink (to a blind horse),** a buen entendedor, pocas palabras bastan. ‖ **to nod one's head,** asentir con la cabeza.
▲ *pt & pp* **nodded,** *ger* **nodding.**
nodal ['nəʊdəl] *adj* nodular.
nodding acquaintance [nɒdɪŋə'kweɪntəns] *n* conocimiento superficial: *I have a nodding acquaintance with him,* lo conozco de hola y adiós.
noddle ['nɒdəl] *n* GB *fam* coco.
node [nəʊd] **1** *n* BOT nudo. **2** ANAT PHYS nudo, nodo.
nodular ['nɒdjʊlə'] *adj* nodular.
nodulated ['nɒdjʊleɪtɪd] *adj* nodular.
nodule ['nɒdjuːl] *n* nódulo.
Noel [nəʊ'el] *n* Navidad *f*.
noggin ['nɒgɪn] **1** *n medida para licores; equivale a* 0,142 *litro*. **2** *fam* (*drink*) copa. **3** *fam* (*head*) coco.
no-go area [nəʊ'gəʊeərɪə] *n* GB zona prohibida.
no-hoper [nəʊ'həʊpə'] *n fam* inútil *mf*.
nohow ['nəʊhaʊ] *adv* de ninguna manera.
noise [nɔɪz] **1** *n* ruido, sonido. **- 2 noises,** *pl* comentarios *mpl*.
● **to make a noise,** hacer ruido. ‖ **to noise sth. abroad,** difundir algo.
■ **big noise,** *fam* pez *m* gordo.
noiseless ['nɔɪzləs] *adj* silencioso,-a.
noiselessly ['nɔɪzləslɪ] *adv* silenciosamente, sin ruido.

noiselessness ['nɔɪzləsnəs] *n* silencio.
noisily ['nɔɪzɪlɪ] *adv* ruidosamente.
noisiness ['nɔɪzɪnəs] *n* ruido.
noisome ['nɔɪsəm] *adj lit* asqueroso,-a.
noisy ['nɔɪzɪ] *adj* ruidoso,-a.
▲ *comp* **noisier,** *superl* **noisiest.**
nomad ['nəʊmæd] *n* nómada *mf*.
nomadic [nəʊ'mædɪk] *adj* nómada.
no-man's-land ['nəʊmænzlænd] *n* tierra de nadie.
nom de plume [nɒmdə'pluːm] *n* seudónimo.
▲ *pl* **noms de plume.**
nomenclature [nəʊ'meŋklətʃə] *n* nomenclatura.
nominal ['nɒmɪnəl] **1** *adj* nominal. **2** (*price*) simbólico,-a.
nominalize ['nɒmɪnəlaɪz] *t* nominalizar.
nominally ['nɒmɪnəlɪ] *adv* nominalmente.
nominate ['nɒmɪneɪt] **1** *t* nombrar: *he was nominated team captain,* lo nombraron capitán del equipo. **2** (*propose*) proponer: *I nominate Neil as captain,* yo propongo a Neil como capitán.
nomination [nɒmɪ'neɪʃən] **1** *n* (*appointment*) nombramiento. **2** (*proposal*) nominación *f*, propuesta.
nominative ['nɒmɪnətɪv] **1** *adj* nominativo,-a. **- 2** *n* nominativo.
nominee [nɒmɪ'niː] **1** *n* (*person chosen*) nominado,-a. **2** (*person proposed*) persona propuesta, candidato,-a.
nonaddictive [nɒnə'dɪktɪv] *adj* que no crea dependencia.
nonagenarian [nɒnədʒə'neərɪən] **1** *adj* nonagenario,-a. **- 2** *n* nonagenario,-a.
nonagon ['nɒnəgɒn] *n* eneágono.
nonagression [nɒnə'greʃən] *n* no agresión *f*.
■ **nonagression pact,** pacto de no agresión.
nonalcoholic [nɒnælkə'hɒlɪk] *adj* no alcohólico,-a, sin alcohol.
nonaligned [nɒnə'laɪnd] *adj* no alineado,-a.
nonalignment [nɒnə'laɪnmənt] *n* no alineamiento.
nonbeliever [nɒnbɪ'liːvə'] *n* no creyente *mf*.
nonbiological [nɒnbaɪə'lɒdʒɪkəl] *adj* no biológico,-a.
nonchalance ['nɒnʃələns] **1** *n* (*lack of worry*) despreocupación *f*. **2** (*calmness*) serenidad *f*, ecuanimidad *f*. **3** (*indifference*) indiferencia.
nonchalant ['nɒnʃələnt] **1** *adj* (*not worried*) despreocupado,-a. **2** (*calm*) sereno,-a ecuánime. **3** (*not interested*) indiferente.
noncombatant [nɒn'kɒmbətənt] *n* no combatiente *mf*.
noncommissioned officer [nɒnkəmɪʃənd'ɒfɪsə'] *n* suboficial *mf*.
noncommittal [nɒnkə'mɪtəl] *adj* (*person*) evasivo,-a; (*answer*) no comprometedor,-ra.
noncompetitive [nɒnkɒm'petɪtɪv] *adj* no competitivo,-a.
noncompliance [nɒnkɒm'plaɪəns] *n* no cumplimiento.
non compos mentis [nɒnkɒmpəs'mentɪs] *adj* que tiene las facultades mentales perturbadas.
nonconductor [nɒnkən'dʌktə'] *n* no conductor *m*.
nonconformism [nɒnkən'fɔːmɪzəm] *n* inconformismo.
nonconformist [nɒnkən'fɔːmɪst] **1** *adj* disidente. **- 2** *n* disidente *mf*. **3** REL miembro de cualquiera de las Iglesias que se escindieron de la Anglicana.
nonconformity [nɒnkən'fɔːmɪtɪ] *n* disidencia.
noncontributory [nɒnkən'trɪbjʊtərɪ] *adj* no contributivo,-a.

noncooperation [nɒnkəʊpəˈreɪʃən] *n* no cooperación *f.*

noncustodial [nɒnkəˈstəʊdɪəl] **1** *adj* (*parent*) *que no tiene custodia legal de sus hijos.* **2** (*sentence*) *que no implica ingresión en prisión.*

nondairy [nɒnˈdeərɪ] *adj* no lácteo,-a.

nondescript [ˈnɒndɪskrɪpt] *adj* soso,-a, insulso,-a, anodino,-a, insípido,-a.

nondiscrimination [nɒndɪskrɪmɪˈneɪʃən] *n* no discriminación *f.*

nondrinker [nɒnˈdrɪŋkəʳ] *n* abstemio,-a: *he's a non drinker,* no bebe alcohol.

nondrip [nɒnˈdrɪp] *adj* que no gotea.

nondriver [nɒnˈdraɪvəʳ] *n persona que no sabe conducir: I'm a nondriver,* no conduzco.

none [nʌn] **1** *pron* ninguno,-a: *none of the keys opens the door,* ninguna de las llaves abre la puerta; *none of them could do it,* nadie supo hacerlo; *I wanted nutmeg, but they had none,* quería nuez moscada, pero no tenían; *it's none of your business!,* ¡no tiene nada que ver contigo!, ¡no es asunto tuyo! – **2** *adv* de ningún modo: *he's none the worse for his ordeal,* no le ha afectado esa mala experiencia.

● **none but,** únicamente, solamente, sólo: *none but the strongest survived,* sobrevivieron sólo los más fuertes. ‖ **none other than,** nada menos que. ‖ **to have none of,** no tolerar, no permitir.

nonentity [nɒˈnentɪtɪ] *n* nulidad *f.*

▲ *pl* **nonentities.**

nonessential [nɒnɪˈsenʃəl] *adj* no esencial.

nonetheless [nʌnðəˈles] *adv* no obstante.

nonevent [nɒnɪˈvent] *n* fracaso.

nonexecutive director [nɒnɪgzekjʊtɪvdaɪˈrektəʳ] *n* director,-ra no ejecutivo,-a.

nonexistent [nɒnɪgˈzɪstənt] *adj* inexistente.

nonfattening [nɒnˈfætənɪŋ] *adj* que no engorda.

nonferrous [nɒnˈferəs] *adj* no ferroso,-a.

nonfiction [nɒnˈfɪkʃən] *n* no ficción *f.*

nonflammable [nɒnˈflæməbəl] *adj* ininflamable.

noninfectious [nɒnɪnˈfekʃəs] *adj* no infeccioso,-a.

noninflammable [nɒnɪnˈflæməbəl] *adj* ininflamable, ignífugo,-a.

noninterference [nɒnɪntəˈfɪərəns] *n* no injerencia.

nonintervention [nɒnɪntəˈvenʃən] *n* no intervención *f.*

non-iron [nɒnˈaɪən] *adj* que no necesita plancha.

nonmember [nɒnˈmembəʳ] *n* no socio,-a.

non-negotiable [nɒnnɪˈgəʊʃɪəbəl] *adj* no negociable.

no-no [ˈnəʊnəʊ] *n fam* cosa prohibida: *nude bathing is definitely a no-no,* bañarse desnudo está completamente prohibido.

no-nonsense [nəʊˈnɒnsens] *adj* práctico,-a.

nonoperational [nɒnɒpəˈreɪʃənəl] **1** *adj* no operativo,-a. **2** MIL no operacional.

nonpareil [ˈnɒnpəreɪl] **1** *adj* sin par, incomparable. – **2** *n* (*person*) persona sin par; (*thing*) cosa sin par.

nonparticipation [nɒnpɑːtɪsɪˈpeɪʃən] *n* no participación *f.*

nonpartisan [nɒnˈpɑːtɪzæn] *adj* imparcial.

nonpayment [nɒnˈpeɪmənt] *n* impago, falta de pago.

nonplus [nɒnˈplʌs] *t* dejar perplejo,-a.

▲ *pt & pp* **nonplussed,** *ger* **nonplussing.**

non-profit-making [nɒnˈprɒfɪtmeɪkɪŋ] *adj* sin fines lucrativos.

nonproliferation [nɒnprəlɪfəˈreɪʃən] *n* no proliferación *f.*

nonrenewable [nɒnrɪˈnjuːəbəl] *adj* no renovable.

nonresident [nɒnˈrezɪdənt] *adj* no residente *mf.*

● *"open to nonresidents",* "abierto al público".

nonresidential [nɒnrezɪˈdenʃəl] *adj* no residencial.

nonrestrictive [nɒnrɪˈstrɪktɪv] *adj* no restrictivo,-a.

nonreturnable [nɒnrɪˈtɜːnəbəl] *adj* no retornable.

nonsense [ˈnɒnsəns] *n* tonterías *fpl: don't talk nonsense!,* ¡no digas tonterías!

nonsensical [nɒnˈsensɪkəl] *adj* absurdo,-a.

non sequitur [nɒnˈsekwɪtəʳ] *n* incongruencia.

nonshrinkable [nɒnˈʃrɪŋkəbəl] *adj* que no encoge.

nonskid [ˈnɒnˈskɪd] *adj* antiderrapante.

nonslip [ˈnɒnˈslɪp] *adj* antideslizante.

nonsmoker [nɒnˈsməʊkəʳ] *n* no fumador,-ra.

nonsmoking [nɒnˈsməʊkɪŋ] *adj* de no fumadores.

nonstandard [nɒnˈstændəd] *adj* no estándar.

nonstarter [nɒnˈstɑːtəʳ] *n* (*horse*) *caballo que no toma la salida en una carrera.*

● **to be a nonstarter,** GB *fam* ser un,-a inútil, estar condenado,-a al fracaso.

nonstick [ˈnɒnˈstɪk] *adj* antiadherente.

nonstop [ˈnɒnˈstɒp] **1** *adj* (*continuous*) continuo,-a. **2** (*flight, etc.*) directo,-a, sin escalas. – **3** *adv* sin parar.

nontaxable [nɒnˈtæksəbəl] *adj* no imponible.

nontoxic [nɒnˈtɒksɪk] *adj* no tóxico,-a.

nontransferable [nɒntrænsˈfɜːrəbəl] *adj* intransferible.

nonunion [nɒnˈjuːnjən] *adj* no sindicado,-a.

nonverbal [nɒnˈvɜːbəl] *adj* no verbal.

nonviolence [nɒnˈvaɪələns] *n* no violencia.

nonviolent [nɒnˈvaɪələnt] *adj* no violento,-a.

nonvoter [nɒnˈvəʊtəʳ] *n* persona que no vota.

nonvoting [nɒnˈvəʊtɪŋ] **1** *adj* que no vota. **2** (*share*) que no da derecho a voto.

nonwhite [nɒnˈwaɪt] **1** *adj* de color. – **2** *n* persona de color.

noodle [ˈnuːdəl] *n* fideo.

nook [nʊk] *n* rincón *m.*

noon [nuːn] *n* mediodía *m.*

noonday [ˈnuːndeɪ] *n* mediodía *m.*

no-one [ˈnəʊwʌn] *pron* nadie: *no-one went to the party,* no fue nadie a la fiesta.

▲ *También se escribe no one.*

noose [nuːs] **1** *n* lazo. **2** (*hangman's*) soga, dogal *m.*

nope [nəʊp] *interj fam* !no¡.

no-place [ˈnəʊpleɪs] *adv* US → **nowhere.**

nor [nɔːʳ] **1** *conj* ni: *neither you nor I,* ni tú ni yo; *I neither know nor care,* ni lo sé ni me importa. **2** tampoco: *nor do I,* yo tampoco.

Nordic [ˈnɔːdɪk] *adj* nórdico,-a.

norm [nɔːm] *n* norma.

normal [ˈnɔːməl] *adj* normal.

normalcy [ˈnɔːməlsɪ] *n* normalidad *f.*

normality [nɔːˈmælɪtɪ] *n* normalidad *f.*

normalize [ˈnɔːməlaɪz] **1** *t* normalizar. – **2** *i* normalizarse.

normally [ˈnɔːməlɪ] *adv* normalmente.

Norman [ˈnɔːmən] **1** *adj* normando,-a. **2** (*church etc*) románico,-a. – **3** *n* normando,-a.

Normandy [ˈnɔːməndɪ] *n* Normandía.

normative [ˈnɔːmətɪv] *adj* normativo,-a.

Norse [nɔːs] **1** *adj* nórdico,-a. – **2** *n* (*language*) nórdico.

Norseman [ˈnɔːsmən] *n* vikingo.

▲ *pl* **Norsemen** [ˈnɔːsmən].

north [nɔːθ] **1** *n* norte *m: to the north of London,* al norte de Londres; *in the north of Scotland,* en el norte de Es-

cocia. – **2** *adj* del norte: *I live in north London,* vivo en el norte de Londres. – **3** *adv* al norte, hacia el norte: *we're travelling north,* viajamos hacia el norte; *they've moved north,* se han trasladado al norte; *it's north of Cambridge,* está al norte de Cambridge.
■ **North Pole,** Polo Norte. ‖ **the North Country,** GB el norte *m.*

northbound ['nɔːθbaʊnd] *adj* con dirección norte, que va hacia el norte.

Northcountryman [nɔːθ'kʌntrɪmən] *n* norteño.
▲ *pl Northcountrymen* [nɔːθ'kʌntrɪmən].

northeast [nɔːθ'iːst] **1** *n* nordeste *m,* noreste *m.* – **2** *adj* del nordeste. – **3** *adv* al nordeste, hacia el nordeste.

northeaster [nɔːθ'iːstəʳ] *n (wind)* viento del nordeste; *(storm)* temporal *m* del nordeste.

northeasterly [nɔːθ'iːstəlɪ] **1** *adj* del nordeste, del noreste. – **2** *n* viento del nordeste.

northeastern [nɔːθ'iːstən] *adj* del nordeste, del noreste.

northeastward [nɔːθ'iːstwəd] *adv* hacia el nordeste.

northeastwards [nɔːθ'iːstwədz] *adv* hacia el nordeste.

northerly ['nɔːðəlɪ] **1** *adj* del norte, septentrional. – **2** *n* viento del norte.

northern ['nɔːðən] *adj* del norte, septentrional.
■ **Northern Lights,** aurora boreal.

northerner ['nɔːðənəʳ] *n* norteño,-a.

northernmost ['nɔːðənməʊst] *adj* más septentrional.

northward ['nɔːθwəd] *adj* hacia el norte.

northwards ['nɔːθwədz] *adj* hacia el norte.

northwest [nɔːθ'west] **1** *n* noroeste *m.* – **2** *adj* del noroeste. – **3** *adv* al noroeste, hacia el noroeste.

northwester [nɔːθ'westəʳ] *n (wind)* viento del noroeste; *(storm)* temporal *m* del noroeste.

northwesterly [nɔːθ'westəlɪ] **1** *adj* del noroeste. – **2** *n* viento del noroeste.

northwestern [nɔːθ'westən] *adj* del noroeste.

northwestward [nɔːθ'westwəd] *adv* hacia el noroeste.

northwestwards [nɔːθ'westwədz] *adv* hacia el noroeste.

Norway ['nɔːweɪ] *n* Noruega.

Norwegian [nɔː'wiːdʒən] **1** *adj* noruego,-a. – **2** *n (person)* noruego,-a. **3** *(language)* noruego.

nose [nəʊz] **1** *n* nariz *f.* **2** *(of animal)* hocico. **3** *(sense)* olfato. **4** *(of car etc)* morro.
◆ **to nose around** *i* curiosear. ‖ **to nose forward** *i (car)* avanzar poco a poco. ‖ **to nose out** *i (car)* salir poco a poco.
● **it's as plain as the nose on your face,** está tan claro como el agua. ‖ **just follow your nose,** *(go straight ahead)* sigue todo recto; *(follow instinct)* guíate por el instinto. ‖ **to blow one's nose,** sonarse. ‖ **to get up sb.'s nose,** GB *fam* fastidiar a algn. ‖ **to have a nose for sth.,** tener olfato para algo. ‖ **to keep one's nose clean,** GB *fam* no meterse en líos. ‖ **to pay through the nose,** pagar un dineral. ‖ **to poke/stick one's nose into sth.,** meter las narices en algo. ‖ **to put sb.'s nose out of joint,** molestar a algn., ofender a algn. ‖ **to turn one's nose up at sth.,** hacer ascos de algo. ‖ **under sb.'s very nose / right under sb.'s nose,** ante las propias narices de algn.

nosebag ['nəʊzbæg] *n* morral *m.*

nosebleed ['nəʊzbliːd] *n* hemorragia nasal.

nosecone ['nəʊzkəʊn] *n* morro.

nosedive ['nəʊzdaɪv] **1** *n* picado. – **2** *i* descender en picado, bajar en picado.

nosegay ['nəʊzgeɪ] *n* ramillete *m* de flores.

nosey ['nəʊzɪ] *adj fam* → **nosy**.

nosh [nɒʃ] **1** *n* GB *sl* papeo. – **2** *i* papear.

nosh-up ['nɒʃʌp] *n* GB *sl* comilona.

nostalgia [nɒ'stældʒɪə] *n* nostalgia, añoranza.

nostalgic [nɒ'stældʒɪk] *adj* nostálgico,-a.

nostalgically [nɒ'stældʒɪklɪ] *adv* con nostalgia, con añoranza.

nostril ['nɒstrəl] *n* fosa nasal.

nostrum ['nɒstrəm] *n* panacea.

nosy ['nəʊzɪ] *adj fam* curioso,-a, entrometido,-a.
■ **nosy parker,** metomentodo *mf.*
▲ *comp nosier, superl nosiest.*

not [nɒt] *adv* no: *I did not steal it,* no lo robé; *she told me not to tell anyone,* me dijo que no lo dijera a nadie; *I hope/suppose not,* espero/supongo que no; *are you coming or not?,* ¿vienes o no?
● **not likely!,** ¡ni hablar! ‖ **not that ...,** no es que ...: *where is he?, not that I mind, of course,* ¿dónde está?, no es que me importe, claro está. ‖ **not to say ...,** por no decir ...
▲ *La forma contracta es* **n't:** *isn't, aren't, doesn't.*

notability [nəʊtə'bɪlɪtɪ] *n* notabilidad *f.*

notable ['nəʊtəbəl] *adj* notable.

notably ['nəʊtəblɪ] *adv* notablemente, especialmente.

notarize ['nəʊtəraɪz] *t* US autenticar, legalizar.

notary ['nəʊtərɪ] *n* notario,-a.
▲ *pl notaries.*

notation [nəʊ'teɪʃən] *n* notación *f.*

notch [nɒtʃ] **1** *n* muesca. **2** *fig* punto: *this film is several notches above his previous ones,* esta película está varios puntos por encima de sus anteriores. **3** US desfiladero. – **4** *t* hacer muescas en.
◆ **to notch up** *t insep* apuntarse.

note [nəʊt] **1** *n* MUS nota; *(key)* tecla. **2** *(message)* nota. **3** *(money)* billete *m:* *£1000 in used five pound notes,* mil libras en billetes usados de cinco libras. – **4** *t (notice)* notar, advertir: *I noted a certain reluctance on John's part,* noté cierta reticencia por parte de John. **5** *(pay special attention)* fijarse en: *note that the plural of "child" is "children",* fijaos en que el plural de "child" es "children"; *please note that VAT is not included,* advierta que el IVA no está incluido. **6** *(write down)* apuntar, anotar. – **7 notes,** *npl* apuntes *mpl.*
● **of note,** digno,-a de mención, de importancia. ‖ **to compare notes,** cambiar impresiones. ‖ **to make a note of,** apuntar. ‖ **to take notes,** tomar apuntes.

notebook ['nəʊtbʊk] *n* libreta, cuaderno.

noted ['nəʊtɪd] *adj* conocido,-a, célebre.

notelet ['nəʊtlət] *n* tarjeta.

notepad ['nəʊtpæd] *n* bloc *m* de notas.

notepaper ['nəʊtpeɪpəʳ] *n* papel *m* de cartas.

noteworthy ['nəʊtwɜːðɪ] *adj* digno,-a de mención.

nothing ['nʌθɪŋ] **1** *n* nada: *there's nothing left,* no queda nada; *it's nothing special,* no es nada del otro jueves; *it's nothing more than a cold,* no es más que un resfriado; *it's nothing to be ashamed of,* no es para avergonzarse; *he's nothing if not cheerful,* antes que nada es alegre; *it's nothing short of brilliant,* es sencillamente brillante; *there's nothing (else) for it but to leave,* no me queda más remedio que marchar; *Magic Johnson's got nothing on you,* a tu lado Magic Johnson no es nadie; *the police have got nothing on me,* la policía no tiene nada contra mí. – **2** *adv* de ningún modo, de ninguna manera: *it's nothing like a pheasant,* no se parece en nada a un faisán.

● **for nothing,** *fam* gratis. ‖ **nothing but ...,** únicamente ..., solo ... ‖ **nothing doing,** *fam* ni hablar. ‖ **nothing else,** nada más. ‖ **nothing much,** nada de interés. ‖ **there's nothing to it,** es facilísimo. ‖ **to say nothing of ...,** por no hablar de ...

nothingness ['nʌθɪŋnəs] *n* la nada.

notice ['nəʊtɪs] **1** *n* (*sign*) letrero: *there's a notice which says "No parking",* hay un letrero que pone "Prohibido aparcar". **2** (*announcement*) anuncio: *there's a notice in the paper about a lost dog,* hay un anuncio en el diario acerca de un perro extraviado. **3** (*criticism*) crítica, reseña, recensión *f: the play got very good notices,* la obra fue muy bien recibida por la crítica, la obra tenía muy buenas críticas. **4** (*attention*) atención *f: it totally escaped my notice,* se me escapó por completo; *it has been brought to my notice that ...,* se me ha informado que ... **5** (*warning*) aviso: *they gave him a month's notice to quit the flat,* le dieron un plazo de un mes para abandonar el piso. – **6** *t* notar, fijarse en, darse cuenta de. – **7** *i fam* (*show*) verse: *don't worry, the stain doesn't notice,* no te preocupes, la mancha no se ve.

● **to hand in one's notice,** presentar la dimisión. ‖ **to take no notice of,** no hacer caso de. ‖ **until further notice,** hasta nuevo aviso. ‖ **without notice,** sin previo aviso.

noticeable ['nəʊtɪsəbəl] *adj* que se nota, evidente.

noticeably ['nəʊtɪsəblɪ] *adv* de manera evidente, sensiblemente: *he was noticeably affected by the scene,* se le vio sensiblemente afectado por la escena.

noticeboard ['nəʊtɪsbɔːd] *n* tablón *m* de anuncios.

notifiable [nəʊtɪ'faɪəbəl] *adj* de declaración médica obligatoria.

notification [nəʊtɪfɪ'keɪʃən] *n* notificación *f.*

notify ['nəʊtɪfaɪ] *t* notificar, avisar.
▲ *pt & pp* **notified,** *ger* **notifying.**

notion ['nəʊʃən] **1** *n* noción *f,* idea, concepto. – **2 notions,** *npl* us mercería *f sing.*

notional ['nəʊʃənəl] *adj* nocional.

notoriety [nəʊtə'raɪətɪ] *n* mala fama.

notorious [nəʊ'tɔːrɪəs] *adj pej* célebre: *a notorious criminal,* un conocido criminal.

notoriously [nəʊ'tɔːrɪəslɪ] *adv* notoriamente.

notwithstanding [nɒtwɪθ'stændɪŋ] **1** *adv* no obstante. – **2** *prep* a pesar de.

nougat ['nuːgɑː] *n* turrón *m* blando.

nought [nɔːt] *n* cero: *nought point six six,* cero coma sesenta y seis.
■ **noughts and crosses,** tres en raya *m.*

noun [naʊn] *n* nombre *m,* substantivo.
■ **noun phrase,** sintagma *m* nominal.

nourish ['nʌrɪʃ] *t* nutrir, alimentar.

nourishing ['nʌrɪʃɪŋ] *adj* nutritivo,-a.

nourishment ['nʌrɪʃmənt] *n* nutrición *f,* alimentación *f.*

nous [naʊs] *n fam* sentido común, cacumen *m,* caletre *m.*

nouveau riche [nuːvəʊ'riːʃ] *n* nuevo,-a rico,-a.
▲ *pl* **nouveaux riches** [nuːvəʊ'riːʃ].

Nov ['nəʊvembəʳ] *abbr* (*November*) noviembre *m.*

nova ['nəʊvə] *n* ASTRON nova.
▲ *pl* **novae** ['nəʊviː] o **novas.**

Nova Scotia [nəʊvə'skəʊʃə] *n* Nueva Escocia.

novel[1] ['nɒvəl] *adj* original, novedoso,-a: *what a novel idea!,* ¡qué idea más original!

novel[2] ['nɒvəl] *n* novela.

novelette [nɒvəl'et] *n* novela corta (*generalmente rosa*).

novelist ['nɒvəlɪst] *n* novelista *mf.*

novella [nəʊ'velə] *n* novela corta.
▲ *pl* **novellas** o **novelle** [nəʊ'veliː].

novelty ['nɒvəltɪ] **1** *n* novedad *f: the novelty soon wore off,* pronto dejó de ser novedad. **2** (*trinket*) chuchería *f.*
▲ *pl* **novelties.**

November [nəʊ'vembəʳ] *n* noviembre *m.*
▲ *véase también* **May.**

novice ['nɒvɪs] **1** *n* novato,-a. **2** REL novicio,-a.

noviciate [nə'vɪʃɪət] *n* → **novitiate.**

novitiate [nə'vɪʃɪət] *n* noviciado.

now [naʊ] **1** *adv* (*at the present*) ahora; (*used contrastively*) ya: *where do you work now?,* ¿dónde trabajas ahora?; *I'm ready now,* ya estoy listo. **2** (*immediately*) ya, ahora mismo: *do it now!,* ¡hazlo ya! **3** (*in past*) ya, entonces. **4** (*introductory*) bueno, vamos a ver, veamos: *now, let's begin,* bueno, empecemos. – **5 now (that),** *conj* ahora que, ya que: *now (that) we're all here, we can begin,* ya que estamos todos, podemos empezar.

● **by now,** ya: *she'll be in Mexico by now,* ya debe de estar en Méjico. ‖ **for now,** por el momento. ‖ **from now on,** de ahora en adelante. ‖ **just now,** (*at this moment*) en estos momentos, ahora mismo; (*a short while ago*) hace un momento, ahora mismo: *I can't help you just now,* ahora mismo no puedo ayudarte; *have you seen Ann? – she was here just now,* ¿has visto a Ann? –estaba aquí hace un momento. ‖ **now and then,** de vez en cuando. ‖ **now now,** vale, basta, ya está bien: *now, now, don't fight,* vale ya, no os peleéis. ‖ **right now,** ahora mismo.

nowadays ['naʊədeɪz] *adv* hoy día, hoy en día, actualmente.

nowhere ['nəʊweəʳ] *adv* (*position*) en ninguna parte, en ningún sitio, en ningún lugar; (*direction*) a ninguna parte, a ningún sitio: *where are you going? –nowhere special,* ¿dónde vas? –a ningún sitio en especial; *there's nowhere to hide,* no hay donde esconderse; *she has nowhere else to go,* no tiene otro sitio donde ir; *that will get you nowhere,* eso no te llevará a ninguna parte, eso no te ayudará en nada; *my keys were nowhere to be found,* no encontraba mis llaves por ninguna parte.

● **in the middle of nowhere,** en el quinto pino. ‖ **nowhere near,** muy lejos de: *I've nowhere near finished,* estoy muy lejos de acabar; *it's nowhere near as good as the other,* no es ni de lejos tan bueno como el otro.

nowise ['nəʊwaɪz] *adv arch* de ninguna manera.

noxious ['nɒkʃəs] *adj* nocivo,-a.

noxiousness ['nɒkʃəsnəs] *n* nocividad *f.*

nozzle ['nɒzəl] *n* boca, boquilla.

nr [nɪəʳ] *abbr* (*near*) cerca de.

NSPCC ['en'es'piː'siː'siː] *abbr* GB (*National Society for the Prevention of Cruelty to Children*) sociedad nacional para la protección de los niños.

NT ['næfənət'trʌst] *abbr* GB (*National Trust*) organización que vela por el patrimonio nacional, tanto natural como arquitectónico.

Nth [nθ] *abbr* (*North*) norte; (*abbreviation*) N.

nth [enθ] *adj fam* enésimo,-a.
● **to the nth degree,** a la enésima potencia.

nuance [njuː'ɑːns] *n* matiz *m.*

nub [nʌb] *n* meollo, clave *f.*
● **the nub of the matter,** el quid de la cuestión.

nubile ['njuːbaɪl] *adj* núbil.

nuclear ['njuːklɪəʳ] *adj* nuclear.
■ **nuclear bomb,** bomba nuclear. ‖ **nuclear capability,** potencial *m* nuclear. ‖ **nuclear capacity,** capacidad *f* nuclear. ‖ **nuclear disarmament,** desarme *m*

nuclear. ‖ **nuclear energy,** energía nuclear. ‖ **nuclear facility,** planta de energía nuclear. ‖ **nuclear family,** familia nuclear. ‖ **nuclear fission,** fisión f nuclear. ‖ **nuclear fusion,** fusión f nuclear. ‖ **nuclear physics,** física nuclear. ‖ **nuclear power,** energía nuclear. ‖ **nuclear power station,** central f nuclear. ‖ **nuclear reaction,** reacción f nuclear. ‖ **nuclear reactor,** reactor m nuclear. ‖ **nuclear war,** guerra nuclear. ‖ **nuclear waste,** residuos nucleares. ‖ **nuclear weapon,** arma nuclear. ‖ **nuclear winter,** invierno nuclear.

nuclear-free [nju:klɪəˈfri:] adj no nuclearizado,-a, libre de energía nuclear, desnuclearizado,-a.

nuclei [nju:ˈklɪaɪ] npl → **nucleus.**

nucleic [nju:ˈkleɪk] adj nucleico,-a.
■ **nucleic acid,** ácido nucleico.

nucleus [ˈnju:klɪəs] n núcleo.
▲ pl nuclei.

nude [nju:d] 1 adj desnudo,-a. – 2 n desnudo m.
● **in the nude,** desnudo,-a.

nudge [nʌdʒ] 1 n (with elbow) codazo. 2 empujón m suave. – 3 t (with elbow) dar un codazo a: he nudged me and gave me a funny look, me dio un codazo y me dirigió una mirada extraña. 4 empujar suavemente: I just nudged the bike with my car and it fell over, tan solo le di un empujoncito a la bici con el coche y se cayó.

nudism [ˈnju:dɪzəm] n nudismo.

nudist [ˈnju:dɪst] 1 adj nudista. – 2 n nudista mf.

nudity [ˈnju:dɪtɪ] n desnudez f.

nugatory [ˈnju:gətərɪ] adj insignificante.

nugget [ˈnʌgɪt] n pepita.

nuisance [ˈnju:səns] 1 n molestia, fastidio, lata. 2 (person) pesado,-a.
● **to make a nuisance of os.,** dar la lata.

nuke [nju:k] 1 n fam bomba nuclear. – 2 t fam atacar con arma nuclear.

null [nʌl] adj nulo,-a.
● **null and void,** nulo,-a, sin validez, sin efecto.

nullification [nʌlɪfɪˈkeɪʃən] n anulación f.

nullify [ˈnʌlɪfaɪ] t anular.
▲ pt & pp nullified, ger nullifying.

nullity [ˈnʌlɪtɪ] n nulidad f.
▲ pl nullities.

numb [nʌm] 1 adj entumecido,-a, insensible. – 2 t entumecer. 3 (anaesthetize) anestesiar. 4 fig consternar.
● **to be numb with cold,** estar helado,-a de frío. ‖ **to be numb with fear,** estar paralizado,-a de miedo.

number [ˈnʌmbəʳ] 1 n número: if I give you my number, you can call me, si te doy mi número, me puedes llamar; a large number of people, un gran número de personas; I thought my number was on that one!, ¡pensé que esa bala era para mí!; I thought my number was up!, ¡creí que me había llegado la hora! 2 (on car) número de matrícula, matrícula: did you get his number?, ¿le cogiste la matrícula? 3 (of magazine etc) número. 4 (song) tema m: she sang a few Gershwin numbers, cantó algunos temas de Gershwin. 5 (group) grupo: two of that number died of malaria, dos de ellos murieron de malaria. 6 LING número: adjectives agree with the noun in number and gender, los adjetivos concuerdan con el substantivo en número y en género. 7 fam (garment) modelo: Vicky turned up in a nice little red leather number, Vicky se presentó con un modelito de cuero rojo. – 8 t numerar: the tickets are not numbered, los billetes no están numerados; his days are numbered, tiene los días contados. 9 (count) contar: I number her among my friends, la cuento entre mis amigos.

◆ **to number off** i numerarse.
● **a number of ...,** varios,-as ... ‖ **any number of ...,** muchísimos,-as ... ‖ **number one,** principal, más importante. ‖ **to be number one,** ser el número uno, ser el mejor. ‖ **to look after number one,** mirar por lo suyo. ‖ **to have sb.'s number,** tener calado,-a a algn. ‖ **... without number,** un sinfín de ...
■ **Number Ten,** el nº 10 de Downing Street: la residencia oficial del primer ministro británico.

number-crunching [ˈnʌmbəkrʌntʃɪŋ] n fam cálculo a gran escala.

numbering [ˈnʌmbərɪŋ] n numeración f.
■ **numbering machine,** numerador m.

numberless [ˈnʌmbələs] adj innumerables, incontables.

numberplate [ˈnʌmbəpleɪt] n GB placa de la matrícula.

numbness [ˈnʌmnəs] 1 n entumecimiento. 2 fig parálisis f.

numbskull [ˈnʌmskʌl] n → **numskull.**

numeracy [ˈnju:mərəsɪ] n conocimiento básico de las matemáticas.

numeral [ˈnju:mərəl] n número, cifra.

numerate [ˈnju:mərət] adj que tiene conocimientos de matemáticas.

numeration [nju:məˈreɪʃən] n numeración f.

numerator [ˈnju:məreɪtəʳ] n numerador m.

numerical [nju:ˈmerɪkəl] adj numérico,-a.

numerically [nju:ˈmerɪkəlɪ] adv numéricamente.

numerologist [nju:meˈrɒlədʒɪst] n numerólogo,-a.

numerology [nju:meˈrɒlədʒɪ] n numerología.

numerous [ˈnju:mərəs] adj numeroso,-a.

numinous [ˈnju:mɪnəs] adj numinoso,-a.

numismatic [nju:mɪzˈmætɪk] adj numismático,-a.

numismatics [nju:mɪzˈmætɪks] n numismática.

numismatist [nju:ˈmɪzmətɪst] n numismático,-a.

numskull [ˈnʌmskʌl] n fam tonto,-a, imbécil mf.

nun [nʌn] n monja, religiosa.

nuncio [ˈnʌnsɪəʊ] n nuncio apostólico.
▲ pl nuncios.

nunnery [ˈnʌnərɪ] n convento (de monjas).
▲ pl nunneries.

nuptial [ˈnʌpʃəl] 1 adj fml nupcial. – 2 **nuptials,** npl fml casamiento, nupcias fpl.

nurse [nɜ:s] 1 n enfermero,-a. 2 (children's) niñera. – 3 t (look after) cuidar. 4 (suckle) amamantar. 5 (hold) acunar. 6 (feeling) guardar.
● **to nurse a cold,** intentar curarse de un resfriado. ‖ **to nurse a grudge/grievance against sb.,** guardar rencor a algn.

nursemaid [ˈnɜ:smeɪd] n niñera.

nursery [ˈnɜ:sərɪ] 1 n (in house) cuarto de los niños. 2 (kindergarten) guardería. 3 (for plants) vivero.
■ **nursery nurse,** enfermero,-a puericultor,-ora. ‖ **nursery rhyme,** canción f infantil, poema m infantil. ‖ **nursery school,** parvulario. ‖ **nursery slope,** pista para principiantes.
▲ pl nurseries.

nurseryman [ˈnɜ:sərɪmən] n horticultor m.
▲ pl nurserymen [ˈnɜ:sərɪmən].

nursing [ˈnɜ:sɪŋ] n profesión f de enfermera, enfermería.
■ **nursing home,** clínica.

nurture [ˈnɜ:tʃəʳ] 1 t nutrir, alimentar. 2 (child) criar.

nut [nʌt] 1 n BOT fruto seco: a selection of nuts: hazelnuts, walnuts, almonds, peanuts and cashews, un surtido de

frutos secos: avellanas, nueces, almendras, cacahuetes y anacardos. **2** TECH tuerca: *tighten this nut with a spanner,* aprieta esta tuerca con una llave inglesa. **3** *fam (head)* coco. **4** fanático,-a: *he's a real soccer nut,* es un fanático del fútbol. **5** *fam (nutcase)* chalado,-a, chiflado,-a. **– 6 nuts,** *npl sl (testicles)* huevos *mpl.* **– 7** *adj* loco,-a, chalado,-a, chiflado,-a: *she must be nuts to go out with him,* debe de estar loca para salir con él.
● **to be a tough nut to crack,** ser un hueso duro de roer. ‖ **to be off one's nut,** estar chalado,-a. ‖ **to do one's nut,** subirse por las paredes. ‖ **to be nuts about** sth./sb., estar loco,-a por algo/algn.
■ **nuts and bolts,** lo básico.
nut-brown ['nʌt'braʊn] *adj* de color avellana.
nutcase ['nʌtkeɪs] *n fam* chalado,-a.
nutcrackers ['nʌtkrækəz] *npl* cascanueces *m inv.*
nuthatch ['nʌthætʃ] *n* trepador *m* azul.
nuthouse ['nʌthaʊs] *n fam* manicomio.
nutmeg ['nʌtmeg] *n* nuez *f* moscada.
nutrient ['njuːtrɪənt] **1** *n* nutriente *m.* **– 2** *adj* nutritivo,-a.
nutrition [njuːˈtrɪʃən] *n* nutrición *f.*
nutritional [njuːˈtrɪʃənəl] *n* nutricional.

nutritionist [njuːˈtrɪʃənɪst] *n* dietista *mf.*
nutritious [njuːˈtrɪʃəs] *adj* nutritivo,-a.
nutritive ['njuːtrɪtɪv] *adj* nutritivo,-a.
nutshell ['nʌtʃel] *n* cáscara.
● **in a nutshell,** en pocas palabras.
nutter ['nʌtəʳ] *n fam* chalado,-a.
nutty ['nʌtɪ] **1** *adj* CULIN que sabe a nuez. **2** *fam* chalado,-a.
● **as nutty as a fruitcake,** como una cabra.
▲ *comp* **nuttier,** *superl* **nuttiest.**
nuzzle ['nʌzəl] *i (animal)* acariciar con el hocico.
◆ **to nuzzle up to** *t insep* arrimarse a.
NW [nɔːθˈwest] *abbr (northwest)* noroeste *m;* (*abbreviation*) NO.
nylon ['naɪlɒn] **1** *n* nailon *m.* **– 2 nylons,** *npl* medias *fpl* de nailon.
nymph [nɪmf] *n* ninfa.
nympho ['nɪmfəʊ] *n fam* ninfómana.
▲ *pl* **nymphos.**
nymphomania [nɪmfəˈmeɪnɪə] *n* ninfomanía.
nymphomaniac [nɪmfəˈmeɪnɪæk] *n* ninfómana.

O

O, o [əʊ] *n* (*the letter*) O, o *f*.

O [əʊ] **1** *n* (*the letter*) O, o. **2** (*as number*) cero.

oaf [əʊf] *n fam* patán *m*, palurdo,-a, zoquete *mf*, zopenco,-a.

oafish ['əʊfɪʃ] *adj* torpe, bruto,-a.

oak [əʊk] **1** *n* BOT roble *m*. **2** (*wood*) roble *m*. – **3** *adj* de roble.

■ **oak apple**, agalla.

oaken ['əʊkən] *adj lit* de roble.

OAP ['əʊ'eɪ'piː] *abbr* GB (*old-age pensioner*) pensionista *mf*.

oar [ɔːʳ] *n* remo.

● **to stick one's oar in**, entrometerse, meter las narices.

oarsman ['ɔːzmən] *n* remero.

▲ *pl* **oarsmen** ['ɔːzmən].

oarswoman ['ɔːzwʊmən] *n* remera.

▲ *pl* **oarswomen** ['ɔːzwɪmɪn].

oasis [əʊ'eɪsɪs] *n* oasis *m*.

▲ *pl* **oases** [əʊ'eɪsiːz].

oat [əʊt] **1** *n* (*plant*) avena. – **2** **oats**, *npl* (*cereal*) avena *f sing*. – **3** *n* (*porridge*) copos *mpl* de avena.

● **to be off one's oats**, no tener ganas de comer. ‖ **to get one's oats**, *sl* echarse polvos.

oatcake ['əʊtkeɪk] *n* torta de avena.

oath [əʊθ] **1** *n* JUR juramento. **2** (*swearword*) palabrota, juramento.

● **on my oath**, lo juro. ‖ **to be on oath / be under oath**, estar bajo juramento. ‖ **to put sb. under oath**, tomarle juramento a algn. ‖ **to swear an oath / take an oath**, jurar, prestar juramento.

■ **oath of allegiance**, juramento de fidelidad, juramento de lealtad.

oatmeal ['əʊtmiːl] **1** *n* (*flour*) harina de avena. **2** US (*porridge*) copos *mpl* de avena.

oats [əʊts] *npl* → **oat**.

obdurate ['ɒbdjərət] *n fml* (*stubborn*) obstinado,-a, terco,-a; (*unyielding*) inflexible.

obedience [ə'biːdɪəns] *n* obediencia.

obedient [ə'biːdɪənt] *adj* obediente.

● **your obedient servant**, su humilde servidor,-ra.

obediently [ə'biːdɪəntlɪ] *adv* obedientemente.

obelisk ['ɒbəlɪsk] *n* obelisco.

obese [əʊ'biːs] *adj* obeso,-a.

obesity [əʊ'biːsɪtɪ] *n* obesidad *f*.

obey [ə'beɪ] **1** *t* (*gen*) obedecer; (*orders*) acatar. **2** (*law*) cumplir. – **3** *i* (*gen*) obedecer.

obituary [ə'bɪtjʊərɪ] *n* necrología, obituario.

■ **obituary column**, sección *f* necrológica. ‖ **obituary notice**, nota necrológica.

▲ *pl* **obituaries**.

object ['ɒbdʒekt] **1** *n* (*thing*) objeto, cosa. **2** (*aim, purpose*) objetivo, objeto, fin *m*, propósito. **3** (*focus of feelings*) objeto: *he was an object of ridicule,* fue objeto de burlas;

she was an object of pity, daba lástima. **4** (*obstacle*) inconveniente *m*. **5** LING complemento: *direct/indirect object,* complemento directo/indirecto. – **6** *t* objetar: *she objected that ...,* objetó que ... – **7** *i* (*oppose*) oponerse (**to**, a), poner reparos (**to**, a): *I object to the use of the term "chairman",* me opongo al uso del término "presidente". **8** (*disapprove, mind*) molestar: *do you object to my smoking?,* ¿le molesta que fume? **9** JUR protestar.

■ **object glass / object lens**, objetivo. ‖ **object lesson**, ejemplo práctico, perfecta demostración *f*.

▲ (*verbo*) [əb'dʒekt].

objection [əb'dʒekʃən] **1** *n* (*argument against*) objeción *f*, reparo. **2** (*disapproval*) inconveniente *m*.

● **to raise objections**, poner reparos, poner inconvenientes.

objectionable [əb'dʒekʃənəbəl] *adj* (*unacceptable*) inaceptable; (*unpleasant*) desagradable, ofensivo,-a.

objective [əb'dʒektɪv] **1** *adj* objetivo,-a: *an objective report,* un informe objetivo. – **2** *n* (*purpose*) objetivo, fin *m*. **3** (*lens*) objetivo.

objectively [əb'dʒektɪvlɪ] *adv* objetivamente.

objectivity [əb'dʒektɪvɪtɪ] *n* objetividad *f*.

objector [əb'dʒektəʳ] *n* objetor,-ra.

obligate ['ɒblɪgeɪt] *t fml* obligar.

obligation [ɒblɪ'geɪʃən] *n* obligación *f*, compromiso.

● **to be under an obligation to sb.**, tener una obligación con algn. ‖ **to be under no obligation to do sth.**, no tener ninguna obligación de hacer algo. ‖ **to meet one's obligations**, cumplir sus obligaciones.

obligatory [ɒ'blɪgətərɪ] *adj* obligatorio,-a.

oblige [ə'blaɪdʒ] **1** *t* (*compel*) obligar: *I felt obliged to attend,* me veía obligado a asistir. **2** (*do a favour*) hacer un favor a, ayudar a: *could you oblige me by closing the window?,* ¿me haría el favor de cerrar la ventana? – **3** *i* (*do a favour*) hacer un favor, ayudar: *I'd be happy to oblige,* me encantaría ayudar.

● **much obliged!**, ¡muy agradecido,-a!

obliging [ə'blaɪdʒɪŋ] *adj* servicial, complaciente.

oblique [ə'bliːk] **1** *adj* (*line, angle*) oblicuo,-a. **2** *fig* (*hint, reference*) indirecto,-a. – **3** *n* barra.

obliterate [ə'blɪtəreɪt] **1** *t* (*destroy*) destruir, arrasar; (*eliminate*) eliminar. **2** (*erase, blot out*) borrar, obliterar.

obliteration [əblɪtə'reɪʃən] **1** *n* (*destruction*) destrucción *f*; (*elimination*) eliminación *f*. **2** (*effacing*) borradura.

oblivion [ə'blɪvɪən] **1** *n* (*obscurity*) olvido. **2** (*unconsciousness*) inconsciencia.

oblivious [ə'blɪvɪəs] *adj* inconsciente (**of**, de), ajeno,-a (**of**, a): *he was totally oblivious of what was happening,* estaba totalmente ajeno de lo que estaba ocurriendo.

oblong ['ɒblɒŋ] **1** *adj* oblongo,-a, alargado,-a. – **2** *n* rectángulo.

obnoxious [əb'nɒkʃəs] *adj* (*person*) repugnante, repelente, detestable, odioso,-a; (*smell*) nocivo,-a, repugnante.

oboe ['əʊbəʊ] *n* oboe *m*.

oboist [ˈəʊbəʊɪst] *n* oboe *mf*, oboísta *mf*.
obscene [bbˈsiːn] 1 *adj* (*indecente*) obsceno,-a, indecente, escabroso,-a. 2 (*scandalous*) escandaloso,-a.
obscenity [əbˈsenɪtɪ] 1 *n* (*indecency*) obscenidad *f*, indecencia. 2 (*word, expression, action*) obscenidad *f*.
▲ *pl obscenities*.
obscure [əbsˈkjʊəʳ] 1 *adj* (*unclear*) obscuro,-a, oscuro,-a, poco claro,-a. 2 (*vague, indistinct*) vago,-a, confuso,-a; (*hidden*) recóndito,-a. 3 (*little known - person*) poco conocido,-a, oscuro,-a; (- *village*) recóndito,-a, perdido,-a: *it's by an obscure nineteenth century poet,* es de un poeta poco conocido del siglo diecinueve. – 4 *t* (*make unclear, difficult to understand*) ofuscar, obscurecer; (*confuse*) confundir. 5 (*hide*) ocultar; (*conceal, cover*) oscurecer, obscurecer.
obscurity [əbˈskjʊərɪtɪ] 1 *n* (*state*) oscuridad *f*, olvido. 2 (*darkness*) oscuridad *f*.
obsequious [əbˈsiːkwɪəs] *adj* servil.
observable [əbˈzɜːvəbəl] *adj* visible, observable, apreciable.
observance [əbˈzɜːvəns] 1 *n* observancia. – 2 **observances,** *npl* prácticas *fpl* religiosas.
observant [əbˈzɜːvənt] *adj* observador,-ra: *she's very observant,* se fija en todo.
observation [bbzəˈveɪʃən] 1 *n* (*watching, study*) observación *f*; (*surveillance*) vigilancia. 2 (*remark*) observación *f*, comentario.
● **to be under observation,** (*by police etc*) estar bajo vigilancia; (*in hospital*) estar en observación. ‖ **to escape observation,** pasar inadvertido,-a. ■ **observation post,** puesto de observación.
observatory [əbˈzɜːvətərɪ] *n* observatorio.
▲ *pl observatories*.
observe [əbˈzɜːv] 1 *t* (*see, watch*) observar, ver; (*in surveillance*) vigilar. 2 (*law*) cumplir, respetar; (*custom*) observar; (*religious festival*) guardar. 3 *fml* (*say*) señalar. – 4 *i* observar.
observer [əbˈzɜːvəʳ] *n* observador,-ra.
obsess [əbˈses] *t* obsesionar.
obsessed [əbˈsest] *adj* obsesionado,-a (**by/with**, con),.
obsession [əbˈseʃən] *n* obsesión *f* (**with/about**, con).
obsessional [əbˈseʃənəl] *adj* obsesivo,-a.
obsessive [əbˈsesɪv] 1 *adj* obsesivo,-a: *she's obsessive about cleanliness,* tiene obsesión con la limpieza. – 2 *n* obsesivo,-a.
obsolescent [bbsəˈlesənt] *adj* obsolescente.
obsolete [ˈbbsəliːt] *adj* obsoleto,-a.
obstacle [ˈbbstəkəl] 1 *n* obstáculo. 2 *fig* obstáculo, impedimento.
■ **obstacle race,** carrera de obstáculos.
obstetric [əbˈstetrɪk] *adj* obstétrico,-a.
obstetrician [bbsteˈstrɪʃən] *n* tocólogo,-a, obstetra *mf*.
obstetrics [bbˈstetrɪks] *n* obstetricia, tocología.
obstinacy [ˈbbstɪnəsɪ] *n* (*stubbornness*) obstinación *f*, terquedad *f*, testarudez *f*.
obstinate [ˈbbstɪnət] 1 *adj* (*person*) obstinado,-a, tenaz, terco,-a; (*problem, thing*) tenaz, pertinaz. – 2 *n* (*illness, etc*) pertinaz, rebelde, persistente.
obstinately [ˈbbstɪnətlɪ] *adv* obstinadamente.
obstreperous [əbˈstrepərəs] *adj* escandaloso,-a.
obstruct [əbˈstrʌkt] 1 *t* (*block - gen*) obstruir; (- *pipe etc*) atascar, bloquear; (- *view*) tapar. 2 (*make difficult*) dificultar; (*hinder*) obstaculizar. 3 SP obstruir, bloquear.
obstruction [əbˈstrʌkʃən] 1 *n* (*gen*) obstrucción *f*. 2 (*hindrance*) estorbo, obstáculo, impedimento. 3 SP obstrucción *f*.

obstructionism [əbˈstrʌkʃənɪzəm] *n fml* obstruccionismo.
obstructionist [əbˈstrʌkʃənɪst] *n* obstruccionista *mf*.
obstructive [əbˈstrʌktɪv] *adj* (*policy, measure*) obstruccionista.
obtain [əbˈteɪn] 1 *t* (*get, acquire*) obtener, conseguir. – 2 *i fml* (*be valid, exist*) prevalecer, regir.
obtainable [əbˈteɪnəbəl] *adj* obtenible: *it's no longer obtainable,* ya no se puede conseguir.
obtrude [əbˈtruːd] 1 *t fml* (*impose*) imponer (**on/upon,** a). 2 *fml* (*push out, stick out*) extender. – 3 *i fml* entrometerse, (**on/upon,** en).
obtrusion [əbˈtruːʒən] *n fml* intrusión *f*.
obtrusive [əbˈtruːsɪv] *adj* (*noise*) molesto,-a; (*smell*) penetrante; (*colour*) llamativo,-a; (*building, presence*) demasiado prominente.
obtuse [əbˈtjuːs] *adj fml* (*stupid*) obtuso,-a.
■ **obtuse angle,** ángulo obtuso. ‖ **obtuse triangle,** triángulo obtusángulo.
obverse [ˈbbvɜːs] 1 *n fml* (*back*) anverso. 2 *fml* (*opposite*) contrario. – 3 *adj* del anverso.
obviate [ˈbbvɪeɪt] *t* obviar, evitar.
obvious [ˈbbvɪəs] *adj* (*clear*) obvio,-a, evidente, patente, claro,-a: *for obvious reasons,* por razones obvias.
obviously [ˈbbvɪəslɪ] *adv* obviamente, evidentemente, claramente: *obviously!,* ¡claro!, ¡por supuesto!
occasion [əˈkeɪʒən] 1 *n* (*time*) ocasión *f*; (*event*) acontecimiento: *on the occasion in question,* en la ocasión en cuestión. 2 (*opportunity*) ocasión *f*, oportunidad *f*: *if the ocassion arises,* si se presenta la ocasión. 3 (*reason, motive*) ocasión *f*, motivo. – 4 *t fml* ocasionar, causar.
● **on occasion,** de vez en cuando. ‖ **on the occasion of,** con motivo de. ‖ **to have occasion to do sth.,** tener motivo de hacer algo. ‖ **to rise to the occasion,** estar a la altura de las circunstancias, dar la talla. ‖ **to take the occasion to do sth.,** aprovechar la oportunidad para hacer algo.
occasional [əˈkeɪʒənəl] *adj* (*not frequent*) esporádico,-a, eventual: *he smokes the occasional cigar,* de vez en cuando fuma un puro.
■ **occasional showers,** chubascos aislados. ‖ **occasional table,** mesa auxiliar.
occasionally [əˈkeɪʒənəlɪ] *adv* de vez en cuando, ocasionalmente.
Occident [ˈbksɪdənt] *n* occidente *m*.
occidental [bksɪˈdentəl] *adj* occidental.
occlusion [əˈkluːʒən] *n* oclusión *f*.
occult [ˈbkʌlt] *adj* oculto,-a.
● **the occult,** las ciencias *fpl* ocultas, el ocultismo.
occupancy [ˈbkjəpənsɪ] *n* ocupación *f*.
occupant [ˈbkjəpənt] *n* (*gen*) ocupante *mf*; (*tenant*) inquilino,-a.
occupation [bkjəˈpeɪʃən] 1 *n* (*job*) ocupación *f*, profesión *f*. 2 (*pastime*) pasatiempo. 3 (*act, state of occupying*) ocupación *f*.
occupational [bkjəˈpeɪʃənəl] *adj* ocupacional, profesional.
● **it's an occupational hazard,** son gajes del oficio. ■ **occupational therapy,** terapia ocupacional. ‖ **occupational therapist,** terapeuta *mf* ocupacional.
occupied [ˈbkjəpaɪd] *adj* ocupado,-a.
● **to keep sb. occupied,** mantener a algn. ocupado,-a.
occupier [ˈbkjəpaɪəʳ] *n* GB (*gen*) ocupante *mf*; (*tenant*) inquilino,-a.
occupy [ˈbkjəpaɪ] 1 *t* (*live in*) ocupar, habitar, vivir en. 2 (*take possession of*) ocupar, tomar posesión de, apode-

rarse de. **3** (*take up, fill - space*) ocupar; (*- time*) ocupar, llevar.

● **to occupy os. in doing sth.**, ocupar el tiempo haciendo algo, entretenerse haciendo algo.

▲ *pt* & *pp* **occupied**, *ger* **occupying**.

occur [əˈkɜːʳ] **1** *i* (*happen - event, incident*) ocurrir, suceder, tener lugar; (*- change*) producirse. **2** *fml* (*be found, exist*) existir, darse, encontrarse. **3** (*come to mind*) ocurrir, ocurrirse: *it never occurred to me to ask*, no se me ocurrió preguntar.

▲ *pt* & *pp* **occurred**, *ger* **occurring**.

occurrence [əˈkʌrəns] **1** *n* (*event, incident*) suceso: *it's an everyday occurrence*, es un hecho cotidiano. **2** *fml* (*frequency*) incidencia, frecuencia; (*existing amount*) cantidad *f*.

ocean [ˈəʊʃən] **1** *n* océano. – **2** *adj* oceánico,-a: *ocean currents*, corrientes oceánicas.

● **oceans of,** *fam* la mar de, un montón de.

ocean-going [ˈəʊʃənɡəʊɪŋ] *adj* de alta mar, de altura.

Oceania [əʊʃɪˈɑːnɪə] *n* Oceanía.

Oceanian [əʊʃɪˈɑːnɪən] **1** *adj* de Oceanía. – **2** *n* nativo,-a de Oceanía, habitante *mf* de Oceanía.

oceanic [əʊʃɪˈænɪk] *adj fml* oceánico,-a.

oceanographer [əʊʃəˈnɒɡrəfəʳ] *n* oceanógrafo,-a.

oceanography [əʊʃənˈɒɡrəfɪ] *n* oceanografía.

ocelot [ˈɒsəlɒt] *n* ocelote *m*.

ochre [ˈəʊkəʳ] **1** *adj* (de color) ocre. – **2** *n* ocre *m*.

■ **red ocre,** almagre *m*. ‖ **yellow ocre,** ocre *m* amarillo.

o'clock [əˈklɒk] *adv*: *it's one o'clock*, es la una; *it's two o'clock*, son las dos; *at three o'clock*, a las tres.

Oct [ˈɒktəʊbəʳ] *abbr* (*October*) octubre.

octagon [ˈɒktəɡən] *n* octágono, octógono.

octagonal [ɒkˈtæɡənəl] *adj* octagonal, octogonal.

octane [ˈɒkteɪn] *n* octano.

■ **octane number / octane rating,** octanaje *m*.

octave [ˈɒktɪv] *n* octava.

octet [ɒkˈtet] *n* octeto.

October [ɒkˈtəʊbəʳ] *n* octubre *m*.

▲ See also **May.**

octogenarian [ɒktəʊdʒəˈneərɪən] *n* octogenario,-a.

octopus [ˈɒktəpəs] *n* pulpo.

ocular [ˈɒkjələʳ] *adj* ocular.

oculist [ˈɒkjəlɪst] *n* oculista *mf*.

odd [ɒd] **1** *adj* (*strange*) extraño,-a, raro,-a: *the odd thing is that ...*, lo raro es que ... **2** (*number*) impar. **3** (*approximately*) y pico: *thirty odd people*, unas treinta y pico personas; *he must be forty odd*, tendrá cuarenta y tantos años. **4** (*left over, spare*) suelto,-a, desparejado,-a. **5** (*left over, spare*) suelto,-a, de más: *have you got any odd coins?*, ¿tienes algunas monedas sueltas? **6** (*occasional*) ocasional: *she does the odd class now and again*, da alguna que otra clase de vez en cuando. – **7** **odds,** *npl* (*probability, chances*) probabilidades *fpl*, posibilidades *fpl*: *the odds are that ...*, lo más probable es que ...; *the odds are against her winning*, lleva las de perder; *the odds are in your favour*, llevas ventaja, tienes las de ganar. **8** (*in betting*) apuestas *fpl*: *the odds are ten to one*, las apuestas están diez a uno.

● **against (all) the odds,** contra todo pronóstico. ‖ **it makes no odds,** lo mismo da, da lo mismo. ‖ **to be at odds with sb.,** estar reñido,-a con algn., estar peleado,-a con algn. ‖ **to be the odd man out,** (*be over*) estar de más; (*be different*) ser la excepción. ‖ **to fight against the odds,** luchar contra fuerzas superiores. ‖ **to lay odds,** ofrecer puntos de ventaja. ‖ **to pay over the odds,** pagar más de la cuenta. ‖ **what's the odds?,** ¿qué más da?, ¿qué importa?

■ **odd jobs,** trabajillos *mpl*. ‖ **odds and ends,** (*bits and pieces*) cositas *fpl*, cosas *fpl* sueltas; (*trinkets*) chucherías *fpl*.

oddball [ˈɒdbɔːl] **1** *n* (*person*) bicho raro, estrafalario,-a, excéntrico,-a. – **2** *adj* estrafalario,-a, excéntrico,-a.

oddity [ˈɒdɪtɪ] **1** *n* (*thing*) cosa rara, rareza, curiosidad *f*; (*person*) bicho raro, estrafalario,-a. **2** (*strangeness*) rareza, singularidad *f*, peculiaridad *f*.

▲ *pl* **oddities.**

odd-jobman [ɒdˈdʒɒbmæn] *n* hombre *m* que hace trabajillos.

▲ *pl* **odd-jobmen** [ɒdˈdʒɒbmen].

odd-looking [ˈɒdlʊkɪŋ] *adj* de apariencia extraña.

oddly [ˈɒdlɪ] *adv* de manera extraña, extrañamente.

● **oddly enough,** por extraño que parezca, curiosamente.

oddness [ˈɒdnəs] *n* (*strangeness*) rareza, peculiaridad *f*; (*eccentricity*) excentricidad *f*.

odds [ɒdz] *npl* → **odd.**

odds-on [ˈɒdzɒn] *adj* muy probable, casi seguro,-a: *it's odds-on they'll be late*, lo más probable es que lleguen tarde; *Red Rum is the odds-on favourite,* Red Rum es el favorito en las apuestas.

ode [əʊd] *n* oda.

odious [ˈəʊdɪəs] *adj* odioso,-a, detestable, repugnante.

odometer [əʊˈdɒmɪtəʳ] *n* us auto cuentakilómetros *m*.

odontologist [ɒdɒnˈtɒlədʒɪst] *n* odontólogo,-a.

odontology [ɒdɒnˈtɒlədʒɪ] *n* odontología.

odor [ˈəʊdəʳ] *n* us → **odour.**

odoriferous [əʊdərˈɪfərəs] *adj lit* odorífero,-a, odorífico,-a.

odorous [ˈəʊdərəs] *adj fml* oloroso,-a, fragante.

odour [ˈəʊdəʳ] *n* (*smell*) olor *m*; (*fragrance*) perfume *m*, fragancia.

odourless [ˈəʊdələs] *adj* inodoro,-a.

odyssey [ˈɒdɪsɪ] *n* odisea.

OECD [ˈəʊiːsiːˈdiː] *abbr* (*Organization for Economic Co-operation and Development*) Organización *f* para la Cooperación y el Desarrollo Económico; (*abbreviation*) OCDE *f*.

Oedipus [ˈiːdɪpəs] *n* Edipo.

■ **Oedipus complex,** complejo de Edipo.

oesophagus [iːˈsɒfəɡəs] *n* esófago.

▲ *pl* **oesophagi** [iːˈsɒfəɡaɪ].

oestrogen [ˈiːstrədʒən] *n* estrógeno.

of [ɒv, *unstressed* əv] **1** *prep* (*belonging to*) de: *a friend of mine*, un amigo mío; *a colleague of John's*, un compañero de John. **2** (*made from*) de: *shoes of Spanish leather*, zapatos de piel española. **3** (*containing*) de: *a bag of crisps*, una bolsa de patatas; *a bottle of wine*, una botella de vino. **4** (*showing a part, a quantity*) de: *a kilo of apples*, un kilo de manzanas; *a sheet of paper*, una hoja de papel. **5** (*partitive use*) de: *a member of the team*, un miembro del equipo; *the two of us*, nosotros dos. **6** (*dates, distance*) de: *the 7th of August*, el 7 de agosto; *the first of May*, el uno de mayo; *within a mile of here*, a menos de una milla de aquí. **7** (*apposition*) de: *the city of London*, la cuidad de Londres. **8** (*by*) de: *the works of Shakespeare*, las obras de Shakespeare. **9** (*originating from, living in*) de: *the people of Liverpool*, los habitantes de Liverpool. **10** (*depicting*) de: *a photo of my boyfriend*, una foto de mi novio; *a map of Europe*, un mapa de Europa. **11** (*cause*) de: *of one's own free will*, por su propia voluntad; *she died of aids*, murió de sida. **12** (*connected with*) de: *the Queen of England*, la reina de Inglaterra; *the estimated time of arrival*, la hora de llegada prevista.

13 (*with, having*) de: *a child of five,* un niño de cinco años; *a matter of importance,* un asunto de importancia. **14** (*description*) de: *how kind of you to buy me flowers,* qué amable de tu parte comprarme flores. **15** (*after superlative*) de: *best of all was the food,* lo mejor de todo fue la comida; *most of all,* más que nada.

off [ɒf] **1** prep (*movement*) de: *it fell off the table,* se cayó de la mesa; *he got off the bus,* bajó del autobús. **2** (*indicating removal*) de: *he cut a branch off the tree,* cortó una rama del árbol. **3** (*distance, situation*) diferentes traducciones: *a narrow street off the main road,* una callejuela que sale a la carretera; *the kitchen's off the hallway,* el pasillo da a la cocina; *the ship sank off Malpica,* el barco se hundió a la altura de Malpica. **4** (*away from*) diferentes traducciones: *the ship went off course,* el barco se desvió de su rumbo; *we're a long way off finding a cure,* estamos lejos de encontrar una cura; *you need something to take your mind off it,* necesitas algo que te distraiga. **5** (*not wanting*) *I'm off coffee,* ya no tomo café; *he's off his food,* no tiene apetito. **6** (*not at work*): *she comes off duty at 10.00pm,* acaba el turno a las 10.00; *why don't you take the day off work?,* ¿por qué no te tomas el día libre? **7** fam (*from*) a: *I bought it off Eva,* se lo compré a Eva; *he borrowed some money off me,* me pidió dinero prestado. – **8** adv (*departure*): *he ran off,* se fue corriendo; *the car drove off at top speed,* el coche se fue a toda pastilla; *I'm off,* me voy; *be off with you!,* ¡lárgate! **9** (*showing distance*) a: *the village is three miles off,* el pueblo está a tres millas; *Christmas is still a long way off,* aún falta mucho para Navidad. **10** (*in theatre*) en off: *voices off,* voces en off. **11** (*removed*) fuera: *hands off!,* ¡fuera las manos!; *the leg fell off,* se cayó la pata; *leave the lid off,* no pongas la tapa; *she sat there with her shoes off,* se quedó allí sentada descalza. **12** (*reduced in price*) menos: *70% off!,* ¡70% menos! **13** (*disconnected, not working*) diferentes traducciones: *turn the light off,* apaga la luz; *have you turned the TV off?,* ¿has apagado la TV?; *she turned the tap off,* cerró el grifo. **14** (*free, on holiday*) libre: *can I have the afternoon off?,* ¿puedo tomarme la tarde libre? – **15** adj (*event*) cancelado,-a, suspendido,-a: *the wedding's off,* la boda se ha suspendido. **16** (*not turned on - gas, water*) cerrado,-a; (*- electricity*) apagado,-a: *the gas is off,* el gas está cerrado; *the TV's off,* la TV está apagada. **17** (*impolite, unfriendly*) descortés, poco amable; (*below standard*) malo,-a: *he's having an off day,* tiene un mal día; *he charged you full price - that's a bit off,* te cobró el precio íntegro - qué descortés. **18** (*food - bad*) malo,-a, pasado,-a; (*- unavailable*) acabado,-a: *the milk's off,* la leche está agria; *soup's off I'm afraid,* me temo que se ha acabado la sopa. **19** GB AUTO del lado del conductor. – **20** the off, n SP (*start - gen*) principio, comienzo; (*- of race*) salida.

● *off and on / on and off,* de vez en cuando, a ratos. ‖ *off the top of one's head,* improvisando, sin pensarlo. ‖ *on the off chance,* por si acaso, si por casualidad. ‖ *right off / straight off,* acto seguido. ‖ *to be off for sth.,* andar de algo, tener algo: *how are you off for money?,* ¿cómo andas de dinero?; *we're well off for time,* tenemos bastante tiempo. ‖ *to be well/badly off,* andar bien/mal de dinero.

■ *off season,* temporada baja.

offal [ˈɒfəl] n (*of cattle, pigs*) asaduras fpl, menudos mpl; (*of chicken*) menudillos mpl.

offbeat [ˈɒfbiːt] adj poco convencional.

off-centre [ˈɒfˈsentəʳ] adj descentrado,-a.

off-colour [ˈɒfˈkʌləʳ] **1** adj (*ill*) indispuesto,-a, pachucho,-a: *you look a little off colour,* tienes mala cara. **2** (*risqué*) subido,-a de tono.

▲ Se escribe *off colour* cuando no se antepone a un sustantivo.

offence [əˈfens] **1** n JUR delito, infracción f: *a traffic offence,* una infracción de tráfico. **2** (*insult*) ofensa: *no offence intended,* sin ánimo de ofenderle. **3** fml (*offensive thing*) atentado: *the monument is an offence to the eye,* el monumento es un atentado a la vista. **4** fml (*attack*) ofensiva, ataque m: *weapons of offence,* armas ofensivas.

● *to commit an offence,* cometer un delito, cometer una infracción. ‖ *to cause offence to sb.,* ofender a algn. ‖ *to take offence at sth.,* ofenderse por algo, sentirse ofendido,-a por algo.

offend [əˈfend] **1** t (*insult, hurt*) ofender: *I never meant to offend anyone,* no estaba en mi ánimo ofender a nadie; *she'll be offended if we don't go,* se ofenderá si no vamos. **2** (*cause displeasure to*) disgustar: *that building offends the eye,* aquel edificio hace daño a la vista. – **3** i fml (*do wrong to*) atentar (**against**, a). **4** JUR fml (*commit crime*) cometer un delito, delinquir.

● *to be easily offended,* ser muy susceptible.

offender [əˈfendəʳ] **1** n JUR (*gen*) infractor,-ra; (*criminal*) delincuente mf. **2** (*culprit*) culpable mf.

offending [əˈfendɪŋ] adj (*causing problems*) problemático,-a; (*unpleasant*) desagradable; (*controversial*) controvertido,-a, polémico,-a.

offense [ˈɒfens] **1** n US → **offence. 2** US SP ataque m, ofensiva.

offensive [əˈfensɪv] **1** adj (*insulting*) ofensivo,-a, insultante. **2** (*disgusting - gen*) repugnante; (*- smell*) desagradable. **3** (*attacking*) ofensivo,-a. – **4** n MIL ofensiva.

● *to be on the offensive,* estar a la ofensiva. ‖ *to go on the offensive,* pasar a la ofensiva. ‖ *to take the offensive,* tomar la ofensiva.

offensively [əˈfensɪvlɪ] adv de manera ofensiva.

offer [ˈɒfəʳ] **1** t (*gen*) ofrecer: *she offered us a drink,* nos ofreció una copa. **2** (*show willingness*) ofrecerse (**to**, para): *he offered me a lift to the airport,* se ofreció para llevarme al aeropuerto. **3** (*propose*) proponer, sugerir. **4** (*provide*) proporcionar, ofrecer, brindar. **5** (*prayer, praise, sacrifice, etc*) ofrecer (**up**, -). – **6** i (*show willingness*) ofrecerse: *she never even offered to help,* ni siquiera se ofreció para ayudar. **7** fml (*occur, arise*) presentarse. **8** (*propose marriage*) proponer matrimonio (**to**, a). – **9** n (*gen*) oferta, ofrecimiento; (*proposal*) propuesta: *she accepted his kind offer to help,* aceptó su amable oferta de ayuda; *an offer of marriage,* una propuesta de matrimonio. **10** (*bid, amount offered*) oferta. **11** COMM oferta.

● *or nearest offer,* a convenir, negociable. ‖ *to be on offer,* (*at reduced price*) estar de oferta; (*available*) disponible. ‖ *to be open to offers,* aceptar ofertas. ‖ *to make an offer for sth.,* hacer una oferta por algo. ‖ *to make sb. an offer they can't refuse,* hacerle una oferta muy tentadora a algn. ‖ *to offer itself,* presentarse. ‖ *to take sb. up on an offer,* aceptar la oferta de algn.

offering [ˈɒfərɪŋ] **1** n (*act*) ofrecimiento. **2** (*thing offered*) ofrenda; (*gift*) regalo. **3** REL ofrenda.

offertory [ˈɒfətərɪ] n REL (*part of service*) ofertorio; (*collection*) colecta.

▲ pl *offertories.*

offhand [ɒfˈhænd] **1** adj (*abrupt*) brusco,-a; (*inconsiderate*) descortés, desatento,-a, desconsiderado,-a. **2** (*easygoing, relaxed*) informal. – **3** adv de improviso: *I'm not sure of the exact figures off-hand,* sin mirar, no estoy seguro de las cifras exactas.

office [ˈɒfɪs] **1** n (*room*) despacho, oficina; (*building*) oficina; (*staff*) oficina. **2** GB POL ministerio: *the Foreign Of-*

fice, el Ministerio de Asuntos Exteriores. **3** (*post, position*) cargo. **4** REL oficio.
● **to be in office,** estar en el poder. ‖ **to hold office,** ocupar un cargo. ‖ **to leave office,** dimitir, dejar el cargo. ‖ **to seek office,** aspirar a un cargo. ‖ **through sb.'s good offices,** gracias a los buenos oficios de algn.
■ **doctor's office,** US consultorio, consulta. ‖ **office block,** edificio de oficinas. ‖ **office boy,** recadero. ‖ **office holder,** titular *mf* del cargo. ‖ **office hours,** horas *fpl* de oficina. ‖ **office junior,** auxiliar *mf* de oficina. ‖ **office work,** trabajo de oficina. ‖ **office worker,** oficinista *mf.*

officer ['ɒfɪsəʳ] **1** *n* MIL oficial *mf.* **2** (*police officer*) agente *mf.* **3** (*in government*) oficial *mf,* funcionario,-a. **4** (*of club, society*) directivo,-a.

official [ə'fɪʃəl] **1** *adj* (*gen*) oficial: *official residence,* residencia oficial. – **2** *n* funcionario,-a, oficial *mf: party official,* representante del partido.

officialese [əfɪʃəl'iːz] *n* jerga burocrática.

officially [ə'fɪʃəlɪ] *adv* oficialmente.

officiate [ə'fɪʃɪeɪt] **1** *i* (*gen*) ejercer. **2** REL oficiar.

officious [ə'fɪʃəs] *adj* (*too eager*) oficioso,-a; (*interfering*) entrometido,-a.

offing ['ɒfɪŋ] **in the offing,** *phr* en perspectiva.

off-key [ɒf'kiː] **1** *adj* MUS desafinado,-a. **2** *fig* desentonado,-a, discordante.

off-licence ['ɒflaɪsəns] *n* GB tienda de bebidas alcohólicas.

off-load [ɒf'ləʊd] **1** *t* (*unload*) descargar. **2** (*get rid of*) endilgar (**onto**, a), deshacerse (**onto**, de).

off-peak ['ɒfpiːk] *adj* (*times, hours*) fuera de las horas punta, de menor consumo: *off-peak electricity,* electricidad a tarifa reducida.

offprint ['ɒfprɪnt] *n* separata.

off-putting ['ɒfpʊtɪŋ] *adj* GB *fam* (*disconcerting*) desconcertante; (*unpleasant*) desagradable; (*annoying*) molesto,-a.

offset [ɒf'set] **1** *t* (*compensate for*) compensar. **2** (*in printing*) imprimir en offset. – **3** *n* (*in printing*) offset *m.*
● **to offset sth. against sth.,** deducir algo de algo.
▲ (*verbo*) *pt & pp* **offset,** *ger* **offsetting;** (*sustantivo*) ['ɒfset].

offshoot ['ɒfʃuːt] **1** *n* BOT renuevo, retoño, vástago. **2** *fig* (*of family*) rama; (*of organization, company*) ramificación *f,* filial *f.*

offshore [ɒf'ʃɔːʳ] **1** *adj* (*at sea*) a poca distancia de la costa: *offshore drilling,* perforación cerca de la costa. **2** (*breeze*) terral, de tierra. **3** (*overseas*) en el extranjero. – **4** *adv* mar adentro.

offside [ɒf'saɪd] **1** *adj* SP fuera de juego. **2** GB AUTO del lado del conductor. – **3** *adv* SP en fuera de juego. – **4** *n* GB AUTO lado del conductor.

offspring ['ɒfsprɪŋ] **1** *n fml* (*child*) descendiente *mf,* vástago *mf;* (*children*) progenitura, descendencia, prole *f.* **2** (*animal - one*) cría; (*- several*) crías *fpl.* **3** *fig* (*outcome, result*) consecuencia, resultado.
▲ *pl* **offspring.**

offstage [ɒf'steɪdʒ] **1** *adj* entre bastidores, de fuera del escenario. – **2** *adv* fuera del escenario.

off-the-cuff [ɒfðə'kʌf] *adj* improvisado,-a.

off-the-peg [ɒfðə'peg] *adj* (*clothes*) de confección.

off-the-record [ɒfðə'rekɔːd] *adj* extraoficial, confidencial.

off-white [ɒf'waɪt] **1** *adj* de color hueso, blancuzco,-a. – **2** *n* color *m* hueso.

often ['ɒfən, 'ɒftən] *adv* (*frequently*) a menudo, con frecuencia: *we often go to the theatre,* vamos al teatro a

menudo; *how often do you go to the dentist?,* ¿cada cuánto vas al dentista?; *I visit them as often as I can,* los visito siempre que puedo.
● **more often than not,** la mayoría de las veces.

ogle ['əʊgəl] **1** *t* comerse con los ojos. – **2** *i* comerse con los ojos (**at,** a).

ogre ['əʊgəʳ] *n* ogro.

oh [əʊ] *interj* ¡oh!, ¡ay!, ¡vaya!: *oh, my God!,* ¡Dios mío!; *oh, really?,* ¿de veras?; *oh, look!,* ¡eh, mira!

ohm [əʊm] *n* ohmio, ohm *m.*

OHMS ['əʊ'eɪtʃ'em'es] *abbr* GB (*On His/Her Majesty's Service*) al servicio de su majestad.

oil [ɔɪl] **1** *n* (*gen*) aceite *m: sunflower oil,* aceite de girasol. **2** (*petroleum*) petróleo: *crude oil,* crudo. **3** ART (*painting*) óleo, pintura al óleo. – **4** *t* engrasar, lubricar, lubrificar. – **5** **oils,** *npl* (*paints*) óleo: *she paints in oils,* pinta al óleo.
● **to be no oil painting,** no ser ninguna belleza. ‖ **to oil sb.'s palm,** untar la mano a algn. ‖ **to oil the wheels,** preparar el terreno. ‖ **to pour oil on troubled waters,** templar los ánimos. ‖ **to strike oil,** (*find oil*) encontrar petróleo; (*become rich*) hacer fortuna.
■ **oil drum,** bidón *m.* ‖ **oil gauge,** indicador *m* del nivel de aceite. ‖ **oil gun,** pistola de engrase. ‖ **oil industry,** industria petrolera. ‖ **oil lamp,** lámpara de aceite. ‖ **oil painting,** cuadro al óleo, óleo. ‖ **oil rig,** plataforma petrolífera. ‖ **oil slick,** marea negra. ‖ **oil tanker,** petrolero. ‖ **oil well,** pozo petrolífero.

oil-bearing ['ɔɪlbeərɪŋ] *adj* petrolífero,-a.

oilcan ['ɔɪlkæn] *n* aceitera.

oilcloth ['ɔɪlklɒθ] *n* hule *m.*

oilfield ['ɔɪlfiːld] *n* yacimiento petrolífero.

oilfired ['ɔɪlfaɪəd] *adj* de fuel-oil.

oilskin ['ɔɪlskɪn] **1** *n* hule *m.* – **2** **oilskins,** *npl* chubasquero *m sing,* traje *m sing* de hule.

oily ['ɔɪlɪ] **1** *adj* (*food*) aceitoso,-a, grasiento,-a; (*skin, hair*) graso,-a; (*rag*) manchado,-a de aceite. **2** *pej* (*manner*) empalagoso,-a.
▲ *comp* **oilier,** *superl* **oiliest.**

ointment ['ɔɪntmənt] *n* ungüento, pomada.

okay [əʊ'keɪ] **1** *interj* ¡vale!, ¡de acuerdo! – **2** *adj* correcto,-a, bien: *are you okay?,* ¿estás bien?; *is it okay if Paul comes?,* ¿te importa que venga Paul? – **3** *adv* bien, bastante bien: *he's doing okay at school,* va bien en el colegio. – **4** *n* visto bueno, aprobación *f.* – **5** *t* dar el visto bueno a: *the boss okayed it,* el jefe ha dado el visto bueno.

old [əʊld] **1** *adj* (*person*) viejo,-a, mayor: *an old man,* un anciano, un hombre mayor, un viejo; *I'm getting old,* me estoy haciendo viejo; *she's a year older than you,* te lleva un año, es un año mayor que tú, tiene un año más que tú. **2** (*thing*) viejo,-a, antiguo,-a; (*wine*) añejo,-a; (*clothes*) usado,-a: *the old part of the city,* el casco antiguo de la ciudad; *the good old days,* los viejos tiempos. **3** (*long-established, familiar*) viejo,-a: *he's an old friend,* es un viejo amigo. **4** (*former*) antiguo,-a: *in my old job,* en mi antiguo trabajo. **5** (*experienced, veteran*) viejo,-a, veterano,-a. – **6 the old,** *n* las personas *fpl* mayores, los ancianos *mpl.*
● **any old how,** de cualquier manera. ‖ **any old thing,** cualquier cosa. ‖ **as old as the hills,** más viejo,-a que Matusalén. ‖ **how old are you?,** ¿cuántos años tienes?, ¿qué edad tienes? ‖ **of old,** de antaño. ‖ **to be ... years old,** tener ... años. ‖ **to be old hat,** no ser ninguna novedad.
■ **old age,** vejez *f.* ‖ **old age pensioner,** pensionista *mf* (*de la tercera edad*). ‖ **old boy,** (*ex-pupil*) ex-alumno,

antiguo alumno; (*old man*) abuelo, viejecito; (*form of address*) viejo. ‖ **old folk,** ancianos *mpl.* ‖ **old girl,** (*ex-pupil*) ex-alumna, antigua alumna; (*old woman*) abuela, viejecita. ‖ **old hand,** veterano,-a. ‖ **old lady,** (*woman*) vieja, señora mayor; (*mother*) vieja; (*wife*) parienta. ‖ **old maid,** solterona. ‖ **old man,** (*father*) viejo; (*husband*) marido. ‖ **old people's home,** residencia de ancianos. ‖ **Old Testament,** Antiguo Testamento. ‖ **old wives' tale,** cuento de viejas. ‖ **the Old World,** el viejo mundo.

olden ['əʊldən] *adj* antiguo,-a: *in olden times,* en tiempos antiguos, antaño.

older ['əʊldəʳ] **1** *adj* (*comparative*) → **old.** **2** (*elder*) mayor.

old-established [əʊldɪˈstæblɪʃt] *adj* antiguo,-a.

old-fashioned [əʊldˈfæʃənd] *adj* (*outdated - gen*) anticuado,-a, pasado,-a de moda; (*- person*) chapado,-a a la antigua.

old-time ['əʊldtaɪm] *adj* antiguo,-a.

old-timer [əʊldˈtaɪməʳ] **1** *n* (*in job etc*) veterano,-a. **2** US (*old man*) viejo.

old-world ['əʊldwɜːld] *adj* (*of past*) tradicional, de los tiempos antiguos; (*quaint*) pintoresco,-a.

oleander [əʊlɪˈændəʳ] *n* вот adelfa.

olfactory [ɒlˈfæktərɪ] *adj* olfativo,-a, olfatorio,-a.

■ olfactory nerve, nervio olfativo.

oligarchy ['ɒlɪgɑːkɪ] *n* oligarquía.

▲ *pl* **oligarchies.**

olive ['ɒlɪv] **1** *n* (*tree, wood*) olivo. **2** (*fruit*) aceituna, oliva. **3** (*colour*) verde *m* oliva. – **4** *adj* (*paint*) color aceituna; (*skin*) aceitunado,-a. **5** (*olive-growing*) olivarero,-a.

● **to hold out the olive branch,** tender la mano en son de paz.

■ **olive branch,** rama de olivo. ‖ **olive grove,** olivar *m.* ‖ **olive oil,** aceite *m* de oliva. ‖ **olive tree,** olivo.

Olympiad [əˈlɪmpɪæd] *n* Olimpíada, Olimpiada.

Olympic [əˈlɪmpɪk] **1** *adj* olímpico,-a. – **2 the Olympics,** *npl* los Juegos Olímpicos, la Olimpíada *f sing.*

■ Olympic Games, Juegos *mpl* Olímpicos.

Oman [əʊˈmæn] *n* Omán.

Omani [əʊˈmɑːnɪ] **1** *adj* omaní. – **2** *n* omaní *mf.*

omelet ['ɒmlət] *n* US → **omelette.**

omelette ['ɒmlət] *n* tortilla.

■ plain omelette, tortilla francesa.

omen ['əʊmən] *n* agüero, presagio, augurio: *it's a good omen,* es un buen presagio, es de buen agüero.

ominous ['ɒmɪnəs] *adj* (*foreboding evil*) de mal agüero, siniestro,-a; (*prophetic*) agorero,-a; (*threatening*) amenazador,-ra, amenazante; (*worrying*) inquietante.

omission [əʊˈmɪʃən] *n* omisión *f.*

omit [əʊˈmɪt] **1** *t* (*not include, leave out*) omitir, suprimir; (*forget to include*) olvidar incluir. **2** (*fail to do*) omitir, pasar por alto, dejar de; (*forget*) olvidarse.

▲ *pt & pp* **omitted,** *ger* **omitting.**

omnibus ['ɒmnɪbəs] **1** *n* dated (*bus*) ómnibus *m.* **2** (*collection*) antología.

omnipotence [ɒmˈnɪpətəns] *n fml* omnipotencia.

omnipotent [ɒmˈnɪpətənt] *adj fml* omnipotente.

omnipresent [ɒmnɪˈprezənt] *adj fml* omnipresente.

omniscient [ɒmˈnɪsɪənt] *adj fml* omnisciente.

omnivore ['ɒmnɪvɔːʳ] *n* zool omnívoro,-a.

omnivorous [ɒmˈnɪvərəs] **1** *adj* zool fml omnívoro,-a. **2** *fml* (*person*) voraz.

on [ɒn] **1** *prep* (*covering or touching*) sobre, encima de, en: *put it on the floor,* ponlo en el suelo; *it's on the table,* está encima de la mesa; *on page 45,* en la página 45; *the ball hit me on the head,* el balón me dio en la cabeza.

2 (*supported by, hanging from*) en: *she put the picture on the wall,* colgó el cuadro en la pared; *lean on me,* apóyate en mí. **3** (*to, towards*) a, hacia: *the army was advancing on Berlin,* el ejército avanzaba hacia Berlín; *on the right/left,* a la derecha/izquierda. **4** (*at the edge of*) en: *a village on the coast,* un pueblo de la costa; *it's on the border,* está en la frontera. **5** (*concerning*) sobre: *a tax on alcohol,* un impuesto sobre el alcohol. **6** (*travelling expressions*) de: *we went on a journey,* nos fuimos de viaje, hicimos un viaje; *he's on a business trip,* está de viaje de negocios; *I was on my way to work,* iba de camino al trabajo. **7** (*days, dates, times*) no se traduce: *on Saturday,* el sábado; *on Saturdays,* los sábados; *on November 3rd,* el tres de noviembre; *on Christmas Day,* el día de Navidad. **8** (*at the time of, just after*) al: *on arrival,* al llegar; *on discovering the body,* al descubrir el cadáver. **9** (*as a result of*) diferentes traducciones: *on your advice,* siguiendo tus consejos; *based on a true story,* basado en una historia real. **10** (*as means of transport*) a, en: *on foot, on horseback, on a bicycle,* a pie, a caballo, en bicicleta; *on the train, on the bus, on the underground,* en el tren, en el autobús, en el metro. **11** (*regarding, about*) sobre, de: *a talk on birds,* una charla sobre aves; *a book on art,* un libro de arte. **12** (*by means of*) por: *on the radio, on the TV,* por la radio, por la tele; *I'm speaking on the phone,* estoy hablando por teléfono. **13** (*using*) con: *how do you get by on your pension?,* ¿cómo te las arreglas con tu pensión?; *cars run on petrol,* los coches funcionan con gasolina. **14** (*state, process*) diferentes traducciones: *it's on fire,* se está quemando; *it's on sale now,* ya está a la venta; *she's on a diet,* está a régimen; *crime is on the increase,* los delitos van en aumento; *on strike,* en huelga. **15** (*working for, belonging to*) diferentes traducciones: *he's on the committee,* forma parte de la comisión; *on the staff,* en plantilla; *whose side are you on?,* ¿de parte de quién estás? **16** (*in possession of*) con: *he was caught with drugs on him,* lo cogieron con drogas; *have you got any money on you?,* ¿llevas dinero? **17** (*paid for by*) pagado por: *the drinks are on me!,* ¡invito yo!; *it's on the house,* paga la casa. **18** (*by comparison with*) respecto a: *sales are up on last year,* las ventas han aumentado respecto al año pasado. – **19** *adv* (*not stopping*) sin parar: *she kept on talking,* siguió hablando; *on with the show! the show must go on!,* ¡que siga el espectáculo! **20** (*movement forward*) diferentes traducciones: *walk on until you get to the church,* sigue hasta que llegues a la iglesia; *it's time we were moving on,* es hora de que nos vayamos. **21** (*clothes - being worn*) puesto,-a: *she had a cap on,* llevaba puesta una gorra; *put a jumper on,* ponte un jersey; *keep your coat on,* no te quites el abrigo. **22** (*working*) diferentes traducciones: *who left the TV on?,* ¿quién dejó la TV encendida?; *don't leave the tap on!,* ¡no dejes el grifo abierto!; *could you put a record on?,* ¿podrías poner un disco? **23** (*happening*) diferentes traducciones: *is there anything good on TV?,* ¿dan algo bueno por la tele?; *what time is the film on?,* ¿a qué hora ponen la película?; *have we got anything on this weekend?,* ¿tenemos plan para este fin de semana? – **24** *adj* (*in use*) diferentes traducciones: *is the heating on?,* ¿está puesta la calefacción?; *all the lights were on,* todas las luces estaban encendidas. **25** (*happening*) diferentes traducciones: *the strike's on,* la huelga sigue convocada; *is the party still on?,* ¿se hace la fiesta?; *the match is on after all,* después de todo, el partido se celebra. **26** (*performing*) diferentes traducciones: *you're on next!,* ¡sales tú el próximo!; *they're bringing the sub on,* hacen salir a jugar el suplente.

● **and so on,** y así sucesivamente. ‖ **from that day on,** a partir de aquel día. ‖ **it's not on,** no hay derecho, eso no vale. ‖ **to be on about,** hablar de: *what on earth is he on about?,* ¿de qué diablos está hablando? ‖ **to be on at sb.,** dar la lata a algn. ‖ **to be on for sth.,** apuntarse a algo. ‖ **to go on and on about sth.,** seguir dale que dale con algo. ‖ **to have sth. on sb.,** tener algo contra algn. ‖ **you're on!,** ¡trato hecho!

once [wʌns] **1** *adv* (*one time*) una vez: *once a week,* una vez por semana; *he didn't write to me once,* no me escribió ni una sola vez. **2** (*formerly*) antes, en otro tiempo: *once I would've stayed up all night,* antes no me habría acostado en toda la noche. − **3** *conj* una vez que, en cuanto: *once everyone gets here, we can start,* una vez que lleguen todos, podemos empezar. − **4** *n* vez *f: just this once,* sólo esta vez.

● **all at once,** de repente. ‖ **at once,** (*at the same time*) a la vez, de una vez; (*immediately*) en seguida, inmediatamente, ahora mismo. ‖ **just for once,** por una vez. ‖ **once again,** otra vez. ‖ **once and for all,** de una vez para siempre, de una vez por todas. ‖ **once bitten, twice shy,** el gato escaldado del agua fría huye. ‖ **once in a blue moon,** de Pascuas a Ramos. ‖ **once in a while,** de vez en cuando. ‖ **once more,** una vez más. ‖ **once or twice,** un par de veces. ‖ **once upon a time,** érase una vez.

once-over ['wʌnsəuvə'] *n fam* vistazo.

● **to give sth. the once-over,** echar un vistazo a algo.

oncology [ɒŋ'kɒlədʒɪ] *n* oncología.

oncoming ['ɒnkʌmɪŋ] **1** *adj* (*traffic*) que viene en dirección contraria. **2** (*event, season*) venidero,-a, futuro,-a.

one [wʌn] **1** *adj* (*stating number*) un, una: *I've got one brother,* tengo un hermano; *there's one biscuit left,* queda una galleta; *one hundred,* cien. **2** (*unspecified, a certain*) un, una, algún,-una: *one day in January,* un día de enero; *come for supper one evening,* ven a cenar una noche. **3** (*only, single*) único,-a: *the one way to get on in life,* la única manera de tener éxito en la vida; *the one and only James Brown,* el inimitable James Brown. **4** (*same*) mismo,-a: *in one direction,* en la misma dirección; *one and the same thing,* la misma cosa. **5** (*with names*) un,-a tal: *one Bill Burroughs,* un tal Bill Burroughs. − **6** *pron* (*thing*) uno,-a: *a red one,* uno,-a rojo,-a; *this one,* éste,-a; *that one,* ése,-a, aquél,-la; *which one?,* ¿cuál?; *the small one,* el pequeño, la pequeña; *the other one,* el otro, la otra. **7** (*drink*) una copa: *let's have a quick one,* tomemos una copa rápida; *you've had one too many,* has bebido más de la cuenta. **8** (*person*) el, la: *he's the one who I was telling you about,* es él de quien te estaba hablando; *she's the one I paid the money to,* es a ella a quien le pagué el dinero; *you're one of the family,* eres de la familia. **9** (*any person, you*) uno, una: *one can't think of everything,* uno no puede pensar en todo; *one has to be patient,* hay que tener paciencia; *one never knows,* nunca se sabe. − **10** *n* (*number*) uno: *my son is one today,* mi hijo cumple un año hoy; *there's only one left,* sólo queda uno.

● **all in one,** de una (sola) pieza. ‖ **a one,** un caso: *you are a one!,* ¡eres un caso! ‖ **a right one,** un,-a idiota. ‖ **as one / as one man,** como un solo hombre, todos a la vez. ‖ **at one with,** en armonía con. ‖ **in one,** (*combined, together*) a la vez, todo en uno; (*in only one attempt*) de una vez, de un golpe; (*in one mouthful*) de un trago. ‖ **neither one thing nor the other,** ni carne ni pescado. ‖ **one after another / one after the other,** uno,-a detrás de otro,-a. ‖ **one and all,** todos,-as, todo el mundo. ‖ **one another,** el uno al otro: *we help one an-*

other, nos ayudamos mutuamente; *they love one another,* se quieren. ‖ **one at a time,** de uno en uno. ‖ **one by one,** de uno,-a en uno,-a, uno,-a tras otro,-a. ‖ **to be one to ...,** ser dado,-a a ...,** ser de los/las que ...: *I'm not one to gossip,* no me gusta chismorrear, no soy de las que chismorrean.

one-act ['wʌnækt] *adj* (*of play*) de un (solo) acto.

one-armed ['wʌnɑːmd] *adj* manco,-a.

■ **one-armed bandit,** máquina tragaperras.

one-eyed ['wʌnaɪd] *adj* tuerto,-a.

one-handed ['wʌnhændɪd] **1** *adj* (*one-armed*) manco,-a. − **2** *adv* con una sola mano.

one-horse town ['wʌnhɔːs'taʊn] *n fam* pueblucho, pueblo de mala muerte.

one-legged ['wʌnlegɪd] *adj* cojo,-a, con una sola pierna.

one-man ['wʌnmæn] *adj* individual, de un solo hombre: *one-man show,* espectáculo con un solo artista.

■ **one-man band,** (*musician*) hombre *m* orquesta; (*business*) empresa llevada por una sola persona.

oneness ['wʌnnəs] *n* (*unity*) unidad *f.*

one-night stand ['wʌnnaɪt'stænd] **1** *n* (*show*) representación *f* única. **2** *fam* (*sexual encounter*) ligue *m* de una sola noche; (*person*) ligue *m* de una sola noche.

one-off ['wʌnɒf] **1** *adj* GB *fam* único,-a, irrepetible. − **2** *n* GB *fam* cosa única, fuera *mf* de serie.

one-parent family ['wʌnpeərənt'fæmɪlɪ] *n* familia monoparental.

one-piece ['wʌnpiːs] *adj* de una sola pieza.

onerous ['ɒnərəs] *adj* (*debt*) oneroso,-a; (*task, duty*) pesado,-a.

oneself [wʌn'self] **1** *pron* (*reflexive*) se; (*emphatic*) uno,-a mismo,-a; (*after prep*) sí mismo,-a: *to wash oneself,* lavarse; *to enjoy oneself,* divertirse; *to talk to oneself,* hablar para sí, hablar a solas. **2** (*alone*) solo,-a: *one will have to do it oneself,* uno tendrá que hacérselo solo. **3** (*one's usual self*) el de siempre, la de siempre.

● **(all) by oneself,** solo,-a. ‖ **to oneself,** para sí, para sí solo,-a.

one-sided ['wʌn'saɪdɪd] **1** *adj* (*contest*) desigual. **2** (*view, account*) parcial. **3** (*agreement*) unilateral.

one-time ['wʌntaɪm] *adj* (*former*) antiguo,-a, ex-.

one-to-one ['wʌntuwʌn] **1** *adj* (*corresponding exactly*) con una correspondencia mutua, de uno a uno. **2** (*individual*) individualizado,-a, personal.

one-track ['wʌntræk] *adj fam* obsesivo,-a: *you've got a one-track mind!,* ¡no piensas más que en una cosa!

one-upmanship [wʌn'ʌpmənʃɪp] *n arte de imponerse a los demás.*

one-way ['wʌnweɪ] **1** *adj* (*street*) de sentido único, de dirección única. **2** (*ticket*) de ida.

one-woman ['wʌnwumən] *adj* de una sola mujer: *a one-woman show,* espectáculo con una sola artista.

ongoing ['ɒngəʊɪŋ] *adj* (*continuing*) en curso, actual, que sigue; (*developing*) en desarrollo: *ongoing negotiations,* negociaciones en curso.

onion ['ʌnɪən] *n* cebolla.

● **to know one's onions,** saber uno,-a lo que se trae entre manos.

■ **onion soup,** sopa de cebolla.

onionskin ['ʌnɪənskɪn] *n* papel *m* cebolla.

online ['ɒnlaɪn] **1** *adj* COMPUT en línea. − **2** *adv* COMPUT en línea.

onlooker ['ɒnlukə'] *n* espectador,-ra, curioso,-a: *a crowd of onlookers,* un grupo de curiosos.

only ['əʊnlɪ] **1** *adj* (*sole*) único,-a: *the only problem is that ...,* el único problema es que ...; *Marbella is the only pla-*

ce to go on honeymoon, Marbella es el único sitio para pasar la luna de miel. – **2** *adv* (*just, merely*) sólo, solamente: *he's only a child,* sólo es un niño; *it only cost a pound,* sólo costó una libra; *they arrived home, only to discover that they'd been burgled,* llegaron a casa y se encontraron con que habían entrado a robar. **3** (*exclusively*) sólo, solamente, únicamente: *we only want to know where you were yesterday,* sólo queremos saber dónde estuviste ayer; *only my mother knows,* mi madre es la única que lo sabe. – **4** *conj* pero: *it's like yoghurt, only better,* es como el yogur, pero mejor.
● **not only ... but also,** no solamente ... sino también. ‖ **only just,** (*a moment before*) acabar de; (*almost not, scarcely*) por poco: *I've only just arrived,* justo acabo de llegar; *he only just caught the plane,* por poco se le escapa el avión. ‖ **only too ...,** muy ...: *I'd be only too pleased to go,* me encantaría ir.
■ **only child,** hijo,-a único,-a.

ono [ɔːˈnɪərɪstˈɒfəˈ] *abbr* GB (**or nearest offer**) u oferta aproximada.

onomatopoeia [ɒnəmætəˈpiːə] *n* onomatopeya.

onrush [ˈɒnrʌʃ] *n* (*of people*) oleada, avalancha; (*of water*) riada, crecida.

onset [ˈɒnset] *n* (*beginning - of war, winter*) comienzo, principio, llegada; (*- of disease, fever*) aparición *f*.

onshore [ɒnˈʃɔːʳ] **1** *adj* (*on land*) en tierra. – **2** *adv* (*towards land*) tierra adentro.

onslaught [ˈɒnslɔːt] *n* ataque *m* violento, arremetida, embestida.

onstage [ɒnˈsteɪdʒ] **1** *adj* en escena. – **2** *adv* a escena.

onto [ˈɒntʊ] **1** *prep* (*movement*) a, en: *it fell onto the floor,* cayó al suelo; *put it onto the plate,* ponlo en el plato. **2** (*new subject*) a: *how did we get onto football?,* ¿cómo es que hemos empezado a hablar de fútbol?; *let's move onto a different subject,* cambiemos de tema.
● **to be onto sb.,** (*pursue*) andar tras algn., sospechar de algn.; (*talk to*) hablar con algn.; (*nag*) dar la lata a algn.: *the police are onto him,* la policía anda tras él, la policía sospecha de él; *Mum's been onto me again about smoking,* mamá me ha dado la lata para que deje de fumar; *have you been onto the manufacturers yet?,* ¿ya has hablado con los fabricantes? ‖ **to be onto sth.,** dar con algo: *he thinks he's onto something big,* cree que ha dado con algo gordo; *you're onto a good thing there!,* ¡qué bien te lo montas!

onus [ˈəʊnəs] *n* responsabilidad *f*: *the onus is on you to prove you're innocent,* te incumbe a ti probar que eres inocente.

onward [ˈɒnwəd] **1** *adj* hacia adelante: *the onward march of time,* el avance inexorable del tiempo. – **2** *adv* US → **onwards**.

onwards [ˈɒnwədz] *adv* GB adelante, hacia adelante: *from now onwards,* a partir de ahora, de ahora en adelante.

onyx [ˈɒnɪks] *n* ónice *m*.

oodles [ˈuːdəlz] *npl* montones *mpl*, cantidad *f* sing.

oomph [ʊmf] *n* brío.

oops [uːps] *interj* ¡ay!, ¡uy!

ooze[1] [uːz] **1** *i* rezumar: *blood oozed from the wound,* rezumaba sangre de la herida. – **2** *t* rezumar: *the wound oozed blood,* la herida rezumaba sangre. **3** *fig* rebosar, irradiar: *he oozes charm,* irradia encanto.

ooze[2] [uːz] *n* cieno, lodo.

op[1] [ɒp] *n fam* operación *f*, intervención *f*.

op[1] [ɒp] *n* MUS → **opus**.

opacity [əʊˈpæsɪtɪ] **1** *n* (*non-transparency*) opacidad *f*. **2** (*obscurity*) oscuridad *f*.

opal [ˈəʊpəl] *n* ópalo.

opaque [əʊˈpeɪk] **1** *adj* (*not transparent*) opaco,-a. **2** (*difficult to understand, obscure*) obscuro,-a, oscuro,-a, poco claro,-a.

op cit [ˈɒpˈsɪt] *abbr* (*opere citato*) obra citada; (*abbreviation*) ob. cit.

OPEC [ˈəʊpek] *abbr* (**Organization of Petroleum Exporting Countries**) Organización *f* de los Países Exportadores de Petróleo; (*abbreviation*) OPEP *f*.

open [ˈəʊpən] **1** *adj* (*not closed - gen*) abierto,-a; (*- wound*) abierto,-a, sin cicatrizar: *the road is now open to traffic,* la carretera ya está abierta al tráfico; *I can't keep my eyes open,* no puedo mantener los ojos abiertos. **2** (*not enclosed*) abierto,-a: *the open sea,* el mar abierto. **3** (*not covered - gen*) descubierto,-a: *an open sewer,* una alcantarilla al descubierto; *an open car,* un coche descapotable. **4** (*not fastened, not folded*) abierto,-a; (*not buttoned*) desabrochado,-a, abierto,-a: *the book lay open,* el libro estaba abierto; *a blouse open at the neck,* una blusa con el cuello desabrochado. **5** (*ready for customers*) abierto,-a; (*ready to start being used*) inaugurado,-a: *many shops are now open on Sundays,* muchas tiendas están abiertas los domingos; *the new school was declared open,* la nueva escuela fue inaugurada oficialmente. **6** (*not settled*) sin resolver; (*not decided*) sin decidir, sin concretar: *an open question,* una cuestión sin resolver; *keep your options open,* deja todas las puertas abiertas; *let's leave the matter open,* dejemos el asunto sin concretar. **7** (*available*) vacante. **8** (*not hidden, not limited*) abierto,-a, franco,-a, manifiesto,-a: *a state of open war,* un estado de guerra abierta. **9** (*frank, honest*) abierto,-a, sincero,-a, franco,-a: *I'll be open with you,* te seré sincero. **10** (*that anyone can enter*) abierto,-a, libre: *an open championship,* un campeonato abierto; *this meeting is open to the public,* esta reunión está abierta al público. **11** GB (*cheque*) abierto,-a. **12** (*cloth, texture, weave*) abierto,-a. **13** LING (*vowel*) abierto,-a. – **14** *n* SP (*competition*) open *m*. – **15** *t* (*gen*) abrir: *open your mouth,* abre la boca; *have you opened your present?,* ¿has abierto tu regalo? **16** (*book, newspaper*) abrir; (*map*) abrir, desplegar: *she opened the book,* abrió el libro; *open your hands,* abre las manos. **17** (*start - gen*) abrir; (*meeting*) abrir, dar comienzo a; (*debate*) abrir, iniciar; (*bidding, negotiations*) iniciar; (*talks, conversation*) entablar: *I'd like to open a bank account,* quisiera abrir una cuenta bancaria; *she opened the congress with a speech,* abrió el congreso con un discurso. **18** (*begin, set up*) abrir, montar, poner; (*inaugurate, declare open*) abrir, inaugurar: *Princess Diana opened a new hospital,* la Princesa Diana inauguró un nuevo hospital; *we're going to open a business,* vamos a montar un negocio. **19** (*tunnel, road, mine, etc*) abrir. – **20** *i* (*gen*) abrir, abrirse: *the door opened,* la puerta se abrió; *the cut's opened up again,* la herida se ha vuelto a abrir. **21** (*spread out, unfold*) abrirse: *the roses are opening,* las rosas se están abriendo; *his parachute failed to open,* su paracaídas no se abrió. **22** (*start - conference, play, book*) comenzar, empezar; (*film*) estrenarse: *the film opens on Friday,* la película se estrena el viernes; *the book opens with a robbery,* el libro comienza con un atraco. **23** (*begin business*) abrir: *what time do the banks open?,* ¿a qué hora abren los bancos? – **24** *open to,* *adj* (*susceptible*) susceptible a, expuesto,-a; (*receptive*) abierto,-a a; (*available*) posible: *we're open to suggestions,* estamos abiertos a todo tipo de sugerencias; *that statement is open to misunderstanding,* esa afirmación puede malinterpretarse; *I'm open to offers,* estoy dispuesto a recibir ofertas; *there are two options open to you,* tienes dos opciones. **– 25 the open,** *n (the outdoors, open air)* campo, aire *m* libre.

◆ **to open into / open onto** *t insep* dar a: *the back door opens onto the patio,* la puerta trasera da al patio. ‖ **to open out 1** *i (develop - person)* volverse más abierto,-a; (*- flower*) abrirse. **2** *(become wider)* ensancharse; (*unfold*) abrirse. ‖ **to open up 1** *t sep (make available)* abrir (**to,** a). **– 2** *i (become available)* abrirse (**to,** a). **3** (*unlock*) abrir: *police! open up!,* ¡policía! ¡abran! **4** *(speak more freely)* abrirse.

● **to be an open book,** *fig* ser como un libro abierto. ‖ **in the open air,** al aire libre. ‖ **open sesame!,** ¡ábrete sésamo! ‖ **to lay os. (wide) open to sth.,** exponerse a algo. ‖ **to be out in the open,** estar al aire libre; *fig* saberse, estar a la luz. ‖ **to bring sth. (out) into the open,** hacer público algo, sacar algo a la luz. ‖ **to keep an open mind,** tener una actitud abierta. ‖ **to keep one's eyes open,** estar ojo avizor. ‖ **to keep open house,** tener las puertas abiertas a todo el mundo. ‖ **to open fire,** abrir fuego (**on/at,** contra). ‖ **to open sb.'s eyes to sth.,** abrirle los ojos a algn., hacerle ver algo a algn.

■ **open day,** jornada de puertas abiertas. ‖ **open letter,** carta abierta. ‖ **open market,** mercado libre, mercado abierto. ‖ **open prison,** prisión *f* de régimen abierto. ‖ **open season,** temporada de caza. ‖ **open secret,** secreto a voces. ‖ **the Open University,** ≈ Universidad Nacional de Educación a Distancia.

open-air [ˈəʊpəneəʳ] *adj* al aire libre.

■ **open-air swimming pool,** piscina descubierta.

open-and-shut [ˈəʊpənənʃʌt] *adj* claro,-a, evidente: *it's an open-and-shut case,* es un caso clarísimo.

opencast [ˈəʊpənkɑːst] *adj* GB a cielo abierto.

open-door [ˈəʊpəndɔːʳ] *adj (policy - on imports)* no proteccionista; (*- on immigration*) de puertas abiertas.

open-ended [əʊpənˈendɪd] *adj (indefinite - contract)* de duración indefinida; (*- discussion*) abierto,-a.

opener [ˈəʊpənəʳ] *n* abridor *m*.

● **for openers,** para empezar.

open-eyed [əʊpənˈaɪd] *adj* con los ojos abiertos.

open-handed [əʊpənˈhændɪd] *adj (generous)* generoso,-a, dadivoso,-a.

open-heart [ˈəʊpənhɑːt] *adj (surgery)* a corazón abierto.

open-hearted [əʊpənˈhɑːtɪd] *adj (kind)* de gran corazón; (*candid*) abierto,-a, franco,-a, sincero,-a.

opening [ˈəʊpənɪŋ] **1** *n (ceremony - gen)* inauguración *f*; (*- of Parliament*) apertura. **2** *(beginning, first part)* apertura, comienzo; *(in chess)* apertura: *the opening of the film,* el comienzo de la película. **3** CINEM THEAT estreno. **4** (*process of opening, unfolding*) apertura. **5** *(hole)* abertura; *(space)* hueco; (*gap*) brecha; *(clearing)* claro: *an opening in the clouds,* un claro en las nubes. **6** *(chance)* oportunidad *f* (**for,** para). **7** *(vacancy)* vacante *f* (**for,** para): *there are few openings in journalism,* hay pocas posibilidades de abrirse camino en el periodismo. **– 8** *adj (initial)* inicial: *opening remarks,* comentarios iniciales.

■ **opening hours,** *(of shop)* horario comercial; *(of office)* horario de atención al público. ‖ **opening night,** noche *f* de estreno. ‖ **opening scene,** primera escena. ‖ **opening speech,** discurso inaugural. ‖ **opening time,** GB *hora de apertura de los pubs.*

openly [ˈəʊpənlɪ] *adv (not secretly)* abiertamente; *(publicly)* públicamente, en público.

open-minded [əʊpənˈmaɪndɪd] *adj (person)* abierto,-a, de actitud abierta; (*approach*) abierto,-a, imparcial.

open-mindedness [əʊpənˈmaɪndɪdnəs] *n (of person)* actitud *f* abierta; (*of approach*) imparcialidad *f*.

open-mouthed [əʊpənˈmaʊðd] *adj* boquiabierto,-a.

open-necked [əʊpənˈnekθ] *adj* desabrochado,-a en el cuello.

openness [ˈəʊpənnəs] *n (frankness)* franqueza; (*receptiveness*) actitud *f* abierta.

open-plan [ˈəʊpənplæn] *adj* de planta abierta.

openwork [ˈəʊpənwɜːk] *n (in lace, cloth)* calado; (*in metal*) enrejado.

opera [ˈɒpərə] *n* ópera.

■ **opera glasses,** indiscretos *mpl*. ‖ **opera house,** ópera, teatro de la ópera. ‖ **opera singer,** cantante *mf* de ópera.

operable [ˈɒpərəbəl] *adj* MED operable.

operate [ˈɒpəreɪt] **1** *t (machine etc)* hacer funcionar, manejar, operar; *(controls)* manejar, accionar. **2** *(manage, run - business)* dirigir, manejar, llevar; (*- factory*) explotar. **3** *(system, method, policy)* aplicar. **– 4** *i (function - machine etc)* funcionar: *the security system operates well,* el sistema de seguridad funciona bien. **5** *(carry on trade)* operar; *(work)* trabajar: *a Sunday service will operate over the Christmas holidays,* habrá un servicio dominical durante las fiestas de Navidad. **6** *(produce effect, be in action)* actuar, obrar: *this law operates against in our favour,* esta ley está a nuestro favor. **7** *(soldiers, police, etc)* operar: *police patrols operate in this area,* patrullas de policía operan en esta zona. **8** MED operar (**on,** a), intervenir (**on,** a): *he's being operated on now,* lo están operando ahora; *she was operated on for cancer,* la operaron de cáncer.

operatic [ɒpəˈrætɪk] *adj* de ópera, operístico,-a.

operating [ˈɒpəreɪtɪŋ] **1** *adj* COMM *(losses, costs)* de explotación. **2** TECH *(conditions)* de funcionamiento.

■ **operating room,** US quirófano. ‖ **operating system,** COMPUT sistema *m* operativo. ‖ **operating table,** mesa de operaciones. ‖ **operating theatre,** GB quirófano.

operation [ɒpəˈreɪʃən] **1** *n* MED operación *f*, intervención *f*: *I've got to have an operation,* me tengo que operar, me tienen que operar. **2** *(of machine - gen)* funcionamiento; (*- by person*) manejo; *(of system)* uso: *the operation of computers,* el funcionamiento de los ordenadores. **3** *(activity)* operación *f*; *(planned campaign)* campaña: *a rescue operation,* una operación de rescate. **4** COMM *(enterprise, company)* operación *f*. **5** MIL operación *f*. **6** MATH operación *f*.

● **to be in operation,** *(machine)* estar en funcionamiento; *(system, rule, law)* regir. ‖ **to come into operation,** *(machine)* entrar en funcionamiento; *(plan)* ponerse en marcha.

■ **operations room,** MIL centro de operaciones.

operational [ɒpəˈreɪʃənəl] **1** *adj (ready for use)* operativo,-a, listo,-a para usar; *(in use)* en uso. **2** *(occurring in practice)* de operación, operativo,-a.

● **to become operational,** entrar en funcionamiento.

operative [ˈɒpərətɪv] **1** *adj (in force)* vigente; *(effective)* operativo,-a; *(operating, in use)* en funcionamiento: *the scheme has been operative since 1992,* el programa está en funcionamiento desde 1992. **2** MED operatorio,-a, quirúrgico,-a. **– 3** *n (worker)* operario,-a; *(spy)* agente *mf*.

● **to become operative,** entrar en vigor.

■ **the operative word,** la palabra clave.

operator [ˈɒpəreɪtəʳ] **1** *n (of equipment, machine)* operario,-a. **2** *(of switchboard)* operador,-ra, telefonista *mf*. **3** COMM *(person)* empresario,-a; *(company)* empresa, compañía: *tour operator,* operador turístico.

● **to be a smooth operator,** ser muy listo,-a.

operetta [ɒpəˈretə] *n* opereta.

ophtalmologist [ɒfθæl'mɒlədʒɪst] *n* oftalmólogo,-a, oculista *mf*.

opine [əʊ'paɪn] *t fml* opinar.

opinion [ə'pɪnɪən] **1** *n* (*belief*) opinión *f*, parecer *m*: *what's your opinion of the new goalkeeper?*, ¿qué opinas del nuevo portero?; *public opinion is against it*, la opinión pública está en contra. **2** (*evaluation, estimation*) opinión *f*, concepto. **3** (*professional judgement, advice*) opinión *f* profesional.
● **in my opinion**, en mi opinión, a mi juicio, a mi parecer. ‖ **to be a matter of opinion**, ser discutible. ‖ **to be of the opinion that ...**, opinar que ... ‖ **to have a difference of opinion with sb.**, discrepar con algn. ‖ **to have a high/low opinion of sb.**, tener buen/mal concepto de algn.
■ **opinion poll**, encuesta.

opinionated [ə'pɪnɪəneɪtɪd] *adj* dogmático,-a.

opium ['əʊpɪəm] *n* opio.
■ **opium addict**, opiómano,-a. ‖ **opium poppy**, BOT adormidera.

Oporto [ə'pɔːtəʊ] *n* Oporto.

opossum [ə'pɒsəm] *n* zarigüeya.

opp ['ɒpəzɪt] *abbr* (*opposite*) enfrente.

opponent [ə'pəʊnənt] *n* adversario,-a, oponente *mf*.

opportune ['ɒpətjuːn] *adj* oportuno,-a.

opportunism [ɒpə'tjuːnɪzəm] *n* oportunismo.

opportunist [ɒpə'tjuːnɪst] *n* oportunista *mf*.

opportunity [ɒpə'tjuːnɪtɪ] **1** *n* (*gen*) oportunidad *f*, ocasión *f*: *she was given the opportunity to go to the States*, le dieron la oportunidad de ir a los Estados Unidos; *if I get an opportunity*, si se me presenta la ocasión; *at the earliest opportunity*, cuanto antes. **2** (*prospect*) perspectiva.
● **to take the opportunity to do sth. / take the opportunity of doing sth.**, aprovechar (la oportunidad) para hacer algo.
▲ *pl* **opportunities**.

oppose [ə'pəʊz] *t* (*disagree with*) oponerse a, estar en contra de; (*fight against*) oponerse a, combatir, luchar contra: *most residents opposed the scheme*, la mayoría de los vecinos se opusieron al proyecto.

opposed [ə'pəʊzd] *adj* opuesto,-a, contrario,-a.
● **as opposed to**, a diferencia de, en contraposición a. ‖ **to be opposed to sth.**, estar en contra de algo, oponerse a algo.

opposing [ə'pəʊzɪŋ] *adj* contrario,-a, opuesto,-a: *the opposing team*, el equipo contrario.

opposite ['ɒpəzɪt] **1** *adj* (*facing*) de enfrente: *she lives on the opposite side of the road*, vive al otro lado de la calle. **2** (*contrary, different*) opuesto,-a, contrario,-a: *in the opposite direction*, en dirección contraria; *the opposite sex*, el sexo opuesto. – **3** *prep* enfrente de, frente a: *the building opposite the cinema*, el edificio enfrente del cine; *we sat opposite each other*, nos sentamos uno frente al otro. – **4** *adv* enfrente: *the family who live opposite*, la familia que vive enfrente. – **5** *n* lo contrario, lo opuesto: *the opposite of big is small*, lo contrario a grande es pequeño; *opposites attract*, los polos opuestos se atraen.
● **to take the opposite view**, tomar la actitud contraria.
■ **opposite number**, POL homólogo,-a.

opposition [ɒpə'zɪʃən] **1** *n* (*resistance*) oposición *f*, resistencia: *there's a lot of opposition to the reforms*, hay mucha resistencia a las reformas. **2** (*rivals - in sport*) adversarios *mpl*; (*- in business*) competencia. **3** (*contrast*)

contraposición *f*. **4 the Opposition**, POL la oposición *f*: *the leader of the Opposition*, el líder de la oposición.
● **to be in opposition to sb./sth.**, oponerse a algn./algo.

oppress [ə'pres] **1** *t* (*rule*) oprimir. **2** (*make uncomfortable*) agobiar; (*make anxious*) agobiar, oprimir.

oppression [ə'preʃən] **1** *n* (*persecution*) opresión *f*. **2** (*feeling*) agobio.

oppressive [ə'presɪv] **1** *adj* (*regime etc*) opresivo,-a. **2** (*heat*) agobiante, sofocante; (*atmosphere, climate*) agobiante; (*situation*) agobiante, opresivo,-a.

oppressor [ə'presəʳ] *n* opresor,-ra.

opt [ɒpt] *i* optar (**for**, por): *she opted to study medicine*, optó por estudiar medicina.
◆ **to opt out** *i* (*person*) abandonar, dejar de participar; (*school, hospital*) *dejar de depender de las autoridades locales y pasar a financiarse del gobierno central: he opted out of the pension scheme*, se dio de baja del plan de pensiones.

optative ['ɒptətɪv] *adj* optativo,-a.

opthalmic [ɒf'θælmɪk] *adj* (*nerve, artery*) oftálmico,-a; (*clinic*) oftalmológico,-a.
■ **ophthalmic optician**, oculista *mf*. ‖ **ophthalmic surgeon**, cirujano,-a oftalmólogo,-a.

opthalmology [ɒfθæl'mɒlədʒɪ] *n* oftalmología.

optic ['ɒptɪk] *adj* óptico,-a.
■ **optic nerve**, nervio óptico.

optical ['ɒptɪkəl] *adj* óptico,-a.
■ **optical character recognition**, reconocimiento óptico de caracteres. ‖ **optical fibre**, fibra óptica. ‖ **optical illusion**, ilusión *f* óptica.

optician [ɒp'tɪʃən] *n* óptico,-a, oculista *mf*.

optics ['ɒptɪks] *n* óptica.

optimal ['ɒptɪməl] *adj* óptimo,-a.

optimism ['ɒptɪmɪzəm] *n* optimismo.

optimist ['ɒptɪmɪst] *n* optimista *mf*.

optimistic [ɒptɪ'mɪstɪk] *adj* optimista.

optimistically [ɒptɪ'mɪstɪklɪ] *adv* con optimismo.

optimize ['ɒptɪmaɪz] *t* optimizar.

optimum ['ɒptɪməm] **1** *adj* óptimo,-a. – **2** *n* lo óptimo, lo ideal *m*.

option ['ɒpʃən] **1** *n* (*choice*) opción *f*, posibilidad *f*: *I have no option*, no tengo opción, no tengo alternativa; *he chose the soft option*, eligió la opción más fácil. **2** COMM (*right to buy or sell*) opción *f* (**on**, a): *he has an option on the house*, tiene opción a comprar la casa. **3** (*optional extra*) extra *m*. **4** EDUC (*optional subject*) asignatura optativa.
● **to keep one's options open**, dejar todas las puertas abiertas.

optional ['ɒpʃənəl] *adj* (*gen*) opcional, facultativo,-a; (*course, subject*) optativo,-a.
■ **optional extra**, extra *m* opcional.

opulence ['ɒpjələns] *n* opulencia.

opulent ['ɒpjələnt] *adj* opulento,-a.

opus ['əʊpəs] *n* MUS opus *m*.

or [ɔːʳ] **1** *conj* (*alternative - gen*) o; (*- before word beginning with* o *or* ho) u: *tea or coffee*, té o café; *seven or eight*, siete u ocho. **2** (*with negative*) ni: *she can't sing or dance*, no sabe cantar ni bailar. **3** (*otherwise*) o: *come on, or we'll be late!*, ¡date prisa o llegaremos tarde!
● **or rather**, o mejor dicho. ‖ **or so**, más o menos: *five pounds or so*, unas cinco libras.

oracle ['ɒrəkəl] *n* oráculo.

oral ['ɔːrəl] **1** *adj* (*spoken - gen*) oral; (*tradition*) transmitido,-a oralmente. **2** MED (*contraceptive*) oral; (*hygiene*) bucal. – **3** *n* (*exam*) examen *m* oral.

orally [ˈɔːrəlɪ] **1** *adv* (*in speech*) oralmente, verbalmente. **2** (*through the mouth*) por la boca, por vía oral.
● **to be taken orally,** tómese por vía oral.
orange [ˈɒrɪndʒ] **1** *n* (*fruit*) naranja. **2** (*colour*) naranja *m*. – **3** *adj* naranja, de color naranja.
■ **orange blossom,** azahar *m*. ‖ **orange grove,** naranjal *m*. ‖ **orange juice,** zumo de naranja. ‖ **orange tree,** naranjo.
orangeade [ɒrɪndʒˈeɪd] *n* naranjada.
Orangeman [ˈɒrɪndʒmən] *n* POL oranjista *m* (*protestante unionista de Irlanda del Norte*).
orang-outang [ɔːræŋuːˈtæŋ] *n* → **orang-utan**.
orang-utan [ɔːræŋuːˈtæŋ] *n* orangután *m*.
oration [ɔːˈreɪʃən] *n* oración *f*, discurso.
orator [ˈɒrətəʳ] *n* orador,-ra.
oratorical [ɒrəˈtɒrɪkəl] *adj* oratorio,-a.
oratory[1] [ˈɒrətərɪ] *n* (*art of speaking*) oratoria.
oratory[2] [ˈɒrətərɪ] *n* REL (*chapel*) oratorio, capilla.
▲ *pl* **oratories**.
orb [ɔːb] **1** *n* (*jewelled ball*) orbe *m*. **2** *fml lit* (*sphere*) esfera; (*sun*) el sol *m*; (*moon*) la luna. **3** *lit* (*eye*) ojo.
orbit [ˈɔːbɪt] **1** *n* ASTRON órbita. **2** (*area of influence*) órbita, esfera de influencia, ámbito. – **3** *t* girar alrededor de, orbitar alrededor de. – **4** *i* orbitar, girar.
● **to go into orbit,** entrar en órbita.
orbital [ˈɔːbɪtəl] *adj* orbital, orbitario,-a.
■ **orbital road,** carretera de circunvalación.
orchard [ˈɔːtʃəd] *n* huerto.
■ **apple orchard,** manzanal *m*.
orchestra [ˈɔːkɪstrə] *n* orquesta.
■ **chamber orchestra,** orquesta de cámara. ‖ **orchestra pit,** foso de la orquesta. ‖ **orchestra stalls,** US THEAT platea.
orchestral [ɔːˈkestrəl] *adj* (*music*) orquestal; (*musician*) de orquesta.
orchestrate [ˈɔːkɪstreɪt] **1** *t* MUS orquestar. **2** (*campaign etc*) organizar, montar, orquestar.
orchestration [ɔːkɪˈstreɪʃən] **1** *n* MUS orquestación *f*. **2** (*of campaign etc*) organización *f*, orquestación *f*.
orchid [ˈɔːkɪd] *n* BOT orquídea.
ordain [ɔːˈdeɪn] **1** *t* REL (*priest*) ordenar: *he was ordained in 1990,* se ordenó en 1990. **2** *fml* (*decree*) decretar, ordenar; (*predestine*) predestinar: *it was ordained by fate,* el destino quiso que fuera así.
ordeal [ɔːˈdiːl] *n* (*bad experience*) mala experiencia, terrible experiencia; (*suffering*) sufrimiento, suplicio.
● **to go through an ordeal,** pasar por una experiencia terrible.
order [ˈɔːdəʳ] **1** *n* (*sequence*) orden *m*, serie *f*: *in alphabetical/chronological order,* por orden alfabético/cronológico; *you've put them in the wrong order,* los has ordenado mal. **2** (*condition, organization*) orden *m*, concierto: *she put her affairs in order,* puso sus asuntos en orden. **3** (*fitness for use*) condiciones *fpl*, estado: *the car's in good working order,* el coche funciona bien; *the house is in good order,* la casa está en buenas condiciones. **4** (*obedience, authority, discipline*) orden *m*, disciplina: *the teacher must keep order in the class,* el profesor debe mantener el orden en la clase. **5** (*system*) orden *m*: *the existing order,* el orden actual. **6** (*rules, procedures, etc*) orden *m*, procedimiento: *a point of order,* una cuestión de procedimiento. **7** (*command*) orden *f*: *until futher orders,* hasta nueva orden. **8** COMM (*request, goods*) pedido: *I placed an order for 5 boxes,* encargué 5 cajas; *the waiter took our order,* el camarero tomó nota de lo que queríamos. **9** (*written instruction*) orden *f*: *a court order,* una

orden *f* judicial. **10** (*classes*) orden *f*: *the military order,* la orden militar; *the lower orders,* las clases bajas. **11** BIOL ZOOL orden *m*. **12** (*group, society*) orden *f*; (*badge, sign worn*) condecoración *f*, orden *f*: *the monastic orders,* las órdenes monásticas; *a Masonic order,* una orden masónica; *the Order of the Garter,* la Orden de la Jarretera. **13** ARCH orden *m*. **14** (*kind, sort*) orden *m*: *of the highest order,* de primer orden. – **15** *t* (*command*) ordenar, mandar: *he ordered the soldiers to shoot,* ordenó a los soldados que dispararan; *the doctor ordered me to stay in bed,* el médico me mandó quedarme en cama. **16** (*ask for*) pedir, encargar: *I've ordered a cake for his birthday,* he encargado un pastel para su cumpleaños; *could you order me a taxi?,* ¿me podrías llamar un taxi?; *we ordered two coffees,* pedimos dos cafés. **17** (*arrange, put in order, organize*) ordenar, poner en orden. – **18** *i* (*request to bring, ask for*) pedir: *have you ordered yet?,* ¿ya han pedido?
◆ **to order about / order around** *t sep* mandonear, dar órdenes. ‖ **to order off** *t sep* SP expulsar. ‖ **to order out** *t sep* mandar salir.
● **by order of,** por orden de. ‖ **in order,** (*tidy, acceptable*) en orden; (*valid*) en regla; (*ready*) dispuesto,-a, listo,-a: *everything in order?,* ¿todo en orden?; *is your passport in order?,* ¿tienes el pasaporte en regla? ‖ **in order that,** para que, a fin de que. ‖ **in order to,** para, a fin de. ‖ **of the order of,** del orden de, alrededor de. ‖ **"last orders, please!",** grito del camarero que indica que el bar va a cerrar y que hay que pedir la última consumición. ‖ **out of order,** (*not working*) que no funciona; (*not in sequence*) desordenado,-a; (*not according to rules*) fuera de lugar; (*unacceptable*) mal: *the lift is out of order,* el ascensor no funciona. ‖ **to be on order,** estar pedido,-a. ‖ **to be under orders (to do sth.),** tener orden (de hacer algo). ‖ **to do sth. to order,** hacer algo por encargo. ‖ **to take holy orders,** recibir las órdenes sagradas.
■ **order book,** libro de pedidos. ‖ **order form,** hoja de pedido. ‖ **the order of the day,** el orden del día.
ordered [ˈɔːdəd] *adj* ordenado,-a.
orderliness [ˈɔːdəlɪnəs] *n* orden *m*.
orderly [ˈɔːdəlɪ] **1** *adj* (*tidy*) ordenado,-a, metódico,-a. **2** (*well-behaved*) disciplinado,-a. – **3** *n* MIL ordenanza *m*. **4** (*in hospital*) camillero,-a.
ordinal [ˈɔːdɪnəl] **1** *adj* ordinal. – **2** *n* ordinal *m*.
■ **ordinal number,** número ordinal.
ordinance [ˈɔːdɪnəns] *n fml* ordenanza, decreto.
ordinarily [ˈɔːdənərɪlɪ] **1** *adv* (*usually*) generalmente. **2** (*in an ordinary way*) de manera normal.
ordinary [ˈɔːdɪnrɪ] *adj* (*usual, normal*) normal, usual, habitual; (*average*) normal, corriente, común: *an ordinary person,* una persona normal y corriente; *the ordinary citizen,* el ciudadano de a pie, el hombre de la calle.
● **above the ordinary,** sobresaliente. ‖ **in the ordinary way,** normalmente, en circunstancias normales. ‖ **out of the ordinary,** fuera de lo común, excepcional.
■ **ordinary seaman,** marinero. ‖ **ordinary shares,** acciones *fpl* ordinarias.
ordinate [ˈɔːdɪnət] *n* MATH ordenada.
ordination [ɔːdɪˈneɪʃən] *n* ordenación *f*.
ordnance [ˈɔːdnəns] *n* MIL (*artillery*) artillería; (*supplies*) pertrechos *mpl*.
■ **Ordnance Survey,** GB *servicio oficial de cartografía*.
ore [ɔːʳ] *n* mineral *m*, mena: *iron ore / copper ore,* mineral de hierro / mineral de cobre.
oregano [ɒrɪˈgɑːnəʊ] *n* orégano.
organ [ˈɔːgən] **1** *n* ANAT órgano. **2** (*agency*) organismo; (*periodical*) órgano. **3** MUS órgano.

■ **barrel organ,** organillo.
organ-grinder [ˈɔːgəngraɪndəʳ] *n* organillero,-a.
organic [ɔːˈgænɪk] **1** *adj* (*living*) orgánico,-a: *organic matter,* materia orgánica. **2** (*without chemicals*) biológico,-a, ecológico,-a. **3** MED *fml* orgánico,-a. **4** *fml* (*made of different parts*) orgánico,-a; (*integral*) integral, integrante.
■ **organic chemistry,** química orgánica.
organically [ɔːˈgænɪklɪ] **1** *adv* MED físicamente. **2** (*food*) biológicamente.
organism [ˈɔːgənɪzəm] *n* organismo.
organist [ˈɔːgənɪst] *n* organista *mf.*
organization [ɔːgənaɪˈzeɪʃən] *n* organización *f.*
organizational [ɔːgənaɪˈzeɪʃənəl] *adj* organizativo,-a, de organización.
organize [ˈɔːgənaɪz] **1** *t* (*arrange*) organizar: *they organized a coach trip,* organizaron una excursión en autocar. **2** (*make a system*) ordenar, organizar: *she organized the books alphabetically,* ordenó los libros alfabéticamente. – **3** *i* organizar.
organized [ˈɔːgənaɪzd] *adj* (*gen*) organizado,-a.
● **to get organized,** organizarse.
■ **organized crime,** el crimen *m* organizado.
organizer [ˈɔːgənaɪzəʳ] *n* organizador,-ra.
orgasm [ˈɔːgæzəm] *n* orgasmo.
orgy [ˈɔːdʒɪ] *n* (*wild party*) orgía.
▲ *pl orgies.*
orient [ˈɔːrɪənt] *t* US → **orientate**.
Orient [ˈɔːrɪənt] **the Orient,** *n* el oriente *m.*
oriental [ɔːrɪˈentəl] **1** *adj* oriental. – **2** *n* oriental *mf.*
orientate [ˈɔːrɪənteɪt] *t* orientar.
● **to orientate os.,** orientarse.
orientation [ɔːrɪenˈteɪʃən] *n* orientación *f.*
orienteering [ɔːrɪənˈtɪərɪŋ] *n* orientación *f.*
orifice [ˈɒrɪfɪs] *n* orificio.
origin [ˈɒrɪdʒɪn] **1** *n* origen *m: what is your country of origin?,* ¿cuál es tu país de origen? – **2 origins,** *npl* origen *m sing: they were of humble origins,* eran de origen humilde.
original [əˈrɪdʒɪnəl] **1** *adj* (*first, earliest*) original, originario,-a, primero,-a. **2** (*not copied*) original: *bring the original documents,* trae los originales. **3** (*new, different*) original: *how original!,* ¡qué original! – **4** *n* original *m: the original is in the Prado,* el original está en el Prado.
● **in the original,** en versión original.
■ **original sin,** pecado original.
originality [ərɪdʒɪˈnælɪtɪ] *n* originalidad *f.*
originally [əˈrɪdʒɪnəlɪ] **1** *adv* (*in the beginning*) originariamente, en un principio. **2** (*in a new way*) de manera original, con originalidad.
originate [əˈrɪdʒɪneɪt] **1** *t* (*create*) originar, crear, dar lugar a. – **2** *i* (*arise*) tener su origen (**in,** en), originarse (**in,** en), provenir (**in,** en), provenir (**in,** de).
oriole [ˈɔːrɪəʊl] (*golden*) oriole, *n* ORN oropéndola.
Orkney [ˈɔːknɪ] **1** *n* las Islas *fpl* Órcadas. – **2 the Orkneys,** *npl* las Islas *fpl* Órcadas.
■ **the Orkney Islands,** las Islas Orcadas.
ornament [ˈɔːnəmənt] **1** *n* (*decoration*) ornamento, adorno; (*object*) adorno. – **2** *t* adornar, engalanar, decorar.
ornamental [ɔːnəˈmentəl] *adj* ornamental, decorativo,-a.
ornate [ɔːˈneɪt] **1** *adj* (*richly decorated*) ornamentado,-a, elaborado,-a; (*prose, verse, style*) florido,-a. **2** *pej* (*overdecorated, too complicated*) recargado,-a.
ornithologist [ɔːnɪˈθɒlədʒɪst] *n* ornitólogo,-a.
ornithology [ɔːnɪˈθɒlədʒɪ] *n* ornitología.

orphan [ˈɔːfən] **1** *n* huérfano,-a. – **2** *t* dejar huérfano,-a.
● **to be orphaned,** quedar huérfano,-a.
orphanage [ˈɔːfənɪdʒ] *n* orfanato.
orthodox [ˈɔːθədɒks] *adj* ortodoxo,-a.
orthodoxy [ˈɔːθədɒksɪ] *n* ortodoxia.
orthography [ɔːˈθɒgrəfɪ] *n* ortografía.
orthopaedic [ɔːθəʊˈpiːdɪk] *adj* MED ortopédico,-a.
orthopaedics [ɔːθəʊˈpiːdɪks] *n* ortopedia.
orthopaedist [ɔːθəʊˈpiːdɪst] *n* ortopedista *mf.*
orthopedic [ɔːθəʊˈpiːdɪk] *adj* US → **orthopaedic**.
orthopedics [ɔːθəʊˈpiːdɪks] *n* US → **orthopaedics**.
orthopedist [ɔːθəʊˈpiːdɪst] *n* → **orthopaedist**.
oscillate [ˈɒsɪleɪt] **1** *i* TECH oscilar. **2** (*vacillate*) oscilar, vacilar.
oscillation [ɒsɪˈleɪʃən] *n* oscilación *f.*
oscillator [ˈɒsɪleɪtəʳ] *n* oscilador *m.*
Oslo [ˈɒzləʊ] *n* Oslo.
osmosis [ɒzˈməʊsɪs] *n* ósmosis *f,* osmosis *f.*
osprey [ˈɒsprɪ] *n* ORN águila pescadora.
ostensible [ɒˈstensɪbəl] *adj* (*apparent*) aparente; (*alleged*) pretendido,-a, fingido,-a.
ostensibly [ɒˈstensɪblɪ] *adv* aparentemente, en apariencia.
ostentation [ɒstenˈteɪʃən] *n* ostentación *f.*
ostentatious [ɒstenˈteɪʃəs] *adj* ostentoso,-a.
osteopath [ˈɒstɪəpæθ] *n* MED osteópata *mf.*
ostracize [ˈɒstrəsaɪz] **1** *t* (*from society*) condenar al ostracismo. **2** (*from group*) aislar, excluir, hacer el vacío a.
ostrich [ˈɒstrɪtʃ] *n* avestruz *m.*
other [ˈʌðəʳ] **1** *adj* (*additional*) otro,-a: *I have one other idea,* tengo otra idea; *are there any other questions?,* ¿hay más preguntas?, ¿alguna pregunta más? **2** (*different*) otro,-a: *we'll go some other time,* iremos otro día; *people from other countries,* gente de otros países. **3** (*second, remaining*) otro,-a: *it's on the other side of the street,* está al otro lado de la calle. – **4** *pron* otro,-a: *with a gun in one hand and an axe in the other,* con una pistola en una mano y una hacha en la otra; *some ate everything, others ate nothing at all,* algunos comieron de todo, otros no comieron nada. – **5** *adv* (*different*) otro,-a: *he's never behaved other than badly,* siempre se ha portado mal. – **6 other than,** *prep* (*except*) aparte de, salvo: *there was nobody other than the teacher,* aparte del profesor, no había nadie.
● **among others,** entre otros,-as. ‖ **every other day etc,** un día sí, otro no. ‖ **one after the other,** uno tras otro. ‖ **or other,** u otro,-a: *I'll find out somehow or other,* de una manera u otra, me enteraré; *for some reason or other,* por alguna razón. ‖ **the other day etc,** el otro día etc.
■ **my other half,** mi media naranja.
otherwise [ˈʌðəwaɪz] **1** *adv* (*differently*) de otra manera, de manera distinta: *she couldn't do otherwise,* no podía obrar de otra manera; *except where otherwise stated,* excepto donde se indique lo contrario. **2** (*apart from that, in other respects*) aparte de eso, por lo demás: *but otherwise he's perfectly fine,* pero aparte de eso está perfectamente. – **3** *conj* (*if not*) si no, de no ser así, de lo contrario: *I must go, otherwise I'll be late,* me tengo que ir, si no, llegaré tarde. – **4** *adj* distinto,-a: *the truth is otherwise,* la verdad es distinta.
● **to be otherwise engaged,** tener otro compromiso.
otter [ˈɒtəʳ] *n* nutria.
Ottoman [ˈɒtəmən] **1** *adj* otomano,-a. – **2** *n* (*person*) otomano,-a.
Ouagadougou [uːægæˈduːguː] *n* Uagadugú.

ouch [aʊtʃ] *interj* ¡ay!

ought [ɔːt]. **1** ought to, *aux (moral obligation)* deber: *you ought to be ashamed of yourself*, debería darte vergüenza; *you ought to have helped them*, debiste ayudarles. **2** *(recommendation)* deber, tener que: *you ought to hear him sing!*, ¡tendrías que oírlo cantar! **3** *(expectation)* deber de: *they ought to be home by now*, ya deberían de estar en casa, seguramente ya estarán en casa; *you ought to get the job*, lo más seguro es que consigas el trabajo.

ounce [aʊns] **1** *n (weight)* onza. **2** *fam (small quantity)* pizca.

▲ Equivale a 28,35 gramos.

our [ˈaʊəʳ] *adj* nuestro,-a: *our house*, nuestra casa; *our children*, nuestros hijos.

■ Our Father, Padrenuestro *m*. ‖ Our Lady, Nuestra Señora *f*.

ours [ˈaʊəz] *pron* (el) nuestro, (la) nuestra: *this table must be ours*, esta mesa debe de ser la nuestra; *a friend of ours*, un amigo nuestro.

ourselves [aʊəˈselvz] **1** *pron (reflexive)* nos: *we made ourselves comfortable*, nos pusimos cómodos. **2** *(emphatic)* nosotros,-as mismos,-as: *we did it ourselves*, lo hicimos nosotros mismos.

● by ourselves, *(alone)* a solas, solos,-as; *(without help)* solos,-as.

oust [aʊst] **1** *t (from position, job, etc)* desbancar. **2** *(from land, property)* expulsar, desalojar.

out [aʊt] **1** *adv (outside)* fuera, afuera: *she's out in the garden*, está en el jardín; *I locked myself out*, me quedé fuera sin llaves; *could you wait out there?*, ¿podrías esperar allí fuera?; *is it cold out?*, ¿hace frío en la calle? **2** *(move outside)* fuera: *I was just on my way out*, estaba a punto de salir; *get out!*, ¡fuera!; *she ran out*, salió corriendo; *they've gone out*, han salido. **3** *(not in)* fuera: *there's no answer, they must be out*, no contestan, deben de haber salido; *shall we eat out?*, ¿comemos fuera? **4** *(expressing distance)* en: *they live out in the country*, viven en el campo; *out at sea*, en alta mar; *out in the Sudan*, en Sudán; *they went to live out east*, se fueron a vivir a oriente. **5** *(expressing removal)* diferentes traducciones: *he tore a page out from the book*, arrancó una página del libro; *I've had a tooth out*, me han sacado una muela; *she got out a handkerchief*, sacó un pañuelo. **6** *(showing disappearance)* diferentes traducciones: *rub that word out*, borra esa palabra; *our money ran out*, se nos acabó el dinero; *this grease stain won't come out*, esta mancha de grasa no sale. **7** *(available, existing)* diferentes traducciones: *when will her new book be out?*, ¿cuándo saldrá su nuevo libro?; *the film comes out next month*, la película se estrenará el mes que viene; *it's the best sandwich out*, es el mejor bocadillo que hay. **8** *(known)* diferentes traducciones: *your secret's out*, tu secreto ha salido a la luz; *the news is out*, se sabe la noticia. **9** *(flowers)* en flor: *(sun, stars, etc)* que ha salido: *the tulips are out*, los tulipanes están en flor; *the sun's out*, ha salido el sol, brilla el sol, hace sol. **10** *(protruding)* que se sale: *a nail sticking out*, un clavo que sobresale; *his stomach sticks out*, le sale la barriga; *she held out her hand*, tendió la mano; *don't put your tongue out!*, ¡no saques la lengua! **11** *(clearly, loudly)* en voz alta: *he called out to me*, me llamó en voz alta; *she said it out loud*, lo dijo en voz alta. **12** *(to the end)* hasta el final; *(completely)* completamente, totalmente: *hear me out*, escúchame hasta el final; *the house was burnt out*, la casa fue destruida totalmente por las llamas; *we've sold out of sugar*, hemos vendido todo el azúcar. **13** RAD *(end of message)* fuera. – **14** *adj (extinguished)* apagado,-a: *the lights are out*, las luces están apagadas; *they put the fire out*, apagaron el fuego. **15** *(unconscious)* inconsciente; *(asleep)* dormido,-a: *she passed out*, se desmayó; *the boxer knocked his opponent out*, el boxeador dejó K.O. a su contrincante; *he went out like a light*, se durmió como un tronco. **16** SP *(defeated)* eliminado,-a; *(out of play)* fuera: *he's out!*, ¡han eliminado!; *his volley was out*, su volea ha ido fuera. **17** *(wrong, not accurate)* equivocado,-a: *my calculation was out by £5*, mi cálculo tenía un error de 5 libras. **18** *(not fashionable)* pasado,-a de moda: *white socks are out*, los calcetines blancos ya no se llevan. **19** *(out of order)* estropeado,-a: *the photocopier's out*, la fotocopiadora no funciona. **20** *(unacceptable)* prohibido,-a. **21** *(on strike)* en huelga: *the miners are out again*, los mineros vuelven a estar en huelga. **22** *(tide)* bajo,-a. **23** *(over, finished)* acabado,-a: *before the year is out*, antes de que acabe el año; *school's out*, han terminado las clases. – **24** *prep fam (out of)* por: *she ran out the door*, salió por la puerta; *I threw it out the window*, lo tiré por la ventana. **25** out of, *(away from, no longer in)* fuera de: *they're out of town*, están fuera de la ciudad; *he's just got out of bed*, se acaba de levantar; *she walked out of the meeting*, abandonó la reunión; *it fell out of his pocket*, cayó de su bolsillo. **26** *(from a state of)* fuera de: *out of danger*, fuera de peligro; *out of control*, fuera de control; *out of print*, agotado,-a; *out of earshot*, fuera del alcance del oído. **27** *(not involved in)* fuera de: *they are out of the cup*, han quedado fuera de la copa. **28** *(from among)* de: *eight smokers out of ten*, ocho de cada diez fumadores; *she got five out of ten in French*, sacó (un) cinco sobre diez en francés. **29** *(without)* sin: *we're out of tea*, se nos ha acabado el té, nos hemos quedado sin té; *out of money*, sin dinero; *out of breath*, sin aliento; *I'm out of practice*, me falta práctica; *he's out of work*, está parado, está sin trabajo. **30** *(because of)* por: *out of spite*, por despecho; *out of respect*, por respeto. **31** *(using, made from)* de: *made out of wood*, hecho,-a de madera; *the suit is made out of wool*, el traje es de lana. **32** *(from)* de: *out of a tin*, de una lata; *out of a book*, de un libro.

● out of favour, en desgracia. ‖ out of sight, out of mind, ojos que no ven, corazón que no siente. ‖ out of sorts, indispuesto,-a. ‖ out of this world, extraordinario,-a. ‖ out with it!, ¡dilo ya!, ¡suéltalo ya! ‖ to feel out of it, sentirse excluido,-a. ‖ to be out and about, *(from illness)* estar recuperado,-a. ‖ to be out for sth., querer algo: *he's out for your blood*, va a por ti; *she's only out for your money*, sólo quiere tu dinero. ‖ to be out of one's head / be out of one's mind, estar loco,-a. ‖ to be out to lunch, US estar loco,-a. ‖ to be out to do sth., estar decidido,-a a hacer algo: *they're out to win*, están decididos a vencer; *he's out to get me*, va a por mí.

■ out tray, bandeja de salidas.

out-and-out [ˈaʊtənaʊt] *adj* empedernido,-a, redomado,-a.

outback [ˈaʊtbæk] *n (in Australia)* interior *m*.

outbid [aʊtˈbɪd] *t* pujar más que, ofrecer más que.

▲ *pt & pp* outbid, *ger* outbidding.

outboard motor [aʊtbɔːdˈməʊtəʳ] *n* MAR motor *m* fueraborda, fueraborda *m*.

outbound [ˈaʊtbaʊnd] *adj* que parte, que sale.

outbreak [ˈaʊtbreɪk] **1** *n (of violence, fighting)* brote *m*; *(of war)* estallido; *(of hostilities)* comienzo. **2** *(of disease)* brote *m*, epidemia; *(of spots)* erupción *f*.

outbuilding [ˈaʊtbɪldɪŋ] *n (gen)* dependencia; *(shed)* cobertizo; *(stable)* establo; *(barn)* granero.

outburst [ˈaʊtbɜːst] **1** *n (of emotion)* explosión *f*, arrebato, arranque *m*: *there was an outburst of applause*, el público irrumpió en aplausos. **2** (*of activity*) explosión *f*.

outcast ['aʊtkɑːst] **1** *n* marginado,-a, proscrito,-a. – **2** *adj* marginado,-a.

outcome ['aʊtkʌm] *n* (*result*) resultado; (*consequences*) consecuencias *fpl*.

outcry ['aʊtkraɪ] *n* protesta: *there was a public outcry,* hubo una ola de protestas.
▲ *pl* **outcries**.

outdated [aʊt'deɪtɪd] *adj* anticuado,-a, pasado,-a de moda.

outdid [aʊt'dɪd] *pt* → **outdo**.

outdo [aʊt'duː] *t* (*person, team*) superar, ganar, sobrepasar; (*result, achievement*) superar, mejorar.
● **not to be outdone,** para no ser menos.
▲ *pt* **outdid**, *pp* **outdone**.

outdone [aʊt'dʌn] *pp* → **outdo**.

outdoor [aʊt'dɔːʳ] **1** *adj* (*gen*) exterior, al aire libre; (*swimming pool*) descubierto,-a; (*shoes, clothes*) de calle. – **2 outdoors,** *adv* fuera, al aire libre.
● **the great outdoors,** *n* el aire *m* libre, la naturaleza.
‖**to be the outdoor type,** ser el tipo de persona a la que le gusta la vida al aire libre.

outer ['aʊtəʳ] *adj* exterior, externo,-a.
■ **outer space,** espacio exterior. ‖ **outer suburbs,** afueras *fpl*.

outermost ['aʊtəməʊst] *adj* (*outer*) exterior; (*furthest away*) más remoto,-a.

outfit ['aʊtfɪt] **1** *n* (*kit, equipment*) equipo, juego. **2** (*clothes*) conjunto; (*uniform*) uniforme *m*; (*fancy dress*) disfraz *m*. **3** *fam* (*group of people*) grupo, equipo; (*business*) negocio; (*organization*) organización *f*.

outgoing [aʊt'gəʊɪŋ] **1** *adj* (*departing*) saliente. **2** (*sociable*) sociable, extrovertido,-a. – **3 outgoings,** *npl* gastos *mpl*.

outgrow [aʊt'grəʊ] **1** *t* (*clothes etc*) hacerse demasiado grande para: *he's outgrown his shoes,* se le han quedado pequeños los zapatos. **2** (*habit*) superar, dejar atrás. **3** (*grow faster than*) crecer más rápido que.
▲ *pt* **outgrew** [aʊt'gruː], *pp* **outgrown** [aʊt'grəʊn].

outhouse ['aʊthaʊs] **1** *n* GB → **outbuilding**. **2** US (*outside toilet*) servicio exterior.

outing ['aʊtɪŋ] *n* (*trip*) salida, excursión *f*.
● **to go on an outing,** ir de excursión.

outlandish [aʊt'lændɪʃ] *adj* (*strange, unusual*) extravagante, estrafalario,-a; (*crazy*) descabellado,-a.

outlast [aʊt'lɑːst] *t* (*gen*) durar más que; (*outlive*) sobrevivir a.

outlaw ['aʊtlɔː] **1** *n* forajido,-a, proscrito,-a. – **2** *t* prohibir, declarar ilegal.

outlay ['aʊtleɪ] **1** *n* (*spending*) desembolso; (*amount spent*) gasto, inversión *f*. – **2** *t* desembolsar.
▲ (*verbo*) [aʊt'leɪ], *pt* & *pp* **outlaid**.

outlet ['aʊtlet] **1** *n* (*opening - gen*) salida; (*for water*) desagüe *m*. **2** *fig* (*for emotions*) válvula de escape. **3** COMM (*shop*) punto de venta; (*market*) mercado, salida de mercado.

outline ['aʊtlaɪn] **1** *n* (*outer edge*) contorno; (*shape*) perfil *m*. **2** (*sketch*) boceto, esbozo; (*of map*) trazado. **3** (*draft*) bosquejo, esquema *m*; (*summary*) resumen *m*. – **4** *t* **1** (*draw lines of*) perfilar; (*sketch*) bosquejar; (*map*) trazar. **5** (*describe roughly*) dar una idea general de; (*summarize*) hacer un resumen de, resumir.
● **to be outlined against the sky,** perfilarse en el cielo.

outlive [aʊt'lɪv] *t* sobrevivir a.
● **to outlive its usefulness,** dejar de ser útil, ya no tener razón de ser.

outlook ['aʊtlʊk] **1** *n* (*view*) vista, panorama *m*. **2** (*point of view, attitude*) punto de vista (**on,** ante). **3** (*prospect*) perspectiva, panorama *m*. **4** METEOR previsión *f* meteorológica.

outlying ['aʊtlaɪɪŋ] **1** *adj* (*remote*) alejado,-a, distante. **2** (*suburban*) periférico,-a.

outmanoeuvre [aʊtmə'nuːvəʳ] *t* (*opponent*) superar estratégicamente, mostrarse más hábil que.

outmoded [aʊt'məʊdɪd] *adj* anticuado,-a, pasado,-a de moda.

outnumber [aʊt'nʌmbəʳ] *t* superar en número, ser más que.

out-of-date [aʊtəv'deɪt] *adj* (*fashion*) pasado,-a de moda; (*technology*) desfasado,-a, obsoleto,-a; (*food, ticket*) caducado,-a.

out-of-doors [aʊtəv'dɔːz] *adj* → **outdoors**.

out-of-pocket [aʊtəv'pɒkɪt] **out-of-pocket expenses,** *npl* gastos varios.
● **to be out of pocket,** perder dinero.

out-of-the-way [aʊtəvðə'weɪ] **1** *adj* (*distant*) alejado,-a, distante. **2** (*uncommon*) poco corriente, insólito,-a.

outpatient ['aʊtpeɪʃənt] *n* MED paciente externo,-a.

outpost ['aʊtpəʊst] *n* MIL avanzada.

outpouring ['aʊtpɔːrɪŋ] **1** *n* torrente *m*. – **2 outpourings,** *npl* desahogo *m sing*.

output ['aʊtpʊt] **1** *n* (*gen*) producción *f*; (*of machine*) rendimiento. **2** ELEC salida. **3** COMPUT salida.
■ **output device,** dispositivo de salida.

outrage ['aʊtreɪdʒ] **1** *n* (*anger, resentment*) indignación *f* (**at,** ante): *he felt a sense of outrage,* se sintió ultrajado. **2** (*violent action*) atrocidad *f*; (*terrorist act*) atentado. **3** (*scandal*) escándalo; (*insult*) ultraje *m*, agravio. – **4** *t* (*make angry*) ultrajar, indignar; (*shock*) escandalizar.
● **to be outraged at sth.,** indignarse ante algo.

outrageous [aʊt'reɪdʒəs] **1** *adj* (*shocking - gen*) escandaloso,-a, indignante; (*crime*) atroz; (*language*) injurioso,-a; (*price*) escandaloso,-a, exorbitante, abusivo,-a. **2** (*unconventional*) extravagante, estrafalario,-a.

outran [aʊt'ræn] *pp* → **outrun**.

outrider ['aʊtraɪdəʳ] *n* escolta *mf*.

outright [aʊt'raɪt] **1** *adj* (*total - gen*) absoluto,-a, total; (*refusal, denial*) rotundo,-a, total, categórico,-a; (- *winner, victory, loser*) indiscutible; (*majority*) absoluto,-a. **2** (*direct - attack*) declarado,-a, abierto,-a; (- *lie*) descarado,-a. – **3** *adv* (*completely - refuse*) rotundamente, categóricamente, terminantemente; (*ban*) totalmente, terminantemente; (*win*) indiscutiblemente. **4** (*directly - ask, say*) directamente, abiertamente, sin reserva. **5** (*instantly*) en el acto.
● **to buy sth. outright,** comprar algo en su totalidad.
▲ (*adverbo*) [aʊt'raɪt].

outrun [aʊt'rʌn] **1** *t* (*run faster than*) correr más rápido que, dejar atrás. **2** *fig* superar.
▲ *pt* **outran,** *pp* **outrun,** *ger* **outrunning**.

outsell [aʊt'sel] *t* venderse más que.
▲ *pt* & *pp* **outsold**.

outset ['aʊtset] *n* comienzo, principio.
● **at the outset,** al principio. ‖ **from the outset,** de entrada, desde el principio.

outshine [aʊt'ʃaɪn] *t* eclipsar.
▲ *pt* & *pp* **outshone**.

outside [aʊt'saɪd] **1** *n* (*exterior part*) exterior *m*, parte *f* exterior: *from the outside,* desde fuera; *on the outside,* por fuera. **2** GB AUTO derecha: *you have to overtake on the outside,* hay que adelantar por la derecha. – **3** *prep* (*gen*) fuera de: *outside Spain,* fuera de España; *a demonstra-*

tion outside the French Embassy, una manifestación delante de la embajada francesa. **4** (*beyond*) más allá de, fuera de: *outside working hours,* fuera del horario laboral. **5** (*other than*) aparte de, fuera de. **– 6** *adv* (*gen*) fuera, afuera: *let's go outside,* vamos fuera; *it's warm outside,* hace bastante calor fuera. **– 7** *adj* (*exterior*) exterior. **8** (*external*) externo,-a: *an outside opinion,* una opinión independiente. **9** (*remote*) remoto,-a. **10** (*greatest possible*) mayor, sumo,-a, más alto,-a.
● **at the outside,** como máximo, como mucho.
■ **outside broadcast,** transmisión *f* desde fuera de los estudios. ‖ **outside call,** llamada exterior. ‖ **outside lane,** GB AUTO carril *m* de la derecha; SP calle *f* exterior. ‖ **outside left,** SP extremo izquierda. ‖ **outside line,** línea exterior. ‖ **outside right,** SP extremo derecha. ‖ **the outside world,** el mundo exterior.
▲ (*adjetivo*) [ˈaʊtsaɪd].

outsider [aʊtˈsaɪdəʳ] **1** *n* (*person - not involved*) persona de fuera; (*- not accepted*) persona marginada; (*- stranger*) extraño,-a, forastero,-a, desconocido,-a; (*- intruder*) intruso,-a. **2** (*unlikely winner - athlete etc*) competidor,-ra con pocas probabilidades de ganar; (*- horse*) caballo con pocas probabilidades de ganar; (*- politician*) candidato,-a con pocas probabilidades de ganar.

outsize [ˈaʊtsaɪz] *adj* (*clothing*) de talla muy grande; (*object*) de gran tamaño, enorme.

outskirts [ˈaʊtskɜːts] *npl* afueras *fpl,* alrededores *mpl,* extrarradio *m sing.*

outsmart [aʊtˈsmɑːt] *t* burlar, engañar.

outsold [aʊtˈsəʊld] *pt & pp →* **outsell.**

outspoken [aʊtˈspəʊkən] *adj* directo,-a, franco,-a.
● **to be an outspoken critic of sth.,** criticar algo abiertamente. ‖ **to be very outspoken,** no tener pelos en la lengua.

outspread [aʊtˈspred] *adj* (*wing*) extendido,-a, desplegado,-a; (*arm*) abierto,-a.

outstanding [aʊtˈstændɪŋ] **1** *adj* (*excellent*) destacado,-a, notable, sobresaliente; (*exceptional*) excepcional, extraordinario,-a, singular. **2** (*conspicuous*) destacado,-a. **3** (*debt*) sin pagar, pendiente; (*problem*) pendiente, por resolver; (*work*) pendiente, por hacer.

outstay [aʊtˈsteɪ] **to outstay one's welcome,** *phr* quedarse más de lo debido, abusar de la hospitalidad de algn.

outstretched [aʊtˈstretʃt] *adj* extendido,-a.

outstrip [aʊtˈstrɪp] **1** *t* (*run faster than*) correr más rápido que, dejar atrás. **2** (*become greater than*) sobrepasar.
▲ *pt & pp* **outstripped,** *ger* **outstripping.**

outtake [ˈaʊteɪk] *n* CINEM toma falsa.

outvote [aʊtˈvəʊt] *t* (*person*) derrotar; (*proposal etc*) vencer.
● **to be outvoted,** perder la votación.

outward [ˈaʊtwəd] **1** *adj* (*appearance*) exterior; (*sign*) externo,-a, show. **2** (*journey, flight*) de ida. **– 3** *adv* US → **outwards.**

outwardly [ˈaʊtwədlɪ] **1** *adv* (*apparently*) aparentemente, en apariencia. **2** (*externally*) por fuera.

outwards [ˈaʊtwəðʒ] *adv* (*gen*) hacia fuera, hacia afuera; (*attention etc*) hacia el exterior.

outweigh [aʊtˈweɪ] **1** *t* (*weigh more than*) pesar más que. **2** *fig* superar: *the advantages far outweigh the disadvantages,* las ventajas superan con creces las desventajas.

outwit [aʊtˈwɪt] *t* burlar, ser más listo,-a que.
▲ *pt & pp* **outwitted,** *ger* **outwitting.**

outworn [aʊtˈwɔːn] *adj* (*gen*) anticuado,-a; (*phrase, metaphor*) trillado,-a, manido,-a.

ova [ˈəʊvə] *npl →* **ovum.**

oval [ˈəʊvəl] **1** *adj* oval, ovalado,-a. **– 2** *n* óvalo.

ovary [ˈəʊvərɪ] *n* ovario.
▲ *pl* **ovaries.**

ovation [əʊˈveɪʃən] *n* ovación *f.*
● **to give sb. a standing ovation,** ovacionar a algn.

oven [ˈʌvən] *n* horno.
● **it's like an oven in here!,** ¡esto es un horno! ‖ **to have a bun in the oven,** estar embarazada.
■ **oven glove,** manopla *f* para el horno.

ovenproof [ˈʌvənpruːf] *adj* refractario,-a.

ovenware [ˈʌvənweəʳ] *n* vajilla refractaria.

over [ˈəʊvəʳ] **1** *adv* (*down*) diferentes traducciones: *the boy fell over,* el niño se cayó; *I knocked the glass over,* tiré la copa (de un golpe). **2** (*from one side to another*) diferentes traducciones: *turn over the page,* dar la vuelta a la página; *the car turned over,* el coche volcó; *he bent over,* se inclinó. **3** (*across*) diferentes traducciones: *let's cross over,* crucemos al otro lado; *we jumped over,* saltamos al otro lado; *over here/there,* aquí/allí; *why don't you come over to dinner?,* ¿por qué no vienes a cenar a casa?; *she's over from Spain,* ha venido de España. **4** (*showing transfer*) diferentes traducciones: *he went over to the enemy,* se pasó al enemigo; *she signed everything over to me,* lo puso todo a mi nombre. **5** (*everywhere, throughout*) en todas partes: *the lake is frozen over,* el lago está completamente helado; *it's black all over,* está todo negro; *she's travelled the world over,* ha viajado por todo el mundo; *I ache all over,* me duele todo. **6** (*again*) otra vez: *I repeated the message over,* repetí el mensaje otra vez; *let's start over (again),* volvamos a empezar; *over and over (again),* repetidas veces, una y otra vez. **7** (*remaining*) sobrante: *are there any strawberries (left) over?,* ¿sobran fresas?, ¿quedan fresas?; *did you have any money over?,* ¿te sobró algún dinero? **8** (*too much*) de más: *it's 50 grams over,* pesa 50 gramos de más. **9** (*more*) más; (*older*) mayor: *a hundred people or over,* cien personas o más; *children of twelve and over,* niños mayores de doce años. **10** RAD (*finished*) corto: *over and out!,* ¡corto y fuera! **– 11** *prep* (*above, higher than*) encima de: *a sign over the door,* un letrero encima de la puerta; *a plane flew over the area,* un avión sobrevoló la zona. **12** (*covering, on top of*) sobre, encima de: *he put his hand over his mouth,* se tapó la boca con la mano; *I put a blanket over her feet,* le tapé los pies con una manta; *he wore a jacket over his sweater,* llevaba una americana encima del jersey. **13** (*across*) sobre; (*on the other side of*) al otro lado de: *a bridge over the river Trent,* un puente sobre el río Trent; *the shop over the road,* la tienda de enfrente; *he lives over the border,* vive al otro lado de la frontera. **14** (*during*) durante: *over the past 25 years,* durante los últimos 25 años; *we talked about it over lunch,* hablamos de ello durante la comida. **15** (*throughout*) por: *we travelled all over Italy,* viajamos por toda Italia. **16** (*by the agency of*) por: *over the radio,* por la radio; *over the phone,* por teléfono. **17** (*more than*) más de: *she's over thirty,* tiene más de treinta años. **18** (*about*) por: *an argument over money,* una discusión por dinero. **19** (*recovered from*) recuperado,-a de: *he's over the flu,* se ha recuperado de la gripe. **20** (*indicating control*) sobre; (*superior*) por encima de: *she has control over the class,* controla la clase; *he has only the managing director over him,* sólo tiene al director ejecutivo por encima de él. **– 21** *adj* (*ended*) acabado,-a, terminado,-a: *the game is over,* la partida ha acabado. **– 22** *n* SP (*in cricket*) serie de seis lanzamientos.
● **over and above,** además de. ‖ **to be over and done with,** haber acabado.

overact [əʊvər'ækt] **1** *t* exagerar, interpretar sobreactuando. – **2** *i* exagerar, sobreactuar.

overall ['əʊvərɔːl] **1** *adj* (*total - cost*) global, total; (*- length*) total. **2** (*general*) general. – **3** *adv* (*in total*) en total: *what will it cost overall?*, ¿cuánto costará en total? **4** (*generally, on the whole*) en conjunto, por lo general, en términos generales. – **5** *n* GB (*work coat*) guardapolvo, bata. – **6 overalls,** *npl* mono *m* sing.
▲ (*adverbio*) [əʊvər'ɔːl].

overambitious [əʊvəræm'bɪʃəs] *adj* demasiado ambicioso,-a.

overanxious [əʊvər'æŋʃəs] *adj* demasiado ansioso,-a.

overate [əʊvə'reɪt] *pt* → **overeat**.

overawe [əʊvər'ɔː] *t* intimidar.
● **to be overawed,** sobrecogerse.

overbalance [əʊvə'bæləns] *i* perder el equilibrio.

overbearing [əʊvə'beərɪŋ] *adj pej* (*domineering*) dominante, autoritario,-a.

overboard ['əʊvəbɔːd] *adv* por la borda: *man overboard!*, ¡hombre al agua!
● **t2o fall overboard,** caer al agua. ‖ **to go overboard,** pasarse.

overbook [əʊvə'bʊk] *t* aceptar demasiadas reservas para: *the hotel was overbooked,* habían aceptado demasiadas reservas para el hotel.

overbooking [əʊvə'bʊkɪŋ] *n* sobrecontratación *f*.

overburden [əʊvə'bɜːdən] *t* sobrecargar (**with,** de), agobiar (**with,** de).

overcame [əʊvə'keɪm] *pt* → **overcome**.

overcast ['əʊvəkɑːst] *adj* METEOR nublado,-a, cubierto,-a.

overcharge [əʊvə'tʃɑːdʒ] **1** *t* (*charge too much*) cobrar demasiado (**for,** por): *I was overcharged by 5 pounds,* me cobraron cinco libras de más. **2** (*overload*) sobrecargar. – **3** *i* cobrar de más (**for,** por).

overcoat ['əʊvəkəʊt] *n* abrigo.

overcome [əʊvə'kʌm] **1** *t* (*defeat*) vencer. **2** (*overwhelm*) agobiar, abrumar, invadir, apoderarse de, vencer: *he was overcome by sleep,* el sueño se apoderó de él; *they were overcome by fumes,* murieron asfixiados por el humo; *she was overcome by grief,* estaba deshecha por el dolor. **3** (*surmount*) superar, dominar, vencer: *we managed to overcome the problem,* logramos superar el problema. – **4** *i* (*triumph*) vencer: *we shall overcome,* venceremos.
▲ *pt* **overcame,** *pp* **overcome.**

overcrowded [əʊvə'kraʊdɪd] *adj* (*room, place, etc*) abarrotado,-a, atestado,-a (de gente); (*country*) superpoblado,-a.

overcrowding [əʊvə'kraʊdɪŋ] *n* (*of prisons etc*) hacinamiento; (*of country*) superpoblación *f*.

overdeveloped [əʊvədɪ'veləpt] **1** *t* (*photo*) sobrerrevelado,-a. – **2** *adj* (*muscle, imagination*) excesivamente desarrollado,-a.

overdo [əʊvə'duː] **1** *t* (*exaggerate*) exagerar, pasarse con: *she overdid her makeup,* se pasó con el maquillaje. **2** CULIN (*overcook*) cocer demasiado, asar demasiado; (*use too much*) pasarse con: *don't overdo the ginger,* no te pases con el jengibre.
● **to overdo it,** exigirse demasiado: *you've been overdoing it a bit lately,* te has estado exigiendo demasiado últimamente.
▲ *pt* **overdid** [əʊvə'dɪd], *pp* **overdone.**

overdone [əʊvə'dʌn] **1** *pp* → **overdo.** – **2** *adj* CULIN demasiado hecho,-a.

overdose ['əʊvədəʊs] *n* sobredosis *f*.

overdraft ['əʊvədrɑːft] *n* (*amount*) descubierto: *she's got an overdraft of 500 pounds,* tiene un descubierto de 500 libras.

overdraw [əʊvə'drɔː] **1** *t* girar en descubierto. – **2** *i* girar en descubierto.
● **to be overdrawn,** (*person*) tener un descubierto; (*account*) estar en descubierto.

overdressed [əʊvə'drest] *adj* demasiado arreglado,-a.

overdrive ['əʊvədraɪv] *n* superdirecta.
● **to go into overdrive,** ponerse a trabajar a toda marcha.

overdue [əʊvə'djuː] **1** *adj* (*late*) atrasado,-a: *the baby's a week overdue,* el bebé debería haber nacido hace una semana; *the train is an hour overdue,* el tren lleva una hora de retraso. **2** COMM (*left unpaid*) vencido,-a y sin pagar.

overeat [əʊvə'riːt] *i* comer en exceso, comer demasiado.
▲ *pt* **overate,** *pp* **overeaten** [əʊvə'riːtən].

overestimate [əʊvər'estɪmeɪt] **1** *t* sobreestimar. – **2** *n* sobreestimación *f*.

overexpose [əʊvərɪks'pəʊʒd] *t* (*photo*) sobreexponer.

overexposure [əʊvərɪks'pəʊʒə'] *n* (*photo*) sobreexposición *f*.

overflew [əʊvə'fluː] *pt* → **overfly**.

overflow ['əʊvəfləʊ] **1** *n* (*of river etc*) desbordamiento; (*excess liquid*) líquido que sale: *there's an overflow from the cistern,* la cisterna se desborda; *put a bucket underneath to catch the overflow,* pon un cubo debajo para coger el agua que sale. **2** (*of people*) exceso. **3** (*pipe*) tubo de desagüe; (*hole*) rebosadero. – **4** *i* (*river*) desbordarse; (*bath etc*) rebosar: *the bath is overflowing,* la bañera está rebosando. **5** (*people*) rebosar: *the church was so full that people were overflowing into the street,* la iglesia estaba tan llena que la gente rebosaba por la calle. **6** (*be full of*) rebosar (**with,** de): *the dustbin is overflowing,* el cubo de la basura está lleno a rebosar; *she was overflowing with love,* estaba rebosante de amor. – **7** *i* (*liquid*) salirse de: *the water overflowed the banks of the river,* el agua se salió del cauce del río.
● **to be full to overflowing,** estar lleno,-a hasta el borde.
■ **overflow pipe,** tubo de desagüe.
▲ (*verbo*) [əʊvə'fləʊ].

overfly [əʊvə'flaɪ] *t* sobrevolar.
▲ *pt* **overflew,** *pp* **overflown** [əʊvə'fləʊn].

overgrown [əʊvə'grəʊn] **1** *adj* (*garden etc*) cubierto,-a (**with,** de). **2** (*in size*) demasiado,-a grande.

overhang [əʊvə'hæŋ] **1** *t* sobresalir por encima de, colgar por encima de. – **2** *i* sobresalir, colgar por encima. – **3** *n* saliente *m*.
▲ (*sustantivo*) ['əʊvəhæŋ].

overhaul ['əʊvəhɔːl] **1** *n* revisión *f* general, puesta a punto. – **2** *t* revisar, poner a punto.
▲ (*verbo*) [əʊvə'hɔːl].

overhead ['əʊvəhed] **1** *adj* (*cable*) aéreo,-a; (*railway*) elevado,-a; (*lighting*) desde arriba. **2** SP (*kick etc*) por encima de la cabeza. – **3** *adv* arriba, por encima de la cabeza. – **4 overheads,** *npl* COMM gastos *mpl* generales.
■ **overhead projector,** retroproyector *m*.
▲ (*adverbio*) [əʊvə'hed].

overhear [əʊvə'hɪə'] *t* oír por casualidad, oír sin querer.
▲ *pt & pp* **overheard** [əʊvə'hɜːd].

overheat [əʊvə'hiːt] *i* recalentarse, calentarse demasiado.

overhung [əʊvə'hʌŋ] *pp* → **overhang.**

overindulge [əʊvəɪn'dʌldʒ] **1** *i* excederse. – **2** *t* consentir demasiado, mimar demasiado.
● **to overindulge in sth.,** abusar de algo.
overjoyed [əʊvə'dʒɔɪd] *adj* rebosante de alegría.
overkill ['əʊvəkɪl] *n fig* exceso, exageración *f*.
overland ['əʊvəlænd] **1** *adj* por tierra. – **2** *adv* por tierra.
▲ *(adverbio)* [əʊvə'lænd].
overlap [əʊvə'læp] **1** *i (tiles etc)* superponerse, solaparse.
2 *fig (activities etc)* coincidir parcialmente; *(courses etc)* tener elementos en común. – **3** *n* superposición *f*: *there should be an overlap of 4cms,* deben solaparse cuatro centímetros. **4** *fig (coincidence)* coincidencia; *(repetition)* repetición *f* de elementos.
▲ *pt & pp* **overlapped,** *ger* **overlapping.**
overleaf [əʊvə'liːf] *adv* al dorso: *see overleaf,* véase al dorso.
overload [əʊvə'ləʊd] **1** *t* sobrecargar **(with,** de): *don't overload the system,* no sobrecargues el sistema; *students are overloaded with work,* los estudiantes están agobiados de trabajo. – **2** *n* sobrecarga.
▲ *(sustantivo)* ['əʊvələʊd].
overlook [əʊvə'lʊk] **1** *t (not notice)* pasar por alto; *(disregard)* no tener en cuenta. **2** *(ignore)* hacer la vista gorda a; *(excuse)* disculpar. **3** *(have a view of)* dar a, tener vistas a.
overly ['əʊvəlɪ] *adv* demasiado.
overmanned [əʊvə'mænd] *adj* con demasiado personal.
overmanning [əʊvə'mænɪŋ] *n* exceso de personal.
overnight [əʊvə'naɪt] **1** *adv (during the night)* durante la noche; *(at night)* por la noche: *it rained overnight,* llovió durante la noche; *we decided to stay there overnight,* decidimos pasar la noche allí. **2** *fam (suddenly)* de la noche a la mañana. – **3** *adj (during the night)* de la noche; *(for the night)* de una noche: *an overnight stay,* una estancia de una (sola) noche. **4** *fam (sudden)* repentino,-a: *the group was an overnight success,* el grupo saltó a la fama de la noche a la mañana.
■ **overnight bag,** bolsa de viaje.
overpaid [əʊvə'peɪd] **1** *pt & pp →* **overpay.** – **2** *adj* que cobra un sueldo excesivo.
overpass ['əʊvəpæs] *n* US AUTO paso elevado.
overpay [əʊvə'peɪ] *t* pagar demasiado, pagar en exceso.
▲ *pt & pp* **overpaid.**
overpopulated [əʊvə'pɒpjəleɪtɪd] *adj* superpoblado,-a.
overpopulation [əʊvə'pɒpjəleɪʃən] *n* superpoblación *f*.
overpower [əʊvə'paʊə'] **1** *t (defeat)* vencer, reducir, dominar. **2** *fig (affect strongly - heat)* agobiar, sofocar; *(-smell)* marear; *(- emotion)* abrumar.
overpowering [əʊvə'paʊərɪŋ] *adj (heat)* aplastante, agobiante; *(smell)* muy fuerte; *(emotion)* abrumador,-ra; *(person)* apabullante.
overproduce [əʊvəprə'djuːs] *t* producir en exceso.
overproduction [əʊvəprə'dʌkʃən] *n* superproducción *f*.
overran [əʊvə'ræn] *pt →* **overrun.**
overrate [əʊvə'reɪt] *t* sobreestimar, sobrevalorar.
overrated [əʊvə'reɪtɪd] *adj* sobreestimado,-a, sobrevalorado,-a.
overreach [əʊvə'riːtʃ] **to overreach os.,** *t* intentar hacer demasiado, sobreesforzarse.
overreact [əʊvərɪ'ækt] *i* reaccionar de forma exagerada.
overreaction [əʊvərɪ'ækʃən] *n* reacción *f* exagerada.
override [əʊvə'raɪd] **1** *t (be more important than)* contar más que, ser más importante que. **2** *(not accept - verdict)* invalidar, anular; *(- advice)* hacer caso omiso de. **3** TECH cancelar. – **4** *n* TECH anulación de automatismo.

▲ *pt* **overrode,** *pp* **overridden** [əʊvə'rɪdən].
overriding [əʊvə'raɪdɪŋ] *adj (most important)* primordial, principal.
overrode [əʊvə'rəʊd] *pp →* **override.**
overrule [əʊvə'ruːl] **1** *t (verdict)* invalidar, anular; *(objection)* rechazar, no aceptar. **2** *(person)* imponerse a: *the umpire overruled the line judge,* el árbitro se impuso al juez de línea.
overrun [əʊvə'rʌn] **1** *t (invade)* invadir. **2** *(time, budget)* exceder, rebasar. – **3** *i (exceed - in time)* durar más de lo previsto; *(- in money)* rebasar el presupuesto.
● **to be overrun with sth.,** estar plagado,-a de algo, estar infestado,-a de algo.
▲ *pt* **overran,** *pp* **overrun,** *ger* **overrunning.**
oversaw [əʊvə'sɔː] *pt →* **oversee.**
overseas [əʊvə'siːz] **1** *adj (person)* extranjero,-a; *(trade)* exterior; *(investment)* en el extranjero. – **2** *adv* en ultramar.
● **to go overseas,** ir al extranjero. ‖ **to live overseas,** vivir en el extranjero.
oversee [əʊvə'siː] *t* supervisar.
▲ *pt* **oversaw,** *pp* **overseen** [əʊvə'siːn].
overseer ['əʊvəsɪə'] *n (gen)* supervisor,-ra; *(foreman)* capataz *m*.
overshadow [əʊvə'ʃædəʊ] *t fig* eclipsar, hacer sombra a.
overshoot [əʊvə'ʃuːt] *t (turning)* pasarse de; *(runway)* salirse de.
● **to overshoot the mark,** pasarse de la raya.
▲ *pt & pp* **overshot** [əʊvə'ʃɒt].
oversight ['əʊvəsaɪt] *n* descuido: *through oversight,* por descuido.
oversimplify [əʊvə'sɪmplɪfaɪ] *t* simplificar demasiado, simplificar excesivamente.
▲ *pt & pp* **oversimplified,** *ger* **oversimplifying.**
oversize [əʊvə'saɪz] *adj →* **oversized.**
oversized [əʊvə'saɪzd] *adj* demasiado grande.
oversleep [əʊvə'sliːp] *i* quedarse dormido,-a, no despertarse a tiempo.
▲ *pt & pp* **overslept** [əʊvə'slept].
overspend [əʊbə'spend] **1** *i* exceder el presupuesto **(on,** de). – **2** *n* déficit *m* presupuestario.
overspill ['əʊvəspɪl] *n* excedente *m* de población.
overstaffed [əʊvə'stɑːft] *adj* con exceso de personal.
overstate [əʊvə'steɪt] *t* exagerar.
overstatement ['əʊvəsteɪtmənt] *n* exageración *f*.
overstay [əʊvə'steɪ] *t →* **outstay.**
overstep [əʊvə'step] *t* pasar de.
● **to overstep the mark,** pasarse de la raya.
▲ *pt & pp* **overstepped,** *ger* **overstepping.**
overt ['əʊvɜːt, əʊ'vɜːt] *adj (obvious)* manifiesto,-a, patente; *(deliberate)* abierto,-a.
overtake [əʊvə'teɪk] **1** *t* GB AUTO *(gen)* adelantar, pasar, AM rebasar: *we overtook a sports car,* adelantamos un coche deportivo. **2** *(surpass)* superar, sobrepasar: *supply overtook demand,* la oferta superó la demanda. **3** *(happen suddenly to)* adelantarse a; *(surprise)* sorprender: *events have overtaken us,* los acontecimientos se nos han adelantado; *disaster overtook the making of the film,* el desastre se abatió sobre el rodaje de la película. – **4** *i* GB AUTO adelantar, AM rebasar.
▲ *pt* **overtook,** *pp* **overtaken** [əʊvə'teɪkən].
overtax [əʊvə'tæks] **1** *t* FIN gravar en exceso. **2** *fig (person)* exigir demasiado a; *(patience, strength)* poner a prueba.
● **to overtax os.,** esforzarse demasiado.
over-the-counter [əʊvəðə'kaʊntə'] *adj (medicine etc)* que se puede comprar sin receta médica.

overthrow [əʊvə'θrəʊ] 1 *t* (*government, regime, etc*) derribar, derrocar. **- 2** *n* (*defeat*) derrocamiento.
▲ (*verbo*) *pt* **overthrew** [əʊvə'θruː], pp **overthrown** [əʊvə'θrəʊn] (sustantivo) ['əʊvəθrəʊ].
overtime ['əʊvətaɪm] 1 *n* (*extra work, extra hours*) horas *fpl* extras. **2** US SP prórroga.
● **to work overtime,** hacer horas extras.
overtire [əʊvə'taɪəʳ] *t* cansar demasiado.
overtly [əʊ'vɜːtlɪ] *adv* abiertamente.
overtone ['əʊvətəʊn] *n* insinuación *f,* connotación *f: the play has political overtones,* la obra tiene connotaciones políticas.
overtook [əʊvə'tʊk] *pp* → **overtake.**
overture ['əʊvətjʊəʳ] 1 *n* MUS obertura. **2** (*approach - gen*) propuesta; (*- sexual*) insinuación *f.*
▲ En 2 normalmente *pl.*
overturn [əʊvə'tɜːn] 1 *t* (*vehicle*) volcar; (*boat*) hacer zozobrar; (*furniture*) dar la vuelta a. **2** (*government*) derrocar, derribar. **3** *fig* (*ruling*) anular. **- 4** *i* (*vehicle*) volcar; (*boat*) zozobrar.
overview ['əʊvəvjuː] *n* perspectiva general.
overweight [əʊvə'weɪt] *adj* (*thing*) demasiado pesado,-a; (*person*) demasiado gordo,-a: *she's overweight by a few pounds,* pesa unas libras de más.
overwhelm [əʊvə'welm] 1 *t* (*physically - defeat*) arrollar, aplastar: *they were overwhelmed by the enemy,* fueron aplastados por el enemigo. **2** *fig* (*emotionally*) abrumar: *I was overwhelmed by their kindness,* me abrumaron con sus atenciones; *we've been overwhelmed by the public's response,* la reacción del público nos ha dejado abrumados.
overwhelming [əʊvə'welmɪŋ] 1 *adj* (*defeat, victory*) aplastante, arrollador,-ra; (*majority*) aplastante; (*generosity*) abrumador,-ra. **2** (*desire, need*) irresistible.
overwhelmingly [əʊvə'welmɪŋlɪ] 1 *adv* (*strongly, completely*) de manera aplastante. **2** (*predominantly*) en su abrumadora mayoría.
overwork [əʊvə'wɜːk] 1 *t* (*person, animal*) hacer trabajar demasiado. **2** (*word, phrase, etc*) usar demasiado. **- 3** *i* trabajar demasiado. **- 4** *n* trabajo excesivo.
overworked [əʊvə'wɜːkt] 1 *adj* (*person, animal*) sobreexplotado,-a: *I'm overworked and underpaid,* trabajo mucho y me pagan poco. **2** (*word, phrase, etc*) muy gastado,-a, trillado,-a.
overwrought [əʊvə'rɔːt] *adj* (*tense, upset*) muy nervioso,-a, con los nervios destrozados.
ovulate ['ɒvjəleɪt] *i* ovular.
ovulation [ɒvjə'leɪʃən] *n* ovulación *f.*
ovum ['əʊvəm] *n* óvulo.
▲ *pl* **ova.**
owe [əʊ] *t* (*gen*) deber: *you owe me 10 pounds,* me debes 10 libras; *you owe me an explanation,* me debes una explicación; *you owe it to yourself,* te lo mereces.
owing ['əʊɪŋ] 1 *adj* (*due*) debido,-a: *the money owing to me,* el dinero que se me debe. **- 2 owing to,** *prep* debido a, a causa de.

owl [aʊl] *n* ORN búho, lechuza.
■ **barn owl,** lechuza común. ‖ **eagle owl,** búho real. ‖ **little owl,** mochuelo. ‖ **tawny owl,** cárabo.
own [əʊn] 1 *adj* propio,-a: *it's all my own work,* lo he hecho todo yo; *they grow their own vegetables,* cultivan sus propios verduras; *he saw it with his own eyes,* lo vio con sus propios ojos; *it's her own fault,* la culpa es de ella misma. **- 2** *pron* propio,-a: *would you like to borrow mine or do you have your own?,* ¿quieres que te deje el mío o ya tienes uno propio?; *where's my dinner? - get your own!,* ¿dónde está mi comida? - ¡prepárala tú mismo!; *for reasons of his own,* por razones personales. **- 3** *t* (*possess*) poseer, ser dueño,-a de, tener: *he owns this land,* es dueño de estas tierras; *who owns that house?,* ¿de quién es aquella casa? **4** (*confess*) reconocer, admitir. **- 5** *i* (*confess, admit*) reconocer (**to, -**).
◆ **to own up** *i* confesarlo, admitir tener la culpa: *no-one has owned up breaking the vase,* nadie ha confesado haber roto el jarrón.
● **on one's own,** (*alone*) solo,-a; (*without help*) uno,-a mismo,-a. ‖ **to come into one's own,** (*do well*) lucirse; (*receive recognition*) ser reconocido,-a; (*show true qualities*) demostrar lo que se vale. ‖ **to get one's own back,** vengarse, tomarse la revancha. ‖ **to hold one's own,** defenderse, saber defenderse.
■ **own brand,** marca propia. ‖ **own goal,** gol *m* en propia portería.
owner ['əʊnəʳ] *n* dueño,-a, propietario,-a.
ownership ['əʊnəʃɪp] *n* propiedad *f,* posesión *f: in private ownership,* de propiedad privada; *under new ownership,* bajo nueva dirección.
ox [ɒks] *n* buey *m.*
▲ *pl* **oxen** ['ɒksən].
oxidation [ɒksɪ'deɪʃən] *n* US oxidación *f.*
oxide ['ɒksaɪd] *n* óxido.
oxidization [ɒksɪdaɪ'zeɪʃən] *n* GB oxidación *f.*
oxidize ['ɒksɪdaɪz] 1 *t* oxidar. **- 2** *i* oxidarse.
Oxon ['ɒksɒn] *abbr* (*Oxoniensis*) de la Universidad de Oxford.
oxtail ['ɒksteɪl] *n* rabo de buey.
oxyacetylene [ɒksɪə'setəliːn] *n* oxiacetileno.
■ **oxyacetylene torch,** soplete *m* oxiacetilénico.
oxygen ['ɒksɪdʒən] *n* oxígeno.
■ **oxygen mask,** mascarilla de oxígeno. ‖ **oxygen tent,** cámara de oxígeno.
oxygenate ['ɒksɪdʒəneɪt] *t* oxigenar.
oyster ['ɔɪstəʳ] *n* (*shellfish*) ostra: *the oyster industry,* la industria ostrícola.
■ **oyster bed / oyster farm,** criadero de ostras.
oz [aʊns] *abbr* (*ounce*) onza.
▲ *pl* **oz** o **ozs.**
ozone ['əʊzəʊn] *n* ozono.
■ **ozone layer,** capa del ozono.
ozone-friendly ['əʊzəʊnfrendlɪ] *adj* que no daña la capa de ozono

P

P, p [piː] *n* (*the letter*) P, p *f*.
● **to mind one's Ps and Qs,** *fam* ir con cuidado.
p¹ [peɪdʒ] *abbr* (*page*) página; (*abbreviation*) p., pág.
p² [piː, 'penɪ, pens] *abbr* GB FAM (*penny, pence*) penique *m*, peniques *mpl*.
P ['kɑːpɑːk] *abbr* (*Parking, car park*) aparcamiento; (*abbreviation*) P.
PA¹ ['piː'eɪ] *abbr* (*personal assistant*) ayudante *mf* personal.
PA² ['piː'eɪ] *abbr* (*Press Association*) asociación nacional de prensa.
PA³ ['piː'eɪ] *abbr* (*public address*) megafonía, sistema *m* de megafonía.
pa [pər'ænəm] *abbr* (*per annum*) al año.
pace [peɪs] **1** *n* (*rate, speed*) marcha, ritmo, velocidad *f*: *at her own pace,* a su ritmo. **2** (*step*) paso. – **3** *t* (*room, floor*) ir de un lado a otro de. **4** (*set speed for*) marcar el ritmo a.
◆ **to pace off / pace out** *t sep* medir a pasos.
● **at a snail's pace,** a paso de tortuga. ‖ **to keep pace with sb.,** llevar el mismo ritmo que algn., seguir el ritmo de algn. ‖ **to pace up and down,** ir de un lado a otro. ‖ **to put sb. through their paces,** poner a algn. a prueba. ‖ **to quicken one's pace,** acelerar el paso. ‖ **to set the pace,** (*speed*) marcar el paso; (*example*) marcar la pauta.
pacemaker ['peɪsmeɪkə'] **1** *n* SP liebre *f*. **2** MED marcapasos *m*.
pacific [pə'sɪfɪk] **1** *adj lit* pacífico,-a. **2 Pacific,** del pacífico: *he went to live on a Pacific island,* se fue a vivir a una isla del pacífico.
■ **the Pacific (Ocean),** el (océano) Pacífico.
pacification [pæsɪfɪ'keɪʃən] *n* pacificación *f*.
pacifism ['pæsɪfɪzəm] *n* pacifismo.
pacifist ['pæsɪfɪst] **1** *adj* pacifista. – **2** *n* pacifista *mf*.
pacify ['pæsɪfaɪ] **1** *t* (*person*) calmar, tranquilizar, apaciguar. **2** (*country*) pacificar.
▲ *pt & pp* **pacified,** *ger* **pacifying.**
pack¹ [pæk] **1** *n* (*parcel*) paquete *m*; (*bundle*) fardo, bulto; (*rucksack*) mochila. **2** US (*packet - gen*) paquete *m*; (*of cigarettes*) paquete *m*, cajetilla. **3** GB (*of cards*) baraja. **4** *pej* (*of thieves*) banda, partida. **5** (*of lies*) sarta. **6** (*of wolves, dogs*) manada; (*of hounds*) jauría. **7** SP (*in rugby*) delanteros *mpl*. – **8** *t* (*goods - as parcel*) empaquetar; (*- in container*) envasar; (*- for transport*) embalar. **9** (*suitcase*) hacer; (*clothes etc*) poner, meter: *I haven't packed my case yet,* aún no he hecho la maleta; *did you pack my swimming costume?,* ¿pusiste mi bañador? **10** (*fill*) atestar, abarrotar, llenar: *the disco was packed with young people,* la discoteca estaba abarrotada de jóvenes. **11** (*press down*) apretar. – **12** *i* (*suitcase etc*) hacer las maletas, hacer el equipaje: *he hasn't packed yet,* aún no ha hecho las maletas. **13** (*people*) apiñarse, apretarse, meterse.

◆ **to pack in** *t sep* (*attract*) atraer: *the show is packing them in!,* ¡el espectáculo es un exitazo! ‖ **to pack off** *t sep* (*send*) enviar, mandar. ‖ **to pack up 1** *i* (*stop, give up*) dejarlo. **2** (*machine*) estropearse; (*car*) averiarse. – **3** *t sep* (*belongings - in case*) meter en la maleta; (*gather together*) recoger.
● **pack it in!,** ¡déjalo ya!, ¡basta ya! ‖ **to pack a hard punch,** (*of boxer*) pegar duro; (*have powerful effect*) pegar fuerte. ‖ **to pack one's bags,** (*belongings*) hacer las maletas; (*leave*) marcharse.
■ **pack ice,** banco de hielo.
pack² [pæk] *t* (*jury, committee*) llenar de partidarios.
package ['pækɪdʒ] **1** *n* (*parcel*) paquete *m*. **2** (*proposals*) paquete *m*; (*agreement*) acuerdo. – **3** *t* (*goods - in parcel*) empaquetar; (*in container*) envasar; (*for transport*) embalar.
■ **package deal,** convenio general, acuerdo global. ‖ **package holiday / package tour,** viaje *m* organizado.
packaging ['pækɪdʒɪŋ] *n* embalaje *m*.
packed [pækt] *adj* (*with people*) lleno,-a, atestado,-a de gente, abarrotado,-a, repleto,-a; (*with facts, information, etc*) lleno,-a: *the theatre was packed out,* el teatro estaba de bote en bote; *this film is packed with surprises,* esta película está llena de sorpresas.
■ **packed lunch,** comida fría para llevar.
packer ['pækə'] *n* (*person*) empaquetador,-ra, embalador,-ra; (*company*) envasadora.
packet ['pækɪt] **1** *n* (*small box - gen*) paquete *m*, cajita; (*of cigarettes*) paquete *m*, cajetilla; (*envelope*) sobre *m*. **2** *fam* (*large amount of money*) dineral *m*.
● **to cost a packet,** costar un ojo de la cara, costar un riñón. ‖ **to make a packet,** ganar una fortuna.
packhorse ['pækhɔːs] *n* caballo de carga.
packing ['pækɪŋ] *n* (*material*) embalaje *m*.
● **to do one's packing,** hacer la maleta. ‖ **to send sb. packing,** mandar a paseo a algn.
■ **packing case,** caja de embalar.
pact [pækt] *n* pacto.
● **to make a pact with sb.,** hacer un pacto con algn.
pad¹ [pæd] **1** *n* (*cushioning*) almohadilla, cojinete *m*. **2** (*inkpad*) tampón *m*. **3** (*of paper*) taco, bloc *m*. **4** (*of animal*) almohadilla. **5** (*platform*) plataforma. **6** *fam dated* (*house*) casa; (*flat*) piso. – **7** *t* (*chair etc*) acolchar, rellenar, guatear; (*garment*) poner hombreras a.
◆ **to pad out** *t sep* (*speech etc*) meter paja en.
■ **knee pad,** rodillera. ‖ **launch pad,** plataforma de lanzamiento. ‖ **pad of cotton,** algodón *m*. ‖ **sanitary pad,** compresa. ‖ **shin pad,** espinilla.
▲ (*verbo*) *pt & pp* **padded,** *ger* **padding.**
pad² [pæd] *i* andar sin hacer ruido.
▲ *pt & pp* **padded,** *ger* **padding.**
padded ['pædɪd] *adj* (*chair etc*) acolchado,-a, guateado,-a; (*envelope, cell*) acolchado,-a; (*garment*) con hombreras; (*bra*) con relleno.
■ **padded shoulders,** hombreras *fpl*.

padding ['pædɪŋ] 1 n (*material*) relleno, acolchado. 2 (*in speech, writing, etc*) paja.

paddle[1] ['pædəl] 1 n (*oar*) pala, remo, canalete m. 2 (*blade on paddle wheel*) álabe m, paleta. – 3 t (*boat, canoe*) remar con pala, remar con canalete. – 4 i remar con pala, remar con canalete.
● **to paddle one's own canoe,** *fig* arreglárselas uno,-a solo,-a.
■ **paddle boat / paddle steamer,** vapor m de ruedas.
‖ **paddle wheel,** rueda hidráulica de paletas.

paddle[2] ['pædəl] 1 i (*walk or play in water*) mojarse los pies, chapotear. – 2 n chapoteo.
● **to go for a paddle,** mojarse los pies, chapotear.

paddling pool ['pædəlɪŋpuːl] n piscina para niños, piscina infantil.

paddock ['pædək] 1 n (*field*) potrero, prado. 2 SP (*in race course*) paddock m.

paddy ['pædɪ] n arrozal m.
▲ pl *paddies.*

padlock ['pædlɒk] 1 n candado. – 2 t cerrar con candado.

padre ['pɑːdrɪ] n MIL capellán m.

paediatric [piːdɪ'ætrɪk] adj pediátrico,-a.

paediatrician [piːdɪ'ætrɪʃən] n pediatra mf.

paediatrics [piːdɪ'ætrɪks] n pediatría.

paedophile ['piːdəfaɪl] n pedófilo,-a.

paedophilia [piːdə'fɪlɪə] n pedofilia.

pagan ['peɪgən] 1 adj pagano,-a. – 2 n pagano,-a.

page[1] [peɪdʒ] n (*of book*) página; (*of newspaper*) plana, página.
● **on the front page,** en primera plana.

page[2] [peɪdʒ] 1 n (*boy servant, at wedding*) paje m; (*in hotel, club*) botones m. 2 HIST escudero. – 3 t (*over loudspeaker*) llamar por megafonía, llamar por altavoz; (*on pager*) llamar por el buscapersonas.

pageant ['pædʒənt] n (*show*) espectáculo; (*procession*) desfile m; (*on horses*) cabalgata.

pageantry ['pædʒəntrɪ] n pompa, boato.

pageboy ['peɪdʒbɔɪ] 1 n (*boy servant, at wedding*) paje m; (*in hotel, club*) botones m. 2 (*hairstyle*) estilo paje.

pager ['peɪdʒəʳ] n buscapersonas m, busca m.

pagoda [pə'gəʊdə] n pagoda.

paid [peɪd] 1 pt & pp → **pay**. – 2 adj (*purchase, holiday*) pagado,-a; (*work*) remunerado,-a.
● **to put paid to sth.,** acabar con algo.

paid-up ['peɪdʌp] adj (*member*) que ha pagado la cuota, que está al corriente de los pagos.

pail [peɪl] n cubo.

pain [peɪn] 1 n (*physical*) dolor m: *he was in great pain,* sufría mucho; *I've got a pain in my stomach,* me duele el estómago; *she screamed with pain,* gritó de dolor. 2 (*mental suffering*) sufrimiento, pena, dolor m. 3 (*annoying thing*) lata, fastidio, pesadez f; (*person*) pesado,-a, pelmazo. – 4 t doler, dar pena o apenar. – 5 pains, npl (*effort*) esfuerzos mpl, esmero; (*trouble*) molestia.
● **on pain of,** so pena de. ‖ **to be a pain in the neck,** ser un,-a pesado,-a, ser un pelmazo, ser un coñazo. ‖ **to be at pains to do sth.,** afanarse por hacer algo. ‖ **to take pains over sth.,** esforzarse en algo, esmerarse en algo. ‖ **to take pains to do sth.,** esforzarse en hacer algo, esmerarse en hacer algo.
■ **aches and pains,** achaques mpl.

pained [peɪnd] adj (*hurt*) afligido,-a, apenado,-a, dolido,-a; (*look, expression*) de pena.

painful ['peɪnfʊl] 1 adj (*physically*) doloroso,-a; (*mentally*) angustioso,-a, doloroso,-a. 2 fam (*very bad*) malísimo,-

a, pésimo,-a; (*embarrassing*) de pena, penoso,-a, lamentable.

painfully ['peɪnfʊlɪ] 1 adv (*causing pain*) dolorosamente, con dolor. 2 (*extremely*) terriblemente: *he's painfully shy,* es terriblemente tímido.
● **to be painfully aware of sth.,** tener plena conciencia de algo.

painkiller ['peɪnkɪləʳ] n analgésico, calmante m.

painless ['peɪnləs] 1 adj (*without pain*) indoloro,-a, sin dolor. 2 (*without distress*) sencillo,-a, sin complicaciones, llevadero,-a.

painlessly ['peɪnləslɪ] 1 adv (*without pain*) sin (causar) dolor. 2 (*without distress*) sin complicaciones.

pains [peɪnz] npl → **pain**.

painstaking ['peɪnzteɪkɪŋ] adj (*person*) meticuloso,-a, minucioso,-a; (*care, research*) esmerado,-a, concienzudo,-a.

painstakingly ['peɪnzteɪkɪŋlɪ] adv minuciosamente.

paint [peɪnt] 1 n pintura: *we'll have to give it another coat of paint,* tendremos que darle otra mano de pintura. – 2 t (*gen*) pintar: *we're going to paint the walls yellow,* vamos a pintar las paredes de amarillo. – 3 i (*gen*) pintar: *she paints in oils,* pinta al óleo.
● **to paint one's face,** pintarse, maquillarse. ‖ **to paint the town red,** irse de juerga. ‖ "**wet paint**", "recién pintado".

paintbox ['peɪntbɒks] n caja de pinturas.

paintbrush ['peɪntbrʌʃ] 1 n (*for walls etc*) brocha. 2 (*artist's*) pincel m.

painter[1] ['peɪntəʳ] 1 n ART pintor,-ra. 2 (*decorator*) pintor,-ra de brocha gorda.

painter[2] ['peɪntəʳ] n MAR amarra.

painting ['peɪntɪŋ] 1 n ART (*picture*) pintura, cuadro. 2 (*activity*) pintura.

paint-stripper ['peɪntstrɪpəʳ] n quitapinturas m.

paintwork ['peɪntwɜːk] n pintura.

pair [peəʳ] 1 n (*of shoes, socks, gloves, etc*) par m; (*of cards*) pareja: *I've only got one pair of hands!,* ¡sólo tengo dos manos!; *a pair of brown eyes,* dos ojos castaños. 2 (*of people, animals*) pareja: *shut up, the pair of you!,* ¡callaos, vosotros dos! – 3 t (*people*) emparejar; (*animals*) aparear. – 4 i (*animals*) aparearse.
◆ **to pair off** 1 t sep emparejar (**with,** con). – 2 i formar pareja (**with,** con). ‖ **to pair up** 1 t sep emparejar. – 2 i formar pareja (**with,** con).
● **in pairs,** de dos en dos.
■ **a pair of knickers,** unas bragas. ‖ **a pair of pants,** (*men's*) unos calzoncillos. ‖ **a pair of pyjamas,** un pijama. ‖ **a pair of scissors,** unas tijeras. ‖ **a pair of tights,** un panty, unos pantys. ‖ **a pair of trousers,** unos pantalones.

pajamas [pə'dʒæməz] npl US → **pyjamas**.

Pakistan [pɑːkɪ'stɑːn] n Paquistán m, Pakistán m.

Pakistani [pɑːkɪ'stɑːnɪ] 1 adj paquistaní, pakistaní. – 2 n paquistaní mf, pakistaní mf.

pal [pæl] n fam amigo,-a, colega mf, compinche mf.

palace ['pæləs] n palacio.

palatable ['pælətəbəl] 1 adj (*tasty*) sabroso,-a. 2 (*acceptable*) aceptable; (*pleasant*) agradable.

palatal ['pælətəl] 1 adj LING palatal. – 2 n LING palatal f.

palate ['pælət] n (*gen*) paladar m.

palatial [pə'leɪʃəl] adj magnífico,-a, suntuoso,-a, grandioso,-a.

palaver [pə'lɑːvəʳ] n fam (*fuss*) lío, follón m.

pale[1] [peɪl] 1 adj (*complexion, skin*) pálido,-a; (*colour*) claro,-a, pálido,-a; (*light*) débil, tenue. – 2 i palidecer.

● **to pale before sth. / pale beside sth.**, palidecer al lado de algo, parecer nimio,-a comparado,-a con algo. ‖ **to turn pale**, ponerse pálido,-a, palidecer. ■ **pale ale**, GB *tipo de cerveza rubia suave.*

pale[2] [peɪl] *n (stake)* estaca.
● **to be beyond the pale**, ser inaceptable, ser intolerable.

paleness ['peɪlnəs] *n* palidez *f.*

paleolithic [pælɪəʊ'lɪθɪk] *adj* paleolítico,-a.

Palestine ['pælɪstaɪn] *n* Palestina.

Palestinian [pælɪ'stɪnɪən] **1** *adj* palestino,-a. – **2** *n* palestino,-a.

palette ['pælət] *n* paleta.
■ **palette knife**, espátula.

paling ['peɪlɪŋ] *n (fence)* empalizada, estacada, valla.
▲ *A menudo se emplea en pl con el mismo significado.*

palisade [pælɪ'seɪd] **1** *n (fence)* palizada, estacada. – **2 palisades**, *npl* US *(cliffs)* acantilado *m sing.*

pall[1] [pɔːl] **1** *n (cloth on coffin)* paño mortuorio. **2** US *(coffin)* féretro. **3** *fig (of smoke)* cortina.

pall[2] [pɔːl] *i (become boring)* dejar de gustar, hacerse pesado,-a, cansar, aburrir: *the idea of doing nothing soon palled on us,* la idea de no hacer nada pronto dejó de gustarnos.

pallbearer ['pɔːlbeərəʳ] *n* portador,-ra del féretro.

pallet[1] ['pælət] *n* TECH paleta.

pallet[2] ['pælət] *n (mattress)* jergón *m; (bed)* camastro.

palliative ['pælɪətɪv] *adj* paliativo,-a.

pallid ['pælɪd] *adj* pálido,-a.

pallor ['pæləʳ] *n* palidez *f.*

pally ['pælɪ] *adj* amigo,-a: *they're very pally all of a sudden,* de repente son muy amigos.
● **to be pally with sb.**, ser muy amigo,-a de algn.
▲ *comp* **pallier**, *superl* **palliest.**

palm[1] [pɑːm] *n* BOT *(tree)* palmera; *(leaf)* palma.
■ **Palm Sunday**, Domingo de Ramos.

palm[2] [pɑːm] **1** *n* ANAT palma. – **2** *t (touch ball)* dar con la mano a.
◆ **to palm off** *t sep* endosar (**on/onto**, a).
● **to have sb. in the palm of one's hand**, tener a algn. en la palma de la mano. ‖ **to grease sb.'s palm**, untarle la mano a algn., untar a algn. ‖ **to read sb.'s palm**, leerle la mano a algn.

palmist ['pɑːmɪst] *n* quiromántico,-a.

palmistry ['pɑːmɪstrɪ] *n* quiromancia.

palpable ['pælpəbəl] *adj* palpable.

palpably ['pælpəblɪ] *adv* palpablemente.

palpate ['pælpeɪt] *t* MED palpar.

palpitate ['pælpɪteɪt] *i (heart)* palpitar.

palpitation [pælpɪ'teɪʃən] *n* palpitación *f.*

paltry ['pɔːltrɪ] *adj* insignificante.
▲ *comp* **paltrier**, *superl* **paltriest.**

pampas ['pæmpəs] *npl* GEOG pampa *f sing.*

pamper ['pæmpəʳ] *t* mimar, consentir.

pamphlet ['pæmflət] *n* folleto.

pan[1] [pæn] **1** *n (saucepan)* cacerola, cazuela, cazo; *(cooking pot)* olla. **2** *(of lavatory)* taza. **3** *(of scales)* platillo. **4** *(for washing gravel)* batea. – **5** *t (soil, gravel)* cribar con batea, lavar con batea. **6** *fam (criticize)* poner por los suelos. – **7** *i* extraer oro.
◆ **to pan out** *i fam (turn out)* salir, resultar.
■ **pots and pans**, batería de cocina, cacharros *mpl* (de cocina). ‖ **frying pan**, sartén *f.*
▲ *(verbo) pt & pp* **panned**, *ger* **panning.**

pan[2] [pæn] **1** *t* CINEM tomar una panorámica de. – **2** *i* CINEM tomar una panorámica.

▲ *pt & pp* **panned**, *ger* **panning.**

panacea [pænə'sɪə] *n* panacea.

panache [pə'næʃ] *n* garbo, salero.

panama ['pænəmɑː] *n (hat)* panamá *m.*

Panama ['pænəmɑː] *n* Panamá.
■ **Panama Canal**, Canal *m* de Panamá.

Panamanian [pænə'meɪnɪən] **1** *adj* panameño,-a. – **2** *n* panameño,-a.

pancake ['pænkeɪk] *n* tortita, crepe *f.*
■ **Pancake Day**, martes *m* de Carnaval. ‖ **pancake landing**, AV aterrizaje *m* de emergencia.

panchromatic [pænkrəʊ'mætɪk] *adj* pancromático,-a.

pancreas ['pæŋkrɪəs] *n* páncreas *m.*

panda ['pændə] *n* oso panda *m,* panda *m.*
■ **panda car**, GB coche *m* patrulla.

pandemonium [pændə'məʊnɪəm] *n* pandemónium *m.*

pander ['pændəʳ] *i (person)* consentir (**to**, a), complacer (**to**, a); *(wishes etc)* acceder (**to**, a).

p and p [piːən'piː] *abbr* GB *(postage and packing)* gastos de embalaje y envío.
▲ *También se escribe* **p & p.**

pane [peɪn] *n* cristal *m,* vidrio.

panel ['pænəl] **1** *n (of door, wall, car body, etc)* panel *m; (on ceiling)* artesón *m.* **2** *(of controls, instruments)* tablero. **3** *(group of people)* panel *m; (team)* equipo. **4** *(jury)* jurado. **5** *(in garment)* pieza. **6** ART tabla. – **7** *t* revestir con paneles.
■ **panel beater**, planchista *mf.*
▲ *(verbo) pt & pp* **panelled** (US **paneled**), *ger* **panelling** (US **paneling**).

panelled ['pænəld] *adj (door, wall, etc)* con paneles; *(ceiling)* artesonado,-a.

panelling ['pænəlɪŋ] *n (of door, wall, etc)* paneles *mpl; (on ceiling)* artesonado.

panellist ['pænəlɪst] *n (in discussion etc)* participante *mf,* contertulio,-a; *(judge)* miembro *mf* del jurado; *(contestant)* concursante *mf.*

pang [pæŋ] **1** *n (of pain, hunger)* punzada; *(of childbirth)* dolores *mpl* (de parto). **2** *fig (of emotion)* punzada, remordimiento.

panic ['pænɪk] **1** *n* pánico: *panic spread throughout the crowd,* el pánico cundió entre la gente. – **2** *t* infundir pánico a. – **3** *i* entrarle el pánico a, aterrarse: *I panicked,* me entró el pánico; *don't panic!,* ¡tranquilo!
● **to be panic stations**, reinar el pánico. ‖ **to get into a panic**, dejarse llevar por el pánico.
■ **panic button**, botón *m* de alarma.
▲ *(verbo) pt & pp* **panicked.**

panicky ['pænɪkɪ] *adj fam (person)* muy nervioso,-a, asustadizo,-a; *(reaction, feeling)* aterrador,-ra, de pánico.
● **to get panicky**, dejarse llevar por el pánico.

panic-striken ['pænɪkstrɪkən] *adj* preso,-a de pánico, aterrorizado,-a.

pannier ['pænɪəʳ] *n (on animal)* alforja; *(on bicycle)* bolsa.

panorama [pænə'rɑːmə] **1** *n (view)* panorama *m.* **2** CINEM TV panorámica.

panoramic [pænə'ræmɪk] *adj* panorámico,-a.

panpipes ['pænpaɪps] *npl* MUS zampoña *f sing.*

pansy ['pænzɪ] **1** *n* BOT pensamiento. **2** *fam pej (effeminate man)* mariquita *m.*
▲ *pl* **pansies.**

pant [pænt] **1** *n* jadeo. – **2** *i* jadear, resoplar.
● **to pant for breath**, intentar recobrar el aliento.

pantechnicon [pæn'teknɪkən] *n* camión *m* de mudanzas.

pantheism ['pænθɪɪzəm] *n* panteísmo.

pantheist ['pænθɪɪst] **1** adj panteísta. – **2** n (person) panteísta mf.

pantheon ['pænθɪən] n ARCH panteón m.

panther ['pænθə'] n pantera.

panties ['pæntɪz] npl bragas fpl, braguitas fpl.

pantomime ['pæntəmaɪm] **1** n (mime) pantomima. **2** GB (play) representación musical navideña basada en cuentos de hadas.

pantry ['pæntrɪ] n despensa.
▲ pl pantries.

pants [pænts] **1** npl GB (underpants - men's) calzoncillos mpl; (- women's) bragas fpl. **2** US (trousers) pantalón m, pantalones mpl.

papa [pə'pɑː] n dated papá m.

papacy ['peɪpəsɪ] n papado, pontificado.

papal ['peɪpəl] adj papal, pontificio.

papaya [pə'paɪə] n (tree) papayo; (fruit) papaya.

paper ['peɪpə'] **1** n (material) papel m: take a sheet of paper, coge una hoja de papel. **2** (newspaper) periódico, diario. **3** (examination) examen m. **4** (essay, written work) trabajo (escrito); (for conference) ponencia. – **5** t empapelar. – **6** papers, – npl (documents) papeles mpl, documentos mpl. **7 the papers**, los periódicos mpl, la prensa.
● **on paper**, (in theory) en teoría, sobre el papel; (written down) por escrito. ‖ **not to be worth the paper it's written on**, ser papel mojado. ‖ **to put sth. down on paper**, poner algo por escrito.
■ **brown paper**, papel m de estraza. ‖ **call-up papers**, llamamiento m sing a filas. ‖ **identity papers**, documentación f. ‖ **paper handkerchief**, kleenex m, pañuelo de papel. ‖ **paper mill**, fábrica de papel. ‖ **paper money**, papel m moneda. ‖ **paper round**, reparto de periódicos. ‖ **paper shop**, quiosco. ‖ **paper tiger**, tigre m de papel. ‖ **question paper**, EDUC cuestionario. ‖ **white paper**, libro blanco. ‖ **writing paper**, papel m de escribir.

paperback ['peɪpəbæk] n libro en rústica.

paperboy ['peɪpəbɔɪ] n repartidor m de periódicos.

paperclip ['peɪpəklɪp] n clip m, sujetapapeles m.

papergirl ['peɪpəɡɜːl] n repartidora de periódicos.

paperknife ['peɪpənaɪf] n cortapapeles m.

paperweight ['peɪpəweɪt] n pisapapeles m.

paperwork ['peɪpəwɜːk] n papeleo.

papier-mâché [pæpɪeɪ'mæʃeɪ] n cartón m piedra.

papist ['peɪpɪst] **1** adj pej papista. – **2** n pej papista mf.

paprika ['pæprɪkə] n pimentón m dulce, paprika.

Papua ['pæpjʊə] n Papúa.
■ **Papua New Guinea**, Papúa Nueva Guinea.

Papuan ['pæpjʊən] **1** adj papú,-úa. – **2** n papú,-úa.

papyrus [pə'paɪərəs] n papiro.
▲ pl papyri [pə'paɪraɪ] o papyruses.

par [pɑː'] **1** n (parity) igualdad f. **2** SP (in golf) par m. **3** FIN (par value) par f; (par of exchange) tipo de cambio.
● **to be on a par with sb./sth.**, estar al mismo nivel que algn./algo, correr parejas con algn./en algo: the two goalkeepers are on a par, los dos porteros están al mismo nivel. ‖ **to be par for the course**, ser lo normal. ‖ **to be up to par**, ser del nivel adecuado. ‖ **to feel below par**, sentirse mal, estar en baja forma.

para ['pærəɡrɑːf] abbr (paragraph) párrafo.

parable ['pærəbəl] n parábola.

parabola [pə'ræbələ] n MATH parábola.

parabolic [pærə'bɒlɪk] adj parabólico,-a.

parachute ['pærəʃuːt] **1** n paracaídas m. – **2** t lanzar en paracaídas. – **3** i saltar en paracaídas, lanzarse en paracaídas.

■ **parachute jump**, salto en paracaídas.

parachutist ['pærəʃuːtɪst] n paracaidista mf.

parade [pə'reɪd] **1** n (procession) desfile m: fashion parade, desfile de modelos. **2** MIL desfile m. – **3** t MIL hacer desfilar. **4** (flaunt - knowledge, wealth) alardear, hacer alarde de. – **5** i (gen) desfilar. **6** MIL pasar revista.
◆ **to parade about / parade around** i pavonearse.
● **to be on parade**, MIL pasar revista. ‖ **to make a parade of sth.**, hacer alarde de algo.
■ **parade ground**, plaza de armas. ‖ **shopping parade**, zona comercial.

paradigm ['pærədaɪm] n paradigma m.

paradigmatic [pærədɪɡ'mætɪk] adj paradigmático,-a.

paradise ['pærədaɪs] n paraíso: a shopper's paradise, el paraíso de los compradores.

paradox ['pærədɒks] n paradoja.

paradoxical [pærə'dɒksɪkəl] adj paradójico,-a.

paraffin ['pærəfɪn] **1** paraffin (oil), n GB queroseno. **2** paraffin (wax), GB parafina.
■ **liquid paraffin**, aceite m de parafina. ‖ **paraffin lamp**, lámpara de petróleo.

paragon ['pærəɡən] n modelo, dechado.
● **a paragon of virtue**, un dechado de virtudes.

paragraph ['pærəɡrɑːf] n párrafo.
● **full stop, new paragraph**, punto y aparte.

Paraguay [pærə'ɡwaɪ] n Paraguay.

Paraguayan [pærə'ɡwaɪən] **1** adj paraguayo,-a. – **2** n paraguayo,-a.

parakeet ['pærəkiːt] n periquito, perico.

parallel ['pærəlel] **1** adj paralelo,-a (to/with, a). **2** fig (similar) paralelo,-a (to/with, a), análogo,-a (to/with, a). – **3** n MATH paralela. **4** GEOG paralelo. **5** (similarity) paralelo, paralelismo: there is a certain parallel, existe un cierto paralelismo. – **6** t ser paralelo a a, ser análogo,-a a a.
● **in parallel**, ELEC en paralelo. ‖ **to draw a parallel between**, establecer un paralelo entre, establecer un paralelismo entre. ‖ **without parallel**, sin comparación, sin parangón.
■ **parallel bars**, SP (barras) paralelas.

parallelogram [pærə'leləɡræm] n paralelogramo.

paralyse ['pærəlaɪz] t (gen) paralizar.
● **to be paralysed**, MED estar paralizado,-a, ser paralítico,-a: he's paralysed from the neck down, está paralizado del cuello hacia abajo. ‖ **to be paralysed with fear**, quedarse paralizado,-a de miedo.

paralysis [pə'ræləsɪs] **1** n MED parálisis f. **2** fig paralización f.

paralytic [pærə'lɪtɪk] **1** adj MED paralítico,-a. – **2** n MED paralítico,-a.
● **to be paralytic**, (drunk) estar como una cuba.

paralyze ['pærəlaɪz] t US → **paralyse**.

parameter [pə'ræmɪtə'] n parámetro.

paramilitary [pærə'mɪlɪtərɪ] adj paramilitar.

paramount ['pærəmaʊnt] adj supremo,-a, primordial, sumo,-a: of paramount importance, de suma importancia.

paranoia [pærə'nɔɪə] n paranoia.

paranoiac [pærə'nɔɪk] **1** adj paranoico,-a. – **2** n paranoico,-a.

paranoid ['pærənɔɪd] **1** adj paranoico,-a. – **2** n paranoico,-a.
● **to be paranoid about sth.**, estar obsesionado,-a con algo.

paranormal [pærə'nɔːməl] adj paranormal.

parapet ['pærəpɪt] n parapeto.

paraphernalia [pærəfə'neɪlɪə] n parafernalia.
paraphrase ['pærəfreɪz] 1 n paráfrasis f. – 2 t parafrasear.
paraplegia [pærə'pliːdʒə] n MED paraplejía.
paraplegic [pærə'pliːdʒɪk] 1 adj MED parapléjico,-a. – 2 n MED parapléjico,-a.
parasite ['pærəsaɪt] n parásito,-a.
parasitic [pærə'sɪtɪk] adj (plant, animal, etc) parásito,-a; (disease) parasitario,-a.
parasol [pærə'sɒl] n sombrilla.
paratrooper ['pærətruːpə'] n MIL paracaidista mf.
paratroops ['pærətruːps] npl MIL paracaidistas mpl.
parboil ['paːbɔɪl] t cocer a medias, sancochar.
parcel ['paːsəl] 1 n (package) paquete m. 2 (piece of land) parcela.
◆ to **parcel out** t sep (gen) repartir, dividir; (land) parcelar. ‖ to **parcel up** t sep empaquetar, embalar.
■ **parcel bomb**, paquete m bomba. ‖ **parcel post**, servicio de paquetes postales.
parched [paːtʃt] 1 adj (very dry - land, earth) agostado,-a, reseco,-a; (- throat, mouth) reseco,-a. 2 (thirsty) muerto,-a de sed.
parchment ['paːtʃmənt] n pergamino.
■ **parchment paper**, papel m pergamino.
pardon ['paːdən] 1 n (forgiveness) perdón m. 2 JUR indulto. – 3 t (forgive) perdonar: *pardon me for interrupting*, perdone que le interrumpa. 4 JUR indultar.
● if you'll **pardon the expression**, con perdón. ‖ I **beg your pardon!**, fml ¡perdone! ‖ I **beg your pardon?**, fml ¿cómo dice? ‖ **pardon?**, (for repetition) ¿cómo dice?, ¿cómo? ‖ **pardon me!**, (sorry) ¡perdón!, ¡perdone!, ¡Vd. perdone! ‖ to **ask sb.'s pardon**, pedirle perdón a algn. ‖ to **pardon sb. sth.**, perdonarle algo a algn.
pardonable ['paːdənəbəl] adj perdonable, disculpable.
pare [peə'] 1 t (fruit) pelar, mondar. 2 (nails) cortar.
◆ to **pare down** t sep reducir, recortar.
parent ['peərənt] 1 n (father) padre m; (mother) madre f. – 2 **parents**, npl padres mpl.
■ **parent company**, casa madre, casa matriz, casa central.
parentage ['peərəntɪdʒ] n familia, origen m.
● of unknown **parentage**, de padres desconocidos.
parental [pə'rentəl] adj (of both parents) de los padres; (parental) paterno,-a; (maternal) materno,-a.
parenthesis [pə'renθəsɪs] n paréntesis m.
● in **parenthesis**, entre paréntesis.
▲ pl **parentheses**.
parenthetical [pærən'θetɪkəl] adj entre paréntesis.
parenthood ['peərənthʊd] n (being a parent) ser padre, ser madre; (fatherhood) paternidad f; (motherhood) maternidad f: *the joys of parenthood*, la alegría de tener hijos.
■ planned **parenthood**, planificación f familiar.
par excellence [paːr'eksələns] adv por excelencia.
pariah [pə'raɪə] n paria m.
parings ['peərɪŋz] npl (of fruit) mondas fpl, mondaduras fpl; (of nails) cortes mpl.
Paris ['pærɪs] n París.
parish ['pærɪʃ] 1 n REL parroquia. 2 GB (civil) municipio.
■ **parish church**, iglesia parroquial. ‖ **parish council**, consejo parroquial, consejo municipal. ‖ **parish priest**, párroco.
parishioner [pə'rɪʃənə'] n feligrés,-esa.
Parisian [pə'rɪzɪən] 1 adj parisino,-a. – 2 n parisino,-a.
parity ['pærɪtɪ] 1 n (equality) igualdad f, paridad f. 2 FIN paridad f.

park [paːk] 1 n (gen) parque m, jardín m público; (surrounding country house) jardines mpl. – 2 t (car) aparcar, estacionar: *I'm parked opposite*, he aparcado enfrente. 3 (books, belongings, etc) dejar, poner. – 4 i aparcar, estacionar.
● to **park os.**, sentarse.
■ national **park**, parque m nacional. ‖ **park bench**, banco.
parka ['paːkə] n anorak m, parka.
parking ['paːkɪŋ] n (act) aparcamiento, estacionamiento: *I'm really bad at parking*, soy muy malo aparcando.
● "no **parking**", "prohibido aparcar".
■ **parking attendant**, guardacoches mf. ‖ **parking brake**, US freno de mano. ‖ **parking lights**, US luces fpl de estacionamiento. ‖ **parking lot**, US aparcamiento, parking m. ‖ **parking meter**, parquímetro. ‖ **parking place / parking space**, (gen) aparcamiento, sitio para aparcar; (private) plaza de parking. ‖ **parking ticket**, multa (por estacionamiento indebido).
parkland ['paːklænd] n jardines mpl.
parkway ['paːkweɪ] n US avenida, alameda, paseo.
parky ['paːkɪ] adj fam fresco,-a: *it's a bit parky*, hace fresquito.
▲ comp **parkier**, superl **parkiest**.
parlance ['paːləns] n fml lenguaje m, habla.
parley ['paːlɪ] 1 n dated discusión f, negociación f. – 2 i dated negociar, parlamentar.
parliament ['paːləmənt] 1 n (assembly) parlamento. 2 **Parliament**, GB (body) Parlamento; (period) legislatura.
■ Member of **Parliament**, Diputado,-a.
parliamentarian [paːləmən'teərɪən] n parlamentario,-a.
parliamentary [paːlə'mentərɪ] adj parlamentario,-a.
parlor ['paːlə'] n US → **parlour**.
parlour ['paːlə'] 1 n US (shop) salón m, tienda. 2 dated (room in house) salón m, salita.
■ beauty **parlour**, salón m de belleza. ‖ **parlour game**, juego de salón.
parochial [pə'rəʊkɪəl] 1 adj (of parish) parroquial. 2 pej (narrow) provinciano,-a, pueblerino,-a.
parody ['pærədɪ] 1 n parodia. – 2 t parodiar.
▲ (sustantivo) pl **parodies**; (verbo) pt & pp **parodied**, ger **parodying**.
parole [pə'rəʊl] 1 n libertad f condicional. – 2 t poner en libertad condicional.
● to **be (out) on parole**, estar en libertad condicional. ‖ to **be released on parole**, concederle a uno la libertad condicional.
paroxysm ['pærəksɪzəm] n paroxismo.
parquet ['paːkeɪ] n parqué m: *parquet floor*, suelo de parqué.
parrot ['pærət] n loro, papagayo.
● to **be as sick as a parrot**, estar muerto,-a de rabia. ‖ to **repeat sth. parrot fashion**, repetir algo como un loro.
parry ['pærɪ] 1 t (blow) parar, desviar. 2 (question etc) esquivar, eludir. – 3 n parada.
▲ (sustantivo) pl **parries**; (verbo) pt & pp **parried**, ger **parrying**.
parse [paːz] t LING analizar sintácticamente, analizar gramaticalmente.
parsimonious [paːsɪ'məʊnɪəs] adj fml mezquino,-a, tacaño,-a, parsimonioso,-a.
parsimony ['paːsɪmənɪ] n fml mezquindad f, tacañería, parsimonia.
parsley ['paːslɪ] n perejil m.

parsnip ['paːsnɪp] n chirivía.
parson ['paːsən] n REL párroco, cura m.
■ **parson's nose**, CULIN rabadilla (del pollo).
parsonage ['paːsənɪdʒ] n casa del párroco.
part [paːt] 1 n (gen) parte f: we spent part of the day on the beach, pasamos parte del día en la playa; which part of London are you from?, ¿de qué parte de Londres eres?; the fire devastated part of the castle, el incendio asoló parte del castillo; he's like part of the family, es como de la familia; you must be able to work as part of a team, hay que saber trabajar en equipo; now comes the difficult part, ahora viene lo difícil. 2 (component) pieza. 3 (of serial, programme) capítulo; (of serialized publication) fascículo, entrega. 4 (measure) parte f. 5 CINEM THEAT papel m: she plays the part of Scarlett, hace el papel de Scarlett; a bit part, un papel secundario. 6 (role, share, involvement) papel m, parte f: he admitted his part in the crime, confesó su parte en el crimen; I want no part in your dodgy deals, no quiero saber nada de tus negocios sucios. 7 MUS parte f. 8 US (parting) raya. – 9 adv en parte: he's part Irish, part Spanish, es mitad irlandés, mitad español. – 10 adj parcial. – 11 t (separate) separar (from, de): till death us do part, hasta que la muerte nos separe. – 12 i (separate) separarse; (say goodbye) despedirse: they parted as friends, se separaron amistosamente. 13 (open - lips, curtains) abrirse. – 14 parts, npl (area) zona, parajes mpl, lugares mpl: you're not from these parts, are you?, no eres de por aquí, ¿verdad? 15 (abilities) facetas fpl: a man/woman of many parts, un hombre/una mujer de muchas facetas.
◆ to part with t insep desprenderse de, separarse de.
● for my part, por mi parte, en cuanto a mí. ‖ in part, en parte. ‖ on the part of sb. / on sb.'s part, de parte de algn. ‖ the best part of / the better part of, la mayor parte de, casi todo,-a. ‖ to be part and parcel of sth., formar parte de algo. ‖ to look the part, encajar bien en el papel. ‖ to part company with, (leave) despedirse de; (separate) separarse de; (disagree) no estar de acuerdo con. ‖ to play a part in, (in play etc) desempeñar un papel en; (in project etc) intervenir en algo, influir en algo, tener que ver con algo: various factors played a part in our decision, diversos factores influyeron en nuestra decisión. ‖ to part one's hair, hacerse la raya. ‖ to take part in sth., participar en algo, tomar parte en algo. ‖ to take sb.'s part, ponerse de parte de algn. ‖ to take sth. in good part, tomarse bien algo.
■ foreign parts, el extranjero. ‖ part exchange, parte f del pago. ‖ part of speech, parte f de la oración. ‖ part owner, copropietario,-a.
partake [paː'teɪk] partake of, i fml (eat) comer; (drink) beber.
partial ['paːʃəl] 1 adj (not complete) parcial. 2 (biased) parcial.
● to be partial to sth., ser aficionado,-a a algo, tener debilidad por algo.
partiality [paːʃɪ'ælɪtɪ] 1 n (bias) parcialidad f. 2 (liking) afición f (for, a), debilidad f (for, por).
partially ['paːʃəlɪ] 1 adv (partly) parcialmente. 2 (with bias) con parcialidad.
participant [paː'tɪsɪpənt] n (gen) participante mf; (in competition) concursante mf.
participate [paː'tɪsɪpeɪt] i participar (in, en).
participation [paːtɪsɪ'peɪʃən] n participación f.
participle ['paːtɪsɪpəl] n participio.
■ past participle, participio pasado. ‖ present participle, participio presente.

particle ['paːtɪkəl] n partícula.
particular [pə'tɪkjʊləʳ] 1 adj (special) particular, especial: for no particular reason, por nada en especial, por nada en particular. 2 (specific) concreto, particular: in this particular case, en este caso concreto. 3 (fussy) exigente, especial: she's very particular about food, es muy especial para la comida. – 4 particulars, npl (of event, thing) detalles mpl, pormenores mpl; (of person) datos mpl personales.
● in particular, en particular.
particularly [pə'tɪkjʊləlɪ] adv especialmente, particularmente.
parting ['paːtɪŋ] 1 n (leaving) despedida; (separation) separación f. 2 (in hair) raya. – 3 adj de despedida: her parting words, sus palabras de despedida.
● the parting of the ways, el momento de la despedida.
■ parting shot, último comentario (antes de marcharse).
partisan [paːtɪ'zæn] 1 n (supporter) partidario,-a. 2 MIL partisano,-a. – 3 adj partidista.
partition [paː'tɪʃən] 1 n (act) partición f, división f. 2 (wall) tabique m; (screen) mampara. – 3 t partir, dividir.
◆ to partition off t sep dividir con un tabique, separar con un tabique.
partly ['paːtlɪ] adv parcialmente, en parte: what he said is partly true, lo que ha dicho es en parte verdad; it's partly my fault, en parte es culpa mía.
partner ['paːtnəʳ] 1 n (in an activity) compañero,-a; (in dancing, tennis, cards, etc) pareja. 2 COMM socio,-a, asociado,-a. 3 (spouse) cónyuge mf; (husband) marido; (wife) mujer f; (in relationship) pareja, compañero,-a. – 4 t acompañar, ser pareja de.
■ junior partner, socio,-a adjunto,-a. ‖ partner in crime, cómplice mf.
partnership ['paːtnəʃɪp] 1 n COMM (company) sociedad f. 2 (working relationship) asociación f.
● to go into partnership with sb., asociarse con algn.
partook [paː'tʊk] pt → partake.
partridge ['paːtrɪdʒ] n perdiz f, perdiz f pardilla.
▲ pl partridges o partridge.
part-time [paːt'taɪm] 1 adj (work, job) de media jornada, a tiempo parcial. – 2 adv media jornada, a tiempo parcial.
part-timer [paːt'taɪməʳ] n (worker) trabajador,-ra a tiempo parcial; (student) estudiante mf a tiempo parcial.
party ['paːtɪ] 1 n (celebration) fiesta: birthday party, fiesta de cumpleaños. 2 POL partido. 3 (group) grupo: a party of schoolchildren, un grupo de escolares. 4 JUR parte f, interesado,-a. – 5 adj (dress) de fiesta; (mood, atmosphere) festivo,-a. 6 POL (member, leader) del partido. – 7 i (go to parties) ir a fiestas; (have fun) divertirse.
● to be party to a crime, ser cómplice de un delito. ‖ to be party to sth., hacerse cómplice de algo.
■ guilty party, el/la culpable. ‖ innocent party, el/la inocente. ‖ party line, (on telephone) línea compartida; (in politics) línea del partido. ‖ party politics, política de partido. ‖ party political broadcast, emisión f de propaganda política, espacio de propaganda electoral. ‖ party spirit, (party mood) espíritu m festivo; (loyalty) partidismo. ‖ party piece, numerito. ‖ party wall, pared f medianera. ‖ tea party, merienda. ‖ third party, tercera persona.
▲ (sustantivo) pl parties; (verbo) pt & pp partied, ger partying.
pass [paːs] 1 n GEOG (in mountains - gen) puerto, paso (de montaña); (narrow) desfiladero. 2 (official permit) pase m,

permiso. **3** (*in exam*) aprobado. **4** SP pase *m*. **– 5** *t* (*go past - gen*) pasar; (*person*) cruzarse con: *do you pass the library on your way to work?*, ¿pasas por la biblioteca de camino al trabajo?; *I passed her in the street*, me crucé con ella en la calle. **6** (*overtake*) adelantar. **7** (*cross - border, frontier*) pasar, cruzar. **8** (*give, hand*) pasar: *pass me that screwdriver*, pásame ese destornillador; *they passed the hat round*, pasaron la gorra. **9** (*move*) pasar: *he passed a comb through his hair*, se pasó el cepillo por el pelo. **10** SP (*ball*) pasar. **11** (*exam, test, examinee*) aprobar; (*bill, law, motion*) aprobar; (*censor*) pasar. **12** (*time*) pasar: *we looked at some photos to pass the time*, miramos unas fotos para pasar el rato. **13** (*say, utter - opinion*) expresar, dar; (*- remark, comment*) hacer. **– 14** *i* (*go past - gen*) pasar; (*procession*) desfilar; (*people*) cruzarse: *I was just passing*, pasaba por aquí; *we moved aside to let them pass*, nos apartamos para dejarlos pasar. **15** (*overtake*) adelantar. **16** (*move, go*) pasar: *we passed through Zaragoza*, pasamos por Zaragoza; *the cyclists pass along this route*, los ciclistas pasan por esta ruta. **17** SP pasar la pelota, pasar el balón, hacer un pase. **18** (*be transferred to*) pasar (**to**, a). **19** (*change*) cambiar (**from**, de). **20** (*of time*) pasar, transcurrir. **21** (*come to an end - pain, feeling*) pasarse; (*storm*) pasar. **22** (*exam, test*) aprobar; (*bill, motion*) ser aprobado,-a. **23** (*be acceptable*) pasar; (*be tolerated*) consentir: *let it pass*, déjalo correr. **24** (*happen*) ocurrir, acontecer, suceder: *it came to pass that ...*, sucedió que ...

◆ to pass away *i* (*die*) pasar a mejor vida. ‖ **to pass by 1** *i* pasar: *she watched the people passing by*, miraba pasar a la gente. **– 2** *t sep* pasar de largo: *do you ever get the feeling life is passing us by?*, ¿no tienes la impresión de que la vida se nos escapa? ‖ **to pass down** *t sep* (*hand down - heirloom*) pasar; (*tradition, story*) transmitir. ‖ **to pass for** *t insep* pasar por. ‖ **to pass off 1** *i* (*happen*) pasar, transcurrir. **2** (*stop*) parar; (*disappear*) pasarse. **– 3** *t sep* (*succeed in presenting*) hacer pasar (**as**, por). ‖ **to pass on 1** *t sep* (*information*) pasar, dar; (*infection*) contagiar. **– 2** *i* (*die*) pasar a mejor vida. **3** (*proceed*) pasar (**to**, a). ‖ **to pass out 1** *i* (*faint*) desmayarse, perder el conocimiento. **2** MIL graduarse. **– 3** *t sep* (*distribute*) repartir. ‖ **to pass over 1** *t sep* (*ignore, overlook*) pasar por alto, dejar de lado, olvidar. **– 2** *t insep* (*cross*) atravesar, cruzar. ‖ **to pass through 1** *i* estar de paso. **– 2** *t insep* pasar por, atravesar. ‖ **to pass up** *t sep* (*opportunity*) dejar pasar, dejar escapar, desperdiciar; (*offer*) rechazar.

● **to make a pass at sb.**, intentar ligar con algn. ‖ **to pass judgment on**, juzgar. ‖ **to pass sentence**, dictar sentencia, fallar. ‖ **to pass the time of day (with sb.)**, pasar el rato con algn. ‖ **to pass water**, orinar. ‖ **to pass wind**, expulsar ventosidades.

■ press pass, pase *m* de prensa. ‖ bus pass, abono de autobús.

passable ['pɑːsəbəl] **1** *adj* (*acceptable*) pasable, aceptable. **2** (*road, bridge*) transitable.

passably ['pɑːsəblɪ] *adv* aceptablemente.

passage ['pæsɪdʒ] **1** *n* (*in street*) pasaje *m*; (*alleyway*) callejón *m*; (*narrow*) pasadizo *m*. **2** (*in building - corridor*) pasillo. **3** (*way, movement - gen*) paso; (*of vehicle*) tránsito, paso. **4** (*of time*) paso, transcurso. **5** MAR (*journey*) travesía, viaje *m*; (*fare*) pasaje *m*. **6** LIT MUS pasaje *m*. **7** (*of law, bill, etc*) aprobación *f*. **8** ANAT conducto.

● **to grant sb. a safe passage**, darle a algn. un salvoconducto.

■ back passage, ANAT recto.

passageway ['pæsɪdʒweɪ] *n* (*corridor*) pasillo.

passbook ['pɑːsbʊk] *n* libreta de ahorros, cartilla de ahorros.

passé [pæˈseɪ] *adj* pasado,-a de moda.

passenger ['pæsɪndʒəʳ] *n* viajero,-a, pasajero,-a.

passer-by [pɑːsəˈbaɪ] *n* transeúnte *mf*.

▲ *pl* passers-by.

passing ['pɑːsɪŋ] **1** *adj* (*fashion, thought*) pasajero,-a; (*remark, reference*) de pasada; (*glance*) rápido,-a. **2** (*vehicle*) que pasa. **– 3** *n* (*of time*) paso, transcurso.

● **in passing**, de pasada: *he just mentioned it in passing*, lo mencionó de pasada.

passion ['pæʃən] **1** *n* (*gen*) pasión *f*; (*vehemence*) ardor *m*, vehemencia: *she has a passion for Mozart*, le apasiona Mozart; *passions were running high*, los ánimos estaban exaltados; *crime of passion*, crimen pasional. **2** the Passion, REL la Pasión *f*.

● **to be in a passion**, estar fuera de sí. ‖ **to fly into a passion**, montar en cólera.

■ passion fruit, granadilla, maracuyá *m*.

passionate ['pæʃənət] *adj* (*gen*) apasionado,-a; (*vehement*) ardiente, ferviente, vehemente.

passionately ['pæʃənətlɪ] *adv* (*gen*) apasionadamente; (*intensely*) fervientemente.

passionflower ['pæʃənflaʊəʳ] *n* BOT pasionaria.

passive ['pæsɪv] **1** *adj* (*gen*) pasivo,-a. **– 2** *n* LING voz *f* pasiva: *in the passive*, en (voz) pasiva.

passively ['pæsɪvlɪ] *adv* (*gen*) pasivamente.

passiveness ['pæsɪvnəs] *n* pasividad *f*.

passivity [pæˈsɪvətɪ] *n* pasividad *f*.

passkey ['pɑːskiː] *n* llave *f* maestra.

Passover ['pɑːsəʊvəʳ] *n* Pascua (judía).

passport ['pɑːspɔːt] **1** *n* (*gen*) pasaporte *m*. **2** *fig* pasaporte *m* (**to**, a).

password ['pɑːswɜːd] *n* contraseña.

past [pɑːst] **1** *adj* (*gone by in time*) pasado,-a; (*former*) anterior: *past presidents*, los anteriores presidentes. **2** (*gone by recently*) último,-a: *the past few days*, los últimos días. **3** (*finished, over*) acabado,-a, terminado,-a: *summer is past*, el verano ha terminado; *the danger is past*, el peligro ha pasado. **4** LING pasado,-a: *the past tense*, el pasado, el pretérito. **– 5** *n* (*former times*) pasado: *in the past*, en el pasado, antes, antiguamente; *that's all in the past now*, eso ya es historia; *typewriters are a thing of the past*, las máquinas de escribir pertenecen al pasado. **6** (*of person*) pasado; (*of place*) historia. **– 7** *prep* (*farther than, beyond*) más allá de; (*by the side of*) por (delante de): *it's just past the cinema*, está un poco más allá del cine; *she walked past the school*, pasó por delante de la escuela; *he walked straight past me*, pasó de largo por mi lado. **8** (*in time*) y: *it's five past six*, son las seis y cinco; *it's half past nine*, son las nueve y media. **9** (*older than*) más de: *he's past forty*, pasa de los cuarenta (años); *she's past retirement age*, ya ha pasado la edad de la jubilación. **10** (*beyond the limits of*): *it's past my comprehension*, me resulta incomprensible; *I'm past caring*, me trae sin cuidado; *I wouldn't put it past him*, no me extrañaría que lo hiciera, no me extraña tratándose de él. **– 11** *adv*: *they went past without stopping*, pasaron de largo; *a few joggers ran past*, pasaron unos haciendo footing.

● **in times past**, antaño, antiguamente. ‖ **to be a past master at sth.**, ser experto,-a en algo. ‖ **to be past it**, estar para el arrastre, estar muy carroza.

■ the past / the past tense, el pasado, el pretérito.

pasta ['pæstə] *n* pasta, pastas *fpl*.

paste [peɪst] **1** *n* (*mixture*) pasta; (*glue*) engrudo. **2** CULIN pasta, paté *m*: *anchovy paste*, paté de anchoas. **3** (*jew-*

ellery) bisutería. **– 4** *t* (*stick*) pegar; (*put paste on*) engomar, encolar.
● **to paste sth. on a wall,** pegar algo en una pared.
■ **tomato paste,** tomate *m* concentrado.
pasteboard ['peɪstbɔːd] *n* cartón *m*.
pastel ['pæstəl] **1** *n* (*chalk*) pastel *m*; (*drawing*) dibujo al pastel. **2** (*colour*) color *m* pastel; (*tone*) tono pastel. **– 3** *adj* (*drawing*) al pastel; (*colour, tone, shade, etc*) pastel.
paste-up ['peɪstʌp] *n* maqueta.
pasteurization [pæstjəraɪ'zeɪʃən] *n* pasteurización *f*.
pasteurized ['pɑːstjəraɪzd] *adj* pasteurizado,-a.
pastiche [pæ'stiːʃ] *n* pastiche *m*.
pastille ['pæstɪl] *n* pastilla.
pastime ['pɑːstaɪm] *n* pasatiempo.
pasting ['peɪstɪŋ] *n fam* paliza.
● **to give sb. a pasting,** dar una paliza a algn.
pastor ['pɑːstəʳ] *n* REL pastor *m*.
pastoral ['pɑːstərəl] **1** *adj* (*rustic*) pastoril, bucólico,-a. **2** REL pastoral.
pastry ['peɪstrɪ] **1** *n* (*dough*) masa. **2** (*cake*) pasta, bollo. ▲ *pl* **pastries**.
pastrycook ['peɪstrɪkʊk] *n* pastelero,-a, repostero,-a.
pasture ['pɑːstʃəʳ] **1** *n* pasto. **– 2** *t* apacentar, pastar. **– 3** *i* pacer, pastar.
● **to move on to pastures new,** buscar nuevos horizontes. ‖ **to put cattle out to pasture,** pastorear el ganado, apacentar el ganado.
pasty[1] ['pæstɪ] *n* CULIN empanadilla.
pasty[2] ['peɪstɪ] **1** *adj* (*pale*) pálido,-a. **2** (*like paste*) pastoso,-a.
▲ *comp* **pastier**, *superl* **pastiest**.
pat[1] [pæt] **1** *n* (*tap*) golpecito, palmadita; (*touch*) toque *m*; (*caress*) caricia. **2** (*of butter*) porción *f*. **– 3** *t* (*tap*) dar palmaditas a; (*touch*) tocar; (*caress*) acariciar.
● **to pat sb. on the back / give sb. a pat on the back,** felicitar a algn., darle una palmadita en la espalda a algn.
▲ (*verbo*) *pt* & *pp* **patted**, *ger* **patting**.
pat[2] [pæt] **1** *adv* de memoria. **– 2** *adj* (*answer*) fácil; (*excuse*) preparado,-a.
● **to know sth. off pat,** saberse algo al dedillo. ‖ **to learn sth. off pat,** aprender algo de memoria.
Pat ['petɪənt] *abbr* (*patent*) patente *f*; (*abbreviation*) Pat.
patch [pætʃ] **1** *n* (*to mend clothes*) remiendo, parche *m*. **2** (*over eye*) parche *m*. **3** (*area on surface - gen*) trozo, lugar *m*, zona; (- *of colour, damp, etc*) mancha; (- *of road*) trecho, tramo. **4** (*plot of land*) parcela. **5** GB *fam* (*territory*) territorio. **– 6** *t* (*mend*) remendar; (*put patch on*) poner un parche a.
◆ **to patch up 1** *t sep* (*garment*) remendar, poner un parche a. **2** (*quarrel*) resolver; (*marriage*) salvar.
● **not to be a patch on,** no tener ni punto de comparación con. ‖ **to go through a bad patch,** pasar por una mala racha, atravesar una mala racha.
patchwork ['pætʃwɜːk] **1** *n* labor *f* de retales. **2** *fig* (*of fields*) mosaico. **– 3** *adj* de retales.
patchy ['pætʃɪ] *adj* (*colour*) desigual, disparejo,-a; (*performance*) desigual, irregular, con altibajos; (*knowledge*) incompleto,-a, parcial.
▲ *comp* **patchier**, *superl* **patchiest**.
pâté ['pæteɪ] *n* paté *m*.
patent ['peɪtənt] **1** *n* COMM patente *f*. **– 2** *adj* (*obvious*) patente, evidente. **3** COMM patentado. **– 4** *t* COMM patentar.
● **to take out a patent on sth.,** sacar una patente de algo, patentar algo.
■ **patent medicine,** específico. ‖ **patent leather,** cha-

rol *m*: **patent leather shoes,** zapatos de charol. ‖ **Patent Office,** Registro de la propiedad industrial.
▲ En *Patent Office* ['pætnət].
patently ['peɪtəntlɪ] *adv* evidentemente.
● **to be patently obvious,** estar clarísimo.
paternal [pə'tɜːnəl] *adj* (*fatherly*) paternal; (*on father's side*) paterno,-a, por parte de padre.
paternalism [pə'tɜːnəlɪzəm] *n* paternalismo.
paternalistic [pətɜːnə'lɪstɪk] *adj* paternalista.
paternity [pə'tɜːnɪtɪ] *n* paternidad *f*.
■ **paternity suit,** JUR demanda de paternidad.
path [pɑːθ] **1** *n* (*track*) camino, sendero, senda: *keep to the path*, seguir el camino; *they cleared a path through the forest*, abrieron un camino por el bosque. **2** (*course of bullet, missile*) trayectoria; (*of flight*) rumbo; (*of moon, sun*) recorrido, trayectoria: *she walked into the path of an approaching car*, se cruzó en el camino de un coche que se acercaba.
● **to be on the right path,** ir bien encaminado,-a. ‖ **to lead sb. up the garden path,** llevar a algn. al huerto.
pathetic [pə'θetɪk] **1** *adj* (*rousing pity*) patético,-a. **2** (*awful, hopeless*) malísimo,-a, pésimo,-a: *you're pathetic!*, ¡eres inútil!
pathetically [pə'θetɪklɪ] **1** *adv* (*pitiably*) patéticamente. **2** *fam* (*badly, hopelessly*) que da lástima, que da pena.
● **to say sth. pathetically,** decir algo con voz lastimera.
pathological [pæθə'lɒdʒɪkəl] *adj* patológico,-a.
pathologist [pə'θɒlədʒɪst] *n* patólogo,-a.
pathology [pə'θɒlədʒɪ] *n* patología.
pathos ['peɪθɒs] *n* patetismo.
pathway ['pɑːθweɪ] *n* camino, sendero.
patience ['peɪʃəns] **1** *n* (*quality*) paciencia: *I lost my patience*, perdí la paciencia; *you need patience to do a jigsaw*, hace falta paciencia para hacer un puzzle. **2** (*card game*) solitario.
● **patience is a virtue,** la paciencia es la madre de la ciencia. ‖ **to have the patience of a saint,** tener más paciencia que un santo. ‖ **to play patience,** hacer solitarios. ‖ **to try sb.'s patience,** poner a prueba la paciencia de algn.
patient ['peɪʃənt] **1** *adj* (*person - gen*) paciente; (*long-suffering*) sufrido,-a: *be patient with him*, ten paciencia con él; *she's very patient*, tiene mucha paciencia. **– 2** *n* paciente *mf*, enfermo,-a.
patiently ['peɪʃəntlɪ] *adv* pacientemente, con paciencia.
patina ['pætɪnə] *n* pátina.
patio ['pætɪəʊ] *n* patio.
▲ *pl* **patios**.
patriarch ['peɪtrɪɑːk] *n* patriarca *m*.
patriarchal [peɪtrɪ'ɑːkəl] *adj* patriarcal.
patriarchy ['peɪtrɪɑːkɪ] *n* patriarcado.
▲ *pl* **patriarchies**.
patricide ['pætrɪsaɪd] **1** *n* (*crime*) parricidio. **2** (*person*) parricida *mf*.
patrimony ['pætrɪmənɪ] *n* patrimonio.
patriot ['peɪtrɪət] *n* patriota *mf*.
patriotic [pætrɪ'ɒtɪk] *adj* patriótico,-a.
patriotism ['pætrɪətɪzəm] *n* patriotismo.
patrol [pə'trəʊl] **1** *n* (*act*) patrulla, ronda; (*person, group*) patrulla. **– 2** *t* (*area*) patrullar por, estar de patrulla en. **– 3** *i* patrullar.
● **to be on patrol,** patrullar, estar de patrulla.
■ **patrol boat,** patrullera. ‖ **patrol car,** coche *m* patrulla.
▲ (*verbo*) *pt* & *pp* **patrolled** (US **patroled**), *ger* **patrolling** (US **patroling**).

patrolman [pə'trəʊlmən] *n* US policía *m*, guardia *m*.
▲ *pl* **patrolmen** [pə'trəʊlmən].

patron ['peɪtrən] **1** *adj* (*customer*) cliente,-a habitual, parroquiano,-a. **2** (*sponsor - of charity, cause*) patrocinador,-ra; (*of arts*) mecenas *m*.
■ **patron saint,** patrón,-ona, santo,-a patrón,-ona.

patronage ['pætrənɪdʒ] **1** *n* (*sponsorship - of charity, cause*) patrocinio; (*of arts*) mecenazgo. **2** (*custom*) clientela, parroquia. **3** POL *pej* enchufe *m*, influencias *fpl*.

patronize ['pætrənaɪz] **1** *t* (*shop, hotel*) ser cliente,-a (habitual) de; (*club, cinema*) frecuentar. **2** (*sponsor - gen*) patrocinar; (*arts*) proteger, formentar. **3** *pej* (*condescend to*) tratar con condescendencia.

patronizing ['pætrənaɪzɪŋ] *adj pej* condescendiente.

patter[1] ['pætə'] **1** *n* (*of rain*) repiqueteo, golpeteo; (*of footsteps*) ruido. – **2** *i* (*rain*) repiquetear, golpear; (*feet, person*) corretear, trotar.
● **the patter of tiny feet,** pasitos de niño.

patter[2] ['pætə'] *n fam* (*talk*) parloteo, palabrería, labia.

pattern ['pætən] **1** *n* (*decorative design*) diseño, dibujo; (*on fabric*) diseño, estampado. **2** (*way something develops*) orden *m*, estructura, pauta: *behaviour pattern,* patrón de conducta; *the illness followed its usual pattern,* la enfermedad siguió las pautas normales; *a pattern began to emerge after the third murder,* después del tercer asesinato se empezaron a detectar ciertos rasgos en común. **3** (*example, model*) ejemplo, modelo. **4** (*for sewing, knitting*) patrón *m*; (*sample*) muestra.
● **to pattern os. on sb.,** imitar a algn., seguir el ejemplo de algn., tomar a algn. como modelo. ‖ **to pattern sth. on sth.,** inspirarse algo en algo, tomar algo como modelo para algo.
■ **pattern book,** (*of wallpaper, fabrics*) muestrario, libro de muestras; (*of dress patterns*) revista de patrones.

patterned ['pætənd] *adj* (*gen*) con dibujos, decorado,-a; (*fabric*) estampado,-a.

paunch ['pɔːntʃ] *n* panza, barriga.

paunchy ['pɔːntʃɪ] *adj* barrigón,-ona, panzudo,-a.
▲ *comp* **paunchier;** *superl* **paunchiest.**

pauper ['pɔːpə'] *n* pobre *mf*, indigente *mf*.
■ **pauper's grave,** fosa común.

pause [pɔːz] **1** *n* (*gen*) pausa; (*silence*) silencio; (*rest*) descanso: *without pausing,* sin interrupción; *there was a slight pause in the conversation,* la conversación se interrumpió por un instante. **2** MUS pausa. – **3** *i* (*gen*) hacer una pausa; (*stop moving*) detenerse.
● **to pause for breath,** parar para recobrar el aliento.

pave [peɪv] *t* (*with concrete - road*) pavimentar; (*with flagstones*) enlosar; (*with stones*) empredrar, adoquinar; (*with bricks*) enladrillar.
● **to pave the way for sb./sth.,** preparar el terreno para algn./algo.

pavement ['peɪvmənt] **1** *n* GB acera. **2** US calzada, pavimento.

pavilion [pə'vɪljən] **1** *n* (*at exhibition*) pabellón *m*. **2** GB SP vestuarios *mpl*.

paving ['peɪvɪŋ] *n* (*paved area - on road*) pavimento; (*of flagstones*) enlosado; (*of stones*) empedrado, adoquinado; (*of bricks*) enladrillado.
■ **paving stone,** baldosa, losa.

paw [pɔː] **1** *n* ZOOL (*foot*) pata; (*claw - of big cats*) zarpa, garra. **2** *fam* (*person's hand*) manaza, zarpa, garra. – **3** *t* (*animal*) tocar con la pata; (*lion*) dar zarpazos. **4** *pej* (*person*) manosear, sobar.
● **to paw the ground,** (*horse*) piafar.

pawn[1] [pɔːn] **1** *n* (*in chess*) peón *m*. – **2** *t fig* (*unimportant person*) juguete *m*, marioneta, títere *m*.

● **to be sb.'s pawn,** *fig* ser un juguete en manos de algn.

pawn[2] [pɔːn] **1** *n* (*pledge*) prenda. – **2** *t* empeñar.
● **in pawn,** en prenda. ‖ **to place/put sth. in pawn,** entregar algo en prenda, empeñar algo.

pawnbroker ['pɔːnbrəʊkə'] *n* prestamista *mf*.

pawnshop ['pɔːnʃɒp] *n* monte *m* de piedad, casa de empeños.

pawpaw ['pɔːpɔː] *n* GB BOT (*fruit*) papaya; (*tree*) papayo.

pay [peɪ] **1** *n* (*wages*) paga, sueldo, salario: *equal pay,* igualdad de salarios. – **2** *t* (*gen*) pagar; (*bill, debt*) pagar, saldar: *I paid him 10 pounds to mend my bike,* le pagué 10 libras para que me arreglara la bici; *how much did you pay for that dress?,* ¿cuánto te costó ese vestido?, ¿cuánto pagaste por ese vestido?; *he still hasn't paid me for the meal,* aún no me ha pagado la comida; *I wouldn't go out with him if you paid me,* no saldría con él ni que me pagaran. **3** (*make, give - attention*) prestar; (*homage, tribute*) rendir; (*respects*) presentar, ofrecer; (*compliment, visit, call*) hacer. **4** FIN (*make, give - interest, dividends*) dar. **5** (*be worthwhile*) compensar, convenir: *it'll pay you to keep your mouth shut,* te conviene no decir ni pío. – **6** *i* (*gen*) pagar: *you don't have to pay to go in,* no hay que pagar para entrar; *I'll pay for it,* yo lo pagaré; *the company paid for him to go to New York,* la empresa le pagó el viaje a Nueva York; *this kind of work pays very well,* este tipo de trabajo está muy bien pagado. **7** *fig* (*suffer*) pagar (**for,** -): *he'll pay for this!,* ¡me las pagará!; *I paid dearly for my haste,* pagué muy cara mi prisa. **8** (*be profitable - business etc*) ser rentable, ser factible. **9** (*be worthwhile*) compensar, convenir: *crime doesn't pay,* el crimen no compensa.
◆ **to pay back 1** *t sep* (*money*) devolver, reembolsar; (*loan, mortgage*) pagar: *I'll pay you back tomorrow,* te devolveré el dinero mañana. **2** *fig* (*take revenge on*) hacer pagar a: *I'll pay you back for this!,* ¡te haré pagar por esto! ‖ **to pay in** *t sep* (*money, cheque*) ingresar: *she paid the money into her account,* ingresó el dinero en su cuenta. ‖ **to pay off** *t* (*debt*) saldar, liquidar, cancelar; (*loan*) pagar; (*mortgage*) acabar de pagar. **2** (*worker*) liquidar el sueldo a, dar el finiquito a. – **3** *i* (*be successful*) dar resultado; (*prove worthwhile*) valer la pena. ‖ **to pay out 1** *t sep* (*money - spend*) desembolsar (**on,** en); (*- give out*) pagar. **2** (*rope*) ir soltando. – **3** *i* pagar ‖ **to pay up** *i* pagar.
● **to be in sb.'s pay,** ser empleado,-a de algn., estar a sueldo de algn. ‖ **to get paid,** cobrar: *how much do you get paid?,* ¿cuánto cobras? ‖ **to pay in advance,** pagar por adelantado. ‖ **to pay cash / pay in cash,** pagar al contado, pagar en efectivo. ‖ **to pay by cheque,** pagar con talón, pagar con cheque. ‖ **to pay in instalments,** pagar a plazos. ‖ **to pay one's way,** pagar su parte. ‖ **to pay through the nose,** pagar un dineral. ‖ **there will be hell to pay,** se va a armar la gorda.
■ **overtime pay,** dinero de horas extras. ‖ **pay cheque,** sueldo, cheque *m* del sueldo. ‖ **pay claim,** reivindicación *f* salarial. ‖ **pay packet,** sobre *m* de la paga. ‖ **pay phone,** teléfono público. ‖ **pay rise,** aumento de sueldo. ‖ **pay slip,** nómina, hoja de salario.
▲ *pt & pp* **paid.**

payable ['peɪəbəl] *adj* pagadero,-a.
● **to make a cheque payable to sb.,** extender un talón a favor de algn., extender un talón a nombre de algn.

payday ['peɪdeɪ] *n* día *m* de paga.

PAYE ['piː'eɪ'waɪ'iː] *abbr* GB (*pay as you earn*) recaudación *de impuestos mediante retenciones practicadas sobre el sueldo.*

payee [peɪ'iː] *n* beneficiario,-a.
paying guest ['peɪɪŋ'gest] *adj* huésped,-a de pago.
paymaster ['peɪmɑːstə'] *n* (oficial *mf*) pagador,-ra.
■ **Paymaster General,** GB *funcionario,-a encargado,-a del pago de sueldos a los funcionarios.*
payment ['peɪmənt] **1** *n* (*paying*) pago: *on payment of,* mediante pago de. **2** (*amount paid*) pago, remuneración *f*: *she wanted no payment for her work,* no quería cobrar por su trabajo. **3** (*instalment*) plazo. **4** (*reward*) pago, recompensa.
■ **annual payment,** anualidad *f*, pago anual. ‖ **down payment,** entrada, pago inicial. ‖ **monthly payment,** mensualidad *f*, pago mensual.
payoff ['peɪɒf] **1** *n* (*payment - gen*) pago; (*of debt*) liquidación *f*; (*of redundancy money*) indemnización *f*. **2** *fam* (*bribe*) soborno. **3** (*climax, outcome*) desenlace *m*, resultado.
payroll ['peɪrəʊl] *n* (*gen*) nómina.
● **to be on the payroll,** estar en nómina, estar en plantilla.
pc¹ [pɜː'sent] *abbr* (*per cent*) por ciento; (*abbreviation*) p.c.
pc² ['pəʊstkɑːd] *abbr* (*postcard*) tarjeta postal, postal *f*.
pc³ ['piː'siː] *abbr* (*personal computer*) ordenador *m* personal; (*abbreviation*) PC.
PC ['piː'siː] *abbr* GB (*Police Constable*) agente *mf* de policía.
pct [pɜː'sent] *abbr* (*per cent*) por ciento; (*abbreviation*) p.c.
pd [peɪd] *abbr* (*paid*) pagado,-a.
PE ['piː'iː] *abbr* (*physical education*) educación física.
pea [piː] *n* guisante *m*.
● **to be alike as two peas in a pod,** parecerse como dos gotas de agua.
■ **pea green,** verde *m* guisante.
peace [piːs] **1** *n* (*not war*) paz *f*. **2** (*tranquility*) paz *f*, tranquilidad *f*, sosiego: *he doesn't give me a moment's peace,* no me deja en paz ni un momento; *I just want a bit of peace and quiet,* sólo quiero un poco de paz (y de tranquilidad).
● **at peace / in peace,** en paz. ‖ **"rest in peace",** "descanse en paz". ‖ **to hold one's peace,** guardar silencio: *speak now or forever hold your peace,* hable ahora o calle para siempre. ‖ **to keep the peace,** JUR mantener el orden. ‖ **to make one's peace with sb.,** hacer las paces con algn. ‖ **to make peace,** (*people*) hacer las paces; (*countries*) firmar la paz.
■ **breach of the peace,** alteración *f* del orden público. ‖ **Peace Corps,** Cuerpo de Paz. ‖ **peace movement,** movimiento pacifista. ‖ **peace of mind,** tranquilidad *f* de espíritu, serenidad *f*. ‖ **peace offering,** prenda de paz, ofrenda de paz. ‖ **peace talks,** negociaciones *fpl* por la paz. ‖ **peace treaty,** tratado de paz.
peaceable ['piːsəbəl] *adj* pacífico,-a.
peaceful ['piːsfʊl] **1** *adj* (*non-violent*) pacífico,-a, no violento,-a. **2** (*calm*) tranquilo,-a, sosegado,-a.
peacefulness ['piːsfʊlnəs] *n* (*quietness*) paz *f*, tranquilidad *f*, sosiego.
peace-keeping ['piːskiːpɪŋ] *adj* de paz, pacificador,-ra.
■ **peace-keeping forces,** fuerzas *fpl* de paz, fuerzas *fpl* pacificadoras.
peace-loving ['piːslʌvɪŋ] *adj* amante de la paz, pacífico,-a.
peacemaker ['piːsmeɪkə'] *n* pacificador,-ra, conciliador,-ra.
peacetime ['piːstaɪm] *n* tiempos *mpl* de paz.
peach [piːtʃ] **1** *n* (*fruit*) melocotón *m*. **2** (*colour*) (color *m*) melocotón *m*. – **3** *adj* de color melocotón.

■ **peach tree,** melocotonero.
peacock ['piːkɒk] *n* pavo real.
peahen ['piːhen] *n* pava real.
peak [piːk] **1** *n* GEOG (*of mountain*) pico; (*summit*) cima, cumbre *f*. **2** *fig* (*highest point*) cumbre *f*, cúspide *f*, punto álgido; (*climax*) apogeo, punto culminante. **3** (*of cap*) visera. – **4** *adj* (*maximum*) máximo,-a: *peak rate,* tarifa máxima; *during peak periods,* durante las horas de mayor consumo. – **5** *i* (*demand, sales, etc*) alcanzar su nivel más alto, alcanzar su punto máximo; (*career*) alcanzar su apogeo; (*athlete*) alcanzar su mejor momento.
■ **peak hours,** horas *fpl* punta. ‖ **peak season,** temporada alta.
peaked [piːkt] *adj* (*cap*) con visera.
peaky ['piːkɪ] *adj fam* pálido,-a, paliducho,-a.
▲ *comp* **peakier,** *superl* **peakiest.**
peal [piːl] **1** *n* (*of bells*) repique *m*. – **2** *t* (*bells*) repicar, tocar a vuelo. – **3** *i* (*bells*) repicar, tocar a vuelo.
■ **a peal of thunder,** un trueno: *peals of laughter,* carcajadas *fpl*.
peanut ['piːnʌt] **1** *n* cacahuete *m*. – **2 peanuts,** *npl* (*small amount*) una miseria.
■ **peanut butter,** mantequilla de cacahuete.
pear [peə'] *n* (*fruit*) pera.
■ **pear tree,** peral *m*.
pearl [pɜːl] **1** *n* perla: *are those pearls real or cultured?,* ¿esas perlas son auténticas o cultivadas?; *he gave her a string of pearls,* le regaló un collar de perlas. **2** *fig* (*thing of value, beauty, etc*) joya. – **3** *adj* (*necklace etc*) de perlas; (*button*) de nácar, de madreperla.
■ **pearl barley,** cebada perlada. ‖ **pearl diver,** pescador,-ra de perlas. ‖ **pearl grey,** gris *mpl* perla. ‖ **pearl oyster,** ostra perlífera.
pearly ['pɜːlɪ] *adj* nacarado,-a, perlado,-a: *pearly teeth,* dientes de perla.
■ **the Pearly Gates,** las puertas del Paraíso.
▲ *comp* **pearlier,** *superl* **pearliest.**
pear-shaped ['peəʃeɪpt] *adj* en forma de pera.
peasant ['pezənt] **1** *adj* campesino,-a, rural. – **2** *n* (*gen*) campesino,-a. **3** *pej* (*uncultured person*) inculto,-a, palurdo,-a.
peashooter ['piːʃuːtə'] *n* canuto, cerbatana.
peat [piːt] *n* turba.
■ **peat bog,** turbera.
peaty ['piːtɪ] *adj* turboso,-a.
▲ *compo* **peatier,** *superl* **peatiest.**
pebble ['pebəl] *n* guija, guijarro, china, piedrecita.
pebbly ['pebəlɪ] *adj* (*beach*) guijarroso,-a.
pecan ['piːkæn] *n* (*nut*) pacana; (*tree*) pacanero.
peck [pek] **1** *n* (*of bird*) picotazo; (*kiss*) beso, besito. – **2** *t* (*bird*) picotear; (*kiss*) dar un besito a. – **3** *i* (*bird*) picotear (**at, -**).
● **to peck at one's food,** picar la comida.
pecker ['pekə'] **to keep one's pecker up,** *phr* no desanimarse.
pecking order ['pekɪŋɔːdə'] *n* jerarquía.
peckish ['pekɪʃ] *adj fam* algo hambriento,-a.
● **to feel peckish,** tener un poco de hambre.
pectin ['pektɪn] *n* pectina.
pectoral ['pektərəl] **1** *adj* pectoral. – **2 pectorals,** *npl* músculos *mpl* pectorales, pectorales *mpl*.
peculiar [pɪ'kjuːlɪə'] **1** *adj* (*strange*) extraño,-a, raro,-a; (*unwell*) indispuesto,-a. **2** (*particular*) característico,-a (**to,** de), propio,-a (**to,** de).
peculiarity [pɪkjuːlɪ'ærɪtɪ] **1** *n* (*oddity*) rareza, cosa extraña, singularidad *f*. **2** (*distinctive feature, characteristic*) característica, peculiaridad *f*, particularidad *f*.

▲ *pl* peculiarities.
peculiarly [pɪˈkjuːlɪərlɪ] 1 *adv* (*strangely*) de forma rara, de forma extraña. 2 (*especially, more than usually*) especialmente, particularmente. 3 (*exclusively*) peculiarmente, típicamente.
pecuniary [pɪˈkjuːnɪərɪ] *adj fml* (*motives, advantage*) pecuniario,-a; (*problems*) monetario,-a, financiero,-a.
pedagogical [pedəˈɡɒdʒɪkəl] *adj* pedagógico,-a.
pedagogy [ˈpedəɡɒdʒɪ] *n* pedagogía.
pedal [ˈpedəl] 1 *n* (*gen*) pedal *m*. – 2 *i* pedalear. – 3 *t* (*bicycle, boat*) dar a los pedales de, impulsar pedaleando.
 ■ **pedal bin,** cubo de la basura con pedal.
 ▲ (*verbo*) *pt & pp* **pedalled** (US **pedaled**), *ger* **pedalling** (US **pedaling**).
pedalo [ˈpedələʊ] *n* patín *m*.
 ▲ *pl* pedalos *o* pedaloes.
pedant [ˈpedənt] *n* pedante *mf*.
pedantic [pəˈdæntɪk] *adj* pedante.
pedantry [ˈpedəntrɪ] *n* pedantería.
peddle [ˈpedəl] 1 *t* COMM vender de puerta en puerta. – 2 *i* COMM vender de puerta en puerta.
 ● **to peddle drugs,** traficar con drogas, pasar droga.
peddler [ˈpedləʳ] 1 *n* US → **pedlar.** 2 (*drug pusher*) traficante *mf* de drogas.
pederast [ˈpedəræst] *n* pederasta *m*.
pedestal [ˈpedɪstəl] *n* pedestal *m*.
 ● **to put sb. on a pedestal,** poner a algn. sobre un pedestal.
 ■ **pedestal table,** mesa con pie central.
pedestrian [pəˈdestrɪən] 1 *n* peatón,-ona. – 2 *adj* (*dull*) pedestre.
 ■ **pedestrian crossing,** paso de peatones. ‖ **pedestrian precinct,** zona peatonal.
pediatric [piːdɪˈætrɪk] *adj* US pediátrico,-a.
pediatrician [piːdɪəˈtrɪʃən] *n* US pediatra *mf*.
pediatrics [piːdɪˈætrɪks] *n* US pediatría.
pedicure [ˈpedɪkjʊəʳ] *n* pedicura.
 ● **to have a pedicure,** hacerse los pies, arreglarse los pies.
pedigree [ˈpedɪɡriː] 1 *n* (*of animals*) pedigrí *m*; (*of people*) linaje *m*. 2 (*family tree*) árbol *m* genealógico. – 3 *adj* de raza.
pedlar [ˈpedləʳ] *n* vendedor,-ra ambulante, buhonero,-a.
pee [piː] 1 *n fam* pis *m*, pipí *m*. – 2 *i fam* hacer pis, hacer pipí.
 ● **to have a piss,** hacer pis, hacer pipí.
peek [piːk] 1 *n* ojeada, miradita. – 2 *i* mirar (a hurtadillas).
 ● **to have a peek at / take a peek at,** echar una ojeada a, echar una miradita a.
peel [piːl] 1 *n* (*skin - gen*) piel *f*; (- *of orange, lemon, etc*) corteza, cáscara, monda, mondadura. – 2 *t* pelar, quitar la piel de. – 3 *i* (*skin*) pelarse; (*paint*) desconcharse; (*wallpaper*) despegarse.
 ◆ **to peel back** *t sep* quitar, despegar. ‖ **to peel off** 1 *t sep* (*fruit*) pelar, quitar la piel de; (*clothes*) quitarse. – 2 *i* (*skin*) pelarse; (*paint*) desconcharse; (*wallpaper*) despegarse.
 ● **to keep one's eyes peeled,** estar ojo avizor.
peeler [ˈpiːləʳ] *n* (*potato peeler*, *n* pelapatatas *m*.
peelings [ˈpiːlɪŋz] *npl* peladuras *fpl*, mondaduras *fpl*.
peep[1] [piːp] 1 *n* (*look*) ojeada, vistazo. – 2 *i* espiar, atisbar, mirar a hurtadillas.
 ● **to have a peep at / take a peep at,** echar una ojeada a, echar un vistazo a.

peep[2] [piːp] *n* (*noise*) pío: *I don't want to hear another peep out of you!,* ¡que no te oiga decir ni pío!
peephole [ˈpiːphəʊl] *n* mirilla.
peeping Tom [piːpɪŋˈtɒm] *n pej* mirón *m*.
peepshow [ˈpiːpʃəʊ] *n* (*machine*) mundonuevo, cosmorama *m*.
peer[1] [pɪəʳ] *i* (*look closely*) mirar detenidamente (**at,** -); (*shortsightedly*) mirar con ojos de miope (**at,** -).
peer[2] [pɪəʳ] 1 *n* (*equal*) par *mf*, igual *mf*; (*contemporary*) coetáneo,-a. 2 GB (*noble*) par *mf*, noble *mf*.
 ● **to be a life peer,** tener un título de nobleza vitalicio. ‖ **to be made a peer,** adquirir un título de nobleza.
 ■ **peer group,** grupo paritario. ‖ **peer pressure** / **peer group pressure,** presión *f* que ejercen los compañeros.
peerage [ˈpɪərɪdʒ] 1 *n* (*rank*) título nobiliario. 2 **the peerage,** (*nobility*) la nobleza.
 ● **to give sb. a peerage,** otorgar a algn. un título de nobleza.
peeress [ˈpɪəres] *n* paresa.
peerless [ˈpɪələs] *adj* sin par, sin igual, incomparable.
peeve [piːv] *t fam* (*annoy*) fastidiar, molestar, dar rabia a.
peeved [piːvd] *adj fam* (*annoyed*) fastidiado,-a, molesto,-a, picado,-a, mosqueado,-a.
peevish [ˈpiːvɪʃ] *adj fam* (*irritable*) malhumorado,-a.
peevishly [ˈpiːvɪʃlɪ] *adv* con mal humor, de mala manera.
peg [peɡ] 1 *n* (*for hanging clothes on*) percha, colgador *m*. 2 TECH clavija. – 3 *t* (*clothes*) tender (**out,** -); (*tent*) fijar con estacas (**down,** -). 4 (*prices*) fijar, estabilizar.
 ◆ **to peg out** 1 *i fam* (*die*) estirar la pata, palmarla. – 2 *t sep* (*boundary*) marcar con estacas.
 ● **to buy clothes off the peg,** comprar ropa de confección. ‖ **to take sb. down a peg or two,** bajarle los humos a algn.
 ■ **tent peg,** estaca, estaquilla. ‖ **tuning peg,** clavija.
 ▲ (*verbo*) *pt & pp* **pegged,** *ger* **pegging.**
pejorative [pəˈdʒɒrətɪv] *adj* peyorativo,-a, despectivo,-a.
Pekinese [piːkəˈniːz] 1 *adj* pequinés,-esa. – 2 *n* (*person*) pequinés,-esa. 3 (*dog*) (perro) pequinés *m*.
Peking [piːˈkɪŋ] *n* Pekín.
pelican [ˈpelɪkən] *n* pelícano.
 ■ **pelican crossing,** GB paso de peatones.
pellet [ˈpelɪt] 1 *n* (*small ball*) bolita. 2 (*piece of shot*) perdigón *m*.
pell-mell [pelˈmel] *adv* (*untidily*) desordenadamente, sin orden ni concierto; (*in a hurry*) precipitadamente, en tropel.
pelmet [ˈpelmɪt] *n* GB galería (de cortina).
pelt[1] [pelt] 1 *t* tirar, lanzar, arrojar: *they pelted him with eggs,* le tiraron huevos; *he was pelted with questions,* lo bombardearon a preguntas. – 2 *i* (*rain*) llover a cántaros (**down,** -). 3 (*run*) correr a toda prisa, correr a toda pastilla; (*move fast*) ir a toda máquina, ir como un bólido.
 ● **to pelt sb. with stones,** apedrear a algn.
pelt[2] [pelt] *n* (*skin*) piel *f*, pellejo.
pelvic [ˈpelvɪk] *adj* pélvico,-a.
pelvis [ˈpelvɪs] *n* pelvis *f*.
pen[1] [pen] 1 *n* (*gen*) pluma; (*ballpoint*) bolígrafo, boli *m*. – 2 *t* (*write - gen*) escribir; (*article*) redactar; (*verse*) componer.
 ● **to live by the pen,** ganarse la vida con la pluma. ‖ **to put pen to paper,** tomar la pluma, escribir.

■ **fountain pen,** pluma estilográfica, estilográfica. ‖ **felt-tip pen,** rotulador *m.* ‖ **pen name,** seudónimo.
▲ (*verbo*) *pt & pp* **penned,** *ger* **penning.**

pen² [pen] *n* (*for animals*) corral *m;* (*for sheep*) aprisco, redil *m.*
◆ **to pen in / pen up** *t sep* encerrar, acorralar.

pen³ [pen] *n* US *fam* (*penitentiary*) chirona, talego.

penal ['piːnəl] *adj* penal.
■ **penal code,** código penal. ‖ **penal offence,** infracción *f* penal, delito penal. ‖ **penal servitude,** GB trabajos *mpl* forzados.

penalize ['piːnəlaɪz] **1** *t* (*punish*) castigar, sancionar. **2** SP penalizar. **3** (*put at a disadvantage*) perjudicar.

penalty ['penəltɪ] **1** *n* (*gen*) pena, castigo; (*fine*) multa. **2** SP (*gen*) castigo (máximo); (*football*) penalti *m.* **3** (*disadvantage*) desventaja, inconveniente *m.*
● **to pay the penalty for sth.,** pagar las consecuencias de algo, cargar con las consecuencias de algo.
■ **death penalty,** pena de muerte. ‖ **penalty area,** SP área de penalti, área de castigo. ‖ **penalty clause,** JUR cláusula de penalización. ‖ **penalty kick,** SP penalti *m.*
▲ *pl* **penalties.**

penance ['penəns] *n* penitencia.
● **to do penance for sth.,** hacer penitencia por algo.

pence [pens] *npl* → **penny.**

penchant ['pɒnʃɒn] *n* inclinación *f* (**for,** por), afición *f* (**for,** por).

pencil ['pensəl] **1** *n* lápiz *m: write in pencil,* escribir con lápiz. – **2** *t* (*write*) escribir con lápiz; (*draw*) dibujar con lápiz.
◆ **to pencil in** *t sep* apuntar provisionalmente, anotar provisionalmente.
■ **eyebrow pencil,** lápiz *m* de cejas. ‖ **pencil case,** plumero, estuche *m* de lápices. ‖ **pencil drawing,** dibujo a lápiz. ‖ **pencil sharpener,** sacapuntas *m.* ‖ **pencil skirt,** falda tubo.
▲ (*verbo*) *pt & pp* **pencilled** (US **penciled**), *ger* **pencilling** (US **penciling**).

pendant ['pendənt] *n* colgante *m.*

pending ['pendɪŋ] **1** *adj* (*waiting to be decided or settled*) pendiente; (*imminent*) próximo,-a, inminente. – **2** *prep* (*until*) hasta; (*while awaiting*) en espera de.

pendulum ['pendjʊləm] *n* péndulo.

penetrate ['penɪtreɪt] **1** *t* (*gen*) penetrar en; (*clothing*) atravesar, traspasar; (*organization*) infiltrarse en. **2** (*see into*) penetrar (en), calar (en). **3** (*understand*) penetrar, entender. – **4** *i* (*gen*) penetrar (**into,** en), entrar (**into,** en); (*clothing*) atravesar (**through,** -). **5** (*sink in*) causar impresión, hacer mella en.

penetrating ['penɪtreɪtɪŋ] *adj* (*gen*) penetrante; (*mind*) penetrante, perspicaz; (*sound*) penetrante, agudo,-a.

penetration [penɪ'treɪʃən] **1** *n* (*gen*) penetración *f.* **2** (*insight*) penetración *f,* perspicacia, agudeza.

penfriend ['penfrend] *n* amigo,-a por correspondencia: *I've got a penfriend in Sweden,* me carteo con un amigo en Suecia.

penguin ['peŋgwɪn] *n* pingüino.

penicillin [penɪ'sɪlɪn] *n* penicilina.

peninsula [pə'nɪnsjʊlə] *n* península.
■ **the Iberian Peninsula,** la Península Ibérica.

peninsular [pə'nɪnsjʊləʳ] *adj* peninsular.
■ **the Peninsular War,** la Guerra de Independencia Española.

penis ['piːnɪs] *n* ANAT pene *m.*
▲ *pl* **penises** o **penes** ['piːniːz].

penitence ['penɪtəns] **1** *n* REL penitencia. **2** (*sorrow*) arrepentimiento.

penitent ['penɪtənt] **1** *adj* REL penitente. **2** (*sorry*) arrepentido,-a. – **3** *n* REL penitente *mf.*

penitentiary [penɪ'tenʃərɪ] *n* US penitenciaría, cárcel *f,* prisión *f,* penal *m.*
▲ *pl* **penitentiaries.**

penknife ['pennaɪf] *n* cortaplumas *m,* navaja.
▲ *pl* **penknives** ['pennaɪvz].

pennant ['penənt] **1** *n* (*gen*) banderín *m.* **2** MAR gallardete *m.*

penniless ['penɪləs] *adj* pobre, sin dinero.
● **to be penniless,** estar sin un céntimo, estar sin un duro.

Pennines ['penaɪnz] **the Pennines,** *n* los (montes) Peninos.

Pennsylvania [pensɪl'veɪnɪə] *n* Pensilvania.

penny ['penɪ] **1** *n* GB penique *m: a fifty pence piece,* una moneda de cincuenta peniques. **2** US centavo.
● **a penny for your thoughts,** ¿en qué estás pensando? ‖ **in for a penny, in for a pound,** de perdidos, al río. ‖ **the penny dropped,** caí (*cayó etc*) en la cuenta. ‖ **to be two a penny / be ten a penny,** haber a montones. ‖ **to cost a pretty penny,** costar un dineral. ‖ **not to have a penny to one's name,** estar sin un duro, no tener dónde caerse muerto,-a. ‖ **to spend a penny,** ir al servicio. ‖ **to turn up like a bad penny,** aparecer en todas partes.
▲ *pl* **pence.**

penny-pinching ['penɪpɪntʃɪŋ] *adj* tacaño,-a, cicatero,-a.

penpal ['penpæl] *n* US amigo,-a por correspondencia.

pension ['penʃən] *n* pensión *f.*
◆ **to pension off** *t sep* jubilar.
● **to be on a pension / draw a pension,** cobrar una pensión.
■ **pension fund,** fondo de pensiones. ‖ **pension plan / pension scheme,** plan *m* de jubilación. ‖ **retirement pension,** jubilación *f,* pensión *f.* ‖ **widow's pension,** pensión *f* de viudedad, viudedad *f.*

pensioner ['penʃənəʳ] *n* jubilado,-a, pensionista *mf.*

pensive ['pensɪv] *adj* (*thoughtful*) pensativo,-a, meditabundo,-a; (*melancholy*) melancólico,-a.

pensively ['pensɪvlɪ] *adv* (*thoughtfully*) con aire pensativo; (*sadly*) con aire melancólico.

pentagon ['pentəgən] *n* pentágono.
■ **the Pentagon,** US el Pentágono.

pentathlon [pen'tæθlən] *n* pentatlón *m.*

Pentecost ['pentɪkɒst] *n* Pentecostés *m.*

penthouse ['penthaʊs] *n* ático, sobreático.

pent-up [pent'ʌp] **1** *adj* (*confined*) encerrado,-a. **2** (*repressed - emotions*) contenido,-a, reprimido,-a.

penultimate [pɪ'nʌltɪmət] *adj* penúltimo,-a.

penury ['penjʊrɪ] *n* penuria, miseria, pobreza.
● **to live in penury,** vivir en la miseria.

peony ['piːənɪ] *n* BOT peonía.
▲ *pl* **peonies.**

people ['piːpəl] **1** *npl* (*gen*) gente *f,* personas *fpl: a lot of people,* mucha gente; *most people,* la mayoría de la gente; *over a hundred people,* más de cien personas; *people say that ...,* dicen que ..., se dice que ... **2** (*citizens*) ciudadanos *mpl;* (*inhabitants*) habitantes *mpl: power to the people!,* ¡poder para el pueblo! **3** (*family*) familia, gente *f.* – **4** *n* (*nation, race*) pueblo, nación *f.* – **5** *t* poblar.
■ **old people,** los viejos *mpl,* los ancianos *mpl,* la gente *f* mayor. ‖ **people's republic,** república popular. ‖ **the common people,** la gente *f* corriente. ‖ **young people,** los jóvenes *mpl,* la juventud *f,* la gente *f* joven.

pep [pep] *n fam* energía, vitalidad *f.*
◆ **to pep up** *t sep* (*gen*) animar; (*person*) dar ánimos a.
■ **pep pill,** estimulante *m.* ‖ **pep talk,** discurso enardecedor.
pepper ['pepəʳ] **1** *n* (*spice*) pimienta. **2** (*vegetable*) pimiento. – **3** *t* CULIN poner pimienta a, echar pimienta a.
◆ **to pepper with 1** *t sep* (*hit, pelt*) acribillar a. **2** *fig* (*intersperse*) salpicar de.
■ **pepper mill,** molinillo de pimienta. ‖ **pepper pot,** pimentero.
peppercorn ['pepəkɔːn] *n* grano de pimienta.
peppermint ['pepəmɪnt] **1** *n* BOT menta. **2** (*sweet*) caramelo de menta.
■ **peppermint tea,** infusión *f* de menta.
peppery ['pepərɪ] **1** *adj* CULIN (*taste*) a pimienta; (*spicy*) picante. **2** *fig* (*person*) colérico,-a, enojadizo,-a.
peptic ['peptɪk] *adj* MED péptico,-a.
■ **peptic ulcer,** úlcera estomacal.
per [pɜːʳ] *prep* por: *100 miles per hour,* 100 millas por hora; *it works out at 15 pounds per person,* sale a 15 libras por persona; *per day,* por día, al día.
● **as per,** de acuerdo con, según. ‖ **as per usual,** como de costumbre. ‖ **per annum,** por año, al año. ‖ **per cent,** por ciento: *100 per cent,* cien por cien.
perceive [pə'siːv] *t* (*see*) percibir, ver; (*notice*) notar; (*realize*) darse cuenta de.
percentage [pə'sentɪdʒ] *n* porcentaje *m.*
perceptible [pə'septəbəl] *adj* (*visible*) perceptible, visible; (*audible*) perceptible, audible; (*noticeable*) sensible, apreciable.
perceptibly [pə'septəblɪ] *adv* (*visibly*) perceptiblemente, visiblemente; (*noticeably*) sensiblemente, apreciablemente.
perception [pə'sepʃən] **1** *n* (*sense*) percepción *f.* **2** (*insight*) perspicacia, agudeza. **3** (*way of understanding*) idea.
perceptive [pə'septɪv] *adj* (*person*) perspicaz, agudo,-a.
perch[1] [pɜːtʃ] *n* (*fish*) perca.
▲ *pl* **perch** o **perches**.
perch[2] [pɜːtʃ] **1** *n* (*for bird*) percha. **2** (*high position*) posición *f* elevada, posición *f* privilegiada; (*pedestal*) pedestal *m.* – **3** *t* poner, colocar. – **4** *i* (*bird*) posarse (**on,** en); (*person*) sentarse (**on,** en).
● **to be perched,** estar encaramado,-a.
percolate ['pɜːkəleɪt] **1** *t* (*coffee*) hacer (en una cafetera eléctrica). – **2** *i* (*gen*) filtrarse; (*coffee*) hacerse. **3** (*news etc*) difundirse.
■ **percolated coffee,** café *m* hecho en una cafetera eléctrica.
percolator ['pɜːkəleɪtəʳ] *n* cafetera eléctrica.
percussion [pɜː'kʌʃən] *n* percusión *f.*
■ **percussion instrument,** instrumento de percusión.
percussionist [pe'kʌʃənɪst] *n* percusionista *nf.*
peregrine ['perɪgrɪn] **peregrine (falcon),** *n* ORN halcón *m* peregrino.
peremptory [pə'remptərɪ] *adj* (*person, manner*) autoritario,-a, imperioso,-a; (*command*) perentorio,-a, imperioso,-a.
perennial [pə'renɪəl] **1** *adj* (*plant*) perenne, vivaz. **2** (*problem*) perenne, perpetuo,-a, eterno,-a; (*subject*) eterno,-a, de siempre. – **3** *n* BOT planta perenne, planta vivaz.
perfect ['pɜːfɪkt] **1** *adj* (*gen*) perfecto,-a; (*behaviour, reputation*) intachable. **2** (*ideal*) perfecto,-a, ideal. **3** (*absolute, utter - fool*) perdido,-a, redomado,-a; (- *gentleman*) consumado; (- *waste of time*) auténtico,-a: *he's a perfect stranger to me,* me es totalmente desconocido. **4** LING perfecto,-a. – **5** *n* LING perfecto. – **6** *t* perfeccionar.

▲ (*verbo*) [pə'fekt].
perfection [pə'fekʃən] **1** *n* (*state, quality*) perfección *f.* **2** (*act*) perfeccionamiento.
● **to do sth. to perfection,** hacer algo a la perfección.
perfectionist [pə'fekʃənɪst] *n* perfeccionista *mf.*
perfectly ['pɜːfɪktlɪ] **1** *adv* (*exactly, faultlessly*) perfectamente, a la perfección. **2** (*absolutely*) completamente, totalmente: *that's perfectly obvious,* eso está clarísimo; *you know perfectly well that ...,* sabes perfectamente bien que ...
perfidious [pə'fɪdɪəs] *adj* pérfido,-a.
perfidy ['pɜːfɪdɪ] *n* perfidia.
perforate ['pɜːfəreɪt] *t* perforar.
perforation [pɜːfə'reɪʃən] **1** *n* MED perforación *f.* **2** (*on stamps etc*) perforado.
perform [pə'fɔːm] **1** *t* (*task*) ejecutar, llevar a cabo; (*function*) desempeñar, hacer, cumplir; (*experiment*) realizar; (*operation*) practicar; (*miracle*) hacer. **2** MUS THEAT (*piece of music*) interpretar, tocar; (*song*) cantar; (*play*) representar, dar; (*role*) interpretar, representar; (*sumersault, trick*) hacer, ejecutar. – **3** *i* MUS THEAT (*actor*) actuar; (*singer*) cantar; (*musician*) tocar, interpretar; (*dancer*) bailar; (*company*) dar una representación. **4** (*machine*) funcionar, marchar; (*car*) andar, ir; (*person*) trabajar.
performance [pə'fɔːməns] **1** *n* (*of task*) ejecución *f,* realización *f;* (*of function, duty*) ejercicio, desempeño. **2** (*session - at theatre*) representación *f,* función *f;* (- *at cinema*) función *f;* (- *of circus, show, etc*) número, espectáculo. **3** (*action - of song, of musician*) interpretación *f;* (- *of play*) representación *f;* (- *of actor*) interpretación *f,* actuación *f;* (- *of team*) actuación *f.* **4** (*of machine*) funcionamiento; (*of car*) prestaciones *fpl;* (*of worker*) rendimiento, desempeño. **5** (*fuss*) lío, follón *m.*
performer [pə'fɔːməʳ] *n* THEAT artista *mf,* actor *m,* actriz *f;* MUS intérprete *mf.*
performing arts [pəfɔːmɪŋ'ɑːts] *npl* artes *fpl* interpretativas.
perfume ['pɜːfjuːm] **1** *n* perfume *m.* – **2** *t* perfumar.
perfunctory [pə'fʌŋktərɪ] *adj* (*examination, inspection, search*) superficial, somero,-a; (*greeting*) mecánico,-a.
perhaps [pə'hæps] *adv* quizá, quizás, tal vez, a lo mejor: *perhaps, perhaps not,* puede que sí, puede que no; *perhaps so, perhaps not,* tal vez sí, tal vez no; *perhaps they've got lost,* quizá se hayan perdido; *perhaps he'll come later,* a lo mejor viene luego.
peril ['perəl] *n* (*danger*) peligro.
● **at one's own peril,** por su cuenta y riesgo.
perilous ['perɪləs] *adj* (*dangerous*) peligroso,-a; (*risky*) arriesgado,-a.
perilously ['perɪləslɪ] *adv* peligrosamente.
perimeter [pə'rɪmɪtəʳ] *n* perímetro.
period ['pɪərɪəd] **1** *n* (*length of time*) período, periodo: *he spends long periods abroad,* pasa largos períodos en el extranjero; *tests carried out during a six-month period,* pruebas realizadas durante un período de seis meses. **2** (*epoch*) época. **3** GEOL período. **4** EDUC (*lesson*) clase *f.* **5** (*menstruation*) regla, período. **6** US (*full stop*) punto. – **7** *adj* (*dress, furniture*) de época.
■ **free period,** EDUC hora libre. ‖ **period costume,** traje *m* de época. ‖ **period pains,** dolores *mpl* menstruales. ‖ **sunny periods,** intervalos *mpl* de sol. ‖ **the post-war period,** la posguerra.
periodic [pɪərɪ'ɒdɪk] *adj* periódico,-a.
■ **periodic table,** CHEM tabla periódica.
periodical [pɪərɪ'ɒdɪkəl] **1** *adj* periódico,-a. – **2** *n* publicación *f* periódica.

periodically [pɪərɪ'ɒdɪklɪ] adv periódicamente.
peripatetic [perɪpə'tetɪk] adj itinerante.
peripheral [pə'rɪfərəl] 1 adj (zone etc) periférico,-a. 2 (secondary) secundario,-a.
periphery [pə'rɪfərɪ] 1 n (of city) periferia. 2 (of society) margen m.
periscope ['perɪskəʊp] n periscopio.
perish ['perɪʃ] 1 i (die) perecer, fallecer. 2 (decay - food) estropearse; (- rubber) deteriorarse. – 3 t (rubber) deteriorar.
perishable ['perɪʃəbəl] 1 adj perecedero,-a. – 2 perishables, npl productos mpl perecederos.
perishing ['perɪʃɪŋ] it's perishing, adj GB fam hace un frío que pela.
peritonitis [perɪtə'naɪtəs] n MED peritonitis f.
periwinkle ['perɪwɪŋkəl] 1 n BOT vincapervinca. 2 ZOOL bígaro, caracol m de mar.
perjure ['pɜːdʒəʳ] to perjure os., i jurar en falso, perjurar.
perjurer ['pɜːdʒərəʳ] n perjuro,-a.
perjury ['pɜːdʒərɪ] n perjurio.
● to commit perjury, cometer perjurio, jurar en falso, perjurar.
perk [pɜːk] 1 n fam (benefit) beneficio, extra m; (money, goods) gajes mpl. – 2 t → **percolate**. – 3 i → **percolate**.
◆ to perk up 1 t sep animar, reanimar. – 2 i (person) animarse, reanimarse.
perky ['pɜːkɪ] adj animado,-a, alegre.
▲ comp perkier, superl perkiest.
perm [pɜːm] n fam (in hair) permanente f.
● to have a perm, hacerse la permanente. ‖ to have one's hair permed, hacerse la permanente. ‖ to perm sb.'s hair, hacer la permanente a algn.
permanence ['pɜːmənəns] n permanencia.
permanent ['pɜːmənənt] 1 adj (lasting - gen) permanente; (dye, ink) indeleble; (scar) imborrable; (damage) irreparable. 2 (job, address) fijo,-a.
■ permanent wave, permanente f.
permanently ['pɜːmənəntlɪ] adv (gen) permanentemente, de forma permanente; (damaged) irreparablemente; (disfigured, stained, etc) para siempre.
permanganate [pə'mæŋgəneɪt] n permanganato.
permeable ['pɜːmɪəbəl] adj permeable (to, a).
permeate ['pɜːmɪeɪt] 1 t (liquid) penetrar, calar; (smell, smoke) impregnar. 2 fig (mood, desire) extenderse por. – 3 i penetrar (through, a través de) (into, en).
permissible [pɜː'mɪsəbəl] adj (allowed) permisible, lícito,-a; (acceptable) aceptable.
permission [pə'mɪʃən] n (gen) permiso; (authorization) autorización f.
● to ask for permission to do sth., pedir permiso para hacer algo. ‖ to give sb. permission to do sth., dar a algn. permiso para hacer algo.
permissive [pə'mɪsɪv] adj permisivo,-a.
permit ['pɜːmɪt] 1 n (gen) permiso; (licence) permiso, licencia; (pass) pase m. – 2 t (gen) permitir; (authorize) autorizar: he was not permitted access to the meeting, no se le permitió la entrada a la reunión; smoking is not permitted, no se permite fumar; the girl's parents did not permit her to go out, los padres de la niña no le permitían salir. – 3 i permitir: weather permitting, si el tiempo lo permite.
■ residence permit, permiso de residencia. ‖ work permit, permiso de trabajo.
▲ (verbo) [pɜː'mɪt], pt & pp permitted, ger permitting.

permutation [pɜːmjʊ'teɪʃən] 1 n MATH permutación f. 2 GB fam (in football pools) combinación f.
pernicious [pɜː'nɪsəs] adj fml pernicioso,-a.
pernickety [pɜː'nɪkətɪ] adj fam (person) quisquilloso,-a; (job) delicado,-a.
peroxide [pə'rɒksaɪd] n peróxido.
perpendicular [pɜːpən'dɪkjʊləʳ] 1 adj MATH perpendicular (to, a). 2 (upright) vertical. – 3 n perpendicular f.
perpetrate ['pɜːpɪtreɪt] t fml perpetrar, cometer.
perpetrator ['pɜːpɪtreɪtəʳ] n autor,-ra.
perpetual [pə'petjʊəl] adj (permanent) perpetuo,-a, eterno,-a; (continual) continuo,-a, constante.
perpetually [pə'petjʊəlɪ] adv (permanently) perpetuamente; (continually) continuamente, constantemente.
perpetuate [pə'petjʊeɪt] t perpetuar.
perpetuity [pɜːpɪ'tjuːtɪ] n perpetuidad f.
● in perpetuity, a perpetuidad.
perplex [pə'pleks] t dejar perplejo,-a, desconcertar.
perplexed [pə'plekst] adj perplejo,-a, confuso,-a.
perplexing [pə'pleksɪŋ] adj desconcertante.
perplexity [pə'pleksɪtɪ] n perplejidad f.
pers ['pɜːsən, 'pɜːsənəl] 1 abbr (person) persona. 2 (personal) personal.
per se [pɜː'seɪ] adv en sí, de por sí.
persecute ['pɜːsɪkjuːt] t (for beliefs) perseguir; (hound, harass) atormentar, acosar.
persecution [pɜːsɪ'kjuːʃən] n persecución f.
■ persecution complex, manía persecutoria.
persecutor ['pɜːsɪkjuːtəʳ] n perseguidor,-ra.
perseverance [pɜːsɪ'vɪərəns] n perseverancia.
persevere [pɜːsɪ'vɪəʳ] i perseverar (at/in/with, en).
persevering [pɜːsɪ'vɪərɪŋ] adj perseverante.
Persia ['pɜːʒə] n Persia.
Persian ['pɜːʒən] 1 adj persa. – 2 n (person) persa mf. 3 (language) persa m.
persist [pə'sɪst] 1 i (person) persistir (in, en). 2 (pain, loyalty, belief) persistir; (rain) continuar.
● to persist in doing sth., insistir en hacer algo, empeñarse en hacer algo.
persistence [pə'sɪstəns] 1 n (continuation) persistencia. 2 (determination, insistence) perseverancia, empeño.
persistent [pə'sɪstənt] 1 adj (person) persistente, insistente. 2 (cough, pain, fog) persistente; (rain) continuo,-a, persistente; (denials, rumours, warnings) continuo,-a, constante, repetido,-a.
person ['pɜːsən] 1 n (gen) persona: who was the first person to fly a plane?, ¿quién fue la primera persona que pilotó un avión?; he's a really nice person, es una persona muy simpática; she was murdered by a person or persons unknown, fue asesinada por una persona o personas no identificadas. 2 LING persona.
● in person, en persona, personalmente. ‖ person to person, personalmente. ‖ to have on one's person / have about one's person, llevar encima.
▲ El plural más usual es people, pero persons se emplea en el lenguaje jurídico.
persona [pə'səʊnə] n (character) personaje m.
personable ['pɜːsənəbəl] adj (good looking) bien parecido,-a; (pleasant) amable, afable.
personage ['pɜːsənɪdʒ] n fml personaje m.
personal ['pɜːsənəl] 1 adj (private) personal, privado,-a: my personal life, mi vida privada; for personal reasons, por motivos personales; personal call, llamada particular. 2 (own) particular, personal: she's got a personal trainer, tiene un entrenador particular. 3 (individual)

personal: *it's a personal opinion,* es una opinión personal. **4** (*physical - appearance*) personal; (*hygiene*) íntimo,-a, personal. **5** (*in person*) en persona: *the actor made a personal appearance,* el actor apareció en persona; *the Prime Minister made a personal visit,* el Primer Ministro realizó una visita de carácter privado; *I'll give it my personal attention,* me encargaré de ello personalmente. **6** (*rude*) ofensivo,-a.
● **to get personal,** hacer alusiones personales.
■ **personal assistant,** secretario,-a personal. ‖ **personal best,** SP mejor marca. ‖ **personal column,** sección *f* de anuncios *mpl* personales. ‖ **personal computer,** ordenador *m* personal. ‖ **personal effects,** efectos *mpl* personales. ‖ **personal pronoun,** pronombre *m* personal. ‖ **personal property,** propiedad *f* privada. ‖ **personal stereo,** walkman *m*.

personality [pɜːsə'nælɪtɪ] **1** *n* (*nature*) personalidad *f*. **2** (*famous person*) personaje *m*.
▲ *pl* **personalities.**

personalize ['pɜːsənəlaɪz] *t* personalizar.

personally ['pɜːsənəlɪ] **1** *adv* (*in person*) personalmente, en persona. **2** (*for my part*) personalmente. **3** (*as a person*) como persona.
● **to take sth. personally,** ofenderse.

personification [pɜːsɒnɪfɪ'keɪʃən] *n* personificación *f*: *she's the personification of friendliness,* es la simpatía personificada.

personify [pɜː'sɒnɪfaɪ] *t* personificar.
▲ (*verbo*) *pt* & *pp* **personified,** *ger* **personifying.**

personnel [pɜːsə'nel] *n* personal *m*.
■ **personnel department,** departamento de personal, sección *f* de personal. ‖ **personnel manager,** jefe,-a de personal.

person-to-person ['pɜːsəntə'pɜːsən] *adj* (*call*) de persona a persona.

perspective [pə'spektɪv] **1** *n* ART perspectiva: *it's out of perspective,* no está en perspectiva. **2** *fig* (*view, angle*) perspectiva.
● **to get/keep things in perspective,** tratar de ver las cosas objetivamente, tratar de ver las cosas con cierta perspectiva.

Perspex ['pɜːspeks] *n* plexiglás *m*.

perspicacious [pɜːspɪ'keɪʃəs] *adj fml* perspicaz.

perspicacity [pɜːspɪ'kæsɪtɪ] *n fml* perspicacia.

perspiration [pɜːspɪ'reɪʃən] *n* transpiración *f,* sudor *m*.

perspire [pə'spaɪəʳ] *i* transpirar, sudar.

persuade [pə'sweɪd] *t* persuadir, convencer: *she's easily persuaded,* se deja convencer fácilmente.
● **to persuade sb. to do sth.,** convencer a algn. para que haga algo. ‖ **to persuade sb. not to do sth.,** disuadir a algn. de hacer algo. ‖ **to persuade sb. that ...,** convencer a algn. de que ...

persuasion [pə'sweɪʒən] **1** *n* (*act*) persuasión *f*: *I didn't need much persuasion to go out with them,* no hubo que insistirme mucho para que saliera con ellos. **2** (*ability*) persuasiva. **3** REL (*belief*) creencia.
● **to use persuasion on sb.,** persuadir a algn.
■ **powers of persuasion,** poder *m* de persuasión.

persuasive [pə'sweɪsɪv] *adj* (*person, manner*) persuasivo,-a; (*argument, excuse*) convincente.

persuasively [pə'sweɪsɪvlɪ] *adv* de modo persuasivo.

pert [pɜːt] **1** *adj* US (*hat, dress*) coqueto,-a. **2** (*cheeky*) fresco,-a; (*girl*) pizpireta.

pertain [pɜː'teɪn] **1** *i fml* (*connected with*) estar relacionado,-a (**to,** con). **2** JUR (*belong to*) pertenecer (**to,** a).

pertinacious [pɜːtɪ'neɪʃəs] *adj fml* pertinaz.

pertinence ['pɜːtɪnəns] *n fml* pertinencia.

pertinent ['pɜːtɪnənt] *adj fml* pertinente (**to,** a).
● **to be pertinent to sth.,** guardar relación con algo, estar relacionado,-a con algo.

perturb [pə'tɜːb] *t* perturbar, inquietar.

perturbing [pə'tɜːbɪŋ] *adj* inquietante, perturbador,-ra.

Peru [pə'ruː] *n* Perú.

perusal [pə'ruːzəl] *n* (*careful reading*) lectura detenida.

peruse [pə'ruːz] **1** *t* (*read carefully*) leer detenidamente. **2** (*browse*) leer por encima.

Peruvian [pə'ruːvɪən] **1** *adj* peruano,-a. – **2** *n* (*person*) peruano,-a.

pervade [pɜː'veɪd] *t* (*smell*) penetrar,; (*idea, feeling, mood*) extenderse, dominar.

pervasive [pɜː'veɪsɪv] *adj* (*smell*) penetrante; (*influence, mood*) extendido,-a, dominante.

perverse [pə'vɜːs] **1** *adj* (*delight, desire, pleasure, etc*) perverso,-a, malsano,-a. **2** (*person - stubborn*) terco,-a, obstinado,-a; (*contrary*) puñetero,-a.

perversion [pə'vɜːʃən] **1** *n* (*sexual*) perversión *f*. **2** (*distortion*) tergiversación *f,* distorsión *f*.

perversity [pə'vɜːsɪtɪ] *n* (*wickedness*) perversidad *f*; (*stubbornness*) terquedad *f,* obstinación *f* malsana.
▲ *pl* **perversities.**

pervert ['pɜːvɜːt] **1** *n* (*sexual*) pervertido,-a. – **2** *t* (*corrupt*) pervertir. **3** (*truth, justice*) tergiversar, distorsionar.
▲ (*verbo*) [pə'vɜːt].

pessimism ['pesɪmɪzəm] *n* pesimismo.

pessimist ['pesɪmɪst] *n* pesimista *mf*.

pessimistic [pesɪ'mɪstɪk] *adj* pesimista.
● **to be pessimistic about sth.,** ser pesimista respecto a algo.

pest [pest] **1** *n* ZOOL insecto nocivo, animal *m* nocivo; AGR plaga. **2** *fam* (*person*) pelma *mf,* pesado,-a; (*thing*) lata, rollo.
■ **pest control,** (*of insects*) desinsectación *f*; (*of rats*) desratización *f*.

pester ['pestəʳ] *t* molestar.
● **to pester sb. for sth.,** dar la lata a algn. para algo. ‖ **to pester sb. to do sth.,** dar la lata a algn. para que haga algo.

pesticide ['pestɪsaɪd] *n* pesticida.

pestilence ['pestɪləns] *n arch* pestilencia.

pestilent ['pestɪlənt] **1** *adj* (*of pestilence*) mortal. **2** *fam* (*irritating*) molesto,-a, latoso,-a, pesado,-a.

pestle ['pesəl] *n* mano *f* (de mortero), maja.

pet [pet] **1** *n* (*tame animal*) animal *m* de compañía, mascota. – **2** *adj* (*kind person*) sol, cielo; (*term of affection*) cariño, cielo. **3** (*tame*) domesticado,-a. **4** (*favourite - theory, subject, etc*) preferido,-a, favorito,-a. – **5** *t* (*animal*) acariciar. – **6** *i fam* tocarse y besuquearse.
■ **pet hate:** *politics is her pet hate,* lo que más odia es la política. ‖ **pet name,** nombre *m* cariñoso. ‖ **pet shop,** tienda de animales. ‖ **teacher's pet,** enchufado,-a.
▲ *pt* & *pp* **petted,** *ger* **petting.**

petal ['petəl] *n* pétalo.

peter out [piːtər'aʊt] *i* (*supplies*) acabarse, agotarse; (*enthusiasm, interest*) decaer, irse apagando; (*track, path*) perderse; (*engine*) pararse.

petite [pə'tiːt] *adj* (*woman*) menuda, chiquita.

petition [pə'tɪʃən] **1** *n* petición *f,* solicitud *f*: *I signed a petition against experiments on live animals,* firmé una petición en contra de la experimentación con seres vivos. **2** JUR demanda. – **3** *t* presentar una petición a, elevar una petición a, presentar una solicitud a. – **4** *i* solicitar (**for,** -).

● **to petition for divorce,** presentar una demanda de divorcio.

petrel ['petrəl] *n* ORN paíño, petrel *m*.

petrify ['petrɪfaɪ] **1** *t fam* (*terrify*) petrificar, aterrorizar. **2** GEOL petrificar. **– 3** *i* GEOL petrificarse.

● **to be petrified,** quedarse de piedra.

▲ (*verbo*) *pt* & *pp* **petrified,** *ger* **petrifying.**

petrochemical [petrəʊˈkemɪkəl] **1** *adj* petroquímico,-a. **– 2** *n* producto petroquímico.

petrodollar ['petrəʊdɒləʳ] *n* petrodólar *m*.

petrol ['petrəl] *n* gasolina.

■ **petrol bomb,** cóctel *m* molotov. || **petrol can,** bidón *m* de gasolina. || **petrol pump,** surtidor *m* de gasolina. || **petrol station,** gasolinera. || **petrol tank,** depósito de gasolina.

petroleum [pəˈtrəʊlɪəm] *n* petróleo.

■ **petroleum jelly,** vaselina.

petticoat ['petɪkəʊt] *n* (*underskirt*) enaguas *fpl*; (*slip*) enagua, combinación *f*.

pettiness ['petɪnəs] *n* mezquindad *f*, pobreza *f* de espíritu.

petty ['petɪ] **1** *adj* (*trivial*) insignificante, nimio,-a, sin importancia. **2** (*mean*) mezquino,-a.

■ **petty cash,** dinero para gastos *mpl* menores. || **petty officer,** suboficial *m* de marina. || **petty theft,** hurto. || **petty thief,** ladronzuelo,-a.

▲ *comp* **pettier,** *superl* **pettiest.**

petulance ['petjʊləns] *n* mal humor *m*, mal genio.

petulant ['petjʊlənt] *adj* malhumorado,-a.

petunia [pɪˈtjuːnɪə] *n* petunia.

pew [pjuː] *n* banco de iglesia.

● **take a pew!,** ¡siéntate!

pewter ['pjuːtəʳ] *n* peltre *m*.

phalanx ['fælæŋks] *n* falange *f*.

phallic ['fælɪk] *adj* fálico,-a.

phallus ['fæləs] *n* falo.

phantom ['fæntəm] **1** *n* (*ghost*) fantasma *m*. **2** (*illusion*) fantasía. **– 3** *adj* (*ghostly*) fantasmal. **4** (*imaginary*) ilusorio,-a, imaginario,-a.

Pharaoh ['feərəʊ] *n* faraón *m*.

pharmaceutical [fɑːməˈsjuːtɪkəl] *adj* farmacéutico,-a.

pharmachology [fɑːməˈkɒlədʒɪ] *n* farmacología.

pharmacist ['fɑːməsɪst] *n* farmacéutico,-a.

pharmacy ['fɑːməsɪ] *n* farmacia.

▲ *pl* **pharmacies.**

pharyngitis [færɪnˈdʒaɪtɪs] *n* faringitis *f*.

pharynx ['færɪŋks] *n* faringe *f*.

phase [feɪz] **1** *n* (*gen*) fase *f*; (*stage*) etapa: *the phases of the moon,* las fases de la luna; *it's just a phase she's going through,* ya se le pasará. **– 2** *t* escalonar, realizar por etapas.

◆ **to phase in** *t sep* introducir paulatinamente, introducir progresivamente. || **to phase out** *t sep* retirar paulatinamente, retirar progresivamente.

● **to be in phase,** estar sincronizado,-a. || **to be out of phase,** estar desfasado,-a.

phased [feɪzd] *adj* (*gradual*) progresivo,-a, gradual.

PhD ['piːˈeɪtʃˈdiː] *abbr* (*Doctor of Philosophy - person*) doctor,-ra (*en cualquier especialidad académica*); (*- degree*) doctorado.

pheasant ['fezənt] *n* faisán *m*.

phenomenal [fɪˈnɒmɪnəl] *adj* fenomenal, extraordinario,-a.

phenomenon [fɪˈnɒmɪnən] *n* fenómeno.

▲ *pl* **phenomenons** *o* **phenomena** [fɪˈnɒmɪnə].

phew [fjuː] *interj* ¡uf!

phial [faɪəl] *n* frasco.

Philadelphia [fɪləˈdelfɪə] *n* Filadelfia.

philanderer [fɪˈlændərəʳ] *n* tenorio.

philanthropic [fɪlənˈθrɒpɪk] *adj* filantrópico,-a.

philanthropist [fɪˈlænθrəpɪst] *n* filántropo,-a.

philanthropy [fɪˈlænθrəpɪ] *n* filantropía.

philately [fɪˈlætəlɪ] *n* filatelia.

philharmonic [fɪlɑːˈmɒnɪk] *adj* filarmónico,-a.

Philippine ['fɪlɪpiːn] *adj* filipino,-a.

■ **Philippine Sea,** Mar *m* de Filipinas.

Philippines ['fɪlɪpiːnz] *n* Filipinas.

Philistine ['fɪlɪstaɪn] **1** *adj* filisteo,-a. **– 2** *n* filisteo,-a.

philologist [fɪˈlɒlədʒɪst] *n* filólogo,-a.

philology [fɪˈlɒlədʒɪ] *n* filología.

philosopher [fɪˈlɒsəfəʳ] *n* filósofo,-a.

philosophic [fɪləˈsɒfɪk] *adj* → **philosophical.**

philosophical [fɪləˈsɒfɪkəl] **1** *adj* (*study, work, argument*) filosófico,-a. **2** (*person, attitude*) resignado,-a.

● **to be philosophical about sth.,** tomarse algo con filosofía.

philosophize [fɪˈlɒsəfaɪz] *i* filosofar.

philosophy [fɪˈlɒsəfɪ] *n* filosofía.

phlegm [flem] *n* flema.

phlegmatic [flegˈmætɪk] *adj* flemático,-a.

phobia ['fəʊbɪə] *n* fobia.

Phoenicia [fəˈnɪʃə] *n* Fenicia.

Phoenician [fəˈnɪʃən] **1** *adj* fenicio,-a. **– 2** *n* (*person*) fenicio,-a. **3** (*language*) fenicio.

phoenix ['fiːnɪks] *n* fénix *m*.

phone [fəʊn] **1** *n fam* teléfono. **– 2** *t* llamar (por teléfono), telefonear. **– 3** *i* llamar (por teléfono), telefonear.

▲ *Véase también* **telephone.**

phonecard ['fəʊnkɑːd] *n* tarjeta telefónica.

phone-in ['fəʊnɪn] *n* RAD TV programa *m* en el que el público participa activamente por teléfono.

phoneme ['fəʊniːm] *n* fonema *m*.

phonetic [fəˈnetɪk] *adj* fonético,-a.

phonetics [fəˈnetɪks] *n* fonética.

phoney ['fəʊnɪ] **1** *adj fam* (*gen*) falso,-a; (*accent*) fingido,-a. **– 2** *n fam* (*person*) farsante *mf*; (*thing*) falsificación *f*, imitación *f*.

▲ *comp* **phonier,** *superl* **phoniest.**

phonology [fəˈnɒlədʒɪ] *n* fonología.

phony ['fəʊnɪ] *adj* → **phoney.**

▲ *comp* **phonier,** *superl* **phoniest.**

phosphate ['fɒsfeɪt] *n* fosfato.

phosphorescent [fɒsfəˈresənt] *adj* fosforescente.

phosphorus ['fɒsfərəs] *n* fósforo.

photo ['fəʊtəʊ] *n fam* foto *f*.

photocopier ['fəʊtəʊkɒpɪəʳ] *n* fotocopiadora.

photocopy ['fəʊtəʊkɒpɪ] **1** *n* fotocopia *f*. **– 2** *t* fotocopiar.

▲ (*sustantivo*) *pl* **photocopies;** (*verbo*) *pt* & *pp* **photocopied,** *ger* **photocopying.**

photoelectric [fəʊtəʊɪˈlektrɪk] *adj* fotoeléctrico,-a.

■ **photoelectric cell,** célula fotoeléctrica, fotocélula.

photogenic [fəʊtəʊˈdʒenɪk] *adj* fotogénico,-a.

photograph ['fəʊtəgrɑːf] **1** *n* fotografía, foto *f*: *colour fotograph,* fotografía en color. **– 2** *t* fotografiar.

● **to have one's photograph taken,** sacarse una fotografía. || **to photograph well/badly,** salir bien/mal en las fotografías. || **to take a photograph of sth./sb.,** fotografiar algo/a algn., hacer/sacar/tomar una fotografía de algo/algn.

■ **photograph album,** álbum *m* de fotografías.
photographer [fə'tɒɡrəfə'] *n* fotógrafo,-a.
photographic [fəʊtə'ɡræfɪk] *adj* fotográfico,-a.
photography [fə'tɒɡrəfɪ] *n* fotografía.
photosensitive [fəʊtəʊ'sensɪtɪv] *adj* fotosensible.
photostat ['fəʊtəʊstæt] **1** *n* fotocopia. – **2** *t* fotocopiar.
▲ (*verbo*) *pt & pp* **photostatted** *o* **photostated,** *ger* **photostatting** *o* **photostating.**
photosynthesis [fəʊtəʊ'sɪnθəsɪs] *n* fotosíntesis *f*.
phrasal verb [freɪzəl'vɜːb] *n* verbo compuesto.
phrase [freɪz] **1** *n* LING frase *f*, locución *f*. **2** (*expression*) frase *f*, expresión *f*; (*idiom*) modismo. **3** MUS frase *f*. – **4** *t* (*express*) expresar. **5** MUS frasear.
■ **phrase book,** guía de conversación para el viajero.
phraseology [freɪzɪ'ɒlədʒɪ] *n* fraseología.
phrasing ['freɪzɪŋ] *n* MUS fraseo.
phrenology [frə'nɒlədʒɪ] *n* frenología.
Phrygia ['frɪdʒɪə] *n* Frigia.
Phrygian ['frɪdʒɪən] **1** *adj* frigio,-a. – **2** *n* (*person*) frigio,-a. **3** (*language*) frigio.
physical ['fɪzɪkəl] **1** *adj* (*of the body*) físico,-a. **2** (*material - world*) material. **3** (*of physics*) físico,-a. **4** *fam euph* (*rough*) duro,-a: *it was a very physical game,* fue un partido muy duro. – **5** *n* (*medical examination*) reconocimiento médico.
■ **physical chemistry,** fisicoquímica. ‖ **physical education,** educación *f* física. ‖ **physical examination,** reconocimiento médico. ‖ **physical geography,** geografía física. ‖ **physical jerks,** GB ejercicios *mpl* físicos.
physically ['fɪzɪklɪ] **1** *adv* (*bodily*) físicamente. **2** (*of nature*) materialmente.
● **to be physically disabled / be physically handicapped,** ser minusválido,-a. ‖ **to be physically fit,** estar en forma.
physician [fɪ'zɪʃən] *n* médico,-a.
physicist ['fɪzɪsɪst] *n* físico,-a.
physics ['fɪzɪks] *n* física.
physiological [fɪzɪə'lɒdʒɪkəl] *adj* fisiológico,-a.
physiology [fɪzɪ'ɒlədʒɪ] *n* fisiología.
physiotherapist [fɪzɪəʊ'θerəpɪst] *n* fisioterapeuta *mf*.
physiotherapy [fɪzɪəʊ'θerəpɪ] *n* fisioterapia.
physique [fɪ'ziːk] *n* físico.
pi [paɪ] *n* MATH pi *f*.
pianist ['pɪənɪst] *n* pianista *mf*.
piano [pɪ'ænəʊ] **1** *n* piano. – **2** *adv* piano.
● **to play the piano,** tocar el piano.
■ **grand piano,** piano de cola. ‖ **piano accordion,** acordeón *m* piano. ‖ **piano stool,** taburete *m* de piano.
▲ (*sustantivo*) *pl* **pianos**; (*adverbio*) ['pjɑːnəʊ].
piccolo ['pɪkələʊ] *n* flautín *m*.
▲ *pl* **piccolos**.
pick[1] [pɪk] **1** *n* (*tool*) pico, piqueta. **2** (*plectrum*) púa, plectro.
pick[2] [pɪk] **1** *n* (*choice*) elección *f*, selección *f*: *here's my pick of this month's videos,* he aquí mi selección personal de los vídeos del mes; *take your pick,* elige el que quieras, escoge el que quieras. – **2** *t* (*choose - gen*) elegir, escoger; (*team*) seleccionar. **3** (*flowers, fruit, cotton, etc*) coger, recoger. **4** (*remove pieces from - gen*) escarbar, hurgar; (*spots*) tocarse. **5** (*remove from - hair etc*) quitar. **6** (*open - lock*) forzar, abrir con una ganzúa. **7** US (*pluck - guitar etc*) puntear. **8** (*of birds*) picotear.
◆ **to pick at** *t insep* (*gen*) tocar; (*food*) comer sin ganas. ‖ **to pick off** *t sep* (*shoot*) matar uno a uno. ‖ **to pick on** *t insep* (*victimize*) meterse con; (*choose for task*) elegir, escoger. ‖ **to pick out 1** *t sep* (*choose*) elegir, escoger. **2** (*see,*

discern) distinguir; (*recognize*) reconocer. **3** MUS tocar de oído. ‖ **to pick up 1** *t sep* (*lift*) levantar; (*from floor*) recoger; (*take*) coger; (*stitch*) coger; (*telephone*) descolgar: *don't forget to pick up all your litter,* no os olvidéis de recoger toda la basura; *she picked up the child and gave her a cuddle,* cogió a la niña y la abrazó. **2** (*learn - language*) aprender; (*- habit*) adquirir, coger; (*- news, gossip*) descubrir, enterarse de: *he went to London and picked up English in no time,* se fue a Londres y aprendió inglés enseguida. **3** (*illness, cold*) pescar, pillar. **4** (*acquire, get*) conseguir, encontrar. **5** (*collect - person*) recoger, pasar a buscar; (*- hitchhiker*) coger; (*- thing*) recoger: *I'll pick you up at 9.00 pm,* te vendré a buscar a las nueve. **6** *fam* (*man, woman*) ligar con, ligarse. **7** (*arrest*) detener. **8** (*on radio*) captar, recibir. **9** (*resume - conversation*) reanudar. **10** (*reprimand*) reprender (**for,** por); (*correct*) corregir; (*notice*) darse cuenta de. – **11** *i* (*improve - health, weather, acting*) mejorar; (*economy, business*) reputarse; (*prices*) subir. **12** (*resume*) seguir, continuar. ‖ **to pick up on** *t sep* (*news*) hacer reseña de; (*point*) volver a; (*mistake*) señalar.
● **the pick of,** lo mejor de. ‖ **to pick a fight with sb.,** buscar camorra con algn. ‖ **to pick a hole in sth.,** agujerear algo. ‖ **to pick and choose,** ser muy exigente. ‖ **to pick holes in sth.,** *fig* encontrar defectos en algo. ‖ **to pick one's nose,** hurgarse la nariz. ‖ **to pick one's teeth,** mondarse los dientes, escarbarse los dientes. ‖ **to pick os. up,** (*stand up*) levantarse, ponerse de pie; (*after illness*) reponerse. ‖ **to pick sb.'s brains,** explotar los conocimientos de algn. ‖ **to pick sb.'s pocket,** robar algo del bolsillo de algn. ‖ **to pick a winner,** (*horse*) pronosticar el ganador; (*choose well*) elegir bien, escoger bien. ‖ **to pick up speed,** coger velocidad, acelerar la marcha. ‖ **to pick up the bill,** pagar la cuenta.
■ **the pick of the bunch,** el/la mejor de todos,-as.
pickax ['pɪkæks] *n* US → **pickaxe.**
pickaxe ['pɪkæks] *n* GB pico, piqueta.
picker ['pɪkə'] *n* recolector,-ra.
picket ['pɪkɪt] **1** *n* IND (*group*) piquete *m*; (*individual*) miembro de un piquete. **2** MIL piquete *m*. **3** (*stick*) estaca. – **4** *t* (*factory etc*) formar un piquete frente a. – **5** *i* formar parte de un piquete.
■ **picket fence,** vallado. ‖ **picket line,** piquete *m*.
pickings ['pɪkɪŋz] **1** *npl* (*leftovers*) restos *mpl*, sobras *fpl*. **2** (*profits*) ganancias *fpl*.
pickle ['pɪkəl] **1** *t* encurtir, conservar en vinagre. – **2** *n* CULIN (*food*) conserva en vinagre. – **3 pickles,** *npl* (*vegetables*) encurtidos *mpl*.
● **to be in a pickle,** estar en un apuro, estar metido,-a en un berenjenal.
pickled ['pɪkəld] **1** *adj* (*food*) en vinagre, encurtido,-a. **2** *fam* (*drunk*) borracho,-a.
picklock ['pɪklɒk] *n* ganzúa.
pick-me-up ['pɪkmiːʌp] *n* tónico, reconstituyente *m*.
pickpocket ['pɪkpɒkɪt] *n* carterista *mf*, ratero,-a.
pick-up ['pɪkʌp] **1** *n* (*on record player*) brazo (del tocadiscos), fonocaptor *m*. **2** *fam* (*person*) ligue *m*.
■ **pick-up point,** punto de recogida. ‖ **pick-up truck,** furgoneta, camioneta.
picnic ['pɪknɪk] **1** *n* picnic *m*. – **2** *i* (*go on a picnic*) ir de picnic; (*eat*) hacer un picnic.
● **to be no picnic,** no ser nada fácil. ‖ **to go on a picnic / go for a picnic,** ir de picnic.
■ **picnic site / picnic spot,** zona para picnics, merendero.
picnicker ['pɪknɪkə'] *n* excursionista *mf*.
Pict [pɪkt] *n* picto,-a.

Pictish ['pɪktɪʃ] **1** *adj* picto,-a. – **2** *n* picto.

pictorial [pɪk'tɔːrɪəl] **1** *adj* (*magazine*) ilustrado,-a; (*record, account*) en imágenes. **2** ART pictórico,-a.

picture ['pɪktʃəˈ] **1** *n* (*painting*) pintura, cuadro; (*portrait*) retrato; (*drawing*) dibujo, grabado; (*illustration*) ilustración *f*, lámina; (*photograph*) fotografía, foto *f*: *she drew a picture of the church*, hizo un dibujo de la iglesia; *he painted her picture*, la retrató; *I took a picture of them*, les saqué una foto. **2** (*account, description*) descripción *f*; (*mental picture*) imagen *f*, idea, impresión *f*. **3** TV (*quality of image*) imagen *f*. **4** GB (*film*) película. – **5** *t* (*imagine*) imaginarse, verse: *I can't picture them married*, no me los imagino casados. **6** (*paint*) pintar; (*draw*) dibujar. – **7 the pictures,** *npl* GB el cine: *we went to the pictures*, fuimos al cine.

● **to be a picture of health,** rebosar salud. ‖ **to be (as pretty as) a picture,** ser precioso,-a. ‖ **to be pictured,** (*in press*) aparecer en la foto. ‖ **to get the picture,** entender, enterarse. ‖ **to put sb. in the picture,** poner a algn. al corriente.

■ **picture book,** libro ilustrado. ‖ **picture frame,** marco. ‖ **picture postcard,** tarjeta postal. ‖ **picture window,** ventanal *m*.

picturesque [pɪktʃə'resk] *adj* pintoresco,-a.

piddling ['pɪdəlɪŋ] *adj fam* (*amount*) insignificante; (*matter*) de poca monta.

pidgin ['pɪdʒɪn] *n* lengua híbrida utilizada como lengua franca comercial.

pie [paɪ] *n* CULIN (*sweet*) pastel *m*, tarta; (*savoury*) pastel *m*, empanada.

● **pie in the sky,** pura fantasía, castillos en el aire.
■ **pie chart,** gráfico circular, gráfica circular.

piebald ['paɪbɔːld] **1** *adj* picazo. – **2** *n* picazo, caballo picazo.

piece [piːs] **1** *n* (*bit – large*) trozo, pedazo; (*small*) cacho; (*of broken glass*) fragmento. **2** (*part, component*) pieza, parte *f*: *a thirty-piece dinner service*, una vajilla de treinta piezas; *a three-piece suite*, un tresillo. **3** (*coin*) moneda. **4** (*in board games*) ficha. **5** ART MUS pieza: *a 30-piece orchestra*, una orquesta de 30 músicos. **6** (*in newspaper*) artículo. **7** (*item, example of*) pieza: *a piece of advice*, un consejo; *a piece of chalk*, una tiza; *a piece of clothing*, una prenda de vestir; *a piece of furniture*, un mueble; *a piece of information*, una información; *a piece of jewellery*, una joya, una alhaja; *a piece of land*, un terreno, una parcela; *a piece of luck*, un golpe de suerte; *a piece of luggage*, un bulto; *a piece of news*, una noticia; *a piece of paper*, un papel; *a piece of work*, un trabajo.

◆ **to piece together** *t sep* (*facts, events*) reconstruir; (*torn letter etc*) recomponer; (*jigsaw*) hacer.
● **in one piece,** (*unharmed*) sano,-a y salvo,-a. ‖ **to be a piece of cake,** ser pan comido. ‖ **to be in pieces,** (*broken*) estar hecho,-a pedazos; (*dismantled*) estar desmontado,-a. ‖ **to break sth. in pieces,** hacer algo pedazos. ‖ **to fall to pieces,** hacerse pedazos. ‖ **to give sb. a piece of one's mind,** decirle cuatro verdades a algn. ‖ **to go to pieces,** (*break down*) perder el control; (*crack up*) quedarse deshecho,-a, venirse abajo. ‖ **to pull sth./sb. to pieces,** destrozar algo/a algn., criticar duramente algo/a algn., hacer trizas algo/a algn. ‖ **to pick up the pieces,** volver a empezar, rehacer su vida. ‖ **to say one's piece,** decir su parte. ‖ **to take sth. to pieces,** desmontar algo.

piecemeal ['piːsmiːl] **1** *adv* (*gradually*) poco a poco, por etapas; (*unsystematically*) de manera poco sistemática. – **2** *adj* (*gradual*) gradual; (*unsystematic*) poco sistemático,-a.

piecework ['piːswɜːk] *n* trabajo a destajo.

● **to be on piecework / do piecework,** trabajar a destajo.

pieceworker ['piːswɜːkəˈ] *n* trabajador,-ra a destajo.

pied [paɪd] *adj* de varios colores.

pier [pɪəˈ] **1** *n* (*landing place*) muelle *m*, embarcadero. **2** (*with amusements etc*) paseo sobre un muelle con atracciones, chiringuitos, etc. **3** ARCH (*pillar*) pilar *m*, estribo.

pierce [pɪəs] **1** *t* (*make hole in*) perforar, agujerear; (*go through*) atravesar, traspasar. **2** (*of light, sound*) penetrar, traspasar.

● **to have one's ears pierced,** hacerse agujeros en las orejas.

piercing ['pɪəsɪŋ] *adj* (*sound*) agudo,-a; (*scream*) desgarrador,-ra; (*look*) penetrante; (*wind*) cortante.

piety ['paɪətɪ] *n* piedad *f*.

pig [pɪg] **1** *n* ZOOL cerdo, puerco, marrano. **2** *pej* (*ill-mannered person*) cerdo, puerco, cochino; (*glutton*) glotón,-ona, tragón,-ona, comilón,-ona. **3** (*difficult thing*) mierda: *a pig of a day*, una mierda de día. **4** *sl* (*policeman*) madero. – **5 the pigs,** *npl sl* la pasma *f sing*, la bofia *f sing*.

◆ **to pig out** *i* US pegarse un atracón (**on,** de).
● **pigs might fly,** cuando las ranas críen pelo. ‖ **to buy a pig in a poke,** darle a algn. gato por liebre. ‖ **to make a pig of os.,** pegarse un atracón, darse un atracón, ponerse las botas. ‖ **to make a pig's ear of sth.,** hacer una verdadera chapuza con algo.
■ **pig farm,** granja porcina. ‖ **pig iron,** hierro en lingotes.

pigeon ['pɪdʒɪn] **1** *n* ORN paloma. **2** CULIN SP pichón *m*.

● **it's my (*your/his/her etc*) pigeon,** es asunto mío (*tuyo/suyo etc*).
■ **pigeon fancier,** colombófilo,-a. ‖ **pigeon loft,** palomar *m*.

pigeonhole ['pɪdʒɪnhəʊl] **1** *n* casilla. – **2** *t* encasillar.

pigeon-toed [pɪdʒɪn'təʊd] *adj* patituerto,-a.

piggery ['pɪgərɪ] *n* (*farm*) granja porcina; (*sty*) pocilga.
▲ *pl* **piggeries**.

piggy ['pɪgɪ] *n* cerdito.
■ **piggy bank,** hucha (en forma de cerdito).
▲ *pl* **piggies**.

piggyback ['pɪgɪbæk] *adv* a cuestas.

● **to give sb. a piggyback,** llevar a algn. a cuestas.

pig-headed [pɪg'hedɪd] *adj* terco,-a, testarudo,-a, cabezudo,-a.

piglet ['pɪglət] *n* cerdito, cochinillo, lechón *m*.

pigment ['pɪgmənt] *n* pigmento.

pigmentation [pɪgmən'teɪʃən] *n* pigmentación *f*.

pigmy ['pɪgmɪ] *n* → **pygmy**.
▲ *pl* **pigmies**.

pigskin ['pɪgskɪn] *n* piel *f* de cerdo.

pigsty ['pɪgstaɪ] *n* pocilga.
▲ *pl* **pigsties**.

pigtail ['pɪgteɪl] *n* coleta.

pike¹ [paɪk] *n* (*weapon*) pica.

pike² [paɪk] *n* (*fish*) lucio.

pilchard ['pɪltʃəd] *n* sardina.

pile¹ [paɪl] **1** *n* (*heap*) montón *m*, pila. **2** *fam* (*a lot of*) montón *m*, pila: *I've got a pile of essays to mark*, tengo que corregir un montón de redacciones. **3** *fam* (*large building*) mole *m*. – **4** *t* (*form a pile*) amontonar, apilar. **5** (*fill*) llenar, colmar: *the sink was piled high with dishes*, el fregadero estaba lleno de platos; *a plate piled high with food*, un plato colmado de comida. – **6 piles of,** *npl* montones *mpl* de.

◆ **to pile in** 1 *i* (*squeeze in*) meterse; (*vehicle*) subir. **2** (*crowd*) entrar en tropel. ‖ **to pile into** 1 *t insep* (*squeeze in*) meterse en. **2** (*attack*) arremeter contra. ‖ **to pile on** 1 *t sep* poner un montón de. – **2** *i* (*crowd*) subir en tropel. ‖ **to pile out** *i* (*crowd*) salir en tropel. ‖ **to pile up** 1 *i* (*accumulate* - *gen*) amontonarse, acumularse; (- *money*) acumularse. **2** (*crash*) chocar en cadena. – **3** *t sep* (*books, boxes, logs, etc*) amontonar, apilar. **4** (*riches, debts*) acumular.

● **to make a pile,** (*get rich*) hacer fortuna, forrarse. ‖ **to pile it on,** exagerar. ‖ **to pile on the agony,** cargar las tintas. ‖ **to put things into a pile,** amontonar cosas.

pile² [paɪl] *n* ARCH pilote *m*, pilar *m*.

pile³ [paɪl] *n* (*on carpet*) pelo: **thick pile,** pelo largo.

pile-driver [ˈpaɪldraɪvəʳ] *n* martinete *m*.

piles [paɪlz] *npl* MED almorranas *fpl*, hemorroides *fpl*.

pile-up [ˈpaɪlʌp] *n* AUTO choque *m* en cadena.

pilfer [ˈpɪlfəʳ] 1 *t* hurtar. – **2** *i* hurtar.

pilgrim [ˈpɪlgrɪm] *n* peregrino,-a.

pilgrimage [ˈpɪlgrɪmɪdʒ] *n* peregrinación *f*, romería.

● **to go on a pilgrimage / make a pilgrimage,** ir en peregrinación.

pill [pɪl] 1 *n* (*gen*) píldora, pastilla. **2 the pill,** la píldora (anticonceptiva).

● **to be on the pill,** tomar la píldora.

pillage [ˈpɪlɪdʒ] 1 *n* pillaje *m*, saqueo. – **2** *t* pillar, saquear. – **3** *i* pillar, saquear.

pillar [ˈpɪləʳ] 1 *n* ARCH pilar *m*, columna. **2** (*of smoke*) columna. **3** (*person*) pilar *m*, baluarte *m*.

● **to go from pillar to post,** ir de la Ceca a la Meca, ir de Herodes a Pilatos.

■ **pillar box,** buzón *m*.

pillbox [ˈpɪlbɒks] 1 *n* (*for pills*) pastillero. **2** (*hat*) casquete *m*.

pillion [ˈpɪlɪən] *n* asiento trasero (de una moto).

● **to ride pillion,** ir de paquete.

pillory [ˈpɪlərɪ] 1 *n* picota. – **2** *t* poner en la picota. **3** *fig* burlarse de, ridiculizar.

▲ (*sustantivo*) *pl* **pillories**; (*verbo*) *pt & pp* **pilloried**, *ger* **pillorying**.

pillow [ˈpɪləʊ] *n* almohada.

pillowcase [ˈpɪləʊkeɪs] *n* funda de almohada.

pillowslip [ˈpɪləʊslɪp] *n* funda de almohada.

pilot [ˈpaɪlət] 1 *n* AV piloto *mf*. **2** MAR práctico *mf*. **3** RAD TV programa *m* piloto. – **4** *adj* piloto, experimental. – **5** *t* AV MAR pilotar. **6** (*guide*) dirigir. **7** (*test*) poner a prueba.

● **to pilot a bill through Parliament,** lograr la aprobación de un proyecto de ley.

■ **pilot light,** piloto.

pimento [pɪˈmentəʊ] *n* pimiento morrón.

▲ *pl* **pimentos**.

pimp [pɪmp] *n* chulo, macarra *m*, proxeneta *mf*.

pimple [ˈpɪmpəl] *n* (*spot*) grano.

pimply [ˈpɪmplɪ] *adj* lleno,-a de granos.

▲ *comp* **pimplier**, *superl* **pimpliest**.

pin [pɪn] 1 *n* (*gen*) alfiler *m*. **2** (*badge, brooch*) insignia, pin *m*, alfiler *m*. **3** TECH (*peg, dowel*) clavija, espiga; (*cotter pin*) chaveta; (*bolt*) perno. **4** MED clavo. **5** ELEC polo: *a two-pin plug,* una clavija de dos patillas, una clavija bipolar. **6** (*on grenade*) anilla. **7** SP (*in bowling*) bolo; (*in golf*) banderín *m*. – **8** *t* (*garment, hem, seam*) prender (con alfileres); (*papers etc together*) sujetar (con un alfiler); (*notice on board etc*) clavar (**up,** -); (*hair*) recoger (**up,**-). **9** (*person*) inmovilizar; (*arms*) sujetar. – **10 pins,** *npl fam* (*legs*) patas *fpl*.

◆ **to pin down** 1 *t sep* (*person*) inmovilizar, sujetar. **2**

(*force - decision*) hacer que se comprometa; (- *position*) hacer que se defina. ‖ **to pin on** *t sep* (*hopes*) poner en, depositar en, cifrar en; (*blame*) hacer cargar con; (*crime*) endosar a. ‖ **to pin up** *t sep* clavar (con chinchetas), sujetar (con alfileres).

● **you could've heard a pin drop,** se podía oír el vuelo de una mosca. ‖ **not to care two pins / not give two pins,** importarle a uno un bledo, importarle a uno un pepino.

■ **drawing pin,** chincheta. ‖ **hair pin,** horquilla. ‖ **pins and needles,** hormigueo. ‖ **pin money,** dinero para gastos personales. ‖ **safety pin,** imperdible *m*.

▲ (*verbo*) *pt & pp* **pinned**, *ger* **pinning**.

pinafore [ˈpɪnəfɔːʳ] *n* (*apron*) delantal *m*.

■ **pinafore dress,** pichi *m*.

pinball [ˈpɪnbɔːl] *n* flipper *m*.

pincers [ˈpɪnsəz] 1 *npl* (*tool*) tenazas *fpl*. **2** (*on crab etc*) pinzas *fpl*.

pinch [pɪntʃ] 1 *n* (*nip*) pellizco. **2** (*small amount*) pizca. – **3** *t* (*nip*) pellizcar; (*shoes*) apretar. **4** *fam* (*steal*) birlar, afanar, robar. – **5** *i* (*shoes*) apretar.

● **at a pinch,** (*if necessary*) si fuera necesario; (*at the most*) como máximo. ‖ **if it comes to the pinch,** en caso de apuro. ‖ **to feel the pinch,** pasar apuros, pasar estrecheces. ‖ **to pinch os.,** pellizcarse.

pinched [pɪntʃt] 1 *adj* (*face - drawn*) cansado,-a, ojeroso,-a; (- *worried*) preocupado,-a. **2** (*short of*) escaso,-a (**for,** de), apretado,-a (**for,** de).

● **to be pinched with cold,** estar muerto,-a de frío. ‖ **to have a pinched look,** tener mala cara.

pincushion [ˈpɪnkʊʃən] *n* acerico.

pine¹ [paɪn] 1 *n* BOT (*tree, wood*) pino. – **2** *adj* de pino.

■ **pine cone,** piña. ‖ **pine forest,** pinar *m*. ‖ **pine needle,** aguja de pino. ‖ **pine nut,** piñón *m*.

pine² [paɪn] *i* estar triste, sufrir.

◆ **to pine away** *i* consumirse, morirse de pena.

● **to pine for sb.,** añorar a algn., echar mucho de menos a algn. ‖ **to pine for sth.,** suspirar por algo, anhelar algo.

pineapple [ˈpaɪnæpəl] *n* piña.

ping [pɪŋ] 1 *n* (*sound*) sonido metálico. – **2** *adj* de pino.

‖ **to be in the pink,** (*healthy*) estar en plena forma, rebosar salud; (*happy*) estar feliz de la vida. ‖ **to go pink / turn pink,** ponerse colorado,-a.

ping-pong [ˈpɪŋpɒŋ] *n* tenis *m* de mesa, ping-pong *m*.

pinion¹ [ˈpɪnɪən] *n* TECH piñón *m*.

pinion² [ˈpɪnjən] 1 *t* (*person*) inmovilizar, sujetar; (*arms*) maniatar. **2** (*bird*) cortar las alas a.

pink¹ [pɪŋk] 1 *adj* (*de color*) rosa, rosado,-a. **2** POL rojillo,-a. – **3** *n* (*colour*) (color *m*) rosa *m*. **4** BOT clavel *m*, clavellina.

● **to be in the pink,** (*healthy*) estar en plena forma, rebosar salud; (*happy*) estar feliz de la vida. ‖ **to go pink / turn pink,** ponerse colorado,-a.

■ **pink gin,** ginebra con angostura.

pink² [pɪŋk] 1 *t* SEW cortar con tijeras dentadas. – **2** *i* AUTO (*engine*) picar.

pinkie [ˈpɪŋkɪ] *n* US *fam* meñique *m*, dedo meñique.

pinking shears [ˈpɪŋkɪŋʃɪəz] *npl* tijeras *fpl* dentadas.

pinkish [ˈpɪŋkɪʃ] *adj* rosáceo,-a.

pinnacle [ˈpɪnəkəl] 1 *n* (*of building*) pináculo. **2** (*of mountain*) cima, cumbre *f*. **3** *fig* cumbre *f*.

pinny [ˈpɪnɪ] *n fam* delantal *m*.

▲ *pl* **pinnies**.

pinpoint [ˈpɪnpɔɪnt] 1 *t* (*position*) localizar; (*cause, origin, time*) establecer con exactitud, precisar exactamente; (*fact*) señalar. – **2** *n* puntito.

● **pinpoint accuracy,** precisión *f* milimétrica.

pinprick ['pɪnprɪk] **1** n (sensation) pinchazo; (hole) agujerito. **2** (annoying thing) pequeño inconveniente m.

pinstripe ['pɪnstraɪp] **1** n (stripe) raya fina, raya diplomática; (cloth) tela de raya diplomática. – **2** adj (suit) de raya diplomática.

pinstriped ['pɪnstraɪpt] adj de raya diplomática.

pint [paɪnt] **1** n (measurement) pinta. **2 a pint,** fam (of beer) una cerveza, una jarra.

● **to go for a pint,** ir a tomar una cerveza.

▲ en Gran Bretaña equivale a 0,57 litros; en Estados Unidos equivale a 0,47 litros.

pint-sized ['paɪntsaɪzd] adj fam muy pequeño,-a, pequeñito,-a.

pin-up ['pɪnʌp] n foto f.

pioneer [paɪə'nɪəʳ] **1** n (settler) pionero,-a. **2** (first person, originator) pionero,-a, precursor,-ra, iniciador,-ra. – **3** t (policy, industry) promover; (technique) iniciar, ser el/la primero,-a en aplicar.

pioneering [paɪə'nɪərɪŋ] adj pionero,-a.

pious ['paɪəs] **1** adj (devout - person) piadoso,-a, pío,-a, devoto,-a. **2** pej (person) beato,-a, santurrón,-ona; (apology, platitude) de beato.

● **a pious hope,** una esperanza infundada.

piously ['paɪəslɪ] **1** adv (devoutly) píamente, piadosamente. **2** (hypocritically) hipócritamente.

pip[1] [pɪp] n (seed) pepita.

pip[2] [pɪp] **1** n (sound) señal f (corta). **2** (on dice, domino) punto. **3** GB MIL (on uniform) estrella.

● **to give sb. the pip,** GB sacar de quicio a algn.

pip[3] [pɪp] t (hit with a shot) dar, alcanzar.

● **to be pipped at the post,** perder por un pelo. ‖ **to pip sb. at the post,** ganar a algn. en el último momento.

▲ pt & pp **pipped,** ger **pipping.**

pipe [paɪp] **1** n (for water, gas, etc) tubería, cañería, conducto. **2** MUS (wind instrument) caramillo; (of organ) tubo, cañón m. **3** (for smoking) pipa: he smokes a pipe, fuma en pipa. – **4** t (water, gas) llevar por tuberías; (oil) conducir por oleoducto. **5** CULIN (with cream, icing) poner con manga. **6** SEW ribetear. – **7** i MUS (pipe) tocar el caramillo; (pipes) tocar la gaita. – **8 pipes,** npl gaita f sing.

◆ **to pipe down** i callarse. ‖ **to pipe up** i decir inesperadamente, salir con.

● **put that in your pipe and smoke it!,** ¡chúpate ésa! ■ **pipe cleaner,** limpiapipas m. ‖ **piped music,** hilo musical. ‖ **pipe dream,** quimera, sueño imposible. ‖ **pipes of Pan,** flauta f sing de Pan.

pipeline ['paɪplaɪn] n (for water) tubería, cañería, conducto; (for gas) gasoducto; (for oil) oleoducto.

● **to be in the pipeline,** (being dealt with) estar en trámite; (being prepared) estar proyectado,-a, tener en proyecto.

piper ['paɪpəʳ] n gaitero,-a.

piping ['paɪpɪŋ] **1** n (for water, gas, etc) tubería, cañería. **2** SEW ribete m. **3** CULIN adorno, decoración f (hecho con manga).

● **piping hot,** bien caliente, muy caliente.

pipit ['pɪpɪt] n ORN bisbita.

piquancy ['pɪkənsɪ] n (spice) gusto picante.

piquant ['piːkənt] **1** adj (taste) picante. **2** fig (exciting) estimulante, intrigante.

pique [piːk] **1** n resentimiento, despecho. – **2** t (offend) picar, herir. **3** (arouse - curiosity) picar; (- interest) despertar.

● **in a fit of pique,** por despecho. ‖ **to be piqued by sth.,** estar resentido,-a por algo.

piracy ['paɪərəsɪ] n piratería.

piranha [pɪ'rɑːnə] n (fish) piraña.

pirate ['paɪərət] **1** n pirata m. – **2** adj pirata. – **3** t piratear.

■ **pirate radio,** emisora pirata.

pirouette [pɪrʊ'et] n pirueta. – **2** i hacer piruetas, piruetear.

Pisces ['paɪsiːz] n Piscis m.

piss [pɪs] **1** n taboo meada. – **2** i sl mear.

◆ **to piss about / piss around 1** i sl (play the fool) hacer el tonto, hacer tonterías; (idle) gandulear, perder el tiempo. – **2** t sep sl (waste sb.'s time) hacer perder tiempo a; (take for a ride) tomar el pelo a. ‖ **to piss down i** sl (rain heavily) llover a cántaros. ‖ **to piss off 1** i sl largarse, irse a la mierda. – **2** t sep sl cabrear, poner de mala leche.

● **to have a piss,** sl mear. ‖ **to take the piss out of sb./sth.,** sl cachondearse de algn./algo.

pissed [pɪst] **1** adj GB sl (drunk) trompa, bolinga, mamado,-a. **2** US sl (annoyed) cabreado,-a.

■ **pissed off,** GB cabreado,-a.

pistachio [pɪs'tɑːʃɪəʊ] n pistacho.

■ **pistachio tree,** pistachero.

▲ pl **pistachios.**

pistol ['pɪstəl] n pistola.

● **to hold a pistol to sb.'s head,** fig poner a algn. entre la espada y la pared.

piston ['pɪstən] n TECH pistón m, émbolo.

■ **piston ring,** aro de pistón. ‖ **piston rod,** biela.

pit[1] [pɪt] **1** n (hole) hoyo, foso; (large) hoya; (grave) fosa. **2** (mine) mina, pozo. **3** (in garage) foso. **4** (mark - on metal, glass) señal f, marca; (- on skin) picadura, cicatriz f. **5** THEAT (stalls) patio de butacas, platea; (for orquestra) foso de la orquesta. – **6** t (mark) picar, marcar. – **7 the pit,** n (hell) el infierno. – **8 the pits,** npl (in motor racing) los boxes mpl.

● **to be the pits,** ser terrible, ser fatal. ‖ **to work down the pit,** trabajar en las minas. ‖ **to pit one's strength against sb.,** medirse con algn., enfrentarse a algn., competir con algn. ‖ **to pit one's wits against sb.,** medirse con algn. intelectualmente.

■ **pit of the stomach,** boca del estómago. ‖ **pit worker,** minero.

▲ (verbo) pt & pp **pitted,** ger **pitting.**

pit[2] [pɪt] **1** n US (seed) pepita; (stone) hueso. – **2** t US quitar las pepitas a, deshuesar.

▲ (verbo) pt & pp **pitted,** ger **pitting.**

pitch[1] [pɪtʃ] **1** n MUS (of sound) tono; (of instrument) diapasón m. **2** SP (field) campo, terreno; (throw) lanzamiento. **3** (degree, level) grado, punto, extremo: their argument reached such a pitch that I had to intervene, su discusión llegó a tal extremo que tuve que intervenir. **4** (position, site) lugar m, sitio; (in market) puesto. **5** MAR (movement) cabezada. **6** (slope of roof) pendiente f. – **7** t MUS (note, sound) entonar: the song was pitched too high, la canción tenía un tono demasiado alto. **8** fig (aim, address) dirigir (at, a); (set) dar un tono a: they pitched the leaflet at a simple level, le dieron al folleto un tono accesible. **9** (throw) tirar, arrojar; (in baseball) lanzar, pichear. **10** (tent) plantar, armar, montar; (camp) montar, hacer. – **11** i (fall) caerse. **12** AV MAR cabecear. **13** SP (in baseball) lanzar.

◆ **to pitch in** i fam (lend a hand) dar una mano, echar una mano, arrimar el hombro; (start work) ponerse a trabajar; (eat) atacar. ‖ **to pitch into** t insep fam (attack) atacar, arremeter contra.

● **to be at fever pitch,** estar al rojo vivo.

pitch[2] [pɪtʃ] n (tar) brea, pez f.

pitch-black [pɪtʃ'blæk] *adj* muy oscuro,-a, (oscuro,-a) como boca de lobo.

pitch-dark [pɪtʃ'dɑːk] *adj* → **pitch-black**.

pitched [pɪtʃt] *adj* (*roof*) en pendiente, inclinado,-a.
■ pitched battle, batalla campal.

pitcher[1] ['pɪtʃəʳ] 1 *n* (*of clay*) cántaro. 2 US jarro, jarra.

pitcher[2] ['pɪtʃəʳ] *n* SP pítcher *mf*, lanzador,-ra.

pitchfork ['pɪtʃfɔːk] *n* AGR horca.

piteous ['pɪtɪəs] *adj* (*cry*) lastimero,-a; (*sight, condition*) lastimoso,-a.

pitfall ['pɪtfɔːl] *n* (*difficulty*) dificultad *f*, escollo; (*danger*) peligro, riesgo.

pith [pɪθ] 1 *n* (*of bone, plant*) médula; (*of orange*) piel *f* blanca. 2 *fig* meollo.

pithead ['pɪthed] *n* (*of mine*) bocamina.

pithy ['pɪθɪ] 1 *adj* (*bone, plant*) meduloso,-a. 2 (*description, comment, etc*) conciso,-a y contundente.
▲ *comp* pithier, superl pithiest.

pitiable ['pɪtɪəbəl] *adj* (*arousing pity*) lastimoso,-a.

pitiful ['pɪtɪfʊl] 1 *adj* (*arousing pity - sight*) lastimoso,-a; (*cry*) lastimero,-a. 2 (*arousing contempt*) lamentable.

pitifully ['pɪtɪfəlɪ] 1 *adv* (*sadly*) que da pena, lastimosamente. 2 (*deplorably*) lamentablemente.

pitiless ['pɪtɪləs] 1 *adj* (*killer, tyrant, etc*) despiadado,-a. 2 *fig* (*sun, wind, tec*) implacable.

pittance ['pɪtəns] *n* miseria.

pitter-patter ['pɪtəpætəʳ] *n* repiqueteo.

pituitary [pɪ'tjuːɪtərɪ] *adj* pituitario,-a.
■ pituitary gland, glándula pituitaria.

pity ['pɪtɪ] 1 *n* (*compassion*) piedad *f*, compasión *f*: *she gave him some money out of pity*, le dio dinero por compasión. 2 (*regret*) lástima, pena: *it's a pity there are so few people*, es una pena que haya tan poca gente; *it's a pity about the car*, es una pena lo del coche. − 3 *t* (*feel pity for*) compadecerse de, tener lástima de, dar lástima: *I pity you if he catches you!*, ¡pobre de ti como te pille!
● for pity's sake!, ¡por amor de Dios! ‖ more's the pity, por desgracia, desgraciadamente. ‖ to have pity on sb. / take pity on sb., compadecerse de algn., tener piedad de algn., tener compasión de algn. ‖ what a pity!, ¡qué lástima!, ¡qué pena!
▲ (*sustantivo*) *pl* pities; (*verbo*) *pt* & *pp* pitied; *ger* pitying.

pitying ['pɪtɪɪŋ] *adj* compasivo,-a, de lástima.

pivot ['pɪvət] 1 *n* pivote *m*. 2 *fig* eje *m* central. − 3 *t* pivotar, girar sobre su eje.
● to pivot on, (*hinge on*) girar sobre; (*depend on*) depender de.

pixie ['pɪksɪ] *n* duendecillo.

pizza ['piːtsə] *n* pizza.
■ pizza parlour, pizzería.

Pk [pɑːk] *abbr* (*Park*) Parque *m*.

pkt ['pækɪt] *abbr* (*packet*) paquete *m*.

placard ['plækɑːd] *n* pancarta.

placate [plə'keɪt] *t* aplacar, apaciguar, calmar.

place [pleɪs] 1 *n* (*particular position, part*) lugar *m*, sitio: *we visited lots of different places*, fuimos a muchos sitios diferentes; *this looks like the place*, me parece que es aquí. 2 (*proper position*) lugar *m*, sitio; (*suitable place*) lugar *m* adecuado, sitio adecuado: *put the book back in its place*, devuelve el libro a su sitio; *this isn't the place to discuss business*, éste no es el lugar más indicado para hablar de negocios. 3 (*building*) lugar *m*, sitio; (*home*) casa, piso: *let's go to my place*, vamos a mi casa. 4 (*in book*) página: *I've lost my place*, he perdido la página. 5 (*seat*) asiento, sitio; (*at table*) cubierto: *can you save my place?*, ¿me guardas el sitio?; *everybody go back to their places*, todo el mundo a su sitio. 6 (*position, role, rank*) lugar *m*; (*duty*) obligación *f*: *there will always be a place for you here*, siempre habrá un lugar para ti aquí; *if I were in your place*, yo en tu lugar; *it's not my place to tell you what to do*, yo no soy quién para decirte lo que tienes que hacer. 7 (*in race, contest*) puesto, lugar *m*, posición *f*; (*in queue*) turno: *our horse finished in last place*, nuestro caballo llegó el último. 8 (*job*) puesto; (*at university, on course*) plaza; (*on team*) puesto. − 9 *t* (*put - gen*) poner; (*- carefully*) colocar: *she placed the vase on the shelf*, puso el florero en el estante. 10 (*find home, job for*) colocar. 11 (*rank, class*) poner, situar. 12 (*remember - face, person*) recordar; (*- tune, accent*) identificar: *I recognize his face, but I can't quite place him*, me suena su cara, pero no sé de qué.
● all over the place, por todas partes, por todos lados. ‖ a place in the sun, una posición destacada. ‖ in place, en su sitio. ‖ in place of sb. / in sb.'s place, en el lugar de algn. ‖ in the first place ..., en primer lugar ... ‖ out of place, fuera de lugar. ‖ there's no place like home, no hay nada como estar en casa. ‖ to be placed first (*second etc*), ocupar el primer (*segundo etc*) puesto, llegar el primero (*segundo etc*). ‖ to change places with sb., cambiar de sitio con algn. ‖ to fall into place / fit into place / slot into place, encajar, cuadrar: *things are beginning to fall into place*, las cosas empiezan a cuadrar. ‖ to have friends in high places, tener amigos influyentes. ‖ to give place to sth., dar paso a algo. ‖ to go from place to place, ir de un lugar a otro, ir de un sitio a otro, ir de un lado a otro. ‖ to go places, llegar lejos. ‖ to hold sth. in place, sujetar algo. ‖ to know one's place, saber el lugar que le corresponde a uno. ‖ to place a bet, hacer una apuesta. ‖ to place an order, hacer un pedido. ‖ to place one's trust in sb., depositar su confianza en algn. ‖ to put os. in sb.'s place, ponerse en el lugar de algn. ‖ to put sb. in his place, poner a algn. en su sitio. ‖ to take place, tener lugar. ‖ to take second place, pasar a un segundo plano. ‖ to take the place of, ocupar el sitio de, reemplazar, sustituir.
■ decimal place, MATH punto decimal. ‖ place of birth, lugar *m* de nacimiento. ‖ place of residence, domicilio. ‖ place of worship, lugar *m* de culto. ‖ place mat, individual *m*. ‖ place name, topónimo.

placebo [plə'siːbəʊ] *n* placebo.
▲ *pl* placebos o placeboes.

placement ['pleɪsmənt] *n* colocación *f*.

placenta [plə'sentə] *n* placenta.
▲ *pl* placentas o placentae [plə'sentiː].

placid ['plæsɪd] *adj* plácido,-a, apacible, tranquilo,-a.

plagiarism ['pleɪdʒərɪzəm] *n* plagio.

plagiarize ['pleɪdʒəraɪz] *t* plagiar.

plague [pleɪg] 1 *n* (*of insects etc*) plaga. 2 MED peste *f*. − 3 *t* (*pester*) acosar, asediar: *they plagued her with questions*, la acosaron a preguntas. 4 (*afflict*) afligir, asolar, plagar, atormentar: *a scheme plagued by problems*, un proyecto plagado de problemas; *she was plagued by doubts*, estaba atormentada por las dudas.
● to avoid sb. like the plague, huir de algn. como de la peste.

plaice [pleɪs] *n* (*fish*) platija.
▲ *pl* plaice.

plaid [plæd] 1 *n* (*material*) tejido escocés; (*pattern*) cuadros *mpl* escoceses. − 2 *adj* escocés,-esa.

plain [pleɪn] 1 *adj* (*clear*) claro,-a, evidente: *he made it quite plain*, lo dejó muy claro. 2 (*straightforward*) franco,-

a, directo,-a: *we need to do some plain speaking*, tenemos que hablar con franqueza; *tell me in plain language*, dímelo en lenguaje corriente; *the plain truth*, la pura verdad. **3** (*simple, ordinary*) sencillo,-a; (*without pattern*) liso,-a. **4** (*unattractive*) poco agraciado,-a, feúcho,-a. **5** (*chocolate*) sin leche; (*flour*) sin levadura. – **6** *adv* (*absolutely*) totalmente. **7** (*clearly*) claramente, francamente. – **8** *n* GEOG llanura. **9** (*in knitting*) punto del derecho.
● **in plain clothes**, vestido,-a de paisano. ‖ **in plain English**, en términos sencillos, en cristiano. ‖ **to be (all) plain sailing**, ser coser y cantar. ‖ **to make os. plain**, explicarse.

plainly ['pleɪnlɪ] **1** *adv* (*clearly - explain, speak*) claramente; (*remember*) perfectamente. **2** (*obviously - gen*) claramente, obviamente; (*- upset, angry*) evidentemente. **3** (*simply*) sencillamente, con sencillez.

plainness ['pleɪnnəs] **1** *n* (*clearness*) claridad *f*. **2** (*simplicity*) sencillez *f*. **3** (*unattractiveness*) fealdad *f*.

plain-spoken [pleɪn'spəʊkən] *adj* franco,-a.

plaintiff ['pleɪntɪf] *n* demandante *mf*, querellante *mf*.

plaintive ['pleɪntɪv] *adj* lastimero,-a, triste.

plait [plæt] **1** *n* trenza. – **2** *t* trenzar.

plan [plæn] **1** *n* (*scheme, arrangement*) plan *m*, proyecto: *a change of plan*, un cambio de planes; *development plan*, plan de desarrollo; *what are your plans for the weekend?*, ¿qué planes tienes para el fin de semana? **2** (*map, drawing, diagram*) plano; (*design*) proyecto; (*for essay*) esquema *m*: *have you seen the plans for the new opera house?*, ¿has visto los planos de la nueva ópera? – **3** *t* (*make plans*) planear, proyectar, planificar; (*intend*) pensar, tener pensado: *they plan to get married next year*, tienen planeado casarse el año que viene; *we're planning to spend Christmas with my parents*, pensamos pasar las navidades con mis padres; *everything turned out as planned*, todo salió como estaba planeado. **4** (*make a plan of - house, garden, etc*) hacer los planos de, diseñar, proyectar; (*- economy, strategy*) planificar. – **5** *i* (*make preparations*) hacer planes; (*intend*) pensar: *we've planned for about 20 people*, tenemos previsto (que vendrán) unas 20 personas; *we hadn't planned on rain!*, ¡no contábamos con que lloviera!; *I'd planned on going away this weekend*, había pensado salir fuera este fin de semana.
● **to go according to plan**, salir como estaba previsto, salir según lo previsto. ‖ **to plan for the future**, hacer planes para el futuro.
▲ (*verbo*) *pt* & *pp* **planned**, *ger* **planning**.

plane¹ [pleɪn] **1** *n* MATH (*surface*) plano. **2** *fig* (*level, standard*) nivel *m*. **3** *fam* (*aircraft*) avión *m*: *they went by plane*, fueron en avión. – **4** *adj* plano,-a. – **5** *i* (*glide*) planear.
■ **plane geometry**, geometría plana. ‖ **plane ticket**, billete *m* de avión.

plane² [pleɪn] **1** *n* (*tool*) cepillo. – **2** *t* cepillar.
◆ **to plane down** *t sep* desbastar.

plane³ [pleɪn] **1** *n* **plane (tree)**, *n* BOT plátano.

planet ['plænət] *n* planeta *m*.

planetarium [plænɪ'teərɪəm] *n* planetario.
▲ *pl* **planetariums** o **planetaria** [plænɪ'teərɪə].

planetary ['plænətərɪ] *adj* planetario,-a.

plank [plæŋk] **1** *n* (*of wood*) tablón *m*, tabla. **2** POL (*principle*) punto fundamental.

plankton ['plæŋktən] *n* plancton *m*.

planner ['plænə'] *n* planificador,-ra.
■ **town planner**, urbanista *mf*.

planning ['plænɪŋ] *n* planificación *f*.
■ **planning permission**, permiso de obras.

plant¹ [plɑːnt] **1** *n* BOT planta. – **2** *t* (*flowers, trees*) plantar; (*seeds, vegetables*) sembrar; (*bed, garden, etc*) plantar (**with**, de). **3** (*bomb*) colocar; (*blow*) plantar; (*kiss*) dar, plantar. **4** (*ideas, doubt*) inculcar, meter.
● **to plant one's feet**, plantar los pies. ‖ **to plant os.**, plantarse. ‖ **to plant sth. on sb.**, colocarle algo a algn. a escondidas para comprometerlo.
■ **plant life**, flora. ‖ **plant pot**, maceta, tiesto.

plant² [plɑːnt] *n* IND (*factory*) planta, fábrica; (*machinery*) equipo, maquinaria.

plantain¹ ['plæn'teɪn] *n* BOT (*weed*) llantén *m*.

plantain² ['plæn'teɪn] *n* (*fruit*) plátano grande; (*tree*) plátano.

plantation [plæn'teɪʃən] *n* (*for crops*) plantación *f*.

planter ['plɑːntə'] *n* (*plantation owner*) hacendado,-a.

plaque [plæk] *n* placa.

plasma ['plæzmə] *n* plasma *m*.

plaster ['plɑːstə'] **1** *n* (*powder, mixture - gen*) yeso; (*for walls*) revoque *m*, enlucido. **2** MED escayola: *he's got his arm in plaster*, tiene el brazo escayolado. – **3** *t* (*wall, ceiling*) enyesar, enlucir. **4** (*cover, spread*) cubrir (**with**, de).
■ **plaster cast**, ART vaciado de yeso; MED escayolado. ‖ **plaster of Paris**, yeso de mate. ‖ **sticking plaster**, esparadrapo, tirita.

plasterboard ['plɑːstəbɔːd] *n* cartón *m* yeso.

plastered ['plɑːstəd] *adj fam* (*drunk*) borracho,-a, trompa, como una cuba.

plasterer ['plɑːstərə'] *n* yesero,-a.

plastic ['plæstɪk] **1** *adj* (*bag, cup, spoon, etc*) de plástico,-a. **2** (*malleable*) moldeable. – **3** *n* plástico. **4** *fam* (*credit cards*) tarjetas de crédito.
■ **plastic surgery**, cirugía plástica. ‖ **plastic surgeon**, cirujano,-a plástico,-a. ‖ **the plastic arts**, las artes *fpl* plásticas. ‖ **the plastics industry**, la industria del plástico.

Plasticine ['plæstɪsiːn] *n* GB plastilina.

plate [pleɪt] **1** *n* (*dish, plateful*) plato; (*for church offering*) platillo, bandeja. **2** (*sheet of metal, glass*) placa; (*thin layer*) lámina. **3** (*metal covered with gold*) chapa de oro; (*with silver*) chapa de plata. **4** (*dishes, bowls - of gold*) vajilla de oro; (*- of silver*) vajilla de plata. **5** (*illustration*) grabado, lámina. **6** (*dental*) dentadura postiza. – **7** *t* (*gen*) chapar; (*with gold*) dorar; (*with silver*) platear.
● **to have a lot on one's plate**, tener mucha faena, tener muchas cosas entre manos. ‖ **to give/hand sth. to sb. on a plate**, poner algo a algn. en bandeja.
■ **hot plate**, placa eléctrica. ‖ **number plate**, matrícula. ‖ **plate glass**, cristal *m* cilindrado, vidrio cilindrado. ‖ **plate rack**, escurreplatos *m*.

plateau ['plætəʊ] **1** *n* GEOG meseta. **2** (*state*) estancamiento.
● **to reach a plateau**, estancarse.
▲ *pl* **plateaus** o **plateaux** ['plætəʊz].

platform ['plætfɔːm] **1** *n* (*gen*) plataforma; (*for speaker*) tribuna, estrado; (*for band*) estrado. **2** (*railway*) andén *m*, vía. **3** POL programa *m*.

platinum ['plætɪnəm] *n* platino.
■ **platinum blonde**, rubia platina.

platitude ['plætɪtjuːd] *n* tópico, lugar *m* común.

platonic [plə'tɒnɪk] *adj* platónico,-a.

platoon [plə'tuːn] *n* MIL pelotón *m*.

platter ['plætə'] *n* (*dish*) fuente *f*.

platypus ['plætɪpəs] *n* ornitorrinco.

plausible ['plɔːzɪbəl] *adj* (*statement, excuse, etc*) plausible, admisible, verosímil; (*person*) convincente.

play [pleɪ] **1** *n* (*recreation*) juego: *all work and no play*, mucho trabajo y nada de diversión; *children at play*, niños

jugando. **2** SP (action) juego; (match) partido; (move) jugada: **rain has stopped play,** la lluvia ha interrumpido el juego. **3** THEAT obra (de teatro), pieza (teatral). **4** (free and easy movement, slack) juego. **5** (action, effect, interaction) juego. **– 6** t (game, sport) jugar a: **some played cards while the others played football,** algunos jugamos a cartas mientras otros jugaron a fútbol; **do you play the Stock Exchange?,** ¿juegas a la Bolsa? **7** SP (compete against) jugar contra; (in position) jugar de; (ball) pasar; (card) jugar; (piece) mover: **Arsenal are playing Manchester tomorrow,** el Arsenal juega contra el Manchester mañana; **have you played David at tennis?,** ¿has jugado al tenis con David? **8** MUS tocar: **she plays the piano,** toca el piano; **play us something on the guitar,** tócanos algo a la guitarra. **– 9** n (joke, trick) gastar, hacer: **they played a dirty trick on me,** me jugaron una mala pasada. **– 10** t THEAT (part) hacer el papel de, hacer de; (play) representar, dar: **she plays the part of Juliet,** hace de Julieta; **they're playing King Lear at the Royal,** representan el Rey Lear en el Royal. **11** (record, song, tape) poner. **12** (direct - light, water) dirigir. **– 13** i (amuse oneself) jugar (**at,** a), (**with,** con). **14** SP (at game) jugar: **he plays for England,** juega con la selección inglesa. **15** THEAT (cast) actuar, trabajar; (show) ser representado,-a. **16** (pretend) pretender, jugar a: **what are you playing at?,** ¿qué pretendes?, ¿a qué estás jugando? **17** MUS tocar. **18** (move) recorrer.
◆ **to play about** i juguetear. ‖ **to play along** i hacer el juego a, seguir la corriente a. ‖ **to play around** i (gen) juguetear; (have affairs) tener líos. ‖ **to play back** t sep (volver a) poner. ‖ **to play down** t sep minimizar, quitar importancia a. ‖ **to play off** 1 t sep oponer (**against,** a). **– 2** i jugar el desempate. ‖ **to play on** t insep aprovecharse de, explotar. ‖ **to play up** 1 t sep (cause trouble) dar la lata a, fastidiar. **– 2** i (machine) no funcionar bien; (child) dar guerra, portarse mal. **3** (flatter) halagar (**to,** a), dar coba (**to,** a).
● **a play on words,** un juego de palabras. ‖ **to be in play,** estar dentro de juego. ‖ **to be out of play,** estar fuera de juego. ‖ **to be played out,** estar agotado,-a, estar rendido,-a. ‖ **to bring sth. into play,** poner algo en juego. ‖ **to come into play,** entrar en juego. ‖ **to give full play to sth.,** dar rienda suelta a algo. ‖ **to make a play for sth./sb.,** intentar conseguir algo/conquistar a algn. ‖ **to play by ear,** (music) tocar de oído. ‖ **to play dead,** hacerse el/la muerto,-a. ‖ **to play for time,** tratar de ganar tiempo. ‖ **to play hard to get,** hacerse el duro, hacerse el/la interesante. ‖ **to play into sb.'s hands,** hacerle el juego a algn. ‖ **to play it by ear,** (improvise) decidir sobre la marcha, improvisar. ‖ **to play it cool,** hacer como si nada. ‖ **to play one's cards right,** jugar bien sus cartas. ‖ **to play safe / play it safe,** ir a lo seguro, no arriesgarse. ‖ **to play the fool,** hacer el indio, hacer el tonto. ‖ **to play the game,** jugar limpio. ‖ **to play truant,** hacer novillos, hacer campana. ‖ **to play with an idea,** dar vueltas a una idea. ‖ **to play with fire,** jugar con fuego.
■ **fair play / foul play,** juego limpio / juego sucio.
play-act ['pleɪækt] i hacer teatro.
playbill ['pleɪbɪl] n cartel m.
playboy ['pleɪbɔɪ] n playboy m.
player ['pleɪəʳ] **1** n SP jugador,-ra. **2** THEAT (actor) actor m; (actress) actriz f.
■ **trumpet player,** trompetista mf.
playful ['pleɪful] adj (person, animal) juguetón,-ona, travieso,-a; (mood) juguetón,-ona.
playground ['pleɪgraʊnd] n patio de recreo.
playgroup ['pleɪgruːp] n jardín m de infancia, guardería.

playhouse ['pleɪhaʊs] **1** n (theatre) teatro. **2** (for children) casita.
playing card ['pleɪŋkɑːd] n carta, naipe m.
playing field ['pleɪŋfiːld] n campo deportivo.
playmate ['pleɪmeɪt] n compañero,-a de juego, amiguito,-a.
play-off ['pleɪɒf] n SP partido de desempate.
playpen ['pleɪpen] n parque m (para niños).
playroom ['pleɪruːm] n cuarto de juego, cuarto de jugar.
playschool ['pleɪskuːl] n jardín m de infancia, guardería.
plaything ['pleɪθɪŋ] n juguete m.
playtime ['pleɪtaɪm] n recreo.
playwright ['pleɪraɪt] n dramaturgo,-a.
PLC ['piː'el'siː] abbr GB (Public Limited Company) Sociedad Anónima; (abbreviation) S.A.
▲ También se escribe plc.
plea [pliː] **1** n fml (request) petición f, súplica. **2** fml (excuse) excusa, pretexto. **3** JUR alegato, declaración f.
● **on the plea of,** so pretexto de. ‖ **to enter a plea of guilty/not guilty,** declararse culpable/inocente. ‖ **to make a plea for mercy,** rogar clemencia, suplicar clemencia.
plead [pliːd] **1** i suplicar (**with,** -). **– 2** t (give as excuse) alegar.
pleading ['pliːdɪŋ] **1** adj (tone, voice, look) suplicante. **– 2** n súplica, ruego. **– 3 pleadings,** npl JUR defensa f sing, alegato m sing.
pleasant ['plezənt] **1** adj (gen) agradable; (surprise) grato,-a. **2** (person) simpático,-a, amable.
pleasantry ['plezəntrɪ] n cumplido.
● **to exchange pleasantries,** intercambiar cumplidos.
▲ pl pleasantries.
please [pliːz] **1** t (make happy, be agreeable to) agradar, gustar, complacer; (satisfy) contentar, complacer: **you can't please everyone,** no se puede complacer a todos; **there's no pleasing her,** no hay forma de contentarla; **he's easy to please,** se contenta con cualquier cosa. **– 2** i (satisfy) contentar, complacer, satisfacer. **3** (choose, want, like) querer: **you can do as you please,** puedes hacer lo que quieras; **come this way, if you please,** haga el favor de pasar por aquí. **– 4** interj por favor: **quiet, please,** silencio, por favor; **yes, please,** sí, por favor.
● **please do!,** ¡desde luego!, ¡sí, cómo no!, ¡no faltaba más! ‖ **please yourself,** haz lo que quieras. ‖ **to be hard to please,** ser exigente.
pleased [pliːzd] adj (happy) contento,-a; (satisfied) satisfecho,-a: **I'm so pleased to see you,** me alegro mucho de verte; **he looks very pleased with himself,** parece muy satisfecho de sí mismo; **I'd be only too pleased to,** lo haría con mucho gusto; **we are pleased to inform you that ...,** tenemos el placer de comunicarles que ..., nos complace comunicarles que ...
● **pleased to meet you!,** ¡encantado,-a!, ¡mucho gusto!
pleasing ['pliːzɪŋ] adj (pleasant) agradable; (gratifying) grato,-a; (satisfying) satisfactorio,-a.
pleasurable ['pleʒərəbəl] adj agradable, placentero,-a.
pleasure ['pleʒəʳ] n placer m: **it's a pleasure to be here,** es un placer estar aquí; **it gives me great pleasure to ...,** tengo el placer de ..., tengo el gusto de ...
● **my pleasure,** ha sido un placer. ‖ **to be detained at Her Majesty's pleasure,** quedar detenido,-a a disposición del Estado. ‖ **to have the pleasure of ...,** te-

ner el placer de ..., tener gusto de ...: *may I have the pleasure of this dance,* ¿me concede este baile? ‖ **to take pleasure in doing sth.,** disfrutar haciendo algo. ‖ **with pleasure,** con mucho gusto.
■ **pleasure boat,** barco de recreo. ‖ **pleasure cruise,** crucero de placer. ‖ **pleasure trip,** viaje *m* de placer.

pleat [pliːt] 1 *n* pliegue *m.* – 2 *t* plisar.

pleb [pleb] *n pej* ordinario,-a.

plebeian [plɪˈbiːən] 1 *adj* HIST plebeyo,-a. 2 *pej* ordinario,-a.

plebiscite [ˈplebɪsɪt] *n* plebiscito.
● **to hold a plebiscite,** celebrar un plebiscito.

plectrum [ˈplektrəm] *n* púa, plectro.
▲ *pl* **plectrums** *o* **plectra** [ˈplektrə].

pledge [pledʒ] 1 *n* (*promise*) promesa. 2 (*token*) prenda, señal *f: as a pledge of our friendship,* en señal de nuestra amistad. 3 (*security, guarantee*) garantía, prenda. – 4 *t* (*promise*) prometer: *he pledged allegiance to the king,* juró fidelidad al rey. 5 (*pawn*) empeñar, dar en prenda.
● **to pledge sb. to secrecy,** hacer jurar a algn. guardar el secreto. ‖ **to take the pledge,** jurar no probar el alcohol.

plenary [ˈpliːnərɪ] *adj* (*session, meeting*) plenario,-a; (*power, authority*) pleno,-a.

plenipotentiary [plenɪpəˈtenʃərɪ] 1 *adj* plenipotenciario,-a. – 2 *n* plenipotenciario,-a.

plentiful [ˈplentɪful] *adj* abundante: *apples are plentiful in winter,* en invierno hay manzanas en abundancia.

plenty [ˈplentɪ] 1 *n* abundancia. – 2 *pron* mucho,-a, muchos,-as: *we've got plenty of time,* tenemos tiempo de sobra; *there's plenty of food,* hay mucha comida. – 3 *adv* US *fam* muy.
● **in plenty,** en abundancia. ‖ **years of plenty,** años *mpl* de abundancia.

plethora [ˈpleθərə] *n* plétora (**of,** de).

pleurisy [ˈpluərɪsɪ] *n* pleuresía.

pliable [ˈplaɪəbəl] *adj* flexible.

pliant [ˈplaɪənt] *adj* flexible.

pliers [ˈplaɪəz] (**pair of**) **pliers,** *npl* alicates *mpl,* tenazas *fpl.*

plight [plaɪt] *n* situación *f* grave.

plimsolls [ˈplɪmsəlz] *npl* GB playeras *fpl,* zapatillas *fpl* de lona.

plinth [plɪnθ] *n* (*of column, pillar*) plinto; (*of statue*) peana.

plod [plɒd] 1 *i* (*walk slowly*) andar con paso lento, andar con paso pesado. 2 (*work steadily*) hacer laboriosamente.
◆ **to plod away** *i* perseverar (**at,** en).
▲ *pt* & *pp* **plodded,** *ger* **plodding.**

plodder [ˈplɒdəʳ] *n* persona tenaz.

plodding [ˈplɒdɪŋ] *adj* tenaz, laborioso,-a.

plonk[1] [plɒŋk] 1 *n* ruido sordo. – 2 *t fam* dejar caer: *she plonked herself down on the sofa,* se dejó caer en el sofá.

plonk[2] [plɒŋk] *n* GB *fam* vinaza.

plop [plɒp] 1 *n* plaf *m.* – 2 *adv* plaf. – 3 *i* hacer plaf (al caer).

plot[1] [plɒt] 1 *n* (*conspiracy*) conspiración *f,* complot *m.* 2 (*of book, film, etc*) trama, argumento. – 3 *t* (*plan secretly*) tramar, urdir. 4 (*course, position*) trazar. – 5 *i* conspirar, tramar, maquinar: *they plotted to kill the king,* conspiraron para matar al rey.
● **the plot thickens,** la historia se complica.
▲ (*verbo*) *pt* & *pp* **plotted,** *ger* **plotting.**

plot[2] [plɒt] *n* (*of land*) parcela, terreno; (*for building*) solar *m.*

plotter [ˈplɒtəʳ] *n* conspirador,-ra.

plough [plaʊ] 1 *n* AGR arado. – 2 *t* (*land etc*) arar. – 3 *i* arar la tierra.
◆ **to plough back** *t sep* (*profits*) reinvertir. ‖ **to plough into** *t insep* (*crash*) estrellarse contra. ‖ **to plough through** 1 *t insep* (*mud, snow, etc*) abrirse camino a través de; (*sea*) surcar. 2 *fig* (*finish*) tratar de acabar; (*do with difficulty*) hacer laboriosamente.
■ **the Plough,** el Carro, la Osa Mayor.

ploughman [ˈplaʊmən] *n* arador *m,* labrador *m.*
■ **ploughman's lunch,** plato de queso, ensalada, encurtidos *y* pan.

plover [ˈplʌvəʳ] *n* ORN chorlito.

plow [plaʊ] *n* US → **plough.**

plowman [ˈplaʊmən] *n* US → **ploughman.**

ploy [plɔɪ] *n* truco, ardid *m,* treta, estratagema.

pluck [plʌk] 1 *n* valor *m,* ánimo, coraje *m,* arrojo. – 2 *t* (*gen*) arrancar; (*flower, fruit*) coger. 3 (*bird*) desplumar. – 4 *n* MUS puntear.
● **to pluck one's eyebrows,** depilarse las cejas. ‖ **to pluck up courage,** armarse de valor, cobrar ánimo.

plucky [ˈplʌkɪ] *adj* valiente.
▲ *comp* **pluckier,** *superl* **pluckiest.**

plug [plʌg] 1 *n* (*for bath, sink, etc*) tapón *m.* 2 ELEC (*on lead*) enchufe *m,* clavija; (*socket*) enchufe *m,* toma de corriente. 3 (*publicity*) publicidad *f.* 4 (*of tobacco*) rollo. – 5 *t* (*hole etc*) tapar (**up, -**). 6 (*publicize*) dar publicidad a, promocionar.
◆ **to plug away** *t insep* perseverar (**at,** en). ‖ **to plug in** 1 *t sep* enchufar: *plug it in,* enchúfalo. – 2 *i* enchufarse. ‖ **to plug into** *t sep* enchufar a: *plug the radio into the mains,* enchufa la radio a la corriente.
● **to give sth. a plug,** dar publicidad a algo, promocionar algo.
■ **sparking plug,** bujía.
▲ (*verbo*) *pt* & *pp* **plugged,** *ger* **plugging.**

plughole [ˈplʌghəʊl] *n* desagüe *m.*

plum [plʌm] 1 *n* (*fruit*) ciruela. 2 (*colour*) color *m* ciruela. – 3 *adj fam* fantástico,-a: *a plum job,* un chollo.
■ **plum pudding,** budín *m* de pasas. ‖ **plum tree,** ciruelo.

plumage [ˈpluːmɪdʒ] *n* plumaje *m.*

plumb [plʌm] 1 *n* (*lead weight used in building*) plomada. 2 (*for depth-sounding*) sonda. – 3 *adj* ARCH a plomo, vertical. – 4 *adv* ARCH a plomo, verticalmente. 5 (*exactly*) justo, de lleno. 6 US (*quite, absolutely*) completamente: *plum crazy,* loco,-a de remate. – 7 *t* ARCH aplomar. 8 (*water*) sondar. 9 *fig* (*mystery*) descifrar.
◆ **to plumb in** *t sep* instalar, conectar.
● **to be out of plumb,** no estar a plomo. ‖ **to plumb the depths of despair,** estar completamente desesperado,-a.
■ **plumb line,** plomada.

plumber [ˈplʌməʳ] *n* fontanero,-ra.

plumbing [ˈplʌmɪŋ] 1 *n* (*occupation*) fontanería. 2 (*system*) tubería, cañería.

plume [pluːm] *n* penacho.

plummet [ˈplʌmɪt] 1 *i* (*bird, plane*) caer en picado. 2 *fig* (*prices*) caer en picado, desplomarse, bajar vertiginosamente; (*morale*) caer a plomo.

plump[1] [plʌmp] *adj* (*person*) regordete, rollizo,-a; (*baby*) rechoncho,-a; (*animal*) gordo,-a.
◆ **to plump up** *t sep* (*pillow etc*) ahuecar, sacudir.

plump[2] [plʌmp] **to plump for,** *t* optar por, decidirse por.

plunder [ˈplʌndəʳ] 1 *n* (*action*) pillaje *m,* saqueo. 2 (*loot*) botín *m.* – 3 *t* saquear, pillar.

plunge [plʌndʒ] **1** *n* (*dive*) zambullida, chapuzón *m*. **2** (*fall*) caída, descenso. – **3** *i* (*dive*) lanzarse, zambullirse, tirarse de cabeza; (*fall*) caer, hundirse, precipitarse. **4** (*drop - prices etc*) caer en picado, desplomarse. **5** MAR cabecear. – **6** *t* (*immerse*) sumergir, hundir; (*thrust*) clavar, meter; (*in despair, poverty etc*) sumir: *Henry plunged the knife into his back,* Henry le clavó el cuchillo en la espalda; *the tragic news plunged her into despair,* la trágica noticia la sumió en la desesperación; *the neighbourhood was plunged into darkness,* el barrio quedó sumido en la oscuridad.
● **to take the plunge,** dar el paso decisivo.

plunger [ˈplʌndʒəʳ] **1** *n* (*for drain etc*) desatascador *m*. **2** TECH (*piston*) émbolo.

plunging [ˈplʌndʒɪŋ] *adj* (*neckline*) escotado,-a.

pluperfect [pluːˈpɜːfɪkt] *n* LING pluscuamperfecto.

plural [ˈpluərəl] **1** *adj* plural. – **2** *n* plural *m*.

pluralism [ˈpluərəlɪzəm] *n* pluralismo.

plurality [pluəˈrælɪtɪ] **1** *n* pluralidad *f*. **2** US POL mayoría relativa.

plus [plʌs] **1** *prep* más: *four plus five is nine,* cuatro más cinco son nueve. – **2** *adj* (*ion, number*) positivo,-a: *the temperature is plus five degrees,* la temperatura es de cinco grados. **3** (*and more*) más de, algo más de: *a house costs £60,000 plus,* una casa cuesta algo más de 60.000 libras. **4** (*advantageous*) positivo,-a. – **5** *n* MATH (*sign*) signo más. **6** (*advantage*) ventaja, factor *m* positivo, pro.
■ **plus sign,** signo más.

plush [plʌʃ] **1** *n* felpa, peluche *m*. – **2** *adj fam* lujoso,-a.

Pluto [ˈpluːtəʊ] *n* Plutón *m*.

plutonium [pluːˈtəʊnɪəm] *n* plutonio.

ply[1] [plaɪ] **1** *t* (*of ship*) navegar por. **2** (*tool*) manejar. – **3** *i* (*ship, bus, etc*) hacer el trayecto, navegar: *ferries that ply between Dover and Calais,* transbordadores que hacen el trayecto de Dover a Calais.
◆ **to ply with** *t sep* (*drink, food*) no parar de ofrecer; (*questions*) asediar a, acosar a.
● **to ply for hire,** (*taxi*) ir en busca de clientes. ‖ **to ply one's trade,** ejercer su oficio.
▲ (*verbo*) *pt* & *pp* **plied,** *ger* **plying.**

ply[2] [plaɪ] *n* (*of wood*) chapa; (*of paper*) capa; (*of wool*) cabo; *four-ply wool,* lana de cuatro cabos.
▲ *pl* **plies.**

plywood [ˈplaɪwʊd] *n* contrachapado, madera contrachapada.

pm [ˈpiːˈem] *abbr* (*post meridiem*) después del mediodía: *at 4 pm,* a las cuatro de la tarde.
▲ En Estados Unidos también se escribe *PM.*

PM [ˈpiːˈem] *abbr* GB FAM (*Prime Minister*) Primer,-a Ministro,-a.

PMT [ˈpiːˈemˈtiː] *abbr* (*premenstrual tension*) tensión premenstrual.

pneumatic [njuːˈmætɪk] *adj* neumático,-a.

pneumonia [njuːˈməʊnɪə] *n* pulmonía.

PO[1] [petɪˈɒfɪsəʳ] *abbr* (*Petty Officer*) contramaestre *m*.

PO[2] [ˈpəʊstəlˈɔːdəʳ] *abbr* (*postal order*) giro postal; (*abbreviation*) g.p.

PO[3] [ˈpəʊstˈɒfɪs] *abbr* (*Post Office*) correos *mpl*.

poach[1] [pəʊtʃ] **1** *i* (*for game*) cazar en vedado, cazar furtivamente; (*for fish*) pescar en vedado, pescar furtivamente. – **2** *t* (*game*) cazar en vedado, cazar furtivamente; (*fish*) pescar en vedado, pescar furtivamente. **3** (*take, steal*) robar.

poach[2] [pəʊtʃ] *t* CULIN (*fish*) hervir; (*eggs*) escalfar.

poacher [ˈpəʊtʃəʳ] *n* (*of game*) cazador,-ra furtivo,-a; (*of fish*) pescador,-ra furtivo,-a.

pocket [ˈpɒkɪt] **1** *n* (*gen*) bolsillo: *he put his hand in his pocket,* echó mano al bolsillo; *prices to suit every pocket,* precios para todos los bolsillos. **2** (*small area - of air*) bolsa; (*- of resistence*) foco. **3** (*on snooker table*) tronera. – **4** *adj* (*dictionary, camera, etc*) de bolsillo. – **5** *t* (*put in pocket*) meterse en el bolsillo, guardarse en el bolsillo. **6** (*keep, take dishonestly*) embolsar, quedarse con: *he pocketed the change,* se quedó con el cambio.
● **to live in each other's pockets,** estar uno encima del otro. ‖ **to be out of pocket,** (*lose*) salir perdiendo; (*have to pay*) tener que poner de su propio bolsillo: *it left me £50 out of pocket,* salí perdiendo 50 libras. ‖ **to pay for sth. out of one's own pocket,** pagar algo con su propio dinero. ‖ **to pick sb.'s pocket,** robarle algo a algn.
■ **pocket calculator,** calculadora de bolsillo. ‖ **pocket handkerchief,** pañuelo. ‖ **pocket money,** (*for children*) paga, semanada.

pocketbook [ˈpɒkɪtbʊk] **1** *n* US bolso. **2** (*notebook*) libreta (de bolsillo).

pocketful [ˈpɒkɪtful] *n* bolsillo.

pocketknife [ˈpɒkɪtnaɪf] *n* navaja.

pocket-sized [ˈpɒkɪtsaɪzd] *adj* de bolsillo, (de) tamaño bolsillo.

pockmark [ˈpɒkmɑːk] *n* (*on face, skin*) viruela; (*hole*) agujero.

pockmarked [ˈpɒkmɑːkt] *adj* (*face, skin*) picado,-a de viruelas; (*surface, building*) lleno,-a de agujeros.

pod [pɒd] *n* BOT vaina.

podgy [ˈpɒdʒɪ] *adj* gordinflón,-ona, regordete,-a.
▲ *comp* **podgier,** *superl* **podgiest.**

podium [ˈpəʊdɪəm] *n* podio.
▲ *pl* **podiums** o **podia** [ˈpəʊdɪə].

poem [ˈpəʊəm] *n* poema *m*, poesía.

poet [ˈpəʊət] *n* poeta *mf*.

poetic [pəʊˈetɪk] *adj* poético,-a.
● **poetic justice,** justicia divina. ‖ **poetic licence,** licencia poética.

poetry [ˈpəʊətrɪ] *n* poesía.
● **to be poetry in motion,** ser pura poesía.
■ **poetry reading,** recital *m* de poesía.

pogrom [ˈpɒgrəm] *n* pogromo.

poignancy [ˈpɔɪnjənsɪ] *n* (*sorrow*) tristeza; (*pathos*) patetismo.

poignant [ˈpɔɪnjənt] *adj* (*moving*) conmovedor,-ra; (*sad*) triste, patético,-a.

point [pɔɪnt] **1** *n* (*sharp end - of knife, nail, pencil*) punta. **2** (*place*) punto, lugar *m*: *meeting point,* punto de encuentro, punto de reunión. **3** (*moment*) momento, instante *m*, punto: *at no point,* en ningún momento; *at this point,* en este momento; *at that point,* en aquel momento, entonces. **4** (*state, degree*) punto, extremo: *he was offhand to the point of rudeness,* estuvo tan brusco que llegó a ser grosero. **5** (*on scale, graph, compass*) punto; (*on thermometer*) grado: *what's the boiling point of water?,* ¿cuál es el punto de ebullición del agua? **6** SP (*score, mark*) punto, tanto: *he won on points,* ganó por puntos. **7** FIN entero: *the financial index is up two points,* el índice ha subido dos enteros. **8** (*item, matter, idea, detail*) punto: *I'd like to raise a point,* quisiera plantear una cuestión; *she made some interesting points,* hizo unas observaciones interesantes; *I see your point,* ya veo lo que quieres decir, entiendo lo que quieres decir; *point taken!,* ¡de acuerdo!; *he's got a point,* tiene cierta razón (en lo que dice). **9** (*central idea, meaning*) idea, significado: *you've missed the point,* no has captado la idea; *that's*

not the point, no se trata de eso. **10** (*purpose, use*) sentido, propósito: *what's the point?,* ¿para qué?; *what's the point of ...,* ¿qué sentido tiene ...; *there's no point in ...,* no vale la pena ... **11** (*quality, ability*) cualidad *f*: *he has his good points and bad points,* tiene cualidades y defectos. **12** GEOG punta, cabo. **13** MATH (*in geometry*) punto (de intersección). **14** (*on compass*) punto (cardinal). **15** (*in decimals*) coma: *5 point 6,* cinco coma seis. – **16** *i* (*show*) señalar: *the girl pointed at the clown,* la niña señaló al payaso con el dedo. **17** *fig* (*indicate*) indicar: *it all points to blackmail,* todo indica que se trata de un chantaje. – **18** *t* (*with weapon*) apuntar: *he pointed a gun at me,* me apuntó con una pistola. **19** (*direct*) señalar, indicar. **20** (*wall, house*) ajuntar. – **21** points, *npl* GB (*on railway*) agujas *fpl*.
◆ to point out **1** *t sep* (*show*) señalar: *point your boss out,* señala a tu jefe. **2** (*mention*) señalar, hacer notar; (*warn*) advertir.
● at the point of a gun, a punta de pistola. ‖ in point of fact, de hecho, en realidad. ‖ not to put too finer point on it, hablando en plata. ‖ to be beside the point, no venir al caso. ‖ to be on the point of doing sth., estar a punto de hacer algo. ‖ to be to the point, ser relevante y conciso,-a. ‖ to come to the point, ir al grano. ‖ to dance on points, bailar de puntas. ‖ to get to the point, ir al grano. ‖ to make a point of doing sth., proponerse hacer algo, poner empeño en hacer algo. ‖ to reach the point of no return, no poder echarse atrás. ‖ up to a point, hasta cierto punto.
■ point of order, moción *f* de orden. ‖ point of view, punto de vista. ‖ sore point, tema *mf* delicado. ‖ strong point, punto fuerte *m*. ‖ weak point, punto débil.

point-blank [pɔɪnt'blæŋk] **1** *adj* (*refusal*) categórico,-a, rotundo,-a; (*question*) directo,-a. **2** (*shot*) a quemarropa, a bocajarro. – **3** *adv* (*refuse*) categóricamente, rotundamente; (*ask*) de golpe y porrazo. **4** (*shoot*) a quemarropa.

pointed ['pɔɪntɪd] **1** *adj* (*sharp*) puntiagudo,-a; (*shoes*) en punta. **2** *fig* (*comment*) intencionado,-a, significativo,-a; (*wit*) mordaz.

pointedly ['pɔɪntɪdlɪ] *adv* (*significantly*) con intención, de un modo significativo; (*cuttingly*) con mordacidad.

pointer ['pɔɪntə'] **1** *n* (*on dial, scale, etc*) aguja; (*for blackboard, etc*) puntero. **2** (*dog*) perro de muestra. **3** (*piece of advice, suggestion*) consejo, sugerencia; (*clue*) pista.

pointless ['pɔɪntləs] *adj* (*meaningless*) sin sentido; (*useless*) inútil: *it's pointless,* no tiene sentido, no sirve de nada.

pointsman ['pɔɪntsmən] *n* GB guardagujas *m*.

poise [pɔɪz] **1** *n* (*bearing*) porte *m*, elegancia, garbo. **2** (*self-assurance*) aplomo, desenvoltura. – **3** *t* colocar en equilibrio. – **4** *i* (*bird*) cernerse.

poised [pɔɪzd] **1** *adj* (*balanced*) en equilibrio, equilibrado,-a; (*in air*) suspendido,-a. **2** (*ready*) listo,-a, preparado,-a. **3** (*self-controlled*) sereno,-a, dueño,-a de sí mismo,-a.

poison ['pɔɪzən] **1** *n* veneno. – **2** *t* (*harm, kill - person, animal*) envenenar; (*make ill*) intoxicar; (*river*) contaminar; (*arrow, dart*) envenenar. **3** (*corrupt*) envenenar, corromper.
● what's your poison?, ¿qué quieres tomar? ‖ to take poison, envenenarse.
■ poison ivy, hiedra venenosa. ‖ rat poison, raticida *m*, matarratas *m*.

poisoning ['pɔɪzənɪŋ] *n* envenenamiento.
● to die of poisoning, morir envenenado,-a.

■ blood poisoning, envenenamiento de la sangre.

poisonous ['pɔɪzənəs] **1** *adj* (*plant, berry, snake*) venenoso,-a; (*drugs, gas*) tóxico,-a. **2** *fig* (*doctrine, ideas*) pernicioso,-a; (*remark, person*) venenoso,-a.

poison-pen letter [pɔɪzən'penletə'] *n* anónimo.

poke [pəʊk] **1** *n* (*jab*) empujón *m*, golpe *m*; (*with elbow*) codazo; (*with sharp object*) pinchazo. – **2** *t* (*jab - with finger*) dar con la punta del dedo; (*- with elbow*) dar un codazo a; (*- with pointed object*) dar un pinchazo a. **3** (*insert*) meter. **4** (*fire*) atizar. **5** (*show*) asomar: *he poked his head round the door,* asomó la cabeza por la puerta.
◆ to poke about / poke around *i* fisgonear. ‖ to poke out **1** *t sep* sacar: *you nearly poked my eye out!,* ¡casi me sacas el ojo! – **2** *i* asomar.
● to poke fun at sb., burlarse de algn. ‖ to poke one's nose into sb. else's business, meterse en asuntos ajenos.

poker[1] ['pəʊkə'] *n* (*for fire*) atizador *m*.
● as stiff as a poker, más tieso,-a que un palo.

poker[2] ['pəʊkə'] *n* (*card game*) póquer *m*.

poker-faced ['pəʊkəfeɪst] *adj* de rostro impasible.

poky ['pəʊkɪ] *adj fam* minúsculo,-a, diminuto,-a: *a poky little room,* un cuartucho.
▲ *comp* pokier, *superl* pokiest.

Poland ['pəʊlənd] *n* Polonia.

polar ['pəʊlə'] *adj* polar.
■ polar bear, oso polar.

polarity [pəʊ'lærɪtɪ] *n* polaridad *f*.
▲ *pl* polarities.

polarization [pəʊləraɪ'zeɪʃən] *n* polarización *f*.

polarize ['pəʊləraɪz] **1** *t* polarizar. – **2** *i* polarizarse.

Polaroid ['pəʊlərɔɪd] *adj* polaroid.

pole[1] [pəʊl] *n* (*stick, post*) poste *m*, palo, pértiga: *telegraph pole,* poste telegráfico; *tent pole,* palo de tienda.
■ pole vault, salto con pértiga.

pole[2] [pəʊl] *n* ELEC GEOG polo.
● to be poles apart, ser polos opuestos.
■ pole star, estrella polar. ‖ South Pole, Polo Sur.

Pole [pəʊl] *n* polaco,-a.

poleaxe ['pəʊlæks] **1** *n* (*for war*) hacha de guerra; (*for slaughtering*) hacha. – **2** *t* derribar, tumbar.
● to be poleaxed, *fig* quedarse de piedra, quedarse de una pieza.

polecat ['pəʊlkæt] *n* turón *m*.

polemic [pə'lemɪk] **1** *n* polémica. – **2** polemics, *npl* polémica *f sing*.

polemical [pə'lemɪkəl] *adj* polémico,-a.

police [pə'liːs] **1** *npl* (*body*) policía *f sing*; (*officers*) policías *mpl*. – **2** *t* (*keep order in*) mantener el orden en; (*keep watch on*) vigilar; (*area*) patrullar: *the march was heavily policed,* hubo un gran despliegue policial en la manifestación.
● to join the police, hacerse policía.
■ police car, coche *m* patrulla. ‖ police constable, policía *mf*, agente *mf*. ‖ police dog, perro policía. ‖ police force, cuerpo de policía. ‖ police headquarters, jefatura de policía. ‖ police state, estado policial. ‖ police station, comisaría.

policeman [pə'liːsmən] *n* policía *m*, agente *m* de policía, guardia *m*.

policewoman [pə'liːswumən] *n* policía *f*, agente *f* de policía, guardia *f*.

policy ['pɒlɪsɪ] **1** *n* POL política: *the government's policy on immigration,* la política del gobierno respecto a la inmigración. **2** (*course of action, plan*) política, estrategia: *it's company policy,* es la política de la empresa. **3** (*insurance*) póliza (de seguros).

● **to do sth. as a matter of policy,** tener por norma hacer algo.
■ **policy holder,** asegurado,-a.
▲ *pl* **policies**.
polio ['pəʊlɪəʊ] *n* poliomielitis *f*, polio *f*.
polish ['pɒlɪʃ] **1** *n* (*for furniture*) cera (para muebles); (*for shoes*) betún *m*; (*for floors*) cera, abrillantador *m* (de suelos); (*for nails*) esmalte *m*. **2** (*shine*) lustre *m*, brillo. **3** (*action*) pulimento. **4** *fig* (*refinement*) refinamiento, brillo. – **5** *t* (*floor, furniture*) sacar brillo a, encerar; (*shoes*) limpiar; (*silver, cutlery*) sacar brillo a; (*nails*) pintar con esmalte; (*stone*) pulir. **6** *fig* (*refine*) pulir (**up**, -), perfeccionar (**up**, -).
◆ **to polish off** *t sep* (*work*) despachar, terminar con; (*food*) zamparse, tragarse.
Polish ['pəʊlɪʃ] **1** *adj* polaco,-a. – **2** *n* (*person*) polaco,-a. **3** (*language*) polaco. – **4** **the Polish,** *npl* los polacos *mpl*.
polished ['pɒlɪʃt] **1** *adj* (*wood*) brillante; (*metal*) pulido,-a, lustroso,-a. **2** (*manners*) refinado,-a, elegante; (*performance, style*) pulido,-a.
polite [pə'laɪt] *adj* cortés, educado,-a, cumplido,-a, correcto,-a: *he was very polite to me,* me trató con cortesía; *she only said it to be polite,* lo dijo solo como cumplido.
● **in polite society,** en la buena sociedad, entre gente educada.
politely [pə'laɪtlɪ] *adv* cortésmente, educadamente, correctamente.
politeness [pə'laɪtnəs] *n* cortesía, educación *f*.
political [pə'lɪtɪkəl] *adj* (*gen*) político,-a: *students are becoming more and more political,* a los estudiantes les interesa cada vez más la política.
■ **political asylum,** asilo político. ‖ **political prisoner,** preso,-a político,-a. ‖ **political science,** ciencias *fpl* políticas.
politically [pə'lɪtɪkəlɪ] *adv* políticamente.
■ **politically correct,** políticamente correcto,-a.
politician [pɒlɪ'tɪʃən] *n* político,-a.
politics ['pɒlɪtɪks] **1** *n* (*gen*) política: *he's active in politics,* es militante (político). **2** (*science*) ciencias *fpl* políticas. – **3** *npl* (*view, opinions*) opiniones *fpl* políticas, ideas *fpl* políticas.
● **to go into politics,** dedicarse a la política. ‖ **to talk politics,** hablar de política.
polka ['pɒlkə] *n* (*dance*) polca.
■ **polka dot,** lunar *m*.
poll [pəʊl] **1** *n* (*voting*) votación *f*; (*number of votes cast*) votos *mpl*: *there's been a heavy poll,* el índice de participación ha sido muy alto. **2** (*survey*) encuesta, sondeo. – **3** *t* (*votes - obtain*) obtener. **4** (*ask opinion*) sondear, encuestar. – **5** **the polls,** *npl* las elecciones *fpl*, los comicios *mpl*: *a defeat at the polls,* una derrota electoral.
● **to go to the polls,** acudir a las urnas. ‖ **to take a poll on sth.,** someter algo a votación.
■ **poll tax,** GB ≈ contribución *f* urbana.
pollen ['pɒlən] *n* polen *m*.
■ **pollen count,** índice m de polen en el aire.
pollinate ['pɒlɪneɪt] *t* polinizar.
polling ['pəʊlɪŋ] *n* votación *f*.
■ **polling booth,** cabina electoral.
pollutant [pə'luːtənt] *n* contaminante *m*.
pollute [pə'luːt] *t* contaminar.
pollution [pə'luːʃən] *n* contaminación *f*.
polo ['pəʊləʊ] *n* SP polo.
■ **polo neck,** (*of sweater*) cuello cisne.
polo-neck ['pəʊləʊnek] *adj* (*sweater*) de cuello alto, de cuello cisne.

poltergeist ['pɒltəgaɪst] *n* duende *m*.
polyester [pɒlɪ'estə'] *n* poliéster *m*.
polygamous [pə'lɪgəməs] *adj* polígamo,-a.
polygamy [pɒ'lɪgəmɪ] *n* poligamia.
polyglot ['pɒlɪglɒt] **1** *adj* polígloto,-a. – **2** *n* (*person*) polígloto,-a.
polygon ['pɒlɪgɒn] *n* polígono.
polymer ['pɒlɪmə'] *n* polímero.
Polynesia [pɒlɪ'niːzɪə] *n* Polinesia.
polyp ['pɒlɪp] *n* pólipo.
polyphonic [pɒlɪ'fɒnɪk] *adj* polifónico,-a.
polystyrene [pɒlɪ'staɪriːn] *n* poliestireno *m*.
polytechinic [pɒlɪ'teknɪk] *n* escuela politécnica, politécnico.
polythene ['pɒlɪθiːn] *n* polietileno.
■ **polythene bag,** bolsa de plástico.
polyunsaturated [pɒlɪʌn'sætʃəreɪtɪd] *adj* poliinsaturado,-a.
polyurethane [pɒlɪ'jʊərəθeɪn] *n* poliuretano.
pomegranate ['pɒmɪgrænət] *n* BOT (*fruit*) granada; (*tree*) granado.
pomp [pɒmp] *n* pompa.
● **pomp and circumstance,** pompa y solemnidad.
pompom ['pɒmpɒm] *n* borla, pompón *m*.
pomposity [pɒm'pɒsɪtɪ] *n* pomposidad *f*.
pompous ['pɒmpəs] *adj* (*person*) pedante, presumido,-a, presuntuoso,-a; (*speech, language, style*) pomposo,-a, ampuloso,-a, rimbombante; (*occasion, ceremony*) pomposo,-a; (*building*) ostentoso,-a, imponente.
poncho ['pɒntʃəʊ] *n* poncho.
▲ *pl* **ponchos**.
pond [pɒnd] *n* estanque *m*.
ponder ['pɒndə'] **1** *t* considerar, cavilar sobre. – **2** *i* reflexionar (**on/over,** sobre), meditar (**on/over,** sobre).
ponderous ['pɒndərəs] *adj* pesado,-a.
pong [pɒŋ] **1** *n* GB *fam* peste *f*, tufo. – **2** *i* GB *fam* apestar.
pontiff ['pɒntɪf] *n* pontífice *m*.
pontificate [pɒn'tɪfɪkeɪt] *i* pontificar.
pontoon[1] [pɒn'tuːn] *n* pontón *m*.
■ **pontoon bridge,** puente *m* de pontones.
pontoon[2] [pɒn'tuːn] *n* GB (*card game*) veintiuna.
pony ['pəʊnɪ] *n* poney *m*, poni *m*.
■ **pony trekking,** excursión *f* en poney.
▲ *pl* **ponies**.
ponytail ['pəʊnɪteɪl] *n* cola de caballo.
poodle ['puːdəl] *n* caniche *m*.
poof [pʊf] *n sl pej* marica *m*.
pooh [puː] *interj* (*expressing contempt*) ¡bah!; (*expressing disgust*) ¡puf!
pooh-pooh [puː'puː] *t* (*idea, suggestion*) descartar, desechar, desdeñar.
pool[1] [puːl] **1** *n* (*of water, oil, blood, etc*) charco; (*of light*) foco. **2** (*pond*) estanque *m*; (*in river*) pozo.
pool[2] [puːl] **1** *n* (*common fund of money*) fondo común; (*in gambling*) bote *m*. **2** (*common supply of services*) servicios *mpl* comunes; (*of resources*) fondo; (*of vehicles*) parque *m*. **3** US (*snooker*) billar *m* americano. – **4** *t* (*funds, money*) reunir, juntar; (*ideas, resources*) poner en común. – **5** **the pools,** *npl* las quinielas *fpl*.
● **to do the pools,** hacer una quiniela.
poor [pʊə'] **1** *adj* (*person, family, country*) pobre. **2** (*inadequate*) pobre, escaso,-a; (*bad quality*) malo,-a; (*inferior*) inferior: *you've got a poor memory,* tienes mala memoria; *he's in poor health,* está mal de salud; *that joke was in poor taste,* ese chiste era de mal gusto; *she's a*

poor judge of character, no sabe juzgar a las personas; *they took a poor view of my decision,* vieron mi decisión con malos ojos. **3** (*unfortunate*) pobre: *poor Edward,* el pobre Edward; *you poor thing!,* ¡pobrecito! – **4 the poor,** *npl* los pobres *mpl.*

poorly ['pʊəlɪ] **1** *adj* (*ill*) indispuesto,-a, pachucho,-a. – **2** *adv* (*badly*) mal: *poorly dressed,* mal vestido,-a; *they're poorly paid,* les pagan muy poco.

pop¹ [pɒp] **1** *n* (*of cork*) taponazo. **2** *fam* (*drink*) gaseosa. – **3** *t* (*burst*) hacer reventar; (*cork*) hacer saltar. **4** (*put*) poner, meter: *she popped the letter in the postbox,* metió la carta en el buzón; *pop your coat on,* ponte el abrigo. – **5** *i* (*burst*) estallar, reventar; (*cork*) saltar. **6** (*go quickly*) ir rápidamente: *she's just popped out for a minute,* acaba de salir un momento; *I'm just popping over to Kate's,* voy un momento a casa de Kate; *I'll pop in later,* pasaré luego.
◆ **to pop off** *i euph* (*die*) estirar la pata, palmarla. ‖ **to pop up** *i* (*appear*) aparecer.
● **to go pop,** (*burst*) reventar; (*bang*) hacer pum. ‖ **to pop the question,** declararse.
▲ (*verbo*) *pt* & *pp* **popped,** *ger* **popping.**

pop² [pɒp] *n fam* (*music*) música pop.
■ **pop singer,** cantante *mf* pop. ‖ **pop festival,** festival *m* de música pop. ‖ **pop art,** pop-art *m.*

pop³ [pɒp] *n* US *fam* (*dad*) papá *m.*

pop⁴ [pɒpjʊ'leɪʃən] *abbr* (*population*) nº de habitantes.

popcorn ['pɒpkɔːn] *n* palomitas *fpl* de maíz.

pope [pəʊp] *n* papa *m.*

poplar ['pɒplə'] *n* BOT álamo.

poplin ['pɒplɪn] *n* popelín *m.*

popper ['pɒpə'] *n* GB SEW corchete *m.*

poppy ['pɒpɪ] *n* amapola.
▲ *pl* **poppies.**

populace ['pɒpjʊləs] *n* (*people*) pueblo; (*masses*) populacho.

popular ['pɒpjʊlə'] **1** *adj* (*well-liked* - *gen*) popular; (- *person*) estimado,-a; (- *resort, restaurant*) muy frecuentado,-a; (*fashionable*) de moda; (*name*) común,-una: *she's popular with her workmates,* les cae muy bien a sus compañeras de trabajo; *he's very popular with the ladies,* tiene mucho éxito con las mujeres; *we're not very popular with the neighbours,* los vecinos no nos tienen mucha simpatía. **2** (*of or for general public*) popular; (*belief, notion*) generalizado,-a; (*prices*) popular, económico,-a.
● **by popular demand / by popular request,** a petición del público.
■ **the popular press,** la prensa popular.

popularity [pɒpjʊ'lærɪtɪ] *n* popularidad *f.*

popularize ['pɒpjʊləraɪz] *t* (*make popular*) popularizar, hacer popular; (*make accessible*) vulgarizar, divulgar.

popularly ['pɒpjʊləlɪ] *adv* popularmente: *she is popularly known as Fergie,* es más conocida como Fergie.

populate ['pɒpjʊleɪt] *t* poblar.

population [pɒpjʊ'leɪʃən] *n* población *f: what is the population of Scotland?,* ¿cuántos habitantes tiene Escocia?
■ **population explosion,** explosión *f* demográfica.

populous ['pɒpjʊləs] *adj* populoso,-a.

porcelain ['pɔːsəlɪn] **1** *n* porcelana. – **2** *adj* de porcelana.

porch [pɔːtʃ] **1** *n* (*of church*) pórtico; (*of house*) porche *m,* entrada. **2** US (*veranda*) terraza.

porcupine ['pɔːkjʊpaɪn] *n* puerco espín.

pore¹ [pɔː'] *n* ANAT poro.

pore² [pɔː'] **to pore over,** *t* leer detenidamente, estudiar minuciosamente.

pork [pɔːk] *n* carne *f* de cerdo.
■ **pork butcher,** charcutero,-a. ‖ **pork chop,** chuleta de cerdo. ‖ **pork pie,** empanada de carne de cerdo.

pornographic [pɔːnə'græfɪk] *adj* pornográfico,-a.

pornography [pɔː'nɒgrəfɪ] *n* pornografía.

porous ['pɔːrəs] *adj* poroso,-a.

porpoise ['pɔːpəs] *n* marsopa.

porridge ['pɒrɪdʒ] *n* gachas *fpl* de avena.
■ **porridge oats,** copos *mpl* de avena.

port¹ [pɔːt] **1** *n* (*harbour, town*) puerto. – **2** *adj* portuario,-a.
● **to come into / put into port,** tomar puerto.
■ **fishing port,** puerto pesquero. ‖ **port of call,** puerto de escala. ‖ **port of registry,** puerto de matrícula.

port² [pɔːt] *n* AV MAR (*left side*) babor *m.*

port³ [pɔːt] *n* (*wine*) vino de Oporto, oporto.

portable ['pɔːtəbəl] *adj* portátil.

Port-au-Prince [pɔːtəʊ 'prɪns] *n* Puerto Príncipe.

portend [pɔː'tend] *t fml* augurar, presagiar.

portent ['pɔːtent] *n fml* augurio, presagio.

portentous [pɔː'tentəs] **1** *adj fml* (*ominous*) agorero,-a, profético,-a. **2** *pej* (*solem*) solemne.

porter ['pɔːtə'] **1** *n* (*in hotel, block of flats*) portero,-a; (*in public building, school*) conserje *m;* (*in hospital*) camillero. **2** (*at station, airport*) mozo, maletero. **3** US mozo de los coches-cama.

portfolio [pɔːt'fəʊlɪəʊ] **1** *n* (*flat case*) carpeta. **2** POL cartera: *minister without portfolio,* ministro,-a sin cartera.
▲ *pl* **portfolios.**

porthole ['pɔːthəʊl] *n* portilla.

portion ['pɔːʃən] *n* (*gen*) porción *f,* parte *f;* (*of food*) ración *f.*
◆ **to portion out** *t sep* repartir, dividir.

portly ['pɔːtlɪ] *adj* corpulento,-a.
▲ *comp* **portlier,** *superl* **portliest.**

portrait ['pɔːtreɪt] *n* retrato.
● **to paint sb.'s portrait,** retratar a algn.
■ **portrait painter,** retratista *mf.*

portray [pɔː'treɪ] **1** *t* (*painting*) representar, retratar. **2** (*describe*) describir, retratar. **3** (*act*) interpretar.

portrayal [pɔː'treɪəl] **1** *n* (*painting*) representación *f.* **2** (*description*) descripción *f.* **3** (*acting*) interpretación *f.*

Portugal ['pɔːtjʊgəl] *n* Portugal.

Portuguese [pɔːtjʊ'giːz] **1** *adj* portugués,-esa. – **2** *n* (*person*) portugués,-esa. **3** (*language*) portugués *m.* – **4 the Portuguese,** *npl* los portugueses *mpl.*

pos ['pɒzɪtɪv] *abbr* (*positive*) positivo,-a.

pose [pəʊz] **1** *n* (*position, stance*) postura, pose *f,* actitud *f.* **2** *pej* (*affectation*) pose *f,* afectación *f.* – **3** *t* (*problem, question, etc*) plantear; (*threat*) representar. – **4** *i* (*for painting, photograph*) posar. **5** *pej* (*behave affectedly*) presumir, hacer pose.
● **to pose as,** hacerse pasar por.

poser ['pəʊzə'] **1** *n* (*question*) pregunta difícil; (*problem*) dilema *m.* **2** (*person*) presumido,-a.

poseur ['pəʊzə'] *n* → **poser.**

posh [pɒʃ] **1** *adj* GB *fam* (*place, area*) elegante, de lujo; (*person*) de clase alta; (*accent*) refinado,-a. **2** GB *pej* (*gen*) pijo,-a.
● **to talk posh,** hablar con acento refinado.

position [pə'zɪʃən] **1** *n* (*place*) posición *f: what's the exact position of the plane?,* ¿cuál es la posición exacta del avión? **2** (*right place*) sitio, lugar *m: they manoeuvred the piano into position,* colocaron el piano en su lugar. **3** (*posture*) postura, posición *f: he was sitting in a very uncomfortable position,* estaba sentado en una postura

muy incómoda. **4** (*on scale, in competition*) posición *f*, lugar *m*, puesto; (*social standing*) categoría social, posición *f*. **5** (*job*) puesto: *she applied for the position of manager,* solicitó el puesto de gerente. **6** (*situation, circumstances*) situación *f*, lugar *m*: *you've put me in a difficult position,* me has puesto en una situación difícil; *put yourself in my position,* ponte en mi lugar. **7** (*opinion, point of view*) postura, posición *f*: *I think you know my position,* creo que ya conoces mi postura, creo que ya sabes lo que opino. **8** SP posición *f*. **–** **9** *t* (*put in place*) colocar, poner; (*troops, police*) situar, apostar.
● **to be in position,** estar en su sitio. ‖ **to be in a position to do sth.,** estar en condiciones de hacer algo. ‖ **to be out of position,** estar fuera de lugar. ‖ **to position os.,** situarse.

positive ['pɒzɪtɪv] **1** *adj* (*gen*) positivo,-a. **2** (*definite - proof, evidence*) concluyente, definitivo,-a; (*- refusal, decision*) categórico,-a; (*- answer*) firme; (*- instruction, order*) preciso,-a. **3** (*effective - criticism, advice*) constructivo,-a; (*- attitude, experience*) positivo,-a. **4** (*quite certain*) seguro,-a (**about**, de): *I'm absolutely positive,* estoy segurísimo. **5** *fam* (*absolute, complete, real*) auténtico,-a, verdadero,-a. **–** **6** *n* LING MATH positivo.
● **to think positive,** ser positivo,-a.
■ **positive discrimination,** discriminación *f* positiva.

positively ['pɒzɪtɪvlɪ] **1** *adv* (*with certainty*) categóricamente; (*definitely*) de forma decisiva, sin duda. **2** (*optimistically*) positivamente; (*actively*) activamente; (*favourably*) favorablemente. **3** *fam* (*absolutely*) verdaderamente, realmente: *the weather was positively awful!,* ¡hizo un tiempo malísimo!

possess [pə'zes] **1** *t* (*own*) poseer, tener. **2** (*take over - anger, fear*) apoderarse de: *whatever possessed you to buy that?,* ¿cómo se te ocurrió comprar eso?, ¿qué te dio por comprar eso?

possessed [pə'zest] *adj* (*by devil*) poseído,-a, poseso,-a, endemoniado,-a.

possession [pə'zeʃən] **1** *n* (*ownership*) posesión *f*, poder *m*; (*of arms*) tenencia. **2** (*thing owned*) bien *m*, posesión *f*: *all my personal possessions,* todas mis pertenencias. **3** SP posesión *f* de la pelota.
● **to be in possession of sth.,** estar en posesión de algo. ‖ **to come into possession of sth.,** llegar algo a su poder, llegar algo a sus manos. ‖ **to have sth. in one's possession,** tener algo (en su poder).

possessive [pə'zesɪv] **1** *adj* (*person*) posesivo,-a; (*selfish*) egoísta. **2** LING posesivo,-a. **– 3** *n* LING posesivo.

possessor [pə'zesə] *n* poseedor,-ra.

possibility [pɒsɪ'bɪlɪti] **1** *n* (*likelihood*) posibilidad *f*: *there's a strong possibility that I may be in London next week,* es muy posible que esté en Londres la semana que viene; *there's not much possibility of that happening!,* ¡eso es poco probable! **2** (*something possible*) posibilidad *f*: *we've studied all the possibilities,* hemos explorado todas las posibilidades. **– 3** possibilities, *npl* (*potential*) posibilidades *fpl*, potencial *m*: *the house has possibilities,* la casa tiene posibilidades.
▲ *pl* possibilities.

possible ['pɒsɪbəl] **1** *adj* posible: *I'll do everything possible,* haré todo lo posible; *it's not possible,* es imposible; *is it possible to book in advance?,* ¿se puede reservar con anticipación? **– 2** *n* posible candidato,-a.
● **as far as possible,** en lo posible, dentro de lo posible. ‖ **as much as possible,** todo lo posible. ‖ **as soon as possible,** cuanto antes, lo antes posible. ‖ **if (at all) possible,** si es posible, a ser posible.

possibly ['pɒsɪblɪ] **1** *adv* (*reasonably, conceivably*) posiblemente: *you can't possibly have finished already!,* ¡no es posible que ya hayas acabado!; *if I possibly can,* si me es posible. **2** (*in requests*): *could you possibly give me a lift to the station?,* ¿me podría llevar a la estación? **3** (*perhaps*) posiblemente, quizás, puede ser.

post¹ [pəʊst] **1** *n* (*of wood*) estaca, poste *m*. **– 2** *t* (*notice, list*) fijar, poner, exponer.
● **"post no bills",** "prohibido fijar carteles".
■ **goal post,** poste *m*, palo. ‖ **finishing post,** poste *m* de llegada.

post² [pəʊst] **1** *n* (*job*) puesto, empleo; (*important position*) cargo. **2** MIL puesto. **– 3** *t* MIL destinar, apostar. **4** (*employee*) destinar, mandar.
● **to take up one's post,** (*job*) ocupar el cargo, entrar en funciones.

post³ [pəʊst] **1** *n* GB (*mail*) correo; (*collection*) recogida; (*delivery*) reparto: *is there anything for me in the post?,* ¿hay alguna carta para mí en el correo?; *you'll catch the post if you hurry,* llegarás a la recogida si te das prisa; *it's in the post,* ya está enviado. **– 2** *t* GB (*send - letter, parcel*) enviar por correo, mandar por correo, echar al correo; (*put in postbox*) echar al buzón. **3** (*enter - in ledger*) anotar.
● **to keep sb. posted,** mantener a algn. al corriente, tener a algn. al corriente. ‖ **to post sth. to sb.,** mandar algo a algn. (por correo).
■ **post office,** Correos, oficina de correos. ‖ **post office box,** apartado de correos.

postage ['pəʊstɪdʒ] *n* franqueo, porte *m*.
■ **postage and packaging,** gastos *mpl* de envío. ‖ **postage paid,** franco de porte. ‖ **postage stamp,** sello postal.

postal ['pəʊstəl] *adj* (*charges, worker, district, etc*) postal; (*application, booking, vote*) por correo.
■ **postal order,** giro postal. ‖ **postal service,** servicio postal.

postbag ['pəʊstbæg] **1** *n* (*sack*) saca (de correos). **2** GB (*letters*) cartas *fpl*, correspondencia.

postbox ['pəʊstbɒks] *n* GB buzón *m*.

postcard ['pəʊstkɑːd] *n* tarjeta postal, postal *f*.

postcode ['pəʊstkəʊd] *n* GB código postal.

postdate [pəʊst'deɪt] *t* poner fecha posterior a.

poster ['pəʊstə] *n* póster *m*, cartel *m*.

poste restante [pəʊstrɪ'stænt] *n* lista de correos.

posterior [pɒ'stɪərɪə] **1** *adj* posterior. **– 2** *n fam* trasero, pompis *m*.

posterity [pɒs'terɪtɪ] *n* posteridad *f*.

post-free [pəʊst'friː] **1** *adj* porte pagado. **– 2** *adv* a porte pagado.

postgraduate [pəʊst'grædjʊət] **1** *n* postgraduado,-a. **– 2** *adj* de postgrado.

posthaste [pəʊst'heɪst] *adv* a toda prisa.

posthumous ['pɒstjʊməs] *adj* póstumo,-a.

posthumously ['pɒstjʊməslɪ] *adv* póstumamente, después de la muerte.

postman ['pəʊstmən] *n* cartero.

postmark ['pəʊstmɑːk] **1** *n* matasellos *m*. **– 2** *t* timbrar, matasellar.

postmaster ['pəʊstmɑːstə] *n* jefe *m* de oficina de correos.
■ **Postmaster General,** Director,-ra General de Correos.

postmistress ['pəʊstmɪstrəs] *n* jefa de la oficina de correos.

postmortem [pəʊst'mɔːtəm] *n* autopsia.

postnatal [pəʊst'neɪtəl] *adj* postnatal, (de) posparto.
■ **postnatal depression,** depresión *f* posparto.

postpone [pəs'pəʊn] *t* aplazar, posponer.

postponement [pəs'pəʊnmənt] *n* aplazamiento.
postscript ['pəʊstskrɪpt] *n* posdata *f*.
postulate ['pɒstjʊleɪt] *t* postular.
posture ['pɒstʃəʳ] **1** *n* (*way of holding body*) postura; (*position of body*) postura, pose *f*. **2** (*attitude*) postura. – **3** *i* hacer poses, adoptar poses.
postwar ['pəʊstwɔːʳ] *adj* de la posguerra, de posguerra: *the postwar period*, la posguerra.
postwoman ['pəʊstwʊmən] *n* cartera.
posy ['pəʊzɪ] *n* ramillete *m*.
▲ *pl* **posies**.
pot[1] [pɒt] **1** *n* CULIN (*container*) pote *m*, tarro; (*for cooking*) olla, puchero; (*earthenware*) vasija; (*teapot*) tetera; (*coffee pot*) cafetera. **2** (*of paint*) bote *m*. **3** (*flower pot*) maceta, tiesto. **4** (*chamber pot*) orinal *m*. – **5** *t* (*plant*) plantar en una maceta, plantar en un tiesto. **6** (*shoot game*) cazar. **7** SP (*pocket ball in billiards*) meter (en la tronera). – **8** the **pot**, *n* (*in card games*) el bote.
● **to go to pot**, echarse a perder, irse al traste. ‖ **to have pots of money**, estar forrado,-a. ‖ **to make pots of money**, forrarse.
■ **pots and pans**, batería de cocina, cacharros *mpl* (de cocina). ‖ **pot shot**, tiro al azar.
pot[2] [pɒt] *n fam* (*marijuana*) maría, hierba.
potable ['pəʊtəbəl] *adj fml* potable.
potash ['pɒtæʃ] *n* potasa.
potassium [pə'tæsɪəm] *n* potasio.
potato [pə'teɪtəʊ] *n* patata.
■ **potato chip,** US patata frita (de bolsa).
▲ *pl* **potatoes**.
potbellied ['pɒtbəlɪd] *adj* (*fat*) barrigón,-ona, panzudo,-a.
potbelly ['pɒtbelɪ] *n* barriga, panza.
▲ *pl* **potbellies**.
potency ['pəʊtənsɪ] *n* potencia, fuerza.
potent ['pəʊtənt] *adj* potente, fuerte.
potentate ['pəʊtənteɪt] *n* potentado.
potential [pə'tenʃəl] **1** *adj* potencial, posible. – **2** *n* potencial *m*.
● **to have potential**, ser prometedor,-ra. ‖ **to realize one's full potential**, realizarse plenamente.
potentially [pə'tenʃəlɪ] *adv* en potencia.
pothole ['pɒthəʊl] **1** *n* GEOL cueva. **2** (*in road*) bache *m*.
potholer ['pɒthəʊləʳ] *n* GB espeleólogo,-a.
potholing ['pɒthəʊlɪŋ] *n* GB espeleología.
potion ['pəʊʃən] *n* poción *f*, pócima.
■ **love potion**, filtro.
potluck [pɒt'lʌk] **to take potluck**, *n* conformarse con lo que haya.
potpourri [pəʊ'pʊərɪ] *n* (*gen*) popurrí *m*.
potted ['pɒtɪd] **1** *adj* CULIN en conserva. **2** (*plant*) en maceta, en tiesto. **3** (*of account, version, etc*) resumido,-a.
■ **potted meat / potted shrimps**, paté *m* de carne / paté *m* de camarones.
potter[1] ['pɒtəʳ] *n* alfarero,-a.
■ **potter's wheel**, torno de alfarero.
potter[2] ['pɒtəʳ] **to potter about / potter around**, *i* entretenerse: *I've been pottering about in the garden*, me he entretenido trabajando en el jardín.
pottery ['pɒtərɪ] *n* (*craft*) alfarería, cerámica; (*place*) alfarería, taller *m* de cerámica; (*objects*) cerámica, loza.
potty[1] ['pɒtɪ] *adj* GB *fam* (*crazy*) chiflado,-a.
● **to drive sb. potty**, volver loco,-a a algn.
potty[2] ['pɒtɪ] *n* orinal *m*.
▲ *pl* **potties**.

potty-trained ['pɒtɪtreɪnd] *adj* (*child*) que ya no lleva pañales.
pouch [paʊtʃ] **1** *n* (*gen*) bolsa (pequeña); (*for tobacco*) petaca; (*for ammunition*) morral *m*. **2** ZOOL bolsa abdominal.
pouf [puːf] *n* → **pouffe**.
pouffe [puːf] *n* (*seat*) puf *m*.
poultice ['pəʊltɪs] *n* cataplasma, emplasto.
poultry ['pəʊltrɪ] *n* (*birds*) aves *fpl* de corral; (*food*) carne *f* de ave, aves *fpl*, volatería.
■ **poultry farm**, granja avícola. ‖ **poultry farming**, avicultura.
pounce [paʊns] **1** *n* salto. – **2** *i* saltar (**on**, sobre), abalanzarse (**on**, sobre).
pound[1] [paʊnd] **1** *t* (*crush*) machacar. **2** (*strike, beat*) aporrear, golpear. – **3** *i* (*strike, beat*) aporrear (**at/on**, -), golpear (**at/on**, -); (*of waves*) batir (**against**, contra). **4** (*heart*) palpitar, latir con fuerza; (*music, sound*) resonar, retumbar. **5** (*walk heavily*) andar con pasos pesados.
pound[2] [paʊnd] **1** *n* FIN libra: *pound sterling*, libra esterlina; *a five-pound note*, un billete de cinco libras. **2** (*weight*) libra: *sixteen ounces make a pound*, una libra son dieciséis onzas; *half a pound of tomatoes*, media libra de tomates.
▲ Como medida de peso, equivale a 454 gramos.
pound[3] [paʊnd] *n* (*enclosure - for dogs*) perrera; (*- for cars*) depósito.
pounding ['paʊndɪŋ] **1** *n* (*of heart*) palpitación *f*, latidos *mpl* fuertes. **2** (*hammering*) golpes *mpl*, aporreo; (*of waves*) embate *m*. **3** (*beating*) paliza, zurra.
pour [pɔːʳ] **1** *t* (*liquid*) verter, echar; (*substance*) echar; (*money*) invertir; (*drink*) servir: *she poured the orange juice into a jug*, vertió el zumo de naranja en una jarra; *pour the rest of the milk away*, tira la leche que quedaba; *I've poured you a cup of tea*, te he servido una taza de té; *he poured himself a drink*, se sirvió una copa. – **2** *i* (*blood*) manar, salir; (*water, sweat*) chorrear: *the sweat was pouring off him*, chorreaba de sudor. **3** *fig* moverse en tropel: *people poured out of the station*, la gente salía en tropel de la estación; *offers are pouring in*, las ofertas llegan a raudales.
● **to pour (down/with rain)**, llover a cántaros: *it's pouring*, está lloviendo a cántaros. ‖ **to pour one's heart out to sb.**, desahogarse con algn. ‖ **to pour scorn on sth.**, despreciar algo, burlarse de algo.
pouring ['pɔːrɪŋ] *adj* (*rain*) torrencial.
pout [paʊt] **1** *n* puchero, mohín *m*. – **2** *i* hacer pucheros, hacer un mohín.
poverty ['pɒvətɪ] *n* (*gen*) pobreza: *extreme poverty*, miseria.
● **to live below the poverty line**, no tener ni el mínimo necesario para vivir.
■ **poverty line**, umbral *m* de la pobreza.
poverty-striken ['pɒvətɪstrɪkən] *adj* necesitado,-a, muy pobre.
POW ['piː'əʊ'dʌbəljuː] *abbr* (*prisoner of war*) prisionero,-a de guerra.
powder ['paʊdəʳ] **1** *n* (*dust*) polvo; (*cosmetic, medicine*) polvos *mpl*: *talcum powder*, polvos de talco. – **2** *t* (*put powder on*) poner polvos, empolvar. **3** (*pulverize*) pulverizar, reducir a polvo.
● **to powder one's nose**, *euph* lavarse las manos.
■ **powder compact**, polvera. ‖ **powder keg**, polvorín *m*. ‖ **powder puff**, borla. ‖ **powder room**, lavabo de señoras, tocador *m*.
powdered ['paʊdəd] *adj* (*milk, eggs*) en polvo.

powdery ['paʊdərɪ] *adj* como polvo, polvoriento,-a: *powdery snow,* nieve en polvo.
power ['paʊəʳ] **1** *n* (*strength, force*) fuerza; (*of sun, wind*) potencia, fuerza; (*of argument*) fuerza. **2** (*ability, capacity*) poder *m,* capacidad *f: I've done everything in my power,* he hecho todo lo posible; *it's beyond his power,* no está en sus manos; *she has the power to predict the future,* es capaz de predecir el futuro. **3** (*faculty*) facultad *f: he lost the power of speech,* perdió el habla; *she has great powers of concentration,* tiene una gran capacidad de concentración. **4** (*control, influence, authority*) poder *m;* (*of country*) poderío, poder *m: the power of the media,* el poder de los medios de comunicación; *he has some sort of power over her,* ejerce algún poder sobre ella; *the power of veto,* el derecho de veto; *the police have been granted special powers,* se ha concedido a la policía poderes especiales. **5** (*nation*) potencia; (*person, group*) fuerza: *world powers,* potencias mundiales; *the powers of darkness,* las fuerzas del mal. **6** PHYS (*capacity, performance*) potencia; (*energy*) energía. **7** ELEC electricidad *f,* corriente *f.* **8** MATH potencia: *six to the power of four,* seis elevado a la cuarta potencia. – **9** *t* propulsar, impulsar: *buses are powered by diesel engines,* los autobuses funcionan con diesel; *it's powered by electricity,* funciona con electricidad.
● **the powers that be,** las autoridades *fpl.* ‖ **to be in power,** estar en el poder. ‖ **to come to power,** llegar al poder. ‖ **to do sb. a power of good,** hacer a algn. mucho bien. ‖ **to have sb. in one's power,** tener a algn. en su poder. ‖ **to rise to power,** subir al poder. ‖ **to seize/take power,** tomar el poder, hacerse con el poder.
■ **nuclear power,** energía nuclear. ‖ **power base,** zona de influencia. ‖ **power cut,** apagón *m,* corte *m* del suministro eléctrico. ‖ **power drill,** taladradora mecánica. ‖ **power failure,** corte *m* del suministro eléctrico. ‖ **power of attorney,** JUR poder notarial *m,* procuración *f.* ‖ **power point,** enchufe *m,* toma de corriente. ‖ **power saw,** sierra mecánica, motosierra. ‖ **power station,** central *f* eléctrica. ‖ **power steering,** dirección *f* asistida. ‖ **power struggle,** lucha por el poder. ‖ **solar power,** energía solar.
powerboat ['paʊəbəʊt] *n* lancha motora.
powerful ['paʊəful] **1** *adj* (*strong - athlete, body, current*) fuerte; (*- blow, engine, machine*) potente. **2** (*influential - enemy, nation, ruler*) poderoso,-a. **3** (*effective - performance, image*) impactante; (*- argument, speech*) poderoso,-a, convincente; (*drug*) potente, fuerte.
powerfully ['paʊəfʊlɪ] *adv* (*hit*) con fuerza; (*argue*) convincentemente.
● **to be powerfully built,** ser de complexión fuerte.
powerhouse ['paʊəhaʊs] **1** *n* ELEC central *f* eléctrica. **2** *fig* (*person*) persona dinámica; (*thing*) fuerza motriz, motor *m.*
powerless ['paʊələs] *adj* impotente.
● **to be powerless to do sth.,** no poder hacer nada para hacer algo.
powerlessness ['paʊələsnəs] *n* impotencia.
pox [pɒks] *n* viruela.
poxy ['pɒksɪ] *adj sl* malísimo,-a.
▲ *comp* **poxier***; superl* **poxiest***.*
pp ['peɪdʒɪz] *abbr* (*pages*) páginas *fpl;* (*abbreviation*) pgs.
ppm ['pɑːtspə'mɪljən] *abbr* (*parts per million*) partes por millón; (*abbreviation*) ppm.
PR ['piː'ɑː] *abbr* (*public relations*) relaciones públicas.
practibility [præktɪkə'bɪlɪtɪ] *n* factibilidad *f,* practibilidad *f.*

practicable ['præktɪkəbəl] *adj* factible, practicable.
practical ['præktɪkəl] **1** *adj* (*gen*) práctico,-a; (*useful*) práctico,-a, útil; (*sensible*) práctico,-a, realista: *for all practical purposes,* en la práctica. **2** (*person - sensible*) práctico,-a, sensato,-a, realista; (*good with hands*) hábil, mañoso,-a. **3** (*real*) real, verdadero,-a. – **4** *n* (*lesson*) clase *f* práctica.
■ **practical joke,** broma.
practicality [præktɪ'kælɪtɪ] **1** *n* (*of suggestion, plan*) factibilidad *f.* – **2 practicalities,** *npl* aspectos *mpl* prácticos.
▲ *pl* **practicalities***.*
practically ['præktɪkəlɪ] **1** *adv* (*almost*) casi, prácticamente: *it cost us practically nothing,* no nos costó casi nada; *he smoked practically all the time,* fumaba prácticamente todo el tiempo. **2** (*in a practical way*) de manera práctica, con sentido práctico.
practice ['præktɪs] **1** *n* (*repeated exercise*) práctica; (*training*) entrenamiento; (*rehearsal*) ensayo: *I'm out of practice,* me falta práctica. **2** (*action, reality*) práctica: *in practice,* en la práctica. **3** (*custom, habit*) costumbre *f: standard practice,* es (lo) normal; *as was his usual practice,* como de costumbre. **4** (*exercise of profession*) ejercicio; (*place - of doctor*) consultorio, consulta; (*- of lawyer*) bufete *m,* gabinete *m.* – **5** *t* US → **practise***.*
● **practice makes perfect,** la práctica hace al maestro. ‖ **to be in practice,** (*doctor*) ejercer la medicina; (*lawyer*) ejercer la abogacía. ‖ **to make a practice of doing sth.,** tener como norma hacer algo. ‖ **to put sth. into practice,** poner algo en práctica, llevar algo a la práctica.
■ **piano practice,** ejercicios *mpl* de piano: *teaching practice,* prácticas *fpl* de magisterio.
practise ['præktɪs] **1** *t* GB (*do repeatedly - language, serve, scales*) practicar; (*song, act*) ensayar. **2** GB (*religion, belief, economy*) practicar: *you should practise what you preach,* deberías predicar con el ejemplo. **3** GB (*profession*) ejercer. – **4** *i* GB (*gen*) practicar: *to practise law,* ejercer la abogacía; *to practise medicine,* ejercer la medicina. **5** GB SP entrenar; GB MUS THEAT ensayar. **6** GB (*professionally*) ejercer (**as***,* de/como).
practised ['præktɪst] *adj* GB experto,-a.
● **to be practised in sth.,** tener mucha práctica en algo, tener mucha experiencia en algo.
practising ['præktɪsɪŋ] *adj* GB (*doctor, lawyer*) que ejerce, en ejercicio; (*Catholic etc*) practicante.
practitioner [præk'tɪʃənəʳ] *n* (*medical*) médico,-a.
pragmatic [præg'mætɪk] *adj* pragmático,-a.
pragmatics [præg'mætɪks] *n* pragmática.
pragmatism ['prægmətɪzəm] *n* pragmatismo.
pragmatist ['prægmətɪst] *n* pragmatista *mf.*
Prague [prɑːg] *n* Praga.
prairie ['preərɪ] *n* pradera, llanura.
praise [preɪz] **1** *n* alabanza, elogio, loa: *he had nothing but praise for his son,* no tenía más que elogios para su hijo; *the minister spoke in praise of her colleagues,* la ministra habló elogiando a sus colegas. **2** REL alabanza: *songs of praise,* cánticos de alabanza; *praise be to God!,* ¡alabado sea Dios! – **3** *t* elogiar. **4** REL alabar: *praise the Lord!,* ¡alabado sea Dios!
● **to praise sb. to the skies,** poner a algn. por las nubes. ‖ **to sing the praises of,** alabar, elogiar, cantar las excelencias de.
praiseworthy ['preɪzwɜːðɪ] *adj* digno,-a de elogio, loable.
praline ['prɑːliːn] *n* praliné *m.*
pram [præm] *n* GB cochecito de niño.

prance [prɑːns] **1** i (*horse*) hacer cabriolas. **2** (*child*) brincar (**about**, -), ir dando brincos; (*show off*) pavonearse: *she was prancing around in front of the mirror,* andaba pavoneándose delante del espejo.

prank [præŋk] n (*trick*) broma; (*of child*) travesura.
● to play a prank on sb., gastar una broma a algn.

prat [præt] n GB *fam* imbécil *mf*.

prattle ['prætəl] **1** n (*of adult*) cháchara, parloteo; (*of baby*) balbuceo. – **2** i (*adult*) charlar, parlotear; (*baby*) balbucear.

prawn [prɔːn] n (*large*) langostino; (*medium*) gamba; (*small*) camarón *m*.
■ prawn cocktail, cóctel *m* de gambas.

pray [preɪ] **1** i orar, rezar: *let us pray,* oremos. – **2** t rezar, rogar.
● to pray for sb./sth., rezar por algn./algo. ‖ to pray for sth. to happen, rezar para que pase algo, rogar para que pase algo.

prayer [preəʳ] n REL (*request*) oración f, rezo, plegaria; (*action*) oración f, rezo: *our prayers were answered,* nuestras pregarias fueron atendidas.
● to say one's prayers, rezar, orar.
■ evening prayers, oficio de vísperas. ‖ morning prayers, oficio de maitines. ‖ prayer book, devocionario. ‖ the Lord's Prayer, el Padrenuestro.

preach [priːtʃ] **1** t REL (*gospel*) predicar; (*sermon*) dar, hacer. **2** (*advocate*) aconsejar. – **3** i REL predicar.
● to preach at/to sb., *pej* sermonear a algn.

preacher ['priːtʃəʳ] **1** n (*person who preaches*) predicador,-ra. **2** US (*minister*) pastor,-ra.

preamble [priː'æmbəl] n preámbulo.

prearrange [priːə'reɪndʒ] t arreglar de antemano, acordar de antemano.

prearranged [priːə'reɪndʒd] adj (*signal, place, time*) convenido,-a.

precarious [prɪ'keəriəs] adj precario,-a.

precaution [prɪ'kɔːʃən] n precaución f: *take these tablets as a precaution against malaria,* toma estas pastillas como precaución contra el paludismo.
● to take precautions, (*gen*) tomar precauciones; (*in sex*) usar anticonceptivos. ‖ to take the precaution of doing sth., tener la precaución de hacer algo.

precautionary [prɪ'kɔːʃənərɪ] adj preventivo,-a.

precede [prɪ'siːd] **1** t preceder a, anteceder a. – **2** i preceder.

precedence ['presɪdəns] n (*order of importance*) precedencia; (*priority*) preferencia, prioridad f.
● in order of precedence, por orden de preferencia. ‖ to take precedence over sb./sth., tener prioridad sobre algn./algo.

precedent ['presɪdənt] adj precedente *m*.
● to set a precedent, sentar un precedente. ‖ without precedent, sin precedente.

preceding [prɪ'siːdɪŋ] adj (*year, week*) anterior; (*paragraph*) anterior, precedente.

precept ['priːsept] n precepto.

precinct ['priːsɪŋkt] **1** n (*of cathedral, hospital, etc*) recinto. **2** GB (*part of town*) zona. **3** US (*police district*) distrito policial; (*election precinct*) distrito electoral, circunscripción f. – **4** precincts, *npl* recinto *m sing*.

precious ['preʃəs] **1** adj (*jewel, stone, metal*) precioso,-a. **2** (*moment, memory, possession*) preciado,-a, querido,-a. **3** *iron* queridísimo,-a, maldito,-a. – **4** n (*term of endearment*) tesoro, vida.
● precious few, poquísimos,-as. ‖ precious little, poquísimo,-a. ‖ to be precious to sb., tenerle mucho cariño a algn./algo: *she's very precious to me,* le tengo mucho cariño.

precipice ['presɪpɪs] n precipicio.
● to be on the edge of a precipice, *fig* estar al borde del abismo.

precipitate [prɪ'sɪpɪteɪt] **1** t *fml* (*hasten*) precipitar. **2** CHEM precipitar. – **3** i CHEM precipitarse. – **4** n CHEM precipitado. – **5** adj *fml* precipitado,-a. ▲ (*adjetivo*) adj [prɪ'sɪpɪtət].

precipitation [prɪsɪpɪ'teɪʃən] **1** n *fml* (*haste*) precipitación f. **2** CHEM precipitación f. **3** METEOR precipitaciones fpl.

precipitous [prɪ'sɪpɪtəs] adj (*steep*) escarpado,-a.

précis ['preɪsiː] **1** n resumen *m*. – **2** t resumir, hacer un resumen de.

precise [prɪ'saɪs] **1** adj (*exact*) preciso,-a, exacto,-a. **2** (*meticulous*) meticuloso,-a, minucioso,-a.

precisely [prɪ'saɪslɪ] adv (*exactly*) precisamente, exactamente; (*accurately*) con precisión: *at nine o'clock precisely,* a las nueve en punto.
● precisely!, ¡exacto!, ¡eso es!

precision [prɪ'sɪʒən] n precisión f, exactitud f.
■ precision instrument, instrumento de precisión.

preclude [prɪ'kluːd] t *fml* (*prevent - gen*) impedir, evitar; (*- possibility*) excluir.
● to preclude sb. from doing sth., impedir a algn. hacer algo, impedir que algn. haga algo.

precocious [prɪ'kəʊʃəs] adj precoz.

precociousness [prɪ'kəʊʃəsnəs] n precocidad f.

precocity [prɪ'kɒsɪtɪ] n precocidad f.

preconceived [priːkən'siːvd] adj preconcebido,-a.

preconception [priːkən'sepʃən] n (*idea*) idea preconcebida.

precondition [priːkən'dɪʃən] n condición f previa.

precook [priː'kʊk] t precocinar.

precursor [prɪ'kɜːsəʳ] n *fml* precursor,-ra.

predate [priː'deɪt] **1** t (*precede*) preceder, ser anterior a. **2** (*put earlier date on*) poner fecha anterior a, antedatar.

predator ['predətəʳ] n ZOOL depredador *m*, predador *m*.

predatory ['predətərɪ] **1** adj ZOOL depredador,-ra, predador,-ra. **2** *fig* (*person*) depredador,-ra.

predecease [priːdɪ'siːs] t morir antes que.

predecessor ['priːdɪsesəʳ] n predecesor,-ra, antecesor,-ra.

predestination [priːdestɪ'neɪʃən] n predestinación f.

predestine [priː'destɪn] t predestinar.
● to be predestined to do sth., estar predestinado,-a a hacer algo.

predetermination [priːdɪtɜːmɪ'neɪʃən] n predeterminación f.

predetermine [priːdɪ'tɜːmɪn] t predeterminar.

predicament [prɪ'dɪkəmənt] n apuro, aprieto.

predicate ['predɪkət] **1** n LING predicado. – **2** t *fml* (*declare, assert*) afirmar; (*base*) basar (**on**, en).

predicative [prɪ'dɪkətɪv] adj LING predicativo,-a.

predict [prɪ'dɪkt] t predecir, pronosticar.

predictable [prɪ'dɪktəbəl] adj (*results, weather*) previsible: *he's so predictable,* siempre hace lo mismo, siempre dice lo mismo.

predictably [prɪ'dɪktəblɪ] adv de manera previsible, como era de esperar.

prediction [prɪ'dɪkʃən] n predicción f, pronóstico.

predilection [priːdɪ'lekʃən] n *fml* predilección f (**for**, por), preferencia (**for**, por).

predispose [priːdɪs'pəʊz] t *fml* predisponer (**to**, a).

predisposition [priːdɪspə'zɪʃən] n predisposición f (**to**, a), propensión f (**to**, a).

predominance [prɪ'dɒmɪnəns] 1 n (in strength, numbers, amount) predominio. 2 (in power, influence) predominio, primacía, supremacía.
predominant [prɪ'dɒmɪnənt] adj predominante, prevalente.
predominantly [prɪ'dɒmɪnəntlɪ] adv predominantemente, en su mayoría.
predominate [prɪ'dɒmɪneɪt] 1 i (in numbers etc) predominar. 2 (in power, influence) ejercer primacía (**over**, sobre), ejercer supremacía (**over**, sobre).
pre-eminence [priː'emɪnəns] n preeminencia.
pre-eminent [priː'emɪnənt] adj preeminente.
pre-empt [priː'empt] 1 t (forestall) adelantarse a. 2 (acquire) apropiarse de.
pre-emptive [priː'emptɪv] adj (attack, strike) preventivo,-a.
preen [priːn] t (of bird) arreglar con el pico.
● to preen os., (bird) arreglarse con el pico; (person) acicalarse.
pre-establish [priːɪ'stæblɪʃ] t establecer de antemano.
pre-established [priːɪ'stæblɪʃt] adj preestablecido,-a.
prefab ['priːfæb] n fam casa prefabricada.
prefabricated [priː'fæbrɪkeɪtɪd] adj prefabricado,-a.
preface ['prefəs] 1 n prefacio, prólogo. – 2 t prologar.
● to preface sth. with sth. / preface sth. by doing sth., introducir algo con algo / introducir algo haciendo algo.
prefect ['priːfekt] 1 n (official) prefecto. 2 GB EDUC monitor,-ra.
prefer [prɪ'fɜːʳ] 1 t preferir: she prefers coffee to tea, prefiere el café al té; he prefers swimming to running, prefiere nadar a correr; I'd prefer them to come on Sunday, preferiría que vinieran el domingo. 2 JUR (charge) presentar, formular.
▲ (verbo) pt & pp preferred, ger preferring.
preferable ['prefərəbəl] adj preferible (**to**, a).
preferably ['prefərəblɪ] adv preferentemente, de preferencia.
preference ['prefərəns] n preferencia (**for**, por).
● in preference to, antes que. ‖ to give preference to sb., dar preferencia a algn. ‖ to have a preference for sth., preferir algo.
■ preference shares / preference stock, FIN acciones fpl preferentes.
preferential [prefə'renʃəl] adj preferente.
● to give preferential treatment to sb., dar trato preferente a algn.
prefix ['priːfɪks] n LING prefijo.
pregnancy ['pregnənsɪ] n embarazo.
■ pregnancy test, prueba de embarazo.
pregnant ['pregnənt] 1 n (woman) embarazada; (animal) preñada: she's six months pregnant, está embarazada de seis meses. – 2 adj (pause, silence) muy significativo,-a.
● to be pregnant with sth., lit estar preñado,-a de algo. ‖ to get pregnant, quedarse embarazada.
preheat ['priːhiːt] t precalentar.
prehistoric [priːhɪ'stɒrɪk] n prehistórico,-a.
prehistorical [priːhɪ'stɒrɪkəl] adj prehistórico,-a.
prehistory [priː'hɪstərɪ] n prehistoria.
prejudge [priː'dʒʌdʒ] t (situation) prejuzgar; (person) juzgar de antemano.
prejudice ['predʒədɪs] 1 n (unfavourable bias) prejuicio; (favourable) predisposición f: racial prejudice, prejuicio racial. 2 JUR (injury, harm) perjuicio. – 3 t (influence, bias) predisponer (**against**, contra), (**in favor of**, a favor de). 4 (harm) perjudicar.

● to the prejudice of, JUR en perjuicio de, detrimento de. ‖ without prejudice to, JUR sin perjuicio de.
prejudiced ['predʒʊdɪst] adj parcial.
● to be prejudiced against/in favour of, estar predispuesto,-a en contra de/a favor de.
prejudicial [predʒə'dɪʃəl] adj perjudicial (**to**, para).
prelate ['prelət] n prelado.
preliminary [prɪ'lɪmɪnərɪ] 1 adj preliminar. – 2 preliminaries, npl preliminares mpl, prolegómenos mpl.
■ preliminary heat / preliminary round, SP eliminatoria.
prelude ['preljuːd] n (gen) preludio.
● a prelude to sth., un preludio de algo.
premarital [priː'mærɪtəl] adj prematrimonial.
premature [premə'tjʊəʳ] adj (gen) prematuro,-a.
● to be premature in doing sth., precipitarse en hacer algo, hacer algo antes de tiempo.
prematurely [premə'tjʊərlɪ] adv antes de tiempo.
● to be born prematurely, ser prematuro,-a.
premeditate [prɪ'medɪteɪt] t premeditar.
premeditated [priː'medɪteɪtɪd] adj premeditado,-a.
premenstrual [priː'menstruəl] adj premenstrual.
premier ['premɪəʳ] 1 adj primero,-a, principal. – 2 n POL primer,-a ministro,-a.
première ['premɪeəʳ] 1 CINEM THEAT estreno. – 2 t CINEM THEAT estrenar.
premise ['premɪs] n premisa.
premises ['premɪsɪz] npl local m.
● on the premises, dentro del local. ‖ out the premises, fuera del local.
premiss ['premɪs] n → premise.
premium ['priːmɪəm] n FIN (insurance) prima; (extra cost) recargo.
● to be at a premium, (stocks, shares) estar sobre la par; (in great demand) estar muy solicitado,-a. ‖ to put a premium on sth., dar mucha importancia a algo.
■ Premium Bonds, bonos mpl del estado.
premonition [priːmə'nɪʃən] n presentimiento, premonición f.
prenatal [priː'neɪtəl] adj prenatal.
preoccupation [priːɒkjʊ'peɪʃən] n (worry) preocupación f; (obsession) obsesión f, manía.
preoccupied [priː'ɒkjʊpaɪd] adj (worried) preocupado,-a; (wrapped up) absorto,-a, ensimismado,-a.
preoccupy [priː'ɒkjʊpaɪ] t (worry) preocupar; (think about too much) pensar demasiado en, darle demasiadas vueltas a.
▲ (verbo) pt & pp preoccupied, ger preoccupying.
prep [prep] n GB EDUC (homework) deberes mpl; (study period) hora de estudio.
■ prep school, → preparatory school.
prepaid [priː'peɪd] 1 t → prepay. – 2 adj (envelope) franqueado,-a; (reply) pagado,-a por adelantado.
preparation [prepə'reɪʃən] 1 n (action) preparación f. 2 (substance) preparado. – 3 preparations, npl preparativos mpl (**for**, para).
● in preparation for, en preparación para.
preparatory [prɪ'pærətərɪ] adj preparatorio,-a, preliminar.
● preparatory to, antes de, previo,-a a.
■ preparatory school, GB escuela de primaria privada; US colegio de secundaria privado.
prepare [prɪ'peəʳ] 1 t (gen) preparar; (report) redactar: this meal is easy to prepare, esta comida es fácil de preparar; have you prepared your parents for the news?, ¿has preparado a tus padres para la noticia? – 2 i prepararse (**for**, para).

● **to prepare os.**, prepararse.

prepared [prɪ'peəd] 1 *adj* (*gen*) preparado,-a; (*ready*) preparado,-a, listo,-a. 2 (*willing*) dispuesto,-a (**to,** a).
● "**be prepared**", "siempre listos". ‖ **to be prepared for sth.**, (*gen*) estar preparado,-a para algo; (*expect*) contar con algo, haber previsto algo.

prepay [priː'peɪ] *t* pagar por adelantado.
▲ *pt & pp* **prepaid,** *ger* **prepaying.**

prepayment [priː'peɪmənt] *n* pago por adelantado.

preponderance [prɪ'pɒndərəns] *n fml* preponderancia.

preponderant [prɪ'pɒndərənt] *adj fml* preponderante.

preposition [prepə'zɪʃən] *n* preposición *f*.

prepossessing [priːpə'zesɪŋ] *adj fml* atractivo,-a, agradable.

preposterous [prɪ'pɒstərəs] *adj* absurdo,-a, ridículo,-a.

prerecord [priːrɪ'kɔːd] *t* pregrabar, grabar de antemano.

prerecorded [priːrɪ'kɔːdɪd] *adj* pregrabado,-a.

prerequisite [priː'rekwɪzɪt] 1 *n* requisito previo, condición *f* previa. – 2 *adj* indispensable.

prerogative [prɪ'rɒgətɪv] *n* prerrogativa, privilegio.

Pres ['prezɪdənt] *abbr* (*President*) Presidente,-a; (*abbreviation*) Pres.

presage ['presɪdʒ] *t lit* presagiar.

Presbyterian [prezbɪ'tɪərɪən] 1 *adj* presbiteriano,-a. – 2 *n* presbiteriano,-a.

presbytery ['prezbɪtərɪ] 1 *n* (*local court*) presbiterio. 2 (*priest's house*) casa parroquial. 3 (*in church*) presbiterio.
▲ *pl* **presbyteries.**

preschool [priː'skuːl] *adj* preescolar.

prescribe [prɪs'kraɪb] 1 *t* (*medicine, drugs, etc*) recetar; (*holiday, rest*) recomendar: *do not exceed the prescribed dose,* no exceder la dosis recomendada. 2 *fml* (*order*) prescribir.

prescription [prɪs'krɪpʃən] *n* receta (médica): *it's only available on prescription,* sólo se vende con receta médica.
● **to make out a prescription,** extender una receta. ‖ **to make up a prescription / fill a prescription,** preparar una receta.
■ **prescription charge,** *precio fijo de los medicamentos recetados.*

prescriptive [prɪ'skrɪptɪv] 1 *adj fml* preceptivo,-a. 2 LING normativo,-a.

presence ['prezəns] 1 *n* (*gen*) presencia; (*attendance*) asistencia: *I'd rather we didn't discuss this in his presence,* preferiría que no habláramos de esto delante de él. 2 (*spirit*) espíritu *m*.
● **in the presence of sb.,** en presencia de algn. ‖ **to have presence,** tener presencia. ‖ **to make one's presence felt,** hacerse sentir.
■ **presence of mind,** presencia de ánimo, aplomo.

present[1] ['prezənt] 1 *adj* (*in attendance*) presente: *those present,* los presentes. 2 (*current*) actual. 3 LING presente. – 4 *n* (*now*) presente *m*, actualidad *f*. 5 **the present,** LING presente *m*.
● **at present,** actualmente, en este momento. ‖ **for the present,** de momento, por el momento, por ahora. ‖ **present company excepted,** exceptuando a los presentes. ‖ **there's no time like the present,** no dejes para mañana lo que puedas hacer hoy. ‖ **to be present,** (*at event, class, etc*) estar presente, asistir; (*see*) presenciar.

present[2] [prɪ'zent] 1 *t* (*make presentation*) entregar, hacer entrega de; (*give - as gift*) regalar; (*- formally*) obsequiar: *the winner was presented with a medal,* le entregaron

una medalla al ganador. 2 (*offer - report, petition, bill, cheque*) presentar; (*- argument, ideas, case*) presentar, exponer. 3 *fml* (*offer - apologies, respects*) presentar; (*- compliments, greetings*) dar. 4 (*give - difficulty, problem*) plantear; (*constitute*) suponer, constituir, ser; (*provide*) presentar, ofrecer: *this presented us with a new problem,* esto nos planteó un nuevo problema. 5 (*introduce*) presentar: *may I present Mr Brown?,* le presento al Sr. Brown. 6 (*play*) representar; (*programme*) presentar. – 7 *n* (*gift*) regalo; (*formal*) obsequio: *he gave me a present,* me hizo un regalo.
● **to make sb. a present of sth.,** regalar algo a algn.
‖ **to present itself,** (*opportunity*) presentarse. ‖ **to present os.,** presentarse.
▲ (*sustantivo*) ['prezənt].

presentable [prɪ'zentəbəl] *adj* presentable.
● **to make os. presentable,** arreglarse.

presentation [prezən'teɪʃən] 1 *n* (*of awards, prizes, gifts*) entrega. 2 (*of document, cheque, ticket*) presentación *f*. 3 (*way of presenting*) presentación *f*. 4 (*of play*) representación *f*.
■ **presentation ceremony,** ceremonia de entrega. ‖ **presentation copy,** ejemplar *m* gratuito.

present-day ['prezəntdeɪ] *adj* actual, de hoy en día.

presenter [prɪ'zentə'] *n* RAD presentador,-ra, locutor,-ra; TV presentador,-ra.

presentiment [prɪ'zentɪmənt] *n* presentimiento.

presently ['prezəntlɪ] 1 *adv* GB (*soon*) pronto, dentro de poco, enseguida. 2 US (*at present*) actualmente, en este momento.

preservation [prezə'veɪʃən] *n* (*of wildlife*) conservación *f*, preservación *f*; (*of food, works of art, buildings*) conservación *f*.
● **to be in a good/poor state of preservation,** estar en buen/mal estado.
■ **preservation order,** orden *f* de protección.

preservative [prɪ'zɜːvətɪv] *n* CULIN conservante *m*.

preserve [prɪ'zɜːv] 1 *n* CULIN (*fruit*) conserva; (*jam*) confitura, mermelada. 2 (*hunting area*) coto, vedado. 3 (*activity*) dominio, terreno; (*responsibility*) incumbencia. – 4 *t* (*building, manuscript, wood, leather*) conservar; (*specimen*) conservar, preservar; (*food*) conservar; (*fruit*) poner en conserva; (*standards, dignity, sense of humour*) mantener. 5 (*save, protect*) proteger. 6 SP (*game, fishing, etc*) proteger.

preset [priː'set] *t* programar.

preshrunk [priː'ʃrʌŋk] *adj* ya lavado,-a.

preside [prɪ'zaɪd] *i* presidir (**over,** -).

presidency ['prezɪdənsɪ] *n* presidencia.
▲ *pl* **presidencies.**

president ['prezɪdənt] 1 *n* (*of state, society*) presidente,-a. 2 US (*of bank, corporation*) director,-ra.

presidential [prezɪ'denʃəl] *adj* presidencial.

press [pres] 1 *n* (*newspapers*) prensa: *the gutter press,* la prensa sensacionalista, la prensa amarilla; *the quality press,* la prensa seria. 2 (*printing machine*) prensa, imprenta. 3 (*for grapes, flowers*) prensa: *trouser press,* prensa para pantalones. 4 (*act of pressing*) presión *f*; (*of hand*) apretón *m*; (*act of ironing*) planchado: *at the press of a botton,* con sólo apretar un botón; *give this shirt a quick press,* dale un planchado a esta camisa. – 5 *t* (*push down - button, switch*) pulsar, apretar, presionar; (*- accelerator*) pisar; (*- key on keyboard*) pulsar; (*- trigger*) apretar. 6 (*squeeze - hand*) apretar. 7 (*crush - fruit*) exprimir, estrujar; (*- grapes, olives, flowers*) prensar. 8 (*clothes*) planchar, planchar a vapor. 9 (*record*) imprimir. 10 (*urge, put pressure on*) presionar, instar; (*insist on*) insistir en, exigir: *they*

pressed me to report the theft, insistieron en que denunciara el robo; *they pressed me for an answer,* me exigían una respuesta. – 11 *i (push)* apretar, presionar: *press down on the lever,* presiona la palanca. 12 *(crowd)* apretujarse, apiñarse. 13 *(urge, pressurize)* presionar, insistir; *(time)* apremiar: *we are pressing for a peaceful solution,* estamos presionando para que se resuelva de forma pacífica.
◆ **to press ahead / press on** *i* seguir adelante.
● **at the time of going to press,** al cierre de la edición. ‖ **to go to press,** entrar en prensa. ‖ **to have a good/bad press,** tener buena/mala prensa. ‖ **to press a point,** recalcar un punto. ‖ **to press charges against sb.,** presentar cargos contra algn., formular cargos contra algn. ‖ **to press home an advantage,** aprovechar una ventaja.
■ **press agency,** agencia de prensa. ‖ **press conference,** conferencia de prensa, rueda de prensa. ‖ **press cutting,** recorte *m* de prensa. ‖ **press box,** tribuna de prensa. ‖ **press release,** comunicado de prensa. ‖ **press stud,** botón *m* de presión.
pressed [prest] *adj* CULIN *(ham, chicken)* embutido,-a.
● **to be pressed for sth.,** andar escaso,-a de algo, andar corto,-a de algo. ‖ **to be hard pressed to do sth.,** costarle mucho a algn. hacer algo.
press-gang ['presgæŋ] *t* obligar.
● **to press-gang sb. into doing sth.,** obligar a algn. a hacer algo.
pressing ['presɪŋ] 1 *adj (engagement, need)* urgente, apremiante; *(request, person)* insistente. – 2 *n (of records)* prensado.
pressman ['presmən] *n* periodista *m*.
▲ *pl* **pressmen** ['presmen].
press-up ['presʌp] *n* flexión *f*.
pressure ['preʃə'] 1 *n* PHYS TECH *(force, weight)* presión *f*. 2 METEOR presión *f*: *high pressure usually means good weather,* las altas presiones suelen significar buen tiempo. 3 MED tensión *f* arterial, tensión: *she has high/low blood pressure,* tiene la tensión alta/baja. 4 *(forcible influence)* presión *f*: *the pressure of public opinion,* la presión de la opinión pública. 5 *(stress)* tensión *f*: *he's under a lot of pressure,* está sometido a una gran presión. – 6 *t* US *(pressurize)* apretar.
● **to do sth. under pressure,** hacer algo presionado,-a (por algn.). ‖ **to bring pressure to bear on sb.,** ejercer presión sobre algn. ‖ **to put pressure on sb. (to do sth.),** presionar a algn. (para que haga algo).
■ **pressure cooker,** olla a presión, olla exprés. ‖ **pressure gauge,** manómetro. ‖ **pressure group,** grupo de presión.
pressure-cook ['preʃəkʊk] *t* cocinar en olla a presión, cocinar en olla exprés.
pressurize ['preʃəraɪz] 1 *t* AV TECH presurizar: *pressurized cabin,* cabina presurizada. 2 GB *(force)* presionar.
● **to pressurize sb. into doing sth.,** presionar a algn. para que haga algo.
prestige [pres'tiːʒ] *n* prestigio.
prestigious [pres'tɪdʒəs] *adj* prestigioso,-a.
presumably [prɪ'zjuːməblɪ] *adv* se supone que, es de suponer: *presumably you can afford it?,* ¿supongo que te lo puedes permitir?
presume [prɪ'zjuːm] 1 *t* suponer, imaginarse, presumir: *I presume so,* supongo que sí. – 2 *i* suponer. 3 *(venture to)* atreverse a.
● **to presume on sb.'s generosity,** abusar de la generosidad de algn.
presumed [prɪ'zjuːmd] *adj* presunto,-a, supuesto,-a: *presumed innocent,* presunto inocente; *missing, presumed dead,* desaparecido, dado por muerto.

presumption [prɪ'zʌmpʃən] 1 *n (assumption - gen)* suposición *f*, presunción *f*; *(- of innocence)* presunción *f*. 2 *(boldness)* atrevimiento, osadía, audacia, presunción *f*.
presumptuous [prɪ'zʌmptjʊəs] *adj* atrevido,-a, audaz, impertinente.
presuppose [priːsə'pəʊz] *t* presuponer.
presupposition [priːsʌpə'zɪʃən] *n* suposición *f*, presunción *f*.
pretence [prɪ'tens] 1 *n (deception, make-believe)* fingimiento, apariencia, fachada: *it's all pretence,* es una fachada; *they kept up a pretence of normality,* mantuvieron una apariencia de normalidad. 2 *(pretext)* pretexto. 3 *fml (claim)* pretensión *f*.
● **to keep up/make a pretence of doing sth.,** fingir hacer algo.
■ **false pretences,** JUR fraude *m*, estafa.
pretend [prɪ'tend] 1 *t (feign)* fingir, aparentar: *she pretended that she didn't care,* fingió que no le importaba; *the children pretended to be asleep,* los niños fingían estar dormidos. 2 *(claim)* pretender. – 3 *i (feign)* fingir. 4 *(claim)* pretender. – 5 *adj (make-believe)* de mentirijillas.
pretender [prɪ'tendə'] *n* pretendiente *mf* **(to,** a).
pretense [prɪ'tens] *n* US → **pretence.**
pretension [prɪ'tenʃən] 1 *n (claim)* pretensión *f*. 2 *fml (pretentiousness)* presunción *f*, pretensiones *fpl*.
pretensiousness [prɪ'tenʃəsnəs] *n* presunción *f*, pretensiones *fpl*.
pretentious [prɪ'tenʃəs] *adj (claiming importance)* pretencioso,-a,; *(showy)* presuntuoso,-a.
preterite ['pretərɪt] *n* LING pretérito.
pretext ['priːtekst] *n* pretexto.
● **on/under the pretext of,** so pretexto de.
pretty ['prɪtɪ] 1 *adj (girl, baby)* bonito,-a, guapo,-a, mono,-a; *(thing)* bonito,-a mono,-a: *what a pretty little girl!,* ¡qué niña más bonita!; *it was not a pretty sight,* no era nada agradable. – 2 *adv* bastante: *I'm pretty sure,* estoy bastante seguro,-a.
● **pretty much,** más o menos. ‖ **pretty well,** casi.
▲ *comp* **prettier,** *superl* **prettiest.**
pretzel ['pretsəl] *n* galleta salada.
prevail [prɪ'veɪl] 1 *i (exist, be widespread - custom, belief, attitude)* predominar, imperar; *(- conditions)* predominar. 2 *(win through, defeat)* prevalecer **(against/over,** sobre), imponerse **(against/over,** sobre).
● **to prevail on sb. to do sth.,** convencer a algn. para que haga algo, persuadir a algn. para que haga algo.
prevailing [prɪ'veɪlɪŋ] *adj (wind)* predominante; *(custom, fashion, style)* imperante, preponderante; *(law)* vigente.
prevalent ['prevələnt] *adj (frequent, common - gen)* frecuente, corriente; *(- disease)* extendido,-a.
prevaricate [prɪ'værɪkeɪt] *i* andarse con rodeos, buscar evasivas.
prevarication [prɪværɪ'keɪʃən] 1 *n* evasivas *fpl*. 2 JUR prevaricación *f*.
prevent [prɪ'vent] *t (gen)* impedir; *(avoid - accident)* evitar; *(- illness)* prevenir.
● **to prevent sb. from doing sth.,** impedir a algn. hacer algo. ‖ **to prevent sth. from happening,** impedir que pase algo.
preventable [prɪ'ventəbəl] *adj* evitable.
prevention [prɪ'venʃən] *n* prevención *f*.
● **prevention is better than cure,** más vale prevenir que curar.
preventive [prɪ'ventɪv] 1 *adj* preventivo,-a: *preventive medicine,* medicina preventiva. – 2 *n* medida preventiva.

preview ['priːvjuː] **1** *n* (*advance showing of film*) preestreno. **2** (*trailer*) tráiler *m*, avance *m*. **3** (*foretaste*) anticipo. – **4** *t* (*see in advance*) ver de preestreno. **5** (*give a preview of*) ofrecer un anticipo de.

previous ['priːvɪəs] *adj* previo,-a, anterior: *the previous day,* el día anterior; *previous experience,* experiencia previa; *a previous engagement,* un compromiso previo.
● **previous to,** antes de, anterior a.
■ **previous convictions,** antecedentes *mpl* penales.

previously ['priːvɪəslɪ] *adv* antes, anteriormente, previamente.

prewar ['priːwɔːʳ] *adj* de antes de la guerra: *the pre-war period,* la preguerra.

prey [preɪ] **1** *n* (*animal*) presa. **2** *fig* presa, víctima.
◆ **to prey on** *t insep* (*animal*) alimentarse de; (*person*) explotar a, aprovecharse de.
● **to be prey to sth.,** ser presa de algo, ser víctima de algo. ‖ **to fall prey to sth.,** caer víctima de algo, caer presa de algo. ‖ **to prey on sb.'s mind,** preocupar mucho a algn.
■ **bird of prey,** ave *f* de presa, ave *f* de rapiña.

price [praɪs] **1** *n* (*gen*) precio; (*amount, cost*) importe *m*; (*value*) valor *m*: *what's the price of this jacket?,* ¿qué precio tiene esta chaqueta? **2** *fig* (*cost, sacrifice*) precio. – **3** *t* (*fix price of*) tener un precio; (*value*) valorar, tasar; (*mark price on*) poner el precio a: *these shirts are highly priced,* estas camisas son muy caras.
● **at a price,** a un precio caro. ‖ **at any price,** a toda costa, cueste lo que cueste, a cualquier precio. ‖ **not at any price,** por nada del mundo. ‖ **price control,** control *m* de precios. ‖ **to go down in price,** bajar de precio. ‖ **to go up in price,** subir de precio. ‖ **to pay a high price for sth.,** pagar algo muy caro,-a. ‖ **to price os. out of the market,** perder clientes por poner precios muy altos.
■ **price list,** lista de precios. ‖ **price reduction,** descuento, rebaja. ‖ **price tag,** etiqueta. ‖ **set price,** precio fijo.

priceless ['praɪsləs] *adj* que no tiene precio, inestimable.

pricey ['praɪsɪ] *adj fam* caro,-a.
▲ *comp* **pricier,** *superl* **priciest.**

prick [prɪk] **1** *n* (*pain*) pinchazo; (*hole*) agujero. **2** *fig* (*of conscience*) remordimiento. **3** *sl* (*penis*) polla, picha. **4** *sl* (*obnoxious person*) gilipollas *mf*. – **5** *t* (*with needle, pin, fork*) pinchar. – **6** *fig* (*conscience*) remorder **7** *i* (*pin, thorn*) pinchar; (*itch, sting*) escocer, picar.
● **to prick up one's ears,** (*animal*) levantar las orejas; (*person*) aguzar el oído.

prickle ['prɪkəl] **1** *n* (*thorn*) pincho, espina, púa; (*spine*) púa, pincho. **2** (*sensation*) picor *m*. – **3** *t* pinchar, picar. – **4** *i* pinchar, picar.

prickly ['prɪklɪ] **1** *adj* (*plant*) espinoso,-a; (*animal*) con púas; (*wool, sweater*) que pica: *a prickly sensation,* un picor. **2** (*irritable, touchy*) enojadizo,-a, irritable, difícil.
■ **prickly heat,** sarpullido por causa del calor. ‖ **prickly pear,** (*fruit*) higo chumbo; (*plant*) chumbera.
▲ *comp* **pricklier,** *superl* **prickliest.**

pricy ['praɪsɪ] *adj* → **pricey.**
▲ *comp* **pricier,** *superl* **priciest.**

pride [praɪd] **1** *n* (*gen*) orgullo; (*self-respect*) amor *m* propio: *she's their pride and joy,* es su orgullo. **2** (*arrogance*) soberbia, orgullo. **3** (*group of lions*) manada.
● **to have pride of place / take pride of place,** ocupar el lugar de honor. ‖ **to pride os. on sth.,** enorgullecerse de algo. ‖ **to take pride in / take a pride in,** (*be proud of*) estar orgulloso,-a de, enorgullecerse

de; (*take seriously*) tomar en serio; (*take care over*) preocuparse por.
■ **false pride,** vanidad *f*.

priest [priːst] *n* sacerdote *m*, cura *m*.

priestess ['priːstes] *n* sacerdotisa.

priesthood ['priːsthʊd] *n* (*clergy*) clero; (*office*) sacerdocio.
● **to enter the priesthood,** hacerse sacerdote, ordenarse sacerdote.

priestly ['priːstlɪ] *adj* sacerdotal.
▲ *comp* **priestlier,** *superl* **priestliest.**

prig [prɪg] *n pej* mojigato,-a.

priggish ['prɪgɪʃ] *adj* mojigato,-a.

prim [prɪm] *adj* (*stiffly formal*) remilgado,-a, formal; (*prudish*) gazmoño,-a: *prim and proper,* remilgado,-a.
▲ *comp* **primmer,** *superl* **primmest.**

primacy ['praɪməsɪ] *n* primacía.

prima donna [priːmə'dɒnə] *n* diva.

primaeval [praɪ'miːvəl] *adj* → **primeval.**

prima facie [praɪmə'feɪʃɪ] *adv* a primera vista.

primal ['praɪməl] **1** *adj* (*first, original*) primario,-a. **2** (*most important*) primordial.

primarily [praɪ'merəlɪ] *adv* principalmente, ante todo.

primary ['praɪmərɪ] **1** *adj* (*main*) principal, fundamental. **2** (*first, basic*) primario,-a. – **3** *n* US POL primaria.
■ **primary education,** enseñanza primaria. ‖ **primary school,** escuela primaria. ‖ **primary school teacher,** maestro,-a, maestro,-a de escuela.
▲ (*sustantivo*) *pl* **primaries.**

primate¹ ['praɪmeɪt] *n* REL primado.

primate² ['praɪmeɪt] *n* ZOOL primate *m*.

prime [praɪm] **1** *adj* (*main, chief*) principal, primero,-a; (*major*) primordial. **2** (*first-rate - meat*) de primera (calidad); (*example, location*) excelente. **3** MATH primo. – **4** *n* (*best time of life*) flor *f* de la vida. – **5** *t* (*engine, pump, bomb*) cebar; (*surface, wood*) imprimar, preparar. **6** *fig* (*person*) preparar, enseñar.
● **to be in one's prime / be in the prime of life,** estar en la flor de la vida.
■ **prime cost,** coste *m* de producción. ‖ **Prime Minister,** primer,-a ministro,-a. ‖ **prime time,** horas *fpl* de máxima audiencia.

primer ['praɪməʳ] *n* (*paint*) imprimación *f*.

primeval [praɪ'miːvəl] *adj* primitivo,-a.
■ **primeval forests,** bosques *mpl* vírgenes.

primitive ['prɪmɪtɪv] **1** *adj* (*man, tribe, culture*) primitivo,-a; (*tool, method, shelter*) rudimentario,-a, primitivo,-a. – **2** *n* ART (*artist*) primitivo,-a; (*work*) obra primitiva.

primrose ['prɪmrəʊz] **1** *n* BOT primavera, prímula. **2** (*colour*) amarillo claro.
■ **primrose yellow,** (de color) amarillo claro.

Primus ['praɪməs] *n* hornillo de camping.

prince [prɪns] *n* príncipe *m*.
■ **Prince Charming,** Príncipe *m* Azul.

princess ['prɪnses] *n* princesa.

principal ['prɪnsɪpəl] **1** *adj* principal. – **2** *n* EDUC director,-ra. **3** THEAT protagonista *mf*, primera figura. **4** FIN capital *m*, principal *m*. **5** JUR autor,-ra.
■ **principal boy,** THEAT actriz *que representa el papel del protagonista principal masculino.*

principality [prɪnsɪ'pælɪtɪ] *n* principado.
▲ *pl* **principalities.**

principally ['prɪnsɪpəlɪ] *adv* principalmente, sobre todo.

principle ['prɪnsɪpəl] **1** *n* (*basic idea, rule, law*) principio; (*basis*) base *f*. **2** (*moral rule*) principio: *it's a matter of principle,* es cuestión de principios.

● **in principle,** en principio. ‖ **on principle,** por principio.

print [prɪnt] **1** n (lettering) letra: *in large print,* en letra grande; *in small print,* en letra menuda, en letra pequeña; *I saw it in print,* lo vi impreso. **2** (photo) copia; (picture) grabado. **3** (printed fabric) estampado. **4** (mark - of finger, foot) huella, marca. – **5** t (book, page, poster, etc) imprimir; (publish) publicar, editar. **6** (photo - negative) imprimir; (- copy) sacar una copia de. **7** (write clearly) escribir con letra de imprenta. **8** (fabric) estampar. **9** (make impression) marcar; (mentally) grabar.
◆ **to print out** t sep imprimir.
● **in print,** (published) publicado,-a; (available) a la venta. ‖ **out of print,** agotado,-a.

printed [ˈprɪntɪd] adj impreso,-a.
■ **printed matter,** impresos mpl.

printer [ˈprɪntəʳ] n (person) impresor,-ra; (machine) impresora.
■ **printer's,** (firm) imprenta. ‖ **printer's error,** error m de imprenta.

printing [ˈprɪntɪŋ] **1** n (act, process) impresión f; (industry) imprenta. **2** (number of copies) tirada. **3** (writing) letra de imprenta.
■ **printing press,** prensa. ‖ **printing works,** imprenta f sing.

print-out [ˈprɪntaʊt] n COMPUT impresión f.

prior[1] [ˈpraɪəʳ] adj anterior, previo,-a: *I have to refuse because of a prior engagement,* no puedo aceptar debido a un compromiso previo; *they raised the rent without prior warning,* subieron el alquiler sin previo aviso.
● **prior to,** antes de. ‖ **to have a prior claim on/to sth.,** tener prioridad sobre algo.

prior[2] [ˈpraɪəʳ] n REL prior m.

prioress [ˈpraɪərəs] n REL priora.

priority [praɪˈɒrɪtɪ] **1** n (gen) prioridad f. **2** GB AUTO preferencia. – **3** adj prioritario,-a.
● **to get one's priorities right,** saber uno lo que más le importa en la vida. ‖ **to give priority to sth.,** dar prioridad a algo. ‖ **to have/take priority over sth.,** tener prioridad sobre algo.
▲ pl priorities.

priory [ˈpraɪərɪ] n priorato.
▲ pl priories.

prise [praɪz] t GB (open) abrir con palanca; (lift up) levantar con palanca: *I prised it open with a chisel,* lo abrí (haciendo palanca) con un cincel.
◆ **to prise out** t sep fig (information) sonsacar, arrancar.

prism [ˈprɪzəm] n prisma.

prismatic [prɪzˈmætɪk] adj prismático,-a.
■ **prismatic binoculars,** prismáticos mpl.

prison [ˈprɪzən] n prisión f, cárcel f: *he's in prison,* está en la cárcel; *she was sent to prison for 5 years,* fue condenada a 5 años de cárcel.
● **to be sent to prison for sth.,** meter a algn. en la cárcel por algo, encarcelar a algn. por algo.
■ **prison camp,** campamento para prisioneros. ‖ **prison cell,** celda. ‖ **prison population,** población f penitenciaria, reclusos mpl. ‖ **prison warder,** carcelero,-a.

prisoner [ˈprɪzənəʳ] **1** n (in jail) preso,-a, recluso,-a; (captive) prisionero,-a. **2** MIL prisionero,-a.
● **to hold/keep sb. prisoner,** tener a algn. prisionero,-a. ‖ **to take sb. prisoner,** hacer a algn. prisionero,-a.
■ **prisoner of war,** prisionero,-a de guerra.

prissy [ˈprɪsɪ] adj remilgado,-a, melindroso,-a.
▲ comp prissier, superl prissiest.

pristine [ˈprɪstiːn] n (original) prístino,-a; (unspoilt) inmaculado,-a; (as if new) perfecto,-a, impecable.

privacy [ˈpraɪvəsɪ] n intimidad f, vida privada, privacidad f.
● **in the privacy of one's own home,** en la intimidad del hogar.

private [ˈpraɪvət] **1** adj (own, for own use - property, house, class) particular; (- letter, income) personal. **2** (confidential) privado,-a, confidencial. **3** (not state-controlled) privado,-a; (school) privado,-a, de pago. **4** (not official) privado,-a, personal. **5** (person) reservado,-a. – **6** n MIL soldado raso.
● **in private,** (privately) en privado; (undisturbed, alone) en la intimidad.
■ **private citizen,** particular mf. ‖ **private detective,** detective mf privado,-a. ‖ **private eye,** detective mf privado,-a. ‖ **private individual,** particular mf. ‖ **private investigator,** detective mf privado,-a. ‖ **private parts,** euph partes fpl pudendas, intimidades fpl.

privately [ˈpraɪvətlɪ] **1** adv (in private) en privado; (undisturbed, alone) en la intimidad. **2** (personally) personalmente: *privately, he was scared,* en el fuero interno, tenía miedo. **3** (not by state) de forma privada: *it's privately owned,* es de particulares; *he wants his son privately educated,* quiere que su hijo vaya a un colegio privado.

privation [praɪˈveɪʃən] n privación f.
● **to endure privation / suffer privation,** pasar privaciones, pasar apuros.

privatization [praɪvətaɪˈzeɪʃən] n privatización f.

privatize [ˈpraɪvətaɪz] t privatizar.

privet [ˈprɪvɪt] n BOT alheña.

privilege [ˈprɪvɪlɪdʒ] n (special right) privilegio; (honour) privilegio, honor m: *parliamentary privilege,* inmunidad parlamentaria.

privileged [ˈprɪvɪlɪdʒd] adj privilegiado,-a.
● **to be privileged to do sth.,** tener el privilegio de hacer algo, tener el honor de hacer algo.

privy [ˈprɪvɪ] **1** n fam (toilet) retrete m. – **2** adj arch privado,-a.
● **to be privy to sth.,** estar enterado,-a de algo, tener conocimiento de algo.
■ **the Privy Council,** GB el Consejo Privado que asesora al monarca. ‖ **Privy Councillor,** Consejero,-a Privado,-a.
▲ (sustantivo) pl privies.

prize[1] [praɪz] **1** n (gen) premio. – **2** adj (having won a prize) premiado,-a; (excellent) de primera, selecto,-a. **3** fam (complete, utter) de remate, perfecto,-a.
● **to win first prize,** (gen) ganar el primer premio; (in lottery) tocarle el gordo.
■ **prize day,** (día m de la) entrega de premios. ‖ **prize money,** premio (en metálico).

prize[2] [praɪz] t apreciar, valorar.

prize[3] [praɪz] t US → **prise.**

prizefight [ˈpraɪzfaɪt] n combate m de boxeo profesional.

prizefighter [ˈpraɪzfaɪtəʳ] n boxeador m profesional.

prize-giving [ˈpraɪzgɪvɪŋ] n entrega de premios.

prizewinner [ˈpraɪzwɪnəʳ] n ganador,-ra.

prizewinning [ˈpraɪzwɪnɪŋ] adj premiado,-a, galardonado,-a.

pro[1] [prəʊ] n pro m: *the pros and cons,* los pros y contras.

pro[2] [prəʊ] n fam profesional mf.
▲ pl pros.

probability [prɒbəˈbɪlɪtɪ] n probabilidad f: *in all probability they'll be late,* es muy probable que lleguen tarde.

▲ *pl* probabilities.
probable ['prɒbəbəl] *adj* probable, posible.
probably ['prɒbəblɪ] *adv* probablemente: *it'll probably rain*, es probable que llueva; *he's probably gone out with his friends*, habrá salido con sus amigos.
probate ['prəʊbeɪt] **1** *n* JUR *(process)* legalización *f* de un testamento. **2** JUR *(copy)* copia legalizada de un testamento. **– 3** *t* JUR legalizar.
probation [prə'beɪʃən] **1** *n* JUR libertad *f* condicional. **2** *(in employment)* período de prueba.
● **to be on probation**, JUR estar en libertad condicional.
■ **probation officer**, *persona que se encarga de la vigilancia de los que están en libertad provisional.*
probationary [prə'beɪʃənərɪ] *adj* de prueba.
probationer [prə'beɪʃənəʳ] **1** *n (in employment)* persona a prueba. **2** JUR persona en libertad condicional.
probe [prəʊb] **1** *n* MED sonda. **2** *(investigation)* investigación *f*. **– 3** *t* MED sondar. **4** *(investigate - gen)* investigar; *(public opinion)* sondear; *(mind)* explorar. **– 5** *i* investigar **(into, -)**.
probing ['prəʊbɪŋ] *adj (question)* agudo,-a, perspicaz.
probity ['prəʊbɪtɪ] *n fml* probidad *f*.
problem ['prɒbləm] *n* problema *m*: *the housing problem*, el problema de la vivienda; *he's got a drink problem*, tiene problemas con la bebida; *no problem!*, ¡no hay problema!, ¡ningún problema!
● **to get to the root of a problem**, llegar a la raíz de un problema.
■ **problem child**, niño,-a difícil. ‖ **problem page**, consultorio (sentimental).
problematic [prɒblə'mætɪk] *adj* problemático,-a, difícil.
problematical [prɒblə'mætɪkəl] *adj* problemático,-a, difícil.
proboscis [prə'bɒsɪs] *n* probóscide *f*.
▲ *pl* **proboscises** *o* **proboscides** [prə'bɒsiːdiːz].
procedure [prə'siːdʒəʳ] *n (set of actions)* procedimiento; *(step)* trámite *m*, gestión *f*.
proceed [prə'siːd] **1** *i (continue)* seguir, continuar: *she then proceeded to complain about my driving*, entonces pasó a quejarse de mi manera de conducir; *we decided to proceed with the plan as agreed*, decidimos seguir con el plan tal y como habíamos acordado. **2** *(progress)* marchar. **3** *fml (go along)* avanzar, circular; *(go towards)* dirigirse a.
● **to proceed against sb.**, proceder contra algn.
proceedings [prə'siːdɪŋz] **1** *npl (events at meeting, ceremony, etc)* actos *mpl*. **2** JUR *(lawsuit)* proceso *sing*. **3** *(minutes)* actas *fpl*.
● **to start/institute proceedings against sb.**, proceder contra algn., entablar un proceso contra algn.
proceeds ['prəʊsiːdz] *npl* beneficios *mpl*, ganancias *fpl*.
process[1] ['prəʊses] **1** *n (set of actions, changes)* proceso: *the process of growing old*, el envejecimiento. **2** *(method)* procedimiento, proceso. **3** JUR *(lawsuit)* acción *f* judicial; *(summons)* demanda. **– 4** *t (raw material, food)* procesar, tratar; *(film)* revelar. **5** *(deal with)* ocuparse de, tramitar. **6** COMPUT procesar, tratar.
● **in process**, en curso. ‖ **in the process**, *(as a result)* con ello: *she won the race, but pulled a muscle in the process*, ganó la carrera, pero con ello se hizo un tirón. ‖ **in the process of time**, con el tiempo. ‖ **to be in the process of doing sth.**, estar en vías de hacer algo, estar haciendo algo.
process[2] [prə'ses] **1** *i (gen)* desfilar. **2** REL ir en procesión.

processing ['prəʊsesɪŋ] **1** *n (treatment)* procesamiento, tratamiento; *(of film)* revelado. **2** COMM FIN JUR tramitación *f*. **3** COMPUT procesamiento, tratamiento.
procession [prə'seʃən] **1** *n (gen)* desfile *m*. **2** REL procesión *f*.
processor ['prəʊsesəʳ] **1** *n (for food)* robot *m* de cocina. **2** COMPUT procesador *m*.
proclaim [prə'kleɪm] **1** *t (announce)* proclamar, declarar. **2** *fml (reveal)* revelar.
proclamation [prɒklə'meɪʃən] *n* proclamación *f*.
proclivity [prə'klɪvɪtɪ] *n fml* proclividad *f*, propensión *f*, tendencia.
▲ *pl* **proclivities**.
procrastinate [prə'kræstɪneɪt] *i* aplazar una decisión.
procrastination [prəʊkræstɪ'neɪʃən] *n* dilación *f*.
procreate ['prəʊkrɪeɪt] *i* procrear.
procreation [prəʊkrɪ'eɪʃən] *n* procreación *f*.
procure [prə'kjʊəʳ] **1** *t (obtain)* conseguir, obtener. **2** *(women for prostitution)* llevar a la prostitución. **– 3** *i (for prostitution)* alcahuetear, chulear.
prod [prɒd] **1** *n (with finger, sharp object)* golpecito, pinchazo. **2** *fig (encouragement)* pinchazo, empujón *m*, estímulo; *(reminder)* toque *m*. **– 3** *t (with object)* pinchar; *(with finger)* dar golpecitos a. **4** *fig (encourage)* pinchar, empujar, estimular; *(remind)* recordar. **– 5** *i* pinchar **(at, -)**.
● **to give sb. a prod**, empujar a algn.
▲ *(verbo)* *pt* & *pp* **prodded**, *ger* **prodding**.
prodigal ['prɒdɪgəl] *adj* pródigo,-a.
prodigious [prə'dɪdʒəs] *adj (great)* prodigioso,-a; *(huge)* enorme.
prodigy ['prɒdɪdʒɪ] *n* prodigio.
▲ *pl* **prodigies**.
produce [prə'djuːs] **1** *t (gen)* producir; *(manufacture)* producir, fabricar. **2** *(give birth to)* tener. **3** *(show)* enseñar, presentar; *(bring out)* sacar. **4** *(cause)* producir, causar. **5** *(film)* producir; *(play)* poner en escena, dirigir; *(tv programme)* realizar. **– 6** *n* productos *mpl*: *produce of Spain*, productos de España.
▲ *(noun)* ['prɒdjuːs].
producer [prə'djuːsəʳ] **1** *n (gen)* productor,-ra; *(manufacturer)* fabricante *mf*. **2** *(film)* productor,-ra; *(play)* director,-ra de escena; *(tv programme)* realizador,-ra.
product ['prɒdʌkt] **1** *n (gen)* producto. **2** *(result)* producto, fruto, resultado.
production [prə'dʌkʃən] **1** *n (gen)* producción *f*; *(manufacture)* fabricación *f*, producción *f*: *mass production*, fabricación en serie. **2** *(showing)* presentación *f*: *on production of your passes*, al presentar sus pases. **3** THEAT *(show produced)* producción *f*. **4** *(of film)* producción *f*; *(of play)* producción *f*, puesta en escena; *(of tv programme)* realización *f*. **– 5** *adj* de producción.
● **to go into production**, empezar a fabricarse. ‖ **to take sth. out of production**, dejar de fabricar algo.
■ **production line**, cadena de montaje.
productive [prə'dʌktɪv] **1** *adj (gen)* productivo,-a. **2** *(useful)* positivo,-a, productivo,-a, fructífero,-a.
productively [prə'dʌktɪvlɪ] *adv* productivamente.
● **to spend one's time productively**, aprovechar el tiempo.
productivity [prɒdʌk'tɪvɪtɪ] *n* productividad *f*.
■ **productivity agreement**, acuerdo sobre productividad. ‖ **productivity bonus**, prima por productividad.
Prof [prə'fesəʳ] *abbr (Professor)* catedrático,-a de universidad.

profane [prə'feɪn] 1 adj fml (irreverent) sacrílego,-a; (language) blasfemo,-a. 2 fml (secular) profano,-a. – 3 t profanar.
profanity [prə'fænɪtɪ] n blasfemia.
▲ pl profanities.
profess [prə'fes] 1 t (faith, religion) profesar. 2 (state) proclamar, manifestar, declarar. 3 (claim) pretender: I don't profess to be an expert, no pretendo ser (ningún) experto.
professed [prə'fest] 1 adj (Christian, Muslim) profeso,-a; (supporter, monarchist) declarado,-a. 2 (claimed, alleged) pretendido,-a, supuesto,-a.
profession [prə'feʃən] 1 n (occupation) profesión f: he's a baker by profession, es panadero de profesión; the medical profession, el cuerpo médico. 2 (declaration) declaración f, afirmación f.
■ profession of faith, profesión f de fe.
professional [prə'feʃənəl] 1 adj (gen) profesional: they argue for a professional army, abogan por un ejército profesional. – 2 n profesional mf.
● to go professional / turn professional, volverse profesional. ‖ to take professional advice, asesorarse por un,-a profesional.
professionalism [prə'feʃənəlɪzəm] n profesionalidad f, profesionalismo.
professionally [prə'feʃənəlɪ] adv (as paid occupation) profesionalmente; (in professional way) con profesionalidad, como un profesional, de manera profesional; (by professional person) por un,-a experto,-a, por un,-a profesional.
professor [prə'fesə'] n GB catedrático,-a; US profesor,-ra universitario,-a.
proffer ['profə'] t (gift, assistance, apology) ofrecer; (thanks, resignation, advice) dar.
proficiency [prə'fɪʃənsɪ] n competencia.
proficient [prə'fɪʃənt] adj muy competente: she's proficient in French, domina el francés.
profile ['prəʊfaɪl] 1 n (side view) perfil m: in profile, de perfil. 2 (description) perfil m; (written) reseña; (biography) reseña biográfica.
● to keep a low profile, intentar pasar desapercibido,-a.
profit ['profɪt] 1 n COMM ganancia, beneficio: gross profit, beneficio bruto; net profit, beneficio neto. 2 fml (advantage) provecho.
● to make a profit, sacar beneficios, tener ganancias. ‖ to profit from sth., sacar provecho de algo, beneficiarse de algo. ‖ to sell sth. at a profit, vender algo con ganancia.
■ profit and loss account, cuenta de ganancias y pérdidas. ‖ profit margin, margen m de ganancias, margen m de beneficios.
profitability [profɪtə'bɪlɪθɪ] n rentabilidad f.
profitable ['profɪtəbəl] 1 adj COMM rentable. 2 (beneficial) provechoso,-a.
profitably ['profɪtəblɪ] 1 adv (do business) de manera rentable, con rentabilidad; (sell) con ganancia, con beneficio. 2 (in a worthwhile way) provechosamente.
profiteer [profɪ'tɪə'] 1 n especulador,-ra. – 2 i especular.
profit-making ['profɪtmeɪkɪŋ] adj (business) rentable; (charity) con fines lucrativos.
profit-sharing ['profɪtʃeərɪŋ] adj participación f en los beneficios.
profligate ['proflɪgət] 1 adj fml (wasteful) despilfarrador,-ra. 2 fml (immoral) disoluto,-a, libertino,-a.
profound [prə'faʊnd] adj profundo,-a.

profundity [prə'fʌndɪtɪ] n profundidad f.
▲ pl profundities.
profuse [prə'fjuːs] adj (gen) profuso,-a; (bleeding) intenso,-a: profuse apologies, disculpas excesivas.
profusely [prə'fjuːslɪ] adv (gen) profusamente; (thank, apologise) efusivamente.
● to sweat profusely, sudar mucho.
profusion [prə'fjuːʒən] n profusión f, abundancia.
progenitor [prəʊ'dʒenɪtə'] n (ancestor) progenitor,-ra; (forerunner) precursor,-ra.
progeny ['prodʒənɪ] n progenie f, prole f.
prognosis [prog'nəʊsɪs] n pronóstico.
prognosticate [prog'nostɪkeɪt] t pronosticar.
program ['prəʊgræm] 1 n COMPUT programa m. 2 US → programme. – 3 t COMPUT programar. 4 US → programme.
▲ (verbo) pt & pp programmed, ger programming.
programer ['prəʊgræmə'] n US → programmer.
programme ['prəʊgræm] 1 n (gen) programa m; (plan) plan m. – 2 t (gen) programar; (activities) programar, planear.
programmer ['prəʊgræmə'] n programador,-ra.
progress ['prəʊgres] 1 n (advance) progreso, avance m; (development) desarrollo. – 2 i (advance) progresar, avanzar, adelantar; (develop) desarrollar. 3 (improve - gen) mejorar, hacer progresos; (- patient) mejorar.
● to be in progress, (work) estar en curso, estar en marcha; (meeting, match, etc) haber empezado. ‖ to make progress, (pupil) adelantar, hacer progresos, progresar; (patient) mejorar.
■ progress report, informe m sobre la marcha de los trabajos, informe m sobre la marcha de los estudios.
▲ (verbo) [prəʊ'gres].
progression [prə'greʃən] 1 n (development) evolución f, avance m. 2 (series) serie f. 3 (math mus) progresión f.
progressive [prə'gresɪv] 1 adj (increasing) progresivo,-a. 2 (favouring progress) progresista. – 3 n progresista mf.
progressively [prə'gresɪvlɪ] adv progresivamente, cada vez más.
prohibit [prə'hɪbɪt] 1 t (forbid) prohibir: smoking is prohibited, está prohibido fumar. 2 (prevent) impedir.
● to prohibit sb. from doing sth., prohibir a algn. hacer algo.
prohibition [prəʊɪ'bɪʃən] 1 n prohibición f. 2 Prohibition, la Ley f seca, la Prohibición f.
prohibitive [prə'hɪbɪtɪv] adj prohibitivo,-a.
project ['prodʒekt] 1 n (gen) proyecto. 2 EDUC trabajo, estudio. – 3 t (gen) proyectar. 4 (extrapolate) extrapolar. – 5 i sobresalir, resaltar.
● to project os., proyectarse.
▲ (verbo) [prə'dʒekt].
projectile [prə'dʒektaɪl] n proyectil m.
projection [prə'dʒekʃən] 1 n (gen) proyección f. 2 (protuberance) saliente m, resalto.
projectionist [prə'dʒekʃənɪst] n operador,-ra de cine.
projector [prə'dʒektə'] n proyector m.
prolapse [prəʊ'læps] n prolapso.
proletarian [prəʊlə'teərɪən] adj proletario,-a.
proletariat [prəʊlə'teərɪət] n proletariado.
proliferate [prə'lɪfəreɪt] i proliferar.
proliferation [prəlɪfə'reɪʃən] n proliferación f.
prolific [prə'lɪfɪk] adj prolífico,-a.
prolix ['prəʊlɪks] adj fml prolijo,-a.
prologue ['prəʊlɒg] n prólogo.
prolong [prə'lɒŋ] t prolongar, alargar, extender.

prolongation [prəʊlɒŋ'geɪʃən] *n* prolongación *f*, alargamiento, extensión *f*.

prom [prɒm] 1 *n* GB → **promenade**. 2 US baile *m* del colegio.

promenade [prɒmə'nɑːd] 1 *n* GB (*at seaside*) paseo marítimo. 2 *fml* (*walk*) paseo. – 3 *i* pasearse.
■ **promenade concert**, GB concierto sinfónico en que parte del público está de pie. ‖ **promenade deck**, cubierta de paseo.

prominence ['prɒmɪnəns] *n* (*conspicuousness*) prominencia; (*importance*) importancia.

prominent ['prɒmɪnənt] *adj* (*conspicuous*) prominente; (*important*) importante, destacado,-a; (*projecting*) prominente, saliente.

prominently ['prɒmɪnəntlɪ] *adv* (*conspicuously*) muy a la vista.
● **to figure prominently in sth.**, destacar en algo, desempeñar un papel importante en algo.

promiscuity [prɒmɪ'skjuːɪtɪ] *n* promiscuidad *f*.

promiscuous [prə'mɪskjʊəs] *adj* promiscuo,-a.

promise ['prɒmɪs] 1 *n* (*pledge*) promesa. 2 (*expectation, hope*) esperanza, esperanzas *fpl*. – 3 *t* prometer: *you promised to help me*, prometiste ayudarme; *he promised not to tell anyone*, prometió no decírselo a nadie. 4 (*seem likely*) prometer. – 5 *i* (*gen*) prometer; (*swear*) jurar: *I promise*, te lo prometo.
● **to make a promise**, prometer. ‖ **to break a promise**, faltar a una promesa. ‖ **to keep a promise**, cumplir una promesa. ‖ **to promise the moon**, prometer el oro y el moro, prometer la luna. ‖ **to show promise**, ser prometedor,-ra.
■ **the Promised Land**, la Tierra Prometida.

promising ['prɒmɪsɪŋ] *adj* prometedor,-ra.

promontory ['prɒməntərɪ] *n* promontorio.
▲ *pl* **promontories**.

promote [prə'məʊt] 1 *t* (*in rank*) promover, ascender. 2 (*encourage*) promover, fomentar. 3 COMM (*product*) promocionar.
● **to be promoted**, SP subir (de categoría).

promoter [prə'məʊtə'] *n* promotor,-ra.

promotion [prə'məʊʃən] 1 *n* (*in rank*) promoción *f*, ascenso. 2 COMM promoción *f*. 3 (*encouragement*) promoción *f*, fomento.
● **to get promotion**, ser ascendido,-a.

prompt [prɒmpt] 1 *adj* (*quick*) pronto,-a, rápido,-a; (*punctual*) puntual. – 2 *adv* en punto. – 3 *t* (*cause, incite*) instar, incitar, mover; (*cause, lead to*) provocar, dar lugar a: *what prompted you to say that?*, ¿qué te instó a decir eso?; *the scandal prompted calls for his resignation*, el escándalo provocó llamadas pidiendo su dimisión. 4 THEAT apuntar. – 5 *n* THEAT (*line*) apunte *m*.

prompter ['prɒmptə'] *n* THEAT apuntador,-ra.

promptly ['prɒmptlɪ] *adv* (*quickly*) rápidamente; (*punctually*) puntualmente, en punto.

prone [prəʊn] *adj* (*face down*) boca abajo.
● **to be prone to sth.**, ser propenso,-a a algo.

prong [prɒŋ] *n* diente *m*, punta.

pronoun ['prəʊnaʊn] *n* LING pronombre *m*.

pronounce [prə'naʊns] 1 *t* LING pronunciar. 2 (*declare*) declarar. – 3 *i* pronunciarse (**on**, sobre).
● **to pronounce sentence**, JUR dictar sentencia, pronunciar un fallo.

pronounced [prə'naʊnst] *adj* pronunciado,-a, marcado,-a, acusado,-a.

pronouncement [prə'naʊnsmənt] *n* declaración *f*.

pronunciation [prənʌnsɪ'eɪʃən] *n* pronunciación *f*.

proof [pruːf] 1 *n* (*evidence*) prueba: *we need conclusive proof*, necesitamos pruebas concluyentes. 2 (*trial copy, print*) prueba. 3 (*alcohol*) graduación *f* alcohólica: *this beer is 5% proof*, esta cerveza tiene 5 grados. – 4 *t* impermeabilizar.
● **the proof of the pudding is in the eating**, no se puede juzgar algo hasta que se haya probado. ‖ **to be proof against sth.**, ser a prueba de algo.

proofread ['pruːfriːd] 1 *t* corregir. – 2 *i* corregir pruebas.

proofreader ['pruːfriːdə'] *n* corrector,-ra de pruebas.

prop[1] [prɒp] 1 *n* (*support*) puntal *m*. 2 *fig* apoyo, sostén *m*. 3 SP (*in rugby*) pilar *mf*. – 4 *t* apoyar (**against**, en/contra). 5 *fig* apoyar, sostener.
◆ **to prop up** 1 *t sep* (*wall, building*) sostener, apuntalar. 2 (*regime*) apoyar; (*industry, business*) mantener a flote.
▲ (*verbo*) *pt & pp* **propped**, *ger* **propping**.

prop[2] [prɒp] *n* THEAT accesorio.

propaganda [prɒpə'gændə] *n* propaganda.

propagate ['prɒpəgeɪt] 1 *t* propagar. – 2 *i* propagarse.

propagation [prɒpə'geɪʃən] *n* propagación *f*.

propane ['prəʊpeɪn] *n* propano.

propel [prə'pel] *t* propulsar, impulsar.
▲ (*verbo*) *pt & pp* **propelled**, *ger* **propelling**.

propeller [prə'pelə'] *n* hélice *f*.

propelling pencil [prəpelɪŋ'pensəl] *n* portaminas *m*.

propensity [prə'pensɪtɪ] *n* propensión *f* (**to**, a).
▲ *pl* **propensities**.

proper ['prɒpə'] 1 *adj* (*suitable*) adecuado,-a, apropiado,-a; (*correct*) correcto,-a: *the proper time*, el momento oportuno. 2 *fam* (*real, genuine*) verdadero,-a, de verdad; (*as it should be*) como Dios manda, como es debido. 3 *fam* (*thorough*) auténtico,-a, todo,-a: *he's a proper gentleman*, es todo un caballero. 4 (*respectable*) correcto,-a, decente. 5 (*strictly called - comes after noun*) propiamente dicho,-a.
● **to be proper to**, ser propio,-a de.
■ **proper name / proper noun**, nombre propio.

properly ['prɒpəlɪ] 1 *adv* (*properly*) bien, adecuadamente. 2 (*correctly*) bien, correctamente; (*as one should*) como es debido. 3 *fam* (*thoroughly*) totalmente.
● **properly speaking**, propiamente dicho,-a, en sentido estricto: *very properly*, con toda razón.

property ['prɒpətɪ] 1 *n* (*possessions, ownership*) propiedad *f*. 2 (*buildings, land*) propiedad *f*, bienes *mpl*; (*estate*) finca. 3 *fml* (*building*) inmueble *m*. 4 (*quality*) propiedad *f*. 5 THEAT accesorio.
● **to be public property**, ser del dominio público.
■ **lost property**, objetos *mpl* perdidos. ‖ **private property**, propiedad *f* privada. ‖ **property developer**, promotor,-ra inmobiliario,-a.
▲ *pl* **properties**.

prophecy ['prɒfəsɪ] *n* profecía.
▲ *pl* **prophecies**.

prophesy ['prɒfəsaɪ] 1 *t* predecir. 2 REL profetizar. – 3 *i* profetizar, hacer profecías.
▲ *pt & pp* **prophesied**, *ger* **prophesying**.

prophet ['prɒfɪt] *n* profeta *m*.

prophetess ['prɒfɪtes] *n* profetisa.

prophetic [prə'fetɪk] *adj* profético,-a.

prophylactic [prɒfɪ'læktɪk] 1 *adj* profiláctico,-a. – 2 *n* MED profiláctico. 3 US (*condom*) profiláctico, preservativo, condón *m*.

propitiate [prə'pɪʃɪeɪt] *i fml* propiciar.

propitious [prə'pɪʃəs] *adj fml* propicio,-a, favorable.

proponent [prə'pəʊnənt] *n* defensor,-ra.

proportion [prə'pɔ:ʃən] 1 *n* (*ratio*) proporción *f*. 2 (*part*) parte *f*; (*percentage*) porcentaje *m*. 3 (*correct relation*) proporción *f*. – 4 proportions, *npl* dimensiones *fpl*, proporciones *fpl*.
● to be in proportion / be out of proportion, estar proporcionado,-a / no estar proporcionado,-a. ‖ to be in proportion to/with sth. / be out of proportion to/ with sth., guardar proporción con algo / no guardar proporción con algo. ‖ to blow sth. up out of all proportion, exagerar algo desmesuradamente. ‖ to get/ keep things in proportion, guardar el sentido de la medida. ‖ to get things out of proportion, exagerar las cosas. ‖ to have a sense of proportion, tener sentido de la medida.
proportional [prə'pɔ:ʃənəl] *adj* proporcional (to, a).
■ proportional representation, representación *f* proporcional.
proportionate [prə'pɔ:ʃənət] *adj* proporcionado,-a (to, con), en proporción (to, a).
proposal [prə'pəuzəl] *n* propuesta: *proposal of marriage,* proposición de matrimonio, propuesta de matrimonio.
propose [prə'pəuz] 1 *t* (*suggest*) proponer. 2 (*intend*) pensar. – 3 *i* declararse, proponer matrimonio a: *he proposed to me,* me pidió la mano, me propuso matrimonio.
● to propose a toast, proponer un brindis.
proposed [prə'pəuzd] *adj* propuesto,-a.
proposer [prə'pəuzə'] *n* proponente *mf*.
proposition [prɒpə'zıʃən] 1 *n* (*suggestion*) proposición *f*, propuesta; (*offer*) oferta. 2 (*assertion*) proposición *f*. – 3 *t* hacer proposiciones deshonestas.
propound [prə'paund] *t* exponer, proponer.
proprietary [prə'praiətəri] *adj* patentado,-a.
proprietor [prə'praiətə'] *n* propietario,-a, dueño,-a.
propriety [prə'praiəti] 1 *n* (*correctness*) corrección *f*, decoro, decencia. 2 (*suitability*) conveniencia. – 3 proprieties, *npl* convenciones *fpl* sociales.
▲ *pl* proprieties.
propulsion [prə'pʌlʃən] *n* propulsión *f*.
pro rata [prəu'rɑ:tə] 1 *adj* prorrateado,-a. – 2 *adv* a prorrata, proporcionalmente.
prosaic [prəu'zeɪk] *adj* prosaico,-a.
proscribe [prəu'skraɪb] *t* proscribir.
prose [prəuz] 1 *n* LIT prosa. 2 EDUC traducción *f* inversa.
■ prose writer, prosista *mf*.
prosecute ['prɒsɪkju:t] 1 *t* JUR procesar, enjuiciar. – 2 *i* JUR (*bring a charge*) entablar una acción judicial; (*be prosecutor*) llevar la acusación.
prosecution [prɒsɪ'kju:ʃən] 1 *n* JUR (*action*) procesamiento, acción *f* judicial; (*court case*) proceso, juicio. 2 the prosecution, JUR (*person*) la parte acusadora, la acusación.
■ witness for the prosecution, testigo *mf* de cargo.
prosecutor ['prɒsɪkju:tə'] *n* JUR fiscal *mf*, acusador,-ra.
prospect ['prɒspekt] 1 *n* (*picture in mind*) perspectiva: *the prospect of moving house,* la perspectiva de mudarse. 2 (*possibility, hope*) posibilidad *f*, probabilidad *f*: *there isn't much prospect of my finishing this today,* no hay muchas posibilidades de que acabe esto hoy; *there is no prospect of an agreement,* no hay posibilidad de acuerdo. 3 *fml* (*wide view*) panorama *m*, vista, perspectiva. – 4 *t* prospectar, explorar. – 5 *i* buscar (for, -): *to prospect for oil,* buscar petróleo. – 6 prospects, *npl* (*chance of success, outlook*) perspectivas *fpl*; (*future*) futuro *m* sing, porvenir *m* sing: *a job with prospects,* un trabajo con porvenir.

● to be a prospect for sth., (*person*) tener probabilidades de algo.
▲ (*verbo*) [prə'spekt].
prospective [prə'spektɪv] *adj* (*future*) futuro,-a; (*possible*) posible, eventual.
prospector [prə'spektə'] *n* prospector,-ra, explorador,-ra.
prospectus [prə'spektəs] *n* prospecto.
prosper ['prɒspə'] *i* prosperar.
prosperity [prɒ'sperɪtɪ] *n* prosperidad *f*.
prosperous ['prɒspərəs] *adj* próspero,-a.
prostate ['prɒsteɪt] *n* próstata.
prostitute ['prɒstɪtju:t] 1 *n* (*gen*) prostituta; (*vulgar*) puta. – 2 *t* prostituir.
● to prostitute os., prostituirse.
■ male prostitute, prostituto.
prostitution [prɒstɪ'tju:ʃən] *n* prostitución *f*.
prostrate ['prɒstreɪt] 1 *adj* postrado,-a. – 2 *t* postrar.
● to prostrate os., postrarse.
▲ (*verbo*) [prɒ'streɪt].
prostration [prɒs'treɪʃən] *n* postración *f*.
protagonist [prə'tægənɪst] *n* protagonista *mf*.
protect [prə'tekt] *t* (*gen*) proteger; (*interests*) proteger, salvaguardar.
● to protect against / protect from, proteger contra / proteger de.
protection [prə'tekʃən] *n* (*gen*) protección *f*; (*shelter*) protección *f*, amparo.
■ protection money, *dinero que se paga a gángsters a cambio de protección*. ‖ protection racket, chantaje *m*.
protectionism [prə'tekʃənɪzəm] *n* proteccionismo.
protective [prə'tektɪv] *adj* (*gen*) protector,-ra; (*clothing*) de protección.
protector [prə'tektə'] *n* (*person*) protector,-ra; (*thing*) protector *m*.
protégé ['prəutəʒeɪ] *n* protegido.
protégée ['prəutəʒeɪ] *n* protegida.
protein ['prəuti:n] *n* proteína.
protest ['prəutest] 1 *n* (*gen*) protesta; (*complaint*) queja; (*demonstration*) manifestación *f* de protesta: *we refused to eat in protest,* nos negamos a comer en señal de protesta. – 2 *t* protestar de: *he protested his innocence,* protestó de su inocencia. – 3 *i* protestar (about, de), (against, contra), (at, por): *they protested about the working conditions,* protestaron de las condiciones de trabajo.
● under protest, bajo protesta. ‖ to make a protest about sth., protestar por algo.
■ protest song, canción *f* (de) protesta.
▲ (*verbo*) [prə'test].
Protestant ['prɒtɪstənt] 1 *adj* protestante. – 2 *n* protestante *mf*.
Protestantism ['prɒtɪstəntɪzəm] *n* protestantismo.
protestation [prɒtes'teɪʃən] *n* (*protest*) protesta; (*declaration*) declaración *f*.
protester [prə'testə'] *n* manifestante *mf*.
protocol ['prəutəkɒl] *n* protocolo.
proton ['prəutɒn] *n* protón *m*.
prototype ['prəutətaɪp] *n* prototipo.
protracted [prə'træktɪd] *adj* prolongado,-a.
protractor [prə'træktə'] *n* transportador *m*.
protrude [prə'tru:d] *i fml* sobresalir, salir.
protruding [prə'tru:dɪŋ] *adj* (*gen*) salido,-a, saliente, prominente; (*teeth*) salido,-a; (*jaw, chin*) prominente; (*eyes*) saltón,-ona.

protuberance [prə'tjuːbərəns] *n fml* protuberancia.
proud [praud] **1** *adj* (*gen*) orgulloso,-a: *I'm proud of you,* estoy orgulloso de ti. **2** (*arrogant*) orgulloso,-a, arrogante, altanero,-a, soberbio,-a. **3** *fml* (*splendid*) soberbio,-a, imponente.
● **to be proud of sb./sth.,** estar orgulloso,-a de algn./algo, enorgullecerse de algn./algo. ‖ **to be proud to do sth.,** tener el honor de hacer algo. ‖ **to do sb. proud,** tratar a algn. a cuerpo de rey.
proudly ['praudlɪ] *adv* (*with satisfaction*) orgullosamente, con orgullo; (*arrogantly*) arrogantemente, con arrogancia.
● **to proudly present,** tener el honor de presentar.
prove [pruːv] **1** *t* (*show to be true*) probar, demostrar: *they couldn't prove that he killed her,* no pudieron probar que la había matado él. **2** (*turn out to be*) demostrar: *she proved herself to be a competent swimmer,* demostró ser una nadadora competente. – *i* (*turn out*) resultar: *the information proved correct,* la información resultó (ser) correcta.
● **to prove os.,** dar pruebas de valor, demostrar su valía. ‖ **to prove sb. right,** dar a algn. la razón, demostrar que algn. tiene razón.
▲ *pp* **proved** *o* **proven**.
proven ['pruːvən] **1** *pp* → **prove**. – **2** *adj* probado,-a, comprobado,-a.
Provençal [prɒvɒn'saːl] **1** *adj* provenzal. – **2** *n* (*person*) provenzal *mf*. **3** (*language*) provenzal *m*.
Provence [prə'vɒns] *n* Provenza.
proverb ['prɒvɜːb] *n* proverbio, refrán *m*.
proverbial [prə'vɜːbɪəl] *adj* proverbial.
provide [prə'vaɪd] **1** *t* (*supply - gen*) proveer, suministrar, proporcionar; (*information, facts, etc*) proporcionar, facilitar: *the government cannot provide jobs for everyone,* el gobierno no puede proporcionar empleo a todos; *light refreshments will be provided,* se ofrecerá un pequeño refrigerio; *he provided us with all the information,* nos facilitó toda la información. **2** *fig* (*answer, example*) ofrecer, dar; (*opportunity*) brindar, dar. **3** (*of law, rule, clause*) estipular. – **4** *i* proveer.
◆ **to provide against** *t insep* tomar precauciones contra. ‖ **to provide for 1** *t insep* (*family*) mantener. **2** (*make arrangements for*) tomar precauciones contra; (*of bill, constitution*) prever.
● **to provide os. with sth.,** proveerse de algo.
provided [prə'vaɪdɪd] **provided (that),** *conj* siempre que, con tal que, a condición de que.
providence ['prɒvɪdəns] *n* providencia.
provident ['prɒvɪdənt] *adj* previsor,-ra.
providential [prɒvɪ'denʃəl] *adj fml* providencial.
providing [prə'vaɪdɪŋ] *conj* → **provided**.
province ['prɒvɪns] **1** *n* (*region*) provincia. **2** *fig* terreno, campo, competencia.
● **that's not my province,** eso no es de mi competencia.
provincial [prə'vɪnʃəl] **1** *adj* (*government*) provincial; (*town*) de provincia(s). **2** *pej* provinciano,-a, pueblerino,-a. – **3** *n pej* provinciano,-a.
provision [prə'vɪʒən] **1** *n* (*supply - gen*) suministro, abastecimiento; (*of funds*) provisión *f*. **2** (*preparation*) previsiones *fpl*: *they made provision against bad weather,* tomaron precauciones por si hacía mal tiempo. **3** JUR (*stipulation*) disposición *f*; (*condition*) condición *f*: *under the provisions of the agreement,* según lo que estipula el acuerdo. – **4 provisions,** *npl* (*food*) provisiones *fpl*, víveres *mpl*.

● **to make provision for the future,** (*gen*) prever el futuro; (*money*) ahorrar para el futuro. ‖ **to make provision for sb.,** atender las necesidades de algn., asegurar el porvenir de algn. ‖ **with the provision that ...,** con tal de que ..., con la condición de que ...
provisional [prə'vɪʒənəl] *adj* provisional.
proviso [prə'vaɪzəu] *n* condición *f*.
● **with the proviso that,** con la condición de que.
▲ *pl* **provisos**.
provocation [prɒvə'keɪʃən] *n* provocación *f*.
provocative [prə'vɒkətɪv] *adj* (*controversial*) provocador,-ra; (*sexy*) provocativo,-a.
provocatively [prə'vɒkətɪvlɪ] *adv* (*controversially*) de forma provocadora; (*sexily*) de forma provocativa.
provoke [prə'vəuk] **1** *t* (*make angry*) provocar, irritar: *he's not easily provoked,* no se irrita fácilmente. **2** (*cause*) provocar.
● **to provoke sb. into doing sth. / provoke sb. to do sth.,** provocar a algn. a que haga algo.
provoking [prə'vəukɪŋ] **1** *adj* provocador,-ra. **2** (*irritating*) irritante.
provost ['prɒvəst] **1** *n* GB EDUC rector,-ra. **2** GB REL deán *m*. **3** (*in Scotland*) alcalde,-esa.
prow [prau] *n* proa.
prowess ['prauəs] *n fml* destreza, habilidad *f*.
prowl [praul] **1** *i* merodear, rondar. – **2** *t* merodear por, rondar por. – **3** *n* merodeo.
● **to be on the prowl / go on the prowl,** merodear, rondar.
prowler ['praulə'] *n* merodeador,-ra.
proximity ['prɒksɪmɪtɪ] *n fml* proximidad *f*.
● **in the proximity of,** en las proximidades de, cerca de.
proxy ['prɒksɪ] **1** *n* (*authority*) poder *m*. **2** (*person*) apoderado,-a.
● **by proxy,** por poderes.
▲ *pl* **proxies**.
prude [pruːd] *n* gazmoño,-a, mojigato,-a.
prudence ['pruːdəns] *n* prudencia.
prudent ['pruːdənt] *adj* prudente.
prudish ['pruːdɪʃ] *adj* remilgado,-a, mojigato,-a, gazmoño,-a.
prune¹ [pruːn] *n* ciruela pasa.
prune² [pruːn] **1** *t* (*hedge, rosebush, etc*) podar. **2** (*essay, novel, etc*) acortar; (*budget, costs, etc*) reducir, recortar.
pruning ['pruːnɪŋ] *n* poda.
■ **pruning knife,** podera.
prurient ['pruərɪənt] *adj fml* lascivo,-a.
Prussia ['prʌʃə] *n* Prusia.
Prussian ['prʌʃən] **1** *adj* pruso,-a. – **2** *n* pruso,-a.
pry [praɪ] **1** *i* curiosear, husmear, fisgonear. – **2** *t* → **prise**.
● **to pry into sth.,** entrometerse en algo.
▲ (*verbo*) *pt & pp* **pried,** *ger* **prying**.
prying ['praɪɪŋ] *adj* entrometido,-a, husmeador,-ra.
PS ['piː'es] *abbr* (*postscript*) posdata; (*abbreviation*) P.S., P.D.
psalm [saːm] *n* salmo.
pseud [sjuːd] *n fam* farsante *mf*.
pseudonym ['suːdənɪm] *n* seudónimo, pseudónimo.
psych [saɪk] **to psych (out),** *t* desconcertar, poner nervioso,-a a.
◆ **to psych up** *t sep* mentalizar.
● **to psych os. up,** mentalizarse.
psyche ['saɪkɪ] *n* psique *f*, psiquis *f*.

psychedelic [saɪkɪ'delɪk] *adj* psicodélico,-a, sicodélico,-a.

psychiatric [saɪkɪ'ætrɪk] *adj* psiquiátrico,-a, siquiátrico,-a.

psychiatrist [saɪ'kaɪətrɪst] *n* psiquiatra *mf*, siquiatra *mf*.

psychiatry [saɪ'kaɪətrɪ] *n* psiquiatría, siquiatría.

psychic ['saɪkɪk] 1 *adj* (*mental*) psíquico,-a, síquico,-a. 2 (*knowing*) clarividente. – 3 *n* médium *mf*.

psychoanalyse [saɪkəʊ'ænəlaɪz] *t* psicoanalizar, sicoanalizar.

psychoanalysis [saɪkəʊə'nælɪsɪs] *n* psicoanálisis *m*, sicoanálisis *m*.

psychoanalyst [saɪkəʊ'ænəlɪst] *n* psicoanalista *mf*, sicoanalista *mf*.

psychological [saɪkə'lɒdʒɪkəl] *adj* psicológico,-a, sicológico,-a.

psychologist [saɪ'kɒlədʒɪst] *n* psicólogo,-a, sicólogo,-a.

psychology [saɪ'kɒlədʒɪ] *n* psicología, sicología.

psychopath ['saɪkəʊpæθ] *n* psicópata *mf*, sicópata *mf*.

psychosis [saɪ'kəʊsɪs] *n* psicosis *f*, sicosis *f*.
▲ *pl* **psychoses** [saɪ'kəʊsiːz].

psychosomatic [saɪkəʊsə'mætɪk] *adj* psicosomático,-a, sicosomático,-a.

psychotherapy [saɪkəʊ'θerəpɪ] *n* psicoterapia, sicoterapia.

psychotic [saɪ'kɒtɪk] *adj* psicótico,-a, sicótico,-a. – 2 *n* psicótico,-a, sicótico,-a.

pt¹ [pɑːt] *abbr* (*part*) parte *f*.

pt² [paɪnt] *abbr* (*pint*) pinta.

pt³ [pɔɪnt] *abbr* (*point*) punto.

PT ['piː'tiː] *abbr* (*physical training*) educación física.

PTA ['piː'tiː'eɪ] *abbr* (*Parent-Teacher Association*) asociación de padres de alumnos y profesores.

Pte ['praɪvət] *abbr* (*Private*) soldado raso.

PTO ['piː'tiː'əʊ] *abbr* (*please turn over*) sigue.

pub [pʌb] *n* bar *m*, pub *m*, taberna.

pub-crawl ['pʌbkrɔːl] *n* ruta de bares.
● **to go on a pub-crawl**, ir de tascas, ir de bares, ir de copeo.

puberty ['pjuːbətɪ] *n* pubertad *f*.

pubescent [pjuː'besənt] *adj* pubescente.

pubic ['pjuːbɪk] *adj* púbico,-a.
■ **pubic hair**, vello púbico.

pubis ['pjuːbɪs] *n* pubis *m*.

public ['pʌblɪk] 1 *adj* público,-a. – 2 **the public**, *n* el público.
● **in public**, en público. ‖ **to be in the public eye**, ser objeto de interés público. ‖ **to be public knowledge**, ser del dominio público. ‖ **to go public**, COMM salir a bolsa. ‖ **to make public**, hacer público,-a.
■ **public company**, empresa pública, sociedad *f* anónima. ‖ **public convenience**, servicios *mpl*, aseos *mpl*. ‖ **public holiday**, fiesta nacional. ‖ **public house**, bar *m*, pub *m*. ‖ **public opinion**, opinión *f* pública. ‖ **public prosecutor**, fiscal *mf*. ‖ **public relations**, relaciones *fpl* públicas. ‖ **public school**, GB colegio privado; US colegio público. ‖ **public sector**, sector *m* público. ‖ **public speaker**, orador,-ra. ‖ **public speaking**, oratoria. ‖ **public transport**, transporte *m* público. ‖ **public utility**, servicio público.

public-address system [pʌblɪkə'dresɪstəm] *n* (sistema *m* de) megafonía.

publican ['pʌblɪkən] *n* patrón,-ona de un bar, dueño,-a de un bar, tabernero,-a.

publication [pʌblɪ'keɪʃən] *n* publicación *f*.

publicist ['pʌblɪsɪst] *n* publicista *mf*.

publicity [pʌ'blɪsɪtɪ] *n* publicidad *f*.
■ **publicity stunt**, truco publicitario. ‖ **publicity campaign**, campaña publicitaria.

publicize [pʌblɪ'saɪz] 1 *t* (*make public*) divulgar, hacer público,-a, dar a conocer. 2 (*advertise*) promocionar, hacer publicidad de.

public-spirited [pʌblɪk'spɪrɪtɪd] *adj* de espíritu cívico.

publish ['pʌblɪʃ] 1 *t* (*book, newspaper*) publicar, editar; (*article*) publicar. 2 (*make known*) divulgar, hacer público,-a.

publisher ['pʌblɪʃəʳ] *n* (*person*) editor,-ra; (*company*) editorial *f*.

publishing ['pʌblɪʃɪŋ] *n* (*profession*) industria editorial.
■ **publishing company / publishing house**, casa editorial, editorial *f*.

puce [pjuːs] 1 *adj* castaño,-a rojizo,-a. – 2 *n* castaño rojizo.

puck [pʌk] *n* SP disco.

pucker ['pʌkəʳ] 1 *n* (*in fabric*) frunce *m*, fruncido, pliegue *m*; (*on brow*) arruga. – 2 *t* (*face, lips, brow*) fruncir, arrugar. – 3 *i* (*lips, brow*) fruncirse, arrugarse.

pudding ['pʊdɪŋ] 1 *n* CULIN (*sweet*) budín *m*, pudín *m*; (*savoury*) pastel *m*. 2 GB *fam* (*dessert*) postre *m*: *what's for pudding?*, ¿qué hay de postre?
■ **black pudding**, morcilla. ‖ **rice pudding**, arroz *m* con leche.

puddle ['pʌdəl] *n* charco.

puerile ['pjʊəraɪl] *adj* pueril.

Puerto Rican [pweətəʊ'riːkən] 1 *adj* puertorriqueño,-a, portorriqueño,-a. – 2 *n* puertorriqueño,-a, portorriqueño,-a.

Puerto Rico [pweətəʊ'riːkəʊ] *n* Puerto Rico.

puff [pʌf] 1 *n* (*of wind, air*) soplo, racha, ráfaga; (*of smoke*) bocanada. 2 (*action*) soplo, soplido; (*at cigarette, pipe*) calada, chupada. 3 *fam* (*breath*) aliento: *I'm out of puff*, estoy sin aliento. – 4 *t* (*blow - gen*) soplar; (- *smoke*) echar. – 5 *i* (*pipe, cigarette*) chupar (**at/on**, -), dar caladas (**at/on**, a). 6 (*pant*) jadear, resoplar. 7 (*train*) echar humo, echar vapor.
◆ **to puff out** 1 *t sep* (*cheeks, chest*) hinchar, inflar; (*feathers, cushion*) ahuecar. 2 (*make out of breath*) dejar sin aliento. ‖ **to puff up** 1 *t sep* (*cheeks, chaest*) inflar, hinchar; (*cushion, feathers*) ahuecar. – 2 *i* hincharse.
■ **puff pastry**, hojaldre *m*, pasta hojaldrada.

puffed [pʌft] 1 *adj* (*sleeve*) abombado,-a; (*rice*) inflado,-a. 2 (*out of breath*) agotado,-a, sin aliento. 3 **puffed up**, (*swollen*) hinchado,-a.

puffin ['pʌfɪn] *n* ORN frailecillo (común).

puffy ['pʌfɪ] *adj* hinchado,-a.
▲ *comp* **puffier**, *superl* **puffiest**.

pug [pʌg] *n* (*dog*) doguillo.
■ **pug nose**, nariz *f* chata.

pugnacious [pʌg'neɪʃəs] *adj* pugnaz, agresivo,-a.

pug-nosed ['pʌgnəʊzd] *adj* de nariz chata.

puke ['pjuːk] *i fam* devolver, vomitar.

pull [pʊl] 1 *n* (*tug*) tirón *m*. 2 (*of moon, current*) fuerza. 3 (*attraction*) atracción *f*; (*influence*) influencia. 4 (*on bottle*) sorbo; (*on cigarette*) calada, chupada. 5 (*prolonged effort*) paliza. 6 (*single impression, proof*) prueba. – 7 *t* (*draw*) tirar de; (*drag*) arrastrar: *the horse was pulling a cart*, el caballo tiraba una carreta; *he pulled the curtains*, corrió las cortinas; *pull up a chair*, coge una silla. 8 (*tug forcefully*) tirar de, dar un tirón a: *don't pull my hair!*, ¡no me tires el pelo!; *have you pulled the chain?*, ¿has ti-

rado de la cadena?; *he pulled off his boots,* se quitó las botas. **9** (*remove, draw out*) sacar: *he pulled a gun,* sacó una pistola. **10** (*damage - muscle*) sufrir un tirón: *I pulled a muscle,* me dio un tirón. **11** (*operate - trigger*) apretar. **12** *fam* (*attract - crowd, audience*) atraer; (*boy, girl*) ligarse, ligar con. **– 13** *i* (*tug*) tirar (**at/on,** de): *he pulled with all his strength,* tiró con todas sus fuerzas. **14** (*on pipe, cigarette*) chupar, dar caladas a. **15** (*of vehicle - veer*) tirar.
◆ **to pull apart 1** *t sep* (*separate*) separar; (*pull to pieces*) destrozar, hacer pedazos. **2** (*criticize*) poner por los suelos, echar por tierra. ‖ **to pull away 1** *i* (*car, bus*) arrancar; (*train*) salir de la estación. **– 2** *t sep* separar, apartar. ‖ **to pull down** *t sep* derribar, tirar (abajo). ‖ **to pull in 1** *t sep* (*crowd*) atraer. **2** (*money*) sacar, ganar. **– 3** *i* (*train*) entrar en la estación; (*bus, car*) parar. ‖ **to pull off 1** *t sep* (*carry out*) llevar a cabo; (*achieve*) conseguir, lograr. **– 2** *t insep* (*of car etc*) salir de. ‖ **to pull out 1** *t sep* (*gun, tooth, plug, etc*) sacar; (*troops*) retirar. **– 2** *i* (*train*) salir de la estación; (*bus, car*) salir: *a car pulled out suddenly,* un coche salió de repente. **3** (*withdraw*) retirarse. ‖ **to pull over** *i* hacerse a un lado. ‖ **to pull through** *i* reponerse. ‖ **to pull together 1** *i* trabajar juntos. **– 2 to pull os. together,** *t sep* calmarse. ‖ **to pull up 1** *t sep* (*draw up*) subir, levantar; (*plant, weed*) arrancar. **2** (*scold*) regañar. **– 3** *i* (*bus, car*) detenerse, parar.
● **to go (out) on the pull,** salir a ligar. ‖ **to pull a face,** hacer una mueca. ‖ **to pull a fast one (on sb.),** hacer una mala jugada a algn. ‖ **to pull a gun on sb.,** amenazar a algn. con una pistola. ‖ **to pull one's socks up,** *fig* espabilarse, poner un poco de empeño. ‖ **to pull one's weight,** hacer su parte del trabajo. ‖ **to pull sb.'s leg,** tomar el pelo a algn. ‖ **to pull strings,** tocar teclas. ‖ **to pull the wool over sb.'s eyes,** engañar a algn. ‖ **to pull up one's roots,** desarraigarse.
pullet ['pulɪt] *n* pollo.
pulley ['pulɪ] *n* polea.
Pullman ['pulmən] *n* coche-cama *m*.
pull-out ['pulaut] *n* suplemento, separata.
pullover ['puləuvə'] *n* pullover *m*, jersey *m*.
pulmonary ['pʌlmənərɪ] *adj* pulmonar.
pulp [pʌlp] **1** *n* (*of fruit*) pulpa, carne *f*; (*of vegetable*) pulpa; (*of wood, paper*) pasta, pulpa. **2** (*substance*) papilla. **3** *pej* (*books, magazines, etc*) literatura barata, basura. **– 4** *t* (*wood, paper*) hacer pasta de, hacer pulpa de; (*fruit*) reducir a pulpa.
● **to beat sb. to a pulp,** hacer papilla a algn.
pulpit ['pulpɪt] *n* púlpito.
pulsate [pʌl'seɪt] *i* (*pulse*) latir, palpitar; (*vibrate*) vibrar, palpitar.
pulsation [pʌl'seɪʃən] *n* (*of heart*) latido; (*of blood*) pulsación *f*.
pulse[1] [pʌls] **1** *n* ANAT pulso. **2** PHYS pulsación *f*. **– 3** *i* palpitar, latir.
● **to take sb.'s pulse,** tomarle el pulso a algn.
■ **pulse rate,** número de pulsaciones.
pulse[2] [pʌls] *n* BOT legumbre *f*.
pulverize ['pʌlvəraɪz] *t* pulverizar.
puma ['pjuːmə] *n* puma *m*.
pumice stone ['pʌmɪsstəun] *n* piedra pómez.
pummel ['pʌməl] *t* aporrear.
▲ (*verbo*) *pt* & *pp* **pummelled** (US **pummeled**), *ger* **pummelling** (US **pummeling**).
pump[1] [pʌmp] **1** *n* (*machine*) bomba: *bicycle pump,* bomba de aire, bombín *m*. **2** (*act*) bombeo. **– 3** *t* bombear: *he pumped air into the tyre,* infló el neumático con una bomba; *the water is pumped from the well,* el agua se saca del pozo con una bomba. **– 4** *i* (*of heart*) latir.

◆ **to pump up** *t sep* inflar.
● **to pump iron,** hacer pesas. ‖ **to pump money into sth.,** invertir dinero en algo. ‖ **to pump sb. for information,** (tratar de) sonsacar información a algn. ‖ **to pump sb.'s hand,** darle un fuerte apretón de manos a algn.
pump[2] [pʌmp] **1** *n* (*plimsoll*) zapatilla de lona, playera; (*for dancing*) zapatilla de ballet. **2** US (*shoe*) zapato de salón.
pumpkin ['pʌmpkɪn] *n* calabaza.
pun [pʌn] *n* juego de palabras, retruécano.
punch[1] [pʌntʃ] **1** *n* (*blow*) puñetazo, golpe *m*; (*in boxing*) pegada. **2** *fig* fuerza, garra, empuje *m*. **– 3** *t* dar un puñetazo a, pegar a.
● **to pack a punch,** (*in boxing*) pegar fuerte, pegar duro, tener buena pegada; (*speech etc*) pegar fuerte. ‖ **not to pull any punches,** no tener pelos en la lengua.
■ **punch line,** remate *m* (de un chiste).
punch[2] [pʌntʃ] **1** *n* (*for making holes*) perforadora, taladro; (*in leather*) punzón *m*; (*for tickets*) máquina de picar billetes. **– 2** *t* (*make a hole in*) perforar; (*leather*) punzar; (*ticket*) picar.
punch[3] [pʌntʃ] *n* (*drink*) ponche *m*.
Punch [pʌntʃ] *n* polichinela *m*, títere *m*.
■ **Punch and Judy show,** función *f* de polichinelas.
punchball ['pʌntʃbɔːl] *n* GB SP balón *m* para pegar puñetazos, punching ball *m*.
punchbowl ['pʌntʃbəul] *n* ponchera.
punch-drunk ['pʌntʃdrʌŋk] *adj* grogui, aturdido,-a.
punching bag ['pʌntʃɪŋbæg] *n* US SP saco de arena.
punch-up ['pʌntʃʌp] *n fam* riña, pelea.
punctilious [pʌŋk'tɪlɪəs] *adj fml* puntilloso,-a.
punctual ['pʌŋktjuəl] *adj* puntual.
punctuality [pʌŋktju'ælɪtɪ] *n* puntualidad *f*.
punctually ['pʌŋktjuəlɪ] *adv* puntualmente.
punctuate ['pʌŋktjueɪt] **1** *t* LING puntuar. **2** (*interrupt*) interrumpir. **– 3** *i* LING puntuar.
punctuation [pʌŋktju'eɪʃən] *n* puntuación *f*.
■ **punctuation mark,** signo de puntuación.
puncture ['pʌŋktʃə'] **1** *n* pinchazo: *his bike's got a puncture,* su bici tiene una rueda pinchada; *he had a puncture,* se le pinchó una rueda. **– 2** *t* (*tyre, ball, etc*) pinchar. **3** MED puncionar. **– 4** *i* pincharse.
■ **punctured lung,** pulmón *m* perforado.
pundit ['pʌndɪt] *n* experto,-a.
pungency ['pʌndʒənsɪ] **1** *n* (*of smell, taste*) acritud *f*. **2** (*of remark*) mordacidad *f*.
pungent ['pʌndʒənt] **1** *adj* (*smell, taste*) acre. **2** (*remark*) mordaz.
punish ['pʌnɪʃ] *t* castigar.
punishable ['pʌnɪʃəbəl] **1** *adj* punible, castigable. **2** JUR delictivo,-a.
● **punishable by death,** penado,-a con la muerte.
punishing ['pʌnɪʃɪŋ] *adj* (*severe*) duro,-a; (*exhausting*) agotador,-ra.
punishment ['pʌnɪʃmənt] **1** *n* (*gen*) castigo. **2** *fig* (*wear and tear*) trote *m*.
● **to make the punishment fit the crime,** adecuar el castigo al crimen. ‖ **to take a lot of punishment,** *fig* haber sido muy castigado,-a.
■ **capital punishment,** pena de muerte, pena capital. ‖ **corporal punishment,** castigo físico.
punitive ['pjuːnɪtɪv] *adj* punitivo,-a.
punk [pʌŋk] **1** *n* (*person*) punk *mf*, punki *mf*; (*music*) punk *m*. **2** US (*lout*) gamberro,-a.
punnet ['pʌnɪt] *n* cestita.

punt¹ [pʌnt] 1 *n* (*boat*) batea. – 2 *i* ir en batea.
punt² [pʌnt] *i* GB *fam* apostar.
punt³ [punt] *n* (*currency*) libra irlandesa.
punter¹ ['pʌntəʳ] 1 *n fam* (*in betting*) jugador,-ra. 2 (*customer*) cliente,-a.
puny ['pjuːnɪ] *adj* enclenque, endeble, canijo,-a.
   ▲ *comp* **punier,** *superl* **puniest**
pup [pʌp] *n* (*dog*) cachorro,-a; (*seal, otter*) cría.
pupa ['pjuːpə] *n* pupa, crisálida.
   ▲ *pl* **pupas** *o* **pupae** ['pjuːpiː].
pupil¹ ['pjuːpəl] *n* EDUC alumno,-a.
pupil² ['pjuːpəl] *n* ANAT pupila.
puppet ['pʌpɪt] 1 *n* títere *m*, marioneta. 2 *fig* títere *m*.
   ■ **puppet show,** teatro de títeres, teatro de marionetas.
puppeteer [pʌpə'tɪəʳ] *n* titiritero,-a.
puppy ['pʌpɪ] *n* cachorro,-a.
   ■ **puppy fat,** gordura infantil. ‖ **puppy love,** amor *m* adolescente.
   ▲ *pl* **puppies**.
purchase ['pɜːtʃəs] 1 *n fml* compra, adquisición *f*. – 2 *t fml* comprar, adquirir.
   ● **to get a purchase on sth.,** (*grip*) agarrar algo bien.
   ■ **purchase price,** precio de compra. ‖ **purchase tax,** impuesto sobre la venta. ‖ **purchasing power,** poder *m* adquisitivo.
purchaser ['pɜːtʃəsəʳ] *n fml* comprador,-ra.
pure ['pjuəʳ] *adj* (*gen*) puro,-a: *it was pure chance,* fue pura casualidad.
   ● **pure and simple,** puro,-a y simple.
   ■ **pure new wool,** pura lana virgen.
purebred [pjuə'bred] 1 *adj* de pura sangre, de pura raza. – 2 *n* (*horse*) caballo de purasangre, pura *m* sangre.
purée ['pjuəreɪ] 1 *n* puré *m*. – 2 *t* hacer un puré de.
purely ['pjuəlɪ] *adv* simplemente, sencillamente: *it's purely a routine check,* es simplemente una revisión de rutina.
   ● **purely and simply,** pura y simplemente.
purgative ['pɜːgətɪv] 1 *n* MED purgante *m*. – 2 *adj* MED purgante.
purgatory ['pɜːgətərɪ] *n* purgatorio.
purge [pɜːdʒ] 1 *n* purga. – 2 *t* (*cleanse*) purgar. 3 POL purgar, hacer una purga en, depurar.
purification [pjuərɪfɪ'keɪʃən] *n* (*gen*) purificación *f*; (*of water*) depuración *f*, purificación *f*.
purifier ['pjuərɪfaɪəʳ] *n* (*gen*) purificador *m*; (*of water*) depurador *m*, purificador *m*.
purify ['pjuərɪfaɪ] *t* (*gen*) purificar; (*water*) depurar, purificar.
   ▲ *pt & pp* **purified,** *ger* **purifying**.
puritan ['pjuərɪtən] 1 *adj* puritano,-a. – 2 *n* puritano,-a.
purity ['pjuərɪtɪ] *n* pureza.
purl [pɜːl] 1 *n* punto del revés. – 2 *t* hacer punto del revés.
purple ['pɜːpəl] 1 *adj* púrpura, morado,-a. – 2 *n* (*color m*) púrpura, (*color m*) morado.
purport [pɜː'pɔːt] 1 *n fml* significado, sentido. – 2 *t fml* pretender.
purpose ['pɜːpəs] 1 *n* (*aim, intention*) propósito, intención *f*, fin *m*; (*reason*) razón *f*, motivo: *what is the purpose of your visit?,* ¿cuál es el motivo de su visita?; *she went with the express purpose of causing a scene,* fue con el propósito expreso de montar una escena. 2 (*use*) uso, utilidad *f*: *make sure you put it to good purpose,* asegúrate de aprovecharlo. 3 (*determination*) resolución *f*.
   ● **to no purpose,** inútilmente, en vano. ‖ **to have a**

purpose in life, tener una meta en la vida. ‖ **to have a sense of purpose,** tener una razón de ser. ‖ **to serve a purpose,** servir de algo, servir para algo. ‖ **to serve no purpose,** no servir para nada, ser inútil. ‖ **on purpose,** a propósito, adrede, a posta.
purpose-built ['pɜːpəsbɪlt] *adj* construido,-a especialmente, hecho,-a especialmente.
purposeful ['pɜːpəsfʊl] *adj* (*resolute*) decidido,-a, resuelto,-a.
purposefully ['pɜːpəsfʊlɪ] *adv* con determinación, resueltamente.
purposeless ['pɜːpəsləs] *adj* sin sentido.
purposely ['pɜːpəslɪ] *adv* a propósito, adrede.
purr [pɜːʳ] 1 *n* (*of cat*) ronroneo. – 2 *i* (*of cat*) ronronear.
purse [pɜːs] 1 *n* GB monedero, portamonedas *m*. 2 US bolso. 3 (*funds*) fondos *mpl*. 4 (*prize*) premio en efectivo, premio en metálico. – 5 *t* (*lips*) fruncir.
   ● **to hold the purse strings,** administrar el dinero.
purser ['pɜːsəʳ] *n* MAR contador,-ra.
pursue [pə'sjuː] 1 *t* (*chase*) perseguir; (*follow*) seguir. 2 (*seek*) buscar; (*strive for*) esforzarse por conseguir, luchar por. 3 (*carry out - policy*) llevar a cabo; (*- matter*) investigar. 4 (*continue with - studies*) seguir, dedicarse a; (*- profession, career*) ejercer.
pursuer [pə'sjuːəʳ] *n* perseguidor,-ra.
pursuit [pə'sjuːt] 1 *n* (*chase*) persecución *f*; (*hunt*) caza. 2 (*search*) búsqueda, busca; (*striving*) lucha. 3 (*activity*) actividad *f*.
   ● **in hot pursuit (of),** pisando los talones (a).
   ■ **leisure pursuit,** pasatiempo.
purveyor [pɜː'veɪəʳ] *n fml* proveedor,-ra, abastecedor,-ra.
pus [pʌs] *n* pus *m*.
push [pʊʃ] 1 *n* (*shove*) empujón *m*: *we had to give the car a push,* tuvimos que empujar el coche; *at the push of a button,* con sólo apretar un botón. 2 MIL ofensiva. 3 (*drive*) empuje *m*, dinamismo. – 4 *t* (*shove*) empujar: *the car broke down and I had to push it,* el coche se averió y tuve que empujarlo; *they pushed her in the water,* la empujaron al agua; *he pushed his way forward,* se abrió paso a empujones. 5 (*press - button, bell, etc*) pulsar, apretar. 6 (*persuade forcefully*) empujar, presionar; (*harass*) apretar, presionar, exigir: *they pushed her into marrying him,* la empujaron a casarse con él; *they're pushing me for an answer,* me están exigiendo una respuesta; *you're pushing yourself too hard,* te estás exigiendo demasiado. 7 (*promote, try to sell*) promocionar. 8 *fam* (*drugs*) pasar, vender, traficar con. – 9 *i* (*shove*) empujar: *push harder!,* ¡empuja más!; *stop pushing!,* ¡no empujes! 10 (*move forward*) abrirse paso: *they just pushed past me,* me apartaron de un empujón. 11 (*pressurize*) presionar, exigir: *they're pushing for reforms,* están exigiendo reformas.
   ◆ **to push about / push around** *t sep* intimidar, atropellar. ‖ **to push ahead** *i* seguir adelante. ‖ **to push in** *i* (*in queue*) colarse. ‖ **to push off** 1 *i fam* (*go away*) largarse. 2 (*in boat*) desatracar. ‖ **to push on** *i* seguir, continuar. ‖ **to push over** *t sep* (*person*) hacer caer, tirar; (*thing*) volcar. ‖ **to push through** *t sep* (*legislation, bill*) hacer aprobar; (*student*) ayudar.
   ● **at a push,** si fuera necesario. ‖ **if it comes to the push,** en último caso. ‖ **to be (hard) pushed for sth.,** andar escaso,-a de algo, andar corto,-a de algo. ‖ **to be pushed to do sth.,** tenerlo difícil para hacer algo. ‖ **to be pushing thirty, forty, etc,** rondar los treinta, cuarenta, etc. ‖ **to give sb. the push,** (*from job*) poner a algn. de patitas en la calle, echar a algn.; (*end rela-*

tionship) dejar a algn. ‖ **to push and shove,** dar empujones. ‖ **to push one's luck,** arriesgarse demasiado, forzar la suerte.

pushbike ['puʃbaɪk] *n fam* bicicleta.

pushchair ['puʃtʃeə'] *n* GB cochecito de niño, sillita de niño.

pusher ['puʃə'] *n fam* (*of drugs*) camello, traficante *mf* (de drogas).

pushover ['puʃəʊvə'] *n fam* (*person*) incauto,-a, presa fácil.
● it's a pushover, está chupado,-a, es pan comido.

push-start ['puʃstɑːt] *t* arrancar empujando.
● to give a car a push-start, arrancar un coche empujando.

push-up ['puʃʌp] *n* US flexión *f.*

pushy ['puʃɪ] *adj fam* agresivo,-a, insistente.
▲ *comp* pushier, *superl* pushiest.

puss [pus] *n fam* minino,-a, gatito,-a.

pussycat ['pusɪkæt] *n fam* minino,-a, gatito,-a.

pussyfoot ['pusɪfʊt] 1 *i* andar sigilosamente. 2 *fig* no comprometerse.

pussy willow ['pusɪwɪləʊ] *n* BOT sauce *m* blanco.

pustule ['pʌstjuːl] *n* pústula.

put [put] 1 *t* (*gen*) poner; (*place*) colocar; (*add*) echar, añadir; (*place inside*) meter, poner: *where did you put the matches?,* ¿dónde has puesto las cerillas?; *she put the vase on the table,* puso el florero en la mesa; *don't put too much salt in it,* no le eches demasiada sal; *I put the letter in the envelope,* metí la carta en el sobre; *she put her arms round him,* lo abrazó; *Fred put his head round the door,* Fred asomó la cabeza por la puerta. 2 (*write, mark*) poner, apuntar, escribir: *what did you put for number six?,* ¿qué pusiste en el número seis? 3 (*cause to be*) poner: *this puts me in a difficult position,* esto me pone en una situación difícil; *he put other people's lives in danger,* puso la vida de otras personas en peligro; *what's put you in such a bad mood,* ¿qué te ha puesto de tan mal humor? 4 (*rate, classify*) poner: *I'd put him among the top ten cyclists,* yo lo pondría entre los diez mejores ciclistas; *she puts her family before her job,* antepone su familia al trabajo. 5 (*express*) expresar, decir: *how shall I put it?,* ¿cómo te lo diría?; *you put that very well,* lo has expresado muy bien. 6 (*calculate, estimate*) calcular: *I'd put the cost at 100 pounds,* yo diría que cuesta 100 libras; *she put his age at 50,* le echó 50 años. 7 SP (*shot*) lanzar. – 8 *i* MAR: *the ship put about,* el barco viró en redondo; *the ship put in at Southampton,* el barco hizo escala en Southampton; *the ship put out to sea,* el barco se hizo a la mar.
◆ **to put about** *t sep* (*news, rumour*) hacer correr: *she put it about that ...,* hizo correr la voz de que ... ‖ **to put across** *t sep* (*idea, message, case*) comunicar, hacer entender; (*oneself*) comunicarse, hacerse entender. ‖ **to put aside** *t sep* (*place to one side*) dejar a un lado, apartar; (*save - money*) ahorrar; (*reserve - item, goods*) reservar, apartar, guardar; (*- time*) reservar. 2 (*disregard - differences*) dejar de lado. ‖ **to put away** 1 *t sep* (*clothes, toys, dishes*) guardar (en su sitio); (*save - money*) ahorrar. 2 (*lock up - criminal, mad person*) encerrar. 3 (*eat copiously*) zamparse. ‖ **to put back** 1 *t sep* (*replace, return*) devolver a su sitio. 2 (*clock*) atrasar, retrasar; (*postpone, delay*) aplazar, posponer. 3 (*drink*) beberse. ‖ **to put by** *t sep* ahorrar. ‖ **to put down** 1 *t sep* (*set down - gen*) dejar; (*- phone*) colgar; (*- baby*) acostar: *I couldn't put the book down,* no podía dejar de leer el libro. 2 (*payment*) entregar, dejar (en depósito); (*deposit*) dejar. 3 (*rebellion*) sofocar. 4 (*animal*) sacrificar. 5 (*write*) apuntar, anotar,

escribir. 6 (*humilliate*) humillar, rebajar: *don't put yourself down,* no te menosprecies. – 7 *i* AV aterrizar. ‖ **to put down for** *t sep* (*register - for school*) inscribir; (*for trip, dinner, etc*) apuntar. ‖ **to put down to** *t sep* (*attribute*) atribuir a. ‖ **to put forward** 1 *t sep* (*idea, theory, plan*) proponer, presentar; (*proposal, suggestion*) hacer; (*candidate*) proponer. 2 (*clock, meeting, wedding*) adelantar. ‖ **to put in** 1 *t sep* (*instal, fit*) instalar, poner. 2 (*include, insert*) poner, incluir; (*say*) agregar. 3 (*enter, submit - claim, request, bid*) presentar. 4 (*spend time working*) trabajar, hacer. ‖ **to put in for** *t insep* (*apply*) solicitar. ‖ **to put off** 1 *t sep* (*postpone*) aplazar, posponer: *I keep putting off going to the dentist,* sigo aplazando la visita al dentista; *never put off until tomorrow what you can do today,* nunca dejes para mañana lo que puedas hacer hoy. 2 (*distract*) distraer. 3 (*discourage*) desanimar, disuadir, quitar las ganas a: *the price of the tickets has put a lot of people off,* el precio de las entradas ha disuadido a mucha gente; *don't be put off by his manner,* no dejes que su actitud te desanime. ‖ **to put on** 1 *t sep* (*clothes*) poner, ponerse: *put your coat on,* ponte el abrigo; *put your clothes on,* vístete. 2 (*expression, attitude*) fingir, adoptar: *he's not sorry, he's just putting it on,* no lo lamenta, está fingiendo. 3 (*gain, increase*) aumentar: *she's put on a lot of weight,* ha engordado mucho. 4 (*present - show*) presentar, montar; (*- exhibition*) organizar. 5 (*provide, add - train etc*) poner: *they've put on extra trains for the match,* han puesto más trenes para el partido. 6 (*switch on - light, television*) encender; (*- music, radio*) poner: *I'll put the kettle on,* pondré agua a hervir. 7 (*add - gen*) añadir; (*- tax*) gravar con un impuesto; (*- bet*) apostar por: *they put a tax on windows,* gravaron las ventanas con un impuesto; *he put £5 on the favourite,* apostó 5 libras por el favorito; *this will put millions on the price,* esto aumentará el precio millones. ‖ **to put onto** *t sep* (*put in touch with*) poner en contacto con. ‖ **to put out** 1 *t sep* (*fire, light, cigarette*) apagar. 2 (*put outside - cat, washing, rubbish*) sacar. 3 (*extend - hand*) tender, alargar; (*- tongue*) sacar; (*dislocate*) dislocar. 4 (*inconvenience*) molestar; (*upset, offend, annoy*) molestar, ofender: *don't put yourself out on my account,* no te molestes por mí. 5 (*publish, issue*) publicar; (*broadcast*) difundir. ‖ **to put over** *t sep* → **put across**. ‖ **to put through** 1 *t sep* (*phone - connect*) pasar, poner (**to,** con): *could you put me through to accounts?,* ¿me puede poner con contabilidad? 2 (*cause to undergo*) someter a, hacer pasar por. 3 (*complete, conclude - reform, business*) llevar a cabo. ‖ **to put to** 1 *t sep* (*present, submit - proposal, case*) presentar, exponer; (*ask - question*) hacer; (*ask to vote on*) someter a votación. 2 (*cause to experience*) causar, ocasionar: *I don't want to put you to any trouble,* no quiero causarte ninguna molestia. ‖ **to put together** 1 *t sep* (*pieces*) armar, montar; (*team*) formar; (*meal etc*) preparar, hacer. 2 (*combine*) juntar, reunir: *he earns more than both of us put together,* gana más que nosotros dos juntos. ‖ **to put up** 1 *t sep* (*provide accommodation for*) alojar, hospedar: *we can put you up,* puedes quedarte a dormir en casa. 2 (*erect - tent*) armar; (*- building, fence*) levantar, construir. 3 (*shelves, picture, decorations*) colocar; (*curtains, notice, poster*) colgar. 4 (*raise - hand*) levantar; (*flag*) izar; (*hair*) recoger; (*umbrella*) abrir. 5 (*increase - price etc*) aumentar, subir. 6 (*present - candidate*) presentar, proponer. – 7 *t* (*resistance, struggle*) ofrecer, oponer: *they put up a good fight,* ofrecieron mucha resistencia. 8 (*money*) poner, aportar. ‖ **to put up to** *t sep* incitar, empujar: *who put you up to it?,* ¿quién te incitó a hacerlo? ‖ **to put up with** *t insep* soportar, aguantar. ‖ **to put upon** *t insep* explotar: *I'm* *fed up with being put upon,* estoy harta de que me exploten.

● **to be hard put to do sth.,** serle difícil a uno hacer algo. ‖ **to not know where to put os.,** no saber dónde ponerse, no saber dónde esconderse. ‖ **to put an end to sth.,** acabar con algo, poner fin a algo. ‖ **to put in a good word for sb.,** recomendar a algn. ‖ **to not put it past sb. (to do sth.),** creer a algn. muy capaz (de hacer algo). ‖ **to put one over on sb.,** engañar a algn. ‖ **to put paid to sth.,** estropear algo. ‖ **to put sth. right,** arreglar algo. ‖ **to put sb. on the train, plane, etc,** acompañar a algn. al tren, al avión, etc. ‖ **to put sb. to bed,** acostar a algn. ‖ **to put sb. to death,** ejecutar a algn. ‖ **to put sb. up to sth.,** incitar a algn. a hacer algo. ‖ **to put sth. out to contract,** subcontratar algo. ‖ **to put sth. to good use,** hacer buen uso de algo. ‖ **to put the blame on sb.,** echar la culpa a algn. ‖ **to put two and two together,** atar cabos. ‖ **to put sth. up for sale,** poner algo en venta. ‖ **to stay put,** quedarse quieto,-a.

▲ *pt & pp put, ger putting.*

putative ['pjuːtətɪv] *adj fml* putativo,-a.
put-down ['pʊtdaʊn] *n* corte *m*.
putrefaction [pjuːtrɪ'fækʃən] *n* putrefacción *f*.
putrefy ['pjuːtrɪfaɪ] *i* pudrirse.

▲ *pt & pp putrefied, ger putrefying.*

putrid ['pjuːtrɪd] *adj* (*rotting*) putrefacto,-a, podrido,-a.
putsch [pʊtʃ] *n* golpe *m* de estado.
putt [pʌt] **1** *n* tiro al hoyo. – **2** *t* tirar al hoyo. – **3** *i* tirar al hoyo.
putter ['pʌtəʳ] *n* (*in golf*) putter *m*.
putty ['pʌtɪ] *n* masilla.

● **to be putty in sb.'s hands,** ser dominado,-a por algn.: *she was putty in his hands,* hacía con ella lo que quería, la tenía en el bolsillo.

▲ *pl putties.*
put-up job ['pʊtʌp'dʒɒb] *n fam* montaje *m*.
puzzle ['pʌzəl] **1** *n* (*jigsaw*) puzzle *m*; (*toy*) rompecabezas *m*; (*riddle*) adivinanza, acertijo; (*crossword*) crucigrama *m*. **2** (*mystery*) misterio, enigma *m*. – **3** *t* dejar perplejo,-a, extrañar.

◆ **to puzzle out** *t sep* (*problem*) resolver; (*mystery*) descifrar: *they couldn't puzzle it out,* no lograron entenderlo.

● **to puzzle about/over sth.,** darle vueltas a algo (en la cabeza).

puzzled ['pʌzəld] *adj* (*confused*) perplejo,-a, desconcertado,-a; (*face, expression*) de perplejidad.
puzzling ['pʌzəlɪŋ] *adj* extraño,-a.
PVC ['piː'viː'siː] *abbr* (*polyvinyl chloride*) cloruro de polivinilo; (*abbreviation*) PVC *m*.
Pvt ['praɪvət] *abbr* US (*Private*) soldado raso.
PW ['piː'dʌbəljuː] *abbr* GB (*Policewoman*) mujer *f* policía.
pygmy ['pɪgmɪ] **1** *adj* pigmeo,-a, enano,-a. – **2** *n* (*small person*) pigmeo,-a, enano,-a. **3** Pygmy, pigmeo,-a.

▲ *pl pygmies.*
pyjamas [pə'dʒɑːməz] *npl* pijama *m sing.*
pylon ['paɪlən] **1** *n* ELEC torre *f* (de tendido eléctrico). **2** ARCH pilón *m*, pilar *m*.
pyramid ['pɪrəmɪd] *n* pirámide *f*.
pyre ['paɪəʳ] *n* pira.
Pyrenean [pɪ'rniːən] *adj* pirenaico,-a.
Pyrenees [pɪrə'niːz] the Pyrenees, *n* los Pirineos *mpl.*
Pyrex ['paɪreks] **1** *n* pírex *m*. – **2** *adj* de pírex.

▲ *Es marca registrada.*
pyromaniac [paɪrəʊ'meɪnɪæk] *n* pirómano,-a.
pyrotechnics [paɪrəʊ'tek.nɪks] **1** *n* pirotecnia. – **2** *npl* fuegos *mpl* artificiales.
python ['paɪθən] *n* pitón *m*

Q

Q, q [kjuː] *n* (*the letter*) Q, q *f*.

Qatar [kæˈtɑːʳ] *n* Qatar.

QC [ˈkjuːˈsiː] *abbr* (*Queen's Counsel*) ≈ abogado,-a del Estado.

QED [ˈkjuːˈiːˈdiː] *abbr* MATH (*quod erat demonstrandum*) lo que había que demostrar.

qt [kwɔːt] *abbr* (*quart*) cuarto de galón.

quack [kwæk] **1** *n* graznido. **2** (*doctor*) curandero,-a. **– 3** *i* graznar.

quackery [ˈkwækəri] *n fam* curanderismo, curandería.

quad [kwɒd] **1** *n* GB patio interior. **2** *fam* (*quadruplet*) cuatrillizo,-a.

quadrangle [ˈkwɒdræŋgəl] **1** *n* patio interior. **2** (*in geometry*) cuadrángulo.

quadrant [ˈkwɒdrənt] *n* cuadrante *m*.

quadraphonic [kwɒdrəˈfɒnɪk] *adj* cuadrafónico,-a.

quadratic [kwɒˈdrætɪk] *adj* MATH cuadrático,-a, de segundo grado.

■ quadratic equation, ecuación *f* de segundo grado.

quadrilateral [kwɒdrɪˈlætərəl] **1** *n* cuadrilátero. **– 2** *adj* cuadrilátero,-a.

quadruped [ˈkwɒdrʊped] *n fml* cuadrúpedo.

quadruple [ˈkwɒdrəpəl] **1** *n* cuádruplo. **– 2** *adj* cuádruple. **– 3** *t* cuadruplicar. **– 4** *i* cuadruplicarse.

quadruplet [ˈkwɒdrəplət, kwɒˈdruːplɪt] *n* cuatrillizo,-a.

quadruplicate [kwɒˈdruːplɪkət, kwɒˈdruːplɪkeɪt] **1** *n* cuadruplicado. **– 2** *adj* cuadruplicado,-a: *in quadruplicate*, por cuadruplicado. **– 3** *t* cuadruplicar.

▲ (*verbo*) [kwɒˈdruːplɪkeɪt].

quaff [kwɒf] *t lit* beber a tragos.

quagmire [ˈkwɒgmaɪəʳ] **1** *n* cenagal *m*. **2** *fig* atolladero.

quail [kweɪl] **1** *n* codorniz *f*. **– 2** *i* acobardarse, encogerse.

quaint [kweɪnt] **1** *adj* pintoresco,-a, típico,-a. **2** (*odd*) singular, original. **3** (*strange*) raro,-a, extraño,-a.

■ quaint fellow, tipo raro.

quake [kweɪk] **1** *n fam* terremoto. **– 2** *i* temblar: *he quaked with fear*, temblaba de miedo.

● to quake at the knees, temblarle las piernas a algn.

Quaker [ˈkweɪkəʳ] **1** *adj* REL cuáquero,-a. **– 2** *n* cuáquero,-a.

Quakerism [ˈkweɪkərɪzəm] *n* cuaquerismo.

qualification [kwɒlɪfɪˈkeɪʃən] **1** *n* (*for job*) requisito. **2** (*ability*) aptitud *f*, capacidad *f*. **3** (*paper*) diploma *m*, título. **4** (*reservation*) reserva, salvedad *f*. **5** (*restriction*) limitación *f*. **6** (*act of qualifying*) graduación *f*: *she soon found a job after qualification*, no tardó mucho en encontrar trabajo después de graduarse.

qualified [ˈkwɒlɪfaɪd] **1** *adj* (*for job*) capacitado,-a. **2** (*with qualifications*) titulado,-a: *qualified nurse*, enfermera,-o titulada,-o. **3** (*limited, modified*) limitado,-a, restringido,-a: *a qualified agreement*, un acuerdo limitado.

qualify [ˈkwɒlɪfaɪ] **1** *t* (*entitle, make eligible*) capacitar, dar derecho, habilitar: *her excellent grades qualified her for a grant*, sus excelentes notas le dieron derecho a una

beca. **2** (*modify*) modificar, matizar, puntualizar. **3** LING calificar. **– 4** *i* reunir las condiciones necesarias: *I'm afraid you don't qualify for a pension*, me temo que usted no reúne las condiciones necesarias para percibir una pensión. **5** (*obtain degree*) obtener el título (**as**, de). **6** SP clasificarse: *he qualified for the finals*, se clasificó para las finales.

▲ *pt & pp* qualified, *ger* qualifying.

qualifying [ˈkwɒlɪfaɪɪŋ] *adj* eliminatorio,-a, clasificatorio,-a.

qualitative [ˈkwɒlɪtətɪv] *adj* cualitativo,-a.

quality [ˈkwɒlɪtɪ] **1** *n* (*degree of excellence*) calidad *f*: *of good quality*, de buena calidad; *of poor quality*, de poca calidad. **2** (*attribute*) cualidad *f*: *she has many qualities*, tiene muchas cualidades.

■ quality control, control *m* de calidad. ‖ quality goods, género de calidad, productos *mpl* de calidad. ‖ quality newspapers, prensa *f* no sensacionalista.

▲ *pl* qualities.

qualm [kwɑːm] **1** *n* (*doubt*) duda *f*; (*worry*) inquietud *f*, ansia: *she has qualms about aborting*, tiene dudas de si abortar o no. **2** (*scruple*) escrúpulo *m*.

● to have no qualms about doing sth., no tener escrúpulos en hacer algo.

■ qualms of conscience, remordimientos *mpl* de conciencia.

quandary [ˈkwɒndəri] **1** *n* (*dilemma*) dilema *m*. **2** (*difficulty*) apuro *m*.

● to be in a quandry, estar en un dilema.

▲ *pl* quandaries.

quango [ˈkwæŋgəʊ] *n* POL organización *f* no gubernamental semi-autónoma.

▲ *pl* quangos.

quantify [ˈkwɒntɪfaɪ] *t* cuantificar.

▲ *pt & pp* quantified, *ger* quantifying.

quantitative [ˈkwɒntɪtətɪv] *adj* cuantitativo,-a.

quantity [ˈkwɒntɪtɪ] **1** *n* cantidad *f*. **2** MATH cantidad *f*.

■ quantity surveyor, aparejador *m*.

▲ *pl* quantities.

quantum [ˈkwɒntəm] *n* PHYS quántum *m*.

■ quantum theory, teoría de los quanta.

quarantine [ˈkwɒrəntiːn] **1** *n* cuarentena: *to be in quarantine*, estar en cuarentena. **– 2** *t* poner en cuarentena.

quark [kwɑːk] *n* TECH quark *m*.

quarrel [ˈkwɒrəl] **1** *n* riña, disputa, pelea. **2** (*disagreement*) desacuerdo. **3** (*complaint*) queja: *I have no quarrel with him*, no tengo ninguna queja de él, no tengo nada contra él. **– 4** *i* (*argue*) reñir, pelearse, disputar, discutir: *she is always quarreling with her mother*, siempre está discutiendo con su madre.

● to pick a quarrel with sb., meterse con algn., buscar pelea con algn.

▲ (*verbo*) *pt & pp* quarrelled (US quarreled), *ger* quarrelling (US quarreling).

quarrelsome [ˈkwɒrəlsəm] *adj* pendenciero,-a, peleón,-ona, camorrista.

quarry ['kwɒrɪ] **1** *n* cantera. **2** (*in hunting*) presa. – **3** *t* extraer.
▲ (*sustantivo*) *pl* **quarries**; (*verbo*) *pt* & *pp* **quarried**, *ger* **quarrying**.
quart [kwɔːt] *n* cuarto de galón.
● **to put a quart into a pint pot,** hacer algo imposible.
▲ *en Gran Bretaña equivale a 1,14 litros; en Estados Unidos equivale a 0,95 litro.*
quarter ['kwɔːtəʳ] **1** *n* cuarto. **2** (*area*) barrio: *the old quarter*, el casco antiguo; *the Latin Quarter*, el barrio latino. **3** (*time*) cuarto: *it's a quarter to one,* es la una menos cuarto. **4** (*weight*) cuarto de libra: *a quarter of sugar,* un cuarto de libra de azúcar. **5** (*of moon*) cuarto. **6** (*three months*) trimestre *m*. **7** US (*amount*) veinticinco centavos; (*coin*) moneda de veinticinco centavos. – **8** *t* dividir en cuatro. **9** (*reduce*) reducir a la cuarta parte. **10** HIST descuartizar. **11** (*lodge*) alojar. – **12 quarters,** *npl* alojamiento *m sing*.
● **at close quarters,** desde muy cerca. ‖ **from all quarters,** de todas partes. ‖ **to give no quarter,** no dar cuartel.
■ **first quarter,** cuarto creciente. ‖ **last quarter,** cuarto menguante. ‖ **officer's quarters,** residencia *f sing* de oficiales.
quarterdeck ['kwɔːtədek] *n* MAR alcázar *m*.
quarterfinal [kwɔːtə'faɪnəl] **1** *n* (*sport*) cuarto de final. – **2 quarterfinals,** *npl* cuartos *mpl* de final *f*.
quarterfinalist [kwɔːtə'faɪnəlɪst] *n* (*sport*) cuartofinalista *mf*.
quarterlight ['kwɔːtəlaɪt] *n* GB AUT ventanilla.
quarterly ['kwɔːtəlɪ] **1** *adj* trimestral. – **2** *adv* trimestralmente. – **3** *n* revista trimestral.
▲ (*sustantivo*) *pl* **quarterlies**.
quartermaster ['kwɔːtəmɑːstəʳ] **1** *n* (*in army*) oficial *m* de intendencia. **2** (*in navy*) cabo de la marina.
quartet [kwɔː'tet] *n* (*mus*) cuarteto.
quartette [kwɔː'tet] *n* → **quartet**.
quarto ['kwɔːtəʊ] **1** *adj* (*paper size*) en cuarto. – **2** *n* (*book*) libro en cuarto.
▲ (*sustantivo*) *pl* **quartos**.
quartz [kwɔːts] *n* cuarzo.
■ **quartz watch,** reloj *m* de cuarzo.
quash [kwɒʃ] **1** *t* (*uprising*) sofocar, aplastar. **2** JUR anular, invalidar.
quasi ['kwɑːzɪ, 'kweɪzaɪ] *adv* casi, cuasi.
■ **quasi contract,** JUR cuasi contrato.
quatrain ['kwɒtreɪn] *n* LIT cuarteto.
quaver ['kweɪvəʳ] **1** *n* MUS (*note*) corchea. **2** MUS (*voice*) trémolo. **3** (*trembling*) temblor *m*. – **4** *i* temblar: *her voice quavered,* le temblaba la voz.
quavering ['kweɪvərɪŋ] *adj* tembloroso,-a, trémulo,-a,: *quavering voice,* voz trémula.
quay [kiː] *n* muelle *m*.
quayside ['kiːsaɪd] *n* muelle *m*.
queasiness ['kwiːzɪnəs] *n* náuseas *fpl*.
queasy ['kwiːzɪ] **1** *adj* mareado,-a. **2** (*conscience*) delicado,-a, escrupuloso,-a.
● **to feel queasy,** sentirse mal, tener náuseas: *she felt queasy throughout the crossing,* se sintió mal durante toda la travesía.
▲ *comp* **queasier,** *superl* **queasiest**.
Quechua ['ketʃwə] **1** *adj* quechua – **2** *n* (*person*) quechua *mf*. **3** (*language*) quechua *m*.
queen [kwiːn] **1** *n* reina. **2** (*cards, chess*) dama, reina; (*chess*) reina. **3** *sl* loca, maricona. – **4** *t* (*pawn*) coronar.

● **to queen it,** pavonearse.
■ **queen bee,** abeja reina. ‖ **Queen Mother,** reina madre.
queenly ['kwiːnlɪ] *adj* regio,-a, de reina.
queer [kwɪəʳ] **1** *adj* raro,-a, extraño,-a. **2** (*ill*) malucho,-a. **3** *fam* gay. **4** (*mad*) loco,-a, chiflado,-a. – **5** *n fam* gay *m*, marica *m*, maricón *m*. – **6** *t fam* fastidiar, estropear.
● **in queer street,** (*in debt*) endeudado,-a, en deuda; (*in trouble*) en apuros. ‖ **to queer sb.'s pitch,** fastidiarle los planes a algn.
queerness ['kwɪənəs] *n* rareza.
quell [kwel] **1** *t* (*rebellion*) sofocar. **2** (*fears*) disipar.
quench [kwentʃ] **1** *t* (*thirst*) saciar. **2** (*fire*) apagar.
querulous ['kwerjʊləs] *adj fml* quejumbroso,-a.
query ['kwɪərɪ] **1** *n* pregunta, duda. **2** LING signo de interrogación. **3** *fig* interrogante *m*. – **4** *t* (*doubt*) poner en duda. **5** (*ask*) preguntar.
▲ (*sustantivo*) *pl* **queries**; (*verbo*) *pt* & *pp* **queried**, *ger* **querying**.
quest [kwest] *n* búsqueda, busca.
● **in quest of,** en busca de: *in quest of the Holy Grail,* en busca del Santo Grial.
question ['kwestʃən] **1** *n* pregunta. **2** (*in exam*) pregunta, problema *m*. **3** (*problem, issue*) cuestión *f*, problema *m*: *the Basque question,* el problema del País Vasco. **4** (*topic, matter*) cuestión *f*, asunto: *there is still the question of expenses,* todavía queda el asunto de los gastos. – **5** *t* hacer preguntas a, interrogar: *she questioned the girl,* le hizo preguntas a la niña; *the detained are being questioned about the holdup,* están interrogando a los detenidos sobre el atraco. **6** (*cast doubt on*) cuestionar, poner en duda.
● **it's a question of,** se trata de, es cuestión de: *it's a question of time,* es cuestión de tiempo. ‖ **out of the question,** imposible, impensable. ‖ **that is the question,** de eso se trata, he aquí la dificultad. ‖ **to call into question,** poner en duda, dudar de. ‖ **without question,** sin rechistar: *she did it without question,* lo hizo sin rechistar.
■ **question mark,** (*punctuation mark*) signo de interrogación, interrogación *f*, interrogante *m*; (*doubt*) interrogante *m*. ‖ **question tag,** coletilla.
questionable ['kwestʃənəbəl] **1** *adj* (*debatable*) cuestionable, discutible: *his authority is questionable,* su autoridad es discutible. **2** (*doubtful*) dudoso,-a, sospechoso,-a.
● **of questionable taste,** de gusto dudoso.
questioner ['kwestʃənəʳ] *n* interrogador,-ra.
questioning ['kwestʃənɪŋ] **1** *adj* inquisitivo,-a, interrogativo,-a: *she gave him a questioning glance,* le lanzó una mirada inquisitiva. – **2** *n* preguntas *fpl*, interrogatorio: *the Police brought him in for questioning,* la policía lo detuvo para someterlo a un interrogatorio.
questionnaire [kwestʃə'neəʳ] *n* cuestionario.
queue [kjuː] **1** *n* (GB) cola. – **2** *i* hacer cola: *nowadays you have to queue up for everything,* hoy en día hay que hacer cola para todo.
● **to jump the queue,** colarse.
queue-jumper ['kjuːdʒʌmpəʳ] *n fam* persona que se cuela.
quibble ['kwɪbəl] **1** *n* (*difficulty*) pega, objeción *f*. **2** (*subtlety*) sutileza. **3** (*evasion*) evasiva, subterfugio. – **4** *i* poner pegas, sutilizar: *he's always quibbling about something,* siempre pone pegas a todo. **5** *fam* buscarle tres pies al gato.
quibbler ['kwɪbələʳ] *n* sofista *mf*, polemista *mf*, porfiador,-ra.

quibbling ['kwɪbəlɪŋ] *n* sutilezas *fpl*, sofistería, sofismos *mpl*.

quiche [kiːʃ] *n* quiche *f*.

quick [kwɪk] **1** *adj (fast)* rápido,-a: *let's have a quick look*, echemos un vistazo; *I would appreciate a quick reply*, agradecería una respuesta pronta; *he let me have it cheap for a quick sale*, me lo dejó barato porque lo quería vender rápido; *let's have a quick snack*, comamos algo rápido; *be quick or you'll miss it!*, ¡rápido o lo perderás!, ¡date prisa o lo perderás! **2** *(clever)* espabilado,-a, despierto,-a, listo,-a.
● **as quick as lightning**, como un rayo, como una bala. ‖ **quick march!**, MIL ¡de frente! ‖ **to be quick on the uptake**, captar algo en seguida. ‖ **to be quick to anger**, tener mal genio. ‖ **to be quick to take offence**, enfadarse por nada. ‖ **to cut sb. to the quick**, herir a algn. en lo vivo. ‖ **to have a quick one**, *fam* echar un trago, tomar una copita. ‖ **to have a quick temper**, tener un genio vivo.

quick-acting ['kwɪkˈæktɪŋ] *adj* de acción *f* rápida, superrápido,-a.

quick-change artist [kwɪkˈtʃeɪndʒɑːtɪst] *n* THEAT transformista *m*.

quicken ['kwɪkən] **1** *t (speed up)* acelerar: *he quickened his pace*, aceleró el paso. **– 2** *i (speed up)* acelerarse.

quickening ['kwɪkənɪŋ] *n* MED movimientos *mpl* del feto.

quickie ['kwɪkɪ] *n fam* algo hecho con rapidez: *let's have a quickie before we go*, tomemos una copita rápidamente antes de marchar.

quicklime ['kwɪklaɪm] *n* cal *f* viva.

quickly ['kwɪklɪ] *adv* rápido, rápidamente, de prisa, pronto.

quickness ['kwɪknəs] *n (speed)* velocidad *f*, rapidez *f*; *(wit)* agudeza, viveza, inteligencia.

quicksand ['kwɪksænd] *n* arenas *fpl* movedizas.

quick-sighted [kwɪkˈsaɪtɪd] *adj* de vista aguda.

quicksilver ['kwɪksɪlvə'] *n* mercurio.

quick-tempered [kwɪkˈtempəd] *adj* de genio vivo, irascible.

quick-witted [kwɪkˈwɪtɪd] *adj* agudo,-a, listo,-a, perspicaz.

quid[1] [kwɪd] *n* GB *fam (money)* libra esterlina: *it cost me ten quid*, me costó diez libras.
▲ *pl* quid.

quid[2] [kwɪd] *n* mascada de tabaco.

quiet ['kwaɪət] **1** *adj (silent)* callado,-a, silencioso,-a: *he kept quiet all night*, estuvo callado toda la noche. **2** *(peaceful, calm)* tranquilo,-a, sosegado,-a: *this is a very quiet village*, éste es un pueblo muy tranquilo. **3** FIN apagado,-a, poco activo,-a: *business was very quiet in the shop today*, las ventas han sido muy flojas en la tienda. **4** *(unobtrusive)* callado,-a, reservado,-a. **5** *(tranquil, without fuss)* tranquilo,-a: *they spent a quiet evening at home*, pasaron una velada tranquila en casa. **– 6** *n (silence)* silencio. **7** *(calm)* tranquilidad *f*, calma, sosiego. **– 8** *t* US calmar, silenciar: *she quieted the baby down*, calmó a la criatura. **– 9** *i* US calmarse.
● **on the quiet**, a la chita callando, a hurtadillas, en secreto, sigilosamente: *he did it on the quiet*, lo hizo en secreto.

quieten ['kwaɪətən] **1** *t (silence)* callar; *(calm)* tranquilizar, calmar. **2** *(calm down)* tranquilizar. **– 3** *i (silence)* callarse; *(calm)* calmarse, tranquilizarse.

quietism ['kwaɪətɪzəm] *n* REL quietismo.

quietist ['kwaɪətɪst] *n* REL quietista *mf*.

quietly ['kwaɪətlɪ] **1** *adv (silently)* silenciosamente, sin hacer ruido; *(not loudly)* bajo: *she always speaks quietly*, siempre habla en voz baja. **2** *(calmly)* tranquilamente. **3** *(discreetly)* discretamente, con discreción. **4** *(simply)* sencillamente, con sencillez.

quietness ['kwaɪətnəs] **1** *n (silence)* silencio, paz *f*. **2** *(calm)* tranquilidad *f*, sosiego. **3** *(discretion)* discreción *f*, intimidad *f*.

quiff [kwɪf] *n* GB *(of hair)* copete *m*.

quill [kwɪl] **1** *n (feather)* pluma. **2** *(porcupine)* púa. **3** *(part of feather)* cañón *m* de pluma. **4** *(pen)* pluma.

quilt [kwɪlt] **1** *n* colcha, edredón *m*. **– 2** *t* acolchar.

quince [kwɪns] *n* membrillo.
■ **quince jelly**, carne *f* de membrillo.

quinine ['kwɪniːn], US ['kwaɪnaɪn] *n* quinina.

quins [kwɪnz] *n* POL *fam (all boys, mixed)* quintillizos; *(all girls)* quintillizas.

quinsy ['kwɪnzɪ] *n* MED anginas *fpl*.

quint [kwɪnt] *n* US *fam* quintillizo,-a.

quintessence [kwɪnˈtesəns] *n* quintaesencia.

quintessential [kwɪntɪˈsenʃəl] *adj* fundamental, primordial.

quintet [kwɪnˈtet] *n* MUS quinteto.

quintuple ['kwɪntjupəl, kwɪnˈtjuːpəl] **1** *adj* quíntuplo,-a. **– 2** *n* quíntuplo. **– 3** *t* quintuplicar. **– 4** *i* quintuplicarse.

quintuplet ['kwɪntjuplət, kwɪnˈtjuːplət] *n* quintillizo,-a.

quip [kwɪp] **1** *n (remark)* agudeza, ocurrencia, pulla, salida. **2** *(joke)* chiste *m*. **– 3** *i* bromear.
▲ *(verbo)* pt & pp **quipped**, ger **quipping**.

quire [kwaɪ'] *n* mano de papel.

quirk [kwɜːk] **1** *n (oddity)* manía, rareza, peculiaridad *f*. **2** *(in writing)* rasgo. **3** *(of fate)* avatar *m*, vicisitud *f*.

quirky ['kwɜːkɪ] *adj* raro,-a.
▲ *comp* **quirkier**, superl **quirkiest**.

quisling ['kwɪzlɪŋ] *n* colaboracionista *mf*.

quit [kwɪt] **1** *t* dejar, abandonar: *he quit his job*, dejó el trabajo. **2** *(stop)* dejar de: *she quit smoking*, dejó de fumar. **– 3** *i* marcharse, irse.
● **to be quits**, estar iguales, estar en paz. ‖ **to call it quits**, hacer las paces, estar en paz.
▲ pt & pp **quit**, ger **quitting**.

quite [kwaɪt] **1** *adv (rather)* bastante: *it was quite a good game*, fue un partido bastante bueno; *they played quite well*, jugaron bastante bien; *they're quite difficult exercises*, son ejercicios bastante difíciles; *there are quite a few people here*, hay bastante gente aquí. **2** *(totally)* completamente, del todo: *I quite understand*, lo entiendo perfectamente; *you've quite ruined it*, lo has destrozado completamente; *it isn't quite finished*, no está terminado del todo. **3** *(exceptional)* excepcional, increíble, original: *he's quite a comedian*, es un cómico increíble; *our trip was quite something*, nuestro viaje fue algo excepcional. **4** *(exactly)* exactamente: *it isn't quite what I was looking for*, no es exactamente lo que buscaba.
● **quite so!**, ¡exactamente!

quiver[1] ['kwɪvə'] **1** *n (for arrows)* carcaj *m*, aljaba. **2** *(tremble of lips, voice)* temblor *m*; *(of eyelids)* parpadeo; *(shiver)* estremecimiento. **– 3** *i* temblar, estremecerse.

quiver[2] ['kwɪvə'] *n (for arrows)* carcaj *m*, aljaba.

quivering ['kwɪvərɪŋ] *adj* tembloroso,-a.

quixotic [kwɪkˈsɒtɪk] *adj* quijotesco,-a.

quiz [kwɪz] **1** *n* RAD TV concurso. **2** *(enquiry)* encuesta; *(exam)* examen *m*. **– 3** *t* preguntar, interrogar.

quizmaster ['kwɪzmɑːstə'] *n* moderador,-ra.

quizzical [ˈkwɪzɪkəl] **1** *adj* (*bemused*) burlón,-ona: *she gave me a quizzical smile,* me sonrió burlonamente. **2** (*enquiring*) curioso,-a: *he had a quizzical look on his face,* su mirada reflejaba curiosidad.

quoin [ˈkɔɪn] *n* ARCH piedra angular.

quoit [kwɔɪt] **1** *n* (*ring*) tejo. – **2 quoits,** *npl* (*game*) tejo *m sing.*

quorum [ˈkwɔːrəm] *n* quórum *m.*

quota [ˈkwəʊtə] **1** *n* (*share*) cuota, parte *f.* **2** (*fixed limit*) cupo.

quotation [kwəʊˈteɪʃən] **1** *n* LING cita. **2** FIN cotización *f.* **3** COMM presupuesto.
  ■ **quotation marks,** comillas *fpl.*

quote [kwəʊt] **1** *n* LING cita. **2** (*price - gen*) presupuesto; (*- for shares*) cotización *f.* – **3** *t* citar, entrecomillar. **4** (*price*) dar, ofrecer. **5** FIN cotizar.
  ● **to ask for a quote,** pedir un presupuesto. ‖ **to give sb. a quote,** dar un presupuesto a algn. ‖ **to quote sb. a price,** ofrecer un precio a algn.

quotidian [kwəʊˈtɪdɪən] *adj fml* cotidiano,-a.

quotient [ˈkwəʊʃənt] **1** *n* MATH cociente *m.* **2** (*degree*) coeficiente *m,* grado.
  ■ **intelligence quotient,** coeficiente intelectual *m,* coeficiente *m* de inteligencia.

qv [ˈkjuːˈviː] *abbr* (*quod vide*) véase; (*abbreviation*) v

R

R, r [ɑː] *n (the letter)* R, r *f*.
■ **the three Rs,** *fam* lectura, escritura y aritmética.
R¹ [reks] *abbr (Rex)* rey.
R² [rɪ'dʒaɪnə] *abbr (Regina)* reina.
R³ ['rɪvə'] *abbr (River)* río.
R⁴ ['redʒɪstəd'treɪdmɑːk] *abbr (registered trademark)* marca registrada.
r [raɪt] *abbr (right)* derecho,-a; *(abbreviation)* dcho,-a.
RA ['ɑːr'eɪ] **1** *abbr* GB *(Royal Academy)* Real Academia de las Artes. **2** GB *(Royal Academician)* miembro de la Real Academia de las Artes.
rabbi ['ræbaɪ] *n* rabí *m*, rabino.
rabbinical [rə'bɪnɪkəl] *adj* rabínico,-a.
rabbit ['ræbɪt] *n* conejo.
● **to rabbit on,** no parar de hablar.
■ **rabbit hole,** madriguera de conejos. ‖ **rabbit hutch,** conejera. ‖ **rabbit punch,** golpe *m* en la nuca. ‖ **rabbit warren,** madriguera de conejos.
rabble ['ræbəl] *n* populacho.
rabble-rouser ['ræbəlrauzə'] *n pej* demagogo,-a.
rabble-rousing ['ræbəlrauzɪŋ] **1** *n* demagogia. – **2** *adj* demagógico,-a.
rabid ['ræbɪd] **1** *adj (having rabies)* rabioso,-a. **2** *fig* fanático,-a.
rabies ['reɪbiːz] *n* rabia.
RAC ['ɑːr'eɪ'siː] *abbr* GB *(Royal Automobile Club)* automóvil club británico.
raccoon [rə'kuːn] *n* mapache *m*.
race¹ [reɪs] *n (people)* raza.
■ **race relations,** relaciones *fpl* raciales. ‖ **race riot,** disturbio racial.
race² [reɪs] **1** *n* SP carrera. **2** *(current)* corriente *f* fuerte; *(channel)* canal *m*. – **3** *i (compete)* competir, correr. **4** *(go fast)* correr, ir deprisa. **5** *(heart)* latir deprisa. **6** *(engine)* acelerarse. – **7** *t (person)* competir con, echar una carrera a. **8** *(engine)* acelerar.
● **to run a race,** participar en una carrera.
■ **race against time,** carrera contra reloj. ‖ **race meeting,** las carreras *fpl*. ‖ **the races,** las carreras *fpl*.
racecourse ['reɪskɔːs] *n* GB hipódromo.
racegoer ['reɪsgəʊə'] *n* aficionado,-a a las carreras.
racehorse ['reɪhɔːs] *n* caballo de carreras.
racer ['reɪsə'] *n (person)* corredor,-ra; *(bicycle)* bicicleta de carreras; *(car)* coche *m* de carreras; *(horse)* caballo de carreras.
racetrack ['reɪstræk] **1** *n (for cars)* circuito; *(for cycles)* velódromo. **2** *(for people)* pista, pista de atletismo. **3** *(for horses)* hipódromo; *(for greyhounds)* canódromo.
racial ['reɪʃəl] *adj* racial.
■ **racial discrimination,** discriminación *f* racial.
racialism ['reɪʃəlɪzəm] *n* racismo.
racialist ['reɪʃəlɪst] **1** *adj* racista. – **2** *n* racista *mf*.
racing ['reɪsɪŋ] **1** *n* carreras *fpl*. – **2** *adj* de carreras.
racism ['reɪsɪzəm] *n* racismo.

racist ['reɪsɪst] **1** *adj* racista. – **2** *n* racista *mf*.
rack¹ [ræk] **1** *n* estante *m*. **2** AUTO baca. **3** *(on train)* rejilla. **4** *(for torture)* potro. – **5** *t* atormentar: *I was racked by doubts,* me atormentaban las dudas.
● **to rack one's brains,** devanarse los sesos.
■ **clothes rack,** perchero. ‖ **magazine rack,** revistero. ‖ **plate rack,** escurreplatos *m*. ‖ **roof rack,** baca.
rack² [ræk] *n (destruction)* ruina.
● **to go to rack and ruin,** venirse abajo.
racket¹ ['rækɪt] *n* SP raqueta.
racket² ['rækɪt] **1** *n (din)* alboroto, ruido. **2** *fam (fraud)* timo. **3** *fam (business)* asunto, negocio.
● **to make a racket,** armar barullo.
racketeer [rækə'tɪə'] *n* timador,-ra.
racketeering [rækɪ'tɪərɪŋ] *n* crimen *m* organizado.
raconteur [rækɒn'tɜː'] *n* anecdotista *mf*.
racoon [rə'kuːn] *n* mapache *m*.
racquet ['rækɪt] *n* raqueta.
racy ['reɪsɪ] *adj (lively)* vivo,-a, animado,-a; *(risqué)* atrevido,-a.
▲ *comp* **racier**, *superl* **raciest**.
RADA ['rɑːdə] *abbr* GB *(Royal Acadamy of Dramatic Art)* ≈ Real Academia de las Artes Dramáticas.
radar ['reɪdɑː'] *n* radar *m*.
■ **radar trap,** control *m* de velocidad por radar.
radial ['reɪdɪəl] *adj* radial.
■ **radial tyre,** neumático radial.
radiance ['reɪdɪəns] *n* resplandor *m*.
radiant ['reɪdɪənt] *adj* radiante.
radiate ['reɪdɪeɪt] **1** *t (emit)* irradiar, radiar. – **2** *i (be emitted)* irradiar. **3** *(spread out)* salir.
radiation [reɪdɪ'eɪʃən] *n* radiación *f*.
■ **radiation sickness,** enfermedad *f* provocada por la radiación.
radiator ['reɪdɪeɪtə'] *n* radiador *m*.
■ **radiator grille,** rejilla del radiador, calandra.
radical ['rædɪkəl] **1** *adj* radical. – **2** *n* radical *mf*.
radicalize ['rædɪkəlaɪz] **1** *t* radicalizar. – **2** *i* radicalizarse.
radically ['rædɪkəlɪ] *adv* radicalmente.
radii ['reɪdɪaɪ] *npl* → **radius**.
radio ['reɪdɪəʊ] **1** *n* radio *f*. – **2** *t (person)* llamar por radio; *(message)* enviar por radio, comunicar por radio. – **3** *i* llamar por radio.
■ **radio alarm,** radio-despertador *m*. ‖ **radio beacon,** radiobaliza. ‖ **radio frequency,** radiofrecuencia. ‖ **radio ham,** radioaficionado,-a. ‖ **radio programme,** programa *m* de radio. ‖ **radio station,** emisora de radio. ‖ **radio telescope,** radiotelescopio.
▲ *pl* **radios**.
radioactive [reɪdɪəʊ'æktɪv] *adj* radiactivo,-a.
■ **radioactive waste,** residuos *mpl* radiactivos.
radioactivity [reɪdɪəʊæk'tɪvɪtɪ] *n* radiactividad *f*.
radiocarbon [reɪdɪəʊ'kɑːbən] *n* radiocarbono.
■ **radiocarbon dating,** datación *f* por radiocarbono.

radio-controlled [ˌreɪdɪəʊkən'trəʊld] *adj* teledirigido,-a.
radiogram ['reɪdɪəʊgræm] *n* radiogramola.
radiographer [reɪdɪ'ɒgrəfəʳ] *n* radiógrafo,-a.
radiography [reɪdɪ'ɒgrəfɪ] *n* radiografía.
▲ *pl radiographies.*
radiologist [reɪdɪ'ɒlədʒɪst] *n* radiólogo,-a.
radiology [reɪdɪ'ɒledʒɪ] *n* radiología.
radiotelephone [reɪdɪəʊ'telɪfəʊn] *n* radioteléfono.
radiotherapist [reɪdɪəʊ'θerəpɪst] *n* radioterapeuta *mf*.
radiotherapy [reɪdɪəʊ'θerəpɪ] *n* radioterapia.
radish ['rædɪʃ] *n* rábano.
radium ['reɪdɪəm] *n* radio.
radius ['reɪdɪəs] *n* radio.
▲ *pl radii.*
radon ['reɪdɒn] *n* radón *m*.
RAF ['ɑːr'eɪ'ef] *abbr* GB (*Royal Air Force*) fuerzas aéreas británicas.
raffia ['ræfɪə] *n* rafia.
raffle ['ræfəl] **1** *n* rifa. – **2** *t* rifar, sortear.
raft [rɑːft] **1** *n* balsa. **2** US *fam* montón *m*.
rafter ['rɑːftəʳ] *n* viga.
rag¹ [ræg] **1** *n* harapo, andrajo, pingajo. **2** (*for cleaning*) trapo. **3** *fam* (*newspaper*) periodicucho.
● **in rags**, harapiento,-a, andrajoso,-a. ‖ **from rags to riches**, de la pobreza a la riqueza. ‖ **to lose one's rag**, perder los estribos. ‖ **to be like a red rag to a bull**, enfurecer a algn., sacar a algn. de sus casillas.
■ **rag doll**, muñeca de trapo. ‖ **rag trade**, la industria de la confección.
rag² [ræg] **1** *n* broma pesada. – **2** *t* gastar bromas a.
■ **rag week**, *semana en la que los estudiantes universitarios recaudan fondos con fines benéficos.*
ragamuffin ['rægəmʌfɪn] *n* pilluelo,-a.
rag-and-bone man [rægən'bəʊnmæn] *n* trapero.
ragbag ['rægbæg] *n fam* mezcolanza, batiburrillo.
rage [reɪdʒ] **1** *n* rabia, furor *m*, cólera. – **2** *i* (*person*) rabiar, estar hecho,-a una furia. **3** (*fire etc*) arder sin control; (*storm, sea*) bramar, rugir; (*debate etc*) seguir candente.
● **to be in a rage**, estar furioso,-a. ‖ **to be all the rage**, hacer furor. ‖ **to fly into a rage**, montar en cólera.
ragged ['rægɪd] **1** *adj* (*person*) andrajoso,-a, harapiento,-a. **2** (*clothes*) roto,-a, deshilachado,-a. **3** (*edge*) irregular. **4** *fig* desigual.
raging ['reɪdʒɪŋ] **1** *adj* (*headache, thirst*) terrible. **2** (*sea*) embravecido,-a; (*storm*) feroz, violento,-a.
raglan ['ræglən] *adj* raglán.
ragout [ræ'guː] *n* ragú *m*.
ragtime ['rægtaɪm] *n* ragtime *m*.
raid [reɪd] **1** *n* MIL incursión *f*, ataque *m*. **2** (*by police*) redada. **3** (*robbery*) atraco. – **4** *t* hacer una incursión en. **5** (*police*) hacer una redada en. **6** (*rob*) atracar, asaltar.
raider ['reɪdəʳ] **1** *n* (*robber*) atracador,-ra, asaltante *mf*. **2** MIL invasor,-ra.
rail¹ [reɪl] **1** *n* barra. **2** (*handrail*) pasamano, barandilla, baranda. **3** (*for train*) raíl *m*, carril *m*, riel *m*. **4** (*the railway*) ferrocarril *m*.
● **by rail**, por ferrocarril. ‖ **to go off the rails**, irse por el mal camino, descarriarse.
■ **rail strike**, huelga de ferroviarios.
rail² [reɪl] **to rail against**, *t* despotricar contra.
railcard ['reɪlkɑːd] *n* tarjeta de descuento *para viajar en tren.*
railing ['reɪlɪŋz] *n* verja.
▲ *También se usa en plural sin cambio de significado.*

railroad ['reɪlrəʊd] **1** *n* US → **railway**. – **2** *t* (*person*) presionar: *they railroaded him into selling the farm,* lo presionaron para que vendiera la granja. **3** (*measure, bill*) tramitar sin debate: *they railroaded the bill through parliament,* el proyecto se tramitó sin el debido debate.
railway ['reɪlweɪ] *n* ferrocarril *m*.
■ **railway carrriage**, vagón *m*. ‖ **railway engine**, máquina de tren, locomotora. ‖ **railway line**, vía férrea, vía del tren. ‖ **railway station**, estación *f* de ferrocarril, estación *f* de trenes. ‖ **railway track**, vía férrea.
railwayman ['reɪlweɪmən] *n* ferroviario.
▲ *pl railwaymen* ['reɪlweɪmən].
rain [reɪn] **1** *n* lluvia: *it looks like rain,* parece que va a llover; *don't go out in the rain,* no salgas, que llueve. – **2** *i* llover: *it's raining,* llueve, está lloviendo; *arrows rained down from the walls,* cayó una lluvia de flechas desde la muralla. – **3** *t fig* cubrir: *she rained gifts upon them,* les cubrió de regalos. – **4 the rains**, *npl* la estación *f sing* de las lluvias.
● **come rain or shine**, pase lo que pase, llueva o truene. ‖ **it never rains but it pours**, las desgracias nunca vienen solas, siempre llueve sobre mojado. ‖ **to be as right as rain**, estar perfectamente, estar como nuevo,-a. ‖ **to be rained off**, suspenderse por la lluvia, cancelarse por la lluvia.
■ **rain forest**, selva tropical. ‖ **rain gauge**, pluviómetro.
rainbow ['reɪnbəʊ] *n* arco iris *m*.
raincheck ['reɪntʃek] *n vale canjeable por una nueva entrada que se da cuando un acontecimiento deportivo se suspende por la lluvia.*
● **to take a raincheck on sth.**, dejar algo para más adelante: *I'll take a raincheck on lunch, thank you,* dejaré la comida para otro día, si no te importa.
raincoat ['reɪnkəʊt] *n* impermeable *m*.
raindrop ['reɪndrɒp] *n* gota de lluvia.
rainfall ['reɪnfɔːl] **1** *n* precipitación *f*. **2** (*quantity*) pluviosidad *f*.
rainproof ['reɪnpruːf] *adj* impermeable.
rainstorm ['reɪnstɔːm] *n* temporal *m* de lluvias.
rainwater ['reɪnwɔːtəʳ] *n* agua de lluvia.
rainy ['reɪnɪ] *adj* lluvioso,-a: *another rainy day,* otro día de lluvia.
● **to save for a rainy day**, ahorrar para los tiempos difíciles.
■ **rainy season**, estación *f* de las lluvias.
▲ *comp rainier, superl rainiest.*
raise [reɪz] **1** *t* (*lift up*) levantar: *raise your hands,* levantad la mano; *he never raises his voice,* nunca levanta la voz; *let us raise our glasses to the victor,* brindemos por el vencedor. **2** (*move to a higher position*) subir: *he raised the mirror because he had to stoop to shave,* subió el espejo porque tenía que agacharse para afeitarse. **3** (*build, erect*) erigir, levantar. **4** (*increase*) subir, aumentar: *VAT will be raised again,* el IVA subirá otra vez. **5** (*improve*) mejorar. **6** (*laugh, smile, etc*) provocar; (*doubt, fear*) suscitar. **7** (*children*) criar, educar; (*animals*) criar. **8** (*matter, point*) plantear. **9** (*funds*) recaudar; (*enough money*) conseguir, reunir; (*team, army*) formar: *they raised £20,000 for the new church,* recaudaron veinte mil libras para la nueva iglesia; *she somehow manages to raise the rent every month,* de algún modo consigue el dinero para pagar el alquiler cada mes; *he raised an army of beggars,* formó un ejército de mendigos. **10** (*by radio*) comunicar con. **11** (*at cards*) subir: *I'll raise you twenty,* te subo veinte. – **12** *n* US aumento de sueldo.
raisin ['reɪzən] *n* pasa.

raison d'être [reɪzɒn'detrə] n razón f de ser.
raja ['rɑːdʒə] n rajá m.
rajah ['rɑːdʒə] n rajá m.
rake[1] [reɪk] **1** n (tool) rastrillo. – **2** t (garden) rastrillar; (leaves) recoger con el rastrillo. **3** (with gun) barrer. **4** (search) registrar. **5** (fire) hurgar.
◆ **to rake up 1** t sep (leaves) recoger con el rastrillo. **2** (past) desenterrar.
● **to be raking it in,** estar forrándose. ‖ **to be as thin as a rake,** estar como un fideo, estar como un palillo.
rake[2] [reɪk] n (dissolute man) libertino, calavera m.
rake[3] [reɪk] n (slope) inclinación f.
raked [reɪkt] adj (sloping) inclinado,-a.
rake-off ['reɪkɒf] n sl tajada.
rakish[1] [reɪkɪʃ] adj (dissolute) libertino,-a.
rakish[2] [reɪkɪʃ] adj (jaunty) desenfadado,-a.
rally ['rælɪ] **1** n (public gathering) reunión f; (political) mitin m; (demonstration) manifestación f. **2** (car race) rally m. **3** (in tennis) intercambio (de golpes). – **4** i (recover) reponerse, recuperarse. – **5** t (bring together) unir.
◆ **to rally round 1** t insep unirse, juntarse. – **2** i formar una piña.
▲ (sustantivo) pl **rallies**; (verbo) pt & pp **rallied,** ger **rallying.**
ram [ræm] **1** n zool carnero. **2** tech pisón m. – **3** t tech apisonar. **4** (cram) apretar, embutir; (stick in) clavar, hincar. **5** (crash into) chocar contra.
● **to ram sth. home,** dejar algo bien claro. ‖ **to ram sth. down sb.'s throat,** machacar algo a algn.
▲ pt & pp **rammed,** ger **ramming.**
RAM [ræm] abbr (random access memory) memoria de acceso aleatorio; (abbreviation) RAM f.
ramble ['ræmbəl] **1** n excursión f. – **2** i ir de excursión. **3** (digress) divagar.
● **to ramble on about sth.,** divagar sin parar sobre algo.
rambler ['ræmblər] **1** n (walker) excursionista mf. **2** (rose) trepador m.
rambling ['ræmblɪŋ] **1** adj (speech etc) confuso,-a, incoherente. **2** (house etc) laberíntico,-a. – **3** n (activity) excursionismo. – **4** ramblings, npl desvaríos mpl.
● **to go rambling,** ir de excursión.
ramekin ['ræmɪkɪn] n molde m individual.
ramification [ræmɪfɪ'keɪʃən] n ramificación f.
ramp [ræmp] **1** n (slope) rampa. **2** (steps) escalerilla. **3** GB (speed bump) badén m, guardia m tumbado. **4** US (slip road) vía de acceso.
rampage [ræm'peɪdʒ] i comportarse como un loco.
● **to go on the rampage,** causar destrozos.
rampant ['ræmpənt] **1** adj (uncontrolled) incontrolado,-a; (widespread) extendido,-a. **2** (in heraldry) rampante.
rampart ['ræmpɑːt] n muralla.
ramrod ['ræmrɒd] n baqueta.
ramshackle ['ræmʃækəl] adj destartalado,-a.
ran [ræn] pt → **run.**
ranch [rɑːntʃ] n rancho, hacienda.
■ **ranch house,** (type of house) bungalow m; (house on ranch) hacienda.
rancher ['rɑːntʃər] n ranchero,-a.
rancid ['rænsɪd] adj rancio,-a.
rancor ['ræŋkər] n US → **rancour.**
rancorous ['ræŋkərəs] adj rencoroso,-a.
rancour ['ræŋkər] n rencor m.
rand [rænd] n rand m.
▲ pl **rand.**
random ['rændəm] adj aleatorio,-a.
● **at random,** al azar.

■ **random access memory,** memoria de acceso directo.
randy ['rændɪ] adj fam cachondo,-a.
▲ comp **randier,** superl **randiest.**
rang [ræŋ] pp → **ring.**
range [reɪndʒ] **1** n (choice) gama, surtido, variedad f; (of products) gama; (of clothes) línea. **2** (reach) alcance m: **this missile has a range of 1,000 miles,** este misil tiene un alcance de mil millas; **it's out of my price range,** no está al alcance de mi bolsillo, es demasiado caro para mí. **3** (of mountains) cordillera, sierra. **4** US (prairie) pradera. **5** (for shooting) campo de tiro. **6** (of voice) registro. **7** (stove) cocina económica. **8** US (cooker) cocina. **9** (of car, plane) autonomía. – **10** i variar, oscilar: **they range from ... to...,** van desde ... hasta ... **11** (wander) vagar (**over,** por). – **12** t (arrange) colocar, disponer. **13** (travel) recorrer, viajar por.
rangefinder ['reɪndʒfaɪndər] n telémetro.
ranger ['reɪndʒər] **1** n guardabosques mf. **2** US (police officer) policía mf montado,-a; (soldier) soldado mf de las tropas de asalto.
Rangoon [ræŋ'guːn] n Rangún.
rank[1] [ræŋk] **1** n (line) fila. **2** MIL (in hierarchy) graduación f, rango. – **3** i (be) figurar, estar: **it ranks as one of the finest hotels in Wales,** está entre los mejores hoteles del País de Gales. – **4** t (classify) clasificar, considerar: **I rank him with the best,** lo considero entre los mejores; **she is ranked second in Europe,** está clasificada la segunda de Europa, es la segunda en el ranking europeo.
● **to pull rank,** abusar de su autoridad. ‖ **to break ranks,** romper filas. ‖ **to close ranks,** cerrar filas.
■ **the rank and file,** las bases fpl.
rank[2] [ræŋk] **1** adj (plants) exuberante. **2** (smelly) fétido,-a. **3** (complete) total, completo,-a.
ranking ['ræŋkɪŋ] n clasificación f, ranking m.
rankle ['ræŋkəl] i doler.
ransack ['rænsæk] **1** t (plunder) saquear. **2** (search) registrar.
ransom ['rænsəm] **1** n rescate m. – **2** t rescatar.
● **to hold to ransom,** pedir rescate por; fig chantajear.
■ **ransom money,** rescate m.
rant [rænt] i vociferar, desgañitarse, gritar: **he ranted on at them about sin for over an hour,** les estuvo vociferando sobre el pecado más de una hora; **he was ranting and raving about the youth of today,** estuvo desgañitándose sobre la juventud de hoy.
rap [ræp] **1** n golpe m seco. **2** mus rap m. – **3** i golpear, dar golpes. **4** mus cantar rap.
● **to take the rap,** pagar el pato, cargar con las culpas.
▲ pt & pp **rapped,** ger **rapping.**
rapacious [rə'peɪʃəs] adj fml rapaz, codicioso,-a.
rape[1] [reɪp] **1** n violación f. – **2** t violar.
rape[2] [reɪp] n BOT colza.
rapeseed ['reɪpsiːd] n semilla de colza.
■ **rapeseed oil,** aceite m de colza.
rapid ['ræpɪd] **1** adj rápido,-a. – **2** rapids, npl rápidos mpl.
rapidity [rə'pɪdɪtɪ] n rapidez f.
rapidly ['ræpɪdlɪ] adv rápidamente, rápido.
rapier ['reɪpɪər] n estoque m.
rapist ['reɪpɪst] n violador,-ra.
rapper ['ræpər] n cantante mf de rap, rapero,-a.
rapport [ræ'pɔː] n compenetración f, entendimiento.
rapprochement [ræ'prɒʃəmɑːn] n acercamiento.
rapt [ræpt] adj absorto,-a, embelesado,-a.

rapture ['ræptʃəʳ] *n* éxtasis *m*, arrobamiento.
● **to go into raptures over/about sth.**, arrobarse por algo, extasiarse por algo.
rapturous ['ræptʃərəs] *adj* (*welcome*) muy entusiasta; (*applause*) calurosísimo,-a; (*feeling*) extático,-a.
rare [reəʳ] **1** *adj* (*uncommom*) poco común, poco frecuente, raro,-a. **2** (*air*) enrarecido,-a. **3** CULIN poco hecho,-a.
■ **rare earth**, tierra rara. ‖ **rare gas**, gas *m* raro.
rarebit ['reəbɪt] *n* tostada con queso.
rarefied ['reərɪfaɪd] *adj* enrarecido,-a.
rarely ['reəlɪ] *adv* raras veces, rara vez, pocas veces.
raring ['reərɪŋ] *adj fam* con unas ganas locas de: *she was raring to start*, tenía unas ganas locas de empezar.
rarity ['reərɪtɪ] *n* rareza.
▲ *pl* **rarities**.
rascal ['rɑːskəl] *n* bribón *m*, pillo, pillín,-ina.
rash¹ [ræʃ] **1** *n* MED sarpullido, erupción *f* cutánea. **2** (*series*) sucesión *f*, serie *f*.
rash² [ræʃ] *adj* imprudente, precipitado,-a.
rasher ['ræʃəʳ] *n* loncha.
rashly ['ræʃlɪ] *adj* precipitadamente, sin reflexionar.
rashness ['ræʃnəs] *n* impetuosidad *f*, precipitación *f*.
rasp [rɑːsp] **1** *n* escofina. – **2** *t* raspar. **3** (*say*) decir con voz áspera.
raspberry ['rɑːzbərɪ] **1** *n* frambuesa. **2** *fam* (*noise*) pedorreta.
● **to blow a raspberry at sb.**, hacer una pedorreta a algn.
■ **raspberry cane**, frambueso.
▲ *pl* **raspberries**.
rasping ['rɑːspɪŋ] *adj* (*voice*) áspero,-a.
Rastafarian [ræstəˈfeərɪən] **1** *adj* rastafariano,-a. – **2** *n* rastafari *mf*.
rat [ræt] **1** *n* rata. **2** *fam* canalla *m*.
● **to rat on sb.**, chivar a algn. ‖ **like a drowned rat**, hecho,-a una sopa. ‖ **to rat on a promise**, romper una promesa. ‖ **to smell a rat**, olerse algo raro: *I smell a rat*, aquí hay gato encerrado.
■ **rat race**, *competitividad despiadada*. ‖ **rat poison**, raticida *m*.
ratatouille [rætəˈtuːɪ] *n* CULIN ≈ pisto.
ratbag ['rætbæg] *n* GB persona desagradable.
ratchet ['rætʃɪt] *n* trinquete *m*.
rate [reɪt] **1** *n* tasa, índice *m*: *the rate of growth has slowed down*, la tasa de crecimiento ha disminuido. **2** (*speed*) velocidad *f*, ritmo: *at the rate he's going he'll finish by Tuesday*, al paso que lleva, acabará el martes; *at this rate there'll be no woods left*, a este paso no quedará bosque, como sigamos así no quedará bosque. **3** (*price*) tarifa, precio: *we were paid at the standard rate*, nos pagaron según la tarifa habitual. – **4** *t* (*consider*) considerar: *I rate this her best book yet*, creo que éste es su mejor libro hasta la fecha; *how do you rate your chances for the race?*, ¿qué oportunidad crees que tienes en la carrera? **5** (*deserve*) merecer: *the fire rated no more than three lines in the local paper*, el incendio mereció tan solo tres líneas en el diario local. **6** (*fix value*) tasar. – **7** **rates**, *npl* GB contribución *f sing* urbana.
● **at any rate**, (*anyway*) de todos modos; (*at least*) por lo menos, al menos. ‖ **at the rate of**, a razón de. ‖ **first/second rate**, de primera/segunda (categoría).
■ **interest rate**, tipo de interés. ‖ **rate of inflation**, tasa de inflación.
rateable value ['reɪtəbəlˈvæljuː] *n* GB valor *m* catastral.
ratepayer ['reɪtpeɪəʳ] *n* GB contribuyente *mf*.
rather ['rɑːðəʳ] **1** *adv* (*a little*) algo; (*fairly*) bastante; (*very*) muy: *she's rather reserved*, es algo reservada; *it's rather*

warm today, hace bastante calor hoy; *I rather enjoyed myself*, me lo pasé bastante bien; *I found it rather disgusting*, lo encontré muy desagradable. **2** (*showing preference*): *I'd rather go out*, preferiría salir; *would you rather stay in?*, ¿preferirías quedarte en casa?; *I'd rather stay in than go out*, preferiría quedarme en casa más que salir; *I'd rather drink white than red*, preferiría beber blanco mejor que tinto; *rather than put my foot in it, I said nothing*, antes que meter la pata, preferí no decir nada. **3** (*more precisely*) o mejor dicho; (*not*) y no: *there was a river, or rather a stream*, había un río, o mejor dicho un arroyo; *it will cost thousands rather than hundreds of pounds*, costará miles más que cientos de libras; *it was Jane rather than Esther who invited me*, fue Jane y no Esther quien me invitó; *it disappointed rather than angered me*, más que enojarme me decepcionó.
ratification [rætɪfɪˈkeɪʃən] *n* ratificación *f*.
ratify ['rætɪfaɪ] *t* ratificar.
▲ *pt & pp* **ratified**, *ger* **ratifying**.
rating ['reɪtɪŋ] **1** *n* (*evaluation*) valoración *f*, tasación *f*. **2** (*position on scale*) clasificación *f*, posición *f*. **3** MAR marinero. – **4** **ratings**, *npl* TV índice *m sing* de audiencia.
ratio ['reɪʃɪəʊ] *n* razón *f*, relación *f*, proporción *f*: *in a ratio of three to two*, en una proporción de tres a dos.
▲ *pl* **ratios**.
ration ['ræʃən] **1** *n* ración *f*. – **2** *t* racionar. – **3** **rations**, *npl* víveres *mpl*.
● **to be on rations**, sufrir racionamientos.
■ **ration book**, cartilla de racionamiento.
rational ['ræʃənəl] *adj* racional.
rationale [ræʃəˈnɑːl] *n* razón *f*, lógica.
rationalization [ræʃənəlaɪˈzeɪʃən] *n* racionalización *f*.
rationalize ['ræʃənəlaɪz] *t* racionalizar.
rationally ['ræʃənəlɪ] *adv* racionalmente.
rationing ['ræʃənɪŋ] *n* racionamiento.
ratted ['rætɪd] *adj fam* borracho,-a.
● **to get ratted**, coger una cogorza.
rattle ['rætəl] **1** *n* (*object*) carraca, matraca; (*baby's*) sonajero; (*rattlesnake's*) cascabel *m*. **2** (*noise*) ruido; (*of train*) traqueteo; (- *of rattlesnake*) cascabeleo; (*vibration*) vibración *f*. – **3** *t* hacer sonar, hacer vibrar: *the ghost rattled his chains*, el fantasma hizo sonar sus cadenas; *the wind rattled the windows*, el viento hacía vibrar la ventana. – **4** *i* sonar, vibrar: *the window rattled in the wind*, la ventana vibraba con el viento. – **5** *t fam* poner nervioso,-a.
◆ **to rattle off** *t sep* (*say*) decir a toda prisa; (*write*) escribir a toda prisa. ‖ **to rattle on** *i* hablar sin parar. ‖ **to rattle through** *t insep* despachar rápidamente.
rattlesnake ['rætəlsneɪk] *n* serpiente *f* de cascabel.
ratty ['rætɪ] **1** *adj* GB *fam* malhumorado,-a. **2** US (*person*) desastrado,-a; (*thing*) destartalado,-a; (*clothes*) andrajoso,-a, raído,-a.
▲ *comp* **rattier**, *superl* **rattiest**.
raucous ['rɔːkəs] *adj* (*loud*) escandaloso,-a; (*shrill*) estridente.
raunchy ['rɔːntʃɪ] *adj fam* sexy.
▲ *comp* **raunchier**, *superl* **raunchiest**.
ravage ['rævɪdʒ] **1** *t* devastar, asolar. – **2** **ravages**, *npl* estragos *mpl*.
rave [reɪv] **1** *i* delirar. **2** (*rage*) despotricar (**against**, contra). **3** *fam* entusiasmarse: *the critics are raving about the film*, los críticos están entusiasmados con la película. – **4** *n* GB fiesta *con música de baile y que puede durar toda la noche*.
■ **rave review**, crítica muy favorable.

raven ['reɪvən] *n* cuervo.

ravenous ['rævənəs] *adj* (*appetite*) voraz; (*person*) hambriento,-a: *I'm absolutely ravenous,* tengo una hambre devoradora.

ravenously ['rævənəslɪ] *adv* vorazmente: *I'm ravenously hungry,* tengo una hambre devoradora.

raver ['reɪvəʳ] *n* juerguista *mf,* marchoso,-a.

rave-up ['reɪvʌp] *n fam* juerga.

ravine [rə'viːn] *n* barranco.

raving ['reɪvɪŋ] **1** *adj* de atar. – **2** **ravings,** *npl* desvaríos *mpl.*

● **raving mad,** loco,-a de atar.

ravioli [rævɪ'əʊlɪ] *n* raviolis *mpl.*

ravish ['rævɪʃ] **1** *t* (*rape*) violar. **2** (*delight*) extasiar, embelesar, encantar.

ravishing ['rævɪʃɪŋ] *adj* encantador,-ra: *a ravishing beauty,* una belleza deslumbrante.

ravishingly ['rævɪʃɪŋlɪ] *adv: ravishing beautiful,* de una belleza deslumbrante.

raw [rɔː] **1** *adj* (*uncooked*) crudo,-a. **2** (*unprocessed*) bruto,-a; (*unrefined*) sin refinar; (*untreated*) sin tratar. **3** (*inexperienced*) novato,-a. **4** (*weather*) crudo,-a.

■ **raw deal,** trato injusto. ‖ **raw material,** materia prima.

Rawlplug ['rɔːlplʌg] *n* taco.

▲ **Es marca registrada.**

ray[1] [reɪ] *n* (*of light*) rayo: *a ray of hope,* un resquicio de esperanza.

ray[2] [reɪ] *n* (*fish*) raya.

ray[3] [reɪ] *n* (*note*) re *m.*

rayon ['reɪɒn] *n* rayón *m.*

raze [reɪz] *t* arrasar.

razor ['reɪzəʳ] **1** *n* (*cutthroat*) navaja de afeitar; (*safety*) maquinilla de afeitar. **2** (*electric*) máquina de afeitar.

■ **razor blade,** hoja de afeitar.

razorbill ['reɪzəbɪl] *n* alca común.

razor-sharp ['reɪzə'ʃɑːp] *adj* (*blade*) afiladísimo,-a; (*wit*) agudísimo,-a.

razor-shell ['reɪzəʃel] *n* navaja.

razzle ['ræzəl] *n* juerga.

● **to go on the razzle,** ir de juerga.

razzmatazz [ræzəmə'tæz] *n* jaleo, revuelo, bulla, alboroto.

RC ['ɑː'siː, 'rəʊmən'kæθəlɪk] *abbr* (**Roman Catholic**) católico,-a.

Rd [rəʊd] *abbr* (**Road**) calle; (*abbreviation*) c/.

re [riː] *prep* respecto a, con referencia a.

R.E. ['ɑːr'iː] *abbr* (*religious education*) educación religiosa.

reach [riːtʃ] **1** *n* alcance *m*: *he has a long reach,* tiene un largo alcance. – **2** *t* (*arrive in/at, get to*) llegar a: *we reached Málaga at dawn,* llegamos a Málaga al amanecer; *have you reached a decision?,* ¿has llegado a una decisión?; *no news has reached us yet,* todavía no hemos recibido ninguna noticia. **3** (*rise to, fall to*) alcanzar: *the temperature reached 45 degrees,* la temperatura alcanzó 45 grados; *fruit prices have reached a new low,* el precio de la fruta ha alcanzado su valor más bajo. **4** (*be able to touch*) alcanzar, llegar a: *I can't reach the switch,* no llego al interruptor. **5** (*contact*) contactar, localizar: *have you got an address where I can reach you?,* ¿tienes una dirección donde pueda contactar contigo? **6** (*pass*) alcanzar: *could you reach me that hammer?,* ¿podrías alcanzarme ese martillo? – **7** *i* (*be long enough*) llegar: *the rope doesn't reach,* la cuerda no llega. **8** (*extend*) extenderse: *the gardens reach down to the river,* los jar-

dines se extienden hasta el río. **9** (*take*) extender la mano, tender la mano: *he reached for the telephone,* tendió la mano para coger el teléfono. – **10 reaches,** *npl* (*of river*) parte *f,* tramo.

● **beyond the reach of,** fuera del alcance de. ‖ **out of reach of,** fuera del alcance de: *keep out of the reach of children,* guardar fuera del alcance de los niños. ‖ **within reach of,** (*at hand*) al alcance de; (*near*) cerca de: *within easy reach of the shops,* cerca de las tiendas.

react [rɪ'ækt] *i* reaccionar: *how did he react to the news?,* ¿cómo reaccionó ante la noticia?; *they reacted to the robberies by installing alarms,* su reacción ante los robos fue la de instalar alarmas.

reaction [rɪ'ækʃən] *n* reacción *f.*

reactionary [rɪ'ækʃənərɪ] **1** *adj* reaccionario,-a. – **2** *n* reaccionario,-a.

▲ (*sustantivo*) *pl* **reactionaries.**

reactivate [rɪ'æktɪveɪt] *t* reactivar.

reactive [rɪ'æktɪv] *adj* reactivo,-a.

reactor [rɪ'æktəʳ] *n* reactor *m.*

read [riːd] **1** *t* (*gen*) leer: *have you read his latest novel?,* ¿has leído su última novela?; *she reads the Times,* lee el Times; *read me a story,* léeme un cuento; *a gypsy read my palm,* una gitana me leyó la mano. **2** (*meter*) hacer la lectura de: *I've come to read the electricity meter,* vengo a hacer la lectura del contador de la luz. **3** (*interpret*) interpretar; (*decipher*) descifrar: *he read the signs correctly,* interpretó bien los indicios; *the situation as I read it ...,* la situación tal como la veo yo ...; *it's very hard to read your writing,* es muy difcil descifrar tu letra; *I wouldn't read too much into it,* no le daría demasiada importancia. **4** (*at university*) estudiar: *she read politics at Oxford,* estudió política en Oxford. **5** (*instrument*) indicar, marcar: *the thermometer read 37 degrees,* el termómetro marcaba 37 grados. **6** (*sign, notice*) decir, poner: *"Closed for holidays" read the sign on the door,* "Cerrado por vacaciones" decía el letrero en la puerta. – **7** *i* (*gen*) leer: *he never learned to read,* nunca aprendió a leer; *have you read about the accident in the paper?,* ¿has leído lo del accidente en el diario? **8** (*text, passage*): *this text reads like a translation,* este texto suena como una traducción; *the last sentence doesn't read at all well,* la última frase está muy mal redactada. – **9** *n: this book is an excellent read,* este libro es buenísimo; *I gave it a quick read,* lo leí por encima.

◆ **to read back** *t sep* volver a leer. ‖ **to read on** *i* seguir leyendo. ‖ **to read off** *t sep* leer, leer uno,-a por uno,-a. ‖ **to read out** *t sep* leer en voz alta. ‖ **to read through** *t sep* (*first time*) leer detenidamente; (*again*) repasar. ‖ **to read up on** *t insep* investigar, buscar datos sobre.

● **to be well read / widely read,** tener una gran cultura. ‖ **to take sth. as read,** dar algo por sentado.

▲ *pt & pp* **read** [red].

readable ['riːdəbl] **1** *adj* (*handwriting*) legible. **2** (*style*) ameno,-a.

readdress [riə'dres] *t* remitir a una nueva dirección.

reader ['riːdəʳ] **1** *n* (*person - gen*) lector,-ra; (*- of proofs*) corrector,-ra. **2** (*at university*) profesor,-ra adjunto,-a. **3** (*book*) libro de lectura. **4** (*apparatus*) lector *m.*

readership ['riːdəʃɪp] **1** *n* (*of newspaper*) lectores *mpl.* **2** (*at university*) puesto de profesor,-ra adjunto,-a.

readies ['redɪz] *npl* → **ready.**

readily ['redɪlɪ] **1** *adv* (*easily*) fácilmente: *it's cheap and readily available,* es barato y fácil de conseguir. **2** (*willingly*) de buena gana.

readiness ['redɪnəs] **1** *n* (*willingness*) buena disposición *f,* buena voluntad *f: his readiness to help surprised us* *all*, nos sorprendió a todos su buena disposición para ayudar. **2** (*preparedness*) preparación *f*: *they tidied up in readiness for the inspection*, hicieron limpieza para la inspección.

reading ['riːdɪŋ] **1** *n* lectura: *reading is my favourite pastime*, la lectura es mi pasatiempo preferido. **2** (*of bill, law*) presentación *f*. **3** (*of instrument*) indicación *f*, lectura. **4** (*interpretation*) interpretación *f*.
■ **reading glasses**, gafas *fpl* para leer. ‖ **reading lamp**, lámpara para leer. ‖ **reading matter**, material *m* de lectura. ‖ **reading room**, sala de lectura.

readjust [riːəˈdʒʌst] **1** *t* (*modify*) reajustar. – **2** *i* (*readapt*) readaptarse.

readjustment [riːəˈdʒʌstmənt] **1** *n* (*modification*) reajuste *m*. **2** (*readaptation*) readaptación *f*.

readout ['riːdaʊt] *n* lectura.

ready ['redɪ] **1** *adj* (*prepared*) preparado,-a, listo,-a: *are you ready to begin?*, ¿estás listo para empezar?; *I don't feel ready for marriage yet*, todavía no me siento preparado para casarme. **2** (*willing*) dispuesto,-a: *she's always ready to help*, siempre está dispuesta a ayudar. **3** (*quick*) rápido,-a; (*easy*) fácil: *there is no ready answer to that question*, no hay respuesta fácil a esa pregunta; *she's always ready with an excuse*, siempre tiene una excusa a punto. – **4** *t* preparar. – **5** **readies**, *npl* GB *fam* dinero.
● **at the ready**, listo,-a, preparado,-a. ‖ **to get ready**, prepararse. ‖ **to get sth. ready**, preparar algo. ‖ **to make ready**, preparar. ‖ **ready, steady, go!**, ¡preparados, listos, ya!
■ **ready cash**, dinero en efectivo. ‖ **ready reckoner**, baremo.
▲ (*verbo*) *pt & pp* **readied**, *ger* **readying**.

ready-cooked [redɪˈkʊkt] *adj* precocinado,-a.

ready-made [redɪˈmeɪd] *adj* hecho,-a, confeccionado,-a.

ready-mix ['redmɪks] *adj* (*cake etc*) de sobre.

ready-salted [redɪˈsɔːltɪd] *adj* con sal.

reaffirm [riːəˈfɜːm] **1** *t* (*restate*) reafirmar. **2** (*strengthen*) fortalecer.

reafforest [riːəˈfɒrɪst] *t* GB reforestar.

reafforestation [riːəfɒrɪˈsteɪʃən] *n* GB reforestación *f*, repoblación *f* forestal.

real [rɪəl] **1** *adj* real, verdadero,-a: *there is a real threat of war*, la amenaza de la guerra es real; *he never knew his real father*, nunca conoció a su verdadero padre. **2** (*genuine*) auténtico,-a: *it's real caviar*, es caviar auténtico; *they're made of real leather*, son de piel legítima. – **3** *adv* US *fam* muy: *he was real friendly*, era muy simpático.
● **in real life**, en la vida real. ‖ **in the real world**, en el mundo real. ‖ **in real terms**, en términos reales. ‖ **for real**, de veras. ‖ **get real!**, pero, ¿tú en qué mundo vives?
■ **real ale**, cerveza tradicional. ‖ **real estate**, bienes *mpl* inmuebles. ‖ **real time**, tiempo real. ‖ **the real McCoy**, lo auténtico.

realign [riːəˈlaɪn] *t* (*bring back into line*) realinear; (*restructure*) reestructurar; (*readjust*) reajustar.

realignment [riːəˈlaɪnmənt] *n* (*bringing back into line*) realineamiento; (*restructuring*) reestructuración *f*; (*readjustment*) reajuste *m*.

realism ['rɪəlɪzəm] *n* realismo.

realist ['rɪəlɪst] *n* realista *mf*.

realistic [rɪəˈlɪstɪk] *adj* realista.

realistically [rɪəˈlɪstɪkəlɪ] *adv* (*practically*) de manera realista.

reality [rɪˈælɪtɪ] *n* realidad *f*.
● **in reality**, en realidad.

realizable ['rɪəlaɪzəbəl] *adj* realizable.

realization [rɪəlaɪˈzeɪʃən] **1** *n* (*of plan*) realización *f*. **2** FIN realización *f*. **3** (*understanding*) comprensión *f*.

realize ['rɪəlaɪz] **1** *t* (*understand*) darse cuenta de, comprender: *he soon realized that he was alone*, pronto se dio cuenta de que estaba solo. **2** (*know*) saber: *I didn't realize that you were here*, no sabía que estabas aquí. **3** (*carry out*) realizar: *she realized her ambition of marrying a duke*, realizó su ambición de casarse con un duque. **4** (*sell*) realizar, vender; (*fetch*) reportar: *they realized their assets*, realizaron su activo; *the charity concert realized £100,000*, el concierto benéfico reportó cien mil libras.

really ['rɪəlɪ] **1** *adv* (*in fact*) en realidad: *I'll tell you what really happened*, te explicaré lo que pasó en realidad; *did you really say that?*, ¿de verdad dijiste eso? **2** (*very*) muy, realmente: *it was really interesting*, fue muy interesante. **3** (*showing interest*) ¿ah sí?, ¿en serio? ¿de verdad?; (*showing surprise*) ¿de verdad?, ¡no me digas!; (*showing annoyance*) ¡vaya!

realm [relm] **1** *n* (*kingdom*) reino. **2** (*field*) campo, terreno.

real-time ['rɪəltaɪm] *adj* de tiempo real.

realtor ['rɪəltɔːr] *n* agente *mf* inmobiliario,-a.

ream [riːm] *n* resma.

reanimate [rɪˈænɪmeɪt] *t* reanimar.

reap [riːp] *t* cosechar.
● **to reap the benefits**, cosechar beneficios.

reaper ['riːpər] **1** *n* (*person*) segador,-ra. **2** (*machine*) segadora.

reappear [riːəˈpɪər] *i* reaparecer.

reappearance ['riːəpɪərəns] *n* reaparición *f*.

reappraisal [riːəˈpreɪzəl] *n* revaluación *f*.

reappraise [riːəˈpreɪz] *t* revaluar.

rear[1] [rɪər] **1** *adj* trasero,-a, de atrás. – **2** *n* (*back part*) parte *f* de atrás. **3** (*of room*) fondo. **4** *fam* (*of person*) trasero.
● **to bring up the rear**, cerrar la marcha.
■ **rear admiral**, contraalmirante *m*. ‖ **rear entrance**, puerta de atrás. ‖ **rear seat**, asiento de atrás. ‖ **rear wheel**, rueda trasera.

rear[2] [rɪə] **1** *t* (*raise*) criar. **2** (*lift up*) levantar: *racism has once again reared its ugly head*, el racismo ha vuelto a mostrar su siniestro rostro. – **3** **to rear (up)**, *i* encabritarse.

rearguard ['rɪəgɑːd] *n* retaguardia.
● **to fight a rearguard action**, MIL cubrir la retirada; (*make a last effort*) hacer un último intento.

rearm [riːˈɑːm] **1** *t* rearmar. – **2** *i* rearmarse.

rearmament [riːˈɑːməmənt] *n* rearme *m*.

rearmost ['rɪəməʊst] *adj* último,-a.

rearrange [riːəˈreɪndʒ] **1** *t* (*objects*) colocar de otra manera. **2** (*event*) cambiar la fecha de, cambiar la hora de.

rearrangement [riːəˈreɪndʒmənt] **1** *n* (*of objects*) cambio de lugar. **2** (*of event*) cambio de fecha, cambio de hora.

rearview mirror [rɪəvjuːˈmɪrə] *n* retrovisor *m*.

reason ['riːzən] **1** *n* (*cause*) razón *f*, motivo: *the reason why I'm late is that ...*, la razón por la que llego tarde es que ...; *I see no reason to doubt his word*, no veo ninguna razón en dudar de su palabra; *what is the reason for this?*, ¿a qué se debe esto? **2** (*faculty*) razón *f*: *he lost his reason*, perdió la razón. – **3** *t* deducir, llegar a la conclusión de que: *I reasoned that she would return to the scene of the crime*, deduje que volvería al lugar del crimen. – **4** *i* razonar: *it's impossible to reason with him*, es imposible razonar con él.

● **by reason of,** en virtud de. ‖ **it stands to reason,** es lógico, es de lógica. ‖ **to have reason to believe that ...,** tener razones para creer que ... ‖ **to listen to reason,** atender a razones. ‖ **to see reason,** entrar en razón. ‖ **within reason,** dentro de lo razonable.

reasonable ['riːzənəbəl] **1** *adj* (*gen*) razonable: *he's a very reasonable person,* es una persona muy razonable; *their prices are quite reasonable,* sus precios son razonables. **2** (*acceptable*) pasable, aceptable: *the weather was reasonable, but not wonderful,* el tiempo era pasable, pero no maravilloso.

reasonably ['riːzənəblɪ] **1** *adv* (*gen*) razonablemente: *it's reasonably priced,* tiene un precio razonable. **2** (*quite*) bastante: *it's reasonably cheap,* no es muy caro.

reasoning ['riːzənɪŋ] *n* razonamiento.

reassemble [riːəˈsembəl] **1** *t* (*parts*) volver a montar. **2** (*people*) volver a reunir. – **3** *i* (*people*) reunirse.

reassurance [riːəˈʃʊərəns] **1** *n* (*feeling*) tranquilidad *f,* consuelo: *I was in need of reassurance,* necesitaba consuelo. **2** (*words*) palabras *fpl* tranquilizadoras: *despite all our reassurances, she insisted on carrying a gun,* a pesar de todos nuestros intentos por tranquilizarla, se empeñó en llevar una pistola.

reassure [riːəˈʃʊəʳ] **1** *t* (*comfort*) tranquilizar, dar confianza a: *the manager tried to reassure the workers about the company's future,* el director intentó tranquilizar a los trabajadores sobre el futuro de la compañía. **2** (*assure again*) volver a asegurar.

reassuring [riːəˈʃʊərɪŋ] *adj* tranquilizador,-ra.

reawakening [riːəˈweɪkənɪŋ] *n* renacer *m.*

rebate ['riːbeɪt] **1** *n* (*of tax*) devolución *f.* **2** (*discount*) descuento.

rebel ['rebəl] **1** *adj* rebelde. – **2** *n* rebelde *mf.* – **3** *i* rebelarse (**against,** contra).
▲ (*verbo*) [rɪˈbel], pt & pp *rebelled,* ger *rebelling.*

rebellion [rɪˈbeliən] *n* rebelión *f.*

rebellious [rɪˈbeliəs] *adj* rebelde.

rebelliousness [rɪˈbeliənəs] *n* rebeldía.

rebirth [riːˈbɜːθ] *n* renacimiento.

reborn [riːˈbɔːn] **to be reborn,** *phr* renacer, volver a nacer.

rebound ['riːbaʊnd] **1** *n* rebote *m: I hit the ball on the rebound,* pegué a la pelota de rebote. – **2** *i* rebotar. – **3 to rebound on sb.,** *phr* volverse contra algn.: *his plans rebounded on him,* le salió el tiro por la culata.
● **to marry on the rebound,** casarse por despecho.
▲ (*verbo*) [rɪˈbaʊnd].

rebuff [rɪˈbʌf] **1** *n* rechazo. – **2** *t* rechazar.
● **to meet with a rebuff,** ser rechazado,-a.

rebuild [riːˈbɪld] *t* reconstruir.
▲ *pt & pp rebuilt* [riːˈbɪlt].

rebuke [rɪˈbjuːk] **1** *n* reprimenda. – **2** *t* reprender.

rebut [rɪˈbʌt] *t* refutar.
▲ *pt & pp rebutted,* ger *rebutting.*

rebuttal [rɪˈbʌtəl] *n* refutación *f.*

recalcitrance [rɪˈkælsɪtrəns] *n* obstinación *f.*

recalcitrant [rɪˈkælsɪtrənt] *adj* recalcitrante.

recall [rɪˈkɔːl] **1** *n* (*memory*) memoria: *she has total recall,* tiene una memoria infalible. **2** (*withdrawal*) retirada. **3** (*of parliament*) convocación *f* extraordinaria. – **4** *t* (*remember*) recordar: *I can't recall exactly what happened,* no recuerdo exactamente lo que pasó. **5** (*withdraw*) retirar. **6** (*parliament*) convocar de manera extraordinaria.
● **to sound recall,** tocar retreta.
▲ (*verbo*) [rɪˈkɔːl].

recant [rɪˈkænt] **1** *i* retractarse. – **2** *t* retractarse de.

recap ['riːkæp] **1** *n fam* resumen *m.* – **2** *t fam* resumir. – **3** *i fam* resumir.
▲ *pt & pp recapped,* ger *recapping.*

recapitulate [riːkəˈpɪtjʊleɪt] **1** *t* recapitular, resumir. – **2** *i* recapitular, resumir.

recapitulation [riːkəpɪtjʊˈleɪʃən] *n* recapitulación *f,* resumen *m.*

recapture [riːˈkæptʃəʳ] **1** *n* (*of person*) nueva detención *f;* (*of territory*) reconquista. – **2** *t* (*person*) volver a detener, volver a capturar; (*territory*) reconquistar, volver a tomar. **3** *fig* recuperar.

recast [riːˈkɑːst] **1** *t* (*do again*) rehacer. **2** (*metals*) refundir. **3** (*play, film*) cambiar el reparto de; (*actor*) dar otro papel a; (*role*) asignar a otro actor, asignar a otra actriz.
▲ *pt & pp recast.*

recd [rɪˈsiːvd] *abbr* COMM (*received*) recibido,-a.
▲ También se escribe *rec'd.*

recede [rɪˈsiːd] **1** *i* (*move back*) retirarse. **2** (*be left behind*) retroceder, irse retrocediendo. **3** (*fears, danger*) alejarse; (*memories, possibilities*) desvanecerse.

receipt [rɪˈsiːt] **1** *n* (*document*) recibo: *could I have a receipt, please?,* ¿podría darme un recibo? **2** (*act of receiving*) recepción *f,* recibo: *your order will be dispatched on receipt of payment,* su pedido será enviado en cuanto recibamos el pago. – **3 receipts,** *npl* COMM ingresos *mpl,* recaudación *f sing.*
● **to be in receipt of,** acusar recibo de.

receive [rɪˈsiːv] **1** *t* (*gen*) recibir: *we received your letter last week,* recibimos tu carta la semana pasada; *he was received by the president,* lo recibió el presidente. **2** (*wound*) sufrir: *he received a blow to the head,* sufrió un golpe en la cabeza. **3** (*radio signal*) recibir: *are you receiving me, Halifax?,* ¿me reciben, Halifax? **4** (*stolen goods*) comerciar con: *he was charged with receiving stolen watches,* lo acusaron de comerciar con relojes robados. – **5** *i* (*in tennis etc*) estar al resto. – **6** *t* (*welcome*) recibir, acoger: *they were received into the church,* fueron admitidos en el seno de la iglesia.
● **to be on the receiving end,** ser la víctima, ser quien le toca recibir. ‖ **to be well/badly received,** tener una buena/mala acogida.
■ **received pronunciation,** pronunciación *f* estándar. ‖ **received wisdom,** sabiduría popular.

receiver [rɪˈsiːvəʳ] **1** *n* (*of telephone*) auricular *m.* **2** (*of stolen goods*) perista *mf.* **3** JUR síndico,-a, síndico,-a de quiebras. **4** RAD TV receptor *m.* **5** (*in American football*) receptor,-ra.
● **to call in the receiver,** declarar suspensión de pagos. ‖ **to pick up the receiver,** descolgar el teléfono. ‖ **to put down the receiver,** colgar el teléfono.

receivership [rɪˈsiːvəʃɪp] *n* quiebra, bancarrota.
● **to go into receivership,** declarar suspensión de pagos.

recent ['riːsənt] *adj* reciente: *in recent months/years,* en los últimos meses/años.

recently ['riːsəntlɪ] **1** *adv* (*lately*) recientemente, últimamente: *I've seen a lot of her recently,* últimamente la he visto bastante. **2** (*a short time ago*) hace poco: *until recently everyone thought it was impossible,* hasta hace poco todos pensaron que era imposible.

receptacle [rɪˈseptəkəl] *n* receptáculo, recipiente *m.*

reception [rɪˈsepʃən] **1** *n* (*gen*) recepción *f.* **2** (*welcome*) acogida. **3** (*party*) recepción *f;* (*after wedding*) banquete *m.*
■ **reception class,** primera clase *f* (*en la escuela primaria*). ‖ **reception desk,** recepción *f.* ‖ **reception room,**

(in public place) salón m; (in house) sala de estar, sala, comedor o cualquier estancia donde se reciba a la gente.
receptionist [rɪ'sepʃənɪst] n recepcionista mf.
receptive [rɪ'septɪv] adj receptivo,-a.
receptor [rɪ'septəʳ] n receptor m.
recess ['riːses] 1 n (in wall) hueco. 2 (rest) descanso. 3 POL período de vacaciones. 4 (secret place) recoveco.
recession [rɪ'seʃən] n recesión f.
recharge [riː'tʃɑːdʒ] t recargar.
rechargeable [riː'tʃɑːdʒəbəl] adj recargable.
recherché [rə'ʃeʃeɪ] adj rebuscado,-a.
recidivism [rɪ'sɪdɪvɪzəm] n reincidencia.
recidivist [rɪ'sɪdɪvɪst] 1 adj reincidente. – 2 n reincidente mf.
recipe ['resəpɪ] 1 n receta. 2 fig fórmula.
■ **recipe book,** (personal collection) recetario; (cookery book) libro de cocina.
recipient [rɪ'sɪpɪənt] 1 n (gen) persona que recibe: recipients of medals are asked to rise, se ruega se pongan en pie los que hayan recibido una medalla. 2 (of letter etc) destinatario,-a. 3 (of transplant) receptor,-ra.
reciprocal [rɪ'sɪprəkəl] adj recíproco,-a.
reciprocate [rɪ'sɪprəkeɪt] 1 i corresponder. – 2 t (invitation) devolver, corresponder a.
reciprocity [resɪ'prɒsɪtɪ] n reciprocidad f.
recital [rɪ'saɪtəl] n recital m.
recitation [resɪ'teɪʃən] 1 n (of poetry) recitación f. 2 (of list) enumeración f.
recite [rɪ'saɪt] 1 t (poetry) recitar. 2 (list) enumerar.
reckless ['rekləs] 1 adj (hasty) precipitado,-a. 2 (careless) imprudente, temerario,-a.
■ **reckless driving,** conducción f temeraria.
recklessly ['rekləslɪ] adv imprudentemente, temerariamente, de manera temeraria.
recklessness ['rekləsnəs] n (haste) imprudencia, temeridad f.
reckon ['rekən] 1 t (estimate) calcular: the organizers reckon there were about 10,000 people there, los organizadores calculan que había unas 10.000 personas. 2 (calculate) calcular: how are pensions reckoned in this country?, ¿cómo se calculan las pensiones en este país? 3 (regard) considerar: it's reckoned to be the finest coffee in the world, está considerado el mejor café del mundo. 4 (think) creer, considerar: I reckon he's finished as a footballer, yo creo que está acabado como futbolista.
◆ **to reckon on** t insep contar con: you can reckon on it costing at least £2,000, puedes contar con que costará al menos 2000 libras. ‖ **to reckon up** t sep calcular, sumar. ‖ **to reckon with** 1 t insep (expect) esperar: I never reckoned with so much traffic, no esperaba tanto tráfico. 2 (take into account) tener en cuenta: they're still a force to be reckoned with, aún son una fuerza a tener en cuenta. 3 (deal with) vérselas con: you touch me and you'll have my cousin to reckon with, si me tocas tendrás que vérselas con mi primo. ‖ **to reckon without** t insep no tener en cuenta, no contar con.
reckoning ['rekənɪŋ] n cálculos mpl: by my reckoning, ..., según mis cálculos, ...
■ **the day of reckoning,** el día m del juicio final.
reclaim [rɪ'kleɪm] 1 t (money, right, etc) reclamar. 2 (land) ganar (al mar). 3 (recycle) reciclar. 4 (baggage) recoger.
reclamation [reklə'meɪʃən] 1 n (of land) rescate m. 2 (of waste) reciclaje m.
recline [rɪ'klaɪn] 1 t (lean back) reclinar; (rest) apoyar. – 2 i reclinarse, recostarse.

reclining [rɪ'klaɪnɪŋ] adj reclinable.
recluse [rɪ'kluːs] n ermitaño,-a.
● to live the life of a recluse, vivir recluido,-a.
reclusive [rɪ'kluːsɪv] adj solitario,-a.
recognition [rekəg'nɪʃən] n reconocimiento.
● in recognition of, en reconocimiento a. ‖ to change beyond all recognition, ser irreconocible.
recognizable [rekəg'naɪzəbəl] adj reconocible.
recognizably [rekəg'naɪzəblɪ] adv de manera apreciable.
recognize ['rekəgnaɪz] t reconocer.
recoil ['riːkɔɪl] 1 n (of gun) culatazo, retroceso. – 2 i (person - move back) retroceder; (- feel disgust) sentir repugnancia: she recoils from all forms of cruelty, le repugna la crueldad en todas sus formas. 3 (gun) retroceder, dar un culatazo.
▲ (verbo) [rɪ'kɔɪl].
recollect [rekə'lekt] t recordar.
recollection [rekə'lekʃən] n recuerdo.
recommence [rekə'mens] 1 t reanudar. – 2 i reanudarse.
recommend [rekə'mend] 1 t recomendar: what do you recommend?, ¿qué me recomiendas? 2 (advise) recomendar, aconsejar, sugerir.
recommendation [rekəmen'deɪʃən] 1 n recomendación f. 2 (advice) consejo, sugerencia.
recompense ['rekəmpens] 1 n recompensa. 2 JUR indemnización f. – 3 t recompensar. 4 JUR indemnizar.
reconcile ['rekənsaɪl] 1 t (people) reconciliar. 2 (ideas) conciliar.
● to reconcile os. to sth., resignarse a algo.
reconciliation [rekənsɪlɪ'eɪʃən] n reconciliación f.
recondite ['rekəndaɪt] adj recóndito,-a.
recondition [riːkən'dɪʃən] t revisar totalmente.
reconnaissance [rɪ'kɒnɪsəns] n reconocimiento.
reconnoiter [rekə'nɔɪtəʳ] t US → **roconnoitre**.
reconnoitre [rekə'nɔɪtəʳ] 1 t reconocer. – 2 i hacer un reconocimiento.
reconquer [riː'kɒŋkəʳ] t reconquistar.
reconquest [riː'kɒŋkwest] n reconquista.
reconsider [riːkən'sɪdəʳ] t reconsiderar.
reconsideration [riːkɒnsɪdə'reɪʃən] n revisión f, reconsideración f.
reconstitute [riː'kɒnstɪtjuːt] 1 t (food) reconstituir. 2 (group) reconstituir, reorganizar.
reconstruct [riːkəns'trʌkt] t reconstruir.
reconstruction [riːkən'strʌkʃən] n reconstrucción f.
record ['rekɔːd] 1 n (written evidence) constancia, constancia escrita: there is no record of his ever having married, no queda constancia de que se haya casado nunca; it's the driest spring on record, es la primavera más seca de la que se tiene constancia. 2 (note) relación f: he keeps a record of everything he spends, lleva una relación de todo lo que gasta. 3 (facts about a person) historial m. 4 MUS disco. 5 SP récord m, marca, plusmarca. – 6 t (write down) anotar, apuntar, tomar nota de: he recorded all the details in his diary, anotaba todos los detalles en su diario; the lady's reply is not recorded, no queda constancia de lo que contestó la señora. 7 (voice, music) grabar: the interview was recorded on tape, la entrevista fue grabada en una cinta. 8 (instrument, gauge) registrar: winds in excess of 110 miles per hour were recorded, se registraron vientos de más de 110 millas por hora. – 9 adj récord: they built it in record time, lo construyeron en un tiempo récord. – 10 records, npl (files) archivos mpl: all our records were des-

troyed in the fire, todos nuestros archivos fueron destruidos en el incendio. ● **off the record,** confidencialmente. ‖ **to be on record as saying that ...,** haber declarado públicamente que ... ‖ **to break a record,** batir un récord. ‖ **to have a record,** tener antecedentes. ‖ **to hold the record,** ostentar el récord. ‖ **to set a record,** establecer un récord. ‖ **to set the record straight,** dejar las cosas claras. ■ **medical record,** historial *m* médico. ‖ **record breaker,** plusmarquista *mf.* ‖ **record card,** ficha. ‖ **record company,** casa discográfica. ‖ **record holder,** plusmarquista *mf.* ‖ **record library,** fonoteca, discoteca. ‖ **record player,** tocadiscos *m.* ‖ **record token,** vale *para comprar discos, casetes, etc.* ▲ (*verbo*) [rɪ'kɔːd].

record-breaking ['rekɔːdbreɪkɪŋ] *adj* récord, que bate todos los récords.

recorded [rɪ'kɔːdɪd] *adj* (*written*) anotado,-a, apuntado,-a; (*on tape etc*) grabado,-a. ■ **recorded delivery,** correo certificado.

recorder [rɪ'kɔːdəʳ] *n* MUS flauta. ■ **cassette recorder,** casete *m.*

recording [rɪ'kɔːdɪŋ] *n* grabación *f.* ■ **recording studio,** estudio de grabación.

recount [rɪ'kaʊnt] *t* (*narrate*) contar, relatar.

re-count ['riːkaʊnt] **1** *n* recuento. – **2** *t* (*count again*) volver a contar, hacer el recuento de. ▲ (*verbo*) [riː'kaʊnt].

recoup [rɪ'kuːp] *t* (*gen*) recuperar; (*losses*) resarcirse de.

recourse [rɪ'kɔːs] *n* recurso. ● **to have recourse to,** recurrir a. ‖ **without recourse to,** sin recurrir a.

recover [rɪ'kʌvəʳ] **1** *t* recuperar. – **2** *i* recuperarse, reponerse. ● **to recover consciousness,** recobrar el conocimiento.

re-cover [riː'kʌvəʳ] *t* (*furniture*) retapizar; (*book*) volver a forrar.

recoverable [rɪ'kʌvərəbəl] *adj* recuperable.

recovery [rɪ'kʌvərɪ] *n* recuperación *f.*

recreate [riːkrɪ'eɪt] *t* recrear.

recreation [rekrɪ'eɪʃən] **1** *n* (*free time*) esparcimiento. **2** (*hobby*) pasatiempo. **3** (*in school*) recreo. ■ **recreation ground,** parque *m* infantil. ‖ **recreation room,** (*in institution*) sala de recreo; (*in house*) sala de juegos.

re-creation [riːkrɪ'eɪʃən] *n* recreación *f.*

recreational [rekrɪ'eɪʃənəl] *adj* de recreo.

recriminate [rɪ'krɪmɪneɪt] *t* recriminar.

recrimination [rɪkrɪmɪ'neɪʃən] *n* recriminación *f.*

recriminatory [rɪ'krɪmɪnətərɪ] *adj* recriminatorio,-a.

recruit [rɪ'kruːt] **1** *n* (*soldier*) recluta *m*; (*to group*) nuevo miembro, nuevo componente *m*; (*to company*) nuevo,-a empleado,-a, nuevo fichaje *m.* – **2** *t* (*soldier*) reclutar; (*employee*) contratar; (*member*) conseguir. – **3** *i* (*soldiers*) alistar reclutas; (*employees*) contratar empleados; (*members*) buscar socios.

recruitment [rɪ'kruːtmənt] *n* (*of soldiers*) reclutamiento; (*of employees*) contratación *f*; (*of members*) búsqueda de socios.

recta ['rektə] *npl* → **rectum.**

rectangle ['rektæŋgəl] *n* rectángulo.

rectangular [rekt'æŋgjuləʳ] *adj* rectangular.

rectifiable [rektɪ'faɪəbəl] *adj* rectificable.

rectification [rektɪfɪ'keɪʃən] *n* rectificación *f.*

rectify ['rektɪfaɪ] *t* rectificar, corregir.

rectilinear [rektɪ'lɪnɪəʳ] *adj* rectilíneo,-a.

rectitude ['rektɪtjuːd] *n* rectitud *f.*

rector ['rektəʳ] **1** *n* (*of church*) párroco. **2** (*of university*) rector,-ra.

rectory ['rektərɪ] *n* rectoría.

rectum ['rektəm] *n* recto. ▲ *pl* **rectums** o **recta.**

recumbent [rɪ'kʌmbənt] *adj* recostado,-a, yacente.

recuperate [rɪk'uːpəreɪt] **1** *t* (*get back*) recuperar. – **2** *i* (*from illness*) recuperarse, reponerse.

recuperation [rɪkuːpər'eɪʃən] *n* recuperación *f.*

recur [rɪ'kɜːʳ] *i* repetirse, reproducirse.

recurrence [rɪ'kʌrəns] *n* repetición *f.*

recurrent [rɪ'kʌrənt] **1** *adj* MATH periódico,-a. **2** MED recurrente.

recurring [rɪ'kɜːrɪŋ] **1** *adj* (*gen*) recurrente. **2** MATH periódico,-a.

recyclable [riː'saɪkləbəl] *adj* reciclable.

recycle [riː'saɪkəl] *t* reciclar.

recycling [riː'saɪkəlɪŋ] *n* reciclaje *m.* ■ **recycling plant,** planta de reciclaje.

red [red] **1** *n* (*colour*) rojo *m.* **2** (*left winger*) rojo,-a. – **3** *adj* rojo,-a: *she was dressed all in red,* iba vestida toda de rojo. **4** (*hair*) pelirrojo,-a. ● **to be in the red,** estar en descubierto. ‖ **to turn red,** ponerse colorado,-a, sonrojarse. ■ **red admiral,** vanesa roja. ‖ **red alert,** alerta roja. ‖ **Red Army,** Ejército Rojo. ‖ **red blood cell,** glóbulo rojo. ‖ **red cabbage,** col *f* lombarda. ‖ **red card,** tarjeta roja. ‖ **red carpet,** alfombra roja: *they rolled out the red carpet for him,* lo recibieron con todos los honores. ‖ **red corpuscle,** glóbulo rojo. ‖ **Red Crescent,** Media Luna Roja. ‖ **Red Cross,** Cruz *f* Roja. ‖ **red deer,** ciervo común. ‖ **red giant,** gigante *f* roja. ‖ **red herring,** pista falsa. ‖ **Red Indian,** piel roja *mf.* ‖ **red light,** semáforo en rojo. ‖ **red meat,** carne *f* roja. ‖ **red pepper,** pimiento rojo. ‖ **Red Riding Hood,** Caperucita Roja. ‖ **red route,** *calle donde el estacionamiento está terminantemente prohibido.* ‖ **Red Sea,** Mar *m* Rojo. ‖ **red tape,** papeleo burocrático. ‖ **red wine,** vino tinto.

red-blooded ['red'blʌdɪd] *adj* viril: *he's a real red-blooded male,* es un macho de pelo en pecho.

redbreast ['redbrest] *n* petirrojo.

red-brick ['redbrɪk] *adj* de ladrillo rojo. ■ **red-brick university,** GB *universidad de provincias construida a finales del siglo XIX.*

redcurrant [red'kʌrənt] *n* grosella.

redden ['redən] **1** *t* enrojecer. – **2** *i* (*gen*) enrojecerse; (*blush*) ponerse rojo,-a, sonrojarse.

reddish ['redɪʃ] *adj* rojizo,-a.

redecorate [riː'dekəreɪt] *t* (*paint*) repintar; (*paper*) reempapelar.

redeem [rɪ'diːm] **1** *t* rescatar, salvar: *the film had not a single feature to redeem it,* la película no tenía ni una sola cosa que la salvara. **2** (*from pawn*) desempeñar. **3** (*voucher*) canjear. **4** (*promise*) cumplir. **5** REL redimir. ● **to redeem os.,** conseguir el perdón, reparar el mal que uno ha hecho.

redeemable [rɪ'diːməbəl] *adj* (*debt*) amortizable; (*pawned item*) redimible; (*voucher*) canjeable.

redeemer [rɪ'diːməʳ] *n* redentor,-ra. ■ **The Redeemer,** el Redentor *m.*

redeeming [rɪ'diːmɪŋ] *adj* redentor,-ra: *her sole redeeming feature is ...,* lo único que la salva es ...

redemption [rɪ'dempʃən] **1** *n* (*of debt*) pago. **2** (*of voucher*) canje *m.* **3** REL redención *f.*

● **to be beyond redemption,** ser irredimible, no tener remedio.
redeploy [riːdɪ'plɔɪ] t transferir, trasladar.
redeployment [riːdɪ'plɔɪmənt] n transferencia, traslado.
redevelop [riːdɪ'veləp] t reurbanizar.
redevelopment [riːdɪ'veləpmənt] n reurbanización f.
red-haired ['red'heəd] adj pelirrojo,-a.
red-handed [red'hændɪd] adj con las manos en la masa, in fraganti.
redhead ['redhed] n pelirrojo,-a.
red-hot [red'hɒt] adj al rojo vivo, candente.
redial [riː'daɪəl] 1 t volver a marcar. – 2 n rellamada.
▲ (sustantivo) ['riːdaɪəl].
redid [riː'dɪd] pt → **redo**.
redirect [riːdaɪ'rekt] t (traffic) desviar; (letter) remitir.
rediscover [riːdɪs'kʌvə'] t redescubrir.
rediscovery [riːdɪs'kʌvərɪ] n redescubrimiento.
red-letter day [red'letədeɪ] n día m memorable.
red-light district [red'laɪtdɪstrɪkt] n barrio chino.
redness ['rednəs] n rojez f.
redo [riː'duː] t rehacer, volver a hacer.
▲ pt **redid**, pp **redone**, ger **redoing**.
redouble [riː'dʌbəl] t redoblar, reduplicar.
redoubtable [rɪ'dautəbəl] adj temible.
redpoll ['redpɒl] n pardillo sizerín.
redress [rɪ'dres] 1 n reparación f. – 2 t reparar, corregir.
● **to redress the balance,** restablecer el equilibrio.
redshank ['redʃæŋk] n archibebe m común.
redskin ['redskɪn] n piel roja mf.
redstart ['redstɑːt] n colirrojo.
reduce [rɪ'djuːs] 1 t (gen) reducir, disminuir: *they're going to reduce the staff,* van a reducir la plantilla; *the house was reduced to ashes,* la casa se redujo a cenizas. 2 (price etc) rebajar.
● *"reduce speed now",* "disminuya la velocidad". ‖ **to be reduced to doing sth.,** no tener más remedio que hacer algo, verse obligado,-a a hacer algo: *he was reduced to begging,* se vio obligado a pedir limosna. ‖ **to be reduced to sth.,** verse sumido,-a en algo: *the country was reduced to poverty,* el país se vio sumido en la pobreza. ‖ **to reduce sb. to tears,** hacer llorar a algn.
reduced [rɪ'djuːst] adj (gen) reducido,-a; (price) rebajado, reducido,-a.
reduction [rɪ'dʌkʃən] n (gen) reducción f; (fall) disminución f; (in price) rebaja.
redundancy [rɪ'dʌndənsɪ] 1 n (dismissal) despido. 2 (superfluity) superfluidad f. 3 LING redundancia.
redundant [rɪ'dʌndənt] 1 adj (dismissed) despedido,-a. 2 (superfluous) superfluo,-a. 3 LING redundante.
● **to be made redundant,** perder el empleo, ser despedido,-a.
reduplicate [riː'djuːplɪkeɪt] t reduplicar.
reduplication [riːdjuːplɪ'keɪʃən] n reduplicación f.
redwing ['redwɪŋ] n zorzal m alirrojo.
redwood ['redwʊd] n secuoya.
re-echo [riː'ekəʊ] 1 i resonar. – 2 t repetir.
reed [riːd] 1 n (plant) caña, junco. 2 MUS lengüeta.
redbed ['riːdbed] n cañaveral m.
reeducate [riː'edjʊkeɪt] t reeducar.
reedy ['riːdɪ] adj (voice) aflautado,-a.
▲ comp **reedier**, superl **reediest**.
reef [riːf] n arrecife m.
■ **reef knot,** nudo de rizo.

reefer ['riːfə'] n sl porro, canuto.
reek [riːk] 1 n peste m, tufo. – 2 i apestar, heder.
reel¹ [riːl] 1 n (of thread, cotton) carrete m; (of camera film) carrete m, rollo; (of cine film) bobina; (of wire, tape) rollo. 2 (for fishing) carrete m.
◆ **to reel in** t sep (line) recoger, cobrar; (fish) cobrar, sacar del agua. ‖ **to reel off** t sep recitar.
reel² [riːl] 1 i (stagger) tambalearse: *he reeled back and almost fell into the water,* se tambaleó y por poco se cae al agua; *he's still reeling from the £15,000 fine,* aún no se ha recuperado de la multa de quince mil libras. 2 (spin round) dar vueltas: *my head was reeling,* la cabeza me daba vueltas.
reel³ [riːl] n baile tradicional escocés.
re-elect [riːɪ'lekt] t reelegir.
re-election [riːɪ'lekʃən] n reelección f.
re-employ [riːɪm'plɔɪ] t volver a contratar.
reenact [riːɪ'nækt] t (event) volver a representar; (crime) reconstruir.
reenactment [riːɪ'næktmənt] n (event) representación f; (crime) reconstrucción f.
re-enter [riː'entə'] t volver a entrar en, reingresar en.
re-entry [riː'entrɪ] n reingreso.
▲ pl **re-entries**.
reeve [riːv] n (in Canada) presidente,-ta mf del concejo.
re-examination [riːɪgzæmɪ'neɪʃən] n (of evidence) nuevo examen m; (of patient) nuevo reconocimiento; (of witness) nuevo interrogatorio.
re-examine [riːɪg'zæmɪn] t (evidence, patient, student) volver a examinar, reexaminar; (witness) volver a interrogar.
ref¹ ['refərəns] abbr (reference) referencia; (abbreviation) ref.
ref² [ref] n fam (abbr of referee) árbitro,-a.
refectory [rɪ'fektərɪ] n refectorio.
▲ pl **refectories**.
refer [rɪ'fɜː'] 1 t (send) remitir, mandar, enviar: *I'm going to refer you to a specialist,* voy a mandarlo a un especialista; *I refer you to my article in ...,* te remito a mi artículo en ... – 2 i (allude to) referirse (**to,** a): *who are you referring to?,* ¿a quién te refieres? 3 (mention, name) hacer referencia (**to,** a): *he referred to a Mr Fletcher,* hizo referencia a un tal Sr Fletcher. 4 (consult) consultar (**to,** -): *he referred constantly to his notes,* consultaba constantemente sus apuntes. 5 (describe) calificar (**to,** de); (call) llamar (**to,** a): *he was referred to as an opportunist,* lo calificaron de oportunista; *she refers to him as "the Fox",* lo llama "el Zorro".
referee [refə'riː] 1 n SP árbitro,-a. 2 (for job) persona que da referencias personales sobre alguien. – 3 t arbitrar.
reference ['refərəns] 1 n referencia, mención f: *I can find no reference to his wife,* no encuentro mención alguna a su esposa. 2 (for job) referencias fpl.
● **for future reference,** para consultas en el futuro. ‖ **to make reference to,** hacer referencia a, mencionar. ‖ **with reference to,** referente a, con relación a.
■ **reference book,** libro de consulta. ‖ **reference library,** biblioteca de consulta.
referendum [refə'rendəm] n referéndum m.
▲ pl **referendums** o **referenda** [refə'rendə].
referral [rɪ'fɜːrəl] n remisión f.
refill ['riːfɪl] 1 n (for pen etc) recambio; (for lighter) carga: *your glass is empty, would you like a refill?,* tu copa está vacía, ¿quieres que te la llene? – 2 t (glass, pen) volver a llenar; (lighter) recargar.
▲ (verbo) [riː'fɪl].

refillable [riːˈfɪləbəl] *adj* recargable.
refine [rɪˈfaɪn] 1 *t* (*purify*) refinar. 2 (*polish, perfect*) pulir, perfeccionar.
refined [rɪˈfaɪnd] 1 *adj* (*product*) refinado,-a. 2 (*person, behaviour*) refinado,-a, fino,-a.
refinement [rɪˈfaɪnmənt] 1 *n* (*genteelness*) refinamiento. 2 (*improvement*) mejora. 3 (*process of refining*) refinado.
refinery [rɪˈfaɪnərɪ] *n* refinería.
  ▲ *pl refineries.*
refining [rɪˈfaɪnɪŋ] *n* refinado.
refit [ˈriːfɪt] 1 *n* reacondicionamiento. – 2 *t* reacondicionar.
  ▲ *pt & pp refitted, ger refitting.*
reflation [riːˈfleɪʃən] *n* reflación *f.*
reflect [rɪˈflekt] 1 *t* reflejar: *my face was reflected in the lake,* mi cara se reflejaba en el lago. – 2 *i* (*think*) reflexionar (**on,** sobre): *I reflected a great deal before acting,* reflexioné mucho antes de actuar.
  ◆ **to reflect on** *t insep* perjudicar: *this in no way reflects on your reputation,* esto no perjudica de ningún modo tu reputación.
reflection [rɪˈflekʃən] 1 *n* (*image*) reflejo. 2 (*thought*) reflexión *f.* 3 (*aspersion*) descrédito.
  ● **on reflection, ...,** pensándolo bien, ...
reflector [rɪˈflektəʳ] *n* (*gen*) reflector *m*; (*on car*) catafaro.
reflex [ˈriːfleks] *n* reflejo.
  ■ **reflex action,** acto reflejo. ‖ **reflex camera,** cámara réflex.
reflexive [rɪˈfleksɪv] *adj* reflexivo,-a.
reflexology [riːflksˈɒlədʒɪ] *n* reflexoterapia.
refloat [riːˈfləʊt] *t* reflotar.
reforest [riːˈfɒrɪst] *t* reforestar.
reforestation [riːfɒrɪˈsteɪʃən] *t* reforestación *f,* repoblación *f* forestal.
reform [rɪˈfɔːm] 1 *n* reforma. – 2 *t* reformar.
reformat [riːˈfɔːmæt] *t* reformatear.
reformation [refəˈmeɪʃən] *n* reforma.
reformatory [rɪˈfɔːmətərɪ] *n* reformatorio.
reformer [rɪˈfɔːməʳ] *n* reforamador,-ra.
reformist [rɪˈfɔːmɪst] 1 *adj* reformista. – 2 *n* reformista *mf.*
refract [rɪˈfrækt] 1 *t* refractar. – 2 *i* refractarse.
refractory [rɪˈfræktərɪ] *adj* refractario,-a.
refrain¹ [rɪˈfreɪn] *n* MUS estribillo.
refrain² [rɪˈfreɪn] *i* abstenerse (**from,** de): *please refrain from doing that,* por favor, absténgase de hacer eso.
refresh [rɪˈfreʃ] *t* refrescar.
refresher course [rɪˈfreʃəkɔːs] *n* cursillo de reciclaje.
refreshing [rɪˈfreʃɪŋ] *adj* (*gen*) refrescante; (*rest, sleep*) reparador,-ra.
refreshment [rɪˈfreʃmənt] *n* refresco, refrigerio.
refrigerant [rɪˈfrɪdʒərənt] *n* refrigerante *m.*
refrigerate [rɪˈfrɪdʒəreɪt] *t* refrigerar.
refrigeration [rɪfrɪdʒəˈreɪʃən] *n* refrigeración *f.*
refrigerator [rɪˈfrɪdʒəreɪtəʳ] *n* frigorífico, nevera.
refuel [riːˈfjʊəl] 1 *t* (*vehicle*) poner carburante a. 2 (*emotions*) reavivar. – 3 *i* repostar.
refuge [ˈrefjuːdʒ] *n* refugio.
  ● **to seek refuge,** buscar refugio. ‖ **to take refuge,** refugiarse, guarecerse.
refugee [refjuˈdʒiː] *n* refugiado,-a.
  ■ **refugee camp,** campamento de refugiados.
refund [ˈriːfʌnd] 1 *n* reembolso. – 2 *t* reembolsar.
  ▲ (*verbo*) [riːˈfʌnd].
refurbish [riːˈfɜːbɪʃ] *t* remozar, renovar.

refusal [rɪˈfjuːzəl] 1 *n* (*negative reply*) negativa, respuesta negativa. 2 (*rejection*) rechazo.
  ● **to meet with refusal,** ser rechazado,-a.
  ■ **first refusal,** primera opción *f.*
refuse¹ [ˈrefjuːs] *n* basura.
  ■ **refuse collection,** recogida de basuras. ‖ **refuse collector,** basurero,-a. ‖ **refuse dump / refuse tip,** vertedero. ‖ **refuse worker,** basurero,-a.
refuse² [rɪˈfjuːz] 1 *t* (*reject*) rehusar, rechazar, no aceptar: *my offer was refused,* mi oferta fue rechazada. 2 (*withhold*) negar, denegar, no conceder: *they refused me a visa,* me denegaron el visado. – 3 *i* negarse (**to,** a): *he refused to sing,* se negó a cantar.
refutation [refjuˈteɪʃən] *n* refutación *f.*
refute [rɪˈfjuːt] *t* refutar.
regain [rɪˈgeɪn] 1 *t* (*recover*) recobrar, recuperar. 2 (*get back to*) volver a.
  ● **to regain consciousness,** volver en sí.
regal [ˈriːgəl] *adj* regio,-a.
regale [rɪˈgeɪl] 1 *t* (*present with*) agasajar (**with,** con). 2 (*entertain*) entretener (**with,** con).
regalia [rɪˈgeɪlɪə] *n* galas *fpl.*
regally [ˈriːgəlɪ] *adv* regiamente.
regard [rɪˈgɑːd] 1 *n* respeto, consideración *f: he has no regard for people's feelings,* no respeta los sentimientos de los demás. – 2 *t* (*consider*) considerar: *it's regarded as his finest work,* se considera su mejor obra; *I regard the matter closed,* doy por cerrado el asunto. 3 (*look at*) mirar, contemplar. 4 (*heed*) hacer caso a. – 5 **regards,** *npl* recuerdos *mpl.*
  ● **as regards,** con respecto a, por lo que se refiere a. ‖ **with regard to,** con respecto a. ‖ **to hold in high regard,** tener en gran estima. ‖ **without regard to,** sin hacer caso de.
regarding [rɪˈgɑːdɪŋ] *prep* tocante a, respecto a.
regardless [rɪˈgɑːdləs] 1 *adv fam* a pesar de todo. – 2 **regardless of,** *prep fam* sin tener en cuenta.
regatta [rɪˈgætə] *n* regata.
regd [ˈredʒɪstəd] *abbr* (*registered*) registrado,-a.
regency [ˈriːdʒensɪ] *n* regencia.
regenerate [rɪˈdʒenəreɪt] 1 *t* regenerar. – 2 *i* regenerarse.
regeneration [rɪdʒenəˈreɪʃən] *n* regeneración *f.*
regent [ˈriːdʒənt] *n* regente *mf.*
reggae [ˈregeɪ] *n* reggae *m.*
regime [reɪˈʒiːm] *n* régimen *m.*
  ▲ *También se escribe régime.*
regiment [ˈredʒɪmənt] 1 *n* regimiento. – 2 *t* MIL regimentar. 3 *fig* disciplinar, reglamentar.
regimental [redʒɪˈmentəl] *adj* del regimiento.
regimentation [redʒɪmenˈteɪʃən] *n* reglamentación *f.*
region [ˈriːdʒən] *n* región *f.*
  ● **in the region of,** aproximadamente, alrededor de.
regional [ˈriːdʒənəl] *adj* regional.
regionalism [ˈriːdʒənəlɪzəm] *n* regionalismo.
regionalist [ˈriːdʒənəlɪst] 1 *adj* regionalista. – 2 *n* regionalista *mf.*
register [ˈredʒɪstəʳ] 1 *n* (*gen*) registro; (*in school*) lista: *would you sign the register, please?,* ¿quiere firmar el registro, por favor?; *the teacher took the register,* la profesora pasó lista. – 2 *t* (*put on record, list*) registrar; (*car, student*) matricular; (*birth, death, marriage*) inscribir en el registro: *I registered the car in my sister's name,* matriculé el coche en nombre de mi hermana; *she registered the death of her father,* inscribió la muerte de su padre en el registro. 3 (*show – reading*) registrar, indicar, mar-

car; (- *feeling*) mostrar, reflejar: *this gauge registers internal pressure*, este manómetro indica la presión interior; *his face registered disappointment*, su cara mostraba decepción. **4** (*make known*) hacer constar: *I wish to register my disapproval*, quisiera hacer constar mi desaprobación; *I wish to register a complaint*, quisiera presentar una queja. **5** (*letter*) certificar. – **6** *i* (*for classes*) matricularse; (*at congress, with doctor*) inscribirse; (*at hotel*) registrarse. **7** (*make impact*): *it didn't register until later who she was*, no caí en la cuenta de quién era hasta más tarde.
■ **register office**, registro civil.

registered ['redʒɪstəd] **1** *adj* (*person*) inscrito,-a; (*student*) matriculado,-a. **2** (*letter*) certificado,-a. **3** (*car, etc*) matriculado,-a; (*ship*) de bandera: *a Taiwanese registered tanker*, un petrolero de bandera taiwanesa.
■ **registered nurse**, enfermero,-a diplomado,-a. ‖ **registered office**, sede *f* social. ‖ **registered post**, correo certificado. ‖ **registered trademark**, marca registrada.

registrar [redʒɪs'trɑːʳ] **1** *n* (*in office*) registrador,-ra; (*at university*) secretario,-a general. **2** (*doctor*) médico,-a interno,-a.

registration [redʒɪs'treɪʃən] **1** *n* (*of birth, death marriage*) inscripción *f*; (*of patent etc*) registro. **2** (*enrolment*) inscripción *f*; (*of student*) matrícula.
■ **registration number**, AUTO matrícula.

registry ['redʒɪstrɪ] *n* registro.
■ **registry office**, registro civil: *it'll be a registry office wedding*, nos casaremos por lo civil.

regress [rɪ'gres] *i* sufrir una regresión.

regression [rɪ'greʃən] *n* regresión *f*.

regressive [rɪ'gresɪv] *adj* regresivo,-a.

regret [rɪ'gret] **1** *n* (*remorse*) remordimiento. **2** (*sadness*) pesar *m*. – **3** *t* (*feel sorry*) lamentar, arrepentirse de: *I don't regret leaving her*, no me arrepiento de haberla dejado. **4** (*express one's sadness*) lamentar: *I regret to inform you that ...*, lamento informarle que ...; *we regret to announce the death of ...*, lamentamos comunicar la muerte de ... **5** (*miss*) echar de menos, echar en falta. – **6** **regrets**, *npl* excusas *mpl*: *she sends her regrets*, manda sus excusas.

regretful [rɪ'gretful] *adj* arrepentido,-a.

regrettable [rɪ'gretəbəl] *adj* lamentable.

regrettably [rɪ'gretəblɪ] *adv* lamentablemente.

regroup [riː'gruːp] **1** *t* reagrupar. – **2** *i* reagruparse.

regular ['regjʊləʳ] **1** *adj* (*gen*) regular: *the buses on this route are very regular*, los autobuses de esta línea son muy regulares; *I submit regular reports to my boss*, a mi jefe le presento informes regularmente; *regular attendance is essential*, la asistencia regular es imprescindible. **2** (*normal*) normal, usual, de siempre: *our regular milkman will be back next week*, el lechero de siempre volverá la semana que viene. **3** (*habitual*) habitual, asiduo,-a: *he's one of our regular customers*, es uno de nuestros clientes habituales. **4** (*normal in size*) de tamaño normal: *do you want regular or giant?*, ¿quiere tamaño normal o gigante? **5** US (*pleasant*) simpático,-a; (*honest*) legal. – **6** *fam* cliente *mf* habitual.
● **as regular as clockwork**, con una regularidad cronométrica.
■ **regular army**, ejército regular. ‖ **regular soldier**, soldado profesional.

regularity [regjʊ'lærətɪ] *n* regularidad *f*.

regularize ['regjʊləraɪz] *t* regularizar.

regularly ['regjʊləlɪ] *adv* regularmente, con regularidad.

regulate ['regjʊleɪt] **1** *t* (*control*) regular, controlar; (*adjust*) regular. **2** (*impose rules*) reglamentar, regular.

regulation [regjʊ'leɪʃən] **1** *n* (*control*) regulación *f*. **2** (*rule*) regla.

regulator ['regjʊleɪtəʳ] *n* regulador *m*.

regurgitate [rɪ'gɜːdʒɪteɪt] **1** *t* (*food*) regurgitar. **2** (*information*) repetir maquinalmente.

regurgitation [rɪgɜːdʒɪ'teɪʃən] **1** *n* (*of food*) regurgitación *f*. **2** (*of information*) repetición *f* maquinal.

rehabilitate [riːhə'bɪlɪteɪt] *t* rehabilitar.

rehabilitation [riːhəbɪlɪ'teɪʃən] *n* rehabilitación *f*.
■ **rehabilitation centre**, centro de rehabilitación.

rehash ['riːhæʃ] **1** *n* refrito. – **2** *t* refundir.

rehearsal [rɪ'hɜːsəl] *n* ensayo.

rehearse [rɪ'hɜːs] *t* ensayar.

reheat [rɪ'hiːt] *t* recalentar.

rehouse [riː'haʊz] *t* realojar.

reign [reɪn] **1** *n* reinado. – **2** *i* reinar.

reigning ['reɪnɪŋ] *adj* (*gen*) actual; (*king etc*) reinante.

reimburse [riːɪm'bɜːs] *t* reembolsar.

reimbursement [riːɪm'bɜːsmənt] *n* reembolso.

rein [reɪn] **1** *n* rienda. – **2 reins**, *npl* (*child's*) andadores *mpl*.
◆ **to rein in** *t sep* refrenar.
● **to give free rein to**, dar rienda suelta a. ‖ **to keep a tight rein on**, controlar estrictamente, llevar un estricto control de. ‖ **to take the reins**, tomar las riendas.

reincarnation [riːɪnkɑː'neɪʃən] *n* reencarnación *f*.

reindeer ['reɪndɪəʳ] *n* reno.
▲ *pl* **reindeer** *o* **reindeers**.

reinforce [riːɪn'fɔːs] *t* reforzar.
■ **reinforced concrete**, hormigón *m* armado.

reinforcement [riːɪn'fɔːsmənt] *n* refuerzo.

reinstate [riːɪn'steɪt] *t* (*to job*) readmitir.

reinstatement [riːɪn'steɪtmənt] *n* readmisión *f*.

reinterpret [riːɪn'tɜːprɪt] *t* reinterpretar.

reinterpretation [riːɪntɜːprɪ'teɪʃən] *n* reinterpretación *f*.

reintroduce [riː'ntrədjuːs] *t* reintroducir.

reintroduction [riːɪntrə'dʌkʃən] *n* reintroducción *f*.

reissue [riː'ɪʃuː] **1** *n* (*of book*) reedición *f*; (*of stamp*) nueva emisión *f*. – **2** *t* (*book*) reeditar; (*stamp*) volver a emitir.

reiterate [riː'ɪtəreɪt] *t* reiterar.

reiteration [riːɪtə'reɪʃən] *n* reiteración *f*.

reject ['riːdʒekt] **1** *n* (*thing*) artículo defectuoso; (*person*) marginado,-a. – **2** *t* (*gen*) rechazar, no aceptar; (*in law*) desestimar.
▲ (*verbo*) [rɪ'dʒekt].

rejection [rɪ'dʒekʃən] *n* (*gen*) rechazo; (*negative reply*) respuesta negativa.
● **to meet with rejection**, ser rechazado,-a.

rejoice [rɪ'dʒɔɪs] *i* alegrarse, regocijarse.

rejoicing [rɪ'dʒɔɪsɪŋ] **1** *n* alegría, regocijo. **2** (*public*) fiestas *fpl*.

rejoin[1] [riː'dʒɔɪn] **1** *t* (*put back together*) volver a juntar. **2** (*go back to - group, family*) volver a juntarse con; (- *team*) volver a incorporarse a; (- *army*) volver a alistarse en; (- *road, path*) volver a tomar.

rejoin[2] [rɪ'dʒɔɪn] *t* (*answer*) replicar.

rejoinder [rɪ'dʒɔɪndəʳ] *n* réplica.

rejuvenate [rɪ'dʒuːvəneɪt] *t* rejuvenecer.

rejuvenating [rɪ'dʒuːvəneɪtɪŋ] *adj* rejuvenecedor,-ra.

rejuvenation [rɪdʒuːvə'neɪʃən] *n* rejuvenecimiento *f*.

rekindle [riː'kɪndəl] *t* reavivar.

re-laid [riː'leɪd] *pt & pp* → **re-lay**.

relapse [rɪ'læps] **1** *n* MED recaída. **2** (*crime*) reincidencia. – **3** *i* MED recaer. **4** (*crime*) reincidir.

● **to suffer a relapse,** tener una recaída.
relate [rɪ'leɪt] **1** *t* (*tell*) relatar, contar. **2** (*connect*) relacionar (**to**, con). – **3** *i* (*connect*) relacionarse, estar relacionado: *how does this relate to your work?,* ¿esto, cómo está relacionado con tu trabajo?
related [rɪ'leɪtɪd] **1** *adj* (*connected*) relacionado,-a. **2** (*relatives*) emparentado,-a. **3** (*plants, animals, languages, etc*) de la misma familia.
relation [rɪ'leɪʃən] **1** *n* (*connection*) relación *f.* **2** (*family*) pariente *mf.*
● **in relation to,** con relación a. ‖ **to bear no relation to,** no guardar ninguna relación con.
relationship [rɪ'leɪʃənʃɪp] **1** *n* (*connection*) relación *f.* **2** (*between people*) relaciones *fpl.*
relative ['relətɪv] **1** *adj* relativo,-a. – **2** *n* pariente *mf,* familiar *mf.*
● **relative to,** con relación a.
relatively ['relətɪvlɪ] *adv* relativamente.
relativity [relə'tɪvɪtɪ] *n* relatividad *f.*
relax [rɪ'læks] **1** *t* (*gen*) relajar. **2** (*grip, hold*) aflojar. **3** (*rules, control*) suavizar, relajar. – **4** *i* (*gen*) relajarse. **5** (*grip, hold*) aflojarse.
relaxation [riːlæk'seɪʃən] **1** *n* (*gen*) relajación *f.* **2** (*of grip, hold*) aflojamiento. **3** (*of rules, control*) suavización *f,* relajación *f.* **4** (*rest*) descanso. **5** (*recreation*) esparcimiento.
relaxed [rɪ'lækst] **1** *adj* (*person*) relajado,-a. **2** (*atmosphere*) distendido,-a.
relaxing [rɪ'læksɪŋ] *adj* relajante.
relay ['riːleɪ] **1** *n* relevo. **2** ELEC relé *m.* – **3** *t* (*pass on*) transmitir. **4** RAD TV retransmitir.
■ **relay race,** carrera de relevos. ‖ **relay station,** estación *f* repetidora.
▲ (*verbo*) [rɪ'leɪ].
re-lay [riː'leɪ] **1** *t* (*carpet*) volver a poner. **2** (*cable*) volver a tender.
▲ *pt & pp* **re-laid**, *ger* **re-laying**.
release [rɪ'liːs] **1** *n* (*setting free*) liberación *f,* puesta en libertad. **2** (*relief*) alivio. **3** (*of film*) estreno; (*of record*) lanzamiento. **4** (*of gas etc*) emisión *f.* **5** (*new thing - film*) estreno, novedad *f* cinematográfica; (- *record*) nuevo disco, novedad *f* discográfica. **6** (*statement*) comunicado. – **7** *t* (*set free*) liberar, poner en libertad. **8** (*let go of*) soltar. **9** (*brake etc*) soltar; (*shutter*) disparar. **10** (*bring out - film*) estrenar; (- *record*) sacar. **11** (*gas etc - give out*) emitir; (- *give off*) desprender. **12** (*statement, information*) hacer público, dar a conocer.
● **to release from jail,** excarcelar.
relegate ['relɪgeɪt] *t* relegar.
● **to be relegated,** SP descender.
relegation [relɪ'geɪʃən] **1** *n* relegación *f.* **2** SP descenso.
relent [rɪ'lent] **1** *i* (*person*) ablandarse, ceder. **2** (*storm*) amainar.
relentless [rɪ'lentləs] *adj* implacable, inexorable.
relentlessly [rɪ'lentləslɪ] *adv* implacablemente.
relevance ['reləvəns] **1** *n* (*connection*) relación *f.* **2** (*importance*) relevancia, importancia.
relevant ['reləvənt] **1** *adj* (*connected*) pertinente: *that is not relevant to the question,* eso no tiene nada que ver con la cuestión. **2** (*important*) relevante, importante.
reliability [rɪlaɪə'bɪlɪtɪ] *n* fiabilidad *f.*
reliable [rɪ'laɪəbəl] **1** *adj* (*person*) fiable, de fiar. **2** (*news etc*) fidedigno,-a. **3** (*machine*) fiable.
reliably [rɪ'laɪəblɪ] *adv: I am reliably informed that ...,* fuentes fidedignas me informan que ..., sé de buena tinta que ...

reliance [rɪ'laɪəns] *n* dependencia.
reliant [rɪ'laɪənt] **to be reliant on,** *phr* depender de.
relic ['relɪk] **1** *n* REL reliquia. **2** (*custom*) vestigio.
relief [rɪ'liːf] **1** *n* (*from pain etc*) alivio. **2** (*help*) auxilio, socorro, ayuda. **3** (*person*) relevo. **4** (*lifting of siege*) liberación *f.* **5** GEOG relieve *m.*
● **to breathe a sigh of relief / heave a sigh of relief,** dar un suspiro de alivio. ‖ **to throw into relief,** poner en relieve. ‖ **what a relief!,** ¡qué alivio!
■ **relief fund,** fondo de ayuda. ‖ **relief map,** mapa *m* físico. ‖ **relief road,** vía de descongestión.
relieve [rɪ'liːv] **1** *t* (*lessen*) aliviar: *this will relieve the pain,* esto aliviará el dolor. **2** (*take over from*) relevar. **3** (*help*) socorrer, ayudar. **4** (*lift siege of*) liberar.
● **to relieve sb. of sth.,** (*take away*) llevar; (*steal*) robar, quitar: *let me relieve you of your bags,* déjeme que le lleve las bolsas; *they relieved me of my watch,* me quitaron el reloj; *he was relieved of his duties as director,* lo despidieron de su puesto de director. ‖ **to relieve os.,** hacer sus necesidades.
relieved [rɪ'liːvd] *adj* aliviado,-a.
religion [rɪ'lɪdʒən] *n* religión *f.*
religious [rɪ'lɪdʒəs] *adj* religioso,-a.
religiously [rɪ'lɪdʒəslɪ] *adv* religiosamente.
relinquish [rɪ'lɪŋkwɪʃ] *t* renunciar a.
relish ['relɪʃ] **1** *n* gusto, deleite *m.* **2** CULIN condimento. – **3** *t* disfrutar de: *I don't relish the idea,* no me gusta la idea, no me hace gracia la idea.
relocate [riːləʊ'keɪt] **1** *t* trasladar. – **2** *i/*trasladarse.
relocation [riːləʊ'keɪʃən] *n* traslado.
reluctance [rɪ'lʌktəns] *n* renuencia.
reluctant [rɪ'lʌktənt] *adj* renuente, reacio,-a.
● **to be reluctant to do sth.,** estar poco dispuesto,-a a hacer algo.
rely [rɪ'laɪ]. **1 to rely on,** *t* (*trust*) confiar en, contar con. **2** (*depend on*) depender de.
remade [riː'meɪd] *pt & pp* → **remake.**
remain [rɪ'meɪn] **1** *i* (*stay*) quedarse, permanecer. **2** (*be left*) quedar, sobrar. **3** (*continue*) seguir, continuar, permanecer. – **4 remains,** *npl* restos *mpl.*
● **it only remains for me to ...,** solo me queda ... ‖ **it remains to be seen whether ...,** queda por ver si ..., está por ver si ...
remainder [rɪ'meɪndəʳ] *n* resto.
remaining [rɪ'meɪnɪŋ] *adj* restante.
remake ['riːmeɪk] **1** *n* nueva versión *f.* – **2** *t* hacer una nueva versión de.
▲ (*verbo*) [riː'meɪk], *pt & pp* **remade.**
remand [rɪ'mɑːnd] *n* prisión *f* preventiva.
● **to be on remand,** estar en prisión preventiva. ‖ **to remand sb. in custody,** decretar prisión preventiva contra algn. ‖ **to remand sb. on bail,** poner en libertad bajo fianza.
■ **remand centre / remand home,** *centro penitenciario donde los menores aguardan juicio.*
remark [rɪ'mɑːk] **1** *n* observación *f,* comentario. – **2** *t* (*say*) observar, comentar. **3** (*notice*) advertir.
◆ **to remark on** *t insep* comentar.
remarkable [rɪ'mɑːkəbəl] **1** *adj* (*exceptional*) extraordinario,-a, excepcional. **2** (*odd*) extraño,-a; (*surprising*) sorprendente, curioso,-a.
remarkably [rɪ'mɑːkəblɪ] *adv* extraordinariamente.
remarry [riː'mærɪ] **1** *t* (*priest*) volver a casar; (*bride, groom*) volver a casarse con. – **2** *i* volver a casarse.
remediable [rɪ'miːdɪəbəl] *adj* remediable.
remedial [rɪ'miːdɪəl] **1** *adj* (*classes*) de recuperación. **2** (*treatment*) de rehabilitación.

remedy [ˈremədɪ] **1** *n* remedio. – **2** *t* remediar.

remember [rɪˈmembəʳ] **1** *t* recordar, acordarse de: *I don't remember where I put it,* no me acuerdo de dónde lo puse; *I remember seeing it in the office,* recuerdo haberlo visto en el despacho. **2** (*commemorate*) recordar: *on this day we remember the dead of two world wars,* en este día recordamos los caídos de dos guerras mundiales. – **3** *i* acordarse, recordar.
● **as far as I remember,** que yo recuerde. ‖ **remember me to ...,** recuerdos a ... de mi parte. ‖ **to remember to do sth.,** acordarse de hacer algo.

remembrance [rɪˈmembrəns] **1** *n* conmemoración *f.* **2** (*keepsake*) recuerdo.
● **in remembrance of,** para conmemorar.
■ **Remembrance Day,** *día en que se recuerda a los caídos de las dos guerras mundiales.*

remind [rɪˈmaɪnd] *t* recordar: *remind me to phone her,* recuérdame que la llame; *he reminds me of Richard,* me recuerda a Richard.
● **that reminds me, ...,** a propósito, ..., ahora que me acuerdo, ...

reminder [rɪˈmaɪndəʳ] **1** *n* (*note*) recordatorio. **2** (*of payment due*) aviso. **3** (*keepsake*) recuerdo.

reminisce [remɪˈnɪs] *i* rememorar.

reminiscences [remɪˈnɪsənsɪz] *npl* memorias *fpl.*

reminiscent [remɪˈnɪsənt] *adj* nostálgico,-a.
● **to be reminiscent of,** recordar: *it's reminiscent of basil,* recuerda albahaca.

remiss [rɪˈmɪs] *adj* negligente.

remission [rɪˈmɪʃən] *n* remisión *f.*
● **to go into remission,** entrar en remisión.

remit [rɪˈmɪt] **1** *t* remitir. – **2** *n* competencia, atribuciones *fpl.*
▲ (*sustantivo*) [ˈriːmɪt].

remittance [rɪˈmɪtəns] *n* envío.

remnant [ˈremnənt] **1** *n* resto. **2** (*cloth*) retal *m.* **3** (*of past*) vestigio.

remonstrance [rɪˈmɒnstrəns] *n* protesta.

remonstrate [rɪˈmənstreɪt] *i* protestar, quejarse: *I remonstrated with my brother for not phoning,* me quejé a mi hermano porque no había llamado por teléfono.

remorse [rɪˈmɔːs] *n* remordimiento.

remorseful [rɪˈmɔːsfʊl] *adj* arrepentido,-a.

remorseless [rɪˈmɔːsləs] **1** *adj* (*pitiless*) despiadado,-a. **2** (*inexorable*) implacable.

remote [rɪˈməʊt] **1** *adj* (*far away*) remoto,-a, lejano,-a. **2** (*lonely*) aislado,-a, apartado,-a. **3** (*person*) distante, inaccesible. **4** (*possibility*) remoto,-a, muy pequeño,-a: *his chances of winning are very remote,* sus posibilidades de ganar son muy remotas.
● **not the remotest idea,** ni la más mínima idea.
■ **remote control,** mando a distancia.

remote-controlled [rɪməʊtkənˈtrəʊld] *adj* teledirigido,-a.

remotely [rɪˈməʊtlɪ] *adv* remotamente: *I'm not remotely interested,* no me interesa en lo más mínimo.

remoteness [rɪˈməʊtnəs] **1** *n* (*distance*) lejanía, lo lejano. **2** (*loneliness*) lo aislado, lo apartado.

remould [ˈriːməʊld] *n* neumático recauchutado.

remount [riːˈmaʊnt] **1** *t* (*horse etc*) volver a subir a. **2** (*picture, photo*) volver a montar.

removable [rɪˈmuːvəbəl] *adj* (*gen*) que se puede quitar; (*lining, sleeve*) separable; (*legs, wheels*) desmontable.

removal [rɪˈmuːvəl] **1** *n* (*getting rid of*) eliminación *f*; (*surgically*) extirpación *f.* **2** (*moving*) traslado; (*to another house*) traslado, mudanza. **3** (*from post*) destitución *f.*

■ **removal van,** camión *m* de mudanzas.

remove [rɪˈmuːv] **1** *t* (*get rid of - gen*) quitar, eliminar; (*surgically*) extirpar. **2** (*take out, take off*) quitar. **3** (*move*) trasladar. **4** (*dismiss*) destituir. – **5** *i* (*change houses*) trasladarse.
● **to be far removed from,** tener muy poco que ver con.

remover [rɪˈmuːvəʳ] **1** *n* (*product*) producto que quita algo. **2** (*person*) empleado,-a de mudanzas: *the removers came at 7.30,* los de las mudanzas se presentaron a las 7.30.
■ **hair remover,** depilatorio. ‖ **nail varnish remover,** quitaesmaltes *m.* ‖ **paint remover,** quitapinturas *m.*

remunerate [rɪˈmjuːnəreɪt] *t* remunerar.

remuneration [rɪˈmjuːnəreɪʃən] *t* remuneración *f.*

remunerative [rɪˈmjuːnərətɪv] *adj* remunerativo,-a.

renaissance [rəˈneɪsəns] **1** *n* renacimiento. **2 the Renaissance,** el Renacimiento. – **3 Renaissance,** *adj* renacentista, del Renacimiento.

renal [ˈriːnəl] *adj* renal.

rename [riːˈneɪm] *t* renombrar.

rend [rend] *t* desgarrar.
▲ *pt & pp* **rent.**

render [ˈrendəʳ] **1** *t* (*give*) prestar, dar: *for services rendered to the nation,* por servicios prestados al país. **2** (*make*) hacer, convertir en: *this technology has been rendered obsolete,* esta tecnología ha quedado obsoleta. **3** (*translate*) traducir. **4** (*song*) cantar; (*music*) interpretar. **5** (*wall*) enlucir. **6** (*fat*) derretir.
● **to render an account of,** justificar, presentar una factura por. ‖ **to render homage to,** rendir homenaje a. ‖ **to render thanks to,** dar gracias a.

rendering [ˈrendərɪŋ] **1** *n* (*of song*) interpretación *f.* **2** (*translation*) traducción *f.* **3** (*wall covering*) enlucido.

rendezvous [ˈrɒndɪvuː] **1** *n* cita. **2** (*place*) lugar *m* de reunión. – **3** *i* encontrarse.
▲ (*sustantivo*) *pl* **rendezvous.**

rendition [renˈdɪʃən] *n* interpretación *f.*

renegade [ˈrenɪɡeɪd] *n* renegado,-a.

renege [rɪˈneɪɡ] *i* faltar a su palabra: *they reneged on their promise,* faltaron a su promesa.

renew [rɪˈnjuː] **1** *t* (*gen*) renovar; (*contract, permit, etc*) prorrogar: *he renewed his passport,* renovó su pasaporte. **2** (*start again*) reanudar. **3** (*replace*) sustituir, cambiar.

renewable [rɪˈnjuːəbəl] *adj* (*gen*) renovable; (*contract, permit, etc*) prorrogable.

renewal [rɪˈnjuːəl] **1** *n* renovación *f.* **2** (*new start*) reanudación *f.* **3** (*replacement*) sustitución *f*, cambio.

rennet [ˈrenɪt] *n* cuajo.

renounce [rɪˈnaʊns] *t* renunciar a.

renouncement [rɪˈnaʊnsmənt] *n* renuncia.

renovate [ˈrenəveɪt] *t* (*building*) reformar, renovar.

renovation [renəˈveɪʃən] *n* reforma, renovación *f.*

renown [rɪˈnaʊn] *n* renombre *m*, fama.

renowned [rɪˈnaʊnd] *adj* renombrado,-a, famoso,-a.

rent[1] [rent] **1** *n* (*for flat etc*) alquiler *m.* **2** (*for land*) arriendo. – **3** *t* (*flat*) alquilar: *we rented the flat from the mayor,* alquilamos el piso al alcalde; *she rented her flat to a French couple,* alquiló su piso a una pareja francesa. **4** (*land*) arrendar.
◆ **to rent out** *t sep* alquilar.
● **"for rent",** "se alquila".
■ **rent book,** *libro que da constancia del alquiler pagado y la fecha de pago.* ‖ **rent boy,** chapero.

rent[2] [rent] **1** *pt & pp* → **rend.** – **2** *n* rasgadura.

rental [ˈrentəl] **1** *n* (*for flat etc*) alquiler *m.* **2** (*for land*) arriendo.

rented ['rentɪd] *adj* de alquiler, alquilado,-a.
rent-free [rent'friː] 1 *adj* gratuito. – 2 *adv* gratuitamente, gratis.
renunciation [rɪnʌnsɪ'eɪʃən] *n* renuncia.
reopen [riː'əʊpən] 1 *t* (*open again*) reabrir, volver a abrir. 2 (*restart*) reanudar. – 3 *i* volver a abrir, reabrir.
reopening [riː'əʊpənɪŋ] 1 *n* (*new opening*) reapertura. – 2 *t* (*restart*) reanudación *f*.
reorder [riː'ɔːdəʳ] 1 *t* (*goods*) volver a pedir, pedir de nuevo. 2 (*items in list*) reordenar, volver a ordenar.
reorganization [riːɔːgənaɪ'zeɪʃən] *n* reorganización *f*.
reorganize [riː'ɔːgənaɪz] *t* reorganizar.
reorient [riː'ɔːrɪent] *t* → **reorientate**.
reorientate [riː'ɔːrɪenteɪt] *t* reorientar.
reorientation [riːɔːrɪen'teɪʃən] *n* reorientación *f*.
rep¹ [rep] *n* (*abbr of representative*) representante *mf*.
rep² [rep] *n* (*abbr of repertory*) repertorio.
repaid [riː'peɪd] *pt & pp* → **repay**.
repair [rɪ'peəʳ] 1 *t* reparación *f*. – 2 *t* reparar, arreglar. ● **in good repair / bad repair,** en buen estado / mal estado. ‖ "closed for repairs", "cerrado por obras". ‖ **to be beyond repair,** no tener arreglo.
repairable [rɪ'peərəbəl] *adj* reparable.
reparation [repə'reɪʃən] 1 *n* reparación *f*. – 2 reparations, *npl* POL indemnización *f sing*. ● **to make reparation to sb. for sth.,** indemnizar a algn. por algo.
repartee [repɑː'tiː] *n* (*reply*) respuestas *fpl* ingeniosas; (*ability*) agudeza verbal, ingenio verbal.
repast [rɪ'pɑːst] *n* ágape *m*.
repatriate [riː'pætrɪeɪt] *t* repatriar.
repatriation [riːpætrɪ'eɪʃən] *n* repatriación *f*.
repay [riː'peɪ] *t* devolver: *have they repaid the loan?,* ¿han devuelto el préstamo?; *I'll repay you next month,* te lo devolveré el mes que viene; *they repaid my kindness with treachery,* pagaron mi bondad con traición. ▲ *pt & pp* **repaid,** *ger* **repaying.**
repayable [riː'peɪəbəl] *adj* pagadero,-a.
repayment [riː'peɪmənt] *n* pago.
repeal [rɪ'piːl] 1 *n* abrogación *f*, derogación *f*, revocación *f*. – 2 *t* abrogar, derogar, revocar.
repeat [rɪ'piːt] 1 *n* (*gen*) repetición *f*. 2 (*on television*) reposición *f*. – 3 *t* repetir: *could you repeat the question, please?,* ¿podría repetir la pregunta, por favor? – 4 *i* repetir.
repeatedly [rɪ'piːtɪdlɪ] *adv* repetidamente, repetidas veces.
repel [rɪ'pel] 1 *t* (*gen*) repeler. 2 (*disgust*) repugnar, repeler.
repellent [rɪ'pelənt] 1 *adj* repelente. – 2 *n* (*lotion*) loción *f* anti-insectos; (*stick*) barra anti-insectos; (*spray*) espray *m* anti-insectos.
repent [rɪ'pent] 1 *i* arrepentirse. – 2 *t* arrepentirse de.
repentance [rɪ'pentəns] *n* arrepentimiento.
repentant [rɪ'pentənt] *adj* arrepentido,-a.
repercussion [riːpə'kʌʃən] *n* repercusión *f*.
repertoire ['repətwɑːʳ] *n* repertorio.
repertory ['repətərɪ] *n* repertorio. ■ **repertory company,** compañía de repertorio.
repetition [repə'tɪʃən] *n* repetición *f*.
repetitious [repə'tɪʃəs] *adj* repetitivo,-a.
repetitive [rɪ'petɪtɪv] *adj* repetitivo,-a.
rephrase [riː'freɪz] *t* expresar de otra manera.
replace [rɪ'pleɪs] 1 *t* (*put back*) devolver a su sitio. 2 (*substitute*) reemplazar, sustituir; (*change*) cambiar.

● **to replace the receiver,** colgar el teléfono.
replacement [rɪ'pleɪsmənt] 1 *n* (*act*) sustitución *f*, reemplazo: *his replacement is long overdue,* hace tiempo que debía sustituirse. 2 (*person*) sustituto,-a. 3 (*thing*) otro,-a: *I'll never find a replacement for that vase I broke,* nunca encontraré otro jarrón para sustituir ése que se me rompió. 4 (*spare part*) recambio, pieza de recambio.
replay ['riːpleɪ] 1 *n* (*of film sequence*) repetición *f* de la jugada. 2 (*match*) partido de desempate. – 3 *t* (*tape, film*) volver a poner. 4 (*match*) volver a jugar. ▲ (*verbo*) [riː'pleɪ].
replenish [rɪ'plenɪʃ] 1 *t* (*stocks*) reponer. 2 (*glass etc*) rellenar, llenar de nuevo.
replete [rɪ'pliːt] *adj* repleto,-a.
replica ['replɪkə] *n* réplica.
replicate ['replɪkeɪt] 1 *t* reproducir. – 2 *i* reproducirse.
reply [rɪ'plaɪ] 1 *n* respuesta, contestación *f*: *I knocked for ages, but there was no reply,* estuve llamando durante un buen rato, pero no contestó nadie. – 2 *i* responder (**to,** a), contestar (**to,** a). ● **in reply to,** en respuesta a.
report [rɪ'pɔːt] 1 *n* (*informative document*) informe *m*: *the government commissioned a report on national security,* el gobierno encargó un informe sobre la seguridad nacional. 2 (*school report*) boletín *m* escolar, informe *m* escolar. 3 (*piece of news*) noticia: *reports are coming in of an earthquake in Tibet,* nos están llegando noticias de un terremoto en el Tibet. 4 (*news story*) reportaje *m*: *and now a report on otter breeding in Devon,* y ahora un reportaje sobre la cría de nutrias en Devon. 5 (*rumour*) rumor *m*: *there are reports of a royal divorce,* corren rumores de un divorcio real. 6 (*of gun*) estampido. – 7 *i* (*give information*) informar (**on,** sobre): *the committee will report on its progress each month,* el comité informará de sus progresos cada mes; *he has reported on several wars,* ha hecho reportajes sobre varias guerras. 8 (*go in person*) presentarse, personarse: *I reported to the commanding officer,* me presenté al comandante. – 9 *t* (*say, inform*) decir: *forty people report seeing the UFO,* cuarenta personas dicen haber visto el ovni; *her condition is reported to be serious,* según se informa, su condición es grave. 10 (*to authority*) informar de: *I shall report you to your superiors,* informaré de usted a sus superiores; *he reported the breakdown to the maintenance department,* dio parte de la avería al departamento de mantenimiento. 11 (*to police - crime*) denunciar; (*- accident*) dar parte de: *you should have reported the accident,* debiste dar parte del accidente. ■ **report card,** boletín *m* de notas.
reportedly [rɪ'pɔːtɪdlɪ] *adv* según se informa, según se dice.
reported speech [rɪpɔːtɪd'spiːtʃ] *n* estilo indirecto.
reporter [rɪ'pɔːtəʳ] *n* reportero,-a, periodista *mf*.
repose [rɪ'pəʊz] 1 *n* reposo. – 2 *i* reposar, descansar.
reposession [riːpə'zeʃən] *n* recuperación *f*.
repository [rɪ'pɒzɪtərɪ] *n* depósito.
repossess [riːpə'zes] *t* recuperar, recuperar la posesión de.
reprehensible [reprɪ'hensɪbəl] *adj* reprensible.
represent [reprɪ'zent] *t* representar.
representation [reprɪzen'teɪʃən] *n* representación *f*. ● **to make representations to,** elevar una protesta a, presentar una queja a.
representative [reprɪ'zentətɪv] 1 *adj* representativo,-a. – 2 *n* representante *mf*. 3 US POL diputado,-a.

repress [rɪ'pres] *t* reprimir.
repressed [rɪ'prest] *adj* reprimido,-a.
repression [rɪ'preʃən] *n* represión *f.*
repressive [rɪ'presɪv] *adj* represivo,-a.
reprieve [rɪ'priːv] **1** *n* aplazamiento de la ejecución de una sentencia. **2** *fig* respiro, tregua. – **3** *t* conceder un aplazamiento de la ejecución de una sentencia a.
reprimand ['reprɪmɑːnd] **1** *n* reprimenda, reprensión *f.* – **2** *t* reprender.
reprint ['riːprɪnt] **1** *n* reimpresión *f.* – **2** *t* reimprimir.
▲ (*verbo*) [riː'prɪnt].
reprisal [rɪ'praɪzəl] *n* represalia.
reprise [rɪ'priːz] *n* repetición *f.*
reproach [rɪ'prəʊtʃ] **1** *n* reproche *m.* – **2** *t* reprochar (**for**, -): *she reproached him for his apathy,* le reprochó su desidia.
reproachful [rɪ'prəʊtʃfʊl] *adj* de reproche.
reprobate ['reprəbeɪt] *n* libertino,-a.
reprocess [riː'prəʊses] *t* reprocesar.
reprocessing [riː'prəʊsesɪŋ] *n* reprocesado, reprocesamiento.
reproduce [riːprə'djuːs] **1** *t* reproducir. – **2** *i* reproducirse.
reproduction [riːprə'dʌkʃən] *n* reproducción *f.*
reproductive [riːprə'dʌktɪv] *adj* reproductor,-ra.
reprogram [riː'prəʊgræm] *t* reprogramar.
reproof [rɪ'pruːf] *n* reprobación *f,* reprensión *f.*
reprove [rɪ'pruːv] *t* reprobar, reprender.
reproving [rɪ'pruːvɪŋ] *adj* reprobatorio,-a.
reptile ['reptaɪl] *n* reptil *m.*
reptilian [rep'tɪlɪən] *adj* de los reptiles.
republic [rɪ'pʌblɪk] *n* república.
republican [rɪ'pʌblɪkən] **1** *adj* republicano,-a. – **2** *n* republicano,-a.
repudiate [rɪ'pjuːdɪeɪt] **1** *t* (*reject*) rechazar. **2** (*deny*) negar. **3** (*disown*) repudiar.
repudiation [rɪpjuːdɪ'eɪʃən] **1** *n* (*rejection*) rechazo. **2** (*denial*) negación *f.* **3** (*disowning*) repudio.
repugnance [rɪ'pʌgnəns] *n* repugnancia.
repugnant [rɪ'pʌgnənt] *adj* repugnante.
repulse [rɪ'pʌls] **1** *t* (*reject*) rechazar. **2** (*drive back*) repulsar.
repulsion [rɪ'pʌlʃən] *n* repulsión *f.*
repulsive [rɪ'pʌlsɪv] *adj* repulsivo,-a.
reputable ['repjutəbəl] *adj* acreditado,-a, de confianza.
reputation [repju'teɪʃən] *n* reputación *f,* fama.
● **to have a reputation for ...,** tener fama de ...
repute [rɪ'pjuːt] *n* reputación *f,* fama.
reputed [rɪ'pjuːtɪd] **1** *adj* (*supposed*) presunto,-a, supuesto,-a: *she married him because of his reputed fortune,* se casó con él por su presunta fortuna. **2** (*respected*) respetado,-a, acreditado,-a: *they're a highly reputed firm,* es una empresa muy respetada.
reputedly [rɪ'pjuːtɪdlɪ] *adv* según se dice.
request [rɪ'kwest] **1** *n* solicitud *f,* petición *f: catalogues available on request,* pida su catálogo. **2** (*on radio*) canción *f.* – **3** *t* (*gen*) pedir, solicitar; (*officially*) rogar: *you are requested not to feed the animals,* se ruega no dar comida a los animales. **4** (*on radio*) pedir: *this song has been requested by Michael of Beverley,* esta canción la ha pedido Michael de Beverley.
● **at the request of,** a petición de. ‖ **to make a request for,** pedir.
■ **last request,** último deseo. ‖ **request stop,** parada discrecional.

requiem ['rekwɪem] *n* réquiem *m.*
require [rɪ'kwaɪəʳ] **1** *t* requerir, exigir. **2** (*need*) necesitar, requerir.
● **to be required to do sth.,** estar obligado,-a a hacer algo.
requirement [rɪ'kwaɪəmənt] **1** *n* (*demand*) requisito. **2** (*need*) necesidad *f.*
requisite ['rekwɪzɪt] **1** *adj* requerido,-a, necesario,-a. – **2** *n* requisito.
requisition [rekwɪ'zɪʃən] **1** *n* MIL requisa. – **2** *t* requisar.
reran [riː'ræn] *pt* → **rerun.**
reread [riː'riːd] *t* releer.
▲ *pt & pp* **reread** [riː'red].
rerecord [riːrɪ'kɔːd] *t* volver a grabar.
reroute [riː'ruːt] *t* desviar.
rerun ['riːrʌn] **1** *n* (*repetition*) repetición *f;* (TV *programme*) reposición *f;* (*film*) reestreno. – **2** *t* (*repeat*) repetir; (TV *programme*) reponer; (*film*) reestrenar.
▲ (*verbo*) [riː'rʌn], *pt* **reran,** *pp* **rerun,** *ger* **rerunning.**
resale ['riːseɪl] *n* reventa.
resat [riː'sæt] *pt & pp* → **resit.**
reschedule [riː'ʃedjuːl] *t* (*repayment*) renegociar; (*time*) cambiar la hora de; (*date*) cambiar la fecha de.
rescind [rɪ'sɪnd] *t* rescindir.
rescue ['reskjuː] **1** *n* rescate *m.* – **2** *t* rescatar (**from,** de).
● **to come to sb.'s rescue,** acudir en auxilio de algn.
■ **rescue attempt,** intento de rescate. ‖ **rescue operation,** operación *f* de rescate. ‖ **rescue team,** equipo de salvamento.
rescuer ['reskjʊəʳ] *n* salvador,-ra.
research [rɪ'sɜːtʃ] **1** *n* investigación *f: he's conducting research into bilingualism,* está investigando el bilingüismo; *research shows that ...,* las investigaciones muestran que ... – **2** *i* investigar (**into,** -). – **3** *t* documentar.
■ **research and development,** investigación *f* y desarrollo.
researcher [rɪ'sɜːtʃəʳ] *n* investigador,-ra.
resemblance [rɪ'zembləns] *n* parecido, semejanza.
● **to bear a strong resemblance to,** tener un gran parecido con. ‖ **to bear no resemblance to,** no tener ningún parecido con.
resemble [rɪ'zembəl] *t* parecerse a.
resent [rɪ'zent] *t* ofenderse por, tomarse a mal: *I resent her interference,* me molestan sus injerencias.
resentful [rɪ'zentfʊl] *adj* resentido,-a, ofendido,-a.
resentment [rɪ'zentmənt] *n* resentimiento, rencor *m.*
reservation [rezə'veɪʃən] **1** *n* (*gen*) reserva. **2** (*central*) reservation, (*in road*) mediana.
● **to make a reservation,** hacer una reserva. ‖ **without reservation,** sin reservas.
reserve [rɪ'zɜːv] **1** *n* (*gen*) reserva. – **2** *t* reservar.
● **to reserve the right to do sth.,** reservarse el derecho de hacer algo.
■ **reserve currency,** divisa de reserva. ‖ **reserve price,** precio mínimo. ‖ **reserve team,** equipo de reserva.
reserved [rɪ'zɜːvd] *adj* reservado,-a.
reservist [rɪ'zɜːvɪst] *n* reservista *mf.*
reservoir ['rezəvwɑːʳ] **1** *n* (*lake*) embalse *m.* **2** (*store*) reserva.
reset [riː'set] **1** *t* (*programmer, computer*) reinicializar; (*mechanism*) rearmar. **2** (*clock*) poner en hora. **3** (*bone*) componer. **4** (*book*) recomponer.
▲ *pt & pp* **reset,** *ger* **resetting.**
resettle [riː'setəl] **1** *t* (*person*) reasentar. – **2** *i* (*person*) reasentarse; (*land*) repoblarse.

resettlement [riː'setəlmənt] *n* (*of person*) reasentamiento; (*of land*) repoblación *f*.
reshape [riː'ʃeɪp] *t* dar nueva forma a, reestructurar, rehacer.
reshuffle [riː'ʃʌfəl] **1** *n* (*of cabinet*) remodelación *f*. – **2** *t* (*cabinet*) remodelar. **3** (*cards*) volver a barajar.
reside [rɪ'zaɪd] *i* residir.
residence ['rezɪdəns] *n* residencia.
● **to take up residence**, instalarse.
resident ['rezɪdənt] **1** *adj* residente. – **2** *n* (*gen*) residente *mf*; (*of area*) vecino,-a; (*in hotel*) huésped,-da.
■ **residents' association**, asociación *f* de vecinos.
residential [rezɪ'denʃəl] *adj* residencial.
■ **residential care**, *sistema de cuidados a domicilio para los enfermos*.
residual [rɪ'zɪdjʊəl] *adj* residual.
residue ['rezɪdjuː] *n* residuo.
resign [rɪ'zaɪn] **1** *i* dimitir (**from**, de), presentar la dimisión: *he says he's going to resign,* dice que presentará la dimisión. – **2** *t* dimitir de: *she resigned her post as manager,* dimitió de su puesto de directora.
● **to resign os. to sth.**, resignarse a algo.
resignation [rezɪg'neɪʃən] **1** *n* (*from post*) dimisión *f*. **2** (*acceptance*) resignación *f*.
● **to hand in one's resignation**, presentar la dimisión.
resigned [rɪ'zaɪnd] *adj* resignado,-a.
resilience [rɪ'zɪlɪəns] **1** *n* (*flexibility*) elasticidad *f*. **2** (*strength*) fuerza, resistencia.
resilient [rɪ'zɪlɪənt] **1** *adj* (*flexible*) elástico,-a. **2** (*strong*) fuerte, resistente.
resin ['rezɪn] *n* resina.
resist [rɪ'zɪst] **1** *t* (*not give in to*) resistir, resistirse a: *they resisted the attack for three weeks,* resistieron el ataque durante tres semanas; *I couldn't resist buying it,* no pude resistir la tentación de comprarlo; *I can't resist liqueur chocolates,* no puedo resistirme a los bombones de licor. **2** (*oppose*) oponer resistencia a.
resistance [rɪ'zɪstəns] **1** *n* (*gen*) resistencia. **2** (*opposition*) oposición *f*.
● **to put up resistance**, oponer resistencia. ‖ **to take the line of least resistance**, seguir el camino más fácil.
resistant [rɪ'zɪstənt] *adj* resistente.
resistor [rɪ'zɪstəʳ] *n* resistencia.
resit ['riːsɪt] **1** *n* examen *m* de repesca. – **2** *t* volver a presentarse a.
▲ (*verbo*) [riː'sɪt], *pt & pp* **resat**, *ger* **resitting**.
resolute ['rezəluːt] *adj* resuelto,-a, firme, decidido,-a.
resolutely ['rezəluːtlɪ] *adv* resueltamente.
resolution [rezə'luːʃən] **1** *n* (*gen*) resolución *f*. **2** (*decision*) decisión *f*, determinación *f*.
resolve [rɪ'zɒlv] **1** *n* resolución *f*. – **2** *t* resolver.
resonance ['rezənəns] *n* resonancia.
resonant ['rezənənt] *adj* resonante.
resort [rɪ'zɔːt] **1** *n* (*place*) lugar *m* de vacaciones. **2** (*recourse*) recurso. – **3** *i* recurrir (**to**, a): *it can be achieved without resorting to violence,* se puede conseguir sin recurrir a la violencia.
● **as a last resort**, como último recurso.
■ **tourist resort**, centro turístico.
resound [rɪ'zaʊnd] *i* resonar.
resounding [rɪ'zaʊndɪŋ] **1** *adj* retumbante. **2** *fig* rotundo,-a: *it was a resounding success,* tuvo un éxito clamoroso.
resource [rɪ'zɔːs] *n* recurso.

resourceful [rɪ'zɔːsfʊl] *adj* ingenioso,-a.
respect [rɪ'spekt] **1** *n* (*admiration, consideration*) respeto. **2** (*aspect*) respecto: *in some respects the old one is better,* en algunos sentidos el antiguo está mejor. – **3** *t* respetar.
● **to have no respect for**, no respetar. ‖ **to pay one's respects to sb.**, presentar sus respetos a algn. ‖ **to pay one's last respects to sb.**, rendir el último homenaje a algn., dar el último adiós a algn. ‖ **with all due respect**, con el debido respeto. ‖ **with respect to**, con respecto a.
respectability [rɪspektə'bɪlɪtɪ] *n* respetabilidad *f*.
respectable [rɪ'spektəbəl] **1** *adj* (*gen*) respetable. **2** (*decent*) decente, presentable.
respectably [rɪ'spektəblɪ] *adv* de manera respetable.
respectful [rɪ'spektfʊl] *adj* respetuoso,-a.
respectfully [rɪ'spektfʊlɪ] *adv* respetuosamente.
respecting [rɪ'spektɪŋ] *prep* con respecto a.
respective [rɪ'spektɪv] *adj* respectivo,-a.
respectively [rɪ'spektɪvlɪ] *adv* respectivamente.
respiration [respɪ'reɪʃən] *n* respiración *f*.
respiratory ['respərətərɪ] *adj* respiratorio,-a.
■ **respiratory system**, sistema *m* respiratorio.
respire ['rɪspaɪəʳ] *i* respirar.
respite ['rɪspaɪt] *n* respiro.
resplendent [rɪ'splendənt] *adj* resplandeciente.
respond [rɪ'spɒnd] *i* responder.
response [rɪ'spɒns] **1** *n* (*gen*) respuesta. **2** (*reaction*) reacción *f*. **3** REL responso.
● **in response to**, en respuesta a.
responsibility [rɪspɒnsɪ'bɪlɪtɪ] *n* responsabilidad *f*.
● **to accept responsibility for**, responsabilizarse de. ‖ **to claim responsibility for**, reivindicar.
responsible [rɪ'spɒnsəbəl] **1** *adj* (*gen*) responsable. **2** (*in control*) responsable, encargado,-a: *she's responsible for ordering materials,* ella es la responsable de pedir materiales. **3** (*position*) de responsabilidad: *it's a very responsible job,* es un trabajo de mucha responsabilidad.
responsibly [rɪ'spɒnsəblɪ] *adv* con responsabilidad.
responsive [rɪ'spɒnsɪv] *adj* que reacciona, que muestra interés.
● **to be responsive**, responder: *this car has very responsive steering,* la dirección de este coche responde muy bien.
rest[1] [rest] **1** *n* (*repose*) descanso, reposo: *I need a rest,* necesito descansar. **2** (*peace*) paz *f*, tranquilidad *f*: *they don't give me a moment's rest,* no me dejan tranquilo ni un momento. **3** (*support*) soporte *m*; (*in snooker etc*) diablo; (*for head*) reposacabezas *m*; (*for arms*) apoyabrazos *m*. – **4** *t* (*relax*) descansar: *take off your boots and rest your feet,* quítate las botas y descansa los pies. **5** (*lean*) apoyar: *rest the shotgun against the tree,* apoya la escopeta contra el árbol; *rest your head on my shoulder,* apoya la cabeza en mi hombro. – **6** *i* (*relax*) descansar: *this tablet will help you to rest,* esta pastilla te ayudará a descansar. **7** (*be calm*) quedarse tranquilo,-a: *I shall not rest until I know the answer,* no me quedaré tranquilo hasta que sepa la respuesta. **8** (*depend*) depender (**on**, de): *his whole argument rests on one piece of evidence,* todo su argumento depende de una sola prueba. – **9** *t* (*lean*) apoyar.
● **at rest**, en reposo. ‖ **give it a rest!**, ¡déjalo ya!, ¡basta ya! ‖ **Rest in peace**, Descanse en paz. ‖ **to come to rest**, pararse. ‖ **to lay to rest**, enterrar. ‖ **to set sb.'s mind at rest**, tranquilizar a algn.
■ **rest cure**, cura de reposo. ‖ **rest room**, US servicios

mpl. ‖ **rest home,** *(for the ill)* casa de reposo; *(for the elderly)* asilo.

rest² [rest] **1** *i* quedar: *the matter won't rest here,* el asunto no quedará así; *you may rest assured that ...,* puede tener la seguridad de que ... – **2 the rest,** *n* el resto: *I spent half of the money and put the rest in the bank,* gasté la mitad del dinero y metí el resto en el banco; *we'll eat one trout and freeze the rest,* comeremos una de las truchas y congelaremos las otras; *Tom came, but the rest stayed at home,* vino Tom, pero los demás se quedaron en casa.

◆ **to rest with** *t insep* ser responsabilidad de, corresponder a: *the decision rests with the supreme court,* la decisión corresponde al tribunal supremo; *it rests with you to decide,* te toca a ti decidir.

restart [riː'staːt] **1** *t (activity)* reanudar, reiniciar; *(from the beginning)* volver a empezar. **2** *(machine)* volver a poner en marcha; *(engine)* volver a arrancar.

restate [riː'steɪt] *t* volver a exponer.

restatement [riː'steɪtmənt] *n* repetición *f.*

restaurant ['restərɒnt] *n* restaurante *m.*

■ **restaurant car,** vagón *m* restaurante.

restaurateur [restərə'tɜːʳ] *n* restaurador,-ra.

rested ['restɪd] *adj* descansado,-a.

restful ['restfʊl] *adj* relajante.

resting place ['restɪnpleɪs] *n* última morada.

restitution [restɪ'tjuːʃən] *n* restitución *f.*

● **to make restitution to sb. for sth.,** indemnizar a algn. por algo.

restive ['restɪv] *adj* inquieto,-a.

restless ['restləs] *adj* inquieto,-a.

● **to grow restless,** impacientarse. ‖ **to spend a restless night,** pasar una noche agitada.

restlessly ['restləslɪ] *adv* con impaciencia.

restlessness ['restləsnəs] *n* inquietud *f.*

restock [riː'stɒk] **1** *t (shop etc)* reabastecer. **2** *(lake)* repoblar.

restoration [restə'reɪʃən] **1** *n (gen)* restauración *f.* **2** *(return)* devolución *f.*

restorative [rɪ'stɒrətɪv] **1** *adj* reconstituyente. – **2** *n* reconstituyente *m.*

restore [rɪ'stɔːʳ] **1** *t (gen)* restaurar. **2** *(return)* devolver. **3** *(order)* restablecer.

restorer [rɪ'stɔːrəʳ] **1** *n (person)* restaurador,-ra. **2** *(for hair)* tónico capilar.

restrain [rɪ'streɪn] *t* contener.

● **to restrain os. from doing sth.,** contenerse para no hacer algo. ‖ **to restrain sb. from doing sth.,** impedir que algn. haga algo.

restrained [rɪ'streɪnd] *adj (person)* comedido,-a; *(style)* sobrio,-a.

restraint [rɪ'streɪnt] **1** *n (restriction)* restricción *f,* limitación *f.* **2** *(moderation)* moderación *f.*

restrict [rɪ'strɪkt] *t* restringir, limitar.

● **to restrict os. to sth.,** limitarse a algo.

restricted [rɪ'strɪktɪd] **1** *adj (limited)* restringido,-a, limitado,-a. **2** *(confidential)* confidencial.

restriction [rɪ'strɪkʃən] *n* restricción *f.*

restrictive [rɪ'strɪktɪv] *adj* restrictivo,-a.

restructure [riː'strʌktʃəʳ] *t* reestructurar.

restructuring [riː'strʌktʃərɪn] *n* reestructuración *f.*

result [rɪ'zʌlt] **1** *n* resultado: *the result was a draw,* el resultado fue un empate. **2** *(consequence)* consecuencia: *as a result of his injuries he died,* murió a consecuencia de las heridas. – **3 to result from,** *i* resultar de.

◆ **to result in** *t insep* producir, causar.

resultant [rɪ'zʌltənt] *adj* resultante.

resume [rɪ'zjuːm] **1** *t (begin again)* reanudar. **2** *(take over again)* volver a asumir. – **3** *i* continuar.

● **to resume one's seat,** volver a sentarse.

résumé ['rezjuːmeɪ] **1** *n (summary)* resumen *m.* **2** US *(curriculum vitae)* currículo, currículum vitae *m.*

resumption [rɪ'zʌmpʃən] *n* reanudación *f.*

resurface [riː'sɜːfəs] **1** *t (road)* repavimentar. – **2** *i (return to surface)* volver a la superficie. **3** *(reappear)* volver a surgir.

resurgence [rɪ'sɜːdʒəns] *n* resurgimiento.

resurgent [rɪ'sɜːdʒənt] *adj* renaciente.

resurrect [rezə'rekt] *t* resucitar.

resurrection [rezə'rekʃən] *n* resurrección *f.*

resuscitate [rɪ'sʌsɪteɪt] *t* resucitar, reanimar.

resuscitation [rɪsʌsɪ'teɪʃən] *n* resucitación *f.*

retail ['riːteɪl] **1** *n* venta al detall, venta al por menor. – **2** *t* vender al detall, vender al por menor. – **3** *i* venderse, venderse al por menor: *they retail at around £50,* su precio de venta es de unas cincuenta libras. – **4** *adv* al detall, al por menor.

■ **retail outlet,** punto de venta. ‖ **retail price,** precio de venta al público. ‖ **retail price index,** índice *m* de precios al consumo.

retailer ['riːteɪləʳ] *n* detallista *mf,* minorista *mf.*

retain [rɪ'teɪn] **1** *t (keep - power, moisture)* retener; *(- heat, charge)* conservar. **2** SP *(lead)* mantener; *(title)* revalidar: *Hill retained his lead throughout the race,* Hill mantuvo la primera posición durante toda la carrera. **3** *(possessions)* guardar. **4** *(remember)* retener, recordar. **5** *(hold back)* contener. **6** *(employ)* contratar.

retainer [rɪ'teɪnəʳ] **1** *n (servant)* criado,-a. **2** *(fee)* cuota fija *(que se paga para disponer de los servicios de un profesional).*

retake ['riːteɪk] **1** *n (of scene)* nueva toma. **2** *(exam)* examen *m* de recuperación. – **3** *t (scene)* volver a filmar. **4** *(exam)* volver a presentarse a; *(subject)* volver a examinarse de. **5** *(territory)* retomar.

▲ *(verbo)* [riː'teɪk] *pt* **retook,** *pp* **retaken** [riː'teɪkən].

retaliate [rɪ'tælɪeɪt] *i* tomar represalias (**against,** contra).

retaliation [rɪtælɪ'eɪʃən] *n* represalias *fpl.*

● **in retaliation for,** como represalia por.

retard [rɪ'tɑːd] *t* retardar, retrasar.

retarded [rɪ'tɑːdɪd] *adj* retrasado,-a.

retch [retʃ] *i* tener arcadas, tener náuseas.

retell [riː'tel] *t* volver a contar.

▲ *pt & pp* **retold.**

retention [rɪ'tenʃən] **1** *n (gen)* retención *f.* **2** *(memory)* retentiva.

retentive [rɪ'tentɪv] *adj* retentivo,-a.

rethink [riː'θɪŋk] **1** *t* repensar, reconsiderar, replantearse. – **2** *n* replanteamiento: *I'll have to have a rethink about it,* tendré que repensármelo.

▲ *(verbo) pt & pp* **rethought;** *(sustantivo)* ['riːθɪŋk].

rethought [riː'θɔːt] *pt & pp* → **rethink.**

reticence ['retɪsəns] *n* reticencia, reserva.

reticent ['retɪsənt] *adj* reticente.

retina ['retɪnə] *n* retina.

▲ *pl* **retinas** o **retinae** ['retɪniː].

retinue ['retɪnjuː] *n* séquito.

retire [rɪ'taɪəʳ] **1** *t (from work)* jubilar. – **2** *i (from work)* jubilarse. **3** *(withdraw)* retirarse. **4** *(go to bed)* acostarse.

retired [rɪ'taɪəd] *adj* jubilado,-a.

retirement [rɪ'taɪəmənt] *n* jubilación *f.*

retiring [rɪ'taɪərɪn] **1** *adj (shy)* retraído,-a, tímido,-a. **2** *(from post)* saliente.

retold [riːˈtəʊld] *pt & pp* → **retell**.
retook [riːˈtʊk] *pt* → **retake**.
retort[1] [riˈtɔːt] **1** *n* réplica. − **2** *t* replicar.
retort[2] [riˈtɔːt] *n* CHEM retorta.
retouch [riːtʌtʃ] *t* retocar.
retrace [riˈtreɪs] *t* desandar, volver sobre.
● **to retrace one's steps**, volver sobre sus pasos.
retract [riˈtrækt] **1** *t* (*statement, promise*) retractarse de. **2** (*claws*) retraer. **3** (*undercarriage*) replegar. − **4** *i* (*claws*) retraerse. **5** (*undercarriage*) replegarse.
retractable [riˈtræktəbəl] *adj* (*claws*) retráctil; (*undercarriage*) replegable.
retractile [riˈtræktaɪl] *adj* retráctil.
retraction [riˈtrækʃən] *n* (*gen*) retracción *f*; (*of undercarriage*) repliegue *m*.
retrain [riːˈtreɪn] *t* reciclar.
retraining [riːˈtreɪnɪŋ] *n* reciclaje *m*.
retread [ˈriːtred] **1** *n* neumático recauchutado. − **2** *t* recauchutar.
retreat [riˈtriːt] **1** *n* (*withdrawal*) retirada. **2** (*place*) retiro, refugio. − **3** *i* (*withdraw*) retirarse. **4** (*back down*) dar marcha atrás.
● **to beat a retreat**, batirse en retirada.
retrench [riːˈtrentʃ] *i* reducir gastos, economizar.
retrenchment [riːˈtrentʃmənt] *i* reducción *f* de gastos.
retrial [riːˈtraɪəl] *n* nuevo juicio.
retribution [retrɪˈbjuːʃən] *n* justo castigo.
retrieval [riˈtriːvəl] *n* recuperación *f*.
● **beyond retrieval**, irreparable.
retrieve [riˈtriːv] **1** *t* (*gen*) recuperar. **2** (*situation*) salvar, remediar. **3** (*in hunting*) cobrar.
retriever [riˈtriːvəˈ] *n* perro cobrador.
retroactive [retrəʊˈæktɪv] *adj* retroactivo,-a.
retrograde [ˈretrəgreɪd] *adj* retrógrado,-a.
retrogress [retrəʊˈgres] *i* (*go back*) retroceder; (*worsen*) empeorar.
retrogressive [retrəʊˈgresɪv] *adj* retrógrado,-a.
retrospect [ˈretrəʊspekt] **in retrospect**, *phr* retrospectivamente.
retrospective [retrəˈspektɪv] **1** *adj* (*exhibition etc*) retrospectivo,-a. **2** (*law*) retroactivo,-a.
return [riˈtɜːn] **1** *n* (*coming or going back*) vuelta, regreso: *on his return, he found the safe empty*, a su regreso, encontró la caja vacía. **2** (*giving back*) devolución *f*: *I would appreciate the return of my money*, agradecería que me devolvieran el dinero. **3** SP (*of ball*) devolución *f*; (*of service*) resto. **4** (*reappearance*) reaparición *f*. **5** (*on keyboard*) retorno. **6** (*profit*) beneficio. **7** (*ticket*) billete *m* de ida y vuelta. − **8** *i* (*come back, go back*) volver, regresar: *he's returning tomorrow*, vuelve mañana. **9** (*reappear*) reaparecer. − **10** *t* (*give back*) devolver: *have you returned your room key?*, ¿ha devuelto la llave de su habitación? **11** SP (*ball*) devolver; (*serve*) restar. **12** POL (*elect*) elegir. **13** (*verdict*) pronunciar. **14** (*interest*) producir. − **15** **returns**, *npl* resultados *mpl* electorales.
● **by return of post**, a vuelta de correo. ‖ **in return for**, a cambio de. ‖ **many happy returns (of the day)!**, ¡feliz cumpleaños! ‖ **return to sender**, devuélvase al remitente.
■ **income tax return**, declaración *f* de la renta. ‖ **return match**, partido de vuelta. ‖ **return ticket**, billete *m* de ida y vuelta.
returnable [riˈtɜːnəbəl] *adj* retornable.
reunification [riːjuːnɪfɪˈkeɪʃən] *n* reunificación *f*.
reunify [riːˈjuːnɪfaɪ] *t* reunificar.

reunion [riːˈjuːnɪən] *n* reencuentro.
reunite [riːjuːˈnaɪt] *t* (*parts*) reunir.
● **to be reunited with**, volver a encontrarse con.
reusable [riːˈjuːzəbəl] *adj* reutilizable.
reuse [riːˈjuːz] *t* reutilizar.
rev [rev] **1** *n fam* (*abbr of revolution*) revolución *f*. − **2** *t fam* acelerar. − **3** *i fam* acelerar el motor.
■ **rev counter**, cuentarrevoluciones *m*.
Rev [ˈrevərənd] *abbr* (*Reverend*) Reverendo; (*abbreviation*) R., Rev., Revdo.
revalue [riːˈvæljuː] *t* revalorizar.
revamp [riːˈvæmp] *t* renovar.
Revd [ˈrevərənd] *abbr* (*Reverend*) Reverendo; (*abbreviation*) R., Rev., Revdo.
reveal [riˈviːl] **1** *t* (*make known*) revelar. **2** (*show*) dejar ver, mostrar.
revealing [riˈviːlɪŋ] *adj* revelador,-ra.
reveille [riˈvælɪ] *n* MIL diana.
revel [ˈrevəl] **to revel in**, *phr* disfrutar mucho con, deleitarse en.
▲ *pt & pp revelled* (US *reveled*), *ger revelling* (US *reveling*).
revelation [revəˈleɪʃən] *n* revelación *f*.
reveler [ˈrevələˈ] *n* US juerguista *mf*.
reveller [ˈrevələˈ] *n* juerguista *mf*.
revelry [ˈrevəlrɪ] *n* juerga.
▲ *pl revelries*.
revenge [riˈvendʒ] **1** *n* venganza. − **2** *t* vengar.
● **to revenge os.**, vengarse. ‖ **to take revenge on sb. for sth.**, vengarse de algn. por algo. ‖ **in revenge for**, como venganza por.
revengeful [riˈvendʒfʊl] *adj* vengativo,-a.
revenue [ˈrevənjuː] *n* ingresos *mpl*, renta.
reverberate [riˈvɜːbəreɪt] *t* resonar, retumbar.
reverberation [rɪvɜːbəˈreɪʃən] *n* resonancia, retumbo.
revere [riˈvɪəˈ] *t* reverenciar.
reverence [ˈrevərəns] *n* reverencia.
reverend [ˈrevərənd] **1** *adj* reverendo,-a. − **2** **Reverend**, *n* reverendo.
■ **Reverend Mother**, reverenda madre *f*.
reverent [ˈrevərənt] *adj* reverente.
reverie [ˈrevərɪ] *n* ensueño.
reversal [riˈvɜːsəl] **1** *n* (*in order*) inversión *f*. **2** (*change*) cambio completo. **3** (*setback*) revés *m*.
reverse [riˈvɜːs] **1** *adj* inverso,-a. − **2** *n* (*back - of coin, paper*) reverso; (*- of cloth*) revés *m*. **3** (*of decision*) revocación *f*. **4** AUTO marcha atrás. **5** (*setback*) revés *m*. − **6** *t* (*positions, roles*) invertir. **7** (*decision*) revocar. **8** (*vehicle*) dar marcha atrás a: *you have to reverse the car out of the garage*, tienes que sacar el coche del garaje marcha atrás. − **9** *i* AUTO poner marcha atrás, dar marcha atrás: *she reversed into a wall*, chocó con un muro dando marcha atrás. − **10** **the reverse**, *n* lo contrario: *quite the reverse!*, ¡todo lo contrario!
● **in reverse order**, en orden inverso. ‖ **to reverse the charges**, llamar a cobro revertido.
■ **the reverse side**, (*of coin, paper*) reverso; (*of cloth*) revés *m*.
reversible [riˈvɜːsɪbəl] *adj* reversible.
reversion [riˈvɜːʒən] *n* reversión *f*.
revert [riˈvɜːt] **1** *i* volver (**to**, a). **2** JUR revertir.
review [riˈvjuː] **1** *n* (*magazine, show*) revista. **2** MIL revista. **3** (*examination*) examen *m*. **4** (*of film, book, etc*) crítica. − **5** *t* (*troops*) pasar revista a. **6** (*examine*) examinar. **7** (*film, book, etc*) hacer una crítica de.
● **under review**, bajo revisión.

reviewer [rɪ'vjuːəʳ] n crítico,-a.
revile [rɪ'vaɪl] t injuriar, vilipendiar.
revise [rɪ'vaɪz] 1 t revisar. 2 (correct) corregir. 3 (change) modificar. 4 (examination topic) repasar. – 5 i (for exam) repasar.
revision [rɪ'vɪʒən] 1 n revisión f. 2 (correction) corrección f. 3 (change) modificación f. 4 (for exam) repaso.
revisionism [rɪ'vɪʒənɪzəm] n revisionismo.
revisionist [rɪ'vɪʒənɪst] 1 adj revisionista. – 2 n revisionista mf.
revisit [riː'vɪzɪt] t volver a visitar.
revitalization [riːvaɪtəlaɪ'zeɪʃən] n revitalización f.
revitalize [riː'vaɪtəlaɪz] t revitalizar.
revival [rɪ'vaɪvəl] 1 n (rebirth) renacimiento. 2 (of economy) reactivación f. 3 (of play) reestreno.
revive [rɪ'vaɪv] 1 t reanimar, reavivar, despertar. 2 (economy) reactivar. 3 (play) reestrenar. 4 MED reanimar, hacer volver en sí. – 5 i MED volver en sí.
revoke [rɪ'vəʊk] t revocar.
revolt [rɪ'vəʊlt] 1 n (rising) revuelta, rebelión f. – 2 i (rise) sublevarse (**against**, contra), rebelarse (**against**, contra). – 3 t (disgust) repugnar.
revolting [rɪ'vəʊltɪŋ] adj repugnante, asqueroso,-a.
revolution [revə'luːʃən] n revolución f.
revolutionary [revəl'uːʃənərɪ] 1 adj revolucionario,-a. – 2 n revolucionario,-a.
revolutionize [revə'luːʃənaɪz] t revolucionar.
revolve [rɪ'vɒlv] 1 i girar: the Earth revolves around the Sun, la Tierra gira alrededor del Sol; her whole life revolves around her family, su vida entera gira en torno a su familia. – 2 t hacer girar.
revolver [rɪ'vɒlvəʳ] n revólver m.
revolving [rɪ'vɒlvɪŋ] adj giratorio,-a.
■ revolving door, puerta giratoria.
revue [rɪ'vjuː] n revista.
revulsion [rɪ'vʌlʃən] n revulsión f.
reward [rɪ'wɔːd] 1 n recompensa. – 2 t recompensar.
● as a reward for, en recompensa por.
rewarding [rɪ'wɔːdɪŋ] adj gratificante.
rewind [riː'waɪnd] t rebobinar.
▲ pt & pp rewound.
rewire [riː'waɪəʳ] t cambiar la instalación eléctrica de.
reword [riː'wɜːd] t expresar de otra manera.
rewound [riː'waʊnd] pt & pp → rewind.
rewrite [riː'raɪt] 1 t volver a escribir. – 2 n nueva versión f.
▲ (verbo) pt rewrote [riː'rəʊt], pp rewritten [riː'rɪtən]; (sustantivo) ['riːraɪt].
Reykjavik ['reɪkjəvɪk] n Reykjavik.
rhapsody ['ræpsədɪ] n rapsodia.
● to go into rhapsodies over sth., extasiarse con algo.
rhd ['raɪthænd'draɪv] abbr (right hand drive) (coche) con el volante a la derecha.
rhea [rɪə] n ñandú m.
rheostat ['rɪəstæt] n reóstato.
rhesus ['riːsəs] n rhesus m.
■ rhesus factor, factor m rhesus. || rhesus monkey, macaco rhesus. || rhesus positive / negative, rhesus m positivo / negativo.
rhetoric ['retərɪk] n retórica.
rhetorical [rɪ'tɒrɪkəl] adj retórico,-a.
■ rhetorical question, pregunta retórica.
rheumatic [ruː'mætɪk] adj reumático,-a.
rheumatism ['ruːmətɪzəm] n reumatismo, reuma m, reúma m.

rheumatoid arthritis [ruːmətɔɪdɑː'θraɪtəs] n reumatismo articular.
Rhine [raɪn] n el Rin m.
rhinestone ['raɪnstəʊn] n estrás m.
rhino [raɪ'nɒsərəs] n rinoceronte m.
▲ pl rhino o rhinos.
rhinoceros [raɪ'nɒsərəs] n rinoceronte m.
▲ pl rhinoceroses o rhinoceros.
rhizome ['raɪzəʊm] n rizoma m.
Rhodes [rəʊdʒ] n Rodas.
Rhodesia [rəʊ'diːʃə] n Rhodesia.
Rhodesian [rəʊ'diːʃən] 1 adj rhodesiano,-a. – 2 n rhodesiano,-a.
rhododendron [rəʊdə'dendrən] n rododendro.
rhombus ['rɒmbəs] n rombo.
▲ pl rhombuses o rhombi ['rɒmbaɪ].
Rhône [rəʊn] n el Ródano m.
rhubarb ['ruːbɑːb] n ruibarbo.
rhyme [raɪm] 1 n rima. – 2 i rimar (**with**, con).
● without rhyme or reason, sin ton ni son.
rhythm ['rɪðəm] n ritmo.
rhythmic ['rɪðmɪk] adj rítmico,-a.
rib[1] [rɪb] n costilla.
■ rib cage, caja torácica.
rib[2] [rɪb] t burlarse de.
▲ pt & pp ribbed, ger ribbing.
ribald ['rɪbəld] adj grosero,-a, obsceno,-a.
ribbed [rɪbd] adj acanalado,-a.
ribbon ['rɪbən] 1 n cinta. 2 (for hair) lazo.
riboflavin [raɪbəʊ'fleɪvɪn] n riboflavina.
rice [raɪs] n arroz m.
■ rice field, arrozal m.
rich [rɪtʃ] 1 adj rico,-a. 2 (luxurious) suntuoso,-a, lujoso,-a. 3 (fertile) fértil. 4 (food) fuerte, pesado,-a. 5 (voice) sonoro,-a. – 6 riches, npl riqueza f sing.
richness ['rɪtʃnəs] 1 n (wealth) riqueza; (sumptuousness) suntuosidad f. 2 (fertility) fertilidad f. 3 (of voice) sonoridad f. 4 (of colour) viveza.
rickets ['rɪkɪts] npl raquitismo m sing.
rickety ['rɪkətɪ] 1 adj desvencijado,-a. 2 (unsteady) tambaleante.
ricochet ['rɪkəʃeɪ] 1 n rebote m. – 2 i rebotar.
rid [rɪd] t librar.
● to get rid of, deshacerse de, desembarazarse de.
▲ pt & pp rid o ridded ['rɪdɪd], ger ridding.
riddance ['rɪdəns] n liberación f.
● good riddance!, ¡ya era hora de que se fuera!
ridden ['rɪdən] pp → ride.
riddle ['rɪdəl] 1 n acertijo, adivinanza. 2 (sieve) criba. – 3 t cribar. 4 (with bullets) acribillar.
ride [raɪd] 1 n (on bicycle, horse) paseo. 2 (in car) paseo, vuelta; (on bus, train) viaje m, trayecto. – 3 i (on horse) montar a caballo; (on bicycle) ir en bicicleta. 4 (in vehicle) viajar. – 5 t (horse) montar. 6 (bicycle) montar en, andar en: can you ride a bike?, ¿sabes andar en bici?
◆ to ride on t insep depender de. || to ride out t sep aguantar hasta el final de.
● to take sb. for a ride, tomar el pelo a algn. || to ride the storm, capear el temporal.
▲ (verbo) pt rode, pp ridden, ger riding.
rider ['raɪdəʳ] 1 n (on horse - man) jinete m, (woman) amazona. 2 (on bicycle) ciclista mf. 3 (on motorcycle) motorista mf. 4 (clause) cláusula adicional.
ridge [rɪdʒ] 1 n GEOG cresta. 2 (of roof) caballete m.
ridicule ['rɪdɪkjuːl] 1 n ridículo. – 2 t ridiculizar, poner en ridículo.

ridiculous [rɪˈdɪkjʊləs] *adj* ridículo,-a.
ridiculousness [rɪˈdɪkjʊləsnəs] *n* ridiculez *f*.
riding [ˈraɪdɪŋ] *n* equitación *f*.
rife [raɪf] *adj* abundante.
● **to be rife,** abundar.
riffraff [ˈrɪfræf] *n* chusma.
rifle[1] [ˈraɪfəl] *n* rifle *m*, fusil *m*.
rifle[2] [ˈraɪfəl] *t* hurgar (**through**, en).
rift [rɪft] *n* hendedura, grieta. **2** *fig* ruptura.
rig [rɪg] **1** *n* rig *m*, plataforma petrolífera. **– 2** *t* MAR aparejar. **3** *fam* (*fix*) amañar.
◆ **to rig up** *t sep* improvisar.
▲ *pt & pp* **rigged,** *ger* **rigging.**
rigging [ˈrɪgɪŋ] *n* aparejo, jarcia.
right [raɪt] **1** *adj* (*not left*) derecho,-a: *my right leg hurts,* me duele la pierna derecha; *I've lost my right shoe,* he perdido el zapato del pie derecho. **2** (*correct*) correcto,-a: *that's not the right answer,* ésa no es la respuesta correcta. **3** (*just*) justo,-a: *it's not right that he should suffer,* no es justo que sufra él. **4** (*suitable*) apropiado,-a, adecuado,-a: *I don't think he's the right person for the job,* no creo que sea la persona adecuada para el puesto; *that hat doesn't look right,* ese sombrero no queda bien. **5** *fam* (*total*) auténtico,-a, total: *he's a right idiot,* es un idiota total. **6** *fam* (*okay*) bien: *this watch hasn't been right since it was repaired,* este reloj no ha ido bien desde que lo repararon; *you don't look right,* no tienes buena cara. **– 7** *adv* a la derecha, hacia la derecha: *turn right at the traffic lights,* en el semáforo, gira a la derecha. **8** (*correctly*) bien, correctamente: *you can't do anything right,* no haces nada bien. **9** (*exactly*) justo: *they arrived right after the explosion,* llegaron justo después de la explosión; *it hit him right in the eye,* le dio de lleno en el ojo; *she's right next to you,* está justo a tu lado; *right at the end,* al final de todo. **10** (*well*) bueno, bien: *right, I'm going to bed,* bueno, yo me voy a la cama. **11** *fam* (*very*) muy: *she's not right happy,* no está muy contenta. **– 12** *n* (*not left*) derecha: *in Spain they drive on the right,* en España conducen por la derecha. **13** (*entitlement*) derecho: *you have no right to do that,* no tienes derecho a hacer eso. **– 14** *t* corregir. **15** MAR enderezar.
● **all right!,** ¡bien!, ¡conforme!, ¡vale! ‖ **it serves you** (*him, etc*) **right,** te (*le, etc*) está bien empleado. ‖ **right away,** en seguida. ‖ **to be right,** tener razón: *he's absolutely right,* tiene toda la razón. ‖ **to get it right,** acertar. ‖ **to put right,** arreglar, corregir.
■ **right and wrong,** el bien y el mal. ‖ **right angle,** ángulo recto. ‖ **right of way,** JUR derecho de paso; AUTO prioridad *f*. ‖ **right wing,** POL derecha.
righteous [ˈraɪtʃəs] **1** *adj* recto,-a, justo,-a. **2** (*justified*) justificado,-a.
righteousness [ˈraɪtʃəsnəs] *n* rectitud *f*.
rightful [ˈraɪtfʊl] *adj* legítimo,-a.
rightfully [ˈraɪtfʊlɪ] *adv* legítimamente.
right-hand [ˈraɪthænd] *adj* derecho,-a.
● **right-hand drive,** con el volante a la derecha.
■ **right-hand man,** brazo derecho.
right-handed [raɪtˈhændɪd] *adj* diestro,-a.
rightist [ˈraɪtɪst] **1** *adj* de derechas, derechista. **– 2** *n* derechista *mf*.
rightly [ˈraɪtlɪ] *adv* correctamente.
● **rightly or wrongly,** con razón o sin ella.
right-minded [raɪtˈmaɪndɪd] *adj* recto,-a.
rightness [ˈraɪtnəs] **1** *n* (*honesty*) rectitud *f*, honradez *f*. **2** (*justice*) justicia.

right-wing [ˈraɪtwɪŋ] *adj* POL de derechas, derechista.
right-winger [raɪtˈwɪŋər] *n* derechista *mf*.
rigid [ˈrɪdʒɪd] *adj* rígido,-a.
rigidity [rɪˈdʒɪdɪtɪ] *n* rigidez *f*.
rigmarole [ˈrɪgmərəʊl] *n* lío.
rigor [ˈrɪgər] *n* US → **rigour.**
rigorous [ˈrɪgərəs] *adj* riguroso,-a.
rigorously [ˈrɪgərəslɪ] *adv* con rigor, rigurosamente.
rigour [ˈrɪgər] *n* rigor *m*.
rig-out [ˈrɪgaʊt] *n* atuendo.
rile [raɪl] *t fam* poner nervioso,-a, irritar.
rim [rɪm] **1** *n* (*gen*) borde *m*, canto. **2** (*of wheel*) llanta. **3** (*of spectacles*) montura.
rind [raɪnd] *n* corteza.
ring[1] [rɪŋ] **1** *n* (*for finger*) anillo, sortija. **2** (*hoop*) anilla, aro. **3** (*circle*) círculo; (*of people*) corro; (*of criminals*) red *f*. **4** (*of circus*) pista, arena. **5** (*for boxing*) ring *m*, cuadrilátero; (*for bullfighting*) ruedo. **– 6** *t* (*put a ring on*) anillar. **7** (*draw a ring round*) marcar con un círculo. **8** (*encircle*) rodear.
■ **ring road,** cinturón *m* de ronda.
ring[2] [rɪŋ] **1** *n* (*of bell*) tañido, toque *m*; (*of doorbell*) llamada. **2** (*phonecall*) llamada. **– 3** *i* (*bell*) sonar. **4** (*ears*) zumbar. **– 5** *t* (*call*) llamar. **6** (*bell*) tocar.
◆ **to ring off** *i* colgar. ‖ **to ring out** *i* resonar. ‖ **to ring up** *t sep* llamar por teléfono, telefonear.
▲ *pt* **rang,** *pp* **rung.**
ringing [ˈrɪŋɪŋ] **1** *n* campaneo, repique *m*. **2** (*in ears*) zumbido.
ringleader [ˈrɪŋliːdər] *n* cabecilla *mf*.
ringlet [ˈrɪŋlət] *n* rizo.
ringmaster [ˈrɪŋmɑːstər] *n* maestro de ceremonias.
ringside [ˈrɪŋsaɪd] **1** *n* primera fila. **– 2** *adj* de primera fila: *we had ringside seats,* estuvimos sentados en la primera fila.
ringworm [ˈrɪŋwɜːm] *n* tiña.
rink [rɪŋk] *n* pista de patinaje.
■ **ice rink,** pista de hielo.
rinse [rɪns] **1** *t* (*clothes, hair*) aclarar. **2** (*dishes, mouth*) enjuagar. **– 3** *n* (*of clothes*) aclarado. **4** (*of dishes*) enjuague *m*. **5** (*for hair*) tinte *m*.
riot [ˈraɪət] **1** *n* (*in street*) disturbio. **2** (*in prison*) motín *m*. **– 3** *i* (*in street*) provocar disturbios. **4** (*in prison*) amotinarse.
● **to run riot,** provocar disturbios.
■ **riot police,** policía antidisturbios.
rioter [ˈraɪətər] **1** *n* (*in street*) alborotador,-ra. **2** (*in prison*) amotinado,-a.
riotous [ˈraɪətəs] **1** *adj* (*behaviour*) revoltoso,-a. **2** (*living*) desenfrenado,-a.
rip [rɪp] **1** *n* rasgón *m*, desgarrón *m*. **– 2** *t* rasgar, desgarrar. **– 3** *i* rasgarse, desgarrarse.
◆ **to rip off** *t sep* arrancar. **2** *fam* timar. ‖ **to rip up** *t sep* romper, hacer pedazos.
▲ *pt & pp* **ripped,** *ger* **ripping.**
RIP [ˈɑːraɪˈpiː] *abbr* (*rest in peace, requiescat in pace*) en paz descanse; (*abbreviation*) E.P.D.
ripcord [ˈrɪpkɔːd] *n* cordón *m* de apertura.
ripe [raɪp] *adj* maduro,-a.
● **the time is ripe,** es el momento oportuno.
ripen [ˈraɪpən] **1** *t* madurar. **– 2** *i* madurar.
ripeness [ˈraɪpnəs] *n* madurez *f*.
rip-off [ˈrɪpɒf] *n fam* timo.
riposte [rɪˈpɒst] **1** *n* respuesta, réplica. **– 2** *i* responder, replicar.
ripple [ˈrɪpəl] **1** *n* (*on water*) onda. **2** (*sound*) murmullo. **– 3** *t* rizar. **– 4** *i* rizarse.

rise [raɪz] **1** *n* ascenso, subida. **2** (*increase*) aumento. **3** (*slope*) subida, cuesta. **– 4** *i* ascender, subir. **5** (*increase*) aumentar. **6** (*stand up*) ponerse de pie. **7** (*get up*) levantarse. **8** (*sun*) salir. **9** (*river*) nacer. **10** (*level of river*) crecer. **11** (*mountains*) elevarse.
● **to give rise to,** dar origen a. ‖ **to rise to the occasion,** ponerse a la altura de las circunstancias.
▲ *pt* **rose,** *pp* **risen** ['rɪzən].

risible ['rɪzɪbəl] *adj* ridículo,-a.

rising ['raɪzɪŋ] **1** *n* (*rebellion*) levantamiento. **– 2** *adj* (*prices*) en aumento. **3** (*sun*) naciente. **4** (*land*) en pendiente.
■ **rising damp,** humedad *f*.

risk [rɪsk] **1** *n* riesgo, peligro. **– 2** *t* arriesgar.
● **to put sth. at risk,** poner algo en riesgo. ‖ **to risk doing sth.,** correr el riesgo de hacer algo. ‖ **to risk one's neck,** jugarse el tipo. ‖ **to run a risk,** correr un riesgo. ‖ **to take a risk,** correr un riesgo.

risky ['rɪskɪ] *adj* arriesgado,-a.
▲ *comp* **riskier,** *superl* **riskiest.**

risqué ['rɪskeɪ] *adj* atrevido,-a.

rissole ['rɪsəʊl] *n* croqueta.

rite [raɪt] *n* rito.
■ **last rite,** extremaunción *f*.

ritual ['rɪtjʊəl] **1** *adj* ritual. **– 2** *n* ritual *m*.

ritzy ['rɪtsɪ] *adj* de película.
▲ *comp* **ritzier,** *superl* **ritziest.**

rival ['raɪvəl] **1** *adj* competidor,-ra, rival. **– 2** *n* competidor,-ra, rival *mf*. **– 3** *t* competir con, rivalizar con.

rivalry ['raɪvəlrɪ] *n* rivalidad *f*.
▲ *pl* **rivalries.**

river ['rɪvəʳ] *n* río.

river-bank ['rɪvəbæŋk] *n* ribera, orilla.

river-bed ['rɪvəbed] *n* lecho.

riverside ['rɪvəsaɪd] *n* ribera, orilla.

rivet ['rɪvɪt] **1** *n* remache *m*. **– 2** *t* remachar. **3** *fig* fijar, absorber.
● **to be riveted to the spot,** quedarse clavado,-a.

riveting ['rɪvɪtɪŋ] *adj fig* fascinante.

rly ['reɪlweɪ] *abbr* (*railway*) ferrocarril; (*abbreviation*) FC.

rm [ruːm] *abbr* (*room*) habitación; (*abbreviation*) Hab.

RM [ɑːr'em] *abbr* GB (*Royal Marines*) Infantería Real de Marina.

RN¹ ['ɑːr'en] *abbr* (*Registered Nurse*) enfermera diplomada.

RN² ['ɑːr'en] *abbr* GB (*Royal Navy*) Armada Real.

RNIB ['ɑːr'en'aɪ'biː] *abbr* GB (*Royal National Institute for the Blind*) ≈ Organización Nacional de Ciegos Españoles; (*abbreviation*) ONCE *f*.

roach¹ [rəʊtʃ] *n* (*fish*) pardilla.

roach² [rəʊtʃ] **1** *n* US *fam* cucaracha. **2** *n sl* (*of joint*) colilla de porro.

road [rəʊd] **1** *n* carretera. **2** (*way*) camino.
● **in the road,** *fam* estorbando el paso.
■ **road accident,** accidente *m* de tráfico. ‖**road hog,** conductor,-ra desconsiderado,-a y agresivo,-a. ‖ **road network,** red *f* viaria. ‖ **road safety,** seguridad *f* vial. ‖ **road sign,** señal *f* de tráfico. ‖ **road tax,** impuesto de circulación. ‖ **road works,** obras *fpl*.

roadblock ['rəʊdblɒk] *n* control *m* policial.

roadroller ['rəʊdrəʊləʳ] *n* apisonadora.

roadside ['rəʊdsaɪd] *n* borde *m* de la carretera.

roadway ['rəʊdweɪ] *n* calzada.

roadworthy ['rəʊdwɜːðɪ] *adj* AUTO en buen estado.

roam [rəʊm] **1** *t* vagar por. **– 2** *i* vagar.

roaming ['rəʊmɪŋ] *adj* errante.

roar [rɔːʳ] **1** *n* (*of bull, person*) bramido. **2** (*of lion, sea*) rugido. **3** (*of traffic*) estruendo. **4** (*of crowd*) griterío, clamor *m*. **– 5** *i* (*bull, person*) bramar. **6** (*lion, sea*) rugir.
● **to roar with laughter,** reírse a carcajadas.

roaring ['rɔːrɪŋ] **1** *adj* (*fire*) crepitante. **2** *fig* tremendo,-a, enorme: *it was a roaring success,* tuvo un éxito clamoroso.
● **to do a roaring trade,** hacer un negocio redondo.

roast [rəʊst] **1** *adj* asado,-a. **– 2** *n* asado. **– 3** *t* (*meat*) asar. **4** (*coffee, nuts, etc*) tostar. **– 5** *i* (*meat*) asarse. **6** (*person*) achicharrarse.
■ **roast beef,** rosbif *m*. ‖ **roast potato,** patata al horno.

roasting ['rəʊstɪŋ] *adj* abrasador,-ra.

rob [rɒb] **1** *t* robar: *they robbed my boss,* le robaron a mi jefe; *he was robbed of his money,* le robaron el dinero. **2** (*bank*) atracar; (*shop*) asaltar, robar.
▲ *pt & pp* **robbed,** *ger* **robbing.**

robber ['rɒbəʳ] **1** *n* ladrón,-ona. **2** (*of bank*) atracador,-ra.

robbery ['rɒbərɪ] **1** *n* robo. **2** (*of bank*) atraco.
▲ *pl* **robberies.**

robe [rəʊb] **1** *n* (*dressing gown*) bata. **2** (*ceremonial*) vestidura, toga. **3** (*dress*) vestido.
■ **bath robe,** albornoz *m*.

robin ['rɒbɪn] *n* petirrojo.

robot ['rəʊbɒt] *n* robot *m*.

robotic [rə'bɒtɪk] *adj* robótico,-a.

robotics [rə'bɒtɪks] *n* robótica.

robust [rəʊ'bʌst] *adj* robusto,-a, fuerte.

rock [rɒk] **1** *n* (*gen*) roca. **2** US piedra. **3** MUS rock *m*, música rock. **– 4** *t* (*chair*) mecer. **5** (*baby*) acunar. **6** (*upset*) sacudir, convulsionar. **– 7** *i* (*chair*) mecerse.
● **on the rocks,** arruinado,-a; (*drink*) con hielo. ‖ **rock solid,** sólido,-a como una roca.
■ **rock and roll,** rock and roll *m*, rocanrol *m*. ‖ **rock bottom,** fondo: *we've reached rock bottom,* hemos tocado fondo. ‖ **rock concert,** concierto de rock. ‖ **rock singer,** cantante *mf* de rock. ‖ **the Rock of Gibraltar,** el Peñón *m* de Gibraltar.

rock-bottom [rɒk'bɒtəm] *adj* (*gen*) bajísimo,-a; (*price*) de regalo, regalado,-a, imbatible.

rock-climber ['rɒkklaɪməʳ] *n* escalador,-ra.

rock-climbing ['rɒkklaɪmɪŋ] *n* escalada en roca.

rocker ['rɒkəʳ] **1** *n* (*mechanism*) balancín *m*. **2** (*chair*) mecedora. **3** (*person*) roquero,-a.
● **to be off one's rocker,** *fam* estar mal de la cabeza, estar chiflado,-a.

rockery ['rɒkərɪ] *n* jardín *m* de rocalla.

rocket ['rɒkɪt] **1** *n* (*missile*) cohete *m*. **2** *fam* bronca. **– 3** *i* (*rise*) dispararse.
● **to give sb. a rocket,** echar una bronca a algn.
■ **rocket launcher,** lanzacohetes *m*.

rock-hard [rɒk'hɑːd] *adj* como una piedra.

Rockies ['rɒkɪz] **the Rockies,** *n* las Montañas *fpl* Rocosas.

rocking-chair ['rɒkɪŋtʃeəʳ] *n* mecedora.

rocking-horse ['rɒkɪŋhɔːs] *n* caballo de balancín.

rock'n'roll [rɒkən'rəʊl] *n fam* rock and roll *m*, rocanrol *m*.

rocky ['rɒkɪ] *adj* rocoso,-a.
▲ *comp* **rockier,** *superl* **rockiest.**

rod [rɒd] **1** *n* (*thin*) vara. **2** (*thick*) barra.

rode [rəʊd] *pt* → **ride.**

rodent ['rəʊdənt] *n* roedor *m*.

rodeo ['rəʊdɪəʊ] *n* rodeo.
▲ *pl* **rodeos.**

roe¹ [rəʊ] *n* (*eggs*) hueva.
roe² [rəʊ] *n* (*deer*) corzo,-a.
■ **roe deer**, corzo,-a.
roebuck ['rəʊbʌk] *n* corzo.
rogue [rəʊg] *n* bribón,-ona, pillo,-a.
roguish ['rəʊgɪʃ] *adj* pillo,-a.
role [rəʊl] *n* papel *m*: *what role did you play in all this?*, ¿cuál ha sido tu papel en todo esto?; *she played the role of Titania*, interpretó el papel de Titania.
rôle [rəʊl] *n* → **role**.
role-play ['rəʊlpleɪ] *n* dramatización *f*.
roll [rəʊl] **1** *n* (*gen*) rollo: *a roll of sticky tape*, un rollo de cinta adhesiva. **2** (*of film*) carrete *m*. **3** (*list*) lista. **4** (*of bread*) bollo, panecillo; (*sandwich*) bocadillo: *a cheese roll, please*, un bocadillo de queso, por favor. **5** (*movement*) balanceo. **6** (*of thunder*) fragor *m*; (*of drum*) redoble *m*. – **7** *t* (*ball, coin*) hacer rodar: *he rolled the coin across the table*, hizo rodar la moneda por la mesa. **8** (*flatten*) allanar, apisonar. **9** (*into a ball*) enroscar. **10** (*paper*) enrollar. – **11** *i* (*thunder*) retumbar; (*drum*) redoblar. **12** (*ball, coin*) rodar: *the ball rolled down the hill*, la pelota fue rodando colina abajo. **13** (*into a ball*) enroscarse. **14** (*paper*) enrollarse. **15** (*wallow*) revolcarse.
◆ **to roll by** *i* pasar *lentamente*. ‖ **to roll out** *t sep* (*pastry*) extender, estirar. ‖ **to roll over 1** *t sep* dar la vuelta a. – **2** *i* darse la vuelta. ‖ **to roll up 1** *t sep* enrollar. **2** (*into a ball*) enroscar. – **3** *i* enrollarse. **4** (*into a ball*) enroscarse.
● **roll on ...!**, ¡que venga ...!, ¡ojalá fuese ...!: *roll on Friday!*, ¡ojalá fuese viernes! ‖ **to roll one's eyes**, poner los ojos en blanco. ‖ **to roll up one's sleeves**, arremangarse. ‖ **to call the roll**, pasar lista. ‖ **to be rolling in it**, *fam* estar forrado,-a.
roll-call ['rəʊlkɔːl] **to take roll-call**, *phr* pasar lista.
rolled-up ['rəʊldʌp] *adj* arrollado,-a.
roller ['rəʊlə'] **1** *n* (*for painting*) rodillo. **2** (*wave*) ola grande. **3** (*for hair*) rulo.
■ **roller blind**, persiana enrollable. ‖ **roller coaster**, montaña rusa. ‖ **roller hockey**, hockey *m* sobre patines. ‖ **roller skate**, patín *m* de ruedas. ‖ **roller skating**, patinaje *m* sobre ruedas.
roller-skate ['rəʊləskeɪt] *i* patinar sobre ruedas.
rolling ['rəʊlɪŋ] *adj* ondulante.
■ **rolling stock**, material *m* rodante. ‖ **rolling pin**, rodillo.
roll-neck ['rəʊlnek] **1** *adj* → **roll-necked**. – **2** *n* jersey *m* de cuello vuelto.
roll-necked ['rəʊlnekt] *adj* de cuello vuelto.
roll-on ['rəʊlɒn] *adj* roll-on.
ROM [rɒm] *abbr* (*read-only memory*) memoria sólo de lectura; (*abbreviation*) ROM *f*.
Roman ['rəʊmən] **1** *adj* romano,-a. – **2** *n* romano,-a.
■ **Roman Catholic**, católico,-a. ‖ **Roman Catholicism**, catolicismo. ‖ **Roman numeral**, número romano.
romance [rəʊ'mæns] **1** *n* romance *m*. **2** (*novel*) novela romántica. **3** (*quality*) lo romántico. **4** (*affair*) idilio.
Romance [rəʊ'mæns] *adj* románico,-a.
Romania [ruː'meɪnɪə] *n* Rumanía.
Romanian [ruː'meɪnɪən] **1** *adj* rumano,-a. – **2** *n* (*person*) rumano,-a. **3** (*language*) rumano.
romantic [rəʊ'mæntɪk] *adj* romántico,-a.
romanticism [rəʊ'mæntɪsɪzəm] *n* romanticismo.
romanticize [rəʊ'mæntɪsaɪz] *t* idealizar.
Romany ['rəʊmənɪ] **1** *adj* gitano,-a. – **2** *n* (*persona*) gitano,-a. **3** (*language*) caló *m*.

▲ (*sustantivo*) *pl* **Romanies**.
Rom Cath ['rəʊmən'kæθəlɪk] *abbr* (*Roman Catholic*) católico,-a; (*abbreviation*) Cat.
Rome [rəʊm] *n* Roma.
● **when in Rome, do as the Romans do**, allá donde fueres, haz lo que vieres.
romp [rɒmp] **1** *i* jugar, retozar. – **2** *n* jugueteo.
rompers ['rɒmpəz] *npl* pelele *m sing*.
roof [ruːf] **1** *n* tejado; (*tiled*) techado. **2** (*of mouth*) cielo. **3** (*of car etc*) techo. – **4** *t* techar.
● **to go through the roof**, (*person*) subirse por las paredes; (*prices*) ponerse por las nubes. ‖ **to hit the roof**, subirse por las paredes.
■ **flat roof**, azotea.
roofing ['ruːfɪŋ] *n material para techar*.
■ **roofing tile**, teja.
roofless ['ruːfləs] *adj* sin tejado.
rooftop ['ruːftɒp] *n* tejado.
rook [rʊk] **1** *n* (*bird*) grajo. **2** (*in chess*) torre *f*.
rookery ['rʊkərɪ] *n* colonia de grajos.
▲ *pl* **rookeries**.
rookie ['rʊkɪ] *n fam* novato,-a.
room [ruːm] **1** *n* habitación *f*, AM pieza: *a single room for two nights*, una habitación individual para dos noches. **2** (*space*) espacio, sitio, lugar *m*: *there's no room for a garage*, no hay sitio para un garaje; *make room for me*, hazme sitio; *there's a lot of room for improvement*, podría mejorar mucho. – **3** *i* (*lodge*) alojarse. **4** (*share a room*) compartir una habitación.
■ **room temperature**, temperatura ambiente.
roomful ['ruːmfʊl] *n* habitación *f* llena: *a roomful of screaming kids*, una habitación llena de niños chillando.
rooming-house ['ruːmɪŋhaʊs] *n* US casa de huéspedes.
roommate ['ruːmmeɪt] *n* compañero,-a de habitación.
room-service ['ruːmsɜːvɪs] *n* servicio de habitaciones.
roomy ['ruːmɪ] *adj* espacioso,-a, amplio,-a.
▲ *comp* **roomier**, *superl* **roomiest**.
roost [ruːst] **1** *n* percha. – **2** *i* posarse.
● **to rule the roost**, llevar la batuta.
rooster ['ruːstə'] *n* gallo.
root¹ [ruːt] **1** *n* raíz *f*. – **2** *t* arraigar. – **3** *i* arraigar.
◆ **to root out** *t sep* erradicar.
● **to take root**, arraigar, echar raíces. ‖ **to put down roots**, echar raíces. ‖ **to be rooted to the spot**, quedarse clavado,-a.
■ **root vegetable**, tubérculo.
root² [ruːt] **to root about / root around**, *i* hurgar.
root³ [ruːt] **to root for**, *t* animar, alentar.
rope [rəʊp] **1** *n* (*gen*) cuerda; (*thicker*) soga. – **2** *t* atar (*con cuerdas*), amarrar.
◆ **to rope in** *t sep fam* enganchar. ‖ **to rope off** *t sep* acordonar.
● **to give sb. plenty of rope**, dar a algn. rienda suelta. ‖ **to have sb. on the ropes**, tener a algn. contra las cuerdas. ‖ **to know the ropes**, estar al tanto. ‖ **to learn the ropes**, ponerse al tanto.
ropey ['rəʊpɪ] **1** *adj fam* (*naff*) de pacotilla. **2** *fam* (*ill*) pachucho,-a.
▲ *comp* **ropier**, *superl* **ropiest**.
ropy ['rəʊpɪ] *adj* → **ropey**.
▲ *comp* **ropier**, *superl* **ropiest**.
rosary ['rəʊzərɪ] *n* rosario.
● **to say the rosary**, rezar el rosario.
▲ *pl* **rosaries**.

rose¹ [rəʊz] **1** *n* (*flower*) rosa. **2** (*bush*) rosal *m*. **3** (*colour*) rosa *m*. **4** (*of shower etc*) alcachofa.
■ **rose garden**, rosaleda. ‖ **rose window**, rosetón *m*.

rose² [rəʊz] *pt* → **rise**.

rosé [ˈrəʊzeɪ] *n* vino rosado, rosado.

rosebud [ˈrəʊzbʌd] *n* capullo de rosa.

rose-coloured [ˈrəʊzkʌləd] *adj* de color rosa.
● **to see things through rose-coloured glasses**, ver las cosas de color de rosa.

rosehip [ˈrəʊzhɪp] *n* escaramuza.

rosemary [ˈrəʊzmərɪ] *n* romero.

rosette [rəʊˈzet] *n* escarapela.

rose-water [ˈrəʊzwɔːtəʳ] *n* agua de rosas.

rosewood [ˈrəʊzwʊd] *n* palisandro.

roster [ˈrɒstəʳ] *n* lista.

rostrum [ˈrɒstrəm] *n* tribuna.
▲ *pl* **rostrums** o **rostra** [ˈrɒstrə].

rosy [ˈrəʊzɪ] **1** *adj* (*colour*) rosado,-a, sonrosado,-a. **2** (*future*) prometedor,-ra.
▲ *comp* **rosier**, *superl* **rosiest**.

rot [rɒt] **1** *n* (*decay*) putrefacción *f*. **2** (*rubbish*) tonterías *fpl*. **– 3** *t* pudrir. **– 4** *i* pudrirse.
▲ *pt & pp* **rotted**, *ger* **rotting**.

rota [ˈrəʊtə] *n* lista.

rotary [ˈrəʊtərɪ] *adj* rotatorio,-a.

rotate [rəʊˈteɪt] **1** *t* (*spin*) hacer girar, dar vueltas a. **2** (*alternate*) alternar. **– 3** *i* (*spin*) girar, dar vueltas. **4** (*alternate*) alternarse.

rotating [rəʊˈteɪtɪŋ] *adj* giratorio,-a, rotativo,-a.

rotation [rəʊˈteɪʃən] *n* rotación *f*.

rote [rəʊt] **by rote**, *phr* de memoria.

rotor [ˈrəʊtəʳ] *n* rotor *m*.

rotten [ˈrɒtən] **1** *adj* (*decayed*) podrido,-a. **2** (*tooth*) picado,-a. **3** *fam* (*thing*) malísimo,-a; (*person*) malo,-a.

rotter [ˈrɒtəʳ] *n fam* sinvergüenza *mf*.

rotund [rəˈtʌnd] *adj* (*fat*) regordete,-a.

rouble [ˈruːbəl] *n* rublo.

rouge [ruːʒ] *n* colorete *m*.

rough [rʌf] **1** *adj* (*not smooth*) áspero,-a, basto,-a. **2** (*road*) lleno,-a de baches. **3** (*edge*) desigual. **4** (*terrain*) escabroso,-a. **5** (*sea*) agitado,-a. **6** (*weather*) tempestuoso,-a. **7** (*wine*) áspero,-a. **8** (*rude*) rudo,-a. **9** (*violent*) violento,-a; (*dangerous*) peligroso,-a. **10** (*approximate*) aproximado,-a. **11** *fam* (*bad*) fatal.
● **to have a rough time of it**, pasarlo mal. ‖ **to play rough**, jugar duro. ‖ **to rough it**, vivir sin comodidades. ‖ **to sleep rough**, dormir al raso. ‖ **to take the rough with the smooth**, estar a las duras y a las maduras.
■ **rough copy / rough version**, borrador *m*. ‖ **rough diamond**, diamante *m* en bruto.

roughage [ˈrʌfɪdʒ] *n* fibra.

rough-and-ready [rʌfənˈredɪ] **1** *adj* (*crude*) rudimentario,-a. **2** (*improvised*) improvisado,-a. **3** (*person*) campechano,-a.

roughen [ˈrʌfən] *t* poner áspero,-a.

roughly [ˈrʌflɪ] **1** *adv* (*about*) aproximadamente; (*more or less*) más o menos. **2** (*not gently*) bruscamente.

roughneck [ˈrʌfnek] *n fam* matón *m*.

roughness [ˈrʌfnəs] **1** *n* (*of surface*) aspereza; (*of manner*) brusquedad *f*. **2** (*violence*) violencia.

roughshod [ˈrʌfʃɒd] **to ride roughshod over**, *phr* no hacer el más mínimo caso de, ignorar completamente.

roulette [ruːˈlet] *n* ruleta.
■ **Russian roulette**, ruleta rusa.

round [raʊnd] **1** *adj* redondo,-a: *a round bathtub*, una bañera redonda. **– 2** *n* (*circle*) círculo. **3** (*series*) serie *f*, tanda; (*one of a series*) ronda. **4** sp (*stage of competition*) ronda; (*boxing*) asalto; (*of golf*) partido: *she was knocked out in the first round*, la eliminaron en la primera ronda; *he went three rounds with Murphy*, duró tres asaltos con Murphy. **5** (*of drinks*) ronda. **6** (*of policeman etc*) ronda. **7** (*for gun*) cartucho. **8** (*of bread*) rebanada: *two rounds of toast*, dos tostadas. **– 9** *adv* (*in circles*): *it goes round and round*, da vueltas y vueltas; *she turned round*, se dio la vuelta. **10** (*about*) por ahí: *I've been waiting round all day*, he estado esperando todo el día. **11** (*to somebody's house*) a casa: *they came round to see me*, vinieron a casa a verme; *she invited me round*, me invitó a casa. **– 12** *prep* alrededor de: *they sat round the fire*, se sentaron alrededor del fuego; *he went round the field*, dio la vuelta al campo; *have you lived round here long?*, ¿hace mucho que vives por aquí? **– 13** *t* doblar: *the ship rounded Cape Horn*, el barco dobló el cabo de Hornos.
◆ **to round down** *t sep* redondear (*a la baja*). ‖ **to round off** *t sep* completar, acabar. ‖ **to round on** *t insep* volverse contra. ‖ **to round up** **1** *t sep* (*number*) redondear (*al alza*). **2** (*cattle*) acorralar. **3** (*people*) reunir, juntar.
● **all the year round**, durante todo el año. ‖ **round the clock**, día y noche, las veinticuatro horas. ‖ **round the corner**, a la vuelta de la esquina. ‖ **the other way round**, al revés. ‖ **to have round shoulders**, tener las espaldas cargadas. ‖ **to go round**, dar vueltas.
■ **round table**, mesa redonda. ‖ **round trip**, viaje *m* de ida y vuelta. ‖ **round number**, número redondo.

roundabout [ˈraʊndəbaʊt] **1** *adj* indirecto,-a. **– 2** *n* tiovivo. **3** AUTO rotonda.

rounded [ˈraʊndɪd] *adj* redondeado,-a.

rounders [ˈraʊndəz] *n especie de béisbol infantil.

round-shouldered [raʊndˈʃəʊldəd] *adj* cargado,-a de espaldas.

roundsman [ˈraʊndzmən] *n* repartidor *m*.
▲ *pl* **roundsmen** [ˈraʊndzmən].

round-the-clock [ˈraʊndðəklɒk] *adj* de veinticuatro horas.

round-up [ˈraʊndʌp] **1** *n* (*of cattle*) rodeo. **2** (*by police*) redada. **3** (*summary*) resumen *m*.

rouse [raʊz] **1** *t* (*wake*) despertar. **2** (*provoke*) provocar. **– 3** *i* despertarse.

rousing [ˈraʊzɪŋ] **1** *adj* (*stirring*) apasionante, enardecedor,-ra. **2** (*moving*) conmovedor,-ra.

rout [raʊt] **1** *n* derrota total. **– 2** *t* derrotar *de forma aplastante*.

route [ruːt] **1** *n* ruta, camino, vía. **2** (*of bus*) línea, trayecto. **– 3** *t* mandar. **– 4 Route**, *n* us carretera nacional.

routine [ruːˈtiːn] **1** *n* rutina. **2** (*act*) número. **– 3** *adj* (*monotonous*) rutinario,-a. **4** (*everyday*) de rutina.

rove [rəʊv] *i* vagar, errar.

roving [ˈrəʊvɪŋ] *adj* errante.
● **to have a roving eye**, ser muy ligón,-ona.

row¹ [raʊ] **1** *n* (*fight*) riña, pelea. **2** (*din, racket*) jaleo: *they were making a real row*, armaban un jaleo increíble. **– 3** *i* pelearse.

row² [rəʊ] *n* (*line*) fila, hilera.

row³ [rəʊ] **1** *n* (*in a boat*) paseo en bote, vuelta en bote. **– 2** *i* (*of boat*) remar. **– 3** *t* impeler mediante remos.

rowan [ˈraʊən, ˈrəʊən] *n* serbal *m*.

rowboat [ˈrəʊbəʊt] *n* bote *m* de remos.

rowdy [ˈraʊdɪ] **1** *adj* (*causing trouble*) alborotador,-ra. **2** (*noisy*) ruidoso,-a. **– 3** *n* (*troublemaker*) camorrista *mf*.
▲ (*adjetivo*) *comp* **rowdier**, *superl* **rowdiest**; (*sustantivo*) *pl* **rowdies**.

rower ['rəʊəʳ] *n* remero,-a.
rowing ['rəʊɪŋ] *n* remo.
■ rowing boat, bote *m* de remos.
rowlock ['rɒlək] *n* escálamo, tolete *m*.
royal ['rɔɪəl] 1 *adj* real. - 2 the Royals, *npl* la familia real.
■ royal blue, azul *m* real. ‖ royal flush, escalera real. ‖ Royal Highness, Alteza Real. ‖ royal jelly, jalea real. ‖ the Royal Air Force, *las fuerzas aéreas británicas.* ‖ the Royal Navy, *la marina de guerra británica.*
royalist ['rɔɪəlɪst] 1 *adj* monárquico,-a. - 2 *n* monárquico,-a.
royally ['rɔɪəlɪ] *adv* magníficamente.
royalty ['rɔɪəltɪ] 1 *n* realeza. 2 (*people*) miembros *mpl* de la familia real. - 3 royalties, *npl* (*gen*) royalties *mpl*; (*of writer*) derechos *mpl* de autor.
▲ *pl* royalties.
RRP ['ɑːrˈɑːrˈpiː] *abbr* (**recommended retail price**) precio recomendado de venta al público.
RSC ['ɑːrˈesˈsiː] *abbr* GB (*Royal Shakespearian Company*) compañía real shakesperiana.
RSPB ['ɑːrˈesˈpiːˈbiː] *abbr* GB (*Royal Society for the Protection of Birds*) *sociedad protectora de las aves.*
RSPCA ['ɑːrˈesˈpiːˈsiːˈeɪ] *abbr* GB (*Royal Society for the Prevention of Cruelty to Animals*) ≈ Sociedad Protectora de Animales; (*abbreviation*) SPA.
RSVP ['ɑːrˈesˈviːˈpiː] *abbr* (*répondez s'il vous plaît*) se ruega contestación; (*abbreviation*) S. R. C.
Rt. Hon [raɪtˈɒnərəbəl] *abbr* GB POL (*Right Honourable*) su Señoría.
Rt. Rev [raɪtˈrevərənd] *abbr* REL (*Right Reverend*) muy reverendo,-a.
▲ *También se escribe Rt. Revd.*
rub [rʌb] 1 *n* friega: *give it a quick rub,* frótalo un poquito. - 2 *t* (*gen*) frotar; (*hard*) restregar: *he rubbed his hands together because of the cold,* se frotó las manos por el frío. - 3 *i* rozar.
◆ to rub off 1 *t sep* quitar *frotando.* - 2 *i* quitarse. 3 *fig* pegarse: *his manners seem to have rubbed off on his wife,* parece que sus modales se le han pegado a su mujer. ‖ to rub out 1 *t sep* borrar. - 2 *i* borrarse.
● to rub it in, *fam* insistir. ‖ to rub shoulders with, codearse con. ‖ to rub sb. up the wrong way, sacar de quicio a algn.
▲ *pt & pp rubbed, ger rubbing.*
rubber ['rʌbəʳ] 1 *n* caucho, goma. 2 (*eraser*) goma de borrar. 3 US *fam* goma, preservativo.
■ rubber band, goma elástica. ‖ rubber plant, ficus *m*. ‖ rubber stamp, tampón *m*.
rubbery ['rʌbərɪ] 1 *adj* (*rubber-like*) gomoso,-a. 2 (*chewy*) correoso,-a.
rubbish ['rʌbɪʃ] 1 *n* (*refuse*) basura. 2 *fam* (*thing*) birria, porquería. 3 (*nonsense*) tonterías *fpl*.
■ rubbish bin, cubo de la basura. ‖ rubbish dump, vertedero, basurero.
rubbishy ['rʌbɪʃɪ] *adj fam* de pacotilla.
rubble ['rʌbəl] *n* escombros *mpl*.
rubella [ruːˈbelə] *n* rubéola.
rubicund ['ruːbɪkʌnd] *adj* rubicundo,-a.
ruble ['ruːbəl] *n* → **rouble**.
rubric ['ruːbrɪk] *n* rúbrica.
ruby ['ruːbɪ] *n* rubí *m*.
▲ *pl* rubies.
RUC ['ɑːˈjuːˈsiː] *abbr* GB (*Royal Ulster Constabulary*) *cuerpo de policía de Irlanda del Norte.*
rucksack ['rʌksæk] *n* mochila.
ructions ['rʌkʃənz] *npl fam* follón *m sing.*

rudder ['rʌdəʳ] *n* timón *m*.
rudderless ['rʌdələs] *adj* sin timón.
ruddy ['rʌdɪ] 1 *adj* (*colour*) colorado,-a. 2 GB *fam* maldito,-a.
▲ *comp* ruddier, *superl* ruddiest.
rude [ruːd] 1 *adj* (*person*) maleducado,-a, grosero,-a; (*behaviour*) grosero,-a; (*word*) malsonante. 2 (*improper*) grosero,-a. 3 (*crude*) rudo,-a, tosco,-a.
rudely ['ruːdlɪ] *adv* groseramente.
rudeness ['ruːdnəs] 1 *n* (*of person*) falta de educación; (*of behaviour*) grosería. 2 (*simplicity*) rudeza, tosquedad *f*. 3 (*impropriety*) grosería.
rudiment ['ruːdɪmənt] *n* rudimento.
rudimentary [ruːdɪˈmentrɪ] *adj* rudimentario,-a.
rue[1] [ruː] *t* (*regret*) lamentar, arrepentirse de.
rue[2] [ruː] *n* (*plant*) ruda.
rueful ['ruːfʊl] 1 *adj* (*repentant*) arrepentido,-a. 2 (*sad*) afligido,-a, triste, compungido,-a.
ruefully ['ruːfʊlɪ] *adv* con arrepentimiento.
ruff [rʌf] 1 *n* (*collar*) gorguera. 2 ZOOL collarín *m*.
ruffian ['rʌfɪən] *adj* rufián *m*.
ruffle ['rʌfəl] 1 *n* (*on shirt front*) chorrera. 2 (*on cuffs*) volante *m*. - 3 *t* (*disturb - gen*) agitar; (*- feathers*) erizar; (*- hair*) despeinar, alborotar. 4 (*annoy*) irritar, alterar, hacer perder la calma.
ruffled ['rʌfəld] 1 *adj* (*hair*) despeinado,-a, alborotado,-a; (*feathers*) erizado,-a. 2 (*person*) alterado,-a.
● to get ruffled, alterarse.
rug [rʌg] *n* alfombra, alfombrilla.
● to pull the rug out from under sb.'s feet, fastidiar los planes a algn.
rugby ['rʌgbɪ] *n* rugby *m*.
■ rugby ball, pelota de rugby. ‖ rugby league, rugby *m* a trece. ‖ rugby union, rugby *m* a quince.
rugged ['rʌgɪd] 1 *adj* (*terrain*) escabroso,-a, agreste; (*mountain*) escarpado,-a. 2 (*features*) duro,-a.
rugger ['rʌgəʳ] *n* → **rugby**.
ruin [ruːɪn] 1 *n* ruina: *we saw the ruins of a monastery,* vimos un monasterio en ruinas. - 2 *t* arruinar. 3 (*spoil*) estropear.
● to fall into ruins, caer en la ruina.
ruined ['ruːɪnd] 1 *adj* arruinado,-a. 2 (*spoilt*) estropeado,-a. 3 (*building*) en ruinas.
ruinous ['ruːɪnəs] *adj* ruinoso,-a.
rule [ruːl] 1 *n* (*regulation*) regla, norma. 2 (*control*) dominio. 3 (*of monarch*) reinado; (*by government*) gobierno. 4 (*measure*) regla. - 5 *t* (*govern*) gobernar; (*reign*) reinar en. 6 (*decree*) decretar, dictaminar. 7 (*draw*) trazar. - 8 *i* (*govern*) gobernar; (*reign*) reinar. 9 (*decree*) decretar, dictaminar.
◆ to rule out *t sep* excluir, descartar.
● as a rule, por lo general, por regla general. ‖ to work to rule, hacer una huelga de celo. ‖ as a rule of thumb, como regla general.
ruled [ruːld] *adj* rayado,-a.
ruler ['ruːləʳ] 1 *n* gobernante *mf*, dirigente *mf*. 2 (*monarch*) soberano,-a, monarca *mf*. 3 (*instrument*) regla.
ruling ['ruːlɪŋ] 1 *adj* (*in charge*) dirigente; (*governing*) en el poder; (*reigning*) reinante. - 2 *n* JUR fallo.
rum [rʌm] *n* ron *m*.
■ rum baba, baba al ron.
Rumania [ruːˈmeɪnɪə] *n* → **Romania**.
Rumanian [ruːˈmeɪnɪən] *adj-n* → **Romanian**.
rumble ['rʌmbəl] 1 *n* (*gen*) ruido sordo; (*of thunder*) estruendo; (*of stomach*) borborigmo. - 2 *i* (*gen*) hacer un

ruido sordo; (*thunder*) retumbar; (*stomach*) hacer ruidos, sonar.

rumbling [ˈrʌməlɪŋ] **1** *n* (*gen*) ruido sordo; (*of thunder*) retumbos *mpl*; (*of stomach*) borborigmos *mpl*. – **2 rumblings,** *npl* (*of discontent*) indicios *mpl*: *there were rumblings of discontent,* hubo muestras de descontento.

ruminant [ˈruːmɪnənt] **1** *adj* rumiante. – **2** *n* rumiante *m.*

ruminate [ˈruːmɪneɪt] **1** *i* (*animal*) rumiar. **2** (*person*) rumiar, cavilar.

rummage [ˈrʌmɪdʒ] *i* revolver (*buscando*): *I found this while I was rummaging through her drawers,* encontré esto mientras revolvía entre sus cajones.

rummy [ˈrʌmɪ] *n* rummy *m.*

rumor [ˈruːmə^r] *t-n* US → **rumour**.

rumour [ˈruːmə^r] **1** *n* rumor *m.* – **2** *t* rumorear.
● it is rumoured that ..., corre el rumor de que ...

rump [rʌmp] **1** *n* (*of animal*) ancas *fpl*; (*of horse*) grupa; (*of cow*) cadera. **2** (*of person*) trasero.
■ **rump steak,** filete *m* de cadera.

rumple [ˈrʌmpəl] **1** *t* arrugar. **2** (*hair*) despeinar.

rumpus [ˈrʌmpəs] *n fam* jaleo, follón *m.*
● **to kick up a rumpus,** armar un jaleo.
■ **rumpus room,** US cuarto de los niños.

run [rʌn] **1** *n* carrera. **2** (*trip*) viaje *m*; (*for pleasure*) paseo: *we went for a run in the car,* dimos una vuelta en el coche. **3** (*sequence*) racha: *I've had a run of bad luck,* he tenido una racha de mala suerte. **4** (*ski run*) pista. **5** (*in stocking*) carrera. **6** (*demand*) gran demanda: *there's been a run on olive oil,* ha habido una gran demanda de aceite de oliva; *there was a run on the lira,* la lira sufrió una gran presión. **7** THEAT permanencia en cartel: *the play closed after an eight-month run,* la obra dejó de representarse después de ocho meses en cartelera. **8** (*in cricket*) carrera: *he scored 50 runs,* marcó 50 carreras. **9** (*in printing*) tirada. **10** (*at cards*) escalera. – **11** *i* (*gen*) correr: *run faster!,* ¡corre más deprisa!; *I ran up the hill,* subí corriendo la colina. **12** (*flow*) correr: *a stream runs through the garden,* corre un arroyo por el jardín; *blood ran down his leg,* la sangre le corría por la pierna; *don't leave the tap running,* no dejes el grifo abierto; *your nose is running,* tienes mocos. **13** (*operate*) funcionar: *it runs on petrol,* funciona con gasolina; *the engine's running,* el motor está en marcha. **14** (*trains, buses*) circular: *this train doesn't run on Sundays,* este tren no circula los domingos; *buses run every half hour,* hay un autobús cada media hora; *the buses are running late,* los autobuses llevan retraso. **15** (*in election*) presentarse: *the general has decided not to run for president,* el general ha decidido no presentarse como candidato para la presidencia. **16** (*play*) estar en cartel; (*contract etc*) seguir vigente: *this play ran for four years on Broadway,* esta obra estuvo en cartel durante cuatro años en Broadway; *my contract runs until October,* mi contrato sigue vigente hasta octubre. **17** (*colour*) correrse: *I washed it and the colours ran,* lo lavé y se destiñó, lo lavé y los colores se corrieron. – **18** *t* (*gen*) correr: *I ran more than a mile,* corrí más de una milla. **19** (*race*) correr en, participar en: *she ran the 100 metres hurdles,* corrió en la carrera de los cien metros vallas. **20** (*take by car*) llevar, acompañar: *could you run me to school?,* ¿me podrías acompañar al colegio en coche? **21** (*manage*) llevar, dirigir, regentar: *she runs a café near the cinema,* lleva una cafetería cerca del cine. **22** (*organize*) organizar, montar: *we're running a competition,* organizamos una competición. **23** (*operate*) hacer funcionar. **24** (*pass, submit to*) pasar: *he ran his fingers through her hair,*

pasó sus dedos por su cabello; *I ran my eye over the names,* eché un vistazo a los nombres; *have you run this data through the computer?,* ¿has pasado estos datos por el ordenador?; *we'll run a check on it,* lo comprobaremos; *they ran several tests on me,* me sometieron a varias pruebas. **25** (*publish*) publicar: *they ran a series of articles on wine,* publicaron una serie de artículos sobre el vino. **26** (*water*) dejar correr: *run the tap until the water gets hot,* deja correr el agua hasta que salga caliente.
◆ **to run across 1** *t insep* (*cross over*) cruzar corriendo. **2** (*find*) encontrar, tropezar con. ‖ **to run after** *t insep* perseguir. ‖ **to run along** *i* irse. ‖ **to run away** *i* irse corriendo, escaparse. ‖ **to run away with** *t insep* escaparse con: *he ran away with my daughter,* se fugó con mi hija; *don't run away with the idea that ...,* no te vayas a creer que ...; *you let your imagination run away with you,* te dejas llevar por la imaginación. ‖ **to run down 1** *t sep* (*knock down*) atropellar: *he was run down by a tram,* lo atropelló un tranvía. **2** (*criticize*) criticar: *she runs everybody down,* critica a todo el mundo. **3** (*battery*) agotar. – **4** *t insep* bajar corriendo. – **5** *i* bajar corriendo. **6** (*battery*) agotarse. **7** (*clock*) pararse: *my watch has run down,* se me ha parado el reloj. ‖ **to run in 1** *t sep* (*car*) rodar. **2** (*criminal*) detener. – **3** *i* entrar corriendo. ‖ **to run into 1** *t insep* entrar corriendo en. **2** (*car*) chocar con. **3** (*meet*) tropezar con. ‖ **to run off 1** *t sep* (*print*) imprimir. – **2** *i* irse corriendo. ‖ **to run off with** *t insep* escaparse con, llevarse. ‖ **to run out 1** *i* salir corriendo. **2** (*be used up - gen*) acabarse; (*- stocks*) agotarse: *time is running out for us,* se nos está acabando el tiempo; *I've run out of sugar,* se nos ha acabado el azúcar. **3** (*contract*) caducar. ‖ **to run over 1** *t sep* (*knock down*) atropellar. – **2** *i* (*overflow*) rebosar. **3** (*spill*) derramar. ‖ **to run through 1** *t insep* (*rehearse*) ensayar; (*do again*) repasar. **2** (*read*) echar un vistazo a. ‖ **to run up 1** *t insep* (*ascend*) subir corriendo. – **2** *t sep* (*debts*) acumular. **3** (*flag*) izar. – **4** *i* (*ascend*) subir corriendo.
● **in the long run,** a la larga. ‖ **to be on the run,** haber fugado, haber huido. ‖ **to break into a run,** echarse a correr. ‖ **to go for a run,** ir a correr. ‖ **to have the run of sth.,** tener algo a su entera disposición. ‖ **to run in the family,** venir de familia. ‖ **to run short of sth.,** ir mal de algo: *we're running short of money,* se nos está acabando el dinero.
■ **a run for one's money:** *he's had a good run for his money,* no le ha ido mal, no se puede quejar; *she won the match, but I gave her a run for her money,* ella ganó el partido, pero la hice trabajar.
▲ *pt* ran, *pp* run, *ger* running.

runabout [ˈrʌnəbaʊt] *n* coche *m* pequeño.

runaway [ˈrʌnəweɪ] **1** *n* (*prisoner*) fugitivo,-a; (*horse*) desbocado,-a. **2** (*out of control*) incontrolado,-a; (*inflation*) galopante. **3** (*tremendous*) aplastante; (*success*) clamoroso,-a. – **4** *n* (*adult*) fugitivo,-a; (*youngster*) joven fugado,-a.

rundown [ˈrʌndaʊn] *n* resumen *m.*
● **to give sb. a rundown on sth.,** poner a algn. al corriente de algo.

run-down [rʌnˈdaʊn] **1** *adj* (*person*) agotado,-a. **2** (*area*) venido,-a a menos, decaído,-a.

rung¹ [rʌŋ] *pp* → **ring**.

rung² [rʌŋ] *n* escalón *m.*

run-in [ˈrʌnɪn] *n fam* roce *m.*

runner [ˈrʌnə^r] **1** *n* corredor,-ra. **2** (*of sledge*) patín *m*; (*of skate*) cuchilla. **3** (*carpet*) alfombrilla. **4** (*on furniture*) tapete *m.*

runner-up [rʌnər'ʌp] *n* subcampeón,-ona.
▲ *pl* *runners-up.*
running ['rʌnɪŋ] **1** *n* (*action*) el correr; (*sport*) atletismo: *running is good for you,* el correr es bueno para la salud. **2** (*management*) dirección *f.* – **3** *adj* (*water*) corriente. **4** (*continuous*) contínuo,-a. – **5** *adv* seguido,-a: *five days running,* cinco días seguidos.
● **to be in the running,** tener posibilidades de ganar. ‖ **to be out of the running,** no tener posibilidades de ganar.
■ **running board,** estribo. ‖ **running commentary,** comentario en directo. ‖ **running costs,** (*of car*) gastos *mpl* de mantenimiento; (*of company*) gastos *mpl* de operación. ‖ **running mate,** US POL candidato,-a a la vicepresidencia. ‖ **running shoes,** zapatillas *fpl* para correr. ‖ **running track,** pista de atletismo.
runny ['rʌnɪ] **1** *adj* (*liquid*) líquido,-a; (*egg*) poco hecho. **2** (*nose*) que moquea.
▲ *comp* **runnier,** *superl* **runniest.**
run-off ['rʌnɒf] *n* (*match*) partido de desempate; (*race*) carrera de desempate.
run-of-the-mill [rʌnəvðə'mɪl] *adj* corriente y moliente.
runproof ['rʌnpruːf] *adj* indesmallable.
runt [rʌnt] **1** *n* (*animal*) animal más pequeño de una camada. **2** *fam* (*person*) piltrafa.
run-through ['rʌnθruː] *n* ensayo.
run-up ['rʌnʌp] **1** *n* (*period before*) etapa preliminar: *the run-up to the elections,* el periodo pre-electoral. **2** (*before jumping etc*) carrerilla: *he took a run-up and leapt over the fence,* tomó carrerilla y saltó la valla.
runway ['rʌnweɪ] *n* pista de aterrizaje.
rupee [ruː'piː] *n* rupia.
rupture ['rʌptʃə'] **1** *n* (*hernia*) hernia. **2** (*breakage*) rotura; (*burst*) reventón *m.* **3** *fig* ruptura. – **4** *t* (*break*) romper; (*burst*) reventar. – **5** *i* (*break*) romperse; (*burst*) reventarse.
● **to rupture os.,** herniarse.
rural ['rʊərəl] *adj* rural.
ruse [ruːz] *n* ardid *m,* astucia.
rush¹ [rʌʃ] **1** *n* prisa: *I'm in no rush,* no tengo prisa; *the train doesn't leave until six, there's no rush,* el tren no sale hasta las seis, no hay prisa. **2** (*movement*) movimiento impetuoso, avance *m* impetuoso: *she made a rush for the door,* se precipitó hacia la puerta. – **3** *t* (*hurry - person*) apresurar, dar prisa a, meter prisa a; (- *job etc*) hacer demasiado deprisa: *don't rush me,* no me apresures; *if you rush your work, you'll make mistakes,* si trabajas demasiado deprisa, cometerás errores; *she got up late and had to rush her breakfast,* se levantó tarde y tuvo que desayunar corriendo. **4** (*send quickly*) enviar urgentemente, mandar urgentemente; (*take quickly*) llevar rápidamente: *medical supplies were*

rushed to the war zone, material médico fue enviado urgentemente a la zona de guerra; *they rushed her to hospital,* la llevaron urgentemente al hospital. **5** (*attack*) abalanzarse sobre, arremeter contra. **6** *fam* cobrar: *how much did they rush you for that?,* ¿cuánto te cobraron por eso? – **7** *i* ir deprisa, precipitarse, apresurarse: *don't rush!,* ¡no vayas tan deprisa!; *she rushed out of the room,* salió corriendo de la sala; *he rushed to help us,* se apresuró a ayudarnos; *we rushed through our lunch,* comimos a toda prisa.
◆ **to rush in** *i* entrar corriendo. ‖ **to rush out** *i* salir corriendo.
● **to be rushed off one's feet,** ir de culo. ‖ **to rush into sth.,** hacer algo precipitadamente: *you should never rush into marriage,* no debes casarte sin pensarlo muy bien.
■ **rush job,** trabajo urgente: *it was a bit of a rush job, I'm afraid,* me temo que lo hice deprisa y corriendo.
rush² [rʌʃ] *n* (*plant*) junco.
rusk [rʌsk] *n* galleta.
russet ['rʌsɪt] **1** *n* marrón *m* rojizo. – **2** *adj* de color marrón rojizo.
Russia ['rʌʃə] *n* Rusia.
Russian ['rʌʃən] **1** *adj* ruso,-a. – **2** *n* (*person*) ruso,-a. **3** (*language*) ruso.
rust [rʌst] **1** *n* óxido, herrumbre *m.* – **2** *t* oxidar. – **3** *i* oxidar.
rustic ['rʌstɪk] *adj* rústico,-a.
rustle ['rʌsəl] **1** *n* (*of leaves etc*) crujido. – **2** *t* (*leaves etc*) hacer crujir. – **3** *i* (*leaves etc*) crujir. – **4** *t* (*cattle*) robar. – **5** *i* (*cattle*) robar ganado.
rustler ['rʌsələ'] *n* cuatrero,-a.
rustling ['rʌsəlɪŋ] **1** *n* (*noise*) crujido. **2** (*theft*) robo de ganado.
rustproof ['rʌstpruːf] *adj* inoxidable.
rusty ['rʌstɪ] **1** *adj* (*metal*) oxidado,-a. **2** *fig* oxidado,-a, olvidado,-a.
▲ *comp* **rustier,** *superl* **rustiest.**
rut [rʌt] **1** *n* surco. **2** ZOOL celo.
● **to be in a rut,** ser esclavo,-a de la rutina. ‖ **to get out of a rut,** salir de la rutina.
ruthless ['ruːθləs] *adj* cruel, despiadado,-a.
ruthlessly ['ruːθləslɪ] *adj* despiadadamente, sin piedad.
ruthlessness ['ruːθləsnəs] *n* crueldad *f.*
Rwanda [rʊ'ændə] *n* Ruanda.
Rwandan [rʊ'ændən] **1** *adj* ruandés,-esa. – **2** *n* ruandés,-esa.
rye [raɪ] *n* centeno.
■ **rye bread,** pan *m* de centeno. ‖ **rye grass,** ballica.

S

S, s [es] *n (the letter)* S, s *f.*
S [sauθ] *abbr (south)* sur *m; (abbreviation)* S.
Sabbath ['sæbəθ] *n (Christian)* domingo; *(Jewish)* sábado.
sabbatical [sə'bætɪkəl] **1** *n (year)* año sabático; *(term)* trimestre *m* sabático. **– 2** *adj* sabático,-a.
● **to be on sabbatical,** tener un año sabático.
saber ['seɪbəʳ] *n* US → **sabre.**
sable ['seɪbəl] **1** *n (animal, fur)* marta cebellina. **– 2** *adj (coat)* de marta cebellina. **3** *fml (colour)* negro,-a.
sabotage ['sæbətɑːʒ] **1** *n* sabotaje *m.* **– 2** *t* sabotear.
saboteur [sæbə'tɜːʳ] *n* saboteador,-ra.
sabre ['seɪbəʳ] *n* sable *m.*
saccharin ['sækərɪn] *n* sacarina.
saccharine ['sækəriːn] **1** *adj (very sweet)* muy dulce. **2** *fig* empalagoso,-a, azucarado,-a.
sachet ['sæʃeɪ] *n* bolsita, sobrecito.
sack¹ [sæk] **1** *n (bag)* saco. **2** US *fam (bed)* catre *m*, sobre *m*, piltra. **– 3** *t* GB *fam* despedir a, echar a.
◆ **to sack out** *i* US irse al catre, irse al sobre.
● **to get the sack,** ser despedido,-a. ‖ **to give sb. the sack,** despedir a algn., echar del trabajo a algn. ‖ **to hit the sack,** irse al catre, irse al sobre.
sack² [sæk] **1** *t* MIL saquear. **– 2** *n* MIL saqueo.
sackcloth ['sækklɒθ] *n* arpillera.
● **in sackcloth and ashes,** con túnica de penitente.
sackful ['sækful] *n* saco.
● **by the sackful,** a montones.
sacking ['sækɪŋ] **1** *n (material)* arpillera. **2** *(dismissal)* despido.
sacrament ['sækrəmənt] *n* sacramento.
● **to receive the sacrament,** comulgar.
■ **the Blessed Sacrament / the Holy Sacrament,** el Santísimo Sacramento.
sacramental [sækrə'mentəl] *adj* sacramental.
sacred ['seɪkrəd] *adj* sagrado,-a, sacro,-a.
● **is nothing sacred?,** ¿no se respeta nada? ‖ **sacred to sb./sth.,** dedicado,-a a algn./algo.
■ **sacred cow,** vaca sagrada. ‖ **sacred music,** música religiosa.
sacredness ['seɪkrədnəs] *n* carácter *m* sagrado, santidad *f.*
sacrifice ['sækrɪfaɪs] **1** *n (gen)* sacrificio. **2** *(offering)* ofrenda. **– 3** *t (offer as sacrifice)* sacrificar. **4** *(give up)* sacrificar, renunciar a.
● **to make sacrifices,** hacer sacrificios, sacrificarse.
sacrificial [sækrɪ'fɪʃəl] *adj* de sacrificio.
● **sacrificial lamb,** chivo expiatorio.
sacrilege ['sækrɪlɪdʒ] *n* sacrilegio.
sacrilegious [sækrɪ'lɪdʒəs] *adj* sacrílego,-a.
sacristan ['sækrɪstən] *n* sacristán,-ana.
sacristy ['sækrɪstɪ] *n* sacristía.
▲ *pl* **sacristies.**
sacrosanct ['sækrəusæŋkt] *adj* sacrosanto,-a.

sacrum ['sækrəm] *n* ANAT sacro.
▲ *pl* **sacra.**
sad [sæd] **1** *adj (unhappy)* triste: *you look very sad,* estás muy triste; *we'll be sad to see you go,* será una pena perderte; *I was sad to hear about your father's death,* sentí mucho saber lo de la muerte de tu padre. **2** *(deplorable)* lamentable: *it's a sad state of affairs,* es una situación lamentable.
● **sad to say,** por desgracia, desgraciadamente. ‖ **to make sb. sad,** entristecer a algn., dar pena a algn.
▲ *comp* **sadder,** *superl* **saddest.**
sadden ['sædən] **1** *t* entristecer. **– 2** *i* entristecerse.
saddle ['sædəl] **1** *n (for horse)* silla (de montar); *(of bicycle etc)* sillín *m.* **– 2** *t* ensillar (**up,** -). **– 3** *i* ensillar (**up,** -).
◆ **to saddle with** *t sep* cargar con.
● **to be in the saddle,** llevar las riendas.
saddlebag ['sædəlbæg] *n* alforja.
saddler ['sædələʳ] *n* guarnicionero,-a.
saddlery ['sædələrɪ] **1** *n (equipment)* guarniciones *fpl.* **2** *(workshop)* guarnicionería.
sadism ['seɪdɪzəm] *n* sadismo.
sadist ['seɪdɪst] *n* sádico,-a.
sadistic [sə'dɪstɪk] *adj* sádico,-a.
sadly ['sædlɪ] **1** *adv (in sad manner)* tristemente. **2** *(regrettably)* lamentablemente. **3** *(unfortunately)* desgraciadamente.
● **to be sadly mistaken,** estar muy equivocado,-a.
sadness ['sædnəs] *n* tristeza.
sadomasochism [seɪdəu'mæsəkɪzəm] *n* sadomasoquismo.
safari [sə'fɑːrɪ] *n* safari *m.*
● **to be on safari,** estar de safari.
■ **safari jacket,** sahariana. ‖ **safari park,** safari *m*, reserva.
safe [seɪf] **1** *adj (gen)* seguro,-a; *(out of danger)* a salvo, fuera de peligro: *be careful, the banisters aren't very safe,* ten cuidado, la barandilla no es muy segura; *it's not safe to play in the road,* es peligroso jugar en la calle; *she's a safe driver,* conduce con cuidado; *your secret's safe with me,* guardaré tu secreto; *don't worry, you'll be safe here,* no te preocupes, aquí estarás a salvo. **2** *(unharmed)* ileso,-a, indemne: *the missing boy has been found safe,* se ha encontrado sano y salvo al niño desaparecido. **3** *(not risky - method, investment, choice)* seguro,-a; *(subject)* no polémico,-a. **– 4** *n* caja fuerte, caja de caudales, caja de seguridad.
● **to be a safe bet,** ser seguro,-a. ‖ **as safe as houses,** completamente seguro,-a. ‖ **better safe than sorry,** más vale prevenir que curar. ‖ **in safe hands,** en buenas manos. ‖ **it's safe to say that ...,** se puede decir con seguridad que ... ‖ **safe and sound,** sano,-a y salvo,-a. ‖ **to be on the safe side,** para mayor seguridad, por si acaso. ‖ **to play (it) safe,** ir sobre seguro, jugar sobre seguro.

■ **safe house,** piso franco. ‖ **safe seat,** GB POL escaño asegurado. ‖ **safe sex,** sexo seguro.

safe-breaker ['seɪfbreɪkəʳ] *n* ladrón,-ona de cajas fuertes.

safe-conduct [seɪf'kɒndʌkt] *n* salvoconducto.

safe-deposit ['seɪfdɪpɒzɪt] *n* (*in bank*) cámara acorazada.

■ **safe-deposit box,** caja de seguridad.

safeguard ['seɪfgɑːd] **1** *n* salvaguardia; (*protection*) protección *f* (**against,** contra); (*guarantee*) garantía, salvaguarda. – **2** *t* salvaguardar, proteger (**against,** contra), resguardar (**against,** de).

safekeeping [seɪf'kiːpɪŋ] *n* custodia: *I gave it to him for safekeeping,* se lo di para que estuviera a buen recaudo.

● **in sb.'s safekeeping,** bajo la custodia de algn.

safely ['seɪflɪ] **1** *adv* (*for certain*) con toda seguridad, sin temor a equivocarse: *we can safely say that ...,* podemos decir con toda seguridad que ... **2** (*without mishap*) sin contratiempos, sin accidentes, sin percances: *we got home safely,* llegamos a casa sin ningún percance; *drive safely,* conduce con cuidado. **3** (*securely*) de manera segura: *we'll soon have him safely locked up,* pronto lo tendremos bien encerrado.

● **to arrive safely,** llegar a buen puerto.

safety ['seɪftɪ] *n* seguridad *f*: *there's safety in numbers,* es más seguro ir en grupo; *for safety reasons,* por razones de seguridad.

■ **safety belt,** cinturón *m* de seguridad. ‖ **safety catch,** seguro, cierre *m* de seguridad. ‖ **safety chain,** cadenilla de seguridad. ‖ **safety check,** revisión *f* de seguridad. ‖ **safety curtain,** telón *m* de seguridad. ‖ **safety fuse,** fusible *m* de seguridad. ‖ **safety glass,** vidrio inastillable. ‖ **safety lamp,** lámpara de seguridad. ‖ **safety match,** cerilla, fósforo. ‖ **safety measure,** medida de seguridad. ‖ **safety net,** red *f* de protección, red *f* de seguridad. ‖ **safety pin,** imperdible *m*. ‖ **safety precaution,** medida de seguridad. ‖ **safety razor,** maquinilla de afeitar. ‖ **safety regulations,** normas *fpl* de seguridad. ‖ **safety valve,** válvula de seguridad.

saffron ['sæfrən] **1** *n* (*plant, condiment*) azafrán *m*. – **2** *adj* (*colour*) de color azafrán.

sag [sæg] **1** *i* (*shelf, branch, beam, ceiling*) combarse; (*roof, bed*) hundirse; (*wall*) pandear, pandearse. **2** (*flesh*) colgar. **3** (*demand, prices, etc*) caer, bajar. **4** *fig* (*spirits*) flaquear, decaer. – **5** *n* (*in beam, wall, ceiling, shelf*) combadura; (*in roof*) hundimiento; (*in mattress, chair*) hundimiento. **6** (*in prices, profuts, etc*) baja, caída.

▲ *pt & pp* **sagged,** *ger* **sagging.**

saga ['sɑːgə] *n* saga.

sagacious [sə'geɪʃəs] *adj* sagaz, perspicaz.

sagacity [sə'gæsətɪ] *n* sagacidad *f*.

sage¹ [seɪdʒ] **1** *adj* sabio,-a. – **2** *n* sabio,-a.

sage² [seɪdʒ] *n* BOT salvia.

■ **sage green,** verde *m* salvia, verdigris *m*. ‖ **sage and onion stuffing,** relleno de salvia y cebolla.

sagging ['sægɪŋ] **1** *adj* (*roof*) hundido,-a; (*wall*) pandeado,-a; (*beam, wood*) combado,-a. **2** (*breasts*) caído,-a.

Sagittarian [sædʒɪ'teərɪən] **1** *adj* sagitario,-a. – **2** *n* sagitario,-a.

Sagittarius [sædʒɪ'teərɪəs] *n* Sagitario.

sago ['seɪgəʊ] *n* sagú *m*.

■ **sago palm,** sagú *m*.

Sahara [sə'hɑːrə] *n* Sáhara *m*.

■ **Western Sahara,** Sáhara Occidental.

Saharan [sə'hɑːrən] *adj* sahariano,-a, saharaui.

said [sed] **1** *pt & pp* → **say.** – **2** *adj* JUR (*aforementioned*) susodicho,-a, arriba citado,-a.

sail [seɪl] **1** *n* (*canvas*) vela. **2** (*trip*) paseo en barco; (*journey*) viaje *m* en barco. **3** (*ship*) velero, barco de vela. **4** (*of windmill*) aspa. – **5** *t* (*travel*) navegar; (*cross*) cruzar en barco: *she sailed the Atlantic single-handed,* cruzó el Atlántico sola. **6** (*control ship*) gobernar. – **7** *i* (*ship, boat*) navegar; (*person*) ir en barco, navegar: *I'd love to sail round the world,* me encantaría dar la vuelta al mundo en barco. **8** (*begin journey*) zarpar, hacerse a la mar.

◆ **to sail into** *t insep* arrebatar contra.

● **in full sail,** a toda vela, con las velas desplegadas. ‖ **to be under sail,** moverse (por el viento). ‖ **to set sail,** zarpar, hacerse a la mar. ‖ **to sail close to the wind,** (*in ship*) navegar de bolina; *fig* jugársela. ‖ **to sail through sth.,** *fig* encontrar algo muy fácil: *she sailed through the exam,* aprobó el examen sin ningún problema. ‖ **to sail under false colours,** expresar opiniones falsas.

sailboard ['seɪlbɔːd] *n* tabla de vela, tabla de windsurf.

sailcloth ['seɪlklɒθ] *n* lona.

sailing ['seɪlɪŋ] **1** *n* (*skill*) navegación *f*. **2** (*sport*) vela, navegación *f* a vela: *we go sailing every weekend,* hacemos vela todos los fines de semana. **3** (*departure*) salida; (*crossing*) travesía.

● **to be plain sailing,** ser coser y cantar.

■ **sailing boat,** barco de vela, velero. ‖ **sailing ship,** buque *m* de vela, velero.

sailor ['seɪləʳ] *n* marinero.

● **to be a bad sailor,** marearse fácilmente. ‖ **to be a good sailor,** no marearse.

■ **sailor hat,** gorra marinera. ‖ **sailor suit,** traje *m* de marinero.

saint [seɪnt] **1** *n* (*person*) santo,-a. **2** Saint, (*before most masculine names*) san; (*before masculine names beginning with Do- or To-*) santo; (*before feminine names*) santa: *Saint Paul,* San Pablo; *Saint Thomas,* Santo Tomás.

■ **All Saint's Day,** Día *m* de Todos los Santos. ‖ **saint's day,** santo, onomástica.

saintliness ['seɪntlɪnəs] *n* santidad *f*.

saintly ['seɪntlɪ] *adj* santo,-a.

▲ *comp* **saintlier,** *superl* **saintliest.**

sake¹ [seɪk] *n* bien *m*: *for your own sake,* por tu propio bien; *for the kids' sake,* por los niños; *for the sake of peace,* en aras de la paz.

● **for God's sake!,** ¡por el amor de Dios!, ¡por Dios! ‖ **for goodness' sake!,** ¡por el amor de Dios! ‖ **for Heaven's sake!,** ¡por el amor de Dios! ‖ **for old times' sake,** por los viejos tiempos. ‖ **for Pete's sake!,** ¡por Dios! ‖ **for the sake of,** por (el bien de). ‖ **for the sake of argument,** por decir algo, pongamos por caso. ‖ **just for the sake of it,** porque sí. ‖ **to talk for talking's sake,** hablar por hablar.

sake² ['sɑːkɪ] *n* (*drink*) sake *m*.

salable ['seɪləbəl] *adj* US → **saleable.**

salacious [sə'leɪʃəs] *adj* salaz.

salad ['sæləd] *n* ensalada.

■ **potato salad,** ensaladilla. ‖ **salad bowl,** ensaladera. ‖ **salad cream,** salsa para ensalada (*tipo mahonesa*). ‖ **salad days,** años *mpl* de juventud. ‖ **salad dressing,** aliño, aderezo.

salamander ['sæləmændəʳ] *n* salamandra.

salami [sə'lɑːmɪ] *n* salami *m*.

salaried ['sælərɪd] *adj* asalariado,-a.

salary ['sælərɪ] **1** *n* sueldo, salario. – **2** *adj* salarial.

▲ *pl* **salaries.**

sale [seɪl] **1** *n* (*act, transaction*) venta: *I made a sale,* hice una venta, vendí algo. **2** (*special offer*) rebajas *fpl,* liquidación *f: I bought it in a sale,* lo compré en las rebajas. **3** (*auction*) subasta. – **4 sales,** *npl* (*amount sold*) venta, ventas *fpl: sales are up this month,* las ventas han subido este mes. **5** (*reductions*) rebajas *fpl.*
● **for sale,** en venta. ‖ **"for sale",** (*sign on house etc*) "se vende". ‖ **on sale,** (*available*) en venta, a la venta; (*reduced*) rebajado,-a. ‖ **on sale or return,** en depósito. ‖ **to put sth. up for sale,** poner algo a la venta, poner algo en venta.
■ **clearance sale,** liquidación *f.* ‖ **sale goods,** artículos *mpl* rebajados. ‖ **sale price,** precio rebajado, precio de rebaja. ‖ **sales department,** departamento comercial, departamento de ventas. ‖ **sales manager,** jefe,-a de ventas, gerente *mf* de ventas, director,-ra comercial. ‖ **sales pitch/talk,** charlatanería (*de un,-a vendedor,-ra*). ‖ **sales tax,** impuesto sobre las ventas.
saleable ['seɪləbəl] *adj* vendible.
salesclerk ['seɪlzklɑːk] *n* US dependiente,-a.
salesgirl ['seɪlzgɜːl] *n* dependienta.
salesman ['seɪlzmən] **1** *n* (*gen*) vendedor *m*; (*in shop*) dependiente *m.* **2** (*travelling*) representante *m.*
▲ *pl* **salesmen** ['seɪlsmən].
salesperson ['seɪlzpɜːsən] **1** *n* (*gen*) vendedor,-ra; (*in shop*) dependiente,-a. **2** (*travelling*) representante *mf.*
▲ *pl* **salespeople** ['seɪlzpiːpəl].
salesroom ['seɪlzruːm] *n* US sala de subastas.
saleswoman ['seɪlzwʊmən] **1** *n* (*gen*) vendedora; (*in shop*) dependienta. **2** (*travelling*) representanta *f.*
▲ *pl* **saleswomen** ['seɪlzwɪmɪn].
Salic ['sælɪk] *adj* sálico,-a.
salient ['seɪlɪənt] **1** *adj* (*angle*) saliente, saledizo,-a. **2** (*feature*) sobresaliente, destacado,-a. – **3** *n* (*angle*) saliente *m.*
saline ['seɪlaɪn] *adj* salino,-a.
saliva [sə'laɪvə] *n* saliva.
salivary [sə'laɪvərɪ] *adj* salival.
■ **salivary glands,** glándulas *fpl* salivales.
sallow² ['sæləʊ] *adj* cetrino,-a.
sallowness ['sæləʊnəs] *n* color *m* cetrino, palidez *f.*
sally ['sælɪ] **1** *n* MIL salida. **2** (*remark*) agudeza, réplica.
◆ **to sally forth / sally out 1** *i* MIL hacer una salida. **2** (*gen*) salir a buen paso, emprender la marcha.
▲ (*sustantivo*) *pl* **sallies**; (*verbo*) *pt* & *pp* **sallied,** *ger* **sallying**.
salmon ['sæmən] **1** *n* (*fish*) salmón *m.* **2** (*colour*) color *m* salmón, salmón *m.*
■ **salmon fishing,** pesca del salmón. ‖ **salmon pink,** rosa *m* salmón, rosa *m* asalmonado. ‖ **salmon trout,** trucha asalmonada, reo. ‖ **smoked salmon,** salmón *m* ahumado.
salmonella [sælmə'nelə] *n* (*bacteria*) salmonelosis *f.*
salon ['sælɒn] *n* (*shop*) salón *m.*
■ **beauty salon,** salón *m* de belleza. ‖ **hairdressing salon,** peluquería.
saloon [sə'luːn] **1** *n* US taberna, bar *m.* **2** (*public room*) sala; (*on ship*) salón *m.* **3 saloon** (*car*), GB (*car*) berlina. **4 saloon** (**bar**), GB (*in pub*) *parte de un pub más cómoda y mejor decorada donde las bebidas salen un poco más caras que en la parte más sencilla.*
salsa ['sælsə] *n* MUS salsa.
salt [sɔːlt] **1** *n* (*gen*) sal *f.* – **2** *adj* salado,-a. – **3** *t* (*preserve, cure*) salar, conservar en sal, curar. **4** (*season*) echar sal a, salar. **5** (*on road*) echar sal en. – **6 salts,** *npl* sales *fpl.*
◆ **to salt away** *t sep* (*money*) guardar.
● **to be the salt of the earth,** ser la sal de la tierra. ‖

to be worth one's salt, merecer el pan que se come. ‖ **to rub salt into the wounds,** hurgar en la herida. ‖ **to take sth. with a pinch of salt,** creer algo con reservas.
■ **common salt,** sal *f* común. ‖ **cooking salt,** sal *f* de cocina. ‖ **Epsom salts,** epsomita *f,* sal *f* de la Higuera. ‖ **salt beef,** *carne de vaca curada en sal.* ‖ **salt flat,** salina. ‖ **salt lake,** lago de agua salada. ‖ **salt lick,** bloque *m* de sal, salegar *m.* ‖ **salt marsh,** marisma. ‖ **salt mine,** mina de sal, salina. ‖ **salt pork,** tocino. ‖ **salt shaker,** US salero. ‖ **sea salt,** sal *f* marina. ‖ **smelling salts,** sales *fpl* (aromáticas). ‖ **table salt,** sal *f* fina, sal *f* de mesa.
SALT [sɔːlt] *abbr* (*Strategic Arms Limitation Talks*) conversaciones *fpl* para la limitación de armas estratégicas.
saltcellar ['sɔːltselə'] *n* salero.
salted ['sɔːltɪd] *adj* salado,-a.
salt-free ['sɔːltfriː] *adj* sin sal.
saltiness ['sɔːltɪnəs] *n* (*water*) salubridad *f*; (*sea*) salinidad *f*; (*food*) sabor *m* salado.
saltpan ['sɔːltpæn] *n* salina.
saltpeter ['sɔːltpiːtə'] *n* US → **saltpetre**.
saltpetre ['sɔːltpiːtə'] *n* salitre *m.*
saltwater ['sɔːltwɔːtə'] *adj* de agua salada.
salty ['sɔːltɪ] **1** *adj* (*food*) salado,-a. **2** *fig* (*racy*) salado,-a, picante, atrevido,-a.
▲ *comp* **saltier,** *superl* **saltiest**.
salubrious [sə'luːbrɪəs] **1** *adj fml* (*health-giving*) salubre, sano,-a, saludable. **2** (*respectable - gen*) sano,-a; (- *area*) recomendable.
salutary ['sæljʊtərɪ] *adj* (*experience*) beneficioso,-a; (*warning*) útil.
salute [sə'luːt] **1** *n* MIL (*gesture*) saludo; (*firing of guns*) salva. **2** (*greeting*) saludo, salutación *f.* – **3** *t* (*gen*) saludar. **4** (*honour, applaud*) aplaudir, aclamar. – **5** *i* MIL saludar.
● **in salute,** como saludo. ‖ **to take the salute,** presidir el desfile.
Salvadoran [sælvə'dɔːrən] *adj-n* → **Salvadorian**.
Salvadorian [sælvə'dɔːrɪən] **1** *adj* salvadoreño,-a. – **2** *n* salvadoreño,-a.
salvage ['sælvɪdʒ] **1** *n* (*recovery*) salvamento, rescate *m.* **2** (*things recovered*) objetos *mpl* recuperados, material *m* recuperado. **3** JUR (*compensation*) derecho de salvamento. – **4** *t* salvar, rescatar, recuperar.
salvation [sæl'veɪʃən] *n* salvación *f.*
Salvation Army [sælveɪʃən'ɑːmɪ] *n* Ejército de Salvación.
salve [sælv] **1** *n* (*ointment*) pomada, ungüento, bálsamo. **2** (*comfort*) alivio, bálsamo. – **3** *t* (*apply salve*) curar con pomada, curar. **4** *fml* (*soothe, appease*) aliviar.
● **to salve one's conscience,** aliviarse la conciencia. ‖
■ **lip salve,** protector *m* de labios, crema protectora de labios.
salver ['sælvə'] *n* (*gen*) salvilla; (*silver*) bandeja (de plata).
salvo ['sælvəʊ] *n* (*of guns, applause*) salva.
▲ *pl* **salvos** o **salvoes**.
Samaria [sə'meərɪə] *n* Samaria.
Samaritan [sə'mærɪtən] **1** *adj* samaritano,-a. – **2** *n* (*person*) samaritano,-a. **3** (*language*) samaritano. – **4 the Samaritans,** *npl* ≈ el teléfono de la esperanza.
samba ['sæmbə] *n* (*dance*) samba.
same [seɪm] **1** *adj* (*not different*) mismo,-a: *the same day,* el mismo día; *the same thing,* lo mismo. **2** (*alike*) mismo,-a, igual, idéntico,-a: *he's wearing the same tie as you,* lleva una corbata igual que la tuya; *you men are all the same!,* ¡los hombres sois todos iguales! – **3** *pron* COMM (*previously mentioned thing*) el mismo, la misma: *es-*

timate for repairing door and varnishing of same, presupuesto para reparar la puerta y barnizar la misma. **4 the same,** lo mismo: *it won't be the same without you,* no será lo mismo sin ti. **5** (*same person*) el mismo, la misma: *are you Phil Rogers? - The same!,* ¿es usted Phil Rogers? - ¡El mismo!; *the very same,* el mismísimo, la mismísima. **– 6** *adv* igual, del mismo modo: *they talk the same,* hablan igual.
● **all the same,** a pesar de todo. ‖ **at the same time,** (*simultaneously*) a la vez, al mismo tiempo; (*however*) sin embargo, aun así. ‖ **in the same breath,** inmediatamente después. ‖ **it's all the same to me,** me da igual, me da lo mismo. ‖ **just the same,** a pesar de todo. ‖ **on the same wavelength,** en la misma onda. ‖ **one and the same,** el mismo, la misma, lo mismo. ‖ **same difference,** es igual. ‖ **same here,** yo también. ‖ **thanks all the same,** gracias de todas maneras. ‖ **the same again, please,** lo mismo de antes, por favor, otro por favor. ‖ **the same as,** igual que, como. ‖ **the same old story,** la misma historia de siempre. ‖ **the same to you!,** ¡igualmente! ‖ **to amount the same thing,** venir a ser lo mismo. ‖ **to be in the same boat,** estar en el mismo barco, estar en la misma situación. ‖ **to be of the same mind,** opinar lo mismo.

sameness [ˈseɪmnəs] **1** *n* (*similarity*) igualdad *f*, identidad *f*. **2** (*monotony*) monotonía, uniformidad *f*.

Samoa [səˈməʊə] *n* Samoa.
■ **Western Samoa,** Samoa Occidental.

Samoan [səˈməʊən] **1** *adj* samoano,-a. **– 2** *n* (*person*) samoano,-a. **3** (*language*) samoano.

samosa [sæˈməʊzə] *n* CULIN samosa (*empanadilla hindú rellena de carne o verduras*).

sampan [ˈsæmpæn] *n* sampán *m*.

sample [ˈsɑːmpəl] **1** *n* (*gen*) muestra: *would you like a free sample?,* ¿quieres una muestra gratuita? **2** (*of food, drink*) muestra, cata, degustación *f*. **– 3** *t* (*place, activity*) probar. **4** (*dish*) probar, degustar; (*wine*) catar, probar, degustar. **5** (*opinion*) sondear.

sampler [ˈsɑːmplə^r] **1** *n* SEW dechado. **2** MUS sampleador *m*.

samurai [ˈsæmjʊraɪ] *n* samurái *m*, samuray *m*.
▲ *pl* samurai.

sanatorium [sænəˈtɔːriəm] *n* sanatorio.
▲ *pl* sanatoriums *o* sanatoria [sænəˈtɔːriə].

sanctify [ˈsæŋktɪfaɪ] *t* santificar, consagrar.
▲ *pt & pp* sanctified, *ger* sanctifying.

sanctimonious [sæŋktɪˈməʊniəs] *adj pej* santurrón,-ona, mojigato,-a.

sanctimoniousness [sæŋktɪˈməʊniəsnəs] *n* santurronería, mojigatería, beatería.

sanction [ˈsæŋkʃən] **1** *n fml* (*permission*) sanción *f*, autorización *f*, permiso. **2** (*penalty*) sanción *f*; (*weapon*) arma. **– 3** *t fml* (*authorize*) sancionar, autorizar. **– 4** **sanctions,** *npl* POL (*measures*) sanciones *fpl*.

sanctity [ˈsæŋktɪtɪ] *n* (*sacredness*) santidad *f*, carácter *m* sagrado: *the sanctity of marriage,* la santidad del matrimonio.

sanctuary [ˈsæŋktjʊəri] **1** *n* REL (*sacred palce*) santuario; (*chancel*) presbiterio. **2** (*gen*) refugio, protección *f*; (*asylum*) asilo. **3** (*for animals*) reserva.
● **to take sanctuary,** refugiarse.
▲ *pl* sanctuaries.

sanctum [ˈsæŋktəm] **1** *n* (*holy place*) lugar *m* sagrado. **2** *fig* lugar *m* privado.
■ **inner sanctum,** sanctasantórum *m*.

sand [sænd] **1** *n* (*gen*) arena. **– 2** *t* (*smooth*) lijar (**down,** -). **3** (*sprinkle with sand*) enarenar. **– 4** **sands,** *npl* (*beach*) playa *f sing*; (*sandbank*) banco *m sing* de arena.

■ **sand castle,** castillo de arena. ‖ **sand dune,** duna. ‖ **sand pie,** flan *m* de arena. ‖ **sand trap,** (*in golf*) búnker *m*.

sandal [ˈsændəl] *n* sandalia.

sandalwood [ˈsændəlwʊd] *n* BOT sándalo.

sandbag [ˈsændbæg] **1** *n* saco terrero. **– 2** *t* (*protect*) proteger con sacos terreros.
▲ *pt & pp* sandbagged, *ger* sandbagging.

sandbank [ˈsændbæŋk] *n* banco de arena.

sandboy [ˈsændbɔɪ] **as happy as a sandboy,** *phr* como un niño con zapatos nuevos.

sander [ˈsændə^r] *n* (*machine*) lijadora.

sandman [ˈsændmæn] *n* ser imaginario que trae el sueño a los niños.

sandpaper [ˈsændpeɪpə^r] **1** *n* papel *m* de lija. **– 2** *t* lijar.

sandpit [ˈsændpɪt] *n* GB cajón *m* de arena.

sandstone [ˈsændstəʊn] *n* arenisca.

sandstorm [ˈsændstɔːm] *n* tempestad *f* de arena.

sandwich [ˈsænwɪdʒ] **1** *n* (*French bread*) bocadillo; (*sliced bread*) sandwich *m*: *double-decker sandwich,* sandwich de dos pisos. **– 2** *t* encajonar (**between,** entre).
■ **sandwich board,** cartel *m* anunciador, cartelones *mpl*. ‖ **sandwich course,** GB EDUC curso teórico-práctico (*en que se alternan las clases teóricas con períodos de prácticas en la industria*). ‖ **sandwich man,** hombre *m* anuncio.

sandy [ˈsændɪ] **1** *adj* (*beach etc*) arenoso,-a, de arena. **2** (*hair*) rubio,-a oscuro,-a.
▲ *comp* sandier, *superl* sandiest.

sane [seɪn] **1** *adj* (*person*) cuerdo,-a; (*mind*) sano,-a. **2** *fig* (*solution, decision, etc*) sensato,-a.

sang [sæŋ] *pt* → **sing**.

sang-froid [sɒŋˈfrwɑː] *n* sangre *f* fría.

sanguinary [ˈsæŋgwɪnəri] **1** *adj fml* (*bloody*) sangriento,-a. **2** *fml* (*bloodthirsty*) sanguinario,-a.

sanguine [ˈsæŋgwɪn] **1** *adj fml* (*in attitude*) optimista. **2** *fml* (*complexion*) sanguíneo,-a.

sanitarium [sænɪˈteəriəm] *n* US → **sanatorium**.

sanitary [ˈsænɪtəri] **1** *adj* (*to do with health*) sanitario,-a, de sanidad. **2** (*hygienic*) higiénico,-a.
■ **sanitary inspector,** inspector,-ra de sanidad. ‖ **sanitary napkin / sanitary pad / sanitary towel,** compresa.

sanitation [sænɪˈteɪʃən] **1** *n* (*public health*) sanidad *f* (pública); (*hygiene*) higiene *f*. **2** (*plumbing*) sistema *m* de saneamiento; (*sewage system*) alcantarillado.

sanity [ˈsænɪtɪ] **1** *n* (*health of mind*) cordura. **2** (*good sense*) sensatez *f*, juicio.

sank [sæŋk] *pt* → **sink**.

Sanskrit [ˈsænskrɪt] **1** *n* sánscrito. **– 2** *adj* sánscrito,-a.

Santa Claus [sæntəˈklɔːz] *n* Papá *m* Noel, San Nicolás.

Saône [səʊn] *n* el Saona *m*.

sap[1] [sæp] **1** *n* BOT savia. **2** *fig* (*energy, vigour*) energía, vigor *m*. **3** *US fam* (*person*) bobo,-a, inocentón,-ona.

sap[2] [sæp] **1** *n* MIL zapa. **– 2** *t* (*weaken*) debilitar, agotar, minar.
● **to be sapped,** quedarse agotado,-a.
▲ *pt & pp* sapped, *ger* sapping.

sapling [ˈsæplɪŋ] *n* BOT árbol *m* joven.

sapper [ˈsæpə^r] *n* MIL zapador,-ra.

sapphire [ˈsæfaɪə^r] **1** *n* zafiro. **– 2** *adj* zafirino,-a, zafíreo,-a, azul zafiro.

Saracen [ˈsærəsən] **1** *adj* sarraceno,-a. **–2** *n* (*person*) sarraceno,-a.

Saragossa [særəˈgɒsə] *n* Zaragoza.

sarcasm ['sɑːkæzəm] *n* sarcasmo, sorna.
sarcastic [sɑː'kæstɪk] *adj* sarcástico,-a.
sarcophagus [sɑː'kɒfəgəs] *n* sarcófago.
▲ *pl* **sarcophaguses** *o* **sarcophagi** [sɑː'kɒfəgaɪ].
sardine [sɑː'diːn] *n* sardina.
● **to be packed like sardines,** estar como sardinas en lata.
Sardinia [sɑː'dɪnɪə] *n* Cerdeña.
Sardinian [sɑː'dɪnɪən] **1** *adj* sardo,-a. – **2** *n* (*person*) sardo,-a. **3** (*language*) sardo.
sardonic [sɑː'dɒnɪk] *adj* sardónico,-a.
sarge [sɑːdʒ] *n* MIL *fam* → **sargeant**.
sari ['sɑːrɪ] *n* sari *m*.
sarong [sə'rɒŋ] *n* sarong *m*.
sartorial [sɑː'tɔːrɪəl] **1** *adj fml* (*dress*) de sastre. **2** ANAT sartorio,-a.
■ **sartorial elegance,** elegancia en el vestir.
sartorius [sɑː'tɔːrɪəs] *n* ANAT sartorio.
▲ *pl* **sartorii** [sɑː'tɔːrɪaɪ].
sash[1] [sæʃ] **1** *n* (*waistband*) faja. **2** MIL (*waist*) fajín *m*; (*shoulder*) banda.
sash[2] [sæʃ] *n* (*frame*) marco de ventana.
■ **sash window,** ventana de guillotina.
Sassenach ['sæsənæx] *n pej* (*English person*) inglés,-esa.
sassy ['sæsɪ] **1** *adj* US *fam* (*rude*) descarado,-a, fresco,-a. **2** US *fam* (*bold*) atrevido,-a.
▲ *comp* **sassier**, *superl* **sassiest**.
sat [sæt] *pt & pp* → **sit**.
Sat ['sætədɪ] *abbr* (*Saturday*) sábado; (*abbreviation*) sáb.
Satan ['seɪtən] *n* Satán *m*, Satanás *m*.
satanic [sə'tænɪk] *adj* satánico,-a.
satchel ['sætʃəl] *n* cartera (*de colegial*), mochila (*de colegial*).
satellite ['sætəlaɪt] *n* satélite *m*.
■ **satellite broadcasting,** TV retransmisión *f* vía satélite. ‖ **satellite dish,** TV antena parabólica. ‖ **satellite state,** POL país *m* satélite, nación *f* satélite. ‖ **satellite television,** televisión *f* vía satélite.
satiate ['seɪʃɪeɪt] *t* saciar.
satiation [seɪʃɪ'eɪʃən] *n* saciedad *f*.
satin ['sætɪn] **1** *n* satén *m*, raso. – **2** *adj* (*made of satin*) de satén, de raso. **3** (*finish*) satinado,-a.
satire ['sætaɪəʳ] *n* sátira.
satirical [sə'tɪrɪkəl] *adj* satírico,-a.
satirist ['sætərɪst] *n* satírico,-a, escritor,-ra satírico,-a.
satirize ['sætəraɪz] *t* satirizar.
satisfaction [sætɪs'fækʃən] **1** *n* (*contentment*) satisfacción *f*, complacencia: *he expressed his satisfaction with the service,* expresó su satisfacción por el servicio; *everyone needs job satisfaction,* todo el mundo necesita sentirse realizado en su trabajo. **2** (*fulfilment*) satisfacción *f*, cumplimiento. **3** (*response to complaint*) satisfacción *f*.
satisfactory [sætɪs'fæktərɪ] **1** *adj* satisfactorio,-a. **2** EDUC suficiente.
satisfied ['sætɪsfaɪd] **1** *adj* satisfecho,-a, complacido,-a, contento,-a: *another satisfied customer,* otro cliente satisfecho; *we'd be satisfied with steak and chips,* nos contentaríamos con un bistec con patatas. **2** (*convinced*) convencido,-a.
satisfy ['sætɪsfaɪ] **1** *t* (*please, make happy*) satisfacer, complacer, contentar: *does nothing satisfy you?,* ¿no hay nada que te satisfaga? **2** (*fulfil - need etc*) satisfacer; (*requirement*) cumplir, satisfacer: *do you satisfy the entry conditions?,* ¿cumples los requisitos de admisión? **3**

(*convince*) convencer: *you must satisfy the jury that you are innocent,* debes convencer al jurado de tu inocencia.
▲ *pt & pp* **satisfied**, *ger* **satisfying**.
satisfying ['sætɪsfaɪɪŋ] *adj* (*gen*) satisfactorio,-a; (*meal*) bueno,-a, delicioso,-a.
satsuma [sæt'suːmə] *n* BOT satsuma.
saturate ['sætʃəreɪt] **1** *t* (*fill*) saturar (**with**, de). **2** (*soak*) empapar (**with**, de).
saturated ['sætʃəreɪtɪd] **1** *adj* (*full*) saturado,-a. **2** (*wet*) empapado,-a: *I got absolutely saturated!,* ¡me quedé totalmente empapado!
■ **saturated fat,** grasa saturada.
saturation [sætʃə'reɪʃən] *n* saturación *f*.
■ **saturation bombing,** MIL bombardeo de saturación. ‖ **saturation point,** punto de saturación.
Saturday ['sætədɪ] *n* sábado: *a week on Saturday,* del sábado en una semana; *every other Saturday,* cada dos sábados, un sábado sí y otro no; *every Saturday,* todos los sábados; *last Saturday,* el sábado pasado; *next Saturday,* el sábado que viene, el próximo sábado; *on a Saturday,* en sábado; *on Saturday,* el sábado; *on Saturday morning/afternoon/evening/night,* el sábado por la mañana/tarde/tarde/noche; *on Saturdays,* los sábados; *the following Saturday,* el sábado siguiente; *the Saturday after next,* del sábado en ocho días; *the Saturday before last,* el sábado antepasado; *this Saturday,* este sábado.
Saturn ['sætɜːn] *n* Saturno.
satyr ['sætəʳ] *n lit* sátiro.
sauce [sɔːs] **1** *n* CULIN salsa: *fish in parsley sauce,* pescado con salsa de perejil. **2** *fam* (*cheek*) frescura, descaro.
● **what is sauce for the goose is sauce for the gander,** lo que es bueno para uno es bueno para el otro.
■ **sauce boat,** salsera. ‖ **tomato sauce,** ketchup *m*, salsa de tomate.
saucepan ['sɔːspən] *n* (*gen*) cazo, cacerola; (*large*) olla.
saucer ['sɔːsəʳ] *n* platillo.
saucy ['sɔːsɪ] **1** *adj fam* descarado,-a, fresco,-a. **2** (*risqué*) picante. **3** (*jaunty*) coqueto,-a, gracioso,-a.
▲ *comp* **saucier**, *superl* **sauciest**.
Saudi ['saʊdɪ] **1** *adj* saudí, saudita. – **2** *n* saudí *mf*, saudita *mf*.
■ **Saudi Arabia,** Arabia Saudita.
sauna ['sɔːnə] *n* sauna.
saunter ['sɔːntəʳ] **1** *i* pasear, pasearse. – **2** *n* paseo, vuelta.
sausage ['sɒsɪdʒ] *n* (*uncooked*) salchicha; (*cured*) salchichón *m*; (*spicy*) chorizo.
■ **sausage dog,** perro salchicha. ‖ **sausage meat,** carne *f* de salchicha. ‖ **sausage roll,** salchicha envuelta en hojaldre.
sauté ['səʊteɪ] **1** *t* saltear. – **2** *adj* salteado,-a.
▲ *pt & pp* **sautéed** *o* **sautéd**, *ger* **sautéing**.
savage ['sævɪdʒ] **1** *adj* (*ferocious*) feroz; (*cruel*) cruel; (*violent*) violento,-a, salvaje; (*severe*) severo,-a, duro,-a: *a savage attack,* un ataque duro; *savage cuts in public spending,* recortes drásticos en el gasto público. **2** *pej* (*primitive*) salvaje, primitivo,-a. – **3** *n pej* salvaje *mf*. – **4** *t* (*animal*) embestir (contra), atacar salvajemente. **5** *fig* (*criticize*) atacar violentamente, arremeter contra, poner por los suelos.
savageness ['sævɪdʒnəs] *n* (*ferocity*) ferocidad *f*; (*cruelty*) crueldad *f*, brutalidad *f*; (*violence*) violencia; (*severeness*) severidad *f*.

515

scalding

savagery [ˈsævɪdʒrɪ] *n* (*cruel act*) salvajada; (*cruelty*) crueldad *f*, brutalidad *f*.
savanna [səˈvænə] *n* → **savannah**.
savannah [səˈvænə] *n* sabana.
save [seɪv] **1** *t* (*rescue*) salvar (**from**, de), rescatar (**from**, de); (*preserve*) salvar (**from**, de): *you saved my life!*, ¡me has salvado la vida! **2** REL salvar. **3** (*not spend - money*) ahorrar: *I've saved $200 towards my holidays*, he ahorrado $200 para las vacaciones. **4** (*not waste - fuel, work, money*) ahorrar; (*time*) ahorrar, ahorrarse, ganar: *we must all make an effort to save water*, todos debemos esforzarnos por ahorrar agua. **5** (*keep, put by - food, strength*) guardar, reservar; (*- stamps*) coleccionar: *save me a seat*, guárdame un asiento; *he's saving his strength for later*, se guarda las fuerzas para luego. **6** (*avoid*) evitar, ahorrar: *it saved us a lot of trouble*, nos evitó muchas molestias, nos ahorró muchas molestias. **7** SP (*goal*) parar. **8** COMPUT guardar, archivar. – **9** *i* (*not spend*) ahorrar (**up**, -): *we're saving up to buy a flat*, ahorramos para comprar un piso. **10** REL salvar. – **11** *n* SP parada. – **12** *prep fml* (*except*) salvo, excepto.
◆ **to save on** *t insep* ahorrar: *we're going to have to save on electricity*, tendremos que ahorrar electricidad.
● **God save the Queen**, Dios salve a la Reina. ‖ **to save sb.'s bacon**, salvarle el pellejo a algn. ‖ **to save face**, salvar las apariencias. ‖ **to save one's breath**, no gastar saliva. ‖ **to save one's hide/neck/skin**, salvar el pellejo. ‖ **to save the day**, salvar la situación.
saver [ˈseɪvəʳ] *n* (*person*) ahorrador,-ra.
saving [ˈseɪvɪŋ] **1** *n* (*of time, money*) ahorro, economía. – **2** savings, *npl* ahorros *mpl*.
● **to be sb.'s saving grace**, ser el único mérito que tiene algn., ser lo que le salva a algn.
■ **savings account**, cuenta de ahorros. ‖ **savings bank**, caja de ahorros.
savior [ˈseɪvjəʳ] *n* US → **saviour**.
saviour [ˈseɪvjəʳ] **1** *n* salvador,-ra. **2 the Saviour / Our Saviour**, REL El Salvador *m*.
savor [ˈseɪvəʳ] *t* → **savour**.
savory [ˈseɪvərɪ] **1** *n* BOT ajedrea. – **2** *adj* US → **savoury**.
savour [ˈseɪvəʳ] **1** *n* (*taste, flavour*) sabor *m*, gusto. **2** *fig* (*interest*) interés *m*. – **3** *t* saborear.
◆ **to savour of** *t insep* saber a, oler a.
savour-faire [sævwɑːˈfeəʳ] *n* don *m* de la diplomacia, desenvoltura.
savoury [ˈseɪvərɪ] **1** *adj* (*salty*) salado,-a; (*tasty*) sabroso,-a. **2** (*respectable, wholesome*) saludable, sano,-a. – **3** *n* entrante *m* salado, canapé *m*.
savvy [ˈsævɪ] **1** *n fam* sentido común, conocimiento práctico, entendimiento. – **2** *i fam* entender, comprender, captar.
saw¹ [sɔː] *pt* → **see**.
saw² [sɔː] **1** *n* (*tool*) sierra, serrucho. – **2** *t* serrar, aserrar, cortar con una sierra: *they sawed the tree down*, talaron el árbol con una sierra; *this is where they saw the wood up*, es aquí donde se aserra la madera. – **3** *i* serrar, cortar.
■ **mechanical saw**, sierra mecánica.
▲ *pt* sawed, *pp* sawed *o* sawn [sɔːn].
sawdust [ˈsɔːdʌst] *n* serrín *m*.
sawhorse [ˈsɔːhɔːs] *n* (*frame*) burro, caballete *m*.
sawmill [ˈsɔːmɪl] *n* aserradero, serrería *f*.
sawn [sɔːn] *pp* → **saw**.
sawn-off shotgun [sɔːnɒfˈʃɒtɡʌn] *n* escopeta de cañones recortados.
Saxon [ˈsæksən] **1** *adj* sajón,-ona. – **2** *n* (*person*) sajón,-ona.

Saxony [ˈsæksənɪ] *n* Sajonia.
saxophone [ˈsæksəfəʊn] *n* saxofón *m*.
saxophonist [sækˈsɒfənɪst] *n* saxofonista *mf*, saxo *mf*.
say [seɪ] **1** *t* (*gen*) decir; (*express*) expresar; (*state*) afirmar, declarar: *what did he say?*, ¿qué dijo?, ¿qué ha dicho?; *could you say that again?*, ¿podrías repetir eso?; *first she said yes and then no*, primero dijo que sí y luego que no; *I thought you said you could cook!*, ¡no habías dicho que sabías cocinar!; *she said to be here at 9.00 pm*, dijo que teníamos que estar aquí a las 9.00; *they say he killed her*, dicen que la mató. **2** (*prayer*) rezar; (*poem, lines*) recitar. **3** (*newspaper, sign, etc*) decir; (*clock, meter, etc*) marcar: *what does the guidebook say?*, ¿qué dice la guía?, ¿qué pone en la guía?; *what time does your watch say?*, ¿qué hora marca tu reloj? **4** (*think*) pensar, opinar, decir: *what do you say?*, ¿qué opinas?; *I say we keep looking*, creo que deberíamos seguir buscando; *what do you say we have a break?*, ¿qué te parece si hacemos un descanso?; *what would you say to an ice-cream?*, ¿te apetece un helado? **5** (*suppose*) suponer, poner, decir: *say you found a wallet, what would you do?*, supongamos que encuentras una cartera, ¿qué harías?; *come round at, say, 8.00pm*, pásate hacia las 8.00, ¿te parece?; *shall we say Saturday then?*, ¿quedamos el sábado, pues? – **6** *n* opinión *f*: *I didn't have much say in the matter*, no tuve ni voz ni voto en el asunto. – **7** *interj* US *fam* ¡oye!, ¡oiga!
● **having said that ...**, a pesar de eso ..., no obstante ... ‖ **I say!**, (*calling sb.*) ¡oiga!, ¡oye!; (*surprise*) ¡caramba!, ¡caray! ‖ **I'll say!**, ¡ya lo creo! ‖ **it goes without saying that ...**, por supuesto que ..., huelga decir que ... ‖ **it is said that ...**, dicen que ..., se dice que ... ‖ **never say die**, no rendirse. ‖ **not to have a lot to say for os.**, no tener mucho que decir. ‖ **not to say ...**, por no decir ... ‖ **not to say much for sb./sth.**, decir mal de algn./algo. ‖ **say no more!**, (*interrupting*) ¡basta!; (*I understand*) ¡no me digas más! ‖ **say when!**, ¡ya me dirás basta! ‖ **that is to say**, es decir. ‖ **the least said the better**, cuanto menos decimos, mejor. ‖ **to have one's say**, dar su opinión, hablar. ‖ **to not say a dicky-bird**, no decir ni pío. ‖ **to say a lot for sb./sth.**, decir mucho en favor de algn./algo. ‖ **to say nothing of ...**, por no decir nada de ..., por no mencionar ... ‖ **to say the least**, como mínimo. ‖ **to say to os.**, decir para sí. ‖ **when all is said and done**, al fin y al cabo. ‖ **you can say that again!**, ¡y que lo digas!, ¡ya lo creo! ‖ **you don't say!**, ¡no me digas! ‖ **you said it!**, ¡ya lo creo!; ¡dímelo a mí!
▲ *pt & pp* said.
saying [ˈseɪɪŋ] *n* dicho, decir *m*.
say-so [ˈseɪsəʊ] *n fam* (*permission*) visto bueno, aprobación *f*, permiso *f*.
● **on sb.'s say-so**, porque lo diga algn.
scab [skæb] **1** *n* MED costra, postilla. **2** *fam pej* (*blackleg*) esquirol *m*.
scabbard [ˈskæbəd] *n* vaina.
scabby [ˈskæbɪ] *adj* MED costroso,-a, lleno,-a de costras.
▲ *comp* scabbier, *superl* scabbiest.
scabies [ˈskeɪbiːz] *n* MED sarna.
scads [skædz] *npl fam* montones *mpl*.
scaffold [ˈskæfəʊld] **1** *n* (*framework*) andamio. **2** (*for execution*) patíbulo, cadalso.
scaffolding [ˈskæfəldɪŋ] *n* andamiaje *m*.
scald [skɔːld] **1** *n* escaldadura. – **2** *t* (*burn*) escaldar. **3** (*heat*) calentar. **4** (*instrument, recipient*) esterilizar; (*vegetables*) escaldar.
scalding [ˈskɔːldɪŋ] *adj* (*extremely hot*) hirviente, hirviendo.

scale¹ [skeɪl] **1** *n* (*of fish, reptile*) escama. **2** (*on skin*) escama. **3** (*in kettle etc*) sarro, incrustaciones *fpl.* – **4** *t* (*fish*) escamar, quitar las escamas a.
◆ **to scale off** *i* desconcharse.

scale² [skeɪl] **1** *n* (*measure*) escala: *a metric scale,* una escala métrica. **2** (*size, amount*) escala, magnitud *f*: *changes on an unprecedented scale,* cambios a una escala sin precedentes; *the scale of the tragedy,* la magnitud de la tragedia. **3** MUS escala. – **4** *t* (*climb up*) escalar.
◆ **to scale down** *t sep* (*reduce*) reducir la escala de; (*proportionately*) reducir proporcionalmente. ‖ **to scale up** *t sep* (*increase*) ampliar la escala de; (*proportionately*) ampliar proporcionalmente.
● **on a large scale,** a gran escala. ‖ **out of scale,** fuera de escala. ‖ **to scale,** a escala.
■ **pay scale,** escala de salarios. ‖ **scale drawing,** dibujo a escala. ‖ **scale model,** maqueta. ‖ **social scale,** escala social.

scale³ [skeɪl] **1** *n* (*pan*) platillo. – **2** *i* SP (*weigh*) pesar. – **3** **scales,** *npl* (*for weighing in shop, kitchen*) balanza; (*bathroom, large weights*) báscula. **4** **the Scales,** Libra *f sing.*
● **to tip the scales in sb.'s favour,** inclinar la balanza a favor de algn.

scallop [ˈskɒləp] **1** *n* (*mollusc*) vieira, concha de peregrino. **2** (*shell*) concha de peregrino, venera. **3** SEW festón *m.* – **4** *t* SEW festonear. **5** US CULIN guisar al gratén.

scalp [skælp] **1** *n* ANAT cuero cabelludo. **2** (*war trophy*) cabellera. **3** *fam fig* (*as trophy*) trofeo, cabellera. – **4** *t* arrancar el cuero cabelludo a. **5** *fam* (*cut hair short*) rapar.
● **to be after sb.'s scalp,** querer vengarse de algn., ir a por algn.

scalpel [ˈskælpəl] **1** *n* (*surgeon's*) bisturí *m*; (*for dissecting*) escalpelo. **2** (*tool*) escoplo, gubia.

scaly [ˈskeɪlɪ] **1** *adj* (*fish etc*) escamoso,-a, con escamas. **2** (*kettle etc*) lleno,-a de sarro, lleno,-a de incrustaciones.
▲ *comp* **scalier,** *superl* **scaliest.**

scam [skæm] *n fam* timo, estafa, chanchullo.

scamp [skæmp] *n fam* diablillo,-a, pilluelo,-a, bribón,-ona, granuja *mf.*

scamper [ˈskæmpəʳ] *i* corretear.

scampi [ˈskæmpɪ] *n* colas *fpl* de cigala rebozadas.

scan [skæn] **1** *t* (*examine - gen*) escrutar, escudriñar; (*- horizon*) otear; (*- with searchlight*) barrer. **2** (*glance at*) echar un vistazo a, recorrer con la vista. **3** TECH (*with radar*) explorar. **4** MED escanear, pasar por el escáner. **5** (*poetry*) escandir, medir. – **6** *i* (*poetry*) seguir las reglas de la métrica. – **7** *n* TECH (*with radar*) exploración *f.* **8** MED (*gen*) exploración *f* ultrasónica; (*in gynaecology etc*) ecografía.
▲ *pt & pp* **scanned,** *ger* **scanning.**

scandal [ˈskændəl] **1** *n* (*outrage*) escándalo; (*disgrace*) vergüenza. **2** (*gossip*) chismes *mpl*, chismorreo.

scandalize [ˈskændəlaɪz] *t* escandalizar.
● **to be scandalized,** escandalizarse.

scandalous [ˈskændələs] *adj* escandaloso,-a.

Scandinavia [skændɪˈneɪvɪə] *n* Escandinavia.

Scandinavian [skændɪˈneɪvɪən] **1** *adj* escandinavo,-a. – **2** *n* escandinavo,-a.

scanner [ˈskænəʳ] **1** *n* TECH (*radar*) antena direccional. **2** MED escáner *m.*

scansion [ˈskænʃən] *n* (*poetry*) medida.

scant [skænt] *adj* escaso,-a.

scantily [ˈskæntɪlɪ] *adv* escasamente.
● **to be scantily dressed,** ir ligero,-a de ropa.

scanty [ˈskæntɪ] *adj* (*gen*) escaso,-a; (*meal*) parco,-a, insuficiente; (*clothes*) ligero,-a.

▲ *comp* **scantier,** *superl* **scantiest.**

scapegoat [ˈskeɪpɡəʊt] *n fig* cabeza de turco, chivo expiatorio.

scapula [ˈskæpjʊlə] *n* ANAT escápula.

scar [skɑːʳ] **1** *n* cicatriz *f*, señal *f*. **2** *fig* marca, huella, señal *f*. – **3** *t* (*mark with scar*) marcar con una señal; (*leave scar*) dejar una cicatriz. **4** *fig* marcar, señalar. – **5** *i* (*heal*) cicatrizar (**over,** -).
● **to be scarred for life,** quedarle a uno la cicatriz. ‖ **to scar sb. for life,** *fig* marcar a algn. para siempre.
▲ *pt & pp* **scarred,** *ger* **scarring.**

scarce [skeəs] **1** *adj* (*not plentiful*) escaso,-a. **2** (*rare*) raro,-a, contado,-a. – **3** *adv lit* apenas.
● **to be scarce,** faltar, escasear, haber poco,-a: *water is scarce,* hay poca agua, el agua escasea. ‖ **to make os. scarce,** esfumarse, largarse.

scarcely [ˈskeəslɪ] **1** *adv* (*hardly*) apenas: *I scarcely know them,* apenas los conozco; *scarcely had I sat down when the phone rang,* apenas me hube sentado cuando sonó el teléfono. **2** (*surely not*) ni mucho menos: *you can scarcely expect me to believe that!,* ¡no esperarás que crea eso ni mucho menos!

scarcity [ˈskeəsətɪ] *n* escasez *f*, falta.

scare [skeəʳ] **1** *n* (*fright*) susto: *what a scare you gave me!,* ¡vaya susto me has dado! **2** (*widespread alarm*) alarma, pánico: *there was a bomb scare,* hubo una amenaza de bomba; *the news caused quite a scare,* la noticia sembró el pánico. – **3** *t* asustar, espantar: *did I scare you?,* ¿te he asustado? – **4** *i* asustarse, espantarse: *she scares easily,* se asusta fácilmente.
◆ **to scare away** / **scare off** *t sep* espantar, ahuyentar.
● **to scare sb. to death** / **scare sb. out of their wits,** dar un susto de muerte a algn. ‖ **to scare the living daylights out of sb.,** dar un susto de muerte a algn.
■ **scare story,** historia alarmista.

scarecrow [ˈskeəkrəʊ] *n* espantapájaros *m*, espantajo.

scared [skeəd] *adj* asustado,-a, espantado,-a.
● **to be scared,** tener miedo (**of,** a/de): *I'm scared of spiders,* tengo miedo a las arañas, las arañas me dan miedo; *she's scared to go out after dark,* tiene miedo de salir después del anochecer. ‖ **to be scared out of one's wits,** sufrir un susto mortal, caerse del susto. ‖ **to be scared stiff,** estar muerto,-a de miedo.

scaremonger [ˈskeəmʌŋɡəʳ] *n* alarmista *mf.*

scarf [skɑːf] *n* (*small*) pañuelo; (*silk*) fular *m*; (*long, woolen*) bufanda.
▲ *pl* **scarfs** o **scarves** [skɑːvz].

scarlet [ˈskɑːlət] **1** *adj* escarlata. – **2** *n* escarlata *m.*
■ **scarlet fever,** escarlatina. ‖ **scarlet woman,** *pej* mujer *f* de la calle, mujer *f* de la vida.

scarp [skɑːp] *n* escarpa, pendiente *f.*

scarper [ˈskɑːpəʳ] *i* GB *fam* largarse, abrirse.

scary [ˈskeərɪ] *adj fam* (*situation etc*) espantoso,-a; (*film, story*) de miedo, de terror.
▲ *comp* **scarier,** *superl* **scariest.**

scathing [ˈskeɪðɪŋ] *adj* mordaz, cáustico,-a.
● **to be scathing about sb./sth.,** criticar duramente a algn./algo.

scatter [ˈskætəʳ] **1** *t* (*crowd, birds*) dispersar. **2** (*papers, cushions, etc*) esparcir, desparramar; (*ashes*) esparcir; (*seeds*) sembrar a voleo, esparcir; (*money*) desparramar, derrochar. – **3** *i* (*crowd, birds*) dispersarse; (*small things*) desparramarse, diseminarse.
● **a scatter of,** *n* unos,-as cuantos,-as, algunos,-as.

scatterbrain [ˈskætəbreɪn] *n* cabeza *mf* de chorlito, despistado,-a, alocado,-a.

scatterbrained ['skætəbreɪnd] *adj* (*person*) despistado,-a, alocado,-a; (*idea etc*) descabellado,-a.

scattered ['skætəd] *adj* esparcido,-a, disperso,-a: *there were cushions scattered about the floor*, había cojines esparcidos por el suelo; *there are a few scattered villages*, hay algunos pueblos aislados.
■ **scattered population**, población *f* diseminada. ‖ **scattered showers**, chubascos *mpl* aislados.

scattering ['skætərɪŋ] **a scattering of**, *phr* (*singular*) un poco; (*plural*) unos,-as pocos,-as, algunos,-as: *there was a only scattering of people*, hubo muy poca gente; *a scattering of snow*, un poco de nieve.

scatty ['skætɪ] *adj* (*slightly mad*) tocado,-a, loco,-a, chalado,-a; (*scatterbrained*) despistado,-a, alocado,-a.
▲ *comp* **scattier**, *superl* **scattiest**.

scavenge ['skævɪndʒ] **1** *i* (*animal, bird - search*) rebuscar (**for**, -); (*- feed on*) comer (**on**, -). **2** (*person - search*) hurgar, escarbar; (*find*) encontrar en la basura, rescatar de la basura: *that tramp scavenges through the dustbins*, aquel vagabundo hurga en la basura; *the poor scavenge food from the rubbish tip*, los pobres encuentran comida en el vertedero.

scavenger ['skævɪndʒə'] **1** *n* (*animal*) animal *m* carroñero; (*bird*) ave *f* carroñera. **2** (*person*) rebuscador,-ra, trapero,-a.

scenario [sɪ'nɑːrɪəʊ] **1** *n* CINEM guión *m*; THEAT argumento. **2** (*situation*) (*posible*) situación *f*, panorama *m*.
▲ *pl* **scenarios**.

scene [siːn] **1** *n* (*place*) lugar *m*, escenario; (*sight, picture*) escena: *the scene of the crime*, el lugar del crimen; *a change of scene*, un cambio de aires, un cambio de ambiente; *there were scenes of violence*, hubo escenas de violencia. **2** (*in play, book*) escena: *Act III, Scene 1*, Acto Tercero, Escena Primera; *the love scene*, la escena de amor. **3** (*stage setting*) decorado, escenario: *a rural scene*, un decorado rural. **4** (*emotional outburst*) escena, escándalo. **5** (*sphere*) ámbito, mundo, panorama *m*: *the music scene*, el mundo musical; *discos are not really my scene*, a mí no me van las discotecas.
● **to come on the scene**, llegar, aparecer, presentarse. ‖ **to create/make a scene**, hacer una escena, armar un escándalo, montar un número. ‖ **to set the scene**, (*describe*) describir la escena; (*prepare, help*) crear el ambiente, preparar el terreno.

scenery ['siːnərɪ] **1** *n* (*landscape*) paisaje *m*. **2** THEAT (*on stage*) decorado.

sceneshifter ['siːnʃɪftə'] *n* tramoyista *mf*.

scenic ['siːnɪk] **1** *adj* (*picturesque*) pintoresco,-a. **2** THEAT escénico,-a.
■ **scenic route**, ruta panorámica.

scent [sent] **1** *n* (*gen*) olor *m*; (*pleasant smell*) aroma *m*, perfume *m*, fragancia. **2** (*perfume*) perfume *m*. **3** (*track, trail*) pista, rastro. – **4** *t* (*animal*) olfatear. **5** *fig* (*suspect*) presentir, intuir. **6** (*perfume*) perfumar (**with**, de).
● **to be on the scent of sb./sth.**, seguir/estar sobre la pista de algn./algo. ‖ **to put/throw sb. off the scent**, despistar a algn.

scepter ['septə'] *n* US → **sceptre**.

sceptic ['skeptɪk] *n* escéptico,-a.

sceptical ['skeptɪkəl] *adj* escéptico,-a.
● **to be sceptical about sth.**, dudar de algo.

scepticism ['skeptɪsɪzəm] *n* escepticismo.

sceptre ['septə'] *n* cetro.

schedule ['ʃedjuːl, *te* 'skedjʊəl] **1** *n* (*programme*) programa *m*: *a work schedule*, un programa de trabajo; *he's got a tight schedule today*, hoy tiene una jornada apre-

tada. **2** (*list - gen*) lista; (*- of prices*) tarifa; (*inventory*) inventario. **3** US (*timetable*) horario. – **4** *t* programar, fijar: *I've scheduled the meeting for 2.00 pm*, he programado la reunión para las 2.00.
● **according to schedule**, según lo previsto. ‖ **on schedule**, (*flight*) a la hora (prevista); (*work*) al día. ‖ **to be ahead of schedule**, ir adelantado,-a. ‖ **to be behind schedule**, llevar retraso, ir atrasado,-a.

scheduled ['ʃedjuːld, *te* 'skedʒʊəld] *adj* previsto,-a, programado,-a.
■ **scheduled flight**, vuelo regular.

scheduling ['ʃedjuːlɪŋ *te* 'skedʒʊəlɪŋ] *n* RAD TV programación *f*; COMM organización *f*.

schematic [skiː'mætɪk] *adj* esquemático,-a.

scheme [skiːm] **1** *n* (*plan*) plan *m*, programa *m*; (*project*) proyecto; (*idea*) idea. **2** (*system, order*) sistema *m*, orden *m*; (*arrangement*) disposición *f*, combinación *f*: *a colour scheme*, una combinación de colores. **3** (*plot*) complot *m*, conspiración *f*; (*trick*) ardid *m*, estratagema, truco. – **4** *i* (*plot*) conspirar, intrigar, confabularse: *the rebels schemed against the government*, los rebeldes conspiraron contra el gobierno; *he's scheming to get rid of me*, está intrigando para deshacerse de mí. – **5** *t* (*plan deviously*) tramar, maquinar: *his opponents schemed the president's downfall*, sus adversarios maquinaron la ruina del presidente.
● **the scheme of things**, (*organized system*) el sistema; (*world*) el orden establecido.
■ **pension scheme**, plan *m* de jubilación.

schemer ['skiːmə'] *n* intrigante *mf*, maquinador,-ra, conspirador,-ra.

scheming ['skiːmɪŋ] **1** *adj* intrigante, maquinador,-ra. – **2** *n* intrigas *fpl*, maquinaciones *fpl*.

schism ['skɪzəm] *n* cisma *m*.

schizophrenia [skɪtsəʊ'friːnɪə] *n* esquizofrenia.

schizophrenic [skɪtsəʊ'frenɪk] **1** *adj* esquizofrénico,-a. – **2** *n* esquizofrénico,-a.

schlep [ʃlep] *t* US *fam* (*drag*) arrastrar.
▲ *pt & pp* **schlepped**, *ger* **schlepping**.

schmaltz [ʃmælts] *n* *fam* sentimentalismo, sensiblería.

schmuck [ʃmʌk] *n* US *fam* (*fool*) tonto,-a, gilipollas *mf*.

schnapps [ʃnæps] *n* licor *m*, aguardiente *m*.

schnitzel ['ʃnɪtsəl] *n* US CULIN escalopa de ternera.

scholar ['skɒlə'] **1** *n* (*learned person*) erudito,-a; (*specialist*) especialista *mf*, experto,-a: *he's a Greek scholar*, es helenista; *Latin scholar*, latinista. **2** (*scholarship holder*) becario,-a; (*pupil*) alumno,-a, estudioso,-a. **3** (*good learner*) estudiante *mf*; (*clever person*) intelectual *mf*.

scholarly ['skɒləlɪ] **1** *adj* (*person*) erudito,-a, culto,-a; (*behaviour*) estudioso,-a, meticuloso,-a. **2** (*journal etc*) erudito,-a, académico,-a.

scholarship ['skɒləʃɪp] **1** *n* (*grant, award*) beca. **2** (*learning*) erudición *f*.

scholastic [skə'læstɪk] **1** *adj* (*of schools*) escolar, académico,-a; (*of teaching*) docente. **2** (*of scholasticism*) escolástico,-a.

scholasticism [skə'læstɪsɪzəm] *n* escolasticismo, escolástica.

school[1] [skuːl] **1** *n* (*gen, primary*) escuela, colegio; (*secondary*) colegio, instituto: *what are you going to do when you leave school?*, ¿qué harás cuando dejes el colegio? **2** (*lessons*) clase *f*: *let's meet after school*, quedemos después de clase. **3** (*students*) alumnos *mpl*, alumnado. **4** (*university department*) facultad *f*. **5** US (*university*) universidad *f*. **6** (*course*) curso, cursillo. **7** (*group of artists etc*) escuela: *the Dutch school of painting*, la escuela pictó-

rica holandesa. **– 8** *t* (*teach*) enseñar; (*train*) educar, formar. **9** (*discipline*) disciplinar.
● **to be one of the old school,** ser de la vieja escuela, estar chapado,-a a la antigua.
■ **art school,** escuela de bellas artes. ‖ **comprehensive school,** instituto de enseñanza secundaria (*para alumnos de cualquier nivel académico*). ‖ **convent school,** colegio de monjas. ‖ **drama school,** academia de arte dramático. ‖ **language school,** academia de idiomas, escuela de idiomas. ‖ **primary school,** escuela primaria. ‖ **school age,** edad *f* escolar. ‖ **school holidays,** vacaciones *fpl* escolares. ‖ **school of thought,** corriente *f* de opinión. ‖ **school uniform,** uniforme *m* escolar. ‖ **school year,** año escolar.
school[2] [sku:l] *n* (*of fish*) banco.
schoolbook ['sku:lbʊk] *n* libro de texto.
schoolboy ['sku:lbɔɪ] *n* alumno, colegial *m*, escolar *m*.
schoolchild ['sku:ltʃaɪld] *n* alumno,-a, colegial,-la, escolar *mf*.
▲ *pl* **schoolchildren** ['sku:ltʃɪldrən].
schooldays ['sku:ldeɪz] *npl* años *mpl* de colegio, tiempos *mpl* del colegio.
schoolfellow ['sku:lfeləʊ] *n* compañero,-a de clase.
schoolgirl ['sku:lgɜ:l] *n* alumna, colegiala, escolar *f*.
schooling ['sku:lɪŋ] *n* educación *f*, estudios *mpl*, escolaridad *f*.
school-leaver ['sku:lli:və[r]] *n* *alumno,-a que está a punto de dejar la escuela o que acaba de dejarla.*
schoolmarm ['sku:lmɑ:m] **1** *n* *fam* (*woman - domineering*) marimandona, sargenta; (*- prim*) mujer estricta. **2** us *fam* (*schoolmistress*) profesora, maestra.
schoolmaster ['sku:lmɑ:stə[r]] *n* (*secondary school*) profesor *m*; (*primary school*) maestro.
schoolmate ['sku:lmeɪt] *n* compañero,-a de clase.
schoolmistress ['sku:lmɪstrəs] *n* (*secondary school*) profesora; (*primary school*) maestra.
schoolroom ['sku:lru:m] *n* aula, clase *f*.
schoolteacher ['sku:lti:tʃə[r]] *n* (*secondary school*) profesor,-ra; (*primary school*) maestro,-a.
schoolyard ['sku:lja:d] *n* patio de recreo.
schooner ['sku:nə[r]] **1** *n* MAR goleta. **2** (*glass - for sherry*) copa; (*- for beer*) jarra.
sciatic [saɪˈætɪk] *adj* MED ciático,-a.
sciatica [saɪˈætɪkə] *n* MED ciática.
science ['saɪəns] **1** *n* (*gen*) ciencia. **2** (*subject*) ciencias *fpl*.
■ **science fiction,** ciencia-ficción *f*.
scientific [saɪənˈtɪfɪk] *adj* científico,-a.
scientist ['saɪəntɪst] *n* científico,-a.
sci-fi ['saɪfaɪ] *n* *fam* → **science fiction**.
scintillate ['sɪntɪleɪt] **1** *i* (*sparkle*) centellear, destellar. **2** *fig* brillar, chispear.
scintillating ['sɪntɪleɪtɪŋ] *adj* brillante.
scissors ['sɪzəz] **1** *npl* tijeras *fpl*. **– 2** *n* SP (*wrestling*) (llave *f* de) tijera; (*high jump*) (salto de) tijera.
● **a pair of scissors,** unas tijeras.
sclerosis [sklɪəˈrəʊsɪs] *n* MED esclerosis *f*.
▲ *pl* **scleroses**.
scoff[1] [skɒf] **1** *i* (*mock*) mofarse (**at,** de), burlarse (**at,** de). **– 2 scoffs,** *npl* mofas *fpl*, burlas *fpl*.
scoff[2] [skɒf] **1** *t* *fam* (*eat greedily*) tragarse, zamparse, engullir, jalarse, devorar. **– 2** *n* *fam* (*food*) papeo, manduca.
scoffing ['skɒfɪŋ] *adj* (*mocking*) burlón,-ona.
scold [skəʊld] **1** *t* reñir, regañar. **– 2** *n* *dated* (*complaining person*) quejica *mf*, regañón,-ona, refunfuñón,-ona.
scolding ['skəʊldɪŋ] *n* regañina, reprimenda.

scone [skəʊn, skɒn] *n* CULIN bollo (*que se suele comer con mantequilla, mermelada, nata, etc*).
scoop [sku:p] **1** *n* (*for flour, rice, etc*) pala; (*for ice-cream*) cucharón *m*. **2** (*amount*) palada, cucharada. **3** (*news story*) primicia (informativa). **4** (*large profit*) golpe *m* financiero. **– 5** *t* (*take out*) sacar con una pala. **6** (*beat rival*) vencer, pisar; (*get news first*) dar la primicia. **7** (*win*) ganar; (*make profit*) forrarse. **8** SP (*in hockey, golf*) levantar.
◆ **to scoop out 1** *t sep* (*take out*) sacar con pala. **2** (*hollow out*) vaciar, hacer un hueco en. ‖ **to scoop up** *t sep* recoger, levantar.
scooter ['sku:tə[r]] *n* (*child's*) patinete *m*, patineta; (*motorized*) escúter *m*, Vespa.
scope [skəʊp] **1** *n* (*area, range - gen*) alcance *m*; (*- of book, undertaking*) ámbito; (*ability, field*) competencia, campo: *that is beyond the scope of this report,* eso queda fuera del alcance de este informe; *we need to widen the scope of the course,* hay que ampliar el ámbito del curso. **2** (*opportunity*) oportunidad *f*; (*room*) posibilidades *fpl*: *there is scope for creativity in this job,* este trabajo te ofrece muchas posibilidades para expresar tu creatividad.
scorch [skɔ:tʃ] **1** *t* (*singe*) chamuscar, socarrar. **2** (*burn*) quemar, abrasar. **– 3** *i* (*singe*) chamuscarse. **4** GB *fam* (*travel fast*) ir a toda velocidad. **– 5** *n* chamusquina, quemadura (superficial).
■ **scorch mark,** chamusquina, quemadura (superficial).
scorched [skɔ:tʃt] *adj* quemado,-a, abrasado,-a.
■ **scorched earth policy,** MIL política de tierra quemada.
scorcher ['skɔ:tʃə[r]] *n* *fam* (*hot day*) día *m* abrasador.
scorching ['skɔ:tʃɪŋ] *adj* abrasador,-ra.
● **to be scorching hot,** abrasar.
score [skɔ:[r]] **1** *n* SP (*gen*) tanteo; (*in golf, cards*) puntuación *f*: *what's the score?,* ¿cómo van?; *what's my score?,* ¿cuántos puntos tengo?; *there is still no score,* todavía no se ha inaugurado el marcador; *the final score was 3-0,* el resultado final fue 3-0; *what's the highest score you can get?,* ¿cuál es la puntuación más alta que se puede conseguir? **2** (*in exam, test*) nota, calificación *f*, puntuación *f*. **3** (*notch, cut*) muesca, corte *m*, marca; (*scratch*) rasguño. **4** MUS (*written version*) partitura; (*of film, play, etc*) música. **5** (*twenty*) veinte, veintena. **– 6** *t* SP (*goal*) marcar, hacer, meter; (*point*) ganar; (*run*) hacer, realizar: *who scored the winning goal?,* ¿quién marcó el gol decisivo?; *if you answer this question correctly, you score 50 points,* si contestas esta pregunta correctamente, ganas 50 puntos. **7** (*in exam, test*) sacar, obtener, conseguir. **8** (*give points to*) dar, puntuar: *the judge scored the gymnast 9.9,* el juez dio a la gimnasta una puntuación de 9,9; *this question scores 10 points,* esta pregunta vale 10 puntos. **9** (*achieve, succeed*) tener, conseguir, lograr: *we have scored an important victory,* hemos logrado una victoria importante. **10** MUS (*write*) escribir, componer; (*arrange*) hacer un arreglo de, arreglar. **11** (*notch - wood*) hacer una muesca en, hacer cortes en; (*- paper*) rayar, marcar. **12** SP (*obtain drugs*) ligar, pillar. **– 13** *i* SP (*gen*) marcar (un tanto); (*goal*) marcar (un gol); (*point*) puntuar, conseguir puntos: *he has yet to score this season,* aún no ha marcado ningún gol; *all the contestants have scored extremely well,* todos los concursantes han conseguido muchos puntos. **14** (*record points etc*) llevar el marcador, tantear. **15** (*have success*) tener éxito. **16** *sl* (*get off with*) ligar (**with,** con); (*do to bed with*) acostarse (**con,** with). **17** *sl* (*obtain drugs*) ligar droga, pillar droga. **– 18 scores,** *npl* (*very many*) muchísimos,-as, montones *mpl* de.

◆ **to score off** *t insep* triunfar a costa de. ‖ **to score out/through** *t sep* tachar, rayar.

● **by the score,** muchísimos,-as. ‖ **on more scores than one,** en más de un sentido. ‖ **on that score,** por lo que se refiere a eso, a ese respecto. ‖ **to keep the score,** seguir el marcador. ‖ **to know the score,** estar al tanto. ‖ **to pay/settle an old score,** ajustar cuentas pendientes, saldar cuentas pendientes.

scoreboard ['skɔːbɔːd] *n* marcador *m*.

scorecard ['skɔːkaːd] *n* SP (*golf*) tarjeta; (*at match, race*) ficha.

scorekeeper ['skɔːkiːpəʳ] *n* encargado,-a del marcador.

scorer ['skɔːrəʳ] **1** *n* (*scorekeeper*) encargado,-a del marcador, persona que lleva el marcador. **2** (*goal striker*) goleador,-ra: *who was the scorer?,* ¿quién marcó el gol?

scorn [skɔːn] **1** *n* desdén *m*, desprecio. – **2** *t* desdeñar, despreciar, menospreciar.

● **to pour scorn on sth.,** despreciar algo, menospreciar algo.

scornful ['skɔːnfʊl] *adj* desdeñoso,-a.

Scorpio ['skɔːpɪəʊ] *n* Escorpión *mf*.

scorpion ['skɔːpɪən] *n* escorpión *m*, alacrán *m*.

Scot [skɒt] **1** *n* escocés,-esa. **2** HIST escoto,-a.

scotch [skɒtʃ] *t* (*idea, plan*) frustrar, echar por tierra; (*rumour*) acallar, poner fin a.

Scotch [skɒtʃ] **1** *adj* escocés,-esa. – **2** *n* (*whisky*) whisky *m* escocés.

■ **Scotch broth,** potaje *m* (*hecho de caldo de carne, verduras y cebada*). ‖ **Scotch egg,** huevo a la escocesa, (*huevo duro envuelto en una capa de carne de salchicha, empanado y frito*). ‖ **Scotch tape,** US cinta adhesiva, celo. ‖ **Scotch terrier,** terrier *m* escocés. ‖ **Scotch whisky,** whisky *m* escocés.

scot-free [skɒt'friː] *adj fam* impune.

● **to get off scot-free,** quedar impune, salir impune.

Scotland ['skɒtlənd] *n* Escocia.

Scots [skɒts] *adj* escocés,-esa.

Scotsman ['skɒtsmən] *n* escocés *m*.

▲ *pl Scotsmen* ['skɒtsmən].

Scotswoman ['skɒtswʊmən] *n* escocesa.

▲ *pl Scotswomen* ['skɒtswɪmɪn].

Scottish ['skɒtɪʃ] **1** *adj* escocés,-esa. – **2 the Scottish,** *npl* los escoceses *mpl*.

scoundrel ['skaʊndrəl] *n* sinvergüenza *mf*.

scour¹ [skaʊəʳ] *t* (*search - countryside*) recorrer; (*- building*) registrar.

scour² [skaʊəʳ] **1** *t* (*clean*) fregar, restregar. **2** (*erode*) erosionar.

scourer ['skaʊrəʳ] *n* estropajo.

scourge [skɜːdʒ] **1** *n* (*whip*) azote *m*. **2** *fig* (*thing*) azote *m*, calamidad *f*, flagelo; (*person*) verdugo. – **3** *t* (*flog*) azotar. **4** *fml fig* afligir, azotar.

Scouse [skaʊs] **1** *n* GB *fam* (*person*) persona de Liverpool. **2** GB *fam* (*dialect*) dialecto de Liverpool. – **3** *adj* GB de Liverpool.

scout [skaʊt] **1** *n* MIL (*person*) explorador,-ra; (*plane*) avión *m* de reconocimiento. **2** (*boy*) scout *m*. **3** (*talent spotter*) cazatalentos *mf*. **4** (*act of scouting*) busca, búsqueda. – **5** *i* MIL reconocer el terreno. **6** (*look for*) buscar (**about/around,** -), andar en busca de (**about/around,** -).

■ **scout camp,** acampada de scouts. ‖ **scout troop,** grupo scout.

scouting ['skaʊtɪŋ] **1** *n* (*activities*) actividades *fpl* de los scouts. **2** (*movement*) escultismo.

scoutmaster ['skaʊtmaːstəʳ] *n* jefe *m* de un grupo de scouts.

scowl [skaʊl] **1** *i* fruncir el ceño. – **2** *n* ceño (fruncido).

scrabble ['skræbəl] *i* (*among stones etc*) escarbar; (*in bag etc*) hurgar; (*on floor etc*) rebuscar.

scrag [skræg] **1** *n* CULIN pescuezo. – **2** *t fam* (*attack roughly*) dar una paliza a.

▲ *pt & pp scragged, ger scragging.*

scraggly ['skrægəlɪ] *adj fam* (*untidy*) descuidado,-a; (*poor*) de mala calidad; (*uneven*) escabroso,-a.

▲ *comp scragglier, superl scraggliest.*

scraggy ['skrægɪ] *adj pej* flacucho,-a, enjuto,-a, escuálido,-a.

▲ *comp scraggier, superl scraggiest.*

scram [skræm] *i fam* largarse: *scram!,* ¡lárgate!, ¡largo de aquí!

▲ *pt & pp scrammed, ger scramming.*

scramble ['skræmbəl] **1** *n* (*difficult climb*) subida escabrosa; (*difficult walk*) caminata difícil. **2** (*struggle*) lucha, pelea; (*confusion*) confusión *f*, barullo. **3** SP (*motorcycle race*) carrera de motocross. – **4** *i* (*climb*) trepar (**over,** por) (**up,** a), subir gateando; (*crawl*) gatear, arrastrarse; (*clamber*) moverse rápidamente: *the children scrambled over the rocks,* los niños gatearon por las rocas; *they scrambled to their feet,* se levantaron apresuradamente. **5** (*struggle*) pelearse (**for,** por), luchar (**for,** para): *people scrambled to get out,* la gente se peleó para salir; *we scrambled for seats,* nos peleamos por encontrar asiento. **6** MIL (*plane*) despegar de repente. – **7** *t* (*mix, jumble*) revolver, mezclar. **8** (*eggs*) revolver. **9** (*message*) cifrar, poner en cifra, codificar. **10** MIL (*plane*) hacer que despegue de repente.

scrambling ['skræmbəlɪŋ] *n* SP motocross *m*.

scrap¹ [skræp] **1** *n* (*of paper, cloth, etc*) trozo, trocito, pedazo; (*of news, conversation*) fragmento, migaja: *scraps of fabric,* retales. **2** (*of metal*) chatarra. **3** (*in negatives*) pizca, ápice *m*: *there's not a scrap of truth in it,* no hay ni un ápice de verdad. – **4** *t* (*throw away*) desechar; (*cars etc*) convertir en chatarra, desguazar. **5** *fig* (*idea*) descartar; (*plan*) abandonar. – **6 scraps,** *npl* (*gen*) restos *mpl*; (*of food*) sobras *fpl*.

■ **scrap (metal) dealer,** chatarrero,-a. ‖ **scrap metal,** chatarra. ‖ **scrap paper,** papel *m* de borrador. ‖ **scrap yard,** (*gen*) parque de chatarra, chatarrería; (*for cars*) cementerio de coches.

▲ *pt & pp scrapped, ger scrapping.*

scrap² [skræp] **1** *n fam* (*fight*) pelea. – **2** *i* pelearse.

▲ *pt & pp scrapped, ger scrapping.*

scrapbook ['skræpbʊk] *n* álbum *m* de recortes.

scrape [skreɪp] **1** *n* (*act*) raspado; (*sound*) chirrido. **2** (*on skin*) rasguño, arañazo; (*on object*) raspadura, roce *m*. **3** *fam* (*fix, jam*) lío, apuro, aprieto. – **4** *t* (*surface, paint, etc*) raspar (**away/off,** -), rascar (**away/off,** -); (*vegetables*) raspar: *he scraped the paint off the door,* raspó la pintura de la puerta. **5** (*graze skin*) arañarse, hacerse un rasguño en, rasparse: *he fell and scraped his knee,* se cayó y se arañó la rodilla. **6** (*rub against*) rozar, raspar, rascar: *I scraped the car against the wall,* he rozado el coche con el muro; *he scraped his nails down the blackboard,* rascó la pizarra con las uñas. – **7** *i* (*grate*) chirriar. **8** (*rub against*) raspar, rozar, pasar rozando. **9** (*economize*) hacer economías, ahorrar.

◆ **to scrape along / scrape by** *i* ir tirando, arreglárselas, apañárselas. ‖ **to scrape in** *i* (*job, university*) entrar por los pelos; (*political party*) ganar por los pelos. ‖ **to scrape through** *t insep* (*exam*) aprobar de chiripa, aprobar por los pelos; (*round of competition*) pasar por los pelos. ‖ **to scrape together / scrape up** *t sep* reunir a duras penas, ir arañando.

● **to get into a scrape,** meterse en un lío. ‖ **to scrape a living,** ganar lo justo para vivir. ‖ **to scrape sth. clean,** dejar algo limpio,-a, limpiar algo. ‖ **to scrape the (bottom of the) barrel,** tocar fondo.

scraper ['skreɪpəʳ] 1 *n* (*tool*) rasqueta, rascador *m*. 2 (*for shoes*) limpiabarros *m*.

scrapheap ['skræphiːp] *n* vertedero.

● **to find os. on the scrapheap,** encontrarse rechazado,-a y sin futuro. ‖ **to throw sth. on the scrapheap,** desechar algo.

scraping ['skreɪpɪŋ] *npl* raspaduras *fpl*.

scrappy ['skræpɪ] 1 *adj* (*report, speech*) deshilvanado,-a; (*book, structure*) incompleto,-a, fragmentario,-a; (*education*) rudimentario,-a; (*match*) irregular. 2 US *fam* (*agressive*) camorrista, luchador,-ra.

▲ *comp* **scrappier,** *superl* **scrappiest.**

scratch [skrætʃ] 1 *n* (*on skin*) arañazo, rasguño; (*on paintwork, furniture*) arañazo, raspadura, marca, señal *m*; (*on record, photo*) raya: *we escaped without a scratch,* salimos ilesos; *there's a scratch on this record,* este disco está rayado. 2 (*noise*) chirrido. 3 SP (*start line*) línea de salida. – 4 *adj* (*improvised*) improvisado,-a: *we put together a scratch team,* improvisamos un equipo. 5 (*without handicap*) sin hándicap: *scratch golfer,* golfista sin hándicap. – 6 *t* (*with nail, claw*) arañar, rasguñar; (*paintwork, furniture, record*) rayar; (*with initials etc*) grabar: *be careful the cat doesn't scratch you!,* ¡ojo que no te arañe el gato! 7 (*part of body*) rascar: *could you scratch my back?,* ¿me puedes rascar la espalda?; *she scratched her leg,* se rascó la pierna 8 SP retirar. 9 (*idea*) descartar; (*plan*) abandonar. – 10 *i* (*animal*) arañar, rascar, rasguñar; (*pen*) raspear; (*wool, sweater, towel*) raspar, picar: *does your cat scratch?,* ¿tu gato araña?; *the dog is scratching at the door,* el perro está arañando la puerta; *this jumper scratches,* este jersey pica. 11 (*itch*) rascarse: *stop scratching!,* ¡deja de rascarte! 12 SP retirarse.

◆ **to scratch out** *t sep* (*erase*) tachar, borrar.

● **to be/come up to scratch,** dar la talla, ser del nivel requerido. ‖ **to scratch one's head,** (*think*) calentarse la cabeza, darle vueltas en la cabeza. ‖ **to scratch sb.'s eyes out,** sacarle los ojos a algn. ‖ **to scratch the surface of sth.,** tratar algo muy por encima: *this article doesn't even scratch the surface of the problem,* este artículo no profundiza en el problema. ‖ **to start from scratch,** empezar de cero, partir de cero. ‖ **you scratch my back and I'll scratch yours,** favor con favor se paga, hoy por ti y mañana por mí.

■ **scratch card,** rasca rasca *m*. ‖ **scratch pad,** US bloc *m* de notas. ‖ **scratch test,** MED cutirreacción *f*.

▲ *comp* **scratchier,** *superl* **scratchiest.**

scrawl [skrɔːl] 1 *n* (*writing*) garabato, garabatos *mpl*. – 2 *t* garabatear, garrapatear. – 3 *i* garabatear, hacer garabatos.

scrawny ['skrɔːnɪ] *adj pej* flacucho,-a, huesudo,-a, escuálido,-a.

▲ *comp* **scrawnier,** *superl* **scrawniest.**

scream [skriːm] 1 *n* (*of pain, fear*) grito, chillido, alarido; (*of laughter*) carcajada. 2 *fig* (*screech*) chirrido. 3 *fam* (*funny person*) persona divertida, persona graciosa; (*funny thing*) cosa divertida: *your cousin's a scream,* tu primo es la monda, tu primo es divertidísimo; *it was a scream,* fue la monda, fue para mondarse (de risa). – 4 *t* gritar, decir a gritos, vocear: *he screamed out a warning,* dio un aviso a gritos; *she just screamed insults at me,* simplemente me lanzó insultos. 5 *fig* (*headlines*) anunciar. – 6 *i* (*gen*) gritar, berrear, chillar, pegar un

grito; (*wind, siren, etc*) aullar: *she screamed for help,* pidió socorro a gritos; *he screamed at me to run,* me gritó para que corriera; *the patient screamed with pain,* el paciente lanzó gritos de dolor; *the baby won't stop screaming,* el bebé no para de berrear; *he was screaming with laughter,* se mondaba de risa, se tronchaba de risa. 7 *fig* (*need*) pedir (a gritos), clamar (a gritos).

● **to scream the place down,** desgañitarse.

screech [skriːtʃ] 1 *n* (*of person*) grito, alarido, chillido; (*of tyres, brakes, birds, etc*) chirrido; (*of siren*) aullido. – 2 *t* gritar, decir a gritos, chillar. – 3 *i* (*person*) chillar; (*tyres, brakes, bird, etc*) chirriar; (*siren*) aullar; (*gate*) rechinar: *the police car screeched to a halt,* el coche patrulla paró en seco con un chirrido.

■ **screech owl,** lechuza.

screed [skriːd] 1 *n* GB *fam pej* mucha palabrería. – 2 **screeds,** *pl* (*pages*) páginas *fpl*.

screen [skriːn] 1 *n* (*partition - folding*) biombo; (- *of wood, glass*) mampara; (*fireguard*) pantalla. 2 (*for window*) alambrera, mosquitera, mosquitero. 3 (*protection, cover*) cortina, pantalla: *a screen of trees,* una cortina de árboles; *the video shop is a screen for illegal goings-on,* la tienda de videos sirve de pantalla para actividades ilegales. 4 (*of TV, for projection*) pantalla. 5 (*cinema in complex*) sala. 6 (*sieve*) tamiz *m*, criba. – 7 *t* (*protect, shelter*) proteger (**from,** de), abrigar; (*hide, conceal*) tapar, ocultar: *the trees screened the house from onlookers,* los árboles protegían la casa de curiosos; *she screened her face with her hand,* se tapó la cara con la mano; *this groyne will screen us against the wind,* este espigón nos protegerá del viento. 8 *fig* (*protect - gen*) proteger, abrigar, amparar; (- *criminal*) encubrir. 9 MED (*examine*) someter a una exploración médica: *all women must be screened for cancer,* todas las mujeres deben someterse a una revisión para prevenir el cáncer. 10 (*test*) investigar, someter a una investigación: *all applicants will be screened,* todos los candidatos serán sometidos a una investigación; *the government screens all its employees,* el gobierno investiga a todos sus empleados. 11 (*film - gen*) proyectar; (- *first time*) estrenar; (- *on* TV) emitir. 12 (*sieve*) cribar, tamizar, pasar por el tamiz. – 13 *the screen,* *n* la pantalla, el cine: *stars of the screen,* estrellas de la pantalla; *I'd like to write for the screen,* me gustaría escribir para el cine.

◆ **to screen off** *t insep* aislar, separar (con un biombo/ una mampara). ‖ **to screen out** *t sep* eliminar, rechazar.

■ **screen door,** puerta mosquitera. ‖ **screen test,** prueba.

screening ['skriːnɪŋ] 1 *n* (*of film*) proyección *f*; (*first time*) estreno; (*on* TV) emisión *f*. 2 MED exploración *f*, revisión *f*. 3 (*of candidates etc*) selección *f*, investigación *f*.

screenplay ['skriːnpleɪ] *n* guión *m*.

screenwriter ['skriːnraɪtəʳ] *n* guionista *mf*.

screw [skruː] 1 *n* (*metal pin*) tornillo. 2 (*propeller*) hélice *f*. 3 (*turn*) vuelta. 4 *sl* (*prison warder*) carcelero,-a. 5 GB *sl* (*pay, wages*) paga, sueldo. 6 *taboo* (*sexual act*) polvo. – 7 *t* (*fasten with screws*) atornillar; (*tighten*) enroscar, apretar: *screw this hinge on the door,* atornilla esta bisagra en la puerta; *screw the two pieces together,* une las dos piezas con tornillos; *screw the bulb in well,* enrosca bien la bombilla; *screw the lid on tight,* enrosca bien la tapa. 8 (*crumple*) arrugar: *she screwed the piece of paper into a ball,* hizo una bola con el papel. 9 (*cheat, swindle*) timar; (*overcharge*) clavar; (*get money out of*) sacar: *you were well and truly screwed!,* ¡te han timado de verdad!; *how much did they screw you for?,* ¿cuánto te clavaron?; *I'll screw you for every penny you've got!,* ¡te

sacaré hasta el último penique! **10** *taboo* (*have sex with*) joder, follar, tirarse. – **11** *i* (*turn, tighten*) atornillarse, enroscarse. **12** (*have sex*) echar un polvo, joder, follar.
◆ **to screw up** **1** *t sep* (*paper*) arrugar; (*face*) torcer; (*eyes*) cerrar, entornar. **2** *sl* (*ruin - interview, exam*) cagarla; (*plans*) fastidiar; (*- person*) traumatizar: *I really screwed up driving test,* la cagué en el examen de conducir; *the bad weather really screwed up my plans for the weekend,* el mal tiempo fastidió mis planes para el fin de semana. – **3** *i sl* (*make a mess*) meter la pata, cagarla.
● **to have a screw loose,** faltarle un tornillo a uno. ‖ **screw that!,** *sl* ¡a joderse! ‖ **screw you!,** *sl* ¡jódete!, ¡vete a la mierda! ‖ **to be screwed up,** (*person*) tener muchos traumas, estar neurótico,-a. ‖ **to have one's head screwed on,** tener la cabeza bien sentada. ‖ **to screw up one's courage,** armarse de valor.
screwball ['skruːbɔːl] **1** *n* US *fam* (*crazy person*) excéntrico,-a, chiflado,-a, loco,-a; (*idea etc*) chalado,-a, descabellado,-a, disparatado,-a. **2** US SP *fam* (*baseball*) torniquete *m*, tirabuzón *m*.
screwdriver ['skruːdraɪvəʳ] **1** *n* (*tool*) destornillador *m*. **2** (*cocktail*) destornillador *m*, vodka *m* con naranja.
screw-top ['skruːtɒp] *adj* con tapón de rosca, con tapa de rosca.
screwy ['skruːɪ] *adj fam* (*crazy*) loco,-a, chalado,-a, excéntrico,-a.
▲ *comp* **screwier,** *superl* **screwiest**.
scribble ['skrɪbəl] **1** *n* garabato, garabatos *mpl.* – **2** *t* garabatear, garrapatear. – **3** *i* garabatear, hacer garabatos.
scribbler ['skrɪbələʳ] *n pej* escritorzuelo,-a.
scribbling ['skrɪbəlɪŋ] *n* garabatos *mpl.*
■ **scribbling block/pad,** bloc *m* de notas.
scribe [skraɪb] **1** *n* (*copier*) escribiente *mf*, amanuense *mf*; (*writer, journalist*) escribidor,-ra. **2** (*in Biblical times*) escriba *m*.
scrimmage ['skrɪmɪdʒ] **1** *n* (*fight*) escaramuza (**on**, en), refriega. **2** US SP escaramuza. – **3** *i* escaramuzar, pelearse.
scrimp [skrɪmp] *i* hacer economías, escatimar (**on**, en).
● **to scrimp and save,** hacer grandes economías, ir arañando, apretarse el cinturón.
script [skrɪpt] **1** *n* (*of film etc*) guión *m*. **2** (*writing*) escritura; (*text*) texto; (*handwriting*) letra. **3** GB EDUC (*in exam*) escrito, examen *m.* – **4** *t* (*film*) escribir un guión de; (*text*) redactar.
scripture ['skrɪptʃəʳ] *n* escritura, escrito.
Scripture ['skrɪptʃəʳ] **the Scripture,** *n* REL Sagrada Escritura.
■ **Holy Scriptures,** Sagradas Escrituras *fpl.*
scriptwriter ['skrɪptraɪtəʳ] *n* guionista *mf.*
scroll [skrəʊl] **1** *n* (*of parchment*) pergamino, rollo (de pergamino). **2** ART ARCH voluta. – **3** *t* COMPUT correr, desplazar.
◆ **to scroll down** *i* COMPUT desplazarse hacia abajo. ‖ **to scroll up** *i* (*comput*) desplazarse hacia arriba.
scrooge [skruːdʒ] *n fam pej* tacaño,-a, avaro,-a, roña *mf.*
scrotum ['skrəʊtəm] *n* ANAT escroto.
▲ *pl* **scrotums** *o* **scrota** ['skrəʊtə].
scrounge [skraʊndʒ] **1** *i fam* (*gen*) gorrear (**from/off**, a), gorronear, vivir de gorra; (*money*) dar sablazos, sablear, vivir de sablazos. – **2** *t* (*gen*) gorrear (**from/off**, a), gorronear (**from/off**, a); (*money*) dar sablazos (**from/off**, a), sablear (**from/off**, a): *he scrounges fags off his friends,* gorronea pitillos a sus amigos; *she's always scrounging money off me,* siempre me sablea.

● **to be on the scrounge,** andar pidiendo. ‖ **to scrounge off sb.,** vivir a costa de algn.
scrounger ['skraʊndʒəʳ] *n fam* (*gen*) gorrón,-ona, sablista *mf*; (*from State*) parásito,-a.
scrub¹ [skrʌb] *n* (*undergrowth*) maleza.
scrub² [skrʌb] **1** *t* (*clean - floor, dishes*) fregar bien, estregar, restregar; (*- clothes, wall*) lavar bien, frotar bien: *she was on her knees, scrubbing the floor,* estaba de rodillas fregando el suelo. **2** *fam* (*cancel*) cancelar, abandonar. – **3** *i* fregar bien (**at**, -). – **4** *n* (*cleaning*) fregado, lavado: *give the floor a good scrub,* friega bien el suelo.
◆ **to scrub off** *t sep* quitar frotando, quitar fregando. ‖ **to scrub up** *i* lavarse (las manos).
▲ *pt & pp* **scrubbed,** *ger* **scrubbing**.
scrubber ['skrʌbəʳ] **1** *n* US (*for cleaning*) estropajo. **2** GB *fam pej* fulana, golfa, furcia.
scrubbing brush ['skrʌbɪŋbrʌʃ] *n* (*for floors*) estregadera, cepillo de fregar.
scruff¹ [skrʌf] *n* (*neck*) cogote *m*, pescuezo.
scruff² [skrʌf] *n fam* (*untidy person*) desaliñado,-a, zarrapastroso,-a, desaseado,-a.
scruffy ['skrʌfɪ] *adj* desaliñado,-a, zarrapastroso,-a, desaseado,-a.
▲ *comp* **scruffier,** *superl* **scruffiest**.
scrum [skrʌm] **1** *n* SP (*rugby*) melé *f.* **2** *fam* (*struggle*) refriega, follón *m.*
◆ **to scrum down** *i* SP formar una melé, hacer una melé.
■ **scrum half,** media melé.
▲ *pt & pp* **scrummed,** *ger* **scrumming**.
scrummage ['skrʌmɪdʒ] **1** *n* SP (*rugby*) melé *f.* **2** *fam* refriega, follón *m.* – **3** *i* formar una melé, hacer una melé.
scrumptious ['skrʌmpʃəs] *adj fam* delicioso,-a, de rechupete.
scrumpy ['skrʌmpɪ] *n* (*cider*) sidra fuerte.
scrunch ['skrʌntʃ] **1** *t* (*crumple - paper*) estrujar (**up**, -). **2** (*crunch food*) mascar, ronchar, ronzar. **3** (*make noise*) hacer crujir. – **4** *i* (*make noise*) crujir, ronchar, ronzar. – **5** *n* (*noise*) crujido.
scruple ['skruːpəl] **1** *n* escrúpulo. – **2** *i* vacilar en.
● **to be without scruple,** no tener escrúpulos. ‖ **to not scruple to do sth.,** no tener ningún escrúpulo en hacer algo.
scrupulous ['skruːpjʊləs] **1** *adj* (*meticulous*) escrupuloso,-a, meticuloso,-a, puntilloso,-a. **2** (*honest*) escrupuloso,-a, concienzudo,-a, honrado,-a.
scrupulously ['skruːpjʊləslɪ] *adv* escrupulosamente: *scrupulously clean,* impecable.
scrupulousness ['skruːpjʊləsnəs] *n* escrupulosidad *f*, escrúpulos *mpl.*
scrutineer [skruːtɪˈnɪəʳ] *n* GB escrutador,-ra.
scrutinize ['skruːtɪnaɪz] *t* (*document*) escudriñar, examinar a fondo, inspeccionar; (*face*) escrutar, escudriñar.
scrutiny ['skruːtɪnɪ] **1** *n* (*examination*) examen *m* profundo. **2** GB POL escrutinio.
● **to be under scrutiny,** ser analizado,-a.
scuba ['skjuːbə] *n* equipo de submarinismo.
■ **scuba diving,** submarinismo, buceo con botellas de oxígeno.
scuff [skʌf] **1** *t* (*scrape floor, furniture*) rayar, dejar marcas en; (*shoes*) raspar, rayar. **2** (*drag feet*) arrastrar. – **3** *i* (*shuffle*) andar arrastrando los pies. – **4** *n* raya, marca.
scuffle ['skʌfəl] **1** *n* (*fight*) refriega, escaramuza, riña, pelea. – **2** *i* reñir (**with**, con), pelearse (**with**, con).
scull [skʌl] **1** *n* (*oar*) remo de cuple. **2** (*small boat*) bote *m* de scull. – **3** *t* impulsar remando. – **4** *i* remar.

scullery ['skʌlərɪ] *n* fregadero, trascocina.
▲ *pl* **sculleries**.
sculpt [skʌlpt] **1** *t* esculpir. – **2** *i* esculpir.
sculptor ['skʌlptə'] *n* escultor,-ra.
sculptress ['skʌlptrəs] *n* escultora.
sculpture ['skʌlptʃə'] **1** *n* escultura. – **2** *t* esculpir (**in**, **en**).
scum [skʌm] **1** *n* (*froth*) espuma; (*on pond*) verdín *m*. **2** *pej* (*people*) escoria; (*individual*) canalla *m*.
● **the scum of the earth,** la escoria de la sociedad.
scupper ['skʌpə'] **1** *t* GB (*ship*) hundir adrede, echar a pique. **2** *fam* (*plan, chance*) desbaratar, frustar, hundir, echar a pique. – **3** *n* (*on ship*) cañería de desagüe, imbornal *m*.
● **to be scuppered,** (*plans*) frustrarse, irse a pique; (*person*) estar acabado,-a.
scurf [skɜːf] *n* caspa.
scurrilous ['skʌrɪləs] *adj* (*abusive, insulting*) difamatorio,-a, caluminoso,-a; (*coarse, obscene*) grosero,-a.
scurry ['skʌrɪ] **1** *i* (*run*) correr, corretear; (*hurry*) apresurarse: *everyone scurried for shelter,* todos corrieron para ponerse a cubierto. – **2** *n* (*movement, act*) correteo, movimiento; (*sound*) ruido.
◆ **to scurry away / scurry off** *i* escabullirse.
▲ *pt & pp* **scurried,** *ger* **scurrying.**
scurvy ['skɜːvɪ] **1** *n* MED escorbuto. – **2** *adj* (*mean, despicable*) despreciable, vil, ruin.
▲ *comp* **scurvier,** *superl* **scurviest.**
scuttle¹ ['skʌtəl] **1** *i* (*run*) correr, corretear. – **2** *n* correteo, movimiento.
◆ **to scuttle away/off** *i* escabullirse.
scuttle² ['skʌtəl] *n* (*for coal*) cubo de carbón.
scuttle³ ['skʌtəl] **1** *n* MAR escotilla. – **2** *t* (*sink ship*) barrenar, hundir adrede, echar a pique. **3** *fam* (*plan etc*) desbaratar, frustrar, hundir, echar a pique.
scythe [saɪð] **1** *n* guadaña. – **2** *t* guadañar, segar (con la guadaña). – **3** *i* guadañar.
SE [saʊθ 'iːst] *abbr* (**southeast**) sudeste *m*, sureste *m*; (*abbreviation*) SE.
sea [siː] **1** *n* mar *m & f*: *we love swimming in the sea,* nos encanta nadar en el mar; *the sea is calm/rough today,* la mar está serena/picada hoy; *a heavy/light sea,* una mar gruesa/llana. **2** *fig* mar *m*, multitud *f*: *a sea of faces,* un mar de caras. – **3** *adj* marítimo,-a, de mar.
● **at sea,** en el mar. ‖ **by the sea,** a orillas del mar. ‖ **out to sea,** mar adentro. ‖ **to be all at sea,** estar perdido,-a, estar confundido,-a. ‖ **to find one's sea legs,** acostumbrarse al mar, no marearse. ‖ **to go by sea,** ir en barco. ‖ **to go to sea,** hacerse marinero. ‖ **to put (out) to sea,** zarpar, hacerse a la mar. ‖ **to send sth. by sea,** enviar algo por mar.
■ **sea air,** aire *m* marino. ‖ **sea anemone,** anémona de mar. ‖ **sea bass,** lubina, róbalo. ‖ **sea bird,** ave *f* marina. ‖ **sea bream,** pagro, pargo. ‖ **sea breeze,** brisa marina. ‖ **sea captain,** capitán *m* de barco. ‖ **sea change,** cambio radical, metamorfosis *f*. ‖ **sea cow,** manatí *m*. ‖ **sea dog,** lobo de mar. ‖ **sea fog,** bruma. ‖ **sea green,** verde *m* mar. ‖ **sea horse,** caballito de mar, hipocampo. ‖ **sea kale,** col *f* marina. ‖ **sea legs,** equilibrio. ‖ **sea level,** nivel *m* del mar. ‖ **sea lion,** león *m* marino. ‖ **sea mile,** milla marina (6000 pies ó 1000 brazas ó 1828,8 metros). ‖ **sea mist,** bruma. ‖ **sea pink,** armenia marítima. ‖ **sea power,** (*country*) potencia naval; (*power*) poderío naval. ‖ **sea trout,** trucha de mar, reo. ‖ **sea urchin,** erizo de mar. ‖ **sea wall,** dique *m*, rompeolas *m*, malecón *m*, espigón *m*.

seabed ['siːbed] *n* fondo del mar, fondo marino.
seaboard ['siːbɔːd] *n* US costa, litoral *m*.
seaborne ['siːbɔːn] *adj* transportado,-a por vía marítima.
seafarer ['siːfeərə'] *n* marinero.
seafaring ['siːfeərɪŋ] *adj* marinero,-a.
seafood ['siːfuːd] *n* marisco, mariscos *mpl*.
■ **seafood restaurant,** marisquería.
seafront ['siːfrʌnt] *n* (*area*) puerto; (*beach*) playa; (*promenade*) paseo marítimo.
■ **seafront restaurant,** restaurante *m* frente al mar.
seagoing ['siːgəʊɪŋ] *adj* de alta mar.
sea-green ['siːgriːn] *adj* verdemar.
seagull ['siːgʌl] *n* gaviota.
seal¹ [siːl] **1** *n* ZOOL foca. – **2** *i* cazar focas.
seal² [siːl] **1** *n* (*official stamp*) sello: *wax seal,* sello de lacre; *the royal seal,* el sello real. **2** (*on letter*) sello; (*on bottle etc*) precinto; (*airtight*) cierre *m* hermético; (*on window, door*) burlete *m*. – **3** *t* (*with offical stamp*) sellar; (*with wax*) lacrar, sellar con lacre: *the document is signed and sealed,* el documento está firmado y sellado. **4** (*close*) cerrar; (*bottle etc*) precintar; (*make airtight*) cerrar herméticamente; (*window, door*) sellar, poner burletes a: *parcels must be well sealed,* se debe cerrar bien los paquetes. **5** (*coat with sealant*) sellar, impermeabilizar. **6** (*settle, make formal*) sellar, concluir.
◆ **to seal in** *t sep* encerrar. ‖ **to seal off** *t sep* (*block entry to*) acordonar, cerrar el acceso a.
● **to give one's seal of approval to sth.,** aprobar algo, dar su aprobación a algo, dar el visto bueno a algo. ‖ **to seal sb.'s fate,** decidir el destino de algn. ‖ **to set the seal on sth.,** (*complete*) culminar algo, ratificar algo.
sealant ['siːlənt] *n* sellador *m*.
sealing ['siːlɪŋ] *n* caza de focas: *a sealing expedition,* una expedición para cazar focas.
sealing wax ['siːlɪŋwæks] *n* lacre *m*.
sealskin ['siːlskɪn] **1** *n* piel *f* de foca. – **2** *adj* de piel de foca.
seam [siːm] **1** *n* SEW costura. **2** TECH juntura, junta. **3** GEOL (*of mineral*) veta, filón *m*: *coal seam,* veta de carbón.
● **to be bursting at the seams,** (*with people*) rebosar de gente; (*with things*) estar hasta los topes; (*with food*) estar a punto de reventar. ‖ **to come apart at the seams,** (*clothes*) descoserse; (*plans etc*) fracasar, irse a pique, venirse abajo.
seaman ['siːmən] *n* marinero, marino.
▲ *pl* **seamen** ['siːmən].
seamanship ['siːmənʃɪp] *n* náutica.
seamless ['siːmləs] *adj* SEW sin costura.
seamstress ['semstrəs] *n* costurera.
seamy ['siːmɪ] *adj* sórdido,-a: *the seamy side of life,* el lado más sórdido de la vida.
▲ *comp* **seamier,** *superl* **seamiest.**
séance ['seɪɑːns] *n* sesión *f* de espiritismo.
seaplane ['siːpleɪn] *n* hidroavión *m*.
seaport ['siːpɔːt] *n* puerto marítimo, puerto de mar.
seaquake ['siːkweɪk] *n* maremoto.
sear [sɪə'] **1** *t* (*scorch, burn*) quemar, chamuscar, abrasar. **2** MED cauterizar. **3** CULIN freír rápidamente, rehogar. **4** (*dry up plant*) abrasar, secar, achicharrar. **5** *fig* (*affect*) afectar mucho, marcar.
● **to be seared on one's memory,** estar grabado,-a en la memoria.
search [sɜːtʃ] **1** *n* (*gen*) búsqueda (**for,** de); (*of building*) registro; (*of person*) cacheo; (*of records, files, etc*) inspec-

ción f, examen m. **– 2** t (gen) buscar (**for**, -); (records, files) buscar en, examinar; (building, suitcase, etc) registrar; (person) cachear, registrar: *volunteers are searching the woods for the missing child,* unos voluntarios están registrando el bosque en busca del niño desaparecido; *they searched the house for clues,* registraron la casa buscando pistas; *the police searched the suspects,* la policía cacheó a los sospechosos. **– 3** i (gen) buscar (**through,** entre); (pockets) registrar: *I've searched everywhere,* he buscado en todas partes; *doctors are searching for a cure,* los médicos buscan una cura.
◆ **to search out** t *sep* averiguar, descubrir, encontrar. ● **in search of,** en busca de. ‖ **search me!,** ¡yo qué sé!, ¡ni idea! ‖ **to search one's conscience,** examinar la conciencia. ‖ **to search one's memory,** hacer memoria. ■ **search party,** equipo de rescate. ‖ **search warrant,** orden f de registro.
searcher ['sɜːtʃəʳ] n buscador,-ra.
searching ['sɜːtʃɪŋ] adj (look) penetrante; (question) agudo,-a; (examination) profundo,-a.
searchlight ['sɜːtʃlaɪt] n reflector m, proyector m.
searing ['sɪərɪŋ] **1** adj (heat) abrasador,-ra; (pain) punzante. **2** fig (emotive) emotivo,-a; (strong) virulento,-a.
seascape ['siːskeɪp] n ART marina.
seashell ['siːʃel] n concha (de mar).
seashore ['siːʃɔːʳ] n (coast) costa, orilla del mar; (beach) playa.
seasick ['siːsɪk] adj mareado,-a.
● **to get seasick,** marearse.
seasickness ['siːsɪknəs] n mareo.
seaside ['siːsaɪd] n playa, costa.
■ **seaside resort,** lugar m de veraneo en la costa. ‖ **seaside town,** ciudad f costera.
season ['siːzən] **1** n (of year) estación f; (time) época; (for sport, theatre, social activity) temporada; (of films) ciclo: *the dry/rainy season,* la estación seca/de las lluvias; *the football/fishing season,* la temporada futbolística/de pesca; *the mating season,* la época de celo, la época de apareamiento, el celo; *the tourist season,* la temporada turística. **– 2** t (food) sazonar (**with,** con), condimentar (**with,** con). **3** (wood) secar. **4** fig (person) avezar, acostumbrar. **– 5** i (wood) secarse.
● **to be in season,** (fresh food) estar en sazón, ser la temporada de; (animal on heat) estar en celo; (game) ser temporada de: *strawberries are in season,* es temporada de fresas. ‖ **to go in season,** ir en temporada alta. ‖ **to go off/out of season,** ir en temporada baja. ‖ Seasons Greetings, Felices Pascuas. ■ **season ticket,** abono. ‖ **season ticket holder,** abonado,-a.
seasonable ['siːzənəbəl] **1** adj (weather) propio,-a de la época del año, propio,-a de la estación. **2** (opportune, timely) oportuno,-a.
seasonal ['siːzənəl] adj estacional, temporal: *seasonal worker,* temporero,-a.
seasonally ['siːzənəlɪ] adv estacionalmente.
■ **seasonally ajusted figures,** cifras fpl que tienen en cuenta las variaciones estacionales.
seasoned ['siːzənd] **1** adj (food) sazonado,-a (**with,** con), condimentado,-a (**with,** con): *highly seasoned,* picante. **2** (wood) seco,-a. **3** fig (person) experimentado,-a, curtido,-a, avezado,-a. **4** fig (conversation) salpicado,-a (**with,** de).
seasoning ['siːzənɪŋ] n CULIN condimento, aderezo.
seat [siːt] **1** n (chair – gen) asiento; (– in cinema, theatre) butaca: *the back/front seat of the car,* el asiento de de-

trás/delante del coche; *I'd like a window seat,* quisiera un asiento al lado de la ventanilla; *give up your seat to an elderly person,* cede tu asiento a un anciano. **2** (place) plaza; (at theatre, opera, stadium) localidad f; (ticket) entrada, localidad f: *there are no seats left on that flight,* no quedan plazas en aquel vuelo; *do you think we can get seats for "Cats"?,* ¿crees que podemos encontrar entradas para "Cats"? **3** (of cycle) sillín m; (of toilet) asiento; (of trousers) fondillos mpl; (of chair) fondo; (bottom, buttocks) trasero, pompis m. **4** (centre) sede f, centro: *seat of learning,* centro de estudios. **5** POL (in parliament) escaño; (constituency) distrito electoral: *he has a seat on the council,* es miembro del consejo. **– 6** t (sit) sentar. **7** (accomodate) tener sitio para; (theatre, hall, etc) tener cabida para.
● **please be seated,** siéntese/siéntense por favor. ‖ **to be in the driving/driver's seat,** dirigir, controlar. ‖ **to remain seated,** quedarse sentado,-a. ‖ **to seat os.,** sentarse. ‖ **to take a back seat,** pasar a segundo plano, mantenerse al margen. ‖ **to take a seat,** sentarse, tomar asiento. ■ **seat belt,** cinturón m de seguridad.
seater ['siːtəʳ] n: *a three-seater sofa,* un sofá de tres plazas; *he bought a two-seater car,* se compró un coche de dos plazas, se compró un biplaza.
seating ['siːtɪŋ] n asientos mpl: *seating arrangement/ plan,* plan de asientos; *seating capacity,* aforo, cabida.
seaward ['siːwəd] adj (facing sea) que da al mar, hacia el mar; (coming from sea) del mar.
seawards ['siːwədz] adv hacia el mar.
seaway ['siːweɪ] **1** n (course) vía marítima. **2** (river, waterway) canal m.
seaweed ['siːwiːd] n alga (marina).
seaworthy ['siːwɜːðɪ] adj (boat) en condiciones de navegar.
sebaceous [sɪ'beɪʃəs] adj sebáceo,-a.
sec[1] [sek] n fam (second) segundo, momento.
sec[2] [sek] n fam (secretary) secretario,-a.
secateurs [sekə'tɜːz] npl podadera, tijeras fpl de podar.
secede [sɪ'siːd] i separarse (**from,** de), independizarse (**from,** de).
secession [sɪ'seʃən] n secesión f.
seclude [sɪ'kluːd] t aislar, apartar, retirar.
● **to seclude os.,** aislarse, apartarse, retirarse.
secluded [sɪ'kluːdɪd] adj aislado,-a, apartado,-a.
seclusion [sɪ'kluːʒən] n (act of secluding) aislamiento, reclusión f; (privacy) intimidad f.
● **in seclusion,** aislado,-a.
second[1] ['sekənd] **1** n (time) segundo: *Christie's time was 9.9 seconds,* Christie hizo un tiempo de 9,9 segundos. **2** fam momento, momentito: *have you got a second?,* ¿tienes un momento?; *I'll be back in a second,* enseguida vuelvo.
■ **second hand,** (of watch) segundero.
second[2] [sɪ'kɒnd] t GB trasladar temporalmente.
second[3] ['sekənd] **1** adj (gen) segundo,-a; (another) otro,-a: *it's the second largest city in England,* es la segunda ciudad más grande de Inglaterra; *Birmingham is second only to London in population,* sólo Londres tiene más habitantes que Birmingham; *every second day/week/ month/year,* cada dos días/semanas/meses/años. **– 2** pron segundo,-a: *they've got one baby and now she's expecting a second,* tienen un bebé y ya espera el segundo. **– 3** n (in series) segundo,-a. **4** GB EDUC (degree) ≈ notable m. **5** AUTO (gear) segunda: *in second,* en segunda. **6** SP (boxing) segundo, mánager m, cuidador m. **7**

524

MUS segunda. – **8** *adv* segundo, en segundo lugar: *he came second,* llegó segundo, quedó en segundo lugar. – **9** *t* (*motion, proposal*) apoyar, secundar. **10** *fam* (*agree*) estar de acuerdo con. – **11 seconds,** *npl* COMM artículos *mpl* con tara, artículos *mpl* defectuosos. **12** (*food*) segunda ración *f*: *who wants seconds?,* ¿quién quiere repetir?

● **on second thoughts,** pensándolo bien. ‖ **to be second nature to sb.,** serle completamente natural a algn.: *don't worry, it'll soon become second nature to you,* no te preocupes, pronto te parecerá una cosa muy natural. ‖ **to be second to none,** no tener igual. ‖ **to have a second string to one's bow,** tener otra alternativa. ‖ **to have second helpings,** repetir. ‖ **to have second thoughts (about sth.),** entrarle dudas a uno (sobre algo), cambiar de idea (sobre algo). ‖ **to play second fiddle,** ser segundón,-ona, desempeñar un papel secundario.

■ **second class,** segunda clase. ‖ **Second Coming,** Segundo Advenimiento. ‖ **second floor,** GB segundo piso; US primer piso. ‖ **second generation,** segunda generación *f*. ‖ **second half,** segundo tiempo. ‖ **second language,** segundo idioma. ‖ **second lieutenant,** alférez *mf*. ‖ **second name,** apellido. ‖ **second person,** segunda persona. ‖ **second sight,** clarividencia. ‖ **Second World War,** Segunda Guerra *f* Mundial.

▲ *Véase también* **sixth.**

secondary ['sekəndərɪ] *adj* secundario,-a: *that's a secondary matter,* eso es un asunto secundario.

■ **secondary education,** enseñanza secundaria. ‖ **secondary colour,** color *m* secundario. ‖ **secondary picketing,** piquetes *mpl* de apoyo. ‖ **secondary school,** colegio de enseñanza secundaria, instituto de bachillerato.

second-best [sekənd'best] *adj* segundo,-a mejor: *my second-best dress,* mi segundo mejor vestido.

● **to come off second-best,** quedar en segundo lugar. ‖ **to settle for second-best,** conformarse con una segunda alternativa.

second-class [sekənd'klɑːs] **1** *adj* (*ticket, carriage*) de segunda (clase); (*citizen*) de segunda categoría, de segunda clase; (*goods*) de calidad inferior. **2** (*mail, postage, stamp, etc*) ordinario,-a.

■ **second-class (honours) degree,** ≈ notable *m* (*título universitario que corresponde a la segunda o tercera nota más alta*).

second-degree [sekəndɪ'griː] *adj* MED de segundo grado.

■ **second-degree burns,** quemaduras *fpl* de segundo grado.

seconder ['sekəndəʳ] *n* persona que secunda una moción etc.

second-guess [sekənd'ges] **1** *t* US *fam* (*criticize, evaluate with hindsight*) cuestionar posteriormente. **2** US *fam* (*anticipate, predict*) intentar adivinar, anticiparse a, adelantarse a.

second-hand [sekənd'hænd] **1** *adj* (*used, not new*) de segunda mano, usado,-a, viejo,-a: *we bought a second-hand car,* compramos un coche de segunda mano. **2** (*news, information*) de segunda mano. – **3** *adv* (*buy*) de segunda mano: *I often buy things second-hand,* suelo comprar cosas de segunda mano. **4** (*learn, find out*) por terceros: *I got the news second-hand,* me enteré de la noticia por terceros.

■ **second-hand bookshop,** librería de viejo. ‖ **second-hand dealer,** chamarilero,-a.

second-in-command ['sekəndɪnkə'mɑːnd] **1** *n* AV MAR segundo de a bordo. **2** COMM segundo,-a en jefe, número dos.

secondly ['sekəndlɪ] *adv* en segundo lugar.

secondment [sɪ'kɒndmənt] *n* GB traslado temporal.

● **to be on secondment,** ser trasladado,-a temporalmente.

second-rate [sekənd'reɪt] *adj* de segunda categoría, de calidad inferior.

second-string [sekənd'strɪŋ] *adj* SP suplente, de reserva.

secrecy ['siːkrəsɪ] **1** *n* (*gen*) secreto, sigilo: *in secrecy,* en secreto, con sigilo. **2** (*ability to keep secrets*) discreción *f*, reserva.

● **to swear sb. to secrecy,** hacer que algn. jure guardar un secreto.

secret ['siːkrət] **1** *adj* (*gen*) secreto,-a: *this is my secret hiding-place,* este es mi escondite secreto; *she's a secret gin drinker,* bebe ginebra en secreto. – **2** *n* (*gen*) secreto; (*something confided*) secreto, confidencia *f*: *our affair must remain a secret,* tenemos que mantener en secreto nuestra relación. **3** (*method, key*) secreto, clave *f*: *what's the secret of your success?,* ¿cuál es el secreto de tu éxito?

● **in secret,** en secreto. ‖ **open secret,** secreto a voces. ‖ **to be in (on) the secret,** estar al tanto, estar en el ajo, estar al corriente. ‖ **to keep a secret,** guardar un secreto: *can you keep a secret?,* ¿sabes guardar un secreto? ‖ **to keep sth. secret,** mantener algo en secreto. ‖ **to let sb. in on a secret,** revelar un secreto a algn., compartir un secreto con algn. ‖ **to make no secret of sth.,** no tratar de esconder algo.

■ **secret agent,** agente *mf* secreto,-a, espía *mf*. ‖ **secret ballot,** votación *f* secreta. ‖ **secret police,** policía secreta. ‖ **secret service,** servicio secreto.

secretarial [sekrɪ'teərɪəl] *adj* de secretario,-a.

■ **secretarial college,** escuela de secretariado. ‖ **secretarial course,** curso de secretariado.

secretariat [sekrɪ'teərɪət] *n* secretaría, secretariado.

secretary ['sekrətərɪ] **1** *n* secretario,-a. **2** (*non-elected official*) ministro,-a; (*representative below ambassador*) ministro,-a plenipotenciario,-a.

■ **Secretary of State,** GB ministro,-a con cartera; US ministro,-a de Asuntos *m* Exteriores.

▲ *pl* **secretaries.**

secretary-general [sekrətərɪ'dʒenərəl] *n* secretario general.

▲ *pl* **secretaries-general.**

secrete [sɪ'kriːt] **1** *t* (*emit liquid*) secretar, segregar. **2** *fml* (*hide*) ocultar, esconder.

secretion [sɪ'kriːʃən] **1** *n* (*of liquid*) secreción *f*. **2** *fml* (*hiding*) ocultación *f*.

secretive ['siːkrətɪv] *adj* (*gen*) sigiloso,-a, hermético,-a; (*quiet*) reservado,-a, callado,-a.

secretly ['siːkrətlɪ] *adv* en secreto, a escondidas.

sect [sekt] *n* secta.

sectarian [sek'teərɪən] *adj* sectario,-a.

sectarianism [sek'teərɪənɪzəm] *n* sectarismo.

section ['sekʃən] **1** *n* (*of newspaper, orchestra, department*) sección *f*; (*of furniture, book*) parte *f*; (*of road*) tramo; (*of orange*) gajo. **2** (*of population, community*) sector *m*; (*of army*) sección *f*. **3** (*of document, law*) artículo, apartado. **4** ARCH ART GEOM sección *f*, corte *m*: *cross section,* sección transversal. **5** MED sección *f*. **6** US (*land*) milla cuadrada. – **7** *t* MED (*cut*) cortar, seccionar. **8** (*divide*) dividir.

sectional ['sekʃənəl] **1** *adj* (*furniture etc*) desmontable, modular. **2** (*interests*) de grupo; (*rivalry*) entre facciones. **3** (*diagram, plan*) en sección.

sector ['sektə] *n* (*gen*) sector *m*: *the public/private sector,* el sector público/privado; *a considerable sector of the population,* un sector importante de la población.

secular ['sekjʊləʳ] **1** adj (education) laico,-a; (art, music) profano,-a. **2** (clergy, priest) seglar, secular.

secularism ['sekjʊlərɪzəm] n laicismo.

secularize ['sekjʊləraɪz] t secularizar.

secure [sɪ'kjʊəʳ] **1** adj (job, income, etc) seguro,-a; (relationship etc) estable: *he wanted a nice secure job,* quería un trabajo bueno y seguro; *you have a secure future here,* tiene el futuro asegurado aquí. **2** (ladder, shelf, foothold) firme; (stronghold) seguro,-a; (window, door) bien cerrado,-a; (rope, knot) seguro,-a, bien sujeto,-a; (base, foundation) sólido,-a. – **3** t (make safe) asegurar; (protect) salvaguardar, proteger (**from**, de), (**against**, contra). **4** (fasten - rope, knot) sujetar, fijar; (- window, door, etc) asegurar, cerrar bien. **5** (obtain) obtener, conseguir. **6** FIN (loan) garantizar, avalar.

securely [sɪ'kjʊəlɪ] adv bien: *the door was securely locked,* la puerta estaba bien cerrada con llave.

security [sɪ'kjʊərətɪ] **1** n (safety, confidence) seguridad f: *job security,* seguridad laboral; *children need love and security,* los niños necesitan amor y seguridad. **2** (protection) seguridad f: *national security,* la seguridad nacional; *there was tight security for the President's visit,* se adoptaron fuertes medidas de seguridad para la visita del Presidente. **3** FIN (guarantee) fianza, garantía, aval m. – **4** securities, npl COMM valores mpl, títulos mpl: *government securities,* bonos del Estado.
● **to lend money on security,** prestar dinero sobre fianza. || **to stand security for sb.,** salir fiador,-ra de algn., garantizar a algn.
■ **the Security Council,** el Consejo de Seguridad. || **security forces,** fuerzas fpl de seguridad. || **security guard,** guarda mf jurado,-a. || **security leak,** fuga (de información), filtración f. || **security risk,** riesgo para la seguridad, peligro para la seguridad. || **security service,** servicio de seguridad. || **security van,** furgoneta blindada. || **social security,** seguridad f social.
▲ pl *securities*.

sedan [sɪ'dæn] **1** n US (car) berlina. **2 sedan (chair),** silla de manos, palanquín m.

sedate¹ [sɪ'deɪt] adj sosegado,-a, sereno,-a, tranquilo,-a.

sedate² [sɪ'deɪt] t MED administrar sedantes a, sedar.

sedation [sɪ'deɪʃən] n sedación f.
● **to be under sedation,** estar bajo,-a el efecto de los sedantes. || **to put sb. under sedation,** administrarle un sedante a algn., sedar a algn.

sedative ['sedətɪv] **1** n sedante m, calmante m. – **2** adj sedante.

sedentary ['sedəntərɪ] adj sedentario,-a.

sediment ['sedɪmənt] **1** n (gen) sedimento. **2** (of wine) hez f, poso.

sedimentary [sedɪ'mentərɪ] adj sedimentario,-a.

sedimentation [sedɪmen'teɪʃən] n sedimentación f.

sedition [sɪ'dɪʃən] n sedición f.

seditious [sɪ'dɪʃəs] adj sedicioso,-a.

seduce [sɪ'djuːs] **1** t (sexually) seducir. **2** fml (tempt, entice) tentar, seducir: *he was seduced into buying a new car,* lo tentaron para que comprara un coche nuevo; *the sunshine seduced me away from my books,* dejé los libros atraído por el sol.

seducer [sɪ'djuːsəʳ] n seductor,-ra.

seduction [sɪ'dʌkʃən] n (sexual) seducción f.

seductive [sɪ'dʌktɪv] adj (person, voice, look) seductor,-ra; (clothing) provocativo,-a; (offer) tentador,-ra.

see¹ [siː] **1** t (gen) ver: *I can't see anything,* no veo nada; *did you see who it was?,* ¿has visto quién era?; *you can see the sea from here,* desde aquí se ve el mar; *have you seen any good films lately?,* ¿has visto una buena película últimamente?; *see page 123,* véase la página 123; *she could see that he hadn't listened to a single word,* veía que no había escuchado ni una sola palabra; *I can see you're busy,* ya veo que estás ocupado; *we don't know what she sees in him,* no sabemos qué es lo que ve en él; *this year sees the cinema's centenary,* este año se celebra el centenario del cine. **2** (meet, visit) ver; (receive) ver, atender; (go out with) salir con: *guess who I saw on Saturday?,* ¿a que no sabes a quién vi el sábado?; *you should see a doctor,* deberías ir al médico; *I'm seeing Pat on Friday,* he quedado con Pat el viernes; *I want to see the manager,* quiero ver al director; *they've been seeing each other for a month,* hace un mes que salen juntos. **3** (understand) comprender, entender, ver: *do you see what I mean?,* ¿entiendes lo que quiero decir?; *I can see why you're worried,* entiendo por qué estás preocupado; *I don't see why I have to go,* no entiendo por qué tengo que ir yo; *I can see your point,* entiendo tu punto de vista. **4** (visualize, imagine) imaginarse, ver; (envisage) creer: *I can't see him working in a factory,* no me lo imagino trabajando en una fábrica; *I can't see Dad lending you the money,* no creo que papá te vaya a dejar el dinero; *I can't see that it matters,* no creo que tenga importancia; *they saw it coming,* lo vieron venir. **5** (find out, discover) ver; (learn) oír, leer: *I'll see what I can do,* veré lo que puedo hacer; *go and see what she's up to,* vete a ver qué hace; *I see that Chirac has won the French elections,* veo que Chirac ha ganado las elecciones francesas; *I see in the paper that Major did badly in the local elections,* he leído que a Major le fueron mal las elecciones locales. **6** (ensure, check) asegurarse de, procurar: *see that you arrive on time,* procura llegar a la hora; *see that he gets complete rest,* asegúrate de que tenga reposo completo; *could you see that all the doors are locked?,* ¿podría asegurarse de que todas las puertas estén cerradas con llave? **7** (accompany) acompañar: *he saw me home,* me acompañó a casa; *we saw her to her car,* la acompañamos a su coche; *I saw the old lady across the road,* ayudé a la anciana a cruzar la calle. **8** (in cards) ver, ir. – **9** i (gen) ver: *she can't see without her glasses,* no ve sin las gafas; *I can't see to read,* no veo para leer; *she can see into the future,* ve el futuro. **10** (find out, discover) ver: *we'll have to see,* ya veremos. **11** (understand) entender, ver: *oh, I see,* ah, ya veo.
◆ **to see about 1** t insep (deal with) arreglar, organizar: *I must see about the tickets,* debo arreglar lo de las entradas. **2** (consider) ver, pensar: *I'll have to see about that,* tendré que pensarlo. || **to see in** t insep (celebrate) celebrar: *we saw in the New Year together,* celebramos el Año Nuevo juntos. || **to see off 1** t sep (say goodbye to) despedir: *they came to the airport to see me off,* vinieron al aeropuerto a despedirme. **2** (chase off) ahuyentar; (remain firm) resistir. || **to see out 1** t sep (last) durar; (survive) sobrevivir: *have we got enough wood to see the week out?,* ¿tenemos suficiente leña para aguantar toda la semana? **2** (go to door with) acompañar hasta la puerta: *I can see myself out,* no hace falta que me acompañéis hasta la puerta. || **to see round/over** t insep (house etc) visitar, recorrer. || **to see through** t insep (person) calar, verle el plumero a; (trick, game, scheme, etc) no creerse: *we saw through his trick,* su trampa no nos engañó. – **2** t sep (support) ayudar a salir de un apuro, ayudar a sobrellevar; (last) alcanzar, llegar: *my parents saw me through a bad time,* mis padres me

ayudaron a sobrellevar una mala época; *have you got enough money to see you through the month?*, ¿tienes suficiente dinero para llegar a final de mes? **3** (*not abandon until finished*) terminar, llevar a buen término. ‖ **to see to** t *insep* (*deal with*) atender a, ocuparse de, encargarse de: *could you see to the baby?*, ¿podrías ocuparte del niño?; *I'll see to it personally*, me ocuparé personalmente; *see to it that she gets the message, won't you?*, asegúrate de que reciba el recado, ¿vale? ● **I'll be seeing you!**, ¡hasta luego! ‖ **let me see/let's see**, a ver, vamos a ver. ‖ **seeing is believing**, ver para creer. ‖ **see you around**, ya nos veremos. ‖ **see you later/soon/Monday!**, ¡hasta luego/pronto/el lunes! ‖ **to be seeing things**, ver visiones. ‖ **to have seen better days**, haber conocido tiempos mejores. ‖ **to see for os.**, comprobarlo uno,-a mismo,-a. ‖ **to see a lot of sb.**, ver a algn. a menudo. ‖ **to see one's way (clear) to doing sth.**, poder hacer algo, estar dispuesto,-a a hacer algo. ‖ **to see reason**, ver la razón. ‖ **to see red**, ponerse rojo,-a (de ira). ‖ **to see stars**, ver las estrellas. ‖ **to see the back/last of sb.**, perder a algn. de vista. ‖ **to see the joke**, verle la gracia, entender el chiste. ‖ **to see the light**, ver la luz. ‖ **not to see the point**, no ver el sentido, no ver para qué. ‖ **we'll soon see about that!**, ¡ya lo veremos! ‖ *you see*, (*in explanations*) verás; (*in questions*) ¿sabes?, ¿ves? ▲ *pt* **saw**, *pp* **seen**, *ger* **seeing**.

see² [siː] *n* REL sede *f*.

seed [siːd] **1** *n* BOT (*gen*) semilla; (*for planting*) semilla, simiente *f*; (*of fruit*) pepita: *sunflower seeds*, pipas. **2** SP (*tennis*) cabeza *mf* de serie. – **3** t (*plant seeds*) sembrar (**with**, de). **4** (*remove seed*) despepitar. **5** SP (*tennis*) preseleccionar: *a seeded player*, un,-a (jugador,-ra) cabeza de serie. – **6** i (*produce seed*) granar. ● **to go/run to seed**, (*plant*) granar; (*person*) descuidarse, abandonarse, echarse a perder. ‖ **to plant/sow the seeds of sth.**, sembrar las semillas de algo. ■ **seed pearl**, aljófar *m*. ‖ **seed potato**, patata de siembra.

seedbed ['siːdbed] **1** *n* semillero, almácigo,-a. **2** *fig* semillero, hervidero, caldo de cultivo.

seedcake ['siːdkeɪk] *n* torta de semillas de alcaravea.

seedless ['siːdləs] *adj* sin pepitas, sin semillas.

seedling ['siːdlɪŋ] *n* planta de semillero.

seedy ['siːdɪ] **1** *adj* (*place*) cutre, sórdido,-a, de mala muerte; (*person*) desastrado,-a: *a seedy-looking character*, un individuo con mala pinta. **2** *fam* (*unwell*) pachucho,-a. ▲ *comp* **seedier**, *superl* **seediest**.

seeing ['siːɪŋ] **1** *n* (*vision*) visión *f*. – **2 seeing (as/that)**, *conj* visto que, en vista de que, dado que, ya que. ■ **seeing eye dog**, US perro lazarillo, perro guía.

seek [siːk] **1** t (*look for, try to obtain*) buscar: *the homeless seek food and shelter*, la gente sin techo busca comida y alojamiento; *they sought revenge*, querían vengarse, buscaban venganza. **2** (*ask for*) pedir, solicitar: *you should seek advice from a lawyer*, deberías consultar a un abogado. **3** (*attempt, try*) tratar de, intentar: *they seek to reduce costs*, intentan reducir gastos. – **4** i (*look for, try to obtain*) buscar (**after/for**, -), ir en busca de. ◆ **to seek out** t *sep* buscar. ● **to seek one's fortune**, probar fortuna. ▲ *pt* & *pp* **sought**.

seeker ['siːkə'] *n* buscador,-ra.

seem [siːm] i (*appear*) parecer: *it seemed like a good idea at the time*, parecía una buena idea entonces; *she seems nice*, parece maja; *things are not always what*

they seem, las apariencias engañan; *do whatever seems best*, haz lo que mejor te parezca; *you seem to think I'm made of money*, parece que crees que tengo mucho dinero; *it seems like there's going to be a storm*, parece que va a haber una tormenta; *I can't seem to relax*, no logro relajarme; *I seem to remember that he was a photographer*, creo recordar que era fotógrafo. ● **so it seems**, eso parece.

seeming ['siːmɪŋ] *adj* aparente.

seemingly ['siːmɪŋlɪ] **1** *adv* (*used with adjective*) aparentemente. **2** (*used separately*) al parecer, según parece.

seemly ['siːmlɪ] *adj fml dated* correcto,-a, apropiado,-a.

seen [siːn] *pp* → **see**.

seep [siːp] i filtrarse: *there was water seeping through the ceiling*, se filtraba agua por el techo.

seepage ['siːpɪdʒ] *n* (*of water*) filtración *f*; (*of gas*) fuga, escape *m*.

seer ['sɪə'] *n* vidente *mf*.

seesaw ['siːsɔː'] **1** *n* (*for children*) balancín *m*, subibaja *m*. **2** (*movement*) vaivén *m*, oscilación *f*. – **3** i (*move*) oscilar, vacilar: *seesawing prices*, precios oscilantes.

seethe [siːð] **1** i (*liquid*) hervir, bullir. **2** *fig* (*be angry*) rabiar, estar furibundo,-a, estar furioso,-a. **3** *fig* (*be crowded*) bullir. ● **to seethe with people**, estar a rebosar, ser (como) un hervidero.

see-through ['siːθruː] *adj* transparente.

segment ['segmənt] *n* (*gen*) segmento; (*of orange*) gajo.

segregate ['segrɪgeɪt] t segregar.

segregation [segrɪ'geɪʃən] *n* segregación *f*.

Seine [seɪn] *n* el Sena *m*.

seismic ['saɪzmɪk] *adj* sísmico,-a. ■ **seismic wave**, onda sísmica.

seismograph ['saɪzməgrɑːf] *n* sismógrafo.

seismologist [saɪz'mɒlədʒɪst] *n* sismólogo,-a.

seismology [saɪz'mɒlədʒɪ] *n* sismología.

seize [siːz] **1** t (*grab*) asir, agarrar, coger: *he seized my arm*, me agarró del brazo. **2** (*opportunity*) aprovechar. **3** JUR (*impound*) incautar, embargar; (*confiscate*) confiscar, decomisar. **4** (*take control of*) tomar, apoderarse de. **5** (*person - arrest*) detener; (- *take hostage*) secuestrar. **6** *fig* (*strong feelings*) apoderarse de, acometer: *panic seized the guests*, el pánico se apoderó de los invitados. ◆ **to seize on/upon** t *insep* aprovechar, valerse de. ‖ **to seize up** i (*machine, engine*) agarrotarse; (*traffic*) paralizarse. ● **to be seized with sth.**, (*pain, fear, panic, etc*) apoderarse algo de uno: *he was seized with anger*, la ira se apoderó de él; *she was seized with the desire to run away*, sintió ganas de escapar.

seizure ['siːʒə'] **1** *n* JUR (*impoundment*) incautación *f*, embargo; (*confiscation*) confiscación *f*, decomiso. **2** (*of power, territory*) toma. **3** MED ataque *m* (de apoplejía): *epileptic seizure*, ataque epiléptico; *heart seizure*, ataque cardíaco.

seldom ['seldəm] *adv* raramente, rara vez, pocas veces: *we seldom eat out*, pocas veces comemos fuera.

select [sɪ'lekt] **1** t (*thing*) escoger, elegir; (*team, player, candidate*) seleccionar. – **2** *adj* (*audience etc*) selecto,-a; (*club, area, etc*) selecto,-a, exclusivo,-a, distinguido,-a; (*fruit, wine*) selecto,-a, de primera calidad. ■ **select committee**, GB POL comisión *f* de investigación, comisión *f* investigadora.

selected [sɪ'lektɪd] *adj* (*gen*) escogido,-a; (*team, player, candidate*) seleccionado,-a.

■ **selected works,** LIT obras *fpl* escogidas.

selection [sɪˈlekʃən] **1** *n (people or things chosen)* selección *f*; *(choosing)* elección *f*. **2** *(range to choose from)* surtido, gama.

selective [sɪˈlektɪv] **1** *adj (specific)* selectivo,-a; *(not general)* parcial: *selective strike,* huelga parcial; *selective weed killer,* herbicida selectivo. **2** *(discriminating, choosy)* exigente, selectivo,-a: *I'm very selective in my reading,* soy muy selectivo con lo que leo; *she's very selective about the people she goes out with,* es muy selectiva con la gente con quien sale.

■ **selective service,** US MIL servicio militar obligatorio.

selectively [sɪˈlektɪvlɪ] **1** *adv (chosen)* selectivamente; *(not generally)* parcialmente. **2** *(carefully)* de forma selectiva, con criterio selectivo.

selectivity [sɪlekˈtɪvətɪ] **1** *n (gen)* selectividad *f*, criterio selectivo. **2** RAD selectividad *f*.

selector [sɪˈlektəʳ] **1** *n (person)* seleccionador,-ra. **2** *(device)* selector *m*.

selenium [sɪˈliːnɪəm] *n* CHEM selenio.

self [self] **1** *n* ser *m*, uno,-a mismo,-a, sí mismo,-a: *one's better self,* su lado bueno; *one's true self,* su verdadero carácter; *he was his usual self again,* volvió a ser él mismo. **2** *(one's own interest)* sí mismo,-a: *he thinks only of self,* sólo piensa en sí mísmo. **3** *(in psychology)* yo: *my other self,* mi otro yo.
▲ *pl selves.*

self-absorbed [selfəbˈsɔːbd] *adj* absorto,-a en sí mismo,-a.

self-acting [selfˈæktɪŋ] *adj* automático,-a.

self-addressed [selfəˈdrest] *adj* con el nombre y la dirección.

■ **self-addressed envelope,** sobre respuesta.

self-adhesive [selfədˈhiːsɪv] *adj* autoadhesivo,-a, autoadherente.

self-appointed [selfəˈpɔɪntɪd] *adj* autoproclamado,-a.

self-assembly [selfəˈsemblɪ] *adj* para montar uno,-a mismo,-a.

self-assertive [selfəˈsɜːtɪv] *adj* seguro,-a de sí mismo,-a.

self-assertiveness [selfəˈsɜːtɪvnəs] *n* seguridad *f* en sí mismo,-a.

self-assurance [selfəˈʃʊərəns] *n* seguridad *f*, confianza en sí mismo,-a.

self-assured [selfəˈʃʊəd] *adj* seguro,-a de sí mismo,-a.

self-catering [selfˈkeɪtərɪŋ] *adj* sin servicio de comidas.

self-centered [selfˈsentəd] *adj* US → **self-centred.**

self-centred [selfˈsentəd] *adj* egocéntrico,-a.

self-cleaning [selfˈkliːnɪŋ] *adj* auto-limpiable.

self-closing [selfˈkləʊzɪŋ] *adj* de cierre automático.

self-composed [selfkəmˈpəʊzd] *adj* sereno,-a, compuesto,-a.

self-confessed [selfkənˈfest] *adj* confeso,-a.

self-confidence [selfˈkɒnfɪdəns] *n* seguridad *f*, confianza en sí mismo,-a.

self-confident [selfˈkɒnfɪdənt] *adj* seguro,-a de sí mismo,-a.

self-conscious [selfˈkɒnʃəs] **1** *adj (nervous)* cohibido,-a, tímido,-a. **2** *(conscious)* consciente de la propia identidad.

● **to be self-conscious about sth.,** estar acomplejado,-a por algo.

self-contained [selfkənˈteɪnd] **1** *adj (flat etc)* independiente, con entrada propia. **2** *(person - independent)* independiente; *(- reserved)* reservado,-a.

self-control [selfkənˈtrəʊl] *n* dominio de sí mismo,-a, autocontrol *m*.

● **to exercise/show self-control,** autocontrolarse, dominarse. ‖ **to lose one's self-control,** perder el autocontrol, descontrolarse.

self-deception [selfdɪˈsepʃən] *n* autoengaño.

self-defeating [selfdɪˈfiːtɪŋ] *adj* contraproducente.

self-defence [selfdɪˈfens] *n* defensa personal, autodefensa.

● **to act in self-defence,** actuar en defensa propia.

self-denial [selfdɪˈnaɪəl] *n* abnegación *f*, sacrificio.

self-destruct [selfdɪˈstrʌkt] *i* autodestruirse.

self-determination [selfdɪtɜːmɪˈneɪʃən] *n* autodeterminación *f*.

self-discipline [selfˈdɪsɪplɪn] *n* autodisciplina.

self-drive [selfˈdraɪv] *adj* sin chófer.

self-educated [selfˈedjʊkeɪtɪd] *adj* autodidacta.

self-effacing [selfɪˈfeɪsɪŋ] *adj* modesto,-a, humilde.

self-employed [selfɪmˈplɔɪd] *adj* autónomo,-a, que trabaja por cuenta propia.

self-esteem [selfɪˈstiːm] *n* amor *m* propio.

self-evident [selfˈevɪdənt] *adj* evidente, patente, obvio,-a, manifiesto,-a.

self-explanatory [selfɪkˈsplænətrɪ] *adj* que se explica por sí mismo,-a, muy claro,-a.

self-fulfilling [selffʊlˈfɪlɪŋ] *adj que se cumple únicamente porque se cree que se va a cumplir.*

self-governing [selfˈgʌvənɪŋ] *adj* autónomo,-a.

self-government [selfˈgʌvənmənt] *n* autonomía, autogobierno.

self-help [selfˈhelp] *n* autoayuda.

■ **self-help group,** grupo de autoayuda.

self-importance [selfɪmˈpɔːtəns] *n* engreimiento, presunción *f*.

self-important [selfɪmˈpɔːtənt] *adj* engreído,-a, presumido,-a.

self-imposed [selfɪmˈpəʊzd] *adj* autoimpuesto,-a, voluntario,-a.

self-indulgence [selfɪnˈdʌldʒəns] *n* tendencia a permitirse excesos, indulgencia consigo mismo,-a.

self-indulgent [selfɪnˈdʌldʒənt] *adj* que se permite excesos, indulgente consigo mismo,-a.

self-interest [selfˈɪntrəst] *n* interés *m* propio.

selfish [ˈselfɪʃ] *adj* egoísta.

selfishness [ˈselfɪʃnəs] *n* egoísmo.

selfless [ˈselfləs] *adj* desinteresado,-a.

self-locking [selfˈlɒkɪŋ] *adj* de cierre automático.

self-made [selfˈmeɪd] *adj (man, woman)* que ha llegado donde está por sus propios esfuerzos, que se ha hecho a sí mismo,-a.

self-opinionated [selfəˈpɪnjəneɪtɪd] *adj* testarudo,-a, terco,-a.

self-pity [selfˈpɪtɪ] *n* autocompasión *f*, lástima de sí mismo,-a.

self-portrait [selfˈpɔːtreɪt] *n* autorretrato.

self-possessed [selfpəˈzest] *adj* sereno,-a, dueño,-a de sí mismo,-a.

self-preservation [selfprezəˈveɪʃən] *n* supervivencia: *the instinct for self-preservation,* el instinto de supervivencia.

self-raising flour [selfreɪzɪŋˈflaʊəʳ] *n* harina con levadura.

self-reliance [selfrɪˈlaɪəns] *n* independencia, autosuficiencia.

self-reliant [selfrɪˈlaɪənt] *adj* independiente, autosuficiente.

self-respect [selfrɪˈspekt] *n* amor *m* propio, dignidad *f*.

self-respecting [selfrɪ'spektɪŋ] *adj* que se precie.
self-restraint [selfrɪ'streɪnt] *n* dominio de sí mismo,-a, autocontrol *m*.
self-righteous [self'raɪtʃəs] *adj* petulante.
self-righteousness [self'raɪtʃəsnəs] *n* petulancia.
self-rising flour [selfraɪzɪn'flauə'] *n* US → **self-raising flour**.
self-rule [self'ruːl] *n* autonomía, autogobierno.
self-sacrifice [self'sækrɪfaɪs] *n* sacrificio, abnegación *f*.
selfsame ['selfseɪm] *adj* mismísimo,-a.
self-satisfied [self'sætɪsfaɪd] *adj* satisfecho,-a de sí mismo,-a, ufano,-a, engreído,-a.
self-service [self'sɜːvɪs] **1** *adj* de autoservicio. – **2** *n* autoservicio.
self-sufficiency [selfsə'fɪʃənsɪ] *n* autosuficiencia.
self-sufficient [selfsə'fɪʃənt] *adj* autosuficiente.
self-taught [self'tɔːt] *adj* autodidacta.
sell [sel] **1** *t* (*gen*) vender: *we're selling our flat,* vendemos nuestro piso; *sorry, we don't sell stamps,* lo siento, pero no vendemos sellos; *he sold his bike to his neighbour,* vendió la bici a su vecino. **2** *fam* (*convince*) convencer de: *you've got to sell your ideas to the voters,* tienes que convencer a los votantes de tus ideas. – **3** *i* (*product*) venderse: *the tickets are selling well,* las entradas se están vendiendo bien; *these plants sell at a pound each,* estas plantas se venden a una libra cada una. – **4** *n* GB *fam* (*deception*) estafa, engaño.
◆ **to sell off** *t sep* (*gen*) vender; (*cheaply*) liquidar. ‖ **to sell out 1** *i* (*be disloyal*) claudicar, venderse. **2** COMM (*sell all of*) agotarse (**of**, -), acabarse (**of**, -): *we've sold out of that size,* se nos ha acabado esa talla, no nos queda esa talla. **3** (*sell business*) vender el negocio. – **4** *t sep* COMM (*sell all of*) agotar, agotar las existencias de. ‖ **to sell up** *i* vender el negocio, venderlo todo.
● **to be sold on sth.,** estar entusiasmado,-a por algo.
‖ **to be sold out,** estar agotado,-a: *the concert was sold out,* se habían agotado las entradas para el concierto; *"sold out",* "agotadas las existencias". ‖ **to sell like hot cakes,** venderse como rosquillas. ‖ **to sell os.,** venderse. ‖ **to sell one's body,** vender el cuerpo. ‖ **to sell one's soul to the devil,** venderle el alma al diablo. ‖ **to sell sb. a pup,** venderle a algn. una moto. ‖ **to sell sb. down the river,** traicionar a algn. ‖ **to sell sb. short,** (*cheat*) timar a algn.; (*underestimate*) subestimar a algn., no reconocer el valor de algn.
▲ *pt & pp* **sold**.
sell-by date ['selbaɪdeɪt] *n* fecha límite de venta.
seller ['selə'] *n* (*person*) vendedor,-ra.
● **to be a good/bad seller,** (*product*) venderse bien/mal.
■ **seller's market,** mercado favorable al vendedor,-ra.
selling ['selɪŋ] *n* ventas *fpl*.
■ **selling point,** atractivo comercial. ‖ **selling price,** precio de venta.
sellotape ['seləteɪp] **1** *n* GB celo, cinta adhesiva. – **2** *t* pegar con celo, fijar con celo.
sell-out ['selaut] **1** *n* (*performance*) éxito de taquilla. **2** *fam* (*betrayal*) traición *f*, engaño.
selvage ['selvɪdʒ] *n* orillo.
selvedge ['selvɪdʒ] *n* orillo.
selves [selvz] *npl* → **self**.
semantic [sɪ'mæntɪk] *adj* semántico,-a.
semantics [sɪ'mæntɪks] *n* semántica.
semaphore ['seməfɔː'] **1** *n* (*device*) semáforo; (*system*) código de señales. – **2** *t* transmitir por semáforo.
semblance ['sembləns] *n fml* apariencia: *we must establish some semblance of order,* hay que establecer cierta apariencia de orden.

semen ['siːmən] *n* semen *m*.
semester [sɪ'mestə'] *n* semestre *m*.
semiautomatic [semɪɔːtə'mætɪk] *adj* semi-automático,-a.
semibreve ['semɪbriːv] *n* MUS semibreve *f*, redonda.
semicircle ['semɪsɜːkəl] *n* semicírculo.
semicircular [semɪ'sɜːkjulə'] *adj* semicircular.
semicolon [semɪ'kəulən] *n* punto y coma *m*.
semiconductor [semɪkən'dʌktə'] *n* semiconductor *m*.
semiconscious [semɪ'kɒnʃəs] *adj* semiconsciente.
semidarkness [semɪ'dɑːknəs] *n* penumbra.
● **in semidarkness,** en penumbra.
semidetached [semɪdɪ'tætʃt] **1** *adj* pareado,-a. – **2** *n* (*house*) casa pareada.
semifinal [semɪ'faɪnəl] *n* semifinal *f*.
semifinalist [semɪ'faɪnəlɪst] *n* semifinalista *mf*.
seminal ['semɪnəl] **1** *adj* (*producing semen*) seminal. **2** *fig* (*influential*) fundamental, de gran influencia.
seminar ['semɪnɑː'] *n* EDUC seminario.
seminary ['semɪnərɪ] *n* REL seminario.
▲ *pl* **seminaries**.
semiofficial [semɪə'fɪʃəl] *adj* semioficial.
semiotics [semɪ'ɒtɪks] *n* semiótica.
semiprecious [semɪ'preʃəs] *adj* semiprecioso,-a.
semiquaver ['semɪkweɪvə'] *n* MUS semicorchea.
semiskilled [semɪ'skɪld] *adj* semicualificado,-a.
semiskimmed [semɪ'skɪmd] *adj* semidesnatado,-a, semidescremado,-a.
Semite ['siːmaɪt] *n* semita *mf*.
Semitic [sɪ'mɪtɪk] *adj* semita, semítico,-a.
semitone ['semɪtəun] *n* semitono.
semivowel ['semɪvauəl] *n* semivocal *f*.
semolina [semə'liːnə] *n* sémola.
senate ['senət] **1** *n* POL senado. **2** EDUC claustro.
senator ['senətə'] *n* senador,-ra.
send [send] **1** *t* (*gen*) enviar, mandar; (*telex, telegram*) enviar, poner; (*radio signal, radio message*) transmitir, emitir: *send me the results,* envíame los resultados; *he sent me some flowers,* me mandó flores; *Nicola's sent us a postcard,* Nicola nos ha mandado una postal; *Polly sends her love,* Polly manda recuerdos de su parte. **2** (*order to go*) mandar, enviar: *the doctor sent me to a specialist,* el médico me mandó a un especialista; *he sent his brother to get some cigarettes,* mandó a su hermano a comprar tabaco; *the company is sending me on a training course,* la empresa me manda a hacer un curso de formación. **3** (*drive, cause to move*) mandar; (*rocket, ball*) lanzar: *the explosion sent pieces of glass flying everywhere,* la explosión lanzó trozos de cristal por los aires; *the punch sent me reeling,* el puñetazo me dejó tambaleante; *the news sent a shiver down her spine,* la noticia le dio escalofríos. **4** (*cause to become*) volver, hacer: *the noise sent her mad,* el ruido la volvió loca; *the lecture sent me to sleep,* la conferencia me hizo dormir; *her comments sent him into a rage,* sus comentarios lo pusieron furioso. **5** *fam dated* (*excite, thrill*) transportar, chiflar. – **6** *i* (*send a message*) avisar: *he sent to say that he'd arrived safely,* mandó aviso de que había llegado sano y salvo.
◆ **to send away** *t sep* despachar: *I sent them away,* les dije que se fueran. ‖ **to send away for** *t insep* pedir por correo. ‖ **to send back 1** *t sep* (*goods etc*) devolver. **2** (*person*) hacer volver. ‖ **to send down 1** *t sep* (*gen*) mandar; (*prices*) hacer bajar. **2** GB (*student*) expulsar; (*criminal*) enchironar, entalegar. ‖ **to send for 1** *t insep* (*person*) llamar a, hacer llamar a. **2** (*thing*) pedir, encargar. ‖ **to**

send in 1 *t sep* (*application, request*) mandar, enviar. **2** (*troops, police*) enviar; (*visitor*) hacer pasar. ‖ **to send off 1** *t sep* (*letter etc*) enviar, mandar; (*goods*) despachar, mandar. **2** GB SP (*footballer etc*) expulsar. ‖ **to send off for** *t insep* pedir por correo. ‖ **to send on** *t sep* (*letter*) hacer seguir; (*luggage etc*) enviar, mandar (por adelantado). ‖ **to send out 1** *t sep* (*leaflets, invitations*) enviar, mandar; (*goods*) despachar, mandar. **2** (*radio signals*) emitir, transmitir, dar. **3** (*light, smoke, heat*) emitir. **4** (*person*) echar, hacer salir. ‖ **to send out for** *t insep* (*food etc*) mandar traer, mandar por, mandar a comprar. ‖ **to send up 1** *t sep* (*gen*) hacer subir; (*rocket, flare*) lanzar. **2** GB *fam* (*satirize*) parodiar, burlarse de.
● **to send sb. away with a flea in their ear,** despachar a algn. con las orejas gachas. ‖ **to send sb. packing,** mandar a algn. a paseo, mandar a algn. a freír espárragos. ‖ **to send sb. to Coventry,** hacerle el vacío a algn. ‖ **to send word,** mandar aviso, enviar un mensaje, avisar: *he sent word that he was well,* mandó aviso de que estaba bien.
▲ *pt & pp* **sent**.

sender ['sendə'] *n* remitente *mf*.
sendoff ['sendɒf] *n fam* despedida.
send-up ['sendʌp] *n* sátira, parodia.
● **to do a send-up of sb.,** imitar a algn., parodiar a algn.
Senegal [senɪ'gɔːl] *n* Senegal.
Senegalese [senɪgə'liːz] **1** *adj* senegalés,-esa. – **2** *n* senegalés,-esa. – **3 the Senegalese,** *npl* los senegaleses *mpl*.
senile ['siːnaɪl] *adj* senil.
● **to go senile,** chochear.
■ **senile dementia,** demencia senil.
senility [sɪ'nɪlətɪ] *n* senilidad *f*.
senior ['siːnɪə'] **1** *adj* (*in age*) mayor: *he's five years senior to me,* es cinco años mayor que yo. **2** (*in rank*) superior; (*with longer service*) más antiguo,-a, de mayor antigüedad: *she is senior to me,* es mi superior. – **3** *n* (*in age*) mayor *mf*; (*in rank*) superior *fm*: *you're two years my senior,* eres dos años mayor que yo. **4** GB EDUC mayor *mf*; US EDUC estudiante *mf* del último curso.
■ **senior citizen,** jubilado,-a, persona de la tercera edad. ‖ **senior high (school),** US *instituto donde se estudian los tres últimos cursos de la enseñanza media.* ‖ **senior lecturer,** GB profesor,-ra titular. ‖ **senior management,** altos cargos *mpl*. ‖ **senior officer,** MIL oficial,-la de alta graduación. ‖ **senior partner,** socio,-a mayoritario,-a. ‖ **the Senior Service,** GB la marina, la armada.
Senior ['siːnɪə'] *adj* padre: *John Williams, Senior,* John Williams, padre.
seniority [siːnɪ'ɒrɪtɪ] *n* (*in length of service*) antigüedad *f*; (*in rank*) superioridad *f*, jerarquía; (*in age*) el hecho de ser mayor.
sensation [sen'seɪʃən] **1** *n* (*feeling*) sensación *f*; (*ability to feel*) sensibilidad *f*: *it gave me a tingling sensation,* me dio una sensación de cosquilleo; *he had no sensation in his leg,* no se sentía la pierna. **2** (*interest, excitement, etc*) sensación *f*; (*success*) éxito.
● **to be a sensation,** ser (todo) un éxito. ‖ **to cause a sensation,** causar sensación.
sensational [sen'seɪʃənəl] **1** *adj fam* (*wonderful*) sensacional. **2** (*exaggerated*) sensacionalista; (*causing interest, excitement, etc*) que causa sensación.
sensationalism [sen'seɪʃənəlɪzəm] *n* sensacionalismo.
sensationalist [sen'seɪʃənəlɪst] **1** *adj* sensacionalista. – **2** *n* sensacionalista *mf*.

sensationalize [sen'seɪʃənəlaɪz] *t* sensacionalizar.
sense [sens] **1** *n* (*faculty*) sentido: *sense of smell,* sentido del olfato. **2** (*feeling - of well-being, loss*) sensación *f*; (*awareness, appreciation - of justice, duty*) sentido: *I had the sense someone was watching me,* tenía la sensación de que alguien me miraba; *he has an exaggerated sense of his own importance,* se cree más importante de lo que es; *he's got no sense of humour,* no tiene sentido del humor; *sense of direction,* sentido de la orientación; *dress sense,* gusto para vestirse; *business sense,* visión para los negocios. **3** (*wisdom, judgement*) sentido común, juicio, sensatez *f*, seso: *he had the (good) sense to turn off the electricity,* tuvo la sensatez de desconectar la corriente; *I thought you had more sense,* creía que tenías más sentido común. **4** (*reason, purpose*) sentido: *what's the sense in driving there?,* ¿qué sentido tiene conducir hasta allí?; *there's no sense in crying,* ¿de qué sirve llorar? **5** (*meaning - gen*) sentido; (*- of word*) significado, acepción *f*: *in every sense of the word,* en todos los sentidos; *this word has 9 different senses,* esta palabra tiene 9 significados diferentes. – **6** *t* (*feel, perceive*) sentir, percibir, presentir, intuir; (*apprehend, detect*) percibir, darse cuenta de: *I sensed that she wanted to leave,* intuí que quería marcharse; *animals can sense danger,* los animales perciben el peligro. **7** (*machine*) detectar. – **8 senses,** *npl* (*normal state of mind*) juicio *m sing*.
● **in a sense,** hasta cierto punto, en cierto sentido. ‖ **in no sense,** de ninguna manera. ‖ **to be out of one's senses,** no estar en sus cabales. ‖ **to bring sb. to their senses,** hacer a algn. entrar en razón. ‖ **to come to one's senses,** recobrar el juicio. ‖ **to have a sense of occasion,** tener sentido de la ocasión. ‖ **to make sense,** (*have clear meaning*) tener sentido; (*be sensible*) ser razonable, ser sensato,-a. ‖ **to make sense out of sth.,** entender algo. ‖ **to see sense,** entrar en razón. ‖ **to take leave of one's senses,** perder el juicio. ‖ **to talk sense,** hablar con juicio.
■ **sense organ,** órgano del sentido.
senseless ['sensləs] **1** *adj* (*unconscious*) inconsciente, sin conocimiento: *he was beaten senseless,* lo golpearon hasta dejarlo inconsciente. **2** (*foolish, pointless*) absurdo,-a, sin sentido, insensato,-a: *senseless violence,* violencia sin sentido.
● **to be bored senseless,** aburrirse mortalmente.
sensibility [sensɪ'bɪlətɪ] **1** *n* sensibilidad *f*. – **2 sensibilities,** *npl* susceptibilidad *f sing*, sensibilidad *f sing*.
sensible ['sensəbəl] **1** *adj* (*person*) sensato,-a; (*behaviour, decision*) razonable, prudente; (*choice*) acertado,-a: *it was a very sensible thing to do,* fue lo más sensato que podías hacer; *that's the most sensible suggestion I've heard all day,* esa es la sugerencia más razonable que he oído en todo el día. **2** (*clothes*) práctico,-a, cómodo,-a. **3** *dated* (*noticeable*) apreciable, perceptible.
sensitive ['sensɪtɪv] **1** *adj* (*person - perceptive*) sensible (**to,** a), consciente (**to,** de): *she's very sensitive to her pupils' needs,* es muy consciente de las necesidades de sus alumnos. **2** (*person - touchy*) susceptible (**to,** a), preocupado,-a (**about,** por): *he's very sensitive about his baldness,* está muy preocupado por su calvicie. **3** (*teeth, paper, instrument, film*) sensible (**to,**-a); (*skin*) sensible, delicado,-a. **4** (*issue*) delicado,-a. **5** (*document*) confidencial.
sensitivity [sensɪ'tɪvɪtɪ] **1** *n* (*gen*) sensibilidad *f* (**to,** a/ frente a): *his remark showed a crass lack of sensitivity,* su comentario mostró una falta extrema de sensibilidad. **2** (*touchiness*) susceptibilidad *f* (**to,** a). **3** (*of skin, issue*) delicadeza.

sensitize ['sensɪtaɪz] **1** *t* (*to problem*) sensibilizar, concienciar. **2** TECH sensibilizar.
sensor ['sensə'] *n* TECH sensor *m*, detector *m*.
sensory ['sensərɪ] *adj* sensorial.
sensual ['sensjʊəl] *adj* sensual.
sensuality [sensju'ælətɪ] *n* sensualidad *f*.
sensuous ['sensjʊəs] *adj* sensual.
sent [sent] *pt* & *pp* → **send**.
sentence ['sentəns] **1** *n* (*gen*) frase *f*; (*in grammar*) oración *f*. **2** JUR sentencia, fallo. – **3** *t* JUR condenar. **4** *fig* condenar, predestinar.
● to be under sentence of death, estar condenado,-a a muerte. ‖ to pass sentence, dictar sentencia. ‖ to pass/pronounce sentence on sb., imponer una pena a algn.
■ death sentence, pena de muerte.
sententious [sen'tenʃəs] *adj* sentencioso,-a.
sentiment ['sentɪmənt] **1** *n* (*sentimentality*) sentimentalismo, sensiblería. **2** *fml* (*feeling*) sentimiento. **3** *fml* (*opinion*) opinión *f*, parecer *m*: *my sentiments exactly*, estoy totalmente de acuerdo.
sentimental [sentɪ'mentəl] **1** *adj* sentimental: *it's of sentimental value*, tiene valor sentimental. **2** *pej* sentimentaloide, sensiblero,-a.
sentimentality [sentɪmen'tælətɪ] *n* sentimentalismo, sensiblería.
sentinel ['sentɪnəl] *n dated* centinela *m*.
sentry ['sentrɪ] *n* centinela *m*.
● to be on sentry duty, estar de guardia, hacer guardia.
■ sentry box, garita de centinela. ‖ sentry duty, guardia.
▲ *pl* **sentries**.
Seoul [səʊl] *n* Seúl.
Sep [sep'tembə'] *abbr* (*September*) setiembre, septiembre.
sepal ['sepəl] *n* BOT sépalo.
separable ['sepərəbəl] *adj* separable.
separate ['sepərət] **1** *t* (*gen*) separar (**from**, de); (*divide*) dividir: *I stepped in to separate the two boys*, intervine para separar a los dos chicos; *break the egg and separate the white from the yolk*, rompe el huevo y separa la clara de la yema; *the Channel separates England from France*, el Canal de la Mancha separa Inglaterra de Francia. **2** (*distinguish*) distinguir, separar. – **3** *i* (*gen*) separarse: *they separated after being married for ten years*, se separaron después de diez años de matrimonio. **4** (*mayonnaise etc*) cortarse. – **5** *adj* (*apart*) separado,-a: *keep the sheeps separate from the goats*, mantén a las ovejas separadas de las cabras; *political prisoners are kept separate from the others*, los presos políticos están separados de los demás. **6** (*not shared*) separado,-a, individual: *they have separate bank accounts*, tienen cuentas bancarias separadas; *we had separate rooms*, cada uno tenía su habitación. **7** (*different, distinct*) distinto,-a, diferente: *it's happened on three separate occasions*, ha pasado en tres ocasiones distintas; *that is a separate issue*, eso es un tema aparte, eso es otro tema; *this word has five separate meanings*, esta palabra tiene cinco significados distintos; *put the olives on a separate plate*, pon las aceitunas en un plato aparte. – **8** **separates**, *npl* (*clothes*) prendas de mujer que combinan con otras, pero que se venden sueltas.
● to go one's separate ways, irse cada uno por su lado. ‖ to lead separate lives, hacer cada uno su propia vida. ‖ to send sth. under separate cover, mandar algo por separado.

▲ (*adjetivo*) ['sepərət].
separated ['sepəreɪtɪd] *adj* separado,-a.
separately ['sepərətlɪ] **1** *adv* (*apart*) por separado, aparte: *could you wrap the perfume separately?*, ¿podría envolver el perfume aparte? **2** (*individually*) por separado: *we paid separately*, pagamos por separado.
separation [sepə'reɪʃən] *n* separación *f*.
separatism ['sepərətɪzəm] *n* separatismo.
separatist ['sepərətɪst] *n* separatista *mf*.
Sephardi [se'fɑːdɪ] *n* sefardí *mf*, sefardita *mf*.
▲ *pl* **Sephardim** [se'fɑːdɪm].
Sephardic [se'fɑːdɪk] *adj* sefardita.
sepia ['siːpɪə] **1** *n* sepia *m*. – **2** *adj* sepia.
sepsis ['sepsɪs] *n* MED sepsia.
September [sep'tembə'] *n* septiembre *m*, setiembre *m*.
▲ *Véase también* **May**.
septet [sep'tet] *n* MUS septeto.
septic ['septɪk] *adj* séptico,-a.
● to go septic, infectarse.
■ septic tank, pozo séptico, pozo negro.
septicaemia [septɪ'siːmɪə] *n* septicemia.
septicemia [septɪ'siːmɪə] *n* US → **septicaemia**.
sepulchre ['sepəlkə'] *n* sepulcro.
sequel ['siːkwəl] **1** *n* (*result, consequence*) secuela. **2** (*book, film, etc*) segunda parte *f*, continuación *f*.
sequence ['siːkwəns] **1** *n* (*order*) secuencia, orden *m*: *the sequence of events*, la secuencia de los hechos. **2** (*series*) secuencia, serie *f*, sucesión *f*; (*in maths*) secuencia; (*of cards*) escalera. **3** TV CINEM secuencia.
■ sequence of tenses, LING concordancia de los tiempos verbales.
sequester [sɪ'kwestə'] **1** *t fml* (*seclude*) aislar. **2** JUR (*sequestrate*) embargar, secuestrar.
sequestration [siːkwe'streɪʃən] *n* JUR embargo, secuestro.
sequin ['siːkwɪn] *n* lentejuela.
sequoia [sɪ'kwɔɪə] *n* secoya, secuoya.
Serb [sɜːb] **1** *n* (*person*) serbio,-a. – **2** *adj* serbio,-a.
Serbia ['sɜːbɪə] *n* Serbia.
Serbian ['sɜːbɪən] **1** *n* (*person*) serbio,-a. **2** (*dialect*) serbio. – **3** *adj* serbio,-a.
Serbo-Croat [sɜːbəʊ'krəʊæt] *n* (*language*) serbocroata *m*.
Serbo-Croatian [sɜːbəʊkrəʊ'eɪʃən] *n* → **Serbo-Croat**.
serenade [serə'neɪd] **1** *n* serenata. – **2** *t* dar una serenata a.
serene [sə'riːn] *adj* sereno,-a, tranquilo,-a.
serenely [sə'riːnlɪ] *adv* serenamente, con serenidad.
serenity [sə'renɪtɪ] *n* serenidad *f*.
serf [sɜːf] *n* siervo,-a.
serge [sɜːdʒ] *n* sarga.
sergeant ['sɑːdʒənt] **1** *n* MIL sargento *mf*. **2** (*of police*) cabo *mf*.
■ sergeant major, sargento mayor, brigada *m*.
serial ['sɪərɪəl] **1** *adj* consecutivo,-a, en serie: *in serial order*, en orden consecutivo. **2** RAD TV (*in parts*) seriado,-a, en capítulos. – **3** *n* RAD TV (*gen*) serie *f*, serial *m*; (*soap opera*) radionovela, telenovela. **4** (*book*) novela por entregas.
■ serial killer, asesino,-a en serie. ‖ serial number, número de serie. ‖ serial processing, procesamiento en serie.
serialization [sɪərɪəlaɪ'zeɪʃən] *n* adaptación *f* (*para la radio o televisión en capítulos*).
serialize ['sɪərɪəlaɪz] *t* seriar, adaptar (*para la radio o televisión en capítulos*).

series [ˈsɪəriːz] **1** *n* (*gen*) serie *f*, sucesión *f*. **2** (*of films, lectures, concerts, etc*) ciclo; (*of books*) colección *f*. **3** RAD TV serie *f*, serial *m*. **4** SP serie *f*.
● **in series,** TECH en serie.
▲ *pl* **series**.

serigraph [ˈserɪgræf] *n* serigrafía.

serigraphy [səˈrɪgrəfɪ] *n* serigrafía.

serious [ˈsɪərɪəs] **1** *adj* (*solemn, earnest*) serio,-a: *you look very serious,* estás muy serio; *you can't be serious!,* ¡no lo dices en serio!, ¡no hablas en serio!; *are you serious about leaving your job?,* ¿en serio quieres dejar el trabajo?; *I'll give it some serious consideration,* lo consideraré seriamente; *we must get down to some serious work,* tenemos que ponernos a trabajar en serio. **2** (*causing concern, severe*) grave, serio,-a: *she has a serious illness,* padece una enfermedad grave; *no serious damage was caused,* no hubo daños importantes; *serious crime is on the increase,* los delitos de mayor gravedad van en aumento; *things are getting serious,* las cosas se están poniendo serias.

seriously [ˈsɪərɪəslɪ] **1** *adv* (*in earnest*) en serio: *don't take things so seriously,* no te tomes las cosas tan en serio; *are you seriously saying that we have to leave?,* ¿lo dices en serio que nos tenemos que marchar? **2** (*severely*) seriamente, gravemente: *seriously wounded,* herido,-a de gravedad; *smoking can seriously damage your health,* fumar perjudica seriamente la salud.
● **seriously though,** bromas aparte, (hablando) en serio. ‖ **to take os. seriously,** darse importancia.

seriousness [ˈsɪərɪəsnəs] **1** *n* (*severity*) seriedad *f*, gravedad *f*. **2** (*earnestness, solemnity*) seriedad *f*.
● **in all seriousness,** hablando (muy) en serio, bromas aparte.

sermon [ˈsɜːmən] *n* sermón *m*.

sermonize [ˈsɜːmənaɪz] *i* sermonear.

serous [ˈsɪərəs] *adj* seroso,-a.

serpent [ˈsɜːpənt] *n* lit serpiente *f*.

serrated [səˈreɪtɪd] *adj* dentado,-a, serrado,-a.

serum [ˈsɪərəm] *n* MED suero.
▲ *pl* **serums** o **sera**.

servant [ˈsɜːvənt] **1** *n* (*domestic*) criado,-a, sirviente *mf*. **2** *fig* servidor,-ra.

serve [sɜːv] **1** *t* (*work for*) servir (**as,** de): *she served the company loyally for fifty years,* sirvió fielmente a la empresa durante cincuenta años; *he has served his country,* ha servido a la patria. **2** (*customer*) servir, atender; (*food, drink*) servir: *are you being served?,* ¿le atienden?; *dinner is served at 8.00 pm,* se sirve la cena a les 8.00; *we can't serve alcohol after 11.00 pm,* no podemos servir alcohol después de las 11.00; *this dish serves two,* este plato es para dos. **3** (*be useful to*) servir, ser útil: *this penknife will serve my purpose,* esta navaja me servirá; *it serves many different purposes,* sirve para varias cosas. **4** (*provide with service*) prestar servicio a: *the new hospital will serve the whole region,* el nuevo hospital prestará servicio a toda la región; *Barcelona is served by a good public transport system,* Barcelona dispone de un buen sistema de transporte público. **5** (*complete period of time - apprenticeship*) hacer; (*- sentence*) cumplir: *he served a three-year apprenticeship,* hizo un aprendizaje de tres años; *she served six months for stealing,* cumplió una condena de seis meses por robo. **6** JUR (*summons, writ, court order, etc*) entregar, hacer entrega de: *he was served with a summons,* fue citado para comparecer ante del juez, recibió una citación judicial. **7** (*tennis*) sacar, servir. – **8** *i* (*work for*) servir: *my father served in the army,* mi padre sirvió en el ejército; *she served on*

a parliamentary committee, fue miembro de la comisión parlamentaria. **9** (*in shop*) atender; (*food, drink*) servir: *who wants to serve?,* ¿quién quiere servir?; *she's learning to serve at table,* aprende a servir la mesa. **10** (*be useful to*) servir (**as,** de): *this small room can serve as my study,* esta habitación pequeña puede servirme de estudio; *let this serve as a reminder to us all,* que esto nos sirva de recuerdo a todos; *his remark only served to make things worse,* su comentario sólo sirvió para empeorar las cosas; *this will serve as an example,* esto servirá de ejemplo. **11** (*tennis*) servir, sacar. – **12** *n* (*tennis*) saque *m*.
◆ **to serve out 1** *t sep* (*food*) servir. **2** (*complete period of time*) cumplir, hacer. ‖ **to serve up 1** *t sep* (*excuse etc*) ofrecer. **2** (*meal, food*) servir.
● **if my memory serves me right/well,** si no me falla la memoria, si mal no recuerdo. ‖ **to serve at mass,** ayudar en misa. ‖ **to serve sb. right,** tenerlo bien merecido algn.: *it serves you right,* lo tienes bien merecido. ‖ **to serve time,** cumplir una condena.

server [ˈsɜːvə] **1** *n* (*cutlery*) cubierto de servir. **2** (*tray*) bandeja, salvilla. **3** REL (*at mass*) monaguillo. **4** SP jugador,-ra que tiene el saque.

service [ˈsɜːvɪs] **1** *n* (*attention to customer*) servicio: *the service here is terribly slow,* el servicio aquí es muy lento; *is service included?,* ¿el servicio está incluido? **2** (*organization, system, business*) servicio: *there's a good bus service,* hay un buen servicio de autobuses; *there's a 24-hour service,* hay un servicio permanente, hay un servicio las 24 horas. **3** (*work, duty*) servicio: *a life of public service,* una vida de servicio al pueblo; *he has twenty years' service in the army,* lleva veinte años de servicio en el ejército; *he died on active service,* murió en acto de servicio; *she went into (domestic) service,* se puso a trabajar de criada. **4** (*use*) servicio: *you'll get excellent service from this model,* este modelo te dará un servicio excelente; *this machine is not in service,* esta máquina no funciona. **5** (*maintenance of car, machine*) revisión *f*. **6** REL oficio, oficio religioso: *wedding service,* ceremonia de boda. **7** (*of dishes*) vajilla; (*for tea, coffee*) juego. **8** (*tennis*) saque *m*, servicio. **9** JUR entrega, citación *f*, notificación *f*. – **10** *adj* (*for use of workers*) de servicio: *service entrance,* entrada de servicio. **11** (*military*) de militar: *service family,* familia de militar. – **12** *t* (*car, machine*) revisar, hacer una revisión de: *I must get the car serviced,* tengo que llevar el coche a revisión. **13** (*organization, group*) atender, servir. **14** (*debt, loan*) pagar los intereses de. – **15 services,** *npl* (*work, act, help*) servicios *mpl*: *the services of a lawyer,* los servicios de un abogado; *he was commended for his services to industry,* lo alabaron por sus servicios a la industria. **16 the services,** MIL las fuerzas *fpl* armadas: *which of the services were you in?,* ¿en qué cuerpo estuviste?
● **at your service,** a su disposición, para servirle. ‖ **how can I be of (any) service (to you)?,** ¿en qué puedo servirle? ‖ **it's all part of the service,** está incluido en el servicio. ‖ **to do sb. a service,** hacer un favor a algn.
■ **service area,** área de servicio. ‖ **service charge,** (*on bill*) servicio; (*in banking*) comisión *f*; (*for flat*) gastos *mpl* de comunidad. ‖ **service flat,** apartamento con servicios incluidos. ‖ **service industry/sector,** sector *m* de servicios. ‖ **service road,** vía de acceso. ‖ **service station,** estación *f* de servicio.

serviceable [ˈsɜːvɪsəbəl] **1** *adj* (*in usable condition*) útil, utilizable, servible. **2** (*durable, hard-wearing*) práctico,-a, duradero,-a.

serviceman [ˈsɜːvɪsmən] *n* militar *m*.
▲ *pl* **servicemen** [ˈsɜːvɪsmən].
servicewoman [ˈsɜːvɪswʊmən] *n* militar *f*.
▲ *pl* **servicewomen** [ˈsɜːvɪswɪmɪn].
serviette [sɜːvɪˈet] *n* GB servilleta.
servile [ˈsɜːvaɪl] *adj* servil.
serving [ˈsɜːvɪŋ] *n* porción *f*, ración *f*.
■ **serving dish**, fuente *f*. ‖ **serving spoon**, cuchara de servir.
servitude [ˈsɜːvɪtjuːd] *n* servidumbre *f*.
servo [ˈsɜːvəʊ] *n fam* servomecanismo.
■ **servo brakes**, servofrenos *mpl*.
▲ *pl* **servos**.
servoassisted [ˈsɜːvəʊəsɪstɪd] *adj* servoasistido,-a.
■ **servoassisted brakes**, servofrenos *mpl*.
servomechanism [ˈsɜːvəʊmekənɪzəm] *n* servomecanismo.
servomotor [ˈsɜːvəʊməʊtəʳ] *n* servomotor *m*.
sesame [ˈsesəmɪ] *n* BOT sésamo, ajonjolí *m*.
■ **sesame oil**, aceite *m* de sésamo. ‖ **sesame seeds**,
semillas *fpl* de sésamo.
session [ˈseʃən] **1** *n* (*formal meeting*) sesión *f*, junta, reunión *f*; (*sitting*) sesión *f*. **2** (*period of time, activity*) sesión
f: *a training session*, una sesión de entrenamiento. **3**
EDUC (*year*) año académico, curso académico; (*term*) trimestre *m*.
● **to be in session**, (*court*) estar en juicio, estar en sesión; (*parliament*) estar en período de sesiones.
set¹ [set] **1** *n* (*of golf clubs, brushes, tools, etc*) juego; (*books,
poems*) colección *f*; (*of turbines*) equipo, grupo; (*of stamps*)
serie *f*: *chess set*, juego de ajedrez; *set of cutlery*, cubertería; *set of dishes*, vajilla; *set of saucepans*, batería
de cocina; *set of teeth*, dentadura; *tea set*, juego de té;
a boxed set, un juego en estuche. **2** ELEC (*apparatus*)
aparato: *they bought a TV set*, compraron un televisor;
a wireless set, una radio. **3** MATH conjunto. **4** SP (*tennis*)
set *m*. **5** MUS (*performance*) actuación *f*: *the set included
several new songs*, la actuación incluía varias cancio-
nes nuevas; *the band played a short set*, la banda tocó
pocos temas. **6** (*of people*) grupo; (*clique*) pandilla, camarilla. **7** (*of pupils*) grupo.
● **to make a dead set at**, (*attack*) emprenderla con;
(*seduce*) proponerse ligar con.
set² [set] **1** *n* (*in hairdressing*) marcado: *shampoo and set,
please*, lavar y marcar, por favor. **2** CINEM THEAT TV (*scenery*) decorado; (*place of filming*) plató *m*: *all actors must
be on the set at 9.00 am*, todos los actores deben estar
en el plató a las 9.00. **3** (*position, posture*) postura, posición *f*. – **4** *adj* (*placed*) situado,-a: *a village set on a hill*,
un pueblo situado sobre una colina; *the cottage is set
in beautiful countryside*, la casita está enclavada en un
paisaje precioso. **5** (*fixed, arranged*) fijo,-a, determinado,-a, establecido,-a: *we've got set hours of work*, tenemos un horario fijo de trabajo; *meals are served at
set times*, se sirven las comidas a horas determinadas;
my day never follows a set pattern, no tengo ninguna
rutina establecida durante el día. **6** (*rigid, stiff*) rígido,-
a, forzado,-a; (*opinion*) inflexible; (*idea*) fijo,-a. **7** EDUC (*of
book*) prescrito,-a. **8** (*ready, prepared*) listo,-a (**for/to**,
para), preparado,-a (**for/to**, para); (*likely*) probable: *is
everyone set to go?*, ¿todos estáis listos para salir?; *the
Socialists seem set to win again*, parece que los socialistas volverán a ganar. – **9** *t* (*put, place*) poner, colocar:
she set the divorce papers (down) before him, le puso
los papeles de divorcio delante. **10** (*prepare - trap*) - tender, preparar; (*- table*) poner; (*- camera, video*) preparar;
(*- clock, watch, oven, etc*) poner: *set the table for dinner,*

pon la mesa para la cena; *I've set the alarm clock for
6.00 am*, he puesto el despertador a las 6.00. **11** (*date,
time*) fijar, señalar, acordar; (*example*) dar; (*rule, record,
limit*) establecer; (*precedent*) sentar; (*fashion*) imponer,
dictar: *have you set a date for the wedding?*, ¿has fijado
una fecha para la boda?; *you should set a good example*,
deberías dar buen ejemplo. **12** (*price*) fijar; (*value*) poner: *he sets a minimum price on his services*, fija un precio mínimo para sus servicios; *high values are set on
safety*, se valora mucho la seguridad. **13** (*jewel, stone*)
montar, engastar. **14** (*text for printing*) componer. **15**
MED (*broken bone*) componer; (*joint*) encajar. **16** (*exam,
test, problem*) poner; (*homework*) mandar, poner; (*task*)
asignar; (*text*) prescribir; (*target, aim*) fijar, proponer: *the
teacher set them some difficult questions in the exam*, el
profesor les puso unas preguntas difíciles en el examen. **17** (*story, action*) ambientar: *the novel is set in Madrid*, la novela está ambientada en Madrid; *the action is
set in 1930s Spain*, la acción se desarrolla en la España
de los años treinta. **18** (*provoke, start off*) poner, hacer:
you've set me thinking, me has hecho pensar; *this will
certainly set tongues wagging*, esto sí que dará que hablar. **19** (*provide music for*) arreglar, poner música a. **20**
(*hair*) marcar. **21** (*make firm - jelly*) cuajar; (*- cement*) hacer
fraguar; (*- teeth*) apretar. – **22** *i* (*sun, moon*) ponerse. **23**
(*liquid, jelly*) cuajar, cuajarse; (*cement*) fraguarse, endurecerse; (*glue*) endurecerse; (*bone*) soldarse.
◆ **to set about** **1** *t insep* (*begin*) empezar a, ponerse a.
2 (*attack*) atacar, agredir. ‖ **to set against** **1** *t sep* (*cause
to oppose*) enemistar con, poner en contra de. **2** (*balance,
compare*) contraponer, sopesar, comparar con; (*subtract
from*) desgravar: *the drop in unemployment must be set
against the rise in inflation*, el descenso del paro debe
contrastarse con el alza de la inflación. ‖ **to set apart**
t sep (*distinguish*) distinguir (**from**, de), hacer diferente
(**from**, de). ‖ **to set aside** **1** *t sep* (*save - money*) guardar,
ahorrar; (*- time*) dejar; (*reserve*) reservar. **2** (*disregard*) dejar de lado. **3** JUR (*quash, overturn*) anular. ‖ **to set back**
1 *t sep* (*at a distance*) apartar, retirar. **2** (*delay*) retrasar,
atrasar. **3** *fam* (*cost*) costar. ‖ **to set down** **1** *t sep* (*write*)
poner por escrito, escribir. **2** GB (*passenger*) dejar. **3** (*establish*) establecer, fijar. ‖ **to set forth** *i* emprender marcha, partir. ‖ **to set in** *i* (*bad weather*) empezar, comenzar;
(*problems etc*) surgir; (*infection, disease*) declararse. ‖ **to set
off** **1** *i* (*begin journey*) salir, ponerse en camino. – **2** *t sep*
(*bomb*) hacer estallar, hacer explotar; (*alarm*) hacer sonar; (*firework*) lanzar, tirar. **3** (*cause, start*) hacer empezar,
provocar, desencadenar. **4** (*enhance*) hacer resaltar,
realzar. ‖ **to set on** **1** *t sep* (*cause to attack*) echar: *I'll set
the dog on you*, te echaré el perro. – **2** *t insep* (*attack*)
atacar, agredir. ‖ **to set out** **1** *i* (*begin journey*) partir, salir
(**for**, para). **2** (*intend*) proponerse (**to**, -), tener la intención de, querer: *he set out to do something different*, se
propuso hacer algo diferente. – **3** *t sep* (*arrange*) disponer, exponer. **4** (*explain*) exponer. ‖ **to set to** *i* ponerse a, empezar a. ‖ **to set up** **1** *t sep* (*statue*) levantar,
erigir; (*roadblock*) colocar; (*tent, stall*) montar; (*machine,
equipment*) montar, armar. **2** *fam* (*drinks*) poner, servir. **3**
(*business*) montar, poner; (*school, trust fund*) fundar; (*inquiry*) abrir; (*committee*) crear. **4** (*provide with*) proveer de:
we're set up with everything we need, estamos provis-
tos de todo lo que necesitamos; *you're set up for life!*,
¡tienes el porvenir asegurado! **5** *fam* (*make healthier*)
ayudar a reponerse. **6** GB *fam* (*frame*) tender una trampa
a: *we've been set up!*, ¡nos han tendido una trampa! **7**
(*establish person*) establecerse (**as**, como): *she set herself
up as a freelance journalist*, se estableció como perio-

dista independiente; *he set his brother up in business,* ayudó a su hermano a establecerse. **8** (*claim to be*) pretender ser. **– 9** *i* establecerse (**as,** como): *he set up as a painter,* se estableció como pintor; *they've decided to set up in business,* han decidido montar un negocio.
● **to be all set,** estar listo,-a, estar preparado,-a. ‖ **to be dead set against sth.,** oponerse rotundamente a algo. ‖ **to be set in one's ways,** tener unas costumbres muy arraigadas, ser reacio,-a al cambio. ‖ **to be set on doing sth.,** estar empeñado,-a en hacer algo, estar resuelto,-a a hacer algo. ‖ **to set fire to sth.,** prender fuego a algo. ‖ **to set free,** poner en libertad, liberar. ‖ **to set one's heart on sth.,** querer algo más que nada. ‖ **to set sb.'s mind at rest,** tranquilizar a algn. ‖ **to set the ball rolling / to set things in motion,** poner las cosas en marcha. ‖ **to set the pace,** marcar el paso. ‖ **to set the tone,** marcar las pautas.
■ **set lunch,** menú *m* del día. ‖ **set phrase,** frase *f* hecha. ‖ **set square,** cartabón *m*, escuadra.
▲ *pt & pp set.*

setback ['setbæk] *n* revés *m*, contratiempo.

sett [set] **1** *n* (*of badger*) madriguera de tejón, tejonera. **2** (*paving stone*) adoquín *m*.

settee [se'tiː] *n* sofá *m*.

setter ['setə'] *n* (*dog*) setter *m*.

setting ['setɪŋ] **1** *n* (*of sun*) puesta. **2** (*of jewel*) engaste *m*, montura. **3** (*background*) marco, entorno; (*of film, novel*) escenario. **4** (*of machine, device, etc*) ajuste *m*, posición *f*. **5** (*place at table*) cubierto. **6** MUS arreglo, versión *f*.
■ **setting lotion,** (*for hair*) fijador *m*.

setting-up [setɪŋ'ʌp] *n* creación *f*, fundación *f*.

settle¹ ['setəl] **1** *t* (*establish*) instalar, colocar; (*make comfortable*) poner cómodo,-a, acomodar: *he settled himself on the sofa,* se puso cómodo en el sofá. **2** (*decide on, fix*) acordar, decidir, fijar: *we haven't settled where we're going yet,* todavía no hemos decidido adónde vamos; *I've got to settle my affairs,* tengo que poner mis asuntos en orden; *that's settled then,* queda decidido entonces; *that settles it!,* ¡ya está!, ¡se acabó! **3** (*sort out - problem, dispute*) resolver, solucionar; (*- differences*) resolver, arreglar; (*- score*) arreglar, ajustar: *we need to settle an argument,* tenemos que resolver una discusión. **4** (*calm - nerves*) calmar; (*- stomach*) asentar; (*- weather*) arreglar, asentar. **5** (*pay - debt*) pagar; (*- account*) saldar, liquidar. **6** (*colonize*) colonizar, poblar. **7** (*cause to sink - sediment*) depositar; (*- dust*) asentar. **– 8** *i* (*make one's home in*) establecerse, afincarse, instalarse. **9** (*make os. comfortable*) ponerse cómodo,-a (**into,** en), acomodarse (**into,** en): *she settled back in the armchair,* se puso cómoda en el sillón. **10** (*bird, fly, etc*) posarse; (*dust*) asentarse; (*snow*) cuajar; (*cloud, fog*) caer. **11** (*sediment, dregs*) precipitarse, depositarse; (*liquid*) asentarse, clarificarse; (*earth, ground*) asentarse. **12** (*calm down - person*) calmarse, tranquilizarse; (*- weather*) serenarse. **13** (*pay*) pagar, saldar la cuenta, saldar la deuda. **14** JUR resolver: *they settled out of court,* llegaron a un acuerdo amistoso. **15** *fig* (*silence, stillness, etc*) caer.
◆ **to settle down 1** *i* (*establish a home*) instalarse, afincarse, establecerse; (*lead settled way of life - gen*) empezar a llevar una vida asentada; (*- wild person*) sentar (la) cabeza. **2** (*calm down*) calmarse, tranquilizarse; (*get back to normal*) normalizarse, volver a la normalidad. **3** (*get comfortable*) ponerse cómodo,-a, acomodarse, instalarse. ‖ **to settle down to 1** *t insep* (*get used to*) adaptarse a, acostumbrarse a. **– 2** *i* (*begin seriously, give attention to*) ponerse a. ‖ **to settle for** *t insep* (*accept*) conformarse con, aceptar. ‖ **to settle in 1** *i* (*get used to*) acostum-

brarse, adaptarse. **2** (*move in*) instalarse. ‖ **to settle on 1** *t insep* (*decide on*) decidirse por; (*choose*) escoger; (*agree on*) ponerse de acuerdo sobre. **– 2** *t sep* JUR (*transfer*) ceder a, transferir a. ‖ **to settle up 1** *i* (*pay and receive what is owed*) arreglar (las) cuentas. **2** (*pay bill*) pagar, saldar la cuenta (**with,** con).

settle² ['setəl] *n* (*wooden bench*) banco.

settled ['setəld] *adj* (*habits, life*) ordenado,-a; (*weather*) estable.

settlement ['setəlmənt] **1** *n* (*village*) poblado, pueblo, asentamiento; (*colony*) colonia. **2** (*colonization*) colonización *f*, población *f*. **3** (*agreement*) acuerdo, convenio; (*solution*) resolución *f*, solución *f*: *the unions have reached a settlement with the management,* los sindicatos han llegado a un acuerdo con la patronal; *a pay settlement,* un acuerdo salarial. **4** (*of bill, debt*) pago; (*of account*) liquidación *f*. **5** (*formal gift, money, property*) donación *f* (**on,** a).

settler ['setlə'] *n* poblador,-ra, colono *mf*, colonizador,-ra.

set-to [set'tuː] *n* riña, pelea.
▲ *pl set-tos.*

setup ['setʌp] **1** *n* (*arrangement, organization*) sistema *m*, situación *f*: *it's a nice little setup you've got here!,* ¡lo tenéis todo muy bien montado aquí! **2** *fam* (*trick*) montaje *m*.

seven ['sevən] **1** *adj* siete. **– 2** *n* siete *m*.
▲ *Véase también* **six.**

seventeen [sevən'tiːn] **1** *adj* diecisiete. **– 2** *n* diecisiete *m*.
▲ *Véase también* **sixteen.**

seventeenth [sevən'tiːnθ] **1** *adj* decimoséptimo,-a. **– 2** *adv* en decimoséptimo lugar. **– 3** *n* (*in series*) decimoséptimo,-a. **4** (*fraction*) decimoséptimo; (*one part*) decimoséptima parte *f*.
▲ *Véase también* **sixth.**

seventh ['sevənθ] **1** *adj* séptimo,-a. **– 2** *adv* en séptimo lugar. **– 3** *n* (*in series*) séptimo,-a. **4** (*fraction*) séptimo; (*one part*) séptima parte *f*.
● **to be in seventh heaven,** estar en la gloria.
▲ *Véase también* **sixth.**

seventies ['sevəntɪz] *the seventies,* *npl* los años *mpl* setenta.
● **to be in one's seventies,** tener entre setenta y ochenta años, tener setenta y tantos años.
▲ *Véase también* **sixties.**

seventieth ['sevəntɪəθ] **1** *adj* septuagésimo,-a. **– 2** *adv* en septuagésimo lugar. **– 3** *n* (*in series*) septuagésimo,-a. **4** (*fraction*) septuagésimo; (*one part*) septuagésima parte *f*.
▲ *Véase también* **sixtieth.**

seventy ['sevəntɪ] **1** *adj* setenta. **– 2** *n* setenta *m*.
▲ *Véase también* **sixty.**

sever ['sevə'] **1** *t* (*cut*) cortar. **2** (*relations, ties*) romper; (*communications*) cortar. **– 3** *i* (*break*) romperse.

several ['sevərəl] **1** *adj* (*some*) varios,-as: *we've had several complaints,* hemos recibido varias quejas; *we've been there several times,* hemos ido varias veces. **2** *fml* (*different, separate*) distintos,-as, diversos,-as. **– 3** *pron* (*some*) varios,-as: *several of us have phoned,* varios de nosotros hemos llamado.

severance ['sevərəns] *n* ruptura.
■ **severance pay,** indemnización *f* por cese.

severe [sɪ'vɪə'] **1** *adj* (*person, punishment, treatment*) severo,-a. **2** (*pain*) agudo,-a; (*injury, illness, damage*) grave, serio,-a. **3** (*climate, winter*) duro,-a, severo,-a; (*shortage*) grave; (*setback*, *blow*) severo,-a, duro,-a; (*criticism*) severo,-a. **4** (*competition*, *test*) duro,-a, difícil. **5** (*architecture*) austero,-a.

severely [sɪ'vɪəlɪ] **1** *adv* (*strictly*) severamente, con severidad. **2** (*seriously*) gravemente: *severely injured*, gravemente herido, herido de gravedad; *severely disabled*, gravemente incapacitado. **3** (*harshly*) duramente. **4** (*austerely*) austeramente.

severeness [sɪ'vɪənəs] *n* → **severity**.

severity [sɪ'verətɪ] **1** *n* (*of person, punishment, criticism*) severidad *f*. **2** (*of pain*) agudeza, intensidad *f*; (*of illness, wound*) gravedad *f*; (*of climate*) rigor *m*. **3** (*of style*) austeridad *f*.

Seville [sə'vɪl] *n* Sevilla.

sew [səʊ] **1** *t* coser (**onto**, a). – **2** *i* coser.
◆ **to sew up 1** *t sep* (*hole, tear, etc*) coser; (*mend*) remendar. **2** (*wound*) coser, suturar. **3** *fam* (*arrange, settle*) arreglar, acordar: *you've got everything sewn up!*, ¡lo tienes todo arreglado!
▲ *pt sewed, pp sewed o sewn* [səʊn].

sewage ['sjuːɪdʒ] *n* aguas *fpl* residuales, aguas *fpl* negras.
■ **sewage disposal**, tratamiento de aguas residuales. ‖ **sewage farm**, planta depuradora. ‖ **sewage system**, alcantarillado. ‖ **sewage works**, depuradora, planta depuradora, depuradora de aguas residuales.

sewer [sjʊəʳ] **1** *n* alcantarilla, cloaca. – **2 sewers**, *npl* alcantarillado.

sewerage ['sjuːərɪdʒ] *n* (*system*) alcantarillado.

sewing ['səʊɪŋ] *n* costura.
■ **sewing machine**, máquina de coser.

sewn [səʊn] *pp* → **sew**.

sex [seks] **1** *n* sexo: *the opposite sex*, el sexo opuesto. – **2** *t* TECH sexar.
● **to have sex with sb.**, tener relaciones sexuales con algn.
■ **sex act**, acto sexual. ‖ **sex appeal**, sex-appeal *m*, atractivo sexual. ‖ **sex education**, educación *f* sexual. ‖ **sex life**, vida sexual. ‖ **sex maniac**, maníaco sexual, obseso. ‖ **sex object**, objeto sexual. ‖ **sex offender**, delincuente *m* sexual. ‖ **sex organ**, órgano sexual. ‖ **sex shop**, sex-shop *m*. ‖ **sex symbol**, símbolo sexual, sex-symbol *mf*.

sexagenarian [seksədʒə'neərɪən] *n* sexagenario,-a.

sexism ['seksɪzəm] *n* sexismo.

sexist ['seksɪst] **1** *adj* sexista. – **2** *n* sexista *mf*.

sexless ['seksləs] *adj* asexual, asexuado,-a.

sexologist [sek'sɒlədʒɪst] *n* sexólogo,-a.

sexology [sek'sɒlədʒɪ] *n* sexología.

sextet [seks'tet] *n* MUS sexteto.

sexton ['sekstən] *n* REL sacristán *m*.

sextuplet [sek'stjuːplət] *n* sextillizo,-a.

sexual ['seksjʊəl] *adj* sexual.
■ **sexual abuse**, abusos deshonestos. ‖ **sexual discrimination**, discriminación *f* sexual. ‖ **sexual harassment**, acoso sexual. ‖ **sexual intercourse**, relaciones *fpl* sexuales.

sexuality [seksjʊ'ælətɪ] *n* sexualidad *f*.

sexually ['sekʃʊəlɪ] *adv* sexualmente.
■ **sexually transmitted disease**, enfermedad *f* de transmisión sexual.

sexy ['seksɪ] *adj* (*sexually attractive*) sexy; (*erotic*) erótico,-a.
▲ *comp sexier, superl sexiest*.

Seychelles [seɪ'ʃelz] **the Seychelles**, *n* las Seychelles *fpl*.

shabbiness ['ʃæbɪnəs] *n* (*poor condition*) aspecto lastimoso, mal aspecto; (*of people*) pobreza, aspecto lastimoso; (*of clothes*) pobreza, vejez *f*.

shabby ['ʃæbɪ] **1** *adj* (*clothes*) gastado,-a, raído,-a, desharrapado,-a; (*furniture*) de aspecto lastimoso; (*place*) desvencijado,-a, destartalado,-a. **2** (*person - in old clothes*) mal vestido,-a, pobremente vestido,-a; (*unkept*) desaseado,-a. **3** (*treatment*) mezquino,-a.
▲ *comp shabbier, superl shabbiest*.

shack [ʃæk] *n* choza.
◆ **to shack up with** *i* irse a vivir con, juntarse con.

shackle ['ʃækəl] **1** *t* poner grilletes a. **2** *fig* poner trabas a, coartar, constreñir. – **3 shackles**, *npl* grilletes *mpl*, grillos *mpl*. **4** *fig* ataduras *fpl*, trabas *fpl*.
● **to throw off one's shackles**, librarse de las ataduras, librarse de las trabas.

shade [ʃeɪd] **1** *n* (*shadow*) sombra: *a temperature of 30 degrees in the shade*, una temperatura de 30 grados a la sombra. **2** (*for lamp*) pantalla; (*for eye*) visera; (*blind*) persiana. **3** (*of colour*) tono, matiz *m*. **4** (*small bit*) poquito. **5** *fig* (*of meaning*) matiz *m*. – **6** *t* (*shelter from light*) proteger de la luz, resguardar de la luz. **7** (*screen*) tapar. **8** ART (*darken*) sombrear (**in**, -). – **9** *i* (*change gradually*) convertirse (**into**, en). – **10 shades**, *npl fam* gafas *fpl* de sol.
● **to put sb./sth. in the shade**, hacer sombra a algn./ algo, eclipsar a algn./algo.

shading ['ʃeɪdɪŋ] *n* sombreado.

shadow ['ʃædəʊ] **1** *n* (*dark shape*) sombra. **2** (*trace*) sombra, vestigio. **3** (*follower*) sombra. **4** (*under eyes*) ojera. – **5** *adj* GB POL de la oposición, en la sombra. – **6** *t* (*follow*) seguir la pista a. **7** (*cast shadow on*) hacer sombra. – **8 shadows**, *npl* (*darkness*) oscuridad *f sing*: *there was someone standing in the shadows*, había alguien en la oscuridad.
● **to be afraid of one's own shadow**, tener miedo hasta de su propia sombra. ‖ **to be a shadow of one's former self**, no ser ni sombra de lo que había sido. ‖ **to cast a shadow**, hacer sombra. ‖ **to cast a (long) shadow**, *fig* ensombrecer (**over**, -). ‖ **to live in sb.'s shadow**, vivir eclipsado,-a por algn. ‖ **without a shadow of doubt**, sin lugar a dudas, sin sombra de duda.
■ **Shadow Cabinet**, gabinete *m* de la oposición. ‖ **shadow mask**, máscara perforada con ranuras. ‖ **shadow play**, sombras *fpl* chinescas.

shadow-box ['ʃædəʊbɒks] *i* boxear con un adversario imaginario.

shadowy ['ʃædəʊɪ] **1** *adj* (*dark*) oscuro,-a; (*dim*) vago,-a, impreciso,-a, borroso,-a. **2** (*mysterious*) misterioso,-a.

shady ['ʃeɪdɪ] **1** *adj* (*place*) a la sombra; (*tree*) que da sombra. **2** *fam* (*person*) sospechoso,-a; (*deal, past*) turbio,-a.
▲ *comp shadier, superl shadiest*.

shaft [ʃɑːft] **1** *n* (*of axe, tool, golf club*) mango; (*of arrow*) astil *m*; (*of lance, spear*) asta; (*of cart*) vara. **2** ARCH fuste *m*. **3** TECH eje *m*. **4** (*of mine*) pozo; (*of lift*) hueco. **5** (*of light*) rayo. **6** *fig* (*sharp remark*) salida: *shaft of wit*, agudeza.

shag[1] [ʃæg] *n* (*tobacco*) tabaco picado.

shag[2] [ʃæg] *n* ORN cormorán *m* moñudo.

shag[3] [ʃæg] **1** *n* GB *taboo* (*sex*) polvo. – **2** *t* GB *taboo* (*screw*) follar, tirarse a. **3** GB *sl* (*exhaust*) agotar (**out**, -), reventar (**out**, -).
● **to be shagged (out)**, estar hecho,-a polvo. ‖ **to have a shag**, echar un polvo.
▲ *pt & pp shagged, ger shagging*.

shaggy ['ʃægɪ] **1** *adj* (*hair, beard*) desgreñado,-a, greñudo,-a, enmarañado,-a; (*eyebrows*) poblado,-a. **2** (*coat, mat*) peludo,-a; (*dog*) lanudo,-a, peludo,-a.
■ **shaggy dog story**, chiste *m* largo y malo.
▲ *comp shaggier, superl shaggiest*.

shah [ʃɑː] *n* sha *m*.

shake [ʃeɪk] **1** n sacudida: *he said "no" with a shake of the head,* dijo que no con la cabeza; *give the cough mixture a good shake,* agita bien el jarabe. **2** us fam (*milk-shake*) batido. – **3** t (*move - carpet, person*) sacudir; (- *bottle, dice*) agitar; (- *building*) hacer temblar: *he shook her roughly,* la sacudió bruscamente; *shake well before use,* agítese bien antes de usar. **4** (*upset, shock*) afectar, impresionar, conmocionar: *the news shook her badly,* la noticia le afectó mucho. **5** (*weaken*) debilitar, minar: *nothing could shake her faith,* nada podía debilitar su fe. – **6** i (*gen*) temblar: *the whole room seemed to shake,* parecía que temblaba toda la habitación; *she was shaking with fear,* temblaba de miedo; *my voice was shaking,* me temblaba la voz. – **7 the shakes,** npl (*trembling*) temblequera; (*feverish*) tiritera: *he always gets the shakes the morning after,* siempre le entra la temblequera a la mañana siguiente.
◆ **to shake out** t sep sacudir. ‖ **to shake up 1** t sep (*liquid*) agitar. **2** (*shock, upset*) afectar, impresionar, conmocionar. **3** (*rearrange*) reorganizar; (*rouse*) espabilar.
● **in two shakes (of a lamb's tail),** en un santiamén. ‖ **let's shake!,** ¡chócala!, ¡choca esos cinco! ‖ **to be no great shakes,** no ser nada del otro mundo, no ser nada del otro jueves. ‖ **to shake a leg,** darse prisa, apresurarse. ‖ **to shake hands,** darse la mano, estrecharse la mano. ‖ **to shake hands with sb. / shake sb.'s hand / shake sb. by the hand,** darle la mano a algn., estrecharle la mano a algn. ‖ **to shake in one's shoes,** temblar de miedo. ‖ **to shake like a leaf,** temblar como una hoja. ‖ **to shake on a deal,** cerrar un trato con un apretón de manos. ‖ **to shake one's fist (at sb.),** amenazar (a algn.) con el puño. ‖ **to shake one's head,** negar con la cabeza, decir que no con la cabeza. ‖ **to shake with cold,** tiritar de frío. ‖ **to shake with laughter,** troncharse de risa.
▲ pt *shook,* pp *shaken* | ['ʃeɪkən].

shaken ['ʃeɪkən] **1** pp → **shake**. – **2** adj (*of liquid*) agitado,-a: *I like my vermouth shaken not stirred,* me gusta el vermú agitado y no removido.
● **to be shaken up by sth.,** estar muy afectado,-a por algo.

shaker ['ʃeɪkəʳ] n (*for cocktails*) coctelero; (*for salt*) salero.

Shakespearian [ʃeɪk'spɪrɪən] adj shakesperiano,-a.

shake-up ['ʃeɪkʌp] n COMM reorganización f.

shaky ['ʃeɪkɪ] **1** adj (*hand, voice*) tembloroso,-a; (*writing*) temblón,-ona; (*step*) inseguro,-a; (*health*) débil, delicado,-a. **2** (*ladder, table, etc*) cojo,-a, inestable, poco firme. **3** fig (*argument etc*) sin fundamento; (*government, currency*) débil; (*theory, start*) flojo,-a: *you're treading on very shaky ground,* estás pisando terreno poco firme; *his French is a bit shaky,* anda flojo en francés; *the team got off to a shaky start this season,* el equipo empezó la temporada jugando con poca confianza.
▲ comp *shakier,* superl *shakiest.*

shale [ʃeɪl] n esquisto, pizarra.

shall [ʃæl, unstressed ʃəl] **1** aux (*future*): *I shall go tomorrow,* iré mañana; *we shall see them on Sunday,* los veremos el domingo; *I shan't mention any names,* no daré nombres. **2** (*questions, offers, suggestions*): *shall I close the window?,* ¿cierro la ventana?; *shall I make some tea?,* ¿hago un poco de té?, ¿quieres que haga un poco de té?; *what shall we do today?,* ¿qué hacemos hoy?; *I'll carry it, shall I?,* lo llevaré yo, ¿quieres?; *let's go to the beach, shall we?,* vamos a la playa, ¿te parece? **3** fml (*emphatic, command*): *we shall overcome,* venceremos; *you shall leave immediately,* te irás enseguida.
▲ En *1* y *2 se* emplea sólo para la 1ª pers del sing y pl.

shallot [ʃə'lɒt] n chalota.

shallow ['ʃæləʊ] **1** adj (*water, pond, etc*) poco profundo,-a; (*dish, bowl*) llano,-a, plano,-a: *let's go down the shallow end,* vamos a la parte poco profunda; *shallow grave,* tumba poco profunda; *shallow breathing,* respiración superficial. **2** fig superficial: *a very shallow argument,* un razonamiento muy superficial. – **3** shallows, npl bajío m sing.

shallowness ['ʃæləʊnəs] **1** n (*of water*) poca profundidad f, falta de profundidad f. **2** fig superficialidad f.

sham [ʃæm] **1** n (*piece of deceit, pretence*) farsa, simulacro: *their marriage was a sham,* su matrimonio fue una farsa; *the deal was a complete sham,* el trato fue un completo simulacro. **2** (*person*) farsante mf, impostor,-ra. – **3** adj (*interest, sympathy, emotion*) falso,-a, simulado,-a; (*illness*) fingido,-a; (*jewellery, antiques*) falso,-a, de imitación. – **4** t fingir, simular: *she used to sham illness,* solía fingir que estaba enferma. – **5** i fingir, fingirse.
▲ pt & pp *shammed,* ger *shamming.*

shamble ['ʃæmbəl] i andar arrastrando los pies.

shambles ['ʃæmbəlz] n fam (*mess*) desastre m, caos m: *the house is in a shambles!,* ¡la casa está hecha un desastre!, ¡la casa está patas arriba!; *the rehearsal was a complete shambles!,* ¡el ensayo fue un caos total!

shambolic [ʃæm'bɒlɪk] adj fam caótico,-a, desastroso,-a.

shame [ʃeɪm] **1** n (*disgrace, humiliation*) vergüenza; (*dishonour*) deshonra: *he felt shame at having hit her,* le dio vergüenza haberle pegado; *have you no shame?,* ¿es que no tienes vergüenza? **2** (*pity*) pena, lástima: *it seems a shame to waste it,* es una pena tirarlo; *what a shame you couldn't go,* qué pena que no pudieras ir. – **3** t avergonzar, deshonrar.
● **shame on you!,** ¡qué vergüenza! ‖ **to bring shame on sb./sth.,** deshonrar a algn./algo. ‖ **to put sb. to shame,** (*be superior to*) dejar a algn. en evidencia, hacer pasar vergüenza a algn.

shamefaced [ʃeɪm'feɪst] adj avergonzado,-a.

shameful ['ʃeɪmfʊl] adj vergonzoso,-a.

shameless ['ʃeɪmləs] adj (*person*) desvergonzado,-a, sinvergüenza; (*behaviour*) descarado,-a.
● **to be shameless about sth.,** no darle ninguna vergüenza a uno hacer algo.

shamelessness ['ʃeɪmləsnəs] n desvergüenza, descaro.

shammy ['ʃæmɪ] n gamuza.
▲ pl *shammies.*

shampoo [ʃæm'puː] **1** n (*product*) champú m. **2** (*act*) lavado. – **3** t (*hair*) lavar, lavarse (con champú); (*carpet*) limpiar.
▲ (*sustantivo*) pl *shampoos;* (*verbo*) pt & pp *shampooed,* ger *shampooing.*

shamrock ['ʃæmrɒk] n trébol m.

shandy ['ʃændɪ] n GB clara, cerveza con limonada.
▲ pl *shandies.*

shanghai [ʃæŋ'haɪ] t dated secuestrar (*a un hombre y forzarlo a trabajar como marinero*).
● **to shanghai sb. into doing sth.,** (*trick*) engañar a algn. para que haga algo; (*force*) presionar a algn. para que haga algo.

shank [ʃæŋk] **1** n (*of anchor, key*) tija; (*of tool, drill, golf club*) mango; (*of screw*) vástago, tallo, varilla. **2** CULIN (*of meat*) pierna. – **3** shanks, npl ANAT espinillas fpl, canillas fpl.
● **on Shanks's pony,** en el coche de San Fernando.

shan't [ʃɑːnt] aux → **shall not.**

shanty[1] ['ʃæntɪ] n (*song*) saloma.

shanty² [ˈʃæntɪ] *n* (*shack*) chabola.
▲ *pl* shanties.

shantytown [ˈʃæntɪtaʊn] *n* chabolas *fpl*, barrio de chabolas.

shape [ʃeɪp] **1** *n* (*form, appearance*) forma: *what shape is it?*, ¿qué forma tiene?, ¿de qué forma es?; *geometric shapes*, formas geométricas; *in the shape of a heart*, en forma de corazón. **2** (*outline, shadow*) figura, bulto. **3** (*state - of thing*) estado; (*- of person*) forma, condiciones *fpl*: *the team is in good shape*, el equipo está en buena forma; *he goes jogging to keep in shape*, hace footing para mantenerse en forma; *she's in no shape to go to work*, no está en condiciones de ir a trabajar. **4** (*framework, character*) conformación *f*, configuración *f*. – **5** *t* (*gen*) dar forma a; (*clay*) modelar. **6** (*character*) formar; (*future, destiny*) decidir, determinar: *early experiences shape a person's character*, las primeras experiencias forman el carácter de una persona.
◆ **to shape up 1** *i* (*project*) tomar forma; (*plan*) desarrollarse; (*person*) hacer progresos: *the football team is shaping up well*, el equipo de fútbol hace progresos; *things are shaping up nicely*, la cosas están tomando buen cariz. **2** (*behave better*) espabilarse, despabilarse.
● **in all shapes and sizes**, de todas las formas: *sofas come in all shapes and sizes*, hay sofás de muy diversos tipos. ‖ **in any shape or form**, del tipo que sea: *we oppose violence in any shape or form*, nos oponemos a la violencia sea de la forma que sea. ‖ **in shape**, (*fit*) en forma. ‖ **in the shape of**, (*physically*) bajo la forma de; (*figuratively*) en forma de: *the devil appeared to her in the shape of a snake*, se le apareció el diablo bajo la forma de una serpiente; *government aid in the shape of tax reductions*, ayudas del gobierno en forma de bonificaciones impositivas; *help came in the shape of my next-door neighbour*, la ayuda se me presentó en la persona de mi vecino. ‖ **out of shape**, (*unfit*) en baja forma; (*deformed*) deformado,-a. ‖ **the shape of things to come**, lo que nos espera. ‖ **to get (os.) into shape**, ponerse en forma. ‖ **to knock/lick sb./sth. into shape**, poner a algn./algo en forma. ‖ **to take shape**, tomar forma.

shaped [ʃeɪpt] *adj* en forma de, con forma de: *this potato is very strangely shaped*, esta patata tiene una forma muy rara; *it is shaped like a swan*, tiene forma de cisne; *she has a pear-shaped body*, tiene el cuerpo en forma de pera.

shapeless [ˈʃeɪpləs] *adj* informe, sin forma.

shapelessness [ˈʃeɪpləsnəs] *n* falta de forma.

shapely [ˈʃeɪplɪ] *adj* (*body*) curvilíneo,-a; (*legs*) torneado,-a.

share [ʃeəʳ] **1** *n* (*portion*) parte *f*: *you've already eaten your share!*, ¡ya te has comido tu parte!; *you'll get your share of the winnings*, recibirás tu parte de las ganancias; *she's had her share of bad luck*, ha tenido su parte de mala suerte. **2** FIN (*held by shareholder*) acción *f*; (*held by partner*) participación *f*. – **3** *t* (*have or use with others*) compartir; (*have in common*) compartir, tener en común: *can you share one book between two?*, ¿podéis compartir un libro entre los dos?; *I used to share a bedroom with my sister*, compartía una habitación con mi hermana; *let's share a taxi*, compartamos un taxi. **4** (*tell news, feelings, etc*) compartir: *she wanted to share her secret with someone*, quería compartir el secreto con alguien. **5** (*divide*) repartir, dividir: *the profits are shared out among the workers*, se reparten los beneficios entre los trabajadores; *share the cake between everyone*, divide el pastel entre todos. – **6** *i* compartir: *there's only one bed*

so you'll have to share, sólo hay una cama así que tendréis que compartirla.
● **a problem shared is a problem halved**, las penas compartidas son menos penas. ‖ **to share and share alike**, compartir las cosas. ‖ **to do one's share**, hacer su parte. ‖ **to go shares**, pagar a medias.
■ **share capital**, capital *m* social. ‖ **share price**, cotización *f*.

shareholder [ˈʃeəhəʊldəʳ] *n* accionista *mf*.

share-out [ˈʃeəraʊt] *n* reparto.

shark¹ [ʃɑːk] *n* ZOOL tiburón *m*.

shark² [ʃɑːk] *n fam* (*swindler*) estafador,-ra, timador,-ra.
■ **loan shark**, usurero,-a.

sharp [ʃɑːp] **1** *adj* (*knife etc*) afilado,-a; (*needle, pencil*) puntiagudo,-a; (*features*) anguloso,-a. **2** (*angle*) agudo,-a; (*bend*) cerrado,-a; (*slope*) empinado,-a; (*turn, rise, fall*) brusco,-a. **3** (*outline*) definido,-a; (*photograph etc*) nítido,-a; (*contrast*) marcado,-a. **4** (*mind, wit*) perspicaz; (*eyes, ears*) agudo,-a, bueno,-a; (*reflexes*) rápido,-a: *keep a sharp eye on those two*, ten bien vigilados a esos dos. **5** (*person - clever*) listo,-a, vivo,-a; (*- quick-witted*) avispado,-a, despabilado,-a, despierto,-a: *it was very sharp of you to spot that*, fuiste muy listo al darte cuenta. **6** (*pain*) agudo,-a, fuerte; (*cry, noise*) agudo,-a, estridente; (*frost*) fuerte; (*wind*) cortante, penetrante. **7** (*taste*) ácido,-a; (*smell*) acre. **8** (*change etc*) brusco,-a, repentino,-a, súbito,-a. **9** (*blow*) seco,-a. **10** (*criticism*) mordaz; (*rebuke*) severo,-a; (*retort*) cortante; (*temper*) arisco,-a, violento,-a; (*tone*) seco,-a. **11** (*unscrupulous*) astuto,-a, mañoso,-a. **12** MUS (*key*) sostenido,-a; (*too high*) desafinado,-a: *F sharp*, fa sostenido. – **13** *adv* (*exactly*) en punto: *at ten o'clock sharp*, a las diez en punto. **14** (*abruptly*) bruscamente: *the car stopped sharp*, el coche se paró bruscamente; *turn sharp left*, gira a la izquierda. **15** MUS (*too high*) demasiado alto,-a. – **16** *n* MUS sostenido.
● **look sharp!**, ¡date prisa!, ¡espabílate! ‖ **to be as sharp as a needle**, ser un lince. ‖ **to be a sharp dresser**, tener mucho estilo para vestirse. ‖ **to have a sharp tongue**, tener una lengua mordaz.
■ **sharp practice**, mañas *fpl*, tejemanejes *mpl*.

sharp-edged [ʃɑːpˈedʒd] *adj* afilado,-a.

sharpen [ˈʃɑːpən] **1** *t* (*knife, claws*) afilar; (*pencil*) sacar punta a. **2** *fig* (*feeling, intelligence*) agudizar; (*desire*) avivar; (*appetite*) abrir; (*awareness*) sensibilizar. – **3** *i* (*voice*) agudizarse; (*tone*) hacerse más mordaz.
● **to sharpen one's wits**, espabilarse, despabilarse.

sharpener [ˈʃɑːpənəʳ] *n* (*for knife*) afilador *m*; (*for pencil*) sacapuntas *m*.

sharp-eyed [ʃɑːpˈaɪd] *adj* que tiene vista de lince.

sharpish [ˈʃɑːpɪʃ] *adv fam* (*quickly, briskly*) rápidamente, pronto: *you'd better get over here sharpish*, más vale que vengas pronto aquí.

sharply [ˈʃɑːplɪ] **1** *adv* (*abruptly, suddenly*) bruscamente, repentinamente. **2** (*acutely*) agudamente. **3** (*clearly*) marcadamente, claramente. **4** (*harshly*) mordazmente, con severidad.

sharpness [ˈʃɑːpnəs] **1** *n* (*of knife*) lo afilado; (*of point*) lo puntiagudo; (*of features*) lo anguloso. **2** (*of taste*) acidez *f*. **3** (*abruptness, suddeness*) brusquedad *f*. **4** (*of image etc*) nitidez *f*. **5** (*of pain*) agudeza, intensidad *f*. **6** (*harshness*) mordacidad *f*, severidad *f*.

sharpshooter [ˈʃɑːpʃuːtəʳ] *n* tirador,-ra de primera.

sharp-sighted [ʃɑːpˈsaɪtɪd] *adj* → **sharp-eyed**.

sharp-tongued [ʃɑːpˈtʌŋd] *adj* de lengua viperina, de lengua mordaz.

sharp-witted [ʃɑːpˈwɪtɪd] *adj* avispado,-a, perspicaz.

shat [ʃæt] pp → **shit**.

shatter [ˈʃætəʳ] **1** t (break into small pieces) romper, hacer añicos, hacer pedazos. **2** fig (health) destrozar, quebrantar, minar; (nerves) destrozar; (hopes, confidence) frustrar, destruir. **3** fam (shock) conmocionar, afectar, dejar destrozado,-a. **4** fam (exhaust) dejar hecho,-a polvo, reventar. – **5** i (break - gen) romperse, hacerse añicos, hacerse pedazos; (- glass) astillarse, estallar (en pedazos).

shattered [ˈʃætəd] **1** adj (broken) hecho,-a añicos, hecho,-a pedazos. **2** fig (hopes, confidence) destruido,-a. **3** (shocked) destrozado,-a: when his mother died, Tony was shattered, cuando murió su madre, Tony quedó destrozado; I was shattered by the news, la noticia me dejó destrozado. **4** (exhausted) agotado,-a, hecho,-a polvo, reventado,-a.

shattering [ˈʃætərɪŋ] **1** adj (experience, news, etc) terrible, demoledor,-ra; (loss) terrible, tremendo,-a. **2** (defeat) aplastante; (blow) demoledor,-ra. **3** (exhausting) agotador,-ra.

shatterproof [ˈʃætəpruːf] adj inastillable.

shave [ʃeɪv] **1** n afeitado. – **2** t (face, legs, underarms) afeitar; (head) rapar: you've shaved off your beard, te has afeitado la barba; she shaves her legs, se afeita las piernas. **3** (wood) cepillar. **4** fig (reduce - costs) recortar. **5** fam (touch slightly) rozar. – **6** i (person) afeitarse: he shaves every morning, se afeita cada mañana.
● **to have a close shave**, fig salvarse por los pelos. ‖ **to have a shave**, afeitarse.
■ **wet shave**, afeitado con espuma.

shaven [ˈʃeɪvən] adj (face, chin) afeitado,-a; (head) rapado,-a.

shaver [ˈʃeɪvəʳ] n máquina de afeitar.
■ **electric shaver**, máquina de afeitar.

shaving [ˈʃeɪvɪŋ] **1** n (of face) afeitado. – **2 shavings**, npl (wood) virutas fpl.
■ **shaving brush**, brocha de afeitar. ‖ **shaving cream**, crema de afeitar. ‖ **shaving foam**, espuma de afeitar.

shawl [ʃɔːl] n chal m, mantón m.

she [ʃiː] **1** pron ella: ask Linda, she'll help you, pregunta a Linda, ella te ayudará; she's called Nina, se llama Nina; she's happy, está contenta. – **2** n (animal) hembra; (baby) niña: she's had the baby! Is it a he or a she?, ¡ya ha nacido el bebé! ¿Es niño o niña?

she- [ʃiː] pref hembra: she-bear, osa; she-wolf, loba.

sheaf [ʃiːf] **1** n (of corn, barley, etc) gavilla. **2** (of papers, banknotes, etc) fajo. **3** (of arrows) haz m.
▲ pl **sheaves**.

shear [ʃɪəʳ] **1** t (sheep) esquilar, trasquilar (off, -). **2** lit (hair) cortar (off, -). **3** TECH (bolt, shaft) romper. – **4** i TECH (break) romperse (off, -); (cut) cortar. – **5 shears**, npl (gen) tijeras fpl (grandes); (for hedges) podadera f sing; (for metal) cizalla f sing, cizallas fpl.
● **to be shorn of sth.**, ser despojado,-a de algo, quedarse sin algo.
▲ pt **sheared**, pp **sheared** o **shorn**.

shearer [ˈʃɪərəʳ] n esquilador,-ra, trasquilador,-ra.

shearing [ˈʃɪərɪŋ] n esquileo, esquila.

shears [ʃɪəz] npl → **shear**.

sheath [ʃiːθ] **1** n (for sword) vaina; (for knife, scissors) funda; (for cable) forro, cubierta. **2** BOT vaina. **3** (condom) preservativo, condón m. **4** (dress) vestido tubo.
■ **sheath knife**, cuchillo de monte.
▲ pl **sheaths** [ʃiːðz].

sheathe [ʃiːð] **1** t (sword) envainar; (knife) enfundar. **2** (cable etc) revestir; (building) cubrir.

sheathing [ˈʃiːðɪŋ] n (for building) cubierta.

sheaves [ʃiːvz] npl → **sheaf**.

shebang [ʃɪˈbæŋ] **the whole shebang**, phr todo el tinglado.

she'd [ʃiːd] **1** contr she had. **2** she would.

shed¹ [ʃed] n (in garden, for bicycles) cobertizo; (workman's hut) cabaña; (for cattle) establo; (industrial) nave f.
■ **coal shed**, carbonera.

shed² [ʃed] **1** t (leaves, horns, skin) mudar; (clothes) quitarse, despojarse de; (workers, jobs) deshacerse de; (load, weight) perder: the snake sheds its skin, la serpiente muda la piel; the lorry shed its load, el camión perdió la carga; she shed 10 kilos, perdió 10 kilos de peso. **2** fig (inhibitions etc) liberarse de. **3** (water) repelar. **4** (blood, tears, etc) derramar: without shedding blood, sin derramiento de sangre. **5** (light, warmth) emitir.
▲ pt & pp **shed**, ger **shedding**.

sheen [ʃiːn] n brillo, lustre m.

sheep [ʃiːp] n oveja.
● **like sheep**, como borregos. ‖ **the black sheep of the family**, la oveja negra de la familia. ‖ **to make sheep's eyes at sb.**, hacerle ojitos a algn.
■ **sheep farming**, cría de ovejas, ganado ovino.
▲ pl **sheep**.

sheep-dip [ˈʃiːpdɪp] n (bath) baño desinfectante (para ovejas); (liquid) desinfectante m (para ovejas).

sheepdog [ˈʃiːpdɒg] n perro pastor.
■ **sheepdog trial**, concurso de perros pastores.

sheepfold [ˈʃiːpfəʊld] n redil m, aprisco.

sheepish [ˈʃiːpɪʃ] adj (embarrassed) avergonzado,-a, abochornado,-a; (lacking initiative) borrego,-a.

sheepishly [ˈʃiːpɪʃlɪ] adv con vergüenza, con bochorno.

sheepskin [ˈʃiːpskɪn] **1** n (skin, leather) piel f de zamarro, piel f de carnero. **2** (parchment) pergamino.
■ **sheepskin jacket**, zamarra, pelliza. ‖ **sheepskin rug**, alfombra de piel de oveja.

sheer¹ [ʃɪəʳ] **1** adj (total, utter) total, absoluto,-a, puro,-a: by sheer coincidence, por pura casualidad; out of sheer desperation, por pura desesperación; a sheer waste of time, una pérdida total de tiempo. **2** (cliff) escarpado,-a; (drop) vertical. **3** (stockings etc) muy fino,-a.

sheer² [ʃɪəʳ] i MAR desviarse (**away/off**, -).
◆ **to sheer away** i (topic, subject) evitar, eludir (**from,-**); (person) esquivar (**from,** -). ‖ **to sheer off** i desviarse.

sheet [ʃiːt] **1** n (on bed) sábana: bottom/top sheet, sábana bajera/encimera; fitted sheet, sábana ajustable. **2** (of paper) hoja; (of metal) lámina, chapa; (of glass) lámina, placa; (of tin) hoja. **3** (of ice) capa, placa; (of water) expansión f; (of flames, rain) cortina. **4** fam (newspaper) periódico. – **5** i (rain heavily) diluviar, llover a cántaros.
■ **sheet lightning**, relámpagos mpl difusos. ‖ **sheet metal**, chapa de metal. ‖ **sheet music**, hojas pl de partitura, papel pautado.

sheik [ʃeɪk] n → **sheikh**.

sheikh [ʃeɪk] n jeque m.

shelduck [ˈʃeldʌk] n ORN tarro.

shelf [ʃelf] **1** n (in bookcase, cupboard) estante m, balda, anaquel m; (on wall) estante m, anaquel m, repisa, balda; (in oven) parrilla, rejilla. **2** GEOL (in rock) promontorio, saliente m; (underwater) plataforma.
● **to be left on the shelf**, (of unmarried woman) quedarse para vestir santos.
■ **continental shelf**, plataforma continental. ‖ (set of) **shelves**, estantería. ‖ **shelf life**, tiempo que puede permanecer expuesto para su venta un producto perecedero.
▲ pl **shelves**.

shell [ʃel] **1** *n* (*of egg, nut*) cáscara; (*of pea*) vaina; (*of tortoise, lobster, etc*) caparazón *m*; (*of snail, oyster, etc*) concha: *the children were collecting shells on the beach,* los niños recogían conchas en la playa. **2** (*of building*) armazón *m*, esqueleto, estructura; (*of vehicle*) armazón *m*; (*of ship*) casco. **3** MIL (*for explosives*) proyectil *m*, obús *m*; (*cartridge*) cartucho. – **4** *t* (*nuts, egg*) pelar; (*peas*) desvainar; (*mussels etc*) quitar la concha a. **5** MIL bombardear.
◆ **to shell out 1** *t sep fam* (*money*) soltar, aflojar. – **2** *i fam* apoquinar.
● **it's as easy as shelling peas,** es coser y cantar. ‖ **to come out of one's shell,** salir del cascarón. ‖ **to go/retire/withdraw into one's shell,** retraerse.
■ **shell shock,** neurosis *f* de guerra. ‖ **shell suit,** chándal *m*.
she'll [ʃiːl] *contr* she will, she shall.
shellac [ʃəˈlæk] **1** *n* laca. – **2** *t* (*varnish*) laquear. **3** US (*defeat*) dar una paliza a.
shellfire [ˈʃelfaɪəˈ] *n* MIL fuego de artillería.
shellfish [ˈʃelfɪʃ] *n* (*individual*) marisco; (*as food*) marisco, mariscos *mpl*.
▲ *pl* **shellfish.**
shelling [ˈʃelɪŋ] *n* MIL bombardeo.
shell-shocked [ˈʃelʃɒkt] *adj* MED traumatizado,-a por la guerra, que padece neurosis de guerra.
shelter [ˈʃeltəˈ] **1** *n* (*protection*) abrigo, protección *f*, cobijo: *the climbers sought shelter from the storm,* los montañeros buscaron abrigo para protegerse de la tormenta; *everyone ran for shelter,* todos corrieron a refugiarse, todos corrieron para ponerse a cubierto; *the school provided shelter for the people who had been made homeless,* la escuela dio cobijo a la gente que se había quedado sin casa. **2** (*place - gen*) refugio, cobijo; (*- for homeless etc*) asilo, refugio; (*- in mountains*) refugio. – **3** *t* (*protect - from weather, danger, etc*) abrigar, proteger, resguardar; (*- from persecution, harm*) dar refugio a, dar cobijo a, amparar: *these trees should shelter us from the rain,* esos árboles nos resguardarán de la lluvia; *the monk sheltered an escaped prisioner,* el monje dio refugio a un fugitivo. – **4** *i* (*from weather etc*) resguardarse, guarecerse; (*from danger*) refugiarse: *the climbers sheltered in a cave,* los alpinistas se guarecieron en una cueva; *we sheltered from the rain,* nos resguardamos de la lluvia.
● **to take shelter,** refugiarse (**from,** de).
sheltered [ˈʃeltəd] **1** *adj* (*place*) abrigado,-a. **2** (*life, childhood, etc*) protegido,-a: *she's had a very sheltered life,* ha llevado una vida muy entre algodones.
■ **sheltered accommodation / sheltered housing,** viviendas *fpl* vigiladas (*para ancianos y minusválidos*).
shelve[1] [ʃelv] **1** *t* (*put on shelf*) poner en el estante, poner en la estantería. **2** *fig* (*postpone, abandon*) aparcar, archivar, dar carpetazo a.
shelve[2] [ʃelv] *i* (*slope*) bajar, descender.
shelves [ʃelvz] *npl* → **shelf.**
shelving [ˈʃelvɪŋ] *n* estanterías *fpl*.
shepherd [ˈʃepəd] **1** *n* pastor *m*. – **2** *t* (*guide, direct*) guiar, conducir.
■ **shepherd's pie,** CULIN pastel *m* de carne (*hecho de carne picada cubierta de una capa de puré de patatas*).
shepherdess [ˈʃepədes] *n* pastora.
sherbet [ˈʃɜːbət] **1** *n* GB (*sweets*) polvos *mpl* picapica, sidral *m*. **2** US (*sorbet*) sorbete *m*.
sheriff [ˈʃerɪf] **1** *n* US sheriff *mf*, alguacil,-la. **2** GB gobernador,-ra civil, representante *mf* de la corona en un condado. **3** (*in Scotland*) juez *mf* presidente, juez *mf* principal de un distrito o condado.

sherry [ˈʃerɪ] *n* jerez *m*.
▲ *pl* **sherries.**
she's [ʃiːz] **1** *contr* she is. **2** she has.
Shetland [ˈʃetlənd] *adj* Shetland.
■ **Shetland pony,** poney *m* Shetland. ‖ **Shetland wool,** lana Shetland.
Shetlander [ˈʃetləndəˈ] *n* nativo,-a de las islas shetland, habitante *mf* de las islas Shetland.
Shetlands [ˈʃetləndz] **the Shetlands,** *n* las islas *fpl* Shetland.
Shia [ˈʃiːə] **1** *n* (*branch of Islam*) Shiísmo. **2** (*Shiite*) chiíta *mf*, shií *mf*.
Shiah [ˈʃiːə] *n* → **Shia.**
shield [ʃiːld] **1** *n* MIL escudo. **2** (*for protection*) escudo: *riot shield,* escudo antidisturbios. **3** (*trophy, prize*) placa (*en forma de escudo*). **4** TECH pantalla protectora. **5** (*of animal*) caparazón *m*. **6** *fig* barrera. – **7** *t* (*protect*) proteger (**from,** de): *you should shield the plants from the wind,* deberías proteger las plantas del viento; *she shielded her eyes from the sun,* se protegió los ojos del sol.
shift [ʃɪft] **1** *n* (*change*) cambio: *a shift in policy,* un cambio de política; *a shift in political opinions,* un cambio en las opiniones políticas; *a shift away from traditional industries towards the service sector,* un alejamiento de las industrias tradicionales hacia el sector de servicios. **2** (*of war, workers*) turno: *the day/night shift,* el turno de día/de noche; *he works a ten-hour shift,* hace un turno de diez horas; *they work in shifts,* trabajan por turnos. **3** (*on keyboard*) tecla de las mayúsculas. **4** *dated* (*trick, scheme, expedient*) expediente *m*, recurso. **5** (*dress*) vestido suelto; (*undergarment, chemise*) enagua. – **6** *t* (*change*) cambiar; (*move*) desplazar, mover: *he shifted his feet,* movió sus pies; *they couldn't shift the piano,* no podían mover el piano; *come on! shift yourself,* ¡venga! ¡muévete! **7** (*transfer*) traspasar, transferir: *don't shift the blame onto me!,* ¡no me cargues la culpa a mí!; *the royal wedding has shifted attention away from the political scandals,* la boda real ha distraído la atención de los escándalos políticos. **8** GB *fam* (*remove, get rid of*) quitar; (*sell*) vender: *this new detergent will shift any stain,* este nuevo detergente quitará cualquier mancha; *we've not shifted much today,* hoy no hemos vendido mucho. **9** US (*change gear*) cambiar. – **10** *i* (*change*) cambiar: *the wind shifted,* el viento cambió de dirección. **11** (*move*) moverse, cambiar de sitio, desplazarse; (*cargo*) correrse: *he shifted uneasily in his seat,* se movía intranquilo en el asiento. **12** US (*change gear*) cambiar de marcha. **13** GB *fam* (*move fast*) volar.
● **to make shift with sth.,** arreglárselas con algo. ‖ **to shift for os.,** arreglárselas sólo. ‖ **to shift one's ground,** cambiar de posición.
■ **shift key,** tecla de las mayúsculas. ‖ **shift worker,** trabajador,-ra por turnos.
shiftily [ˈʃɪftɪlɪ] *adv* de manera sospechosa.
shiftless [ˈʃɪftləs] *adj* perezoso,-a, vago,-a, holgazán,-ana.
shiftwork [ˈʃɪftwɜːk] *n* trabajo por turnos.
shifty [ˈʃɪftɪ] *adj* (*person*) sospechoso,-a; (*behaviour*) furtivo,-a.
▲ *comp* **shiftier,** *superl* **shiftiest.**
Shiite [ˈʃiːaɪt] **1** *n* chiíta *mf*, shií *mf*. – **2** *adj* chiíta, shií.
shilling [ˈʃɪlɪŋ] *n* chelín *m*.
shimmer [ˈʃɪməˈ] **1** *n* (*tremulous light*) luz *f* trémula, reflejo trémulo; (*shining*) brillo, resplandor *m*. – **2** *i* (*shine*) relucir, brillar; (*in water*) rielar.
shimmering [ˈʃɪmərɪŋ] *adj* reluciente, brillante.

shin [ʃɪn] 1 *n* ANAT espinilla, canilla. 2 CULIN (*of beef*) jarrete *m*.
◆ **to shin down** *i* deslizarse por. ‖ **to shin up** *i* trepar.
■ **shin guard / shin pad**, espinillera.
▲ *pt & pp* **shinned**, *ger* **shinning**.
shinbone [ˈʃɪnbəʊn] *n* ANAT tibia.
shindig [ˈʃɪndɪg] 1 *n fam* (*party*) fiesta, juerga. 2 → **shindy**.
shindy [ˈʃɪndɪ] *n fam* (*noisy disturbance*) jaleo, escándalo.
● **to kick up a shindy**, armar un jaleo.
▲ *pl* **shindies**.
shine [ʃaɪn] 1 *n* brillo, lustre *m*: *the table has a lovely shine*, la mesa tiene un brillo precioso; *he gave his shoes a good shine*, sacó brillo a sus zapatos. – 2 *i* (*sun, light, eyes*) brillar; (*metal, glass, shoes*) relucir, brillar; (*face*) resplandecer, irradiar: *she rubbed the medals until they shone*, frotó las medallas hasta que relucieron; *her eyes shone with happiness*, le brillaban los ojos de alegría; *his honesty shines through*, irradia honestidad. 3 *fig* (*excel*) sobresalir (**at**, en), destacar (**at**, en), brillar (**at**, en): *he shines at tennis*, destaca en tenis; *now is your chance to shine*, ahora tienes la oportunidad de brillar. – 4 *t* (*light, lamp*) dirigir: *don't shine the light in my eyes*, no me dirijas la luz a los ojos. 5 (*polish*) sacar brillo a; (*shoes*) limpiar.
● **to take a shine to sb.**, tomarle cariño a algn., prendarse de algn. ‖ **to take a shine to sth.**, gustarle algo, prendarle algo, tener el ojo echado a algo.
▲ *pt & pp* **shone**, *en* 5 *pt & pp* **shined**.
shiner [ˈʃaɪnəʳ] *n fam* (*black eye*) ojo morado, ojo a la funerala.
shingle¹ [ˈʃɪŋgəl] *n* (*pebbles*) guijarros *mpl*.
■ **shingle beach**, playa de guijarros.
shingle² [ˈʃɪŋgəl] 1 *n* (*roof tile*) tablilla. 2 US (*name plate*) placa. – 3 *t* (*roof*) cubrir con tablillas.
● **to hang one's shingle**, US empezar un negocio, establecerse.
shingles [ˈʃɪŋgəlz] *n* MED herpes *m*, culebrilla.
shingly [ˈʃɪŋglɪ] *adj* de guijarros.
▲ *comp* **shinglier**, *superl* **shingliest**.
shining [ˈʃaɪnɪŋ] 1 *adj* (*metal, glass*) brillante, reluciente; (*eyes*) brillante, luminoso,-a; (*face, sun*) radiante; (*hair, furniture*) lustroso,-a. 2 *fig* (*outstanding*) destacado,-a, ilustre, magnífico,-a.
shinty [ˈʃɪntɪ] *n* SP hóckey *m* (escocés) sobre hierba.
shiny [ˈʃaɪnɪ] *adj* (*coin, leather, glass*) brillante, reluciente; (*hair, shoes*) lustroso,-a; (*material, trousers*) brillante; (*face, nose*) brillante.
▲ *comp* **shinier**, *superl* **shiniest**.
ship [ʃɪp] 1 *n* (*gen*) barco, buque *m*, navío, embarcación *f*. 2 *fam dated* (*aircraft, spacecraft*) nave *f*. – 3 *t* (*send - gen*) enviar, mandar; (*- by ship*) enviar por barco, mandar por barco, transportar (en barco); (*carry*) transportar: *we had our luggage shipped to England*, mandamos nuestro equipaje a Inglaterra por barco. 4 (*take on board*) embarcar, traer a bordo.
◆ **to ship off** *t sep* (*person*) despachar.
● **like ships that pass in the night**, como extraños. ‖ **on board ship**, a bordo. ‖ **when one's ship comes home**, cuando lleguen las vacas gordas, cuando toque la lotería. ‖ **to abandon ship / jump ship**, abandonar el barco. ‖ **to ship oars**, levantar los remos. ‖ **to ship water**, hacer agua.
■ **passenger ship**, buque *m* de pasajeros. ‖ **ship's company**, tripulación *f*.
▲ *pt & pp* **shipped**, *ger* **shipping**.
shipboard [ˈʃɪpbɔːd] *n* de a bordo.
● **on shipboard**, a bordo.

shipbuilder [ˈʃɪpbɪldəʳ] *n* constructor,-ra naval, empresa de construcción naval.
shipbuilding [ˈʃɪpbɪldɪŋ] *n* construcción *f* naval.
shipload [ˈʃɪpləʊd] *n* cargamento, carga.
shipmate [ˈʃɪpmeɪt] *n* compañero,-a de a bordo.
shipment [ˈʃɪpmənt] 1 *n* (*act*) embarque *m*, envío, transporte *m* (marítimo). 2 (*load*) consignación *f*, remesa.
shipowner [ˈʃɪpəʊnəʳ] *n* armador,-ra, naviero,-a.
shipper [ˈʃɪpəʳ] *n* (*gen*) consignador,-ra; (*exporter*) exportador,-ra.
shipping [ˈʃɪpɪŋ] 1 *n* (*business*) transporte *m* (en barco); (*sending*) envío, embarque *m*. 2 (*ships*) barcos *mpl*, buques *mpl*, embarcaciones *fpl*; (*of one country*) flota; (*tonnage*) tonelaje *m* (de buques).
■ **shipping agent**, consignatario,-a, agente *mf* marítimo,-a. ‖ **shipping charge**, gastos *mpl* de envío, gastos *mpl* de expedición. ‖ **shipping company**, empresa naviera. ‖ **shipping forecast**, parte *m* meteorológico para marineros. ‖ **shipping lane**, ruta de navegación. ‖ **shipping line**, compañía naviera. ‖ **shipping magnate**, magnate *mf* de la navegación.
shipshape [ˈʃɪpʃeɪp] 1 *adj* limpio,-a y ordenado,-a, en perfecto orden. – 2 *adv* limpio,-a y ordenado,-a, en perfecto orden.
shipwreck [ˈʃɪprek] *n* naufragio.
● **to be shipwrecked**, naufragar: *shipwrecked sailors*, marineros náufragos.
shipyard [ˈʃɪpjɑːd] *n* astillero.
shire [ˈʃaɪəʳ] 1 *n* GB *arch* (*county*) condado. – 2 **the Shires**, *npl* los condados *mpl* rurales.
■ **shire horse**, caballo de tiro, percherón *m*.
shirk [ʃɜːk] 1 *t* (*duty etc*) esquivar, eludir. – 2 *i* gandulear, haraganear.
shirker [ˈʃɜːkəʳ] *n* gandul,-la, haragán,-ana, vago,-a.
shirt [ʃɜːt] *n* (*gen*) camisa; (*for sport*) camiseta.
● **keep your shirt on!**, ¡no te sulfures! ‖ **to have the shirt off sb.'s back**, ser capaz de robarle a su propia madre. ‖ **to put one's shirt on sth.**, jugarse hasta la camisa en algo.
shirtsleeve [ˈʃɜːtsliːv] *n* manga de camisa.
● **in shirtsleeves**, en mangas de camisa.
shirt-tail [ˈʃɜːteɪl] *n* faldón *m* de camisa.
shirty [ˈʃɜːtɪ] *adj fam* agresivo,-a, grosero,-a, borde.
● **to get shirty**, sulfurarse, ponerse borde.
▲ *comp* **shirtier**, *superl* **shirtiest**.
shit [ʃɪt] 1 *n fam* (*faeces*) mierda. – 2 *interj fam* ¡mierda! – 3 *n fam* (*nonsense*) imbecilidades *fpl*, gilipolleces *pl*: *you talk shit*, no dices más que gilipolleces. 4 *fam* (*worthless thing*) mierda; (*contemptible person*) cabrón,-ona, mierda *mf*: *that film was a load of shit*, esa película era una mierda. – 5 *i fam* cagar. – 6 *adj fam* de mierda. – 7 **the shits**, *npl fam* diarrea, cagalera.
● **to be in the shit**, estar jodido,-a. ‖ **to be shit hot**, ser cojonudo,-a, ser de puta madre. ‖ **to beat the shit out of sb.**, moler a algn. a palos. ‖ **to not give a shit**, importarle a uno un carajo. ‖ **to have a shit**, cagar. ‖ **to scare the shit out of sb.**, acojonar a algn. ‖ **to shit one's pants**, cagarse encima. ‖ **to shit os.**, (*accidentally*) cagarse encima; (*be scared*) cagarse de miedo. ‖ **when the shit hits the fan**, cuando la mierda empiece a salpicar.
▲ *pt & pp* **shitted** *o* **shit**, *ger* **shitting**.
shitty [ˈʃɪtɪ] 1 *adj fam* (*bad*) de mierda: *a shitty book*, una porquería de libro; *she felt shitty*, se encontraba fatal, estaba hecha polvo. 2 *fam* (*contemptible*) ruin, vil: *what a shitty thing to do*, qué putada.

▲ *comp* **shittier,** superl **shittiest.**

shiver ['ʃɪvəʳ] **1** *n* (*with cold*) escalofrío, tiritón *m*, estremecimiento; (*with fear*) escalofrío. **– 2** *i* (*with cold*) temblar, tiritar; (*with fear*) estremecerse. **– 3** the shivers, *npl* escalofríos *mpl*.

● to send shivers down sb.'s spine, darle escalofríos a algn.

shivery ['ʃɪvərɪ] *adj* (*with cold*) estremecido,-a; (*feverish*) destemplado,-a.

shoal[1] [ʃəʊl] *n* (*underwater sandbank*) banco de arena.

shoal[2] [ʃəʊl] *n* (*of fish*) banco, cardumen *m*. **– 2** shoals, *npl fam* montones *mpl*.

shock[1] [ʃɒk] **1** *n* (*jolt, blow*) choque *m*, impacto, golpe *m*; (*of explosion etc*) sacudida; (*electric*) descarga. **2** (*upset, distress*) conmoción *f*, golpe *m*; (*fright, scare*) susto: *his death came as a real shock to them,* su muerte les cogió totalmente por sorpresa; *you gave me quite a shock,* me has dado un buen susto; *you're in for a shock,* te vas a llevar un susto. **3** MED shock *m*, choque *m*: *she's still in a state of shock,* sigue en estado de shock. **– 4** *t* (*upset*) conmocionar, conmover, afectar, sacudir: *France was shocked by the news of his illness,* la noticia de su enfermedad conmocionó a Francia. **5** (*startle*) asustar, sorprender, sobresaltar; (*scandalize*) escandalizar, horrorizar. **– 6** *i* impresionar, impactar.

■ shock absorber, amortiguador *m*. ‖ shock therapy / shock treatment, electrochoque *m*. ‖ shock troops, tropas *fpl* de choque, tropas *fpl* de asalto. ‖ shock wave, onda expansiva.

shock[2] [ʃɒk] *n* (*of hair*) mata.

shock[3] [ʃɒk] *n* AGR gavilla.

shocked [ʃɒkt] *adj* horrorizado,-a, escandalizado,-a: *some viewers may be shocked,* puede que algunos espectadores se escandalicen.

shocker ['ʃɒkəʳ] **1** *n* (*bad thing*) desastre *m*: *the match was a shocker,* el partido fue un desastre. **2** (*surprise*) bombazo.

shockheaded ['ʃɒkhedɪd] *adj* greñudo,-a.

shocking ['ʃɒkɪŋ] **1** *adj* (*horrific*) terrible, horroroso,-a, horrible. **2** (*disgraceful, offensive*) chocante, escandaloso,-a, vergonzoso,-a. **3** *fam* (*very bad*) espantoso,-a, pésimo,-a. **4** (*colour*) chillón,-ona: *shocking pink,* rosa chillón, rosa fosforito.

shockproof ['ʃɒkpruːf] *adj* a prueba de golpes.

shod [ʃɒd] *pt & pp* → **shoe.**

shoddy ['ʃɒdɪ] **1** *adj* (*work*) chapucero,-a; (*thing*) de pacotilla, de mala calidad. **2** (*treatment*) mezquino,-a.

▲ *comp* **shoddier,** superl **shoddiest.**

shoe [ʃuː] **1** *n* zapato: *what size shoe do you take?,* ¿qué número calzas?; *I need a new pair of shoes,* necesito unos zapatos nuevos. **2** (*for horse*) herradura. **3** (*of brake*) zapata. **– 4** *t* (*horse*) herrar.

● to put os. in sb. else's shoes, ponerse en el lugar de algn.

■ shoe leather, cuero para zapatos. ‖ shoe polish, betún *m*. ‖ shoe shop, zapatería.

▲ *pt & pp* **shod.**

shoebrush ['ʃuːbrʌʃ] *n* cepillo para los zapatos.

shoehorn ['ʃuːhɔːn] *n* calzador *m*.

shoelace ['ʃuːleɪs] *n* cordón *m* (de zapato).

shoemaker ['ʃuːmeɪkəʳ] *n* zapatero,-a.

shoeshine ['ʃuːʃaɪn] *n* limpieza de zapatos: *would you like a shoeshine?,* ¿le limpio los zapatos?

■ shoeshine boy, limpiabotas *m*.

shoestring ['ʃuːstrɪŋ] **1** *n* (*shoelace*) cordón *m* (de zapatos). **2** (*small amount of money*) poquísimo dinero.

● to do sth. on a shoestring, hacer algo con poquísimo dinero.

shoetree ['ʃuːtriː] *n* horma.

shone [ʃɒn, ʃə ʃəʊn] *pt & pp* → **shine.**

shoo [ʃuː] **1** *interj* ¡fuera!, ¡zape! **– 2** to shoo away, *t* ahuyentar, espantar.

shook [ʃʊk] *pt* → **shake.**

shoot [ʃuːt] **1** *n* BOT (*gen*) brote *m*, retoño, renuevo; (*of vine*) sarmiento. **2** GB (*hunting party*) cacería; (*land*) coto de caza. **3** CINEM rodaje *m*, filmación *f*. **– 4** *t* (*person, animal*) pegar un tiro a, pegar un balazo a; (*hit, wound*) herir (de bala); (*kill*) matar de un tiro, matar a tiros; (*by firing squad*) fusilar; (*hunt*) cazar: *she shot her husband,* le pegó un tiro a su marido; *she was shot in the back,* recibió un balazo en la espalda; *he was shot dead,* lo mataron a tiros. **5** (*fire - missile*) lanzar; (*- arrow, bullet, weapon*) disparar; (*- glance*) lanzar: *she can shoot a gun,* sabe disparar una pistola; *this gun doesn't shoot real bullets,* esta pistola no dispara balas de verdad; *they shot questions at her,* la bombardearon a preguntas. **6** (*film*) rodar, filmar; (*photograph*) fotografiar, sacar una foto de. **7** (*rapids*) salvar; (*bridge*) pasar por debajo de; (*traffic lights*) saltarse. **8** (*bolt*) echar, correr. **9** *sl* (*heroin*) chutarse, picarse, pincharse. **– 10** *i* (*fire weapon*) disparar (**at,** a/sobre); (*hunt with gun*) cazar: *don't shoot!,* ¡no disparen!; *he shot at a rabbit,* disparó a un conejo; *we're being shot at!,* ¡nos están disparando! **11** SP (*aim at goal*) tirar, disparar, chutar. **12** (*move quickly*) pasar volando, salir disparado,-a: *the car shot past us,* el coche nos pasó volando; *the pain shot up my arm,* el dolor me recorrió todo el brazo; *he shot out of the room,* salió disparado de la habitación; *they shot off somewhere,* salieron disparados a alguna parte; *the record shot to the top of the charts,* el disco subió directamente al número uno de la lista de éxitos. **13** CINEM rodar, filmar. **14** BOT brotar.

◆ to shoot down **1** *t sep* (*aircraft*) derribar, abatir; (*person*) matar a tiros. **2** *fig* (*argument, idea, etc*) rebatir; (*person*) poner por los suelos. ‖ to shoot up **1** *i* (*prices, costs*) dispararse; (*flames, hands*) alzarse; (*plant, child*) crecer mucho; (*buildings*) aparecer de la noche a la mañana. **2** *sl* (*heroin*) chutarse, picarse, pincharse.

● to shoot for the moon, pedir la luna. ‖ to shoot it out (with sb.), resolverlo a tiros (con algn.), emprenderla a tiros (con algn.). ‖ to shoot pool, jugar al billar. ‖ to shoot one's mouth off, irse de la lengua. ‖ to shoot on sight, disparar en el acto. ‖ to shoot one's bolt, echar el resto. ‖ to shoot os., pegarse un tiro. ‖ to shoot os. in the foot, salirle a algn. el tiro por la culata. ‖ to shoot to kill, disparar a matar.

▲ *pt & pp* **shot.**

shooter ['ʃuːtəʳ] *n sl* pistola, pipa.

shooting ['ʃuːtɪŋ] **1** *n* (*shots*) disparos *mpl*, tiros *mpl*; (*continuous*) tiroteo; (*wounding*) incidente *m*; (*killing*) asesinato; (*execution*) fusilamiento. **2** (*hunting*) caza. **3** CINEM rodaje *m*, filmación *f*. **– 4** *adj* (*of pain*) punzante.

● the whole shooting match, todo el tinglado, toda la pesca.

■ shooting brake, GB AUTO coche *m* familiar. ‖ shooting gallery, (*at targets*) barraca de tiro al blanco, caseta de tiro al blanco; (*drugs*) lugar *m* donde se reúnen muchos drogadictos. ‖ shooting iron, US pistola, pipa. ‖ shooting lodge, pabellón *m* de caza. ‖ shooting season, temporada de caza. ‖ shooting star, estrella fugaz. ‖ shooting stick, bastón *m* taburete.

shoot-out ['ʃuːtaʊt] *n* tiroteo.

shop [ʃɒp] **1** *n* (*gen*) tienda; (*business*) comercio, negocio: *I'm going to the shop,* voy a la tienda; *the shops open at*

9.00 am, las tiendas abren a las 9.00 horas. **2** (*workshop*) taller *m*. – **3** *i* (*gen*) hacer compras, hacer la compra, comprar: *we usually shop on Saturday mornings,* normalmente hacemos la compra los sábados por la mañana; *I was shopping for a new coat,* quería comprarme un abrigo nuevo. – **4** *t* GB *fam* (*inform on*) delatar, denunciar, vender.

◆ **to shop around** *i* ir de tienda en tienda y comparar precios.

● **all over the shop,** por todas partes. ‖ **to keep shop,** tener una tienda. ‖ **to set up shop,** poner un negocio, abrir un negocio. ‖ **to shut up shop,** cerrar (el negocio). ‖ **to talk shop,** hablar del trabajo. ‖ **to work one's way up from the shop floor,** empezar desde abajo. ■ **assembly shop,** taller *m* de montaje. ‖ **paint shop,** taller *m* de pintura. ‖ **repair shop,** taller *m* de reparaciones. ‖ **shop assistant,** dependiente,-a. ‖ **shop floor,** (*part of factory*) taller *m*; (*workers*) obreros *mpl,* trabajadores *mpl.* ‖ **shop steward,** enlace *mf* sindical. ‖ **shop window,** escaparate *m*.

▲ *pt & pp* **shopped,** *ger* **shopping.**

shopfitter [ˈʃɒpfɪtəʳ] *n* instalador,-ra comercial.
shopfitting [ˈʃɒpfɪtɪŋ] *n* instalación *f* comercial.
shopgirl [ˈʃɒpɡɜːl] *n* dependienta.
shopkeeper [ˈʃɒpkiːpəʳ] *n* tendero,-a.
shoplift [ˈʃɒplɪft] *i* hurtar (en las tiendas).
shoplifter [ˈʃɒplɪftəʳ] *n* mechero,-a.
shoplifting [ˈʃɒplɪftɪŋ] *n* ratería, hurto (en las tiendas).
shopper [ˈʃɒpəʳ] *n* comprador,-ra.
shopping [ˈʃɒpɪŋ] *n* (*purchases*) compra, compras *fpl;* (*activity*) compra: *I had a bit of shopping to do,* tuve que hacer unas compras.

● **to do the shopping,** hacer la compra. ‖ **to go on a shopping spree,** ir a la compra loca. ‖ **to go shopping,** ir de compras, ir de tiendas, ir a comprar. ■ **shopping bag,** bolsa de la compra. ‖ **shopping basket,** cesta de la compra. ‖ **shopping centre,** centro comercial. ‖ **shopping list,** lista de la compra. ‖ **shopping mall,** US centro comercial. ‖ **shopping precinct,** zona comercial. ‖ **shopping trolley,** carrito (de la compra).

shopsoiled [ˈʃɒpsɔɪld] *adj* (*damaged*) deteriorado,-a; (*dirty*) sucio,-a.
shopworn [ˈʃɒpwɔːn] *adj* US → **shopsoiled.**
shore¹ [ʃɔːʳ] **1** *n* (*of sea, lake*) orilla; (*coast*) costa; (*beach*) playa. – **2 shores,** *npl* tierra *f sing,* país *m sing,* tierras *fpl.*

● **on shore,** en tierra. ‖ **to go on shore,** (*sailors*) bajar a tierra; (*passengers*) desembarcar. ■ **shore leave,** permiso para bajar a tierra.

shore² [ʃɔːʳ] **1** *n* puntal *m*. – **2** *t* (*building, tunnel*) apuntalar (**up,** -). **3** *fig* (*company, prices*) sostener, apuntalar; (*argument, case*) apoyar, reforzar.

shoring [ˈʃɔːrɪŋ] *n* apuntalamiento.
shorn [ʃɔːn] *pp* → **shear.**
short [ʃɔːt] **1** *adj* (*not long*) corto,-a; (*not tall*) bajo,-a: *we'll take the shortest route,* iremos por el camino más corto; *it's only a short journey,* es sólo un viajecito; *he's got short hair,* lleva el pelo corto; *you're shorter than me,* eres más bajito que yo; *Jo is short for Joanne,* Jo es el diminutivo de Joanne. **2** (*brief - of time*) breve, corto,-a: *the days are shorter in winter,* los días son más cortos en invierno; *it was a very short interview,* fue una entrevista muy breve; *a short time ago,* hace poco (tiempo); *in a short while,* dentro de un ratito; *you've got a short memory,* tienes mala memoria. **3** (*deficient*) esca-

so,-a: *water was short,* escaseaba el agua; *we're still £50 short,* todavía nos faltan £50; *he collapsed two miles short of the finishing line,* sufrió un colapso cuando faltaban dos millas para llegar a la meta. **4** (*curt*) seco,-a, brusco,-a, cortante: *I was very short with her,* fui muy brusco con ella; *he's got a short temper,* tiene mal genio. **5** CULIN (*pastry*) quebradizo,-a. **6** FIN (*bill, exchange*) a corto plazo. **7** LING breve. – **8** *adv* (*abruptly*) bruscamente: *the car stopped short,* el coche se paró bruscamente. – **9** *n* (*drink*) copa, chupito. **10** CINEM cortometraje *m,* corto. **11** ELEC cortocircuito. – **12** *t* ELEC *fam* provocar un cortocircuito. – **13** *i* ELEC *fam* tener un cortocircuito.

● **at short notice,** con poca antelación. ‖ **for short,** para abreviar. ‖ **in short,** en pocas palabras. ‖ **in the short term,** a corto plazo. ‖ **short and sweet,** cortito,-a. ‖ **short of,** a menos que, salvo que: *short of calling a strike …,* a menos que convoquemos una huelga … ‖ **to be caught short / be taken short,** entrarle ganas a algn. de ir al lavabo. ‖ **to be in short supply,** haber escasez de, escasear. ‖ **to be short of sth.,** andar escaso,-a de algo, estar falto,-a de algo: *I'm a bit short of money,* ando algo escaso de dinero, tengo poco dinero; *he was short of breath,* le faltaba la respiración, le faltaba el aliento. ‖ **to be short on sth.,** tener poco,-a de algo: *he's short on tact,* tiene poco tacto, le falta tacto. ‖ **to cut sb. short,** interrumpir a algn. ‖ **to cut sth. short,** acortar algo, abreviar algo: *she had to cut her holiday short,* tuvo que acortar sus vacaciones. ‖ **to fall short of sth.,** no alcanzar algo, estar por debajo de algo: *the number of jobs created falls short of the government's target,* el número de puestos de trabajo creados está por debajo del objetivo del gobierno. ‖ **to get sb. by the short hairs/short and curlies,** pillar a algn. ‖ **to have sb. by the short hairs/short and curlies,** tener a algn. bien agarrado. ‖ **to give sb. short measure/weight,** no dar el peso exacto. ‖ **to go short (of sth.),** pasarse sin (algo), faltarle a uno (algo): *we were poor, but we never went short of food,* éramos pobres, pero nunca nos faltó comida. ‖ **to run short of sth.,** acabarse algo: *we're running short of coffee,* se nos está acabando el café. ■ **short circuit,** cortocircuito. ‖ **short cut,** (*route*) atajo; (*method*) método fácil, fórmula mágica. ‖ **short list,** lista de preseleccionados. ‖ **short order,** US comida rápida. ‖ **short story,** cuento. ‖ **short subject,** US cortometraje *m*. ‖ **short time,** jornada reducida. ‖ **short wave,** onda corta.

shortage [ˈʃɔːtɪdʒ] *n* falta, escasez *f*: *water shortage,* escasez de agua; *the housing shortage,* la falta de viviendas; *there's a shortage of language teachers,* no hay suficientes profesores de idiomas; *there was no shortage of volunteers,* no faltaban voluntarios.
shortbread [ˈʃɔːtbred] *n* galleta hecha de mantequilla tipo *mantecado.*
shortcake [ˈʃɔːtkeɪk] *n* GB CULIN → **shortbread;** US CULIN tarta de frutas.
short-change [ʃɔːtˈtʃeɪndʒ] **1** *t* (*give wrong change*) dar mal el cambio a, dar de menos (en el cambio) a. **2** *fam* (*cheat*) estafar, engañar.
short-circuit [ʃɔːtˈsɜːkɪt] **1** *t* ELEC provocar un cortocircuito en. **2** *fig* (*bypass*) pasar por encima de. – **3** *i* ELEC tener un cortocircuito.
shortcomings [ˈʃɔːtkʌmɪŋz] *npl* defectos *mpl,* puntos *mpl* flacos.
shortcrust pastry [ˈʃɔːtkrʌstˈpeɪstrɪ] *n* pasta quebradiza.
shorten [ˈʃɔːtən] **1** *t* (*gen*) acortar; (*text*) abreviar; (*prison sentence*) reducir. – **2** *i* acortarse.

shortening [ˈʃɔːtənɪŋ] *n* CULIN (*butter*) mantequilla; (*lard*) manteca.
shortfall [ˈʃɔːtfɔːl] *n* déficit *m* (**of/in**, en).
short-haired [ˈʃɔːthead] *adj* de pelo corto.
▲ *Se escribe* **short haired** [ʃɔːtˈhead] *cuando no se antepone a un sustantivo.*
shorthand [ˈʃɔːthænd] *n* taquigrafía.
■ **shorthand typing**, taquimecanografía. ‖ **shorthand typist**, taquimecanógrafo,-a, taquimeca *mf*.
short-handed [ʃɔːtˈhændɪd] **to be short-handed**, *phr* no tener personal suficiente.
short-list [ˈʃɔːtlɪst] *t* incluir en la lista de preselecciónados.
short-lived [ˈʃɔːtlɪvd] *adj* efímero,-a, fugaz, pasajero,-a.
shortly [ˈʃɔːtlɪ] **1** *adv* (*soon*) dentro de poco, en breve: *shortly after/before*, poco después/antes. **2** (*impatiently*) bruscamente, de manera brusca.
shortness [ˈʃɔːtnəs] **1** *n* (*of thing, distance*) lo corto; (*of person*) baja estatura; (*of period*) brevedad *f*. **2** (*lack*) falta.
short-range [ˈʃɔːtreɪndʒ] **1** *adj* MIL de corto alcance. **2** (*forecast, plan, project, etc*) a corto plazo.
shorts [ʃɔːts] **1** *npl* pantalones *mpl* cortos, shorts *mpl*: *a pair of shorts*, un pantalón corto. **2** US (*underpants*) calzonzillos *mpl*.
short-sighted [ˈʃɔːtsaɪtɪd] **1** *adj* MED miope, corto,-a de vista. **2** (*plan, policy, etc*) corto,-a de miras, estrecho,-a de miras.
short-sightedness [ʃɔːtˈsaɪtɪdnəs] **1** *n* MED miopía. **2** (*of plan, policy, etc*) falta de visión.
short-sleeved [ˈʃɔːtsliːvd] *adj* de manga corta.
short-staffed [ˈʃɔːtstɑːft] **to be short-staffed**, *phr* no tener personal suficiente.
short-tempered [ˈʃɔːttempəd] *adj* de mal genio.
short-term [ˈʃɔːttɜːm] *adj* a corto plazo.
short-wave [ˈʃɔːtweɪv] *adj* de onda corta.
short-winded [ʃɔːtˈwɪndɪd] *adj* corto,-a de resuello.
shot¹ [ʃɒt] **1** *pt & pp* → **shoot**. – **2** *adj* (*of textiles*) tornasolado,-a. **3** *fam* (*exhausted*) deshecho,-a.
● **to get shot of sth./sb.**, quitarse algo/a algn. de encima, deshacerse de algo/algn.
shot² [ʃɒt] **1** *n* (*act, sound*) tiro, disparo, balazo: *I thought I heard a shot*, creo haber oído un disparo; *he fired six shots*, disparó seis veces; *an exchange of shots*, un tiroteo; *a warning shot*, un disparo al aire. **2** (*projectile*) bala, proyectil *m*; (*pellets*) perdigones *mpl*; (*large iron ball*) peso. **3** (*person*) tirador,-ra: *he's a crack shot*, es un tirador de élite. **4** SP (*in football*) tiro (a gol), chut *m*, chute *m*; (*in tennis, golf, cricket, etc*) golpe *m*; (*in basketball*) tiro. **5** (*attempt, try*) tentativa, intento: *why don't you have a shot at it?*, ¿por qué no lo intentas?; *he'd like a shot at the title*, le gustaría intentar ganar el título. **6** *fam* (*injection*) inyección *f*, pinchazo. **7** (*drink*) trago, chupito. **8** (*photo*) foto *f*; (*cinema*) toma.
● **a cheap shot**, un golpe bajo. ‖ **a long shot**, una posibilidad remota. ‖ **a shot in the arm**, un estímulo, una inyección. ‖ **a shot in the dark**, un intento a ciegas, un palo de ciego. ‖ **like a shot**, (*without hesitation*) sin pensárselo dos veces, sin dudar, sin vacilar un solo momento. ‖ **not by a long shot**, ni mucho menos. ‖ **to be off like a shot**, salir disparado,-a, salir como una bala. ‖ **to call the shots**, mandar.
■ **shot put**, SP lanzamiento de peso.
shotgun [ˈʃɒtɡʌn] *n* escopeta.
● **to have a shotgun wedding**, casarse de penalty.
shot-putter [ˈʃɒtpʊtəʳ] *n* lanzador,-ra de peso.
should [ʃʊd] **1** *aux* (*duty, advisability, recommendation*) deber: *you should see the dentist*, deberías ir al dentista;

children should be seen and not heard, los niños deberían verse y no escucharse; *you should have phoned me*, deberías haberme llamado. **2** (*probability*) deber de: *the clothes should be dry now*, la ropa ya debe de estar seca; *there shouldn't be any problem*, no debe de haber ningún problema; *this should be interesting*, esto promete ser interesante. **3** (*subjunctive, conditional*): *if you should see Janet by any chance*, si por casualidad vieras a Janet; *should you change your mind*, si cambiaras de opinión; *it's strange that you should say that*, es extraño que digas eso; *it has been decided that you should go*, se ha decidido que fueras tú. **4** (*conditional, 1st person*): *I should like to ask a question*, quisiera hacer una pregunta; *I should be grateful if you could reply ...*, le agradecería que contestara ...; *I should buy it if I were you*, yo en tu lugar lo compraría. **5** (*tentative statement*): *I should think so*, me imagino que sí; *I shouldn't think so*, no creo. **6** (*disbelief, surprise*): *and who should be in the bar but Gary Linekerl*, ¿y quién te parece que estaba en el bar? ¡Gary Lineker!; *how should I knowl*, ¡yo qué sé!
● **I should have thought ...**, hubiera pensado ... ‖ **I should think so tool**, ¡faltaría más!, ¡era lo menos que podía hacer!
shoulder [ˈʃəʊldəʳ] **1** *n* ANAT hombro: *she looked over her shoulder*, miró por encima del hombro. **2** (*of garment*) hombro: *padded shoulders*, hombreras. **3** (*of meat*) paletilla. **4** (*of hill, mountain*) ladera; (*of road*) arcén *m*, andén *m*. – **5** *t* (*duty, responsibility*) cargar con. **6** (*load*) ponerse al hombro, echarse al hombro. **7** (*push*) empujar con el hombro. – **8 shoulders**, *npl* ANAT hombros *mpl*, espalda *f sing*.
● **a shoulder to cry on**, un paño de lágrimas. ‖ **shoulder to shoulder**, hombro con hombro. ‖ **to cry on sb.'s shoulders**, desahogarse con algn. ‖ **to give sb. the cold shoulder**, volver la espalda a algn., dar de lado a algn., hacerle el vacío a algn. ‖ **to look over sb.'s shoulder**, vigilar a algn. ‖ **to put one's shoulder to the wheel**, arrimar el hombro. ‖ **to rub shoulders with sb.**, codearse con algn. ‖ **to shoulder one's way in/past/through**, abrirse paso a empujones. ‖ **to stand head and shoulders above sth.**, estar muy por encima de algo.
■ **shoulder bag**, bolso (de bandolera). ‖ **shoulder blade**, omóplato. ‖ **shoulder pad**, hombrera. ‖ **shoulder patch/flash**, galón *m*. ‖ **shoulder strap**, (*of garment*) tirante *m*; (*of bag*) correa.
shoulder-high [ˈʃəʊldəhaɪ] **1** *adj* a la altura del hombro. – **2** *adv* a hombros, en hombros.
shoulder-length [ˈʃəʊldəlenθ] *adj* (*que llega*) hasta los hombros.
shout [ʃaʊt] **1** *n* grito: *shouts of delight*, gritos de alegría; *give me a shout*, avísame, pégame un grito. **2** GB *fam* (*turn to buy drink*) ronda: *it's your shout*, te toca a ti invitar. – **3** *t* gritar (**out**, -): *get outl he shouted*, ¡fuera! gritó. – **4** *i* gritar: *there's no need to shout!*, ¡no hace falta que grites!; *I don't like it when you shout at me*, no me gusta que me grites.
◆ **to shout down** *t sep* abuchear.
● **to shout for help**, pedir auxilio a gritos, pedir socorro a gritos. ‖ **to shout os. hoarse**, gritar hasta quedarse ronco,-a, gritar hasta quedarse afónico,-a. ‖ **to shout sth. from the rooftops**, divulgar algo a los cuatro vientos.
shouting [ˈʃaʊtɪŋ] *n* gritos *mpl*, vocerío.
● **it's all over bar the shouting**, esto ya es asunto concluido. ‖ **to have a shouting match**, pelearse a gritos.

shove [ʃʌv] **1** n empujón m: *we had to give the car a shove,* tuvimos que dar un empujón al coche. **- 2** t *(push)* empujar: *he shoved me out of the way,* me apartó a empujones; *she shoved the plate away,* apartó el plato de un empujón. **3** *(put casually)* meter: *shove it in the cupboard,* métenlo en el armario; *he shoved the letter in his pocket,* se metió la carta en el bolsillo. **- 4** i *(push)* empujar, dar empujones: *don't shovel,* ¡no empujes!; *everyone was pushing and shoving to see the actor,* todos andaban dando empujones para ver al actor.
◆ **to shove off 1** i *fam* largarse. **2** MAR desatracar. ‖ **to shove over / shove up** i *fam* correrse.

shovel [ˈʃʌvəl] **1** n *(tool)* pala. **2** *(machine)* excavadora, pala mecánica. **- 3** t mover con pala, quitar con pala, echar con pala.
● **to shovel food into one's mouth,** zamparse la comida.
▲ pt & pp **shovelled,** ger **shovelling.**

shoveler [ˈʃʌvələʳ] n pato cuchara.

shovelful [ˈʃʌvəlfʊl] n palada.

show [ʃəʊ] **1** n THEAT *(entertainment)* espectáculo; *(performance)* función f: *let's go and see a show,* vayamos a ver un espectáculo; *they perform two shows a day,* hacen dos funciones diarias. **2** RAD TV programa m, show m. **3** *(exhibition)* exposición f. **4** *(display)* muestra, demostración f: *a show of strength,* una demostración de fuerza, una exhibición de fuerza; *a show of hands,* una votación a mano alzada. **5** *(outward appearance, pretence)* apariencia: *she made a show of interest,* fingió estar interesada. **6** *(ostentation, pomp)* alarde m: *it's all for show,* es pura fachada, todo es para aparentar. **7** *fam (organization)* negocio, cotarro: *who runs this show?,* ¿quién manda aquí? **- 8** t *(display -gen)* enseñar; *(- things for sale)* mostrar, enseñar: *I showed her my photos,* le enseñé mis fotos; *she showed me some beautiful jewellery,* me mostró unas joyas preciosas. **9** *(point out)* indicar, señalar: *do you want me to show you the way?,* ¿quieres que te indique el camino? **10** *(reveal - feelings)* demostrar, expresar; *(- interest, enthusiasm, etc)* demostrar, mostrar: *she rarely shows his feelings,* raras veces demuestra sus sentimientos; *they showed great kindness to me,* se mostraron muy amables conmigo; *he showed no mercy,* no fue clemente; *you should show some respect for your elders,* deberías guardar más respeto a tus mayores. **11** *(allow to be seen)* dejar ver: *black doesn't show the dirt,* el negro no deja ver la suciedad. **12** *(measurement etc)* marcar; *(profit, loss)* indicar, registrar, arrojar: *the clock showed 4.25,* el reloj marcaba las 4.25; *the thermometer shows a temperature of 20 degrees,* el termómetro marca una temperatura de 20 grados; *figures out today show that inflation is up by 2%,* cifras publicadas hoy indican que la inflación ha subido un 2%. **13** *(teach)* enseñar; *(explain)* explicar: *she showed us how it works,* nos enseñó cómo funciona; *I'll show him!,* ¡se va a enterar! **14** *(prove, demonstrate)* demostrar: *this work shows real talent,* este trabajo demuestra mucho talento; *research has shown that the common cold can be cured,* las investigaciones han demostrado que se puede curar el resfriado común. **15** *(depict, present)* representar, mostrar: *this photo shows him swimming in the sea,* en esta foto está nadando en el mar; *this painting shows a rural scene,* este cuadro muestra una escena rural; *motorways are shown in red,* las autopistas están señaladas en rojo. **16** *(guide)* llevar, acompañar: *I'll show you to your room,* le acompañaré a tu habitación; *will you show Mr. Smith out please?,* ¿quieres acompañar al Sr. Smith a la puerta

por favor?; *he showed me round the factory,* me mostró la fábrica. **17** *(painting etc)* exponer, exhibir; *(film)* dar, poner, pasar, proyectar; *(slides)* pasar, proyectar; *(on TV)* dar, poner: *they're showing "Dracula" at the Rex,* dan "Drácula" en el Rex; *are they showing the match live?,* ¿dan el partido en directo? **- 18** i *(be perceptible)* verse, notarse: *the stain doesn't show,* no se ve la mancha; *she was nervous but didn't let it show,* estaba nerviosa pero no se le notaba; *I did it quickly - yes, it shows!,* lo hice deprisa - ¡sí, se nota! **19** CINEM poner, dar, echar, proyectar, exhibir: *what's showing at the Odeon?,* ¿qué dan en el Odeon?, ¿qué echan en el Odeon?; *now showing at a cinema near you,* ahora se exhibe en un cine muy cerca de ti. **20** *fam (appear, turn up)* aparecer, presentarse: *he didn't show,* no se presentó.
◆ **to show off 1** i *(gen)* fardar, fanfarronear, presumir, lucirse; *(child)* hacerse el/la gracioso,-a. **- 2** t *sep (set off)* hacer resaltar, realzar. **3** *(flaunt, parade)* hacer alarde de, presumir de, fardar con, lucirse con. ‖ **to show up 1** t *sep (make visible - gen)* hacer resaltar, hacer destacar; *(- defect, inadequacy, etc)* revelar, sacar a la luz, poner de manifiesto. **2** *fam (embarrass)* dejar en ridículo, poner en evidencia. **- 3** i *(be visible)* notarse, verse. **4** *fam (arrive)* acudir, presentarse, aparecer.
● *it just goes to show!,* ¡hay que ver! ‖ *let's get this show on the road!,* ¡manos a la obra! ‖ *the show must go on,* el espectáculo debe continuar. ‖ *time will show,* el tiempo lo dirá. ‖ *to be all show,* ser puro teatro, ser fingido,-a. ‖ *to be on show,* estar expuesto,-a. ‖ *to have nothing to show for sth.,* no reportarle a uno ningún beneficio: *he had nothing to show for a life's work except a stupid watch,* lo único que tenía como recompensa a una vida dedicada al trabajo era un estúpido reloj. ‖ *to have something to show for sth.,* tener algo que recompensa: *at least you've got something to show for it,* al menos tienes algo que te compensa el esfuerzo que has hecho; *and what have you got to show for it?,* ¿y qué tienes como recompensa?, ¿y qué beneficio te ha reportado? ‖ *to put on/ up a good show,* hacer un buen papel, estar muy bien. ‖ *to show a leg,* levantarse. ‖ *to show one's age,* notársele los años a uno. ‖ *to show one's face,* asomar la cara. ‖ *to show one's teeth,* mostrar los dientes, enseñar los dientes. ‖ *to show sb. the door,* echar a algn. (a la calle). ‖ *to show signs of sth.,* dar señales de algo, dar muestras de algo. ‖ *to show the way, (set an example)* dar ejemplo. ‖ *to steal the show,* llevarse la palma.
■ *agricultural show,* feria del campo. ‖ *boat show,* salón m náutico. ‖ *fashion show,* desfile m de modelos. ‖ *horse show,* concurso hípico. ‖ *quiz show,* programa m concurso. ‖ *show business,* el mundo del espectáculo. ‖ *show house,* casa piloto. ‖ *show trial,* juicio amañado (para influir en la opinión pública).
▲ pt **showed,** pp **showed** o **shown.**

showcase [ˈʃəʊkeɪs] **1** n *(cabinet)* vitrina. **2** *(opportunity, setting)* escaparate m: *the festival has become a showcase for new directors,* el festival se ha convertido en un escaparate para los nuevos directores. **- 3** t exhibir.

showdown [ˈʃəʊdaʊn] n enfrentamiento, confrontación f.

shower [ˈʃaʊəʳ] **1** n METEOR chubasco, chaparrón m. **2** *(of stones, blows, insults, etc)* lluvia. **3** *(in bathroom)* ducha. **4** US *(party)* fiesta de obsequio. **- 5** t *(sprinkle)* espolvorear; *(spray)* rociar: *they showered the bride and groom with confetti,* les tiraron confeti a los novios. **6** *fig (bestow, heap)* inundar, colmar, llover: *he showered her with ex-*

pensive gifts, la inundó de regalos caros; *honours were showered on him,* lo colmaron de honores, le llovieron honores. – **7** *i* (*rain*) llover; (*objects*) caer, llover. **8** (*in bath*) ducharse.
● **to have a shower / take a shower,** ducharse.
■ **shower cap,** gorro de baño. ‖ **shower gel,** gel *m* de baño, gel *m* de ducha.

showerproof ['ʃaʊəpruːf] *adj* impermeable.

showery ['ʃaʊərɪ] *adj* lluvioso,-a.

showgirl ['ʃaʊgɜːl] *n* (*singer*) corista; (*dancer*) bailarina.

showground ['ʃaʊgraʊnd] *n* real *m*, recinto ferial.

showing ['ʃaʊɪŋ] **1** *n* (*of film*) pase *m*, sesión *f*, proyección *f*; (*of paintings*) exhibición *f*. **2** (*performance*) actuación *f*; (*result*) resultado: *on its current showing,* según los últimos resultados.

showjumper ['ʃaʊdʒʌmpəʳ] *n* jinete *mf*.

showjumping ['ʃaʊdʒʌmpɪŋ] *n* (*gen*) hípica; (*event*) concurso *f* hípico.

showman ['ʃaʊmən] **1** *n* (*manager*) empresario (de espectáculos). **2** (*entertainer*) artista *m*, showman *m*.
▲ *pl* **showmen** ['ʃaʊmən].

showmanship ['ʃaʊmənʃɪp] *n* teatralidad *f*.

shown [ʃaʊn] *pp* → **show**.

show-off ['ʃaʊɒf] *n fam* fanfarrón,-ona, fardón,-ona.

showpiece ['ʃaʊpiːs] **1** *n* (*in exhibition*) joya, objeto de valor. **2** (*fine example*) modelo (de su género).

showplace ['ʃaʊpleɪs] *n* (*place of interest*) lugar *m* de interés turístico; (*impressive building*) edificio de interés turístico.

showroom ['ʃaʊruːm] **1** *n* COMM exposición *f*. **2** ART sala de exposiciones.

showy ['ʃaʊɪ] *adj* (*thing*) llamativo,-a, vistoso,-a; (*person*) ostentoso,-a.
▲ *comp* **showier,** *superl* **showiest.**

shrank [ʃræŋk] *pt* → **shrink.**

shrapnel ['ʃræpnəl] *n* metralla.

shred [ʃred] **1** *n* (*gen*) triza; (*of cloth*) jirón *m*; (*of paper*) tira; (*of tobaco*) brizna, hebra. **2** *fig* (*bit*) pizca: *not a shred of truth,* ni pizca de verdad; *without a shred of evidence,* sin la más mínima prueba. – **3** *t* (*paper*) hacer trizas, triturar; (*vegetables - cut in strips*) cortar en tiras; (*- grate*) rallar.
● **in shreds,** (*clothes*) hecho,-a jirones; (*reputation etc*) hecho,-a trizas, destrozado,-a. ‖ **to tear sth./sb. to shreds,** hacer trizas algo/a algn.
▲ *pt & pp* **shredded,** *ger* **shredding.**

shredder ['ʃredəʳ] *n* (*for paper*) trituradora; (*for vegetables*) rallador *m*.

shrew [ʃruː] **1** *n* ZOOL musaraña. **2** *fig* (*woman*) arpía, bruja, fiera.

shrewd [ʃruːd] **1** *adj* (*person - gen*) astuto,-a, sagaz; (*clear-sighted*) perspicaz; (*- wise*) sabio,-a. **2** (*decision*) muy acertado,-a; (*move*) hábil, inteligente; (*assessment, remark, guess*) perspicaz; (*guess*) razonable.

shrewdness ['ʃruːdnəs] *n* (*gen*) astucia, sagacidad *f*; (*clear-sightedness*) perspicacia; (*wisdom*) juicio.

shriek [ʃriːk] **1** *n* chillido, grito agudo: *shriek of laughter,* carcajada; *shriek of pain,* alarido de dolor. – **2** *i* chillar, gritar: *the children shrieked with laughter,* los niños chillaban de risa. – **3** *t* chillar, gritar.
● **to shriek with laughter,** reírse a carcajadas.

shrift [ʃrɪft] *short* **shrift,** *n* trato indiferente.
● **to get short shrift,** (*person*) ser echado,-a con cajas destempladas, ser despachado,-a sin rodeos; (*idea etc*) ser desechado,-a de plano. ‖ **to give short shrift,** (*person*) echar con cajas destempladas, despachar sin rodeos; (*idea etc*) desestimar de plano.

shrike [ʃraɪk] *n* alcaudón *m*.

shrill [ʃrɪl] **1** *adj* (*voice, words, people*) agudo,-a, chillón,-ona, estridente; (*sound, whistle*) agudo,-a, estridente, penetrante. **2** (*demand, protest, criticism*) frenético,-a, estridente. – **3** *i* (*whistle*) pitar; (*phone, alarm*) sonar; (*person, voice*) chillar.

shrimp [ʃrɪmp] **1** *n* camarón *m*, gamba. **2** *pej* (*person*) enano,-a, renacuajo,-a. – **3** *i* pescar camarones.
● **to go shrimping,** ir a pescar camarones.
■ **shrimp cocktail,** cóctel *m* de gambas.

shrine [ʃraɪn] *n* REL (*holy place*) santuario, lugar *m* sagrado; (*chapel*) capilla; (*remote*) ermita; (*tomb*) sepulcro; (*reliquary*) relicario.

shrink [ʃrɪŋk] **1** *t* (*clothes etc*) encoger. – **2** *i* (*clothes*) encoger, encogerse; (*meat*) achicarse, reducirse: *my jumper's shrunk,* mi jersey (se) ha encogido. **3** (*savings, numbers, profits, etc*) disminuir, reducirse. **4** (*move back*) retroceder, echarse atrás. – **5** *n fam* (*psychiatrist*) psiquiatra *mf*, loquero,-a.
● **to shrink from doing sth.,** no tener valor para hacer algo, acobardarse ante algo.
▲ *pt* **shrank,** *pp* **shrunk.**

shrinkage ['ʃrɪŋkɪdʒ] **1** *n* (*of clothes*) encogimiento; (*of metal*) contracción *f*. **2** (*of savings, numbers, etc*) disminución *f*, reducción *f*.

shrinking violet [ʃrɪŋkɪŋ'vaɪələt] *n fam* persona muy tímida.

shrink-wrap ['ʃrɪŋkræp] *t* empaquetar en plástico, envolver en plástico.
▲ *pt & pp* **shrink-wrapped,** *ger* **shrink-wrapping.**

shrivel ['ʃrɪvəl] **1** *t* (*plant*) secar, marchitar; (*skin*) arrugar. – **2** *i* (*plant*) secarse, marchitarse; (*skin*) arrugarse.
▲ *pt & pp* **shrivelled** (US **shriveled**), *ger* **shrivelling** (US **shriveling**).

shroud [ʃraʊd] **1** *n* REL mortaja, sudario. **2** *fig* (*of mist, secrecy*) velo. – **3** *t fig* envolver.
● **to be shrouded in sth.,** estar envuelto,-a en un velo de algo.

Shrove Tuesday [ʃrəʊv'tjuːzdɪ] *n* martes *m* de carnaval.

shrub [ʃrʌb] *n* arbusto, mata.

shrubbery ['ʃrʌbərɪ] *n* arbustos *mpl*, matas *fpl*.
▲ *pl* **shrubberies.**

shrug [ʃrʌg] **1** *t* encoger. – **2** *i* encogerse de hombros. – **3** *n* encogimiento de hombros.
➧ **to shrug off** *t sep* quitar importancia a, no hacer caso de.
● **to shrug one's shoulders,** encogerse de hombros.
▲ *pt & pp* **shrugged,** *ger* **shrugging.**

shrunk [ʃrʌŋk] *pp* → **shrink.**

shrunken ['ʃrʌŋkən] *adj* (*gen*) encogido,-a; (*body*) consumido,-a, empequeñecido,-a; (*size, head*) reducido,-a.

shudder ['ʃʌdəʳ] **1** *n* (*of person*) escalofrío, estremecimiento. **2** (*of machine, engine*) vibración *f*, sacudida. – **3** *i* (*person*) estremecerse, temblar (**with**, de): *I shudder to think of it,* me dan escalofríos sólo de pensarlo. **4** (*machinery, vehicle*) vibrar, dar sacudidas.
● **to give sb. the shudders,** dar un escalofrío a algn.; poner los pelos de punta a algn. ‖ **to shudder to a halt,** pararse de una sacudida.

shuffle ['ʃʌfəl] **1** *n* (*walk*) arrastre *m*. **2** (*of cards*) barajeo: *give the cards a shuffle,* baraja las cartas. – **3** *t* (*feet - drag*) arrastrar; (*- move*) mover. **4** (*cards*) barajar; (*papers*) revolver. – **5** *i* (*walk*) andar arrastrando los pies; (*in seat*) revolverse.

shun [ʃʌn] *t* (*person*) rechazar, rehuir; (*responsibility, publicity*) rehuir, evitar.

▲ *pt & pp* shunned, *ger* shunning.

shunt [ʃʌnt] **1** *t* (*train, railway carriage*) cambiar de vía. **2** ELEC derivar. **3** *fam* (*person*) apartar, relegar, trasladar; (*object*) empujar, mover: *he's been shunted off to another branch,* se lo han quitado de encima mandándolo a otra sucursal. – **4** *n* (*shunting*) maniobra, empujón *m*. **5** ELEC derivación *f*. **6** MED derivación *f*. **7** *fam* (*crash*) choque *m*.

shunting ['ʃʌntɪŋ] *n* maniobras *fpl*.
■ shunting engine, máquina auxiliar. ‖ shunting yard, estación *f* de maniobras.

shush [ʃʊʃ] **1** *interj* ¡chis!, ¡chitón! – **2** *t* callar, hacer callar.

shut [ʃʌt] **1** *t* (*gen*) cerrar: *shut your eyes,* cierra los ojos; *he shut his finger in the door,* se pilló el dedo en la puerta. – **2** *i* (*gen*) cerrar, cerrarse: *the door won't shut,* le puerta no se cierra; *the shops shut at 5.30 pm,* las tiendas cierran a las 5.30 horas. – **3** *adj* (*closed*) cerrado,-a.
◆ to shut away *t sep* (*isolate*) encerrar. ‖ to shut down **1** *t sep* (*factory, business*) cerrar; (*machinery*) desconectar, apagar. – **2** *i* (*factory, business*) cerrar. ‖ to shut in *t sep* (*enclose, imprison*) encerrar. ‖ to shut off **1** *t sep* (*gas, electricity, water*) cortar, cerrar; (*machinery, engine*) desconectar, apagar. **2** (*isolate*) aislar (**from**, de). **3** (*view, light, etc*) tapar. – **4** *i* (*gas, electricity, water*) cortarse, cerrarse; (*machinery, engine*) desconectarse, apagarse. ‖ to shut out **1** *t sep* (*exclude*) excluir, no dejar participar. **2** (*stop entering - person, animal*) dejar fuera; (*- light, heat, noise*) no dejar entrar; (*lock out*) cerrar la puerta a. **3** *fig* (*thought, feeling, etc*) no pensar en, ahuyentar. ‖ to shut up **1** *t sep* (*close*) cerrar. **2** (*confine*) encerrar. **3** *fam* (*quieten*) callar, hacer callar. – **4** *i* (*close*) cerrar. **5** (*keep quiet*) callarse: *shut up!,* ¡cállate!
● to shut one's ears to sth., hacer oídos sordos a algo. ‖ to shut one's mouth/gob/trap/face, cerrar el pico. ‖ to shut the door in sb.'s face, dar a algn. con la puerta en las narices. ‖ to shut the door on sth., negarse a pensar en algo, no querer saber nada de algo. ‖ to shut up shop, cerrar (el negocio).
▲ *pt & pp* shut, *ger* shutting.

shutdown ['ʃʌtdaʊn] *n* (*of factory etc*) cierre *m*; (*of power*) corte *m*; (*of machinery*) parada.

shuteye ['ʃʌtaɪ] *n fam* dormir *m*.
● to get some/a bit of shuteye, echar una cabezada, dormir un poco.

shut-in ['ʃʌtɪn] **1** *adj* (*gen*) encerrado,-a; (*patient*) confinado,-a en casa. – **2** *n* US MED enfermo,-a confinado,-a en casa.

shutout ['ʃʌtaʊt] **1** *n* (*lockout*) cierre *m* patronal. **2** US SP partido en que sólo marca un equipo.

shutter ['ʃʌtə'] **1** *n* (*on window*) postigo, contraventana; (*of shop*) cierre *m*. **2** (*of camera*) obturador *m*. – **3** *t* (*close shutters*) cerrar los postigos, cerrar las contraventanas.
● to put up the shutters, (*for day*) cerrar, echar el cierre; (*for ever*) cerrar el negocio.
■ shutter speed, tiempo de exposición.

shuttered ['ʃʌtəd] *adj* (*with shutters closed*) con las contraventanas cerradas; (*with shutters*) con contraventanas.

shuttle ['ʃʌtl] **1** *n* AV puente *m* aéreo. **2** (*spacecraft*) transbordador *m* espacial. **3** (*bus, train*) servicio regular de enlace. **4** (*in weaving*) lanzadera. **5** *fam* (*shuttlecock*) volante *m*. – **6** *t* trasladar, transportar. – **7** *i* (*plane*) volar regularmente; (*bus, train*) viajar, ir regularmente.
● to shuttle back and forth, ir y venir.
■ shuttle service, servicio regular de enlace.

shuttlecock ['ʃʌtlkɒk] *n* volante *m*.

shy¹ [ʃaɪ] **1** *adj* (*person - timid*) tímido,-a; (*- bashful*) vergonzoso,-a; (*- reserved*) reservado,-a; (*- unsociable, ner-*

vous) huraño,-a: *don't be shy,* no seas tímido, no tengas vergüenza, no te cortes. **2** (*animal*) asustadizo,-a, huraño,-a. – **3** *i* (*horse*) espantarse (**at,** de), respingar, asustarse.
◆ to shy away from *t insep* (*avoid*) huir de, rehuir.
● once bitten, twice shy, gato escaldado del agua fría huye. ‖ to be shy about doing sth., darle vergüenza a uno hacer algo. ‖ to be shy of doing sth., (*wary, cautious*) tener miedo de hacer algo, no atreverse a hacer algo. ‖ to be shy of sth., (*lacking, short*) andar escaso,-a de algo, faltar algo: *we're still one person shy,* todavía nos falta una persona.
▲ *comp* shyer *o* shier, *superl* shyest *o* shiest.

shy² [ʃaɪ] *t* (*throw*) tirar, lanzar.
▲ *pt & pp* shied, *ger* shying.

shyly ['ʃaɪlɪ] *adv* tímidamente, con timidez.

shyness ['ʃaɪnəs] *n* timidez *f*.

shyster ['ʃaɪstə'] *n* US *fam* (*gen*) estafador,-ra, timador,-ra; (*lawyer*) picapleitos *mf*.

Siam [saɪˈæm] *n* Siam.

Siamese [saɪəˈmiːz] **1** *adj* siamés,-esa. – **2** *n* (*person*) siamés,-esa. **3** (*language*) siamés *m*. – **4** the Siamese, *npl* los siameses *mpl*.
■ Siamese cat, gato siamés. ‖ Siamese twin, hermano,-a siamés,-esa.

Siberia [saɪˈbɪərɪə] *n* Siberia.

Siberian [saɪˈbɪərɪən] *adj* siberiano,-a.

sibilant ['sɪbɪlənt] **1** *n* LING sibilante *f*. – **2** *adj* sibilante.

sibling ['sɪblɪŋ] *n fml* (*brother*) hermano; (*sister*) hermana: *sibling rivalry,* rivalidad entre hermanos.

Sicilian [sɪˈsɪlɪən] **1** *adj* siciliano,-a. – **2** *n* siciliano,-a.

Sicily ['sɪsəlɪ] *n* Sicilia.

sick [sɪk] **1** *adj* (*ill*) enfermo,-a. **2** (*nauseated, queasy*) mareado,-a. **3** (*fed up*) harto,-a; (*worried*) preocupado,-a: *I'm sick and tired of your moaning,* estoy más que harto de tus quejas; *I bet you're sick of the sight of grapes!,* ¡seguro que estás harto de ver uvas!; *we were worried sick,* estábamos muy preocupados. **4** (*morbid - mind, person*) morboso,-a; (*- joke, humour*) de muy mal gusto, negro,-a. – **5** *n* GB (*vomit*) vómito. **6** the sick, *npl* los enfermos *mpl*.
◆ to sick up *t sep* GB vomitar, devolver.
● to be off sick, estar ausente por enfermedad. ‖ to be sick, (*vomit*) vomitar, devolver. ‖ to be as sick as a parrot, estar destrozado,-a. ‖ to call in sick, llamar diciendo que se está enfermo,-a. ‖ to feel sick, estar mareado,-a, tener náuseas. ‖ to go sick, darse de baja por enfermedad. ‖ to make sb. sick, (*angry*) reventar a algn., dar rabia a algn.: *it makes you sick!,* ¡da rabia!; *you make me sick!,* ¡me das asco! ‖ to report sick, dar parte de enfermedad, coger la baja por enfermedad. ‖ to take sick, *dated* enfermar, caer enfermo,-a, ponerse enfermo,-a.
■ sick bag, bolsa para el mareo. ‖ sick headache, jaqueca, migraña. ‖ sick leave, baja por enfermedad. ‖ sick note, (*doctor's*) baja; (*parent's*) nota. ‖ sick pay, *sueldo que se cobra cuando se está de baja por enfermedad.*

sickbay ['sɪkbeɪ] *n* enfermería.

sickbed ['sɪkbed] *n* lecho de enfermo.

sicken ['sɪkən] **1** *t* (*make ill*) poner enfermo,-a; (*revolt, disgust*) dar asco, dar rabia. – **2** *i* caer enfermo,-a, ponerse enfermo,-a, enfermar.
● to be sickening for sth., estar incubando algo, tener síntomas de algo.

sickening ['sɪkənɪŋ] **1** *adj* (*disgusting*) repugnante, asqueroso,-a; (*horrifying*) escalofriante, horrible; (*nauseat-*

ing) nauseabundo,-a. **2** *(annoying)* irritante, exasperante: *it's sickening,* da rabia.

sickle ['sɪkəl] *n* hoz *f.*

sickly ['sɪklɪ] **1** *adj (person)* enfermizo,-a; *(pale)* pálido,-a, paliducho,-a. **2** *(smell, taste)* empalagoso,-a, dulzón,-ona; *(smile)* forzado,-a; *(colour)* horrible, asqueroso,-a.
▲ *comp* **sicklier,** *superl* **sickliest.**

sickness ['sɪknəs] **1** *n (illness)* enfermedad *f.* **2** *(nausea)* náuseas *fpl,* ganas *fpl* de vomitar.
■ **sickness benefit,** subsidio de enfermedad.

sickroom ['sɪkruːm] *n* enfermería.

side [saɪd] **1** *n (gen)* lado; *(of coi, cube, record)* cara; *(of written page)* carilla: *there's a garage at the side of the house,* hay un garaje al lado de la casa; *write on one side of the paper only,* sólo escribir en una cara del papel; *the right/wrong side of the material,* el derecho/revés de la tela; *he's from the other side of town,* es del otro lado de la cuidad; *let's cross over to the other side,* crucemos al otro lado; *they sat on either side of the table,* se sentaron a ambos lados de la mesa; *they drive on the right-hand side of the road,* conducen por la derecha; *it's on the left-hand side,* está a mano izquierda. **2** *(of hill, mountain)* ladera, falda. **3** *(of body)* lado, costado; *(of animal)* ijada, ijar *m: I've got a pain in my right side,* me duele el lado derecho; *she was lying on her side,* estaba echada de lado; *she never left his side,* no dejó nunca de estar con él; *come and sit by my side,* ven y siéntate a mi lado; *a side of beef,* media res. **4** *(edge - gen)* borde *m; (- of lake, river, etc)* orilla; *(- of page)* margen *m: flowers grow at the side of the path,* crecen flores a los lados del sendero; *she made notes at the side of the page,* tomó notas en el margen de la página. **5** *(aspect)* aspecto, faceta, lado; *(position, opinion, point of view)* lado, parte *f,* punto de vista: *a new side to his character,* una nueva faceta de su carácter; *try and look on the bright side,* trata de ver el lado bueno de las cosas; *look at it from my side,* míralo desde mi punto de vista; *the practical side of things,* el aspecto práctico de las cosas; *listen to both sides before you decide,* escucha los dos partes antes de decidir; *I've kept my side of the bargain,* he cumplido con mi parte del trato; *one side of the story,* una versión de la historia. **6** *(participant in war, argument, debate, etc)* lado, parte *f,* bando; *(party)* partido: *whose side are you on?,* ¿de qué parte estás?, ¿de parte de quién estás?; *I'm on your side,* estoy de tu parte, estoy de tu lado; *both sides are as bad as each other,* los dos bandos son igual de malos. **7** SP equipo. **8** *(line of descent)* parte *f,* lado: *on his mother's side,* por parte de su madre. **9** GB TV *fam* canal *m.* – **10** *adj* lateral: *use the side door,* utiliza la puerta lateral.
◆ **to side against** *t insep* ponerse contra. ‖ **to side with** *t insep* ponerse de parte de.
● **by the side of,** junto a. ‖ **on/from all sides,** por los cuatro costados. ‖ **on/from every side,** por los cuatro costados. ‖ **on the side,** *(in addition to main job)* como trabajo extra: *he makes a bit of money on the side by giving private classes,* gana algún dinero extra dando clases particulares. ‖ **side by side,** juntos,-as, uno,-a al lado del/de la otro,-a. ‖ **this side of ...,** *(place)* sólo en ...; *(time)* antes de ...: *this side of the year 2000,* antes del año 2000. ‖ **to be on the right/wrong side of fifty,** tener menos/más de cincuenta años. ‖ **to be on the big/small side,** ser más bien grande/pequeño,-a. ‖ **to come down on sb.'s side,** *(gen)* ponerse de parte de algn.; JUR fallar a favor de algn. ‖ **to get on the wrong side of sb.,** ganarse la antipatía de algn. ‖ **to have sth. on one's side,** tener ventaja en algo. ‖ **to keep**

on the right side of sb., tratar de llevarse bien con algn. ‖ **to let the side down,** fallar a algn., hacer quedar mal a algn. ‖ **to put sth. on/to one side,** guardar algo, reservar algo, dejar algo a un lado. ‖ **to take sb. on(to) one side,** llamar a algn. aparte. ‖ **to take sides with sb.,** ponerse de parte de algn.
■ **side dish,** guarnición *f,* acompañamiento. ‖ **side drum,** tambor *m.* ‖ **side effect,** efecto secundario. ‖ **side issue,** tema secundario. ‖ **side street,** calle *f* lateral. ‖ **side view,** vista de perfil.

sideboard ['saɪdbɔːd] *n (furniture)* aparador *m.*

sideboards ['saɪdbɔːdz] *npl* patillas *fpl.*

sideburns ['saɪdbɜːnz] *npl* US → **sideboards.**

sidecar ['saɪdkɑːʳ] *n* sidecar *m.*

sidekick ['ʃaɪdkɪk] *n* US *fam* compinche *m,* amigote *m,* colega *mf.*

sidelight ['saɪdlaɪt] *n* AUTO piloto, luz *f* lateral.

sideline ['saɪdlaɪn] **1** *n* SP línea de banda. **2** *(extra job)* empleo suplementario, trabajo extra; *(extra business)* negocio suplementario; *(product)* línea suplementaria.
● **to sit/stand on the sidelines,** *fig* mantenerse al margen. ‖ **to wait on the sidelines,** *fig* esperar en la sombra.

sidelong ['saɪdlɒŋ] **1** *adj (glance etc)* de soslayo, de reojo. – **2** *adv* de lado.

sidereal [saɪ'dɪərɪəl] *adj* sideral, sidéreo,-a.

side-saddle ['saɪdsædəl] **1** *n* silla de amazona. – **2** *adv* a la amazona.

sideshow ['saɪdʃəʊ] **1** *n (at fair)* puesto de feria, barraca. **2** *fig (less important activity)* acción *f* secundaria.

sidestep ['saɪdstep] **1** *t (question, issue)* eludir, esquivar. – **2** *i* SP *(boxing)* dar un quiebro, hacerse a un lado.
▲ *pt & pp* **sidestepped,** *ger* **sidestepping.**

sidetrack ['saɪdtræk] *t (distract)* distraer; *(divert)* hacer desviar del tema.
● **to get sidetracked,** *(distracted)* distraerse, entretenirse; *(diverted)* desviarse del tema.

sidewalk ['saɪdwɔːk] *n* US acera.

sideways ['saɪdweɪz] **1** *adj (movement, step)* lateral; *(look, glance)* de soslayo, de reojo. – **2** *adv* de lado.
● **to knock sb. sideways,** dejar anonadado,-a a algn. ‖ **to step sideways,** dar un paso hacia un lado.

siding ['saɪdɪŋ] *n (railway)* apartadero, vía muerta.

sidle ['saɪdəl] *i* moverse sigilosamente.
● **to sidle up to sb.,** acercarse sigilosamente a algn.

siege [siːdʒ] **1** *n* MIL sitio, cerco. **2** *(by criminals, journalists)* asedio.
● **to be under seige,** estar sitiado,-a. ‖ **to lay siege to,** *gen* sitiar, cercar, poner sitio a; *fig* asediar, acosar. ‖ **to raise the seige,** levantar el sitio.

sienna [sɪ'enə] *n* (tierra de) siena.

Sierra Leone [sɪeərəlɪ'əʊn] *n* Sierra Leona.

Sierra Leonean [sɪeərəlɪ'əʊnɪən] **1** *adj* sierraleonés,-esa. – **2** *n* sierraleonés,-esa.

siesta [sɪ'estə] *n* siesta.
● **to have a siesta,** echar la siesta, dormir la siesta.

sieve [sɪv] **1** *n (fine)* tamiz *m; (coarse)* criba; *(for liquids)* colador *m.* – **2** *t (fine)* tamizar, pasar por el tamiz; *(coarse)* cribar.
● **to have a memory like a sieve,** tener muy mala memoria.

sift [sɪft] **1** *t (sieve)* tamizar, cribar. **2** *(sprinkle)* espolvorear.
● **to sift through sth.,** *fig* examinar algo cuidadosamente.

sifter ['sɪftəʳ] *n (sieve)* tamiz *m; (sprinkler)* espolvoreador *m.*

sigh [saɪ] **1** n (of person) suspiro. – **2** i (person) suspirar (**for**, por); (wind) susurrar, gemir: she sighed with relief, suspiró aliviada.
● **to breathe/heave a sigh of relief,** dar un suspiro de alivio, respirar aliviado,-a.

sight [saɪt] **1** n (faculty) vista: his sight is failing, le está fallando la vista. **2** (range of vision) vista: don't let him out of your sight!, ¡no lo pierdas de vista!; we waited until he was out of sight, esperamos hasta que hubo desaparecido; get out of my sight!, ¡fuera de mi vista! **3** (act of seeing, view) vista: it was her first sight of the country-side, fue la primera vez que veía el campo; he faints at the sight of blood, se desmaya cuando ve sangre; it was love at first sight, fue amor a primera vista. **4** (thing seen, spectacle) espectáculo: it was a sight to behold, fue un regalo para la vista; it was a sorry sight, fue un triste espectáculo; you look a sight!, ¡tienes una pinta horrorosa!, ¡estás horroroso! **5** (on gun) mira. – **6** t (bird, animal) observar, ver; (person) ver; (land) divisar. – **7** a sight, n fam (a great deal) mucho: a sight better, mucho mejor; a sight more expensive, mucho más caro. – **8** sights, npl (of city) monumentos mpl, lugares mpl de interés: we're going to see the sights, vamos a hacer un recorrido turístico de la cuidad.
● **in one's sights,** en la mira. ‖ **in/within sight,** a la vista. ‖ **in the sight of God,** ante Dios. ‖ **out of sight,** US (very good) alucinante. ‖ **out of sight, out of mind,** ojos que no ven, corazón que no siente. ‖ **sight unseen,** sin haberlo visto antes. ‖ **to be a sight for sore eyes,** dar gusto verlo. ‖ **to catch sight of,** ver, divisar. ‖ **to come into sight,** aparecer. ‖ **to hate/loathe the sight of sb.,** no poder ni ver a algn. ‖ **to keep out of sight,** no dejarse ver, esconderse. ‖ **to know sb. by sight,** conocer a algn. de vista. ‖ **to lose sight of sb./ sth.,** perder a algn./algo de vista. ‖ **to raise one's sights,** aspirar a más, apuntar más alto. ‖ **to set one's sights on sth.,** tener la mira puesta en algo. ‖ **to take a sight,** apuntar.

sighted ['saɪtɪd] adj vidente.
● **to be partially sighted,** tener visión parcial, tener problemas de vista.

sighting ['saɪtɪŋ] n observación f: there have been several sightings of the wanted man, se ha visto al hombre buscado en varias ocasiones.

sightless ['saɪtləs] adj ciego,-a, invidente.

sightly ['saɪtlɪ] adj atractivo,-a, agradable a la vista.

sight-read ['saɪtriːd] **1** t repentizar. – **2** i repentizar.

sight-reading ['saɪtriːdɪŋ] n repentización f.

sightseeing ['saɪtsiːɪŋ] n visita turística, turismo.
● **to go sightseeing,** visitar los monumentos y lugares de interés.
■ **sightseeing tour,** excursión f turística, recorrido turístico.

sightseer ['saɪtsɪəʳ] n turista mf, visitante mf.

sign [saɪn] **1** n (symbol) signo, símbolo. **2** (gesture) gesto, seña; (signal) señal f: wait until I give the sign, espera hasta que dé la señal; he made signs to us to go away, no hizo señales para que nos fuéramos. **3** (indication) señal f, indicio, muestra; (proof) prueba; (trace) rastro: it's a sure sign of rain, es un claro indicio de lluvia; that must be a good sign, eso debe de ser (una) buena señal; talking to oneself is the first sign of madness, hablar solo es el primer signo de locura; there was no sign of them anywhere, no se los veía por ninguna parte, no había ni rastro de ellos; there are no signs of life in this village, no hay señales de vida en este pueblo; she's showing signs of improvement, da muestras de mejoría; all the

signs are that ..., todo parece indicar que ... **4** (board) letrero; (notice) anuncio, aviso; (over shop) letrero, rótulo. – **5** t (letter, document, cheque, etc) firmar: sign your name here, please, firme aquí, por favor; the two countries signed a treaty, los dos países firmaron un tratado. **6** (player, group) fichar (**on/up**, -): Spurs have signed a new player, los Spurs han fichado un nuevo jugador. **7** (gesture) hacer una seña/señal: he signed me to shut up, me hizo una señal para que me callara. – **8** i (write name) firmar. **9** (player, group) fichar (**for/with**, por): Laudrup signed for Real Madrid, Laudrup fichó por el Real Madrid. **10** US (use sign language) comunicarse por señas, hablar por señas.
◆ **to sign away** t sep ceder. ‖ **to sign for** t insep (goods, parcel, etc) firmar el recibo de. ‖ **to sign in** i firmar el registro. ‖ **to sign off** i despedirse. ‖ **to sign on 1** t sep (worker) contratar. – **2** i (student) matricularse; (soldier) alistarse. **3** GB fam (unemployed person - first time) apuntarse al paro; (- periodically) sellar. ‖ **to sign out** i firmar el registro. ‖ **to sign over** t sep ceder mediante un escrito. ‖ **to sign up 1** t sep (soldier) reclutar; (worker) contratar. – **2** i (soldier) alistarse; (student) matricularse, inscribirse.
● **as a sign of,** como muestra de. ‖ **a sign of the times,** un signo de los tiempos que corren; ‖ **to make the sign of the cross,** hacer la señal de la cruz. ‖ **to sign one's own death warrant,** firmar su propia sentencia de muerte.
■ **plus sign,** signo de más. ‖ **sign language,** lenguaje m por señas. ‖ **sign of the zodiac,** signo del zodíaco. ‖ **traffic sign,** señal f de tráfico.

signal ['sɪgnəl] **1** n (gen) señal f: hand signal, señal con la mano; traffic signal, señal de tráfico; a red light is the signal for danger, una luz roja es la señal de peligro. **2** US (telephone) señal f: busy signal, señal de comunicar. **3** RAD TV señal f. **4** (railway) señal f. – **5** adj (achievement, triumph, success, etc) señalado,-a, destacado,-a, notable; (failure) rotundo,-a. – **6** t (indicate) indicar, señalar, marcar; (forecast) pronosticar: it signals a definite change in policy, indica sin duda un cambio de política; it signalled the end of an era, marcó el fin de una época. **7** (gesture) hacer señas: he signalled the waiter to bring the bill, le hizo una seña al camarero para que trajera la cuenta. **8** AUTO indicar. – **9** i (gesture) hacer señas, hacer una seña: she was signalling to us frantically, nos hacía señas frenéticamente; the teacher signalled for silence, el profesor hizo una seña para que callaran. **10** AUTO poner el intermitente.
■ **signal box,** garita de señales.

signalman ['sɪgnəlmən] n (railway) guardavía m.
▲ pl signalmen ['sɪgnəlmən].

signatory ['sɪgnətərɪ] n fml firmante mf, signatario,-a.
▲ pl signatories.

signature ['sɪgnɪtʃəʳ] n (name) firma.
■ **signature tune,** sintonía.

signboard ['saɪnbɔːd] n (sign) letrero; (noticeboard) tablón m de anuncios; (hoarding) cartelera.

signet ['sɪgnət] n sello.
■ **signet ring,** (anillo) sello.

significance [sɪg'nɪfɪkəns] **1** n (meaning) significado. **2** (importance) importancia, trascendencia: it's of no significance, no tiene importancia.

significant [sɪg'nɪfɪkənt] **1** adj (meaningful - gen) significativo,-a; (look etc) elocuente, expresivo,-a. **2** (important) importante, trascendente, considerable.

significantly [sɪg'nɪfɪkəntlɪ] **1** adv (considerably, notably) considerablemente, apreciablemente. **2** (meaningfully - used alone) lo cual es significativo.

signify ['sɪɡnɪfaɪ] 1 *t fml* (*mean*) significar; (*denote*) indicar, ser indicio de. 2 *fml* (*show, make known*) mostrar, expresar.
▲ *pt & pp signified, ger signifying.*
signing ['saɪnɪŋ] *n* GB (*of player, group*) fichaje *m*.
signpost ['saɪnpəʊst] 1 *n* poste *m* indicador. – 2 *t* (*route*) señalizar.
signwriter ['saɪnraɪtə'] *n* rotulista *mf*.
Sikh [siːk] 1 *n* sij *mf*. – 2 *adj* sij.
silage ['saɪlɪdʒ] *n* ensilado, ensilaje *m*.
silence ['saɪləns] 1 *n* (*gen*) silencio: *a deathly silence,* un silencio sepulcral; *we walked in silence,* caminamos en silencio; *they observed a two-minute silence,* guardaron dos minutos de silencio. – 2 *t* (*person*) acallar, hacer callar; (*protest, opposition, criticism*) apagar, silenciar.
● **to reduce sb. to silence,** dejar a algn. sin habla. ‖ **silence is golden,** el silencio es oro.
silencer ['saɪlənsə'] *n* silenciador *m*.
silent ['saɪlənt] 1 *adj* (*thing, place, taciturn person*) silencioso,-a. 2 (*not speaking*) callado,-a: *please remain silent,* guarden silencio por favor; *he was silent for a moment,* se quedó callado un momento; *you have the right to remain silent,* tiene derecho a guardar silencio; *the law is silent on this point,* la ley no dice nada sobre este punto. 3 (*film, consonant*) mudo,-a; (*prayer*) silencioso,-a: *the letter "p" is silent,* la "p" no se pronuncia.
● **the silent majority,** la mayoría silenciosa. ‖ **to be silent,** callarse.
■ **silent partner,** socio,-a comanditario,-a.
silently ['saɪləntlɪ] *adv* (*without making a noise*) silenciosamente; (*without talking*) en silencio.
silhouette [sɪluːˈet] *n* silueta.
● **to see sth. in silhouette,** ver la silueta de algo. ‖ **to be silhouetted against sth.,** recortarse contra algo.
silica ['sɪlɪkə] *n* sílice *f*.
silicate ['sɪlɪkeɪt] *n* silicato.
silicon ['sɪlɪkən] *n* silicio.
■ **silicon chip,** chip *m* (de silicio).
silicone ['sɪlɪkəʊn] *n* silicona.
■ **silicone implant,** implantación *f* de silicona.
silicosis [sɪlɪˈkəʊsɪs] *n* silicosis *f*.
silk [sɪlk] 1 *n* (*gen*) seda: *raw/pure silk,* seda cruda/natural. 2 GB JUR fiscal *mf*. – 3 *adj* de seda. – 4 **silks,** *npl* (*jockeys' shirts*) colores *mpl*.
● **to take silk,** GB JUR nombrarse fiscal. ‖ **you can't make a silk purse from/out of a sow's ear,** no se puede pedir peras al olmo.
■ **silk screen,** serigrafía.
silken ['sɪlkən] *adj* (*like silk*) sedoso,-a; (*of silk*) de seda.
silk-screen printing ['sɪlkskriːnprɪntɪŋ] *n* serigrafía.
silkworm ['sɪlkwɜːm] *n* gusano de seda.
silky ['sɪlkɪ] *adj* (*cloth, hair, fur, etc*) sedoso,-a; (*voice*) aterciopelado,-a; (*skin*) suave.
▲ *comp silkier, superl silkiest.*
sill [sɪl] *n* (*of window*) alféizar *m*, antepecho; (*on vehicle*) solera de puerta.
silliness ['sɪlɪnəs] 1 *n* (*quality*) estupidez *f*, necedad *f*. 2 (*act*) tontería, bobada.
silly ['sɪlɪ] 1 *adj* (*stupid*) tonto,-a, estúpido,-a, necio,-a, bobo,-a; (*ridiculous*) ridículo,-a: *how silly of me!,* ¡qué tonto soy!; *you look really silly in those boots,* estás ridícula con esas botas. 2 (*unimportant*) trivial, sin importancia. 3 *fam* (*senseless*) atontado,-a: *he knocked me silly,* me dejó atontado. – 4 *n* tonto,-a, bobo,-a.
● **to do sth. silly,** hacer una tontería. ‖ **to drink os. silly,** pillar una borrachera. ‖ **to make sb. look silly,** dejar a algn. en ridículo.

■ **silly season,** período veraniego en que los periódicos están llenos de noticias triviales.
▲ *comp sillier, superl silliest.*
silly-billy ['sɪlɪbɪlɪ] *n fam* tonto,-a, bobo,-a.
silo ['saɪləʊ] *n* silo.
▲ *pl silos.*
silt [sɪlt] *n* cieno, limo, légamo.
◆ **to silt up** 1 *i* encenagarse. – 2 *t sep* encenagar.
silver ['sɪlvə'] 1 *n* (*metal*) plata: *sterling silver,* plata de ley. 2 (*coins*) monedas *fpl* (de plata). 3 (*articles, ornaments, etc*) plata; (*tableware*) vajilla de plata. – 4 *adj* (*made of silver*) de plata. 5 (*in colour*) plateado,-a; (*hair*) canoso,-a, cano,-a. – 6 *t* (*metal*) dar un baño de plata a, platear.
■ **silver birch,** BOT abedul *m*. ‖ **silver foil / silver paper,** papel *m* de plata. ‖ **silver medal,** medalla de plata. ‖ **silver plate,** (*layer*) plateado; (*objects*) artículos *mpl* plateados. ‖ **silver screen,** el cine *m*. ‖ **silver wedding,** bodas *fpl* de plata.
silverfish ['sɪlvəfɪʃ] *n* lepisma.
silver-plated [sɪlvəˈpleɪtɪd] *adj* plateado,-a.
silversmith ['sɪlvəsmɪθ] *n* platero,-a, orfebre *mf*.
silverware ['sɪlvəweə'] *n* plata, vajilla de plata.
silvery ['sɪlvərɪ] 1 *adj* (*colour, material*) plateado,-a; (*hair*) canoso,-a, cano,-a. 2 (*sound*) argentino,-a.
similar ['sɪmɪlə'] *adj* parecido,-a (**to,** a), similar (**to,** a), semejante (**to,** a): *these artists have similar styles,* estos artistas tienen estilos parecidos; *the two flats are similar in size,* los dos pisos son de tamaño parecido; *those boys are very similar,* esos chicos se parecen mucho; *I have a similar problem to yours,* tengo un problema parecido al tuyo.
■ **similar triangle,** triángulo semejante.
similarity [sɪmɪˈlærətɪ] 1 *n* (*likeness - betwen things*) semejanza, parecido, similitud *f*; (*- between people*) parecido. 2 (*common feature*) característica común.
▲ *pl similarities.*
similarly ['sɪmɪləlɪ] 1 *adv* (*in a similar way*) de modo parecido, de modo similar; (*equally*) igualmente. 2 (*also, likewise*) del mismo modo, asimismo.
simile ['sɪmɪlɪ] *n* símil *m*.
simmer ['sɪmə'] 1 *t* CULIN hervir a fuego lento. – 2 *i* CULIN hervir a fuego lento. 3 (*person*) hervir, estar a punto de estallar (**with,** de). 4 (*violence, quarrel*) fermentar.
◆ **to simmer down** *i* calmarse, tranquilizarse.
simper ['sɪmpə'] 1 *n* sonrisa afectada. – 2 *i* sonreír con afectación.
simpering ['sɪmpərɪŋ] 1 *adj* melindroso,-a. – 2 *n* melindres *mpl*.
simple ['sɪmpəl] 1 *adj* (*easy, straightforward*) sencillo,-a, fácil, simple: *a simple solution,* una solución sencilla; *it's not as simple as that,* no es tan sencillo como eso; *this is simple,* esto es fácil. 2 (*plain, not elaborate*) sencillo,-a, simple: *a simple dress,* un vestido sencillo; *simple food,* comida sencilla. 3 (*not compound*) simple, sencillo,-a: *a simple sentence,* una frase simple; *a simple form of life,* una forma de vida sencilla. 4 (*plain, pure, nothing more than*) sencillo,-a, puro,-a, mero,-a: *for the simple reason that ...,* por la sencilla razón que ...; *simple greed,* pura codicia. 5 (*unsophisticated, ordinary*) simple, sencillo,-a: *simple people,* gente sencilla; *simple tastes,* gustos sencillos. 6 (*genuine, sincere*) sencillo,-a; (*foolish*) tonto,-a; (*naive, easily deceived*) ingenuo,-a, inocente, simple; (*backward, weak-minded*) simple, corto,-a de alcances: *she's simple enough to believe anything,* es tan ingenua que se cree cualquier cosa.
■ **simple fracture,** fractura simple. ‖ **simple interest,** interés *m* simple.

simple-minded [sɪmpəl'maɪndɪd] *adj* simple, ingenuo,-a.

simpleton ['sɪmpəltən] *n dated* simplón,-ona.

simplicity [sɪm'plɪsətɪ] **1** *n* (*easiness, incomplexity*) sencillez *f*, simplicidad *f*. **2** (*lack of sophistication*) sencillez *f*, naturalidad *f*. **3** (*foolishness*) simpleza; (*naivety*) ingenuidad *f*.
● **to be simplicity itself,** ser de lo más sencillo.

simplification [sɪmplɪfɪ'keɪʃən] *n* simplificación *f*.

simplify ['sɪmplɪfaɪ] *t* simplificar.
▲ *pt & pp* simplified, *ger* simplifying.

simplistic [sɪm'plɪstɪk] *adj* simplista.

simply ['sɪmplɪ] **1** *adv* (*easily, plainly, modestly*) simplemente, sencillamente: *to put it simply,* para decirlo sencillamente; *she lives very simply,* vive muy sencillamente. **2** (*only*) simplemente, solamente, sólo; (*just, merely*) meramente: *their job is simply to keep watch,* su trabajo consiste simplemente en vigilar; *it's simply a question of luck,* sólo es cuestión de suerte; *I did it simply because I felt like it,* lo hice simplemente porque me dio la gana; *I simply don't know,* sencillamente, no lo sé. **3** (*really, absolutely*) francamente, realmente: *simply awful,* francamente horrible; *simply scrumptious,* francamente delicioso; *you simply must come to my party!,* ¡tienes que venir a mi fiesta!

simulate ['sɪmjəleɪt] *t* (*reproduce*) simular; (*imitate*) imitar; (*feign*) fingir, simular.

simulated ['sɪmjəleɪtɪd] *adj* (*flight, conditions, attack*) simulado,-a; (*leather etc*) de imitación, sintético,-a; (*jewels*) de imitación, artificiales: *a simulated nuclear explosion,* un simulacro de explosión nuclear.

simulation [sɪmjə'leɪʃən] *n* (*reproduction*) simulación *f*, simulacro.

simulator ['sɪmjəleɪtə'] *n* simulador *m*.

simultaneous [sɪməl'teɪnɪəs] *adj* simultáneo,-a: *simultaneous translation,* traducción simultánea.
■ **simultaneous equations,** MATH sistema *m* de ecuaciones.

simultaneously [sɪmə'teɪnɪəslɪ] *adv* simultáneamente, a la vez.

sin [sɪn] **1** *n* pecado: *mortal sin,* pecado mortal; *it's a sin to waste all that food,* es un pecado tirar toda esa comida. **- 2** *i* pecar (**against,** contra).
● **for one's sins,** para su castigo. ‖ **to be as ugly as sin,** ser feo,-a como un pecado. ‖ **to live in sin,** vivir en concubinato, vivir amancebado,-a, vivir en pecado.
▲ *pt & pp* sinned, *ger* sinning.

since [sɪns] **1** *adv* desde entonces: *he left 10 years ago and I haven't seen him since,* se marchó hace 10 años y desde entonces no lo he visto; *she arrived in 1988 and has lived here ever since,* llegó en 1988 y vive aquí desde entonces; *I've long since stopped worrying about my weight,* hace mucho que dejé de preocuparme por mi peso. **- 2** *prep* desde: *I've been here since four o'clock,* llevo aquí desde las cuatro; *he's worked there since 1980,* trabaja allí desde 1980; *I haven't seen her since last summer,* no la veo desde el verano pasado; *how long is it since your party?,* ¿cuánto (tiempo) hace de tu fiesta?; *since when do you call the shots round here?,* ¿desde cuándo mandas tú por aquí? **- 3** *conj* (*time*) desde que: *he hasn't worked since he had the accident,* no trabaja desde que tuvo el accidente; *it's years since I went to the theatre,* hace años que no voy al teatro; *since moving here, she's taken up painting,* desde que se trasladó aquí, ha empezado a pintar; *how long is it since we had a holiday?,* ¿cuánto hace que no tenemos

vacaciones? **4** (*because, seeing that*) ya que, puesto que: *since you're going to the shop ...,* ya que vas a la tienda ...; *since you haven't got any money ...,* ya que tú no tienes dinero ...

sincere [sɪn'sɪə'] *adj* sincero,-a.

sincerely [sɪn'sɪəlɪ] *adv* sinceramente.
● **Yours sincerely,** (*in letter*) (le saluda) atentamente.

sincerity [sɪn'serətɪ] *n* sinceridad *f*: *in all sincerity,* con toda sinceridad.

sine [saɪn] *n* MATH seno.

sinecure ['saɪnɪkjʊə'] *n* sinecura.

sinew ['sɪnju:] **1** *n* (*tendon*) tendón *m*; (*in meat*) nervio. **- 2** sinews, *npl fig* fuerza *f sing*, vigor *m sing*.

sinewy ['sɪnjuɪ] *adj* nervudo,-a.

sinful ['sɪnfʊl] **1** *adj* (*person*) pecador,-ra. **2** (*thought, act*) pecaminoso,-a. **3** *fam* (*waste*) escandaloso,-a.

sing [sɪŋ] **1** *t* (*gen*) cantar. **- 2** *i* (*person, bird*) cantar; (*wind, kettle, bullet*) silbar; (*ears, insect*) zumbar. **3** US *sl* cantar.
◆ **to sing along** *i* cantar. ‖ **to sing out 1** *i* (*sing loudly*) cantar fuerte. **2** (*shout*) gritar. ‖ **to sing up** *i* cantar fuerte.
● **to sing a baby to sleep,** arrullar a un niño (cantando). ‖ **to sing a different song/tune,** cambiar de opinión. ‖ **to sing sth's/sb.'s praises,** alabar algo/a algn.
▲ *pt* sang, *pp* sung.

Singapore [sɪŋgə'pɔ:'] *n* Singapur.

singe [sɪndʒ] **1** *t* chamuscar: *he singed his eyebrows,* se chamuscó las cejas. **- 2** *n* quemadura (superficial).

singer ['sɪŋə'] *n* (*gen*) cantante *mf*; (*in choir*) cantor,-ra: *jazz singer,* cantante de jazz.

singing ['sɪŋɪŋ] *n* (*act*) canto, cantar *m*; (*songs*) canciones *fpl*; (*of kettle*) silbido; (*in ears*) zumbido: *he loves singing in the shower,* le encanta cantar en la ducha; *she has a fine singing voice,* tiene buena voz.
■ **singing lesson,** clase *f* de canto.

single ['sɪŋgəl] **1** *adj* (*only one*) solo,-a, único,-a: *we heard a single scream,* oímos un solo grito; *a single blow,* un solo golpe; *not a single person came,* no vino ni una sola persona. **2** (*composed of one part*) simple, sencillo,-a: *single figures,* cifras de un solo dígito; *a single flower,* una flor simple; *a single yellow line,* una línea amarilla sencilla. **3** (*for one person*) individual. **4** (*separate, individual*) cada: *she copied every single word,* copió cada palabra; *every single day,* todos los días; *it's the single most important cause,* es la causa más importante. **5** (*unmarried*) soltero,-a. **- 6** *n* GB (*single ticket*) billete *m* de ida, billete *m* sencillo. **7** (*record*) (*disco*) sencillo, single *m*. **8** SP (*in cricket*) tanto; (*in baseball*) sencillo. **9** US (*one dollar bill*) billete *m* de un dólar. **- 10** singles, *npl* SP (*in tennis, badminton*) individuales *mpl*.
◆ **to single out 1** *t sep* (*choose*) escoger, seleccionar. **2** (*distinguish*) distinguir, destacar, resaltar.
● **in single file,** en fila india.
■ **single combat,** combate *m* singular. ‖ **single cream,** nata líquida. ‖ **single parent,** (*mother*) madre *f* soltera; (*father*) padre *m* soltero. ‖ **single room,** habitación *f* individual.

single-breasted [sɪŋgəl'brestɪd] *adj* (*jacket, suit*) recto,-a, sin cruzar.

single-decker [sɪŋgəl'dekə'] *n* autobús *m* de un solo piso.

single-handed [sɪŋgəl'hændɪd] **1** *adj* sin ayuda, solo,-a. **- 2** *adv* sin ayuda, solo,-a.

single-minded [sɪŋgəl'maɪndɪd] *adj* resuelto,-a, decidido,-a.

singleness ['sɪŋgəlnəs] singleness of purpose, *phr* resolución *f*, determinación *f*.

single-parent ['sɪŋgəlpeərənt] *adj* (*family*) monoparental.

single-sex ['sɪŋgəlseks] *adj* (*school - for boys*) sólo para niños; (*- for girls*) sólo para niñas.

singlet ['sɪŋglət] *n* GB (*vest*) camiseta.

singly ['sɪŋglɪ] *adv* (*separately*) por separado; (*one by one*) uno por uno, individualmente.

sing-song ['sɪŋsɒŋ] **1** *adj* (*voice, tone*) cantarín,-ina. **– 2** *n* (*voice, tone*) sonsonete *m*. **3** (*singing session*) ocasión informal en que la gente se pone a cantar: *we had a sing-song in the pub,* nos pusimos a cantar en el pub.

singular ['sɪŋgjʊləʳ] **1** *adj* GRAM singular. **2** *fml* (*outstanding*) extraordinario,-a, excepcional, singular. **3** *fml* (*unique, unusual*) único,-a, extraño,-a, singular. **– 4** *n* LING singular *m*.

● **in the singular,** en singular.

singularity [sɪŋjə'lærətɪ] *n fml* singularidad *f*.
▲ *pl* **singularities**.

singularly ['sɪŋgjələlɪ] *adv fml* extraordinariamente, excepcionalmente, singularmente.

Sinhalese [sɪnhæ'liːz] **1** *adj* cingalés,-esa. **– 2** *n* (*person*) cingalés,-esa. **3** (*language*) cingalés *m*. **– 4** **the Sinhalese,** *npl* los cingaleses *mpl*.

sinister ['sɪnɪstəʳ] *adj* siniestro,-a.

sink [sɪŋk] **1** *n* (*in kitchen*) fregadero, pila; (*in bathroom*) lavabo, lavamanos *m*. **– 2** *t* (*ship*) hundir, echar a pique. **3** *fig* (*hopes, plans*) acabar con. **4** (*hole, shaft, tunnel*) cavar, excavar; (*well*) abrir; (*post, pipe, cable*) enterrar; (*knife*) clavar, hundir; (*teeth*) hincar (**into,** en). **5** (*forget*) olvidar, dejar a un lado. **6** (*invest*) invertir (**into,** en). **7** GB *fam* (*drink*) soplar. **8** SP (*snooker, golf*) meter. **– 9** *i* (*ship*) hundirse, irse al pique; (*stone, wood, etc*) hundirse. **10** (*land, building*) hundirse. **11** (*sun, moon*) ponerse. **12** (*figures, prices, value*) bajar; (*water, level*) descender, bajar: *his voice sank to a whisper,* su voz se convirtió en un susurro. **13** *fig* (*hopes etc*) venirse abajo: *my heart sank,* se me cayó el alma a los pies. **14** (*person*) dejarse caer: *he sank bank into an armchair,* se dejó caer en un sillón; *she sank to her knees,* cayó de rodillas. **15** (*decline*) hundirse (**into,** en), caer (**into,** en): *she sank into a deep depression,* cayó en una profunda depresión; *they sank into poverty,* se hundieron en la miseria; *how could you sink so low?,* ¿cómo has podido caer tan bajo?; *he has sunk in our estimation,* ha bajado en nuestra estima. **16** (*deteriorate*) empeorar: *the patient is sinking fast,* el paciente está empeorando rápidamente.

◆ **to sink in** **1** *i* (*liquids*) penetrar. **2** *fig* (*words*) causar impresión; (*news, idea, fact*) hacer impacto: *I don't think it's sunk in yet,* no creo que lo haya asimilado todavía.

● **to leave sb. to sink or swim,** abandonar a algn. a su suerte. ‖ **to be sunk,** (*finished*) estar perdido,-a. ‖ **to be sunk in thought,** estar sumido,-a en sus pensamientos. ‖ **to sink one's differences,** hacer las paces.
▲ *pt* **sank,** *pp* **sunk**.

sinker ['sɪŋkəʳ] *n* plomo.

sinking ['sɪŋkɪŋ] *n* MAR hundimiento.
● **that sinking feeling,** esa desazón.
■ **sinking fund,** fondo de amortización.

sinuous ['sɪnjʊəs] *adj* sinuoso,-a, serpenteante.

sinus ['saɪnəs] *n* seno.

sip [sɪp] **1** *n* sorbo. **– 2** *t* sorber, beber a sorbos. **– 3** *i* beber a sorbos (**at,** -).
▲ *pt & pp* **sipped,** *ger* **sipping**.

siphon ['saɪfən] *n* (*gen*) sifón *m*.
◆ **to siphon off** *t sep* (*liquid*) sacar con sifón; (*funds, traffic*) desviar.

sir [sɜːʳ] **1** *n fml* (*gen*) señor *m*: *yes, sir,* sí, señor. **2** MIL (*to captain*) mi capitán; (*to general*) mi general; (*to lieutenant*) mi teniente: *sir,* ¡a la orden!, ¡a sus órdenes! **3** (*title*) sir *m*: *Sir Winston Churchill,* Sir Winston Churchill.
● **Dear Sir,** (*in letter*) muy señor mío, muy señores míos, estimado señor.

sire ['saɪəʳ] **1** *t* (*beget*) engendrar, ser padre de. **– 2** *n* (*animal*) macho.

siren ['saɪərən] *n* (*gen*) sirena.

sirloin ['sɜːlɔɪn] *n* solomillo.

sissy ['sɪsɪ] *n fam pej* (*effeminate*) afeminado,-a, mariquita *mf*; (*cowardly*) miedica *mf*, gallina *mf*.
▲ *pl* **sissies**.

sister ['sɪstəʳ] **1** *n* (*relative*) hermana. **2** (*comrade*) hermana, compañera. **3** GB enfermera jefe. **4** REL (*nun*) hermana, monja; (*before name*) Sor. **5** (*company, organization*) hermana.
■ **sister ship,** barco gemelo.

sisterhood ['sɪstəhʊd] *n* hermandad *f*.

sister-in-law ['sɪstərɪnlɔː] *n* cuñada, hermana política.
▲ *pl* **sisters-in-law**.

sisterly ['sɪstəlɪ] *adj* (*propio,-a*) de hermana.

sit [sɪt] **1** *t* (*child etc*) sentar (**down, -**): *she sat him down on the table,* lo sentó en la mesa; *he sat himself down,* se sentó. **2** (*room, hall, etc*) tener cabida para; (*table*) ser para: *the theatre seats 200 people,* el teatro tiene cabida para 200 personas. **3** GB EDUC (*exam*) presentarse a. **– 4** *i* (*action*) sentarse (**down, -**): *I sat next to Anna,* me senté junto a Anna; *sit down, please,* siéntese, por favor; *sit!,* ¡siéntate! **5** (*be seated*) estar sentado,-a: *they were sitting on the floor,* estaban sentados en el suelo; *she was sitting at the table,* estaba sentada a la mesa; *David usually sits there,* normalmente David se sienta allí. **6** (*village, building*) ubicarse, hallarse, estar, situarse; (*object*) estar; (*clothes*) sentar, quedar: *the village sits on top of the hill,* el pueblo está situado encima de la colina; *the book sat on the shelf,* el libro estaba en el estante; *that dress sits well on you,* aquel vestido te sienta bien. **7** (*person*) quedarse: *don't just sit there!,* ¡no te quedes allí sentado!; *he can't sit still,* no puede quedarse quieto. **8** ART (*model*) posar (**for,** para). **9** (*bird*) posarse (**on,** en); (*hen on eggs*) empollar (**on, -**). **10** (*be a member*) ser miembro (**on,** de), formar parte (**on,** de): *he sits on a jury,* es miembro de un jurado. **11** (*parliament etc*) reunirse (en sesión): *the House sat until 2.00 am,* la Cámara estuvo reunida hasta las 2.00. **– 12** *t* GB POL (*represent*) representar (**for,** a), ser diputado,-a (**for,** por). **– 13** *i fam* (*babysit*) hacer de canguro (**for,** a).

◆ **to sit about / sit around** *i fam* (*be lazy*) holgazanear, hacer el vago; (*wait*) esperar sentado,-a. ‖ **to sit back** **1** *i* (*lean back*) recostarse; (*relax*) ponerse cómodo,-a. **2** (*take no active part*) cruzarse de brazos: *he just sat back and did nothing,* se cruzó de brazos, no levantó ni un dedo para ayudar. ‖ **to sit by** *i* (*do nothing*) quedarse sin hacer nada, estarse quieto,-a. ‖ **to sit for** *t insep* GB EDUC (*exam*) presentarse a. ‖ **to sit in for** *t insep* (*take place*) sustituir a. ‖ **to sit in on** *i* (*attend*) asistir a (sin participar), estar presente en. ‖ **to sit on** **1** *t insep fam* (*delay*) retener; (*keep secret*) mantener oculto,-a. **2** (*silence*) hacer callar; (*discipline, control*) poner en su sitio. ‖ **to sit out** **1** *t sep* (*stay until end*) aguantar (hasta el final); (*wait until over*) esperar que acabe. **2** (*not dance*) no bailar. ‖ **to sit through** *t insep* (*stay until end*) aguantar (hasta el final). ‖ **to sit up** **1** *i* (*in bed*) incorporarse (en la cama); (*straight*) ponerse derecho. **2** (*stay up late*) quedarse levantado,-a, no acostarse: *don't sit up for me,* no me esperes levantado. **– 3** *t sep* (*child etc*) sentar.

● **to sit in judgement on,** enjuiciar a. ‖ **to sit on one's hands,** cruzarse de brazos, estar mano sobre mano. ‖ **to sit on sb.'s tail,** pisarle los talones a algn. ‖ **to sit on the fence,** ver los toros desde la barrera, nadar entre dos aguas. ‖ **to sit tight,** mantenerse en sus trece, quedarse en un sitio. ‖ **to sit up and take notice,** prestar atención.
▲ *pt* & *pp* **sat,** *ger* **sitting.**

sit-down ['sɪtdaʊn] **1** *n* (*protest*) sentada; (*strike*) huelga de brazos cruzados. **2** (*rest*) breve descanso.
■ **sit-down meal,** comida servida en la mesa.

site [saɪt] **1** *n* (*location*) situación *f*, emplazamiento, colocación *f*. **2** (*area, land*) terreno, lugar *m*, solar *m*. – **3** *t* situar, ubicar, emplazar.
● **on site,** en el recinto.
■ **archeological site,** yacimiento arqueológico.

sit-in ['sɪtɪn] *n* (*protest*) sentada; (*strike*) huelga de brazos cruzados.

siting ['saɪtɪŋ] *n* emplazamiento.

sitter ['sɪtə'] **1** *n* ART modelo *mf*. **2** (*baby sitter*) canguro *mf*. **3** (*hen*) gallina clueca. **4** (*easy thing to do*) cosa muy fácil, cosa chupada: *he missed a sitter,* falló un gol cantado.

sitting ['sɪtɪŋ] **1** *n* (*of meal*) turno; (*of committee, for portrait*) sesión *f*. – **2** *adj* (*position*) sentado,-a.
● **in a sitting / at a single sitting,** de una sentada, de un tirón. ‖ **sitting duck,** presa fácil, blanco seguro. ‖ **to be sitting pretty,** estar bien situado,-a, estar en una posición aventajada.
■ **sitting member,** POL miembro *mf* activo,-a. ‖ **sitting room,** GB sala de estar, salón *m*, living *m*. ‖ **sitting target,** blanco fácil. ‖ **sitting tenant,** inquilino,-a (con derecho a propiedad).

situate ['sɪtjʊeɪt] *t fml* situar, ubicar, emplazar.

situated ['sɪtjʊeɪtɪd] *adj* (*of building etc*) situado,-a, ubicado,-a.
● **to be well/badly situated,** (*person*) estar en una buena/mala situación: *how are you situated for money?,* ¿cómo andas de dinero?

situation [sɪtjʊ'eɪʃən] **1** *n* (*circumstances*) situación *f*: *the current political situation,* la situación política actual; *we're in a very difficult situation,* estamos en una situación muy difícil. **2** *dated* (*job, position*) empleo, puesto. **3** (*location*) situación *f*, ubicación *f*.
● **"situations vacant",** "demandas de trabajo".
■ **situation comedy,** telecomedia.

sit-up ['sɪtʌp] *n* SP abdominal *m*.

six [sɪks] **1** *adj* seis: *it costs six pounds,* cuesta seis libras; *turn to page six,* pasa a la página seis; *six hundred,* seiscientos,-as; *six thousand,* seis mil. – **2** *n* seis *m*: *she's six years old,* tiene seis años; *it's six o'clock,* son las seis; *six and six are twelve,* seis más seis son doce; *the six of diamonds,* el seis de diamantes; *all six of them,* todos seis. **3** SP (*in cricket*) seis puntos *mpl*.
● **it's six of one and half a dozen of the other,** (*not important*) viene a ser lo mismo, da lo mismo, da igual; (*both people's fault*) los dos tienen parte de la culpa. ‖ **six of the best,** una paliza. ‖ **to be at sixes and sevens,** estar confuso,-a, estar hecho,-a un lío. ‖ **to knock sb. for six,** dejar anonadado,-a a algn.

sixfold ['sɪksfəʊld] **1** *adj* séxtuplo,-a. – **2** *adv* por seis, seis veces.

six-pack ['sɪkspæk] *n* (*of beer*) paquete *m de* seis botellas o latas *de cerveza.*

sixpence ['sɪkspəns] *n* GB *dated* moneda de seis peniques.

sixteen [sɪks'tiːn] **1** *adj* dieciséis. – **2** *n* dieciséis *m*.
▲ *Véase también* **six.**

sixteenth [sɪks'tiːnθ] **1** *adj* decimosexto,-a. – **2** *adv* en decimosexto lugar. – **3** *n* (*in series*) decimosexto,-a. **4** (*fraction*) decimosexto; (*one part*) decimosexta parte *f*.
■ **sixteenth note,** US semicorchea.
▲ *Véase también* **sixth.**

sixth [sɪksθ] **1** *adj* sexto,-a: *the sixth floor,* la sexta planta, el sexto piso; *it's their sixth wedding anniversary,* es su sexto aniversario de boda; *the sixth century,* el siglo sexto; *tomorrow's her sixth birthday,* mañana cumple seis años. – **2** *adv* sexto, en sexto lugar: *he came sixth,* llegó en sexto lugar. – **3** *n* (*in series*) sexto,-a; (*day*) el seis, el día seis: *Henry the Sixth,* Enrique sexto; *Arencón was sixth,* Arencón fue sexto, Arencón quedó sexto; *the sixth of June,* el seis de junio; *January the sixth,* el seis de enero; *I'm arriving on the sixth,* llego el día seis; *your fax of the sixth,* su fax del día seis. **4** (*fraction*) sexto; (*one part*) sexta parte *f*: *five sixths of the population,* cinco sextos de la población, cinco de cada seis habitantes; *one sixth of the pupils,* una sexta parte del alumnado, uno de cada seis alumnos.
■ **sixth form,** GB EDUC ≈ COU. ‖ **sixth form college,** GB EDUC ≈ *instituto para estudiantes de* COU. ‖ **sixth former,** GB EDUC ≈ estudiante *mf* de COU. ‖ **sixth sense,** sexto sentido.

sixties ['sɪkstɪz] **the sixties,** *npl* los años *mpl* sesenta.
● **to be in one's sixties,** (*person*) tener entre sesenta y setenta años, tener sesenta y tantos años. ‖ **to be in the sixties,** (*temperature*) estar comprendido entre sesenta y setenta grados: *temperatures will be in the sixties,* habrá temperaturas de entre sesenta y setenta grados Fahrenheit.
■ **sixties music,** música de los años sesenta.

sixtieth ['sɪkstɪəθ] **1** *adj* sexagésimo,-a: *it's his sixtieth birthday,* es su sexagésimo cumpleaños, es su sesenta cumpleaños. – **2** *adv* en sexagésimo lugar: *he finished sixtieth,* quedó en sexagésimo lugar. – **3** *n* (*in series*) sexagésimo,-a: *he was sixtieth,* fue sexagésimo, quedó en sexagésimo lugar. **4** (*fraction*) sexagésimo; (*one part*) sexagésima parte *f*.

sixty ['sɪkstɪ] **1** *adj* sesenta: *he's sixty,* tiene sesenta años; *there were about sixty people,* había unas sesenta personas; *sixty per cent of the population,* el sesenta por ciento de la población. – **2** *t* sesenta *m*.

sizable ['saɪzəbəl] *adj* → **sizeable.**

size[1] [saɪz] **1** *n* (*gen*) tamaño; (*magnitude*) magnitud *f*: *it's the size of an egg,* es del tamaño de un huevo; *the size of the problem,* la magnitud del problema. **2** (*of clothes*) talla; (*of shoes*) número; (*of person*) talla, estatura: *what size are you?,* ¿qué talla tienes?; ¿qué talla gastas?; *what size (shoes) are you?,* ¿qué número calzas?; *she's a size 12,* gasta la talla 12; *I need the next size,* necesito una talla más grande. – **3** *t* (*sort according to size*) poner la talla a.
◆ **to size up** *t sep* (*situation, problem*) evaluar; (*person*) juzgar.
● **that's about the size of it,** es más o menos así. ‖ **to cut sb. down to size,** bajarle los humos a algn. ‖ **to try sth. on for size,** probarse algo para ver cómo le queda la talla.

size[2] [saɪz] **1** *n* (*sticky substance for paper, cloth*) cola, apresto. – **2** *t* encolar, aprestar.

sizeable ['saɪzəbəl] *adj* (*house, estate, etc*) (*bastante*) grande, de proporciones considerables; (*sum*) considerable; (*problem*) importante.

sizzle ['sɪzəl] **1** *i* chisporrotear, crepitar. – **2** *n* chisporroteo.

sizzler ['sɪzələ'] *n fam* (*hot day*) día *m* abrasador.

ska [skɑː] *n* MUS ska *m*.

skate[1] [skeɪt] **1** *n* (*gen*) patín *m*; (*ice skate*) patín *m* de hielo; (*roller skate*) patín *m* de rueda. – **2** *i* patinar.
◆ **to skate over** *t insep* (*problem, delicate issue*) tratar muy por encima. ‖ **to skate round** *t insep* (*problem, difficulty*) evitar, esquivar.
● **to get/put one's skates on,** darse prisa, moverse.
‖ **to skate on thin ice,** pisar un terreno peligroso.

skate[2] [skeɪt] *n* (*fish*) raya.

skateboard ['skeɪtbɔːd] *n* monopatín *m*.

skater ['skeɪtə^r] *n* patinador,-ra.

skating ['skeɪtɪŋ] *n* patinaje *m*.
● **to go skating,** ir a patinar.
■ **ice skating,** patinaje *m* sobre hielo. ‖ **skating rink,** pista de patinaje.

skedaddle [skɪˈdædəl] *i* pirarse.

skein [skeɪn] **1** *n* (*of yarn*) madeja. **2** (*of geese*) bandada.

skeletal ['skelɪtəl] **1** *adj* ANAT esquelético,-a, óseo,-a. **2** (*emaciated*) esquelético,-a, escuálido,-a. **3** (*report etc*) escueto,-a.

skeleton ['skelɪtən] **1** *n* (*of person, animal*) esqueleto. **2** (*of building, ship*) armazón *m*, estructura. **3** (*outline, plan*) esquema *m*, bosquejo, esbozo. – **4** *adj* (*staff*) reducido,-a; (*service*) mínimo,-a, básico,-a.
● **to have a skeleton in the cupboard,** tener un secreto vergonzoso que ocultar.
■ **skeleton key,** llave *f* maestra.

skeptic ['skeptɪk] *n* US → **sceptic**.

skeptical ['skeptɪkəl] *adj* US → **sceptical**.

sketch [sketʃ] **1** *n* (*drawing*) dibujo; (*preliminary drawing*) bosquejo, esbozo. **2** (*outline, rough idea*) esquema *m*, esbozo; (*rough draft*) boceto, borrador *m*. **3** THEAT TV sketch *m*. – **4** *t* (*draw*) dibujar; (*preliminary drawing*) bosquejar, hacer un bosquejo de. **5** (*outline*) esbozar. – **6** *i* hacer bosquejos, hacer bocetos.
◆ **to sketch in/out** *t sep* (*outline*) trazar las líneas generales de, dar un resumen de.
■ **character sketch,** breve descripción *f* de un personaje. ‖ **sketch map,** croquis *m*.

sketch-book ['sketʃbʊk] *n* bloc *m* de dibujo.

sketch-pad ['sketʃpæd] *n* bloc *m* de dibujo.

sketchy ['sketʃi] *adj* (*coverage, account*) incompleto,-a, sin detalles; (*knowledge*) básico,-a; (*memory*) vago,-a, impreciso,-a.
▲ *comp* **sketchier,** *superl* **sketchiest**.

skewer ['skjʊə^r] **1** *n* CULIN pincho, brocheta, broqueta. – **2** *t* ensartar (en un pincho etc).

ski [skiː] **1** *n* (*equipment*) esquí *m*. – **2** *i* esquiar.
● **to ski down,** bajar esquiando.
■ **ski boots,** botas de esquiar. ‖ **ski instructor,** monitor,-ra de esquí. ‖ **ski jump,** (*slope*) pista de saltos; (*competition*) saltos *mpl* de esquí. ‖ **ski lift,** telesquí *m*. ‖ **ski pants,** pantalón *m sing* de esquí. ‖ **ski pole / ski stick,** bastón *m* de esquí. ‖ **ski resort,** estación *f* de esquí. ‖ **ski slope,** pista de esquí. ‖ **ski run,** pista de esquí.

skibob ['skibɒb] *n* esquibob *m*, skibob *m*.

skid [skɪd] **1** *n* AUTO patinazo, resbalón *m*, derrapaje *m*. – **2** *i* patinar, derrapar.
● **to be on the skids,** ir cuesta abajo. ‖ **to go into a skid,** patinar, derrapar. ‖ **to put the skids under sb./sth.,** (*cause to fail*) poner zancadillas a algn./algo. ‖ **to skid to a halt,** frenar patinando.
■ **skid row,** US barrios *mpl* bajos, barriadas *fpl*. ‖ **skid marks,** AUTO señales *fpl* de los neumáticos en el asfalto.

▲ *pt & pp* **skidded,** *ger* **skidding**.

skidpan ['skɪdpæn] *n* GB pista resbaladiza donde los conductores practican el patinaje.

skier ['skɪə^r] *n* esquiador,-ra.

skiff [skɪf] *n* MAR esquife *m*.

skiing ['skiːɪŋ] *n* esquí *m*.
● **to go skiing,** ir a esquiar.

skilful ['skɪlfʊl] *adj* (*gen*) diestro,-a, hábil; (*with hands*) mañoso,-a; (*with words*) hábil.
● **to be skilful at sth.,** ser hábil para algo, tener habilidad para algo.

skilfully ['skɪlfʊli] *adv* hábilmente, con destreza.

skill [skɪl] **1** *n* (*ability*) habilidad *f*, destreza; (*talent*) talento, don *m*, dotes *fpl*: *he acted with great skill,* actuó con gran habilidad; *the work shows artistic skill,* la obra demuestra talento artístico. **2** (*technique*) técnica, arte *m*. – **3** **skills,** *npl* (*expertise*) capacidad *f sing*, aptitudes *fpl*: *a person with secretarial skills,* una persona que sepa mecanografía; *a person with computer skills,* una persona que sepa informática.

skilled [skɪld] **1** *adj* (*specialized - worker*) cualificado,-a, especializado,-a; (- *work*) especializado,-a, de especialista. **2** (*able*) hábil, diestro,-a; (*expert*) experto,-a.

skillful ['skɪlfʊl] *adj* US → **skilful**.

skim [skɪm] **1** *t* (*milk*) desnatar, descremar (**off,** a); (*soup*) espumar (**off,** a). **2** (*move over surface*) pasar (casi) rozando: *the plane skimmed the ground,* el avión volaba a ras de suelo. **3** (*read quickly*) hojear, leer por encima. – **4** (*move over surface*) pasar (casi) rozando (**across/over,** -). **5** (*read quickly*) hojear (**through/over,** -), leer por encima (**through/over,** -).
● **to skim stones,** hacer cabrillas.
■ **skim milk,** leche *f* desnatada, leche *f* descremada.
▲ *pt & pp* **skimmed,** *ger* **skimming**.

skimmed [skɪmd] *adj* (*milk*) desnatado,-a, descremado,-a.

skimmer ['skɪmə^r] *n* (*spoon*) espumadera.

skimp [skɪmp] **1** *t* escatimar. – **2** *i* escatimar (**on,** -).

skimpy ['skɪmpi] *adj* (*dress*) ligero,-a, cortísimo,-a; (*meal*) escaso,-a, pobre.
▲ *comp* **skimpier,** *superl* **skimpiest**.

skin [skɪn] **1** *n* (*of person*) piel *f*; (*of face*) cutis *m*, piel *f*; (*complexion*) tez *f*: *she has light/dark skin,* tiene la piel clara/morena; *skin problems,* problemas en la piel. **2** (*of animal*) piel *f*, pellejo; (*pelt*) piel *f*; (*hide*) cuero (curtido). **3** (*of fruit, vegetable*) piel *f*; (*hard*) cáscara, corteza; (*peeling*) monda, mondadura. **4** (*of sausage*) pellejo. **5** (*on paint*) telilla, capa fina; (*on milk, custard, etc*) nata. **6** TECH (*of plane etc*) revestimiento. – **7** *t* (*animal, fish*) desollar, despellejar. **8** (*fruit, vegetable*) pelar. **9** (*elbow, knee*) arañar, rascar, hacerse un rasguño en.
● **it's no skin off my nose,** a mí me da lo mismo, a mí me trae sin cuidado. ‖ **to be all skin and bone(s),** estar en los huesos. ‖ **by the skin of one's teeth,** por los pelos. ‖ **to get under sb.'s skin,** (*annoy*) irritar a algn., crispar (los nervios) a algn., sacar a algn. de quicio. ‖ **to have a thick skin,** ser poco sensible. ‖ **to have a thin skin,** ser muy susceptible. ‖ **to jump out of one's skin,** llevarse un susto. ‖ **to save one's own skin,** salvar el pellejo. ‖ **to skin sb. alive,** desollar vivo,-a a algn.
■ **skin care,** cuidado de la piel. ‖ **skin cream,** crema para la piel. ‖ **skin disease,** enfermedad *f* de la piel, dermatosis *f*. ‖ **skin diving,** buceo, submarinismo. ‖ **skin graft,** injerto cutáneo. ‖ **skin test,** cutirreacción *f*.

▲ *pt* & *pp* skinned, *ger* skinning.
skin-deep [skɪn'diːp] *adj* superficial.
skin-diver ['skɪndaɪvə'] *n* buceador,-ra, submarinista *mf*.
skinflint ['skɪnflɪnt] *n fam* tacaño,-a.
skinful ['skɪnfʊl] **to have had a skinful,** *n* estar como una cuba.
skinhead ['skɪnhed] *n* cabeza *mf* rapada, skin *mf*.
skinny ['skɪnɪ] *adj fam* flaco,-a, flacucho,-a, delgaducho,-a, enjuto,-a.
▲ *comp* skinnier, *superl* skinniest.
skinny-dip ['skɪnɪdɪp] *i* bañarse desnudo,-a.
skinny-dipping ['skɪnɪdɪpɪŋ] **to go skinny-dipping,** *phr* ir a bañarse desnudo,-a.
skint [skɪnt] *adj* pelado,-a.
● **to be skint,** estar sin blanca, estar sin un duro.
skintight ['skɪntaɪt] *adj* (*clothes*) muy ceñido,-a, muy ajustado,-a.
skip¹ [skɪp] **1** *n* salto, brinco. – **2** *i* (*move, jump*) saltar, brincar; (*with rope*) saltar a la comba. **3** (*jump, flit*) saltar: *the book skips from one subject to another,* el libro salta de un tema a otro. **4** *fam* (*leave*) largarse: *he skipped off without a word,* se largó sin decir nada. – **5** *t* (*miss, omit*) saltarse: *she skipped a few pages,* se saltó unas páginas; *I skipped lunch today,* no he comido hoy; *we'll skip dessert,* pasamos del postre. **6** *fam* (*fail to attend*) faltar a: *the boy's been skipping classes,* el niño ha faltado a clase.
● **skip it!,** ¡déjalo!
▲ *pt* & *pp* skipped, *ger* skipping.
skip² [skɪp] *n* (*container*) contenedor *m*, container *m*.
skipper ['skɪpə'] **1** *n* MAR patrón,-ona, capitán,-ana. **2** SP capitán,-ana. – **3** *t* capitanear.
skipping ['skɪpɪŋ] *n* comba.
■ **skipping rope,** comba, cuerda de saltar.
skirmish ['skɜːmɪʃ] **1** *n* MIL escaramuza. **2** (*fight*) refriega, pelea, trifulca; (*argument*) escaramuza, riña, discusión *f*. – **3** *i* (*fight*) pelear; (*argue*) reñir, discutir.
skirt [skɜːt] **1** *n* (*garment*) falda: *a straight skirt or a pleated one?,* ¿una falda recta o plisada? **2** (*machinery guard*) cubierta. – **3** *t* (*go round - town, hill*) rodear; (*- lake, coast*) bordear. **4** *fig* (*problem*) esquivar, eludir (**round,** -).
skirting ['skɜːtɪŋ] skirting (**board**), *n* GB zócalo, rodapié *m*.
skit [skɪt] *n* LIT sátira, parodia; THEAT sketch *m* satírico.
skittish ['skɪtɪʃ] **1** *adj* (*person*) caprichoso,-a, frívolo,-a. **2** (*animal*) excitable, asustadizo,-a.
skittle ['skɪtəl] **1** *n* (*wooden pin*) bolo. – **2** skittles, *npl* bolos *mpl*, boliche *m sing*: *let's play skittles,* juguemos a los bolos.
skive [skaɪv] *i* GB *fam* (*avoid work*) escaquearse.
◆ **to skive off** *i* (*avoid work*) escaquearse; (*leave early*) pirarse, escurrirse.
● **to skive off schoolk,** hacer novillos.
skiver ['skaɪvə'] *n* vago,-a.
skivvies ['skɪvɪz] *npl* US paños *mpl* menores.
skivvy ['skɪvɪ] **1** *n* GB *fam* (*female servant*) fregona, sirvienta. – **2** *i* servir, trabajar como una esclava.
▲ *pl* skivvies.
skulduggery [skʌl'dʌgərɪ] *n* tejemanejes *mpl*, trapicheo.
skulk [skʌlk] *i* (*hide*) esconderse, estar escondido,-a; (*prowl*) merodear, rondar; (*lurk, lie in wait*) estar al acecho.
skull [skʌl] **1** *n* ANAT cráneo. **2** (*symbol*) calavera. **3** *fam* (*head*) coco, calavera, tarro.

● **skull and crossbones,** bandera pirata.
skullcap ['skʌlkæp] *n* (*garment*) casquete *m*; (*of priest*) solideo.
skunk [skʌŋk] **1** *n* ZOOL mofeta. **2** *fam* (*person*) sinvergüenza *mf*, canalla *mf*.
sky [skaɪ] *n* (*gen*) cielo; (*firmament*) firmamento.
● **the sky's the limit,** todo es posible. ‖ **to praise sth./ sb. to the skies,** poner algo/a algn. por las nubes.
■ **sky blue,** azul *m* celeste.
sky-blue ['skaɪbluː] *adj* azul celeste.
skydive ['skaɪdaɪv] *i* practicar el paracaidismo.
skydiver [skaɪ'daɪvə'] *n* paracaidista *mf*.
skydiving ['skaɪdaɪvɪŋ] *n* paracaidismo.
sky-high [skaɪ'haɪ] **1** *adv* por las nubes, por los aires: *prices have gone sky-high,* los precios se han puesto por las nubes. – **2** *adj* por las nubes, astronómico,-a.
● **to blow sth. sky-high,** hacer volar algo por los aires.
skylark ['skaɪlɑːk] *n* ORN alondra.
skylight ['skaɪlaɪt] *n* tragaluz *m*, claraboya.
skyline ['skaɪlaɪn] **1** *n* (*horizon*) horizonte *m*. **2** (*of city*) perfil *m*.
skyscraper ['skaɪskreɪpə'] *n* rascacielos *m*.
slab [slæb] **1** *n* (*of stone*) losa; (*of cake*) trozo; (*of chocolate*) tableta. **2** (*in mortuary*) mesa de autopsias.
slack¹ [slæk] **1** *adj* (*not taut*) flojo,-a: *a slack rope,* una cuerda floja. **2** (*careless, lax*) descuidado,-a; (*negligent*) negligente; (*sloppy*) despreocupado,-a, dejado,-a: *slack security led to an escape,* la deficiente seguridad causó la fuga; *discipline is slack,* hay poca disciplina; *don't get slack in your work,* no descuides tu trabajo. **3** (*not busy - trade, demand*) flojo,-a: *business is slack,* hay poco trabajo. – **4** *n* (*part of rope, wire etc*) parte *f* floja. – **5** *i fam pej* (*be lazy*) gandulear, holgazanear.
◆ **to slack off** *i* (*activity*) aflojar (el ritmo de trabajo); (*speed*) reducir, disminuir.
● **to take up the slack,** (*rope*) tensar la cuerda; (*industry*) reactivar la productividad, aumentar la productividad.
■ **slack season,** temporada baja.
slack² [slæk] *n* (*coal*) cisco.
slacken ['slækən] **1** *t* (*rope, grip*) aflojar; (*reins*) soltar. **2** (*speed*) reducir, disminuir; (*pace*) aflojar, reducir, aminorar. – **3** *i* (*rope, grip*) aflojarse; (*wind, rain*) amainar. **4** (*trade, demand*) aflojar, flaquear, decaer; (*speed*) reducirse, disminuir.
◆ **to slacken off / slacken up** *i* (*activity*) aflojar (el ritmo de trabajo); (*speed*) reducirse, disminuir.
slacker ['slækə'] *n fam* vago,-a, gandul,-la, holgazán,-ana.
slackness ['slæknəs] **1** *n* (*of rope*) flojedad *f*. **2** (*carelessness, laxness*) descuido; (*negligence*) negligencia; (*laziness*) pereza, gandulería. **3** (*of trade*) inactividad *f*, estancamiento.
slacks [slæks] *npl dated* pantalón *m*, pantalones *mpl*.
slag [slæg] **1** *n* (*of metal etc*) escoria. **2** GB *sl pej* fulana, puta.
◆ **to slag off** *t sep* GB *fam* (*person*) poner verde a, hablar mal de; (*thing*) poner por los suelos.
■ **slag heap,** escorial *m*.
▲ *pt* & *pp* slagged, *ger* slagging.
slain [sleɪn] *pp* → **slay.**
slake [sleɪk] **1** *t* (*thirst*) saciar, apagar, aplacar. **2** *fig* satisfacer. **3** CHEM (*lime*) apagar.
■ **slaked lime,** cal *f* apagada, cal *f* muerta.
slalom ['slɑːləm] *n* SP slalom *m*, eslalon *m*.
slam¹ [slæm] **1** *n* (*of lid, book, etc*) golpe *m*; (*of door*) portazo. – **2** *t* (*shut forcefully*) cerrar de golpe: *she slammed*

the door in my face, me dio con la puerta en las narices. **3** (throw noisily) arrojar, lanzar: she slammed the book down on the table, arrojó el libro sobre la mesa. **4** fig (criticize) criticar duramente, atacar violentamente. **5** (defeat) dar una paliza a. – **6** i cerrarse de golpe: the door slammed shut, la puerta se cerró de un portazo.
● to slam on the brakes, AUTO dar un frenazo. ‖ to slam the door, dar un portazo. ‖ to slam the phone down, colgar de golpe.
▲ pt & pp slammed, ger slamming.
slam² [slæm] n (in bridge) slam m.
■ grand slam, gran slam m.
slammer ['slæmə'] n sl (prison) chirona, trullo.
slander ['slɑːndə'] **1** n (smear) difamación f. **2** JUR calumnia. – **3** t difamar. **4** JUR calumniar.
● to bring an action against sb. for slander, querellarse contra algn. por difamación. ‖ to sue sb. for slander, demandar a algn. por difamación.
slanderer ['slɑːndərə'] **1** n difamador,-ra. **2** JUR calumniador,-ra.
slanderous ['slɑːndərəs] **1** adj difamatorio,-a. **2** JUR calumnioso,-a.
slang [slæŋ] **1** n argot m, jerga: "slammer" is slang for prison, en argot "trullo" quiere decir cárcel. – **2** adj de jerga, de argot. – **3** t fam insultar.
slanging match ['slæŋɪŋmætʃ] n fam intercambio de insultos.
slangy ['slæŋɪ] adj muy coloquial, vulgar.
▲ comp slangier, superl slangiest.
slant [slɑːnt] **1** n (gen) inclinación f; (slope) declive m, pendiente f. **2** (point of view) enfoque m, punto de vista, perspectiva; (bias) sesgo. – **3** t (slope) inclinar. **4** fig (news, report, etc) enfocar subjetivamente, presentar tendenciosamente. – **5** i (slope) inclinarse.
● on a slant / on the slant, inclinado,-a.
slanted ['slɑːntɪd] adj (biased) tendencioso,-a.
slanting ['slɑːntɪŋ] adj (sloping) inclinado,-a.
slap [slæp] **1** n (gen) palmada; (smack) cachete m; (in face) bofetada, bofetón m. – **2** adv (straight) de lleno: we drove slap into a wall, dimos de lleno contra una pared. **3** (right) justo: they've built a huge hotel slap in the middle of the port, han construido un hotel enorme justo en medio del puerto. – **4** t (gen) pegar (con la mano); (in face) abofetear, dar una bofetada a. **5** (place, put) tirar, arrojar: I slapped the form down on the counter, arrojé el formulario sobre el mostrador.
◆ to slap around t sep (hit) pegar. ‖ to slap down t sep (force into silence) hacer callar. ‖ to slap on t sep (add to price) añadir a, aumentar.
● a slap in the face, (rebuff) un desaire, una bofetada. ‖ a slap on the wrist, un tirón de orejas. ‖ to slap make-up on one's face, embadurnarse la cara de maquillaje. ‖ to slap paint on a wall, dar una mano de pintura en la pared. ‖ to slap sb. on the back, dar a algn. una palmadita en la espalda.
▲ pt & pp slapped, ger slapping.
slap-bang ['slæpbæŋ] adv → slap.
slapdash ['slæpdæʃ] adj fam (careless) descuidado,-a; (work) chapucero,-a.
slaphappy ['slæphæpɪ] adj fam (person) despreocupado,-a; (work) descuidado,-a.
slapped [slæpt] pt pp → slap.
slapstick ['slæpstɪk] n bufonadas fpl, payasadas fpl.
■ slapstick comedy, astracanada.
slap-up ['slæpʌp] adj fam excelente.
■ slap-up meal, comilona, banquete m.

slash [slæʃ] **1** n (with sword) tajo; (with knife) cuchillada; (with razor) navajazo; (with whip) latigazo. **2** GB sl meada. **3** fam (oblique) barra oblicua. – **4** t (with sword) dar un tajo a; (with knife) acuchillar, rajar; (with whip) azotar: vandals have slashed all the seats, unos gamberros han rajado todos los asientos; she slashed her wrists, se cortó las venas. **5** fig (prices, wages) rebajar, reducir; (budget) recortar: prices slashed, precios de remate. – **6** i (swipe) golpear (at, -).
● to have a slash, sl mear.
slat [slæt] n tablilla, listón m.
slate¹ [sleɪt] **1** n (gen) pizarra. **2** GB (credit) cuenta. **3** US POL lista de candidatos. – **4** t (roof) empizarrar. **5** US POL (choose) elegir: he's slated to be the next director, lo han elegido para ser el próximo director. **6** US (plan, schedule) programar: the meeting is slated for Tuesday, le reunión está programada para el martes.
● to put sth. on sb.'s slate, apuntar algo en la cuenta de algn. ‖ to wipe the slate clean, hacer borrón y cuenta nueva.
■ slate quarry, pizarral m. ‖ slate roof, tejado de pizarra.
slate² [sleɪt] t GB fam (criticize) poner por los suelos, criticar duramente.
slaughter ['slɔːtə'] **1** n (of animals) matanza; (of people) carnicería, matanza. – **2** t (animals) matar, sacrificar; (people) matar brutalmente; (in large numbers) masacrar, exterminar. **3** fam (defeat) dar una paliza a.
slaughterhouse ['slɔːtəhaʊs] n matadero.
Slav [slɑːv] **1** n (person) eslavo,-a. – **2** adj eslavo,-a.
slave [sleɪv] **1** n esclavo,-a: he's a slave to drink, es esclavo de la bebida. – **2** i trabajar como una bestia (at, en), trabajar como un negro (at, en): she's slaving away at the accounts, está trabajando como una bestia en las cuentas.
■ slave driver, negrero,-a, tirano,-a. ‖ slave labour, (slaves) los esclavos; (hard work) trabajo de negros. ‖ slave trade, trata de esclavos.
slaver¹ ['sleɪvə'] n arch (ship) barco negrero; (person) negrero,-a.
slaver² ['slævə'] i (drool) babear: she slavered over the baby, se le caía la baba con el niño.
slavery ['sleɪvərɪ] n esclavitud f.
● to be sold into slavery, ser vendido,-a como esclavo,-a.
Slavic ['slɑːvɪk] adj → Slavonic.
slavish ['sleɪvɪʃ] **1** adj (servile) esclavo,-a, servil. **2** (copy, imitation, remake) poco original, calcado,-a, imitativo,-a; (obedience, devotion) ciego,-a.
Slavonic [slə'vɒnɪk] **1** adj eslavo,-a. – **2** n (language) eslavo.
slay [sleɪ] t lit matar, asesinar.
▲ pt slew, pp slain.
sleaze [sliːz] n sordidez f.
■ sleaze politics, política de trapicheo.
sleazy ['sliːzɪ] adj sórdido,-a.
▲ comp sleazier, superl sleaziest.
sled [sled] n US → sledge.
sledge [sledʒ] **1** n GB trineo. – **2** i ir en trineo.
sledgehammer ['sledʒhæmə'] n almádena.
sleek [sliːk] **1** adj (hair, fur) liso,-a, lustroso,-a. **2** (appearance) impecable, elegante; (vehicle) de líneas elegantes.
sleep [sliːp] **1** n sueño: I'm going to have a little sleep, voy a dormir un poco; I need eight hours' sleep, necesito dormir ocho horas; he talks in his sleep, habla dormido. **2** (in eyes) legaña. – **3** i (gen) dormir: I slept well, he dor-

mido bien; *he slept for ten hours,* durmió diez horas. –
4 *t (accommodate)* tener camas para, poder alojar a: *the
bungalow sleeps six,* en el bungalow hay camas para
seis personas.
◆ **to sleep around** *i fam* acostarse con cualquiera. ‖
to sleep in *i (sleep late)* quedarse en la cama, dormir
hasta tarde. ‖ **to sleep out** *i (sleep outdoors)* dormir al
aire libre, dormir al raso. ‖ **to sleep through** *t insep (not
hear)* no oír; *(be asleep)* seguir durmiendo. ‖ **to sleep together** *i (sleep in same bed)* dormir juntos,-as; *(have sex)*
tener relaciones sexuales. ‖ **to sleep with** *t insep* acostarse con.
● **sleep tight,** que duermas bien, que descanses. ‖ **to
cry os. to sleep,** llorar hasta quedarse dormido,-a. ‖
to get to sleep, conciliar el sueño. ‖ **to go to sleep,**
(fall asleep) dormirse; *(become numb)* dormirse, entumecerse: *my foot's gone to sleep,* se me ha dormido el pie.
‖ **to lose sleep over sth.,** perder el sueño por algo. ‖
to put an animal to sleep, sacrificar un animal. ‖ **to
put a patient to sleep,** dormir a un paciente. ‖ **to
sleep like a log / sleep like a top,** dormir como un
tronco, dormir como un lirón. ‖ **to sleep it off,** *(hangover)* dormir la mona; *(meal)* reponerse. ‖ **to sleep on
it,** consultarlo con la almohada. ‖ **to sleep rough,** dormir al raso.
▲ *pt & pp* **slept***.*

sleeper [ˈsliːpəʳ] **1** *n (person)* durmiente *mf.* **2** *(train)* tren
m con coches cama; *(sleeping car)* coche-cama *m*; *(berth)*
litera. **3** *(beam of wood on track)* traviesa. **4** GB *(earring)*
arete *m*, aro, pendiente *m.* **5** US *(late/unexpected success)*
éxito inesperado.
● **to be a light sleeper / be a heavy sleeper,** tener
el sueño ligero / tener el sueño pesado.

sleepily [ˈsliːpɪlɪ] *adv* con voz soñolienta, medio dormido,-a.

sleepiness [ˈsliːpɪnəs] *n* somnolencia, soñolencia.

sleeping [ˈsliːpɪŋ] *adj* durmiente, dormido,-a.
● **let sleeping dogs lie,** mejor no remover el asunto.
■ **sleeping bag,** saco de dormir. ‖ **Sleeping Beauty,**
la Bella durmiente. ‖ **sleeping car,** coche-cama *m.* ‖
sleeping partner, socio,-a comanditario,-a. ‖ **sleeping pill / sleeping tablet,** somnífero. ‖ **sleeping policeman,** AUTO badén *m.* ‖ **sleeping sickness,** encefalitis *f* letárgica, enfermedad *f* del sueño.

sleepless [ˈsliːpləs] *adj* insomne.
● **to have a sleepless night,** pasar la noche en blanco.

sleeplessness [ˈsliːpləsnəs] *n* insomnio.

sleepwalker [ˈsliːpwɔːkəʳ] *n* sonámbulo,-a.

sleepwalking [ˈsliːpwɔːkɪŋ] *n* sonambulismo.

sleepy [ˈsliːpɪ] **1** *adj (drowsy)* soñoliento,-a, somnoliento,-a, adormecido,-a. **2** *(quiet, not busy)* tranquilo,-a.
● **to be sleepy / feel sleepy,** tener sueño. ‖ **to get
sleepy,** entrarle sueño a uno. ‖ **to look sleepy,** tener
cara de sueño. ‖ **to make sleepy,** darle sueño a uno.
▲ *comp* **sleepier,** *superl* **sleepiest***.*

sleepyhead [ˈsliːpɪhed] *n fam* dormilón,-ona.

sleet [sliːt] **1** *n* aguanieve *f.* – **2** *i* caer aguanieve.

sleeve [sliːv] **1** *n (of garment)* manga. **2** *(of record)* funda.
3 TECH manguito.
● **to have sth. up one's sleeve,** guardarse una carta
en la manga.

sleeveless [ˈsliːvləs] *adj (garment)* sin mangas.

sleigh [sleɪ] *n* trineo.
■ **sleigh bell,** cascabel *m.*

sleight [slaɪt] **sleight of hand,** *phr* prestidigitación *f,*
juego de manos.

slender [ˈslendəʳ] **1** *adj (person)* delgado,-a, esbelto,-a;
(waist, wineglass) delgado,-a, fino,-a. **2** *fig (hope, chance)*
ligero,-a, remoto,-a; *(income, majority)* escaso,-a: *a person of slender means,* una persona de escasos recursos;
he won by a slender margin, ganó por un estrecho margen.

slept [slept] *pt & pp* → **sleep***.*

sleuth [sluːθ] *n* detective *mf,* sabueso *mf.*

slew [sluː] *pt* → **slay***.*

slice [slaɪs] **1** *n (of bread)* rebanada; *(thin - ham etc)* lonja,
loncha; *(- meat)* tajada; *(- of salami, lemon, etc)* rodaja. **2**
(portion - of cake, pie) porción *f,* trozo; *(- of melon etc)* raja.
3 *fig (share)* parte *f; (proportion)* proporción *f.* **4** *(kitchen
tool)* pala, paleta. **5** SP *(in golf)* slice *m; (in tennis)* golpe
m con efecto. – **6** *t (cut up)* cortar a rebanadas, cortar
a lonjas, cortar a rodajas: *she sliced up the ham,* cortó
el jamón en lonchas; *he sliced the apple in two,* partió
la manzana por la mitad. **7** *(cut off)* cortar: *can you slice
me a piece of cake?,* ¿puedes cortarme un trozo de pastel? **8** *(cut with knife)* cortar: *she sliced her finger,* se cortó
el dedo. **9** SP dar efecto a. – **10** *i* SP dar efecto a la pelota.
● **to be the best thing since sliced bread,** ser lo mejor que hay, ser de lo mejorcito que hay.
■ **sliced bread,** pan *m* de molde.

slick [slɪk] **1** *adj (skilful)* mañoso,-a, hábil, diestro,-a;
(smooth) fluido,-a: *a slick changeover,* un relevo rápido.
2 *(attractive)* ingenioso,-a, logrado,-a; *(effective)* eficaz,
impresionante: *a slick advertising campaign,* una campaña publicitaria muy lograda. **3** *pej (glib - person)* despabilado,-a, con mucha labia; *(- answer, excuse)* fácil,
simplista: *he's a slick operator,* es un listillo, es un tipo
despabilado, tiene un pico de oro. **4** US *(slippery)* resbaladizo,-a. – **5** *n* marea negra.
◆ **to slick down** *t sep (hair)* alisar.

slicker [ˈslɪkəʳ] **1** *n* US *fam (person)* chulo,-a, presuntuoso,-a. **2** US *(raincoat)* impermeable *m.*

slide [slaɪd] **1** *n (act of sliding)* deslizamiento, desliz *m;
(slip)* resbalón *m.* **2** *(in playground)* tobogán *m.* **3** FIN
(drop, fall) baja, caída, bajón *m.* **4** *(photo)* diapositiva. **5**
(of microscope) platina, portaobjetos *m.* **6** MUS *(on instrument)* vara, corredera. **7** GB *(for hair)* pasador *m.* – **8** *t
(gen)* deslizar, pasar; *(furniture)* correr: *I slid the coin into
his pocket,* le deslicé la moneda en el bolsillo; *she slid
her glass across the table,* deslizó la copa sobre la
mesa. – **9** *i (slip deliberately)* deslizar, deslizarse; *(slip accidentally)* resbalar: *she slid on the ice,* resbaló en el hielo; *the children were sliding down the slope,* los niños
se deslizaban por la cuesta. **10** *(move quietly)* deslizarse:
the drawer slid open, el cajón se abrió con facilidad; *he
slid into the room,* entró sigilosamente en la habitación.
11 FIN *(fall)* bajar.
◆ **to slide into** *t insep (gradually pass into)* caer en. ‖ **to
slide over** *t insep (avoid)* esquivar, eludir.
● **to let sth. slide,** no ocuparse de algo, tener algo
abandonado,-a.
■ **slide projector,** proyector *m* de diapositivas. ‖ **slide
rule,** MATH regla de cálculo. ‖ **slide show,** proyección
f de diapositivas.
▲ *pt & pp* **slid** [slɪd]*.*

sliding [ˈslaɪdɪŋ] **1** *adj (door, window)* corredero,-a. **2** *(roof)*
corredizo,-a.
■ **sliding scale,** FIN escala móvil.

slight [slaɪt] **1** *adj (small in degree)* pequeño,-a, ligero,-a;
(not serious, unimportant) leve, insignificante: *she has a
slight French accent,* tiene un ligero acento francés; *a
slight change of plan,* un pequeño cambio de planes; *I*

haven't the slightest idea, no tengo la menor idea. **2** *(person - small)* menudo,-a; *(- slim)* delgado,-a; *(- frail)* delicado,-a. **– 3** *n (affront)* desaire *m,* desprecio. **– 4** *t (scorn)* despreciar, menospreciar. **5** *(snub, insult)* desairar, ofender, insultar.

● **not in the slightest,** en absoluto.

slighting ['slaɪtɪŋ] **1** *adj (scornful)* despreciativo,-a, menospreciativo,-a. **2** *(offensive)* ofensivo,-a.

slightly ['slaɪtlɪ] *adv (a little)* ligeramente, un poco, algo: *serve slightly chilled,* sírvase ligeramente frío; *he's slightly taller,* es un poco más alto; *I know him slightly,* apenas lo conozco.

● **to be slightly built,** ser de complexión menuda.

slim [slɪm] **1** *adj (person, build)* delgado,-a, esbelto,-a; *(waist, object)* fino,-a. **2** *(chance, hopes, prospect)* remoto,-a; *(evidence)* insuficiente; *(profit)* escaso,-a, exiguo,-a. **– 3** *i* adelgazar, hacer régimen: *I'm slimming,* estoy a régimen.

◆ **to slim down** *t sep* reducir.

▲ *(adjetivo) comp* **slimmer***, superl* **slimmest***; (verbo) pt & pp* **slimmed***, ger* **slimming***.*

slime [slaɪm] **1** *n (mud)* limo, cieno. **2** *(of snail)* baba.

slimmer ['slɪmə'] *n* persona que está a régimen.

slimming ['slɪmɪŋ] **1** *adj (diet, pills)* para adelgazar, adelgazante; *(food)* que no engorda, de bajo contenido calorífico. **– 2** *n (process)* adelgazamiento.

slimy ['slaɪmɪ] **1** *adj (muddy)* limoso,-a; *(sticky)* viscoso,-a, pegajoso,-a; *(of snail)* baboso,-a. **2** *(person)* zalamero,-a, cobista.

▲ *comp* **slimier***, superl* **slimiest***.*

sling [slɪŋ] **1** *n* MED cabestrillo. **2** *(catapult)* honda; *(child's)* tirador *m.* **3** *(device for lifting, carrying)* cuerda; *(for baby)* canguro. **– 4** *t fam (throw)* tirar, arrojar, lanzar: *sling it in the bin,* tíralo a la basura. **5** *(lift, support)* colgar: *a rope had been slung between two trees,* se había colgado una cuerda entre dos árboles.

◆ **to sling out** *t sep (thing)* echar, tirar (a la basura); *(person)* echar (a la calle).

● **to sling one's hook,** largarse.

▲ *pt & pp* **slung***.*

slink [slɪŋk] *i (move secretly)* moverse sigilosamente; *(in shame)* moverse avergonzado,-a.

◆ **to slink away / slink off** *i* escabullirse, escurrirse.

▲ *pt & pp* **slunk***.*

slinky ['slɪŋkɪ] *adj (garment)* ceñido,-a, ajustado,-a; *(movement)* sensual, provocativo,-a.

▲ *comp* **slinkier***, superl* **slinkiest***.*

slip[1] [slɪp] **1** *n (of paper)* papelito, trocito de papel. **2** BOT *(cutting)* esqueje *m.*

■ **slip of a girl,** chiquilla.

slip[2] [slɪp] **1** *n (slide)* resbalón *m; (trip)* traspiés *m,* tropezón *m.* **2** *(mistake)* error *m,* equivocación *f; (moral)* desliz *m.* **3** *(women's underskirt)* combinación *f; (petticoat)* enaguas *fpl.* **– 4** *i (slide)* resbalar; *(fall, get away, escape)* caer: *my foot slipped,* se me fue el pie; *she slipped on the ice,* resbaló en el hielo; *this bag keeps slipping off my shoulder,* este bolso se me cae del hombro; *the ball slipped through his fingers,* la pelota le resbaló de las manos. **5** AUTO *(clutch, tyre)* patinar. **6** *(move - quickly)* ir de prisa; *(- secretly)* escabullirse: *he slipped out when no-one was looking,* se escabulló cuando no miraba nadie; *she's just slipped out for a minute,* ha salido un momento. **7** *(decline)* decaer, empeorar. **– 8** *t (pass, give, put)* pasar, deslizar, dar a escondidas: *he slipped the doorman a fiver,* deslizó en la mano del portero un billete de cinco libras; *she slipped the note into her bag,* disimuladamente metió la nota en el bolso. **9** *(overlook, for-*

get) escaparse: *it completely slipped my mind,* se me olvidó por completo; *in case it slipped your notice,* por si se te ha pasado por alto. **10** *(get free from)* soltarse de: *the dog slipped its leash,* el perro se soltó de la correa.

◆ **to slip away 1** *i (time)* pasar, irse. **2** *(person)* irse. ‖ **to slip by** *i (time)* pasar, transcurrir. ‖ **to slip into** *t insep (clothes)* ponerse. ‖ **to slip off** *t sep (clothes)* quitarse. ‖ **to slip on** *t sep (clothes)* ponerse. ‖ **to slip out** *i (secret, comment, etc)* escaparse: *it just slipped out,* se me escapó. ‖ **to slip out of** *t insep (clothes)* quitarse. ‖ **to slip up** *i (make a mistake)* equivocarse, cometer un error; *(blunder)* cometer un desliz, meter la pata.

● **a slip of the pen,** un lapsus. ‖ **a slip of the tongue,** un lapsus linguae. ‖ **there's many a slip 'twixt the cup and the lip,** del dicho al hecho hay mucho trecho. ‖ **to be slipping,** estar perdiendo facultades, no ser lo que uno era antes. ‖ **to give sb. the slip,** dar esquinazo a algn. ‖ **to let an opportunity slip through one's fingers,** dejar escapar una oportunidad. ‖ **to let sth. slip,** escapársele algo a uno. ‖ **to slip a disc,** dislocarse una vértebra. ‖ **to slip anchor,** levar anclas.

■ **slipped disc,** vértebra dislocada. ‖ **slip road,** pista de aceleración.

slipknot ['slɪpnɒt] *n* nudo corredizo.

slip-on ['slɪpɒn] **1** *adj (shoes)* sin cordones; *(garment)* de quita y pon. **– 2 slip-ons,** *npl (shoes)* zapatos *mpl* sin cordones.

slipper ['slɪpə'] **1** *n* zapatilla. **2** TECH zapata, patín *m.*

slippery ['slɪpərɪ] **1** *adj (surface)* resbaladizo,-a, resbaloso,-a; *(fish, soap)* escurridizo,-a. **2** *fam (person)* astuto,-a, que no es de fiar.

● **to be a slippery customer,** no ser de fiar, ser un,-a granuja. ‖ **to be on the slippery slope,** andar sobre terreno pantanoso.

slipshod ['slɪpʃɒd] *adj (careless)* descuidado,-a; *(manual work)* chapucero,-a.

slipstream ['slɪpstriːm] *n* estela.

slip-up ['slɪpʌp] *n (mistake)* error *m,* descuido; *(blunder)* desliz *m,* metedura de pata.

slipway ['slɪpweɪ] *n* MAR grada.

slit [slɪt] **1** *n (opening)* abertura, hendedura; *(cut)* corte *m,* raja: *a skirt with a slit up the back,* una falda con un corte detrás; *eyes like slits,* ojos achinados. **– 2** *t (cut)* cortar, rajar, hender.

● **to slit open an envelope,** rasgar un sobre. ‖ **to slit sb.'s throat,** degollar a algn.

▲ *pt & pp* **slit***, ger* **slitting***.*

slither ['slɪðə'] *i (snake)* deslizarse; *(person)* resbalar; *(car)* patinar.

slithery ['slɪðərɪ] *adj* resbaladizo,-a.

sliver ['slɪvə'] *n (of wood, glass)* astilla; *(of ham etc)* loncha fina, tajada fina.

slob [slɒb] *n fam (dirty, untidy)* dejado,-a; *(lazy)* vago,-a; *(slovenly)* desaseado,-a: *you fat slob!,* ¡cerdo!, ¡guarro!

slobber ['slɒbə'] **1** *i (dribble)* babear. **– 2** *n fam* baba.

◆ **to slobber over 1** *t insep fam (drool over)* babosear, caerse la baba con. **2** *fam (kiss)* besuquear.

sloe [sləʊ] *n* BOT *(shrub)* endrino; *(fruit)* endrina.

■ **sloe gin,** ginebra de endrinas.

slog [slɒg] **1** *n* GB *fam (hard work)* paliza, gran esfuerzo; *(hard walk)* caminata: *digging is a real slog,* cavar es un auténtica paliza. **2** SP *(hard hit)* golpe *m.* **– 3** *i* GB *fam* sudar tinta **(away, -),** trabajar como un negro **(away, -):** *he's still slogging away in the garden,* aún está trabajando como un negro en el jardín. **4** *(walk)* caminar

con dificultad, caminar con gran esfuerzo. – **5** t SP (*hit*) golpear.
● **to slog one's way through sth.**, conseguir hacer algo a duras penas.
▲ *pt* & *pp* **slogged**, *ger* **slogging**.

slogan ['sləʊgən] *n* slogan *m*, eslogan *m*, lema *m*.

slogger ['slɒgəˈ] **1** *n* (*hard worker*) currante *mf*, trabajador,-ra. **2** SP bateador,-ra.

sloop [sluːp] *n* MAR balandro.

slop [slɒp] **1** t (*spill*) derramar, verter: *she slopped paint everywhere,* derramó pintura por todas partes. – **2** i derramarse, verterse: *water was slopping about everywhere,* el agua se derramaba por todas partes. – **3** *n* (*liquid food*) gachas *fpl*; (*swill*) bazofia *f*. **4** (*liquid waste from tea, coffee*) posos *mpl* de té, posos *mpl* de café; (*dirty water*) aguachirle *m*, lavazas *fpl*, líquido de desecho. **5** (*human waste - solid*) excrementos *mpl*; (*- liquid*) orina. **6** CINEM LIT (*slush*) sentimentalismo, sensiblería.
▲ *pt* & *pp* **slopped**, *ger* **slopping**.

slope [sləʊp] **1** *n* (*incline*) cuesta, pendiente *f*; (*upward*) subida; (*downward*) bajada, declive *m*: *a steep slope,* una cuesta empinada. **2** (*of mountain*) ladera, falda, vertiente *f*; (*of roof*) vertiente *f*. **3** (*for skiing*) pista de esquí, pista. – **4** i inclinarse: *my handwriting slopes to the right,* tengo la letra inclinada hacia la derecha.
◆ **to slope off** i largarse, escabullirse.

sloping ['sləʊpɪŋ] *adj* (*ground*) en pendiente, inclinado,-a; (*roof, handwriting*) inclinado,-a; (*shoulder*) caído,-a.

sloppily ['slɒpɪlɪ] **1** *adv* (*carelessly*) de modo descuidado, de cualquier manera. **2** (*sentimentally*) de modo empalagoso.

sloppy ['slɒpɪ] **1** *adj* (*garment*) muy ancho,-a. **2** (*messy, careless - gen*) descuidado,-a; (*- manual work*) chapucero,-a; (*- appearance, dress*) desaliñado,-a, dejado,-a. **3** (*sentimental*) empalagoso,-a, sentimentaloide. – **4** *n* (*kiss*) baboso,-a.
▲ *comp* **sloppier**, *superl* **sloppiest**.

slosh [slɒʃ] **1** t (*splash*) salpicar: *he sloshed some paint on the floor,* salpicó el suelo de pintura. **2** GB *fam* (*hit*) cascar, zurrar, pegar. – **3** i agitarse: *the water sloshed over the sides,* el agua se salía por los lados.

sloshed [slɒʃt] *adj fam* borracho,-a.
● **to get sloshed,** pillar una trompa, coger una trompa, agarrar un pedo, coger un pedo.

slot [slɒt] **1** *n* (*for coin*) ranura; (*groove*) muesca; (*opening*) rendija, abertura. **2** (*programme*) espacio; (*position, place*) puesto, hueco: *he's got an hour-long slot on local radio,* tiene un espacio de una hora en una emisora local. – **3** t (*insert*) insertar, introducir: *slot the coin in the machine,* insertar la moneda en la máquina.
◆ **to slot in 1** t *sep* (*fit in*) meter: *I can slot you in on Friday,* te puedo hacer un hueco para el viernes. – **2** i (*fit together*) encajar. ‖ **to slot together** i encajar.
■ **slot machine,** (*vending machine*) distribuidor *m* automático; (*for gambling*) máquina tragaperras. ‖ **slot meter,** contador *m*.
▲ (*verbo*) *pt* & *pp* **slotted**, *ger* **slotting**.

sloth [sləʊθ] **1** *n fml* (*laziness, idleness*) pereza, indolencia. **2** ZOOL perezoso.

slothful ['sləʊθfʊl] *adj fml* perezoso,-a, indolente.

slotted ['slɒtɪd] *adj* con ranura, con ranuras.
■ **slotted spatula / slotted spoon,** US espumadera. ‖ **slotted screw,** tornillo con ranura en la cabeza.

slouch [slaʊtʃ] **1** i (*walk*) andar con los hombros caídos, andar arrastrando los pies; (*sit*) sentarse con los hombros caídos: *don't slouch!,* ¡ponte derecho!; *there he*

was, slouching in an armchair, allí estaba, repantigado en un sillón. – **2** *n* (*posture*) andar *m* desgarbado.
● **to be no slouch,** no ser manco,-a.

slough[1] [slaʊ] **1** *n* (*swamp, marsh*) cenagal *m*. **2** *fml lit* (*emotional state, despair*) pozo, abismo.

slough[2] [slʌf] **1** *n* (*of snake*) muda. – **2** t (*snake*) mudar de (**off, -**).
◆ **to slough off** t *sep fig* (*responsibility, habit, etc*) deshacerse de, librarse de, abandonar.

Slovak ['sləʊvæk] **1** *adj* eslovaco,-a. – **2** *n* (*person*) eslovaco,-a. **3** (*language*) eslovaco.

Slovakia [sləʊ'vækɪə] *n* Eslovaquia.

Slovakian [sləʊ'vækɪən] *adj* → **Slovak**.

slovenly ['slʌvənlɪ] *adj* (*careless*) descuidado,-a, dejado,-a; (*scruffy*) desaliñado,-a, desaseado,-a.

slow [sləʊ] **1** *adj* (*gen*) lento,-a: *a slow recovery,* una recuperación lenta; *it's slow going,* avanzamos poco a poco. **2** (*clock, watch*) atrasado,-a: *my watch is slow,* mi reloj va atrasado, mi reloj atrasa. **3** (*dull, not active*) aburrido,-a, pesado,-a: *the film is a bit slow,* la película es un poco aburrida; *business is slow,* no hay mucho trabajo. **4** (*not quick to learn*) lento,-a, torpe; (*thick*) corto,-a de alcances: *he's a slow learner,* le cuesta aprender; *I'm a bit slow today,* estoy un poco espeso hoy. – **5** *adv* despacio, lentamente: *drive slow!,* ¡conduce despacio! – **6** t (*vehicle, machine*) reducir la marcha de; (*production, progress*) retrasar, retardar; (*person*) hacer ir más lento, retrasar. – **7** i (*gen*) ir más despacio; (*vehicle*) reducir la velocidad; (*pace*) aminorar el paso; (*person*) tomarse las cosas con calma.
◆ **to slow down 1** t *sep* hacer ir más despacio. – **2** i (*gen*) ir más despacio; (*vehicle*) reducir la velocidad; (*person*) aminorar el paso.
● **in a slow oven,** a fuego lento. ‖ **to be slow about/ in doing sth.,** tardar en hacer algo. ‖ **to be slow off the mark,** ser un poco lento,-a de reflejos. ‖ **to be slow to do sth.,** tardar en hacer algo. ‖ **to go slow,** (*workers*) hacer una huelga de celo.
■ **slow lane,** carril *m* lento.

slowcoach ['sləʊkəʊtʃ] *n fam* tortuga *mf*.

slowdown ['sləʊdaʊn] *n* (*workers*) huelga de celo.

slowly ['sləʊlɪ] *adv* despacio, lentamente.

slowness ['sləʊnəs] **1** *n* (*gen*) lentitud *f*. **2** (*dullness*) pesadez *f*. **3** (*of person*) torpeza.

slowpoke ['sləʊpəʊk] *n* US tortuga *mf*.

slow-witted ['sləʊ'wɪtɪd] *adj* lento,-a, torpe, corto,-a (de luces).

slowworm ['sləʊwɜːm] *n* lución *m*.

sludge [slʌdʒ] **1** *n* (*mud*) fango, cieno, lodo, barro; (*sediment*) sedimento, residuos *mpl*. **2** (*sewage*) aguas *fpl* residuales.

slug[1] [slʌg] *n* ZOOL babosa.

slug[2] [slʌg] **1** *n* (*bullet*) posta, bala. **2** (*drink*) trago, traguito. **3** (*token*) ficha.

slug[3] [slʌg] t (*hit*) pegar un porrazo a.
● **to slug it out,** liarse a puñetazos.
▲ *pt* & *pp* **slugged**, *ger* **slugging**.

sluggish ['slʌgɪʃ] **1** *adj* (*river, engine*) lento,-a; (*person*) perezoso,-a, holgazán,-ana. **2** COMM (*market, trade*) inactivo,-a, flojo,-a.

sluggishness ['slʌgɪʃnəs] **1** *n* (*slowness*) lentitud *f*; (*laziness*) pereza, aletargamiento. **2** COMM (*inactivity*) inactividad *f*.

sluice [sluːs] **1** *n* (*gate, valve*) compuerta, esclusa; (*waterway*) canal *m*. – **2** t (*wash*) lavar a chorro (**down/out, -**), regar (**down/out, -**), lavar con abundante agua (**down/ out, -**). – **3** i (*water*) correr a raudales.

sluicegate ['sluːsgeɪt] n esclusa, compuerta.

slum [slʌm] 1 n (place, house, etc) casuca, casucha, tugurio. 2 fam (tip) pocilga. – 3 i fam visitar los barrios bajos. – 4 slums, npl (area) barrios mpl bajos.
● to slum it, (accept lower standard of living) vivir con lo mínimo.
■ slum clearance programme, proyecto de erradicación de viviendas inhabitables.
▲ pt & pp slummed, ger slumming.

slumber ['slʌmbəʳ] 1 n lit (sleep) sueño; (deep sleep) sopor m. – 2 i dormir.

slummy ['slʌmɪ] adj sórdido,-a, miserable.
▲ comp slummier, superl slummiest.

slump [slʌmp] 1 n (recession) crisis f económica, recesión f económica; (drop in demand etc) bajón m, baja repentina, caída repentina. 2 us sp (of person, player, team) bajón m, mala racha. – 3 i (economy) hundirse; (sales, demand, etc) bajar en picado, caer en picado, caer de repente; (prices) desplomarse. 4 (fall, flop down) caer, derrumbarse; (faint) desmayarse: he slumped to the floor, se desplomó en el suelo; she slumped into the armchair, se derrumbó en el sillón; they found him slumped over the steering wheel, lo encontraron desplomado sobre el volante.

slung [slʌŋ] pt & pp → **sling**.

slunk [slʌŋk] pt & pp → **slink**.

slur [slɜːʳ] 1 n (stigma) mancha; (slanderous remark) calumnia, difamación f; (insult) afrenta. 2 (way of speaking) dificultad f al hablar. 3 mus ligado. – 4 t (letters, words) comerse, tragarse, pronunciar mal. 5 mus ligar. 6 (slander - reputation) manchar, mancillar; (- person) calumniar, difamar.
● to cast a slur on sb., injuriar a algn., difamar a algn.
║ to cast a slur on sb.'s reputation, manchar la reputación de algn.
▲ pt & pp slurred, ger slurring.

slurp [slɜːp] 1 t sorber ruidosamente, beber ruidosamente. – 2 i sorber ruidosamente, beber ruidosamente. – 3 n sorbetón m.

slush [slʌʃ] 1 n (melting snow) aguanieve f, nieve f derretida; (muddy snow) nieve f fangosa. 2 fam sentimentalismo, sensiblería. 3 (drink) granizado.
■ slush fund, us fondos mpl para sobornos.

slushy ['slʌʃɪ] 1 adj (snow) medio derretido,-a, fangoso,-a; (street) cubierto,-a de nieve derretida, cubierto,-a de nieve fangosa. 2 (sentimental) sentimentaloide, sensiblero,-a.
▲ comp slushier, superl slushiest.

slut [slʌt] 1 n pej (whore) fulana, ramera, puta. 2 pej (slovenly woman) guarra, marrana.

sly [slaɪ] 1 adj (cunning) astuto,-a, ladino,-a, taimado,-a; (deceitful) tramposo,-a: he's a sly old fox!, ¡es muy zorro! 2 (secretive, knowing) furtivo,-a: a sly smile, una sonrisa maliciosa. 3 (mischievous, playful) travieso,-a, pícaro,-a; (underhand) malicioso,-a.
● on the sly, a escondidas, a hurtadillas, por lo bajo.
▲ comp slyer o slier, superl slyest o sliest.

slyboots ['slaɪbuːts] n zorro,-a.

slyly ['slaɪlɪ] 1 adv (cunningly) con astucia, astutamente. 2 (secretively) furtivamente. 3 (mischievously) con picardía; (underhandedly) con malicia, maliciosamente.

smack¹ [smæk] 1 n (slap) bofetada, tortazo, azote m; (blow) golpe m: I'll give you a smack on the bottom, te daré un azote en el culo. 2 fam (loud kiss) besote m, beso sonoro. 3 (loud noise) ruido sonoro, chasquido. – 4 t (slap) dar una bofetada a, abofetear, pegar a: she

smacked his bottom, le pegó en el culo. 5 (strike) golpear. – 6 adv fam (with force) de lleno, directamente: he ran smack into the door, dio de lleno contra la puerta. 7 fam (exactly) justo.
● to have a smack at doing sth., probar algo, intentar algo. ║ to smack one's lips, relamerse.

smack² [smæk] 1 n (flavour) sabor m; (smell) olor m. 2 (hint, suggestion) pizca. 3 sl (heroin) caballo.
◆ to smack of t insep (gen) oler a.

smack³ [smæk] n mar barca de pesca.

smacker ['smækəʳ] 1 n fam (kiss) besazo. 2 gb libra; us dólar m.

small [smɔːl] 1 adj (not large) pequeño,-a, chico,-a: this skirt is too small for me, esta falda me va pequeña; we live in a small flat, vivimos en un piso pequeño; it's just a small present, sólo es un regalito; get the small table, coge la mesita. 2 (in height) bajo,-a, pequeño,-a: he's a small man, es un hombre bajito; she's quite small for her age, es bastante pequeña para su edad. 3 (young) joven, pequeño,-a: when I was small, cuando era pequeño; small children, niños pequeños. 4 (reduced - sum, number) reducido,-a, módico,-a; (slight, scant) escaso,-a, poco,-a: I want you to work in small groups, quiero que trabajéis en grupos reducidos; we paid small attention, prestamos poca atención; it's small comfort, es un triste consuelo. 5 (small-scale) pequeño,-a: small business, pequeño comercio; small investor, pequeño inversor. 6 (unimportant, trivial) sin importancia, de poca importancia, insignificante: you've made a few small mistakes, has hecho unos errores sin importancia. 7 (not capital) minúscula: with a small t, con t minúscula. 8 (mean, petty) mezquino,-a. – 9 adv pequeño: cut it up small, córtalo en trocitos. – 10 smalls, npl dated (underwear) paños mpl menores, ropa f sing interior.
● a small fortune, un dineral m. ║ (it's) small wonder that ..., no me extraña (nada) que ... ║ in a small voice, con la boca pequeña. ║ in the small hours, a altas horas de la madrugada. ║ it's a small world, el mundo es un pañuelo. ║ the small of the back, la región f lumbar. ║ to have a small appetite, no ser de mucho comer. ║ to feel small, sentirse humillado,-a. ║ to make sb. look small, dejar a algn. en ridículo, humillar a algn.
■ small ads, anuncios mpl por palabras, pequeños anuncios mpl. ║ small arms, armas mpl portátiles. ║ small change, cambio, monedas fpl sueltas. ║ small fry, gente f de poca monta. ║ small print, letra menuda, letra pequeña. ║ small screen, pequeña pantalla. ║ small talk, charla, charloteo.

smallholder ['smɔːlhəʊldəʳ] n (landowner) minifundista mf; (grower) pequeño,-a agricultor,-ra.

smallholding ['smɔːlhəʊldɪŋ] n (estate) minifundio; (farm) granja pequeña, parcela.

smallish ['smɔːlɪʃ] adj más bien pequeño,-a.

small-minded [smɔːl'maɪndɪd] adj (narrow-minded) de miras estrechas; (petty) mezquino,-a.

smallness ['smɔːlnəs] n (size) pequeñez f; (lack of importance) insignificancia.

smallpox ['smɔːlpɒks] n viruela.

small-scale ['smɔːl'skeɪl] adj a pequeña escala, en pequeña escala.

small-time ['smɔːl'taɪm] adj de poca monta.

small-town ['smɔːltaʊn] adj provinciano,-a, pueblerino,-a.

smarmy ['smɑːmɪ] adj zalamero,-a, cobista.
▲ comp smarmier, superl smarmiest.

smart [smɑːt] 1 adj (elegant) elegante, fino,-a; (chic) fino,-a, de buen tono: you look very smart today, vas muy ele-

gante hoy, estás muy elegante hoy. **2** US (*clever*) listo,- a, inteligente; (*sharp*) agudo,-a, vivo,-a; (*impudent*) fresco,-a, descarado,-a: *he thinks he's so smart,* se cree muy listo; *don't get smart with me!,* ¡no te pases de listo conmigo! **3** (*quick, brisk*) rápido,-a, ligero,-a; (*forceful*) seco,- a, fuerte. **– 4** i (*sting*) escocer, picar: *the smoke made my eyes smart,* el humo me escocía los ojos. **5** (*suffer*) sufrir, dolerse: *she smarted from their cruel remarks,* sus comentarios crueles la hirieron en lo más vivo.
● **to smart from sth.,** (*be bitter*) resentirse de algo. ‖ **smart alec(k),** listillo, sabelotodo.

smart-arse ['smɑːtɑːs] *n sl* listillo,-a, sabihondo,-a, sabelotodo *mf*.

smarten ['smɑːtən] *t* (*person, house*) arreglar (**up,** -).
● **to smarten up one's ear/ideas,** despabilarse, espabilarse. ‖ **to smarten os. (up),** arreglarse.

smartly ['smɑːtlɪ] **1** *adv* (*elegantly*) elegante, elegantemente, con elegancia. **2** (*cleverly*) inteligentemente; (*sharply*) con agudeza. **3** (*quickly*) rápidamente; (*forcefully*) con fuerza.

smartness ['smɑːtnəs] **1** *n* (*elegance*) elegancia, buena presencia; (*chic*) buen tono. **2** (*cleverness*) inteligencia; (*sharpness*) agudeza.

smarty-pants ['smɑːtɪpænts] *n fam* listillo,-a, sabihondo,-a, sabelotodo *mf*.

smash [smæʃ] **1** *n* (*noise*) estrépito, estruendo. **2** (*collision*) choque *m* violento, colisión *f*. **3** (*blow*) golpe *m*. **4** SP (*tennis*) smash *m*, mate *m*. **5** (*success, hit*) exitazo, gran éxito. **– 6** *t* (*break*) romper; (*shatter*) hacer pedazos, hacer añicos; (*destroy - car, room, etc*) destrozar: *the vandals smashed the place up,* los vándalos destrozaron el local. **7** (*hit forcefully*) romper; (*crash, throw violently*) estrellar (**into,** contra): *he smashed the door in,* tiró la puerta abajo; *she smashed her fist through the table,* rompió la mesa de un puñetazo; *the waves smashed the little boat against the rocks,* las olas estrellaron la barquita contra las rocas. **8** (*defeat*) vencer, derrotar, aplastar; (*destroy*) destrozar, destruir; (*break up*) desarticular, desmantelar; (*beat*) batir, superar. **9** SP (*in tennis*) hacer un mate, dar un mate. **– 10** i (*break*) romperse; (*shatter*) hacerse pedazos, hacerse añicos: *the mirror smashed into tiny pieces,* el espejo se hizo añicos. **11** (*crash*) estrellarse (**into,** contra), chocar (**into,** contra): *they smashed into a tree,* chocaron contra un árbol.
● **to smash sb.'s face,** partirle la cara a algn. ‖ ■ **smash hit,** gran éxito, exitazo.

smash-and-grab [smæʃən'græb] *n* robo relámpago.

smashed [smæʃt] *adj fam* (*drunk*) borracho,-a.
● **to get smashed,** emborracharse, agarrar un pedo, ponerse ciego,-a.

smasher ['smæʃəʳ] *n fam* (*person*) tío,-a bueno,-a; (*thing*) maravilla.
● **to be a real smasher,** estar como un tren.

smashing ['smæʃɪŋ] *adj* GB *fam* estupendo,-a, fantástico,-a, genial, fenomenal: *we had a smashing time,* lo pasamos bomba.

smash-up ['smæʃʌp] *n* (*crash*) choque *m* violento, colisión *f*; (*accident*) accidente *m*.

smattering ['smætərɪŋ] *n* nociones *fpl*: *he has a smattering of French,* habla un poco de francés.

smear [smɪəʳ] **1** *n* (*smudge, stain*) mancha. **2** MED frotis *m*. **3** *fig* (*defamation*) calumnia. **– 4** *t* (*spread - butter, ointment*) untar; (*- grease, paint*) embadurnar: *he smeared butter on the bread,* untó el pan con mantequilla; *she smeared suntan lotion all over her body,* se embadurnó todo el cuerpo con bronceador. **5** (*make dirty*) manchar; (*smudge*) borrar: *the child had ice-cream smeared all*

round his mouth, el niño tenía toda la boca manchada de helado. **6** *fig* (*defame*) calumniar, difamar. **– 7** i (*smudge*) correrse.
■ **smear campaign,** campaña de difamación. ‖ **smear test,** MED citología.

smell [smel] **1** *n* (*sense*) olfato. **2** (*odour*) olor *m*; (*perfume*) perfume *m*, aroma *m*: *I love the smell of roses,* me encanta el olor a rosas; *this fish has a funny smell,* este pescado huele raro; *there's a smell of gas,* huele a gas; *poo! what a smell!,* ¡qué peste! **– 3** *t* oler: *I can smell burning,* huelo a quemado; *smell this perfume,* huele este perfume. **4** *fig* olfatear: *she smelt danger,* olfateaba el peligro. **– 5** i (*sense*) oler. **6** (*have particular smell*) oler (a): *it smells like orange,* huele a naranja; *this food smells delicious,* esta comida huele muy bien; *the room smelt of smoke,* la habitación olía a humo; *you smell of beer,* hueles a cerveza; *his feet smell,* le huelen los pies; *his breath smells,* tiene mal aliento.
◆ **to smell out 1** *t sep* (*discover by smelling*) husmear. **2** (*stink*) apestar.
● **to have a smell of sth.,** olerse algo. ‖ **I smell a rat,** aquí hay gato encerrado.
▲ *pt & pp* **smelled** *o* **smelt**.

smelling salts ['smelɪŋsɔːlts] *npl* sales *fpl* aromáticas.

smelly ['smelɪ] *adj* apestoso,-a, maloliente, pestilente, hediondo,-a: *you've got smelly feet,* te huelen los pies.
▲ *comp* **smellier,** *superl* **smelliest**.

smelt[1] [smelt] *t* (*melt*) fundir.

smelt[2] [smelt] *pp →* **smell**.

smelter ['smeltəʳ] *n* (*furnace*) fundición *f*, altos hornos *mpl*.

smile [smaɪl] **1** *n* sonrisa. **– 2** i (*gen*) sonreír: *he smiled at me,* me sonrió. **– 3** *t* (*say with a smile*) decir sonriendo.
◆ **to smile on** i sonreír a.
● **to be all smiles,** no parar de sonreír. ‖ **to wipe the smile off sb.'s face,** quitarle las ganas de sonreír a algn.

smiling ['smaɪlɪŋ] *adj* sonriente, risueño,-a.

smirk [smɜːk] **1** *n* (*self-satisfied*) sonrisa satisfecha, sonrisa de satisfacción; (*foolish*) sonrisa boba. **– 2** i (*with self-satisfaction*) sonreír con satisfacción; (*foolishly*) sonreír bobamente.

smite [smaɪt] **1** *t arch* (*hit*) golpear, pegar. **2** *arch* (*afflict*) aquejar. **3** *arch* (*punish*) castigar.
▲ *pt* **smote,** *pp* **smitten**.

smith [smɪθ] *n* herrero,-a.

smithereens [smɪðə'riːnz] *npl* añicos *mpl*.
● **to smash sth. to smithereens,** hacer algo añicos, hacer algo trizas, hacer algo pedazos.

smithy ['smɪðɪ] *n* herrería.
▲ *pl* **smithies**.

smitten ['smɪtən] **1** *pp →* **smite**. **– 2** *adj* (*besotted*) locamente enamorado,-a.
● **to be smitten with sb.,** (*besotted*) estar locamente enamorado,-a de algn., estar loco,-a por algn. ‖ **to be smitten by/with sth.,** estar entusiasmado,-a con algo. ‖ **to be smitten (down) by/with sth.,** (*illness*) estar aquejado,-a de algo. ‖ **to be smitten with sth.,** (*affected*) estar lleno,-a de algo, sentir mucho algo: *he was smitten with remorse,* le remordía la conciencia.

smock [smɒk] **1** *n* (*blouse*) blusón *m*; (*for pregnant women*) blusón de premamá, vestido premamá. **2** (*overall*) bata, guardapolvo.

smocking ['smɒkɪŋ] *n* SEW nido de abeja.

smog [smɒg] *n* niebla tóxica, smog *m*.

smoke [sməʊk] **1** *n* (*gen*) humo. **2** *fam* (*cigarette*) cigarillo, cigarro, pitillo. **– 3** *t* (*person*) fumar: *he smokes a pipe,* fuma en pipa. **4** (*meat, fish*) ahumar. – **5** *i* (*person*) fumar. **6** (*fire, chimney, etc*) echar humo, humear.

◆ **to smoke out** *t sep* (*insects*) ahuyentar con humo; (*people*) desalojar con bombas fumígenas.

● **the Smoke,** GB Londres. ‖ **there's no smoke without fire,** cuando el río suena, agua lleva. ‖ **to go up in smoke,** (*books, paintings, etc*) quemarse, ser destruido,-a por un incendio; (*project, campaign, etc*) irse en humo, quedar en agua de borrajas. ‖ **to have a smoke,** fumar: *I'm going outside for a smoke,* salgo a fumarme un cigarillo.

■ **smoke alarm / smoke detector,** detector *m* de humo. ‖ **smoke bomb,** bomba fumígena. ‖ **smoke screen,** cortina de humo. ‖ **smoke signal,** señal *f* de humo.

smoked [sməʊkt] *adj* CULIN ahumado,-a.

smokeless [ˈsməʊkləs] *adj* sin humo.

■ **smokeless fuel,** combustible *m* sin humo. ‖ **smokeless zone,** zona libre de humos.

smoker [ˈsməʊkəʳ] **1** *n* (*person*) fumador,-ra: *she's a heavy smoker,* fuma mucho. **2** (*on train*) vagón *m* de fumadores.

■ **smoker's cough,** tos *f* de fumador.

smokestack [ˈsməʊkstæk] *n* chimenea.

smoking [ˈsməʊkɪŋ] **1** *adj* humeante, que echa humo. – **2** *n* fumar *m*: *smoking is bad for you,* fumar es malo; *smoking damages your health,* fumar es perjudicial para la salud.

● "**no smoking**", "prohibido fumar".

■ **smoking compartment,** compartimiento de fumadores. ‖ **smoking jacket,** batín *m*.

smoky [ˈsməʊkɪ] **1** *adj* (*chimney, fire, etc*) humeante, que echa humo; (*room*) lleno,-a de humo; (*atmosphere*) cargado,-a de humo. **2** (*food, colour*) ahumado,-a.

▲ *comp* **smokier,** *superl* **smokiest**.

smolder [ˈsməʊldəʳ] *i* US → **smoulder**.

smooch [smuːtʃ] **1** *i* (*kiss and cuddle*) besuquearse. **2** (*dance*) bailar agarrado.

smooth [smuːð] **1** *adj* (*surface, texture, tyre*) liso,-a; (*skin*) suave; (*road*) llano,-a, uniforme; (*sea*) tranquilo,-a, en calma. **2** (*liquid mixture, sauce*) sin grumos. **3** (*wine, beer, etc*) suave. **4** (*style etc*) fluido,-a. **5** (*journey, flight*) tranquilo,-a; (*take-off, landing, stop*) suave; (*take-over, transition*) sin problemas, sin obstáculos, sin complicaciones. **6** *pej* (*person*) zalamero,-a, meloso,-a. – **7** *t* (*gen*) alisar; (*with sandpaper*) lijar; (*polish*) pulir: *he smoothed down his hair,* se alisó el pelo.

◆ **to smooth away 1** *t sep* (*problems etc*) allanar. **2** (*wrinkles*) hacer desaparecer.

● **as smooth as a baby's bottom,** suave como el culito de un bebé. ‖ **to be a smooth operator,** ser un tipo muy hábil. ‖ **to be a smooth talker,** tener un pico de oro. ‖ **to smooth the path/way,** preparar el terreno, allanar el terreno. ‖ **to smooth things over,** limar asperezas.

smoothie [ˈsmuːðɪ] *n fam* tipo zamalero, pelota *m*, cobista *m*.

smoothly [ˈsmuːðlɪ] **1** *adv* (*without problems*) sin problemas, sobre ruedas: *everything is running smoothly,* todo va sobre ruedas, todo va como una seda. **2** (*of movement*) suavemente.

smoothness [ˈsmuːðnəs] **1** *n* (*softness*) suavidad *f*; (*flatness*) llaneza, lisura, uniformidad *f*. **2** (*lack of problems*) tranquilidad *f*. **3** (*of movement*) suavidad *f*. **4** (*flattery*) zalamería.

smooth-running [ˈsmuːðˈrʌnɪŋ] *adj* que funciona bien.

smooth-talking [ˈsmuːðˈtɔːkɪŋ] *adj* zalamero,-a, con mucha labia.

smote [sməʊt] *pt* → **smite**.

smother [ˈsmʌðəʳ] **1** *t* (*asphyxiate*) asfixiar, ahogar: *she smothered him with a pillow,* lo asfixió con una almohada. **2** (*put out - fire*) sofocar, extinguir, apagar. **3** (*stifle - yawn, cough, laughter*) contener, reprimir; (*suppress - opposition*) acallar: *the terrorist attack has smothered all hopes for peace,* el atentado terrorista ha echado por tierra todas las esperanzas de paz. **4** (*cover*) cubrir (**in/with,** de); (*heap*) colmar (**in/with,** de): *the wall is smothered with graffiti,* la pared está cubierta de grafitis; *the cake was smothered with cream,* el pastel estaba cubierto de nata; *they smothered her with love,* la colmaron de amor. – **5** *i* (*asphyxiate*) asfixiarse, ahogarse.

smoulder [ˈsməʊldəʳ] **1** *i* (*fire*) arder sin llama. **2** *fig* (*passion*) arder; (*anger*) consumir.

smouldering [ˈsməʊldərɪŋ] **1** *adj fig* (*passion, eyes*) ardiente; (*hatred*) latente. **2** (*ashes*) humeante.

smudge [smʌdʒ] **1** *n* (*stain - gen*) mancha; (*- of ink*) borrón *m*. – **2** *t* (*gen*) manchar; (*writing*) emborronar. – **3** *i* (*ink, paint, etc*) correrse.

smudgy [ˈsmʌdʒɪ] *adj* (*dirty*) manchado,-a; (*writing*) emborronado,-a; (*blurred*) borrado,-a.

▲ *comp* **smudgier,** *superl* **smudgiest**.

smug [smʌg] *adj* engreído,-a, satisfecho,-a, pagado,-a de sí mismo,-a, suficiente.

▲ *comp* **smugger,** *superl* **smuggest**.

smuggle [ˈsmʌgəl] **1** *t* (*illegally*) pasar de contrabando: *he smuggled tobacco into the country,* entraba tabaco de contrabando en el país. **2** (*sneak*) pasar a escondidas.

● **to smuggle sth. through customs,** pasar algo de contrabando por la aduana.

smuggler [ˈsmʌgələʳ] *n* contrabandista *mf*.

smuggling [ˈsmʌgəlɪŋ] *n* contrabando.

smugly [ˈsmʌglɪ] *adv* con engreimiento, con (aire de) suficiencia.

smugness [ˈsmʌgnəs] *n* engreimiento, suficiencia.

smut [smʌt] **1** *n* (*of soot*) hollín *m*, carbonilla; (*stain*) mancha de tizne, mancha de hollín. **2** *fam* (*filthy talk*) obscenidades *fpl*; (*jokes*) chistes *mpl* verdes; (*books etc*) pornografía.

smutty [ˈsmʌtɪ] **1** *adj* (*dirty with smut*) manchado,-a, sucio,-a; (*with soot*) tiznado,-a. **2** (*filthy - talk*) obsceno,-a; (*- joke*) verde; (*- book etc*) pornográfico,-a.

▲ *comp* **smuttier,** *superl* **smuttiest**.

snack [snæk] **1** *n* (*light meal*) bocado, piscolabis *m*, tentempié *m*, refrigerio; (*in afternoon*) merienda. – **2** *i* comer, comerse. – **3 snacks,** *npl* (*gen*) cosas *fpl* para picar; (*in bar*) tapas *fpl*.

● **to have a snack,** comer algo ligero, tomarse un piscolabis. ‖ **to snack on sth.,** comer algo.

■ **snack bar,** cafetería, bar *m*.

snag [snæg] **1** *n* (*difficulty*) pega, problema *m*, inconveniente *m*: *the only snag is the price,* la única pega es el precio. **2** (*tear, hole, thread*) enganchón *m*, desgarrón *m*, rasgón *m*, siete *m*. **3** (*sharp projection*) saliente *m*; (*tree stump*) tocón *m*. – **4** *t* (*catch, tear*) enganchar.

▲ *pt & pp* **snagged,** *ger* **snagging**.

snail [sneɪl] *n* caracol *m*.

● **at a snail's pace,** a paso de tortuga.

snake [sneɪk] **1** *n* (*big*) serpiente *f*; (*small*) culebra. – **2** *i fig* (*river, road, etc*) serpentear.

■ **snake charmer,** encantador,-ra de serpientes. ‖ **snake in the grass,** traidor,-ra, judas *m*. ‖ **snakes and ladders,** (el juego de) la oca.

snakebite ['sneɪkbaɪt] 1 *n* mordedura de serpiente. 2 GB (*drink*) cerveza con sidra (y grosella negra).
snakeskin ['sneɪkskɪn] *n* piel *f* de serpiente.
snaky ['sneɪkɪ] *adj* sinuoso,-a, tortuoso,-a.
▲ *comp* snakier, *superl* snakiest.
snap [snæp] 1 *n* (*sharp noise*) ruido seco; (*of fingers, branch*) chasquido. 2 *fam* (*snapshot*) foto *f*, instantánea. 3 (*card game*) juego de naipes infantil. 4 *fam* (*eagerness, zip*) afán *m*, brío, energía. 5 US (*easy thing to do*) cosa tirada: *it's a snap,* está chupado, está tirado. 6 US (*press-stud*) broche *m* a presión. – 7 *adj* (*decision etc*) precipitado,-a, repentino,-a. – 8 *interj* GB ¡toma!, ¡caramba! – 9 *t* (*break*) partir en dos, romper en dos. 10 (*close*) cerrar de golpe: *she snapped her bag shut,* cerró el bolso de golpe. 11 (*click*) chasquear: *he snapped his fingers,* chasqueó los dedos. 12 (*say sharply*) decir bruscamente. 13 *fam* (*photograph*) sacar una foto de. – 14 *i* (*break*) romperse, partirse. 15 *fig* (*person*) perder los nervios, sufrir una crisis nerviosa: *she snapped under the strain of too much work,* sufrió una crisis nerviosa por exceso de trabajo. 16 (*say sharply*) regañar (**at**, a), hablar con brusquedad (**at**, a): *there's no need to snap!,* ¡no hace falta morder! 17 (*bite*) morder (**at**, -): *the dog snapped at his ankles,* el perro le quiso morder los tobillos.
◆ **to snap up** *t sep* (*bargain*) llevarse; (*offer*) agarrar, no dejar escapar.
● **snap to it!,** ¡rápido!, ¡muévete! ‖ **to go snap,** romperse. ‖ **to snap one's fingers at,** burlarse de. ‖ **to snap out of it,** animarse, reaccionar. ‖ **to snap sb.'s head off,** echarle un rapapolvo a algn. ‖ **to snap shut,** cerrarse de golpe.
▲ (*verbo*) *pt* & *pp* snapped, *ger* snapping.
snapdragon ['snæpdrægən] *n* BOT dragón *m*.
snappish ['snæpɪʃ] *adj* (*person*) irritable, irascible; (*dog*) que muerde, mordedor,-ra.
snappy ['snæpɪ] 1 *adj* (*quick*) rápido,-a; (*brisk, lively*) enérgico,-a, vivo,-a: *make it snappy!,* ¡date prisa!, ¡rápido! 2 (*stylish*) elegante. 3 (*short-tempered*) irritable, irascible.
● **to be a snappy dresser,** vestir con elegancia.
▲ *comp* snappier, *superl* snappiest.
snapshot ['snæpʃɒt] *n* foto *f*, instantánea.
snare[1] [sneəʳ] 1 *n* (*trap - for animal*) lazo, trampa, cepo; (- *for person*) trampa. – 2 *t* (*catch - animal*) coger con lazo, cazar con trampa; (- *person*) atrapar, cazar; (*trick*) engañar.
snare[2] [sneəʳ] *n* MUS bordón *m*.
■ **snare drum,** tambor *m* (con bordón).
snarl[1] [snɑːl] 1 *n* (*growl*) gruñido. – 2 *i* (*growl*) gruñir (**at**, a). – 3 *t* (*say*) gruñir.
snarl[2] [snɑːl] 1 *n* (*in wool*) maraña, enredo. 2 (*confused state*) enredo, maraña, lío.
◆ **to snarl up** 1 *t sep* (*wool*) enmarañar, enredar; (*traffic*) atascar; (*plans*) enredar. – 2 *i* (*traffic*) atascarse.
snarl-up ['snɑːlʌp] *n* (*gen*) enredo, maraña; (*in traffic*) atasco.
snatch [snætʃ] 1 *n* (*grab*) arrebatamiento. 2 *fam* (*theft*) robo, hurto. 3 (*of song, conversation*) fragmento. – 4 *t* (*grab*) arrebatar, arrancar, coger; (*steal*) robar; (*kidnap*) secuestrar: *he snatched the paper out of my hand,* me arrancó el papel de la mano; *my bag's been snatched,* me han robado el bolso. 5 (*sleep, food, etc*) coger, pillar; (*opportunity etc*) aprovechar: *try and snatch a few hours' sleep,* trata de dormir unas horas; *I'll snatch a bite to eat later,* pillaré algo de comer después. – 6 *i* arrebatar, quitar: *don't snatch!,* ¡no me lo quites!
◆ **to snatch at** 1 *t insep* (*ball, branch, etc*) tratar de coger. – 2 *t sep* (*opportunity etc*) aprovechar.

● **in snatches,** a ratos.
snazzy ['snæzɪ] *adj fam* (*stylish*) elegante; (*flashy*) vistoso,-a, llamativo,-a.
▲ *comp* snazzier, *superl* snazziest.
sneak [sniːk] 1 *n* GB *fam* acusica *mf*, acusón,-ona, chivato,-a, soplón,-ona. – 2 *adj* (*attack, visit, etc*) sorpresa; (*look*) furtivo,-a. – 3 *t* (*take out*) sacar (a escondidas); (*take in*) pasar (a escondidas), colar (de extranjis): *she sneaked a camera into the concert,* coló una cámara (de extranjis) en el concierto; *I sneaked a look at the answers,* miré las respuestas de reojo. – 4 *i* (*move*) moverse sigilosamente: *they sneaked past the guard,* pasaron desapercibidos delante del guardia; *she sneaked out the back way,* salió a hurtadillas por la parte de atrás; *where did you two sneak off to?,* ¿dónde os habéis escabullido? 5 (*tell tales*) acusar (**on**, a), chivarse (**on**, de).
◆ **to sneak up** *i* acercarse sigilosamente, acercarse a hurtadillas: *I wish you wouldn't sneak up on me like that!,* ¡no me gusta que te me acerques así, tan sigilosamente!
■ **sneak preview,** preestreno. ‖ **sneak thief,** ladronzuelo,-a, ratero,-a.
sneakers ['sniːkəz] *npl* US zapatillas *fpl* de deporte, bambas *fpl,* playeras *fpl.*
sneaking ['sniːkɪŋ] 1 *adj* (*secret*) secreto,-a: *he has a sneaking admiration for her,* en el fondo la admira. 2 (*vague, slight*) ligero,-a: *I have a sneaking suspicion that ...,* tengo la sensación de que ...
sneaky ['sniːkɪ] 1 *adj* (*secretive*) sigiloso,-a, furtivo,-a. 2 (*deceitful*) solapado,-a, cuco,-a, artero,-a.
▲ *comp* sneakier, *superl* sneakiest.
sneer [snɪəʳ] 1 *n* (*look*) cara de desprecio; (*smile*) sonrisa burlona, sonrisa socarrona. 2 (*remark*) comentario desdeñoso, comentario despreciativo. – 3 *i* (*mock*) burlarse (**at**, de), mofarse (**at**, de); (*scorn*) desdeñar, despreciar.
sneering ['snɪərɪŋ] 1 *adj* (*mocking*) burlón,-ona; (*sarcastic*) socarrón,-ona, sarcástico,-a. 2 (*scornful*) desdeñoso,-a, despreciativo,-a.
sneeze [sniːz] 1 *n* estornudo. – 2 *i* estornudar.
● **it's not to be sneezed at,** no es de despreciar.
snide [snaɪd] *adj* (*sarcastic*) sarcástico,-a; (*scornful*) despectivo,-a.
sniff [snɪf] 1 *n* aspiración: *she said with a loud sniff,* dijo aspirando por la nariz. 2 (*inhalation*) aspiración *f* (por la nariz), inhalación *f*: *have a sniff of this,* huele esto; *one sniff of the gas is enough,* una inhalación del gas es suficiente. – 3 *i* (*with a cold*) sorber (por las narices), sorberse los mocos: *stop sniffing!,* ¡deja de sorberte los mocos! 4 (*when crying*) resollar. – 5 *t* (*person - gen*) oler; (- *suspiciously*) olfatear, husmear, olisquear; (*animal*) olfatear, husmear, olisquear. 6 (*say proudly*) decir con desdén; (*complainingly*) gimotear. 7 (*drugs*) esnifar; (*glue*) esnifar, inhalar; (*vapour, snuff, smelling salts*) aspirar (por la nariz), inhalar.
◆ **to sniff at** 1 *t insep* (*person*) oler; (*animal*) olfatear, husmear, olisquear. 2 (*turn nose up at*) despreciar, desdeñar: *it's not to be sniffed at,* no es (como) para despreciarlo. ‖ **to sniff out** 1 *t insep* (*drugs etc*) descubrir husmeando, descubrir olfateando. 2 (*secret, plot, etc*) oler, olerse.
sniffer dog ['snɪfədɒg] *n* perro rastreador.
sniffle ['snɪfəl] 1 *n* (*slight cold*) resfriado. – 2 *i* (*with cold*) sorberse los mocos; (*when crying*) lloriquear.
● **to have the sniffles,** estar resfriado,-a.
snifter ['snɪftəʳ] 1 *n* GB *fam* (*drink*) trago, copa. 2 US (*brandy glass*) copa de coñac.

● **to have a snifter,** echar un trago.
snigger ['snɪgə'] **1** *n* risa disimulada, risilla. – **2** *i* reír disimuladamente, reír por lo bajo.
● **to snigger at sb./sth.,** reírse de algn./algo, burlarse de algn./algo.
sniggering ['snɪgərɪŋ] *n* risillas *fpl*.
snip [snɪp] **1** *n* (*cut with scissors*) tijeretazo, tijeretada; (*action, noise*) tijereteo. **2** (*small piece cut off*) recorte *m*. **3** GB *fam* (*bargain*) ganga, chollo. – **4** *t* tijeretear.
◆ **to snip off** *t sep* cortar con tijeras.
▲ (*verbo*) *pt & pp* **snipped,** *ger* **snipping.**
snipe [snaɪp] **1** *i* (*shoot*) disparar (desde un escondite) (**at,** sobre). **2** *fig* (*criticize*) criticar. – **3** *n* ORN agachadiza.
sniper ['snaɪpə'] *n* MIL francotirador,-ra.
snippet ['snɪpɪt] **1** *n* (*small piece cut off*) recorte *m*, trocito. **2** (*of conversation etc*) fragmento.
snitch [snɪtʃ] **1** *t* (*steal*) birlar, afanar, mangar. – **2** *i* (*inform on*) chivarse (**on,** de), acusar (**on,** a).
snivel ['snɪvəl] **1** *i* lloriquear. – **2** *n* lloriqueo.
▲ *pt & pp* **snivelled** (US **sniveled**), *ger* **snivelling** (US **sniveling**).
snivelling ['snɪvəlɪŋ] **1** *adj* llorón,-ona. – **2** *n* lloriqueo.
snob [snɒb] *n pej* snob *mf*, esnob *mf*.
■ **snob appeal / snob value,** toque *m* de distinción.
snobbery ['snɒbərɪ] *n* snobismo, esnobismo.
snobbish ['snɒbɪʃ] *adj* snob, esnob.
snobby ['snɒbɪ] *adj* snob, esnob.
▲ *comp* **snobbier,** *superl* **snobbiest.**
snog [snɒg] **1** *i* besuquearse. – **2** *n* besuqueo.
● **to have a snog,** besuquearse.
▲ (*verbo*) *pt & pp* **snogged,** *ger* **snogging.**
snooker ['snuːkə'] **1** *n* snooker *m*, billar *m* ruso. – **2** *t* SP interponer una bola en la línea de tiro del jugador contrario. **3** GB *fam* poner en un aprieto.
● **to be snookered,** estar arreglado,-a, estar con el agua al cuello.
snoop [snuːp] **1** *i* (*search, investigate*) husmear, fisgar, fisgonear, curiosear. **2** (*pry*) entrometerse, meterse (**into,** en). – **3** *n* (*person*) fisgón,-ona.
● **to have a snoop about/around,** husmear, fisgonear, curiosear.
snooper ['snuːpə'] *n* fisgón,-ona.
snooty ['snuːtɪ] *adj fam* altivo,-a, presumido,-a, altanero,-a, arrogante, engreído,-a.
▲ *comp* **snootier,** *superl* **snootiest.**
snooze [snuːz] **1** *n fam* cabezada, siestecilla. – **2** *i fam* dormitar, echar una cabezada.
● **to have a snooze,** echar una cabezada, echar una siestecilla.
snore [snɔː'] **1** *n* ronquido. – **2** *i* roncar.
snoring ['snɔːrɪŋ] *n* ronquidos *mpl*.
snorkel ['snɔːkəl] **1** *n* (*of swimmer*) tubo de respiración; (*of submarine*) esnórquel *m*. – **2** *i* bucear con tubo de respiración.
▲ *pt & pp* **snorkelled** (US **snorkeled**), *ger* **snorkelling** (US **snorkeling**).
snorkelling ['snɔːkəlɪŋ] *n* buceo (con tubo de respiración).
● **to go snorkelling,** bucear con tubo de respiración.
snort [snɔːt] **1** *i* (*make noise - person*) resoplar, bufar; (- *animal*) resoplar. **2** (*say angrily etc*) bramar, gruñir. – **3** *t* (*drugs*) esnifar. – **4** *n* (*person*) resoplido, bufido; (*animal*) resoplido. **5** *fam* (*drink*) trago. **6** (*of drugs*) esnifada.
snot [snɒt] *n fam* mocos *mpl*.
snotty ['snɒtɪ] **1** *adj fam* (*child*) mocoso,-a; (*adult*) altivo,-a, altanero,-a. **2** (*nose, hanky*) lleno,-a de mocos.

▲ *comp* **snottier,** *superl* **snottiest.**
snotty-nosed ['snɒtɪnəʊzd] *adj* (*child*) mocoso,-a; (*adult*) altivo,-a, altanero,-a.
snout [snaʊt] **1** *n* (*of animal*) morro, hocico. **2** GB *fam* (*of person*) napias *mf*, narizotas *mf*. **3** (*of gun, bottle, etc*) morro. **4** GB *sl* (*tobacco*) tabaco. **5** GB *sl* (*informer*) soplón,-ona, chivato,-a.
snow [snəʊ] **1** *n* METEOR (*gen*) nieve *f*; (*snowfall*) nevada. **2** TV nieve *f*. **3** *sl* (*cocaine*) nieve *f*. – **4** *i* nevar: *it's snowing,* está nevando. – **5** *t* US *fam* (*influence*) convencer, impresionar.
● **to be snowed in/up,** estar aislado,-a por la nieve, quedar aislado,-a por la nieve. ‖ **to be snowed under with sth.,** (*work*) estar agobiado,-a por algo, estar desbordado,-a por algo; (*applications*) haber recibido una lluvia de solicitudes.
■ **snow blindness,** ceguera de la nieve. ‖ **snow leopard,** onza. ‖ **snow line,** límite *m* de las nieves perpetuas. ‖ **snow report,** informe *m* sobre el estado de la nieve. ‖ **snow shower,** nevada. ‖ **Snow White,** Blancanieves *f*.
snowball ['snəʊbɔːl] **1** *n* bola de nieve. – **2** *i* tirar bolas de nieve. **3** (*of plan, project*) aumentar rápidamente.
snow-blind ['snəʊblaɪnd] *adj* cegado,-a por la nieve.
snowbound ['snəʊbaʊnd] *adj* aislado,-a por la nieve, bloqueado,-a por la nieve.
snow-capped ['snəʊkæpt] *adj* coronado,-a de nieve, nevado,-a.
snow-covered ['snəʊkʌvəd] *adj* cubierto,-a de nieve, nevado,-a.
snowdrift ['snəʊdrɪft] *n* ventisquero.
snowdrop ['snəʊdrɒp] *n* BOT campanilla de invierno.
snowfall ['snəʊfɔːl] *n* nevada.
snowflake ['snəʊfleɪk] *n* copo de nieve.
snowman ['snəʊmæn] *n* muñeco de nieve.
snowmobile ['snəʊməbiːl] *n* moto *f* para la nieve.
snowplough ['snəʊplaʊ] *n* quitanieves *m*.
snowplow ['snəʊplaʊ] *n* US → **snowplough**.
snowshoe ['snəʊʃuː] *n* raqueta (de nieve).
snowstorm ['snəʊstɔːm] *n* nevasca, ventisca, tormenta de nieve.
snowsuit ['snəʊsuːt] *n* US traje *m* de invierno para niños.
snow-white [snəʊ'waɪt] *adj* blanco,-a como la nieve.
snowy ['snəʊɪ] **1** *adj* (*full of snow - mountain etc*) nevado,-a; (- *region, climate*) de mucha nieve; (- *day*) de nieve; (- *season*) de las nieves. **2** (*pure white*) blanco,-a como la nieve, níveo,-a.
▲ *comp* **snowier,** *superl* **snowiest.**
Snr ['siːnɪə'] *abbr* (*senior*) padre.
snub [snʌb] **1** *n* (*of person*) desaire *m*; (*of offer*) rechazo. – **2** *t* (*person*) desairar; (*offer*) rechazar. – **3** *adj* (*nose*) respingón,-ona, chato,-a.
● **to be snubbed,** sufrir un desaire.
▲ (*verbo*) *pt & pp* **snubbed,** *ger* **snubbing.**
snub-nosed ['snʌb'nəʊzd] *adj* de nariz chata, de nariz respingona.
snuff[1] [snʌf] *n* (*tobacco*) rapé *m*: *a pinch of snuff,* un pellizco de rapé.
● **to take snuff,** tomar rapé.
snuff[2] [snʌf] *t* (*extinguish candle*) apagar (**out,** -); (*cut off wick*) cortar.
◆ **to snuff out** *t sep* (*rebellion*) sofocar; (*hopes*) acabar con.
● **to snuff it,** estirar la pata, liar el petate, diñarla.
snuffbox ['snʌfbɒks] *n* caja de rapé, tabaquera.

snuffle ['snʌfəl] **1** *n* (*act, sound*) sorbo por las narices, resuello. **– 2** *i* (*make sniffing noises*) resoplar; (*breathe noisily*) respirar ruidosamente.

snug [snʌg] **1** *adj* (*cosy*) cómodo,-a; (*warm*) calentito,-a. **2** (*tightfitting*) ajustado,-a, ceñido,-a. **– 3** *n* GB (*in pub*) saloncito.

snuggle ['snʌgəl] *i* acurrucarse: *they snuggled up together in bed,* se acurrucaron juntos en la cama; *snuggle up to me,* arrímate a mí.

snugly ['snʌglɪ] **1** *adv* (*cosily*) cómodamente; (*warmly*) calentito,-a. **2** (*tightly*) perfectamente: *these jeans fit very snugly,* estos vaqueros me quedan ajustados.

so [səʊ] **1** *conj* (*therefore*) así que, por lo tanto, de manera que: *she was tired, so she went to bed,* estaba cansada, así que se fue a la cama. **2** (*to express purpose*) para, para que: *speak up so that everyone can hear,* habla fuerte para que todos te oigan; *he took off his shoes so as not to make any noise,* se quitó los zapatos para no hacer ruido. **– 3** *adv* (*introductory*) así que, pues, bueno: *so you've decided to come,* así que has decidido venir; *so I made a mistake! what about it?,* ¡pues me he equivocado! ¿y qué?; *so, what now?,* bueno, ¿ahora qué? **4** (*very - before adj or adv*) tan; (*- before noun or with verb*) tanto,-a: *she's so bored,* está tan aburrida; *it's so cold,* hace tanto frío; *don't drive so fast,* no vayas tan rápido, no corras tanto; *he was so hungry that he ate the lot,* tenía tanta hambre que se lo comió todo; *he isn't so clever as he looks,* no es tan listo como parece. **5** (*unspecified number or amount, limit*) tanto,-a: *I can only do so much,* no puedo hacer más; *it'll take a month or so,* tardará un mes más o menos, tardará un mes o así; *why don't you say that you earn so much?,* ¿por qué no dices que ganas tanto?; *so much noise/food,* tanto ruido/tanta comida; *so many boys/girls,* tantos niños/tantas niñas. **6** (*thus, in this way*) así, de esta manera, de este modo: *he's about so tall,* es así de alto; *cut the fish, like so,* corta el pescado así; *of all the stupid people I know, no-one is more so than you,* de todas las personas estúpidas que conozco, no hay ninguna como tú. **7** (*to avoid repetition*) que sí: *I think/hope so,* creo/espero que sí; *I'm afraid so,* me temo que sí; *I told you so,* ya te lo dije; *and quite rightly so,* y con mucha razón; *if so,* en este caso, de ser así. **8** (*to express agreement, also*) también: *so am I/so do I/so can I/so have I,* yo también; *it's snowing - so it is,* está nevando - así es; *so I see,* ya veo; *so it seems,* así parece. **– 9** *adj* (*factual, true*) así: *it can't be so,* no puede ser; *that just isn't so,* eso no es verdad.

● **and so on (and so forth),** y así sucesivamente, etcétera. ‖ **just so / exactly so,** perfecto, en orden. ‖ **so be it,** así sea. ‖ **so long!,** ¡hasta luego!, ¡hasta pronto! ‖ **so much for sth.:** *so much for new technology!,* ¡vaya nueva tecnología!; *so much for your advice!,* ¡vaya consejo que me diste! ‖ **so there!,** ¡ea!, ¡para que sepas! ‖ **so what?,** ¿y qué?

soak [səʊk] **1** *t* (*put in liquid*) poner en remojo, remojar; (*saturate*) empapar. **– 2** *i* (*washing, dried pulses*) estar en remojo: *leave it to soak,* déjalo en remojo. **3** (*bathe*) bañarse. **4** (*penetrate*) empapar, calar: *the blood had soaked through his shirt,* la sangre le había empapado la camisa. **– 5** *n* remojón *m*. **6** *fam* (*drunkard*) borracho,-a.

◆ **to soak up** *t sep* (*liquid*) absorber; (*sun, atmosphere*) empaparse de; (*information*) embeber.

soaked [səʊkt] *adj* empapado,-a, calado,-a.

● **soaked to the skin,** calado,-a hasta los huesos. ‖ **to get soaked,** empaparse, quedarse empapado,-a.

soaking ['səʊkɪŋ] **1** *n* remojón *m*. **– 2** *adj* empapado,-a, calado,-a.

so-and-so ['səʊənsəʊ] **1** *n fam* fulano,-a: *she's always going on about Mrs So-and-so,* siempre habla de la señora Fulana de tal. **2** *euph* sinvergüenza *mf*: *which so-and-so has drunk all the beer?,* ¿qué sinvergüenza se ha bebido toda la cerveza?

▲ *pl* **so-and-sos.**

soap [səʊp] **1** *n* jabón *m*: *a bar/cake/tablet of soap,* una pastilla de jabón. **– 2** *t* enjabonar, jabonar.

■ **soap dish,** jabonera. ‖ **soap flakes,** jabón *m* en escamas. ‖ **soap opera,** TV telenovela, culebrón *m*; RAD radionovela. ‖ **soap powder,** jabón *m* en polvo.

soapbox ['səʊpbɒks] *n* tribuna improvisada.

● **to get on one's soapbox,** ponerse a pontificar.

soapsuds ['səʊpsʌdz] *npl* jabonaduras *fpl,* espuma *f sing.*

soapy ['səʊpɪ] **1** *adj* (*water*) jabonoso,-a; (*hands etc*) enjabonado,-a; (*taste, smell*) parecido,-a al jabón. **2** *fam pej* (*ingratiating*) falso,-a, zalamero,-a.

▲ *comp* **soapier;** *superl* **soapiest.**

soar [sɔːr] **1** *i* (*bird, plane - fly*) volar; (*- rise*) remontar el vuelo, remontarse; (*- glide*) planear. **2** *fig* (*prices, costs, etc*) dispararse. **3** (*building*) elevarse, alzarse.

soaring ['sɔːrɪŋ] **1** *adj* (*bird, plane*) que planea, que vuela. **2** *fig* (*prices*) en alza; (*temperature*) en aumento. **3** (*building*) altísimo,-a.

sob [sɒb] **1** *n* sollozo. **– 2** *i* sollozar. **– 3** *t* decir sollozando, decir entre sollozos.

● **to sob one's heart out,** llorar a lágrima viva.

■ **sob story,** tragedia, dramón *m*.

▲ (*verbo*) *pt & pp* **sobbed,** *ger* **sobbing.**

sobbing ['sɒbɪŋ] *n* sollozos *mpl.*

sober ['səʊbər] **1** *adj* (*not drunk*) sobrio,-a. **2** (*person*) serio,-a, formal; (*attitude*) sobrio,-a, moderado,-a, sensato,-a. **3** (*colour*) discreto,-a, sobrio,-a.

◆ **to sober down 1** *i* serenarse, calmarse, atemperarse, moderarse. **– 2** *t sep* serenar, calmar, atemperar, moderar. ‖ **to sober up 1** *i* pasársele la borrachera a uno, despejarse. **– 2** *t sep* despejar.

sobering ['səʊbərɪŋ] *adj* moderador,-ra: *it's a sobering thought,* te hace pensar, da mucho que pensar.

● **to have a sobering effect on sb.,** moderar los ánimos a algn.

soberly ['səʊbəlɪ] **1** *adv* (*moderately*) con moderación, con sobriedad; (*seriously*) con seriedad. **2** (*dress*) de forma sobria, con sobriedad.

sober-minded [səʊbər'maɪndɪd] *adj* serio,-a, formal.

sobriety [sə'braɪətɪ] *n* (*seriousness*) seriedad *f*; (*moderation*) moderación *f*, sobriedad *f*; (*good sense*) sensatez *f*.

Soc.[1] ['səʊsəlɪst] *abbr* (*Socialist*) socialista.

Soc.[2] [sə'saɪətɪ] *abbr* (*Society*) sociedad.

so-called ['səʊkɔːld] *adj* llamado,-a, supuesto,-a.

soccer ['sɒkər] *n* fútbol *m*.

■ **soccer match,** partido de fútbol. ‖ **soccer player,** futbolista *mf*, jugador,-ra de fútbol.

sociable ['səʊʃəbəl] *adj* (*person*) sociable, tratable, afable, amistoso,-a, simpático,-a; (*behaviour*) sociable.

social ['səʊʃəl] **1** *adj* (*gen*) social. **2** *fam* (*sociable*) sociable. **– 3** *n* (*informal meeting*) acto social, reunión *f* (*social*); (*party*) fiesta; (*dance*) baile *m*.

● **to be a social drinker,** beber sólo en compañía. ‖ **to have a good social life,** llevar una buena vida social, tener una buena vida social.

■ **social class,** clase *f* social. ‖ **social climber,** arribista *mf*, trepa *mf*. ‖ **social democracy,** socialdemocracia. ‖ **Social Democrat,** socialdemócrata *mf*. ‖ **social sciences,** ciencias *fpl* sociales. ‖ **social securi-**

ty, seguridad f social. ‖ **social security benefit,** subsidio de la seguridad social. ‖ **the social services,** los servicios mpl sociales. ‖ **social studies,** ciencias fpl sociales. ‖ **social work,** asistencia social, trabajo social. ‖ **social worker,** asistente,-a social.

socialism [ˈsəʊʃəlɪzəm] n socialismo.

socialist [ˈsəʊʃəlɪst] 1 adj socialista. – 2 n socialista mf.

socialistic [səʊʃəˈlɪstɪk] adj socialista.

socialite [ˈsəʊʃəlaɪt] n vividor,-ra, mundano,-a.

socialization [səʊʃəlaɪˈzeɪʃən] n socialización f.

socialize [ˈsəʊʃəlaɪz] 1 i (mix socially) relacionarse, alternar; (at party) circular, mezclarse con la gente: *he's not one for socializing,* no le gusta mucho hacer vida social. – 2 t TECH (adapt to society) socializar. 3 US POL (nationalize) nacionalizar.

socially [ˈsəʊʃəlɪ] adv socialmente: *socially acceptable,* admisible, bien visto,-a; *socially unacceptable,* no admisible, mal visto,-a.

society [səˈsaɪətɪ] 1 n (community, people) sociedad f: *a multi-racial society,* una sociedad multirracial; *consumer society,* la sociedad de consumo; *Western society,* la sociedad occidental. 2 (fashionable group, upper class) (alta) sociedad f. 3 (organization, club) sociedad f, asociación f, club m, círculo. 4 fml (company) compañía.
● **to be a danger to society,** ser un peligro para la sociedad. ‖ **to be introduced into society,** ser presentado,-a en sociedad.
■ **society news,** ecos mpl de sociedad. ‖ **society wedding,** boda de sociedad.
▲ pl *societies.*

sociobiology [səʊsɪəʊbaɪˈɒlədʒɪ] n sociobiología.

socioeconomic [səʊsɪəʊekəˈnɒmɪk] adj socioeconómico,-a.

sociological [səʊsɪəˈlɒdʒɪkəl] adj sociológico,-a.

sociologist [səʊsɪˈɒlədʒɪst] n sociólogo,-a.

sociology [səʊsɪˈɒlədʒɪ] n sociología.

sociopolitical [səʊsɪəʊpəˈlɪtɪkəl] adj sociopolítico,-a.

sock[1] [sɒk] n calcetín m: *a pair of socks,* unos calcetines
● **to pull one's socks up,** hacer un esfuerzo, esforzarse. ‖ **to put a sock in it,** cerrar el pico.
■ **ankle sock,** calcetín m corto. ‖ **knee-length sock,** calcetín m largo.

sock[2] [sɒk] 1 n (blow) puñetazo, tortazo. – 2 t pegar un puñetazo a, dar un tortazo a: *sock him one!,* ¡dale una!
● **to sock it to sb.,** darle caña a algn.

socket [ˈsɒkɪt] 1 n ANAT (of eye) cuenca, órbita; (of joint) glena. 2 ELEC (for plug) enchufe m, toma de corriente; (for light bulb) portalámparas m.
■ **socket wrench,** llave f de tubo.

sod[1] [sɒd] n fml (earth) tepe m, terrón m; (turf) césped f.

sod[2] [sɒd] 1 n fam (bastard) cabrón,-ona: *what a sod!,* ¡qué cabrón!; *you lazy sod!,* ¡qué vago eres!; *you lucky sod!,* ¡qué suerte tienes, tío! 2 fam (wretch) desgraciado,-a: *poor sod,* pobre (tío). 3 fam (difficult job) rollo, coñazo: *this bike is a sod to start,* esta moto es un coñazo para arrancar. – 4 t taboo jorobar, joder: *sod it!,* ¡mierda!; *sod the landlord!,* ¡qué se joda el propietario!; *sod the elections!,* ¡a la mierda con las elecciones!; *sod this for a game of soldiers!,* ¡a la mierda con esto!
◆ **to sod off** i taboo irse a la mierda, irse a tomar por culo.
● **sod all,** ni golpe, ni brote: *I've done sod all today,* hoy no he pegado ni golpe. ‖ **not to give a sod,** importarle un carajo a uno, importarle un huevo a uno: *I don't give a sod,* me importa un huevo.

soda [ˈsəʊdə] 1 n CHEM sosa, soda. 2 (soda water) soda, sifón m. 3 US (pop) refresco: *orange soda / lemon soda,*

naranjada / limonada. 4 (ice-cream soda) soda con helado y almíbar.
■ **soda cracker,** US galleta salada. ‖ **soda pop,** refresco. ‖ **soda siphon,** sifón m. ‖ **soda water,** soda, sifón m.

sodden [ˈsɒdən] adj (soaked) empapado,-a.

sodding [ˈsɒdɪŋ] adj taboo puñetero,-a.

sodium [ˈsəʊdɪəm] n CHEM sodio.
■ **sodium bicarbonate,** bicarbonato sódico, bicarbonato de sosa. ‖ **sodium chloride,** cloruro sódico, cloruro de sodio.

sodomy [ˈsɒdəmɪ] n sodomía.

sofa [ˈsəʊfə] n sofá m.
■ **sofa bed,** sofá cama m.

Sofia [ˈsəʊfɪə] n Sofía.

soft [sɒft] 1 adj (not hard) blando,-a; (spongy) esponjoso,-a; (flabby) fofo,-a: *soft bed,* cama mullida; *soft cheese,* queso blando; *soft metal,* metal dulce. 2 (skin, hair, fur, etc) suave. 3 (light, music, colour) suave; (words) tierno,-a; (breeze, steps, knock) ligero,-a; (outline) difuminado,-a: *in a soft voice,* en voz baja. 4 fam (easy) fácil: *a soft job,* un chollo. 5 (person - lenient) blando,-a, indulgente; (- weak) débil; (- gentle, kind) dulce; (- easily upset) sensiblero,-a: *you're too soft on/with the kids,* eres demasiado blando con los niños. 6 (water) blando,-a. 7 LING (consonant) suave.
● **to be soft in the head,** ser tonto,-a del culo, ser estúpido,-a. ‖ **to be soft on sb.,** (attracted) gustarle algn. a uno: *he's soft on Louise,* le gusta Louise. ‖ **to have a soft spot for sb.,** tener debilidad por algn., tenerle cariño a algn.
■ **soft copy,** datos mpl contenidos en la memoria del ordenador. ‖ **soft currency,** moneda débil. ‖ **soft drink,** refresco, bebida no alcohólica. ‖ **soft drug,** droga blanda. ‖ **soft furnishings,** (tejidos mpl para) cortinas, fundas de sofá, etc. ‖ **soft landing,** aterrizaje m suave. ‖ **soft option,** camino fácil. ‖ **soft palate,** velo del paladar. ‖ **soft pedal,** MUS pedal m suave. ‖ **soft porn,** pornografía blanda. ‖ **soft sell,** venta basada en la persuasión. ‖ **soft soap,** coba. ‖ **soft toy,** muñeco de peluche, animal m de peluche.

soft-boiled [ˈsɒftˈbɔɪld] adj (egg) pasado,-a por agua.

soften [ˈsɒfən] 1 t (leather, heart) ablandar; (skin) suavizar; (light, sound, colour) atenuar, suavizar; (voice) bajar. – 2 i (leather, heart, butter) ablandarse; (skin) suavizarse; (light, sound, colour) atenuarse, suavizarse; (voice) bajar; (attitude) volverse menos intransigente, volverse más tolerante.
◆ **to soften up** 1 t sep (person) ablandar. 2 MIL debilitar.
● **to soften one's position,** adoptar una postura menos intransigente. ‖ **to soften up one's attitude,** adoptar una actitud menos intransigente. ‖ **to soften the blow,** amortiguar el golpe.

softener [ˈsɒfənə] n (for water) suavizador m; (for fabric) suavizante m.

soft-headed [ˈsɒftˈhedɪd] adj bobo,-a, tonto,-a.

soft-hearted [ˈsɒftˈhɑːtɪd] adj tierno,-a, compasivo,-a, bondadoso,-a.

softie [ˈsɒftɪ] 1 n fam (sentimental) sentimental mf. – 2 adj fam (weak) blandengue mf.

softly [ˈsɒftlɪ] 1 adv (gently) suavemente; (tenderly) dulcemente. 2 (quietly - speak, play music) bajito,-a; (- move) sin hacer ruido. 3 (weakly, leniently) con indulgencia.
● **to be softly lit,** estar suavemente iluminado,-a.

softly-softly [ˈsɒftlɪˈsɒftlɪ] adj (manner, approach) cauteloso,-a.

softness ['sɒftnəs] 1 *n* (*gen*) blandura, lo blando. 2 (*of hair, fabric, skin*) suavidad *f*. 3 (*weakness*) debilidad *f*; (*leniency*) blandura.

soft-pedal [sɒft'pedəl] *t fam* (*play down*) minimizar la importancia de, restar importancia a.
▲ *pt* & *pp* **soft-pedalled** (us **soft-pedaled**), *ger* **soft-pedalling** (us **soft-pedaling**).

soft-soap [sɒft'səup] *t fam* dar jabón a, dar coba a.
● **to soft-soap sb. into doing sth.**, engatusar a algn. para que haga algo.

soft-spoken [sɒft'spəukən] *adj* de voz dulce, de voz suave.

software ['sɒftweəʳ] *n* COMPUT software *m*.

softwood ['sɒftwʊd] *n* (*wood*) madera de coníferas; (*tree*) conífera.

softy ['sɒftɪ] *n* → **softie**.
▲ *pl* **softies**.

soggy ['sɒgɪ] 1 *adj* (*wet*) empapado,-a, saturado,-a. 2 (*too soft*) pastoso,-a, gomoso,-a.
▲ *comp* **soggier**, *superl* **soggiest**.

soil [sɔɪl] 1 *n* (*earth*) tierra. 2 *fml* (*country, territory*) tierra: **on British soil**, en suelo británico. – 3 *t* (*dirty*) ensuciar; (*stain*) manchar. 4 *fig* (*reputaion*) manchar. – 5 *i* ensuciarse.

soiled [sɔɪld] *adj* (*dirty*) sucio,-a; (*stained*) manchado,-a.

soirée ['swɑːreɪ] *n fml* velada.

sojourn ['sɒdʒɜːn] 1 *n lit* estancia. – 2 *i lit* morar, pasar una temporada.

solace ['sɒlɪs] 1 *n* (*comfort*) consuelo, solaz *m*; (*source of comfort*) consuelo. – 2 *t lit* consolar.
● **to take solace in sth.**, consolarse con algo.

solar ['səʊləʳ] *adj* solar.
■ **solar cell**, célula solar. ‖ **solar energy**, energía solar. ‖ **solar plexus**, plexo solar. ‖ **the solar system**, el sistema *m* solar. ‖ **solar year**, año solar.

solarium [sə'leərɪəm] *n* solario, solárium *m*.
▲ *pl* **solaria** o **solariums**.

sold [səʊld] *pt* & *pp* → **sell**.

solder ['sɒldəʳ] 1 *n* soldadura. – 2 *t* soldar.

soldering iron ['sɒldərɪŋaɪən] *n* soldador *m*.

soldier ['səʊldʒəʳ] *n* (*not officer*) soldado; (*military man*) militar *m*.
◆ **to soldier on** *i* seguir adelante (a pesar de todo), seguir al pie del cañón.
● **a soldier of fortune**, un mercenario.
■ **old soldier**, veterano, excombatiente *m*.

sole¹ [səʊl] *n* (*fish*) lenguado.

sole² [səʊl] 1 *adj* (*only, single*) único,-a. 2 (*exclusive*) exclusivo,-a.

sole³ [səʊl] 1 *n* (*of foot*) planta; (*of shoe, sock*) suela. – 2 *t* poner suela a.

solecism ['sɒləsɪzəm] *n fml* solecismo.

solely ['səʊllɪ] 1 *adv* (*only*) solamente, únicamente. 2 (*exclusively*) exclusivamente.

solemn ['sɒləm] 1 *adj* (*ceremony, oath, etc*) solemne. 2 (*expression*) serio,-a.

solemnity [sə'lemnɪtɪ] 1 *n* solemnidad *f*. – 2 **solemnities**, *npl* ceremonial *m sing*.
▲ *pl* **solemnities**.

solemnize ['sɒləmnaɪz] *t* solemnizar.

sol-fa ['sɒlfɑː] *n* solfeo.

solicit [sə'lɪsɪt] 1 *t* (*request*) pedir, solicitar. 2 (*of prostitute*) abordar (buscando clientes). – 3 *i* (*request*) pedir, solicitar. 4 (*of prostitute*) ejercer la prostitución, abordar a clientes.

solicitor [sə'lɪsɪtəʳ] 1 *n* GB JUR abogado,-a. 2 US JUR oficial *mf* de justicia.

Solicitor General [səlɪsɪtə'dʒenərəl] 1 *n* GB procurador,-ra de la Corona. 2 US Subsecretario,-a de Justicia.

solicitous [sə'lɪsɪtəs] 1 *adj fml* (*eager, kind, helpful*) solícito,-a. 2 *fml* (*concerned, anxious*) preocupado,-a (**about/ for**, por), inquieto,-a (**about/for**, por).

solicitude [sə'lɪsɪtjuːd] 1 *n fml* (*eagerness, kindness*) solicitud *f*. 2 *fml* (*concern, anxiousness*) preocupación *f* (**for**, por).

solid ['sɒlɪd] 1 *adj* (*not liquid or gas*) sólido,-a: *solid food*, alimentos sólidos; *solid fuel*, combustible sólido. 2 (*not hollow*) macizo,-a: *solid tyres*, neumáticos macizos. 3 (*dense, compact*) compacto,-a: *solid rock*, roca sólida; *a solid mass*, una masa compacta. 4 (*unmixed*) puro,-a, macizo,-a: *solid gold*, oro macizo; *a solid oak door*, una puerta de roble macizo. 5 (*strong*) sólido,-a, fuerte: *solid grounds for believing he's dead*, razones sólidas para creer que está muerto; *on solid ground*, en tierra firme; *a man of solid build*, un hombre de complexión fuerte; *a solid meal*, una comida consistente. 6 (*reliable*) sólido,-a, de confianza, de fiar: *a solid argument*, un argumento sólido; *a good solid worker*, un trabajador serio y responsable. 7 (*unanimous*) unánime: *solid support*, apoyo unánime; *a solid Labour stronghold*, un firme baluarte laborista. 8 (*continuous*) seguido,-a, entero,-a; (*unbroken*) continuo,-a: *we waited for two solid hours*, esperamos dos horas enteras; *a solid yellow line*, una línea amarilla continua. 9 TECH (*three-dimensional*) tridimensional. – 10 *n* CHEM PHYS MATH sólido. – 11 **solids**, *npl* (*food*) alimentos *mpl* sólidos, sólidos *mpl*: *milk solids*, sólidos lácteos.
● **as solid as a rock**, firme como una roca. ‖ **to become solid**, solidificarse.
■ **solid figure**, cuerpo sólido. ‖ **solid geometry**, geometría del espacio.

solidarity [sɒlɪ'dærətɪ] *n* solidaridad *f*.

solidify [sə'lɪdɪfaɪ] 1 *t* solidificar. – 2 *i* solidificarse.
▲ *pt* & *pp* **solidified**, *ger* **solidifying**.

solidity [sə'lɪdɪtɪ] 1 *n* (*firmness, strength*) solidez *f*, resistencia. 2 (*reliability*) seriedad *f*, formalidad *f*. 3 (*substance*) solidez *f*, substancia, sustancia. 4 (*unanimity*) unanimidad *f*.

solidly ['sɒlɪdlɪ] 1 *adv* (*firmly, substancially*) sólidamente: *solidly built*, de construcción sólida. 2 (*continuously*) contínuamente, sin parar: *it rained solidly*, llovió sin parar. 3 (*unanimously*) unánimemente.

solidness ['sɒlɪdnəs] *n* → **solidity**.

solid-state [sɒlɪd'steɪt] *adj* ELEC de estado sólido, transistorizado,-a.

soliloquy [sə'lɪləkwɪ] *n* soliloquio.
▲ *pl* **soliloquies**.

solitaire ['sɒlɪteəʳ] *n* (*gen*) solitario.

solitary ['sɒlɪtərɪ] 1 *adj* (*alone*) solitario,-a. 2 (*secluded, remote*) apartado,-a, retirado,-a. 3 (*only, sole*) solo,-a, único,-a: *not a solitary soul*, ni un alma. – 4 *n sl* (*solitary confinement*) incomunicación *f*.
● **to be in solitary confinement**, estar incomunicado,-a.
■ **solitary confinement**, incomunicación *f*.

solitude ['sɒlɪtjuːd] *n* soledad *f*.

solo ['səʊləʊ] 1 *n* MUS solo: *a guitar solo*, un solo de guitarra. 2 AV vuelo en solitario. 3 (*card game*) solitario. – 4 *adj* MUS (*performance, album*) en solitario; (*instrument*) solo; (*piece*) para solista. 5 (*attempt, flight*) en solitario. – 6 *adv* MUS (*play, sing*) solo,-a. 7 (*fly*) en solitario.
▲ (*sustantivo*) *pl* **solos**.

soloist ['səʊləʊɪst] *n* MUS solista *mf*.

Solomon [ˈsɒləmən] *n* Salomón.
■ **Solomon Islands,** Islas Salomón.
solstice [ˈsɒlstɪs] *n* solsticio.
soluble [ˈsɒljəbəl] 1 *adj* (*substance*) soluble. 2 *fml* (*problem etc*) soluble.
solution [səˈluːʃən] 1 *n* (*to problem*) solución *f*: *the solution to all my problems,* la solución de todos mis problemas. 2 CHEM solución *f*.
solvable [ˈsɒlvəbəl] *adj* soluble, que tiene solución.
solve [sɒlv] *t* (*problem*) resolver, solucionar; (*case, equation*) resolver: *we've got a problem that needs solving,* tenemos un problema que hay que solucionar.
solvent [ˈsɒlvənt] 1 *adj* (*not in debt*) solvente. 2 (*that can dissolve*) soluble. – 3 *n* solvente *m*, disolvente *m*.
Somali [səˈmɑːlɪ] 1 *adj* somalí. – 2 *n* somalí *mf*.
Somalia [səˈmɑːlɪə] *n* Somalia.
somber [ˈsɒmbəʳ] *adj* US → **sombre**.
sombre [ˈsɒmbəʳ] 1 *adj* (*colour, place*) sombrío,-a; (*day, weather*) gris, triste; (*sky*) cubierto,-a. 2 (*person*) sombrío,-a, triste, serio,-a; (*statement, occasion, thought*) pesimista, grave.
some [sʌm] 1 *adj* (*with plural noun*) unos,-as, algunos,-as; (*a few*) unos,-as cuantos,-as, unos,-as pocos,-as: *there were some flowers on the table,* había unas flores en la mesa; *would you like some biscuits?,* ¿quieres galletas? 2 (*with singular noun*) algún, alguna; (*a little*) algo de, un poco de: *would you like some coffee?,* ¿quieres café?; *he needs some money,* necesita dinero. 3 (*certain*) cierto,-a, alguno,-a: *unlike some people I know,* no como algunas personas que conozco; *some days are better than others,* algunos días son mejores que otros; *I like some classical music,* me gusta alguna música clásica; *in some ways,* en cierto modo; *to some extent,* hasta cierto punto. 4 (*unknown, unspecified*) algún, alguna: *some day,* algún día, un día de éstos; *for some reason or another,* por alguna razón u otra; *there's some bloke at the door,* hay un tipo en la puerta; *some other time,* otra vez, otro día. 5 (*quite a lot of*) bastante: *she's been gone some time,* hace ya bastante tiempo que se ha ido; *it's some distance away,* queda bastante lejos; *some years ago,* hace algunos años. 6 *fam iron* (*none, not at all*) valiente, menudo,-a: *some help that was!,* ¡valiente ayuda!; *some friend you are!,* ¡valiente amigo eres tú!, ¡menudo amigo eres! 7 *fam* (*quite a, a fine*) menudo,-a: *that was some meal!,* ¡menuda comida!, ¡ésa sí que era una comida!, ¡vaya comilona!; *he's quite some guy!,* ¡menudo tío! – 8 *pron* (*unspecified number*) unos,-as, algunos,-as: *there are no potatoes - I'll have to buy some,* no quedan patatas - tendré que comprar; *keys? - I saw some on the table,* ¿llaves? - he visto unas sobre la mesa. 9 (*unspecified amount*) *no se traduce: you'll need plenty of money - I've got some,* te hará falta mucho dinero - ya tengo; *if you want more paper, there's some in the drawer,* si te hace falta más papel, hay un en el cajón. 10 (*certain ones*) ciertos,-as, algunos,-as; (*a certain part*) algo, un poco, parte *f*: *some say it was suicide,* algunos dicen que se suicidó; *some of my friends,* algunos amigos míos; *some of the money,* parte del dinero; *I agree with some of what she said,* estoy de acuerdo con parte de lo que ha dicho. – 11 *adv* (*approximately, about*) unos,-as, alrededor de, aproximadamente: *there were some twenty people,* había unas veinte personas; *some 100 miles away,* a unas cien millas de aquí. 12 US *fam* (*rather, a little*) un poco: *they waited some,* esperaron un poco; *he likes her some,* le gusta bastante.
somebody [ˈsʌmbədɪ] *pron* alguien: *somebody must have lost it,* alguien debe de haberlo perdido; *she thinks she's somebody,* se cree alguien.

● **somebody else,** otro,-a, otra persona. ‖ **to be a somebody,** ser todo un personaje, ser alguien.
somehow [ˈsʌmhaʊ] 1 *adv* (*in some way*) de algún modo, de alguna manera: *don't worry, I'll manage somehow,* no te preocupes, me las apañaré como sea; *somehow, he managed to get to London,* de algún modo, logró llegar a Londres. 2 (*for some reason*) por alguna razón: *I don't think he's quite my type somehow,* no sé por qué, pero no creo que sea mi tipo; *somehow it doesn't seem to matter anymore,* no sé por qué, pero ya no importa tanto.
someone [ˈsʌmwʌn] *pron* → **somebody**.
someplace [ˈsʌmpleɪs] *adv* → **somewhere**.
somersault [ˈsʌməsɔːlt] 1 *n* (*by acrobat*) salto mortal; (*by child*) voltereta; (*by car*) vuelta de campana. – 2 *i* (*acrobat*) dar un salto mortal; (*child*) dar volteretas; (*car*) dar una vuelta de campana.
something [ˈsʌmθɪŋ] 1 *pron* algo: *I've got something to tell you,* tengo que decirte algo; *can I ask you something?,* ¿puedo preguntarte una cosa?; *would you like something to drink?,* ¿quieres tomar algo? 2 (*a thing of value*) algo: *there's something in what he says,* hay algo de verdad en lo que dice; *there's something strange about this place,* este sitio tiene algo extraño; *at least they didn't take much, that's something,* al menos no se llevaron mucho, algo es algo. 3 (*in vague or ill-defined statements*) algo: *something like that,* algo así, algo por el estilo; *her name's Janet something or other,* se llama Janet no sé qué más; *he must be thirty something,* tendrá unos treinta y tantos; *do you want a sandwich or something?,* ¿quieres un bocadillo o algo así?; *are you drunk or something?,* ¿estás borracho o qué?; *it came as something of a surprise,* me pilló un poco por sorpresa. – 4 *adv*: *it costs something like 100 pounds,* cuesta unas cien libras; *the pain is something terrible,* duele una barbaridad.

● **something else,** otra cosa. ‖ **to be something else,** (*special*) ser algo extraordinario,-a.
sometime [ˈsʌmtaɪm] 1 *adv* algún día: *sometime next week,* algún día de la semana que viene; *phone me sometime,* llámame algún día; *sometime or another,* tarde o temprano. – 2 *adj fml* (*former*) antiguo,-a, ex-.
sometimes [ˈsʌmtaɪmz] *adv* a veces, de vez en cuando: *sometimes I walk,* a veces voy a pie; *she phones me sometimes,* me llama de vez en cuando.
somewhat [ˈsʌmwɒt] *adv* algo, un tanto: *needless to say, we were somewhat shocked,* huelga decir que quedamos algo escandalizados.
somewhere [ˈsʌmweəʳ] 1 *adv* (*in some place*) en alguna parte; (*to some place*) a alguna parte: *there should be a phone box round here somewhere,* debe de haber un teléfono por aquí en alguna parte; *I must have dropped it somewhere between here and the car,* se me debe de haber caído en algún sitio entre aquí y el coche. 2 (*approximately*) más o menos, alrededor de: *somewhere in the region of a million pounds,* alrededor de un millón de libras; *somewhere between 150 and 200 people,* más o menos entre 150 y 200 personas; *they live somewhere near Birmingham,* viven cerca de Birmingham. – 3 *pron* un lugar, un sitio: *he's looking for somewhere to stay,* busca algún sitio donde quedarse.

● **somewhere else,** (*in*) en otra parte, en otro sitio; (*to*) a otra parte, a otro sitio. ‖ **to get somewhere,** empezar a hacer progresos, empezar a marchar la cosa.
somnabulist [sɒmˈnæmbjəlɪst] *n* sonámbulo,-a.
somnambulism [sɒmˈnæmbjəlɪzəm] *n* sonambulismo.

somnolence ['sɒmnələns] *n* somnolencia.
somnolent ['sɒmnələnt] *adj* somnoliento,-a, soñolien-to,-a.
son [sʌn] *n* hijo: *eldest son / youngest son,* hijo mayor / hijo menor.
● **the son and heir,** el heredero. ‖ **son of a bitch,** *taboo* hijo de puta.
sonar ['səʊnɑːʳ] *n* (*abbr of sound navigation and ranging*) sonar *m.*
sonata [sə'nɑːtə] *n* sonata.
song [sɒŋ] *n* (*gen*) canción *f*; (*art, of bird*) canto: *sing us a song,* cántanos una canción.
● (*going*) **for a song,** regalado,-a. ‖ **to burst into song,** ponerse a cantar. ‖ **to make a song and dance about sth.,** armar un revuelo por algo.
songbird ['sɒŋbɜːd] *n* pájaro cantor, ave *f* canora.
songbook ['sɒŋbʊk] *n* cancionero.
songwriter ['sɒŋraɪtəʳ] *n* compositor,-ra (de cancio-nes).
sonic ['sɒnɪk] *adj* sónico,-a.
■ **sonic boom /sonic bang,** estampido sónico.
son-in-law ['sʌnɪnlɔː] *n* yerno, hijo político.
▲ *pl* sons-in-law.
sonnet ['sɒnɪt] *n* soneto.
sonny ['sʌnɪ] *n* hijo, hijito.
sonorous ['sɒnərəs] *adj* sonoro,-a.
soon [suːn] **1** *adv* (*within a short time*) pronto, dentro de poco: *write soon,* escríbeme pronto; *it'll soon be over,* falta poco para que se acabe; *we must be going soon,* nos tenemos que ir dentro de poco; *soon after lunch,* poco después de comer; *we'll soon be home,* pronto estaremos en casa; *see you soon,* hasta pronto. **2** (*early*) pronto, temprano: *it's too soon to tell,* es demasiado pronto para saberlo; *you spoke too soon,* hablaste an-tes de tiempo; *must you leave so soon?,* ¿ya te mar-chas?; *how soon can you get here?,* ¿cuándo puedes estar aquí? **3** (*expressing preference, readiness, willingness*): *I'd (just) as soon eat in as ...,* preferiría comer en casa que ...; *I'd just as soon not, if you don't mind,* preferiría que no, si no te importa.
● **as soon as,** en cuanto, tan pronto como: *as soon as we hear anything, we'll let you know,* en cuanto sepa-mos algo, te lo haremos saber; *I'll leave as soon as I can,* me iré en cuanto pueda. ‖ **as soon as possible,** cuanto antes, lo más pronto posible. ‖ **not a moment too soon,** no antes de tiempo. ‖ **soon afterwards,** poco después.
sooner ['suːnəʳ] **1** *adv* (*earlier*) más temprano. **2** (*rather*) antes: *I'd sooner die!,* ¡antes morir!, ¡antes la muerte!; *sooner you than me!,* ¡mejor tú que yo!; *he'd sooner read than watch TV,* preferiría leer que mirar la tele; *I'd sooner go alone,* preferiría ir sola. **3** **no sooner,** (*im-mediately after*) nada más, apenas: *no sooner had she fall-en asleep than the phone rang,* apenas se había dormido cuando empezó a sonar el teléfono; *no sooner had we unpacked our picnic than it began to rain,* nada más sacar las cosas del picnic empezó a llover.
● **no sooner said than done,** dicho y hecho. ‖ **soon-er or later,** tarde o temprano. ‖ **the sooner the bet-ter,** cuanto antes mejor.
soot [sʊt] *n* hollín *m.*
soothe [suːð] **1** *t* (*calm*) calmar, tranquilizar, aplacar; (*quieten*) acallar. **2** (*ease pain*) aliviar, calmar.
soothing ['suːðɪŋ] *adj* (*medicine*) calmante; (*ointment*) balsámico,-a; (*bath, music*) relajante; (*tone, words*) tran-quilizador,-ra.

sooty ['sʊtɪ] **1** *adj* (*dirty*) cubierto,-a de hollín, tiznado,-a. **2** (*black*) negro,-a como el hollín.
▲ *comp* sootier, *superl* sootiest.
sophism ['sɒfɪzəm] *n* sofisma *m.*
sophist ['sɒfɪst] *n* sofista *mf.*
sophisticated [sə'fɪstɪkeɪtɪd] *adj* sofisticado,-a.
sophistication [səfɪstɪ'keɪʃən] *n* sofisticación *f.*
sophistry ['sɒfɪstrɪ] **1** *n* (*art*) sofistería. **2** (*argument*) so-fisma *m.*
▲ *pl* sophistries.
sophomore ['sɒfəmɔːʳ] *n* US EDUC estudiante *mf* de se-gundo año.
soporific [sɒpə'rɪfɪk] *adj* soporífero,-a, soporífico,-a.
sopping ['sɒpɪŋ] *adj* *fam* empapado,-a: *you're sopping wet!,* ¡estás como una sopa!
soppy ['sɒpɪ] *adj* *fam* sensiblero,-a, sentimentaloide.
● **to be soppy about sb./sth.,** caérsele a uno la baba por algn./algo.
▲ *comp* soppier, *superl* soppiest.
soprano [sə'prɑːnəʊ] **1** *n* soprano *mf,* tiple *mf.* – **2** *adj* (*instrument*) soprano,-a; (*voice*) de soprano.
▲ *pl* sopranos.
sorbet ['sɔːbeɪ] *n* sorbete *m.*
sorcerer ['sɔːsərəʳ] *n* hechicero, brujo.
sorceress ['sɔːsərəs] *n* hechicera, bruja.
sorcery ['sɔːsərɪ] *n* hechicería, brujería.
sordid ['sɔːdɪd] **1** *adj* (*dishonourable*) sórdido,-a, vergon-zoso,-a, bochornoso,-a: *a sordid affair,* un asunto ver-gonzoso; *all the sordid details,* los detalles escabrosos. **2** (*squalid*) sórdido,-a, miserable.
sordidness ['sɔːdɪdnəs] *n* sordidez *f.*
sore [sɔːʳ] **1** *adj* (*aching*) dolorido,-a; (*painful*) doloroso,-a; (*inflamed*) inflamado,-a: *I've got a sore throat,* tengo dolor de garganta, me duele la garganta; *he felt sore all over,* le dolía todo; *her legs are sore,* le duelen las piernas. **2** US *fam* (*angry*) enfadado,-a (**about,** por), pi-cado,-a (**about,** por): *she's still sore at him,* todavía está enfadada con él. **3** *lit* (*great*) enorme, gran; (*serious*) gra-ve; (*urgent*) urgente. – **4** *n* MED llaga, úlcera.
■ **sore point,** asunto delicado, asunto espinoso.
sorely ['sɔːlɪ] *adv* (*very much, greatly*) muy; (*deeply*) profun-damente; (*seriously*) gravemente; (*urgently*) urgente-mente: *we shall miss him sorely,* le echaremos mucho de menos.
● **to be sorely tempted to do sth.,** estar muy ten-tado,-a de hacer algo.
soreness ['sɔːnəs] *n* (*pain*) dolor *m.*
sorghum ['sɔːgəm] *n* sorgo.
sorrel[1] ['sɒrəl] *n* ZOOL alazán *m.*
sorrel[2] ['sɒrəl] *n* BOT acedera.
sorrow ['sɒrəʊ] **1** *n* (*grief*) pena, pesar *m,* dolor *m.* **2** (*cause of sadness*) disgusto. – **3** *i* llorar (**at/over/for,** por).
sorrowful ['sɒrəʊfʊl] *adj* afligido,-a, apenado,-a, triste.
sorry ['sɒrɪ] **1** *adj* (*pitiful, wretched*) triste, lamentable: *a sorry sight,* un triste espectáculo; *in a sorry state,* en un estado lamentable. – **2** *interj* (*apology*) ¡perdón!, ¡dis-culpe! **3** GB (*for repetition*) ¿perdón?, ¿cómo?
● **to be sorry,** (*grieved, feeling sadness*) sentir: *I'm very sorry to hear about your uncle,* siento mucho lo de tu tío; *I'm sorry you didn't get the job,* siento que no hayas conseguido el trabajo; *I'm sorry,* lo siento; *sorry I'm late,* siento llegar tarde; *he's very sorry about what hap-pened,* siente mucho lo ocurrido; *you'll be sorry,* lo la-mentarás; *I'm sorry to trouble you,* perdone que le moleste, siento molestarle. ‖ **to feel sorry for sb.,** compadecer: *she felt sorry for him,* le compadecía; *he*

was feeling sorry for himself, se compadecía de sí mismo. ‖ **to say sorry,** disculparse, pedir perdón.
▲ *comp* **sorrier,** *superl* **sorriest.**

sort [sɔːt] **1** *n* (*type, kind*) clase *f,* tipo, género, suerte *f;* (*make, brand*) marca: *what sort of novels do you prefer?,* ¿qué tipo de novelas prefieres?; *we've got three sorts of tea,* tenemos tres clases de té; *there are all sorts of board games,* hay toda clase de juegos de mesa; *it's not really your sort of film,* no es el tipo de película que te gusta; *I know you like that sort of thing,* sé que te gustan esas cosas. **2** *fam* (*person*) tipo,-a, tío,-a: *he's a good sort,* es buen tío; *he's a strange sort,* es un tipo raro; *I know your sort,* ya sé de qué pie calzas. **– 3** *t* (*classify*) clasificar. **4** (*repair*) arreglar. **– 5** *i* (*check*) revisar (**through,** -).
◆ **to sort out 1** *t sep* (*classify*) clasificar; (*put in order*) ordenar, poner en orden. **2** (*separate*) separar (**from,** de). **3** (*solve - problem*) arreglar, solucionar; (- *misunderstanding*) aclarar. **4** (*arrange*) organizar, arreglar; (*set - date*) fijar: *have you sorted out how much I owe you?,* ¿has calculado cuánto te debo? **5** (*deal with - person*) meter en vereda, meter en cintura: *I'll sort them out!,* ¡yo les arreglaré!
● **a sort of,** una especie de: *she was wearing a sort of kimono,* llevaba una especie de quimono; *he's a sort of journalist,* es una especie de periodista. ‖ **it takes all sorts (to make a world),** de todo hay en la viña del Señor. ‖ **of a sort / of sorts,** una especie de: *it was a meal of sorts,* fue una especie de comida. ‖ **nothing of the sort,** nada semejante: *you said she was mean, but she's nothing of the sort,* me dijiste que era tacaña, pero no lo es en absoluto. ‖ **out of sorts,** (*unwell*) pachucho,-a; (*moody*) de mal humor. ‖ **sort of,** en cierto modo: *I sort of expected it,* en cierto modo me lo esperaba; *it's sort of strange,* es un poco raro; *I was sort of hoping that you'd come with me,* en cierto modo esperaba que me acompañaras; *did you like it? - well, sort of,* ¿te ha gustado? - bueno, en cierto modo sí. ‖ **to sort os. out,** poner sus pensamientos en orden.
sortie [ˈsɔːti] *n* MIL salida.
sorting [ˈsɔːtɪŋ] *n* clasificación *f.*
■ **sorting office,** sala de batalla.
sort-out [ˈsɔːtaʊt] **to have a sort-out,** *phr* ordenar.
so-so [ˈsəʊsəʊ] *adv fam* así así, regular, de aquella manera.
soufflé [ˈsuːfleɪ] *n* CULIN soufflé *m.*
sought [sɔːt] *pt & pp →* **seek.**
sought-after [ˈsɔːtɑːftəʳ] *adj* (*person*) solicitado,-a; (*object*) codiciado,-a.
soul [səʊl] **1** *n* REL alma, espíritu *m.* **2** (*spirit*) espíritu *m;* (*feeling, character*) carácter *m,* personalidad *f: he puts his heart and soul into his music,* se entrega a su música en cuerpo y alma; *you've got no soul,* no tienes sensibilidad. **3** (*person*) alma, persona: *don't tell a soul,* no se lo digas a nadie; *there wasn't a soul to be seen,* no había ni un alma; *she's a dear old soul,* es una viejecita encantadora; *some poor soul,* algún pobre diablo. **4** MUS soul *m,* música soul.
● **to be the life and soul of the party,** ser el alma de la fiesta. ‖ **to be the soul of sth.,** ser algo personificado,-a: *she's the soul of discretion,* es la discreción personificada. ‖ **upon my soul!,** ¡Santo Dios!, ¡Dios mío!
■ **soul brother,** US hermano. ‖ **soul food,** US cocina tradicional de los negros del Sur de los EEUU. ‖ **soul mate,** alma gemela. ‖ **soul music,** música soul. ‖ **soul sister,** US hermana.

soul-destroying [ˈsəʊldɪstrɔɪɪŋ] *adj* (*boring*) tedioso,-a, monótono,-a; (*demoralizing*) desmoralizador,-ra, degradante.
soulful [ˈsəʊlfʊl] *adj* conmovedor,-ra, emotivo,-a.
soulless [ˈsəʊlləs] *adj* (*building, place*) sin carácter, sin personalidad; (*person*) desalmado,-a.
soul-searching [ˈsəʊlsɜːtʃɪŋ] *n* introspección *f,* examen *m* de conciencia.
sound¹ [saʊnd] **1** *adj* (*healthy*) sano,-a: *of sound mind,* en su sano juicio, en pleno uso de sus facultades; *safe and sound,* sano,-a y salvo,-a. **2** (*solid*) sólido,-a, firme; (*in good condition*) en buen estado. **3** (*sensible*) sensato,-a, acertado,-a; (*valid*) sólido,-a, lógico,-a, razonable; (*responsible*) responsable, formal, de fiar; (*reliable, safe*) seguro,-a: *a sound piece of advice,* un bueno consejo; *he's got a sound grasp of Italian,* domina el italiano; *her knowledge of modern history is sound,* sus conocimientos de historia moderna son sólidos; *a sound investment,* una inversión segura. **4** (*thorough*) completo,-a; (*severe*) severo,-a: *a sound training,* una formación sólida; *a sound examination,* un examen a fondo; *a sound beating,* una buena paliza. **5** (*of sleep*) profundo,-a.
● **to be as sound as a bell,** (*person*) estar sano,-a; (*thing*) estar en perfectas condiciones, estar en perfecto estado. ‖ **to be sound asleep,** estar profundamente dormido,-a.
sound² [saʊnd] **1** *t* MAR sondar. **2** MED (*gen*) sondar; (*chest*) auscultar. **– 3** *n* MED sonda.
◆ **to sound out** *t sep* (*discover opinions*) sondear, tantear: *sound him out and let me know what he thinks,* tantéalo y dime lo que piensa.
sound³ [saʊnd] *n* GEOG estrecho, brazo de mar.
sound⁴ [saʊnd] **1** *n* (*gen*) sonido; (*musical*) sonido, son *m;* (*noise*) ruido: *I heard the sound of voices,* oí (unas) voces; *the sound of the guitar,* el son de la guitarra; *the sound was so bad we couldn't hear the singer,* el sonido era tan malo que no oímos al cantante; *without a sound,* sin hacer ruido; *the speed of sound,* la velocidad del sonido; *I was born within the sound of Bow bells,* desde donde nací se oyen las campanas de la iglesia de Bow. **2** TV (*volume*) volumen *m: turn the sound up/down,* sube/baja el volumen. **3** (*impression, idea*) idea: *I don't like the sound of this,* esto se está poniendo feo, esto me da mala espina; *I quite like the sound of that,* podría estar bien; *by/from the sound of it, he's getting on fine,* por lo visto las cosas le van bien. **– 4** *t* (*bell, horn, trumpet*) tocar, hacer sonar; (*alarm*) dar (la señal de); (*retreat*) tocar. **5** LING pronunciar. **– 6** *i* (*bell, horn, alarm, etc*) sonar, resonar. **7** (*seem*) parecer; (*give impression*) sonar: *how does that sound?,* ¿qué te parece eso?; *it sounds lovely,* me parece estupendo; *it sounds as if she knows what she's doing,* parece que sabe lo que hace; *you sound like you've got a cold,* parece que estés resfriado; *you sound different,* tu voz suena distinta; *he sounds just like my brother,* es igual que mi hermano; *does this sentence sound right to you?,* ¿te suena bien esta frase?; *it sounds like Mozart,* (me) suena a Mozart; *it sounds like a lie,* me huele a mentira. **8** LING pronunciarse, sonar.
◆ **to sound off** *i* (*express opinions*) hablar a gritos; (*complain*) quejarse (**about,** de), protestar (**about,** por).
■ **sound barrier,** barrera del sonido. ‖ **sound check,** prueba de sonido. ‖ **sound effects,** efectos *mpl* sonoros. ‖ **sound engineer,** ingeniero,-a de sonido. ‖ **sound wave,** onda sonora.
sounding¹ [ˈsaʊndɪŋ] **1** *n* MAR sondeo. **– 2 soundings,** *npl* MAR (*measurements*) sondeos *mpl.* **3** (*testing opinions*) sondeos *mpl.*

sounding² ['saʊndɪŋ] *adj* (*resounding, resonant*) resonante.

■ **sounding board,** MUS (*on instrument*) caja de resonancia; (*over pulpit, stage*) tornavoz *m*; (*to test ideas, policy, etc*) caja de resonancia.

soundless ['saʊndləs] *adj* silencioso,-a, mudo,-a.

soundly ['saʊndlɪ] **1** *adv* (*sleep*) profundamente. **2** (*thoroughly, severely*) completamente: *we were soundly beaten,* nos dieron una buena paliza. **3** (*solidly*) sólidamente.

soundness ['saʊndnəs] **1** *n* (*physical solidity*) solidez *f*; (*good condition*) buen estado. **2** (*validity*) solidez *f*; (*sensibleness*) sensatez *f*.

soundproof ['saʊndpruːf] **1** *adj* insonorizado,-a, a prueba de sonidos. – **2** *t* insonorizar.

soundproofing ['saʊndpruːfɪŋ] **1** *n* (*action*) insonorización *f*. **2** (*material*) aislante *m* acústico.

soundtrack ['saʊndtræk] *n* banda sonora.

soup [suːp] *n* CULIN (*gen*) sopa; (*clear, thin*) caldo, consomé *m*.

◆ **to soup up 1** *t sep* (*car, motorbike, engine*) trucar. **2** *fam* (*film, play, book*) modernizar, popularizar.

● **in the soup,** en un apuro, en un aprieto. ‖ **from soup to nuts,** US de cabo a rabo.

■ **soup dish,** plato sopero. ‖ **soup kitchen,** comedor *m* popular, olla común. ‖ **soup spoon,** cuchara sopera. ‖ **soup tureen,** sopera.

souped-up ['suːptʌp] **1** *adj* (*car, motorbike, engine*) trucado,-a. **2** *fam* (*film, play, book*) popular, refrito,-a.

sour ['saʊə⁻] **1** *adj* (*fruit*) ácido,-a, agrio,-a; (*milk*) cortado,-a, agrio,-a; (*wine*) agrio,-a. **2** (*person*) amargado,-a, avinagrado,-a; (*behaviour, expression*) agrio,-a, avinagrado,-a. – **3** *t* (*milk*) agriar, cortar. **4** (*person, relationship*) amargar. – **5** *i* (*milk*) agriarse, cortarse; (*wine*) agriarse. **6** (*person, character*) amargarse, avinagrarse.

● **sour grapes!,** ¡mala suerte!, ¡te aguantas! ‖ **to turn sour / go sour,** (*milk*) agriarse, cortarse; (*wine*) agriarse; (*relationship etc*) estropearse, echarse a perder.

source [sɔːs] **1** *n* (*of river*) fuente *f*, nacimiento. **2** (*origin, cause*) fuente *f*, origen *m*: *source of income,* fuente de ingresos; *energy sources,* fuentes de energía; *source of the rumour,* el origen del rumor; *the source of the trouble,* la causa del problema. **3** (*person, thing supplying information*) fuente *f*: *reliable sources,* fuentes fidedignas. **4** MED (*of infection*) foco.

sourly ['saʊəlɪ] *adv* agriamente, con amargura.

sourness ['saʊənəs] **1** *n* (*of fruit*) acidez *f*, agrura; (*of milk*) agrura. **2** (*of person*) amargura, acritud *f*.

sourpuss ['saʊəpʊs] *n fam* amargado,-a.

souse [saʊs] **1** *t* CULIN (*fish*) escabechar; (*meat*) adobar. **2** (*soak in water*) empapar; (*plunge in water*) sumergir; (*pour water over*) mojar.

soused [saʊst] **1** *adj fam* (*drunk*) como una cuba. **2** (*fish*) en escabeche.

south [saʊθ] **1** *n* sur *m*: *in the south,* en el sur; *to the south of,* al sur de. – **2** *adj* sur, del sur, meridional: *south coast,* costa sur; *south wind,* viento del sur. – **3** *adv* (*direction*) hacia el sur; (*location*) al sur: *birds fly south,* los pájaros vuelan hacia el sur; *the house faces south,* la casa está orientada al sur; *it's south of the river,* está al sur del río. – **4** *the South,* el Sur *m*, el sur *m*.

● **down south,** (*location*) al sur; (*direction*) hacia el sur.

■ **South American,** sudamericano,-a. ‖ **the South Pacific,** el Pacífico Sur. ‖ **the South Pole,** el Polo Sur. ‖ **the South Seas,** los mares del Sur. ‖ **South Wales,** Gales del Sur.

southbound ['saʊθbaʊnd] *adj* que va hacia el sur, que va en dirección sur, con rumbo al sur.

southeast [saʊθˈiːst] **1** *n* sudeste *m*. – **2** *adj* sudeste, del sudeste. – **3** *adv* (*direction*) hacia el sudeste; (*location*) al sudeste.

southeasterly [saʊθˈiːstəlɪ] *adj* del sudeste.

southeastern [saʊθˈiːstən] *adj* sudeste, del sudeste.

southerly ['sʌðəlɪ] *adj* (*direction*) hacia el sur; (*location*) al sur; (*wind*) del sur.

southern ['sʌðən] *adj* del sur, meridional, austral: *in southern Spain,* en el sur de España, en la España meridional.

■ **Southern Europe,** Europa del Sur. ‖ **southern hemisphere,** hemisferio austral. ‖ **southern lights,** la aurora austral.

southerner ['sʌðənə⁻] *n* sureño,-a, meridional *mf*.

southernmost ['sʌðənməʊst] *adj* más meridional, más austral: *the southernmost tip of the island,* el extremo más meridional de la isla.

southward ['saʊθwəd] **1** *adj* hacia el sur, en dirección sur. – **2** *adv* (*direction*) hacia el sur; (*location*) al sur.

southwards ['saʊθwədz] *adv* (*direction*) hacia el sur; (*location*) al sur.

southwest [saʊθˈwest] **1** *n* suroeste *m*. – **2** *adj* suroeste, del suroeste. – **3** *adv* (*direction*) hacia el suroeste; (*location*) al suroeste.

southwesterly [saʊθˈwestəlɪ] *adj* del suroeste.

southwestern [saʊθˈwestən] *adj* del suroeste.

souvenir [suːvəˈnɪə⁻] *n* recuerdo (**of,** de).

sou'wester [saʊˈwestə⁻] *n* (*hat*) sueste *m*.

sovereign ['sɒvrɪn] **1** *n* soberano,-a. **2** GB (*coin*) rano. – **3** *adj* soberano,-a.

sovereignty ['sɒvrɪntɪ] *n* soberanía.

soviet ['səʊvɪət] **1** *n* (*council*) soviet *m*. **2** **Soviet,** (*person*) soviético,-a. – **3** *adj* soviético,-a.

■ **Soviet Union,** Unión *f* Soviética.

sow¹ [saʊ] *n* ZOOL cerda, puerca.

sow² [səʊ] *t* (*gen*) sembrar (**with,** de).

▲ *pp* **sowed** o **sown.**

sower ['səʊə⁻] *n* (*person*) sembrador,-ra; (*machine*) sembradora.

sowing ['səʊɪŋ] *n* siembra.

sown [səʊn] *pp* → **sow.**

soy [sɔɪ] *n* US soja.

■ **soy sauce,** salsa de soja.

soya ['sɔɪə] *n* GB soja.

■ **soya bean,** soja.

sozzled ['sɒzəld] *adj fam* (*drunk*) borracho,-a, trompa, mamado,-a.

● **to get sozzled,** pillar una trompa.

spa [spaː] **1** *n* (*resort*) balneario; (*baths*) baños *mpl*, termas *fpl*. **2** US (*jacuzzi*) jacuzzi *m*. **3** US (*gymnasium*) gimnasio.

■ **spa resort,** estación *f* balnearia.

space [speɪs] **1** *n* PHYS espacio: *astronauts travel in space,* los astronautas viajan por el espacio. **2** (*continuous expanse*) espacio: *space and time,* espacio y tiempo; *she was staring into space,* miraba al vacío, tenía la mirada perdida. **3** (*room, unoccupied area*) espacio, sitio, lugar *m*: *can we make space for one more person?,* ¿podemos hacer sitio para otra persona?; *it takes up too much space,* ocupa demasiado espacio; *there isn't enough space for everything,* no cabe todo. **4** (*gap, empty place*) espacio, hueco: *open spaces,* espacios abiertos; *a parking space,* un sitio para aparcar; *write in the blank spaces,* escribir en los espacios en blanco; *the word "space" takes five spaces,* la palabra "space" ocupa

cinco espacios. **5** (*in time*) espacio, lapso: *in the space of an hour*, en el espacio de una hora; *in a short space of time*, en poco tiempo. – **6** *t* espaciar (**out**, -).
■ **advertising space**, espacio publicitario. ‖ **space age**, era espacial. ‖ **space agency**, agencia espacial. ‖ **space capsule**, cápsula espacial. ‖ **space flight**, vuelo espacial. ‖ **space lab**, laboratorio espacial. ‖ **space probe**, sonda espacial. ‖ **space programme**, programa *m* de vuelos espaciales. ‖ **space shuttle**, transbordador *m* espacial. ‖ **space station**, estación *f* espacial. ‖ **space travel**, viajes *mpl* por el espacio, viajes *mpl* espaciales.
space-age ['speɪseɪdʒ] *adj* de la era espacial.
space-bar ['speɪsbaːʳ] *n* espaciador *m*.
spacecraft ['speɪskraːft] *n* nave *f* espacial.
▲ *pl* **spacecraft**
spaced out [speɪst'aʊt] **1** *adj* (*separated*) separado,-a, distanciado,-a. **2** *fam* (*stoned*) colocado,-a, flipado,-a.
spaceman ['speɪsmən] *n* astronauta *m*.
spaceship ['speɪsʃɪp] *n* nave *f* espacial.
spacewoman ['speɪswʊmən] *n* astronauta *f*.
spacing ['speɪsɪŋ] *n* espacio.
■ **in double space**, a doble espacio.
spacious ['speɪʃəs] *adj* espacioso,-a, amplio,-a.
spade[1] [speɪd] *n* (*playing card - international pack*) pica; (- *Spanish pack*) espada.
spade[2] [speɪd] *n* (*for digging*) pala.
● **to call a spade a spade**, llamar al pan, pan y al vino, vino.
spaghetti [spə'getɪ] *n* espaguetis *mpl*.
■ **spaghetti bolognese**, espaguetis *mpl* a la boloñesa.
Spain [speɪn] *n* España.
spam [spæm] *n* fiambre.
span[1] [spæn] *pp* → **spin**.
span[2] [spæn] *n* (*of horses*) tronco; (*of oxen*) yunta.
span[3] [spæn] **1** *n* (*of wings*) envergadura; (*of arch, bridge*) luz *f*, ojo; (*of hand*) palmo. **2** (*of time*) espacio, período, lapso: *over a span of five years*, durante un período de cinco años, en un lapso de cinco años; *they have a life span of twelve years*, tienen una vida de doce años. – **3** *t* (*cross*) atravesar, cruzar. **4** (*extend over*) abarcar, extenderse a: *a career spanning 50 years in showbusiness*, una trayectoria que abarca 50 años en el mundo del espectáculo; *football has a history spanning over a 100 years*, la historia del fútbol abarca más de 100 años.
▲ (*verbo*) *pt* & *pp* **spanned**, *ger* **spanning**.
spangle ['spæŋgəl] *n* lentejuela.
Spaniard ['spænjəd] *n* (*person*) español,-la.
spaniel ['spænjəl] *n* perro de aguas, perro de lanas, spaniel *m*.
Spanish ['spænɪʃ] **1** *adj* español,-la. – **2** *n* (*person*) español,-la. **3** (*language*) español *m*, castellano. – **4 the Spanish**, *npl* los españoles *mpl*.
■ **the Spanish Armada**, la Armada Invencible. ‖ **the Spanish Embassy**, la Embajada de España. ‖ **Spanish America**, Hispanoamérica. ‖ **Spanish fly**, cantárida. ‖ **Spanish guitar**, guitarra clásica.
Spanish-American [spænɪʃə'merɪkən] *adj* hispanoamericano,-a.
■ **the Spanish-American War**, la Guerra de Cuba.
Spanish-speaking ['spænɪʃspiːkɪŋ] *adj* de habla española, hispanohablante.
spank [spæŋk] *t* zurrar, pegar, dar azotes a.
spanking[1] ['spæŋkɪŋ] *n* zurra, azotaina, paliza.
spanking[2] ['spæŋkɪŋ] **1** *adj* (*lively - gen*) vivaz, rápido,-a; (- *breeze*) fuerte. – **2** *adv* muy: *spanking new*, flamante; *spanking clean*, limpísimo,-a.

spanner ['spænəʳ] *n* llave *f* de tuerca.
● **to put/throw a spanner in the works**, meter un palo en la rueda, sabotearlo todo.
spar[1] [spaːʳ] **1** *i* (*boxing*) entrenarse. **2** (*argue*) discutir.
▲ *pt* & *pp* **sparred**, *ger* **sparring**.
spar[2] [spaːʳ] *n* (*mineral*) espato.
spar[3] [spaːʳ] *n* MAR palo, verga.
spare [speəʳ] **1** *adj* (*reserve*) de repuesto; (*free*) libre; (*extra*) de sobra: *a spare key*, una llave de repuesto; *the spare room*, el cuarto de los invitados; *a spare moment*, un momento libre; *we've got a spare ticket*, tenemos una entrada de sobra; *have you got any spare change?*, ¿tienes algo suelto? **2** (*thin, lean*) enjuto,-a. – **3** *n* (*spare part*) recambio, repuesto. – **4** *t* (*do without*) prescindir de, pasar sin: *we can't spare anyone today*, no podemos prescindir de nadie hoy; *can you spare a few coins?*, ¿te sobran algunas monedas?; *I can't spare the time*, no tengo tiempo; *can you spare me five minutes?*, ¿tienes cinco minutos?; *puedes dedicarme cinco minutos?* **5** (*begrudge*) escatimar: *no expense was spared*, no repararon en gastos; *no trouble was spared*, no escatimaron esfuerzos. **6** (*save, relieve*) ahorrar, evitar: *I wanted to spare myself the trouble*, quería ahorrarme la molestia; *spare me the gory details*, ahórrate los detalles escabrosos. **7** *lit* (*not harm, not kill, show mercy*) perdonar: *we prayed that his life might be spared*, rogamos para que le perdonaran la vida; *he tried to spare her feelings*, procuró no herir sus sentimientos.
● **to go spare**, (*become angry*) cabrearse, enloquecer; (*be leftover*) sobrar. ‖ **to spare**, de sobra: *have you got any bread to spare?*, ¿tienes algo de pan de sobra? ‖ **to spare a thought for sb.**, pensar un momento en algn. ‖ **to spare sb.'s blushes**, ahorrarle un bochorno a algn., no hacer que algn. pase vergüenza.
■ **spare part**, (pieza de) recambio, pieza de repuesta. ‖ **spare time**, tiempo libre. ‖ **spare tyre**, (*wheel*) rueda de recambio; (*stomach*) michelín *m*. ‖ **spare wheel**, rueda de recambio.
spare-part ['speəpaːt] *adj* MED de transplantes.
sparerib [speə'rɪb] *n* CULIN costilla de cerdo.
sparing ['speərɪŋ] *adj* (*frugal*) frugal; (*economical*) económico,-a.
● **to be sparing with food**, economizar comida. ‖ **to be sparing with praise**, escatimar elogios. ‖ **to be sparing with words**, ser parco,-a en palabras.
sparingly ['speərɪŋlɪ] *adv* (*eat*) frugalmente; (*use*) en poca cantidad, con moderación.
spark [spaːk] **1** *n* (*from fire, electrical*) chispa. **2** (*trace*) chispa, pizca. **3** (*cause, trigger*) chispazo. – **4** *i* echar chispas, chispear.
◆ **to spark off** *t insep* (*conflict, riot, etc*) hacer estallar, provocar, desencadenar, desatar; (*interest*) despertar, suscitar.
■ (**the**) **sparks fly**, armarse la gorda.
■ **bright spark**, (*clever person*) listillo,-a. ‖ **spark plug**, AUTO bujía.
sparking plug ['spaːkɪŋplʌg] *n* AUTO bujía.
sparkle ['spaːkəl] **1** *n* (*of diamond, glass*) centelleo, destello, brillo; (*of eyes*) brillo. **2** *fig* (*liveliness*) viveza; (*wit*) brillo. – **3** *i* (*diamond, glass*) centellear, destellar, brillar; (*eyes*) brillar, chispear; (*firework*) echar chispas, chispear. **4** *fig* (*person*) brillar, lucirse; (*conversation*) brillar.
sparkler ['spaːkələʳ] **1** *n* (*firework*) bengala. **2** *fam* (*gem*) brillante *m*.
sparkling ['spaːkəlɪŋ] **1** *adj* (*diamond, glass*) centelleante, brillante; (*eyes*) brillante, chispeante: *sparkling clean*, limpio,-a como un espejo. **2** *fig* (*person, conversation, performance*) brillante, chispeante.

■ **sparkling wine,** vino espumoso.

sparring partner ['spɑːrɪŋpɑːtnəʳ] n (boxing) sparring m, compañero de entrenamiento.

sparrow ['spærəʊ] n ORN gorrión m.

sparrowhawk ['spærəʊhɔːk] n ORN gavilán m.

sparse [spɑːs] adj (vegetation) escaso,-a, poco denso,-a; (population) disperso,-a, esparcido,-a; (hair) ralo,-a; (information) escaso,-a.

sparsely ['spɑːslɪ] adv escasamente: scarcely furnished, con pocos muebles; scarcely populated, escasamente poblado.

Sparta ['spɑːtə] n Esparta.

Spartan ['spɑːtən] I adj espartano,-a. – 2 n (person) espartano,-a.

spasm ['spæzəm] I n MED espasmo. 2 (of coughing, laughing, etc) ataque m, acceso; (of anger) arrebato, acceso.
● in spasms, a rachas.

spasmodic [spæz'mɒdɪk] I adj MED espasmódico,-a. 2 (irregular) irregular, intermitente.

spasmodically [spæz'mɒdɪklɪ] adv de forma irregular, a rachas.

spastic ['spæstɪk] I n MED espástico,-a. 2 pej (clumsy, incompetent person) inútil mf, patoso,-a, torpe. – 3 adj MED espástico,-a. 4 pej (clumsy, incompetent) inútil, patoso,-a, torpe.

spat[1] [spæt] n (gaiter) polaina.

spat[2] [spæt] n fam (quarrel) rencilla.

spat[3] [spæt] pt & pp → **spit**.

spate [speɪt] I n (of letters, orders) avalancha; (of accidents, bad luck) racha; (of activities, protests) serie f; (of words) torrente m. 2 GB (of river) avenida, crecida.
● to be in (full) spate, (river) estar crecido,-a; (talker) estar en pleno discurso.

spatial ['speɪʃəl] adj espacial, del espacio.

spatter ['spætəʳ] I t (splash) salpicar (with, de); (sprinkle) rociar (with, de): the car spattered me with mud as it went past, al pasar, el coche me salpicó de barro. – 2 i salpicar. – 3 n (spattered spot) salpicadura, manchita; (small amount) pizca: a spatter of rain, unas gotas.

spatula ['spætjʊlə] n (gen) espátula; (in kitchen) pala, paleta.

spawn [spɔːn] I n ZOOL huevas fpl, freza. 2 BOT micelio. – 3 t fig generar, producir, engendrar. – 4 i ZOOL frezar, desovar.

spay [speɪ] t esterilizar.

speak [spiːk] I i (gen) hablar: could you speak more slowly please?, ¿podrías hablar más despacio, por favor?; I need speak to you about next year's budget, necesito hablar contigo acerca del presupuesto del año que viene; nobody spoke for five minutes, nadie habló durante cinco minutos; she didn't want to speak about it, no quería hablar de ello; I don't know him to speak to, sólo lo conozco de vista; they're not speaking (to each other), no se hablan, no se dirigen la palabra. 2 (make speech) pronunciar un discurso: we've invited Preston to speak at the meeting, hemos invitado a Preston a hablar en la reunión; she can speak on any subject, sabe hablar de cualquier tema; he spoke for/in favor of the motion, habló en favor de la moción. 3 (on phone) hablar: Laura speaking!, ¡Laura al habla!; can I speak to Karen please?, ¿me puedes poner con Karen por favor?, ¿me pasas con Karen por favor?; speaking!, ¡al habla!, ¡soy yo!, ¡yo mismo,-a! – 4 t (utter, say) decir: he spoke the truth, dijo la verdad; we didn't speak a word, no dijimos palabra; she spoke her lines confidently, recitó su papel con seguridad. 5 (language) hablar: do you speak En-

glish?, ¿hablas inglés?; Spanish spoken, se habla español.
◆ **to speak for** t insep (state views, wishes of) hablar en nombre de: I'm speaking for everyone, hablo en nombre de todos; the lawyer spoke for the defence, el abogado habló en nombre de la defensa. ‖ **to speak out** i (speak openly) hablar claro: she spoke out against experiments on animals, denunció los experimentos con animales. ‖ **to speak up** I i (speak more loudly) hablar más fuerte. 2 (give opinion) defender: we must speak up for our beliefs, hemos de defender nuestras creencias.
● generally/roughly speaking, en términos generales. ‖ personally speaking, personalmente. ‖ so to speak, por así decirlo. ‖ speak for yourself!, ¡eso lo dirás tú!, ¡eso lo dirás por ti! ‖ speak now or forever hold your peace, hable ahora o guarde silencio para siempre. ‖ to be nothing to speak of, no ser nada especial, no ser nada del otro mundo. ‖ to be spoken for, (reserved) estar reservado,-a; (engaged) estar comprometido,-a. ‖ to speak for itself/themselves, ser evidente, hablar por sí solo. ‖ speaking of ..., a propósito de ... ‖ to speak ill of sb. / speak well of sb., hablar mal de algn./hablar bien de algn. ‖ to speak in public, hablar en público. ‖ to speak in tongues, hablar en lenguas desconocidas. ‖ to speak one's mind, hablar claro, hablar sin rodeos. ‖ to speak out of turn, hablar fuera de lugar. ‖ to speak volumes, decirlo todo.
▲ pt spoke, pp spoken.

speakeasy ['spiːkiːzɪ] n US taberna clandestina.
▲ pl speakeasies.

speaker ['spiːkəʳ] I n (gen) persona que habla, el que habla, la que habla; (in dialogue) interlocutor,-ra; (in public) orador,-ra; (lecturer) conferenciante mf. 2 (of language) hablante mf. 3 (loudspeaker) altavoz m. 4 the Speaker, GB POL el/la Presidente,-a de la Cámara de los Comunes; US POL el/la presidente,-a de la Cámara de los Representantes: Mr/Madam Speaker, Señor/Señora presidente,-a.

speaking ['spiːkɪŋ] adj hablante: a speaking part, un papel hablado.
● to not be on speaking terms, no hablarse, estar peleados: we're not on speaking terms, no nos hablamos, estamos peleados.
■ speaking clock, información f horaria.

spear [spɪəʳ] I n (gen) lanza; (javelin) jabalina; (harpoon) arpón m. 2 BOT punta: asparagus spears, puntas de espárragos. – 3 t (with fork) pinchar; (with harpoon) arponear; (impale with spear) atravesar con una lanza.

spearhead ['spɪəhed] I n (person, group) punta de lanza, vanguardia. – 2 t encabezar.

spearmint ['spɪəmɪnt] n menta verde.

spec [spek] on spec, phr GB fam por si acaso, para probar suerte: I didn't know if he was in, I just called round on spec, no sabía si estaba en casa, me pasé por si acaso.

special ['speʃəl] I adj (not ordinary or usual) especial; (exceptional) extraordinario,-a: for special occasions, para ocasiones especiales; a special case, un caso especial; a special friend, un amigo íntimo; what's so special about today?, ¿qué tiene hoy de especial?; there's nothing special about him, no tiene nada de extraordinario. 2 (specific) específico,-a, particular: my special interest is ..., mi interés particular es ...; a special tool for ..., una herramienta especial para ... – 3 n (train) tren m especial. 4 RAD TV programa m especial. 5 US COMM (special offer) oferta especial.
● on special, de oferta. ‖ today's special, plato del día.

■ **special agent,** agente *mf* secreto,-a. ‖ Special Branch, GB Servicio de Seguridad del Estado. ‖ special delivery, *(letter)* correo urgente; *(parcel)* entrega inmediata. ‖ special edition, edición *f* especial, número especial, número extraordinario. ‖ special effects, efectos *mpl* especiales. ‖ special issue, extraordinario. ‖ special licence, dispensa matrimonial. ‖ special needs, EDUC atención *f* diferenciada. ‖ special offer, oferta (especial). ‖ Special Olympics, Juegos Paralímpicos *mpl.* ‖ special powers, poderes *mpl* extraordinarios. ‖ special school, escuela especial.

specialist ['speʃəlɪst] **1** *n (expert)* especialista *mf* (**in,** en). **2** MED especialista *mf: heart specialist,* especialista de corazón, cardiólogo,-a. – **3** *adj* especializado,-a.

speciality [speʃɪ'ælɪtɪ] *n* especialidad *f.*
▲ *pl* **specialities.**

specialization [speʃəlaɪ'zeɪʃən] *n (of study)* especialidad *f;* (*act*) especialización *f.*

specialize ['speʃəlaɪz] *i* especializarse (**in,** en).

specialized ['speʃəlaɪzd] *adj* especializado,-a.

specially ['speʃəlɪ] *adv (particularly)* especialmente, particularmente; *(on purpose)* expresamente: *do you like figs? - not specially,* ¿te gustan los higos? - no especialmente; *specially for you,* especialmente para ti; *we went there specially to see it,* fuimos allí expresamente para verlo; *this is a specially difficult problem,* un problema particularmente difícil.

specialty ['speʃəltɪ] *n* US → **speciality.**
▲ *pl* **specialties.**

species ['spiːʃiːz] *n* especie *f.*
▲ *pl* **species.**

specific [spə'sɪfɪk] **1** *adj (particular, not general)* específico,-a; *(definite)* concreto,-a: *for a specific purpose,* para un uso específico; *a specific example,* un ejemplo concreto. **2** *(exact, detailed, precise)* preciso,-a; *(clear in meaning)* explícito,-a: *can't you be a bit more specific?,* ¿no puedes ser un poco más preciso? – **3** *n* MED *(drug)* específico. – **4 specifics,** *npl (particulars, details)* datos *mpl* (concretos).
● **to be specific to sth.,** ser específico,-a de algo, ser propio,-a de algo.
■ **specific gravity,** peso específico.

specifically [spə'sɪfɪkəlɪ] **1** *adv (particularly)* específicamente, expresamente: *specifically designed for ...,* expresamente diseñado para ... **2** *(exactly, clearly)* explícitamente, expresamente: *I specifically told you not to go near the river,* te dije explícitamente que no te acercaras al río. **3** *(namely)* concretamente, en concreto.

specification [spesɪfɪ'keɪʃən] **1** *n (act)* especificación *f.* **2** *(requirement)* especificación *f;* (*condition*) requisito. – **3 specifications,** *npl (details)* detalles *mpl;* (*instructions*) instrucciones *fpl.*

specify ['spesɪfaɪ] *t* especificar, precisar, concretar: *the instructions specify that ...,* las instrucciones especifican que ...; *unless otherwise specified,* a menos que se especifique lo contrario.
▲ *pt & pp* **specified,** *ger* **specifying.**

specimen ['spesɪmən] **1** *n (sample)* espécimen *m,* muestra: *urine specimen,* muestra de orina. **2** *(example)* ejemplar *m: specimen copy,* ejemplar de muestra; *a fine specimen,* un buen ejemplar. **3** *fam pej (person)* tipo,-a: *a strange specimen,* un bicho raro.

specious ['spiːʃəs] *adj fml* engañoso,-a, especioso,-a.

speck [spek] **1** *n (of dust, soot)* mota; *(stain)* manchita; *(dot)* punto negro. **2** *(trace)* pizca.

speckled ['spekəld] *adj* moteado,-a, con motas.

specs [speks] *npl fam →* **spectacles.**

spectacle ['spektəkəl] **1** *n (show, display)* espectáculo. – **2 spectacles,** *npl* gafas *fpl: a pair of spectacles,* unas gafas.
● **to make a spectacle of os.,** hacer el ridículo, ponerse en ridículo.

spectacular [spek'tækjələʳ] **1** *adj* espectacular, impresionante. – **2** *n* TV gran espectáculo, programa *m* especial.

spectate [spek'teɪt] *i* mirar.

spectator [spek'teɪtəʳ] **1** *n* espectador,-ra. – **2 the spectators,** *npl* el público *m sing.*
■ **spectator sport,** deporte *m* espectáculo.

specter ['spektəʳ] *n* US → **spectre.**

spectre ['spektəʳ] *n* espectro, fantasma *m.*

spectrum ['spektrəm] **1** *n* PHYS espectro. **2** *(range)* espectro, gama.
▲ *pl* **spectra.**

speculate ['spekjəleɪt] **1** *i (conjecture)* especular, hacer conjeturas (**on/about,** sobre). **2** FIN especular (**in,** en/con).
● **to speculate on the stock market,** jugar a la bolsa, especular en la bolsa.

speculation [spekjə'leɪʃən] **1** *n (conjecture)* especulación *f,* conjetura, suposición *f.* **2** FIN especulación *f.*

speculator ['spekjəleɪtəʳ] *n* especulador,-ra.

sped [sped] *pt & pp →* **speed.**

speech [spiːtʃ] **1** *n (faculty, act)* habla. **2** *(spoken language, way of speaking)* habla, manera de hablar: *children's speech,* el habla de los niños. **3** *(formal talk)* discurso, alocución *f;* (*informal talk*) charla; *(lecture)* conferencia; *(lines in play)* diálogo: *he gave a speech on/about birdwatching,* dio una charla sobre ornitología. **4** LING oración *f: part of speech,* parte de la oración; *direct/indirect speech,* estilo directo/indirecto.
● **freedom of speech,** libertad *f* de expresión. ‖ **to give/make a speech,** pronunciar un discurso.
■ **speech day,** día *m* del reparto de premios. ‖ **speech defect,** defecto del habla. ‖ **speech impediment,** impedimento del habla. ‖ **speech therapist,** logopeda *mf,* foniatra *mf.* ‖ **speech therapy,** logopedia, foniatría.

speechless ['spiːtʃləs] *adj (flabbergasted)* boquiabierto,-a, estupefacto,-a; *(dumb)* mudo,-a: *he was speechless with anger,* enmudeció de ira; *I was left speechless,* me quedé sin habla.

speed [spiːd] **1** *n (rate of movement)* velocidad *f;* (*quickness*) rapidez *f;* (*haste*) prisa: *the speed of light,* la velocidad de la luz; *what speed were you doing?,* ¿a qué velocidad ibas?; *our cruising speed will be around 600 mph,* nuestra velocidad de crucero será de unas 600 millas por hora; *everything was prepared with amazing speed,* se preparó todo con una rapidez alucinante; *the forward's speed is his forte,* la rapidez del delantero es su fuerte. **2** *(sensitivity of film)* sensibilidad *f,* velocidad *f;* (*time of shutter*) tiempo de exposición, abertura. **3** *(gear)* marcha, velocidad *f: a five-speed gearbox,* una caja de cambios de cinco marchas, una caja de cambios de cinco velocidades. **4** *sl (drug)* speed *m,* anfetas *fpl.* – **5** *i (go fast)* ir corriendo, ir a toda prisa, ir a toda velocidad: *the car sped away/off,* el coche se alejó a toda prisa; *they were speeding along,* iban a toda velocidad; *the days sped by,* los días pasaron volando. **6** *(break limit)* ir a exceso de velocidad. – **7** *t (hurry - process, matter)* acelerar. **8** *(take quickly)* hacer llegar rápidamente.
◆ **to speed up 1** *t sep (process, matter, production)* ace-

lerar; (*person*) apresurar, meter prisa a. **– 2** *i* (*vehicle*) acelerar; (*person, process, production*) acelerarse, apresurarse, darse prisa.
● **at speed,** a gran velocidad. ‖ **at top speed / at full speed,** a toda velocidad. ‖ **God speed,** vaya con Dios. ‖ **to pick up speed / gather speed,** ganar velocidad, coger velocidad. ‖ **to speed sb. on their way,** despedir a algn., desearle buen viaje a algn.
■ **speed bump,** US badén *m*. ‖ **speed limit,** velocidad máxima, límite *m* de velocidad. ‖ **speed trap,** control *m* de velocidad.
▲ *pt & pp* **speeded** *o* **sped.**
speedboat ['spiːdbəʊt] *n* lancha rápida.
speeding ['spiːdɪŋ] *n* AUTO exceso de velocidad.
speedometer [spɪ'dɒmɪtəʳ] *n* AUTO velocímetro, cuentakilómetros *m*.
speedway ['spiːdweɪ] **1** *n* (*racing*) carreras *fpl* de moto. **2** (*track*) pista de carreras, circuito.
speedwell ['spiːdwel] *n* BOT verónica.
speedy ['spiːdɪ] *adj* (*quick*) rápido,-a, veloz; (*prompt*) pronto,-a, rápido,-a.
● **to wish sb. a speedy recovery,** desearle una pronta mejoría a algn.
▲ *comp* **speedier,** *superl* **speediest.**
spell¹ [spel] *n* (*magical*) hechizo, encanto.
● **to cast/put a spell on sb.,** hechizar a algn., embrujar a algn. ‖ **to fall under sb.'s spell,** estar hechizado,- a por algn.
spell² [spel] **1** *n* (*period of time*) temporada, período; (*short period*) rato: *a spell in hospital,* una temporada hospitalizado; *I had a spell as a waitress,* trabajé una temporada de camarera; *she's going through a bad spell,* está pasando una mala racha. **2** METEOR período, ola, racha: *sunny spells,* períodos de sol; *a cold spell,* una ola de frío. **3** MED (*dizziness*) mareo; (*of coughing*) acceso. **4** (*turn*) turno, tanda. **– 5** *t* US (*take sb.'s turn*) relevar.
● **to take spells at (doing) sth.,** turnarse para hacer algo.
spell³ [spel] **1** *t* (*orally*) deletrear; (*written*) escribir correctamente: *how do you spell it?,* ¿cómo se escribe?; *do you spell it with one N or two?,* ¿se escribe con una N o con dos?; *could you spell your name for me?,* ¿me podría deletrear su nombre?; *D-O-G spells dog,* dog se deletrea D-O-G. **2** *fig* (*mean*) significar, representar; (*bring*) traer, acarrear; (*foretell*) anunciar, augurar, presagiar: *the drought spelt disaster,* la sequía significó un desastre; *this new law spells trouble,* esta nueva ley traerá problemas. **– 3** *i* saber escribir correctamente: *you can't spell,* haces faltas de ortografía.
◆ **to spell out** *t sep* (*word*) deletrear. **2** (*explain in detail*) explicar con detalle, detallar, pormenorizar: *do I have to spell it out for you?,* ¿te lo tengo que explicar con detalle?
▲ *pt & pp* **spelled** *o* **spelt.**
spellbound ['spelbaʊnd] *adj* hechizado,-a, embelesado,-a.
spelling ['spelɪŋ] *n* ortografía.
■ **spelling mistake,** falta de ortografía.
spelt [spelt] *pt & pp* → **spell.**
spelunker [spə'lʌŋkəʳ] *n* US espeleólogo,-a.
spelunking [spə'lʌŋkɪŋ] *n* US espeleología.
spend [spend] **1** *t* (*money*) gastar (**on,** en): *I've spent a lot this month,* he gastado mucho este mes; *he spends all his money on records,* gasta todo su dinero en discos. **2** (*pass time*) pasar: *we spent the weekend there,* pasamos allí el fin de semana; *she spent the day sunbathing,*

(se) pasó el día tomando el sol. **3** (*devote time/energy*) dedicar (**on,** a), invertir (**on,** en): *I'd like to spend more time with my family,* me gustaría dedicar más tiempo a mi familia; *you should spend more time on your homework,* deberías dedicar más tiempo a tus deberes. **4** (*use up, exhaust*) gastar, agotar: *the storm spent its force,* la tormenta perdió su fuerza. **– 5** *i* (*money*) gastar.
▲ *pt & pp* **spent.**
spender ['spendəʳ] *n* gastador,-ra, derrochador,-ra.
spending ['spendɪŋ] *n* gasto, gastos *mpl*: *they are threatening big cuts in government spending,* amenazan con grandes recortes en el gasto público.
■ **public spending,** gasto público. ‖ **spending cuts,** recortes *mpl* en el presupuesto. ‖ **spending money,** dinero de bolsillo. ‖ **spending power,** poder *m* adquisitivo.
spendthrift ['spendθrɪft] *n* derrochador,-ra, despilfarrador,-ra, manirroto,-a.
spent [spent] **1** *pt & pp* → **spend. – 2** *adj* (*used*) usado,- a, gastado,-a: *a spent match,* una cerilla usada. **3** (*exhausted*) agotado,-a; (*finished*) acabado,-a.
■ **a spent force,** una fuerza acabada.
sperm [spɜːm] *n* esperma *mf*.
■ **sperm bank,** banco de esperma. ‖ **sperm whale,** cachalote *m*.
spermatozoon [spɜːmətə'zəʊən] *n* espermatozoide *m*.
▲ *pl* **spermatozoa.**
spermicide ['spɜːmɪsaɪd] *n* espermicida.
spew [spjuː] **1** *t* (*flames, lava, smoke, etc*) arrojar, vomitar. **2** **to spew (up),** GB fam vomitar, devolver. **– 3** *i* salir a borbotones. **4** GB *fam* vomitar, devolver, arrojar.
sphere [sfɪəʳ] **1** *n* (*shape*) esfera. **2** (*area, range, extent*) esfera, ámbito: *sphere of influence,* ámbito de influencia; *in the sphere of economics,* en el ámbito económico.
spherical ['sferɪkəl] *adj* esférico,-a.
spheroid ['sfɪərɔɪd] *n* esferoide *m*.
sphincter ['sfɪŋktəʳ] *n* esfínter *m*.
sphinx [sfɪŋks] *n* esfinge *f*.
spice [spaɪs] **1** *n* especia. **2** *fig* sazón *m*, sal *f*, salsa, sabor *m*. **– 3** *t* CULIN sazonar, condimentar. **4** (*story etc*) echar salsa a (**up,** -).
spick-and-span [spɪkən'spæn] *adj* (*of room, house, etc*) limpísimo,-a, pulcro,-a; (*of person*) impecable, acicalado,-a.
spicy ['spaɪsɪ] **1** *adj* CULIN (*seasoned*) sazonado,-a, condimentado,-a; (*hot*) picante. **2** *fig* (*story etc*) picante.
▲ *comp* **spicier,** *superl* **spiciest.**
spider ['spaɪdəʳ] *n* araña.
■ **spider plant,** BOT cinta. ‖ **spider's web,** telaraña.
spiel [spiːl] *n* fam rollo.
spigot ['spɪgət] **1** *n* (*tap*) espita; (*stopper*) bitoque *m*. **2** US (*tap*) grifo.
spike¹ [spaɪk] **1** *n* (*sharp point*) punta, pincho; (*sharp-pointed object*) objeto puntiagudo. **2** (*on running shoe*) clavo. **– 3** *t* (*with shoes*) clavar. **4** (*drink*) echar alcohol a. **– 5** **spikes,** *npl* (*running shoes*) zapatillas *fpl* de clavos.
● **to spike sb.'s guns,** echar por tierra los planes de algn.
■ **spike heel,** tacón *m* de aguja.
spike² [spaɪk] *n* BOT espiga.
spiky ['spaɪkɪ] **1** *adj* (*gen*) puntiagudo,-a; (*hedgehog*) erizado,-a; (*hair*) de punta. **2** *fam* (*easily offended*) susceptible.
▲ *comp* **spikier,** *superl* **spikiest.**
spill¹ [spɪl] *n* (*for lighting fires, lamps, pipes - of wood*) astilla; (*of paper*) trozo de papel enrollado.

spill² [spɪl] **1** *n* (*act, amount of spilling*) derrame *m*, derramamiento. **2** *fam* (*fall*) caída. **– 3** *t* (*liquid*) derramar, verter; (*knock over*) volcar: *I've spilt some wine on the carpet,* he derramado vino sobre la alfombra; *he spilt coffee down/on his shirt,* se manchó la camisa de café. **– 4** *i* (*liquid*) derramarse, verterse: *the water spilt all over the floor,* el agua se derramó por todo el suelo. **5** (*people*) salir en tropel: *passengers spilled out onto the platform,* los pasajeros salieron al andén en tropel.
◆ **to spill over** *i* (*liquid*) salirse, desbordarse; (*people*) rebosar; (*conflict*) extenderse: *the pub was full and people spilled over into the street,* el pub estaba lleno y la gente rebosaba por la calle.
● **to spill blood,** derramar sangre. ‖ **to spill the beans,** descubrir el pastel.
▲ *pt & pp* spilled *o* spilt.
spillage ['spɪlɪdʒ] *n* derrame *m*.
spin [spɪn] **1** *n* (*turn*) vuelta, giro, revolución *f*. **2** (*of washing machine*) centrifugado. **3** SP (*of ball*) efecto. **4** AER barrena; AUTO patinazo. **5** (*ride, trip*) vuelta, paseo (en coche o en moto): *let's go for a spin in the car,* demos una vuelta en coche. **6** *fam* (*panic*) pánico, miedo. **– 7** *t* (*make turn*) hacer girar, dar vueltas a: *we spun a coin,* hicimos girar una moneda. **8** (*washing*) centrifugar. **9** (*ball*) darle efecto a. **10** (*cotton, wool, etc*) hilar; (*spider's web*) tejer. **– 11** *i* (*turn*) girar, dar vueltas: *the wheel spun round and round,* la rueda daba vueltas (y más vueltas); *my head was spinning,* la cabeza me daba vueltas; *the blow sent him spinning,* el golpe lo mandó a rodar. **12** (*washing machine*) centrifugar. **13** (*cotton, wool, etc*) hilar. **14** AER caer en barrena; AUTO patinar. **15** (*move rapidly*) girar(se), darse la vuelta: *he spun round suddenly,* (se) giró de repente; *the car span off the road,* el coche salió de la carretera dando vueltas; *they were spinning along at 100 mph,* rodaban a 100 millas por hora.
◆ **to spin out** *t sep* (*holiday, speech*) prolongar, alargar; (*time, money*) estirar.
● **to be in a flat spin,** estar hecho,-a un lío. ‖ **to go into a spin,** AER caer en barrena. ‖ **to put spin on a ball,** darle efecto a una pelota. ‖ **to spin sb. a yarn,** pegarle un rollo a algn. ‖ **to spin a story / spin a tale,** contar una historia.
■ **spin bowler,** (*in cricket*) lanzador,-ra rápido,-a.
▲ *pt* spun *o* span, *pp* spun, *ger* spinning.
spina bifida [spaɪnəˈbɪfɪdə] *n* espina bífida.
spinach ['spɪnɪdʒ] **1** *n* BOT espinaca. **2** CULIN espinacas *fpl*.
spinal ['spaɪnəl] *adj* espinal, vertebral.
■ **spinal column,** columna vertebral. ‖ **spinal cord,** médula espinal.
spindle ['spɪndəl] **1** *n* (*rod for spinning*) huso. **2** TECH (*part of machine*) eje *m*; (*of lathe*) mandril *m*.
spindly ['spɪndlɪ] *adj* (*leg*) largo y delgado,-a; (*person*) larguirucho,-a, zanquilargo,-a; (*plant*) alto,-a.
▲ *comp* spindlier, *superl* spindliest.
spin-dry [spɪn'draɪ] *t* centrifugar.
▲ *pt & pp* spin-dried, *ger* spin-drying.
spin-dryer [spɪn'draɪəʳ] *n* secador *m* centrífugo, centrifugadora.
spine [spaɪn] **1** *n* ANAT columna vertebral, espina dorsal, espinazo. **2** (*of book*) lomo. **3** ZOOL (*of hedgehog etc*) púa. **4** BOT espina.
spine-chilling ['spaɪntʃɪlɪŋ] *adj* horripilante, escalofriante, espeluznante.
spineless ['spaɪnləs] **1** *adj* (*invertebrate*) invertebrado,-a. **2** *fig* (*weak*) débil, sin carácter.
spinet [spɪ'net] *n* MUS espineta.

spinner ['spɪnəʳ] **1** *n* (*thread*) hilandero,-a. **2** (*spin-dryer*) secador centrífugo, centrifugadora. **3** (*bowler*) lanzador,-ra rápido,-a. **4** (*bait for fish*) cuchara.
spinney ['spɪnɪ] *n* bosquecillo, soto.
spinning ['spɪnɪŋ] *n* (*action*) hilado; (*art*) hilandería.
■ **spinning jenny,** máquina de hilar. ‖ **spinning top,** peonza, trompo. ‖ **spinning wheel,** rueca, torno de hilar.
spin-off ['spɪnɔːf] **1** *n* (*product*) producto derivado; (*result*) resultado indirecto. **2** US TV programa *m* derivado.
spinster ['spɪnstəʳ] *n* soltera.
● **to be an old spinster,** ser una vieja solterona.
spiny ['spaɪnɪ] *adj* espinoso,-a.
▲ *comp* spinier, *superl* spiniest.
spiral ['spaɪərəl] **1** *n* espiral *f*. **– 2** *adj* espiral, en espiral. **– 3** *i* (*move in a spiral*) moverse en espiral: *the plane began to spiral down,* el avión empezó a caer en espiral. **4** (*increase rapidly*) dispararse: *spiralling prices,* precios en alza vertiginosa.
■ **inflationary spiral,** espiral *f* inflacionista. ‖ **spiral staircase,** escalera de caracol.
spire ['spaɪəʳ] *n* aguja.
spirit¹ ['spɪrɪt] **1** *n* CHEM alcohol *m*. **– 2** **spirits,** *npl* (*alcoholic drink*) bebidas *fpl* alcohólicas, licores *mpl*.
■ **spirit lamp,** lámpara de alcohol. ‖ **spirit level,** nivel *m* de aire.
spirit² ['spɪrɪt] **1** *n* (*soul*) espíritu *m*, alma; (*ghost*) fantasma *m*: *his spirit lives on,* su espíritu perdura; *evil spirit,* espíritu maligno. **2** (*person*) ser *m*, alma: *kindred spirits,* almas gemelas. **3** (*force, vigour*) vigor *m*, energía; (*personality*) carácter *m*; (*courage*) valor *m*; (*vitality, liveliness*) ánimo, vitalidad *f*: *she played with great spirit,* jugó con gran energía; *try as they might, they couldn't break his spirit,* por mucho que lo interaran, no pudieron quebrantarle el espíritu. **4** (*mood, attitude*) espíritu *m*, humor *m*: *he approached the challenge in the right spirit,* abordó el reto con buen humor; *the party spirit,* el espíritu festivo. **5** (*central quality, real or intended meaning*) espíritu *m*, sentido: *the spirit of the law,* el espíritu de la ley. **– 6 spirits,** *npl* (*mood, feelings*) moral *f sing*, humor *m sing*: *she's in good spirits,* está de buen humor; *he's in high spirits,* está animado; *you're in low spirits today,* estás deprimido hoy.
◆ **to spirit away / spirit off** *t sep* llevarse como por arte de magia.
● **in spirit,** en espíritu. ‖ **that's the spirit!,** ¡eso es!, ¡así me gusta! ‖ **the spirit is willing but the flesh is weak,** las intenciones son buenas, pero la carne es débil. ‖ **to enter into the spirit of things,** meterse en el ambiente. ‖ **to raise sb.'s spirits,** subirle la moral a algn.
■ **the Holy Spirit,** el Espíritu Santo.
spirited ['spɪrɪtɪd] **1** *adj* (*attack, reply*) enérgico,-a, vigoroso,-a; (*attempt*) valiente: *the orquestra gave a spirited performance,* la orquestra tocó con brío. **2** (*person*) animado,-a; (*horse*) fogoso,-a.
spiritual ['spɪrɪtjʊəl] **1** *adj* espiritual. **– 2** *n* (*song*) espiritual *m* negro.
● **one's spiritual home,** su patria espiritual.
spiritualism ['spɪrɪtjʊəlɪzəm] *n* espiritismo.
spiritualist ['spɪrɪtjʊəlɪst] *n* espiritista *mf*.
spirituality [spɪrɪtjʊ'ælətɪ] *n* espiritualidad *f*.
spit¹ [spɪt] **1** *n* CULIN asador *m*, espetón *m*. **2** GEOG (*of sand*) banco; (*of land*) punta, lengua.
spit² [spɪt] **1** *n* (*saliva*) saliva, esputo. **– 2** *t* (*gen*) escupir. **– 3** *i* (*gen*) escupir (**at**, a), (**on**, en). **4** (*rain*) chispear: *it's spitting with rain,* caen gotas. **5** (*sputter*) chisporrotear.

◆ **to spit out** 1 *t sep* (*gen*) escupir. **2** *fig* (*say sharply*) soltar: *spit it out!*, ¡suéltalo ya!

● **spit and polish**, pulcritud *f* y limpieza. ‖ **to be the spit of sb. / be the spitting image of sb.**, ser el vivo retrato de algn.

▲ *pt & pp* **spat**.

spite [spaɪt] 1 *n* (*ill will*) rencor *m*, ojeriza. – **2** *t* fastidiar: *he did it to spite me*, lo hizo para fastidiarme.

● **in spite of**, a pesar de, pese a: *we went to the zoo in spite of the bad weather*, fuimos al zoo a pesar del mal tiempo; *in spite of the fact that she felt ill, she went to work*, a pesar de que se encontraba mal, se fue a trabajar. ‖ **in spite of os.**, a pesar suyo. ‖ **out of spite**, por despecho.

spiteful [ˈspaɪtfʊl] *adj* (*person*) rencoroso,-a, malévolo,-a; (*comment*) malicioso,-a; (*tongue*) viperino,-a.

spitefully [ˈspaɪtfʊlɪ] *adv* con rencor, por despecho.

spitefulness [ˈspaɪtfʊlnəs] *n* rencor *m*, despecho.

spittle [ˈspɪtəl] *n* saliva, baba.

spittoon [spɪˈtuːn] *n* escupidera.

spiv [spɪv] *n* GB *sl pej* chanchullero.

splash [splæʃ] 1 *n* (*noise*) chapoteo, chapaleo. **2** (*spray*) salpicadura, rociada. **3** (*small amount*) gota, chorrito, poco. **4** *fig* (*of light, colour, etc*) mancha. – **5** *t* (*gen*) salpicar (**with**, de), rociar (**with**, de): *she splashed water on her face*, se echó agua en la cara; *don't splash me!*, ¡no me salpiques!; *you've splashed oil on my shirt*, me has salpicado la camisa de aceite. **6** *fam* (*of news, story, etc*) sacar, salir: *the newspaper splashed the story all over the front page*, el periódico sacó la historia (en grandes titulares) en la portada. – **7** *i* (*of liquid*) salpicar, esparcirse: *the rain splashed against/on the window*, la lluvia salpicaba el cristal; *water splashed everywhere*, todo se salpicó de agua. **8** (*move noisily*) chapotear (**about/around**, -): *they love splashing around in the puddles*, les encanta chapotear en los charcos. – **9** *interj* ¡plaf!

◆ **to splash down** *i* amarar, amerizar. ‖ **to splash out** 1 *i fam* darse un lujo, gastarse un dineral: *we decided to splash out on a new car*, decidimos darnos un lujo y comprar un coche nuevo. – **2** *t sep fam* (*money*) derrochar, gastarse: *we splashed out $500 on a new video*, nos gastamos $500 en un vídeo nuevo.

● **to make a splash**, causar sensación.

splashdown [ˈsplæʃdaʊn] *n* amerizaje *m*, amaraje *m*.

splat [splæt] *adv* ¡paf!

▲ *pt & pp* **splatted**, *ger* **splatting**.

splatter [ˈsplætəʳ] 1 *t* salpicar. – **2** *i* salpicar.

splay [spleɪ] 1 *t* (*fingers*) abrir, separar; (*pipe*) extender, ensanchar. **2** ARCH (*window, door*) construir un derrame en. – **3** *i* (*fingers*) separarse (**out**, -); (*pipe*) extenderse, ensancharse. – **4** *adj* (*of feet*) plano,-a.

spleen [spliːn] 1 *n* ANAT bazo. **2** *lit* (*anger*) cólera, ira.

● **to vent one's spleen on sb./sth.**, descargar su cólera contra algn./algo.

splendid [ˈsplendɪd] 1 *adj* (*excellent*) estupendo,-a, maravilloso,-a. **2** (*magnificent*) espléndido,-a, magnífico,-a.

splendidly [ˈsplendɪdlɪ] *adv* estupendamente, maravillosamente.

splendor [ˈsplendəʳ] *n* US → **splendour**.

splendour [ˈsplendəʳ] *n* esplendor *m*.

splice [splaɪs] 1 *t* (*rope*) empalmar. **2** CINEM montar.

● **to get spliced**, casarse.

splicer [ˈsplaɪsəʳ] *n* CINEM máquina de montaje, montadora.

splint [splɪnt] *n* tablilla.

● **to be in splints**, estar entablillado,-a.

splinter [ˈsplɪntəʳ] 1 *n* (*of wood*) astilla; (*of metal, bone, stone*) esquirla; (*of glass*) fragmento. – **2** *t* astillar, hacer astillas. – **3** *i* astillarse, hacerse astillas. **4** POL escindirse (**off**, -).

■ **splinter group**, grupo disidente, facción *f*.

split [splɪt] 1 *n* (*crack, cut, break*) grieta, hendidura, raja. **2** (*tear - in garment*) desgarrón *m*, rasgón *m*; (*- in seam*) descosido. **3** (*division - gen*) división *f*, ruptura, cisma *m*; (*- in politics*) escisión *f*, cisma *m*, ruptura. **4** (*division, sharing out*) reparto. – **5** *adj* (*cracked*) partido,-a, hendido,-a, rajado,-a; (*torn*) desgarrado,-a, rasgado,-a: *split lip*, labio partido; *split seam*, descosido. **6** (*divided - gen*) dividido,-a; (*- in politics*) dividido,-a, escindido,-a: *the party is split on this issue*, el partido está dividido por este tema. – **7** *t* (*crack, break*) agrietar, hender; (*cut*) partir: *he's splitting logs*, está partiendo troncos; *she split the coconut open*, abrió el coco. **8** (*tear - garment*) rajar, desgarrar; (*- seam*) descoser: *he split his trousers*, rompió los pantalones. **9** PHYS (*atom*) desintegrar. **10** (*divide, separate*) dividir (**up**, -); (*political party etc*) dividir, escindir: *she split the class (up) into two groups*, dividió la clase en dos grupos; *the issue of the prison has split the community*, el asunto de la cárcel ha dividido a la comunidad. **11** (*share*) repartir, dividir: *we had to split the prize money between 10 people*, tuvimos que repartir el premio entre 10 personas; *let's split the cost*, paguemos a medias. – **12** *i* (*crack*) agrietarse, henderse, rajarse; (*in two parts*) partirse: *this wood splits easily*, esta madera se parte fácilmente. **13** (*tear - garment*) rajarse, desgarrarse; (*- seams*) descoserse: *his trousers split*, se le descosieron los pantalones. **14** (*divide - gen*) dividirse (**up**, -); (*- in politics*) dividirse, escindirse: *the river splits in two here*, aquí el río se divide en dos; *the students split up into small groups*, los estudiantes se dividieron en grupos pequeños; *the coalition split over the issue of abortion*, la coalición se escindió por el tema del aborto. **15** *fam* (*tell tales*) acusar, soplar, chivarse (**on**, de): *don't split on me*, no me soples. **16** *sl* (*leave*) largarse, abrirse, pirárselas: *let's split*, larguémonos.

◆ **to split away / split off** 1 *t sep* (*branch, rock etc*) romper, desprender. – **2** *i* (*branch, rock, etc*) romperse, desprenderse. **3** (*group*) escindirse, separarse (**from**, de): *some radicals have split off from the official group*, algunos radicales se han escindido del grupo oficial. ‖ **to split up** 1 *t sep* (*friends, lovers*) separar: *I'm going to have to split you two up*, voy a tener que separaros. – **2** *i* (*crowd, meeting*) dispersarse; (*couple*) separarse, romper: *Hugh and Liz split up ages ago*, Hugh y Liz rompieron hace mucho; *she split up with him last year*, cortó con él el año pasado.

● **in a split second**, en una fracción de segundo, en menos de un segundo. ‖ **to do the splits**, abrir las piernas en cruz. ‖ **to split hairs**, rizar el rizo, buscarle tres pies al gato. ‖ **to split one's head open**, romperse la crisma, partirse la crisma. ‖ **to split one's sides laughing**, partirse de risa, troncharse de risa. ‖ **to split the difference**, partir la diferencia.

■ **cream split / jam split**, pastelito relleno de nata / pastelito relleno de mermelada. ‖ **split decision**, decisión *f* no unánime. ‖ **split ends**, (*of hair*) puntas *fpl* abiertas. ‖ **split infinitive**, LING infinitivo con un adverbio intercalado entre el "to" y el verbo. ‖ **split peas**, guisantes *mpl* secos. ‖ **split pin**, chaveta. ‖ **split personality**, desdoblamiento de personalidad. ‖ **split ring**, llavero. ‖ **split shift**, horario partido.

▲ *pt & pp* **split**, *ger* **splitting**.

split-level [ˈsplɪtˈlevəl] *adj* (*room, flat*) en dos niveles; (*oven*) con el grill en la parte superior.

split-screen ['splɪtskriːn] *adj* con pantalla dividida.
split-second [splɪt'sekənd] *adj* (*very rapid*) instantáneo,- a; (*accurate*) perfecto,-a: *split-second timing,* sincronización *f* perfecta.
splitting ['splɪtɪŋ] *adj* (*headache*) terrible, muy fuerte.
splodge [splɒdʒ] *n fam* mancha, borrón *m*.
splotch [splɒtʃ] *n fam* mancha, borrón *m*.
splurge [splɜːdʒ] **1** *t fam* despilfarrar (**on**, en), derrochar (**on**, en), gastarse (**on**, en). – **2** *i* gastarse un dineral (**on**, en). – **3** *n* derroche *m*.
● **to go on a splurge,** salir a gastar a lo loco.
splutter ['splʌtə'] **1** *n* (*of flame*) chisporreteo; (*of engine*) ruido; (*of person*) barboteo, farfulleo. – **2** *t* (*person*) mascullar, farfullar. – **3** *i* (*person*) farfullar, barbotar: *she spluttered with indignation,* farfulló de indignación; *he was coughing and spluttering,* tosía y resoplaba. **4** (*fire, candle, fat, etc*) chisporrotear, crepitar. **5** (*of engine*) petardear, renquear.
spoil [spɔɪl] **1** *t* (*ruin*) estropear, echar a perder, arruinar: *that's spoilt the whole plan,* eso ha estropeado todo el plan; *people who drop litter spoil the countryside,* las personas que tiran papeles afean el campo; *he spoilt all our fun,* nos aguó la fiesta; *it'll spoil your appetite,* te quitará el apetito. **2** (*invalidate*) anular. **3** (*make child selfish*) mimar, consentir; (*indulge*) complacer: *her parents spoil her terribly,* sus padres la miman muchísimo; *everyone likes being spoilt,* a todos nos gusta que nos mimen; *spoil yourself,* date un gusto. – **4** *i* (*food*) estropearse, echarse a perder. – **5** spoils, *npl* botín *m sing*.
● **to be spoiling for a fight,** andar buscando pelea, andar buscando camorra. ‖ **to be spoilt for choice,** tener demasiadas cosas para elegir.
▲ *pt & pp* spoiled *o* spoilt [spɔɪlt].
spoilsport ['spɔɪlspɔːt] *n* aguafiestas *mf*.
spoilt [spɔɪlt] **1** *pp* spoilt. – **2** *adj* (*food etc*) estropeado,-a. **3** (*child*) mimado,-a, consentido,-a. **4** (*ballot paper*) nulo,-a.
spoke[1] [spəʊk] *n* (*of wheel*) radio, rayo.
● **to put a spoke in sb.'s wheel,** poner trabas a algn.
spoke[2] [spəʊk] *pt* → **speak**.
spoken ['spəʊkən] **1** *pp* → **speak**. – **2** *adj* hablado,-a, oral.
spokesman ['spəʊksmən] *n* portavoz *m*.
spokesperson ['spəʊkspɜːsən] *n* portavoz *mf*.
spokeswoman ['spəʊkswʊmən] *n* portavoz *f*.
sponge [spʌndʒ] **1** *n* (*gen*) esponja. **2** GB CULIN bizcocho. – **3** *t* (*clean*) lavar con esponja, limpiar con esponja, pasar una esponja por: *sponge down the walls,* pase una esponja por las paredes; *she sponged the wound,* limpió la herida con una esponja. **4** *fam* (*scrounge*) gorronear, gorrear, sablear: *he sponged a fiver from me,* me gorroneó cinco libras. – **5** *i fam* (*scrounge*) vivir de gorra, gorrear, dar sablazos.
◆ **to sponge off / sponge on** *t insep fam* (*scrounge*) vivir a costa de.
● **to give sth. a sponge,** pasar una esponja por algo. ‖ **to throw in/up the sponge,** arrojar la toalla.
■ **sponge bag,** bolsa de aseo, neceser *m*. ‖ **sponge cake,** bizcocho. ‖ **sponge pudding,** budín *m*.
sponger ['spʌndʒə'] *n fam pej* gorrón,-ona, sablista *mf*.
spongy ['spʌndʒɪ] *adj* esponjoso,-a.
▲ *comp* spongier, *superl* spongiest.
sponsor ['spɒnsə'] **1** *n* (*gen*) patrocinador,-ra, sponsor *mf*; (*for arts*) mecenas *mf*. **2** FIN avalador,-ra, garante *mf*. **3** REL (*godfather*) padrino; (*godmother*) madrina. **4** (*of law,*

bill, motion) proponente *mf*. – **5** *t* (*gen*) patrocinar; (*studies, research*) subvencionar: *this team is sponsored by a hi-fi company,* una empresa de alta fidelidad patrocina este equipo. **6** (*support*) apoyar, respaldar. **7** FIN avalar, garantizar. **8** REL apadrinar.
sponsorship ['spɒnsəʃɪp] **1** *n* (*gen*) patrocinio. **2** FIN aval *m*, garantía. **3** (*support*) apoyo, respaldo.
spontaneity [spɒntə'neɪtɪ] *n* espontaneidad *f*.
spontaneous [spɒn'teɪnɪəs] *adj* espontáneo,-a.
spoof [spuːf] **1** *n* (*parody*) parodia, burla. **2** (*hoax*) engaño, broma. – **3** *t* (*parody*) parodiar. **4** (*trick*) engañar.
spooky ['spuːkɪ] *adj fam* escalofriante, espeluznante, horripilante.
▲ *comp* spookier, *superl* spookiest.
spool [spuːl] *n* carrete *m*, bobina.
spoon [spuːn] **1** *n* (*gen*) cuchara; (*small*) cucharilla, cucharita; (*large*) cucharón *m*. **2** (*spoonful - gen*) cucharada; (*- small*) cucharadita. – **3** *t* (*lift and move*) sacar con cuchara; (*serve*) servir con cuchara. – **4** *i* US *fam* (*kiss*) besuquearse.
● **to be born with a silver spoon in one's mouth,** nacer entre algodones.
spoonerism ['spuːnərɪzəm] *n* confusión entre palabras debido a un trastocamiento de letras.
spoon-fed ['spuːnfed] *adj* mimado,-a.
spoon-feed ['spuːnfiːd] **1** *t* (*baby*) dar de comer con cuchara. **2** *fig* (*pupil*) dar la lección masticada a.
▲ *pt & pp* spoon-fed.
spoonful ['spuːnfʊl] *n* cucharada.
▲ *pl* spoonfuls *o* spoonsful.
sporadic [spə'rædɪk] *adj* esporádico,-a.
spore [spɔː'] *n* BIOL espora.
sporran ['spɒrən] *n* escarcela que llevan los escoceses encima de la falda.
sport [spɔːt] **1** *n* (*gen*) deporte *m*: *do you play much sport?,* ¿practicas mucho deporte?; *what's your favourite sport?,* ¿cuál es tu deporte preferido? **2** (*person*) buena persona: *be a sport,* sé bueno. **3** (*fun*) diversión *f*: *they hunt for sport,* cazan por diversión; *he said it in sport,* lo dijo en broma. **4** *fam* (*fellow*) amigo,-a. – **5** *t* (*wear proudly*) lucir: *she was sporting a new dress,* lucía un vestido nuevo. – **6** *i* (*frolic*) retozar, juguetear.
● **the sport of kings,** el deporte de los reyes, la hípica. ‖ **to be good at sport,** ser buen,-na deportista. ‖ **to make sport of sb.,** burlarse de algn.
sporting ['spɔːtɪŋ] **1** *adj* (*of sports*) deportivo,-a; (*of country sports*) de caza: *sporting event,* prueba deportiva. **2** (*fair, generous*) caballeroso,-a, deportivo,-a.
● **a sporting chance,** bastantes posibilidades *fpl*.
sports [spɔːts] **1** *npl* deportes *mpl*. – **2** *n* (*meeting*) competición *f* deportiva. – **3** *adj* deportivo,-a, de deportes: *sports commentator,* comentarista deportivo,-a; *sports programme,* programa de deportes.
■ **sports car,** (coche *m*) deportivo. ‖ **sports centre/ complex,** polideportivo. ‖ **sports day,** día dedicado a competiciones deportivas escolares. ‖ **sports ground,** campo de deportes. ‖ **sports jacket,** chaqueta (de) sport. ‖ **sports scholarship,** beca deportiva.
sportsman ['spɔːtsmən] *n* deportista *m*.
▲ *pl* sportsmen ['spɔːtsmən].
sportsmanlike ['spɔːtsmənlaɪk] *adj* deportivo,-a.
sportsmanship ['spɔːtsmənʃɪp] *n* deportividad *f*, espíritu *m* deportivo.
sportswear ['spɔːtsweə'] *n* (*for sport*) ropa de deporte; (*casual*) ropa (de) sport.
sportswoman ['spɔːtswʊmən] *n* deportista *f*.
▲ *pl* sportswomen ['spɔːtswɪmɪn].

sporty ['spɔːtɪ] *adj fam* deportivo,-a, aficionado,-a a los deportes.
▲ *comp* **sportier,** *superl* **sportiest.**
spot [spɒt] **1** *n* (*dot*) punto; (*on fabric*) lunar *m*, mota; (*on animal*) mancha. **2** (*mark, stain*) mancha. **3** (*blemish, pimple*) grano. **4** (*place*) sitio, lugar *m*: *what a lovely spot for a picnic!,* ¡qué lugar más bonito para un picnic!; *this is the exact spot where he was killed,* este es el lugar exacto donde lo mataron; *a night spot,* un local nocturno; *accident black spot,* punto negro; *trouble spot,* punto conflictivo. **5** (*area of body*) punto; (*flaw*) mancha: *weak spot,* punto débil, punto flaco. **6** (*fix, trouble*) lío, aprieto, apuro: *I'm in a tight spot,* estoy en un aprieto. **7** RAD TV (*place in broadcast*) espacio: *she has a guest spot on a radio programme,* aparece como invitada en un programa de radio. **8** *fam* (*small amount*) poquito, poquitín *m*; (*drop*) gota: *a spot of rain,* un poco de lluvia; *a spot of lunch,* algo de comer; *a spot of bother,* un problemilla, un pequeño disgusto. **9** (*position*) puesto. **10** *fam* (*spotlight*) foco. **11** US *fam* (*banknote*) billete *m.* – **12** *t* (*notice*) darse cuenta de, notar; (*see*) ver; (*recognize*) reconocer; (*find*) encontrar, descubrir; (*catch out*) pillar: *we spotted him in the crowd,* lo vimos entre la multitud; *can you spot the mistake?,* ¿puedes descubrir el error?; *a golden eagle has been spotted near here,* han visto un águila real cerca de aquí; *she was spotted leaving his apartment,* la vieron salir de su apartamento; *he was spotted by the Arsenal manager,* fue descubierto por el entrenador del Arsenal. **13** (*mark with spots*) motear; (*stain*) manchar, salpicar. – **14** *i* GB METEOR (*rain, spit*) chispear, lloviznar. – **15** *adj* COMM (*price, cash*) contante, al contado.
● **on the spot,** (*at once, then and there*) en ese mismo momento, en el acto, allí mismo; (*at the place of the action*) en el lugar del los hechos, en el lugar del crimen; (*without moving away*) en el lugar: *he was killed on the spot,* murió en el acto; *the police were on the spot within minutes,* la policía llegó al lugar a los pocos minutos. ‖ **to see spots before one's eyes,** ver manchas. ‖ **to knock spots off sb.,** (*defeat*) vencer fácilmente a algn.; (*surpass*) dejar atrás a algn. ‖ **to put sb. on the spot,** poner a algn. en un aprieto. ‖ **to spot the winner,** elegir el ganador.
■ **penalty spot,** punto de penalty. ‖ **spot cash,** dinero contante. ‖ **spot check,** control *m* hecho al azar. ‖ **spot fine,** multa que se paga en el acto. ‖ **spot welding,** soldadura por puntos.
▲ (*verbo*) *pt* & *pp* **spotted,** *ger* **spotting.**
spot-check ['spɒtʃek] *t* realizar un control al azar, realizar una inspección al azar.
spotless ['spɒtləs] **1** *adj* (*very clean*) limpísimo,-a, impecable. **2** *fig* (*reputation*) intachable.
spotlight ['spɒtlaɪt] **1** *n* (*lamp*) foco, proyector *m*, reflector *m*; (*beam*) luz *f* de foco. – **2** *t* iluminar, enfocar. **3** (*draw attention to*) poner de relieve, destacar.
● **to be in the spotlight,** ser objeto de la atención pública, ser el blanco de las miradas.
spot-on [spɒt'ɒn] *adj* perfecto,-a, exacto,-a.
spotted ['spɒtɪd] *adj* (*with dots*) con puntos; (*fabric*) de lunares; (*speckled*) moteado,-a; (*stained*) manchado,-a; (*animal*) con manchas.
■ **spotted dick,** GB CULIN *pudín de sebo con pasas cocido al vapor.*
spotter ['spɒtəʳ] *n* observador,-ra.
■ **spotter plane,** avión *m* de reconocimiento. ‖ **train spotter,** aficionado,-a a los trenes.
spotty ['spɒtɪ] *adj* (*person, face, complexion*) con granos, lleno,-a de granos.

▲ *comp* **spottier,** *superl* **spottiest.**
spot-weld ['spɒtweld] *t* soldar por puntos.
spouse [spauz] *n* cónyuge *mf.*
spout [spaut] **1** *n* (*of jug*) pico; (*of fountain*) surtidor *m*, caño; (*of roof-gutter*) canalón *m*; (*of teapot*) pitorro. **2** (*jet of water*) chorro. – **3** *t* (*liquid*) echar, arrojar. **4** *fam pej* (*poetry*) declamar; (*nonsense*) soltar. – **5** *i* (*liquid*) salir a chorros, chorrear. **6** (*of whale*) expulsar chorros de agua. **7** *fam pej* (*verse etc*) perorar, declamar.
● **to be up the spout,** (*plans etc*) fastidiarse, irse a pique; (*pregnant*) estar embarazada.
sprain [spreɪn] **1** *n* MED torcedura. – **2** *t* torcer: *she sprained her ankle,* se torció el tobillo.
sprang [spræŋ] *pt* → **spring.**
sprat [spræt] *n* (*fish*) espadín *m.*
sprawl [sprɔːl] **1** *i* (*person*) tumbarse, echarse, repantigarse, repanchingarse: *he sprawled out on the settee,* se repantigó en el sofá; *he sent him sprawling,* lo tiró al suelo, lo tumbó; *she went sprawling,* cayó de bruces. **2** (*city, suburbs, etc*) extenderse. – **3** *n* (*mass*) extensión *f.*
■ **urban sprawl,** crecimiento urbano descontrolado.
sprawled [sprɔːld] *adj* (*person*) tumbado,-a, echado,-a.
sprawling ['sprɔːlɪŋ] **1** *adj* (*mass*) extendido,-a; (*city, suburbs*) de crecimiento descontrolado. **2** (*handwriting*) garabateado,-a.
spray¹ [spreɪ] *n* (*of flowers*) ramita, ramillete *m.*
spray² [spreɪ] **1** *n* (*of water*) rociada; (*from sea*) espuma; (*from aerosol*) pulverización *f.* **2** (*aerosol*) spray *m*; (*atomizer*) atomizador *m*, vaporizador *m*; (*for plants*) pulverizador *m*: *fly spray,* insecticida en spray; *nasal spray,* pulverizador nasal. – **3** *t* (*water*) rociar; (*perfume*) atomizar; (*plants*) pulverizar; (*crops*) fumigar; (*paint*) pintar a pistola, pintar con pistola. – **4** *i* (*water*) rociar.
● **to spray with bullets,** acribillar a balazos.
■ **spray can,** aerosol *m.* ‖ **spray gun,** pistola pulverizadora. ‖ **spray paint,** pintura spray.
spread [spred] **1** *n* (*gen*) extensión *f*; (*of ideas, news*) difusión *f*, diseminación *f*, divulgación *f*; (*of disease, fire*) propagación *f*; (*of nuclear weapons*) proliferación *f*; (*of terrorism, crime*) aumento. **2** (*scope*) extensión *f*, envergadura; (*range*) gama, abanico. **3** (*of wings, sails*) envergadura. **4** CULIN (*paste*) pasta (para untar): *cheese spread,* queso para untar. **5** *fam* (*large meal*) comilona, banquetazo. **6** (*in press*) extensión *f*: *full-page spread,* plana entera; *two-page spread,* doble página. **7** US (*ranch*) finca. – **8** *t* (*lay out*) extender, tender; (*unfold*) desplegar; (*scatter*) esparcir: *spread out the map on the ground,* extiende el mapa en el suelo; *the bird spread out its wings,* el pájaro desplegó las alas; *she emptied her purse and spread the contents out on the table,* vació su monedero y esparció el contenido sobre la mesa. **9** (*butter etc*) untar, extender; (*paint, glue, etc*) extender, repartir. **10** (*news, ideas, etc*) difundir, divulgar; (*rumour*) hacer correr; (*disease, fire*) propagar; (*panic, terror*) sembrar. **11** (*wealth, work, cost*) distribuir, repartir: *you can spread the payments over three years,* se puede pagar en tres años. – **12** *i* (*stretch out*) extenderse; (*open out, unfold*) desplegarse; (*widen*) ensancharse: *wash that stain out or it will spread,* quita esa mancha, si no se extenderá; *the desert spreads for miles and miles,* el desierto se extiende a lo largo de muchas millas; *a smile spread across her face,* una sonrisa apareció en su rostro. **13** (*butter etc*) extenderse. **14** (*news, ideas, etc*) difundirse, diseminarse, divulgarse; (*rumour*) correr; (*disease, fire*) propagarse; (*panic, fear*) cundir: *the fire spread quickly,* el incendio se propagó con rapidez; *we must stop this virus from spreading,* hay que impedir que se

extienda este virus; *the news spread like wildfire,* la noticia corrió como la pólvora. **15** (*in time*) extenderse.
▲ *pt & pp* **spread.**
spread-eagled [spred'iːɡəld] *adj* con los brazos y piernas abiertos, despatarrado,-a.
spree [spriː] *n* juerga, jarana, parranda.
● **to go on a spree,** ir de juerga. ‖ **to go on a shopping/spending spree,** hacer muchas compras.
sprig [sprɪɡ] *n* ramita, ramito.
sprightly ['spraɪtlɪ] *adj* (*lively*) animado,-a, vivaz; (*energetic*) enérgico,-a; (*nimble*) ágil.
▲ *comp* **sprightlier,** *superl* **sprightliest.**
spring [sprɪŋ] **1** *n* (*season*) primavera. *everything comes to life in spring,* todo renace en primavera. **2** (*of water*) manantial *m,* fuente *f; hot springs,* aguas termales. **3** (*of mattress, seat*) muelle *m;* (*of watch, lock, etc*) resorte *m;* (*of car*) ballesta. **4** (*elasticity*) elasticidad *f;* (*active, healthy quality*) energía, brío. **5** (*leap, jump*) salto, brinco. **– 6** *i* (*jump*) saltar: *she sprang out of bed,* saltó de la cama; *the cat was ready to spring,* el gato estaba listo para atacar; *he sprang to his feet,* se levantó de un salto; *the soldier sprang to attention,* el soldado se puso firme; *they sprang into action,* entraron en acción; *we sprang to their aid,* corrimos en su ayuda. **7** (*appear*) aparecer (de repente): *where did you spring from?,* ¿de dónde has salido?; *tears sprang to her eyes,* se le llenaron los ojos de lágrimas. **– 8** *t* (*operate mechanism*) accionar. **9** *fig* (*news, surprise*) espetar (**on,** a), soltar: *he sprang the news on me,* me espetó la noticia; *we decided to spring a surprise on him,* decidimos darle una sorpresa; *I hate to spring this on you at such short notice,* siento mucho soltarte esto con tan poca antelación. **10** *fam* (*help escape, set free*) soltar.
◆ **to spring from** *t insep* (*result from, originate from*) surgir de, provenir de. ‖ **to spring up** *i* (*gen*) aparecer, surgir; (*friendship*) nacer; (*wind*) levantarse; (*plants*) brotar; (*buildings, towns, etc*) elevarse, levantarse: *a couple of problems have sprung up,* han surgido un par de problemas; *Chinese restaurants are springing up everywhere,* aparecen restaurantes chinos por todas partes.
● **to spring a leak,** (empezar a) hacer agua. ‖ **to spring forth,** brotar, surgir. ‖ **to spring open,** abrirse de (un) golpe. ‖ **to spring (in)to life,** (*engine*) ponerse en marcha; (*person, animal*) animarse. ‖ **to spring to mind,** ocurrirse: *nothing springs to mind,* no se me ocurre nada.
■ **spring fever,** fiebre *f* de primavera. ‖ **spring chicken,** (*young chicken*) pollo tomatero; (*young person*) pollo. ‖ **spring onion,** cebolleta. ‖ **spring roll,** rollito de primavera. ‖ **spring tide,** marea viva.
▲ *pt* **sprang,** *pp* **sprung.**
springboard ['sprɪŋbɔːd] *n* trampolín *m.*
spring-clean [sprɪŋ'kliːn] *t* hacer una limpieza general de, limpiar a fondo.
spring-cleaning [sprɪŋ'kliːnɪŋ] *n* limpieza general, limpieza a fondo.
spring-like ['sprɪŋlaɪk] *adj* primaveral.
springtime ['sprɪŋtaɪm] *n* primavera.
springy ['sprɪŋɪ] *adj* (*mattress*) elástico,-a; (*step*) ligero,-a, ágil.
▲ *comp* **springier,** *superl* **springiest.**
sprinkle ['sprɪŋkəl] **1** *t* (*with water*) rociar (**with,** de/con), salpicar (**with,** de/con). **2** (*with flour, sugar, etc*) espolvorear (**with,** de/con). **3** *fig* salpicar (**with,** de/con).
sprinkler ['sprɪŋkələ'] **1** *n* (*on hose*) aspersor *m.* **2** (*for fires*) extintor *m.* **3** (*for sugar, flour, etc*) espolvoreador *m.*
sprinkling ['sprɪŋkəlɪŋ] *n* (*small amount*) poco: *there was a sprinkling of rain,* cayeron unas gotas; *a sprinkling of cottages,* algunas casitas.

sprint [sprɪnt] **1** *n* SP sprint *m,* esprint *m.* **2** (*dash*) carrera corta: *we made a sprint for the train,* corrimos para coger el tren. **– 3** *i* SP esprintar, sprintar: *he sprinted for the line,* esprintó hasta la meta. **4** (*dash*) correr a toda velocidad.
■ **sprint finish,** esprint *m* final.
sprinter ['sprɪntə'] *n* esprinter *mf,* sprinter *mf.*
sprocket ['sprɒkɪt] *n* TECH diente *m* de engranaje.
■ **sprocket wheel,** rueda dentada.
sprog [sprɒɡ] *n* GB *fam* (*child*) niño,-a, chaval,-la.
sprout [spraʊt] **1** *n* BOT (*shoot*) brote *m,* retoño. **– 2** *i* (*bud, leaf*) brotar, salir; (*branch*) echar brotes; (*plant*) echar retoños, retoñar. **3** *fig* surgir, aparecer, crecer rápidamente. **– 4** *t* (*leaves, shoots*) echar; (*beard etc*) salir.
■ **(Brussels) sprouts,** coles *fpl* de Bruselas.
spruce[1] [spruːs] *adj* (*neat*) pulcro,-a, acicalado,-a; (*smart*) apuesto,-a.
◆ **to spruce up** *t sep* acicalar, arreglar.
spruce[2] [spruːs] *n* BOT picea.
▲ *pl* **spruces** o **spruce.**
sprung [sprʌŋ] **1** *pp* → **spring. – 2** *adj* (*mattress*) de muelles.
spry [spraɪ] *adj* (*active*) activo,-a; (*lively*) vivaz, lleno,-a de vida; (*energetic*) enérgico,-a, dinámico,-a.
▲ *comp* **sprier,** *superl* **spriest.**
spud [spʌd] *n fam* patata.
spun [spʌn] **1** *pt & pp* → **spin. – 2** *adj* hilado,-a: *spun glass,* lana de vidrio; *spun silk,* seda hilada; *spun silver / spun gold,* hilo de plata / hilo de oro; *spun sugar,* caramelo hilado.
spunk [spʌŋk] **1** *n fam* (*courage, spirit*) valor *m,* agallas *fpl.* **2** GB *sl* (*semen*) leche *f.*
spunky ['spʌŋkɪ] *adj fam* (*plucky*) valiente.
▲ *comp* **spunkier,** *superl* **spunkiest.**
spur [spɜː'] **1** *n* (*horserider's*) espuela. **2** ZOOL (*of cock*) espolón *m.* **3** *fig* (*stimulus, incentive*) aguijón *m,* espuela, acicate *m.* **4** GEOG espolón *m,* estribación *f.* **5** (*railway track, road*) ramal *m.* **– 6** *t* (*horse*) espolear, picar con las espuelas. **7** *fig* (*stimulate*) estimular, incitar, aguijonear, alentar: *we spurred them on to victory,* los incitamos a la victoria.
● **on the spur of the moment,** sin pensarlo.
▲ (*verbo*) *pt & pp* **spurred,** *ger* **spurring.**
spurious ['spjʊərɪəs] *adj* falso,-a, espurio,-a.
spurn [spɜːn] *t fml* (*disdain*) desdeñar, despreciar; (*reject*) rechazar.
spurt [spɜːt] **1** *n* (*of liquid*) chorro. **2** *fig* (*of speed, effort, activity etc*) racha, ataque *m,* esfuerzo: *he put on a sudden spurt,* aceleró de repente; *final spurt,* esfuerzo final. **– 3** *i* (*liquid*) chorrear, salir a chorro. **4** *fig* (*make an effort*) hacer un último esfuerzo, esforzarse; (*accelerate*) acelerar: *the runner spurted for the line,* el corredor aceleró hasta la meta.
sputter ['spʌtə'] **1** *i* (*fire, fat, candle*) chisporrotear. **2** (*engine*) petardear, renquear.
sputum ['spjuːtəm] *n* MED esputo.
▲ *pl* **sputa.**
spy [spaɪ] **1** *n* (*gen*) espía *mf.* **– 2** *i* espiar (**on,** a): *he was spying for the enemy,* espiaba para el enemigo; *someone had been spying on them,* alguien los había estado espiando. **– 3** *t lit* divisar, descubrir, ver.
◆ **to spy out** *t insep* (*activities*) investigar; (*person*) espiar.
● **I spy with my little eye ...,** veo, veo ... ‖ **to play I spy,** jugar al veo-veo. ‖ **to spy out the land,** reconocer la tierra, explorar la tierra.
■ **industrial spy,** espía *mf* industrial. ‖ **police spy,**

confidente *mf*, soplón,-ona. ‖ **spy ring,** red *f* de espionaje. ‖ **spy story,** historia de espías.
▲ *(sustantivo) pl* **spies;** *(verbo) pt & pp* **spied,** *ger* **spying.**
spyglass [ˈspaɪɡlɑːs] *n* catalejo.
spyhole [ˈspaɪhəʊl] *n* mirilla.
spying [ˈspaɪɪŋ] *n* espionaje *m*.
sq [skweəʳ] *abbr* (*square*) cuadrado,-a.
Sq [skweəʳ] *abbr* (*Square*) Plaza; *(abbreviation)* Pza., Plza.
Sqn Ldr [ˈskwɒdrənˈliːdəʳ] *abbr* (*Squadron Leader*) Comandante de escuadrilla; *(abbreviation)* Cte.
squabble [ˈskwɒbəl] **1** *n* disputa, riña, pelea. – **2** *i* disputar, reñir, pelearse (**over,** por) (**about,** sobre).
squabbling [ˈskwɒbəlɪŋ] *n* riñas *fpl*, disputas *fpl*, peleas *fpl*.
squad [skwɒd] **1** *n* MIL pelotón *m*. **2** *(of police)* brigada. **3** SP *(team)* equipo; *(national)* selección *f*.
■ **drugs squad,** brigada de estupefacientes. ‖ **squad car,** coche *m* patrulla.
squadron [ˈskwɒdrən] *n* *(of soldiers)* escuadrón *m*; *(of planes)* escuadrilla; *(of ships)* escuadra.
■ **squadron leader,** comandante *m* (de escuadrilla).
squalid [ˈskwɒlɪd] **1** *adj* *(dirty, unpleasant)* sucio,-a, mugriento,-a, asqueroso,-a; *(poor)* miserable. **2** *(sordid)* sórdido,-a.
squall[1] [skwɔːl] **1** *n* *(wind)* ráfaga; *(storm)* borrasca, chubasco, tormenta. **2** *fig (noisy argument)* bronca.
squall[2] [skwɔːl] **1** *n* *(cry, scream, yell)* chillido, berrido. – **2** *i* chillar, berrear.
squalor [ˈskwɒləʳ] **1** *n* *(dirtiness)* suciedad *f*, mugre *f*. **2** *(poverty)* miseria.
squander [ˈskwɒndəʳ] *t* *(money)* derrochar, malgastar, despilfarrar, tirar; *(fortune)* dilapidar; *(opportunity, time)* desperdiciar, desaprovechar.
square [skweəʳ] **1** *n* *(shape)* cuadrado; *(on fabric)* cuadro; *(on chessboard, graph paper, crossword)* casilla. **2** *(in town)* plaza; *(in barracks)* patio; *(block of houses)* manzana. **3** MATH cuadrado. **4** *(tool)* escuadra. **5** *fam (old-fashioned person)* carroza *mf*; *(conservative)* carca *mf*. – **6** *adj* *(in shape)* cuadrado,-a; *(forming right angle)* en ángulo recto, a escuadra: *a square table,* una mesa cuadrada; *a square jaw,* una mandíbula cuadrada; *the flat is 100 metres square,* el piso mide 100 metros cuadrados. **7** MATH cuadrado,-a. **8** *fam (fair)* justo,-a, equitativo,-a; *(honest)* honesto,-a, franco,-a: *a square deal,* un trato justo; *I'll be square with you,* seré franco contigo. **9** *(equal in points)* igual, empatado,-a; *(not owing money)* en paz. **10** *(tidy)* ordenado,-a, en orden. **11** *(old-fashioned)* carroza; *(conservative)* carca. – **12** *adv* directamente: *it landed square in the middle of the lake,* cayó justo en medio del lago; *she hit him square on the nose,* le dio de lleno en la nariz. – **13** *t (make square)* cuadrar (**with,** con): *he squared his shoulders,* se puso derecho, sacó el pecho. **14** MATH cuadrar, elevar al cuadrado: *4 squared is 16,* el cuadrado de 4 es 16. **15** *(settle - debts, accounts)* saldar, pagar; *(- matters)* arreglar: *I want to square my account,* quiero pagar mi cuenta; *I'll square it with the teacher,* lo arreglaré con el profesor. **16** *(equalize)* empatar: *after a hard struggle they managed to square the match,* después de luchar mucho consiguieron empatar. **17** *(agree, reconcile)* conciliar: *you must square your alibi with the facts,* tienes que hacer cuadrar tu coartada con los hechos; *I can't square it with my conscience,* mi conciencia no me lo permite. **18** *fam (bribe)* sobornar. – **19** *i (agree)* cuadrar (**with,** con), concordar (**with,** con): *his story doesn't square with the facts,* su versión no cuadra con los hechos.

◆ **to square off** *t sep (wood, corner)* cuadrar; *(paper)* cuadricular. ‖ **to square up 1** *i fam (settle debts)* ajustar cuantas, saldar cuentas. **2** *(fighters)* ponerse en guardia. ‖ **to square up to** *t insep* hacer frente a.
● **a square peg in a round hole,** gallina en corral ajeno. ‖ **to be all square with sb.,** estar en paz con algn. ‖ **to get a square deal,** recibir un trato justo. ‖ **to get square with sb.,** ajustar cuentas con algn. ‖ **to go back to square one,** volver al punto de partida, partir de cero. ‖ **to square the circle,** cuadrar el círculo.
■ **square brackets,** corchetes *mpl*. ‖ **square dance,** baile *m* de figuras. ‖ **square meal,** comida decente, buena comida. ‖ **square metre,** metro cuadrado. ‖ **square root,** raíz *f* cuadrada.
squared [ˈskweəd] *adj (paper)* cuadriculado,-a.
squarely [ˈskweəlɪ] *adv* directamente, de lleno: *I looked him squarely in the face,* lo miré directamente a la cara.
squash[1] [skwɒʃ] **1** *n (in crowd)* apiñamiento, agolpamiento, apretujón *m*: *it's a bit of a squash,* estamos un poco apretados. **2** *(drink)* bebida de frutas, concentrado de frutas. **3** SP squash *m*. – **4** *t (crush, flatten)* aplastar, chafar, esparruchar: *try not to squash the strawberries,* procura no chafar las fresas. **5** *(squeeze)* meter apretando, apretar, apiñar: *can you squash a couple more things in?,* ¿puedes meter un par de cosas más? **6** *fig (crush - person)* apabullar, aplastar, desairar; *(- rumour, dissent, rebellion)* hacer callar, acallar, aplastar; *(- argument, plan, proposal)* echar por tierra, dar al traste con: *she felt squashed by his remark,* su comentario la dejó apabullada; *he squashed all rumours of resignation,* acalló todos los rumores de dimisión. – **7** *i (crush, flatten)* aplastarse, chafarse, espachurrarse. **8** *(squeeze)* meterse apretando, apretujarse: *we all squashed into the car,* nos apretujamos todos en el coche.
◆ **to squash up** *i* apretarse, apretujarse.
■ **squash rackets,** *(game)* squash *m*.
squash[2] [skwɒʃ] *n* BOT calabaza.
squashy [ˈskwɒʃɪ] *adj* blando,-a, fofo,-a, esponjoso,-a.
▲ *comp* **squashier,** *superl* **squashiest.**
squat [skwɒt] **1** *adj (person)* rechoncho,-a y bajo,-a, achaparrado,-a; *(building)* achaparrado,-a. – **2** *n (crouching position)* en cuclillas. **3** *(house occupied by squatters)* vivienda ocupada, esquat *m*, edificio ocupado ilegalmente; *(action of squatting)* ocupación *f* ilegal. – **4** *i (crouch)* agacharse, ponerse en cuclillas: *squat down behind the sofa,* agáchate detrás del sofá. **5** *(in building)* ocupar ilegalmente.
▲ *(adjetivo) comp* **squatter,** *superl* **squattest;** *(verbo) pt & pp* **squatted,** *ger* **squatting.**
squatter [ˈskwɒtəʳ] *n* ocupante *mf* ilegal, okupa *mf*.
squaw [skwɔː] *n* india norteamericana.
squawk [skwɔːk] **1** *n (of bird)* graznido, chillido. **2** *(complaint)* queja. – **3** *i (bird)* graznar, chillar. **4** *(complain loudly)* gruñir, rezongar.
squeak [skwiːk] **1** *n (of mouse)* chillido; *(of wheel, hinge, etc)* chirrido, rechinamiento; *(of shoes)* crujido. – **2** *i (mouse)* chillar; *(wheel, hinge, etc)* chirriar, rechinar; *(shoes)* chirriar.
● **a narrow squeak,** por los pelos. ‖ **not a squeak,** ni pío.
squeaky [ˈskwiːkɪ] *adj (gen)* chirriante; *(voice)* chillón,-ona; *(shoes)* que crujen.
● **squeaky clean,** super limpio,-a, reluciente.
▲ *comp* **squeakier,** *superl* **squeakiest.**
squeal [skwiːl] **1** *n (of animal, person)* chillido, grito; *(of tyres, brakes)* chirrido: *squeals of delight,* chillidos de regocijo; *squeals of protest,* gritos de protesta. – **2** *i (an-*

imal, person) chillar; (*tyres, brakes*) chirriar. **3** *fam* (*inform on*) cantar, chivarse: *the boy squealed on his friends,* el chico delató a sus amigos. – **4** *t* (*say*) decir chillando, chillar, gritar.

squeamish ['skwiːmɪʃ] **1** *adj* (*easily made to feel sick*) remilgado,-a, delicado,-a; (*easily upset*) muy sensible, impresionable: *don't go to see this film if you're sqeamish,* no vayas a ver esta película si eres impresionable; *the sight of blood makes me squeamish,* tengo horror a la sangre. **2** (*easily shocked morally*) escrupuloso,-a.

squeeze [skwiːz] **1** *n* (*pressure - gen*) estrujón *m*, presión *f*; (*- of hand*) apretón *m*; (*hug*) abrazo: *I gave her hand a squeeze,* le di un apretón de manos. **2** (*small amount*) unas gotas: *a squeeze of lemon,* unas gotas de limón. **3** (*of crowd*) apretujón *m*, apiñamiento: *it was a tight squeeze in the tube today,* hoy íbamos como sardinas en lata en el metro. **4** COMM FIN (*difficult situation*) restricciones *fpl*: *credit squeeze,* restricciones de crédito. – **5** *t* (*gen*) apretar; (*lemon, orange*) exprimir; (*sponge*) estrujar; (*cloth*) retorcer, escurrir: *he squeezed my hand,* me apretó la mano. **6** (*fit in*) meter: *can you squeeze one more person in?,* ¿puede meter a una persona más?; *it's a job to squeeze all these clothes into the suitcase,* cuesta meter toda esta ropa en la maleta; *we can squeeze you in at 5.00pm,* podemos hacerle un hueco a las 5.00. **7** (*force out*) extraer, sacar: *squeeze all the water out of the cloth,* escurre bien el trapo; *they're trying to squeeze money out of me,* tratan de sacarme dinero. – **8** *i* (*force into, through, etc*) meterse: *she managed to squeeze in,* consiguió meterse; *can I squeeze past?,* ¿puedo pasar?
◆ **to squeeze up** *i* apretujarse.
● **to put the squeeze on sb.,** apretar a algn. ‖ **to squeeze out of business,** obligar a abandonar un negocio.

squeezer ['skwiːzəʳ] *n* exprimidor *m*.

squelch [skweltʃ] **1** *i* (*move*) chapotear: *he squelched up the path,* subió el camino chapoteando. – **2** *n* chapoteo.

squib [skwɪb] *n* petardo.

squid [skwɪd] *n* (*gen*) calamar *m*; (*small*) chipirón *m*.
■ **fried squid,** CULIN calamares *mpl* a la romana.
▲ *pl* squid *o* squids.

squiffy ['skwɪfɪ] *adj fam* achispado,-a, piripi.
▲ *comp* squiffier, *superl* squiffiest.

squiggle ['skwɪgəl] *n* (*line*) garabato.

squiggly ['skwɪglɪ] *adj* (*writing*) garabateado,-a; (*line*) serpenteante.

squint [skwɪnt] **1** *n* MED bizquera, estrabismo: *he's got a squint,* es bizco. **2** *fam* (*quick look*) vistazo, ojeada, miradita: *have a squint at this,* echa un vistazo a esto. – **3** *i* MED bizquear, ser bizco,-a. **4** (*in sunlight*) entrecerrar los ojos.

squire [skwaɪəʳ] **1** *n dated* (*landowner*) terrateniente *m*, hacendado, señor *m*. **2** HIST (*knight's armour-carrier*) escudero. **3** GB *fam* jefe *m*.

squirm [skwɜːm] **1** *i* (*twist*) retorcerse. **2** (*feel embarrassment*) sentirse incómodo,-a: *I squirmed with embarrassment,* me dio mucha vergüenza.

squirrel ['skwɪrəl] *n* ardilla.

squirt [skwɜːt] **1** *n* (*of liquid*) chorro, chorrito. **2** *fam pej* (*person*) mequetrefe *mf*. – **3** *t* echar un chorro de: *squirt a little oil into the lock,* echa un chorrito de aceite en la cerradura; *my nephew loves squirting water at me,* a mi sobrino le encanta rociarme con agua. – **4** *i* salir a chorros: *water started squirting out everywhere,* el agua empezó a salir a chorros por todas partes.

Sr[1] ['siːnɪəʳ] *abbr* (*Senior*) → **Snr**.

Sr[2] ['sɪstəʳ] *abbr* (*Sister*) Hermana; (*abbreviation*) Hna.

Sri Lanka [sriːˈlæŋkə] *n* Sri Lanka.

SS ['esˈes] *abbr* (*steamship*) buque de vapor, vapor.

SS. [seɪnts] *abbr* (*Saints*) Santos, Santas; (*abbreviation*) Stos., Stas.

st [stəʊn] *abbr* GB (*stone*) unidad de peso que equivale a 6,350 *kilogramos*.

St[1] [seɪnt] *abbr* (*Saint*) San, Santo, Santa; (*abbreviation*) S., Sto. Sta.

St[2] [striːt] *abbr* (*Street*) calle; (*abbreviation*) c/.

stab [stæb] **1** *n* (*with knife*) puñalada, navajazo. **2** (*of pain*) punzada. – **3** *t* (*with knife*) apuñalar, acuchillar: *he's been stabbed in the stomach,* lo han apuñalado en el estómago; *she was stabbed to death,* la mataron a puñaladas.
◆ **to stab** *at i* (*jab - with finger*) golpear, dar con el dedo; (*- with pointed object*) pinchar, clavar.
● **a stab in the back,** una puñalada trapera. ‖ **to have a stab at sth.,** intentar hacer algo. ‖ **to stab sb. in the back,** apuñalar a algn. por la espalda.
■ **stab wound,** puñalada.
▲ (*verbo*) *pt* & *pp* stabbed, *ger* stabbing.

stabbing ['stæbɪŋ] **1** *adj* (*pain*) punzante. – **2** *n* apuñalamiento.

stability [stəˈbɪlɪti] *n* estabilidad *f*.

stabilize ['steɪbəlaɪz] **1** *t* estabilizar. – **2** *i* estabilizarse.

stabilizer ['steɪbəlaɪzəʳ] **1** *n* (*on plane, ship, bicycle*) estabilizador *m*. **2** (*in food*) estabilizante *m*.

stable[1] ['steɪbəl] **1** *adj* (*unchanging*) estable, constante; (*firm*) sólido,-a, estable; (*secure*) fijo,-a, estable, seguro,-a; (*person - sane*) equilibrado,-a: *she needs a stable relationship,* necesita una relación estable; *the patient is in a stable condition,* el paciente está en estado estacionario. **2** CHEM estable.

stable[2] ['steɪbəl] **1** *n* (*for horses*) cuadra, caballeriza; (*for other animals*) establo. **2** (*training establishment for horses*) cuadra; (*school, theatre, club, etc*) escuela. – **3** *t* (*put in stable*) encerrar en una cuadra; (*keep in stable*) guardar en una cuadra.
● **to close/lock/shut the stable door after the horse has bolted,** tomar precauciones cuando ya no hay remedio.
■ **stable boy / stable girl,** mozo de cuadra / moza de cuadra.

stack [stæk] **1** *n* (*pile, heap*) montón *m*, pila: *a stack of newspapers,* un montón de periódicos; *a stack of rifles,* un pabellón (de fusiles). **2** (*of grass, grain, etc*) almiar *m*. **3** (*chimney*) cañón de chimenea. – **4** *t* (*pile up*) apilar, amontonar; (*fill*) llenar: *stack the dishes on the draining board,* apila los platos en el escurridor; *we have to stack the chairs,* tenemos que amontonar las sillas. **5** *fam* (*in cards*) arreglar: *you stacked the cards!,* ¡has arreglado la baraja! – **6 stacks,** *npl fam* montón *m*, montones *mpl*. **7** (*in library*) estanterías *fpl*.
◆ **to stack up** *i* US (*compare, match*) comparar, equiparar (**against,** con).
● **to be stacked with sth.,** estar lleno,-a de algo. ‖ **to have the cards/odds stacked against sb.,** serle las circunstancias desfavorables a algn., estar todo en contra de algn.
■ **stack system,** equipo de música.

stadium ['steɪdɪəm] *n* estadio.
▲ *pl* stadiums *o* stadia.

staff [stɑːf] **1** *n* (*personnel - gen*) personal *m*, empleados *mpl*, plantilla; (*- teachers*) profesorado, personal docente: *she's a member of staff,* es una empleada; *we've got*

a staff of twenty, tenemos una plantilla de veinte personas; *Mary is going to join the staff,* Mary se va a incorporar a la plantilla; *some staff have complained about the noise,* algunos (de los) empleados se han quejado del ruido. **2** MIL estado mayor. **3** *(stick)* bastón *m*; *(of shepherd)* cayado; *(of bishop)* báculo; *(flagpole)* asta. **4** MUS pentagrama *m*. – **5** *t* proveer de personal: *the office is well staffed,* en la oficina trabaja mucha gente; *the centre is staffed by volunteers,* en el centro trabajan voluntarios.
● **the staff of life,** el pan de cada día.
■ **general staff,** MIL estado mayor. ‖ **staff entrance,** entrada del personal. ‖ **staff meeting,** EDUC reunión *f* de profesores, claustro. ‖ **staff nurse,** enfermero,-a cualificado,-a. ‖ **staff of office,** bastón *m* de mando.

staffroom ['stɑːfruːm] *n* EDUC sala de profesores.

stag [stæg] *n* ZOOL ciervo, venado.
■ **stag beetle,** ciervo volante. ‖ **stag party / stag night,** despedida de soltero.

stage [steɪdʒ] **1** *n* *(point, period)* etapa, fase *f*: *at this stage of the negotiations,* a estas alturas de las negociaciones; *corrections can be done at a later stage,* se pueden hacer las correcciones más adelante; *the project is still in its early stages,* el proyecto está aún en pañales; *it's just a stage she's going through,* ya superará esa fase. **2** *(of journey, race)* etapa; *(day's journey)* jornada. **3** *(in theatre)* escenario, escena; *(raised platform)* plataforma, tablado, estrado: *what time do you go on stage?,* ¿a qué hora sales al escenario? **4** *fig (scene of action)* escena. **5** *(of rocket)* fase *f*. **6** *fam (stagecoach)* diligencia. – **7** *t* THEAT poner en escena, montar, representar. **8** *(hold, carry out)* llevar a cabo, efectuar; *(arrange)* organizar, montar. – **the stage,** *n (the theatre)* el teatro, las tablas *fpl*: *she's always wanted to go on the stage,* siempre ha querido ser actriz; *his novel has been adapted for the stage,* se ha adaptado su novela para el teatro.
● **by stages / in stages,** por etapas. ‖ **to set the stage for sth.,** crear el marco para algo.
■ **stage direction,** acotación *f*. ‖ **stage door,** entrada de artistas. ‖ **stage fright,** miedo a salir a escena, miedo escénico. ‖ **stage manager,** director,-ra de escena. ‖ **stage name,** nombre *m* artístico. ‖ **stage whisper,** aparte *m*.

stagecoach ['steɪdʒkəʊtʃ] *n* diligencia.
stagehand ['steɪdʒhænd] *n* tramoyista *mf*.
stage-manage [steɪdʒ'mænɪdʒ] *t* orquestar, arreglar, montar.
stage-struck ['steɪdʒstrʌk] *adj* apasionado,-a por el teatro.
stagey ['steɪdʒɪ] *adj* → **stagy**.
stagger ['stægəʳ] **1** *i (walk unsteadily)* tambalearse: *he staggered out of the pub,* salió tambaleándose del pub; *she staggered out of bed and into the bathroom,* se levantó tambaleando y entró en el baño. – **2** *t (hours, work)* escalonar. **3** *(amaze)* asombrar, pasmar. – **4** *n (unsteady walk)* tambaleo.
staggered ['stægəd] **1** *adj (amazed)* asombrado,-a, pasmado,-a. **2** *(hours, holidays)* escalonado,-a.
■ **staggered start,** salida escalonada.
staggering ['stægərɪŋ] *adj (amazing)* asombroso,-a, pasmoso,-a.
staging ['steɪdʒɪŋ] **1** *n* THEAT montaje *m*, puesta en escena. **2** *(scaffolding)* andamiaje *m*.
■ **staging post,** escala.
stagnant ['stægnənt] **1** *adj (of water)* estancado,-a. **2** *fig* paralizado,-a, inactivo,-a, estancado,-a: *stagnant customs,* costumbres anquilosadas.

stagnate [stæg'neɪt] *i (gen)* estancarse; *(person)* quedarse estancado,-a, anquilosarse.
stagnation [stæg'neɪʃən] *n (of water)* estancamiento; *(person)* anquilosamiento.
stagy ['steɪdʒɪ] *adj* teatral, efectista, exagerado,-a.
▲ *comp* **stagier**, *superl* **stagiest**.
staid [steɪd] *adj (person)* serio,-a, tradicional; *(manner, clothes)* sobrio,-a, formal.
stain [steɪn] **1** *n (gen)* mancha: *blood stain,* mancha de sangre. **2** *(dye)* tinte *m*, tintura. – **3** *t (gen)* manchar: *tea and coffee stain your teeth,* el té y el café manchan los dientes. **4** *(dye)* teñir. – **5** *i* mancharse.
■ **stain remover,** quitamanchas *m*.
stained [steɪnd] *adj* manchado,-a *(with,* de).
■ **stained glass,** vidrio de colores. ‖ **stained glass window,** vidriera de colores.
stainless ['steɪnləs] *adj (spotless)* sin mancha.
■ **stainless steel,** acero inoxidable.
stair [steəʳ] **1** *n (single step)* escalón *m*, peldaño. **2** *lit* escalera. – **3 stairs,** *npl* escalera *f sing*: *he was sitting at the bottom of the stairs,* estaba sentado al pie de la escalera; *I was going up/down the stairs,* subía/baja la escalera; *a flight of stairs,* un tramo de escalera.
● **above stairs,** la parte de la casa donde vivían los señores. ‖ **below stairs,** la parte de la casa donde trabajaba el servicio.
staircase ['steəkeɪs] *n* escalera.
stairway ['steəweɪ] *n* escalera.
stairwell ['steəwel] *n* caja de la escalera, hueco de la escalera.
stake¹ [steɪk] **1** *n (stick)* estaca, palo; *(post)* poste *m*; *(for plant, tree)* rodrigón *m*; *(in surveying)* jalón *m*. – **2** *t (fasten, support - gen)* sujetar con estacas, apoyar con estacas **(up,** -); *(- plant, tree)* arrodrigar; *(in surveying)* jalonar.
◆ **to stake out 1** *t sep (mark, enclose)* cercar con estacas, marcar con estacas, delimitar con estacas. **2** *fam (watch secretly)* vigilar secretamente, vigilar a escondidas.
● **to be burnt at the stake,** morir en la hoguera. ‖ **to pull up stakes,** US marcharse, desarraigarse. ‖ **to stake a claim to sth.,** reivindicar algo, reclamar el derecho a algo.
stake² [steɪk] **1** *n (bet)* apuesta: *the stakes were high,* había mucho en juego. **2** *(investment, share)* interés *m*, participación *f*: *the minister has a stake in that company,* el ministro tiene intereses en esa empresa. – **3** *t (bet)* apostar, jugar(se); *(risk)* arriesgar, jugarse: *I wouldn't stake my life on it,* no me jugaría la vida por eso; *he stakes his reputation on it,* se juega la reputación en ello. **4** *(give financial support to)* invertir en. – **5 stakes,** *npl (prize money)* premio *m sing*: *they were playing for very high stakes,* jugaban fuerte. **6** *(horse race)* carrera *f sing* de caballos.
● **to be at stake,** *(at risk)* estar en juego; *(in danger)* estar en peligro.
■ **popularity stakes,** índice *m* de popularidad.
stalactite ['stæləktaɪt] *n* estalactita.
stalagmite ['stæləgmaɪt] *n* estalagmita.
stale [steɪl] **1** *adj (food - gen)* no fresco,-a, pasado,-a; *(- bread, cake)* duro,-a; *(tobacco)* rancio,-a; *(wine, beer)* picado,-a. **2** *(air)* viciado,-a; *(smell)* a cerrado. **3** *(news)* viejo,-a, pasado,-a; *(joke)* trillado,-a. **4** *(person)* quemado,-a, cansado,-a, harto,-a.
stalemate ['steɪlmeɪt] **1** *n (chess)* tablas *fpl*. **2** *fig* punto muerto, impasse *m*.
● **to end in stalemate,** *(chess)* quedar en tablas; *(impasse)* acabar en un punto muerto.

staleness [ˈsteɪlnəs] **1** *n* (*of food*) ranciedad *f*; (*of bread*) dureza. **2** (*of air*) lo viciado. **3** (*of news, joke*) lo añejo, lo viejo. **4** (*of person*) anquilosamiento.

Stalinist [ˈstɑːlɪnɪst] **1** *adj* estalinista. − **2** *n* (*person*) estalinista *mf*.

stalk¹ [stɔːk] **1** *t* (*hunt - animals*) acechar; (*- hunter*) cazar al acecho; (*- detective, killer, etc*) acechar, cazar, perseguir; (*menace - danger, famine, disease, etc*) asolar: *an animal stalking its prey,* un animal que acecha su presa; *fear stalked the city,* el miedo asolaba la ciudad. − **2** *i* (*walk - proudly*) andar con paso majestuoso; (*- angrily*) andar indignado,-a: *she stalked out,* salió indignada.

stalk² [stɔːk] **1** *n* BOT (*of plant*) tallo; (*of fruit*) rabo, rabillo; (*of cabbage*) troncho. **2** ZOOL pedúnculo.

● **to have one's eyes on stalks,** salírsele a uno los ojos de las órbitas.

stall¹ [stɔːl] **1** *i fam* (*delay*) andar con rodeos, contestar con evasivas: *he's stalling for time,* nos está entreteniendo para ganar tiempo. − **2** *t fam* (*delay*) entretener; (*put off*) aplazar, dar largas a.

■ **stalling tactics,** maniobras *fpl* dilatorias.

stall² [stɔːl] **1** *n* (*in market*) puesto, tenderete *m*; (*at fair*) caseta, barraca. **2** (*for animal - stable*) establo; (*- stable compartment*) compartimiento (en un establo). **3** (*row of seats*) sillería. **4** (*small room, compartment*) compartimiento. − **5** *t* AUTO hacer calar: *learner drivers often stall their cars,* a los conductores novatos se les cala el coche a menudo. **6** (*put animal in stall*) encerrar en establo; (*keep in stall*) guardar en establo. − **7** *i* AUTO calarse, pararse. − **8** stalls, *npl* (*in theatre*) platea *f sing.*

■ **choir stalls,** sillería del coro. ‖ **finger stall,** dedil *m.* ‖ **shower stall,** ducha.

stallholder [ˈstɔːlhəʊldəʳ] *n* persona que tiene un puesto de mercado.

stallion [ˈstælɪən] *n* semental *m*, garañón *m*.

stalwart [ˈstɔːlwət] **1** *adj dated* (*strong*) fuerte, fornido,-a. **2** (*staunch, loyal*) leal, fiel. − **3** *n* partidario,-a incondicional.

stamen [ˈsteɪmən] *n* BOT estambre *m*.

stamina [ˈstæmɪnə] *n* (*endurance*) resistencia, aguante *m*.

stammer [ˈstæməʳ] **1** *n* tartamudeo. − **2** *i* tartamudear. − **3** *t* (*say with a stammer*) decir tartamudeando, farfullar.

● **to have a stammer,** tartamudear.

stammerer [ˈstæmərəʳ] *n* tartamudo,-a.

stammering [ˈstæmərɪŋ] *adj* tartamudeante.

stamp [stæmp] **1** *n* (*postage*) sello; (*fiscal*) timbre *m*; (*trading stamp*) cupón *m*, vale *m*. **2** (*tool - gen*) sello; (*- rubber*) sello de goma, tampón *m*; (*- metal*) cuño, troquel *m*. **3** (*seal, mark*) sello. **4** (*with foot - act*) patada, pisotada, pisotón *m*; (*- sound*) paso. **5** *fml* (*distinguishing mark*) impronta, huella, marca. **6** *fml* (*kind, sort*) clase *f*, índole *f.* − **7** *t* (*letter*) franquear: *a stamped addressed envelope,* un sobre franqueado. **8** (*passport, document*) sellar, marcar con sello; (*metal, coin*) cuñar, troquelar. **9** *fig* (*impress - event*) grabar, estampar; (*- personality, authority, influence*) imprimir, dejar: *the date is stamped on my memory,* tengo la fecha grabada en la memoria; *he stamped his personality on the game,* dejó su impronta en el juego. **10** (*characterize - positively*) caracterizar, marcar, demostrar; (*- negatively*) tildar: *this act stamps her as a heroine,* este acto nos demuestra que es una heroína. **11** (*with foot*) dar una patada en; (*in dancing*) zapatear. − **12** *i* (*with foot*) dar patadas, patear, patalear; (*in dancing*) zapatear. **13** (*walk noisily*) pisar fuerte.

◆ **to stamp on 1** *t insep* (*crush with foot*) pisar, pisotear.

2 (*suppress*) sofocar, aplastar. ‖ **to stamp out 1** *t sep* (*eliminate - racism, violence, etc*) acabar con, erradicar; (*- rebellion, epidemic, etc*) sofocar, aplastar. **2** (*extinguish, put out*) apagar (con los pies).

■ **stamp album,** álbum *m* de sellos. ‖ **stamp collecting,** filatelia. ‖ **stamp collector,** filatelista *mf*, coleccionista *mf* de sellos. ‖ **stamp duty,** impuesto del timbre. ‖ **stamp machine,** máquina expendedora de sellos.

stampede [stæmˈpiːd] **1** *n* estampida, desbandada, espantada: *there was a stampede for the exit,* todos se precipitaron hacia la salida. − **2** *i* (*cattle*) salir en estampida; (*people*) salir en desbandada. − **3** *t* hacer salir en estampida.

● **to stampede sb. into doing sth.,** empujar a algn. a hacer algo.

stamping ground [ˈstæmpɪŋɡraʊnd] *n fam* territorio.

stance [stæns] **1** *n* (*way of standing*) postura. **2** (*opinion, attitude*) postura (**on**, respecto a), posición *f* (**on**, respecto a), actitud *f* (**on**, respecto a).

stand [stænd] **1** *n* (*position*) lugar *m*, sitio *m*; (*attitude, opinion*) posición *f*, postura; (*defence, resistence*) resistencia: *she took up her stand by the window,* se colocó en su sitio al lado de la ventana; *we took a stand against the proposal,* adoptamos una postura contraria a la propuesta; *Custer's last stand,* la última batalla de Custer. **2** (*of lamp, sculpture, etc*) pie *m*, pedestal *m*, base *f.* **3** (*stall - market*) puesto, tenderete *m*; (*- at exhibition*) stand *m*; (*- at fair*) caseta, barraca. **4** (*for taxis*) parada. **5** SP (*in stadium*) tribuna. **6** US (*witness box*) estrado: *he took the stand,* subió al estrado. − **7** *i* (*person - be on one's feet*) estar de pie, estar; (*- get up*) ponerse de pie, levantarse; (*- remain on one's feet*) quedarse de pie; (*- take up position*) ponerse: *stand still,* ¡estáte quieto,-a!, ¡no te muevas!; *stand over there,* ponte allí; *she was standing in the queue,* estaba en la cola; *they were standing at the bar,* estaban en la barra; *he was too weak to stand,* estaba demasiado débil para tenerse en pie; *there were no seats and we had to stand,* no quedaban asientos y tuvimos que quedarnos de pie; *don't just stand there!,* ¡no te quedes allí parado! **8** (*measure - height*) medir; (*- value, level*) marcar, alcanzar: *he stands six feet,* mide dos metros; *the building stands over 40 metres high,* el edificio mide 40 metros de altura; *inflation stands at 6%,* la inflación alcanza el 6%; *the score stands at 2-0,* el marcador señala 2-0. **9** (*thing - be situated*) estar, encontrarse, haber: *a temple once stood here,* antes aquí había un templo; *in the corner stands a grand piano,* hay un piano de cola en el rincón; *the train stands at platform one,* el tren que está en el andén número uno; *the car has stood in the garage for years,* el coche lleva años en el garaje; *few buildings were left standing,* pocos edificios quedaban en pie. **10** (*remain valid*) seguir en pie, seguir vigente: *my offer still stands,* mi oferta sigue en pie; *what I said still stands,* lo que dije sigue siendo válido; *the court ruling stands,* el fallo es válido. **11** (*be in a certain condition*) estar: *that house has stood empty for ages,* hace mucho tiempo que esa casa está vacía; *the machines stand idle,* las máquinas están paradas; *I stand corrected,* tienes (toda) la razón; *he stands high in their opinion,* tienen muy buena opinión de él, le tienen mucho respeto; *I stand accused of murder,* se me acusa de asesinato. **12** (*be in particular situation*) estar: *how do things stand between you and your boss?,* ¿cómo están las cosas entre tu jefe y tú?; *as things stand,* tal (y) como están las cosas. **13** (*take attitude, policy*) adoptar una postura: *where do you stand on abortion?,* ¿cuál es tu posición sobre el aborto?; *we want to know how you stand on this issue,* queremos saber cuál es tu postura sobre este tema. **14** *(be likely to)* poder: *we stand to win a lot of money,* podríamos ganar mucho dinero; *he stands to lose a fortune,* podría llegar a perder una fortuna. **15** *(liquid)* estancar; *(mixture)* reposar: *the water lay standing in pools,* había charcos de agua; *leave the mixture to stand,* dejar reposar la mezcla. **16** POL *(run)* presentarse: *she's going to stand for election,* va a presentarse como candidata. − **17** *t (place)* poner, colocar: *she stood the photo on the mantelpiece,* colocó la foto en la repisa; *I stood the boy on a box so he could see the procession,* puso el niño encima de un caja para que viera el desfile; *stand it against the wall,* ponlo contra la pared. **18** *fam (bear, tolerate)* aguantar, soportar; *(endure, withstand)* soportar, resistir: *I can't stand the sight of him,* no puedo ni verlo; *she couldn't stand the noise any longer,* no podía aguantar más el ruido; *my nerves won't take much more,* mis nervios no aguantarán mucho más; *he can't stand opera,* no soporta la ópera; *I can't stand being made to wait,* no soporto que me hagan esperar; *will it stand the test of time?,* ¿resistirá el paso del tiempo?; *it won't stand close examination,* no resistirá un examen minucioso. **19** *fam (invite)* invitar: *I'll stand you a drink,* te invitaré a una copa.

◆ **to stand aside** *i (move to one side)* apartarse, quitarse de en medio; *(take no part)* no tomar parte, mantenerse al margen. ‖ **to stand back** *i (move back)* apartarse, echarse hacia atrás, alejarse; *(be objective)* distanciarse **(from,** de). ‖ **to stand by 1** *i (do nothing)* cruzarse de brazos, quedarse sin hacer nada. **2** *(be ready for action - gen)* estar preparado,-a, estar listo,-a; *(- troops)* estar en estado de alerta. − **3** *t insep (not desert)* no abandonar, respaldar, apoyar, defender. **4** *(keep to - decision)* atenerse a; *(- promise)* cumplir: *I stand by what I said before,* mantengo lo que he dicho antes. ‖ **to stand down 1** *i (withdraw)* retirarse; *(resign)* dimitir. **2** JUR *(leave witness box)* retirarse, abandonar el estrado. ‖ **to stand for 1** *t insep (mean)* significar, querer decir; *(represent)* representar: *what does I.B.A. stand for?,* ¿qué significan las siglas I.B.A.?; *we hate everything he stands for,* odiamos todo lo que representa. **2** *(support, be in favour of)* defender, apoyar, ser partidario,-a de: *our party stands for freedom and democracy,* nuestro partido defiende la libertad y la democracia. **3** *(tolerate)* tolerar, permitir, consentir: *I won't stand for that kind of behaviour,* no toleraré ese tipo de comportamiento. ‖ **to stand in for** *t insep (substitute, deputize)* sustituir, suplir: *could you stand in for me this afternoon?,* ¿me podrías sustituir esta tarde? ‖ **to stand out 1** *i (building, etc)* destacar, sobresalir. **2** *(person, qualities)* destacarse, sobresalir. **3** *(be firm in opposition)* oponerse **(against,** a). ‖ **to stand over** *t insep (supervise, watch closely)* vigilar a, velar a. ‖ **to stand to 1** *i* MIL estar en estado de alerta. − **2** *t sep* MIL poner en estado de alerta. ‖ **to stand up 1** *i (get up)* ponerse de pie, levantarse; *(be standing)* estar de pie: *stand up straight,* ponte derecho; *everyone stood up when he entered the room,* todos se pusieron de pie cuando entró en la sala; *he can fall asleep standing up,* es capaz de dormirse de pie. **2** *(withstand)* resistir **(to,** -), soportar **(to,** -): *this material will stand up to wear and tear,* esta tela es muy resistente; *that won't stand up in court,* eso no convencerá a ningún tribunal. − **3** *t sep (place upright)* poner en posición vertical. **4** *fam (fail to keep appointment)* dejar plantado,-a a, dar un plantón a: *I've been stood up,* me ha dejado plantada. ‖ **to stand up for** *t insep (defend)* defender; *(support)* apoyar: *you've*

got to learn to stand up for yourself, tienes que aprender a defenderte tu solo; *stand up for your rights,* lucha por tus derechos, defiende tus derechos. ‖ **to stand up to** *t insep (resist, defend os.)* hacer frente a, resistir a: *when are you going to stand up to him?,* ¿cuándo le vas a hacer frente?

● **"no standing",** US AUTO "prohibido estacionarse". ‖ **"stand and deliver!",** "la bolsa o la vida". ‖ **to do sth. standing on one's head,** hacer algo con los ojos cerrados. ‖ **to know where one stands,** saber a qué atenerse. ‖ **to make a stand against,** *(gen)* oponer resistencia a; *(mil)* resistir a. ‖ **not to stand a chance,** no tener ni la más remota posibilidad. ‖ **to stand bail (for sb.),** salir fiador,-ra (por algn.). ‖ **to stand clear (of sth.),** apartarse (de algo): *stand clear of the doors!,* ¡apártense de las puertas! ‖ **to stand fast / stand firm,** mantenerse firme. ‖ **to stand guard over,** vigilar. ‖ **to stand in the way of,** impedir, obstaculizar, poner trabas a: *we don't want to stand in the way of progress,* no queremos impedir el progreso. ‖ **to stand on ceremony,** ser muy ceremonioso,-a. ‖ **to stand one's ground,** mantenerse firme, seguir en sus trece. ‖ **to stand on one's head,** hacer el pino. ‖ **to stand on one's own two feet,** apañárselas solo,-a. ‖ **to stand out a mile,** saltar a la vista. ‖ **to stand sb. in good stead,** resultarle muy útil a algn. ‖ **to stand sth. on its head,** dar la vuelta a algo, poner algo patas arriba. ‖ **to stand to attention,** estar firmes, cuadrarse. ‖ **to stand to reason,** ser lógico,-a. ‖ **to stand trial,** ser procesado,-a. ‖ **to stand up and be counted,** dar la cara por sus principios.

■ **cake stand,** bandeja para pasteles. ‖ **coat stand / hat stand,** perchero. ‖ **newspaper stand,** quiosco.

▲ *pt & pp* **stood.**

standard [ˈstændəd] **1** *n (level, degree)* nivel *m*; *(quality)* cualidad *f*: *your work is of a very high standard,* tu trabajo es de muy buena calidad; *the hygiene in this restaurant does not reach the standard required,* la higiene de este restaurante no alcanza el nivel exigido; *he sets very high standards,* exige un nivel muy alto. **2** *(criterion, yardstick)* criterio, valor *m*: *by European standards,* según criterios europeos; *by any standard,* desde cualquier punto de vista. **3** *(norm, rule)* norma, regla, estándar *m*: *rigorous safety standards,* normas de seguridad rigurosas. **4** *(flag)* estandarte *m*, bandera; *(of ship)* pabellón *m*. **5** *(official measure)* patrón *m*: *the gold standard,* el patrón oro. **6** MUS tema *m* clásico, clásico. − **7** *adj* normal, estándar: *it is standard practice,* es la norma, es la práctica habitual; *standard model,* modelo estándar; *standard size,* tamaño normal; *standard English,* inglés estándar. **8** *standards, npl (moral principles)* principios *mpl,* valores *mpl.*

● **to be up to / be below standard,** satisfacer los requisitos / no satisfacer los requisitos.

■ **standard lamp,** lámpara de pie. ‖ **standard of living,** nivel *m* de vida. ‖ **standard time,** hora oficial.

standard-bearer [ˈstændədbeərəʳ] *n* MIL abanderado.

standardization [stændədaɪˈzeɪʃən] *n* normalización *f*, estandarización *f*.

standardize [ˈstændədaɪz] *t* normalizar, estandarizar.

standby [ˈstændbaɪ] **1** *n (person)* suplente *mf*, sustituto,-a, reserva *mf*. **2** *(thing)* recurso: *we only use it as a standby for emergencies,* sólo recurrimos a ello en casos de emergencia.

● **to be on standby,** *(passenger)* estar en la lista de espera; *(soldier)* estar de retén.

■ **standby generator,** grupo electrógeno auxiliar. ‖ **standby ticket,** billete *m* standby.

stand-in ['stændɪn] 1 *n* suplente *mf*, sustituto,-a (**for**, de). 2 CINEM doble *mf*.

standing ['stændɪn] 1 *adj* (*not sitting*) de pie: *standing room only!*, ¡no quedan asientos! 2 (*upright, vertical*) derecho,-a, recto,-a, vertical. 3 (*permanent - committee, body*) permanente; (- *rule*) fijo,-a; (- *invitation*) abierto,-a. – 4 *n* (*status*) estatus *m*, status *m*, posición *f*; (*prestige, reputation*) prestigio: *a woman of some standing in the community*, una mujer que tiene cierto estatus en la comunidad; *a judge of considerable standing*, un juez de mucho prestigio. 5 (*duration*) duración *f*; (*in job*) antigüedad *f*: *an alliance of long standing*, una alianza duradera.
● **to be a standing joke**, provocar siempre las risas de todo el mundo: *Mary's coffee is a standing joke*, todo el mundo siempre se ríe del café que hace Mary.
■ **standing army**, ejército permanente. ‖ **standing order**, FIN orden *f* permanente de pago. ‖ **social standing**, estatus *m* social. ‖ **standing ovation**, ovación *f* calurosa. ‖ **standing start**, SP salida parada.

stand-offish [stænd'ɒfɪʃ] *adj fam* estirado,-a, altivo,-a, distante.

stand-offishness [stæns'ɒfɪʃnəs] *n fam* altivez *f*, distancia, reserva.

standpipe ['stændpaɪp] *n* (*in street*) tubo vertical.

standpoint ['stændpɔɪnt] *n* punto de vista.

standstill ['stændstɪl] **at a standstill**, *phr* parado,-a, paralizado,-a.
● **to bring to a standstill**, (*car, traffic, machine*) parar; (*industry, activity, production*) paralizar: *the strike brought the country to a standstill*, la huelga provocó la paralización del país. ‖ **to come to a standstill**, (*car, traffic*) pararse; (*industry, productivy, production*) paralizarse.

stand-up ['stændʌp] 1 *adj* (*meal*) tomado,-a de pie. 2 (*collar*) levantado,-a.
■ **stand-up fight**, pelea. ‖ **stand-up comedian**, humorista *mf* que explica chistes.

stank [stæŋk] *pt* → **stink**.

stanza ['stænzə] *n* estrofa.

staple[1] ['steɪpəl] 1 *adj* (*food, ingredient*) básico,-a; (*product, export*) principal: *they live on a staple diet of rice*, se alimentan principalmente de arroz. 2 (*usual*) típico,-a, de siempre. – 3 *n* (*main food*) alimento básico; (*main product*) producto principal; (*main thing*) elemento principal.
■ **staple commodity**, artículo de primera necesidad.

staple[2] ['steɪpəl] 1 *n* (*fastener*) grapa. – 2 *t* grapar.

stapler ['steɪplə'] *n* grapadora.

star [stɑː'] 1 *n* (*gen*) estrella; (*person*) estrella, astro: *the sky is full of stars*, el cielo está lleno de estrellas. – 2 *i* CINEM protagonizar (**in**, -): *she's starred in many films*, ha protagonizado muchas películas. – 3 *t* CINEM tener como protagonista a, presentar como estrella: *the film starred Fred Scutttle*, el protagonista de la película fue Fred Scutttle. 4 (*mark with star*) marcar con un asterisco. – 5 **stars**, *npl* (*horoscope*) horóscopo *m sing*: *what do my stars say?*, ¿qué dice mi horóscopo?
● **to see stars**, ver estrellas.
■ **star attraction**, atracción *f* estelar. ‖ **star pupil**, alumno,-a estrella. ‖ **star role**, papel *m* estelar. ‖ **star sign**, signo del zodíaco. ‖ **star witness**, testigo *mf* principal. ‖ **the morning star / evening star**, el lucero del alba / el lucero de la tarde. ‖ **the star of David**, la estrella de David. ‖ **the Stars and Stripes**, la bandera de los Estados Unidos.

starboard ['stɑːbəd] *n* MAR estribor *m*.

starch [stɑːtʃ] 1 *n* (*for laundry, in rice*) almidón *m*; (*in potatoes*) fécula. – 2 *t* (*laundry*) almidonar.

starchy ['stɑːtʃi] *adj* (*food*) feculento,-a; (*person*) rígido,-a, estirado,-a, almidonado,-a.
▲ *comp* **starchier**, *superl* **starchiest**.

stardom ['stɑːdəm] *n* estrellato.
● **to rise to stardom**, convertirse en estrella, alcanzar el estrellato.

stardust ['stɑːdʌst] *n* polvo de estrellas.

stare [steə'] 1 *n* mirada fija. – 2 *i* mirar fijamente (**at**, -), clavar la vista (**at**, en): *he's staring at you*, te está mirando fijamente; *stop staring at me!*, ¡deja de mirarme así!; *what are you staring at?*, ¿qué miras?; *it's rude to stare*, ¡no mires!, es de mala educación.
● **to stare into space**, mirar al vacío. ‖ **to stare sb. in the face**, (*be obvious*) estar delante de las narices de algn., saltar a la vista; (*seem certain*) estar muy cerca: *the answer was staring me in the face*, tenía la respuesta delante de las narices; *death was staring him in the face*, estaba a un paso de la muerte. ‖ **to stare sb. out**, mirar fijamente a algn. hasta que aparte la vista.

starfish ['stɑːfɪʃ] *n* estrella de mar.

stark [stɑːk] 1 *adj* (*landscape*) desolado,-a, desierto,-a, inhóspito,-a; (*climate*) duro,-a, severo,-a, crudo,-a; (*décor, room*) sobrio,-a, austero,-a: *stark poverty*, miseria. 2 *fig* (*realism, truth, facts, etc*) crudo,-a, puro,-a y duro,-a: *the stark reality is that ...*, la realidad pura y dura es que ...; *in stark contrast*, en marcado contraste. 3 (*complete, utter*) absoluto,-a.
● **stark raving mad / stark staring mad**, loco,-a de remate. ‖ **stark naked**, completamente desnudo,-a, en cueros.

starkers ['stɑːkəz] *adj* completamente desnudo,-a, en cueros.

starkly ['stɑːklɪ] 1 *adv* (*portray*) crudamente; (*contrast*) marcadamente. 2 (*clear, obvious*) absolutamente.

starlet ['stɑːlət] *n* aspirante *f* a estrella.

starlight ['stɑːlaɪt] *n* luz *f* de las estrellas.

starling ['stɑːlɪn] *n* ORN estornino.

starlit ['stɑːlɪt] *adj* iluminado,-a por las estrellas.

starry ['stɑːrɪ] *adj* estrellado,-a, sembrado,-a de estrellas.
▲ *comp* **starrier**, *superl* **starriest**.

starry-eyed [stɑːrɪ'aɪd] *adj* (*idealistic*) idealista, ilusionado,-a; (*in love*) enamorado,-a, arrobado,-a.

start [stɑːt] 1 *n* (*gen*) principio, comienzo, inicio: *the film is a bit slow at the start*, la película es un poco lenta al principio; *it was boring from start to finish*, fue un rollo desde el principio hasta el final; *we knew it wouldn't last from the start*, sabíamos desde el principio que no duraría; *we need to make an early start*, tenemos que empezar temprano; *they wanted her to get a good start in life*, querían que tuviera una buena base. 2 SP (*of race*) salida; (*advantage*) ventaja: *the athletes lined up at the start*, los atletas se alinearon a la salida; *they gave us a five-minute start*, nos dieron cinco minutos de ventaja. 3 (*fright, jump*) susto, sobresalto: *what a start you gave me!*, ¡qué susto me has pegado!; *she woke up with a start*, se despertó sobresaltada. – 4 *t* (*begin - gen*) empezar, comenzar, iniciar; (- *conversation*) entablar: *what time do you start work?*, ¿a qué hora empiezas a trabajar?; *I'm starting a new job next week*, empiezo un nuevo trabajo la semana que viene; *they started fighting*, empezaron a pelearse; *it's starting to snow*, empieza a nevar; *she started to cry*, empezó a llorar, arrancó a llorar. 5 (*cause to begin - fire, epidemic*) provocar; (- *ar-*

gument, fight, war, etc) empezar, iniciar: *she started a new fashion,* empezó una nueva moda; *they think the fire was started,* creen que el incendio fue provocado; *the referee started the match,* el árbitro dio comienzo al partido; *you've started me thinking,* me has hecho pensar, me has dado que pensar. **6** (*set up - business*) montar, poner; (*- organization*) fundar, establecer, crear. **7** (*set in motion - machine*) poner en marcha; (*- vehicle*) arrancar, poner en marcha. **– 8** *i* (*begin*) empezar, comenzar: *what time does it start?,* ¿a qué hora comienza?; *let's start by welcoming our guest,* empecemos por dar la bienvenida a nuestro invitado; *don't start, honey,* no empieces, cariño; *the trouble started after the match,* los problemas empezaron después del partido; *prices start at a pound,* precios a partir de una libra; *starting from Tuesday,* a partir del martes, empezando el martes. **9** (*be set up - business*) ser fundado,-a, fundarse, crearse. **10** (*begin to operate*) ponerse en marcha, empezar a funcionar; (*car*) arrancar. **11** (*begin journey*) salir, partir, ponerse en camino: *we started for home,* nos pusimos en camino a casa. **12** (*jump*) asustarse, sobresaltarse: *she starts at the slightest noise,* se asusta con el más mínimo ruido.
◆ **to start back** *i* emprender el viaje de vuelta. ‖ **to start off** **1** *i* (*begin*) empezar, comenzar: *we'll start off with soup,* empezaremos con sopa; *he started off by saying that ...,* empezó diciendo que ... **2** (*leave*) salir, ponerse en camino. **– 3** *t sep* empezar, ayudar a empezar: *who's going to start the discussion off?,* ¿quién quiere empezar el debate?; *I'll start you off with an example,* os ayudaré a empezar con un ejemplo; *don't start him off on football!,* ¡no le des pie para que empiece a hablar de fútbol! ‖ **to start on 1** *t insep* empezar, ponerse a: *we need to start on the painting,* hay que empezar a pintar. **2** (*complain*) empezar a quejarse (**about,** de); (*criticize*) meterse con. ‖ **to start out 1** *i* (*leave*) salir, ponerse en camino. **2** (*begin*) empezar, comenzar: *he started out as a delivery man,* empezó trabajando de repartidor. ‖ **to start over** *i* us volver a empezar. ‖ **to start up 1** *t sep* (*car*) arrancar; (*engine*) poner en marcha; (*business*) montar, poner en marcha; (*conversation*) entablar. **– 2** *i* (*car*) arrancar; (*engine*) ponerse en marcha; (*orchestra*) empezar a tocar; (*music*) empezar a sonar.
● **for a start,** para empezar. ‖ **to get off to a bad start,** empezar mal. ‖ **to get off to a good start,** empezar bien. ‖ **to get started,** empezar. ‖ **to make a fresh start,** volver a empezar. ‖ **to make a start on sth.,** empezar algo. ‖ **to start a family,** tener hijos. ‖ **to start with,** (*firstly*) para empezar, en primer lugar; (*at the beginning*) al principio.
starter ['stɑːtəʳ] **1** *n* sp (*official*) juez *mf* de salida. **2** sp (*competitor*) competidor,-ra, participante *mf.* **3** AUTO motor *m* de arranque. **4** CULIN *fam* primer plato, entrante *m.*
● **for starters,** para empezar. ‖ **to be a late starter,** (*child*) ser tardío,-a en el desarrollo. ‖ **to be under starter's orders,** *estar en la línea de salida a la espera de que el juez dé las órdenes pertinentes.*
■ **starter home,** *casa pequeña que se compra para obtener acceso al mundo de la vivienda.*
starting ['stɑːtɪŋ] *adj* FIN inicial.
■ **starting block,** bloque *m* de salida. ‖ **starting date,** fecha de comienzo. ‖ **starting gate,** cajones *mpl* de salida. ‖ **starting pistol,** pistola de fogueo. ‖ **starting point,** punto de partida. ‖ **starting post,** línea de salida. ‖ **starting price,** FIN precio inicial; sp *precio de las últimas apuestas antes de empezar una carrera.* ‖ **starting salary,** sueldo inicial.

startle ['stɑːtəl] *t* asustar, sobresaltar: *you startled me!,* ¡me has asustado!
startling ['stɑːtəlɪŋ] **1** *adj* (*frightening*) alarmante, sobrecogedor,-ra. **2** (*amazing*) sorprendente, asombroso,-a.
start-up ['stɑːtʌp] *adj* us (*costs etc*) inicial, de puesta en marcha.
starvation [stɑː'veɪʃən] *n* hambre *f,* inanición *f.*
● **to die of starvation,** morirse de hambre, morirse de inanición.
■ **starvation wages,** sueldo de hambre.
starve [stɑːv] **1** *i* (*feel hungry*) pasar hambre; (*die*) morirse de hambre: *thousands of people are starving,* miles de personas se están muriendo de hambre; *I'm starving!,* ¡estoy muerto de hambre! **– 2** *t* (*deprive of food*) privar de comida a, hacer pasar hambre a. **3** *fig* privar (**of,** de): *these kids are starved of love,* estos niños están privados de amor; *schools are being starved of resources,* las escuelas tienen una necesidad apremiante de recursos.
● **to starve sb. to death,** matar de hambre a algn., hacer morir de hambre a algn. ‖ **to starve to death,** morirse de hambre.
starving ['stɑːvɪŋ] *adj* hambriento,-a, famélico,-a, muerto,-a de hambre.
stash [stæʃ] **1** *n* alijo. **– 2 to stash (away),** *t* esconder, guardar en un lugar seguro.
state [steɪt] **1** *n* (*condition*) estado: *the state of the economy,* el estado de la economía; *a state of shock,* un estado de shock; *it's in a bad/good state of repair,* está en mal/buen estado; *a terrible state of affairs,* una situación terrible; *look at the state of this room!,* ¡mira cómo está la habitación! **2** POL (*government*) estado: *affairs/matters of state,* asuntos del estado; *Church and State,* la Iglesia y el Estado. **3** (*country, division of country*) estado: *a member state of EEC,* un país miembro de la CEE; *one-party state,* estado de partido único; *head of state,* jefe de estado. **4** (*ceremony, pomp*) ceremonia, pompa, solemnidad *f.* **– 5** *adj* POL estatal, del estado: *it came under state ownership,* pasó a ser propiedad del estado. **– 6** *t* (*say, declare, express*) exponer, declarar, afirmar: *please state your name,* diga su nombre por favor; *she's not afraid to state her views,* no tiene miedo de dar su opinión; *he stated the facts clearly and simply,* expuso los hechos clara y simplemente; *the document states the conditions,* el documento establece las condiciones. **7** (*specify*) fijar.
● **to be in a state about sth.,** estar nervioso,-a por algo. ‖ **to be in no fit state to do sth.,** no estar en condiciones de hacer algo. ‖ **to get (os.) into a state about sth.,** ponerse nervioso,-a por algo. ‖ **to lie in state,** estar de cuerpo presente. ‖ **to state the obvious,** estar de más decir(lo).
■ **state benefit,** subsidio del estado. ‖ **state capitalism,** capitalismo del estado. ‖ State Department, us Ministerio de Asuntos Exteriores. ‖ **state education,** enseñanza pública. ‖ **state institution,** institución *f* estatal. ‖ **state occasion,** ocasión *f* de estado. ‖ **state of emergency,** estado de emergencia. ‖ **state of mind,** estado de ánimo. ‖ **state school,** escuela estatal, escuela pública. ‖ **state secret,** secreto de estado. ‖ **state visit,** visita de estado. ‖ **the state opening of Parliament,** la apertura del Parlamento. ‖ **the States,** los Estados *mpl* Unidos.
stated ['steɪtɪd] *adj* (*specified*) indicado,-a, señalado,-a.
stateless ['steɪtləs] *adj* apátrida.
stately ['steɪtlɪ] *adj* majestuoso,-a, imponente.
■ **stately home,** casa solariega, casa señorial.

statement ['steɪtmənt] **1** *n* (*gen*) declaración *f*, afirmación *f*; (*official*) comunicado: *a statement of fact*, una declaración de hecho; *the government have issued a statement*, el gobierno ha hecho público un comunicado; *a sworn statement*, una declaración jurada. **2** FIN estado de cuentas, extracto de cuenta.
● **to make a statement,** JUR prestar declaración.
state-of-the-art [steɪtəfðɔɪ'ɑːt] *adj* ultimísimo,-a, más avanzado,-a.
■ **state-of-the-art technology,** tecnología punta.
stateroom ['steɪtruːm] *n* (*on ship*) camarote *m*; (*in palace*) salón *m*.
statesman ['steɪtsmən] *n* estadista *m*, hombre *m* de estado.
▲ *pl* **statesmen** ['steɪtsmən].
statesmanlike ['steɪtsmənlaɪk] *adj* propio,-a de un estadista.
statesmanship ['steɪtʃmənʃɪp] *n* (*skill*) habilidad *f* política; (*management*) arte *m* de gobernar.
static ['stætɪk] **1** *adj* PHYS TECH estático,-a. **2** (*not moving, not changing*) estacionario,-a. **- 3** *n* RAD TV interferencias *fpl*, parásitos *mpl*. **4 statics,** PHYS estática.
■ **static electricity,** electricidad *f* estática.
station ['steɪʃən] **1** *n* (*railway*) estación *f* (de ferrocarril); (*underground*) estación *f* de metro; (*bus, coach*) estación *f*, terminal *f*. **2** RAD emisora, estación *f*, radio *f*; TV canal *m*. **3** AGR granja: *a sheep station*, una granja de ganado ovino. **4** (*social rank*) condición *f* social, posición *f* social. **5** MIL puesto: *action stations!,* ¡zafarrancho de combate!, ¡a sus puestos de combate! **- 6** *t* (*put*) colocar, emplazar, instalar. **7** MIL estacionar, apostar.
● **to have ideas above one's station,** tener delirios de grandeza. ∥ **to marry above/beneath one's station,** casarse con alguien de posición social superior/ inferior a la suya. ∥ **to station os.,** colocarse.
■ **station wagon,** coche *m* familiar, ranchera. ∥ **weather station,** estación *f* meteorológica.
stationary ['steɪʃənərɪ] **1** *adj* (*not moving, still*) estacionario,-a, parado,-a, detenido,-a. **2** (*unchanging*) estacionario,-a. **3** (*cannot be moved*) fijo,-a.
stationer ['steɪsənəʳ] *n* dueño,-a de una papelería.
■ **stationer's (shop),** papelería.
stationery ['steɪʃənərɪ] *n* (*paper*) papel *m* de escribir; (*pen, ink, etc*) artículos *mpl* de escritorio.
stationmaster ['steɪʃənmɑːstəʳ] *n* jefe *m* de estación.
statistic [stə'tɪstɪk] *n* estadística.
statistical [stə'tɪstɪkəl] *adj* estadístico,-a.
statistically [stæ'tɪstɪkəlɪ] *adv* estadísticamente.
statistician [stætɪ'stɪʃən] *n* estadístico,-a.
statistics [stə'tɪstɪks] **1** *n* (*science*) estadística. **- 2** *npl* (*data*) estadísticas *fpl*.
statue ['stætjuː] *n* estatua.
statuesque [stætjʊ'esk] *adj* escultural.
statuette [stætjʊ'et] *n* estatuilla, figurilla.
stature ['stætʃəʳ] **1** *n* (*height*) estatura, talla. **2** *fig* (*standing*) talla.
status ['steɪtəs] **1** *n* (*official position, condition*) situación *f*, condición *f*, posición *f*: *what's his status in the organization?,* ¿cuál es su posición en la organización?; *what is your legal status?,* ¿cuál es su situación legal?; *he had diplomatic status,* tenía condición de diplomático. **2** (*prestige, social standing*) estatus *m*, status *m*, prestigio (social).
■ **marital staus,** estado civil. ∥ **status quo,** statu quo *m*. ∥ **status symbol,** símbolo de prestigio.
statute ['stætjuːt] *n* estatuto, decreto, ley *f*.
● **by statute,** por ley.

■ **statute book,** código de leyes. ∥ **statute law,** derecho escrito.
statutory ['stætjətərɪ] *adj* (*referring to statute*) estatutario,-a; (*penalty*) establecido,-a por la ley, reglamentario,-a; (*right, obligation*) legal; (*holiday*) legalmente establecido,-a.
■ **statutory rape,** US JUR estupro.
staunch[1] [stɔːntʃ] *adj* (*loyal*) incondicional, acérrimo,-a.
staunch[2] [stɔːntʃ] *t* (*blood*) restañar.
stave [steɪv] **1** *n* (*of barrel*) duela. **2** MUS pentagrama *m*.
◆ **to stave in** **1** *t sep* romper. **- 2** *i* romperse. ∥ **to stave off** *t sep* (*disaster, defeat*) evitar.
● **to stave off hunger,** engañar el hambre.
▲ *verbo pt & pp* **staved** *o* **stove.**
staves [steɪvz] **1** *npl* → **staff. 2** → **stave.**
stay[1] [steɪ] *n* MAR (*guy rope*) estay *m*, viento.
stay[2] [steɪ] **1** *n* (*prop, support*) sostén *m*, soporte *m*, puntal *m*. **2** (*in corset*) ballena.
stay[3] [steɪ] **1** *n* (*time*) estancia, permanencia: *we made an overnight stay in Bilbao,* pasamos la noche en Bilbao, hicimos noche en Bilbao. **- 2** *i* (*remain*) quedarse, permanecer: *I can't stay long,* no puedo quedarme mucho rato; *stay there!,* ¡quédate allí!; *she had to stay late at work,* tuvo que quedarse hasta tarde en el trabajo; *why don't you stay for dinner?,* ¿por qué no te quedas a cenar?; *let's stay at home,* quedémonos en casa. **- 3** *t* (*continue to be*) seguir: *if it stays sunny,* si el tiempo sigue soleado; *he couldn't stay awake,* no podía mantenerse despierto; *it stays light until 10.00 pm in summer,* es de día hasta las 10.00 de la noche en verano. **- 4** *i* (*reside temporarily*) alojarse, hospedarse: *they stayed at a hotel,* se alojaron en un hotel; *Helen's coming to stay for a week,* Helen vendrá a pasar una semana en casa; *she stayed the night at a friend's,* se quedó a dormir en casa de una amiga. **- 5** *t fml* (*stop*) detener; (*delay*) aplazar, suspender; (*calm*) calmar: *he managed to stay our fears,* logró calmar nuestros temores; *they've stayed the execution,* han suspendido la ejecución; *we must stay the spread of this disease,* hay que detener la propagación de esta enfermedad.
◆ **to stay away** *i* alejarse (**from,** de), mantenerse lejos (**from,** de), no acercarse (**from,** a). ∥ **to stay behind** *i* quedarse. ∥ **to stay down** *i* (*food*) quedarse en el estómago; (*price*) mantenerse bajo,-a. ∥ **to stay in** *i* quedarse en casa, no salir. ∥ **to stay on** *i* (*remain*) quedarse, permanecer; (*remain in place*) quedarse en su sitio: *she stayed on at school to retake her exams,* se quedó en el instituto para volver a presentarse a los exámenes. ∥ **to stay out** *i* (*gen*) quedarse fuera; (*strikers*) seguir en huelga: *young people often stay out all night,* muchas veces los jóvenes pasan toda la noche fuera. ∥ **to stay out of** *t insep* no meterse en: *I want you to stay out of trouble,* no quiero que te metas en líos. ∥ **to stay up** *i* (*not go to bed*) quedarse levantado,-a, no acostarse; (*remain in position*) mantenerse, no caerse: *he stays up late watching TV,* se queda levantado mirando la tele; *these socks won't stay up,* estos calcetines se me caen.
● **to be here to stay,** formar parte de la vida. ∥ **to stay put,** quedarse. ∥ **to stay the course,** (*race, studies*) terminar la carrera; (*not give up*) resistir hasta el final.
■ **stay of execution,** JUR suspensión de cumplimiento de la sentencia.
stay-at-home ['steɪəthəʊm] *n fam* persona casera.
stayer ['steɪəʳ] *n* (*person*) persona de mucha resistencia; (*horse*) caballo de fondo.
staying power ['steɪɪŋpaʊəʳ] *n* resistencia, aguante *m*.
stead [sted] *n* lugar *m*.
● **in sb.'s stead,** en lugar de algn. ∥ **to stand sb. in good stead,** resultarle muy útil a algn.

steadfast ['stedfɑːst] **1** *adj fml* (*refusal*) firme, rotundo,-a, categórico,-a; (*friend*) leal, incondicional: *he was steadfast in his resolve*, se mantuvo firme en sus propósitos. **2** (*steady, not moving*) constante, inmóvil: *a steadfast gaze*, una mirada fija.

steadfastly ['stedfɑːstlɪ] **1** *adv* (*refuse*) rotundamente, categóricamente; (*persevere, resist*) tenazmente; (*love, admire*) incondicionalmente. **2** (*gaze*) fijamente.

steadfastness ['stedfɑːstnəs] *n* (*resolution*) firmeza, resolución *f*; (*perseverance*) perseverancia, tenacidad *f*; (*loyalty*) lealtad *f*.

steadily ['stedɪlɪ] **1** *adv* (*grow, improve, rise*) constantemente, a un ritmo constante; (*rain, work*) sin parar: *prices have been rising steadily*, los precios han estado subiendo a un ritmo constante; *she's breathing steadily*, respira regularmente; *the situation is getting steadily worse*, la situación sigue empeorando. **2** (*gaze, stare*) fijamente; (*walk*) con paso seguro, decididamente; (*speak*) firmemente.

steadiness ['stedɪnəs] **1** *n* (*of hand, gait*) firmeza. **2** (*of prices*) estabilidad *f*; (*of demand*) lo constante. **3** (*of character*) formalidad *f*, seriedad *f*.

steady ['stedɪ] **1** *adj* (*table, ladder, etc*) firme, seguro,-a; (*gaze*) fijo,-a; (*voice*) tranquilo,-a, firme: *hold the ladder steady*, aguanta firme la escalera; *you need a steady hand*, hace falta un pulso firme. **2** (*regular, constant - heartbeat, pace*) regular; (- *demand, speed, improvement, decline, increase*) constante; (- *flow, rain*) continuo,-a; (- *rhythm*) regular, constante; (- *prices, currency*) estable: *steady progress*, progresos continuos; *steady breathing*, respiración regular; *a steady stream of customers*, un flujo continuo de clientes. **3** (*regular - job*) fijo,-a, estable; (- *income*) regular, fijo,-a: *she has a steady boyfriend*, tiene novio. **4** (*student*) aplicado,-a; (*worker, person*) serio,-a, formal. − **5** *interj* ¡cuidado!, ¡ojo! − **6** *n* (*boyfriend*) novio; (*girlfriend*) novia. − **7** *t* (*hold firm - ladder, table, etc*) sujetar, sostener; (*stabilize*) estabilizar: *steady the ladder for me*, sujétame la escalera. **8** (*person, nerves*) calmar, tranquilizar. − **9** *i* (*market, prices*) estabilizarse.
● *to be as steady as a rock*, ser sólido,-a como una roca. ‖ *to go steady on sth.*, tener cuidado con algo: *go steady on the sherry*, no te pases con el jerez. ‖ *to go steady (with sb.)*, ser novio,-a (de algn.): *are they going steady?*, ¿son novios?
▲ (adjetivo) *comp* **steadier**, *superl* **steadiest**; (verbo) *pt & pp* **steadied**, *ger* **steadying**.

steak [steɪk] **1** *n* (*of beef*) bistec *m*, filete *m*; (*of meat*) filete *m*; (*of salmon*) rodaja. **2** (*meat for stewing*) carne *f* de vaca para estofar.
■ *steak and kidney pie*, pastel *m* de carne con riñones. ‖ *rump steak*, filete de cadera. ‖ *sirloin steak*, filete de solomillo. ‖ *T-bone steak*, entrecot *m*.

steal[1] [stiːl] *n us fam* (*bargain*) ganga, regalo.

steal[2] [stiːl] **1** *t* robar, hurtar: *my car's been stolen*, me han robado el coche; *he had his wallet stolen*, le robaron la cartera; *he stole it from a tourist*, se lo robó a un turista; *she stole it from the shop*, lo robó en la tienda; *he stole a kiss from her*, le robó un beso. − **2** *i* (*rob*) robar, hurtar. **3** (*move quietly, creep*) moverse con sigilo: *he stole up on her*, se le acercó sigilosamente; *they stole away*, se escabulleron; *she stole into the room*, entró sigilosamente en la habitación.
● *to steal a glance at sb./sth.*, echar una mirada furtiva a algn./algo. ‖ *to steal a march on sb.*, ganarle la mano a algn., adelantarse a algn. ‖ *to steal sb.'s heart*, robarle el corazón a algn. ‖ *to steal sb.'s thunder*, quitarle la primicia a algn. ‖ *to steal the scene / steal the show*, acaparar la atención de todos.

▲ *pt* **stole**, *pp* **stolen**.

stealing ['stiːlɪŋ] *n* (*theft*) robo.

stealth [stelθ] *n fml* cautela, sigilo: *they entered the building by stealth*, entraron sigilosamente en el edificio.

stealthily ['stelθɪlɪ] *adv* a hurtadillas, sigilosamente.

stealthy ['stelθɪ] *adj* sigiloso,-a, furtivo,-a.
▲ *comp* **stealthier**, *superl* **stealthiest**.

steam [stiːm] **1** *n* (*gen*) vapor *m*. − **2** *t* CULIN (*vegetables*) cocer al vapor. − **3** *i* (*boat*) echar vapor; (*soup, drink, etc*) humear.
◆ *to steam up i* (*window, glasses*) empañarse. ‖ *to steam off t sep* quitar con vapor, despegar con vapor: *you can steam the stamp off*, puedes quitar el sello con vapor.
● *full steam ahead!*, ¡avante toda!, ¡a todo vapor! ‖ *to get steamed up*, indignarse (*about*, por). ‖ *to do sth. under one's own steam*, hacer algo por sus propios medios. ‖ *to get up steam*, (*person*) acelerarse; (*project etc*) coger impulso; (*engine etc*) dar presión, cobrar velocidad. ‖ *to go full steam ahead*, ir viento en popa. ‖ *to let off steam*, desfogarse, desahogarse. ‖ *to run out of steam*, quedar agotado,-a, quemarse. ‖ *to steam a letter open*, abrir una carta con vapor.
■ *steam bath*, baño de vapor. ‖ *steam engine*, (*locomotive*) locomotora de vapor, máquina de vapor; (*engine*) motor *m* de vapor. ‖ *steam iron*, plancha de vapor.

steamboat ['stiːmbəʊt] *n* vapor *m*.

steamer ['stiːmə'] **1** *n* MAR vapor *m*, buque *m* de vapor. **2** CULIN olla a vapor.

steaming ['stiːmɪŋ] *adj* (*heat*) húmedo,-a; (*liquid*) humeante.

steamroller ['stiːmrəʊlə'] **1** *n* (*vehicle*) apisonadora. − **2** *t fam* (*crush, defeat*) aplastar.
● *to steamroller sb. into doing sth.*, forzar a algn. a hacer algo, obligar a algn. a hacer algo.

steamship ['stiːmʃɪp] *n* vapor *m*, buque *m* de vapor *m*.

steamy ['stiːmɪ] **1** *adj* (*full of steam*) lleno,-a de vapor; (*window, glass*) empañado,-a. **2** (*erotic*) erótico,-a; (*passionate*) apasionado,-a, tórrido,-a.
▲ *comp* **steamier**, *superl* **steamiest**.

steed [stiːd] *n* corcel *m*.

steel [stiːl] **1** *n* (*gen*) acero. − **2** *adj* (*knife, girder, etc*) de acero.
● *to have nerves of steel*, tener nervios de acero. ‖ *to steel one's heart*, endurecerse. ‖ *to steel os. against sth.*, hacerse fuerte para hacer frente a algo. ‖ *to steel os. for sth.*, armarse de valor para algo.
■ *steel band*, MUS banda de percusión del Caribe. ‖ *steel industry*, industria siderúrgica. ‖ *steel mill*, acería, acerería. ‖ *steel wool*, estropajo de acero.

steelworker ['stiːlwɜːkə'] *n* trabajador,-ra de una acería, acerería.

steelworks ['stiːlwɜːks] *npl* acería, acerería.

steely ['stiːlɪ] **1** *adj* (*stare, look*) duro,-a; (*determination*) férreo,-a; (*character*) frío,-a. **2** (*colour*) acerado,-a, metálico,-a.
▲ *comp* **steelier**, *superl* **steeliest**.

steep[1] [stiːp] **1** *t* (*soak - washing*) remojar; (- *dried food*) poner en remojo; (- *fruit*) macerar. − **2** *i* (*fruit*) macerarse.
● *to be steeped in sth.*, *fig* estar empapado,-a de algo: *a city steeped in history*, una ciudad empapada de historia.

steep[2] [stiːp] **1** *adj* (*hill, slope, stairs*) empinado,-a; (*rise, drop*) abrupto,-a, brusco,-a. **2** *fam* (*price, fee*) excesivo,-a; (*demand*) excesivo,-a, poco razonable: *they charged me*

£100 - *that's a bit steep!*, me cobraron £100 - ¡eso es un poco excesivo!; *it's a bit steep to expect me to do all the food*, esperar que yo haga toda la comida es demasiado.

steeple ['stiːpəl] *n* aguja, chapitel *m*.

steeplechase ['stiːpəlʃeɪs] *n* carrera de obstáculos.

steeplejack ['stiːpəldʒæk] *n* reparador,-ra de chimeneas, torres, campanarios, etc.

steer[1] [stɪəʳ] *n* buey *m*.

steer[2] [stɪəʳ] **1** *t* (*gen*) dirigir, guiar; (*vehicle*) conducir, dirigir; (*ship*) gobernar; (*conversation*) llevar. – **2** *i* (*vehicle*) ir al volante; (*ship*) llevar el timón, estar al timón.
● **to steer clear of sth.**, evitar algo.

steering ['stɪərɪŋ] *n* dirección *f*: *assisted steering*, dirección asistida.
■ **steering column**, columna de (la) dirección. ‖ **steering committee**, comité *m* directivo, comisión *f* directiva. ‖ **steering lock**, (*device*) seguro antirrobo; (*when turning*) radio de giro. ‖ **steering wheel**, volante *m*.

stem [stem] **1** *n* BOT (*of plant, flower*) tallo; (*of leaf*) pecíolo; (*of fruit*) pedúnculo. **2** (*of glass*) pie *m*; (*of tobacco pipe*) boquilla, caña. **3** LING raíz *f*, radical *m*. – **4** *t* (*stop - gen*) frenar, detener, parar; (*- bleeding*) contener, parar.
◆ **to stem from** *t insep* provenir de, ser el resultado de.
● **from stem to stern**, MAR de proa a popa.
▲ (*verbo*) *pt* & *pp* **stemmed**, *ger* **stemming**.

stench [stentʃ] *n* hedor *m*, peste *f*, fetidez *f*.

stencil ['stensəl] **1** *n* (*template*) plantilla; (*design, pattern*) estarcido. **2** (*for typewriter*) cliché *m*, matriz *f*. – **3** *t* (*design, pattern*) dibujar utilizando una plantilla. **4** (*duplicate*) multicopiar.
● **to cut a stencil**, hacer un cliché.
▲ *pt* & *pp* **stencilled** (us **stenciled**), *ger* **stencilling** (us **stenciling**).

stenographer [stəˈnɒɡrəfəʳ] *n* us taquígrafo,-a.

stenography [stəˈnɒɡrəfɪ] *n* us taquigrafía.

step [step] **1** *n* (*gen*) paso; (*sound*) paso, pisada: *he walks with quick steps*, anda con paso rápido; *she took a step forward*, dio un paso adelante; *I heard steps outside*, oí pasos fuera; *I retraced my steps*, volví sobre mis pasos; *we're learning a new step at dancing classes*, estamos aprendiendo un nuevo paso en las clases de baile. **2** (*distance*) paso: *it's quite a step to the swimming pool*, hay una buena caminata hasta la piscina; *it's only a step to the library from my house*, la biblioteca está a un paso de mi casa. **3** (*move, act*) paso: *what's the next step?*, ¿cuál es el próximo paso?; *a step in the right direction*, un paso hacia adelante; *the first step on the road to victory*, el primer paso hacia la victoria; *a major step forward for mankind*, un paso gigantesco para la humanidad. **4** (*measure*) medida; (*formality*) gestión *f*, trámite *m*: *we've taken all the necessary steps*, hemos tomado todas las medidas necesarias. **5** (*degree on scale, stage in process*) peldaño, escalón *m*, paso: *she's gone up another step on the career ladder*, ha ascendido otro peldaño en la escala profesional. **6** (*stair*) escalón *m*, peldaño, grada; (*of ladder*) escalón *m*, travesaño; (*of vehicle*) estribo: *mind the step*, cuidado con el escalón. – **7** *i* (*move, walk*) dar un paso, andar: *step this way*, pase por aquí; *he stepped into the house*, entró en la casa; *she stepped off the plane*, se bajó del avión. **8** (*tread*) pisar: *he stepped in a puddle*, pisó un charco; *you stepped on my foot*, me pisaste. – **9 steps**, *npl* GB (*stepladder*) escalera de tijera. **10** (*outdoor*) escalinata; (*indoor*) escalera; (*of plane*) escalerilla: *a flight of steps*, un tramo de escalera.

◆ **to step aside** *i* hacerse a un lado, apartarse. ‖ **to step back** *i* retroceder, dar un paso atrás. ‖ **to step down** *i* (*from position, job*) renunciar (**from,** a), dimitir (**from,** de). ‖ **to step forward** *i* (*volunteer*) ofrecerse. ‖ **to step in** *i* (*intervene*) intervenir. ‖ **to step out 1** *i* GB (*start walking fast*) apretar el paso. **2** US (*go outside, go somewhere*) salir. ‖ **to step up** *t sep* (*increase - gen*) aumentar; (*- campaign*) intensificar; (*- security*) reforzar.
● **every step of the way**, en todo momento, desde principio a fin. ‖ **step by step**, paso a paso, poco a poco. ‖ **step on it!, step on the gas!**, ¡date prisa!, ¡pisa a fondo! ‖ **to be in step / keep in step**, (*walking*) llevar el paso; (*dancing*) llevar el compás. ‖ **to be one step ahead**, llevar la ventaja. ‖ **to be out of step**, (*walking*) no llevar el paso; (*dancing*) no llevar el compás. ‖ **to step into sb.'s shoes**, pasar a ocupar el puesto de algn. ‖ **to step into the breach**, llenar el hueco. ‖ **to watch one's step**, (*be careful*) andar con cuidado; (*when walking*) mirar por dónde camina.
■ **a step up**, un ascenso.

stepbrother ['stepbrʌðəʳ] *n* hermanastro.

stepchild ['steptʃaɪld] *n* hijastro,-a.

stepdaughter ['stepdɔːtəʳ] *n* hijastra.

stepfather ['stepfɑːðəʳ] *n* padrastro.

stepladder ['steplædəʳ] *n* escalera de tijera.

stepmother ['stepmʌðəʳ] *n* madrastra.

steppe [step] *n* GEOG estepa.

stepping-stone ['stepɪŋstəʊn] **1** *n* pasadera. **2** *fig* trampolín *m*.

stepsister ['stepsɪstəʳ] *n* hermanastra.

stepson ['stepsʌn] *n* hijastro.

stereo ['sterɪəʊ] **1** *n* (*system*) equipo estereofónico; (*sound*) estéreo. – **2** *adj* estereofónico,-a.
▲ *pl* **stereos**.

stereophonic [sterɪəˈfɒnɪk] *adj* estereofónico,-a.

stereotype ['sterɪətaɪp] **1** *n* estereotipo. – **2** *t* estereotipar.

stereotyped ['sterɪətaɪpt] *adj* estereotipado,-a.

sterile ['steraɪl] **1** *adj* (*barren*) estéril. **2** (*germ-free*) esterilizado,-a.

sterility [stəˈrɪlɪtɪ] *n* esterilidad *f*.

sterilization [sterəlaɪˈzeɪʃən] *n* esterilización *f*.

sterilize ['sterəlaɪz] *t* esterilizar.

sterilizer ['sterəlaɪzəʳ] *n* esterilizador *m*.

sterling ['stɜːlɪŋ] **1** *n* FIN libra esterlina, libras *fpl* esterlinas. – **2** *adj fml* (*excellent*) excelente.
■ **sterling silver**, plata de ley. ‖ **the pound sterling**, la libra esterlina.

stern[1] [stɜːn] *n* MAR popa.

stern[2] [stɜːn] *adj* (*treatment, measures*) austero,-a, severo,-a; (*person*) severo,-a; (*look, face, etc*) severo,-a, adusto,-a, ceñudo,-a; (*job, task*) duro,-a: *stern resolve*, resolución firme.
● **to be made of sterner stuff**, ser más fuerte.

sternly ['stɜːnlɪ] *adv* severamente, duramente.

sternness ['stɜːnnəs] *n* severidad *f*, austeridad *f*.

sternum ['stɜːnəm] *n* ANAT esternón *m*.
▲ *pl* **sternums** o **sterna**.

steroid ['sterɔɪd] *n* esteroide *m*.

stethoscope ['steθəskəʊp] *n* estetoscopio.

stetson ['stetsən] *n* sombrero tejano.

stevedore ['stiːvədɔːʳ] *n* estibador *m*.

stew [stjuː] **1** *n* CULIN estofado, guisado, guiso. – **2** *t* (*meat*) estofar, guisar; (*fruit*) hacer una compota de. – **3** *i* (*meat, fruit*) cocerse lentamente. **4** *fam* (*swelter*) ahogarse de calor.

● **to be in a stew**, estar nervioso,-a. ‖ **to get into a stew**, ponerse nervioso,-a. ‖ **to let sb. stew**, dejar sufrir a algn. ‖ **to stew in one's own juice**, sufrir.

steward ['stjuːəd] **1** n (on ship) camarero; (on plane) auxiliar m de vuelo. **2** (manager of estate) administrador m. **3** (of club, college, hotel) mayordomo, maitre m. **4** GB (in horse racing) comisario de carreras; (in athletics) juez m; (at demonstration etc) oficial mf.

stewardess ['stjuːədes] n (on ship) camarera; (on plane) azafata, auxiliar f de vuelo.

stewed [stjuːd] adj fam (drunk) borracho,-a.

stick¹ [stɪk] **1** t (insert pointed object) clavar, hincar: *she stuck the fork into the sausage*, clavó el tenedor en la salchicha; *he stuck the needle in his finger*, se clavó la aguja en el dedo. **2** fam poner, meter: *stick it over there*, ponlo allí; *he stuck the letter in his pocket*, metió la carta en el bolsillo; *stick my name down*, apúntame, apunta mi nombre; *he stuck his head out the window*, asomó la cabeza por la ventana; *she's always sticking her nose in*, siempre anda metiendo la nariz. **3** (fix) colocar, fijar; (with glue) pegar, fijar: *he stuck the stamp on the envelope*, fijó el sello en el sobre; *they stick their photos in an album*, pegan sus fotos en un álbum; *she's stuck posters all over her wall*, ha colocado pósters por toda la pared. **4** fam (bear) aguantar, soportar: *I can't stick her*, no la aguanto; *I don't know how you stick this heat*, no sé cómo aguantas este calor. **– 5** i (penetrate) clavarse: *there was a drawing pin sticking in the tyre*, había una chincheta clavada en el neumático; *your elbow's sticking in me!*, ¡me estás clavando el codo! **6** (fix, become attached) pegarse: *this stamp won't stick*, este sello no pega; *this glue sticks to your hands*, esta cola se pega a las manos; *the omelette stuck to the pan*, la tortilla se pegó a la sartén. **7** (jam - drawer, key in lock) atascarse; (- machine part, lock) atrancarse, encasquillarse; (- vehicle in mud) atascarse, atollarse: *the car horn stuck*, el claxon se atascó; *the bone stuck in her throat*, se le atravesó la espina en la garganta. **8** (remain) quedarse: *the phrase stuck in my mind*, la frase se me quedó grabada en la memoria; *and the name just stuck*, y me quedé con el nombre. **9** (in cards) plantarse.

◆ **to stick about / stick around** i fam quedarse. ‖ **to stick at** t insep perseverar, perseguir en, seguir con. ‖ **to stick by** t insep (friend) mantenerse fiel a; (promise) cumplir con. ‖ **to stick out 1** i (project, protrude) salir, sobresalir; (be noticeable) resaltar, destacarse. **2** fam (be obvious) ser obvio,-a, ser evidente. **– 3** t sep (tongue, hand) sacar. **4** (endure) aguantar: *we stuck it till out the end*, aguantamos hasta el final. ‖ **to stick out for** t insep empeñarse en conseguir. ‖ **to stick to 1** t insep (principles) atenerse a; (promise) cumplir con; (plans) seguir con; (text, rules) ceñirse a. **2** (limit oneself) limitarse. ‖ **to stick together** i mantenerse unido,-a, no separarse. ‖ **to stick up 1** i (project, protrude) salir, sobresalir; (hair) ponerse de punta, erizarse. **– 2** t sep (poster etc) fijar, poner, colocar. **3** (hands) levantar: *stick 'em up!*, ¡arriba las manos! **4** (bank) atracar. ‖ **to stick up for** t insep defender. ‖ **to stick with** t insep seguir con.

● **to make stick**, (accusation, charge) probar: *do you think they'll be able to make the murder charge stick?*, ¿crees que podrán probar que es culpable del asesinato? ‖ **to get stuck into sth.**, meterse de lleno en algo. ‖ **to stick at nothing**, no pararse en barras. ‖ **to stick one's neck out**, jugarse el tipo. ‖ **to stick out a mile / stick out like a sore thumb**, saltar a la vista. ‖ **to stick to one's guns**, mantenerse en sus trece.

▲ pt & pp **stuck**.

stick² [stɪk] **1** n (piece of wood) trozo de madera, palo; (twig) ramita; (for punishment) palo, vara. **2** (for walking) bastón m. **3** (for plants) rodrigón m, tutor m. **4** MUS (baton) batuta; (drumstick) palillo. **5** SP (for hockey) palo. **6** (of celery) rama; (of rhubarb) tallo; (of licorice, rock) barrita, tira; (of dynamite) cartucho; (of wax, of soap) barra: *a stick of chalk*, una tiza; *a stick of chewing gum*, un chicle. **7** (of furniture) mueble m. **8** GB fam (person) tipo,-a. **– 9 sticks**, npl (for fire) astillas fpl, leña f sing. **10** (remote area) lugar m sing apartado: *they live out in the sticks*, viven en el quinto pino.

● **the big stick**, POL mano f dura. ‖ **to be in a cleft stick**, estar en una encrucijada. ‖ **to get hold of the wrong end of the stick**, coger el rábano por las hojas. ‖ **to give sb. stick**, (criticize) criticar severamente a algn.; (make fun of) burlarse de algn., cachondearse de algn.: *we gave him some stick about his new girlfriend*, nos cachondeamos de él por su nueva novia; *the government has come in for a lot of stick*, el gobierno ha sido objeto de duras críticas.

■ **stick figure**, figura de palotes. ‖ **stick insect**, insecto palo.

sticker ['stɪkə'] **1** n (label) etiqueta adhesiva; (with slogan, picture) pegatina. **2** (person) persona tenaz.

stickiness ['stɪkɪnəs] **1** n (gen) pegajosidad f, lo pegajoso. **2** fig (of situation) dificultad f, lo delicado, lo espinoso.

sticking ['stɪkɪŋ]. **1 sticking plaster**, n (small) tirita; (on roll) esparadrapo. **– 2 sticking point**, n escollo.

stick-in-the-mud ['stɪkɪnðəmʌd] n fam persona chapada a la antigua, carroza mf.

stickleback ['stɪkəlbæk] n (fish) espinoso, espinosillo.

stickler ['stɪklə'] n persona quisquillosa: *she's a stickler for details*, es muy detallista, repara mucho en los detalles; *he's a stickler for discipline*, insiste mucho en la disciplina.

stick-on ['stɪkɒn] adj adhesivo,-a.

stick-up ['stɪkʌp] n fam atraco, asalto, robo a mano armada.

sticky ['stɪkɪ] **1** adj (gen) pegajoso,-a; (label) adhesivo,-a; (weather) bochornoso,-a; (hand) pringoso,-a. **2** fam (situation) difícil, peliagudo,-a: *we're going through a sticky patch*, pasamos por una época difícil.

● **to be on a sticky wicket**, estar en un aprieto. ‖ **to be sticky about doing sth.**, poner pegas para hacer algo. ‖ **to come to a sticky end**, acabar mal. ‖ **to have sticky fingers**, tener los dedos largos.

▲ comp **stickier**, superl **stickiest**.

stiff [stɪf] **1** adj (hair, fabric) rígido,-a, tieso,-a; (card, collar, brush, lock) duro,-a. **2** (joint) entumecido,-a; (muscle) agarrotado,-a: *he's got a stiff neck*, tiene tortícolis; *I feel stiff after yesterday's work-out*, tengo agujetas después del entrenamiento de ayer. **3** (door, window) difícil de abrir, difícil de cerrar. **4** (not liquid) espeso,-a, consistente. **5** (person, manner) estirado,-a, tieso,-a; (smile) forzado,-a. **6** fig (climb, test, etc) difícil, duro,-a; (breeze) fuerte; (sentence, punishment) severo,-a: *there's stiff competition for the post*, hay mucha competencia por el puesto. **7** fam (price, fee) excesivo,-a. **8** fam (drink) fuerte, cargado,-a. **– 9** n sl (corpse) fiambre m.

● **to keep a stiff upper lip**, poner a mal tiempo buena cara. ‖ **to be bored stiff**, aburrirse como una ostra. ‖ **to be frozen stiff**, estar helado,-a hasta los huesos. ‖ **to be scared stiff**, estar muerto,-a de miedo. ‖ **to be worried stiff**, estar preocupadísimo,-a.

stiffen ['stɪfən] **1** t (card, fabric) reforzar; (collar) almidonar; (paste) endurecer. **2** fig (resistance, morale) fortalecer.

– 3 *i* (*material*) ponerse tieso,-a; (*mixture*) espesarse. **4** (*muscles, joints*) agarrotarse; (*person*) ponerse tenso,-a; (*corpse*) ponerse rígido,-a. **5** *fig* (*resistance, morale*) fortalecerse.

stiffly [ˈstɪflɪ] *adv* (*move, turn*) rígidamente, con rigidez; (*smile, greet, etc*) fríamente, con frialdad.

stiff-necked [stɪfˈnekt] *adj* (*stubborn*) terco,-a, testarudo,-a.

stiffness [ˈstɪfnəs] **1** *n* (*gen*) rigidez *f*, dureza; (*of muscles*) agarrotamiento; (*of joints*) entumecimiento. **2** (*severity*) severidad *f*, dureza. **3** (*formality*) frialdad *f*.

stifle [ˈstaɪfəl] **1** *t* (*suffocate*) sofocar. **2** (*extinguish*) sofocar. **3** (*repress - rebellion, opposition*) reprimir, sofocar, ahogar; (- *sound, noise*) amortiguar, sofocar, ahogar; (- *tears, cries*) ahogar; (- *yawn, anger*) reprimir, contener; (- *growth*) frenar. **– 4** *i* ahogarse, sofocarse.

stifling [ˈstaɪfəlɪŋ] *adj* (*gen*) sofocante, agobiante: *a stifling hot day,* un día sofocante.

stigma [ˈstɪgmə] *n* (*gen*) estigma *m*.

stigmatize [ˈstɪgmətaɪz] *t* estigmatizar.
● **to stigmatize sb. as sth.,** tildar a algn. de algo.

stile [staɪl] *n dos escalones de madera para pasar por encima de una cerca.*

stiletto [stɪˈletəʊ] **1** *n* (*small dagger*) estilete *m*. **– 2** stilettos, *npl* (*shoes*) zapatos *mpl* de tacón de aguja.
■ **stiletto heel,** tacón *m* de aguja.
▲ *pl* **stilettos.**

still¹ [stɪl] **1** *n* (*distillation apparatus*) alambique *m*. **2** (*place*) destilería.

still² [stɪl] **1** *adj* (*not moving*) quieto,-a, inmóvil; (*stationary*) parado,-a; (*water*) manso,-a; (*air*) en calma. **2** (*tranquil, calm*) tranquilo,-a; (*peaceful*) sosegado,-a; (*subdued*) callado,-a, apagado,-a; (*silent*) silencioso,-a. **3** (*not fizzy - water*) sin gas; (*soft drink*) sin burbujas. **– 3** *adv* (*so far*) todavía, aún: *I still remember it,* aún lo recuerdo; *we've still got ten pounds left,* todavía nos quedan diez libras; *do they still live in the same house?,* ¿aún viven en la misma casa?; *she still hasn't learnt to drive,* aún no ha aprendido a conducir; *they're still arguing,* siguen discutiendo; *I still don't get it,* sigo sin entenderlo. **5** (*even*) aún, todavía: *that would be better still,* eso sería aún mejor; *today it's hotter still,* hoy hace aún más calor. **6** (*even so, nevertheless*) a pesar de todo, con todo, no obstante, sin embargo: *but that still doesn't excuse your behaviour,* pero aun así, eso no justifica tu comportamiento; *we still love you, no matter what,* a pesar de todo, te seguimos queriendo; *it was worth it,* no obstante, valía la pena. **7** *fml* (*besides, yet, in addition*) aún, todavía: *still more,* aún más. **8** (*quiet, without moving*) quieto,-a: *keep still,* estáte quieto; *stand still,* no te muevas. **– 4** *n lit* (*calm, silence*) silencio, quietud *f*, tranquilidad *f*: *in the still of the night,* en la quietud de la noche. **10** CINEM (*photograph*) fotograma *m*.
● **still waters run deep,** del agua mansa líbreme Dios.
■ **still life,** ART naturaleza muerta, bodegón *m*.

stillbirth [ˈstɪlbɜːθ] *n* mortinato,-a.

stillborn [ˈstɪlbɔːn] *adj* mortinato,-a, nacido,-a muerto,-a.

stillness [ˈstɪlnəs] **1** *n* (*calm*) calma, quietud *f*, tranquilidad *f*. **2** (*silence*) silencio.

stilt [stɪlt] *n* (*for walking*) zanco; (*for houses*) pilote *m*.

stilted [ˈstɪltɪd] *adj pej* (*style, language*) rebuscado,-a; (*manner*) afectado,-a; (*conversation*) forzado,-a.

stimulant [ˈstɪmjələnt] **1** *n* (*drug*) estimulante *m*. **2** (*stimulus*) estímulo, incentivo, acicate *m*.

stimulate [ˈstɪmjəleɪt] *t* (*activate*) estimular; (*encourage*) animar, alentar.

stimulating [ˈstɪmjəleɪtɪŋ] *adj* (*gen*) estimulante; (*inspiring*) inspirador,-ra.

stimulation [stɪmjəˈleɪʃən] *n* (*stimulus*) estímulo; (*action*) estimulación *f*.

stimulus [ˈstɪmjələs] *n* estímulo.
▲ *pl* **stimuli** [ˈstɪmjəliː].

sting [stɪŋ] **1** *n* (*organ - of bee, wasp*) aguijón *m*; (- *of scorpion*) uña; (- *of plant*) pelo urticante. **2** (*action, wound*) picadura: *a jellyfish sting is very painful,* una picadura de medusa duele mucho. **3** (*pain*) escozor *m*, picazón *f*: *this cream will take the sting away,* esta pomada quitará el escozor. **4** *fig* (*of remorse*) punzada: *the sting of conscience,* el gusanillo de la conciencia. **5** US (*trick*) timo, golpe *m*. **– 6** *t* (*gen*) picar: *if you keep still it won't sting you,* si no te mueves, no te picará; *he's been stung by a wasp,* le ha picado una avispa; *the smoke stung her eyes,* le picaban los ojos por el humo. **7** *fig* (*remark*) herir en lo más hondo; (*conscience*) remorder: *his words really stung me,* sus palabras me hirieron en lo más vivo. **8** (*provoke*) incitar, provocar (**into/to,** a). **9** (*overcharge, swindle*) clavar: *they stung me for £50,* me clavaron £50. **– 10** *i* (*insects, nettles, etc*) picar; (*substance*) escocer. **11** (*be painful*) escocer.
● **to have a sting in the tail,** *fig* esconder algo malo.
‖ **to take the sting out of sth.,** *fig* quitar hierro a algo.
▲ *pt & pp* **stung.**

stinginess [ˈstɪndʒɪnəs] *n* tacañería.

stinging [ˈstɪŋɪŋ] *adj* (*words*) mordaz, hiriente.
■ **stinging nettle,** ortiga. ‖ **stinging pain,** escozor *m*.

stingray [ˈstɪŋreɪ] *n* (*fish*) raya venosa.

stingy [ˈstɪndʒɪ] *n* (*person*) tacaño,-a, roñoso,-a, agarrado,-a, rácano,-a; (*amount*) escaso,-a, mezquino,-a: *don't be so stingy with the chips!,* ¡no seas tan rácano con las patatas!
▲ *comp* **stingier,** *superl* **stingiest.**

stink [stɪŋk] **1** *n* (*smell*) peste *f*, hedor *m*, hediondez *f*, fetidez *f*: *what a stink!,* ¡qué peste! **2** *fam* (*fuss, trouble*) escándalo, lío, follón *m*: *the leaked document caused a real stink,* el documento filtrado provocó un auténtico escándalo; *she made a stink about the noise,* armó un lío por el ruido. **– 3** *i* apestar (**of,** a), heder (**of,** a): *that cheese stinks,* aquel queso apesta; *it stinks of cats,* apesta a gatos; *he stinks of whisky,* huele a whisky que apesta. **4** *fam* (*seem bad or dishonest*) dar asco: *the whole affair stinks,* todo el asunto da asco; *I think your idea stinks,* me parece una idea pésima.
◆ **to stink out** **1** *t sep* (*fill with bad smell*) apestar, dejar hediondo,-a: *his cigar stank the whole house out,* su puro apestó toda la casa. **2** (*drive away*) hacer salir.
● **to create/kick up/make/raise a stink,** armar un lío, armar un escándalo.
■ **stink bomb,** bomba fétida.
▲ *pt* **stank** o **stunk,** *pp* **stunk.**

stinker [ˈstɪŋkəʳ] *n fam* (*unpleasant person*) canalla *mf*; (*difficult thing*) cosa dificilísima; (*bad day*) día *m* de perros; (*bad cold*) resfriado muy fuerte.

stinking [ˈstɪŋkɪŋ] **1** *adj* (*smelly*) hediondo,-a, fétido,-a, apestoso,-a. **2** (*unpleasant, very bad*) horroroso,-a, asqueroso,-a: *keep your stinking money!,* ¡quédate con tu maldito dinero!
● **to be stinking rich,** estar podrido,-a de dinero.

stint [stɪnt] **1** *n* (*period of work*) período, temporada; (*shift*) turno, tanda; (*fixed amount of work*) parte *f*: *I had a stint as a barman,* trabajé de camarero durante una temporada; *have you done your stint?,* ¿has hecho tu parte?

– 2 *t* (*food*) escatimar. **3** (*deprive*) privar: *don't stint yourself of food,* no te prives de comida. **– 4** *i* escatimar (**on,** -): *don't stint on the garlic,* no escatimes el ajo.
● **without stint,** generosamente.
stipend ['staɪpend] *n* estipendio, salario.
stipple ['stɪpəl] *n* puntear.
stipulate ['stɪpjəleɪt] *t* estipular, especificar.
stipulation [stɪpjə'leɪʃən] *n* estipulación *f*, condición *f*.
stir¹ [stɜːʳ] **1** *n* (*act*) acción *f* de agitar: *give it a stir,* remuévelo. **2** (*slight movement*) movimiento: *a stir of excitement,* una leve agitación. **3** *fig* (*public excitement, commotion*) revuelo: *it caused a great stir,* provocó un gran revuelo. **– 4** *t* (*liquid, mixture*) remover, revolver: *has this tea been stirred?,* ¿has removido este té?; *stirring all the time,* sin dejar de remover; *stir the milk into the mixture,* incorpora la leche a la mezcla removiéndola. **5** (*move slightly*) mover, agitar: *the wind stirred the leaves,* el viento movía las hojas; *stir yourself!,* ¡muévete! **6** (*curiosity, interest, etc*) despertar, excitar; (*anger*) provocar; (*imagination*) avivar, estimular; (*emotions*) conmover: *the poem stirred everyone,* el poema conmovió a todos; *his words stirred us to action,* sus palabras nos incitaron a la acción; *her plight stirred my sympathy,* su grave situación despertó mi compasión. **– 7** *i* (*move*) moverse, agitarse; (*wake up*) despertarse; (*get up*) levantarse: *he stirred in his sleep,* se movía mientras dormía; *the baby hasn't stirred all evening,* el bebé no se ha despertado en toda la noche; *he didn't stir from the armchair,* no se movió del sillón; *nobody stirs before ten o'clock,* nadie se levanta antes de las diez. **8** (*feelings*) despertarse: *memories began to stir within her,* los recuerdos empezaron a despertarse en su mente. **9** *fam* (*cause trouble*) armar lío, meter cizaña.
◆ **to stir up 1** *t sep* (*unrest, revolt, etc*) provocar; (*hatred*) fomentar, promover; (*trouble*) provocar, crear; (*memories*) despertar; (*passions*) excitar: *the workers are being stirred up by outside agitators,* agitadores ajenos están provocando a los obreros; *she loves stirring things up,* le encanta liar las cosas. **2** (*mud, waters, dust*) remover.
● **to stir sb.'s blood,** excitar a algn. ‖ **to stir one's stumps,** moverse.
stir² [stɜːʳ] *n sl dated* (*prison*) cárcel *f*, chirona.
stir-crazy [stɜː'kreɪzɪ] *adj* loco,-a.
stir-fry ['stɜːfraɪ] *t* CULIN freír en poco aceite sin dejar de removerlo.
▲ *pt & pp* **stir-fried,** *ger* **stir-frying.**
stirrer ['stɜːrəʳ] *n fam* (*person*) liante *mf*, follonero,-a.
stirring ['stɜːrɪŋ] *adj* (*moving*) conmovedor,-ra; (*rousing, exciting*) emocionante.
stirrup ['stɪrəp] *n* estribo.
■ **stirrup pump,** bomba de mano.
stitch [stɪtʃ] **1** *n* (*in sewing*) puntada; (*in knitting*) punto. **2** MED punto (*de sutura*). **3** (*sharp pain*) punzada; (*when running etc*) flato. **– 4** SEW coser (**on,** a), (**up,** -). **5** MED suturar (**up,** -). **– 6** *i* SEW coser.
◆ **to stitch up 1** *t sep* (*complete satisfactorily*) arreglar, acabar: *we'll soon have it stitched up,* pronto lo tendremos todo arreglado. **2** *fam* (*double-cross*) engañar, traicionar: *we've been stitched up,* nos han engañado.
● **a stitch in time saves nine,** un remiendo a tiempo ahorra ciento. ‖ **to be in stitches,** troncharse de risa. ‖ **to have not got a stitch on,** estar en cueros. ‖ **to have sb. in stitches,** hacer que algn. se tronce de risa, hacer que algn. se parta de risa.
stoat [stəʊt] *n* armiño.
stock [stɒk] **1** *n* (*supply*) reserva: *coal stocks,* reservas de carbón; *they laid in stocks of food for the winter,* se abas-

tecieron de provisiones para el invierno. **2** COMM (*goods*) existencias *fpl*, stock *m*; (*variety*) surtido: *we're getting our new stock in next week,* tendremos el nuevo stock la semana que viene; *we're selling off the old stock,* estamos liquidando el stock antiguo. **3** FIN (*company's capital*) capital *m* social. **4** AGR (*livestock*) ganado. **5** CULIN (*broth*) caldo. **6** BOT (*flower*) alhelí *m*. **7** (*trunk, main part of tree*) tronco; (*of vine*) cepa. **8** (*plant from which cuttings are grown*) planta madre; (*stem onto which another plant is grafted*) patrón *m*. **9** (*descent - of person*) linaje *m*, estirpe *m*; (*- of animal*) raza. **10** *fml* (*standing, status*) prestigio; (*popularity*) popularidad *f*. **11** (*of gun*) culata; (*of tool, whip, fishing rod*) mango. **– 12** *adj* COMM (*goods, size*) corriente, normal, de serie, estándar. **13** *pej* (*excuse, argument, response*) de siempre, típico,-a, de costumbre; (*greeting, speech*) consabido,-a; (*phrase, theme*) trillado,-a, gastado,-a, muy visto,-a. **– 14** *t* COMM (*keep supplies of*) tener en stock; (*sell*) vender: *we stock all sizes,* tenemos todas las tallas; *do you stock textbooks?,* ¿venden libros de texto? **15** (*provide with a supply*) abastecer de, surtir de, proveer de; (*fill - larder etc*) llenar (**with,** de); (*- lake, pond*) poblar: *the shop is well-stocked with exotic food,* la tienda tiene un buen surtido de comida exótica; *we're well stocked up with tinned food,* tenemos más que suficientes latas de comida; *he stocks shelves at the supermarket,* llena los estantes en el supermercado; *a well-stocked larder,* una despensa llena. **– 16 stocks,** *npl* FIN (*shares*) acciones *fpl*, valores *mpl*.
◆ **to stock up** *i* abastecerse (**on/with,** de/con), aprovisionarse (**on/with,** de/con): *we must stock up on food for Christmas,* hay que abastecerse de alimentos para Navidad.
● **to be out of stock,** estar agotado,-a. ‖ **to have sth. in stock,** tener algo en stock, tener algo en existencias. ‖ **to take stock,** COMM hacer el inventario. ‖ **to take stock of sth.,** *fig* evaluar algo, hacer balance de algo.
■ **government stock,** papel de estado. ‖ **stock certificate,** US FIN título de acciones. ‖ **stock company,** THEAT compañía de repertorio; FIN sociedad *f* anónima. ‖ **stock cube,** pastilla de caldo. ‖ **stock exchange,** bolsa (de valores). ‖ **stock market,** bolsa, mercado bursátil.
stockade [stɒ'keɪd] *n* (*fence*) empalizada, estacada.
stockbreeder ['stɒkbriːdəʳ] *n* ganadero,-a.
stockbreeding ['stɒkbriːdɪŋ] *n* ganadería, cría del ganado.
stockbroker ['stɒkbrəʊkəʳ] *n* corredor,-ra de bolsa, agente *mf* de bolsa, bolsista *mf*.
■ **stockbroker belt,** *zona residencial de alta categoría en las afueras de una cuidad.*
stockbroking ['stɒkbrəʊkɪŋ] *n* correduría de valores: *stockbroking firm,* agencia de valores y bolsa.
stockholder ['stɒkhəʊldəʳ] *n* US accionista *mf.*
Stockholm ['stɒkhəʊm] *n* Estocolmo.
stocking ['stɒkɪŋ] *n* media: *a pair of stockings,* unas medias, un par de medias.
● **in one's stocking(ed) feet,** descalzo,-a.
■ **stocking stitch,** punto de media.
stockist ['stɒkɪst] *n* almacenista *mf*, proveedor,-ra, distribuidor,-ra.
stockman ['stɒkmən] *n* ganadero.
stockpile ['stɒkpaɪl] **1** *n* reservas *fpl*. **– 2** *t* (*gen*) almacenar; (*accumulate*) acumular, hacer acopio de.
stockpot ['stɒkpɒt] *n* olla, marmita.
stockroom ['stɒkruːm] *n* almacén *m*, depósito.
stocks [stɒks] **1** *npl* HIST (*wooden frame*) cepo. **2** MAR (*framework*) grada de construcción, astillero.

● **to be on the stocks,** estar en construcción.
stock-still [stɒk'stɪl] *adv* inmóvil.
stocktaking ['stɒkteɪkɪŋ] **1** *n* COMM inventario. **2** (*review*) balance *m*.
stocky ['stɒkɪ] *adj* (*heavily-built*) robusto,-a, fornido,-a; (*strong, solid*) cuadrado,-a; (*squat*) bajito,-a.
▲ *comp* **stockier,** *superl* **stockiest**.
stockyard ['stɒkjɑːd] *n* corral *m* de ganado.
stodge [stɒdʒ] *n* comida indigesta, mazacote *m*.
stodgy ['stɒdʒɪ] **1** *adj* (*food*) indigesto,-a, pesado,-a. **2** (*book, person*) pesado,-a, aburrido,-a.
▲ *comp* **stodgier,** *superl* **stodgiest**.
stoical ['stəʊɪkəl] *adj* estoico,-a.
stoicism ['stəʊɪsɪzəm] *n* estoicismo.
stoke [stəʊk] **1** *t* (*fire - add fuel to*) alimentar, echar carbón a, echar leña a; (*- poke*) atizar, avivar. **2** *fig* (*feeling*) avivar, alimentar.
◆ **to stoke up 1** *i* (*add fuel to fire*) alimentar el fuego; (*poke fire*) atizar el fuego, avivar el fuego. **2** *fam* (*fill up*) llenarse (**on,** de), atiborrarse (**on,** de). – **3** *t sep fig* (*feeling*) avivar, alimentar.
stoker ['stəʊkə'] *n* fogonero,-a.
stole[1] [stəʊl] *pt* → **steal**.
stole[2] [stəʊl] *n* (*garment*) estola.
stolen ['stəʊlən] *pp* → **steal**.
stolid ['stɒlɪd] *adj* (*impassive*) impasible, imperturbable.
stomach ['stʌmək] **1** *n* ANAT estómago. **2** *fam* (*belly*) barriga; (*abdomen*) abdomen *m*, vientre *m*: *a feeling in the pit of my stomach,* un presentimiento en la boca del estómago. – **3** *t fig* (*bear, endure*) aguantar, soportar, tragar; (*eat, drink*) tolerar.
● **on a full stomach,** cuando acabas de comer. ‖ **on an empty stomach,** en ayunas, con el estómago vacío. ‖ **to have no stomach for sth.,** (*appetite*) no tener ganas de comer algo, no apetecerle comer algo; (*liking*) no gustarle algo a uno; (*afraid*) tener miedo de algo, no atreverse a hacer algo. ‖ **to lie on one's stomach,** tumbarse boca abajo. ‖ **to turn sb.'s stomach,** revolverle el estómago a algn.
■ **stomach pump,** bomba estomacal. ‖ **stomach upset,** trastorno gástrico.
stomach-ache ['stʌməkeɪk] *n* dolor *m* de estómago.
stomp [stɒmp] *i fam* pisar fuerte.
stone [stəʊn] **1** *n* (*gen*) piedra. **2** (*on grave*) lápida. **3** (*of fruit*) hueso. **4** MED cálculo, piedra. **5** GB (*measure of weight*) unidad de peso que equivale a 6,348 *kg*: *she weighs 9 stones,* pesa 57 kilos. – **6** *adj* de piedra, pétreo,-a. – **7** *t* (*person*) apedrear, lapidar. **8** (*fruit*) deshuesar.
● **a rolling stone gathers no moss,** piedra movediza nunca moho la cobija. ‖ **at a stone's throw,** a tiro de piedra. ‖ **stone the crows! / stone me!,** ¡caray! ‖ **to leave no stone unturned,** no dejar piedra por mover.
■ **Stone Age,** Edad *f* de Piedra.
stonechat ['stəʊntʃæt] *n* ORN tarabilla.
stone-cold [stəʊn'kəʊld] *adj* helado,-a.
● **to be stone-cold sober,** no haber bebido ni una gota.
stoned [stəʊnd] **1** *adj sl* (*on drugs*) ciego,-a, flipado,-a, colocado,-a. **2** *sl* (*drunk*) trompa, mamado,-a.
● **to get stoned,** (*on drugs*) colocarse; (*drunk*) emborracharse.
stone-dead [stəʊn'ded] *adj* tieso,-a, muerto,-a.
stone-deaf [stəʊn'def] *adj* sordo,-a como una tapia.
stonemason ['stəʊnmeɪsən] *n* (*stone cutter*) cantero,-a; (*builder*) mampostero,-a.
stonewall ['stəʊnwɔːl] **1** *i* (*gen*) poner obstáculos, utilizar tácticas obstruccionistas. **2** POL practicar el obs-

truccionismo. **3** (*in cricket*) jugar a la defensiva. – **4** *t* obstaculizar, poner obstáculos a.
stoneware ['stəʊnweə'] *n* gres *m*, cerámica de gres.
stone-washed [stəʊn'wɒʃt] *adj* lavado,-a a la piedra.
stonework ['stəʊnwɜːk] *n* mampostería.
stony ['stəʊnɪ] **1** *adj* (*ground, beach*) pedregoso,-a. **2** *fig* (*look, silence*) frío,-a, glacial.
● **to fall on/upon stony ground,** caer en oídos sordos.
▲ *comp* **stonier,** *superl* **stoniest**.
stony-broke [stəʊnɪ'brəʊk] *adj* sin blanca, pelado,-a, sin un duro.
stood [stʊd] *pt* & *pp* → **stand**.
stooge [stuːdʒ] **1** *n* THEAT comparsa *mf*. **2** *pej* (*person*) títere *mf*, pelele *mf*.
stool [stuːl] **1** *n* (*seat*) taburete *m*, banqueta. **2** MED (*faeces*) deposición *f*, heces *fpl*.
● **to fall between two stools,** quedarse entre dos aguas.
stoolpigeon ['stuːlpɪdʒɪn] *n sl* (*informer*) soplón,-ona; (*decoy*) señuelo.
stoop[1] [stuːp] *n* US (*porch*) entrada.
stoop[2] [stuːp] **1** *n* (*of person*) encorvamiento, encorvadura; (*of shoulders*) espaldas *fpl* encorvadas: *he walks with a stoop,* anda encorvado. – **2** *i* (*bend*) inclinarse (**down,** -), agacharse (**down,** -). **3** (*have a stoop*) andar encorvado,-a, ser cargado,-a de espaldas.
◆ **to stoop to** *t insep fig* (*lower os.*) rebajarse a: *he'd stoop to anything,* se rebajaría a cualquier cosa.
● **to stoop so low (as to do sth.),** llegar tan bajo (como para hacer algo).
stop [stɒp] **1** *n* (*halt*) parada, alto: *the vehicle came to a stop,* el vehículo se paró; *work has been at a stop for weeks,* hace semanas que el trabajo está parado. **2** (*stopping place*) parada: *bus stop,* parada de autobús; *which stop do you want to get off at?,* ¿dónde quieres bajar? **3** (*on journey*) parada; (*break, rest*) descanso, pausa: *we make two stops on this route,* hacemos dos paradas en este recorrido; *let's make a stop for lunch,* hagamos una parada para comer; *our first stop was in Paris,* nuestra primera parada fue en París. **4** (*punctuation mark*) punto; (*in telegram*) stop *m*. **5** MUS (*on organ*) registro; (*knob*) botón *m* de registro; (*on wind instrument*) llave *f*. **6** (*in camera*) diafragma *m*. – **7** *t* (*halt - vehicle, person*) parar, detener; (*- machine, ball*) parar: *he stopped the car outside the station,* detuvo el coche delante de la estación; *she stopped a passing taxi,* paró un taxi que pasaba; *he was stopped by police at the airport,* la policía lo detuvo en el aeropuerto; *stop that man! he's taken my bag!,* ¡detened a ese hombre! ¡me ha robado el bolso! **8** (*end, interrupt - production*) parar, paralizar; (*- inflation, advance*) parar, contener; (*- conversation, play*) interrumpir; (*pain etc*) poner fin a, poner término a, acabar con. **9** (*pay, match, holidays*) suspender; (*cheque*) cancelar; (*money from wages*) retener: *the referee stopped the match,* el árbitro suspendió el partido; *they stopped £10 from my wages,* me retuvieron £10 del sueldo. **10** (*cease*) dejar de, parar de: *has it stopped raining?,* ¿ha dejado de llover?; *he stopped smoking,* dejó de fumar; *she stopped work to have a baby,* dejó de trabajar para tener un niño; *stop crying!,* ¡para de llorar!; *do you ever stop talking?,* ¿no paras de hablar jamás?; *stop it!,* ¡basta ya! **11** (*prevent*) impedir, evitar: *they tried to stop me (from) going,* trataron de impedir que fuera; *no-one could stop her (from) seeing him,* nadie pudo impedir que lo viera; *the students stopped the theatre being closed,* los estudiantes impidieron que se cerrara el

teatro; *nothing can stop us now,* nada nos puede parar ahora; *what's stopping you?,* ¿por qué no lo haces?, ¿qué te lo impide?; *you must stop the bleeding,* hay que parar la hemorragia. **12** *(block - hole)* tapar, taponar (**up,** -); *(- gap)* rellenar (**up,** -); *(- tooth)* empastar (**up,** -): *I've got to stop a leak in the pipe,* tengo que taponar un escape en la cañería. **13** MUS *(string, key)* apretar; *(hole)* cubrir. – **14** *i (halt)* parar, pararse, detener, detenerse: *does this bus stop at the station?,* ¿este autobús para en la estación?; *the train stopped in a tunnel,* el tren se paró en un túnel; *we stopped for a rest,* paramos para descansar; *she stopped to look in a shop window,* paró para mirar en un escaparate; *my watch has stopped,* se me ha parado el reloj; *his heart stopped,* se le paró el corazón; *she never stops,* no para nunca. **15** *(cease)* acabarse, terminar, cesar: *the shouting suddenly stopped,* de repente se acabaron los gritos; *the fighting has stopped,* han cesado los combates; *the rain has stopped,* ha dejado de llover, ya no llueve. **16** GB *fam* *(stay)* quedarse: *no, I'm not stopping long,* no, no me quedo mucho rato; *are you stopping for lunch?,* ¿te quedas a comer?; *we stopped at a hotel,* nos quedamos en un hotel.

◆ **to stop behind** *i* quedarse. ‖ **to stop by** *i (visit)* pasar: *tell Dave to stop by and see me one day,* dile a Dave que pase a verme un día. ‖ **to stop in** *i* quedarse en casa, no salir. ‖ **to stop off** *i (interrupt journey)* parar: *we stopped off in Tarragona,* paramos en Tarragona. ‖ **to stop out** *i* no volver a casa. ‖ **to stop over 1** *i (interrupt journey)* parar; *(overnight)* pasar la noche, hacer noche. **2** AER hacer escala. ‖ **to stop up 1** *i (go to bed late)* no acostarse. – **2** *t sep* taponar.

● **stop thief!,** ¡al ladrón! ‖ **to come to a stop,** pararse, hacer un alto. ‖ **to pull out all the stops,** tocar todos los registros. ‖ **to put a stop to sth.,** poner fin a algo. ‖ **to stop a bullet,** recibir un balazo. ‖ **to stop at nothing (to do sth.),** no pararse en barras (para hacer algo), no tener miramientos (para hacer algo). ‖ **to stop dead in one's tracks,** pararse en seco. ‖ **to stop os.,** contenerse. ‖ **to stop short,** pararse en seco. ‖ **to stop short of sth.,** no llegar a: *he insulted him, but he stopped short of hitting him,* lo insultó, pero no llegó a pegarle. ‖ **to stop the rot,** cortar por lo sano. ‖ **to stop the show,** causar sensación. ‖ **to stop to think,** detenerse a pensar. ‖ **without stopping,** sin parar, sin cesar.

■ **stop press,** noticias *fpl* de última hora. ‖ **stop sign,** stop *m.*

▲ *(verbo) pt & pp* **stopped,** *ger* **stopping.**

stopcock ['stɒpkɒk] *n* llave *f* de paso.

stopgap ['stɒpgæp] *n (thing)* recurso provisional, medida provisional; *(person)* sustituto,-a.

stoplight ['stɒplaɪt] *n* us semáforo.

stopover ['stɒpəʊvə'] *n (stop)* parada; *(on flight)* escala; *(stay)* estancia.

stoppage ['stɒpɪdʒ] **1** *n (of work)* paro, suspensión *f; (strike)* huelga. **2** *(in production, play)* interrupción *f.* **3** *(cancellation, withholding)* suspensión *f.* **4** *(blockage)* obstrucción *f.* – **5 stoppages,** npl *(money from wages)* retenciones *fpl,* deducciones *fpl.*

stopper ['stɒpə'] *n* tapón *m.*

stopping ['stɒpɪŋ] *adj* GB *(of train)* que para en todas las estaciones.

stop-press [stɒp'pres] *adj (news)* de última hora.

stopwatch ['stɒpwɒtʃ] *n* cronómetro.

storage ['stɔːrɪdʒ] **1** *n (act)* almacenaje *m,* almacenamiento. **2** *(place)* almacén *m,* depósito, guardamuebles

m. **3** *(cost)* (gastos *mpl* de) almacenaje *m.* **4** COMPUT almacenamiento.

● **to be in storage,** estar guardado,-a. ‖ **to keep sth. in cold storage,** guardar algo en frío. ‖ **to put sth. into storage,** guardar algo.

■ **storage battery,** acumulador *m.* ‖ **storage capacity,** capacidad *f* de almacenamiento. ‖ **storage heater,** acumulador *m* de calor. ‖ **storage space,** sitio para guardar cosas. ‖ **storage tank,** tanque *m* de almacenamiento. ‖ **storage unit,** armario.

store [stɔːr'] **1** *n (supply - gen)* reserva, provisión *f; (- of wisdom, knowledge)* reserva; *(- of jokes etc)* colección *f: he has a secret store of whisky,* tiene una reserva secreta de whisky. **2** *(warehouse)* almacén *m,* depósito. **3** US *(shop)* tienda. – **4** *t (put away)* almacenar (**up,** -); *(keep)* guardar; *(amass)* acumular, hacer acopio de: *we store the goods in the garage,* almacenamos las mercancías en el garage; *I've already stored my winter clothes away,* ya he guardado la ropa de invierno; *squirrels store up nuts for the winter,* las ardillas almacenan frutos secos para el invierno. **5** COMPUT almacenar. **6** *(put in storage)* guardar, almacenar, mandar a un depósito. **7** *fig (trouble etc)* ir acumulando (**up,** -), ir almacenando (**up,** -). **8** *(fill with supplies)* abastecer (**with,** de). – **9 stores,** npl *(provisions)* provisiones *fpl,* víveres *mpl.* **10** MIL *(supplies, equipment)* pertrechos *mpl; (place)* intendencia *f sing.*

● **to be in store,** estar en depósito, estar en un guardamuebles. ‖ **to be sth. in store (for sb.),** esperarle algo a algn., aguardarle algo a algn. ‖ **to have sth. in store for sb.,** tenerle algo preparado para algn.: *I have a surprise in store for you,* te tengo preparada una sorpresa, tengo una sorpresa para ti; *what does the future have in store for us?,* ¿qué nos depara el futuro? ‖ **to keep sth. in store,** guardar algo de reserva. ‖ **to set store by sth.,** valorar algo mucho.

■ **general stores,** colmado.

storehouse ['stɔːhaʊs] *n* almacén *m,* depósito.

storekeeper ['stɔːkiːpə'] *n* us tendero,-a.

storeroom ['stɔːruːm] *n (gen)* almacén *m,* depósito; *(for food)* despensa.

storey ['stɔːrɪ] *n* piso, planta: *a ten-storey building,* un edificio de diez pisos; *a multi-storey car park,* un aparcamiento de varias plantas.

stork [stɔːk] *n* cigüeña.

storm [stɔːm] **1** *n (thunderstorm)* tormenta; *(at sea)* tempestad *f,* temporal *m; (with wind)* borrasca: *there's a storm brewing,* se prepara una tormenta; *the storm broke,* se desató la tormenta. **2** *fig (uproar)* revuelo, escándalo; *(of missiles, insults)* lluvia, torrente *m: a storm of protest,* una ola de protestas; *a storm of applause,* una salva de aplausos. – **3** *t (attack)* asaltar, tomar por asalto: *they stormed the palace,* asaltaron el palacio. **4** *(say angrily)* bramar. – **5** *i (go or move angrily)* andar airado,-a: *he stormed out,* salió airado; *she stormed off,* se marchó hecha una furia; *he stormed in,* entró como un vendaval. **6** *(shout angrily)* echar pestes, vociferar, rabiar, despotricar.

● **to ride out the storm / weather the storm,** capear el temporal. ‖ **to take by storm,** MIL tomar por asalto; THEAT MUS cautivar.

■ **a storm in a teacup,** una tempestad en un vaso de agua. ‖ **storm cloud,** nubarrón *m.* ‖ **storm door,** contrapuerta. ‖ **storm petrel,** petrel *m,* ave *f* de las tempestades. ‖ **storm trooper,** soldado de las tropas de asalto. ‖ **storm troops,** tropas *fpl* de asalto. ‖ **storm warning,** aviso de tormenta. ‖ **storm window,** contraventana.

stormy ['stɔːmɪ] 1 adj (weather) tormentoso,-a. 2 fig (meeting, discussion) acalorado,-a; (relationship) tormentoso,-a, con muchos altibajos.
▲ comp **stormier**, superl **stormiest**.

story[1] ['stɔːrɪ] n US → **storey**.

story[2] ['stɔːrɪ] 1 n (gen) historia; (tale) cuento, relato; (account) relato: *it's a love story*, es una historia de amor; *tell me a story*, cuéntame un cuento; *the book tells the story of Cinderella*, el libro relata la historia de la Cenicienta; *that's my story and I'm sticking to it*, ésa es mi historia y a ella me atengo; *a success story*, una historia de éxito; *I want to hear your side of the story*, quiero oír tu versión de los hechos. 2 (anecdote) anécdota; (joke) chiste m. 3 (rumour) rumor m; (lie) mentira, cuento: *don't tell stories*, no digas mentiras. 4 (newspaper article) artículo; (newsworthy item) artículo de interés periodístico: *that would make a good story*, eso sería una buena noticia. 5 (story-line, narrative, plot) argumento, trama.
● *but that's another story*, pero eso es otro cantar. ‖ *it's a long story*, es largo de contar. ‖ *so the story goes*, según cuenta la historia, según dicen. ‖ *that's the story of my life!*, ¡siempre me pasa lo mismo! ‖ *to cut a long story short*, en resumidas cuentas, en pocas palabras.
▲ pl **stories**.

storybook ['stɔːrɪbʊk] n libro de cuentos.

storyteller ['stɔːrɪtelə'] n cuentista mf.

stout [staut] 1 adj euph (fat) corpulento,-a, robusto,-a. 2 (strong) sólido,-a, fuerte. 3 (determined, resolute) firme, resuelto,-a, tenaz; (brave) valiente: *with a stout heart*, valientemente, resueltamente. – 4 n (beer) cerveza negra.

stout-hearted [staut'hɑːtɪd] adj valiente, resuelto,-a.

stove[1] [stəʊv] 1 n (for heating) estufa. 2 (cooker) cocina; (cooking ring) hornillo; (oven) horno.
■ oil stove, estufa de petróleo.

stove[2] [stəʊv] pp → **stave**.

stow [stəʊ] 1 t (put away, store) guardar, poner, colocar. 2 MAR (cargo) estibar, arrumar, cargar.
◆ to stow away i (on ship, plane) viajar de polizón.

stowage ['stəʊɪdʒ] n MAR (act) estiba; (space) bodega.

stowaway ['stəʊəweɪ] n polizón mf.

straddle ['strædəl] 1 t (on horse, fence, etc) sentarse a horcajadas sobre. 2 (bridge, town) extenderse sobre. – 3 n SP (high-jumping technique) tijereta.

strafe [streɪf] t bombardear.

straggle ['strægəl] 1 i (spread untidily) extenderse, desparramarse; (grow) crecer desordenadamente. 2 (lag behind) rezagarse, ir rezagado,-a.

straggler ['stræglə'] n (person) rezagado,-a.

straggly ['strægli] adj (of town, houses) disperso,-a, esparcido,-a; (of plant) que crece desordenadamente; (of hair) desgreñado,-a.
▲ comp **stragglier**, superl **straggliest**.

straight [streɪt] 1 adj (not curved - gen) recto,-a; (- hair) liso,-a: *a straight road*, una carretera recta; *can you walk in a straight line?*, ¿puedes caminar en línea recta? 2 (level, upright) derecho,-a, recto,-a: *backs straight!*, ¡espalda recta!; *is my tie straight?*, ¿tengo la corbata recta?; *the picture isn't straight*, el cuadro no está recto; *sit with your back straight*, siéntate erguido. 3 (tidy, neat) en orden, arreglado,-a: *I must get the house straight*, tengo que ordenar la casa. 4 (honest - person) honrado,-a, de confianza; (sincere) sincero,-a, franco,-a: *be straight with me*, sea sincero conmigo; *give me a straight answer*, dame una respuesta clara; *let's do some*

straight talking, hablemos claro. 5 (direct - question) directo,-a; (- refusal, rejection) categórico,-a, rotundo,-a: *he gave me a straight "no" for an answer*, su respuesta fue un "no" rotundo. 6 (correct, accurate) correcto,-a: *let me get this straight*, a ver si lo he entendido; *have you got your facts straight?*, ¿tienes la información correcta? 7 (consecutive) seguido,-a: *he worked for five days straight*, trabajó cinco días seguidos; *31 straight wins*, 31 victorias consecutivas; *she got straight A's*, sacó sobresaliente en todo. 8 (drink) solo,-a. 9 (play, actor, etc) serio,-a, dramático,-a. 10 (person - conventional) convencional; (- heterosexual) heterosexual; (non-drug user) que no toma droga. 11 fam (not in debt) solvente. – 12 adv (in a straight line) recto,-a: *he was staring straight ahead*, miraba al frente; *go straight on*, sigue todo recto; *it's straight in front of you*, está delante de tus narices; *he can't shoot straight*, no es un tirador certero. 13 (not in a curve) derecho,-a, recto,-a: *sit up straight*, ponte derecho. 14 (directly) directamente: *he went straight to the fridge*, se fue directamente a la nevera; *come straight home*, vuelve directamente a casa; *she went straight from school to university*, pasó directamente del instituto a la universidad; *go straight to bed*, vete directamente a la cama; *the car was coming straight at me*, el coche venía directo hacia mí. 15 (immediately) en seguida: *straight after lunch*, inmediatamente después de comer; *I'll come straight back*, volveré en seguida. 16 (frankly) francamente, con franqueza: *tell him straight (out)*, díselo sin rodeos; *get straight to the point*, ve al grano. 17 (clearly) claro, con claridad: *I can't think straight*, no puedo pensar bien. – 18 n SP (in race) recta: *he sped down the final straight*, bajó la recta final a gran velocidad. 19 (in cards) escalera. 20 fam (conventional person) carca mf; (heterosexual) heterosexual mf; (non-drug user) persona que no se droga.
● as straight as an arrow/die, (line, direction) derecho,-a como una vela; (person) honrado,-a. ‖ the straight and narrow, el buen camino. ‖ straight from the shoulder, sin rodeos. ‖ straight away, en seguida. ‖ straight off, sin pensarlo, en el acto. ‖ straight up, en serio. ‖ to go straight, (criminal) reformarse. ‖ to keep a straight face, contener la risa. ‖ to play straight (with sb.), jugar limpio (con algn.). ‖ to put/set the record straight, dejar las cosas claras, aclarar las cosas, poner las cosas en su lugar. ‖ to put/set sb. straight (about sth.), explicar los hechos a algn. ‖ to vote a/the straight ticket, US POL votar a/ por candidatos del mismo partido para todos los cargos.
■ straight choice, alternativa clara. ‖ straight fight, mano a mano m. ‖ straight profit, beneficio limpio. ‖ straight swap, cambio directo.

straightaway [streɪtə'weɪ] adv en seguida, inmediatamente.

straighten ['streɪtən] 1 t (wire) enderezar; (- tie, skirt, picture) poner bien, poner recto,-a; (- hair) estirar, alisar: *straighten your tie*, ponte bien la corbata. 2 (tidy) ordenar (up, -), arreglar (up, -). – 3 i (road) hacerse recto,-a.
◆ to straighten out 1 t sep (problem) resolver, solucionar; (confusion, misunderstanding) aclarar; (affair) arreglar. 2 (person) resolver los problemas de. ‖ to straighten up i (person) ponerse derecho,-a.

straight-faced ['streɪt'feɪst] adj serio,-a, sin reírse.

straightforward [streɪt'fɔːwəd] 1 adj (honest) honrado,-a; (sincere, open) sincero,-a, franco,-a, abierto,-a. 2 (simple, easy) sencillo,-a, simple; (clear) claro,-a: *it's quite straightforward*, es bastante sencillo; *in straightforward language*, en lenguaje llano.

　　　　　　　　　　　　　　　　　　strawberry

strain¹ [streɪn] **1** *n* (*race, breed*) raza; (*descent*) linaje *m*; (*of plant, virus*) cepa. **2** (*streak*) vena: *a strain of madness,* una vena de loco.

strain² [streɪn] **1** *n* PHYS (*tension*) tensión *f*; (*pressure*) presión *f*; (*weight*) peso: *the rope broke under the strain,* la cuerda se rompió debido a la tensión; *breaking strain,* tensión máxima. **2** (*stress, pressure*) tensión *f*, estrés *m*; (*effort*) esfuerzo; (*exhaustion*) agotamiento: *she's been under a lot of strain lately,* ha estado sometida a muchas tensiones últimamente; *the move put a lot of strain on them,* la mudanza los sometió a muchas tensiones; *I find it a constant strain,* me resulta un esfuerzo continuo; *mental strain,* tensión nerviosa. **3** (*tension*) tirantez *f*, tensión *f*: *the latest crisis has put more strain on Franco-Spanish relations,* la última crisis ha aumentado la tirantez en las relaciones francoespañolas. **4** MED torcedura, esguince *m*. – **5** *t* (*stretch*) estirar, tensar. **6** (*damage, weaken - muscle*) torcer(se), hacerse un esguince en; (- *back*) hacerse daño en; (- *voice, eyes*) forzar; (*ears*) aguzar; (- *heart*) cansar: *I strained my back,* me hice daño en la espalda; *she strained her ears to hear,* aguzó el oído para escuchar. **7** (*stretch - patience, nerves, credulity*) poner a prueba; (- *resources*) estirar al máximo; (- *relations*) someter a demasiada tensión, crear tirantez en: *it strained my patience,* puso a prueba mi paciencia; *he strained his authority,* abusó de su autoridad. **8** (*filter - liquid*) colar; (- *vegetables, rice*) escurrir. – **9** *i* (*make great efforts*) esforzarse, hacer un gran esfuerzo. – **10 strains,** *npl* MUS son *m* *sing,* compás *m* *sing.*

◆ **to strain at** *t* *insep* tirar de.

● **to strain at the leash,** tirar de la correa. ‖ **to strain os.,** esforzarse: *don't strain yourself,* ¡no te esfuerces!

strained [streɪnd] **1** *adj* (*tense, unfriendly*) tenso,-a, tirante; (*unnatural, forced, artificial*) forzado,-a. **2** (*stressed, anxious*) tenso,-a, estresado,-a; (*tires*) cansado,-a; (*eyes, voice*) forzado,-a.

■ **strained muscle,** esguince *m.*

strainer [ˈstreɪnəʳ] *n* colador *m.*

strait [streɪt] **1** *n* GEOG estrecho. – **2 straits,** *npl* (*difficulties*) aprietos *mpl,* apuros *mpl.*

● **to be in dire straits / be in desperate straits,** estar en un gran aprieto. ‖ **to be in financial straits,** pasar apuros económicos.

straitened [ˈstreɪtənd] **to be in straitened circumstances,** *phr* *fml* pasar estrecheces, pasar apuros.

straitjacket [ˈstreɪtdʒækɪt] **1** *n* camisa de fuerza. **2** *fig* control *m,* limitaciones *fpl.*

strait-laced [streɪtˈleɪst] *adj* *pej* puritano,-a, remilgado,-a, mojigato,-a.

strand¹ [strænd] *n* *lit* (*beach*) playa.

strand² [strænd] **1** *n* (*of thread*) hebra, hilo; (*of rope, string*) ramal *m;* (*of hair*) pelo; (*of pearls*) sarta. **2** *fig* (*of story, argument*) hilo, línea.

strand³ [strænd] **1** *t* MAR (*ship, whale, fish*) varar. **2** *fig* (*person*) abandonar.

● **to be (left) stranded,** (*boat etc*) quedar varado,-a, quedar encallado,-a; (*person*) quedarse varado,-a, quedarse colgado,-a. ‖ **to leave sb. stranded,** abandonar a algn., dejar a algn. en la estacada, dejar a algn. tirado,-a.

strange [streɪndʒ] **1** *adj* (*odd, bizarre*) extraño,-a, raro,-a: *it's strange that she hasn't arrived yet,* es extraño que no aún haya llegado; *how strange!,* ¡qué raro!; *what strange clothes he's wearing!,* ¡qué ropa más rara lleva!; *I feel a bit strange,* me encuentro un poco raro; *the strange thing is that no-one said anything,* lo raro es que nadie dijera nada. **2** (*unknown*) desconocido,-a; (*unfa-*

miliar) nuevo,-a: *strange people,* gente desconocida; *he was strange to the job,* no estaba acostumbrado al trabajo.

● **strange to say,** aunque parezca mentira.

strangely [ˈstreɪndʒlɪ] *adv* extrañamente, de forma extraña: *strangely enough,* aunque parezca extraño.

strangeness [ˈstreɪndʒnəs] **1** *n* (*oddness*) rareza, extrañeza. **2** (*newness*) novedad *f.*

stranger [ˈstreɪndʒəʳ] *n* (*unknown person*) extraño,-a, desconocido,-a; (*outsider*) forastero,-a.

● **to be no stranger to sth.,** conocer algo bastante bien, no serle desconocido,-a algo a algn.

strangle [ˈstræŋgəl] **1** *t* (*kill*) estrangular. **2** *fig* (*stifle*) sofocar, ahogar: *this collar is strangling me!,* ¡el cuello de esta camisa me está ahogando!

strangled [ˈstræŋgəld] *adj* (*cry etc*) ahogado,-a.

stranglehold [ˈstræŋgəlhəʊld] **1** *n* SP (*wrestling*) llave *f* al cuello. **2** *pej* (*firm control*) poder *m,* dominio.

● **to have a stranglehold on sb.,** tener a algn. dominado,-a.

strangler [ˈstræŋgələʳ] *n* estrangulador,-ra.

strangulate [ˈstræŋgjəleɪt] *t* MED estrangular.

strangulation [stræŋgjəˈleɪʃən] *n* estrangulación *f.*

strap [stræp] **1** *n* (*on watch, camera*) correa; (*on bag*) asa; (*on shoe*) tira; (*on dress etc*) tirante *m*: *I bought a watch strap,* compré una correa de reloj. – **2** *t* (*fasten*) atar con correa. **3** (*bandage*) vendar.

● **to give sb. the strap,** azotar a algn. con correa, darle a algn. con la correa. ‖ **to strap os. in,** ponerse el cinturón de seguridad.

▲ (*verbo*) *pt* & *pp* **strapped,** *ger* **strapping.**

strapless [ˈstræpləs] *adj* sin tirantes.

strapping [ˈstræpɪn] *adj* (*big, strong*) fornido,-a, robusto,-a.

Strasbourg [ˈstræzbʊəg] *n* Estrasburgo.

strata [ˈstrɑːtə] *npl* → **stratum.**

stratagem [ˈstrætədʒəm] *n* estratagema.

strategic [strəˈtiːdʒɪk] *adj* estratégico,-a.

strategical [strəˈtiːdʒɪkəl] *adj* estratégico,-a.

strategist [ˈstrætədʒɪst] *n* estratega *mf.*

strategy [ˈstrætədʒɪ] *n* estrategia.

▲ *pl* **strategies.**

stratification [strætɪfɪˈkeɪʃən] *n* estratificación *f.*

stratify [ˈstrætɪfaɪ] *t* estratificar.

▲ *pt* & *pp* **stratified,** *ger* **stratifying.**

stratosphere [ˈstrætəsfɪəʳ] *n* estratosfera.

stratum [ˈstrɑːtəm] **1** *n* GEOL estrato. **2** (*level, class*) estrato, nivel *m.*

▲ *pl* **strata.**

straw [strɔː] **1** *n* (*dried stalk(s)*) paja. **2** (*for drinking*) paja, pajita. – **3** *adj* de paja.

● **a straw in the wind,** un indicio de cómo pueden ir las cosas. ‖ **that's the last straw!,** ¡eso ya es el colmo!, ¡lo que faltaba para el duro! ‖ **the straw that broke the camel's back,** la gota que colmó el vaso. ‖ **to clutch/grasp at straws,** agarrarse a un clavo ardiente/aferrarse a una esperanza vana. ‖ **to draw/get the short straw,** tocarle a uno bailar con la más fea. ‖ **to not care/give a straw for sth.,** importarle algo un pepino/bledo a uno.

■ **straw hat,** sombrero de paja. ‖ **straw man,** hombre de paja. ‖ **straw poll / straw vote,** US POL sondeo informal de opinión.

strawberry [ˈstrɔːbərɪ] *n* (*gen*) fresa; (*large*) fresón *m.*

■ **strawberry blonde,** (*colour*) rubio rojizo; (*person*) pelirroja. ‖ **strawberry jam,** mermelada de fresa. ‖

strawberry mark, antojo. ‖ strawberry tree, madroño.

▲ *pl* strawberries.

straw-coloured [ˈstrɔːkʌləd] *adj* pajizo,-a, de color de paja.

stray [streɪ] **1** *adj* (*lost*) perdido,-a, extraviado,-a; (*animal*) callejero,-a. **2** (*isolated, odd*) perdido,-a: *stray bullet,* bala perdida; *a few stray tourists,* algún que otro turista; *a few stray hairs,* algunos pelos sueltos. – **3** *n* (*animal*) animal *m* extraviado. – **4** *i* (*get lost*) extraviarse, perderse; (*wander away*) desviarse, apartarse, alejarse; (*from group*) separarse, apartarse, alejarse: *I don't want you straying off on your own,* no quiero que te separes del grupo; *some sheep have strayed from the flock,* algunas ovejas se han descarriado; *they strayed from the path,* se desviaron del camino. **5** *fig* (*digress, wander*) divagar, apartarse del tema, desviarse del tema: *he strayed away from the subject,* se desviaba del tema; *let your thoughts stray,* deja vagar tus pensamientos; *my eyes kept straying from the page,* mis ojos no hacían más que apartarse de la página.

■ streak of lightning, rayo, relámpago.

streak [striːk] **1** *n* (*line - gen*) raya, lista; (- *in mineral*) veta, filón *m*, vena; (- *in hair*) mecha; (- *in meat*) veta, nervio. **2** (*element of genius, madness, etc*) vena: *mad streak,* vena de locura; *mean streak,* lado mezquino, vena mezquina. **3** (*period*) racha: *winning streak,* buena racha; *losing streak,* mala racha. – **4** *t* (*mark with streaks*) rayar, surcar (**with**, de): *a face streaked with tears,* una cara surcada de lágrimas; *white marble streaked with grey,* mármol blanco con vetas grises; *I've had my hair streaked,* me he hecho mechas (en el pelo). – **5** *i* (*move fast*) pasar como un rayo. **6** (*run naked*) correr desnudo,-a por un lugar público.

■ streak of lightning, rayo, relámpago.

streaker [ˈstriːkə^r] *n* persona que corre desnuda por un lugar público.

streaky [ˈstriːkɪ] *adj* (*hair*) con mechas desiguales; (*paint*) no uniforme.

■ streaky bacon, GB CULIN tocino entreverado.

▲ *comp* streakier, *superl* streakiest.

stream [striːm] **1** *n* (*brook*) arroyo, riachuelo. **2** (*current*) corriente *f*. **3** (*flow of liquid*) flujo, chorro, río; (*of blood, air*) chorro; (*of lava, tears*) torrente *m*; (*of light*) raudal *m*. **4** *fig* (*of people*) oleada, torrente *m*; (*of vehicles, traffic*) desfile *m* continuo, caravana; (*of abuse, excuses, insults*) torrente *m*, sarta. **5** GB EDUC clase *f*, grupo, nivel *m* (*de alumnos seleccionados según su nivel académico*). – **6** *i* (*flow, pour out*) manar, correr, chorrear; (*gush*) salir a chorros: *tears streamed down her face,* las lágrimas le corrían por la cara; *blood was streaming from the wound,* salía mucha sangre de la herida; *the sun streamed through the window,* el sol entraba a raudales por la ventana; *a streaming cold,* un catarro muy fuerte. **7** *fig* (*people, vehicles, etc*) desfilar: *people streamed out of the station,* la gente salía a raudales de la estación. **8** (*hair, banner, scarf*) ondear. – **9** *t* (*liquid*) derramar. **10** GB EDUC poner en grupos según su nivel académico.

■ stream of consciousness, monólogo interior.

streamer [ˈstriːmə^r] *n* (*decoration*) serpentina; (*flag*) banderín *m*.

streaming [ˈstriːmɪŋ] *n* GB EDUC selección *f* por niveles.

streamline [ˈstriːmlaɪn] **1** *n* (*contour*) línea aerodinámica. – **2** *t* (*car*) aerodinamizar. **3** (*system, method, organization*) racionalizar.

streamlined [ˈstriːmlaɪnd] **1** *adj* (*car*) de líneas aerodinámicas. **2** (*organization*) racionalizado,-a.

street [striːt] *n* calle *f*: *we were walking down the street,* íbamos por la calle; *it's just across the street,* está al otro lado de la calle; *there's a bank in the High Street,* hay un banco en la calle mayor.

● at street level, a nivel de la calle. ‖ not to be in the same street as sb., no llegarle a algn. a la suela del zapato. ‖ to be right up sb.'s street, venirle a algn. de perlas, ser ideal para algn. ‖ to walk the streets, (*homeless*) estar sin vivienda, estar sin techo; (*prostitute*) hacer la carrera, trabajar la calle. ‖ to be streets ahead of sb., dar cien vueltas a sb.

■ one-way street, calle de sentido único. ‖ street corner, esquina. ‖ street credibilty / street cred, imagen *f; wearing white socks will do nothing for your street cred,* los calcetines blancos no mejoran en nada tu imagen. ‖ street directory, guía de calles, callejero. ‖ street lighting, alumbrado público. ‖ street map, plano de la ciudad. ‖ street plan, plano de la ciudad. ‖ street market, mercadillo. ‖ street theatre, teatro callejero. ‖ street musician, músico,-a callejero,-a. ‖ street value, valor *m* (en el mercado).

streetcar [ˈstriːtkaː^r] *n* US tranvía.

streetlamp [ˈstriːtlæmp] *n* farol *m*, farola.

streetlight [ˈstriːtlaɪt] *n* farol *m*, farola.

streetwalker [ˈstriːtwɔːkə^r] *n* prostituta callejera.

streetwise [ˈstriːtwaɪz] *adj fam* espabilado,-a, despabilado,-a, avispado,-a.

strength [streŋθ] **1** *n* (*of person - physical*) fuerza, fuerzas *fpl*, fortaleza; (- *stamina*) resistencia, aguante *m*: *you should eat spinach to build up your strength,* deberías comer espinacas para aumentar tu fuerza; *he pushed with all his strength,* empujó con todas sus fuerzas; *we need to get our strength back,* necesitamos recobrar las fuerzas; *by sheer strength,* a viva fuerza. **2** (*intellectual, spiritual*) fortaleza, entereza, firmeza: *he showed great strength of character,* demostró gran fortaleza de carácter; *strength of will,* fuerza de voluntad. **3** (*of machine, object*) resistencia; (*of wind, current*) fuerza; (*of light, sound, magnet, lens*) potencia. **4** (*of solution*) concentración *f*; (*of drug*) potencia; (*of alcohol*) graduación *f*. **5** (*of currency*) valor *m*, fortaleza; (*of economy*) solidez *f*, fortaleza. **6** (*of argument, evidence, story*) fuerza, validez *f*, credibilidad *f*; (*of emotion, conviction, colour*) intensidad *f*; (*of protest*) energía: *her statement lends strength to his story,* su declaración da credibilidad a su historia. **7** (*strong point*) punto fuerte, virtud *f*; (*ability, capability*) capacidad *f*; (*advantage*) ventaja: *her strength as a teacher lies in her patience,* su capacidad como profesora estriba en su paciencia; *tolerance is one of his many strengths,* la tolerancia es uno de sus muchos fuertes; *unity is their strength,* la unidad es su punto fuerte; *the strengths and weaknesses of the film,* las virtudes y defectos de la película. **8** (*power, influence*) poder *m*, potencia: *the strength of the miners,* el poder de los mineros. **9** (*force in numbers*) fuerza numérica, número: *the strength of the workforce,* el número de trabajadores.

● in great strength, en gran número. ‖ to be on the strength, (*be a member*) formar parte del personal. ‖ to do sth. on the strength of sth., hacer algo basándose en algo. ‖ to be at full strength, estar con la plantilla completa. ‖ to be under strength, estar corto,-a de personal. ‖ to go from strength to strength, ir ganando fuerzas, marchar viento en popa.

■ strength of feeling, ánimos *mpl: there is great strength of feeling over this issue,* los ánimos están exacerbados por este tema.

strengthen [ˈstreŋθən] **1** *t* (*wall, glass, defence, etc*) reforzar; (*muscle*) fortalecer. **2** (*character, faith, love*) fortalecer; (*support*) aumentar; (*relationship, ties*) consolidar, fortalecer; (*resolve, determination*) redoblar, intensificar. – **3** *i* (*muscle*) fortalecerse. **4** (*economy, currency*) reforzarse, fortalecerse; (*relationship*) consolidarse, reforzarse, fortalecerse; (*support, opposition, feeling*) intensificarse, aumentar.

strenuous ['strenjʊəs] **1** *adj* (*requiring effort*) extenuante, fatigoso,-a, agotador,-ra. **2** (*denial*) enérgico,-a, vigoroso,-a; (*protest*) vehemente; (*opposition*) tenaz; (*supporter*) acérrimo,-a.

strenuously ['strenjʊəslɪ] *adv* enérgicamente, vigorosamente.

stress [stres] **1** *n* MED tensión *f* (nerviosa), estrés *m*: *he's under a lot of stress,* está muy estresado; *his problems are stress related,* sus problemas están relacionados con el estrés. **2** (*pressure*) presión *f*, tensión *f*: *the stresses and strains of modern life,* las tensiones y presiones de la vida moderna. **3** TECH tensión *f*. **4** (*emphasis*) hincapié *m* (**on**, en), énfasis *m* (**on**, en). **5** LING (*on word*) acento (tónico). – **6** *t* (*emphasize*) hacer hincapié en, poner énfasis en, subrayar, enfatizar. **7** LING (*word*) acentuar.
● **to lay great stress on sth.,** hacer mucho hincapié en algo, poner mucho énfasis en algo.
■ **stress mark,** acento.

stressed [strest] **1** *adj* MED (*person*) estresado,-a. **2** PHYS (*object*) tensado,-a.
● **to be stressed out,** sufrir del estrés, estar estresado,-a.

stressful ['stresfʊl] *adj* estresante, de mucho estrés.

stretch [stretʃ] **1** *n* (*of land, water*) extensión *f*; (*of road*) tramo, trecho: *a beautiful stretch of coastline,* un hermoso trecho de costa. **2** (*elasticity*) elasticidad *f*. **3** (*act of stretching*) estiramiento: *he had a good stretch,* se estiró, se desperezó. **4** (*period of time*) período, tiempo, intervalo; (*in prison*) condena: *he did a two-year stretch for robbery,* cumplió condena de dos años por robo. **5** SP (*of race track*) recta. – **6** *t* (*extend - elastic, clothes, rope*) estirar; (*- canvas*) extender; (*- shoes*) ensanchar; (*- arm, leg*) alargar, estirar, extender; (*- wings*) desplegar, extender. **7** (*make demands on, made to use all abilities*) exigir a: *he's not being stretched at school,* no le exigen lo suficiente en la escuela; *I like being stretched in my job,* me gusta que me exijan en mi trabajo. **8** (*strain - money, resources*) estirar, emplear al máximo; (*- patience*) abusar; (*- meaning*) forzar, distorsionar: *you're stretching my patience,* estás abusando de mi paciencia; *it's stretching it a bit to say it's brilliant,* decir que es brillante es exagerar. – **9** *i* (*elastic*) estirarse; (*fabric*) dar de sí; (*shoes*) ensancharse, dar de sí; (*person, animal - gen*) estirarse; (*person - when tired*) desperezarse. **10** (*extend - land, sea, etc*) extenderse (**out**, -); (*- in time*) alargarse, prolongarse: *the beach stretches for miles and miles,* la playa se extiende a lo largo de millas y millas. **11** (*reach*) llegar (**to,** para), alcanzar (**to,** para). – **12** *adj* (*material, jeans, etc*) elástico,-a.
◆ **to stretch out 1** *i* (*person - gen*) estirarse; (*- lie down*) tumbarse. – **2** *t sep* (*arm, leg*) alargar, estirar, extender. **3** (*money, resources*) estirar.
● **to stretch a point,** hacer una excepción. ‖ **to stretch one's legs,** (*walk*) estirar las piernas. ‖ **at a stretch,** de un tirón, sin parar. ‖ **at full stretch,** a tope, al máximo. ‖ **not by any stretch of the imagination,** de ningún modo, ni por asomo.

stretcher ['stretʃəʳ] *n* camilla.

stretcher-bearer ['stretʃəbeərəʳ] *n* camillero,-a.

stretchmarks ['stretʃmɑːks] *n* estrías *fpl*.

stretchy ['stretʃɪ] *adj* elástico,-a.
▲ *comp* **stretchier,** *superl* **stretchier.**

strew [struː] *t lit* (*scatter*) esparcir, desparramar; (*lie scattered*) sembrar, cubrir: *papers were strewn all over the floor,* había papeles desparramados por todo el suelo.
● **to be strewn with sth.,** (*conversation*) estar lleno,-a de algo.
▲ *pp* **strewed** *o* **strewn** [struːn].

striated [straɪ'eɪtɪd] *adj* estriado,-a.

striation [straɪ'eɪʃən] *n* (*state*) estriación *f*; (*stripe*) estría.

stricken ['strɪkən] **1** *adj* (*afflicted - with grief*) afligido,-a, acongojado,-a; (*- with illness*) aquejado,-a; (*- by disaster*) afectado,-a, asolado,-a: *she was stricken with remorse,* le remordió mucho la conciencia. **2** (*damaged*) destrozado,-a.

strict [strɪkt] **1** *adj* (*severe - person*) severo,-a, estricto,-a; (*- discipline*) riguroso,-a, severo,-a, estricto,-a; (*- rule, law, order, etc*) estricto,-a, riguroso,-a, rígido,-a: *they're strict vegetarians,* son vegetarianos estrictos; *a strict upbringing,* una educación estricta. **2** (*exact, precise*) estricto,-a, riguroso,-a; (*complete, total*) absoluto,-a: *in the strict sense of the word,* en el sentido estricto de la palabra; *in strict secrecy,* en el más absoluto secreto; *in the strictest confidence,* en la más absoluta confianza.

strictly ['strɪktlɪ] **1** *adv* (*severely*) severamente, estrictamente, de manera estricta. **2** (*rigorously, rigidly*) estrictamente; (*categorically*) terminantemente: *bathing is strictly prohibited,* bañarse está terminantemente prohibido. **3** (*exactly, precisely*) estrictamente, exactamente; (*completely*) totalmente, del todo, absolutamente: *to be strictly accurate,* para ser precisos; *strictly confidential,* absolutamente/estrictamente confidencial. **4** (*exclusively*) exclusivamente.
● **strictly speaking,** en rigor, en sentido estricto, en realidad.

strictness ['strɪktnəs] *n* (*severity*) severidad *f*; (*rigorousness*) rigurosidad *f*, rigidez *f*.

stride [straɪd] **1** *n* (*long step*) zancada; (*gait*) paso, manera de andar. **2** (*advance, development*) progresos *mpl*: *we're making great strides,* estamos haciendo grandes progresos. – **3** *i* andar a zancadas: *he strode into her office,* entró resueltamente en su oficina. – **4 strides,** *npl fam* (*trousers*) pantalón *m sing*, pantalones *mpl*.
● **to get into one's stride,** coger el ritmo. ‖ **to take sth. in one's stride,** tomarse algo con calma, tomarse algo muy bien.
▲ *pt* **strode,** *pp* **stridden** ['strɪdən].

strident ['straɪdənt] *adj* (*voice, sound*) estridente; (*protest*) fuerte.

strife [straɪf] *n* conflictos *mpl*, luchas *fpl*: *industrial strife,* conflictos laborales.

strike [straɪk] **1** *n* (*by workers, students, etc*) huelga. **2** SP (*blow - gen*) golpe *m*; (*- in tenpin bowling*) pleno; (*- in baseball*) strike *m*. **3** (*find*) hallazgo; (*of oil, gold, etc*) descubrimiento. **4** MIL ataque *m*: *air strike,* ataque aéreo. – **5** *t* (*hit*) pegar, golpear: *he struck her with the back of his hand,* le pegó con el dorso de la mano; *I struck the ball as hard as I could,* golpeé la pelota con todas mis fuerzas. **6** (*knock against, collide with*) dar contra, chocar contra; (*ball, stone*) pegar contra, dar contra; (*lightning, bullet, torpedo*) alcanzar: *he was struck on the head by a rock,* una roca le dio en la cabeza; *she struck her head against the low ceiling,* dio con la cabeza contra el techo bajo; *the tree was struck by lightning,* el árbol fue alcanzado por un rayo. **7** (*disaster, earthquake*) golpear, sobrevenir; (*disease*) atacar, golpear: *the town has been struck by tragedy,* el pueblo ha sido golpeado por la tragedia. **8** (*gold, oil*) descubrir, encontrar, dar con; (*track, path*) dar con. **9** (*coin, medal*) acuñar. **10** (*match*) encender. **11** (*of*

clock) dar, tocar: *the clock struck one,* el reloj dio la una. **12** MUS (*note*) dar; (*chord*) tocar. **13** (*bargain, deal*) cerrar, hacer; (*balance*) encontrar, hallar; (*agreement*) llegar a: *he struck a bargain with the owner,* hizo un trato con el propietario; *they've managed to strike a balance,* han logrado encontrar un punto medio. **14** (*pose, attitude*) adoptar. **15** (*give impression*) parecer, dar la impresión de: *Michael strikes me as a very sensible young man,* Michael me parece un joven muy sensato; *it struck me as strange that ...,* me pareció muy extraño que ... **16** (*occur to*) ocurrírsele a; (*remember*) acordarse de: *a terrible thought struck me,* se me ocurrió algo terrible; *it suddenly struck her that it was their anniversary,* de repente se acordó de que era su aniversario. **17** (*render*) dejar: *he was struck dumb,* se quedó mudo. **18** (*cause fear, terror, worry*) infundir: *the scream struck terror into them,* el grito les infundió terror. **19** (*take down - sail, flag*) arriar; (*- tent, set*) desmontar. **20** (*cutting*) plantar. **– 21** *i* (*attack - troops, animal, etc*) atacar; (*- disaster, misfortune*) sobrevenir, ocurrir; (*- disease*) atacar, golpear; (*- lightning*) alcanzar, caer: *the killer has struck again,* el asesino ha vuelto a atacar; *then disaster struck,* entonces sobrevino el desastre. **22** (*workers etc*) declararse en huelga, hacer huelga: *the air-traffic controllers threatened to strike,* los controladores aéreos amenazaron con hacer huelga; *they struck for more pay,* hicieron huelga por un aumento de sueldo. **23** (*clock*) dar la hora.
◆ **to strike back 1** *i* (*gen*) devolver el golpe. **2** MIL contraatacar. ‖ **to strike down** *t sep* (*by illness, disease*) abatir, fulminar. ‖ **to strike off 1** *t sep* (*name from list*) tachar. **2** JUR (*doctor, lawyer, etc*) inhabilitar para ejecer. ‖ **to strike on** *t insep* (*discover*) dar con, encontrar. ‖ **to strike out 1** *t sep* (*remove, cross out*) tachar. **– 2** *i* (*attack, hit out*) arremeter (**at**, contra). **3** (*set off*) emprender el camino. ‖ **to strike up 1** *t insep* (*friendship*) entablar, trabar; (*conversation*) entablar, iniciar. **– 2** *i* (*band*) empezar a tocar.
● **strike a light!,** ¡caray! ‖ **to be on strike,** estar en huelga. ‖ **to call a strike,** convocar una huelga. ‖ **to go on strike,** declararse en huelga. ‖ **to strike a chord,** sonarle a uno. ‖ **to strike a chord with sb.,** estar en sintonía con algn. ‖ **to strike a note of sth.,** expresar algo. ‖ **to strike at the heart of sth.,** dar con el meollo de algo. ‖ **to strike camp,** levantar el campamento. ‖ **to strike (it) lucky,** tener suerte. ‖ **to strike the eye,** saltar a la vista. ‖ **to strike out on one's own,** (*become independent*) volar con sus propias alas; (*set up own business*) ponerse a trabajar por su propia cuenta. ‖ **to strike it rich,** hacerse rico,-a. ‖ **to strike while the iron's hot,** actuar de inmediato. ‖ **within striking distance,** a un paso.
■ **general strike,** huelga general. ‖ **lucky strike,** golpe *m* de suerte. ‖ **sit-down strike,** sentada. ‖ **strike fund,** caja de resistencia. ‖ **strike pay,** subsidio de huelga.
▲ *pt & pp* **struck**.

strikebound [ˈstraɪkbaʊnd] *adj* paralizado,-a por una huelga.

strikebreaker [ˈstraɪkbreɪkəʳ] *n* esquirol *mf*, rompehuelgas *mf*.

striker [ˈstraɪkəʳ] **1** *n* IND huelguista *mf*. **2** SP (*football*) delantero,-a; (*cricket*) bateador,-ra.

striking [ˈstraɪkɪŋ] **1** *adj* (*eye-catching*) llamativo,-a; (*stunning*) atractivo,-a. **2** (*similarity, resemblance*) sorprendente, asombroso,-a; (*feature etc*) impresionante, destacado,-a. **3** (*on strike*) en huelga.

string [strɪŋ] **1** *n* (*cord*) cuerda, cordel *m*; (*lace*) cordón *m*; (*of puppet*) hilo. **2** (*on instrument, racket*) cuerda. **3** (*of garlic, onions*) ristra; (*of pearls, beads*) sarta, hilo. **4** (*of vehicles*) fila, hilera; (*of hotels*) cadena; (*of events*) serie *f*, cadena, sucesión *f*; (*of lies, complaints*) sarta; (*of insults*) retahíla: *a string of best sellers,* una serie de best-sellers; *a string of wins,* una serie de victorias. **– 5** *t* (*beads*) ensartar, enhebrar. **6** (*guitar, racket*) encordar. **7** (*beans*) quitar la hebra a. **– 8 the strings,** *npl* MUS los instrumentos *mpl* de cuerda.
◆ **to string along 1** *i* (*accompany*) pegarse, venir. **– 2** *t sep* (*mislead*) tomar el pelo a. ‖ **to string out** *t sep* (*spread in a line*) colocar a intervalos. ‖ **to string together** *t sep* (*words, phrases*) ensartar, hilar. ‖ **to string up** *t sep* (*hang*) colgar.
● **no strings attached,** sin (ningún) compromiso. ‖ **to have sb. on a string,** tener a algn. en un puño. ‖ **to have two strings to one's bow,** ser una persona de recursos. ‖ **to pull strings,** tocar teclas. ‖ **to pull strings for sb.,** enchufar a algn.
■ **string bag,** bolsa de red. ‖ **string band,** orquesta de cuerda. ‖ **string orchestra,** orquestra de cuerda. ‖ **string quartet,** cuarteto de cuerda. ‖ **string vest,** camiseta de malla.
▲ *pt & pp* **strung**.

stringed [strɪŋd] *adj* (*instrument*) de cuerda.

stringent [ˈstrɪndʒənt] **1** *adj* (*laws, rules, conditions*) severo,-a, estricto,-a, riguroso,-a. **2** FIN severo,-a, difícil: *a stringent economic climate,* un clima económico difícil.

string-pulling [ˈstrɪŋpʊlɪŋ] *n fam* enchufismo.

stringy [ˈstrɪŋɪ] **1** *adj* (*beans*) fibroso,-a, con hebras; (*meat*) nervudo,-a. **2** (*hair*) greñudo,-a. **3** (*person, arms*) nervudo,-a.
▲ *comp* **stringier**, *superl* **stringiest**.

strip¹ [strɪp] **1** *t* (*person*) desnudar, quitarle la ropa a; (*bed*) quitar la ropa de; (*room, house*) vaciar; (*wallpaper, paint*) quitar; (*leaves, bark*) arrancar: *he was stripped and searched,* lo desnudaron y cachearon; *we'll have to strip the paint (off) first,* primero tendremos que quitar la pintura; *the thieves stripped the house bare,* los ladrones desvalijaron la casa. **2** (*property, rights, titles*) despojar (**of**, de): *the major was stripped of his rank,* el comandante fue despojado de su graduación. **3** (*engine*) desarmar, desmontar (**down**, -); (*ship*) desaparejar. **– 4** *i* (*undress*) desnudarse (**off**, -), quitarse la ropa; (*perform striptease*) hacer un striptease. **– 5** *n* (*striptease*) striptease *m*.
● **to strip sb. naked,** desnudar a algn. ‖ **to strip to the buff,** desnudarse (completamente).
■ **strip club / strip joint,** club *m* de striptease. ‖ **strip poker,** variedad del póquer en la que los jugadores, al perder, se van quitando la ropa. ‖ **strip search,** cacheo obligando a desnudarse.
▲ *pt & pp* **stripped**, *ger* **stripping**.

strip² [strɪp] **1** *n* (*of paper, leather*) tira; (*of land*) franja; (*of metal*) tira, cinta. **2** SP (*colours, kit*) equipo. **3** (*airstrip*) pista (de aterrizaje). **4 strip (cartoon),** (*cartoon*) historieta, tira cómica.
■ **strip lighting,** alumbrado fluorescente. ‖ **strip mining,** US explotación *f* a cielo abierto.

stripe [straɪp] **1** *n* (*gen*) raya, lista: *our cat is black with a white stripe,* nuestro gato es negro con una raya negra. **2** MIL galón *m*. **3** (*kind, type*) tipo, clase *f*. **– 4** *t* pintar a rayas, dibujar a rayas.

striped [straɪpt] *adj* rayado,-a, a rayas: *a striped shirt,* una camisa a rayas.

stripper [ˈstrɪpəʳ] **1** *n* (*person*) artista *mf* de striptease. **2** (*liquid*) quitapinturas *m*; (*tool*) rasqueta.

striptease [ˈstrɪpˈtiːz] *n* striptease *m*.

stripy [ˈstraɪpɪ] *adj* rayado,-a, a rayas.
▲ *comp* **stripier**, *superl* **stripiest**.

strive [straɪv] *i* esforzarse, procurar.
● **to strive after/for sth.**, esforzarse por conseguir algo.
▲ *pt* **strove**, *pp* **striven** ['strɪvən].
strobe [strəʊb] *n* estroboscopio.
■ **strobe lighting**, luces *fpl* estroboscópicas.
strode [strəʊd] *pt* → **stride**.
stroke [strəʊk] **1** *n* (*blow*) golpe *m*: *a stroke of the cane*, un palmetazo; *a stroke of the whip*, un latigazo; *a stroke of the axe*, un hachazo. **2** (*caress*) caricia. **3** SP (*in tennis, cricket, golf*) golpe *m*, jugada; (*in billiards*) tacada; (*in rowing*) remada; (*in swimming - movement*) brazada; (*- style*) estilo. **4** SP (*oarsman*) cabo. **5** (*of pen*) trazo; (*of brush*) pincelada. **6** (*of bell*) campanada: *on the stroke of midnight*, al dar las doce de la noche. **7** (*of engine*) tiempo; (*of piston*) carrera. **8** MED ataque *m* de apoplejía, derrame *m* cerebral. **9** (*oblique*) barra (oblicua). – **10** *t* (*caress*) acariciar: *she stroked the cat*, acarició el gato. **11** (*ball*) dar un golpe a.
● **at a/one stroke**, de (un) golpe, de un plumazo. ‖ **a stroke of genius**, una genialidad *f*. ‖ **a stroke of luck**, un golpe *m* de suerte. ‖ **to not do a stroke of work**, no dar golpe, no pegar golpe. ‖ **to put sb. off their stroke**, distraer a algn.
stroll [strəʊl] **1** *n* paseo, vuelta. – **2** *i* pasear, dar un paseo, dar una vuelta.
● **to go for a stroll**, dar un paseo, dar una vuelta.
stroller ['strəʊləʳ] **1** *n* (*pushchair*) cochecito, sillita de niño. **2** (*person*) paseante *mf*.
strong [strɒŋ] **1** *adj* (*physically - person*) fuerte; (*- consitution*) robusto,-a: *you're not strong enough*, no tienes bastante fuerza. **2** (*material, furniture, shoes, etc*) fuerte, resistente. **3** (*country, army*) poderoso,-a, fuerte. **4** (*beliefs, views, principles*) firme; (*faith*) firme, sólido,-a; (*support*) mucho, firme. **5** (*argument, evidence*) contundente, convincente; (*influence*) grande; (*protest*) enérgico,-a. **6** (*colour*) fuerte, intenso,-a, vivo,-a; (*food, drink*) fuerte; (*tea, coffee*) fuerte, cargado,-a; (*light*) brillante. **7** (*resemblance, accent*) fuerte, marcado,-a. **8** (*chance, likelihood, probability*) bueno,-a: *she's in with a strong chance*, tiene muchas posibilidades. **9** (*wind, current*) fuerte. **10** (*good - team*) fuerte; (*- cast*) sólido,-a. **11** COMM FIN (*currency etc*) fuerte, en alza. – **12** *adv* fuerte.
● **to be as strong as a horse/an ox**, ser fuerte como un toro/un roble. ‖ **to be going strong**, (*business*) ir fuerte; (*machine etc*) marchar bien; (*elderly person*) estar en plena forma. ‖ **to be strong on sth.**, ser bueno,-a en algo. ‖ **to be 20 (etc) strong**, (*of team etc*) contar con 20 (etc) miembros. ‖ **to have a strong stomach**, tener buen estómago.
■ **strong language**, palabras *fpl* duras, lenguaje *m* fuerte. ‖ **strong point**, fuerte *m*. ‖ **strong room**, cámara acorazada.
strong-arm ['strɒŋɑːm] *adj* de mano dura.
strongbox ['strɒŋbɒks] *n* caja fuerte.
stronghold ['strɒŋhəʊld] **1** *n* MIL fortaleza. **2** *fig* baluarte *m*.
strongly ['strɒŋlɪ] **1** *adv* (*solidly*) sólidamente. **2** (*firmly*) firmemente; (*completely*) totalmente, profundamente; (*fervently*) con fervor, con ardor; (*forcefully*) enérgicamente, con insistencia: *the exhibition is strongly recommended*, recomiendan mucho la exposición; *I'm strongly in favour of the proposal*, estoy totalmente a favor de la propuesta; *he strongly advised me to buy the property*, me recomendó con insistencia que comprara la propiedad. **3** (*intensely*) mucho, muy: *it smells strongly of mint*, huele mucho a menta.

● **to be strongly built**, ser de complexión fuerte. ‖ **to feel strongly about sth.**, tener opiniones muy contundentes acerca de algo.
strongly-worded [strɒŋlɪ'wɜːdɪd] *adj* (*letter*) duro,-a.
strong-minded [strɒŋ'maɪndɪd] *adj* resuelto,-a, decidido,-a.
strongroom ['strɒŋruːm] *n* cámara acorazada.
strong-willed ['strɒŋ'wɪld] *adj* tenaz, decidido,-a, obstinado,-a.
strontium ['strɒntɪəm] *n* estroncio.
stroppy ['strɒpɪ] *adj* GB *fam* borde, de mala uva.
▲ *comp* **stroppier**, *superl* **stroppiest**.
strove [strəʊv] *pt* → **strive**.
struck [strʌk] *pt & pp* → **strike**.
● **to be struck on sb.**, estar loco,-a por algn.
structural ['strʌktʃərəl] *adj* (*gen*) estructural.
■ **structural engineer**, ingeniero,-a de estructuras. ‖ **structural fault**, defecto de construcción.
structuralism ['strʌktʃərəlɪzəm] *n* estructuralismo.
structuralist ['strʌktʃərəlɪst] **1** *n* estructuralista *mf*. – **2** *adj* estructuralista.
structure ['strʌktʃəʳ] **1** *n* (*organization, composition*) estructura. **2** (*thing constructed*) construcción *f*; (*building*) edificio. – **3** *t* (*arguemnt, essay, report, etc*) estructurar; (*event*) planificar.
struggle ['strʌgəl] **1** *n* (*gen*) lucha; (*physical fight*) pelea, forcejeo: *she put up a real struggle*, opuso mucha resistencia; *they gave in without a struggle*, se dieron por vencidos sin oponer resistencia; *it was a struggle to bring up two children on my own*, me costó mucho criar a dos niños yo sola; *it's a struggle to make ends meet*, cuesta Dios y ayuda llegar a fin de mes. – **2** *i* (*fight*) luchar; (*physically*) forcejear: *he struggled to get loose*, luchó por liberarse; *she struggled with her assailant*, forcejeó con su asaltante. **3** (*strive*) luchar (**for**, por), esforzarse (**for**, por); (*suffer*) pasar apuros; (*have difficulty*) costar, tener problemas: *a country struggling for independence*, un país que lucha por la independencia. **4** (*move with difficulty*) con dificultad: *he struggled to his feet*, se levantó con dificultad; *she struggled up the stairs*, subió la escalera con dificultad.
■ **armed struggle**, lucha armada. ‖ **class struggle**, lucha de clases.
strum [strʌm] **1** *t* rasguear. – **2** *i* rasguear (**on**, -).
▲ *pt & pp* **strummed**, *ger* **strumming**.
strung [strʌŋ] *pt & pp* → **string**.
● **to be highly strung**, estar muy nervioso,-a, estar muy tenso,-a.
strut [strʌt] **1** *n* ARCH (*rod, bar*) puntal *m*, riostra. **2** (*way of walking*) contoneo, pavoneo. – **3** *i* pavonearse, contonearse: *the peacock strutted in front of us*, el pavo real se contoneaba delante nuestro; *Jagger struts around the stage*, Jagger se pavonea por el escenario.
▲ *pt & pp* **strutted**, *ger* **strutting**.
strychnine ['strɪkniːn] *n* estricnina.
stub [stʌb] *n* (*of cigarette*) colilla; (*of pencil, candle*) cabo; (*of cheque etc*) matriz *f*.
◆ **to stub out** *t sep* apagar.
● **to stub one's toe on sth.**, darse con el dedo del pie contra algo.
▲ *pt & pp* **stubbed**, *ger* **stubbing**.
stubble ['stʌbəl] **1** *n* (*in field*) rastrojo. **2** (*on chin*) barba incipiente.
stubborn ['stʌbən] **1** *adj* (*person, animal*) terco,-a, testarudo,-a, tozudo,-a, obstinado,-a; (*refusal, resistance*) obcecado,-a. **2** (*stain, cough, etc*) rebelde.

stubbornness ['stʌbənnəs] *n* testarudez *f*, terquedad *f*, tozudez *f*, obstinación *f*.

stubby ['stʌbɪ] *adj* corto,-a y rechoncho,-a: *stubby fingers*, dedos regordetes; *a stubby tail*, un rabo cortito y gordito.
▲ *comp* **stubbier**, *superl* **stubbiest**.

stucco ['stʌkəʊ] *n* estuco.
▲ *pl* **stuccoes** *o* **stuccos**.

stuck [stʌk] **1** *pt & pp* → **stick**. – **2** *adj* (*not able to move*) atascado,-a: *the drawer's got stuck*, el cajón se ha atascado; *the car was stuck in the mud*, el coche estaba atascado en el fango; *the lift got stuck between floors*, el ascensor se quedó atascado entre dos plantas. **3** (*trapped*) atrapado,-a; (*in routine*) estancado,-a: *I got stuck in a traffic jam*, me quedé atrapado en un atasco; *she's stuck at home all day*, está metida en casa todo el día. **4** *fam* (*stumped*) atascado,-a; (*in difficulties*) en apuros: *he's stuck on the third question*, está atascado en la tercera pregunta; *she's never stuck for an answer*, siempre tiene una respuesta.
● **to be stuck on sb.**, estar loco,-a por algn. ‖ **to get stuck with sb./sth.**, tener que cargar con algn./algo: *I got stuck with my niece*, tuve que cargar con mi sobrina. ‖ **to get stuck in/into sth.**, (*work etc*) meterse de lleno en algo, emprender algo en serio; (*food*) atacar.

stuck-up [stʌk'ʌp] *adj fam* creído,-a, estirado,-a.

stud¹ [stʌd] **1** *n* (*on shirt*) gemelo; (*earring*) pendiente *m* (*en forma de bolita*). **2** (*on football boots*) taco; (*on clothing, belt*) tachuela, tachón *m*; (*on furniture*) tachuela; (*on shield*) tachón *m*; (*in road*) clavo. – **3** *t* (*decorate - with studs*) tachonar (**with**, de); (*- with jewels*) incrustar (**with**, de). **4** *fig* (*dot*) salpicar (**with**, de).
▲ (*verbo*) *pt & pp* **studded**, *ger* **studding**.

stud² [stʌd] **1** *n* (*animal*) semental *m*. **2** *pej* (*man*) semental *m*.
■ **stud farm**, cuadra, caballeriza.

studded ['stʌdɪd] *adj* (*sky*) tachonado,-a; (*speech etc*) salpicado,-a; (*crown*) con incrustaciones.

student ['stjuːdənt] **1** *n* (*university*) estudiante *mf*, universitario,-a; (*school*) alumno,-a. **2** *fml* (*scholar*) estudioso,-a. – **3** *adj* estudiantil.
■ **students' union**, (*association*) federación *f* de estudiantes; (*building*) sede *f* de la federación de estudiantes. ‖ **student nurse**, estudiante *mf* de enfermería. ‖ **student teacher**, profesor,-ra en prácticas.

studied ['stʌdɪd] *adj* (*style etc*) estudiado,-a, afectado,-a, falso,-a; (*insult, indifference, etc*) calculado,-a.

studio ['stjuːdɪəʊ] **1** *n* RAD TV estudio. **2** (*artist's*) estudio, taller *m*. – **3 studios**, *npl* CINEM estudios *mpl*.
■ **studio apartment / studio flat**, estudio. ‖ **studio audience**, público invitado. ‖ **studio couch**, sofá-cama *m*.
▲ *pl* **studios**.

studious ['stjuːdɪəs] **1** *adj* (*fond of studying*) estudioso,-a, aplicado,-a. **2** *fml* (*careful*) esmerado,-a; (*deliberate*) deliberado,-a.

studiously ['stjuːdɪəslɪ] *adv* deliberadamente, cuidadosamente.

study ['stʌdɪ] **1** *n* (*act of studying*) estudio; (*investigation, research*) investigación *f*, estudio: *she devotes a lot of time to study*, dedica mucho tiempo al estudio. **2** (*room*) despacho, estudio. – **3** *t* (*gen*) estudiar; (*university subject*) estudiar, cursar; (*investigate, research*) estudiar, investigar. **4** (*scrutinize*) estudiar, examinar. – **5** *i* estudiar: *he's studying to be a lawyer*, estudia para abogado; *they're studying for their exams*, están preparando los exámenes. – **6 studies**, *npl* (*work*) estudios *mpl*; (*subjects*) estudios *mpl*, asignaturas *fpl*.

■ **study group**, grupo de trabajo. ‖ **study guide**, manual *m* de estudio.
▲ (*sustantivo*) *pl* **studies**; (*verbo*) *pt & pp* **studied**.

stuff [stʌf] **1** *n fam* (*matter, material, substance*) materia, material *m*: *it's made of a kind of plastic stuff*, está hecho de un tipo de material plástico; *what's that stuff on your shirt?*, ¿qué es eso que tienes en la camisa?; *do you like cauliflower? - no, I can't stand the stuff*, ¿te gusta la coliflor? - no, no la aguanto; *do you call this stuff lasagne?*, ¿a esto lo llamas lasaña? **2** *fam* (*things, possesions*) cosas *fpl*, trastos *mpl*: *put your stuff over there*, pon tus cosas por allí. **3** *fam* (*content*) cuento, rollo, cosas *fpl*: *I've heard all that stuff before*, ya he oído todo ese rollo; *don't give me all that macho stuff!*, ¡no me vengas con esos cuentos de macho!; *we just talked about work and stuff*, sólo hablamos de trabajo y cosas por el estilo. – **4** *t* (*fill - container, bag, box*) llenar (**with**, de); (*- cushion, toy, food*) rellenar (**with**, de); (*- hole*) tapar: *have you stuffed the turkey?*, ¿has rellenado el pavo?; *we stuffed as much as we could in the car*, metimos cuanto pudimos en el coche; *he stuffed his pockets full of sweets*, se llenó los bolsillos de caramelos; *don't stuff her full of nonsense*, no la llenes de tonterías. **5** (*dead animal*) disecar. **6** (*push carelessly, shove*) meter, poner: *he stuffed the letter in his pocket*, metió la carta en el bolsillo. **7** *fam* (*beat, thrash*) dar una paliza a. **8** *sl* (*sod*) meter: *you can stuff your job!*, ¡métete el trabajo donde te quepa!
● **that's the stuff!**, ¡así es!, ¡así me gusta! ‖ **to do one's stuff**, hacer lo suyo. ‖ **to know one's stuff**, saber de lo que uno está hablando. ‖ **to stuff one's face**, hartarse de comida, atiborrarse, ponerse morado,-a.
■ **stuff and nonsense**, tonterías *fpl*.

stuffed [stʌft] **1** *adj* (*full*) relleno,-a; (*crammed*) atiborrado,-a: *peppers stuffed with mincemeat*, pimientos rellenos de carne picada; *I'm stuffed!*, ¡estoy lleno! **2** (*animal*) disecado,-a.
● **get stuffed!**, ¡vete a tomar por culo!, ¡vete a la porra!
■ **stuffed shirt**, estirado,-a. ‖ **stuffed toy**, muñeco de peluche.

stuffed up ['stʌftʌp] *adj* con la nariz tapada.
● **to be stuffed up**, estar congestionado,-a, estar acatarrado,-a. ‖ **to have a stuffed-up nose**, tener la nariz tapada.

stuffing ['stʌfɪŋ] *n* relleno.
● **to knock the stuffing out of sb.**, dejar hecho,-a polvo a algn.

stuffy ['stʌfɪ] **1** *adj* (*room*) mal ventilado,-a; (*atmosphere*) cargado,-a. **2** (*person*) estirado,-a, remilgado,-a; (*institution*) tradicional; (*ideas, manners*) formal, serio,-a, convencional.
▲ *comp* **stuffier**, *superl* **stuffiest**.

stultify ['stʌltɪfaɪ] **1** *t fml* (*make dull*) atrofiar. **2** *fml* (*negate*) anular, invalidar.
▲ *pt & pp* **stultified**, *ger* **stultifying**.

stumble ['stʌmbəl] **1** *n* tropezón *m*, traspié *m*, tropicón *m*. – **2** *i* (*trip*) tropezar (**on/over**, con), dar un traspié: *I stumbled on the step*, tropecé con el escalón. **3** (*walk unsteadily*) tambalearse: *he stumbled around in the dark*, iba tambaleándose en la oscuridad. **4** (*while speaking*) atrancarse, atascarse: *she stumbled over a long word*, se atrancó con una palabra larga.
◆ **to stumble across / stumble on** *t insep* dar con, tropezar con.

stumbling block ['stʌmbəlɪŋblɒk] *n* escollo, tropiezo.

stump [stʌmp] **1** *n* (*of tree*) tocón *m*, cepa; (*of pencil, candle*) cabo; (*of arm, leg*) muñón *m*. **2** SP (*cricket*) estaca, palo.

– **3** t fam (baffle) desconcertar, confundir, dejar perplejo,-a a. – **4** i (move heavily) pisar fuerte.
◆ **to stump up** I t insep fam soltar, aflojar, apoquinar. – **2** i fam soltar la pasta, aflojar la mosca.
stumpy ['stʌmpɪ] adj rechoncho,-a, achaparrado,-a.
▲ comp stumpier, superl stumpiest.
stun [stʌn] **1** t (make unconscious) dejar sin sentido; (daze) aturdir, atontar, pasmar. **2** (surprise) sorprender, dejar atónito,-a, dejar pasmado,-a; (shock) atolondrar, aturdir, dejar anonadado,-a.
▲ pt & pp stunned, ger stunning.
stung [stʌŋ] pt & pp → sting.
stunk [stʌŋk] pt & pp → stink.
stunned [stʌnd] **1** adj (unconscious) sin sentido; (dazed) aturdido,-a. **2** (amazed, shocked) atónito,-a, pasmado,-a, anonadado,-a: we were stunned by the news, nos quedamos anonadados con la noticia.
stunner ['stʌnə'] n fam (woman) mujer f guapísima.
stunning ['stʌnɪŋ] **1** adj (surprising) alucinante, apabullante; (shocking) asombroso,-a. **2** (beautiful, impressive) impresionante, imponente, fenomenal.
stunningly ['stʌnɪŋlɪ] adv increíblemente.
stunt¹ [stʌnt] t (growth) atrofiar.
stunt² [stʌnt] **1** n (dangerous act) proeza; (in film) escena peligrosa. **2** (trick) truco, maniobra: it's just a publicity stunt, no es más que un truco publicitario.
● **to pull a stunt,** cometer una estupidez.
■ **stunt man / stunt woman,** doble mf, especialista mf.
stunted ['stʌntɪd] adj (tree, body) raquítico,-a; (growth) atrofiado,-a.
stupefaction [stjuːpɪ'fækʃən] n estupefacción f.
stupefy ['stjuːpɪfaɪ] **1** t (alcohol, drugs) atontar, aturdir, aletargar. **2** (amaze) dejar pasmado,-a, dejar estupefacto,-a.
▲ pt & pp stupefied.
stupendous [stjuː'pendəs] **1** adj (wonderful) estupendo,-a, fabuloso,-a, formidable. **2** (enormous) tremendo,-a; (unusual) extraordinario,-a, increíble.
stupid ['stjuːpɪd] **1** adj tonto,-a, bobo,-a, imbécil, estúpido,-a: how stupid of me!, ¡qué tonto soy!, ¡mira que soy tonta!; don't be so stupid!, ¡no seas tan tonto! **2** (senseless) atontado,-a. **3** fam (annoying) maldito,-a. – **4** n tonto,-a, imbécil mf.
■ **a stupid thing to say / a stupid thing to do,** una estupidez f, una tontería.
stupidity [stjuː'pɪdɪtɪ] n estupidez f, tontería.
stupor ['stjuːpə'] n estupor m: in a drunken stupor, borracho,-a perdido,-a.
sturdiness ['stɜːdɪnəs] **1** n (solidness) robustez f, fuerza, solidez f. **2** (determination) tenacidad f.
sturdy ['stɜːdɪ] **1** adj (strong) robusto,-a, fuerte; (solid) sólido,-a. **2** (opposition, resistence, defence) enérgico,-a, férreo,-a, tenaz, inquebrantable.
▲ comp sturdier, superl sturdiest.
sturgeon ['stɜːdʒən] n esturión m.
stutter ['stʌtə'] **1** n tartamudeo: he has a stutter, tartamudea. – **2** i tartamudear. – **3** t decir tartamudeando, balbucear.
stutterer ['stʌtərə'] n tartamudo,-a.
sty¹ [staɪ] n (for pigs) pocilga.
sty² [staɪ] n → stye.
▲ pl sties.
stye [staɪ] n (in eye) orzuelo.
style [staɪl] **1** n (gen) estilo: in the Gothic style, de estilo gótico. **2** (type, model) modelo, diseño: we have all the latest styles, tenemos todos los últimos modelos. **3** (of hair) peinado. **4** (fashion) moda: it's the latest style, es la última moda; that's out of style now, ya está pasado de moda. **5** fml (correct title) título. **6** BOT estilo. – **7** t (gen) diseñar; (hair) peinar. **8** fml (name, title) llamar.
● **to be sb.'s style,** ir con algn., irle a algn.: pink's not my style, el rosa no me va. ‖ **to do sth. in style,** hacer algo a lo grande.
styling ['staɪlɪŋ] n diseño.
■ **styling mousse,** espuma moldeadora.
stylish ['staɪlɪʃ] **1** adj (elegant) elegante, con mucho estilo. **2** (fashionable) a la moda, de última moda.
stylist ['staɪlɪst] **1** n (hairdresser) estilista mf, peluquero,-a. **2** (writer) estilista mf.
stylistic [staɪ'lɪstɪk] adj estilístico,-a.
stylistics [staɪ'lɪstɪks] n estilística.
stylized ['staɪlaɪzd] adj estilizado,-a.
stylus ['staɪləs] **1** n (of record player) aguja. **2** (for writing) estilo.
▲ pl styluses o styli.
stymie ['staɪmɪ] **1** t fam frustrar. – **2** n fam apuro, lío.
styptic ['stɪptɪk] **1** n astringente m. – **2** adj astringente.
■ **styptic pencil,** barrita astringente.
suave [swɑːv] adj (charming, polite) afable, cortés; (slick, ingratiating) zalamero,-a.
sub [sʌb] **1** n (submarine) submarino. **2** SP (substitute) sustituto,-a, suplente mf. **3** (subscription) cuota, subscripción f, suscripción f. **4** (subeditor) redactor,-ra. **5** GB (advance from wages) anticipo. – **6** i (act as substitute) sustituir (**for,** a). – **7** t GB (give an advance) anticipar, dar un anticipo. **8** (subedit) corregir, revisar.
▲ (verbo) pt & pp subbed, ger subbing.
sub- [sʌb] pref sub.
subaltern ['sʌbəltən] n MIL alférez m.
subaqua [sʌb'ækwə] adj de submarinismo.
subcommittee ['sʌbkəmɪtɪ] n subcomisión f, subcomité m.
subconscious [sʌb'kɒnʃəs] **1** adj subconsciente. – **2** the subconscious, n el subconsciente m.
subconsciously [sʌb'kɒnʃəslɪ] adv de forma subconsciente, de manera subconsciente.
subcontinent [sʌb'kɒntɪnənt] n subcontinente m.
subcontract [sʌb'kɒntrækt] **1** n subcontrato. – **2** t subcontratar (**to,** a).
▲ verb |sʌbkən'trækt|.
subcontractor [sʌbkən'træktə'] n subcontratista mf.
subculture ['sʌbkʌltʃə'] n subcultura.
subcutaneous [sʌbkjuː'teɪnɪəs] adj subcutáneo,-a.
subdivide [sʌbdɪ'vaɪd] t subdividir (**into,** en).
subdivision ['sʌbdɪvɪʒən] n subdivisión f.
subdue [səb'djuː] **1** t (nation, people) someter, dominar, sojuzgar. **2** (feelings, passions, etc) contener, dominar. **3** (sound, colour, light) atenuar, suavizar.
subdued [səb'djuːd] **1** adj (person, emotion) callado,-a, apagado,-a. **2** (tone, voice) bajo,-a; (light) tenue; (colour) apagado,-a.
subedit [sʌb'edɪt] t corregir, revisar.
subeditor [sʌb'edɪtə'] n redactor,-ra.
subgroup ['sʌbgruːp] n subgrupo.
subheading [sʌb'hedɪŋ] n subtítulo.
subhuman [sʌb'hjuːmən] adj infrahumano,-a.
subject ['sʌbdʒekt] **1** n (theme, topic) tema m: what's your opinion on the subject?, ¿qué opinas del tema?; while we're on the subject of money, ya que hablamos de dinero. **2** EDUC asignatura. **3** (citizen) súbdito, ciudadano,-

a. **4** LING sujeto. **5** (*cause*) objeto (**of/for**, de). **6** (*of experiment*) sujeto. – **7** *adj* (*subordinate, governed*) sometido,- a. – **8** *t* (*bring under control*) someter, sojuzgar (**to**, a). – **9 subject to**, *adj* (*bound by*) sujeto,-a a: *we are all subject to the law,* todos estamos sujetos a la ley. **10** (*prone to - floods, subsidence*) expuesto,-a a; (*- change, delay*) susceptible de, sujeto,-a a; (*- illness*) propenso,-a a. – **11** *prep* (*conditional on*) previo,-a, supeditado,-a a: *subject to approval,* previa aprobación.
◆ **to subject to** *t sep* someter a: *the prisoners were subjected to torture,* los presos fueron sometidos a tortura.
● **to change the subject,** cambiar de tema.
■ **subject matter,** (*topic*) tema *m*, materia; (*contents*) contenido.
▲ *verb* [səb'dʒekt].
subjection [səb'dʒekʃən] *n* (*act*) sujeción *f* (**of**, de); (*state*) sometimiento (**to**, a).
subjective [səb'dʒektɪv] *adj* subjetivo,-a.
subjectivity [sʌbdʒek'tɪvɪtɪ] *n* subjetividad *f*.
sub judice [sʌb'dʒuːdɪsɪ] *adj* JUR pendiente de resolución.
subjugate ['sʌbdʒəgeɪt] *t* sojuzgar, subyugar.
subjugation [sʌbdʒə'geɪʃən] *n* subyugación *f*.
subjunctive [səb'dʒʌŋktɪv] **1** *adj* LING subjuntivo,-a. – **2** *n* LING subjuntivo.
sublease [sʌb'liːs] *t* → **sublet**.
sublet [sʌb'let] **1** *t* realquilar, subarrendar. – **2** *i* realquilar, subarrendar.
▲ *pt & pp* **sublet**, *ger* **subletting**.
sublieutenant [sʌblə'tenənt] *n* MAR alférez *m* de navío.
sublimate ['sʌblɪmeɪt] *t* sublimar.
sublime [sə'blaɪm] **1** *adj* (*beauty, music, compliment, etc*) sublime. **2** *fam* (*food, performance*) maravilloso,-a, sensacional. **3** *pej* (*indifference, ignorance, etc*) sumo,-a, supremo,-a, absoluto,-a, total. – **4 the sublime,** *n* lo sublime.
● **from the sublime to the ridiculous,** de un extremo a otro.
subliminal [sʌb'lɪmɪnəl] *adj* subliminal.
sub-machine-gun [sʌbmə'ʃiːngʌn] *n* ametralladora, metralleta.
submarine ['sʌbməriːn] **1** *n* submarino. – **2** *adj* submarino,-a.
submariner [sʌb'mærɪnəʳ] *n* submarinista *mf*.
submerge [səb'mɜːdʒ] **1** *t* sumergir (**in**, en). – **2** *i* sumergirse.
● **to submerge os. in sth.,** sumergirse en algo.
submerged [səb'mɜːdʒd] *adj* (*wreck, rock, submarine*) sumergido,-a.
● **to be submerged in work etc,** estar agobiado,-a de trabajo etc.
submersible [səb'mɜːsəbəl] *adj* submergible.
submersion [səb'mɜːʃən] *n* sumersión *f*.
submission [səb'mɪʃən] **1** *n* (*subjection*) sumisión *f* (**to**, a). **2** SP (*in wrestling*) rendición *f*. **3** (*presentation*) presentación *f*: *the last day for submission of applications,* el último día para la presentación de solicitudes. **4** (*report*) informe *m*; (*proposal*) propuesta.
submissive [səb'mɪsɪv] *adj* sumiso,-a, dócil.
submissiveness [səb'mɪsɪvnəs] *n* sumisión *f*.
submit [səb'mɪt] **1** *t* (*present*) presentar. **2** (*subject*) someter (**to**, a). **3** JUR (*suggest*) sostener. – **4** *i* (*admit defeat, surrender*) rendirse, ceder; (*to demand, wishes*) acceder: *they eventually submitted to the enemy,* finalmente se rindieron al enemigo.
▲ *pt & pp* **submitted**, *ger* **submitting**.
subnormal [sʌb'nɔːməl] **1** *adj* (*person*) subnormal, retrasado,-a. **2** (*temperatures*) por debajo de lo normal.

subordinate [sə'bɔːdɪnət] **1** *adj* (*lower, less important*) subordinado,-a (**to**, a), secundario,-a. **2** LING subordinado,-a. – **3** *n* (*person*) subordinado,-a, subalterno,-a. – **4** *t* subordinar (**to**, a), supeditar (**to**, a).
■ **subordinate cause,** oración *f* subordinada.
▲ En acepción **2** (*verbo*) [sə'bɔːdɪneɪt].
subordination [səbɔːdɪ'neɪʃən] *n* subordinación *f*.
suborn [sə'bɔːn] *t* *fml* sobornar.
subpoena [səb'piːnə] **1** *n* JUR citación *f*. – **2** *t* JUR citar.
subscribe [səb'skraɪb] **1** *i* (*to newspaper etc*) suscribirse (**to**, a), abonarse (**to**, a). **2** (*to charity*) hacer donaciones, contribuir con donativos (**to**, a). **3** (*to opinion, theory*) suscribir (**to**, -), estar de acuerdo (**to**, con): *he subscribes to the view that ...,* él es de la opinión de que ... **4** FIN (*shares*) suscribir (**for**, -). – **5** *t* (*contribute*) contribuir, donar. **6** *fml* (*sign*) suscribir: *I subscribed my name to the petition,* suscribí la petición, firmé la petición.
subscriber [səb'skraɪbəʳ] *n* (*to newspaper etc*) suscriptor,-ra, abonado,-a; (*to telephone service, cable television*) abonado,-a.
● **to be a subscriber to a charity,** contribuir a una organización benéfica.
subscription [səb'skrɪpʃən] *n* (*to newspaper etc*) suscripción *f*, abono; (*to club*) cuota; (*to charity*) donativo, donación *f*.
● **to take out a subscription to sth.,** suscribirse a algo.
subsection ['sʌbsekʃən] *n* JUR (*in document, text*) artículo.
subsequent ['sʌbsɪkwənt] *adj* subsiguiente, posterior.
● **subsequent to,** posterior a.
subsequently ['sʌbsɪkwəntlɪ] *adv* posteriormente.
subservient [səb'sɜːvɪənt] **1** *adj* (*submissive*) servil (**to**, a). **2** *fml* (*subordinate*) supeditado,-a (**to**, a).
subside [səb'saɪd] **1** *i* (*land, building, road*) hundirse. **2** *fig* (*person*) dejarse caer. **3** (*storm, wind*) amainar; (*floods*) decrecer, bajar; (*pain, fever*) disminuir; (*noise, applause*) irse apagando; (*anger, excitement*) calmarse.
subsidence [səb'saɪdəns] *n* (*of land, building*) hundimiento.
subsidiary [səb'sɪdɪərɪ] **1** *adj* (*role, interest, issue*) secundario,-a. **2** (*income*) adicional, extra; (*payment, loan*) subsidiario,-a. – **3** *n* COMM filial *f*.
■ **subsidiary company,** empresa filial. ‖ **subsidiary subject,** EDUC asignatura complementaria.
▲ (*sustantivo*) *pl* **subsidiaries**.
subsidize ['sʌbsɪdaɪz] *t* (*gen*) subvencionar; (*exports*) primar.
subsidized ['sʌbsɪdaɪzd] *adj* subvencionado,-a.
subsidy ['sʌbsɪdɪ] *n* subvención *f*, subsidio.
▲ *pl* **subsidies**.
subsist [səb'sɪst] *i* subsistir.
● **to subsist on,** subsistir a base de.
subsistence [səb'sɪstəns] *n* subsistencia.
● **to live at subsistence level,** vivir con lo justo para subsistir.
■ **subsistence allowance,** dietas *fpl*. ‖ **subsistence crop,** cultivo de subsistencia. ‖ **subsistence farming,** agricultura de subsistencia. ‖ **subsistence wage,** sueldo miserable, sueldo de hambre.
subsoil ['sʌbsɔɪl] *n* subsuelo.
substance ['sʌbstəns] **1** *n* (*matter*) sustancia. **2** (*real matter, solid content*) sustancia, solidez *f*: *matters of substance,* temas fundamentales/importantes; *there is no substance in the rumour,* el rumor no es fundado, el rumor carece de fundamento. **3** (*essence, gist*) esencia, sustancia: *the substance of his argument,* la esencia de

su argumento. **4** (*wealth*) riqueza: *a man of substance,* un hombre acaudalado.

substandard [sʌb'stændəd] *adj* de calidad inferior.

substantial [səb'stænʃəl] **1** *adj* (*solid*) sólido,-a, fuerte. **2** (*large - sum, increase, loss, damage*) importante, considerable; (*- difference, change*) sustancial, notable. **3** (*meal - large*) abundante; (*nourishing*) sustancioso,-a. **4** (*wealthy*) acaudalado,-a. **5** *fml* (*real, tangible*) sustancial.
● **to be in substantial agreement,** estar de acuerdo en los puntos esenciales.

substantially [səb'stænʃəlɪ] **1** *adv* (*solidly*) sólidamente. **2** (*considerably*) de manera considerable; (*noticeably*) notablemente, sustancialmente. **3** (*essentially*) esencialmente, fundamentalmente; (*largely, mainly*) en gran parte.

substantiate [səb'stænʃɪeɪt] *t* (*gen*) confirmar, corroborar; (*accusation*) probar.

substantive ['sʌbstəntɪv] **1** *adj fml* (*research, information, evidence*) sustantivo,-a; (*matter, issue*) fundamental. – **2** *n* LING sustantivo.

substitute ['sʌbstɪtjuːt] **1** *n* (*person*) sustituto,-a, suplente *mf*: *Barnes came on as a substitute for the injured player,* Barnes sustituyó al jugador lesionado. **2** (*thing*) sucedáneo (**for,** de): *a sugar substitute,* un sucedáneo del azúcar; *oil can be used as a substitute for butter,* se puede sustituir la mantequilla por aceite; *there's no substitute for being actually there,* no hay nada como estar allí. – **3** *t* sustituir, reemplazar: *substitute fresh fruit for cakes and sweets,* sustituye los pasteles y dulces por fruta fresca; *the manager substituted Green for Watson,* el entrenador sustituyó a Watson por Green. – **4** *i* sustituir, suplir (**for,** a): *can you substitute for me tomorrow?,* ¿me puedes sustituir mañana?

substitution [sʌbstɪ'tjuːʃən] *n* sustitución *f*.

substratum [sʌb'strɑːtəm] *n* substrato.
▲ *pl* substrata.

subterfuge ['sʌbtəfjuːdʒ] *n* subterfugio.

subterranean [sʌbtə'reɪnɪən] *adj* subterráneo,-a.

subtitle ['sʌbtaɪtəl] **1** *n* subtítulo. – **2** *t* subtitular, poner subtítulos a.

subtle ['sʌtəl] **1** *adj* (*person - tactful*) delicado,-a, discreto,-a: *try being a bit more subtle,* procura tener más delicadeza. **2** (*colour, difference, hint, joke*) sutil; (*taste*) delicado,-a, ligero,-a; (*lighting*) tenue, sutil. **3** (*remark, mind*) agudo,-a, perspicaz; (*plan, argument, analysis*) ingenioso,-a; (*irony*) fino,-a.

subtlety ['sʌtəltɪ] **1** *n* (*delicacy, fine difference*) sutileza *f*. **2** (*tact*) delicadeza. – **3** *adj* (*perceptiveness*) agudeza, perspicacia; (*ingenuity*) sutileza.
▲ *pl* subtleties.

subtly ['sʌtəlɪ] **1** *adv* (*delicately*) sutilmente. **2** (*tactfully*) con delicadeza. **3** (*perceptively*) con agudeza, perspicazmente; (*ingeniously*) ingeniosamente.

subtotal [sʌb'təʊtəl] *n* subtotal *m*.

subtract [səb'trækt] *t* restar (**from,** de): *subtract five from nine,* resta cinco de nueve.

subtraction [səb'trækʃən] *n* resta.

subtropical [sʌb'trɒpɪkəl] *adj* subtropical.

suburb ['sʌbɜːb] *n* barrio residencial.
■ **the suburbs,** las afueras *fpl*.

suburban [sə'bɜːbən] *adj* (*area*) de los barrios residenciales; (*attitude*) convencional.

suburbia [sə'bɜːbɪə] *n* los barrios *mpl* residenciales.

subversion [sʌb'vɜːʃən] *n* subversión *f*.

subversive [sʌb'vɜːsɪv] **1** *adj* subversivo,-a. – **2** *n* (*person*) elemento subversivo.

subvert [sʌb'vɜːt] *t* subvertir.

subway ['sʌbweɪ] **1** *n* GB (*underpass*) paso subterráneo. **2** US (*underground*) metro.

subzero [sʌb'zɪːrəʊ] *adj* bajo cero.

succeed [sək'siːd] **1** *i* (*be successful - person*) tener éxito, triunfar; (*- plan, marriage*) salir bien; (*- strike*) surtir efecto, dar resultado. **2** (*manage*) lograr, conseguir: *she aimed to swim a mile and succeeded,* se propuso nadar una milla y lo consiguió; *at least we succeeded in raising public awareness,* al menos conseguimos sensibilizar a los ciudadanos. **3** (*throne*) subir (**to,** a); (*title*) heredar (**to,** -). – **4** *t* (*take place of*) suceder a. **5** *fml* (*follow after*) suceder a.
● **if at first you don't succeed, try, try, try again,** el que la sigue la consigue. ‖ **to succeed in life,** triunfar en la vida.

succeeding [sək'siːdɪŋ] *adj* subsiguiente.

success [sək'ses] **1** *n* (*good result, achievement*) éxito: *they met with success,* tuvieron éxito; *that's the key to success,* eso es la clave del éxito. **2** (*successful person, thing*) éxito: *the novel was a great success,* la novela fue un gran éxito.
● **to make a success of sth.,** sacar adelante algo con éxito.

successful [sək'sesfʊl] *adj* (*person, career, film*) de éxito; (*plan, performance, attempt*) acertado,-a, logrado,-a; (*business*) próspero,-a; (*marriage*) feliz; (*meeting*) satisfactorio,-a, positivo,-a: *the successful candidate,* el candidato (que resulte) seleccionado.
● **to be successful in doing sth.,** conseguir hacer algo. ‖ **to be successful in life,** triunfar en la vida.

successfully [sək'sesfʊlɪ] *adv* con éxito, satisfactoriamente.

succession [sək'seʃən] **1** *n* (*act of following*) sucesión *f*: *three months in succession,* tres meses seguidos, tres meses consecutivos; *three goals in rapid succession,* tres goles consecutivos. **2** (*series*) serie *f*, sucesión *f*. **3** (*to post, throne*) sucesión *f*.

successive [sək'sesɪv] *adj* sucesivo,-a, consecutivo,-a: *he's won five successive championships,* ha ganado cinco campeonatos consecutivos; *successive governments,* sucesivos gobiernos.

successively [sək'sesɪvlɪ] *adv* sucesivamente.

successor [sək'sesə'] *n* sucesor,-ra.

succinct [sək'sɪŋkt] *adj* sucinto,-a, conciso,-a.

succinctly [sək'sɪŋtlɪ] *adv* sucintamente.

succinctness [sək'sɪŋtnəs] *n* concisión *f*.

succulent ['sʌkjələnt] **1** *adj* (*juicy*) suculento,-a. **2** BOT carnoso,-a. – **3** *n* BOT planta carnosa, suculenta.

succumb [sə'kʌm] *i* sucumbir (**to,** a).

such [sʌtʃ] **1** *adj* (*of that sort*) tal, semejante: *there's no such thing,* no existe tal cosa; *in such cases,* en tales casos. **2** (*so much, so great*) tal, tanto,-a: *he's always in such a hurry,* siempre anda con tanta prisa; *there were such a lot of people,* había tanta gente. – **3** *adv* (*so very*) tan: *it was such a boring film that ...,* era una película tan aburrida que ...; *she's such a clever woman,* es una mujer tan inteligente. – **4** *pron* (*of that specified sort*) tal: *he acts like a child and I treat him as such,* se comporta como un niño y lo trato como tal; *the disaster was such that ...,* el desastre fue tal que ...
● **as such,** (*strictly speaking*) propiamente dicho; (*that way*) como tal. ‖ **at such and such a time,** a tal hora. ‖ **in such a way that ...,** de tal manera que ... ‖ **such as,** (*like, for example*) como. ‖ **such as?,** ¿por ejemplo? ‖ **such is life!,** ¡así es la vida!

suchlike ['sʌtʃlaɪk] 1 *adj* por el estilo. – 2 *pron* (*things*) cosas *fpl* por el estilo; (*people*) gente *f* por el estilo.

suck [sʌk] 1 *t* (*person - liquid*) sorber; (*- lollipop, pencil, thumb, etc*) chupar; (*insect -blood, nectar*) chupar, succionar: *he's ten years old and still sucks his thumb,* tiene diez años y aún se chupa el dedo. 2 (*vacuum cleaner*) aspirar (**in**, -); (*pump*) succionar, aspirar (**in**, -); (*plant*) absorber (**up**, -). 3 (*draw powerfully*) arrastrar: *the current sucked him under,* la corriente se lo tragó. – 4 *i* (*person*) chupar (**at/on**, -); (*baby*) mamar (**at**, -); (*vacuum cleaner*) aspirar (**up**,-); (*pump*) succionar, aspirar. 5 us *sl* (*be very bad*) ser terrible, ser una mierda. – 6 *n* chupada.
● **to be sucked into sth.,** verse arrastrado,-a a algo, verse involucrado,-a en algo. ‖ **to suck up to sb.,** hacerle la pelota a algn.

sucker ['sʌkə'] 1 *n* ZOOL ventosa. 2 BOT chupón *m*, mamón *m*. 3 (*rubber disc*) ventosa. 4 *fam* (*person*) primo,-a, bobo,-a, imbécil *mf*.
● **to be a sucker for sth.,** tener debilidad por algo.

sucking pig ['sʌkɪŋpɪg] *n* cochinillo, lechón *m*.

suckle ['sʌkəl] 1 *t* amamantar, dar de mamar a. – 2 *i* mamar.

suckling ['sʌkəlɪŋ] *n* lactante *mf*.

sucrose ['sjuːkrəʊz] *n* sacarosa.

suction ['sʌkʃən] *n* (*sticking together*) succión *f*; (*of water, air*) aspiración *f*.
■ **suction cup,** ventosa. ‖ **suction pump,** bomba de aspiración.

Sudan [suːˈdæn] (the) Sudán, *n* Sudán.

Sudanese [suːdəˈniːz] 1 *adj* sudanés,-esa. – 2 *n* sudanés,-esa. – 3 **the Sudanese,** *npl* los sudaneses *mpl*.

sudden ['sʌdən] 1 *adj* (*quick*) súbito,-a, repentino,-a. 2 (*unexpected*) inesperado,-a, imprevisto,-a. 3 (*abrupt*) brusco,-a.
● **all of a sudden,** de repente, de pronto, de golpe.
■ **sudden death,** muerte *f* súbita.

suddenly ['sʌdənlɪ] 1 *adv* (*unexpectedly*) de repente, de pronto. 2 (*abruptly*) abruptamente.

suddenness ['sʌdənnəs] 1 *n* (*quickness*) lo repentino, lo súbito. 2 (*unexpectedness*) lo imprevisto, lo inesperado. 3 (*abruptness*) brusquedad *f*.

suds [sʌdz] *npl* jabonaduras *fpl*, espuma *f sing* (de jabón).

sue [suː] 1 *t* JUR demandar. – 2 *i* JUR entablar una demanda (**for**, por).
● **to sue for damages,** demandar por daños y perjuicios. ‖ **to sue for divorce,** solicitar el divorcio. ‖ **to sue for libel,** entablar juicio por difamación. ‖ **to sue for peace,** hacer un llamamiento a la paz.

suede [sweɪd] 1 *n* ante *m*, gamuza. – 2 *adj* de ante, de gamuza.

suet ['suːɪt] *n* sebo.

suffer ['sʌfə'] 1 *t* (*gen*) sufrir; (*pain*) padecer, sufrir; (*hunger*) padecer, pasar; (*losses*) sufrir, registrar: *they suffered a humiliating defeat,* sufrieron una derrota humillante. 2 (*bear, tolerate*) aguantar, soportar, tolerar: *we had to suffer the consequences,* tuvimos que atenernos a las consecuencias. – 3 *i* (*gen*) sufrir: *she's suffered enough already,* ya ha sufrido bastante; *she suffered in silence,* sufrió en silencio. 4 (*be affected - work, studies, etc*) verse afectado,-a; (*- health*) resentirse: *if you smoke, your health will suffer,* si fumas, perjudicará tu salud.
● **not to suffer fools gladly,** no aguantar a los imbéciles. ‖ **to suffer for sth.,** sufrir las consecuencias de algo. ‖ **to suffer from,** (*illness*) sufrir de, padecer; (*shock*) sufrir los efectos de; (*effects*) resentirse de: *he's suffering from exhaustion,* está agotado.

sufferance ['sʌfərəns] **on sufferance,** *phr* a regañadientes.

sufferer ['sʌfərə'] *n* enfermo,-a: *AIDS sufferers,* las víctimas del sida; *arthritis sufferers,* los artríticos; *cancer sufferers,* los cancerosos.

suffering ['sʌfərɪŋ] *n* (*affliction*) sufrimiento, aflicción *f*; (*grief*) pena, dolor *m*; (*pain*) dolor *m*.

suffice [səˈfaɪs] 1 *t fml* ser suficiente. – 2 *i* bastar, ser suficiente (**for**, para).
● **suffice it to say (that) ...,** basta con decir que ...

sufficient [səˈfɪʃənt] *adj* suficiente, bastante: *we don't have sufficient information,* no tenemos suficiente información.
● **to be sufficient,** bastar.

sufficiently [səˈfɪʃəntlɪ] *adv* (lo) suficientemente, lo suficiente: *it's not sufficiently cooked,* no está suficientemente cocido.

suffix ['sʌfɪks] *n* sufijo.

suffocate ['sʌfəkeɪt] 1 *t* asfixiar, ahogar. – 2 *i* asfixiarse, ahogarse.

suffocating ['sʌfəkeɪtɪŋ] 1 *adj* (*heat*) sofocante, agobiante; (*smoke, fumes*) asfixiante. 2 *fig* asfixiante.

suffocation [sʌfəˈkeɪʃən] *n* asfixia, ahogo.

suffrage ['sʌfrɪdʒ] *n* sufragio.

suffragette [sʌfrəˈdʒet] *n* sufragista.

suffuse [səˈfjuːz] *t* (*colour*) teñir; (*light*) bañar.

sugar ['ʃʊgə'] 1 *n* azúcar *m* & *f*: *do you take sugar?,* ¿quieres azúcar? 2 us *fam* (*form of address*) cariño, cielo. – 3 *t* azucarar.
● **to sugar the pill,** dorar la píldora.
■ **brown sugar,** azúcar *m* moreno. ‖ **castor sugar,** azúcar *m* extrafino. ‖ **sugar beet,** remolacha azucarera. ‖ **sugar bowl,** azucarero, azucarera. ‖ **sugar cane,** caña de azúcar. ‖ **sugar cube,** terrón *m* de azúcar. ‖ **sugar daddy,** *viejo rico que regala cosas a una mujer joven.* ‖ **sugar lump,** terrón *m* de azúcar. ‖ **sugar tongs,** pinzas *fpl* para el azúcar.

sugar-coated [ʃʊgəˈkəʊtɪd] *adj* cubierto,-a de azúcar.

sugared ['ʃʊgəd] *adj* azucarado,-a.
■ **sugared almond,** peladilla.

sugary ['ʃʊgərɪ] 1 *adj* (*of/like sugar*) azucarado,-a; (*sweet*) dulce. 2 *fig* (*insincere*) almibarado,-a, meloso,-a; (*sentimental*) sensiblero,-a, empalagoso,-a.
▲ *comp* **sugarier,** *superl* **sugariest**.

suggest [səˈdʒest] 1 *t* (*propose*) sugerir, proponer; (*advise*) sugerir, aconsejar: *I'd like to suggest Kate for the job,* quisiera proponer a Kate para el puesto; *he suggested going for a drink,* sugirió que fuéramos a tomar algo; *I suggest that we leave,* sugiero que nos marchemos. 2 (*imply*) insinuar: *are you suggesting that I'm a thief?,* ¿insinúas que soy un ladrón? 3 (*indicate*) indicar: *the evidence suggests that he's guilty,* las pruebas indican que es culpable. 4 (*evoke*) evocar, sugerir.

suggestible [səˈdʒestəbəl] *adj* sugestionable, influenciable.

suggestion [səˈdʒestʃən] 1 *n* (*proposal*) sugerencia, propuesta: *I'd like to make a suggestion,* quisiera hacer una sugerencia; *we're open to suggestions,* aceptamos sugerencias. 2 (*insinuation*) insinuación *f*. 3 (*indication, hint*) indicio; (*slight trace*) sombra, traza, asomo, nota: *with the suggestion of a smile,* esbozando una sonrisa; *with the suggestion of an accent,* con un (leve) deje; *with a suggestion of ginger,* con un saborcillo a jengibre. 4 (*in psychology*) sugestión *f*.

suggestive [səˈdʒestɪv] *adj* (*with sexual connotations*) provocativo,-a, insinuante.

605 **summery**

● **to be suggestive of sth.**, *(indicative)* parecer indicar algo; *(evocative)* evocar algo: *the painting is suggestive of a Mediterranean country,* el cuadro evoca un país mediterráneo.

suggestively [sə'dʒestɪvlɪ] *adv* de manera provocativa, de manera insinuante.

suicidal [suːɪ'saɪdəl] *adj* suicida: *suicidal tendencies,* tendencias suicidas; *a suicidal policy,* una política suicida; *it would be suicidal to call an election now,* sería una verdadera locura convocar elecciones ahora.

suicide ['suːɪsaɪd] **1** *n (act)* suicidio: *she attempted suicide,* intentó suicidarse; *her attempted suicide,* su intento de suicidio. **2** *(person)* suicida *mf*. **3** *fig* suicidio.
● **to commit suicide,** suicidarse.

suit [suːt] **1** *n (man's)* traje *m; (woman's)* traje *m* de chaqueta: *he was wearing a three-piece suit,* vestía un terno. **2** JUR pleito, juicio. **3** *(in cards)* palo. – **4** *t (be convenient, acceptable)* convenir a, venir bien a; *(please)* satisfacer, agradar, contentar: *does Tuesday suit you?,* ¿el martes te viene bien?; *she can be very sweet when it suits her,* puede ser encantadora cuando le conviene. **5** *(be right for)* ir bien a, sentar bien a; *(look good on)* quedar bien a, favorecer: *this hot weather doesn't suit me,* este calor no me sienta bien; *red suits you,* el rojo te favorece mucho. **6** *(adapt)* adaptar **(to,** a), ajustar **(to,** a).
● **suit yourself!,** ¡como quieras! ‖ **to be sb.'s strongest suit,** ser el fuerte de algn. ‖ **to bring/file a suit against sb.,** demandar a algn., entablar una demanda contra algn. ‖ **to follow suit,** seguir su ejemplo, hacer lo mismo. ‖ **to suit os.,** hacer lo que a uno le apetece. ‖ **to suit sb. down to the ground,** venirle a algn. de perlas.
■ **suit of armour,** armadura.

suitability [suːtə'bɪlɪtɪ] **1** *n (appropriateness)* lo apropiado, lo apropiado; *(for job)* idoneidad *f*. **2** *(propriety)* lo apropiado, lo apto. **3** *(convenience)* conveniencia.

suitable ['suːtəbəl] **1** *adj (appropriate)* adecuado,-a **(for,** para), apropiado,-a **(for,** para); *(for job, post)* adecuado,-a, indicado,-a, idóneo,-a: *a suitable present for a ten-year-old boy,* un regalo adecuado para un niño de diez años; *clothes suitable for hot weather,* ropa apropiada para el calor. **2** *(acceptable, proper)* apropiado,-a, apto,-a: *will this skirt be suitable?,* ¿esta falda será apropiada?; *the film is suitable for children,* la película es apta para niños. **3** *(convenient)* conveniente.

suitably ['suːtəblɪ] **1** *adv (qualified)* adecuadamente; *(dressed)* apropiadamente, de manera adecuada. **2** *(correctly)* como es debido, como corresponde.

suitcase ['suːtkeɪs] *n* maleta.

suite [swiːt] **1** *n (of furniture)* juego. **2** *(in hotel)* suite *f*. **3** MUS suite *f*. **4** *(retinue)* séquito, comitiva. **5** COMPUT juego.
■ **dining-room suite,** (juego de) comedor *m*.

suited ['suːtɪd] *adj* apropiado,-a **(for,** para), adecuado,-a **(for,** para): *he's ideally suited to the job,* es idóneo para el trabajo; *you would be better suited to a job outdoors,* te convendría más un trabajo al aire libre; *they are ideally suited,* están hechos el uno para el otro.

suitor ['sjuːtəʳ] **1** *n (wooer)* pretendiente *mf*. **2** JUR *(plaintiff)* demandante *mf*, querellante *mf*.

sulfate ['sʌlfeɪt] *n* US → **sulphate**.
sulfide ['sʌlfaɪd] *n* US → **sulphide**.
sulfur ['sʌlfəʳ] *n* US → **sulphur**.

sulk [sʌlk] **1** *i* enfurruñarse, estar de mal humor: *she's sulking,* está enfurruñada. – **2** *n* malhumor *m*.

● **to be in a sulk,** enfurruñarse. ‖ **to have the sulks,** enfurruñarse, poner morros.

sulky ['sʌlkɪ] *adj (look, mood)* malhumorado,-a; *(person)* con tendencia a enfurruñarse.
▲ *comp* **sulkier,** *superl* **sulkiest**.

sullen ['sʌlən] **1** *adj (person, mood)* hosco,-a, arisco,-a, huraño,-a; *(face)* adusto,-a. **2** *lit (sky, weather)* sombrío, triste.

sullenness ['sʌlənnəs] *n* malhumor *m*.

sully ['sʌlɪ] **1** *t (dirty)* ensuciar. **2** *fig (tarnish, spoil)* manchar, mancillar.
▲ *pt & pp* **sullied,** *ger* **sullying**.

sulphate ['sʌlfeɪt] *n* sulfato.
■ **copper sulphate,** sulfato de cobre.

sulpher ['sʌlfəʳ] *n* azufre *m*.

sulphide ['sʌlfaɪd] *n* sulfuro.

sulphuric [sʌl'fjʊərɪk] *adj* sulfúrico,-a.
■ **sulphuric acid,** ácido sulfúrico.

sulphurous ['sʌlfərəs] *adj (smell)* a azufre; *(solution)* de azufre.

sultan ['sʌltən] *n* sultán *m*.

sultana [sʌl'tɑːnə] **1** *n (raisin)* pasa de Esmirna. **2** *(woman)* sultana.

sultanate ['sʌltəneɪt] *n* sultanato.

sultry ['sʌltrɪ] **1** *adj (weather)* bochornoso,-a, sofocante. **2** *(person)* sensual.
▲ *comp* **sultrier,** *superl* **sultriest**.

sum [sʌm] **1** *n* MATH *(calculation)* cuenta; *(addition)* suma, adición *f*. **2** *(amount of money)* suma (de dinero), cantidad *f* (de dinero): *a large sum of money,* una suma importante de dinero. **3** *(total amount)* suma, total *m*. – **4** **sums,** *npl* aritmética *f sing*, cálculos *mpl*.
◆ **to sum up 1** *t sep (summarize)* resumir, hacer un resumen de, sintetizar. **2** *(size up - situation)* evaluar; *(- person)* catalogar. – **3** *i (summarize)* resumir; *(of judge)* recapitular: *to sum up ...,* en resumen ..., resumiendo ..., en resumidas cuentas ...
● **in sum,** en suma, en resumen. ‖ **to do one's sums,** hacer cuentas.
■ **the sum total,** suma, total *m*.

Sumer ['suːmə] *n* Sumeria.

Sumerian [suː'mɪərɪən] **1** *adj* sumerio,-a. – **2** *n (person)* sumerio,-a. **3** *(language)* sumerio.

summarily ['sʌmerɪlɪ] *adv* sumariamente.

summarize ['sʌməraɪz] *t* resumir, hacer un resumen de.

summary ['sʌmərɪ] **1** *n (gen)* resumen *m*. – **2** *adj* JUR *(justice, punishment)* sumario,-a: *summary trial,* juicio sumario. **3** *(immediate - dismissal)* inmediato,-a. **4** *(brief - account)* breve, corto,-a.
● **in summary,** en resumen.
▲ *pl* **summaries**.

summer ['sʌməʳ] **1** *n (gen)* verano: *I love going to the beach in summer,* me encanta ir a la playa en verano; *they always spend the summer in Alicante,* siempre veranean en Alicante; *in high summer,* en pleno verano. **2** *lit* abril *m: a girl of 16 summers,* una chica de 16 abriles. – **3** *adj (gen)* de verano; *(summery)* veraniego,-a.
■ **summer camp,** colonia de vacaciones. ‖ **summer holidays,** vacaciones *fpl* de verano. ‖ **summer school,** curso de verano. ‖ **summer time,** horario de verano.

summerhouse ['sʌməhaus] *n* cenador *m*.

summertime ['sʌmətaɪm] *n* verano, estío.
● **in (the) summertime,** en verano.

summery ['sʌmərɪ] *adj* de verano, veraniego,-a.
▲ *comp* **summerier,** *superl* **summeriest**.

summing-up [sʌmɪŋ'ʌp] *n* JUR recapitulación *f*.
summit ['sʌmɪt] **1** *n* (*of mountain, carrer*) cumbre *f*, cita. **2** (*meeting*) cumbre *f*.
■ **summit conference**, cumbre *f*.
summon ['sʌmən] **1** *t* (*person*) llamar; (*meeting, parliament*) convocar. **2** JUR citar, emplazar.
◆**to summon up 1** *t insep* (*courage*) armarse de; (*strength*) reunir, cobrar; (*support*) lograr, obtener; (*resources, help*) reunir, conseguir. **2** (*memories, thoughts*) evocar.
summons ['sʌmənz] **1** *n* (*call*) llamamiento. **2** JUR citación *f* (judicial). – **3** *t* JUR citar, emplazar.
● **to serve a summons on sb.**, entregarle una citación a algn.
sumo ['suːməʊ] sumo (wrestling), *n* SP sumo.
■ **sumo wrestler**, luchador *m* de sumo.
sumptuous ['sʌmptjʊəs] *adj* (*gen*) suntuoso,-a; (*meal*) opíparo,-a.
sumptuousness ['sʌmptjʊəsnəs] *n* suntuosidad *f*.
sun [sʌn] *n* (*gen*) sol *m*: *she loves sitting in the sun,* le encanta sentarse al sol; *you've caught the sun,* te ha cogido el sol; *the sun's in my eyes,* me da el sol en los ojos; *we didn't have much sun,* no tuvimos muchos días de sol.
● **everything under the sun**, de todo. ‖ **there's nothing new under the sun**, no hay nada nuevo bajo el sol. ‖ **to call sb. all the names under the sun**, decirle a algn. de todo. ‖ **to sun os.**, tomar el sol.
■ **sun blind**, persiana. ‖ **sun block**, filtro solar. ‖ **sun deck**, cubierta superior. ‖ **sun lamp**, lámpara solar. ‖ **sun lounge**, jardín *m* de invierno. ‖ **sun lounger**, tumbona. ‖ **sun visor**, visera.
▲ (*verbo*) *pt & pp* **sunned**, *ger* **sunning**.
Sun ['sʌndɪ] *abbr* (*Sunday*) domingo; (*abbreviation*) dom.
sunbaked ['sʌnbeɪkt] *adj* (*place*) quemado,-a por el sol, calcinado,-a; (*brick*) secado,-a por el sol.
sunbathe ['sʌnbeɪð] *i* tomar el sol.
sunbather ['sʌnbeɪðə'] *n* persona que toma el sol.
sunbathing ['sʌnbeɪðɪŋ] *n* baños *mpl* de sol: *he hates sunbathing,* odia tomar el sol.
sunbeam ['sʌnbiːm] *n* rayo de sol.
sunbed ['sʌnbed] *n* cama solar.
sunburn ['sʌnbɜːn] *n* quemadura de sol.
sunburnt ['sʌnbɜːnt] *adj* (*burnt*) quemado,-a (por el sol); (*tanned*) bronceado,-a, moreno,-a.
sundae ['sʌndɪ] *n* CULIN *copa de helado con fruta, almendras, jarabe y nata montada.*
Sunday ['sʌndɪ] *n* domingo.
● **in a month of Sundays**, en mucho tiempo. ‖ **in one's Sunday best**, vestido,-a de domingo, endomingado,-a.
■ **Sunday driver**, dominguero,-a. ‖ **Sunday newspaper**, periódico dominical. ‖ **Sunday school**, catequesis *f*. ‖ **Sunday trading / Sunday opening**, apertura de las tiendas los domingos.
▲ *See also* **Saturday**.
sundial ['sʌndaɪəl] *n* reloj *m* de sol.
sundown ['sʌndaʊn] *n* US puesta de(l) sol.
● **at sundown**, al atardecer.
sundress ['sʌndres] *n* vestido de tirantes.
sun-dried ['sʌndraɪd] *adj* secado,-a al sol.
sundry ['sʌndrɪ] **1** *adj* diversos,-as, varios,-as. – **2** sundries, *npl* COMM (*goods*) artículos *mpl* diversos; (*expenses*) gastos *mpl* diversos.
● **all and sundry**, todo el mundo.
sunflower ['sʌnflaʊə'] *n* girasol *m*.
■ **sunflower seed**, semilla de girasol, pipa.

sung [sʌŋ] *pp* → **sing**.
sunglasses ['sʌnglɑːsɪz] *npl* gafas *fpl* de sol.
sun-god ['sʌngɒd] *n* dios *m* del Sol.
sunhat ['sʌnhæt] *n* pamela, sombrero de ala ancha.
sunk [sʌŋk] *pp* → **sink**.
sunken ['sʌnkən] **1** *adj* (*ship, treasure*) hundido,-a, sumergido,-a; (*eyes, cheeks*) hundido,-a. **2** (*terrace, bath*) a un nivel más bajo.
sunlight ['sʌnlaɪt] *n* sol *m*, luz *f* del sol.
sunlit ['sʌnlɪt] *adj* soleado,-a.
sunny ['sʌnɪ] **1** *adj* (*room, house, etc*) soleado,-a; (*day*) de sol. **2** *fig* (*person*) alegre, risueño,-a; (*future*) risueño,-a.
● **to be sunny**, hacer sol.
▲ *comp* **sunnier**, *superl* **sunniest**.
sunray ['sʌnreɪ] *n* rayo de sol.
sunrise ['sʌnraɪz] *n* (*sun-up*) salida del sol; (*dawn*) amanecer *m*, alba *m*.
sunroof ['sʌnruːf] **1** *n* AUTO capota, techo corredizo. **2** (*on building*) azotea.
sunset ['sʌnset] *n* (*sundown*) puesta de(l) sol, ocaso; (*twilight*) crepúsculo, atardecer *m*.
sunshade ['sʌnʃeɪd] **1** *n* (*parasol*) sombrilla. **2** (*awning*) toldo.
sunshine ['sʌnʃaɪn] **1** *n* sol *m*, luz *f* de sol: *Brighton had eight hours of sunshine yesterday,* ayer tuvieron ocho horas de sol en Brighton. **3** GB *fam* (*friendly form of address*) corazón, majo,-a; (*sarcastic*) guapo,-a.
sunspot ['sʌnspɒt] **1** *n* ASTRON mancha solar. **2** *fam* (*place*) lugar de veraneo donde hace mucho sol.
sunstroke ['sʌnstrəʊk] *n* insolación *f*.
suntan ['sʌntæn] *n* bronceado, moreno.
● **to get a suntan**, broncearse, ponerse moreno,-a.
■ **suntan cream / suntan lotion**, crema bronceadora. ‖ **suntan oil**, aceite *m* bronceador.
sun-tanned ['sʌntænd] *adj* bronceado,-a, moreno,-a.
suntrap ['sʌntræp] *n* lugar *m* muy soleado, solana.
sun-up ['sʌnʌp] *n* US (*sunrise*) salida de sol; (*dawn*) amanecer *m*, alba *m*.
sup [sʌp] **1** *t* GB (*drink*) beber a sorbos. – **2** *i arch* (*have supper*) cenar (**on/off,** -).
▲ *pt & pp* **supped**, *ger* **supping**.
super ['suːpə'] **1** *adj fam* genial, súper, fenomenal, de primera. – **2** *n* GB (*superintendent*) comisario,-a de policía. **3** US (*superintendent*) portero,-a.
superabundance [suːpərə'bʌndəns] *n fml* superabundancia.
superabundant [suːpərə'bʌndənt] *adj fml* superabundante.
superannuated [suːpər'ænjʊeɪtɪd] *adj fml* anticuado,-a.
superannuation [suːpərænjuː'eɪʃən] *n* GB (*pension*) pensión *f*, jubilación *f*.
■ **superannuation scheme**, plan *m* de jubilación.
superb [suː'pɜːb] *adj* estupendo,-a, magnífico,-a, espléndido,-a, soberbio,-a.
superbly [suː'pɜːblɪ] *adv* estupendamente, magníficamente, espléndidamente, soberbiamente.
supercharge ['suːpətʃɑːdʒ] *t* AUTO sobrealimentar.
supercharger ['suːpətʃɑːdʒə'] *n* AUTO sobrealimentador *m*.
supercilious [suːpə'sɪlɪəs] *adj* (*condescending*) altanero,-a; (*disdainful*) desdeñoso,-a.
superciliousness [suːpə'sɪlɪəsnəs] *n* (*condescension*) altanería; (*disdain*) desdén *m*.
superconductivity [suːpəkɒndək'tɪvɪtɪ] *n* superconductividad *f*.

superconductor [suːpəkən'dʌktəʳ] n superconductor m.

superficial [suːpə'fɪʃəl] adj (gen) superficial.

superficiality [suːpəfɪʃɪ'ælɪtɪ] n superficialidad f.

superficially [suːpə'fɪʃəlɪ] adv superficialmente.

superfine ['suːpəfaɪn] adj (in size, quality) extrafino,-a.

superfluous [suː'pɜːfluəs] adj (gen) superfluo,-a; (remark, comment) de más.

● to be superfluous, sobrar, estar de más.

superhuman [suːpə'hjuːmən] adj sobrehumano,-a.

superimpose [suːpəɪm'pəʊz] t sobreponer, superponer.

superintendent [suːpərɪn'tendənt] 1 n (person in charge - gen) director,-ra, inspector,-ra, supervisor,-ra. 2 GB (in police) comisario,-a de policía. 3 US (in apartment building) portero,-a, conserje mf. 4 (of park) encargado,-a.

superior [suː'pɪərɪəʳ] 1 adj (gen) superior (to, a): a superior brand, una marca superior; a superior artist, un gran artista. 2 pej (attitude, tone, smile) de superioridad: a superior look, una mirada de superioridad; she's so superior, tiene aires de superioridad. – 3 n (senior) superior mf.

● to be superior in number, superar en número.

■ Mother Superior, Madre Superiora. ‖ superior officer, (oficial m) superior m.

superiority [suːpɪərɪ'ɒrɪtɪ] n superioridad f.

■ superiority complex, complejo de superioridad.

superlative [suː'pɜːlətɪv] 1 adj (excellent) superlativo,-a, de primera, excelente, excepcional. 2 LING superlativo,-a. – 3 n LING superlativo.

superman ['suːpəmæn] n superhombre m.

▲ pl supermen.

supermarket [suːpə'mɑːkɪt] n supermercado, autoservicio.

supernatural [suːpə'nætʃərəl] 1 adj sobrenatural. – 2 the supernatural, n lo sobrenatural m.

supernova [suːpə'nəʊvə] n supernova.

▲ pl supernovae o supernovas.

superpower ['suːpəpaʊəʳ] n superpotencia.

supersede [suːpə'siːd] t (replace) reemplazar, substituir, suplantar.

supersonic [suːpə'sɒnɪk] adj supersónico,-a.

superstar ['suːpəstɑːʳ] n superestrella.

superstition [suːpə'stɪʃən] n superstición f.

superstitious [sjuːpə'stɪʃəs] adj supersticioso,-a.

superstore ['suːpəstɔːʳ] n hipermercado.

superstructure ['suːpəstrʌktʃəʳ] n superestructura.

supertanker ['suːpətæŋkəʳ] n superpetrolero.

supertax ['suːpətæks] n impuesto adicional (pagado por los que tienen ingresos muy altos).

supervene [suːpə'viːn] i fml sobrevenir.

supervise ['suːpəvaɪz] 1 t (watch over) vigilar. 2 (keep check on) supervisar; (run) dirigir: the foreman supervises the work in the factory, el capataz supervisa el trabajo en la fábrica.

supervision [suːpə'vɪʒən] n supervisión f.

supervisor ['suːpəvaɪzəʳ] 1 n (gen) supervisor,-ra. 2 GB EDUC director,-ra de tesis.

supervisory [suːpə'vaɪzərɪ] adj de supervisor,-ra.

superwoman ['suːpəwʊmən] n supermujer f.

▲ pl superwomen.

supine ['suːpaɪn] 1 adj fml (position) supino,-a. 2 fig (attitude) pasivo,-a.

supper ['sʌpəʳ] n cena.

● to have supper, cenar.

supper-time ['sʌpətaɪm] n hora de cenar.

supplant [sə'plɑːnt] t suplantar, reemplazar, sustituir.

supple ['sʌpəl] adj (body, fingers) flexible, ágil; (material) flexible; (mind) ágil; (movement) natural.

supplement ['sʌplɪmənt] 1 n (charge) suplemento: a £5.00 supplement, un suplemento de £5.00. 2 (dietary) complemento. 3 LIT suplemento. – 4 t complementar: he supplements his income by working in a bar, trabaja en un bar para complementar sus ingresos.

▲ (verbo) [ˈsʌplɪment].

supplementary [sʌplɪ'mentərɪ] 1 adj (gen) suplementario,-a, adicional. 2 MATH suplementario,-a.

■ supplementary benefit, GB subsidio complementario concedido a los más pobres.

suppleness ['sʌpəlnəs] n flexibilidad f, agilidad f.

supplicant ['sʌplɪkənt] n fml suplicante mf.

supplicate ['sʌplɪkeɪt] 1 t fml suplicar. – 2 i fml suplicar (for, -).

supplication [sʌplɪ'keɪʃən] n fml súplica.

supplier [sə'plaɪəʳ] n COMM proveedor,-ra, abastecedor,-ra.

supply [sə'plaɪ] 1 n (provision) suministro: the electricity/water supply, el suministro de electricidad/agua. 2 COMM (provision - to markets, areas, etc) abastecimiento; (- to individuals, houses, shops, etc) suministro. 3 (amount availabe) reserva: the world's food supply, la reserva alimentaria del mundo; I've got my own supply of biscuits, tengo mi propia reserva de galletas. – 4 t (goods, materials) suministrar: this company supplies gas to its customers, esta empresa suministra gas a los clientes; who supplies arms to the Serbian forces?, ¿quién suministra armas a las fuerzas serbias? 5 (a person, company, city, etc) abastecer (with, de), proveer (with, de): they supply the whole town with fruit, abastecen de fruta a toda la cuidad; this reservoir supplies the whole area with water, este pantano abastece de agua a toda la región; the company supplies all employees with a uniform, la empresa provee a todos los empleados de un uniforme. 6 (give - information, proof, facts) facilitar, proporcionar. 7 MIL (with provisions) aprovisionar. 8 fml (need, requirement) satisfacer. – 9 supplies, npl (food) provisiones fpl, víveres mpl; (stock) existencias fpl, stock m: office supplies, material de oficina. 10 MIL pertrechos mpl.

● to be in short supply, escasear.

■ supply and demand, la oferta y la demanda. ‖ supply teacher, profesor,-ra suplente.

▲ (sustantivo) pl supplies, (verbo) pt & pp supplied, ger supplying.

support [sə'pɔːt] 1 n (physical - gen) apoyo, sostén m; (- thing worn on body) protector m. 2 (of building) soporte m, puntal m. 3 (moral) apoyo, respaldo: you have our full support, cuentas con nuestro total apoyo; he was a great support to me when my father died, me apoyó mucho cuando se murió mi padre. 4 (financial) ayuda económica, apoyo económico; (sustenance) sustento; (person) sostén m: the scheme is run without government support, el proyecto funciona sin ninguna ayuda gubernamental; he had no means of support, no tenía ninguna fuente de ingresos. 5 (supporters) afición f. 6 (evidence) pruebas fpl. – 7 t (roof, bridge, etc) sostener; (weight) aguantar, resistir; (part of body) sujetar: I don't think that shelf can support so many books, no creo que esa estantería aguante tantos libros. 8 (back, encourage) apoyar, respaldar, ayudar; (cause, motion, proposal) apoyar, estar de acuerdo con: my parents have always supported me in everything I've done, mis padres siempre me han apoyado en todo lo que he hecho. 9 SP (follow) seguir; (*encourage*) animar: *which team do you support?*, ¿de qué equipo eres? **10** (*keep, sustain*) mantener, sustentar, sostener; (*feed*) alimentar. **11** (*corroborate, substantiate*) confirmar, respaldar, apoyar, respaldar. **12** *fml* (*endure*) soportar, tolerar.

● **in support,** (*in reserve*) de apoyo. ‖ **in support of sb./ sth.,** en apoyo de algn./algo, a favor de algn./algo. ‖ **to drum up support for sb./sth.,** conseguir apoyo para algn./algo. ‖ **to support os.,** ganarse la vida.

■ **support group,** POL grupo de apoyo; MUS grupo telonero.

supporter [sə'pɔːtəʳ] **1** *n* POL partidario,-a. **2** SP (*gen*) seguidor,-ra; (*fan*) hincha *mf*, forofo,-a. – **3 supporters,** *npl* SP la afición *f sing*.

■ **supporters' club,** peña deportiva.

supporting [sə'pɔːtɪŋ] *adj* CINEM THEAT (*part, role*) secundario,-a.

supportive [sə'pɔːtɪv] **to be supportive,** *phr* apoyar, dar apoyo.

suppose [sə'pəʊz] **1** *t* (*assume, imagine*) suponer, imaginarse: *I suppose you heard about the bomb,* supongo que te habrás enterado de la bomba; *I suppose Terry sent you,* supongo que te habrá enviado Terry; *I don't suppose you've got any serviettes?,* ¿no tendrás servilletas, por casualidad? **2** (*in polite requests*): *I don't suppose you could lend me £10, could you?,* no podrías dejarme £10, ¿no? **3** (*believe*) creer: *what do you suppose will happen now?,* ¿qué crees que pasará ahora?; *we all supposed her to be Spanish,* todos creíamos que era española. **4** (*postulate*) suponer: *let's suppose that ...,* supongamos que ... **5** *fml* (*presuppose*) suponer. – **6** *conj* (*hypothesis*) ¿y si ...?, pongamos por caso, supongamos: *suppose she's right?,* ¿y si tiene razón?; *suppose you miss the flight,* supongamos que pierdes el vuelo; *just suppose you'd won,* pongamos por caso que hubieras ganado. **7** (*making suggestions*) ¿y si ...?, ¿qué tal si ...?: *suppose we leave now?,* ¿y si nos fuéramos ya?; *suppose we wait until tomorrow?,* ¿qué tal si esperamos hasta mañana?

● **I suppose not,** supongo que no. ‖ **I suppose so,** supongo que sí.

supposed [sə'pəʊzd] *adj* supuesto,-a.

● **to be supposed to,** (*supposition, reputation*) se supone que, dicen que; (*obligation, responsibility*) deber, tener que; (*intention*) se supone que: *it's supposed to be a good restaurant,* dicen que es un restaurante muy bueno; *you're supposed to be in bed,* deberías estar en la cama; *what's that supposed to mean?,* ¿qué quieres decir con eso?, ¿y eso qué se supone que quiere decir?; *it was supposed to be a surprise,* se suponía que iba a ser una sorpresa.

supposedly [sə'pəʊsədlɪ] *adv* supuestamente.

supposing [sə'pəʊzɪŋ] **1** *conj* (*hypothesis*) ¿y si ...?, suponiendo: *supposing it rains,* ¿y si llueve?; *supposing somebody saw you,* ¿y si te vio alguien?; *supposing I have to work late,* suponiendo que tenga que trabajar hasta tarde. **2** (*making suggestions*) ¿i si ...?, ¿qué tal si ...?: *supposing I have a word with her,* ¿y si yo hablo con ella?

supposition [sʌpə'zɪʃən] *n* suposición *f*, supuesto *m*: *it's pure supposition,* no son más que suposiciones.

suppository [sə'pɒzɪtərɪ] *n* supositorio.

▲ *pl suppositories.*

suppress [sə'pres] *t* (*gen*) suprimir; (*feelings, laugh, yawn, etc*) contener, reprimir; (*news, truth, evidence*) callar, ocultar; (*revolt, rebellion*) sofocar, reprimir.

suppression [sə'preʃən] *n* (*gen*) supresión *f*; (*of feelings*) represión *f*, inhibición *f*; (*of truth, evidence, information*)

ocultación *f*; (*of book*) prohibición *f*; (*of revolt*) represión *f*.

suppressor [sə'presəʳ] **1** *n* (*person, thing*) el/la/lo que suprime. **2** RAD TV supresor *m*.

suppurate ['sʌpjəreɪt] *i* supurar.

suppuration [sʌpjə'reɪʃən] *n* supuración *f*.

supranational [suːprə'næʃənəl] *adj* supranacional.

supremacist [suː'preməsɪst] *n* supremacista *mf*.

supremacy [suː'preməsɪ] *n* supremacía.

supreme [suː'priːm] *adj* (*highest*) supremo,-a, sumo,-a; (*greatest*) supremo,-a: *supreme authority,* suma autoridad; *a supreme effort,* un esfuerzo supremo.

● **to make the supreme sacrifice,** hacer el supremo sacrificio.

■ **the Supreme Being,** el Ser Supremo. ‖ **Supreme Commander,** MIL Comandante *m* Supremo. ‖ **the Supreme Court,** JUR el Tribunal *m* Supremo.

supremely [suː'priːmlɪ] *adv* sumamente.

supremo [su'priːməʊ] *n* GB *fam* gran jefe,-a.

▲ *pl supremos.*

surcharge ['sɜːtʃɑːdʒ] **1** *n* recargo, sobretasa. – **2** *t* (*person*) aplicar un recargo a.

sure [ʃʊəʳ] **1** *adj* (*positive, certain*) seguro,-a (**about/of,** de); (*convinced*) convencido,-a: *I think so, but I'm not sure,* creo que sí, pero no estoy seguro; *I'm quite sure,* estoy absolutamente seguro; *are you sure of your facts?,* ¿estás seguro de lo que dices?; *I'm not sure about the style,* el estilo no me convence del todo; *he felt sure of winning,* se sentía seguro de que iba a ganar; *are you sure you won't stay for supper?,* ¿seguro que no te quedarás a cenar?; *she's not sure how it works,* no sabe muy bien cómo funciona. **2** (*certain, inevitable*) seguro,-a: *one thing is sure ...,* lo que es seguro es una cosa ...; *it's sure to be sunny,* seguro que hará sol; *he's sure to win,* seguro que ganará. **3** (*reliable*) seguro,-a. – **4** *adv* (*of course*) claro, por supuesto: *do you want to come? –sure,* ¿quieres venir? –claro que sí. **5** US (*as intensifier*) realmente, de verdad: *he sure is handsome!,* ¡qué guapo es!; *it sure is hot!,* ¡qué calor hace!

● **as sure as eggs is eggs,** (tan seguro) como que dos y dos son cuatro. ‖ **as sure as I'm standing here,** palabra de honor. ‖ **for sure,** seguro: *we don't know for sure,* no estamos seguros; *I can't say for sure,* no te lo puedo decir; *that's for sure!,* ¡de eso no cabe duda! ‖ **sure enough,** efectivamente, en efecto. ‖ **sure thing,** claro, por supuesto. ‖ **to be sure of os.,** estar seguro,-a de sí mismo,-a. ‖ **to be sure of sb.,** poder confiar en algn. ‖ **to be sure to,** no olvidarse de, no dejar de: *be sure to lock the door,* no te olvides de cerrar la puerta con llave. ‖ **to make sure,** asegurarse (**of,** de): *make sure that the money's there,* asegúrate de que el dinero esté allí; *I'll just make sure,* voy a asegurarme.

sure-fire ['ʃʊəfaɪəʳ] *adj fam* segurísimo,-a, infalible.

sure-footed [ʃʊə'fʊtɪd] *adj* de pie firme.

surely ['ʃʊəlɪ] **1** *adv* (*doubtless*) seguramente, sin duda: *this is surely her best novel,* ésta es sin duda su mejor novela. **2** (*as intensifier*): *surely you haven't forgotten!,* ¡no se te habrá olvidado!; *he surely doesn't expect me to do it!,* ¡no puede ser que espere que lo haga yo!; *surely not!,* ¡no puede ser! **3** (*in a sure manner*) con seguridad: *slowly but surely,* sin prisas pero sin pausas. **4** US (*certainly*) por supuesto, desde luego, claro (que sí).

surety ['ʃʊərɪ] **1** *n* (*person*) fiador,-ra, garante *mf*. **2** (*money*) fianza, garantía.

● **to stand surety for sb.,** ser fiador,-ra de algn.

▲ *pl sureties.*

surf [sɜːf] **1** *n* (*waves*) olas *fpl*, oleaje *m*; (*foam*) espuma. – **2** *i* hacer surf.

surface ['sɜːfəs] **1** *n* (*gen*) superficie *f*; (*of road*) firme *m*: *the moon's surface,* la superficie de la luna. **2** *fig* (*exterior*) apariencia: *beneath her calm surface,* bajo su calmada apariencia: *he only looks at the surface of things,* sólo mira las cosas muy superficialmente. – **3** *adj* (*gen*) superficial. – **4** *t* (*cover road*) pavimentar; (*with asphalt*) asfaltar. – **5** *i* (*submarine etc*) salir a la superficie; (*problems etc*) aflorar, aparecer, surgir. **6** (*from bed*) asomarse, dejarse ver; (*after disappearance*) reaparecer.

● **on the surface,** en apariencia, a primera vista. ‖ **to come/rise to the surface,** (*problem etc*) aflorar, surgir. ■ **surface area,** superficie *f*, area (de la superficie). ‖ **surface mail,** correo de superficie: *by surface mail,* por vía terrestre o marítima. ‖ **surface tension,** tensión *f* superficial. ‖ **surface worker,** trabajador,-ra en superficie.

surface-to-air [sɜːfəstʊˈeəʳ] *adj* tierra-aire.
■ **surface-to-air missile,** mísil *m* tierra-aire.

surfboard ['sɜːfbɔːd] *n* tabla de surf.

surfeit ['sɜːfɪt] *n fml* exceso.

surfer ['sɜːfəʳ] *n* surfista *mf*.

surfing ['sɜːfɪŋ] *n* surf *m*.

surge [sɜːdʒ] **1** *n* (*of sea*) oleada, oleaje *m*, marejada; (*of people*) oleada, marea. **2** (*increase - in demand etc*) aumento; (*- of support*) oleada; (*- of anger*) arranque *m*. – **3** *i* (*sea, wave*) levantarse, hincharse; (*people, crowd*) ir en tropel, avanzar a manadas. **4** (*increase*) aumentar bruscamente.

● **to surge up inside sb.,** (*anger etc*) invadir a algn., apoderarse de algn.

surgeon ['sɜːdʒən] *n* cirujano,-a.
■ **brain surgeon,** neurocirujano,-a. ‖ **heart surgeon,** cardiocirujano,-a.

surgery ['sɜːdʒərɪ] **1** *n* (*operating*) cirugía: *plastic surgery,* cirugía estética. **2** GB (*place*) consultorio, consulta; (*time*) consulta: *surgery hours are from 9 to 3,* las horas de consulta son de 9 a 3.

● **to undergo surgery,** ser operado,-a, ser sometido,-a a una intervención quirúrgica.

▲ *pl surgeries.*

surgical ['sɜːdʒɪkəl] *adj* (*instrument, treatment*) quirúrgico,-a.
■ **surgical appliance,** aparato ortopédico. ‖ **surgical knife,** bisturí *m*. ‖ **surgical spirit,** alcohol *m* de 90°.

Surinam [sʊərɪˈnæm] *n* Surinam.

surly ['sɜːlɪ] *adj* (*bad-tempered*) hosco,-a, arisco,-a, malhumorado,-a; (*bad-mannered*) maleducado,-a.

▲ *comp surlier, superl surliest.*

surmise [sɜːˈmaɪz] **1** *n fml* conjetura, suposición *f*. – **2** *t fml* suponer, figurarse.

surmount [sɜːˈmaʊnt] **1** *t* (*overcome*) superar, vencer. **2** ARCH rematar, coronar.

surmountable [sɜːˈmaʊntəbəl] *adj* superable.

surname ['sɜːneɪm] *n* apellido.

surpass [sɜːˈpɑːs] *t* (*better*) superar; (*exceed*) superar, sobrepasar: *the holiday surpassed all our expectations,* las vacaciones superaron todas nuestras expectativas.

surplice ['sɜːplɪs] *n* sobrepelliz *f*.

surplus ['sɜːpləs] **1** *n* (*of goods, produce*) excedente *m*, sobrante *m*; (*of budget*) superávit *m*: *a food surplus,* un excedente de alimentos; *trade surplus,* superávit en la balanza comercial. – **2** *adj* sobrante, excedente: *surplus labour,* mano de obra excedente.

■ **surplus stock,** saldos *mpl*. ‖ **army surplus,** excedentes *mpl* del ejército.

surprise [səˈpraɪz] **1** *n* sorpresa: *what a surprise!,* ¡qué sorpresa!; *to my surprise,* para mi sorpresa. – **2** *adj* (*visit, result*) inesperado,-a; (*attack, party*) sorpresa. – **3** *t* (*cause surprise to*) sorprender. **4** (*catch unawares*) sorprender, coger desprevenido,-a.

● **to come as a surprise,** ser una sorpresa. ‖ **to take sb. by surprise,** coger desprevenido,-a a algn.

surprised [səˈpraɪzd] *adj* (*person*) sorprendido,-a; (*look*) de sorpresa.

● **to be surprised,** sorprenderse, llevarse una sorpresa: *I'm surprised to see you here!,* ¡me sorprende verte aquí!; *I'm surprised (that) Julie passed,* me sorprende que Julie haya aprobado; *I wouldn't be surprised if it rained,* no me extrañaría que lloviese; *I'm surprised at you!,* ¡me sorprendes!

surprising [səˈpraɪzɪŋ] *adj* sorprendente.

surprisingly [səˈpraɪzɪŋlɪ] *adv* sorprendentemente: *surprisingly enough ...,* para sorpresa de todos ...; *not surprisingly ...,* como es lógico ...

surreal [səˈrɪəl] *adj* surrealista.

surrealism [səˈrɪəlɪzəm] *n* surrealismo.

surrealist [səˈrɪəlɪst] **1** *n* surrealista *mf*. – **2** *adj* surrealista.

surrealistic [sərɪəˈlɪstɪk] *adj* surrealista.

surrender [səˈrendəʳ] **1** *n* (*capitulation*) rendición *f*; (*submission*) sumisión *f*, claudicación *f*. **2** (*giving up - of arms*) entrega; (*- of rights*) renuncia. – **3** *t* MIL (*weapons, town*) rendir, entregar. **4** *fml* (*passport, ticket, etc*) entregar; (*claim, right, priviledge*) renunciar a, ceder. – **5** *i* rendirse, entregarse.

● **to surrender os. to sth.,** dejarse vencer por algo.

surreptitious [sʌrəpˈtɪʃəs] *adj* subrepticio,-a, furtivo,-a.

surrogacy ['sʌrəgəsɪ] *n* alquiler *m* de úteros.

surrogate ['sʌrəgeɪt] *n fml* (*gen*) sustituto,-a.
■ **surrogate mother,** madre *f* de alquiler.

surround [səˈraʊnd] **1** *t* (*encircle*) rodear (**with,** de): *police surrounded the building,* la policía rodeó el edificio. – **2** *n* marco, borde *m*.

● **to be surrounded by sth.,** estar rodeado,-a de algo.

surrounding [səˈraʊndɪŋ] **1** *adj* circundante: *the surrounding countryside,* el campo circundante. – **2** **surroundings,** *npl* (*of town, city, etc*) alrededores *mpl*, cercanías *fpl*. **3** (*environment*) entorno *m*, ambiente *m*.

surtax ['sɜːtæks] *n* recargo.

surveillance [sɜːˈveɪləns] *n* vigilancia.
● **to keep sb. under surveillance,** mantener a algn. bajo vigilancia.

survey ['sɜːveɪ] **1** *n* (*investigation - of opinion*) sondeo, encuesta; (*- of prices, trends, etc*) estudio; (*written report*) informe *m*. **2** (*of land*) inspección *f*, reconocimiento; (*in topography*) medición *f*: *an aerial survey,* un reconocimiento aéreo. **3** (*general view*) visión *f* general, visión *f* de conjunto. **4** GB (*of house, building*) inspección *f*, peritaje *m*. – **5** *t* (*contemplate, look at*) contemplar, mirar. **6** (*study - gen*) examinar, analizar; (*- prices, trends, etc*) estudiar, hacer una encuesta sobre; (*investigate - people*) encuestar, hacer un sondeo de. **7** (*- land*) hacer un reconocimiento de; (*in topography*) medir. **8** (*house, building*) inspeccionar, hacer un peritaje de.

▲ *verbo* [səˈveɪ].

surveying [sɜːˈveɪɪŋ] *n* agrimensura, topografía.

surveyor [səˈveɪəʳ] *n* (*of land*) agrimensor,-ra, topógrafo,-a; (*of house, building*) perito,-a.

survival [səˈvaɪvəl] **1** *n* (*gen*) supervivencia: *survival of the fittest,* la ley del más fuerte. **2** (*relic*) reliquia, vestigio (**from,** de).

survive

610

■ **survival kit,** equipo para emergencias.
survive [sə'vaɪv] **1** i (gen) sobrevivir; (custom, tradition) sobrevivir, perdurar; (book, painting) conservarse: *he survived on bread and water,* sobrevivió a base de pan y agua; *the amount I earn is hardly enough to survive on,* lo que gano apenas me alcanza para sobrevivir. **2** fam (cope, get by) ir tirando, arreglárselas: *don't worry, we'll survive,* no te preocupes, nos las arreglaremos. – **3** t (disaster) sobrevivir a: *few people survived the earthquake,* pocas personas sobrevivieron al terremoto; *somehow he survived the accident,* de alguna manera salió con vida del accidente. **4** (person) sobrevivir a.
survivor [sə'vaɪvəʳ] n superviviente mf, sobreviviente mf.
susceptibility [səseptə'bɪlɪtɪ] **1** n (vunerability - gen) vunerabilidad f (**to,** frente a); (- to illness) propensión f (**to,** a). – **2 susceptibilities,** npl (feelings) sentimientos mpl, susceptibilidades fpl.
▲ pl **susceptibilities.**
susceptible [sə'septɪbəl] **1** adj (easily influenced) sugestionable; (impressionable) susceptible, sensible, impresionable (**to,** a); (prone to illness) propenso,-a (**to,** a). **2** JUR fml susceptible (**of,** de).
suspect ['sʌspekt] **1** adj (suspicious) sospechoso,-a; (dubious, questionable) dudoso,-a: *his statement is suspect,* su declaración es de dudosa autenticidad. – **2** n (person) sospechoso,-a. – **3** t (believe guilty) sospechar de; (mistrust) recelar de, desconfiar de, dudar de: *surely you don't suspect me!,* ¡no puede ser que sospeches de mí!; *he is suspected of murdering his wife,* se sospecha que asesinó a su mujer. **4** (think true) sospechar: *he suspected murder,* sospechaba que había sido un asesinato. **5** (suppose, guess) imaginarse, creer: *I suspected as much,* me lo imaginaba.
▲ (verbo) [sə'spekt].
suspected [sə'spektɪd] adj (criminal etc) presunto,-a; (disease, illness) posible, no confirmado,-a.
suspend [sə'spend] **1** t (stop temporarily) suspender; (postpone) posponer, aplazar: *building work has been suspended,* se han suspendido las obras. **2** (remove) suspender. **3** (hang) suspender, colgar.
suspended [sə'spendɪd] adj (gen) suspendido,-a.
■ **suspended animation,** muerte f aparente. ‖ suspended sentence, JUR condena condicional.
suspender [sə'spendəʳ] **1** n GB (for stocking) liga. – **2** suspenders, npl US (braces) tirantes mpl.
■ **suspender belt,** liguero.
suspense [sə'spens] n (anticipation) incertidumbre f; (intrigue) suspense m, intriga.
● **to keep sb. in suspense,** tener a algn. con en vilo, tener a algn. sobre ascuas.
suspension [sə'spenʃən] **1** n (halt) suspensión f; (postponement) aplazamiento, postergación f. **2** (of employee, player) suspensión f; (of pupil) expulsión f. **3** CHEM suspensión f. **4** TECH suspensión f.
■ **suspension bridge,** puente m colgante.
suspicion [sə'spɪʃən] **1** n (gen) sospecha; (mistrust) recelo, desconfianza; (doubt) duda; (hunch) presentimiento: *I have my suspicions,* tengo mis sospechas; *the boy's movements aroused our suspicions,* los movimientos del chico despertaron nuestras sospechas. **2** (slight trace) pizca, asomo, atisbo.
● **to arrest sb. on suspicion,** detener a algn. como sospechoso,-a. ‖ **to be above suspicion,** estar por encima de toda sospecha. ‖ **to be under suspicion,** estar bajo sospecha.
suspicious [sə'spɪʃəs] **1** adj (arousing suspicion) sospechoso,-a: *he's a very suspicious-looking bloke,* es un tipo

muy sospechoso. **2** (distrustful, wary) receloso,-a, desconfiado,-a, suspicaz: *she's suspicious of strangers,* desconfía de extraños.
● **to be suspicious of/about sb./sth.,** desconfiar de algn./algo.
suspiciously [sə'spɪʃəslɪ] **1** adv (arousing suspicion) sospechosamente: *it looks suspiciously like arson,* tiene todo el aspecto de un incendio provocado. **2** (having suspicions) con recelo, con desconfianza.
suss [sʌs] t GB sl (realize) darse cuenta de; (see through) calar: *he never sussed what was going on,* nunca cayó en la cuenta de lo que estaba pasando; *I've got you sussed!,* ¡te tengo calado!
◆ **to suss out** t sep GB sl (see through) calar; (understand) entender.
sustain [sə'steɪn] **1** t (keep alive - gen) sustentar; (- spirits, hope) mantener: *a coffee won't sustain you,* un café no te sustentará. **2** (maintain - gen) sostener; (- interest, conversation) mantener; (- work) continuar: *the film doesn't sustain the audience's interest,* la película no mantiene el interés del público. **3** MUS (note) sostener. **4** fml (suffer - loss, injury, wound, etc) sufrir. **5** fml (hold up) sostener. **6** JUR admitir.
● **objection sustained,** se admite la protesta.
sustainable [sə'steɪnəbəl] adj sostenible.
sustained [sə'steɪnd] **1** adj (effort) sostenido,-a; (applause, attack) prolongado,-a; (work, growth) continuo,-a. **2** MUS (note) sostenido,-a.
sustenance ['sʌstɪnəns] n sustento, alimento.
svelte [svelt] adj (slim) esbelto,-a.
SW¹ ['ʃɔːtweɪv] abbr (short wave) onda corta; (abbreviation) OC.
SW² [sauθ] abbr (southwest) sudoeste, suroeste; (abbreviation) S.
swab [swɒb] **1** n MED (cotton wool) algodón m; (gauze) gasa. **2** MED (specimen) frotis m, muestra. **3** (cleaning cloth) paño, bayeta, trapo; (mop) fregona. – **4** t MED (wound) limpiar. **5** MAR (deck) limpiar, fregar.
▲ pt & pp **swabbed,** ger **swabbing.**
swaddle ['swɒdəl] t envolver.
swag [swæg] n (stolen goods) botín m.
swagger ['swægəʳ] **1** i pavonearse, chulearse: *he swaggered around showing off his trophy,* se pavoneaba luciendo su trofeo. – **2** n pavoneo: *he walked off with a swagger,* se marchó con aire arrogante.
swaggeringly ['swægərɪŋlɪ] adv con chulería, con fanfarronería.
Swahili [swɑː'hiːlɪ] n swahili m, suajili m.
swallow¹ ['swɒləʊ] **1** n (of drink, food) trago. – **2** t (food etc) tragar: *the snake swallowed the dog whole,* la serpiente se tragó el perro entero. **3** fig (be taken in by) tragarse: *she's so gullible, she'll swallow anything,* es tan crédula, se tragará cualquier cosa. – **4** i tragar.
◆ **to swallow up** t sep (engulf) tragarse, engullir. **2** (use up) consumir, tragarse, comerse, absorber.
● **to swallow one's pride,** tragarse el orgullo. ‖ **to swallow one's words,** desdecirse de sus palabras. ‖ **to swallow the bait,** tragar el anzuelo.
swallow² ['swɒləʊ] n ORN golondrina.
● **one swallow does not make a summer,** una golondrina no hace verano.
■ **swallow dive,** salto del ángel.
swam [swæm] pt → **swim.**
swamp [swɒmp] **1** n pantano, ciénaga. – **2** t (land) inundar, anegar; (boat) hundir. **3** fig (inundate) inundar (**with/ by,** de); (overwhelm) agobiar, abrumar (**with/by,** de);

we've been swamped with applications, hemos recibido una avalancha de solicitudes.

swampy ['swɒmpɪ] *adj* pantanoso,-a.

▲ *comp* **swampier,** *superl* **swampiest.**

swan [swɒn] **1** *n* ORN cisne *m.* – **2** *i* pavonearse: *she swans about the office as if she owned the place,* se pavonea por la oficina como si fuese suya; *they're swanning off to Greece!,* ¡se van a Grecia por la cara!

▲ *(verbo) pt & pp* **swanned,** *ger* **swanning.**

swank [swæŋk] **1** *n fam (behaviour)* farol *m,* fanfarronada. **2** *(person)* fafarrón,-ona, fardón,-ona. – **3** *i fam* fanfarronear, fardar.

swanky ['swæŋkɪ] **1** *adj* US *fam (posh)* de lujo. **2** *pej (person)* fanfarrón,-ona, fardón,-ona.

▲ *comp* **swankier,** *superl* **swankiest.**

swan-song ['swɒnsɒŋ] *n* canto del cisne.

swap [swɒp] **1** *n* canje *m,* cambalache *m.* – **2** *t fam* cambiar, intercambiar: *he swapped his skates for a videogame,* cambió sus patines por un videojuego; *can I swap places with you?,* ¿te puedo cambiar el sitio? – **3** *i* hacer un intercambio, cambiar.

◆ **to swap over / swap round** *t sep* cambiar (de sitio).

▲ *pt & pp* **swapped,** *ger* **swapping.**

swarm [swɔːm] **1** *n (of bees)* enjambre *m.* **2** *fig (of people)* enjambre *m,* nube *f,* multitud *f.* – **3** *i (bees)* enjambrar. **4** *fig (people)* aglomerarse, apiñarse, arremolinarse: *they swarmed round the food like bees round a honey pot,* se apiñaban alrededor de la comida como abejas alrededor de un bote de miel.

◆ **to swarm with** *t insep* rebosar de, estar plagado,-a de: *Barcelona is swarming with tourists,* Barcelona está plagada de turistas.

swarthy ['swɔːðɪ] *adj* moreno,-a, de tez morena.

▲ *comp* **swarthier,** *superl* **swarthiest.**

swashbuckling ['swɒʃbʌklɪŋ] *adj (person)* bravucón,-ona; *(film)* de capa y espada.

swastika ['swɒstɪkə] *n* esvástica, cruz *f* gamada.

swat [swɒt] **1** *t (try to hit)* aplastar; *(kill)* matar. – **2** *n (blow)* golpe *m;* *(with hand)* manotazo.

● **to take a swat at sth.,** dar un golpe a algo.

▲ *pt & pp* **swatted,** *ger* **swatting.**

swath [swɔːθ] *n (of grass, land)* franja.

swathe¹ [sweɪð] *n* → **swath.**

swathe² [sweɪð] *t (wrap)* envolver, vendar.

◆ **to swathe in** *t sep fig* envolver.

swatter ['swɒtə'] *n* matamoscas *m.*

sway [sweɪ] **1** *n (movement)* balanceo, vaivén *m,* movimiento. **2** *fig (influence)* dominio, influencia **(over,** sobre). – **3** *t (swing)* balancear, bambolear: *she swayed her body in time to the music,* bamboleaba el cuerpo al compás de la música. **4** *fig (influence)* influir en, influenciar, convencer: *the closing speech swayed the crowd,* el discurso final arrastró a las masas; *don't let yourself be swayed,* no te dejes influenciar. – **5** *i (person, tree, ladder)* balancearse, bambolearse; *(tower)* bambolearse; *(crops)* mecerse; *(person - totter)* tambalearse: *the trees were swaying in the wind,* los árboles se balanceaban con el viento; *he swayed a little as he walked,* caminaba tambaleándose un poco. **6** *fig (waver)* vacilar **(between,** entre), oscilar **(between,** entre).

● **to hold sway,** *(ideas, beliefs)* prevalecer; *(person)* dominar. ‖ **to hold sway over sb.,** dominar a algn.

Swaziland ['swɑːzɪlænd] *n* Swazilandia.

swear [sweə'] **1** *t (declare formally)* jurar; *(vow)* juramentar: *he swore allegiance to the constitution,* juró lealtad a la constitución; *I swear to tell the truth,* juro decir la ver-

dad; *she had to swear an oath,* tuvo que hacer un juramento. **2** *fam (state firmly)* jurar: *I swear I didn't do it,* juro que no lo hice; *I could've sworn I heard the phone,* hubiera jurado que oí el teléfono. – **3** *i (declare formally)* jurar, prestar juramento: *do you swear on the Bible?,* ¿lo juras sobre la Biblia? **4** *(curse)* decir palabrotas, soltar tacos; *(blaspheme)* jurar, blasfemar: *he twisted his ankle and swore loudly,* se torció el tobillo y soltó un taco; *the players swear at each other all the time,* los jugadores se insultan continuamente; *don't swear at me!,* ¡no me insultes!

◆ **to swear by** *t insep fam* tener una fe absoluta en. ‖ **to swear in** *t sep (in court)* tomarle juramento a. ‖ **to swear to** *t insep* jurar.

● **to be sworn in,** *(in court)* prestar juramento; *(in post)* jurar un cargo. ‖ **to swear blind,** jurar y perjurar. ‖ **to swear like a trooper,** jurar como un carretero. ‖ **to swear sb. to secrecy,** hacer que algn. jure guardar un secreto.

▲ *pt* **swore,** *pp* **sworn.**

swear-word ['sweəwɜːd] *n* palabrota, taco.

sweat [swet] **1** *n (perspiration)* sudor *m:* *the sweat was pouring off him,* estaba sudando a chorros. **2** *fam (hard work)* paliza: *this job is a real sweat,* este trabajo es una auténtica paliza. **3** *fam (anxious state)* nerviosismo: *she's in a sweat because she hasn't finished the essay,* está muy nerviosa porque no ha acabado la redacción; *don't get in a sweat about it,* no te pongas nervioso por ello. – **4** *i (perspire)* sudar. **5** *(cheese)* exudar humedad. **6** *(work hard)* sudar la gota gorda. **7** *fam (worry)* estar preocupado,-a, sufrir: *let's make them sweat a bit,* hagamos que pasen un mal rato. – **8** *t* GB CULIN *(cook gently)* rehogar.

◆ **to sweat out** *t sep (illness, cold)* quitarse sudando; *(toxins)* eliminar.

● **by the sweat of one's brow,** con el sudor de su frente. ‖ **to be all of/in a sweat,** *(wet)* estar empapado,-a de sudor; *(anxious)* estar muy nervioso,-a. ‖ **to be in a cold sweat,** tener un sudor frío. ‖ **no sweat,** ningún problema. ‖ **to sweat blood,** sudar sangre, sudar tinta, sudar la gota gorda. ‖ **to sweat it out,** *(exercise)* sudar la gota gorda; *(suffer until end)* aguantar. ‖ **to sweat one's guts out,** echar los bofes.

■ **sweat gland,** glándula sudorípara.

sweatband ['swetbænd] **1** *n* SP *(around head)* cinta; *(around wrist)* muñequera. **2** *(in hat)* faja interior.

sweated ['swetɪd] **sweated labour,** *n (work)* trabajo mal pagado; *(workers)* mano de obra explotada.

sweater ['swetə'] *n* suéter *m,* jersey *m.*

sweatshirt ['swetʃɜːt] *n* sudadera.

sweatshop ['swetʃɒp] *n fábrica o taller donde se explota a los trabajadores.*

sweaty ['swetɪ] *adj (person, clothes)* sudoroso,-a, sudado,-a; *(day, weather)* borchornoso,-a; *(work)* que hace sudar.

▲ *comp* **sweatier,** *superl* **sweatiest.**

swede [swiːd] *n* BOT nabo sueco.

Swede [swiːd] *n (person)* sueco,-a.

Sweden ['swiːdən] *n* Suecia.

Swedish ['swiːdɪʃ] **1** *adj* sueco,-a. – **2** *n (language)* sueco. – **3 the Swedish,** *npl* los suecos *mpl.*

sweep [swiːp] **1** *n (with broom)* barrido: *the floor needs a good sweep,* el suelo necesita un buen barrido. **2** *(of arm)* movimiento amplio, gesto amplio; *(with weapon)* golpe *m.* **3** *(curve)* curva; *(area, stretch)* extensión *f.* **4** *fig (range, extent)* abanico, alcance *m.* **5** *(by police, rescuers)* peinado, rastreo. **6** *fam (chimney cleaner)* deshollinador,-ra. **7** *fam (sweepstake)* → **sweepstake.** – **8** *t (room, floor)*

barrer; (*chimney*) deshollinar: *she swept the kitchen floor*, barrió el suelo de la cocina. **9** (*with hand*) quitar de un manotazo: *he swept the papers off his desk*, quitó los papeles de su escritorio de un manotazo. **10** (*move over*) azotar, barrer: *violent storms swept the north of the country*, tormentas violentas azotaron el norte del país. **11** (*remove by force*) arrastrar, llevarse: *the swimmers were swept out to sea by the current*, la corriente arrastró a los nadadores mar adentro; *I was swept along by the crowd*, la multitud me arrastró. **12** (*pass over*) recorrer: *her eyes swept the horizon*, sus ojos recorrieron el horizonte. **13** *fig* (*spread through*) recorrer, extenderse por: *a new fashion is sweeping Spain*, una nueva moda está haciendo furor en España; *rumours of a royal visit swept the village*, rumores de una visita real recorrieron el pueblo. **14** (*touch lightly*) rozar, pasar por: *her gown swept the floor*, su vestido largo rozó el suelo. – **15** *i* (*with broom*) barrer. **16** (*move quickly*) pasar rápidamente: *the limousine swept past*, la limusina pasó rápidamente; *she swept into the room*, entró rápidamente en la habitación; *the fire swept through the building*, el fuego se propagó rápidamente por todo el edificio; *huge waves swept over the rocks*, olas enormes azotaban las rocas. **17** (*extend*) recorrer, extenderse: *the road sweeps down to the sea*, la carretera baja hasta llegar al mar; *the river sweeps round the bend*, el río se extiende por toda la curva.
◆ **to sweep aside 1** *t sep* (*objection etc*) rechazar; (*suggestion*) descartar. **2** (*object*) apartar (bruscamente). ‖ **to sweep away 1** *t sep* (*priviledge etc*) erradicar. **2** (*by flood, storm*) arrastrar, llevarse. ‖ **to sweep up 1** *t sep* (*room etc*) barrer; (*dust etc*) (barrer y) recoger. **2** (*object, person*) recoger, levantar. – **3** *i* barrer, limpiar.
● **to sweep sb. off his/her feet**, hacerle perder la cabeza a algn. ‖ **to sweep sth. under the carpet**, ocultar algo. ‖ **to make a clean sweep of things**, barrer con todo, hacer tabla rasa. ‖ **to sweep the board**, llevarse todos los premios.
▲ *pt & pp* **swept**.
sweeper ['swiːpəʳ] **1** *n* (*person*) barrendero,-a. **2** (*machine*) barredora; (*carpet sweeper*) cepillo mecánico. **3** GB SP (*in football*) defensa *mf* escoba, líbero *mf*.
sweeping ['swiːpɪŋ] **1** *adj* (*broad*) amplio,-a; (*very general*) muy general: *don't make such sweeping statements*, no generalices tanto. **2** (*overwhelming*) arrollador,-ra, aplastante; (*far-reaching*) radical; (*huge*) enorme.
sweepings ['swiːpɪŋz] *npl* (*dirt, dust, etc*) basura.
sweepstake ['swiːpsteɪk] *n* (*bet*) apuesta en que el ganador se lleva todo el dinero apostado; (*horse race*) carrera de caballos en que se hace este tipo de apuestas.
sweet [swiːt] **1** *adj* (*taste*) dulce; (*sugary*) azucarado,-a: *I don't like sweet things*, no me gusta lo dulce; *as sweet as honey*, dulce como la miel. **2** (*pleasant*) agradable; (*smell*) fragante, bueno,-a; (*sound, music, voice*) melodioso,-a, suave, dulce: *these flowers smell sweet*, estas flores huelen muy bien; *sweet dreams*, felices sueños. **3** (*air*) limpio,-a; (*water*) dulce. **4** (*charming*) encantador,-ra, simpático,-a; (*cute*) rico,-a, mono,-a; (*gentle*) dulce: *she's such a sweet person*, es una persona tan encantadora; *he has a very sweet nature*, tiene un carácter muy dulce; *how sweet of you!*, ¡qué detalle!; *what a sweet little kitten!*, ¡qué gatito tan mono! – **5** *n* GB (*candy*) caramelo, golosina; (*chocolate*) bombón *m*. **6** GB (*dessert*) postre *m*. **7** (*form of address*) cariño, cielo, amor *m*, vida.
● **to be sweet on sb.**, gustarle mucho algn. a alguien. ‖ **to have a sweet tooth**, ser goloso,-a. ‖ **to keep sb. sweet**, tener a algn. contento,-a.

■ **sweet corn**, maíz *m* tierno. ‖ **sweet pea**, guisante *m* de olor. ‖ **sweet pepper**, pimiento morrón. ‖ **sweet potato**, boniato, batata. ‖ **sweet shop**, tienda de golosinas, confitería, bombonería. ‖ **sweet talk**, zalamerías *fpl*.
sweet-and-sour ['swiːtənsaʊəʳ] *adj* CULIN agridulce.
sweetbreads ['swiːtbredz] *npl* mollejas *fpl*, lechecillas *fpl*.
sweeten ['swiːtən] **1** *t* (*drink etc*) endulzar, azucarar; (*air, breath*) refrescar. **2** *fig* (*person*) endulzar (el carácter de); (*temper*) aplacar, calmar. **3** *fam* (*make more attractive*) hacer más apetecible.
◆ **to sweeten up** *t sep* ablandar.
● **to sweeten the pill**, dorar la píldora.
sweetener ['swiːtənəʳ] **1** *n* (*in food, drink*) edulcorante *m*, dulcificante *m*. **2** *fam* (*bribe*) soborno.
sweetheart ['swiːthɑːt] **1** *n* (*dear, love*) cariño, tesoro, amor *m*. **2** (*loved one*) novio,-a.
sweetie ['swiːtɪ] **1** *n fam* (*sweet*) caramelo. **2** *fam* (*person*) encanto, cielo, amor *m*, sol *m*. **3** US (*from of address*) vida, cariño, amor *m*, tesoro.
sweetly ['swiːtlɪ] **1** *adv* (*smile*) dulcemente, con dulzura; (*offer*) amablemente. **2** (*work, run*) perfectamente, a la perfección; (*kick, hit*) acertadamente.
sweetmeat ['swiːtmiːt] *n* dulce *m*.
sweetness ['swiːtnəs] *n* (*taste*) dulzor *m*; (*smell*) fragancia; (*sound*) suavidad *f*; (*character*) dulzura, simpatía.
● **to be all sweetness and light**, estar hecho,-a un encanto.
sweet-talk ['swiːttɔːk] *t* engatusar, camelar.
● **to sweet-talk sb. into doing sth.**, camelar a algn. para que haga algo.
sweet-tempered ['swiːt'tempəd] *adj* amable, dulce.
sweet-toothed ['swiːt'tuːθt] *adj* goloso,-a.
swell [swel] **1** *n* (*of sea*) marejada, oleaje *m*. **2** MUS (*crescendo*) crescendo. – **3** *adj* US *fam* (*excellent*) fenomenal, bárbaro,-a, estupendo,-a. – **4** *i* (*gen*) hincharse (**up**, -); (*sea*) levantarse; (*river*) crecer, subir. **5** (*grow - in number*) crecer, aumentar; (*- louder*) hacerse más fuerte. – **6** *t* (*gen*) hinchar; (*river*) hacer crecer. **7** (*increase in number*) aumentar, engrosar.
▲ *pp* **swollen**.
swelling ['swelɪŋ] *n* (*swollen place*) hinchazón *f*, bulto; (*condition*) tumefacción *f*.
swelter ['sweltəʳ] *i* ahogarse de calor.
sweltering ['sweltərɪŋ] *adj* sofocante, asfixiante.
swept [swept] *pt & pp* → **sweep**.
sweptback ['sweptbæk] *adj* (*wing*) en flecha; (*hair*) peinado,-a hacia atrás.
swerve [swɜːv] **1** *n* AUTO viraje *m* brusco, desvío brusco. **2** SP (*by player*) regate *m*; (*of ball*) efecto. – **3** *i* AUTO virar bruscamente, dar un viraje brusco. **4** SP (*player*) dar un regate, regatear; (*ball*) llevar efecto. **5** *fig* (*veer, deviate*) desviarse (**from**, de).
swift [swɪft] **1** *adj* (*runner, horse*) rápido,-a, veloz. **2** (*reaction, reply*) pronto,-a, rápido,-a. – **3** *n* ORN vencejo común.
swift-footed ['swɪft'futɪd] *adj* rápido,-a.
swiftly ['swɪftlɪ] *adv* (*speedily*) rápidamente, velozmente; (*promptly*) pronto, rápidamente.
swiftness ['swɪftnəs] **1** *n* (*speed*) velocidad *f*, rapidez *f*. **2** (*promptness*) prontitud *f*, rapidez *f*.
swig [swɪg] **1** *n* trago. – **2** *t fam* beber (a grandes tragos).
▲ *pt & pp* **swigged**, *ger* **swigging**.
swill [swɪl] **1** *n* (*pig food*) bazofia; (*rubbish*) basura, porquería. **2** (*rinse*) enjuague *m*; (*wash*) lavada. – **3** *t* (*rinse -*

mouth, dish, etc) enjuagar (**out**, -); (- area) regar (**down**, -); (- deck) baldear (**down**, -): *swill your mouth out*, enjuágate la boca. **4** fam (drink) beber a tragos, pimplar. **– 5** i (liquid) moverse (**around/over**, -).

swim [swɪm] **1** n baño. **– 2** i (gen) nadar: *she's learning to swim*, está aprendiendo a nadar; *he goes swimming every day*, va a nadar cada día; *we had to swim across*, tuvimos que cruzar nadando. **3** (be covered in liquid) nadar (**in**, en), flotar (**in**, en); (be overflowing) estar cubierto,-a ((**with**, de), estar inundado,-a: *the meat was swimming in fat*, la carne nadaba en grasa; *the floor was swimming with water*, el suelo estaba cubierto de agua. **4** (spin, whirl) dar vueltas: *my head is swimming*, la cabeza me da vueltas. **– 5** t (cross river) cruzar a nado, cruzar nadando; (cover distance) nadar, hacer; (use particular stroke) nadar: *she swam a mile when she was 10*, nadó una milla cuando tenía 10 años; *can you swim butterfly?*, ¿sabes nadar (estilo) mariposa? **•** *to be in the swim*, estar al tanto, estar en la onda. **‖** *to go for a swim*, ir a nadar. **‖** *to have a swim*, bañarse, nadar. **‖** *to swim with the tide*, seguir la corriente. **‖** *to swim against the tide*, ir contra la corriente. ▲ pt **swam**, pp **swum**, ger **swimming**.

swimmer ['swɪməʳ] n nadador,-ra.
swimming ['swɪmɪŋ] n natación f. **•** *to go swimming*, ir a nadar. **■** *swimming baths*, piscina f cubierta. **‖** *swimming pool*, piscina. **‖** *swimming trunks*, bañador m (de hombre).
swimmingly ['swɪmɪŋlɪ] adv a las mil maravillas.
swimsuit ['swɪmsuːt] n bañador m, traje m de baño.
swimwear ['swɪmweəʳ] n bañadores mpl, trajes mpl de baño.
swindle ['swɪndəl] **1** n (fiddle) estafa; (con) timo. **– 2** t estafar, timar. **•** *to swindle sb. out of sth.*, estafar algo a algn.
swindler ['swɪndləʳ] n estafador,-ra, timador,-ra.
swine [swaɪn] **1** n arch (pig) cerdo, puerco, cochino. **2** fam (person) cerdo,-a, canalla mf, marrano,-a. **■** *swine fever*, peste f porcina. ▲ En 1 pl **swine**, en 2 **swines**.
swineherd ['swaɪnhɜːd] n arch porquerizo,-a.
swing [swɪŋ] **1** n (movement) balanceo, vaivén m; (of pendulum) oscilación f, vaivén m; (of hips) contoneo. **2** (plaything) columpio. **3** (change, shift) giro, viraje m, cambio. **4** SP (in golf, boxing) swing m. **5** MUS (jazz style) swing m; (rhythm) ritmo. **– 6** i (hanging object) balancearse, bambolearse; (pendulum) oscilar; (arms, legs) menearse; (child on swing) columpiarse; (on a pivot) mecerse: *the lightbulb was swinging from a flex*, la bombilla se balanceaba de un cable; *the gate was swinging in the wind*, la puerta se mecía con el viento. **7** (drive) girar, doblar; (walk) caminar con energía; (jump) saltar: *the car swung into the drive*, el coche dobló por el camino de entrada; *the monkey swung from tree to tree*, el mono saltaba de árbol en árbol. **8** (shift) cambiar, oscilar, virar: *the electorate has swung to the right*, el electorado ha virado a la derecha; *her moods swing drastically*, tiene muchos cambios de humor. **9** (music, party) tener ritmo; (party) estar muy animado,-a. **– 10** t (gen) balancear, bambolear; (arms, legs) balancear; (child on swing) columpiar, balancear; (object on rope) hacer oscilar: *she swung her bag as she walked along*, balanceaba la bolsa al andar; *she swings her hips*, se contonea. **11** (cause to move) hacer girar: *he swung the rucksack onto his back*, se echó la mochila a la espalda. **12** (change) cambiar: *they are* trying to swing public opinion, intentan cambiar la opinión pública. **13** fam (arrange, achieve) arreglar: *I'll see if I can swing it for you to come*, miraré de arreglarlo para que puedas venir; *he managed to swing the deal*, logró cerrar el trato. **◆** *to swing around / swing round* **1** i (person) girar (sobre los talones), volverse bruscamente; (vehicle) dar un viraje, girar, virar (en redondo). **– 2** t sep (vehicle) hacer girar en redondo. **‖** *to swing at* t insep intentar pegarle a, intentar darle a. **•** *in full swing*, en plena marcha, en pleno apogeo. **‖** *it's swings and roundabouts*, lo que se pierde acá se gana allá. **‖** *to get into the swing of sth.*, coger el ritmo de algo, cogerle el tranquillo a algo. **‖** *to go with a swing*, ir sobre ruedas. **‖** *to swing for sth.*, colgarle algo a algn. **‖** *to swing into action*, ponerse en marcha. **‖** *to swing open/shut*, (door) abrirse/cerrarse (de golpe). **‖** *to swing the lead*, (intentar) escaquearse, poner excusas para no trabajar. **‖** *to take a swing at sb./sth.*, asestar un golpe a algn./algo, intentar darle a algn./algo. **■** *swing bridge*, puente m giratorio. **‖** *swing door*, puerta giratoria. ▲ pt & pp **swung**.

swingeing ['swɪndʒɪŋ] adj GB (fine etc) severo,-a, salvaje; (attack) duro,-a, feroz.
swinger ['swɪŋəʳ] **1** n fam dated (raver) moderno,-a. **2** fam dated (sexually) desinhibido,-a.
swinging ['swɪŋɪŋ] **1** adj fam (trendy) moderno,-a; (full of life) con mucha marcha. **2** fam (sexually) desinhibido,-a.
swipe [swaɪp] **1** n (blow) golpe m: *she took a swipe at the ball*, intentó darle a la pelota. **2** (verbal attack) ataque m. **– 3** t pegarle a, darle a. **4** fam (pinch) birlar, mangar, afanar. **– 5** i asestar un golpe (**at**, a), intentar darle (**at**, a).
swirl [swɜːl] **1** n (gen) remolino; (of smoke, cream) voluta; (of skirt) vuelo. **2** (pattern) espiral f. **– 3** i (whirl) arremolinarse; (person) girar, dar vueltas. **– 4** t arremolinar.
swish [swɪʃ] **1** n (of water) susurro, rumor m; (of whip, cane) silbido, chasquido; (of skirt, curtain) frufrú m, crujido, ruido; (of animal's tail) sacudida. **– 2** adj fam (smart) muy elegante, elegantón,-ona. **– 3** t (whip, cane) chasquear; (skirt) hacer crujir; (tail) menear, sacudir. **– 4** i (water) susurrar; (whip, cane) dar un chasquido, producir un silbido; (skirt) crujir, hacer frufrú.
Swiss [swɪs] **1** adj suizo,-a. **– 2** n suizo,-a. **– 3** the Swiss, npl los suizos mpl. **■** *the Swiss Guard*, la Guardia Suiza. **‖** *Swiss roll*, CULIN brazo de gitano.
switch [swɪtʃ] **1** n ELEC interruptor m, conmutador m. **2** US (on railway) agujas fpl. **3** (change, shift) cambio; (turnround) viraje m: *a switch in policy*, un cambio de política; *he made a switch from teaching to translating*, cambió de la enseñanza a la traducción. **4** (exchange, swap) intercambio, trueque m. **5** (stick) vara; (riding whip) fusta. **6** (hairpiece) trenza postiza. **– 7** t (change) cambiar de; (move) trasladar; (attention) desviar: *she switched jobs*, cambió de trabajo; *they switched production to the other plant*, trasladaron la producción a la otra fábrica; *he managed to switch the conversation to politics*, logró desviar la conversación hacia la política. **8** (exchange) intercambiar: *someone switched their drinks*, alguien intercambió sus copas. **9** RAD TV (setting) poner; (channel) cambiar de: *switch the fan to "low"*, pon el ventilador en "bajo"; *stop switching channels!*, ¡deja de cambiar de canal! **10** (train) desviar, cambiar de vía. **– 11** i (gen) cambiar (**to**, a): *he switched to a different topic*, cambió

a otro tema; *we've switched to a different brand,* hemos cambiado a una marca diferente.
◆ **to switch off 1** *t sep* (*light,* TV, *etc*) apagar; (*current, gas, electricity*) cortar, desconectar; (*engine*) parar. **– 2** *i* (*light, machine, heating*) apagarse; (*engine*) parar; (*person*) distraerse, desconectar, dejar de prestar atención. ‖ **to switch on 1** *t sep* (*light, machine, engine*) encender; (*light, radio,* TV) poner. **– 2** *i* (*gen*) encenderse. ‖ **to switch over** *i* (*gen*) cambiar (**to,** a); (*channel*) cambiar de canal.

switchback ['swɪtʃbæk] **1** *n* (*road*) carretera con muchos cambios de rasante y/o muchas curvas pronunciadas. **2** GB (*rollercoaster*) montaña rusa.

switchblade ['swɪtʃbleɪd] *n* navaja automática.

switchboard ['swɪtʃbɔːd] *n* centralita.
● **to jam the switchboard,** saturar/colapsar la centralita.
■ **switchboard operator,** telefonista *mf.*

Switzerland ['swɪtsələnd] *n* Suiza.

swivel ['swɪvəl] **1** *i* girar, girarse, volverse. **– 2** *t* (*head*) girar; (*chair*) hacer girar.
■ **swivel chair,** silla giratoria.
▲ *pt & pp* **swivelled** (US **swiveled**), *ger* **swivelling** (US **swiveling**).

swizz [swɪz] *n fam* (*swindle, con*) timo, estafa; (*disappointment*) decepción *f,* chasco.

swizzle ['swɪzəl] *n →* **swizz.**
■ **swizzle stick,** agitador *m,* varilla para agitar cócteles.

swollen ['swəʊlən] **1** *pp →* **swell. – 2** *adj* (*ankle, face*) hinchado,-a; (*glands*) inflamado,-a; (*river, lake*) crecido,-a.
● **to have a swollen head,** ser engreído,-a, ser creído,-a.

swoon [swuːn] **1** *n lit* desmayo, desvanecimiento. **– 2** *i lit* (*faint*) desmayarse, desvanecerse. **3** *fig* (*be emotionally affected*) enamorarse (**over,** por).

swoop [swuːp] **1** *i* (*bird*) abalanzarse (**down on,** sobre), abatirse (**down on,** sobre); (*plane*) bajar en picado. **2** *fam* (*police*) hacer una redada (**on,** en). **– 3** *n* (*of bird, plane*) descenso (en picado). **4** *fam* (*by police*) redada.
● **at one fell swoop,** de un golpe, de un tirón, de una sola vez.

swop [swɒp] *n →* **swap.**

sword [sɔːd] *n* espada.
● **they that live by the sword shall die by the sword,** quien a hierro mata, a hierro muere. ‖ **to cross swords with sb.,** pelearse con algn., habérselas con algn. ‖ **to put sb. to the sword,** pasar a algn. a cuchillo.
■ **sword dance,** danza de las espadas.

swordfish ['sɔːdfɪʃ] *n* pez *m* espada.

swordplay ['sɔːdpleɪ] *n* manejo de espada.

swordsman ['sɔːdzmən] *n* espadachín *m,* espada.

swore [swɔːʳ] *pt →* **swear.**

sworn [swɔːn] *pp →* **swear.**

swot [swɒt] **1** *n fam* empollón,-ona. **– 2** *i fam* empollar.
● **to swot up on sth.,** empollar algo.
▲ *pt & pp* **swotted,** *ger* **swotting.**

swum [swʌm] *pp →* **swim.**

swung [swʌŋ] *pt & pp →* **swing.**

sybarite ['sɪbəraɪt] *n lit* sibarita *mf.*

sybaritic [sɪbə'rɪtɪk] *adj lit* sibarita, sibarítico,-a.

sycamore ['sɪkəmɔːʳ] *n* BOT plátano falso, sicómoro.

sycophant ['sɪkəfənt] *n* adulador,-ra.

syllabic [sɪ'læbɪk] *adj* silábico,-a.

syllable ['sɪləbəl] *n* sílaba.

syllabus ['sɪləbəs] *n* programa *m* de estudios.
▲ *pl* **syllabuses** *o* **syllabi.**

syllogism ['sɪlədʒɪzəm] *n* silogismo.

sylph [sɪlf] *n* sílfide *f.*

sylphlike ['sɪlflaɪk] *adj* de sílfide.

sylvan ['sɪlvən] *adj lit* nemoroso,-a.

symbiosis [sɪmbɪ'əʊsɪs] *n* simbiosis *f.*

symbiotic [sɪmbɪ'ɒtɪk] *adj* simbiótico,-a.

symbol ['sɪmbəl] *n* símbolo (**of,** de).

symbolic [sɪm'bɒlɪk] *adj* simbólico,-a.

symbolical [sɪm'bɒlɪkəl] *adj* simbólico,-a.

symbolically [sɪm'bɒlɪklɪ] *adv* simbólicamente, de manera simbólica.

symbolism ['sɪmbəlɪzəm] *n* simbolismo.

symbolize ['sɪmbəlaɪz] *t* simbolizar.

symmetric [sɪ'metrɪk] *adj* simétrico,-a.

symmetrical [sɪ'metrɪkəl] *adj* simétrico,-a.

symmetry ['sɪmɪtrɪ] *n* simetría.

sympathetic [sɪmpə'θetɪk] **1** *adj* (*showing pity, compassion*) compasivo,-a; (*understanding*) comprensivo,-a (**to,** con); (*kind*) amable. **2** (*showing agreement, approval*) favorable (**to,** a): *she was sympathetic to our request,* se mostró favorable a nuestra petición.
● **to be sympathetic to a cause,** simpatizar con una causa.

sympathetically [sɪmpə'θetɪklɪ] *adv* (*showing pity*) compasivamente, con compasión; (*understanding*) comprensivamente, con comprensión; (*kindly*) amablemente.

sympathize ['sɪmpəθaɪz] **1** *i* (*show pity, commiserate*) compadecer, compadecerse (**with,** de); (*understand*) comprender (**with,** -): *I sympathize with you,* te compadezco; *I sympathize with your feelings,* comprendo tus sentimientos. **2** (*support - cause*) simpatizar (**with,** con); (*- request*) mostrarse favorable (**with,** a): *they sympathize with the nationalist cause,* simpatizan con la causa nacionalista.

sympathizer ['sɪmpəθaɪzəʳ] *n* simpatizante *mf.*

sympathy ['sɪmpəθɪ] **1** *n* (*pity, compassion*) compasión *f,* lástima; (*condolences*) condolencia, pésame *m*: *he didn't show much sympathy for my plight,* no mostró mucha compasión por la difícil situación en que me encontraba; *we felt great sympathy for the victims of the tragedy,* sentimos gran compasión por las víctimas de la tragedia; *please accept my deepest sympathy,* le ruego acepte mi más sentido pésame. **2** (*understanding*) comprensión *f*; (*affinity*) afinidad *f*: *there was an unusual bond of sympathy between them,* había un vínculo de afinidad insólito entre ellos. **3** (*agreement, support*) acuerdo: *I'm in sympathy with you,* estoy de acuerdo contigo; *he had no sympathy with our point of view,* no estaba de acuerdo con nuestro punto de vista. **– 4 sympathies,** *npl* (*condolences*) condolencia *f sing,* pésame *m sing.* **5** (*loyalties, leanings*) simpatías *fpl,* tendencias *fpl.*
● **to come out in sympathy (with sb.),** declararse en huelga por solidaridad (con algn.). ‖ **to express one's sympathy,** dar el pésame.
■ **letter of sympathy,** carta de pésame.
▲ *pl* **sympathies.**

symphonic [sɪm'fɒnɪk] *adj* sinfónico,-a.

symphony ['sɪmfənɪ] *n* sinfonía.
■ **symphony orchestra,** orquesta sinfónica.
▲ *pl* **symphonies.**

symposium [sɪm'pəʊzɪəm] *n* simposio.
▲ *pl* **symposiums** *o* **symposia.**

symptom ['sɪmptəm] 1 *n* MED síntoma *m*. 2 (*sign*) síntoma *m*, señal *f*, indicio.
symptomatic [sɪmptə'mætɪk] *adj* sintomático,-a (**of**, de).
synagogue ['sɪnəgɒg] *n* sinagoga.
sync [sɪŋk] *n fam* sincronización *f*.
● to be in sync, CINEM estar sincronizado,-a (**with**, con); POL sintonizar (**with**, con). ‖ to be out of sync, CINEM no estar sincronizado,-a (**with**, con); POL no sintonizar (**with**, con).
synch [sɪŋk] *n* → **sync**.
synchromesh ['sɪŋkrəʊmeʃ] *n* AUTO sincronizador *m* (del cambio de marchas).
synchronization [sɪŋkrənaɪ'zeɪʃən] *n* sincronización *f*.
synchronize ['sɪŋkrənaɪz] *t* sincronizar.
synchronizer ['sɪŋkrənaɪzəʳ] *t* sincronizador *m*.
syncopate ['sɪŋkəpeɪt] *t* sincopar.
syncopation [sɪŋkə'peɪʃən] *n* síncopa.
syncope ['sɪŋkəpɪ] *n* MED síncope *m*.
syndicalism ['sɪndɪkəlɪzəm] *n* sindicalismo.
syndicalist ['sɪndɪkəlɪst] *n* sindicalista *mf*.
syndicate ['sɪndɪkət] 1 *n* (*gen*) corporación *f*, agrupación *f*, empresa: *crime syndicate*, sindicato del crimen. 2 (*news agency*) agencia (de prensa). – 3 *t* (*distribute*) distribuir; (*publish*) publicar.
syndrome ['sɪndrəʊm] *n* síndrome *m*.
synod ['sɪnəd] *n* sínodo.
synonym ['sɪnənɪm] *n* sinónimo.
synonymous [sɪ'nɒnɪməs] *adj* sinónimo,-a (**with**, de).
synopsis [sɪ'nɒpsɪs] *n* sinopsis *f*, resumen *m*.
▲ *pl synopses*.
synoptic [sɪ'nɒptɪk] *adj* sinóptico,-a.

syntactic [sɪn'tæktɪk] *adj* sintáctico,-a.
syntax ['sɪntæks] *n* sintaxis *f inv*.
synthesis ['sɪnθəsɪs] *n* síntesis *f inv*.
▲ *pl syntheses*.
synthesize ['sɪnθəsaɪz] *t* sintetizar.
synthesizer ['sɪnθəsaɪzəʳ] *n* sintetizador *m*.
synthetic [sɪn'θetɪk] 1 *adj* sintético,-a. – 2 *n* fibra sintética.
syphilis ['sɪfɪlɪs] *n* sífilis *f*.
syphon ['saɪfən] *n* → **siphon**.
Syria ['sɪrɪə] *n* Siria.
Syrian ['sɪrɪən] 1 *adj* sirio,-a. – 2 *n* sirio,-a.
syringe [sɪ'rɪndʒ] 1 *n* MED jeringa, jeringuilla. – 2 *t* MED (*ear*) hacer un lavado de.
syrup ['sɪrəp] 1 *n* MED jarabe *m*: *cough syrup*, jarabe para la tos. 2 CULIN almíbar *m*: *golden syrup*, melaza.
syrupy ['sɪrəpɪ] *adj* (*too sweet*) almibarado,-a.
▲ *comp syrupier, superl syrupiest*.
system ['sɪstəm] 1 *n* (*gen*) sistema *m*: *she bought a stereo system*, se compró un equipo de estéreo. 2 (*body*) cuerpo, organismo: *too much fat is not good for the system*, el exceso de grasa no es bueno para el organismo.
● all systems go!, ¡todo bien! ‖ to get sth. out of one's system, desahogarse.
■ systems analysis, análisis *m* de sistemas. ‖ systems analyst, analista *mf* de sistemas.
systematic [sɪstə'mætɪk] *adj* sistemático,-a, metódico,-a.
systematically [sɪstə'mætɪklɪ] *adv* sistemáticamente.
systematize ['sɪstəmataɪz] *t* sistematizar.
systemize ['sɪstəmaɪz] *t* sistematizar.
systolic [sɪs'tɒlɪk] *adj* sistólico,-a.

T

T, t [tiː] *n* (*the letter*) T, t *f*.
ta [taː] *interj* GB *fam* ¡gracias!
tab [tæb] **1** *n* (*flap*) lengüeta; (*on can*) anilla. **2** (*label*) etiqueta. **3** US (*bill*) cuenta. **4** (*on computer*) tabulador *m*.
● **to keep a tab on sth.**, controlar algo. ‖ **to keep tabs on sb.**, vigilar a algn. ‖ **to pick up the tab**, pagar la cuenta.
Tabasco [təˈbæskəʊ] *n* salsa de tabasco.
tabby [ˈtæbɪ] *adj* atigrado,-a.
■ **tabby cat**, gato atigrado.
tabernacle [ˈtæbənækəl] *n* tabernáculo.
table [ˈteɪbəl] **1** *n* (*gen*) mesa. **2** (*chart*) tabla, cuadro. **3** SP clasificación *f*. – **4** *t* GB (*motion, report, etc*) presentar. – **5 tables**, *npl* tablas *fpl*, tablas *fpl* de multiplicar.
● **at table**, en la mesa. ‖ **to be on the table**, (*issue*) estar sobre el tapete. ‖ **to clear the table**, quitar la mesa. ‖ **to drink sb. under the table**, poder beber más que algn. ‖ **to lay the table**, poner la mesa. ‖ **to set the table**, poner la mesa. ‖ **to turn the tables on sb.**, volver las tornas a algn. ‖ **under the table**, bajo mano.
■ **table d'hôte menu**, menú *m* del día, menú *m*. ‖ **table lamp**, lámpara de mesa. ‖ **table manners**, modales *mpl* en la mesa. ‖ **table mat**, salvamanteles *m inv*. ‖ **table of contents**, índice *m* de materias. ‖ **table tennis**, tenis *m* de mesa, ping-pong *m*. ‖ **table wine**, vino de mesa.
tableau [ˈtæbləʊ] *n* cuadro vivo.
▲ *pl* **tableaux** o **tableaus**.
tablecloth [ˈteɪbəlklɒθ] *n* mantel *m*.
tableland [ˈteɪbəllænd] *n* meseta.
tablespoon [ˈteɪbəlspuːn] **1** *n* cucharón *m*. **2** cucharada grande.
tablespoonful [ˈteɪbəlspuːnfʊl] *n* cucharada grande.
tablet [ˈtæblɪt] **1** *n* MED pastilla, comprimido. **2** (*of stone*) lápida. **3** (*of soap*) pastilla.
tableware [ˈteɪblweəʳ] *n* vajilla.
tabloid [ˈtæblɔɪd] *n* periódico de formato pequeño.
■ **tabloid press**, prensa sensacionalista.
taboo [təˈbuː] **1** *n* tabú *m*. – **2** *adj* tabú.
▲ (*sustantivo*) *pl* **taboos**.
tabular [ˈtæbjʊləʳ] *adj* tabular.
tabulate [ˈtæbjʊleɪt] *t* tabular.
tabulation [tæbjʊˈleɪʃən] *n* tabulación *f*.
tabulator [ˈtæbjəleɪtəʳ] *n* tabulador *m*.
tachograph [ˈtækɡrɑːf] *n* tacógrafo.
tachometer [tæˈkɒmɪtəʳ] *n* tacómetro.
tacit [ˈtæsɪt] *adj* tácito,-a.
tacitly [ˈtæsɪtlɪ] *adv* tácitamente.
taciturn [ˈtæsɪtɜːn] *adj* taciturno,-a.
tack [tæk] **1** *n* (*nail*) tachuela. **2** MAR bordada, viraje *m*. **3** (*approach*) táctica. **4** SEW hilván *m*. – **5** *t* (*secure*) clavar con tachuelas. **6** SEW hilvanar. – **7** *i* MAR dar bordadas, virar.

◆ **to tack on** *t sep* añadir.
● **to change tack**, cambiar de táctica.
tackle [ˈtækəl] **1** *n* (*equipment*) equipo, avíos *mpl*, aparejos *mpl*. **2** MAR polea, aparejo. **3** SP (*football*) entrada; (*rugby*) placaje *m*. – **4** *t* (*deal with - problem*) abordar, encarar; (- *task*) emprender; (*person*) hablar con. **5** SP (*football*) entrarle a; (*rugby*) placar.
● **to tackle sb. about/on sth.**, plantarle a algn. algo.
tacky [ˈtækɪ] **1** *adj* (*sticky*) pegajoso,-a. **2** (*in bad taste*) de mal gusto, cutre, hortera.
▲ *comp* **tackier**, *superl* **tackiest**.
tact [tækt] *n* tacto, discreción *f*, delicadeza.
tactful [ˈtæktfʊl] *adj* diplomático,-a, discreto,-a.
tactfully [ˈtæktfʊlɪ] *adv* discretamente, con tacto.
tactic [ˈtæktɪk] *n* táctica.
tactical [ˈtæktɪkəl] *adj* táctico,-a.
■ **tactical voting**, votación *f* táctica.
tactician [tækˈtɪʃən] *n* estratega *mf*.
tactics [ˈtæktɪks] *npl* MIL táctica *f sing*.
tactile [ˈtæktaɪl] *adj* táctil.
tactless [ˈtæktləs] *adj* (*person*) falto,-a de tacto, poco diplomático,-a; (*remark, question*) indiscreto,-a.
tactlessly [ˈtæktləslɪ] *adv* indiscretamente, con poco tacto.
tactlessness [ˈtæktləsnəs] *n* indiscreción *f*, falta de tacto.
tad [tæd] **1** *n* US niño *m*. **2 a tad**, US (*a bit*) un poco.
tadpole [ˈtædpəʊl] *n* renacuajo.
tae kwon do [taɪˈkwɒndəʊ] *n* tae kwon do *m*.
taffeta [ˈtæfɪtə] *n* tafetán *m*.
tag [tæɡ] **1** *n* (*label*) etiqueta. **2** (*on shoelace*) herrete *m*. **3** (*phrase*) coletilla. **4** (*game*) el corre que te pillo. – **5** *t* (*gen*) etiquetar, poner una etiqueta a. **6** (*on animals*) poner una chapa identificativa a.
● **to tag along** *i* pegarse. ‖ **to tag on** *t sep* añadir.
▲ (*verbo*) *pt* & *pp* **tagged**, *ger* **tagging**.
tagliatelle [tæljəˈtelɪ] *n* tallarines *mpl*.
Tagus [ˈteɪɡəs] *n* el Tajo *m*.
tahini [təˈhiːnɪ] *n* pasta de sésamo.
Tahiti [təˈhiːtɪ] *n* Tahití.
Tahitian [təˈhiːʃən] **1** *adj* tahitiano,-a. – **2** *n* (*person*) tahitiano,-a. **3** (*language*) tahitiano.
tail [teɪl] **1** *n* (*gen*) cola; (*of some four-legged animals*) cola, rabo. **2** (*of plane, kite, comet*) cola; (*of shirt, coat*) faldón *m*. **3** (*pursuer*) perseguidor,-ra. – **4** *t* seguir de cerca. – **5 tails**, *npl* (*of coin*) cruz *f sing*. **6** (*suit*) frac *m*.
◆ **to tail away** *i* (*become smaller, fewer*) disminuir; (*become weaker*) irse apagando, debilitarse. ‖ **to tail back** *i* extenderse. ‖ **to tail off** *i* disminuir, mermar.
● **to be on sb.'s tail**, pisarle los talones a algn. ‖ **to have one's tail between one's legs**, tener el rabo entre las piernas. ‖ **to turn tail**, huir.
■ **tail wind**, viento de cola.
tailback [ˈteɪlbæk] *n* (*traffic jam*) caravana, cola, retención *f*.

tailcoat ['teɪlkəʊt] *n* frac *m*.

tail-end [teɪl'end] *n* final *m*, parte *f* final.

tail-gate ['teɪlgeɪt] *n* portón *m* trasero.

tail-light ['teɪllaɪt] *n* luz *f* trasera, piloto.

tailor ['teɪlə'] **1** *n* sastre,-a. – **2** *t* confeccionar. **3** *fig* adaptar.

tailored ['teɪləd] *adj* (*shirt*) entallado,-a; (*suit*) tipo sastre.

tailor-made [teɪlə'meɪd] *adj* hecho,-a a medida.

tailor's ['teɪləz] *n* sastrería.

taint [teɪnt] **1** *t* (*reputation*) mancillar, manchar, empañar; (*food*) contaminar. – **2** *n* mancha, mancilla.

Taiwan [taɪ'wæn] *n* Taiwan.

Taiwanese [taɪwæ'niːz] **1** *adj* taiwanés,-esa. – **2** *n* taiwanés,-esa.

take [teɪk] **1** *n* CINEM toma. – **2** *t* (*carry, bring*) llevar: *take your umbrella, it might rain,* lleva el paraguas, puede que llueva; *she took her grandson a cup of tea,* le llevó una taza de té a su nieto. **3** (*drive, escort*) llevar: *shall I take you to the station?,* ¿quieres que te lleve a la estación?; *they took their children to the cinema,* llevaron a sus hijos al cine. **4** (*remove*) llevarse, quitar, coger: *who's taken my pencil?,* ¿quién ha cogido mi lápiz?; *I think someone's taken my wallet,* creo que alguien me ha quitado la cartera; *she took a chocolate,* cogió un bombón. **5** (*hold, grasp*) tomar, coger: *do you want me to take your suitcase?,* ¿quieres que te coja la maleta?; *he took her by the hand,* la cogió de la mano. **6** (*accept - money etc*) aceptar, coger; (*- criticism, advice, responsibility*) aceptar, asumir; (*- patients, clients*) aceptar: *do you take cheques?,* ¿aceptáis cheques?; *he decided not to take the job,* decidió no aceptar el trabajo; *he'll take it better coming from you,* se lo tomará mejor si se lo dices tú; *the machine only takes pound coins,* la máquina sólo admite monedas de una libra. **7** (*win prize, competition*) ganar; (*earn*) ganar, hacer: *how much have we taken today?,* ¿cuánto hemos hecho hoy de caja?* **8** (*medicine, drugs*) tomar: *have you ever taken drugs?,* ¿has tomado drogas alguna vez?; *do you take sugar?,* ¿te pones azúcar?* **9** (*subject*) estudiar; (*course of study*) seguir, cursar: *I'm taking history this year,* estudio historia este curso; *he took a degree in politics,* se licenció en ciencias políticas. **10** (*teach*) dar clase a: *she takes my son for French,* ella da clases de francés a mi hijo. **11** (*bus, train, etc*) tomar, coger: *she took a taxi because she was late,* cogió un taxi porque llegaba tarde; *take the second on the left,* coja la segunda a la izquierda; *my job takes me all over the world,* mi trabajo me lleva por todo el mundo. **12** (*capture*) tomar, capturar; (*in board games*) comer: *the soldiers have taken the city,* los soldados han tomado la ciudad; *ten men were taken prisoners,* apresaron a diez hombres. **13** (*time*) tardar, llevar: *how long does it take to get to Madrid?,* ¿cuánto se tarda en llegar a Madrid?; *it takes two hours to cook,* tarda dos horas en cocerse; *it took her half an hour to make it,* hacerlo le llevó media hora. **14** (*hold, contain*) tener cabida, acoger: *this plane takes 500 passengers,* este avión tiene cabida para 500 pasajeros; *how many people does your car take?,* ¿cuántas personas caben en tu coche?* **15** (*size of clothes*) usar, gastar; (*size of shoes*) calzar: *what size do you take?,* ¿qué talla usas?, ¿cuál es tu talla?; *what size shoe does he take?,* ¿qué número calza?* **16** (*measurement, temperature, etc*) tomar; (*write down*) anotar. **17** (*need, require*) requerir, necesitar: *it will take two people to carry the fridge,* se necesitarán dos personas para llevar la nevera; *it doesn't take much to frighten her,* no hace falta mucho para que se asuste; *that will take some explaining,* te costará trabajo explicar esto. **18** (*buy*) quedarse con,

llevar(se): *I'll take it,* me lo quedo; *I'll take the red one,* me quedaré con el rojo; *she takes The Guardian,* compra The Guardian. **19** (*bear*) aguantar, soportar: *I can't take any more,* no aguanto más; *you can't take a joke,* no sabes aguantar una broma. **20** (*react*) tomarse; (*interpret*) interpretar: *she took it the wrong way,* lo interpretó mal, se lo tomó a mal; *he took the news very badly,* se tomó la noticia muy mal. **21** (*perform, adopt*) tomar, adoptar; (*exercise*) hacer: *they had to take drastic measures,* tuvieron que tomar medidas drásticas; *don't take any notice,* no hagas caso; *she takes the view that ...,* opina que ...* **22** (*have*) tomar(se): *let's take a break,* tomemos un descanso. **23** (*suppose*) suponer: *I take it that ...,* supongo que ...* **24** (*consider*) considerar, mirar. **25** LING regir: *transitive verbs take a direct object,* los verbos transitivos rigen objeto directo. **26** (*rent*) alquilar: *they have taken a flat in London,* han alquilado un piso en Londres. – **27** *i* (*work - dye*) coger; (*- fire*) prender; (*- cutting*) prender; (*- seed*) germinar. **28** (*fish*) picar. **29** (*in draughts etc*) comer.
◆ **to take after** *t insep* parecerse a: *I take after my mother,* me parezco a mi madre. ‖ **to take apart** **1** *t sep* (*machine etc*) desmontar, deshacer. **2** (*argument*) echar por tierra. ‖ **to take aside** *t sep* llevar a un lado. ‖ **to take away** **1** *t sep* (*remove*) llevarse, quitar. **2** (*subtract*) restar. – **3** *i* (*food*) llevar: *I'd like a sandwich to take away please,* quisiera un bocadillo para llevar, por favor. ‖ **to take back** **1** *t sep* (*accept back*) recibir otra vez, aceptar algo devuelto; (*employee*) readmitir. **2** (*return*) devolver: *this watch doesn't work so I'm taking it back,* este reloj no funciona así que voy a devolverlo. **3** (*retract*) retirar, retractar. **4** (*in time*) hacer recordar. ‖ **to take down** **1** *t sep* (*remove, lower*) quitar, bajar. **2** (*dismantle*) desmontar. **3** (*write down*) apuntar. – **4** *t insep* (*humiliate*) humillar. ‖ **to take for** *t sep* tomar por: *who do you take me for?,* ¿por quién me tomas?; *she took me for someone else,* me confundió con otra persona. ‖ **to take in** **1** *t sep* (*shelter*) dar cobijo a, alojar, recoger. **2** (*deceive*) engañar: *I was completely taken in by his disguise,* su disfraz me engañó completamente. **3** (*grasp*) asimilar, entender, captar. **4** (*include*) incluir, abarcar. **5** (*clothes*) meterle a, estrechar. ‖ **to take off** **1** *t sep* (*clothes*) quitarse. **2** (*remove, detach*) quitar, sacar: *he couldn't take his eyes off her,* no le quitaba la vista de encima. **3** (*force to go*) llevar: *the boy was taken off to the police station,* llevaron al chico a la comisaría. **4** (*have as holiday*) tomarse: *I think I'll take the day off,* creo que me tomaré el día libre. **5** (*imitate*) imitar. **6** (*deduct, discount*) descontar, rebajar. – **7** *i* (*plane*) despegar. **8** (*leave hurriedly*) irse, marcharse: *they just took off without saying a word,* se fueron sin decir palabra. **9** (*become popular*) hacerse popular, tener éxito, ponerse de moda: *video games have really taken off in the last few years,* los videojuegos se han puesto de moda en los últimos años. ‖ **to take on** **1** *t sep* (*decide to do, undertake*) hacerse cargo de, encargarse de, aceptar; (*responsibility*) asumir: *don't take on more than you can handle,* no aceptes más trabajo del que puedes hacer. **2** (*employ*) contratar, coger. **3** (*challenge*) desafiar, enfrentarse con. – **4** *t insep* (*begin to have, assume*) asumir, tomar, adquirir. – **5** *i* (*become upset*) agitarse, ponerse nervioso,-a: *don't take on so,* no te pongas así. ‖ **to take out** **1** *t sep* (*remove, extract, withdraw*) sacar, quitar. **2** (*escort, accompany*) invitar a salir; (*child, dog*) llevar de paseo. **3** (*insurance*) hacerse, sacar; (*licence, patent*) obtener. **4** us llevar comida a casa. **5** (*kill, destroy*) eliminar. ‖ **to take out on** *t sep* tomarla con, desquitarse con, descargarse con: *people often take their anger out*

on the ones they love most, la gente suele desahogar su cólera con los que más quiere. ‖ **to take over 1** *t sep* (*country, party etc*) tomar (posesión de), apoderarse de; (*building*) ocupar. **2** (*company, business*) absorber, adquirir; (*job, post*) hacerse cargo de; (*duty, responsibility*) asumir. – **3** *i* (*assume control*) tomar el poder, hacerse con el poder; (*job*) entrar en funciones, relevar. – **4** *t insep* (*lines, points, argument*) repasar; (*show round*) enseñar, mostrar. ‖ **to take over from** *t insep* relevar, sustituir. ‖ **to take to 1** *t insep* (*person*) tomar cariño a. **2** (*vice*) darse a: *he's taken to drink,* se ha dado a la bebida. **3** (*start to do*) empezar a, aficionarse a. ‖ **to take up 1** *t sep* (*fill, occupy*) ocupar. **2** (*take upstairs*) llevar, subir; (*remove, lift - carpet etc*) quitar, levantar. **3** (*space*) ocupar; (*time*) ocupar, llevar: *cleaning the flat took up all the morning,* limpiar el piso llevó toda la mañana. **4** (*continue*) continuar, reanudar: *let's take up where we left off,* continuemos donde lo dejamos. – **5** *t insep* (*offer*) aceptar. – **6** *t sep* (*start to do*) dedicarse a. **7** (*pursue - point etc*) volver a. **8** (*sew*) acortar. ‖ **to take upon** *t sep* encargarse de. ‖ **to take up on 1** *t sep* (*challenge*) hacer puntualizaciones sobre. **2** (*accept*) aceptar (una oferta). ‖ **to take up with 1** *t insep* (*form relationship with*) empezar a salir con, entrar en relaciones con. – **2** *t sep* (*raise with*) hablar de: *I shall take this up with the manager,* hablaré de esto con el director.

● **not to take no for an answer,** no aceptar una respuesta negativa. ‖ **take it from me,** escucha lo que te digo. ‖ **take it or leave it,** lo tomas o lo dejas. ‖ **take my word for it,** créeme. ‖ **to be hard to take,** ser difícil de aceptar. ‖ **to be on the take,** dejarse sobornar. ‖ **to have what it takes,** tener lo que hace falta. ‖ **to take five,** descansar cinco minutos. ‖ **to take it out of sb.,** dejar a uno sin ganas de nada. ‖ **to take sb. out of himself,** hacer que algn. se olvide de sus propias penas. ‖ **to take sth. as read,** dar algo por sentado,-a.

▲ *pt* **took,** *pp* **taken.**

take-away ['teɪkəweɪ] **1** *n* (*food*) comida para llevar. **2** (*restaurant*) restaurante *m* de comida para llevar.

take-home pay ['teɪkhəʊmpeɪ] *n* sueldo neto.

taken ['teɪkən] **1** *pp* → **take.** – **2** *adj* (*seat*) ocupado,-a: *is this seat taken?,* ¿está ocupado?

● **to be taken ill,** ponerse enfermo, caer enfermo. ‖ **to be taken short,** entrarle ganas a algn. de ir al lavabo. ‖ **to be taken with sb./sth.,** gustarle algn./algo mucho a algn. ‖ **to be taken up with sth.,** estar muy ocupado,-a con algo.

take-off ['teɪkɒf] **1** *n* (*aviation*) despegue *m*. **2** SP salto. **3** (*imitation*) imitación *f*, parodia.

take-out ['teɪkaʊt] *n* US (*food*) comida para llevar.

takeover ['teɪkəʊvəʳ] **1** *n* POL toma del poder, toma de posesión. **2** (*of company*) adquisición *f*.

■ **military takeover,** golpe *m* de estado. ‖ **take-over bid,** oferta pública de adquisición, OPA.

taker ['teɪkəʳ] *n* persona interesada, interesado,-a.

● **any takers?,** ¿alguien quiere? ¿a alguien le interesa?

taking ['teɪkɪŋ] *n* dated atractivo,-a.

● **it's there for the taking,** allí está. ‖ **it's yours for the taking,** es tuyo si quieres.

takings ['teɪkɪŋz] *npl* (*gen*) recaudación *f sing*, caja; (*at box office*) taquilla, entrada.

talc [tælk] *n* talco.

talcum powder ['tælkəmpaʊdəʳ] *n* polvos *mpl* de talco.

tale [teɪl] *n* (*story*) cuento, relato, historia; (*lie*) cuento, mentira.

● **to tell tales,** contar cuentos. ■ **old wife's tale,** cuento de viejas.

talent ['tælənt] **1** *n* (*special ability*) talento, dotes *mpl*. **2** (*talented people*) gente *f* de talento, gente *f* dotada. **3** fam (*attractive people*) gente *f* guapa: *all the men were eyeing up the local talent,* todos los hombres pasaban revista a las chicas del lugar.

■ **talent scout,** cazatalentos *mf inv*.

talented ['tæləntɪd] *adj* de talento, dotado,-a.

talentless ['tæləntləs] *adj* carente de talento, sin talento.

talisman ['tælɪzmən] *n* talismán *m*.

talk [tɔːk] **1** *i* (*gen*) hablar (**to**, con/a): *I'd like to talk to you for a minute,* quisiera hablar contigo un momento; *what were you talking about?,* ¿de qué hablabais?; *everyone was talking at once,* todos hablaban a la vez; *he talks to himself,* habla consigo mismo. **2** (*negotiate*) negociar: *the leaders agreed to talk,* los líderes acordaron negociar. **3** (*gossip*) hablar, chismorrear: *you know how people love to talk,* sabes cómo a la gente le encanta chismorrear. – **4** *t* hablar (**about/of,** de): *let's talk business,* hablemos de negocios; *don't talk nonsense,* no digas tonterías. – **5** *n* (*conversation*) conversación *f*. **6** (*lecture*) charla, conferencia: *she gave a talk on the Spanish Civil War,* dio una charla sobre la Guerra Civil Española. **7** (*rumour*) rumor *m*, voz *f*: *there is talk of his resigning,* se habla de la posibilidad de que dimita. – **8 talks,** *npl* negociaciones *fpl*: *the management and the unions met for talks,* el patronal y los sindicatos se reunieron para negociar.

◆ **to talk back** *i* contestar, contestar de mala manera. ‖ **to talk down 2** *t insep* (*person*) hacer callar. **3** (*aircraft*) dirigir por radio. ‖ **to talk down to** *t insep* hablar con desprecio a, hablar con aires de suficiencia a. ‖ **to talk over** *t sep* discutir, hablar de. ‖ **to talk round 1** *t sep* convencer. – **2** *t insep* dar vueltas a.

● **it's just talk,** son cosas que se dicen, son rumores. ‖ **look who's talking,** quién lo dice, mira quién habla. ‖ **not to have a clue what one is talking about,** no tener la menor idea de qué habla. ‖ **now you're talking,** eso sí que me interesa. ‖ **talk about luck!,** ¡vaya suerte! ‖ **talk of the devil,** hablando del rey de Roma, (por la puerta asoma). ‖ **to be all talk (and no action),** no hacer nada más que hablar. ‖ **to be the talk of the town,** ser la comidilla de todos. ‖ **to know what one is talking about,** hablar con conocimiento de causa. ‖ **to talk big,** fanfarronear, farolear, presumir, exagerar. ‖ **to talk sb. into sth.,** convencer a algn. para que haga algo. ‖ **to talk sb. out of sth.,** disuadir a algn. de hacer algo. ‖ **to talk sense,** hablar con sentido común. ‖ **to talk shop,** hablar del trabajo. ‖ **to talk through one's hat,** decir tonterías, hablar sin pies ni cabeza. ‖ **to talk turkey,** hablar a las claras, hablar con franqueza. ‖ **you can talk,** y tú que lo digas.

■ **pillow talk,** conversación *f* íntima (en la cama). ‖ **talk show,** programa *m* de entrevistas.

talkative ['tɔːkətɪv] *adj* hablador,-ra, parlanchín,-ina, charlatán,-a, locuaz.

talker ['tɔːkəʳ] *n* hablador,-ra.

● **he's a smooth talker,** tiene mucha labia.

talkie ['tɔːkɪ] **1** *n* película sonora. – **2 talkies,** *npl* cine *m sing* sonoro.

talking ['tɔːkɪŋ] **1** *n* hablar *m*: *let me do the talking,* déjame que hable yo. – **2** *adj* que habla.

● **"no talking",** "silencio".

■ **talking book,** libro grabado (para ciegos). ‖ **talking head,** busto parlante. ‖ **talking point,** tema *m* de conversación. ‖ **talking shop,** tertulia.

talking-to [ˈtɔːkɪŋtuː] *n fam* bronca, reprimenda, rapapolvo.
● **to give sb. a right talking-to,** leerle la cartilla a algn., cantarle las cuarenta a algn.

tall [tɔːl] *adj* alto,-a: *she's very tall,* es muy alta; *how tall are you?,* ¿cuánto mides?; *it's 5 metres tall,* mide 5 metros de alto.
● **to be a tall order,** ser muy difícil. ‖ **to walk tall,** andar con la cabeza alta.
■ **tall story,** cuento chino.

tallboy [ˈtɔːlbɔɪ] *n* GB cómoda.

tallow [ˈtæləʊ] *n* sebo.

tally [ˈtælɪ] **1** *n* cuenta. **– 2** *i* concordar, cuadrar.
▲ *(sustantivo) pl* **tallies;** *(verbo) pt & pp* **tallied,** *ger* **tallying.**

talon [ˈtælən] *n* garra.

tamarind [ˈtæmərɪnd] *n* tamarindo.

tamarisk [ˈtæmərɪsk] *n* tamarisco.

tambour [ˈtæmbʊəʳ] *n* tambor *m.*

tambourine [tæmbəˈriːn] *n* pandereta.

tame [teɪm] **1** *adj (by nature)* manso,-a, dócil. **2** *(tamed)* domesticado,-a. **3** *fig* soso,-a, aburrido,-a. **– 4** *t* domar, domesticar.

tamely [ˈteɪmlɪ] *adv* dócilmente.

tamer [ˈteɪməʳ] *n* domador,-ra.

tamper [ˈtæmpəʳ] **to tamper with,** *t (gen)* tocar, manipular; *(lock)* intentar forzar; *(document, figures)* alterar.

tampon [ˈtæmpɒn] *n* tampón *m.*

tan¹ [tæn] **1** *n (colour)* color *m* marrón claro. **2** *(suntan)* bronceado, moreno. **– 3** *adj* marrón claro. **– 4** *t (leather)* curtir. **5** *(skin)* broncear, poner moreno,-a. **– 6** *i* broncearse, ponerse moreno,-a.
● **to tan sb.'s hide,** dar una paliza a algn., zurrar a algn.
▲ *(verbo) pt & pp* **tanned,** *ger* **tanning.**

tan² [ˈtændʒənt] *abbr (tangent)* tangente; *(abbreviation)* tang.

tandem [ˈtændəm] *n* tándem *m.*
● **in tandem,** conjuntamente.

tandoori [tænˈdʊərɪ] **1** *n* tandori *m,* *(método hindú de asar en un horno de barro).* **– 2** *adj* asado,-a al estilo hindú en un horno de barro.

tang [tæŋ] *n (taste)* sabor *m* fuerte; *(smell)* olor *m* fuerte.

tangent [ˈtændʒənt] *n* tangente *f.*
● **to go off at a tangent / fly off at a tangent,** salirse por la tangente.

tangerine [tændʒəˈriːn] **1** *n (fruit)* clementina, mandarina. **2** *(colour)* naranja. **– 3** *adj* naranja.

tangible [ˈtændʒəbəl] *adj* tangible.

Tangier [tænˈdʒɪəʳ] *n* Tánger *m.*

tangle [ˈtæŋɡəl] **1** *n (confused mass)* enredo, maraña, embrollo; *(confusion)* enredo, lío. **– 2** *t* enredar, enmarañar. **– 3** *i* enredarse.
◆ **to tangle up** *t sep* enredarse: *we got ourselves tangled up,* nos hicimos un lío; *he got tangled up in something dangerous,* se vio implicado en un asunto peligroso. ‖ **to tangle with** *t insep* meterse con.

tango [ˈtæŋɡəʊ] **1** *n* tango. **– 2** *i* bailar el tango.
● **it takes two to tango,** es cosa de dos.
▲ *(sustantivo) pl* **tangos;** *(verbo) pt & pp* **tangoed,** *ger* **tangoing.**

tangy [ˈtæŋɡɪ] *adj (smell)* penetrante; *(taste)* ácido,-a, fuerte: *a tangy lemon sorbet,* un sorbete de limón fuerte.
▲ *comp* **tangier,** *superl* **tangiest.**

tank [tæŋk] **1** *n (for water)* depósito, tanque *m;* *(for fuel)* depósito. **2** MIL tanque *m.* **3** US *sl (jail)* chirona.

◆ **to tank up 1** *t sep* llenar el depósito, repostar. **– 2** *i (get drunk)* emborracharse.
■ **fuel tank,** depósito de combustible. ‖ **think tank,** grupo de expertos.

tankard [ˈtæŋkəd] *n* jarra (para cerveza).

tanked up [tæŋktˈʌp] *adj sl (drunk)* borracho,-a.

tanker [ˈtæŋkəʳ] **1** *n (ship)* buque *m* cisterna. **2** *(for oil)* petrolero. **3** *(lorry)* camión *m* cisterna.

tank top [ˈtæŋktɒp] **1** *n* GB chaleco de punto. **2** US camiseta sin mangas.

tanned [tænd] *adj (person)* moreno,-a, bronceado,-a; *(leather)* curtido,-a.

tanner [ˈtænəʳ] **1** *n* curtidor,-ra. **2** *fam dated moneda de seis peniques.*

tannin [ˈtænɪn] *n* tanino.

Tannoy [ˈtænɔɪ] *n* sistema *m* de megafonía: *they heard the message over the Tannoy,* escucharon el mensaje por los altavoces.

tantalize [ˈtæntəlaɪz] *t* atormentar (tentando).

tantalizing [ˈtæntəlaɪzɪŋ] *adj* tentador,-ra.

tantamount [ˈtæntəmaʊnt] *adj* equivalente (**to,** a).

tantrum [ˈtæntrəm] *n* berrinche *m,* rabieta: *kids often throw tantrums,* los niños a menudo cogen berrinches.

Tanzania [tænzəˈnɪə] *n* Tanzania.

Tanzanian [tænzəˈnɪən] **1** *adj* tanzano,-a. **– 2** *n* tanzano,-a.

tap¹ [tæp] **1** *n* grifo: *turn the tap on/off,* abre/cierra el grifo. **2** *(light blow)* golpecito: *she felt a tap on her arm,* sintió un golpecito en el brazo. **3** *(on phone)* micrófono de escucha: *they'd put a tap on her phone,* le habían pinchado el teléfono. **4** *(on barrel)* espita; *(for gas)* llave *f.* **– 5** *t (strike lightly)* golpear suavemente, dar un golpecito a. **6** *(on keyboard)* teclear, pulsar. **7** *(liquid)* sacar. **8** *(resources)* explotar, utilizar. **9** *(telephone)* pinchar, intervenir. **10** *sl (borrow)* sablear: *he tapped me for ten pounds,* me sableó diez libras.
◆ **to tap out 1** *t sep* teclear, escribir a máquina. **2** *(Morse code)* enviar.
● **on tap,** *(beer)* de barril. ‖ **to have sth. on tap,** tener algo al alcance de la mano.
■ **tap water,** agua del grifo.
▲ *pt & pp* **tapped,** *ger* **tapping.**

tap² [tæp] *n* claqué *m.*
■ **tap dance,** claqué *m.* ‖ **tap dancer,** bailarín,-ina de claqué.

tape [teɪp] **1** *n (audio, visual)* cinta. **2** *(recorded material)* grabación *f.* **3** SP cinta de llegada. **4** *(sticky)* cinta adhesiva. **– 5** *t (fasten)* pegar con cinta adhesiva. **6** *(record)* grabar: *John's taped the concert,* John ha grabado el concierto.
● **to have sb. taped,** tener calado,-a a algn. ‖ **to have sth. taped,** *fig* haber cogido el tranquillo a algo.
■ **tape deck,** pletina. ‖ **tape measure,** cinta métrica. ‖ **tape recorder,** magnetófono.

taper [ˈteɪpəʳ] **1** *n* vela *delgada.* **– 2** *t* afilar, estrechar. **– 3** *i* afilarse, estrecharse.
◆ **to taper off** *t insep* ir disminuyendo.

tapestry [ˈtæpɪstrɪ] **1** *n (art)* tapicería. **2** *(cloth)* tapiz *m.*
● **it's part of life's rich tapestry,** ¡son cosas de la vida!
▲ *pl* **tapestries.**

tapeworm [ˈteɪpwɜːm] *n* tenia, solitaria.

tapioca [tæpɪˈəʊkə] *n* tapioca.

tapir [ˈteɪpəʳ] *n* tapir *m.*

tar [tɑːʳ] **1** *n (for roads, in cigarettes)* alquitrán *m.* **2** *(in soap etc)* brea. **– 3** *t* alquitranar.
● **to tar and feather,** emplumar. ‖ **to be tarred with**

the same brush, estar cortados,-as por el mismo patrón, ser de la misma calaña.
▲ (verbo) pt & pp tarred, ger tarring.
taramasalata [tærəməsə'lɑːtə] n taramasalata.
tarantula [tə'ræntjʊlə] n tarántula.
tardily ['tɑːdəlɪ] adv tardíamente.
tardiness ['tɑːdɪnəs] n tardanza, retraso.
tardy ['tɑːdɪ] adj (late) tardío,-a; (slow) lento,-a.
▲ comp tardier, superl tardiest.
tare [teəʳ] n tara.
target ['tɑːgɪt] **1** n (of missile, goal, aim) objetivo: we must meet our sales targets, tenemos que alcanzar nuestros objetivos de ventas. **2** (in shooting, of criticism) blanco: she was the target of repeated attacks, fue el blanco de repetidos ataques. **3** (board) diana. – **4** t (aim at target) apuntar: the missiles are targeted on Sarajevo, los misiles apuntan a Sarajevo. **5** (cause to have effect on) dirigir a, destinar a: a campaign targeted at young people, una campaña dirigida a los jóvenes. – **6** adj (date, figure) fijado,-a; (audience, market) objetivo: target date, fecha prevista; target readership, lectores objetivo.
● to be on target, ir de acuerdo a lo previsto: export figures are on target, las cifras de exportaciones van de acuerdo a lo previsto.
■ target language, idioma m de destino. ‖ target practice, prácticas fpl de tiro. ‖ moving target, blanco móvil.
tariff ['tærɪf] **1** n (list of fixed charges) tarifa. **2** (duty to be paid on imports) arancel m. – **3** adj arancelario,-a.
tarmac ['tɑːmæk] **1** n asfalto. **2** (area) pista. – **3** t asfaltar.
tarn [tɑːn] n lago pequeño de montaña.
tarnish ['tɑːnɪʃ] **1** t (metal) deslustrar; (reputation) empañar, manchar. – **2** i (metal) deslustrarse; (reputation) empañarse, mancharse. – **3** n falta de lustre, falta de brillo.
tarot ['tærəʊ] n tarot m.
■ tarot cards, cartas fpl del tarot.
tarpaulin [tɑːˈpɔːlɪn] n lona.
tarragon ['tærəgən] n estragón m.
tarsus ['tɑːsəs] n ANAT tarso.
▲ pl tarsi.
tart [tɑːt] **1** adj (sour) acre, agrio,-a. **2** (reply) mordaz, áspero,-a, acre. – **3** n (pie) tarta, pastel m. **4** sl pej fulana.
◆ to tart up t sep (building) renovar, remodelar; (person) emperifollar.
● to tart os. up, emperifollarse.
tartan ['tɑːtən] n tela escocesa, tartán m.
tartar ['tɑːtəʳ] **1** n (on teeth) sarro. **2** (in wine) tártaro.
■ tartar sauce, salsa tártara.
Tartar ['tɑːtəʳ] **1** adj tártaro,-a. – **2** n tártaro,-a. **3** tártaro.
task [tɑːsk] n tarea, labor f.
● to take sb. to task over sth., reprender a algn. por algo.
■ task force, destacamento especial.
taskmaster ['tɑːskmɑːstəʳ] n capataz m.
● to be a hard taskmaster, ser muy severo,-a, ser un auténtico tirano.
Tasman ['tæzmən] the Tasman Sea, n el Mar de Tasmania.
Tasmania [tæz'meɪnɪə] n Tasmania.
Tasmanian [tæz'meɪnɪən] **1** adj tasmano,-a. – **2** n tasmano,-a.
tassel ['tæsəl] n borla.
taste [teɪst] **1** n (faculty) gusto. **2** (flavour) sabor m: it's got a sweet taste, tiene un sabor dulce; it is sweet to the

taste, es dulce al paladar; this cheese hasn't got much taste, este queso no tiene sabor; this fish's got a strange taste to it, este pescado tiene un gusto raro; it's an acquired taste, es un gusto adquirido. **3** (small sample) muestra, poquito; (experience) experiencia: have a taste of this cake, prueba este pastel; she had a taste of independence, conoció la independencia. **4** (ability to make good judgements) gusto; (liking) afición f (for, a), gusto (for, por): he's got good taste in clothes, tiene muy buen gusto para vestirse; pop music is not to my taste, la música pop no es de mi gusto. – **5** t (try food) probar; (wine) catar, degustar. **6** (eat, drink) probar: this is the most delicious cake I've ever tasted, es el pastel más delicioso que he probado. **7** (experience) conocer. **8** (perceive flavour) notar: you can taste the pepper in this stew, se nota la pimienta en este estofado. – **9** i saber (of/like, a): what does it taste like?, ¿a qué sabe?; it tastes bitter, tiene un gusto amargo, sabe a amargo.
● to be in bad/poor taste, ser de mal gusto. ‖ to be in good taste, ser de buen gusto. ‖ to give sb. a taste of their own medicine, pagar a algn. con la misma moneda, darle a algn. de su medicina. ‖ to leave a nasty taste in the mouth, dejar un mal sabor de boca. ‖ to taste, al gusto.
■ taste bud, papila gustativa.
tasteful ['teɪstfʊl] adj de buen gusto, elegante.
tastefully ['teɪstfʊlɪ] adv elegantemente.
tasteless ['teɪstləs] **1** adj de mal gusto. **2** (insipid) insípido,-a, soso,-a.
tasty ['teɪstɪ] adj sabroso,-a, rico,-a.
▲ comp tastier, superl tastiest.
ta-ta [tæ'tɑː] interj GB fam ¡adiós!, ¡hasta luego!
Tatar ['tɑːtəʳ] n → **Tartar**.
tattered ['tætəd] adj harapiento,-a, andrajoso,-a,.
tatters ['tætəz] npl (clothes) harapos mpl, andrajos mpl.
● in tatters, (clothes) harapiento,-a, andrajoso,-a, hecho,-a jirones; (nerves, reputation, etc) hecho,-a pedazos, destrozado,-a.
tattle ['tætl] **1** n chismes mpl, habladurías fpl. – **2** i cotorrear. – **3** t US acusar, chivarse.
tattler ['tætləʳ] n soplón,-ona.
tattletale ['tætlteɪl] n US soplón,-ona.
tattoo [tə'tuː] **1** n MIL retreta. **2** (show) espectáculo militar musical. **3** (on skin) tatuaje m. – **4** t tatuar.
▲ (sustantivo) pl tattoos; (verbo) pt & pp tattooed, ger (tattooing).
tatty ['tætɪ] adj (gen) muy usado,-a gastado,-a; (clothes) gastado,-a, raído,-a.
▲ comp tattier, superl tattiest.
taught [tɔːt] pt & pp → **teach**.
taunt [tɔːnt] **1** n mofa, pulla, insulto. – **2** t (mock) bufarse de, mofarse de; (provoke) hostigar, provocar.
Taurus ['tɔːrəs] n ASTROL ASTRON Tauro.
■ Taurus Mountains, Montes mpl Taurus.
taut [tɔːt] adj tirante, tenso,-a.
tauten ['tɔːtən] **1** t tensar. – **2** i tensarse, ponerse tenso,-a, ponerse tirante.
tautness ['tɔːtnəs] n tensión f, tirantez f.
tautology [tɔː'tɒlədʒɪ] n tautología.
tavern ['tævən] n taberna, mesón m.
TAVR ['tiː'eɪ'viː'ɑːʳ] abbr GB (Territorial Army and Volunteer Reserve) ejército de voluntarios reservistas.
tawdry ['tɔːdrɪ] adj hortera, charro,-a.
▲ comp tawdrier, superl tawdriest.
tawny ['tɔːnɪ] adj leonado,-a.
tax [tæks] **1** n impuesto, contribución f: everyone must pay taxes, todo el mundo debe pagar los impuestos;

taxes deducted at source, retenciones fiscales; *she earns £900 before/after tax,* gana novecientas libras brutas/netas. **2** *fig* (*burden, strain*) carga (**on,** sobre), esfuerzo (**on,** para). – **3** *t* (*impose a tax on - goods, profits*) gravar; (*- business, person*) imponer contribuciones a. **4** *fig* (*strain, test*) poner a prueba: *he taxes my patience,* pone a prueba mi paciencia.
● **to be a tax on sth.,** ser una carga para algn. ‖ **to tax sb. with sth.,** acusar a algn. de algo.
■ **income tax,** impuesto sobre la renta. ‖ **property tax,** US impuesto sobre la propiedad inmobiliaria. ‖ **tax allowance,** desgravación f fiscal. ‖ **tax avoidance,** evasión f fiscal. ‖ **tax collector,** recaudador,-ra de impuestos. ‖ **tax cut,** reducción f de impuestos. ‖ **tax disc,** *pegatina que acredita el pago del impuesto de circulación.* ‖ **tax evasion,** fraude m fiscal. ‖ **tax exile,** *persona que fija su residencia en un país extranjero para evitar los impuestos.* ‖ **tax haven,** paraíso fiscal. ‖ **tax inspector,** inspector,-ra de Hacienda. ‖ **tax rebate,** devolución f de impuestos. ‖ **tax return,** declaración f de renta. ‖ **value added tax,** impuesto sobre el valor añadido.
taxable ['tæksəbəl] *adj* imponible, gravable.
■ **taxable income,** renta imponible.
taxation [tæk'seɪʃən] *n* (*taxes*) impuestos mpl; (*system*) sistema m tributario.
tax-deductible ['tæksdɪ'dʌktəbəl] *adj* desgravable.
tax-free ['tæks'friː] *adj* libre de impuestos, exento,-a de impuestos.
taxi ['tæksɪ] **1** *n* taxi *m*. – **2** *i* (*plane*) rodar por la pista.
■ **taxi driver,** taxista *mf*. ‖ **taxi rank,** parada de taxis.
taxidermist ['tæksɪdɜːmɪst] *n* taxidermista *mf*.
taxidermy ['tæksɪdɜːmɪ] *n* taxidermia.
taximeter ['tæksɪmiːtə'] *n* taxímetro.
taxing ['tæksɪŋ] *adj* (*problem*) difícil; (*journey, job*) agotador,-ra.
taxman ['tæksmæn] *n* recaudador,-ra de impuestos.
■ **the Taxman,** Hacienda, el Fisco.
taxonomy [tæk'sɒnəmɪ] *n* taxonomía.
▲ *pl* **taxonomies.**
taxpayer ['tækspeɪə'] *n* contribuyente *mf*.
TB ['tiː'biː] *abbr* (*tuberculosis*) tuberculosis f.
tbsp ['teɪbəlspuːn] *abbr* (*tablespoon*) cucharada.
▲ *pl* **tbsps.**
tea [tiː] **1** *n* (*gen*) té m: *I had a cup of tea,* tomé una taza de té; *will you make some tea?,* ¿quieres hacer un poco de té? **2** (*infusion*) infusión f. **3** (*light meal*) merienda: *we have tea at half past five,* merendamos a las cinco y media. **4** (*full meal*) cena: *what do you want for your tea?,* ¿qué quieres para cenar?
● **not for all the tea in China,** por nada del mundo. ‖ **to be one's cup of tea,** ser del gusto de uno.
■ **tea bag,** bolsita de té. ‖ **tea cloth,** paño (de cocina). ‖ **tea cosy,** cubretetera. ‖ **tea leaf,** (*gen*) hoja de té; (*thief*) ladrón m. ‖ **tea party,** merienda. ‖ **tea service / tea set,** juego de té. ‖ **tea strainer,** colador m (pequeño). ‖ **tea towel,** paño de cocina. ‖ **tea trolley,** carrito.
tea-break ['tiːbreɪk] *n* descanso *para tomar el té.*
tea-caddy ['tiːkædɪ] *n* caja para el té.
▲ *pl* **tea-caddies.**
teach [tiːtʃ] **1** *t* (*gen*) enseñar; (*subject*) dar clases: *he teaches English,* da clases de inglés; *I've been teaching maths for 5 years,* llevo 5 años dando clases de mates; *my mother taught me (how) to read,* mi madre me enseñó a leer; *this course will be taught by Mr Smith,* este curso lo impartirá el Sr. Smith; *I was taught never to*

talk to strangers, me enseñaron a no hablar nunca con extraños. – **2** *i* ser profesor,-ra, dar clases: *he teaches at the university,* es profesor en la universidad.
● **that'll teach you,** así aprenderás. ‖ **to teach school,** US ser profesor,-ra. ‖ **you can't teach an old dog new tricks,** loro viejo no aprende a hablar.
▲ *pt & pp* **taught.**
teacher ['tiːtʃə'] *n* maestro,-a, profesor,-ra.
■ **teacher training,** magisterio, profesorado. ‖ **teacher training college,** escuela de magisterio.
tea-chest ['tiːtʃest] *n* caja para té.
teach-in ['tiːtʃɪn] *n* seminario.
teaching ['tiːtʃɪŋ] **1** *n* enseñanza. – **2** *adj* docente. – **3** **teachings,** *npl* doctrina, enseñanzas *fpl*.
■ **teaching practice,** prácticas *fpl* de magisterio. ‖ **teaching staff,** profesorado, personal m docente.
teacup ['tiːkʌp] *n* taza para té.
teak [tiːk] *n* teca.
teal [tiːl] *n* cerceta común.
team [tiːm] **1** *n* (*gen*) equipo. **2** (*of horses*) tiro; (*of oxen*) yunta. – **3** *adj* de equipo: *he's our team leader,* es el líder de nuestro equipo; *she's a good team worker,* trabaja bien en equipo. – **4** *i* combinar (**with,** con).
◆ **to team up** *t sep* asociarse (**with,** con), unirse (**with,** con): *he teamed up with his cousin,* se asoció con su primo.
■ **team effort,** esfuerzo de equipo. ‖ **team game,** juego de equipo. ‖ **team mate,** compañero,-a de equipo. ‖ **team spirit,** compañerismo, espíritu m de equipo. ‖ **team work,** trabajo de equipo.
teamster ['tiːmstə'] *n* US camionero,-a.
teapot ['tiːpɒt] *n* tetera.
tear¹ [teə'] **1** *n* (*rip*) rasgón m, desgarrón m, rotura. – **2** *t* (*rip, make a hole*) rasgar, desgarrar; (*pull apart, into pieces*) romper, hacer pedazos: *I've torn my shirt,* me he roto la camisa; *tear the piece of paper in half,* rompe el papel en dos; *she tore a hole in her dress,* se hizo un agujero en el vestido; *he tore a muscle,* se desgarró un músculo; *he tore open the parcel,* rompió el paquete para abrirlo. **3** (*remove by force*) arrancar: *the storm tore the roof off the shed,* la tormenta arrancó el techo del cobertizo. – **4** *i* romperse, rasgarse: *this material tears very easily,* esta tela se rompe muy fácilmente. **5** (*rush*) ir a toda velocidad, lanzarse, precipitarse: *they tear across the road,* cruzaron la calle corriendo; *the car tore past me,* el coche me pasó a toda velocidad; *I tore off down the road,* me fui corriendo por la calle.
◆ **to tear apart** *t sep* (*rip up*) despedazar, desgarrar; (*destroy*) destrozar: *the lion tore the deer apart,* el león despedazó al ciervo; *they threatened to tear my flat apart,* amenazaron con destrozarme el piso. **2** *fig* destrozar, desgarrar: *love will tear us apart,* el amor nos destrozará; *the critics tore the play apart,* los críticos dejaron la obra por los suelos. ‖ **to tear at** *t sep* arañar, rasgar. ‖ **to tear away** *t sep* (*snatch*) arrancar; (*force to leave*) arrancar, sacar: *he tore the book away from me,* me arrancó el libro de las manos; *I couldn't tear him away from the television,* no podía arrancarlo de delante de la televisión; *I couldn't tear myself away,* no podía apartarme. ‖ **to tear down** *t sep* (*building*) derribar, tirar abajo: *they have torn down all the old houses,* han derribado todas las casas viejas. ‖ **to tear into** *t insep* (*criticize severely*) arremeter contra. ‖ **to tear off** *t sep* (*pull violently*) arrancar; (*clothes*) quitarse precipitadamente. ‖ **to tear out** *t sep* arrancar: *she tore the page out of the book,* arrancó la página del libro. ‖ **to tear up** *t sep* (*paper*) romper en pedazos, hacer pedazos; (*plant*) arrancar de raíz.

● **to be torn between ...,** debatirse entre ..., no poder escoger entre ... ‖ **to tear to pieces,** (*rip up*) hacer pedazos; (*criticize*) poner por los suelos. ‖ **to be tearing one's hair out,** *fig* estar que se sube por las paredes. ‖ **to tear a strip off sb.,** regañar severamente a algn. ‖ **to tear sb. limb from limb,** despedazar a algn. ■ **wear and tear,** desgaste *m*.
▲ *pt* **tore,** *pp* **torn.**

tear² [tɪəʳ] *n* lágrima: *tears of joy/laughter,* lágrimas de alegría/risa; *the film brought tears to my eyes,* la película me hizo llorar; *we were moved to tears,* se nos saltaron las lágrimas.
● **in tears,** llorando. ‖ **to be bored to tears,** aburrirse como una ostra. ‖ **to burst into tears,** romper en lágrimas. ‖ **to shed tears,** derramar lágrimas.
■ **crocodile tears,** lágrimas *fpl* de cocodrilo. ‖ **tear gas,** gas *m* lacrimógeno.

tearaway [ˈtɛərəweɪ] *n* GB gamberro,-a.
teardrop [ˈtɪədrɒp] *n* lágrima.
tearful [ˈtɪəful] *adj* lloroso,-a.
tearing [ˈtɛərɪŋ] *adj* vertiginoso,-a: *to be in a tearing hurry,* tener muchísima prisa.
tear-jerker [ˈtɪədʒɜːkəʳ] *n* (*film*) dramón *m*; (*song, play etc*) canción *f* lacrimógena; (*play*) obra lacrimógena.
tearoom [ˈtɪːrʊm] *n* salón *m* de té.
tease [tiːz] **1** *t* (*make fun of - playfully*) tomar el pelo a, burlarse de; (*- annoyingly, unkindly*) atormentar, molestar. **2** (*sexually*) provocar, incitar. **3** (*wool etc*) cardar. **– 4** tomar el pelo. **– 5** *n* (*joker*) bromista *mf*. **6** *fam* (*flirt*) coqueta.
◆ **to tease out** *t sep* (*disentangle*) desenredar; (*obtain information*) sacar, sonsacar.
teasel [ˈtiːzəl] *n* cardencha.
teaser [ˈtiːzəʳ] **1** *n* (*puzzle*) rompecabezas *m*. **2** (*person*) bromista *mf*.
teashop [ˈtiːʃɒp] *n* salón *m* de té.
teasing [ˈtiːzɪŋ] *adj* burlón,-ona, guasón,-ona.
teasingly [ˈtiːzɪŋlɪ] *adv* en broma.
teaspoon [ˈtiːspuːn] *n* cucharilla.
teaspoonful [ˈtiːspuːnful] *n* cucharadita.
teat [tiːt] **1** *n* ZOOL tetilla. **2** (*on bottle*) tetina.
teatime [ˈtiːtaɪm] *n* hora del té, hora de la merienda.
technical [ˈteknɪkəl] *adj* técnico,-a.
■ **technical college,** centro de formación profesional. ‖ **technical drawing,** dibujo técnico. ‖ **technical hitch,** fallo técnico, incidente *m* técnico.
technicality [teknɪˈkælɪtɪ] *n* (*detail*) detalle *m* técnico; (*technical term*) tecnicismo.
▲ *pl* **technicalities.**
technically [ˈteknɪkəlɪ] **1** *adv* técnicamente. **2** (*theoretically*) en teoría.
technician [tekˈnɪʃən] *n* técnico,-a.
technique [tekˈniːk] *n* técnica.
technological [teknəˈlɒdʒɪkəl] *adj* tecnológico,-a.
technology [tekˈnɒlədʒɪ] *n* tecnología.
▲ *pl* **technologies.**
teddy bear [ˈtedɪbɛəʳ] *n* osito de peluche.
teddy boy [ˈtedɪbɔɪ] *n* rocker *m*, rockabilly *m*.
tedious [ˈtiːdɪəs] *adj* tedioso,-a, aburrido,-a.
tediousness [ˈtiːdɪəsnəs] *n* tedio, aburrimiento.
tedium [ˈtiːdɪəm] *n* tedio, aburrimiento.
tee [tiː] *n* tee *m*.
◆ **to tee off** *i* dar el primer golpe, golpear desde el tee. ‖ **to tee up** *i* colocar la pelota sobre el tee.
teem¹ [tiːm] *i* (*rain*) llover a cántaros, diluviar: *it's teeming (down),* está lloviendo a cántaros.

teem² [tiːm] *i* (*be abundant in*) abundar (**with,** en), estar lleno,-a (**with,** de).
teenage [ˈtiːneɪdʒ] *adj* adolescente.
teenager [ˈtiːneɪdʒəʳ] *n* adolescente *mf* de 13 a 19 años, quinceañero,-a.
teens [tiːnz] *npl* adolescencia, edad *f* de 13 a 19 años: *he's in his teens,* tiene entre trece y diecinueve años.
teeny [ˈtiːnɪ] *adj fam* pequeñito,-a, chiquitín,-ina.
▲ *comp* **teenier,** *superl* **teeniest.**
teenybopper [ˈtiːnɪbɒpəʳ] *n* chica adolescente a quien le gusta la moda, la música pop, etc.
tee-shirt [ˈtiːʃɜːt] *n* camiseta.
teeter [ˈtiːtəʳ] **1** *i* (*totter*) tambalearse. **2** (*hesitate*) vacilar.
● **to teeter on the edge of sth.,** estar al borde de algo.
teeth [tiːθ] *npl* → **tooth.**
teethe [tiːð] *i* endentecer, echar los dientes.
teething [ˈtiːðɪŋ] *n* dentición *f*.
● **teething troubles,** problemas *mpl* iniciales.
■ **teething ring,** chupador *m*.
teetotal [tiːˈtəʊtəl] *adj* abstemio,-a.
teetotalism [tiːˈtəʊtəlɪzəm] *n* abstinencia de bebidas alcohólicas.
teetotaller [tiːˈtəʊtələʳ] *n* abstemio,-a.
TEFL [ˈtefəl, ˈtiːˈiːˈefˈel] *abbr* (*Teaching of English as a Foreign Language*) la enseñanza del inglés como idioma extranjero.
Teheran [teəˈrɑːn] *n* → **Tehran.**
Tehran [teəˈrɑːn] *n* Teherán.
tel [tel, ˈtelɪfəʊn] *abbr* (*telephone*) teléfono; (*abbreviation*) tel.
telecommunications [telɪkəmjuːnɪˈkeɪʃənz] *npl* telecomunicaciones *fpl*.
telegram [ˈtelɪgræm] *n* telegrama *m*.
telegraph [ˈtelɪgrɑːf] **1** *n* telégrafo. **– 2** *i* telegrafiar.
■ **telegraph line,** cable *m* telegráfico. ‖ **telegraph pole / telegraph post,** poste *m* telegráfico.
teleology [telɪˈɒlədʒɪ] *n* teleología.
telepathic [telɪˈpæθɪk] *adj* telepático,-a.
telepathy [tɪˈlepəθɪ] *n* telepatía.
telephone [ˈtelɪfəʊn] **1** *n* teléfono. **– 2** *t* telefonear, llamar por teléfono. **– 3** *i* hacer una llamada telefónica.
● **to be on the telephone,** (*have a phone*) tener teléfono; (*be speaking*) estar al teléfono, hablar por teléfono. ‖ **you're wanted on the telephone,** te llaman por teléfono.
■ **telephone book,** guía telefónica. ‖ **telephone box / telephone booth,** cabina telefónica. ‖ **telephone call,** llamada telefónica. ‖ **telephone directory,** guía telefónica. ‖ **telephone exchange,** central *f* telefónica. ‖ **telephone number,** número de teléfono. ‖ **telephone operator,** telefonista *mf*.
telephonist [təˈlefənɪst] *n* telefonista *mf*.
telephoto lens [telɪfəʊtəʊˈlenz] *n* teleobjetivo.
teleprinter [ˈtelɪprɪntəʳ] *n* teletipo.
teleprompter [ˈtelɪprɒmptəʳ] *n* autocue *m*, teleprompter *m*.
telesales [ˈtelɪseɪlz] *npl* ventas *fpl* por teléfono.
telescope [ˈtelɪskəʊp] **1** *n* telescopio. **– 2** *t* plegar. **– 3** *i* plegarse.
telescopic [telɪˈskɒpɪk] *adj* (*aerial*) telescópico,-a; (*umbrella*) plegable.
teletext [ˈtelɪtekst] *n* teletexto.
telethon [ˈtelɪθɒn] *n* telemaratón *m*.
teletypewriter [telɪˈtaɪpraɪtəʳ] *n* US teletipo.

tenacity

televise ['telɪvaɪz] *t* televisar.

television ['telɪvɪʒən] **1** *n* (*gen*) televisión *f*: *black and white television,* televisión en blanco y negro; *colour television,* televisión en color; *what's on (the) television?,* ¿qué hay en la televisión?; *do you like watching television?,* ¿te gusta ver la televisión?; *my father works in television,* mi padre trabaja en la televisión. **2** (*set*) televisor *m*.
■ **television licence,** *permiso para tener un televisor.* || **television programme,** programa *m* de televisión. || **television screen,** pantalla de televisión.

telex ['teleks] **1** *n* télex *m*. – **2** *t* enviar por télex.

tell [tel] **1** *t* (*gen*) decir: *tell me your name,* dime tu nombre; *tell me (that) you love me,* dime que me quieres; *why didn't you tell me?,* ¿por qué no me lo dijiste?; *he told me (that) he'd seen you,* me dijo que te había visto; *could you tell me where the station is, please?,* ¿me podría indicar dónde está la estación, por favor?* **2** (*story, joke*) contar; (*truth, lies, secret*) decir: *tell us a joke, Fred,* cuéntanos un chiste, Fred; *telling lies is bad,* mentir es malo, decir mentiras es malo. **3** (*talk about*) hablar de: *tell me all about your family,* háblame de tu familia; *he told us of his travels in China,* nos habló de sus viajes por la China. **4** *fml* comunicar, informar: *we regret to tell you that ...,* lamentamos comunicarle que ... **5** (*assure*) asegurar, garantizar: *it's true, I tell you,* es verdad, te lo aseguro. **6** (*order*) decir, mandar: *he told us to go away,* nos dijo que nos marcháramos; *the boss told me to shut up,* el jefe me mandó callar; *he told me not to be late,* me dijo que no llegara tarde; *you'll do as you're told!,* ¡harás lo que yo te digo! **7** (*show*) indicar; (*in writing*) explicar: *this light tells you when it's on,* esta luz te indica cuándo está en marcha; *this book tells you how to grow orchids,* este libro te explica cómo cultivar orquídeas. **8** (*distinguish*) distinguir: *the teacher can't tell Peter from Paul,* el profesor no puede distinguir a Peter de Paul; *children can't tell right from wrong,* los niños no saben distinguir el bien del mal; *can you tell the difference between Gruyère and Emmental?,* ¿sabes distinguir entre el gruyère y el emmental? **9** (*know*) saber, notarse: *it's difficult to tell what is happening,* es difícil saber lo que está pasando; *you can tell by his voice that he's angry,* se le nota en la voz que está enfadado. **10** (*count - votes*) escrutar; (*- rosary beads*) pasar. – **11** *i* (*reveal secret*) hablar, soplar: *promise you won't tell?,* ¿me prometes que no lo dirás?; *no matter what you do to me, I'll never tell,* podéis hacerme lo que queráis, porque no hablaré. **12** (*have effect*) notarse, hacerse notar: *Induráin's experience began to tell,* la experiencia de Induráin se hizo notar; *the strain is telling on her,* la tensión empieza a afectarle. **13** (*know*) saber: *who can tell?,* ¿quién sabe?; *you can never tell,* nunca se sabe.
◆ **to tell against** *t insep* obrar en contra de: *all the evidence tells against you,* todas las pruebas obran en contra de ti. || **to tell apart** *t sep* (saber) distinguir: *it's impossible to tell them apart,* es imposible distinguirlos. || **to tell off 1** *t sep* regañar, reñir: *she told him off for swearing,* le regañó por decir tacos. **2** MIL destacar. || **to tell on** *t insep* (*inform on*) chivarse de: *he told on his friend for stealing,* se chivó que su amigo había robado.
● **as far as I can tell,** que yo sepa, por lo que yo sé. || **I'll tell you what,** escucha lo que digo. || **I told you so,** ya te lo dije, ya lo decía yo. || **tell me another!,** ¡anda ya!, ¡eso no te lo crees ni tú! || **there's no telling,** no se sabe, vete a saber. || **time will tell,** el tiempo lo dirá. || **to tell sb. where to get off,** cantarle las cuarenta a algn., decirle cuatro cosas a algn. || **to tell the**

time, saber decir la hora. || **you can never tell,** nunca se sabe. || **you're telling me,** a mí me lo dices, ni que lo digas.
▲ *pt & pp* **told.**

teller ['telə'] *n* (*in bank*) cajero,-a.

telling ['telɪŋ] *adj* (*blow*) contundente; (*smile, reaction*) elocuente, expresivo,-a, revelador,-ra.

telling-off [telɪŋ'ɒf] *n fam* bronca, rapapolvo.

tell-tale ['telteɪl] **1** *n* chivato,-a, acusica *mf*. – **2** *adj* revelador,-ra.

telly ['telɪ] *n fam* tele *f*.
▲ *pl* **tellies.**

temerity [tə'merɪtɪ] *n* temeridad *f*.

temp[1] ['temprɪtʃə'] *abbr* (*temperature*) temperatura; (*abbreviation*) temp.

temp[2] [temp] **1** *n* trabajador,-ra temporal. – **2** *i* hacer trabajos eventuales.

temper ['tempə'] **1** *n* (*mood*) humor *m*; (*nature*) genio, temperamento, disposición *f*. **2** (*of metal*) temple *m*. – **3** *t* (*metal*) templar. **4** *fig* atenuar, suavizar.
● **to be in a bad temper,** estar de mal humor. || **to fly into a temper,** ponerse furioso,-a. || **to have a bad temper,** tener mal genio. || **to have a fit of temper,** darle a uno un ataque de furia. || **to have a quick temper,** tener el genio vivo. || **to keep one's temper,** controlarse. || **to lose one's temper,** enfadarse, perder los estribos.

temperament ['tempərəmənt] *n* temperamento.

temperamental [temprə'mentl] *adj* temperamental.

temperance ['tempərəns] *n* (*gen*) moderación *f*; (*from alcohol*) abstinencia.

temperate ['tempərɪt] *adj* (*gen*) moderado,-a; (*climate*) templado,-a.

temperature ['tempərɪtʃə'] *n* temperatura.
● **to have/run a temperature,** tener fiebre. || **to take sb.'s temperature,** tomarle la temperatura a algn.

tempered ['tempəd] *adj* templado,-a.

tempest ['tempɪst] *n* tempestad *f*.

tempestuous [tem'pestjuəs] *adj* tempestuoso,-a.

tempi ['tempiː] *npl* → **tempo.**

template ['templeɪt] *n* plantilla.

temple ['tempəl] **1** *n* (*building*) templo. **2** ANAT sien *f*.

tempo ['tempəʊ] **1** *n* MUS tempo. **2** *fig* ritmo.
▲ *pl* **tempos** *o* **tempi.**

temporary ['tempərərɪ] *adj* temporal, provisional.

temporize ['tempəraɪz] *i* dar largas, intentar ganar tiempo.

tempt [tempt] *t* tentar.
● **to be tempted to do sth.,** estar tentado,-a a hacer algo. || **to tempt fate,** tentar a la suerte. || **to tempt providence,** tentar la suerte. || **to tempt sb. to sth.,** ofrecerle algo a algn., servirle algo a algn.

temptation [temp'teɪʃən] *n* tentación *f*.
● **to yield to temptation,** caer en la tentación.

tempter ['temptə'] *n* tentador,-ra.

tempting ['temptɪŋ] *adj* tentador,-ra.

ten [ten] **1** *n* diez *m*. – **2** *adj* diez.
● **it's ten to one that ...,** te apuesto lo que quieras a que ...: *it's ten to one they don't come,* te apuesto lo que quieras a que no vienen.
▲ *Véase también* **six.**

tenable ['tenəbəl] **1** *adj* (*theory etc*) sostenible, defendible. **2** (*post, office*): *how long is the post tenable for?,* ¿durante cuántos años se puede ocupar el puesto?

tenacious [tə'neɪʃəs] *adj* tenaz.

tenacity [tə'næsɪtɪ] *n* tenacidad *f*.

tenancy ['tenənsɪ] n (period) contrato de alquiler; (possession) arrendamiento.
▲ pl tenancies.
tenant ['tenənt] n inquilino,-a, arrendatario,-a.
tend [tend] 1 t (person) cuidar de, atender; (other) ocuparse de. – 2 i (have tendency) tender (to, a), tener tendencia (to, a): he tends to wander, tiende a digresar; their music tends towards heavy, su música tiende a ser dura; I tend to go on holiday in June, suelo irme de vacaciones en junio; it tends to be very warm in May, suele hacer bastante calor en mayo.
◆ to tend to t insep ocuparse de.
tendency ['tendənsɪ] n tendencia.
▲ pl tendencies.
tendentious [ten'denʃəs] adj tendencioso,-a.
tender[1] ['tendə'] 1 adj (meat etc) tierno,-a. 2 (loving) tierno,-a, cariñoso,-a. 3 (sore) dolorido,-a. 4 (delicate) delicado,-a, sensible.
● at a tender age, a una tierna edad.
tender[2] ['tendə] 1 n COMM (offer) oferta, propuesta. – 2 t presentar, ofrecer. – 3 i hacer una oferta (for, para).
● to put sth. out to tender, sacar algo a concurso algo.
tender[3] ['tendə] 1 n (dinghy) lancha (auxiliar). 2 (of train) ténder m.
tender-hearted ['tendə'hɑːtɪd] adj compasivo,-a, bondadoso,-a.
tenderly ['tendəlɪ] adv con ternura.
tenderness ['tendənəs] n ternura.
tendon ['tendən] n tendón m.
tendril ['tendrəl] n zarcillo.
tenement ['tenəmənt] n casa de vecindad.
tenet ['tenət] n principio, dogma m.
tenfold ['tenfəʊld] adv diez veces.
tenner ['tenə'] n GB fam billete de diez libras esterlinas.
tennis ['tenɪs] n tenis m.
■ tennis court, pista de tenis. ‖ tennis elbow, codo de tenista, sinovitis f del codo.
tenor ['tenə'] 1 adj (voice) de tenor; (instrument) tenor. – 2 n MUS tenor m. 3 fml (sense) tenor m.
tenpin bowling [tenpɪn'bəʊlɪŋ] n bolos mpl.
tense [tens] 1 adj (anxious) tenso,-a. 2 (taut) tirante, tenso,-a. – 3 n GRAM tiempo: write this sentence in the past tense, escribe esta oración en pasado. – 4 t tensar.
● to get tensed up, ponerse nervioso,-a.
tension ['tenʃən] n tensión f.
tent [tent] n tienda de campaña.
tentacle ['tentəkəl] n tentáculo.
tentative ['tentətɪv] 1 adj de prueba, de ensayo, provisional. 2 (person) indeciso,-a.
tentatively ['tentətɪvlɪ] 1 adv provisionalmente, en pruebas. 2 con indecisión, dubitativamente.
tenterhooks ['tentəhʊks] on tenterhooks, phr sobre ascuas.
tenth [tenθ] 1 adj décimo,-a. – 2 adv en décimo lugar. – 3 n (fraction) décimo; (one part) décima parte f.
▲ Véase también sixth.
tent-peg ['tentpeg] n estaquilla.
tenuous ['tenjʊəs] adj tenue, delicado,-a.
tenure ['tenjə'] 1 n (of property) ocupación f. 2 (of position) ejercicio. 3 EDUC titularidad f.
tepee ['tiːpiː] n tipi m.
tepid ['tepɪd] adj tibio,-a.
tequila [tə'kiːlə] n tequila.
term [tɜːm] 1 n EDUC trimestre m. 2 (period of time) período. 3 (expression, word) término: in general terms, en tér-

minos generales. – 4 t calificar de, llamar, denominar. – 5 terms, npl (sense) términos mpl: in political terms, desde el punto de vista político; in real terms, en términos reales. 6 COMM condiciones fpl: the terms of the agreement, las condiciones del acuerdo. 7 (relations) relaciones fpl.
● in the long/short term, a largo/corto plazo. ‖ in terms of, en cuanto a. ‖ on equal terms, en igualdad de condiciones. ‖ to be a contradiction in terms, ser un contrasentido. ‖ to be on first name terms, ≈ tutearse. ‖ to be on good terms with sb., tener buenas relaciones con algn. ‖ to come to terms with sth., llegar a aceptar algo, adaptarse a algo. ‖ to come to terms with sb., llegar a un arreglo con algn.
■ term of office, mandato.
terminal ['tɜːmɪnəl] 1 adj terminal. – 2 n ELEC borne m. 3 COMPUT terminal m. 4 (at airport etc) terminal f.
terminally ['tɜːmɪnəlɪ] terminally ill, adv en fase terminal, desahuciado,-a.
terminate ['tɜːmɪneɪt] 1 t (gen) terminar, poner fin a; (contract) rescindir. 2 (pregnancy) interrumpir. – 3 i terminarse: this train terminates here, éste es el final del recorrido.
termination [tɜːmɪ'neɪʃən] 1 n (gen) terminación f; (contract) rescisión f. 2 (of pregnancy) interrupción f.
termini ['tɜːmɪnaɪ] npl → **terminus**.
terminology [tɜːmɪ'nɒlədʒɪ] n terminología.
terminus ['tɜːmɪnəs] n término.
▲ pl terminuses o termini.
termite ['tɜːmaɪt] n termita.
terrace ['terəs] 1 n (of house, café, bar, etc) terraza. 2 (on hillside) terraza, bancal m. 3 (of houses) hilera de casas. – 4 terraces, npl SP gradas fpl.
■ terraced house, casa adosada.
terracotta [terə'kɒtə] n terracota.
terra firma [terə'fɜːmə] n tierra firme.
terrain [tə'reɪn] n terreno.
terrapin ['terəpɪn] n tortuga de agua dulce.
terrestrial [tə'restrɪəl] adj terrestre.
terrible ['terɪbəl] 1 adj terrible, espantoso,-a, atroz. 2 fam (as intensifier) mucho,-a.
terribly ['terɪblɪ] 1 adv terriblemente. 2 fam (very) muy: I'm terribly sorry, lo siento muchísimo.
terrier ['terɪə'] n terrier m.
terrific [tə'rɪfɪk] 1 adj (wonderful) fabuloso,-a, estupendo,-a. 2 (huge) tremendo,-a.
terrified ['terɪfaɪd] adj aterrorizado,-a.
● to be terrified of sth., darle pánico a uno algo.
terrify ['terɪfaɪ] t aterrar, aterrorizar.
▲ pt & pp terrified, ger terrifying.
terrifying ['terɪfaɪɪŋ] adj aterrador,-ra, espantoso,-a.
territorial [terɪ'tɔːrɪəl] adj territorial.
■ territorial waters, aguas fpl territoriales.
territory ['terɪtərɪ] 1 n (gen) territorio. 2 (zone) zona, área.
▲ pl territories.
terror ['terə'] 1 n (gen) terror m, espanto. 2 fam (child) diablillo.
terrorism ['terərɪzəm] n terrorismo.
terrorist ['terərɪst] 1 n terrorista mf. – 2 adj terrorista.
terrorize ['terəraɪz] t aterrorizar.
● to terrorize sb. into doing sth., atemorizar a algn. para que haga algo.
terror-stricken ['terəstrɪkən] adj aterrorizado,-a.
terse [tɜːs] adj seco,-a, brusco,-a.
tersely ['tɜːslɪ] adv bruscamente.

tertiary ['tɜːʃərɪ] *adj* terciario,-a.
■ **tertiary education,** enseñanza *f* superior.
TESL ['tesəl, 'tiː'iː'es'el] *abbr* (*Teaching of English as a Second Language*) la enseñanza del inglés como segundo idioma.
test [test] **1** *n* (*trial*) prueba. **2** EDUC (*gen*) examen *m*, prueba; (*multiple choice*) test *m*. **3** MED análisis *m*. – **4** *t* (*gen*) probar: *our products are not tested on animals,* nuestros productos no se prueban con animales. **5** (*patience, loyalty*) poner a prueba. **6** EDUC hacerle una prueba a. **7** MED analizar.
● **to stand the test of time,** resistir el paso del tiempo. ‖ **to take a car for a test drive,** probar un coche en carretera.
■ **test case,** *caso que sienta jurisprudencia.* ‖ **test flight,** vuelo de prueba. ‖ **test match,** partido internacional. ‖ **test pilot,** piloto de pruebas. ‖ **test tube,** probeta.
testament ['testəmənt] *n* testamento.
testicle ['testɪkəl] *n* testículo.
testify ['testɪfaɪ] **1** *t* JUR declarar, atestiguar. – **2** *i* (*bear witness*) dar fe (**to,** de). **3** JUR prestar declaración, testificar.
▲ *pt & pp* testified, *ger* testifying.
testimonial [testɪ'məʊnɪəl] **1** *n* (*for job etc*) recomendación *f.* **2** (*homage*) homenaje *m.*
testimony ['testɪmənɪ] *n* testimonio.
▲ *pl* testimonies.
testing ['testɪŋ] **1** *adj* difícil, duro,-a. – **2** *n* pruebas *fpl.*
test-tube baby [testtjuːb'beɪbɪ] *n* niño,-a probeta.
testy ['testɪ] *adj* irritable.
▲ *comp* testier, *superl* testiest.
tetanus ['tetənəs] *n* tétanos *m inv.*
tetchy ['tetʃɪ] *adj* irritable.
▲ *comp* tetchier, *superl* tetchiest.
tête-à-tête [teɪtə'teɪt] *n* conversación *f* privada.
tether ['teðəʳ] **1** *n* (*rope*) cuerda; (*chain*) cadena. – **2** *t* atar.
● **to be at the end of one's tether,** estar hasta la coronilla.
Texan ['teksən] **1** *adj* tejano,-a. – **2** *n* tejano,-a.
Texas ['teksəs] *n* Tejas.
text [tekst] *n* texto.
textbook ['tekstbʊk] *n* libro de texto.
textile ['tekstaɪl] **1** *adj* textil. – **2** *n* textil *m.*
textual ['tekstjʊəl] *adj* textual.
texture ['tekstʃəʳ] *n* textura.
Thai [taɪ] **1** *adj* tailandés,-esa. – **2** *n* (*person*) tailandés,-esa. **3** (*language*) tailandés *m.*
Thailand ['taɪlænd] *n* Tailandia.
Thames [temz] *n* el Támesis *m.*
than [ðæn, *unstressed* ðən] **1** *conj* que: *he is taller than you are,* él es más alto que tú; *you do it better than me,* tú lo haces mejor que yo. **2** (*with numbers*) de: *more than fifty,* más de cincuenta; *more than once,* más de una vez. **3** (*followed by clause*) de lo que: *this is easier than we thought,* esto es más fácil de lo que pensábamos.
thank [θæŋk] *t* dar las gracias a, agradecer: *she thanked me for the flowers,* me agradeció las flores.
● **no, thank you,** no, gracias. ‖ **thank God,** gracias a Dios. ‖ **thank goodness,** gracias a Dios. ‖ **thank heavens,** gracias a Dios. ‖ **thank you,** gracias. ‖ **to have sb. to thank (for sth.),** *iron* tener algn. la culpa de algo: *you've only yourself to thank,* la culpa la tienes tú solito. ‖ **to thank one's lucky stars,** dar gracias al cielo.
thankful ['θæŋkfʊl] *adj* agradecido,-a.
● **to be thankful to sb. for sth.,** estarle agradecido,-a a algn. por algo.

thankfully ['θæŋkfəlɪ] *adv* afortunadamente.
thankless ['θæŋkləs] *adj* ingrato,-a.
thanks [θæŋks] **1** *interj* gracias: *thanks to,* gracias a. – **2** *npl* (*gratitude*) agradecimiento.
● **no, thanks,** no, gracias. ‖ *that's all the thanks I get,* ¿así es como me lo agradeces?
thanksgiving [θæŋks'gɪvɪŋ] *n* acción *f* de gracias.
■ **Thanksgiving Day,** Día *m* de Acción de Gracias.
that [ðæt *unstressed* ðət] **1** *adj* ese, esa; (*remote*) aquel, aquella: *look at that woman,* mira a aquella mujer; *how much is that dress?,* ¿cuánto vale ese vestido?; *what was that noise?,* ¿qué ha sido ese ruido?; *just at that moment,* justo en aquel instante; *have you got that record I lent you?,* ¿tienes aquel disco que te dejé? – **2** *pron* ése *m,* ésa; (*remote*) aquél *m,* aquélla: *who's that?,* ¿quién es ése/ésa?; *this is mine, that is yours,* éste es mío, aquél es tuyo; *this one's much nicer than that,* éste es mucho más bonito que aquél. **3** (*indefinite*) eso; (*remote*) aquello: *what's that?,* ¿qué es eso?; *don't do that,* no hagas eso; *where did you get that?,* ¿dónde has comprado eso?; *that's why I didn't go,* por eso no fui. **4** (*relative*) que: *the man that lives upstairs is a writer,* el hombre que vive arriba es escritor; *I really like the book (that) you gave me,* me encanta el libro que me regalaste; *this is the most difficult job (that) I've ever done,* este es el trabajo más difícil que he hecho. **5** (*with preposition*) que, el/la que, el/la cual: *this is the book (that) I was telling you about,* éste es el libro de que te hablaba; *the day (that) we met,* el día (en el) que nos conocimos. – **6** *conj* que: *I know (that) it's true,* sé que es verdad; *he said (that) he was a policeman,* dijo que era policía; *the problem is that I don't speak French,* el problema es que no hablo francés; *she was so happy (that) she danced in the street,* estaba tan contenta que bailó en la calle; *give me the money so (that) I can buy a present,* dame el dinero para que pueda comprar un regalo. **7** ¡ojalá!: *oh that I were rich,* ojalá fuera rico. – **8** *adv fam* tan, tanto,-a, tantos,-as: *it's not that expensive,* no es tan caro; *it isn't that cold,* no hace tanto frío; *it wasn't that bad,* no fue tan malo.
● **and all that,** y todo eso. ‖ **like that,** así, de aquella manera. ‖ **that is to say,** es decir. ‖ **that's it,** (*that's all*) eso es todo; (*that's right*) eso es; (*that's enough*) se acabó. ‖ **that's life,** así es la vida. ‖ **that's more like it,** ¡ahora!, ¡así me gusta! ‖ **that's right,** así es. ‖ **that's that,** ya está, se acabó. ‖ **who's that?,** (*on 'phone*) ¿quién es?, ¿quién eres?
▲ (*adjetivo y pronombre*) *pl* those.
thatch [θætʃ] **1** *n* (*straw*) paja; (*roof*) tejado de paja. **2** (*hair*) mata. – **3** *t* poner techo de paja a, cubrir con techo de paja.
thatched ['θætʃt] *adj* de paja.
■ **thatched cottage,** casa con tejado de paja. ‖ **thatched roof,** tejado de paja.
thaw [θɔː] **1** *n* deshielo. – **2** *t* (*food*) descongelar; (*snow, ice*) derretir. – **3** *i* (*food*) descongelarse; (*snow, ice*) derretirse. **4** (*person*) ablandarse; (*relations*) distenderse, mejorar.
◆ **to thaw out 1** *i* descongelarse. – **2** *t sep* descongelar.
the [ðə] **1** *def art* el, la; (*plural*) los, las: *the sun is shining,* el sol brilla; *the moon is full,* la luna está llena; *we went to the cinema,* fuimos al cine; *he's from the next village,* es del pueblo al lado; *the Queen of England,* la Reina de Inglaterra; *the river Thames,* el río Támesis; *he's the richest man in the world,* es el hombre más rico del mundo; *the English are not famous for their cooking,* los ingleses no tienen fama por su cocina; *the Browns are*

very friendly, los Brown son muy amables; *Elizabeth the Second,* Elisabeth segunda. **2** (*per*) por: *we are paid by the hour,* nos pagan por horas. **3** (*emphasis*) el, la, los, las: *you're not the Paul Newman, are you?,* no serás el auténtico Paul Newman, ¿verdad? – **4** *adv* (*with comparatives*): *the more you have, the more you want,* cuanto más se tiene, más se quiere; *the sooner the better,* cuanto antes mejor; *the less said, the better,* cuanto menos digas, mejor; *the more the merrier,* cuantos más seamos, más nos divertiremos.
▲ *Delante de una vocal* [ðɪ]; con enfasis [ðiː].

theater [ˈθɪətəʳ] *n* US → **theatre**.

theatre [ˈθɪətəʳ] **1** *n* (*gen*) teatro. **2** MED quirófano. **3** US cine *m.* **4** (*scene of action*) escenario. – **5** *adj* teatral, de teatro.
■ **theatre company,** compañía teatral.

theatregoer [ˈtɪətəɡɔʳ] *n* aficionado,-a al teatro.

theatrical [θɪˈætrɪkəl] *adj* teatral.

thee [ðiː] *pron arch* tú, usted.

theft [θeft] *n* robo, hurto.

their [ðeəʳ] *adj* su; (*plural*) sus: *they took their children and their dog,* se llevaron a sus hijos y al perro; *who wants their present now?,* ¿quién quiere su regalo ahora?; *nobody likes their neighbours,* a nadie le gustan sus vecinos.

theirs [ðeəz] *pron* (el) suyo, (la) suya; (*plural*) (los) suyos, (las) suyas: *that house is theirs,* aquella casa es suya; *our children play with theirs,* nuestros hijos juegan con los suyos; *everyone wants what is theirs by right,* todos quieren lo que es suyo por derecho.

them [ðem, *unstressed* ðəm] **1** *pron* (*direct object*) los, las; (*indirect object*) les; (*before another pronoun*) se: *the Smiths are coming, do you know them?,* vienen los Smith, ¿los conoces?; *I like these shoes so I'll buy them,* me gustan estos zapatos así que me los compraré; *take these flowers and give them to Mary,* coge estas flores y dáselas a Mary; *we'll give them a share of the profits,* les daremos una participación de las ganancias; *I sent them a Christmas card,* les envié una tarjeta de Navidad; *you must tell them,* debes decírselo. **2** (*with preposition, stressed*) ellos, ellas: *don't speak to them,* no hables con ellos; *this is for them,* esto es para ellos; *I took a photo of them,* les saqué una foto; *there were ten of them,* eran diez. **3** *fam* (*used with singular meaning*) lo, la, le: *if anyone arrives, tell them to wait,* si llega alguien, dile que espere.
● **them and us,** ellos y nosotros.

thematic [θɪˈmætɪk] *adj* temático,-a.

theme [θiːm] *n* tema *m.*
■ **theme park,** parque *m* temático. ‖ **theme song,** tema *m* musical. ‖ **theme tune,** sintonía.

themselves [ðəmˈselvz] **1** *pron* (*subject*) ellos mismos, ellas mismas: *they made it themselves,* lo hicieron ellos mismos. **2** (*object*) se: *they looked at themselves in the mirror,* se miraron en el espejo. **3** (*after preposition*) sí mismos,-as: *they are old enough to look after themselves,* son lo bastante mayores como para cuidar de sí mismos.
● **by themselves,** solos,-as: *don't leave the children by themselves,* no dejes a los niños solos.

then [ðen] **1** *adv* (*at that time*) entonces: *I was living in London then,* vivía en Londres entonces. **2** (*next*) luego, después, entonces: *I'll have soup first and then fish,* primero tomaré sopa y después pescado; *first he went to the baker's and then to the supermarket,* primero fue a la panadería y luego al supermercado. **3** (*besides*) además. **4** (*so, therefore*) entonces, así que; (*in that case*) en-

tonces, pues: *you've come back then?,* ¿así que has vuelto?; *if you don't want to go, then don't,* si no quieres ir, pues no vayas. – **5** *adj* (de) entonces: *the then prime minister,* el entonces primer ministro.
● **but then,** pero claro. ‖ **by then,** para entonces. ‖ **from then on,** a partir de entonces, desde entonces. ‖ **now and then,** de vez en cuando. ‖ **now then,** pues bien, ahora bien. ‖ **since then,** desde entonces. ‖ **then again,** también. ‖ **there and then,** en el acto, en el mismo momento. ‖ **until then / till then,** hasta entonces.

thence [ðens] *adv arch* de allí, desde allí.

thenceforth [ðensˈfɔːθ] *adv* desde entonces, a partir de entonces.

theological [θɪəˈlɒdʒɪkəl] *adj* teológico,-a.

theology [θɪˈɒlədʒɪ] *n* teología.

theorem [ˈθɪərəm] *n* teorema *m.*

theoretical [θɪəˈretɪkəl] *adj* teórico,-a.

theoretically [θɪəˈretɪklɪ] *adv* en teoría.

theorize [ˈθɪəraɪz] *i* teorizar.

theory [ˈθɪərɪ] *n* teoría.
● **in theory,** en teoría.
▲ *pl* **theories.**

therapeutic [θerəˈpjuːtɪk] *adj* terapéutico,-a.

therapist [ˈθerəpɪst] *n* terapeuta *mf.*

therapy [ˈθerəpɪ] *n* terapia, terapéutica: *she's having therapy,* está recibiendo terapia.
▲ *pl* **therapies.**

there [ðeəʳ] **1** *adv* allí, allá, ahí: *I often go there on holiday,* voy de vacaciones allí a menudo; *don't just sit there, do something,* no te quedes ahí sentado, haz algo; *it's over there, on the table,* está por allí, en la mesa; *look at that man over there,* mira a aquel hombre de allí; *I went there and back,* fui hasta allí y volví; *let's leave it there,* dejémoslo ahí; *there he comes,* ahí viene. **2** (*in discussion*) acerca de eso: *I agree with you there,* estoy de acuerdo contigo en eso. **3** **there + be,** → **be.**
● **not to be all there,** faltarle a uno un tornillo. ‖ **there and then,** en el momento. ‖ **there you are,** aquí tienes. ‖ **there you go,** ya está. ‖ **there you go again,** ya empiezas otra vez. ‖ **there, there,** vamos, venga, ya está.

thereabouts [ðeərəˈbaʊts] *adv* (*near there*) por ahí, allí cerca; (*mora or less*) más o menos.

thereafter [ðeəˈrɑːftəʳ] *adv* a partir de entonces.

thereby [ˈðeəbaɪ] *adv* por eso, por ello.

therefore [ˈðeəfɔːʳ] *adv* por tanto, por lo tanto, por consiguiente.

therein [ðeərˈɪn] *adv* allí.

theremodynamis [θɜːməʊdaɪˈnæmɪk] **1** *adj* termodinámico,-a. – **2 thermodynamics,** *n* termodinámica.

thereupon [ðeərəˈpɒn] *adv* acto seguido.

therm [θɜːm] *n* termia.

thermal [ˈθɜːməl] **1** *adj* (*stream, bath, spring*) termal; (*underwear*) térmico,-a. **2** PHYS térmico,-a. – **3** *n* corriente *f* térmica. – **4 thermals,** *npl* ropa *sing* interior térmica.

thermometer [θeˈmɒmɪtəʳ] *n* termómetro.

thermos [ˈθɜːmɒs] *n* termo.
▲ *Es marca registrada.*

thermostat [ˈθɜːməstæt] *n* termostato.

thesaurus [θɪˈsɔːrəs] *n* diccionario ideológico.

these [ðiːz] **1** *adj* estos,-as: *these apples are cheaper than those,* estas manzanas son más baratas que aquellas. – **2** *pron* éstos,-as: *which ones do you prefer? –these,* ¿cuáles prefieres? –éstos.

thesis [ˈθiːsɪs] *n* tesis *f inv.*
▲ *plural* **theses** [ˈθiːsiːz].

thespian [ˈθespɪən] 1 *adj* dramático,-a. – 2 *n* actor *m*, actriz *f.*

they [ðeɪ] 1 *pron* (*plural*) ellos,-as: *where are the children?* –*they're in the garden*, ¿dónde están los niños? –están en el jardín; *they like playing*, les gusta jugar; *they're showing "Batman" on the telly*, hacen "Batman" en la tele. 2 *fam* (*singular - substitutes he or she*) él, ella: *if anyone saw the accident, they should go to the police*, si alguien vio el accidente, que vaya a la policía; *I was supposed to meet a friend, but they never turned up*, había quedado con un amigo pero no se presentó.
● **they say that ...**, dicen que ..., se dice que ...

thiamine [ˈθaɪəmiːn] *n* tiamina.

thick [θɪk] 1 *adj* (*solid things*) grueso,-a: *it's a thick book*, es un libro grueso; *it's two inches thick*, tiene dos pulgadas de grosor. 2 (*liquid, gas, vegetation etc*) espeso,-a. 3 (*beard, eyebrows*) poblado,-a. 4 (*cloud, smoke, fog, forest*) denso,-a, espeso,-a. 5 (*fur, hedge*) tupido,-a. 6 *fam* (*stupid*) corto,-a, corto,-a de alcances, de pocas luces; (*unable to think*) espeso,-a. 7 (*accent*) marcado,-a, cerrado,-a; (*of speech, voice*) poco claro,-a. – 8 *adv* espesamente, gruesamente: *cut the bread nice and thick*, corta el pan en rebanadas bien gruesas; *don't spread the jam too thick*, no pongas demasiada mermelada; *the snow lay thick on the ground*, había una capa espesa de nieve en la tierra.
● **thick and fast**, en cantidad: *the snow fell thick and fast*, nevaba copiosamente; *the questions came thick and fast*, llovieron las preguntas. ‖ **through thick and thin**, a las duras y a las maduras, pase lo que pase, contra viento y marea. ‖ **to be as thick as thieves**, estar a partir un piñón, ser como uña y carne. ‖ **to be as thick as two short planks**, ser tan corto como las mangas de un chaleco. ‖ **to be in the thick of sth.**, estar metido,-a de lleno en algo: *she loves being in the thick of things*, a ella le encanta estar en el ajo. ‖ **to be thick with sb.**, ser íntimo,-a amigo,-a de algn. ‖ **to be thick with sth.**, estar lleno,-a de algo. ‖ **to get a thick ear**, recibir una torta. ‖ **to give sb. a thick ear**, dar una torta a algn. ‖ **to have a thick head**, tener resaca, tener la cabeza embotada. ‖ **to have a thick skin**, ser insensible a las críticas. ‖ **to lay it on thick**, (*exaggerate*) exagerar; (*flatter*) dar coba.

thicken [ˈθɪkən] 1 *t* espesar. – 2 *i* espesarse, hacerse más denso,-a.

thicket [ˈθɪkɪt] *n* espesura, matorral *m.*

thickly [ˈθɪklɪ] 1 *adv* → **also thick**. 2 (*populated*) densamente. 3 (*speak*) con voz poco clara.

thickness [ˈθɪknəs] 1 *n* (*in size*) espesor *m*, grosor *m*. 2 (*density - of liquid*) espesura; (*- of fog*) densidad *f*. 3 (*layer*) capa.

thickset [ˈθɪkset] *adj* de complexión grande, fornido,-a.

thick-skinned [ˈθɪkˈskɪnd] *adj* insensible.

thief [θiːf] *n* (*gen*) ladrón,-ona; (*mugger*) atracador,-ra.

thieve [θiːv] 1 *t* robar. – 2 *i* robar.

thieving [ˈθiːvɪŋ] 1 *adj* ladrón,-ona: *keep your thieving hands off!*, ¡quita esas manos de ahí, ladrón! – 2 *n* hurtos *mpl.*

thigh [θaɪ] *n* muslo.

thighbone [ˈθaɪbəʊn] *n* fémur *m.*

thimble [ˈθɪmbəl] *n* dedal *m.*

thimbleful [ˈθɪmbəlfʊl] *n* dedo, dedito.

thin [θɪn] 1 *n* (*person*) delgado,-a, flaco,-a. – 2 *adj* (*thing*) delgado,-a, fino,-a: *thin material*, tela fina; *a thin slice*, una loncha fina. 3 (*liquid - soup, sauce*) poco espeso,-a, claro,-a; (*- rain*) fino,-a. – 4 *n* (*hair*) escaso,-a, fino,-a y

poco abundante; (*vegetation*) poco tupido,-a: *you're getting a bit thin on top*, te estás quedando calvo. – 5 *adj* (*audience, crowd*) poco numeroso,-a; (*response, attendance*) escaso,-a. 6 (*voice*) débil. 7 (*excuse, argument*) pobre, poco convincente. – 8 *adv* finamente: *cut the bread thin*, corta el pan en rebanadas finas. – 9 *t* (*paint*) diluir; (*sauce*) hacer menos espeso,-a. – 10 *i* (*fog, mist*) disiparse. 11 (*audience, crowd, traffic*) hacerse menos denso,-a, disminuir.
◆ **to thin down** 1 *i* adelgazar. – 2 *t sep* (*sauce*) hacer menos espeso,-a, aclarar; (*paint*) diluir. ‖ **to thin out** 1 *t insep* (*crowd, traffic*) mermar, disminuir. – 2 *t sep* (*crops, plants*) entresacar.
● **as thin as a rake**, más flaco,-a que un palo. ‖ **to be thin on the ground**, haber muy poco,-a. ‖ **to have a thin time of it**, pasarlas canutas. ‖ **to wear thin**, (*joke etc*) perder interés; (*patience*) acabarse; (*clothes*) gastarse.
▲ *comp* **thinner**, *superl* **thinnest**.

thing [θɪŋ] 1 *n* (*object*) cosa, objeto: *what's that thing for?*, ¿para qué sirve eso?; *what's that thing doing on the table?*, ¿qué hace eso en la mesa?; *pass me that thing over there*, pásame aquel chisme. 2 (*non-material*) cosa: *a strange thing happened to me today*, me ha pasado una cosa rara hoy; *don't take things so seriously*, no te tomes las cosas tan en serio. 3 (*affair*) asunto: *let's forget the whole thing*, olvidémoslo todo. 4 (*person, creature*) *you poor little thing!*, ¡pobrecito!; *you lucky thing!*, ¡qué suerte! 5 (*action*): *the best thing to do*, lo mejor que puedes hacer; *that was a silly thing to do*, vaya tontería has hecho. 6 *fam* (*preference*): *it's not really my thing*, la verdad es que no es lo mío. 7 (*with negative*) nada: *I can't understand a thing you're saying*, no entiendo nada de lo que dices. 8 **the thing**, (*what*) lo que: *the thing I like most in life*, lo que más me gusta en la vida; *the same thing*, lo mismo; *the terrible thing is that ...*, lo malo es que ...; *the latest thing*, lo último; *the main thing*, lo principal; *the important thing*, lo importante. – 9 **things**, *npl* (*belongings*) cosas *fpl*, ropa *f sing*, equipaje *m sing*: *have you got all your things?*, ¿tienes todas tus cosas?; *I'm going to pack my things*, voy a hacer la maleta.
● **as things stand**, tal y como están las cosas. ‖ **by the look of things**, según parece. ‖ **for one thing**, en primer lugar, para empezar, entre otras cosas. ‖ **how's things?**, ¿qué tal? ‖ **it's a good thing that ...**, menos mal que ... ‖ **it's just one of those things**, son cosas que pasan, así es la vida. ‖ **it's not the done thing**, esto no se hace. ‖ **it's the done thing**, es lo que se hace, es lo correcto. ‖ **it was a close/near thing**, por muy poco, por un pelo. ‖ **just the thing**, justo lo que hace falta. ‖ **last thing**, (*at night*) a última hora. ‖ **next thing**, luego. ‖ **the next thing I knew**, cuando me di cuenta. ‖ **there's no such thing**, no hay tal cosa. ‖ **the thing is ...**, lo que pasa es que ..., resulta que ... ‖ **things ain't what they used to be**, las cosas ya no son lo que eran. ‖ **to be a thing of the past**, ser historia, haber pasado a la historia. ‖ **to be on to a good thing**, tener un chollo. ‖ **to be seeing things**, estar alucinando. ‖ **to do one's own thing**, hacer lo que a uno le da la gana. ‖ **to do the right thing**, hacer bien, hacer lo correcto. ‖ **to have a thing about sb.**, estar obsesionado,-a con algn., haberle dado fuerte a uno con algn. ‖ **to have a thing about sth.**, (*dislike*) tenerle manía a algo. ‖ **to make a big thing out of sth.**, armar un escándalo por algo. ‖ **to say the wrong thing**, meter la pata. ‖ **what with one thing and another**, entre una cosa y otra.

thingamabob [ˈθɪŋəmbɒb] *n fam* chisme *m.*

thingamajig [ˈθɪŋəmədʒɪg] n fam chisme m.

think [θɪŋk] **1** i (use mind) pensar: he thought hard before answering, se lo pensó mucho antes de contestar; nowadays, young people think differently, hoy en día, los jóvenes piensan de otra manera; I wasn't thinking, no pensaba; it makes you think, da que pensar, te hace pensar. **2** (have in mind, consider) pensar: what are you thinking about?, ¿en qué piensas?; I was thinking about the time we went to Brighton, estaba pensando en cuando fuimos a Brighton; you only think about yourself, sólo piensas en ti mismo; I'll think about it, lo pensaré; you always think of everything, siempre piensas en todo; how kind of you to think of me, qué amable de su parte pensar en mí; come to think of it, ..., ahora que lo pienso, ...; what were you thinking of?, ¿en qué estabas pensando? **3** (intend, plan) pensar: we're thinking of going away for the weekend, pensamos salir fuera este fin de semana. **4** (come to mind) ocurrírsele a uno: I hadn't thought of that, no se me había ocurrido. **5** (remember) acordarse (of, de), recordar: I can't think of the title, no me acuerdo del título. **6** (have an opinion) pensar (of, de), opinar (of, de): what do you think of the government?, ¿qué opinas del gobierno?; what did you think of the film?, ¿qué te pareció la película?; I didn't think much of his speech, no me gustó su discurso; well, what do you think?, ¿bueno, qué te parece? **7** (imagine) imaginarse, pensar: just think of it!, ¡fíjate!, ¡imagínate! – **8** t (reflect, ponder) pensar: just think how lucky you are!, ¡piensa en la suerte que tienes! **9** (imagine, suppose) pensar, imaginarse, creer: I thought as much, ya me lo imaginaba; who would have thought it?, ¿quién se lo hubiera imaginado?; anyone would think that ..., cualquiera diría que ...; that's what you think!, ¡eso es lo que tú crees! **10** (expect) pensar, esperar: I never thought I'd see you here, no esperaba verte aquí; it's more difficult than we thought, es más difícil de lo que pensábamos. **11** (believe) creer: I think it's going to rain, creo que lloverá; do you think they'll come?, ¿crees que vendrán?; I think so, creo que sí; I don't think so, creo que no; I thought it started at 8.00, creía que empezaba a las ocho; who do you think you are?, ¿quién te crees que eres? **12** (remember) recordar, acordarse de: I'm trying to recall where I put it, estoy intentando recordar dónde lo puse; I can't think what her name is, no me acuerdo de su nombre. **13** (have an opinion) pensar, opinar: I really don't know what to think, la verdad es que no sé qué pensar.

◆ to think ahead i prevenir. ‖ to think back i hacer memoria. ‖ to think back to i recordar, acordarse de. ‖ to think out t sep (consider carefully) estudiar, pensar bien: have you thought this whole thing out?, ¿lo has pensado bien? ‖ to think over t sep (reflect upon) reflexionar, pensar: I need to think it over, me lo tengo que pensar. ‖ to think through t sep (consider fully) estudiar, considerar: have you thought your decision through?, ¿has reflexionado sobre tu decisión? ‖ to think up t sep (invent - excuse) inventar; (- slogan) idear, crear: he's thought up a way to escape, ha pensado una manera de escapar.

● think nothing of it!, ¡no tiene importancia! ‖ to have a think about sth., pensar algo: I'm going to have a think about this, voy a pensármelo. ‖ to think a lot of sb., estimar mucho a algn., apreciar a algn. ‖ to think aloud / think out loud, pensar en voz alta. ‖ to think better of doing sth., repensarse algo, pensarse algo mejor. ‖ to think big, tener grandes proyectos, ser ambicioso,-a. ‖ to think highly of sb., tener un buen con-

cepto de algn., tener muy buena opinión de algn. ‖ to think nothing of doing sth., hacer algo tan tranquilo,-a. ‖ to think on one's feet, improvisar. ‖ to think the best of sb., pensar bien de algn. ‖ to think the worst of sb., pensar mal de algn. ‖ to think twice about doing sth., pensar algo dos veces antes de hacerlo. ‖ without thinking, sin pensar. ‖ you've got another think coming, estás muy equivocado,-a, lo tienes claro.

▲ pt & pp thought.

thinkable [ˈθɪŋkəbəl] adj pensable, imaginable.

thinker [ˈθɪŋkə] n pensador,-ra.

thinking [ˈθɪŋkɪŋ] **1** n (opinion) opinión f, parecer m. **2** (thought) pensamiento, ideas fpl: good thinking!, ¡buena idea! – **3** adj pensante, inteligente.

● to do some thinking, reflexionar, pensar. ‖ to my way of thinking, a mi parecer, en mi opinión.

thinly [ˈθɪnlɪ] **1** adv → also thin. **2** (sparcely) escasamente, en poca cantidad: a thinly populated area, una región escasamente poblada; sprinkle the seeds thinly, esparza bien las semillas. **3** (scarcely) apenas: a thinly disguised threat, una amenaza apenas velada.

thinner [ˈθɪnə] n (for diluting) disolvente m.

thinness [ˈθɪnnəs] n delgadez f.

third [θɜːd] **1** adj tercero,-a. – **2** adv (in series) tercero, en tercer lugar. – **3** n tercero,-a: Richard III (the Third), Richard III (tercero); the third of November, el tres de noviembre. **4** (fraction) tercio; (one part) tercera parte f. **5** GB EDUC ≈ bien m (título universitario que corresponde a la cuarta nota más alta).

● third time lucky, a la tercera va la vencida. ■ the third degree, un interrogatorio. ‖ third degree burn, quemadura de tercer grado. ‖ third gear, AUTO tercera. ‖ third party, tercero,-a. ‖ third person, LING tercera persona. ‖ the Third World, el tercer mundo. ‖ third world, tercermundista.

▲ Véase también sixth.

third-class [ˈθɜːdklɑːs] **1** adj de tercera clase. – **2** adv (travel) en tercera.

thirdly [ˈθɜːdlɪ] adv en tercer lugar.

third-rate [ˈθɜːdreɪt] adj de tercera (categoría).

thirst [θɜːst] **1** n sed f. **2** fig ansias fpl, afán m, sed f.

◆ to thirst for t insep tener sed de, tener afán de.

thirstily [ˈθɜːstɪlɪ] adv con avidez.

thirsty [ˈθɜːstɪ] **1** adj sediento,-a: I'm thirsty, tengo sed. **2** (work etc) que da sed. **3** fig (eager) ansioso,-a (for, por).

▲ comp thirstier, superl thirstiest.

thirteen [θɜːˈtiːn] **1** n trece m. – **2** adj trece.

▲ Véase también sixteen.

thirteenth [θɜːˈtiːnθ] **1** adj decimotercero,-a. – **2** adv decimotercero lugar. – **3** n (fraction) decimotercero; (one part) decimotercera parte f.

▲ Véase también sixteenth.

thirties [ˈθɜːtɪz] the thirties, npl los años mpl treinta.

● to be in one's thirties, tener entre treinta y cuarenta años, tener treinta y tantos años.

▲ Véase también sixties.

thirtieth [ˈθɜːtɪəθ] **1** adj trigésimo,-a. – **2** adv en trigésimo lugar. – **3** n (fraction) trigésimo; (one part) trigésima parte f.

▲ Véase también sixtieth.

thirty [ˈθɜːtɪ] **1** n treinta m. – **2** adj treinta.

▲ Véase también sixty.

this [ðɪs] **1** adj este, esta: whose is this book?, ¿de quién es este libro?; do you like this shirt?, ¿te gusta esta camisa? – **2** pron éste, ésta; (indefinite) esto: I prefer this

one, prefiero éste; *I was afraid this was going to happen,* me temía que iba a pasar esto. **3** (*on 'phone*): *this is Laura,* soy Laura. − **4** *adv* tan, tanto,-a: *I didn't think it was this far,* no creía que fuera tan lejos; *I've never had this much money before,* nunca había tenido tanto dinero; *she's about this tall,* es así de alta.
● **like this,** así. ‖ **this and that,** nada en particular. ‖ **this is,** (*introducing*) te presento a: *this is my wife,* te presento a mi mujer.

thistle ['θɪsəl] *n* cardo.

thong [θɒŋ] **1** *n* (*strip of leather*) correa. **2** US (*flip-flop*) chancla *f*.

thorax ['θɔːræks] *n* tórax *m inv*.

thorn [θɔːn] *n* espina, pincho.
● **to be a thorn in one's side,** ser una espina que uno tiene clavada.

thorny ['θɔːnɪ] *adj* espinoso,-a.
▲ *comp* **thornier,** *superl* **thorniest**.

thorough ['θʌrə] **1** *adj* (*deep*) profundo,-a, a fondo. **2** (*careful*) cuidadoso,-a, minucioso,-a. **3** (*person*) concienzudo,-a. **4** (*utter, complete*) total, verdadero,-a.

thoroughbred ['θʌrəbred] **1** *n* (*horse*) pura sangre *mf*; (*other animal*) animal *m* de raza. − **2** *adj* (*horse*) de pura sangre; (*other animal*) de raza.

thoroughfare ['θʌrəfeəʳ] *n* vía pública.
● **"no thoroughfare"**, "prohibido el paso".

thoroughgoing ['θʌrəgəʊɪŋ] *adj* profundo,-a, minucioso,-a.

thoroughly ['θʌrəlɪ] **1** *adv* (*carefully*) a fondo, meticulosamente. **2** (*completely*) totalmente, absolutamente.

those [ðəʊz] **1** *adj* esos,-as; (*remote*) aquellos,-as: *could you pass me those plates?,* ¿me podrías pasar esos platos?; *look at those flowers,* mira aquellas flores. − **2** *pron* ésos,-as; (*remote*) aquéllos,-as: *if these are my books, whose are those?,* si estos libros son míos, ¿de quién son aquellos?

thou [ðaʊ] *pron arch* tú.

though [ðəʊ] **1** *conj* aunque, si bien, a pesar de que: *though he doesn't earn very much, he loves his job,* aunque no gana mucho, le encanta su trabajo; *I'll go, though I don't feel like it,* iré, aunque no me apetece; *strange though it may seem,* aunque parezca extraño; *though she tried hard, she failed the exam,* a pesar de esforzarse mucho, suspendió el examen. − **2** *adv* sin embargo, a pesar de todo: *it's expensive - it's worth it though,* es caro - sin embargo, vale lo que cuesta.
● **even though,** aun cuando, a pesar de que.

thought [θɔːt] **1** *pt & pp* → **think**. − **2** *n* pensamiento: *she was deep in thought,* estaba absorta en sus pensamientos; *my thoughts turned to holidays,* empecé a pensar en las vacaciones; *his thoughts were elsewhere,* estaba pensando en otra cosa; *keep your thoughts to yourself,* guárdate tus pensamientos; *she read my thoughts,* me adivinó el pensamiento; *the very thought of it makes me feel sick,* me da náuseas sólo pensarlo. **3** (*consideration*) consideración *f*: *I'll give it some serious thought,* lo pensaré seriamente; *he put a lot of thought into his essay,* pensó mucho la redacción; *spare a thought for the homeless,* piensa en los que no tienen casa. **4** (*idea, opinion*) idea, opinión *f*: *let me know your thoughts on the matter,* hazme saber tu opinión sobre el asunto; *I can't bear the thought of retiring,* no soporto la idea de jubilarme; *you can give up any thought of going abroad,* puedes olvidarte de ir al extranjero; *the thought never crossed my mind,* ni se me ocurrió. **5** (*intention*) intención *f*: *it's the thought that counts,* la intención es lo que cuenta.

● **to have second thoughts,** cambiar de opinión.

thoughtful ['θɔːtfʊl] **1** *adj* (*considerate*) atento,-a, considerado,-a. **2** (*pensive*) pensativo,-a, meditabundo,-a. **3** (*considered*) serio,-a.

thoughtfully ['θɔːtfəlɪ] **1** *adv* (*considerately*) atentamente, amablemente: *they thoughtfully provided some sandwiches,* tuvieron el detalle de darnos unos bocadillos. **2** (*pensively*) pensativamente.

thoughtfulness ['θɔːtfʊlnəs] **1** *n* (*kindness*) amabilidad *f*, consideración *f*, atención *f*. **2** (*pensiveness*) aire *m* pensativo, seriedad *f*.

thoughtless ['θɔːtləs] **1** *adj* (*unthinking*) irreflexivo,-a, descuidado,-a. **2** (*inconsiderate*) desconsiderado,-a, poco considerado,-a.

thoughtlessly ['θɔːtləslɪ] **1** *adv* (*without thinking*) sin pensar, descuidadamente. **2** (*without consideration*) desconsideradamente, con poca consideración.

thoughtlessness ['θɔːtləsnəs] **1** *n* (*carelessness*) irreflexión *f*, descuido. **2** (*lack of consideration*) falta de consideración.

thousand ['θaʊzənd] **1** *n* mil *m*: *there were thousands of people,* había miles de personas. − **2** *adj* mil: *it costs a thousand pesetas,* cuesta mil pesetas.

thousandth ['θaʊzənθ] **1** *adj* milésimo,-a. − **2** *adv* en milésimo lugar. − **3** *n* (*fraction*) milésimo; (*one part*) milésima parte *f*.

Thrace [θreɪs] *n* Tracia.

Thracian ['θreɪʃən] **1** *adj* tracio,-a. − **2** *n* (*person*) tracio,-a. **3** (*language*) tracio.

thrall [θrɔːl] *n* (*slave*) esclavo,-a.

thrash [θræʃ] **1** *t* (*beat*) azotar. **2** (*defeat*) derrotar, dar una paliza a. **3** (*arm, leg, etc*) sacudir.
◆ **to thrash about / thrash around** *i* retorcerse. ‖ **to thrash out** *t sep* (*problem*) discutir; (*agreement*) llegar a un acuerdo sobre.

thrashing ['θræʃɪŋ] *n* zurra, paliza.

thread [θred] **1** *n* SEW hilo, hebra. **2** (*of screw, bolt*) rosca. **3** (*of story*) hilo. − **4** *t* (*needle*) enhebrar. **5** (*beads*) ensartar.
● **to hang by a thread,** pender de un hilo.

threadbare ['θredbeəʳ] *adj* gastado,-a, raído,-a.

threat [θret] *n* amenaza: *a threat to wildlife,* una amenaza para la fauna; *he made threats against me,* me amenazó; *the hospital is under threat of closure,* amenazan con cerrar el hospital.
■ **death threat,** amenaza de muerte. ‖ **empty threat,** amenaza vana. ‖ **nuclear threat,** amenaza nuclear.

threaten ['θretən] **1** *t* amenazar (**with/to**, con): *he threatened me with a knife,* me amenazó con una navaja; *they threatened to kill us,* amenazaron con matarnos; *eagles are threatened with extinction,* las águilas están amenazadas de extinción. − **2** *i* amenazar: *it's threatening to rain,* amenaza llover.

threatening ['θretənɪŋ] *adj* amenazador,-ra, intimidatorio,-a.

threateningly ['θretənɪŋlɪ] *adv* de modo amenazador.

three [θriː] **1** *n* tres *m*. − **2** *adj* tres.
■ **three quarters,** tres cuartos.
▲ *Véase también* **six**.

three-dimensional [θriːdɪ'menʃənəl] *adj* tridimensional.

threefold ['θriːfəʊld] **1** *adj* triple. − **2** *adv* tres veces.

three-legged [θriː'legɪd] *adj* de tres patas.

three-piece ['θriːpiːs] *adj* de tres piezas.
■ **three-piece suit,** terno. ‖ **three-piece suite,** tresillo.

threesome ['θriːsəm] *n* grupo de tres.

thresh [θreʃ] *t* trillar.
thresher ['θreʃəʳ] *n* (*machine*) trilladora; (*person*) trillador,-ra.
threshing ['θreʃɪŋ] *adj* trilla.
■ **threshing floor,** era.
threshold ['θreʃəʊld] **1** *n* umbral *m*. **2** *fig* umbral *m*, límite *m*: *he has a high/low pain threshold,* tolera mucho/poco el dolor.
● **to be on the threshold of ...,** estar en el umbral de ..., estar a las puertas de ...
threw [θruː] *pt* → **throw**.
thrift [θrɪft] *n* economía, frugalidad *f*.
■ **thrift shop,** US *tienda que vende cosas de segunda mano.*
thrifty ['θrɪftɪ] *adj* económico,-a, frugal.
▲ *comp* thriftier, *superl* thriftiest.
thrill [θrɪl] **1** *n* (*excitement*) emoción *f*, ilusión *f*: *it was the thrill of a lifetime,* fue la emoción más grande de mi vida, fue lo más emocionante de mi vida. – **2** *t* (*excite*) entusiasmar, hacer ilusión a, ilusionar: *I was thrilled to hear about your baby,* me hizo mucha ilusión saber lo de tu bebé; *I'm thrilled about the holiday,* me hacen mucha ilusión las vacaciones. – **3** *i* (*de excited*) entusiasmarse.
● **to be thrilled to bits,** emocionarse mucho.
thriller ['θrɪləʳ] *n* (*novel*) novela de suspense; (*film*) película de suspense; (*play*) obra de suspense.
thrilling ['θrɪlɪŋ] *adj* emocionante, apasionante.
thrive [θraɪv] *i* (*plant*) crecer mucho, crecer bien; (*person*) estar estupendamente; (*business*) prosperar: *he seems to thrive on problems,* parece que los problemas le sientan de maravilla.
▲ *pt* throve *o* thrived; *pp* thrived *o* thriven ['θrɪvən].
thriving ['θraɪvɪŋ] *adj* próspero,-a, floreciente.
throat [θrəʊt] *n* garganta: *I've got something stuck in my throat,* tengo algo clavado en la garganta; *he cleared his throat before speaking,* aclaró la voz antes de hablar.
● **to be at each other's throats,** estar peleándose. ‖ **to cut one's own throat,** *fig* actuar en perjuicio propio. ‖ **to jump down sb.'s throat,** arremeter contra algn. ‖ **to ram sth. down sb.'s throat,** *fig* imponer algo a algn.
■ **sore throat,** dolor *m* de garganta.
throaty ['θrəʊtɪ] *adj* ronco,-a, gutural.
▲ *comp* throatier, *superl* throatiest.
throb [θrɒb] **1** *n* (*of heart, pulse*) latido, palpitación *f*; (*of engine, music*) vibración *f*, zumbido. – **2** *i* (*heart, pulse*) latir, palpitar; (*engine, music*) vibrar, zumbar. **3** (*with pain*) dar punzadas: *my head's throbbing,* la cabeza me va a estrellar.
▲ *pt & pp* throbbed, *ger* throbbing.
throes [θrəʊz] **in the throes of,** *phr* en medio de: *they're in the throes of a divorce,* se están divorciando.
thrombosis [θrɒm'bəʊsɪs] *n* trombosis *f inv*.
throne [θrəʊn] *n* trono.
● **to come to the throne,** subir al trono.
■ **throne room,** sala del trono.
throng [θrɒŋ] **1** *n* muchedumbre *f*, multitud *f*. – **2** *i* (*come together*) apiñarse, agolparse; (*enter*) entrar en tropel, entrar en masa. – **3** *t* (*fill*) abarrotar, atestar.
throttle ['θrɒtəl] **1** *n* válvula reguladora. **2** *fam* acelerador *m*. – **3** *t* estrangular, ahogar.
◆ **to throttle back / throttle down 1** *t sep* desacelerar. – **2** *i* disminuir la velocidad.
● **at full throttle,** a toda pastilla.
through [θruː] **1** *prep* por, a través de: *I climbed in through a window,* entré por una ventana; *we drove*

right through France, condujimos por toda Francia; *you have to go through Customs,* hay que pasar por la aduana. **2** (*because of*) por, a causa de: *off work through illness,* de baja por enfermedad. **3** (*from beginning to the end*) durante todo,-a, hasta el final de: *we danced through the night,* bailamos durante toda la noche; *my mother looked after me through my illness,* mi madre me cuidó durante toda la enfermedad; *he read through the book,* leyó todo el libro; *I'd never have got through this crisis without you,* nunca hubiera superado esta crisis sin ti. **4** (*by means of*) por, a través de, mediante: *he got the job through a friend,* consiguió el trabajo a través de un amigo. – **5** *adv* de un lado a otro: *he let me through,* me dejó pasar; *we drove through a red light,* pasamos un semáforo en rojo. **6** (*to the end*) hasta el final: *he read the book through,* leyó todo el libro; *we slept right through,* dormimos de un tirón. **7** GB (*on phone*) conectado,-a: *can you put me through to Helen James?,* ¿me puede poner con Helen James?; *I rang several times, but I couldn't get through,* llamé varias veces, pero estaba comunicando. **8** US terminado,-a, acabado,-a: *are you through?,* ¿has acabado?; *we'll be through at lunchtime,* terminaremos a la hora de comer. – **9** *adj* (*train*) directo,-a; (*traffic*) de paso.
● **to be through with sth./sb.,** haber acabado con algo/algn. ‖ **through and through,** hasta la médula, a ultranza.
■ **no through road,** calle *f* sin salida, cul-de-sac *m*.
throughout [θruː'aʊt] **1** *prep* por todo,-a, en todo,-a: *throughout the world,* en todo el mundo. **2** (*time*) durante todo,-a, a lo largo de: *throughout the year,* durante todo el año. – **3** *adv* (*all over*) por/en todas partes: *the house has central heating throughout,* la casa tiene calefacción central en todas las habitaciones. **4** (*completely*) completamente. **5** (*time*) desde el principio hasta el fin, todo el tiempo.
throve [θrəʊv] *pt* → **thrive**.
throw [θrəʊ] **1** *n* lanzamiento, tiro. **2** (*of dice*) tirada, lance *m*; (*in game*) jugada, turno. – **3** *t* (*gen*) tirar, arrojar, lanzar: *throw me the ball,* tírame la pelota. **4** (*to the floor - rider*) desmontar; (*- wrestler*) derribar. **5** (*head*) echar; (*arms*) extender, abrir: *she threw her head back,* echó la cabeza hacia atrás; *he threw his arms out,* extendió los brazos. **6** *fig* (*kiss*) echar, tirar; (*glance, look*) lanzar, dirigir. **7** *fam* (*party*) organizar, dar, hacer: *they threw a party for her,* le hicieron una fiesta. **8** *fam* (*confuse*) desconcertar: *the first question really threw me,* la primera pregunta me desconcertó del todo. **9** (*light, shadow*) proyectar: *can you throw any light on this?,* ¿puedes tú aclarar esto? **10** (*shape pottery*) formar, hacer. **11** (*extend bridge*) tender, construir.
◆ **to throw about** *t sep* (*money*) derrochar. ‖ **to throw away 1** *t sep* (*get rid of, discard*) tirar. **2** (*waste*) desaprovechar, perder; (*money*) malgastar, derrochar. **3** (*speech*) lanzar al aire. ‖ **to throw back 1** *t sep* (*ball etc*) devolver. **2** (*bedclothes*) echar atrás. ‖ **to throw back on** *t insep* obligar a recurrir a. ‖ **to throw in 1** *t sep fam* (*include*) incluir gratis. **2** SP sacar de banda. ‖ **to throw off 1** *t sep* (*get rid of*) deshacerse de, librarse de. **2** (*confuse, escape, elude*) despistar. **3** (*clothes*) quitarse. ‖ **to throw on** *t sep* (*clothes*) ponerse. ‖ **to throw out 1** *t sep* (*expel*) echar, expulsar: *they threw him out of the club,* lo echaron del club. **2** (*reject*) rechazar: *the proposal was thrown out,* la propuesta fue rechada. **3** (*discard*) tirar, tirar a la basura: *throw that old chair out,* tira esa silla vieja a la basura. ‖ **to throw together 1** *t sep* (*assemble*) juntar de prisa; (*improvise*) improvisar. **2** (*bring into contact*) juntar.

‖ **to throw up** 1 *i* (*vomit*) vomitar, devolver. – **2** *t sep* (*give up, resign*) abandonar, renunciar a. **3** (*produce*) arrojar, dar, aportar; (*reveal*) revelar, poner en evidencia. **4** (*vomit*) vomitar, devolver.
● **to be a stone's throw away,** estar a tiro de piedra.
‖ **to throw down the gauntlet,** lanzar un desafío, arrojar el guante. ‖ **to throw in one's hand,** abandonar la partida. ‖ **to throw in one's lot with,** compartir la suerte con. ‖ **to throw in the sponge,** arrojar la toalla. ‖ **to throw into confusion,** sumir en la confusión. ‖ **to throw one's weight about,** mandonear. ‖ **to throw os. at sb.,** tirarse sobre algn. ‖ **to throw os. into sth.,** lanzarse a algo. ‖ **to throw sth. back at sb./in sb.'s face,** echarle algo en cara a algn.
▲ *pt* **threw** [θruː]; *pp* **thrown** [θrəʊn].
throw-away [ˈθrəʊəweɪ] *adj* (*disposable*) de usar y tirar, desechable; (*spoken casually*) hecho,-a como de pasada.
throw-in [ˈθrəʊɪn] *n* SP saque *m* de banda.
thru [θruː] *prep-adv* US → **through**: *Monday thru Friday,* de lunes a viernes.
thrush [θrʌʃ] *n* ORN tordo.
thrust [θrʌst] **1** *n* (*gen*) empuje *m*, empujón *m*. **2** (*attack*) ataque *m*, avance *m*. **3** (*hostile remark*) ataque *m*, crítica. **4** (*with sword*) estocada; (*with dagger*) puñalada; (*with knife*) cuchillada. **5** (*main point*) idea central, idea clave. – **6** *t* (*shove*) empujar, empujar con violencia. – **7** *i* (*jostle*) dar empujones. – **8** *t* (*push in*) meter. – **9** *i* (*pierce - with sword*) dar estocadas; (*- with other instrument*) clavar.
◆ **to thrust on** *t sep* imponer.
▲ (*verbo*) *pt & pp* **thrust**.
thud [θʌd] **1** *n* ruido sordo. – **2** *i* caer con un ruido sordo.
▲ (*verbo*) *pt & pp* **thudded,** *ger* **thudding**.
thug [θʌg] *n* (*violent man*) matón *m*, gamberro. **2** (*criminal*) gángster *m*, malhechor *m*.
thumb [θʌm] **1** *n* pulgar *m*. – **2** *t* hacer autostop.
◆ **to thumb through** *t insep* hojear.
● **to be all thumbs,** ser un manazas, ser torpe. ‖ **to be under sb.'s thumb,** estar dominado,-a por algn. ‖ **to get the thumbs up,** ser aprobado,-a, recibir la aprobación. ‖ **to get the thumbs down,** ser rechazado,-a. ‖ **to give sth. the thumbs up,** aprobar algo. ‖ **to give sth. the thumbs down,** rechazar algo. ‖ **to have sb. under one's thumb,** tener a algn. en el bolsillo. ‖ **to stick out like a sore thumb,** saltar a la vista. ‖ **to thumb a ride / thumb a lift,** hacer autostop.
thumb-index [ˈθʌmɪndeks] *n* uñero.
thumbnail [ˈθʌmneɪl] *n* uña del pulgar.
■ **thumbnail sketch,** pequeña reseña.
thumbtack [ˈθʌmtæk] *n* US chincheta.
thump [θʌmp] **1** *n* (*blow*) golpe *m*, puñetazo; (*sound*) golpazo. – **2** *t* golpear, pegar un puñetazo. – **3** *i* (*gen*) golpear; (*heart*) latir con fuerza; (*feet*) caminar con pasos pesados.
thumping [ˈθʌmpɪŋ] *adv* enorme, tremendo.
thunder [ˈθʌndəʳ] **1** *n* trueno. – **2** *i* tronar. – **3** *t* (*shout*) bramar, rugir.
● **with a face as black as thunder,** con cara de pocos amigos.
■ **thunder and lightning,** rayos *mpl* y truenos *mpl*.
thunderbolt [ˈθʌndəbəʊlt] *n* rayo.
thunderclap [ˈθʌndəklæp] *n* trueno.
thundercloud [ˈθʌndəklaʊd] *n* nubarrón *m*.
thunderous [ˈθʌndərəs] *adj fig* ensordecedor,-ra, atronador,-ra.
thunderstorm [ˈθʌndəstɔːm] *n* tormenta.

thunderstruck [ˈθʌndərstrʌk] *adj* atónito,-a, pasmado,-a, estupefacto,-a.
thundery [ˈθʌndərɪ] *adj* tormentoso.
Thurs [ˈθɜːzdɪ] *abbr* (*Thursday*) jueves *m*; (*abbreviation*) juev.
▲ *También se escribe* **Thur.**
Thursday [ˈθɜːzdɪ] *n* jueves *m*.
▲ *Véase también* **Saturday.**
thus [ðʌs] **1** *adv* (*in this way, like this*) así, de este modo. **2** (*consequently*) así que, por lo tanto, por consiguiente. **3** (*to this extent*) hasta.
thwart [θwɔːt] *t* desbaratar, frustrar.
thy [ðaɪ] *adj arch* tu.
thyme [taɪm] *n* tomillo.
thyroid [ˈθaɪrɔɪd] *n* tiroides *m*.
■ **tyroid gland,** glándula tiroidea.
tiara [tɪˈɑːrə] **1** *n* (*diadem*) diadema. **2** (*of Pope*) tiara.
Tiber [ˈtaɪbəʳ] *n* el Tíber *m*.
Tiberias [taɪˈbɪərɪəs] **Lake Tiberias,** *n* lago de Tiberiades.
tibia [ˈtɪbɪə] *n* tibia.
tic [tɪk] *n* tic *m*.
tick[1] [tɪk] *n* ZOOL garrapata.
tick[2] [tɪk] **1** *n* (*noise*) tictac *m*. **2** (*mark*) marca, señal *f*. **3** *fam* momento, segundito. – **4** *i* (*clock*) hacer tictac. – *t* señalar, marcar.
◆ **to tick away** *i* transcurrir. ‖ **to tick off** 1 *t sep* marcar, señalar. **2** (*scold*) regañar, reñir. **3** US fastidiar, dar rabia. ‖ **to tick over** 1 *i* AUTO marchar al ralentí, estar en marcha. **2** (*business etc*) ir tirando.
● **what makes sb. tick,** lo que mueve a algn.
tick[3] [tɪk] *n* GB *fam* (*credit*) crédito.
● **to buy sth. on tick,** comprar algo a crédito.
ticker [ˈtɪkəʳ] *n fam* corazón *m*.
ticker-tape [ˈtɪkəteɪp] *n* US cinta de teletipo.
■ **ticker-tape parade,** desfile *m* triunfal.
ticket [ˈtɪkɪt] **1** *n* (*for transport*) billete *m*. **2** (*for concert, cinema, etc*) entrada. **3** (*for library etc*) carnet *m*. **4** (*label*) etiqueta. **5** (*for item deposited*) resguardo. **6** *fam* (*fine*) multa: *I got a speeding ticket,* me pusieron una multa por exceso de velocidad. **7** POL lista de candidatos: *he ran for office on the Republican ticket,* se presentó a las elecciones como candidato republicano.
● **to be just the ticket,** ser justo lo que hace falta.
■ **season ticket,** abono. ‖ **ticket agency,** agencia de localidades. ‖ **ticket collector,** revisor,-ra. ‖ **ticket office,** taquilla, ventanilla. ‖ **ticket-tout,** revendedor,-ra.
ticking[1] [ˈtɪkɪŋ] *n* (*of clock*) tictac *m*.
ticking[2] [ˈtɪkɪŋ] *n* (*material*) cutí *m*.
ticking-off [tɪkɪŋˈɒf] *n fam* bronca, reprimenda.
tickle [ˈtɪkəl] **1** *n* cosquilleo. – **2** *t* (*touch lightly*) hacer cosquillas a; (*itch*) picar. **3** (*amuse*) hacer gracia a, divertir. – **4** *i* (*touch lightly*) hacer cosquillas; (*itch*) picar.
● **to be tickled pink,** estar contentísimo,-a, no caber en sí de gozo.
ticklish [ˈtɪkəlɪʃ] **1** *adj* cosquilloso,-a: *she's really ticklish,* tiene muchas cosquillas. **2** *fig* delicado,-a, peliagudo,-a.
tick-tock [ˈtɪktɒk] *n* tic-tac *m*.
tidal [ˈtaɪdəl] *adj* de la marea.
■ **tidal power,** energía de las mareas. ‖ **tidal wave,** (*gen*) maremoto; *fig* oleada.
tiddler [ˈtɪdləʳ] **1** *n* (*stickleback*) espinoso; (*small fish*) pececillo, pececito. **2** (*child*) niño,-a pequeñito,-a.
tiddly [ˈtɪdlɪ] **1** *adj* GB *fam* (*tipsy*) achispado,-a, piripi. **2** (*small*) pequeñito,-a.

▲ *comp* **tiddlier,** *superl* **tiddliest.**

tide [taɪd] **1** *n* marea: *the tide is in/out,* la marea está alta/ baja; *we got cut off by the tide,* la marea nos aisló. **2** *fig* (*trend*) corriente *f.*

◆ **to tide over** *t sep* ayudar, sacar de un apuro: *can you lend me 20 pounds to tide me over until the end of the month?,* ¿me puedes dejar veinte libras para ayudarme a llegar a fin de mes?

● **to go against the tide,** ir contra (la) corriente. ‖ **to go with the tide,** seguir la corriente.

■ **high tide,** pleamar *f.* ‖ **low tide,** bajamar *f.*

tidemark [ˈtaɪdmɑːk] **1** *n* marca que deja la marea. **2** *fam* (*on bath, neck*) marca de mugre.

tidily [ˈtaɪdɪlɪ] *adv* en orden.

tidiness [ˈtaɪdɪnəs] *n* orden *m.*

tidings [ˈtaɪdɪŋz] *n* noticias *fpl,* nuevas *fpl.*

tidy [ˈtaɪdɪ] **1** *adj* (*place*) ordenado,-a, bien arreglado. **2** (*person - appearance*) arreglado,-a; (*- habits*) metódico,-a. **3** (*considerable*) considerable, bastante. – **4** *n* organizador *m.* – **5** *to* **tidy (up),** *t* ordenar, poner en orden, arreglar. – **6** *i* poner las cosas en orden.

◆ **to tidy away** *t sep* recoger, guardar. ‖ **to tidy out** *t sep* vaciar, limpiar, ordenar.

● **to tidy os. up,** arreglarse.

▲ (adjetivo) *comp* **tidier,** *superl* **tidiest;** (verbo) *pt & pp* **tidied,** *ger* **tidying.**

tie [taɪ] **1** *n* (*of shirt*) corbata. **2** (*for fastening*) cierre *m.* **3** (*rod, beam*) tirante *m.* **4** *fig* (*bond*) lazo, vínculo: *family ties are strong,* los lazos del parentesco son fuertes. **5** *fig* (*restriction*) estorbo, atadura. **6** SP (*draw*) empate *m;* (*match*) encuentro, partido. **7** MUS ligadura. – **8** *t* (*fasten*) atar; (*knot, bow*) hacer. **9** *fig* ligar, vincular, relacionar. **10** (*restrict*) atar. **11** MUS ligar. – **12** *i* (*fasten*) atarse. **13** SP empatar.

◆ **to tie down** *t sep* atar, sujetar. **2** (*restrict*) atar; (*commit oneself*) comprometerse. ‖ **to tie in** *t sep* relacionar, ligar. – **2** *i* concordar, cuadrar. ‖ **to tie up** *t sep* (*fasten*) atar; (*boat*) amarrar. **2** (*link*) conectar, ligar, relacionar. **3** (*occupy*) liar, ocupar: *I'm tied up all afternoon,* estaré ocupado toda la tarde. **4** FIN (*capital*) inmovilizar, invertir. **5** (*finalize*) finalizar, concluir, cerrar.

● **to tie oneself up in knots,** liarse. ‖ **to tie the knot,** casarse.

■ **tie beam,** tirante *m.*

tie-break [ˈtaɪbreɪk] *n* SP tie-break *m.*

tiebreaker [ˈtaɪbreɪkə˙] **1** *n* SP tie-break *m.* **2** (*in quiz*) pregunta del desempate.

tie-dyed [ˈtaɪdaɪd] *adj* teñido,-a.

tie-pin [ˈtaɪpɪn] *n* alfiler *m* de corbata.

tier [tɪə˙] **1** *n* (*in stadium*) grada. **2** (*of cake*) piso. **3** (*in hierarchy*) nivel *m.*

tiered [ˈtɪəd] *adj* (*stadium*) con gradas: *a three-tiered cake,* un pastel de tres pisos; *a two-tiered system,* un sistema de dos niveles.

tie-up [ˈtaɪʌp] **1** *n* (*link, connection*) enlace *m,* conexión *f.* **2** US (*traffic jam*) embotellamiento, atasco.

tiff [tɪf] *n fam* pelea, riña.

tiger [ˈtaɪgə˙] *n* tigre *m.*

■ **tiger lily,** lirio tigrado. ‖ **tiger moth,** mariposa tigre.

tight [taɪt] **1** *adj* (*firmly fastened*) apretado,-a, duro,-a. **2** (*taut*) tensado,-a, tirante, tenso,-a; (*chest*) oprimido. **3** (*clothes*) ajustado,-a, ceñido,-a. **4** (*not leaky*) hermético,-a, impermeable. **5** (*hold*) estrecho,-a, fuerte. **6** (*packed together*) apretado,-a. **7** (*strict - schedule*) apretado,-a; (*-security*) estricto,-a, riguroso,-a. **8** *fam* (*mean*) agarrado,-a, tacaño,-a. **9** *fam* (*drunk*) borracho,-a. **10** (*not easily ob-*

tainable) escaso,-a. **11** (*contest*) reñido,-a. **12** (*bend*) cerrado,-a. – **13** *adv* firmemente, fuerte: *hold (on) tight!,* ¡agárrate fuerte!; *close your eyes tight,* cierra bien los ojos; *hold me tight,* abrázame fuerte; *sit tight,* ¡no te muevas!

● **to be a tight squeeze,** estar apretados,-as.

■ **tight spot,** aprieto.

tighten [ˈtaɪtən] **1** *t* (*gen*) apretar, ajustar; (*rope*) tensar. **2** (*make stricter - security*) hacer más estricto, reforzar; (*-credit*) restringir. – **3** *i* (*gen*) apretarse; (*rope, muscles*) tensarse.

◆ **to tighten up 1** *t sep* intensificar, hacer más estricto,-a. – **2** *i* ponerse más estricto,-a.

● **to tighten one's belt,** apretarse el cinturón.

tight-fisted [taɪtˈfɪstɪd] *adj* tacaño,-a, agarrado,-a.

tight-fitting [taɪtˈfɪtɪŋ] *adj* ceñido,-a, ajustado,-a.

tight-knit [ˈtaɪtnɪt] *adj* muy unido,-a.

tight-lipped [ˈtaɪtˈlɪpt] *adj* (*silent*) callado,-a; (*angry*) con los labios apretados.

tightly [ˈtaɪtlɪ] *adv* → **tight.**

tightness [ˈtaɪtnəs] *n* (*of rope, muscles*) tensión *f;* (*in chest*) opresión *f.*

tightrope [ˈtaɪtrəʊp] *n* cuerda floja.

■ **tightrope walker,** funámbulo,-a.

tights [taɪts] **1** *npl* (*gen*) panties *mpl,* medias *fpl.* **2** (*thick*) leotardos *mpl,* mallas *fpl.*

tigress [ˈtaɪgrəs] *n* tigresa *f.*

tile [taɪl] **1** *n* (*wall*) azulejo; (*floor*) baldosa; (*roof*) teja. – **2** *t* (*wall*) alicatar, poner azulejos a. **3** (*floor*) embaldosar. **4** (*roof*) tejar.

● (*out*) **on the tiles,** de juerga, de marcha.

till [tɪl] **1** *prep* hasta: *why don't you wait till tomorrow,* ¿por qué no te esperas hasta mañana? – **2** *conj* hasta que: *we waited till it stopped raining,* esperamos hasta que dejó de llover. – **3** *n* (*for cash*) caja: *please pay at the till,* pase por caja por favor. – **4** *t* (*cultivate*) labrar, cultivar.

tiller [ˈtɪlə˙] *n* caña del timón.

tilt [tɪlt] **1** *n* inclinación *f,* ladeo *m: the table is at a slight tilt,* la mesa está ligeramente inclinada. **2** (*with lance*) acometida. – **3** *t* inclinar, ladear: *don't tilt your chair backwards,* no inclines la silla hacia atrás; *he looked at me, tilting his head to one side,* me miró, inclinando la cabeza a un lado; *the earth is tilted on its axis,* la tierra está inclinada sobre su eje. – **4** *i* (*slope, shift*) inclinarse: *public opinion has tilted in favour of Labour,* la opinión pública se ha inclinado en favor de los laboristas. **5** (*with lance*) acometer.

◆ **to tilt at** *t insep* arremeter contra.

● **at full tilt,** a toda velocidad. ‖ **to have a tilt at sb.,** arremeter contra algn.

timber [ˈtɪmbə˙] **1** *n* (*wood*) madera (de construcción). **2** (*beam*) viga. **3** (*trees*) árboles *mpl* maderables. – **4** *interj* ¡cuidado, que cae!, ¡allá va!

■ **timber mill,** aserradero.

timberyard [ˈtɪmbəjɑːd] *n* almacén *m* de madera.

time [taɪm] **1** *n* (*period*) tiempo: *I haven't got time to finish this,* no tengo tiempo para acabar esto; *time flies when you're enjoying yourself,* el tiempo vuela cuando uno se lo pasa bien; *what a waste of time,* qué pérdida de tiempo; *in an hour's time,* dentro de una hora. **2** (*short period*) rato: *we spoke for a time,* hablamos durante un rato; *you've been a long time,* has tardado mucho. **3** (*of day*) hora: *it's time to go,* es (la) hora de marchar; *what time is it?,* qué hora es?; *this time next week, we'll be on the beach,* la semana que viene a esta hora, estaremos en la playa; *by the time he gets here, it'll be time to go* *home,* cuando llegue él, será la hora de volver a casa. **4** (*age, period, season*) época: *it's warm for the time of year,* hace bastante calor para la época del año; *in Victorian times,* en la época victoriana; *these are hard times,* son tiempos difíciles. **5** (*occasion*) vez *f: how many times have you been to London?,* ¿cuántas veces has estado en Londres?; *the last time I saw her,...,* la última vez que la vi, ...; *we left at the same time,* salimos a la vez. **6** (*suitable moment*) momento: *this is not really the time to talk about that,* no es el momento de hablar de eso. **7** MUS compás *m: you're out of time,* has perdido el compás. **8** GB la hora de cerrar: *time now please!,* ¡hora de cerrar! **9** *fam* (*imprisonment*) condena: *he did time for robbery when he was young,* cumplió una condena por robo cuando era joven. – **10** *t* (*measure time*) medir la duración de, calcular; SP cronometrar: *he timed his journey to work,* calculó cuánto tarda en llegar al trabajo. **11** (*schedule*) estar previsto,-a: *the plane is timed to arrive at 12 o'clock,* el avión tiene su llegada prevista para las doce horas; *the bomb was timed to explode during the parade,* la bomba estaba preparada para explotar durante el desfile; *you timed that well - I've just made some tea,* has llegado en el momento justo - acabo de hacer té. – **12 times,** *npl* veces *fpl: 4 times 5 is 20,* 4 por 5 son 20, 4 veces 5 son 20; *it's three times more expensive than last year,* es tres veces más caro que el año pasado. ● (*and*) **about time,** ya era hora. ‖ **all the time,** todo el rato, todo el tiempo. ‖ **at all times,** siempre. ‖ **at any time,** en cualquier momento. ‖ **at no time,** nunca. ‖ **at one time,** en un tiempo. ‖ **at the same time,** al mismo tiempo. ‖ **at the time / at that time,** entonces. ‖ **at times,** a veces. ‖ **behind the times,** anticuado,-a. ‖ **behind time,** tarde. ‖ **for the time being,** de momento. ‖ **from time to time,** de vez en cuando. ‖ **in no time (at all),** en seguida. ‖ **in time,** (*in the long run*) con el tiempo; (*not late*) a tiempo. ‖ **in time to the music,** al compás de la música. ‖ **many a time,** a menudo. ‖ **not to give sb. the time of day,** no darle a algn. ni la hora. ‖ **on time,** puntual. ‖ **one/two/three at a time,** de uno en uno/de dos en dos/de tres en tres. ‖ **time after time,** una y otra vez. ‖ **time's up,** se acabó el tiempo, ya es la hora. ‖ **to beat time,** marcar el compás. ‖ **to be ahead of one's time,** adelantarse a su época. ‖ **to be badly/well timed,** (*remark*) ser inoportuno,-a/oportuno,-a. ‖ **to give sb. a hard time,** ponérselo difícil a algn., hacérselo pasar mal a algn. ‖ **to have a bad time,** pasarlas negras. ‖ **to have a good time,** pasarlo bien. ‖ **to have a lot of time for sb.,** caerle bien algn. a uno. ‖ **to have no time for sb./sth.,** no soportar a algn./algo, no tener tiempo para algn./ algo. ‖ **to keep time,** (*to music*) seguir el compás; (*watch*) ir bien, funcionar bien. ‖ **to keep up with the times,** estar al día. ‖ **to move with the times,** estar al día. ‖ **to take one's time,** (*not hurry*) hacer algo con calma; (*be slow*) tardar mucho. ■ **time and motion study,** estudio de productividad. ‖ **time bomb,** bomba de relojería. ‖ **time limit,** límite *m* de tiempo, plazo límite. ‖ **time off,** tiempo libre. ‖ **time out,** descanso. ‖ **time warp,** salto en el tiempo. ‖ **time zone,** huso horario.

time-consuming [ˈtaɪmkənsjuːmɪŋ] *adj* que lleva mucho tiempo.

time-honoured [ˈtaɪmɒnəd] *adj* consagrado,-a.

timekeeper [ˈtaɪmkiːpəʳ] *n* cronometrador,-ra.

time-lag [ˈtaɪmlæg] *n* lapso, intervalo.

timeless [ˈtaɪmləs] *adj* eterno,-a.

timely [ˈtaɪmlɪ] *adj* oportuno,-a.

timepiece [ˈtaɪmpiːs] *n* reloj *m.*

timer [ˈtaɪməʳ] *n* (*machine*) temporizador *m.*

timescale [ˈtaɪmskeɪl] *n* escala de tiempo.

time-served [ˈtaɪmsɜːvd] *adj* que ha seguido el aprendizaje de un oficio.

time-server [ˈtaɪmsɜːvəʳ] *n* oportunista *mf.*

time-share [ˈtaɪmʃeəʳ] **1** *adj* (*property*) en multipropiedad. – **2** *n* (*property*) (sistema *mf* de) multipropiedad *f.*

time-sharing [ˈtaɪmʃeərɪŋ] **1** *n* (*computer*) trabajo a tiempo compartido. **2** (*property*) (sistema *m* de) multipropiedad *f.* – **3** *adj* (*computer*) a tiempo compartido. **4** (*system*) en multipropiedad.

timetable [ˈtaɪmteɪbəl] *n* horario.

timid [ˈtɪmɪd] *adj* tímido,-a.

timidity [tɪˈmɪdɪtɪ] *n* timidez *f.*

timing [ˈtaɪmɪŋ] **1** *n* (*time chosen*) momento escogido; (*judgement*) sentido de la oportunidad: *what good timing!,* ¡qué oportuno! **2** SP (*measurement of time*) cronometraje *m.*
■ **timing gear,** AUTO engranaje *m* de distribución.

tin [tɪn] **1** *n* (*metal*) estaño. **2** (*can*) lata, bote *m.* **3** (*for baking*) molde *m.* – **4** *t* enlatar.
■ **tin hat,** casco. ‖ **tin soldier,** soldadito de plomo. ‖ **tin whistle,** flautín *m.*
▲ (*verbo*) *pt* & *pp* **tinned,** *ger* **tinning.**

tinder [ˈtɪndəʳ] *n* yesca.

tinfoil [ˈtɪnfɔɪl] *n* papel *m* de estaño.

tinge [tɪndʒ] **1** *n* tinte *m,* matiz *f.* – **2** *t* teñir.

tingle [ˈtɪŋgəl] **1** *n* hormigueo. – **2** *i* hormiguear.

tinker [ˈtɪŋkəʳ] **1** *n* (*tinsmith*) hojalatero,a, calderero,-a. **2** (*gypsy*) gitano,-a. **3** (*naughty child*) pícaro,-a, tunante,-a, diablillo,-a. – **4 to tinker with,** *i* (*try to repair*) tratar de arreglar; (*meddle with*) manosear, apañar, tocar.

tinkle [ˈtɪŋkəl] **1** *n* tintineo. – **2** *t* hacer tintinear. – **3** *i* (*ring*) tintinear. **4** GB *fam* (*urinate*) hacer pipí.
● **to give sb. a tinkle,** GB *fam* llamar a algn. por teléfono.

tinny [ˈtɪnɪ] **1** *adj* (*sound*) metálico,-a; (*taste*) a lata. **2** (*cheap, badly made*) de lata.
▲ *comp* **tinnier,** *superl* **tinniest.**

tin-opener [ˈtɪnəʊpənəʳ] *n* abrelatas *m inv.*

tinpot [ˈtɪnpɒt] *adj* insignificante: *tinpot dictator,* dictador,-ra de pacotilla.

tinsel [ˈtɪnsəl] *n* oropel *m.*

tinsmith [ˈtɪnsmɪθ] *n* hojalatero,-a.

tint [tɪnt] **1** *n* tinte *m,* matiz *f.* – **2** *t* teñir, matizar.

tiny [ˈtaɪnɪ] *adj* diminuto,-a.
▲ *comp* **tinier,** *superl* **tiniest.**

tip[1] [tɪp] *n* (*gen*) extremo, punta, cabo; (*of cigarette*) boquilla, filtro: *the tips of one's fingers,* las puntas de los dedos; *the northern tip of the island,* el extremo norte de la isla.
● **from tip to toe,** de pies a cabeza. ‖ **to have sth. on the tip of one's tongue,** tener algo en la punta de la lengua. ‖ **the tip of the iceberg,** la punta del iceberg.

tip[2] [tɪp] **1** *n* (*gratuity*) propina. **2** (*advice*) consejo, truco; (*confidential information*) soplo, confidencia; (*prediction*) pronóstico. – **3** *t* (*give gratuity to*) dar una propina a. **4** (*predict*) pronosticar: *he tipped the horse to win,* pronosticó que ganaría el caballo; *he is widely tipped as the new director,* muchos creen que será el nuevo director.
◆ **to tip off** *t sep* avisar, dar el soplo: *the police were tipped off about the robbery,* la policía recibió el soplo del robo; *the burglars were tipped off and escaped,* avisaron a los ladrones y se escaparon.

tip[3] [tɪp] **1** *n* (*for rubbish*) vertedero, basurero; (*dirty place*) porquería, desorden *m,* revoltijo: *your room is a tip!,* ¡tu habitación está hecha un asco! – **2** *t* (*lean, tilt*) inclinar, ladear. **3** (*pour*) verter; (*throw*) tirar; (*empty*) vaciar: *she tipped the leftovers into the bin,* tiró las sobras a la basura. **4** (*rubbish*) verter. – **5** *i* inclinarse, ladearse.

◆ **to tip over 1** *i* (*overturn*) volcarse, caerse; (*boat*) zozobrar. – **2** *t sep* volcar. ‖ **to tip up 1** *i* (*tilt*) ladearse; (*seats*) levantarse. – **2** *t sep* inclinar.

● **to tip it down,** llover a cántaros. ‖ **to tip one's hat,** quitarse el sombrero. ‖ **to tip the scales / tip the balance,** *fig* inclinar la balanza, decidir la cuestión. ‖ **to tip the scales (at),** (*weigh*) pesar.

▲ (*verbo*) *pt & pp* **tipped,** *ger* **tipping.**

tip-off ['tɪpɒf] *n fam* soplo, aviso.

tipper ['tɪpəʳ] *n* (*vehicle*) volquete *m.*
● **to be a good tipper,** (*person*) dejar buenas propinas.
■ **tipper truck / tipper lorry,** volquete *m.*

tipple ['tɪpəl] *n fam* bebida (alcohólica).

tipster ['tɪpstəʳ] *n* pronosticador,-ra.

tipsy ['tɪpsɪ] *adj* achispado,-a, piripi.
● **to get tipsy,** achisparse.
▲ *comp* **tipsier,** *superl* **tipsiest.**

tiptoe ['tɪptəʊ] *i* caminar de puntillas.
● **on tiptoe,** de puntillas.

tiptop ['tɪptɒp] *adj fam* de primera.

TIR ['tiː'aɪ'ɑːʳ] *abbr* (*transport international routier*) transporte internacional por carretera; (*abbreviation*) TIR.

tirade [taɪ'reɪd] *n* invectiva.

Tirana [tɪ'rɑːnə] *n* Tirana.

tire[1] [taɪəʳ] **1** *t* cansar. – **2** *i* cansarse (**of,** de).
◆ **to tire out** *t sep* agotar.

tire[2] [taɪəʳ] *n US* → **tyre.**

tired [taɪəd] **1** *adj* (*weary*) cansado,-a. **2** (*fed up*) harto,-a (**of,** de).
● **to get tired,** cansarse.

tiredness ['taɪədnəs] *n* cansancio.

tireless ['taɪələs] *adj* incansable.

tiresome ['taɪəsəm] *adj* molesto,-a, pesado,-a.

tiring ['taɪərɪŋ] *adj* cansado,-a, agotador,-ra.

tissue ['tɪʃuː] **1** *n* (*cloth*) tisú *m.* **2** (*handkerchief*) pañuelo de papel, Kleenex. **3** BIOL tejido.
■ **tissue paper,** papel *m* de seda.

tit[1] [tɪt] *n* ORN paro, herrerillo.
● **tit for tat,** donde las dan las toman.
■ **blue tit,** herrerillo común. ‖ **coal tit,** carbonero garrapinos. ‖ **crested tit,** herrerillo capuchino. ‖ **great tit,** carbonero común. ‖ **long-tailed tit,** mito. ‖ **marsh tit,** carbonero palustre. ‖ **willow tit,** carbonero sibilino.

tit[2] [tɪt] *n sl* (*breast*) teta.

titbit ['tɪtbɪt] **1** *n* (*delicacy*) manjar *m*, exquisitez *f.* **2** (*gossip*) chisme *m.*

tithe [taɪð] *n* diezmo.

titillate ['tɪtɪleɪt] *t* excitar.

titivate ['tɪtɪveɪt] **1** *t* emperifollar. – **2** *i* emperifollarse.

title ['taɪtəl] **1** *n* (*gen*) título. **2** JUR título, derecho. **3** SP título, campeonato. – **4** *t* titular. – **5 titles,** *npl* (*film credits*) créditos *mpl.*
■ **title deed,** escritura de propiedad. ‖ **title page,** portada. ‖ **title role,** papel *m* principal.

titled ['taɪtəld] *adj* con título de nobleza.

titleholder ['taɪtəlhəʊldəʳ] *n* campeón,-ona.

titter ['tɪtəʳ] **1** *n* risita. – **2** *i* reírse disimuladamente.

tittle-tattle ['tɪtltætl] *n fam* cotilleo, chismes *mpl.*

titular ['tɪtjʊləʳ] *adj* titular, nominal.

tizzy ['tɪzɪ] **to get in a tizzy,** *phr fam* ponerse nervioso,-a.

▲ *pl* **tizzies.**

TM ['treɪdmɑːk] *abbr* (*trademark*) marca registrada.

TNT ['tiː'en'tiː] *abbr* (*trinitrotoluene*) trinitrotolueno; (*abbreviation*) TNT.

to [tʊ, *unstressed* tə] **1** *prep* (*with place*) a: *we're going to a concert,* vamos a un concierto; *did you go to the bank?,* ¿fuiste al banco?; *he was taken to the police station,* lo llevaron a la comisaría; *I have been to lots of countries,* he estado en muchos países; *I saw her on the way to the airport,* la vi camino del aeropuerto; *they travelled from town to town,* viajaron de ciudad en ciudad; *A is to the north/south/east/west of B,* A está al norte/sur/este/oeste de B; *it's twenty miles to York,* York está a veinte millas de aquí. **2** (*towards*) hacia: *the Labour party has moved to the right,* el partido laborista se ha desplazado hacia la derecha; *it's further to the north,* está más hacia el norte; *he sat with his back to her,* se sentó de espaldas a ella. **3** (*as far as, until*) a, hasta: *from beginning to end,* desde el principio hasta el final; *she can count up to 10,* sabe contar hasta 10; *from Monday to Friday,* de lunes a viernes; *we work from 9 to 5,* trabajamos de 9 a 5; *her hair reaches down to her waist,* el pelo le llega hasta la cintura; *I like all music, from Abba to ZZTop,* me gusta toda la música, desde Abba hasta ZZTop; *it's accurate to within one second,* tiene un margen de error de menos de un segundo. **4** (*of time*) menos: *it's ten to two,* son las dos menos diez; *it's nearly twenty to,* son casi menos veinte; *a quarter to eight,* las ocho menos cuarto; *there are only two weeks to Christmas,* faltan sólo dos semanas para Navidad. **5** (*with indirect object*) a: *I showed the letter to my mother,* le enseñé la carta a mi madre; *she lent the book to her friend,* le dejó el libro a su amiga; *I gave it to him,* se lo di a él. **6** (*for*) de: *the key to the safe,* la llave de la caja fuerte; *he's secretary to the board,* es secretario del consejo de administración; *what's the answer to question 4?,* ¿cuál es la respuesta a la pregunta número 4?; *heir to the throne,* heredero al trono. **7** (*attitude, behaviour*) con, para con: *you've been very kind to us,* has sido muy amable con nosotros; *be nice to her,* pórtate bien con ella; *he was so rude to me,* se mostró muy grosero conmigo. **8** (*in honour of*) a: *we drink to his health,* brindamos a su salud; *a monument to Churchill,* un monumento a Churchill. **9** (*touching*) a, contra: *he put his ear to the wall,* puso la oreja contra la pared; *she clutched her bag to her chest,* se estrechó el bolso contra el pecho. **10** (*accompanied by*) acompañado,-a de: *we danced to the music,* bailamos al compás de la música; *he left to loud shouts of disapproval,* se marchó entre gritos de desaprobación. **11** (*causing sth.*) para: *to my surprise, it was empty,* para mi sorpresa, estaba vacío. **12** (*as seen by*) por lo que respecta: *to a foreigner, it must seem awful,* para un extranjero, debe parecer terrible; *to some people he was a hero, to others a traitor,* para algunos era un héroe, para otros era un traidor. **13** (*indicating comparison*) a: *I prefer tea to coffee,* prefiero el té al café; *that's nothing to what I heard,* eso no es nada comparado con lo que he oído. **14** (*ratio*) a: *they won by fourteen points to ten,* ganaron por catorce puntos a diez; *we lost by three goals to two,* perdimos por tres a dos; *the odds are 50 to 1,* las posibilidades son 50 contra 1. **15** (*per, equivalent*) a, en: *there are 100 pence to the pound,* hay 100 peniques en una libra; *how much does your car do to the gallon?,* ≈ ¿cuánto gasta tu coche a los cien kilómetros? **16** (*according to*) según: *to my way of thinking,* a mi modo de entender; *is it to your taste?,* ¿es de su agrado?; *I did it to the best of my ability,* lo

hice lo mejor posible; *contrary to all appearances,* en contra de todos los indicios. **17** (*result*) a: *wait until the light turns to green,* espera hasta que la luz cambie a verde; *she was reduced to tears,* se deshizo en lágrimas; *the party's rapid rise to power,* la rápida subida al poder del partido; *he smashed it to pieces,* lo hizo pedazos. **18** (*in order to*) para, a fin de: *I worked overtime to earn some extra money,* hice horas extras para ganar más dinero. **19** (*used as object of many verbs*): *she wants you to go away,* quiere que te vayas. **20** (*substituting infinitive*): *would you like to dance? –I'd love to,* ¿te gustaría bailar? –me encantaría; *she didn't want to go, but she had to,* no quería ir, pero no le quedaba más remedio. **– 21** *adv* (*of door*) ajustada: *push the door to,* ajusta la puerta.
● **to and fro,** vaivén, ir y venir.
▲ *Cuando se usa con la raíz del verbo para formar el infinitivo no se traduce: I want to help you, quiero ayudarte; he tried to sell his car, intentó vender su coche.*
toad [təʊd] *n* sapo.
toadstool [ˈtəʊdstuːl] *n* hongo venenoso.
toady [ˈtəʊdɪ] **1** *n* pelota *mf*, cobista *mf*. **– 2** *i* hacer la pelota a, dar coba a.
▲ (*sustantivo*) *pl toadies;* (*verbo*) *pt & pp toadied, ger toadying.*
toast [təʊst] **1** *n* (*food*) pan *m* tostado: *a piece of toast,* una tostada. **2** (*drink*) brindis *m*: *let's drink a toast to the bride and groom,* brindemos por los novios. **– 3** *t* (*cook*) tostar. **4** (*drink*) brindar por, beber a la salud de.
■ **toast rack,** portatostadas *m inv.*
toaster [ˈtəʊstəʳ] *n* tostadora.
toastmaster [ˈtəʊstmɑːstəʳ] *n* maestro de ceremonias.
tobacco [təˈbækəʊ] *n* tabaco.
■ **tobacco pouch,** petaca.
▲ *pl tobaccos o tobaccoes.*
tobacconist [təˈbækənɪst] *n* estanquero,-a.
■ **tobacconist's (shop),** estanco.
Tobago [təˈbeɪgəʊ] *n* Tobago.
toboggan [təˈbɒgən] **1** *n* tobogán (*m*). **– 2** *i* tirarse por un tobogán.
tod [tɒd] **on one's tod,** *phr* solo,-a.
today [təˈdeɪ] **1** *n* hoy *m*. **– 2** *adv* hoy: *I'm leaving a week today,* me voy de aquí una semana. **3** (*nowadays*) hoy en día: *young people today,* los jóvenes de hoy en día.
toddle [ˈtɒdəl] **1** *i* (*child*) dar los primeros pasos. **2** (*person*) andar con paso inseguro.
◆ **to toddle off** *i* marcharse, irse.
toddler [ˈtɒdləʳ] *n* niño,-a (que empieza a andar).
toddy [ˈtɒdɪ] *n bebida hecha generalmente de whisky, agua caliente, azúcar y limón.*
to-do [təˈduː] *n* lío, jaleo.
▲ *pl to-dos.*
toe [təʊ] **1** *n* ANAT dedo del pie. **2** (*of shoe*) puntera; (*of sock*) punta. **– 3** *t* tocar con la punta del pie.
● **to be on one's toes,** estar alerta. ‖ **to keep on one's toes,** mantenerse alerta. ‖ **to step/tread on sb.'s toes,** (*literally*) pisar a algn.; (*offend*) ofender a algn. ‖ **to toe the line,** acatar la disciplina, ser conformista.
toecap [ˈtəʊcæp] *n* puntera.
toenail [ˈtəʊneɪl] *n* uña del dedo del pie.
toff [tɒf] *n fam* pijo,-a, esnob *mf.*
toffee [ˈtɒfɪ] *n* caramelo.
■ **toffee apple,** manzana caramelizada.
toffee-nosed [ˈtɒfɪnəʊzd] *n* presumido,-a, engreído,-a.
tog[1] [tɒg] *t* vestir.
◆ **to tog out / tog up 1** *t sep* vestir. **– 2** *i* vestirse.

tog[2] [tɒg] *n unidad de aislamiento térmico.*
toga [ˈtəʊgə] *n* toga.
together [təˈgeðəʳ] **1** *adv* (*gen*) juntos,-as: *we spend all our time together,* pasamos todo nuestro tiempo juntos; *beat the flour and the sugar together,* batir la harina con el azúcar; *they strove to keep the family together,* lucharon por mantener la familia unida. **2** (*simultaneously*) a la vez, al mismo tiempo: *they answered together,* contestaron a la vez; *problems always come together,* los problemas siempre vienen juntos. **3** (*nonstop*) seguido,-a. **– 4** *adj fam* (*confident, organized, capable*) seguro,-a de sí mismo,-a.
● **to bring together,** reunir, juntar. ‖ **to come together,** juntarse. ‖ **to get it together,** organizarse. ‖ **to go together,** ir juntos,-as. ‖ **together with,** junto con.
togetherness [təˈgeðənəs] *n* unión *f.*
toggle [ˈtɒgəl] *n* botón *m* de madera.
Togo [ˈtəʊgəʊ] *n* Togo.
Togolese [təʊgəˈliːz] **1** *adj* togolés,-esa. **– 2** *n* togolés,-esa.
togs [tɒgz] *npl fam* ropa *f sing.*
toil [tɔɪl] **1** *n* trabajo, esfuerzo. **– 2** *i* afanarse, esforzarse.
toilet [ˈtɔɪlət] **1** *n* (*appliance*) váter *m*, inodoro; (*room*) lavabo, baño. **2** (*public*) servicios *mpl*, aseos *mpl*. **3** (*washing*) aseo personal, higiene *m* personal.
■ **toilet paper,** papel *m* higiénico. ‖ **toilet roll,** rollo de papel higiénico. ‖ **toilet water,** agua de colonia.
toiletries [ˈtɔɪlətrɪz] *npl* artículos *mpl* de aseo.
toilet-train [ˈtɔɪlɪtreɪn] *t enseñar a un,-a niño,-a a a pedir las necesidades.*
token [ˈtəʊkən] **1** *n* (*sign, proof*) señal *f*, prueba. **2** (*memento, souvenir*) detalle *m*, recuerdo. **3** (*coupon*) vale *m*. **4** (*coin*) ficha. **– 5** *adj* simbólico,-a: *a token payment,* un pago simbólico; *they put up token resistance,* presentaron resistencia simbólica.
● **by the same token,** del mismo modo, de la misma manera. ‖ **in token of,** en señal de, en recuerdo de.
told [təʊld] *pt & pp →* **tell.**
tolerable [ˈtɒlərəbəl] **1** *adj* (*endurable*) tolerable, soportable. **2** (*not bad*) regular, pasable.
tolerance [ˈtɒlərəns] *n* tolerancia.
tolerant [ˈtɒlərənt] *adj* tolerante (**of/towards,** con).
tolerate [ˈtɒləreɪt] *t* tolerar, aguantar, suportar: *he doesn't tolerate such behaviour,* no tolera tal comportamiento; *how can you tolerate that noise?,* ¿cómo aguantas aquel ruido?
toll[1] [təʊl] **1** *n* (*payment*) peaje *m*. **2** (*loss*) mortalidad *f*, número de víctimas mortales.
● **to take its toll on,** afectar negativamente: *the damp and cold took their toll on his health,* la humedad y el frío minaron su salud.
toll[2] [təʊl] **1** *n* (*of bell*) tañido. **– 2** *t* tañer, doblar. **– 3** *i* doblar.
tollgate [ˈtəʊlgeɪt] *n* peaje *m.*
Toltec [ˈtɒltek] **1** *adj* tolteca. **– 2** *n* tolteca *mf.*
tom [tɒm] *n* gato (macho).
tomahawk [ˈtɒməhɔːk] *n* hacha de guerra.
tomato [təˈmɑːtəʊ, *je* təˈmeɪtəʊ] *n* tomate *m.*
■ **tomato plant,** tomatera.
▲ *pl tomatoes.*
tomb [tuːm] *n* tumba, sepulcro.
tombola [tɒmˈbəʊlə] *n* tómbola.
tomboy [ˈtɒmbɔɪ] *n* marimacho *f.*
tombstone [ˈtuːmstəʊn] *n* lápida (sepulcral).
tomcat [ˈtɒmkæt] *n* gato (macho).
tome [təʊm] *n* tomo.

tomfoolery [tɒmˈfuːlərɪ] *n* tonterías *fpl*.
Tommy gun [ˈtɒmɪɡʌn] *n* metralleta.
tommyrot [ˈtɒmɪrɒt] *n* tonterías *fpl*.
tomorrow [təˈmɒrəʊ] **1** *n* mañana *f*. – **2** *adv* mañana: *tomorrow morning/afternoon,* mañana por la mañana/ tarde; *see you tomorrow!,* ¡hasta mañana!
tom-tom [ˈtɒmtɒm] *n* tam-tam *m*.
ton [tʌn] **1** *n* tonelada. – **2 tons,** *npl fam* montones *mpl*: *I've got tons of homework to do,* tengo montones de de- beres que hacer.
● **to come down on sb. like a ton of bricks,** arre- meter contra algn. ‖ **to do a ton,** (*car*) ir a 100 millas por hora. ‖ **to weigh a ton,** pesar muchísimo, pesar una tonelada.
tone [təʊn] **1** *n* (*sound, manner of speaking*) tono; (*on phone*) señal *f*: *don't use that tone of voice with me,* no me ha- bles en ese tono; *please leave your message after the tone,* deje su mensaje después de la señal. **2** (*colour*) tonalidad *f*, tono. **3** (*mood, character*) tono, carácter *m*. **4** (*quality, respectability*) buen tono, clase *f*, nivel *m*: *they lower the tone of the area,* ellos hacen bajar el nivel de la zona. **5** MUS tono. **6** (*of muscle*) tono.
◆ **to tone down** *t sep* atenuar, suavizar. ‖ **to tone in with** *i* ir bien con, armonizar con. ‖ **to tone up** *t sep* tonificar.
tone-deaf [ˈtəʊnˈdef] *adj* que no tiene sentido musical, que no tiene oído.
toneless [ˈtəʊnləs] *adj* monótono,-a.
Tonga [ˈtɒŋɡə] *n* Tonga.
Tongan [ˈtɒŋɡən] **1** *adj* tongano,-a. – **2** *n* (*person*) ton- gano,-a. **3** (*language*) tongano.
tongs [tɒŋz] *npl* tenacillas *fpl*, pinzas *fpl*.
tongue [tʌŋ] **1** *n* ANAT lengua. **2** (*language*) lengua, idio- ma *m*. **3** (*of shoe*) lengüeta. **4** (*of bell*) badajo. **5** (*of land, flame*) lengua.
● **cat got your tongue? / have you lost your ton- gue?,** ¿se te ha comido la lengua el gato? ‖ **to get one's tongue round sth.,** poder pronunciar algo. ‖ **to hold one's tongue,** callarse. ‖ **tongue in cheek,** en broma, irónicamente. ‖ **to put one's tongue out / stick one's tongue out,** sacar la lengua. ‖ **to set ton- gues wagging,** dar que hablar. ‖ **with one's tongue hanging out,** con la lengua fuera.
■ **tongue twister,** trabalenguas *m inv*.
tongue-tied [ˈtʌŋtaɪd] *adj* cortado,-a.
tonic [ˈtɒnɪk] **1** *n* MED tónico *m*. **2** MUS tónica. **3** (*drink*) tónica. – **4** *adj* tónico,-a.
■ **tonic water,** tónica.
tonight [təˈnaɪt] **1** *n* esta noche *f*. – **2** *adv* esta noche *f*.
tonnage [ˈtʌnɪdʒ] *n* tonelaje *m*.
tonne [tʌn] *n* tonelada.
tonsil [ˈtɒnsəl] *n* amígdala.
tonsillitis [tɒnsəˈlaɪtəs] *n* amigdalitis *f*.
too [tuː] **1** *adv* (*excessively*) demasiado: *too slow,* demasia- do lento; *too big,* demasiado grande. **2** (*also*) también: *can I come too?,* ¿puedo ir también?; *me too,* yo tam- bién. **3** (*besides*) además. **4** (*very*) muy.
● **too many,** demasiados,-as. ‖ **too much,** demasia- do,-a. ‖ **all too / only too,** demasiado,-a. ‖ **I should think so too!,** ¡era lo menos que podía hacer! ‖ **about time too,** ya era hora. ‖ **to be too much for sb.,** ser demasiado para algn.
took [tʊk] *pt* → **take**.
tool [tuːl] **1** *n* (*gen*) herramienta; (*instrument*) instrumen- to. – **2** *t* (*book*) estampar; (*leather*) labrar. – **3 tools,** *npl* (*gardening etc*) útiles *mpl*.

◆ **to tool up** *t sep* equipar.
■ **tool shed,** cobertizo para las herramientas.
toolbox [ˈtuːlbɒks] *n* caja de herramientas.
toolkit [ˈtuːlkɪt] *n* juego de herramientas.
tool-maker [ˈtuːlmeɪkəʳ] *n* trabajador,-ra que fabrica herra- mientas.
toot [tuːt] **1** *n* AUTO bocinazo. **2** (*on whistle*) pitido. – **3** *t* tocar. – **4** *i* tocar el claxon, tocar la bocina.
tooth [tuːθ] **1** *n* (*gen*) diente *m*; (*molar*) muela; (*front tooth*) incisivo: *he had a tooth out,* le sacaron una muela. **2** (*of comb*) púa. **3** (*of saw*) diente *m*.
● **long in the tooth,** viejo,-a. ‖ **to cut a tooth,** echar los dientes, endentecer. ‖ **to fight tooth and nail,** lu- char con uñas y dientes. ‖ **to get one's teeth into sth.,** hincarle el diente a algo. ‖ **to have a sweet tooth,** ser goloso,-a. ‖ **to set one's teeth on edge,** darle dentera a uno. ‖ **to show one's teeth,** enseñar los dientes.
■ **tooth fairy,** ratoncito Pérez.
▲ *pl* **tooth**.
toothache [ˈtuːθeɪk] *n* dolor *m* de muelas.
toothbrush [ˈtuːθbrʌʃ] *n* cepillo de dientes.
toothless [ˈtuːθləs] *adj* desdentado,-a.
toothpaste [ˈtuːθpeɪst] *n* pasta de dientes.
toothpick [ˈtuːθpɪk] *n* mondadientes *m inv*, palillo.
toothsome [ˈtuːθsəm] *adj* apetitoso,-a, sabroso,-a.
top¹ [tɒp] **1** *n* (*highest/upper part*) parte *f* superior, parte *f* de arriba, parte *f* más alta: *an attic is the room at the top of a house,* el desván es el cuarto en la parte más alta de una casa. **2** (*far end - of street*) final *m*; (*- of table*) cabecera: *I'll meet you at the top of the street,* quedamos al final de la calle. **3** (*of mountain*) cumbre *m*. **4** (*of tree*) copa. **5** (*surface*) superficie *f*. **6** (*of bottle*) tapón *m*; (*of pen*) capuchón *m*. **7** (*highest position*): *she was top of the class,* fue la primera de la clase; *I think you'll make it to the top,* creo que llegarás hasta arriba; *who's the top of the organization?,* ¿quién es el jefe de la organización? **8** (*of list*) cabeza: *who's at the top of the league?,* ¿quién en- cabeza la liga?; *what's top of the list?,* ¿qué es lo pri- mero de la lista? **9** (*of car*) capota. **10** (*clothes*) blusa (corta), camiseta, top *m*; (*of bikini*) parte de arriba. **11** (*beginning*) principio: *let's take it from the top,* hagámos- lo desde el principio. **12** (*gear*) directa. – **13** *adj* (*highest*) de arriba, superior, más alto,-a: *I live on the top floor,* vivo en el último piso. **14** (*best, highest, leading*) mejor, principal: *one of Spain's top directors,* uno de los me- jores directores españoles; *top party officials,* los ca- becillas del partido; *only the top graduates get the top jobs,* sólo los mejores licenciados consiguen los mejores trabajos. **15** (*highest, maximum*) principal, máxi- mo,-a: *the car's top speed,* la velocidad máxima del coche. – **16** *t* (*cover*) cubrir, rematar. **17** (*remove top of plant/fruit*) quitar los rabillos. **18** *sl* (*kill*) cargarse: *he topped himself,* se mató. **19** (*come first, head*) encabezar. **20** (*better, surpass, exceed*) superar. – **21 tops,** *npl* (*of plant*) hojas *fpl*.
◆ **to top off** *i* rematar. ‖ **to top up** *t sep* (*fill up*) acabar de llenar; (*refill*) volver a llenar.
● **at the top of the tree,** *fig* en el cumbre. ‖ **at the top of one's voice,** a voz en grito. ‖ **at top speed,** a toda velocidad. ‖ **from top to bottom,** de arriba abajo. ‖ **from top to toe,** de cabeza a pies. ‖ **on top,** encima de, sobre: *put your things on top,* pon tus cosas encima. ‖ **on top of,** encima de: *don't put your books on top of mine,* no pongas tus libros encima de los míos; *do you get commission on top of your salary?,* ¿ganas una co- misión además de tu sueldo? ‖ **on top of it all / to top it all,** para colmo. ‖ **to be on top of the world,** estar

en la gloria, estar contento,-a y feliz. ‖ **to be over the top,** (*excessive*) ser demasiado. ‖ **to blow one's top,** perder los estribos. ‖ **to come out on top,** salir ganando. ‖ **to get on top of sb.,** agobiar a algn. ‖ **to go over the top,** pasarse. ■ **top brass,** peces *mpl* gordos. ‖ **top copy,** original *m*. ‖ **top dog,** gallito. ‖ **top gear,** directa. ‖ **top hat,** chistera, sombrero de copa. ‖ **top of the bill,** actor *m* principal, actriz *f* principal. ▲ (*verbo*) *pt & pp* **topped,** *ger* **topping.**

top² [tɒp] *n* peonza. ● **to sleep like a top,** dormir como un tronco, dormir como un lirón.

topaz ['təʊpæz] *n* topacio.

topcoat [tɒp'kəʊt] *n dated* abrigo.

top-heavy ['tɒp'hevɪ] *adj* demasiado pesado,-a en la parte superior, inestable.

top-hole [tɒp'həʊl] *adj* excelente.

topic ['tɒpɪk] *n* tema *m*.

topical ['tɒpɪkəl] *adj* actual, de actualidad.

topless ['tɒpləs] *adj* desnudo,-a de cintura para arriba.

topmost ['tɒpməʊst] *adj* más alto,-a.

topnotch [tɒp'nɒtʃ] *adj* de primera.

topographer [tə'pɒgrəfəʳ] *n* topógrafo,-a.

topography [tə'pɒgrəfɪ] *n* topografía.

topping ['tɒpɪŋ] 1 *n* (*for pizza*) ingrediente *m*; (*for ice-cream*) salsa. – **2** *adj* excelente.

topple ['tɒpəl] 1 *t* (*overturn*) volcar, hacer caer. **2** *fig* (*overthrow*) derribar, derrocar. – **3** *i* (*fall*) caerse; (*lose balance*) tambalearse, perder el equilibrio.

top-ranking ['tɒpræŋkɪŋ] *adj* de alto nivel.

tops [tɒps] **the tops,** *npl fam* lo mejor *m sing*.

top-secret [tɒp'siːkrət] *adj* sumamente secreto,-a, confidencial.

topsoil ['tɒpsɔɪl] *n* capa superficial del suelo.

topsy-turvy ['tɒpsɪ'tɜːvɪ] 1 *adv* en desorden, patas arriba. – **2** *adj* confuso,-a, desordenado,-a.

tor [tɔːʳ] *n* colina, peñasco.

torch [tɔːtʃ] 1 *n* (*with naked flame*) antorcha. **2** (*electric*) linterna. – **3** *t* quemar, prender fuego a. ● **to carry a torch for sb.,** estar enamorado,-a de algn. sin ser correspondido,-a. ■ **torch song,** canción *f* de amor.

torchlight ['tɔːtʃlaɪt] **by torchlight,** *phr* (*read*) con una linterna. ■ **torchlight parade,** procesión *f* con antorchas.

tore [tɔːʳ] *pt* → **tear.**

toreador ['tɒrɪədəʳ] *n* torero.

torment ['tɔːmənt] 1 *n* (*gen*) tormento, tortura; (*suffering*) angustia: *she was in torment,* sufría muchísimo. – **2** *t* (*cause to suffer*) atormentar, torturar. **3** (*annoy*) molestar, hacer rabiar, martirizar. ▲ En acepción 2 (*verbo*) [tɔː'ment].

tormentor [tɔː'mentəʳ] *n* atormentador,-ra.

torn [tɔːn] 1 *pp* → **tear.** – **2** *adj* rasgado,-a, roto,-a. ● **that's torn it!,** ¡ahora sí que la he (*has, ha, etc.*) hecho buena!, ¡se ha ido todo al traste! ‖ **to be torn between X and Y,** no poder decidir entre X e Y. ‖ **to be torn by sth.,** estar atormentado,-a por algo.

tornado [tɔː'neɪdəʊ] *n* tornado. ▲ *pl* **tornados** o **tornadoes.**

torpedo [tɔː'piːdəʊ] 1 *n* torpedo. – **2** *t* torpedear. **3** *fig* hacer fracasar. ▲ (*sustantivo*) *pl* **torpedos** o **torpedoes**; (*verbo*) *pt & pp* **torpedoed,** *ger* **torpedoing.**

torpid ['tɔːpɪd] 1 *adj* (*of animal - dormant*) en estado letárgico. **2** (*apathetic, sluggish, lethargic*) apático,-a, letárgico,-a.

torpor ['tɔːpəʳ] *n* letargo.

torrent ['tɒrənt] *n* torrente *m*.

torrential [tə'renʃəl] *adj* torrencial.

torrid ['tɒrɪd] 1 *adj* (*hot, dry*) tórrido,-a. **2** (*passionate*) apasionado,-a.

torsion ['tɔːʃən] *n* torsión *f*.

torso ['tɔːsəʊ] *n* torso. ▲ *pl* **torsos.**

tort [tɔːt] *n* JUR agravio.

tortoise ['tɔːtəs] *n* tortuga (de tierra).

tortoiseshell ['tɔːtəsʃel] 1 *n* carey *m*. **2** (*color*) color *m* carey. – **3** *adj* de carey. **4** (*colour*) de color carey.

tortuous ['tɔːtjʊəs] *adj* tortuoso,-a.

torture ['tɔːtʃəʳ] 1 *n* tortura, tormento. – **2** *t* torturar, atormentar.

torturer ['tɔːtʃərəʳ] *n* torturador,-ra.

Tory ['tɔːrɪ] 1 *n* GB POL conservador,-ra. – **2** *adj* conservador,-ra. ▲ (*sustantivo*) *pl* **Tories.**

tosh [tɒʃ] *n* tonterías *fpl*, bobadas *fpl*.

toss [tɒs] 1 *n* (*shake*) sacudida, movimiento. **2** (*of coin*) sorteo a cara o cruz. – **3** *t* (*move, shake*) mover, agitar, sacudir; (*pancake*) dar la vuelta a; (*salad*) mezclar. **4** (*throw*) arrojar, lanzar, tirar. – **5** *i* moverse, agitarse, sacudirse. ● **not to give a toss about sth.,** no importarle un cojón a algn. ‖ **to toss a coin,** echarlo a cara o cruz. ‖ **to toss and turn (in bed),** revolverse (en la cama), dar vueltas (en la cama). ‖ **to toss for sth.,** jugar algo a cara o cruz.

toss-up ['tɒsʌp] *n*: *it's a toss-up between Smith and Jones,* tanto puede ser Smith como Jones.

tot [tɒt] 1 *n* (*child*) chiquitín,-na. **2** *fam* (*drink*) trago. ◆ **to tot up** *t sep* sumar. ▲ (*verbo*) *pt & pp* **totted,** *ger* **totting.**

total ['təʊtəl] 1 *adj* (*overall*) total; (*complete*) completo,-a, rotundo,-a. – **2** *n* total *m*, suma. – **3** *t* sumar. – **4** *i* sumar, ascender a. ● **in total,** en total.

totalitarian [təʊtælɪ'teərɪən] *adj* totalitario,-a.

totality [təʊ'tælɪtɪ] *n* totalidad *f*.

totalizator ['təʊtəlaɪzeɪtəʳ] *n* totalizador *m*.

totally ['təʊtəlɪ] *adv* totalmente, completamente.

tote [təʊt] 1 *t fam* (*carry*) acarrear. – **2** *n* → **totalizator.**

totem ['təʊtəm] *n* tótem *m*. ■ **totem pole,** tótem *m*.

totter ['tɒtəʳ] *i* tambalearse.

tottering ['tɒtərɪŋ] *adj* (*gen*) tambaleante; (*step*) inseguro,-a.

tottery ['tɒtərɪ] *adj* (*gen*) tambaleante; (*step*) inseguro,-a.

toucan ['tuːkən] *n* tucán *m*.

touch [tʌtʃ] 1 *n* (*gen*) toque *m*; (*light touch*) roce *m*: *it'll fall down at the slightest touch,* caerá al mínimo toque; *I felt a touch on my arm,* sentí que alguien me tocaba el brazo. **2** (*detail*) detalle *m*, toque *m*: *she put the finishing touches to the tree,* dio los últimos toques al árbol. **3** (*sense*) tacto: *it was cold to the touch,* era frío al tacto. **4** (*connection*) contacto, comunicación *f*: *I'll be in touch with you,* estaré en contacto contigo; *I've lost touch with Rob,* he perdido el contacto con Rob. **5** (*slight quantity*) poquito, pizca; (*trace*) punto, asomo: *this soup needs a touch of salt,* falta una pizca de sal en la sopa; *a touch of frost,* un poco de escarcha; *he said with a touch of irony,* dijo con un dejo de ironía; *it's a touch expensive for me,* es un poco caro para mí. **6** MED amago: *I've got a touch of flu,* tengo un amago de gripe. **7** *fam* (*skill,*

ability) habilidad *f*: *you must be losing your touch,* debes de estar perdiendo la habilidad. **8** (*manner, style*) toque *m*, sello: *he plays with a special touch,* juega con un toque especial; *this job requires a personal touch,* este trabajo requiere un toque personal. **9** SP toque *m*. – **10** *t* (*gen*) tocar; (*lightly*) rozar: *look, but don't touch,* mirad, pero no toquéis; *he touched her cheek softly,* le tocó suavemente la mejilla; *his lips touched her hand,* sus labios rozaron su mano. **11** (*eat*) probar: *you haven't touched your food,* no has probado la comida. **12** (*move*) conmover: *she was touched by the kind gift,* se conmovió con el regalo; *the tragedy touched everyone,* la tragedia conmovió a todos. **13** (*equal, rival*) igualar: *nobody can touch him as a harpist,* nadie puede igualarlo como arpista. **14** (*affect*) afectar, tocar: *I think you touched a sore point,* creo que has tocado un punto débil. **15** (*deal with*) tocar, abordar. – **16** *i* tocarse: *their hands touched,* se tocaron las manos.
◆ **to touch down 1** *i* (*plane*) aterrizar. **2** SP hacer un ensayo. ‖ **to touch off** *t sep* provocar, causar. ‖ **to touch on / touch upon** *i* mencionar. ‖ **to touch up 1** *t sep* ART retocar. **2** *sl* manosear, magrear, meter mano a.
● **at a touch,** al primer roce. ‖ **into touch,** SP fuera. ‖ **not to touch sth. with a bargepole,** no querer algo ni regalado,-a, no querer algo ni que le paguen a uno. ‖ **to be an easy/soft touch,** ser fácil sacarle dinero a uno. ‖ **to be in touch with sth.,** estar al corriente de algo. ‖ **to be out of touch,** estar fuera de onda. ‖ **to get in touch,** ponerse en contacto (**with,** con). ‖ **to keep in touch,** mantenerse en contacto (**with,** con). ‖ **to touch bottom,** tocar fondo. ‖ **to touch sb. for money,** sablear, dar un sablazo a algn.: *he touched me for £10,* me sableó diez libras. ‖ **to touch wood,** tocar madera.
touch-and-go ['tʌtʃən'gəʊ] *adj* dudoso,-a: *it was touch-and-go whether he would live or not,* no era seguro si viviría, estaba entre la vida y la muerte.
touchdown ['tʌtʃdaʊn] **1** *n* (*on land*) aterrizaje *m*. **2** (*on sea*) amerizaje *m*. **3** SP ensayo.
touched [tʌtʃt] **1** *adj* (*moved*) conmovido,-a. **2** (*crazy*) tocado,-a.
touchiness ['tʌtʃɪnəs] *n* susceptibilidad *f*.
touching ['tʌtʃɪŋ] *adj* conmovedor,-ra.
touchline ['tʌtʃlaɪn] *n* SP línea de banda.
touch-screen ['tʌtʃskriːn] *n* pantalla táctil.
touchstone ['tʌtʃstəʊn] *n* piedra de toque.
touch-type ['tʌtʃtaɪp] *i* mecanografiar sin mirar las teclas.
touchy ['tʌtʃɪ] **1** *adj* (*person*) susceptible: *she's touchy about her nose,* es muy susceptible cuando se trata de su nariz. **2** (*subject etc*) delicado,-a.
▲ *comp* **touchier**, *superl* **touchiest**.
tough [tʌf] **1** *adj* (*strong*) fuerte, resistente. **2** (*difficult*) duro,-a, arduo,-a. **3** (*rough, violent*) violento,-a. **4** (*severe*) duro,-a, severo,-a. **5** (*meat*) duro,-a. **6** *fam* malo,-a, injusto,-a: *tough luck,* mala suerte. – **7** *n* tipo duro.
● **to be a tough nut to crack,** ser un hueso duro de roer. ‖ **to be as tough as old boots,** ser muy duro,-a. ‖ **to get tough with sb.,** ponerse duro,-a con algn.
■ **tough customer,** cliente *m* difícil.
toughen ['tʌfən] **1** *t* (*muscles, laws*) endurecer; (*person*) hacer más fuerte. – **2** *i* (*muscles, approach*) endurecerse; (*person*) hacerse más fuerte.
toughness ['tʌfnəs] **1** *n* (*strength*) dureza, resistencia. **2** (*difficulty*) dificultad *f*. **3** (*severity*) severidad *f*.
Toulouse [tuːˈluːz] *n* Tolosa.
toupee ['tuːpeɪ] *n* peluquín *m*.

tour [tʊəʳ] **1** *n* viaje *m*, excursión *f*: *we're going on a tour of Britain,* vamos a hacer un viaje por Gran Bretaña. **2** (*round building*) visita. **3** (*by performers*) gira; (*cycling*) vuelta. – **4** *t* (*gen*) recorrer, viajar por. **5** (*building*) visitar. – **6** *i* (*by performers*) hacer una gira.
● **to be on tour,** estar de gira.
■ **coach tour,** viaje *m* en autocar. ‖ **conducted tour,** visita comentada. ‖ **guided tour,** visita con guía. ‖ **package tour,** viaje *m* con todo incluido. ‖ **tour operator,** agente *m* de viajes.
tour de force [tʊədəˈfɔːs] *n* hazaña.
tourism ['tʊərɪzəm] *n* turismo.
tourist ['tʊərɪst] **1** *n* turista *mf*. – **2** *adj* turístico,-a.
■ **tourist class,** clase *f* turística. ‖ **tourist industry,** turismo. ‖ **tourist trap,** sitio que atrae a muchos turistas.
touristy ['tʊərɪstɪ] *adj fam pej* demasiado turístico,-a.
tournament ['tʊənəmənt] *n* torneo.
tourniquet ['tʊənɪkeɪ] *n* torniquete *m*.
tousle ['taʊzəl] *t* despeinar.
tout [taʊt] **1** *n* revendedor,-ra. – **2** *t* revender. – **3** *i* intentar captar clientes: *he's always touting for custom,* siempre anda buscando clientes.
● **to tout one's wares,** intentar vender sus mercancías.
■ **ticket tout,** revendedor,-ra de entradas.
tow [təʊ] **1** *t* remolcar: *if you leave your car there, the police will tow it away,* si dejas el coche allí, se lo llevará la grúa. **2** *n* remolque *m*: *how did you get home? –somebody gave me a tow,* ¿cómo llegaste a casa? –alguien me remolcó.
● **on tow,** de remolque. ‖ **with ... in tow,** acompañado,-a de ..., seguido,-a de ...: *he arrived with his family in tow,* llegó acompañado de su familia.
toward [təˈwɔːd] *prep* US → **towards**.
towards [təˈwɔːdz] **1** *prep* (*in direction of*) hacia: *he ran towards me,* corrió hacia mí; *we have made steps towards reaching an agreement,* estamos cerca de llegar a un acuerdo. **2** (*attitude*) con, para con: *everyone was very friendly towards me,* todos eran muy amables conmigo. **3** (*payment*) para: *the money will go towards (the cost of) a new minibus,* el dinero será para un nuevo minibús; *huge sums have been spent towards improving public safety,* se han gastado cantidades enormes de dinero para mejorar la seguridad ciudadana. **4** (*of time*) hacia, cerca de: *it must have been towards 11.00,* serían cerca de las once; *it was towards the end of 1986,* hacia finales de 1986.
towbar ['təʊbɑːʳ] *n* barra de remolque.
towel ['taʊəl] **1** *n* toalla. – **2** *t* secar con toalla.
● **to throw in the towel,** arrojar la toalla.
■ **towel rail,** toallero.
▲ (*verbo*) *pt & pp* **towelled** (US **toweled**), *ger* **towelling** (US **toweling**).
towelling ['taʊəlɪŋ] *n* felpa.
tower ['taʊəʳ] **1** *n* (*gen*) torre *f*. **2** (*of church*) campanario. – **3** *i* elevarse.
◆ **to tower above / tower over** *t insep* dominar, destacarse sobre.
● **to be a tower of strength,** ser una ayuda valiosa.
■ **ivory tower,** torre *f* de marfil. ‖ **tower block,** bloque *m* (de pisos).
towering ['taʊərɪŋ] **1** *adj* (*tall*) muy alto,-a, elevado,-a, dominante. **2** (*rage*) violento,-a, intenso,-a, extremo,-a. **3** (*person*) destacado,-a, dominante.
town [taʊn] **1** *n* (*large*) ciudad *f*; (*small*) población *f*, municipio, pueblo. **2** (*city centre*) centro: *we're going into*

town, vamos al centro; *he's out of town,* está fuera. **3** (*people*) ciudadanos *mpl,* ciudad *f.* – **4** *adj* urbano,-a, municipal.
● **(out) on the town,** de juerga, de marcha. ‖ **to go to town,** (*do enthusiastically*) dedicarse con entusiasmo, entregarse de pleno; (*spend a lot of money*) tirar la casa por la ventana, no reparar en gastos. ‖ **to paint the town red,** ir de juerga.
■ **town centre,** centro urbano, centro comercial. ‖ **town clerk,** secretario del ayuntamiento. ‖ **town council,** ayuntamiento. ‖ **town crier,** pregonero municipal. ‖ **town hall,** ayuntamiento. ‖ **town house,** (*terraced house*) casa unifamiliar adosada; (*house in city*) casa de la ciudad. ‖ **town planning,** urbanismo.
township ['taʊnʃɪp] **1** *n* (*gen*) municipio, pueblo. **2** (*in South Africa*) distrito segregado.
townspeople ['taʊnzpiːpəl] *npl* ciudadanos *mpl.*
towpath ['taʊpɑːθ] *n* camino de sirga.
towrope ['taʊrəʊp] *n* cable *m* de remolque.
toxic ['tɒksɪk] *n* tóxico,-a.
toxicology [tɒksɪ'kɒlədʒɪ] *n* toxicología.
toxin ['tɒksɪn] *n* toxina.
toy [tɔɪ] **1** *n* juguete *m.* – **2** *adj* de juguete. **3** (*dog*) enano,-a.
◆ **to toy with** *t insep* (*object, food*) jugar con; (*idea*) acariciar; (*affections*) divertirse con: *I've been toying with the idea of emigrating,* he estado pensando en emigrar.
■ **toy soldier,** soldadito de plomo.
toyshop ['tɔɪʃɒp] *n* juguetería.
trace [treɪs] **1** *n* (*mark, sign*) indicio, rastro. **2** (*small amount - material*) pizca, vestigio; (*- non-material*) dejo, asomo, nota. – **3** *t* (*sketch*) trazar, esbozar. **4** (*copy*) calcar. **5** (*find*) encontrar, localizar; (*follow*) seguir la pista de. **6** (*describe development*) describir: *this book traces the history of music,* este libro describe la historia de la música. **7** (*find origin*) encontrar el origen de: *have they traced the cause of the fire?,* ¿han encontrado la causa del incendio?; *they traced the call to a mobile phone,* averiguaron que la llamada provenía de un teléfono móvil. **8** (*go back to*) remontarse a: *she traced her family back to the 16th century,* los orígenes de su familia se remontan al siglo XVI; *the problem can be traced back to his childhood,* el problema se remonta a su infancia.
■ **trace element,** oligoelemento.
tracer ['treɪsəʳ] **1** *n* MIL trazadora. **2** MED trazador *m.*
■ **tracer bullet,** bala trazadora.
trachea [trə'kiːə] *n* ANAT tráquea.
trachoma [trə'kəʊmə] *n* MED tracoma *m.*
tracing ['treɪsɪŋ] *n* calco.
■ **tracing paper,** papel *m* de calco, papel *m* de calcar.
track [træk] **1** *n* (*mark*) pista, huellas *fpl,* rastro; (*of wheels*) rodada. **2** (*of rocket, bullet, etc*) trayectoria. **3** (*path*) camino, senda, sendero. **4** SP pista. **5** (*for motor-racing*) circuito. **6** (*of railway*) vía; (*platform*) andén *m.* **7** (*on record, etc*) tema *m,* corte *m,* canción *f.* **8** (*belt on wheels*) oruga. – **9** *t* (*person, animal*) seguir la pista de. **10** TECH seguir la trayectoria de. – **11** *i* CINEM hacer una toma larga con la cámara en movimiento.
◆ **to track down** *t sep* localizar, encontrar.
● **to be on sb.'s tracks / be on the track of sb.,** seguir la pista de algn. ‖ **to be on the right track,** ir por buen camino. ‖ **to be on the wrong track,** estar equivocado,-a/despistado,-a. ‖ **to have a one-track mind,** no tener más que un solo pensamiento. ‖ **to keep track of,** seguir, mantenerse al tanto de. ‖ **to lose track of,** perder de vista, perder el hilo de. ‖ **to make**

tracks, irse, largarse. ‖ **to stop (dead) in one's tracks,** parar en seco.
■ **track events,** atletismo en pista. ‖ **track record,** historial *m.* ‖ **track and field,** atletismo.
tracker ['trækəʳ] *n* rastreador,-ra.
■ **tracker dog,** perro rastreador.
tracksuit ['træksuːt] *n* chándal *m.*
tract[1] [trækt] *n* (*treatise*) tratado; (*pamphlet*) folleto.
tract[2] [trækt] **1** *n* (*land*) extensión *f.* **2** ANAT tracto.
■ **digestive tract,** tracto digestivo.
tractable ['træktəbəl] *adj* (*person*) tratable, dócil; (*metal*) maleable.
traction ['trækʃən] *n* (*gen*) tracción *f.*
■ **traction engine,** vehículo de tracción.
tractor ['træktəʳ] *n* tractor *m.*
trade [treɪd] **1** *n* (*commerce*) comercio: *there's been an increase in foreign trade,* ha habido un aumento del comercio exterior; *trade picks up at Christmas,* el comercio se recupera en Navidad; *fine weather is good for trade,* el buen tiempo es favorable para el comercio; *we're doing a good trade today,* estamos vendiendo mucho hoy. **2** (*business*) negocio; (*industry*) industria: *my parents are in the antique trade,* mis padres se dedican al negocio de las antigüedades; *the building trade has suffered a decline,* la construcción ha experimentado un descenso; *Spain relies heavily on the tourist trade,* España vive principalmente del turismo. **3** (*occupation*) oficio, profesión *f: he's a carpenter by trade,* es carpintero de oficio; *printing is a dying trade,* el oficio de impresor está desapareciendo. **4** (*people who work in particular industry*) comerciantes *mpl,* gente *f* del negocio: *they give discounts to the trade,* ofrecen descuentos a los comerciantes. – **5** *adj* comercial. – **6** *i* (*do business*) comerciar: *he trades in textiles,* comercia en textiles; *they have stopped trading with Cuba,* han dejado de tener tratos comerciales con Cuba. – **7** *t* (*exchange*) cambiar: *I'll trade my bike for your stereo,* cambiaré mi bici por tu estéreo.
◆ **to trade in** *t sep* dar como parte del pago. ‖ **to trade on** *t* explotar, aprovecharse de.
● **to do a good/brisk/roaring trade in sth.,** hacer un gran negocio con algo, vender algo como pan caliente.
■ **trade cycle,** ciclo comercial. ‖ **trade deficit / trade gap,** déficit *m* comercial. ‖ **trade discount,** descuento comercial. ‖ **trade fair,** feria de muestras. ‖ **trade name,** nombre *m* comercial. ‖ **trade price,** precio al por mayor. ‖ **trade secret,** secreto industrial. ‖ **trade union,** sindicato, gremio obrero. ‖ **trade unionism,** sindicalismo. ‖ **trade unionist,** sindicalista *mf.* ‖ **trade winds,** vientos *mpl* alisios.
trademark ['treɪdmɑːk] *n* marca registrada, marca.
trader ['treɪdəʳ] *n* comerciante *mf.*
tradesman ['treɪdzmən] **1** *n* (*businessman*) comerciante *m;* (*shopkeeper*) tendero. **2** (*deliveryman*) repartidor *m.*
■ **tradesman's entrance,** puerta de servicio.
trading ['treɪdɪŋ] *n* comercio.
■ **trading estate,** polígono industrial. ‖ **trading post,** *establecimiento comercial pequeño en una zona poco habitada.* ‖ **trading stamp,** cupón *m.*
tradition [trə'dɪʃən] *n* tradición *f.*
traditional [trə'dɪʃənəl] *adj* tradicional.
traditionalist [trə'dɪʃənəlɪst] *n* tradicionalista *mf.*
traditionally [trə'dɪʃənəlɪ] *adv* tradicionalmente.
traduce [trə'djuːs] *t* US calumniar, difamar.
traffic ['træfɪk] **1** *n* AUTO tráfico, circulación *f,* tránsito: *there's heavy traffic today,* hay circulación intensa hoy.

2 (*of ships, aircraft*) tráfico. **3** (*of people, goods*) tránsito, movimiento. **4** (*trade*) tráfico: *drug traffic,* tráfico de drogas. – **5** *adj* de la circulación, del tráfico. – **6** *i* traficar (**in,** en): *he trafficked in arms,* traficaba en armas. ■ **traffic jam,** atasco, embotellamiento. ‖ **traffic lights,** semáforo.

trafficker [ˈtræfɪkəʳ] *n* traficante *mf: drug trafficker,* narcotraficante.

tragedy [ˈtrædʒədɪ] *n* tragedia.
▲ *pl* **tragedies**.

tragic [ˈtrædʒɪk] *adj* trágico,-a.

tragically [ˈtrædʒɪkəlɪ] *adv* trágicamente.

tragicomedy [trædʒɪˈkɒmədɪ] *n* tragicomedia.
▲ *pl* **tragicomedies**.

trail [treɪl] **1** *n* (*path*) camino, sendero. **2** (*track, mark, scent*) rastro, pista, huellas *fpl*. **3** (*of rocket, comet*) cola; (*of dust, vapour*) estela; (*of blood*) reguero. – **4** *t* (*follow*) seguir la pista de. **5** (*drag*) arrastrar. – **6** *i* (*lag behind*) ir rezagado,-a, quedarse atrás: *the others trailed way behind,* los demás iban muy rezagados; *this country is trailing behind in space research,* este país está quedando atrás en investigación espacial. **7** (*drag*) arrastrarse. **8** (*plant*) arrastrarse, trepar. **9** (*lose*) perder: *Chelsea are trailing by two goals to nil,* el Chelsea pierde por dos goles a zero; *the socialists are trailing in the opinion polls,* los socialistas pierden según los sondeos de opinión.
◆ **to trail away / trail off** *i* (*voice*) irse apagando.
● **to leave a trail of destruction,** arrasar todo a pasar. ‖ **to trail one's coat,** incitar, provocar.

trailblazer [ˈtreɪlblaɪzəʳ] *n* pionero,-a.

trailer [ˈtreɪləʳ] **1** *n* AUTO remolque *m.* **2** US caravana. **3** CINEM tráiler *m,* avance *m.*

train [treɪn] **1** *n* (*transport*) tren *m: some got on the train and some got off,* unos subieron al tren y otros bajaron; *I changed trains at Miranda,* hice transbordo en Miranda. **2** (*of dress*) cola. **3** (*line - of animals*) recua; (*- of vehicles*) convoy *m.* **4** (*retinue*) grupo, séquito. **5** (*of ideas, thoughts*) serie *f,* hilo; (*of events*) serie *f,* sucesión *f.* – **6** *t* SP entrenar, preparar. **7** (*teach*) enseñar, formar, capacitar: *to train the mind,* formar la mente; *he trained us to fight,* nos enseñó a luchar; *the police are trained to shoot,* se enseña a la policía a disparar. **8** (*one's eye, ear, voice*) educar. **9** MIL adiestrar. **10** (*animal*) enseñar; (*to perform tricks*) amaestrar, adiestrar. **11** (*direct - gun*) apuntar (**on,** a); (*- camera*) enfocar (**on,** a), dirigir (**on,** hacia); (*- plant*) guiar. – **12** *i* SP entrenarse, prepararse: *he was training for the marathon,* se entrenaba para (correr) el maratón. **13** (*teach*) estudiar: *she trained to be a teacher,* estudió magisterio; *he was trained as a nurse,* estudió enfermería. **14** MIL adiestrarse.
● **in train,** en fase de preparación. ‖ **to bring in its train,** acarrear, traer como consecuencia.
■ **train driver,** maquininsta *mf.* ‖ **train set,** juego de trenes. ‖ **train spotter,** coleccionista de números de trenes.

trained [treɪnd] **1** *adj* (*worker - skilled*) calificado,-a, cualificado,-a; (*- qualified*) graduado,-a, diplomado,-a. **2** (*animal*) amaestrado,-a, adiestrado,-a. **3** (*voice, ear*) educado,-a.

trainee [treɪˈniː] **1** *n* (*manual work*) aprendiz,-za. **2** (*professional work*) persona que está haciendo prácticas.
■ **management trainee,** persona que está haciendo prácticas de gerente.

trainer [ˈtreɪnəʳ] **1** *n* SP entrenador,-ra. **2** (*of dogs*) amaestrador,-ra; (*of circus animals*) domador,-ra; (*of race horses*) preparador,-ra. **3** (*aircraft*) entrenador *m.* **4** (*shoe*) zapatilla de deporte.

training [ˈtreɪnɪŋ] **1** *n* formación *f* (profesional), capacitación *f.* **2** SP entrenamiento, preparación *f* física. – **3** *i* MIL instrucción *f.*

● **to be in training (for sth.),** SP entrenarse (para algo).
■ **training college,** instituto de formación profesional. ‖ **training course,** cursillo de capacitación. ‖ **training shoe,** zapatilla de deporte.

traipse [treɪps] *i* recorrerse a pie, patearse.

trait [treɪt] *n* rasgo, característico.

traitor [ˈtreɪtəʳ] *n* traidor,-ra: *he was a traitor to his country,* traicionó a su país.
● **to turn traitor,** pasarse al enemigo.

trajectory [trəˈdʒektərɪ] *n* trayectoria.
▲ *pl* **trajectories**.

tram [træm] *n* tranvía *m.*

tramlines [ˈtræmlaɪnz] **1** *npl* (*of tram*) carriles *mpl* de tranvía. **2** SP (*in tennis*) líneas *fpl* laterales.

tramp [træmp] **1** *n* (*person*) vagabundo,-a. **2** caminata, excursión *f* a pie. **3** US *sl* fulana, puta. – **4** *t* andar por, recorrer a pie. – **5** *i* (*walk*) caminar (con pasos pesados), andar penosamente; (*hike*) recorrer.
■ **tramp steamer,** vapor *m* volandero.

trample [ˈtræmpəl] **1** *t* pisotear: *the tourists trampled the grass,* los turistas pisotearon la hierba; *a child was trampled to death,* un niño murió aplastado. – **2** *i* pisotear (**on/over,** -).

trampoline [ˈtræmpəliːn] *n* cama elástica.

trance [trɑːns] *n* trance *m: she went into a trance,* entró en trance.

tranquil [ˈtræŋkwɪl] *adj* tranquilo,-a.

tranquillity [træŋˈkwɪlətɪ] *n* tranquilidad *f.*

tranquillize [ˈtræŋkwɪlaɪz] *t* tranquilizar.

tranquillizer [ˈtræŋkwɪlaɪzəʳ] *n* tranquilizante *m,* calmante *m: she's on tranquillizers,* toma tranquilizantes.

trans[1] [trænzˈleɪtɪd] *abbr* (*translated*) traducido,-a; (*abbreviation*) trad.

trans[2] [ˈtrænsɪtɪv] *abbr* (*transitive*) transitivo,-a; (*abbreviation*) trans.

transact [trænˈzækt] **1** *t* negociar. – **2** *i* negociar.
● **to transact business with sb.,** hacer negocios con algn.

transaction [trænˈzækʃən] **1** *n* (*deal*) operación *f,* transacción *f.* **2** (*business*) negocio.

transatlantic [trænzətˈlæntɪk] *adj* transatlántico,-a.

transcend [trænˈsend] **1** *t* (*go beyong*) trascender. **2** (*surpass*) superar.

transcendent [trænˈsendənt] *adj* trascendente.

transcendental [trænsenˈdentəl] *adj* trascendental.
■ **transcendental meditation,** meditación *f* transcendental.

transcontinental [trænzkɒntɪˈnentəl] *adj* transcontinental.

transcribe [trænˈskraɪb] *t* transcribir, trascribir.

transcript [ˈtrænskrɪpt] *n* transcripción *f.*

transcription [trænˈskrɪpʃən] *n* transcripción *f: phonetic transcription,* transcripción fonética.

transept [ˈtrænsept] *n* crucero.

transfer [ˈtrænsfɜːʳ] **1** *n* FIN transferencia. **2** JUR (*of property*) traspaso. **3** (*of employee*) traslado. **4** SP (*of player*) traspaso; (*player*) fichaje *m.* **5** (*drawing*) cromo, calcomanía. **6** (*of airline passenger*) transbordo, trasbordo. – *t* FIN transferir: *I've transferred £100 into your account,* he transferido 100 libras a tu cuenta. **8** JUR (*property*) traspasar. **9** (*employee, prisioner*) trasladar: *he was transferred to another branch,* lo trasladaron a otra sucursal. **10** SP (*player*) traspasar. **11** (*data, information, 'phone call*) pasar. – **12** *i* (*employee*) trasladarse: *she's transferred to another department,* se ha trasladado a otro departamento. **13**

(transport) hacer transbordo, cambiar. **14** EDUC cambiar: *I'd like to transfer to another course,* me gustaría cambiar de curso.
■ **transfer fee,** traspaso. ‖ **transfer list,** lista de traspasos.
▲ *(verbo)* [træns'fɜːʳ], pt & pp *transferred,* ger *transferring.*

transferable [træns'fɜːrəbəl] *adj* transferible.
transfiguration [trænsfɪgəˈreɪʃən] *n* transfiguración *f.*
transfigure [trænsˈfɪgəʳ] *t* transfigurar, transformar.
transfix [trænsˈfɪks] **1** *t* *(render motionless)* paralizar. **2** *(impale)* traspasar, atravesar.
● **to be transfixed,** quedarse paralizado,-a.
transform [trænsˈfɔːm] **1** *t* transformar: *this area has been completely transformed,* han transformado esta zona por completo. – **2** *i* transformarse **(into,** en), convertirse **(into,** en).
transformation [trænsfəˈmeɪʃən] *n* transformación *f.*
transformer [trænsˈfɔːməʳ] *n* ELEC transformador *m.*
transfuse [trænsˈfjuːz] *t* hacer una transfusión de.
transfusion [trænsˈfjuːʒən] *n* transfusión *f*: *blood transfusion,* transfusión *f* de sangre.
transgress [trænsˈgres] **1** *t* *(break moral principle)* transgredir, violar. **2** *(go beyond)* traspasar, exceder.
transgression [trænsˈgreʃən] *n* transgresión *f,* violación *f.*
transient [ˈtrænzɪənt] *adj* transitorio,-a, pasajero,-a.
transistor [trænˈzɪstəʳ] *n* transistor *m.*
■ **transistor radio,** transistor *m.*
transit [ˈtrænsɪt] *n* tránsito, paso.
● **in transit,** en tránsito, en el viaje.
■ **transit camp,** campamento provisional. ‖ **transit lounge,** sala de tránsito. ‖ **transit van,** furgoneta. ‖ **transit visa,** visado de tránsito.
transition [trænˈzɪʃən] *n* transición *f.*
transitional [trænˈzɪʃənəl] *adj* transicional.
transitive [ˈtrænsɪtɪv] *adj* transitivo,-a.
transitory [ˈtrænsɪtəɾɪ] *adj* transitorio,-a.
translate [trænsˈleɪt] **1** *t* *(gen)* traducir **(from,** de) **(into,** a): *how do you translate "watch"?,* ¿cómo se traduce "watch"?; *this book has been translated into many languages,* este libro ha sido traducido a muchos idiomas. **2** *(express, explain)* expresar. **3** *(transform)* transformar. – **4** *i* *(person)* traducir; *(word, book, etc)* traducirse.
translation [trænsˈleɪʃən] *n* traducción *f.*
● **to read sth. in translation,** leer algo traducido,-a.
translator [trænsˈleɪtəʳ] *n* traductor,-ra.
translucent [trænzˈluːsənt] *adj* translúcido,-a.
transmission [trænzˈmɪʃən] *n* transmisión *f.*
transmit [trænzˈmɪt] *t* transmitir **(to,** a).
▲ pt & pp *transmitted,* ger *transmitting.*
transmitter [trænzˈmɪtəʳ] *n* transmisor *m.*
transom [ˈtrænsəm] **1** *n* *(traverse)* travesaño. **2** *(separating door from window)* dintel *m.* **3** US *(fanlight)* montante *m.*
transparency [trænsˈpeərənsɪ] **1** *n* *(quality)* transparencia. **2** *(slide)* diapositiva; *(acetate)* transparencia.
▲ pl *transparencies.*
transparent [trænsˈpeərənt] **1** *adj* transparente. **2** *fig* claro,-a, evidente.
transpiration [trænspɪˈreɪʃən] *n* transpiración *f.*
transpire [trænsˈpaɪəʳ] **1** *t* *(plants)* transpirar. – **2** *i* *(become known)* resultar: *it transpired that ...,* resultó ser que ... **3** *fam* *(happen)* pasar, ocurrir: *it is not known exactly what transpired,* no se sabe exactamente lo que ocurrió.
transplant [ˈtrænsplɑːnt] **1** *n* trasplante *m*: *he had a heart transplant,* le hicieron un trasplante de corazón. – **2** *t* trasplantar.

■ **hair transplant,** implante *m* de cabello.
▲ En *acepción 2 (verbo)* [trænsˈplɑːnt].
transport [ˈtrænspɔːt] **1** *n* transporte *m*: *we use public transport,* utilizamos el transporte público; *air transport,* transporte aéreo. – **2** *t* transportar. **3** HIST deportar.
■ **transport café,** restaurante *m* de carretera. ‖ **transport plane,** avión *m* de transporte. ‖ **transport ship,** buque *m* de transporte.
▲ *(verbo)* [trænsˈpɔːt].
transportable [trænsˈpɔːtəbəl] *adj* transportable.
transportation [trænspɔːˈteɪʃən] *n* transporte *m.*
transporter [trænsˈpɔːtəʳ] *n* transportador *m.*
transpose [trænsˈpəʊz] **1** *t* *(words, letters)* transponer, trasponer. **2** MUS transportar.
transsexual [trænsˈsekʃʊəl] *n* transexual *mf.*
transship [trænˈʃɪp] *t* transbordar.
▲ pt & pp *transshipped,* ger *transshipping.*
transversal [trænzˈvɜːsəl] *adj* transversal.
transverse [trænzˈvɜːs] *adj* transversal.
transvestite [trænzˈvestaɪt] *n* travestido,-a, travesti *m,* travestí *m.*
trap [træp] **1** *n* *(gen)* trampa. **2** *fam* *(mouth)* boca: *keep your trap shut,* cállate. **3** *(vehicle)* coche *m* ligero de dos ruedas. **4** *(of drain)* sifón *m.* – **5** *t* *(catch - gen)* atrapar; *(snare - animal)* cazar; *(imprison)* entrampar; *(part of body)* pillar: *they were trapped in the building,* quedaron atrapados en el edificio. **6** SP *(in football)* parar con el pie. **7** *fig* *(trick)* engañar, tender una trampa a: *they trapped me into telling them,* me sacaron la información engañándome. **8** *(heat, light, etc)* retener.
● **to lay a trap / set a trap,** tender una trampa, poner una trampa. ‖ **to fall into a trap,** caer en una trampa.
▲ *(verbo)* pt & pp *trapped,* ger *trapping.*
trapdoor [ˈtræpdɔːʳ] *n* *(gen)* trampilla; *(in theatre)* escotillón *m.*
trapeze [trəˈpiːz] *n* trapecio.
■ **trapeze artist,** trapecista *mf.*
trapezium [trəˈpiːzɪəm] *n* GB trapecio.
trapezoid [ˈtræpɪzɔɪd] *n* GB trapezoide *m.*
trapper [ˈtræpəʳ] *n* cazador,-ra, trampero,-a.
trappings [ˈtræpɪŋz] **1** *npl* *(paraphernalia)* parafernalia, símbolos *mpl*: *he enjoyed all the trappings of success,* disfrutaba de todo aquello que el éxito conlleva. **2** *of horse,* arreos *mpl.*
Trappist [ˈtræpɪst] **1** *n* REL trapense *m.* – **2** *adj* trapense.
trash [træʃ] **1** *n* porquería, basura, bodrio: *this book is pure trash,* este libro es pura basura. **2** US *(rubbish)* basura. **3** US *(people)* gente *f* despreciable.
■ **trash can,** cubo de la basura.
trashy [ˈtræʃɪ] *adj* malo,-a, que no vale para nada.
▲ comp *trashier,* superl *trashiest.*
trauma [ˈtrɔːmə] *n* trauma *m.*
traumatic [trɔːˈmætɪk] *adj* traumático,-a.
travel [ˈtrævəl] **1** *n* viajes *mpl,* viajar *m*: *we share a love of travel,* a los dos nos encanta viajar. – **2** *t* viajar por, recorrer: *he's travelled the whole of Spain,* ha viajado por toda España; *we've travelled 100 kms,* hemos hecho 100 kms. – **3** *i* *(make a journey)* viajar: *I love travelling,* me encanta viajar; *she travels to work by car,* va al trabajo en coche; *they travelled round the world,* dieron la vuelta al mundo. **4** *(move, go)* ir: *do you know what speed you were travelling at?,* ¿sabe a qué velocidad iba?; *light travels faster than sound,* la luz viaja más rápido que el sonido; *news travels fast,* las noticias vuelan. **5** *(go fast)* ir rápido, ir a toda velocidad. **6** *(as*

salesperson) ser viajante, ser representante. **7** (*wine, food, etc*) poderse transportar. – **8 travels,** *npl* (*journeys*) viajes *mpl.*
■ **travel agency,** agencia de viajes. ‖ **travel agent,** agente *mf* de viajes.

travelled [ˈtrævəld] *adj* que ha viajado: *she's a well-travelled person,* es una persona que ha viajado mucho.

traveller [ˈtrævələˈ] **1** *n* (*gen*) viajero,-a. **2** COMM viajante *mf,* representante *mf.* **3** GB *persona que lleva una vida de nómada.*
■ **traveller's cheque,** cheque *m* de viaje.

travelling [ˈtrævəlɪŋ] **1** *adj* (*exhibition etc*) ambulante. **2** (*bag, clock etc*) de viaje. – **3** *n* viajar *m,* viajes *mpl.*
■ **travelling expenses,** gastos *mpl* de viaje. ‖ **travelling salesman,** viajante *mf,* representante *mf.*

travelogue [ˈtrævəlɒg] *n* (*film*) documental *m;* (*lecture*) conferencia sobre viajar.

travel-sick [ˈtrævəlsɪk] *adj* mareado,-a.

travel-sickness [ˈtrævəlsɪknəs] *n* mareo.

traverse [trəˈvɜːs] **1** *t* cruzar, atravesar. – **2** *n* ARCH travesaño. **3** (*mountaineering*) travesía.

travesty [ˈtrævəstɪ] **1** *n* parodia (**of,** de). – **2** *t* parodiar.
▲ (*sustantivo*) *pl* **travesties;** (*verbo*) *pt & pp* **travestied,** *ger* **travestying.**

trawl [trɔːl] **1** *n* (*net*) red *f* de arrastre. – **2** *t* (*fish*) pescar (con red de arrastre). **3** (*search*) buscar (**for,** -). – **4** *i* pescar al arrastre.
■ **trawl line,** palangre *m,* espinel *m.*

trawler [ˈtrɔːləˈ] *n* pesquero de arrastre.

tray [treɪ] **1** *n* (*for food*) bandeja. **2** (*for papers*) caja, cesta. **3** (*in photography*) cubeta.

treacherous [ˈtretʃərəs] **1** *adj* (*person*) traidor,-ra, traicionero,-a. **2** (*dangerous*) muy peligroso,-a, traicionero,-a.

treachery [ˈtretʃərɪ] *n* traición *f.*
▲ *pl* **treacheries.**

treacle [ˈtriːkəl] *n* GB melaza.

tread [tred] **1** *n* (*manner or sound of walking*) paso, pasos *mpl: he walks with a heavy tread,* anda con pasos pesados. **2** (*on tyre*) banda de rodadura, dibujo. **3** (*on stair*) escalón *m.* – **4** *t* (*gen*) pisar, pisotear: *he trod his cigarette into the carpet,* apagó su cigarrillo pisándolo en la moqueta; *the locals tread the grapes,* los del lugar pisan la uva. **5** (*walk on*) andar por; (*make*) hacer. – **6** *i* pisar, poner el pie (**on,** -): *don't tread in that dog muck!,* no pises esa caca!; *you're treading on my foot,* me estás pisando.
● **to tread on sb.'s corns/toes,** ofender a algn. ‖ **to tread the boards,** pisar las tablas. ‖ **to tread warily/carefully/lightly,** andar con pies de plomo. ‖ **to tread water,** pedalear en el agua.
▲ (*verbo*) *pt* **trod,** *pp* **trodden** *o* **trod.**

treadle [ˈtredəl] *n* pedal *m.*

treadmill [ˈtredmɪl] **1** *n* HIST (*punishment*) rueda de castigo. **2** *fig* rutina.

treas [ˈtreʒərəˈ] *abbr* (*treasurer*) tesorero,-a.

treason [ˈtriːzən] *n* traición *f.*

treasure [ˈtreʒəˈ] **1** *n* (*gen*) tesoro, tesoros *mpl.* **2** (*valued person*) tesoro, joya. – **3** *t* (*value, cherish*) apreciar mucho, valorar mucho.
◆ **to treasure up** *t sep* guardar como un tesoro, atesorar.
■ **treasure hunt,** caza del tesoro. ‖ **treasure trove,** tesoro encontrado.

treasurer [ˈtreʒərəˈ] *n* tesorero,-a.

treasury [ˈtreʒərɪ] *n* tesorería.
■ **Treasury Department,** Ministerio de Hacienda. ‖ **Treasury bill,** bono del Tesoro.

▲ *pl* **treasuries.**

treat [triːt] **1** *n* (*meal, drink*) convite *m: it's my treat,* invito yo. **2** (*present*) regalo. **3** (*pleasure*) placer *m,* gusto, deleite *m.* – **4** *t* (*act, behave towards*) tratar: *why don't you treat me like an adult?,* ¿por qué no me tratas como a un adulto?; *I was treated as one of the family,* me trataron como a uno (más) de la familia. **5** (*subject*) tratar: *this will be treated with the utmost confidentiality,* se tratará con total confianza. **6** (*consider, regard*) tomar(se): *he treated it as a joke,* lo tomó en broma. **7** (*invite*) convidar, invitar; (*give*) regalar; (*spoil os.*) permitirse el lujo, darse el gusto: *they treated us to dinner,* nos invitaron a cenar; *she treated the children to a trip to the seaside,* llevó a los niños de excursión a la playa como algo especial; *I treated myself to a new pair of shoes,* me di el gusto de comprarme unos zapatos nuevos. **8** MED (*condition*) tratar, curar; (*person*) atender: *he was treated for hepatitis,* le curaron la hepatitis. **9** TECH (*wood, worm, etc*) tratar (**with,** con).
● **to treat sb. like dirt,** despreciar a algn. ‖ **to work a treat,** funcionar a las mil maravillas.

treatise [ˈtriːtɪs] *n* tratado.

treatment [ˈtriːtmənt] **1** *n* MED tratamiento, cura: *she's undergoing treatment for cancer,* se está sometiendo a un tratamiento contra el cáncer; *he's not responding to treatment,* no responde al tratamiento. **2** (*manner of treating*) trato; (*behaviour*) conducta: *they criticized the treatment of prisioners,* criticaron el trato de los prisioneros. **3** (*process*) tratamiento.
■ **preferential treatment,** trato preferente.

treaty [ˈtriːtɪ] *n* tratado.
▲ *pl* **treaties.**

treble [ˈtrebəl] **1** *adj* (*threefold*) triple. **2** MUS de tiple. – **3** *n* MUS tiple *mf.* – **4** *t* triplicar. – **5** *i* triplicarse.
■ **treble clef,** clave *f* de sol.

tree [triː] *n* árbol *m.*
● **to be at the top of the tree,** estar en la cúspide. ‖ **you can't see the wood for the trees,** los árboles no dejan ver el bosque.
■ **tree surgeon,** arboricultor,-ra. ‖ **tree trunk,** tronco.

treeless [ˈtriːləs] *adj* sin árboles.

tree-lined [ˈtriːlaɪnd] *adj* con árboles en las aceras.

tree-top [ˈtriːtɒp] *n* copa.

trefoil [ˈtrefɔɪl] *n* trébol *m.*

trek [trek] **1** *n* caminata: *it's quite a trek,* queda bien lejos. – **2** *i* caminar, andar.
▲ (*verbo*) *pt & pp* **trekked,** *ger* **trekking.**

trekking [ˈtrekɪŋ] *n* senderismo.

trellis [ˈtrelɪs] *n* (*for plants*) espaldera.

tremble [ˈtrembəl] **1** *n* temblor *m.* – **2** *i* temblar: *she trembled with fear,* temblaba de miedo; *his voice trembled,* le temblaba la voz, su voz temblaba.
● **to be all of a tremble,** temblar como un flan.

tremendous [trɪˈmendəs] **1** *adj* (*huge*) tremendo,-a, inmenso,-a. **2** *fam* (*great*) fantástico,-a, estupendo,-a.

tremor [ˈtreməˈ] *n* temblor *m.*

tremulous [ˈtremjələs] *adj* trémulo,-a, tembloroso,-a.

trench [trentʃ] **1** *n* (*ditch*) zanja. **2** MIL trinchera.
■ **trench coat,** trinchera. ‖ **trench warfare,** guerra de trincheras.

trenchant [ˈtrentʃənt] *adj* cáustico,-a, mordaz.

trend [trend] **1** *n* (*tendency*) tendencia (**to/towards,** hacia), tónica. **2** (*fashion*) moda.
● **to set the trend,** iniciar una moda, imponer un estilo.

trendsetter [ˈtrendsetəˈ] *n* iniciador,-ra de moda.

trendy ['trendɪ] adj fam moderno,-a, de moda: *you look very trendy,* vas a la última.
▲ comp **trendier,** superl **trendiest.**

trepidation [trepɪ'deɪʃən] n turbación f, agitación f: *I asked with trepidation,* pregunté turbado.

trespass ['trespəs] 1 n entrada ilegal. 2 REL pecado. – 3 i (*on land*) entrar sin autorización; (*on patience etc*) abusar de; (*in affairs*) meterse, entrometerse, interferir: *he was fined for trespassing on army land,* lo multaron por entrar ilegalmente en terrenos del ejército. 4 REL pecar (**against**, contra).
● "no trespassing", "prohibido el paso".

trespasser ['trespəsəʳ] n intruso,-a.
● "trespassers will be prosecuted", "prohibido el paso, propiedad privada".

tress [tres] 1 n mechón m. – **2 tresses**, npl melena f sing, cabellera f sing.

trestle ['tresəl] n caballete m.
■ **trestle table**, mesa de caballete.

triad ['traɪæd] n tríada.

trial ['traɪəl] 1 n JUR proceso, juicio: *he went on trial for murder,* lo procesaron por asesinato. 2 (*test*) prueba: *this drug is on trial,* esta droga está a prueba. 3 (*suffering*) aflicción f, sufrimiento; (*trouble*) molestia, problema m: *the trials and tribulations of modern life,* las tribulaciones de la vida moderna; *that child is a trial to his parents,* aquel niño es un problema para sus padres. – **4 trials,** npl sp pruebas fpl.
● **on trial**, a prueba. ‖ **to bring sb. to trial**, procesar a algn. ‖ **to stand trial**, ser procesado,-a.
■ **trial and error**, ensayo y error, prueba y error. ‖ **trial offer**, oferta especial. ‖ **trial period**, período de prueba.

triangle ['traɪæŋgəl] n triángulo.

triangular [traɪ'æŋgjʊləʳ] adj triangular.

tribal ['traɪbəl] adj tribal.

tribe [traɪb] 1 n tribu f. 2 fam (*family*) tribu f, familia.

tribesman ['traɪbzmən] n miembro de una tribu.
▲ pl **tribesmen.**

tribulation [trɪbjʊ'leɪʃən] n tribulación f.

tribunal [traɪ'bjuːnəl] n tribunal m.

tributary ['trɪbjʊtərɪ] 1 n afluente m. – **2** adj tributario,-a.
▲ (*sustantivo*) pl **tributaries.**

tribute ['trɪbjuːt] 1 n (*homage*) homenaje m, tributo. 2 (*payment*) tributo.
● **to pay tribute to sb.**, rendir homenaje a algn.
■ **floral tribute**, ofrenda floral.

trice [traɪs] *in a trice,* phr en un santiamén.

triceps ['traɪseps] npl tríceps m inv.
▲ pl **triceps.**

trick [trɪk] 1 n (*skill, knack*) truco. 2 (*for entertainment*) truco, juego de manos; (*with cards*) juego de naipes; (*by animals*) número. 3 (*deception, ruse*) ardid m, engaño, trampa, truco: *there must be a trick in it,* aquí debe de haber trampa; *you can't fool me with that old trick,* a mí no me engañas con ese viejo truco; *it's a trick of the light,* es un efecto de la luz. 4 (*prank, joke*) broma: *the children are always playing tricks on their friends,* los niños siempre gastan bromas a sus amigos. 5 (*cards won*) baza. 6 (*habit*) hábito, costumbre f, manía. – **7** adj de juguete, de mentira. – **8** t (*deceive*) engañar, burlar: *he realized he'd been tricked,* se dio cuenta de que lo habían engañado.
◆ **to trick out / trick up** i (*decorate*) adornar (**in/with**, con).

● **every trick in the book,** todos los trucos: *he tried every trick in the book,* lo intentó todo. ‖ **how's tricks?,** ¿cómo van las cosas?, ¿qué tal? ‖ **never to miss a trick,** no perderse nada. ‖ **to be up to one's tricks,** hacer de las suyas. ‖ **to do the trick,** funcionar, ser la solución. ‖ **to have a trick up one's sleeve,** guardarse un as en la manga. ‖ **to play a dirty trick on sb.,** jugar una mala pasada a algn. ‖ **to trick sb. into doing sth.,** engañar a algn. para que haga algo: *she tricked him into marrying her,* lo engañó para que se casara con ella. ‖ **to trick sb. out of sth.,** estafar a algn., timar a algn.: *they tried to trick her out of her share of the money,* trataron de estafarle su parte del dinero. ‖ **trick or treat,** US frase de los niños que en Halloween van por las casas pidiendo un regalo a cambio de no hacer una jugarreta.
■ **trick of the trade,** truco del oficio. ‖ **trick photograph,** fotografía trucada. ‖ **trick photography,** trucaje m. ‖ **trick question,** pregunta capciosa.

trickery ['trɪkərɪ] n superchería, engaño.

trickle ['trɪkəl] 1 n goteo, hilo. 2 fig pequeña cantidad f, poco. – **3** i (*liquid*) gotear, salir gota a gota. 4 fig salir (*entrar, llegar, etc*) poco a poco: *refugees have been trickling out of the war zone,* los refugiados han ido saliendo poco a poco de la zona de guerra.

trickster ['trɪkstəʳ] n estafador,-ra, embustero,-a, timador,-ra.

tricky ['trɪkɪ] 1 adj (*person*) taimado,-a, astuto,-a, mañoso,-a. 2 (*problem, situation - difficult*) difícil; (- *delicate*) delicado,-a.
▲ comp **trickier,** superl **trickiest.**

tricolour ['trɪkələʳ] n tricolor f.

tricycle ['traɪsɪkəl] n triciclo.

trident ['traɪdənt] n tridente m.

tried [traɪd] pp → **try.**
● **tried and tested,** de calidad probada.

trier [traɪəʳ] n persona que se esfuerza: *he's a real trier,* se esfuerza al máximo.

trifle ['traɪfəl] 1 n (*unimportant thing*) fruslería, bagatela, nimiedad f, chuchería. 2 (*little money*) poco dinero, insignificancia. 3 GB CULIN postre de bizcocho borracho, fruta, gelatina, crema y nata.
◆ **to trifle with** t insep jugar con: *he's not someone to be trifled with,* es una persona a la que hay que tratar con respeto.
● **a trifle,** un poco, algo.

trifling ['traɪfəlɪŋ] adj insignificante, sin importancia.

trigger ['trɪgəʳ] 1 n (*of gun*) gatillo. 2 (*of camera, machine*) disparador m. – **3 to trigger (off),** t desencadenar, provocar.

trigonometry [trɪgə'nɒmətrɪ] n trigonometría.

trilateral [traɪ'lætərəl] adj trilátero,-a.

trilby ['trɪlbɪ] n sombrero flexible.
▲ pl **trilbies.**

trilingual [traɪ'lɪŋgwəl] adj trilingüe.

trill [trɪl] 1 n (*of birds*) trino, gorjeo. 2 MUS trino. 3 LING vibración f. – **4** i trinar. 5 LING vibrar.

trillion ['trɪlɪən] 1 n GB trillón m. 2 US billón m.

trilogy ['trɪlədʒɪ] n trilogía.
▲ pl **trilogies.**

trim [trɪm] 1 adj (*neat, tidy*) (bien) arreglado,-a, ordenado,-a, cuidado,-a. 2 (*person, figure*) esbelto,-a, delgado,-a: *she has a trim figure,* tiene buen tipo. – **3** n (*cut*) recorte m: *I'd like a trim, please,* ¿me puede cortar las puntas? 4 (*decoration - on clothes*) adornos mpl; (- *along edges*) bordete m; (*upholstery*) tapicería, interior: *a black dress with a red trim,* un vestido negro con un bordete

rojo. **5** MAR asiento, estiba. – **6** t (*make neat*) arreglar; (*cut - hair*) cortar, recortar; (- *hedge etc*) podar: *your hair needs trimming,* tienes que cortarte el pelo. **7** (*reduce by cutting back*) recortar, reducir. **8** (*decorate*) adornar (**with,** con); (*upholster*) tapizar. **9** MAR (*sails*) orientar; (*ship*) equilibrar, asentar.
◆ **to trim off** t *sep* recortar, quitar.
● **to be in trim / in good trim,** estar en forma, estar en buena forma.
▲ (*adjetivo*) *comp* **trimmer,** *superl* **trimmest**; (*verbo*) *pt & pp* **trimmed,** *ger* **trimming.**

trimmings ['trɪmɪŋz] **1** *npl* CULIN (*accompaniments*) guarnición *f sing.* **2** (*decorations*) adornos *mpl.* **3** (*after cutting*) recortes *mpl.*

Trinidad ['trɪnɪdæd] n Trinidad.
■ **Trinidad and Tobago,** Trinidad y Tobago.

Trinity ['trɪnətɪ] **the Trinity,** n REL la Trinidad *f.*
■ **Trinity Sunday,** fiesta de la Trinidad.
▲ *pl* **trinities.**

trinket ['trɪŋkɪt] n chuchería, baratija.

trio ['triːəʊ] n trío.
▲ *pl* **trios.**

trip [trɪp] **1** n (*journey*) viaje *m*: *he's on a trip,* está de viaje. **2** (*excursion*) excursión *f*: *we went on a trip to the seaside,* fuimos de excursión a la playa. **3** (*stumble*) tropezón *m.* **4** *sl* (*on drugs*) viaje *m.* – **5** t hacer tropezar, hacerle una zancadilla a. **6** (*set off - switch, alarm, etc*) activar, hacer que se dispare. – **7** i (*stumble*) tropezar (**over,** con). **8** (*move lightly*) ir con paso ligero. **9** *sl* (*on drugs*) viajar.
◆ **to trip up 1** t *sep* (*make fall*) echar la zancadilla a. **2** (*cause to make a mistake*) hacer equivocar. – **3** i (*fall*) tropezar. **4** (*make a mistake*) equivocarse.
▲ (*verbo*) *pt & pp* **tripped,** *ger* **tripping.**

tripartite [traɪˈpɑːtaɪt] adj tripartito,-a.

tripe [traɪp] **1** n CULIN callos *mpl.* **2** *fam* tonterías *fpl,* bobadas *fpl.*

triple ['trɪpəl] **1** adj triple. – **2** t triplicar. – **3** i triplicarse.
■ **triple jump,** triple salto.

triplet ['trɪplət] **1** n (*child*) trillizo,-a. **2** MUS tresillo.

triplicate ['trɪplɪkət] **1** adj triplicado,-a. – **2** t triplicar.
● **in triplicate,** por triplicado,-a.

tripod ['traɪpɒd] n trípode *m.*

Tripoli ['trɪpəlɪ] n Trípoli.

tripper ['trɪpəʳ] n excursionista *mf.*

trite [traɪt] **1** adj (*subject*) trillado,-a, manido,-a. **2** (*sentiment*) banal.

triumph ['traɪəmf] **1** n triunfo, éxito: *this is a triumph for democracy,* esto es un triunfo para la democracia. **2** (*joy*) júbilo, alegría: *the winners came home in triumph,* los ganadores volvieron a casa triunfantes. – **3** i triunfar (**over,** de/sobre), vencer.

triumphal [traɪˈʌmfəl] adj triunfal.
■ **triumphal arch,** arco de triunfo.

triumphant [traɪˈʌmfənt] adj (*team etc*) triunfador,-ra, victorioso,-a; (*return, entry, etc*) triunfal.

trivia ['trɪvɪə] *npl* trivialidades *fpl.*

trivial ['trɪvɪəl] adj (*unimportant*) trivial, insignificante; (*shallow*) superficial.

triviality [trɪvɪˈælətɪ] n trivialidad *f.*

trivialize ['trɪvɪəlaɪz] t trivializar.

trod [trɒd] *pt & pp* → **tread.**

trodden ['trɒdən] *pp* → **tread.**

Trojan ['trəʊdʒən] **1** n troyano *mf.* – **2** adj troyano,-a.
■ **Trojan horse,** caballo de Troya.

troll [trəʊl] n duende *m.*

trolley ['trɒlɪ] **1** n (*in supermarket, at airport*) carro, carrito. **2** (*in hospital*) cama con ruedas. **3** (*for food*) mesita de ruedas. **4** US tranvía.

● **to be off one's trolley,** estar chiflado,-a.
■ **trolley bus,** trolebús *mf.* ‖ **trolley car,** tranvía *mf.*

trombone [trɒmˈbəʊn] n trombón *m.*

trombonist [trɒmˈbəʊnɪst] n trombón *mf.*

troop [truːp] **1** n (*group*) grupo. **2** MIL tropa. – **3** i ir en tropel. – **4 troops,** *npl* soldados *mpl,* tropas *fpl.*
● **to troop the colour,** desfilar con la bandera.

trooper ['truːpəʳ] n soldado de caballería.

trophy ['trəʊfɪ] n trofeo.
▲ *pl* **trophies.**

tropic ['trɒpɪk] **1** n trópico. – **2 the tropics,** *npl* los trópicos *mpl.*
■ **Tropic of Cancer,** trópico de Cáncer. ‖ **Tropic of Capricorn,** trópico de Capricornio.

tropical ['trɒpɪkəl] adj tropical.

trot [trɒt] **1** n trote *m*: *he broke into a trot,* empezó a trotar. – **2** t hacer trotar. – **3** i (*gen*) trotar, ir al trote; (*on horse*) cabalgar al trote. **4** *fam* (*go*) ir. – **5 the trots,** *npl fam* diarrea *f sing.*
◆ **to trot out 1** t *sep* (*excuses, arguments*) salir con, soltar. **2** (*names, list*) recitar de memoria.
● **on the trot,** (*one after the other*) seguidos,-as; (*continually busy*) siempre ocupado,-a. ‖ **to have the trots,** tener cagalera.

troth [trəʊθ] n fe *f.*
● **by my troth,** a fe mía. ‖ **to plight one's troth,** hacer promesa de matrimonio.

trotter ['trɒtəʳ] n (*horse*) trotón,-ona.
■ **pig's trotter,** mano de cerdo.

troubadour ['truːbədɔːʳ] n trovador *m.*

trouble ['trʌbəl] **1** n (*problems*) problema *m,* *mpl*: *did you have any trouble parking?,* ¿has tenido problemas para aparcar?; *I had the same trouble when I went there,* tuve el mismo problema cuando fui allí; *she has money troubles,* tiene problemas económicos; *the plane had engine trouble,* el avión tenía problemas de motor; *you know what your trouble is, don't you?,* sabes cuál es tu problema, ¿verdad?; *their son is in trouble with the police,* su hijo tiene problemas con la policía; *I'm in real trouble,* estoy metido en un buen lío; *I didn't mean to get you into trouble,* no quise meterte en líos; *that's the least of my troubles,* eso es lo que menos me preocupa. **2** (*inconvenience, bother*) molestia, esfuerzo: *it's no trouble,* no es molestia; *were the children any trouble?,* ¿te han causado alguna molestia los niños?; *I hope I've not put you to any trouble,* espero que no haya sido molestia; *she went to the trouble of preparing a meal,* se molestó en preparar una comida; *at least he took the trouble to reply,* al menos se tomó la molestia de contestar; *it's not worth the trouble,* no vale la pena. **3** MED problema *m,* enfermedad *f*: *he has heart trouble,* tiene problemas de corazón; *what seems to be the trouble?,* ¿qué le pasa? **4** (*unrest, disturbance*) conflictos *mpl,* disturbios *mpl*: *there's been some trouble at the pub,* ha habido jaleo en el pub; *people often talk about the troubles in Northern Ireland,* muchas veces se habla de los conflictos en Irlanda del Norte. – **5** t (*cause worry, distress*) preocupar, inquietar: *what's troubling you?,* ¿qué te preocupa? **6** (*hurt*) dar problemas a, doler: *my back's troubling me,* la espalda me está dando problemas. **7** (*bother*) molestar, incomodar: *I'm sorry to trouble you, but ...,* siento molestarle, pero ...; *may I trouble you for the salt?,* ¿sería tan amable de pasarme la sal?; *don't touble yourself!,* ¡no se moleste! – **8** i molestarse, preocuparse (**about,** por): *he didn't even trouble to look at it,* ni siquiera se molestó en mirarlo.
● **it's more trouble than it's worth,** no merece la

pena. ‖ **that's asking for trouble,** eso es buscársela. ‖ **to get sb. into trouble,** *fam* dejar embarazada a una mujer. ‖ **to look for trouble,** buscarse problemas, buscar camorra.

■ **trouble spot,** punto conflictivo.

troubled ['trʌbəld] **1** *adj* (*person, look*) preocupado,-a, inquieto,-a. **2** (*period*) turbulento,-a, agitado,-a.

trouble-free ['trʌbəlfriː] *adj* sin problemas, tranquilo,-a; (*demonstration etc*) sin incidentes.

troublemaker ['trʌbəlmeɪkəʳ] *n* alborotador,-ra.

troubleshooter ['trʌbəlʃuːtəʳ] *n* (*mediator*) conciliador,-ra, mediador,-ra.

troublesome ['trʌbəlsəm] *adj* (*thing*) molesto,-a, fastidioso,-a; (*person*) difícil, problemático,-a; (*situation*) problemático,-a, conflictivo,-a.

trough [trɒf] **1** *n* (*for drinking*) abrevadero; (*for eating*) comedero, pesebre *m*. **2** (*channel*) canal *m*; (*gutter*) canalón *m*. **3** METEOR depresión *f*, zona de bajas presiones. **4** (*depression - in land*) depresión *f*, hoya; (*between waves*) seno. **5** (*low point in cycle*) parte *f* baja, punto más bajo.

trounce [traʊns] *t* (*thrash*) zurrar, dar una paliza a; (*defeat*) derrotar.

troupe [truːp] *n* compañía, grupo.

trouper ['truːpəʳ] *n* actor *m*, actriz *f*.

trouser ['traʊzə] *adj* del pantalón.

■ **trouser suit,** traje *m* pantalón. ‖ **trouser press,** plancha para pantalones.

trousers ['traʊzəz] *npl* pantalón *m sing*, pantalones *mpl*.

trousseau ['truːsəʊ] *n* ajuar *m* de novia.

▲ *plural* **trousseaus** o **trousseaux**.

trout [traʊt] *n* trucha: *we went trout fishing,* fuimos a pescar truchas.

■ **old trout,** vieja bruja.

trowel ['traʊəl] **1** *n* (*bricklaying tool*) paleta. **2** (*garden tool*) desplantador *m*.

Troy [trɔɪ] *n* Troya.

truancy ['truːənsɪ] *n* ausentismo escolar.

truant ['truːənt] *n* (*from school*) persona que hace novillos.

● **to play truant,** hacer novillos, faltar a clase.

truce [truːs] *n* tregua.

● **to call a truce,** acordar una tregua.

truck [trʌk] **1** *n* (*lorry*) camión *m*. **2** GB (*railway wagon*) vagón *m*. **3** US (*fruit, vegetables*) productos *mpl* agrícolas. **4** (*dealings*) tratos *mpl*.

● **to have no truck with sb.,** no querer saber nada de algn., no tener trato con algn.

■ **truck driver,** camionero,-a. ‖ **truck farm,** huerta.

trucker ['trʌkəʳ] *n* US camionero,-a.

truckle ['trʌkəl] **to truckle (to),** *i* rendirse a, someterse a.

truckload ['trʌkləʊd] *n* (*lorry*) camión *m* lleno; (*railway wagon*) vagón *m* lleno.

● **by the truckload,** a montones, en cantidades industriales.

truculence ['trʌkjʊləns] *n* agresividad *f*, hostilidad *f*.

truculent ['trʌkjʊlənt] *adj* agresivo,-a, hostil.

trudge [trʌdʒ] **1** *i* andar con dificultad. **– 2** *n* caminata (larga y difícil).

true [truː] **1** *adj* (*not false*) verdadero,-a, cierto,-a: *it's true,* es cierto, es verdad. **2** (*genuine, real*) auténtico,-a, genuino,-a, real: *true story,* historia real. **3** (*faithful*) fiel, leal. **4** (*exact*) exacto,-a. **5** (*accurate - aim*) acertado,-a. **6** (*straight, level - wall*) a plomo; (*- surface, level*) a nivel, nivelado,-a; (*- wheel*) centrado,-a. **– 7** *adv* (*truthfully*) sinceramente. **8** (*accurately*) bien: *he aimed true,* apuntó bien.

● **to be out of true,** (*wall*) no estar a plomo; (*surface*) no estar a nivel; (*wheel*) estar descentrado,-a. ‖ **to be true to life,** ser realista. ‖ **to come true,** realizarse, hacerse realidad, cumplirse. ‖ **true to form,** como siempre, como era de esperar.

true-blue ['truːbluː] **1** *adj* leal, fiel. **2** POL hasta la médula.

true-life ['truːlaɪf] *adj* real.

truffle ['trʌfəl] *n* trufa.

truism ['truːɪzəm] *n* perogrullada.

truly ['truːlɪ] **1** *adv* (*really*) verdaderamente, de verdad, realmente. **2** (*sincerely*) sinceramente. **3** (*faithfully*) fielmente, lealmente.

● **yours truly,** (*in letters*) atentamente; (*myself*) servidor,-ra, menda.

trump [trʌmp] **1** *n* (*cards*) triunfo. **– 2** *t* (*cards*) ganar con un triunfo. **– 3** **trumps,** *npl* triunfo: *what are trumps?,* ¿qué triunfan?; *clubs are trumps,* triunfan tréboles.

◆ **to trump up** *t sep* inventar, falsificar.

● **to turn up trumps / come up trumps,** (*be helpful*) ayudar, sacar de un apuro; (*save the day*) salvar la situación; (*not fail*) no fallar: *Dave turned up trumps and lent me some cash,* Dave me sacó de un apuro y me dejó dinero.

■ **trump card,** (*gen*) triunfo; *fig* baza.

trumpet ['trʌmpɪt] **1** *n* MUS trompeta. **– 2** *i* fanfarronear. **3** (*elephant*) barritar.

● **to blow one's own trumpet,** tirarse flores, darse bombo.

trumpeter ['trʌmpɪtəʳ] *n* trompetero,-a.

truncate [trʌŋ'keɪt] **1** *t* truncar. **– 2** *adj* truncado,-a.

truncheon ['trʌntʃən] *n* porra (de policía).

trundle ['trʌndəl] **1** *t* (*move on wheels*) hacer rodar; (*move*) mover (con dificultad). **– 2** *i* (*vehicles*) rodar (con mucho ruido), rodar (pesadamente); (*people*) ir(se) (pesadamente): *the bus trundled up the hill,* el autobús subió la colina con dificultad; *he trundled off to the pub,* se fue pesadamente al bar.

trunk [trʌŋk] **1** *n* (*of tree, body*) tronco. **2** (*large case*) baúl *m*. **3** (*elephant's*) trompa. **4** US AUTO maletero.

■ **trunk call,** conferencia, llamada interurbana. ‖ **trunk line,** (*railway*) línea principal; (*telephone*) línea interurbana. ‖ **trunk road,** carretera principal.

trunks [trʌŋks] *npl* bañador *m sing* (de hombre).

truss [trʌs] **1** *t* (*tie*) atar (**up,** -). **2** ARCH apuntalar. **– 3** *n* MED braguero. **4** ARCH cuchillo de armadura. **5** (*of hay*) haz *m*, lío. **6** (*of tomatoes etc*) racimo; (*of flowers*) ramo.

trust [trʌst] **1** *n* (*confidence*) confianza: *our relationship is based on trust,* nuestra relación se basa en la confianza; *there's been a breach of trust,* ha habido un abuso de confianza. **2** (*responsibility*) responsabilidad *f*: *a position of trust,* un puesto de confianza. **3** FIN (*money, property*) fondo de inversión. **4** JUR (*money or property held or invested for sb.*) fideicomiso. **5** (*foundation*) patronato, fundación *f*. **6** FIN (*cartel*) trust *m*, cartel *m*. **– 7** *t* (*have faith in, rely on*) confiar en, fiarse de: *do you trust me?,* ¿confías en mí?, ¿te fías de mí?; *you can trust him,* es de fiar; *you can't trust what you read,* no te puedes fiar de lo que lees; *I don't trust these newfangled gadgets,* no me fío de estos aparatos tan modernos; *can I trust you to lock up?,* ¿me puedo fiar de que cerrarás con llave?; *she didn't trust me to look after her baby,* no confiaba en mí para que cuidara de su bebé. **8** (*hope, expect*) esperar: *I trust you're all coming to the reunion,* espero que todos vengáis a la reunión. **9** (*entrust*) confiar: *can I trust you with all this money?,* ¿puedo confiarte todo este dinero?; *the child was trusted to my care,* me confiaron el cuidado del bebé. – **10** *i* confiar (**in**, en), tener confianza (**in**, en): *in God we trust,* confiamos en Dios. ● **in trust,** en fideicomiso. ‖ **on trust,** (*without proof*) a ojos cerrados; (*on credit*) a crédito. ‖ **to trust sth. to luck,** dejar algo librado,-a al azar. ‖ **trust you!,** ¡típico! ■ **trust company,** compañía de fideicomiso. ‖ **trust fund,** patronato.

trusted ['trʌstɪd] **1** *adj* (*loyal*) leal, fiel, de confianza. **2** (*remedy*) probado,-a, comprobado,-a.

trustee [trʌs'tiː] **1** *n* (*of money, property*) fideicomisario,-a. **2** (*in bankruptcy*) síndico. **3** (*of institution*) miembro del consejo de administración.

trustful ['trʌstful] *adj* confiado,-a.

trusting ['trʌstɪŋ] *adj* confiado,-a.

trustworthiness ['trʌstwɜːðɪnəs] **1** *n* (*of people*) honradez *f,* formalidad *f.* **2** (*of information*) veracidad *f,* exactitud *f.*

trustworthy ['trʌstwɜːðɪ] **1** *adj* (*person*) digno,-a de confianza, honrado,-a. **2** (*news etc*) fidedigno,-a.

trusty ['trʌstɪ] **1** *adj* fiel, leal. – **2** *n* (*prisoner*) ordenanza *m.*
▲ (*adjetivo*) *comp* **trustier,** *superl* **trustiest;** (*sustantivo*) *pl* **trusties.**

truth [truːθ] **1** *n* (*quality*) verdad *f: the whole truth,* toda la verdad; *the honest truth,* la pura verdad. **2** (*truthfulness*) veracidad *f: the truth of these accounts has not been verified,* no se ha comprobado la veracidad de estas historias.
● **the truth will out,** se pilla antes al mentiroso que al cojo. ‖ **to tell sb. a few home truths,** decirle a algn. cuatro verdades. ‖ **to tell the truth,** decir la verdad.

truthful ['truːθful] **1** *adj* (*account etc*) verídico,-a, veraz. **2** (*person*) sincero,-a, veraz.

truthfully ['truːθfəlɪ] *adv* sinceramente.

truthfulness ['truːθfulnəs] *n* veracidad *f.*

try [traɪ] **1** *n* intento, tentativa: *why don't you give it a try?,* ¿por qué no lo pruebas?; *I think it's worth a try,* creo que vale la pena probarlo; *they gave up after a few tries,* se rindieron después de varios intentos. **2** SP (*rugby*) ensayo. – **3** *t* (*attempt*) intentar: *you tried your best,* hiciste lo que pudiste. **4** (*test, use*) probar, poner a prueba, ensayar; (*food*) probar: *have you ever tried caviar?,* ¿has probado el caviar alguna vez?; *you must try some of our home-made wine,* tienes que probar nuestro vino casero; *why don't we try it with the sofa here and the table over there?,* ¿por qué no lo probamos con el sofá aquí y la mesa allí?; *she tried the door but it was locked,* intentó abrir pero estaba cerrada. **5** JUR juzgar, procesar: *the case was tried before a jury,* el caso fue juzgado por un jurado; *he was tried for murder,* fue procesado por asesinato. **6** (*be a strain on* - *eyes*) cansar; (- *patience, person*) poner a prueba. – **7** *i* (*make an attempt*) intentar: *I don't know if I can do it, but I'll try,* no sé si podré hacerlo, pero lo intentaré; *you're not trying,* no haces ningún esfuerzo; *he tried to swim the Channel but failed,* intentó cruzar el Canal de la Mancha nadando pero no lo logró; *please try to get here on time in future,* procura llegar puntualmente en el futuro; *I tried hard not to laugh,* procuré no reír; *it's trying to snow,* quiere nevar.
◆ **to try for** *i* tratar de obtener. ‖ **to try on** *t sep* (*clothes*) probarse: *would you like to try it on?,* ¿quisiera probárselo? ‖ **to try out** *t sep* probar, ensayar: *try it out on a strand of hair first,* pruébalo en un mechón primero.
● **to try it on with sb.,** ver hasta dónde puede llegar con algn. ‖ **to try one's hand at sth.,** probar algo por primera vez. ‖ **to try one's luck,** probar suerte. ‖ **to try out for sth.,** US hacer una prueba para algo.

▲ (*sustantivo*) *pl* **tries;** (*verbo*) *pt* & *pp* **tried,** *ger* **trying.**

trying ['traɪɪŋ] *adj* molesto,-a, difícil, pesado,-a: *I've had a very trying day,* he tenido un día muy pesado.

tsar [zɑːʳ] *n* zar *m.*

tsarina [zɑː'riːnə] *n* zarina.

tsetse fly ['tsetsɪflaɪ] *n* mosca tsetsé.

tsp ['tiːspuːn] *abbr* (*teaspoon*) cucharadita.
▲ *pl* **tsps.**

tub [tʌb] **1** *n* (*for washing clothes*) balde *m.* **2** (*bath*) bañera, baño. **3** (*food container*) tarrina.

tuba ['tjuːbə] *n* tuba.

tubby ['tʌbɪ] *adj* rechoncho,-a.
▲ *comp* **tubbier,** *superl* **tubbiest.**

tube [tjuːb] **1** *n* (*pipe, container*) tubo. **2** AUTO cámara de aire. **3** **the tube,** la televisión *f.* **4** **the Tube,** (*underground*) el metro.

tubeless ['tjuːbləs] *adj* sin cámara.

tuber ['tjuːbəʳ] *n* tubérculo.

tuberculosis [tjʊbɜːkjʊ'ləʊsɪs] *n* tuberculosis *f inv.*

tubing ['tjuːbɪŋ] *n* tubería: *a piece of tubing,* un tubo.

tubular ['tjuːbjʊləʳ] *adj* tubular.

tuck [tʌk] **1** *n* (*fold*) pliegue *m.* **2** GB (*sweets etc*) golosinas *fpl,* chucherías *fpl.* – **3** **3** (*place*) meter, poner: *she tucked the letter into the envelope,* metió la carta dentro del sobre.
◆ **to tuck away** *t sep* esconder, ocultar: *he's got some money tucked away,* tiene algún dinero guardado; *the cottage is tucked away in the mountains,* la casita está escondida en las montañas. ‖ **to tuck in 1** *i* (*eat*) ponerse a comer, atacar. – **2** *t sep* (*clothes*) meter: *tuck your shirt in,* métete la camisa en los pantalones. **3** (*person*) arropar. ‖ **to tuck into** *t insep* ponerse a comer, atacar. ‖ **to tuck up** *t sep* arropar: *she tucked him up in bed,* lo arropó en la cama.
■ **tuck shop,** tienda de golosinas y chucherías *en una escuela.*

Tues ['tjuːzdɪ] *abbr* (*Tuesday*) martes; (*abbreviation*) mart.

Tuesday ['tjuːzdɪ] *n* martes *m inv.*
▲ *véase también Saturday.*

tuft [tʌft] **1** *n* (*of feathers*) penacho. **2** (*of hair*) mechón *m.* **3** (*of grass*) mata.

tug [tʌg] **1** *n* (*pull*) tirón *m,* estirón *m.* **2** (*boat*) remolcador *m.* – **3** *t* (*pull*) tirar de, dar un estirón de: *stop tugging my hair,* deja de tirarme del pelo. **4** (*boat*) remolcar. – **5** *i* tirar (**at**, de): *she felt someone tugging at her sleeve,* sintió que alguien le tiraba de la manga.
■ **tug of love,** lucha por la custodia de los hijos. ‖ **tug of war,** juego de la cuerda.
▲ (*verbo*) *pt* & *pp* **tugged,** *ger* **tugging.**

tugboat ['tʌgbəʊt] *n* remolcador *m.*

tuition [tjuː'ɪʃən] *n* enseñanza, instrucción *f.*
■ **private tuition,** clases *fpl* particulares. ‖ **tuition fees,** EDUC matrícula.

tulip ['tjuːlɪp] *n* tulipán *m.*

tumble ['tʌmbəl] **1** *n* caída, tumbo: *he took a tumble,* se cayó. – **2** *i* (*fall*) caerse: *he tumbled down the stairs,* cayó escaleras abajo; *she tumbled into bed,* se dejó caer en la cama. **3** (*in acrobatics*) dar voltaretas. **4** (*prices etc*) caer en picado.
◆ **to tumble to** *t insep* comprender, caer en la cuenta. ■ **tumble drier,** secadora.

tumbledown ['tʌmbəldaʊn] *adj* ruinoso,-a, en ruinas.

tumbler ['tʌmbləʳ] **1** *n* (*glass*) vaso. **2** (*acrobat*) volteador,-ra.

tummy ['tʌmɪ] *n fam* barriga, estómago.
■ **tummy ache,** dolor *m* de barriga.

▲ *pl* **tummies**.
tumour ['tjuːməʳ] *n* tumor *m*.
tumult ['tjuːmʌlt] *n* tumulto.
tumultuous [tjuːˈmʌltjʊəs] *adj* tumultuoso,-a.
tun [tʌn] *n* tonel *m*.
tuna ['tjuːnə] *n* atún *m*, bonito.
■ **tuna fish**, atún *m*.
▲ *pl* **tuna** *o* **tunas**.
tundra ['tʌndrə] *n* tundra.
tune [tjuːn] **1** *n* melodía. – **2** *t* MUS afinar. **3** RAD TV sintonizar. **4** (*engine*) poner a punto.
◆ **to tune in to** *t insep* RAD TV sintonizar. ‖ **to tune up** *t sep* afinar.
● **in tune**, afinado,-a. ‖ **out of tune**, desafinado,-a. ‖ **to be in tune with**, *fig* estar en armonía con. ‖ **to be out of tune with**, *fig* no estar en armonía con. ‖ **to call the tune**, llevar la batuta, llevar la voz cantante. ‖ **to change one's tune**, cambiar de opinión. ‖ **to sing in tune**, afinar, cantar bien. ‖ **to sing out of tune**, desafinar, cantar mal. ‖ **to the tune of**, a la melodía de. ‖ **to the tune of**, *fig* por la cantidad de: *he's in debt to the tune of £5000*, tiene una deuda de cinco mil libras.
tuneful ['tjuːnfʊl] *adj* melodioso,-a.
tuneless ['tjuːnləs] *adj* sin armonía.
tuner ['tjuːnəʳ] **1** *n* (*of paino*) afinador,-ra. **2** (*on radio*) sintonizador *m*.
tungsten ['tʌŋstən] *n* tungsteno.
tunic ['tjuːnɪk] **1** *n* (*gen*) túnica. **2** MIL guerrera.
tuning ['tjuːnɪŋ] **1** *n* (*of instrument*) afinación *f*. **2** (*of radio*) sintonización *f*. **3** (*of engine*) puesta a punto.
■ **tuning fork**, diapasón *m*.
Tunis ['tjuːnɪs] *n* Túnez.
Tunisia [tjuːˈnɪsɪə] *n* Túnez.
Tunisian [tjuːˈnsɪən] **1** *adj* tunecino,-a. – **2** *n* tunecino,-a.
tunnel ['tʌnəl] **1** *n* (*gen*) túnel *m*; (*in mine*) galería. – **2** *t* abrir un túnel: *the prisioners tunnelled their way out*, los prisioneros excavaron un túnel para escaparse. – **3** *i* construir un túnel: *they tunnelled through the mountains*, construyeron un túnel a través de las montañas.
■ **tunnel vision**, (*blindness*) ceguera; (*narrow-mindedness*) estrechez *f* de miras.
▲ *pt & pp* **tunnelled** (US **tunneled**), *ger* **tunnelling** (US **tunneling**).
tunny ['tʌnɪ] *n* atún *m*, bonito.
▲ *pl* **tunnies**.
tuppence ['tʌpəns] *n* GB *fam* dos peniques *mpl*.
● **not to give tuppence / not to care tuppence**, importarle a uno un rábano/bledo/comino.
turban ['tɜːbən] *n* turbante *m*.
turbine ['tɜːbaɪn] *n* turbina.
turbo ['tɜːbəʊ] *n* turbo.
turbocharge ['tɜːbəʊtʃɑːdʒ] *t* turboalimentar.
turbocharger ['tɜːbəʊtʃɑːdʒəʳ] *n* turboalimentador *m*.
turbojet ['tɜːbəʊdʒet] *n* turborreactor *m*.
turbot ['tɜːbət] *n* rodaballo.
▲ *pl* **turbot** *o* **turbots**.
turbulence ['tɜːbjʊləns] *n* turbulencia.
turbulent ['tɜːbjʊlənt] *adj* turbulento,-a.
tureen [tjʊˈriːn] *n* sopera.
turf [tɜːf] **1** *n* césped *m*. – **2** *t* cubrir con césped.
◆ **to turf out** *t sep fam* poner de patitas en la calle, echar.
■ **the turf**, las carreras de caballos, el turf *m*. ‖ **turf accountant**, corredor,-ra de apuestas.
turgid ['tɜːdʒɪd] **1** *adj* (*swollen*) hinchado,-a. **2** (*bombastic*) rimbombante.

Turk [tɜːk] *n* (*person*) turco,-a.
turkey ['tɜːkɪ] *n* pavo.
● **to talk turkey**, hablar a las claras.
■ **cold turkey**, *sl* el mono. ‖ **turkey cock**, pavo. ‖ **turkey hen**, pava.
Turkey ['tɜːkɪ] *n* Turquía.
Turkish ['tɜːkɪʃ] **1** *adj* turco,-a. – **2** *n* (*language*) turco. – **3 the Turkish**, *npl* los turcos *mpl*.
■ **Turkish bath**, baño turco. ‖ **Turkish coffee**, café *m* turco. ‖ **Turkish delight**, delicias turcas *fpl*.
turmeric ['tɜːmərɪk] *n* cúrcuma.
turmoil ['tɜːmɔɪl] *n* confusión *f*, agitación *f*.
turn [tɜːn] **1** *n* (*act of turning*) vuelta. **2** (*change of direction*) giro, vuelta; (*bend*) curva, recodo: *take the second turn on the left*, tome la segunda a la izquierda. **3** (*chance, go*) turno: *whose turn is it?*, ¿a quién le toca?; *we took turns at driving*, nos turnamos para conducir; *you have to wait your turn*, tienes que esperar tu turno. **4** (*change*) cambio, giro: *things have taken a turn for the worse*, las cosas han empeorado; *events have taken a strange turn*, los acontecimientos han dado un giro extraño. **5** (*short walk*) vuelta, paseo. **6** (*attack of illness*) ataque *m*; (*shock*) susto. **7** (*act of kindness, favour*) favor *m*. **8** THEAT (*act*) número. – **9** *t* (*rotate*) girar, hacer girar, dar la vuelta a: *turn the key*, gira la llave. **10** (*page*) pasar, volver; (*soil*) revolver; (*ankle*) torcer. **11** (*cause to change direction*) girar, dar la vuelta a: *turn right at the next traffic lights*, gira a la derecha en el próximo semáforo; *he turned the corner*, dobló en la esquina; *about turn!*, ¡media vuelta! **12** (*invert*) darle la vuelta a. **13** (*change*) convertir, transformar, volver; (*milk*) agriar; (*stomach*) revolver: *they turned the cinema into a bingo hall*, convirtieron el cine en un bingo; *Jesus turned the water into wine*, Jesús transformó el agua en vino; *they turned the book into a film*, adaptaron el libro al cine; *it turned her into a different person*, la convirtió en una persona diferente, la convirtió en otra persona. **14** (*pass*) pasar: *it's turned twelve*, pasan de las doce, son más de las doce, son las doce pasadas; *he's turned sixty*, ya ha cumplido los sesenta. **15** (*fold*) doblar. **16** (*shape*) tornear, labrar en un torno. – **17** *i* (*revolve*) girar, dar vueltas: *the wheels turned slowly*, las ruedas giraron despacio. **18** (*change direction - person*) girarse, dar la vuelta, volverse; (*- car*) girar, torcer; (*- plane, ship*) virar; (*- tide*) repuntar: *she turned and looked at me*, se giró y me miró; *I tossed and turned all night long*, me estuve revolviendo toda la noche; *the car turned left*, el coche giró a la izquierda; *the road turns to the right here*, aquí la carretera tuerce a la derecha. **19** (*become*) hacerse, ponerse, volverse; (*milk*) agriarse, cortarse: *my hair's turning grey*, me están saliendo canas; *the traffic light turned green*, el semáforo se puso en verde; *she turns red easily*, se pone colorada fácilmente; *he can turn quite nasty*, a veces se pone frío; *it has turned from a small fishing village into a tourist resort*, de pueblecito de pescadores se ha convertido en centro turístico; *caterpillars turn into butterflies*, las orugas se convierten en mariposas.
◆ **to turn against 1** *t insep* (*cause to dislike*) poner en contra. **2** (*become hostile towards*) ponerse en contra de. ‖ **to turn around / turn round 1** *i* volverse, darse la vuelta. – **2** *t sep* volver, darle la vuelta a. ‖ **to turn away 1** *t sep* (*not let in*) no dejar entrar. – **2** *i* (*look away*) volver la cabeza, volver la espalda. ‖ **to turn back 1** *t sep* (*make return*) hacer retroceder, hacer volver. **2** (*clock*) retrasar. – **3** *i* (*return*) volverse atrás. ‖ **to turn down 1** *t sep* (*reject*) rechazar, no aceptar; (*request*) denegar. **2** (*radio etc*) bajar. **3** (*fold*) doblar. ‖ **to turn in 1** *t sep* (*to police*) entregar

a la policía. – **2** *i fam* (*go to bed*) acostarse. ‖ **to turn off** **1** *t sep* (*electricity*) desconectar; (*light, gas, appliance*) apagar; (*tap*) cerrar. **2** (*dislike*) repugnar, dar asco a: *her false teeth turned me off,* su dentadura postiza me quitó las ganas. – **3** *t insep* (*off road*) salir de: *you turn off the main road after the bridge,* sales de la carretera principal pasado el puente. – **4** *i* (*switch off*) apagarse. **5** (*off road*) salir. ‖ **to turn on 1** *t sep* (*electricity*) conectar; (*light, gas, appliance*) encender; (*tap*) abrir; (*engine*) poner en marcha, encender. **2** (*attack*) atacar, arremeter contra; (*aim, point at*) apuntar, dirigir. **3** *fam* (*excite*) excitar, entusiasmar: *leather turns him on,* el cuero le excita. – **4** *t insep* (*hinge on*) depender de, girar en torno a. – **5** *i* encenderse. ‖ **to turn out 1** *t sep* (*light*) apagar. **2** (*produce*) producir, fabricar. **3** (*empty*) vaciar; (*cake, jelly, etc*) desmoldar. **4** (*expel*) expulsar, echar. – **5** *i* (*prove to be, happen*) salir, resultar: *it all turned out fine in the end,* al final todo salió bien; *she turned out to be a spy,* resultó ser una espía. **6** (*go out*) salir; (*attend*) asistir, acudir; (*crowds*) salir a la calle: *thousands turned out to see the king,* salieron a la calle miles de personas para ver al rey. ‖ **to turn over 1** *t sep* (*invert*) dar la vuelta a, volver, poner al revés. **2** (*idea*) dar vueltas a. **3** (*hand over*) entregar. – **4** *t insep* (*page*) volver. **5** COMM facturar, hacer. – **6** *i* (*person*) darse la vuelta; (*car*) volcar. **7** (*engine*) marchar en vacío, funcionar. ‖ **to turn to 1** *t insep* (*person*) acudir a, recurrir. **2** (*page*) buscar, pasar a; (*subject*) pasar a. **3** (*take up*) dedicarse a, recurrir a, darse a, empezar. ‖ **to turn up 1** *i* (*arrive*) llegar, presentarse; (*appear*) aparecer: *he turned up at midnight,* se presentó a medianoche; *he turned up in Paris,* apareció en París; *that pen I lost never turned up,* ese bolígrafo que perdí nunca apareció; *don't worry, some job's bound to turn up,* no te preocupes, seguro que te saldrá algún trabajo. – **2** *t sep* (*fold*

turnip ['tɜːnɪp] *n* nabo.
turn-off ['tɜːnɒf] **1** *n* (*road*) salida. **2** (*something offputting*): *it's a real turn-off,* te quita las ganas.
turn-on ['tɜːnɒn] *n* (*something exciting*): *I find it a turn-on,* me excita.
turnout ['tɜːnaʊt] **1** *n* (*attendance*) asistencia; (*voters*) número de votantes. **2** (*clearout*) limpieza general. **3** (*appearance*) aspecto.
turnover ['tɜːnəʊvəʳ] **1** *n* (*sales, business*) facturación *f*. **2** (*movement of employees*) movimiento; (*of stock*) rotación *f*. **3** CULIN pastelito relleno.
turnpike ['tɜːnpaɪk] *n* US autopista de peaje.
turnround ['tɜːnraʊnd] **1** *n* (*of passengers*) operación *f* de desembarque y embarque de pasajeros; (*of freight*) operación *f* de descarga y carga. **2** (*reversal of situation*) cambio total.
turnstile ['tɜːnstaɪl] *n* torniquete *m*.
turntable ['tɜːnteɪbəl] **1** *n* (*on record player*) plato giratorio. **2** (*for trains*) plataforma giratoria.
turn-up ['tɜːnʌp] **1** *n* GB (*of trousers*) vuelta. **2** *fam* (*chance occurence*) acontecimiento. ● *that's a turn-up for the books!,* ¡vaya sorpresa!
turpentine ['tɜːpəntaɪn] *n* trementina, aguarrás *m*.
turps [tɜːps] *n* → **turpentine**.
turquoise ['tɜːkwɔɪz] **1** *n* (*gem*) turquesa. **2** (*colour*) azul *m* turquesa. – **3** *adj* azul turquesa.
turret ['tʌrɪt] **1** *n* torrecilla. **2** MIL torreta.
turtle ['tɜːtəl] *n* tortuga marina. ● *to turn turtle,* zozobrar.
turtledove ['tɜːtəldʌv] *n* tórtola.
turtleneck ['tɜːtəlnek] *n* cuello cisne, cuello alto.
tusk [tʌsk] *n* colmillo.

upwards) doblar hacia arriba, levantar; (*shorten*) acortar. **3** (*radio, gas, heat, etc*) subir, poner más fuerte. – **4** *t insep* (*find*) descubrir, encontrar. ● **at every turn,** a cada paso, a cada momento. ‖ **by turns / in turns,** por turnos, sucesivamente. ‖ **in turn,** a su vez, por su parte. ‖ **on the turn,** a punto de cambiar. ‖ **one good turn deserves another,** favor con favor se paga. ‖ **out of turn,** fuera de lugar. ‖ **to be badly turned out,** ir mal vestido,-a. ‖ **to be done to a turn / be cooked to a turn,** estar en su punto. ‖ **to be well turned out,** ir bien vestido,-a. ‖ **to do sb. a good turn,** hacerle un favor a algn. ‖ **to do sb. a bad turn,** hacer un mala pasada a algn. ‖ **to take it in turns,** turnarse. ‖ **to turn free,** dejar en libertad, soltar. ‖ **to turn one's hand to sth.,** dedicarse a algo. ‖ **to turn sb.'s head,** afectar mucho a algn.: *success has turned his head,* el éxito se le ha subido a la cabeza. ‖ **to turn sth. inside out,** (*back to front*) dar la vuelta a; (*make a mess*) revolver: *she turned the jeans inside out,* les dio la vuelta a los tejanos; *they turned the house inside out, but they couldn't find it,* revolvieron toda la casa, pero no lo encontraron. ‖ **turn and turn about,** por turnos.
■ **turn of phrase,** manera de expresarse. ‖ **turn of the century,** finales *mpl* de siglo. ‖ **turn of the screw,** vuelta del tornillo.
turnabout ['tɜːnəbaʊt] *n* giro, cambio.
turnaround ['tɜːnəraʊnd] *n* US → **turnround**.
turncoat ['tɜːnkəʊt] *n* renegado,-a, chaquetero,-a.
turned-up ['tɜːnd'ʌp] *adj* (*nose*) respingón,-ona.
turner ['tɜːnəʳ] *n* tornero.
turning ['tɜːnɪŋ] *n* bocacalle *f*, esquina.
■ **turning lathe,** torno. ‖ **turning point,** punto decisivo.
tussle ['tʌsəl] **1** *n* pelea, lucha. – **2** *i* pelear, luchar: *he tussled with the problem for hours,* peleó con el problema durante horas.
tussock ['tʌsək] *n* mata de hierba.
tutelage ['tjuːtəlɪdʒ] *n* tutela.
tutor ['tjuːtəʳ] **1** *n* (*private teacher*) profesor,-ra particular. **2** (*at university*) profesor,-ra, tutor,-ra. – **3** *t* dar clases particulares a (**in,** de).
tutorial [tjuːˈtɔːrɪəl] *n* clase *f* con grupo reducido.
tutti-frutti [tuːtɪˈfruːtɪ] *n* tutti-frutti *m*.
tutu ['tuːtuː] *n* tutú *m*.
Tuvalu [tuːvəˈluː] *n* Tuvalu.
tuxedo [tʌkˈsiːdəʊ] *n* US esmoquin *m*.
▲ *pl* tuxedos.
TV ['tiːˈviː] *abbr* (*television*) televisión; (*abbreviation*) TV.
twaddle ['twɒdəl] *n fam* tonterías *fpl*.
twang [twæŋ] **1** *n* (*of instrument*) sonido vibrante, tañido. **2** (*through nose*) gangueo. – **3** *t* (*strum*) puntear. – **4** *i* vibrar.
tweak [twiːk] **1** *t* pellizcar. – **2** *n* pellizco.
twee [twiː] *adj* GB *fam pej* cursi.
tweed [twiːd] *n* cheviot *m*.
tweet [twiːt] **1** *n* pío. – **2** *i* piar.
tweeter ['twiːtəʳ] *n* altavoz *f* para altas frecuencias.
tweezers ['twiːzəz] *npl* pinzas *fpl*.
twelfth [twelfθ] **1** *adj* duodécimo,-a. – **2** *adv* en duodécimo lugar. – **3** *n* (*fraction*) duodécimo; (*one part*) duodécima parte *f*.
■ **Twelfth Night,** Noche *f* de Reyes.
▲ *Véase también* **sixteenth**.
twelve [twelv] **1** *n* doce *m*. – **2** *adj* doce.
▲ *Véase también* **six**.

twenties ['twentɪz] the twenties, *npl* los años *mpl* veinte.
● to be in one's twenties, tener entre veinte y treinta años, tener veintitantos años.
▲ Véase también *sixties*.
twentieth ['twentɪəθ] 1 *adj* vigésimo,-a. – 2 *adv* en vigésimo lugar. – 3 *n (fraction)* vigésimo; *(one part)* vigésima parte *f.*
▲ Véase también *sixtieth*.
twenty ['twentɪ] 1 *n* veinte *m.* – 2 *adj* veinte.
▲ Véase también *sixty*.
twice [twaɪs] *adv* dos veces: *I've been to Paris twice*, he estado en París dos veces; *he's twice your age*, te dobla la edad; *twice as big as this one*, el doble de grande que éste.
● twice over, dos veces.
twiddle ['twɪdəl] 1 *t* dar vueltas a, girar. – 2 *i* juguetear **(with**, con). – 3 *n* vuelta.
● to twiddle one's thumbs, *fig* estar mano sobre mano.
twig[1] [twɪg] *n* ramita.
twig[2] [twɪg] *i* caer en la cuenta, darse cuenta.
▲ *(verbo) pt & pp* **twigged,** *ger* **twigging**.
twilight ['twaɪlaɪt] *n* crepúsculo: *at twilight*, al anochecer.
twill [twɪl] *n (fabric)* sarga, tela cruzada.
twin [twɪn] 1 *n* gemelo,-a, mellizo,-a. – 2 *adj* gemelo,-a, mellizo,-a. – 3 *t* hermanar: *Cambridge is twinned with Heidelberg*, Cambridge está hermanada con Heidelberg.
■ twin bed, cama gemela. ‖ twin set, conjunto de jersey y chaqueta. ‖ twin town, ciudad *f* hermanada.
▲ *(verbo) pt & pp* **twinned,** *ger* **twinning**.
twine [twaɪn] 1 *n* bramante *m.* – 2 *t* enroscar, entrelazar. – 3 *i* enroscarse, entrelazarse.
twinge [twɪndʒ] 1 *n (pain)* punzada, dolor *m* agudo. 2 *fig (remorse)* remordimiento.
twinkle ['twɪŋkəl] 1 *n (of light, stars)* centelleo. 2 *(in eye)* brillo. – 3 *i (lights, stars)* centellear, destellar. 4 *(eyes)* brillar.
twinkling ['twɪŋkəlɪŋ] *n* centelleo.
● in the twinkling of an eye, en un abrir y cerrar de ojos.
twirl [twɜːl] 1 *n* giro, vuelta. – 2 *t* girar rápidamente, dar vueltas a. 3 *(twist, fiddle with)* retorcer, juguetear con. – 4 *i* girar rápidamente, dar vueltas.
twist [twɪst] 1 *n (in road)* recodo, vuelta. 2 *(action)* torsión *m.* 3 MED torcedura, esguince *m.* 4 *(dance)* twist *m.* 5 *(development)* giro. 6 *(of thread)* torzal *m;* *(of lemon)* rodajita. – 7 *t (sprain)* torcer: *she's twisted her ankle*, se ha torcido el tobillo. 8 *(screw, coil)* retorcer. 9 *(turn, wind)* girar, dar vueltas a. 10 *(interweave)* entrelazar, trenzar. 11 *(pervert)* tergiversar, torcer: *stop twisting my words!*, ¡no tergiverses mis palabras! – 12 *i (turn)* girarse. 13 *(wind, coil)* enroscarse, enrollarse. 14 *(road)* serpentear. 15 *(writhe)* retorcerse. 16 *(dance)* bailar el twist.
◆ to twist off *t sep* desenroscar.
● to be round the twist, *fam* estar chalado,-a. ‖ to twist sb. round one's little finger, hacer con algn. lo que se quiere, meterse a algn. en el bolsillo. ‖ to twist sb.'s arm, torcerle el brazo a algn.
twisted ['twɪstɪd] *adj* retorcido,-a.
twit [twɪt] *n fam* tonto,-a, imbécil *mf.*
twitch [twɪtʃ] 1 *n (pull)* tirón *m.* 2 *(nervous tic)* tic *m* nervioso. – 3 *t* mover. – 4 *i* moverse nerviosamente, palpitar.

twitchy ['twɪtʃɪ] *adj* nervioso,-a.
▲ *comp* **twitchier,** *superl* **twitchiest**.
twitter ['twɪtəʳ] 1 *n* gorjeo. – 2 *i (bird)* gorjear; *(person)* hablar sin parar.
● to be all of a twitter, estar excitado,-a, estar nervioso,-a.
two [tuː] 1 *n* dos *m.* – 2 *adj* dos.
● in two, en dos, por la mitad. ‖ in twos, de dos en dos. ‖ it takes two, es cosa de dos. ‖ to put two and two together, atar cabos. ‖ that makes two of us, ya somos dos.
two-bit ['tuːbɪt] *adj* de tres al cuatro.
two-edged ['tuːedʒd] *adj* de doble filo.
two-faced ['tuːfeɪst] *adj* hipócrita, falso,-a.
twopence ['tʌpəns] *n* dos peniques *mpl.*
two-piece ['tuːpiːs] *adj* de dos piezas.
two-ply ['tuːplaɪ] *adj (wool)* de dos hebras; *(wood)* de dos capas.
two-seater [tuː'siːtəʳ] *n* biplaza *m.*
twosome ['tuːsəm] *n* pareja, grupo de dos.
two-time ['tuːtaɪm] *t* engañar, poner los cuernos a.
two-tone ['tuːtəʊn] *adj* de dos tonos.
two-way [tuː'weɪ] *adj (street)* de doble sentido.
■ two-way radio, aparato emisor y receptor.
tycoon [taɪ'kuːn] *n* magnate *m.*
type [taɪp] 1 *n (kind)* tipo, clase *f.* 2 *(letter)* letra, carácter *m: in bold type / in heavy type*, en negrita. – 3 *t* escribir a máquina, mecanografiar. – 4 *i* escribir a máquina.
◆ to type up *t sep* pasar a máquina.
typecast ['taɪpkɑːst] 1 *t* encasillar. – 2 *adj* encasillado,-a.
▲ *pt & pp* **typecast**.
typeface ['taɪpfeɪs] *n* tipografía.
typescript ['taɪpskrɪpt] *n* texto escrito a máquina, texto mecanografiado.
typesetter ['taɪpsetəʳ] *n (person)* cajista *mf;* *(machine)* componedora, máquina para componer tipos.
typewriter ['taɪpraɪtəʳ] *n* máquina de escribir.
typewritten ['taɪprɪtən] *adj* escrito,-a a máquina, mecanografiado,-a.
typhoid ['taɪfɔɪd] *n* fiebre *f* tifoidea.
typhoon [taɪ'fuːn] *n* tifón *m.*
typhus ['taɪfəs] *n* tifus *m.*
typical ['tɪpɪkəl] *adj* típico,-a.
typically ['tɪpɪkəlɪ] *adv* típicamente.
typify ['tɪpɪfaɪ] *t* tipificar.
▲ *pt & pp* **typified,** *ger* **typifying**.
typing ['taɪpɪŋ] *n* mecanografía.
■ typing pool, servicio de mecanografía.
typist ['taɪpɪst] *n* mecanógrafo,-a.
typography [taɪ'pɒɡrəfɪ] *n* tipografía.
tyrannical [tɪ'rænɪkəl] *adj* tiránico,-a.
tyrannize ['tɪrənaɪz] *t* tiranizar.
tyranny ['tɪrənɪ] *n* tiranía.
▲ *pl* **tyrannies**.
tyrant ['taɪərənt] *n* tirano,-a.
tyre ['taɪəʳ] *n* neumático.
Tyrol [tɪ'rɒl] *n* Tirol.
Tyrolean [tɪrə'lɪən] 1 *n* tirolés,-esa. 2 tirolés,-esa.
Tyrrhenian [tɪ'riːnɪən] *adj* tirreno,-a.
■ the Tyrrhenian Sea, el (mar) *m* Tirreno.
tzar [zɑːʳ] *n* zar *m,* czar *m.*

U

U, u [juː] *n* (*the letter*) U, u *f.*

UAE ['juːeɪ'iː] *abbr* (*United Arab Emirates*) Emiratos Árabes Unidos; (*abbreviation*) EAU *mpl.*

ubiquitous [juːˈbɪkwɪtəs] *adj* ubicuo,-a, omnipresente.

ubiquity [juːˈbɪkwɪtɪ] *n* ubicuidad *f*, omnipresencia.

udder ['ʌdə'] *n* ubre *f.*

UDR ['juːˈdiːˈɑː'] *abbr* (*Ulster Defense Regiment*) *fuerza paramilitar de Irlanda del Norte.*

UEFA [juːˈeɪfə] *abbr* (*Union of European Football Associations*) Unión de Asociaciones Europeas de Fútbol; (*abbreviation*) UEFA.

ufo ['juːfəʊ] *n fam* ovni *m.*
▲ *pl* **ufos.**

UFO ['juːˈefˈəʊ] *abbr* (*unidentified flying object*) objeto volador no identificado; (*abbreviation*) OVNI *m*, ovni *m.*

Uganda [juːˈgændə] *n* Uganda.

Ugandan [juːˈgændən] **1** *adj* ugandés,-esa. – **2** *n* ugandés,-esa.

ugh [ʌg] *interj* ¡uf!, ¡puf!

ugliness ['ʌglɪnəs] *n* fealdad *f.*

ugly ['ʌglɪ] **1** *adj* feo,-a. **2** (*situation etc*) desagradable. **3** (*custom, vice*) repugnante, asqueroso,-a. **4** (*wound, mood*) peligroso,-a. **5** (*rumour*) inquietante, nada grato.
● **as ugly as sin,** más feo,-a que Picio, más feo,-a que un pecado.
■ **ugly duckling,** patito feo.
▲ *comp* **uglier,** *superl* **ugliest.**

UHF ['juːˈeɪtʃˈef] *abbr* (*ultra high frequency*) frecuencia ultraalta; (*abbreviation*) UHF *f.*

UK ['juːˈkeɪ] *abbr* (*United Kingdom*) Reino Unido; (*abbreviation*) R.U. *m.*

Ukraine [juːˈkreɪn] *n* Ucrania.

Ukranian [juːˈkeɪnɪən] **1** *adj* ucraniano,-a, ucranio,-a. – **2** *n* (*person*) ucraniano,-a, ucranio,-a. **3** (*language*) ucranio.

ulcer ['ʌlsə'] **1** *n* (*external*) llaga. **2** (*in stomach*) úlcera.

ulcerate ['ʌlsəreɪt] **1** *t* ulcerar. – **2** *i* ulcerarse.

ulterior [ʌlˈtɪərɪə'] **1** *adj* (*hidden*) oculto,-a. **2** (*further*) ulterior.

ultimate ['ʌltɪmət] **1** *adj* (*final*) final: *the ultimate decision lies with the manager,* la decisión final corresponde al director. **2** (*basic*) esencial, fundamental. – **3** **the ultimate,** *n* (*good*) el no va más, el último grito; (*bad*) el colmo: *the ultimate in comfort,* el no va más en comodidad; *this is the ultimate in decadence,* esto es el colmo de la decadencia.

ultimately ['ʌltɪmətlɪ] **1** *adv* (*finally*) finalmente. **2** (*basically*) en el fondo.

ultimatum [ʌltɪˈmeɪtəm] *n* ultimátum *m.*
▲ *pl* **ultimatums** o **ultimata** [ʌltɪˈmeɪtə].

ultrafashionable [ʌltrəˈfæʃənəbəl] *adj* a la última moda, muy de moda.

ultramarine [ʌltrəməˈriːn] **1** *n* azul *m* marino, azul *m* de ultramar. – **2** *adj* (*from overseas*) ultramarino,-a, de ultramar.

ultramodern [ʌltrəˈmɒdən] *adj* ultramoderno,-a.

ultrasonic [ʌltrəˈsɒnɪk] *adj* ultrasónico,-a.

ultrasound ['ʌltrəsaʊnd] *n* ultrasonido.

ultraviolet [ʌltrəˈvaɪələt] *adj* ultravioleta.

umbilical [ʌmˈbɪlɪkəl] *adj* umbilical.
■ **umbilical cord,** cordón *m* umbilical.

umbrage ['ʌmbrɪdʒ] *n* resentimiento.
● **to take umbrage at,** ofenderse por, resentirse de.

umbrella [ʌmˈbrelə] **1** *n* paraguas *m.* **2** MIL AV cobertura aérea. **3** *fig* (*protection*) manto, protección *f*; (*patronage*) patrocinio.
■ **beach umbrella,** sombrilla, parasol *m.* ‖ **umbrella stand,** paragüero. ‖ **umbrella organization,** organismo madre.

umpire ['ʌmpaɪə'] **1** *n* árbitro,-a. – **2** *t* arbitrar.

umpteen [ʌmpˈtiːn] *adj fam* un montón de, muchísimos,-as, la tira de: *I've told you umpteen times,* te lo he dicho un montón de veces.

umpteenth [ʌmpˈtiːnθ] *adj* enésimo,-a.

UN ['juːˈen] *abbr* (*United Nations Organization*) Organización de las Naciones Unidas; (*abbreviation*) ONU *f.*

'un [ən] *pron* GB *fam* uno, una: *give us a big 'un,* dame uno grande.
▲ *Véase también* **one.**

unabashed [ʌnəˈbæʃt] **1** *adj* (*shameless*) descarado,-a, desvergonzado,-a. **2** (*unperturbed*) impertubable, inmutable.

unable [ʌnˈeɪbəl] **1** *adj* incapaz.
● **to be unable to do sth.,** no poder hacer algo, ser incapaz de hacer algo: *I'm unable to attend,* no puedo asistir.

unabridged [ʌnəˈbrɪdʒd] *adj* íntegro,-a.
■ **unabridged text,** versión *f* íntegra.

unacceptable [ʌnəkˈseptəbəl] *adj* inaceptable, inadmisible.

unaccommodating [ʌnəˈkɒmədeɪtɪŋ] *adj* (*person*) poco amable, poco servicial, poco sociable.

unaccompanied [ʌnəˈkʌmpənɪd] **1** *adj* (*person*) solo,-a, sin compañía. **2** MUS sin acompañamiento.

unaccomplished [ʌnəˈkʌmplɪʃt] **1** *adj* (*unfinished*) inacabado,-a, incompleto,-a, sin acabar. **2** (*without talent*) sin talento, mediocre. **3** (*ambitions, goals, etc.*) no realizado,-a, no logrado,-a.

unaccountable [ʌnəˈkaʊntəbəl] *adj* inexplicable.

unaccounted for [ʌnəˈkaʊntɪdfɔː'] *adj* (*missing*) faltar: *three documents are still unaccounted for,* todavía faltan tres documentos; *two fishermen are still unaccounted for,* se desconoce aún el paradero de dos pescadores.

unaccustomed [ʌnəˈkʌstəmd] *adj* desacostumbrado,-a, inacostumbrado,-a, no acostumbrado,-a: *she's unaccustomed to hard work,* no esta acostumbrada al trabajo duro.

unacquainted [ʌnəˈkweɪntɪd] *adj* desconocer, ignorar: *he's unacquainted with State matters,* desconoce los asuntos de Estado.

unadulterated [ʌnəˈdʌltəreɪtɪd] *adj* puro,-a.

unadventurous [ʌnədˈventʃərəs] *adj* poco arriesgado,-a, poco atrevido,-a.

unadvisable [ʌnədˈvaɪzəbəl] *adj* poco aconsejable.

unaffected [ʌnəˈfektɪd] **1** *adj* (*unchanged*) no afectado,-a: *this land has been unaffected by the hand of man,* la mano del hombre no ha afectado esta tierra. **2** (*for person*) afable, campechano,-a, natural, sencillo,-a. **3** (*indifferent*) indiferente, inmutable: *he is unaffected by sarcasm,* ni se inmuta ante el sarcasmo. **4** (*style*) llano,-a, sin afectación *f.*

unafraid [ʌnəˈfreɪd] *adj* sin miedo, sin temor, impertérrito,-a: *he is unafraid of anyone,* no le tiene miedo a nadie.

unaided [ʌnˈeɪdɪd] *adv* sin ayuda, solo,-a.

unaknowledged [ʌnəkˈnɒlɪdʒd] *adj* (*not recognized*) no reconocido,-a; (*letter*) sin contestar.

unalterable [ʌnˈɔːltərəbəl] *adj* inalterable, invariable.

unambiguous [ʌnæmˈbɪgjʊəs] *adj* inequívoco,-a, sin ambigüedad *f.*

unambitious [ʌnæmˈbɪʃəs] *adj* poco ambicioso,-a, sin ambición, poco emprendedor.

unanimity [juːnəˈnɪmətɪ] *n* unanimidad *f.*

unanimous [juːˈnænɪməs] *adj* unánime.

unanimously [juːˈnænɪməslɪ] *adv* unánimemente, por unanimidad *f: the law was passed unanimously,* la ley fue aprobada por unanimidad.

unannounced [ʌnəˈnaʊnst] **1** *adj* (*without knocking*) sin avisar, sin llamar: *he came in unannounced,* entró sin llamar. **2** (*without announcement*) sin ser anunciado,-a: *the customer went in unannounced,* el cliente entró sin ser anunciado.

unanswerable [ʌnˈɑːnsərəbəl] **1** *adj* (*question*) incontestable, sin respuesta. **2** (*attack, criticism*) irrebatible, irrefutable.

unanswered [ʌnˈɑːnsəd] **1** *adj* (*of letter*) sin contestar. **2** (*of love*) no correspondido,-a.

unappreciated [ʌnəˈpriːʃɪeɪtɪd] *adj* poco apreciado,-a, poco valorado,-a.

unappreciative [ʌnəˈpriːʃətɪv] *adj* desagradecido,-a.
● **to be unappreciative of,** no agradecer, no apreciar, no valorar.

unapproachable [ʌnəˈprəʊtʃəbəl] **1** *adj* inaccesible. **2** (*of person*) inabordable, intratable, inaccesible.

unarmed [ʌnˈɑːmd] *adj* desarmado,-a, sin armas.
■ **unarmed combat,** lucha a cuerpo limpio.

unashamed [ʌnəˈʃeɪmd] *adj* desvergonzado,-a, descarado,-a.

unasked [ʌnˈɑːskt] **1** *adv* (*voluntarily*) voluntariamente: *he is always ready to lend a hand unasked,* siempre está dispuesto a echar una mano sin que se lo pida. – **2** *adj* (*not asked*) sin preguntar, sin formular: *my question remained unasked,* mi pregunta quedó sin formular. **3** **unasked for,** (*unsolicited*) no solicitado,-a: *I gave him my advice, although it was unasked for,* le di consejos aunque no me los solicitara.

unassailable [ʌnəˈseɪləbəl] **1** *adj* (*fortress*) inexpugnable. **2** (*position*) intacable. **3** (*argument*) irrebatible.

unassuming [ʌnəˈsjuːmɪŋ] *adj* modesto,-a, sin pretensiones.

unattached [ʌnəˈtætʃt] **1** *adj* (*loose*) suelto,-a. **2** (*not engaged or married*) sin compromiso, soltero,-a. **3** (*independent*) libre, independiente. **4** JUR (*of property, etc.*) no embargado,-a.

unattainable [ʌnəˈteɪnəbəl] *adj* inalcanzable, inaccesible.

unattended [ʌnəˈtendɪd] **1** *adj* (*children*) sin vigilar. **2** (*not looked after*) desatendido,-a: *she often left the office unattended,* a menudo dejaba desatendida la oficina. **3** (*alone*) solo,-a.

unattractive [ʌnəˈtræktɪv] *adj* poco atractivo,-a, feo,-a.

unauthorized [ʌnˈɔːθəraɪzd] **1** *adj* (*person*) no autorizado,-a: *no entry to unauthorized personnel,* prohibida la entrada a toda persona ajena al recinto. **2** (*business, etc.*) ilegal, ilícito,-a.

unavailable [ʌnəˈveɪləbəl] **1** *adj* indisponible, no disponible. **2** (*busy*) ocupado,-a: *Mr Smith is unavailable this morning,* el Sr. Smith está ocupado esta mañana. **3** (*out of print*) agotado,-a. **4** (*not for sale*) que no está en venta: *certain commodities are unavailable in the shops,* hay ciertos productos que no están a la venta en las tiendas.

unavoidable [ʌnəˈvɔɪdəbəl] **1** *adj* (*general*) inevitable, ineludible. **2** (*accident*) fortuito,-a.

unaware [ʌnəˈweəʳ] *adj* ignorante, inconsciente.
● **to be unaware of,** ignorar, no darse cuenta, ser inconsciente de: *many people are unaware of their potential,* mucha gente ignora su potencial.

unawareness [ʌnəˈweənəs] *n* ignorancia, inconsciencia.

unawares [ʌnəˈweəz] **1** *adv* desprevenido,-a: *I was caught unawares,* me cogió desprevenido. **2** (*unintentionally*) inconscientemente, sin darse cuenta.

unbalance [ʌnˈbæləns] *t* **1** desequilibrar. **2** trastornar.

unbalanced [ʌnˈbælənst] **1** *adj* desequilibrado,-a. **2** (*mind*) trastornado,-a.

unbar [ʌnˈbɑːʳ] **1** *t* (*door*) desatrancar. **2** *fig* abrir, franquear.
▲ *pt & pp* **unbarred,** *ger* **unbarring**.

unbearable [ʌnˈbeərəbəl] *adj* inaguantable, insoportable, intolerable.

unbeatable [ʌnˈbiːtəbəl] **1** *adj* (*competition*) invencible, sin rival, sin igual. **2** (*price, quality*) insuperable, inigualable, inmejorable.

unbecoming [ʌnbɪˈkʌmɪŋ] **1** *adj* (*unsuitable*) impropio,-a, poco apropiado,-a. **2** (*clothes*) que no sienta bien, poco favorecedor,-ra.

unbelievable [ʌnbɪˈliːvəbəl] *adj* increíble.

unbend [ʌnˈbend] **1** *t* desencorvar, enderezar. **2** *fig* hacerse más amable. – **3** *i fig* relajarse.
▲ *pt & pp* **unbent**.

unbending [ʌnˈbendɪŋ] *adj* inflexible.

unbent [ʌnˈbent] *pt & pp* → **unbend**.

unbiased [ʌnˈbaɪəst] *adj* imparcial.

unbiassed [ʌnˈbaɪəst] *adj* → **unbiased**.

unblinking [ʌnˈblɪŋkɪŋ] **1** *adj* sin pestañear. **2** *fig* imperturbable.

unborn [ʌnˈbɔːn] **1** *adj* aún no nacido,-a, sin nacer, nonato,-a. **2** *fig* futuro,-a, venidero,-a.

unbosom [ʌnˈbʊzəm] **1** *t* descubrir, revelar. **2** deshogarse, abrir su corazón.
● **to unbosom os. to sb.,** abrirle el corazón a algn.

unbounded [ʌnˈbaʊndɪd] **1** *adj* ilimitado,-a, infinito,-a. **2** *fig* desmedido,-a,.

unbreakable [ʌnˈbreɪkəbəl] **1** *adj* irrompible. **2** *fig* inquebrantable. **3** (*horse*) indomable.

unbridled [ʌnˈbraɪdəld] *adj fig* desenfrenado,-a.

unbroken [ʌnˈbrəʊkən] **1** *adj* (*whole*) entero,-a, intacto,-a. **2** (*uninterrupted*) ininterrumpido,-a, continuo,-a. **3** (*record*) imbatido,-a. **4** (*untamed*) indómito,-a, sin domar.

unburden [ʌnˈbɜːdən] *t fml* descargar, aliviar.
● **to unburden os.,** desahogarse, abrir su corazón.

unbusinesslike [ʌnˈbɪznəslaɪk] 1 *adj* (*unmethodical*) poco metódico,-a, desorganizado,-a. 2 (*informal*) informal. 3 (*lacking in business sense*) poco negociante, carente de instinto comercial.

unbutton [ʌnˈbʌtən] 1 *t* desabrochar. – 2 *i fam* relajarse.
● **to unbutton os.**, desahogarse.

uncalled-for [ʌnˈkɔːldfɔːʳ] *adj* (*unjustified*) injustificado,-a, gratuito,-a, fuera de lugar; (*unnecessary*) innecesario,-a: *everyone criticized his uncalled-for attack on the minister,* todos criticaron su ataque injustificado al ministro; *that remark was uncalled for,* ese comentario era innecesario.
▲ *Se escribe* **uncalled for** *cuando no se antepone a un sustantivo.*

uncanny [ʌnˈkænɪ] *adj* misterioso,-a, extraño,-a.
▲ *comp* **uncannier,** *superl* **uncanniest.**

uncared-for [ʌnˈkeədfɔːʳ] 1 *adj* (*appearance*) descuidado,-a, abandonado,-a. 2 (*person*) abandonado,-a, desamparado,-a.
▲ *Se escribe* **uncared for** *cuando no se antepone a un sustantivo.*

uncaring [ʌnˈkeərɪŋ] *adj* indiferente, despreocupado,-a.
unceasing [ʌnˈsiːsɪŋ] *adj* incesante, continuo,-a.
uncertain [ʌnˈsɜːtən] 1 *adj* (*not certain*) incierto,-a, dudoso,-a. 2 (*unspecified*) indeterminado,-a. 3 (*indecisive*) indeciso,-a. 4 (*changeable*) variable.
● **to be uncertain of/about/as to sth.**, no estar seguro de algo: *he is still uncertain as to his participation,* aún no sabe seguro si va a participar, aún no está seguro de si va a participar. ‖ **in no uncertain terms,** claramente, sin rodeos, sin titubeos.

uncertainty [ʌnˈsɜːtəntɪ] *n* incertidumbre *f*, duda.
▲ *pl* **uncertainties.**

unchallenged [ʌnˈtʃælɪndʒd] *adj* incontestado,-a, sin protestar.
unchangeable [ʌnˈtʃeɪndʒəbəl] *adj* inalterable, inmutable.
unchanged [ʌnˈtʃeɪndʒd] *adj* igual, sin alterar.
unchanging [ʌnˈtʃeɪndʒɪŋ] *adj* inalterable.
uncharitable [ʌnˈtʃærɪtəbəl] *adj* poco caritativo,-a, duro,-a.
unchecked [ʌnˈtʃekt] 1 *adj* no comprobado,-a: *the results of the experiment remain unchecked,* los resultados del experimento aún no se han comprobado. 2 (*unrestrained*) libre: *enemy soldiers entered the city unchecked,* soldados enemigos entraron en la ciudad libremente.
uncivil [ʌnˈsɪvəl] *adj* (*rude*) descortés, grosero,-a.
uncivilized [ʌnˈsɪvəlaɪzd] 1 *adj* (*tribe*) incivilizado,-a, salvaje. 2 (*not cultured*) inculto,-a. 3 *fig* intempestivo,-a, poco ortodoxo,-a: *his working timetable is uncivilized,* su horario laboral es poco ortodoxo.
unclaimed [ʌnˈkleɪmd] *adj* sin reclamar, sin dueño.
uncle [ˈʌŋkəl] *n* tío.
■ **Uncle Sam,** el Tío Sam.
unclean [ʌnˈkliːn] 1 *adj* sucio,-a. 2 REL impuro,-a.
unclear [ʌnˈklɪəʳ] *adj* poco claro,-a, confuso,-a.
uncleared [ʌnˈklɪəd] 1 *adj* (*table*) sin quitar. 2 (*ground*) sin desbrozar. 3 COMM que no ha sido despachado,-a por la aduana. 4 (*debt*) impagado,-a. 5 *fig* (*mystery*) que no ha sido resuelto,-a. 6 (*doubt*) no disipado,-a.
■ **uncleared cheque,** talón *m* no compensado.
unclog [ʌnˈklɒg] *t* desatascar, desbloquear.
▲ *pt & pp* **unclogged,** *ger* **unclogging.**
uncoil [ʌnˈkɔɪl] 1 *t* desenrollar. – 2 *i* (*snake*) desenroscarse. 3 (*rope*) desenrollarse.

uncombed [ʌnˈkəʊmd] *adj* (*hair*) despeinado,-a.
uncomfortable [ʌnˈkʌmfətəbəl] 1 *adj* (*physical*) incómodo,-a, poco confortable. 2 (*worrying*) inquietante, preocupante: *I have the uncomfortable feeling that I'm being watched,* tengo la inquietante sensación de que me están vigilando. 3 (*unpleasant*) desagradable. 4 (*awkward*) incómodo,-a, molesto,-a.
● **to feel uncomfortable,** no estar a gusto, sentirse incómodo,-a. ‖ **to make things uncomfortable for sb.**, complicarle la vida a algn.
uncommitted [ʌnkəˈmɪtɪd] *adj* (*ideas, beliefs*) no comprometido,-a; (*politics*) no alineado,-a.
uncommon [ʌnˈkɒmən] 1 *adj* (*rare*) poco común, poco corriente. 2 (*strange*) insólito,-a; (*unusual*) extraordinario,-a, fuera de lo común. 3 (*excessive*) excesivo,-a, desmesurado,-a.
uncommonly [ʌnˈkɒmənlɪ] *adv* extraordinariamente, particularmente.
● **not uncommonly,** con cierta frecuencia.
uncommunicative [ʌnkəˈmjuːnɪkətɪv] *adj* poco comunicativo,-a, cerrado,-a, reservado,-a.
uncomplimentary [ʌnkɒmplɪˈmentərɪ] *adj* poco halagüeño,-a.
uncompromising [ʌnˈkɒmprəmaɪzɪŋ] *adj* inflexible, intransigente.
unconcealed [ʌnkənˈsiːld] *adj* evidente, no disimulado,-a.
unconcerned [ʌnkənˈsɜːnd] *adj* despreocupado, indiferente.
● **unconcerned about,** indiferente a: *she is unconcerned about losing her job,* no le preocupa perder su empleo.
unconditional [ʌnkənˈdɪʃənəl] *adj* incondicional: *he gave her his unconditional support,* le dio su apoyo incondicional.
unconditioned [ʌnkənˈdɪʃənd] *adj* (*reflex*) no condicionado,-a, espontáneo,-a.
unconfirmed [ʌnkənˈfɜːmd] *adj* no confirmado,-a, sin confirmar.
uncongenial [ʌnkənˈdʒiːnɪəl] 1 *adj* (*person*) antipático,-a. 2 (*job*) desagradable.
unconnected [ʌnkəˈnektɪd] *adj* no relacionado,-a, inconexo,-a.
unconscionable [ʌnˈkɒnʃənəbəl] *adj fml* (*excessive*) desmesurado,-a, excesivo,-a.
unconscious [ʌnˈkɒnʃəs] 1 *adj* MED inconsciente: *he was unconscious for five minutes,* estuvo inconsciente durante cinco minutos. 2 (*unaware*) inconsciente. 3 (*not on purpose*) involuntario,-a. – 4 **the unconscious,** *n* el inconsciente.
● **to become unconscious,** perder el conocimiento.
unconsciousness [ʌnˈkɒnʃəsnəs] *n* MED pérdida del conocimiento, inconsciencia.
unconsidered [ʌnkənˈsɪdəd] *adj* (*hasty*) irreflexivo,-a.
unconstitutional [ʌnkɒnstɪˈtjuːʃənəl] *adj* anticonstitucional, inconstitucional.
uncontested [ʌnkənˈtestɪd] *adj* incontestado,-a.
■ **uncontested seat,** POL escaño ganado sin oposición.
uncontrollable [ʌnkənˈtrəʊləbəl] 1 *adj* (*general*) incontrolable. 2 (*people*) ingobernable. 3 (*desire*) irrefrenable, irresistible. 4 (*child*) indisciplinado,-a.
■ **uncontrollable laughter,** ataque *m* de risa.
unconventional [ʌnkənˈvenʃənəl] 1 *adj* poco convencional. 2 (*original*) original.
unconvinced [ʌnkənˈvɪnst] *adj* poco convencido,-a, escéptico,-a.

uncooperative [ʌnkəʊ'ɒpərətɪv] *adj* poco cooperativo,-a.

uncoordinated [ʌnkəʊ'ɔːdɪneɪtɪd] *adj* no coordinado,-a, sin coordinar.

uncork [ʌn'kɔːk] *t* descorchar, destaponar.

uncorrected [ʌnkə'rektɪd] *adj* sin corregir, no corregido,-a.

uncouple [ʌn'kʌpəl] **1** *t* (*railways*) desenganchar. **2** (*wheels*) desacoplar. **3** (*disconnect*) desconectar.

uncouth [ʌn'kuːθ] **1** *adj* (*awkward*) tosco,-a, inculto,-a. **2** (*rude*) grosero,-a, vulgar.

uncover [ʌn'kʌvəʳ] **1** *t* destapar. **2** (*secret*) revelar, descubrir.

uncovered [ʌn'kʌvəd] *adj* destapado, al descubierto.
■ **uncovered cheque,** US talón *m* sin fondos.

uncrossed [ʌn'krɒst] *adj* GB (*cheque*) sin barrar, sin cruzar.

unction ['ʌŋkʃən] **1** *n* REL (*act, ointment*) unción *f*. **2** (*balm*) ungüento. **3** *fig* unción *f*, fervor *m* fingido, zalamería.
■ **extreme unction,** extremaunción *f*.

unctuous ['ʌŋktʃʊəs] *adj fml fig* meloso,-a, zalamero,-a.

uncultivated [ʌn'kʌltɪveɪtɪd] **1** *adj* (*land*) yermo,-a, baldío,-a, sin cultivar. **2** (*person*) inculto,-a.

uncurbed [ʌn'kɜːbd] *adj* (*uncontrolled*) desenfrenado,-a.

uncut [ʌn'kʌt] **1** *adj* sin cortar. **2** (*gem*) en bruto, sin tallar. **3** (*film*) íntegro, sin cortes *mpl*. **4** (*printing, books etc.*) intonso,-a.

undamaged [ʌn'dæmɪdʒd] **1** *adj* (*goods*) en buen estado, sin desperfectos, intacto,-a. **2** (*person*) indemne, ileso,-a. **3** *fig* intacto,-a.

undated [ʌn'deɪtɪd] *adj* sin fecha.

undaunted [ʌn'dɔːntɪd] *adj* (*dauntless*) firme, impávido,-a: *he remained undaunted by the situation,* se mantuvo impávido ante la situación.

undeceive [ʌndɪ'siːv] *t fml* desengañar, desilusionar.

undecided [ʌndɪ'saɪdɪd] **1** *adj* indeciso,-a. **2** (*question*) no resuelto,-a. **3** (*issue*) pendiente.

undecipherable [ʌndɪ'saɪfərəbəl] *adj* indescifrable.

undefeated [ʌndɪ'fiːtɪd] *adj* invicto,-a.

undefended [ʌndɪ'fendɪd] *adj* indefenso,-a.

undefined [ʌndɪ'faɪnd] *adj* indefinido,-a, indeterminado,-a.

undelivered [ʌndɪ'lɪvəd] *adj* sin entregar.
■ **undelivered letter,** carta devuelta.

undeniable [ʌndɪ'naɪəbəl] *adj* innegable, indiscutible.

under ['ʌndəʳ] **1** *prep* (*below*) bajo, debajo de: *it's under the bed,* está debajo de la cama; *the tunnel goes under the Channel,* el túnel pasa por debajo del Canal de la Mancha. **2** (*less than*) menos de: *he earns under two million pesetas a year,* gana menos de dos millones de pesetas al año; *he looks under eighteen to me,* a mi me parece que tiene menos de dieciocho años; *there was nobody under the age of sixty,* no había nadie con menos de sesenta años. **3** (*ruler*) bajo, en el tiempo de: *dancing was banned under Cromwell,* bajo Cromwell estaba prohibido bailar. **4** (*according to*) conforme a, según: *under the terms of the agreement,* según los términos del acuerdo. **5** (*subjecto to, in*) bajo: *he's under arrest,* está detenido, está bajo arresto. **6** (*known by*) con, bajo: *she worked under a false name,* trabajó con un nombre falso. **7** ASTROL bajo: *she was born under Cancer,* nació bajo el signo de Cáncer. – **8** *adv* (*below*) debajo: *he fell into the river and was under for over a minute,* cayó al río y estuvo bajo el agua durante más de un minuto. **9** (*less*) menos: *we have a wide range of watches for £30 or under,* tenemos una amplia gama de relojes por treinta libras o menos.

● **to be under age,** ser menor de edad. ‖ **to be under cover,** (*protected*) estar a cubierto; (*in hiding*) estar en la clandestinidad. ‖ **to be under lock and key,** estar bajo llave. ‖ **to be under repair,** estar en reparación, estar reparándose. ‖ **to be under the doctor,** estar en manos del médico. ‖ **to be under the impression that ...,** tener la impresión de que ... ‖ **to go under,** estrellarse, irse a pique. ‖ **under the circumstances ...,** dadas la circunstancias ...

under- ['ʌndəʳ] *pref* (*below*) infra-, sub-; (*insufficiently*) insuficientemente: *the library is underused,* la biblioteca está infrautilizada.

underarm ['ʌndərɑːm] **1** *adv* SP sin alzar el brazo por encima del hombro. – **2** *adj* SP hecho,-a sin alzar el brazo por encima del hombro. **3** (*of the armpit*) de las axilas: *she bought him some underarm deodorant,* le compró desodorante para las axilas.

undercarriage ['ʌndəkærɪdʒ] *n* AER tren *m* de aterrizaje.

undercharge [ʌndə'tʃɑːdʒ] *t* cobrar menos de lo debido.

underclothes ['ʌndəkləʊðz] *npl* ropa *f sing* interior.

underclothing ['ʌndəkləʊðɪŋ] *n* ropa *f* interior.

undercoat ['ʌndəkəʊt] *n* (*of paint*) primera mano *f*.

undercover [ʌndə'kʌvəʳ] **1** *adj* clandestino,-a, secreto,-a,. – **2** *adv* en la clandestinidad.

undercurrent ['ʌndəkʌrənt] **1** *n* (*in sea*) corriente *f* submarina. **2** *fig* tendencia oculta.

undercut [ʌndə'kʌt] *t* vender más barato que.
▲ *pt & pp* **undercut,** *ger* **undercutting**.

underdeveloped [ʌndədɪ'veləpt] **1** *adj* subdesarrollado,-a. **2** (*of photo*) insuficientemente revelado,-a.

underdevelopment [ʌndədɪ'veləpmənt] *n* subdesarrollo.

underdog ['ʌndədɒg] *n* desvalido,-a, perdedor,-ra.
● **the underdogs,** los de abajo, los desamparados.

underdone [ʌndə'dʌn] *adj* CULIN poco hecho,-a.

underemployed [ʌndərem'plɔɪd] *adj* subempleado,-a.

underemployment [ʌndərem'plɔɪmənt] *n* subempleo.

underestimate [ʌndər'estɪmət] **1** *n* infravaloración *f*, menosprecio. – **2** *t* infravalorar, subestimar.
▲ (*verbo*) [ʌndər'estɪmeɪt].

underexposure [ʌndərɪk'spəʊʒəʳ] *n* (*of photo*) subexposición *f*.

underfed [ʌndə'fed] *adj* subalimentado,-a, desnutrido,-a.

underfoot [ʌndə'fʊt] *adv* debajo de los pies, en el suelo.
● **to trample sth. underfoot,** pisotear algo.

undergo [ʌndə'gəʊ] **1** *t* (*general*) experimentar. **2** (*change*) sufrir. **3** (*test*) pasar por, someterse a: *he has undergone many operations,* se ha sometido a numerosas intervenciones quirúrgicas.
▲ *pt* **underwent,** *pp* **undergone** [ʌndə'gɒn].

undergraduate [ʌndə'grædjʊət] **1** *n* estudiante *mf* universitario,-a no licenciado,-a. – **2** *adj* no graduado,-a, no licenciado,-a.

underground ['ʌndəgraʊnd] **1** *adj* subterráneo,-a. **2** *fig* clandestino,-a. **3** *fig* (*cinema, music*) underground. – **4** *n* (*railway*) metro: *it's quicker on the underground,* es más rápido en metro. **5** (*resistance*) resistencia: *she joined the underground to fight the Germans,* se incorporó a la resistencia para luchar contra los alemanes. – **6** *adv* bajo tierra. **7** *fig* (*secretly*) en la clandestinidad, clandestinamente: *he went underground during the uprising,* durante la revuelta pasó a la clandestinidad.

▲ (*adverbio*) [ˌʌndəˈɡraʊnd].

undergrowth [ˈʌndəɡraʊθ] *n* maleza, monte *m* bajo.

underhand [ˈʌndəhænd] **1** *adj fig* (*method*) ilícito,-a, deshonesto,-a, turbio,-a, poco limpio,-a: *he is always making underhand deals*, siempre está metido en tratos poco limpios. **2** (*trick*) malo. **3** (*attack*) ladino,-a, solapado,-a. **4** (*service*) sacar con la mano por debajo del hombro.

underline [ˌʌndəˈlaɪn] *t* subrayar.

underling [ˈʌndəlɪŋ] **1** *n pej* subordinado,-a, inferior *mf*, mandado,-a. **2** (*follower*) secuaz *m*.

underlying [ˌʌndəˈlaɪɪŋ] **1** *adj* (*hidden*) subyacente. **2** *fig* (*basic*) esencial, fundamental.

undermanned [ˌʌndəˈmænd] **1** *adj* falto,-a de personal, escaso,-a de personal. **2** MAR sin la debida tripulación *f*.

undermentioned [ˌʌndəˈmenʃənd] *adj* abajo citado,-a, abajo mencionado,-a.

undermine [ˌʌndəˈmaɪn] *t* minar, socavar.

underneath [ˌʌndəˈniːθ] **1** *prep* bajo, debajo de. – **2** *adv* abajo, debajo, por debajo. – **3** *adj* de abajo, inferior. – **4** *n* parte *f* inferior, fondo.

undernourished [ˌʌndəˈnʌrɪʃt] *adj* desnutrido,-a, subalimentado,-a.

underpaid [ˌʌndəˈpeɪd] *adj* mal pagado,-a.

underpants [ˈʌndəpænts] *npl* calzoncillos *mpl*, eslip *m* sing.

underpass [ˈʌndəpɑːs] *n* paso subterráneo.

underprivileged [ˌʌndəˈprɪvɪlɪdʒd] **1** *adj* desvalido,-a, marginado,-a, desamparado,-a. – **2 the underprivileged,** *npl* los desvalidos.

underrate [ˌʌndəˈreɪt] **1** *t* (*danger*) subestimar, juzgar mal. **2** (*person*) menospreciar.

undersell [ˌʌndəˈsel] **1** *t* (*at too low a price*) malvender. **2** (*undercut*) vender más barato que.

▲ *pt & pp* **undersold** [ˌʌndəˈsəʊld].

undershirt [ˈʌndəʃɜːt] *n* (*us*) camiseta.

undersigned [ˌʌndəˈsaɪnd] **1** *adj* abajo firmante. – **2** *n* abajo firmante *mf*.

undersized [ˌʌndəˈsaɪzd] **1** *adj* (*thing*) demasiado pequeño,-a, diminuto,-a. **2** (*person*) diminuto,-a. **3** (*baby*) sietemesino,-a.

■ **undersized baby,** bebé *m* sietemesino.

underskirt [ˈʌndəskɜːt] **1** *n* (*modern use*) combinación *f*. **2** (*petticoat*) enaguas *fpl*. **3** (*lining*) forro.

undersold [ˌʌndəˈsəʊld] *pt & pp* → **undersell**.

understaffed [ˌʌndəˈstɑːft] *adj* falto,-a de personal.

understand [ˌʌndəˈstænd] **1** *t* entender, comprender. **2** (*believe*) tener entendido. **3** (*to get on with sb.*) entenderse: *they understand each other very well*, se entienden muy bien. **4** (*take for granted*) sobreentender.

● **to give to understand,** dar a entender.

▲ *pt & pp* **understood**.

understandable [ˌʌndəˈstændəbəl] *adj* comprensible.

understanding [ˌʌndəˈstændɪŋ] **1** *n* (*intelligence*) entendimiento, inteligencia. **2** (*grasp*) comprensión *f*. **3** (*agreement*) acuerdo: *they quickly reached an understanding*, no tardaron nada en llegar a un acuerdo. **4** (*condition*) condición *f*: *I'll lend you the money on the understanding that you pay me back as soon as possible*, te dejaré el dinero a condición de que me lo devuelvas lo antes posible. **5** (*interpretation*) interpretación *f*: *it is my understanding that she'll be back soon*, tengo entendido que ella volverá pronto. – **6** *adj* comprensivo,-a.

understatement [ˌʌndəˈsteɪtmənt] *n* atenuación *f*, eufemismo: *it's an understatement to say that ...*, es quedarse corto decir ...

understood [ˌʌndəˈstʊd] **1** *pt & pp* → **understand**. – **2** *adj* (*assumed*) entendido,-a: *I wish it to be understood that I'm here against my will*, quiero que conste que estoy aquí en contra de mi voluntad. **3** (*agreed on*) convenido,-a. **4** (*implied*) sobreentendido,-a, implícito,-a.

● **to make os. understood,** hacerse entender.

understudy [ˈʌndəstʌdɪ] **1** *n* THEAT suplente *mf*. – **2** *t* THEAT doblar a, aprender un papel para suplir a.

▲ (*sustantivo*) *pl* **understudies**; (*verbo*) *pt & pp* **understudied**, *ger* **understudying**.

undertake [ˌʌndəˈteɪk] **1** *t* (*take on - job, task*) emprender, encargarse de; (*- responsibility*) asumir: *this is a responsibility few would undertake*, poca gente estaría dispuesta a asumir de esta responsabilidad. – **2** *i* (*promise*) comprometerse (**to,** a): *he undertook to supply the materials*, se comprometió a suministrar el material.

▲ *pt* **undertook**, *pp* **undertaken** [ˌʌndəˈteɪkən].

undertaker [ˈʌndəteɪkəʳ] **1** *n* empresario,-a de pompas fúnebres. – **2** *npl* (*undertaker's*) funeraria, pompas *fpl* fúnebres.

undertaking [ˌʌndəˈteɪkɪŋ] **1** *n* (*task*) empresa, tarea. **2** (*responsibility*) responsabilidad *f*, carga. **3** (*promise*) garantía, promesa: *he was unable to give me any such undertaking*, le fue imposible darme tal garantía.

■ **large-scale undertaking,** empresa a gran escala.

under-the-counter [ˌʌndəðəˈkaʊntəʳ] *adj fam* (*buying and selling*) bajo mano, en secreto.

■ **under-the-counter sales,** ventas bajo mano.

undertone [ˈʌndətəʊn] **1** *n* (*low voice*) voz *f* baja, murmullo. **2** (*colour*) color *m* de fondo. **3** *fig* (*suggestion*) fondo, matiz *m*; (*tendency*) corriente *f*.

undertook [ˌʌndəˈtʊk] *pt* → **undertake**.

undervalue [ˌʌndəˈvæljuː] *t* infravalorar, subvalorar.

underwater [ˌʌndəˈwɔːtəʳ] **1** *adj* submarino,-a, subacuático,-a: *underwater sports*, deportes subacuáticos. – **2** *adv* bajo el agua.

underwear [ˈʌndəwɛəʳ] *n* ropa interior.

underweight [ˌʌndəˈweɪt] *adj* (*gen*) de peso insuficiente.

● **to be underweight,** (*gen*) no pesar lo suficiente, tener un peso inferior al debido; (*athlete*) no dar el peso.

underwent [ˌʌndəˈwent] *pt* → **undergo**.

underworld [ˈʌndəwɜːld] **1** *n* (*of criminals*) hampa, bajos fondos *mpl*, inframundo. **2** (*Hades*) el Hades, el averno.

underwrite [ˌʌndəˈraɪt] **1** *t* (*insurance*) asegurar. **2** FIN suscribir. **3** (*guarantee*) garantizar, avalar.

▲ *pt* **underwrote** [ˌʌndəˈrəʊt], *pp* **underwritten** [ˌʌndəˈrɪtən].

underwriter [ˈʌndəraɪtəʳ] **1** *n* (*insurer*) asegurador,-ra. **2** FIN suscriptor,-ra.

underwritten [ˌʌndəˈrɪtən] *pp* → **underwrite**.

underwrote [ˌʌndəˈrəʊt] *pt* → **underwrite**.

undeserved [ˌʌndɪˈzɜːvd] *adj* inmerecido,-a.

undeserving [ˌʌndɪˈzɜːvɪŋ] *adj* (*not meritorious*) de poco mérito, que no merece atención.

● **undeserving of,** indigno,-a de.

undesirable [ˌʌndɪˈzaɪərəbəl] **1** *adj* indeseable. – **2** *n* indeseable *mf*.

undetected [ˌʌndɪˈtektɪd] *adj* (*error*) pasado,-a por alto, no detectado,-a.

● **to pass undetected,** pasar desapercibido,-a.

undetermined [ˌʌndɪˈtɜːmaɪnd] *adj* indeterminado,-a, indefinido,-a.

undeterred [ˌʌndɪˈtɜːd] *adj* sin inmutarse, sin dejarse intimidar por.

● **undeterred by,** sin arredrarse ante, sin dejarse acobardar por.

undeveloped [ʌndɪ'veləpt] **1** *adj* sin desarrollar. **2** (*land*) sin edificar, sin explotar, sin cultivar. **3** (*film*) sin revelar.

undid [ʌn'dɪd] *pt* → **undo**.

undies ['ʌndiːz] *npl fam* bragas *fpl*.

undigested [ʌndaɪ'dʒestɪd] **1** *adj* indigesto,-a. **2** *fig* mal digerido,-a, mal asimilado,-a.

undignified [ʌn'dɪgnɪfaɪd] **1** *adj* (*person*) poco digno,-a. **2** (*act*) poco decoroso,-a.

undiluted [ʌndaɪ'luːtɪd] *adj* no diluido,-a, sin diluir, puro,-a: *pure undiluted orange juice,* puro zumo de naranja natural.

● **to talk undiluted nonsense,** decir solemnes tonterías.

undiplomatic [ʌndɪplə'mætɪk] *adj* poco diplomático,-a, indiscreto,-a.

undiscerning [ʌndɪ'sɜːnɪŋ] *adj* sin discernimiento, poco perspicaz.

undischarged [ʌndɪs'tʃɑːdʒd] **1** *adj* (*bankrupt*) no rehabilitado,-a. **2** (*duty*) no cumplido,-a. **3** (*debt*) sin liquidar. **4** (*rifle, battery*) sin descargar.

undisciplined [ʌn'dɪsɪplɪnd] *adj* indisciplinado,-a.

undisclosed [ʌndɪs'kləʊzd] *adj* sin revelar.

undiscovered [ʌndɪs'kʌvəd] **1** *adj* sin descubrir, no descubierto. **2** (*place*) desconocido,-a.

undiscriminating [ʌndɪs'krɪmɪneɪtɪŋ] **1** *adj* (*not preferential*) indiscriminado,-a, sin discriminación. **2** (*without judgment*) sin discernimiento, poco juicioso,-a.

undisguised [ʌndɪs'gaɪzd] **1** *adj* (*person*) sin disfraz *m*. **2** *fig* franco,-a, abierto,-a, sincero,-a.

undisputed [ʌndɪs'pjuːtɪd] **1** *adj* (*unquestionable*) indiscutible, incuestionable. **2** (*unchallenged*) incontestable.

undisturbed [ʌndɪs'tɜːbd] **1** *adj* (*person*) tranquilo,-a: *she wants to be left undisturbed,* ella quiere que la dejen tranquila. **2** (*objects*) intacto,-a, sin tocar: *the police found the room undisturbed,* la policía encontró la habitación intacta.

undivided [ʌndɪ'vaɪdɪd] **1** *adj* (*whole*) entero,-a, íntegro,-a. **2** (*unanimous*) unánime.

● **to give one's undivided attention to sb./sth.,** prestar toda la atención a algn./algo.

undo [ʌn'duː] **1** *t* (*knot*) deshacer, desatar. **2** (*button*) desabrochar. **3** (*arrangement*) anular. **4** (*destroy*) deshacer, destruir. **5** (*to set right*) enmendar, reparar.

● **to undo the damage,** reparar el daño. ‖ **to leave sth. undone,** dejar algo sin hacer, dejar algo por hacer. ‖ **what is done cannot be undone,** a lo hecho pecho.

▲ *pt undid, pp undone.*

undone [ʌn'dʌn] *adj* (*incomplete*) inacabado,-a: *he left some of the exercises undone,* dejó algunos de los ejercicios sin acabar.

undoubted [ʌn'daʊtɪd] *adj* indudable.

undreamed of [ʌn'driːmdəv, ʌn'dremtəv] *adj* nunca soñado,-a: *we now enjoy freedom and wealth previously undreamed of,* ahora disfrutamos de una libertad y una riqueza nunca soñadas.

undress [ʌn'dres] **1** *t* desnudar. – **2** *i* desnudarse.

undressed [ʌn'drest] *adj* (*naked*) desnudo,-a.

● **to get undressed,** desnudarse, quitarse la ropa.

undue [ʌn'djuː] **1** *adj* (*exaggerated*) excesivo,-a, no justificado,-a. **2** (*not suitable*) indebido,-a.

undulate ['ʌndjʊleɪt] **1** *i* ondular, ondear. – **2** *t* hacer ondear.

undulation [ʌndjʊ'leɪʃən] *n* ondulación *f*.

unduly [ʌn'djuːlɪ] *adv* indebidamente, excesivamente.

undying [ʌn'daɪɪŋ] *adj* imperecedero,-a.

unearned [ʌn'ɜːnd] **1** *adj* (*salary*) no ganado,-a. **2** (*undeserved*) inmerecido,-a.

■ **unearned income,** ingresos *mpl* no salariales. ‖ **unearned increment,** plusvalía.

unearth [ʌn'ɜːθ] **1** *t* desenterrar. **2** *fig* desenterrar, sacar a la luz, descubrir.

unearthly [ʌn'ɜːθlɪ] **1** *adj* (*supernatural*) sobrenatural, de otro mundo. **2** *fam* espantoso,-a, horrible, infernal: *stop making that unearthly row,* deja de hacer ese ruido infernal. **3** (*hour*) intempestivo,-a.

uneasiness [ʌn'iːzɪnəs] **1** *n* (*of person*) inquietud *f*, intranquilidad *f*, desasosiego *m*. **2** (*of situation*) incomodidad *f*, molestia *f*, malestar *m*.

uneasy [ʌn'iːzɪ] **1** *adj* (*worried*) intranquilo,-a, inquieto,-a, preocupado,-a; (*disturbing*) inquietante. **2** (*annoying*) incómodo,-a, molesto,-a.

● **to be uneasy about sth.,** inquietarse por algo, preocuparse por algo.

■ **uneasy sleep,** sueño agitado.

▲ *comp* **uneasier,** *superl* **uneasiest**.

uneconomic [ʌniːkə'nɒmɪk] *adj* poco económico,-a, poco rentable.

uneconomical [ʌniːkə'nɒmɪkəl] *adj* poco rentable, poco económico,-a.

uneducated [ʌn'edjʊkeɪtɪd] *adj* inculto,-a, ignorante.

unemployed [ʌnɪm'plɔɪd] *adj* parado,-a, sin trabajo, en paro.

● **to be unemployed,** estar en paro. ■ **the unemployed,** los parados.

unemployment [ʌnɪm'plɔɪmənt] **1** *n* paro, desempleo. **2** (*percentage*) número de parados.

● **to be on unemployment benefit,** cobrar el paro. ■ **unemployment benefit,** subsidio de desempleo. ‖ **unemployment compensation,** US subsidio de desempleo.

unending [ʌn'endɪŋ] *adj* interminable.

unenthusiastic [ʌnɪnθjuːzɪ'æstɪk] *adj* poco entusiasta.

unenviable [ʌn'envɪəbəl] *adj* poco envidiable.

unequal [ʌn'iːkwəl] **1** *adj* (*not the same*) desigual, distinto,-a; (*pulse*) irregular. **2** (*not adequate*) poco apto, inadecuado,-a.

● **to be unequal to doing sth.,** no estar a la altura para hacer algo, ser incapaz de hacer algo.

unequaled [ʌn'iːkwəld] *adj* US → **unequalled**.

unequalled [ʌn'iːkwəld] *adj* sin igual, sin par.

unequivocal [ʌn'kwɪvəkəl] *adj* inequívoco,-a, claro,-a.

unerring [ʌn'ɜːrɪŋ] *adj* infalible.

UNESCO [juː'neskəʊ] *abbr* (*United Nations Educational, Scientific and Cultural Organization*) Organización de las Naciones Unidas para la Educación, la Ciencia y la Cultura; (*abbreviation*) UNESCO *f*.

unethical [ʌn'eθɪkəl] *adj* poco ético,-a, inmoral.

uneven [ʌn'iːvən] **1** *adj* (*not level*) desigual; (*bumpy*) accidentado,-a: *uneven land,* terreno accidentado. **2** (*varying*) irregular, variable. **3** (*road*) lleno,-a de baches. **4** (*unfairly matched*) desigual: *it was an uneven match,* resultó un partido desigual. **5** MATH impar.

unevenness [ʌn'iːvənnəs] **1** *n* (*of a surface*) desigualdad *f*. **2** (*of progress*) irregularidad *f*.

uneventful [ʌnɪ'ventfʊl] **1** *adj* sin acontecimientos, tranquilo,-a: *he had a very uneventful life,* tuvo una vida muy tranquila. **2** (*routine*) monótono,-a, rutinario,-a.

unexceptionable [ʌnɪk'sepʃənəbəl] *adj fml* irreprochable, intachable.

unexceptional [ʌnɪk'sepʃənəl] *adj* corriente, ordinario,-a.

unexciting [ʌnɪk'saɪtɪŋ] *adj* (*boring*) monótono,-a; (*uninteresting*) sin interés.

unexpected [ʌnɪk'spektɪd] **1** *adj* inesperado,-a. **2** (*event*) imprevisto,-a.

unexplained [ʌnɪks'pleɪnd] *adj* inexplicado,-a: *her whereabouts still remain unexplained,* su paradero sigue siendo un misterio.

unexplored [ʌnɪk'splɔːd] *adj* inexplorado,-a.

unexposed [ʌnɪks'pəʊzd] **1** *adj* (*film*) sin exponer.

unexpurgated [ʌn'ekspɜːgeɪtɪd] *adj* íntegro,-a, sin expurgar.

unfailing [ʌn'feɪlɪŋ] **1** *adj* (*general*) indefectible; (*incessant*) constante. **2** (*patience*) inagotable; (*humour*) inalterable. **3** (*memory*) infalible.

unfair [ʌn'feəʳ] **1** *adj* injusto,-a. **2** (*sport*) sucio,-a.

unfairly [ʌn'feəlɪ] *adv* injustamente.

unfairness [ʌn'feənəs] **1** *n* injusticia. **2** (*competition*) deslealtad *f*; (*sport*) suciedad *f*. **3** (*prices*) exceso, exageración *f*.

unfaithful [ʌn'feɪθfʊl] **1** *adj* (*husband, wife*) infiel. **2** (*friend*) desleal.

unfaithfulness [ʌn'feɪθfʊlnəs] **1** *n* (*of husband, wife*) infidelidad *f*. **2** (*of friend*) deslealtad *f*.

unfamiliar [ʌnfə'mɪlɪəʳ] *adj* (*unknown*) desconocido,-a.
● **to be unfamiliar with,** desconocer, no estar familiarizado,-a con.

unfashionable [ʌn'fæʃənəbəl] *adj* (*fashion, trends, etc.*) pasado,-a de moda; (*ideas, measures*) poco popular.

unfasten [ʌn'fɑːsən] **1** *t* (*vest, button*) desabrochar. **2** (*untie*) desatar. **3** (*open*) abrir.

unfathomable [ʌn'fæðəməbəl] *adj fml* insondable.

unfavorable [ʌn'feɪvərəbəl] *adj us* → **unfavourable**.

unfavorably [ʌn'feɪvərəblɪ] *adv us* → **unfavourably**.

unfavourable [ʌn'feɪvərəbəl] **1** *adj* (*gen*) desfavorable; (*criticism*) adverso,-a. **2** (*winds*) contrario,-a.

unfavourably [ʌn'feɪvərəblɪ] *adv* desfavorablemente.

unfeasible [ʌn'fiːzəbəl] *adj* irrealizable, impracticable.

unfeeling [ʌn'fiːlɪŋ] **1** *adj* (*insensitive*) insensible. **2** (*unsympathetic*) sin compasión *f*.

unfettered [ʌn'fetəd] *adj* sin trabas.

unfinished [ʌn'fɪnɪʃt] *adj* inacabado,-a, incompleto,-a, sin acabar.
■ **unfinished business,** un asunto pendiente.

unfit [ʌn'fɪt] **1** *adj* (*person*) no apto,-a, incapaz: *he is unfit for the job,* no es apto para el trabajo; *I'm unfit to do anything at the moment,* soy incapaz de hacer nada en este momento. **2** (*physically*) incapacitado,-a, inútil. **3** (*injured*) lesionado,-a. **4** (*incompetent*) incompetente.
● **to be unfit,** no estar en forma.

unflagging [ʌn'flægɪŋ] **1** *adj* (*courage*) incansable, infatigable. **2** (*interest*) constante.

unflappable [ʌn'flæpəbəl] *adj fam* imperturbable, flemático,-a.

unflattering [ʌn'flætərɪŋ] *adj* poco halagüeño,-a, poco halagador,-ra.

unflinching [ʌn'flɪntʃɪŋ] **1** *adj* (*determined*) resuelto,-a, decidido,-a. **2** (*unafraid*) impávido,-a.

unfold [ʌn'fəʊld] **1** *t* (*paper*) desplegar; (*sheet*) desdoblar. **2** (*newspaper*) abrir; (*map*) extender. **3** (*outline*) exponer; (*reveal*) revelar. **4** (*secret*) descubrir. – **5** *i* (*open up*) desplegarse, desdoblarse, abrirse; (*landscape*) extenderse: *the sofa unfolds into a double bed,* el sofá se convierte en una cama de matrimonio. **6** (*ideas etc*) desarrollarse.

7 (*secret*) descubrirse, revelarse: *the mystery unfolds,* el misterio se revela.

unforeseeable [ʌnfɔː'siːəbəl] *adj* imprevisible.

unforeseen [ʌnfɔː'siːn] *adj* imprevisto,-a.

unforgettable [ʌnfə'getəbəl] *adj* inolvidable.

unforgivable [ʌnfə'gɪvəbəl] *adj* imperdonable.

unforgiving [ʌnfə'gɪvɪŋ] *adj* implacable, que no perdona.

unfortunate [ʌn'fɔːtʃənət] **1** *adj* (*person*) desgraciado,-a, desafortunado,-a; (*event*) desgraciado,-a. **2** (*remark*) desafortunado,-a.
● **how unfortunate!,** ¡qué mala suerte!, ¡qué pena!

unfortunately [ʌn'fɔːtʃənətlɪ] *adv* desgraciadamente, desafortunadamente, por desgracia.

unfounded [ʌn'faʊndɪd] *adj* (*rumour*) infundado,-a, sin base, sin fundamento; (*complaint*) injustificado,-a.

unfreeze [ʌn'friːz] **1** *t* (*defrost*) descongelar. **2** COMM (*prices, wages etc*) descongelar; (*account, loan*) desbloquear.
▲ *pt* **unfroze,** *pp* **unfrozen.**

unfrequented [ʌnfrɪ'kwentɪd] *adj* poco frecuentado,-a.

unfriendly [ʌn'frendlɪ] *adj* poco amistoso,-a, antipático,-a, hostil.
▲ *comp* **unfriendlier,** *superl* **unfriendliest.**

unfroze [ʌn'frəʊz] *pt* → **unfreeze.**

unfrozen [ʌn'frəʊzən] *pp* → **unfreeze.**

unfruitful [ʌn'fruːtfʊl] **1** *adj* estéril. **2** *fig* infructuoso,-a.

unfulfilled [ʌnfʊl'fɪld] **1** *adj* (*not carried out*) incumplido,-a, frustrado,-a. **2** (*not satisfied*) no satisfecho,-a, insatisfecho,-a. **3** (*ambition*) frustrado,-a; (*dream*) irrealizado,-a.

unfurl [ʌn'fɜːl] **1** *t* desplegar. – **2** *i* desplegarse.

unfurnished [ʌn'fɜːnɪʃt] **1** *adj* sin amueblar, desamueblado,-a. **2** (*flat to let*) vacío,-a.

ungainly [ʌn'geɪnlɪ] **1** *adj* (*awkward*) torpe. **2** (*gait*) desgarbado,-a.
▲ *comp* **ungainlier,** *superl* **ungainliest.**

ungodly [ʌn'gɒdlɪ] **1** *adj* (*behaviour, language*) impío,-a. **2** *fam fig* (*hour*) intempestivo,-a: *she got home at an ungodly hour,* llegó a casa a las tantas de la noche.
▲ *comp* **ungodlier,** *superl* **ungodliest.**

ungovernable [ʌn'gʌvənəbəl] **1** *adj* (*people, country*) ingobernable. **2** (*emotions*) incontrolable, incontenible, irreprimible.

ungracious [ʌn'greɪʃəs] **1** *adj* poco amable, descortés. **2** (*unpleasant*) desagradable.

ungrateful [ʌn'greɪtfʊl] **1** *adj* (*unthankful*) desagradecido,-a. **2** (*thankless*) ingrato,-a.

ungrudging [ʌn'grʌdʒɪŋ] *adj* (*generous - person*) generoso,-a; (- *support*) incondicional.

ungrudgingly [ʌn'grʌdʒɪŋlɪ] *adv* de buena gana, generosamente.

unguarded [ʌn'gɑːdɪd] **1** *adj* (*unprotected*) indefenso,-a, sin protección; (*without guards*) sin vigilancia. **2** (*careless*) desprevenido,-a, descuidado,-a, imprudente. **3** (*frank*) franco,-a.

unhampered [ʌn'hæmpəd] *adj* libre.
● **unhampered by,** sin estorbos.

unhappily [ʌn'hæpɪlɪ] *adv* (*unfortunately*) desgraciadamente; (*miserably*) tristemente, infelizmente.

unhappiness [ʌn'hæpɪnəs] *n* (*wretchedness*) infelicidad *f*, desdicha; (*sadness*) tristeza.

unhappy [ʌn'hæpɪ] **1** *adj* (*sad*) infeliz, triste. **2** (*miserable*) desdichado,-a, desgraciado,-a, infeliz. **3** (*unsuitable*) desafortunado,-a, poco afortunado,-a.
▲ *comp* **unhappier,** *superl* **unhappiest.**

unharmed [ʌn'hɑːmd] *adj* ileso,-a, indemne.
● **to escape unharmed,** salir ileso,-a.
unhealthy [ʌn'helθɪ] **1** *adj* (*place*) malsano,-a, insalubre.
2 (*ill*) enfermizo,-a, enfermo,-a. **3** *fig* (*unnatural*) morboso,-a, malsano,-a.
▲ *comp* **unhealthier,** *superl* **unhealthiest.**
unheard [ʌn'hɜːd] *adj* no oído,-a: *her appeal went unheard,* su apelación no fue atendida.
● **unheard of,** (*preposterous*) inaudito,-a; (*without precedent*) sin precedente.
▲ *unheard of* se escribe con guión (**unheard-of**) cuando califica un sustantivo.
unheeded [ʌn'hiːdɪd] *adj* desatendido,-a: *his words went unheeded,* desoyeron sus palabras.
unhelpful [ʌn'helpfʊl] *adj* (*advice*) inútil, vano,-a; (*person*) poco servicial.
unhesitating [ʌn'hezɪteɪtɪŋ] **1** *adj* (*person*) resuelto,-a, decidido,-a. **2** (*answer*) pronto,-a, inmediato,-a.
unhesitatingly [ʌn'hezɪteɪtɪŋlɪ] *adv* sin dudar, sin vacilar.
unhinge [ʌn'hɪndʒ] **1** *t* desquiciar, sacar de quicio. **2** (*mind*) trastornar; (*person*) trastornar el juicio de.
unhinged [ʌn'hɪndʒd] **1** *adj* (*door*) desquiciado,-a. **2** (*person, mind*) trastornado,-a, desquiciado,-a.
unholy [ʌn'həʊlɪ] **1** *adj* (*place etc*) profano,-a; (*person*) impío,-a. **2** *fam* infernal, terrible: *he got into an unholy mess,* se metió en un lío de mil demonios.
▲ *comp* **unholier,** *superl* **unholiest.**
unhook [ʌn'hʊk] **1** *t* desenganchar. **2** (*take down*) descolgar. **3** (*dress*) desabrochar.
unhoped-for [ʌn'həʊptfɔːʳ] *adj* inesperado,-a.
▲ Se escribe **unhoped for** cuando no se antepone a un sustantivo.
unhurt [ʌn'hɜːt] *adj* ileso,-a, indemne.
unhygienic [ʌnhaɪ'dʒiːnɪk] *adj* antihigiénico,-a.
UNICEF ['juːnɪsef] *abbr* (*United Nations Children's Fund*) Fondo de las Naciones Unidas para la ayuda a la infancia; (*abbreviation*) UNICEF *m*.
unicorn ['juːnɪkɔːn] *n* unicornio.
unidentified [ʌnaɪ'dentɪfaɪd] *adj* no identificado,-a, sin identificar: *unidentified flying object, ufo,* objeto volador no identificado, ovni *m*.
unification [juːnɪfɪ'keɪʃən] *n* unificación *f*.
uniform ['juːnɪfɔːm] **1** *adj* uniforme. **2** (*temperature*) constante. **– 3** *n* uniforme *m*.
● **in uniform,** de uniforme, uniformado,-a.
uniformed ['juːnɪfɔːmd] *adj* uniformado,-a.
uniformity [juːnɪ'fɔːmətɪ] *n* uniformidad *f*.
unify ['juːnɪfaɪ] *t* unificar.
▲ *pt & pp* **unified,** *ger* **unifying.**
unilateral [juːnɪ'lætərəl] *adj* unilateral.
unimaginable [ʌnɪ'mædʒɪnəbəl] *adj* inimaginable.
unimaginative [ʌnɪ'mædʒɪnətɪv] *adj* poco imaginativo,-a, falto,-a de imaginación.
unimpaired [ʌnɪm'peəd] **1** *adj* (*strength*) no disminuido,-a. **2** (*unharmed*) intacto,-a; (*health*) inalterado,-a.
unimportant [ʌnɪm'pɔːtənt] *adj* insignificante, sin importancia, poco importante.
unimpressed [ʌnɪm'prest] *adj* no impresionado,-a.
unimpressive [ʌnɪm'presɪv] **1** *adj* poco impresionante, mediocre, poco convincente. **2** (*not moving*) poco conmovedor,-ra.
uninformed [ʌnɪn'fɔːmd] **1** *adj* mal informado,-a, ignorante. **2** (*opinion*) sin base, sin fundamento.
uninhabitable [ʌnɪn'hæbɪtəbəl] *adj* inhabitable.

uninhabited [ʌnɪn'hæbɪtɪd] **1** *adj* deshabitado,-a. **2** (*deserted*) despoblado,-a.
uninhibited [ʌnɪn'hɪbɪtɪd] *adj* sin inhibición.
uninitiated [ʌnɪ'nɪʃɪeɪtɪd] *adj* no iniciado,-a, lego,-a, ignorante.
uninspired [ʌnɪn'spaɪəd] **1** *adj* (*performance*) aburrido,-a, soso,-a, mediocre, insulso,-a, poco inspirado,-a. **2** (*person*) falto,-a de inspiración, sin inspiración.
uninspiring [ʌnɪn'spaɪərɪŋ] *adj* que no inspira.
unintelligent [ʌnɪn'telɪdʒent] *adj* ininteligente, poco inteligente.
unintelligible [ʌnɪn'telɪdʒəbəl] *adj* ininteligible, incomprensible.
unintentional [ʌnɪn'tenʃənəl] *adj* involuntario,-a.
unintentionally [ʌnɪn'tenʃənəlɪ] *adv* involuntariamente, sin querer: *she did it unintentionally,* lo hizo sin querer.
uninterested [ʌn'ɪntrəstɪd] *adj* no interesado,-a, sin interés, indiferente.
uninteresting [ʌn'ɪntrəstɪŋ] *adj* sin interés, poco interesante.
uninterrupted [ʌnɪntə'rʌptɪd] *adj* ininterrumpido,-a, continuo,-a.
uninvited [ʌnɪn'vaɪtɪd] **1** *adj* (*guest*) no invitado,-a. **2** (*remark*) gratuito,-a, no solicitado,-a.
uninviting [ʌnɪn'vaɪtɪŋ] *adj* (*appearance*) poco atractivo,-a; (*food*) poco apetitoso,-a, poco apetecible.
union ['juːnɪən] **1** *n* unión *f*. **2** *fig* (*marriage*) enlace *m*. **3** (*of workers*) sindicato. **4** TECH unión *f*. **– 5** *adj* sindical, del sindicato.
■ **Union Jack,** la bandera del Reino Unido, la bandera británica. ‖ **the Union,** US los Estados Unidos.
unionization [juːnɪənaɪ'zeɪʃən] *n* sindicación *f*, sindicalización*f*.
unionize [juːnɪə'naɪz] **1** *t* agremiar, sindicalizar. **– 2** *i* agremiarse, sindicalizarse.
unique [juː'niːk] **1** *adj* (*singular*) único,-a. **2** (*outstanding*) extraordinario,-a.
unisex ['juːnɪseks] *adj* unisex.
unison ['juːnɪsən] **1** *n* MUS unisonancia. **2** *fig* (*harmony*) armonía.
● **in unison,** al unísono.
unit ['juːnɪt] **1** *n* unidad *f*. **2** (*furniture*) módulo, elemento. **3** MIL unidad *f*. **4** MATH unidad *f*. **5** TECH grupo. **6** (*centre*) centro; (*department*) servicio. **7** (*team*) equipo.
■ **unit trust,** (Fin) fondo de inversión. ‖ **intensive care unit,** (Med) unidad *f* de cuidados intensivos, unidad *f* de vigilancia intensiva. ‖ **research unit,** centro de investigaciones. ‖ **film unit,** (*cinema* TV) equipo de rodaje.
unite [juː'naɪt] **1** *t* (*join*) unir; (*assemble*) reunir. **– 2** *i* unirse, reunirse.
united [juː'naɪtɪd] *adj* unido,-a.
● **united we stand, divided we fall,** la unión hace la fuerza.
■ **United Kingdom,** Reino Unido. ‖ **United Nations,** Naciones *fpl* Unidas. ‖ **United States of America,** Estados *mpl* Unidos *mpl* de América. ‖ **United Arab Emirates,** Emiratos *mpl* Árabes Unidos.
unity ['juːnɪtɪ] *n* (*union*) unidad *f*; (*harmony*) armonía.
Univ [juː'nɪ'vɜːsɪtɪ] *abbr* (*University*) Universidad; (*abbreviation*) Univ *f*.
universal [juːnɪ'vɜːsəl] *adj* universal.
■ **universal remedy,** panacea. ‖ **universal suffrage,** sufragio universal.
universe ['juːnɪvɜːs] *n* universo.

university [juːnɪ'vɜːsətɪ] 1 *n* universidad *f.* – 2 *adj* universitario,-a.
▲ (*sustantivo*) *pl* **universities.**

unjust [ʌn'dʒʌst] *adj* (*unfair*) injusto,-a; (*unfounded*) sin fundamento, infundado,-a.

unjustifiable [ʌndʒʌstɪ'faɪəbəl] *adj* injustificable.

unjustified [ʌn'dʒʌstɪfaɪd] *adj* injustificado,-a.

unkempt [ʌn'kempt] 1 *adj* (*general*) descuidado,-a. 2 (*hair*) despeinado,-a. 3 (*appearance*) desaliñado,-a.

unkind [ʌn'kaɪnd] 1 *adj* (*unpleasant*) poco amable, desconsiderado,-a. 2 (*cruel*) cruel; (*criticism*) despiadado,-a.

unkindly [ʌn'kaɪndlɪ] *adv* con poca amabilidad, desconsideradamente.
● **to take sth. unkindly,** tomar algo a mal.

unkindness [ʌn'kaɪndnəs] 1 *n* falta de amabilidad *f*, falta de consideración *f*, antipatía. 2 (*cruelty*) crueldad *f.* 3 (*harshness*) severidad *f.*

unknowing [ʌn'nəʊɪŋ] *adj* (*unaware*) inconsciente; (*ignorant*) ignorante.

unknowingly [ʌn'nəʊɪŋlɪ] *adv* (*unwittingly*) inconscientemente, sin darse cuenta.

unknown [ʌn'nəʊn] 1 *adj* desconocido,-a. – 2 *n* lo desconocido.
■ **unknown quantity,** incógnita.

unlabelled [ʌn'leɪbəld] *adj* sin etiqueta.

unlawful [ʌn'lɔːful] *adj* (*illegal*) ilegal; (*illegitimate*) ilegítimo,-a.

unleash [ʌn'liːʃ] 1 *t* (*dog*) soltar. 2 *fig* (*free - gen*) liberar; (*- passions*) dar rienda suelta a, desatar. 3 (*fury*) provocar.

unleavened [ʌn'levənd] *adj* ácimo,-a, sin levadura.
■ **unleavened bread,** pan ácimo.

unless [ən'les] 1 *conj* a menos que, a no ser que. – 2 *prep* salvo, excepto: *this agreement is binding unless otherwise provided,* este acuerdo es obligatorio salvo disposición contraria.

unlike [ʌn'laɪk] 1 *adj* (*different*) diferente a, distinto de; (*not characteristic*) impropio,-a: *he is not unlike his father,* se parece bastante a su padre; *it's unlike him to forget,* es impropio de él olvidarse. – 2 *prep* a diferencia de: *John, unlike his brothers, takes after his mother,* a diferencia de sus hermanos, Juan se parece más a su madre.

unlikelihood [ʌn'laɪklɪhʊd] *n* improbabilidad *f.*

unlikely [ʌn'laɪklɪ] *adj* (*improbable*) improbable, poco probable; (*unexpected, unusual*) inverosímil: *he is unlikely to get the job,* es poco probable que consiga el empleo.

unlimited [ʌn'lɪmɪtɪd] *adj* ilimitado,-a: *her kindness is unlimited,* su bondad no conoce límites.

unlit [ʌn'lɪt] 1 *adj* (*place*) sin luz, no iluminado,-a, oscuro,-a, sin alumbrado. 2 (*fire etc*) sin encender, no encendido,-a.

unload [ʌn'ləʊd] 1 *t* (*gen*) descargar: *they unloaded the lorry in ten minutes,* descargaron el camión en diez minutos. 2 (*get rid of*) deshacerse de: *the robbers unloaded the loot before escaping,* los atracadores se deshicieron del botín antes de fugarse. – 3 *i* descargar: *you can stop here for unloading only,* se puede parar aquí sólo para descargar.

unloading [ʌn'ləʊdɪŋ] *n* descarga.

unlock [ʌn'lɒk] 1 *t* (*door*) abrir (con llave). 2 *fig* (*secret*) revelar; (*enigma*) resolver.

unlooked-for [ʌn'lʊktfɔːʳ] *adj* inesperado,-a, imprevisto,-a.
▲ *Se escribe* unlooked for *cuando no se antepone a un sustantivo.*

unloosen [ʌn'luːsən] 1 *t* (*shoelace*) aflojar, desatar. 2 (*set free*) soltar.

unloved [ʌn'lʌvd] *adj* no amado,-a.

unloving [ʌn'lʌvɪŋ] *adj* poco cariñoso,-a.

unluckily [ʌn'lʌkɪlɪ] *adv* desafortunadamente, desgraciadamente, por desgracia.

unlucky [ʌn'lʌkɪ] 1 *adj* (*unfortunate*) desafortunado,-a, desgraciado,-a. 2 (*fateful*) aciago,-a, nefasto,-a.
● **to be unlucky,** (*person*) tener mala suerte. ‖ **to be unlucky,** (*thing*) traer mala suerte. ‖ **how unlucky!,** ¡qué mala suerte!
▲ *comp* **unluckier,** *superl* **unluckiest.**

unmade [ʌn'meɪd] 1 *adj* (*bed*) sin hacer. 2 (*road*) sin asfaltar.

unmanageable [ʌn'mænɪdʒəbəl] 1 *adj* (*people*) ingobernable; (*child etc*) indomable. 2 (*large object*) inmanejable, poco manejable.

unmanly [ʌn'mænlɪ] *adj* poco viril, afeminado,-a. 2 (*cowardly*) cobarde.

unmanned [ʌn'mænd] *adj* (*spacecraft*) no tripulado,-a, sin tripulación *f.*

unmarked [ʌn'mɑːkt] 1 *adj* (*as new*) en perfecto estado, como nuevo. 2 (*street*) sin letrero. 3 (*uninjured*) ileso,-a, indemne. 4 SP desmarcado,-a.

unmarried [ʌn'mærɪd] *adj* soltero,-a.

unmask [ʌn'mɑːsk] 1 *t* desenmascarar. 2 *fig* (*conspiracy*) descubrir.

unmatched [ʌn'mætʃt] *adj* (*unique*) sin par, sin igual, incomparable.

unmentionable [ʌn'menʃənəbəl] 1 *adj* que no se debe mencionar, indecible.

unmerciful [ʌn'mɜːsɪful] *adj* despiadado,-a, sin piedad.

unmethodical [ʌnme'θɒdɪkəl] *adj* poco metódico,-a.

unmistakable [ʌnmɪs'teɪkəbəl] *adj* inconfundible, inequívoco,-a.

unmistakably [ʌnmɪs'teɪkəblɪ] *adv* sin lugar a dudas.

unmitigated [ʌn'mɪtɪgeɪtɪd] 1 *adj* (*absolute*) absoluto,-a, total; (*liar*) rematado,-a. 2 (*grief*) profundo,-a. 3 (*hatred*) implacable.

unmolested [ʌnmə'lestɪd] *adj* tranquilo,-a.

unmoved [ʌn'muːvd] 1 *adj* (*indifferent*) impasible, indiferente. 2 (*in place*) en su sitio, sin mover. 3 (*unfeeling*) insensible: *he was unmoved by the horror that surrounded him,* era insensible al horror que había a su alrededor.

unmusical [ʌn'mjuːzɪkəl] 1 *adj* (*not harmonious*) poco armonioso,-a. 2 (*without musical skill*) poco dotado,-a para la música, que tiene mal oído; (*without enthusiasm*) poco aficionado,-a a la música.

unnamed [ʌn'neɪmd] 1 *adj* sin nombre. 2 (*anonymous*) anónimo,-a.

unnatural [ʌn'nætʃərəl] 1 *adj* (*afected*) afectado,-a, poco natural. 2 (*perverse*) antinatural, contra natura; (*abnormal*) anormal.

unnecessary [ʌn'nesəsərɪ] *adj* innecesario,-a, inútil.
● **it's unnecessary to add that ...,** huelga decir que ..., sobra añadir que ...

unnerve [ʌn'nɜːv] 1 *t* (*scare*) acobardar. 2 (*to disturb*) desconcertar, turbar.

unnerving [ʌn'nɜːvɪŋ] *adj* desconcertante.

unnoticed [ʌn'nəʊtɪst] *adj* inadvertido,-a, desapercibido,-a.
● **let sth. go unnoticed,** pasar algo por alto, no reparar en algo.

unnumbered [ʌn'nʌmbəd] 1 *adj* sin numerar. 2 (*countless*) innumerable.

UNO ['juː'en'əʊ] *abbr* (*United Nations Organization*) Organización de las Naciones Unidas; (*abbreviation*) ONU *f.*

unobserved [ˌʌnəb'zɜːvd] *adj* desapercibido,-a, inadvertido,-a.

unobtainable [ˌʌnəb'teɪnəbəl] *adj* inalcanzable, inasequible, que no se puede conseguir.

unobtrusive [ˌʌnəb'truːsɪv] *adj* discreto,-a, modesto,-a.

unobtrusively [ˌʌnəb'truːsɪvlɪ] *adv* discretamente, modestamente.

unoccupied [ʌn'ɒkjʊpaɪd] 1 *adj* (*house*) deshabitado,-a. 2 (*person*) desocupado,-a. 3 (*post*) vacante. 4 (*area*) despoblado,-a. 5 (*seat*) libre. 6 MIL no ocupado,-a.

unofficial [ʌnə'fɪʃəl] *adj* extraoficial, oficioso,-a.

unofficially [ʌnə'fɪʃəlɪ] *adv* extraoficialmente.

unopened [ʌn'əʊpənd] *adj* sin abrir.

unorthodox [ʌn'ɔːθədɒks] 1 *adj* (*behaviour etc*) poco ortodoxo,-a, poco convencional. 2 REL heterodoxo,-a, no ortodoxo,-a.

unpack [ʌn'pæk] 1 *t* (*objects*) desempaquetar, desenvolver. 2 (*suitcase*) deshacer. 3 (*boxes*) desembalar. – 4 *i* deshacer las maletas.

unpaid [ʌn'peɪd] 1 *adj* (*bill, debt*) sin pagar, impagado,-a, por pagar, pendiente. 2 (*work*) no retribuido,-a, sin remuneración.
■ **unpaid balance,** FIN saldo deudor. ‖ **unpaid capital,** FIN capital *m* no desembolsado.

unpalatable [ʌm'pælətəbəl] 1 *adj* (*taste*) desagradable al gusto, de mal sabor. 2 *fig* desagradable, difícil de tragar, difícil de aceptar.

unparalleled [ʌn'pærəleld] 1 *adj* (*of quality*) incomparable, sin par. 2 (*unprecedented*) sin precedente.

unpardonable [ʌn'pɑːdənəbəl] *adj* imperdonable.

unpatriotic [ʌnpætrɪ'ɒtɪk] 1 *adj* (*person*) poco patriótico,-a. 2 (*action*) antipatriótico,-a.

unperturbed [ʌnpə'tɜːbd] *adj* impertérrito,-a, impasible, impávido,-a: *he went on with his work unperturbed,* prosiguió con su trabajo sin inmutarse.
● **unperturbed by,** no perturbado,-a por.

unpick [ʌn'pɪk] *t* (*in sewing*) descoser.

unplanned [ʌn'plænd] *adj* imprevisto,-a, inesperado,-a.

unplayable [ʌn'pleɪəbəl] 1 *adj* (*of music*) intocable, que no se puede tocar. 2 (*a ball in sport*) imposible de jugar. 3 (*sports field*) impracticable, que no está en condiciones.

unpleasant [ʌn'plezənt] *adj* (*disagreeble, nasty*) desagradable, molesto,-a. 2 (*unfriendly*) antipático,-a. 3 (*words*) grosero,-a, mal educado,-a: *she made some most unpleasant remarks,* sus comentarios fueron de lo más grosero.

unpleasantness [ʌn'plezəntnəs] 1 *n* lo desagradable: *I found the unpleasantness of the situation most upsetting,* me disgustó mucho lo desagradable de la situación. 2 (*nastiness*) antipatía, carácter *m* desagradable: *his general unpleasantness annoys people,* su antipatía en general molesta a la gente. 3 (*ill feeling*) resentimiento; (*disagreement*) desavenencias *fpl*: *the will caused much unpleasantness in the family,* el testamento provocó mucho resentimiento entre la familia. 4 (*trouble*) problemas *mpl*.

unplug [ʌn'plʌg] *t* desenchufar.
▲ *pt & pp* **unplugged,** *ger* **unplugging.**

unpolished [ʌn'pɒlɪʃt] 1 *adj* (*general*) sin brillo, sin pulir; (*shoes*) sin lustrar. 2 (*gems*) en bruto; (*floors*) no encerado,-a. 3 *fig* poco pulido,-a, tosco,-a.

unpolluted [ʌnpə'luːtɪd] *adj* no contaminado,-a.

unpopular [ʌn'pɒpjələ'] *adj* impopular: *the new measures were very unpopular,* las nuevas medidas sentaron muy mal.
● **to make os. unpopular,** ganarse la antipatía de los demás.

unpopularity [ʌnpɒpjə'lærɪtɪ] *n* impopularidad *f.*

unprecedented [ʌn'presɪdentɪd] 1 *adj* (*without precedent*) sin precedente. 2 (*unheard of*) inaudito,-a.

unpredictable [ʌnprɪ'dɪktəbəl] 1 *adj* imprevisible. 2 (*of person*) de reacciones imprevisibles. 3 (*whimsical*) antojadizo,-a.

unprejudiced [ʌn'predʒədɪst] *adj* imparcial, sin prejuicios.

unprepared [ʌnprɪ'peəd] 1 *adj* (*talk etc*) improvisado,-a. 2 (*not ready*) desprevenido,-a, no preparado,-a: *she caught him quite unprepared,* ella lo cogió totalmente desprevenido.

unprepossessing [ʌnpriːpə'zesɪŋ] *adj* poco atractivo,-a.

unpresentable [ʌnprɪ'zentəbəl] *adj* impresentable.

unpretentious [ʌnprɪ'tenʃəs] 1 *adj* (*simple*) modesto,-a, sencillo,-a. 2 (*humble*) sin pretensiones *fpl*.

unprincipled [ʌn'prɪnsɪpəld] *adj* sin escrúpulos *mpl*, sin principios *mpl*.

unprintable [ʌn'prɪntəbəl] *adj* (*book*) impublicable; (*remark etc*) intranscribible.

unproductive [ʌnprə'dʌktɪv] 1 *adj* (*inefficient*) improductivo,-a. 2 *fig* (*fruitless*) infructuoso,-a.

unprofessional [ʌnprə'feʃənəl] *adj* (*conduct*) no ético,-a, contrario,-a a la ética profesional; (*person*) poco profesional.

unprofitable [ʌn'prɒfɪtəbəl] 1 *adj* (*efficient*) poco rentable. 2 (*fruitless*) infructuoso,-a, poco provechoso,-a. 3 (*business*) improductivo, no lucrativo,-a.

unpronounceable [ʌnprə'naʊsəbəl] *adj* impronunciable.

unprotected [ʌnprə'tektɪd] *adj* indefenso,-a, sin protección.

unprovoked [ʌnprə'vəʊkt] 1 *adj* no provocado,-a. 2 (*attack*) gratuito,-a.

unpublishable [ʌn'pʌblɪʃəbəl] *adj* impublicable.

unpublished [ʌn'pʌblɪʃt] *adj* inédito,-a, no publicado,-a.

unpunished [ʌn'pʌnɪʃt] *adj* (*person*) sin castigo; (*crime*) impune.
● **to go unpunished,** (*person*) no ser castigado,-a; (*offence*) quedar impune.

unqualified [ʌn'kwɒlɪfaɪd] 1 *adj* (*lacking qualification*) sin título; (*incompetent*) incompetente: *he is unqualified to work,* no reúne las condiciones para trabajar; *there is a need for unqualified labour,* se precisa mano de obra no especializada. 2 (*absolute*) incondicional; (*denial*) rotundo,-a. 3 (*endorsement*) sin reserva; (*success*) total, sin paliativos.

unquenchable [ʌn'kwentʃəbəl] 1 *adj fig* inextinguible, inapagable. 2 (*thirst*) insaciable.

unquestionable [ʌn'kwestʃənəbəl] *adj* incuestionable, indiscutible.

unquestioned [ʌn'kwestʃənd] *adj* (*right*) indiscutido,-a, incontrovertido,-a; (*undoubted*) indudable.

unquestioning [ʌn'kwestʃənɪŋ] *adj* (*general*) incondicional; (*loyalty*) ciego,-a.

unquote [ʌn'kwəʊt] *adv* fin de la cita.
● **quote ...unquote,** se abren comillas ...se cierran comillas.

unravel [ʌn'rævəl] **1** t (untangle) desenmarañar, desenredar. **2** fig (mystery, problem) desenmarañar, desembrollar. – **3** i (become untangled) desenredarse, desenmarañarse. **4** (mystery) desenmarañarse, desembrollarse.
▲ pt & pp **unravelled** (US **unraveled**), ger **unravelling** (US unraveling).

unread [ʌn'red] **1** adj (book) sin leer, no leído,-a. **2** (person) poco leído,-a, inculto,-a.

unreadable [ʌn'riːdəbəl] **1** adj (handwriting) ilegible. **2** (book) imposible de leer; (understand) incomprensible.

unreal [ʌn'rɪəl] adj irreal.

unrealistic [ʌnrɪə'lɪstɪk] adj poco realista.

unreasonable [ʌn'riːzənəbəl] **1** adj poco razonable, irrazonable. **2** (irrational) irracional. **3** (excessive) desmesurado,-a, desmedido,-a; (prices) exorbitante. **4** (hour) inoportuno,-a.

unreasoning [ʌn'riːzənɪŋ] adj irracional.

unrecognizable [ʌnrekəg'naɪzəbəl] adj irreconocible.

unrecognized [ʌn'rekəgnaɪzd] adj (leader, talent) no reconocido,-a.
● to go **unrecognized,** pasar desapercibido,-a, pasar sin ser reconocido,-a.

unrecorded [ʌnrɪ'kɔːdɪd] **1** adj (music etc) no grabado,-a, sin grabar. **2** (remark etc) no mencionado,-a; (event) sin registrar. **3** COMM no registrado,-a, sin registrar.

unrefined [ʌnrɪ'faɪnd] **1** adj (product) no refinado,-a, sin refinar. **2** (person) inculto,-a, rudo,-a, tosco,-a, basto,-a.

unrehearsed [ʌnrɪ'hɜːst] **1** adj (not prepared) improvisado,-a. **2** THEAT sin ensayar.

unrelated [ʌnrɪ'leɪtɪd] **1** adj (unconnected) no relacionado,-a, inconexo,-a. **2** (family) sin parentesco: John James and Mary James are unrelated, John James y Mary James no guardan ningún parentesco entre sí.

unrelenting [ʌnrɪ'lentɪŋ] adj (conduct) inexorable, implacable; (fight) encarnizado,-a.

unreliability [ʌnrɪlaɪə'bɪlɪti] **1** n (person) poca formalidad f; (character) inestabilidad f. **2** (information) poca seguridad f; (weather) inseguridad f. **3** (machine) tendencia a averiarse.

unreliable [ʌnrɪ'laɪəbəl] **1** adj (person) de poca confianza, poco formal, que no es de fiar. **2** (information) que no es de fiar, poco seguro,-a. **3** (machine) poco fiable, poco seguro,-a. **4** (news) poco fidedigno,-a: his car is pretty unreliable, su coche es poco seguro.

unrelieved [ʌnrɪ'liːvd] **1** adj (boredom) absoluto,-a, total. **2** (pain) no aliviado,-a. **3** (landscape) monótono,-a.

unremitting [ʌnrɪ'mɪtɪŋ] **1** adj (unceasing) incesante, continuo,-a. **2** (person) incansable.

unrepentant [ʌnrɪ'pentənt] adj impenitente.

unrepresented [ʌnreprɪ'zentɪd] adj no representado,-a, sin representación f.

unrequited [ʌnrɪ'kwaɪtɪd] adj (love) no correspondido,-a.

unreserved [ʌnrɪ'zɜːvd] **1** adj (not booked) no reservado,-a, libre. **2** (unconditional) incondicional, sin reserva. **3** (character) abierto,-a.

unresolved [ʌnrɪ'zɒlvd] **1** adj (problem) sin resolver, no resuelto,-a. **2** (person) irresoluto,-a.

unresponsive [ʌnrɪ'spɒnsɪv] adj insensible.

unrest [ʌn'rest] **1** n (uneasiness) malestar m. **2** (restlessness) inquietud f; (political disturbance) agitación f, disturbios mpl.

unrewarded [ʌnrɪ'wɔːdɪd] adj sin recompensa.

unripe [ʌn'raɪp] adj verde, inmaduro,-a.

unrivaled [ʌn'raɪvəld] adj US → **unrivalled**.

unrivalled [ʌn'raɪvəld] adj único,-a, sin par, sin rival.

unroll [ʌn'rəʊl] **1** t desenrollar. – **2** i desenrollarse.

unruffled [ʌn'rʌfəld] **1** adj (hair) liso,-a. **2** (water) sereno,-a, tranquilo,-a. **3** (person) imperturbable.

unruly [ʌn'ruːli] **1** adj (child) revoltoso,-a, indisciplinado,-a. **2** (hair) rebelde, despeinado,-a.
▲ comp **unrulier**, superl **unruliest**.

unsaddle [ʌn'sædəl] **1** t (horse) desensillar. **2** (horseman) desmontar.

unsafe [ʌn'seɪf] **1** adj (risky) inseguro,-a, arriesgado,-a. **2** (dangerous) peligroso,-a.

unsaid [ʌn'sed] adj sin decir.
● to leave sth. **unsaid,** dejar de decir algo, callar algo.

unsalaried [ʌn'sælərɪd] adj sin sueldo, no remunerado,-a.

unsalted [ʌn'sɔːltɪd] adj sin sal.

unsanitary [ʌn'sænɪtərɪ] adj antihigiénico,-a.

unsatisfactory [ʌnsætɪs'fæktərɪ] adj insatisfactorio,-a, poco satisfactorio,-a: his work is most unsatisfactory, su trabajo deja mucho que desear.

unsatisfied [ʌn'sætɪsfaɪd] adj insatisfecho,-a.

unsatisfying [ʌn'sætɪsfaɪɪŋ] adj (work etc) poco satisfactorio,-a; (meal) insuficiente.

unsavory [ʌn'seɪvərɪ] adj US → **unsavoury**.

unsavoury [ʌn'seɪvərɪ] **1** adj (taste etc) desagradable; (tasteless) insípido,-a. **2** (morally not right) deshonroso,-a, infame, sospechoso,-a; (person) indeseable.

unscathed [ʌn'skeɪðd] adj indemne, ileso,-a.

unscented [ʌn'sentɪd] adj sin perfume.

unscientific [ʌnsaɪən'tɪfɪk] adj poco científico,-a.

unscramble [ʌn'skræmbəl] t (code) descifrar.

unscrew [ʌn'skruː] t destornillar, desatornillar.

unscripted [ʌn'skrɪptɪd] adj no preparado,-a, sin guión previo.

unscrupulous [ʌn'skruːpjələs] adj sin escrúpulos.

unseasonable [ʌn'siːzənəbəl] adj (of weather) atípico,-a, anormal, impropio,-a.

unseasoned [ʌn'siːzənd] **1** adj (food) sin sazonar, sin aderezar. **2** fig inexperimentado,-a, inexperto,-a. **3** (unripe) no maduro,-a, verde.

unseat [ʌn'siːt] **1** t POL quitar el escaño a. **2** POL derribar, derrocar. **3** (horseriding) derribar.

unseconded [ʌn'sekəndɪd] adj (motion) no apoyado,-a; (person) no secundado,-a.

unseemly [ʌn'siːmlɪ] **1** adj indecoroso,-a. **2** (unsuitable) impropio,-a.

unseen [ʌn'siːn] **1** adj (invisible) no visto,-a, invisible; (unnoticed) inadvertido,-a. – **2** n (translation) a libro abierto.
■ the **unseen,** lo invisible m.

unselfish [ʌn'selfɪʃ] adj desinteresado,-a, generoso,-a.

unselfishly [ʌn'selfɪʃlɪ] adv desinteresadamente.

unselfishness [ʌn'selfɪʃnəs] n desinterés m, abnegación f, altruismo m.

unserviceable [ʌn'sɜːvɪsəbəl] adj inservible, inútil.

unsettle [ʌn'setəl] t perturbar, inquietar.

unsettled [ʌn'setəld] **1** adj (weather) inestable, variable, incierto,-a. **2** (person) nervioso,-a, intranquilo; (situation) inestable. **3** (country etc) agitado,-a. **4** (question, matter) pendiente; (account etc) pendiente, sin saldar. **5** (land) sin colonizar, sin poblar.

unshakable [ʌn'ʃeɪkəbəl] adj (faith) firme, inquebrantable; (person) firme, impertérrito,-a.

unshakeable [ʌnˈʃeɪkəbəl] adj → **unshakable**.

unshaven [ʌnˈʃeɪvən] adj sin afeitar.

unshrinkable [ʌnˈʃrɪŋkəbəl] adj inencogible, que no encoge.

unsightly [ʌnˈsaɪtlɪ] adj feo,-a, antiestético,-a, desagradable.
▲ comp unsightlier, superl unsightliest.

unsigned [ʌnˈsaɪnd] adj sin firmar, no firmado,-a.

unskilful [ʌnˈskɪlfʊl] adj torpe, desmañado,-a, inexperto.

unskilled [ʌnˈskɪld] 1 adj (worker) no cualificado,-a. 2 (job) no especializado,-a. 3 (untalented) inexperto,-a.

unskillful [ʌnˈskɪlfʊl] adj → **unskilful**.

unsociable [ʌnˈsəʊʃəbəl] adj insociable, huraño,-a.

unsold [ʌnˈsəʊld] adj no vendido,-a, sin vender.

unsolicited [ʌnsəˈlɪsɪtɪd] adj (not solicited) no solicitado,-a, voluntario,-a; (spontaneous) espontáneo,-a.

unsolved [ʌnˈsɒlvd] adj no resuelto,-a, sin resolver.

unsophisticated [ʌnsəˈfɪstɪkeɪtɪd] 1 adj (not complex) sencillo,-a, poco sofisticado,-a. 2 fig (naïve) ingenuo,-a.

unsound [ʌnˈsaʊnd] 1 adj (goods) defectuoso,-a, imperfecto,-a; (fruit) podrido,-a. 2 (idea) erróneo,-a, falso,-a, equivocado,-a. 3 (unstable) inestable, débil; (not solid) poco sólido,-a. 4 (sleep) ligero,-a. 5 JUR (mentally unstable) demente. 6 COMM poco seguro,-a, especulativo.

unsparing [ʌnˈspeərɪŋ] adj generoso,-a, pródigo,-a.
● unsparing in one's efforts, sin escatimar esfuerzos. ‖ unsparing of praise, pródigo en alabanzas.

unspeakable [ʌnˈspiːkəbəl] 1 adj (ineffable) indecible, inexpresable, inenarrable. 2 (atrocious) atroz, terrible.

unspecified [ʌnˈspesɪfaɪd] adj no especificado,-a, indeterminado,-a, sin especificar.

unspoiled [ʌnˈspɔɪld] 1 adj (undamaged) intacto,-a, conservado,-a, sin estropear. 2 (child) no mimado,-a.

unspoilt [ʌnˈspɔɪlt] adj → **unspoiled**.

unspoken [ʌnˈspəʊkən] 1 adj (tacit) tácito,-a, implícito,-a. 2 (unuttered word) no pronunciado,-a, sobreentendido,-a; (feelings) no expresado,-a.
■ unspoken agreement, un acuerdo tácito.

unstable [ʌnˈsteɪbəl] adj inestable.

unsteady [ʌnˈstedɪ] 1 adj (not firm) inseguro,-a, inestable; (furniture) cojo,-a, inestable. 2 (voice, hand) tembloroso,-a, poco firme. 3 (weather conditions) variable; (pulse) irregular.
● to be unsteady on one's feet, tambalearse, titubear.

unstinting [ʌnˈstɪntɪŋ] adj pródigo,-a.
● to be unstinting in one's efforts, no escatimar esfuerzos. ‖ to be unstinting in one's praise, no escatimar elogios.

unstitch [ʌnˈstɪtʃ] t descoser.
● to come unstitched, descoserse.

unstressed [ʌnˈstrest] adj LING átono,-a, sin acentuar.

unstuck [ʌnˈstʌk] adj despegado,-a.
● to come unstuck, despegarse, desengancharse, desprenderse; fig venirse abajo, fracasar.

unsubstantiated [ʌnsʌbˈstænʃɪeɪtɪd] adj (accusation) no probada,-a, no demostrado,-a; (rumour) infundado,-a.

unsuccessful [ʌnsəkˈsesfʊl] 1 adj fracasado,-a, sin éxito. 2 (useless) vano, inútil, infructuoso,-a; (examination) suspendido,-a. 3 (candidate in elections) derrotado,-a, vencido,-a.
● to be unsuccessful, no tener éxito, fracasar.

unsuccessfully [ʌnsəkˈsesfʊlɪ] adv sin éxito.

unsuitable [ʌnˈsuːtəbəl] 1 adj (gen) no apto,-a, no indicado,-a: this program is unsuitable for children, este

programa no es apto para los niños; she's unsuitable for the job, no es la persona indicada para el trabajo. 2 (thing) inapropiado,-a, impropio,-a, inadecuado,-a; (comment) inoportuno,-a: those shoes are unsuitable for wet weather, esos zapatos no son adecuados para la lluvia. 3 (time) inconveniente: I hope I haven't called at an unsuitable moment, espero que no haya llamado en un momento inoportuno.

unsuited [ʌnˈsuːtɪd] 1 adj (person) no apto,-a; (thing) impropio,-a, inadecuado,-a. 2 (people) incompatible.

unsupported [ʌnsəˈpɔːtɪd] adj (person) sin apoyo, no respaldado,-a, no apoyado,-a; (statement) infundado,-a, sin fundamento.

unsure [ʌnˈʃʊəʳ] adj inseguro,-a, poco seguro,-a.
● to be unsure about sth., dudar de algo. ‖ to be unsure of os., dudar de sí mismo, carecer de confianza en sí mismo.

unsurmountable [ʌnsəˈmaʊntəbəl] adj insuperable.

unsurpassed [ʌnsəˈpɑːst] adj no superado,-a.

unsuspected [ʌnsəsˈpektɪd] adj (not suspected) insospechado,-a; (unknown) desconocido,-a, ignorado,-a.

unsuspecting [ʌnsəsˈpektɪŋ] adj confiado,-a.
● to be unsuspecting of sth., no sospechar algo.

unsweetened [ʌnˈswiːtənd] adj sin azucarar, no azucarado,-a.

unswerving [ʌnˈswɜːvɪŋ] adj (faith, loyalty) firme, inquebrantable: she was unswerving in her work, era constante en su trabajo.

unsympathetic [ʌnsɪmpəˈθetɪk] adj (unfeeling) poco compasivo, sin compasión f, indiferente; (lacking understanding) poco comprensivo,-a: her teacher was quite unsympathetic, la profesora se mostró poco comprensiva; they were unsympathetic to his appeal, se mostraron indiferentes ante su petición.

unsystematic [ʌnsɪstəˈmætɪk] adj sin sistema, poco metódico,-a.

untainted [ʌnˈteɪntɪd] 1 adj (water, food) fresco,-a, no contaminado,-a. 2 fig (reputation) no manchado,-a, no corrompido,-a.
■ untainted love, amor puro.

untangle [ʌnˈtæŋgəl] t desenmarañar, desenredar.

untapped [ʌnˈtæpt] adj (resources) sin explotar.

untarnished [ʌnˈtɑːnɪʃt] 1 adj (metal) sin oxidar. 2 fig sin mancha, sin tacha.

untaxed [ʌnˈtækst] adj libre de impuestos.

untempered [ʌnˈtempəd] adj (metals) sin templar.

untenable [ʌnˈtenəbəl] adj insostenible, indefendible.

untested [ʌnˈtestɪd] 1 adj (not tried out) no probado,-a. 2 (not proved) sin comprobar.

unthinkable [ʌnˈθɪŋkəbəl] adj impensable, inconcebible: it is unthinkable that this should happen, es impensable que esto pase.

untidiness [ʌnˈtaɪdɪnəs] 1 n (general) desorden m. 2 (scruffiness) desaliño, desaseo.

untidy [ʌnˈtaɪdɪ] 1 adj (room, person) desordenado,-a. 2 (scruffy) desaliñado,-a, desaseado,-a; (hair) despeinado,-a.
▲ comp untidier, superl untidiest.

untie [ʌnˈtaɪ] 1 t (unfasten) desatar. 2 (liberate) soltar, desligar.

until [ənˈtɪl] 1 prep hasta: restaurants are open until very late in Spain, en España los restaurantes abren hasta muy tarde. – 2 conj hasta: she won't stop until she gets what she wants, no parará hasta que consiga lo que quiere.

untimely [ʌnˈtaɪmlɪ] 1 adj inoportuno,-a. 2 (premature) prematuro,-a. – 3 adv (early) prematuramente; (inopportunely) inoportunamente.

untiring [ʌnˈtaɪərɪŋ] *adj* incansable, infatigable.
untold [ʌnˈtəʊld] **1** *adj* (*not told*) no contado,-a. **2** *fig* (*uncalculably great*) incalculable, fabuloso,-a, inaudito,-a; (*unspeakable*) indecible, inefable.
untouchable [ʌnˈtʌtʃəbəl] **1** *adj* intocable. – **2** *n* intocable *mf*.
untouched [ʌnˈtʌtʃt] **1** *adj* (*not touched*) intocado,-a, sin tocar: *much of the food remained untouched,* mucha comida quedó sin tocar. **2** (*not affected*) no afectado,-a; (*unmoved*) insensible. **3** (*unhurt*) ileso,-a, indemne. **4** (*photos*) sin retocar.
untoward [ʌnˈtəwɔːd] **1** *adj* *fml* (*unfortunate*) desafortunado,-a; (*adverse*) adverso,-a, contrario,-a. **2** desgraciado,-a.
■ **untoward circumstances,** circunstancias adversas.
untrained [ʌnˈtreɪnd] **1** *adj* inexperto,-a. **2** (*unskilled*) sin formación (profesional), no cualificado,-a; (*nurse*) sin título. **3** (*animals*) no amaestrado,-a; (*sport*) carente de preparación *f*, sin preparar.
untransferable [ʌntrænsˈfɜːrəbəl] *adj* intransferible.
untried [ʌnˈtraɪd] **1** *adj* (*not tested*) no probado,-a. **2** (*inexperienced*) inexperto,-a, no experimentado,-a. **3** JUR no procesado,-a, no juzgado,-a; (*case*) no visto,-a.
untrue [ʌnˈtruː] **1** *adj* falso,-a. **2** (*unfaithful*) infiel, desleal. **3** (*inexact*) inexacto,-a, erróneo,-a.
untrustworthy [ʌnˈtrʌstwɜːði] *adj* (*person*) poco fiable, informal; (*source*) dudoso,-a, no fidedigno,-a.
untruth [ʌnˈtruːθ] *n* (*falsehood*) mentira; (*lacking in truthfulness*) falsedad *f*.
untruthful [ʌnˈtruːθʊl] *adj* (*person*) mentiroso,-a; (*statement*) falso,-a.
untuned [ʌnˈtjuːnd] *adj* MUS desafinado,-a.
unusable [ʌnˈjuːzəbəl] *adj* inservible, inutilizable.
unused [ʌnˈjuːzd] **1** *adj* (*new*) no usado,-a, nuevo,-a, sin estrenar; (*not in use*) que no se utiliza: *unused stamps are often more valuable than used ones,* los sellos no usados a menudo valen más que los usados; *the drill is second-hand, but unused,* el taladro es de segunda mano, pero está sin estrenar; *I need an unused tape,* necesito una cinta virgen. **2** (*unaccustomed*) no acostumbrado,-a, desacostumbrado,-a: *I'm unused to this heat,* No estoy acostumbrado a que haga tanto calor.
▲ En **2** [ʌnˈjuːst].
unusual [ʌnˈjuːʒʊəl] **1** *adj* (*rare, strange*) raro,-a, insólito,-a, extraño,-a, poco común. **2** (*different*) original; (*exceptional*) excepcional, extraordinario,-a: *it's unusual of him to be so punctual,* es extraño que llegue tan puntual; *Spain has many landscapes of unusual beauty,* España goza de numerosos paisajes de excepcional belleza.
● *that's unusual!,* ¡qué raro!, ¡qué extraño!
unusually [ʌnˈjuːʒʊəlɪ] *adv* excepcionalmente, extraordinariamente: *she's an unusually gifted child,* es una niña con unas dotes poco comunes.
unutterable [ʌnˈʌtərəbəl] *adj* indecible, terrible.
unvarying [ʌnˈveərɪŋ] *adj* invariable, constante.
unveil [ʌnˈveɪl] **1** *t* (*uncover*) descubrir. **2** *fig* (*reveal*) descubrir, desvelar; (*secret*) revelar.
unventilated [ʌnˈventɪleɪtɪd] *adj* sin ventilación *f*, sin aire *m*.
unverifiable [ʌnverɪˈfaɪəbəl] *adj* incomprobable, que no puede verificarse.
unvoiced [ʌnˈvɔɪst] **1** *adj* (*untold*) no expresado,-a. **2** LING (*consonant*) sordo,-a; (*vowel*) mudo,-a.
unwaged [ʌnˈweɪdʒd] *adj* (*not paid*) parado,-a, sin trabajo.

■ **the unwaged,** los parados.
unwanted [ʌnˈwɒntɪd] **1** *adj* (*child*) no deseado,-a. **2** (*advice etc*) no solicitado,-a, no pedido,-a. **3** (*superfluous*) superfluo,-a.
unwarranted [ʌnˈwɒrəntɪd] **1** *adj* (*without justificaion*) injustificado,-a; (*remark*) gratuito,-a. **2** (*interference*) indebido,-a. **3** (*unauthorized*) no autorizado,-a.
unwary [ʌnˈweərɪ] *adj* incauto,-a, imprudente.
▲ *comp* **unwarier,** *superl* **unwariest**.
unwashed [ʌnˈwɒʃt] *adj* sin lavar, sucio,-a.
unwavering [ʌnˈweɪvərɪŋ] **1** *adj* (*steady*) constante, firme; (*courage*) inquebrantable. **2** (*look*) fijo,-a.
● **to be unwavering in one's resolve,** ser firme en sus propósitos.
unwelcome [ʌnˈwelkəm] **1** *adj* (*guest*) inoportuno,-a, molesto,-a; (*news*) desagradable. **2** (*uncomfortable*) incómodo,-a.
● **to make sb. feel unwelcome,** hacer que algn. se sienta incómodo,-a.
unwell [ʌnˈwel] *adj* (*sick, ill*) indispuesto,-a, malo,-a.
unwholesome [ʌnˈhəʊlsəm] **1** *adj* (*climate etc*) insalubre, nocivo,-a. **2** (*morally*) malsano,-a, indeseable, depravado,-a.
unwieldly [ʌnˈwiːldlɪ] *adj* → **unwieldy**.
unwieldy [ʌnˈwiːldɪ] **1** *adj* (*hard to handle*) difícil de manejar, poco manejable; (*cumbersome*) abultado,-a, voluminoso,-a. **2** (*heavy*) pesado,-a; (*clumsy*) torpe, patoso,-a.
▲ *comp* **unwieldier,** *superl* **unwieldiest**.
unwilling [ʌnˈwɪlɪŋ] *adj* reacio,-a, poco dispuesto,-a.
● **to be unwilling to do sth.,** no estar dispuesto,-a a hacer algo.
unwillingly [ʌnˈwɪlɪŋlɪ] *adv* de mala gana, a disgusto.
unwillingness [ʌnˈwɪlɪŋnəs] *n* desgana, poca disposición *f*.
unwind [ʌnˈwaɪnd] **1** *t* desenrollar. – **2** *i* desenrollarse. **3** *fam* (*relax*) relajarse.
▲ *pt & pp* **unwound**.
unwise [ʌnˈwaɪz] **1** *adj* (*foolish*) imprudente; (*senseless*) insensato,-a. **2** (*illadvised*) desaconsejable, poco aconsejable.
unwitting [ʌnˈwɪtɪŋ] *adj* inconsciente, involuntario,-a.
unwittingly [ʌnˈwɪtɪŋlɪ] *adv* sin querer, involuntariamente, inconscientemente.
unworkable [ʌnˈwɜːkəbəl] **1** *adj* (*not feasible*) impracticable; (*not possible*) irrealizable. **2** inexplotable.
unworldly [ʌnˈwɜːldlɪ] **1** *adj* poco mundano,-a, poco realista. **2** (*spiritual*) espiritual; (*naïve*) ingenuo,-a.
▲ *comp* **unworldlier,** *superl* **unworldliest**.
unworthy [ʌnˈwɜːði] *adj* indigno,-a, despreciable: *he is unworthy of my trust,* no merece mi confianza; *she is unworthy of such honour,* es indigna de tal honor.
■ **unworthty behaviour,** conducta despreciable.
▲ *comp* **unworthier,** *superl* **unworthiest**.
unwound [ʌnˈwaʊnd] *pt & pp* → **unwind**.
unwrap [ʌnˈræp] *t* (*present*) desenvolver; (*parcel, package*) abrir, deshacer.
▲ *pt & pp* **unwrapped,** *ger* **unwrapping**.
unwritten [ʌnˈrɪtən] **1** *adj* (*not written*) no escrito,-a; (*agreement*) verbal. **2** (*tradition*) oral. **3** JUR (*common law*) no escrito,-a.
■ **unwritten law,** derecho consuetudinario. ‖ **unwritten tradition,** tradición oral.
unyielding [ʌnˈjiːldɪŋ] *adj* inflexible, rígido,-a.
unzip [ʌnˈzɪp] *t* bajar la cremallera de.
▲ *pt & pp* **unzipped,** *ger* **unzipping**.

up [ʌp] **1** *adv* (*upwards*) hacia arriba, arriba: *to sit up in bed,* incorporarse; *he walked up to the top,* subió andando hasta arriba; *he left the book face up on the table,* dejó el libro boca arriba en la mesa. **2** (*out of bed*) levantado,- a: *he isn't up yet,* aún no se ha levantado. **3** (*sun, moon*): *the sun is up,* ha salido el sol. **4** (*roadworks*) levantado,- a, en obras: *"road up",* "carretera en obras". **5** (*towards*) hacia: *he came up and ...,* se acercó y ... **6** (*northwards*) hacia el norte: *we went up to Scotland,* fuimos a Escocia. **7** (*totally finished*) acabado,-a: *eat it up,* acábatelo, cómetelo todo; *your time's up,* se te ha acabado el tiempo. **8** (*into pieces*) a trozos, a porciones, a raciones: *she cut it up into three,* lo cortó en tres trozos. – **9** *prep* (*movement*): *to go up the stairs,* subir la escalera; *to run up the street,* ir corriendo calle arriba. **10** (*position*) en lo alto de: *up a tree,* en lo alto de un árbol. – **11** *t* subir, aumentar: *they've upped the prices,* han subido los precios.
● *it's not up to much, fam* no vale gran cosa. ‖ *it's up to you, fam* es cosa tuya. ‖ *to be on the up and up, fam* ir cada vez mejor. ‖ *to be up in arms,* estar en pie de guerra: *the people are up in arms about the new taxes,* la gente está en pie de guerra por los nuevos impuestos. ‖ *to be up to sth.,* estar haciendo algo; *pej* estar tramando algo. ‖ *to feel up to doing sth.,* sentirse con fuerzas de hacer algo. ‖ *to up and go, fam* coger e irse. ‖ *up to,* hasta. ‖ *up yours!, taboo* ¡métetelo por el culo! ‖ *well up in sth.,* saber mucho de algo. ‖ *what's up?, fam* ¿qué pasa?
■ *ups and downs,* altibajos *mpl.*
▲ (*verbo*) *pt* & *pp* **upped,** *ger* **upping.**

up-and-coming [ʌpən'kʌmɪŋ] *adj* prometedor,-ra, que promete mucho: *she's an up-and-coming actress,* es una actriz con futuro.

up-and-down [ʌpən'daʊn] **1** *adj* (*motion*) vertical; (*varying*) variable. **2** (*eventful*) accidentado,-a; (*period*) con altibajos.

up-and-up [ʌpən'ʌp] *n* GB *fam* en alza.
● *to be on the up-and-up,* estar en alza, ir cada vez mejor.

upbeat ['ʌpbiːt] *adj fam* alegre, esperanzador,-ra: *all his songs have a pretty upbeat message,* todas sus canciones llevan un mensaje muy esperanzador.

upbraid [ʌp'breɪd] *t fml* regañar, reprender, censurar.

upbringing ['ʌpbrɪŋɪŋ] *n* educación *f*: *his parents gave him the best upbringing a child could have,* sus padres le dieron la mejor educación que un niño puede recibir.

upcoming ['ʌpkʌmɪŋ] *adj* próximo,-a.

update ['ʌpdeɪt] **1** *n* actualización *f*, puesta al día. – **2** *t* actualizar, poner al día, modernizar.
▲ (*verbo*) [ʌp'deɪt].

upfront [ʌp'frʌnt] *adj* sincero,-a, franco,-a.

upgrade [ʌp'greɪd] **1** *t* (*promote*) ascender, subir de categoría; (*improve*) mejorar la calidad de, valorar más. – **2** *n* mejora.
● *to be on the upgrade,* ir mejorando, ir a más.
▲ (*sustantivo*) ['ʌpgreɪd].

upheaval [ʌp'hiːvəl] *n fig* trastorno, agitación *f*.

upheld [ʌp'held] *pt* & *pp* → **uphold.**

uphill ['ʌphɪl] **1** *adj* ascendente. **2** *fig* (*task, struggle*) arduo,-a, difícil, duro,-a, penoso,-a. – **3** *adv* cuesta arriba.
▲ (*adverbio*) [ʌp'hɪl].

uphold [ʌp'həʊld] **1** *t* (*opinion*) sostener, mantener; (*to support*) apoyar. **2** (*defend*) defender: *it is the Trade Unions' duty to uphold workers' rights,* el deber de los sindicatos es defender los derechos de los trabajadores. **3** (*confirm*) confirmar.
● *to uphold the laws,* hacer respetar las leyes.
▲ *pt* & *pp* **upheld.**

upholster [up'həʊlstəʳ] *t* tapizar.

upholstery [ʌp'həʊlstəri] *n* tapicería, tapizado.

upkeep ['ʌpkiːp] *n* (*maintenance*) mantenimiento, conservación *f*; (*costs*) gastos *mpl* de mantenimiento.

uplift [ʌp'lɪft] **1** *t* (*lift up*) elevar, levantar; (*soul, voice*) inspirar, elevar, alzar. – **2** *n fig* edificación *f*, inspiración *f*.

uplifting [ʌp'lɪftɪŋ] *adj fig* edificante.

up-market ['ʌpmɑːkɪt] *adj* de calidad *f* superior, de categoría.

upon [ə'pɒn] *prep fml* en, sobre.
▲ *Véase también* **on.**

upper ['ʌpəʳ] **1** *adj* (*position*) superior. **2** (*in geography*) alto,-a: *the upper Amazon,* el alto Amazonas. – **3** *n* (*of shoe*) pala.
● *to get the upper hand,* llevar ventaja, llevar la delantera. ‖ *to be on one's uppers, dated* estar sin blanca, estar sin un duro.
■ *the upper crust,* la flor y nata. ‖ *upper case,* caja alta. ‖ *upper class,* clase *f* alta. ‖ *upper house,* cámara alta.

upper-class [ʌpə'klɑːs] *adj* de (la) clase alta.

uppermost ['ʌpəməʊst] **1** *adj* más alto,-a. **2** *fig* principal, dominante: *the question that is uppermost in his mind,* el asunto que más le preocupa.

uppish ['ʌpɪʃ] *adj* GB *fam* engreído,-a, presumido,-a: *you don't have to be so uppish about it!,* ¡no hace falta presumir tanto de ello!

uppity ['ʌpɪti] *adj* → **uppish.**

upright ['ʌpraɪt] **1** *adj* derecho,-a, vertical. **2** (*honest*) recto,-a, honrado,-a. – **3** *adv* derecho, en posición *f* vertical: *he stood bolt upright when he heard the seargent,* se puso derecho como un palo al oír al sargento. – **4** *n* SP poste *m*, palo.
■ *upright piano,* piano vertical.

uprising [ʌp'raɪzɪŋ] *n* alzamiento, levantamiento, sublevación *f*.

uproar ['ʌprɔːʳ] *n* alboroto, tumulto: *the whole town was in an uproar about the new rates,* toda la ciudad estaba alborotada por los nuevos impuestos municipales.

uproarious [ʌp'rɔːriəs] **1** *adj* (*especially with laughter*) tumultuoso,-a, ruidoso,-a, escandaloso,-a. **2** (*very funny*) graciosísimo,-a, divertidísimo,-a.

uproot [ʌp'ruːt] **1** *t* (*plant etc*) desarraigar, arrancar; (*people*) desarraigar. **2** (*eliminate*) eliminar, extirpar.

upset [ʌp'set] **1** *adj* (*angry*) disgustado,-a, contrariado,- a, enfadado,-a. **2** (*mentally or physically*) trastornado,-a; (*worried*) preocupado,-a. **3** (*nerves*) desquiciado,-a; (*a little unwell*) indispuesto,-a. **4** (*stomach*) trastornado,-a. **5** (*overturned*) volcado,-a; (*spoiled*) desbaratado,-a. – **6** *n* (*reversal*) revés *m*, contratiempo, vuelco; (*slight ailment*) indisposición *f*, malestar *m*. **7** (*emotion, stomach, etc*) trastorno; (*plans etc*) trastorno, perturbación *f*. **8** (*trouble, difficulty*) molestia, dificultad *f*. **9** (*sport*) un resultado inesperado. – **10** *t* (*overturn*) volcar; (*capsize*) hacer zozobrar. **11** (*spill*) derramar. **12** (*shock*) trastornar. **13** (*person*) contrariar; (*worry*) preocupar; (*displease*) disgustar. **14** (*stomach*) trastornar, sentar mal. **15** (*plans*) desbaratar. **16** (*to cause disorder*) desordenar, revolver, poner patas arriba: *he was very upset by his father's death,* la muerte de su padre le afectó muchísimo; *hot food upsets her stomach,* las comidas picantes le sientan mal; *the bad weather upset our plans,* el mal tiempo dio al traste con nuestros planes.

■ **upset price,** COMM precio de salida, precio inicial.
▲ (*sustantivo*) |'ʌpset|; (*verbo*) pt & pp *upset,* ger *upsetting.*
upsetting [ʌp'setɪŋ] *adj* desconcertante, inquietante, preocupante.
upshot ['ʌpʃɒt] *n* (*outcome*) resultado: *what was the upshot of the meeting?,* ¿cuál fue el resultado de la reunión?
upside down [ʌpsaɪd'daʊn] **1** *adv* al revés. **2** *fig* (*disorder*) patas arriba.
upstage [ʌp'steɪdʒ] **1** *adj* THEAT del fondo del escenario. **– 2** *adv* THEAT (*movement*) hacia el fondo del escenario; (*position*) en el fondo del escenario.
upstairs [ʌp'steəz] **1** *adv* (*direction*) al piso de arriba; (*position*) en el piso de arriba. **– 2** *adj* de arriba: *the upstairs bathroom,* al baño de arriba. **– 3** *n* piso de arriba, piso superior: *he went upstairs to bed,* subió a la cama.
▲ (*adjetivo*) |'ʌpsteəz|.
upstanding [ʌp'stændɪŋ] **1** *adj fml fig* honrado,-a, recto,-a. **2** (*strong*) robusto,-a, fuerte.
upstart ['ʌpstɑːt] **1** *n pej* advenedizo,-a, arribista,. **2** (*arrogant*) impertinente *mf,* insolente *mf.*
upstream [ʌp'striːm] **1** *adv* río arriba, aguas arriba: *he lives upstream,* vive río arriba. **2** (*against the current*) a contracorriente, contra la corriente.
upsurge ['ʌpsɜːdʒ] **1** *n* (*increase*) aumento, subida; (*anger*) acceso, arrebato. **2** *fig* (*strong increase in feelings, etc*) resurgimiento, renacimiento; (*of violence*) ola.
uptake ['ʌpteɪk]. **1 to be quick on the uptake,** *phr fam* ser muy listo,-a, pillarlas al vuelo. **2 to be slow on the uptake,** *fam* ser duro,-a de mollera.
uptight [ʌp'taɪt] *adj sl* nervioso,-a, agobiado,-a: *to be uptight,* estar agobiado,-a, agobiarse.
up-to-date [ʌptə'deɪt] **1** *adj* al día. **2** (*modern*) moderno,-a, a la moda; (*informed*) al tanto, al corriente, al día.
upturn ['ʌptɜːn] *n* (*improvement*) mejora; (*increase*) aumento.
upturned ['ʌptɜːnd] **1** *adj* (*nose*) respingón,-na. **2** (*car*) volcado,-a.
upward ['ʌpwəd] **1** *adj* hacia arriba, ascendente. **– 2** *adv* hacia arriba. **– 3** *adj* COMM (*tendency*) al alza *m.*
upwards ['ʌpwədz] **1** *adv* hacia arriba: *from five years upwards,* a partir de los cinco años. **2** *fam* algo más de: *from fifty pounds upwards,* de cincuenta libras para arriba.
● **upwards of,** más de: *there were upwards of 50,000 people at the demonstration,* había más de 50.000 personas en la manifestación. ‖ **face upwards,** boca arriba.
Urals ['juərəlz] *n* los Urales *m.*
uranium [ju'reɪnɪəm] *n* CHEM uranio.
Uranus [ju'reɪnəs] *n* ASTRON Urano.
urban ['ɜːbən] *adj* urbano,-a.
urbane [ɜː'beɪn] *adj* cortés, urbano,-a.
urbanize ['ɜːbənaɪz] *t* urbanizar.
urchin ['ɜːtʃɪn] *n* (*mischievous child*) pilluelo,-a, golfillo,-a.
■ **sea urchin,** ZOOL erizo de mar.
urea [ju'riːə] *n* urea.
urethra [ju'riːθrə] *n* ANAT uretra.
urge [ɜːdʒ] **1** *n* impulso, deseo: *to have the urge to do sth.,* tener unas ganas irrefrenables de hacer algo. **– 2** *t* encarecer, preconizar, instar, insistir: *to urge sb. to do sth.,* instar a algn. a hacer algo. **3** (*incite*) incitar; (*plead*) exhortar: *he urged them not to continue,* les exhortó a que no continuaran. **4** (*encourage*) animar: *the mother urged the child to take part in the play,* la madre animó al niño a que participara en la obra.

● **to urge sb. on,** darle cuerda a algn.
urgency ['ɜːdʒənsɪ] *n* urgencia: *it's a matter of great urgency,* es un asunto muy urgente.
urgent ['ɜːdʒənt] **1** *adj* (*general*) urgente. **2** (*tone, need*) apremiante, perentorio,-a: *it is urgent that I see him,* me urge verlo.
urinal [ju'raɪnəl] **1** *n* (*toilet*) urinario. **2** (*bedpan*) orinal *m.*
urinate ['juərɪneɪt] *i* orinar.
urine ['juərɪn] *n* orina.
urn [ɜːn] **1** *n* urna. **2** (*for tea*) tetera grande.
■ **burial urn,** urna funeraria.
urology [ju'rɒlədʒɪ] *n* MED urología.
Ursa ['ɜːsə] *n* ASTRON Osa.
■ **Ursa Major,** Osa Mayor. ‖ **Ursa Minor,** Osa Menor.
Uruguay ['juərəgwaɪ] *n* Uruguay.
Uruguayan [juərə'gwaɪən] **1** *adj* uruguayo,-a. **– 2** *n* uruguayo,-a.
us [ʌs, ʌz] **1** *pron* nos; (*with preposition*) nosotros,-as: *give us your gun,* danos tu pistola; *come with us,* ven con nosotros; *let us pray,* oremos; *it's us,* somos nosotros. **2** *fam* me: *give us a kiss,* dame un beso; *let's have a look,* déjame ver.
US ['juː'es] *abbr* (*United States*) Estados *mpl* Unidos; (*abbreviation*) EE.UU.
USA[1] ['juː'es'eɪ] *abbr* (*United States of America*) Estados Unidos de América; (*abbreviation*) EE.UU.
USA[2] ['juː'es'ɑːmɪ] *abbr* (*United States Army*) Ejército de los Estados Unidos.
usable ['juːzəbəl] *adj* utilizable, aprovechable: *his old car is no longer usable,* ya no le sirve su coche viejo.
USAF ['juː'es'eəfɔːs] *abbr* (*United States Air Force*) Fuerzas Aéreas de los Estados Unidos; (*abbreviation*) USAF.
usage ['juːsɪdʒ] **1** *n* uso, tratamiento, manejo. **2** (*custom*) uso, costumbre *f,* usanza. **3** LING uso. **4** (*way of speaking*) habla *m,* lenguaje *m.*
use [juːs] **1** *n* uso, empleo, utilización *f: directions for use,* instrucciones de uso, modo de empleo. **2** (*handling*) manejo: *for emergency use only,* utilícese sólo en caso de emergencia. **3** (*usefulness*) utilidad *f: it's not much use,* tiene poca utilidad; *it's no use at all,* no sirve para nada. **4** (*right to use, power to use*) uso: *I have the use of the car,* tengo derecho a utilizar el coche; *she lost the use of her left arm,* perdió el uso del brazo izquierdo. **– 5** *t* usar, utilizar: *what do you use to remove stains?,* ¿qué usas para quitar manchas?; *use your handkerchief,* ¡utiliza el pañuelo!; *don't cross the road, use the subway,* no cruces la carretera, utiliza el paso subterráneo. **6** (*consume*) gastar, consumir: *this car uses a lot of oil,* este coche gasta mucho aceite. **7** (*exploit unfairly*) aprovecharse de. **8** *fam* (*need*) necesitar: *I could use a coffee,* necesito un café. **– 9** *aux* (*past habits*) soler, acostumbrar: *he used to get up early,* solía levantarse temprano; *where did you use to live?,* ¿dónde vivías antes?; *she didn't use to like fish,* antes no le gustaba el pescado; *I used to be fat,* antes estaba gordo.
➔ **to use up** *t sep* gastar, acabar: *we've used up all the wood,* hemos gastado toda la leña.
● **in use,** en uso, que se está utilizando. ‖ *it's no use,* no sirve de nada, es inútil: *it's no use complaining,* no sirve de nada quejarse. ‖ **"not in use",** "no funciona". ‖ **out of use,** desusado,-a. ‖ **to be of use,** ser útil, ser de utilidad. ‖ **what's the use of ...?,** ¿de qué sirve ...?: *what's the use of crying?,* ¿de qué sirve llorar?
▲ De *5 a 9* [juːz]. In *9,* if no habit is involved, translate using the *imperfect.*
useable ['juːzəbəl] *adj* → **usable**

used [juːzd] **1** adj (second-hand) usado,-a, de segunda mano: she doesn't want a used car, she wants a new one, no quiere un coche usado, lo quiere nuevo. **2** (accustomed) acostumbrado,-a.
● to be used to, estar acostumbrado,-a a. ‖ to get used to, acostumbrarse a.
▲ En 2 [ˈjuːst]. Véase también use.

useful [ˈjuːsfʊl] adj útil: this penknife is very useful, esta navaja es muy útil; dictionaries are useful for looking up words, los diccionarios sirven para consultar palabras.
● to come in useful, venir bien, ser útil. ‖ to make os. useful, ser útil, ayudar.

usefulness [ˈjuːsfʊlnəs] n utilidad f, provecho.

useless [ˈjuːsləs] **1** adj inútil: it's useless trying to go on, es inútil intentar seguir. **2** fam (person) inútil, inepto,-a, incompetente: he's useless at football, no sirve para el fútbol, es un negado para el fútbol; he's absolutely useless, es un cero a la izquierda, es un inepto total.

user [ˈjuːzəʳ] n usuario,-a.

usher [ˈʌʃəʳ] **1** n (in court) ujier m, portero. **2** CINEM THEAT acomodador,-ra.
◆ to usher in t sep (guest) hacer pasar; (cinema theatre) acomodar.

USN [ˈjuːˈesˈneɪvi] abbr (United States Navy) Armada de los Estados Unidos; (abbreviation) USN.

USS [ˈjuːˈesˈes] abbr (United States Ship) barco de la armada estadounidense.

USSR [ˈjuːˈesˈesˈɑːʳ] abbr (Union of Soviet Socialist Republics) Unión de Repúblicas Socialistas Soviéticas; (abbreviation) URSS f.

usual [ˈjuːʒʊəl] **1** adj usual, habitual, normal, corriente. **– 2** n lo habitual, lo usual. **3** fam (drink etc) lo de siempre: I'll have the usual, tomaré lo de siempre.
● as usual, como de costumbre, como siempre.

usually [ˈjuːʒʊəlɪ] adv normalmente, por lo general: we usually go away at weekends, normalmente nos vamos fuera los fines de semana.

usurer [ˈjuːʒərəʳ] n usurero,-a.

usurp [juːˈzɜːp] t usurpar.

usurpation [juːzɜːˈpeɪʃən] n usurpación f.

utensil [juːˈtensəl] n utensilio.
■ kitchen utensils, batería f sing, de cocina, menaje m sing de cocina, utensillos mpl de cocina.

uterine [ˈjuːtəraɪn] adj uterino,-a.

uterus [ˈjuːtərəs] n útero.
▲ pl uteruses o uteri [ˈjuːtəraɪ].

utilitarian [juːtɪlɪˈteərɪən] **1** adj (useful) utilitario,-a. **2** (in philosophy) utilitarista. **– 3** n (in philosophy) utilitarista mf.

utility [juːˈtɪlɪtɪ] **1** n utilidad f. **2** (company) empresa de servicio público.
■ utility room, (for storage) trascocina; (for ironing) cuarto de planchar.
▲ pl utilities.

utilize [ˈjuːtɪlaɪz] t fml utilizar.

utmost [ˈʌtməʊst] **1** adj sumo,-a, extremo,-a: he did it with the utmost secrecy, lo hizo con el sigilo más absoluto. **– 2** n máximo.
● to do one's utmost, hacer todo lo posible.

utopia [juːˈtəʊpɪə] n utopía.

utopian [juːˈtəʊpɪən] **1** adj utópico,-a. **– 2** n utopista mf.

utter [ˈʌtəʳ] **1** adj absoluto,-a, completo,-a, total: she's an utter fool, es tonta de remate; what utter nonsense!, ¡vaya tontería! **– 2** t (words) pronunciar, articular, decir; (feelings) expresar. **3** (lies curses etc) soltar; (shouts, cries etc) lanzar, dar. **4** (theatre) proferir; (sounds) emitir: he never uttered her name, jamás pronunció su nombre.

utterance [ˈʌtərəns] n declaración f, pronunciación f.
● to give utterance to, expresar.

utterly [ˈʌtəlɪ] adv totalmente, completamente, del todo: it's utterly impossible, es del todo imposible.

U-turn [ˈjuːtɜːn] **1** n cambio de sentido. **2** fam fig marcha atrás: management has done a U-turn on wage increases, la patronal ha dado marcha atrás a los aumentos salariales.

uvula [ˈjuːvjʊlə] n ANAT úvula, campanilla.
▲ pl uvulas o uvulae [ˈjuːvjuliː].

uvular [ˈjuːvjʊləʳ] adj uvular.

Uzbek [ˈʊzbek] **1** adj uzbeco,-a. **– 2** n (person) uzbeco,-a. **3** (language) uzbeco.

Uzbekistan [ʊzbekɪˈstæn] n Uzbekistán.

V

V, v [viː] **1** *n* (*the letter*) V, v *f.* **2** (*shape*) uve *f*: *she cut the paper in a V*, cortó el papel en forma de uve.

v¹ [vɜːs] *abbr* (**verse**) verso; (*abbreviation*) v.

v² ['vɜːsəs, viː] *abbr* (**versus**) contra.

v³ ['verɪ] *abbr* (**very**) muy.

V [vəʊlt] *symb* (**volt**) voltio; (*symbol*) V.

vac [væk] **1** *n* GB *fam* (*abbr of* **vacation**) vacaciones *fpl.* **2** GB *fam* (*abbr of* **vacuum cleaner**) aspirador *m*, aspiradora. – **3** *t* GB *fam* pasar la aspiradora por.

vacancy ['veɪkənsɪ] **1** *n* (*job*) vacante *f*: *we have a vacancy for a typist*, necesitamos una mecanógrafa; *to fill a vacancy*, ocupar un puesto. **2** (*room*) habitación *f* libre.
● *"no vacancies"*, "completo".
▲ *pl* **vacancies**.

vacant ['veɪkənt] **1** *adj* (*gen*) vacío. **2** (*job*) vacante. **3** (*room*) libre. **4** (*mind, expression*) vacío,-a: *he stared into space with a vacant expression*, se quedó mirando al vacío con la mirada perdida.
● *"situations vacant"*, "ofertas de trabajo", "demandas"

vacate [vəˈkeɪt] **1** *t fml* (*job*) dejar (vacante). **2** *fml* (*flat etc*) desocupar, desalojar: *guests should vacate their rooms by 12 o'clock*, se ruega a los clientes que dejen libres las habitaciones antes de las doce; *everyone must vacate the premises*, todo el mundo debe abandonar el edificio.

vacation [vəˈkeɪʃən] **1** *n* vacaciones *fpl.* – **2** *i* US pasar las vacaciones (**in/at**, en).
● **to be on vacation**, US estar de vacaciones. ‖ **to go on vacation**, US irse de vacaciones. ‖ **to take a vacation**, US tomarse unas vacaciones.
■ **the long vacation**, GB las vacaciones de verano.

vacationer [veɪˈkeɪʃənəʳ] *n* US veraneante *mf.*

vaccinate ['væksɪneɪt] *t* vacunar.

vaccine ['væksiːn] *n* vacuna.
■ **smallpox vaccine**, vacuna contra la viruela.

vacillate ['væsɪleɪt] *t* (*hesitate*) vacilar.

vacua ['vækjʊə].

vacuous ['vækʊəs] **1** *adj fml* (*empty*) vacío,-a. **2** *fml* (*mindless*) necio,-a.

vacuum ['vækjʊəm] **1** *n* vacío. **2** *fam* (**vacuum cleaner**) aspiradora. – **3** *t* limpiar con aspiradora, pasar la aspiradora por.
● **to leave a vacuum**, dejar un vacío.
■ **vacuum cleaner**, aspiradora. ‖ **vacuum flask**, termo.

vacuum-packed ['vækjʊəmpækt] *adj* envasado,-a al vacío.

vagabond ['vægəbɒnd] *n lit* vagabundo,-a.

vagary ['veɪgərɪ] *n fml* capricho: *the vagaries of youth*, los caprichos de la juventud.
▲ *pl* **vagaries**.

vagina [vəˈdʒaɪnə] *n* vagina.
▲ *pl* **vaginas** o **vaginae** [vəˈdʒaɪniː].

vaginae [vəˈdʒaɪniː] *npl* → **vagina**.

vaginal [vəˈdʒaɪnəl] *adj* vaginal.

vagrancy ['veɪgrənsɪ] *n* vagabundería.

vagrant ['veɪgrənt] **1** *adj* vagabundo,-a. – **2** *n* vagabundo,-a.

vague [veɪg] **1** *adj* (*imprecise*) vago,-a, impreciso,-a: *he hasn't the vaguest idea*, no tiene la más mínima idea; *they were vague about it*, no dieron detalles. **2** (*indistinct*) borroso,-a.

vagueness ['veɪgnəs] **1** *n* (*in general*) vaguedad *f*, imprecisión *f*. **2** (*of outline*) lo borroso.

vain [veɪn] **1** *adj* (*conceited*) vanidoso,-a. **2** (*hopeless*) vano,-a, inútil.
● **in vain**, en vano.

valance ['væləns] *n* (*of bed*) cenefa, doselera.

vale [veɪl] *n lit* valle *m.*
■ **vale of tears**, valle *m* de lágrimas.

valence ['veɪləns] *n* US valencia.

Valencian [vəˈlensɪən] **1** *adj* valenciano,-a. – **2** *n* (*person*) valenciano,-a. **3** (*language*) valenciano.

valency ['veɪlənsɪ] *n* GB valencia.
▲ *pl* **valencies**.

valentine ['væləntaɪn] **1** *n* tarjeta *enviada por* San Valentín. **2** (*person*) novio,-a.

valerian [vəˈlɪərɪən] *n* valeriana.

valet ['væleɪ, 'vælɪt] *n* ayuda *m* de cámara.

valiant ['vælɪənt] *adj lit* valiente.

valid ['vælɪd] **1** *adj* válido,-a. **2** (*ticket*) valedero,-a: *the ticket is no longer valid*, el billete está caducado; *valid for two months*, valedero,-a por dos meses.

validate ['vælɪdeɪt] *t fml* validar.

validity [vəˈlɪdɪtɪ] *n* validez *f.*

valise [vəˈliːz] *n* maletín *m*, bolsa de viaje.

Valletta [vəˈletə] *n* La Valetta.

valley ['vælɪ] *n* valle *m.*

valour ['væləʳ] *n* valor *m*, valentía.

valuable ['væljʊəbəl] **1** *adj* valioso,-a, de valor. – **2** *npl* objetos *mpl* de valor.

valuation [væljʊˈeɪʃən] **1** *n* (*act*) valoración *f*. **2** (*price*) valor *m.*

value ['væljuː] **1** *n* valor *m*. – **2** *t* (*estimate value of*) valorar, tasar. **3** (*appreciate*) valorar, apreciar.
● **it's good value for money**, bien vale lo que cuesta. ‖ **of great/little value**, de gran/poco valor. ‖ **of no value**, sin valor. ‖ **to get good value for money**, sacarle jugo al dinero. ‖ **to the value of ...**, por el valor de ...
■ **value added tax**, impuesto sobre el valor añadido. ‖ **value judgment**, juicio de valor.

valueless ['væljuːləs] *adj* sin valor.

valuer ['væljʊəʳ] *n* tasador,-ra.

valve [vælv] **1** *n* (*in general*) válvula. **2** RAD lámpara. **3** ZOOL valva. **4** MUS llave *f.*
■ **safety valve**, válvula de seguridad.

valvular ['vælvjələʳ] *adj* valvular.

vamp [væmp] *n fam* vampiresa.
vampire ['væmpaɪəʳ] *n* vampiro.
■ **vampire bat,** vampiro.
van¹ [væn] **1** *n* camioneta, furgoneta. **2** GB (*on train*) furgón *m*.
■ **breakdown van,** GB grúa. ‖ **delivery van,** furgoneta de reparto. ‖ **prison van,** coche *m* celular. ‖ **removal van,** camión *m* de mudanza.
van² [væn] **in the van,** *adv phr fml* en la vanguardia.
vandal ['vændəl] *n* vándalo,-a.
Vandal ['vændəl] **1** *adj* vándalo,-a. – **2** *n* vándalo,-a.
vandalism ['vændəlɪzəm] *n* vandalismo.
vandalize ['vændəlaɪz] *t* destrozar, destruir.
vane [veɪn] **1** *n* (*weather etc*) veleta. **2** (*of fan etc*) aspa.
vanguard ['vænɡɑːd] *n* vanguardia.
● **to be in the vanguard of,** estar en la vanguardia de.
vanilla [və'nɪlə] *n* vainilla.
vanish ['vænɪʃ] *i* desaparecer.
● **to vanish from sight,** desaparecer de la vista. ‖ **to vanish into thin air,** esfumarse, desaparecer sin dejar rastro.
vanishing point ['vænɪʃɪŋpɔɪnt] *n* punto de fuga.
vanity ['vænɪtɪ] *n* vanidad *f*.
● **out of sheer vanity,** por pura vanidad.
■ **vanity bag / vanity case,** neceser *m*.
▲ *pl* **vanities.**
vanquish ['væŋkwɪʃ] *t lit* vencer.
vantage point ['vɑːntɪdʒpɔɪnt] *n* posición *f* ventajosa, posición *f* estratégica.
Vanuatu ['vænuːætuː] *n* Vanuatu.
vapid ['væpɪd] *adj fml* insípido,-a.
vaporize ['veɪpəraɪz] **1** *t* vaporizar. – **2** *i* vaporizarse.
vaporous ['veɪpərəs] *adj* vaporoso,-a.
vapour ['veɪpəʳ] **1** *n* vapor *m*. **2** (*on windowpane*) vaho.
■ **vapour trail,** estela de humo.
variability [veərə'bɪlɪtɪ] *n* variabilidad *f*.
variable ['veərəbəl] **1** *adj* variable. – **2** *n* variable *f*.
variance ['veərɪəns] **to be at variance,** *phr fml* (*ideas etc*) no concordar; (*person*) estar en desacuerdo (**with,** con).
variant ['veərɪənt] *n* variante *f*.
variation [veərɪ'eɪʃən] *n* variación *f*.
varicose ['værɪkəʊs] *adj* varicoso,-a.
■ **varicose veins,** varices *fpl*.
varied ['veərɪd] *adj* variado,-a, diverso,-a.
variegated ['veərɪɡeɪtɪd] *adj* abigarrado,-a.
variety [və'raɪətɪ] **1** *n* (*diversity*) variedad *f*. **2** (*assortment*) surtido.
● **a wide variety of,** gran diversidad de. ‖ **for a variety of reasons,** por razones diversas. ‖ **variety is the spice of life,** en la variedad está el gusto.
■ **variety show,** (espectáculo de) variedades *fpl*.
▲ *pl* **varieties.**
various ['veərɪəs] **1** *adj* (*different*) diverso,-a, distinto,-a. **2** (*several*) varios,-as.
● **to be many and various,** ser muchos,-as y variados,-as: *the books he reads are many and various,* lee mucho y variado.
varnish ['vɑːnɪʃ] **1** *n* barniz *m*. – **2** *t* barnizar.
■ **nail varnish,** GB esmalte *m* de uñas, laca de uñas.
vary ['veərɪ] **1** *i* variar. – **2** *t* variar de.
● **to vary between ... and ...,** oscilar entre ... y ...
▲ *pt* & *pp* **varied,** *ger* **varying.**
vascular ['væskjələʳ] *adj* vascular.
vase [vɑːz, ʲᵊ veɪs] *n* jarrón *m*, florero.

vasectomy [væ'sektəmɪ] *n* vasectomía.
▲ *pl* **vasectomies.**
Vaseline ['væsɪliːn] *n* vaselina.
▲ Es marca registrada.
vassal ['væsəl] *n* vasallo,-a.
vast [vɑːst] *adj* (*extensive*) vasto,-a, inmenso,-a; (*huge*) inmenso,-a, enorme: *a vast majority of people,* la inmensa mayoría de la gente; *vast sums of money were spent,* se gastaron enormes cantidades de dinero.
vastly ['vɑːstlɪ] *adv* inmensamente, tremendamente.
vastness ['vɑːstnəs] *n* inmensidad *f*.
vat [væt] *n* tina, cuba.
VAT [væt, viː'eɪ'tiː] *abbr* (*value added tax*) impuesto sobre el valor añadido; (*abbreviation*) IVA *m*.
Vatican ['vætɪkən] **1** *adj* vaticano,-a. – **2 the Vatican,** *n* el Vaticano.
■ **Vatican City,** Ciudad *f* del Vaticano. ‖ **Vatican Council,** Concilio Vaticano.
vaudeville ['vɔːdəvɪl] *n* US vodevil *m*.
vault¹ [vɔːlt] **1** *n* (*ceiling*) bóveda. **2** (*in bank*) cámara acorazada. **3** (*for dead*) panteón *m*; (*in church*) cripta. **4** (*cellar*) sótano; (*for wine*) bodega.
vault² [vɔːlt] **1** *t* saltar. – **2** *i* saltar. – **3** *n* (*gymnastics*) salto.
■ **pole vault,** salto de pértiga. ‖ **vaulting horse,** potro. ‖ **vaulting pole,** pértiga.
vaunt [vɔːnt] *i fml* jactarse de.
VC¹ [vaɪs'tʃeəmən] *abbr* (*Vice-Chairman*) Vicepresidente *m*.
VC² [vaɪs'tsɑːnsələʳ] *abbr* (*Vice Chancellor*) Rector *m*.
VC³ [vaɪs'kɒnsəl] *abbr* (*Vice-Consul*) Vicecónsul *m*.
VC⁴ ['viː'siː] *abbr* GB (*Victoria Cross*) máxima condecoración militar británica.
VCR ['viː'siː'ɑːʳ] *abbr* (*video cassette recorder*) grabador *m* de vídeo, vídeo.
VD ['viː'diː] *abbr* (*venereal disease*) enfermedad *f* venérea.
VDU ['viː'diː'juː] *abbr* (*visual display unit*) pantalla.
veal [viːl] *n* ternera.
vector ['vektəʳ] *n* vector *m*.
veer [vɪəʳ] **1** *i* (*ship, car*) virar; (*road*) torcer. **2** (*wind*) cambiar de dirección.
● **to veer from one's course,** desviarse de su camino. ‖ **to veer round,** *fig* cambiar de opinión.
veg [vedʒ] *n* GB *fam* (*abbr of vegetable or vegetables*) verdura, verduras *fpl*.
vegan ['viːɡən] **1** *adj* veganista, vegetariano,-a estricto,-a. – **2** *n* veganista *mf*, vegetariano,-a estricto,-a.
vegetable ['vedʒtəbəl] **1** *n* (*as food*) verdura, hortaliza: *I love vegetables,* me encanta la verdura. **2** (*as plant*) vegetal *m*. **3** *fam* (*person*) vegetal *m*.
■ **the vegetable kingdom,** el reino vegetal. ‖ **vegetable garden,** huerto, huerta.
vegetarian [vedʒɪ'teərɪən] **1** *adj* vegetariano,-a. – **2** *n* vegetariano,-a.
vegetarianism [vedʒɪ'teərɪənɪzəm] *n* vegetarianismo.
vegetate ['vedʒɪteɪt] *i* vegetar.
vegetation [vedʒɪ'teɪʃən] *n* vegetación *f*.
vehemence ['vɪəməns] *n* vehemencia.
vehement ['vɪəmənt] *adj* vehemente.
vehicle ['viːəkəl] **1** *n* TECH vehículo. **2** *fig* medio, vehículo.
■ **armoured vehicle,** vehículo blindado. ‖ **motor vehicle,** vehículo a motor: *the motor vehicle industry,* la industria del automóvil.

vehicular traffic [vɪhɪkjʊləˈtræfɪk] n tránsito rodado.
veil [veɪl] 1 n velo. – 2 t velar.
● to draw a veil over sth., correr un tupido velo sobre algo. ‖ to take the veil, tomar el velo.
veiled [veɪld] adj velado,-a.
vein [veɪn] 1 n ANAT vena. 2 BOT vena, nervio. 3 (of mineral) veta, vena, filón m. 4 (mood) humor m, vena.
● to be in vein, estar en vena.
veined [veɪnd] 1 adj (marble) veteado,-a. 2 (hand) venoso,-a.
vela [ˈviːlə] npl → velum.
velar [ˈviːlər] 1 adj LING velar. – 2 n LING velar f.
velcro [ˈvelkrəʊ] n velcro.
▲ Es marca registrada.
vellum [ˈveləm] n vitela.
■ vellum paper, papel m vitela.
velocity [vəˈlɒsɪtɪ] n velocidad f.
▲ pl velocities.
velodrome [ˈveladrəʊm] n velódromo.
velour [vəˈlʊər] n terciopelo (por urdimbre).
■ velour finish, acabado pana.
velum [ˈviːləm] n velo (del paladar).
▲ pl vela [ˈviːlə].
velvet [ˈvelvɪt] n terciopelo.
velveteen [velvɪˈtiːn] n veludillo, terciopelo.
velvety [ˈvelvɪtɪ] adj aterciopelado,-a.
venal [ˈviːnəl] adj venal.
vendetta [venˈdetə] n vendetta.
vending machine [ˈvendɪŋməʃiːn] n máquina expendedora.
vendor [ˈvendər] n vendedor,-ra.
veneer [vəˈnɪər] 1 n chapa. 2 fig apariencia. – 3 t chapear, chapar.
venerable [ˈvenərəbəl] adj venerable.
venerate [ˈvenəreɪt] t venerar, reverenciar.
veneration [venəˈreɪʃən] n veneración f.
venereal [vəˈnɪərɪəl] adj venéreo,-a.
Venetian [vəˈniːʃən] 1 adj veneciano,-a. – 2 n veneciano,-a.
■ Venetian blind, persiana graduable, persiana veneciana.
Venezuela [venəˈzweɪlə] n Venezuela.
Venezuelan [venəˈzweɪlən] 1 adj venezolano,-a. – 2 n venezolano,-a.
vengeance [ˈvendʒəns] n venganza.
● to take vengeance on sb., vengarse de algn. ‖ with a vengeance, fam a rabiar.
vengeful [ˈvendʒfʊl] adj vengativo,-a.
venial [ˈviːnɪəl] adj venial.
■ venial sin, pecado venial.
Venice [ˈvenɪs] n Venecia.
venison [ˈvenɪsən] n (carne f de) venado.
venom [ˈvenəm] 1 n veneno. 2 fig odio.
venomous [ˈvenəməs] adj venenoso,-a.
■ venomous tongue, fig lengua viperina.
venous [ˈviːnəs] adj venoso,-a.
vent [vent] 1 n (opening) abertura. 2 (hole) orificio, respiradero. 3 (grille) rejilla de ventilación. – 4 t descargar.
● to give vent to, descargar, soltar. ‖ to give vent to one's feelings, desahogarse. ‖ to vent one's anger on sb., descargar su ira en algn.
ventilate [ˈventɪleɪt] t ventilar.
ventilation [ventɪˈleɪʃən] n ventilación f.
■ ventilation shaft, (mining) pozo de ventilación.
ventilator [ˈventɪleɪtər] n ventilador m.

ventricle [ˈventrɪkəl] n ventrículo.
ventriloquist [venˈtrɪləkwɪst] n ventrílocuo,-a.
venture [ˈventʃər] 1 t arriesgar, aventurar. – 2 i arriesgarse: to venture out of doors, atreverse a salir. – 3 n aventura, empresa arriesgada: it's a completely new venture, es algo totalmente nuevo.
● to venture an opinion, aventurar una opinión. ‖ to venture to do sth., atreverse a hacer algo. ‖ nothing ventured, nothing gained, quien no se moja no pasa el río, quien no se aventuró ni perdió ni ganó.
■ business venture, empresa comercial, proyecto comercial. ‖ joint venture, empresa conjunta, proyecto conjunto, operación conjunta. ‖ venture capital, capital m riesgo.
venturesome [ˈventʃəsəm] 1 adj (person) emprendedor,-ra. 2 (action) arriesgado,-a.
venue [ˈvenjuː] 1 n (place) local m. 2 (scene) escenario.
veranda [vəˈrændə] n porche m.
verandah [vəˈrændə] n → veranda.
verb [vɜːb] n verbo.
verbal [ˈvɜːbəl] adj verbal.
■ verbal diarrhoea, verborrea. ‖ verbal noun, gerundio.
verbalize [ˈvɜːbəlaɪz] t GB verbalizar.
verbally [ˈvɜːbəlɪ] adv verbalmente, de palabra.
verbatim [vɜːˈbeɪtɪm] 1 adj textual. – 2 adv textualmente.
verbena [vɜːˈbiːnə] n verbena.
verbiage [ˈvɜːbɪdʒ] n fml verbosidad f.
verbose [vɜːˈbəʊs] adj verboso,-a, locuaz.
verbosity [vɜːˈbɒsɪtɪ] n verbosidad f, verborrea.
verdant [ˈvɜːdənt] adj lit verde.
verdict [ˈvɜːdɪkt] 1 n veredicto, fallo. 2 (opinion) opinión f, juicio: what's your verdict on it?, ¿qué opinas de ello?
verge [vɜːdʒ] 1 n borde m, margen m. 2 (of road) arcén m.
◆ to verge on 1 t insep (condition) rayar en: his behaviour verges on madness, su comportamiento raya en la locura. 2 (age) rondar: he's verging on forty, ronda los cuarenta años.
● on the verge of, al borde de. ‖ to be on the verge of doing sth., estar a punto de hacer algo.
verger [ˈvɜːdʒər] n GB sacristán m.
verifiable [ˈverɪfaɪəbəl] adj verificable.
verification [verɪfɪˈkeɪʃən] n verificación f, comprobación f.
verify [ˈverɪfaɪ] t verificar, comprobar.
▲ pt & pp verified, ger verifying.
verisimilitude [verɪsɪˈmɪlɪtjuːd] n verosimilitud f.
veritable [ˈverɪtəbəl] adj verdadero,-a.
vermicelli [vɜːmɪˈselɪ] n fideos mpl.
vermilion [vəˈmɪlɪən] 1 n bermellón m. – 2 adj bermejo,-a.
vermin [ˈvɜːmɪn] 1 npl (small animals) alimañas fpl. 2 (insects) bichos mpl, sabandijas fpl. 3 (people) gentuza f sing, chusma f sing.
vermouth [ˈvɜːməθ, vɜːˈmuːθ] n vermú m, vermut m.
vernacular [vəˈnækjʊlər] 1 adj vernáculo,-a. – 2 n lengua vernácula.
● to lapse into the vernacular, ponerse a hablar como la gente del lugar.
veronica [vəˈrɒnɪkə] n verónica.
verruca [vəˈruːkə] n verruga.
▲ pl verrucas o verrucae [vəˈruːkiː].
versatile [ˈvɜːsətaɪl] 1 adj (person) polifacético,-a. 2 (object) que tiene muchos usos, de múltiples usos. 3 ZOOL versátil.

versatility [vɜːsə'tɪlɪtɪ] 1 *n* (*of person*) carácter *m* polifacético. 2 (*of object*) múltiples aplicaciones *fpl*. 3 ZOOL versatilidad *f*.

verse [vɜːs] 1 *n* (*poetry*) versos *mpl*, poesía. 2 (*set of lines*) estrofa. 3 (*song, set of lines*) estrofa. 4 (*in Bible*) versículo.
● **in verse**, en verso.
■ **blank verse**, verso libre. ‖ **free verse**, verso libre.

versed [vɜːst] *adj fml* versado,-a.
● **to be (well) versed in sth.**, ser muy versado,-a en algo.

versification [vɜːsɪfɪ'keɪʃən] *n* versificación *f*.

version ['vɜːʒən] 1 *n* versión *f*. 2 MUS interpretación *f*. 3 AUTO modelo: *the sports version*, el modelo deportivo.
■ **stage version**, THEAT adaptación *f* teatral.

versus ['vɜːsəs] 1 *prep* (*against*) contra: *tonight's match is Leeds versus Liverpool*, el partido de esta noche es Leeds contra Liverpool; *the Crown versus Riley*, la corona contra Riley. 2 (*as opposed to*) frente a: *diesel versus petrol*, el gasoil frente a la gasolina.

vertebra ['vɜːtɪbrə] *n* vértebra.
▲ *pl* **vertebrae** ['vɜːtɪbriː].

vertebral ['vɜːtɪbrəl] *adj* vertebral.

vertebrate ['vɜːtɪbrət, 'vɜːtɪbreɪt] 1 *adj* vertebrado,-a. – 2 *n* vertebrado.

vertex ['vɜːteks] *n* vértice *m*.
▲ *pl* **vertexes** *o* **vertices** ['vɜːtɪsiːz].

vertical ['vɜːtɪkəl] *adj* vertical.

vertically ['vɜːtɪkəlɪ] *adv* en vertical, verticalmente.

vertices ['vɜːtɪsiːz] *npl* → **vertex**.

vertigo ['vɜːtɪgəʊ] *n* vértigo.

vervain ['vɜːveɪn] *n* verbena.

verve [vɜːv] *n* brío, vigor *m*, empuje *m*.

very ['verɪ] 1 *adv* (*extremely*) muy: *it's very easy*, es muy fácil, es facilísimo; *to be very hungry/sleepy*, tener mucha hambre/mucho sueño; *very few*, muy pocos,-as, poquísimos,-as; *very little*, muy poco,-a, poquísimo,-a; *very well*, muy bien. 2 (*emphatic*) muy: *at the very latest*, como muy tarde, a más tardar; *at the very least*, como mínimo, por lo menos; *there was another accident in the very same place*, ha habido otro accidente en el mismo lugar exacto. – 3 *adj* (*extreme*) de todo: *at the very end*, al final de todo; *he was at the very back of the library*, estaba al final de todo de la biblioteca. 4 (*precise*) mismo,-a, exacto,-a: *at that very moment*, en aquel mismo instante.
● **it's the very thing**, *fam* es justo lo que necesitas/hace falta. ‖ **the very best**, el/la mejor, lo mejor: *he did the very best he could*, hizo lo mejor que pudo. ‖ **not very**, no mucho: *were the tickets expensive? –not very*, ¿eran caras las entradas? –no mucho. ‖ **the very thought of it!**, ¡sólo con pensarlo!

vesicle ['vesɪkəl] *n* vesícula.

vesicular [ve'sɪkjələ'] *adj* vesicular.

vespers ['vespəz] *npl* vísperas *fpl*.

vessel ['vesəl] 1 *n* (*ship*) nave *f*, buque *m*. 2 (*container*) recipiente *m*, vasija. 3 ANAT vaso.
■ **blood vessel**, vaso sanguíneo. ‖ **cargo vessel**, buque *m* de carga.

vest [vest] 1 *n* GB camiseta. 2 US chaleco. – 3 **to vest with**, *t* conferir a, dar posesión a: *to vest sb. with authority/rights*, conferir autoridad/derechos a algn.
■ **bullet-proof vest**, chaleco antibalas.

vestal ['vestəl] *adj* vestal.
■ **vestal virgin**, vestal *f*.

vested interest [vestɪd'ɪntrəst] *n* derecho adquirido; *fig* interés *m* creado.

● **to have a vested interest in a matter**, *fig* tener intereses personales en un asunto.

vestibule ['vestɪbjuːl] 1 *n* (*entrance hall*) vestíbulo, entrada. 2 ANAT vestíbulo.

vestige ['vestɪdʒ] *n* vestigio.

vestigial [ves'tɪdʒɪəl] *adj* vestigial.

vestment ['vestmənt] *n* vestidura.

vestry ['vestrɪ] *n* sacristía.
▲ *pl* **vestries**.

vet[1] [vet] 1 *n fam* veterinario,-a. – 2 *t* GB investigar, examinar.
▲ (*verbo*) *pt* & *pp* **vetted**, *ger* **vetting**.

vet[2] [vet] *n* US *fam* (*abbr of veteran*) excombatiente *mf*.

veteran ['vetərən] 1 *adj* veterano,-a: *she's quite a veteran traveller*, es toda una viajera avezada. – 2 *n* veterano,-a. 3 (*soldier etc*) excombatiente *mf*.
■ **veteran car**, GB coche *m* de época *construido antes de 1919*. ‖ **veteran soldier**, soldado veterano.

veterinarian [vetərɪ'neərɪən] *n* US veterinario,-a.

veterinary ['vetərɪnərɪ] *adj* veterinario,-a.
■ **veterinary medicine**, veterinaria. ‖ **veterinary surgeon**, GB veterinario,-a.

veto ['viːtəʊ] 1 *n* veto. – 2 *t* vetar; (*forbid*) prohibir, vedar.
● **to impose a veto over sth.**, poner el veto a algo.
■ **power/right of veto**, derecho de veto.
▲ (*sustantivo*) *pl* **vetoes**; (*verbo*) *pt* & *pp* **vetoed**, *ger* **vetoing**.

vex [veks] *t dated* (*annoy*) disgustar, vejar.

vexation [vek'seɪʃən] *n fml* vejación *f*, disgusto.

vexed [vekst] *adj* disgustado,-a: *he was vexed at having to wait so long*, le disgustó tener que esperar tanto.
■ **vexed question**, tema *m* conflictivo, tema *m* controvertido.

VHF ['viː'eɪtʃ'ef] *abbr* (*very high frequency*) frecuencia muy alta; (*abbreviation*) VHF.

VHS ['viː'eɪtʃ'es] *abbr* (*Video Home System*) sistema de vídeo doméstico; (*abbreviation*) VHS.

via ['vaɪə] 1 *prep* (*through*) vía, por: *he will travel via Athens*, viajará vía Atenas. 2 (*by means of*) por medio de, a través de: *I sent a message to Emma via her husband*, le envié un mensaje a Emma a través de su marido.

viability [vaɪə'bɪlɪtɪ] *n* viabilidad *f*.

viable ['vaɪəbəl] *adj* viable, factible.

viaduct ['vaɪədʌkt] *n* viaducto.

vibes [vaɪbz] *npl fam* (*abbr of vibrations*) vibraciones *fpl*.

vibrant ['vaɪbrənt] 1 *adj* (*sound*) vibrante. 2 (*personality*) vital, fuerte; (*city*) animado,-a.

vibraphone ['vaɪbrəfəʊn] *n* vibráfono.

vibrate [vaɪ'breɪt, ʃə 'vaɪbreɪt] 1 *i* vibrar (**with**, con). – 2 *t* hacer vibrar.

vibration [vaɪ'breɪʃən] *n* vibración *f*.

vibrator [vaɪ'breɪtə', ʃə 'vaɪbreɪtə'] *n* vibrador *m*.

viburnum [vaɪ'bɜːnəm] *n* viburno.

vicar ['vɪkə'] 1 *n* (*Anglican*) párroco. 2 (*Catholic*) vicario.
■ **the vicar of Christ**, el vicario de Cristo.

vicarage ['vɪkərɪdʒ] *n* casa del párroco.

vicarious [vɪ'keərɪəs] *adj* experimentado,-a por otro: *he felt vicarious pride when his brother won the prize*, sintió el mismo orgullo que su hermano cuando éste ganó el premio.

vice[1] [vaɪs] *n* vicio.
■ **vice squad**, brigada antivicio.

vice[2] [vaɪs] *n* (*tool*) torno de banco, tornillo de banco.

vice[3] [vaɪs] *pref* vice-.
● **vice admiral**, MIL vicealmirante *m*. ‖ **vice chancellor**, EDUC rector,-ra. ‖ **vice president**, vicepresidente,-ta.

vice-chairman [vaɪs'tʃeəmən] *n* vice-presidente *m*.
▲ *pl* *vice-chairmen* [vaɪs'tʃeəmən].
vicelike ['vaɪslaɪk] *adj* firme, férreo,-a.
● in a vicelike grip, con mano férrea.
vicereine [vaɪs'reɪn] *n* virreina.
viceroy ['vaɪsrɔɪ] *n* virrey *m*.
vice versa [vaɪs'vɜːsə] *adv* viceversa.
vicinity [və'sɪnətɪ] **1** *n* inmediaciones *fpl*. **2** *fml* proximidad *f*.
● in the vicinity of, (*near*) en las inmediaciones de; (*more or less*) alrededor de, aproximadamente.
vicious ['vɪʃəs] **1** *adj* (*cruel*) cruel; (*malicious*) malintencionado,-a. **2** (*violent*) virulento,-a, violento,-a. **3** (*dangerous*) peligroso,-a.
■ vicious circle, círculo vicioso.
vicissitudes [vɪ'sɪsɪtjuːdz] *npl* vicisitudes *fpl*.
victim ['vɪktɪm] *n* víctima.
● to be the victim of, ser víctima de. ‖ to fall victim to ..., caer víctima de ...; *fig* sucumbir ante ...
victimize ['vɪktɪmaɪz] *t* victimizar.
victor ['vɪktə] *n fml* vencedor,-ra.
Victorian [vɪk'tɔːrɪən] **1** *adj* victoriano,-a. – **2** *n* victoriano,-a.
victorious [vɪk'tɔːrɪəs] *adj* victorioso,-a, vencedor,-ra.
■ the victorious team, SP el equipo ganador.
victory ['vɪktərɪ] *n* victoria, triunfo: *it was a sweeping victory,* fue una victoria aplastante.
● to claim victory, cantar victoria. ‖ to snatch victory from the jaws of defeat, ganar por los pelos.
▲ *pl* *victories*.
victuals ['vɪtəlz] *npl* vituallas *fpl*, víveres *mpl*.
vicuña [vɪ'kjuːnə] *n* vicuña.
videlicet [vɪ'diːlɪset] *adv fml* a saber.
video ['vɪdɪəʊ] **1** *n* vídeo. – **2** *t* grabar en vídeo.
■ video camera, videocámara. ‖ video cassette, videocasete *f*. ‖ video cassette recorder, vídeo. ‖ video clip, videoclip *m*. ‖ video club, videoclub *m*. ‖ video game, videojuego. ‖ video nasty, *fam* película de vídeo desagradablemente violenta o pornográfica. ‖ video recorder, vídeo. ‖ video tape, cinta de vídeo, videocinta.
▲ *pl* *videos*.
videodisc ['vɪdɪəʊdɪsk] *n* videodisco.
videophone ['vɪdɪəfəʊn] *n* videoteléfono, videófono.
videorecorder [vɪdɪəʊrɪ'kɔːdə] *n* vídeo.
video-tape ['vɪdɪəʊteɪp] *t* grabar en vídeo.
vie [vaɪ] *i* competir (for, por).
Vienna [vɪ'enə] *n* Viena.
Viennese [vɪə'niːz] **1** *adj* vienés,-esa. – **2** *n* vienés,-esa. – **3** the Viennese, *npl* los vieneses *mpl*.
Vietnam [vɪet'næm] *n* Vietnam.
Vietnamese [vɪetnə'miːz] **1** *adj* vietnamita. – **2** *n* (*person*) vietnamita *mf*. **3** (*language*) vietnamita *m*. – **4** the Vietnamese, *npl* los vietnamitas *mpl*.
view [vjuː] **1** *n* vista, panorama *m*: *a room with a view,* una habitación con vistas; *we may have a bird's-eye view of the mountains,* vimos las montañas a vista de pájaro. **2** (*opinion*) opinión *f*, parecer *m*: *in my view ...,* en mi opinión ..., yo opino que ... – **3** *t* (*consider*) considerar, ver: *I view his policies as a threat to the economy,* considero que su política es una amenaza para la economía. **4** (*regard, think about*) enfocar. **5** (*examine*) ver; (*visit*) visitar. **6** (*watch*) ver; (*critically*) visionar: *this programme has high viewing figures,* este programa tiene un alto índice de audiencia.
● in full view, a la vista de todo el mundo: *in full view of the audience,* a la vista de todo el público. ‖ in view,

en mente, pensado,-a: *what have you in view for the new season?,* ¿qué tiene pensado para la próxima temporada? ‖ in view of, en vista de. ‖ in view of the fact that ...,* dado que ..., en vista de que ... ‖ to be on view, exponerse. ‖ to keep sth./sb. in view, tener algo/a algn. en cuenta. ‖ to take a dim/poor view of sth., *fam* ver algo con malos ojos. ‖ to take the long view (of sth.), planear (algo) a largo plazo. ‖ with a view to, con vistas a, con miras a. ‖ within view, a la vista. ‖ with this in view, ..., teniendo esto en cuenta, ..., con este fin.
■ point of view, punto de vista. ‖ world view, perspectiva global.
viewer ['vjuːə] **1** *n* TV telespectador,-ra, televidente *mf*. **2** (*photography*) visionador *m*.
viewfinder ['vjuːfaɪndə] *n* visor *m*.
viewpoint ['vjuːpɔɪnt] *n* punto de vista.
vigil ['vɪdʒɪl] *n* vela, vigilia; (*religious*) vigilia.
● to keep vigil, velar.
■ all-night vigil, vela nocturna.
vigilance ['vɪdʒɪləns] *n* vigilancia.
vigilant ['vɪdʒɪlənt] *adj* atento,-a.
● to remain vigilant, mantener la vigilancia.
vigilante [vɪdʒɪ'læntɪ] *n* vigilante *mf*.
vigorous ['vɪgərəs] *adj* vigoroso,-a, enérgico,-a.
vigour ['vɪgə] *n* vigor *m*, energía.
Viking ['vaɪkɪŋ] **1** *adj* vikingo,-a. – **2** *n* vikingo,-a.
vile [vaɪl] **1** *adj* vil, despreciable. **2** *fam* (*taste, smell*) queroso,-a. **3** *fam* (*temper*) espantoso: *she's in a vile temper,* está de un humor de perros; *he has a vile temper,* tiene un genio espantoso.
vileness ['vaɪlnəs] *n* vileza.
vilify ['vɪlɪfaɪ] *t* vilipendiar.
▲ *pt & pp* vilified, *ger* vilifying.
villa ['vɪlə] **1** *n* (*for holidays*) chalet *m*; (*in country*) casa de campo. **2** (*Roman*) villa. **3** (*large house*) villa, quinta.
village ['vɪlɪdʒ] **1** *n* (*gen*) pueblo; (*small*) pueblecito.
■ village idiot, tonto del pueblo. ‖ village life, la vida de pueblo.
villager ['vɪlɪdʒə] *n* habitante *m* del pueblo, aldeano,-a.
villain ['vɪlən] **1** *n* (*bad character*) malo,-a, malo,-a de la película. **2** GB *fam* malvado,-a.
● the villain of the piece, *fam* el malo de la película.
villainous ['vɪlənəs] *adj* infame, malvado,-a.
villainy ['vɪlənɪ] *n* vileza, maldad *f*.
▲ *pl* villainies.
vim [vɪm] *n fam* marcha.
vinaigrette [vɪnə'gret] *n* vinagreta.
vindicate ['vɪndɪkeɪt] **1** *t* (*exonerate*) vindicar, exculpar. **2** (*justify*) justificar.
vindication [vɪndɪ'keɪʃən] **1** *n* (*exoneration*) vindicación *f*, exculpación *f*. **2** (*justification*) justificación *f*.
vindictive [vɪn'dɪktɪv] *adj* vengativo,-a, rencoroso,-a: *he has a vindictive streak,* es rencoroso.
vindictively [vɪn'dɪktɪvlɪ] *adv* con rencor.
vine [vaɪn] **1** *n* vid *f*. **2** (*made to climb*) parra.
■ vine grower, viticultor,-ra. ‖ vine growing, viticultura. ‖ vine leaf, hoja de parra. ‖ vine shoot, sarmiento.
vinegar ['vɪnɪgə] *n* vinagre *m*.
■ vinegar bottle, vinagrera. ‖ wine vinegar, vinagre de vino.
vinegary ['vɪnɪgərɪ] **1** *adj* avinagrado,-a: *it has a vinegary taste,* sabe a vinagre. **2** *fig* avinagrado,-a.
vine-growing ['vaɪngrəʊɪŋ] *adj* vitícola.

vineyard ['vɪnjəd] *n* viña, viñedo.
vintage ['vɪntɪdʒ] **1** *n* cosecha: *what vintage is it?*, ¿de qué cosecha es? – **2** *adj* (*wine*) de añada. **3** (*classic*) clásico,-a; (*high-quality*) glorioso,-a, maravilloso,-a: *this has been a vintage year for the theatre in London*, este año ha sido glorioso para el teatro en Londres. **4** *fam* lo mejor de: *this opera is vintage Pavarotti*, esta ópera es de lo mejorcito de Pavarotti.
■ **vintage car**, coche *m* de época *construido entre* 1919 *y* 1930.
vintner ['vɪntnə'] *n dated* vinatero,-a.
vinyl ['vaɪnəl] *n* vinilo.
viola[1] [vɪ'əʊlə] *n* MUS viola.
viola[2] [vaɪ'əʊlə] *n* BOT violeta.
violate ['vaɪəleɪt] *t* violar; (*law*) infringir, transgredir.
violation [vaɪə'leɪʃən] *n* violación *f*; (*of law*) infracción *f*, transgresión *f*.
violator ['vaɪəleɪtə'] *n* infractor,-ra, transgresor,-ra.
violence ['vaɪələns] *n* violencia.
● **to do violence to sth.**, *fml* ir en contra de algo.
violent ['vaɪələnt] *adj* violento,-a.
● **to die a violent death**, morir de muerte violenta. ‖ **to have a violent temper**, ser de carácter violento.
violently ['vaɪələntlɪ] *adv* violentamente.
● **to be violently ill**, vomitarlo todo, echarlo todo. ‖ **to behave violently**, mostrarse violento,-a.
violet ['vaɪələt] **1** *n* BOT violeta *f*. **2** (*colour*) violeta *m*, violado,-a, violáceo,-a. – **3** *adj* (de color) violeta, violado,-a.
■ **shrinking violet**, *fam* mosquita muerta.
violin [vaɪə'lɪn] *n* violín *m*.
violinist [vaɪə'lɪnɪst] *n* violinista *mf*, violín *m*.
violoncello [vaɪələn'tʃeləʊ] *n* violonchelo.
VIP ['viː'aɪ'piː] *abbr* (*very important person*) personaje *m* muy importante; (*abbreviation*) VIP.
■ **VIP lounge**, sala de personalidades. ‖ **VIP treatment**, privilegios *mpl* especiales.
viper ['vaɪpə'] *n* víbora.
virago [vɪ'rɑːgəʊ] *n* virago *f*.
▲ *pl* **viragos** o **viragoes**.
viral ['vaɪrəl] *adj* viral, vírico,-a.
virgin ['vɜːdʒɪn] **1** *n* virgen *mf*: *he's still a virgin*, todavía es virgen. – **2** *adj* virgen.
■ **the Virgin Mary**, la Virgen María. ‖ **virgin birth**, alumbramiento virginal. ‖ **virgin territory**, tierra virgen.
virginal[1] ['vɜːdʒɪnəl] *adj* virginal.
virginal[2] ['vɜːdʒɪnəl] *n* MUS espineta.
Virginia [və'dʒɪnɪə] *n* Virginia.
■ **Virginia creeper**, enredadera de Virginia. ‖ **West Virginia**, Virginia Occidental.
virginity [vɜː'dʒɪnɪtɪ] *n* virginidad *f*.
Virgo ['vɜːgəʊ] *n* Virgo.
virile ['vɪraɪl] *adj* viril, varonil.
virility [və'rɪlɪtɪ] *n* virilidad *f*.
virological [vaɪrə'lɒdʒɪkəl] *adj* virológico,-a.
virologist [vaɪ'rɒlədʒɪst] *n* virólogo,-a.
virology [vaɪ'rɒlədʒɪ] *n* virología.
virtual ['vɜːtʃʊəl] *adj* virtual.
■ **virtual reality**, realidad *f* virtual.
virtually ['vɜːtʃʊəlɪ] *adv* casi, prácticamente: *that's virtually impossible*, eso es prácticamente imposible; *virtually all the shareholders were in agreement*, la práctica totalidad de los accionistas estaba de acuerdo.
virtue ['vɜːtʃuː] **1** *n* virtud *f*. **2** (*advantage*) ventaja.
● **by virtue of**, en virtud de. ‖ **in virtue of**, en virtud

de. ‖ **to make a virtue of necessity**, hacer de la necesidad virtud.
virtuosity [vɜːtʃʊ'ɒsɪtɪ] *n* virtuosismo.
virtuoso [vɜːtʃʊ'əʊzəʊ] *n* virtuoso,-a: *he's a piano virtuoso*, es un virtuoso del piano.
▲ *pl* **virtuosos** o **virtuosi** [vɜːtʃʊ'əʊzɪ].
virtuous ['vɜːtʃʊəs] **1** *adj* virtuoso,-a. **2** *pej* santurrón,-ona.
virulence ['vɪrʊləns] *n* virulencia.
virulent ['vɪrʊlənt] *adj* virulento,-a.
virus ['vaɪərəs] *n* virus *m*.
■ **virus infection**, infección *f* vírica.
visa ['viːzə] **1** *n* visado, *am* visa. – **2** *t* estampar un visado en.
■ **entry visa**, visado de entrada. ‖ **exit visa**, visado de salida.
▲ *pt* & *pp* **visaed**, *ger* **visaing**.
visage ['vɪzɪdʒ] *n* rostro, semblante *m*.
vis-à-vis [viːzɑː'viː] *prep* respecto a, con respecto a, respecto de.
viscera ['vɪsərə] *npl* vísceras *fpl*.
visceral ['vɪsərəl] *adj* visceral.
viscose ['vɪskəʊs] **1** *n* (*textile*) viscosilla. **2** CHEM viscosa.
viscosity [vɪs'kɒsɪtɪ] *n* viscosidad *f*.
viscount ['vaɪkaʊnt] *n* vizconde *m*.
viscountcy ['vaɪkaʊntsɪ] *n* vizcondado *f*.
viscountess ['vaɪkaʊntəs] *n* vizcondesa.
viscous ['vɪskəs] *adj* viscoso,-a.
vise [vaɪs] *n* US → **vice 2**.
visibility [vɪzɪ'bɪlɪtɪ] *n* visibilidad *f*: *there was poor visibility*, había escasa visibilidad.
visible ['vɪzɪbəl] *adj* visible.
Visigoth ['vɪzɪgɒθ] *n* visigodo,-a. – **2** *n* visigodo,-a.
vision ['vɪʒən] **1** *n* (*gen*) visión *f*: *she had visions of losing her husband*, ya se veía sin marido; *to see visions*, ver visiones. **2** (*eyesight*) vista: *to have good vision*, tener buena vista.
● **a man of vision**, un hombre con visión de futuro.
visionary ['vɪʒənərɪ] **1** *adj* (*showing vision*) con visión de futuro. **2** (*unrealistic*) visionario,-a. – **3** *n* visionario,-a.
▲ (*sustantivo*) *pl* **visionaries**.
visit ['vɪzɪt] **1** *t* (*person*) visitar, hacer una visita a. **2** (*place*) visitar, ir a: *they are visiting the city*, están visitando la ciudad. – **3** *i* estar de visita: *Aunt Helen is visiting this week*, la tía Helen pasa la semana con nosotros. – **4** *n* visita: *an official visit*, una visita oficial; *they're on a visit to Florence*, se han ido de viaje a Florencia.
● **to pay sb. a visit**, hacer una visita a algn. ‖ **to visit with sb.**, *us* charlar con algn.
■ **flying visit**, *fam* visita relámpago.
visitation [vɪzɪ'teɪʃən] **1** *n fml* (*official*) visita oficial. **2 the Visitation**, la Visitación.
visiting ['vɪzɪtɪŋ] **1** *adj* (*for visiting*) de visita. **2** (*guest*) visitante.
■ **visiting card**, tarjeta de visita. ‖ **visiting hours**, horas *fpl* de visita. ‖ **visiting lecturer**, profesor,-ra invitado,-a. ‖ **visiting team**, equipo visitante.
visitor ['vɪzɪtə'] **1** *n* (*at home*) invitado,-a, visita: *we've got visitors today*, hoy tenemos visita. **2** (*tourist*) turista *mf*, visitante *mf*: *visitors to this region*, los visitantes de esta región.
■ **visitors' book**, libro de visitas.
visor ['vaɪzə'] *n* visera.
vista ['vɪstə] **1** *n* vista, panorama *m*. **2** *fig* perspectiva.
visual ['vɪʒʊəl] *adj* visual.
■ **visual aid**, medio visual. ‖ **visual arts**, artes *mpl* visuales. ‖ **visual display unit**, pantalla.

visualize ['vɪʒʊəlaɪz] t visualizar.
visually ['vɪʒʊəlɪ] adv visualmente.
vital ['vaɪtəl] 1 adj vital. 2 (essential) esencial, imprescindible. – 3 npl órganos mpl vitales.
● of vital importance, de suma importancia.
■ vital organ, órgano vital. ‖ vital signs, señales fpl de vida. ‖ vital statistics, datos mpl demográficos; fam medidas fpl: Marilyn's vital statistics made her famous, las medidas de Marilyn la hicieron famosa.
vitalism ['vaɪtəlɪzəm] n vitalismo.
vitality [vaɪ'tælɪtɪ] n vitalidad f.
vitally ['vaɪtəlɪ] adv sumamente: vitally important, de suma importancia.
vitamin ['vɪtəmɪn, 'vaɪtəmɪn] n vitamina: with added vitamins, vitaminado,-a.
■ vitamin C, vitamina C. ‖ vitamin content, contenido vitamínico. ‖ vitamin deficiency, avitaminosis f.
vitiate ['vɪʃɪeɪt] t fml viciar.
viticulture ['vɪtɪkʌltʃə'] n viticultura.
vitreous ['vɪtrɪəs] adj vítreo,-a.
vitrify ['vɪtrɪfaɪ] t vitrificar.
▲ pt & pp vitrified, ger vitrifying.
vitriol ['vɪtrɪəl] n vitriolo.
vitriolic [vɪtrɪ'ɒlɪk] adj vitriólico,-a.
vitro ['viːtrəʊ]. 1 in vitro, adj in vitro: in vitro fertilization, fertilización in vitro. – 2 adv in vitro.
vituperation [vɪjuːpə'reɪʃən] n vituperación f.
viva ['vaɪvə] n GB fam (abbr of viva voce) examen m oral.
vivacious [vɪ'veɪʃəs] adj vivaz, animado,-a.
vivacity [vɪ'væsɪtɪ] n vivacidad f.
vivid ['vɪvɪd] 1 adj vivo, intenso,-a. 2 (description) gráfico,-a.
● to have a vivid imagination, tener mucha imaginación.
vividly ['vɪvɪdlɪ] adv vivamente, con viveza.
vividness ['vɪvɪdnəs] n viveza.
viviparous [vɪ'vɪpərəs] adj vivíparo,-a.
vivisection [vɪvɪ'sekʃən] n vivisección f.
vixen ['vɪksən] 1 n zorra. 2 lit arpía.
viz [vɪz] adv (abbr of videlicet) a saber.
V-neck ['viːnek] n cuello de pico.
V-necked ['viːnekt] adj con el cuello de pico.
vocab ['vəʊkæb] n (abbr of vocabulary) vocabulario.
vocabulary [və'kæbjʊlərɪ] n vocabulario.
▲ pl vocabularies.
vocal ['vəʊkəl] 1 adj vocal. 2 fam (noisy) escandaloso,-a.
■ vocal cords, cuerdas fpl vocales.
vocalist ['vəʊkəlɪst] n cantante mf, vocalista mf.
vocalize ['vəʊkəlaɪz] 1 t vocalizar. – 2 i vocalizar. 3 GRAM vocalizarse.
vocation [vəʊ'keɪʃən] n vocación f: one must have a real vocation to become a nurse, hace falta mucha vocación para ser enfermera.
● to lose one's vocation, perder la vocación.
vocational [vəʊ'keɪʃənəl] adj profesional.
■ vocational guidance, orientación f profesional. ‖ vocational guidance counsellor, tutor,-ra.
vocative ['vɒkətɪv] 1 n vocativo. – 2 adj vocativo,-a.
vociferate [və'sɪfəreɪt] i vociferar.
vociferous [və'sɪfərəs] adj vociferante, vocinglero,-a.
vociferously [və'sɪfərəslɪ] adv a (grandes) voces.
vodka ['vɒdkə] n vodka m & f.
vogue [vəʊg] n boga, moda.
● to be all the vogue, estar muy en boga.
■ to be in vogue, estar en boga.

voice [vɔɪs] 1 n voz f: to have a hoarse/weak voice, tener la voz ronca/apagada; she has a high/low voice, tiene la voz aguda/grave; a tenor voice, una voz de tenor; his voice is breaking, le está cambiando la voz; he had little voice in the matter, no tuvo voz ni voto en el asunto. – 2 t expresar: I had no time to voice my opinion, no tuve tiempo de expresar mi opinión. 3 LING sonorizar.
● at the top of one's voice, a voz en grito. ‖ in a loud voice, en voz alta. ‖ in a low/soft voice, en voz baja, a media voz. ‖ the voice of experience, la voz de la experiencia. ‖ the voice of reason, la voz de la razón. ‖ to be in voice, estar en voz. ‖ to give voice to one's feelings, expresar sus sentimientos. ‖ to lose one's voice, quedarse afónico,-a, quedarse sin voz. ‖ to lower/raise one's voice, bajar/levantar la voz. ‖ with one voice, de una voz, a una, a coro.
■ voice box, laringe f. ‖ voice offstage, THEAT voz f en off.
voiced [vɔɪst] adj LING sonoro,-a.
voiceless ['vɔɪsləs] 1 adj (hoarse) afónico,-a. 2 LING sordo,-a.
voice-over [vɔɪs'əʊvə'] n voz f en off.
void [vɔɪd] 1 adj vacío,-a (of, de): void of interest, falto,-a de interés. 2 JUR nulo,-a, inválido,-a. – 3 n vacío. – 4 t (empty) vaciar. 5 JUR anular, invalidar.
● to make sth. void, anular algo.
vol [vɒl, 'vɒljuːm] abbr (volume - book) tomo; (- loudness) volumen m.
volatile ['vɒlətaɪl] adj volátil.
vol-au-vent ['vɒləʊvɒn] n volován m.
volcanic [vɒl'kænɪk] adj volcánico,-a.
volcano [vɒl'keɪnəʊ] n volcán m: a dormant volcano, un volcán inactivo.
▲ pl volcanos o volcanoes.
volcanologist [vɒlkə'nɒlədʒɪst] n vulcanólogo,-a.
volcanology [vɒlkə'nɒlədʒɪ] n vulcanología.
vole [vəʊl] n campañol m.
volition [və'lɪʃən] n volición f, voluntad f.
● of/on one's own volition, por voluntad propia: she left of her own volition, se marchó por voluntad propia.
volley ['vɒlɪ] 1 n MIL descarga: they fired a volley of shots into the field, lanzaron una descarga contra el campo. 2 fig (of stones, curses) aluvión m; (of blows) tanda; (of applause) salva. 3 (tennis) volea. – 4 i MIL lanzar una descarga. 5 (tennis) hacer una volea. – 6 t (sp) volear.
volleyball ['vɒlɪbɔːl] n balonvolea m, voleibol m.
volt [vəʊlt] n voltio.
voltage ['vəʊltɪdʒ] n voltaje m, tensión f: a high voltage fence, una verja de alta tensión.
volte-face [vɒlt'fɑːs] n lit cambio de opinión, giro en redondo.
voltmeter ['vəʊltmiːtə'] n voltímetro.
volubility [vɒljə'bɪlətɪ] n locuacidad f.
voluble ['vɒljəbəl] adj locuaz, hablador,-ra.
volume ['vɒljuːm] 1 n volumen m. 2 (book) tomo.
● to speak volumes, decirlo todo: her silence spoke volumes, su silencio lo decía todo. ‖ to turn down/up the volume, bajar/subir el volumen.
voluminous [və'ljuːmɪnəs] adj voluminoso,-a.
voluntarily ['vɒləntərɪlɪ] adv voluntariamente.
voluntary ['vɒləntərɪ] adj voluntario,-a.
● to take voluntary redundancy, acogerse al despido voluntario.
■ voluntary organization, organización f benéfica. ‖ voluntary society, sociedad f benéfica. ‖ voluntary work, obras fpl benéficas. ‖ voluntary helper/worker, voluntario,-a.

volunteer [vɒlən'tɪəʳ] **1** *n* voluntario,-a. – **2** *t* ofrecer: *to volunteer information/a statement,* facilitar información/una declaración. – **3** *i* ofrecerse (**for**, para): *he volunteered to tidy up the room,* se ofreció para ordenar la habitación. **4** MIL alistarse como voluntario,-a (**for**, en).
■ **volunteer army,** ejército de voluntarios.
voluptuous [və'lʌptjuəs] *adj* voluptuoso,-a.
voluptuousness [və'lʌptjuəsnəs] *n* voluptuosidad *f.*
vomit ['vɒmɪt] **1** *n* vómito. – **2** *i* vomitar, devolver. – **3** *t* vomitar, devolver.
voodoo ['vuːduː] *n* vudú *m.*
voracious [və'reɪʃəs] *adj* voraz.
voracity [və'ræsɪtɪ] *n* voracidad *f.*
vortex ['vɔːteks] **1** *n* vórtice *m.* **2** *fig* vorágine *f.*
▲ *pl* **vortexes** o **vortices** ['vɔːtɪsiːz].
Vosges [vəʊʒ] *n* los Vosgos *mpl.*
vote [vəʊt] **1** *n* voto: *the majority cast their vote for Berlusconi,* la mayoría votó a Berlusconi. **2** (*voting*) voto, votación *f: it was a very close vote,* fue una votación muy reñida. **3** (*right to vote*) sufragio, (derecho al) voto: *young people are given the (right to) vote at age 18,* los jóvenes pueden votar a los 18 años. – **4** *i* votar: *they voted Conservative,* votaron al partido conservador; *vote for Smith!,* ¡vota a Smith! – **5** *t* votar. **6** (*elect*) elegir: *he was voted president,* fue elegido presidente. **7** *fam* considerarse: *the party was voted a complete flop,* la fiesta se consideró un desastre total.
◆ **to vote down** *t sep* votar en contra de. ‖ **to vote through** *t sep* votar a favor de.
● **to be voted into/out of office,** ganar/perder las elecciones. ‖ **to pull in votes,** atraer el voto. ‖ **to vote by a show of hands,** votar a mano alzada. ‖ **to vote on sth. / take a vote on sth.,** someter algo a votación.
■ **vote of censure,** voto de censura. ‖ **vote of confidence,** voto de confianza. ‖ **write-in vote,** votación *f* por escrito.
voter ['vəʊtəʳ] *n* votante *mf.*
voting ['vəʊtɪŋ] *n* votación *f.*
■ **voting paper,** papeleta. ‖ **voting pattern,** tendencia del voto.
votive ['vəʊtɪv] *adj* votivo,-a.
vouch [vaʊtʃ] **to vouch for sb./sth.,** *phr* responder por algn./responder de algo.

voucher ['vaʊtʃəʳ] **1** *n* GB vale *m,* bono. **2** JUR comprobante *m,* justificante *m.*
■ **gift voucher,** cupón *m* de regalo. ‖ **luncheon voucher,** ticket *m* restaurante.
vow [vaʊ] **1** *n* promesa solemne. **2** REL voto. – **3** *t* jurar.
● **to take a vow of chastity/poverty,** hacer voto de castidad/pobreza. ‖ **to take one's vows,** pronunciar sus votos.
■ **vow of silence,** voto de silencio.
vowel ['vaʊəl] *n* vocal *f.*
vox pop [vɒks'pɒp] *n* GB *fam* vox populi *f.*
voyage ['vɔɪɪdʒ] **1** *n* viaje *m;* (*by sea*) viaje *m* en barco; (*crossing*) travesía. – **2** *i fml* viajar.
● **to go on a (sea) voyage,** hacer un viaje en barco.
voyager ['vɔɪədʒəʳ] *n* viajero,-a.
VP [vaɪs'prezɪdənt] *abbr* (*Vice-President*) Vicepresidente *m.*
vs. ['vɜːsəs] *prep* (*abbr of versus*) contra.
V-sign ['viːsaɪn] **1** *n* (*for victory*) señal *f* de la victoria. **2** GB (*as insult*) ≈ corte *m* de mangas.
VSO ['viː'es'əʊ] *abbr* GB (*Voluntary Service Overseas*) *organización que envía voluntarios a prestar ayuda a países del tercer mundo.*
VTOL ['viː'tiː'əʊ'el] *abbr* (*vertical take-off and landing*) de despegue y aterrizaje vertical.
VTR ['viː'tiː'ɑːʳ] *abbr* (*video tape recorder*) grabador *m* de videocinta.
vulcanize ['vʌlkənaɪz] *t* vulcanizar.
vulgar ['vʌlgəʳ] **1** *adj* (*in poor taste*) de mal gusto. **2** (*coarse*) grosero,-a, ordinario,-a. **3** LING vulgar.
■ **vulgar fraction,** fracción *f* común. ‖ **Vulgar Latin,** latín *m* vulgar.
vulgarity [vʌl'gærɪtɪ] **1** *n* (*poor taste*) mal gusto. **2** (*coarseness*) vulgaridad *f,* ordinariez *f,* grosería.
vulgarize ['vʌlgəraɪz] *t* degradar.
vulnerability [vʌlnərə'bɪlətɪ] *n* vulnerabilidad *f.*
vulnerable ['vʌlnərəbəl] *adj* vulnerable.
vulture ['vʌltʃəʳ] *n* buitre *m.*
vulva ['vʌlvə] *n* vulva.
▲ *pl* **vulvas** o **vulvae** ['vʌlviː].

W

W, w ['dʌbəljuː] *n* (*the letter*) W, w *f*.

W¹ [wɒt] *symb* (*Watt*) watt, vatio; (*symbol*) W.

W² [west] *abbr* (*west*) oeste *m*; (*abbreviation*) O.

wacky ['wækɪ] *adj fam* (*person*) loco,-a, chiflado,-a; (*thing*) absurdo,-a, ridículo,-a.
▲ *comp* **wackier**, *superl* **wackiest**.

wad [wɒd] **1** *n* (*of cotton wool*) tapón *m*. **2** (*of notes, papers*) fajo, taco. – **3** *t* (*line, pad*) forrar, acolchar; (*stuff*) rellenar.
▲ *pt & pp* **wadded**, *ger* **wadding**.

wadding ['wɒdɪŋ] *n* (*padding*) relleno, acolchado; (*in quilting*) guata.

waddle ['wɒdəl] **1** *i* anadear. – **2** *n* andar *m* de los patos.

wade [weɪd] **1** *i* caminar por el agua: *he waded out into the lake*, entró caminando en el lago; *I waded across the river*, atravesé el río vadeando. – **2** *t* vadear: *they had to wade the river*, tuvieron que vadear el río.
◆ **to wade in 1** *i* (*get involved*) meterse. **2** (*start work*) ponerse. ‖ **to wade into** *t insep* (*attack*) atacar, arremeter contra. ‖ **to wade through** *t insep* leer (*con dificultad*).

wader ['weɪdəʳ] **1** *n* ORN ave *f* zancuda. – **2 waders**, *npl* botas *fpl* de pescador.

wading bird ['weɪdɪŋbɜːd] *n* ave *f* zancuda.

wafer ['weɪfəʳ] **1** *n* (*for icecream*) barquillo; (*biscuit*) galleta de barquillo. **2** REL hostia.

wafer-thin ['weɪfəˈθɪn] *adj* (*gen*) muy fino,-a, muy delgado,-a; (*majority*) muy escaso,-a.
● **to cut sth. wafer thin**, cortar algo en lonchas muy finas.
▲ *Se escribe* **wafer thin** *cuando no se antepone a un sustantivo.*

waffle¹ ['wɒfəl] *n* CULIN gofre *m*.

waffle² ['wɒfəl] **1** *n* GB *fam* (*writing*) paja; (*talk*) palabrería. – **2** *i* GB *fam* (*write*) meter mucha paja; (*talk*) hablar mucho sin decir nada, parlotear.

waft [wɒft] **1** *t* llevar por el aire. – **2** *i* flotar por el aire, llegar con el aire, irse con el aire: *the scent of roses wafted in from the garden*, un olor de rosas entraba desde el jardín. – **3** *n* (*smell*) bocanada.

wag¹ [wæg] **1** *n* meneo. – **2** *t* menear: *the dog wagged its tail*, el perro meneó la cola; *she wagged her finger at him*, lo amonestó con el dedo. – **3** *i* menearse.
● **tongues will wag**, la gente hablará.
▲ *pt & pp* **wagged**, *ger* **wagging**.

wag² [wæg] *n dated* bromista *mf*, chistoso,-a.

wage [weɪdʒ] **1** *n* sueldo, salario: *the minimum wage*, el salario mínimo; *a weekly wage*, un sueldo semanal. – **2 wages**, *npl* sueldo *m sing*, salario *m sing*: *we demand better wages*, exigimos un salario mejor.
● **to earn a living wage**, ganar lo suficiente para vivir. ‖ **to wage war on**, hacer la guerra a.
■ **day's wage**, jornal *m*. ‖ **wage claim**, reivindicación *f* salarial. ‖ **wage earner**, asalariado,-a. ‖ **wage freeze**, congelación *f* de salarios. ‖ **wage incentive**, prima de rendimiento. ‖ **wage rise**, aumento de sueldo.

wage-packet ['weɪdʒpækɪt] *n* (*envelope*) sobre *m* del sueldo; (*money*) sueldo.

wager ['weɪdʒəʳ] **1** *n dated* apuesta. – **2** *t dated* apostar: *he wagered $10 on a horse*, apostó $10 a un caballo. – **3** *i* apostar.
● **to make a wager**, hacer una apuesta.

waggle ['wægəl] **1** *t fam* menear. – **2** *i fam* menearse. – **3** *n fam* meneo.

waggon ['wægən] *n* GB → **wagon**.

wagon ['wægən] **1** *n* (*cart*) carro; (*covered*) carromato. **2** GB (*railway truck*) vagón *m*. **3** US (*trolley*) carrito, mesa camarera.
● **to be on the wagon**, haber dejado la bebida. ‖ **to go on the wagon**, dejar la bebida.
■ **goods wagon**, vagón *m* de mercancías.

wagon-lit [vægɒnˈliː] *n* coche-cama *m*.
▲ *pl* **wagons-lits**.

wagtail ['wægteɪl] *n* ORN lavandera.

waif [weɪf] *n* niño,-a abandonado,-a.
● **waifs and strays**, niños *mpl* abandonados.

wail [weɪl] **1** *n* (*of pain, grief*) lamento, gemido; (*of siren*) aullido. – **2** *i* (*person - cry*) gemir, llorar; (- *complain*) quejarse (**about/over**, de), lamentarse (**about/over**, de). **3** (*siren*) aullar, ulular; (*wind*) ulular. **4** (*mourn*) plañir.
● **to wail for sb.**, llorar la muerte de algn.

wailing ['weɪlɪŋ] *n* llanto, lamentaciones *fpl*, gemidos *mpl*.
■ **Wailing Wall**, Muro de las Lamentaciones.

waist [weɪst] **1** *n* ANAT cintura. **2** (*of garment*) talle *m*. **3** (*of guitar etc*) parte estrecha.
● **from the waist up**, de (la) cintura para arriba.
■ **waist measurement**, medida de la cintura.

waistband ['weɪstbænd] *n* cinturilla.

waistcoat ['weɪskəʊt] *n* chaleco.

waisted ['weɪstɪd] *adj* de talle ajustado.

waistline ['weɪstlaɪn] **1** *n* ANAT cintura. **2** SEW talle *m*.
● **to watch one's waistline**, guardar la línea.

wait [weɪt] **1** *n* (*gen*) espera; (*delay*) demora: *we're in for a long wait*, nos queda una larga espera; *I hope it was worth the wait*, espero que la espera haya merecido la pena. – **2** *i* esperar (**for**, -), aguardar (**for**, -): *wait for me!*, ¡espérame!; *have you been waiting long?*, ¿hace mucho que esperas?; *we're still waiting to be seen*, aún estamos esperando que nos atiendan; *I waited half an hour for the train*, estuve media hora esperando el tren; *can't it wait until later?*, ¿no puede esperar hasta más tarde?; *I can't wait to meet him*, tengo muchas ganas de conocerlo. – **3** *t* esperar, aguardar: *wait your turn*, espera tu turno, espera que te toque.
◆ **to wait about / wait around** *i* esperar, perder el tiempo. ‖ **to wait on** *t insep* servir. ‖ **to wait up** *i* esperar levantado,-a: *don't wait up for me, I'll be late*, no me esperes levantado,-a, llegaré tarde.
● **"while you wait"**, "en el acto". ‖ **just you wait**, ya

verás. ‖ **to keep sb. waiting,** hacer esperar a algn. ‖ **to wait and see,** esperar a ver qué pasa: *all we can do is wait and see,* lo único que podemos hacer es esperar a ver qué pasa; *where are we going? –wait and see,* ¿dónde vamos? –espera y verás. ‖ **to wait at table,** servir la mesa. ‖ **to wait on sb. hand and foot,** tratar a algn. a cuerpo de rey.

waiter ['weɪtə'] *n* camarero.

waiting ['weɪtɪŋ] *n* espera.
● "**no waiting",** "prohibido estacionar". ‖ **to play a waiting game,** esperar el momento oportuno.
■ **waiting list,** lista de espera. ‖ **waiting room,** sala de espera.

waitress ['weɪtrəs] *n* camarera.

waive [weɪv] *t fml* (*claim, right, etc*) renunciar a; (*rule*) no aplicar.

wake[1] [weɪk] **1** *n* (*for dead*) velatorio. – **2** *t* (*awaken*) despertar (**up,** -): *don't wake the baby (up),* no despiertes al bebé. **3** (*make alert*) despertar (**up,** -), espabilar (**up,** -): *a run round the block will soon wake you up,* una vuelta a la manzana te espabilará en seguida. – **4** *i* (*stop sleeping*) despertarse (**up,** -): *wake up! it's late!,* ¡despiértate! ¡es tarde!; *I usually wake up at eight,* normalmente me despierto a las ocho. **5** (*pay attention*) despertarse, espabilarse: *wake up you lot!,* ¡espabilaos!
◆ **to wake up to** *t insep* (*become aware*) darse cuenta de.
▲ *pt* **woke,** *pp* **woken.**

wake[2] [weɪk] *n* (*in water*) estela.
● **in the wake of sth.,** tras algo. ‖ **to leave sth. in its wake,** dejar una estela de algo.

wakeful [weɪkfʊl] *adj* (*unable to sleep*) desvelado,-a; (*alert, vigilant*) alerta, vigilante.
● **to have a wakeful night,** pasar la noche en blanco.

waken ['weɪkən] **1** *t fml lit* despertar. – **2** *i fml lit* despertarse.

wakey ['weɪkɪ] **wakey! wakey!,** *interj fam* ¡despierta!

Wales [weɪlz] *n* País *m* de Gales.

walk [wɔːk] **1** *n* (*gen*) paseo; (*distance*) camino; (*long*) caminata, excursión *f*; (*sport*) marcha: *I'm going for a walk,* me voy a pasear, voy a dar un paseo; *he took the dog for a walk,* sacó el perro a pasear; *it's about twenty minutes' walk,* está a unos veinte de minutos caminando. **2** (*path, route*) paseo, ruta; (*long*) excursión *f: a book on country walks,* un libro sobre rutas a pie por el campo; *there are some lovely walks in this area,* hay bastantes excursiones bonitas por esta zona. **3** (*gait*) modo de andar, andares *mpl: I recognized you by your walk,* te he reconocido por tu modo de andar. – **4** *i* andar, caminar, pasear: *I'll walk there,* iré andando, iré a pie; *is the baby walking yet?,* ¿ya anda el bebé?; *she walked home,* se fue andando a casa; *we've walked about five miles,* hemos caminado unas cinco millas; *I love walking round the old part of the city,* me encanta pasear por el barrio antiguo de la ciudad; *he just walked off,* se echó a andar y se fue. – **5** *t* (*cover on foot*) ir a pie, ir andando, andar: *is it far? can I walk it?,* ¿está lejos? ¿se puede ir andando?; *he spends all day walking the streets,* pasa todo el día caminando por la calle. **6** (*person*) acompañar; (*animal*) pasear: *he offered to walk me home,* se ofreció para acompañarme a casa.
◆ **to walk away** *i* alejarse. ‖ **to walk away from** *t insep* (*come out unhurt*) salir ileso,-a. ‖ **to walk away with 1** *t insep* (*win easily*) ganar con facilidad, llevarse de calle: *she walked away with first prize,* se llevó el primer premio. **2** *fam* (*steal*) mangar, birlar: *that man's just walked away with my umbrella,* ese hombre acaba de birlarme

el paraguas. ‖ **to walk into 1** *t insep* (*get caught*) caer en: *he walked right into the trap,* cayó directamente en la trampa. **2** (*bump into*) tropezar con. ‖ **to walk off with** *t insep* → **walk away with.** ‖ **to walk out 1** *i* (*leave suddenly*) marcharse. **2** (*go on strike*) ir a la huelga. ‖ **to walk out on** *t insep* (*abandon*) abandonar a.
● **to go for a walk,** dar un paseo. ‖ **to run before one can walk,** precipitarse. ‖ **to walk all over sb.,** tratar muy mal a algn. ‖ **to walk it,** (*win easily*) ganar fácilmente. ‖ **to walk sb. off their feet,** agotar a algn. a fuerza de caminar. ‖ **to walk tall,** ir con la cabeza bien alta.
■ **walk of life,** condición *f* social.

walkabout ['wɔːkəbaʊt] *n* (*of VIP*) paseo informal entre la gente.
● **to go walkabout,** dar un paseo entre la gente: *the king went walkabout on his visit to Tokyo,* el rey dio un paseo entre la gente durante su visita a Tokio.

walker ['wɔːkə'] **1** *n* (*gen*) paseante *mf;* (*hiker*) excursionista *mf.* **2** (*athlete*) marchador,-ra. **3** (*for babies*) andador *m,* tacataca *m,* tacatá *m;* (*for disabled*) andador *m.*

walkie-talkie [wɔːkɪ'tɔːkɪ] *n* walkie-talkie *m.*

walk-in ['wɔːkɪn] *adj* (*cupboard*) empotrado y lo bastante *grande como para entrar en él.*

walking ['wɔːkɪŋ] **1** *n* (*activity*) andar *m,* caminar *m,* pasear *m;* (*hiking*) excursionismo. – **2** *adj* ambulante: *he's a walking encyclopedia,* es una enciclopedia ambulante.
● **to give sb. their walking papers,** *us* poner a algn. de patitas en la calle, echar a algn.
■ **walking pace,** paso de marcha. ‖ **walking shoes,** zapatos *mpl* para caminar. ‖ **walking stick,** bastón *m.* ‖ **walking tour,** excursión *f* a pie.

Walkman ['wɔːkmən] *n* walkman *m.*
▲ **Es marca registrada.**

walk-on ['wɔːkɒn] *adj* (*theatre*) de comparsa.
■ **walk-on part,** papel *m* de comparsa.

walkout ['wɔːkaʊt] *n* (*strike*) huelga.

walkover ['wɔːkəʊvə'] *n fam* (*easy victory*) paseo, triunfo fácil: *the game against Wigan was a walkover,* el partido contra Wigan fue un paseo.

walk-up ['wɔːkʌp] **1** *adj us* sin ascensor. – **2** *n us* bloque *m* de pisos sin ascensor.

walkway ['wɔːkweɪ] *n us* pasaje *m* peatonal.

wall [wɔːl] **1** *n* (*exterior*) muro; (*defensive, city*) muralla; (*garden*) tapia; (*sea*) dique *m.* **2** (*interior*) pared *f;* (*partition*) tabique *m;* (*party*) pared *f* medianera; (*main*) pared *f* maestra: *shall we hang this picture on the wall?,* ¿colgamos este cuadro en la pared? **3** ANAT (*of artery, blood vessel*) pared *f;* (*of abdomen*) pared *f* abdominal. **4** *fig* (*barrier*) barrera, muro. **5** SP barrera. – **6** *t* (*surround with wall*) amurallar.
◆ **to wall in** *t sep* tapiar. ‖ **to wall off** *t sep* tapiar. ‖ **to wall up** *t sep* (*door, window*) tapiar, tabicar, condenar.
● **walls have ears,** las paredes oyen. ‖ **to bang one's head against a brick wall,** darse contra las paredes. ‖ **to have one's back to the wall,** estar en un aprieto, estar en un brete. ‖ **to come up against a brick wall,** encontrarse con una barrera infranqueable. ‖ **to drive sb. up the wall,** volver loco,-a a algn., hacer que algn. se suba por las paredes. ‖ **to go to the wall,** arruinarse, quebrar. ‖ **to go up the wall,** volverse loco,-a, subirse por las paredes.
■ **wall lamp / wall light,** aplique *m.* ‖ **wall map,** mapa *m* mural.

wallaby ['wɒləbɪ] *n* ualabí *m.*
▲ *pl* **wallabies.**

walled [wɔːld] *adj* (*city*) amurallado,-a; (*garden*) tapiado,-a.

wallet ['wɒlɪt] *n* cartera.

wallflower ['wɔːlflauəʳ] *n* BOT alhelí *m*.
● to be a **wallflower**, *fig* hacer de comparsa.

Walloon [wɒ'luːn] **1** *adj* valón,-ona. **– 2** *n* (*person*) valón,-ona. **3** (*language*) valón *m*.

wallop ['wɒləp] **1** *n fam* (*blow*) golpazo. **– 2** *t fam* (*hit hard*) pegar fuerte. **3** *fam* (*defeat*) dar una paliza a.

walloping ['wɒləpɪŋ] **1** *n fam* (*beating*) paliza, zurra; (*defeat*) paliza. **– 2** *adj fam* (*very big*) enorme, colosal.

wallow ['wɒləu] **1** *i* (*animal*) revolcarse (**in**, en); (*ship*) bambolearse. **2** (*person - in luxury etc*) disfrutar (**in**, de), nadar (**in**, en); (*- in grief, self-pity*) sumirse (**in**, en).

wallpaper ['wɔːlpeɪpəʳ] **1** *n* papel *m* pintado. **– 2** *t* empapelar.

wall-to-wall [wɔːltə'wɔːl] *adj* de pared a pared.
■ **wall-to-wall carpeting**, moqueta.

wally ['wɒlɪ] *n fam* idiota *mf*, inútil *mf*.
▲ *pl* **wallies**.

walnut ['wɔːlnʌt] *n* (*fruit*) nuez *f*; (*wood*) nogal *m*.
■ **walnut tree**, nogal *m*.

walrus ['wɔːlrəs] *n* morsa.

waltz [wɔːls] **1** *n* vals *m*. **– 2** *i* (*dance*) valsar, bailar el vals. **3** *fam* (*move casually, confidently*) moverse con desenvoltura, moverse despreocupadamente: *I can't just waltz up to her and ask her out*, no puedo acercarme a ella y pedirle que salga conmigo como si tal cosa.
◆ **to waltz off with 1** *t insep* (*win easily*) llevarse, ganar con facilidad. **2** (*steal*) robar, mangar, birlar.

wan [wɒn] **1** *adj* (*face*) pálido,-a, macilento,-a. **2** (*look, smile*) triste, apagado,-a. **3** *fig* (*light*) débil.
▲ *comp* **wanner**, *superl* **wannest**.

wand [wɒnd] *n* varita.
■ **magic wand**, varita mágica.

wander ['wɒndəʳ] **1** *i* (*roam*) deambular, errar, vagar; (*stroll*) pasear, caminar: *they wandered through the desert*, vagaban por el desierto; *I enjoy wandering around strange cities*, me gusta pasear por ciudades desconocidas; *he wandered into the first pub he saw*, entró tranquilamente en el primer bar que vio. **2** (*stray*) apartarse, desviarse, alejarse; (*get lost*) extraviarse: *don't wander from the path*, no os apartéis del camino; *it seems as though a child has wandered off*, parece que un niño se ha extraviado. **3** (*river, road*) serpentear. **4** (*mind, thoughts*) desviarse, divagar; (*person*) apartarse, desviarse: *her attention kept wandering*, su atención divagaba; *don't wander off the point*, no te desvíes del tema. **– 5** *t* (*streets, area*) vagar por, recorrer: *she was found wandering the streets*, la encontraron vagando por las calles. **– 6** *n* vuelta, paseo.
● to go for a **wander**, ir a dar una vuelta.

wanderer ['wɒndərəʳ] *n* (*traveller*) trotamundos *m*; (*nomad*) nómada *mf*.

wandering ['wɒndərɪŋ] **1** *adj* (*gen*) errante, errabundo,-a; (*itinerant*) ambulante, itinerante; (*nomadic*) nómada. **– 2 wanderings**, *npl* andanzas *fpl*, viajes *mpl*.
■ **wandering Jew**, BOT tradescantia.

wanderlust ['wɒndəlʌst] *n* ansia de viajar.

wane [weɪn] **1** *i* (*moon*) menguar. **– 2** *t* (*strength, influence*) menguar, decrecer; (*emotion, interest*) decaer, decrecer, declinar, disminuir.
● to be on the **wane**, (*moon*) estar menguando; (*power*) estar en decadencia.

wangle ['wæŋgəl] *t fam* conseguir, agenciarse: *I managed to wangle a free ticket to the concert*, me las amañé para agenciarme una entrada para el concierto.

● he **wangled** his way onto the board, se las arregló para entrar en el consejo. ‖ **to wangle out of sth.**, escaquearse de algo.

wank [wæŋk] **1** *n taboo* paja. **– 2** *i* hacerse una paja, meneársela.

wanker ['wæŋkəʳ] *n taboo* gilipollas *mf*, cabrón *m*, mamón,-ona.

want [wɒnt] **1** *n* (*lack*) falta, carencia: *for want of anywhere better to go*, a falta de algún sitio mejor adonde ir; *for want of trying*, no por falta de esfuerzos; *they died from want of food and water*, murieron por falta de comida y agua. **2** (*desire, need*) necesidad *f*: *all their wants were satisfied*, se satisficieron todas sus necesidades. **3** (*poverty*) miseria, indigencia. **– 4** *t* (*gen*) querer: *they want to go home*, quieren irse a casa; *I want you to come with me*, quiero que me acompañes; *what do you want to drink?*, ¿qué quieres beber?; *he wants to be a fireman*, quiere ser bombero; *you don't have to come if you don't want to*, no tienes que venir si no quieres; *how much do you want for the bike?*, ¿cuánto pides por la bici?; *what more do you want?*, ¿qué más quieres? **5** *fam* (*need*) necesitar: *the door wants a coat of paint*, la puerta necesita una mano de pintura; *you want your head examined*, tú estás mal de la cabeza; *I've got a few jobs that want doing*, tengo unos trabajillos que hacer; *it still wants cooking a bit more*, todavía hace falta guisarlo un poco más; *that boy wants a good telling-off*, una bronca no le vendría mal a ese chico. **6** *fam* (*ought to*) deber: *you want to see the doctor*, deberías ir a ver al médico. **7** *fml* (*lack*) necesitar, carecer de, faltar. **8** (*require to be present*) buscar, requerir la presencia de; (*seek, hunt*) buscar: *the boss wants you*, el jefe quiere verte; *you're wanted upstairs*, requieren tu presencia arriba; *he's wanted by the police*, lo busca la policía; *you're wanted on the phone*, te llaman por teléfono. **9** (*desire*) desear, querer.
◆ **to want for** *t insep* carecer de, necesitar: *they've never wanted for anything*, nunca les ha faltado nada. ‖ to want in *i* querer entrar. ‖ **to want out 1** *i* querer salir. **2** (*in plan, project, etc*) querer dejarlo: *it's too risky and I want out*, es demasiado arriesgado y quiero dejarlo.
● in want of sth., necesitar. ‖ to be in want, estar necesitado,-a. ‖ not to want to know (about sth.), no querer saber nada de algo. ‖ to want some doing, exigir mucho esfuerzo.
■ **want ad**, us anuncio pequeño.

wanted ['wɒntɪd] **1** *adj* (*for work*) necesario,-a: *"boy wanted"*, "se necesita mozo". **2** (*by police*) buscado,-a: *"wanted"*, "se busca".

wanting ['wɒntɪŋ] *adj* (*deficient*) deficiente; (*inadequate*) insuficiente.
● to be **wanting** in sth., carecer de algo. ‖ to be found **wanting**, no dar la talla.

wanton ['wɒntən] **1** *adj* (*gratuitous*) gratuito,-a: *wanton cruelty*, crueldad gratuita. **2** *fml* (*unrestrained*) desenfrenado,-a; (*licentious*) disipado,-a, licencioso,-a.

wantonly ['wɒntənlɪ] *adv* sin motivo, gratuitamente.

war [wɔːʳ] **1** *n* guerra: *the Spanish Civil War*, la Guerra Civil Española; *between the wars*, en el período de entreguerras. **– 2** *i arch* guerrear.
● war of nerves, guerra de nervios, guerra psicológica. ‖ war of words, guerra de propaganda. ‖ at war, en guerra. ‖ to declare war on sb./sth., declarar la guerra a algn./algo. ‖ to go to war over sth., emprender la guerra por algo. ‖ to have been in the wars, estar algo maltrecho,-a. ‖ to wage war on sb./sth., hacer la guerra a algn./algo.

■ **cold war,** guerra fría. ‖ **holy war,** guerra santa. ‖ **war baby,** niño,-a, nacido,-a durante la guerra. ‖ **war correspondent,** corresponsal *mf* de guerra. ‖ **war crime,** crimen *m* de guerra. ‖ **war cry,** grito de guerra. ‖ **war dance,** danza guerrera. ‖ **war game,** (*game*) juego de estrategia militar; (*military exercise*) ejercicio de simulacro de combate. ‖ **war hero,** héroe *m* de guerra. ‖ **war memorial,** monumento a los caídos. ‖ **war paint,** (*for war*) pintura de guerra; (*make-up*) maquillaje *m*. ‖ **war zone,** zona de conflicto.

▲ (*verbo*) *pt & pp* **warred,** *ger* **warring.**

warble ['wɔːbəl] **1** *n* gorjeo. – **2** *t* gorjear. – **3** *i* gorjear.

warbler ['wɔːblə'] *n* ORN pájaro cantor, ave *f* cantora.

■ **garden warbler,** curruca mosquitera. ‖ **willow warbler,** mosquitero musical. ‖ **wood warbler,** mosquitero silbador.

ward [wɔːd] **1** *n* (*in hospital*) sala. **2** GB POL distrito electoral. **3** JUR pupilo,-a. **4** (*in lock*) guarda.

◆ **to ward off** **1** *t sep* (*illness*) prevenir; (*danger*) evitar. **2** (*blow*) parar, desviar; (*attack*) rechazar.

■ **ward of court,** pupilo,-a bajo tutela judicial.

warden ['wɔːdən] **1** *n* (*of hostel, home*) encargado,-a. **2** US (*of prison*) alcaide *m*, director,-ra. **3** (*of university*) rector,-ra.

■ **game warden,** guarda *mf* de coto. ‖ **traffic warden,** ≈ guardia *mf* urbano,-a.

warder ['wɔːdə'] *n* GB carcelero.

wardress ['wɔːdrəs] *n* carcelera.

wardrobe ['wɔːdrəub] **1** *n* armario (ropero), guardarropa *m*: *built-in wardrobe,* armario empotrado. **2** (*clothes*) vestuario. **3** (*theatre*) vestuario.

■ **wardrobe master,** encargado del vestuario. ‖ **wardrobe mistress,** encargada del vestuario.

wardroom ['wɔːdruːm] *n* (*on ship*) cámara de oficiales.

wardship ['wɔːdʃɪp] *n* JUR tutela.

warehouse ['weəhaus] **1** *n* almacén *m*, depósito. – **2** *t* almacenar, depositar.

wares [weəz] *npl* mercancías *fpl*.

warfare ['wɔːfeə'] **1** *n* (*war*) guerra. **2** (*conflict, struggle*) lucha, batalla.

■ **germ warfare,** guerra bacteriológica. ‖ **guerrilla warfare,** guerrilla. ‖ **nuclear warfare,** guerra nuclear.

warhead ['wɔːhed] *n* ojiva, cabeza: *nuclear warhead,* cabeza nuclear.

warhorse ['wɔːhɔːs] **1** *n* caballo de guerra. **2** *fig* veterano,-a.

warily ['weərɪlɪ] *adv* con cautela, cautamente.

● **to tread warily,** andar con pies de plomo.

wariness ['weərɪnəs] *n* cautela, precaución *f*.

warlike ['wɔːlaɪk] *adj* belicoso,-a, guerrero,-a.

warm [wɔːm] **1** *adj* (*climate, wind*) cálido,-a; (*day*) caluroso,-a, de calor: *the weather's lovely and warm today,* hoy hace un día caluroso; *when the hot weather arrives,* cuando llegue el calor. **2** (*hands etc*) caliente; (*liquid*) tibio,-a, templado,-a. **3** (*clothing*) de abrigo, que abriga: *this jacket's really warm,* esta chaqueta abriga mucho. **4** (*colour*) cálido,-a. **5** (*welcome, applause, etc*) cálido,-a, caluroso,-a. **6** (*character*) afectuoso,-a. **7** (*scent*) fresco,-a; (*in game*) caliente. – **8** *t* (*gen*) **come in and warm your hands by the fire,** entra y caliéntate las manos junto al fuego. – **9** *i* calentarse: *the soup was warming on the hob,* la sopa se calentaba en la encimera. – **10** **the warm,** *n* el calor *m*: *don't stand out there! come into the warm!,* ¡no te quedes allí fuera! ¡ven al calor!

◆ **to warm over 1** *t sep* US (*reheat*) calentar, recalentar. **2** US (*use again*) volver a utilizar. ‖ **to warm to 1** *t insep*

(*person*) coger simpatía a. **2** (*subject etc*) entusiasmarse con. ‖ **to warm up 1** *t sep* (*food*) calentar, recalentar; (*engine*) calentar. **2** (*audience, party*) animar. – **3** *i* (*food, engine etc*) calentarse. **4** (*audience, party*) animarse. **5** SP hacer ejercicios de calentamiento.

● **as warm as toast,** calentito,-a. ‖ **to get warm,** calentarse. ‖ **to keep warm,** (*person*) abrigarse; (*food*) mantener caliente.

■ **warm front,** frente *m* cálido.

warm-blooded ['wɔːm'blʌdɪd] *adj* de sangre caliente.

▲ *Se escribe* **warm blooded** *cuando no se antepone a un sustantivo.*

warm-hearted ['wɔːm'hɑːtɪd] *adj* afectuoso,-a.

▲ *Se escribe* **warm hearted** *cuando no se antepone a un sustantivo.*

warm-heartedness [wɔːm'hɑːtɪdnəs] *n* afectuosidad *f*, cariño.

warming ['wɔːmɪŋ] *adj* que calienta.

warmly ['wɔːmlɪ] **1** *adv* (*with heat*) con ardor: *the sun shone warmly on my back,* el sol me calentaba la espalda. **2** (*thank*) con efusión; (*recommend*) con entusiasmo; (*welcome, greet*) calurosamente. **3** (*dress*) con ropa de abrigo: *dress warmly,* abrígate bien, ponte ropa caliente.

warmonger ['wɔːmʌŋgə'] *n* belicista *mf*.

warmth [wɔːmθ] **1** *n* (*heat*) calor *m*. **2** *fig* afecto, cordialidad *f*.

warm-up ['wɔːmʌp] *n* SP calentamiento, precalentamiento: *a warm-up lap,* una vuelta de calentamiento; *a warm-up match,* un partido de preparación.

warn [wɔːn] **1** *t* avisar (**of,** de), advertir (**of,** de), prevenir (**about,** sobre), (**against,** contra): *he warned me not to touch it,* me advirtió que no lo tocara; *I warned them to be careful with their wallets,* les advertí que tuvieran cuidado con las carteras; *don't say I didn't warn you,* no puedes decir que no te había avisado; *the police are warning motorists to drive carefully,* la policía está avisando a los conductores que conduzcan con precaución; *you've been warned,* estás avisado, estás sobre aviso. **2** (*instead of punishing*) amonestar.

● **to warn sb. off,** (*tell to go away*) advertir a algn. para que se vaya; (*tell to stop*) advertir a algn. para que deje de hacer algo.

warning ['wɔːnɪŋ] **1** *n* (*of danger*) aviso, advertencia: *let this be a warning to you,* que esto te sirva de escarmiento. **2** (*instead of punishment*) amonestación *f*. **3** (*advance notice*) aviso: *without warning,* sin previo aviso. – **4** *adj* (*shot, glance*) de aviso, de advertencia; (*letter*) admonitorio: *the warning signs of anorexia,* los síntomas de la anorexia.

● **to give sb. fair warning,** avisar a algn. debidamente.

■ **warning light,** piloto.

warp [wɔːp] **1** *t* alabear, combar, torcer. **2** *fig* pervertir, torcer. – **3** *i* alabearse, combarse. – **4** *n* (*in character*) manía. **5** (*in wood*) alabeo. **6** (*thread*) urdimbre *f*.

warpath ['wɔːpæθ] **to be on the warpath,** *phr* (*ready to fight*) estar en pie de guerra; (*angry*) estar furioso,-a, estar buscando guerra.

warped [wɔːpt] **1** *adj* (*bent, twisted*) alabeado,-a, combado,-a, torcido,-a. **2** *fig* pervertido,-a, retorcido,-a: *she has a warped mind,* tiene una mente retorcida.

warplane ['wɔːpleɪn] *n* avión *m* de combate.

warrant ['wɔrənt] **1** *n* JUR orden *f* judicial, mandamiento judicial: *a warrent is out for his arrest,* se ha ordenado su detención. **2** COMM FIN (*voucher*) cédula, bono.

vale *m*. **3** *fml* (*justification*) justificación *f*. – **4** *t fml* (*justify*) justificar; (*deserve*) merecer, ser digno,-a de. **5** (*guarantee*) garantizar.
● **I'll warrant (you)**, se lo aseguro.
■ **death warrant**, sentencia de muerte. ‖ **search warrant**, orden *f* de registro. ‖ **travel warrant**, vale *m* de viaje. ‖ **warrant officer**, suboficial *m*.

warranty ['wɒrəntɪ] **1** *n* COMM (*guarantee*) garantía: *it's still under warranty*, aún está en garantía. **2** *fml* (*authority*) autorización *f*.
▲ *pl* **warranties**.

warren ['wɒrən] **1** *n* conejera. **2** *fig* laberinto.

warring ['wɔːrɪŋ] *adj* (*at war*) en guerra; (*opposing*) opuesto,-a.

warrior ['wɒrɪəʳ] *n* guerrero,-a.

Warsaw ['wɔːsɔː] *n* Varsovia.

warship ['wɔːʃɪp] *n* buque *m* de guerra, barco de guerra.

wart [wɔːt] *n* verruga.
● **warts and all**, con todas sus imperfecciones.
● **wart hog**, jabalí *m* verrugoso.

wartime ['wɔːtaɪm] **1** *n* tiempos *mpl* de guerra. – **2** *adj* de guerra.

wary ['weərɪ] *adj* (*cautious*) cauto,-a, cauteloso,-a, prudente; (*suspicious*) desconfiado,-a.
● **to be wary of sb.**, desconfiar de algn., recelar de algn., dudar de algn. ‖ **to be wary of sth./sb.**, recelar de algo/algn., no fiarse de algo/algn. ‖ **to be wary about doing sth.**, no querer hacer algo, temer hacer algo. ‖ **to keep a wary eye on sb.**, vigilar a algn.
▲ *comp* **warier**, *superl* **wariest**.

was [wɒz, *unstressed* wəz] *pt* → **be**.

wash [wɒʃ] **1** *n* (*act*) lavado: *the car needs a wash*, el coche necesita un lavado; *the colour comes out after six washes*, el tinte desaparece después de seis lavados; *he had a quick wash before dinner*, se lavó rápidamente antes de cenar. **2** (*laundry*) ropa sucia, colada: *I do the weekly wash every Monday*, hago la colada cada lunes. **3** (*of ship*) estela; (*of water*) remolinos *mpl*; (*sound*) chapoteo. **4** MED enjuague *m*. **5** (*thin layer of paint*) capa. **6** (*swill*) bazofia. – **7** *t* (*gen*) lavar; (*dishes*) fregar: *have you washed your hands?*, ¿te has lavado las manos?; *wash dark colours separately*, lavar los colores oscuros por separado; *the cat washed its kittens*, la gata lavó los gatitos; *she hates washing clothes by hand*, odia lavar la ropa a mano; *who's going to wash the dishes?*, ¿quién fregará los platos? **8** (*carry*) llevar, arrastrar: *the dolphin was washed ashore*, el delfín fue arrastrado a la playa. **9** (*flow against, flow past*) lamer, besar: *the waves wash the shore*, las olas lamen la playa. **10** (*form by erosion*) erosionar. **11** (*cover thinly*) bañar. – **12** *i* (*gen*) lavarse: *have you washed behind your ears?*, ¿te has lavado detrás de las orejas?; *I hate washing in cold water*, odio lavarme con agua fría; *this new jumper washes well*, este jersey nuevo se lava bien. **13** (*flow, lap*) batir: *the waves washed against the cliff*, las olas batían contra el acantilado. **14** *fam* (*be believed*) colar: *that won't wash*, eso no cuela.
◆ **to wash away** **1** *t sep* (*destroy and carry away*) llevarse, arrastrar: *the water washed away several cottages*, las aguas se llevaron varias casitas. **2** (*remove*) borrar. ‖ **to wash down** **1** *t sep* (*clean*) lavar, regar. **2** (*with wine etc*) acompañar (**with**, de), regar (**with**, con): *we had fish washed down with a young white wine*, tomamos pescado regado con un vino blanco joven; *wash the tablet down with a glass of water*, toma un vaso de agua para ayudarte a tragar la pastilla. ‖ **to wash off** **1** *t sep* (*re-*

move *by washing*) quitar (lavando): *wash that make-up off at once*, quítate ese maquillaje en seguida. – **2** *i* quitarse lavando. ‖ **to wash out** **1** *t sep* (*remove by washing*) quitar lavando. **2** (*rinse*) enjuagar: *wash your mouth out!*, ¡enjuágate la boca! **3** (*prevent*) imposibilitar, impedir: *rain has washed out all play at Wimbledon today*, la lluvia ha impedido que se jugara en Wimbledon hoy. – **4** *i* quitarse lavando. ‖ **to wash up** **1** *t sep* fregar. **2** arrojar a la playa, arrastrar a la playa. – **3** *i* fregar los platos: *he doesn't mind washing-up*, no le importa fregar los platos. **4** US lavarse las manos y la cara, lavarse rápidamente.
● **to be in the wash**, estar para lavar, estar en la colada: *your white T-shirt's in the wash*, tu camiseta blanca está para lavar. ‖ **to come out in the wash**, (*turn out all right*) salir bien. ‖ **to wash one's dirty linen in public**, lavar los trapos sucios en público. ‖ **to wash one's hair**, lavarse la cabeza, lavarse el pelo. ‖ **to wash one's hands of sth./sb.**, desentenderse de algo/algn. ‖ **to wash os.**, lavarse.
■ **wash house**, lavadero.

washable ['wɒʃəbəl] *adj* lavable.

washbasin ['wɒʃbeɪsən] *n* (*fixed to wall*) lavabo; (*bowl*) palangana.

washboard ['wɒʃbɔːd] *n* tabla de lavar.

washbowl ['wɒʃbəʊl] *n* US palangana.

washcloth ['wɒʃklɒθ] *n* US manopla.

washday ['wɒʃdeɪ] *n* día *m* de la colada.

washed-out ['wɒʃt'aʊt] **1** *adj* (*tired*) agotado,-a, sin energía; (*pale*) pálido,-a. **2** (*faded*) descolorido,-a, desteñido,-a.
▲ *Se escribe* **washed out** *cuando no se antepone a un sustantivo*.

washed-up ['wɒʃt'ʌp] *adj fam* acabado,-a.
▲ *Se escribe* **washed up** *cuando no se antepone a un sustantivo*.

washer ['wɒʃəʳ] **1** *n* TECH (*metal*) arandela; (*rubber*) junta. **2** *fam* (*machine*) lavadora.

washing ['wɒʃɪŋ] **1** *n* (*action*) lavado, el lavar *m*. **2** (*dirty clothes*) colada, ropa sucia, ropa para lavar; (*clean clothes*) colada; (*clothes hanging out*) ropa tendida: *did you hang the washing out?*, ¿tendiste la ropa?; *can you get the washing in?*, ¿puedes recoger la ropa tendida?
● **to do the washing**, lavar la ropa, hacer la colada.
■ **washing line**, tendedero. ‖ **washing machine**, lavadora. ‖ **washing powder**, detergente *m*. ‖ **washing soda**, sosa.

washing-up [wɒʃɪŋ'ʌp] **1** *n* (*action*) fregado, el fregar *m*. **2** (*dishes*) platos *mpl*.
● **to do the washing-up**, fregar los platos.
■ **washing-up bowl**, barreño. ‖ **washing-up liquid**, lavavajillas *m*.

washout ['wɒʃaʊt] *n fam* fracaso.

washroom ['wɒʃruːm] *n* US *euph* servicios *mpl*.

washstand ['wɒʃstænd] *n* lavabo.

washtub ['wɒʃtʌb] *n* tina.

wasp [wɒsp] *n* avispa.
■ **wasp's nest**, avispero. ‖ **wasp waist**, cintura de avispa.

WASP ['wɒsp] *abbr* US (*White, Anglo-Saxon, Protestant*) blanco, anglosajón, protestante.

waspish ['wɒspɪʃ] *adj* (*person, temperament*) irascible, malhumorado,-a; (*comment*) punzante.

wastage ['weɪstɪdʒ] *n* (*waste, loss*) pérdida, merma, desgaste *m*; (*amount wasted*) pérdidas *fpl*.

waste [weɪst] **1** *n* (*gen*) derroche *m*, desperdicio; (*of money, energy*) derroche *m*, despilfarro; (*of time*) pérdida, desperdicio. **2** (*matter*) desechos *mpl*, desperdicios *mpl*; (*rubbish*) basura. – **3** *adj* (*unwanted*) desechado,-a: *the waste paper is recycled,* el papel desechado se recicla. **4** (*land*) yermo,-a, baldío,-a. – **5** *t* (*gen*) desperdiciar, malgastar; (*resources*) derrochar; (*money*) despilfarrar, derrochar; (*time, chance*) desperdiciar, desaprovechar, perder: *don't waste water,* no malgastes agua; *you're wasting your time,* estás perdiendo el tiempo. **6** (*because of disease*) atrofiar, debilitar. – **7 wastes,** *npl* extensiones *fpl* desoladas.

◆ **to waste away** *i* consumirse, demacrarse.

● **to go to waste,** echarse a perder, desperdiciarse. ‖ **to lay waste to,** destrozar, destruir. ‖ **to waste no time in doing sth.,** hacer algo sin demora, no perder un minuto en hacer algo. ‖ **to waste one's breath,** cansarse inútilmente, perder el tiempo, gastar saliva en balde. ‖ **waste not, want not,** no malgastes y no te faltará.

■ **bodily waste,** excrementos *mpl.* ‖ **household waste,** residuos *mpl* domésticos. ‖ **industrial waste,** desechos *mpl* industriales, residuos *mpl* industriales. ‖ **radioactive waste,** desechos *mpl* radioactivos. ‖ **waste disposal,** eliminación *f* de desperdicios. ‖ **waste disposal unit,** triturador *m* de basura. ‖ **waste pipe,** desagüe *m.*

wasted ['weɪstɪd] *adj* (*life, youth*) desperdiciado,-a; (*body*) atrofiado,-a.

wasteful ['weɪstfʊl] *adj* (*person*) pródigo,-a, derrochador,-ra, despilfarrador,-ra; (*process, habit, use*) ruinoso,-a.

wastefulness ['weɪstfʊlnəs] *n* despilfarro, derroche *m.*

wasteland ['weɪstlænd] *n* baldío, yermo.

wastepaper basket [weɪst'peɪpəbɑːskɪt] *n* papelera.

waster ['weɪstə'] *n* (*lazy*) vago,-a.

wasting ['weɪstɪŋ] **wasting disease,** *n* enfermedad *f* que consume.

wastrel ['weɪstrəl] *n* gandul,-la.

watch [wɒtʃ] **1** *n* (*small clock*) reloj *m.* **2** (*look-out*) vigilancia, guardia; (*person*) vigilante *mf,* guardia *mf,* centinela *mf,* guarda *mf.* **3** MAR (*period, body*) guardia; (*individual*) vigía. **4** HIST ronda. – **5** *t* (*look at, observe*) mirar, observar; (*television, sport*) ver: *Mum! watch me!,* ¡mamá! ¡mírame!; *he loves watching the fish in the aquarium,* le encanta mirar los peces en el acuario; *I want to watch the news,* quiero ver las noticias. **6** (*keep an eye on*) vigilar, observar; (*spy on*) espiar, vigilar: *don't worry, I'll watch your luggage,* no te preocupes, yo te vigilaré el equipaje; *she got the feeling someone was watching her,* tenía la sensación de que alguien la espiaba; *watch the time, please,* esté atento al reloj, por favor. **7** (*be careful about*) tener cuidado con, cuidar de: *I have to watch my weight,* tengo que guardar la línea; *watch how you cross the road,* ten cuidado al cruzar la calle; *she watches every penny,* vigila hasta la última peseta que gasta; *watch your language!,* ¡modera tu lenguaje!, ¡cuidado con lo que dices!; *watch where you're going!,* ¡mira por dónde vas! – **8** *i* (*look*) mirar, observar: *he scored just when I wasn't watching,* marcó justo cuando no miraba.

◆ **to watch for** *t insep* (*look and wait for*) esperar, aguardar. ‖ **to watch out for** *t insep* (*look out for, be alert*) estar alerta, estarse al tanto de, estar pendiente de: *the police were watching out for suspects,* la policía estaba alerta buscando sospechosos; *watch out for his new book,* estáte al tanto de su nuevo libro. **2** (*be careful of*) tener cuidado con. ‖ **to watch over** *t insep* (*guard and protect*) vigilar.

● **watch it!,** ¡ojo!, ¡cuidado! ‖ **watch out!,** ¡ojo!, ¡cuidado!, ¡alerta! ‖ **watch this space,** seguid atentos a este espacio. ‖ **to be on watch,** estar de guardia. ‖ **to be on the watch for sb./sth.,** estar al acecho de algn./algo. ‖ **to keep watch,** vigilar. ‖ **to watch one's step,** ir con pies de plomo. ‖ **to watch os.,** (*be careful*) ir con cuidado; (*control one's habits*) controlarse. ‖ **to watch the clock,** estar atento,-a al reloj. ‖ **to watch the world go by,** ver pasar el mundo.

■ **watch chain,** cadena de reloj.

watchdog ['wɒtʃdɒg] **1** *n* perro guardián. **2** *fig* guardián,-ana.

watcher ['wɒtʃə'] *n* observador,-ra, espectador,-ra.

watchful ['wɒtʃfʊl] *adj* vigilante, atento,-a.

watchfulness ['wɒtʃfʊlnəs] *n* vigilancia.

watchmaker ['wɒtʃmeɪkə'] *n* relojero,-a.

watchman ['wɒtʃmən] **1** *n* vigilante *m.* **2** *dated* (*on Spanish street*) sereno.

■ **night watchman,** vigilante nocturno.

watchstrap ['wɒtʃstræp] *n* correa (de reloj).

watchtower ['wɒtʃtaʊə'] *n* atalaya.

watchword ['wɒtʃwɜːd] **1** *n* (*password*) contraseña. **2** (*catchphrase, slogan*) consigna, lema *m.*

water ['wɔːtə'] **1** *n* (*gen*) agua: *can I have a drink of water?,* ¿puedo beber un vaso de agua?; *the water's lovely!,* ¡el agua está buenísima!; *drinking water,* agua potable; *mineral water,* agua mineral; *running water,* agua corriente; *spring water,* agua de manantial. **2** (*tide*) marea: *high/low water,* marea alta/baja. – **3** *t* (*plant, river*) regar. **4** (*animals*) abrevar. – **5** *i* (*eyes*) llorar, lagrimear; (*mouth*) hacerse la boca agua. – **6 waters,** *npl* (*sea etc*) aguas *fpl:* *coastal waters,* aguas costeras; *territorial waters,* aguas jurisdiccionales. **7** (*of pregnant woman*) aguas *fpl:* *her waters have broken,* ha roto aguas.

◆ **to water down 1** *t sep* (*drink*) aguar, mezclar con agua. **2** *fig* descafeinar.

● **a lot of water has flowed under the bridge since then,** ha llovido mucho desde entonces. ‖ **by water,** en barco. ‖ **to spend money like water,** gastar el dinero como si fuera agua. ‖ **to be in deep water,** estar con el agua al cuello. ‖ **to be water off a duck's back,** ser como quien oye llover. ‖ **to be water under the bridge,** ser agua pasada. ‖ **to get into hot water,** meterse en un buen lío. ‖ **to hold water,** estar bien fundado,-a, ser coherente. ‖ **not to hold water,** caer por su propio peso. ‖ **to keep one's head above water,** mantenerse a flote. ‖ **to pass water,** orinar. ‖ **to take the waters,** tomar las aguas. ‖ **under water,** (*flooded*) inundado,-a; (*submerged*) sumergido,-a.

■ **hot water bottle,** bolsa de agua caliente. ‖ **water bird,** ave *f* acuática. ‖ **water biscuit,** galleta seca. ‖ **water bottle,** (*flask*) cantimplora. ‖ **water buffalo,** búfalo acuático. ‖ **water butt,** barril *m* (*que recoge el agua de la lluvia*). ‖ **water cannon,** tanqueta antidisturbios. ‖ **water chestnut,** castaña de agua. ‖ **water closet,** *dated* váter *m,* retrete *m.* **3** **water cycle,** ciclo del agua. ‖ **water hole,** charca. ‖ **water ice,** sorbete *m.* ‖ **water jump,** ría. ‖ **water level,** (*in reservoir*) nivel del agua; (*of ship*) línea de flotación. ‖ **water lily,** nenúfar *m.* ‖ **water line,** línea de flotación. ‖ **water main,** conducción *f* del agua. ‖ **water on the brain,** MED hidrocefalia. ‖ **water on the knee,** MED derrame *m* sinovial. ‖ **water pipe,** cañería. ‖ **water pistol,** pistola de agua. ‖ **water polo,** waterpolo. ‖ **water power,** energía hidráulica. ‖ **water rat,** rata de agua. ‖ **water rate,** tarifa del agua. ‖ **water ski,** (*equipment*) esquí acuático. ‖ **water softener,** ablandador *m* del agua. ‖ **water supply,** abastecimiento de agua, suministro de agua. ‖ **water table,** nivel *m* freático. ‖ **water tank,** depósito de agua. ‖ **water tower,** depósito de agua. ‖ **water vapour,** vapor *m* de agua. ‖ **water wheel,** (*for power*) rueda hidraúlica; (*for irrigation*) noria. ‖ **water wings,** flotadores *mpl.*

waterbed ['wɔːtəbed] *n* colchón *m* de agua.

watercolor ['wɔːtəkʌləʳ] *n* → **watercolour.**

watercolour ['wɔːtəkʌləʳ] **1** *n* acuarela. – **2 watercolours,** *npl* acuarelas *fpl.*

water-cooled ['wɔːtəkuːld] *adj* TECH refrigerado,-a por agua.

watercourse ['wɔːtəkɔːs] **1** *n* (*channel, bed*) lecho, cauce *m,* canal *m.* **2** (*stream*) arroyo; (*river*) río.

watercress ['wɔːtkres] *n* berro.

watered-down ['wɔːtəd'daʊn] **1** *adj* (*drink*) aguado,-a. **2** *fig* descafeinado,-a.
▲ *Se escribe* **watered down** *cuando no se antepone a un sustantivo.*

waterfall ['wɔːtəfɔːl] *n* cascada, salto de agua, catarata.

waterfowl ['wɔːtəfaʊl] *n* ave *f* acuática.
▲ *pl* **waterfowl** *o* **waterfowls.**

waterfront ['wɔːtəfrʌnt] *n* (*port*) puerto, zona del puerto; (*promenade*) paseo marítimo.

watering ['wɔːtərɪŋ] *n* riego.
■ **watering can,** regadera. ‖ **watering hole,** (*for animals*) charca, abrevadero; (*pub*) bar *m.* ‖ **watering place,** (*for animals*) charca, abrevadero; (*spa*) balneario.

waterlogged ['wɔːtəlɒgd] *adj* empapado,-a, anegado,-a.

watermark ['wɔːtəmaːk] *n* filigrana.

watermelon ['wɔːtəmelən] *n* sandía.

watermill ['wɔːtəmɪl] *n* molino de agua.

waterproof ['wɔːtəpruːf] **1** *adj* (*material*) impermeable. **2** (*watch*) sumergible. – **3** *n* (*coat*) impermeable *m.* – **4** *t* impermeabilizar.

watershed ['wɔːtəʃed] **1** *n* GEOG línea divisoria de aguas. **2** *fig* coyuntura crítica, punto decisivo.

waterside ['wɔːtəsaɪd] **1** *n* ribera. – **2** *adj* ribereño,-a.

water-ski ['wɔːtəskiː] **1** *n* esquí *m* acuático. – **2** *i* hacer esquí acuático.

water-skier ['wɔːtəskɪəʳ] *n* esquiador,-ra acuático,-a.

water-skiing ['wɔːtəskiːɪŋ] *n* esquí *m* acuático.

watertight ['wɔːtətaɪt] **1** *adj* estanco,-a, hermético,-a. **2** *fig* irrefutable, irrebatible.

waterway ['wɔːtəweɪ] *n* vía fluvial.
■ **inland waterway,** canal *m* (navegable).

waterworks ['wɔːtəwɜːks] **1** *n* depuradora, planta de tratamiento de aguas. – **2** *npl* GB *fam euph* aparato urinario.
● **to turn on the waterworks,** empezar a llorar.

watery ['wɔːtərɪ] *adj* (*like water*) acuoso,-a; (*soup, milk*) aguado,-a; (*coffee*) flojo,-a, aguado,-a. **2** (*eyes*) lacrimoso,-a; (*smile*) débil; (*colour, sun*) pálido,-a, tenue.
● **to go to a watery grave,** morir ahogado,-a.
▲ *comp* **waterier,** *superl* **wateriest.**

watt [wɒt] *n* ELEC watt *m,* vatio.

wattage ['wɒtɪdʒ] *n* potencia en vatios.

wave [weɪv] **1** *n* (*in sea*) ola. **2** (*in hair*) onda. **3** PHYS onda. **4** (*of hand*) ademán *m,* movimiento; (*in greeting*) saludo con la mano: *with a wave of her hand,* con un movimiento de la mano; *he gave me a wave,* me saludó con la mano. **5** (*steady increase*) ola, oleada: *a mounting wave of anger,* una oleada creciente de ira; *a wave of panic,* una ola de pánico. **6** (*influx*) oleada; (*sudden increase*) oleada, ola: *a wave of strikes/bombings/violence/protest,* una oleada de huelgas/atentados/violencia/protestas;

crime wave, ola de delincuencia. – **7** *i* (*greet*) saludar (con la mano): *he waved at me,* me saludó (con la mano). **8** (*flag*) ondear; (*corn*) ondular. **9** (*hair*) ondular. – **10** *t* (*brandish*) agitar: *she was waving something in the air,* agitaba algo en el aire. **11** (*direct*) indicar con la mano: *the policeman waved them on,* el policía les indicó que siguieran; *she waved him away,* le indicó que se fuera. **12** (*hair*) marcar, ondular.
◆ **to wave aside** *t sep* rechazar, desechar. ‖ **to wave down** *t sep* hacer señales para que pare (*un coche*). ‖ **to wave off** *t sep* despedirse de.
● **to wave goodbye to sb.,** despedirse de algn. con la mano. ‖ **to wave goodbye to sth.,** despedirse de algo.

waveband ['weɪvbænd] *n* RAD banda.

wavelength ['weɪvleŋθ] *n* RAD longitud *f* de onda.
● **to be on different wavelengths,** *fam* no estar en la misma onda.

waver ['weɪvəʳ] **1** *i* (*hesitate, dither*) vacilar, titubear, dudar; (*oscillate*) oscilar (**between,** entre). **2** (*falter - gen*) vacilar, flaquear, flojear; (- *voice*) temblar, fallar: *he never wavered in his loyalty to her,* nunca flaqueó en su lealtad hacia ella. **3** (*flicker*) vacilar, parpadear.

wavering ['weɪvərɪŋ] *adj* (*person*) indeciso,-a, vacilante; (*voice*) tembloroso,-a, trémulo,-a.

wavy ['weɪvɪ] *adj* ondulado,-a.
▲ *comp* **wavier,** *superl* **waviest.**

wax¹ [wæks] **1** *n* (*gen*) cera. **2** (*in ear*) cerumen *m.* – **3** *t* (*polish*) encerar.
■ **paraffin wax,** parafina. ‖ **sealing wax,** lacre *m.* ‖ **wax candle,** vela. ‖ **wax paper,** papel *m* encerado. ‖ **wax polish,** cera para abrillantar.

wax² [wæks] **1** *i* (*moon*) crecer. **2** *dated* (*become*) ponerse.
● **to wax lyrical,** entusiasmarse, exaltarse.

waxen ['wæksən] **1** *adj dated* de cera. **2** *fml* (*of face, complexion*) céreo,-a.

waxwork ['wækswɜːk] **1** *n* figura de cera. – **2 waxworks,** *npl* museo *m sing* de cera.

waxy ['wæksɪ] *adj* céreo,-a.
▲ *comp* **waxier,** *superl* **waxiest.**

way [weɪ] **1** *n* (*right route, road, etc*) camino: *which is the best way to the swimming pool?,* ¿cómo se va a la piscina?, ¿por dónde se va a la piscina?; *do you know the way?,* ¿conoces el camino?, ¿sabes cómo ir?; *she asked me the way to the cathedral,* me preguntó cómo se va a la catedral; *we've gone the wrong way,* nos hemos equivocado de camino. **2** (*direction*) dirección *f*: *which way did he go?,* ¿por dónde se fue?; *which way is the harbour from here?,* ¿por dónde cae el puerto desde aquí?; *come this way, please,* venga por aquí, por favor; *are you going my way?,* ¿vas en la misma dirección que yo?; *look both ways,* mira en las dos direcciones; *she's looking this way,* está mirando hacia aquí; *the way things are going,* tal van las cosas. **3** (*distance*) distancia: *it's a long way to Tipperary,* Tipperary está lejos, Tipperary queda lejos; *we're a good way from home,* estamos lejos de casa; *she slept the whole way,* durmió durante todo el viaje; *Easter is a long way off,* falta mucho para Semana Santa; *we'd come a good way,* habíamos hecho un buen trecho. **4** (*manner, method*) manera, modo: *what's the best way to cook trout?,* ¿cuál es la mejor manera de guisar las truchas?; *you're going about it the wrong way,* lo estás haciendo mal; *you've done your hair a different way,* te has peinado de otro modo; *I had no way of knowing,* no había manera de saberlo; *we don't enjoy life the way we used to,* no disfrutamos de la vida como antes; *let me do it my way,*

déjame hacerlo a mi manera; *OK, you do it your own way,* vale, hazlo como quieras; *have it your own way,* como tú quieras. **5** (*behaviour, custom*) manera, forma, modo: *you dance in a strange way,* bailas de una manera extraña; *it's her way of saying she likes you,* es su manera de decirte que le gustas; *it's just his way,* él es así; *I don't like the way you're laughing,* no me gusta tu modo de reír; *she hates the way he's always late,* odia que él siempre llegue tarde; *the American way of life,* el estilo de vida americano. **6** (*area*) zona, área: *if ever you're over this way,* si alguna vez vienes por aquí; *that's out Romford way, isn't it?,* está por la zona de Romford, ¿verdad? **7** *adv fam* muy: *you're way out,* vas muy equivocado; *he's way ahead of the rest of the group,* está mucho más avanzado que el resto del grupo; *this flat is way too small for us,* este apartamento es demasiado pequeño para nosotros. – **8 ways,** *npl* (*customs*) costumbres *fpl*; (*habits, behaviour*) manías *fpl*.
● **across the way / over the way,** enfrente. ‖ **all the way,** (*distance*) todo el viaje; (*completely*) totalmente. ‖ **along the way,** (*on journey*) por el camino. ‖ **by a long way:** *this flat's not big enough by a long way,* este piso es demasiado pequeño, pero pequeño de verdad. ‖ **by the way,** (*incidentally*) a propósito, por cierto. ‖ **by way of,** (*via*) vía, por vía de, pasando por; (*serving as, as a kind of*) a modo de. ‖ **either way,** en cualquier caso. ‖ **every which way,** por todas partes, en todas direcciones. ‖ **in a bad way,** *fam* mal: *he's in a very bad way,* está muy mal. ‖ **in a big way,** a lo grande, a gran escala, en plan grande. ‖ **in a small way,** a pequeña escala, en plan modesto. ‖ **in a way,** en cierto modo, en cierta manera. ‖ **in any way,** de alguna manera: *can I help in any way?,* ¿puedo ayudar de alguna manera? ‖ **in many ways,** desde muchos puntos de vista, en muchos aspectos: *in many ways, this is her best book,* desde muchos puntos de vista, éste es su mejor libro. ‖ **in more ways than one,** en más de un sentido. ‖ **in no way,** de ninguna manera, de ningún modo. ‖ **in some ways,** en algunos aspectos. ‖ **in the way of,** (*regarding*) en cuanto a, como: *what would you like in the way of dessert?,* ¿qué quieres de postre? ‖ **in this way,** (*thus*) de este modo, de esta manera. ‖ **no two ways about it,** no tiene vuelta de hoja. ‖ **no way!,** ¡ni hablar!, ¡de ninguna manera!: *there's no way I'm going to help her,* de ninguna manera voy a ayudarla yo. ‖ **on one's way / on the way,** por el camino, de camino, de paso: *I should be on my way home,* debería irme a casa; *I'll get some wine on my way,* compraré vino por el camino; *on the way to Madrid,* camino de Madrid; *we're on our way!,* ¡ya estamos en camino!; *is it on your way?,* ¿te pilla de camino?; *something happened on the way here,* ha pasado algo mientras venía hacia aquí; *close the door on your way out,* cierra la puerta al salir. ‖ **one way and another,** en conjunto: *one way and another it's been a good year,* ha sido un buen año. ‖ **one way or the other,** (*somehow*) de algún modo, de una manera u otra, como sea: *don't worry, we'll find it one way or the other,* no te preocupes, lo encontraremos de una manera u otra; *I don't mind one way or the other,* me da exactamente igual, me da lo mismo. ‖ **out of the way,** (*remote*) apartado,-a, remoto,-a; (*exceptional*) excepcional, particular, original. ‖ **over the way,** enfrente. ‖ **that way,** (*direction*) por allá; (*like that*) así. ‖ **that's always the way,** siempre es así. ‖ **that's the way the cookie crumbles,** así es la vida. ‖ **the other way round,** al revés, viceversa. ‖ **the right way up,** cabeza arriba, derecho,-a. ‖ **the wrong way up,** cabeza abajo. ‖ **to be born that way,** ser así, nacer así. ‖ **to be in the way,** estorbar, estar por en medio: *you're in the way!,* ¡estás estorbando!; *move your car, it's in the way,* quita tu coche de en medio, obstruye el paso. ‖ **to be on the way,** (*coming*) estar en camino, estar al llegar, avecinarse: *changes are on the way,* se avecinan cambios; *help is on the way,* la ayuda está de camino; *there's rain on the way,* va a llover. ‖ **to be on the way down,** (*fall*) estar bajando, ir a la baja. ‖ **to be on the way in,** (*coming into fashion*) estar poniéndose de moda. ‖ **to be on the way out,** (*going out of fashion*) en camino de desaparecer, estar pasando de moda. ‖ **to be on the way up,** (*rise*) estar subiendo, ir al alza. ‖ **to be out of sb.'s way,** no pillar a algn. de camino: *I hope it's not out of your way,* espero que no te pille lejos. ‖ **to be set in one's ways,** tener unas costumbres muy arraigadas, ser reacio,-a al cambio. ‖ **to be under way,** (*work*) estar en marcha, estar avanzado,-a; (*meeting, match*) haber empezado. ‖ **to cut both ways / cut two ways,** ser un arma de doble filo, tener ventajas y desventajas. ‖ **to get in the way,** estorbar, molestar, ponerse en medio. ‖ **to get into the way of doing sth.,** coger la costumbre de hacer algo. ‖ **to get one's own way,** salirse con la suya. ‖ **to get out of the way of sth.,** dejarle paso a algo, apartarse del camino de algo. ‖ **to get out of the way,** apartarse del camino, quitarse de en medio. ‖ **to get out of the way of doing sth.,** perder la costumbre de hacer algo. ‖ **to get sth. out of the way,** deshacerse de algo, quitar algo de en medio: *as soon as I've got this essay out of the way,* en cuanto acabe esta redacción. ‖ **to get under way,** (*meeting, match*) empezar; (*travellers, work*) ponerse en marcha. ‖ **to give way,** (*collapse*) ceder, hundirse; (*yield*) ceder (**to,** a); (*when driving*) ceder el paso. ‖ **to go a long way towards sth.,** contribuir en gran medida a algo. ‖ **to go a long way,** (*succeed*) ir lejos; (*be productive*) cundir mucho, dar mucho de sí. ‖ **to go one's own way,** ir a lo suyo, seguir su propio camino. ‖ **to go out of one's way (to do sth.),** desvivirse (por hacer algo). ‖ **to have a way with ...,** tener un don especial para ...: *he has a way with children,* tiene un don especial para los niños. ‖ **to keep out of sb.'s way,** evitar el contacto con algn. ‖ **to keep out of the way,** (*hide*) mantener un perfil bajo; (*step aside*) apartarse. ‖ **to learn sth. the hard way,** aprender algo a las malas. ‖ **to look the other way,** hacer la vista gorda. ‖ **to lose one's way,** perderse, extraviarse. ‖ **to make one's own way in life/in the world,** abrirse paso en la vida/el mundo. ‖ **to make one's way,** dirigirse (**to,** a). ‖ **to make way for sth.,** hacer lugar para algo. ‖ **to my way of thinking,** a mi modo de ver. ‖ **to put sb. in the way of (doing) sth.,** dar a algn. la oportunidad de (hacer) algo. ‖ **to see one's way clear to doing sth.,** ver la manera de hacer algo. ‖ **to stand in the way of sth.,** ser un obstáculo para algo, ser un estorbo para algo. ‖ **to talk one's way out of sth.,** salir de algo a base de labia. ‖ **to work one's way through sth.,** (*crowd etc*) abrirse camino por algo; (*work, book*) hacer algo con dificultad; (*college etc*) costearse los estudios trabajando. ‖ **to work one's way up,** ascender a fuerza de trabajo, subir a base de trabajar. ‖ **way back,** (*in time*) hace muchísimo.
■ **way in,** entrada. ‖ **way out,** (*exit*) salida; (*solution*) solución *f*, remedio. ‖ **ways and means,** medios *mpl*.

wayfarer ['weɪfeərə'] *n fml* caminante *mf*, viajero,-a.

waylay [weɪ'leɪ] **1** *t* (*intercept*) salirle al paso a algn., abordar. **2** (*attack*) atacar por sorpresa.

▲ *pt & pp* **waylaid**, *ger* **waylaying**.

way-out [weɪ'aʊt] *adj fam* estrafalario,-a, exagerado,-a, supermoderno,-a.

wayside ['weɪsaɪd] *n* borde *m* del camino.
● **to fall by the wayside**, quedarse en el camino.

wayward ['weɪwəd] **1** *adj* (*person* - *wilful*) voluntarioso,-a; (- *unruly*) revoltoso,-a, indisciplinado,-a, rebelde; (- *erratic*) voluble, inconstante; (- *capricious*) caprichoso,-a. **2** (*behaviour*) irregular, imprevisible.

wc ['dʌbəljuː'siː] *n* (*abbr of* water closet) váter *m*.

we [wiː, unstressed wɪ] *pron* nosotros,-as: *we're French*, somos franceses; *we study French*, estudiamos francés.

weak [wiːk] **1** *adj* (*gen*) débil; (*person*) débil, endeble; (*light, voice*) débil, ténue; (*team, piece of work*) flojo,-a: *she was weak from hunger*, estaba débil por el hambre; *my legs felt weak*, sentía las piernas débiles; *they've got a weak defence*, tienen una defensa floja; *the film has a very weak plot*, la película tiene un argumento muy flojo; *he's got a weak heart*, tiene el corazón débil; *she gave a weak smile*, sonrió débilmente; *the peseta is weak*, la peseta está débil. **2** (*argument, excuse, etc*) poco convincente, pobre, de poco peso, débil. **3** (*tea, coffee, etc*) aguado,-a, flojo,-a, poco cargado,-a. – **4 the weak**, *npl* los necesitados *mpl*, los inválidos *mpl*.
● **a weak moment**, un momento débil. ‖ **to be weak at/in/on sth.**, ir flojo,-a en algo. ‖ **to be weak in the head**, estar mal de la cabeza. ‖ **to go weak at the knees**, flaquearle a algn. las piernas.
■ **weak spot**, punto flaco, punto débil.

weaken ['wiːkən] **1** *t* (*gen*) debilitar. **2** (*argument*) quitar fuerza a; (*morale*) socavar. – **3** *i* (*person*) debilitarse, desfallecer. **4** (*resolve, influence*) flaquear. **5** (*currency*) aflojar, caer. **6** (*give in*) ceder.

weak-kneed ['wiːk'niːd] *adj fig* medroso,-a, pusilánime.
▲ *Se escribe* **weak kneed** *cuando no se antepone a un sustantivo.*

weakling ['wiːklɪŋ] *n pej* (*physical*) débil *mf*, debilucho,-a, alfeñique *m*; (*moral*) cobarde *mf*.

weakly ['wiːklɪ] **1** *adv* (*gen*) débilmente. **2** (*lamely*) sin convicción.

weak-minded [wiːk'maɪndɪd] **1** *adj* (*indecisive*) indeciso,-a; (*weak-willed*) de poca voluntad. **2** (*mentally deficient*) deficiente mental.
▲ *Se escribe* **weak minded** *cuando no se antepone a un sustantivo.*

weakness ['wiːknəs] **1** *n* (*gen*) debilidad *f*, flaqueza. **2** (*lack of conviction*) falta de peso, pobreza. **3** (*defect, fault, flaw*) flaqueza, punto flaco.
● **to have a weakness for sb./sth.**, tener una debilidad por algn./algo.

weak-willed ['wiːk'wɪld] *adj* de poca voluntad.
▲ *Se escribe* **weak willed** *cuando no se antepone a un sustantivo.*

weal [wiːl] *n* cardenal *m*, equimosis *f inv*.

wealth [welθ] **1** *n* (*riches*) riqueza. **2** *fig* abundancia, profusión *f*.

wealthy ['welθɪ] **1** *adj* rico,-a, adinerado,-a, acaudalado,-a. – **2 the wealthy**, *npl* los ricos *mpl*.
▲ *comp* **wealthier** *superl* **wealthiest**.

wean [wiːn] *t* (*child*) destetar.
● **to wean sb. (away) from sth.**, deshabituar a algn. de algo.

weapon ['wepən] *n* arma.

wear [weə'] **1** *n* (*clothing*) ropa: *evening wear*, traje de noche; *ladies' wear*, ropa para señoras, ropa de señoras;

men's wear, ropa para hombres, ropa de hombres. **2** (*use*) uso: *for everyday wear*, para todos los días. **3** (*deterioration*) desgaste *m*, deterioro: *your jacket's beginning to show signs of wear*, tu cazadora ya empieza a verse deteriorada. **4** (*capacity for being used*) durabilidad *f*: *there's still a lot of wear left in this coat*, este abrigo aún te durará mucho. – **5** *t* (*clothing, jewellery, etc*) llevar, llevar puesto,-a, vestir, usar; (*shoes*) calzar: *is he wearing a tie?*, ¿lleva corbata?; *she was wearing a black dress*, llevaba un vestido negro; *I've got nothing to wear*, no tengo nada que ponerme; *she usually wears her hair up*, suele llevar el pelo recogido. **6** *fam* (*accept, tolerate*) tolerar, aceptar, soportar. **7** (*damage by use*) desgastar: *you've worn holes in your socks*, has hecho agujeros en los calcetines; *they've worn a path across the field*, han señalado un camino por el campo. – **8** *i* (*become damaged by use*) desgastarse: *the carpet is starting to wear*, la moqueta empieza a desgastarse; *the collar on this shirt is worn*, el cuello de esta camisa está gastado. **9** (*endure*) durar: *wool wears well*, la lana dura mucho.
◆ **to wear away 1** *t sep* (*grass, rocks, stone, etc*) erosionar, desgastar. **2** (*inscription*) borrar. – **3** *i* (*stone etc*) erosionarse, desgastarse. **4** (*inscription*) borrarse. ‖ **to wear down 1** *t sep* (*tread, stone, etc*) desgastar. **2** (*person, resistance*) agotar, cansar. – **3** *i* (*heels, teeth*) desgastarse. ‖ **to wear off** *i* (*pain, shock, novelty, etc*) pasar, desaparecer. ‖ **to wear on** *i* (*time*) transcurir, pasar, avanzar. ‖ **to wear out 1** *t sep* (*shoes etc*) gastar, desgastar, romper con el uso. **2** (*person*) agotar, rendir. – **3** *i* (*shoes etc*) gastarse, desgastarse, romperse con el uso.
● **to be the worse for wear**, (*object*) estar deteriorado,-a; (*person*) estar desmejorado,-a, estar maltrecho,-a. ‖ **to wear one's heart on one's sleeve**, ir con el corazón en la mano. ‖ **to wear thin**, (*clothing*) trasparentarse, desgastarse; (*patience*) acabarse. ‖ **to wear smooth**, alisarse. ‖ **to wear the trousers**, llevar los pantalones. ‖ **to wear os. out**, agotarse. ‖ **to wear well**, (*person*) conservarse bien; (*clothes*) durar mucho, dar buen resultado. ‖ **wear and tear**, desgaste *m* natural, deterioro.
▲ *pt* **wore**, *pp* **worn**.

wearable ['weərəbəl] *adj* llevable.

wearily ['wɪərɪlɪ] *adv* con cansancio, cansadamente.

weariness ['wɪərɪnəs] *n* cansancio, fatiga.

wearing ['weərɪŋ] *adj* (*tiring*) cansado,-a, agotador,-ra; (*tiresome*) pesado,-a.

wearisome ['wɪərɪsəm] **1** *adj* (*tiring*) cansado,-a, fatigoso,-a. **2** (*boring*) pesado,-a.

weary ['wɪərɪ] **1** *adj* (*exhausted*) cansado,-a, agotado,-a, fatigado,-a, exhausto,-a. **2** (*fed up*) cansado,-a, harto,-a. **3** (*tiring*) cansado,-a, agotador,-ra, fatigoso,-a. – **4** *t* cansar. – **5** *i* cansarse de.
▲ *comp* **wearier**, *superl* **weariest**.

weasel ['wiːzəl] *n* comadreja.

weather ['weðə'] **1** *n* (*gen*) tiempo: *what's the weather like?*, ¿qué tiempo hace?; *the weather's beautiful*, hace un tiempo estupendo; *we had really good weather*, hizo muy buen tiempo. – **2** *t* (*withstand, survive*) aguantar, soportar, resistir: *we weathered the crisis*, aguantamos la crisis. **3** (*rocks*) erosionar; (*wood*) curar. – **4** *i* (*rocks*) desgastarse; (*wood*) resistir la intemperie.
● **in all weathers**, haga el tiempo que haga. ‖ **to keep a weather eye open for sth.**, estar atento,-a por si se ve algo. ‖ **to make heavy weather of sth.**, costar mucho trabajo hacer algo. ‖ **to weather the storm**, capear el temporal. ‖ **under the weather**, (*unwell*) mal; (*depressed*) deprimido,-a. ‖ **weather permitting**, si el tiempo no lo impide.

■ **weather forecast,** parte *m* meteorológico. ‖ **weather chart / weather map,** mapa *m* meteorológico. ‖ **weather vane,** veleta.

weather-beaten ['weðəbiːtən] **1** *adj* (*building etc*) deteriorado,-a por la intemperie. **2** (*person*) curtido,-a.

weathercock ['weðəkɒk] *n* veleta.

weatherman ['weðəmən] *n* hombre *m* del tiempo.
▲ *pl* **weathermen** ['weðəmen].

weatherproof ['weðəpruːf] *adj* (*clothing*) impermeable; (*house*) impermeabilizado,-a.

weave [wiːv] **1** *n* tejido – **2** *t* (*cloth*) tejer. **3** (*fence, basket, nest, etc*) trenzar, entretejer, tejer. **4** (*one's way*) serpentear, zigzaguear. **5** *fig* (*plot, story*) tramar, urdir, tejer. – **6** *i* (*cloth*) tejer. **7** (*zig-zag about*) serpentear, zigzaguear.
● **to weave in and out,** (*dance*) trenzar: *weave in and out through the traffic*, abrirse paso por entre el tráfico.
▲ *pt* **wove,** *pp* **woven,** *ger* **weaving.**

weaver ['wiːvə'] *n* tejedor,-ra.

weaving ['wiːvɪŋ] *n* (*activity*) tejido.

web [web] **1** *n* (*spider's*) telaraña. **2** *fig* red *f*, sarta, embrollo: *a web of deceit*, una red de engaños. **3** (*of animals' feet*) membrana interdigital.

webbed [webd] *adj* palmeado,-a.

webbing ['webɪŋ] *n* (*on chairs etc*) cinchas *fpl*.

web-footed ['web'fʊtɪd] *adj* palmípedo,-a.

wed [wed] *t* casarse con.
▲ *pt & pp* **wedded** *o* **wed,** *ger* **wedding.**

we'd [wiːd] **1** *contr* we had. **2** we would.

Wed ['wenzdɪ] *abbr* (*Wednesday*) miércoles *m*; (*abbreviation*) miérc.

wedded ['wedɪd] **1** *adj* casado,-a (**to,** con): *he's my lawful wedded husband*, es mi legítimo esposo; *fifty years of wedded bliss*, cincuenta años de felicidad conyugal. **2** (*devoted*) aferrado,-a (**to,** a).

wedding ['wedɪŋ] *n* boda, casamiento: *have you been invited to the wedding?*, ¿te han invitado a la boda?; *it was a lovely wedding*, ha sido una boda preciosa.
● **to have a church wedding,** casarse por la iglesia. ‖ **to have a shotgun wedding,** casarse de penalty.
■ **wedding anniversary,** aniversario de boda. ‖ **wedding breakfast,** banquete *m* nupcial. ‖ **wedding cake,** tarta nupcial. ‖ **wedding day,** día *m* de la boda. ‖ **wedding dress,** traje *m* de novia, vestido de novia. ‖ **wedding invitation,** invitación *f* de boda. ‖ **Wedding March,** marcha nupcial. ‖ **wedding present,** regalo de boda. ‖ **wedding reception,** banquete *m* de bodas. ‖ **wedding ring,** alianza, anillo de boda.

wedge [wedʒ] **1** *n* (*gen*) cuña, calza, calce *m*; (*for splitting*) cuña. **2** (*of cake, cheese*) trozo grande. **3** (*golf*) wedge *m*. – **4** *t* (*force apart*) acuñar, calzar. **5** (*pack tightly*) apretar.
● **the thin edge of the wedge,** solo el principio. ‖ **to be wedged tight,** estar completamente trabado,-a. ‖ **to wedge sth. open,** mantener algo abierto,-a mediante una cuña.

wedlock ['wedlɒk] *n* matrimonio.

Wednesday ['wenzdɪ] *n* miércoles *m inv*.
▲ *Véase también* **Saturday.**

wee[1] [wiː] *adj fam* (*very small*) pequeñito,-a, chiquito,-a: *a wee bit*, un poquitín.
● **the wee hours,** la madrugada.

wee[2] [wiː] **1** *n fam* pipí *m*. – **2** *i fam* hacer pipí.
● **to do a wee / go for a wee,** hacer pipí.

weed [wiːd] **1** *n* BOT (*in garden*) mala hierba; (*in water*) algas *fpl*. **2** *fam pej* (*person*) debilucho,-a, canijo,-a. **3** *fam* (*tobacco*) tabaco, el fumar *m*; (*marijuana*) hierba, maría, hachís *m*. – **4** *t* escardar. – **5** *i* escardar.

◆ **to weed out** *t sep* desherbar, escardar.

weeding ['wiːdɪŋ] *n* escarda.

weedkiller ['wiːdkɪlə'] *n* herbicida *m*.

weedy ['wiːdɪ] *adj pej* debilucho,-a, esmirriado,-a, canijo,-a.
▲ *comp* **weedier,** *superl* **weediest.**

week [wiːk] *n* semana: *this week*, esta semana; *last/next week*, la semana pasada/que viene; *once a week*, una vez por semana, una vez a la semana; *a week today*, de hoy en ocho; *a week ago today*, hoy hace una semana; *during the week*, entre semana; *the week after next*, la semana que viene no sino la otra; *week in, week out*, semana tras semana; *a weeks' holiday*, una semana de vacaciones.
■ **working week,** semana laborable.

weekday ['wiːkdeɪ] *n* día *m* laborable.

weekend ['wiːkend, wiː'kend] **1** *n* fin *m* de semana: *we're going away this weekend*, nos vamos fuera este fin de semana; *what do you do at weekends?*, ¿qué haces los fines de semana? – **2** *i* pasar el fin de semana.
● **long weekend,** puente *m*.

weekender [wiːk'endə'] *n* dominguero,-a.

weekly ['wiːklɪ] **1** *adj* semanal. – **2** *adv* semanalmente, cada semana: *twice weekly*, dos veces por semana. – **3** *n* (*press*) semanario.

weep [wiːp] **1** *i fml* (*person*) llorar. **2** (*wound*) supurar. – **3** *t* (*tears*) derramar.
● **to have a good weep,** llorar a lágrima viva. ‖ **to have a little weep,** llorar un poco. ‖ **to weep for sb.,** llorar a algn. ‖ **to weep for joy,** llorar de alegría.
▲ *pt & pp* **wept.**

weeping ['wiːpɪŋ] **1** *adj* lloroso,-a. – **2** *n* llanto.
■ **weeping willow,** BOT sauce *m* llorón.

weepy ['wiːpɪ] *adj* (*person*) llorón,-ona, lloroso,-a; (*film*) lagrimógeno,-a.
▲ *comp* **weepier,** *superl* **weepiest.**

weevil ['wiːvəl] *n* gorgojo.

weft [weft] *n* trama.

weigh [weɪ] **1** *t* (*gen*) pesar: *she weighed the parcel*, pesó el paquete. **2** *fig* (*consider carefully*) ponderar, sopesar (**up,** -); (*compare carefully*) contraponer (**with/against,** a): *weigh (up) the pros and cons*, sopesar los pros y los contras; *weigh the advantages against the disadvantages*, contraponer las ventajas a las desventajas. – **3** *i* (*gen*) pesar: *how much do you weigh?*, ¿cuánto pesas?; *it doesn't weigh anything*, no pesa nada. **4** (*be important to, have influence on*) influir en, pesar: *his previous record weighed heavily against him*, sus antecedentes penales pesaban mucho contra él.

◆ **to weigh down 1** *t sep* cargar: *she was weighed down with shopping*, iba muy cargada de compras. **2** *fig* agobiar, abrumar, sobrecargar: *he was weighed down with problems*, estaba agobiado de problemas. ‖ **to weigh in 1** *i* SP pesarse: *the jockey weighed in at 60 kg*, el jinete pesó 60 kg. **2** (*join in*) intervenir (**with,** con). ‖ **to weigh on** *t insep* (*worry*) pesar sobre: *the responsibility weighs heavily on my mind*, la responsabilidad pesa mucho sobre mí. ‖ **to weigh out** *t sep* (*food etc*) pesar. ‖ **to weigh up** *t sep* (*consider carefully*) evaluar, ponderar, sopesar: *we have to weigh up the consequences*, hay que evaluar las consecuencias. **2** (*assess*) juzgar, calar: *I just can't weigh him up*, es que no lo llego a entender.
● **to weigh anchor,** levar anclas. ‖ **to weigh the evidence,** sopesar las pruebas. ‖ **to weigh a ton,** pesar una tonelada. ‖ **to weigh one's words,** ponderar las palabras.

weighbridge ['weɪbrɪdʒ] *n* báscula de puente.

weigh-in [ˈweɪɪŋ] *n* SP pesaje *m*.

weight [weɪt] **1** *n* (*gen*) peso: *gross weight / net weight,* peso bruto / peso neto; *it's 10 kilos in weight,* pesa 10 kilos; *feel the weight of this,* sopesa esto; *the columns support the weight of the roof,* las columnas aguantan el peso del tejado. **2** (*of scales, clock, gym*) pesa; (*heavy object*) peso, cosa pesada: *you shouldn't lift heavy weights,* no deberías levantar cosas pesadas. **3** *fig* (*burden, worry*) peso, carga: *that's a weight off my mind,* eso me quita un peso de encima; *the full weight of responsibility fell on her,* ella cargó con toda la responsabilidad. **4** *fig* (*importance, influence*) peso, importancia, influencia: *the weight of the evidence,* el peso de las pruebas; *your support adds weight to the campaign,* tu apoyo da peso a la campaña; *that argument doesn't carry much weight,* ese argumento no tiene mucho peso. **– 5** *t* (*make heavy*) cargar con peso, poner peso en, añadir peso a; (*fishing net*) lastrar. **6** *fig* (*statistics etc*) ponderar.

● **to lose weight,** perder peso, adelgazar. ‖ **to pull one's weight,** poner de su parte. ‖ **to put on weight,** engordar, ganar peso. ‖ **to take the weight off one's feet,** descansar los pies. ‖ **to throw one's weight about/around,** hacer sentir su autoridad.

■ **weight limit,** límite *m* de peso. ‖ **weight training,** entrenamiento con pesas. ‖ **weight watcher,** persona que se cuida la línea. ‖ **weights and measures,** pesos *mpl* y medidas.

weighting [ˈweɪtɪŋ] *n* GB (*extra pay*) suplemento salarial, plus *m*.

weightless [ˈweɪtləs] *adj* ingrávido,-a.

weightlessness [ˈweɪtləsnəs] *n* ingravidez *f*.

weightlifter [ˈweɪtlɪftəʳ] *n* SP levantador,-ra de pesas, halterófilo,-a.

weightlifting [ˈweɪtlɪftɪŋ] *n* levantamiento de pesas, halterofilia.

weighty [ˈweɪtɪ] **1** *adj* (*gen*) pesado,-a. **2** *fig* (*argument*) de peso; (*problem, decision*) importante, grave.
▲ *comp* **weightier,** *superl* **weightiest**.

weir [wɪəʳ] *n* presa.

weird [wɪəd] **1** *adj* (*bizarre*) raro,-a, extraño,-a. **2** (*eerie*) siniestro,-a.

weirdness [ˈwɪədnəs] *n* rareza.

weirdo [ˈwɪədəʊ] *n fam* tipo raro.
▲ *pl* **weirdos**.

welcome [ˈwelkəm] **1** *adj* (*gen*) bienvenido,-a: *all welcome,* todo el mundo es bienvenido; *you're always welcome here,* siempre eres bienvenido aquí, estás en tu casa. **2** (*news, sight, etc*) grato,-a, agradable; (*change*) oportuno,-a, beneficioso,-a: *a welcome break from study,* un oportuno descanso durante el estudio; *a drink would be most welcome right now,* una copa me vendría muy bien ahora mismo. **– 3** *interj* bienvenido,-a (**to, a**): *welcome home!,* ¡bienvenido a casa! **– 4** *n* bienvenida, acogida: *the crowd gave the winners an enthusiastic welcome,* el público acogió a los ganadores con entusiasmo. **– 5** *t* (*greet*) acoger, recibir; (*officially*) dar la bienvenida a. **6** (*approve of, support*) aplaudir, acoger con agrado: *we gladly welcome all suggestions,* agradecemos cualquier sugerencia.

● **to be welcome to ...,** poder ... con toda libertad: *you're welcome to borrow any of my tapes,* puedes coger cualquiera de mis cintas; *if he wants the job, then he's welcome to it!,* si quiere el trabajo, pues que se lo quede. ‖ **to give sb. a warm welcome,** acoger a algn. calurosamente. ‖ **to make sb. welcome,** hacer que algn. se sienta en casa. ‖ **to welcome sth./sb. with**

open arms, acoger algo/a algn. con los brazos abiertos. ‖ **you're welcome,** (*not at all*) no hay de qué, de nada.

welcoming [ˈwelkəmɪŋ] *adj* (*smile*) acogedor,-ra; (*speech*) de bienvenida.

weld [weld] **1** *n* soldadura. **– 2** *t* soldar. **3** *fig* soldar, unir. **– 4** *i* soldarse.

welder [ˈweldəʳ] *n* soldador,-ra.

welding [ˈweldɪŋ] *n* soldadura.

welfare [ˈwelfeəʳ] **1** *n* (*well-being*) bienestar *m*; (*health*) salud *f*. **2** (*care, help*) protección *f*. **3** US (*money*) seguridad *f* social.

● **to be on welfare,** recibir prestaciones de la seguridad social.

■ **welfare payments,** prestaciones *fpl* de la seguridad social. ‖ **welfare state,** estado de bienestar. ‖ **welfare work,** trabajos *mpl* de asistencia social. ‖ **welfare worker,** asistente *mf* social.

we'll [wiːl] *contr* we will.

well[1] [wel] **1** *n* (*for water*) pozo. **2** (*of staircase*) hueco de la escalera; (*of lift*) hueco del ascensor. **3** GB (*in court*) área de los abogados. **– 4** *i* (*tears, blood*) brotar (**up,** -), manar (**up,** -): *tears welled up in her eyes,* se le llenaron los ojos de lágrimas.

■ **oil well,** pozo de petróleo.

well[2] [wel] **1** *adj* (*in good health*) bien: *I'm very well, thank you,* estoy muy bien, gracias; *she doesn't feel very well,* no se encuentra muy bien; *you look very well,* tienes muy buena cara; *he's not a well man,* no está bien de salud; *get well soon,* que te mejores pronto. **2** (*satisfactory, right*) bien: *things are not well at home,* hay problemas en casa. **– 3** *adv* (*gen*) bien: *well played!,* ¡bien jugado!; *they behaved really well,* se portaron muy bien; *I don't know her that well,* no la conozco muy bien; *things are going well for him,* las cosas le van bien; *they treated me extremely well,* me trataron muy bien; *shake well before use,* agítese bien antes de usar; *he's well aware of the problem,* es perfectamente consciente del problema. **4** (*with modals*) bien: *you may well be right,* bien puede que tengas razón; *I might well go away for a few days,* es muy posible que me vaya fuera unos días; *he could well be lying,* bien puede que mienta; *she couldn't very well refuse,* ¿cómo iba a decir que no?; *you may as well tell him, he'll find out anyway,* ¿de qué te sirve no decírselo, se va a enterar de todas maneras. **5** (*much, quite*) bien: *she's well over fifty,* tiene cincuenta años bien cumplidos; *book well in advance,* haz tu reserva con mucha anticipación; *we sat well back in the cinema,* nos sentamos bien atrás en el cine; *it was well after eleven,* eran bien pasadas las once; *the film's well worth seeing,* bien vale la pena ver la película. **– 6** *interj* (*gen*) bueno, bien, pues: *well, I think that ...,* bueno, yo creo que ...; *well I'm not going,* pues no voy; *well why didn't you say so?,* ¿pues, por qué no lo has dicho?; *well, as I said earlier,* bueno, como he dicho antes. **7** (*surprise*) ¡vaya!: *well, well, well, look who it is!,* ¡vaya! ¡mira quién es!

● **all's well that ends well,** bien está lo que bien acaba. ‖ **all well and good,** muy bien, perfecto. ‖ **as well,** (*also, too*) también. ‖ **as well as,** además de, aparte de: *she studies German as well as English,* además de inglés, estudia alemán. ‖ **it's all very well to + inf,** resulta muy fácil + *inf*. ‖ **to be (just) as well to + inf,** no estar de más + *inf,* convenir + *inf: it would be as well to phone first,* sería una buena idea llamar antes. ‖ **to be well in with sb.,** ser muy amigo,-a de algn. ‖ **to be well off for sth.,** tener algo de sobra. ‖ **to be**

well out of sth., tener la suerte de haberse librado de algo. ‖ **to be well up on/in sth.,** estar muy bien informado,-a de algo. ‖ **to do well,** *(business etc)* ir bien, marchar bien, tener éxito; *(person - success)* irle bien las cosas; *(- health)* encontrarse bien, estar bien. ‖ **to do well by sb.,** tratar bien a algn. ‖ **to do well for os.,** prosperar, tener éxito. ‖ **to do well in sth.,** hacer algo bien, irle algo bien a algn.: *he did well in the test,* la prueba le fue bien. ‖ **to do well out of ...,** sacar provecho de ... ‖ **to do well to do sth.,** convenir hacer algo. ‖ **to speak well of sb.,** hablar bien de algn. ‖ **to think well of sb.,** pensar bien de algn. ‖ **very well,** muy bien, bueno. ‖ **well and truly,** completamente. ‖ **well done!,** ¡muy bien!, ¡así se hace! ‖ **well I never!,** ¡vaya!, ¡habráse visto! ‖ **well off,** *(comfortable, rich)* acomodado,-a, rico,-a, pudiente: *you don't know when you're well off,* no te das cuenta de la suerte que tienes.

well-balanced ['wel'bælənst] *adj* equilibrado,-a.
▲ *Se escribe* **well balanced** *cuando no se antepone a un sustantivo.*

well-behaved ['welbɪ'heɪvd] *adj* formal, educado,-a.
▲ *Se escribe* **well behaved** *cuando no se antepone a un sustantivo.*

wellbeing [wel'biːɪŋ] *n* bienestar *m*.

well-bred ['wel'bred] *adj* bien educado,-a.
▲ *Se escribe* **well bred** [wel'bred] *cuando no se antepone a un sustantivo.*

well-built ['wel'bɪlt] **1** *adj (building)* de construcción sólida. **2** *(person)* fornido,-a.
▲ *Se escribe* **well built** *cuando no se antepone a un sustantivo.*

well-chosen ['wel'tʃəʊzən] *adj* acertado,-a.
▲ *Se escribe* **well chosen** *cuando no se antepone a un sustantivo.*

well-disposed ['weldɪs'pəʊzd] *adj* bien dispuesto,-a **(towards,** hacia).
▲ *Se escribe* **well disposed** *cuando no se antepone a un sustantivo.*

well-done ['wel'dʌn] *adj* muy hecho,-a.
▲ *Se escribe* **well done** *cuando no se antepone a un sustantivo.*

well-earned ['wel'ɜːnd] *adj* (bien) merecido,-a.
▲ *Se escribe* **well earned** *cuando no se antepone a un sustantivo.*

well-educated [wel'edjəkeɪtɪd] *adj* culto,-a, instruido,-a.
▲ *Se escribe* **well educated** *cuando no se antepone a un sustantivo.*

well-founded ['wel'faʊndɪd] *adj* bien fundado,-a.
▲ *Se escribe* **well founded** *cuando no se antepone a un sustantivo.*

well-heeled ['wel'hiːld] *adj fam* adinerado,-a.
▲ *Se escribe* **well heeled** *cuando no se antepone a un sustantivo.*

well-informed ['welɪn'fɔːmd] *adj* bien informado,-a.
▲ *Se escribe* **well informed** *cuando no se antepone a un sustantivo.*

wellington ['welɪŋtən] *n* bota de agua.
■ **wellington boots,** botas *fpl* de agua.

well-intentioned ['welɪn'tenʃənd] *adj* bien intencionado,-a.
▲ *Se escribe* **well intentioned** *cuando no se antepone a un sustantivo.*

well-judged ['wel'dʒʌdʒd] *adj* bien calculado,-a.
▲ *Se escribe* **well judged** *cuando no se antepone a un sustantivo.*

well-known [wel'nəʊn] *adj* (bien) conocido,-a.

well-mannered ['wel'mænəd] *adj* educado,-a, cortés.
▲ *Se escribe* **well mannered** *cuando no se antepone a un sustantivo.*

well-meaning ['wel'miːnɪŋ] *adj* bien intencionado,-a.
▲ *Se escribe* **well meaning** *cuando no se antepone a un sustantivo.*

well-nigh ['welnaɪ] *adj* casi.

well-off ['wel'ɒf] *adj* rico,-a, acomodado,-a, pudiente.
▲ *Se escribe* **well off** *cuando no se antepone a un sustantivo.*

well-spoken ['wel'spəʊkən] *adj* con acento culto.
▲ *Se escribe* **well spoken** *cuando no se antepone a un sustantivo.*

well-timed ['wel'taɪmd] *adj* oportuno,-a.
▲ *Se escribe* **well timed** *cuando no se antepone a un sustantivo.*

well-to-do ['weltə'duː] **1** *adj* acomodado,-a, pudiente. **– 2 the well-to-do,** *npl* la gente pudiente.

well-wisher ['welwɪʃəʳ] *n persona que llama o escribe a otra deseándole suerte, una pronta recuperación, etc.*

well-worn ['wel'wɔːn] **1** *adj (clothes)* gastado,-a, raído,-a; *(path)* trillado,-a. **2** *(phrase)* gastado,-a, trillado,-a.
▲ *Se escribe* **well worn** *cuando no se antepone a un sustantivo.*

welly ['welɪ] *n* GB *fam* bota de agua.

Welsh [welʃ] **1** *adj* galés,-esa. **– 2** *n (language)* galés *m*. **– 3 the Welsh,** *npl* los galeses *mpl*.
■ **Welsh dresser,** aparador *m*. ‖ **Welsh rarebit,** CULIN tostada con queso fundido.

Welshman ['welʃmən] *n* galés *m*.
▲ *pl* **Welshmen** ['welʃmən].

Welshwoman ['welʃwumən] *n* galesa.
▲ *pl* **Welshwomen** ['welʃwɪmɪn].

welt [welt] **1** *n (weal)* verdugón *m*, cardenal *m*. **2** *(of shoe)* vira.

welter ['weltəʳ] *n* mezcla confusa, mezcolanza.

welterweight ['weltəweɪt] *n* SP peso wélter, wélter *m*.

wench [wentʃ] *n arch* moza, mozuela.

wend [wend] **to wend one's way,** *phr* dirigir sus pasos **(towards,** hacia).

went [went] *pt* → **go**.

wept [wept] *pt & pp* → **weep**.

were [wɜːʳ] *pt* → **be**.

we're [wɪəʳ] *contr* we are.

werewolf ['wɪəwʊlf] *n* hombre *m*. lobo.
▲ *pl* **werewolves** ['wɪəwʊlvz].

west [west] **1** *n* oeste *m*, occidente *m*: *the sun sets in the west,* el sol se pone por el oeste. **– 2** *adj* occidental, del oeste. **– 3** *adv* al oeste, hacia el oeste: *it faces west,* mira hacia el oeste; *they were pushed west by invading tribes,* fueron empujados hacia el oeste por las tribus invasoras. **– 4 the West,** *n* POL Occidente *m*, los países *mpl* occidentales.
■ **the Far West,** el Lejano Oeste. ‖ **the West Coast,** la costa oeste. ‖ **the West Country,** *zona del sudoeste de Inglaterra.* ‖ **the West End,** *zona céntrica londinense de comercios, teatros y cines.* ‖ **West Indies,** las Antillas. ‖ **West Indian,** antillano,-a.

westbound ['westbaʊnd] *adj* en dirección al oeste.

westerly ['westəlɪ] **1** *adj (point, direction)* oeste: *in a westerly direction,* en dirección al oeste. **2** *(wind)* del oeste.

western ['westən] **1** *adj* del oeste, occidental. **– 2** *n (cinema)* western *m*.

westward ['westwəd] *adj* hacia el oeste.

westwards ['westwədz] *adv* hacia el oeste.

wet [wet] **1** *adj (gen)* mojado,-a; *(damp)* húmedo,-a: *my hair's wet,* tengo el pelo mojado; *take off those wet clothes,* quítate esa ropa mojada. **2** *(weather)* lluvioso,-a: *it was a wet day,* hacía un día de lluvia. **3** *(paint, ink)* fresco,-a: *"wet paint",* "recién pintado". **4** *fam (person)* apocado,-a, soso,-a. **– 5** *n (damp)* humedad *f*. **6** *(rain)* lluvia. **7** *fam (person)* apocado,-a; *(politician)* moderado,-a. **– 8** *t* mojar, humedecer.

● **to get wet**, mojarse. ‖ **to wet os.**, orinarse, mearse encima. ‖ **to wet the bed**, orinarse en la cama. ‖ **to be wet behind the ears**, estar verde. ‖ **wet through**, *(person)* calado,-a hasta los huesos; *(thing)* empapado,-a.

■ **wet blanket**, aguafiestas *mf*. ‖ **wet fish**, pescado fresco. ‖ **wet nurse**, ama de cría, nodriza. ‖ **wet suit**, traje *m* isotérmico.

▲ *(adjetivo) comp* **wetter**, *superl* **wettest**. *(verbo) pt & pp* **wet** *o* **wetted**, *ger* **wetting** wetting.

wetback ['wetbæk] *n* US mojado.

wetness ['wetnəs] *n* humedad *f*.

we've [wi:v] *contr* we have.

whack [wæk] **1** *n (blow)* golpe *m*, porrazo. **2** *fam (share)* parte *f*, porción *f*. *everyone has had their whack*, todos han recibido su parte. **3** *fam (attempt)* tentativa: *I'll have a whack at it*, lo intentaré, probaré suerte. – **4** *t (hit hard - gen)* pegar, zurrar; *(- ball)* golpear fuerte.

whacked [wækt] *adj fam (tired out)* agotado,-a.

whacking ['wækɪŋ] **1** *adj fam* enorme, grandísimo,-a. – **2** *adv fam (very)* muy. – **3** *n (beating)* paliza, zurra.

whale [weɪl] *n* ballena.

● **to have a whale of a time**, pasarlo pipa, pasarlo en grande.

whalebone ['weɪlbəʊn] *n* (barba de) ballena.

whaler ['weɪlə'] *n (gen)* ballenero,-a.

whaling ['weɪlɪŋ] *n* caza de ballenas.

■ **whaling industry**, industria ballenera.

wharf [wɔːf] *n* muelle *m*, embarcadero.

▲ *pl* **wharfs** *o* **wharves**.

what [wɒt] **1** *adj (direct questions)* qué: *what time is it?*, ¿qué hora es?; *what colour is it?*, ¿de qué color es?; *what kind of music do you like?*, ¿qué tipo de música te gusta?; *what film did you see?*, ¿qué película viste? **2** *(indirect questions)* qué: *I don't know what to do*, no sé qué hacer. **3** *(exclamations)* qué: *what a man!*, ¡qué hombre!; *what a smart car!*, ¡qué coche más chulo!; *what a pity!*, ¡qué lástima!; *what beautiful flowers!*, ¡qué flores más preciosas! **4** *(all the)* todo,-a: *what oil we have is here*, todo el aceite que tenemos está aquí; *what little free time she has she spends with her family*, el poco tiempo libre que tiene lo pasa con su familia. – **5** *pron (direct questions)* qué: *what is it?*, ¿qué es?; *what do you do?*, ¿a qué te dedicas?; *what are you doing?*, ¿que haces?; *what's your name?*, ¿cómo te llamas?; *what's that for?*, ¿para qué sirve eso?; *what does this word mean?*, ¿qué significa esta palabra?; *what does she look like?*, ¿cómo es ella?; *what did he say?*, ¿qué dijo? **6** *(indirect questions)* qué: *he didn't know what to say*, no sabía qué decir. **7** lo que: *that's what he told me*, eso es lo que me dijo; *what you need is a nice hot bath*, lo que necesitas es un baño caliente; *show me what you did at school today*, enséñame lo que has hecho en el colegio hoy; *it's just what I wanted*, es justo lo que quería; *what worries me is how we're going to get home*, lo que me preocupa es cómo llegaremos a casa. – **8** *interj* ¡cómo!: *what! you've lost it!*, ¡cómo! ¡lo has perdido!

● **and what not**, y tal, cosas por el estilo. ‖ **guess what?**, ¿sabes qué? ‖ **or what?**, ¿o qué? ‖ **to give sb. what for**, darle a algn. su merecido. ‖ **to know what's what**, saber de qué va la cosa, estar al tanto. ‖ **what about ...?**, ¿qué tal ...?, ¿qué te parece ...?: *what about Friday?*, ¿qué tal el viernes?; *what about the cat?*, ¿y el gato qué?; *what about that drink you owe me?*, ¿qué hay de la copa que me debes?; *what about seeing a film?*, ¿qué te parece ver una película? ‖ **what for?**, *(why)* ¿por qué?; *(for what purpose)* ¿para qué? ‖ **what have**

you, y tal. ‖ **what if ...?**, ¿y si ...?: *what if there's no answer?*, ¿y si no contestan? ‖ **what is it?**, *(what's wrong?)* ¿qué pasa?; *(definition)* ¿qué es? ‖ **what of it?**, ¿y qué? ‖ **what with ... and ...**, entre ... y ..., con lo de ... y ...: *what with one thing and another*, entre una cosa y otra; *what with the wedding, the fire and everything*, con lo de la boda, el incendio y todo. ‖ **what's more**, y además.

what-d'you-call-it ['wɒtdʒəkɔːlɪt] *n fam (thing)* chisme *m*.

whatever [wɒt'evə'] **1** *adj (any)* cualquiera que: *whatever colour you like*, el color que tú quieras. **2** *(at all)* en absoluto: *with no money whatever*, sin absolutamente nada de dinero. – **3** *pron (anything, all that)* (todo) lo que: *do whatever you like*, haz lo que tú quieras. **4** *(no matter what)*: *whatever happens*, pase lo que pase; *don't tell Sally whatever you do*, no se lo digas a Sally bajo ningún concepto; *whatever the cost*, cueste lo que cueste; *he goes out whatever the weather*, él sale haga el tiempo que haga. **5** *(surprise)* qué: *whatever are you doing?*, ¿qué diablos haces? **6** *fam (show indifference)* lo que sea: *do you want pizza or pasta? –Whatever*, ¿quieres pizza o pasta? –Lo que sea.

● **or whatever**, o tal, o cosas por el estilo. ‖ **whatever next?**, ¡habráse visto!, ¡vaya!

whatnot ['wɒtnɒt] **1** *n fam (thing)* chisme *m*. **2** *(furniture)* estantería.

whatsoever [wɒtsəʊ'evə'] *adj* en absoluto: *nothing whatsoever*, nada en absoluto.

wheat [wi:t] *n* trigo.

■ **wheat germ**, germen *m* de trigo.

wheatmeal ['wi:tmi:l] *n* harina integral de trigo.

wheedle ['wi:dəl] *t* engatusar.

● **to wheedle sb. into doing sth.**, engatusar a algn. para que haga algo. ‖ **to wheedle sth. out of sb.**, sonsacar algo a algn.

wheel [wi:l] **1** *n* rueda. **2** *(steering wheel)* volante *m*. – **3** *(push)* empujar. – **4** *i* girar: *she wheeled round*, giró sobre los talones. **5** *(birds)* revolotear. – **6** **wheels**, *npl* coche *m sing*.

◆ **to wheel out** *t sep* sacar.

● **to be at the wheel**, *(car)* estar al volante; *(ship)* llevar el timón. ‖ **to wheel and deal**, trapichear.

■ **big wheel**, noria. ‖ **wheel clamp**, cepo.

wheelbarrow ['wi:lbærəʊ] *n* carretilla de mano.

wheelbase ['wi:lbeɪs] *n* AUTO distancia entre ejes.

wheelchair ['wi:ltʃeə'] *n* silla de ruedas.

wheeler-dealer [wi:lə'di:lə'] *n* trapichero,-a.

wheeling ['wi:lɪŋ] **wheeling and dealing**, *n* trapicheos *mpl*.

wheeze [wi:z] **1** *n (sound)* resuello; *(act)* respiración *f* sibilante. – **2** *i* respirar con dificultad, resollar. – **3** *t* decir resollando.

wheezy ['wi:zɪ] *adj (person)* asmático,-a; *(breathing)* sibilante.

▲ *comp* **wheezier**, *superl* **wheeziest**.

whelk [welk] *n* buccino.

whelp [welp] **1** *n* cachorro,-a. – **2** *i* parir.

when [wen] **1** *adv (direct questions)* cuándo: *when did it happen?*, ¿cuándo pasó?; *when are they coming?*, ¿cuándo vendrán?; *when did she die?*, ¿cuándo murió?; *since when?*, ¿desde cuándo? **2** *(indirect questions)* cuándo: *tell me when you're ready*, dime cuándo estés listo; *I don't know when she went*, no sé cuándo se fue. **3** *(at which, on which)* cuando, en que: *August is the month when everyone goes on holiday*, agosto es el mes en que todo el mundo se va de vacaciones; *there are times when I can't cope,* hay momentos en que no puedo más. – **4** *conj* (*at the time that*) cuando: *when I arrived,* cuando llegué yo; *when I was a student,* cuando era estudiante; *when they had finished eating,* cuando habían acabado de comer; *we were just going out when the phone rang,* estábamos a punto de salir cuando sonó el teléfono. **5** (*whenever*) cuando, siempre que: *when I have a free moment,* cuando tenga un momento libre. **6** (*considering*) cuando, si: *why do you want to move when you've got such a nice house?,* ¿por qué te quieres mudar si tienes una casa tan bonita? **7** (*although*) cuando, aunque: *they said it was an antique when in fact it was a reproduction,* dijeron que era una antigüedad cuando en realidad era una reproducción. – **8** *pron* cuando: *that was when it broke,* fue entonces cuando se rompió.

● **say when,** (*pouring*) me dirás basta.

whence [wens] *adv fml* de dónde.

whenever [wen'evə[r]] **1** *conj* (*at any time, when*) cuando quiera que: *whenever you like,* cuando·quieras. **2** (*every time that*) siempre que: *whenever we have a picnic, it rains,* siempre que vamos de picnic, llueve. – **3** *adv* (*surprise*) cuándo: *whenever do you find the time?,* ¿cuándo encuentras el tiempo?

● **or whenever,** o cuando sea.

where [weə[r]] **1** *adv* (*direct question - place*) dónde; (- *direction*) adónde: *where is it?,* ¿dónde está?; *where did you go?,* ¿adónde fuiste?; *where does she live?,* ¿dónde vive?; *where are you from,* ¿de dónde eres? **2** (*indirect question*) dónde, adónde: *tell me where it is,* dime dónde está. **3** (*at, in or which*) donde, en que; (*to which*) adonde, a donde: *this is where it all happened,* es aquí donde pasó todo. – **4** *conj* donde: *where I come from we don't do that,* de donde soy yo eso no se hace; *that's where you're mistaken,* ahí es donde te equivocas. **5** (*when*) cuando: *where possible,* cuando sea posible.

whereabouts ['weərəbauts] **1** *n* paradero: *his whereabouts is/are unknown,* se desconoce su paradero. – **2** *adv* (*por*) dónde: *whereabouts in London do you live?,* ¿dónde vives en Londres exactamente?

▲ (*adverbio*) [weərə'bauts].

whereas [weər'æz] **1** *conj* mientras que: *he wants a boy whereas I want a girl,* él quiere un niño mientras que yo quiero una niña. **2** *JUR* considerando que.

whereby [weə'bai] *adv fml* por el/la/lo cual: *a system whereby everyone works shifts,* un sistema por el cual todos trabajamos por turnos.

wherein [weə'rɪn] *adv* en donde.

whereupon ['weərəpɒn] *adv* con lo cual.

wherever [weər'evə[r]] **1** *conj* (*in any place, where*) dondequiera que: *sit wherever you like,* siéntate donde quieras. **2** (*everywhere*) dondequiera: *wherever you go,* dondequiera que vayas, vayas dónde vayas. – **3** *adv* (*in questions*) dónde, adónde: *wherever did you put it?,* ¿dónde diablos lo has puesto? **4** (*unspecified place*) en cualquier parte.

● **or wherever,** o donde sea.

wherewithal ['weəwɪðɔːl] *n* medios *mpl*, recursos *mpl*.

whet [wet] **1** *t* (*appetite*) despertar, abrir. **2** *fml* (*knife*) afilar.

▲ *pt & pp* **whetted,** *ger* **whetting**.

whether ['weðə[r]] **1** *conj* si: *I don't know whether I can make it or not,* no sé si podré ir o no; *I'll ask her whether or not she agrees,* le preguntaré si está de acuerdo o no?; *we're not sure whether to go today or tomorrow,* no sabemos si iremos hoy o mañana. **2** (*no matter if*) aun-

que: *I'm going whether you like it or not,* voy a ir te guste o no, voy a ir aunque no te guste; *whether it rains or not,* llueva o no.

● **whether by accident or design,** fuera por accidente o a propósito.

whey [wei] *n* suero.

which [wɪtʃ] **1** *adj* (*direct questions*) qué, cuál, cuáles: *which size?,* ¿qué tamaño/talla?; *which colour do you prefer?,* ¿qué color prefieres?; *which newspaper do you read?,* ¿qué periódico lees?; *which one do you like best?,* ¿cuál te gusta más? **2** (*indirect questions*) qué: *I can't remember which department she's in,* no recuerdo en qué sección trabaja. – **3** *pron* (*questions*) cuál, cuáles: *which do you want?,* ¿cuál quieres?; *which is your car?,* ¿cuál es tu coche?; *which is mine?,* ¿cuál es el mío? **4** (*indirect questions*) cuál: *ask him which is his,* pregúntale cuál·es el suyo. **5** (*defining relative*) que; (*with preposition*) que, el/la que, el/la cual, los/las que, los/las cuales: *the shoes which I bought,* los zapatos que compré; *this is the record I was telling you about,* este es el disco del·que te hablaba; *the shop in which they met,* la tienda donde se conocieron. **6** (*non-defining relative*) el/la cual, los/las cuales: *two glasses, one of which was dirty,* dos copas, una de las cuales estaba sucia. **7** (*referring to a clause*) lo que, lo cual: *he lost, which was sad,* perdió, lo cual era triste.

● **in which case,** en cuyo caso.

whichever [wɪtʃ'evə[r]] **1** *adj* (*any one*) cualquier, el/la que: *take whichever book you like best,* coge el libro que más te guste. **2** (*no matter which*) cualquiera que, no importa: *whichever way you look at it,* no importa cómo lo mires. **3** (*interrogative*) cuál: *whichever coat did you buy?,* ¿cuál de los abrigos compraste? – **4** *pron* cualquiera, el/la que: *take whichever you want,* coge el que quieras. **5** (*interrogative*) cuál: *whichever did you choose?,* ¿cuál escogiste?

whiff [wɪf] **1** *n* (*of air, smoke*) bocanada. **2** (*faint smell*) olor *m* fugaz, olor *m* pasajero, olorcillo: *I caught a whiff of her perfume,* percibí el olor de su perfume. **3** *fam* (*bad smell*) tufo. **4** *fig* (*of scandal etc*) indicio, atisbo, sospecha.

while [wail] **1** *n* (*time*) rato, tiempo: *we talked for a while,* charlamos durante un rato; *it took me a while to get used to the idea,* me llevó un rato hacerme a la idea; *I'll be back in a little while,* enseguida vuelvo; *he left a good while ago,* hace un buen rato que se marchó; *we like to go out once in a while,* nos gusta salir de vez en cuando; *you've been here all the while!,* ¡has estado aquí todo el rato! – **2** *conj* (*when*) mientras: *somebody stole our car while we were on holiday,* nos robaron el coche mientras estábamos de vacaciones; *I met my husband while I was studying in Paris,* conocí a mi marido mientras estudiaba en París; *I'll cook the dinner while you clean the car,* yo haré la comida mientras tú lavas el coche. **3** (*although*) aunque: *while I sympathize with the cause, I cannot support your methods,* aunque simpatizo con la causa, no puedo apoyar tus métodos. **4** (*whereas*) mientras que: *he prefers to go out, while I like staying in,* él prefiere salir mientras que a mí me gusta quedarme en casa.

◆ **to while away** *t sep* pasar: *they whiled away the time reminiscing about the past,* pasaron el rato rememorando el pasado.

▲ → also **worth**.

whilst [wailst] *conj* → **while**.

whim [wɪm] *n* antojo, capricho.

● **on a whim,** por capricho. ‖ **as the whim takes sb.,** según se le antoja a algn.

whimper ['wɪmpəʳ] **1** *n* (*of person*) gimoteo, quejido; (*of dog*) gemido. – **2** *i* (*person*) lloriquear, gimotear; (*dog*) gemir.

whimsical ['wɪmsɪkəl] *adj* (*person, idea, etc*) caprichoso,-a; (*smile*) enigmático,-a; (*story etc*) fantástico,-a.

whine [waɪn] **1** *n* (*of child*) gimoteo, quejido; (*of dog*) gemido. **2** (*of engine*) zumbido, sonido; (*of siren*) aullido. – **3** *i* (*child*) gimotear, lloriquear; (*dog*) gemir. **4** (*complain*) quejarse; (*in pain*) gimotear.

whiner ['waɪnəʳ] *n* (*person*) quejica *mf*.

whinge [wɪndʒ] *i* GB *fam* (*complain*) quejarse (**about**, de).

whining ['waɪnɪŋ] **1** *adj* (*person*) quejica. – **2** *n* (*of child*) gimoteo; (*of dog*) gemidos *mpl*.

whinny ['wɪnɪ] **1** *n* relincho. – **2** *i* relinchar.
▲ (*sustantivo*) *pl* **whinnies**; (*verbo*) *pt* & *pp* **whinnied**, *ger* **whinnying**.

whip [wɪp] **1** *n* (*for animals*) látigo; (*for punishment*) azote *m*; (*for riding*) fusta. **2** POL (*person*) oficial encargado,-a de la disciplina de un partido; (*instruction*) llamada a los miembros de un partido para que asistan a la cámara. **3** CULIN (*dessert*) batido. – **4** *t* (*person*) azotar; (*horse*) fustigar. **5** (*wind*) azotar. **6** CULIN (*ingredients*) batir; (*cream, egg whites*) montar. **7** GB *fam* (*steal*) birlar, mangar. **8** (*act quickly*) hacer algo deprisa: *he whipped out a twenty-pound note,* sacó de repente un billete de veinte libras; *she whipped the toy away from him,* le arrebató el juguete; *the wind whipped some tiles off the roof,* el viento arrastró unas tejas del tejado. – **9** *i* (*move quickly*) ir volando: *I'll just whip to the shop,* voy volando a la tienda.
◆ **to whip up 1** *t sep* (*arouse - enthusiasm etc*) despertar, avivar, animar; (- *help, support*) conseguir; (- *hatred*) fomentar; (- *strife, tension*) provocar, crear. **2** (*prepare quickly*) preparar en un momento, improvisar.
● **to crack the whip**, hacer restallar el látigo. ‖ **to get a fair crack of the whip**, tener la misma oportunidad. ‖ **to have the whip hand**, estar en una posición de control, llevar la batuta.
▲ *pt* & *pp* **whipped**, *ger* **whipping**.

whiplash ['wɪplæʃ] *n* latigazo, trallazo.
■ **whiplash injury**, MED traumatismo cervical.

whippersnapper ['wɪpəʳsnæpəʳ] *n fam* mocoso,-a.

whippet ['wɪpɪt] *n* galgo pequeño.

whipping ['wɪpɪŋ] *n* azotaina, paliza.
● **to give sb. a whipping**, dar una azotaina a algn.
■ **whipping boy**, cabeza de turco. ‖ **whipping cream**, nata para montar.

whip-round ['wɪpraʊnd] *n* GB *fam* colecta.
● **to have a whip-round**, hacer una colecta.

whirl [wɜːl] **1** *n* (*movement*) giro, vuelta. **2** *fig* torbellino: *whirl of activity,* bullicio, ajetreo; *the social whirl,* la vida social; *my mind's in a whirl,* la cabeza me da vueltas. – **3** *i* (*move round*) girar, dar vueltas; (*of dust, leaves, etc*) arremolinarse: *the dancers were whirling round the floor,* los bailarines giraban por la pista; *a whirling snowstorm,* un remolino de viento y nieve. **4** (*move quickly*) ir como un relámpago. **5** *fig* (*of brain, senses*) dar vueltas: *my head was whirling round,* la cabeza me daba vueltas. – **6** *t* (*spin*) hacer girar, dar vueltas a. **7** (*move quickly*) llevar rápidamente.
● **to give sth. a whirl**, (*try*) probar algo, probar suerte con algo.

whirlpool ['wɜːlpuːl] *n* vorágine *m*, remolino.

whirlwind ['wɜːlwɪnd] **1** *n* torbellino, remolino. – **2** *adj* *fig* vertiginoso,-a, relámpago: *a whirlwind romance,* un idilio tormentoso.

whirr [wɜːʳ] **1** *n* zumbido. – **2** *i* zumbar.

whisk [wɪsk] **1** *n* (*quick movement*) movimiento brusco, sacudida: *with a whisk of the tail,* de un coletazo. **2** CULIN (*hand*) batidor *m*; (*electric*) batidora. – **3** *t* (*of animal's tail*) sacudir (la cola). **4** CULIN batir. **5** (*take quickly*) llevar rápidamente: *she was whisked away to safety,* se la llevó fuera del peligro; *they whisked him off in a taxi,* se lo llevaron rápidamente en un taxi.

whisker ['wɪskəʳ] **1** *n* (*single hair*) pelo (de la barba). – **2** whiskers, *npl* (*man's*) patillas *fpl*. **3** (*of cat etc*) bigote *m*, bigotes *mpl*.
● **by a whisker**, por un pelo, por los pelos. ‖ **to think one is the cat's whiskers**, ser un creído,-a, ser engreído,-a, creerse el ombligo del mundo.

whiskey ['wɪskɪ] *n* US → **whisky**.

whisky ['wɪskɪ] *n* GB whisky *m*, güisqui *m*.
▲ *pl* **whiskies**.

whisper ['wɪspəʳ] **1** *n* (*quiet voice*) susurro: *she said in a whisper,* dijo en voz baja. **2** (*rumour*) rumor *m*, voz *f*. – **3** *t* (*gen*) susurrar, decir en voz baja: *she whispered something in my ear,* me susurró algo al oído. **4** (*rumour*) correr la voz, rumorearse: *it is whispered that ...,* se rumorea que ... – **5** *i* (*gen*) susurrar, cuchichear, hablar en voz baja: *stop whispering!,* ¡dejad de cuchichear! **6** (*of wind, leaves*) susurrar.

whispering ['wɪspərɪŋ] *n* (*gen*) cuchicheo; (*of leaves*) murmullo.
■ **whispering campaign**, campaña de difamación. ‖ **whispering gallery**, galería de los murmullos.

whist [wɪst] *n* whist *m*.
■ **whist drive**, reunión *f* para jugar al whist.

whistle ['wɪsəl] **1** *n* (*instrument*) silbato, pito: *the guard blew his whistle,* el jefe del tren tocó el silbato. **2** (*noise*) silbido, pitido; (*of train*) pitido; (*of wind*) silbido. – **3** *t* (*tune*) silbar. – **4** *i* (*person, kettle, wind*) silbar; (*referee, police, train*) pitar: *the referee whistled for half-time,* el árbitro pitó para señalar el descanso. **5** (*call*) llamar con un silbido, silbar; (*protest*) silbar, pitar: *the crowd whistled angrily,* el público pitó enfadado. **6** (*move swiftly*) pasar silbando.
● **to blow the whistle on sb.**, delatar a algn. ‖ **to wet one's whistle**, mojar el gaznate, echarse un trago. ‖ **to whistle for sth.**, esperar algo vanamente.

whistle-stop ['wɪsəlstɒp] *n* US apeadero.
■ **whistle-stop tour**, gira relámpago.

whit [wɪt] *n* pizca, ápice *m*: *you haven't changed a whit,* no has cambiado un ápice.

Whit [wɪt] *n* Pentecostés *m*.
■ **Whit Sunday**, domingo de Pentecostés.

white [waɪt] **1** *adj* blanco,-a: *a white person,* una persona de raza blanca; *white coffee,* café con leche; *white hair,* pelo blanco, pelo cano; *white grapes,* uvas verdes. **2** (*pale*) pálido,-a. – **3** *n* blanco, color *m* blanco. **4** (*person*) blanco,-a. **5** (*of egg*) clara. **6** (*of eye*) blanco. – **7** whites, *npl* (*linen*) ropa *f sing* blanca; (*for tennis*) ropa *f sing* de jugar al tenis.
● **as white as a sheet**, blanco,-a como el papel. ‖ **as white as snow**, más blanco,-a que la nieve. ‖ **to go/turn white**, (*person's face*) palidecer, ponerse pálido,-a; (*hair*) ponerse cano, encanecer; (*person*) quedarse canoso,-a: *she went white overnight,* se quedó canosa de la noche a la mañana. ‖ **to have a white wedding**, casarse de blanco.
■ **white (blood) cell**, glóbulo blanco. ‖ **white Christmas**, Navidad *f* con nieve. ‖ **white corpuscle**, glóbulo blanco. ‖ **white elephant**, elefante *m* blanco. ‖ **white flag**, bandera blanca. ‖ **white heat**, incandescencia. ‖ **white horses**, palomas *fpl*. ‖ **White House**, Casa

Blanca. ‖ **white lead,** albayalde *m*, plomo blanco. ‖ **white lie,** mentira piadosa. ‖ **white meat,** carne *f* blanca. ‖ **White Paper,** libro blanco. ‖ **white pepper,** pimienta blanca. ‖ **white sauce,** (salsa) bechamel *f*. ‖ **white spirit,** aguarrás *m*. ‖ **white stick,** bastón *m* blanco de los ciegos. ‖ **white tie,** (*bow tie*) pajarita blanca. ‖ **white trash,** basura blanca.

whitebait ['waɪtbeɪt] *n* CULIN pescaditos *mpl* (fritos).

white-collar [waɪt'kɒləʳ] *adj* administrativo,-a.
■ **white-collar worker,** empleado,-a administrativo,-a, oficinista *mf*.

white-hot ['waɪt'hɒt] *adj* candente, incandescente.
▲ Se escribe *white hot* cuando no se antepone a un sustantivo.

whiten ['waɪtən] *t* blanquear, emblanquecer.

whiteness ['waɪtnəs] *n* blancura.

whitening ['waɪtənɪŋ] *n* blanco de España.

white-slave trade [waɪt'sleɪvtreɪd] *n* trata de blancas.

white-tie [waɪt'taɪ] *adj* (*party etc*) de etiqueta.

whitewash ['waɪtwɒʃ] **1** *n* cal *f*, lechada, jalbegue *m*. **2** *fig* encubrimiento. – **3** *t* encalar, enjalbegar, blanquear. **4** *fig* encubrir.

whither ['wɪðəʳ] *adv* adónde.

whiting[1] ['waɪtɪŋ] *n* (*fish*) pescadilla.
▲ *pl whiting.*

whiting[2] ['waɪtɪŋ] *n* (*whitening*) blanco de España.

whitish ['waɪtɪʃ] *adj* blanquecino,-a.

Whitsun ['wɪtsən] *n* Pentecostés *m inv*.

Whitsuntide ['wɪtsəntaɪd] *n* Pentecostés *m inv*.

whittle ['wɪtəl] *t* (*sharpen*) afilar, sacar punta a; (*shape*) tallar.
◆ **to whittle away** *t sep* mermar, ir reduciendo, ir disminuyendo. ‖ **to whittle down** *t sep* reducir: *we've whittled the applicants down to three,* hemos conseguido reducir a tres los candidatos.

whiz [wɪz] *n* → **whizz**.

whizz [wɪz] **1** *n* (*sound*) zumbido, silbido. – **2** *i* (*make sound*) zumbar, silbar. **3** (*car, bullet*) pasar zumbando, pasar silbando; (*time*) pasar volando: *the cars whizzed past,* los coches pasaron zumbando; *the days whizz by,* los días pasan volando.
● **to be a whizz at sth.,** ser una hacha en algo.
■ **whizz kid,** joven *mf* dinámico,-a y emprendedor,-ra.

who [huː] **1** *pron* (*direct questions*) quién, quiénes: *who is it?,* ¿quién es?; *who did it?,* ¿quién lo hizo?; *who did you go with?,* ¿con quién fuiste?; *who are you talking to?,* ¿con quién hablas?; *who knows?,* ¿quién sabe? **2** (*indirect questions*) quién, quiénes: *I don't know who they are,* no sé quiénes son. **3** (*defining relative*) que: *you're the only one who can help me,* eres el único que puede ayudarme; *it's the man who called earlier,* es el hombre que llamó antes; *those who want to go,* los que quieran ir; *the boy (who) she loves,* el chico que ama; *the woman who lives next door has just had a baby,* la mujer que vive al lado acaba de tener un niño. **4** (*non-defining relative*) que, quien, quienes, el/la cual, los/las cuales: *the workers, who were on strike, ...,* los trabajadores, los cuales estaban en huelga, ...; *my brother, who lives in England, ...,* mi hermano, que vive en Inglaterra, ...

WHO ['dʌbəljuː'eɪtʃ'əʊ] *abbr* (*World Health Organization*) Organización Mundial de la Salud; (*abbreviation*) OMS *f*.

whoa [wəʊ] *interj* ¡so!

whodunit [huː'dʌnɪt] *n fam* novela u obra de teatro de suspense.

whoever [huː'evəʳ] **1** *pron* (*the person who*) quien, quienquiera que, el que: *go with whoever you like,* vete con quien quieras; *whoever said that is a liar,* el que dijo eso es un mentiroso; *whoever gets home first makes the tea,* el que llegue primero a casa hace el té. **2** (*no matter who*) quienquiera que, cualquiera que: *whoever it is, I'm not in,* quienquiera que sea, no estoy; *whoever you vote for, the result will be the same,* votes a quien votes, el resultado será el mismo. **3** (*questions, exclamations*) quién?: *whoever can that be at this time?,* ¿pero quién será a estas horas?
● **... or whoever,** ... o quien sea.

whole [həʊl] **1** *adj* (*entire, all (the), the full amount of*) entero,-a, íntegro,-a, todo,-a: *the whole day,* todo el día; *a whole bottle,* una botella entera; *the whole truth,* toda la verdad; *in my whole life,* en toda mi vida; *in the whole world,* en el mundo entero; *that's the whole point,* precisamente de eso se trata. **2** (*intact, not broken*) intacto,-a, sano,-a; (*in one piece, complete*) entero,-a: *cook it whole,* guísalo entero. – **3** *n* conjunto, todo: *two halves make a whole,* dos mitades hacen un todo.
● **a whole lot,** mucho,-a, muchos,-as, un montón de: *it's a whole lot better than I expected,* es muchísimo mejor de lo que me esperaba; *a whole lot of things,* un montón de cosas, muchas cosas. ‖ **as a whole,** en conjunto, en su totalidad. ‖ **on the whole,** en general. ‖ **the whole caboodle,** absolutamente todo, todo el tinglado. ‖ **the whole of,** la totalidad de, todo,-a: *the whole of Europe,* toda Europa; *the whole of the summer,* todo el verano. ‖ **to make sb. whole,** curar a algn.
■ **whole milk,** leche *f* entera. ‖ **whole number,** número entero.

wholefood ['həʊlfuːd] *n* alimento integral.

wholehearted [həʊl'hɑːtɪd] *adj* (*support*) absoluto,-a, incondicional; (*attention*) completo,-a; (*sympathy*) sincero,-a; (*effort*) entusiasta.

wholeheartedly [həʊl'hɑːtɪdlɪ] *adv* con entusiasmo, sinceramente, de todo corazón, sin reservas: *I agree wholeheartedly,* estoy completamente de acuerdo.

wholemeal ['həʊlmiːl] *adj* integral.

wholesale ['həʊlseɪl] **1** *adj* COMM al por mayor. **2** (*complete, indiscriminate*) total, general, masivo,-a, sistemático,-a, absoluto,-a: *wholesale slaughter,* matanza indiscriminada; *wholesale redundancies,* despidos masivos. – **3** *adv* COMM al por mayor. **4** (*on a large scale*) de modo general, en su totalidad, en masa, de manera sistemática. – **5** *n* COMM venta al por mayor.

wholesaler ['həʊlseɪləʳ] *n* mayorista *mf*.

wholesome ['həʊlsəm] **1** *adj* (*food*) sano,-a; (*appearance*) sano,-a, saludable. **2** *fig* (*good in effect*) saludable.

wholly ['həʊlɪ] *adv* enteramente, completamente.

whom [huːm] **1** *pron* fml (*direct questions*) a quién/quiénes: *whom did he kill?,* ¿a quién mató?; *to whom should I address it?,* ¿a quién debería ir dirigido? **2** fml (*relative - defining*) que, quien, quienes; (*- after preposition*) quien, quienes, el cual, la cual, los cuales, las cuales: *pupils whom I have taught,* alumnos a quienes he dado clase; *the gentleman whom I saw,* el señor a quien vi; *the man with whom she was seen,* el hombre con quien la vieron; *someone for whom I have the greatest respect,* alguien a quien tengo mucho respeto. **3** (*relative - non-defining*) quien, quienes, el cual, la cual, los cuales, las cuales: *our guest, of whom you must all have heard, ...,* nuestro invitado, de quien todos deben haber oído hablar, ...; *the man, whom she'd met previously, ...,* el hombre, a quien había conocido antes, ...

whoop [huːp] **1** *n* grito (de alegría). – **2** *i* gritar (de alegría).
● **to whoop it up,** pasárselo en grande.

whoopee [wʊ'piː] *interj* ¡hurra!
whooping cough ['huːpɪŋkɒf] *n* MED tos *f* ferina.
whoops [wʊps] *interj* ¡ay!
whopper ['wɒpə'] **1** *n fam* (*large thing*) cosa enorme, cosa descomunal: *I caught a whopper!*, pesqué uno enorme. **2** *fam* (*lie*) trola, bola.
whopping ['wɒpɪŋ] **1** *adj fam* enorme, descomunal. – **2** *adv fam* muy: *a whopping great steak*, un bistec enorme.
whore [hɔː'] *n pej* puta.
whose [huːz] **1** *pron* (*direct questions*) de quién/quiénes: *whose is this?*, ¿de quién es esto? **2** (*indirect questions*) de quién/quiénes: *I don't know whose it is*, no sé de quién es. – **3** *adj* (*direct questions*) de quién/quiénes: *whose dog is this?*, de quién es este perro?; *whose fault is it?*, ¿quién tiene la culpa? **4** (*indirect questions*) de quién/quiénes: *I wonder whose books these are*, me pregunto de quién serán estos libros. **5** (*relative*) cuyo,-a, cuyos,-as: *the woman whose car was stolen*, la mujer cuyo coche fue robado; *that's the man whose wife is in hospital*, ese es el hombre cuya mujer está en el hospital.
why [waɪ] **1** *adv* (*direct questions - for what reason*) por qué; (*- for what purpose*) para qué: *why didn't you go?*, ¿por qué no fuiste?; *why do you hate me?*, ¿por qué me odias?; *why bother?*, ¿por qué molestarse?; *why do you need the money?*, ¿para qué necesitas el dinero? **2** (*indirect questions - for what reason*) por qué; (*- for what purpose*) para qué: *I asked him why he did it*, le pregunté por qué lo hizo; *she wondered why he hadn't come*, se preguntaba por qué no había venido. **3** (*relative*) por eso: *that is why he left*, por eso se fue; *why she kept quiet we'll never know*, nunca sabremos por qué nunca dijo nada. – **4** *interj* ¡vaya!, ¡anda!, ¡toma! – **5** *n* porqué *m*.
● **the whys and (the) wherefores**, el cómo y el porqué. ‖ **why ever?**, ¿por qué demonios? ‖ **why not?**, ¿por qué no?: *why don't we go out for lunch?*, ¿por qué no comemos fuera?; *I don't see why not*, no veo por qué no.
wick [wɪk] *n* mecha.
● **to get on sb.'s wick**, GB tocarle las narices a algn.
wicked ['wɪkɪd] **1** *adj* (*evil - person*) malvado,-a, malo,-a; (*- action*) malo,-a, perverso,-a, inicuo,-a. **2** (*harmful*) peligroso,-a, dañino,-a, nocivo,-a. **3** (*mischievous*) travieso,-a, pícaro,-a. **4** *fam fig* (*very bad - gen*) malísimo,-a; (*- weather*) feo,-a, horrible; (*- temper, price*) terrible; (*- waste*) vergonzoso,-a; (*humour*) cruel. – **5 the wicked**, *npl* los malos.
● **there's no rest for the wicked**, los malos nunca descansan.
wickedly ['wɪkɪðlɪ] **1** *adv* (*evilly*) malvadamente, perversamente. **2** *fam fig* (*very*) terriblemente.
wickedness ['wɪkɪdnəs] *n* maldad *f*.
wicker ['wɪkə'] **1** *n* mimbre *m*. – **2** *adj* de mimbre.
wickerwork ['wɪkəwɜːk] **1** *n* (*articles*) artículos *mpl* de mimbre; (*art*) cestería. – **2** *adj* de mimbre.
wicket ['wɪkɪt] **1** *n* (*in cricket - stumps*) palos *mpl*; (*- pitch*) terreno. **2** (*small door, gate*) postigo, portillo.
● **to be on a sticky wicket**, encontrarse en un apuro.
wicketkeeper ['wɪkɪtkiːpə'] *n* (*cricket*) cátcher *m*.
wide [waɪd] **1** *adj* (*broad*) ancho,-a; (*space, hole, gap*) grande: *a wide road*, una carretera ancha; *a wide hole in the fence*, un agujero grande en la valla; *the wide gap between rich and poor*, la gran diferencia entre ricos y pobres. **2** (*having specified width*) de ancho: *two feet wide*, de dos pies de ancho; *how wide is it?*, ¿cuánto hace de

ancho? **3** (*large - area*) amplio,-a, extenso,-a; (*- knowledge, experience, repercussions*) amplio,-a; (*- coverage, range, support*) extenso,-a: *a wide variety of books*, una gran variedad de libros; *he has wide interests*, tiene intereses muy diversos; *a wide following*, muchos admiradores; *this raises wider issues*, esto plantea cuestiones más generales. **4** (*eyes, smile*) abierto,-a. **5** (*off target*) desviado,-a. – **6** *adv* (*fully - gen*) completamente: *wide awake*, completamente despierto,-a; *wide apart*, muy separados,-as; *the door was wide open*, la puerta estaba abierta de par en par; *open wide! said the dentist*, ¡abre bien la boca! dijo el dentista. **7** (*off target*) desviado.
● **from far and wide**, de todas partes. ‖ **to be/fall wide of the mark**, no dar en el blanco, no acertar. ‖ **to give sb./sth. a wide berth**, evitar a algn./algo. ‖ **to go into sth. with one's eyes wide open**, saber muy bien dónde se está metiendo uno. ‖ **wide open (to sth.)**, (*exposed*) completamente expuesto,-a (a algo).
wide-angle ['waɪdæŋgəl] *adj* amplio,-a.
■ **wide-angle lens**, objetivo gran angular.
wide-awake ['waɪdə'weɪk] **1** *adj* (*fully awake*) completamente despierto,-a. **2** (*alert*) despierto,-a, despabilado,-a, espabilado,-a.
▲ *Se escribe* **wide awake** *cuando no se antepone a un sustantivo.*
wide-eyed ['waɪd'aɪd] **1** *adj* (*surprised*) con los ojos muy abiertos. **2** (*innocent, naive*) inocente, ingenuo,-a.
▲ *Se escribe* **wide eyed** *cuando no se antepone a un sustantivo.*
widely ['waɪdlɪ] **1** *adv* (*over wide area or range of things*) extensamente; (*generally*) generalmente: *it is widely known that ...*, es bien sabido que ...; *he has travelled widely*, ha viajado extensamente; *she is widely read*, ha leído mucho; *these drugs are widely available*, estas drogas se consiguen con facilidad. **2** (*to a large degree*) mucho: *accents vary widely from place to place*, los acentos varían mucho de un sitio a otro.
widen ['waɪdən] **1** *t* (*road etc*) ensanchar. **2** *fig* (*knowledge etc*) ampliar, extender: *the party must widen its appeal among young people*, el partido tiene que extender su popularidad entre los jóvenes. – **3** *i* (*road etc*) ensancharse; (*eyes*) abrirse: *the river widens here*, el río se ensancha aquí. **4** (*project etc*) extenderse; (*difference, gap*) aumentar: *the widening gap between rich and poor*, la diferencia cada vez más grande entre ricos y pobres.
wide-ranging ['waɪd'reɪndʒɪŋ] **1** *adj* (*interests, products, subjects*) múltiples, muy diversos,-as, muy variados,-as; (*discussion*) amplio,-a. **2** (*effects, implications*) de gran alcance; (*survey, study, investigation*) a fondo, de gran alcance.
▲ *Se escribe* **wide ranging** *cuando no se antepone a un sustantivo.*
widespread ['waɪdspred] *adj* (*concern, confusion, unrest, use, belief*) generalizado,-a; (*damage, disease, news*) extenso,-a, extendido,-a.
● **to become widespread**, (*gen*) generalizarse; (*illness, news*) extenderse, difundirse.
widow ['wɪdəʊ] *n* viuda.
widowed ['wɪdəʊd] *adj* enviudado,-a.
● **to be widowed**, enviudar.
widower ['wɪdəʊə'] *n* viudo.
widowhood ['wɪdəʊhʊd] *n* viudez *f*.
width [wɪdθ] **1** *n* (*gen*) anchura: *the width of the street*, la anchura de la calle; *it's ten metres in width*, tiene diez metros de ancho; *measure the width of the room*, mide la anchura de la habitación. **2** (*of material*) ancho. **3** (*of swimming pool*) ancho.
wield [wiːld] **1** *t* (*weapon, tool, etc*) empuñar, blandir, manejar. **2** *fig* (*power, control, etc*) ejercer.

wife [waɪf] *n* esposa, mujer *f.*
● **an old wives' tale,** cuento de viejas.
▲ *pl* **wives.**
wig [wɪg] **1** *n* (*gen*) peluca. **2** JUR peluquín *m.*
● **to wear a wig,** llevar peluca.
wiggle ['wɪgəl] **1** *t* (*gen*) menear; (*hips*) contonearse. – **2** *i* (*gen*) menearse. – **3** *n* meneo.
wiggly ['wɪgəlɪ] *adj* (*wavy*) ondulado,-a; (*moving*) sinuoso,-a.
▲ *comp* **wigglier,** *superl* **wiggliest.**
wigwam ['wɪgwæm] *n* tienda india, tepe *m.*
wild [waɪld] **1** *adj* (*animal*) salvaje, bravío,-a: **wild beast,** fiera; **wild bull,** toro bravo. **2** (*plant, flower*) silvestre; (*vegetation*) salvaje. **3** (*country, landscape*) agreste, bravo,-a, salvaje. **4** (*weather - wind*) furioso,-a, borrascoso,-a; (*sea*) bravo,-a; (*- night*) tempestuoso,-a, de tormenta. **5** (*tribe*) salvaje. **6** (*violent, angry - person*) furioso,-a, colérico,-a, frenético,-a; (*- behaviour*) incontrolado,-a, desenfrenado,-a; (*- blow, attack*) violento,-a, salvaje, brutal: **he's wild with anger,** está loco de furia. **7** (*very excited - person*) loco,-a (**with,** de), alocado,-a; (*very exciting - party etc*) escandaloso,-a, desmadrado,-a: **the crowd went wild,** el público enloqueció; **wild applause,** aplausos fervorosos. **8** (*showing lack of thought - thoughts, talk*) disparatado,-a; (*- guess*) al azar; (*- idea, scheme*) descabellado,-a, desorbitado,-a, loco,-a, alocado,-a; (*- decision*) precipitado,-a, impetuoso,-a; (*- exaggeration, speculation*) enorme. **9** *fam* (*fantastic, crazy*) bárbaro,-a, salvaje. – **10 the wild,** *n* estado salvaje, estado natural, naturaleza: **few gorillas remain in the wild,** quedan pocos gorilas en su hábitat natural; **this species couldn't survive in the wild,** esta especie no podría sobrevivir en estado salvaje. – **11 the wilds,** *npl* las regiones *fpl* salvajes.
● **beyond one's wildest dreams,** más de lo que jamás había soñado. ‖ **to be wild about sth.,** estar loco,-a por algo: **he's wild about football,** está loco por el fútbol; **I'm not wild about the colour,** el color no me entusiasma demasiado. ‖ **to grow wild,** ser silvestre. ‖ **to run wild,** (*animal*) vivir en su estado natural; (*plant, garden*) volver a su estado natural; (*person, child*) desmandarse; (*hooligan etc*) portarse como un salvaje.
■ **wild boar,** jabalí *m.* ‖ **wild card,** comodín *m.* ‖ **the Wild West,** el Lejano Oeste *m.*
wildcat ['waɪldkæt] *n* gato,-a montés.
■ **wildcat strike,** huelga salvaje.
wildebeest ['wɪldɪbiːst] *n* ñu *m.*
wilderness ['wɪldənəs] **1** *n* (*desert*) yermo, desierto; (*wasteland*) páramo. **2** *pej* (*garden*) selva, jungla.
● **in the (political) wilderness,** POL alejado,-a del mundo de la política.
wildfire ['waɪldfaɪə'] *n* fuego incontrolable, fuego arrasador.
● **to spread like wildfire,** correr como la pólvora, extenderse como un reguero de pólvora.
wildfowl ['waɪldfaʊl] *n* ave *f* de caza.
▲ *pl* **wildfowl** *o* **wildfowls.**
wild-goose chase [waɪld'guːstʃeɪs] *n* búsqueda inútil.
wildlife ['waɪldlaɪf] *n* fauna.
■ **wildlife park,** reserva.
wildly ['waɪldlɪ] **1** *adv* (*run etc*) como un loco,-a, frenéticamente; (*talk*) exageradamente, sin ton ni son, incoherentemente; (*applaud*) efusivamente; (*hit*) violentamente, furiosamente. **2** (*guess*) al azar, sin pensar; (*shoot*) sin apuntar, a lo loco. **3** (*very*) muy, totalmente, absolutamente: **wildly exaggerated,** exageradísimo,-a; **wildly inaccurate,** absolutamente errado,-a; **she's wildly happy,** está loca de alegría.

wildness ['waɪldnəs] **1** *n* (*of landscape*) lo agreste; (*of storm, sea, wind*) furia. **2** (*of behaviour*) desenfreno, locura; (*of imagination etc*) extravagancia.
wiles [waɪlz] *npl* (*tricks*) artimañas *fpl,* artificios *mpl*; (*cunning*) astucia.
wilful ['wɪlfʊl] **1** *adj* (*headstrong, obstinate*) voluntarioso,-a, terco,-a. **2** JUR (*intentional*) premeditado,-a, deliberado,-a.
wilfully ['wɪlfʊlɪ] **1** *adv* (*obstinately*) voluntariosamente, tercamente. **2** JUR (*deliberately*) premeditadamente, con alevosía.
will¹ [wɪl] **1** *n* (*control, volition*) voluntad *f*; (*free will*) albedrío: **she's lost the will to live,** ha perdido la voluntad de vivir; **a clash of wills,** un conflicto de voluntades; **he's got a strong will,** tiene mucha voluntad; **it is God's will,** es la voluntad de Dios. **2** JUR testamento, últimas *fpl* voluntades: **he left me this ring in his will,** me dejó este anillo en su testamento; **have you made a will?,** ¿has hecho (tu) testamento? – **3** *t* (*make or intend to happen by power of mind*) desear, querer: **we were willing him to win,** estábamos deseando que ganara; **she willed it to happen,** logró que pasara por fuerza de voluntad. **4** *fml* (*intend, desire*) querer, ordenar, mandar: **if God wills,** si Dios lo quiere. **5** JUR legar, dejar en testamento.
● **against one's will,** contra su voluntad, a pesar suyo. ‖ **at will,** a voluntad. ‖ **of one's own free will,** por voluntad propia. ‖ **where there's a will there's a way,** querer es poder. ‖ **with a will,** con ilusión, con entusiasmo, con ganas.
■ **last will and testament,** última voluntad *f.*
will² [wɪl] **1** *aux* (*future*): **she will be here tomorrow,** estará aquí mañana; **we won't finish today,** no acabaremos hoy; **it won't rain, will it?,** no lloverá, ¿verdad?; **you'll catch it if you hurry,** lo cogerás si te das prisa; **I'll see you next week,** hasta la semana que viene; **I will always love you,** siempre te amaré; **what will you do if she's late?,** ¿qué harás si llega tarde? **2** (*be disposed to, be willing to*): (no), **I won't,** no quiero; **I'll do it,** lo haré (yo); **he won't open the door,** se niega a abrir la puerta; **the car won't start,** el coche no arranca; **I won't have it!,** ¡no lo permito!; **will you stay for dinner?,** ¿quieres quedarte a cenar?; **won't you take a seat?,** ¿quiere sentarse?, siéntese, por favor. **3** (*requests*) querer: **will you do me a favour?,** ¿quieres hacerme un favor?; **you won't forget to tell him, will you?,** no se te olvidará de decírselo, ¿verdad?; **make me a cup of tea, will you?,** hazme una taza de té, ¿quieres? **4** (*general truths, custom*): **accidents will happen,** siempre habrá accidentes; **boys will be boys,** así son los chicos. **5** (*orders, commands*): **will you be quiet!,** ¡quieres callarte!, ¡cállate!; **you will report in my office tomorrow,** preséntese en mi oficina mañana. **6** (*insistence, persistence*) insistir en: **she will play her music at full volume,** insiste en poner la música a tope; **he will leave the door open,** es que no hay manera de que cierre la puerta. **7** (*can, possibility*) poder: **this phone will accept credit cards,** este teléfono va con tarjetas de crédito; **this washing machine will take 5 kgs,** esta lavadora aguanta 5 kilos. **8** (*supposition, must, probability*) deber de: **that'll be John,** será John, debe de ser John; **they'll be home by now,** ya estarán en casa, ya deben de estar en casa. – **9** *i fml dated* (*wish*) querer: **what you will,** lo que quieras.
● **if you will,** si así lo quiere. ‖ **I will,** (*in wedding*) sí, quiero. ‖ **will do,** muy bien, lo haré.
willie ['wɪlɪ] *n fam* pito.
willies ['wɪlɪz] *npl fam* susto.
● **to give sb. the willies,** poner a algn. la piel de ga-

llina, poner a algn. los pelos de punta. ‖ **to put the willies up sb.,** poner a algn. los pelos de punta.

willing ['wɪlɪŋ] **1** *adj* (*without being forced*) complaciente, de gran voluntad, dispuesto,-a; (*eager*) entusiasta: *he's a willing helper,* un ayudante dispuesto; *willing students,* estudiantes entusiastas; *she's very willing,* buena voluntad no le falta. **2** (*ready, prepared, disposed*) dispuesto,-a (**to, a**): *I'm willing to take all the blame,* estoy dispuesto a cargar con toda la culpa; *she's more than willing to lend a hand,* está más que dispuesta a echar una mano. **3** (*given/done gladly*) voluntario,-a.
● **to show willing,** dar pruebas de buena voluntad.

willingly ['wɪlɪŋlɪ] *adv* de buena gana, de buen grado.

willingness ['wɪlɪŋnəs] *n* (*good will*) buena voluntad *f*; (*readiness*) buena disposición *f*.

will-o'-the-wisp [wɪləʊ'wɪsp] *n* fuego fatuo.

willow ['wɪləʊ] *n* sauce *m*.
■ **willow tree,** sauce *m*.

willowy ['wɪləʊɪ] *adj* esbelto,-a.

willpower ['wɪlpaʊəʳ] *n* (fuerza de) voluntad *f*: *she gave up smoking through sheer willpower,* dejó de fumar por pura fuerza de voluntad; *he hasn't got much willpower,* tiene poca voluntad.

willy ['wɪlɪ] *n* → **willie.**
▲ *pl* **willies.**

willy-nilly [wɪlɪ'nɪlɪ] *adv* como sea, quiera o no.

wilt [wɪlt] **1** *t* marchitar, secar. – **2** *i* (*plant*) marchitarse, secarse. **3** (*person - become weak or tired*) debilitarse, decaer, languidecer; (- *lose confidence*) desanimarse.

wily ['waɪlɪ] *adj* astuto,-a, zorro,-a, mañoso,-a.
▲ *comp* **wilier,** *superl* **wiliest.**

wimp [wɪmp] *n fam pej* debilucho,-a, esmirriado,-a, canijo,-a.

win [wɪn] **1** *n* victoria: *five consecutive wins,* cinco victorias consecutivas; *I had a win on the lottery,* gané (algo) en la lotería. – **2** *t* (*gen*) ganar; (*victory*) conseguir, ganar: *the Spaniard won the 1500 metres,* el español ganó los 1500 metros; *who do you think will win the election?,* ¿quién crees que ganará las elecciones?; *you always win at cards,* siempre (me) ganas a las cartas. **3** (*prize, cup, etc*) ganar, llevarse: *we've won the pools!,* ¡hemos sacado una quiniela!; *she won first prize in a competition,* se llevó el primer premio en un concurso; *this performance won him an Oscar,* esta interpretación le valió un Óscar. **4** (*gain, obtain, achieve - gen*) conseguir, obtener, ganar; (- *friendship, respect*) granjearse; (- *sympathy, affection*) ganarse, granjearse; (- *support*) atraer, captar; (- *heart, love*) conquistar: *she won a place at university,* consiguió una plaza en la universidad; *we need to win support for the cause,* hay que captar apoyo para la causa; *he managed to win her friendship,* logró granjearse su amistad. – **5** *i* ganar: *who's winning?,* ¿quién va ganando?; *we won 1-0,* ganamos por 1-0; *my horse won by a head,* mi caballo ganó por una cabeza; *OK! you win!,* ¡vale! ¡tú ganas!
◆ **to win back** *t sep* (*money, love, support*) recuperar; (*land*) reconquistar. ‖ **to win over / win round** *t sep* (*person*) convencer, persuadir; (*supporter*) atraerse, captar, ganarse; (*lover*) conquistar: *we can win them over to our point of view,* podemos persuadirlos para que adopten nuestro punto de vista. ‖ **to win through / win out** *i* conseguir triunfar, triunfar al final.
● **to win hands down,** ganar fácilmente. ‖ **to win the day,** llevarse la palma. ‖ **to win the toss,** ganar el sorteo. ‖ **win or lose,** tanto si ganamos como si perdemos. ‖ **you can't win,** (*certain to lose*) no hay caso.
▲ *pt & pp* **won,** *ger* **winning.**

wince [wɪns] **1** *n* rictus *m*, mueca de dolor. – **2** *i* (*in pain*) hacer un rictus, hacer una mueca de dolor; (*in embarrassment*) hacer una mueca.

winch [wɪntʃ] **1** *n* torno, cabrestante *m*. – **2** *t* levantar con un torno.

wind¹ [wɪnd] **1** *n* METEOR viento, aire *m*: *high winds,* vientos fuertes; *a gust of wind,* una ráfaga de viento; *the wind has dropped,* el viento ha amainado; *there's quite a wind blowing,* hace mucho aire. **2** (*breath*) aliento: *he couldn't get his wind,* le faltaba el aliento. **3** (*flatulence*) gases *mpl*, flato; (*air*) gases *mpl* del estómago. **4** *pej* (*talk*) palabrería. – **5** *adj* MUS de viento: *wind section,* sección de viento. – **6** *t* dejar sin aliento, cortar la respiración: *the ball caught him in the stomach and winded him,* el balón le dio en el estómago y se quedó sin aliento. **7** (*baby*) hacer eructar.
● **like the wind,** como el viento. ‖ **to break wind,** ventosear. ‖ **to get one's second wind,** (*feel strong again*) recobrar el aliento; (*become lively again*) reanimarse. ‖ **to get wind of sth.,** olerse algo. ‖ **to get/have the wind up (about sth.),** arrugarse por algo, encogérsele a uno el ombligo por algo. ‖ **to put the wind up sb.,** espantar a algn., asustar a algn. ‖ **to run/sail before the wind,** navegar viento en popa. ‖ **to take the wind out of sb.'s sails,** bajarle los humos a algn. ‖ **to throw caution to the wind,** liarse la manta a la cabeza. ‖ **to the four winds,** a los cuatro vientos. ‖ **winds of change,** aires de cambio.
■ **wind gauge,** anemómetro. ‖ **wind instrument,** instrumento de viento. ‖ **wind power,** energía eólica. ‖ **wind tunnel,** túnel *m* aerodinámico.

wind² [waɪnd] **1** *t* (*handle*) dar vueltas a, girar. **2** (*on reel*) arrollar, devanar. **3** (*tape, film*) bobinar: *wind it back,* rebobínalo; *wind it on/forward,* avánzalo; *he wound the fishing line in,* cobró el sedal; *she wound the car window up/down,* subió/bajó la ventanilla, cerró/abrió la ventanilla. **4** (*clock*) dar cuerda a (**up, -**). **5** (*bandage, scarf*) envolver; (*wool*) ovillar. – **6** *i* (*road, river*) serpentear, zigzaguear; (*staircase*) formar un espiral: *the road wound up the hill,* la carretera ascendía la colina serpenteando; *the river winds through a fertile valey,* el río serpentea por un fértil valle. – **7** *n* (*bend*) curva, recodo, vuelta.
◆ **to wind down** **1** *i* (*clock*) quedarse sin cuerda. **2** (*person*) relajarse. ‖ **to wind up 1** *t sep* (*business, company*) concluir, cerrar; (*meeting, speech*) clausurar, terminar, acabar. **2** (*annoy*) fastidiar; (*kid*) tomar el pelo, quedarse con: *are you winding me up?,* ¿te estás quedando conmigo? – **3** *i fam* acabar: *we wound up in Paris,* fuimos a parar a París, acabamos en París; *you'll wind up in jail,* darás con tus huesos en la cárcel.
● **to wind one's way,** serpentear.
▲ *pt & pp* **wound.**

windbag ['wɪndbæg] *n* charlatán,-ana.

windbreak ['wɪndbreɪk] *n* protección *f* contra el viento.

windcheater ['wɪndtʃiːtəʳ] *n* cazadora.

winder ['waɪndəʳ] *n* (*of watch*) corona de reloj, ruedecilla.

windfall ['wɪndfɔːl] **1** *n* (*fruit*) fruta caída. **2** *fig* suerte *f* inesperada, ganancia inesperada o caída del cielo.

winding ['waɪndɪŋ] *adj* (*road, river*) sinuoso,-a, tortuoso,-a; (*staircase*) de caracol, espiral.
■ **winding sheet,** mortaja, sudario.

windlass ['wɪndləs] *n* torno.

windmill ['wɪndmɪl] *n* molino de viento.

window ['wɪndəʊ] **1** *n* (*gen*) ventana: *open the window,* abre la ventana; *he was looking out (of) the window,* miraba por la ventana. **2** (*in vehicle, bank, theatre, etc*) ventanilla. **3** (*of shop*) escaparate *m*: *how much is that dress*

in the window?, ¿cuánto cuesta ese vestido del escaparate? **4** (*glass*) cristal *m*: *the ball broke the window*, el balón rompió el cristal; *the windows need cleaning*, hay que limpiar los cristales. **5** COMPUT ventana.
■ **window box**, jardinera. ‖ **window cleaner**, limpiacristales *mf inv*. ‖ **window envelope**, sobre *m* con ventanilla. ‖ **window seat**, asiento junto a la ventanilla. ‖ **window shade**, US persiana.
window-dresser ['wɪndəʊdresəʳ] *n* escaparatista *mf*.
window-dressing ['wɪndəʊdresɪŋ] **1** *n* decoración *f* de escaparates, escaparatismo. **2** *fig* fachada, apariencias *fpl*.
windowpane ['wɪndəʊpeɪn] *n* cristal *m*.
window-shop ['wɪndəʊʃɒp] *i* mirar escaparates.
▲ *pt & pp* window-shopped, *ger* window-shopping.
window-shopping ['wɪndəʊʃɒpɪŋ] **to go window-shopping**, *phr* ir a mirar escaparates.
windowsill ['wɪndəʊsɪl] *n* alféizar *m*.
windpipe ['wɪndpaɪp] *n* tráquea.
windscreen ['wɪndskriːn] *n* AUTO parabrisas *m inv*.
■ **windscreen wiper**, limpiaparabrisas *m inv*.
windshield ['wɪndʃiːld] *n* US → **windscreen**.
windsock ['wɪndsɒk] *n* manga.
windsurf ['wɪndsɜːf] *i* hacer windsurfing.
windsurfer ['wɪndsɜːfəʳ] *n* windsurfista *mf*.
windsurfing ['wɪndsɜːfɪŋ] *n* windsurfing *m*.
windswept ['wɪndswept] *adj* (*place*) azotado,-a por el viento; (*person, hair*) despeinado,-a (por el viento).
wind-up ['waɪndʌp] *n* tomadura de pelo, burla.
windward ['wɪndwəd] **1** *adj* de barlovento. **– 2** *adv* por barlovento. **– 3** *n* barlovento.
● **to windward**, a barlovento.
windy ['wɪndɪ] **1** *adj* (*day, weather*) ventoso,-a; (*place*) expuesto,-a al viento: *it's windy*, hace viento, hace aire. **2** (*speech*) rimbombante.
▲ *comp* windier, *superl* windiest.
wine [waɪn] **1** *n* vino: *red/rosé/white wine*, vino tinto/rosado/blanco. **2** (*colour*) (color *m*) morado, granate *m*.
● **to wine and dine sb.**, dar agasajo a algn., agasajar a algn., tratar a algn. por todo lo alto.
■ **wine bar**, bar *m* cuya especialidad es el vino. ‖ **wine cellar**, bodega. ‖ **wine cooler**, heladera (para el vino). ‖ **wine grower**, vinicultor,-ra. ‖ **wine list**, lista de vinos. ‖ **wine merchant**, vinatero,-a. ‖ **wine producer**, vinicultor,-ra. ‖ **wine taster**, catavinos *mf*. ‖ **wine tasting**, cata de vinos.
wineglass ['waɪnɡlɑːs] *n* copa (para vino).
winemaking ['waɪnmeɪkɪŋ] *n* vinicultura, elaboración *f* de vino.
wine-producing ['waɪnprədjuːsɪŋ] *adj* vinícola, vitícola.
wing [wɪŋ] **1** *n* (*gen*) ala. **2** AUTO aleta. **3** SP (*side*) banda; (*player*) extremo,-a. **– 4** *i* volar. **– 5 wings**, *npl* THEAT bastidores *mpl*.
● **on the wing**, volando. ‖ **to take sb. under one's wings**, tomar a algn. bajo su protección. ‖ **to take wing**, alzar el vuelo. ‖ **to wait in the wings**, esperar la entrada en escena. ‖ **to wing one's way**, ir volando.
■ **wing chair**, sillón *m* con orejas, orejero. ‖ **wing commander**, teniente *m* coronel. ‖ **wing mirror**, (espejo) retrovisor *m* exterior. ‖ **wing nut**, tuerca mariposa. ‖ **wing tip**, punta del ala.
winged ['wɪŋd] *adj* alado,-a, con alas.
winger ['wɪŋəʳ] *n* SP extremo,-a.
wingspan ['wɪŋspæn] *n* envergadura.
wink [wɪŋk] **1** *n* guiño. **– 2** *i* (*person*) guiñar el ojo: *he winked at me*, me guiñó el ojo. **3** (*of light, star*) titilar, parpadear.

◆ **to wink at** *t insep* (*pretend not to notice*) hacer la vista gorda.
● **not to get/have a wink of sleep / not to sleep a wink**, no pegar ojo, pasar la noche en blanco. ‖ **to have/take forty winks**, echar una siestecita, echar una cabezada. ‖ **to tip sb. the wink**, darle el soplo a algn.
winker ['wɪŋkəʳ] *n* GB AUTO intermitente *m*.
winkle ['wɪŋkəl] *n* bígaro, bigarro.
winner ['wɪnəʳ] **1** *n* ganador,-ra, vencedor,-ra. **2** *fam* (*idea etc*) éxito.
● **to be onto a winner**, tener un éxito seguro.
winning ['wɪnɪŋ] **1** *adj* (*person, team, etc*) ganador,-ra. **2** (*ticket, number, etc*) premiado,-a. **3** (*stroke, goal*) decisivo,-a. **4** (*smile, ways*) atractivo,-a, encantador,-ra. **– 5 winnings**, *npl* ganancias *fpl*.
■ **winning post**, meta.
winnow ['wɪnəʊ] *t* aventar.
wino ['waɪnəʊ] *n* *fam* borracho,-a.
▲ *pl* winos.
winsome ['wɪnsəm] *adj fml* atractivo,-a, encantador,-ra.
winter ['wɪntəʳ] **1** *n* invierno. **– 2** *i fml* invernar, pasar el invierno.
● **in the depths of winter**, en pleno invierno.
■ **winter solstice**, solsticio de invierno. ‖ **winter sports**, deportes *mpl* de invierno.
wintertime ['wɪntətaɪm] *n* invierno.
wintry ['wɪntrɪ] **1** *adj* invernal, de invierno. **2** *fig* frío,-a, antipático,-a.
▲ *comp* wintrier, *superl* wintriest.
wipe [waɪp] **1** *t* (*clean*) limpiar; (*dry*) enjugar: *wipe your feet*, límpiate los pies; *wipe the table*, limpia la mesa; *wipe the dishes*, enjuga los platos; *wipe your eyes*, enjúgate los ojos; *wipe your nose*, límpiate las narices; *wipe away her tears*, enjúgale las lágrimas; *wipe that off the blackboard*, borra eso de la pizarra; *wipe the milk (up) off the floor*, limpia la leche del suelo; *he wiped the recording off the tape*, borró la grabación de la cinta. **– 2** *i* (*dishes*) enjugar: *shall I wash or wipe?*, ¿lavo o enjugo? **– 3** *n* (*clean*) lavado, fregado: *just give the table a quick wipe*, pasa un trapo por la mesa. **4** (*cloth*) paño, trapo.
◆ **to wipe out** *t sep* (*destroy - army*) aniquilar; (*- population, species*) exterminar. **2** (*clean inside*) limpiar el interior de. **3** (*cancel - debts*) saldar, liquidar, cancelar; (*- profit*) borrar, anular.
● **to wipe the floor with sb.**, darle una paliza a algn. ‖ **to wipe sth. off the face of the earth**, borrar algo de la faz de la tierra. ‖ **to wipe the slate clean**, hacer borrón y cuenta nueva. ‖ **to wipe the smile off sb.'s face**, quitarle a algn. la sonrisa.
wiper ['waɪpəʳ] *n* AUTO limpiaparabrisas *m inv*.
wire ['waɪəʳ] **1** *n* (*metal*) alambre *m*. **2** ELEC cable *m*, hilo. **3** (*fence*) alambrada, valla. **4** US telegrama *m*. **– 5** *t* (*fasten, join*) atar con alambre. **6** (*house*) hacer la instalación eléctrica de; (*equipment, appliance*) conectar (a la toma eléctrica). **7** US (*telegram*) enviar un telegrama a; (*money*) mandar un giro telegráfico a.
● **to get one's wires crossed**, tener los cables cruzados.
■ **wire brush**, cepillo metálico. ‖ **wire cutters**, cortaalambres *m inv*, cizalla. ‖ **wire netting**, red *f* de alambre, tela metálica. ‖ **wire wool**, estropajo metálico.
wired ['waɪəd] *adj* conectado,-a.
wireless ['waɪələs] **1** *n* (*set*) radio *f*. **2** (*system*) radiofonía.
■ **wireless operator**, radiotelegrafista *mf*.

wiretapping ['waɪətæpɪŋ] *n* intervención *f* de teléfonos.

wiring ['waɪrɪŋ] *n* cableado.

wiry ['waɪərɪ] *adj* (*person*) nervudo,-a; (*hair*) estropajoso,-a.

▲ *comp* **wirier**, *superl* **wiriest**.

wisdom ['wɪzdəm] **1** *n* (*knowledge*) sabiduría, saber *m*. **2** (*good sense - of person*) cordura, (buen) juicio, tino; (*- of action*) prudencia, sabiduría, sensatez *f*.
■ **wisdom tooth**, muela del juicio.

wise[1] [waɪz] **1** *adj* (*learned, knowledgeable*) sabio,-a. **2** (*sensible, prudent - person*) prudente, sensato,-a; (*- action, remark*) prudente; (*- advice*) sabio,-a; (*- decision, choice, move*) atinado,-a, acertado,-a: *you were wise to sell it*, estuviste acertado al venderlo; *it would be wise to wait*, sería prudente esperar.
◆ **to wise up** *i* (*realize, become aware*) darse cuenta; (*become informed*) enterarse; (*wake up*) espabilarse.
● **as wise as an owl**, tan sabio,-a como Salomón. ‖ **to be wise after the event**, hablar a toro pasado. ‖ **to be/get wise to sb.**, calar a algn. ‖ **to be none the wiser**, (*not understand*) seguir sin entender; (*not realize*) no darse cuenta, no enterarse. ‖ **to put sb. wise to sth.**, poner a algn. al tanto de algo.
■ **the Three Wise Men**, los Reyes Magos. ‖ **wise guy**, sabelotodo.

wise[2] [waɪz] *n arch* manera, modo, guisa: *any wise*, de cualquier manera; *in no wise*, de ningún modo; *in this wise*, de esta guisa.

wisecrack ['waɪzkræk] **1** *n fam* ocurrencia, salida, chiste *m*. **- 2** *i* chancear, bromear.

wish [wɪʃ] **1** *t* (*want*) querer, desear: *she wishes she were on holiday*, quisiera estar de vacaciones; *I wish I was rich!*, ¡ojalá fuera rico!; *I wish I hadn't drunk so much*, ojalá no hubiese bebido tanto; *I wish it would stop raining*, ojalá dejara de llover. **2** *fml* (*demand, want*) querer: *I wish to make a complaint*, quisiera formular una queja. **3** (*hope*) desear: *we wish you a Merry Christmas*, te deseamos una Feliz Navidad; *they wished us luck*, nos desearon buena suerte. **- 4** *i* desear (*for*, -): *everything one could wish for*, todo lo que uno pudiera desear. **5** *fml* (*want*) querer: *as you wish*, como quiera. **- 6** *n* deseo: *you have three wishes*, tienes tres deseos; *you went against my wishes*, obraste contra mis deseos; *her wish came true*, su deseo se hizo realidad. **- 7 wishes**, *npl* (*greeting*) deseos *mpl*; (*in letter*) saludos *mpl*, recuerdos *mpl*: *with best wishes for the future*, con mis mejores deseos para el futuro; *with best wishes from ...*, saludos cordiales de ..., recuerdos de ...
◆ **to wish on** *t sep*: *I wouldn't wish that on anyone*, eso no se lo desearía a nadie.
● **to make a wish**, pedir un deseo. ‖ **to wish sb. well / wish sb. all the best**, desear buena suerte a algn. ‖ *wish you were here*, ojalá estuvieras aquí. ‖ *your wish is my command*, sus deseos son órdenes para mí.

wishbone ['wɪʃbəʊn] *n* espoleta.

wishful ['wɪʃful] *adj fml* de ensueño.
● **(to be) wishful thinking**, (hacerse) ilusiones *fpl*.

wishy-washy ['wɪʃɪwɒʃɪ] **1** *adj fam* (*person*) soso,-a, insípido,-a, sin carácter; (*idea*) borroso,-a. **2** (*of drink*) acuoso,-a, aguado,-a, flojo,-a.

wisp [wɪsp] **1** *n* (*of grass, straw, etc*) brizna; (*of hair, wool, etc*) mechón *m*; (*of smoke, cloud*) voluta. **2** (*person*) persona menuda.

wispy ['wɪspɪ] **1** *adj* (*delicate, slight*) tenue, delgado,-a. **2** (*straggly*) desordenado,-a.

▲ *comp* **wispier**, *superl* **wispiest**.

wistful ['wɪstful] *adj* pensativo,-a, nostálgico,-a, melancólico,-a.

wit [wɪt] **1** *n* (*clever humour*) agudeza, ingenio, chispa, sal *f*, gracia. **2** (*intelligence*) inteligencia, presencia de ánimo. **3** (*person*) persona salada, chistoso,-a.
● **to be at one's wit's end**, estar para volverse loco,-a. ‖ **to gather one's wits**, calmarse, tranquilizarse. ‖ **to have one's wits about one**, ser despabilado,-a. ‖ **to keep one's wits about one**, estar despabilado,-a. ‖ **to wit**, es decir.

witch [wɪtʃ] *n* bruja.
■ **witch doctor**, hechicero. ‖ **witch hazel**, (*tree*) hamamélide *f* de Virginia; (*liquid*) solución *f* de hamamélide de Virginia.

witchcraft ['wɪtʃkrɑːft] *n* brujería.

witch-hunt ['wɪtʃhʌnt] *n* caza de brujas.

with [wɪð, wɪθ] **1** *prep* (*accompanying*) con: *come with me*, ven conmigo; *do you live with your parents?*, ¿vives con tus padres?; *she went off with a friend*, se fue con una amiga; *mix the flour with the sugar*, mezclar la harina con el azúcar; *I've got an appointment with the bank manager*, tengo una cita con el director del banco; *they leave their child with a babysitter*, dejan al niño al cuidado de una canguro; *have you brought your swimsuit with you?*, ¿te has traído el bañador? **2** (*having, possessing*) con, de; (*including, and also*) con, incluido: *the man with the beard*, el hombre de la barba; *the woman with glasses*, la mujer de las gafas; *a room with a view*, una habitación con vistas; *a flat with a terrace*, un piso con terraza; *someone with experience*, alguien con experiencia; *he speaks with an accent*, habla con acento; *with wine it cost 3,000 pesetas*, costó 3.000 pesetas vino incluido. **3** (*using, by means of*) con: *cut it with a knife*, córtalo con un cuchillo; *he cleaned it with turps*, lo limpió con aguarrás. **4** (*cover, fill, contain*) de: *you fill it with water*, lo llenas de agua; *the furniture was covered with dust*, los muebles estaban cubiertos de polvo. **5** (*agreeing, in support of*) con: *we're with you all the way!*, ¡estamos contigo hasta el final!; *I agree with Lesley*, estoy de acuerdo con Lesley. **6** (*against*) con: *I've had a row with Daniel*, he discutido con Daniel; *at war with the Serbs*, en guerra con los serbios; *don't argue with your mother!*, ¡no discutas con tu madre! **7** (*because of, on account of*) con: *trembling with fear*, temblando de miedo; *blue with cold*, amoratado de frío; *he split his sides with laughter*, se tronchó de risa; *with things as they are*, tal como están las cosas; *with my luck I'll come last*, con la suerte que tengo llegaré el último. **8** (*indicating manner*) con: *with pleasure*, con mucho gusto; *with ease*, con facilidad; *with a smile*, con una sonrisa. **9** (*in same direction as*) con: *with the flow*, con la corriente. **10** (*at the same time and rate as*) con: *wine improves with age*, el vino mejora con los años. **11** (*regarding, concerning*) con: *this has nothing to do with you*, esto no tiene nada que ver contigo; *the trouble with Ian is that ...*, lo que pasa con Ian es que ...; *he's in love with Ellen*, está enamorado de Ellen; *be patient with her*, sea paciente con ella; *is there something wrong with her?*, ¿le pasa algo? **12** (*in the case of, as regards*) con respecto a, en cuanto a: *with Mrs Smith what happened was that ...*, en el caso de la Señora Smith lo que pasó fue que ... **13** (*as an employee or client of*) en: *she's with the council now*, trabaja en el ayuntamiento ahora; *he's been with the company for fifteen years*, lleva quince años trabajando en esta empresa; *who do you bank with?*, ¿en qué banco tienes una cuenta? **14** (*remaining*): *with only half an hour to go*,

cuando tan sólo falta media hora; *with five laps remaining,* cuando sólo faltan cinco vueltas para el final de la carrera. **15** (*despite, in spite of*) con: *with all his faults,* con todos sus defectos. **16** (*in comparisons*) con: *if we compare this brand with a cheaper one,* si comparamos esta marca con una más barata. **17** (*illness*) con: *he's in bed with flu,* está en cama con la gripe. **18** (*according to*) según, de acuerdo con: *prices vary with the seasons,* los precios varían según la temporada.
● **down with capitalism!,** ¡abajo el capitalismo! ‖ **on with the show!,** ¡que siga el espectáculo! ‖ **to be with sb.,** (*accompany*) estar con algn., acompañar a algn.; (*understand*) seguir a algn., entender a algn. ‖ **with it,** (*fashionable*) de moda; (*alert*) al tanto, al día. ‖ **with that,** con lo cual.

withdraw [wɪð'drɔ:] **1** *t* (*take out*) retirar: *the government is going to withdraw the troops from Northern Ireland,* el gobierno retirará las tropas de Irlanda del Norte; *the miners threatened to withdraw their labour,* los mineros amenazaron con hacer huelga; *she withdrew $100 from the bank,* sacó $100 del banco; *this drug must be withdrawn from the market,* hay que retirar esta droga del mercado. **2** *fml* (*retract, take back - statement*) retractarse de, retirar; (*- offer*) renunciar a; (*- charge, support*) retirar. – **3** *i* (*retire, not take part in*) retirarse: *he withdrew to his room,* se retiró a su habitación; *she withdrew from the race,* se retiró de la carrera.
● **to withdraw into oneself,** retraerse.
▲ *pt* **withdrew,** *pp* **withdrawn.**

withdrawal [wɪð'drɔ:əl] **1** *n* (*gen*) retirada: *a withdrawal of troops,* una retirada de tropas. **2** (*of words*) retractación *f.* **3** (*psychology, behaviour*) retraimiento.
■ **withdrawal symptoms,** síndrome *m* de abstinencia.

withdrawn [wɪð'drɔ:n] **1** *pp* → **withdraw.** – **2** *adj* introvertido,-a, retraído,-a.

withdrew [wɪð'dru:] *pt* → **withdraw.**

wither ['wɪðəʳ] **1** *t* (*plant*) marchitar, secar. **2** (*crush*) fulminar, aplastar, intimidar: *he withered her with a look,* la fulminó con una mirada. – **3** *i* (*plant*) marchitarse (**away,** -), secarse (**away,** -). **4** *fig* (*hopes etc*) desvanecerse, menguar.

withered ['wɪðəd] **1** *adj* (*plant*) marchito,-a, seco,-a. **2** (*skin*) ajado,-a; (*limb*) deformado,-a.

withering ['wɪðərɪŋ] **1** *adj* (*look*) fulminante. **2** (*remark*) mordaz.

withhold [wɪð'həʊld] **1** *t* (*money*) retener; (*information*) ocultar; (*consent, permission*) negar. **2** (*laughter etc*) contener.
▲ *pt & pp* **withheld.**

within [wɪ'ðɪn] **1** *prep fml* (*inside*) dentro de: *within the area shown,* dentro de la zona indicada; *within these walls,* entre estas paredes; *within the party,* en el seno del partido; *within it,* en su interior. **2** (*inside range or limits of*) al alcance de: *within hearing/earshot,* al alcance del oído; *within arm's reach,* al alcance de la mano; *within a 10-mile radius,* en un radio de diez millas; *within the law,* dentro de (los límites de) la ley; *within their one's means/income,* dentro de sus posibilidades/de acuerdo a sus ingresos. **3** (*less than - distance*) a menos de: *within 2 miles of the beach,* a menos de dos millas de la playa; *he got within 3 kilometres of the finishing line,* le faltaban sólo tres kilómetros para llegar a la meta. **4** (*less than - time*) dentro de: *he'll be back within the hour,* volverá dentro de una hora; *he got within seconds of the world record,* se quedó a segundos del récord mundial; *they arrived within a few minutes of each other,* lle-

garon con pocos minutos de diferencia; *within a year of getting married,* menos de un año después de casarse. – **5** *adv fml* dentro, en el interior: *from within,* desde dentro.
● "**apply within**", "razón aquí". ‖ "**enquire within**", "razón aquí". ‖ **within inches of sth.,** a un paso de algo.

with-it ['wɪðɪt] *adj* de moda, a la última moda.

without [wɪ'ðaʊt] **1** *prep* sin: *two nights without sleep,* dos noches sin dormir; *I couldn't have done it without you,* no podría haberlo hecho sin ti; *don't go without saying goodbye,* no te vayas sin decirme adiós; *he left without paying,* se fue sin pagar; *she can't read without glasses,* no puede leer sin gafas. **2** *arch* fuera de: *without the city walls,* extramuros. – **3** *adv* fuera: *from without,* desde fuera. **4** sin: *we'll manage without,* ya nos las apañaremos.
● **to do without / go without,** (*voluntarily*) prescindir de; (*forcibly*) pasarse sin, arreglárselas sin. ‖ **without doubt,** sin duda. ‖ **without so much as +** *ger,* sin siquiera + *inf.*

withstand [wɪð'stænd] *t* (*gen*) resistir; (*pain*) aguantar, soportar.
● **to withstand the test of time,** resistir el paso del tiempo.
▲ *pt & pp* **withstood.**

withstood [wɪð'stʊd] *pt & pp* → **withstand.**

witness ['wɪtnəs] **1** *n* (*person*) testigo *mf: a witness of the accident,* un testigo (presencial) del accidente; *a witness to the will,* un testigo del testamento; *a witness for the defence/prosecution,* un testigo de descargo/cargo. **2** *fml* (*testimony, evidence*) testimonio. – **3** *t* (*see*) presenciar, ver: *he witnessed a murder,* presenció un asesinato; *the attack was witnessed by four people,* cuatro personas presenciaron el ataque; *we are witnessing the end of apartheid,* presenciamos el fin del apartheid. **4** (*document*) firmar como testigo: *I had to witness a contract,* tuve que firmar un contrato como testigo. **5** (*be a sign or proof of*) testimoniar: (*look at the example of*) ver, notar, considerar: *witness the number of recent accidents,* nótese el número de accidentes recientes. – **6** *i* ɪᴜʀ *fml* (*give evidence, testify*) atestiguar (**to,** -), declarar (**to,** -).
● **to be witness to sth.,** ver algo, presenciar algo. ‖ **to bear witness to sth.,** dar fe de algo, atestiguar algo. ‖ **to call sb. as a witness,** citar a algn. como testigo, poner a algn. por testigo.
■ **witness box,** barra de los testigos. ‖ **witness stand,** ᴜs barra de los testigos.

witter ['wɪtəʳ] *i fam* parlotear (**on,** -): *what are you wittering on about?,* ¿de qué estás hablando?

witticism ['wɪtɪsɪzəm] *n* agudeza, ocurrencia, salida.

wittily ['wɪtɪlɪ] *adv* ingeniosamente, con gracia.

wittiness ['wɪtɪnəs] *n* ingenio, agudeza.

wittingly ['wɪtɪŋlɪ] *adv* a sabiendas.

witty ['wɪtɪ] *adj* (*person*) ingenioso,-a, agudo,-a, salado,-a; (*remark*) agudo,-a; (*speech*) gracioso,-a.
▲ *comp* **wittier,** *superl* **wittiest.**

wives [waɪvz] *npl* → **wife.**

wizard ['wɪzəd] **1** *n* (*male witch*) brujo, hechicero. **2** (*genius*) lince *mf,* genio, experto,-a.

wizardry ['wɪzədrɪ] **1** *n* (*magic*) hechicería, magia. **2** (*extraordinary ability*) genio.

wizened ['wɪzənd] *adj* (*skin, face*) arrugado,-a; (*fruit*) seco,-a.

wk [wi:k] *abbr* (*week*) semana; (*abbreviation*) sem.

wobble ['wɒbəl] 1 n (table, chair, ladder) tambaleo, bamboleo; (bicycle) movimiento; (voice, jelly) temblor m. – 2 i (table, chair, ladder) cojear; (bicycle, tooth) moverse; (legs, jelly, voice) temblar; (wheel) bailar; (person) tambalearse, bambolearse, vacilar. – 3 t (table, ladder) mover.

wobbly ['wɒbəlɪ] 1 adj (table, chair, ladder) cojo,-a; (bicycle, tooth) que se mueve; (writing) de trazo poco firme; (voice) tembloroso,-a: *my legs feel all wobbly,* me tiemblan las piernas. 2 (person) débil. – 3 n ataque m, pataleta.
● **to throw a wobbly,** darle a uno un ataque, darle a uno una pataleta.
▲ (adjetivo) comp **wobblier,** superl **wobbliest;** (sustantivo) pl **wobblies.**

woe [wəʊ] 1 n fml dated (sorrow) infortunio, aflicción f, congoja. – 2 **woes,** npl males mpl, penas fpl, desgracias fpl.
● **woe betide sb.,** ay de algn.: *woe betide you if you're late!,* ¡ay de ti si llegas tarde! ‖ **woe is me!,** ¡pobre de mí!

woebegone ['wəʊbɪgɒn] adj fml desconsolado,-a, afligido,-a, angustiado,-a, cariacontecido,-a.

woeful ['wəʊfʊl] 1 adj fml (very sad) afligido,-a, apenado,-a, triste. 2 (deplorable) lamentable, deplorable, penoso,-a, malísimo,-a.

wok [wɒk] n wok m, sartén f china.

woke [wəʊk] pt → **wake.**

woken ['wəʊkən] pp → **wake.**

wolf [wʊlf] 1 n lobo. – 2 **to wolf (down),** t tragarse, zamparse, devorar.
● **a lone wolf,** un lobo solitario. ‖ **a wolf in sheep's clothing,** un lobo con piel de cordero. ‖ **to cry wolf,** gritar "¡al lobo!", dar una falsa alarma. ‖ **to keep the wolf from the door,** no pasar hambre. ‖ **to throw sb. to the wolves,** arrojar a algn. a los lobos.
■ **wolf cub,** lobato, lobezno. ‖ **wolf whistle,** silbido de admiración.
▲ pl **wolves.**

wolfhound ['wʊlfhaʊnd] n perro lobo.

wolfish ['wʊlfɪʃ] adj lobuno,-a.

wolf-whistle ['wʊlfwɪsəl] i silbar de admiración.

woman ['wʊmən] 1 n mujer f, señora: *old woman,* vieja, anciana; *young woman,* joven f. – 2 adj: *woman doctor,* doctora; *woman friend,* amiga; *woman driver,* conductora.
■ **Women's Liberation/Lib,** liberación de la mujer. ‖ **Women's Libber,** defensora de los derechos de la mujer. ‖ **Women's Movement,** movimiento de la liberación de la mujer. ‖ **women's refuge,** centro de acogida para mujeres.
▲ pl **women** ['wɪmɪn].

womanhood ['wʊmənhʊd] n condición f de mujer.
● **to reach womanhood,** hacerse mujer.

womanize ['wʊmənaɪz] i ser un mujeriego.

womanizer ['wʊmənaɪzə'] n mujeriego.

womankind ['wʊmənkaɪnd] n las mujeres fpl.

womanly ['wʊmənlɪ] adj femenino,-a.

womb [wuːm] n útero, matriz f.

wombat ['wɒmbæt] n wombat m.

won [wʌn] pt & pp → **win.**

wonder ['wʌndə'] 1 n (thing) maravilla, milagro: *the seven wonders of the world,* las siete maravillas del mundo; *the wonders of science,* las maravillas de la ciencia. 2 (feeling) admiración f, asombro: *they were filled with wonder,* se quedaron asombrados; *they gazed at the baby in wonder,* contemplaban el bebé maravillados. – 3 adj milagroso,-a: *wonder drug,* remedio milagroso,

panacea. – 4 t fml (be surprised) sorprenderse, extrañarse: *I don't wonder that she left him,* no me extraña que lo haya dejado; *I wonder that he wasn't killed,* fue un milagro que no se matara. 5 (ask oneself) preguntarse: *I wonder what she'll be like,* me pregunto cómo será, tengo curiosidad por saber cómo será; *we were wondering where you'd got to,* nos preguntábamos dónde te habías metido; *I wonder why he did that,* me pregunto por qué lo habrá hecho; *I bet you're wondering who I am,* te estarás preguntando quién soy. 6 (polite request): *I wonder if you can help me,* a ver si puede ayudarme; *I was wondering if you'd care to dance,* estaba pensando si le gustaría bailar. – 7 i (reflect, ponder) pensar (**about,** en); (doubt) tener dudas: *it makes you wonder,* da en qué pensar; *I just wondered,* por curiosidad, por nada; *she couldn't help wondering about what he'd said,* no pudo evitar pensar en lo que le había dicho; *now I'm beginning to wonder,* ahora tengo mis dudas. 8 fml (marvel) asombrarse, maravillarse, admirarse: *we wondered at his brilliance,* nos admiramos de su brillantez; *that's not to be wondered at,* eso no tiene nada de extraño.
● **I shouldn't wonder if** + **indic,** no me extrañaría que + subj. ‖ **it's a wonder (that)** + **indic,** es un milagro que + subj. ‖ **no/little/small wonder (that)** + **indic,** no es de extrañar que + subj. ‖ **to do/work wonders,** hacer milagros. ‖ **wonders will never cease,** ¡qué sorpresa tan grande!
■ **nine days' wonder,** prodigio efímero.

wonderful ['wʌndəfʊl] adj maravilloso,-a, estupendo,-a.
● **to have a wonderful time,** pasarlo de maravilla, pasarlo en grande.

wonderfully ['wʌndəfəlɪ] adv maravillosamente, de maravilla.

wonderland ['wʌndəlænd] n mundo maravilloso.
● **Alice in Wonderland,** Alicia en el País de las Maravillas.

wonderment ['wʌndəmənt] n admiración f, asombro.

wondrous ['wʌndrəs] adj fml maravilloso,-a.

wonky ['wɒŋkɪ] adj (wobbly) poco firme, cojo,-a, tambaleante; (crooked) torcido,-a.
▲ comp **wonkier,** superl **wonkiest.**

wont [wəʊnt] n costumbre f, hábito.
● **as is one's wont,** como es su costumbre. ‖ **to be wont to,** tener la costumbre de, soler.

won't [wəʊnt] contr will not.

woo [wuː] 1 t dated (court) cortejar. 2 (voters) solicitar el apoyo de; (fame, fortune, etc) intentar conseguir.
▲ pt & pp **wooed,** ger **wooing.**

wood [wʊd] 1 n (material) madera. 2 (for fire) leña. 3 (forest) bosque m. 4 SP (golf) palo de madera; (bowling) bola. – 5 **woods,** npl bosque m sing.
● **from the wood,** de barril. ‖ **out of the wood,** estar a salvo. ‖ **you can't see the wood for the trees,** los árboles no dejan ver el bosque. ‖ **touch wood!,** ¡toca madera!
■ **wood pigeon,** paloma torcaz. ‖ **wood pulp,** pulpa de madera. ‖ **wood shavings,** virutas fpl.

woodcarver ['wʊdkɑːvə'] n tallista mf.

woodcarving ['wʊdkɑːvɪŋ] 1 n (craft) tallado en madera. 2 (object) talla en madera.

woodcut ['wʊdkʌt] n grabado en madera.

woodcutter ['wʊdkʌtə'] n leñador,-ra.

wooded ['wʊdɪd] adj arbolado,-a, cubierto,-a de bosques.

wooden ['wʊdən] **1** adj de madera. **2** fig (expression, style) rígido,-a; (movement) tieso,-a; (acting) sin expresión.
● to win the wooden spoon, ser el colista.
■ wooden leg, pata de palo. ‖ wooden spoon, cuchara de palo.

woodland ['wʊdlənd] n bosque m, arbolado, monte m.

woodpecker ['wʊdpekəʳ] n pico, pájaro carpintero.

woodpile ['wʊdpaɪl] n montón m de madera.

woodshed ['wʊdʃed] n leñera.

woodwind ['wʊdwɪnd] **1** n instrumentos mpl de viento de madera. – **2** adj de viento de madera.

woodwork ['wʊdwɜːk] **1** n (craft) carpintería. **2** (of building) maderaje m, maderamen m.

woodworm ['wʊdwɜːm] n carcoma: it has woodworm, está carcomido,-a.

woody ['wʊdɪ] **1** adj (wooded) arbolado,-a. **2** (like wood) leñoso,-a.
▲ comp woodier, superl woodiest.

woof [wʊf] **1** interj (of dog) ¡guau! – **2** i ladrar.

wool [wʊl] **1** n lana: a ball of wool, un ovillo de lana; all/ pure wool, pura lana. – **2** adj (made of wool) de lana. **3** COMM lanero,-a.
● to pull the wool over sb.'s eyes, engañar a algn., dar gato por liebre a algn.

woolen ['wʊlən] adj-n US → **woollen**.

woollen ['wʊlən] **1** adj (made of wool) de lana. **2** COMM lanero,-a. – **3** woollens, npl géneros mpl de lana.

woolly ['wʊlɪ] **1** adj (made of wool) de lana, lanoso,-a, lanudo,-a. **2** (like wool) lanoso,-a, lanudo,-a. **3** fig (idea, argument) confuso,-a, vago,-a; (outline) borroso,-a; (sound) impreciso,-a; (person, mind) espeso,-a. – **4** n (clothing) prenda de lana.
▲ (adjetivo) comp woollier, superl woolliest; (sustantivo) pl woollies.

woolly-headed ['wʊlɪ'hedɪd] adj espeso,-a.
▲ Se escribe woolly headed cuando no se antepone a un sustantivo.

wooly ['wʊlɪ] adj → **woolly**.

woozy ['wuːzɪ] adj fam (dizzy, sick) mareado,-a; (confused, dazed) aturdido,-a, confuso,-a.
▲ comp woozier, superl wooziest.

word [wɜːd] **1** n (gen) palabra: tell me what happened in your own words, explícame con tus propias palabras lo que pasó; I can't find the words to describe it, no encuentro palabras para describirlo; he's a man of few words, es un hombre poco hablador; don't believe a word he says, no creas ni una palabra de lo que dice; he didn't say a word, no dijo ni pío, no dijo ni una palabra; don't breathe a word of this, no digas nada de esto, ni palabra de esto; it's your word against mine, es tu palabra contra la mía. **2** (message, news) noticia: there's been no word, no hay noticias; word came that ..., llegó noticia (de) que ...; he left no word of his new address, no dejó dicha su nueva dirección. **3** (promise) palabra: I give you my word, te doy mi palabra; he's a man of his word, es hombre de palabra. **4** (command) orden f: wait until I give the word, espera hasta que dé la orden; just say the word, no tienes más que pedirlo; his word is law, su palabra es ley. **5** LING palabra, vocablo, voz f. – **6** t expresar, formular, redactar: a well-worded letter, una carta bien redactada. – **7** the word, n (rumour) voz f, rumor m: the word is that Macy's out, corre la voz de que Macy ha salido. **8** the Word, REL el Verbo. – **9** words, npl (lyrics) letra f sing. **10** (discussion, talk) palabras fpl.
● from the word go, desde el principio. ‖ in a word,

en una palabra. ‖ in other words, o sea, es decir, en otras palabras. ‖ mark my words, fíjate en lo que te digo. ‖ not in so many words, no exactamente, no directamente, no con esas palabras. ‖ not to have a good word to say for sb./sth., no decir absolutamente nada en favor de algn./algo. ‖ to be as good as one's word, cumplir su palabra. ‖ to be the last word in sth., ser el último grito en algo. ‖ to break/go back on one's word, faltar a la palabra. ‖ to get a word in edgeways, meter baza. ‖ to have a word with sb., hablar con algn. ‖ to have sb.'s word for it that ..., tener la palabra de algn. que ...: you have my word, tienes mi palabra. ‖ to have the last word, decir la última palabra. ‖ to have words with sb., discutir con algn., tener unas palabras con algn. ‖ to keep one's word, cumplir su palabra. ‖ not to mince one's words, no tener pelos en la lengua. ‖ to put in/say a good word for sb., (intercede) interceder por algn.; (recommend) recomendar a algn. ‖ to put sth. into words, expresar algo con palabras. ‖ to put words in sb.'s mouth, poner palabras en boca de algn. ‖ to take sb. at their word, cogerle la palabra a algn./algo. ‖ to take sb.'s word for it, aceptar lo que algn. le dice, creer a algn., confiar en la palabra de algn.: take my word for it, te lo aseguro. ‖ to take the words out of sb.'s mouth, quitarle la palabra de la boca a algn. ‖ too ... for words, de lo más ... que hay, indescriptiblemente ...: it's too awful for words, es demasiado horrible para explicarlo; I'm too happy for words, no tengo palabras para explicar lo feliz que estoy. ‖ upon my word!, ¡caramba! ‖ without a word, sin decir palabra, sin chistar. ‖ word for word, palabra por palabra. ‖ words fail me, no sé qué decir, no tengo palabras.
■ a word of advice, un consejo. ‖ a word of warning, una advertencia. ‖ word of honour, palabra de honor. ‖ word processing, procesamiento de textos. ‖ word processor, procesador m de textos.

wording ['wɜːdɪŋ] n redacción f, expresión f, palabras fpl, términos mpl.

word-perfect [wɜːd'pɜːfekt] adj (correct in every detail) correcto,-a hasta la última palabra.
● to be word-perfect, (actor, speaker) saber su papel perfectamente; (role, speech) memorizado,-a a la perfección.

wordplay ['wɜːdpleɪ] n juegos mpl de palabras.

wordy ['wɜːdɪ] adj prolijo,-a, verboso,-a.
▲ comp wordier, superl wordiest.

wore [wɔːʳ] pt → **wear**.

work [wɜːk] **1** n (gen) trabajo: I've got a lot of work to do, tengo mucho trabajo que hacer; he put a lot of hard work into that project, trabajó mucho en ese proyecto, puso mucho esfuerzo en ese proyecto; they often take work home to do, muchas veces se llevan trabajo a casa. **2** (employment) empleo, trabajo: she's at work, está en el trabajo; what sort of work do you do?, ¿qué clase de trabajo haces?, ¿a qué te dedicas?; don't be late for work, no llegues tarde al trabajo; what time do you leave work?, ¿a qué hora sales del trabajo?; she's a friend from work, es una compañera de trabajo; I've got the day off work, tengo el día libre. **3** (building work, roadworks) obras fpl: work on the new road will commence in July, se comenzarán las obras de la nueva carretera en julio. **4** (product, results) trabajo, obra: it's all my own work, es obra de mi propia mano; they sell their own work in the market, venden sus trabajos en el mercado; this is an excellent piece of work, esto es un trabajo excelente; this is the work of vandals, esto es cosa de vándalos. **5** (*literary etc*) obra. – **6** *t* (*person*) hacer trabajar: *she works them too hard,* les hace trabajar demasiado. **7** (*machine*) manejar; (*mechanism*) accionar: *do you know how to work the video?,* ¿sabes cómo hacer funcionar el vídeo?; *it's worked by electricity,* funciona con electricidad. **8** (*mine, oil well*) explotar; (*land, fields*) trabajar, cultivar. **9** (*produce*) hacer: *it works miracles,* hace milagros. **10** (*wood, metal, clay*) trabajar; (*dough*) amasar. **11** (*make by work or effort*) trabajar: *he worked his way up in the company,* ascendió en la empresa por su trabajo; *she worked her way through university,* hizo la carrera trabajando; *I worked my way to the front,* me abrí camino hacia adelante. **12** *fam* (*arrange*) arreglar: *he worked it so that he got off with just a fine,* se las arregló para escapar sólo con una multa. **13** (*move gradually*): *he worked the key into the frozen lock,* metió poco a poco la llave en la cerradura helada; *work the fat into the flour,* vaya mezclando la mantequilla con la harina. – **14** *i* (*gen*) trabajar: *she works for an insurance company,* trabaja en una compañía de seguros; *he worked as a waiter,* trabajaba de camarero; *I'm working on a new book,* estoy trabajando en un nuevo libro; *she works hard at her homework,* trabaja mucho en sus deberes, pone mucho esfuerzo en sus deberes; *he's working for his exams,* está estudiando para los exámenes; *they were working away at the design,* estaban ocupados con el diseño. **15** (*machine, system*) funcionar: *the lift's not working,* el ascensor no funciona; *how does this machine work?,* ¿cómo funciona esta máquina? **16** (*medicine, cleaner*) surtir efecto, tener efecto; (*plan*) tener éxito, salir bien, funcionar, resultar: *your plan won't work,* tu plan no saldrá bien; *the special effects work well,* los efectos especiales resultan bien. **17** (*move*): *her dress had worked up,* su vestido se había subido; *they eventually worked round to my way of thinking,* finalmente coincidieron con mi parecer. – **18** works, *npl* (*factory*) fábrica *f sing.* **19** the works, (*parts*) mecanismo *m sing.* **20** *fam* (*everything*) todo, todo el tinglado.

◆ to work in *t sep* (*include*) introducir, incluir, insertar, meter: *I managed to work in a joke about the boss,* conseguí introducir un chiste sobre el jefe. ‖ to work off *t sep* (*anger*) desahogarse; (*debt, loan*) saldar trabajando; (*weight*) rebajar haciendo ejercicio. ‖ to work on **1** *t insep* (*gen*) trabajar en, preparar; (*case*) investigar; (*car etc*) reparar: *I'm working on it,* estoy en ello; *we're working on him,* lo estamos trabajando. **2** (*principle*) atenerse a, guiarse por; (*fact, idea, assumption, etc*) basarse en, partir de. ‖ to work out **1** *t sep* (*calculation, sum*) calcular, hacer. **2** (*plan, scheme*) planear, elaborar, pensar; (*itinerary*) planear; (*details, idea*) desarrollar. **3** (*problem*) solucionar, resolver; (*solution*) encontrar: *can you work out what this message means?,* ¿puedes descifrar este mensaje? **4** (*person*) calar, entender. – **5** *i* (*calculation*) salir (*at,* por), resultar: *it works out at 5,000 pesetas each,* sale por unas 5.000 pesetas cada uno. **6** (*turn out well - things*) salir bien; (*- problem*) resolverse. **7** sp hacer ejercicio. ‖ to work over *t sep* sacudir el polvo a, dar una paliza a. ‖ to work to *t insep* (*budget*) no pasarse de; (*deadline*) respetar, trabajar con miras a. ‖ to work up **1** *t sep* (*excite, rouse*) exaltar, acalorar; (*make nervous*) poner nervioso,-a, emocionar: *the preacher worked the crowd up into a frenzy,* el predicador exaltó al público; *she worked herself up into a right state,* se puso muy nerviosa. **2** (*develop*) hacer, desarrollar: *I've worked up a real appetite,* se me ha abierto el apetito; *they couldn't seem to work up much enthusiasm for the idea,* no se entusiasmaron con la idea. **3** (*increase*) aumentar, fomentar;

(*complete, improve*) desarrollar, elaborar. ‖ to work up to *t insep* (*prepare*) preparar el terreno para.

● it's all in a/the day's work, todo forma parte del trabajo, es el pan nuestro de cada día. ‖ all work and no play makes Jack a dull boy, hay que divertirse de vez en cuando. ‖ it works both ways, es una arma de doble filo. ‖ keep up the good work!, ¡que siga así! ‖ the forces at work, los elementos en juego. ‖ to be in work, tener trabajo, tener un empleo. ‖ to be out of work, estar en el paro, estar sin trabajo, estar parado,-a. ‖ to get down/set to work, ponerse a trabajar, poner manos a la obra. ‖ to get worked up, exaltarse, excitarse, ponerse nervioso,-a. ‖ to give sb. the (full) works, tratar a algn. a lo grande. ‖ to have one's work cut out to do sth., costarle a uno mucho trabajo hacer algo. ‖ to make light/short work of sth., despachar algo deprisa. ‖ to work like a Trojan, trabajar como un negro. ‖ to work loose, soltarse, aflojarse. ‖ to work one's fingers to the bone, dejarse los codos trabajando. ‖ to work os. to death, matarse trabajando. ‖ to work to rule, hacer huelga de celo.

■ public works, obras *fpl* públicas. ‖ road works, obras *fpl* (de carretera). ‖ work basket, costurero, cesto de labor. ‖ work camp, campamento de trabajo. ‖ work experience, experiencia laboral. ‖ work of art, obra de arte. ‖ work station, comput terminal *m* de trabajo. ‖ work surface, encimera.

workable ['wɜːkəbəl] **1** *adj* (*plan, scheme*) factible, viable. **2** (*mine, land*) explotable.

workaday ['wɜːkədeɪ] *adj* (*ordinary*) rutinario,-a; (*everyday*) de cada día.

workaholic [wɜːkə'hɒlɪk] *n fam* adicto,-a al trabajo.

workbench ['wɜːkbentʃ] *n* banco de trabajo.

workbook ['wɜːkbʊk] *n* cuaderno, libreta de ejercicios.

workday ['wɜːkdeɪ] *n* us día *m* laborable.

worker ['wɜːkəʳ] *n* (*gen*) trabajador,-ra; (*manual*) obrero,-a, operario,-a; (*office*) oficinista *mf*, administrativo,-a: *she's a hard worker,* trabaja mucho.

■ worker bee, abeja obrera.

workforce ['wɜːkfɔːs] *n* (*of company, factory, etc*) personal *m*, plantilla; (*of country*) población *f* activa.

work-in ['wɜːkɪn] *n* encierro (en la fábrica etc).

working ['wɜːkɪŋ] **1** *adj* (*clothes, conditions, surface*) de trabajo; (*week, day, life*) laborable: *an eight-hour working day,* una jornada laboral de ocho horas. **2** (*population, partner, etc*) activo,-a; (*person, mother*) que trabaja. – **3** *n* (*machine, model*) que funciona; (*part*) móvil. – **4** *adj* (*majority*) suficiente. **5** (*hypothesis etc*) de trabajo. – **6** *n* (*of machine*) funcionamiento; (*of pit*) explotación *f.* – **7** workings, *npl* (*of mine, quarry*) pozos *mpl.* **8** (*mechanics*) funcionamiento.

● to be in (full) working order, funcionar.

■ working capital, capital *m* activo. ‖ working class, clase *f* obrera, clase *f* trabajadora. ‖ working knowledge, conocimientos *mpl* básicos. ‖ working breakfast/lunch, desayuno/almuerzo/comida de negocios. ‖ working party, grupo de trabajo. ‖ working relationship, relación *f* laboral.

working-class [wɜːkɪŋ'klɑːs] *adj* (*person*) de clase obrera, de clase trabajadora; (*area*) obrero,-a.

workload ['wɜːkləʊd] *n* volumen *m* de trabajo.

workman ['wɜːkmən] *n* (*gen*) trabajador *m*; (*manual*) obrero, operario.

▲ *pl* workmen ['wɜːkmən].

workmanlike ['wɜːkmənlaɪk] *adj* (*person*) concienzudo,-a, hábil, eficiente; (*work*) bien hecho,-a.

workmanship ['wɜːkmənʃɪp] n habilidad f, arte m, destreza, trabajo: a fine piece of workmanship, un trabajo primoroso; shoddy workmanship, trabajo de mala calidad.

workmate ['wɜːkmeɪt] n compañero,-a de trabajo.

work-out ['wɜːkaʊt] n SP entrenamiento.

workplace ['wɜːkpleɪs] n lugar m de trabajo.

workroom ['wɜːkruːm] n taller m.

work-sharing ['wɜːkʃeərɪŋ] n repartición f de trabajo.

workshop ['wɜːkʃɒp] n taller m.

workshy ['wɜːkʃaɪ] adj gandul,-la, holgazán,-ana, vago,-a.

worktop ['wɜːktɒp] n encimera.

work-to-rule [wɜːktə'ruːl] n huelga de celo.

world [wɜːld] **1** n (earth) mundo: I'd love to travel round the world, me encantaría dar la vuelta al mundo; she's the richest woman in the world, es la mujer más rica del mundo; in a perfect world, en un mundo ideal; all over the world, en todo el mundo. **2** (sphere) mundo: the world of show business, el mundo del espectáculo; the animal world, el reino de los animales. **3** (life) mundo, vida: in this world, en esta vida; in the next world, en el otro mundo; she's brought six children into the world, ha traído seis niños al mundo. **4** (people) mundo: in the eyes of the world, a los ojos del mundo; what is the world coming to?, ¿a dónde iremos a parar? **5** (large amount, large number): this will make a world of difference to the disabled, esto cambiará totalmente la vida de los minusválidos; we're worlds apart, somos muy diferentes; a holiday will do you a world of good, unas vacaciones te sentarán de maravilla; he hasn't got a care in the world, no tiene ninguna preocupación. **– 6** adj (population, peace) mundial; (politics, trade) internacional: world record, récord mundial; world power, potencia mundial.

● not to do sth. for (all) the world, no hacer algo por nada del mundo. ‖ a man/woman of the world, un hombre/una mujer de mundo. ‖ it's a small world, el mundo es un pañuelo. ‖ it's not the end of the world, no es el fin del mundo. ‖ out of this world, fenomenal, estupendo,-a, increíble, fantástico,-a. ‖ the outside world, el mundo exterior. ‖ the world is one's oyster, el mundo es suyo, tener el mundo a sus pies. ‖ to be/mean all the world to sb., serlo todo para algn. ‖ to be dead/lost to the world, estar profundamente dormido,-a. ‖ to come down in the world, venir a menos. ‖ to go up in the world, prosperar, mejorar. ‖ to have the best of both worlds, tener todas las ventajas. ‖ to live in a world of one's own, vivir en su propio mundo. ‖ to see the world, ver mundo. ‖ to set the world on fire, comerse el mundo. ‖ to think the world of sb., querer mucho a algn., adorar a algn.

■ the Third World, el Tercer Mundo. ‖ World Bank, Banco Mundial. ‖ world champion, campeón,-ona mundial. ‖ World Cup, el Mundial, los Mundiales. ‖ world music, música étnica. ‖ World War I, primera guerra mundial. ‖ World War II, segunda guerra mundial.

world-class ['wɜːld'klɑːs] adj de categoría mundial.
▲ Se escribe world class cuando no se antepone a un sustantivo.

world-famous ['wɜːld'feɪməs] adj de fama mundial.
▲ Se escribe world famous cuando no se antepone a un sustantivo.

worldliness ['wɜːldlɪnəs] n mundanería.

worldly ['wɜːldlɪ] adj mundano,-a.
■ worldly goods, bienes mpl materiales.

▲ comp worldlier, superl worldliest.

world-weary ['wɜːldwɪərɪ] adj hastiado,-a del mundo.
▲ comp world-wearier, superl world-weariest.

worldwide ['wɜːldwaɪd] **1** adj mundial, universal. **– 2** adv mundialmente.

worm [wɜːm] **1** n (grub, maggot) gusano; (earthworm) lombriz f. **2** pej (person) gusano, canalla. **3** TECH (of screw) tornillo. **– 4** t (make one's way) deslizarse; (insinuate) insinuarse (into, en): he wormed his way under the fence, se deslizó por debajo de la valla; they wormed their way in, se colaron; he wormed his way into her confidence, consiguió ganarse su confianza. **5** MED quitar las lombrices a, desparasitar. **– 6** worms, npl MED lombrices fpl.

◆ to worm out t sep (extract) sacar, sonsacar.

● the early worm catches the bird, a quien madruga Dios le ayuda. ‖ the worm will turn, la paciencia tiene un límite.

■ a can of worms, un problema peliagudo.

worm-eaten ['wɜːmiːtən] adj (wood) carcomido,-a; (fruit) agusanado,-a.

wormy ['wɜːmɪ] **1** adj (like a worm) agusanado,-a. **2** (wood) carcomido,-a; (fruit) agusanado,-a.
▲ comp wormier, superl wormiest.

worn [wɔːn] **1** pp → wear. **– 2** adj (thing) usado,-a, gastado,-a. **3** (person) cansado,-a, fatigado,-a.

worn-out ['wɔːn'aʊt] **1** adj (thing) gastado,-a, estropeado,-a. **2** (person) rendido,-a, agotado,-a.
▲ Se escribe worn out cuando no se antepone a un sustantivo.

worried ['wʌrɪd] adj (person) inquieto,-a, preocupado,-a (about, por); (look, voice) de preocupación.
● to be worried sick, estar muy preocupado,-a. ‖ to get worried, preocuparse.

worrier ['wʌrɪə'] n sufridor,-ra.
● to be a (born) worrier, preocuparse por cualquier cosa.

worry ['wʌrɪ] **1** n (state, feeling) preocupación f, inquietud f, intranquilidad f; (problem) preocupación f, problema m; (responsibility) responsabilidad f: it's a worry to me, me preocupa; money worries, problemas económicos; that's the least of my worries, eso es lo que menos me preocupa. **– 2** t inquietar, preocupar: I don't want to worry you, no quiero preocuparte. **3** (annoy, disturb) molestar. **4** (of dog) acosar, perseguir. **– 5** i inquietarse, preocuparse (about/over, por): there's nothing to worry about, no tiene por qué preocuparse; don't worry about me, no te preocupes por mí.

● not to worry, es igual, no importa, déjalo. ‖ to worry os. about sb./sth., preocuparse por algn./algo.

■ worry beads, sarta de cuentas.

▲ (sustantivo) pl worries; (verbo) pt & pp worried, ger worrying.

worrying ['wʌrɪɪŋ] adj inquietante, preocupante, desconcertante.
● to be the worrying sort, ser de los que se preocupan por cualquier cosa.

worse [wɜːs] **1** adj (comp of bad) peor: it could have been worse, podría haber sido peor; it was much worse than I expected, fue mucho peor de lo que esperaba; they were none the worse for their experience, la experiencia no les ha perjudicado. **– 2** adv (comp of badly) peor; (more intensely) más: they played worse than last week, jugaron peor que la semana pasada. **– 3** n lo peor: there's worse to follow, aún falta lo peor; I've seen worse, he visto casos peores; there's been a change for the worse, ha habido un cambio a peor.

● the worse for wear, (worn, damaged) gastado,-a, viejo,-a; (*tired*) cansado,-a. ‖ **the worse for drink,** borracho,-a. ‖ **to be worse off,** (*financially*) andar peor de dinero; (*physically*) estar peor. ‖ **to get worse,** empeorar. ‖ **to get worse and worse,** ir de mal en peor. ‖ **to go from bad to worse,** ir de mal en peor. ‖ **to make matters worse,** para colmo de desgracias, por si fuera poco. ‖ **worse luck!,** ¡mala suerte! ‖ **worse still,** lo que es peor, peor aún.

worsen ['wɜːsən] **1** *t* empeorar. – **2** *i* empeorarse.

worship ['wɜːʃɪp] **1** *n* REL adoración *f*, veneración *f*, culto; (*service*) culto, oficio: *a place of worship,* templo; *let us join together in holy worship,* unámonos en sagrada adoración; *Sunday worship,* culto dominical. **2** (*devotion, love*) amor *m*, culto, idolatría. – **3** *t* REL adorar, venerar. **4** (*idolize*) rendir culto a, idolatrar. – **5** *i* (*attend church*) ir a misa, ser feligrés,-esa.
● **his** *(your etc)* **Worship,** GB (*form of address - mayor*) el señor alcalde; (*- magistrate*) su señoría.
▲ *pt & pp* **worshipped,** *ger* **worshipping.**

worshipper ['wɜːʃɪpəʳ] *n* adorador,-ra, devoto,-a, fiel.

worst [wɜːst] **1** *adj* (*superl*) peor: *the worst job I've ever had,* el peor empleo que he tenido; *this has been the worst winter on record,* éste ha sido el peor invierno que se recuerda; *the worst part of it is that ...,* lo peor es que ... – **2** *adv* (*superl*) peor: *she is one of the worst dressed women in the world,* es una de la mujeres peor vestidas del mundo; *the elderly are the worst affected by the cold,* los ancianos son los más afectados por el frío. – **3** *n* (*indefinite*) lo peor; (*person*) el/la peor, los/las peores: *the worst is over now,* ya ha pasado lo peor; *we feared the worst,* temíamos lo peor.
● **at (the) worst,** en el peor de los casos. ‖ **if the worst comes to the worst,** si pasa lo peor, en el peor de los casos. ‖ **to be one's own worst enemy,** ser su peor enemigo. ‖ **to come off worst,** salir perdiendo, llevarse la peor parte.
■ **worst case scenario,** el peor de los casos.

worsted ['wʊstəd] *n* SEW estambre *m*.

worth [wɜːθ] **1** *n* (*in money*) valor *m*: *hundreds of pounds' worth of damage,* daños por valor de cientos de libras. **2** (*of person*) valía; (*of thing*) valor *m*. – **3** *adj* (*having certain value*) que vale, que tiene un valor de: *it's worth £10, but I got it for £5,* vale diez libras pero me costó sólo cinco; *how much is that jewel worth?,* ¿cuánto vale esa joya? **4** (*deserving of*) que vale la pena, que merece la pena, digno,-a de, merecedor,-ra de: *it's worth seeing,* vale la pena verlo; *a book worth reading,* un libro que vale la pena leer; *it's worth thinking about,* es digno de consideración; *it's worth a try,* vale la pena intentarlo.
● **if a job's worth doing, it's worth doing well,** si se hace un trabajo, hay que hacerlo bien. ‖ **for all one is worth,** con toda el alma. ‖ **for what it's worth,** por si te sirve de algo. ‖ **it's more than my job's worth,** me arriesgaría el trabajo. ‖ **to not be worth a damn,** no valer nada. ‖ **to be worth one's/its weight in gold,** valer su peso en oro. ‖ **to get one's money's worth,** sacarle jugo al dinero. ‖ **to not be worth the paper it's written on,** ser papel mojado. ‖ **to be worth the trouble/it,** valer la pena, merecer la pena. ‖ **to be worth one's salt,** merecer el pan que se come. ‖ **to be worth sb.'s while,** valer la pena, merecer la pena: *it's not worth your while,* no vale la pena; *I'll make it worth your while,* te lo recompensaré.

worthiness ['wɜːθɪnəs] *n* mérito.

worthless ['wɜːθləs] **1** *adj* (*gen*) sin valor. **2** (*useless*) inútil, sin ningún valor: *this contract is worthless,* este contrato es papel mojado. **3** (*person*) despreciable.

worthlessness ['wɜːθləsnəs] *n* falta de valor.

worthwhile [wɜːθ'waɪl] *adj* (*gen*) que vale la pena, que merece la pena: *it's worthwhile visiting the museum,* vale la pena visitar el museo.

worthy ['wɜːðɪ] **1** *adj* (*deserving*) digno,-a (**of,** de), merecedor,-ra (**of,** de), que vale la pena; (*winner, opponent, successor*) digno,-a: *a building worthy of note,* un edificio digno de ver; *it is worthy of our support,* merece nuestro apoyo; *a worthy winner,* un ganador merecido; *that was a service worthy of Sampras,* ese servicio ha sido digno de Sampras. **2** (*action, cause*) meritorio,-a, bueno,-a, justo,-a; (*effort*) meritorio,-a, encomiable. **3** (*citizen*) honorable, admirable, respetable. – **4** *n iron* prócer *m*, dignitario,-a.
▲ (*adjetivo*) *comp* **worthier,** *superl* **worthiest;** (*sustantivo*) *pl* **worthies.**

would [wʊd] **1** *aux* (*conditional*): *I would love to,* me encantaría; *what would you do with a million pounds?,* ¿qué harías con un millón de libras?; *he would have gone if he'd had time,* habría ido si hubiera tenido tiempo; *she said she'd be here,* dijo que estaría aquí; *I would rather go skiing,* preferiría ir a esquiar; *you would never know she was fifty,* nunca dirías que tiene cincuenta años. **2** (*polite requests*): *would you be so kind as to close the window?,* ¿me haría usted el favor de cerrar la ventana?; *pass me the salt, would you?,* pásame la sal, ¿quieres? **3** (*offers, invitations*): *would you like a drink?,* ¿quieres tomar algo?; *would you like to have dinner with me?,* ¿te gustaría ir a cenar conmigo? **4** (*willingness*): *he wouldn't help me,* se negó a ayudarme, no quiso ayudarme; *the car wouldn't start,* el coche no arrancaba. **5** (*giving advice*): *I wouldn't dwell on it,* yo que tú no pensaría en ello. **6** (*conjecture*): *that would have been in 1978,* debe haber sido en 1978. **7** (*past habit, custom*) soler: *we would often go out together,* a menudo salíamos juntos. **8** (*insistence, persistence*): *you would say that!,* ¡es típico de ti decir eso!; *I think we should go home - you would!,* yo creo que deberíamos volver a casa - ¡típico!
● **so it would appear,** según parece. ‖ **would that I could,** ojalá pudiera.
▲ En 1, 5, 6 y 7 puede contraerse en 'd.

would-be ['wʊdbiː] **1** *adj* (*hopeful*) aspirante a. **2** *pej* (*so-called*) supuesto,-a. **3** (*failed*) frustrado,-a, fracasado,-a.

wound[1] ['waʊnd] *pp* → **wind.**

wound[2] [wuːnd] **1** *n* herida: *a flesh wound,* una herida superficial; *a bullet wound,* una herida de bala. – **2** *t* herir.
● **to open old wounds,** reabrir viejas heridas.

wounded ['wuːndɪd] **1** *adj* herido,-a. – **2 the wounded,** *npl* los heridos.

wounding ['wuːndɪŋ] *adj* hiriente.

wove [wəʊv] *pt* → **weave.**

woven ['wəʊvən] *pp* → **weave.**

wow [waʊ] **1** *interj fam* ¡vaya!, ¡anda!, ¡caramba!, ¡alucine! – **2** *n fam* éxito sensacional, exitazo. – **3** *t* (*fam*) encandilar, enloquecer.

WPC ['dʌbljuːpiː'siː] *abbr* GB (*Woman Police Constable*) agente *f* de policía.

wpm ['wɜːdzpəˈmɪnɪt] *abbr* (*words per minute*) pulsaciones *fpl* por minuto; (*abbreviation*) p.p.m.

WRAC [ræk] *abbr* GB MIL (*Women's Royal Army Corps.*) rama femenina del ejército de tierra británico.

WRAF [ræf] *abbr* GB MIL (*Women's Royal Air Force*) rama femenina de las fuerzas aéreas británicas.

wrangle ['ræŋgəl] **1** *n* disputa, riña. – **2** *i* discutir (**about/over,** por), reñir (**about/over,** por).

wrap [ræp] 1 t (*cover*) envolver: *I love wrapping (up) Christmas presents,* me encanta envolver los regalos de Navidad; *she wrapped a blanket round him,* lo envolvió en una manta; *he wrapped his arms around me,* me estrechó entre sus brazos; *his hand was wrapped in a bandage,* tenía la mano vendada. 2 *fig* (*surround, immerse*) envolver (**in,** de), rodear (**in,** de): *wrapped in mystery,* rodeado de misterio. – 3 *n* (*scarf, shawl*) chal *m*; (*cape*) capa; (*robe*) bata.
◆ **to wrap up** 1 *i* (*wear warm clothes*) abrigarse: *wrap up warm,* abrígate mucho. 2 (*shut up*) callarse, cerrar el pico. – 3 *t sep* (*complete*) conseguir; (*conclude*) concluir, dar fin a: *they wrapped up the deal,* cerraron el trato.
● **to be wrapped up in sth.,** *fig* (*involved*) estar absorto,-a en algo, no pensar más que en algo: *she was wrapped up in her work,* estaba absorta en su trabajo. ‖ **to keep sth. under wraps,** mantener algo en secreto. ‖ **to wrap sb. up in cotton wool,** criar entre algodones.
▲ (*verbo*) *pt & pp* **wrapped,** *ger* **wrapping.**
wrapper [ˈræpəʳ] *n* (*of food*) envoltorio, envoltura; (*of book*) sobrecubierta.
wrapping [ˈræpɪŋ] *n* envoltura, envoltorio.
■ **wrapping paper,** (*plain*) papel *m* de envolver; (*fancy*) papel *m* de regalo.
wrath [rɒθ] *n* cólera, ira.
wreak [riːk] *t* causar, provocar, sembrar.
● **to wreak damage/havoc on sth.,** causar daños en algo, hacer estragos en algo. ‖ **to wreak revenge/ vengeance on sb.,** vengarse de algn.
wreath [riːθ] *n* (*of flowers*) corona.
■ **laurel wreath,** corona de laurel.
wreathe [riːð] *t* (*circle*) envolver; (*adorn*) adornar; (*crown*) coronar.
● **to be wreathed in/with,** (*flowers, leaves*) estar adornado,-a de; (*smoke, mist, etc*) estar envuelto,-a en; (*smiles*) no parar de sonreír.
wreck [rek] 1 *n* MAR (*action*) naufragio; (*ship*) barco naufragado o hundido. 2 (*of car, plane*) restos *mpl*; (*of building*) ruinas *fpl,* escombros *mpl: the car was a complete wreck,* el coche quedó completamente destrozado. 3 *fig* (*person*) ruina: *she's a nervous wreck,* tiene los nervios destrozados; *he looked a complete wreck,* estaba hecho polvo. – 4 *t* MAR (*ship*) hacer naufragar. 5 (*car, plane*) destrozar; (*machine*) desbaratar, estropear. 6 *fig* (*health, career*) arruinar; (*life, marriage*) destrozar; (*hopes*) destruir, echar por tierra; (*plans*) estropear, desbaratar; (*chances*) echar a perder.
wreckage [ˈrekɪdʒ] 1 *n* (*of vehicle*) restos *mpl*; (*of building*) ruinas *fpl,* escombros *mpl.* 2 *fig* ruina.
wrecked [ˈrekt] 1 *adj* MAR (*ship*) naufragado,-a; (*sailor*) náufrago,-a. 2 (*car, plane*) destrozado,-a; (*building*) destruido,-a. – 3 *n fig* (*life, career, hopes*) arruinado,-a, destrozado,-a; (*plans*) estropeado,-a. – 4 *adj fam fig* (*stoned*) ciego,-a, colocado,-a, pasado,-a.
wrecker [ˈrekəʳ] 1 *n* US (*of building*) demoledor,-ra. 2 US (*breakdown van*) grúa.
wren [ren] *n* ORN chochín *m.*
wrench [rentʃ] 1 *n* (*pull*) tirón *m,* arranque *m.* 2 MED torcedura. 3 *fig* separación *f* dolorosa. 4 GB (*tool*) llave *f* inglesa; US llave *f.* – 5 *t* (*pull*) arrancar (de un tirón), arrebatar: *he wrenched the knife from my hand,* me arrancó la navaja de las manos; *she wrenched herself free,* se soltó de un tirón. 6 MED torcer.
wrest [rest] 1 *t* (*object*) arrancar, arrebatar. 2 (*confession*) sonsacar, arrancar; (*victory, control*) conseguir a duras penas.

wrestle [ˈresəl] 1 *i* (*fight*) luchar (**with,** con/contra). 2 *fig* (*problem, conscience*) luchar (**with,** con), lidiar (**with,** con). – 3 *t* luchar contra. – 4 *n* lucha.
wrestler [ˈresləʳ] *n* SP luchador,-ra.
wrestling [ˈresəlɪŋ] *n* lucha.
■ **all-in wrestling,** lucha libre. ‖ **wrestling match,** combate *m* de lucha.
wretch [retʃ] 1 *n* (*unfortunate person*) desdichado,-a, infeliz, desgraciado,-a. 2 *fam* (*rascal*) pillo,-a, pícaro,-a, granuja *mf.* 3 (*bad person*) canalla *mf,* malvado,-a.
wretched [ˈretʃɪd] 1 *adj* (*condition*) miserable, lamentable. 2 (*unhappy*) desdichado,-a, desgraciado,-a. 3 (*ill*) muy mal, fatal. 4 *fam* (*very bad*) horrible, malísimo,-a, espantoso,-a. 5 *fam* (*damned*) maldito,-a, condenado,-a.
wretchedness [ˈretʃɪdnəs] 1 *n* (*unhappiness, misfortune*) desdicha, desgracia. 2 (*of conditions*) miseria.
wriggle [ˈrɪgəl] 1 *i* retorcerse, menearse, moverse: *stop wriggling (about)!,* ¡deja de moverte! – 2 *t* menear, mover. – 3 *n* meneo.
◆ **to wriggle out of** *t insep* (*situation, responsibility*) librarse hábilmente de, ingeniárselas para librarse de, escaquearse de; (*physically*) escabullirse, escaparse de.
● **to wriggle free,** escapar deslizándose, escabullirse.
wriggly [ˈrɪgəlɪ] *adj* sinuoso,-a.
▲ *comp* **wrigglier,** *superl* **wriggliest.**
wring [rɪŋ] 1 *t* (*one's hands*) torcer, retorcer; (*person's hand*) apretar; (*bird's neck*) retorcer. 2 (*clothes*) escurrir (**out,** -), retorcer (**out,** -). 3 *fig* (*heart*) partir. 4 *fig* (*confession, truth, etc*) sonsacar, arrancar, sacar. – 5 *n* (*of clothes*): *give it a good wring,* escúrrelo bien.
● **to wring sb.'s neck,** retorcer el pescuezo a algn.
▲ *pt & pp* **wrung.**
wringer [ˈrɪŋəʳ] *n* escurridor *m,* rodillo.
● **to put sb. through the wringer,** hacer pasar un mal trago a algn.
wringing wet [ˈrɪŋɪŋwet] *adj* (*garment*) empapado,-a; (*person*) calado,-a hasta los huesos.
wrinkle [ˈrɪŋkəl] 1 *n* arruga. – 2 *t* arrugar. – 3 *i* arrugarse.
wrinkled [ˈrɪŋkəld] *adj* arrugado,-a.
wrinkly [ˈrɪŋklɪ] *adj* arrugado,-a.
wrist [rɪst] 1 *n* ANAT muñeca. 2 (*of clothes*) puño.
wristband [ˈrɪstbænd] 1 *n* (*of clothes*) puño. 2 (*sweatband*) muñequera.
wristwatch [ˈrɪstwɒtʃ] *n* reloj *m* de pulsera.
writ [rɪt] *n* mandato judicial, orden *f* judicial, auto.
● **to issue a writ against sb.,** expedir una orden contra algn. ‖ **to serve sb. with a writ, to serve a writ on sb.,** entregar una orden a algn.
write [raɪt] 1 *t* (*gen*) escribir; (*article*) redactar; (*cheque*) extender. – 2 *i* (*gen*) escribir (**about,** sobre): *he writes for a newspaper,* escribe en un periódico; *we write to each other,* nos escribimos.
◆ **to write away for** *t insep* pedir por correo. ‖ **to write back** *i* contestar (por carta). ‖ **to write down** *t sep* (*note*) anotar, apuntar. ‖ **to write in** *t sep* (*gen*) escribir; (*include*) incluir. ‖ **to write in for** *t insep* escribir pidiendo. ‖ **to write into** *t sep* (*include*) incluir. ‖ **to write off** 1 *t sep* (*debt*) anular, saldar. 2 GB (*car*) destrozar. 3 *fig* (*accept as useless or failure*) dar por acabado,-a, dar por perdido,-a: *we mustn't write her off just yet,* no hay que darla por perdida todavía. ‖ **to write off for** *t insep* pedir por correo. ‖ **to write out** 1 *t sep* (*write in full*) escribir (en su forma completa): *write it out neatly,* pásalo a limpio. 2 (*cheque, receipt, etc*) extender. ‖ **to write up** *t sep* (*notes, minutes, etc*) pasar a limpio; (*describe*) redactar, escribir; (*diary etc*) poner al día.

● **to be nothing to write home about,** no ser nada del otro mundo. ‖ **to be written all over sb.'s face,** llevar (algo) escrito en la cara, estar impreso,-a en la cara: *it's written all over your face,* se te nota en la cara. ▲ *pt* **wrote,** *pp* **written,** *ger* **writing.**

write-off ['raɪtɒf] **1** *n* (*car*) ruina, siniestro total. **2** FIN (*debt*) cancelación *f*.

writer ['raɪtə'] **1** *n* (*by profession*) escritor,-ra; (*of book, letter*) autor,-ra. **2** (*of handwriting*): *she's a neat writer,* tiene buena letra.
■ **writer's cramp,** agarrotamiento de la mano por escribir.

write-up ['raɪtʌp] *n fam* (*review*) crítica, reseña.

writhe [raɪð] *i* (*physically*) retorcerse, contorsionarse.

writing ['raɪtɪŋ] **1** *n* (*script*) escritura; (*handwriting*) letra: *can you read my writing?,* ¿entiendes mi letra? **2** (*written work*) composición *f*, trabajo. **3** (*occupation*) profesión *f* de escritor,-ra, trabajo literario; (*activity*) escribir *m*. – **4** **writings,** *npl* obra, escritos *mpl*.
● **in writing,** por escrito. ‖ **the writing on the wall,** los malos presagios.
■ **writing desk,** escritorio. ‖ **writing materials,** objetos *mpl* de escritorio. ‖ **writing paper,** papel *m* de escribir.

written ['rɪtən] **1** *pp* → **write.** – **2** *adj* escrito,-a.
● **the written word,** la palabra escrita.
■ **written consent,** consentimiento por escrito. ‖ **written exam,** examen *m* escrito.

WRNS [renz] *abbr* GB MIL (*Women's Royal Naval Service*) rama femenina de las fuerzas navales británicas.

wrong [rɒŋ] **1** *adj* (*erroneous*) erróneo,-a, equivocado,-a, incorrecto,-a: *a wrong answer,* una respuesta incorrecta; *we're going the wrong way,* nos hemos equivocado de camino, vamos mal; *my watch is wrong,* mi reloj anda mal; *they arrested the wrong man,* detuvieron al hombre que no era, detuvieron al hombre equivocado; *he was driving on the wrong side of the road,* conducía por el carril contrario; *she played a wrong note,* tocó una nota falsa. **2** (*mistaken*) equivocado,-a: *we proved him wrong,* demostramos que estaba equivocado; *that's just where you're wrong,* ahí es donde te equivocas; *I was wrong about you,* te había juzgado mal; *you're wrong in thinking that ...,* te equivocas si piensas que ... **3** (*evil, immoral*) malo,-a; (*unacceptable, unfair*) injusto,-a: *stealing is wrong,* robar es malo; *I've done nothing wrong,* no he hecho nada malo; *you were wrong not to tell me,* hiciste mal en no decírmelo; *it seems all wrong to me,* a mí me parece injusto. **4** (*amiss*) mal: *something's wrong here,* aquí pasa algo; *what's wrong?,* ¿qué pasa?; *is anything wrong?,* ¿pasa algo?; *what's wrong with him?,* ¿qué le pasa? **5** (*unsuitable*) inadecuado,-a, impropio,-a; (*time*) inoportuno,-a: *she's the*

wrong person for the job, no es la persona adecuada para el puesto; *I think I said the wrong thing,* creo que he dicho algo no debía; *he was in the wrong place at the wrong time,* estaba en el sitio equivocado en el momento inoportuno. – **6** *adv* mal, incorrectamente, equivocadamente: *you've spelt it wrong,* lo has escrito mal; *I must have heard wrong,* debo de haber oído mal; *you're doing it wrong,* lo estás haciendo mal. – **7** *n* (*evil, bad action*) mal *m*: *children know right from wrong,* los niños saben distinguir entre el bien y el mal; *she can do no wrong in his eyes,* para él, todo lo que ella hace está bien. **8** (*injustice*) injusticia; (*offence*) agravio: *many wrongs have been done in the name of the church,* se han cometido muchas injusticias en nombre de la iglesia. – **9** *t* (*treat unfairly*) ser injusto,-a con; (*judge unfairly*) juzgar mal; (*offend*) agraviar.
● **to be from the wrong side of the tracks,** ser de los barrios bajos. ‖ **to be in the wrong,** (*mistaken*) estar equivocado,-a; (*at fault*) tener la culpa. ‖ **to be on the wrong side of forty** (*fifty etc*), tener cuarenta (*cincuenta etc*) años bien cumplidos. ‖ **to be wrong,** (*person*) estar equivocado,-a, no tener razón, equivocarse. ‖ **to have/get the wrong number,** (*tel*) confundirse de número, equivocarse de número. ‖ **to get (hold of) the wrong end of the stick,** coger el rábano por las hojas. ‖ **to get sb. wrong,** malinterpretar a algn. ‖ **to get sth. wrong,** equivocarse, no acertar. ‖ **to go down the wrong hole/way,** atragantarse. ‖ **to go wrong,** (*things in general*) salir mal; (*make a mistake*) equivocarse; (*go wrong way*) equivocarse de camino; (*machine, device*) romperse, estropearse; (*plan*) fallar, fracasar. ‖ **to right a wrong,** deshacer un entuerto. ‖ **two wrongs don't make a right,** no se subsana un error cometiendo otro. ‖ **wrong side out,** al revés. ‖ **you can't go wrong,** (*giving directions*) no tiene pérdida.

wrongdoer ['rɒŋduə'] *n* malhechor,-ra.

wrongdoing ['rɒŋduːɪŋ] *n* maldad *f*, fechoría.

wrongful ['rɒŋfʊl] *adj* (*unfair*) injusto,-a; (*illegal*) ilegal: *wrongful dismissal,* despido improcedente.

wrongly ['rɒŋlɪ] **1** *adv* (*incorrectly*) mal, incorrectamente. **2** (*mistakenly*) sin razón, equivocadamente, erróneamente. **3** (*unjustly*) injustamente.

wrote [rəʊt] *pt* → **write.**

wrought [rɔːt] **1** *adj* (*iron*) forjado,-a; (*silver*) labrado,-a. **2** (*made and decorated*) hecho,-a, elaborado,-a, decorado,-a. – **3** *pp arch* → **work.**

wrung [rʌŋ] *pt* & *pp* → **wring.**

wry [raɪ] *adj* irónico,-a, sardónico,-a.

WWF ['wɜːldwaɪldlaɪf'fʌnd] *abbr* (*World Wildlife Fund*) Fondo Mundial para la Naturaleza

X

X, x [eks] *n* (*the letter*) X, x *f*.
xenon ['zenɒn] *n* CHEM xenón *m*.
xenophobia [zenə'fəʊbɪə] *n* xenofobia.
xenophobic [zenə'fəʊbɪk] *adj* xenófobo,-a.
xerography [zɪ'rɒgrəfɪ] *n* xerografía *f*.
Xerox ['zɪərɒks] **1** *n* xerocopia *f*, fotocopia. **– 2** *t* xerocopiar, fotocopiar.
▲ Es marca registrada.
XL ['eks'el] *abbr* (*extra large*) muy grande.

Xmas ['eksməs, 'krɪsməs] *n* → **Christmas**.
X-ray ['eksreɪ] **1** *n* rayo *m* X. **2** (*photograph*) radiografía *f*. **– 3** *t* radiografiar.
xylene ['zaɪliːn] *n* CHEM xileno *m*.
xylograph ['zaɪləgrɑːf] *n* xilografía *f*.
xylography [zaɪ'lɒgrəfɪ] *n* xilografía *f*.
xylophone ['zaɪləfəʊn] *n* xilófono *m*.
xylophonist [zaɪ'lɒfənɪst] *n* xilofonista *mf*.

Y

Y, y [waɪ] n (*the letter*) Y, y f.

yacht [jɒt] **1** n yate m. **2** (*with sails*) velero, yate m.
■ **yacht club,** club m náutico. ‖ **yacht race,** regata.

yachting ['jɒtɪŋ] n deporte m de la vela, vela: *I go yacht-ing at weekends,* hago vela los fines de semana.

yachtsman ['jɒtsmən] n (*for pleasure*) aficionado a la vela; (*as sport*) regatista m.

yachtswoman ['jɒtswʊmən] n (*for pleasure*) aficionada a la vela; (*as sport*) regatista f.
▲ pl **yachtswomen** ['jɒtswɪmɪn].

yack [jæk] i *fam* cotorrear.

yak [jæk] n yac m, yak m.

yam [jæm] n ñame m.

yank [jæŋk] **1** n *fam* tirón m. – **2** t *fam* tirar de: *he yanked me by the hair,* me tiró del pelo.
◆ **to yank out** t *sep* arrancar, sacar de un tirón: *he yanked a page out of the book,* arrancó una página del libro.

Yank [jæŋk] n *pej* yanqui mf.

Yankee ['jæŋkɪ] **1** n *pej* yanqui mf. – **2** adj *pej* yanqui.

Yaoundé [jæ'uːndeɪ] n Yaundé.

yap [jæp] **1** n (*dog*) ladrido, ladrido agudo. – **2** i (*dog*) la-drar. **3** *fam* (*person*) cotorrear.
▲ pt & pp **yapped,** ger **yapping.**

yard [jɑːd] **1** n (*measure*) yarda: *three feet make a yard,* una yarda son tres pies; *a few yards away,* a unos me-tros. **2** GB (*of house*) patio. **3** US (*of house*) jardín m. **4** (*in-dustry*) almacén m. **5** (*naut*) verga.
■ **builder's yard,** almacén m de materiales de cons-trucción. ‖ **goods yard,** almacén m. ‖ **rail goods yard,** depósito de mercancías. ‖ **Scotland Yard,** oficina central de la policía británica en Londres.
▲ En 1 equivale a 0,914 metros.

yardstick ['jɑːdstɪk] n *fig* criterio, norma.

yarn [jɑːn] **1** n hilo. **2** (*story*) cuento.
● **to spin a yarn,** (*story*) contar un cuento; (*lie*) venir con cuentos: *he span me a yarn about being ill,* me vino con el cuento de que estaba enfermo.

yashmak ['jæʃmæk] n velo de musulmana.

yawn [jɔːn] **1** i bostezar. **2** (*gap etc*) abrirse. – **3** n bostezo. **4** *fam* (*boring event*) rollo: *the film was a yawn from start to finish,* la película fue un auténtico rollo.

yd [jɑːd] *abbr* (*yard*) yarda.
▲ pl **yds.**

ye¹ [jiː] *def art* (*on shop signs etc*) → **the.**

ye² [jiː] *pron arch* vos.

yea [jeɪ] **1** adv *arch* sí. – **2** n *arch* sí m.

yeah [jeə] adv *fam* sí.

year [jɪəʳ] **1** n año: *we bought it last year,* lo compramos el año pasado; *he's retiring next year,* se jubila el año que viene; *they come twice a year,* vienen dos veces al año; *we go abroad every other year,* vamos al extranjero cada dos años; *she earns 14,000 pounds a year,* gana 14.000 libras al año; *I've known him for years (and*

years), lo conozco desde hace muchos años; *she's 20 years old,* tiene 20 años; *he's getting on in years,* es un hombre entrado en años. **2** EDUC curso: *I'm in my first year,* hago primero; *first-year students,* alumnos de pri-mer curso.
● **all the year round,** durante todo el año. ‖ **since the year dot,** desde el año de la nana. ‖ **to put years on sb.,** envejecer: *the death of his son has put years on him,* ha envejecido desde la muerte de su hijo. ‖ **to take years off sb.,** rejuvenecer a algn. ‖ **year in, year out,** año tras año.
■ **donkey's years,** siglos mpl: *he's lived there for don-key's years,* vive allí desde hace años. ‖ **financial year,** año económico. ‖ **fiscal year,** año fiscal. ‖ **leap year,** año bisiesto. ‖ **New Year,** Año Nuevo. ‖ **New Year's Eve,** noche f vieja. ‖ **tax year,** año fiscal.

yearbook ['jɪəbʊk] n anuario.

yearling ['jɪəlɪŋ] **1** n primal,-la. – **2** adj primal.

yearly ['jɪəlɪ] **1** adj anual. – **2** adv anualmente.

yearn [jɜːn] i (*desire*) anhelar (**for,** -), ansiar (**for,** -); (*nos-talgically*) añorar: *he yearns for fame and fortune,* anhela fama y fortuna; *she yearned for the days of her youth,* añoraba su juventud.
● **to yearn to do sth.,** suspirar por hacer algn.: *I yearn to hold you in my arms,* suspiro por tenerte en mis bra-zos.

yearning ['jɜːnɪŋ] **1** n (*desire*) anhelo (**for,** de); (*nostalgia*) añoranza (**for,** de). – **2** adj anhelante.

yeast [jiːst] n levadura.

yell [jel] **1** n grito, alarido. – **2** i gritar, dar alaridos.

yellow ['jeləʊ] **1** adj amarillo,-a. **2** (*cowardly*) cobarde. – **3** n amarillo. – **4** t ponerse amarillo. – **5** i amarillear.
■ **yellow card,** (*sp*) tarjeta amarilla. ‖ **yellow fever,** fiebre f amarilla. ‖ **yellow jersey,** (*sp*) maillot m ama-rillo. ‖ **yellow line,** raya amarilla: *you can't park here, there's a double yellow line,* aquí no se puede estacio-nar, hay una doble raya amarilla. ‖ **Yellow Pages,** pá-ginas amarillas. ‖ **yellow peril,** peligro amarillo. ‖ **yellow press,** prensa sensacionalista, prensa amari-lla.

yellowhammer ['jeləʊhæməʳ] n escribano cerillo.

yelp [jelp] **1** n gañido. – **2** i gañir.

Yemen ['jemən] n Yemen.

Yemeni ['jemənɪ] **1** adj yemení. – **2** n yemení mf.

yen [jen] **1** n deseo. **2** FIN yen m.

yeoman ['jəʊmən] n HIST pequeño terrateniente m.
■ **yeoman of the guard,** alabardero de la Torre de Londres.

yes [jes] **1** adv sí. **2** (*answering person*) dime; (*answering phone*) ¿dígame? – **3** n sí m.
● **to say yes,** decir que sí. ‖ **to say yes to sth.,** con-sentir algo, decir que sí a algo.

yes-man ['jesmæn] n persona que, con sus superiores, siempre dice sí a todo.

▲ *pl* **yesmen** [ˈjesmen].

yesterday [ˈjestədɪ] **1** *adv* ayer: *yesterday morning/afternoon,* ayer por la mañana/tarde. – **2** *n* ayer *m.*
● **not to be born yesterday,** no chuparse el dedo, no ser tonto,-a: *she wasn't born yesterday,* no se chupa el dedo.
■ **the day before yesterday,** anteayer.

yesteryear [ˈjestəjɪəʳ] *adv lit* antaño.

yet [jet] **1** *adv* todavía, aún: *we haven't had lunch yet,* todavía no hemos comido; *haven't you finished that book yet?,* ¿aún no has acabado aquel libro? **2** (*until now*) hasta la fecha, hasta ahora: *her most successful record yet,* su disco de más éxito hasta la fecha; *the earliest remains yet discovered,* los restos más antiguos descubiertos hasta ahora. **3** (*even*) aún, todavía: *yet more guests arrived,* llegaron aún más invitados; *yet worse clashes occurred later,* más tarde hubo enfrentamientos aún peores. **4** (*expressing future possibility, hope, etc*) aún: *don't give up, you may win yet,* no te rindas, aún puedes ganar. – **5** *conj* pero, aunque: *a cheap yet effective solution to the problem,* una solución barata pero efectiva para el problema; *she's very friendly, yet I find her a little mysterious,* es muy simpática, aunque la encuentro un poco misteriosa.
● **yet again,** otra vez. ‖ **yet another ...,** otro,-a ... más: *yet another gold medal for Broddle,* otra medalla de oro más para Broddle.

yeti [ˈjetɪ] **1** *n* yeti *m.* **2 the Yeti,** el abominable hombre *m* de las nieves.

yew [juː] *n* tejo.

Yiddish [ˈjɪdɪʃ] **1** *adj* yiddish, jiddish. – **2** *n* (*language*) yiddish *m,* jiddish *m.*

yield [jiːld] **1** *n* (*harvest*) cosecha. **2** FIN (*return*) rendimiento, rédito. – **3** *t* (*produce*) producir, dar: *this new variety yields more fruit,* esta nueva variedad da más fruto. **4** (*give, hand over*) entregar. **5** FIN rendir: *these bonds yield 5% per year,* estos bonos rinden 5% al año. – **6** *i* (*surrender*) rendirse (**to,** ante), ceder (**to,** a): *the Prime Minister yielded to public pressure,* el primer ministro cedió a la presión pública. **7** (*break*) ceder: *he pushed with all his might, but the door would not yield,* empujó con todas sus fuerzas, pero la puerta no cedió. **8** US ceder el paso.
◆ **to yield up** *t sep* (*secrets*) revelar.

yielding [ˈjiːldɪŋ] **1** *adj* (*material*) flexible, blando,-a. **2** (*person*) dócil, complaciente.

yippee [jɪˈpiː] *interj fam* ¡yupi!

YMCA [ˈwaɪemˈsiːˈeɪ] *abbr* (*Young Men's Christian Association*) asociación *f* de jóvenes cristianos.
■ **YMCA hostel,** albergue *m* para chicos jóvenes.

yob [jɒb] *n fam* → **yobbo.**

yobbo [ˈjɒbəʊ] *n fam* gamberro.
▲ *pl* **yobbos.**

yodel [ˈrəʊdəl] *i* cantar a la tirolesa.
▲ *pt & pp* **yodelled** (US **yodeled**), *ger* **yodelling** (US **yodeling**).

yoga [ˈrəʊgə] *n* yoga *m.*

yoghourt [ˈjɒgət] *n* → **yoghurt.**

yoghurt [ˈjɒgət] *n* yogur *m.*

yogurt [ˈjɒgət] *n* → **yoghurt.**
■ **yogurt maker,** yogurtera.

yoke [jəʊk] **1** *n* (*for carrying, pulling*) yugo. **2** (*pair of oxen*) yunta. **3** SEW canesú *m.* **4** *fig* yugo: *they threw off the yoke of slavery,* se quitaron el yugo de la esclavitud. – **5** *t* (*oxen*) uncir. **6** *fig* unir.

yokel [ˈjəʊkəl] *n* paleto,-a.

yolk [jəʊk] *n* yema.

yon [jɒn] *adj arch* aquel, aquella, aquellos,-as.

yonder [ˈjɒndəʳ] **1** *adv arch* allá. – **2** *adj arch* aquel, aquella, aquellos,-as.

yonks [jɒŋks] *n fam* la tira, siglos *mpl: I haven't seen him for yonks,* hace la tira que no lo veo.

you [juː] **1** *pron* (*subject, familiar, singular*) tú: *and what did you say?,* y tú, ¿qué dijiste? **2** (*subject, familiar, plural - men*) vosotros; (- *women*) vosotras: *you two, where are you going?,* vosotros dos, ¿adónde vais? **3** (*subject, polite, singular*) usted, Vd., Ud.: *you must wait here until the doctor arrives,* usted debe esperar aquí hasta que llegue el médico. **4** (*subject, polite, plural*) ustedes, Vds., Uds.: *you must both wait here,* ustedes dos deben esperar aquí. **5** (*subject, impersonal*) se, uno: *you can go by coach or train,* se puede ir en tren o en autocar; *sometimes you just have to say no, don't you?,* a veces, uno tiene que decir que no, ¿verdad? **6** (*object, familiar, singular*) te; (*with prep*) ti; (*if prep is con*) contigo: *I'm going with you, without you I'm lost,* voy contigo, sin ti estoy perdido. **7** (*object, familiar, plural*) os; (*with preposition*) vosotros,-as: *I forgot to invite you,* se me olvidó invitaros; *I'll go with you,* iré con vosotros. **8** (*direct object, polite, singular - man*) lo, le; (- *woman*) la; (*with preposition*) usted: *good morning, sir, can I help you?,* buenos días, señor, ¿puedo ayudarlo?; *I'm sorry madam, I can't hear you,* perdone señora, no la oigo; *this is for you,* esto es para usted; *I wanted to talk to you,* quería hablar con usted. **9** (*direct object, polite, plural - men*) los; (- *women*) las; (*with preposition*) ustedes: *good morning, gentlemen, can I help you?,* buenos días, señores, ¿puedo ayudarlos?; *I'm sorry ladies, I don't understand you,* lo siento señoras, no las entiendo; *gentlemen, this is for you,* señores, esto es para ustedes; *I wanted to talk to you two ladies,* quería hablar con ustedes dos. **10** (*indirect object, polite, singular*) le: *I'll send you a letter,* le mandaré una carta. **11** (*indirect object, polite, plural*) les: *I sent both of you a card,* les mandé una felicitación a los dos. **12** (*object, impersonal*) *cyanide kills you,* el cianuro mata.

young [jʌŋ] **1** *adj* (*gen*) joven; (*brother, sister*) menor: *I'm not as young as I used to be,* ya no soy tan joven; *we're not getting any younger,* nos estamos haciendo viejos; *the night is yet young,* la noche aún es joven; *my young sister,* mi hermana menor. – **2 the young,** *n* (*humans*) los jóvenes *mpl,* la juventud *f,* la gente *f* joven; (*animals*) las crías *fpl.*
● **you're only young once,** sólo se vive una vez. ‖ **to have an old head on young shoulders,** ser maduro,-a para su edad. ‖ **to be young at heart,** ser joven de espíritu.
■ **young lady,** (*woman*) señorita; (*girlfriend*) novia. ‖ **young man,** (*man*) joven *m,* muchacho; (*boyfriend*) novio. ‖ **young woman,** joven *f,* muchacha.

youngish [ˈjʌnɪʃ] *adj* bastante joven.

youngster [ˈjʌŋstəʳ] *n* joven *mf.*

your [jɔːʳ] **1** *adj* (*familiar, singular*) tu, tus; (*plural*) vuestro,-a, vuestros,-as. **2** (*polite*) su, sus. **3** *fml* (*address*) Su: *Your Majesty,* Su Majestad.

yours [jɔːz] **1** *pron* (*familiar, singular*) (el) tuyo, (la) tuya, (los) tuyos, (las) tuyas; (*plural*) (el) vuestro, (la) vuestra, (los) vuestros, (las) vuestras. **2** (*polite*) (el) suyo, (la) suya, (los) suyos, (las) suyas. **3** (*letters*) le saluda ...: *Yours sincerely ...,* le saluda atentamente ...

yourself [jɔːˈself] **1** *pron* (*familiar singular*) te; (*emphatic*) tú mismo,-a. **2** (*polite singular*) se; (*emphatic*) usted mismo,-a.

yourselves [jɔːˈselvz] **1** *pron* (*familiar plural*) os; (*emphatic*) vosotros,-as mismos,-as. **2** (*polite plural*) se; (*emphatic*) ustedes mismos,-as.

youth [juːθ] **1** *n* (*period*) juventud *f.* **2** (*young person*) joven *mf.* **3** (*young people*) juventud *f,* los jóvenes *mpl.*
● to go youth hostelling, hospedarse en albergues juveniles.
■ youth club, club *m* juvenil. ‖ youth hostel, albergue *m* juvenil.
youthful [ˈjuːθfʊl] *adj* joven, juvenil.
youthfulness [ˈjuːθfʊlnəs] *n* juventud *f.*
yowl [jaʊl] **1** *n* aullido. – **2** *i* aullar.
yo-yo [ˈɪʊɪəʊ] *n* yoyo, yoyó *m.*
yr[1] [jɪəʳ] *abbr* (*year*) año.
▲ *pl* yrs.
yr[2] [jɔːʳ] *abbr* (*your*) tu, su.
YTS [ˈwaɪˈtiːˈes] *abbr* (*Youth Training Scheme*) plan de empleo juvenil que combina formación profesional con experiencia laboral.

yucca [ˈjʌkə] *n* yuca.
yucky [ˈjʌkɪ] *adj fam* asqueroso,-a.
▲ *comp* yuckier, *superl* yuckiest.
Yugoslav [ˈjuːgəslɑːv] *n* (*person*) yugoslavo,-a.
Yugoslavia [juːgəˈslɑːvɪə] *n* Yugoslavia.
Yugoslavian [juːgəˈslɑːvɪən] **1** *adj* yugoslavo,-a. – **2** *n* yugoslavo,-a.
Yule [juːl] *n* Navidad *f.*
Yuletide [ˈjuːltaɪd] *n →* **Yule**.
yummy [ˈjʌmɪ] *adj fam* de rechupete.
▲ *comp* yummier, *superl* yummiest.
yuppie [ˈjʌpɪ] *n* yuppie *mf.*
YWCA [ˈwaɪˈdʌbəljuːˈsiːˈeɪ] *abbr* (*Young Women's Christian Association*) asociación de jóvenes cristianas.
■ YWCA hostel, albergue *m* para chicas jóvenes.

Z

Z, z [zed] *n* (*the letter*) Z, z *f*.
Zairean [zɑːˈrɪən] **1** *adj* zaireño,-a. – **2** *n* zaireño,-a.
Zambesi [zæmˈbiːzɪ] *n* el Zambesi *m*.
Zambia [ˈzæmbɪə] *n* Zambia.
Zambian [ˈzæmbɪən] **1** *adj* zambiano,-a. – **2** *n* zambiano,-a.
zany [ˈzeɪnɪ] **1** *adj fam* estrafalario,-a. **2** (*mad*) chiflado,-a.
▲ *comp* **zanier,** *superl* **zaniest.**
zap [zæp] **1** *t fam* (*kill*) cargarse. **2** (*attack*) atacar. – **3** *i* (*hurry*) apretar: *he zapped through lunch,* comió volando. – **4** *n* marcha.
▲ *pt & pp* **zapped,** *ger* **zapping.**
Zapotec [ˈzæpətek] **1** *adj* zapoteca. – **2** *n* (*person*) zapoteca *mf*. **3** (*language*) zapoteca *m*.
zappy [ˈzæpɪ] *adj fam* marchoso,-a.
▲ *comp* **zappier,** *superl* **zappiest.**
Zaire [zɑːˈrə] *n* Zaire.
zeal [ziːl] *n* celo, entusiasmo.
zealot [ˈzelət] *n* fanático,-a.
zealous [ˈzeləs] *adj* (*fanatical*) celoso,-a; (*enthusiastic*) entusiasta.
zebra [ˈziːbrə, ˈzebrə] *n* cebra.
■ **zebra crossing,** paso de peatones, paso de cebra.
zebu [ˈziːbuː, ˈziːbjuː] *n* cebú *m*.
zed [zed] *n* GB zeta.
zee [ziː] *n* US zeta.
Zen [zen] *n* Zen *m*.
zenith [ˈzenɪθ] **1** *n* cénit *m*. **2** *fig* apogeo.
zephyr [ˈzefəʳ] *n* céfiro.
zeppelin [ˈzepəlɪn] *n* zepelín *m*.
zero [ˈzɪərəʊ] *n* cero.
▲ *pl* **zeros** o **zeroes.**
zest [zest] **1** *n* (*eagerness*) brío, entusiasmo. **2** (*spice*) emoción *f*. **3** (*of lemon etc*) cáscara.
zestful [ˈzestfʊl] *adj* entusiasta.
zigzag [ˈzɪgzæg] **1** *n* zigzag *m*. – **2** *i* zigzaguear.
▲ *pt & pp* **zigzagged,** *ger* **zigzagging.**
zilch [zɪltʃ] *n* US *sl* nada, nada de nada.
zillion [ˈzɪljən] *n fam* cantidad *f*, mogollón *m*: *zillions of locusts,* cantidad de langostas.

Zimbabwe [zɪmˈbɑːbweɪ] *n* Zimbabwe.
Zimbabwean [zɪmˈbɑːbwɪən] **1** *adj* zimbabwense, zimbabuo,-a. – **2** *n* zimbabwense *mf*, zimbabuo,-a.
zinc [zɪŋk] *n* cinc *m*, zinc *m*.
Zion [ˈzaɪən] *n* Sión *m*.
Zionism [ˈzaɪənɪzəm] *n* sionismo.
Zionist [ˈzaɪənɪst] **1** *adj* sionista. – **2** *n* sionista *mf*.
zip [zɪp] **1** *n* cremallera. **2** *fam* (*energy*) vigor *m*, energía. **3** *fam* (*hiss*) zumbido.
◆ **to zip by 1** *t insep* pasar como un rayo. – **2** *i* pasar como un rayo. ‖ **to zip past** *t-i* → **zip by.** ‖ **to zip up** *t sep* cerrar con cremallera.
■ **zip code,** US código postal. ‖ **zip fastener,** cremallera.
zipper [ˈzɪpəʳ] *n* US cremallera.
zit [zɪt] *n* US *sl* grano.
zodiac [ˈzəʊdɪæk] *n* zodiaco, zodíaco.
zombie [ˈzɒmbɪ] *n* zombi *mf*, zombie *mf*.
zonal [ˈzəʊnəl] *adj* zonal.
zone [zəʊn] **1** *n* zona. – **2** *t* dividir en zonas.
■ **postal zone,** US distrito postal. ‖ **time zone,** huso horario.
zoning [ˈzəʊnɪŋ] *n* división *f* en zonas.
zonked [zɒŋkt] **1** *adj fam* (*exhausted*) reventado,-a, molido,-a. **2** (*drunk*) ciego,-a, colocado,-a. **3** (*drugged*) colocado,-a, flipado,-a.
zoo [zuː] *n* zoo *m*, parque *m* zoológico, zoológico.
▲ *pl* **zoos.**
zoological [zʊəˈlɒdʒɪkəl] *adj* zoológico,-a.
zoologist [zʊˈɒlədʒɪst] *n* zoólogo,-a.
zoology [zʊˈɒlədʒɪ] *n* zoología.
zoom [zuːm] **1** *n* (*noise*) zumbido. **2** (*lens*) objetivo zoom, zoom *m*. – **3** *i* zumbar. **4** AER empinarse.
◆ **to zoom by 1** *t insep fam* pasar volando. – **2** *i fam* pasar volando. ‖ **to zoom past** *t-i* → **zip by.**
■ **zoom lens,** objetivo zoom.
zucchini [zuːˈkiːnɪ] *n* calabacín *m*.
▲ *pl* **zucchini** o **zucchinis.**

ESPAÑOL-INGLÉS

Abreviaturas usadas en este diccionario

abr	abreviatura	*fig*	figurado
adj	adjetivo	FIN	finanzas
adv	adverbio	FÍS	física
AER	aeronáutica	*fml*	formal
AGR	agricultura	*fpl*	femenino plural
algn.	alguien	*fut*	futuro
AM	español americano	GB	inglés británico
ANAT	anatomía	*gen*	general
arg	argot	GEOG	geografía
ARQ	arquitectura	GEOL	geología
ART	arte	*ger*	gerundio
art	artículo	GRAM	gramática
art def	artículo definido	HIST	historia
art indef	artículo indefinido	*i*	verbo intransitivo
ASTROL	astrología	*imperat*	imperativo
ASTRON	astronomía	*imperf*	imperfecto
AUTO	automóvil	*indic*	indicativo
aux	verbo auxiliar	*inf*	infinitivo
AV	aviación	*interj*	interjección
BIOL	biología	*irón*	irónico
BOT	botánica	JUR	derecho
CINEM	cinematografía	LING	lingüística
COMM	comercio	LIT	literatura
conj	conjunción	*loc*	locución
contr	contracción	*loc adv*	locución adverbial
COST	costura	*m*	masculino
CULIN	cocina	*m & f*	género ambiguo
DEP	deporte	MAR	marítimo
ECON	economía	MAT	matemáticas
EDUC	educación	MED	medicina
ELEC	electricidad	METEOR	meteorología
etc	etcétera	*mf*	género común
euf	eufemístico	MIL	militar
f	femenino	*mpl*	masculino plural
fam	familiar	MÚS	música

neut	neutro	REL	religión
ORN	ornitología	*sím*	símbolo
p	verbo pronominal	*sing*	singular
pers	persona	*subj*	subjuntivo
pey	peyorativo, despectivo	*t*	verbo transitivo
pl	plural	TEAT	teatro
POL	política	TÉC	técnica
pp	participio pasado	TV	televisión
pref	prefijo	US	inglés norteamericano
prep	preposición	ZOOL	zoología
pres	presente	→	véase
pron	pronombre	≈	aproximadamente equivalente a
QUÍM	química		
RAD	radio		

Spanish grammar

Main spelling difficulties
The letters *b* and *v*
The letters *c*, *k*, and *q*.
The letters *c* and *z*
The letters *g* and *j*
The letters *r* and *rr*
The written accent
Diphthongs, triphthongs and hiatus

The article

The noun
Formation of the masculine and feminine
Formation of the plural

The adjective
Formation of the masculine and feminine
Formation of the plural
Comparative and superlative
Demonstrative adjectives
Possessive adjectives

The pronoun
Demonstrative pronouns
Possessive pronouns
Personal pronouns

The preposition
General
Uses of *por* and *para*

The adverb
Position of the adverb

The verb
Moods
Persons
Formation of tenses
Pronominal or reflexive verbs
Passive voice
Uses of *ser* and *estar*

Main spelling difficulties

The letters *b* and *v*.

These two letters are pronounced in exactly the same way. The letter *b* is used in all words in which this sound is followed by a consonant: *bruma, blanco, abstenerse*, but the letter *v* is used after *b*, *d* and *n*: *obvio, advertir, convencer*. Apart from this there are no general rules which govern their use; in case of doubt check in the dictionary.

The letters *c*, *k* and *q*.

These three letters are used to represent the sound [k]. Before the vowels *a*, *o*, *u*, before a consonant, and in some cases at the end of a word *c* is used: *casa, color, cuna, frac*. Before the vowels *e* or *i*, *qu* is written: *querer, quitar*. The letter *k* is used in words of foreign origin in which the original spelling has been maintained: *kitsch*.

The letters *c* and *z*.

These two letters are used to represent the sound [θ]. Before the vowels *e* and *i* the letter *c* is used; before the vowels *a*, *o*, *u* and at the end of a word *z* is used: *cero, cima, zapato, azote, zurra, pez*. There are a few exceptions to this rule: *zigzag, zipizape, ¡zis, zas!* Some words may also be written with either *c* or *z*: *ácimo/ázimo, acimut/azimut, eccema/eczema, ceta/zeta, cinc/zinc*.

Note that a final *z* changes to *c* in the plural: *pez - peces*.

The letters *g* and *j*.

The letter *j* is always pronounced [x] (as in the Scottish "loch"). The letter *g* is pronounced [x] when it is followed by the vowels *e* and *i*, but [g] (as in "golf", "get") when it is followed by the vowels *a*, *o* or *u*.
In the group *gu* + *e/i* the *u* is silent and the pronunciation is [g], but when *gu* is followed by *a* or *o* the *u* is pronounced giving the sound [gw]. The group *gü*, with a dieresis over the *u*, is written only before *e* or *i*, and is pronounced [gw]. To summarize:

the sound [x] is written	*j*	before *a*, *o* and *u*
	j or *g*	before *e* and *i*
the sound [g] is written	*g*	before *a*, *o*, *u*
	gu	before *i* and *e*
the sound [gw] is written	*gu*	before *a* and *o*
	gü	before *e* and *i*.

The letters *r* and *rr*.

The letter *r* is used to represent two different sounds: the one-tap [r] sound when it appears either in the middle of a word or in the final position: *carta, ardor*; and the multiple vibrant [rr] when it appears in initial position or follows the consonants *l*, *n* or *s*: *roca, honra*. The double *rr* always represents the multiple vibrant [rr] sound and is written only between vowels: *barro, borrar*.

The written accent.

Words stressed on the final syllable require a written accent on that syllable when they end in a vowel or the consonants *n* or *s*:

  vendrá, café, jabalí, miró, tabú, sillón, Tomás, chochín
but *calor, carril, merced, sagaz, carcaj*.

Words stressed on the penultimate syllable require a written accent on that syllable whenever the word does not end in a vowel or the consonants *n* or *s*:

  árbol, inútil, fémur, Gómez, fútbol
but *cosa, venden, acento, examen, pisos*.

Words stressed on the antepenultimate syllable or earlier always require a written accent on the stressed syllable:

  pájaro, carámbano, cómpratelo, pagándoselas.

Generally speaking, monosyllabic words do not require written accents, but in some cases one is used to distinguish two different words with the same spelling: *él* (he, him) - *el* (the); *té* (tea) - *te* (the letter T). These will be found in the dictionary.

Note that in the case of adverbs ending in *-mente* any written accent in the root adjective is retained:

  fácil - fácilmente; económico - económicamente

Diphthongs, triphthongs and hiatus.
A group of two vowels that make one syllable is called a diphthong; a group of three is called a triphthong. A diphthong is formed by one weak vowel (*i* or *u*) in combination with one strong vowel (*a*, *e* or *o*). A triphthong is one strong vowel between two weak ones. As far as stress is concerned the general rules apply, with both diphthongs and triphthongs being treated as if they were one syllable. If a stressed dipththong or triphthong requires a written accent (following the rules above), this is placed above the strong vowel: *miércoles*, *acariciéis*.

Hiatus occurs when groups of consecutive vowels do not form diphthongs or triphthongs. In these cases the group is usually made up of strong vowels; the stressed vowel will carry a written accent or not in accordance with the rules above: *neón*, *tebeo*, *traéis*. However, when the stressed vowel is a weak vowel, it is the weak vowel which carries the written accent in order to distinguish the group from a diphthong or triphthong: *María*, *reían*, *frío*.

The combination *ui* is always considered a diphthong: *contribuir*, *ruin*.

The article

	definite		indefinite	
	masculine	feminine	masculine	feminine
singular	*el*	*la*	*un*	*una*
plural	*los*	*las*	*unos*	*unas*

Observations
With reflexive verbs the definite article is equivalent to an English possessive adjective in sentences such as: *me lavo la cara* (I wash my face). *cámbiate de ropa* (change your clothes).

The definite article may acquire the pronominal value of the English "the one" or "the ones": *el del traje azul* (the one in the blue suit).

The masculine article (*el*, *un*) is used with feminine nouns which begin with a stressed *a*- or *ha*-, when these are used in the singular: *el agua*, *un hacha*. Note however that the plural forms are regular: *las aguas*, *unas hachas*. Nouns which behave in this way are marked in the dictionary.

The prepositions *a* and *de* and the article *el* contract to give the forms *al* and *del*.

There is also a neuter article *lo* which may be used with an adjective to signify a general quality:

me gusta lo bello (I like all that is beautiful)
lo extraño es que ... (what is strange is that ..., the strange thing is that ...).

The noun
Gender indication in the dictionary
Unlike their English counterparts, Spanish nouns have grammatical gender. In this dictionary the gender of every Spanish headword is given, but in the translations on the English-Spanish side, unmarked nouns ending in -*o* are to be taken to be masculine and those ending in -*a* are to be taken to be feminine; gender is marked in those cases where this does not apply.

Masculine and feminine forms
In many cases gender is shown by the ending which is added to the root. Nouns denoting men or male animals commonly end in -*o* while their counterparts denoting women and female animals end in -*a*: *chico* - *chica*, *gato* - *gata*.

Masculine nouns ending in a consonant add -*a* to form the feminine: *señor*, *señora*.
Some nouns denoting persons have the same form for both sexes. In these cases the gender is indicated only by the article used: *un pianista* (a male pianist); *una pianista* (a female pianist).

In the case of some nouns denoting animals gender is not indicated by the article but by placing the word *macho* or *hembra* after the noun: *una serpiente* (a snake); *una serpiente macho* (a male snake); *una serpiente hembra* (a female snake).

In some cases a change in gender signifes a change in meaning. For example, *la cólera* means "anger" and *el cólera*, "cholera". Such changes of meaning will be found in the dictionary. However there are a very few words which are either masculine or feminine with no change in meaning whatever. Two examples are *mar* and *azúcar*; one may say *el mar está agitado* or *la mar está agitada*. Words of this type are marked *m* & *f* in the dictionary.

Formation of the plural.
Nouns whose plural is formed by adding *-s* are:
-those ending in an unstressed vowel: *pluma, plumas*.
-those ending in a stressed *-é*: *bebé, bebés*.

Nouns whose plural is formed by adding *-es* are:
-the names of vowels: *a, aes; i, íes; o, oes; u, úes*.
-nouns ending in a consonant or stressed *-í*:

color - colores; anís - anises; jabalí - jabalíes.

When a compound noun is written as separate elements only the first element indicates the plural: *ojos de buey, patas de gallo*.

All irregular plurals are indicated at the appropriate entries in the dictionary.

The adjective
The adjective usually goes after the noun, and agrees with it in gender and number:

un coche rojo; las chicas guapas.

However, indefinite, interrogative and exclamative adjectives are placed before the noun, as are adjectives expressing cardinal numbers:

¡qué vergüenza!; ¿cuántos leones hay?; hay treinta leones.

Formation of the masculine and feminine.
Most adjectives have a double ending, one for the feminine and one for the masculine. The most common are those ending in *-o/-a*, *-or/-ora* and those ending in or *-és/-esa* formed from place names: *guapo,-a, trabajador,-ra, barcelonés,-esa*.
Some, however, have a single ending: those which end in *-a, -e, -i, -í, -n, -l, -r, -s, -z* and *-ista*:

alegre, marroquí, común, fiel, familiar, cortés, capaz.

Formation of the plural.
The adjective follows the same rules as are given for the noun above.

Comparative and superlative.
The comparative is formed with *más ... que* or *menos ... que*:

Pedro es más alto que Alberto
los perros corren menos que los tigres.

When *que* in a comparative expression is followed by a verb, it is replaced by *de lo que*:

esto es más complicado de lo que parece.

The English comparative phrases "as ... as" and "so ... as" are rendered by *tan ... como*:

mi patio es tan grande como el tuyo.
The superlative is formed with *el más ... de* or *el menos ... de*:

el chico más listo de la clase.

The absolute superlative is formed by placing *muy* before the adjective or by adding the suffix *-ísimo/-ísima*:

muy preocupado, preocupadísimo.

Observations

A few adjectives have special forms for the comparative and superlative:

bueno,-a	*mejor*	*óptimo,-a*
malo,-a	*peor*	*pésimo,-a*
grande	*mayor*	*mayor*

Comparative and superlative forms ending in *-or* do not change when forming the feminine singular: *la mejor solución*.

Demonstrative adjectives.

			near me	near you	away from both
masculine		sing	*este*	*ese*	*aquel*
		plur	*estos*	*esos*	*aquellos*
feminine		sing	*esta*	*esa*	*aquella*
		plur	*estas*	*esas*	*aquellas*
neuter		sing	*esto*	*eso*	*aquello*

Possessive adjectives

One possessor			yo		tú		él, ella, usted	
masculine	sing	*mi*	*mío*	*tu*	*tuyo*	*su*	*suyo*	
possession	plur	*mis*	*míos*	*tus*	*tuyos*	*sus*	*suyos*	
feminine	sing	*mi*	*mía*	*tu*	*tuya*	*su*	*suya*	
possession	plur	*mis*	*mías*	*tus*	*tuyas*	*sus*	*suyas*	

Note that the forms on the left are those which precede the noun; those on the right follow it:

es mi pariente - es pariente mía
son sus problemas - son problemas suyos

Several possessors		nosotros,-as	vosotros,-as	ellos,-as, ustedes	
masculine	sing	*nuestro*	*vuestro*	*su*	*suyo*
possession	plur	*nuestros*	*vuestros*	*sus*	*suyos*
feminine	sing	*nuestra*	*vuestra*	*su*	*suya*
possession	plur	*nuestras*	*vuestras*	*sus*	*suyas*

The pronoun
Demonstrative pronouns

			near me	near you	away from both
masculine		sing	*éste*	*ése*	*aquél*
		plur	*éstos*	*ésos*	*aquéllos*
feminine		sing	*ésta*	*ésa*	*aquélla*
		plur	*éstas*	*ésas*	*aquéllas*
neuter		sing	*esto*	*eso*	*aquello*

These are used to convey the distance between the person or thing they represent and the speaker or speakers: *no viajaré en este coche, viajaré en aquél*.

Possessive pronouns

One possessor			yo	tú	él, ella, usted	
masculine possession	sing plur		*mío* *míos*	*tuyo* *tuyos*	*suyo* *suyos*	
feminine possession	sing plur		*mía* *mías*	*tuya* *tuyas*	*suya* *suyas*	

Several possessors			nosotros,-as	vosotros,-as	ellos,-as, ustedes	
masculine possession	sing plur		*nuestro* *nuestros*	*vuestro* *vuestros*	*su* *sus*	*suyo* *suyos*
feminine possession	sing plur		*nuestra* *nuestras*	*vuestra* *vuestras*	*su* *sus*	*suya* *suyas*

Like the adjective, the possessive pronoun agrees with the noun denoting the thing possessed: *esta camisa es mía, la tuya está en el armario.*

Personal pronouns.
The following table shows recommended use, although in colloquial Spanish variations will be encountered.

subject	reflexive	strong object	weak object	
			direct	indirect
yo	*me*	*mí*	*me*	*me*
tú	*te*	*ti*	*te*	*te*
él	*se*	*él*	*lo*	*le*
ella	*se*	*ella*	*la*	*le*
usted m	*se*	*usted*	*lo*	*le*
usted f	*se*	*usted*	*la*	*le*
nosotros,-as	*nos*	*nosotros,-as*	*nos*	*nos*
vosotros,-as	*os*	*vosotros,-as*	*os*	*os*
ellos	*se*	*ellos*	*los*	*les*
ellas	*se*	*ellas*	*las*	*les*
ustedes mpl	*se*	*ustedes*	*los*	*les*
ustedes fpl	*se*	*ustedes*	*las*	*les*

Use
The Spanish subject pronoun is used only for emphasis or to prevent ambiguity as the person of the subject is already conveyed by the verb. When neither of these reasons for its use exists, its presence in the sentence renders the style heavy and is to be avoided.

The strong object pronouns are always used as complements or objects preceded by a preposition:

esta carta es para ti, aquélla es para mí
¿son de ustedes estos papeles?

Weak object pronouns precede a verb or are suffixed to an infinitive, imperative or gerund:

me tienes que obedecer; tienes que llamarnos

When several weak pronouns accompany the verb, whether preceding or following it, the second and first person pronouns come before the third: *póntelo*; *me lo ha dicho*. The pronoun *se* always precedes the others: *pónselo*.

Note that while it is considered acceptable to use *le* as a weak object pronoun instead of *lo* when a man is being referred to, this is incorrect when referring to women or to objects of either gender, the same is true of *les* instead of *los*:

	direct object	indirect object
(el jarrón)	*lo tiró a la basura*	*le quitó el asa*
(Domingo)	*acabo de conocerlo/le*	*le di mil pesetas*
(María)	*la vimos ayer*	*le dio un abrazo*
(la botella)	*la he descorchado*	*le he sacado el tapón*
(los niños)	*hay que escucharlos/les*	*les compraron muchos juguetes*
(Pepe y Jaime)	*los/les invitó a cenar*	*les concedieron un premio*
(las plantas)	*estaba regándolas*	*tendría que quitarles las hojas secas*
(Ana y Fefa)	*las llamé por teléfono*	*les pediré disculpas*

Se may also be an impersonal subject equivalent to the English "one", "you", "they", "people" or the passive voice:

hay tantos accidentes porque se conduce demasiado rápido.

When *le* and *les* precede another third person pronoun they are replaced by *se* as in *se lo mandaron*. It is incorrect to say *le lo mandaron*.

Usted and **ustedes** are the second person pronouns used for courtesy. The accompanying verb is in the third person.

Vos is used in several Latin American countries instead of *tú*.

The preposition
General
The most usual Spanish prepositions are: *a*, *ante*, *bajo*, *cabe*, *con*, *contra*, *de*, *desde*, *en*, *entre*, *hacia*, *hasta*, *para*, *por*, *según*, *sin*, *so*, *sobre*, *tras*. Consult the dictionary for their use.

Uses of *por* and *para*
The basic difference between these prepositions is that *por* looks back to the roots, origins or causes of a thing, while *para* looks forwards to the result, aim, goal or destination.

por is used to express:
- cause, reason, motive (usually to say why something has happened): *lo hizo por amor*.
- the period in which the action takes place: *vendrán por la mañana*.
- the place where the action takes place: *pasean por la calle*.
- the means: *lo enviaron por avión*.
- the agent of the passive voice: *el incendio fue provocado por el portero*.
- substitution, equivalence: *aquí puedes comer por mil pesetas*.
- distribution, proportion: *cinco por ciento*; *trescientas pesetas por persona*.
- multiplication and measurements: *cinco por dos son diez*.
- "in search of" with verbs of movement (*ir*, *venir* ...): *voy por pan*.
- *estar* + *por* + infinitive expresses:
  - an action still to be performed: *la cena está por hacer*.
  - an action on the point of being performed: *estaba por llamarte*.
- *tener/dar* + *por* expresses opinion: *lo dieron por perdido*.

para is used to express:
- purpose: *esto sirve para limpiar los cristales*
- finality, destiny (often in the future): *es para tu padre*, *compra pescado para la cena*.
- direction of movement, i.e. "towards": *salen para Valencia*.
- deadlines: *lo quiero para mañana*.
- comparison: *es muy alta para la edad que tiene*.
- *estar* + *para* + infinitive expresses imminence: *está para llegar*.

The adverb
Position of the adverb
As a rule, when the word to be qualified is an adjective or an adverb, the adverb is placed immediately before it: *un plato bien cocinado*.

When the word to be qualified is a verb, the adverb may be placed before or after it:

hoy iré al mercado; *iré al mercado hoy*.

Negative adverbs are always placed before the verb:

no lo he visto; *nunca volverás a verme*.

Very rarely, adverbs may be placed between the auxiliary verb and the principal verb:

ha llegado felizmente a su destino.

The verb
Moods
Spanish verbs have three moods, the indicative, subjunctive and imperative.

The indicative is generally used to indicate real actions. It is mainly used in independent statements:

los coches circulan por la calzada.

The subjunctive is mainly used in subordinate statements where the actions are considered to be potential or doubtful, but not real: *es posible que venga*; or else necessary or desired: *¡ojalá venga!*

The imperative is used to express orders: *¡Ven!*; *¡Venid pronto!*. In negative imperatives the subjunctive is used: *¡No vengas!*

Persons
The endings of verbs vary according to whether the subject is the first, second or third person, singular or plural (see **Personal pronouns**). While in English it is not possible to omit the subject, it is quite common in Spanish since the ending of the verb indicates the subject.

Formation of tenses
For the formation of all tenses of both regular and irregular verbs see the Spanish verb conjugation tables at the end of this section.

Pronominal or reflexive verbs
Pronominal or reflexive verbs are those which are conjugated with a personal pronoun functioning as a complement, coinciding in person with the subject: for example the verb *cambiar* has a pronominal form which is *cambiarse*: *se cambia de ropa*.

The personal pronouns (*me, te, se, nos, os, se*) are placed before the verb in all tenses and persons of the indicative and subjunctive moods, but are suffixed onto the infinitive, gerund and imperative.

se ducha cada día; *¡dúchate ya!*

In compound tenses the pronoun is placed immediately before the auxiliary verb.

no se ha duchado

The passive voice
The passive voice in Spanish is formed with the auxiliary verb *ser* and the past participle of the conjugating verb:

el cazador hirió al jabalí - el jabalí fue herido por el cazador.

The use of this form of passive statement is less frequent than in English. However, another construction, the reflexive (or impersonal) passive, is quite common:

se vende leña; *se alquilan apartamentos*; *se habla inglés*.

Uses of *ser* and *estar*

The English verb "to be" may be rendered in Spanish by two verbs: *ser* and *estar*.

When followed by a noun:

ser is used without a preposition to indicate occupation or profession:

Jaime es el director de ventas (Jaime is the sales manager)
Eduardo es médico (Eduardo is a doctor).

ser with the preposition *de* indicates origin or possession:

soy de Salamanca (I am from Salamanca).
es de Alberto (it is Alberto's)

ser with *para* indicates destination:

el disco es para Pilar (the record is for Pilar).

estar cannot be followed directly by a noun, it always takes a preposition and the meaning is dictated by the preposition. It is worth noting, however, its special use with *de* to indicate that someone is performing a function which they do not usually perform:

Andrés está de secretario (Andrés is acting as secretary)

Where the verb is followed by an adjective:

ser expresses a permanent or inherent quality:

Jorge es rubio; sus ojos son grandes.

estar expresses a quality which is neither permanent nor inherent:

Mariano está resfriado; el cielo está nublado.

Sometimes both verbs may be used with the same adjective, but there is a change of meaning. For example, **Lorenzo es bueno** means that Lorenzo is a good man but **Lorenzo está bueno** means either that he is no longer ill or, colloquially, that he is good-looking.

Finally, *estar* is used to indicate position and geographical location:

tu cena está en el microondas; Tafalla está en Navarra.

Spanish verb conjugation tables

Models for the conjugation of regular verbs

Simple tenses

1st conjugation - **AMAR**

Pres Ind	amo, amas, ama, amamos, amáis, aman.
Past Ind	amé, amaste, amó, amamos, amasteis, amaron.
Imperf Ind	amaba, amabas, amaba, amábamos, amabais, amaban.
Fut Ind	amaré, amarás, amará, amaremos, amaréis, amarán.
Cond	amaría, amarías, amaría, amaríamos, amaríais, amarían.
Pres Subj	ame, ames, ame, amemos, améis, amen.
Imperf Subj	amara, amaras, amara, amáramos, amarais, amaran; amase, amases, amase, amásemos, amaseis, amasen.
Fut Subj	amare, amares, amare, amáremos, amareis, amaren.
Imperat	ama (tú), ame (él/Vd.), amemos (nos.) amad (vos.) amen (ellos/Vds.).
Gerund	amando.
Past Part	amado,-a.

2nd conjugation - **TEMER**

Pres Ind	temo, temes, teme, tememos, teméis, temen.
Past Ind	temí, temiste, temió, temimos, temisteis, temieron.
Imperf Ind	temía, temías, temía, temíamos, temíais, temían.
Fut Ind	temeré, temerás, temerá, temeremos, temeréis, temerán.
Cond	temería, temerías, temería, temeríamos, temeríais, temerían.
Pres Subj	tema, temas, tema, tememos, temáis, teman.
Imperf Subj	temiera, temieras, temiera, temiéramos, temierais, temieran; temiese, temieses, temiese, temiésemos, temieseis, temiesen.
Fut Subj	temiere, temieres, temiere, temiéremos, temiereis, temieren.
Imperat	teme (tú), tema (él/Vd.), temamos (nos.) temed (vos.) teman (ellos/Vds.).
Gerund	temiendo.
Past Part	temido,-a.

3rd conjugation - **PARTIR**

Pres Ind	parto, partes, parte, partimos, partís, parten.
Past Ind	partí, partiste, partió, partimos, partisteis, partieron.
Imperf Ind	partía, partías, partía, partíamos, partíais, partían.
Fut Ind	partiré, partirás, partirá, partiremos, partiréis, partirán.
Cond	partiría, partirías, partiría, partiríamos, partiríais, partirían.
Pres Subj	parta, partas, parta, partamos, partáis, partan.
Imperf Subj	partiera, partieras, partiera, partiéramos, partierais, partieran; partiese, partieses, partiese, partiésemos, partieseis, partiesen.
Fut Subj	partiere, partieres, partiere, partiéremos, partiereis, partieren.
Imperat	parte (tú), parta (él/Vd.), partamos (nos.) partid (vos.) partan (ellos/Vds.).
Gerund	partiendo.
Past Part	partido,-a.

Note that the imperative proper has forms for the second person (**tú** and **vosotros**) only; all other forms are taken from the present subjunctive.

Compound tenses

Pres Perf	he, has, ha, hemos, habeis, han amado/temido/partido
Pluperf	había, habías, había, habíamos, habíais, habían amado/temido/partido
Fut Perf	habré, habrás, habrá, habremos, habreis, habrán amado/temido/partido
Cond Perf	habría, habrías, habría, habríamos, habríais, habrían amado/temido/partido
Past Anterior	hube, hubiste, hubo, hubimos, hubisteis, hubieron amado/temido/partido
Pres Perf Subj	haya, hayas, haya, hayamos, hayáis, hayan amado/temido/partido
Pluperf Subj	hubiera, hubieras, hubiera, hubiéramos, hubierais, hubieran amado/temido/partido
	hubiese, hubieses, hubiese, hubiésemos, hubieseis, hubiesen amado/temido/partido.

Models for the conjugation of irregular verbs

Only the tenses which present irregularities are given here; other tenses follow the regular models above. Irregularities are shown in bold type.

1. SACAR (c changes to qu before e)
Past Ind	**saqué**, sacaste, sacó, sacamos, sacasteis, sacaron.
Pres Subj	**saque, saques, saque, saquemos, saquéis, saquen**.
Imperat	saca (tú), **saque** (él/Vd.), **saquemos** (nos.), sacad (vos.), **saquen** (ellos/Vds.).

2. MECER (c changes to z before a and o)
Pres Ind	**mezo**, meces, mece, mecemos, mecéis, mecen.
Pres Subj	**meza, mezas, meza, mezamos, mezáis, mezan**.
Imperat	mece (tú), **meza** (él/Vd.), **mezamos** (nos.), meced (vos.), **mezan** (ellos/Vds.).

3. ZURCIR (c changes to z before a and o)
Pres Ind	**zurzo**, zurces, zurce, zurcimos, zurcís, zurcen.
Pres Subj	**zurza, zurzas, zurza, zurzamos, zurzáis, zurzan**.
Imperat	zurce (tú), **zurza** (él/Vd.), **zurzamos** (nos.), zurcid (vos.), **zurzan** (ellos/Vds.).

4. REALIZAR (z changes to c before e)
Past Ind	**realicé**, realizaste, realizó, realizamos, realizasteis, realizaron.
Pres Subj	**realice, realices, realice, realicemos, realicéis, realicen**.
Imperat	realiza (tú), **realice** (él/Vd.), **realicemos** (nos.), realizad (vos.), **realicen** (ellos/Vds.).

5. PROTEGER (g changes to j before a and o)
Pres Ind	**protejo**, proteges, protege, protegemos, protegéis, protegen.
Pres Subj	**proteja, protejas, proteja, protejamos, protejáis, protejan**.
Imperat	protege (tú), **proteja** (él/Vd.), **protejamos** (nos.), proteged (vos.), **protejan** (ellos/Vds.).

6. DIRIGIR (g changes to j before a and o)
Pres Ind	**dirijo**, diriges, dirige, dirigimos, dirigís, dirigen.
Pres Subj	**dirija, dirijas, dirija, dirijamos, dirijáis, dirijan**.
Imperat	dirige (tú), **dirija** (él/Vd.), **dirijamos** (nos.), dirigid (vos.), **dirijan** (ellos/Vds.).

7. LLEGAR (g changes to gu before e)
Past Ind	**llegué**, llegaste, llegó, llegamos, llegasteis, llegaron.
Pres Subj	**llegue, llegues, llegue, lleguemos, lleguéis, lleguen**.
Imperat	llega (tú), **llegue** (él/Vd.), **lleguemos** (nos.), llegad (vos.), **lleguen** (ellos/Vds.).

8. DISTINGUIR (gu changes to g before a and o)
Pres Ind	**distingo**, distingues, distingue, distinguimos, distinguís, distinguen.
Pres Subj	**distinga, distingas, distinga, distingamos, distingáis, distingan**.
Imperat	distingue (tú), **distinga** (él/Vd.), **distingamos** (nos.), distinguid (vos.), **distingan** (ellos/Vds.).

9. DELINQUIR (qu changes to c before a and o)
Pres Ind	**delinco**, delinques, delinque, delinquimos, delinquís, delinquen.
Pres Subj	**delinca, delincas, delinca, delincamos, delincáis, delincan**.
Imperat	delinque (tú), **delinca** (él/Vd.), **delincamos** (nos.), delinquid (vos.), **delincan** (ellos/Vds.).

10. ADECUAR* (unstressed u)
Pres Ind	adecuo, adecuas, adecua, adecuamos, adecuáis, adecuan.
Pres Subj	adecue, adecues, adecue, adecuemos, adecuéis, adecuen.
Imperat	adecua (tú), adecue (él/Vd.), adecuemos (nos.), adecuad (vos.), adecuen (ellos/Vds.).

11. ACTUAR (stressed ú in certain persons of certain tenses)
Pres Ind	**actúo, actúas, actúa**, actuamos, actuáis, **actúan**.
Pres Subj	**actúe, actúes, actúe**, actuemos, actuéis, **actúen**.
Imperat	**actúa** (tú), **actúe** (él/Vd.), actuemos (nos.), actuad (vos.), **actúen** (ellos/Vds.).

12. CAMBIAR* (unstressed i)
Pres Ind	cambio, cambias, cambia, cambiamos, cambiáis, cambian.
Pres Subj	cambie, cambies, cambie, cambiemos, cambiéis, cambien.
Imperat	cambia (tú), cambie (él/Vd.), cambiemos (nos.), cambiad (vos.), cambien (ellos/Vds.).

13. DESVIAR (*stressed* **í** *in certain persons of certain tenses*)
Pres Ind   **desvío, desvías, desvía**, desviamos, desviáis, **desvían**.
Pres Subj   **desvíe, desvíes, desvíe**, desviemos, desviéis, **desvíen**.
Imperat   **desvía** (tú), **desvíe** (él/Vd.), desviemos (nos.), desviad (vos.), **desvíen** (ellos/Vds.).

14. AUXILIAR (**i** *can be stressed* **or** *unstressed*)
Pres Ind   **auxilío, auxilías, auxilía**, auxiliamos, auxiliáis, **auxilían**.
               auxilio, auxilias, auxilia, auxiliamos, auxiliáis, auxilian.
Pres Subj   **auxilíe, auxilíes, auxilíe**, auxiliemos, auxiliéis, **auxilíen**.
               auxilie, auxilies, auxilie, auxiliemos, auxiliéis, auxilien.
Imperat   **auxilía** (tú), **auxilíe** (él/Vd.), auxiliemos (nos.), auxiliad, (vos.), **auxilíen** (ellos/Vds.)
               auxilia (tú), auxilie (él/Vd.), auxiliemos (nos.), auxiliad (vos.), auxilien (ellos/Vds.).

15. AISLAR (*stressed* **í** *in certain persons of certain tenses*)
Pres Ind   **aíslo, aíslas, aísla**, aislamos, aisláis, **aíslan**.
Pres Subj   **aísle, aísles, aísle**, aislemos, aisléis, **aíslen**.
Imperat   **aísla** (tú), **aísle** (él/Vd.), aislemos (nos.), aislad (vos.), **aíslen** (ellos/Vds.).

16. AUNAR (*stressed* **ú** *in certain persons of certain tenses*)
Pres Ind   **aúno, aúnas, aúna**, aunamos, aunáis, **aúnan**.
Pres Subj   **aúne, aúnes, aúne**, aunemos, aunéis, **aúnen**.
Imperat   **aúna** (tú), **aúne** (él/Vd.), aunemos (nos.), aunad (vos.), **aúnen** (ellos/Vds.).

17. DESCAFEINAR (*stressed* **í** *in certain persons of certain tenses*)
Pres Ind   **descafeíno, descafeínas, descafeína**, descafeinamos, descafeináis, **descafeínan**.
Pres Subj   **descafeíne, descafeínes, descafeíne**, descafeinemos, descafeinéis, **descafeínen**.
Imperat   **descafeína** (tú), **descafeíne** (él/Vd.), descafeinemos (nos.), descafeinad (vos.), **descafeínen** (ellos/Vds.).

18. REHUSAR (*stressed* **ú** *in certain persons of certain tenses*)
Pres Ind   **rehúso, rehúsas, rehúsa**, rehusamos, rehusáis, **rehúsan**.
Pres Subj   **rehúse, rehúses, rehúse**, rehusemos, rehuséis, **rehúsen**.
Imperat   **rehúsa** (tú), **rehúse** (él/Vd.), rehusemos (nos.), rehusad (vos.), **rehúsen** (ellos/Vds.).

19. REUNIR (*stressed* **ú** *in certain persons of certain tenses*)
Pres Ind   **reúno, reúnes, reúne**, reunimos, reunís, **reúnen**.
Pres Subj   **reúna, reúnas, reúna**, reunamos, reunáis, **reúnan**.
Imperat   **reúne** (tú), **reúna** (él/Vd.), reunamos (nos.), reunid (vos.), **reúnan** (ellos/Vds.).

20. AMOHINAR (*stressed* **í** *in certain persons of certain tenses*)
Pres Ind   **amohíno, amohínas, amohína**, amohinamos, amohináis, **amohínan**.
Pres Subj   **amohíne, amohínes, amohíne**, amohinemos, amohinéis, **amohínen**.
Imperat   **amohína** (tú), **amohíne** (él/Vd.), amohinemos (nos.), amohinad (vos.), **amohínen** (ellos/Vds.).

21. PROHIBIR (*stressed* **í** *in certain persons of certain tenses*)
Pres Ind   **prohíbo, prohíbes, prohíbe**, prohibimos, prohibís, **prohíben**.
Pres Subj   **prohíba, prohíbas, prohíba**, prohibamos, prohibáis, **prohíban**.
Imperat   **prohíbe** (tú), **prohíba** (él/Vd.), prohibamos (nos.), prohibid (vos.), **prohíban** (ellos/Vds.).

22. AVERIGUAR (*unstressed* **u**; **gu** *changes to* **gü** *before* **e**)
Past Ind   **averigüé**, averiguaste, averiguó, averiguamos, averiguasteis, averiguaron.
Pres Subj   **averigüe, averigües, averigüe, averigüemos, averigüéis, averigüen**.
Imperat   averigua (tú), **averigüe** (él/Vd.), **averigüemos** (nos.), averiguad (vos.), **averigüen** (ellos/Vds.).

23. AHINCAR (*stressed* **í** *in certain persons of certain tenses*; *the* **c** *changes to* **qu** *before* **e**)
Pres Ind   **ahínco, ahíncas, ahínca**, ahincamos, ahincáis, **ahíncan**.
Past Ind   **ahinqué**, ahincaste, ahincó, ahincamos, ahincasteis, ahincaron.
Pres Subj   **ahínque, ahínques, ahínque, ahinquemos, ahinquéis, ahínquen**.
Imperat   **ahínca** (tú), **ahínque** (él/Vd.), **ahinquemos** (nos.), ahincad (vos.), **ahínquen** (ellos/Vds.).

24. ENRAIZAR (*stressed* **í** *in certain persons of certain tenses*; *the* **z** *changes to* **c** *before* **e**)
Pres Ind   **enraízo, enraízas, enraíza**, enraizamos, enraizáis, **enraízan**.
Past Ind   **enraicé**, enraizaste, enraizó, enraizamos, enraizasteis, enraizaron.
Pres Subj   **enraíce, enraíces, enraíce, enraicemos, enraicéis, enraícen**.
Imperat   **enraíza** (tú), **enraíce** (él/Vd.), **enraicemos** (nos.), enraizad (vos.), **enraícen** (ellos/Vds.).

25. CABRAHIGAR (*stressed í in certain persons of certain tenses; the g changes to gu before e*)
Pres Ind   **cabrahígo, cabrahígas, cabrahíga,** cabrahigamos, cabrahigáis, **cabrahígan.**
Past Ind   **cabrahigué,** cabrahigaste, cabrahigó, cabrahigamos, cabrahigasteis, cabrahigaron.
Pres Subj   **cabrahígue, cabrahígues, cabrahígue, cabrahiguemos, cabrahiguéis, cabrahíguen.**
Imperat   **cabrahíga** (tú), **cabrahígue** (él/Vd.), **cabrahiguemos** (nos.), cabrahigad (vos.), **cabrahíguen** (ellos/ Vds.).

26. HOMOGENEIZAR (*stressed í in certain persons of certain tenses, the z changes to c before e*)
Pres Ind   **homogeneízo, homogeneízas, homogeneíza,** homogeneizamos, homogeneizáis, **homogeneízan.**
Past Ind   **homogeneicé,** homogeneizaste, homogeneizó, homogeneizamos, homogeneizasteis, homogeneizaron.
Pres Subj   **homogeneíce, homogeneíces, homogeneíce, homogeneicemos, homogeneicéis, homogeneícen.**
Imperat   **homogeneíza** (tú), **homogeneíce** (él/Vd.), **homogeneicemos** (nos.), homogeneizad (vos.), **homogeneícen** (ellos/Vds.).

27. ACERTAR (*e changes to ie in stressed syllables*)
Pres Ind   **acierto, aciertas, acierta,** acertamos, acertáis, **aciertan.**
Pres Subj   **acierte, aciertes, acierte,** acertemos, acertéis, **acierten.**
Imperat   **acierta** (tú), **acierte** (él/Vd.), acertemos (nos.), acertad (vos.), **acierten** (ellos/Vds.).

28. ENTENDER (*e changes to ie in stressed syllables*)
Pres Ind   **entiendo, entiendes, entiende,** entendemos, entendéis, **entienden.**
Pres Subj   **entienda, entiendas, entienda,** entendamos, entendáis, **entiendan.**
Imperat   **entiende** (tú), **entienda** (él/Vd.), entendamos (nos.), entended (vos.), **entiendan** (ellos/Vds.).

29. DISCERNIR (*e changes to ie in stressed syllables*)
Pres Ind   **discierno, disciernes, discierne,** discernimos, discernís, **disciernen.**
Pres Subj   **discierna, disciernas, discierna,** discernamos, discernáis, **disciernan.**
Imperat   **discierne** (tú), **discierna** (él/Vd.), discernamos (nos.), discernid (vos.), **disciernan** (ellos/Vds.).

30. ADQUIRIR (*i changes to ie in stressed syllables*)
Pres Ind   **adquiero, adquieres, adquiere,** adquirimos, adquirís, **adquieren.**
Pres Subj   **adquiera, adquieras, adquiera,** adquiramos, adquiráis, **adquieran.**
Imperat   **adquiere** (tú), **adquiera** (él/Vd.), adquiramos (nos.), adquirid (vos.), **adquieran** (ellos/Vds.).

31. CONTAR (*o changes to ue in stressed syllables*)
Pres Ind   **cuento, cuentas, cuenta,** contamos, contáis, **cuentan.**
Pres Subj   **cuente, cuentes, cuente,** contemos, contéis, **cuenten.**
Imperat   **cuenta** (tú), **cuente** (él/Vd.), contemos (nos.), contad (vos.), **cuenten** (ellos/Vds.).

32. MOVER (*o changes to ue in stressed syllables*)
Pres Ind   **muevo, mueves, mueve,** movemos, movéis, **mueven.**
Pres Subj   **mueva, muevas, mueva,** movamos, mováis, **muevan.**
Imperat   **mueve** (tú), **mueva** (él/Vd.), movamos (nos.), moved (vos.), **muevan** (ellos/Vds.).

33. DORMIR (*o changes to ue in stressed syllables or to u in certain persons of certain tenses*)
Pres Ind   **duermo, duermes, duerme,** dormimos, dormís, **duermen.**
Past Ind   dormí, dormiste, **durmió,** dormimos, dormisteis, **durmieron.**
Pres Subj   **duerma, duermas, duerma, durmamos, durmáis, duerman.**
Imperf Subj   **durmiera, durmieras, durmiera, durmiéramos, durmierais, durmieran; durmiese, durmieses, durmiese, durmiésemos, durmieseis, durmiesen.**
Fut Subj   **durmiere, durmieres, durmiere, durmiéremos, durmiereis, durmieren.**
Imperat   **duerme** (tú), **duerma** (él/Vd.), **durmamos** (nos.), dormid (vos.), **duerman** (ellos/Vds.).

34. SERVIR (*e weakens to i in certain persons of certain tenses*)
Pres Ind   **sirvo, sirves, sirve,** servimos, servís, **sirven.**
Past Ind   serví, serviste, **sirvió,** servimos, servisteis, **sirvieron.**
Pres Subj   **sirva, sirvas, sirva, sirvamos, sirváis, sirvan.**
Imperf Subj   **sirviera, sirvieras, sirviera, sirviéramos, sirvierais, sirvieran; sirviese, sirvieses, sirviese, sirviésemos, sirvieseis, sirviesen.**
Fut Subj   **sirviere, sirvieres, sirviere, sirviéremos, sirviereis, sirvieren.**
Imperat   **sirve** (tú), **sirva** (él/Vd.), **sirvamos** (nos.), servid (vos.), **sirvan** (ellos/Vds.).

35. HERVIR (*e changes to* **ie** *in stressed syllables or to* **i** *in certain persons of certain tenses*)
Pres Ind   **hiervo, hierves, hierve,** hervimos, hervís, **hierven.**
Past Ind   herví, herviste, **hirvió,** hervimos, hervisteis, **hirvieron.**
Pres Subj   **hierva, hiervas, hierva, hirvamos, hirváis, hiervan.**
Imperf Subj **hirviera, hirvieras, hirviera, hirviéramos, hirvierais, hirvieran; hirviese, hirvieses, hirviese, hirviésemos, hirvieseis, hirviesen.**
Fut Subj   **hirviere, hirvieres, hirviere, hirviéremos, hirviereis, hirvieren.**
Imperat   **hierve** (tú), **hierva** (él/Vd.), **hirvamos** (nos.), hervid (vos.), **hiervan** (ellos/Vds.).

36. CEÑIR (*the* **i** *of certain endings is absorbed by* **ñ**; *the* **e** *changes to* **i** *in certain persons of certain tenses*)
Pres Ind   **ciño, ciñes, ciñe,** ceñimos, ceñís, **ciñen.**
Past Ind   ceñí, ceñiste, **ciñó,** ceñimos, ceñisteis, **ciñeron.**
Pres Subj   **ciña, ciñas, ciña, ciñamos, ciñáis, ciñan.**
Imperf Subj **ciñera, ciñeras, ciñera, ciñéramos, ciñerais, ciñeran; ciñese, ciñeses, ciñese, ciñésemos, ciñeseis, ciñesen.**
Fut Subj   **ciñere, ciñeres, ciñere, ciñéremos, ciñereis, ciñeren.**
Imperat   **ciñe** (tú), **ciña** (él/Vd.), **ciñamos** (nos.), ceñid (vos.), **ciñan** (ellos/Vds.).

37. REÍR (*like* **ceñir,** *but the loss of* **i** *is not due to the influence of any consonant*)
Pres Ind   **río, ríes, ríe,** reímos, reís, **ríen.**
Past Ind   reí, reíste, **rió,** reímos, reísteis, **rieron.**
Pres Subj   **ría, rías, ría, riamos, riáis, rían.**
Imperf Subj **riera, rieras, riera, riéramos, rierais, rieran; riese, rieses, riese, riésemos, rieseis, riesen.**
Fut Subj   **riere, rieres, riere, riéremos, riereis, rieren.**
Imperat   **ríe** (tú), **ría** (él/Vd.), **riamos** (nos.), reíd (vos.), **rían** (ellos/Vds.).

38. TAÑER (*the* **i** *ending is absorbed by* **ñ** *in certain persons of certain tenses*)
Past Ind   tañí, tañiste, **tañó,** tañimos, tañisteis, **tañeron.**
Imperf Subj **tañera, tañeras, tañera, tañéramos, tañerais, tañeran; tañese, tañeses, tañese, tañésemos, tañeseis, tañesen.**
Fut Subj   **tañere, tañeres, tañere, tañéremos, tañereis, tañeren.**

39. EMPELLER (*the* **i** *ending is absorbed by* **ll** *in certain persons of certain tenses*)
Past Ind   empellí, empelliste, **empelló,** empellimos, empellisteis, **empelleron.**
Imperf Subj **empellera, empelleras, empellera, empelléramos, empellerais, empelleran; empellese, empelleses, empellese, empellésemos, empelleseis, empellesen.**
Fut Subj   **empellere, empelleres, empellere, empelléremos, empellereis, empelleren.**

40. MUÑIR (*the* **i** *ending is absorbed by* **ñ** *in certain persons of certain tenses*)
Past Ind   muñí, muñiste, **muñó,** muñimos, muñisteis, **muñeron.**
Imperf Subj **muñera, muñeras, muñera, muñéramos, muñerais, muñeran; muñese, muñeses, muñese, muñésemos, muñeseis, muñesen.**
Fut Subj   **muñere, muñeres, muñere, muñéremos, muñereis, muñeren.**

41. MULLIR (*the* **i** *ending is absorbed by the* **ll** *in certain persons of certain tenses*)
Past Ind   mullí, mulliste, **mulló,** mullimos, mullisteis, **mulleron.**
Imperf Subj **mullera, mulleras, mullera, mulléramos, mullerais, mulleran; mullese, mulleses, mullese, mullésemos, mulleseis, mullesen.**
Fut Subj   **mullere, mulleres, mullere, mulléremos, mullereis, mulleren.**

42. NACER (*c changes to* **zc** *before* **a** *and* **o**)
Pres Ind   **nazco,** naces, nace, nacemos, nacéis, nacen.
Pres Subj   **nazca, nazcas, nazca, nazcamos, nazcáis, nazcan.**
Imperat   nace (tú), **nazca** (él/Vd.), **nazcamos** (nos.), naced (vos.), **nazcan** (ellos/Vds.).

43. AGRADECER (*c changes to* **zc** *before* **a** *and* **o**)
Pres Ind   **agradezco,** agradeces, agradece, agradecemos, agradecéis, agradecen.
Pres Subj   **agradezca, agradezcas, agradezca, agradezcamos, agradezcáis, agradezcan.**
Imperat   agradece (tú), **agradezca** (él/Vd.), **agradezcamos** (nos.), agradeced (vos.), **agradezcan** (ellos/Vds.).

44. CONOCER (*c changes to* **zc** *before* **a** *and* **o**)
Pres Ind   **conozco,** conoces, conoce, conemos, conocéis, conocen.
Pres Subj   **conozca, conozcas, conozca, conozcamos, conozcáis, conozcan.**
Imperat   conoce (tú), **conozca** (él/Vd.), **conozcamos** (nos.), conoced (vos.), **conozcan** (ellos/Vds.).

45. LUCIR (*c changes to* **zc** *before* **a** *and* **o**)
Pres Ind   **luzco**, luces, luce, lucimos, lucís, lucen.
Pres Subj   **luzca, luzcas, luzca, luzcamos, luzcáis, luzcan**.
Imperat   luce (tú), **luzca** (él/Vd.), **luzcamos** (nos.), lucid (vos.), **luzcan** (ellos/Vds.).

46. CONDUCIR (*c changes to* **zc** *before* **a** *and* **o**; *the Preterite is irregular*)
Pres Ind   **conduzco**, conduces, conduce, conducimos, conducís, conducen.
Past Ind   **conduje, condujiste, condujo, condujimos, condujisteis, condujeron**.
Pres Subj   **conduzca, conduzcas, conduzca, conduzcamos, conduzcáis, conduzcan**.
Imperf Subj   **condujera, condujeras, condujera, condujéramos, condujerais, condujeran; condujese, condujeses, condujese, condujésemos, condujeseis, condujesen**.
Fut Subj   **condujere, condujeres, condujere, condujéremos, condujereis, condujeren**.
Imperat   conduce (tú), **conduzca** (él/Vd.), **conduzcamos** (nos.), conducid (vos.), **conduzcan** (ellos/Vds.).

47. EMPEZAR (*e changes to* **ie** *in stressed syllables and* **z** *changes to* **c** *before* **e**)
Pres Ind   **empiezo, empiezas, empieza**, empezamos, empezáis, **empiezan**.
Past ind   **empecé**, empezaste, empezó, empezamos, empezasteis, empezaron.
Pres Subj   **empiece, empieces, empiece, empecemos, empecéis, empiecen**.
Imperat   **empieza** (tú), **empiece** (él/Vd.), **empecemos** (nos.), empezad (vos.), **empiecen** (ellos/Vds.).

48. REGAR (*e changes to* **ie** *in stressed syllables;* **g** *changes to* **gu** *before* **e**)
Pres Ind   **riego, riegas, riega**, regamos, regáis, **riegan**.
Past Ind   **regué**, regaste, regó, regamos, regasteis, regaron.
Pres Subj   **riegue, riegues, riegue, reguemos, reguéis, rieguen**.
Imperat   **riega** (tú), **riegue** (él/Vd.), **reguemos** (nos.), regad (vos.), **rieguen** (ellos/Vds.).

49. TROCAR (*o changes to* **ue** *in stressed syllables;* **c** *changes to* **qu** *before* **e**)
Pres Ind   **trueco, truecas, trueca**, trocamos, trocáis, **truecan**.
Past Ind   **troqué**, trocaste, trocó, trocamos, trocasteis, trocaron.
Pres Subj   **trueque, trueques, trueque, troquemos, troquéis, truequen**.
Imperat   **trueca** (tú), **trueque** (él/Vd.), **troquemos** (nos.), trocad (vos.), **truequen** (ellos/Vds.).

50. FORZAR (*o changes to* **ue** *in stressed syllables;* **z** *changes to* **c** *before* **e**)
Pres Ind   **fuerzo, fuerzas, fuerza**, forzamos, forzáis, **fuerzan**.
Past Ind   **forcé**, forzaste, forzó, forzamos, forzasteis, forzaron.
Pres Subj   **fuerce, fuerces, fuerce, forcemos, forcéis, fuercen**.
Imperat   **fuerza** (tú), **fuerce** (él/Vd.), **forcemos** (nos.), forzad (vos.), **fuercen** (ellos/Vds.).

51. AVERGONZAR (*in stressed syllables* **o** *changes to* **ue** *and* **g** *to* **gü**; **z** *changes to* **c** *before* **e**)
Pres Ind   **avergüenzo, avergüenzas, avergüenza**, avergonzamos, avergonzáis, **avergüenzan**.
Past Ind   **avergoncé**, avergonzaste, avergonzó, avergonzamos, avergonzasteis, avergonzaron.
Pres Subj   **avergüence, avergüences, avergüence**, avergoncemos, avergoncéis, **avergüencen**.
Imperat   **avergüenza** (tú), **avergüence** (él/Vd.), **avergoncemos** (nos.), avergonzad (vos.), **avergüencen** (ellos/Vds.).

52. COLGAR (*o changes to* **ue** *in stressed syllables;* **g** *changes to* **gu** *before* **e**)
Pres Ind   **cuelgo, cuelgas, cuelga**, colgamos, colgáis, **cuelgan**.
Past Ind   **colgué**, colgaste, colgó, colgamos, colgasteis, colgaron.
Pres Subj   **cuelgue, cuelgues, cuelgue, colguemos, colguéis, cuelguen**.
Imperat   **cuelga** (tú), **cuelgue** (él/Vd.), **colguemos** (nos.), colgad (vos.), **cuelguen** (ellos/Vds.).

53. JUGAR (**u** *changes to* **ue** *in stressed syllables and* **g** *changes to* **gu** *before* **e**)
Pres Ind   **juego, juegas, juega**, jugamos, jugáis, **juegan**.
Past Ind   **jugué**, jugaste, jugó, jugamos, jugasteis, jugaron.
Pres Subj   **juegue, juegues, juegue, juguemos, juguéis, jueguen**.
Imperat   **juega** (tú), **juegue** (él/Vd.), **juguemos** (nos.), jugad (vos.), **jueguen** (ellos/Vds.).

54. COCER (*o changes to* **ue** *in stressed syllables and* **c** *changes to* **z** *before* **a** *and* **o**)
Pres Ind   **cuezo, cueces, cuece**, cocemos, cocéis, **cuecen**.
Pres Subj   **cueza, cuezas, cueza, cozamos, cozáis, cuezan**.
Imperat   **cuece** (tú), **cueza** (él/Vd.), **cozamos** (nos.), coced (vos.), **cuezan** (ellos/Vds.).

55. ELEGIR (*e changes to i in certain persons of certain tenses; g changes to j before a and o*)
Pres Ind   **elijo, eliges, elige**, elegimos, elegís, **eligen**.
Past Ind   elegí, elegiste, **eligió**, elegimos, elegisteis, **eligieron**.
Pres Subj   **elija, elijas, elija, elijamos, elijáis, elijan**.
Imperf Subj   **eligiera, eligieras, eligiera, eligiéramos, eligierais, eligieran; eligiese, eligieses, eligiese, eligiésemos, eligieseis, eligiesen**.
Fut Subj   **eligiere, eligieres, eligiere, eligiéremos, eligiereis, eligieren**.
Imperat   **elige** (tú), **elija** (él/Vd.), **elijamos** (nos.), elegid (vos.), **elijan** (ellos/Vds.).

56. SEGUIR (*e changes to i in certain persons of certain tenses; gu changes to g before a and o*)
Pres Ind   **sigo, sigues, sigue**, seguimos, seguís, **siguen**.
Past Ind   seguí, seguiste, **siguió**, seguimos, seguisteis, **siguieron**.
Pres Subj   **siga, sigas, siga, sigamos, sigáis, sigan**.
Imperf Subj   **siguiera, siguieras, siguiera, siguiéramos, siguierais, siguieran; siguiese, siguieses, siguiese, siguiésemos, siguieseis, siguiesen**.
Fut Subj   **siguiere, siguieres, siguiere, siguiéremos, siguiereis, siguieren**.
Imperat   **sigue** (tú), **siga** (él/Vd.), **sigamos** (nos.), seguid (vos.), **sigan** (ellos/Vds.).

57. ERRAR (*e changes to ye in stressed syllables*)
Pres Ind   **yerro, yerras, yerra**, erramos, erráis, **yerran**.
Pres Subj   **yerre, yerres, yerre**, erremos, erréis, **yerren**.
Imperat   **yerra** (tú), **yerre** (él/Vd.), erremos (nos.), errad (vos.), **yerren** (ellos/Vds.).

58. AGORAR (*o changes to ue in stressed syllables and g changes to gü before e*)
Pres Ind   **agüero, agüeras, agüera**, agoramos, agoráis, **agüeran**.
Pres Subj   **agüere, agüeres, agüere**, agoramos, agoréis, **agüeren**.
Imperat   **agüera** (tú), **agüere** (él/Vd.), agoremos (nos.), agorad (vos.), **agüeren** (ellos/Vds.).

59. DESOSAR (*o changes to hue in stressed syllables*)
Pres Ind   **deshueso, deshuesas, deshuesa**, desosamos, desosáis, **deshuesan**.
Pres Subj   **deshuese, deshueses, deshuese**, desosemos, desoséis, **deshuesen**.
Imperat   **deshuesa** (tú), **deshuese** (él/Vd.), desosemos (nos.), desosad (vos.), **deshuesen** (ellos/Vds.).

60. OLER (*o changes to hue in stressed syllables*)
Pres Ind   **huelo, hueles, huele**, olemos, oléis, **huelen**.
Pres Subj   **huela, huelas, huela**, olamos, oláis, **huelan**.
Imperat   **huele** (tú), **huela** (él/Vd.), olamos (nos.), oled (vos.), **huelan** (ellos/Vds.).

61. LEER (*the i ending changes to y before o and e*)
Past Ind   leí, leíste, **leyó**, leímos, leísteis, **leyeron**.
Imperf Subj   **leyera, leyeras, leyera, leyéramos, leyerais, leyeran; leyese, leyeses, leyese, leyésemos, leyeseis, leyesen**.
Fut Subj   **leyere, leyeres, leyere; leyéremos, leyereis, leyeren**.

62. HUIR (*i changes to y before a, e, and o*)
Pres Ind   **huyo, huyes, huye**, huimos, huís, **huyen**.
Past Ind   huí, huiste, **huyó**, huimos, huisteis, **huyeron**.
Pres Subj   **huya, huyas, huya, huyamos, huyáis, huyan**.
Imperf Subj   **huyera, huyeras, huyera, huyéramos, huyerais, huyeran; huyese, huyeses, huyese, huyésemos, huyeseis, huyesen**.
Fut Subj   **huyere, huyeres, huyere, huyéremos, huyereis, huyeren**.
Imperat   **huye** (tú), **huya** (él/Vd.), **huyamos** (nos.), huid (vos.), **huyan** (ellos/Vds.).

63. ARGÜIR (*i changes to y before a, e, and o; gü becomes gu before y*)
Pres Ind   **arguyo, arguyes, arguye**, argüimos, argüís, **arguyen**.
Past Ind   argüí, argüiste, **arguyó**, argüimos, argüisteis, **arguyeron**.
Pres Subj   **arguya, arguyas, arguya, arguyamos, arguyáis, arguyan**.
Imperf Subj   **arguyera, arguyeras, arguyera, arguyéramos, arguyerais, arguyeran; arguyese, arguyeses, arguyese, arguyésemos, arguyeseis, arguyesen**.
Fut Subj   **arguyere, arguyeres, arguyere, arguyéremos, arguyereis, arguyeren**.
Imperat   **arguye** (tú), **arguya** (él/Vd.), **arguyamos** (nos.), argüid (vos.), **arguyan** (ellos/Vds.).

64. ANDAR

Past Ind	anduve, anduviste, anduvo, anduvimos, anduvisteis, anduvieron.
Imperf Subj	anduviera, anduvieras, anduviera, anduviéramos, anduvierais, anduvieran; anduviese, anduvieses, anduviese, anduviésemos, anduvieseis, anduviesen.
Fut Subj	anduviere, anduvieres, anduviere, anduviéremos, anduviereis, anduvieren.

65. ASIR

Pres Ind	asgo, ases, ase, asimos, asís, asen.
Pres Subj	asga, asgas, asga, asgamos, asgáis, asgan.
Imperat	ase (tú), asga (él/Vd.), asgamos (nos.), asid (vos.), asgan (ellos/Vds.).

66. CABER

Pres Ind	quepo, cabes, cabe, cabemos, cabéis, caben.
Past Ind	cupe, cupiste, cupo, cupimos, cupisteis, cupieron.
Fut Ind	cabré, cabrás, cabrá, cabremos, cabréis, cabrán.
Cond	cabría, cabrías, cabría, cabríamos, cabríais, cabrían.
Pres Subj	quepa, quepas, quepa, quepamos, quepáis, quepan.
Imperf Subj	cupiera, cupieras, cupiera, cupiéramos, cupierais, cupieran; cupiese, cupieses, cupiese, cupiésemos, cupieseis, cupiesen.
Fut Subj	cupiere, cupieres, cupiere, cupiéremos, cupiereis, cupieren.
Imperat	cabe (tú), quepa (él/Vd.), quepamos (nos.), cabed (vos.), quepan (ellos/Vds.).

67. CAER

Pres Ind	caigo, caes, cae, caemos, caéis, caen.
Past Ind	caí, caíste, cayó, caímos, caísteis, cayeron.
Pres Subj	caiga, caigas, caiga, caigamos, caigáis, caigan.
Imperf Subj	cayera, cayeras, cayera, cayéramos, cayerais, cayeran; cayese, cayeses, cayese, cayésemos, cayeseis, cayesen.
Fut Subj	cayere, cayeres, cayere, cayéremos, cayereis, cayeren.
Imperat	cae (tú), caiga (él/Vd.), caigamos (nos.), caed (vos.), caigan (ellos/Vds.).

68. DAR

Pres Ind	doy, das, da, damos, dais, dan.
Past Ind	di, diste, dio, dimos, disteis, dieron.
Pres Subj	dé, des, dé, demos, deis, den.
Imperf Subj	diera, dieras, diera, diéramos, dierais, dieran; diese, dieses, diese, diésemos, dieseis, diesen.
Fut Subj	diere, dieres, diere, diéremos, diereis, dieren.
Imperat	da (tú), dé (él/Vd.), demos (nos.), dad (vos.), den (ellos/Vds.).

69. DECIR

Pres Ind	digo, dices, dice, decimos, decís, dicen.
Past Ind	dije, dijiste, dijo, dijimos, dijisteis, dijeron.
Fut Ind	diré, dirás, dirá, diremos, diréis, dirán.
Cond	diría, dirías, diría, diríamos, diríais, dirían.
Pres Subj	diga, digas, diga, digamos, digáis, digan.
Imperf Subj	dijera, dijeras, dijera, dijéramos, dijerais, dijeran; dijese, dijeses, dijese, dijésemos, dijeseis, dijesen.
Fut Subj	dijere, dijeres, dijere, dijéremos, dijereis, dijeren.
Imperat	di (tú), diga (él/Vd.), digamos (nos.), decid (vos.), digan (ellos/Vds.).
Past Part	dicho,-a.

70. ERGUIR

Pres Ind	irgo, irgues, irgue, erguimos, erguís, irguen; yergo, yergues, yergue, erguimos, erguís, yerguen.
Past Ind	erguí, erguiste, irguió, erguimos, erguisteis, irguieron.
Pres Subj	irga, irgas, irga, irgamos, irgáis, irgan; yerga, yergas, yerga, irgamos, irgáis, yergan.
Imperf Subj	irguiera, irguieras, irguiera, irguiéramos, irguierais, irguieran; irguiese, irguieses, irguiese, irguiésemos, irguieseis, irguiesen.
Fut Subj	irguiere, irguieres, irguiere, irguiéremos, irguiereis, irguieren.
Imperat	irgue, yergue (tú), irga, yerga (él/Vd.), irgamos (nos.), erguid (vos.), irgan, yergan (ellos/Vds.).

71. ESTAR

Pres Ind	**estoy**, estás, está, estamos, estáis, están.
Imperf	estaba, estabas, estaba, estábamos, estabais, estaban.
Past Ind	**estuve, estuviste, estuvo, estuvimos, estuvisteis, estuvieron**.
Fut Ind	estaré, estarás, estará, estaremos, estaréis, estarán.
Cond	estaría, estarías, estaría, estaríamos, estaríais, estarían.
Pres Subj	esté, estés, esté, estemos, estéis, estén.
Imperf Subj	**estuviera, estuvieras, estuviera, estuviéramos, estuvierais, estuvieran; estuviese, estuvieses, estuviese, estuviésemos, estuvieseis, estuviesen.**
Fut Subj	**estuviere, estuvieres, estuviere, estuviéremos, estuviereis, estuvieren.**
Imperat	está (tú), esté (él/Vd.), estemos (nos.), estad (vos.), estén (ellos/Vds.).

72. HABER

Pres Ind	**he, has, ha, hemos**, habéis, **han**.
Imperf Subj	había, habías, había, habíamos, habíais, habían.
Past Ind	**hube, hubiste, hubo, hubimos, hubisteis, hubieron.**
Fut Ind	**habré, habrás, habrá, habremos, habréis, habrán.**
Cond	**habría, habrías, habría, habríamos, habríais, habrían.**
Pres Subj	**haya, hayas, haya, hayamos, hayáis, hayan.**
Imperf Subj	**hubiera, hubieras, hubiera, hubiéramos, hubierais, hubieran; hubiese, hubieses, hubiese, hubiésemos, hubieseis, hubiesen.**
Fut Subj	**hubiere, hubieres, hubiere, hubiéremos, hubiereis, hubieren.**
Imperat	**he** (tú), **haya** (él/Vd.), **hayamos** (nos.), habed (vos.), **hayan** (ellos/Vds.).

73. HACER

Pres Ind	**hago**, haces, hace, hacemos, hacéis, hacen.
Past Ind	**hice, hiciste, hizo, hicimos, hicisteis, hicieron.**
Fut Ind	**haré, harás, hará, haremos, haréis, harán.**
Cond	**haría, harías, haría, haríamos, haríais, harían.**
Pres Subj	**haga, hagas, haga, hagamos, hagáis, hagan.**
Imperf Subj	**hiciera, hicieras, hiciera, hiciéramos, hicierais, hicieran; hiciese, hicieses, hiciese, hiciésemos, hicieseis, hiciesen.**
Fut Subj	**hiciere, hicieres, hiciere, hiciéremos, hiciereis, hicieren.**
Imperat	**haz** (tú), **haga** (él/Vd.), **hagamos** (nos.), haced (vos.), **hagan** (ellos/Vds.).
Past Part	**hecho,-a**.

74. IR

Pres Ind	**voy, vas, va, vamos, vais, van**.
Imperf Subj	**iba, ibas, iba, íbamos, ibais, iban**.
Past Ind	**fui, fuiste, fue, fuimos, fuisteis, fueron**.
Pres Subj	**vaya, vayas, vaya, vayamos, vayáis, vayan**.
Imperf Subj	**fuera, fueras, fuera, fuéramos, fuerais, fueran; fuese, fueses, fuese, fuésemos, fueseis, fuesen**.
Fut Subj	**fuere, fueres, fuere, fuéremos, fuereis, fueren**.
Imperat	**ve** (tú), **vaya** (él/Vd.), **vayamos** (nos.), **id** (vos.), **vayan** (ellos/Vds.).

75. OÍR

Pres Ind	**oigo, oyes, oye**, oímos, oís, **oyen**.
Past Ind	oí, oíste, **oyó**, oímos, oísteis, **oyeron**.
Pres Subj	**oiga, oigas, oiga, oigamos, oigáis, oigan**.
Imperf Subj	**oyera, oyeras, oyera, oyéramos, oyerais, oyeran; oyese, oyeses, oyese, oyésemos, oyeseis, oyesen**.
Fut Subj	**oyere, oyeres, oyere, oyéremos, oyereis, oyeren**.
Imperat	**oye** (tú), **oiga** (él/Vd.), **oigamos** (nos.), oíd (vos.), **oigan** (ellos/Vds.).

76. PLACER

Pres Ind	**plazco**, places, place, placemos, placéis, placen.
Past Ind	plací, placiste, plació or **plugo**, placimos, placisteis, placieron or **pluguieron**.
Pres Subj	**plazca, plazcas, plazca, plegue, plazcamos, plazcáis, plazcan.**
Imperf Subj	placiera, placieras, placiera or **pluguiera**, placiéramos, placierais, placieran placiese, placieses, placiese or **pluguiese**, placiésemos, placieseis, placiesen.
Fut Subj	placiere, placieres, placiere or **pluguiere**, placiéremos, placiereis, placieren.
Imperat	place (tú), **plazca** (él/Vd.), **plazcamos** (nos.), placed (vos.), **plazcan** (ellos/Vds.).

77. PODER

Pres Ind	**puedo, puedes, puede**, podemos, podéis, **pueden**.
Past Ind	**pude, pudiste, pudo**, pudimos, pudisteis, **pudieron**.
Fut Ind	**podré, podrás, podrá, podremos, podréis, podrán**.
Cond	**podría, podrías, podría, podríamos, podríais, podrían**.
Pres Subj	**pueda, puedas, pueda**, podamos, podáis, **puedan**.
Imperf Subj	**pudiera, pudieras, pudiera, pudiéramos, pudierais, pudieran; pudiese, pudieses, pudiese, pudiésemos, pudieseis, pudiesen**.
Fut Subj	**pudiere, pudieres, pudiere, pudiéremos, pudiereis, pudieren**.
Imperat	**puede** (tú), **pueda** (él/Vd.), podamos (nos.), poded (vos.), **puedan** (ellos/Vds.).

78. PONER

Pres Ind	**pongo**, pones, pone, ponemos, ponéis, ponen.
Past Ind	**puse, pusiste, puso, pusimos, pusisteis, pusieron**.
Fut Ind	**pondré, pondrás, pondrá, pondremos, pondréis, pondrán**.
Cond	**pondría, pondrías, pondría, pondríamos, pondríais, pondrían**.
Pres Subj	**ponga, pongas, ponga, pongamos, pongáis, pongan**.
Imperf Subj	**pusiera, pusieras, pusiera, pusiéramos, pusierais, pusieran; pusiese, pusieses, pusiese, pusiésemos, pusieseis, pusiesen**.
Fut Subj	**pusiere, pusieres, pusiere, pusiéremos, pusiereis, pusieren**.
Imperat	**pon** (tú), **ponga** (él/Vd.), **pongamos** (nos.), poned (vos.), **pongan** (ellos/Vds.).
Past Part	**puesto,-a**.

79. PREDECIR

Pres Ind	**predigo, predices, predice**, predecimos, predecís, **predicen**.
Past Ind	**predije, predijiste, predijo, predijimos, predijisteis, predijeron**.
Pres Subj	**prediga, predigas, prediga, predigamos, predigáis, predigan**.
Imperf Subj	**predijera, predijeras, predijera, predijéramos, predijerais, predijeran; predijese, predijeses, predijese, predijésemos, predijeseis, predijesen**.
Fut Subj	**predijere, predijeres, predijere, predijéremos, predijereis, predijeren**.
Imperat	**predice** (tú), **prediga** (él/Vd.), **predigamos** (nos.), predecid (vos.), **predigan** (ellos/Vds.).

80. QUERER

Pres Ind	**quiero, quieres, quiere**, queremos, queréis, **quieren**.
Past Ind	**quise, quisiste, quiso, quisimos, quisisteis, quisieron**.
Fut Ind	**querré, querrás, querrá, querremos, querréis, querrán**.
Cond	**querría, querrías, querría, querríamos, querríais, querrían**.
Pres Subj	**quiera, quieras, quiera**, queramos, queráis, **quieran**.
Imperf Subj	**quisiera, quisieras, quisiera, quisiéramos, quisierais, quisieran; quisiese, quisieses, quisiese, quisiésemos, quisieseis, quisiesen**.
Fut Subj	**quisiere, quisieres, quisiere, quisiéremos, quisiereis, quisieren**.
Imperat	**quiere** (tú), **quiera** (él/Vd.), queramos (nos.), quered (vos.), **quieran** (ellos/Vds.).

81. RAER

Pres Ind	rao, **raigo, rayo**, raes, rae, raemos, raéis, raen.
Past Ind	raí, raíste, **rayó**, raímos, raísteis, **rayeron**.
Pres Subj	**raiga, raigas, raiga, raigamos, raigáis, raigan; raya, rayas, raya, rayamos, rayáis, rayan**.
Imperf Subj	**rayera, rayeras, rayera, rayéramos, rayerais, rayeran; rayese, rayeses, rayese, rayésemos, rayeseis, rayesen**.
Fut Subj	**rayere, rayeres, rayere, rayéremos, rayereis, rayeren**.
Imperat	rae (tú), **raiga, raya** (él/Vd.), **raigamos, rayamos** (nos.), raed (vos.), **raigan, rayan** (ellos/Vds.).

82. ROER

Pres Ind	roo, **roigo, royo**, roes, roe, roemos, roéis, roen.
Past Ind	roí, roíste, **royó**, roímos, roísteis, **royeron**.
Pres Subj	roa, roas, roa, roamos, roáis, roan; **roiga, roigas, roiga, roigamos, roigáis, roigan; roya, royas, roya, royamos, royáis, royan**.
Imperf Subj	**royera, royeras, royera, royéramos, royerais, royeran; royese, royeses, royese, royésemos, royeseis, royesen**.
Fut Subj	**royere, royeres, royere, royéremos, royereis, royeren**.
Imperat	roe (tú), roa, **roiga, roya** (él/Vd.), roamos, **roigamos, royamos** (nos.), roed (vos.), roaɳ, **roigan, royan** (ellos/Vds.).

83. SABER

Pres Ind	**sé**, sabes, sabe, sabemos, sabéis, saben.
Past Ind	**supe, supiste, supo, supimos, supisteis, supieron**.
Fut Ind	**sabré, sabrás, sabrá, sabremos, sabréis, sabrán**.
Cond	**sabría, sabrías, sabría, sabríamos, sabríais, sabrían**.
Pres Subj	**sepa, sepas, sepa, sepamos, sepáis, sepan**.
Imperf Subj	**supiera, supieras, supiera, supiéramos, supierais, supieran; supiese, supieses, supiese, supiésemos, supieseis, supiesen**.
Fut Subj	**supiere, supieres, supiere, supiéremos, supiereis, supieren**.
Imperat	sabe (tú), **sepa** (él/Vd.), **sepamos** (nos.), sabed (vos.), **sepan** (ellos/Vds.).

84. SALIR

Pres Ind	**salgo**, sales, sale, salimos, salís, salen.
Fut Ind	**saldré, saldrás, saldrá, saldremos, saldréis, saldrán**.
Cond	**saldría, saldrías, saldría, saldríamos, saldríais, saldrían**.
Pres Subj	**salga, salgas, salga, salgamos, salgáis, salgan**.
Imperat	**sal** (tú), **salga** (él/Vd.), **salgamos** (nos.), salid (vos.), **salgan** (ellos/Vds.).

85. SATISFACER

Pres Ind	**satisfago**, satisfaces, satisface, satisfacemos, satisfacéis, satisfacen.
Past Ind	**satisfice, satisficiste, satisfizo, satisficimos, satisficisteis, satisficieron**.
Fut Ind	**satisfaré, satisfarás, satisfará, satisfaremos, satisfaréis, satisfarán**.
Cond	**satisfaría, satisfarías, satisfaría, satisfaríamos, satisfaríais, satisfarían**.
Pres Subj	**satisfaga, satisfagas, satisfaga, satisfagamos, satisfagáis, satisfagan**.
Imperf Subj	**satisficiera, satisficieras, satisficiera, satisficiéramos, satisficierais, satisficieran; satisficiese, satisficieses, satisficiese, satisficiésemos, satisficieseis, satisficiesen**.
Fut Subj	**satisficiere, satisficieres, satisficiere, satisficiéremos, satisficiereis, satisficieren**.
Imperat	**satisfaz,** satisface (tú), **satisfaga** (él/Vd.), **satisfagamos** (nos.), satisfaced (vos.), **satisfagan** (ellos/Vds.).
Past Part	**satisfecho,-a**.

86. SER

Pres Ind	**soy, eres, es, somos, sois, son**.
Imperf Subj	**era, eras, era, éramos, erais, eran**.
Past Ind	**fui, fuiste, fue, fuimos, fuisteis, fueron**.
Fut Ind	seré, serás, será, seremos, seréis, serán.
Cond	sería, serías, sería, seríamos, seríais, serían.
Pres Subj	sea, seas, sea, seamos, seáis, sean.
Imperf Subj	**fuera, fueras, fuera, fuéramos, fuerais, fueran; fuese, fueses, fuese, fuésemos, fueseis, fuesen**.
Fut Subj	**fuere, fueres, fuere, fuéremos, fuereis, fueren**.
Imperat	**sé** (tú), sea (él/Vd.), seamos (nos.), **sed** (vos.), sean (ellos/Vds.).
Past Part	**sido**.

87. TENER

Pres Ind	**tengo, tienes, tiene**, tenemos, tenéis, **tienen**.
Past Ind	**tuve, tuviste, tuvo, tuvimos, tuvisteis, tuvieron**.
Fut Ind	**tendré, tendrás, tendrá, tendremos, tendréis, tendrán**.
Cond	**tendría, tendrías, tendría, tendríamos, tendríais, tendrían**.
Pres Subj	**tenga, tengas, tenga, tengamos, tengáis, tengan**.
Imperf Subj	**tuviera, tuvieras, tuviera, tuviéramos, tuvierais, tuvieran; tuviese, tuvieses, tuviese, tuviésemos, tuvieseis, tuviesen**.
Fut Subj	**tuviere, tuvieres, tuviere, tuviéremos, tuviereis, tuvieren**.
Imperat	**ten** (tú), **tenga** (él/Vd.), **tengamos** (nos.), tened (vos.), **tengan** (ellos/Vds.).

88. TRAER

Pres Ind	**traigo**, traes, trae, traemos, traéis, traen.
Past Ind	**traje, trajiste, trajo, trajimos, trajisteis, trajeron**.
Pres Subj	**traiga, traigas, traiga, traigamos, traigáis, traigan**.
Imperf Subj	**trajera, trajeras, trajera, trajéramos, trajerais, trajeran; trajese, trajeses, trajese, trajésemos, trajeseis, trajesen**.
Fut Subj	**trajere, trajeres, trajere, trajéremos, trajereis, trajeren**.
Imperat	trae (tú), **traiga** (él/Vd.), **traigamos** (nos.), traed (vos.), **traigan** (ellos/Vds.).

89. VALER

Pres Ind	**valgo**, vales, vale, valemos, valéis, valen.
Fut Ind	**valdré, valdrás, valdrá, valdremos, valdréis, valdrán.**
Cond	**valdría, valdrías, valdría, valdríamos, valdríais, valdrían.**
Pres Subj	**valga, valgas, valga, valgamos, valgáis, valgan.**
Imperat	vale (tú), **valga** (él/Vd.), **valgamos** (nos.), valed (vos.), **valgan** (ellos/Vds.).

90. VENIR

Pres Ind	**vengo, vienes, viene**, venimos, venís, **vienen.**
Past Ind	**vine, viniste, vino, vinimos, vinisteis, vinieron.**
Fut Ind	**vendré, vendrás, vendrá, vendremos, vendréis, vendrán.**
Cond	**vendría, vendrías, vendría, vendríamos, vendríais, vendrían.**
Pres Subj	**venga, vengas, venga, vengamos, vengáis, vengan.**
Imperf Subj	**viniera, vinieras, viniera, viniéramos, vinierais, vinieran; viniese, vinieses, viniese, viniésemos, vinieseis, viniesen.**
Fut Subj	**viniere, vinieres, viniere, viniéremos, viniereis, vinieren.**
Imperat	**ven** (tú), **venga** (él/Vd.), **vengamos** (nos.), venid (vos.), **vengan** (ellos/Vds.).

91. VER

Pres Ind	veo, **ves**, ve, **vemos, veis**, ven.
Past Ind	**vi, viste, vio, vimos, visteis, vieron.**
Imperf Subj	**viera, vieras, viera, viéramos, vierais, vieran; viese, vieses, viese, viésemos, vieseis, viesen.**
Fut Subj	**viere, vieres, viere, viéremos, viereis, vieren.**
Imperat	**ve** (tú), vea (él/Vd.), veamos (nos.), **ved** (vos.), vean (ellos/Vds.).
Past Part	**visto,-a.**

92. YACER

Pres Ind	**yazco, yazgo, yago**, yaces, yace, yacemos, yacéis, yacen.
Pres Subj	**yazca, yazcas, yazca, yazcamos, yazcáis, yazcan; yazga, yazgas, yazga, yazgamos, yazgáis, yazgan; yaga, yagas, yaga, yagamos, yagáis, yagan.**
Imperat	yace, **yaz** (tú), **yazca, yazga, yaga** (él/Vd.), **yazcamos, yazgamos, yagamos** (nos.), yaced (vos.), **yazcan, yazgan, yagan** (ellos/Vds.).

A

A, a¹ f (la letra) A, a.
▲ pl **as** or **aes**.

a¹ **1** prep (dirección) to: *girar a la derecha*, to turn (to the) right; *irse a casa*, to go home; *subir al autobús*, to get on the bus; *caer al mar*, to fall into the sea; *llegar a Barcelona*, to arrive in Barcelona, reach Barcelona. **2** (destino) to, towards. **3** (distancia) away: *a diez kilómetros de casa*, ten kilometres (away) from home. **4** (lugar) at, on: *a la entrada*, at the entrance; *a la izquierda*, on the left; *a mi lado*, at my side, by my side, next to me; *al sol*, in the sun; *al norte/sur/este/oeste*, to the north/south/east/west. **5** (tiempo) at: *a las once*, at eleven; *a los tres días*, three days later; *a tiempo*, in time; *al final*, in the end; *a la mañana siguiente*, (on) the following morning; *¿a cuántos estamos?*, what's the date?; *estamos a 30 de mayo*, it's the thirtieth of May. **6** (modo) by, in: *a ciegas*, blindly; *a oscuras*, in the dark; *a la española*, (in the) Spanish style, in the Spanish way. **7** (instrumento) by, in: *a mano*, by hand; *a lápiz*, in pencil; *a pie*, on foot. **8** (precio) a: *a 100 pesetas el kilo*, a hundred pesetas a kilo. **9** (medida) at: *a 90 kilómetros por hora*, at 90 kilometres an hour; *a docenas*, by the dozen. **10** (finalidad) to: *él vino a vernos*, he came to see us. **11** (complemento directo persona): *vi a Juanita*, I saw Juanita; *encontramos a Pedro*, we met Pedro. **12** (complemento indirecto): *to: dámelo*, give it to me. **13** (como imperativo): *¡a dormir!*, bedtime!; *¡a ver!*, let's see! **14** verbo + a + inf, to: *aprender a nadar*, to learn (how) to swim; *empezaba a nevar*, it began to snow; *voy a venderlo*, I'm going to sell it.
● **a que ...**, I bet ...: *¡a que no lo haces!*, I bet you don't do it!
▲ See also **al**.

a² abr (alias) alias.
a³ abr (área) are.
A¹ abr (Alteza) Highness; (abreviatura) H.
A² sím (amperio) ampère, amp; (símbolo) A.
A³ abr (autopista) motorway; (abreviatura) M.
AA.EE. abr (Asuntos Exteriores) ≈ Foreign Affairs.
abacería f grocer's (shop).
abacero,-a m,f grocer.
abacial adj abbatial.
ábaco m abacus.
abad m abbot.
abadejo m pollack.
abadesa f abbess.
abadía **1** f (edificio) abbey. **2** (dignidad) abbacy.
abajo **1** adv (lugar) below, down: *ahí abajo*, down there. **2** (en una casa) downstairs. **3** (dirección) down, downward: *calle abajo*, down the street. **– 4** interj down with!: *¡abajo el dictador!*, down with the dictator!
abalanzarse **1** p (lanzarse) to rush forward, spring forward. **2** abalanzarse sobre, (persona) to rush at; (león, tigre) to pounce on; (águila etc) to swoop down on.

▲ Conjugation model [4], like *realizar*.
abalizar t to buoy.
abalorio **1** m (collar) string of beads. **2** (cuentecilla) glass bead.
abanderado,-a **1** pp → **abanderar**. **– 2** m,f (portaestandarte) standard bearer. **3** fig leader, champion.
abanderar **1** t (un barco) to register. **2** (una causa) to defend: *siempre abanderó la causa de las mujeres*, she always defended women's rights.
abandonado,-a **1** pp → **abandonar**. **– 2** adj abandoned: *un barco abandonado*, an abandoned ship; *se sintió abandonada*, she felt she had been deserted. **3** (descuidado) neglected: *tiene el despacho abandonado*, his office hasn't been looked after. **4** (desaseado) untidy, unkempt.
abandonar **1** t (desamparar) to abandon, forsake: *la suerte le ha abandonado*, luck has forsaken him. **2** (lugar) to leave, quit: *abandonar el barco*, to abandon ship. **3** (actividad) to give up, withdraw from: *abandonó los estudios en la facultad*, she dropped out of university. **4** (traicionar) to desert. **5** (renunciar) to relinquish, renounce. **6** (descuidar) to neglect. **7** DEP (retirarse) to withdraw from. **– 8** abandonarse, p (descuidarse) to neglect os., let os. go. **9** (entregarse) to give os. up (a, to): *se abandonó a la bebida*, he gave himself up to drink. **10** (ceder) to give in.
abandono **1** m (acción) abandoning, desertion. **2** (idea, actividad) giving up. **3** (descuido) neglect, lack of care. **4** (dejadez) apathy, carelessness. **5** DEP withdrawal: *ganaron por abandono*, they won by default. **6** MAR abandonment.
● **en estado de abandono**, in an abandoned state.
abanicar t to fan.
▲ Conjugation model [1], like *sacar*.
abanico **1** m fan. **2** fig range: *un abanico de posibilidades*, a range of possibilities.
● **en abanico**, fan-shaped. ‖ **abrirse en abanico**, to fan out.
abaniqueo m fanning.
abanto m (ave) vulture.
abaratamiento m reduction in price.
abaratar **1** t to reduce the price of, make cheaper. **– 2** abaratarse, p (precio) to come down, fall; (artículo) to become cheaper, come down in price.
abarca f sandal.
abarcar **1** t (englobar) to cover, embrace: *sus conocimientos abarcan el campo de la psicología*, her knowledge covers the field of psychology. **2** (abrazar) to embrace, get one's arms around. **3** (trabajo) to undertake, take on.
● **quien mucho abarca poco aprieta**, Jack of all trades, master of none.
▲ Conjugation model [1], like *sacar*.
abaritonado,-a adj baritone.

abarquillado,-a 1 *pp* → **abarquillar**. – **2** *adj* warped.

abarquillamiento *m* (*madera*) warping; (*cartón*) curling up.

abarquillar 1 *t* (*madera*) to warp; (*cartón*) to curl up. – **2** abarquillarse, *p* (*madera*) to warp; (*cartón*) to curl up.

abarraganamiento *m* cohabitation.

abarranagarse *p* to cohabit.

abarrancar 1 *i* to run aground. – **2** abarrancarse, *p* (*varar*) to run aground. **3** *fig* to get bogged down, get stuck (**en**, in).

abarrocado,-a *adj* baroque.

abarrotado,-a 1 *pp* → **abarrotar**. – **2** *adj* (*cosas*) packed (**de**, with), crammed (**de**, with); (*personas*) jam-packed (**de**, with), packed (**de**, with).

abarrotar *t* (*cosas*) to pack (**de**, with), cram (**de**, with), fill up (**de**,with); (*personas*) to pack (**de**, with), jam-pack (**de**, with).

abastecedor,-ra 1 *adj* supplying, providing. – **2** *m,f* supplier, purveyor.

abastecer 1 *t* to supply, provide. – **2** abastecerse, *p* (*uso reflexivo*) to stock up (**de/con**, with), lay in supplies (**de/con**, of): *se abastecieron de víveres,* they laid in supplies.
▲ Conjugation model [43], *like agradecer*.

abastecimiento *m* supplying, provision: *quieren mejorar el abastecimiento de agua,* they want to improve the water supply.

abasto 1 *m* (*abastecimiento*) supplying, provision. **2** (*abundancia*) abundance. – **3** abastos, *mpl* provisions, supplies.
● dar abasto, *fam* to be sufficient for: *es que no doy abasto,* I just can't cope, I can't keep up; *no doy abasto para corregir tantos ejercicios,* I've got so many exercises to correct that I just can't cope.

abatanar 1 *t* (*paño*) to full. **2** (*maltratar*) to beat up.

abate *m* father, abbé.

abatible *adj* folding, collapsible: *asiento abatible,* folding seat; *cama abatible,* folding bed.

abatido,-a 1 *pp* → **abatir**. – **2** *adj* (*deprimido*) dejected, depressed. **3** (*despreciable*) despicable, low. **4** (*fruta*) fallen, drooping.

abatimiento *m* dejection, depression.

abatir 1 *t* (*derribar*) to knock down, pull down. **2** (*matar*) to kill; (*herir*) to wound; (*a tiros*) to shoot down. **3** (*bajar*) to lower, take down. **4** (*desanimar*) to depress. **5** (*humillar*) to humiliate. – **6** abatirse, *p* (*ave*) to swoop (**sobre**, down on); (*avión*) to dive (**sobre**, down on). **7** (*ceder*) to give in. **8** (*desanimarse*) to lose heart, become depressed. **9** *fig* (*descender*) to fall upon.

abdicación *f* abdication.

abdicar 1 *t* (*soberanía*) to abdicate, renounce: *abdicó el reino en su hija,* he abdicated in favour of his daughter. **2** (*ideales, ideas*) to give up, renounce. – **3** *i* (*soberanía*) to abdicate: *abdicó en su hija,* he abdicated in favour of his daughter. **4** (*ideales, ideas*) to give up (**de**, -).
▲ Conjugation model [1], *like sacar*.

abdomen *m* abdomen; *fam* belly.

abdominal 1 *adj* abdominal. – **2** abdominales, *mpl* (*ejercicios*) sit-ups.

abducción *f* abduction.

abductor *adj* abductor.

abecé 1 *m* (*abecedario*) ABC, alphabet. **2** (*nociones*) rudiments *pl*, basics *pl*.

abecedario 1 *m* (*alfabeto*) alphabet. **2** (*libro*) spelling book. **3** (*nociones*) rudiments *pl*, basics *pl*.

abedul *m* birch tree, birch.

abeja 1 *f* (*animal*) bee. **2** *fig* (*persona*) busy bee.
■ abeja obrera, worker bee. ‖ abeja reina, queen bee.

abejarrón *m* bumblebee.

abejaruco *m* bee-eater.

abejón 1 *m* (*zángano*) drone. **2** (*abejorro*) bumblebee.

abejorreo *m* buzzing.

abejorro 1 *m* (*himenóptero*) bumblebee. **2** (*coleóptero*) cockchafer. **3** *fig* (*persona*) bore, nuisance.

aberración *f* aberration.

aberrante *adj* aberrant.

aberrar *i* to be mistaken.

abertura 1 *f* (*agujero*) opening, gap; (*grieta*) crack, slit. **2** (*valle*) pass. **3** (*ensenada*) cove, creek.

abertzale 1 *adj* Basque nationalist. – **2** *mf* Basque nationalist.

abestiarse *p* to become brutalized.
▲ Conjugation model [12], *like cambiar*.

abetal *m* fir plantation.

abetar *m* → **abetal**.

abeto *m* fir tree, fir.
■ abeto blanco, silver fir. ‖ abeto falso, spruce. ‖ abeto rojo, spruce.

abiertamente *adv* openly, frankly.

abierto,-a 1 *pp* → **abrir**. – **2** *adj* open, unlocked. **3** (*grifo*) (turned) on: *dejó el grifo abierto,* she left the tap running. **4** *fig* (*sincero*) open, frank. **5** (*tolerante*) open-minded. **6** LING open.
● abierto,-a al mar, seaward-looking. ‖ abierto,-a de par en par, wide open. ‖ quedarse con la boca abierta, *fig* to be left speechless.

abigarrado,-a 1 *pp* → **abigarrar**. – **2** *adj* (*multicolor*) multi-coloured (US multi-colored), many-coloured (US many-colored). **3** (*mezclado*) jumbled, mixed: *un discurso abigarrado,* a disjointed speech, a hotch-potch of a speech.

abisal *adj* abyssal.

Abisinia *f* Abyssinia.

abisinio,-a 1 *adj* Abyssinian. – **2** *m,f* Abyssinian.

abismal *adj* abysmal: *hay una diferencia abismal,* there is a world of a difference.

abismar 1 *t* (*hundir*) to plunge (**en**, into). **2** (*confundir*) to confuse, bewilder. – **3** abismarse, *p* (*sumirse*) to be engrossed (**en**, in), become absorbed (**en**, in).

abismo *m* abyss: *entre tu y yo media un abismo,* we are worlds apart.
● estar al borde del abismo, *fig* to be on the brink of ruin.

abjuración *f* abjuration.

abjurar 1 *t* to abjure, forswear. – **2** *i* to abjure (**de**, -), renounce (**de**, -): *abjuró de su religión,* he renounced his religion.

ablación 1 *f* (*acción geológica*) ablation. **2** (*cirugía*) ablation, wearing away.

ablandamiento *m* softening.

ablandar 1 *t* to soften. **2** *fig* (*persona*) to soothe, soften up, appease. – **3** *i* (*frío*) to get warmer, get milder; (*hielo, nieve*) to melt. – **4** ablandarse, *p* to soften, get softer. **5** (*persona*) to soften up. **6** (*acobardarse*) to lose one's nerve, become frightened. **7** (*frío*) to get warmer/milder; (*nieve, hielo*) to melt.

ablativo *m* ablative (case).

ablución 1 *f* ablution. – **2** abluciones, *fpl* water and wine *sing*.
▲ In *1*, also used in plural with the same meaning.

ablusado,-a *adj* bloused.

abnegación f abnegation, self-denial.
abnegado,-a 1 pp → **abnegar**. – 2 adj selfless, self-sacrificing.
abnegar t to renounce, give up.
▲ Conjugation model [48], like *regar*.
abobado,-a 1 pp → **abobar**. – 2 adj (*tonto*) stupid, silly. 3 (*distraído*) absent-minded. 4 (*pasmado*) bewildered.
abobar 1 t (*atontar*) to make stupid. 2 (*embobar*) to fascinate, amaze.
abocado,-a 1 pp → **abocar**. – 2 adj (*expuesto*) exposed to: *es un proyecto abocado al fracaso,* it's a project that is doomed to failure. 3 (*vino*) medium dry, smooth.
abocar 1 t (*verter*) to pour out. 2 (*asir*) to catch in one's mouth. 3 (*acercar*) to bring near, draw up: *las olas abocaron el barco a la orilla,* the waves washed the boat to the shore. – 4 i MAR to enter (**en**, -): *el barco abocó en el puerto,* the boat entered the harbour. – 5 abocarse, p (*reunirse*) to meet, gather.
▲ Conjugation model [1], like *sacar*.
abocetar t to sketch, outline.
abochornado,-a 1 pp → **abochornar**. – 2 adj ashamed, embarrassed.
abochornar 1 t (*avergonzar*) to shame. 2 (*acalorar*) to make flushed. – 3 abochornarse, p (*avergonzarse*) to become embarrassed. 4 (*planta*) to wilt.
abocinado,-a 1 pp abocinar. – 2 adj trumpet-shaped. 3 ARQ splayed.
abocinar 1 t to shape like a trumpet. 2 ARQ to splay.
abofetear t to slap.
abogacía f legal profession.
abogadillo,-a m,f pey second-rate lawyer, pettifogger.
abogado,-a 1 m,f lawyer, solicitor; (*tribunal supremo*) barrister. 2 fig advocate, champion.
● ejercer de abogado, to practise law, be a lawyer.
■ abogado de oficio, legal -aid lawyer. ‖ abogado defensor, counsel for the defense. ‖ abogado del diablo, devil's advocate. ‖ abogado del Estado, public prosecutor, US attorney general. ‖ abogado laborista, union lawyer.
abogar 1 i to plead. 2 fig to intercede.
● abogar a favor de, to plead for. ‖ abogar por, (*preconizar*) to advocate, propose; (*defender*) to defend; (*luchar por*) to fight for.
▲ Conjugation model [7], like *llegar*.
abolengo m ancestry, lineage.
● de rancio abolengo, of ancient lineage.
abolición f abolition.
abolicionismo m abolitionism.
abolicionista 1 adj abolitionist. – 2 mf abolitionist.
abolir t to abolish.
▲ Used only in forms which include the letter i in their endings: *abolía, aboliré, aboliendo, etc.*
abolladura f (*hundimiento*) dent; (*bollo*) bump.
abollar 1 t to dent. 2 ART to emboss. – 3 abollarse, p to get dented.
abolsado,-a 1 pp → **abolsarse**. – 2 adj baggy.
abolsarse 1 p (*tela*) to be baggy. 2 (*piel*) to pouch.
abombado,-a 1 pp abombar. – 2 adj convex.
abombar 1 t to make convex. 2 fam (*aturdir*) to deafen, confuse. – 3 abombarse, p to become convex.
abominable adj abominable, loathsome.
■ el abominable hombre de las nieves, the abominable snowman.
abominar 1 t to abominate, loathe. – 2 i to abominate (**de**, -), loathe (**de**, -).
abonable adj payable.

abonado,-a 1 pp → **abonar**. – 2 adj (*tierra*) fertilized. 3 FIN paid. – 4 m,f (*al teléfono, a revista*) subscriber; (*a teatro, tren, etc*) season-ticket holder.
abonanzar i (*tormenta*) to clear up; (*tiempo*) to become settled, grow calm.
▲ Conjugation model [4], like *realizar*.
abonar 1 t FIN to pay. 2 (*avalar*) to guarantee, answer for: *les abonó su buena reputación,* their good reputation spoke for itself. 3 (*tierra*) to fertilize. 4 (*subscribir*) to subscribe. – 5 abonarse, p (a revista) to subscribe (**a**, to); (*a teatro, tren, etc*) to buy a season ticket (**a**, for).
● abonar al contado, to pay cash. ‖ abonar en cuenta, to credit.
abonaré m promissory note, credit note, IOU.
abono 1 m (*pago*) payment. 2 (*aval*) guarantee. 3 (*fertilizante*) fertilizer; (*acción*) fertilizing. 4 (a revista) subscription; (*a teatro, tren, etc*) season-ticket.
abordable adj (*lugar*) accessible; (*persona*) approachable; (*asunto*) manageable.
abordaje 1 m (*choque*) collision, fouling. 2 (*ataque*) boarding.
● ¡al abordaje!, stand by to board!
abordar 1 t MAR (*chocar*) to run foul of, collide with; (*atacar*) to board. 2 MAR (*arribar*) to reach port. 3 fig (*persona*) to approach; (*asunto, tema*) to tackle.
aborigen 1 adj aboriginal, native. – 2 m aborigine, native.
▲ pl *aborígenes*.
aborrascarse p to get/grow stormy.
aborrecer 1 t to abhor, hate, detest. 2 (*aves*) to abandon.
▲ Conjugation model [43], like *agradecer*.
aborrecible adj hateful, detestable, loathsome.
aborrecimiento m hate, loathing, hatred.
aborregado,-a 1 pp → **aborregarse**. – 2 adj (*cielo*) covered with fluffy clouds. 3 fam (*persona*) mindless, sheeplike.
aborregarse 1 p (*cielo*) to become covered with fluffy clouds. 2 fam (*persona*) to follow the crowd, become sheeplike.
▲ Conjugation model [7], like *llegar*.
abortar 1 i (*voluntariamente*) to abort, have an abortion; (*involuntariamente*) to miscarry, have a miscarriage. 2 (*fracasar*) to fail, fall through. – 3 t (*interrumpir*) to interrupt.
● hacer abortar, to procure an abortion.
abortista 1 mf (*médico*) abortionist. 2 (*partidario*) pro-abortionist, abortion campaigner.
abortivo,-a 1 adj abortive. – 2 abortivo, m abortifacient.
aborto 1 m (*provocado*) abortion; (*espontáneo*) miscarriage. 2 pey (*persona*) ugly person, freak; (*cosa*) abortion.
abotagado,-a pp-adj → **abotagado**.
abotagarse p → **abotargarse**.
abotargado,-a 1 pp → **abotargarse**. – 2 adj swollen.
abotargamiento m swelling.
abotargarse p to swell up.
abotinado,-a adj high-fronted.
■ zapato abotinado, ankle boot.
abotonar 1 t (*ropa*) to button, button up. – 2 i (*planta*) to bud. – 3 abotonarse, p to do one's buttons up.
abovedado,-a 1 pp → **abovedar**. – 2 adj vaulted, arched.
abovedar t to vault, arch.
aboyar t to buoy.
abra 1 f (*ensenada*) cove, inlet. 2 (*desfiladero*) gorge, mountain pass. 3 (*fisura*) fissure.

abracadabra *m* abracadabra.
abrasado,-a 1 *pp* → **abrasar**. – **2** *adj* burnt.
abrasador,-ra 1 *adj* burning, scorching. **2** *fig* consuming: *pasión abrasadora*, consuming passion.
abrasar 1 *t* (*quemar*) to burn, scorch. **2** (*calentar*) overheat. – **3** *i* to burn (up): *esta sopa abrasa*, this soup is scalding hot. – **4** abrasarse, *p* to burn.
● abrasarse de amores, *fig* to be madly in love. ‖ abrasarse de calor, *fig* to be sweltering. ‖ abrasarse de sed, *fig* to be parched.
abrasión *f* abrasion.
abrasivo,-a 1 *adj* abrasive. – **2** abrasivo, *m* abrasive.
abrazadera *f* clamp, brace.
abrazar 1 *t* to embrace, hug: *se abrazaron*, they embraced each other. **2** (*ceñir*) to clasp. **3** (*incluir*) to include, comprise. **4** (*adoptar*) to adopt. **5** *fig* (*adherirse*) to embrace.
▲ Conjugation model [4], like *realizar*.
abrazo *m* hug, embrace.
● dar un abrazo a algn., to embrace sb. ‖ (muchos) abrazos (de), (*en carta*) with best wishes from. ‖ un abrazo (de), (*en carta*) with best wishes from.
abrebotellas *m* bottle opener.
▲ *pl* abrebotellas.
abrecartas *m* letter-opener, paper-knife.
▲ *pl* abrecartas.
ábrego *m* south-west wind.
abrelatas *m* tin-opener, us can-opener.
▲ *pl* abrelatas.
abrevadero *m* drinking trough.
abrevar *t* to water, to give water to.
abreviación *f* abbreviation.
abreviar 1 *t* (*acortar*) to shorten, cut short. **2** (*texto*) to abridge; (*palabra*) to abbreviate.
● abreviar los trámites, to speed up the formalities. ‖ para abreviar, to cut a long story short.
▲ Conjugation model [12], like *cambiar*.
abreviatura *f* abbreviation: *la abreviatura de etcétera es etc*, etc. is the abbreviation of et caetera.
abridor *m* opener.
abrigadero *m* shelter, sheltered place.
abrigado,-a 1 *pp* → **abrigar**. – **2** *adj* (*lugar*) sheltered, protected; (*persona*) wrapped up: *iba bien abrigada*, she was well wrapped up.
abrigar 1 *t* (*contra el frío*) to wrap up; (*ropa*) to be warm: *abriga bien al niño, que hace mucho frío en la calle*, wrap him up well, it's very cold outside; *este jersey abriga mucho*, this jumper is very warm. **2** (*proteger*) to shelter, protect. **3** *fig* (*sospechas*) to harbour (us harbor), have. **4** *fig* (*esperanzas*) to foster, cherish. **5** abrigarse, (*uso reflexivo*) to wrap os. up.
▲ Conjugation model [7], like *llegar*.
abrigo 1 *m* (*prenda*) coat, overcoat. **2** (*refugio*) shelter.
● al abrigo de, protected from, sheltered from. ‖ al abrigo de la ley, under the protection of the law. ‖ ser de abrigo, *fig* to be undesirable.
■ abrigo de pieles, fur coat. ‖ ropa de abrigo, warm clothing, warm clothes *pl*.
abril 1 *m* April. **2** *fig* springtime. – **3** abriles, *mpl fig* summers: *una chica de veinte abriles*, a girl of twenty summers.
● el abril de la vida, the springtime of one's life.
▲ See also *marzo*.
abrileño,-a *adj* April: *una plácida tarde abrileña*, a peaceful April afternoon.
abrillantador,-ra 1 *m,f* (*persona*) polisher. – **2** abrillantador, *m* (*producto*) polish. **3** (*instrumento*) polishing tool, polisher.

abrillantar 1 *t* to polish, make shine, burnish. **2** *fig* to enhance.
abrir 1 *t* (*gen*) to open: *abre la ventana*, open the window; *abriré esta botella de cava*, I'll open this bottle of cava; *abrid vuestros libros en la página diez*, open your books at page ten; *ya puedes abrir los ojos*, you can open your eyes now; *quisiera abrir una cuenta corriente*, I would like to open a current account. **2** (*con llave*) to unlock: *sacó una llave y abrió la caja*, he took out a key and unlocked the safe. **3** (*cremallera*) to undo: *abrió la cremallera de la maleta*, she undid the zip on the case, she unzipped the case. **4** (*negocio*) to open: *van a abrir un bar en la esquina*, they're going to open a bar on the corner. **5** (*túnel*) to dig; (*agujero*) to make. **6** (*luz*) to switch on, turn on; (*gas, grifo*) to turn on. **7** (*iniciar*) to start, begin: *abrieron una investigación para aclarar la causa del incendio*, they started an investigation into the causes of the fire. **8** (*encabezar*) to head, lead: *un niño con una cruz abría la procesión*, a boy with a cross headed the procession. – **9** abrirse, *p* (*gen*) to open: *la puerta se abre hacia fuera*, the door opens outwards; *le dieron puntos para que no se le abriera la herida*, they gave her stiches so that the wound wouldn't open. **10** (*flor*) to open, come out: *las rosas se están abriendo*, the roses are opening. **11** (*iniciarse*) to begin, start, open: *la película se abre con una escena muy bella*, the film opens with a very beautiful scene. **12** (*extenderse*) to spread out, unfold. **13** (*dar*) to open (a, onto), look (a, onto): *la casa se abre al mar*, the house looks onto the sea. **14** (*ligamentos*) to sprain. **15** *fig* (*sincerarse*) to open out. **16** *arg* (*largarse*) to clear off, be off,: *¡adiós, me abro!*, bye, I'm off!, us I'm out of here!
● abrir fuego, MIL to open fire. ‖ abrir la mano, *fig* to relax standards. ‖ abrir paso, to make way. ‖ abrir un expediente, JUR to start proceedings. ‖ abrir una posibilidad, to open up a possibility: *la nueva ley abre la posibilidad de que los terroristas se reinserten en la sociedad*, the new law makes it possible for terrorists to be reintegrated into society. ‖ abrirle la cabeza a algn., *fam* to smash sb.'s head in. ‖ abrirse paso en la vida, *fig* to make one's way in life. ‖ en un abrir y cerrar de ojos, *fam* in the twinkling of an eye. ‖ no abrir (la) boca, *fig* not to say a word.
▲ *pp* abierto,-a.
abrochar 1 *t* (*camisa*) to button, button up; (*zapato*) to tie up, do up. **2** (*botones*) to do up; (*broche, corchete*) to fasten: *abróchense los cinturones*, please fasten your seat-belts.
abrogación *f* abrogation, repeal.
abrogar *t* to abrogate.
▲ Conjugation model [7], like *llegar*.
abrojal *m* thistle patch.
abrojo *m* BOT thistle.
abroncar 1 *t* (*reprender*) to give a dressing-down (a, to), to tear a strip off. **2** (*abuchear*) to boo, heckle.
▲ Conjugation model [1], like *sacar*.
abrótano *m* southernwood.
abrumado,-a 1 *pp* → **abrumar**. – **2** *adj* overwhelmed: *estaba abrumado de trabajo*, he was snowed under with work.
abrumador,-ra *adj* overwhelming, crushing.
abrumar 1 *t* to overwhelm, crush: *la abrumó con sus atenciones*, his attentions made her feel uncomfortable. – **2** abrumarse, *p* to become misty.
abrupto,-a 1 *adj* (*terreno*) rugged; (*pendiente*) steep, abrupt. **2** (*persona*) abrupt, sudden.
absceso *m* abscess.

abscisa f abscissa.
absentismo I m (laboral) absenteeism. 2 (del terrate-niente) absentee landlordism.
absentista I adj (trabajador) absentee. 2 (terrateniente) absentee landlord.
ábside m apse.
absolución I f REL absolution. 2 JUR acquittal.
absolutamente adv absolutely, completely.
absolutismo m absolutism.
absolutista I adj absolutist. – 2 mf absolutist.
absoluto,-a adj absolute.
● en absoluto, not at all, by no means. ‖ estar pro-hibido,-a en absoluto, to be absolutely forbidden. ‖ nada en absoluto, nothing at all.
absolutorio,-a adj: fallo absolutorio, verdict of acquit-tal, verdict of not guilty; sentencia absolutoria, verdict of acquittal, verdict of not guilty.
absolver t REL to absolve; JUR to acquit.
▲ Conjugation model |32|, like mover, pp absuelto,-a.
absorbencia f absorbency.
absorbente I adj absorbent. 2 fig (trabajo) absorbing, engrossing; (exigente) demanding. 3 fig (persona) over-bearing, domineering. – 4 m absorbent.
absorber I t (líquidos) to absorb, soak up. 2 fig (conoci-mientos) to absorb. 3 fig (consumir) to use up. 4 fig (cau-tivar) to captivate.
absorción f absorption.
absorto,-a I adj (pasmado) amazed, bewildered. 2 (en-simismado) absorbed (en, in), engrossed (en, in): estaba absorta en sus pensamientos, she was lost in thought.
abstemio,-a I adj abstemious, teetotal. – 2 m,f teeto-taller.
abstención f abstention.
abstencionismo m abstentionism.
abstencionista I adj abstentionist. – 2 mf abstention-ist.
abstenerse p to abstain (de, from), refrain (de, from): se abstuvieron de votar, they abstained from voting.
● ante la duda, abstenerse, when in doubt, don't.
▲ Conjugation model |87|, like tener.
abstinencia f abstinence.
■ síndrome de abstinencia, withdrawal symptoms pl.
abstracción I f abstraction. 2 (concentración) concentra-tion.
abstracto,-a adj abstract: en abstracto, in the abstract.
abstraer I t to abstract. – 2 i (prescindir) to leave aside (de, -). – 3 abstraerse, p (ensimismarse) to become lost in thought; (concentrarse) to engross os. (en, in).
▲ Conjugation model |88|, like traer.
abstraído,-a I pp → abstraer. – 2 adj (absorto) ab-sorbed, engrossed. 3 (distraído) absent-minded.
abstruso,-a adj abstruse.
abstuve pt indef → abstenerse.
absuelto,-a I pp → absolver. – 2 adj REL absolved. 3 JUR acquitted.
absurdamente adv absurdly.
absurdidad f absurdity.
absurdo,-a I adj absurd: sería absurdo que dejaras el trabajo, it would be crazy to leave your job. – 2 ab-surdo, m absurdity, nonsense.
abubilla f hoopoe.
abuchear t to boo, jeer at.
abucheo m booing, jeering.
abuelo,-a I abuelo, m grandfather; (familiarmente) grandad, grandpa. 2 (viejo) old man. – 3 abuela, f grandmother; (familiarmente) grandma, granny. 4 (vieja) old woman. – 5 abuelos, mpl grandparents. 6 fig ancestors, forbears.
● éramos pocos y parió la abuela, fam as if that wasn't enough, that was all we needed. ‖ no tener abuela, fam not to be afraid of blowing one's own trumpet. ‖ ¡tu abuela!, fam rubbish!
abuhardillado,-a adj with a sloping roof.
abulense I adj of Ávila, from Ávila. – 2 mf person from Ávila, inhabitant of Ávila.
abulia f apathy, lack of willpower.
abúlico,-a adj apathetic, lacking in willpower.
abultado,-a I pp → abultar. – 2 adj bulky, big.
abultamiento I m (hinchazón) swelling, protuberance. 2 (bulto) bulkiness.
abultar I t to enlarge, increase. 2 fig to exaggerate. – 3 i to be bulky: la caja abulta mucho, the box takes up a lot of space.
abundamiento m abundance.
● a mayor abundamiento, fml furthermore.
abundancia f abundance, plenty.
abundante adj abundant, plentiful.
abundantemente adv abundantly.
abundar I i (haber en cantidad) to abound, be plentiful: las manzanas abundan, there are plenty of apples. 2 abundar en, (tener en cantidad) to be rich in, abound in: esta región abunda en aceite de oliva, this region is rich in olive oil. 3 fig (adherirse) to share, support: yo abundo en la opinión del ministro, I agree with the minister, I share the minister's opinion.
abuñolado,-a adj fritter-shaped.
abuñuelado,-a adj → abuñolado,-a.
abur interj fam cheerio!, see you!
aburguesado,-a I pp → aburguesarse. – 2 adj bour-geois.
aburguesamiento m process of becoming bourgeois.
aburguesarse p to become bourgeois.
aburrido,-a I pp → aburrir. – 2 adj (ser aburrido) boring, tedious; (monótono) dull, dreary. 3 (estar aburrido) bored, weary; (cansado) tired of; (harto) fed up with.
aburrimiento m boredom.
● ¡menudo aburrimiento!, how boring!, what a bore! ‖ ser un aburrimiento, to be a bore.
aburrir I t to bore. – 2 (cansar) to tire. – 3 aburrirse, p to get bored (con/de/por, with).
● aburrirse como una ostra, fam to be bored stiff.
abusar I i (propasarse) to go too far, abuse (de, -): abusar de algn., to take unfair advantage of sb. 2 (usar mal) to misuse (de, -): abusar de la bebida, to drink too much.
abusivamente adv improperly.
abusivo,-a adj excessive, exorbitant.
■ trato abusivo, ill-treatment.
abuso I m abuse, misuse. 2 (injusticia) injustice.
■ abuso de confianza, betrayal of trust, breach of faith. ‖ abusos deshonestos, indecent assault sing.
abusón,-ona I adj fam (fresco) shameless. 2 fam (gorrón) sponging, scrounging. 3 fam (injusto) unfair. – 4 m,f (go-rrón) sponger, scrounger. 5 (injusto) unfair person.
abyección f abjection, wretchedness.
abyecto,-a adj abject, wretched.
a/c abr (a cuenta) on account.
a.C. abr (antes de Cristo) before Christ; (abreviatura) BC.
acá I adv (lugar) here, over here. 2 (tiempo) now, at this time.
● acá y allá, here and there. ‖ de acá para allá, to

and fro, up and down. ‖ **de entonces acá,** since then. ‖ **de un tiempo acá,** lately. ‖ **más acá,** nearer.

acabado,-a 1 *pp*→ **acabar.** – **2** *adj* (*terminado*) finished; (*perfecto*) perfect, complete: *acabado,-a de hacer,* freshly made. **3** *fig* (*malparado*) worn-out, spent: *una persona acabada,* a has-been; *un actor acabado,* a burnt-out actor. – **4 acabado,** *m* finish: *se presenta con tres acabados distintos,* it comes in three different finishes.

acabamiento 1 *m* (*cumplimiento*) completion; (*fin*) end. **2** *euf* (*muerte*) end.

acabar 1 *t* (*gen*) to finish, finish off; (*completar*) to complete: *he acabado el trabajo,* I've finished the work. **2** (*consumir*) to use up: *acabaron las provisiones,* they used up their supplies. – **3** *i* (*gen*) to finish, end; (*pareja*) to split up: *la película acaba con la muerte del rey,* the film ends with the death of the king; *acaba en punta,* it has a pointed end; *Pilar y Juan han acabado,* Pilar and Juan have split up. **4 acabar por** + *gerundio,* to end up + *-ing*: *acabé por comprar el vestido,* I ended up buying the dress. – **5 acabarse,** *p* to end, finish, come to an end; (*no quedar*) to run out: *el partido se acabó con empate a dos goles,* the match ended in a two-all draw; *se acabó la fiesta,* the party's over; *se le acaba el contrato el mes que viene,* his contract runs out next month; *se nos ha acabado el butano,* we've run out of butane.

● **acabar bien,** to have a happy ending. ‖ **acabar con,** (*destruir*) to destroy, put an end to; (*terminar*) to finish, finish off: *la revolución acabó con los privilegios de los aristócratas,* the revolution put an end to the privileges of the aristocrats; *la caída de la bolsa acabó con su fortuna,* the stock market crash ruined him; *¡este chico acabará conmigo!,* this boy will be the death of me! ‖ **acabar de** + *inf,* to have just + *pp*: *no lo toques, acabo de pintarlo ahora mismo,* don't touch it, I've just painted it. ‖ **acabar mal,** (*cosa*) to end badly; (*persona*) to come to a bad end: *como sigas así acabarás mal,* if you carry on like that you'll come to a bad end. ‖ **¡acabáramos!,** *fam* at last! ‖ **no acabar de ...,** *el autobús no acaba de venir,* the bus still hasn't come; *este queso no acaba de gustarme,* I don't really like this cheese. ‖ **¡se acabó!,** that's it!

acabose ser el acabose, *loc fam* to be the limit.

acacia *f* acacia.

academia 1 *f* (*institución*) academy. **2** (*escuela*) school, academy.

■ **Academia de Bellas Artes,** ≈ Royal Academy of Arts. ‖ **academia de comercio,** business school. ‖ **academia de idiomas,** language school. ‖ **academia militar,** military academy. ‖ **La Real Academia Española,** the Spanish Academy.

académicamente *adv* academically.

academicismo *m* academicism.

académico,-a 1 *adj* academic: *no tiene estudios académicos,* he has no academic qualifications. – **2** *m,f* academician, member of an academy.

acaecer *i* to happen, come to pass, occur.
▲ *Conjugation model* |43|, *like agradecer; used only in the 3rd person.*

acalambrarse *p* to get cramps.

acalenturarse *p* to get feverish.

acallar 1 *t* to silence, hush. **2** *fig* (*persona*) to pacify; (*críticas*) to silence.

acaloradamente *adv* warmly; *fig* excitedly.

acalorado,-a 1 *pp* → **acalorar.** – **2** *adj* hot; (*cara*) flushed. **3** *fig* (*persona*) excited, worked up; (*debate*) heated, angry.

acaloramiento 1 *m* heat. **2** *fig* passion.

acalorar 1 *t* to warm up, heat up. **2** *fig* to excite; (*pasiones*) to inflame, arouse. – **3 acalorarse,** *p* to warm up, heat up, get warm, get hot. **4** *fig* (*persona*) to get excited, get worked up; (*debate etc*) to become heated.

acampada *f* camping.

■ **zona de acampada,** camp site.

acampanado,-a *adj* bell-shaped; (*prendas*) flared.

acampar 1 *i* to camp. – **2** *t* to camp.

acanalado,-a 1 *pp* → **acanalar.** – **2** *adj* grooved. **3** ARQ fluted.

acanaladura 1 *f* groove. **2** ARQ fluting.

acanalar 1 *t* to groove. **2** ARQ to flute.

acanallado,-a *adj* low, disreputable.

acantilado,-a 1 *adj* (*costa*) steep, sheer; (*rocoso*) rocky, craggy. **2** (*fondo del mar*) shelving. – **3 acantilado,** *m* cliff.

acanto *m* acanthus.

acantonamiento *m* (*acción*) stationing; (*lugar*) station.

acantonar *t* to station.

acaparador,-ra 1 *adj* hoarding. **2** (*instinto*) acquisitive; (*tendencia*) monopolizing. – **3** *m,f* hoarder. **4** (*monopolizador*) monopolizer.

acaparamiento 1 *m* hoarding. **2** (*monopolio*) monopolizing.

acaparar 1 *t* (*productos*) to hoard; (*mercado*) to corner, buy up. **2** (*monopolizar*) to monopolize, keep for os.: *acapararon la atención de todos,* they commanded the attention of everyone.

acaracolado,-a 1 *adj* spiral-shaped. **2** (*cabello*) very curly, in corkscrew curls.

acaramelado,-a 1 *pp* → **acaramelar.** – **2** *adj* (*sabor*) oversweet. **3** (*color*) caramel-coloured (us caramel-colored). **4** *fig* (*pareja*) lovey-dovey, starry-eyed; (*voz*) syrupy, sugary.

acaramelar 1 *t* to coat with caramel. – **2 acaramelarse,** *p* to become lovey-dovey, become starry-eyed.

acariciador,-ra *adj* caressing: *tenía una voz acariciadora,* he had a sensuous voice.

acariciar 1 *t* to caress, fondle. **2** (*pelo, animal*) to stroke. **3** *fig* (*esperanzas etc*) to cherish; (*idea, plan*) to have in mind. **4 acariciarse,** (*uso recíproco*) to caress each other.
▲ *Conjugation model* |12|, *like cambiar.*

ácaro *m* mite.

acarrear 1 *t* (*transportar*) to carry, transport. **2** *fig* (*producir*) to cause, bring, give rise to: *esto te podría acarrear muchos problemas,* this could cause you a lot of problems.

acarreo *m* carriage, transport: *gastos de acarreo,* freight, carriage, transport costs.

acartonado,-a 1 *pp* → **acartonarse.** – **2** *adj* cardboard-like, stiff. **3** (*piel*) wizened, shrivelled up.

acartonarse 1 *p* to go stiff/hard. **2** (*piel*) to become wizened, shrivel up.

acaso 1 *adv* perhaps, maybe: *acaso esté enfermo,* maybe he's ill; *¿acaso no lo viste?,* didn't you see him? – **2** *m* (*suerte*) chance.

● **por si acaso,** just in case. ‖ **si acaso,** (*en todo caso*) if anything; (*hipótesis*) if: *si acaso lo ves,* if you see him; *no es mala persona, si acaso un poco brusco,* he isn't a bad person, he's just a little brusque.

acatamiento 1 *m* (*respeto*) respect. **2** (*de la ley*) observance.

acatar 1 *t* (*leyes etc*) to obey, observe, comply with. **2** (*respetar*) to respect.

7

acentuado

acatarrado,-a 1 *pp* → **acatarrarse**. − 2 *adj* with a cold: *estaba acatarrada,* she had a cold.
acatarrarse *p* to catch a cold.
acato *m* → **acatamiento**.
acaudalado,-a 1 *pp* → **acaudalar**. − 2 *adj* wealthy, rich, well-off.
acaudalar *t* (*reunir*) to accumulate; (*dinero*) to amass.
acaudillar *t* to lead.
acceder 1 *i* (*consentir*) to consent (**a**, to), agree (**a**, to). 2 (*tener entrada*) to enter: *por aquí se accede al jardín,* this leads to the garden. 3 (*alcanzar*) to accede (**a**, to): *acceder al poder,* to come to power, take office; *acceder a la universidad,* be admitted to university, enter university.
accesibilidad *f* accessibility.
accesible *adj* accessible; (*persona*) approachable.
accésit 1 *m* (*premio*) consolation prize. 2 (*mención*) honourable (US honorable) mention.
▲ *pl* **accésit**.
acceso 1 *m* (*entrada*) access, entry; (*a una ciudad*) approach. 2 (*de tos*) fit; (*de fiebre*) attack, bout. 3 *fig* (*ataque*) fit, outburst. 4 INFORM access: *acceso directo,* random access.
■ *"prohibido el acceso",* "no admittance". ‖ *prueba de acceso,* entrance examination. ‖ *vía de acceso,* slip road.
accesorio,-a 1 *adj* accessory; (*gasto*) incidental. − 2 accesorio, *m* accessory, extra: *accesorios del automóvil,* car accessories.
accidentado,-a 1 *adj* (*persona*) injured. 3 (*con incidentes*) eventful, agitated: *vida accidentada,* stormy/troubled life. 4 (*terreno*) uneven, rough, bumpy. − 5 *m,f* casualty, accident victim.
accidental *adj* accidental: *no fue más que un encuentro accidental,* it was nothing but a chance meeting.
accidentalmente *adv* accidentally.
accidentarse *p* to have an accident.
accidente 1 *m* accident: *sufrir un accidente,* to have an accident. 2 (*terreno*) unevenness, irregularity. 3 MED faint.
● *por accidente,* by chance.
■ *accidente de carretera,* road accident. ‖ *accidente de coche,* car accident. ‖ *accidente de moto,* motorcycle accident. ‖ *accidente de trabajo,* industrial accident. ‖ *accidente de tráfico,* road accident. ‖ *accidentes geográficos,* geographical features.
acción 1 *f* action; (*acto*) act, deed. 2 (*efecto*) effect: *la acción del agua sobre la piel,* the effect of water on the skin. 3 COM share. 4 JUR action, lawsuit. 5 TEAT plot. 6 MIL action.
● *ejercitar una acción contra algn.,* JUR to bring an action against sb. ‖ *entrar en acción,* MIL to go into action. ‖ *ponerse en acción,* to start doing sth.
■ *acción de gracias,* thanksgiving. ‖ *acción de guerra,* act of war. ‖ *campo de acción,* field of action. ‖ *hombre de acción,* man of action. ‖ *película de acción,* adventure film.
accionamiento *m* starting, activation.
accionar 1 *t* (*máquina*) to drive, work, activate. − 2 *i* to gesticulate.
accionariado *m* shareholders *pl*.
accionista *mf* shareholder, stockholder.
acebo *m* holly.
acechanza *f* → **acecho**.
acechar 1 *t* (*vigilar*) to watch, spy on; (*esperar*) to lie in wait for: *acechar la ocasión,* to wait one's chance. 2

(*caza*) to stalk. 3 (*amenazar*) to threaten, lurk: *un gran peligro acecha,* great danger lies ahead.
acecho *m* watching.
● *estar al acecho de,* (*vigilar*) to be on the lookout for; (*esperar*) to lie in wait for.
acecinar 1 *t* to cure, salt. − 2 **acecinarse**, *p fig* (*acartonarse*) to become thin and wizened.
acedar *t* to turn sour.
acedera *f* sorrel.
acedía[1] *f* (*pez*) dab.
acedía[2] 1 *f* (*acidez*) sourness, acidity. 2 MED heartburn.
acéfalo,-a 1 *adj* acephalous. 2 (*sin jefe*) leaderless.
aceitar *t* to oil.
aceite *m* oil.
■ *aceite de girasol,* sunflower oil. ‖ *aceite de maíz,* corn oil. ‖ *aceite de oliva,* olive oil. ‖ *aceite de ricino,* castor oil.
aceitera *f* → **aceitero,-a**.
aceitero,-a 1 *adj* oil. − 2 *m,f* oil merchant. − 3 aceitera, *f* oil bottle. 4 AUTO oil can. − 5 aceiteras, *fpl* oil and vinegar set *sing*, cruet stand.
aceitoso,-a 1 *adj* oily. 2 (*grasiento*) greasy.
aceituna *f* olive.
■ *aceituna rellena,* stuffed olive.
aceitunado,-a *adj* olive-coloured (US olive-colored), olive: *de tez/piel aceitunada,* olive-skinned.
aceitunero,-a 1 *m,f* (*recolector*) olive harvester, olive picker. 2 (*vendedor*) olive seller.
aceituno *m* olive tree.
aceleración *f* acceleration.
■ *poder de aceleración,* AUTO power of acceleration.
acelerada *f* → **acelerado,-a**.
aceleradamente *adv* quickly.
acelerado,-a 1 *pp* → **acelerar**. − 2 *adj* accelerated, fast, quick. − 3 acelerada, *f* acceleration.
acelerador,-ra 1 *adj* accelerating. − 2 acelerador, *m* AUTO accelerator.
● *pisar el acelerador,* to put one's foot on the accelerator.
aceleramiento *m* → **aceleración**.
acelerar 1 *t* to accelerate; (*paso*) to quicken. 2 *fig* to speed up. − 3 **acelerarse**, *p fig* (*azorarse*) to be embarrassed. 4 *fig* (*apresurarse*) to hasten, hurry up.
aceleratriz 1 *adj* accelerative, accelerating. − 2 *f* accelerating force.
acelerón *m* sudden acceleration.
● *dar un acelerón,* AUTO to step on the accelerator, put one's foot down.
acelga *f* chard.
acémila 1 *f* (*mulo*) mule; (*bestia de carga*) packhorse. 2 *fig* (*persona*) clumsy idiot.
acendradamente *adv* purely.
acendrado,-a 1 *pp* → **acendrar**. − 2 *adj* pure, unblemished.
acendrar *t* to purify.
acento 1 *m* (*tilde*) accent (mark). 2 (*tónico*) stress. 3 (*pronunciación*) accent: *acento andaluz,* Andalusian accent. 4 (*énfasis*) emphasis, stress.
● *poner el acento en algo,* to stress sth., emphasize sth.
■ *acento ortográfico,* written accent, accent.
acentor *m* hedge sparrow, dunnock.
acentuación *f* accentuation.
acentuadamente *adv* strongly.
acentuado,-a 1 *pp* → **acentuar**. − 2 *adj* (*con tilde*) accentuated; (*tónico*) stressed. 3 *fig* (*marcado*) strong, marked.

acentual *adj* relating to accents, accentual: *en el dictado cometió muchos errores acentuales,* he made a lot of mistakes with accents in the dictation.

acentuar 1 *t* (*tilde*) to accentuate; (*tónico*) to stress. 2 (*resaltar*) to emphasize, stress. – 3 **acentuarse,** *p* to become more pronounced, become more marked.
▲ *Conjugation model* |11|, *like actuar.*

aceña *f* watermill.

acepción *f* meaning, sense.

acepilladora *f* planer, planing machine.

acepillar 1 *t* (*madera*) to plane, shave. 2 (*tela, prenda*) to brush.

aceptabilidad *f* acceptability.

aceptable *adj* acceptable.

aceptación 1 *f* acceptance. 2 (*aprobación*) approval; (*éxito*) success: *la película tuvo poca aceptación,* the film wasn't popular, the film met with little success.

aceptar 1 *t* to accept, receive. 2 (*aprobar*) to approve of.

acequia *f* irrigation channel, ditch.

acera *f* pavement, us sidewalk.
● **ser de la acera de enfrente,** *fam* to be gay, be queer.

acerado,-a 1 *pp* → **acerar.** – 2 *adj* steel, steely. 3 *fig* (*incisivo*) sharp, incisive.

acerar 1 *t* (*recubrir de acero*) to steel. 2 *fig* (*hacer fuerte*) to strengthen.

acerbamente *adv* bitterly.

acerbo,-a 1 *adj* (*al gusto*) bitter, sour. 2 (*cruel*) cruel, bitter.

acerca acerca de, *adv* about, concerning, on.

acercamiento 1 *m* (*acción*) coming together, bringing together. 2 *fig* (*reconciliación*) bringing together, reconciliation; (*en política*) rapprochement.

acercar 1 *t* to bring near, bring nearer, draw up: *acércate,* come closer; *¿me acercas el agua?,* can you pass the water?; *nos acercó a casa,* she gave us a lift home. 2 *fig* to bring together. – 3 **acercarse,** *p* (*aproximarse*) to be near: *se acerca el verano,* summer is near. 4 (*ir*) to go: *acércate a la esquina,* go to the corner. 5 (*visitar*) to drop in, drop by: *se acercó a vernos,* he dropped by to see us.
▲ *Conjugation model* |1|, *like sacar.*

acerería *f* → **acería.**

acería *f* steelworks, steel mill.

acerico *m* pincushion.

acerillo *m* pincushion.

acero 1 *m* steel. 2 (*espada*) sword, steel. – 3 **aceros,** *mpl* (*valor*) courage *sing,* bravery *sing.*
● **tener (los) nervios de acero,** to have nerves of steel.
■ **acero fundido,** cast steel. ‖ **acero inoxidable,** stainless steel.

acérrimo,-a *adj* (*seguidor*) staunch, steadfast; (*enemigo*) bitter.

acertadamente *adv* rightly, correctly.

acertado,-a 1 *pp* → **acertar.** – 2 *adj* (*opinión etc*) right, correct; (*comentario*) fitting; (*idea, decisión*) clever; (*color*) well-chosen; (*palabra*) exact. 3 (*conveniente*) suitable.
● **estar acertado,-a,** to be wise.

acertante 1 *adj* winning. – 2 *mf* (*concurso, quiniela*) winner; (*problema*) solver.

acertar 1 *t* (*en un objetivo*) to hit. 2 (*dar con lo cierto*) to get right: *sólo acertó cinco preguntas,* she only got five questions right. 3 (*por azar*) to guess correctly; (*concurso, quinielas*) to win. 4 (*encontrar*) to find: *acertó la casa a la primera,* he found the house at the first attempt. – 5 *i*

(*encontrar*) to find: *acertó con el libro enseguida,* he found the book at once. 6 (*dar con lo cierto*) to get right, be right. 7 **acertar a** + *inf,* to happen to + *inf: yo acertaba a estar allí,* I happened to be there.
▲ *Conjugation model* |27|.

acertijo *m* riddle.

acervo 1 *m* (*montón*) heap. 2 (*haber común*) common property.
■ **acervo cultural,** cultural tradition, cultural heritage. ‖ **acervo familiar,** family property.

acetato *m* acetate.

acético,-a *adj* acetic.

acetileno *m* acetylene.

acetona *f* acetone.

acetoso,-a *adj* (*ácido*) sharp; (*avinagrado*) sour.

achabacanar 1 *t* to make vulgar. – 2 **achabacanarse,** *p* to become vulgar.

achacar *t* to impute, attribute.
▲ *Conjugation model* |1|, *like sacar.*

achacoso,-a *adj* ailing, unwell.

achampañado,-a *adj* champagne-style.

achantar 1 *i fam* (*intimidar*) to scare, frighten. – 2 **achantarse,** *p* (*acobardarse*) to get frightened, lose one's nerve. 3 (*esconderse*) to hide. 4 *fam* (*callarse*) to shut up.

achaparrado,-a *adj* squat, stocky.

achaque *m* ailment, complaint.
● **con achaque de,** under the pretext of. ‖ **en achaque de,** in the matter of, on the subject of.

acharolado,-a *adj* varnished.

achatado,-a 1 *pp* → **achatar.** – 2 *adj* flattened.

achatamiento *m* flattening.

achatar 1 *t* to flatten. – 2 **achatarse,** *p* to become flat, go flat.

achicado,-a 1 *pp* → **achicar.** – 2 *adj* childish.

achicar 1 *t* (*amenguar*) to diminish, reduce, make smaller. 2 (*amilanar*) to intimidate. 3 (*agua*) to drain; (*en barco*) to bale out. – 4 **achicarse,** *p* (*amenguarse*) to get smaller. 5 (*amilanarse*) to lose heart.
▲ *Conjugation model* |1|, *like sacar.*

achicharradero *m fam* oven, furnace.

achicharramiento *m* burning, scorching.

achicharrante *adj* burning, scorching, searing, sweltering: *hace un calor achicharrante,* the heat is sweltering.

achicharrar 1 *t* to scorch; (*comida*) to burn: *hace un sol que achicharra,* it's roasting. – 2 *i* (*molestar*) to bother, pester: *le achicharraron a/con preguntas,* he was plagued with questions. – 3 **achicharrarse,** *p* to roast.

achicoria *f* chicory.

achinado,-a *adj* oriental-looking; (*ojos*) slanting.

achispado,-a 1 *pp* → **achispar.** – 2 *adj* tipsy.

achispar 1 *t* to make tipsy. – 2 **achisparse,** *p* to get tipsy/tight.

achocolatado,-a 1 *adj* (*sabor*) chocolate-flavoured (us chocolate-flavored). 2 (*color*) chocolate-coloured (us chocolate-colored).

achubascarse *p* to cloud over, become overcast.

achuchado,-a 1 *pp* → **achuchar.** – 2 *adj fam* difficult.

achuchar 1 *t* (*azuzar*) to nag at: *me anda achuchando para que lave el coche,* she keeps nagging at me to wash the car. 2 (*abrazar*) to hug, squeeze: *había una pareja achuchándose en el rincón,* there was a couple having a cuddle in the corner. 3 (*dar empujones*) to jostle: *a la hora punta en el bus no dejan de achucharte,* at rush

9

acomodaciónacomodación

hour on the bus people are always jostling you. **4** (*empujar*) to shove.

achuchón 1 *m fam* (*empujón*) push, shove: *el delantero apartó al portero de un achuchón,* the forward pushed the goalkeeper aside. **2** *fam* (*indisposición*) ailment: *siempre tiene algún achuchón,* there's always something wrong with him; *le dio un achuchón,* he had a funny turn. **3** *fam* (*abrazo*) hug, squeeze: *la abuela le dio un achuchón al niño,* the old lady hugged the little boy.

achulado,-a 1 *adj* (*presumido*) cocky. **2** (*grosero*) vulgar, crude, common.

aciago *adj* ill-fated, fateful.

aciano *m* cornflower.

acíbar 1 *m* (*planta*) aloe; (*jugo*) aloe, bitter aloes *pl.* **2** *fig* (*amargura*) bitterness, sorrow.

acibarar *t* to embitter.

acicalado,-a 1 *pp* → **acicalar.** – **2** *adj* well-dressed, smart.

acicalamiento *m* smartening up.

acicalar 1 *t* to smarten up. – **2 acicalarse,** *p* to dress up, smarten up.

acicate 1 *m* (*espuela*) spur. **2** *fig* (*incentivo*) spur, incentive, stimulus.

acidez 1 *f* (*sabor*) sourness, sharpness. **2** QUÍM acidity.
■ **acidez de estómago,** heartburn.

acidia *f* idleness, indolence.

acidificar *t* to acidify.
▲ *Conjugation model* [1], *like* **sacar.**

ácido,-a 1 *adj* (*sabor*) sharp, tart. **2** QUÍM acidic. **3** (*tono*) harsh. – **4** **ácido,** *m* QUÍM acid. **5** *arg* (*droga*) acid, LSD.
■ **ácido acético,** acetic acid. ‖ **ácido carbónico,** carbonic acid. ‖ **ácido clorhídrico,** hydrochloric acid. ‖ **ácido nítrico,** nitric acid. ‖ **ácido sulfúrico,** sulphuric acid. ‖ **ácido úrico,** uric acid.

acierto 1 *m* (*adivinación*) correct guess, right answer. **2** (*buena idea*) good choice/idea. **3** (*logro*) good shot. **4** (*tino*) wisdom, good judgement: *con gran acierto,* very wisely. **5** (*casualidad*) chance. **6** (*éxito*) success. **7** (*habilidad*) skill.

ácimo,-a *adj* unleavened.

acimut *m* azimuth.

aclamación *f* acclamation, acclaim.

aclamar *t* to acclaim.

aclaración *f* explanation.

aclarado *m* rinsing, rinse.

aclarar 1 *t* (*cabello, color*) to lighten, make lighter. **2** (*líquido*) to thin (down). **3** (*enjuagar*) to rinse. **4** (*explicar*) to explain; (*poner en claro*) to make clear, clarify. **5** *fig* (*mejorar*) to improve: *las zanahorias aclaran la vista,* carrots improve your eyesight, carrots are good for your eyes. – **6** *i* (*mejorar el tiempo*) to clear (up): *hay una tormenta horrible y no parece que vaya a aclarar,* there's a heavy storm and it doesn't look as if it's going to clear up. – **7 aclararse,** *p* (*entender*) to understand: *no me aclaro con esta lección,* I can't understand this lesson; *es que no me aclaro,* I don't know what's going on. **8** (*explicarse*) to explain os. **9** (*decidirse*) to make up one's mind: *a ver si te aclaras de una vez,* make up your mind once and for all. **10** (*el tiempo*) to clear (up).
● **aclarar la voz,** to clear one's throat.
▲ In *6* and *10* used only in the 3rd person; it does not take a subject.

aclaratorio,-a *adj* explanatory.

aclimatable *adj* able to become acclimatized (**a,** to), US able to become acclimated (**a,** to).

aclimatación *f* acclimatization, US acclimation.

aclimatar 1 *t* to acclimatize (**a,** to), US acclimate (**a,** to). – **2 aclimatarse,** *p* to become acclimatized (**a,** to), become US acclimated (**a,** to). **3** *fig* to get used to.

acné *f* acne.

ACNUR *abr* (*Alto Comisionado de las Naciones Unidas para los Refugiados*) United Nations High Commissioner for Refugees; (*abreviatura*) UNHCR.

acobardar 1 *t* to frighten, unnerve. – **2 acobardarse,** *p* to become frightened, lose one's nerve, shrink back (**ante,** from).

acodado,-a 1 *pp* → **acodar.** – **2** *adj* (*tubería*) elbowed. **3** (*apoyado*) leaning (on one's elbows).

acodalar *t* to prop up, shore up.

acodar 1 *t* (*plantas*) to layer. **2** (*doblar*) to bend. – **3 acodarse,** *p* to lean/rest on one's elbows.

acodo 1 *m* (*planta*) layering. **2** (*moldura*) frame.

acogedor,-ra 1 *adj* (*persona*) welcoming, friendly. **2** (*lugar*) cosy, warm.

acoger 1 *t* (*recibir*) to receive; (*a invitado*) to welcome. **2** (*admitir*) to admit, accept: *la acogieron cuando murieron sus padres,* they took her in when her parents died. **3** (*proteger*) to shelter, protect. **4** (*ideas etc*) to accept, take to. – **5 acogerse,** *p* (*refugiarse*) to take refuge (**a,** in). **6** (*a una ley etc*) to have recourse to; (*amnistía, promesa*) to avail os. of.
▲ *Conjugation model* [5], *like* **proteger.**

acogida *f* → **acogido,-a.**

acogido,-a 1 *pp* → **acoger.** – **2** *m,f* (*en beneficencia*) inmate, resident. – **3 acogida,** *f* reception, welcome. **4** *fig* shelter. **5** (*aceptación*) popularity.
● **tener buena acogida,** to be welcomed.

acogotar 1 *t* (*matar*) to kill *with a blow on the neck.* **2** (*derribar*) to knock down. **3** (*dar miedo*) to frighten, intimidate.

acojonado,-a 1 *pp* → **acojonar.** – **2** *adj tabú* (*asustado*) shit-scared. **3** *tabú* (*asombrado*) gobsmacked.

acojonamiento *m tabú* funk, jitters *pl.*

acojonante *adj tabú* bloody great, bloody terrific.

acojonar 1 *t tabú* (*atemorizar*) to scare (the shit out of), put the wind up. **2** *tabú* (*asombrar*) to amaze, gobsmack: *acojonó a todos con la moto,* they were all gobsmacked by his motorbike. – **3 acojonarse,** *p tabú* to shit os., get the wind up.

acojone *m tabú* funk, jitters *pl.*

acojono *m tabú* funk, jitters *pl.*

acolchado,-a 1 *pp* → **acolchar.** – **2** *adj* (*superficie*) padded; (*prenda*) quilted. – **3 acolchado,** *m* padding, quilting.

acolchar 1 *t* (*prenda*) to quilt. **2** (*superficie*) to pad.

acólito 1 *m* (*eclesiástico*) acolyte; (*monaguillo*) altar boy. **2** *fig* (*seguidor*) acolyte; *irón* minion.

acollar *t* to earth up.

acollarar *t* (*perro*) to put a collar on; (*buey*) to yoke.

acometedor,-ra 1 *adj* (*agresivo*) aggressive. **2** (*emprendedor*) enterprising.

acometer 1 *t* (*embestir*) to attack. **2** (*emprender*) to undertake. **3** (*empezar repentinamente*) to be seized by: *le acometió la risa,* he burst out laughing; *le acometió la duda,* she was nagged by doubt; *le acometió la tos,* she had a coughing fit.

acometida 1 *f* (*ataque*) attack, assault. **2** (*derivación*) connection.

acometividad 1 *f* (*agresividad*) aggression, aggressiveness. **2** (*dinamismo*) enterprise.

acomodación 1 *f* (*colocación conveniente*) arrangement. **2** (*adaptación*) adaptation.

acomodadizo,-a *adj* accommodating, easy-going.

acomodado,-a 1 *pp* → **acomodar**. – 2 *adj* (*conveniente*) suitable. 3 (*rico*) well-to-do, well off. 4 (*precio*) reasonable, moderate. 5 (*ordenado*) arranged. 6 (*adaptado*) adapted.

acomodador,-ra *m,f* (*hombre*) usher; (*mujer*) usherette.

acomodar 1 *t* (*colocar*) to arrange, fit in, find room for. 2 (*adaptar*) to apply, adapt: *podemos acomodar este ejemplo a la nueva teoría,* we can adapt this example to the new theory. 3 (*alojar*) to lodge, accommodate. 4 (*conseguir empleo*) to provide with a job, find a job for: *la acomodó de niñera en Londres,* he found her a job as a nanny in London. 5 (*en un local*) to find a place for. – 6 **acomodarse,** *p* (*instalarse*) to make os. comfortable. 7 (*adaptarse*) to adapt os. (**a/con,** to); (*aceptar*) to accept: *de momento me acomodaré con este sueldo,* for the time being I'll make do with this salary.

acomodaticio,-a 1 *adj* easy-going, accommodating. 2 *pey* pliable.

acomodo 1 *m* (*empleo*) job, employment. 2 (*alojamiento*) accommodation, lodging.

acompañado,-a 1 *pp* → **acompañar**. – 2 *adj* (*persona*) accompanied; (*lugar*) busy, frequented.
● **estar/ir bien/mal acompañado, -a,** to be/go in good/bad company.

acompañamiento 1 *m* accompaniment. 2 (*comitiva*) retinue, escort. 3 (*guarnición de plato*) accompaniment to a main dish, side dish: *bistec con acompañamiento,* steak with vegetables/chips/salad *etc.* 4 MÚS accompaniment.

acompañanta 1 *f* (female) companion, chaperon, chaperone. 2 MÚS (female) accompanist.

acompañante 1 *adj* accompanying. – 2 *mf* companion, escort. 3 MÚS accompanist.

acompañar 1 *t* to accompany, go with: *te acompaño a la puerta,* I'll see you to the door; *nos acompañó al cine,* she came with us to the cinema; *es muy guapa, pero el pelo no la acompaña,* she's very pretty, but her hair lets her down. 2 (*adjuntar*) to enclose, attach. 3 MÚS to accompany. – 4 **acompañarse,** *p* MÚS to accompany os. (**a,** on).
● **acompañar en el sentimiento,** *fml* to express one's condolences to: *le acompaño en el sentimiento,* please accept my condolences.

acompasadamente 1 *adv* (*con ritmo*) rhythmically. 2 (*lentamente*) slowly.

acompasado,-a 1 *pp* → **acompasar**. – 2 *adj* (*rítmico*) rhythmic. 3 (*pausado*) slow, measured.

acompasar 1 *t* MÚS to mark the time of, mark the rhythm of. 2 (*adaptar*) to keep in time, adjust.

acomplejado,-a 1 *pp* → **acomplejar**. – 2 *adj* with a complex: *estar acomplejado por algo,* to have a complex about sth. – 3 *m,f* person with a complex: *ser un acomplejado por algo,* to have a complex about sth.

acomplejar 1 *i* to give a complex. – 2 **acomplejarse,** *p* to develop a complex (**por,** about).

acondicionado,-a 1 *pp* → **acondicionar**. – 2 *adj* equipped, fitted-out: *la casa no está acondicionada para vivir,* the house is not fit to be lived in.

acondicionador *m* conditioner.
■ **acondicionador de aire,** air conditioner. ‖ **acondicionador del cabello,** hair conditioner.

acondicionamiento 1 *m* conditioning, setting up, fitting up. 2 (*mejora*) improvement.

acondicionar 1 *t* to fit up, set up. 2 (*mejorar*) to improve.

acongojado,-a 1 *pp* → **acongojar**. – 2 *adj* distressed, anguished, afflicted.

acongojar 1 *t* to distress, grieve, make suffer. – 2 **acongojarse,** *p* to be distressed/grieved.

aconsejable *adj* advisable: *nada/poco aconsejable,* inadvisable.

aconsejar 1 *t* to advise: *necesita que le aconsejes,* he needs your advice. – 2 **aconsejarse,** *p* to seek advice.

aconsonantar *t* to rhyme.

acontecer *i* to happen, take place.
▲ Conjugation model [43], like *agradecer;* used only in the 3rd person.

acontecimiento *m* event, happening.

acopiar *t* to gather, collect.
▲ Conjugation model [12], like *cambiar.*

acopio 1 *m* (*acción*) storing. 2 (*cosa*) store, stock.
● **hacer acopio de,** to store up.

acoplable *adj* adjustable, adaptable.

acoplador *m* coupler, adapter.

acopladura *f* → **acoplamiento**.

acoplamiento 1 *m* fitting, adaptation. 2 TÉC (*acción*) coupling, connection; (*junta*) joint. 3 ASTRON docking. 4 INFORM handshaking.

acoplar 1 *t* (*juntar*) to fit (together), join, adjust. 2 TÉC to couple, connect. 3 (*aparear*) to mate, pair. – 4 **acoplarse,** *p* to fit, join. 5 (*aparearse*) to mate, pair. 6 ASTRON to dock.

acoquinamiento *m fam* fear, loss of nerve.

acoquinar 1 *t* to frighten, intimidate. – 2 **acoquinarse,** *p* to become frightened, lose one's nerve.

acorazado,-a 1 *pp* → **acorazar**. – 2 *adj* armoured (us armored), armour-plated (us armor-plated). – 3 **acorazado,** *m* battleship.

acorazar 1 *t* (*blindar*) to armour (us armor), armour-plate (us armor-plate). – 2 **acorazarse,** *p* (*endurecerse*) to steel os.
▲ Conjugation model [4], like *realizar.*

acorazonado,-a *adj* heart-shaped.

acorchado,-a 1 *pp* → **acorchar**. – 2 *adj* cork-like. 3 (*insensibilizado*) numb.

acorchar 1 *t* to cover with cork. – 2 **acorcharse,** *p* to become like cork. 3 (*insensibilizarse*) to go numb.

acordado,-a 1 *pp* → **acordar**. – 2 *adj* agreed: *según lo acordado,* as agreed.

acordar 1 *t* to agree. 2 (*decidir*) to decide. 3 (*conciliar*) to reconcile. 4 MÚS to tune. – 5 **acordarse,** *p* to remember (**de,** -): *no se acuerda de nada,* she can't remember anything.
▲ Conjugation model [31], like *contar.*

acorde 1 *adj* in agreement, agreed. – 2 *m* MÚS chord: *a los acordes de la marcha nupcial,* to the strains of the wedding march; *a los acordes del himno nacional,* to the tune of the National Anthem.

acordelar 1 *t* (*medir*) to measure with a string. 2 (*marcar*) to mark out with string.

acordeón *m* accordion.

acordeonista *mf* accordionist.

acordonado,-a 1 *pp* → **acordonar**. – 2 *adj* cordoned off, sealed off.

acordonar 1 *t* (*atar*) to lace, tie. 2 (*rodear*) to surround, draw a cordon around, cordon off.

acorralado,-a 1 *pp* → **acorralar**. – 2 *adj* cornered; (*ganado*) penned in, rounded up.

acorralar 1 *t* to corner; (*ganado*) to pen in, round up.

acortar 1 *t* to shorten, make shorter: *acortar distancias,* to cut down the distance. – 2 *i* to shorten. – 3 **acortarse,** *p fig* to be shy.

acosar *t* to pursue, chase.
● **acosar a preguntas,** to bombard with questions.
acoso 1 *m* pursuit, chase. 2 *fig* hounding.
■ **acoso sexual,** sexual harassment.
acostar 1 *t* (*en cama*) to put to bed. 2 (*estirar*) to lay down. 3 MAR to bring alongside. – 4 **acostarse,** *p* (*estirarse*) to lie down. 5 (*irse a dormir*) to go to bed: *es hora de acostarse,* it's bedtime.
● **acostarse con,** *fam* to sleep with, go to bed with.
▲ Conjugation model [31], like *contar.*
acostumbrado,-a 1 *pp* → **acostumbrar.** – 2 *adj* (*persona*) accustomed (**a,** to), used (**a,** to). 3 (*hecho*) usual, customary: *es lo acostumbrado,* it is the custom.
acostumbrar 1 *t* (*habituar*) to accustom to: *los acostumbró muy pronto,* she got them used to it very soon. 2 (*soler*) to be in the habit of: *no acostumbro (a) fumar por la mañana,* I don't usually smoke in the morning. – 3 **acostumbrarse,** *p* (*habituarse*) to become accustomed (**a,** to), get used (**a,** to).
acotación 1 *f* (*en escrito*) marginal note. 2 TEAT stage direction. 3 (*topográfica*) elevation mark.
acotado,-a[1] 1 *pp* → **acotar**[1]. – 2 *adj* (*terreno*) enclosed.
acotado,-a[2] 1 *pp* → **acotar**[2]. – 2 *adj* (*texto*) annotated.
acotamiento *m* enclosing, demarcation.
acotar[1] 1 *t* (*área*) to enclose, demarcate. 2 *fig* to delimit.
acotar[2] 1 *t* (*poner notas*) to add notes; (*texto*) to annotate. 2 (*topográfia*) to mark with elevations.
acracia *f* anarchy.
ácrata 1 *adj* anarchist. – 2 *mf* anarchist.
acre[1] 1 *adj* (*sabor, olor*) acrid. 2 *fig* (*lenguaje*) bitter, harsh; (*crítica*) biting.
acre[2] *m* (*medida*) acre.
acrecentamiento *m* increase, growth.
acrecentar 1 *t* to increase. – 2 **acrecentarse,** *p* to increase.
▲ Conjugation model [27], like *acertar.*
acrecer 1 *t* to increase. – 2 **acrecerse,** *p* to increase.
▲ Conjugation model [43], like *agradecer.*
acreditación *f* accreditation.
acreditado,-a 1 *pp* → **acreditar.** – 2 *adj* (*prestigioso*) reputable, well-known, prestigious. 3 (*representante, embajador*) accredited.
acreditar 1 *t* (*probar*) to prove: *¿tiene algún documento que acredite su identidad?,* have you any documents which would prove your identity? 2 FIN to credit: *hemos acreditado a su cuenta la suma de 1000 dólares,* we have credited your account with the sum of 1000 dollars. 3 (*embajador*) to accredit. – 4 **acreditarse,** *p* to gain a reputation, make one's name, become famous.
acreditativo,-a *adj* which proves, which gives proof.
acreedor,-ra 1 *adj* deserving: *ser/hacerse acreedor a,* to be worthy of. – 2 *m,f* FIN creditor.
acribillar 1 *t* to riddle, pepper. 2 *fig* to harass, pester: *acribillar a algn. a preguntas,* to bombard sb. with questions.
acrílico,-a *adj* acrylic.
acriminar *t* to incriminate.
acrimonia *f* acrimony.
acrisolado,-a 1 *pp* → **acrisolar.** – 2 *adj fig* (*puro*) pure; (*probado*) tested.
acrisolar 1 *t* (*metal*) to purify. 2 *fig* (*purificar*) to perfect. 3 *fig* (*probar*) to prove, show.
acristalar *t* to glaze.
acritud 1 *f* (*sabor*) sourness, bitterness; (*olor*) acridness. 2 (*dolor*) intensity. 3 *fig* (*mordacidad*) acrimony.

acrobacia 1 *f* acrobatics. 2 *fig* (*equilibrios*) manoeuvre (US maneuver).
▲ In 2, also used in plural with the same meaning.
acróbata *mf* acrobat.
acrobático,-a *adj* acrobatic.
acrobatismo *m* → **acrobacia.**
acrofobia *f* vertigo.
acromático,-a *adj* achromatic.
acrónimo *m* acronym.
acrópolis *f* acropolis.
▲ *pl acrópolis.*
acróstico *m* acrostic.
acta 1 *f* (*relación*) minutes *pl,* record (of proceedings); (*publicación*) transactions *pl.* 2 (*certificado*) certificate, official document.
● **constar en acta,** to be on record, be in the minutes.
‖ **levantar acta,** to draw up the minutes.
■ **acta notarial,** affidavit.
▲ In 1, also used in plural with the same meaning.
actinia *f* sea anemone.
actinio *m* actinium.
actitud *f* (*disposición*) attitude; (*postura*) position.
● **estar en actitud de** + *inf,* to be getting ready to + *inf.*
activación 1 *f* TÉC activation. 2 *fig* (*avivamiento*) livening up, quickening.
activar 1 *t* TÉC to activate; (*acelerar*) to expedite. 2 to enable. 3 *fig* (*avivar*) to liven up, quicken. – 4 **activarse,** *p* to become activated.
actividad *f* activity.
● **estar en plena actividad,** to be in full swing.
activismo *m* activism.
activista 1 *adj* POL activist. – 2 *mf* POL activist.
activo,-a 1 *adj* active: *estar en activo,* to be on active service. – 2 **activo,** *m* FIN asset, assets *pl.*
■ **activo disponible,** liquid assets *pl.* ‖ **activo y pasivo,** assets and liabilities.
acto 1 *m* act, action. 2 (*ceremonia*) ceremony, meeting, public function: *acto inaugural,* opening ceremony. 3 TEAT act. 4 REL Act.
● **acto seguido,** immediately afterwards. ‖ **en acto de servicio,** in action. ‖ **en el acto,** at once.
■ **acto de fe,** act of faith. ‖ **acto reflejo,** reflex action. ‖ **acto sexual,** sexual intercourse. ‖ **Actos de los Apóstoles,** Acts of the Apostles. ‖ **sala de actos,** assembly hall. ‖ **salón de actos,** assembly hall.
actor,-ra 1 *m,f* JUR plaintiff. – 2 **actor,** *m* actor.
■ **la parte actora,** the prosecution.
actriz *f* actress.
■ **primera actriz,** leading lady.
actuación 1 *f* (*en cine, teatro*) performance. 2 (*intervención*) intervention, action. 3 JUR legal proceedings *pl.*
actual 1 *adj* present, current: *dadas las circunstancias actuales,* under the present circumstances. 2 (*actualizado*) up-to-date: *ese es un tema muy actual,* that's a very topical subject. – 3 *m fml* this month: *el doce del actual,* the 12th of this month.
actualidad 1 *f* present (time). 2 (*hechos*) current affairs *pl;* (*estado*) the current state of things: *este programa te da toda la actualidad cinematográfica,* this programme gives you all the latest cinema news.
● **en la actualidad,** at present. ‖ **estar de actualidad,** to be fashionable.
actualización 1 *f* (*puesta al día*) updating, bringing up to date. 2 (*filosofía*) actualization.
actualizar 1 *t* (*poner al día*) to bring up to date, update. 2 (*filosofía*) to actualize.

▲ *Conjugation model* |4|, like *realizar*.

actualmente *adv* (*hoy en día*) nowadays, these days; (*ahora*) at present, at the moment.

actuar 1 *i* (*ejercer*) to act (**como/de**, as): *actuó de secretario el Sr. Soler*, Mr Soler acted as secretary. 2 (*comportarse*) to act: *actuaron como debían*, they did what they had to do. 3 CINEM TEAT to perform, act. – 4 *t* (*poner en acto*) to actuate, work.

▲ *Conjugation model* |11|.

actuario 1 *m* JUR clerk. 2 FIN actuary.

acuadrillar *t* to form into a band.

acuarela *f* watercolour (US watercolor).

acuarelista *mf* watercolourist (US watercolorist).

acuario *m* aquarium.

Acuario *m* Aquarius.

acuartelamiento 1 *m* (*acción*) quartering. 2 (*retención*) confinement to barracks. 3 (*lugar*) barracks (for confinement).

acuartelar 1 *t* MIL (*alojar*) to quarter. 2 (*retener*) to confine to barracks.

acuático,-a *adj* aquatic, water: *animal acuático*, aquatic animal.

acuatinta *f* aquatint.

acuchillar 1 *t* (*seres vivos*) to knife, stab. 2 (*prendas*) to slash. 3 (*madera*) to plane (down).

acuciante *adj* pressing, urgent: *un problema acuciante*, an urgent problem.

acuciar 1 *t* (*dar prisa*) to hurry up. 2 (*agobiar*) to urge on. 3 (*desear*) to long for, yearn for.

▲ *Conjugation model* |12|, like *cambiar*.

acucioso,-a 1 *adj* (*urgente*) urgent. 2 (*diligente*) diligent.

acuclillarse *p* to squat, crouch, crouch down.

acudir 1 *i* (*ir*) to go; (*venir*) to come, arrive. 2 (*presentarse*) to come back: *las lágrimas acudieron a sus ojos*, tears came to her eyes. 3 (*ir a socorrer*) to help, come forward. 4 (*recurrir*) to call on, turn to: *acudir al médico*, to consult one's doctor.

acueducto *m* aqueduct.

acuerdo *m* agreement.

● ¡**de acuerdo!**, all right!, O.K.! ‖ **de acuerdo con**, in accordance with. ‖ **de común acuerdo**, by mutual agreement, by common consent. ‖ **estar de acuerdo**, to agree (**con**, with). ‖ **llegar a un acuerdo**, to come to an agreement. ‖ **ponerse de acuerdo**, to agree. ■ **acuerdo marco**, framework agreement.

acuidad *f fml* acuity, sharpness.

acuífero,-a 1 *adj* aquiferous. – 2 **acuífero**, *m* water table.

acular *t* to back.

acullá *adv fml* far away: *estaba acullá de los mares*, it lay far beyond the sea.

acumulable *adj* accumulable.

acumulación *f* accumulation.

acumulador,-ra 1 *adj* accumulative. – 2 **acumulador**, *m* FÍS accumulator, storage battery.

acumular 1 *t* to accumulate; (*datos*) to gather; (*dinero*) to amass. – 2 **acumularse**, *p* to accumulate, pile up, build up. 3 (*gente*) to gather.

acumulativo,-a *adj* accumulative.

acunar *t* to rock.

acuñación *f* striking, minting.

acuñar 1 *t* (*monedas*) to strike, coin, mint. 2 (*una frase*) to coin. 3 (*poner cuñas*) to wedge.

acuosidad 1 *f* wateriness. 2 (*jugosidad*) juiciness.

acuoso,-a 1 *adj* watery. 2 (*jugoso*) juicy.

acupuntura *f* acupuncture.

acurrucarse *p* to curl up, snuggle up.

▲ *Conjugation model* |1|, like *sacar*.

acusación *f* accusation; JUR charge. ■ **acta de acusación**, indictment. ‖ **acusación particular**, JUR private prosecutor.

acusadamente *adv* markedly.

acusado,-a 1 *pp* → **acusar**. – 2 *adj* accused: *acusada de asesinato*, charged with murder. 3 (*marcado*) marked, noticeable. – 4 *m,f* accused, defendant.

acusador,-ra 1 *adj* accusing. – 2 *m,f* accuser.

acusar 1 *t* (*echar la culpa*) to accuse (**de**, of); JUR to charge (**de**, with). 2 (*manifestar*) to give away. – 3 **acusarse**, *p* (*confesarse*) to confess: *se acusó del crimen*, he confessed (to) the crime. 4 (*acentuarse*) to become more pronounced.

● **acusar recibo de**, to acknowledge receipt of.

acusativo *m* accusative.

acusatorio,-a *adj* accusatory.

acuse acuse de recibo, *m* acknowledgement of receipt.

acusica 1 *adj fam* telltale. – 2 *mf fam* telltale.

acusón,-ona 1 *adj fam* telltale. – 2 *m,f fam* telltale.

acústica *f* → **acústico,-a**.

acústico,-a 1 *adj* acoustic. – 2 **acústica**, *f* acoustics.

ad hoc, loc ad hoc.

adagio 1 *m* (*aforismo*) proverb. 2 MÚS adagio.

adaguar *i* to drink.

▲ *Conjugation model* |22|, like *averiguar*.

adalid 1 *m* (*soldados*) leader. 2 (*tendencia, escuela*) champion.

adamascado,-a *pp* → **adamascar**. 2 *adj* damask.

Adán 1 *m* Adam. 2 **adán**, *fam* untidy man, slovenly man.

● **estar hecho un adán**, to go about in rags.

adaptabilidad *f* adaptability.

adaptable *adj* adaptable.

adaptación *f* adaptation.

adaptado,-a 1 *pp* → **adaptar**. – 2 *adj* adapted.

adaptador *m* adapter.

adaptar 1 *t* (*acomodar*) to adapt. 2 (*ajustar*) to adjust, fit. – 3 **adaptarse**, *p* (*persona*) to adapt os. (**a**, to); (*cosa*) to fit, adjust.

adarga *f* shield.

adarme *m* jot, whit, scrap.

● **por adarmes**, in dribs and drabs.

adarve *m* walkway (*behind a parapet*).

addenda *f* addendum.

adecentar 1 *t* to tidy (up), clean (up). 2 **adecentarse**, (*uso reflexivo*) to tidy os. up.

Adecu *abr* COM (*Asociación para la Defensa de los Consumidores y Usuarios*) ≈ Consumers' Association.

adecuación *f* adaptation.

adecuado,-a 1 *pp* → **adecuar**. – 2 *adj* adequate, suitable, appropriate.

adecuar *t* to adapt, make suitable.

▲ *Conjugation model* |10|.

adefesio 1 *m* (*persona*) freak. 2 (*cosa*) monstrosity.

a. de J.C. *abr* (*antes de Jesucristo*) before Christ; (*abreviatura*) BC.

Adelaida *f* Adelaide.

adelantado,-a 1 *pp* → **adelantado**. – 2 *adj* (*precoz*) precocious. 3 (*aventajado*) advanced. 4 (*desarrollado*) developed. 5 (*reloj*) fast. 6 (*atrevido*) bold, forward.

● **por adelantado**, in advance.

adelantamiento *m* overtaking.

● **hacer un adelantamiento**, to overtake.

adelantar 1 *t* to move forward. **2** (*reloj*) to put forward. **3** (*pasar delante*) to pass; AUTO to overtake. **4** (*dinero*) to pay in advance. – **5** *i* (*progresar*) to make progress. **6** (*reloj*) to be fast. – **7 adelantarse,** *p* (*ir delante*) to go ahead. **8** (*llegar temprano*) to be early. **9** (*anticiparse*) to get ahead (**a**, of). **10** (*reloj*) to gain, be fast.

adelante 1 *adv* forward, further. – **2** *interj* (*pase*) come in! **3** (*siga*) go ahead!, carry on!
● **de aquí en adelante,** from here on. ‖ **en adelante,** henceforth. ‖ **más adelante,** (*tiempo*) later on; (*espacio*) further on. ‖ **seguir adelante,** to keep going, carry on.

adelanto 1 *m* (*avance*) advance: *los adelantos de la ciencia,* the progress of science. **2** (*tiempo*) advance: *llegó con una hora de adelanto,* she arrived an hour in advance; *el primero lleva diez minutos de adelanto al segundo,* the first has ten minutes' lead over the second. **3** COM advance payment.

adelfa *f* oleander, rosebay.

adelgazador,-ra *adj* slimming.

adelgazamiento *m* slimming.

adelgazar 1 *t* (*afinar*) to make slim. – **2** *i* (*perder peso*) to slim, lose weight. – **3 adelgazarse,** *p* to slim, lose weight.
▲ *Conjugation model* [4], *like realizar.*

ademán 1 *m* (*gesto*) gesture, movement. – **2 ademanes,** *mpl* manners.
● **en ademán de,** with the intention of, as if to. ‖ **hacer ademán de,** to look as if one is about to. ‖ **hacer ademanes,** to gesture, make signs.

además 1 *adv* (*también*) also, as well: *necesitarás además ropa de abrigo,* you will also need warm clothing. **2** (*es más*) furthermore, what is more: *¡y además, el coche es mío!,* and what's more, the car's mine!
● **además de,** as well as, in addition to: *además de gordo es feo,* as well as being fat, he's ugly.

Adén *m* Aden.

ADENA *abr* (*Asociación para la Defensa de la Naturaleza*) *association for the protection of nature.*

adenda *f* → **addenda**.

adensar *t* to condense.

adentellar *t* to sink one's teeth into.

adentrarse 1 *p* (*penetrar*) to penetrate (**en**, into), enter deep (**en**, into). **2** *fig* (*profundizar*) to go deeply (**en**, into), study thoroughly (**en**, -), delve (**en**, into).

adentro 1 *adv* inside: *se fueron muy adentro,* they went too far in. – **2 adentros,** *mpl* inward mind *sing*: *para sus adentros,* in his heart.
● **mar adentro,** out to sea.

adepto,-a 1 *adj* who follows, who supports. – **2** *m,f* follower, supporter.

aderezar 1 *t* (*condimentar*) to season; (*ensalada*) to dress; (*bebida*) to prepare, mix. **2** (*preparar*) to prepare. **3** *fig* (*personas*) to make beautiful; (*cosas*) to embellish. – **4 aderezarse,** *p* (*arreglarse*) to dress up, get ready.
▲ *Conjugation model* [4], *like realizar.*

aderezo 1 *m* (*condimento*) seasoning; (*de ensalada*) dressing. **2** (*preparación*) preparation, disposition. **3** (*joyas*) set of jewellery. **4** (*arreos*) harness, trappings *pl*.

adeudar 1 *t* (*deber*) to owe, have a debt of. **2** FIN to debit, charge. – **3 adeudarse,** *p* (*endeudarse*) to get into debt.

adeudo 1 *m* (*deuda*) debt. **2** FIN debit, charge.

a D.g. *abr* (*a Dios gracias*) thanks be to God.

adherencia 1 *f* (*adhesión*) adherence. **2** (*pegajosidad*) adhesion, sticking. **3** AUTO road-holding. – **4 adherencias,** *fpl* MED adhesion.

adherente *adj* adherent, adhesive.

adherir 1 *t* (*pegar*) to stick on. – **2** *i* (*pegarse*) to stick (**a**, to). – **3 adherirse,** *p* (*pegarse*) to stick (**a**, to). **4** *fig* (*unirse*) to adhere to, follow.
▲ *Conjugation model* [35], *like hervir.*

adhesión 1 *f* adhesion, adherence. **2** (*apoyo*) support.

adhesivo,-a 1 *adj* adhesive. – **2 adhesivo,** *m* adhesive.

adicción *f* addiction.
● **crear adicción,** to be addictive.

adición *f* addition.

adicional *adj* additional.

adicionar 1 *t* (*añadir*) to add. **2** (*sumar*) to add up.

adictivo,-a *adj* addictive.

adicto,-a 1 *adj* (*drogas*) addicted (**a**, to). **2** (*dedicado*) fond (**a**, of), keen (**a**, on). **3** (*partidario*) supporting. – **4** *m,f* (*drogas*) addict. **5** (*partidario*) supporter, follower.

adiestramiento *m* training, instruction.

adiestrar *t* to train, instruct.

adinerado,-a 1 *pp* → **adinerarse**. – **2** *adj* rich, wealthy. – **3** *m,f* rich person.

adinerarse *p* *fam* to get rich.

adintelado,-a *adj* flat.

adiós 1 *interj* goodbye!; *fam* bye-bye! **2** (*al cruzarse con alguien*) hello! – **3** *m* goodbye.
● **decir adiós a algo,** *fig* to say goodbye to sth. ‖ **decir adiós con la mano,** to wave goodbye.
▲ *pl adioses.*

adiposidad 1 *f* adiposity. **2** (*gordura*) obesity.

adiposis *f* obesity.

adiposo,-a *adj* adipose.

aditamento 1 *m* (*añadido*) added piece, addition. **2** (*complemento*) accessory.

aditivo,-a 1 *adj* additive. – **2 aditivo,** *m* additive.

adivinación 1 *f* guessing. **2** (*predicción*) divination, forecast.

adivinador,-ra *m,f* fortune-teller.

adivinanza *f* riddle, puzzle.

adivinar 1 *t* (*descubrir*) to guess: *le adivinó el pensamiento,* she read his mind. **2** (*predecir*) to forecast, foretell. **3** (*enigma*) to solve.

adivinatorio,-a *adj* divinatory.

adivino,-a *m,f* fortune-teller.

adjetivación *f* adjectival use.

adjetival *adj* adjectival.

adjetivar 1 *t* to use as an adjective. **2** *fig* to label, describe.

adjetivo,-a 1 *adj* adjective, adjectival. – **2 adjetivo,** *m* adjective.

adjudicación 1 *f* award, awarding. **2** (*en subasta*) sale.

adjudicar 1 *t* (*premio*) to award. **2** (*venta*) to sell, knock down: *¡adjudicado!,* sold! **3** (*obras*) to award a contract to. – **4 adjudicarse,** *p* (*apropiarse*) to appropriate, take over. **5** (*obtener*) to win.
▲ *Conjugation model* [1], *like sacar.*

adjudicatario,-a 1 *adj* contract-winning. – **2** *m,f* (*premio*) prizewinner. **3** (*venta*) successful bidder. **4** (*obras*) contract-winner, contract-winning company.

adjuntar *t* to enclose, attach: *adjunto un folleto,* leaflet enclosed.

adjunto,-a 1 *adj* (*en carta*) enclosed. **2** (*asistente*) assistant. – **3** *m,f* assistant teacher.

adlátere *m* henchman, follower.

adm. *abr* (*administración*) office.

adminículo *m* accessory, gadget.

administración 1 *f* (*gobierno*) administration, authorities *pl*. **2** (*empresa*) administration, management. **3** (*car-*

administrador 14

go) post of administrator, post of manager. **4** (*despacho*) administrator's office, manager's office. **5** (*oficina*) branch. ■ **administración central,** central government. ‖ **administración de Correos,** Post Office. ‖ **administración de Hacienda,** tax office. ‖ **administración de lotería,** lottery office. ‖ **administración militar,** commissariat. ‖ **administración pública,** public administration. ‖ **consejo de administración,** board of directors.
administrador,-ra I *adj* administrating. – **2** *m,f* administrator: *es muy buena administradora,* she knows how to manage money. **3** (*manager*) manager. ■ **administrador,-ra de fincas,** estate agent.
administrar I *t* (*bienes, justicia*) to administer. **2** (*dirigir*) to manage, run. **3** (*suministrar*) to give: *le administró una aspirina,* she gave him an aspirin. – **4 administrarse,** *p* (*manejarse*) to manage one's own money, manage one's own affairs.
administrativo,-a I *adj* administrative. – **2** *m,f* (*funcionario*) official, civil servant; (*de empresa, banco*) office worker.
admirable *adj* admirable.
admirablemente *adv* admirably.
admiración I *f* admiration: *sentía admiración por ella,* he admired her; *les causó admiración,* she impressed them. **2** (*signo*) exclamation mark.
admirador,-ra I *adj* admiring. – **2** *m,f* admirer.
admirar I *t* (*estimar*) to admire. **2** (*sorprender*) to amaze, surprise, astonish. – **3 admirarse,** *p* (*asombrarse*) to be astonished (**de,** at), be amazed (**de,** at).
admirativo,-a *adj* admiring.
admisibilidad *f* admissibility.
admisible *adj* admissible, acceptable.
admisión I *f* admission. **2** (*aceptación*) acceptance. **3** TÉC inlet, intake.
● "*reservado el derecho de admisión*", "the management reserves the right to refuse admission".
■ **plazo de admisión,** closing date.
admitir I *t* (*dar entrada*) to admit, let in. **2** (*aceptar*) to accept, admit: "*no se admiten propinas*", "no tipping", "tipping not allowed"; "*no se admiten cheques*", "no cheques accepted". **3** (*permitir*) to allow: *su obra admite varias interpretaciones,* his work is open to various interpretations. **4** (*reconocer*) to admit. **5** (*tener capacidad*) to hold: *sólo admite cuatro personas,* there's only room for four people.
admón. *abr* (*administración*) office: *admón. de Hacienda,* tax office.
admonición *f* warning, reproof.
admonitorio,-a *adj* warning.
ADN *abr* MED (*ácido desoxirribonucleico*) desoxyribonucleic acid; (*abreviatura*) DNA.
adobado,-a I *pp* → **adobar.** – **2** *adj* marinated, marinaded.
adobar I *t* (*reparar*) to mend. **2** CULIN to marinate, marinade. **3** (*pieles*) to tan. **4** *fig* (*amañar*) to twist.
adobe *m* adobe.
adobo I *m* (*acción*) marinating, marinading. **2** (*salsa*) marinade.
adocenado,-a I *pp* → **adocenarse.** – **2** *adj* commonplace, ordinary.
adocenarse *p* to become commonplace.
adoctrinamiento *m* indoctrination.
adoctrinar *t* to indoctrinate.
adolecer I *i* (*padecer*) to suffer (**de,** from): *adolece de asma,* he suffers from asthma; *adolece del corazón,* she

has a heart problem. **2** (*tener un defecto*) to have a fault: *el discurso adolece de ambigüedad,* the speech is ambiguous.
▲ *Conjugation model* |43|, *like* **agradecer**.
adolescencia *f* adolescence.
adolescente I *adj* adolescent. – **2** *mf* adolescent.
adonde *adv* where.
adónde *adv* where.
adondequiera **adondequiera (que),** *adv* wherever.
adonis *m* handsome young man, Adonis.
▲ *pl* **adonis**.
adopción *f* adoption.
adoptante I *adj* adoptive, foster. – **2** *mf* adoptive parent, foster parent.
adoptar *t* to adopt.
adoptivo,-a *adj* (*hijo*) adopted, adoptive; (*padres*) adoptive: *lo nombraron hijo adoptivo de la ciudad,* he was given the title of honorary citizen.
■ **patria adoptiva,** country of adoption.
adoquín I *m* cobble, paving stone. **2** *fam* (*persona*) idiot, clod.
adoquinado,-a I *pp* → **adoquinar.** – **2** *adj* cobbled. – **3** adoquinado, *m* cobbling, paving.
adoquinar *t* to cobble, pave.
adorable *adj* adorable.
adoración I *f* REL adoration, worship. **2** *fig* adoration, worshipping.
adorador,-ra I *adj* REL worshipping. **2** *fig* adoring. – **3** *m,f* REL worshipper. **4** *fig* adorer, worshipper.
adorar I *t* REL to worship. **2** *fig* to adore.
adormecedor,-ra *adj* sleep-inducing, soporific.
adormecer I *t* to make sleepy. **2** (*calmar*) to soothe. – **3 adormecerse,** *p* (*dormirse*) to doze off. **4** (*entumecerse*) to go to sleep, go numb.
▲ *Conjugation model* |43|, *like* **agradecer**.
adormecido,-a I *pp* → **adormecer.** – **2** *adj* sleepy, drowsy.
adormecimiento I *m* (*sueño*) drowsiness, sleepiness. **2** (*entumecimiento*) numbness.
adormidera *f* opium poppy.
adormilarse *p* to doze, drowse.
adormitarse *p* → **adormilarse**.
adornamiento *m* adornment, decoration.
adornar I *t* to adorn, decorate. **2** *fig* to embellish.
adornista *mf* decorator.
adorno I *m* decoration, adornment. **2** COST trimming; CULIN garnish.
● **de adorno,** decorative.
adosado,-a I *pp* → **adosar.** – **2** *adj* semi-detached: *casas adosadas,* semi-detached houses.
adosar *t* to lean (**a,** against).
adquirido,-a I *pp* → **adquirir.** – **2** *adj* acquired.
adquirir *t* to acquire; (*comprar*) to buy.
▲ *Conjugation model* |30|.
adquisición *f* acquisition; (*compra*) buy, purchase.
adquisitivo,-a *adj* acquisitive.
■ **poder adquisitivo,** buying power, purchasing power.
adrede *adv* deliberately, on purpose, purposely.
adrenalina *f* adrenalin.
adriático,-a *adj* Adriatic.
■ **el (mar) Adriático,** the Adriatic (Sea).
adscribir I *t* (*atribuir*) to attribute. **2** (*destinar*) to appoint to. – **3** *p* (*afiliarse*) to affiliate (**a,** to).
▲ *pp* **adscrito,-a**.

adscripción 1 *f* (*atribución*) ascription. 2 (*destino*) appointment.
adscrito,-a *pp* → **adscribir**.
adsorbente 1 *adj* adsorbent. – 2 *m* adsorbent.
adsorber *t* to adsorb.
adsorción *f* adsorption.
aduana 1 *f* customs *pl*: *el alcohol paga aduana*, there's duty on spirits. 2 (*oficinas*) customs building.
● **pasar (por) la aduana**, to go through customs.
■ **oficial de aduana**, customs officer.
aduanero,-a 1 *adj* customs. – 2 *m,f* customs officer.
aducción *f* adduction.
aducir *t* to adduce, allege.
▲ *Conjugation model* |46|, *like* **conducir**.
aductor 1 *adj* adductive. – 2 *m* adductor.
adueñarse 1 *p* to take possession (**de**, of). 2 *fig* to seize: *la ira se adueñó de Eva*, Eve was seized with anger.
aduje *pt indef* → **aducir**.
adulación *f* adulation, flattery.
adulador,-ra 1 *adj* adulating, flattering. – 2 *m,f* adulator, flatterer.
adular *t* to adulate, flatter, soft-soap.
adulón,-ona 1 *adj* fawning, grovelling. – 2 *m,f* crawler, groveller.
adulteración *f* adulteration.
adulterado,-a 1 *pp* → **adulterar**. – 2 *adj* adulterated.
adulterar *t* to adulterate.
adulterino,-a 1 *adj* adulterine. – 2 *m,f* adulterine child.
adulterio *m* adultery.
adúltero,-a 1 *adj* adulterous. – 2 *m,f* (*hombre*) adulterer; (*mujer*) adulteress.
adultez *f* adulthood.
adulto,-a 1 *adj* adult: *persona adulta*, adult. – 2 *m,f* adult: *los adultos*, the grown-ups.
adustez *f* harshness, severity.
adusto,-a 1 *adj* scorched, burnt, charred. 2 *fig* (*seco*) harsh, stern, severe.
aduzco *pres indic* → **aducir**.
advenedizo,-a 1 *adj* parvenu. – 2 *m,f* parvenu, upstart.
advenimiento 1 *m* advent, coming. 2 (*al trono*) accession.
adventicio-a 1 *adj* (*accidental*) accidental. 2 BIOL adventitious.
adventismo *m* Adventism.
adventista 1 *adj* Adventist. – 2 *m,f* Adventist.
adverbial *adj* adverbial.
adverbializar *t* to use as an adverb.
adverbio *m* adverb.
adversario,-a 1 *adj* opposing. – 2 *m,f* adversary, opponent.
adversativo,-a *adj* adversative.
adversidad *f* adversity, misfortune, setback.
adverso,-a 1 *adj* adverse, unfavourable (US unfavorable). 2 (*opuesto*) opposite. 3 (*adversario*) opposing.
■ **condiciones adversas**, adverse conditions.
advertencia 1 *f* warning. 2 (*consejo*) piece of advice. 3 (*nota*) notice.
● **hacer una advertencia**, to warn.
advertido,-a 1 *pp* → **advertir**. – 2 *adj* capable, knowledgeable.
advertir 1 *t* (*darse cuenta*) to notice, realize: *nadie advirtió su presencia*, nobody noticed she was there. 2 (*llamar la atención*) to warn: *ya te lo advertí*, I told you. 3 (*aconsejar*) to advise. 4 (*informar*) to inform.

▲ *Conjugation model* |35|, *like* **hervir**.
adviento *m* Advent.
advocación *f* invocation.
● **bajo la advocación de**, under the protection of.
adyacencia *f* nearness, proximity.
adyacente *adj* adjacent.
AECC *abr* (*Asociación Española contra el Cáncer*) Spanish cancer association.
AECI *abr* (*Agencia Española de Cooperación Internacional*) Spanish agency for international cooperation.
Aenor *abr* COM (*Asociación Española para Normalización y Racionalización*) ≈ British Standards Institution.
aeración *f* aeration.
aéreo,-a 1 *adj* aerial. 2 AV air.
■ **tráfico aéreo**, air traffic.
aereobús *m* airbus.
aero- *pref* aero-.
aerobic *m* aerobics.
aeróbic *m* aerobics.
aeróbica *f* aerobics.
aerobio,-a 1 *adj* aerobic. – 2 **aerobio**, *m* aerobe.
aeroclub *m* flying club.
aerodeslizador *m* hovercraft.
aerodinámica *f* → **aerodinámico,-a**.
aerodinámico,-a 1 *adj* aerodynamic: *línea aerodinámica*, streamlined. – 2 **aerodinámica**, *f* aerodynamics.
aerodinamizar *t* to streamline.
aeródromo *m* aerodrome, US airfield.
aeroespacial *adj* aerospace.
aerofagia *f* aerophagia.
aerofaro *m* beacon.
aerofotografía *f* aerial photograph.
aerógrafo *m* airbrush.
aerograma *m* aerogram, aerogramme.
aerolínea *f* airline.
aerolito *m* meteorite.
aeromarítimo,-a *adj* air-sea.
aerometría *f* aerometry.
aerómetro *m* aerometer.
aeromodelismo *m* aeroplane modelling.
aeromodelista 1 *adj* aeroplane modelling. – 2 *m,f* aeroplane model-maker.
aeromodelo *m* model aeroplane.
aeronáutica *f* → **aeronáutico,-a**.
aeronáutico,-a 1 *adj* aeronautic, aeronautical. – 2 **aeronáutica**, *f* aeronautics.
aeronaval *adj* air-sea.
aeronave *f* airship.
■ **aeronave espacial**, spaceship.
aeronavegación *f* aerial navigation.
aeroplano *m* aeroplane, US airplane.
aeropostal *adj* airmail.
aeropuerto *m* airport.
aerosol *m* aerosol, spray.
aerostática *f* → **aerostático,-a**.
aerostático,-a 1 *adj* aerostatic. – 2 **aerostática**, *f* aerostatics.
aerostato *m* hot-air balloon.
aeróstato *m* hot-air balloon.
aerotransportado,-a *adj* airborne.
aerovía *f* airway.
AES *abr* (*Acuerdo Económico y Social*) *economic and social agreement*.
a/f *abr* (*a favor*) in favour.

afabilidad *f* affability.
afable *adj* affable, kind.
afamado,-a[1] *adj* hungry.
afamado,-a[2] 1 *pp* → **afamar**. – 2 *adj* famous, well-known.
afamar 1 *t* to make famous. – 2 **afamarse**, *p* to become famous.
afán 1 *m* (*celo*) zeal; (*interés*) keenness, eagerness: *con afán,* keenly. 2 (*esfuerzo*) effort.
afanador,-ra 1 *adj* zealous, eager. – 2 *m,f* zealous person, eager person. 3 *fam* (*ladrón*) thief.
afanar 1 *t fam* (*robar*) to nick, pinch. – 2 **afanarse**, *p* to work with zeal.
● **afanarse en,** to work hard at. ‖ **afanarse por,** to strive to, do one's best to.
afanosamente *adv* keenly, zealously.
afanoso,-a 1 *adj* (*persona*) eager, keen, zealous. 2 (*tarea*) hard, laborious, tough.
afasia *f* aphasia.
afásico,-a 1 *adj* aphasic. – 2 *m,f* aphasic.
afear 1 *t* to make ugly. 2 *fig* (*vituperar*) to reproach: *mi padre me afeaba la conducta,* my father reproached me for my behaviour.
afección 1 *f* (*enfermedad*) complaint, disease: *afección hepática,* liver complaint. 2 (*afición*) fondness.
afeccionarse *p* to take a liking (**a,** to), become fond (**a,** of).
afectación *f* affectation.
afectadamente *adv* affectedly.
afectado,-a 1 *pp* → **afectar**. – 2 *adj* (*gen*) affected. 3 (*emocionado*) affected, upset.
● **estar afectado,-a de,** to be suffering from.
afectar 1 *t* (*aparentar*) to affect: *afectar la voz,* to talk in an affected way. 2 (*impresionar*) to move. 3 (*dañar*) to damage. 4 (*concernir*) to concern. – 5 **afectarse**, *p* (*impresionarse*) to be affected, be moved.
afectísimo,-a suyo,-a afectísimo,-a, *loc fml* (*en correspondencia*) yours faithfully.
afectividad *f* affectivity.
afectivo,-a 1 *adj* (*sensible*) sensitive. 2 (*psicología*) affective.
afecto,-a 1 *adj* (*aficionado*) fond (**a,** of). 2 (*enfermo*) suffering (**de,** from). – 3 **afecto,** *m* affection: *con todo mi afecto,* with all my love.
● **tomarle afecto a algn.,** to become fond of sb.
afectuosamente *adv* affectionately; (*en cartas*) best wishes, best regards.
afectuosidad *f* affection.
afectuoso,-a *adj* affectionate.
afeitado 1 *m* (*pelo*) shave, shaving. 2 (*cuernos*) blunting.
afeitadora *f* electric shaver, electric razor.
afeitar 1 *t* (*pelo*) to shave. 2 (*toro*) to blunt the horns of.
afeite *m arc* make-up.
afelpado,-a *adj* velvety.
afeminación *f* effeminacy.
afeminado,-a 1 *pp* → **afeminar**. – 2 *adj* effeminate. – 3 *m* effeminate man; *fam* sissy.
afeminamiento *m* effeminacy.
afeminar 1 *t* to make effeminate. – 2 **afeminarse**, *p* to become effeminate.
afer *m* → **affaire**.
aferente *adj* afferent.
aféresis *f* aphaeresis.
▲ *pl* **aféresis**.
aferrado,-a 1 *pp* → **aferrar**. – 2 *adj fig* clutching, clinging, holding on to: *aferrado a un principio,* clinging to a principle.

aferramiento 1 *m* clutching, clinging. 2 (*obstinación*) stubbornness.
aferrar 1 *t* to clutch, grasp. – 2 *i* to cling, clutch, grasp. – 3 **aferrarse a,** *p* to clutch to, cling to.
affaire *m* (*caso*) case, affair; (*amoroso*) love affair.
Afganistán *m* Afghanistan.
afgano,-a 1 *adj* Afghan. – 2 *m,f* (*persona*) Afghan. – 3 afgano, *m* (*idioma*) Afghan.
AFI *abr* LING (*Alfabeto Fonético Internacional*) International Phonetic Alphabet; (*abreviatura*) IPA.
afianzamiento *m* strengthening, reinforcement; (*definitivo*) consolidation.
afianzar 1 *t* (*sujetar*) to strengthen, reinforce. 2 *fig* to support, back: *afianzaron el régimen,* they supported the regime. 3 (*dar fianza*) to stand bail for. – 4 **afianzarse**, *p* (*estabilizarse*) to steady os. 5 (*convencerse*) to become surer, become more convinced: *se afianzó en sus convicciones,* he became more convinced that he was right.
▲ *Conjugation model* |4|, *like* **realizar**.
afiche *m* poster.
afición 1 *f* (*inclinación*) liking, penchant: *tener afición por algo,* to be fond of sth. 2 (*ahínco*) interest, zeal: *con mucha afición,* keenly. 3 la afición, the fans *pl,* the supporters *pl.*
aficionado,-a 1 *pp* → **aficionar**. – 2 *adj* keen, fond: *ser aficionado a algo,* to be fond of sth. 3 (*no profesional*) amateur. – 4 *m,f* fan, enthusiast: *los aficionados al teatro,* theatre lovers. 5 (*no profesional*) amateur.
aficionar 1 *t* to make fond (**a,** of). – 2 **aficionarse**, *p* to become fond (**a,** of), take a liking (**a,** to): *se aficionó a la música,* he became a music lover.
afijo,-a 1 *adj* affixed. – 2 afijo, *m* affix.
afiladera *f* grindstone.
afilado,-a 1 *pp* → **afilar**. – 2 *adj* sharp. 3 (*con punta*) pointed. 4 *fig* (*cara, nariz*) long and thin. – 5 afilado, *m* sharpening.
afilador,-ra 1 *adj* sharpening. – 2 afilador, *m* knife-grinder. – 3 afiladora, *f* sharpener.
afiladora *f* → **afilador,-ra**.
afilalápices *m* pencil sharpener.
▲ *pl* **afilalápices**.
afilamiento *m* sharpness.
afilar 1 *t* to sharpen. – 2 **afilarse**, *p* to grow sharp.
afiliación *f* affiliation.
afiliado,-a 1 *pp* → **afiliar**. – 2 *adj* affiliated, member. – 3 *m,f* affiliate, member.
afiliar 1 *t* to affiliate. 2 **afiliarse**, (*uso reflexivo*) to join (**a,** to), become affiliated (**a,** to).
▲ *Conjugation model* |12|, *like* **cambiar**.
afiligranado,-a 1 *pp* → **afiligranar**. – 2 *adj* (*con filigranas*) filigreed. 3 *fig* delicate, dainty, fine.
afiligranar 1 *t* (*hacer filigrana*) to filigree, filagree. 2 *fig* (*hermosear*) to adorn, decorate.
afín 1 *adj* (*semejante*) similar, kindred. 2 (*relacionado*) related. 3 (*próximo*) adjacent, next.
afinación 1 *f* polishing, refining. 2 MÚS tuning.
afinado,-a 1 *pp* → **afinar**. – 2 *adj* (*fino*) polished, refined. 3 MÚS in tune, tuned.
afinador,-ra 1 *m,f* tuner. – 2 afinador, *m* tuning key.
afinar 1 *t* to perfect, polish. 2 MÚS to tune. 3 (*puntería*) to sharpen. 4 (*metales*) to purify, refine.
afincar *t* to settle down, establish os.
▲ *Conjugation model* |1|, *like* **sacar**.
afinidad 1 *f* affinity. 2 QUÍM similarity.

afirmación 1 *f* (*aseveración*) statement, assertion. **2** (*afianzamiento*) strengthening.

afirmado,-a 1 *pp* → **afirmar**. – **2 afirmado**, *m* road surface.

afirmar 1 *t* (*afianzar*) to strenghten, reinforce. **2** (*aseverar*) to state, say, declare. – **3** *i* (*asentir*) to assent. – **4 afirmarse**, *p* (*ratificarse*) to maintain (**en**, -): *se afirmó en su negativa*, she continued to refuse.

afirmativa *f* → **afirmativo,-a**.

afirmativamente *adv* affirmatively: *contestar/responder afirmativamente*, to answer in the affirmative.

afirmativo,-a 1 *adj* affirmative. – **2 afirmativa**, *f* affirmative answer.

● **en caso afirmativo**, if the answer is yes.

aflamencado,-a *adj* flamenco-like.

aflautado,-a *adj* flute-like: *voz aflautada*, high-pitched voice.

aflicción *f* affliction, grief, suffering.

aflictivo,-a *adj* grievous, distressing.

afligido,-a 1 *pp* → **afligir**. – **2** *adj* afflicted, grieved, troubled.

afligir 1 *t* to afflict, grieve, trouble. – **2 afligirse**, *p* to grieve, be distressed.

▲ *Conjugation model* |6|, *like dirigir*.

aflojamiento 1 *m* loosening. **2** *fig* relaxation.

aflojar 1 *t* (*soltar*) to loosen. **2** *fig* (*esfuerzo*) to relax. **3** *fam fig* (*dinero*) to pay up. – **4** *i* (*disminuir*) to let up: *el calor ha aflojado*, the heat has let up. – **5 aflojarse**, *p* to come loose.

● **aflojar la mosca**, *fam* to fork out, cough up.

afloramiento *m* outcrop.

aflorar 1 *i* (*mineral*) to crop out/up, outcrop. **2** *fig* (*aparecer*) to come up to the surface, appear.

afluencia 1 *f* inflow, influx: *afluencia de público*, flow of people. **2** (*abundancia*) affluence.

afluente 1 *adj* (*caudaloso*) flowing, inflowing. – **2** *m* (*río*) tributary.

afluir *i* to flow (**a**, into).

▲ *Conjugation model* |62|, *like huir*.

aflujo *m* afflux.

afmo.,-a *abr* (*afectísimo*) Yours sincerely, Yours faithfully.

afofarse *p* to become flabby.

afonía *f* loss of voice.

afónico,-a *adj* hoarse, voiceless.

● **estar afónico**, to have lost one's voice.

aforado,-a *adj* privileged.

aforismo *m* aphorism.

aforístico,-a *adj* aphoristic.

aforo 1 *m* (*capacidad*) seating capacity. **2** TÉC gauging.

aforrar 1 *t* to line. – **2 aforrarse**, *p* to wrap up warm.

afortunadamente *adv* luckily, fortunately.

afortunado,-a 1 *adj* lucky, fortunate: *fue una pregunta poco afortunada*, it was a rather inappropriate question. **2** (*dichoso*) happy.

● **afortunado en el juego, desgraciado en amores**, lucky at cards, unlucky in love.

afrancesado,-a 1 *pp* → **afrancesar**. – **2** *adj* pro-French, who has gone French. **3** HIST supporting Napoleon. – **4** *m,f* HIST (Spanish) supporter of Napoleon.

afrancesamiento *m* pro-French attitude, Frenchification.

afrancesarse *p* to become Frenchified, acquire French habits.

afrecho *f* bran.

afrenta *f fml* affront, outrage: *hacerle una afrenta a algn.*, to affront sb.

afrentar 1 *t fml* to affront, outrage. – **2 afrentarse**, *p fml* to be ashamed of.

afrentoso,-a 1 *adj fml* (*ofensivo*) offending, offensive. **2** *fml* (*vergonzoso*) shameful, disgraceful.

Africa *f* Africa.

africada *f* → **africado,-a**.

africado,-a 1 *adj* affricative. – **2 africada**, *f* affricate.

africanismo *m* africanism.

africanista *adj* africanist.

africano,-a 1 *adj* African. – **2** *m,f* African.

afrikaans *m* Afrikaans.

afrikáner *mf* Afrikaner.

afro *adj fam* afro.

afro- *pref* afro-.

afroamericano,-a 1 *adj* Afro-American. – **2** *m,f* Afro-American.

afroasiático,-a *adj* Afro-Asian.

afrodisiaco,-a 1 *adj* aphrodisiac. – **2 afrodisiaco**, *m* aphrodisiac.

afrodisíaco,-a *adj-m* → **afrodisiaco,-a**.

afrontamiento *m* confrontation.

afrontar 1 *t* to face, confront: *afrontaron las consecuencias*, they faced up to the consequences. **2** (*poner enfrente*) to face. **3** JUR to confront, bring face to face.

afrutado,-a *adj* fruity.

afta *f* aphtha.

aftoso,-a *adj* related to aphtha.

■ **fiebre aftosa**, foot-and-mouth disease.

afuera 1 *adv* outside: *vengo de afuera*, I've just been outside; *la parte de afuera*, the outside; *salir afuera*, to come/go out. – **2** *interj* out of the way! – **3 afueras**, *mpl* outskirts.

● **más afuera**, further out.

agachadiza *f* snipe.

■ **agachadiza real**, great snipe.

agachar 1 *t* to lower, bow. – **2 agacharse**, *p* (*encogerse*) to cower. **3** (*protegerse*) to duck (down). **4** (*agazaparse*) to crouch (down), squat.

agalla 1 *f* (*de pez*) gill. **2** (*de ave*) temple. **3** BOT gall, gallnut. – **4 agallas**, *fpl fam* courage *sing*, guts, pluck *sing*: *tener agallas*, to have got guts. **5** (*anginas*) sore throat *sing*.

agallegado,-a *adj* Galician-like.

ágape 1 *m* feast, banquet. **2** HIST agape.

agarbanzado,-a 1 *adj* (*color*) beige. **2** (*vulgar*) vulgar.

agarbillar *t* to sheave, sheaf.

agareno,-a *adj* HIST Muslim, Moslem: *un perfil agareno*, an Arab-like profile.

agarrada *f* → **agarrado,-a**.

agarradera 1 *f* (*asa*) handle. – **2 agarraderas**, *fpl* (*influencias*) influence *sing*, pull *sing*.

● **tener buenas agarraderas**, to be well connected, have the right friends.

agarradero 1 *m* (*asa*) handle. **2** (*excusa*) excuse. – **3 agarraderos**, *mpl* (*influencias*) influence *sing*, pull *sing*.

agarrado,-a 1 *pp* → **agarrar**. – **2** *adj fam* stingy, tight.

● **bailar agarrado**, to dance cheek to cheek.

agarrador *m* oven-cloth.

agarrar 1 *t* (*con la mano*) to clutch, seize, grasp: *agárrala fuerte*, hold it tight. **2** *fam* (*pillar*) to catch. **3** *fam* (*conseguir*) to take advantage of: *hay que agarrar las oportunidades*, one has to grasp one's opportunities. – **4 agarrarse**, *p* (*cogerse*) to hold on, cling (**a**, to). **5** (*pegarse*) to stick. **6** *fam* (*pelearse*) to quarrel, fight.

● **agarrar un cabreo,** to fly off the handle. ‖ **agarrar una borrachera,** to get drunk/pissed. ‖ **agarrarla,** to get drunk/pissed. ‖ **agarrarse a un clavo ardiendo,** *fig* to try anything, do anything.

agarre *m* (*neumático*) grip; (*coche*) road holding.

agarrón *m* pull, tug.

agarrotado,-a 1 *pp* (→ **agarrotar**) tight. – 2 *adj* (*apretado*) tight. 3 (*músculo*) stiff. 4 (*motor*) seized up.

agarrotamiento 1 *m* (*atadura*) tightening. 2 (*rigidez*) stiffening. 3 (*de motor*) seizing up.

agarrotar 1 *t* (*atar fuerte*) to tighten, tie up tightly. 2 (*oprimir*) to squeeze. 3 (*músculo*) to stiffen. 4 (*dar garrote*) to garotte. – 5 **agarrotarse,** *p* (*los músculos*) to stiffen. 6 (*encasquillarse*) to seize up.

agasajado,-a 1 *pp* → **agasajar**. – 2 *m,f* guest of honour (*us* honor).

agasajar 1 *t* (*obsequiar*) to smother with attention, treat well. 2 (*dar agasajo*) to wine and dine.

agasajo 1 *m* (*acogida*) warm welcome; (*trato*) kindness. 2 (*regalo*) gift. 3 (*comida*) reception, banquet.

ágata *f* agate.
▲ *Takes* **el** *in singular.*

agateador *m* tree creeper.

agave *f* agave.

agavilladora *f* binder.

agavillar 1 *t* to bind, sheave. – 2 **agavillarse,** *p fig* to get together, form groups.

agazapar 1 *t* to grab (hold of). – 2 **agazaparse,** *p* (*esconderse*) to hide. 3 (*agacharse*) to crouch (down), squat.

agencia *f* agency; (*sucursal*) branch.
■ **agencia de transportes,** carriers *pl.* ‖ **agencia inmobiliaria,** estate agent's, *us* real estate office. ‖ **agencia de turismo,** tourist office. ‖ **agencia de viajes,** travel agency.

agenciarse 1 *p* (*apañarse*) to manage, look after os., cope: *me las agenciaré como pueda,* I'll manage somehow. 2 (*proporcionarse*) to get os.: *se agenció un puesto fenomenal,* he got himself a fantastic job.
▲ *Conjugation model* [12]*, like* **cambiar**.

agencioso,-a *adj* diligent.

agenda 1 *f* (*libro*) diary. 2 (*orden del día*) agenda.

agente 1 *adj* agent. – 2 *mf* agent. – 3 *m* agent.
■ **agente de cambio y bolsa,** stockbroker. ‖ **agente de policía,** (*hombre*) policeman; (*mujer*) policewoman. ‖ **agente de tráfico,** (*hombre*) traffic policeman; (*mujer*) traffic policewoman. ‖ **agente inmobiliario,** estate agent.

agermanado,-a *adj* Germanized.

agigantado,-a 1 *pp* → **agigantar**. – 2 *adj* massive, huge.
● **a pasos agigantados,** by leaps and bounds.

agigantar 1 *t* to enlarge. 2 *fig* to exaggerate. – 3 **agigantarse,** *p* to become huge.

ágil *adj* agile.

agilidad *f* agility: *con agilidad,* swiftly.

agilipollado,-a 1 *pp* → **agilipollarse**. – 2 *adj tabú* stupid, daft.

agilipollarse *p tabú* to become stupid, become daft.

agilización *f* speeding up.

agilizar 1 *t* to make agile. 2 *fig* to speed up.
▲ *Conjugation model* [4]*, like* **realizar**.

ágilmente *adv* swiftly.

agiotaje *m* speculation.

agiotista *mf* speculator.

agitación 1 *f* agitation. 2 *fig* excitement, restlessness.

agitado,-a 1 *pp* → **agitar**. – 2 *adj* (*movido*) agitated, shaken; (*mar*) rough, choppy. 3 (*ansioso*) anxious. 4 (*ajetreado*) hectic.

agitador,-ra 1 *m,f* agitator. – 2 **agitador,** *m* QUÍM agitator.

agitanado,-a 1 *pp* → **agitanarse**. – 2 *adj* gypsy-like.

agitanarse *t* to become gypsy-like.

agitar 1 *t* (*mover*) to agitate, shake; (*pañuelo*) to wave: *"agítese antes de usarlo",* "shake before use". 2 (*intranquilizar*) agitate, excite. – 3 **agitarse,** *p* (*moverse*) to move restlessly. 4 (*inquietarse*) to become agitated/disturbed. 5 (*mar*) to become rough.

aglomeración 1 *f* agglomeration. 2 (*de gente*) crowd.

aglomerado,-a 1 *adj* → **aglomerar**. – 2 **aglomerado,** *m* (*madera*) chipboard. 3 (*combustible*) briquette.

aglomerante *adj* binding material.

aglomerar 1 *t* (*acumular*) to agglomerate, amass. – 2 **aglomerarse,** *p* (*acumularse*) to agglomerate, amass. 3 (*gente*) to crowd.

aglutinación *f* agglutination.

aglutinante 1 *adj* agglutinant, binding. – 2 *m* agglutinant.
■ **lengua aglutinante,** agglutinative language.

aglutinar 1 *t* to agglutinate, bind. 2 *fig* to bring together. – 3 **aglutinarse,** *p* to agglutinate. 4 *fig* to come together.

agnación *f* agnation.

agnado,-a *adj* agnate.

agnosticismo *m* agnosticism.

agnóstico,-a 1 *adj* agnostic. – 2 *m,f* agnostic.

agobiado,-a 1 *pp* → **agobiar**. – 2 *adj* (*doblado*) bent over/down, weighed down. 3 *fig* (*cansado*) exhausted; (*abrumado*) overwhelmed: *agobiado de trabajo,* up to one's eyes in work; *agobiado de problemas,* snowed under with problems.

agobiador,-ra *adj* → **agobiante**.

agobiante 1 *adj* (*cansado*) backbreaking, exhausting. 2 (*abrumador*) overwhelming. 3 (*lugar*) claustrophobic; (*calor*) oppressive. 4 (*persona*) tiresome, tiring.

agobiar 1 *t* (*doblar*) to weigh/bend down. 2 (*abrumar*) to overwhelm. – 3 **agobiarse,** *p* (*angustiarse*) to worry too much, get worked up.
▲ *Conjugation model* [12]*, like* **cambiar**.

agobio *m* burden, fatigue, suffocation.

agolpamiento *m* crowd, crush.

agolparse *p* to crowd, throng: *se le agolpaban las lágrimas en sus ojos,* tears welled up in her eyes.

agonía 1 *f* dying breath, last gasp: *murió después de una larga agonía,* she died after a long illness; *en su agonía,* on her deathbed. 2 (*sufrimiento*) agony, grief, sorrow. – 3 **agonías,** *mf fam* (*quejica*) moaner; (*pesimista*) pessimist.
▲ *In 3, pl* **agonías**.

agónico,-a *adj* dying, death.
● **estar en estado agónico,** to be at death's door.
■ **estertores agónicos,** death rattle.

agonioso,-a *adj* anxious.

agonizante 1 *adj* dying. – 2 *mf* dying person.

agonizar 1 *i* to be dying: *está agonizando,* she could die any moment now. 2 (*acabarse*) to fail, fade away. 3 (*sufrir*) to suffer.
▲ *Conjugation model* [4]*, like* **realizar**.

ágora *f* agora.
▲ *Takes* **el** *in singular.*

agorafobia *f* agoraphobia.
▲ *Takes* **el** *in singular.*

agorar *t* to predict.

agorero,-a 1 *adj* ominous: *¡qué agorera eres!,* what a jinx you are! – **2** *m,f* fortune-teller.
■ **ave agorera,** *fig* bird of ill omen.

agostadero 1 *m* (*lugar*) summer pasture. **2** (*temporada*) summer-pasture season.

agostar 1 *t* to wither, wilt. **2** *fig* to extinguish, kill. – **3 agostarse,** *p* to wither, wilt.

agosto *m* August.
● **hacer su agosto,** *fig* to make a packet/pile, feather one's nest.
▲ See also *marzo*.

agotado,-a 1 *pp* → **agotar.** – **2** *adj* (*cansado*) exhausted, worn out. **3** (*libros*) out of print; (*mercancías*) sold out.

agotador,-ra *adj* exhausting.

agotamiento *m* exhaustion.
■ **agotamiento físico,** physical strain.

agotar 1 *t* (*cansar*) to exhaust, tire/wear out. **2** (*gastar*) to exhaust, use up. – **3 agotarse,** *p* (*cansarse*) to become exhausted, become tired out. **4** (*gastarse*) to run out; COM to be sold out.

agraciado,-a 1 *pp* → **agraciar.** – **2** *adj* (*bello*) attractive, beautiful. **3** (*ganador*) winning. – **4** *m,f* lucky winner.
● **ser poco agraciado, -a,** to be unattractive/plain.

agraciar 1 *t* (*embellecer*) to make more attractive, beautify. **2** *fml* (*conceder*) to bestow, reward with a favour (US favor).
▲ *Conjugation model* |12|, *like* **cambiar.**

agradable *adj* nice, pleasant: *poco agradable,* unpleasant.

agradablemente *adv* nicely, pleasantly.

agradar *i* to please: *esto me agrada,* I like this.

agradecer 1 *t* to thank for, be grateful for. **2** (*uso impersonal*) to be welcome: *siempre se agradece una ayuda,* help is always welcome.
▲ *Conjugation model* |43|.

agradecido,-a 1 *pp* → **agradecer.** – **2** *adj* grateful, thankful: *le quedaría muy agradecido si...,* I should be very much obliged if...

agradecimiento *m* gratefulness, gratitude, thankfulness.

agrado *m* pleasure: *no es de su agrado,* it isn't to his liking.

agramatical *adj* ungrammatical.

agramaticalidad *f* ungrammaticality.

agrandamiento *m* enlargement.

agrandar 1 *t* (*hacer grande*) to enlarge, make larger. **2** (*exagerar*) to exaggerate. – **3 agrandarse,** *p* (*hacerse grande*) to enlarge, become larger. **4** (*acentuarse*) to become more intense.

agranujarse *p* to become a rogue.

agrario,-a *adj* agrarian, land, agricultural.
■ **política agraria,** agricultural policy.

agrarismo *m* agrarianism.

agravamiento *m* aggravation, worsening.

agravante 1 *adj* aggravating. – **2** *m & f* added difficulty. **3** JUR aggravating circumstance.
■ **robo con agravante,** aggravated theft.

agravar 1 *t* to aggravate, worsen. – **2 agravarse,** *p* to get worse, worsen.

agraviante 1 *adj* offending, insulting. – **2** *m,f* offender.

agraviar *t* to offend, insult.
▲ *Conjugation model* |12|, *like* **cambiar.**

agravio *m* offence, insult.

agraz 1 *m* (*uva*) unripe grape, sour grape; (*zumo*) sour grape juice. **2** *fig* (*amargura*) bitterness; (*sinsabor*) unpleasantness.

● **en agraz,** *fig* prematurely, before its time.

agredir *t* to attack.
▲ *Used only in forms which include the letter i in their endings:* *agredía, agrediré, agrediendo.*

agregación 1 *f* (*añadidura*) aggregation. **2** EDUC post of teacher. **3** POL post of attaché; (*oficina*) office of the attaché.

agregado,-a 1 *pp* → **agregar.** – **2** *adj* aggregate. – **3** *m,f* (*profesor de instituto*) secondary-school teacher; (*profesor de universidad*) assistant teacher. **4** POL attaché.

agregaduría 1 *f* EDUC post of teacher. **2** POL post of attaché; (*oficina*) office of the attaché.

agregar 1 *t* (*añadir*) to add. **2** (*unir*) to gather. **3** (*destinar*) to appoint. – **4 agregarse,** *p* (*unirse*) to join.
▲ *Conjugation model* |7|, *like* **llegar.**

agremiar *t* to form into a guild.

agresión *f* aggression, attack.

agresivamente *adv* aggressively.

agresividad *f* aggressiveness.

agresivo,-a *adj* aggressive.

agresor,-ra 1 *adj* attacking. – **2** *m,f* aggressor, attacker.

agreste 1 *adj* (*del campo*) rural, country. **2** (*sin cultivar*) uncultivated, wild. **3** *fig* (*rudo*) uncouth, coarse.

agriado,-a 1 *pp* → **agriar.** – **2** *adj* (*agrio*) sour. **3** *fig* (*amargado*) sour, embittered.

agriamente *adv* sourly.

agriar 1 *t* to sour. **2** *fig* (*persona*) to embitter. – **3 agriarse,** *p* to turn sour.
▲ *Conjugation model* |12|, *like* **cambiar.**

agrícola *adj* agricultural, farming: *las técnicas agrícolas han cambiado,* farming techniques have changed.

agricultor,-ra *m,f* farmer.

agricultura *f* agriculture, farming.

agridulce 1 *adj* bittersweet. **2** CULIN sweet and sour.

agrietamiento *m* cracking; (*de la piel*) chapping.

agrietar 1 *t* to crack; (*piel*) to chap. – **2 agrietarse,** *p* to crack; (*piel*) to get chapped.

agrimensor,-ra *m,f* surveyor.

agrimensura *f* surveying.

agrio,-a 1 *adj* sour. – **2 agrios,** *mpl* citrus fruits.

agrisado,-a *adj* greyish.

agro *m* agriculture.

agronomía *f* agronomy.

agronómico,-a *adj* agronomical, agronomic.

agrónomo,-a 1 *adj* farming. – **2** *m,f* agronomist.

agropecuario,-a *adj* agricultural, farming.

agrumarse *p* to go lumpy.

agrupación 1 *f* grouping, group. **2** (*asociación*) association.

agrupamiento *m* → **agrupación.**

agrupar 1 *t* to group, put into groups. – **2 agruparse,** *p* to group together, form a group. **3** (*asociarse*) to associate.

agrura *f* sourness, tartness.

agua 1 *f* water: *echarse al agua,* to dive in. **2** (*lluvia*) rain. **3** ARQ slope of a roof: *tejado a dos aguas,* pitched roof. – **4 aguas,** *fpl* (*del mar, río*) waters: *aguas arriba,* upstream. **5** (*de brillante*) water *sing*, sparkle *sing*.
● **claro como el agua,** crystal clear. ‖ **como agua de mayo,** a godsend. ‖ **como dos gotas de agua,** like two peas in a pod. ‖ **estar con el agua al cuello,** *fig* to be up to one's neck in it. ‖ **estar entre dos aguas,** to sit on the fence. ‖ **hacérsele la boca agua a uno,** *fig* to make one's mouth water. ‖ **hacerse una cosa agua en la boca,** to melt in one's mouth. ‖ **nunca**

digas de esta agua no beberé, never say never. ‖ romper aguas, to break waters.
■ agua bendita, holy water. ‖ agua corriente, running water. ‖ agua de colonia, (eau de) cologne. ‖ agua de lluvia, rainwater. ‖ agua de mar, seawater. ‖ agua del grifo, tap water. ‖ agua dulce, fresh water. ‖ agua mineral con gas, sparkling mineral water. ‖ agua mineral sin gas, still mineral water. ‖ agua potable, drinking water. ‖ agua salada, salt water. ‖ aguas jurisdiccionales, territorial waters. ‖ aguas menores, *fam* pee *sing.* ‖ aguas residuales, sewage *sing.* ‖ aguas termales, thermal springs.
▲ *Takes el in singular.*

aguacatal *m* avocado plantation.
aguacate *m* (*árbol*) avocado; (*fruto*) avocado (pear).
aguacero *m* heavy shower, downpour.
aguachirle *f* dishwater.
▲ *Takes el in singular.*
aguada *f* → **aguado,-a**.
aguadero *m* drinking trough.
aguadilla *f* → **ahogadilla**.
aguado,-a 1 *pp* → **aguar**. – 2 *adj* watered down, wishy-washy: *leche aguada*, watered-down milk. – 3 **aguada**, *f* fresh water supply. 4 ART gouache.
● hacer aguada, to take on water.
aguador,-ra *m,f* water carrier.
aguaducho *m* flood.
aguafiestas *mf* killjoy, spoilsport, wet blanket.
▲ *pl aguafiestas.*
aguafuerte 1 *m & f* ART etching: *grabar algo al aguafuerte*, to etch sth. 2 QUÍM nitric acid.
▲ *Takes el in singular.*
aguafuertista *mf* etcher.
aguamanil *m* (*jarro*) water jug; (*palangana*) water bowl.
aguamanos *m* water bowl.
▲ *pl aguamanos.*
aguamar *m* jellyfish.
aguamarina *f* aquamarine.
aguamiel *f* hydromel.
▲ *Takes el in singular.*
aguanieve *f* sleet.
▲ *Takes el in singular.*
aguanoso,-a 1 *adj* (*fruto*) watery. 2 (*lugar*) waterlogged.
aguantable *adj* bearable, tolerable.
aguantaderas *fpl fam* patience *sing.*
● tener aguantaderas, to put up with a lot, be tolerant.
aguantar 1 *t* (*contener*) to hold (back). 2 (*sostener*) to hold, support. 3 (*soportar*) to tolerate: *no aguanto más,* I can't stand any more, I can't take any more. – 4 aguantarse, *p* (*contenerse*) to keep back; (*risa, lágrimas*) to hold back. 5 (*resignarse*) to resign os.
● ¡que se aguante!, *fam* that's her/his tough luck!
aguante 1 *m* (*paciencia*) patience, endurance. 2 (*fuerza*) strength.
● tener mucho aguante, (*paciente*) to be very patient; (*resistente*) to be strong, have a lot of stamina.
aguar 1 *t* to water down, add water to. – 2 aguarse, *p* to become flooded.
● aguar la fiesta a algn., to spoil sb.'s fun.
▲ *Conjugation model* [22]*, like averiguar.*
aguardar 1 *t* to wait (for), await: *no sé lo que me aguarda el futuro,* I don't know what the future holds for me. – 2 *i* to wait.
aguardentoso,-a *adj* alcoholic, containing spirits.
■ voz aguardentosa, rough/husky voice.

aguardiente *m* liquor, brandy.
■ aguardiente de caña, rum. ‖ aguardiente de cerezas, cherry brandy.
aguardo *m* hide.
aguarrás *m* turpentine.
aguaza *f* sap.
aguazal *m* puddle.
agudamente *adv* sharply.
agudeza 1 *f* sharpness, keenness; (*dolor*) acuteness. 2 *fig* (*viveza*) wit, wittiness. 3 *fig* (*ingenio*) witticism, witty saying.
agudización 1 *f* sharpening. 2 (*empeoramiento*) worsening.
agudizamiento *m* → **agudización**.
agudizar 1 *t* (*afilar*) to sharpen. 2 (*empeorar*) to worsen, intensify, make more acute. – 3 agudizarse, *p* (*afilarse*) to become sharper. 4 (*empeorar*) to worsen, intensify, become more acute.
▲ *Conjugation model* [4]*, like realizar.*
agudo,-a 1 *adj* (*afilado*) sharp. 2 (*dolor*) acute. 3 *fig* (*ingenioso*) witty; (*mordaz*) sharp. 4 *fig* (*sentido*) sharp, keen. 5 (*voz*) high-pitched. 6 (*sonido*) treble, high. 7 LING (*palabra*) oxytone; (*acento*) acute.
agüera *f* irrigation ditch.
agüero *m* omen, presage.
● ser de mal agüero, to be ill-omened. ‖ ser pájaro de mal agüero, *fig* to be bird of ill omen.
aguerrido,-a 1 *pp* → **aguerrir**. – 2 *adj* hardened.
aguerrir *t* to harden, inure.
▲ *Used only in forms which include the letter i in their endings: aguerría, aguerriré, aguerriendo.*
aguijada *f* goad.
aguijar 1 *t* to goad. 2 *fig* (*apresurar*) to urge on. 3 *fig* (*estimular*) to stimulate.
aguijón 1 *m* ZOOL sting. 2 BOT thorn, prickle. 3 *fig* (*estímulo*) sting, spur. 4 (*espuela*) spur.
aguijonada *f* sting.
aguijonazo 1 *m* (*punzada*) sting. 2 *fig* (*estímulo*) goad.
aguijonear 1 *t* (*punzar*) to goad. 2 *fig* (*estimular*) to spur on.
águila *f* eagle.
● ser un águila, *fig* to be a genius. ‖ tener vista de águila, to be eagle-eyed.
■ águila caudal, golden eagle. ‖ águila culebrera, short-toed eagle. ‖ águila imperial, imperial eagle. ‖ águila pescadora, osprey. ‖ águila ratonera, buzzard. ‖ águila real, golden eagle.
▲ *Takes el in singular.*
aguilando *m* → **aguinaldo**.
aguileño,-a *adj* aquiline: *nariz aguileña,* aquiline/hook nose.
aguilera *f* eyrie.
agüilla *f* watery liquid.
aguilón 1 *m* ARQ gable, gable-end. 2 TÉC jib.
aguilucho 1 *m* (*cría del águila*) eaglet. 2 (*ave*) harrier.
aguinaldo 1 *m* (*de Navidad*) Christmas bonus/box. 2 (*paga extra*) bonus. 3 (*villancico*) Christmas carol.
aguja 1 *f* needle; (*de tricotar*) knitting needle. 2 (*de reloj*) hand; (*de tocadiscos*) stylus. 3 (*de arma*) firing pin. 4 (*obelisco*) obelisk; (*capitel*) spire, steeple. 5 (*de tren*) point, switch. 6 (*pez*) garfish. 7 (*ave*) godwit. 8 (*pastel dulce*) sweet pastry; (*pastel salado*) meat/fish pastry. – 9 agujas, *fpl* ribs: *carne de agujas,* shoulder.
● buscar una aguja en un pajar, to look for a needle in a haystack.
agujereado,-a 1 *pp* → **agujerear**. – 2 *adj* with holes, perforated.

agujerear *t* to pierce, perforate, make holes in.

agujero 1 *m* hole. 2 *fig* (*falta de dinero*) shortfall: *encontraron un agujero de varios millones de pesetas,* they found that several million pesetas were missing.
■ agujero negro, black hole.

agujetas *fpl* stiffness *sing*: *tener agujetas,* to be stiff.

agujetero,-a *m,f* (*fabricante*) needle maker; (*vendedor*) needle seller.

aguoso,-a *adj* → **acuoso,-a**.

agur *interj fam* bye!, see you!

agusanado,-a 1 *pp* → **agusanarse**. – 2 *adj* maggoty, wormy.

agusanarse *p* to get maggoty, get wormy.

agustino,-a 1 *adj* Augustinian. – 2 *m,f* Augustinian.

agutí *m* agouti.

aguzadura *f* sharpening.

aguzanieves *f* pied wagtail.
▲ *pl aguzanieves*.

aguzar 1 *t* (*afilar*) to sharpen. 2 (*estimular*) to spur on, prick. – 3 aguzarse, *p* to become sharper.
▲ *Conjugation model* [4], *like realizar*.
● aguzar el oído, to prick up one's ears. ‖ aguzar la vista, to look attentively. ‖ la necesidad aguza el ingenio, necessity is the mother of invention.

ah 1 *interj* (*caer en la cuenta*) ah!, oh!: *¡ah, ya te entiendo!,* ah, now I see! 2 (*sorpresa, admiración*) oh!

ahechar *t* to sieve, sift.

aherrojar 1 *t* (*encadenar*) to chain, put in irons. 2 (*someter*) to oppress.

aherrumbrar 1 *t* (*color*) to turn rusty red. 2 (*sabor*) to give a metallic taste to. – 3 aherrumbrarse, *p* (*oxidarse*) to rust, go rusty. 4 (*saber a hierro*) to taste of metal.

ahí *adv* there, in that place.
● de ahí que, hence, therefore. ‖ por ahí, (*lugar*) round there; (*aproximadamente*) more or less.

ahijado,-a 1 *pp* → **ahijar**. – 2 *m,f* godchild; (*chico*) godson; (*chica*) goddaughter. 3 (*adoptivo*) adopted child.

ahijamiento *m* adoption.

ahijar 1 *t* to adopt. 2 *fig* to attribute, impute. – 3 ahijarse, *p* to adopt.
▲ *Conjugation model* [15], *like aislar*.

ahilado,-a 1 *pp* → **ahilarse**. – 2 *adj* (*viento*) light, soft. 3 (*voz*) thin, weak.

ahilarse 1 *p* (*adelgazarse*) to lose weight. 2 (*desmayarse*) to faint with hunger. 3 BOT to grow poorly.

ahincado,-a 1 *pp* → **ahincar**. – 2 *adj* efficient.

ahincar 1 *t* to press, urge. – 2 ahincarse, *p* to hurry up.
▲ *Conjugation model* [23].

ahínco *m* eagerness, keenness, enthusiasm: *con ahínco,* eagerly, enthusiastically.

ahíto,-a 1 *adj* (*de comida*) stuffed, full. 2 (*harto*) fed up. – 3 ahíto, *m* indigestion.

ahocicar 1 *t fam* to shut sb. up. – 2 *i fam* (*claudicar*) to give in, yield. 3 (*caer*) to fall flat on one's face.
▲ *Conjugation model* [1], *like sacar*.

ahogadilla *f* ducking: *le hicieron/dieron una ahogadilla,* they ducked her, they gave her a ducking.

ahogadillo *m* → **ahogadilla**.

ahogado,-a 1 *pp* → **ahogar**. – 2 *adj* drowned. 3 (*asfixiado*) asphyxiated, suffocated. 4 *fig* (*deudas etc*) up to one's neck. 5 (*sitio*) stuffy, close. – 6 *m,f* drowned person.

ahogar 1 *t* (*asfixiar*) to choke, suffocate: *la ahogó con un cojín,* he suffocated her with a cushion. 2 (*en el agua*) to drown. 3 (*plantas*) to overwater. 4 (*motor*) to flood. 5 (*fuego*) to put out, extinguish. 6 *fig* (*reprimir*) to stifle, put down: *el presidente ahogó la revolución,* the President put down the revolution; *apenas logró ahogar las lágrimas,* she just managed to hold back her tears. – 7 ahogarse, *p* to be drowned, drown: *se cayó al río y se ahogó,* he fell into the river and drowned. 8 (*sofocarse*) to choke, suffocate: *me estoy ahogando de calor,* the heat's stifling, I can't breathe in this heat. 9 (*motor*) to flood.
● ahogar las penas, to drown one's sorrows. ‖ ahogarse en un vaso de agua, *fig* to make a mountain out of a molehill.
▲ *Conjugation model* [7], *like llegar*.

ahogo 1 *m* (*al respirar*) breathlessness, shortness of breath. 2 (*congoja*) anguish, sorrow, distress. 3 (*penuria*) financial difficulty.

ahombrarse *p fam* to become mannish, become butch.

ahondar 1 *t* (*hacer profundo*) to deepen, make deeper. 2 (*meter en profundidad*) to go deep. – 3 *i* to go deep. 4 (*investigar*) to examine: *ahondar en un problema,* to examine a problem in depth.

ahora 1 *adv* (*en este momento*) now: *ahora no tengo tiempo,* I haven't got time now. 2 (*hace un momento*) just a moment ago: *lo acabo de ver ahora,* I've just seen it. 3 (*dentro de un momento*) in a minute, shortly: *ahora te lo preparo,* I'll get it ready for you in a minute. – 4 *conj* (*adversativa*) however: *gana poco; ahora, tampoco trabaja mucho,* he doesn't earn very much; but then, he doesn't work very hard.
● ahora bien, but, however. ‖ ahora o nunca, now or never. ‖ de ahora en adelante, from now on. ‖ hasta ahora, until now, so far. ‖ por ahora, for the time being.

ahorcado,-a 1 *pp* → **ahorcar**. – 2 *adj* hanged. – 3 *m,f* hanged person.

ahorcajarse *p* to sit astride.

ahorcamiento *m* hanging.

ahorcar *t* to hang: *se ahorcó con el cinturón,* he hanged himself with his belt.
▲ *Conjugation model* [1], *like sacar*.

ahormar 1 *t* (*ajustar*) to shape, form. 2 *fig* to mould.

ahornar *t* to bake.

ahorquillado,-a 1 *pp* → **ahorquillar**. – 2 *adj* forked.

ahorquillar 1 *t* (*sujetar*) to prop up. 2 (*dar forma*) to shape like a fork.

ahorrador,-ra 1 *adj* thrifty. – 2 *m,f* thrifty person.

ahorrar 1 *t* (*dinero, energía, etc*) to save: *hemos de ahorrar energía,* we must save energy; *lo gasta todo, no ahorra nada,* she spends it and and saves nothing. 2 (*molestia, problema*) to save, spare: *esto te ahorrará mucho trabajo,* this will save you a lot of work; *no se lo dije por ahorrarle el disgusto,* I didn't tell him to avoid upsetting him. – 3 ahorrarse, *p* to save os.: *te ahorrarás problemas si lo haces como yo te digo,* you'll save yourself problems if you do it the way I say; *de haber llamado antes me habría ahorrado el viaje,* if I'd phoned first I'd have saved myself the journey; *te podrías haber ahorrado ese comentario,* you could have kept that comment to yourself.

ahorrativo,-a *adj* thrifty.

ahorro 1 *m* saving: *me supone un ahorro de 6000 pesetas al mes,* it represents a saving of 6000 pesetas a month. 2 (*cualidad*) thrift. – 3 ahorros, *mpl* savings: *tengo unos ahorros,* I have some savings.
■ caja de ahorros, savings bank.

ahuecador *m* bustle, crinoline.

ahuecamiento 1 *m* (*acción*) hollowing out. 2 (*de colchón*) fluffing up; (*de tierra*) loosening. 3 (*de voz*) deepening. 4 *fig* (*engreimiento*) conceit, vanity.

ahuecar 1 *t* to hollow out: *ahuecar las manos,* to cup one's hands. 2 (*esponjar*) to fluff up; (*tierra*) to loosen. 3 (*voz*) to deepen. – 4 ahuecarse, *p* (*engreírse*) to become conceited, give os. airs.
▲ *Conjugation model* |1|, *like sacar.*

ahumado,-a 1 *pp* → **ahumar**. – 2 *adj* smoked; (*bacon*) smoky. – 3 ahumado, *m* (*proceso*) smoking.

ahumar 1 *t* (*tratar con humo*) to smoke. 2 (*llenar de humo*) to fill with smoke, smoke out. – 3 *i* (*echar humo*) to give off smoke, smoke. – 4 ahumarse, *p* (*adquirir color*) to blacken, turn black; (*adquirir olor*) to develop a smoky smell; (*adquirir sabor*) to acquire a smoky taste. 5 *fam* (*emborracharse*) to get drunk.
▲ *Conjugation model* |16|, *like aunar.*

ahusado,-a *adj* tapered, tapering.

ahuyentar 1 *t* to drive away, scare away. 2 *fig* to dismiss.

AI *abr* (*Amnistía Internacional*) Amnesty International; (*abreviatura*) AI.

ailanto *m* tree of heaven.

aindiado,-a *adj* Indian-like.

airado,-a 1 *pp* → **airarse**. – 2 *adj* angry, furious, irate.

airar 1 *t* to anger, make furious. – 2 airarse, *p* to get angry.
▲ *Conjugation model* |15|, *like aislar.*

airbag *m* airbag.

aire 1 *m* air. 2 (*viento*) wind; (*corriente*) draught: *hace aire,* it's windy. 3 *fig* (*aspecto*) air, appearance: *tiene un aire cansado,* she looks tired. 4 *fig* (*parecido*) resemblance, likeness: *este niño tiene un aire a su abuelo,* this boy takes after his grandfather; *tienen un aire de familia,* there's a family likeness to them. 5 *fig* (*estilo*) style, manner, way: *lo hizo a su aire,* he did it his way. 6 *fig* (*gracia*) gracefulness, elegance: *Luisa camina con mucho aire,* Luisa walks very gracefully. 7 *fig* (*ambiente*) atmosphere: *había mucha tensión en el aire,* the atmosphere was very tense. 8 MÚS air, melody.
● al aire, (*hacia arriba*) into the air; (*al raso*) uncovered. ‖ al aire libre, in the open air, outdoors. ‖ cambiar de aires, to change one's surroundings, have a change of scenery. ‖ darse aires, to put on airs. ‖ estar en el aire, (*en antena*) to be on the air. ‖ hacerse/darse aire, to fan os. ‖ saltar por los aires, to blow up. ‖ tener aires, to put on airs. ‖ tomar el aire, to take the air, get some fresh air. ‖ vivir del aire, to live on air. ‖ ¡vete a tomar (el) aire!, *fam* get lost!
■ aire acondicionado, air conditioning. ‖ aire puro, clean air.

aireación *f* ventilation.

airear 1 *t* (*ventilar*) to air. 2 *fig* (*un asunto*) to publicize. – 3 airearse, *p* (*tomar el aire*) to take/get some fresh air. 4 (*resfriarse*) to catch a cold.

aireo 1 *m* (*ventilación*) airing. 2 *fig* (*un asunto*) publicizing.

airón 1 *m* (*garza*) heron. 2 (*penacho*) crest, tuft.

airoso,-a 1 *adj* (*lugar*) windy. 2 (*persona*) graceful, elegant.
● salir airoso de una situación, to come out of a situation with flying colours (US colors), be successful.

aislacionismo *m* isolationism.

aislacionista 1 *adj* isolationist. – 2 *mf* isolationist.

aislado,-a 1 *pp* → **aislar**. – 2 *adj* (*suelto*) isolated. 3 TÉC insulated.

aislador,-ora 1 *adj* insulating. – 2 aislador, *m* insulator.

aislamiento 1 *m* (*acción*) isolation. 2 TÉC insulation.

aislante 1 *adj* insulating. – 2 *m* insulator.

aislar 1 *t* (*dejar separado*) to isolate. 2 TÉC to insulate. 3 aislarse, (*uso reflexivo*) to isolate os. (**de,** from).
▲ *Conjugation model* |15|.

ajá *interj* good!

ajado,-a 1 *pp* → **ajar**. – 2 *adj* (*piel*) wizened. 3 (*ropa*) shabby.

ajajá *interj* → **ajá**.

ajamonarse *p* *fam* to get plump.

ajar 1 *t* (*deslucir*) to spoil, wear out. – 2 ajarse, *p* (*persona*) to become worn out, wear os. out. 3 (*piel*) to become wrinkled, wrinkle.

ajardinar *t* to landscape, lay out with gardens.

a. J.C. *abr* → **a. de J.C.**.

ajedrecista *mf* chess player.

ajedrez 1 *m* (*juego*) chess. 2 (*tablero y piezas*) chess set.

ajedrezado,-a *adj* chequered, US checkered.

ajenjo 1 *m* (*planta*) wormwood, absinth, absinthe. 2 (*bebida*) absinth, absinthe.

ajeno,-a 1 *adj* (*de otro*) another's, belonging to other people: *esta semana el equipo juega en campo ajeno,* our team plays away from home this week; *eso sucedió por causas ajenas a nuestra voluntad,* it happened for reasons beyond our control. 2 (*distante*) detached: *se mantuvo ajeno a la conversación,* he didn't get involved in the conversation; *era totalmente ajeno a lo que sucedía,* he was completely unaware of what was happening. 3 (*impropio*) inappropriate, unsuitable: *tuvo un comportamiento ajeno a él,* it's not like him to behave that way. 4 (*extraño*) not involved: *es ajeno al escándalo de las escuchas telefónicas,* he's not involved in the phone tapping affair; *"prohibido el paso a toda persona ajena a la obra",* "workers only".
● meterse en lo ajeno, to meddle in other people's affairs. ‖ vivir a costa ajena, to live off other people.

ajete *m* young garlic.

ajetreado,-a 1 *pp* → **ajetrearse**. – 2 *adj* busy, hectic.

ajetrearse *t* to be busy, bustle about.

ajetreo *m* activity, bustle.

ají *m* AM red pepper, chilli.

ajiaceite *m* garlic and olive oil sauce.

ajicomino *m* garlic and cumin sauce.

ajilimoje 1 *m* garlic and pepper sauce. – 2 ajilimojes, *mpl* things, bits and pieces.

ajilimójili *m* → **ajilimoje**.

ajillo *m*.
● al ajillo, fried with garlic.

ajipuerro *m* wild leek.

ajo *m* garlic.
● estar en el ajo, *fam* *fig* to be involved, be in the thick of it.
■ ajo tierno, young garlic. ‖ cabeza de ajo, head of garlic. ‖ diente de ajo, clove of garlic.

ajoarriero *m* *dish prepared with cod, olive oil, eggs and garlic.*

ajolote *m* axolotl.

ajonjolí *m* sesame.
▲ *pl* ajonjolíes.

ajonuez *m* garlic and nutmeg sauce.
▲ *pl* ajonueces.

ajoqueso *m* stew with garlic and cheese.

ajorca *f* bracelet; (*para el tobillo*) anklet.

ajornalar *t* to employ by the day.

ajuar 1 *m* (*de novia*) trousseau. 2 (*de bebé*) layette. 3 (*muebles*) household furniture, household furnishings *pl*; (*bienes*) property, goods *pl*.

ajumarse *p fam* to get drunk.

ajuntar 1 *t fam* to be friends with: *ahora no te ajunto,* I am not friends with you now. – 2 **ajuntarse,** *p fam (cohabitar)* to cohabit, live together.

ajustado,-a 1 *pp* → **ajustar.** – 2 *adj (precio)* very low, rock-bottom; *(presupuesto)* tight: *nuestros precios son tan ajustados que apenas sacamos ganancia,* our prices are so low that we hardly make a profit; *trabajamos con un presupuesto muy ajustado,* we're on a very tight budget. 3 *(apretado)* tight-fitting, tight: *lleva unos pantalones ajustadísimos,* he wears very tight-fitting trousers.

ajustador,-ra 1 *adj* adjusting, fitting. – 2 *m,f* fitter.

ajustamiento *m* settlement.

ajustar 1 *t (adaptar)* to adjust, regulate. 2 *(apretar)* to tighten. 3 *(encajar)* to fit, fit tight. 4 *(acordar)* to fix, agree on, set. – 5 *i* to fit. – 6 **ajustarse,** *p (ceñirse)* to fit: *la puerta se ajusta perfectamente al marco,* the door is a perfect fit. 7 *(ponerse de acuerdo)* to come to an agreement; *(estar de acuerdo)* to agree with, fit in with: *esto no se ajusta a la verdad,* this is not true; *esto no se ajusta a mi presupuesto,* this is outside my price range.
● **ajustar cuentas,** COM to settle up; *fig* to settle a score. ‖ **ajustarse el cinturón,** to tighten one's belt.

ajuste 1 *m (unión)* adjustment, fitting; TÉC assembly. 2 COM settlement, fixing. 3 *(tipografía)* make-up, composition.
■ **ajuste de cuentas,** *fig* settling of scores.

ajusticiado,-a 1 *pp* → **ajusticiar.** – 2 *adj* executed. – 3 *m,f* executed person.
● **morir ajusticiado,-a,** to be executed.

ajusticiamiento *m* execution.

ajusticiar *t* to execute.
▲ Conjugation model [12], *like cambiar.*

al 1 *contr* → **a.** – 2 **al** + *inf,* *loc* on + *ger*: *me lo encontré al salir de casa,* I met him when I was leaving, I met him on leaving; *al quedarse sin dinero, tuvo que ponerse a trabajar,* when he ran out of money, he had to get down to work.
● **está al caer,** it's about to happen.
▲ Contraction of *a* + *el.*

ala 1 *f* wing: *de dos alas,* two-winged. 2 *(de sombrero)* brim. 3 *(de hélice)* blade. 4 DEP winger. 5 *(de mesa)* leaf, flap. 6 *fam (dinero)* peseta: *me debes dos mil del ala,* you owe me two thousand pesetas. – 7 **alas,** *fpl (atrevimiento)* daring *sing.*
● **ahuecar el ala,** *fam* to beat it, keep out of the way. ‖ **andar con el ala caída,** to be downcast. ‖ **cortarle las alas a algn.,** *fig* to clip sb.'s wings. ‖ **dar alas a algn.,** to encourage sb., egg sb. on. ‖ **volar con sus propias alas,** *fig* to stand on one's own two feet.
▲ Takes *el* en singular.

alabanza 1 *f (elogio)* praise. 2 *(jactancia)* boasting, bragging.

alabar 1 *t (elogiar)* to praise. – 2 **alabarse,** *p (jactarse)* to boast.

alabarda *f* halberd.

alabardado,-a *adj* halberd-shaped.

alabardero 1 *m (soldado)* halberdier. 2 *(claque)* member of the claque, paid applauder.

alabastrino,-a 1 *adj* alabastrine. – 2 **alabastrina,** *f* thin sheet of alabaster.

alabastro *m* alabaster.

álabe 1 *m (rama)* drooping branch. 2 *(de rueda hidráulica)* paddle; *(diente)* tooth.

alabear 1 *t* to warp. – 2 **alabearse,** *p* to warp.

alabeo *m* warp, warping.

alacena *f* cupboard.

alacrán *m* scorpion.

alada *f* → **alado,-a.**

alado,-a 1 *adj (con alas)* winged. 2 *(veloz)* fast, quick. – 3 **alada,** *f (movimiento)* flutter, fluttering.

alagartado,-a *adj* motley.

alambicado,-a 1 *adj (escaso)* given sparingly. 2 *fig (rebuscado)* overcomplicated; *pey* affected.

alambicamiento 1 *m (destilación)* distilling, distillation. 2 *(sutileza)* affectation.

alambicar 1 *t (destilar)* to distil. 2 *(examinar)* to scrutinize. 3 *fig (estilo)* to make over-subtle, subtilize. 4 *fig (reducir ganancias)* to reduce to a minimum.
▲ Conjugation model [1], *like sacar.*

alambique *m* still.

alambrada *f* → **alambrado,-a.**

alambrado,-a 1 *pp* → **alambrar.** – 2 *adj* wire-fenced. – 3 alambrada, *f* wire fence. – 4 **alambrado,** *m* wire fence. 5 → **alambrera.**

alambrar *t* to fence (off) with wire.

alambre *m* wire.
● **estar como un alambre,** to be as thin as a rake.
■ **alambre de púas,** barbed wire.

alambrera 1 *f (para ventana)* wire netting. 2 *(de brasero)* fireguard. 3 *(de comida)* food safe.

alambrista *mf* tightrope walker.

alameda 1 *f* poplar grove. 2 *(paseo)* avenue, promenade, boulevard.

álamo *m* poplar.

alancear *t* to spear.

alano,-a *adj* mastiff, wolfhound.

alar *m* eaves *pl.*

alarde *m* display, bragging, boasting.
● **hacer alarde de,** to flaunt, show off, parade.

alardear *i* to boast, brag, show off.

alardeo *m* → **alarde.**

alargadera 1 *f* TÉC extension. 2 QUÍM adapter.

alargado,-a 1 *pp* → **alargar.** – 2 *adj* long, elongated.

alargador,-ra 1 *adj* lengthening, extending. – 2 alargador, *m* extension lead.

alargamiento 1 *m* lengthening; *(estirado)* stretching. 2 *(prolongaación)* prolongation, extension.

alargar 1 *t* to lengthen. 2 *(estirar)* to stretch. 3 *(prolongar)* to prolong. 4 *(dar)* to hand, pass. – 5 **alargarse,** *p* to lengthen.
▲ Conjugation model [7], *like llegar.*

alargo *m* extension lead.

alarido *m* screech, yell, shriek: *dar un alarido,* to howl.

alarma *f* alarm.
● **dar la alarma,** to give the alarm, raise the alarm.
■ **alarma aérea,** air-raid warning. ‖ **falsa alarma,** false alarm. ‖ **señal de alarma,** alarm (signal). ‖ **voz de alarma,** alarm (call).

alarmado,-a 1 *pp* → **alarmar.** – 2 *adj* alarmed.

alarmante *adj* alarming.

alarmar 1 *t* to alarm. – 2 **alarmarse,** *p* to be alarmed, alarm os.

alarmismo *m* alarmism.

alarmista *mf* alarmist.

alauita *adj* Alaouite: *el país alauita,* Morocco.

alavés,-esa 1 *adj* of Álava, from Álava. – 2 *m,f* person from Álava, inhabitant of Álava.

alazán,-ana 1 *adj* light chestnut, sorrel. – 2 *m,f (caballo)* sorrel horse.

alba 1 *f* dawn, daybreak. **2** REL alb.
● al rayar/romper el alba, at dawn, at daybreak.
▲ Takes *el* in singular.
albaca *f* → **albahaca**.
albacea *mf* JUR *(hombre)* executor; *(mujer)* executrix.
albacetense 1 *adj* of Albacete, from Albacete. – **2** *mf* person from Albacete, inhabitant of Albacete.
albaceteño,-a 1 *adj* of Albacete, from Albacete. – **2** *m,f* person from Albacete, inhabitant of Albacete.
albacora *f* albacore, long-fin tunny.
albahaca *f* basil.
albanés,-esa 1 *adj* Albanian. – **2** *m,f (persona)* Albanian. – **3** albanés, *m (idioma)* Albanian.
Albania *f* Albania.
albañal 1 *m* sewer, drain. **2** *fig* mess.
albañil *m (de ladrillos)* bricklayer; *(en general)* building worker.
albañilería 1 *f (oficio)* bricklaying. **2** *(obra)* brickwork: *techo de albañilería,* brick ceiling.
albar *adj* white.
albarán *m* delivery note, despatch note.
albarca *f* clog.
albarda *f* packsaddle.
albardado,-a 1 *pp* → **albardar**. – **2** *adj (caballo)* with the *back of a different colour* (US *color) from the body.*
albardar *t* to saddle.
albaricoque 1 *m (fruta)* apricot. **2** *(árbol)* apricot tree.
albaricoquero *m* apricot tree.
albariño *m* Albariño wine.
albarrana torre albarrana, *f* watchtower.
albarranilla *f* scilla.
albatros *m* albatross.
▲ *pl albatros.*
albayalde *m* white lead.
albazano,-a *adj* bay.
albedrío *m* will.
■ libre albedrío, free will.
albéitar *m* veterinary surgeon.
alberca *f* reservoir.
albérchiga 1 *f (melocotón)* peach. **2** *(albaricoque)* apricot.
albérchigo *m* → **albérchiga**.
albergar 1 *t (alojar)* to lodge, house, accommodate. **2** *fig (sentimientos)* to cherish, harbour (US harbor). – **3** albergarse, *p* to stay.
▲ *Conjugation model* [7], *like llegar.*
albergue 1 *m (hostal)* hostel. **2** *(refugio)* shelter, refuge.
● dar albergue, to take in, put up.
■ albergue juvenil, youth hostel.
albero,-a 1 *adj (blanco)* white. – **2** albero, *m* dishcloth.
albinismo *m* albinism.
albino,-a 1 *adj* albino. – **2** *m,f* albino.
albis in albis, *loc adv* left in the dark.
● estar in albis, not to have the faintest idea. ‖ quedarse in albis, not to know a thing.
albo,-a *adj lit* white.
albóndiga *f* meatball.
albondiguilla *f* meatball.
albor 1 *m (luz)* dawn. **2** *lit (blancura)* whiteness. – **3** albores, *mpl lit (comienzo)* beginning *sing.*
alborada 1 *f (alba)* dawn, break of day. **2** *(música)* dawn song. **3** *(toque militar)* reveille.
alborear *i* to dawn.
▲ *Used only in the 3rd person; it does not take a subject.*
albornoz *m* bathrobe.
alborotadamente 1 *adv (agitadamente)* excitedly. **2** *(ruidosamente)* noisily.

alborotadizo,-a *adj* excitable.
alborotado,-a 1 *pp* → **alborotar**. – **2** *adj (agitado)* agitated, excited. **3** *(ruidoso)* noisy, rowdy. **4** *(desordenado)* untidy, messy. **5** *(irreflexivo)* reckless, rash.
alborotador,-ra 1 *adj (rebelde)* rebellious, turbulent. **2** *(ruidoso)* noisy, rowdy. **3** *(mar)* rough, tempestuous. – **4** *m,f* troublemaker, agitator.
alborotar 1 *t (agitar)* to agitate, excite. **2** *(desordenar)* to make untidy, turn upside down. **3** *(sublevar)* to incite to rebel. – **4** *i* to make a racket. – **5** alborotarse, *p (excitarse)* to get excited. **6** *(el mar)* to get rough. **7** *(alarmarse)* to be alarmed.
alboroto 1 *m (gritería)* din, racket, row. **2** *(desorden)* uproar, commotion, disturbance. **3** *(sobresalto)* shock, alarm.
alborozado,-a 1 *pp* → **alborozar**. – **2** *adj* overjoyed, jubilant.
alborozar 1 *t* to delight, fill with joy. – **2** alborozarse, *p* to be overjoyed.
▲ *Conjugation model* [4], *like realizar.*
alborozo *m* joy, merriment, gaiety.
albricias 1 *fpl (regalo)* present *sing*, gift *sing.* – **2** *interj* great!, smashing!
albufera *f* lagoon.
álbum *m* album.
▲ *pl álbumes.*
albumen *m* albumen.
▲ *pl albúmenes.*
albúmina *f* albumin.
albur *m* chance: *los albures de la vida,* the ups and downs of life.
albura *f fml* whiteness.
alca *f* razorbill.
alcachofa 1 *f (planta)* artichoke. **2** *(pieza)* rose, sprinkler.
alcahuete,-a 1 *m,f (hombre)* procurer; *(mujer)* procuress, go-between. **2** *(cotilla)* gossipmonger.
alcahuetear 1 *i (chulear)* to procure, pimp. **2** *(chismorrear)* to gossip.
alcahuetería 1 *f (tercería)* procuring. **2** *fam (encubrimiento)* concealment, hiding. **3** *fam (truco)* trick.
alcaide *m* warder, jailer.
alcaldada *f* abuse of authority.
alcalde *m* mayor.
alcaldesa 1 *f (cargo)* lady mayor, mayoress. **2** *(mujer del alcalde)* mayoress.
alcaldía 1 *f (cargo)* mayorship: *primero fue ministro y ahora tiene una alcaldía,* first he was a minister and now he is a mayor. **2** *(oficina)* mayor's office, mayoralty. **3** *(territorio)* land under the jurisdiction of a mayor.
álcali *m* alkali.
alcalinidad *f* alkalinity.
alcalinizar *t* to alkalize.
alcalino,-a *adj* alkaline.
alcaloide *m* alkaloid.
alcalometría *f* alkalometry.
alcamonías *fpl* aromatic seeds.
alcance 1 *m* reach, grasp: *está al alcance de todo el mundo,* it's within everyone's reach. **2** *(de arma)* range. **3** *(trascendencia)* scope, importance. **4** *(inteligencia)* intelligence: *persona de pocos alcances,* person of low intelligence.
alcancía *f* money-box.
alcanfor *m* camphor.
alcanforado,-a 1 *pp* → **alcanforar**. – **2** *adj* camphorated.

alcanforar t to camphorate.
alcanforero m camphor tree.
alcantarilla 1 f (conducto) sewer. 2 (boca) drain.
alcantarillado m sewer system.
alcantarillar t to lay sewers in.
alcanzable adj within reach, attainable.
alcanzar 1 t (gen) to reach: *no alcanzo el libro,* I can't reach the book. 2 (persona) to catch up, catch up with: *los alcanzamos en la esquina,* we'll catch up with them at the corner. 3 (pasar) to pass, hand over: *alcánzame el agua,* pass me some water. 4 (entender) to understand, grasp. 5 (conseguir) to attain, achieve: *alcanzamos los objetivos,* we achieved the goals. 6 (golpear) to hit: *el tiro la alcanzó en el pie,* the shot hit her in the foot. 7 (afectar) to affect: *eso no nos alcanza,* it doesn't affect us. – 8 i (ser suficiente) to be sufficient (**para,** for), be enough (**para,** for), suffice (**para,** for): *eso no alcanza para todos,* that's not enough for all of us. 9 (ser capaz) to manage, succeed: *no alcanzo a verlo,* I can't see it.
▲ *Conjugation model* [4], *like realizar.*
alcaparra 1 f (fruto) caper. 2 (planta) caper bush.
alcaparrón m caper.
alcaraván m stone curlew.
alcaravea f caraway.
alcarraza f clay jar.
alcatraz m gannet.
alcaudón m shrike.
alcayata f hook.
alcazaba f fortress, citadel.
alcázar 1 m (fortaleza) fortress, citadel. 2 (palacio) palace, castle.
alce m elk, moose.
alción m (martín pescador) kingfisher.
alcista 1 adj (en bolsa) bullish, rising: *mercado alcista,* bull market; *tendencia alcista,* upward tendency, upward trend. – 2 mf bull.
alcoba f bedroom.
■ secretos de alcoba, *fig* intimacies.
alcohol 1 m (sustancia) alcohol. 2 (bebida) alcohol, spirits *pl.*
■ alcohol desnaturalizado/metílico/de quemar, methylated spirit.
alcoholemia f alcohol: *tasa/nivel de alcoholemia,* blood alcohol level.
alcoholera f → **alcoholero,-a**.
alcoholero,-a 1 adj alcohol, alcohol-producing. 2 alcoholera, f distillery.
alcohólico,-a 1 adj alcoholic. – 2 m,f alcoholic.
■ Alcohólicos Anónimos, Alcoholics Anonymous.
alcoholímetro m breathalyzer.
▲ *Registered trademark.*
alcoholismo m alcoholism.
alcoholización f alcoholization.
alcoholizado,-a 1 pp → **alcoholizar.** – 2 adj alcoholic. – 3 m,f alcoholic.
alcoholizar 1 t to alcoholize. – 2 alcoholizarse, p to become an alcoholic.
▲ *Conjugation model* [4], *like realizar.*
alcohómetro m breathalyzer.
▲ *Registered trademark.*
alcor m hill.
Alcorán m Koran.
alcornocal m cork-oak grove.
alcornoque 1 m BOT cork oak. 2 fig blockhead, idiot, dimwit.

alcorque m basin, pit.
alcotán m hobby.
alcotana f pickaxe, US pickax.
alcurnia f lineage, ancestry.
● de alta alcurnia, of noble lineage.
alcuza f oil bottle.
alcuzcuz m couscous.
aldaba 1 f (llamador) door knocker. 2 (barra) bar. 3 (pestillo) bolt.
● tener buenas aldabas, *fig* to know the right people, have influence.
aldabada f knock.
aldabazo m loud knock.
aldabilla f latch, hook.
aldabón m large door knocker.
aldabonazo 1 m loud knock: *dar un aldabonazo,* to knock. 2 *fig* shock.
aldea f hamlet, small village.
aldeano,-a 1 adj (de aldea) village. 2 *fig* (rústico) rustic. – 3 m,f villager.
aldehído m aldehyde.
ale interj come on!
aleación f alloy.
alear t (fundir) to alloy.
aleatorio,-a adj random, chance, fortuitous.
alebrestarse 1 p (agazaparse) to lie down flat. 2 *fig* to lose heart.
aleccionador,-ra 1 adj (instructivo) instructive, enlightening. 2 (ejemplar) exemplary.
aleccionamiento 1 m (instrucción) instruction. 2 (adiestramiento) training.
aleccionar 1 t (instruir) to teach, instruct. 2 (adiestrar) to train.
aledaño,-a 1 adj neighbouring (US neighboring), bordering. – 2 aledaños, mpl (de una ciudad) outskirts.
● en los aledaños, in the surrounding area.
alegación f allegation, plea, claim.
alegar t to allege, plead, claim: *alegó diferentes motivos,* he put forward several reasons.
▲ *Conjugation model* [7], *like llegar.*
alegato 1 m (argumento) claim, plea. 2 (razonamiento) reasoned allegation.
alegoría f allegory.
alegórico,-a adj allegorical, allegoric.
alegorizar t to allegorize.
alegrar 1 t (causar alegría) to make happy, make glad, cheer up: *la fiesta me alegró mucho,* the party cheered me up. 2 *fig* (avivar) to brighten (up), enliven. 3 *fam* (achispar) to make tipsy. – 4 alegrarse, p to be pleased, be glad: *me alegro mucho de que hayas venido,* I am very pleased that you have come. 5 *fam* (achisparse) to get tipsy.
alegre 1 adj (contento) happy, glad. 2 (color) bright. 3 (música) lively. 4 (espacio) cheerful, pleasant. 5 *fam* (achispado) tipsy. 6 *euf* (irreflexivo) thoughtless, irresponsible, rash.
■ alegre de cascos, *fam* scatterbrained.
alegremente 1 adv (con alegría) happily, cheerfully. 2 (frívolamente) gaily.
alegreto m allegretto.
alegría 1 f (felicidad) happiness, joy: *¡qué alegría!,* that's wonderful!, how marvellous! 2 *pey* (irresponsabilidad) irresponsibility, thoughtlessness, rashness: *gasta el dinero con una alegría increíble,* she's very rash with money. – 3 alegrías, fpl dance and song typical of Andalusia.

■ **alegría de vivir,** joie de vivre.
alegro m allegro.
alegrón m fam pleasant surprise.
alejado,-a 1 pp → **alejar**. – **2** adj (lejano) far away, remote. **3** (separado) aloof, apart.
alejamiento 1 m (separación) distance, separation. **2** (enajenación) estrangement.
Alejandría f Alexandria.
alejandrino m → **alejandrino, -a**.
alejandrino,-a 1 adj LIT Alexandrine. – **2** alejandrino, m LIT Alexandrine.
alejar 1 t (llevar lejos) to remove, move away. **2** fig (ahuyentar) to keep away: aleja esa idea, get rid of that idea. – **3** alejarse, p to go/move away: se alejaron lentamente, they went away slowly.
alelado,-a 1 pp → **alelar**. – **2** adj (atontado) dazed. **3** (asombrado) astonished, amazed.
alelar 1 t (asombrar) to overwhelm. **2** (confundir) to bewilder. – **3** alelarse, p (asombrarse) to be overwhelmed. **4** (confundirse) to be bewildered.
alelí m → **alhelí**.
aleluya 1 m & f hallelujah, alleluia. – **2** f fam (pareado) couplet. – **3** interj hallelujah!
alemán,-ana 1 adj German. – **2** m,f (persona) German. – **3** alemán, m (idioma) German.
Alemania f Germany.
■ **Alemania Occidental,** West Germany. ‖ **Alemania Oriental,** East Germany.
alentado,-a 1 pp → **alentar**. – **2** adj (valiente) brave, daring. **3** (altanero) haughty, arrogant.
alentador,-ra adj encouraging.
alentar 1 i arc (respirar) to breathe. **2** fig (existir) to exist, live on: en su alma alientan buenos sentimientos, his soul is full of kindness. – **3** t (animar) to encourage. **4** (tener) to harbour (us harbor), cherish: en su corazón alienta esperanzas de encontrarlo, in her heart she cherishes the hope of finding him. – **5** alentarse, p (recuperarse) to get well.
▲ Conjugation model |27|, like **acertar**.
aleonado,-a adj → **leonado,-a**.
alerce m larch.
alérgeno m allergen.
alergia f allergy.
alérgico,-a adj allergic (**a**, to).
alergista mf allergist.
alergólogo,-a m,f allergist.
alero 1 m ARQ eaves pl. **2** (coche) wing.
alerón m aileron.
alerta 1 adv (vigilante) on the alert. – **2** f (atención) alert. – **3** m (señal) alert, warning. – **4** interj look/watch out!
● **dar la (voz de) alerta,** to give the alert. ‖ **en estado de alerta,** on the alert.
alertar 1 t to alert (**de**, to). – **2** i to be alert.
aleta 1 f (de pez) fin; (de mamífero, de nadador) flipper. **2** (de nariz) wing, ala. **3** (de avión) aileron; (de coche) wing.
aletargado,-a 1 pp → **aletargar**. – **2** adj (dormido) lethargic. **3** (amodorrado) drowsy.
aletargamiento 1 m (letargo) lethargy. **2** (modorra) drowsiness, sleepiness.
aletargar 1 t to make drowsy/sleepy. – **2** aletargarse, p to become drowsy/sleepy.
▲ Conjugation model |7|, like **llegar**.
aletear 1 i (ave) to flutter, flap its wings. **2** (pez) to move its fins. **3** (persona) to wave one's arms about.
aleteo 1 m (de alas) fluttering of wings, flapping of wings; (de aleta) moving of fins. **2** (de brazos) waving of the arms. **3** fig (palpitación) palpitation.

aleutiano,-a 1 adj Aleutian. – **2** m,f (persona) Aleutian. – **3** aleutiano, m (idioma) Aleutian.
■ **islas Aleutianas,** Aleutian Islands.
alevín 1 m (pescado) fry, young fish. **2** (principiante) beginner. – **3** mf DEP competitor of the second youngest age group (11 or 12 years old). – **4** adj DEP of the second youngest age group (11 or 12 years old).
alevosía 1 f (premeditación) premeditation: con alevosía, deliberately. **2** (traición) treachery, perfidy.
alevoso,-a 1 adj (premeditado) premeditated. **2** (traidor) treacherous. – **3** m,f person who has commited a premeditated crime.
alexia f alexia.
alfa f alpha.
■ **alfa y omega,** fig alpha and omega, beginning and end.
▲ Takes **el** in singular.
alfabético,-a adj alphabetic, alphabetical.
alfabetización f teaching of basic literacy: campaña de alfabetización, literacy campaign.
alfabetizar 1 t (enseñar) to teach to read and write. **2** (ordenar) to alphabetize, put in alphabetic order.
▲ Conjugation model |4|, like **realizar**.
alfabeto 1 m (abecedario) alphabet. **2** (código) code.
■ **alfabeto Morse,** Morse code.
alfaguara f abundant spring.
alfajor m type of cake.
alfalfa f alfalfa, lucerne.
alfalfal m lucerne field, alfalfa field.
alfalfar m → **alfalfal**.
alfanje 1 m (sable) cutlass. **2** (pez espada) swordfish.
alfanumérico,-a adj alphanumeric.
alfaque m sandbank.
alfar 1 m (obrador) pottery, potter's workshop. **2** (arcilla) clay.
alfarería 1 f (arte) pottery. **2** (taller) potter's workshop. **3** (tienda) pottery shop.
alfarero,-a m,f potter.
alféizar m window-sill, window-ledge.
alfeñicarse 1 p (remilgarse) to become fussy. **2** (adelgazarse) to lose weight.
alfeñique 1 m (pasta) sugar paste. **2** fig (persona) weakling. **3** fig (remilgo) primness, affectation.
alferecía f fam epilepsy.
alférez m second lieutenant.
alfil m bishop.
alfiler 1 m (costura) pin: sujetó la falda con alfileres, she pinned up her dress. **2** (joya) brooch, pin. **3** (del pelo) clip; (de tender ropa) peg. **4** (de corbata) tiepin.
● **no caber ni un alfiler,** to be crammed full, be absolutely packed. ‖ **prendido,-a con alfileres,** fig shaky.
alfilerazo 1 m (punzada) pinprick. **2** fig taunt.
alfiletero m pin box, pin case.
alfombra 1 f carpet, rug. **2** (de baño) bathmat. **3** (alfombrilla) rug, mat.
alfombrado,-a 1 pp → **alfombrar**. – **2** adj carpeted. – **3** alfombrado, m (acción) carpeting. **4** (conjunto de alfombras) carpets pl.
alfombrar t to carpet.
alfombrilla[1] f rug, mat.
alfombrilla[2] f (enfermedad) German measles pl.
alfonsí adj → **alfonsino,-a**.
alfonsino,-a adj Alphonsine.
alforja 1 f (para caballerías) saddlebag; (para el hombro) knapsack. **2** fig provisions pl.

▲ *Also used in plural with the same meaning.*
alga *f* BOT alga; (*marina*) seaweed.
▲ *Takes* **el** *in singular.*
algaida[1] *f* (*maleza*) bush, thicket.
algaida[2] *f* (*duna*) dune.
algalia *f* civet.
algarabía *f* din, racket, noise.
algarada I *f* (*disturbio*) commotion, brawl. **2** MIL raid.
algarroba I *f* (*fruto*) carob bean. **2** (*planta*) vetch.
algarrobal I *m* (*de algarrobas*) vetch plantation. **2** (*de algarrobos*) carob tree plantation.
algarrobo *m* carob tree.
algazara *f* din, row, racket.
álgebra *f* algebra.
▲ *Takes* **el** *in singular.*
algebraico,-a *adj* algebraic.
algidez *f* algidity.
álgido,-a I *adj* (*frío*) icy, very cold. **2** *fig* culminating: *el punto álgido,* the height.
algo I *pron* (*afirmación*) something; (*negación, interrogación*) anything: *vamos a tomar algo,* let's have something to drink; *¿quieres algo?,* do you want anything?; *¿pasa algo?,* is anything wrong?, is anything the matter?; *¿queda algo de café?,* is there any coffee left? – **2** *adv* (*un poco*) a bit, a little, somewhat: *te queda algo grande,* it's a bit too big for you.
● **algo así,** something like that. ‖ **algo es algo,** something is better than nothing.
algodón *m* cotton.
● **criado,-a entre algodones,** pampered.
■ **algodón dulce/de azúcar,** candyfloss, (US cotton candy). ‖ **algodón en rama,** raw cotton. ‖ **algodón hidrófilo,** cotton wool.
algodonal *m* cotton plantation, cotton field.
algodonero,-a I *adj* cotton. – **2** *m,f* cotton grower. – **3** algodonero, *m* (*planta*) cotton plant.
algodonoso,-a *adj* cottony.
algoritmia *f* algorithmics.
algoritmo *m* algorithm.
alguacil *m* bailiff.
■ **alguacil de moscas,** (*araña*) zebra spider.
alguien *pron* (*afirmativo*) somebody, someone; (*interrogativo, negativo*) anybody, anyone: *preguntemos a alguien,* let's ask someone; *¿hay alguien?,* is anyone there?; *¿conoces a alguien que tenga coche?,* do you know anyone with a car?
algún *adj* → **alguno,-a.**
▲ *Used before singular masculine nouns.*
alguno,-a I *adj* (*afirmativo*) some; (*interrogativo, negativo*) any: *alguna noche voy al cine,* some nights I go to the cinema; *no vino persona alguna,* nobody came; *¿ha habido alguna llamada?,* has anyone phoned?, have there been any phone calls?; *el ministro no facilitó dato alguno,* the minister didn't provide any information. – **2** *pron* (*afirmativo*) someone, somebody; (*interrogativo, negativo*) anybody: *que venga alguno que sepa francés,* get someone who speaks French.
● **alguno que otro,** some, a few.
alhaja I *f* jewel, gem. **2** *fig* (*cosa, persona*) gem, treasure: *¡buena/menuda alhaja está hecho!,* he's a fine one!
alhajar I *t* (*adornar*) to adorn with jewels. **2** (*amueblar*) to decorate.
alharaca *f* fuss.
● **hacer alharacas,** to make a fuss.
alhelí *m* wallflower, stock.
▲ *pl* **alhelíes.**

alheña I *f* (*planta*) privet. **2** (*flor*) privet blossom. **3** (*polvo*) henna.
alhóndiga *f* corn exchange.
alhucema *f* lavender.
aliado,-a I *pp* → **aliar.** – **2** *adj* allied. – **3** *m,f* ally.
■ **los Aliados,** the Allies.
alianza I *f* (*pacto*) alliance. **2** (*anillo*) wedding ring.
aliar I *t* to ally. **2 aliarse,** (*uso recíproco*) to become allies, form an alliance (**con,** with).
▲ *Conjugation model* |13|, *like* ***desviar.***
alias I *adv* alias. – **2** *m* alias.
▲ *pl* **alias.**
alicaído,-a I *adj* *fig* (*débil*) weak, feeble. **2** *fig* (*deprimido*) depressed, down.
alicantino,-a I *adj* of Alicante, from Alicante. – **2** *m,f* person from Alicante, inhabitant of Alicante.
alicatado,-a I *pp* → **alicatar.** – **2** *adj* tiled. – **3** alicatado, *m* (*acción*) glazed tiling. **4** (*azulejos*) glazed tiles *pl.*
alicatar I *t* (*revestir*) to tile. **2** (*cortar*) to cut.
alicates *mpl* pliers.
aliciente I *m* (*incentivo*) incentive, inducement. **2** (*atractivo*) attraction, lure, charm.
alicorto,-a I *adj* (*de alas cortas*) with clipped wings. **2** *fig* (*apocado*) without ambition.
alícuota *adj* aliquot.
alienación I *f* (*gen*) alienation. **2** MED derangement, madness.
alienado,-a I *pp* → **alienar.** – **2** *adj* (*loco*) insane, deranged. – **3** *m,f* lunatic: *un alienado mental,* a mentally-ill person.
alienador,-ra *adj* alienating.
alienante *adj* alienating.
alienar I *t* to alienate. **2** MED to derange, drive mad. – **3 alienarse,** *p* to become alienated.
alienígena *mf* → **alienígeno,-a.**
alienígeno,-a I *adj* alien. – **2** alienígena, *mf* alien.
alienista *mf* psychiatrist.
aliento I *m* (*respiración*) breath, breathing. **2** *fig* (*ánimo*) spirit, courage.
● **cobrar aliento,** to get one's breath back. ‖ **dar aliento a algn.,** to encourage sb. ‖ **quedarse sin aliento,** (*respirando mal*) to be breathless, be out of breath; (*sorprendido*) to gasp.
alifafe[1] *m* (*achaque*) complaint, ailment.
alifafe[2] *m* (*de caballo*) windgall.
aligator *m* alligator.
aligátor *m* alligator.
aligeramiento I *m* (*peso*) lightening. **2** (*paso*) quickening. **3** (*dolor*) easing, soothing.
aligerar I *t* (*descargar*) to lighten, make lighter. **2** (*aliviar*) to relieve, ease, soothe. **3** (*apresurar*) to speed up. – **4** *i* (*apresurar*) to speed up.
● **¡aligera!,** *fam* hurry up! ‖ **aligerar el paso,** to quicken one's pace.
aligustre *m* privet.
alijo *m* consignment: *un alijo de armas,* a consignment of smuggled arms, an arms cache.
alimaña I *f* pest. – **2** alimañas, *fpl* vermin.
alimañero *m* gamekeeper, pest controller.
alimentación I *f* (*acción*) feeding. **2** (*alimento*) food; (*dieta*) diet. **3** TÉC feed.
■ **bomba de alimentación,** feed pump.
alimentador,-ra I *adj* feeding. – **2** alimentador, *m* feeder.
alimentar I *t* (*dar alimento*) to feed. **2** (*mantener*) to keep, support: *con su trabajo alimenta a toda su familia,* he

works to keep the whole family. **3** *fig* (*alentar*) to encourage, foster, nurture; (*pasiones*) to feed, fuel, nurture. **4** INFORM TÉC to feed. – **5** *i* (*servir de alimento*) to nourish, be nutritious: *la verdura alimenta mucho,* vegetables are very nutritious. – **6 alimentarse de/con,** *p* to live on: *se alimenta de patatas,* he lives on potatoes.

alimentario,-a *adj* food.

alimenticio,-a **1** *adj* (*nutritivo*) nutritious, nutritive. **2** (*de la comida*) food.
■ **hábitos alimenticios,** eating habits. ‖ **productos alimenticios,** foodstuffs, food products.

alimento **1** *m* (*comida*) food. **2** (*valor nutritivo*) nutritional value, nourishment: *los caramelos tienen poco alimento,* sweets are not very nourishing. **3** *fig* fuel: *los recuerdos eran el alimento de su ilusión,* he lived off his memories.

alimoche *m* Egyptian vulture.

alimón al alimón, *loc adv* together, in collaboration.

alineación **1** *f* (*colocación*) alignment, lining up. **2** (*equipo*) line-up. **3** POL alignment.
■ **política de no alineación,** non-alignment policy.

alineado,-a **1** *pp* → **alinear.** – **2** *adj* aligned, lined-up.
■ **países no alineados,** non-aligned countries.

alineamiento *m* alignment.

alinear **1** *t* (*poner en línea*) to align, line up. **2** DEP to pick, select. **3** MIL to form up. – **4 alinearse,** *p* (*unirse*) to become aligned, align os. (**con,** with). **5** MIL to fall in.

aliñar *t* (*gen*) to season, flavour (US flavor); (*ensalada*) to dress.

aliño *m* (*gen*) seasoning; (*para ensalada*) dressing.

alioli *m* garlic mayonnaise.

aliquebrado,-a **1** *adj* with a broken wing. **2** *fig* (*alicaído*) depressed, dejected.

alirón *interj* come on!

alisador,-ra **1** *adj* smoothing. – **2 alisador,** *m* smoothing tool.

alisamiento *m* smoothing.

alisar **1** *t* to smooth. – **2 alisarse,** *p* to smooth: *se alisó el pelo,* he smoothed his hair down.

aliseda *f* alder grove.

alisios *mpl* Trade Winds.

aliso *m* alder.

alistado,-a **1** *pp* → **alistar.** – **2** *adj* enrolled, enlisted.

alistamiento *m* enlistment, recruitment.

alistar **1** *t* to enlist, recruit. – **2 alistarse,** *p.* to enlist, join up, enrol (US enroll).
● **¡alístate!,** MIL join the army!, join up!

aliteración *f* alliteration.

aliviadero *m* spillway.

aliviador,-ra **1** *adj* comforting. – **2 aliviador,** *m* (*palanca*) lever on a millstone.

aliviar **1** *t* (*aligerar*) to lighten, make lighter. **2** *fig* (*enfermedad, dolor*) to relieve, ease, alleviate, soothe. **3** (*consolar*) to comfort, console. **4** (*apresurar*) to hurry. – **5 aliviarse,** *p* (*dolor*) to get better, diminish.
▲ Conjugation model |12|, like *cambiar.*

alivio **1** *m* (*aligeramiento*) lightening. **2** (*mejoría*) relief: *¡qué alivio!,* what a relief! **3** (*consuelo*) comfort, consolation.
● **ser de alivio,** *fam* (*persona*) to be a fine one; (*cosa*) to be awful: *un resfriado de alivio,* a stinking cold.

aljaba *f* quiver.

aljama **1** *f* (*reunión - mora*) Moorish assembly; (- *judía*) Jewish assembly. **2** (*barrio - mora*) Moorish quarter; (- *judía*) Jewish quarter. **3** (*mezquita*) mosque; (*sinagoga*) synagogue.

aljamía *f* Spanish written in Arabic characters.

aljamiado,-a *adj* written in Spanish with Arabic characters.

aljibe *m* cistern, tank.

aljófar *m* small pearl: *aljófar de rocío,* dewdrop.

aljofifa *f* floorcloth.

allá **1** *adv* (*lugar*) there, over there: *más allá,* further (on); *allá va tu madre,* there goes your mother. **2** (*tiempo*) back: *allá por los años sesenta,* back in the sixties.
● **allá se las componga,** that's his problem. ‖ **allá tú/vosotros,** that's your problem. ‖ **no muy allá,** not very good.

allanamiento **1** *m* (*aplanamiento*) levelling. **2** *fig* smoothing out.
■ **allanamiento de morada,** unlawful entry; (*robo*) housebreaking, breaking and entering.

allanar **1** *t* (*aplanar*) to level, flatten: *allanar un monte,* to level a mountain. **2** (*dificultad etc*) to smooth out, solve, resolve. **3** (*pacificar*) to pacify, subdue: *allanar la revuelta,* to put down the revolt. **4** (*entrar a la fuerza*) to break into: *allanar un domicilio,* to break into a house. – **5 allanarse,** *p* (*nivelarse*) to level out. **6** *fig* (*avenirse*) to agree, comply (**a,** with): *se allanó a las condiciones,* he agreed to the conditions.
● **allanar el terreno,** *fig* to clear the way.

allegado,-a **1** *pp* → **allegar.** – **2** *adj* close, related. – **3** *m,f* (*familia*) relative; (*amigo*) close friend.

allegar **1** *t* (*juntar*) to gather, collect. – **2 allegarse,** *p* (*llegarse*) to go round, come round.
▲ Conjugation model [7], like *llegar.*

allende *adv fml* beyond.

allí **1** *adv* (*lugar*) there, over there: *allí abajo/arriba,* down/up there; *por allí,* over there, round there. **2** (*tiempo*) then, at that moment: *de allí a poco,* shortly afterwards.

alma *f* soul.
● **agradecer a algn. con toda el alma,** to thank sb. from the bottom of one's heart. ‖ **caerse el alma a los pies,** to become disheartened. ‖ **como alma que lleva el diablo,** in a flash. ‖ **con toda el alma,** wholeheartedly, with all one's heart. ‖ **llegar al alma de algn.,** to touch sb., move sb. ‖ **llevar en el alma a algn.,** to love sb. deeply. ‖ **no había ni una alma,** there wasn't a soul, there was nobody there. ‖ **no poder más con su alma,** to be absolutely exhausted. ‖ **parecer una alma en pena,** to look like a ghost. ‖ **partir el alma a algn.,** to break sb.'s heart. ‖ **sentir algo en el alma,** to be deeply sorry about sth. ‖ **ser el alma de la fiesta,** to be the life and soul of the party. ‖ **tener el alma en un hilo,** to have one's heart in one's mouth, be worried sick.
■ **alma de Dios,** *fig* good soul. ‖ **alma en pena,** lost soul. ‖ **almas gemelas,** *fam* kindred spirits.
▲ Takes *el* in singular.

almacén **1** *m* (*local*) warehouse, storehouse. **2** (*habitación*) storeroom. – **3 almacenes,** *mpl* department store *sing.*
■ **grandes almacenes,** department store *sing.*

almacenaje **1** *m* (*almacenamiento*) storage, warehousing. **2** (*coste*) storage charge.

almacenamiento **1** *m* (*acción*) storage, warehousing. **2** (*mercancías*) stock. **3** INFORM storage.

almacenar **1** *t* to store, warehouse. **2** (*acumular*) to store up, keep.

almacenero *m* storekeeper, warehouseman.

almacenista *mf* (*vendedor*) wholesaler; (*propietario*) warehouse owner.

almáciga¹ *f* (*resina*) mastic (resin)..

almáciga² f (*semillero*) seedbed.
almácigo¹ m (*arbusto*) mastic tree.
almácigo² m (*semillero*) seedbed.
almádana f → **almádena**.
almádena f sledgehammer.
almadraba 1 f (*pesca*) tuna fishing, tunny fishing. 2 (*lugar*) tuna-fishing ground, tunny-fishing ground. 3 (*red*) tuna net, tunny net.
almadreña f clog.
almagre m red ochre.
almanaque m almanac.
almario m wardrobe, cupboard.
almazara f oilmill.
almeja f clam.
almena 1 f merlon. – 2 **almenas**, fpl battlements.
almenado,-a adj crenellated: *un castillo almenado*, a crenellated castle.
almenaje m battlements pl.
almenar 1 t to build battlements on. – 2 m torch holder.
almenara 1 f (*fuego*) beacon. 2 (*candelabro*) candelabrum.
almendra 1 f almond. 2 (*semilla*) kernel, stone.
almendrado,-a 1 adj almond-shaped. – 2 **almendrado**, m (*pasta*) almond paste. 3 (*helado*) chocolate and nut-covered ice cream.
almendral m almond grove.
almendro m almond tree.
almendruco m unripe almond.
almeriense 1 adj of Almería, from Almería. – 2 mf person from Almería, inhabitant of Almería.
almete m helmet.
almiar m haystack.
almíbar m syrup.
almibarado,-a 1 pp → **almibarar**. – 2 adj syrupy. 3 fig (*voz*) sugary; (*palabras*) honeyed.
almibarar 1 t to preserve in syrup, cover in syrup. 2 fig to sweeten: *almibarar las palabras,* to use honeyed words.
almidón m starch.
almidonado,-a 1 pp → **almidonar**. – 2 adj fam (*demasiado acicalado*) dressed up to the nines. 3 fam (*estirado*) stuffy, starchy, uptight.
almidonar t to starch.
alminar m minaret.
almiranta 1 f (*barco*) vice-admiral's ship. 2 (*mujer*) admiral's wife.
almirantazgo m admiralty.
almirante m admiral.
almirez m mortar.
almizcle m musk.
almizcleña f → **almizcleño,-a**.
almizcleño,-a 1 adj musky. – 2 **almizcleña**, f grape hyacinth.
almizclera f → **almizclero,-a**.
almizclero,-a 1 adj musky. – 2 **almizclero**, m musk deer. – 3 **almizclera**, f musk rat.
almogávar adj raider.
almohada f pillow.
● *consultar algo con la almohada,* fam to sleep on sth.
almohadazo m blow with a pillow.
almohade adj Almohad, Almohade.
almohadilla 1 f (*gen*) small cushion. 2 cost (*para coser*) sewing cushion; (*para alfileres*) pincushion. 3 (*tampón*) inkpad. 4 (*de animal*) pad. 5 ARQ (*de capitel*) volute cushion.

almohadillado,-a 1 pp → **almohadillar**. – 2 adj (*forrado*) padded. 3 ARQ rusticated. – 4 **almohadillado**, m (*relleno*) padding. 5 ARQ (*acción*) rustication; (*resultado*) rustication, rustic work.
almohadillar 1 t (*forrar*) to pad. 2 (*labrar*) to rusticate.
almohadón 1 m (*gen*) cushion, large pillow. 2 (*funda*) pillow case. 3 ARQ springer.
almoneda 1 f (*subasta*) auction. 2 (*saldo*) clearance.
almorávide 1 adj Almoravid. – 2 mf Almoravid.
almorrana f fam pile.
almorta f grass pea, vetch.
almorzar 1 i (*al mediodía*) to have lunch; (*de desayuno*) to have breakfast; (*a media mañana*) to have elevenses, have a mid-morning snack. – 2 t (*al mediodía*) to have for lunch; (*de desayuno*) to have for breakfast; (*a media mañana*) to have for elevenses, have for a mid-morning snack.
▲ *Conjugation model* [50], *like* **forzar**.
Almte. abr (*almirante*) admiral; (*abreviatura*) Adm.
almuecín m muezzin.
almuédano m muezzin.
almuerzo 1 m (*a mediodía*) lunch. 2 (*a media mañana*) mid-morning snack, elevenses pl. 3 (*desayuno*) breakfast.
alnado,-a m,f stepchild; (*chico*) stepson; (*chica*) stepdaughter.
alocadamente adv foolishly, thoughtlessly.
alocado,-a 1 adj (*distraído*) scatterbrained. 2 (*loco*) crazy, wild, reckless. 3 (*irreflexivo*) thoughtless, rash, impetuous. – 4 m,f (*despistado*) scatterbrain; (*loco*) fool.
alocución f address, speech.
aloe 1 m (*planta*) aloe. 2 (*jugo*) aloes.
áloe m → **aloe**.
aloja f → **alondra**.
alojamiento m lodging, accommodation: *dar alojamiento a algn.,* to give accommodation to sb.
alojar 1 t (*hospedar*) to lodge, put up, accommodate; (*dar vivienda a*) to house: *alojaron a los estudiantes en un albergue,* they put the students up in a youth hostel. 2 MIL to billet, quarter. 3 (*meter*) to put, place. – 4 **alojarse**, p (*persona*) to stay; (*bala etc*) to be lodged: *nos alojamos en un hotel frente al mar,* we stayed in a hotel on the seafront; *la bala se alojó en la cabeza,* the bullet lodged in his head. 5 MIL to be billeted, be quartered.
alomorfo,-a 1 adj allomorphic. – 2 m,f OUÍM allomorph. – 3 **alomorfo**, m LING allomorph.
alón m plucked wing.
alondra f lark.
■ **alondra común**, skylark.
alópata 1 adj allopathic. – 2 mf allopath.
alopatía f allopathy.
alopecia f alopecia.
alotropía f allotropy.
alpaca¹ f (*animal, tela*) alpaca.
alpaca² f (*metal*) nickel silver, German silver, alpaca.
alpargata f rope-soled sandal, espadrille.
alpargatería f (*taller*) espadrille factory; (*tienda*) shoe shop.
alpargatero,-a m,f (*fabricante*) manufacturer of espadrilles; (*vendedor*) espadrille dealer.
Alpes los Alpes, mpl the Alps.
alpestre 1 adj (*alpino*) Alpine. 2 fig (*montañoso*) mountainous, rough.
alpinismo m mountaineering, mountain climbing.
alpinista mf mountaineer, mountain climber.

alpino,-a *adj* Alpine.
alpiste 1 *m* birdseed, canary grass. **2** *fam* (*comida*) food; (*bebida*) booze.
alquería 1 *f* (*granja*) farmstead; (*casa de campo*) farmhouse. **2** (*grupo de casas*) hamlet.
alquilar 1 *t* (*dar en alquiler - período largo*) to rent, rent out, let; (- *período corto*) to hire out: *alquila habitaciones a estudiantes,* she rents out rooms to students, she lets rooms to students; *¿hay algún sitio dónde alquilen esquís?,* is there anywhere that hires out skis? **2** (*recibir en alquiler - período largo*) to rent; (- *período corto*) to hire: *alquilaron una casita,* they rented a cottage; *¿por qué no alquilamos un coche?,* why don't we hire a car?
● *"se alquila despacho",* "office to let".
alquiler 1 *m* (*acción - de casa*) renting, letting; (- *de coche*) hire: *el alquiler de coches es caro,* car hire is expensive. **2** (*cuota - de casa*) rent; (- *de TV etc*) rental: *¿has pagado el alquiler del piso?,* have you paid the rent on the flat?
● *"pisos en alquiler",* "flats to let", us "apartments for rent".
■ **alquiler de úteros,** surrogacy. ‖ **coche de alquiler,** hire car. ‖ **piso de alquiler,** rented flat.
alquimia *f* alchemy.
alquimista *mf* alchemist.
alquitrán *m* tar.
■ **alquitrán de hulla,** coal tar.
alquitranado,-a 1 *pp* → **alquitranar**. – **2** *adj* tarred, tarry. – **3 alquitranado,** *m* (*acción*) tarring. **4** (*pavimento*) tarmac.
alquitranar *t* to tar.
alrededor 1 *adv* (*lugar*) round, around: *mira alrededor,* look around; *a nuestro alrededor,* around us. **2 alrededor de,** (*tiempo*) around: *alrededor de las cuatro,* around four o'clock. **3** (*aproximadamente*) about: *alrededor de veinte,* about twenty. – **4 alrededores,** *mpl* surrounding area *sing: en los alrededores de Sevilla,* in the vicinity of Seville, just outside Seville.
alt. *abr* (*altitud*) altitude; (*abreviatura*) alt.
alta *f* → **alto,-a**.
altamente *adv* highly, extremely.
altaneramente *adv* arrogantly.
altanería *f* arrogance, haughtiness, conceit.
altanero,-a *adj* arrogant, haughty, conceited.
altar *m* altar.
● **elevar a los altares,** to canonize. ‖ **llevar/conducir al altar,** to lead to the altar, marry. ‖ **poner en un altar,** to put on a pedestal.
■ **altar mayor,** high altar.
altavoz *m* loudspeaker.
alterabilidad *f* changeability.
alterable *adj* changeable, volatile.
alteración 1 *f* (*cambio*) alteration, change. **2** (*excitación*) agitation, uneasiness, restlessness. **3** (*alboroto*) disturbance, quarrel, row.
● **alteración del orden público,** breach of the peace, disturbance of the peace.
alterado,-a 1 *pp* → **alterar**. – **2** *adj* upset, shaken.
alterar 1 *t* (*cambiar*) to change, modify, alter: *alteró nuestros planes,* he changed our plans. **2** (*estropear*) to spoil, upset; (*comida*) to make go off, turn bad: *el calor altera la leche,* heat makes milk go off; *drogas que alteran la percepción,* drugs which distort one's perception. **3** (*enfadar*) to annoy, upset: *todo le altera,* the slightest thing upsets him. **4** (*inquietar*) to unnerve, make feel restless. – **5 alterarse,** *p* (*cambiar*) to change. **6** (*deteriorarse*) to go bad, go off. **7** (*enfadarse*) to lose one's temper, get upset.

● **alterar el orden público,** to disturb the peace, cause a breach of the peace.
altercado *m* argument, quarrel.
alternadamente *adv* alternately.
alternador *m* alternator.
alternancia *f* alternation.
alternante *adj* alternating.
alternar 1 *t* (*gen*) to alternate. – **2** *i* (*turnar*) to alternate. **3** (*relacionarse*) to meet people, socialize (**con,** with), mix (**con,** with): *les gusta mucho alternar,* they are very sociable. **4** (*en salas de fiesta, bar*) to entertain. – **5 alternarse,** *p* (*turnarse*) to take turns: *se alternaron para conducir,* they took turns at driving.
alternativa *f* → **alternativo,-a**.
alternativamente *adv* alternatively.
alternativo,-a 1 *adj* alternative. – **2 alternativa,** *f* alternative, option, choice.
● **tomar la alternativa,** to become a fully-fledged bullfighter. ‖ **tomar una alternativa,** to decide, choose.
alterno,-a *adj* alternate, alternating: *días alternos,* alternate days.
Alteza *f* Highness: *Su Alteza Real,* (*hombre*) His Royal Highness; (*mujer*) Her Royal Highness.
altibajos *mpl* ups and downs: *los altibajos de la vida,* the ups and downs of life.
altillo 1 *m* (*encima de un armario*) top cupboard; (*desván*) attic. **2** GEOG hillock.
altilocuente *adj* grandiloquent.
altímetro *m* altimeter.
altiplanicie *f* high plateau.
altiplano *m* high plateau.
altísimo,-a 1 *adj* very high. – **2 El Altísimo,** *m* REL the Almighty.
altisonancia *f* grandiloquence.
altisonante *adj* grandiloquent, pompous.
altísono,-a *adj* → **altisonante**.
altitud *f* height, altitude.
altivamente *adv* arrogantly.
altivez *f* haughtiness, arrogance, conceit.
altiveza *f* → **altivez**.
altivo,-a *adj* haughty, arrogant, conceited.
alto[1] 1 *m* (*parada*) stop: *hicieron un alto para comer,* they stopped for lunch. – **2** *interj* halt!; (*policía*) stop!
● **dar el alto algn.,** MIL to order sb. to halt.
■ **alto el fuego,** cease-fire.
alto,-a[2] 1 *adj* (*persona, edificio, árbol*) tall: *es una mujer muy alta,* she's a very tall woman. **2** (*montaña, pared, techo, precio*) high: *lleva zapatos de tacón alto,* she wears high-heeled shoes; *la marea está alta,* it's high tide; *tiene la presión alta,* he's got high blood pressure. **3** (*elevado*) top, upper: *viven en los pisos altos,* they live on the upper floors. **4** (*importancia*) high, top: *es un alto ejecutivo en la empresa,* he's a top executive in the company. **5** (*voz, sonido*) loud: *lo dijo en voz alta,* she said it aloud; *pon la tele más alta,* turn the telly up. – **6 alto,** *adv* high (up): *colocaron los platos muy alto,* they put the dishes very high up. **7** (*voz*) loud, loudly: *¿podrías hablar más alto?,* could you speak a bit louder? – **8** *m* (*altura*) height: *sólo hace dos metres de alto,* it's only two metres high. **9** (*elevación*) hill, high ground. – **10 alta,** *f* (*de un enfermo*) discharge: *dieron de/el alta al enfermo,* the patient was discharged from hospital. **11** (*de un em-*

pleado) registration *with* Social Security: *la empresa lo dio de alta en la Seguridad Social,* the company registered him with Social Security. **12** (*entrada, admisión*) admission; (*ingreso*) membership: *solicitó el alta en el club,* he applied for membership of the club. **13** (*en el ejército*) enrolment, enlistment.
● **a altas horas de la noche,** late at night. ‖ **en lo alto de,** on the top of. ‖ **pasar por alto,** to pass over. ‖ **por todo lo alto,** *fig* in a grand way. ‖ **tirando alto,** *fig* at the most.
■ **alta cocina,** haute cuisine. ‖ **alta sociedad,** high society. ‖ **alta tecnología,** high technology. ‖ **altas presiones,** high pressure *sing.* ‖ **alto horno,** blast furnace. ‖ **cámara alta,** upper chamber.
▲ In *10, 11, 12* and *13* takes *el* in *singular.*
altozano 1 *m* (*monte*) hillock, hill. **2** (*de una población*) upper part.
altramuz *m* lupin.
altruismo *m* altruism.
altruista 1 *adj* altruistic. **– 2** *mf* altruist.
altura 1 *f* (*gen*) height: *el edificio tiene una altura de 80 metros,* the building is 80 metres high. **2** (*altitud*) altitude. **3** (*nivel*) level, par; (*punto*) point: *¿a qué altura de la calle vives?,* how far up the street do you live?; *hay un buzón en la calle Mayor, a la altura de la zapatería,* there's a post box in the High Street, near the shoe shop; *el petrolero naufragó a la altura de Malpica,* the petrol tanker went down off Malpica. **4** *fig* (*mérito, valía, calidad*) merit, worth; (*dignidad*) dignity, excellence: *todos son profesionales de altura demostrada,* all of them are professionals of proven worth. **– 5 alturas,** *fpl* REL heavens.
● **a estas alturas,** by now, at this stage. ‖ **estar a la altura de,** to measure up to, match up to, be on a par with. ‖ **estar a la altura de las circunstancias,** *fig* to be worthy of the occasion, rise to the occasion. ‖ **quedar a la altura del betún,** *fam* to make a very poor showing, look bad.
alubia *f* bean.
alucinación *f* hallucination.
alucinado,-a 1 *pp* → **alucinar. – 2** *adj arg* amazed, stunned, gobsmacked.
alucinador,-ra *adj* hallucinatory.
alucinamiento *m* hallucination.
alucinante 1 *adj* hallucinatory. **2** *arg* (*extraordinario*) brilliant, fantastic, amazing, incredible, mind-blowing.
alucinar 1 *t* (*producir sensaciones*) to hallucinate. **2** *fig* (*cautivar*) to fascinate, amaze, astound, flip out, stun. **– 3** *i arg* to be amazed, be gobsmacked: *¡alucinas!,* you're out of your mind!, you're crazy!
alucine *m arg* amazing thing: *¡vaya alucine!,* wow!
alucinógeno,-a 1 *adj* hallucinogenic. **– 2** *alucinógeno, m* hallucinogen.
alud *m* avalanche.
aludido,-a 1 *pp* → **aludir. – 2** *adj* above-mentioned, in question.
● **darse por aludido,-a,** to take the hint.
aludir *i* to allude (**a,** to), mention (**a,** -), refer (**a,** to).
alumbrado,-a 1 *pp* → **alumbrar. – 2** *adj* (*iluminado*) lit, lighted. **3** *fam* (*achispado*) tipsy, merry. **– 4 alumbrado,** *m* TÉC lighting, lights *pl*; (*coche*) lights *pl*.
■ **alumbrado público,** street lighting.
alumbramiento 1 *m* (*eléctrico*) lighting. **2** (*nacimiento*) childbirth.
alumbrar 1 *t* (*iluminar*) to light, give light to, illuminate. **2** *fig* (*enseñar*) to enlighten. **– 3** *i* (*iluminar*) to give light.

4 (*parir*) to give birth to. **– 5 alumbrarse,** *p fam* (*embriagarse*) to get tipsy.
alumbre *m* alum.
alúmina *f* alumina.
aluminio *m* aluminium, US aluminum.
aluminosis *f* aluminosis.
aluminoso,-a *adj* aluminous.
alumnado *m* (*de colegio*) pupils *pl*; (*de universidad*) student body.
alumno,-a *m,f* (*de colegio*) pupil; (*de universidad*) student.
■ **alumno externo,** day pupil. ‖ **alumno interno,** boarder. ‖ **antiguo alumno,** (*de colegio*) old boy, former pupil; (*de universidad*) old student, former student.
alunizaje *m* moon landing.
alunizar *i* to land on the moon.
▲ Conjugation model [4], *like* **realizar.**
alusión *f* allusion, reference.
alusivo,-a *adj* allusive (**a,** to), referring (**a,** to).
aluvial *adj* alluvial.
aluvión 1 *m* alluvion: *tierra de aluvión,* alluvial soil. **2** *fig* flood: *un aluvión de insultos,* a barrage of insults; *recibimos un aluvión de solicitudes,* we were inundated with applications, we received a flood of applications.
álveo *m* river-bed, bed.
alveolar *adj* alveolar.
alveolo 1 *m* ANAT alveolus. **2** (*de panal*) cell.
alvéolo *m* → **alveolo.**
alza 1 *f* (*aumento*) rise, increase. **2** (*impresión*) underlay. **3** (*de calzado*) raised insole. **4** (*de rifle*) rear sight, sight.
● **al alza / en alza,** rising. ‖ **estar en alza,** *fig* to be up and coming, be on the rise. ‖ **jugar al alza,** FIN to bull the market.
▲ Takes *el* in *singular.*
alzacuello *m* clerical collar, dog collar.
alzada *f* → **alzado,-a.**
alzado,-a 1 *pp* → **alzar. – 2** *adj* raised, lifted. **3** (*persona*) fraudulently bankrupt. **– 4 alzado,** *m* ARQ elevation. **5** (*diseño*) design, sketch. **6** (*impresión*) gathering. **7** (*robo*) theft. **– 8 alzada,** *f* (*de caballo*) height. **9** JUR appeal.
● **a mano alzada,** by a show of hands.
alzamiento 1 *m* (*aumento*) raising, lifting. **2** (*rebelión*) uprising, insurrection.
alzaprima 1 *f* (*palanca*) lever, crowbar. **2** (*cuña*) wedge. **3** (*de instrumento músico*) bridge.
alzaprimar *t* to lever up.
alzar 1 *t* (*levantar*) to raise, lift: *alzar los precios,* to raise prices; *alzó la mano,* he raised his hand; *no alces la voz,* don't raise your voice. **2** (*construir*) to build, erect. **3** (*un plano*) to draw up, make out. **4** (*quitar*) to remove, take off, take away: *alzar la mesa,* to clear the table. **5** (*una cosecha*) to get in, gather in. **6** (*cortar la baraja*) to cut. **7** REL to elevate. **8** (*en impresión*) to gather. **– 9 alzarse,** *p* (*levantarse*) to rise up, get up. **10** (*sublevarse*) to rise, rebel: *alzarse en rebelión,* to rise up in rebellion. **11** (*sobresalir*) to stand out. **12** JUR to lodge an appeal.
● **alzar el vuelo,** to take off. ‖ **alzar los ojos,** to look up. ‖ **alzar velas,** MAR to hoist sail. ‖ **alzarse con algo,** to run off with sth.: *se alzó con la recaudación,* he ran off with the takings.
▲ Conjugation model [4], *like* **realizar.**
AM *abr* RAD (*modulación de amplitud*) amplitude modulation; (*abreviatura*) AM.
a.m. *abr* (*ante meridiem*) ante meridiem; (*abreviatura*) a.m.
ama 1 *f* (*señora*) lady of the house. **2** (*propietaria*) landlady.
■ **ama de casa,** housewife. ‖ **ama de cría,** wet nurse. ‖ **ama de leche,** wet nurse. ‖ **ama de llaves,** housekeeper.

▲ Takes *el* in singular.

amabilidad *f* kindness, affability: *tenga la amabilidad de ...,* would you be so kind as to ...?

amable *adj* kind, nice: *¿sería usted tan amable de ...?,* would you be so kind as to ...?

amablemente *adv* kindly.

amado,-a 1 *pp* → **amar.** – 2 *adj* loved, beloved. – 3 *m,f* love, sweetheart.

amadrinar 1 *t* (*en bautizo*) to be the godmother to. 2 (*en boda*) to be bridesmaid to. 3 (*en barco*) to launch.

amaestrado,-a 1 *pp* → **amaestrar.** – 2 *adj* (*adiestrado*) trained; (*domado*) tamed: *ratón amaestrado,* performing mouse.

amaestrador,-ra 1 *adj* (*adiestrador*) training; (*domador*) taming. – 2 *m,f* (*adiestrador*) trainer; (*domador*) tamer.

amaestramiento *m* (*adiestramiento*) training; (*doma*) taming.

amaestrar *t* (*adiestrar*) to train; (*domar*) to tame.

amagar 1 *t* (*dejar ver*) to show signs of. 2 (*amenazar*) to threaten: *le amaga un gran riesgo,* great danger is in store for him. 3 (*fingir*) to simulate. – 4 *i* (*ser inminente*) to threaten, be imminent: *amagaba lluvia,* it looked like rain. 5 (*enfermedad*) to show the first signs. – 6 **amagarse,** *p* to hide.

● **amagar y no dar,** to be all bark and no bite.

▲ *Conjugation model* [7], *like* **llegar.**

amago 1 *m* (*amenaza*) threatening. 2 (*señal*) sign, indication: *amago de infarto,* mild heart attack.

amainar 1 *i* (*viento*) to die down, drop. 2 *fig* (*calmarse*) to calm down.

amalgama *f* amalgam.

amalgamación *f* amalgamation.

amalgamar *t* to amalgamate.

amamantamiento *m* breast-feeding, suckling.

amamantar *t* to breast-feed, suckle.

amancebamiento *m* cohabitation, living together.

amancebarse *p* to cohabit, live together.

amanecer 1 *i* to dawn, get light: *en verano amanece pronto,* day breaks early in summer. 2 (*estar*) to be at dawn, be at daybreak: *amanecimos en Barcelona,* we were in Barcelona at dawn. 3 (*despertar*) to wake up: *amanecí muy cansado,* I woke up very tired. – 4 *m* dawn, daybreak.

● **al amanecer,** at daybreak.

▲ *Conjugation model* [43], *like* **agradecer**; *in* 1, *used only in the 3rd person; it does not take a subject.*

amaneradamente *adv* in an affected way.

amanerado,-a 1 *pp* → **amanerar.** – 2 *adj* affected, mannered.

amaneramiento *m* affectation.

amanerar 1 *t* to affect. – 2 **amanerarse,** *p* to become affected. 3 (*afeminarse*) to become effeminate.

amanita *f* amanita.

amansar 1 *t* (*animal*) to tame; (*caballo*) to break in. 2 *fig* (*persona*) to tame, calm down; (*pasión etc*) to soothe, appease. – 3 **amansarse,** *p* to become tame.

amante *adj* loving, fond (**de,** of). – 2 *mf* lover.

amanuense *mf* scribe.

amañado,-a 1 *pp* → **amañar.** – 2 *adj* (*mañoso*) skilful (us skillful). 3 (*falsificado*) faked, fake.

amañar 1 *t* (*falsear*) to fiddle, fix; (*documentos*) to tamper with, doctor; (*cuentas*) to cook; (*elecciones*) to rig. 2 (*componer*) to fix, arrange. – 3 **amañarse,** *p* (*darse maña*) to be skilful (us skillful).

● **amañárselas,** *fam* to manage: *se las amaña muy bien para hacer el mínimo de trabajo,* he always manages to do as little work as possible.

amaño 1 *m* (*disposición*) skill. – 2 **amaños,** *mpl* (*instrumentos*) tools. 3 (*trucos*) tricks.

amapola *f* poppy.

amar 1 *t* to love. 2 **amarse,** (*uso recíproco*) to love each other, be in love (with each other).

amaraje *m* (*hidroavión*) sea landing; (*nave espacial*) splashdown.

amaranto *m* amaranth.

amarar *i* (*hidroavión*) to land at sea; (*nave espacial*) to splash down.

amargado,-a 1 *pp* → **amargar.** – 2 *adj* embittered, resentful: *estar amargado,-a,* to feel very bitter. – 3 *m,f* bitter person.

amargamente *adv* bitterly.

amargar 1 *i* (*tener sabor amargo*) to taste bitter: *este pan amarga,* this bread tastes bitter. – 2 *t* (*hacer amargo*) to make bitter. 3 *fig* (*disgustos etc*) to embitter, make bitter: *los disgustos le amargaron la existencia,* misfortunes made his life a misery. 4 *fig* (*estropear*) to spoil, ruin: *la lluvia nos amargó el día,* the rain put a damper on our day. – 5 **amargarse,** *p* (*volverse amargo*) to become bitter. 6 *fig* to become embittered, become bitter.

● **a nadie le amarga un dulce,** a gift is always welcome. ‖ **amargar la existencia/vida a algn.,** to make sb.'s life a misery.

▲ *Conjugation model* [7], *like* **llegar.**

amargo,-a 1 *adj* (*sabor*) bitter. 2 *fig* (*carácter*) sour; (*experiencia*) bitter, sour, painful. – 3 **amargo,** *m* bitterness.

amargor *m* bitterness.

amargura 1 *f* bitterness. 2 (*dolor*) sorrow, grief, sadness.

amariconado,-a *adj fam* camp.

amarilis *f* amaryllis.

▲ *pl* **amarilis.**

amarillear 1 *i* (*volverse amarillo*) to yellow, go yellow. 2 (*tirar a amarillo*) to be yellowish.

amarillecer *i* to go yellow.

amarillento,-a *adj* yellowish.

amarillez *f* yellowness.

amarillismo *m* sensationalism.

amarillista *adj* sensationalist.

amarillo,-a 1 *adj* yellow. – 2 **amarillo,** *m* yellow.

■ **prensa amarilla,** sensationalist press.

amariposado,-a 1 *adj* butterfly-shaped. 2 *fam* effeminate.

amarizaje *m* → **amaraje.**

amarizar *i* → **amarar.**

amaro *m* clary sage.

amarra 1 *f* mooring rope. – 2 **amarras,** *fpl fam fig* connections: *tiene buenas amarras,* she has good connections, she has friends in high places.

● **soltar las amarras,** MAR to cast off, let go; *fig* to break loose.

amarradero 1 *m* (*poste*) mooring post; (*argolla*) mooring ring. 2 (*lugar*) mooring.

amarraje *m* mooring charges *pl*.

amarrar 1 *t* (*atar*) to tie (up), fasten. 2 MAR to moor, tie up.

amarre *m* mooring.

amartelado,-a 1 *pp* amartelarse. – 2 *adj* lovesick.

● **andar amartelado,-a con,** to be in love with.

amartelar 1 *t* to drive crazy with jealousy. – 2 **amartelarse,** *p* (*enamorarse*) to fall in love; (*acariciarse*) to be all over one another.

amartillar 1 *t* (*arma*) to cock. 2 (*martillear*) to hammer.

amasadera *f* kneading trough.
amasar 1 *t* CULIN to knead; (*cemento*) to mix. 2 *fig* (*reunir*) to amass. 3 *fam* (*urdir*) to cook up.
amasijo 1 *m* (*masa*) dough; (*cemento, yeso*) mixture. 2 *fam* (*mezcolanza*) hotchpotch, jumble.
amateur 1 *adj* amateur. – 2 *mf* amateur.
▲ *pl amateurs.*
amateurismo *m* amateurism.
amatista *f* amethyst.
amatorio,-a *adj* love.
amazacotado,-a 1 *pp* → **amazacotar**. – 2 *adj* (*compacto*) compact, dense: *arroz amazacotado,* stodgy rice. 3 *fig* stodgy.
amazona 1 *f* (*mitología*) Amazon. 2 (*jinete*) horsewoman.
Amazonas el Amazonas, *m* the Amazon.
ambages *mpl* circumlocutions: *dímelo sin ambages,* tell me straight.
● hablar sin ambages, to speak plainly. ‖ ir/andarse con ambages, to beat about the bush.
ámbar *m* amber.
ambarino,-a *adj* amber.
Amberes *m* Antwerp.
ambición *f* ambition, aspiration.
ambicionar *t* to want: *siempre ambicionó ser rico,* it was always his ambition to be rich.
ambiciosamente *adv* ambitiously.
ambicioso,-a 1 *adj* (*plan etc*) ambitious; (*persona*) ambitious, enterprising. – 2 *m,f* ambitious person, go-getter.
ambidextro,-a 1 *adj* ambidextrous. – 2 *m,f* ambidextrous person.
ambidiestro,-a *adj* → **ambidextro, -a.**
ambientación 1 *f* (*ambiente*) atmosphere. 2 (*localización*) setting.
ambientador *m* air freshener.
ambiental 1 *adj* (*del ambiente*) environmental. 2 (*de fondo*) background.
ambientar 1 *t* (*dar ambiente*) to give atmosphere to. 2 (*localizar*) to set. – 3 ambientarse, *p* to adapt, get used (a, to).
ambiente 1 *m* (*aire*) air, atmosphere. 2 (*entorno*) environment, atmosphere: *ambiente familiar,* family environment; *en este pub hay un ambiente muy bueno,* this pub has a really good atmosphere; *no hay mucho ambiente de noche,* there is not much going on at night.
● cambiar de ambiente, to have a change of scene.
■ temperatura ambiente, (*técnicamente*) ambient temperature; (*en casa*) room temperature.
ambigú *m* buffet, buffet supper.
▲ *pl ambigúes.*
ambiguamente *adv* ambiguously.
ambigüedad *f* ambiguity.
ambiguo,-a *adj* ambiguous.
ámbito 1 *m* (*espacio*) sphere, space: *en el ámbito nacional,* nationwide; *en el ámbito de la región,* within the region; *de ámbito local,* local. 2 (*marco*) field: *en el ámbito de la informática,* in the computer science field; *fuera del ámbito de mis capacidades,* beyond my capabilities.
ambivalencia *f* ambivalence.
ambivalente *adj* ambivalent.
ambos,-as 1 *adj* both: *por ambos lados,* on both sides. – 2 *pron* both: *me gustan ambos,* I like both of them, I like them both.
ambrosía *f* ambrosia.
ambulancia *f* ambulance.

ambulante *adj* itinerant, travelling: *biblioteca ambulante,* mobile library; *es una enciclopedia ambulante,* he's a walking encyclopedia.
ambulatorio,-a 1 *adj* ambulatory. – 2 ambulatorio, *m* surgery, clinic.
ameba *f* amoeba (US ameba).
amedrentar 1 *t* to frighten, scare. – 2 amedrentarse, *p* (*asustarse*) to be frightened, be scared; (*acobardarse*) to become intimidated.
amelgar *t* to furrow.
amelonado,-a 1 *adj* melon-shaped. 2 *fam* lovesick.
amén[1] *m* REL amen.
● decir amén a todo/todos, *fam* to agree with everything/everybody. ‖ en un decir amén, *fam* in the twinkling of an eye.
▲ *pl amenes.*
amén[2] amén de, *loc adv* (*excepto*) except for; (*además de*) in addition to, as well as.
amenamente *adv* entertainingly.
amenaza *f* threat, menace.
amenazador,-ra *adj* threatening, menacing.
amenazadoramente *adv* threateningly.
amenazante *adj* threatening, menacing.
amenazar 1 *t* (*coaccionar*) to threaten: *lo amenazaron con el despido,* they threatened to sack him. 2 (*presagiar*) to threaten: *el edificio amenaza ruina,* the building is on the verge of collapse. – 3 *i* (*coaccionar*) to threaten: *amenaza con suicidarse,* she's threatening to kill herself. 4 *fig* (*presagiar*) to threaten: *amenazaba lluvia,* it looked like rain.
● amenazar de muerte a algn., to threaten to kill sb.
▲ *Conjugation model* [4], *like realizar.*
amenguar 1 *t* (*disminuir*) to reduce. 2 (*deshonrar*) to dishonour (US dishonor), defame.
▲ *Conjugation model* [22], *like averiguar.*
amenidad *f* amenity, pleasantness, agreeableness.
amenizar *t* to liven up, make entertaining, make enjoyable.
▲ *Conjugation model* [4], *like realizar.*
ameno,-a *adj* lively, entertaining, enjoyable.
amenorrea *f* amenorrhoea (US amenorrhea).
América *f* America.
■ América Central, Central America. ‖ América del Norte, North America. ‖ América del Sur, South America. ‖ América Latina, Latin America.
americana *f* → **americano,-a.**
americanada *f fam* (*película etc*) typical American effort; (*acontecimiento*) Hollywood-style affair.
americanismo *m* (*palabra*) Spanish-American word; (*expresión*) Spanish-American expression.
americanista *mf* Americanist.
americanización *f* Americanization.
americanizar *t* to Americanize.
▲ *Conjugation model* [4], *like realizar.*
americano,-a 1 *adj* American. – 2 *m,f* American. – 3 americana, *f* jacket.
americio *m* americium.
amerindio,-a 1 *adj* Amerindian, American Indian. – 2 *m,f* Amerindian, American Indian.
ameritar *t* to deserve.
amerizaje *m* → **amaraje.**
amerizar *i* → **amarar.**
▲ *Conjugation model* [4], *like realizar.*
ametralladora *f* machine gun.
ametrallar 1 *t* to machine-gun. 2 *fig* (*acosar*) to chase, pursue, besiege.

ametropía *f* ametropia.
amianto *m* asbestos.
amiba *f* amoeba (US ameba).
amida *f* amide.
amigable *adj* amicable, friendly.
amigablemente *adv* amicably.
amigacho,-a *m,f fam* mate, friend.
amigarse *p* (*amancebarse*) to live together.
amígdala *f* tonsil.
amigdalitis *f* tonsillitis.
▲ *pl amigdalitis.*
amigo,-a **1** *adj* (*amigable*) friendly: *es muy amigo de Julio,* he's very friendly with Julio. **2** (*aficionado*) fond (**de,** of): *no es muy amiga de discotecas,* she's not keen on discos. – **3** *m,f* friend: *una amiga mía,* a friend of mine; *son amigos íntimos,* they are close friends. **4** (*novio*) boyfriend; (*novia*) girlfriend. **5** (*amante*) lover.
● **hacerse amigo,-a de,** to make friends with. ‖ **hacerse amigos,-as,** to become friends.
amigote *m fam* pal, mate, chum.
amiguete *m fam* → **amigote.**
amiguismo *m* contacts *pl,* string-pulling.
amiguito,-a *m,f fam* (*gen*) lover; (*mujer*) mistress.
amilanado,-a **1** *pp* → **amilanar.** – **2** *adj* (*asustado*) frightened. **3** (*desanimado*) discouraged, depressed.
amilanamiento **1** *m* (*miedo*) fear. **2** (*desánimo*) discouragement, depression.
amilanar **1** *t* (*asustar*) to frighten. **2** (*desanimar*) to discourage, depress, daunt. – **3** **amilanarse,** *p* (*asustarse*) to be frightened. **4** (*desanimarse*) to be discouraged, be daunted, become depressed.
amina *f* amine.
amino *m* amino.
aminoácido *m* amino acid.
aminoración *f* reduction, decrease: *aminoración de la velocidad,* reduction in speed.
aminorar *t* to reduce, decrease.
● **aminorar el paso,** to slow down.
amistad **1** *f* friendship. – **2** **amistades,** *fpl* friends.
● **trabar amistad con algn.,** to make friends with sb. ‖ **hacer amistades,** to make friends.
amistosamente *adv* amicably.
amistoso,-a *adj* friendly: *partido amistoso,* friendly match.
amnesia *f* amnesia, loss of memory: *amnesia temporal,* blackout.
amnésico,-a **1** *adj* amnesic. – **2** *m,f* amnesiac.
amniótico,-a *adj* amniotic.
amnistía *f* amnesty.
amnistiar *t* to amnesty, grant an amnesty to.
▲ *Conjugation model* [13], *like desviar.*
amo **1** *m* (*señor*) master. **2** (*dueño*) owner. **3** (*jefe*) boss.
● **hacerse el amo,** *fig* to be the boss (**de,** of), rule the roost.
amoblar *t* to furnish.
▲ *Conjugation model* [31], *like contar.*
amodorrado,-a **1** *pp* → **amodorrarse.** – **2** *adj* sleepy, drowsy.
amodorramiento *m* sleepiness, drowsiness.
amodorrar **1** *t* to make drowsy, make sleepy. – **2** **amodorrarse,** *p* (*adormecerse*) to feel drowsy, feel sleepy; (*dormirse*) to fall into a stupor.
amohinar **1** *t* (*molestar*) to annoy. – **2** **amohinarse,** *p* (*enfadarse*) to get angry.
amojamado,-a *adj* wizened, wrinkled.

amojonamiento *m* marking out.
amojonar *t* to mark out.
amolado,-a **1** *pp* → **amolar.** – **2** *adj* sharpened, ground. – **3** amolado, *m* sharpening, grinding.
amolar **1** *t* to sharpen, grind: *amoló el cuchillo,* he ground the knife sharp. **2** *fam* (*molestar*) to bother, annoy.
▲ *Conjugation model* [31], *like contar.*
amoldable *adj* adaptable: *es una chica amoldable a todo,* she adapts to everything.
amoldamiento **1** *m* adapting, adjusting. **2** *fig* adaptation.
amoldar **1** *t* to adapt, adjust. – **2** **amoldarse,** *p* to adapt, adjust (**a,** to): *se amoldó a las costumbres españolas,* he adapted himself to Spanish customs.
amollar **1** *i* (*ceder*) to yield, give in. **2** MAR to pay out. – **3** *t* MAR to pay out.
amonarse *p fam* to get drunk.
amonedar *t* to coin, mint.
amonestación **1** *f* (*reprensión*) reprimand, admonition, admonishment. **2** (*advertencia*) warning. **3** DEP caution, booking. – **4** amonestaciones, *fpl* banns.
amonestar **1** *t* (*reprender*) to reprimand, admonish. **2** (*advertir*) to warn. **3** DEP to caution, book. **4** (*en una boda*) to publish the banns of.
amoniacal *adj* ammoniacal.
amoniaco *m* ammonia.
amoníaco *m* ammonia.
amonio *m* ammonium.
amonita *f* ammonite.
amontillado,-a *m* pale dry, amontillado.
amontonado,-a **1** *pp* → **amontonar.** – **2** *adj* heaped up, piled up.
amontonamiento **1** *m* (*acción*) heaping, piling. **2** (*montón*) heap, pile, stack.
amontonar **1** *t* to heap up, pile up. **2** (*juntar*) to collect, gather, accumulate. – **3** **amontonarse,** *p* to heap up, pile up. **4** (*gente*) to crowd together. **5** *fam* to live together.
amor **1** *m* (*gen*) love: *amor a los padres,* love for one's parents; *amor a la pintura,* love of painting; *es mi amor,* she's my love. **2** (*cuidado*) loving care; (*devoción*) devotion: *lo arregló con mucho amor,* she mended it lovingly. – **3** **amores,** *mpl* (*asuntos*) love affairs, loves.
● **al amor de la lumbre,** by the fireside. ‖ **amor con amor se paga,** one good turn deserves another. ‖ **con/de mil amores,** *fam* willingly, with pleasure. ‖ **hacer el amor,** to make love. ‖ **por amor al arte,** *fam* for the sake of it. ‖ **¡por el amor de Dios!,** for God's sake! ■ **amor cortés,** courtly love. ‖ **amor libre,** free love. ‖ **amor propio,** self-esteem.
amoragar *t* to barbecue.
▲ *Conjugation model* [7], *like llegar.*
amoral *adj* amoral.
amoralidad *f* amorality.
amoratado,-a **1** *pp* → **amoratarse.** – **2** *adj* (*de frío*) blue with cold. **3** (*de un golpe*) bruised, black and blue.
amoratarse **1** *p* (*por frío*) to turn blue. **2** (*por un golpe*) to turn black and blue.
amorcillo *m* Cupid.
amordazar *t* (*persona*) to gag; (*perro*) to muzzle.
▲ *Conjugation model* [4], *like realizar.*
amorfo,-a **1** *adj* amorphous. **2** *fig* (*persona*) characterless, insipid, weak.
amorío *m* love affair, fling.

amorosamente *adv* lovingly.
amoroso,-a *adj* loving, affectionate.
amortajamiento *m* shrouding.
amortajar *t* to shroud, wrap in a shroud.
amortiguación *f* (*de golpe*) cushioning; (*de dolor*) alleviation, easing; (*de ruido*) muffling; (*de luz*) subduing, dimming.
amortiguador,-ra 1 *adj* (*de golpe*) cushioning, softening; (*de dolor*) alleviating, mitigating; (*de ruido*) muffling; (*de luz*) subduing. – **2 amortiguador,** *m* AUTO shock absorber. **3** TÉC damper.
amortiguamiento *m* → **amortiguación**.
amortiguar *t* (*golpe*) to cushion; (*dolor*) to alleviate, ease, soothe; (*ruido*) to muffle; (*luz*) to subdue, dim.
▲ *Conjugation model* [22], *like* **averiguar**.
amortizable *adj* redeemable.
amortización 1 *f* (*pago*) redemption. **2** (*recuperación*) amortization, depreciation, writing off.
amortizar 1 *t* (*pagar*) to repay, pay off. **2** (*recuperar - lo pagado*) to get one's money's worth out of; (*- lo invertido*) to get a return on, recoup: *después de poco tiempo ya habíamos amortizado el lavaplatos,* we soon got our money's worth out of the dishwasher, the dishwasher soon paid for itself.
▲ *Conjugation model* [4], *like* **realizar**.
amoscarse *p fam* to get angry.
▲ *Conjugation model* [1], *like* **sacar**.
amostazar *t fam* to make angry, annoy.
▲ *Conjugation model* [4], *like* **realizar**.
amotinado,-a 1 *pp* → **amotinar**. – **2** *adj* rebel, riotous, insurgent. **3** MIL mutinous. – **4** *m,f* rioter, insurgent. **5** MIL mutineer.
amotinamiento *m* (*civil*) riot, rioting; (*militar*) mutiny; (*político*) insurrection.
amotinar 1 *t* to incite to rebellion. **2** MIL to incite to mutiny. – **3 amotinarse,** *p* to rebel, rise up, riot. **4** MIL to mutiny.
amovible *adj* removable, detachable.
amovilidad *f* removability, detachability.
ampararse 1 *t* (*proteger*) to protect, shelter. **2** (*ayudar*) to help; (*favorecer*) to favour (US favor). – **3 ampararse,** *p* (*protegerse*) to take shelter, protect os. **4** (*acogerse*) to avail os. of the protection (**en,** of), seek protection (**en,** in).
amparo *m* protection, shelter.
● **al amparo de,** under the protection of.
ampelis *m* waxwing.
▲ *pl* **ampelis**.
amperaje *m* amperage.
ampere *m* → **amperio**.
amperímetro *m* ammeter.
amperio *m* ampère.
ampliable *adj* (*gen*) extendable, expandable: *un capital inicial de 500.000 pesetas, ampliable a 5.000.000,* a starting capital of 500,000 pesetas which may be increased to 5,000,000.
ampliación 1 *f* enlargement, extension. **2** ARQ extension. **3** (*fotografía*) enlargement.
■ **ampliación de capital,** increase in capital. ‖ **ampliación de estudios,** furthering of studies.
ampliado,-a 1 *pp* → **ampliar**. – **2** *adj* ARQ extended. **3** (*fotografía*) enlarged.
ampliadora *f* enlarger.
ampliamente *adv* largely.
ampliar 1 *t* to enlarge, extend. **2** ARQ to build an extension onto. **3** (*fotografía*) to enlarge. **4** (*capital*) to in-

crease. **5** (*estudios*) to further. **6** (*tema, idea*) to develop, expand on.
▲ *Conjugation model* [13], *like* **desviar**.
amplificación *f* amplification.
amplificador,-ra 1 *adj* amplifying. – **2 amplificador,** *m* amplifier.
amplificar *t* to amplify.
▲ *Conjugation model* [1], *like* **sacar**.
amplio,-a 1 *adj* (*extenso*) large: *amplia mayoría,* large majority. **2** (*espacioso*) roomy, spacious. **3** (*ancho*) wide, broad. **4** (*holgado*) loose.
● **en el sentido más amplio de la palabra,** in the broadest sense of the word.
amplitud 1 *f* (*extensión*) extent, range. **2** (*espacio*) room, space, spaciousness. **3** (*anchura*) width. **4** (*holgadura*) looseness. **5** FÍS amplitude.
● **de gran amplitud,** *fig* far-reaching.
■ **amplitud de miras,** broad-mindedness.
ampolla 1 *f* MED blister. **2** (*burbuja*) bubble. **3** (*vasija*) flask, bottle. **4** (*tubito*) ampoule, phial.
ampulosidad *f* pomposity, bombast.
ampuloso,-a *adj* inflated, pompous, bombastic.
amputación 1 *f* amputation. **2** *fig* cutting out.
amputar 1 *t* to amputate. **2** *fig* to cut out.
Amsterdam *m* Amsterdam.
amueblar *t* to furnish.
● **sin amueblar,** unfurnished.
amuermado,-a 1 *pp* → **amuermar**. – **2** *adj fam* (*aburrido*) bored. **3** (*atontado*) sleepy, dopey, groggy. **4** (*deprimido*) down, depressed.
amuermar 1 *t fam* (*aburrir*) to bore. **2** (*atontar*) to make feel sleepy, make feel dopey, make feel groggy. **3** (*deprimir*) to depress, get down. – **4 amuermarse,** *p* (*aburrirse*) to get bored. **5** (*atontarse*) to feel sleepy, feel dopey, feel groggy. **6** (*deprimirse*) to get depressed.
amujerado,-a *adj* effeminate.
amulatado,-a *adj* like a mulatto.
amuleto *m* amulet, charm.
■ **amuleto de la suerte,** lucky charm.
amura 1 *f* (*proa*) bow. **2** (*cabo*) tack.
amurallado,-a 1 *pp* → **amurallar**. – **2** *adj* walled.
amurallar *t* to wall.
amurriarse *p* to get angry.
▲ *Conjugation model* [12], *like* **cambiar**.
anabaptismo *m* Anabaptism.
anabaptista 1 *adj* Anabaptist. – **2** *mf* Anabaptist.
anabólico,-a *adj* anabolic.
anabolismo *m* anabolism.
anabolizante *adj* anabolic.
anacarado,-a *adj* pearly.
anacardo *m* (*árbol*) cashew tree; (*fruto*) cashew nut.
anacoluto *m* anacoluthon.
anaconda *f* anaconda.
anacoreta *mf* anchorite, anchoret.
anacrónico,-a *adj* anachronistic, anachronic.
anacronismo *m* anachronism.
ánade *m* duck.
■ **ánade friso,** gadwall. ‖ **ánade rabudo,** pintail. ‖ **ánade real,** mallard. ‖ **ánade silbón,** wigeon.
anaerobio,-a 1 *adj* anaerobic. – **2 anaerobio,** *m* anaerobe, anaerobium.
anáfora *f* anaphora.
anagrama *m* anagram.
anal *adj* anal.
anales *mpl* annals.

analfabetismo *m* illiteracy.
analfabeto,-a 1 *adj* illiterate. **2** *fig* stupid. **– 3** *m,f* illiterate person. **4** *fig* stupid person, ignoramous: *es una analfabeta,* she's stupid.
analgesia *f* analgesia.
analgésico,-a 1 *adj* analgesic. **– 2 analgésico,** *m* analgesic, painkiller.
análisis *m* analysis.
■ análisis de orina, urine test. ‖ análisis de sangre, blood test.
▲ *pl análisis.*
analista *mf* analyst.
analítica *f →* **analítico,-a.**
analíticamente *adv* analytically.
analítico,-a 1 *adj* analytic, analytical. **– 2 analítica,** *f* analytics.
analizable *adj* analyzable.
analizador,-ra 1 *adj* analyzing. **– 2 analizador,** *m* analyzer.
analizar *t* to analyze.
▲ *Conjugation model* [4], *like realizar.*
análogamente *adv* analogously.
analogía *f* analogy.
analógicamente *adv* analogically.
analógico,-a *adj* analogical.
analogismo *m* analogism.
análogo,-a *adj* analogous, similar.
ananá *f* pineapple.
▲ *pl ananaes.*
ananás *f* pineapple.
▲ *pl ananases.*
anaquel *m* shelf.
anaranjado,-a 1 *adj* orangey. **– 2 anaranjado,** *m* orangey colour (us color).
anarco *mf fam* anarchist.
anarcosindicalismo *m* anarcho-syndicalism.
anarquía *f* anarchy.
anárquicamente *adv* anarchically.
anárquico,-a *adj* anarchic, anarchical.
anarquismo *m* anarchism.
anarquista 1 *adj* anarchist. **– 2** *mf* anarchist.
anarquizante *adj* anarchistic.
anatema *m* anathema.
● lanzar anatemas contra, to curse, hurl abuse at.
anatematizar 1 *t* to anathematize. **2** *fig* to curse.
▲ *Conjugation model* [4], *like realizar.*
anatomía *f* anatomy.
anatómicamente *adv* anatomically.
anatómico,-a *adj* anatomical, anatomic.
anatomista *mf* anatomist.
anca *f* haunch.
■ ancas de rana, frogs' legs.
▲ *Takes el in singular.*
ancestral *adj* ancestral, ancient.
ancestro *m* ancestor.
ancho,-a 1 *adj* (gen) broad, wide. **2** (prenda - holgada) loose-fitting; (- grande) too big: *me gusta la ropa ancha,* I like loose fitting clothes; *la falda le está ancha,* the skirt is too big for her. **– 3 ancho,** *m* (anchura) breadth, width: *¿qué ancho tiene?,* how wide is it?; *tiene cuatro metros de ancho,* it's four metres wide. **4** (en costura) width.
● a sus anchas, *fam* comfortable, at ease. ‖ a lo ancho, breadthwise, across. ‖ estar más ancho,-a que largo,-a, to be full of os. ‖ estar muy ancho,-a, to

have plenty of space, have plenty of room. ‖ **ponerse más ancho,-a que largo,-a,** to swell with pride. ‖ **quedarse tan ancho,-a,** *fam* to behave as if nothing had happened, not bat an eyelid.
anchoa *f* anchovy.
anchura *f* breadth, width.
■ anchura de pecho/cintura/caderas, bust/waist/hip measurement.
anchuroso,-a *adj* wide, broad; (espacioso) spacious.
ancianidad *f* old age.
anciano,-a 1 *adj* very old, elderly, aged. **– 2** *m,f* old person, elderly person. **– 3 los ancianos,** *mpl* old people, the elderly.
ancla *f* anchor.
● echar anclas, to drop anchor.
▲ *Takes el in singular.*
anclaje 1 *m* MAR anchorage. **2** TÉC anchor.
anclar 1 *i* MAR to anchor. **– 2** *t* TÉC to anchor.
áncora *f* anchor.
▲ *Takes el in singular.*
ancorar *t-i →* **anclar.**
andadas *fpl fam* old ways.
● volver a las andadas, to go back to one's old tricks.
andaderas *fpl* baby-walker *sing.*
andado,-a 1 *pp →* **andar. – 2** *adj* (común) common. **3** (gastado) worn out.
andador,-ra 1 *adj* (aficionado) fond of walking; (rápido) fast-walking. **– 2** *m,f* (bueno) good walker; (rápido) fast walker. **– 3 andador,** *m* (para niños) baby-walker; (para viejos) walking frame.
andadura 1 *f* (viaje) journey. **2** (trayectoria - de persona) career; (- de organización etc) activity, functioning: *este libro resume la andadura de la asociación,* this book summarizes the activities of the association.
● iniciar su andadura / comenzar su andadura, (persona) to start out; (organización) to start up: *inició su andadura teatral como figurante,* he began his theatrical career as an extra, he started out in the theatre as an extra; *la cooperativa inició su andadura en 1987,* the cooperative started up in 1987.
Andalucía *f* Andalusia.
andalucismo 1 *m* LING (palabra) Andalusian word; (expresión) Andalusian expression. **2** POL Andalusian nationalism.
andalucista *adj* Andalusian nationalist.
andalusí *adj* of Moorish Spain.
andaluz,-za 1 *adj* Andalusian. **– 2** *m,f* (persona) Andalusian. **– 3 andaluz,** *m* (dialecto) Andalusian.
andamiaje *m* scaffolding.
andamio *m* scaffold.
andana *f* row, line.
● llamarse andana, *fam* to wash one's hands of a matter.
andanada 1 *f* MAR broadside. **2** (represión) reprimand, rebuke. **3** (en plaza de toros) covered stand.
● echar/soltar una andanada, *fig* to say sth. out of the blue.
andante 1 *adj* walking. **– 2** *m* MÚS andante.
■ caballero andante, knight errant.
andanza 1 *f* event, occurrence. **2 andanzas,** *fpl* adventures.
andar 1 *i* (moverse) to walk: *andaba por la calle principal,* I was walking along the main street; *está cerca, iremos andando,* it's not far, we'll walk. **2** (trasladarse) to move: *este coche anda despacio,* this car goes very slowly. **3** (funcionar) to work, run, go: *este reloj no anda,* this

watch doesn't work; *el coche anda muy bien,* the car goes very well. **4** (*estar*) to be: *¿cómo andas?,* how are you?, how's it going?; *anda por los cincuenta,* he's around fifty years old; *¿cómo andas de dinero?,* how are you for money? **5** (*juntarse*) to mix (**con,** with). – **6** *t* to walk: *no puede andar ni cien metros,* she can't even walk a hundred yards. – **7** *m* walk, gait. – **8** ¡*anda!, interj* well!, oh!; ¡*anda ya!,* come off it!; *bésame, anda,* go on, give me a kiss.

● andar a gatas, to crawl. ‖ no andarse con rodeos, to get straight to the point. ‖ andar de puntillas, to tiptoe. ‖ andar con cien ojos, to keep one's wits about one. ‖ andar con rodeos, to beat about the bush. ‖ andar con cuidado / andarse con cuidado, to be careful. ‖ andar por las nubes, to be absent-minded. ‖ andarse por las ramas, *fig* to beat about the bush. ‖ dime con quién andas y te diré quién eres, a man is known by the company he keeps. ‖ todo se andará, all in good time.

▲ *Conjugation model* [64].

andares *mpl* walk *sing,* gait *sing.*

andariego,-a **1** *adj* (*que anda*) fond of walking. **2** (*que viaja*) fond of travelling (US traveling). – **3** *m,f* (*andador*) good walker. **4** (*viajero*) person who likes travelling (US traveling).

andarín,-ina **1** *adj* good at walking. – **2** *m,f* good walker, tireless walker.

andas *fpl* portable platform *sing.*

● llevar a algn. en andas, *fig* to pamper sb.

andén *m* platform.

Andes los Andes, *mpl* the Andes.

andino,-a **1** *adj* Andean. – **2** *m,f* Andean.

andoba *mf arg* (*hombre*) guy; (*mujer*) bird.

Andorra *m* Andorra.

andorrano,-a **1** *adj* Andorran. – **2** *m,f* Andorran.

andrajo *m* rag, tatter.

andrajoso,-a *adj* ragged, in tatters.

androceo *m* androecium.

andrógeno *m* androgen.

andrógino,-a *adj* androgynous, androgyne.

androide *m* android.

andrómina *f* lie, trick.

andullo **1** *m* (*hoja*) rolled tobacco leaf. **2** (*manojo*) bunch of tobacco leaves.

andurrial *m* out-of-the-way place.

▲ *Also used in plural with the same meaning.*

anea *f* bulrush, reed mace.

anécdota *f* anecdote.

anecdotario *m* collection of anecdotes.

anecdótico,-a *adj* anecdotic, anecdotal.

anegación *f* flooding.

anegadizo,-a *adj* subject to flooding.

anegamiento *m* → **anegación.**

anegar **1** *t* (*inundar*) to flood. **2** (*ahogar*) to drown. – **3** anegarse, *p* (*inundarse*) to be flooded, flood. **4** (*ahogarse*) to be drowned.

● anegarse en llanto/lágrimas, to fill with tears, dissolve into tears.

▲ *Conjugation model* [7], *like* **llegar.**

anejo,-a **1** *adj* adjoining, attached (**a,** to). – **2** anejo, *m* annexe (US annex).

anélido *m* annelid.

anemia *f* anaemia (US anemia).

anémico,-a **1** *adj* anaemic (US anemic). – **2** *m,f* anaemia (US anemia) sufferer, anaemic (US anemic) person.

anemómetro *m* anemometer.

anemona *f* anemone.

■ anemona de mar, sea anemone.

anémona *f* → **anemona.**

anemone *f* → **anemona.**

anestesia *f* anaesthesia (US anesthesia).

anestesiar *t* to anaesthetize (US anesthetize).

▲ *Conjugation model* [12], *like* **cambiar.**

anestésico,-a **1** *adj* anaesthetic (US anesthetic). – **2** anestésico, *m* anaesthetic (US anesthetic).

anestesista *mf* anaesthetist (US anesthesiologist).

aneurisma *m* aneurysm.

anexar *t* to annex.

anexión *f* annexion, annexation.

anexionar *t* to annex.

anexionismo *m* annexationism, annexionism.

anexionista **1** *adj* annexationist, annexionist. – **2** *mf* annexationist, annexionist.

anexo,-a **1** *adj* adjoining, attached (**a,** to). – **2** anexo, *m* annexe (US annex).

anfeta *m arg* → **anfetamina.**

anfetamina *f* amphetamine.

anfibio,-a **1** *adj* amphibious. – **2** anfibio, *m* amphibian. – **3** los anfibios, *mpl* amphibia *pl.*

anfíbol *m* amphibole.

anfibología *f* amphibology.

anfiteatro **1** *m* amphitheatre (US amphitheater). **2** (*en universidad*) lecture theatre (US theater). **3** CINEM TEAT circle.

anfitrión,-ona *m,f* (*hombre*) host; (*mujer*) hostess.

ánfora *f* amphora.

anfractuosidad **1** *f* (*desigualdad*) roughness. **2** (*torcido*) twisting, turning.

angarillas *fpl* portable platform *sing.*

ángel *m* angel.

● ángel caído, fallen angel. ‖ tener ángel, to be charming.

■ ángel custodio/de la guarda, guardian angel.

angélica *f* angelica.

angelical *adj* angelic, angelical.

angélico,-a *adj* angelic, angelical.

angelito *m fam* (*diminutivo*) little angel.

● estar hecho,-a un angelito, *irón* to be a fine one! ¡menudo angelito está él hecho!, butter wouldn't melt in his mouth!

angelote **1** *m fam* (*niño*) chubby child. **2** *fam* (*adulto*) angel.

ángelus *m* Angelus.

▲ *pl* ángelus.

angina *f* angina.

● tener anginas, to have a sore throat.

■ angina de pecho, angina pectoris.

angioma *m* angioma.

angiospermo,-a **1** *adj* angiospermous. – **2** *f* angiosperma, angiosperm.

anglicanismo *m* Anglicanism.

anglicano,-a **1** *adj* Anglican. – **2** *m,f* Anglican.

■ la Iglesia Anglicana, the Anglican Church, the Church of England.

anglicismo *m* Anglicism.

anglicista *mf* Anglicist, Anglist.

anglo,-a **1** *adj* Anglian. – **2** *m,f* Angle, Anglian.

angloamericano,-a **1** *adj* Anglo-American. – **2** *m,f* Anglo-American.

angloárabe **1** *adj* Anglo-Arab. – **2** *mf* Anglo-Arab.

anglófilo,-a **1** *adj* Anglophile. – **2** *m,f* Anglophile.
anglófobo,-a **1** *adj* Anglophobe. – **2** *m,f* Anglophobe.
anglófono,-a **1** *adj* English-speaking. – **2** *m,f* English speaker.
anglomanía *f* Anglomania.
anglosajón, -ona **1** *adj* Anglo-Saxon. – **2** *m,f* (*persona*) Anglo-Saxon. – **3 anglosajón,** *m* (*idioma*) Anglo-Saxon.
Angola *f* Angola.
angoleño,-a **1** *adj* Angolan. – **2** *m,f* Angolan.
angora *f* angora.
angorina *f* artificial angora.
angosto,-a *adj* narrow.
angostura **1** *f* (*estrechez*) narrowness. **2** (*bebida*) angostura.
angra *f* cove, inlet, creek.
ángstrom *m* angstrom.
angstromio *m* → **ángstrom**.
anguiforme *adj* snake-shaped.
anguila *f* eel.
■ **anguila de mar,** conger eel.
angula *f* elver.
angular *adj* angular.
■ (*objetivo*) **gran angular,** (*fotografía*) wide-angle lens.
ángulo **1** *m* angle: *formar ángulo con,* to be at an angle to. **2** (*rincón*) corner.
● **en ángulo con,** at an angle to.
■ **ángulo de tiro,** elevation. ‖ **ángulo recto,** right angle.
anguloso,-a *adj* angular.
angustia **1** *f* anguish, affliction, distress: *¡qué angustia!,* how distressing! **2** (*física*) sickness, nausea.
■ **angustia vital,** anxiety state, angst.
angustiadamente *adv* with anguish, with distress.
angustiado,-a **1** *pp* → **angustiar**. – **2** *adj* (*afligido*) distressed, upset; (*preocupado*) worried, anxious.
angustiar **1** *t* (*afligir*) to distress, upset. **2** (*preocupar*) to worry, make anxious. – **3 angustiarse,** *p* (*afligirse*) to become distressed, get upset. **4** (*preocuparse*) to worry, get anxious.
▲ *Conjugation model* [12], *like* *cambiar*.
angustioso,-a *adj* (*situación*) distressing, worrying; (*mirada*) anguished.
anhelante *adj* longing, yearning.
anhelar *t* to long for, yearn for: *anhela ser famosa,* she longs to be famous.
anhelo *m* longing, yearning.
anhelosamente *adv* longingly.
anheloso,-a *adj* longing.
anhídrido *m* anhydride.
anhidro,-a *adj* anhydrous.
anidar **1** *i* (*pájaro*) to nest, make one's nest. **2** *fig* to live, dwell: *el miedo anida en su corazón,* fear lingers in her heart. – **3** *t* *fig* to shelter.
anilina *f* aniline, anilin.
anilla **1** *f* (*aro*) ring. – **2 anillas,** *fpl* DEP rings.
■ **anilla de lata,** ringpull.
anillado,-a **1** *pp* → **anillar**. – **2** *adj* (*con anillos*) ringed. **3** (*con forma de anillos*) annular, ring-shaped. **4** (*ave*) ringed. – **5 anillado,** *m* (*ave*) ringing.
anillar **1** *t* (*dar forma*) to make into a ring. **2** (*sujetar*) to ring. **3** (*ave*) to ring.
anillo **1** *m* ring. **2** ASTRON ring. **3** ARQ annulet. **4** (*de gusano*) annulus; (*de culebra*) coil.
● **caérsele a algn. los anillos,** to be beneath sb. ‖ **venir como anillo al dedo,** to be just what sb. needed, suit sb. fine.

■ **anillo de boda,** wedding ring. ‖ **anillo de pedida/ prometida,** engagement ring.
ánima **1** *f* soul. **2** (*de arma*) bore. – **3 ánimas,** *fpl* (*toque*) evening bell *sing*.
■ **ánima bendita,** soul in Purgatory.
▲ *Takes* **el** *in singular.*
animación **1** *f* (*actividad*) activity, movement, bustle. **2** (*viveza*) liveliness: *dar animación,* to liven up. **3** CINEM animation.
animadamente *adv* cheerfully, animatedly.
animado,-a **1** *pp* → **animar**. – **2** *adj* (*movido*) animated, lively, jolly. **3** (*concurrido*) bustling, full of people. **4** (*alegre*) cheerful, in high spirits, excited.
animador,-ra **1** *adj* cheering, encouraging. – **2** *m,f* (*artista*) entertainer. **3** (*de un equipo*) cheerleader.
animadversión *f* antagonism, hostility, ill will, animosity.
● **sentir animadversión por algn.,** to feel hostile towards sb.
animal **1** *adj* animal. **2** *fig* (*basto*) rough; (*necio*) ignorant, stupid; (*grosero*) rude, coarse, uncouth. – **3** *m* animal. **4** *fig* (*basto*) rough person, brute, lout; (*necio*) dunce; (*grosero*) rude person: *¡animal!,* you brute!
■ **animal de carga,** beast of burden. ‖ **animal doméstico,** pet. ‖ **reino animal,** animal kingdom.
animalada *f* (*acción*) stupid thing to do; (*dicho*) stupid thing to say: *eso es una animalada,* that's incredibly stupid.
animalidad *f* animality.
animalizar **1** *t* to animalize. – **2 animalizarse,** *p* (*embrutecerse*) to become stupid, become rude.
▲ *Conjugation model* [4], *like* *realizar.*
animalucho *m* *fam* (*persona*) ugly brute.
animar **1** *t* (*alegrar a algn.*) to cheer up. **2** (*alegrar algo*) to brighten up, liven up. **3** (*alentar*) to encourage. – **4 animarse,** *p* (*persona*) to cheer up. **5** (*fiesta etc*) to brighten up, liven up. **6** (*decidirse*) to make up one's mind: *anímate a venir,* say that you'll come.
anímico,-a *adj*.
■ **estado anímico,** frame of mind, state of mind.
animismo *m* animism.
animista **1** *adj* animistic. – **2** *mf* animist.
ánimo **1** *m* (*espíritu*) spirit; (*mente*) mind; (*alma*) soul. **2** (*intención*) intention, purpose: *sin ánimo de ofender,* no offence intended. **3** (*valor*) courage: *no tengo ánimos de nada,* I don't feel up to anything. **4** (*aliento*) encouragement. – **5** *interj* cheer up!
● **con ánimo de,** with the intention of. ‖ **dar ánimos a algn.,** to encourage sb. ‖ **hacerse el ánimo de,** to get used to the idea of, come to terms with.
■ **estado de ánimo,** frame of mind, state of mind.
animosamente *adv* (*con atrevimiento*) bravely; (*con decisión*) resolutely.
animosidad *f* animosity, ill will, hostility.
animoso,-a *adj* (*atrevido*) brave, courageous; (*decidido*) determined.
aniñado,-a **1** *pp* → **aniñarse**. – **2** *adj* childlike; *pey* childish.
aniñarse *p* to grow childish, become childish.
anión *m* anion.
aniquilación *f* annihilation, destruction.
aniquilador,-ra *adj* annihilating, destructive.
aniquilamiento *m* → **aniquilación**.
aniquilar *t* to annihilate, destroy: *aniquilar al enemigo,* to wipe out the enemy.
anís **1** *m* (*planta*) anise; (*grano*) aniseed. **2** (*bebida*) anisette. **3** (*confite*) aniseed ball.

● **no ser grano de anís,** *fam* to be no trifle.
anisado,-a 1 *pp* → **anisar**. – **2** *adj* flavoured (US flavored) with aniseed.
anisar *t* to flavour (US flavor) with aniseed.
anisete *m* anisette.
aniversario *m* anniversary.
Ankara *f* Ankara.
ano *m* anus.
anoche *adv* (*late*) last night; (*early*) yesterday evening.
● **antes de anoche,** the night before last.
anochecer 1 *i* to get dark: *cuando anocheció,* when it got dark. **2** to be at nightfall, reach at nightfall: *anochecimos en Burgos,* we were in Burgos at dusk. – **3** *m* nightfall, dusk, evening.
● **al anochecer,** at nightfall, at dusk.
▲ *Conjugation model* |43|, *like* **agradecer**; *in 1, used only in the 3rd person; it does not take a subject.*
anochecido,-a 1 *pp* → **anochecer**. – **2** anochecido, *adv* night, dark. – **3** anochecida, *f* nightfall, dusk.
anodinamente *adv* dully, insipidly.
anodino,-a 1 *adj* MED anodyne. **2** (*ineficaz*) ineffective, inefficient. **3** (*soso*) insipid, dull. – **4** anodino, *m* MED anodyne.
ánodo *m* anode.
anomalía *f* anomaly.
anómalo,-a *adj* anomalous.
anona *f* soursop.
anonadación *f* → **anonadamiento**.
anonadamiento *m* (*pasmo*) amazement, astonishment.
anonadante *adj* (*que sorprende*) amazing, astonishing, astounding.
anonadar *t* (*sorprender*) to amaze, astonish, astound, dumbfound, take aback, leave speechless.
anonadado,-a *adj* dumbfounded, speechless.
● **dejar anonadado,-a a algn.,** to dumbfound sb., amaze sb., take sb. aback, leave sb. speechless.
anónimamente *adv* anonymously.
anonimato *m* anonymity.
● **permanecer en el anonimato,** to remain anonymous, remain nameless.
anónimo,-a 1 *adj* (*desconocido*) anonymous. **2** (*sociedad*) limited, US incorporated. – **3** anónimo, *m* (*carta*) anonymous letter; (*obra*) anonymous work. **4** (*anonimato*) anonymity.
anorak *m* anorak.
▲ *pl* anoraks.
anorexia *f* anorexia.
anoréxico,-a *adj* anorexic.
anormal 1 *adj* (*no normal*) abnormal. **2** (*inhabitual*) unusual: *comportamiento anormal,* abnormal behaviour. **3** MED subnormal. – **4** *mf* MED subnormal person.
anormalidad *f* abnormality.
anormalmente *adv* abnormally, unusually.
anotación 1 *f* (*acotación*) annotation. **2** (*nota*) note. **3** (*apunte*) noting.
anotar 1 *t* (*acotar*) to annotate, add notes to. **2** (*apuntar*) to take down, jot down, make a note of.
anovelado,-a *adj* novel-like.
anovulación *f* anovulation.
anovulatorio,-a 1 *adj* anovular, anovulatory. – **2** anovulatorio, *m* anovulant.
anquilosado,-a 1 *pp* → **anquilosar**. – **2** *adj* anchylosed, ankylosed. **3** *fig* stagnated, paralysed.
anquilosamiento 1 *m* anchylosis, ankylosis. **2** *fig* stagnation, paralysis.

anquilosar 1 *t* to anchylose, ankylose. – **2** anquilosarse, *p* to anchylose, ankylose. **3** *fig* to stagnate, be paralysed.
anquilosis *f* anchylosis, ankylosis.
▲ *pl* anquilosis.
anquilostoma *f* hookworm.
ánsar *m* goose.
■ **ánsar común,** greylag goose.
ansia 1 *f* (*ansiedad*) anxiety; (*angustia*) anguish. **2** (*deseo*) eagerness, longing, yearning: *tener ansia de poder,* to be longing for power. **3** MED sick feeling.
▲ *Takes* **el** *in singular.*
ansiado,-a 1 *pp* → **ansiar**. – **2** *adj* longed-for.
ansiar *t* to long for, yearn for: *ansiaba la paz,* she longed for peace.
▲ *Conjugation model* |13|, *like* **desviar**.
ansiedad 1 *f* anxiety. **2** MED nervous tension.
● **con ansiedad,** anxiously.
ansiosamente 1 *adv* (*con desasosiego*) anxiously, desperately. **2** (*con deseo*) eagerly, longingly. **3** (*con avaricia*) greedily.
ansioso,-a 1 *adj* (*desasosegado*) anguished, anxious, desperate. **2** (*deseoso*) eager, longing (**por/de,** to): *estaba ansioso de verla,* he couldn't wait to see her, he was dying to see her. **3** (*avaricioso*) greedy, covetous.
anta *f* elk, moose.
antagónico,-a *adj* antagonistic.
antagonismo *m* antagonism.
antagonista 1 *adj* antagonistic. – **2** *mf* antagonist.
antaño *adv* formerly, in olden times, long ago: *las costumbres de antaño,* age-old traditions.
antañón,-ona *adj fam* very old.
Antártida *f* Antarctica.
ante[1] 1 *prep* before, in the presence of. **2** (*considerando*) in the face of: *ante estas circunstancias,* under the circumstances.
● **ante todo,** (*primero*) first of all; (*por encima de*) above all.
ante[2] 1 *m* ZOOL elk, moose. **2** (*piel*) suede.
anteanoche *adv* the night before last.
anteayer *adv* the day before yesterday.
antebrazo *m* forearm.
antecámara *f* antechamber, anteroom.
antecedente 1 *adj* antecedent, previous, preceeding. – **2** *m* precedent. **3** GRAM antecedent. **4** MED history. – **5** antecedentes, *mpl* record *sing*.
● **estar en antecedentes,** to be well informed. ‖ **poner en antecedentes,** to put in the picture. ‖ **tener malos antecedentes,** to have a bad record.
■ **antecedentes penales,** criminal record *sing*, police record *sing*, record *sing*: *el acusado no tiene antecedentes penales,* the accused has no previous convictions.
anteceder *t* to precede, come before.
antecesor,-ra 1 *m,f* (*en un cargo*) predecessor. **2** (*antepasado*) ancestor.
antecocina *f* scullery.
antedata *f* antedate.
antedatar *t* to antedate.
antedicho,-a 1 *adj* aforesaid, aforementioned. – **2** *m,f* person mentioned before, aforementioned person.
antediluviano,-a 1 *adj* antediluvian. **2** *fig* as old as the hills.
antefirma *f fml* title of signatory.
antelación *f* precedence: *con cinco días de antelación,* five days beforehand.

● **con antelación,** in advance. ‖ **con antelación a,** before, prior to. ‖ **con la debida antelación,** *fml* well in advance, in good time. ‖ **con mucha antelación,** long in advance, long beforehand, in good time. ‖ **con poca antelación,** at short notice.

antemano de antemano, *loc adv* beforehand, in advance.

antemeridiano,-a *adj* ante meridiem.

antena 1 *f* RAD TV aerial, antenna. 2 ANAT antenna, feeler.
● **estar en antena,** to be on the air.
■ **antena parabólica,** satellite dish.

anteojeras *fpl* blinkers, us blinders.

anteojo 1 *m* telescope. – 2 **anteojos,** *mpl* (*binóculos*) binoculars, field glasses. 3 (*gafas*) glasses, spectacles.

antepalco *m* anteroom to a box in a theatre.

antepasado,-a 1 *adj* previous, prior. – 2 **antepasado,** *m* ancestor. – 3 **antepasados,** *mpl* forefathers, forbears.

antepatio *m* forecourt.

antepecho 1 *m* (*pretil*) parapet, guardrail. 2 (*de ventana*) windowsill.

antepenúltimo,-a *adj* antepenultimate: *el episodio antepenúltimo,* the second from last episode.

anteponer 1 *t* (*poner delante*) to place in front (**a**, of), put in front (**a**, of); (*poner antes*) to put before. 2 (*preferir*) to prefer (**a**, to).
▲ *Conjugation model* [78], *like* ***poner****; pp* ***antepuesto,-a***.

anteportada *f* half title.

anteproyecto 1 *m* preliminary plan, draft. 2 JUR first draft, discussion document.
■ **anteproyecto de ley,** draft bill.

antepuesto,-a *pp* → **anteponer**.

antepuse *pt indef* → **anteponer**.

antera *f* anther.

anterior 1 *adj* (*tiempo*) previous, preceding, before: *el día anterior,* the day before; *la noche anterior al examen,* the night before the exam. 2 (*lugar*) front: *la parte anterior,* the front part. – 3 *mf* the previous one.

anterioridad *f* priority.
● **con anterioridad,** previously. ‖ **con anterioridad a,** prior to, before.

anteriormente *adv* previously, before.

antes 1 *adv* (*tiempo*) before, earlier: *llámame antes de salir,* ring me before you leave; *llegué antes que él,* I arrived before him; *antes del partido,* before the match; *deberías estar allí antes de las nueve,* you should be there before nine; *bébete el café antes de que se enfríe,* drink your coffee before it gets cold. 2 (*en el pasado*) before, in the past. 3 (*lugar*) in front, before. – 4 *conj* on the contrary, quite the opposite, rather: *no la aborrece, antes la ama,* he doesn't hate her, on the contrary he loves her. – 5 *adj* before.
● **antes bien,** on the contrary: *no se acobardó, antes bien se encaró con su enemigo,* he didn't shrink back, on the contrary, he stood up to his enemy. ‖ **antes de J.C.,** before Christ. ‖ **antes de nada,** first of all. ‖ **lo antes posible,** as soon as possible.

antesala *f* anteroom, antechamber.
● **hacer antesala,** to wait. ‖ **en la antesala de,** *fig* on the verge of.

antever 1 *t* (*ver antes*) to see before. 2 (*prever*) to foresee.
▲ *Conjugation model* [91], *like* ***ver****; pp* ***antevisto,-a***.

antevíspera *f* two days before.

antevisto *pp* → **antever**.

antiabortista 1 *adj* anti-abortionist. – 2 *mf* anti-abortionist, antiabortion compaigner.

antiácido,-a 1 *adj* antacid. – 2 **antiácido,** *m* antacid.

antiadherente *adj* nonstick.

antiaéreo,-a *adj* anti-aircraft.

antialcohólico,-a 1 *adj* teetotal. – 2 *m,f* teetotaller.

antialcoholismo *m* antialcoholism.

antiatómico,-a *adj* fall-out: *refugio antiatómico,* fall-out shelter.

antibalas *adj* bullet-proof.

antibiótico,-a 1 *adj* antibiotic. – 2 **antibiótico,** *m* antibiotic.

anticanceroso,-a *adj* anti-cancer.

anticarro *adj* antitank.

anticatarral *adj* anticatarrhal.

anticiclón *m* anticyclone, high pressure area.

anticiclónico,-a *adj* anticyclonic.

anticipación *f* anticipation, advance.
● **con anticipación,** in advance.

anticipadamente *adv* in advance.

anticipado,-a 1 *pp* → **anticipar**. – 2 *adj* brought forward; (*temprano*) early: *gracias anticipadas,* thanks in advance; *pago anticipado,* advance, advance payment.
● **por anticipado,** COM in advance.

anticipar 1 *t* to anticipate, advance, bring forward. 2 (*dinero*) to advance. – 3 **anticiparse,** *p* (*llegar antes*) to come early. 4 (*adelantarse*) to beat to it: *él se me anticipó,* he beat me to it.

anticipo 1 *m* foretaste, preview. 2 (*adelanto*) advance, advance payment.

anticlerical 1 *adj* anticlerical. – 2 *mf* anticlerical.

anticlericalismo *m* anticlericalism.

anticlinal *m* anticline.

anticoagulante 1 *adj* anticoagulant. – 2 **anticoagulante,** *m* anticoagulant.

anticomunismo *m* anticommunism.

anticomunista 1 *adj* anticommunist. – 2 *mf* anticommunist.

anticoncepción *f* contraception.

anticonceptivo,-a 1 *adj* contraceptive. – 2 **anticonceptivo,** *m* contraceptive.

anticonformismo *m* non-conformism.

anticonformista 1 *adj* non-conformist. – 2 *mf* non-conformist.

anticongelante 1 *adj* antifreeze. – 2 **anticongelante,** *m* antifreeze.

anticonstitucionalmente *adv* unconstitutionally.

anticonstitucional *adj* unconstitutional.

anticorrosivo,-a 1 *adj* anticorrosive. – 2 **anticorrosivo,** *m* anticorrosive.

anticristo *m* Antichrist.

anticuado,-a *adj* antiquated, old-fashioned, obsolete, out-of-date.

anticuario *m* (*conocedor*) antiquary, antiquarian; (*comerciante*) antique dealer.

anticuarse *p* to become antiquated, become obsolete.
▲ *Conjugation model* [10], *like* ***adecuar***.

anticuerpo *m* antibody.

antidemocrático,-a *adj* (*no democrático*) undemocratic; (*que ataca la democracia*) antidemocratic.

antideportivo,-a *adj* unsportsmanlike, unsporting.

antidepresivo,-a 1 *adj* antidepressant. – 2 **antidepresivo,** *m* antidepressant.

antideslizante 1 *adj* (*neumático*) anti-skid; (*suelo*) non-slip. – 2 *m* anti-skid device.

antideslumbrante *adj* anti-glare, anti-dazzle.

antidetonante *adj* antiknock.

antidiabético,-a 1 *adj* antidiabetic. − **2 antidiabético,** *m* diabetic preparation.
antidoping *adj* anti-doping, anti-drug.
antídoto *m* antidote.
antidroga *adj* anti-drug.
antieconómico,-a *adj* uneconomical.
antiespasmódico,-a *adj* antispasmodic.
antiestético,-a *adj* ugly, unsightly, unattractive.
antifascismo *m* anti-fascism.
antifascista *mf* anti-fascist.
antifaz *m* mask.
antifebril *adj* antifebrile.
antifederal *adj* antifederal.
antifeminismo *m* antifeminism.
antifeminista *adj* antifeminist.
antífona *f* antiphon.
antigás máscara/careta antigás, *f* gas mask.
antígeno,-a 1 *adj* antigenic. − **2 antígeno,** *m* antigen.
antigripal 1 *adj* flu. − **2** *m* flu remedy.
Antigua *f* Antigua.
antigualla *f pey* antique, relic.
antiguamente *adv* in the old days, in the past.
antigubernamental *adj* anti-government.
antigüedad 1 *f* (*período*) antiquity: *este jarrón tiene 200 años de antigüedad,* this vase is 200 years old. **2** (*en empleo*) seniority. **3** (*objeto*) antique.
● en la antigüedad, in olden days, in former times.
■ tienda de antigüedades, antique shop.
antigüeño,-a 1 *adj* Antiguan. − **2** *m,f* Antiguan.
antiguo,-a 1 *adj* (*gen*) ancient, old; (*coche*) vintage, old. **2** (*en empleo*) senior. **3** (*pasado*) old-fashioned. **4** (*anterior*) former: *el antiguo primer ministro,* the former Prime Minister. − **5 los antiguos,** *mpl* the ancients.
● a la antigua, in an old-fashioned way. ‖ de antiguo, since ancient times.
antihéroe *m* antihero.
antihigiénico,-a *adj* unhygienic, unhealthy.
antihistamínico,-a 1 *adj* antihistamine. − **2 antihistamínico,** *m* antihistamine.
antiimperialismo *m* anti-imperialism.
antiinflacionista *adj* anti-inflationary.
antiinflamatorio,-a 1 *adj* anti-inflammatory. − **2 antiinflamatorio,** *m* anti-inflammatory.
Antillas *fpl* Antilles.
■ Grandes Antillas, Greater Antilles. ‖ Pequeñas Antillas, Lesser Antilles.
antilogaritmo *m* antilogarithm.
antílope *m* antelope.
antimagnético,-a *adj* antimagnetic.
antimateria *f* antimatter.
antimilitarismo *m* antimilitarism.
antimilitarista 1 *adj* antimilitarist, antimilitaristic. **2** *mf* antimilitarist.
antimísil 1 *adj* antimissile. − **2** *m* antimissile.
antimonárquico,-a *adj* antimonarchical.
antimonio *m* antimony.
antinatural *adj* unnatural, contrary to nature.
antiniebla luces antiniebla, *fpl* foglamps.
▲ *pl* antiniebla.
antinomia *f* antinomy.
antinómico,-a *adj* antinomic.
antinuclear *adj* antinuclear.
antioxidante 1 *adj* (*para alimentos*) antioxidant; (*para metales*) antirust. − **2** *m* (*para alimentos*) antioxidant; (*para metales*) antirust substance.

antipapa *m* antipope.
antiparlamentario,-a *adj* antiparliamentary.
antiparras *fpl fam* specs, glasses.
antipatía *f* antipathy, dislike, aversion.
● coger antipatía a algn., to take a dislike to sb. ‖ tener antipatía a algn., to dislike sb.
antipático,-a 1 *adj* unfriendly, unpleasant, unkind: *Eva me cae antipática,* I don't like Eva. − **2** *m,f* unpleasant person.
antipatriota *mf* unpatriotic person.
antipatriótico,-a *adj* unpatriotic.
antipedagógico,-a *adj* pedagogically unsound.
antipirético,-a 1 *adj* antipyretic. − **2 antipirético,** *m* antipyretic.
antípoda 1 *adj* antipodean, antipodal. − **2** *mf* (*persona*) antipodean. − **3** *m* & *f* (*punto*) antipode, antipodes *pl.*
▲ In 3 also used in plural with the same meaning.
antiprogresista *adj* 1 antiprogressive. **2** *mf* antiprogressive person.
antiquísimo,-a *adj* very old, ancient.
antirrábico,-a *adj* anti-rabies, anti-rabic.
antirreglamentario,-a *adj* DEP against the rules.
antirrepublicano,-a *adj* anti-Republican.
antirreumático,-a 1 *adj* anti-rheumatoid. − **2 antirreumático,** *m* anti-rheumatoid drug.
antirrevolucionario,-a 1 *adj* antirevolutionary. − **2** *m,f* antirevolutionary.
antirrobo *adj* anti-theft.
■ alarma antirrobo, (*para casa*) burglar alarm; (*para coche*) anti-theft device, car alarm.
▲ *pl* antirrobo.
antisemita 1 *adj* anti-Semitic. − **2** *mf* anti-Semite.
antisemítico,-a *adj* anti-Semitic.
antisemitismo *m* anti-Semitism.
antiséptico,-a 1 *adj* antiseptic. − **2 antiséptico,** *m* antiseptic.
antisísmico,-a *adj* earthquake-proof.
antisocial *adj* 1 antisocial. **2** *mf* antisocial person.
antitanque *adj* antitank.
▲ *pl* antitanque.
antiterrorista *adj* antiterrorist.
antítesis *f* antithesis.
▲ *pl* antítesis.
antitetánico,-a 1 *adj* anti-tetanus. − **2 antitetánica,** *f* tetanus injection.
antitético,-a *adj* antithetic, antithetical.
antitóxico,-a *adj* antitoxic.
antitoxina *f* antitoxin.
antituberculoso,-a *adj* antitubercular.
antivirus 1 *m* (*fármaco*) antiviral drug. **2** INFORM antivirus.
antojadizo,-a *adj* capricious, fanciful, whimsical.
antojarse 1 *p* (*encapricharse*) to feel like, fancy, take a fancy to: *se le antojó un patinete,* she fancied a scooter; *cuando se le antoje,* when he feels like it, when it appeals to him. **2** (*suponer*) to think, imagine, suppose, seem: *se me antoja que no vendrá,* I have the feeling that she won't come.
● hacer lo que se le antoja, to do what one fancies.
antojo 1 *m* (*capricho*) whim, fancy; (*de embarazada*) craving. **2** (*en la piel*) birthmark.
● a su (*mi, tu, etc*) antojo, arbitrarily.
antología *f* anthology.
● de antología, *fig* remarkable, outstanding.
antológico,-a *adj* anthological.
antonimia *f* antonymy.

antónimo,-a 1 *adj* antonymous. – **2 antónimo,** *m* antonym.

antonomasia *f* antonomasia.
● **por antonomasia,** par excellence.

antorcha 1 *f* torch. **2** *fig* guiding light.

antracita *f* anthracite.

ántrax *m* anthrax.
▲ *pl* **ántrax.**

antro 1 *m* (*caverna*) cavern. **2** (*tugurio*) dump, hole, dive.
■ **antro de perdición,** den of vice.

antropocéntrico,-a *adj* anthropocentric.

antropocentrismo *m* anthropocentrism.

antropofagia *f* anthropophagy, cannibalism.

antropófago,-a 1 *adj* anthropophagic, cannibalistic. – **2** *m,f* anthropophagite, cannibal.

antropoide 1 *adj* anthropoid, anthropoidal. – **2** *mf* anthropoid.

antropología *f* anthropology.

antropológico,-a *adj* anthropological.

antropólogo,-a *m,f* anthropologist.

antropomórfico,-a *adj* anthropomorphic.

antropomorfismo *m* anthropomorphism.

antropomorfo,-a 1 *adj* anthropomorphic. – **2** *m,f* anthropomorphist.

antroponimia *f* anthroponymy.

antropónimo *m* anthroponym.

anual *adj* annual, yearly: *gastos anuales,* yearly expenses.

anualidad *f* annual payment, annuity.

anualmente *adv* annually, yearly.

anuario *m* yearbook.

anubarrado,-a *adj* cloudy, overcast.

anublar *t* to cloud (over).

anudadura 1 *f* (*acción*) knotting, tying, fastening. **2** (*nudo*) knot.

anudamiento *m* → **anudadura.**

anudar 1 *t* (*atar*) to knot, tie, fasten. **2** *fig* to join, tie together. – **3 anudarse,** *p* to tie, knot.
● **anudarse la voz/lengua,** to become tongue-tied.

anuencia *f* consent, approval.

anuente *adj* consenting, consentient.

anulable *adj* cancellable (US cancelable).

anulación 1 *f* (*gen*) annulment, cancellation; (*de ley*) repeal; (*de sentencia*) quashing, overturning. **2** DEP (*de gol*) disallowing.
■ **anulación de matrimonio,** annulment of marriage.

anular¹ 1 *adj* ring-shaped. – **2** *m* ring finger.

anular² 1 *t* (*matrimonio*) to annul; (*una ley*) to repeal; (*una sentencia*) to quash. **2** (*un pedido, viaje*) to cancel; (*un contrato*) to invalidate, cancel. **3** DEP (*un gol*) to disallow. **4** *fig* (*desautorizar*) to deprive of authority. – **5 anularse,** *p* to lose one's authority.

anunciación *f* REL Annunciation.

anunciador,-ra 1 *adj* announcing. **2** (*publicidad*) advertising: *la empresa anunciadora,* the advertising agency. – **3** *m,f* announcer. **4** (*publicista*) advertiser.

anunciante *adj* → **anunciador,-ra.**

anunciar 1 *t* (*avisar*) to announce, make public. **2** (*hacer publicidad*) to advertise. – **3 anunciarse,** *p* to put an advert (**en,** in).
▲ *Conjugation model* [12], *like* **cambiar.**

anuncio 1 *m* (*aviso*) announcement; (*signo*) sign. **2** (*publicidad*) advertisement, advert, ad: *pusimos un anuncio en el diario,* we put an ad in the paper. **3** (*valla publicitaria*) hoarding, US billboard. **4** (*cartel*) poster, notice.

■ **anuncios económicos / anuncios clasificados,** classified adverts, small ads. ‖ **anuncios por palabras,** classified adverts, small ads.

anverso 1 *m* (*de moneda*) obverse. **2** (*de página*) recto.

anzuelo 1 *m* fish-hook. **2** *fig* lure, bait.
● **echar el anzuelo,-a,** to try to hook. ‖ **tragar/morder/picar el anzuelo,** to swallow the bait.

añadido,-a 1 *pp* → **añadir.** – **2** *adj* added. – **3** añadido, *m* (*postizo*) switch, hairpiece. **4** (*añadidura*) addition, addendum.

añadidura *f* addition, addendum.
● **por añadidura,** besides, in addition.

añadir *t* to add (**a,** to): *añádele un poco de sal,* add a bit of salt (to it).

añagaza 1 *f* (*señuelo*) decoy, stool pigeon, lure. **2** *fig* (*ardid*) lure, trick.

añal 1 *adj* (*anual*) annual. **2** (*animal*) year-old. – **3** *mf* (*animal*) yearling.

añejar 1 *t* (*envejecer*) to age. **2** (*vino, queso*) to mature; (*jamón*) to cure. – **3 añejarse,** *p* (*mejorar*) to improve with age, mature. **4** (*estropearse*) to deteriorate.

añejo,-a 1 *adj* (*vino, queso*) mature; (*jamón*) cured. **2** (*viejo*) old.

añicos *mpl* bits, pieces.
● **hacer añicos,** to smash to pieces. ‖ **hacerse añicos,** to shatter, smash to bits.

añil 1 *adj* indigo, blue. – **2** *m* (*arbusto*) indigo plant. **3** (*color*) indigo. **4** (*substancia*) blue.

año 1 *m* year: *el año pasado,* last year; *el año que viene,* next year; *una vez al año,* once a year; *los años sesenta,* the sixties; *en estos últimos años,* in recent years. – **2** *mpl* years, age *sing: ¿cuántos años tienes?,* how old are you?; *tengo 20 años,* I'm 20 years old.
● **del año de la pera/de María Castaña,** old-fashioned, ancient. ‖ **en mis** (*tus, sus, etc*) **años mozos,** in my (*his, her, etc*) youth. ‖ **entrado,-a en años,** getting on. ‖ **estar a años luz de,** *fig* to be miles away from. ‖ **estar de buen año,** to be in good shape. ‖ **hace años,** a long time ago, years ago. ‖ **¡por muchos años!,** (*cumpleaños*) many happy returns!; (*brindis*) here's to your health!
■ **año civil,** calendar year. ‖ **año escolar,** school year. ‖ **año fiscal,** tax year. ‖ **año luz,** light year.

añojo *m* (*becerro*) yearling calf; (*cordero*) yearling lamb.

añoranza *f* longing (**de,** for), yearning (**de,** for), nostalgia (**de,** for): *sentir añoranza de su país,* to be homesick.

añorar 1 *t* (*gen*) to long for, miss, yearn for. **2** (*país*) to be homesick for, miss. **3** (*persona fallecida*) to mourn. – **4** *i* to pine.

añoso,-a *adj* very old, ancient.

aojar *t* to cast the evil eye on.

aorta *f* aorta.

aovado,-a 1 *pp* → **aovar.** – **2** *adj* egg-shapped, oval.

aovar *i* to lay eggs.

aovillarse *p* to curl up.

ap. *abr* (*aparte*) new paragraph.

apabullamiento *m* bewilderment, confusion.

apabullante *adj* (*victoria, éxito*) resounding, overwhelming; (*persona*) overpowering.

apabullar 1 *t* (*dejar confuso*) to bewilder, confuse. **2** (*abrumar*) to overwhelm.

apacentadero *m* pasture.

apacentamiento *m* pasturing, grazing.

apacentar 1 *t* (*pacer*) to graze, put out to pasture. **2** (*alimentar*) to feed. **3** *fig* (*instruir*) to teach. **4** *fig* (*alimentar* *pasiones etc*) to gratify. – **5 apacentarse,** *p* to pasture, graze.

▲ *Conjugation model* |27|, *like* **acertar.**

apache 1 *adj* Apache. – **2** *mf* Apache.

apachurrar *t* to squash, flatten.

apaciaguador,-ra 1 *adj* pacifying. – **2** *m,f* pacifier.

apacibilidad *f* gentleness, calmness, mildness.

apacible *adj* (*pesona*) gentle, calm, placid; (*vida*) quiet, peaceful; (*clima, tiempo*) mild; (*mar*) calm.

apaciguamiento *m* pacification, appeasement.

apaciguar 1 *t* to pacify, appease, placate, calm down. – **2 apaciguarse,** *p* (*persona*) to calm down; (*tormenta*) to abate; (*mar*) to become calm.

▲ *Conjugation model* |22|, *like* **averiguar.**

apadrinamiento 1 *m* (*de bautizo*) function of godfather. **2** (*de boda*) function of best man. **3** (*de duelo*) function of second. **4** (*mecenazgo*) sponsoring, patronage. **5** (*apoyo*) support, backing.

apadrinar 1 *t* (*en bautizo*) to act as godfather to. **2** (*en boda*) to be the best man for. **3** (*en duelo*) to act as second to. **4** (*artista*) to sponsor.

apagadizo,-a *adj* slow to burn.

apagado,-a 1 *pp* → **apagar.** – **2** *adj* (*luz etc*) out, off. **3** (*persona*) spiritless, lifeless. **4** (*voz*) sad; (*mirada*) expressionless, lifeless. **5** (*color*) dull. **6** (*volcán*) extinct.

apagar 1 *t* (*fuego*) to extinguish, put out. **2** (*luz*) to turn out, turn off, put out. **3** (*televisión etc*) to switch off, turn off: *apaga la radio,* turn the radio off. **4** (*color*) to soften. **5** *fig* (*dolor*) to soothe; (*pena*) to heal. **6** *fig* (*sed*) to quench. – **7 apagarse,** *p* (*luz*) to go out; (*televisión*) to go off. **8** (*emoción*) to fade, wane. **9** *fig* (*morirse*) to pass away.

● **apaga y vámonos,** let's call it a day.

▲ *Conjugation model* |7|, *like* **llegar.**

apagavelas *m* candle snuffer.

▲ *pl* **apagavelas.**

apagón *m* power cut, blackout.

apaisado,-a 1 *adj* oblong. **2** INFORM landscape.

apalabrar 1 *t* (*concertar*) to make a verbal agreement on: *apalabrar una venta,* to make a verbal agreement on a sale. **2** (*contratar*) to engage verbally.

Apalaches los (montes) Apalaches, *mpl* the Appalachians.

apalancado,-a 1 *pp* → **apalancar.** – **2** *adj arg* settled.

apalancamiento 1 *m* (*acción*) leverage. **2** *arg* (*pereza*) laziness.

apalancar 1 *t* (*levantar*) to lever up; (*abrir*) to lever open: *apalancó la puerta,* he levered the door open. – **2 apalancarse,** *p arg* to settle os., settle down: *se apalancó ante la tele,* she settled down in front of the telly. **3** *arg* to get stuck in a rut.

▲ *Conjugation model* |1|, *like* **sacar.**

apalanque *m arg* laziness.

apaleado,-a 1 *pp* → **apalear.** – **2** *adj* beaten.

apaleamiento *m* beating, hitting, thrashing.

apalear[1] 1 *t* (*pegar*) to beat, cane, thrash. **2** (*varear*) to thresh.

apalear[2] *t* (*grano*) to winnow.

apaleo 1 *m* (*acción*) winnowing. **2** (*época*) winnowing time.

apantanar *t* to flood.

apañado,-a 1 *pp* → **apañar.** – **2** *adj* (*ordenado*) tidy; (*limpio*) clean; (*arreglado*) well-dressed, smart. **3** (*hábil*) skilful (us skilfull), clever; (*mañoso*) handy. **4** (*apropiado*) suitable.

● **estar apañado,-a / ir apañado,-a,** *fam* to be in for

a shock, have had it: *estamos apañados si no nos llega el dinero,* we've had it if the money doesn't arrive.

apañar 1 *t* (*ordenar*) to tidy; (*limpiar*) to clean. **2** (*recoger*) to collect. **3** *fam* (*robar*) to steal, snatch, nick, lift, swipe. **4** (*ataviar*) to smarten up. **5** (*remendar*) to patch, mend. **6** (*componer*) to fix, arrange: *apañamos una comida,* we threw a a meal together. – **7 apañarse,** *p* to manage, get by, make do: *ya se apañará sola,* she'll manage on her own. **8** to cohabit.

● **apañárselas,** to manage, get by.

apaño 1 *m* (*remiendo, compostura*) repair, mend, patch. **2** (*acuerdo*) agreement, deal. **3** (*habilidad*) skill. **4** *fam* (*lío amoroso*) (love) affair, fling; (*amante*) lover.

● **tener un apaño,** *fam* to have a bit on the side.

aparador 1 *m* (*escaparate*) shop window. **2** (*mueble*) sideboard, cupboard, buffet.

aparato 1 *m* (*mecanismo*) (piece of) apparatus, set; (*eléctrico*) appliance: *aparatos eléctricos,* equipment. **2** (*dispositivo*) device; (*instrumento*) instrument. **3** (*teléfono*) telephone: *está al aparato,* he's on the phone. **4** (*avión*) plane. **5** (*exageración*) exaggeration. **6** (*ostentación*) pomp, display, show: *con mucho aparato,* very pompously. **7** (*tormenta*) flashes of lightning *pl: una tormenta con gran aparato (eléctrico),* a storm with tremendous flashes of lightning.

■ **aparato auditivo,** hearing aid. ‖ **aparato de radio,** radio set. ‖ **aparato de televisión,** television set. ‖ **aparato digestivo,** ANAT digestive system. ‖ **aparato ortopédico,** orthopedic aid. ‖ **el aparato del estado,** the State apparatus.

aparatosamente 1 *adv* (*con ostentación*) showily, ostentatiously. **2** (*con exageración*) with exaggeration.

aparatosidad 1 *f* (*pomposidad*) pomposity, ostentation, showiness, show. **2** (*exageración*) exaggeration.

aparatoso,-a 1 *adj* (*ostentoso*) pompous, showy, ostentatious. **2** (*exagerado*) exaggerated. **3** (*caída, accidente*) spectacular.

aparcacoches *m* doorman, parking attendant.

▲ *pl* **aparcacoches.**

aparcamiento 1 *m* (*acción*) parking. **2** (*en la calle*) place to park, parking place. **3** (*parking*) car park, us parking lot.

aparcar 1 *t* to park. **2** *fig* (*tema*) to put on one side. – **3** *i* to park.

● **"prohibido aparcar",** "no parking".

▲ *Conjugation model* |1|, *like* **sacar.**

aparcería *f* sharecropping.

aparcero,-a *m,f* sharecropper.

apareamiento 1 *m* (*de cosas*) pairing off, matching up. **2** (*de animales*) mating.

aparear 1 *t* (*cosas*) to pair off, match up. **2** (*animales*) to mate. – **3 aparearse,** (*uso recíproco*) to mate.

aparecer 1 *i* to appear: *no aparece en la lista de invitados,* she's not on the guest list. **2** (*dejarse ver*) to show up, turn up: *ya apareció el dinero,* the money finally turned up: *espero que no aparezca por mi casa,* I hope he doesn't show his face near my house. **3** (*en el mercado*) to come out (**en**, onto): *ya ha aparecido su nuevo libro,* her new book has just been published. – **4 aparecerse,** *p* to appear: *se le apareció la Virgen,* the Virgin appeared to her.

▲ *Conjugation model* |43|, *like* **agradecer.**

aparecido,-a 1 *pp* → **aparecer.** – **2** *m,f* ghost, spectre (us specter).

aparejado,-a 1 *pp* → **aparejar.** – **2** *adj* suitable, fit.

● **ir aparejado,-a con,** to go along with. ‖ **llevar/traer aparejado,-a,** to entail.

aparejador,-ra *m,f* (*de obras*) clerk of works; (*perito*) quantity surveyor.

aparejar 1 *t* (*preparar*) to prepare, get ready. 2 (*caballos*) to harness. 3 (*barcos*) to rig out.

aparejo 1 *m* (*equipo*) gear, equipment. 2 (*arreos*) harness. 3 (*jarcias, velas*) rigging. 4 (*polea*) block and tackle. 5 (*en construcción*) bond.
■ aparejo de pesca, fishing tackle.

aparentar 1 *t* (*simular*) to pretend, affect: *aparenta indiferencia,* she pretends not to care, she affects indifference. 2 (*tener aspecto de*) to look: *no aparenta la edad que tiene,* he doesn't look his age. – 3 *i* to show off.

aparente 1 *adj* apparent. 2 (*conveniente*) suitable. 3 (*lucido*) showy, smart.

aparentemente *adv* apparently.

aparición 1 *f* appearance. 2 (*visión*) apparition.

apariencia *f* appearance, aspect.
● en apariencia, apparently, by all appearances. ‖ guardar las apariencias, *fig* to keep up appearances. ‖ tener apariencia de, to look like.

apartado,-a 1 *pp* → **apartar**. – 2 *adj* (*alejado*) remote, distant; (*aislado*) isolated, cut off. 3 (*retirado*) retired: *apartado de la política,* retired from politics. – 4 apartado, *m* post-office box. 5 (*párrafo*) section.
● mantenerse apartado,-a de algo/algn., to keep away from sth./sb.

apartamento *m* small flat, apartment.

apartamiento 1 *m* (*separación*) removal; (*retirada*) withdrawal. 2 (*apartamento*) small flat, apartment.

apartar 1 *t* (*alejar*) to move away: *aparta la planta del sol,* move the plant out of the sun; *¿puedes apartar la moto?,* can you move your motorbike?; *apartó la mirada,* she looked away. 2 (*separar*) to separate; (*preservar de*) to protect from, keep away from: *peleaban con tanta violencia que nadie pudo apartarlos,* they were fighting so fiercely that nobody could separate them; *lo que haga falta para apartar al menor del peligro,* whatever is necessary to protect the child from danger. 3 (*reservar*) to put aside, set aside: *te he apartado un trozo de pastel,* I've put a piece of cake aside for you, I've saved you a piece of cake. 4 (*de un cargo*) to remove: *ha sido apartado del servicio activo,* he has been removed from active service. – 5 apartarse, *p* (*alejarse*) to move away: *apártate de allí,* get away from there. 6 (*separarse*) to withdraw, move away: *se apartó del tema,* she veered off the subject.
● apartar los ojos de, to take one's eyes off. ‖ "se aparta género", "a deposit secures any item".

aparte 1 *adv* apart, aside, separately: *eso se paga aparte,* you'll have to pay for that separately. – 2 *adj* (*distinto*) special: *eso es caso aparte,* that's completely different. – 3 *m* TEAT aside. 4 LING paragraph: *punto y aparte,* full stop, new paragraph.

apartheid *m* apartheid.

aparthotel *m* serviced flats, US apartment hotel.

apasionadamente *adv* passionately, ardently.

apasionado,-a 1 *pp* → **apasionar**. – 2 *adj* passionate, enthusiastic, fervent. – 3 *m,f* lover, enthusiast: *es un apasionado del boxeo,* he's a boxing fanatic.
● apasionado,-a por, very fond of.

apasionamiento *m* passion, enthusiasm.

apasionante *adj* exciting, fascinating.

apasionar 1 *t* to excite, fascinate, thrill: *me apasiona el queso,* I adore cheese; *me apasiona la música clásica,* I'm very fond of classical music. – 2 apasionarse, *p* to get excited, become enthusiastic (**por/de**, about). 3

(*enamorarse*) to fall head over heels in love (**por/de**, with).

apatía *f* apathy.

apático,-a 1 *adj* apathetic. – 2 *m,f* apathetic person.

apátrida 1 *adj* stateless. – 2 *mf* stateless person.

apdo. *abr* (*apartado*) post-office box; (*abreviatura*) PO Box.

apeadero *m* halt.

apear 1 *t* (*desmontar*) to take down. 2 (*terreno*) to survey. 3 ARQ to prop up. 4 *fam* to dissuade. – 5 apearse, *p* (*del tren, autobús, etc*) to get off; (*del coche*) to get out of; (*del caballo*) to dismount.

apechugar *i* to grin and bear it, lump it: *no nos gusta, pero nos toca apechugar,* we're not happy about it, but we have to lump it; *no pienso apechugar con todo el trabajo,* I don't intend to get lumbered with all the work.
▲ *Conjugation model* [7], *like* **llegar**.

apedrear 1 *t* (*tirar piedras*) to throw stones at. 2 (*matar a pedradas*) to stone (to death). – 3 *i* (*granizar*) to hail. – 4 apedrearse, *p* (*estropearse por granizo*) to be damaged by hail.
▲ *In 3, used only in the 3rd person; it does not take a subject.*

apegado,-a 1 *pp* → **apegarse**. – 2 *adj* attached (**a**, to).

apegarse *p* to become very fond (**a**, of), get attached (**a**, to).
▲ *Conjugation model* [7], *like* **llegar**.

apego *m* attachment, affection, liking, fondness.
● tomar apego a, to become attached to.

apelable *adj* appealable.

apelación 1 *f* JUR appeal. 2 (*llamamiento*) appeal, call. 3 *fig* help.
● interponer apelación, to appeal. ‖ no tener apelación, to be helpless.
■ recurso de apelación, appeal.

apelar 1 *i* JUR to appeal: *apelar de una sentencia,* to appeal against a sentence. 2 *fig* (*recurrir*) to resort to: *tuvo que apelar a sus padres,* he had to go to his parents.

apelativo,-a 1 *adj* appellative. – 2 apelativo, *m* appellative, name.

apellidar 1 *t* to call. – 2 apellidarse, *p* to be called, have as a surname.

apellido *m* family name, surname, (US last name).
● con nombre y apellidos, *fig* with all the details.

apelmazado,-a 1 *pp* → **apelmazar**. – 2 *adj* (*comida*) heavy, stodgy; (*colchón*) lumpy; (*libro, estilo*) dense, stodgy; (*lana*) matted.

apelmazar 1 *t* to compress, squeeze together. – 2 apelmazarse, *p* (*comida*) to go stodgy; (*colchón*) to go lumpy; (*lana*) to get matted. 3 (*gente*) to crowd, throng.
▲ *Conjugation model* [4], *like* **realizar**.

apelotonar 1 *t* (*amontonar*) to pile up, put into a pile; (*gente*) to cluster. 2 (*hacer una pelota*) to roll into a ball. – 3 apelotonarse, *p* (*gente*) to crowd together.

apenado,-a 1 *pp* → **apenar**. – 2 *adj* troubled.

apenar 1 *t* to make sad, sadden, grieve. – 2 apenarse, *p* to be grieved, be upset.

apenas 1 *adv* (*casi no*) scarcely, hardly: *apenas bebió,* he hardly drank anything; *apenas lo conozco,* I hardly know him. 2 (*con dificultad*) only just: *el niño apenas subió la escalera,* the boy only just made it up the stairs. 3 (*tan pronto como*) as soon as, no sooner: *apenas entramos, sonó el teléfono,* no sooner had we had come in than the phone rang.
● apenas si, hardly: *apenas si se oía,* it could hardly be heard.

apencar *i fam* → **apechugar**.
▲ *Conjugation model* |1|, *like* *sacar*.
apéndice 1 *m* appendix. 2 *fig* (*persona*) lapdog.
apendicectomía *f* appendectomy.
apendicitis *f* appendicitis.
▲ *pl* *apendicitis*.
Apeninos los (montes) Apeninos, *mpl* the Apennines.
apeo 1 *m* (*de finca*) surveying. 2 (*de árbol*) felling. 3 (*apuntalamiento*) propping-up.
apercibimiento 1 *m* (*preparación*) preparation. 2 JUR warning.
apercibir 1 *t* (*preparar*) to prepare, get ready. 2 (*avisar*) to warn. – 3 **apercibirse**, *p* (*darse cuenta*) to notice (**de**, -).
apergaminado,-a 1 *pp* → **apergaminarse**. – 2 *adj* parchment-like. 3 (*piel*) wrinkled; (*cara*) wizened.
■ **papel apergaminado**, parchment paper.
apergaminarse *p* to wrinkle, become wizened.
aperiódico,-a *adj* aperiodic.
aperitivo,-a 1 *adj* appetizing. – 2 **aperitivo**, *m* (*bebida*) apéritif. 3 (*comida*) appetizer, snack.
apero 1 *m* implement. – 2 **aperos**, *mpl* (*aperos*) equipment *sing*, tools.
■ **aperos de labranza**, farming implements.
aperreado,-a 1 *pp* → **aperrear**. – 2 *adj fam* lousy, wretched: *una vida aperreada*, a dog's life.
aperrear 1 *t* (*agobiar*) to wear out, exhaust. – 2 **aperrearse**, *p* (*trabajar mucho*) to overwork. 3 (*emperrarse*) to become stubborn.
apertura 1 *f* (*comienzo*) opening, beginning. 2 POL liberalization.
■ **sesión de apertura**, opening session.
aperturismo *m* progressiveness.
aperturista 1 *adj* progressive. – 2 *mf supporter of progressive political ideas*.
apesadumbrado,-a 1 *pp* → **apesadumbrar**. – 2 *adj* sad, distressed.
apesadumbrar *t* to sadden, distress.
apestado,-a 1 *pp* → **apestar**. – 2 *adj* (*olor*) foul, pestilential. 3 MED plague-ridden. 4 *fig* (*en cantidad*) infested (**de**, with), crawling (**de**, with).
apestar 1 *i* (*oler mal*) to stink. – 2 *t* (*causar la peste*) to infect with the plague.
apestoso,-a 1 *adj* stinking: *un olor apestoso*, a foul smell. 2 *fam* (*fastidioso*) annoying.
apétalo,-a *adj* apetalous.
apetecer 1 *i* (*agradar*) to feel like, fancy: *¿te apetece ir al teatro?*, do you fancy going to the theatre?; *¿qué os apetece tomar?*, what would you like? – 2 *t fig* (*desear*) to long for, yearn for: *apetecer la fama*, to long for fame.
▲ *Conjugation model* |43|, *like* *agradecer*.
apetecible 1 *adj* (*empleo*) desirable; (*idea*) appealing. 2 (*comida*) tasty, appetizing.
apetencia 1 *f* (*apetito*) appetite, hunger. 2 *fig* (*deseo*) longing, craving, desire.
apetito *m* appetite.
● **abrir el apetito**, to whet one's appetite. ‖ **tener apetito**, to be hungry.
■ **apetito carnal/sexual**, sexual appetite.
apetitoso,-a 1 *adj* (*aspecto de comida*) appetizing; (*comida*) tasty, delicious. 2 (*oferta*) tempting.
API *abr* (*Agente de la Propiedad Inmobiliaria*) estate agent.
apiadar 1 *t* to inspire pity in, move to pity. – 2 **apiadarse**, *p* to take pity (**de**, on).

apical *adj* apical.
ápice 1 *m* (*punta*) apex. 2 *fig* tiny bit, speck, iota.
● **ni un ápice**, not one bit.
apícola *adj* apicultural, beekeeping.
apicultor,-ra *m,f* beekeeper, apiculturist, apiarist.
apicultura *f* beekeeping, apiculture.
apilamiento *m* piling up, heaping up.
apilar 1 *t* to pile up, heap up. – 2 **apilarse**, *p* to pile up, heap up.
apiñado,-a 1 *pp* → **apiñar**. – 2 *adj* crammed together, packed.
apiñamiento *m* cramming, packing.
apiñar 1 *t* (*apretar*) to pack, press together, jam. – 2 **apiñarse**, *p* to crowd (**en**, into).
apio *m* celery.
apiolar *t* to catch.
apisonador,-ra 1 *adj* rolling. – 2 **apisonadora**, *f* steamroller, roadroller.
apisonar *t* to roll.
apizarrado,-a *adj* slaty, slate-coloured (US slate-colored).
aplacamiento *m* placation, calming.
aplacar 1 *t* to placate, calm, soothe. – 2 **aplacarse**, *p* (*persona*) to calm down; (*viento*) to abate, die down.
▲ *Conjugation model* |1|, *like* *sacar*.
aplanador,-ra *adj* levelling (US leveling), smoothing.
aplanamiento *m* levelling (US leveling), smoothing.
aplanar 1 *t* (*igualar*) to smooth, level, make even. 2 *fig* (*deprimir*) to depress, dishearten. – 3 **aplanarse**, *p* (*desanimarse*) to become depressed, become disheartened.
aplastamiento 1 *m* flattening, squashing. 2 *fig* (*moral*) crushing.
aplastante *adj* crushing, overwhelming.
■ **triunfo/victoria aplastante**, (*electoral*) landslide victory.
aplastar 1 *t* (*gen*) to flatten, squash, crush. 2 *fig* (*destruir*) to crush, destroy: *aplastar al enemigo*, to crush the enemy. – 3 **aplastarse**, *p* to be flattened, be squashed, be crushed.
aplatanado,-a 1 *pp* → **aplatanar**. – 2 *adj fam* apathetic, lazy.
aplatanamiento *m fam* apathy, laziness.
aplatanarse *p fam* to become apathetic.
aplaudir 1 *t* to clap, applaud. 2 *fig* (*aprobar*) to applaud, approve.
aplauso 1 *m* applause: *¡un aplauso para el señor Martín!*, a round of applause for Mr Martín! 2 *fig* (*aprobación*) applause, praise, acclaim.
aplazado,-a 1 *pp* → **aplazar**. – 2 *adj* postponed, put off.
■ **pago aplazado**, deferred payment.
aplazamiento *m* (*gen*) adjournment, postponement; (*de pago*) deferment.
aplazar *t* (*gen*) to adjourn, postpone, put off; (*un pago*) to defer.
▲ *Conjugation model* |4|, *like* *realizar*.
aplicable *adj* applicable.
aplicación 1 *f* (*gen*) application. 2 (*adorno*) appliqué.
aplicado,-a 1 *pp* → **aplicar**. – 2 *adj* (*estudioso*) studious, diligent, hard-working: *es un alumno aplicado*, he's a hard-working pupil.
■ **ciencias aplicadas**, applied sciences.
aplicar 1 *t* (*gen*) to apply: *aplicó una pomada sobre la herida*, she put some ointment on the wound; *aplicó el método que había aprendido de su padre*, he applied the

method he had learned from his father; *para pedidos superiores a 250 se aplica un descuento del 10%*, for orders over 250 there is a 10% discount; *en este caso la cláusula 5 no se aplica,* in this case clause 5 is not applicable. **2** (*destinar*) to assign. – **3 aplicarse,** *p* (*esforzarse*) to apply os., work hard.
▲ Conjugation model [1], like *sacar.*

aplique **1** *m* (*adorno*) appliqué. **2** (*lámpara*) wall light, wall lamp.

aplomar 1 *t* to plumb. – **2 aplomarse,** *p* to compose os.

aplomo *m* assurance, composure, self-possession.

apocado,-a 1 *pp →* **apocar.** – **2** *adj* (*intimidado*) intimidated, frightened. **3** (*tímido*) shy, timid.

apocalipsis *m* apocalypse.
▲ *pl* **apocalipsis.**

apocalíptico,-a *adj* apocalyptic.

apocamiento *m* timidity, lack of self-confidence.

apocar 1 *t* (*intimidar*) to intimidate, frighten. **2** (*humillar*) to humiliate, belittle. – **3 apocarse,** *p* (*intimidarse*) to be intimidated.
▲ Conjugation model [1], like *sacar.*

apocopar *t* to apocopate.

apócope *m* apocope, apocopation.

apócrifo,-a *adj* apocryphal.

apodar 1 *t* to call, nickname. – **2 apodarse,** *p* to be nicknamed.

apoderado,-a 1 *pp →* **apoderar.** – **2** *adj* authorized. **3** JUR with power of attorney (*para,* to). – **4** *m,f* agent, representative. **5** (*de torero, deportista*) manager.

apoderar *t* to authorize, empower. **2** JUR to grant power of attorney. – **3 apoderarse,** *p* to take possession (**de,** of), seize (**de,** -): *el miedo se apoderó de él,* he was seized by fear.

apodo *m* nickname.

apódosis *f* apodosis.
▲ *pl* **apódosis.**

apófisis *f* apophysis.
▲ *pl* **apófisis.**

apogeo 1 *m* ASTRON apogee. **2** *fig* (*punto culminante*) summit, height, climax, peak.
● **estar en pleno apogeo,** to be at its height.

apolillado,-a 1 *pp →* **apolillar.** – **2** *adj* moth-eaten.

apolilladura *f* moth hole.

apolillar 1 *t* to eat away at, make holes in. – **2 apolillarse,** *p* to become moth-eaten.

apolíneo,-a *adj* Apollonian.

apoliticismo *m* apoliticism.

apolítico,-a *adj* apolitical.

apologética *f →* **apologético,-a.**

apologético,-a 1 *adj* apologetic. – **2 apologética,** *f* apologetics.

apología *f* apology, defence (US defense).

apologista *mf* apologist.

apólogo *m* apologue.

apoltronado,-a 1 *pp →* **apoltronarse.** – **2** *adj* lazy, idle.

apoltronamiento *m* laziness, idleness.

apoltronarse 1 *p* (*vegetar*) to grow lazy, get lazy, become idle. **2** (*sentarse*) to sit back, lounge about.

apoplejía *f* apoplexy, stroke.

apoplético,-a 1 *adj* apoplectic. – **2** *m,f* apoplectic.

apoquinar *t fam* to cough up, fork out.

aporcar *t* to earth up.
▲ Conjugation model [1], like *sacar.*

aporreado,-a 1 *pp →* **aporrear.** – **2** *adj* (*pobre*) hard up for money.

aporrear *t* (*persona*) to beat, hit, thrash; (*puerta*) to bang on; (*piano*) to bang (away) on.

aporreo *m* (*golpe*) beating, thrashing; (*de puerta*) banging; (*de piano*) thumping.

aportación *f* contribution.

aportar[1] **1** *t* (*contribuir*) to contribute. **2** (*proporcionar*) to give, provide.
● **aportar su granito de arena,** to do one's bit.

aportar[2] *i* (*llegar a puerto*) to reach port.

aporte *m* contribution.

aportillar *t* to breach, make a breach in.

aposentamiento 1 *m* (*acción*) housing, lodging. **2** (*aposento*) room. **3** (*hospedaje*) lodgings *pl.*

aposentar 1 *t* (*alojar*) to lodge. – **2 aposentarse,** *p* to lodge, stay.

aposento 1 *m* (*cuarto*) room. **2** (*hospedaje*) lodgings *pl.*
● **tomar aposento en,** to put up at.

aposición *f* apposition.

apósito *m* dressing.

aposta *adv* on purpose, deliberately, intentionally.

apostadero 1 *m* MIL post, station. **2** MAR naval station.

apostador,-ra 1 *adj* betting. – **2** *m,f* punter, person who places a bet.

apostante *adj-mf →* **apostador.**

apostar[1] **1** *t* to bet, stake: *te apuesto dos mil pesetas a que no gana,* I bet you two thousand pesetas that she won't win; *apostó todo su dinero por Red Rum,* he bet all his money on Red Rum. – **2** *i* to bet: *apostó por él,* she bet on him; *apuesto a que sí llega tarde,* I bet he'll be late. – **3 apostarse,** *p* to bet.
▲ Conjugation model [31], like *contar.*

apostar[2] *t* (*situar*) to post, station.

apostasía *f* apostasy.

apóstata *mf* apostate.

apostatar *i* to apostatize.

apostilla 1 *f* note, comment. **2** JUR apostille.

apostillar *t* to add notes, annotate.

apóstol 1 *m* apostle. **2** *fig* (*defensor*) apostle, champion.

apostolado *m* apostolate.

apostólico,-a 1 *adj* (*de los apóstoles*) apostolic. **2** (*del papa*) apostolic, papal: *la bendición apostólica,* the papal blessing.

apostrofar 1 *t* to apostrophize. **2** (*reñir*) to reprimand, tell off.

apóstrofe 1 *m & f* GRAM apostrophe. **2** (*reprimenda*) reprimand, rebuke.

apóstrofo *m* apostrophe.

apostura 1 *f* (*aspecto*) appearance, look. **2** (*buen aspecto*) good bearing.

apotegma *m* apothegm, maxim.

apotema *f* apothem.

apoteósico,-a *adj* enormous, tremendous.

apoteosis 1 *f* apotheosis. **2** (*de un espectáculo*) grand finale.
▲ *pl* **apoteosis.**

apoyar 1 *t* to lean, rest: *apoyar la cabeza,* to rest one's head. **2** (*fundar*) to base, found: *apoya su teoría en pruebas concluyentes,* he bases his theory on hard evidence. **3** *fig* (*defender algo*) to support; (*defender a alguien*) to back, support: *sus padres le apoyan en todo,* her parents support everything she does. – **4 apoyarse,** *p* (*descansar*) to lean (**en,** on), rest (**en,** on), stand (**en,** on): *la estatua se apoya en un pilar,* the statue stands on a column; *apóyate en mí,* lean on me; *se apoya demasiado en sus padres,* he relies too much on his parents. **5** (*dar el brazo*) to hold on (**en,** to). **6** *fig* (*basarse*) to be based (**en,** on): *¿en qué te apoyas para decir eso?,* what do you base your arguments on?

apoyatura *f* appoggiatura.

apoyo 1 *m* support. **2** *fig* support, backing, help.
■ **punto de apoyo,** fís fulcrum; *fig* base.

apreciable 1 *adj* (*perceptible*) appreciable, noticeable. **2** (*estimable*) valuable, precious.

apreciación 1 *f* (*valorización*) appreciation, appraisal, evaluation. **2** (*juicio*) appraisal, assessment; (*percepción*) perception. **3** (*opinión*) view, opinion. **4** (*en valor*) appreciation.

apreciado,-a *adj* valued, appreciated.

apreciar 1 *t* (*valorar*) to appraise (**en,** at). **2** (*sentir aprecio*) to regard highly, hold in high esteem: *apreciar a algn.,* to be fond of sb. **3** (*reconocer valor*) to appreciate. **4** (*percibir*) to notice, see, percieve: *no sabe apreciar la diferencia,* he can't tell the difference. – **5 apreciarse,** *p* (*notarse*) to be noticed, be noticeable: *pueden apreciarse grietas en las paredes,* one can see cracks in the walls.
▲ *Conjugation model* [12], *like* **cambiar.**

apreciativo,-a *adj* appreciative.

aprecio *m* esteem, regard.
● **sentir aprecio por algn.,** to be fond of sb.

aprehender 1 *t* (*apresar*) to apprehend. **2** (*confiscar*) to seize. **3** (*percibir*) to understand.

aprehensión 1 *f* (*captura*) apprehension, arrest. **2** (*de contrabando*) seizure. **3** (*percepción*) comprehension, understanding.

apremiador,-ra *adj* urgent, pressing.

apremiante *adj* urgent, pressing.

apremiar 1 *t* (*compeler*) to urge, press, compel, put pressure on. **2** (*dar prisa*) to hurry, rush: *no me apremies,* don't rush me. **3** JUR to compel, constrain. – **4** *i* to be urgent: *el tiempo apremia,* time is short, time is running out, time presses on.
▲ *Conjugation model* [12], *like* **cambiar.**

apremio 1 *m* pressure, urgency: *por apremio de tiempo,* because time is short. **2** JUR writ.
■ **apremio de pago,** demand for payment.

aprender 1 *t* to learn: *así aprenderás a no decir mentiras,* that'll teach you not to tell lies. **2** (*memorizar*) to learn by heart. – **3 aprenderse,** *p* to learn, learn by heart.

aprendiz,-za *m,f* apprentice, trainee: *aprendiza de peluquera,* trainee hairdresser.

aprendizaje 1 *m* (*situación*) apprenticeship. **2** (*tiempo*) training period. **3** (*en pedagogía*) learning.

aprensión *f* (*miedo*) apprehension; (*asco*) squeamishness: *si te da aprensión, no lo comas,* if you're not sure about it, don't eat it.
● **con aprensión,** apprehensively, nervously. ‖ **sentir aprensión,** to feel apprehensive.

aprensivo,-a 1 *adj* apprehensive. – **2** *m,f* apprehensive.

apresamiento *m* seizure, capture.

apresar 1 *t* (*tomar por fuerza*) to seize, capture. **2** (*asir*) to clutch.

aprestar 1 *t* (*preparar*) to get ready, prepare. **2** (*tejidos*) to size.

apresto 1 *m* (*preparación*) preparation. **2** (*tejidos*) sizing; (*material*) size.

apresuración *f* haste, hurry.

apresuradamente *adv* hurriedly, in a hurry, in great haste.

apresurado,-a 1 *pp* → **apresurar.** – **2** *adj* (*persona*) in a hurry. **3** (*cosa*) hurried, rushed, quick.

apresuramiento *m* haste, hurry.

apresurar 1 *t* to hurry up, speed up, accelerate. – **2 apresurarse,** *p* to hurry, hurry up.
● **apresurar el paso,** to quicken one's pace.

apretado,-a 1 *pp* → **apretar.** – **2** *adj* (*objeto*) tight. **3** (*en un espacio*) jammed; (*personas*) crowded, cramped. **4** (*ocupado*) busy: *un día muy apretado,* a very busy day. **5** (*difícil*) tight, difficult.
● **estar/ir apretado,-a de dinero,** to be short of money.

apretar 1 *t* (*estrechar*) to squeeze, hug. **2** (*tornillo*) to tighten; (*cordones, nudo*) to do up tight. **3** (*comprimir*) to compress, press together, pack tight. **4** (*activar*) to press, push: *si aprietas este botón sonará la alarma,* if you press this button the alarm will go off. **5** *fig* (*acosar*) to keep on at; (*presionar*) to put pressure on, pressurize. – **6** *i fig* (*aumentar*) to increase, get worse: *el calor aprieta,* it's getting hotter and hotter. **7** (*prendas*) to fit tight, be tight on: *esta falda me aprieta,* this skirt is too tight on me. **8** (*esforzarse*) to work hard: *tendrás que apretar en tus estudios,* you'll have to study a lot harder, you'll have to pull your socks up. – **9 apretarse,** *p* (*apiñar*) to narrow, tighten. **10** (*agolparse*) to crowd together; (*acercarse*) to squeeze up.
● **apretar a correr,** to start running. ‖ **apretar el paso,** to quicken one's pace. ‖ **apretar la mano a algn.,** to shake sb.'s hand. ‖ **apretar el gatillo,** to pull the trigger.
▲ *Conjugation model* [27], *like* **acertar.**

apretón 1 *m* squeeze. – **2 apretones,** *mpl* crush *sing.*
■ **apretón de manos,** handshake.

apretujado,-a *adj* squashed, cramped.

apretujar 1 *t* to squeeze, crush. – **2 apretujarse,** *p* to squeeze together, cram together.

apretujón *m fam* squeeze, crush.

apretura 1 *f* (*aglomeración*) crowd. **2** *fig* (*aprieto*) tight spot, fix. **3** (*escasez*) scarcity. **4** (*apremio*) urgency.
● **pasar apreturas,** to suffer hardship.
▲ *Also used in plural with the same meaning.*

aprieto *m* tight spot, difficulty, scrape, fix.
● **poner a algn. en un aprieto,** to put sb. in an awkward situation. ‖ **salir del aprieto,** to get out of trouble.

apriorismo *m* apriorism.

apriorístico,-a *adj* aprioristic.

aprisa *adv* quickly.

aprisco *m* sheepfold.

aprisionar 1 *t* (*encarcelar*) to imprison, put in prison. **2** (*sujetar*) to hold tight.

aprobación *f* (*gen*) approval; (*ley*) passing.
● **dar su (*mi, tu, etc*) aprobación,** to give one's consent, approve.

aprobado,-a 1 *pp* → **aprobar.** – **2** *adj* approved, passed. – **3 aprobado** *m* EDUC pass (mark).
● **sacar/tener un aprobado,** to get a pass.

aprobar 1 *t* (*gen*) to approve; (*ley*) to pass. **2** (*estar de acuerdo*) to approve of. **3** EDUC (*examen, asignatura*) to pass. – **4** *i* to pass.
▲ *Conjugation model* [31], *like* **contar.**

aprobatorio,-a *adj* approving, approbatory.

aprontar 1 *t* (*disponer*) to get ready quickly. **2** (*entregar*) to hand over immediately.

apropiación *f* appropriation.
■ **apropiación indebida,** JUR theft.

apropiado,-a 1 *pp* → **apropiar**. – 2 *adj* suitable, fitting, appropriate.
apropiar 1 *t* (*acomodar*) to make suitable, adapt. – 2 **apropiarse**, *p* to appropriate (**de**, -), take possession (**de**, of).
▲ Conjugation model [12], *like* **cambiar**.
aprovechable *adj* usable.
aprovechadamente *adv* profitably.
aprovechado,-a 1 *pp* → **aprovechar**. – 2 *adj* (*tiempo*) well used, well spent. 3 (*espacio*) well-planned. 4 (*diligente*) diligent, studious, hardworking. 5 (*que saca provecho de todo*) thrifty, economical, resourceful. 6 *pey* (*egoísta*) selfish; (*gorrón*) sponging, scrounging. – 7 *m,f fam* (*gorrón*) sponger, scrounger; (*oportunista*) opportunist.
● **mal aprovechado,-a**, wasted.
aprovechamiento 1 *m* (*uso*) use, exploitation: *el aprovechamiento de los recursos naturales,* the exploitation of natural resources. 2 (*provecho*) improvement, progress.
aprovechar 1 *t* (*emplear útilmente*) to make good use of, make the most of. 2 (*sacar provecho*) to benefit from, take advantage of: *aprovechar la oportunidad/ocasión,* to seize the opportunity. – 3 *i* to be useful, make the most of it: *eso no aprovecha para nada,* that's useless. 4 (*avanzar*) to improve, progress. – 5 **aprovecharse**, *p* (*de alguien*) to take advantage (**de**, of); (*de algo*) to make the most (**de**, of).
● **¡que aproveche!**, enjoy your meal!
aprovechón,-ona *m,f fam* scrounger, sponger, freeloader.
aprovisionamiento *m* supply, supplying, provision.
aprovisionar 1 *t* to supply, provide (**de/con,** with): *aprovisionaron el fuerte de víveres,* they supplied the fort with provisions. – 2 **aprovisionarse,** *p* to stock up (**de**, on/with).
aproximación 1 *f* (*gen*) approximation. 2 (*acercamiento*) bringing together; (*de países*) rapprochement. 3 (*lotería*) consolation prize.
● **ni por aproximación,** *fam* far from it.
aproximadamente *adv* approximately, roughly, around, about.
aproximado,-a 1 *pp* → **aproximar**. – 2 *adj* approximate, estimated.
■ **cálculo aproximado**, rough estimate.
aproximar 1 *t* to bring near, put near: *aproxima la mesita al sofá,* put the coffee table nearer the sofa; *el accidente los aproximó más,* the accident brought them closer together. – 2 **aproximarse**, *p* to come near, come closer: *aproxímate,* come closer; *el verano se aproxima,* summer is getting nearer.
aproximativo,-a *adj* approximate, rough.
áptero,-a *adj* apterous.
aptitud 1 *f* (*habilidad*) aptitude, ability: *demuestra aptitud para la música,* he has a gift for music. 2 (*idoneidad*) suitability, aptness.
apto,-a 1 *adj* (*apropiado*) suitable, appropriate; *no es apto para este trabajo,* he's not suitable for this job. 2 (*capaz*) capable, able. 3 (*físicamente*) fit.
● **apto,-a para todos los públicos**, CINEM U-certificate film, US rated G. ‖ **no apto,-a,** CINEM for adults only.
apuesta *f* bet, wager.
apuesto,-a *adj* (*gen*) good-looking; (*hombre*) handsome.
apuntado,-a 1 *pp* → **apuntar**. – 2 *adj* (*en punta*) pointed, sharp. 3 (*anotado*) written down, taken down.

apuntador,-ra *m,f* TEAT prompter.
apuntalamiento *m* propping-up, underpinning.
apuntalar *t* to prop (up), shore up, underpin.
apuntar 1 *t* (*señalar*) to point (**a**, at): *es feo apuntar con el dedo,* it's rude to point (with one's finger); *apuntó que ...,* she pointed out that ... 2 (*arma*) to aim: *¡apunten!,* take aim! 3 (*anotar*) to note down, make a note of: *se lo apunto en cuenta,* I'll put it on your account, I'll charge it to your account; *la apuntamos en la lista,* we put her on the list. 4 (*estar encaminado*) to be aimed (**a**, at), be designed (**a**, to). 5 (*insinuar*) to suggest, indicate. 6 (*sujetar*) to stitch, pin lightly, tack lightly. 7 TEAT to prompt. 8 *fam* (*en un examen*) to whisper the answer to. – 9 *i* to begin to appear: *cuando apunta el día,* when day breaks. 10 TEAT to prompt. – 11 **apuntarse**, *p* (*inscribirse*) to enrol. 12 *fam* (*participar*) to take part (**a**, in): *¿te apuntas?,* are you game?
● **apuntarse un tanto,** to score a point.
apunte 1 *m* note. 2 (*dibujo*) sketch. 3 (*apuntador*) prompter; (*voz del apuntador*) prompt; (*libreto del apuntador*) prompt book. – 4 **apuntes,** *mpl* (*de clase*) notes.
● **sacar un apunte,** to do a sketch. ‖ **tomar apuntes,** to take notes.
apuntillar *t* to finish off.
apuñalar *t* to stab.
apuradamente *adv* with difficulty.
apurado,-a 1 *pp* → **apurar**. – 2 *adj* (*avergonzado*) embarrassed. 3 (*necesitado*) in need: *apurado,-a de dinero,* hard up for money; *apurado,-a de tiempo,* in a hurry, pushed for time. 4 (*dificultoso*) awkward, difficult. 5 (*exacto*) accurate, precise.
■ **afeitado apurado**, close shave. ‖ **situación apurada,** tight spot, jam.
apurar 1 *t* (*terminar*) to finish up: *apurar una copa,* to drain a glass; *apuraron dos botellas de vino,* they polished off two bottles of wine. 2 (*apremiar*) to urge, put pressure on: *si me apuras ...,* if you insist ..., if you push me ... 3 (*purificar*) to purify. 4 (*averiguar*) to investigate. 5 AM (*dar prisa*) to hurry, rush. – 6 **apurarse**, *p* (*preocuparse*) to get worried, be worried. 7 AM (*darse prisa*) to hurry, rush.
apuro 1 *m* fix, tight spot; (*de dinero*) hardship. 2 (*vergüenza*) embarrassment.
● **estar/encontrarse en un apuro,** to be in a tight spot. ‖ **pasar apuros,** (*económicos*) to be hard up; (*dificultades*) to be in a tight spot. ‖ **¡qué apuro!,** how embarrassing!
aqueado,-a 1 *pp* → **aquejar**. – 2 *adj* suffering (**de**, from).
aquejar *t* to afflict, affect: *le aqueja una enfermedad desconocida,* he is suffering from an unknown illness.
aquel,-ella 1 *adj* that: *aquel coche,* that car. 2 **aquellos,-as**, those: *aquellas casas,* those houses.
aquél,-élla 1 *pron* that one; (*el anterior*) the former: *aquél es el mío,* that one is mine; *Nacho y Cristina han encontrado trabajo, aquél con una multinacional japonesa y ésta con una empresa alemana,* Nacho and Cristina have found jobs, the former with a Japanese multinational and the latter with a German firm. 2 **aquéllos,-as**, those; (*los anteriores*) the former. – 3 **aquél,** *m fam* (*donaire*) something: *ella tiene un aquél,* she's got something about her.
● **aquél que ...,** he who ... ‖ **todo aquél que ...,** anyone who ..., whoever ...
aquelarre *m* witches' sabbath.
aquella *adj* → **aquel**.

aquélla *pron* → **aquél**.

aquello *pron* that, it: *aquello fue impresionante,* that was great; *aquello no tiene remedio,* it's hopeless; *aquello de que no tiene dinero es mentira,* it's not true that he hasn't got any money.

● **por aquello de,** so as not to: *cogió un taxi por aquello de no llegar tarde,* he took a taxi so as not to arrive late.

aquellos,-as *adj pl* → **aquel,-ella**.

aquéllos,-as *pron pl* → **aquél,-éllas**.

aquí 1 *adv* (*lugar*) here: *por aquí por favor,* this way please. 2 (*tiempo*) now: *de aquí en adelante,* from now on; *de aquí tres meses,* in three months' (time).

● **de aquí para allá,** back and forth, to and fro. ‖ **de aquí (que),** hence. ‖ **hasta aquí podíamos llegar,** *fig* that's the end of it.

aquiescencia *f* acquiescence.

aquietar *t* to calm down, pacify.

aquilatamiento 1 *m* (*oro, perlas, etc*) assay. 2 *fig* (*valoración*) assessment, evaluation.

aquilatar 1 *t* (*oro, perlas, etc*) to assay. 2 *fig* (*evaluar*) to assess.

aquileño,-a *adj* → **aguileño,-a**.

aquilino,-a *adj* → **aguileño,-a**.

aquilón 1 *m lit* (*polo norte*) North Pole. 2 *lit* (*viento norte*) north wind.

ara *f* (*altar*) altar; (*piedra*) altar stone.

● **en aras de,** *fml* for the sake of: *en aras de la paz,* so as to keep the peace.

árabe 1 *adj* (*gen*) Arab; (*de Arabia*) Arabian. – 2 *m,f* Arab.

■ **alfabeto árabe,** Arabic alphabet.

arabesco *m* arabesque.

Arabia *f* Arabia.

■ **Arabia Saudita,** Saudi Arabia.

arábigo,-a 1 *adj* Arabic, Arabian. – 2 **arábigo,** *m* Arabic.

■ **números arábigos,** arabic numerals.

árabigo,-a *adj* Arabic.

■ **goma árabiga,** gum Arabic. ‖ **número árabigo,** Arabic numeral.

arabismo *m* Arabic expression.

arabista *mf* Arabist.

arabizar *t* to arabize.

▲ *Conjugation model* [4], *like realizar*.

arácnido *m* arachnid.

arada 1 *f* (*acción*) ploughing (us plowing). 2 (*tierra*) ploughed (us plowed).

arado *m* plough (us plow).

arador *m* ploughman (us plowman).

Aragón *m* Aragon.

aragonés,-esa 1 *adj* Aragonese. – 2 *m,f* Aragonese.

aragonesismo *m* Aragonese expression.

Aral el Mar de Aral, *m* the Aral Sea.

arameo,-a 1 *adj* Aramaean, Aramean. – 2 *m,f* (*persona*) Aramaean, Aramean. – 3 **arameo,** *m* (*idioma*) Aramaic.

arancel *m* tariff, customs duty.

arancelario,-a *adj* tariff, duty.

■ **derechos arancelarios,** customs duties.

arándano *m* bilberry, blueberry.

arandela *f* washer.

araña 1 *f* (*arácnido*) spider. 2 (*pez*) weever. 3 (*planta*) love-in-a-mist. 4 (*lámpara*) chandelier.

■ **araña de mar,** spider crab. ‖ **tela de araña,** spider's web.

arañar 1 *t* (*raspar*) to scratch. 2 *fig* (*recoger*) to scrape together. – 3 **arañarse,** *p* to scratch.

arañazo *m* scratch.

arao *m* guillemot.

arar *t* to plough (us plow).

araucanismo *m* Araucanian expression.

araucano,-a 1 *adj* Araucanian. – 2 *m,f* Araucanian.

araucaria *f* araucaria, monkey puzzle tree.

arbitraje 1 *m* (*desacuerdo*) arbitration. 2 DEP (*fútbol, boxeo*) refereeing; (*cricket, tenis*) umpiring.

arbitral *adj* of the referee: *decisión arbitral,* referee's ruling.

■ **sentencia arbitral,** JUR judgement by arbitration.

arbitrar 1 *t* to arbitrate. 2 DEP (*en fútbol, boxeo*) to referee; (*en cricket, tenis*) to umpire. 3 (*obtener*) to contrive; (*reunir*) to collect: *arbitrar fondos,* to raise funds.

arbitrariamente *adv* arbitrarily.

arbitrariedad 1 *f* (*acción*) arbitrary act. 2 (*condición*) arbitrariness.

arbitrario,-a *adj* arbitrary.

arbitrio 1 *m* (*voluntad*) will; (*juicio*) judgement. 2 (*decisión*) power, choice. 3 (*medio*) mean. – 4 **arbitrios,** *mpl* taxes.

● **dejar algo al arbitrio de algn.,** to leave sth. to sb.'s discretion.

arbitrista *mf* armchair politician.

árbitro,-a 1 *m,f* arbiter, arbitrator. 2 DEP (*fútbol, boxeo*) referee; (*cricket, tenis*) umpire.

árbol 1 *m* BOT tree. 2 TÉC axle, shaft. 3 MAR mast. 4 (*gráfico*) tree (diagram).

● **los árboles no dejan ver el bosque,** you can't see the wood for the trees.

■ **árbol del amor,** Judas tree. ‖ **árbol del cielo,** tree of Heaven. ‖ **árbol frutal,** fruit tree.

arbolado,-a 1 *pp* → **arbolar**. – 2 *adj* wooded, with trees. 3 (*mar*) very high. – 4 **arbolado,** *m* woodland.

arboladura *f* masts and spars *pl*.

arbolar 1 *t* MAR to mast. 2 (*enarbolar*) to hoist; (*esgrimir*) to brandish. – 3 **arbolarse,** *p* (*encabritarse*) to rear up.

arboleda *f* grove, wood, copse, spinney.

arboledo *m* woodland.

arborecer *i* to grow.

▲ *Conjugation model* [43], *like agradecer*.

arbóreo,-a *adj* arboreal.

■ **vegetación arbórea,** trees *pl*.

arborescente *adj* arborescent.

arboricida 1 *adj* tree-killing. – 2 *m* treekiller.

arborícola *adj* arboreal.

arboricultor,-ra *m,f* arboriculturist.

arboricultura *f* arboriculture.

arboriforme *adj* tree-shaped.

arbotante *m* flying buttress.

arbustivo,-a *adj* bushlike.

arbusto *m* shrub, bush.

arca 1 *f* chest. 2 (*caja de caudales*) strongbox, safe.

■ **arca de Noé,** Noah's ark. ‖ **arcas públicas,** Treasury *sing*.

▲ *Takes* **el** *in singular*.

arcabucero *m* arquebusier.

arcabuz *m* arquebus.

arcada 1 *f* (*conjunto de arcos*) arcade. 2 (*de puente*) arch. 3 (*vómitos*) retching.

arcaduz *m* pipe, conduit.

arcaico,-a *adj* archaic.

arcaísmo *m* archaism.

arcaizante *adj* archaistic.

arcángel *m* archangel.

arcano,-a 1 *adj* arcane. – 2 **arcano,** *m* secret, mystery.

arce *m* maple (tree).
■ **arce menor,** common maple, field maple. ‖ **arce real,** Norway maple. ‖ **arce rojo,** red maple.
arcediano *m* archdeacon.
arcén *m* side of the road, verge; (*de autopista*) hard shoulder.
archi- *pref* really, very, extremely: *archimillonario,-a,* multimillionaire; *archiconocido,-a,* really famous; *archisabido,-a,* extremely well-known.
archibebe *m* redshank.
archicofradía *f* archconfraternity.
archidiácono *m* archdeacon.
archidiócesis *f* archdiocese.
▲ *pl archidiócesis.*
archiduque,-esa *m,f* (*hombre*) archduke; (*mujer*) archduchess.
archimandrita *m* archimandrite.
archipiélago *m* archipelago.
archivador,-ra 1 *m,f* (*en archivo*) archivist; (*en oficina*) filing clerk. – 2 archivador, *m* (*mueble*) filing cabinet; (*carpeta*) file.
archivar 1 *t* (*ordenar*) to file (away). 2 INFORM to save. 3 (*arrinconar*) to shelve. 4 *fam* (*guardar*) to put (away).
archivero,-a *m,f* archivist.
archivo 1 *m* (*informe, ficha*) file. 2 (*documentos*) files *pl,* archives *pl.* 3 INFORM file. 4 (*lugar*) archive. 5 (*archivador*) filing cabinet. 6 *fig* (*modelo*) model, example.
archivolta *f* archivolt.
arcilla *f* clay.
arcilloso,-a *adj* clayey, clayish, clay-like.
arcipreste *m* archpriest.
arco 1 *m* ARQ arch. 2 MAT ELÉC arc. 3 MÚS DEP bow.
■ **arco apuntado,** lancet arch, pointed arch. ‖ **arco de herradura,** horseshoe arch. ‖ **arco de medio punto,** semicircular arch. ‖ **arco de triunfo,** triumphal arch. ‖ **arco iris,** rainbow. ‖ **arco voltaico,** electric arc.
arcón *m* large chest.
arder 1 *i* to burn; (*completamente*) to burn down; (*sin llama*) to smoulder: *el edificio está ardiendo,* the building is in flames. 2 (*resplandecer*) to glow. 3 *fig* to burn. – 4 *t* to burn.
● **arder de pasión,** *fig* to burn with passion. ‖ **arder en guerras,** *fig* to be ravaged by war. ‖ **la cosa está que arde,** *fam* things are getting pretty hot.
ardid *m* scheme, trick.
ardiente 1 *adj* (*encendido*) burning, hot, scalding. 2 *fig* (*intenso*) passionate, ardent; (*fervoroso*) eager.
ardientemente *adv* ardently, fervently.
ardilla *f* squirrel.
ardite me importa un ardite, *loc* I don't give a damn.
ardor 1 *m* burning sensation, burn; (*calor*) heat. 2 *fig* (*ansia*) ardour (US ardor), fervour (US fervor).
● **con ardor,** passionately.
■ **ardor de estómago,** heartburn.
ardorosamente *adv* ardently, passionately.
ardoroso,-a 1 *adj* burning, hot. 2 *fig* ardent, passionate.
arduo,-a *adj* arduous, very difficult, awkward.
área 1 *f* (*zona*) area, zone. 2 (*medida*) are. 3 (*superficie*) area.
■ **área de castigo,** DEP penalty area. ‖ **área de gol,** DEP goal area. ‖ **área de servicio,** (*en autopista*) service area.
▲ *Takes el in sing.*
arena 1 *f* sand: *playa de arena,* sandy beach. 2 (*de circo romano*) arena. 3 (*plaza de toros*) bullring.
■ **arenas movedizas,** quicksand *sing.*
arenal *m* sands *pl,* sandy area.

arenga *f* harangue.
● **echar/dirigir/pronunciar una arenga,** to harangue.
arengar *t* to harangue.
▲ *Conjugation model* [7], *like* **llegar.**
arenilla 1 *f* fine sand. – 2 **arenillas,** *fpl* (*cálculos*) stones.
arenisca *f* sandstone.
arenoso,-a *adj* sandy.
arenque *m* herring.
■ **arenque ahumado,** kipper, kippered herring.
aréola *f* areola.
areómetro *m* hydrometer.
arete 1 *m* (*anillo*) small ring. 2 (*pendiente*) earring. 3 (*pez*) red gurnard.
argamasa *f* mortar.
Argel 1 *m* (*ciudad*) Algiers. 2 (*país*) Algeria.
argelino,-a 1 *adj* Algerian. – 2 *m,f* Algerian.
argentado,-a 1 *adj* (*bañado en plata*) silver-plated. 2 LIT silvery.
argentán *m* nickel silver, German silver.
argénteo,-a 1 *adj* TÉC silver-plated. 2 *lit* silver, silvery.
argentífero,-a *adj* argentiferous.
argentina *f* → **argentino,-a.**
Argentina *f* Argentina, the Argentine.
argentinismo *m* Argentinian expression.
argentino,-a 1 *adj* Argentinian. – 2 *m,f* Argentinian.
argolla 1 *f* (*aro*) (large) ring. 2 *fig* shackles *pl.*
argón *m* argon.
argonauta *m* argonaut.
argot 1 *m* (*popular*) slang. 2 (*técnico*) jargon.
argucia *f* sophism, phallacy.
argüir 1 *t* (*deducir*) to deduce, conclude. 2 (*probar*) to prove. 3 (*reprochar*) to reproach. – 4 *i* (*discutir*) to argue (**contra,** with).
▲ *Conjugation model* [63].
argumentación 1 *f* (*proceso*) arguing, argument. 2 (*argumento*) argument.
argumentar 1 *t* (*deducir*) to deduce. – 2 *i* (*discutir*) to argue (**contra,** with).
argumentista *mf* scriptwriter.
argumento 1 *m* argument. 2 (*de novela, obra, etc*) plot.
arguyo *pres indic* → **argüir.**
aria *f* aria.
aridecer 1 *t* to dry up. – 2 *i* to dry up. – 3 **aridecerse,** *p* to dry up.
aridez 1 *f* aridity. 2 *fig* dryness.
árido,-a 1 *adj* arid. 2 *fig* dry. – 3 **áridos,** *mpl* dry goods.
Aries *m* Aries.
▲ *pl Aries.*
ariete 1 *m* (*fútbol*) centre (US center) forward. 2 (*máquina*) battering ram.
ario,-a *adj* Aryan.
arisco,-a 1 *adj* (*persona - altiva*) unsociable, unfriendly; (*- áspera*) surly, gruff; (*- huidiza*) shy. 2 (*animal*) unfriendly.
arista 1 *f* (*línea*) edge. 2 (*filamento del trigo*) beard. 3 ARQ (*de viga*) arris; (*de bóveda*) groin. 4 (*de montaña*) arête. – 5 **aristas,** *fpl fig* (*dificultades*) difficulties.
aristocracia *f* aristocracy.
aristócrata *mf* aristocrat.
aristocrático,-a *adj* aristocratic.
aristotélico,-a *adj* Aristotelian.
aritmética *f* → **aritmético,-a.**
aritmético,-a 1 *adj* arithmetical, arithmetic. – 2 **aritmética,** *f* arithmetic.

arlequín *m* Harlequin.
arlequinada *f* piece of clowning, piece of buffoonery.
arlequinesco,-a *adj* grotesque, ridiculous.
arma I *f* weapon, arm. – **2 armas,** *fpl (profesión)* army *sing; (fuerzas armadas)* armed forces; *(empresa militar)* military combat *sing.* **3** *(heráldica)* arms, armorial bearings.
● **alzarse en armas,** to rise up in arms. ‖ **pasar por las armas,** to execute. ‖ **presentar armas,** to present arms. ‖ **rendir armas,** to surrender. ‖ **ser de armas tomar,** *fig* to be formidable. ‖ **tomar las armas,** to take up arms.
■ **arma blanca,** knife. ‖ **arma corta,** small arm. ‖ **arma de artillería,** artillery. ‖ **arma de doble filo,** *fig* double-edged sword. ‖ **arma de fuego,** firearm. ‖ **arma homicida,** murder weapon. ‖ **arma nuclear,** nuclear weapon. ‖ **licencia de armas,** firearms licence (US license).
▲ Takes *el* in singular.
armada *f* navy, naval forces *pl.*
■ **la Armada Invencible,** the Spanish Armada.
armadía *f* raft.
armadijo *m* snare, trap.
armadillo *m* armadillo.
armado,-a I *pp →* **armar.** – **2** *adj* armed: *ir armado,-a,* to be armed. **3** *(en mecánica)* mounted, assembled.
armador,-ra *m,f* shipowner.
armadura I *f (traje)* suit of armour (US armor). **2** *(armazón)* frame. **3** ARQ framework.
armamentismo *m* arms build-up.
armamentista I *adj* arms. **2** *mf (partidario)* rearmament supporter. **3** *(fabricante)* arms manufacturer.
■ **la carrera armamentista,** the arms race.
armamento I *m (acción)* armament, arming. – **2** armamentos, *mpl (armas)* armaments, arms.
armañac *m* Armagnac.
armar I *t (dar armas)* to arm: *armaron al pueblo,* they armed the people. **2** *(cargar)* to load; *(bayoneta)* to fix. **3** *(montar - mueble)* to assemble; *(- tienda)* to pitch, put up; *(- trampa)* to set. **4** *(preparar)* to arrange, prepare; *(organizar)* to organize. **5** *fam (causar, originar)* to cause, kick up, create: *armó un lío tremendo,* he kicked up a tremendous fuss. **6** *(embarcación)* to fit out. **7** *(tela)* to stiffen. **8** TÉC to reinforce. – **9** armarse, *p (proveerse)* to provide os. (**de,** with), arm os. (**de,** with): *se armó de pintura y pincel y se puso a pintar,* he provided himself with paint and paintbrush and began to paint. **10** *(producirse)* to be, break out: *se armó un jaleo,* there was a right row.
● **armarla,** *fam* to cause trouble, kick up a fuss. ‖ **armarse de paciencia,** to summon up patience. ‖ **armarse de valor,** to pluck up courage. ‖ **va a armarse la gorda,** *fam* there's going to be real trouble.
armario *m (para ropa)* wardrobe, US closet; *(de cocina)* cupboard.
■ **armario empotrado,** built-in wardrobe, built-in cupboard.
armatoste I *m (cosa)* monstrosity; *(máquina)* useless contraption. **2** *(persona)* useless great oaf.
armazón I *m & f* frame, framework; *(de madera)* timberwork. **2** ARQ shell; *(de escultura)* armature.
armella *f* eyebolt.
Armenia *f* Armenia.
armenio,-a I *adj* Armenian. – **2** *m,f (persona)* Armenian. – **3** armenio, *m (idioma)* Armenian.
armería I *f (tienda)* gunsmith's (shop). **2** *(oficio)* gunsmith's craft. **3** *(museo)* armoury (US armory), museum of arms.

armero,-a *m,f* armourer (US armorer); *(de armas de fuego)* gunsmith.
■ **maestro armero,** armourer (US armorer).
armiñado,-a I *adj (de armiño)* ermine-trimmed. **2** *(blanco)* white.
armiño *m* ermine.
armisticio *m* armistice.
armonía *f* harmony.
armónica *f →* **armónico,-a.**
armónicamente *adv* in harmony, harmoniously.
armónico,-a I *adj* harmonic. – **2** armónico, *m* MÚS harmonic. – **3** armónica, *f* harmonica, mouth organ.
armonio *m* harmonium.
armoniosamente *adv* harmoniously.
armonioso,-a *adj* harmonious.
armonización *f* harmonizing.
armonizar I *t* to harmonize. – **2** *i* to harmonize.
▲ Conjugation model [4], like *realizar.*
ARN *abr* MED *(ácido ribonucleico)* ribonucleic acid; *(abreviatura)* RNA.
arnés I *m (armadura)* armour (US armor). – **2** arneses, *mpl* harness *sing,* trappings.
árnica *f* arnica.
aro[1] I *m* hoop, ring. **2** *(juego)* hoop. **3** *(servilletero)* serviette ring, US napkin ring. **4** *(sortija)* ring. **5** *(pendiente)* earring, sleeper.
● **entrar/pasar por el aro,** to knuckle under.
aro[2] *m (planta)* cuckoo-pint.
aroma *m* aroma; *(del vino)* bouquet.
aromático,-a *adj* aromatic, fragrant.
aromatización *f* scenting, perfuming.
aromatizador *m* air freshener.
aromatizante *adj* scenting, perfuming: *hierbas aromatizantes,* aromatic herbs.
aromatizar *t* to scent, perfume.
▲ Conjugation model [4], like *realizar.*
arpa *f* harp.
▲ Takes *el* in singular.
arpado,-a *adj* serrated.
arpegio *m* arpeggio.
arpeo *m* grappling iron.
arpía I *f* harpy. **2** *fam fig* dragon, old witch, harpy.
arpillera *f* sackcloth, burlap, hessian, sacking.
arpista *mf* harpist.
arpón *m* harpoon.
arponar *t* to harpoon.
arponear *t* to harpoon.
arponero,-a *m,f* harpooner.
arquear[1] I *t (doblar)* to arch, bend, curve. – **2** arquearse, *p* to arch, bend, curve.
arquear[2] *t (pesar)* to measure the tonnage of.
arqueo[1] *m (curvatura)* bending, curving.
arqueo[2] *m* MAR *(medición)* gauging; *(cabida)* tonnage.
arqueo[3] *m* COM checking, cashing up.
● **hacer el arqueo,** to cash up.
arqueolítico,-a *adj* Stone-Age.
arqueología *f* archaeology (US archeology).
arqueológico,-a *adj* archaeological (US archeological).
arqueólogo,-a *m,f* archaeologist (US archeologist).
arquería *f* arcade.
arquero,-a *m,f* archer.
arqueta *f* small chest.
arquetípico,-a *adj* archetypal.
arquetipo *m* archetype.

arquitecto,-a *m,f* architect.
arquitectónico,-a *adj* architectural, architectonic.
arquitectura *f* architecture.
arquitrabe *m* architrave.
arquivolta *f* archivolt.
arrabal 1 *m* poor area, working-class area (*on the edge of town*). – 2 **arrabales,** *mpl* outskirts.
arrabalero,-a 1 *adj* (*del arrabal*) of or from a poor area. 2 *pey* (*grosero*) vulgar, common, ill-bred. – 3 *m,f pey* (*grosero*) vulgar person, common person, ill-bred person.
arrabio *m* cast iron.
arracada *f* dangly earring.
arracimarse *p* to cluster together, bunch together.
arraigadamente *adv* firmly, securely.
arraigado,-a 1 *pp →* **arraigar.** – 2 *adj* (deeply) rooted.
arraigar 1 *i* to take root. – 2 *t* (*fijar*) to establish, strengthen. – 3 **arraigarse,** *p* (*establecerse*) to settle down.
▲ Conjugation model |7|, like *llegar.*
arraigo 1 *m* (*acción*) act of taking root. 2 *fig* (*raíces*) roots: *con mucho arraigo,* deeply-rooted.
arramblar 1 *t* (*cubrir de arena*) to cover with sand. – 2 *i fam* (*llevarse*) to make off (**con,** with): *arrambló con todo,* he made off with everything.
arrancaclavos *m* claw hammer, nail extractor.
▲ *pl* *arrancaclavos.*
arrancada *f* jerk, jolt.
arrancador,-ra 1 *adj* uprooting. – 2 **arrancadora,** *f* lifter, picker.
arrancadora *f →* **arrancador,-ra.**
arrancar 1 *t* (*árbol*) to uproot; (*flor*) to pull up. 2 (*plumas, cejas*) to pluck; (*cabello, diente*) to pull out; (*con violencia - página*) to tear out. 3 (*arrebatar*) to snatch, grab: *me arrancó el bolso,* he snatched my bag. 4 (*obtener - aplausos, sonrisa*) to get; (- *confesión, información*) to extract. 5 (*rescatar*) to rescue, save: *intentaron arrancarle de la droga,* they tried to get him off drugs. 6 (*coche*) to start. – 7 *i* (*partir*) to begin, start. 8 (*salir*) to go, leave. 9 (*coche*) to start; (*tren*) to pull out. 10 *fig* (*provenir*) to stem (**de,** from).
● **arrancar a correr,** to break into a run.
▲ Conjugation model |1|, like *sacar.*
arranchar *t* to skirt.
arranque 1 *m* TÉC starting mechanism. 2 (*comienzo*) start. 3 *fig* (*arrebato*) outburst, fit: *un arranque de furia,* a fit of rage. 4 ARQ (*de escalera*) foot; (*de arco*) base. 5 (*decisión, valentía*) courage, determination. 6 (*ocurrencia ingeniosa*) joke, witticism.
● **en un arranque,** *fig* impulsively.
■ **motor de arranque,** starter motor. ‖ **punto de arranque,** beginning.
arrapiezo 1 *m* (*andrajo*) rag, tatter. 2 (*niño*) whippersnapper, urchin.
arras *fpl* 13 *coins given by bridegroom to bride during the wedding ceremony.*
arrasado,-a 1 *pp →* **arrasar.** – 2 *adj* (*devastado*) devastated, destroyed. 3 (*allanado*) levelled, smooth.
arrasar 1 *t* (*destruir*) to raze, destroy. 2 (*allanar*) to level, smooth. – 3 *i* (*disco, libro, película*) to be a smash hit, sweep the board; (*deportista*) to sweep to victory.
● **arrasar con,** (*gen*) to sweep away; (*comer*) to polish off; (*destrozar*) to destroy; (*robar*) to get away with, make off with.
arrastradamente *adv* miserably.
arrastradizo,-a *adj* trailing, dragging.
arrastrado,-a 1 *pp →* **arrastrar.** – 2 *adj* wretched, miserable.

● **ir arrastrado,-a,** to be hard up.
arrastrar 1 *t* (*gen*) to drag, pull: *no arrastres los pies,* don't drag your feet. 2 (*corriente, aire*) to sweep along. 3 *fig* to sway, win over, draw: *este grupo arrastra a muchas quinceañeras,* this group draws lots of teenage girls; *lo arrastra la pasión por el teatro,* he lives for the theatre. 4 (*traer como consecuencia*) to cause, bring, lead to. 5 (*tener*) to have: *arrastra ese catarro desde hace un mes,* she's had that cold for a month; *arrastran muchos problemas,* they've got lots of problems. – 6 *i* to drag, trail. – 7 **arrastrarse,** *p* to drag os., to crawl. 8 *fig* (*humillarse*) to creep, crawl.
arrastre 1 *m* (*acción*) dragging, pulling. 2 (*telesquí*) drag lift. 3 (*en naipes*) lead.
● **estar para el arrastre,** *fam* (*persona*) to be on one's last legs, be done for; (*objeto*) to be done for.
■ **materiales de arrastre,** trawling gear *sing.*
arrayán *m* myrtle.
arre *interj fam* gee up!, giddy up!
arrea *interj fam* goodness me!
arrear 1 *t* (*animales*) to spur on, urge on. 2 (*apresurar*) to hurry up. 3 *fam* (*pegar*) to hit: *le arreó una bofetada,* she slapped him round the face. – 4 *i fam* to hurry.
arrebatado,-a 1 *pp →* **arrebatar.** – 2 *adj* (*impetuoso*) rash, impetuous. 3 (*encolerizado*) furious, enraged. 4 (*ruborizado*) blushing, flushed.
arrebatador,-ra *adj fig* captivating, fascinating.
arrebatamiento *m →* **arrebato.**
arrebatar 1 *t* (*quitar*) to grab, snatch: *le arrebató el papel de las manos,* she snatched the paper out of his hands; *esa enfermedad le arrebató la vida,* that illness cost him his life. 2 *fig* (*cautivar*) to captivate, fascinate. 3 (*agostar*) to wither. – 4 **arrebatarse,** *p* (*enfurecerse*) to become furious; (*exaltarse*) to get carried away. 5 (*agostarse*) to wither. 6 (*cocer muy deprisa*) to burn, overcook.
arrebato *m* (*arranque*) fit, outburst: *en un arrebato de celos mató a su amante,* in a sudden fit of jealousy he killed his lover.
arrebol 1 *m* (*de nubes*) red glow. 2 (*de mejillas*) glow, redness. – 3 **arreboles,** *mpl* (*nubes*) red clouds.
arrebolada *f* red clouds *pl.*
arrebolar 1 *t* (*enrojecer*) to give a red glow to. 2 (*persona*) to make turn red. – 3 **arrebolarse,** *p* (*enrojecer*) to glow red. 4 (*persona*) to blush.
arrebujar 1 *t* (*arrugar*) to crumple: *arrebujó su ropa y salió de la habitación,* he screwed up his clothes and left the room. 2 (*arropar*) to wrap up.
arrechucho 1 *m* (*indisposición*) ailment. 2 (*arranque*) outburst, fit. 3 (*empujón*) push, shove.
arreciar *i* to get stronger, get worse: *la tormenta arreció y la vela mayor se rompió,* the storm got worse and the mainsail broke.
▲ Conjugation model |12|, like *cambiar.*
arrecife *m* reef.
arrecirse *p* to be stiff with cold, be numb.
▲ Used only in forms which include the letter *i* in their endings: *arrecía, arreciré, arreciendo.*
arredrar 1 *t* to intimidate, frighten, daunt: *las huelgas no arredran al gobierno,* the government isn't intimidated by strikes. – 2 **arredrarse,** *p* to be frightened.
arreglado,-a 1 *pp →* **arreglar.** – 2 *adj* (*solucionado*) settled, fixed, sorted out: *ya está todo arreglado,* everything is settled, everything is sorted out. 3 (*ordenado*) tidy, neat, arranged, orderly: *lleva una vida muy arreglada,* he has an orderly life. 4 (*bien vestido*) well-dressed, smart: *iba muy arreglado,* he was dressed very smartly. 5 (*precio*) reasonable.

● **¡estamos arreglados,-as!,** *fam* that's all we needed!

arreglar 1 *t* (*gen*) to settle, sort out, fix: *el tiempo lo arregla todo,* time heals all wounds. 2 (*ordenar*) to tidy up, clear up. 3 (*reparar*) to mend, fix, repair: *tienes que llevar el video a arreglar,* you have to take the video to be repaired. 4 MÚS to arrange. 5 *fam* to sort out: *¡ya te arreglaré!,* I'll teach you!, I'll sort you out. – 6 **arreglarse,** *p* (*componerse*) to get ready, dress up; (*cabello*) to do: *arréglate el pelo,* do your hair. 7 (*solucionarse*) to get sorted out, work out; (*pareja*) to get back together again.
● **arreglárselas,** to manage, cope: *arréglatelas como puedas,* do the best you can; *tuvo que arreglárselas solo,* he had to look after himself; *¿cómo te las arreglas para tener tantas novias?,* how do you manage to have so many girlfriends?

arreglista *mf* arranger.

arreglo 1 *m* (*acuerdo*) arrangement, aggreement, settlement. 2 (*reparación*) repair. – 3 *f* (*orden*) order, tidiness. – 4 *m* (*limpieza*) cleaning, tidying; (*personal*) cleanliness. 5 MÚS arrangement.
● **con arreglo a,** according to, in accordance with: *con arreglo al plan,* according to the plan. ‖ **llegar a un arreglo,** to come to an arrangement, reach an agreement. ‖ **no tener arreglo,** (*cosa*) to be beyond repair; (*asunto*) to have no solution; (*persona*) to be hopeless: *ese reloj no tiene arreglo,* that watch is beyond repair; *¡no tienes arreglo!,* you're hopeless! ‖ **arreglo de cuentas,** settling of scores, settling-up.

arrejuntarse *p fam* to shack up together, live together.

arrellanarse *p* to sit back, settle down.

arremangar 1 *t* to roll up. – 2 **arramangarse,** *p* to roll up one's sleeves. 3 **arremangarse,** *fig* to get serious, get down to it: *vamos, arremángate que hay que terminar el trabajo,* come on, get down to it, we've got to finish this job.
▲ *Conjugation model* [7], *like llegar.*

arremeter 1 *i* (*gen*) to attack, charge; (*el toro*) to charge. 2 (*verbalmete*) to attack.

arremetida *f* attack, onslaught.

arremolinarse 1 *p* (*formar remolinos*) to whirl round. 2 *fig* (*gente*) to crowd together, cram together.

arrendable 1 *adj* rentable. 2 JUR leasable.

arrendador,-ra 1 *adj* renting, leasing. – 2 *m,f* lessor; (*hombre*) landlord; (*mujer*) landlady.

arrendajo 1 *m* ORN jay. 2 *fam* mimic.

arrendamiento 1 *m* renting, leasing, letting. 2 (*precio*) rent.
■ **contrato de arrendamiento,** lease.

arrendar *t* (*dar en alquiler*) to let, lease; (*tomar en alquiler*) to rent, lease.
▲ *Conjugation model* [27], *like acertar.*

arrendatario,-a 1 *adj* renting, leasing. – 2 *m,f* (*que da en arriendo*) leaseholder, lessee. 3 (*inquilino*) tenant.

arreos 1 *mpl* (*de caballerías*) harness *sing*, trappings. 2 (*adornos*) adornment *sing*.

arrepanchingarse *p fam* to lounge, sprawl out.
▲ *Conjugation model* [7], *like llegar.*

arrepentida *f* → **arrepentido,-a.**

arrepentido,-a 1 *pp* → **arrepentirse.** – 2 *adj* regretful, repentant: *está arrepentida de lo que dijo,* she's sorry about what she said. – 3 *m,f* penitent. – 4 **arrepentida,** *f euf* reformed prostitute.

arrepentimiento *m* regret, repentance: *después le vino el arrepentimiento,* afterwards he felt sorry.

arrepentirse 1 *p* (*gen*) to regret (**de,** -): *se arrepintió de haber llegado tarde,* he regretted having arrived late. 2

REL to repent (**de,** of): *se arrepintió de sus pecados,* he repented of his sins.
▲ *Conjugation model* [35], *like hervir.*

arrestado,-a 1 *pp* → **arrestar.** – 2 *adj* arrested, detained.

arrestar 1 *t* to arrest, detain. 2 (*poner en prisión*) to imprison, jail, put in prison.

arresto 1 *m* arrest. – 2 **arrestos,** *mpl* (*ímpetu*) daring *sing*, guts.
● **tener arrestos,** to be bold, be daring. ‖ **estar bajo arresto,** to be under arrest.
■ **arresto mayor,** close arrest. ‖ **arresto menor,** open arrest.

arriar 1 *t* (*velas*) to lower. 2 (*bandera*) to strike.
▲ *Conjugation model* [13], *like desviar.*

arriate *m* flower bed.

arriba 1 *adv* up; (*encima*) on (the) top: *ponlo más arriba,* put it higher up. 2 (*piso*) upstairs: *vive arriba,* he/she lives upstairs. 3 (*en escritos*) above: *véase más arriba,* see above. – 4 *interj* up!: *¡arriba la República!,* long live the Republic!, up the Republic!
● **de arriba abajo,** from top to bottom. ‖ **hacia arriba,** upwards.

arribada *f* arrival.

arribar *i* (*gen*) to arrive; (*barco*) to reach port, dock.

arribismo *m* arrivisme, social climbing.

arribista 1 *adj* ambitious, self-seeking. – 2 *mf* arriviste, social climber, parvenu.

arribo *m* arrival.

arriendo *m* lease; (*de un piso*) renting.
● **dar en arriendo,** to let out on lease. ‖ **tomar en arriendo,** to take on lease.

arriero *m* muleteer.

arriesgado,-a 1 *pp* → **arriesgar.** – 2 *adj* (*peligroso*) risky, dangerous. 3 (*temerario*) bold, daring, fearless.

arriesgar 1 *t* to risk; (*dinero*) to stake: *arriesgó mucho dinero con esa operación,* he staked a lot of money on that transaction. 2 (*aventurar*) to venture: *arriesgó una hipótesis absurda,* she ventured an outrageous theory. – 3 **arriesgarse,** *p* (*uso reflexivo*) to risk: *se arriesgó mucho y fracasó,* he took many risks and failed.
● **arriesgar el pellejo,** *fam* to risk one's neck. ‖ **arriesgarse a hacer algo,** to dare to do sth., risk doing sth.
▲ *Conjugation model* [7], *like llegar.*

arrimadero 1 *m* (*de pared*) wainscot. 2 (*estribo*) support.

arrimadizo,-a 1 *adj fig* parasitic. – 2 *m,f fig* parasite.

arrimar 1 *t* (*acercar*) to move closer. – 2 **arrimarse,** *p* to move close, get close. 3 *fam* to cohabit, live together.
● **arrimar a algn.,** *fig* to seek sb.'s protection. ‖ **arrimar al sol que más calienta,** *fig* to get on the winning side.

arrimo 1 *m* (*apoyo*) support, protection. 2 *fig* (*ayuda*) help.
● **al arrimo de,** under the protection of.

arrinconado,-a 1 *pp* → **arrinconar.** – 2 *adj* put away, laid aside, forgotten. 3 (*persona*) forsaken.

arrinconar 1 *t* (*poner en un rincón*) to put in a corner. 2 (*retirar*) to lay aside, put away. 3 (*acorralar*) to corner: *arrinconó a su enemigo en el callejón,* he cornered his enemy in the alley. 4 *fig* (*desatender*) to neglect: *arrinconó a sus abuelos,* he neglected his grandparents. – 5 **arrinconarse,** *p* (*aislarse*) to isolate os.

arriñonado,-a *adj* kidney-shaped.

arriscado,-a 1 *adj* (*con riscos*) craggy, cliffy, rugged. 2 (*arriesgado*) risky, dangerous. 3 (*atrevido*) daring, bold.

arritmia *f* arrhythmia.

arroba *f* (*medida de peso*) measure of weight equal to 11.502 kg, 25.3 lbs; (*medida de capacidad*) variable liquid measure.
● **por arrobas,** heaps of, stacks of, loads of: *había comida por arrobas,* there was heaps of food.
arrobamiento *m* rapture, ecstasy, enthralment (US enthrallment).
arrobar 1 *t* to rapture, enthral (US enthrall). – **2 arrobarse,** *p* to go into raptures, be enthralled.
arrobo *m* → **arrobamiento.**
arrocero,-a 1 *adj* rice. – **2** *m,f* (*cultivador*) rice grower; (*vendedor*) rice seller.
arrodillado,-a 1 *pp* → **arrodillarse.** – **2** *adj* on one's knees, kneeling down.
arrodillarse *p* to kneel down, get down on one's knees.
arrogación *f* arrogation.
arrogancia 1 *f* (*orgullo*) arrogance. **2** (*gallardía*) gallantry, valour (US valor), bravery.
arrogante 1 *adj* (*orgulloso*) arrogant. **2** (*gallardo*) gallant, valiant, brave.
arrogar 1 *t* JUR to adopt. – **2 arrogarse,** *p* to arrogate, assume, take upon os.
▲ *Conjugation model* [7], *like* **llegar.**
arrojadizo,-a *adj* for throwing.
■ **arma arrojadiza,** projectile, missile.
arrojado,-a 1 *pp* → **arrojar.** – **2** *adj* thrown, thrown out. **3** (*osado*) bold, fearless, daring.
arrojar 1 *t* (*tirar*) to throw, fling: *lo arrojararon al mar,* he was flung into the sea. **2** (*echar con violencia*) to throw out, kick out: *le arrojaron a la calle,* he was kicked out on the street. **3** (*vomitar*) to vomit, throw up. **4** (*emitir - humo*) to send out, belch out; (- *olor*) to give off; (- *lava*) to spew out. **5** (*cuentas etc*) to show, produce, give. – **6** *i* to vomit. – **7 arrojarse,** *p* to throw os.: *se arrojó sobre él,* she jumped on him.
● *"prohibido arrojar basuras",* "no dumping".
arrojo *m* boldness, dash, bravery, daring.
arrollable *adj* rollable.
arrollador,-ra *adj* overwhelming, irresistible: *fue un éxito arrollador,* it was a resounding success; *tiene una personalidad arrolladora,* she's got an overpowering personality.
arrollamiento 1 *m* (*acción*) rolling (up). **2** (*atropello*) running over, knocking down. **3** *fig* (*aplastamiento*) crushing, routing.
arrollar 1 *t* (*envolver*) to roll (up). **2** (*el viento*) to sweep away. **3** (*al enemigo*) to crush, rout. **4** (*atropellar*) to run over.
arropamiento *m* wrapping up.
arropar *t* to wrap up: *cada noche arropa a los niños en la cama,* every night she tucks her children up in bed.
arrope *m* boiled must, grape syrup.
arrostrar 1 *t* (*afrontar*) to face: *arrostraron al enemigo,* they faced the enemy. **2** (*emprender*) to brave.
arroyada 1 *f* (*cauce*) stream bed. **2** (*surco*) channel, gully. **3** (*crecida*) flood, flooding.
arroyar *t* to channel.
arroyo 1 *m* (*corriente de agua*) stream, brook. **2** (*en la calle*) gutter. **3** *fig* (*corriente*) flood, stream: *de sus ojos salía un arroyo de lágrimas,* a flood of tears rolled down her cheeks.
● **poner (a algn.) en el arroyo,** *fig* to chuck (sb.) out. ‖ **sacar (a algn.) del arroyo,** *fig* to drag (sb.) from the gutter.
arroyuelo *m* small stream, brook.
arroz *m* rice.
■ **arroz blanco,** (*seco*) white rice; (*hervido*) boiled rice. ‖

arroz con leche, rice pudding. ‖ **arroz integral,** brown rice.
arrozal *m* rice field, rice plantation.
arruga *f* (*piel*) wrinkle; (*ropa*) crease.
arrugamiento *m* (*piel*) wrinkling; (*ropa*) creasing.
arrugar 1 *t* (*piel*) to wrinkle; (*ropa*) to crease; (*papel*) to crumple (up). – **2 arrugarse,** *p* (*piel*) to wrinkle; (*ropa*) to crease; (*papel*) to crumple (up). **3** *fam* (*acobardarse*) to get the wind up.
● **arrugar el ceño/entrecejo,** to frown.
▲ *Conjugation model* [7], *like* **llegar.**
arruinado,-a 1 *pp* → **arruinar.** – **2** *adj* bankrupt, broke. **3** (*estropeado*) ruined.
arruinar 1 *t* to bankrupt, ruin. **2** (*estropear*) to damage: *la tormenta ha arruinado la cosecha,* the storm has ruined the crops. – **3 arruinarse,** *p* to be bankrupt, be ruined.
arrullador,-ra 1 *adj* (*sonido*) lulling. **2** (*ave*) cooing.
arrullar 1 *t* (*ave*) to coo. **2** (*adormecer*) to lull. – **3 arrullarse,** *p* *fig* (*acariciarse*) to bill and coo.
arrullo 1 *m* (*de ave*) cooing. **2** (*nana*) lullaby. **3** (*ropa bebé*) baby wrap. **4** (*de enamorados*) billing and cooing.
arrumaco *m* *fam* (*caricia*) caress; (*palabra cariñosa*) sweet nothing.
● **hacerse arrumacos,** to pet. ‖ **ir con arrumacos a algn.,** to flatter sb.
▲ *Also used in plural with the same meaning.*
arrumar 1 *t* to stow. – **2 arrumarse,** *p* to cloud over.
arrumazón *f* stowing.
arrumbar[1] 1 *t* (*apartar*) to put away, lay aside. **2** *fig* (*persona*) to neglect, ignore.
arrumbar[2] *i* MAR to set course (**hacia,** for).
arsenal 1 *m* MAR shipyard. **2** (*de armas*) arsenal. **3** *fig* (*cantidad*) storehouse, mine.
arsénico *m* arsenic.
art. *abr* (*artículo*) article; (*abreviatura*) art.
arte 1 *m* art. **2** (*habilidad*) craft, skill. **3** (*astucia*) cunning. **4** (*pesca*) fishing gear.
● **con malas artes,** by evil means.
artefacto 1 *m* device, appliance; (*explosivo*) explosive device. **2** (*en arqueología*) artefact.
artejo 1 *m* (*nudillo*) knuckle. **2** (*de artrópodos*) article.
artemisa *f* artemisia.
arteramente *adv* cunningly, artfully.
arteria *f* artery.
■ **arteria carótida,** carotid artery. ‖ **arteria coronaria,** coronary artery.
artería *f* craftiness, artfulness.
arterial *adj* arterial.
arterioesclerosis *f* arteriosclerosis.
▲ *pl* **arterioesclerosis.**
arteriola *f* arteriole.
arteriopatía *f* arteriopathy.
arteriosclerosis *f* arteriosclerosis.
▲ *pl* **arteriosclerosis.**
arteriosclerósico,-a *adj* arteriosclerotic.
arteriosclerótico,-a *adj* arteriosclerotic.
artero,-a *adj* artful, crafty.
artesa *f* trough.
artesanado *m* craftsmen *pl.*
artesanal *adj* (*objeto*) handmade; (*comida*) homemade.
■ **actividades artesanales,** arts and crafts. ‖ **industria artesanal,** craft industry.
artesanía 1 *f* (*calidad*) craftsmanship. **2** (*arte, obra*) crafts *pl,* handicrafts *pl.*

■ **objeto de artesanía,** handmade object. ‖ **obra de artesanía,** piece of craftsmanship.

artesano,-a 1 *adj* handmade. – **2** *m,f (hombre)* craftsman; *(mujer)* craftswoman.

artesiano,-a *adj* artesian.
■ **pozo artesiano,** artesian well.

artesón 1 *m (artesa)* trough. **2** *(parte del artesonado)* coffer. **3** *(artesonado)* coffered ceiling.

artesonado,-a 1 *adj* panelled, coffered. – **2 artesonado,** *m* panelled ceiling, coffered ceiling.

ártico,-a 1 *adj* Arctic. – **2 el Ártico,** *m* the Arctic.
■ **el Círculo Ártico,** the Arctic Circle. ‖ **el océano Ártico,** the Arctic Ocean.

articulación 1 *f* LING articulation. **2** ANAT joint, articulation. **3** TÉC joint.

articulado,-a 1 *pp* → **articular.** – **2** *adj (lenguaje)* articulate. **3** *(objeto)* articulated. – **4 articulado,** *m* articles *pl.*

articular 1 *adj* articulated. – **2** *t* to articulate. **3** JUR to article.

articulatorio,-a *adj* articulatory.

articulista *mf* columnist.

artículo 1 *m* article. **2** *(mercancía)* article, product.
● **hacer el artículo,** *fam* to plug sth. ‖ **in artículo mortis,** in articulo mortis.
■ **artículo de fe,** REL article of faith. ‖ **artículo de fondo,** leading article, editorial. ‖ **artículo definido/determinado,** LING definite article. ‖ **artículo indefinido/indeterminado,** LING indefinite article. ‖ **artículos alimenticios,** foodstuffs. ‖ **artículos de consumo,** consumer goods. ‖ **artículos de limpieza,** cleaning products. ‖ **artículos de primera necesidad,** basic commodities.

artífice 1 *mf (artista)* craftsman, artist. **2** *(autor)* author: *Pepe ha sido el artífice de todo esto,* this is all Pepe's doing. – **3** *m fig* architect: *él ha sido el artífice de este éxito,* he's the man behind this success story.

artificial *adj* artificial.

artificialmente *adv* artificially.

artificiero,-a *m,f* artificier, armourer (US armorer).

artificio 1 *m (habilidad)* skill, dexterity. **2** *(mecanismo)* device. **3** *(falta de naturalidad)* affectation: *su novela tiene demasiado artificio,* her novel was written in an affected style. **4** *(engaño)* artifice, trick.
■ **artificio pirotécnico,** firework.

artificiosamente 1 *adv (hábilmente)* skilfully (US skillfully). **2** *(afectadamente)* in an affected way. **3** *(con disimulo)* slyly, craftily.

artificioso,-a 1 *adj (hábil)* skilful (US skillful), dexterous. **2** *(afectado)* affected. **3** *fig (disimulado)* sly, crafty.

artillería *f* artillery.
■ **artillería antiaérea,** anti-aircraft guns *pl.* ‖ **artillería de campaña,** field guns *pl.* ‖ **artillería pesada,** heavy artillery.

artillero *m* artilleryman.

artilugio 1 *m (mecanismo)* device, gadget. **2** *fig (trampa)* trick, scheme.

artimaña *f* artifice, trick, ruse.

artista *mf* artist.
■ **artista de cine,** film star.

artísticamente *adv* artistically.

artístico,-a *adj* artistic.

artrítico,-a *adj* arthritic.

artritis *f* arthritis.
▲ *pl* **artritis.**

artrópodo *m* arthropod.

artrosis *f* arthrosis.
▲ *pl* **artrosis.**

arveja *f* AM chickpea.

arvejo *m* AM chickpea.

arvicultura *f* cereal farming.

Arz. *abr (arzobispo)* archbishop; *(abreviatura)* Abp.

arzobispado *m* archbishopric.

arzobispal *adj* of the archbishop, relating to the archbishop.

arzobispo *m* archbishop.

arzón *m* saddle tree.

Arzpo. *abr (arzobispo)* archbishop; *(abreviatura)* Abp.

as 1 *m (naipes)* ace. **2** *(dados)* one. **3** *fig* ace, star, wizard: *Fangio fue un as del volante,* Fangio was an ace driver.

asa *f* handle.
▲ Takes *el* in singular.

asadero,-a 1 *adj* (for) roasting. – **2 asadero,** *m fig* oven.

asado,-a 1 *pp* → **asar.** – **2** *adj* roast, roasted. – **3 asado,** *m* roast.
● **asado,-a de calor,** *fig* roasting, boiling hot. ‖ **bien asado,-a,** well done. ‖ **poco asado,-a,** underdone, rare.

asador 1 *m (utensilio)* roaster. **2** *(establecimiento)* grill room, grill house.

asadura *f* offal; *(de ave)* giblets *pl.*
● **echar las asaduras,** *fam* to make a tremendous effort.
▲ Also used in plural with the same meaning.

asaetado,-a 1 *pp* → **asaetar.** – **2** *adj* arrow-shaped.

asaetar 1 *t (disparar)* to shoot arrows at. **2** *(herir)* to wound with arrows; *(matar)* to kill with arrows. **3** *fig (molestar)* to bother, pester.
● **asaetar a algn. a preguntas,** *fig* to bombard sb. with questions.

asalariado,-a 1 *pp* → **asalariar.** – **2** *adj* salaried. – **3** *m,f* wage earner, salaried worker.

asalariar *t* to employ.
▲ *Conjugation model* [12], *like* **cambiar.**

asalmonado,-a *adj* salmon-coloured (US salmon-colored).

asaltador,-ra 1 *adj* assaulting, attacking. – **2** *m,f* attacker; *(en robo)* raider, robber.

asaltante 1 *adj* assaulting, attacker. – **2** *mf* attacker; *(en robo)* raider, robber.

asaltar 1 *t* to assault, attack; *(para robar)* to raid, rob. **2** *(abordar)* to approach, come up to. **3** *fig (surgir)* to assail: *me asaltó la duda de si había dicho la verdad,* doubts sprang to my mind as to whether he had told the truth or not.

asalto 1 *m* assault, attack; *(con robo)* raid, robbery. **2** *(boxeo)* round.
● **asalto a mano armada,** armed robbery. ‖ **tomar por asalto,** to take by storm.

asamblea *f* assembly, meeting.
■ **asamblea general,** general meeting.

asambleísta *mf* member of an assembly, member of a meeting.

asar 1 *t (cocer)* to roast. **2** *fig (importunar)* to annoy, pester. – **3 asarse,** *p (cocerse)* to roast. **4** *fig (pasar calor)* to be roasting, be boiling hot.
● **asar a la parrilla,** to grill. ‖ **asar al horno,** to roast.

asaz 1 *adv lit (muy)* extremely, exceedingly, very: *su muerte fue asaz dolorosa,* her death was extremely painful. **2** *lit (bastante)* rather, quite.

asbesto *m* asbestos.

ascendencia 1 *f* ancestry, ancestors *pl:* *era alemán, pero de ascendencia polaca,* he was German, but of Polish descent. **2** *(influencia)* ascendancy.

ascendente 1 *adj* ascending, ascendant. – **2** *m* ascendant.
ascender 1 *t* to promote. – **2** *i* (*subir*) to climb. **3** (*de categoría*) to be promoted (**a**, to). **4** (*sumar*) to amount (**a**, to).
▲ *Conjugation model* |28|, *like* **entender**.
ascendiente 1 *adj* ascending, ascendant. – **2** *mf* (*antepasado*) ancestor. – **3** *m* (*influencia*) ascendancy, power.
ascensión *f* (*subida*) climb, climbing.
■ día de la Ascensión, REL Ascension Day.
ascensional *adj* ascendant, upward.
ascensionista *mf* (*en globo*) balloonist; (*alpinista*) mountaineer.
ascenso 1 *m* (*subida*) climb, ascent. **2** (*aumento*) rise (**de**, in). **3** (*promoción*) promotion.
ascensor *m* lift, US elevator.
ascensorista *mf* lift attendant, US elevator operator.
asceta *mf* ascetic.
ascética *f* → **ascético,-a**.
asceticismo *m* asceticism.
ascético,-a 1 *adj* ascetic. – **2** **ascética**, *f* asceticism.
asco *m* disgust, repugnance.
● coger asco a algo, to get sick of sth. ‖ dar asco, to be disgusting: *dejó la cocina que daba asco,* he left the kitchen in a terrible mess. ‖ dar asco a algn., to make sb. sick: *me da asco ese sitio,* this place makes me feel sick, this place is disgusting. ‖ estar hecho,-a un asco, (*cosa*) to be filthy, look a real mess; (*persona*) to be filthy, be in a right state. ‖ hacer ascos a algo, to turn up one's nose at sth. ‖ ¡qué asco!, how disgusting!, how revolting!
ascua *f* live coal.
● arrimar el ascua a su sardina, *fam* to look after number one. ‖ estar en/sobre ascuas, to be on tenterhooks. ‖ tener a algn. sobre/en ascuas, to keep sb. on tenterhooks.
▲ *Takes* el *in singular.*
aseado,-a 1 *pp* → **asear**. – **2** *adj* clean, neat, tidy.
asear 1 *t* (*adecentar*) to clean, tidy up. – **2** asearse, *p* (*arreglarse*) to wash, get washed.
asechanza *f* trap.
asediar 1 *t* to besiege, lay siege to. **2** *fig* to besiege, pester, harass.
▲ *Conjugation model* |12|, *like* **cambiar**.
asedio 1 *m* siege. **2** *fig* harassment: *los famosos tienen que soportar el asedio de fotógrafos y periodistas,* famous people have to put up with harassment by photographers and reporters.
asegurado,-a 1 *pp* → **asegurar**. – **2** *adj* (*con seguro*) insured: *el coche está asegurado contra incendio,* the car is insured against fire. **3** (*garantizado*) secure: *tiene el futuro asegurado,* his future is secure. **4** (*seguro*) secured, tightened: *el tornillo está bien asegurado,* the screw is well tightened. – **5** *m,f* (*tomador de un seguro*) the insured person.
asegurador,-ra 1 *adj* insuring, insurance: *compañía aseguradora,* insurance company. – **2** *m,f* insurer.
asegurar 1 *t* (*fijar*) to secure. **2** COM to insure. **3** (*garantizar*) to assure, guarantee: *te aseguro que lo haré,* I assure you that I'll do it. – **4** asegurarse, *p* (*cerciorarse*) to make sure: *asegúrate de cerrar la ventana,* make sure you close the window. **5** COM to insure os.
asemejar 1 *t* to make alike, make similar. – **2** asemejarse a, *p* to look like, be like: *se asemeja a su padre en la nariz,* he's got his father's nose.
asenso *m* assent, consent.
● dar asenso, to assent.

asentaderas *fpl fam* bottom *sing*, buttocks.
asentado,-a 1 *pp* → **asentar**. – **2** *adj* (*situado*) placed, situated. **3** (*firme*) firm, secure.
asentamiento 1 *m* (*poblado*) settlement. **2** MIL emplacement.
asentar 1 *t* (*establecer*) to establish; (*apoyar*) to base. **2** (*colocar - gen*) to locate; (*- colonos*) to settle: *todos los edificios asentados en la Villa Olímpica cuentan con aparcamiento propio,* all buildings in the Olympic Village have their own parking facilities; *estas tribus estaban firmemente asentadas en la península,* these tribes were firmly settled in the peninsula. **3** (*fijar*) to fix, set. **4** (*calmar*) to calm, settle: *toma esto para asentar el estómago,* take this to settle your stomach. **5** (*anotar*) to enter, note down. **6** (*golpes*) to deal. – **7** asentarse, *p* (*establecerse*) to settle: *muchos judíos se han asentado en los territorios ocupados,* many Jews have settled in the occupied territories; *una empresa japonesa ha decidido asentarse en Sevilla,* a Japanese company has decided to set up in Seville. **8** (*aves*) to perch.
● asentar las bases, to lay the foundations.
▲ *Conjugation model* |27|, *like* **acertar**.
asentimiento *m* assent, consent, acquiescence.
asentir *i* to assent, agree; (*con la cabeza*) to nod.
▲ *Conjugation model* |35|, *like* **hervir**.
aseo 1 *m* (*acción*) cleaning, tidying up. **2** (*limpieza*) cleanliness, tidiness. **3** (*habitación*) bathroom, toilet.
■ aseo personal, personal cleanliness, personal hygiene. ‖ cuarto de aseo, bathroom.
asépalo,-a *adj* without sepals, asepalous.
asepsia 1 *f* asepsis. **2** *fig* (*frialdad*) coldness, indifference.
aséptico,-a 1 *adj* aseptic. **2** *fig* cold, indifferent.
asequible *adj* accesible: *a un precio asequible,* at a reasonable price; *la casa que ha comprado no es asequible para todo el mundo,* the house he bought is not within everybody's reach.
aserción *f* assertion, statement.
aserradero *m* sawmill.
aserrado,-a 1 *adj* serrated. – **2** aserrado, *m* sawing.
aserrador,-ra 1 *pp* → **aserrar**. – **2** *adj* sawing. – **3** aserrador, *m* sawyer. – **4** aserradora, *f* power saw.
aserradura 1 *f* (*acción*) sawing. **2** (*corte*) saw cut. – **3** aserraduras, *fpl* sawdust *sing*.
aserrar *t* to saw (up).
▲ *Conjugation model* |27|, *like* **acertar**.
aserrín *m* sawdust.
asertivamente *adv* assertively.
asertivo,-a *adj* assertive:
aserto *m* → **aserción**.
asesinar 1 *t* to kill, murder. **2** (*magnicidio*) to assassinate.
asesinato 1 *m* killing, murder. **2** (*magnicidio*) assassination.
asesino,-a 1 *adj* murderous: *no hallaron el arma asesina,* they couldn't find the murder weapon. – **2** *m,f* killer; (*hombre*) murderer; (*mujer*) murderess.
asesor,-ra 1 *adj* advisory. – **2** *m,f* adviser, consultant.
■ asesor, -ra de imagen, image consultant. ‖ asesor,-ra fiscal, tax advisor.
asesoramiento 1 *m* (*acción*) advising. **2** (*consejo*) advice.
asesorar 1 *t* (*dar consejo*) to advise, give advice. **2** *com* to act as a consultant to. – **3** asesorarse, *p* (*tomar consejo*) to take advice, consult (**de**, -): *se asesoró de expertos para tomar una decisión,* he got expert advice before making a decision.
asesoría 1 *f* (*cargo*) consultancy. **2** (*oficina*) consultant's office.

asestar 1 *t* (*arma*) to aim. **2** (*golpe*) to deal, give. **3** (*tiro*) to fire.
● **asestar una puñalada,** to stab. ‖ **asestar un puñetazo,** to punch.
aseveración *f* asseveration, assertion.
aseverar *t* to asseverate, affirm.
asexuado,-a *adj* asexual.
asexual *adj* asexual.
asfaltado,-a 1 *pp* → **asfaltar.** – **2** asfaltado, *m* (*acción*) asphalting. **3** (*pavimento*) asphalt, asphalted surface.
asfaltadora *f* asphalt layer.
asfaltar *t* to asphalt.
asfáltico,-a *adj* asphalt, containing asphalt.
asfalto *m* asphalt.
● **en el asfalto,** *fig* on the road.
asfixia *f* asphyxia, suffocation, asphyxiation.
asfixiado,-a 1 *pp* → **asfixiar.** – **2** *adj fam* broke, up to one's neck.
asfixiador,-ra *adj* → **asfixiante.**
asfixiante *adj* asphyxiating, suffocating: *hace un calor asfixiante,* it's stiflingly hot.
asfixiar 1 *t* to asphyxiate, suffocate. – **2 asfixiarse,** *p* to asphyxiate, suffocate.
▲ *Conjugation model* [12], *like* **cambiar.**
asgo *pres indic* → **asir.**
así 1 *adv* (*de esta manera*) thus, (in) this way. **2** (*de esa manera*) (in) that way: *por decirlo así,* so to speak; *y así sucesivamente,* and so on. **3** (*tanto*) as: *así usted como yo,* both you and I. **4** (*por tanto*) therefore. **5** (*tan pronto como*) as soon as: *así que lo sepa,* as soon as I know. – **6** *adj* such: *un hombre así,* a man like that, such a man.
● **así así,** so-so. ‖ **así que,** so: *llovía, así que cogimos el paraguas,* it was raining, so we took our umbrella. ‖ **así sea,** so be it.
Asia *f* Asia.
asiático,-a 1 *adj* Asian. – **2** *m,f* Asian.
asibilar *t* to make sibilant.
asidero 1 *m* (*asa*) handle. **2** *fig* (*excusa*) excuse, pretext.
asiduidad *f* assiduity, frequency.
● **con asiduidad,** frequently, regularly.
asiduo,-a 1 *adj* assiduous, frequent, regular. – **2** *m,f* regular: *es un asiduo del cine,* he's a regular cinema-goer.
asiento 1 *m* (*silla etc*) seat. **2** (*emplazamiento*) site. **3** (*sedimento*) sediment. **4** *fig* (*orden*) establishment. **5** COM entry, registry. **6** (*de vasija*) bottom. **7** ARQ settling.
● **tomar asiento,** to take a seat.
■ **asiento abatible,** reclining seat. ‖ **asiento delantero,** front seat. ‖ **asiento trasero,** rear seat, back seat.
asignación 1 *f* (*acción*) assignment, allocation. **2** (*nombramiento*) appointment, assignment. **3** (*remuneración*) allocation, allowance; (*sueldo*) wage, salary.
asignar 1 *t* to assign, allot, allocate. **2** (*nombrar*) to appoint, assign.
asignatura *f* subject.
■ **asignatura pendiente,** (*en el colegio*) subject which has to be retaken; (*en la política etc*) unresolved issue, issue which still has to be tackled, unfinished business.
asilado,-a 1 *pp* → **asilar.** – **2** *m,f person who lives in a home or in care.*
■ **asilado,-a político,-a,** political refugee. ‖ **condición de asilado,** refugee status.
asilar 1 *t* POL to give political asylum to, grant political asylum to. **2** (*recoger*) to give shelter to, take in. **3** (*internar*) to put in a home, take into care.
asilo 1 *m* (*institución*) asylum, home, institution. **2** *fig* (*protección*) protection, assistance.

● **dar asilo,** to shelter.
■ **asilo de ancianos,** old people's home. ‖ **asilo político,** political asylum: *pidió asilo político,* she asked for political asylum; *le concedieron asilo político,* she was granted political asylum.
asimetría *f* asymmetry.
asimétrico,-a *adj* asymmetric, asymmetrical.
asimiento 1 *m* (*acción*) grasping, holding, seizing. **2** (*efecto*) attachment.
asimilación *f* assimilation.
asimilar *t* to assimilate.
asimilativo,-a *adj* assimilative, assimilating.
asimismo 1 *adv* (*también*) also, as well: *asimismo afirmó que ...,* he also stated that ... **2** (*de esta manera*) likewise. **3** (*además*) moreover.
asíndeton *m* GRAM asyndeton.
asíntota *f* MAT asymptote.
asir 1 *t* (*agarrar*) to grab, seize, grasp, take hold of. – **2** (*arraigar*) to take root. – **3 asirse,** *p* (*agarrarse*) to hold on (**a,** to), cling (**a,** to).
● **asirse a una idea,** *fam* to cling to an idea.
▲ *Conjugation model* [65].
Asiria *f* Assyria.
asirio,-a 1 *adj* Assyrian. – **2** *m,f* Assyrian. – **3** asirio, *m* (*idioma*) Assyrian.
asistencia 1 *f* (*presencia*) attendance, presence: *el presidente aún no ha confirmado su asistencia,* the president's attendance has not yet been confirmed; *la reunión contó con la asistencia de todos los ediles,* all the councillors were present at the meeting. **2** (*público*) audience: *hubo mucha asistencia al concierto,* there was a large audience at the concert. **3** (*ayuda*) assistance, help, aid: *la Cruz Roja realizó una veintena de asistencias,* the Red Cross dealt with around twenty cases. **4** DEP (en baloncesto, fútbol) pass. – **5 asistencias,** *fpl* (*conjunto de personas*) assistants, helpers.
● **con la asistencia de,** (*presencia*) in the presence of; (*ayuda*) with the assistance of.
■ **asistencia económica,** financial aid. ‖ **asistencia jurídica,** legal aid. ‖ **asistencia médica,** medical assistance. ‖ **asistencia social,** social assistance. ‖ **asistencia técnica,** technical backup. ‖ **falta de asistencia,** absence.
asistenta *f* cleaning lady.
asistente 1 *adj* (*que está*) attending: *el público asistente aplaudió durante veinte minutos,* the audience applauded for twenty minutes. **2** (*que ayuda*) assistant. – **3** *mf* (*que está*) member of the audience: *los asistentes al acto se quejaron del retraso,* those present at the ceremony complained about the delay. **4** (*que ayuda*) assistant: *el director dio la carta a su asistente para que la tradujera,* the director gave the letter to his assistant to translate. – **5** *m* MIL batman.
■ **asistente social,** social worker.
asistido,-a 1 *pp* → **asistir.** – **2** *adj* assisted.
● **asistido,-a por ordenador,** computer-assisted.
asistir 1 *i* to attend, be present: *la niña asiste a la escuela cada día,* the little girl goes to school every day; *sólo asistieron diez personas,* only ten people were present. – **2** *t* (*servir*) to serve, wait on: *los criados asistieron a los invitados durante la recepción,* the servants waited on the guests during the reception. **3** (*ayudar*) to help, assist; (*a los enfermos*) to attend, care for: *el médico que la atendió era mi hermano,* the doctor who attended her was my brother.
● **me (te, le, etc) asiste la razón,** *fml* I am (*you are, he*

is, *etc*) correct. ‖ me *(te, le, etc)* asiste el derecho de
..., I have (*you have, he has, etc*) the right to ...
asma *f* asthma.
▲ Takes **el** in singular.
asmático,-a 1 *adj* asthmatic. – 2 *m,f* asthmatic person,
person suffering from asthma.
asnal *adj* asinine, of an ass, of a donkey.
asno 1 *m* ass, donkey. 2 *fam* (*persona*) ass, idiot.
asociación *f* association.
■ **asociación de ideas,** association of ideas. ‖ asociación de vecinos, residents' association.
asociacionismo *m* associationism.
asociado,-a 1 *pp* → **asociar**. – 2 *adj* associated, associate. – 3 *m,f* associate, partner.
asociamiento *m* association.
asociar 1 *t* to associate (**a/con,** with), connect, link: *asociaba aquel olor a su juventud,* he associated that smell
with his youth. 2 COM to take into partnership. – 3 asociarse, *p* (*relacionarse*) to be associated (**a/con,** with):
aquella música se asociaba con una época particular,
that music was associated with a particular period. 4
COM to collaborate, form a partnership, become partners.
▲ Conjugation model [12], *like* cambiar.
asociativo,-a *adj* associative.
asolación *f* devastation, destruction, razing.
asolador,-ra *adj* razing, ravaging, devastating.
asolamiento *f* → **asolación**.
asolanar *t* to dry up, parch.
asolapar 1 *t* (*tejas*) to overlap. 2 *fig* to cloak, hide.
asolar *t* (*epidemia*) to ravage; (*ejército*) to lay waste to, raze;
(*incendio, tempestad*) to devastate.
▲ Conjugation model [31], *like* contar.
asolear 1 *t* to expose to the sun, put in the sun. – 2
asolearse, *p* (*persona*) to sunbathe, expose os. to the
sun; (*objeto*) to be exposed to sunlight.
asomar 1 *i* (*empezar a aparecer*) to appear, begin to show,
come out: *todas las mañanas asoma el sol por el Este,*
every morning the sun rises in the East. – 2 *t* (*mostrar*)
to show, put out, stick out: *te asoma la combinación por
debajo de la falda,* your slip's showing; *el chico asomó
la cabeza por la ventana,* the boy stuck his head out of
the window. – 3 asomarse, *p* (*a ventana*) to stick one's
head out (**a,** of), lean out (**a,** of); (*a balcón*) to come out
(**a,** onto): *varios vecinos se asomaron a la ventana para
ver qué pasaba,* several neighbours stuck their heads
out of their windows to see what was happening. 4
(*aparecer*) to appear: *personas que se asoman a la pantalla televisiva,* people who appear on our television
screens; *las calles están casi desiertas, pero aún se asoma algún borracho,* the streets are almost deserted, but
the odd drunk is still to be seen.
asombrado,-a 1 *pp* → **asombrar**. – 2 *adj* amazed, astonished, surprised: *me quedé asombrada,* I was
amazed.
asombrar 1 *t* to amaze, astonish, surprise. – 2 asombrarse, *p* to be astonished, be amazed, be surprised:
nos asombramos de su altura, we were amazed at her
height.
asombro *m* amazement, astonishment, surprise.
asombrosamente *adv* amazingly, astonishingly.
asombroso,-a *adj* amazing, astonishing, surprising.
asomo *m* sign, trace, hint: *lo hizo sin el menor asomo de
interés,* he did it without the slightest interest; *sin el
menor asomo de duda,* without a shadow of a doubt.
● ni por asomo, by no means.

asonada *f* putsch.
asonancia *f* assonance.
asonante *adj* assonant.
asordar *t* to deafen.
aspa 1 *f* (*cruz*) cross. 2 (*de molino*) sail; (*de ventilador*) blade;
(*armazón*) arms *pl.*
● en forma de aspa, X-shaped.
▲ Takes **el** in singular.
aspar 1 *t* to crucify. 2 *fig* (*molestar*) to annoy, pester.
● ¡que me aspen si ...!, *fam* I'll be damned if ...! ‖
¡que te aspen!, *fam* get lost!
aspaventar *t* to frighten, scare.
▲ Conjugation model [27], *like* acertar.
aspaventero,-a 1 *adj* fussy, theatrical, exaggerated. –
2 *m,f* fussy person, theatrical person.
aspaventoso,-a *adj* fussy, theatrical, exaggerated.
aspaviento *m* fuss.
● hacer aspavientos, to make a great fuss.
aspecto 1 *m* (*faceta*) aspect, side, angle: *en el aspecto
político,* from a political point of view, politically. 2
(*apariencia*) look, appearance: *¿qué aspecto tenía?,* what
did he look like?; *no tienes muy buen aspecto,* you don't
look too good; *este pastel tiene buen aspecto,* this cake
looks delicious.
● en el aspecto de que, in the sense that, in that.
ásperamente 1 *adv* roughly. 2 *fig* harshly.
aspereza *f* roughness, coarseness, asperity.
asperillo *m* slightly bitter taste, slightly sour taste.
asperjar 1 *t* to sprinkle. 2 REL to sprinkle with holy water.
áspero,-a 1 *adj* (*cosa*) rough, coarse. 2 *fig* (*persona*) surly.
3 (*clima, tiempo*) harsh.
asperón *m* sandstone.
aspersión *f* sprinkling.
aspersor *m* sprinkler.
aspersorio *m* aspergillum.
áspid *m* asp.
áspide *m* asp.
aspidistra *f* aspidistra.
aspillera *f* loophole.
aspiración 1 *f* (*al respirar*) inhalation, breathing in. 2
LING aspiration. 3 TÉC intake. 4 *fig* (*ambición*) aspiration,
ambition: *su única aspiración fue ser feliz,* being happy
was his only ambition.
■ aspiración de aire, intake of air, air intake.
aspirado,-a 1 *pp* → **aspirar**. – 2 *adj* aspirated. – 3 aspirada, *f* LING aspirate.
aspirador,-ra 1 *adj* sucking: *bomba aspiradora,* suction
pump. – 2 aspirador, *m* vacuum cleaner, Hoover. – 3
aspiradora, *f* vacuum cleaner, Hoover.
● pasar la aspiradora, to vacuum, hoover.
aspiradora *f* → **aspirador,-ra**.
aspirante 1 *adj* suction. – 2 *mf* candidate, applicant.
■ bomba aspirante, suction pump.
aspirar 1 *t* (*al respirar*) to inhale, breathe in. 2 (*absorber*)
to suck in, draw in. 3 LING to aspirate. – 4 *i fig* (*desear*)
to aspire (**a,** to): *aspiraba a convertirse en una estrella
de cine,* he aspired to becoming a film star.
aspirina *f* aspirin.
▲ Registered trademark.
asquear *t* to disgust, revolt, make sick.
asquerosamente 1 *adv* (*desagradablemente*) disgusting-
ly. 2 (*suciamente*) filthily.
asquerosidad *f* filthy thing, revolting thing: *¡menuda
asquerosidad!,* how revolting!

asqueroso,-a 1 *adj* (*sucio*) dirty, filthy. 2 (*desagradable*) disgusting, revolting, foul. 3 (*que siente asco*) squeamish. – 4 *m,f* (*sucio*) filthy person, revolting person. 5 (*que siente asco*) squeamish person.

asta 1 *f* (*de bandera*) staff, pole. 2 (*de lanza*) shaft; (*pica*) lance, pike. 3 (*cuerno*) horn.
● **bandera a media asta**, flag at half-mast.
▲ Takes *el* in singular.

astado,-a 1 *adj* horned. – 2 **astado**, *m* bull.

ástato *m* astatine.

astenia *f* asthenia.

asténico,-a 1 *adj* asthenic. – 2 *m,f* asthenic.

asterisco *m* asterisk.

asteroide 1 *adj* asteroid. – 2 *m* asteroid.

astifino,-a *adj* narrow-horned.

astigmático,-a 1 *adj* astigmatic. – 2 *m,f* person with astigmatism.

astigmatismo *m* astigmatism.

astil 1 *m* (*de herramienta*) handle. 2 (*de flecha*) shaft. 3 (*de balanza*) arm, beam. 4 (*de pluma*) quill.

astilla *f* splinter, chip.
● **de tal palo, tal astilla**, like father, like son. ‖ **hacer astillas**, *fig* to smash to smithereens.

astillar *t* to splinter.

astillero *m* shipyard, dockyard.

astilloso,-a *adj* brittle, easily splintered.

astracán *m* astrakhan.

astracanada *f* theatrical farce.

astrágalo 1 *m* ANAT astragalus. 2 ARQ astragal.

astral *adj* astral.
■ **carta astral**, birth chart, individual horoscope.

astringencia *f* astringency.

astringente 1 *adj* astringent. – 2 *m* astringent.

astringir *t* to astringe, constrict.
▲ *Conjugation model* [6], *like* **dirigir**.

astro *m* star.
■ **el astro rey**, *lit* the sun. ‖ **astro de la pantalla**, *fig* film star.

astrofísica *f* → **astrofísico,-a**.

astrofísico,-a 1 *adj* astrophysical. – 2 **astrofísica**, *f* astrophysics.

astrolabio *m* astrolabe.

astrología *f* astrology.

astrológico,-a *adj* astrological.

astrólogo,-a *m,f* astrologer.

astronauta *mf* astronaut.

astronáutica *f* → **astronáutico,-a**.

astronáutico,-a 1 *adj* astronautical. – 2 **astronáutica**, *f* astronautics.

astronave *f* spaceship, spacecraft.

astronomía *f* astronomy.

astronómico,-a 1 *adj* astronomical, astronomic. 2 *fig* astronomical.

astrónomo,-a *m,f* astronomer.

astroso,-a 1 *adj* (*desastrado*) shabby, ragged, untidy. 2 (*despreciable*) contemptible. 3 (*desdichado*) unfortunate.

astucia *f* astuteness, cunning, shrewdness. 2 (*treta*) trick, ruse.

asturianismo *m* (*palabra*) Asturian word; (*expresión*) Asturian expression.

asturiano,-a 1 *adj* Asturian. – 2 *m,f* Asturian.

Asturias *m* Asturias.

astutamente *adv* astutely, cunningly.

astuto,-a *adj* astute, cunning, shrewd.

asueto *m* time off, free time, rest: *mi tarde de asueto,* my afternoon off; *los meses de asueto,* the holiday months.

asumir *t* to assume, take on, take upon os.: *el coronel asumió el mando de las tropas,* the colonel assumed command of the troops.

asunceno,-a 1 *adj* of Asunción, from Asunción. – 2 *m,f* person from Asunción, inhabitant of Asunción.

asunceño,-a 1 *adj* of Asunción, from Asunción. – 2 *m,f* person from Asunción, inhabitant of Asunción.

asunción *f* assumption, taking on.

asuntillo *m fam irón pey* business, affair.

asunto 1 *m* (*cuestión*) matter, issue; (*tema*) subject; (*de obra*) theme: *no quiero hablar del asunto,* I don't want to discuss the matter. 2 (*negocio*) affair, business: *no es asunto tuyo,* it's none of your business. 3 (*aventura*) affair, love affair.
■ **asuntos a tratar**, agenda *sing*. ‖ **asuntos exteriores**, POL Foreign Affairs.

asustadizo,-a *adj* easily frightened, easily scared.

asustado,-a *adj* frightened, scared.

asustar 1 *t* to frighten, scare. – 2 **asustarse**, *p* to be frightened, be scared: *mi bebé se asusta del ruido,* my baby is frightened of noise.

atabal *m* kettledrum.

atacador,-ra 1 *adj* attacking, assailing. – 2 *m,f* attacker, assailant. – 3 **atacador**, *m* ramrod.

atacante 1 *adj* attacking, assailing. – 2 *mf* attacker, assailant.

atacar 1 *t* (*asaltar*) to attack, assault, assail. 2 (*criticar*) to attack, criticize. 3 (*afectar*) to attack, affect: *esas pastillas pueden atacar al estómago,* those pills can upset your stomach. 4 QUÍM MÚS to attack.
● **atacar los nervios**, to get on one's nerves.
▲ *Conjugation model* [1], *like* **sacar**.

atadero 1 *m* (*cuerda*) cord, rope; (*cadena*) chain. 2 (*anilla*) halter ring, hitching hook.

atadijo *m fam* bundle.

atado,-a 1 *pp* → **atar**. – 2 *adj* (*tímido*) shy, timid. – 3 **atado**, *m* bundle.
● **estar todo atado y bien atado**, to be all sewn up.

atador,-ra 1 *adj* binding. – 2 **atadora**, *f* binder.

atadora *f* → **atador,-ra**.

atadura 1 *f* (*acción*) tying, binding, fastening. 2 (*cosa*) binding, string, cord. 3 *fig* (*unión*) tie. 4 *fig* (*impedimento*) tie, hindrance.

atafagar 1 *t* (*sofocar*) to suffocate. 2 (*molestar*) to annoy, pester.
▲ *Conjugation model* [7], *like* **llegar**.

ataguía *f* coffer-dam, caisson.

ataharre *m* crupper.

atahorma *f* short-toed eagle.

atajar 1 *i* to take a shortcut. – 2 *t* (*interrumpir*) to interrupt. 3 (*entorpecer el paso*) to halt.

atajo 1 *m* (*camino*) shortcut. 2 (*rebaño*) herd. 3 *fig* (*grupo*) bunch: *son un atajo de vagos,* they're a bunch of layabouts.
● **echar por el atajo / tirar por el atajo**, *fig* to take a shortcut, take the easiest way out. ‖ **no hay atajo sin trabajo**, shortcuts don't help in the long run, there are no gains without pains.

atalaje *m* → **atelaje**.

atalaya 1 *f* (*torre*) watchtower, lookout; (*mirador*) vantage point. – 2 *m* (*persona*) watcher, lookout.

atalayar 1 *t* (*vigilar*) to watch, watch over, observe. 2 *pey* (*espiar*) to spy on.

atañedero,-a *adj* concerning (**a**, -).

atañer *i* to concern (**a**, -).
▲ *Conjugation model* [38], *like* **tañer**; *used only in the 3rd person*.

ataque 1 *m* attack. **2** MED fit.
■ **ataque aéreo**, air raid. ‖ **ataque de nervios**, nervous breakdown.

atar 1 *t* to tie: *le ataron las manos con una cuerda,* they tied her hands with a rope; *se ató el pelo,* she tied her hair back. **2** *fig* to tie down: *un negocio ata mucho,* a business really ties you down.
● **atar cabos**, *fig* to put two and two together. ‖ **atar corto a algn.**, to keep sb. on a tight rein.

atarantado,-a 1 *adj* (*aturdido*) stunned, dazed. **2** (*inquieto*) restless.

ataraxia *f* ataraxia, ataraxy.

atarazana *f* shipyard, dockyard.

atardecer 1 *i* to get dark, grow dark. – **2** *m* evening, dusk.
▲ Conjugation model [43], *like* **agradecer**; *in 1, used only in the 3rd person; it does not take a subject.*

atareado,-a 1 *pp →* **atarear**. – **2** *adj* busy, occupied.

atarear 1 *t* to keep busy, assign a task to. – **2 atarearse**, *p* to be busy, work hard.

atarugar 1 *t fam* (*atestar*) to stuff, pack, cram. **2** *fig* (*hacer callar*) to shut up. – **3 atarugarse**, *p* (*avergonzarse*) to feel confused, feel embarrassed; (*cortarse*) to stop short, become tongue-tied. **4** (*atragantarse*) to choke.

atascadero *m fig* obstacle.

atascar 1 *t* (*bloquear*) to block up, clog. **2** *fig* (*obstaculizar*) to hamper, hinder, obstruct. – **3 atascarse**, *p* (*bloquearse*) to get blocked, get blocked up, get clogged: *la tubería se atascó con la porquería,* the pipe got blocked up with dirt. **4** (*mecanismo*) to jam, get jammed, get stuck. **5** *fig* (*estancarse*) to get tangled up, get bogged down.
▲ Conjugation model [1], *like* **sacar**.

atasco 1 *m* (*acción*) obstruction, blockage. **2** (*de tráfico*) traffic jam.

ataúd *m* coffin.

ataviar 1 *t* (*arreglar*) to dress up. **2** (*adornar*) to adorn, deck.
▲ Conjugation model [13], *like* **desviar**.

atávico,-a *adj* atavistic.

atavío 1 *m* (*adorno*) decoration, adornment, ornament. **2** (*vestido*) dress, attire.

atavismo *m* atavism.

atediar *t* to bore.
▲ Conjugation model [12], *like* **cambiar**.

ateísmo *m* atheism.

ateleje 1 *m* (*caballos*) team of horses. **2** (*arreos*) harness.

atemorizar 1 *t* to frighten, scare. – **2 atemorizarse**, *p* to be frightened, be scared.
▲ Conjugation model [4], *like* **realizar**.

atemperación 1 *f* (*moderación*) moderation, restraint, tempering. **2** (*acomodación*) adjustment, accommodation.

atemperar 1 *t* (*moderar*) to moderate, temper. **2** (*acomodar*) to adjust (**a**, to), accommodate (**a**, to).

Atenas *f* Athens.

atenazado,-a 1 *pp →* **atenazar**. – **2** *adj fig* gripped, tormented: *estaba atenazado por la angustia,* he was seized by anguish.

atenazar *t fig* to torture, torment.
▲ Conjugation model [4], *like* **realizar**.

atención 1 *f* (*gen*) attention: *le encanta ser el centro de la atención,* he loves being the centre of attention; *lo hace sólo para que le prestes atención,* she's only doing it to get attention; *es imposible atraer su atención,* it's impossible to get his attention. **2** (*detalle*) nice thought:

fue una atención por su parte, it was a nice thought, it was very kind of him. – **3** ¡**atención!**, *interj* (*gen*) your attention please!; (*cuidado*) watch out!, look out!: *¡atención a los dedos!,* mind your fingers!
● **a la atención de algn.**, (*en cartas*) for the attention of sb. ‖ **colmar muchas atenciones con algn.**, to smother sb. with attentions, make a fuss of sb. ‖ **en atención a**, bearing in mind, taking into account. ‖ **en atención a que ...**, in view of the fact that ..., given that ... ‖ **llamar la atención**, to attract attention: *procura no llamar la atención,* try not to attract attention; *lo que más me llamó la atención fue que no llevara uniforme,* what I noticed most was that he wasn't wearing a uniform. ‖ **llamar la atención a algn.**, to take sb. to task. ‖ **prestar atención**, to pay attention (**a**, to). ‖ **tener una atención con algn.**, to think of sb.

atender 1 *t* (*servir - cliente*) to serve, attend to, see to: *¿ya la atienden a usted?,* are you being served? **2** (*cuidar*) to take care of, look after: *el médico que me había atendido no estaba,* the doctor who had treated me wasn't there. **3** (*negocio*) to take care of; (*teléfono*) to answer. **4** (*consejo, advertencia*) to heed, pay attention to; (*ruego, deseo, protesta*) to attend to; (*instrucción*) to follow, carry out. – **5** *i* (*prestar atención*) to pay attention (**a**, to), attend (**a**, to): *atiende, que te concierne a ti,* pay attention, this concerns you; *el perro atiende a la voz de su dueño,* the dog always obeys its master. **6** (*cumplir con*) to meet (**a**, -), fulfil (us fulfill) (**a**, -). **7** (*tener en cuenta*) to bear in mind.
● **atender por,** to answer to the name of: *el perro perdido atiende por "Canelo",* the dog answers to the name of "Canelo".
▲ Conjugation model [28], *like* **entender**.

atendible *adj* worthy of attention, worthy of consideration.

ateneo *m* athenaeum (US atheneum).

atenerse 1 *p* (*ajustarse*) to abide (**a**, by), comply (**a**, with). **2** (*acogerse*) to rely (**a**, on).
▲ Conjugation model [87], *like* **tener**.

ateniense 1 *adj* Athenian. – **2** *m,f* Athenian.

atentado 1 *m* (*ataque*) attack, assault: *eso puede considerarse un atentado contra su vida,* it can be considered an attempt on his life. **2** (*afrenta*) affront.
■ **atentado terrorista**, terrorist attack.

atentamente 1 *adv* attentively, carefully. **2** (*amablemente*) politely; (*en carta*) sincerely, faithfully: *"le saluda atentamente",* "yours sincerely", "yours faithfully".

atentar atentar a / atentar contra, *i* to commit a crime against.
▲ Conjugation model [27], *like* **acertar**.

atento,-a 1 *adj* attentive. **2** (*amable*) polite, courteous.
● **estar atento,-a a algo**, (*prestar atención*) to pay attention to sth.; (*estar alerta*) to be on the alert for sth., keep an eye out for sth., be on the lookout for.

atenuación 1 *f* attenuation, lessening. **2** JUR extenuation.

atenuante 1 *adj* attenuating. **2** JUR extenuating. – **3** *m* JUR extenuating circumstance.

atenuar 1 *t* to attenuate. **2** JUR to extenuate.
▲ Conjugation model [11], *like* **actuar**.

ateo,-a 1 *adj* atheistic. – **2** *m,f* atheist.

aterciopelado,-a *adj* velvety, velvet: *tenía una voz aterciopelada,* she had a velvety voice.

aterido,-a 1 *pp →* **aterirse**. – **2** *adj* stiff with cold, numb.

aterimiento *m* stiffness from the cold, numbness.

aterirse *p* to be stiff with cold, be numb with cold: *caminé un rato, aterido de frío,* I walked a short distance, numb with cold.

▲ Used only in infinitive and participle.

atérmico,-a adj heatproof.

aterrada f landfall.

aterrador,-ra adj terrifying, frightful.

aterraje 1 m (avión) landing. 2 (barco) landfall.

aterramiento m fear, terror.

aterrar[1] 1 t (asustar) to terrify. – 2 **aterrarse**, p to be terrified.

aterrar[2] 1 t (derribar) to pull down, demolish. 2 (cubrir de tierra) to cover with earth. – 3 i (avión) to land. 4 (barco) to stand inshore.

▲ Conjugation model [27], like acertar.

aterrizaje m landing.

■ **aterrizaje forzoso**, emergency landing. ‖ **aterrizaje violento**, crash landing.

aterrizar 1 i to land. 2 fig to show up, arrive.

▲ Conjugation model [4], like realizar.

aterronar 1 t to cake, harden. – 2 **aterronarse**, p to go lumpy, cake, harden.

aterrorizar 1 t to terrify. 2 MIL POL to terrorize. – 3 **aterrorizarse**, p to be terrified.

▲ Conjugation model [4], like realizar.

atesoramiento m hoarding, accumulation, storing up.

atesorar 1 t (acumular) to hoard, accumulate, store up. 2 fig to possess.

atestación f attestation, testimony.

atestado[1] 1 m JUR affidavit, statement. – 2 **atestados**, mpl testimonials.

atestado,-a[2] 1 pp → **atestar**[2]. – 2 adj packed (**de**, with), crammed (**de**, with).

atestar[1] t JUR to testify.

atestar[2] 1 t (atiborrar) to cram (**de**, with), pack (**de**, with). – 2 **atestarse**, p (de comida) to stuff os. (**de**, with).

▲ Conjugation model [27], like acertar.

atestiguación f attestation, testimony.

atestiguar 1 t JUR to testify to, bear witness to, give evidence of: algunos testigos atestiguaron que los ladrones huyeron en coche, some witnesses testified that the thieves got away by car; el amigo atestiguó su inocencia, his friend testified to his innocence. 2 (ofrecer muestras) to attest, testify, vouch for: tu sinceridad atestigua que eres una buena persona, your sincerity vouches for the fact that you are an honest person.

▲ Conjugation model [22], like averiguar.

atetar t to suckle.

atezado,-a 1 pp → **atezar**. – 2 adj (por el sol) tanned. 3 (color negro) black, blackened.

atezar 1 t (broncear) to tan, burn. 2 (ennegrecer) to blacken, turn black. – 3 **atezarse**, p (broncearse) to get tanned.

▲ Conjugation model [4], like realizar.

atiborrado,-a 1 pp → **atiborrar**. – 2 adj full (**de**, of), stuffed (**de**, with), packed (**de**, with).

atiborrar 1 t (llenar) to pack, cram, stuff (**de**, with). – 2 **atiborrarse**, p fam (de comida) to stuff os. (**de**, with).

ático 1 m (vivienda) penthouse, attic flat. 2 ARQ attic, loft.

atiesar t to stiffen, tighten, stretch taut.

atigrado,-a adj (con rayas) striped; (gato) tabby.

atildado,-a 1 pp → **atildar**. – 2 adj smart, neat, spruce.

atildamiento 1 m (acicalamiento) elegance, tidiness. 2 fig (crítica) censure.

atildar 1 t (tipografía) to mark with a tilde. 2 (acicalar) to tidy, clean up; (persona) to dress up. 3 fig (criticar) to criticize, censure, find fault with. 4 **atildarse**, p (uso reflexivo) to spruce os. up, smarten os. up, get dressed up.

atinadamente adv correctly, sensibly, rightly.

atinado,-a 1 pp → **atinar**. – 2 adj (correcto) right, accurate, correct; (pertinente) pertinent: esa fue una decisión muy atinada, that was a very wise decision. 3 (persona) sensible.

atinar 1 i (dar con) to hit upon, find: si no atinas con la calle, llámame, if you can't find the street, call me. 2 (acertar) to get it right, be right, succeed: nadie ha atinado a presentar un programa político coherente, nobody has managed to present a coherent political programme; atiné en el blanco, I hit the target.

atiparse p fam to stuff os. (**de**, with).

atípico,-a adj atypical.

atiplado,-a 1 pp → **atiplar**. – 2 adj high-pitched.

atiplar 1 t (subir el tono) to raise the pitch of. – 2 **atiplarse**, p to go squeaky.

atirantar t (poner tirante) to tighten, tauten.

atiriciarse p to contract jaundice.

atisbador,-ra 1 adj prying, nosy. – 2 m,f observer, snooper, spy.

atisbar 1 t (observar) to spy on, observe, watch. 2 fig (vislumbrar) to make out, discern.

atisbo 1 m (acción) spying, watching. 2 fig (indicio) inkling, slight sign: mientras haya un atisbo de vida, el médico no abandonará al enfermo, while there's the slightest flicker of life, the doctor will not give up on the patient.

atizador m poker.

atizar 1 t (fuego) to poke; (vela) to snuff. 2 fig (pasiones) to rouse, excite; (rebelión) to stir up. 3 (dar - golpe) give, deal. – 4 **atizarse**, p fam (zamparse - comida) to put away; (- bebida) to knock back.

● **¡atiza!**, wow!

▲ Conjugation model [4], like realizar.

atizonar t to blight.

atlante m Atlas.

atlántico,-a adj Atlantic.

■ **el (océano) Atlántico**, the Atlantic (Ocean).

atlantismo m NATOism.

atlantista adj pro-NATO.

atlas m atlas.

▲ pl atlas.

atleta mf athlete.

atlético,-a adj athletic.

atletismo m athletics.

atmósfera f atmosphere.

atmosférico,-a adj atmospheric, atmospherical.

atoar t to tow.

atocha f esparto.

atochal m esparto field.

atocinar 1 t (abrir) to slice up. 2 fam (asesinar) to do in, carve up. – 3 **atocinarse**, p fam (enfadarse) to get het up. 4 fam (enamorarse) to fall madly in love.

atolladero 1 m (atascadero) morass, quagmire. 2 fig (aprieto) fix, jam.

● **estar en un atolladero**, to be in a jam. ‖ **sacar a algn. del atolladero**, to get sb. out of a fix. ‖ **salir del atolladero**, to get out of a jam.

atollar t to obstruct, block up.

atolón m atoll.

atolondradamente 1 adv (con desatino) recklessly. 2 (con aturdimiento) in a bewildered way, in a stunned way.

atolondrado,-a 1 pp → **atolondrar**. – 2 adj (desatinado) scatterbrained, reckless, silly. 3 (aturdido) stunned, bewildered.

atolondramiento 1 m (desatino) recklessness, silliness. 2 (aturdimiento) confusion, bewilderment.

atolondrar 1 *t* to confuse, stun, bewilder. – 2 **atolondrarse,** *p* to be confused, be stunned, be bewildered.

atómico,-a *adj* atomic.

atomización *f* atomization, spraying.

atomizador *m* atomizer, spray, scent spray.

atomizar *t* to atomize, spray.

▲ Conjugation model |4|, like *realizar*.

átomo 1 *m* atom. 2 *fig* atom, particle, speck.

● **ni un átomo de,** not a trace of.

■ **átomo de vida,** spark of life.

atonal *adj* atonal.

atonía 1 *f* MED atony. 2 (*apatía*) apathy, lethargy.

atónito,-a *adj* astonished, amazed: *escuchó las noticias atónito,* he listened to the news in amazement.

átono,-a *adj* atonic, unstressed.

atontadamente 1 *adv* (*tontamente*) foolishly, recklessly. 2 (*confusamente*) in a bewildered way, in a stunned way.

atontado,-a 1 *pp* → **atontar**. – 2 *adj* (*aturdido*) stunned, confused, bewildered. 3 (*tonto*) stupid, silly, foolish.

atontamiento *m* bewilderment, stupefaction.

atontar 1 *t* (*volver tonto*) to make stupid, stupefy, turn into a vegetable. 2 (*aturdir*) to confuse, bewilder, stun; (*con un golpe*) to stun, daze; (*marear*) to make dopey. – 3 **atontarse,** *p* (*volverse tonto*) to go stupid, turn into a vegetable. 4 (*aturdirse*) to get confused, be bewildered; to become groggy, begin to feel groggy.

atontolinado,-a *pp-adj* → **atontado,-a**.

atontolinar *t* → **atontar**.

atorar 1 *t* (*obstruir*) to obstruct, block. – 2 **atorarse,** *p* (*atascarse*) to get stuck, get jammed. 3 *fig* to get tongue-tied: *estaba tan emocionado que cuando tuvo que hablar se atoró,* he was so overcome by emotion that when he had to speak he got tongue-tied.

atormentador,-ra 1 *adj* tormenting. – 2 *m,f* (*hombre*) tormentor; (*mujer*) tormentress.

atormentar 1 *t* (*torturar*) to torture. 2 *fig* (*causar disgusto*) to torment, harass. – 3 **atormentarse,** *p* (*sufrir*) to torment os.

atornillador *m* screwdriver.

atornillar *t* to screw on, screw down, screw together.

atortolado,-a 1 *pp* → **atortolar**. – 2 *adj* starry-eyed, lovey-dovey.

atortolar 1 *t* (*aturdir*) to confuse. 2 (*turbar*) to disturb. 3 (*intimidar*) to intimidate, scare.

atortujar *t* to squash, flatten.

atosigador,-ra 1 *adj* harassing, pressing. – 2 *m,f* oppressor, tormentor.

atosigamiento *m* harassment.

atosigar *t* to harass, pester.

▲ Conjugation model |4|, like *realizar*.

atrabancar 1 *t* to rush over, hurry over. – 2 **atrabancarse,** *p* to get into a jam.

▲ Conjugation model |1|, like *sacar*.

atrabiliario,-a 1 *adj* bad-tempered, moody. – 2 *m,f* bad-tempered person, moody person.

atrabilis *f fig* bad temper, moodiness.

▲ *pl atrabilis*.

atracadero *m* landing place, wharf, berth.

atracador,-ra *m,f* (*de banco*) (bank) robber; (*en la calle*) attacker, mugger, thief.

atracar 1 *t* (*robar - banco, tienda*) to hold up, rob; (*- persona*) to mug. 2 (*de comida*) to stuff, fill. – 3 *i* MAR (*a otra nave*) to come alongside; (*a tierra*) to tie up, dock, berth. – 4 **atracarse,** *p* (*de comida*) to gorge os. (**de,** on), stuff os. (**de,** with); (*de bebida*) to guzzle os. (**de,** -).

▲ Conjugation model |1|, like *sacar*.

atracción 1 *f* (*gen*) attraction: *sentía atracción por él,* she felt attracted to him. – 2 **atracciones,** *fpl* (*de feria*) rides *pl*.

■ **parque de atracciones,** funfair.

atraco *m* hold-up, robbery.

● **¡esto es un atraco!,** *fig* this is daylight robbery!

■ **atraco a mano armada,** JUR armed robbery.

atracón *m fam* binge, blowout.

● **darse/pegarse un atracón,** to make a pig of os.

atractivamente *adv* attractively.

atractivo,-a 1 *adj* attractive, charming, appealing. – 2 atractivo, *m* attraction, charm, appeal: *el nuevo modelo tiene mucho atractivo,* the new model is very attractive.

atraer 1 *t* (*gen*) to attract. 2 (*captivar*) to captivate, charm: *no me atrae el tema de la obra,* the subject of the play doesn't appeal to me.

▲ Conjugation model |88|, like *traer*.

atrafagar 1 *i* to bustle about, be busy. – 2 **atrafagarse,** *p* to bustle about, be busy.

▲ Conjugation model |7|, like *llegar*.

atragantarse 1 *p* (*no poder tragar*) to choke (**con,** on), swallow the wrong way: *se atragantó con un hueso de aceituna,* he choked on an olive stone. 2 (*atravesarse*) to get stuck in one's throat: *se le atragantó una espina,* he got a fish bone stuck in his throat. 3 *fig* (*causar fastidio*) to turn off: *tengo a ese tipo atragantado,* I can't stand that bloke.

atraigo *pres indic* → **atraer**.

atraillar 1 *t* (*atar*) to put on a leash. 2 *fig* (*dominar*) to control.

▲ Conjugation model |15|, like *aislar*.

atraje *pt indef* → **atraer**.

atramparse 1 *p* (*caer en una trampa*) to be trapped, fall into a trap. 2 (*bloquearse*) to get clogged, get blocked up.

atrancar 1 *t* (*puerta*) to bar, bolt. 2 (*obstruir*) to obstruct, block up. – 3 **atrancarse,** *p* (*atascarse*) to get stuck. 4 (*al leer*) to stumble over one's words.

▲ Conjugation model |1|, like *sacar*.

atrapamoscas *f* flytrap, flycatcher.

▲ *pl atrapamoscas*.

atrapar *t* to seize, capture, catch.

atraque 1 *m* (*acción*) mooring. 2 (*muelle*) mooring place, berth; (*de nave espacial*) link-up.

atrás 1 *adv* back: *dio un salto atrás,* she jumped back. 2 (*tiempo*) ago: *días atrás,* several days ago. – 3 *interj* stand back!, move back!

● **ir hacia atrás,** to go backwards.

atrasado,-a 1 *pp* → **atrasar**. – 2 *adj* (*desfasado*) outdated: *el sistema impositivo es injusto y atrasado,* the tax system is unjust and outdated. 3 (*pago*) overdue. 4 (*reloj*) slow: *este reloj anda atrasado,* this clock is slow. 5 (*país*) backward, underdeveloped; (*alumno*) slow, backward: *es un país intelectualmente atrasado,* it's an intelectually backward country.

atrasar 1 *t* (*gen*) to delay, postpone, put back; (*reloj*) to put back. – 2 *i* (*reloj*) to be slow. – 3 **atrasarse,** *p* (*tren etc*) to be late. 4 (*quedarse atrás*) to fall behind: *el corredor se atrasó en el último kilómetro de la carrera,* the runner fell behind in the last kilometre of the race.

● **atrasarse en los pagos,** to fall behind, be in arrears.

atraso 1 *m* delay. 2 (*de reloj*) slowness: *el tren lleva mucho atraso,* the train is very late. 3 (*de un país*) backwardness. – 4 **atrasos,** *mpl* COM arrears.

atravesado,-a 1 *pp* → **atravesar**. – 2 *adj* (*cruzado*) crossed, laid across. 3 (*algo bizco*) cross-eyed. 4 (*animal cruzado*) mongrel, crossbred. 5 *fig* (*maligno*) wicked, bloody-minded.
● **tener a algn. atravesado,-a,** *fig* to find sb. unbearable: *le tengo atravesada,* I can't stand her.

atravesar 1 *t* (*cruzar*) to cross, go across, go over; (*pasar por*) to go through, pass through: *no sé cómo vamos a atravesar el río,* I don't know how we're going to cross the river; *atravesaron el lago a nado,* they swam across the lake; *la vi al atravesar la puerta principal,* I saw her as I went through the main door. 2 (*experimentar - gen*) to go through, experience; (*enfermedad etc*) to suffer: *está atravesando una mala racha,* she's going through a bad patch; *España atravesó grandes dificultades económicas,* Spain experienced great economic difficulties; *atravesó una grave enfermedad,* he suffered a serious illness. 3 (*poner oblicuamente*) to put across, lay across: *han atravesado un camión en la calle para cortar el tráfico,* they've put a lorry across the street to stop the traffic. 4 (*con bala etc*) to go through; (*con espada*) to run through: *la bala me atravesó el hombro,* the bullet went through my shoulder; *el príncipe atravesó el corazón del dragón con su espada,* the prince ran his sword through the dragon's heart. 5 (*situación*) to go through. – 6 **atravesarse,** *p* (*estar atravesado*) to be in the way, be across. 7 (*inmiscuirse*) to interfere, meddle.
● **atravesarse algn. a uno,** *fam* not to be able to bear sb., not to be able to stand sb.
▲ *Conjugation model* |27|, *like* **acertar**.

atrayente *adj* attractive.

atreguar *t* to agree to a truce.

atreverse *p* to dare, venture: *¿te atreves?,* are you game?; *me atrevo con todos,* I'll take everyone on; *¡a que no te atreves!,* I dare you!
● **atreverse a hacer algo,** to dare to do sth. ‖ **atreverse con algn.,** to be cheeky to sb., to be insolent to sb. ‖ **atreverse con algo,** to take sth. on.

atrevido,-a 1 *pp* → **atreverse**. – 2 *adj* (*osado*) daring, bold. 3 (*insolente*) insolent, impudent. 4 (*indecoroso*) daring, risqué.

atrevimiento 1 *m* (*osadía*) daring, boldness. 2 (*insolencia*) effrontery, insolence, impudence.

atrezo *m* props *pl*.

atrezzo *m* → **atrezo**.

atribución 1 *f* (*acción*) attribution. 2 (*poder*) power, authority.

atribuible *adj* attributable (**a,** to).

atribuir 1 *t* to attribute (**a,** to), ascribe. – 2 **atribuirse,** *p* to assume.
▲ *Conjugation model* |62|, *like* **huir**.

atribuladamente *adv* sadly.

atribulado,-a 1 *pp* → **atribular**. – 2 *adj* sad, distressed.

atribular 1 *t* to grieve, afflict, distress. – 2 **atribularse,** *p* to be grieved, be afflicted, be distressed.

atributivo,-a *adj* attributive.

atributo *m* attribute, quality.

atrición *f* attrition, sorrow.

atril *m* (*para libros*) lectern, bookrest; (*para música*) music stand.

atrincheramiento *m* entrenchment.

atrincherar 1 *t* to entrench, dig a trench. – 2 **atrincherarse,** *p* to entrench os.

atrio 1 *m* (*patio*) atrium. 2 (*vestíbulo*) vestibule, entrance hall.

atrípedo,-a *adj* black-footed.

atrirrostro,-a *adj* black-beaked.

atrito,-a *adj* contrite.

atrochar *i* to take a short cut.

atrocidad 1 *f* (*barbaridad*) atrocity, outrage. 2 (*disparate - acción*) something stupid, foolish thing; (*- dicho*) silly remark, stupid remark: *es una atrocidad salir sin abrigo con el frío que hace,* it's madness to go out without a coat in this cold weather.

atrofia *f* atrophy.

atrofiar 1 *t* to atrophy. – 2 **atrofiarse,** *p* to atrophy.
▲ *Conjugation model* |12|, *like* **cambiar**.

atronado,-a 1 *pp* → **atronar**. – 2 *adj* rash, thoughtless, reckless.

atronador,-ra *adj* thundering, deafening.

atronamiento *m* daze, stunned state.

atronar 1 *t* (*asordar*) to deafen. 2 (*aturdir*) to stun, daze.

atropar *t* to group together.

atropelladamente *adv* hastily, hurriedly.

atropellado,-a 1 *pp* → **atropellar**. – 2 *adj* (*persona*) hasty, rash. 3 (*comportamiento*) abrupt, brusque.

atropellador,-ra *adj* brusque, impetuous, hasty.

atropellar 1 *t* AUTO to knock down, run over. 2 (*arrollar*) to trample over. 3 (*empujar*) to push, jostle. 4 *fig* (*oprimir*) to oppress; (*sentimientos*) to outrage, offend, affront; (*derechos*) to disregard, violate. – 5 **atropellarse,** *p* to rush, hurry.

atropello 1 *m* (*accidente*) accident, collision; (*de coche*) knocking down, running over. 2 (*apresuramiento*) haste. 3 (*agravio*) outrage, abuse; (*de derecho*) violation. – 4 **atropellos,** *mpl* pushing and shoving *sing*.
● **con atropello,** in a hurry, in a rush.

atropina *f* atropine.

atroz 1 *adj* (*bárbaro*) atrocious, outrageous. 2 *fam* (*enorme*) enormous, huge, awful.

atrozmente 1 *adv* atrociously, outrageously. 2 *fam* dreadfully, tremendously.

ATS *abr* MED (*ayudante técnico sanitario*) medical auxiliary.

atta. *abr* COM (*atenta*) letter: *su atta. del 2 de febrero,* your letter of February 2nd.

atuendo *m* attire, dress, outfit.

atufar 1 *t* (*apestar*) to stink, smell awful. – 2 *t* (*asfixiar*) to choke. 3 *fig* (*enojar*) to annoy. – 4 **atufarse,** *p* (*vino*) to turn sour. 5 (*marearse*) to feel sick; (*asfixiarse*) to choke. 6 *fig* (*enojarse*) to get angry, get annoyed.

atufo *m* anger, annoyance.

atún *m* tuna, tuna fish, tunny.

atunero,-a 1 *adj* tuna. – 2 **atunero,** *m* tuna fisherman.

aturdidamente 1 *adv* (*con confusión*) stunningly. 2 (*con atolondramiento*) recklessly.

aturdido,-a 1 *pp* → **aturdir**. – 2 *adj* (*confundido*) stunned, dazed, bewildered. 3 (*atolondrado*) reckless, harebrained.

aturdimiento 1 *m* (*confusión*) confusion, bewilderment. 2 (*por un golpe*) daze. 3 (*atolondramiento*) recklessness, thoughtlessness. 4 (*torpeza*) clumsiness, awkwardness.

aturdir 1 *t* (*por golpe*) to stun, daze; (*por ruido*) to deafen; (*por droga*) to stupefy. 2 *fig* (*atolondrar*) to stun, dumbfound; (*confundir*) to bewilder, confuse. – 3 **aturdirse,** *p* (*atolondrarse*) to be stunned, be confused, be bewildered.

aturrullar 1 *t* to confuse, bewilder. – 2 **aturrullarse,** *p* to get confused, get bewildered.

atusar 1 *t* (*recortar*) to trim. 2 (*alisar*) to smooth (down), comb. – 3 **atusarse,** *p* (*acicalarse*) to overdress.

atutía f tutty, crude zinc oxide.
atuve pt indef → **atenerse**.
auca f wild goose.
audacia f audacity, boldness, daring.
audaz adj audacious, bold, daring.
audazmente adv audaciously, boldly.
audible adj audible.
audición 1 f (acción) hearing; (radio, televisión) reception. 2 TEAT audition: *les hicieron una audición,* they had an audition, they were auditioned. 3 MÚS concert.
audiencia 1 f (recepción) audience, hearing. 2 (entrevista) formal interview. 3 JUR high court. 4 (público) audience.
■ índice de audiencia, ratings pl.
audífono m hearing aid, deaf aid.
audímetro m audience-monitoring device.
audiometría f audiometry.
audiómetro m audiometer.
audiovisual 1 adj audio-visual. – 2 m audio-visual.
auditar t to audit.
auditivo,-a 1 adj auditory: *el nervio auditivo,* the auditory nerve. – 2 auditivo, m (auricular) earpiece, receiver.
auditor,-ra 1 m,f FIN auditor. – 2 adj auditing. – 3 auditor, m MIL legal adviser. – 4 auditora, f firm of auditors.
auditoría 1 f (proceso) auditing, audit. 2 (empleo de auditor,-ra) auditorship.
auditorio 1 m (público) audience. 2 (lugar) auditorium, hall.
auditórium m auditorium, hall.
auge 1 m (del mercado) boom. 2 (de precios) boost. 3 (de fama etc) peak, summit. 4 ASTRON apogee.
● cobrar auge, to gain importance, become important. ‖ estar en auge, to be on the increase, be thriving, be booming.
augita f augite.
auguración f augury, auguration.
augural adj augural.
augurar t to augur.
augurio m augury.
augusto,-a adj august, magnificent, majestic.
aula f (en escuela) classroom; (en universidad) lecture room.
▲ Takes el in singular.
aulaga f gorse, furze.
áulico,-a 1 adj court, courtly. – 2 m,f courtier.
aullador,-ra adj howling, yelling, baying.
aullar i to howl, yell, bay.
▲ Conjugation model [16], like aunar.
aullido m howl, yell.
aúllo m howl, yell.
aumentador,-ra 1 adj augmenting, increasing. – 2 aumentador, m ELEC booster.
aumentar 1 t to augment, increase; (precios) to put up; (producción) to step up. 2 (óptica) to magnify. 3 (fotos) to enlarge. 4 (sonido) to amplify. – 5 i to rise, go up. – 6 aumentarse, p to increase, be on the increase; (precios) to go up, rise.
aumentativo,-a adj augmentative.
aumento 1 m increase, growth. 2 (óptica) magnification. 3 (fotos) enlargement. 4 (sonido) amplification. 5 (salario) rise, US raise.
● ir en aumento, to be on the increase. ‖ aumento de precios, rise in prices.
aun 1 adv even: *aun los tontos lo saben,* even a fool knows that; *te compraré la camiseta y aun el pantalón si sacas*

buenas notas, I'll buy you the T-shirt and even the trousers if you get good marks. – 2 conj (+ infinitivo o participio) although, even though: *aun llegando tarde, lo recibieron amablemente,* although he was late, he was given a warm reception; *aun muerto nos podría causar problemas,* even though he's dead he could still cause us problems.
● aun así, even so, even then. ‖ aun cuando, although, even though. ‖ aun más, even more.
aún adv (afirmación) still; (negación, interrogación) yet: *aún estamos esperando tu respuesta,* we are still waiting for your answer; *aún no ha llamado,* he hasn't phoned yet.
aunar t to unite, combine, join.
● aunar esfuerzos, to join forces.
▲ Conjugation model [16].
aunque 1 conj (valor concesivo) although, though; (con énfasis) even if, even though: *aunque estoy enfermo no faltaré,* although I'm ill I won't miss it; *aunque haga buen tiempo no saldré,* even if it's a fine day I won't go out. 2 (valor adversativo) but: *es duro, aunque justo,* he's tough but fair.
aúpa interj up!, get up!
au pair f au pair.
aupar 1 t (levantar) to help up. 2 fig (alabar) to praise.
▲ Conjugation model [16], like aunar.
aura 1 f (aire) gentle breeze. 2 (halo) aura. 3 fig (aplauso) applause, acclamation.
▲ Takes el in singular.
áureo,-a adj golden.
aureola f aureole, halo.
auréola f aureole, halo.
áurico,-a adj auric.
aurícula f auricle.
auricular 1 adj auricular, of the ear. – 2 m (teléfono) receiver, earpiece. 3 (dedo) little finger. – 4 auriculares, mpl earphones, headphones.
aurífero,-a adj auriferous.
auriga m ASTRON charioteer, wagoner.
aurora f dawn, daybreak.
■ aurora boreal/borealis, aurora borealis, northern lights pl.
auscultación f sounding, auscultation.
auscultar t to sound (with a stethoscope).
ausencia f absence.
● brillar por su ausencia, to be conspicuous by one's absence.
ausentarse 1 p (faltar) to be absent. 2 (irse) to leave.
ausente 1 adj absent. 2 (distraído) lost in thought. – 3 mf absentee. 4 JUR missing person.
ausentismo m absenteeism.
auspiciar 1 t (proteger) to protect. 2 (augurar) to augur.
▲ Conjugation model [12], like cambiar.
auspicio m auspice.
austeramente 1 adv (sobriamente) austerely. 2 (severamente) severely, sternly.
austeridad 1 f (sobriedad) austerity. 2 (severidad) severity.
austero,-a 1 adj (sobrio) austere. 2 (severo) severe, stern.
austral 1 adj south, southern. – 2 m (moneda) austral (monetary unit of Argentina).
Australasia f Australasia.
australasiano,-a 1 adj Australasian. – 2 m,f Australasian.
Australia f Australia.
australiano,-a 1 adj Australian. – 2 m,f (persona) Australian.

australopiteco *m* australopithecine.
Austria *f* Austria.
austriaco,-a *adj-m,f* → **austríaco,-a**.
austríaco,-a 1 *adj* Austrian. – 2 *m,f* Austrian.
austro *m* south wind.
autarquía¹ *f* (*autosuficiencia*) autarky.
autarquía² *f* (*autocracia*) autarchy.
autárquico,-a¹ *adj* (*autosuficiente*) autarkic.
autárquico,-a² *adj* (*autocrático*) autarchic.
auténtica *f* → **auténtico,-a**.
autenticación *f* authentication; (*legalización*) legalization.
auténticamente 1 *adv* authentically. 2 (*realmente*) really, truly.
autenticar *t* to authenticate; (*legalizar*) to authorize, legalize.
▲ Conjugation model [1], like *sacar*.
autenticidad *f* authenticity.
auténtico,-a 1 *adj* authentic, genuine, real: *con chocolate auténtico,* with real chocolate. – 2 **auténtica,** *f* (*certificado*) certificate; (*copia legalizada*) certified copy.
autentificar *t* to authenticate.
▲ Conjugation model [1], like *sacar*.
autentizar *t* to authenticate.
▲ Conjugation model [4], like *realizar*.
autillo *m* scops owl.
autismo *m* autism.
autista *mf* autistic person.
autístico,-a *adj* autistic.
auto¹ *m* (*coche*) car.
auto² 1 *m* JUR decree, writ. 2 LIT mystery play, religious play. – 3 *autos, mpl* papers, documents.
● **estar en autos,** *fam* to be in the know.
■ **auto de prisión,** arrest warrant.
autoadhesivo,-a *adj* self-adhesive.
autoanálisis *m* self-analysis.
▲ *pl autoanálisis*.
autobiografía *f* autobiography.
autobiográfico,-a *adj* autobiographical.
autobomba *f* fire engine.
autobombearse *p fam* to blow one's own trumpet.
autobombo *m fam* self-praise, blowing one's own trumpet.
autobús *m* bus.
autocamión *m* lorry.
autocar *m* coach.
autociclo *m* motorcycle.
autocine *m* drive-in.
autoclave *f* autoclave, sterilizer.
autocontrol *m* self-control.
autocopista *f* stencilling machine.
autocracia *f* autocracy.
autócrata *mf* autocrat.
autocrático,-a *adj* autocratic.
autocrítica *f* self-criticism.
autóctono,-a *adj* indigenous.
autodefensa *f* self-defence (US self-defense).
autodeterminación *f* self-determination.
autodidacta *mf* → **autodidacto,-a**.
autodidacto,-a 1 *adj* self-taught. – 2 **autodidacta,** *mf* self-taught person.
autodirección *f* automatic pilot, autopilot.
autodisciplina *f* self-discipline.
autodominio *m* self-control.

autódromo *m* motor racing track.
autoescuela *f* driving school, school of motoring.
autoestop *m* → **autostop**.
autoestopista *mf* → **autostopista**.
autofinanciación *f* self-finance, self-financing.
autógeno,-a *adj* autogenous.
autogestión *f* self-management.
autogiro *m* autogyro, helicopter.
autogobierno *m* self-government.
autógrafo,-a 1 *adj* autographic. – 2 **autógrafo,** *m* autograph.
autohipnosis *f* self-hypnosis, autohypnosis.
▲ *pl autohipnosis*.
autoinculpación *f* self-incrimination.
autoinducción *f* self-induction.
autolesión *f* self-inflicted pain, self-inflicted injury.
autómata *m* automaton.
automáticamente *adv* automatically.
automaticidad *f* automaticity.
automático,-a *adj* automatic.
automatismo *m* automatism.
automatización *f* automation.
automatizar *t* to automate.
▲ Conjugation model [4], like *realizar*.
automoción *f* motoring.
automodelismo *m* model cars *pl*.
automotor,-ra 1 *adj* self-propelled. – 2 **automotor,** *m* diesel train.
automóvil *m* automobile, car.
automovilismo 1 *m* motoring. 2 DEP motor racing.
automovilista *mf* motorist, driver.
automovilístico,-a *adj* car.
automutilación *f* self-mutilation.
autonomía 1 *f* (*gen*) autonomy. 2 (*capacidad para funcionar sin recargar*) range: *el nuevo avión tiene una autonomía de 3000 km,* the new plane has a range of 3000 km; *este coche tiene una autonomía de 550 km,* this car can go 550 km on one tank of petrol; *el teléfono tiene una autonomía de 9 horas,* the telephone will work for 9 hours without a recharge.
autonómicamente *adv* autonomously.
autonómico,-a *adj* autonomous, self-governing.
autonomista *adj* autonomist.
autónomo,-a 1 *adj* (*región*) autonomous. 2 (*trabajador*) self-employed. – 3 *m,f* COM self-employed person.
autopiloto *m* automatic pilot, autopilot.
autopista *f* motorway, US highway.
autopolinización *f* self-pollination.
autopropulsado,-a *adj* self-propelled.
autopropulsión *f* self-propulsion.
autopsia 1 *f* autopsy, postmortem. 2 *fig* postmortem.
autopullman *m* Pullman coach.
autor,-ra 1 *m,f* (*escritor*) writer, author; (*hombre*) author; (*mujer*) authoress. 2 (*inventor*) inventor. 3 (*responsable - gen*) person responsible; (*- de delito*) perpetrator: *el autor del disparo,* the person who fired the gun; *el autor del proyecto,* the person behind the project; *el autor del diseño de la casa,* the designer of the house; *el autor de las pinturas murales,* the painter of the murals; *los autores del atentado,* those who committed the attack; *se confesó autora de la muerte de su padre,* she confessed to murdering her father; *ha sido detenido como presunto autor del homicidio de Juan Sella,* he has been arrested charged with the murder of Juan Sella.
autoría 1 *f* (*de obra*) authorship. 2 (*de delito*) responsibility: *nadie ha reivindicado la autoría del atentado,* nobody

has claimed responsibility for the attack; *el detenido confesó la autoría del delicto,* the man arrested admitted committing the crime.

autoridad *f* authority.

autoritario,-a *adj* authoritarian.

autoritarismo *m* authoritarianism.

autoritativo,-a *adj* authoritative.

autorizable *adj* authorizable.

autorización *f* authorization.

autorizadamente *adv* with authorization.

autorizado,-a 1 *pp* → **autorizar**. – 2 *adj (oficial)* authorized, official. 3 *(experto)* authoritative, expert.

autorizar 1 *t* to authorize. 2 JUR to legalize. 3 *(aprobar)* to approve of, give authority to.
▲ *Conjugation model* [4], *like realizar.*

autorretrato *m* self-portrait.

autoservicio 1 *m (restaurante)* self-service restaurant, cafeteria. 2 *(supermercado)* supermarket.

autostop *m* hitch-hiking.
● hacer autostop, to hitch-hike.

autostopista *mf* hitch-hiker.

autosuficiencia *f* self-sufficiency.

autosuficiente *adj* self-sufficient.

autosugestión *f* autosuggestion.

autovacuna *f* autovaccine.

autovía *f* dual carriageway, US highway.

auxiliador,-ra 1 *adj* helping. – 2 *m,f* helper.

auxiliar 1 *adj* auxiliary, assistant. – 2 *m (persona)* auxiliary, assistant. 3 GRAM *(verbo)* auxilliary. – 4 *t (ayudar)* to help, assist; *(a un enfermo)* to attend; *(a un país)* to give aid to.
■ auxiliar administrativo, administrative assistant. ‖ auxiliar de vuelo, flight attendant.
▲ *Conjugation model* [14].

auxilio 1 *m* help, aid, assistance, relief. – 2 *interj* help!
■ primeros auxilios, first aid *sing.*

a/v *abr (a vista)* at sight, on sight.

Av. *abr (avenida)* avenue; *(abreviatura)* Av, Ave.

avadar *t* to make fordable.

aval *m* endorsement, guarantee.

avalancha *f* avalanche.

avalar *t* to guarantee, endorse.

avalentonarse *p* to boast.

avalista *mf* guarantor.

avalorar 1 *t (evaluar)* to value (**en**, at), assess (**en**, at), estimate (**en**, at). 2 *(animar)* to encourage.

avaluación *f* valuation.

avaluar *t* to value, assess.
▲ *Conjugation model* [11], *like actuar.*

avance 1 *m (acción)* advance. 2 *(pago)* advance payment; *(balance)* balancing; *(presupuesto)* estimate. 3 *(de película)* trailer.
■ avance informativo, TV news preview, US news brief.

avante *adv* ahead, forward.

avanzada *f* → **avanzado,-a**.

avanzadilla *f* scout, patrol.

avanzado,-a 1 *pp* → **avanzar**. – 2 *adj* advanced. – 3 avanzada, *f* MIL advance guard.
● de avanzada edad, advanced in years, elderly.

avanzar 1 *i* to advance, go forward. – 2 *t (mover adelante)* to advance, move forward. 3 *(dinero)* to advance. 4 *(promover)* to promote. 5 *(una propuesta)* to put forward. – 6 avanzarse, *p (adelantarse)* to go forward, advance; *(día, noche)* to draw in.
▲ *Conjugation model* [4], *like realizar.*

avanzo *m (cómputos)* balancing; *(presupuesto)* estimate.

avaricia *f (tacañería)* avarice, meanness, miserliness; *(codicia)* greed, avarice.
● con avaricia, *fam* extremely: *es feo con avaricia,* he's as ugly as sin.

avariciosamente *adv* avariciously, greedily.

avaricioso,-a *adj* → **avariento,-a**.

avariento,-a *adj (tacaño)* avaricious, mean, miserly; *(codicioso)* greedy, avaricious.

avaro,-a 1 *adj (tacaño)* avaricious, miserly, mean; *(codicioso)* greedy, avaricious. – 2 *m,f (tacaño)* miser; *(codicioso)* greedy person.

avasallador,-ra *adj* overwhelming, overpowering.

avasallamiento *m* subjection, subjugation, domination.

avasallar *t* to subjugate, subdue.

avatar *m* change, transformation.
■ los avatares de la vida, the ups and downs of life.
▲ *Also used in plural with the same meaning.*

Avda. *abr (avenida)* avenue; *(abreviatura)* Av, Ave.

ave *f* bird.
● ser ave nocturna, *fig* to be a nightbird.
■ ave de paso, bird of passage. ‖ ave de rapiña, bird of prey. ‖ aves de corral, poultry *sing.*
▲ *Takes el in singular.*

AVE *abr (Alta Velocidad Española)* Spanish high-speed train.
▲ *Used in masculine.*

avechucho 1 *m* hideous bird. 2 *fam* eyesore.

avecinarse *p* to approach (**a**, -).

avecindarse *p* to settle, take up residence.

avefría *f* lapwing, common plover.

avejentarse *p* to age (prematurely).

avejigarse *p* to blister.
▲ *Conjugation model* [7], *like llegar.*

avellana *f* hazelnut.

avellanal *m* hazel wood, hazel plantation.

avellanedo *m* hazel wood, hazel plantation.

avellano 1 *m (árbol)* hazelnut tree. 2 *(madera)* hazel wood.

avemaría *f* Ave Maria, Hail Mary.
● en un avemaría, in a twinkling, in a jiffy. ‖ saber algo como el avemaría, *fam* to know sth. backwards.

avena *f* oats *pl.*

avenado,-a 1 *pp* → **avenar**. – 2 *adj* half-crazy, rather mad.

avenal *m* oatfield.

avenamiento *m* draining, drainage.

avenar *t* to drain.

avendré *fut* → **avenir**.

avenencia *f* agreement, accord; *(comercial)* deal.

avengo *pres indic* → **avenir**.

avenida *f* → **avenido,-a**.

avenido,-a 1 *pp* → **avenir**. – 2 bien/mal avenido,-a, *loc* in agreement/disagreement, on good/bad terms. – 3 avenida, *f (calle)* avenue. 4 *(riada)* flood, spate. 5 *(concurrencia)* gathering, meeting.

avenimiento 1 *m* agreement, compromise. 2 *(concilio)* harmony, understanding.

avenir 1 *t* to reconcile, bring together: *el juez consiguió avenir a los vecinos,* the judge helped the neighbours to reconcile their differences. – 2 avenirse, *p (llevarse bien)* to be on good terms, get on well: *yo tengo buen carácter y me avengo con cualquiera,* I'm good-natured and I get on well with everyone. 3 *(estar de acuerdo)* to agree (**a**, to), be in agreement (**a**, with): *al final se avi-*

nieron a abrir la puerta, they finally agreed to open the door.
▲ *Conjugation model* |90|, *like* ***venir***.
aventador,-ra I *adj* winnowing. – **2** *m,f* winnower. – **3** aventadora, *f* winnowing machine.
aventadora *f* → ***aventador,-ra***.
aventajado,-a I *pp* → ***aventajar***. – **2** *adj* (*sobresaliente*) outstanding, exceptional; (*en cabeza*) in the lead. **3** (*provechoso*) advantageous, favourable (US favorable).
aventajar I *t* (*exceder*) to surpass, beat: *nadie lo aventaja en amabilidad,* nobody can be kinder than him. **2** (*ir en cabeza*) to lead, be ahead; (*llegar*) to come first, come ahead (**a,** of).
aventamiento *m* winnowing.
aventar I *t* AGR to winnow. **2** (*viento*) to blow away; (*el fuego*) to blow (on), fan; (*cenizas*) to cast to the wind.
▲ *Conjugation model* |27|, *like* ***acertar***.
aventura I *f* adventure. **2** (*riesgo*) hazard, risk. **3** (*relación amorosa*) (love) affair.
aventurado,-a I *pp* → ***aventurar***. – **2** *adj* (*arriesgado*) dangerous, risky. **3** (*atrevido*) daring, bold: *es aventurado decir que todos son iguales,* it's going too far to say they're all alike.
aventurar I *t* (*poner en peligro*) to hazard, risk. **2** (*idea, opinión, etc*) to venture, dare, hazard. – **3 aventurarse,** *p* to venture, dare.
aventurero,-a I *adj* adventurous. – **2** *m,f* (*hombre*) adventurer; (*mujer*) adventuress.
● **de espíritu aventurero,** adventurous, venturesome.
aventurismo *m* adventurism.
avergonzado,-a I *pp* → ***avergonzar***. – **2** *adj* embarrassed, ashamed.
avergonzar I *t* (*causar vergüenza*) to shame, put to shame; (*turbar*) to embarrass. – **2 avergonzarse,** *p* to be ashamed (**de,** of), be embarrassed (**de,** about).
▲ *Conjugation model* |51|.
avería I *f* (*en productos*) damage. **2** TÉC failure. **3** AUTO breakdown: *esta mañana he tenido una avería,* my car broke down this morning.
averiado,-a I *pp* → ***averiar***. – **2** *adj* (*en productos*) damaged. **3** TÉC faulty, not working, out of order: *la máquina está averiada,* the machine is out of order, the machine is not working. **4** AUTO broken down.
averiar I *t* (*productos*) to damage, spoil. **2** TÉC to cause to malfunction. **3** AUTO to cause a breakdown to. – **4 averiarse,** *p* (*productos*) to get damaged. **5** TÉC to malfunction, go wrong. **6** AUTO to break down.
▲ *Conjugation model* |13|, *like* ***desviar***.
averiguable *adj* verifiable.
averiguación *f* inquiry, investigation.
averiguar *t* to inquire, investigate, find out about: *averigua quién viene,* find out who's coming.
▲ *Conjugation model* |22|.
averío I *m* (*pajarera*) aviary. **2** (*bandada*) flock of birds.
averno *m* lit Hades.
averroísmo *m* Averroism.
aversión *f* aversion.
● **sentir aversión por,** to loathe.
avestruz *m* ostrich.
avetorillo *m* little bittern.
avetoro *m* bittern.
avezado,-a I *pp* → ***avezar***. – **2** *adj* seasoned, experienced: *es un hombre avezado a estos avatares,* he's a man who's used to such ups and downs.
avezar I *t* to accustom, familiarize. – **2 avezarse,** *p* (*acostumbrarse*) to get used to (**a,** to), get accustomed (**a,** to).

▲ *Conjugation model* |4|, *like* ***realizar***.
aviación I *f* aviation. **2** MIL air force.
■ **accidente de aviación,** air crash.
aviado,-a *pp* → ***aviar***.
● **estar/ir aviado,-a,** *fam* to be in trouble, be up the creek: *¡estaríamos aviados!,* that's all we needed!
aviador,-ra *m,f* aviator, flier; (*hombre*) airman; (*mujer*) airwoman.
aviar I *t* (*proveer*) to provide (**de,** with), supply. **2** (*arreglar*) to tidy; (*ordenar*) to put in order. **3** (*apresurar*) to hurry up: *¡venga, avía!,* come on, hurry up! **4** (*preparar*) to prepare, get ready. – **5 aviarse,** *p* (*prepararse*) to prepare os. **6** (*arreglárselas*) to manage, get by: *con esto me avío,* I'll manage with this.
▲ *Conjugation model* |13|, *like* ***desviar***.
avícola *adj* poultry.
avicultor,-ra *m,f* poultry keeper, poultry farmer.
avicultura *f* aviculture; (*de aves de corral*) poultry keeping, poultry farming.
ávidamente *adv* eagerly.
avidez *f* avidity, eagerness.
ávido,-a *adj* avid, eager: *el chico estaba ávido de aventuras,* the boy was thirsty for adventure.
aviejar *t* to age prematurely.
aviento *m* (*bieldo*) winnowing rake; (*horca*) pitchfork.
avieso,-a *adj* perverse, evil, wicked.
avifauna *f* avifauna.
avinagrado,-a I *pp* → ***avinagrar***. – **2** *adj* vinegary, sour.
■ **carácter avinagrado,** sour character.
avinagrar I *t* to turn sour, embitter. – **2 avinagrarse,** *p* to turn sour. **3** *fig* to become sour, become bitter.
avío I *m* (*arreglo*) preparation, tidying. **2** (*comida*) provisions *pl.* **3** (*provecho*) profit, benefit: *tu ayuda no nos hace avío,* your help isn't needed. – **4 avíos,** *mpl* (*instrumentos*) gear *sing,* tackle *sing,* equipment *sing.*
avión[1] *m* aeroplane (US airplane), plane, aircraft.
● **ir/viajar en avión,** to fly, go by plane. ‖ **por avión,** (*correo*) airmail.
■ **avión a reacción,** jet (plane).
avión[2] *m* ORN martin.
avioneta *f* light plane, light aircraft.
avisacoches *m* parking attendant.
▲ *pl* ***avisacoches***.
avisado,-a I *pp* → ***avisar***. – **2** *adj* (*advertido*) warned. **3** (*astuto*) shrewd; (*prudente*) wise, prudent.
avisador,-ra I *adj* warning. – **2 avisador,** *m* (*alarma*) warning device. **3** (*mensajero*) messenger.
avisar I *t* (*informar*) to inform, notify, announce: *nos avisó con una semana de antelación,* she gave us a week's notice; *avísanos cuando llegues,* let us know when you arrive; *avisa al portero,* tell the porter. **2** (*advertir*) to warn: *te aviso que no digas nada a nadie,* I warn you not to say anything to anybody. **3** (*mandar llamar*) to call for: *tuvimos que avisar al médico,* we had to send for the doctor; *avisó a la policía,* he notified the police.
● **"se avisa grúa",** "cars will be towed away".
aviso I *m* (*información*) notice. **2** (*advertencia*) warning.
● **andar/estar sobre aviso,** (*estar atento*) to be on the alert, keep one's eyes open; (*estar enterado*) to know what's going on, be in on it; (*estar avisado*) to have been warned. ‖ **hasta nuevo aviso,** until further notice. ‖ **mandar aviso,** to send word. ‖ **poner sobre aviso,** to forewarn. ‖ **sin previo aviso,** without prior notice.
avispa *f* wasp.
avispado,-a I *pp* → ***avispar***. – **2** *adj* clever, smart, sharp.

avispar 1 *t* to smarten up, quicken. **– 2 avisparse,** *p* to smarten up, quicken.
avispero 1 *m* (*conjunto de avispas*) swarm of wasps. **2** (*nido de avispas*) wasp's nest. **3** *fig* (*lío*) tight spot, mess. **4** MED carbuncle.
avistar *t* to see, sight.
avitaminosis *f* avitaminosis, vitamin deficiency.
▲ *pl avitaminosis.*
avituallamiento *m* provisioning.
avituallar *t* to provision (**de,** with), supply with food.
avivado,-a 1 *pp* → **avivar. – 2** *adj fig* enlivened, quickened; (*enfado, pasión*) stirred, aroused.
avivar 1 *t* (*fuego*) to stoke (up). **2** (*anhelos, deseos*) to enliven. **3** (*pasiones, dolor*) to intensify. **4** (*paso*) to quicken. **5** (*colores, luz*) to brighten up. **– 6** *i* to become brighter, become livelier. **– 7 avivarse,** *p* to become brighter, become livelier.
avizor estar ojo avizor, *loc* to be on the alert, be on the lookout.
avizorar *t* to watch, spy on.
avoceta *f* avocet.
avutarda *f* great bustard.
axial *adj* axial.
axil *adj* axial.
axila 1 *f* (*del cuerpo*) armpit, underarm. **2** MED axilla. **3** (*de planta*) axil.
axilar *adj* axillar, axillary.
axiología *f* axiology.
axioma *m* axiom.
axiomático,-a *adj* axiomatic.
axis *m* axis.
▲ *pl axis.*
axoideo,-a *adj* axoidal.
ay 1 *interj* (*dolor*) ouch!, ow! **2** (*pena*) alas!: ¡*ay de mí!,* woe is me!, poor me! **3** (*temor*) oh!: ¡*ay! ¡qué miedo!,* oh God!, I'm terrified! **– 4** *m* (*quejido*) moan, groan; (*suspiro*) sigh.
● ¡ay de mí!, woe is me! ‖ ¡ay de ti *(si etc)* como ...!, (*amenaza*) I'll give it to you (*him etc*) if ...!, you're (*he's etc*) in for it if ...!
aya 1 *f arc* (*ama*) wet nurse. **2** (*niñera*) nanny. **3** (*institutriz*) governess.
ayatollah *m* ayatollah.
ayer 1 *adv* (*el día anterior*) yesterday. **2** (*en el pasado*) in the past, formerly: *ahora estás de acuerdo, pero ayer no,* now you agree but you didn't use to. **– 3** *m* past.
● antes de ayer, the day before yesterday. ‖ ayer por la mañana/tarde, yesterday morning/afternoon. ‖ ayer por la noche, last night. ‖ de ayer a hoy, overnight. ‖ parece que fue ayer, it seems like only yesterday.
ayo *m arc* private tutor.
ayotera *f* gourd, pumpkin.
Ayte. *abr* (*ayudante*) assistant; (*abreviatura*) asst.
ayuda 1 *f* help, aid, assistance. **2** (*lavativa*) enema.
● ir en ayuda de algn., to come to sb.'s assistance. ‖ prestar ayuda, to help (**a,** -).
■ ayuda de cámara, valet.
ayudante 1 *mf* assistant. **2** MIL adjutant.
■ ayudante de dirección, CINEM TEAT production assistant. ‖ ayudante técnico sanitario, nurse.
ayudantía *f* assistantship. **2** MIL adjutancy.
ayudar 1 *t* to help, aid, assist: ¿*en qué podemos ayudarte?,* how can we help you? **– 2 ayudarse,** *p* (*apoyarse*) to make use (**de/con,** of).

ayunar *i* to fast.
ayunas. 1 en ayunas, *loc* on an empty stomach: *tómalo en ayunas,* take it on an empty stomach. **2** *fig* in the dark.
● quedarse en ayunas, *fig* to be in the dark.
ayuno *m* fast, fasting.
● guardar ayuno, to fast.
ayuntamiento 1 *m* (*corporación*) town council, city council. **2** (*edificio*) town hall, city hall.
■ ayuntamiento carnal, *fml* sexual intercourse.
azabache *m* jet.
● negro,-a como el azabache, jet-black.
azada *f* hoe.
azadón *m* mattock.
azafata 1 *f* (*de avión*) air hostess, stewardess. **2** (*de congresos*) hostess.
azafrán *m* saffron.
azafranado,-a *adj* saffron-coloured (us saffron-colored).
azagaya *f* assegai.
azahar *m* (*de naranjo*) orange blossom; (*de limonero*) lemon blossom.
■ agua de azahar, orange-flower water.
azalea *f* azalea.
azar 1 *m* chance. **2** (*percance*) misfortune, accident.
● al azar, at random. ‖ por puro azar, by pure chance.
■ juegos de azar, games of chance. ‖ los azares de la vida, the ups and downs of life.
azarado,-a 1 *pp* → **azararse. – 2** *adj* embarrassed.
azaramiento *m* embarrassment.
azarar 1 *t* to embarrass. **– 2 azararse,** *p* to be embarrassed.
azarbe *m* trench, irrigation ditch.
azarosamente *adv* hazardously.
azaroso,-a *adj* risky, hazardous, dangerous.
Azerbaiyán *m* Azerbaijan.
azerbaiyano,-a 1 *adj* Azerbaijani. **– 2** *m,f* (*persona*) Azerbaijani. **– 3** azerbaiyano, *m* (*idioma*) Azerbaijani.
azerí 1 *adj* Azerbaijani. **– 2** *mf* Azerbaijani.
ázimo,-a *adj* unleavened.
■ pan ázimo, unleavened bread.
ázoe *m arc* nitrogen.
azófar *m* brass.
azogado,-a 1 *pp* → **azogar. – 2** *adj* restless.
azogar 1 *t* to quicksilver, coat with quicksilver; (*espejos*) to silver. **– 2 azogarse,** *p* (*contraer la enfermedad*) to suffer from mercurialism. **3** *fig* (*agitarse*) to move restlessly.
azogue *m* mercury, quicksilver.
azolvar *t* to block, obstruct.
azor *m* goshawk.
azorado,-a 1 *pp* → **azorar. – 2** *adj* embarrassed.
azoramiento *m* embarrassment.
azorar 1 *t* to embarrass. **– 2 azorarse,** *p* to be embarrassed.
azorrarse *p* to feel drowsy, feel dopey.
azotado,-a 1 *pp* → **azotar. – 2** *adj* whipped, flogged. **3** *fig* whipped, lashed.
azotaina *f fam* spanking, smacking.
● dar una azotaina, to spank, smack.
azotar 1 *t* (*con látigo*) to whip, flog. **2** (*golpear*) to beat down on. **3** (*viento, olas*) to lash. **4** *fig* (*peste, hambre, etc*) to ravage.
azotazo *m fam* smack.
azote 1 *m* (*instrumento*) whip, scourge. **2** (*golpe*) lash, stroke (of the whip). **3** (*manotada*) smack. **4** (*del viento, del agua*) lashing. **5** *fig* scourge.

azotea *f* flat roof.
- ● estar mal de la azotea, *fam* to have a screw loose.

azteca 1 *adj* Aztec. – **2** *mf* Aztec.

aztequismo *m* (*palabra*) Aztec word; (*expresión*) Atzec expression.

azúcar *m* & *f* sugar.
- ■ azúcar blanco, refined sugar. ‖ azúcar cande/candi, sugar-candy, candy-sugar. ‖ azúcar de caña, cane sugar. ‖ azúcar de lustre, icing sugar. ‖ azúcar moreno/negro, brown sugar. ‖ terrón de azúcar, lump of sugar.

azucarado,-a 1 *pp* → **azucarar**. – **2** *adj* (*con azúcar*) sugared, sweetened. **3** (*como el azúcar*) sugar-like; (*dulce*) sweet. **4** *fig* sugary.

azucarar 1 *t* to sugar, sweeten. **2** (*bañar*) to coat with sugar, ice with sugar.

azucarera *f* → **azucarero,-a**.

azucarero,-a 1 *adj* sugar. – **2** *m* & *f* (*vasija*) sugar bowl. – **3** azucarera, *f* (*fábrica*) sugar factory.

azucarillo 1 *m* (*terrón*) sugar lump. **2** (*pasta*) lemon candy.

azucena *f* white lily.

azuela *f* adze.

azufaifa *f* jujube.

azufaifo *m* jujube tree.

azufrado,-a 1 *pp* → **azufrar**. – **2** *adj* sulphurous (US sulfurous).

azufrador,-ra 1 *adj* sulphur-bleached (US sulfur-bleached). – **2** *m,f* sulphur bleacher (US sulfur bleacher). – **3** azufrador, *m* linen drier, linen dryer.

azufrar *t* to sulphur (US sulfur), sulphurate (US sulfurate).

azufre *m* sulphur (US sulfur).

azufroso,-a *adj* sulphurous (US sulfurous).

azul 1 *adj* blue. – **2** *m* blue.
- ■ azul celeste, sky blue, light blue. ‖ azul cielo, sky blue, light blue. ‖ azul eléctrico, electric blue. ‖ azul marino, navy blue. ‖ azul turquesa, turquoise. ‖ sangre azul, blue blood.

azulado,-a 1 *pp* → **azular**. – **2** *adj* blue, bluish.

azular *t* to blue.

azularse *p* to turn blue.

azulear *i* to be bluish, have a bluish tinge.

azulejero,-a *m,f* tiler.

azulejo[1] *m* (*pájaro*) bluebird.

azulejo[2] *m* (*baldosa*) tile, glazed tile.

azulenco,-a *adj* bluish.

azulete *m* blue: *dar azulete,* to blue.

azulgrana 1 *m* Barcelona player. – **2** *adj* DEP of Barcelona Football Club.
- ▲ *pl* azulgrana.

azulino,-a *adj* bluish.

azumbre *m* & *f* liquid measure equivalent to 2.016 litres.

azur 1 *adj* azure. – **2** *m* azure.

azurita *f* azurite.

azuzar *t* to egg on.
- ● azuzar los perros a algn., to set the dogs on sb.

B

B, b *f* (*la letra*) B, b.
baba 1 *f* (*de animal, adulto*) spittle, saliva; (*de niño*) dribble.
2 (*de caracol, babosa*) slime.
● **caérsele a uno la baba,** *fam* to drool: *se le cae la baba con su nieta,* he drools over his granddaughter. ∥ **tener mala baba,** to have a bad temper.
babear 1 *i* (*adulto, animal*) to slobber, slaver; (*niño*) to dribble. **2** *fig* to drool, slobber.
babel *m & f* bedlam.
Babel torre de Babel, *f* Tower of Babel.
babélico,-a 1 *adj* (*confuso*) confused; (*difícil de entender*) unintelligible.
babeo *m* (*de adulto, animal*) slobbering, slavering; (*de niño*) dribbling.
babero 1 *m* bib. **2** (*babi*) child's overall.
babi *m* child's overall.
Babia estar en Babia, *loc* to have one's head in the clouds.
babieca 1 *adj* stupid. – **2** *mf* fool.
babilla *f* stifle.
Babilonia *f* Babylon.
babilónico,-a 1 *adj* Babylonian. – **2** *m,f* Babylonian. –
3 *m* (*idioma*) Babylonian.
babilonio,-a *adj-m,f* → **babilónico,-a**.
bable *m* Asturian dialect.
babor *m* port.
● **a babor,** to port, on the port side.
babosa *f* → **baboso,-a**.
babosear *t* to dribble over, slobber over.
baboseo *m* dribbling, slobbering.
baboso,-a 1 *adj* (*adulto, animal*) slobbering, slavering; (*niño*) dribbling, dribbly: *ese niño es muy baboso,* that child dribbles a lot. **2** *fam fig* sloppy. – **3** *m,f* (*joven*) kid: *mira cómo fuman, y no son más que unos babosos,* look at them smoking, and they're no more than kids. – **4** babosa, *f* slug.
babucha *f* slipper.
babuino *m* baboon.
baca *f* rack, roof rack, luggage rack.
bacalada *f* salted cod.
bacaladero,-a 1 *adj* cod: *la pesca bacaladera es su principal industria,* cod fishing is their main industry. – **2** bacaladero, *m* cod boat.
bacaladilla *f* blue whiting.
bacalao *m* cod.
● **cortar el bacalao,** to be the boss, give the orders, wear the trousers. ∥ ¡**te conozco bacalao!,** you can't fool me!
■ **bacalao salado,** salt cod.
bacanal 1 *adj* Bacchanalian. – **2** *f* orgy.
bacará *m* bacarrat.
bacarrá *m* bacarrat.
bache 1 *m* (*en carretera*) pothole. **2** (*de aire*) air pocket. **3** *fig* bad patch.

bachiller *mf* person who has the Spanish certificate of secondary education.
bachillerato *m*.
■ **bachillerato unificado polivalente,** Spanish certificate of secondary education.
bacía *f* barber's bowl.
bacilar *adj* bacillary.
bacilo *m* bacillus.
bacín *m* chamber pot.
backgammon *m* backgammon.
bacon *m* bacon.
bacón *m* → **bacon**.
bacteria *f* bacterium: *las bacterias provocan varias enfermedades,* bacteria cause a number of diseases.
bacteriano,-a *adj* bacterial.
bactericida 1 *adj* bactericidal. – **2** *m* bactericide.
bacteriología *f* bacteriology.
bacteriológico,-a *adj* bacteriological.
bacteriólogo,-a *m,f* bacteriologist.
báculo 1 *m* (*palo*) staff. **2** (*de obispo*) crosier. **3** *fig* support: *los hijos serán nuestro báculo en la vejez,* the children will be our staff in our old age.
■ **báculo pastoral,** crosier.
badajo *m* clapper.
badajocense 1 *adj* of Badajoz, from Badajoz. – **2** *mf* person from Badajoz, inhabitant of Badajoz.
badajoceño,-a 1 *adj* of Badajoz, from Badajoz. – **2** *m,f* person from Badajoz, inhabitant of Badajoz.
badana 1 *f* (*piel*) sheepskin. **2** (*persona*) lazybones, layabout.
● **zurrar la badana a algn.,** to beat sb. up.
badén 1 *m* (*bache*) pothole. **2** (*vado*) ford. **3** (*canal*) channel. **4** (*obstáculo*) speed bump.
badil *m* fire shovel.
bádminton *m* badminton.
baffle *m* loudspeaker.
bafle *m* loudspeaker.
bagaje *m* baggage.
■ **bagaje cultural,** experience, background.
bagatela *f* bagatelle, trifle.
Bagdad *f* Baghdad.
bagre *m* catfish.
bah *interj* bah!
Bahamas las Bahamas, *fpl* the Bahamas.
bahameño,-a 1 *adj* Bahamian. – **2** *m,f* Bahamian.
bahía *f* bay.
■ **Gran Bahía Australiana,** Great Australian Bight.
Bahrein *m* Bahrein.
bahreiní 1 *adj* Bahreini. – **2** *mf* Bahreini.
bailable 1 *adj* danceable: *tócanos algo que sea bailable,* play something we can dance to.
bailador,-ra 1 *adj* dancing: *una cabra bailadora,* a dancing goat. – **2** *m,f* dancer.

bailaor,-ra *m,f* flamenco dancer.

bailar 1 *t* to dance: *bailamos un vals,* we danced a waltz. 2 *(hacer girar)* to spin: *bailó una moneda en la mesa,* she spun a coin on the table. – 3 *i* to dance: *¿bailas?,* do you want to dance?, would you like to dance?; *baila conmigo,* dance with me. 4 *(girar)* to spin: *mira cómo baila la peonza,* look how the top spins. 5 *(ser grande)* to be too big: *me bailan estos zapatos,* these shoes are too big for me. 6 *(moverse; cosa)* to wobble; *(persona)* to move about, fidget: *esta silla baila,* this chair wobbles. 7 *(estar suelto)* to be loose: *este tornillo baila,* this screw is loose.
● **bailar al son que le tocan,** to swim with the tide. ‖ **ir a bailar,** to go dancing. ‖ **otro,-a que tal baila,** he's *(she's)* no different. ‖ **que me *(te, le, etc)* quiten lo bailado,** they can't take the memories away from me *(you, him, her, etc).* ‖ **sacar a algn. a bailar,** to ask sb. to dance.
▲ Conjugation model [15], *like aislar.*

bailarín,-ina 1 *adj (que baila)* dancing; *(que gusta de bailar)* who likes dancing: *es muy bailarina,* she loves dancing. – 2 *m,f* dancer.

baile 1 *m* dance. 2 *(de etiqueta)* ball. 3 *(sala)* dancehall.
■ **baile clásico,** ballet. ‖ **baile de disfraces,** masked ball. ‖ **baile de salón,** ballroom dancing. ‖ **baile de San Vito,** St Vitus' Dance.

bailón,-ona 1 *adj* who likes dancing: *es muy bailona,* she loves dancing. – 2 *m,f* keen dancer.

bailongo *m fam* bop.

bailotear *i fam* to bop, jig about.

bailoteo *m fam* jigging about.

baja *f* → **bajo-a.**

bajada 1 *f (disminución)* drop, fall: *esto representa una bajada del 10%,* this represents a drop of 10%; *ha habido una bajada en la cotización de la peseta,* there has been a fall in the value of the peseta; *sufrió una bajada de tensión,* her blood pressure dropped; *subidas y bajadas,* ups and downs. 2 *(descenso)* descent; *(de telón, barrera)* lowering: *mientras subía, no pensaba más que en la bajada,* all the while I was climbing up I could think of nothing but the descent; *no crucen la vía después de la bajada de la barrera,* do not cross the line after the barrier has come down. 3 *(camino)* way down. 4 *(en carretera etc)* slope, hill.
■ **bajada de bandera,** minimum fare.

bajamar *f* low tide.

bajar 1 *t (coger algo de un lugar alto)* to get down, take down: *bajó un libro de la estantería,* he took a book down from the shelf. 2 *(dejar más abajo)* to lower: *¿has bajado las persianas?,* have you lowered the blinds?; *ese cuadro está muy alto, bájalo un poco,* that picture's too high, bring it down a bit; *se bajó los pantalones para que le pusieran una inyección,* he took his trousers down so that they could give him an injection. 3 *(reducir)* to lower, reduce, bring down: *esto te bajará la tensión,* this will lower your blood pressure; *nuestro objetivo es bajar la inflación,* our aim is to reduce inflation; *han bajado los impuestos directos,* they've cut down direct taxes; *quieren bajar el precio de los libros,* they want to bring down the price of books. 4 *(reducir en intensidad)* to lower; *(voz)* to lower; *(sonido, luz, gas)* to turn down: *baja la voz, que te van a oír,* lower your voice, they'll hear you; *baja la tele un poco, no te oigo,* turn the telly down, I can't hear you; *baja la calefacción, hace calor,* turn the heating down, it's hot. 5 *(alargar)* to lengthen, let down: *la modista me bajó un poco la falda,* the dressmaker let my skirt down a bit. 6 *(recorrer*

de arriba abajo) to go down, come down: *bajamos la escalera,* we went down the stairs; *bajamos andando/corriendo,* we walked/ran down. – 7 *i (ir abajo - acercándose)* to come down; *(- alejándose)* to go down: *¡baja de ahí ahora mismo!,* come down from there right now!; *¿bajas en ascensor o por la escalera?,* are you going down in the lift or by the stairs?; *bajó corriendo/volando,* he ran/ flew down. 8 *(reducirse)* to fall, drop, come down: *ha bajado la temperatura,* the temperature has dropped; *los precios han bajado,* prices have come down; *la peseta sigue bajando,* the peseta continues to fall. 9 *(hinchazón)* to go down; *(fiebre)* to go down, come down. 10 *(marea)* to go out. 11 *(apearse - de coche)* to get out *(de,* of*)*; *(de bicicleta, caballo)* to get off *(de, -)*; *(de avión, tren, autobús)* to get off *(de, -).* – 12 **bajarse,** *p (ir abajo - acercándose)* to come down; *(- alejándose)* to go down. 13 *(apearse - de coche)* to get out *(de, -)*; *(bicicleta, caballo)* to get off *(de, -)*; *(avión, tren, autobús)* to get off *(de, -).* 14 *(agacharse)* to bend down, bend over. – 15 **baja,** *f (descenso)* fall, drop: *la baja del precio del petróleo,* the fall in the price of oil; *el dólar sigue a la baja,* the dollar continues to fall. 16 MIL casualty: *el ejército sufrió pocas bajas,* the army suffered few casualties. 17 *(por enfermedad)* sick leave; *(justificante)* medical certificate, doctor's note.
● **bajarse la cabeza,** to bow one's head. ‖ **no bajar de ...,** to be at least ..., not be less than ...: *ese coche no baja de los tres millones,* that car must cost at least three million.

bajel *m lit* vessel.

bajero,-a 1 *adj* lower, bottom. – 2 **bajera,** *f* bottom sheet.

bajeza 1 *f (acción)* base action, despicable act, vile deed: *cometió la bajeza de abandonarla,* he was despicable enough to abandon her. 2 *fig* baseness: *bajeza moral,* moral baseness.

bajini *adv* → **bajinis.**

bajinis por lo bajinis, *loc (disimuladamente)* on the sly; *(en voz baja)* in a low voice.

bajío *m* sandbank.

bajista 1 *adj* downward: *sigue la tendencia bajista,* the downward trend continues. – 2 *mf (músico)* bass player.

bajo,-a 1 *adj (gen)* low: *una casa baja,* a low house; *precios bajos,* low prices; *el río está bajo,* the river is low; *pon la música, pero baja,* put the music on low. 2 *(persona)* short, not tall: *su padre es muy bajo,* her father is very short. 3 *(cabeza)* bowed, held low; *(ojos)* lowered, downcast: *rezaba con la cabeza baja,* she prayed with her head bowed. 4 *(marea)* out: *la marea está baja,* the tide is out. 5 *(despreciable)* despicable, contemptible, base. 6 *(territorio, río)* lower: *la baja Navarra,* Lower Navarre. 7 *(época)* later: *la Baja Edad Media,* the Later Middle Ages. 8 *(inferior)* poor, low: *es de baja calidad,* it's poor quality; *tu rendimiento es muy bajo,* your performance is very poor. – 9 **bajo,** *m (piso)* ground floor, US first floor. 10 *(de prenda)* bottoms *pl,* US cuff. 11 MÚS bass. – 12 *mf* MÚS *(músico)* bass player; *(cantante)* bass. – 13 *adv (en el aire)* low: *el avión vuela bajo para evitar el radar,* the plane flies low to avoid the radar. 14 *(voz)* softly, quietly, in a low voice: *habla muy bajo,* she speaks very quietly. – 15 *prep* under: *pasamos la noche bajo las estrellas,* we spent the night under the stars; *bajo ningún concepto,* under no circumstances; *bajo el yugo del dictador,* under the yoke of the dictator. 16 *(temperatura)* below: *10 grados bajo cero,* 10 degrees below zero. – 17 **bajos,** *mpl (planta baja)* ground floor; *(sótano)* basement.
● **por lo bajo,** *(disimuladamente)* on the sly; *(en voz baja)*

in a low voice; (*sin exagerar*) conservatively. ‖ **dar de baja,** (*a enfermo*) to give a sick note to; (*a socio de club*) to expel; (*a soldado*) to declare missing. ‖ **darse de baja,** (*de un club*) to cancel one's membership, leave, drop out; (*en una suscripción*) to cancel one's subscription; (*por enfermedad*) to take sick leave. ‖ **estar de baja,** (*enfermo*) to be off sick; (*pasado*) to be dropping, on the way out. ‖ **estar en baja,** to be dropping, on the way out: *los concursos televisivos están en baja,* television quiz shows are on the way out. ‖ **ser baja,** (*deportista*) to be injured, not be playing; (*militar*) to be reported missing: *Osuna es baja para el partido de mañana,* Osuna is out of tomorrow's game.
■ **bajas pasiones,** animal passions. ‖ **bajos.** ‖ **bajos fondos,** underworld *sing.*

bajón 1 *m* sharp fall, sharp drop, slump: *la bolsa ha dado un considerable bajón,* there has been a sharp fall in share prices. **2** (*de ánimos*) depression. **3** (*de salud*) relapse: *tuvo un bajón,* he suffered a relapse. **4** MÚS bassoon.

bajonista *mf* bassoonist.

bajorrelieve *m* bas-relief.

bajura *f.*
■ **pesca de bajura,** inshore fishing. ‖ **pescador de bajura,** inshore fisherman.

bakelita *f* bakelite.

bala 1 *f* bullet: *tiene una herida de bala,* he has a bullet wound; *recibió una herida de bala,* he was hit by a bullet; *el coche presentaba dos impactos de bala,* the car had been hit by two bullets. **2** (*paquete*) bale.
● **como una bala,** *fam* like a shot: *mi moto nueva va como una bala,* my new motorbike goes like a bullet.
■ **bala de cañón,** cannonball. ‖ **bala rasa,** good-for-nothing. ‖ **bala perdida,** stray bullet; *fig* birdbrain.

balacera *f* AM shootout.

balada *f* ballad.

baladí *adj* trivial.
▲ *pl* **baladíes.**

balalaica *f* balalaika.

balance 1 *m* (*movimiento*) rocking. **2** COM (*operación*) balance; (*hoja*) balance sheet. **3** (*cálculo*) total: *el balance provisional es de quince muertos,* the provisional death toll is fifteen. **4** (*resultado*) outcome, result: *el balance de la reunión ha sido positivo,* on balance, the meeting was successful. **5** (*equilibrio*) balance.
● **hacer un balance de,** to take stock of, weigh up, evaluate.
■ **balance acústico,** sound balance.

balancear 1 *t* (*mecer*) to rock; (*columpio, brazo*) to swing. – **2** *i* (*mecer*) to rock; (*columpio, brazo*) to swing. – **3** **balancearse,** *p* (*mecerse*) to rock; (*columpio, brazo*) to swing.

balanceo *m* (*gen*) swinging; (*suave*) rocking.

balancín 1 *m* (*mecedora*) rocking chair. **2** (*columpio*) seesaw. **3** (*de motor*) rocker arm. **4** (*de volatinero*) balance pole.

balandra *f* sloop.

balandrista *mf* (*hombre*) yachtsman; (*mujer*) yachtswoman.

balandro *m* yacht.

balano *m* → **bálano.**

bálano *m* glans penis.

balanza 1 *f* (*aparato*) scales *pl.* **2** COM balance.
● **inclinar la balanza a favor de ...,** to tip the scales in favour (US favor) of ...
■ **balanza comercial,** trade balance, balance of trade. ‖ **balanza de pagos,** balance of payments.

balar *i* to bleat, baa.

balarrasa *mf* good-for-nothing.

balasto *m* ballast.

balaustrada *f* balustrade; (*en escalera*) banister.

balaustre *m* → **balaústre.**

balaústre *m* baluster.

balazo 1 *m* shot: *lo mataron de un balazo,* he was shot dead; *murió acribillado a balazos,* he was riddled with bullets. **2** (*herida*) bullet wound.

balboa *f* balboa (*monetary unit of Panama*).

balbucear 1 *i* to babble. – **2** *t* to babble: *balbuceó una excusa tonta,* he babbled some stupid excuse.

balbuceo *m* babbling.

balbuciente 1 *adj* stammering. **2** *fig* tentative, uncertain, hesitant: *después de unos comienzos balbucientes ...,* after a tentative start, ...

balbucir *i* → **balbucear.**

Balcanes los Balcanes, *mpl* the Balkans.

balcánico,-a *adj* Balkan.

balcón 1 *m* (*en edificio*) balcony. **2** (*mirador*) vantage point: *desde su balcón en lo alto del peñasco ...,* from his vantage point at the top of the rocky crag ...

balda *f* shelf.

baldado,-a 1 *adj* (*inválido*) crippled. **2** *fam* (*cansado*) shattered.

baldaquín *m* baldachin, baldaquin, canopy.

baldaquino *m* → **baldaquín.**

baldar 1 *t* (*lisiar*) to cripple. **2** *fam* (*cansar*) to wear out.

balde *m* bucket, pail.
● **de balde,** free, for nothing. ‖ **en balde,** in vain.

baldear *t* to wash down, swill down, sluice down.

baldeo *m* washing down, swilling down, sluicing down.

baldío,-a 1 *adj* (*tierra - sin cultivar*) uncultivated; (*- estéril*) barren. **2** (*vano*) vain, useless: *todos sus esfuerzos resultaron baldíos,* all his efforts were in vain. – **3 baldío,** *m* wasteland.

baldón 1 *m* (*insulto*) insult, affront, slur. **2** (*deshonra*) disgrace.

baldosa *f* floor tile.

baldosín *m* tile, wall tile.

balear 1 *adj* Balearic. – **2** *mf* Balearic islander.
■ **Islas Baleares,** Balearic Islands.

baleárico,-a *adj* Balearic.

balido *m* bleat, baa: *se oyeron los balidos de las ovejas,* you could hear the bleating of the sheep.

balín *m* pellet.

balística *f* → **balístico,-a.**

balístico,-a 1 *adj* ballistic. – **2 balística,** *f* ballistics.

baliza 1 *f* (*de mar*) buoy. **2** (*de tierra*) beacon.

balizar *t* to mark.

ballena 1 *f* (*animal*) whale. **2** (*material*) whalebone; (*tira de corsé*) stay.
■ **ballena azul,** blue whale.

ballenato *m* whale calf.

ballenero,-a 1 *adj* whaling. – **2** *m.f* (*persona*) whaler. – **3 ballenero,** *m* (*barco*) whaling ship, whaler, whaleboat.

ballesta 1 *f* (*arma*) crossbow. **2** AUTO spring.

ballestero *m* crossbowman.

ballet *m* ballet.
▲ *pl* **ballets.**

balneario,-a 1 *adj* spa. – **2 balneario,** *m* spa, health resort.

balompié *m* football, soccer, US soccer.

balón 1 *m* DEP ball; (*de fútbol*) ball, football; (*de voleibol*) ball, volleyball; (*de rugby*) ball, rugby ball; (*de baloncesto*) ball, basketball. **2** (*para gas*) cylinder.

■ **balón de medicina**, medicine ball. ‖ **balón de oxígeno**, oxygen cylinder; *fig* shot in the arm, boost.
baloncestista *mf* basketball player.
baloncesto *m* basketball.
balonmanista *mf* handball player.
balonmano *m* handball.
balonvolea *m* volleyball.
balsa 1 *f* pool. 2 MAR raft.
● **como una balsa de aceite**, (*mar*) like a millpond; *fig* very peaceful.
balsámico,-a *adj* balsamic.
bálsamo 1 *m* balsam, balm. 2 *fig* comfort.
báltico,-a *adj* Baltic.
■ el (*mar*) Báltico, the Baltic (Sea).
baluarte 1 *m* (*fortificación*) bastion. 2 *fig* bastion, stronghold.
bamba 1 *f* (*baile*) bamba. 2 (*pastel*) cream bun. 3 (*zapato*) pump, US sneaker.
bambalina *f* drop cloth, drop.
● **entre bambalinas**, in the wings.
bamboleante *adj* swaying.
bambolear 1 *i* to sway. – 2 **bambolearse**, *p* to sway.
bamboleo *m* swaying.
bambolla *f* pretence (US pretense).
bambú *m* bamboo.
▲ *pl* **bambúes** or **bambús**.
banal *adj* trivial.
banalidad *f* triviality.
banalización *f* trivialization.
banalizar *t* to trivialize.
banana *f* banana.
bananero,-a 1 *adj* banana: *hay muchas plantaciones bananeras*, there are a lot of banana plantations. – 2 bananero, *m* banana tree.
banano *m* banana tree.
banca 1 *f* COM banking; (*bancos*) (the) banks *pl*. 2 (*asiento*) bench. 3 (*en juego*) bank.
● **hacer saltar la banca**, to break the bank.
bancada 1 *f* (*banco*) long bench. 2 (*superficie*) work surface.
bancal 1 *m* (*en pendiente*) terrace. 2 (*en llano*) plot.
bancario,-a *adj* (*de un banco*) bank; (*de los bancos*) banking.
■ **agencia bancaria**, bank branch. ‖ **entidad bancaria**, bank. ‖ **grupo bancario**, banking group. ‖ **operaciones bancarias**, banking business *sing*. ‖ **sistema bancario**, banking system.
bancarrota *f* bankruptcy.
● **caer en bancarrota**, to go bankrupt. ‖ **estar en bancarrota**, to be bankrupt.
banco 1 *m* bank. 2 (*asiento*) bench; (*de iglesia*) pew. 3 (*mesa*) bench, work bench. 4 (*de peces*) shoal.
■ **banco de carpintero**, workbench. ‖ **banco de datos**, data bank. ‖ **banco de hielo**, ice floe. ‖ **banco de imágenes**, image bank. ‖ **banco de memoria**, memory bank. ‖ **banco de niebla**, fog bank. ‖ **banco de órganos**, organ bank. ‖ **banco de prueba**, test bench. ‖ **banco de sangre**, blood bank. ‖ **banco de semen**, sperm bank.
banda[1] 1 *f* (*faja*) sash. 2 (*lista*) band. 3 (*tira*) strip. 4 (*lado*) side. 5 (*en billar*) cushion.
● **cerrarse en banda**, to dig one's heels in. ‖ **coger por banda a algn. / pillar en banda a algn.**, to lay one's hands on sb.
■ **banda de frecuencia**, radio band. ‖ **banda mag-**

nética, magnetic strip. ‖ **banda sonora**, sound track. ‖ **banda transportadora**, conveyor belt. ‖ **línea de banda**, touchline. ‖ **saque de banda**, DEP throw-in.
banda[2] 1 *f* (*músicos*) band. 2 (*maleantes*) gang. 3 (*pájaros*) flock.
■ **banda armada**, (*delincuentes*) armed gang; (*terroristas*) terrorist group. ‖ **banda de música**, band. ‖ **banda de rock**, rock group. ‖ **banda municipal**, town band. ‖ **banda terrorista**, terrorist group.
bandada 1 *f* (*de pájaros*) flock; (*de insectos*) swarm; (*de peces*) shoal. 2 (*de personas*) horde: *llegaron en bandadas*, they arrived in their thousands.
bandazo *m* lurch.
● **dar bandazos**, to lurch.
bandear 1 *i* to move from side to side. – 2 **bandearse**, *p* to manage, cope, get by: *aunque las cosas no nos van muy bien, nos bandeamos*, although things are not too good, we get by.
bandeja *f* (*gen*) tray; (*para diapositivas*) magazine.
● **dejar algo a algn. en bandeja**, to hand sth. to sb. on a plate. ‖ **poner algo a algn. en bandeja**, *fig* to hand sth. to sb. on a plate. ‖ **pasar la bandeja**, to pass round the hat.
bandera *f* flag: *la bandera del barco es griega*, the ship sails under the Greek flag.
● **arriar la bandera**, to strike one's colours (US colors), surrender. ‖ **de bandera**, *fig* fantastic, great. ‖ **hasta la bandera**, jam-packed: *se llenará hasta la bandera*, it will be jam-packed. ‖ **izar la bandera**, to raise the flag. ‖ **jurar bandera**, to swear allegiance to the flag.
■ **bandera a cuadros**, chequered flag. ‖ **bandera blanca**, white flag. ‖ **bandera nacional**, national flag. ‖ **bandera negra**, Jolly Roger.
bandería *f* faction, party.
banderilla 1 *f* (*tauromaquia*) banderilla (*barbed dart stuck into the bull's back*). 2 (*tapa*) pickled onion, carrot, gherkin, pepper, etc. on a cocktail stick.
banderillear *t* to stick banderillas into the bull's back.
banderillero *m* banderillero.
banderín *m* pennant.
■ **banderín de córner**, corner flag.
banderita *f* little flag.
■ **el día de la banderita**, flag day.
banderola *f* pennant, banderole.
bandidaje *m* banditry.
bandido,-a *m,f* bandit.
bando[1] 1 *m* (*facción*) faction, party, camp. 2 (*de aves*) flock; (*de insectos*) swarm; (*de peces*) shoal.
● **pasar al otro bando / pasarse al otro bando**, to go over to the other side.
bando[2] *m* (*edicto*) edict, proclamation.
bandolera *f* → **bandolero,-a**.
bandolerismo *m* banditry.
bandolero,-a 1 bandolero, *m,f* bandit. – 2 bandolera, *f* bandolier.
● **en bandolera**, slung crossways over the shoulder.
bandoneón *m* type of large accordeon.
bandurria *f* bandurria, (*small guitar-like instrument with six pairs of strings*).
Bangladesh *m* Bangladesh.
bangladesí 1 *adj* Bangladeshi. – 2 *mf* Bangladeshi.
banjo *m* banjo.
banquero,-a *m,f* banker.
banqueta 1 *f* (*taburete*) stool; (*para los pies*) footstool. 2 (*banco*) little bench.

banquete *m* banquet, feast.
■ **banquete de bodas,** wedding reception. ‖ **banque-te de gala,** gala reception. ‖ **banquete nupcial,** wedding breakfast.
banquetear *i* to banquet.
banquillo 1 *m* (*en tribunal*) dock: *el procesado se sentó en el banquillo de los acusados,* the accused sat in the dock. 2 (*en deporte*) bench.
banquisa *f* ice field.
bantú 1 *adj* Bantu. – 2 *mf* (*persona*) Bantu. – 3 *m* (*idioma*) Bantu.
▲ *pl* bantúes *or* bantús.
bañador *m* (*gen*) swimsuit; (*de mujer*) swimming costume, bathing costume; (*de hombre*) swimming trunks *pl.*
bañar 1 *t* (*gen*) to bathe: *la cálida luz del sol bañaba toda la estancia,* warm sunlight bathed the whole room. 2 (*lavar*) to bath: *¿vas a bañar al bebé?,* are you going to bath the baby?; *me baño cada manaña,* I have a bath every morning. 3 (*cubrir*) to coated; (*en oro etc*) to plate: *bañó los pasteles en chocolate,* she coated the cakes in chocolate; *este anillo está bañado en oro,* this ring is gold-plated. – 4 **bañarse,** *p* to bathe; (*nadar*) to have a swim, go for a swim: *se bañaban desnudos,* they were bathing naked; *me voy a bañar, hace calor,* I'm going for a swim, it's hot.
bañera *f* bath, bathtub.
bañista *mf* bather, swimmer.
baño 1 *m* (*gen*) bath; (*en piscina, mar*) dip, swim: *me voy a dar un baño caliente,* I'm going to have a hot bath; *se dio un baño en el lago,* he went for a dip in the lake; *toma muchos baños de sol,* she sunbathes a lot; *dicen que los baños de lodo son buenos,* they say mud baths are good. 2 (*cuarto*) bathroom; (*servicio*) toilet. 3 (*bañera*) bath, bathtub. 4 (*capa*) coat, coating; (*de oro etc*) plating: *la galleta tiene un baño de chocolate,* the biscuit is coated in chocolate; *este anillo tiene un baño de oro,* this ring is gold plated. – 5 **baños,** *mpl* (*balneario*) spa *sing.*
■ **baño de María, →** **baño María.** ‖ **baño de pie,** footbath. ‖ **baño de sangre,** bloodbath. ‖ **baño de vapor,** steam bath. ‖ **baño María,** bain-marie. ‖ **baño turco,** Turkish bath. ‖ **traje de baño,** swimsuit.
baptista 1 *adj* Baptist. – 2 *mf* Baptist.
baptisterio *m* baptistry.
baquelita *f* bakelite.
baqueta 1 *f* (*de arma*) ramrod. 2 (*de tambor*) drumstick.
baqueteado,-a 1 *pp →* **baquetear.** – 2 *adj* (*experimentado*) experienced. 3 (*maltratado*) abused, mistreated, ill-treated.
baquetear *t* to mistreat, ill-treat, abuse.
baqueteo *m* ill-treatment, mistreatment.
báquico,-a 1 *adj* (*de Baco*) Bacchic, Bacchanalian. 2 Bacchanalian.
bar 1 *m* (*cafetería*) café, snack bar; (*de bebidas alcohólicas*) bar. 2 FÍS bar.
▲ *pl* bares.
barahúnda *f* (*ruido*) racket, din; (*caos*) chaos, pandemonium.
baraja 1 *f* (*naipes*) pack, deck. 2 (*gama*) range.
● **jugar con dos barajas,** to be a double-dealer. ‖ **o jugamos todos o rompemos la baraja,** if we don't all pull our weight, we might as well call it off.
barajar 1 *t* (*naipes*) to shuffle. 2 *fig* (*considerar - posibilidades etc*) to consider; (*- cifra*) to talk about. 3 (*problema*) to solve; (*obstáculo*) to overcome.
baranda *f* handrail, banister.

barandal *m* handrail.
barandilla *f* handrail, banister.
baratija *f* trinket, knick-knack.
baratillo 1 *m* (*tienda*) junk shop; (*mercado*) flea market. 2 (*baratijas*) junk.
barato,-a 1 *adj* cheap. – 2 **barato,** *adv* cheaply, cheap.
baratura *f* cheapness: *teniendo en cuento su baratura ...,* bearing in mind how cheap it is ...
baraúnda *f →* **barahúnda.**
barba 1 *f* ANAT chin. 2 (*pelo*) beard.
● **con toda la barba,** true, real: *es un caballero con toda la barba,* he's a real gentleman, he's every inch a gentleman. ‖ **dejarse barba,** to grow a beard. ‖ **en las barbas de algn.,** right under sb.'s nose. ‖ **hacer la barba a algn.,** to shave sb.; (*molestar*) to annoy sb.; (*adular*) to fawn on. ‖ **por barba,** per head, a head, each. ‖ **reírse en las barbas de algn.,** to laugh in sb.'s face. ‖ **subirse a las barbas de algn.,** to get cheeky with sb.
■ **barba cerrada,** thick beard, bushy beard. ‖ **barba de ballena,** whalebone. ‖ **barba de chivo,** goatee beard.
barbacana 1 *f* (*aspillera*) embrasure. 2 (*torre*) barbican.
barbacoa *f* barbecue.
barbado,-a *adj* bearded, with a beard.
Barbados *m* Barbados.
barbaridad 1 *f* (*crueldad - cualidad*) cruelty; (*- acto*) atrocity, act of cruelty. 2 (*disparate*) piece of nonsense. 3 *una barbaridad,* *fam* (*mogollón*) loads *pl,* tons *pl:* *acudieron una barbaridad de niños,* thousands of kids turned up; *bebe una barbaridad,* he drinks a hell of a lot; *pesa una barbaridad,* it weighs a ton.
● **¡qué barbaridad!,** how awful!, how terrible!
barbarie 1 *f* (*rusticidad*) ignorance. 2 (*crueldad - cualidad*) cruelty, savagery, brutality; (*- acto*) atrocity, act of cruelty.
barbarismo *m* barbarism.
bárbaro,-a 1 *adj* HIST barbarian. 2 (*cruel*) barbaric, savage, cruel. 3 (*temerario*) daring. 4 *fam* (*grande*) enormous, tremendous. 5 *fam* (*espléndido*) fantastic, terrific: *nos dieron una comida bárbara,* they gave us a fantastic lunch. – 6 *m,f* HIST barbarian. – 7 **bárbaro,** *adv:* *lo pasamos bárbaro,* we had a great time.
barbechar *t* to plough.
barbecho *m* fallow land.
● **dejar en barbecho,** to leave fallow.
barbería *f* barber's shop, barber's.
barbero *m* barber.
barbiblanco,-a *adj →* **barbicano,-a.**
barbicano,-a *adj* grey-bearded.
barbicastaño,-a *adj* brown-bearded.
barbilampiño,-a *adj* beardless.
barbilla *f* chin.
barbiquejo *m →* **barboquejo.**
barbitúrico *m* barbiturate.
barbo *m* barbel.
■ **barbo de mar,** red mullet.
barboquejo *m* chinstrap.
barbotar *t* to splutter.
barboteo *m* spluttering.
barbudo,-a 1 *adj* bearded. – 2 *m,f* (*hombre*) bearded man; (*mujer*) bearded lady.
barbuquejo *m →* **barboquejo.**
barca *f* boat, small boat.
● **en la misma barca,** in the same boat.

barcarola *f* barcarole.
barcaza *f* lighter.
barcelonés,-esa 1 *adj* of Barcelona, from Barcelona. –
2 *m,f* person from Barcelona, inhabitant of Barcelona.
barcelonista 1 *adj relating to Barcelona football club.* – 2 *mf*
Barcelona supporter.
barco *m* (*gen*) boat; (*grande*) ship.
■ **barco cisterna,** tanker. ‖ **barco de guerra,** warship.
‖ **barco de pasajeros,** passenger ship. ‖ **barco de
pesca,** fishing boat. ‖ **barco de vapor,** steamer. ‖ **barco de vela,** sailing boat. ‖ **barco escuela,** training
ship. ‖ **barco mercante,** merchant ship.
bardana *f* burdock.
bardo *m* bard.
baremo *m* ready reckoner. 2 (*tarifas*) scale, table.
bargueño *m* bureau.
baricentro *m* barycentre (us barycenter).
bario *m* barium.
barisfera *f* barysphere.
barítono *m* baritone.
barloventear *i* to ply to windward.
barlovento *m* windward.
■ **Islas de Barlovento,** Windward Islands.
barman *m* barman, us bartender.
▲ *pl* **bármanes.**
barnacla 1 *f* (*ave*) barnacle goose. 2 (*crustáceo*) barnacle.
barniz 1 *m* (*para madera*) varnish; (*para cerámica*) glaze. 2
(*noción*) smattering, general idea.
barnizado,-a 1 *pp* → **barnizar.** – 2 *adj* varnished.
barnizador,-ra 1 *adj* varnishing. – 2 *m,f* varnisher.
barnizar *t* (*madera*) to varnish; (*cerámica*) to glaze.
▲ *Conjugation model* [4], *like realizar.*
barométrico,-a *adj* barometric.
barómetro *m* barometer.
barón *m* baron.
baronesa *f* baroness.
baronía *f* barony.
barquero,-a *m,f* (*hombre*) boatman; (*mujer*) boatwoman.
barquilla *f* basket, gondola.
barquillero,-a 1 *m,f* (*fabricante*) wafer maker. 2 (*vendedor*)
wafer seller.
barquillo *m* (*gen*) wafer; (*cucurucho*) cornet.
barra 1 *f* (*en bar, cafetería*) bar: *hay que pagar en la barra,*
you have to pay at the bar. 2 (*vara*) bar; (*para cortinas*)
rod; (*de bicicleta*) crossbar. 3 (*de helado*) block. 4 (*de pan*)
loaf. 5 (*en tribunal*) bar, rail. 6 (*signo de puntuación*) slash,
solidus. 7 (*de arena*) sandbar.
● **no reparar en barras,** to stop at nothing.
■ **barra americana,** hostess bar. ‖ **barra de carmín,**
→ **barra se labios.** ‖ **barra de equilibrio,** → **barra
fija.** ‖ **barra de labios,** lipstick. ‖ **barra espaciadora,**
space bar. ‖ **barra fija,** DEP horizontal bar, beam. ‖ **barra inversa,** backslash. ‖ **barra libre,** free bar. ‖ **barras
paralelas,** parallel bars. ‖ **barras paralelas asimétricas,** asymmetric bars.
barrabás *m* scoundrel.
barrabasada *f* dirty trick.
barraca 1 *f* (*casita*) cottage (*typical in Valencia and Murcia*).
2 (*puesto*) stall; (*caseta de feria*) booth. 3 (*chabola*) shack.
barracón *m* hut, large hut.
barracuda *f* barracuda.
barragana *f* mistress.
barranco 1 *m* (*precipicio*) precipice. 2 (*torrentera*) gully;
(*más profunda*) ravine.
barranquillero,-a 1 *adj* of Barranquilla, from Barranquilla. – 2 *m,f* person from Barranquilla, inhabitant of
Barranquilla.

barraquismo *m* slums *pl.*
barreminas *m* minesweeper.
▲ *pl* **barreminas.**
barrena *f* (*gen*) drill; (*manual*) gimlet.
● **entrar en barrena,** to go into a spin.
barrenar 1 *t* to drill. 2 (*desbaratar*) to foil, thwart.
barrendero,-a *m,f* road sweeper.
barreno 1 *m* (*barrena*) large drill. 2 (*agujero*) drill hole,
bore hole; (*para carga*) blast hole.
barreño *m* large bowl.
barrer 1 *t* (*suelo*) to sweep; (*hojas, migas, etc*) to sweep up:
barre el suelo antes de fregarlo, sweep the floor before
you mop it; *barrió las migas,* she swept up the crumbs.
2 (*dejar sin nada*) to clean out: *entraron ladrones y les
barrieron la casa,* burglars broke in and cleaned them
out. 3 (*limpiar*) to sweep away: *el viento barrió las nubes
del cielo,* the wind swept the clouds from the sky. 4
(*derrotar*) to trounce, wipe the floor with: *Lewis barrió a
todos sus rivales,* Lewis wiped the floor with his rivals.
– 5 *i* (*arrasar*) to sweep the board: *la canción española
barrió,* the Spanish song swept the board.
● **barrer hacia dentro,** to look after number one. ‖
barrer para casa, to look out for one's own interests.
barrera 1 *f* (*gen*) barrier. 2 (*en plaza de toros - valla*) barrier;
(*asientos*) front row. 3 *fig* obstacle.
● **poner barreras,** to hinder (**a, -**). ‖ **mirar los toros
desde la barrera,** to sit on the fence.
■ **barrera aduanera,** customs barrier. ‖ **barrera del
sonido,** sound barrier.
barretina *f* Catalan cap.
barriada *f* area.
barrica *f* cask, *medium-sized* barrel.
barricada *f* barricade.
● **levantar barricadas,** to erect barricades.
barrido 1 *m* (*limpieza*) sweep, sweeping: *el suelo necesita
un barrido,* the floor needs a sweep. 2 (*exploración automática*) scan, scanning. 3 (*con cámara*) pan, panning.
barriga *f* belly, stomach, tummy.
● **echar barriga,** to get a paunch. ‖ **tocarse la barriga,** to sit on one's backside, twiddle one's thumbs.
■ **dolor de barriga,** stomach-ache.
barrigón,-ona *adj* big-bellied.
barrigudo,-a *adj* big-bellied.
barril *m* barrel, keg.
● **de barril,** draught.
barrilete 1 *m* (*de revólver*) chamber. 2 (*carpintería*) clamp.
3 (*barril pequeño*) small barrel.
barrillo *m* pimple, spot.
barrio *m* neighbourhood (us neighborhood); (*zona*) district, area: *es un barrio muy tranquilo,* it's a very quiet
neighbourhood; *no vive en este barrio,* she doesn't live
round here.
● **de barrio,** local: *el cine de barrio,* the local cinema.
‖ **irse al otro barrio,** *fam* to kick the bucket.
■ **barrio chino,** red-light district. ‖ **barrio comercial,**
business district. ‖ **barrio histórico,** old town. ‖ **barrio
latino,** Latin Quarter. ‖ **barrio periférico,** suburb. ‖
barrio popular, working-class area. ‖ **barrio residencial,** residential area. ‖ **barrios bajos,** slums.
barriobajero,-a 1 *adj* common, vulgar, low. – 2 *m,f*
common person.
barritar *i* to trumpet.
barrito *m* trumpet.
barrizal *m* quagmire.
barro¹ 1 *m* (*lodo*) mud. 2 (*arcilla*) clay: *objetos de barro,*
earthenware *sing.* 3 (*objeto*) earthenware object.

● **de barro,** earthenware.
barro² *m* (*grano*) spot, pimple.
barroco,-a 1 *adj* ART baroque. 2 *fig* ornate. – 3 **barroco,** *m* baroque.
barroquismo *m* baroque style.
barroso,-a *adj* muddy.
barrote 1 *m* bar. 2 (*de escalera, silla*) rung.
barruntar *t* (*sospechar*) to suspect; (*presentir*) to sense, have a feeling.
barrunto 1 *m* (*sospecha*) suspicion; (*presentimiento*) feeling, presentiment, foreboding. 2 (*indicio*) sign.
bartola a la bartola, *adv* carelessly.
● **tumbarse a la bartola / echarse a la bartola,** to lounge about.
bártulos *mpl* things, stuff *sing*.
● **liar los bártulos,** to pack up, pack one's bags.
barullo *m* noise, din, racket.
basa *f* base.
basalto *m* basalt.
basamento *m* base, plinth.
basar 1 *t* to base (**en,** on). – 2 **basarse,** *p* (*cosa*) to be based (**en,** on); (*persona*) to base oneself on: *nuestra economía no puede basarse únicamente en el turismo,* our economy cannot be based solely on tourism; *me baso en lo que he leído,* I base myself on what I have read; *¿en qué se basa para decir tales cosas?,* what grounds does he have for saying such things?
basca 1 *f* nausea. 2 *fam* (*pandilla*) crowd.
báscula 1 *f* (*gen*) scales *pl;* (*de farmacia*) weighing machine. 2 (*para vehículos*) weighbridge.
basculante 1 *adj* tilting. 2 (*camión*) tip-up.
bascular 1 *i* to tilt. 2 (*oscilar*) to swing. 3 (*variar*) to swing, alternate.
base 1 *f* (*gen*) base: *la base de la torre,* the base of the tower. 2 *fig* basis: *las cereales son la base de nuestra agricultura,* cereals form the basis of our agriculture; *si partimos de la base de que ...,* if we start from the premise that ... 3 QUÍM base, alkali. 4 MAT base. 5 (*en béisbol*) base. – 6 **bases,** *fpl* (*de concurso*) rules. 7 **las bases,** (*de partido etc*) grass roots, rank and file.
● **a base de,** (*por*) through, by means of, using; (*de*) consisting of: *se hizo rico a base de trabajar mucho,* he became rich through hard work; *una dieta a base de hortalizas y pescado,* a diet consisting of vegetables and fish. ‖ **a base de bien,** *fam* really well. ‖ **en base a,** based on, on the basis of.
■ **base aérea,** air base. ‖ **base de datos,** database. ‖ **base de datos documental,** documentary database. ‖ **base de datos relacional,** relational database. ‖ **base de lanzamiento,** launch site. ‖ **base de operaciones,** operational headquarters. ‖ **base imponible,** taxable income. ‖ **base naval,** naval base.
básico,-a 1 *adj* (*gen*) basic. 2 (*imprescindible*) essential, indispensable.
Basilea *f* Basel, Basle.
basílica *f* basilica.
basilisco *m* basilisk.
● **ponerse hecho,-a un basilisco,** to hit the roof, blow one's top.
basket *m* → **baloncesto.**
básquet *m* → **baloncesto.**
basset *m* basset hound.
▲ *pl* bassets.
basta¹ *f* tacking stitch.
basta² *interj* enough!, stop it!
● **¡basta de ...!,** that's enough ...!, no more ...!

bastante 1 *adj* enough, sufficient: *¿tienes bastante dinero?,* have you got enough money? 2 (*abundante*) quite a lot of: *había bastante gente,* there were quite a lot of people. – 3 *adv* enough: *son lo bastante ricos como para poder permitírselo,* they're rich enough to be able to afford it. 4 (*un poco*) fairly, quite: *es bastante alto,* it's fairly high; *nada bastante bien,* she swims quite well; *está bastante lejos,* it's quite a long way. 5 (*tiempo*) some time, quite a while: *hace bastante que no lo veo,* I haven't seen him for some time.
bastar 1 *i* to be enough, be sufficient, suffice: *mi sueldo no basta para pagar el alquiler,* my wage is not enough to pay the rent. – 2 **bastarse a sí mismo,** *p* to be self-sufficient.
● **bastar con,** to be enough: *es muy concentrado, basta con una gota,* it's highly concentrated, one drop is enough.
bastardía *f* bastardy.
bastardillo,-a *adj* italic.
● **en bastardilla,** in italics.
■ **letra bastardilla,** italic type.
bastardo,-a 1 *adj* illegitimate, bastard. 2 (*despreciable*) base, mean. – 3 *m,f* bastard.
bastedad *f* coarseness.
basteza *f* crudeness, vulgarity.
bastidor 1 *m* frame. 2 (*de lienzo*) stretcher. 3 (*de coche*) chassis. 4 TEAT wing.
● **entre bastidores,** in the wings; *fig* behind the scenes.
bastilla *f* tacked hem.
bastimento 1 *m* supplies *pl,* provisions *pl.* 2 MAR vessel.
bastión *m* bastion.
basto¹ 1 *m* ≈ club. – 2 **bastos,** *mpl* ≈ clubs: *el as de bastos,* ≈ the ace of clubs.
● **pintan bastos,** things are getting tough.
basto,-a² 1 *adj* (*grosero*) coarse, rough. 2 (*sin pulimentar*) rough, unpolished.
bastón 1 *m* stick, walking stick, US cane. 2 (*de esquí*) stick, ski stick. 3 (*insignia*) baton.
● **empuñar el bastón,** to take charge.
bastonazo *m* blow with a stick.
bastoncillo 1 *m* ANAT rod. 2 (*de algodón*) cotton bud.
bastonera *f* umbrella stand.
basura 1 *f* (*cosa*) rubbish, US garbage. 2 (*persona despreciable*) swine.
● **bajar la basura / sacar la basura,** to put the rubbish out. ‖ **tirar a la basura,** to throw away.
basurero 1 *m* (*persona*) dustman, US garbage man. 2 (*lugar*) tip, rubbish dump.
bata 1 *f* (*prenda ligera*) housecoat; (*albornoz*) dressing gown, US robe. 2 (*de trabajo*) overall; (*de médicos etc*) white coat.
batacazo *m* (*golpe*) thump, bump, bang, crash; (*caída*) heavy fall: *tropezó y se dio un buen batacazo contra el suelo,* he tripped and fell to the floor with a thud.
batalla *f* battle.
● **de batalla,** *fam* ordinary, everyday: *zapatos de batalla,* everyday shoes.
■ **batalla campal,** pitched battle.
batallador,-ra 1 *adj* fighting: *es muy batalladora,* she's a real fighter. – 2 *m,f* fighter.
batallar *i* to battle, fight.
batallón 1 *m* MIL battalion. 2 (*multitud*) horde.
batata *f* BOT sweet potato.
bate *m* bat.
batea 1 *f* (*barco*) flat-bottomed boat. 2 (*bandeja*) tray. 3 (*artesa*) trough.

bateador,-ra 1 *m,f* (*en béisbol*) batter. 2 (*en cricket - hombre*) batsman; (*- mujer*) batswoman.
batear 1 *i* to bat. – 2 *t* to hit.
batel *m* skiff.
batería 1 *f* (*eléctrica*) battery. 2 MIL battery. 3 TEAT footlights *pl*. 4 (*conjunto de cosas*) set; (*de preguntas*) barrage. 5 MÚS drums *pl*. – 6 *mf* drummer.
● aparcar en batería, to park at right-angles to the kerb. ‖ recargar las baterías, to recharge one's batteries.
■ batería antiaérea, anti-aircraft battery. ‖ batería de cocina, pots and pans *pl*.
batiborrillo *m* → **batiburrillo**.
batiburrillo *m* jumble, hotchpotch.
batida *f* → **batido,-a**.
batido,-a 1 *pp* → **batir**. – 2 *adj* (*camino*) well-worn, well-trodden, beaten. 3 (*seda*) shot. – 4 **batido**, *m* CULIN beaten eggs. 5 (*bebida*) milk shake. – 6 **batida**, *f* (*de cazadores*) beat; (*de policía*) search.
batidor,-ra 1 *m,f* (*de caza*) beater. – 2 **batidor**, *m* CULIN (*manual*) whisk. – 3 **batidora**, *f* blender, mixer.
batidora *f* → **batidor,-ra**.
batiente 1 *adj* beating. – 2 *m* (*marco - de puerta*) jamb; (*-de ventana*) frame. 3 (*hoja de puerta*) leaf. 4 (*de piano*) damper. 5 (*en costa*) wave-beaten spot.
● reírse a mandíbula batiente, to laugh one's head off.
batín *m* short dressing gown.
batintín *m* gong.
batir 1 *t* (*huevos*) to beat; (*nata, claras*) to whip. 2 (*palmas*) to clap. 3 (*metales*) to beat. 4 (*alas*) to flap, beat. 5 (*derribar*) to knock down. 6 (*vencer*) to beat, defeat. 7 DEP (*marca, récord*) to break. 8 (*explorar*) to reconnoitre; (*registrar*) to comb, search. 9 (*cazador*) to beat. – 10 batirse, *p* to fight.
● batirse en duelo, to fight a duel. ‖ batirse en retirada, to retreat.
batiscafo *m* bathyscaphe, bathyscaph.
batista *f* cambric, batiste.
batracio,-a 1 *adj* batrachian. – 2 **batracio**, *m* batrachian.
Batuecas estar en las Batuecas, *loc* to have one's head in the clouds.
baturrillo *m* jumble, hotchpotch.
baturro,-a 1 *adj* Aragonese. – 2 *m,f* (*gen*) person from Aragon; (*del campo*) Aragonese peasant.
batuta *f* baton.
● bajo la batuta de ..., conducted by ... ‖ llevar la batuta, to be the boss.
baúl *m* (*cofre*) chest; (*de viaje*) trunk.
bauprés *m* bowsprit.
▲ *pl* baupreses.
bausán *m* dummy.
bautismal *adj* baptismal.
bautismo 1 *m* (*de niño*) baptism, christening. 2 (*de barco*) naming.
■ bautismo de fuego, baptism of fire.
bautista *mf* Baptist.
bautisterio *m* baptistry.
bautizar 1 *t* to baptize, christen. 2 (*poner nombre a*) to name. 3 (*el vino*) to water down.
▲ *Conjugation model* |4|, *like realizar*.
bautizo *m* (*de niño*) baptism, christening; (*de barco*) naming.
bauxita *f* bauxite.

bávaro,-a 1 *adj* Bavarian. – 2 *m,f* Bavarian.
Baviera *f* Bavaria.
baya *f* berry.
bayeta 1 *f* baize. 2 (*paño*) cloth.
bayo,-a 1 *adj* bay, whitish yellow. – 2 **bayo**, *m* (*caballo*) bay.
bayoneta *f* bayonet.
● calar las bayonetas, to fix bayonets.
bayonetazo *m* (*embestida*) bayonet thrust; (*herida*) bayonet wound.
baza 1 *f* (*naipes*) trick. 2 (*ventaja*) asset, advantage. 3 (*ocasión*) chance.
● meter baza, *fig* to butt in, stick one's oar in. ‖ no poder meter baza, not to be able to get a word in edgeways.
bazar 1 *m* (*oriental*) bazaar. 2 (*tienda*) electrical goods and hardware shop.
bazo *m* spleen.
bazofia 1 *f* (*restos de comida*) scraps *pl*, leftovers *pl*. 2 (*comida mala*) pigswill. 3 (*basura*) rubbish: ¡vaya bazofia de película!, what a rubbishy film!
bazooka *m* & *f* → **bazuca**.
bazuca *m* & *f* bazooka.
Bco. *abr* (*banco*) bank.
be *f* *name of the letter b*.
● tener las tres bes, to be good value and good quality.
beatería 1 *f* piousness, devoutness. 2 *pey* sanctimoniousness.
beatificación *f* beatification.
beatificar *t* to beatify.
▲ *Conjugation model* [1], *like sacar*.
beatífico,-a *adj* beatific.
beatitud *f* beatitude.
beato,-a 1 *adj* (*beatificado*) blessed. 2 (*devoto*) devout; *pey* sanctimonious. 3 (*feliz*) happy. – 4 *m,f* (*persona beatificada*) beatified person.
bebé *m* baby.
■ bebé probeta, test-tube baby.
bebedero,-a 1 *adj* drinkable: agua bebedera, drinking water. – 2 **bebedero**, *m* (*abrevadero*) water trough. 3 (*pico de vasija*) spout. 4 (*vasija*) drinking dish.
bebedizo,-a 1 *adj* drinkable. – 2 **bebedizo**, *m* potion.
bebedor,-ra 1 *adj* hard-drinking. – 2 *m,f* hard drinker.
beber 1 *t* to drink: no quiero beber nada, I don't want anything to drink. 2 *i* to drink. 3 (*emborracharse*) to drink, drink heavily: bebe mucho, he's a heavy drinker.
● beber a algo/algn., to drink to sth./sb. ‖ beber a la salud de algn., to toast sb. ‖ beber los vientos por, *fig* to long for. ‖ beber por algo/algn., to drink to sth./sb.
bebercio *m* *arg* booze, drink.
bebible *adj* drinkable.
bebida *f* → **bebido,-a**.
bebido,-a 1 *pp* → **beber**. – 2 *adj* merry, tipsy. – 3 **bebida**, *f* drink, beverage.
● darse a la bebida, to take to drink, hit the bottle.
■ bebida alcohólica, alcoholic drink. ‖ bebida no alcohólica, non-alcoholic drink.
bebistrajo *m* *fam* witch's brew.
beca *f* (*gen*) grant; (*concedida por méritos*) scholarship, award.
becada *f* woodcock.
becar *t* (*gen*) to award a grant to; (*por méritos*) to award a scholarship to.

▲ *Conjugation model* [1], *like* **sacar**.
becario,-a *m,f* grant holder, scholarship holder.
becerra *f* → **becerro,-a**.
becerrada *f* bullfight (*with bulls of up to three years*).
becerro,-a 1 *m,f* calf (*up to one year old*). – 2 **becerro**, *m* (*en tauromaquia*) young bull (*up to four years old*). 3 (*piel*) calfskin.
bechamel *f* béchamel sauce, white sauce.
becuadro *m* natural, natural sign.
bedel,-la *m,f* porter.
beduino,-a 1 *adj* Bedouin. – 2 *m,f* Bedouin.
befa *f* → **befo,-a**.
befar *t* to jeer at, taunt.
befo,-a 1 *adj* (*belfo*) thick-lipped. 2 (*zambo*) knock-kneed. – 3 **befa**, *f* jeer, taunt.
begonia *f* begonia.
beicon *m* bacon.
beige 1 *adj* beige. – 2 *m* beige.
béisbol *m* baseball.
beisbolero,-a *m,f* baseball player.
bejuco *m* liana.
bel *m* bel.
Belcebú *m* Beelzebub.
beldad *f* beauty.
belén 1 *m* REL nativity scene, crib. 2 *fig* mess.
● **meterse en belenes**, to get into a fix.
Belén *m* Bethlehem.
belfo,-a 1 *adj* thick-lipped. – 2 **belfo**, *m* thick lip.
belga 1 *adj* Belgian. – 2 *m,f* Belgian.
Bélgica *f* Belgium.
Belgrado *m* Belgrade.
Belice *m* Belize.
belicense 1 *adj* Belizean. – 2 *m,f* Belizean.
beliceño,-a 1 *adj* → **belicense**.
belicismo *m* warmongering.
belicista 1 *adj* pro-war. – 2 *mf* warmonger.
bélico,-a *adj* military.
■ **conflicto bélico,** armed conflict, war. ‖ **material bélico,** military equipment.
belicoso,-a *adj* bellicose, aggressive.
beligerancia *f* belligerence.
beligerante 1 *adj* belligerent: *las parte beligerantes,* the warring parties. – 2 *mf* belligerent person.
belio *m* bel.
bellaco,-a 1 *adj* (*malo*) wicked. 2 (*astuto*) cunning, sly. – 3 *m,f* villain, rogue.
belladona *f* deadly nightshade, belladonna.
bellaquería *f* wickedness, roguery.
belleza *f* beauty.
bello,-a *adj* beautiful. 2 (*bueno*) fine, noble.
■ **bellas artes,** fine arts.
bellota *f* acorn.
bemol 1 *adj* MÚS flat. – 2 *m* MÚS flat. – 3 **bemoles**, *mpl* arg guts.
● **tener bemoles,** arg (*ser difícil*) to be tough, be tricky; (*ser demasiado*) to be too much, be rich.
benceno *m* benzene.
bencina *f* benzine.
bendecir 1 *t* to bless. 2 (*alabar*) to praise.
● **bendecir la mesa,** to say grace.
▲ *Conjugation model* [79], *like* **predecir**.
bendición 1 *f* blessing. – 2 **bendiciones,** *fpl* wedding ceremony *sing*.
■ **bendición de la mesa,** grace.

bendito,-a 1 *adj* (*bienaventurado*) blessed. 2 *irón* (*maldito*) damned, blessed. 3 (*feliz*) happy: *¡bendita la hora en que la conocí!,* happy the hour I met her! 4 (*poco inteligente*) simple. – 5 *m,f* simple soul.
● **¡bendito sea Dios!,** *fam* thank Goodness!
benedictino,-a 1 *adj* Benedictine. – 2 *m,f* Benedictine.
benefactor,-ra 1 *adj* beneficent. – 2 *m,f* (*hombre*) benefactor; (*mujer*) benefactress.
beneficencia *f* beneficence, charity.
beneficiado,-a 1 *pp* → **beneficiar**. – 2 beneficiado, *m* beneficiary, incumbent.
● **salir beneficiado,-a de algo,** to do well out of sth.
‖ **verse beneficiado,-a con algo,** to benefit from sth.
beneficiar 1 *t* to benefit, favour (US favor). 2 (*mina*) to work. 3 COM to sell below par. – 4 **beneficiarse,** *p* to benefit. 5 COM to profit.
● **beneficiarse a algn.,** to have it off with sb. ‖ **beneficiarse de algo,** to do well out of sth., benefit from sth.
▲ *Conjugation model* [12], *like* **cambiar**.
beneficiario,-a *m,f* beneficiary.
beneficio 1 *m* (*ganancia*) profit. 2 (*bien*) benefit.
● **en beneficio de,** for the good of, for the benefit of, in the interest of: *todo lo hace en beneficio propio,* everything he does is for his own good; *la derecha ha perdido escaños en beneficio de la izquierda,* the right has lost seats to the left. ‖ **a beneficio de,** in aid of. ‖ **sacar beneficio de,** to profit from.
■ **beneficio bruto,** gross profit. ‖ **beneficio neto,** clear profit.
beneficioso,-a *adj* beneficial.
benéfico,-a *adj* charitable.
■ **causa benéfica,** charitable cause, charity. ‖ **función benéfica,** charity performance.
benemérito,-a *adj* worthy, distinguished.
■ **la Benemérita,** the Spanish Civil Guard.
beneplácito *m* approval: *contamos con el beneplácito del ministro,* we have the minister's approval.
benevolencia 1 *f* benevolence, kindness. 2 (*comprensión*) understanding.
benevolente *adj* → **benévolo**.
benévolo,-a 1 *adj* benevolent, kind. 2 (*comprensivo*) understanding.
bengala 1 *f* (*de aviso etc*) flare. 2 (*para fiestas etc*) sparkler.
Bengala *f* Bengal.
■ **golfo de Bengala,** Bay of Bengal.
bengalí,-a 1 *adj* Bengali. – 2 *m,f* (*persona*) Bengali. – 3 **bengalí,** *m* (*idioma*) Bengali.
benigno,-a 1 *adj* (*persona*) benign, gentle. 2 (*tumor*) benign. 3 (*clima*) mild.
benimeño,-a 1 *adj* Beninese. – 2 *m,f* Beninese.
Benín *m* Benin.
benjamín,-ina 1 *m,f* (*en familia - gen*) youngest child; (*hijo*) youngest son; (*hija*) youngest daughter. 2 (*en grupo*) youngest person. 3 DEP *competitor of the youngest age group* (9 or 10 years old). – 4 *adj* DEP *of the youngest age group* (9 or 10 years old).
beodo,-a 1 *adj* drunk. – 2 *m,f* drunk, drunkard.
berberecho *m* cockle, common cockle.
Berbería *f* Barbary.
berberisco,-a 1 *adj* Berber. – 2 *m,f* Berber.
berbiquí *m* brace: *berbiquí y barrena,* brace and bit.
▲ *pl* **berbiquíes**.
bereber 1 *adj* Berber. – 2 *mf* (*persona*) Berber. – 3 *m* (*idioma*) Berber.
beréber *adj-mf* → **bereber**.

berebere *adj-mf* → **bereber**.
berenjena *f* aubergine, US eggplant.
berenjenal 1 *m* aubergine field, US eggplant field. 2 *fig* mess.
● **meterse en un berenjenal,** to get os. into a mess.
bergamota *f* bergamot.
bergante *m* scoundrel, rascal.
bergantín *m* brigantine, brig.
beriberi *m* beriberi.
berilio *m* beryllium.
berilo *m* beryl.
Berlín *m* Berlin.
berlina 1 *f* (*carruaje*) berlin. 2 AUTO four-door saloon.
berlinés,-esa 1 *adj* of Berlin, from Berlin. – 2 *m,f* Berliner.
bermejo,-a *adj* reddish.
bermellón *m* vermilion.
bermudas *mpl* Bermudas, Bermuda shorts.
Bermudas las Bermudas, *fpl* Bermuda.
Berna *f* Bern, Berne.
bernés,-esa 1 *adj* of Bern, from Bern. – 2 *m,f* person from Bern, inhabitant of Bern.
berrear 1 *i* (*becerro*) to bellow. 2 (*persona*) to bawl; (*niño*) to howl, bawl.
berreo 1 *m* (*de niño*) bawling. 2 (*de becerro*) bellowing.
berrido 1 *m* (*de becerro*) bellow. 2 (*de persona*) howl: *le despertaron los berridos del bebé,* the baby's bawling woke him.
berrinche *m* rage, tantrum, anger.
● **coger un berrinche,** to throw a tantrum.
berro *m* watercress.
berza 1 *f* cabbage. – 2 **berzas,** *mf* idiot, moron.
berzal *m* cabbage patch.
berzotas *mf* idiot, moron.
besamanos 1 *m* (*ceremonia*) royal audience. 2 (*saludo*) hand kissing.
besamel 1 *adj* bechamel. – 2 *f* béchamel, béchamel sauce, white sauce.
■ **salsa besamel,** white sauce, béchamel sauce.
besar 1 *t* to kiss. – 2 **besarse,** *p* (*uso recíproco*) to kiss. 3 *fam* (*chocar*) to collide.
beso 1 *m* kiss. 2 *fam* (*choque*) bump.
● **comerse a besos,** to smother with kisses. ‖ **dar un beso a,** to kiss, give a kiss. ‖ **tirarle un beso a algn.,** to blow sb. a kiss.
■ **beso de Judas,** kiss of Judas. ‖ **beso de la muerte,** kiss of death.
bestia 1 *f* (*animal*) beast. – 2 *mf* (*persona - bruto*) brute; (- *ignorante*) ignorant fool; (- *torpe*) clumsy oaf. – 3 *adj* (*bruto*) brutish. 4 (*ignorante*) ignorant; (*grosero*) rude; (*torpe*) clumsy. 5 (*asombroso*) fantastic, amazing.
● **a lo bestia,** (*fuerte*) hard; (*a lo loco*) like a madman; (*rápido*) like mad; (*en cantidad*) in enormous amounts.
■ **mala bestia,** nasty piece of work.
bestial 1 *adj* (*brutal*) beastly, bestial. 2 *fam* (*enorme*) enormous. 3 *fam* (*extraordinario*) great, fantastic.
bestialidad 1 *f* bestiality, brutality. 2 (*tontería*) stupidity. 3 *fam* (*gran cantidad*) tons *pl*, loads *pl*, stacks *pl*: *una bestialidad de comida,* tons of food.
bestiario *m* bestiary.
best-seller *m* best-seller.
besucón,-ona 1 *adj* fond of kissing: *es muy besucón,* he's always kissing you. – 2 *m,f* person who's always kissing.
besugo 1 *m* (*pez*) sea bream. 2 (*persona*) idiot.
● **sostener un diálogo para besugos,** *fig* to talk at cross purposes.

besuguera *f* shallow oval oven dish (*for cooking sea bream*).
besuquear 1 *t* to kiss again and again. – 2 **besuquearse,** *p* (*uso recíproco*) to smooch, neck, snog.
besuqueo *m* smooching, necking, snogging.
beta *f* beta.
■ **rayo beta,** beta ray.
Bética *f* → **bético,-a**.
bético,-a 1 *adj* HIST Andalusian. 2 DEP *relating to Real Betis Balompié football club*. – 3 *m,f* HIST Andalusian. – 4 DEP Betis supporter. – 5 **Bética,** *f* HIST Andalusia.
betún 1 *m* (*para zapatos*) shoe polish. 2 QUÍM bitumen.
bezo 1 *m* (*labio*) thick lip. 2 (*de herida*) edge.
bezudo,-a *adj* thick-lipped.
Bhután *m* Bhutan.
bhutanés,-esa 1 *adj* Bhutanese. – 2 *m,f* Bhutanese.
bianual *adj* biannual.
biatlón *m* biathlon.
biberón *m* baby's bottle, feeding bottle.
Biblia *f* Bible.
bíblico,-a *adj* biblical.
bibliobús *m* mobile library.
bibliófilo,-a *m,f* bibliophile, book lover.
bibliografía *f* bibliography.
bibliográfico,a *adj* bibliographic, bibliographical.
bibliógrafo,-a *m,f* bibliographer.
biblioteca 1 *f* library. 2 (*mueble*) bookcase, bookshelf.
bibliotecario,-a *m,f* librarian.
bibliotecología *f* librarianship.
biblioteconomía *f* librarianship.
BIC *abr* (*Brigada de Investigación Criminal*) ≈ Criminal Investigation Department; (*abreviatura*) CID.
bicameral *adj* bicameral.
bicarbonato *m* bicarbonate.
■ **bicarbonato sódico,** bicarbonate of soda.
bicéfalo,-a *adj* two-headed, bicephalous.
bicentenario,-a 1 *adj* two-hundred-year-old. – 2 **bi**centenario, *m* bicentenary, US bicentennial.
bíceps *m* biceps.
▲ *pl* **bíceps**.
bicha *f* snake.
bicharraco *m* *fam* loathsome creature.
bichero *m* boathook.
bicho 1 *m* (*animal*) animal, creature; (*insecto*) bug, creepy-crawly. 2 (*persona*) odd character; (*niño*) little devil, little monkey.
■ **bicho raro,** oddball, weirdo.
bici *f* *fam* bike.
bicicleta *f* bicycle.
■ **bicicleta de carreras,** racing bike. ‖ **bicicleta de montaña,** mountain bike.
biciclo *m* penny-farthing.
bicoca *f* *fam* (*ganga*) bargain; (*chollo*) cushy number.
bicolor *adj* two-coloured (US two-colored).
bidé *m* bidet.
bidimensional *adj* two-dimensional.
bidón *m* (*normal*) drum; (*pequeño*) can.
biela *f* AUTO connecting rod.
Bielorrusia *f* Byelorussia.
bielorruso,-a 1 *adj* Byelorussian. – 2 *m,f* (*persona*) Byelorussian. – 3 **bielorruso,** *m* (*idioma*) Byelorussian.
bien 1 *adv* (*gen*) well: *canta bien,* she sings well; *la casa está bien construida,* the house is well built; *trabaja bien,* her work is good, she does a good job; *todo eso*

está muy bien, pero ..., that's all very well, but ... **2** *(como es debido)* properly, right: *si no pronuncias bien, no te van a entender,* if you don't pronounce the words properly, they won't understand you; *siéntate bien,* sit properly; *¡pórtate bien!,* behave yourself!; *no está bien que hagan eso,* it's not right for them to do that. **3** *(acertadamente)* right, correctly: *contestó bien a todas las preguntas,* she answered all the questions correctly. **4** *(con éxito)* successfully. **5** *(de acuerdo)* O.K., all right: *ven mañana a las dos, –bien,* come tomorrow at two, –all right. **6** *(de buena gana)* willingly, gladly: *bien me iría contigo si no tuviera que trabajar,* I'd gladly go with you if I didn't have to work. **7** *(mucho)* very: *quiero un vaso de leche bien fría,* I want a glass of nice cold milk; *ha pagado bien caro su error,* he has paid dearly for his mistake; *dale bien fuerte,* hit it good and hard; *es bien sencillo,* it's really simple. **8** *(fácilmente)* easily: *bien se ve que ...,* it is easy to see that ...; *bien podrías haberme avisado,* you might have warned me. **9** *(de gusto, olor, aspecto, etc)* good, nice, lovely: *esta cerveza está muy bien,* this beer's very good; *la comida estaba bien,* the food was nice; *quiero uno que esté bien,* I want a good one. **10** *(de salud)* well: *¿te encuentras bien?,* are you feeling all right? **11** *(físicamente)* good-looking: *su novio está muy bien,* her boyfriend's very good-looking. – **12** *adj (acomodado)* well-off. – **13** *m* good: *el bien siempre triunfa sobre el mal,* good always triumphs over evil. **14** *(bienestar)* benefit: *lo hice por el bien de todos,* I did it for the good of everyone. – **15 bienes,** *mpl* property *sing,* possessions. – **16 bien ... bien,** *conj* either ... or: *se lo enviaremos bien por correo, bien por mensajero,* we'll send it to you either by post or by messenger.
● **en bien de,** for the sake of. ‖ **estarle bien algo a algn.,** to serve sb. right: *lo han despedido y le está bien,* he's got the sack and it serves him right; *le está bien lo que le ha pasado,* he deserves what happened to him. ‖ **hacer bien,** to do good. ‖ **bien que,** although. ‖ **tener a bien de hacer algo,** to be good enough to do sth. ‖ **¡ya está bien!,** that's enough!
■ **bien de consumo,** consumer item. ‖ **bienes de consumo,** consumer goods. ‖ **bien de equipo,** capital asset. ‖ **bienes de equipo,** capital goods, capital assets. ‖ **bienes inmuebles,** real estate *sing.* ‖ **bienes muebles,** movables, personal property *sing.* ‖ **gente bien,** *fam* the upper classes *pl.* ‖ **hombre de bien,** honest man.

bienal **1** *adj* biennial. – **2** *f* biennial exhibition, biennial festival, biennale.

bienamado,-a *adj* well-beloved.

bienaventurado,-a **1** *adj* REL blessed. **2** *(afortunado)* fortunate.

bienaventuranza **1** *f* happiness, bliss. – **2 Bienaventuranzas,** *fpl* REL Beatitudes *pl.*

bienestar *m* well-being, comfort.

bienhablado,-a *adj* well-spoken, polite.

bienhechor,-ra **1** *adj* beneficent, beneficial. – **2** *m,f* *(hombre)* benefactor; *(mujer)* benefactress.

bienintencionado,-a *adj* well-intentioned.

bienio **1** *m* *(periodo)* two-year period, biennium. **2** *(aumento)* two-yearly increment.

bienoliente *adj* sweet-smelling.

bienquisto,-a *adj* liked, well-liked.

bienvenida *f* → **bienvenido,-a.**

bienvenido,-a **1** *adj* welcome: *tus consejos serán bienvenidos,* your advice will be welcome; *hola María, ¡bienvenida a Barcelona!,* hello María, welcome to Barcelona! – **2 bienvenida,** *f* welcome.

● **dar la bienvenida a,** to welcome.

bies *m* bias binding.
● **al bies,** on the bias.

bifásico,-a *adj* two-phase.

bífido,-a *adj* forked.

bifocal *adj* bifocal.
■ **gafas bifocales,** bifocals.

bifurcación **1** *f* bifurcation. **2** *(de la carretera)* fork; *(de ferrocarril)* junction.

bifurcado,-a **1** *pp* → **bifurcarse.** – **2** *adj* forked.

bifurcarse *p* to fork, branch off.
▲ Conjugation model [1], like *sacar.*

bigamia *f* bigamy.

bígamo,-a **1** *adj* bigamous. – **2** *m,f* bigamist.

bígaro *m* winkle.

big bang *m* big bang.

bigote **1** *m* moustache (US mustache). **2** *(de gato)* whiskers *pl.*

bigotera **1** *f* *(compás)* bow compass. **2** *(protector)* moustach protector. **3** *(bocera)* moustache (US mustache).

bigotudo,-a *adj* mustachioed: *le gustan los bigotudos,* she likes men with moustaches.

bigudí *m* curler.
▲ *pl* bigudíes *or* bigudís.

bikini *m* → **biquini.**

bilabial **1** *adj* bilabial. – **2** *f* bilabial.

bilateral *adj* bilateral.

bilbaíno,-a **1** *adj* of Bilbao, from Bilbao. – **2** *m,f* person from Bilbao, inhabitant of Bilbao.

biliar *adj* biliary, bile.

biliario,-a *adj* → **biliar.**

bilingüe *adj* bilingual.

bilingüismo *m* bilingualism.

bilioso,-a *adj* bilious.

bilis **1** *f* bile. **2** *fig* spleen.
● **descargar la bilis contra,** *fig* to vent one's spleen on.
▲ *pl* bilis.

billar **1** *m* billiards. **2** *(mesa)* billiard table. – **3 billares,** *mpl* billiard room.
■ **billar americano,** pool.

billetaje *m* tickets *pl.*

billete **1** *m* *(moneda)* note, US bill: *un billete de cinco mil pesetas,* a five-thousand peseta note. **2** *(de transporte, sorteo, teatro, etc)* ticket.
■ **billete de ida,** one-way ticket. ‖ **billete de ida y vuelta,** return ticket, US round-trip ticket.

billetera *f* wallet, US billford.

billetero *m* purse, US change purse.

billón *m* billion, US trillion.

bimensual *adj* twice-monthly, bi-monthly.

bimestral *adj* every two months.

bimestre *m* period of two months.

bimotor,-a **1** *adj* twin-engined. – **2** *m* twin-engined plane.

binario,-a *adj* binary.

bingo **1** *m* *(juego)* bingo. **2** *(sala)* bingo hall.
● **¡bingo!,** bingo!

binguero,-a **1** *adj* fond of bingo. – **2** *m,f* *(jugador)* bingo player; *(trabajador)* person who works in a bingo hall.

binocular **1** *adj* binocular. – **2 binoculares,** *mpl* field glasses, binoculars.

binóculo *m* pince-nez.

binomio *m* binomial.

biodegradable *adj* biodegradable.

biofísica *f* → **biofísico,-a.**

biofísico,-a 1 *adj* biophysical. – **2** *m,f* (*persona*) biophysicist. – **3 biofísica**, *f* (*ciencia*) biophysics.
biografía *f* biography.
biográfico,-a *adj* biographical.
biógrafo,-a *m,f* biographer.
biología *f* biology.
biológico,-a *adj* biological.
biólogo,-a *m,f* biologist.
biomasa *f* biomass.
biombo *m* screen, folding screen.
biometría *f* biometry.
biométrico,-a *adj* biometric.
biónica *f* → **bionico,-a**.
biónico,-a 1 *adj* bionic. – **2 biónica**, *f* bionics.
biopsia *f* biopsy.
bioquímica *f* → **bioquímico,-a**.
bioquímico,-a 1 *adj* biochemical. – **2** *m,f* (*persona*) biochemist. – **3 bioquímica**, *f* (*ciencia*) biochemistry.
biorritmo *m* biorhythm.
biosfera *f* biosphere.
bióxido *m* dioxide.
bipartidismo *m* two-party system.
bipartidista *adj* two-party.
bipartito,-a *adj* bipartite.
bípedo,-a 1 *adj* biped. – **2 bípedo**, *m* biped.
biplano *m* biplane.
bipolar *adj* bipolar.
biquini 1 *m* (*traje de baño*) bikini. **2** CULIN (*en Cataluña*) toasted ham and cheese sandwich.
birdie *m* DEP birdie.
birlar *t fam* to pinch, nick.
birlibirloque **por arte de birlibirloque**, *loc* as if by magic.
Birmania *f* Burma.
birmano,-a 1 *adj* Burmese. – **2** *m,f* (*persona*) Burmese. – **3 birmano**, *m* (*idioma*) Burmese.
birra *f fam* beer.
birreactor,-ra 1 *adj* twin-jet. – **2 birreactor**, *m* twin-jet plane.
birreta *f* biretta.
birrete 1 *m* → **birreta**. **2** tasselled cap *worn by judges, lawyers or professors.*
birria 1 *f fam* (*cosa fea*) monstrosity. **2** (*cosa mala*) rubbish: *este libro es una birria*, this book is rubbish.
biruje *m fam* → **biruji**.
biruji *m fam* chilly wind.
bis 1 *adv* (*en dirección*): *viven en el 23 bis*, they live at 23A. **2** MÚS repeat, bis. – **3** *m* encore.
▲ In *3 pl* **bises**.
bisabuelo,-a *m,f* great-grandparent; (*hombre*) great-grandfather; (*mujer*) great-grandmother.
bisagra *f* hinge.
bisar *t* to repeat.
bisbisar *i* → **bisbisear**.
bisbisear *i* to whisper.
bisbiseo *m* whispering.
bisbita *f* pipit.
■ **bisbita común**, meadow pipit. ‖ **bisbita campestre**, tawny pipit. ‖ **bisbita arbóreo**, tree pipit.
biscote *m* piece of melba toast.
bisección *f* bisection.
bisector,-triz 1 *adj* bisecting. – **2 bisectriz**, *f* bisector, bisectrix.
bisectriz *f* → **bisector,-triz**.

bisel *m* bevel.
biselado,-a 1 *pp* → **biselar**. – **2** *adj* bevelled (US beveled). – **3 biselado**, *m* bevelling (US beveling).
biselar *t* to bevel.
bisemanal *adj* twice-weekly.
bisexual 1 *adj* bisexual. – **2** *mf* bisexual.
bisiesto *adj* leap, bisextile.
■ **año bisiesto**, leap year.
bisilábico,-a *adj* → **bisílabo,-a**.
bisílabo,-a *adj* two-syllabled.
bismuto *m* bismuth.
bisnieto,-a *m,f* great-grandchild; (*chico*) great-grandson; (*chica*) great-granddaughter: *tiene quince bisnietos,* she has fifteen greatgrandchildren.
bisojo,-a *adj* cross-eyed.
bisonte *m* bison.
bisoñé *m* toupee, hairpiece.
bisoñez *f* inexperience.
bisoño,-a 1 *adj* inexperienced. – **2** *m,f* novice.
bisté *m* steak.
bistec *m* steak.
bisturí *m* scalpel.
▲ *pl* **bisturíes** *or* **bisturís**.
bisutería *f* costume jewellery (US jewelry).
bit *m* bit.
▲ *pl* **bits**.
bitácora *f* binnacle.
bíter *m* bitters *pl*.
bitoque *m* bung, spigot.
bituminoso,-a *adj* bituminous.
biunívoco,-a *adj* one-to-one.
bivalente *adj* bivalent, divalent.
bivalvo,-a 1 *adj* bivalve, bivalvular. – **2 bivalvo**, *m* bivalve.
Bizancio *m* Byzantium.
bizantino,-a 1 *adj* Byzantine. **2** *fig* (*discusión*) idle. **3** *fig* (*decadente*) decadent.
bizarría 1 *f* (*valor*) bravery. **2** (*generosidad*) generosity.
bizarro,-a 1 *adj* (*valiente*) courageous. **2** (*generoso*) generous.
bizco,-a 1 *adj* cross-eyed. – **2** *m,f* cross-eyed person.
bizcocho *m* sponge, sponge cake.
biznieto,-a *m,f* → **bisnieto,-a**.
bizquear 1 *i* to squint, be cross-eyed. – **2** *t* (*guiñar*) to wink at.
bizquera *f* squint.
blanca *f* → **blanco,-a**.
Blancanieves *f* Snow White.
blanco,-a 1 *adj* white. **2** (*complexión*) fair-skinned: *tiene la piel muy blanca*, she has very fair skin, she's very fair-skinned. – **3** *m,f* (*gen*) white; (*hombre*) white man; (*mujer*) white woman. – **4 blanco**, *m* (*color*) white. **5** (*objetivo*) target, mark; *fig* object: *fue el blanco de todas sus críticas,* he was the target of all their criticism. **6** (*hueco*) blank, gap; (*en escrito*) blank space. **7** (*vino*) white wine. – **8 blanca**, *f* MÚS minim.
● **dar en el blanco**, to hit the mark; *fig* to hit the nail on the head. ‖ **blanco y negro**, black and white: *una película en blanco y negro,* a black and white film. ‖ **en blanco**, blank: *me dio un cheque en blanco,* he gave me a blank cheque. ‖ **estar sin blanca**, to be flat broke. ‖ **más blanco,-a que la nieve**, as white as snow. ‖ **no tener ni blanca**, to be flat broke. ‖ **pasar la noche en blanco**, to have a sleepless night. ‖ **quedarse en blanco**, (*no entender*) to fail to grasp the point; (*olvidarlo*

todo) to forget everything: *me quedé en blanco,* my mind went blank.
■ **blanco de España,** whiting. || **blanco del ojo,** white of the eye.

blancor *m* whiteness.

blancura *f* whiteness.

blancuzco,-a *adj* whitish, off-white.

blandengue 1 *adj* (*débil*) weak, feeble. 2 (*fofo*) flabby.

blandir *t* to brandish, wave.
▲ *Used only in forms which include the letter i in their endings: blandía, blandiré, blandiendo etc.*

blando,-a 1 *adj* (*gen*) soft. 2 (*poco severo*) soft, lenient. 3 *fig* (*benigno*) gentle, mild. 4 (*cobarde*) cowardly.

blanducho,-a *adj* flabby.

blandura 1 *f* softness. 2 *fig* (*dulzura*) gentleness, sweetness.

blanduzco,-a *adj* soft.

blanqueador,-ra 1 *adj* whitening. – 2 blanqueador, *m* (*cal*) whitewash. 3 (*para la ropa*) whitener.

blanquear 1 *t* to whiten, make white. 2 (*con cal*) to whitewash. 3 (*con lejía*) to bleach. 4 (*dinero*) to launder. 5 (*verduras*) to blanch. 6 (*pulir*) to polish. – 7 *i* to whiten, turn white.

blanquecino,-a *adj* whitish, off-white.

blanqueo 1 *m* whitening. 2 (*con cal*) whitewashing. 3 (*de dinero*) laundering.

blasfemar 1 *i* (*contra Dios*) to blaspheme (**contra,** against). 2 (*decir palabrotas*) to swear, curse.

blasfemia 1 *f* (*contra Dios*) blasphemy. 2 (*palabrota*) curse.

blasfemo,-a 1 *adj* blasphemous. – 2 *m,f* blasphemer.

blasón 1 *m* (*heráldica*) heraldry. 2 (*escudo*) coat of arms. 3 (*figura*) blazon, device. 4 *fig* honour (US honor), glory.
● **hacer blasón de,** to boast about, vaunt.

blasonar 1 *t* to emblazon. – 2 *i* to boast.

blástula *f* blastula.

bledo *m* common amaranth.
● **me importa un bledo,** *fam* I couldn't care less, I couldn't give a damn.

blenorragia *f* blennorrhagia.

blenorrea *f* blennorrhoea (US blennhorea).

blindado,-a 1 *pp* → **blindar.** – 2 *adj* armoured (US armored), armour-plated (US armor-plated).
■ **coche blindado,** bullet-proof car; (*furgoneta*) security van. || **puerta blindada,** reinforced door.

blindaje 1 *m* armour (US armor), armour-plating (US armor-plating). 2 (*de puerta*) reinforcing.

blindar 1 *t* to armour-plate (US armor-plate). 2 (*puerta*) to reinforce.

bloc *m* notepad, pad.
▲ *pl* **blocs.**

blocar *t* DEP to block.

blonda *f* → **blondo,-a.**

blondo,-a 1 *adj* (*rubio*) blond. – 2 blonda, *f* (*encaje*) blond lace. 3 (*para tarta*) doily.

bloque 1 *m* block. 2 (*papel*) pad, notepad. 3 POL bloc.
● **en bloque,** en bloc.
■ **bloque de pisos,** block of flats.

bloquear 1 *t* to block: *los manifestantes bloquearon la carretera,* the demonstrators blocked the road; *el portero bloqueó el balón,* the goalkeeper blocked the ball; *esto podría bloquear el proceso de paz,* this could block the peace process. 2 MIL to blockade. 3 (*precios, cuentas,*) to freeze. 4 (*mecanismo*) to jam; (*coche etc*) to immobilize. – 5 **bloquearse,** *p* (*persona*) to have a mental block.

bloqueo 1 *m* (*gen*) blocking. 2 MIL blockade. 3 (*precios, cuenta*) freezing.
■ **bloqueo económico,** trade boycott, economic boycott. || **bloqueo mental,** mental block. || **bloqueo naval,** naval blockade.

blues *m* blues.
▲ *pl* **blues.**

bluff *m* bluff.
▲ *pl* **bluffs.**

blusa *f* blouse.

blusón *m* loose blouse, smock.

boa 1 *f* (*serpiente*) boa. – 2 *m* (*prenda*) boa, feather boa.
■ **boa constrictor,** boa constrictor.

boato *m* pomp, ostentation.

bobada *f* silliness, foolishness.
● **decir bobadas,** to talk nonsense. || **hacer bobadas,** to act the fool.

bobalicón,-ona 1 *adj* simple. – 2 *m,f* simpleton.

bobear 1 *i* (*hablar*) to talk nonsense. 2 (*actuar*) to play the fool.

bobería *f* → **bobada.**

bóbilis de bóbilis bóbilis, *adv* for nothing.

bobina 1 *f* reel, bobbin. 2 ELEC coil.

bobinado *m* winding.

bobinar *t* to wind.

bobo,-a 1 *adj* silly, foolish. – 2 *m,f* fool.

boca 1 *f* ANAT mouth. 2 (*de río*) mouth. 3 (*abertura*) entrance, opening: *hay una boca de metro en la esquina,* there's an entrance to the underground on the corner.
● **abrir boca,** to whet one's appetite. || **hacer boca,** to whet one's appetite. || **andar en boca de todos,** to be the talk of the town, be on everyone's lips. || **arreglarse la boca,** to have one's teeth seen to. || **boca abajo,** face downwards. || **boca arriba,** face upwards. || **callarse la boca,** to shut up, shut one's mouth. || **correr de boca en boca,** to be the talk of the town, be common knowledge. || **en boca cerrada no entran moscas,** silence is golden. || **hacérsele la boca agua a algn.,** to make sb.'s mouth water. || **me lo has quitado de la boca,** you've taken the words right out of my mouth. || **no abrir boca,** not to say a word. || **no decir esta boca es mía,** not to say a word. || **por la boca muere el pez,** silence is golden.
■ **boca a boca,** kiss of life, mouth-to-mouth resuscitation. || **boca de incendios,** fire hydrant. || **boca de riego,** hydrant. || **boca del estómago,** pit of the stomach.

bocacalle 1 *f* entrance to a street: *tuerce por la primera bocacalle a la derecha,* take the first turning on the right. 2 (*calle secundaria*) side street.

bocadillo 1 *m* sandwich. 2 (*en cómics*) speech balloon.

bocado 1 *m* mouthful. 2 (*piscolabis*) snack, bite to eat. 3 (*mordedura*) bite. 4 (*de caballo*) bit.
● **no probar bocado,** not to eat a thing. || **pegar un bocado a,** to bite.
■ **bocado de Adán,** Adam's apple. || **bocado de rey,** titbit, US tidbit, delicacy.

bocajarro. 1 a bocajarro, *loc* (*disparar*) at point-blank range. 2 (*decir algo*) point-blank.

bocallave *f* keyhole.

bocamanga *f* cuff.

bocana *f* entrance.

bocanada 1 *f* (*de humo*) puff; (*de aire*) breath; (*de viento*) gust; (*de frío*) blast. 2 (*de líquido*) mouthful.

bocata *m* *fam* sandwich, sarnie.

bocazas *mf* bigmouth.
▲ *pl* **bocazas.**

bocera 1 f (*escoriación*) crack in the lips 2 (*mancha*) moustache (US mustache). – 2 **boceras,** mf bigmouth.
▲ In 2 pl *boceras.*

boceto m sketch; (*proyecto*) outline.

bocha 1 f (*bola*) bowl. – 2 **bochas,** fpl (*juego*) bowls.

bochinche m (*conmoción*) fuss, uproar; (*ruido*) racket, din, row.

bochorno 1 m (*calor*) sultry weather, close weather, muggy weather, stifling heat; (*viento*) hot wind. 2 fig (*rubor*) embarrassment, shame.

bochornoso,-a 1 adj (*sofocante*) hot, sultry, muggy. 2 fig (*vergonzoso*) disgraceful, shameful.

bocina 1 f (*de coche*) horn; (*de fábrica*) siren. 2 (*instrumento músico*) horn. 3 (*para ampliar la voz*) megaphone. 4 (*de gramófono*) horn.
● **tocar la bocina,** to blow one's horn, sound one's horn.

bocinazo 1 m hoot. 2 (*grito*) scream.
● **pegarle un bocinazo a algn.,** (*en coche*) to blow one's horn at sb.; (*gritar*) to scream at sb., shout at sb.

bocio m goitre.

bock m beer glass.
▲ pl *bocks.*

bocoy m large cask, large barrel.

boda f marriage, wedding.
■ **bodas de plata,** (*de matrimonio*) silver wedding *sing*; (*de ente*) twenty-fifth anniversary, silver jubilee. ‖ **bodas de oro,** (*de matrimonio*) golden wedding *sing*; (*de ente*) fiftieth anniversary, golden jubilee.

bodega 1 f (*almacén*) wine cellar. 2 (*tienda*) wine shop. 3 (*fábrica*) winery. 4 (*de barco*) hold.

bodegón m still-life painting.

bodeguero,-a 1 m,f (*de almacén*) cellarman. 2 (*vendedor*) wine merchant. 3 (*productor*) winemaker, wine producer.

bodoque 1 m (*adorno*) raised embroidery work. – 2 mf dimwit.

bodrio m fam rubbish, trash: *¡qué bodrio!,* what a load of rubbish!; *¡vaya bodrio de película!,* what a useless film!

body m body.
▲ pl *bodies.*

BOE abr (*Boletín Oficial del Estado*) Official Gazette.

bóer mf Boer.
▲ pl *bóers.*

bofe m lights pl.
● **echar los bofes,** to slog one's guts out.

bofetada f slap, slap in the face.
● **darle una bofetada a algn.,** to slap sb. in the face. ‖ **no tener ni media bofetada,** to be a weed.

bofetón m hard slap.

bofia la bofia, f arg the fuzz pl, the cops pl.

boga f vogue.
● **estar en boga,** to be in fashion.

bogar 1 i to row. 2 (*navegar*) to sail.
▲ Conjugation model [7], like **llegar.**

bogavante m lobster.

Bogotá m Bogotá.

bogotano,-a 1 adj of Bogotá, from Bogotá. – 2 m,f person from Bogotá, inhabitant of Bogotá.

bohardilla f → **buhardilla.**

bohemia f → **bohemio,-a.**

Bohemia f Bohemia.

bohemio,-a 1 adj (*vida etc*) bohemian. 2 (*de Bohemia*) Bohemian. – 3 m,f (*artista etc*) bohemian. 4 (*persona de Bohemia*) Bohemian. – 5 **la bohemia,** f Bohemian lifestyle.

bohío m AM hut.

boicot 1 m (*no participación*) boycott. 2 (*sabotaje*) sabotage.
▲ pl *boicots.*

boicotear 1 t (*no participar*) to boycott. 2 (*sabotear*) to sabotage.

boicoteo m → **boicot.**

boina f beret.

boite f nightclub.
▲ pl *boites.*

boj 1 m (*árbol*) box tree. 2 (*madera*) boxwood.
▲ pl *bojes.*

bol m bowl.
▲ pl *boles.*

bola 1 f (*gen*) ball. 2 fam fib, lie.
● **no rascar bola,** (*incompetente*) to make a mess of everything; (*gandul*) not to do a stroke.
■ **bola de nieve,** snowball. ‖ **bola de cristal,** crystal ball.

bolardo m bollard.

bolchevique 1 adj Bolshevik. – 2 mf Bolshevik.

bolcheviquismo m Bolshevism.

bolchevismo m Bolshevism.

bolera f → **bolero,-a 1.**

bolero,-a[1] 1 adj lying. – 2 m,f liar. – 3 **bolera,** f bowling alley.

bolero,-a[2] 1 m,f bolero dancer. – 2 **bolero,** m (*baile*) bolero. 3 (*prenda*) bolero, bolero jacket.

boleta f AM ticket.

boletería 1 f AM (*de teatro*) box office. 2 (*de estación*) ticket office.

boletero,-a m,f AM ticket seller.

boletín 1 m (*revista*) periodical. 2 (*de noticias*) bulletin, news bulletin. 3 (*impreso*) form. 4 (*de colegio*) report.

boleto 1 m ticket. 2 (*quiniela*) coupon.

boli m fam ballpen, biro.

boliche 1 m (*bola pequeña*) jack. 2 (*juego de bolos*) bowling, skittles pl. 3 (*bolera*) bowling alley. 4 (*juguete*) cup-and-ball game.

bólido 1 m ASTRON meteor, fireball. 2 fam racing car.
● **ir de bólido,** to be rushed off one's feet.

bolígrafo m ball-point pen, ball-point, biro.

bolillo m bobbin.

bolinga adj fam pissed.

bolívar m bolivar (*monetary unit of Venezuela*).

Bolivia f Bolivia.

boliviano,-a 1 adj Bolivian. – 2 m,f Bolivian. – 3 **boliviano,** m (*moneda*) boliviano.

bollera f → **bollero,-a.**

bollería 1 f (*establecimiento*) bakery. 2 (*bollos*) pastries pl.

bollero,-a 1 m,f (*fabricante*) baker, pastry-cook; (*vendedor*) pastry-seller. – 2 **bollera,** f pey (*lesbiana*) dyke.

bollo 1 m (*de pan*) bread roll, roll, breadbun; (*dulce*) pastry, bun. 2 (*abolladura*) dent. 3 (*chichón*) bump.
● **no está el horno para bollos,** fig this is not the right time.

bolo 1 m skittle, ninepin. 2 (*necio*) dunce, idiot. – 3 **bolos,** mpl skittles.
■ **bolo alimenticio,** bolus.

bolsa[1] 1 f (*gen*) bag: *¿tiene una bolsa de plástico?,* have you got a plastic bag? 2 (*bajo los ojos*) bag. 3 (*beca*) grant, scholarship. 4 (*en prenda*) pocket. 5 (*de pobreza, fraude, etc*) pocket. 6 (*para dinero*) purse. 7 (*premio*) purse. 8 (*de canguro etc*) pouch. 9 AM jacket.

bolsa

● ¡la bolsa o la vida!, your money or your life!
■ bolsa de agua caliente, hot-water bottle. ‖ bolsa de aguas, amniotic sac. ‖ bolsa de aire, air pocket. ‖ bolsa de aseo, toilet bag. ‖ bolsa de basura, rubbish bag, bin liner, us garbage bag. ‖ bolsa de deportes, sports bag. ‖ bolsa de estudios, scholarship. ‖ bolsa de viaje, travelling bag (us traveling bag).

bolsa[2] 1 *f* stock exchange. 2 (*valores*) share prices: *la bolsa ha subido dos puntos,* share prices are up two points.
■ bolsa de trabajo, (*en periódico*) job section, situations vacant.

bolsillo *m* pocket.
● de bolsillo, pocket: *una calculadora de bolsillo,* a pocket calculator. ‖ rascarse el bolsillo, to dip into one's pocket. ‖ sacar el dinero de su propio bolsillo, *fig* to pay it out of one's own pocket. ‖ tener a algn. en el bolsillo, *fig* to have sb. eating out of one's hand, be able to twist sb. round one's little finger.

bolsín *m* kerb market.

bolso *m* (*gen*) bag; (*de señora*) handbag, us purse.
■ bolso de mano, bag: *se puede llevar un solo bolso de mano,* you may take only one piece of hand luggage.

bomba[1] 1 *f* (*explosivo*) bomb: *pusieron una bomba en el hotel,* they planted a bomb in the hotel. 2 (*noticia*) bombshell.
● a prueba de bomba, bombproof. ‖ pasarlo bomba, to have a whale of a time.
■ bomba atómica, atomic bomb. ‖ bomba de cobalto, cobalt bomb. ‖ bomba de gas lacrimógeno, tear-gas canister. ‖ bomba de hidrógeno, hydrogen bomb. ‖ bomba de mano, hand grenade. ‖ bomba de neutrones, neutron bomb. ‖ bomba de relojería, time bomb. ‖ bomba incendiaria, incendiary bomb, incendiary device. ‖ bomba nuclear, nuclear bomb.

bomba[2] *f* pump.
■ bomba de agua, water pump. ‖ bomba de gasolina, fuel pump.

bombacho,-a 1 *adj* loose-fitting, baggy. – 2 bombachos, *mpl* baggy trousers.

bombardear 1 *t* (*con artillería*) to bombard, shell; (*desde el aire*) to bomb. 2 *fig* to bombard: *me bombardearon a preguntas,* they bombarded me with questions.

bombardeo *m* (*con artillería*) bombardment, shelling; (*desde el aire*) bombing.

bombardero *m* bomber.

bombardino *m* euphonium.

bombazo 1 *m* (*explosión*) bomb blast, explosion. 2 (*cosa inesperada*) bombshell. 3 (*exitazo*) smash hit, smash.

bombear *t* (*agua*) to pump.

bombeo *m* pumping.

bombero,-a *m* (*gen*) firefighter; (*hombre*) fireman; (*mujer*) firewoman.

bombilla *f* light bulb, bulb.

bombín 1 *m* (*sombrero*) bowler, bowler hat. 2 (*de cerradura*) cylinder.

bombo 1 *m* (*tambor*) bass drum. 2 (*elogio*) build-up, hype. 3 (*para sorteo*) drum.
● a bombo y platillo, with a great song and dance. ‖ dar bombo, to praise excessively. ‖ hacer un bombo a algn., to get sb. pregnant.

bombón 1 *m* chocolate. 2 *fam* knock-out.

bombona *f* cylinder.
■ bombona de butano, butane cylinder.

bombonera *f* chocolate box.

bombonería *m* sweet shop, us candy store.

bonachón,-ona 1 *adj* kind, good-natured. – 2 *m,f* kind soul.

bonaerense 1 *adj* of Buenos Aires, from Buenos Aires. – 2 *mf* person from Buenos Aires, inhabitant of Buenos Aires.

bonancible *adj* (*tiempo*) fair, settled; (*mar*) calm; (*viento*) light.

bonanza 1 *f* (*mar*) calm sea. 2 (*tiempo*) fair weather. 3 *fig* prosperity.

bondad 1 *f* goodness. 2 (*afabilidad*) kindness. 3 (*amabilidad*) kindness.
● tener la bondad de + *inf,* to be kind enough to + *inf: tenga la bondad de decirle que ...,* please tell him that ...

bondadoso,-a *adj* kind, good, good-natured.

bonete 1 *m* REL biretta, cap. 2 EDUC college cap. 3 (*de rumiante*) reticulum.

bongó *m* bongo.

boniato *m* sweet potato.

bonificación 1 *f* (*descuento*) discount. 2 (*cosa extra*) bonus. 3 (*mejoría*) improvement.

bonificar 1 *t* COM to allow, discount. 2 (*mejorar*) to improve.
▲ Conjugation model [1], like sacar.

bonísimo,-a *superl* → **bueno,-a**.

bonito,-a *adj* lovely, nice.

bonito *m* (*pez*) bonito, Atlantic bonito.

Bonn *m* Bonn.

bono 1 *m* FIN bond. 2 (*vale*) voucher. 3 (*billete*) ticket: *he comprado un bono mensual,* I've bought a monthly ticket.
■ bono del Tesoro, Treasury bond. ‖ bono del Estado, Government bond. ‖ bono de caja, bank bond.

bonobús *m* multiple-journey bus ticket.

bonoloto *m* Spanish state-run lottery.

bonotrén *m* multiple-journey train ticket.

bonzo *m* bonze.
● quemarse a lo bonzo, to set fire to os.

boñiga *f* cow dung.

boñigo *m* cowpat.

boom *m* boom.

boomerang *m* → **bumerán**.

boqueada *f* gasp.
● dar la última boqueada, to breathe one's last.

boquear 1 *i* (*inspirar*) to gasp. 2 (*expirar*) to breathe one's last. 3 (*estar moribundo*) to be at death's door. – 4 *t* (*pronunciar*) to utter.

boquera *f* crack in the lips.

boquerón *m* (*pez*) anchovy.

boquete *m* hole.
● abrir un boquete en, to make a hole in.

boquiabierto,-a 1 *adj* open-mouthed, agape. 2 (*embobado*) dumbfounded, flabbergasted, agape. 3 (*sin poder hablar*) speechless.

boquilla 1 *f* (*de pipa, instrumento*) mouthpiece. 2 (*de tubo*) nozzle. 3 (*sujetacigarrillos*) cigarette holder. 4 (*filtro de cigarrillo*) tip. 5 (*de cigarro puro*) lit end.

bórax *m* borax.

borbollón *m* bubbling.
● a borbollones, fiercely, furiously: *el petróleo salía a borbollones,* the oil gushed out.

Borbón *m* Bourbon.

borbónico,-a 1 *adj* Bourbon. – 2 *m,f* Bourbonist.

borborigmo *m* borborygmus, rumbling of the stomach.

borbotar *i* → **borbotear**.

borbotear *i* to bubble.

borboteo *m* bubbling.
borbotón *m* → **borbollón**.
borceguí *m* ankle boot.
borda *f* MAR gunwale.
 ● **irse por la borda,** to go down the drain. ‖ **tirar por la borda,** to throw overboard; *fig* to throw away.
bordada *f* tack.
bordado,-a 1 *pp* → **bordar.** – 2 *adj* embroidered. – 3 bordado, *m* embroidering, embroidery.
bordador,-ra *m,f* embroiderer.
bordadura *f* embroidery.
bordar 1 *t* to embroider. 2 *fig* to perform exquisitely.
borde[1] 1 *adj* (*tonto*) stupid: *¡no seas borde!,* don't be so stupid! 2 (*antipático*) unpleasant; (*malhumorado*) stroppy. 3 (*planta - silvestre*) wild. – 4 *mf* idiot.
borde[2] 1 *m* (*extremo*) edge. 2 (*de vaso, copa*) rim. 3 (*de barco, carretera*) side; (*de río*) bank; (*de mar*) shore. 4 (*de prenda*) hem.
 ● **estar al borde de,** to be on the verge of.
bordear 1 *t* to skirt, go round. 2 (*aproximarse*) to border on, verge on: *esto bordea el ridículo,* this is verging on the ridiculous.
bordelés,-esa 1 *adj* of Bordeaux, from Bordeaux. – 2 *m,f* person from Bordeaux, inhabitant of Bordeaux.
bordillo *m* kerb.
bordo *m* MAR board.
 ● **a bordo,** on board.
bordón 1 *m* (*palo*) staff. 2 (*cuerda*) bass string. 3 (*verso*) refrain.
boreal *adj* boreal, northern.
bóreas *m* north wind.
Borgoña *f* Burgundy. – 2 borgoña, *m* (*vino*) Burgundy.
borgoñés,-esa *adj-m,f* → **borgoñón,-ona.**
borgoñón,-ona 1 *adj* Burgundian. – 2 *m,f* Burgundian.
bórico,-a *adj* boric.
borla 1 *f* tassel. 2 (*de gorra*) pompom. 3 (*para polvos*) powder puff.
borne *m* terminal.
boro *m* boron.
borona 1 *f* (*mijo*) millet. 2 (*maíz*) maize.
borrachera *f* drunken state: *llevaba encima tal borrachera que no sabía dónde estaba,* she was so drunk she didn't know where she was; *¡estoy harta de tus borracheras!,* I'm fed up of you getting drunk!
 ● **coger una borrachera / enganchar una borrachera / pillar una borrachera,** to get drunk.
borrachín,-ina *m,f* boozer.
borracho,-a 1 *adj* (*persona*) drunk. 2 (*pastel*) soaked in alcoholic syrup. – 3 *m,f* drunkard, drunk. – 4 borracho, *m* sponge soaked in alcoholic syrup.
 ● **borracho,-a como una cuba,** blind drunk.
borrador 1 *m* (*escrito*) rough version, first draft: *aquí tienes el borrador del contrato,* here's the draft contract. 2 (*croquis*) rough sketch. 3 (*de pizarra*) duster. 4 (*goma*) eraser, GB rubber. 5 (*libro*) rough book.
borradura *f* erasure.
borraja *f* borage.
borrajear 1 *t* (*escribir*) to scribble. – 2 *i* (*dibujar*) to doodle.
borrar 1 *t* (*lo escrito*) to erase, rub out; (*superficie*) to clean: *borra esa palabra,* rub out that word; *borra la pizarra,* clean the blackboard. 2 (*cinta*) to erase. 3 INFORM to delete. 4 (*tachar*) to cross out, cross off: *me han borrado de la lista,* they've crossed me off the list. 5 (*dar de baja*) to cancel the membership of: *si no paga la cuota lo bo-*

rraremos del club, if he doesn't pay the fee we'll cancel his membership; *me he borrado del club de golf,* I've resigned from the golf club. – 6 **borrarse,** *p* to disappear.
borrasca 1 *f* (*ciclón*) depression, low-presssure area. 2 (*tormenta*) storm. 3 (*en un negocio etc*) bad spell, bad patch.
borrascoso,-a 1 *adj* stormy. 2 *fig* tempestuous.
borrego,-a 1 *m,f* lamb. 2 (*ignorante*) moron.
 ● **como borregos,** like sheep.
borrico,-a 1 *m,f* (*animal*) ass, donkey. 2 *fam* (*persona*) ass, dimwit.
borriquete *m* sawhorse.
borrón 1 *m* (*mancha*) blot, ink blot. 2 *fig* blemish. 3 (*boceto*) rough sketch.
 ● **hacer borrón y cuenta nueva,** to wipe the slate clean.
borronear 1 *t* (*escribir*) to scribble. 2 (*dibujar*) to doodle.
borroso,-a *adj* (*visión*) blurred, hazy; (*foto*) blurred; (*idea etc*) vague, hazy.
boscaje *m* thicket.
boscoso,-a *adj* wooded.
Bosnia *f* Bosnia.
 ■ **Bosnia Herzegovina,** Bosnia Herzegovina.
bosnio,-a 1 *adj* Bosnian. – 2 *m,f* Bosnian.
bosque *m* (*pequeño*) wood; (*grande*) forest.
bosquejar 1 *t* (*trazar rasgos*) to sketch, outline. 2 (*explicar sin detalles*) to outline, give an outline of.
bosquejo *m* (*dibujo*) sketch; (*plan etc*) outline.
bosquimán *adj-mf* → **bosquimano,-a.**
bosquimano,-a 1 *adj* Bushman. – 2 *m,f* (*persona*) Bushman. – 3 **bosquimano,** *m* (*idioma*) bosquimano.
bostezar *i* to yawn.
 ▲ *Conjugation model* [4], *like realizar.*
bostezo *m* yawn.
bostoniano,-a 1 *adj* Bostonian. – 2 *m,f* Bostonian.
bota[1] *f* boot.
 ● **ponerse las botas,** *fam* to stuff os.
 ■ **botas de agua,** gum boots, US rubber boots, wellingtons boots, wellingtons. ‖ **botas de esquí / botas de esquiar,** ski boots. ‖ **botas militares,** jackboots.
bota[2] *f* (*de vino*) wineskin.
botadura *f* launch, launching.
botafumeiro *m* censer.
botalón *m* boom.
botana *f* AM snack.
botánica *f* → **botánico,-a.**
botánico,-a 1 *adj* botanical. – 2 *m,f* botanist. – 3 botánica, *f* botany.
botanista *mf* botanist.
botar 1 *i* (*pelota*) to bounce. 2 (*persona*) to jump, jump up and down. – 3 *t* (*pelota*) to bounce. 4 (*barco*) to launch. 5 *fam* (*persona - del trabajo*) to fire, sack; (- *de un local*) to throw out, kick out, boot out.
 ● **está que bota,** he's hopping mad.
botarate 1 *m* (*tonto*) fool, harebrain. 2 AM spendthrift.
botavara *f* boom.
bote[1] *m* MAR small boat.
 ■ **bote salvavidas,** lifeboat.
bote[2] *m* (*salto*) bounce.
 ● **a bote pronto,** off the top of one's head. ‖ **dar botes,** (*persona*) to jump up and down; (*pelota*) to bounce. ‖ **dar botes de alegría,** to jump for joy.
bote[3] 1 *m* (*lata*) tin, can. 2 (*tarro*) jar. 3 (*para propinas*) jar for tips, box for tips. 4 (*fondo*) kitty. 5 (*premio*) jackpot.

● **tener a algn. en el bote,** to have sb. eating out of one's hand.
■ **bote de humo,** smoke canister.
bote⁴ de bote en bote, *loc* jam-packed.
botella 1 *f* bottle. **2** (*de gas*) cylinder.
botellazo *m* blow with a bottle.
botellero *m* bottle rack, wine rack.
botellín *m* small bottle.
botepronto *m* drop kick.
botica *f* pharmacy, chemist's.
● **hay de todo, como en botica,** there's everything imaginable.
boticario,-a *m,f* pharmacist, chemist; US druggist.
botija *f* earthenware pitcher.
botijo *m* earthenware jar (*with spout and handle for drinking*).
botín¹ 1 *m* (*zapato*) ankle boot. **2** (*cubierta*) gaiter.
botín² 1 *m* (*de guerra*) spoils *pl*, booty: *repartieron el botín,* they divided up the spoils. **2** (*de robo*) haul: *se llevaron un botín de ocho millones,* they got away with eight million.
■ **botín de guerra,** spoils *pl* of war.
botina *f* ankle boot.
botiquín *m* first-aid kit.
Botnia *f* Bothnia.
■ **golfo de Botnia,** Gulf of Bothnia.
botón 1 *m* (*gen*) button: *se me ha descosido un botón,* one of my buttons has come off; *pulsa el botón rojo,* press the red button. **2** (*tirador*) knob: *el botón de la puerta es de latón,* the doorknob is made of brass. **3** BOT bud. – **4** botones, *mf* (*de hotel*) bellboy, US bellhop; (*recadero - chico*) errand boy; (*- chica*) errand girl.
■ **botón de muestra,** sample. ‖ **botón de oro,** buttercup.
botonadura *f* buttons *pl*.
Botsuana *f* Botswana.
botsuanés,-esa 1 *adj* Botswanan. – **2** *m,f* Botswanan.
botulismo *m* botulism.
boutique *f* boutique.
bóveda *f* vault.
■ **bóveda celeste,** vault of heaven. ‖ **bóveda craneal,** cranial vault. ‖ **bóveda de cañón,** barrel vault. ‖ **bóveda por arista,** groin vault. ‖ **bóveda de crucería,** ribbed vault.
bóvido,-a 1 *adj* bovine. – **2** los bóvidos, *mpl* the bovidae.
bovino,-a 1 *adj* bovine. – **2** bovino, *m* bovine. – **3** bovinos, *mpl* cattle.
box 1 *m* (*de caballo*) stall. **2** (*en carrera de coches*) pit: *el piloto tuvo que entrar en los boxes,* the driver had to make a pit stop.
▲ *pl* boxes.
boxeador,-ra *m,f* boxer.
boxear *i* to box.
boxeo *m* boxing.
bóxer *m* (*perro*) boxer.
▲ *pl* bóxers.
boya 1 *f* MAR buoy. **2** (*corcho*) float.
boyante 1 *adj* MAR buoyant. **2** *fig* prosperous, successful, flourishing.
boyar *t* to float.
boyardo,-a *m,f* boyar.
boyero,-a *m,f* oxherd.
boy scout *m* boy scout.
▲ *pl* boy scouts.

bozal *m* muzzle.
bozo *m* fuzz.
bracear 1 *i* to wave one's arms about. **2** (*nadar*) to swim. **3** *fig* (*forcejear*) to struggle.
bracero *m* labourer (US laborer).
bracete de bracete, *loc* arm-in-arm.
braga 1 *f* (*prenda*) panties *pl*, knickers *pl*. **2** *fam* rubbish: *esa película es una braga, no vayas a verla,* that film's rubbish, don't go to see it.
● **estar hecho,-a una braga,** to be shattered, be knackered. ‖ **pillar a algn. en bragas,** to catch sb. with their trousers down.
▲ In 1 usually used in plural.
bragado,-a 1 *adj* (*malintencionado*) malicious. **2** (*firme*) determined.
bragadura *m* crotch.
bragazas *m* *fam* henpecked husband.
▲ *pl* bragazas.
braguero *m* truss.
bragueta *f* fly, flies *pl*.
braguetazo *m* *fam* marriage for money.
● **pegar el braguetazo,** to marry for money.
brahmán *m* Brahman, Brahmin.
brahmánico,-a *adj* Brahmanic, Brahminic.
brahmanismo *m* Brahmanism, Brahminism.
braille *m* braille.
bramante *m* string.
bramar 1 *i* (*toro, ciervo*) to bellow. **2** (*persona - de cólera*) to roar, bellow; (*- de dolor*) to howl.
bramido 1 *m* (*de toro, ciervo*) bellow. **2** (*de persona - de cólera*) bellow, roar; (*- de dolor*) howl.
brandi *m* brandy.
▲ *pl* brandis.
brandy *m* brandy.
▲ *pl* brandys.
branquia *f* gill.
branquial *adj* branchial.
braquial *adj* brachial.
brasa *f* ember, live coal.
● **a la brasa,** barbecued.
brasero *m* brazier.
Brasil *m* Brazil.
brasileño,-a 1 *adj* Brazilian. – **2** *m,f* Brazilian.
bravata 1 *f* (*amenaza*) threat. **2** (*fanfarronada*) boast: *déjate de bravatas,* stop boasting, stop showing off.
braveza 1 *f* (*valor*) bravery. **2** (*violencia*) violence. **3** (*fiereza*) ferocity.
bravío,-a 1 *adj* (*animal*) wild, fierce. **2** (*planta*) wild. **3** (*persona*) uncouth. **4** (*aguas*) rough, wild.
bravo,-a 1 *adj* (*valiente*) brave, courageous. **2** (*fiero*) fierce, ferocious. **3** (*bueno*) fine, excellent. **4** (*mar*) rough. **5** (*enojado*) angry, violent. – **6** ¡bravo!, *interj* well done!, bravo!
● **por las bravas,** by force.
■ **toro bravo,** fighting bull.
bravucón,-ona 1 *adj* bragging. – **2** *m,f* braggart.
bravuconada *m* piece of bravado.
bravuconear *i* to brag.
bravura 1 *f* (*valentía*) bravery, courage. **2** (*fiereza*) fierceness, ferocity.
braza 1 *f* (*medida*) fathom. **2** (*natación*) breaststroke.
brazada 1 *f* (*natación*) stroke. **2** (*cantidad*) armful.
brazado *m* armful.
brazal *m* armband.
brazalete *m* bracelet, bangle.

brazo 1 *m* (*de persona*) arm. 2 (*de vestido*) arm, sleeve. 3 (*de silla, cruz, balanza*) arm. 4 (*de animal*) foreleg. 5 (*de río, candelabro, árbol*) branch. 6 (*de grúa*) jib. – 7 **brazos,** *mpl* hands, workers.
● **a brazo partido,** (*sin armas*) hand to hand; (*con empeño*) tooth and nail. ‖ **asidos,-as del brazo / cogidos,-as del brazo,** arm in arm. ‖ **con los brazos abiertos,** with open arms. ‖ **cruzarse de brazos,** to fold one's arms; *fig* to sit back and do nothing. ‖ **estar hecho,-a un brazo de mar,** to be dressed to kill. ‖ **no dar su brazo a torcer,** not to give way, stand one's ground, stand firm. ‖ **ser el brazo derecho de algn.,** (*hombre*) to be sb.'s right-hand man; (*mujer*) to be sb.'s right-hand woman.
■ **brazo armado,** military wing, military arm. ‖ **brazo de gitano,** ≈ swiss roll, us jelly roll. ‖ **brazo de mar,** inlet. ‖ **brazo político,** political wing.

brea *f* tar, pitch.

brebaje *m* brew, potion.

breca *f* pandora.

brecha 1 *f* break, opening. 2 *fig* breach.
● **abrir una brecha en,** to break through. ‖ **estar en la brecha,** to be there.

brécol *m* broccoli.

brega 1 *f* (*lusha*) struggle, fight. 2 (*riña*) quarrel.

bregar 1 *i* (*luchar*) to fight (**con,** against), struggle (**con,** against). 2 (*ajetrearse*) to work hard (**con,** at). – 3 *t* (*amasar*) to knead.
▲ *Conjugation model* [7], *like* **llegar**.

brema *f* bream.

breña *f* scrub.

breñal *m* scrubland.

Bretaña 1 *f* (*británica*) Britain. 2 (*francesa*) Brittany.
■ **Gran Bretaña,** Great Britain.

brete *m* difficult position, tight spot, fix, jam.
● **estar en un brete,** to be in a fix, be in a tight spot. ‖ **poner a algn. en un brete,** to put sb. in a difficult position, put sb. on the spot.

bretón,-ona 1 *adj* Breton. – 2 *m,f* (*persona*) Breton. – 3 **bretón,** *m* (*idioma*) Breton.

breva 1 *f* (*higo*) early fig. 2 (*cigarro*) flat cigar.
● **¡no caerá esa breva!,** fat chance!, I should be so lucky!

breve 1 *adj* short, brief. – 2 *f* MÚS breve. – 3 **breves,** *fpl* (*en periódico*) news-in-brief section *sing*.
● **en breve,** soon, shortly. ‖ **en breves momentos,** soon, shortly.

brevedad *f* brevity, briefness.
● **con la mayor brevedad,** as soon as possible.

breviario 1 *m* REL breviary. 2 (*compendio*) compendium.

brezal *m* moor, heath.

brezo *m* heather, heath.

bribón,-ona 1 *m,f* (*sinvergüenza*) rotter. 2 (*niño*) rascal, little rascal.

bribonada *f* dirty trick.

bricolaje *m* do-it-yourself, DIY.

brida 1 *f* (*de caballo*) bridle. 2 TÉC flange.

bridge *m* bridge.

brigada 1 *f* (*unidad militar*) brigade. 2 (*de policía*) squad; (*de otros efectivos*) team. – 3 *m* (*soldado*) warrant officer.

brigadier *m* brigadier.

brillante 1 *adj* (*extraordinario*) brilliant: *un alumno brillante,* a brilliant student. 2 (*pelo, metal, zapatos*) shiny; (*ojos*) sparkling; (*luz, color*) bright; (*pintura*) gloss. – 3 *m* (*diamante*) diamond.

brillantemente *adv* brilliantly.

brillantez *f* brilliance.

brillantina *f* brilliantine.

brillar 1 *i* (*luz, sol, luna, pelo, zapatos*) to shine. 2 (*ojos*) to sparkle; (*estrella*) to twinkle; (*metal, dientes*) to gleam; (*cosa húmeda*) to glisten. 3 *fig* to be outstanding.

brillo 1 *m* (*gen*) shine. 2 (*de estrella*) twinkling; (*de ojos*) sparkle; (*de pelo, zapatos*) shine; (*de cosa húmeda*) glistening. 3 (*en televisor*) brightness. 4 *fig* brilliance.
● **sacar brillo a / dar brillo a,** to shine, polish.

brincar *i* (*cabra etc*) to skip; (*pájaro*) to hop; (*persona*) to leap, bound.
● **brincar de alegría,** to jump for joy. ‖ **estar algn. que brinca,** to be hopping mad.
▲ *Conjugation model* [1], *like* **sacar**.

brinco *m* (*de cabra*) skip, hop; (*de pájaro*) hop; (*de persona*) leap, bound.
● **dar un brinco,** to skip, hop. ‖ **dar brincos,** to jump up and down.

brindar 1 *i* to toast (**por,** to), drink (**por,** to): *¡brindemos por el futuro!,* let's drink to the future! – 2 *t* (*ofrecer*) to offer, provide: *esto nos brinda muchas posibilidades,* this offers us many possibilities; *brindar a algn. una cosa,* to offer sth. to sb. – 3 **brindarse,** *p* to offer (**a,** to), volunteer (**a,** to): *se brindó a prestarme ayuda,* he offered to help me.

brindis *m* toast.
▲ *pl* **brindis**.

brío 1 *m* (*espíritu*) spirit, verve; (*de motor*) go. 2 (*pujanza*) strength. 3 (*resolución*) determination. 4 (*valentía*) courage.

brioche *m* brioche.

brioso,-a *adj* (*gen*) spirited; (*motor*) lively.

brisa *f* breeze.
■ **brisa marina,** sea breeze.

brisca *f* Spanish card game.

británico,-a 1 *adj* British. – 2 *m,f* British person, Briton, Britisher.

brizna *f* (*gen*) bit; (*hebra*) strand; (*de hierba*) blade.

broca *f* (*barrena*) drill, bit.

brocado *m* brocade.

brocal *m* (*de pozo*) parapet.

brocha *f* brush, paintbrush: *pintor de brocha gorda,* house painter.
■ **brocha de afeitar,** shaving brush.

brochada *f* brushstroke.

brochazo *m* brushstroke.

broche 1 *m* (*cierre*) fastener. 2 (*joya*) brooch.

brocheta *f* skewer.

bróculi *m* broccoli.

broma *f* joke: *no es broma,* I'm not joking, it's not a joke.
● **bromas aparte,** joking apart. ‖ **decir algo en broma,** to joke about sth.: *lo decía en broma,* I was joking. ‖ **entre bromas y veras,** half jokingly. ‖ **gastar una broma a algn.,** to play a joke on sb. ‖ **no estar para bromas,** not to be in the mood for messing about. ‖ **tomar algo a broma,** to treat sth. as a joke, not take sth. seriously.
■ **broma de mal gusto,** sick joke. ‖ **broma pesada,** practical joke.

bromear *i* to joke.

bromista 1 *adj* fond of joking. – 2 *mf* joker.

bromo *m* bromine.

bromuro *m* bromide.

bronca *f* → **bronco,-a**.

bronce 1 *m* bronze. 2 (*medal*) bronze, bronze medal.

bronceado,-a 1 *pp* → **broncear**. – 2 *adj* bronzed. 3 (*piel*) tanned. – 4 **bronceado,** *m* tan, suntan.

bronceador,-ra 1 *adj* tanning. – 2 **bronceador,** *m* (*crema*) suntan cream, suntan lotion; (*aceite*) suntan oil.

broncear 1 *t* (*metal*) to bronze. 2 (*persona*) to tan, suntan. – 3 **broncearse,** *p* to tan, get a tan: *me bronceo fácilmente,* I tan very quickly, I soon tan.

bronco,-a 1 *adj* (*superficie*) rough; (*terreno*) rugged. 2 (*voz*) rough, gruff; (*tos*) rasping; (*sonido*) harsh. 3 (*persona*) rude, surly. – 4 **bronca,** *f* (*lío*) row. 5 (*riña*) quarrel; (*discusión*) argument; (*pelea*) fight. 6 (*reprimenda*) telling-off. 7 (*protesta del público*) noisy protests *pl*, jeers *pl*, jeering.
● **armar una bronca,** to kick up a fuss. ‖ **echar una bronca a algn.,** to tell sb. off, give sb. a telling-off.

broncopulmonar *adj* bronchopulmonary.

bronquial *adj* bronchial.

bronquio *m* bronchus.

bronquítico,-a *adj* bronchitic.

bronquitis *f* bronchitis.
▲ *pl* **bronquitis**.

brontosaurio *m* brontosaurus.

broquel *m* shield.

broqueta *f* skewer.

brotar 1 *i* (*plantas - nacer*) to sprout; (- *echar brotes*) to come into bud. 2 (*agua*) to spring; (*sangre*) to flow; (*lágrimas*) to well up. 3 (*estallar*) to break out. 4 *fig* to spring: *imágenes que brotan del lado oscuro del hombre,* images that spring from the darker side of man.
● **hacer brotar,** to bring forth.

brote 1 *m* (*renuevo*) shoot, sprout. 2 (*estallido*) outbreak: *se ha producido un brote de neumonía,* there has been an outbreak of pneumonia.

broza 1 *f* (*hojas*) dead leaves; (*ramitas*) dead twigs. 2 (*maleza*) scrub, brush. 3 (*suciedad*) dirt. 4 (*desperdicios*) rubbish. 5 (*palabras, paja*) waffle.

brucelosis *f* brucellosis.
▲ *pl* **brucelosis**.

bruces de bruces, *adv* face downwards.
● **caerse de bruces,** to fall flat on one's face.

bruja *f* → **brujo,-a**.

Brujas *f* Bruges.

brujería *f* witchcraft, sorcery.

brujo,-a 1 *adj* enchanting. – 2 **brujo,** *m* wizard, sorcerer. – 3 **bruja,** *f* (*hechicera*) witch. 4 (*mujer - fea*) old hag; (- *malintencionada*) witch.

brújula *f* compass.

bruma *f* mist.

brumoso,-a *adj* misty.

Brunei *m* Brunei.

bruno,-a *adj* dark brown.

bruñido,-a 1 *pp* → **bruñir**. – 2 *adj* burnished. – 3 **bruñido,** *m* burnishing.

bruñir *t* to burnish, polish.
▲ *Conjugation model* [40], *like* **muñir**.

bruscamente *adv* sharply.

brusco,-a 1 *adj* (*repentino*) sudden. 2 (*persona*) brusque, abrupt.

Bruselas *f* Brussels.

bruselense 1 *adj* of Brussels, from Brussels. – 2 *mf* person from Brussels, inhabitant of Brussels.

brusquedad 1 *f* (*de carácter*) brusqueness, abruptness. 2 (*rapidez*) suddenness.
● **con brusquedad,** sharply.

brut *adj* brut.

brutal 1 *adj* (*cruel*) brutal, savage. 2 *fig* (*enorme*) enormous, colossal. 3 *fig* (*magnífico*) terrific, fantastic.

brutalidad 1 *f* (*crueldad*) brutality. 2 (*necedad*) stupid thing. 3 (*cantidad*) tremendous amount.

brutalmente *adv* brutally.

bruto,-a 1 *adj* (*cruel*) brutal. 2 (*necio*) stupid, thick. 3 (*tosco*) rough, coarse. 4 (*torpe*) clumsy. 5 (*grosero*) rude. 6 (*sueldo etc*) gross. 7 (*peso*) gross. 8 (*piedra*) rough, uncut. 9 (*petróleo*) crude. – 10 *m,f* (*persona - violenta*) brute, beast; (*necio*) ignoramus; (*grosero*) rude person. – 11 **bruto,** *m* (*animal*) beast.

BSO *abr* CINEM (*Banda Sonora Original*) original soundtrack; (*abreviatura*) OST.

bubónico,-a *adj* bubonic.

bucal *adj* oral, mouth.

bucanero *m* buccaneer.

Bucarest *m* Bucharest.

búcaro 1 *m* (*florero*) vase. 2 (*para beber*) earthenware drinking jar.

buceador,-ra *m,f* diver.

bucear 1 *i* (*en el agua*) to dive. 2 *fig* (*investigar*) to delve into.

buceo *m* diving.

buche 1 *m* (*de aves*) crow, crop. 2 *fam* (*del hombre*) belly. 3 (*pecho*) bosom. 4 (*lo que cabe en la boca*) mouthful.

bucle 1 *m* curl, ringlet. 2 INFORM loop.

bucólico,-a *adj* bucolic.

Buda *m* Buddha.

Budapest *m* Budapest.

budín *m* pudding.

budismo *m* Buddhism.

budista 1 *adj* Buddhist. – 2 *mf* Buddhist.

buen *adj* → **bueno,-a**.
▲ *Used before a sing masculine noun:* **buen chico** / **chico bueno**.

buenamente *adv*: *haz lo que buenamente puedas,* just do what you can, do as much as you can, do the best you can.

buenaventura 1 *f* (*futuro*) fortune, future. 2 (*buena suerte*) good fortune.
● **decirle a algn. la buenaventura,** to tell sb's fortune.

bueno,-a 1 *adj* (*gen*) good: *es una película muy buena,* it's a very good film; *los niños buenos obedecen a sus padres,* good children obey their parents; *lo que necesitas es una buena taza de café,* what you need is a nice cup of coffee. 2 (*persona - amable*) kind; (- *agradable*) nice, polite. 3 (*tiempo*) good, nice: *hizo un día muy bueno,* the weather was very good. 4 (*apropiado*) right, suitable; (*correcto*) right: *no es bueno para los niños pequeños,* it's not suitable for small children; *esta llave no es la buena,* this key isn't the right one. 5 (*de salud*) well: *¿ya estás buena?,* are you better now? 6 (*grande*) big; (*considerable*) considerable: *un buen número de participantes,* quite a few participants. – 7 *¡bueno!, interj* (*sorpresa*) well, very well; (*de acuerdo*) all right!
● **de buenas a primeras,** *fam* all of a sudden, just like that. ‖ **estar bueno,-a,** to be in good health; *fam* to be good-looking. ‖ **estar de buen ver,** to be good-looking. ‖ **por la buenas,** willingly. ‖ *¡ésta sí que es buena!, fam* that's a good one!
■ **buen humor,** good humour (US humor). ‖ **buenas noches,** good evening. ‖ **buenas tardes,** good afternoon. ‖ **buenos días,** good morning. ‖ **la buena mesa,** good food. ‖ **la buena vida,** the good life.
▲ *See also* **buen**.

buey *m* ox, bullock.
■ **carne de buey,** beef. ‖ **buey de mar,** crab. ‖ **buey marino,** sea cow.

búfalo *m* buffalo.

bufanda *f* scarf.

bufar 1 *i* (*toro*) to snort. **2** (*persona*) to be fuming: *bufar de coraje*, to be fuming with rage.

bufé *m* buffet.
■ **bufé libre**, self-service buffet meal.
▲ *pl bufés*.

bufete 1 *m* (*mesa*) writing desk. **2** (*de abogado*) lawyer's office: *abrir bufete*, to set up as a lawyer.

buffet *m* → **bufé**.
▲ *pl buffets*.

bufido *m* snort: *entró en el despacho dando bufidos*, he came raging into the office.

bufo,-a *adj* comic, farcical, clownish.
● **hacer bufa de**, to make fun of.
■ **ópera bufa**, comic opera.

bufón,-ona 1 *adj* buffoon. – **2** *m,f* buffoon, jester.

bufonada *f* piece of buffoonery.
● **hacer bufonadas**, to clown around.

bufonesco,-a *adj* comical, clownish.

buganvilla *f* bougainvillaea.

buharda 1 *f* (*ventana*) dormer window. **2** (*desván*) attic.

buhardilla 1 *f* → **buharda**.

búho *m* owl.
■ **búho real**, eagle owl.

buhonería 1 *f* (*actividad*) peddling, hawking. **2** (*mercancías*) wares.

buhonero,-a *m,f* pedlar, hawker.

buitre *m* (*ave y persona*) vulture.

buitrear *t* to scrounge.

bujarrón 1 *adj fam* queer. – **2** *m fam* queer.

bujía 1 *f* (*de motor*) spark-plug. **2** (*vela*) candle. **3** (*candelero*) candlestick.

bula 1 *f* (*documento*) bull, papal bull.

bulbo *m* bulb.
■ **bulbo raquídeo**, medulla oblongata.

bulboso,-a *adj* bulbous.

buldog *m* bulldog.

bulerías *fpl* song and dance from Andalusia.

bulevar *m* boulevard.

Bulgaria *f* Bulgaria.

búlgaro,-a 1 *adj* Bulgarian. – **2** *m,f* (*persona*) Bulgarian. – **3** búlgaro, *m* (*idioma*) Bulgarian.

bulimia *f* bulimia.

bulla 1 *f* (*ruido*) din, uproar, racket, row. **2** (*multitud*) crowd.

bullabesa *f* bouillabaisse.

bullanga *f* racket.

bullanguero,-a 1 *adj* (*alborotador*) noisy, rowdy. **2** (*juerguista*) fun-loving. – **3** *m,f* (*alborotador*) rowdy. **4** (*juerguista*) fun-lover.

bullicio 1 *m* (*ruido*) noise, racket. **2** (*tumulto*) bustle, hustle and bustle, hurly-burly.

bullicioso,-a 1 *adj* (*ruidoso*) noisy. **2** (*animado*) lively; (*con ajetreo*) busy.

bullir 1 *i* (*líquido - hervir*) to boil; (- *agitarse*) to bubble up; (*mar*) to seethe; (*calle etc*) to swarm with, seethe with. **2** (*insectos*) to swarm; (*gente*) to bustle about.
▲ Conjugation model [41], like *mullir*.

bulo *m* false rumour (US rumor), unfounded rumour (US rumor).

bulto 1 *m* (*tamaño*) volume, size, bulk. **2** (*forma*) shape, form. **3** (*abultamiento - en cosa*) bulge; (- *en piel*) lump: *el pañuelo te hace un bulto en el bolsillo*, your handkerchief makes a bulge in your pocket; *tiene un bulto en el pe-cho*, she has a lump on her breast. **4** (*equipaje*) piece of luggage, item of luggage; (*fardo*) bundle; (*paquete*) package.
● **a bulto**, roughly. ‖ **de bulto**, serious, important. ‖ **hacer bulto**, to take up space.

bumerán *m* boomerang.

bumerang *m* → **bumerán**.

bungalow *m* bungalow.
▲ *pl bungalows*.

búnker *m* bunker.
▲ *pl búnkers*.

buñuelo *m* fritter: *buñuelos de bacalao*, cod fritters.

BUP *abr* EDUC (*Bachillerato Unificado Polivalente*) ≈ General Certificate of Secondary Education studies.

buque *m* MAR ship, vessel.
■ **buque cisterna**, tanker. ‖ **buque de cabotaje**, coaster. ‖ **buque de carga**, cargo ship. ‖ **buque de guerra**, warship. ‖ **buque de vapor**, steamer. ‖ **buque de vela**, sailboat. ‖ **buque escuela**, training ship. ‖ **buque factoría**, factory ship. ‖ **buque insignia**, flagship. ‖ **buque mercante**, merchant ship. ‖ **buque tanque**, tanker.

buqué *m* bouquet.

burbuja *f* bubble.
● **con burbujas**, (*bebida*) fizzy. ‖ **sin burbujas**, (*bebida*) still.

burbujear *i* to bubble.

burbujeo *m* bubbling.

burdégano *m* hinny.

burdel *m* brothel.

burdeos 1 *adj* maroon, burgundy. – **2** *m* (*color*) maroon, burgundy. **3** (*vino - en general*) Bordeaux; (- *tinto*) claret.

Burdeos *m* Bordeaux.

burdo,-a 1 *adj* (*tejido*) coarse, rough. **2** (*persona*) coarse, crude.

bureo ir de bureo, *loc fam* to go out on the town.

bureta *f* burette (US buret).

burgalés,-esa 1 *adj* of Burgos, from Burgos. – **2** *m,f* person from Burgos, inhabitant of Burgos.

burger *m fam* burger-bar.

burgo *m* walled town.

burgomaestre *m* burgomaster.

burgués,-esa 1 *m,f* bourgeois, middle-class. **2** member of the middle-class.

burguesía *f* bourgeoisie, middle class.
■ **alta burguesía**, upper middle-class.

buril *m* burin.

burilar *t* to engrave.

Burkina Faso *m* Burkina-Faso.

burla 1 *f* (*mofa*) mockery, gibe. **2** (*broma*) joke. **3** (*engaño*) deception, trick.
● **en son de burla**, in fun, tongue in cheek. ‖ **entre burlas y veras**, half-jokingly.

burladero *m* barrier behind which a bullfighter may take refuge from the bull.

burlador,-ra 1 *adj* mocking, deceiving. – **2** burlador, *m* ladies' man.

burlar 1 *t* to deceive, trick. **2** (*eludir*) to dodge, evade. – **3** burlarse, *p* to mock (de, -), make fun (de, of), laugh (de, at).

burlesco,-a *adj* burlesque, comical.

burlete *m* draught excluder.

burlón,-ona 1 *adj* mocking. – **2** *m,f* joker.

buró *m* writing desk, bureau.

burocracia 1 *f* bureaucracy. **2** *pey* red tape.

burócrata *mf* bureaucrat.

burocrático,-a *adj* bureaucratic.

burrada 1 *f* drove of asses. 2 *fig* foolishness, blunder. 3 **una burrada,** *fam* (*cantidad*) loads *pl*, lots *pl*, tons *pl*: *había una burrada de gente,* there were loads of people; *gasté una burrada,* I spent a fortune. – 4 *loc adv fam* a lot: *me gusta una burrada,* I love it.
● **decir burradas,** to talk rubbish, talk nonsense.

burro,-a 1 *adj* stupid. – 2 *m,f* (*animal*) donkey, ass. 3 (*persona ignorante*) ass. – 4 **burro,** *m* (*de carpintero*) sawhorse.
● **apearse del burro / bajarse del burro,** to climb down. ‖ **no ver tres en un burro,** to be as blind as a bat. ‖ **no verse tres en un burro,** to be pitch dark.
■ **burro de carga,** workhorse.

bursátil *adj* stock-exchange: *las autoridades bursátiles de Londres,* the London stock-exchange authorities.

burundés,-esa 1 *adj* Burundian. – 2 *m,f* Burundian.

Burundi *m* Burundi.

bus 1 *m* AUTO bus. 2 INFORM bus.
▲ *pl* buses.

busca 1 *f* search, hunt. – 2 *m fam* bleeper, pager.
● **ir en busca de,** to search for, hunt for.

buscador,-ra 1 *adj* searching. – 2 *m,f* searcher, seeker. – 3 **buscador,** *m* (*anteojo*) finder.

buscapersonas *m* bleeper, pager.

buscapiés *m* jumping jack, cracker.
▲ *pl* buscapiés.

buscapleitos *mf* troublemaker.
▲ *pl* buscapleitos.

buscar 1 *t* (*gen*) to look for, search for: *busco un hombre que se llama Pedro,* I'm looking for a man called Pedro; *la policía busca un hombre de unos treinta años,* the police are searching for a man of about thirty; *hay que buscar una solución al problema,* we have to find a solution to the problem. 2 (*en lista, índice etc*) to look up: *búscalo en el diccionario,* look it up in the dictionary. 3 (*ir a coger*) to go and get, fetch: *ves a buscar pan,* go and get some bread; *busca un médico, ¡rápido!,* fetch a doctor, quick! 4 (*recoger*) to pick up: *iré a buscarte a la estación,* I'll pick you up at the station, I'll meet you at the station; *a la una voy a buscar a los chicos al colegio,* at one o'clock I go to pick the children up from school. 5 (*intentar conseguir*) to try to achieve: *no sé qué buscan con esto,* I don't know what they're trying to achieve with this. – 6 *i* (*mirar*) to look: *he buscado en todas partes,* I've looked everywhere.
● **buscársela,** *fam* to be looking for trouble: *se la estaba buscando y la encontró,* she was looking for trouble and she found it. ‖ **buscarse la vida,** *fam* to try and earn one's living. ‖ *"se busca ...",* *"... wanted".*
▲ *Conjugation model* [1], *like sacar.*

buscavidas 1 *mf* go-getter. 2 (*chismoso*) snooper, busybody.
▲ *pl* buscavidas.

buscón,-ona 1 *m,f* (*ladrón*) petty thief. – 2 **buscona,** *f* whore.

buscona *f* → **buscón,-ona.**

búsqueda *f* search.

busto 1 *m* (*figura*) bust. 2 (*pecho - de mujer*) bust; (*- de hombre*) chest.

butaca 1 *f* (*sillón*) armchair. 2 TEAT seat.

butacón *m* easy chair.

butano *m* butane.

buten de buten, *loc* great, fantastic.

butifarra *f type of* pork sausage.

buzo *m* diver.

buzón *m* letter-box, US mailbox.
● **echar una carta al buzón,** to post a letter.

byte *m* INFORM byte

C

C, c f (la letra) C, c.
C¹ sím (Celsius) Celsius; (símbolo) C.
C² sím (centígrado) centigrade; (símbolo) C.
c/¹ abr (calle) street, road; (abreviatura) St., Rd.
c/² abr (cargo) cargo, freight.
c/³ abr (cuenta) account; (abreviatura) a/c, acc, acct.
C/ abr (calle) street, road; (abreviatura) St., Rd.
c. abr (capítulo) chapter; (abreviatura) ch.
C. abr (compañía) Company; (abreviatura) Co.
Cª. abr (compañía) Company; (abreviatura) Co.
ca interj not at all!, not a bit of it!, never!
cabal 1 adj (exacto) exact, precise: aquí hay diez mil pesetas cabales, there are exactly ten thousand pesetas. 2 (completo) complete: el juego de ajedrez no está cabal, the chess set isn't complete. 3 fig (persona) honest, upright.
● a carta cabal, totally, through and through: es sincero a cartà cabal, he's totally sincere. ‖ estar en sus cabales, to be in one's right mind.
cábala 1 f (ciencia oculta) cabala, cabbala. 2 fig (conjetura) guess, divination. 3 fig (intriga) plot.
● hacer cábalas sobre algo, fig to speculate about sth.
▲ In 2 also used in plural with the same meaning.
cabalgada 1 f (tropa) troop of riders. 2 (correría) cavalry raid.
cabalgadura 1 f (bestia en que se cabalga) mount. 2 (bestia de carga) beast of burden.
cabalgar 1 i (sobre un animal) to ride (**en/sobre,** -): cabalgó sobre un caballo blanco, she rode a white horse. 2 (sobre otra cosa) to straddle (**sobre,** -), sit astride (**sobre,** -): el niño cabalgaba sobre la silla, the boy sat astride the chair. – 3 t to ride. 4 (cubrir a una hembra) to cover, mount.
▲ Conjugation model [7], like llegar.
cabalgata f cavalcade.
■ la cabalgata de los Reyes Magos, the procession of the Three Wise Men.
cabalista 1 mf cabalist, cabbalist. 2 fig intriguer, schemer.
cabalístico,-a 1 adj cabalist, cabbalistic. 2 fig hidden, occult.
caballa f mackerel.
caballada f drove of horses.
caballar adj equine, horse.
■ raza caballar, equine race.
caballeresco,-a adj chivalrous, knightly.
caballería 1 f (cabalgadura) mount. 2 MIL cavalry. 3 HIST chivalry, knighthood.
■ caballería andante, knight-errantry. ‖ caballería ligera, light cavalry. ‖ libros de caballerías, novels of chivalry.
caballeriza 1 f (cuadra) stable. 2 (personal) stable hands pl, grooms pl. 3 (conjunto de caballos) stud.

caballerizo m groom, stableboy, stableman.
■ caballerizo mayor del rey, Master of the King's Horses.
caballero,-a 1 adj riding, mounted: caballero en su rocín, riding a nag. 2 fig (obstinado) obstinate, stubborn: es caballero en su propósito, he's very determined. – 3 caballero, m gentleman, sir: camisas de caballero, men's shirts, gentlemen's shirts. 4 HIST knight, cavalier. 5 (hombre generoso, cortés) gentleman. 6 (noble) gentleman.
● armar caballero a algn., to knight sb.
caballerosamente adv chivalrously.
caballerosidad f chivalry.
caballeroso,-a adj chivalrous, noble.
caballete 1 m (de pintor) easel. 2 ARQ ridge. 3 TÉC trestle. 4 (de nariz) bridge.
caballista 1 mf (que entiende de caballos) horse expert. 2 (que monta bien) good rider.
caballito 1 m small horse. – 2 caballitos, mpl (tiovivo) merry-go-round sing, US carrousel sing.
■ caballito de mar, sea horse. ‖ caballito del diablo, dragonfly.
caballo 1 m ZOOL horse. 2 TÉC horsepower. 3 (ajedrez) knight. 4 (naipes) queen. 5 arg (heroína) junk, horse, scag, smack.
● a caballo, on horseback. ‖ montar a caballo, to ride. ‖ a caballo entre ..., fig halfway between ... ‖ a caballo regalado no le mires el dentado, fig don't look a gift horse in the mouth.
■ caballo de batalla, fig hobbyhorse. ‖ caballo de carreras, racehorse. ‖ caballo de tiro, cart horse.
caballón m ridge.
caballuno,-a adj horsey, horse-like.
cabalmente adv exactly.
cabaña 1 f (choza) cabin, hut, shack. 2 (conjunto de ganados) livestock: la cabaña pirenaica, Pyrenean livestock.
cabañal 1 adj animal. – 2 m hamlet.
■ camino cabañal, animal track.
cabaré m cabaret, nightclub.
▲ pl cabarés.
cabaret m cabaret, nightclub.
▲ pl cabarets.
cabaretera f cabaret entertainer.
cabe¹ prep arc next to.
cabe² m fam header.
cabecear 1 i (mover la cabeza) to move one's head; (para negar) to shake one's head. 2 (dar cabezadas) to nod. 3 (inclinarse) to lean, slope. 4 MAR to pitch. – 5 t DEP to head.
cabeceo m (movimiento de la cabeza) nodding, shaking; (negación) shaking. 2 (al dormirse) nodding, nod. 3 MAR pitching.
cabecera 1 f (gen) top, head. 2 (de cama) headboard. 3 (de mesa) head. 4 (de un río) source, headwaters pl. 5 (de

un periódico) headline; (*de un libro*) headband. **6** (*de una iglesia*) sanctuary.
■ libro de cabecera, bedside book.
cabecero *m* headrest.
cabecilla *mf* leader.
cabellera 1 *f* hair, head of hair. **2** (*de cometa*) tail.
cabello 1 *m* hair. – **2 cabellos,** *mpl* (*barbas de la mazorca*) corn silk *sing*.
■ cabello de ángel, (*dulce*) sweet pumpkin preserve; (*pasta de sopa*) vermicelli.
cabelludo,-a 1 *adj* (*persona*) hairy. **2** (*planta, fruta*) downy.
■ cuero cabelludo, scalp.
caber 1 *i* (*encajar*) to fit (**en,** into): *cabe ahí arriba,* it'll fit up there; *no cabe más en la maleta,* there isn't room for anything else in the suitcase; *en esta lata caben diez litros,* this can holds ten litres. **2** (*pasar*) to fit, go: *el sofá no cabe por la puerta,* the sofa won't go through the door. **3** (*ser posible*) to be possible: *cabe la posibilidad de que vengan,* they might come; *cabe decir que ...,* it's possible to say that ..., it can be said that ...; *no cabe ningun cambio,* no changes may be made. **4** *fml* (*corresponder*) to have: *me cupo el honor de recibirlos,* I had the honour of welcoming them. **5** MAT to go: *ocho entre dos caben a cuatro,* two into eight goes four times, eight divided by two is four.
● dentro de lo que cabe, all things considered, considering. ‖ no cabe duda, there is no doubt. ‖ no caber en sí de gozo, *fig* to be beside os. with joy. ‖ no me cabe en la cabeza, *fig* I can't believe it, I can't understand it. ‖ si cabe, if possible.
▲ Conjugation model |66|.
cabestrar *t* to halter.
cabestrillo *m* sling: *llevaba el brazo en cabestrillo,* she had her arm in a sling.
cabestro 1 *m* (*dogal*) halter. **2** (*animal*) leading ox.
cabeza 1 *f* (*gen*) head: *diez mil por cabeza,* ten thousand a head; *dos mil cabezas de ganado,* two thousand head of cattle. **2** *fig* (*juicio*) good judgement; (*talento*) talent, intelligence: *tiene una buena cabeza,* she's intelligent. **3** (*de región*) main town. – **4** *m* (*jefe*) head, leader: *el cabeza de familia,* the head of the family.
● a la cabeza de, at the front of, at the top of: *a la cabeza de la lista,* at the top of the list. ‖ andar de cabeza / ir de cabeza, to be rushed off one's feet: *andamos de cabeza estos días,* we've been rushed off our feet for the past few days. ‖ andar de cabeza por algn., to be crazy about sb. ‖ cabeza abajo, upside down. ‖ cabeza arriba, the right way up, upright. ‖ calentarse la cabeza por algo, to get worked up about sth. ‖ de cabeza, (*mentalmente*) in one's head; (*de memoria*) from memory. ‖ darse de cabeza contra algo, to bang one's head against sth. ‖ de pies a cabeza, from head to toe, from top to toe. ‖ estar mal de la cabeza, *fig* not to be right in the head. ‖ írsele a uno la cabeza, *fig* to feel dizzy. ‖ meterse algo en la cabeza, *fam* to get sth. into one's head. ‖ no levantar cabeza, *fam* (*en deporte*) not to find form; (*en negocios*) not to get off the ground. ‖ no tener ni pies ni cabeza, *fig* to be absurd, make no sense. ‖ pasarle a algn. por la cabeza, *fig* to occur to sb. ‖ perder la cabeza, *fig* to lose one's head. ‖ quitarle a algn. algo de la cabeza, *fig* to talk sb. out of sth. ‖ quitarse algo de la cabeza, to get sth. out of one's head, forget sth.; (*pensar*) to rack one's brains. ‖ ser un cabeza dura, to be stubborn. ‖ subirse algo a la cabeza, *fig* to go to one's head. ‖ tengo la cabeza como un bombo, *fam* my head is

splitting. ‖ tirarse de cabeza, to dive head first (**a/en,** into). ‖ traer a algn. de cabeza / llevar a algn. de cabeza, to drive sb. crazy, drive sb. mad. ‖ volver la cabeza, to look round.
■ cabeza cuadrada, *fam fig* bigot. ‖ cabeza de ajo, bulb of garlic. ‖ cabeza de chorlito, *fam fig* scatterbrain. ‖ cabeza de espárrago, asparagus tip. ‖ cabeza de lista, main candidate. ‖ cabeza de partido, administrative capital. ‖ cabeza de puente, bridgehead. ‖ cabeza de turco, scapegoat. ‖ cabeza hueca, scatterbrain. ‖ cabeza loca, *fam* scatterbrain. ‖ cabeza rapada, skinhead.
cabezada 1 *f* (*golpe recibido*) blow on the head; (*golpe dado*) butt, head butt. **2** (*saludo, al dormirse*) nod. **3** (*correaje*) cavesson. **4** MAR pitch, pitching.
● dar cabezadas, *fam* to nod. ‖ darse de cabezadas, *fam* to rack one's brains. ‖ echar una cabezada, *fam* to have a snooze.
cabezal 1 *m* TÉC head, headstock. **2** (*de tocadiscos*) pickup. **3** (*almohada*) pillow. **4** (*vendaje*) compress.
cabezazo 1 *m* (*golpe recibido*) blow on the head; (*golpe dado*) butt. **2** DEP header.
● dar un cabezazo, DEP to head the ball.
cabezón,-ona 1 *adj fam* (*de cabeza grande*) with a big head. **2** *fam fig* (*terco*) pigheaded, stubborn. – **3** *m,f fam* (*de cabeza grande*) person with a big head. **4** *fam fig* (*terco*) pigheaded person, stubborn person.
cabezonada *f fam* pigheaded action.
cabezonería 1 *f fam* (*obstinación*) pigheadedness, stubbornness. **2** *fam* (*cabezonada*) pigheaded action.
cabezota 1 *adj fam fig* (*terco*) pigheaded, stubborn. – **2** *mf fam* (*de cabeza grande*) person with a big head. – **3** *m,f fam fig* (*terco*) pigheaded person, stubborn person.
cabezudo,-a 1 *adj* (*de cabeza grande*) bigheaded. **2** *fig* (*terco*) pigheaded, stubborn. **3** *fig* (*vino*) heady. – **4** cabezudo, *m* bigheaded dwarf *in a procession*. **5** (*pez*) mullet.
cabezuela 1 *f* (*harina*) second-grade flour. **2** BOT flower head.
cabida 1 *f* capacity, room, space: *el salón tiene cabida para cincuenta personas,* the hall holds fifty people; *aquí no hay cabida para los gandules,* there's no room for idlers here. **2** (*extensión*) area, extension.
● dar cabida a, to leave room for.
cabildada *f fam* abuse of authority.
cabildear *i* to scheme, intrigue.
cabildeo *m* scheming, intriguing.
cabildo 1 *m* (*de iglesia*) chapter. **2** (*ayuntamiento*) town council; (*sala del ayuntamiento*) town hall; (*junta del ayuntamiento*) council meeting.
cabina 1 *f* (*gen*) cabin, booth. **2** (*de barco, avión*) cabin.
■ cabina de proyección, projection room. ‖ cabina telefónica, telephone box, US telephone booth.
cabizbajo,-a *adj* crestfallen.
cable¹ *m* (*maroma*) cable.
● echarle un cable a algn., *fam* to give sb. a hand.
cable² *m* (*cablegrama*) cablegram, cable.
cablegrafiar *t* to cable, send a cable.
▲ Conjugation model |13|, like *desviar*.
cablegrama *m* cablegram, cable.
cablevisión *f* cablevision.
cabo 1 *m* (*extremo*) end, stub. **2** (*parte pequeña*) bit, piece: *un cabo de cuerda,* a bit of string. **3** *fig* end: *al cabo de un mes,* in a month's time; *cambió de residencia al cabo de un mes,* he moved house a month later. **4** (*cuerda*) rope, line. **5** GEOG cape. **6** MIL corporal.
● al cabo, finally. ‖ atar cabos / juntar cabos, *fig* to

put two and two together. ‖ **de cabo a rabo,** from head to tail. ‖ **estar al cabo (de la calle),** *fig* to be in on it, know what's going on. ‖ **llevar a cabo,** to carry out. ‖ **no dejar cabo suelto,** *fig* to leave no loose ends.
■ **Cabo de Buena Esperanza,** Cape of Good Hope. ‖ **Cabo Cañaveral,** Cape Canaveral. ‖ **Cabo de Hornos,** Cape Horn. ‖ **Cabo Verde,** Cape Verde. ‖ **Ciudad del Cabo,** Cape Town.

cabonera *f →* **carbonero,-a.**

cabotaje *m* cabotage, coastal traffic.
■ **barco de cabotaje,** coaster.

caboverdiano,-a 1 *adj* Cape Verdean. – **2** *m,f* Cape Verdean.

cabra *f* goat.
● **estar como una cabra,** *fam* to be off one's rocker, be nuts.
■ **cabra montés,** wild goat, chamois.

cabracho *m* scorpion fish.

cabrahigar *t to hang skewered wild figs on a fig tree in the belief that the tree will produce more fruit.*
▲ *Conjugation model* [25].

cabrahígo *m* (*higuera*) wild fig tree; (*fruto*) wild fig.

cabrales *m type of blue cheese.*
▲ *pl* **cabrales.**

cabré *fut →* **caber.**

cabreado,-a 1 *pp →* **cabrear.** – **2** *adj fam* furious, pissed off.

cabrear 1 *t fam* to annoy, make angry. – **2 cabrearse,** *p fam* to get angry, get worked up.

cabreo *m fam* anger.
● **agarrar un cabreo / coger un cabreo / pillar un cabreo,** *fam* to fly off the handle, hit the roof. ‖ **tener un cabreo / llevar un cabreo,** *fam* to be in a foul mood, be pissed off.

cabrero *m* goatherd.

cabrestante *m* capstan.

cabria *f* gin.

cabrilla 1 *f* (*trípode*) sawhorse. – **2 cabrillas,** *fpl* (*manchas*) scorch marks on the legs. **3** (*pequeñas olas*) white horses, whitecaps.
● **hacer cabrillas,** to play ducks and drakes, skim stones. ‖ **jugar a salta cabrilla,** to play leapfrog.

cabrillear 1 *i* (*formar olas*) to break into white horses. **2** (*rielar*) to glisten.

cabrio *m* joist.

cabrío,-a 1 *adj* caprine, goatish. – **2 cabrío,** *m* (*rebaño*) herd of goats.
■ **macho cabrío,** he-goat, billy goat.

cabriola 1 *f* (*brinco*) caper, skip. **2** (*salto de caballo*) capriole. **3** *fig* (*voltereta*) somersault.

cabriolé *m arc* cabriolet.

cabritilla *f* kid, kidskin.

cabrito 1 *m* ZOOL kid. **2** *arg* (*cabrón*) bugger, bastard. **3** *fig* (*que consiente el adulterio*) cuckold.

cabrón,-ona 1 *m,f tabú* (*hombre*) bastard; (*mujer*) bitch. – **2 cabrón,** *m* ZOOL he-goat, billy goat. **3** *tabú* (*que consiente el adulterio*) cuckold.

cabronada *f tabú* dirty trick.
● **hacer una cabronada a algn.,** *tabú* to do the dirty on sb., play a dirty trick on sb.

cabronazo *m tabú* bastard, fucker.

cabuchón *m* cabochon.

cabujón *m* cabochon.

cabuya *f* agave, pita.

caca 1 *f fam euf* (*excremento*) shit: *¿has hecho caca?,* have you been to the toilet?; *el niño ha hecho caca,* the ba-

by's dirtied his nappy. **2** *fam* (*en lenguaje infantil*) pooh, poopoo: *deja eso que es caca,* leave it, it's dirty. **3** *fig* shit, rubbish: *esa película es una caca,* that film is shitty, that film is rubbish.

cacahual *m* cacao plantation.

cacahuate *m →* **cacahuete.**

cacahuete 1 *m* (*planta*) groundnut. **2** (*fruto*) peanut.

cacahuey *m →* **cacahuete.**

cacao 1 *m* BOT cacao. **2** (*polvo, bebida*) cocoa. **3** *fam* (*jaleo*) mess, cockup.
● **tener un cacao mental,** *fam* to be confused, US be screwed up.

cacaotal *m* cacao plantation.

cacareado,-a 1 *pp →* **cacarear.** – **2** *adj* hackneyed.

cacarear 1 *i* (*gallina*) to cluck; (*gallo*) to crow. – **2** *t fam fig* to crow about, brag about.

cacareo *m* (*de gallina*) clucking; (*de gallo*) crowing. – **2** *mf fam fig* boasting, bragging.

cacatúa 1 *f* (*ave*) cockatoo. **2** *fam fig* (*mujer fea, vieja*) old hag, old bag.

cacera *f* irrigation ditch.

cacereño,-a 1 *adj* of Cáceres, from Cáceres. – **2** *m,f* person from Cáceres, inhabitant of Cáceres.

cacería *f* hunting, hunt.
● **ir de cacería,** to go hunting.

cacerola *f* saucepan, casserole.

cacha 1 *f* (*de una arma*) butt. **2** *fam* thigh. – **3 cachas,** *m fam* (*hombre musculoso*) hunk.
● **estar cachas,** *fam* to be muscly. ‖ **estar metido,-a en algo hasta las cachas,** to be up to one's eyeballs in sth.

cachalote *m* cachalot, sperm whale.

cacharrazo *m fam* blow, punch.

cacharrería *f* pottery shop.

cacharrero,-a *m,f* pottery dealer.

cacharro 1 *m* (*de cocina*) crock, piece of crockery. **2** *fam* (*cosa*) thing, piece of junk: *¿qué es ese cacharro?,* what's that thing over there? **3** *fam pey* (*coche*) banger.

cachava *f* children's game similar to croquet.

cachaza 1 *f* (*lentitud*) slowness, sluggishness. **2** (*flema*) phlegm. **3** (*aguardiente*) rum.

cachazudo,-a 1 *adj* (*lento*) slow, sluggish. **2** (*flemático*) phlegmatic.

cachear *t* to search, frisk.

cachemir 1 *adj* Kashmiri. – **2** *mf* Kashmiri. – **3** cachemir, *m* (*tejido*) cashmere.

Cachemira 1 *f* Kashmir. **2** cachemira, (*tejido*) cashmere.

cacheo *m* searching, frisking.

cachet 1 *m* (*elegancia*) cachet. **2** (*cotización de un artista*) fee.
▲ *pl* **cachets.**

cachetada *f* slap.

cachete 1 *m* (*bofetada*) slap. **2** (*golpe*) blow, punch. **3** (*carrillo*) cheek.

cachetero 1 *m* (*puñal*) dagger. **2** (*en tauromaquia*) person who finishes off the bull with a dagger.

cachicuerno,-a *adj* with a horn handle.

cachifollar *t fam* to squash, flatten.

cachimba *f* pipe.

cachipolla *f* mayfly, ephemera.

cachiporra *f* club, truncheon.

cachiporrazo *m* blow with a club, clubbing.

cachirulo 1 *m* (*en Aragón*) neckerchief. – **2 cachirulos,** *mpl fam* things.

cachivache *m fam* thing, piece of junk, knick-knack.

cacho m *fam* bit, piece.
● ¡cacho de bestia/animal!, you beast! ‖ ser un cacho de pan, to be an angel, be a dear.
cachondearse p *fam* to take the mickey (**de,** out of), make fun (**de,** of): *¿te estás cachondeando de mí?,* are you taking the mickey out of me?
cachondeo 1 m *fam* (*jarana*) messing about. **2** *fam* (*burla*) joke.
● armar cachondeo, *fam* to lark about. ‖ estar de cachondeo, to be joking. ‖ irse de cachondeo, to go out on the town. ‖ tomarse algo a cachondeo, *fam* to treat sth. as a joke.
cachondo,-a 1 *adj* (*excitado*) hot, randy, horny. **2** *fam* funny.
cachorrillo m small pistol.
cachorro,-a m,f (*de perro*) pup, puppy; (*de gato*) kitten; (*de león, oso, zorro, tigre*) cub; (*de otros mamíferos*) young.
cachucha 1 f (*bote*) small rowing boat. **2** (*gorra*) cap.
cacica 1 f (*jefa india*) chief, cacique. **2** POL local political boss.
▲ See also *cacique.*
cacique 1 m (*jefe indio*) chief, cacique. **2** POL local political boss. **3** *fig* (*déspota*) tyrant.
▲ See also *cacica.*
caciquil *adj pey* despotic.
caciquismo 1 m POL caciquism. **2** *fig* (*despotismo*) despotism.
caco m *fam* thief.
cacofonía f cacophony.
cacofónico,-a *adj* cacophonous, cacophonic.
cacosmia f cacosmia.
cacto m cactus.
cactus m cactus.
▲ *pl* cactus.
cacumen m *fam fig* brains *pl.*
cada 1 *adj* (*de dos*) each; (*de varios*) every: *cada uno lleva su abrigo,* they're each wearing their coat, each of them is wearing his coat; *cada cuatro días,* every four days; *ocho de cada diez,* eight out of (every) ten. **2** *fam* (*intensificador*) such: *¡dice cada cosa!,* he says such strange things!; *¡le pegó cada grito!,* she really shouted at him!
● a cada cual lo suyo, (*recibir*) everyone should get their fair share; (*pagar*) everyone should pay their own way. ‖ a cada paso, at every step. ‖ ¿cada cuánto?, how often?: *¿cada cuánto vais al cine?,* how often do you go to the cinema? ‖ cada día, every day. ‖ cada vez más, more and more, increasingly: *es cada vez más difícil de entender,* it's more and more difficult to understand.
cadalso 1 m (*patíbulo*) scaffold. **2** (*plataforma*) platform.
cadáver 1 m (*de persona*) corpse, cadaver, body, dead body. **2** (*de animal*) body, carcass.
cadavérico,-a 1 *adj* cadaverous. **2** *fig* deathly pale, cadaverous.
cadena 1 f (*gen*) chain; (*de perro*) leash, lead. **2** (*grupo de empresas*) chain: *una cadena de hoteles,* a chain of hotels. **3** (*industrial*) line. **4** (*montañosa*) range. **5** (*musical*) music centre (US center). **6** TV channel. **7** RAD chain of stations. **8** *fig* (*serie*) series, sequence: *una cadena de acontecimientos,* a series of events. – **9** cadenas, *fpl* AUTO tyre (US tire) chains.
● tirar de la cadena (del wáter), to flush the toilet. ‖ trabajar en cadena, to work on the production line. ■ cadena de fabricación, production line. ‖ cadena de montaje, assembly line. ‖ cadena montañosa, mountain range. ‖ cadena perpetua, life imprison-

ment. ‖ reacción en cadena, chain reaction. ‖ trabajo en cadena, assembly-line work.
cadencia 1 f cadence, rhythm. **2** MÚS cadenza.
cadencioso,-a 1 *adj* rhythmic, rhythmical. **2** *fig* measured, even.
cadeneta 1 f (*labor de punto*) chain stitch. **2** (*de libro*) headband. **3** (*tira de papel de colores*) paper chain.
cadenilla f small chain.
cadera f hip.
● con las manos en las caderas, hands on hips.
cadete m cadet.
cadi mf DEP caddie.
cadí m (*juez musulmán*) cadi.
cadmio m cadmium.
caducado,-a *adj* out of date, no longer valid.
caducar 1 i (*documento etc*) to expire: *mi pasaporte caduca este año,* my passport expires this year. **2** (*alimento*) to expire: *caduca a los dos meses,* use within two months of purchase. **3** (*período de tiempo*) to run out, lapse: *el plazo para recoger los premios caduca en una semana,* the period in which prizes may be collected lapses in a week.
▲ Conjugation model [1], *like* sacar.
caduceo m caduceus.
caducidad f expiry: *la fecha de caducidad del plazo,* the closing date; *la fecha de caducidad del yogur,* the sell-by date of the yoghurt; *la fecha de caducidad del carné,* the licence expiry date.
caduco,-a 1 *adj* (*pasado*) past its sell-by date, out-of-date. **2** JUR expired, lapsed. **3** (*decrépito*) decrepit, senile. **4** BOT deciduous.
caer 1 i (*gen*) to fall: *caer de espalda,* to fall on one's back; *caer de rodillas,* to fall on one's knees. **2** (*derrumbar*) to fall down, collapse: *cayó el edificio,* the building collapsed. **3** (*hallarse*) to be: *el camino cae a la derecha,* the road is on the right; *cae por allá abajo,* it's somewhere down there. **4** (*coincidir fechas*) to fall on, be: *el día cuatro cae en jueves,* the fourth falls on a Thursday. **5** (*premio*) to go (**en,** to): *el premio cayó en Oviedo,* the prize went to Oviedo. **6** *fam* (*entender*) to understand, get it: *ya caigo,* I see, I get it; *no caigo,* I don't get it. **7** (*perder posición*) to fall: *el ministro cayó,* the minister fell. **8** MIL (*rendirse*) to surrender; (*morir*) to fall, die. **9** (*el sol*) to set; (*el día*) to draw in; (*el viento*) to drop. **10** COST (*descolgar*) to dip: *el vestido cae de un lado,* your dress dips at one side. – **11** caerse, p (*gen*) to fall, fall down: *se cayó por las escaleras,* he fell down the stairs; *se ha caído algo,* you've dropped something. **12** (*desprenderse*) to fall out: *se le cae el pelo,* he's losing his hair; *el cuadro se cayó de la pared,* the picture fell off the wall.
● al caer el día, in the evening. ‖ al caer la noche, at nightfall. ‖ caer bien, (*sentar*) to agree; (*prenda*) to suit; (*persona*) to like: *no me cae bien la nata,* cream doesn't agree with me; *ese vestido te cae muy bien,* that dress really suits you; *cae bien a todo el mundo,* everyone likes her. ‖ caer mal, (*sentar*) not to agree with; (*prenda*) not to suit; (*persona*) not to like: *Juan me cae mal,* I don't like Juan. ‖ caer en cama, *fig* to fall ill. ‖ caer en la cuenta de, to realize. ‖ caer en la tentación, *fig* to give in to temptation. ‖ caer en manos de, *fig* to fall into the hands of. ‖ caer en un error, *fig* to make a mistake. ‖ caer sobre, to throw os. on. ‖ caerse a pedazos, *fig* to fall to pieces. ‖ caerse de sueño, *fig* to be dead on one's feet, be ready to drop. ‖ caerse de viejo,-a, *fig* to be falling apart with age. ‖ caerse redondo,-a, *fig* to collapse. ‖ dejar caer, to drop: *dejé*

caer el vaso, I dropped the glass. ‖ **dejarse caer por,** *fig* to drop by, come round: *déjate caer por casa,* come round and see us. ‖ **estar al caer,** (*llegar*) to be about to arrive; (*ocurrir*) to be on the way: *Elena está al caer,* Elena will be here any minute. ‖ **no tener dónde caerse muerto,-a,** *fam* to have nothing to one's name.

▲ *Conjugation model* |67].

café 1 *m* (*gen*) coffee: *¿te apetece un café?,* do you fancy a coffee?, do you fancy a cup of coffee? **2** (*cafetería*) café, coffee bar, coffee shop.

■ **café americano,** large black coffee. ‖ **café con leche,** white coffee. ‖ **café molido,** ground coffee. ‖ **café solo,** black coffee. ‖ **café soluble,** instant coffee. ‖ **café torrefacto,** high-roast coffee. ‖ **grano de café,** coffee bean.

cafeína *f* caffeine.

cafetal *m* coffee plantation.

cafetera *f* → **cafetero,-a**.

cafetería *f* snack bar, coffee bar; (*en un tren*) buffet car.

cafetero,-a 1 *adj* coffee. **2** *fam* (*persona*) coffee-loving: *Elena es muy cafetera,* Elena loves coffee. – **3** *cafetera, f* (*para hacer café*) coffee-maker. **4** (*para servir café*) coffeepot. **5** *fam* (*coche viejo*) old banger, old crock.

● **estar como una cafetera,** *fam* to be barmy, be nuts. ■ **cafetera exprés,** expresso-coffee machine.

cafeto *m* coffee.

cáfila 1 *f* (*personas*) crowd. **2** (*animals*) herd, flock.

cafre 1 *adj fig* (*bárbaro*) brutal, barbarous. **2** *fig* (*rústico*) rough, coarse. – **3** *mf fig* (*bárbaro*) savage, beast. **4** *fig* (*rústico*) rough person.

caftán *m* caftan, kaftan.

cagada *f tabú* → **cagado,-a**.

cagado,-a 1 *pp* → **cagar**. – **2** *adj fam fig* (*cobarde*) coward. – **3** *m,f fam fig* chicken. – **4** **cagada,** *f tabú* (*mierda*) shit, crap. **5** *tabú fig* (*equivocación*) fuck-up, cockup.

● **estar cagado,-a (de miedo),** *fam* to be shit-scared.

cagafierro *m* slag.

cagajón *m* dung.

cagalera *f fam* (*diarrea*) the runs *pl*.

● **tener cagalera,** *fam* (*diarrea*) to have the runs; (*miedo*) to be shit-scared.

cagar 1 *i tabú* to shit. – **2** *t tabú* to shit. – **3** *i tabú* (*echar a perder*) to ruin, spoil, mess up, muck up, cock up: *¡ya la has cagado!,* you've really cocked it up now! – **4** **cagarse,** *p tabú* to shit os. **5** *tabú fig* (*acobardarse*) to be shit-scared.

● **cagarse de miedo,** *tabú* to be shit-scared. ‖ *¡me cago en diez!,* *tabú* damn it! ‖ *¡me cago en la leche!,* *tabú* fuck! ‖ *¡me cago en la mar!,* *tabú* damn it!

▲ *Conjugation model* |7], like **llegar**.

cagarruta 1 *f* (*excremento*) sheep dirt, goat dirt. **2** *fig* (*hombre insignificante*) little shit.

cagón,-ona 1 *adj fam* loose-bowelled (us loose-boweled): *es muy cagón,* he's always going to the toilet. **2** *fam fig* (*cobarde*) wet, wimpy, weedy. – **3** *m,f fam* loose-bowelled (us loose-boweled) person: *mi hijo es un cagón,* my little boy is always dirtying his nappy. **4** *fam fig* (*cobarde*) chicken, wimp, weed.

cagueta *mf fam* chicken, coward.

▲ *Also used in plural with the same meaning.*

caída *f* → **caído,-a**.

caído,-a 1 *pp* → **caer**. – **2** *adj* (*gen*) fallen. **3** (*hombros*) sloping. **4** *fig* (*desanimado*) downhearted, crestfallen. – **5** **caída,** *f* (*acción de caer*) fall, falling. **6** (*pérdida*) loss: *la caída del cabello,* hair loss. **7** (*de precios, temperatura*) fall, drop: *ha habido una fuerte caída de ventas,* sales have

fallen sharply. **8** (*de un terreno*) slope. **9** (*del sol*) setting. **10** (*de tejidos*) body, hang: *una tela con mucha caída,* a material with a lot of body. **11** COST (*ancho*) width; (*largo*) length. **12** *fig* downfall, fall: *la caída del Imperio,* the fall of the Empire. – **13** **los caídos,** *mpl* the fallen.

● **a la caída del sol,** at sunset. ‖ **caído,-a de hombros,** with sloping shoulders. ‖ **caído,-a del cielo,** *fig* out of the blue.

■ **caída de ojos,** demure look. ‖ **caída libre,** free fall.

caigo *pres indic* → **caer**.

caimán *m* alligator, caiman, cayman.

Caín *m* Cain.

● **pasar las de Caín,** *fam* to go through hell.

cairel 1 *m* (*postizo*) wig. **2** (*pasamanería*) fringe.

Cairo el Cairo, *m* Cairo.

caja 1 *f* (*gen*) box. **2** (*de madera*) chest; (*grande*) crate. **3** (*de bebidas*) case. **4** (*en comercio*) cash desk, till; (*en banco*) cashier's desk; (*en supermarcado*) checkout: *robaron la caja,* they robbed the till. **5** (*féretro*) coffin. **6** AUTO body. **7** (*tipografía*) case. **8** (*banco*) bank: *caja de ahorros,* savings bank. **9** TÉC housing, casing. **10** (*de piano*) case; (*de violín*) body.

● **echar a algn. con cajas destempladas,** *fam* to send sb. packing. ‖ **entrar en caja,** MIL to be called up. ‖ **hacer (la) caja,** to cash up. ‖ **pagar en caja,** to pay at the cash desk.

■ **caja alta/baja,** (*en impresión*) upper/lower case. ‖ **caja craneana,** ANAT cranium, skull. ‖ **caja de cambios,** AUTO gearbox. ‖ **caja de caudales,** strongbox, safe. ‖ **caja de colores,** paintbox. ‖ **caja de empalmes,** ELEC junction box. ‖ **caja de herramientas,** toolbox. ‖ **caja de música,** musical box. ‖ **caja fuerte,** safe. ‖ **caja negra,** AV black box. ‖ **caja postal de ahorros,** post office savings bank. ‖ **caja registradora,** cash register. ‖ **la caja tonta,** *fam* the goggle-box.

cajero,-a *m,f* cashier.

■ **cajero automático,** cash point, automatic cash dispenser.

cajetilla 1 *f* (*de tabaco*) packet, us pack. **2** (*de cerillas*) box.

cajista *mf* typesetter.

cajón 1 *m* (*en mueble*) drawer. **2** (*caja grande*) crate. **3** (*casilla*) stall. **4** (*entre estantes*) shelf space.

● **ser de cajón,** *fam* to be self-evident, be obvious.

■ **cajón de sastre,** *fig* jumble.

cake *m* fruit cake.

cal¹ *f* lime.

● **cerrar a cal y canto,** (*puerta etc*) to shut tight; (*joyas etc*) to lock away. ‖ **de cal y canto,** *fig* strong, tough. ‖ **una de cal y otra de arena,** *fam* six of one and half a dozen of the other.

■ **cal apagada / cal muerta,** slaked lime. ‖ **cal viva,** quicklime.

cal² *abr* (*caloría*) calorie; (*abreviatura*) cal.

cala¹ 1 *f* (*exploración*) test boring. **2** (*pedazo de una fruta*) slice, sample. **3** (*de un buque*) hold. **4** (*supositorio*) suppository. **5** *fam* peseta.

cala² 1 *f* (*ensenada*) cove, creek. **2** (*paraje para pescar*) fishing ground.

cala³ *f* (*planta*) arum lily.

calabacín 1 *m* (*pequeño*) courgette, us zucchini. **2** (*grande*) marrow, us squash.

calabaza 1 *f* gourd, pumpkin. **2** *fig* (*cabeza humana*) hard nut, bonce. **3** *fam* (*persona*) plonker.

● **dar calabazas a algn.,** *fam* (*suspender un examen*) to fail sb.; (*rechazar un pretendiente*) to turn sb. down, send sb. packing.

calabazada f (golpe) blow on the head.
calabazar m gourd field, pumpkin field.
calabobos m drizzle.
▲ pl calabobos.
calabozo 1 m (prisión) jail, prison. 2 (celda) cell.
calabrote m hawser, warp.
calada f fam (de cigarrillo) drag, puff; (de porro) hit, toke.
caladero m fishing ground.
calado,-a 1 pp → calar. – 2 adj fam soaked. – 3 calado, m (de un barco) draught (us draft). 4 (del agua sobre el fondo) depth. 5 cost openwork, embroidery.
● estar calado,-a hasta los huesos, to be soaked to the skin.
calafate m caulker.
calafatear t to caulk.
calamar m squid.
■ calamares a la romana, squid fried in batter.
calambre 1 m (contracción) cramp: le dio un calambre en la pantorrilla, she got a cramp in her calf muscle. 2 (descarga eléctrica) electric shock.
calamidad 1 f (desgracia) calamity, disaster. 2 fig (persona) dead loss, good-for-nothing.
● ser una calamidad / estar hecho,-a una calamidad, fam to look a sight.
calamitoso,-a adj calamitous, disastrous.
cálamo 1 m (tallo) reed, stalk. 2 (flauta) reed pipe. 3 (eje de pluma) quill, calamus.
calamón m (ave) sultana bird.
calamorra f fam head, nut.
calandrado m calendering.
calandrar t to calender.
calandria[1] 1 f (ave) calandra lark. – 2 mf (persona que se finge enferma) malingerer.
calandria[2] 1 f (máquina para satinar) calender. 2 (máquina para levantar pesos) treadmill.
calaña 1 f (muestra, patrón) sample, pattern. 2 fig (calidad, naturaleza) nature, disposition. 3 pey kind, type, sort: esos hombres son de la misma calaña, those men are all the same type.
calar[1] 1 adj calcareous. – 2 m limestone quarry.
calar[2] 1 t (mojar) to soak through, soak, drench: el agua caló el jersey, the water soaked through the jumper. 2 (agujerear) to go through, pierce, puncture. 3 (el sombrero) to jam on. 4 cost to do openwork. 5 téc to do fretwork on. 6 (la bayoneta) to fix. 7 (las velas) to strike; (las redes) to lower. 8 fig (penetrar) to have an effect on: lo que vimos caló hondo en nosotros, what we saw affected us deeply. 9 fam to rumble, find out: ¡te han calado!, they have got your number! – 10 i mar to draw. – 11 calarse, p (mojarse) to get soaked. 12 (sombrero) to pull down. 13 auto to stop, stall.
calavera 1 f (cabeza del esqueleto) skull. – 2 m fig (hombre) madcap, tearaway, reckless fellow.
calaverada f reckless escapade, madcap escapade.
calcado,-a 1 pp → calcar. – 2 calcado, m tracing.
● ser calcado,-a a algn., fig to be the spitting image of sb.
calcáneo m calcaneus.
calcañal m heel.
calcañar m heel.
calcaño m heel.
calcar 1 t to trace. 2 fig (imitar) to copy, imitate.
▲ Conjugation model [1], like sacar.
calcáreo,-a adj calcareous.
calce 1 m (llanta) rim. 2 (cuña) wedge.

calcedonia f chalcedony.
calcés m masthead.
▲ pl calceses.
calceta 1 f (prenda) stocking. 2 (punto) knitting.
● hacer calceta, to knit.
calcetín m sock.
calcetón m long heavy sock.
cálcico,-a adj calcium, calcic.
calcificación f calcification.
calcificar 1 t to calcify. – 2 calcificarse, p to calcify.
▲ Conjugation model [1], like sacar.
calcina f concrete.
calcinación f calcination.
calcinamiento m calcination.
calcinar 1 t to calcine. 2 fig to burn. – 3 calcinarse, p to calcinate.
calcio m calcium.
calcita f calcite.
calco 1 m (de dibujo) tracing. 2 (copia) copy. 3 fig (imitación) imitation, copy.
calcografía f chalcography.
calcomanía f transfer.
calcopirita f chalcopyrite.
calculable adj calculable.
calculador,-ra 1 adj calculating. – 2 m,f calculator.
■ calculadora de bolsillo, pocket calculator.
calcular 1 t to calculate, work out: calcular una suma, to calculate a figure. 2 (evaluar) to estimate, calculate: calcular los daños, to estimate the damage. 3 (suponer) to think, suppose, figure, guess: calculo que vendrá mañana, I suppose she'll come tomorrow.
● calculando por lo bajo, at the lowest estimate.
cálculo 1 m calculation, estimate. 2 (conjetura) conjecture, reckoning: según sus cálculos, by her reckoning. 3 mat calculus. 4 med gallstone. – 5 cálculos, mpl med gallstones.
■ cálculo biliar, med bile stone. ‖ cálculo mental, mat mental arithmetic. ‖ regla de cálculo, slide rule.
Calcuta f Calcutta.
caldas fpl thermal springs.
caldeamiento m heating, warming.
caldear 1 t (calentar) to warm, heat. 2 fig (excitar) to heat up, warm up. – 3 caldearse, p (calentarse) to get warm, become hot. 4 fig (excitarse) to warm up.
caldeo,-a 1 adj Chaldean. – 2 m,f Chaldean.
caldera 1 f boiler. 2 (caldero) cauldron.
■ las calderas de Pedro Botero, fam fig hell.
calderada 1 f boilerful. 2 (de caldero) cauldronful.
calderería 1 f (oficio) boilermaking. 2 (tienda) boilermaker's shop.
calderero,-a m,f boilermaker.
caldereta 1 f (pequeña caldera) small boiler, small cauldron. 2 (guisado de pescado) fish stew. 3 (guisado de cordero) lamb stew.
calderilla f small change.
caldero 1 m (caldera) small cauldron. 2 (contenido) cauldronful.
calderón 1 m (en imprenta) paragraph mark. 2 mús pause.
caldo 1 m culin stock, broth. 2 (sopa) consommé. – 3 caldos, mpl (vinos) wines.
● gallina vieja hace buen caldo, fig there's many a good tune played on an old fiddle.
■ caldo de carne, beef tea. ‖ caldo de cultivo, biol culture medium; fig breeding ground. ‖ caldo de gallina, chicken stock. ‖ caldo de pescado, fish stock.

caldoso,-a *adj* runny, watery.
calé 1 *adj* gypsy. – **2** *mf* gypsy.
calefacción *f* heating.
■ calefacción central, central heating.
calefactor 1 *m* (*persona*) heating engineer. **2** (*máquina*) heater.
caleidoscópico,-a *adj* kaleidoscopic.
caleidoscopio *m* kaleidoscope.
calendario *m* calendar.
■ calendario académico, school year.
calendas *fpl* calends, kalends.
caléndula *f* calendula.
calentador,-ra 1 *adj* heating. – **2 calentador**, *m* heater.
■ calentador de agua, water heater.
calentamiento 1 *m* heating. **2** DEP warming-up.
■ ejercicios de calentamiento, warm-up exercises.
calentar 1 *t* (*comida, habitación, cuerpo*) to warm up; (*agua, horno*) to heat. **2** DEP to warm up, tone up. **3** *fig* (*exaltar*) to heat up, inflame: *calentar el ambiente*, to heat up the atmosphere. **4** *fig* (*irritar*) to annoy. **5** *fam* (*excitar sexualmente*) to arouse, turn on. **6** *fam* (*pegar*) to tan, warm. – **7 calentarse**, *p* to get hot, get warm. **8** *fig* (*enfadarse*) to get heated, get annoyed. **9** *fig* (*exaltarse*) to get excited. **10** *fam* (*excitarse sexualmente*) to get horny, get randy.
● calentar el asiento, *fig* to warm the chair. ‖ calentarse los sesos / calentarse los cascos, *fig* to get hot under the collar.
▲ *Conjugation model* [27], *like* **acertar**.
calentón,-ona 1 *adj fam* horny, randy. – **2** *m,f fam* randy person.
calentorro,-a *adj-m,f* → **calentón,-ona**.
calentura *f* fever, temperature: *tiene calentura*, she has a fever.
calenturiento,-a *adj* feverish.
■ mente calenturienta, (*exaltada*) hothead; (*excitada*) dirty mind.
caleño,-a 1 *adj* of Cali, from Cali. – **2** *m,f* person from Cali, inhabitant of Cali.
calera *f* → **calero,-a**.
calero,-a 1 *adj* limestone. – **2** *m,f* lime burner. – **3 calera**, *f* (*cantera*) limestone quarry. **4** (*horno*) lime kiln.
calesa *f arc* calash, calèche.
calesera 1 *f* (*prenda*) type of bolero jacket. **2** (*canción*) Andalusian song.
caletre *m fam* common sense.
calibrado *m* boring, gauging (US gaging).
calibrador 1 *m* (*instrumento para calibrar*) gauge (US gage), callipers *pl* (US calipers). **2** (*tubo*) bore.
■ calibrador micrométrico, vernier gauge, calliper rule.
calibrar 1 *t* (*graduar*) to calibrate. **2** (*medir*) to gauge (US gage), gage, bore. **3** *fig* (*estudiar*) to gauge (US gage), weigh up, judge.
calibre 1 *m* (*de arma*) calibre. **2** TÉC bore, gauge (US gage). **3** *fig* (*importancia*) importance.
calicanto *m* stonework, masonry.
calicata *f* bore.
caliche 1 *m* (*costrilla de cal*) flake. **2** (*maca en una fruta*) bruise.
calidad 1 *f* quality: *vino de calidad*, good-quality wine; *carne de mala calidad*, poor-quality meat. **2** (*cualidad*) kind, types: *distintas calidades de papel*, different types of paper. **3** (*condición*) rank, capacity: *en calidad de ministro*, as a Minister.

● de calidad superior, superior. ‖ de primera calidad, first-class.
■ calidad de vida, quality of life. ‖ control de calidad, quality control.
cálido,-a *adj* warm: *un clima cálido*, a warm climate.
calidoscópico,-a *adj* kaleidoscopic.
calidoscopio *m* kaleidoscope.
calientabraguetas *f tabú* prick teaser.
▲ *pl calientabraguetas*.
calientapiés *m* foot warmer.
▲ *pl calientapiés*.
calientaplatos *m* hotplate.
▲ *pl calientaplatos*.
caliente 1 *adj* (*mayor intensidad*) hot; (*menor intensidad*) warm. **2** *fig* (*acalorado*) heated, spirited. **3** *fam fig* (*lujurioso*) hot, randy.
● en caliente, (*ahora*) right now; (*entonces*) there and then: *lo haré ahora en caliente, antes de que se me olvide*, I'll do it now, while it's still fresh in my mind.
califa *m* caliph.
califato *m* caliphate.
calificable *adj* qualifiable.
calificación 1 *f* (*gen*) qualification. **2** (*nota*) mark.
■ libro de calificaciones, school report.
calificado,-a 1 *pp* → **calificar**. – **2** *adj* (*con los requisitos necesarios*) qualified. **3** (*de autoridad, mérito*) eminent, well-known. **4** (*trabajador*) skilled.
calificador,-ra *adj* examining.
calificar 1 *t* (*determinar las cualidades*) to describe, qualify: *calificaron la película de aburrida*, they described the film as boring. **2** EDUC to mark, grade. **3** (*llamar*) to call: *lo calificó de idiota*, he called him an idiot. **4** LING to qualify. – **5 calificarse**, *p* (*probar su nobleza*) to give proof of nobility.
▲ *Conjugation model* [1], *like* **sacar**.
calificativo,-a 1 *adj* GRAM qualifying: *adjetivo calificativo*, qualifying adjective. – **2 calificativo**, *m* epithet. **3** GRAM qualifier.
California *f* California.
californiano,-a 1 *adj* Californian. – **2** *m,f* Californian.
calígine 1 *f lit* (*oscuridad*) darkness. **2** *lit* (*bochorno*) stifling heat.
caligrafía 1 *f* (*arte*) calligraphy. **2** (*escritura de una persona*) handwriting.
■ ejercicios de caligrafía, handwriting exercises.
caligrafiar *t* to calligraph.
▲ *Conjugation model* [13], *like* **desviar**.
caligráfico,-a *adj* calligraphic.
calígrafo,-a *adj* calligrapher.
calima *f* haze, mist.
calimocho *m fam* drink made with wine and Coca-Cola.
calimoso,-a *adj* hazy, misty.
calina *f* haze, mist.
calinoso,-a *adj* hazy, misty.
caliqueño *m* cheap cigar.
calistenia *f* callisthenics.
cáliz 1 *m* REL chalice. **2** BOT calyx. **3** *lit* (*copa*) cup.
caliza *f* → **calizo,-a**.
calizo,-a 1 *adj* lime. – **2 caliza**, *f* limestone.
callada *f* → **callado,-a**.
calladamente *adv* silently.
callado,-a 1 *pp* → **callar**. – **2** *adj* (*silencioso*) silent, quiet. **3** (*reservado*) reserved, quiet. – **4 callada**, *f* silence.
● dar la callada por respuesta, to say nothing in reply, ignore the other person's request. ‖ más callado,-

a que un muerto, *fam* as quiet as a mouse. ‖ tener algo callado, to keep sth. quiet: *¡eso lo tenías bien callado!,* you really kept that one quiet!

callandito 1 *adv fam (en silencio)* quietly, silently. **2** *fam (con sigilo)* on the quiet, on the sly.

callando *adv* → **callandito**.

callar 1 *i (no hablar)* to be quiet, keep quiet: *calló porque no quería pelearse,* she kept quiet because she didn't want to quarrel. **2** *(dejar de hablar)* to stop talking, shut up: *cuando calló todos aplaudieron,* when he stopped talking everybody clapped; *¡quieres callar!,* will you shut up! **3** *(un ruido)* to stop. – **4** *t (esconder)* to keep to os., not mention: *él calló su opinión,* he kept his opinion to himself.

● a la chita callando, *fam* on the quiet, on the sly. ‖ ¡calla!, *fig* never!, no! ‖ ¡cállate!, keep quiet!, be quiet! ‖ quien calla otorga, silence gives consent.

calle 1 *f* street, road. **2** DEP lane.

● dejar a algn. en la calle, *(sin trabajo)* to fire sb.; *(sin casa)* to leave sb. homeless. ‖ doblar la calle, to turn the corner. ‖ echar a algn. de patitas en la calle, to throw sb. out, kick sb. out. ‖ echar/tirar por la calle de en medio, *fig* to go ahead regardless/take the middle course. ‖ hacer la calle, *(prostituta)* to walk the streets. ‖ llevar a algn. por la calle de la amargura, to give sb. a tough time. ‖ quedarse en la calle, *(sin trabajo)* to be left jobless; *(sin casa)* to be homeless.

calleja *f* narrow street.

callejear *i* to wander (about) the streets.

callejeo *m* wandering about.

callejero,-a 1 *adj (que gusta de callejear)* fond of wandering about. **2** *(relativo a la calle)* street, in the street: *fiesta callejera,* street party; *motín callejero,* street riot. – **3** callejero, *m (de calles)* street directory; *(de teléfonos)* telephone directory *classified by streets.*

callejón *m* back street, back alley.

● en un callejón sin salida, *fig* at an impasse, deadlocked. ■ callejón sin salida, cul-de-sac, dead end, blind alley.

callejuela *f* narrow street, lane.

callicida *mf* corn remover.

callista *mf* chiropodist.

callo 1 *m* MED callus, corn. **2** *fam (persona fea)* ugly sight. – **3** callos, *mpl* CULIN tripe *sing.*

callosidad *f* callosity, callus.

calloso,-a *adj* callous.

calma 1 *f* calmness, calm, tranquillity (US tranquility). **2** COM slack period, lull. **3** *fam (cachaza)* slowness, phlegm: *tiene mucha calma,* she's very calm. **4** *(tiempo)* calm weather.

● estar en calma, to be calm. ‖ perder la calma, to lose one's patience. ‖ tomárselo con calma, to take it easy.

■ calma chicha, dead calm.

calmante 1 *adj* soothing, sedative, tranquillizing (US tranquilizing). – **2** *m* sedative, tranquillizer (US tranquilizer).

calmar 1 *t (persona)* to calm (down). **2** *(dolor)* to relieve, soothe. – **3** *i (estar en calma)* to fall calm. – **4** calmarse, *p (persona)* to calm down. **5** *(dolor etc)* to abate, ease off.

calmo,-a *adj* uncultivated.

calmoso,-a 1 *adj (tranquilo)* calm, quiet. **2** *(flemático)* phlegmatic. **3** *(lento)* slow, sluggish.

caló *m* gypsy language.

▲ *pl* caló.

calor 1 *m* heat, warmth: *hace calor,* it is hot; *tengo calor,* I'm hot. **2** *fig (actividad)* heat: *en el calor del debate,* in the heat of the debate. **3** *fig (afecto)* warmth.

● al calor de, *fig* under the wing of: *fue criado al calor de sus abuelos,* he was brought up under his grandparents' wing. ‖ entrar en calor, to get warm; DEP to warm up.

■ calor natural, natural heat. ‖ el calor del hogar, *fig* the warmth of home.

caloría *f* calorie, calory.

calórico,-a *adj* caloric, calorific.

calorífero,-a 1 *adj* heat-producing. – **2** calorífero, *m* heater, radiator.

calorífico,-a *adj* calorific.

calorífugo,-a 1 *adj (que no transmite el calor)* heat-resistant. **2** *(incombustible)* uninflammable.

calorimetría *f* calorimetry.

calorímetro *m* calorimeter.

calostro *m* colostrum.

calta *f* marsh marigold.

calumnia 1 *f* calumny. **2** JUR slander.

calumniador,-ra 1 *adj* calumnious, calumniatory. **2** JUR slanderous. – **3** *m,f* calumniator. **4** JUR slanderer.

calumniar 1 *t* to calumniate. **2** JUR to slander.

▲ *Conjugation model* |12|, *like* cambiar.

calumnioso,-a *adj* calumnious, slanderous.

calurosamente *adv* warmly: *nos recibió calurosamente,* we were warmly received.

caluroso,-a 1 *adj (tiempo)* warm, hot. **2** *fig* warm, enthusiastic: *nos dieron una bienvenida calurosa,* we were given a warm welcome.

calva *f* → **calvo,-a**.

calvados *m* Calvados.

calvario 1 *m* Calvary. **2** *(Vía Crucis)* stations *pl* of the Cross. **3** *fig (sufrimiento)* ordeal, calvary.

calvero 1 *m (de un bosque)* clearing. **2** *(gredal)* claypit.

calvez *f* baldness.

calvicie *f* baldness.

calvinismo *m* Calvinism.

calvinista 1 *adj* Calvinist. – **2** *mf* Calvinist.

calvo,-a 1 *adj (persona)* bald. **2** *(terreno)* bare, barren. – **3** *m,f* bald person. – **4** calva, *f (de la cabeza)* bald patch. **5** *(de un bosque)* clearing.

calza 1 *f (prenda de vestir)* breeches *pl.* **2** *(cuña)* wedge, scotch. **3** *fam (media)* stocking.

▲ *In 1 and 3, also used in plural with the same meaning.*

calzada *f* → **calzado,-a**.

calzado,-a 1 *pp* → **calzar**. – **2** *adj* wearing shoes, with shoes on: *iba calzado para la lluvia,* he was wearing the right shoes for rain. **3** REL calced. – **4** calzado, *m* footwear, shoes *pl.* – **5** calzada, *f* road, roadway, US pavement.

■ industria del calzado, footwear industry. ‖ tienda de calzado, shoe shop.

calzador *m* shoehorn.

calzar 1 *t (poner calzado)* to put shoes on: *tienes que calzar al niño,* you have to put the child's shoes on. **2** *(llevar calzado)* to wear: *calza botas,* she wears boots; *¿qué número calzas?,* what size do you take?; *calzo el 40,* I take size 40. **3** *(hacer zapatos)* to make shoes: *aquel zapatero me calza,* that shoemaker makes my shoes. **4** *(poner una cuña)* to wedge, scotch. **5** *(colocar los neumáticos)* to put tyres (US tires) on. – **6** calzarse, *p (forma reflexiva)* to put (one's) shoes on: *me calcé y me fui,* I put my shoes on and left.

▲ *Conjugation model* [4], *like* realizar.

calzo 1 *m* (*calce*) wedge, scotch. – **2 calzos,** *mpl* (*de caballo*) stockings.
calzón *m desus* trousers *pl.*
calzonazos *m fam* henpecked husband.
▲ *pl* calzonazos.
calzoncillos *mpl* underpants, pants, briefs.
cama 1 *f* (*gen*) bed. **2** *fig* (*de animales*) lair.
● **estar en cama,** to be confined to bed, stay in bed. ‖ **guardar cama,** to be confined to bed, stay in bed. ‖ **hacer cama,** to be confined to bed, stay in bed. ‖ **hacer la cama,** to make the bed. ‖ **irse a la cama,** to go to bed. ‖ **llevarse a algn. a la cama,** *fam* to get sb. into bed. ‖ **meterse en la cama,** (*acostarse*) to go to bed; (*meterse dentro*) to get into bed.
■ **cama de matrimonio,** double bed. ‖ **cama doble,** double bed. ‖ **cama elástica,** trampoline. ‖ **cama individual,** single bed. ‖ **cama turca,** divan, couch.
camachuelo *m* bullfinch.
camada 1 *f* (*gen*) litter; (*de pájaros*) brood. **2** (*capa -gen*) layer; (- *de ladrillos*) course: *tres camadas de manzanas,* three layers of apples. **3** *fig* (*banda*) gang, band.
camafeo *m* cameo.
camal *m* (*cabestro*) halter.
camaleón *m* chameleon.
camaleónico,-a *adj fig* chameleon-like.
camama *f fam* lie, trick.
camándula 1 *f* (*rosario*) rosary. **2** *fig* (*marrullería*) trick.
camandulero,-a 1 *adj fam* hypocritical. – **2** *m,f fam* hypocrite.
cámara 1 *f* (*sala, pieza*) chamber, room. **2** (*institución*) chamber. **3** (*para el grano*) granary. **4** POL house. **5** (*de rueda*) inner tube. **6** MÚS chamber. **7** TÉC chamber. **8** CINEM TV camera. **9** ANAT cavity. – **10** *mf* (*hombre*) cameraman; (*mujer*) camerawoman. – **11 cámaras,** *fpl* (*diarrea*) diarrhoea *sing* (US diarrhea).
● **a cámara lenta,** in slow motion.
■ **cámara acorazada,** strongroom. ‖ **cámara alta,** POL upper house. ‖ **cámara baja,** POL lower house. ‖ **cámara de aire,** air chamber. ‖ **cámara de cine,** cinecamera, (US movie camera). ‖ **cámara de comercio,** chamber of commerce. ‖ **cámara de gas,** gas chamber. ‖ **Cámara de los Comunes,** House of Commons. ‖ **Cámara de los Diputados,** Chamber of Deputies. ‖ **Cámara de los Lores,** House of Lords. ‖ **cámara fotográfica,** camera. ‖ **cámara frigorífica,** cold-storage room. ‖ **cámara mortuoria,** funeral chamber. ‖ **cámara nupcial,** bridal suite. ‖ **música de cámara,** chamber music.
camarada 1 *mf* (*de trabajo*) colleague, fellow worker, workmate; (*de colegio*) schoolmate, schoolfellow. **2** POL comrade.
camaradería 1 *f* (*gen*) companionship, friendship, camaraderie. **2** POL comradeship.
camarera *f* → **camarero,-a**.
camarero,-a 1 *m,f* (*de bar, restaurante - hombre*) waiter; (*mujer*) waitress. **2** (*detrás de la barra - hombre*) barman; (*mujer*) barmaid. **3** (*en barco, avión - hombre*) steward; (*mujer*) stewardess. – **4 camarera,** *f* (*de hotel*) chambermaid. **5** (*sirvienta*) maid, servant. **6** (*de una reina*) lady-in-waiting.
camareta *f* deck cabin.
camarilla 1 *f* clique. **2** POL pressure group, lobby.
camarín *m* small chapel.
camarlengo *m* camerlengo, camerlingo.
camarón *m* prawn, common prawn.
camarote *m* cabin.

camastro *m* rickety old bed.
camastrón,-ona 1 *adj fam* sly, cunning. – **2** *m,f fam* crafty person, sly old fox.
cambalache *m pey* swap, exchange.
cambalachear *t* to swap, exchange.
cámbaro *m* crawfish, crayfish.
cambiante 1 *adj* (*gen*) changing. **2** (*carácter*) moody. – **3** *mf* (*cambista*) moneychanger. – **4 cambiantes,** *mpl* (*reflejos*) glitters, gleams.
cambiar 1 *t* (*gen*) to change: *han cambiado las sillas,* the chairs have been changed. **2** (*intercambiar*) to exchange: *cambiar impresiones,* to exchange views; *cambiar sellos,* to swap stamps. **3** (*de sitio*) to shift, move. **4** (*dar cambio de moneda*) to change, give change for: *¿me puedes cambiar un billete de cinco mil?,* can you change a five-thousand peseta note for me? **5** (*moneda extranjera*) to change, exchange. **6** (*alterar*) to change: *cambiar la risa en llanto,* to change laughter into tears. – **7** *i* (*gen*) to change: *has cambiado mucho,* you have changed a lot. **8** (*viento*) to veer. **9** (*la velocidad de un automóvil*) to change, change gear. – **10 cambiarse,** *p* (*mudarse de ropa*) to change, get changed: *tengo que cambiarme para la cena,* I have to get changed for dinner. **11** (*mudarse de casa*) to move: *nos hemos cambiado de barrio,* we have moved to another district.
● **cambiar de chaqueta,** *fig* to change sides. ‖ **cambiar de dueño/manos/mano,** to change hands. ‖ **cambiar de idea/opinión/parecer,** to change one's mind. ‖ **cambiar de sitio,** to move, change places. ‖ **cambiar de táctica,** to change tactics, change strategy. ‖ **cambiar de tema,** to change the subject. ‖ **cambiar los papeles,** to reverse the roles.
▲ *Conjugation model* [12].
cambiazo 1 *m* (*cambio*) change. **2** *fam* (*estafa*) switch.
● **dar el cambiazo a algn.,** to pull a fast one on sb. by making a switch: *la maleta no era suya - le habían dado el cambiazo,* the suitcase wasn't his - they'd switched it for another one.
cambio 1 *m* change, changing: *un cambio de tiempo,* a change in the weather. **2** (*intercambio*) exchange, exchanging: *cambio de impresiones,* exchange of views. **3** (*dinero suelto*) change, loose change; (*vuelta*) change: *¿me puedes dar cambio de mil pesetas?,* can you change a thousand pesetas?; *me has dado mal el cambio,* you've given me the wrong change. **4** (*acciones*) price, quotation; (*divisas*) exchange rate. **5** (*tren*) switch. **6** AUTO gear change.
● **a cambio de,** in exchange for: *me dio dos libros a cambio del disco,* he gave me two books in exchange for the record. ‖ **a las primeras de cambio,** *fig* at the first opportunity. ‖ **en cambio,** on the other hand, but, whereas: *tú no puedes cantar, en cambio él sí,* you can't sing, but he can.
■ **caja de cambio,** AUTO gearbox. ‖ **cambio automático,** AUTO automatic transmission. ‖ **cambio de la guardia,** changing of the guard. ‖ **cambio de marchas,** (*acción*) gear change; (*caja*) gearbox. ‖ **cambio de planes,** change of plans. ‖ **casa de cambio,** bureau de change. ‖ **letra de cambio,** COM bill of exchange. ‖ **libre cambio,** COM free trade.
cambista *mf* moneychanger.
Camboya *f* Cambodia.
camboyano,-a 1 *adj* Cambodian. – **2** *m,f* (*persona*) Cambodian. – **3 camboyano,** *m* (*idioma*) Cambodian.
cámbrico,-a *adj* Cambrian.
camelar 1 *t fam* (*galantear*) to flirt with. **2** *fam* (*engañar*) to cajole, sweet-talk, get round: *ha camelado a su padre*

para que le compre una moto, he's talked his father into buying him a motorbike. – **3 camelarse,** *p fam* to cajole, sweet-talk, get round.

camelear *t fam* to fool, take in.

camelia *f* camellia.

camellero *m* cameleer, camel-driver.

camello 1 *m* ZOOL camel. **2** *arg* (*drogas*) drug pusher, pusher, dope dealer.

camelo 1 *m fam* (*galanteo*) courting, flirting. **2** *fam* (*engaño*) hoax, sham. **3** *fam* (*cuento*) cock-and-bull story.

camembert *m* Camembert.

camerino *m* dressing room.

camero,-a *adj* three-quarter size: *sábana camera,* three-quarter bed sheet.
■ **cama camera,** three-quarter bed.

Camerún *m* Cameroon.

camerunés,-esa 1 *adj* Cameroonian. – **2** *m,f* Cameroonian.

camilla 1 *f* (*para enfermos*) stretcher. **2** (*cama*) small bed. **3** (*mesa camilla*) round table with a brazier underneath.

camillero,-a *m,f* stretcher-bearer.

caminante *mf* traveller (US traveler), walker.

caminar 1 *i* (*andar*) to walk: *caminamos durante cuatro horas,* we walked for four hours. **2** (*viajar*) to travel: *caminar a Sevilla,* to travel to Seville. **3** *fig* (*seguir su curso*) to move, make its way: *los planetas caminan alrededor del sol,* the planets move around the sun. – **4** *t* (*recorrer*) to cover, travel: *he caminado cinco kilómetros,* I have covered five kilometres.

caminata *f* long walk, trek.

caminero *adj* road.

camino 1 *m* (*vía*) path, track. **2** (*ruta*) way, route: *encontramos a Juan de camino a casa,* we met Juan on our way home. **3** (*viaje*) journey: *dos horas de camino,* a two-hour journey. **4** *fig* (*medio*) way.
● **a medio camino,** half-way. ‖ **abrir camino,** to clear the way (**a,** for). ‖ **abrir el camino,** to clear the way (**a,** for). ‖ **abrirse camino,** to make one's way: *se abrió camino entre la gente,* she made her way through the people. ‖ **abrirse camino en la vida,** to get on in life. ‖ **coger de camino / pillar de camino,** to be on the way: *tu casa nos pilla de camino,* your house is on our way. ‖ **estar en camino,** to be on the way. ‖ **ir camino de,** to be on one's way to. ‖ **ir por (el) buen/mal camino,** *fig* to be on the right/wrong track. ‖ **llevar buen camino,** to be on the right track. ‖ **llevar camino de,** to be on the way to, be heading for, look set to: *lleva camino de convertirse en un gran atleta,* he's on his way to becoming a great athlete. ‖ **ponerse en camino,** to set off (on a journey).
■ **camino de herradura,** bridle path. ‖ **camino de rosas,** *fig* bed of roses. ‖ **camino forestal,** forest track. ‖ **el Camino de Santiago,** ASTRON the Milky Way. ‖ **el camino del éxito,** *fig* the road to success.

camión *m* lorry, US truck.
● **estar como un camión,** *fam* to be gorgeous, be a knockout.
■ **camión cisterna,** tanker. ‖ **camión de la basura,** refuse lorry, US garbage truck. ‖ **camión de mudanzas,** removal van. ‖ **camión frigorífico,** refrigerator lorry, (US refrigerator truck).

camionaje *m* haulage, cartage.

camionero,-a *m,f* lorry driver, US truck driver.

camioneta *f* van.

camisa 1 *f* (*prenda*) shirt. **2** (*de la culebra*) slough. **3** (*de frutos*) skin. **4** TÉC (*de horno*) lining; (*de cilindro*) sleeve. **5** (*de libro*) jacket. **6** (*carpeta*) folder.

● **cambiar de camisa,** *fig* to change sides. ‖ **dejar a algn. sin camisa,** *fig* to leave sb. penniless, leave sb. very short of money. ‖ **en mangas de camisa,** in one's shirtsleeves. ‖ **jugarse hasta la camisa,** *fig* to put one's shirt on it. ‖ **meterse en camisa de once varas,** *fig* to meddle in other people's business. ‖ **no llegarle a algn. la camisa al cuerpo,** *fam* to be terrified. ‖ **perder hasta la camisa,** to lose one's shirt.
■ **camisa de dormir,** nightgown, nightdress. ‖ **camisa de fuerza,** straitjacket.

camisería 1 *f* (*tienda*) shirt shop, outfitter's shop. **2** (*industria*) shirt industry.

camisero,-a 1 *adj* shirt: *blusa camisera,* shirt blouse; *vestido camisero,* shirtwaister. – **2** *m,f* outfitter, shirt maker.

camiseta 1 *f* (*ropa interior*) vest, US undershirt. **2** (*niqui*) T-shirt. **3** DEP shirt, jersey.
● **sudar la camiseta,** *fam* to sweat blood: *sudamos la camiseta para ganar el partido,* we sweated blood to win the match.

camisola 1 *f arc* (*camisa*) camisole. **2** (*camiseta deportiva*) shirt, jersey.

camisón *m* nightdress, nightgown, nightie.

camomila *f* camomile.

camorra *f fam* row, quarrel, fight.
● **armar camorra,** *fam* to kick up a row. ‖ **buscar camorra,** *fam* to look for trouble.

camorrista 1 *adj* quarrelsome, rowdy. – **2** *mf* troublemaker.

camp *adj* camp.

campal batalla campal, *f* pitched battle.

campamento 1 *m* (*acción de acampar*) camping. **2** (*lugar*) camp. **3** (*tropa acampada*) camp.
■ **campamento de trabajo,** work camp. ‖ **campamento de verano,** summer camp.

campana 1 *f* (*gen*) bell. **2** (*de chimenea*) mantelpiece. **3** *fam* (*extractora*) extractor hood, (US stove extractor hood).
● **a toque de campana,** *fig* to the sound of bells. ‖ **dar una vuelta de campana,** to overturn, roll over. ‖ **echar las campanas al vuelo,** *fig* to set all the bells ringing. ‖ **oír campanas y no saber dónde,** *fig* not to have a clue. ‖ **tañer las campanas / tocar las campanas,** to ring the bells.
■ **campana de buzo,** diving bell. ‖ **campana de cristal,** bell jar, bell glass.

campanada 1 *f* stroke of a bell, peal of a bell, ring of a bell. **2** *fig* (*escándalo*) scandal, sensation.
● **dar la campanada,** *fig* to cause a sensation, cause a scandal.

campanario *m* belfry, bell tower.

campanear 1 *i* to ring the bells. – **2 campanearse,** *p* (*contonearse*) to sway, swagger.

campaneo 1 *m* peal of the bells. **2** (*contoneo*) sway, swagger.

campanero,-a 1 *m,f* (*que toca*) bell-ringer. **2** (*que hace*) bell founder.

campaniforme *adj* campanulate, bell-shaped.

campanilla 1 *f* (*gen*) small bell; (*de mano*) handbell. **2** (*adorno*) tassel. **3** ANAT uvula. **4** BOT bell flower.
● **de (muchas) campanillas,** *fam* very important, outstanding: *es un pintor de muchas campanillas,* he's a very important painter.

campanillear *i* to ring the bells.

campanilleo *m* ringing.

campanillero *m* bellringer.

campanilo *m* campanile.

campante 1 *adj fam* (*despreocupado*) cool, unconcerned: *se quedó tan campante cuando vio que había suspendido,* she didn't bat an eyelid when she knew she had failed. 2 *fam* (*ufano*) proud, self-satisfied: *iba tan campante con su coche nuevo,* he was so proud of his new car.

campanudo,-a 1 *adj* (*forma de campana*) bell-shaped. 2 (*escrito, orador*) pompous.

campaña 1 *f* (*conjunto de actividades*) campaign. 2 (*campo plano*) plain. 3 (*expedición militar*) expedition.
● **de campaña,** MIL field: *uniforme de campaña,* field uniform.
■ **campaña electoral,** election campaign. ‖ **campaña publicitaria,** advertising campaign. ‖ **misa de campaña,** open-air mass. ‖ **tienda de campaña,** tent.

campañol *m* vole.

campar 1 *i* (*sobresalir*) to excel, stand out. 2 (*acampar*) to camp.

campear 1 *i* (*salir a pacer*) to graze. 2 (*sobresalir*) to stand out, appear.

campechanería *f fam* openness, informality.

campechanía *f fam* → **campechanería**.

campechano,-a 1 *adj fam* (*franco, alegre*) frank, open, good-humoured (US good-humored). 2 *fam* (*sencillo*) unaffected, natural.

campeón,-ona *m,f* champion.

campeonato *m* championship.
● **de campeonato,** *fam* great, fantastic: *me llevé un susto de campeonato,* I got a terrible fright.

camperas *fpl* → **campero,-a**.

campero,-a 1 *adj* country, rural. 2 (*al descubierto*) openair. - 3 **camperas,** *fpl* (*botas*) Spanish leather boots.

campesinado *m* peasantry, peasants *pl.*

campesino,-a 1 *adj* country, rural. - 2 *m,f* peasant; (*hombre*) countryman; (*mujer*) countrywoman.

campestre *adj* country, rural.

camping *m* camp site.
● **hacer camping / ir de camping,** to go camping.
▲ *pl* campings.

campiña 1 *f* (*campo*) countryside. 2 (*cultivo*) stretch of cultivated land.

campista *mf* camper.

campo 1 *m* (*campiña*) country, countryside: *vivir en el campo,* to live in the country. 2 (*agricultura*) field: *los campos de maíz,* the cornfields; *trabajar el campo,* to work the land. 3 DEP MIL field. 4 ELEC FÍS field. 5 (*espacio*) space; *fig* field, scope: *en el campo de la medicina,* in the field of medicine.
● **dejarle a algn. el campo libre,** *fig* to leave the field open for sb. ‖ **ir a campo traviesa/través,** to cut across the fields.
■ **campo de batalla,** battlefield. ‖ **campo de concentración,** concentration camp. ‖ **campo de fútbol,** football pitch. ‖ **campo de golf,** golf course, golf links *pl.* ‖ **campo de tenis,** tennis court. ‖ **campo de tiro,** shooting range. ‖ **campo deportivo,** playing field. ‖ **campo visual,** visual field. ‖ **campo magnético,** magnetic field. ‖ **casa de campo,** country house. ‖ **trabajo de campo,** fieldwork.

camposanto *m* cemetery.

campus *m* campus.
■ **campus universitario,** university campus.
▲ *pl* campus.

camuesa *f* pippin.

camueso *m* pippin tree.

camuflaje *m* camouflage.

camuflar 1 *t* to camouflage. 2 *fig* to hide, cover up.

can *m lit* dog.

cana *f* → **cano,-a**.

Canadá *m* Canada.

canadiense 1 *adj* Canadian. - 2 *m,f* Canadian.

canal 1 *m* (*artificial*) canal. 2 (*natural*) channel. - 3 *m & f* (*de tejado*) gutter. 4 TÉC channel. 5 (*animal*) open carcass.
● **abrir en canal,** to slit open.
■ **Canal de la Mancha,** English Channel. ‖ **Canal de Panamá,** Panama Canal. ‖ **canal de riego,** irrigation canal.

canaladura *f* flute.

canalete *m* paddle.

canalización 1 *f* (*acción*) canalization, channelling (US channeling). 2 (*tubería*) piping. 3 *fig* (*de opiniones*) directing; (*de dinero*) channelling (US channeling).

canalizar 1 *t* (*agua, área*) to canalize. 2 (*riego*) to channel. 3 *fig* (*opiniones*) to direct; (*dinero*) to channel.
▲ Conjugation model [4].

canalla 1 *f pey* (*chusma*) riffraff, mob, rabble. - 2 *m pey* (*hombre ruin*) rascal, scoundrel, swine, rotter.

canallada *f* dirty trick.

canallesco,-a *adj pey* rotten, despicable.

canalón 1 *m* (*por el borde del tejado*) gutter; (*hacia el suelo*) drainpipe. - 2 **canalones,** *mpl* (*pasta*) cannelloni.

canana *f* cartridge belt.

canapé 1 *m* (*sofá*) couch, sofa. 2 CULIN canapé.
▲ *pl* canapés.

Canarias Islas Canarias, *fpl* Canary Islands.

canario,-a 1 *adj* GEOG Canarian. - 2 *m,f* Canarian. - 3 canario, *m* (*pájaro*) canary.

canasta 1 *f* (*cesto*) basket. 2 (*juego de cartas*) canasta. 3 (*en baloncesto*) basket.

canastero,-a 1 *m,f* (*que hace*) basket maker. 2 (*que vende*) basket dealer.

canastilla 1 *f* (*cestilla*) small basket. 2 (*de bebé*) layette.

canasto 1 *m* (*cesto*) basket, hamper. - 2 canastos, *interj* good heavens!

cáncamo *m* eyebolt.

cancamusa *f fam* trick.

cancán 1 *m* MÚS cancan. 2 (*prenda*) frilly petticoat.

cancel 1 *m* (*contrapuerta*) storm door. 2 (*construcción*) screen.

cancela *f* ironwork gate.

cancelación *f* cancellation.

cancelar 1 *t* (*anular*) to cancel. 2 (*saldar una deuda*) to settle, pay.

cáncer 1 *m* cancer. 2 Cáncer, ASTROL ASTRON Cancer.
▲ In *1 pl* cánceres; in *2 pl* Cáncer.

cancerarse *p* to become cancerous.

cancerbero 1 *m* (*perro de tres cabezas*) Cerberus. 2 *fig* (*portero o guarda severo*) ogre. 3 DEP *fig* goalkeeper.

cancerígeno,-a *adj* carcinogenic.

canceroso,-a *adj* cancerous.

cancha 1 *f* (*gen*) ground; (*tenis*) court. 2 (*para peleas de gallos*) cockpit.

cancho *m* boulder, rock.

cancilla *f* gate.

canciller *m* chancellor.

cancillería *f* chancellery, chancellory.

canción *f* song.
● **¡estamos siempre con la misma canción!,** *fam* here we go again!

cancionero 1 *m* (*poemas*) collection of poems. 2 MÚS songbook.

candado *m* padlock.
candar *t* to padlock.
candeal *adj* white: *pan/trigo candeal,* white bread/wheat.
candela 1 *f* (*vela*) candle. 2 (*lumbre*) fire. 3 (*flor del castaño*) blossom. 4 FÍS candle, candela.
candelabro *m* candelabra, candelabrum.
candelero *m* candlestick.
● **estar en el candelero,** *fig* to be at the top, be very popular.
candente 1 *adj* (*enrojecido por el fuego*) incandescent, red-hot; (*blanqueado por el fuego*) candescent, white-hot. 2 *fig* (*cuestión, tema*) burning, pressing.
candi *adj* crystallized, candied.
■ **azúcar candi,** candy sugar.
candidato,-a *m,f* candidate.
candidatura 1 *f* (*aspiración*) candidacy, candidature: *presentó su candidatura,* she put forward her candidature. 2 (*lista de candidatos*) list of candidates.
candidez *f* ingenuousness, innocence.
cándido,-a 1 *adj* ingenuous, innocent. 2 *lit* (*níveo*) white, snowy.
candil *m* oil lamp.
candileja 1 *f* (*candil*) oil lamp. – 2 **candilejas,** *fpl* footlights.
candonga *f* → **candongo,-a.**
candongo,-a 1 *adj fam* (*zalamero*) coaxing. 2 *fam* (*holgazán*) lazy, idle. – 3 *m,f fam* (*zalamero*) coaxer. 4 *fam* (*holgazán*) layabout, lazybones. – 5 **candonga,** *f fam* (*zalamería*) blarney. 6 *fam* (*burla*) teasing, joking. 7 (*mula de tiro*) draught mule.
candor 1 *m lit* (*suma blancura*) whiteness. 2 *fig* innocence.
candoroso,-a *adj* innocent, pure.
caneca *f* earthenware flask.
canela *f* → **canelo,-a.**
canelo,-a 1 *adj* cinnamon. – 2 **canelo,** *m* cinnamon tree. – 3 **canela,** *f* cinnamon.
● **ser canela fina,** *fig* to be exquisite, be excellent.
canelón 1 *m* (*canalón*) gutter (on a roof). 2 (*labor de pasamanería*) cord. – 3 **canelones,** *mpl* (*pasta*) cannelloni.
canesú *m* (*de vestido*) bodice; (*de camisa*) yoke.
▲ *pl* **canesúes.**
cangilón *m* (*vaso en forma de cántaro*) pitcher; (*de molino*) bucket.
cangreja *f* brig sail.
cangrejo *m* (*de mar*) crab; (*de río*) freshwater crayfish.
● **estar rojo,-a como un cangrejo,** *fam* to be as red as a lobster. ‖ **ir/andar como los cangrejos,** *fam* to take one step forward and two backwards.
canguelo *m arg* funk.
● **tener canguelo,** *arg* to have the wind up.
canguro 1 *m* ZOOL kangaroo. – 2 *mf fam* baby-sitter.
caníbal 1 *adj* cannibal. 2 *fig* (*hombre cruel*) savage. – 3 *mf* cannibal.
canibalismo *m* cannibalism.
canica *f* marble: *jugar a las canicas,* to play marbles.
caniche *m* poodle.
canicie *f* whiteness, greyness.
canícula *f* dog days *pl.*
canijo,-a *adj fam* weak, puny.
canilla 1 *f* ANAT long bone; (*de ave*) wing bone. 2 (*de barril*) tap. 3 (*carrete*) reel, bobbin.
canillera *f* (*espinillera*) shin guard.
canino,-a 1 *adj* canine. – 2 **canino,** *m* canine.
● **tener hambre canina,** *fam* to be starving.
canje *m* exchange.

canjeable *adj* exchangeable.
canjear *t* to exchange.
cannabis *m* cannabis.
cano,-a 1 *adj* white, grey (US gray): *un hombre de pelo cano,* a white-haired man, a grey-haired man. – 2 **cana,** *f* grey hair, white hair: *me están saliendo canas,* I'm starting to go grey, I've got some grey hairs.
● **echar una cana/canita al aire,** *fam* to let one's hair down. ‖ **peinar canas,** *fam* to be getting on, be getting old.
canoa *f* canoe; (*bote*) boat.
canódromo *m* greyhound track, dog track.
canon 1 *m* (*regla*) canon, norm. 2 MÚS REL canon. 3 (*prestación*) royalty. – 4 **cánones,** *mpl* rules: *lo hizo como mandan los cánones de la medicina,* he did it in accordance with the rules of medicine.
▲ *pl* **cánones.**
canónico,-a *adj* canonical: *derecho canónico,* canon law; *matrimonio canónico,* canonical marriage.
canóniga *f fam* nap before a meal.
canónigo *m* canon.
canonización *f* canonization.
canonizar *t* to canonize.
▲ *Conjugation model* [4], *like* **realizar.**
canonjía 1 *f* canonry. 2 *fig* sinecure.
canoro,-a *adj* musical: *ave canora,* songbird.
canoso,-a *adj* grey-haired (US gray-haired), white-haired: *un hombre canoso,* a white-haired man, a grey-haired man; *el pelo canoso,* white hair, grey (US gray) hair.
canotié *m* straw hat, boater.
▲ *pl* **canotiés.**
canotier *m* → **canotié.**
cansado,-a 1 *pp* → **cansar.** – 2 *adj* (*gen*) tired, weary: *estoy cansada,* I'm tired. 3 (*que fatiga*) tiring: *es un trabajo muy cansado,* it's a very tiring job. 4 (*pesado*) boring, tiresome. 5 (*harto*) tired (**de,** of), fed up (**de,** with).
● **tener la vista cansada,** to have eyestrain.
cansancio *m* tiredness, weariness.
● **estar muerto,-a de cansancio,** *fig* to be dead tired, be exhausted.
cansar 1 *t* (*causar cansancio*) to tire, tire out, make tired: *este trabajo me cansa mucho,* this work tires me out; *esta letra cansa la vista,* this writing strains my eyes. 2 (*molestar*) to annoy; (*aburrir*) to tire, bore: *me cansan sus discursos,* I'm fed up with his speeches; *¿no te cansa ver la televisión cada día?,* don't you get tired of watching TV every day? 3 (*tierra*) to exhaust. – 4 *i* (*causar cansancio*) to be tiring: *eso que haces cansa mucho,* what you do is very tiring. 5 (*aburrir*) to be boring: *¡cómo cansan esas clases!,* those clases bore me stiff! – 6 **cansarse,** *p* (*padecer cansancio*) to get tired, tire: *se cansa enseguida,* she gets tired easily. 7 *fig* (*hartarse*) to get tired (**de,** of), get fed up (**de,** with): *me cansé de sus chistes y me fui,* I got tired of their jokes and I left.
cansino,-a *adj* slow, weary.
cantable 1 *adj* singable. – 2 *m* cantabile.
Cantabria *f* Cantabria.
cantábrico,-a *adj* Cantabrian.
■ **mar Cantábrico,** Bay of Biscay.
cántabro,-a 1 *adj* Cantabrian. – 2 *m,f* Cantabrian.
cantada *f fam* blunder.
cantador,-ra *m,f* singer.
cantaleta *f* → **cantilena.**
cantamañanas *mf fam* bullshitter.
▲ *pl* **cantamañanas.**

cantante 1 *adj* singing. – **2** *mf* singer.
● **llevar la voz cantante,** *fig* to rule the roost.
cantaor,-ra *m,f* flamenco singer.
cantar 1 *t* to sing: *cantó una canción preciosa,* she sang a beautiful song. **2** *fig* (*alabar*) to praise, sing the praises of: *cantaron las excelencias de sus vinos,* they sang the praises of their wines. **3** *fig* (*misa*) to sing, say. **4** (*en juegos de naipes*) to call. **5** *fam* (*confesar*) to tell, reveal, confess; (*delatar*) to give away: *el hombre cantó todo lo que sabía sobre el asesinato a la policía,* the man told the police everything he knew about the murder. – **6** *i* to sing: *cantaron a dos voces,* they sang a duet. **7** (*pájaros*) to sing, chirp; (*insectos*) to chirp. **8** *fam* (*confesar*) to spill the beans, talk, confess. **9** *fam* (*oler mal*) to stink: *le cantan los pies,* his feet stink. – **10** *m* song.
● **cantar como una almeja,** *fam* to stick out like a sore thumb. ‖ **cantarlas claras,** *fam* to tell sb. straight. ‖ **cantarle a algn. las cuarenta,** *fam* to give sb. a piece of one's mind. ‖ **cantarle a algn. las verdades,** *fig* to give sb. a piece of one's mind. ‖ **en menos que canta un gallo,** *fam* in a flash, before you could say Jack Robinson. ‖ *¡eso es otro cantar!,* *fam* that's a totally different thing, that's a different kettle of fish. ‖ **ser coser y cantar,** *fam* to be as easy as pie, be child's play: *aquel examen fue coser y cantar,* that exam was as easy as pie.
■ **cantar de gesta,** chanson de geste. ‖ **Cantar de los Cantares,** Song of Songs, Song of Solomon.
cántara *f* liquid measure *of* 16.13 *litres, equivalent to* 3.5 *gallons.*
cantarela *f* first string of a violin or guitar.
cantárida *f* Spanish fly.
cantarín,-ina 1 *adj fam* (*persona*) fond of singing: *Ana es muy cantarina,* Ana loves singing. **2** *fam* (*voz*) sing-song.
cántaro 1 *m* (*vasija*) pitcher. **2** (*contenido*) pitcherful.
● **llover a cántaros,** *fig* to rain cats and dogs.
cantata *f* cantata.
cantautor,-ra *m,f* singer-songwriter.
cante 1 *m* MÚS singing. **2** *fam fig* blunder. **3** *fam fig* (*ragañina*) scolding.
● *¡vaya cante!,* *fam* what a clanger!
■ **cante hondo / cante jondo,** flamenco singing.
cantera 1 *f* (*de piedra*) quarry. **2** *fig* breeding ground. **3** DEP *fig* young players *pl.*
cantería 1 *f* (*arte*) hewing of stone. **2** (*obra*) stonework.
cantero *m* stonemason.
cántico *m* canticle.
cantidad 1 *f* (*gen*) quantity; (*de dinero*) amount, sum: *había una gran cantidad de libros,* there were a large number of books; *tuvieron que pagar una gran cantidad,* they had to pay a large sum of money. – **2** *adv fam* a lot: *llovía cantidad,* it was pouring with rain.
● **cantidad de,** *fam* lots of, loads of: *había cantidad de comida,* there was loads of food. ‖ **en cantidad,** *fam* tons, loads: *había flores en cantidad,* there were tons of flowers.
■ **cantidades industriales,** *fam* tons, loads.
cantiga *f* → **cántiga.**
cántiga *f* song, ballad.
cantil *m* (*en tierra*) cliff; (*en mar*) shelf.
cantilena 1 *f* (*canción*) song, ballad. **2** *fam* (*repetición*) refrain, story: *la misma cantilena,* the same old story.
cantillo 1 *m* (*piedrecilla*) small stone. – **2 cantillos,** *mpl* (*juego*) jacks.
cantimplora *f* water bottle.
cantina 1 *f* (*comedor*) canteen. **2** (*de estación*) buffet.

cantinela *f* → **cantilena.**
cantinero,-a *m,f* bar attendant.
canto[1] 1 *m* (*arte*) singing. **2** (*canción*) song. **3** LIT canto.
● **al canto del gallo,** at daybreak, at cock-crow.
canto[2] 1 *m* (*extremo*) edge: *de canto,* sideways; *tiene tres centímetros de canto,* it's three centimetres thick. **2** (*cuchillo*) blunt edge. **3** (*esquina*) corner. **4** (*piedra*) stone, pebble.
● **al canto,** *fam* for sure: *si llegamos tarde, bronca al canto,* if we are late there'll be a row for sure. ‖ **darse con un canto en los dientes,** *fam* to be thankful for small mercies. ‖ **faltar el canto de un duro,** *fam* to come very close to, to be on the verge of: *le faltó el canto de un duro para caerse del árbol,* he came very close to falling out of the tree. ‖ **por el canto de un duro,** by inches.
■ **canto rodado,** (*grande*) boulder; (*pequeño*) pebble.
cantón *m* canton.
cantonera *f* → **cantonero,-a.**
cantonero,-a 1 *adj* idling, loafer. – **2** *m,f* idler, loafer. – **3 cantonera,** *f* (*pieza*) corner piece.
cantor,-ra 1 *adj* singing. – **2** *m,f* singer.
● **pájaro cantor,** songbird.
cantueso *m* type of lavender.
canturrear *i* to hum.
canturreo *m* humming.
canturriar *i* to hum.

▲ *Conjugation model* [12]*, like* ***cambiar.***

cánula *f* cannula.
canutas **pasarlas canutas,** *loc fam* to have a hard time.
canutero *m* (*alfiletero*) pin box.
canutillo *m* bobbin, reel.
canuto 1 *m* (*tubo*) tube. **2** BOT internode. **3** *arg* (*porro*) joint.
caña 1 *f* (*planta*) reed. **2** (*tallo*) cane, stem. **3** ANAT bone marrow. **4** (*de calzado*) leg: *botas de media caña,* calf-length boots. **5** (*de pescar*) rod. **6** (*de cerveza*) small glass of draught beer.
● **darle / meterle caña a algn./algo,** *fam* (*coche*) to step on the gas, put one's foot down; (*persona*) to beat sb. up, have a go at sb.
■ **caña de azúcar,** sugar cane.
cañacoro *m* canna.
cañada 1 *f* GEOG glen, dell, hollow. **2** (*sendero*) cattle track.
cañafístola *f* cassia.
cañafístula *f* cassia.
cañamazo 1 *m* (*estopa*) tow. **2** (*tela*) burlap, tow cloth. **3** *fig* (*proyecto*) project.
cáñamo 1 *m* BOT hemp. **2** (*tela*) hempen cloth.
■ **cáñamo indio,** cannabis.
cañamón *m* hemp seed.
cañaveral *m* cane plantation.
cañería *f* piping.
cañí 1 *adj* (*de raza gitana*) gypsy. **2** (*típico, folclórico*) typically Spanish, stereotypically Spanish: *la España cañí,* clichéd Spain. – **3** *m,f* gypsy.
▲ *pl* **cañís.**
cañizal *m* cane plantation.
cañizar *m* cane plantation.
cañizo *m* framework of interwoven canes.
caño 1 *m* (*tubo*) tube. **2** (*chorro*) jet. **3** (*galería de mina*) gallery. **4** (*canal*) navigation channel.
cañón 1 *m* (*de artillería*) gun; (*antiguamente*) cannon. **2** (*de arma*) barrel. **3** (*tubo*) tube, pipe. **4** (*de chimenea*) flue. **5**

GEOG canyon. **6** (*foco*) spotlight. **7** (*de pluma*) quill. **– 8** *adj fam* terrific, great, fabulous: *esa chica está cañón,* that girl is gorgeous. **– 9** *adv fam* very much: *lo pasamos cañón,* we had a great time.
● **estar al pie del cañón,** *fig* to be working away, be hard at it.
cañonazo 1 *m* (*disparo*) gunshot. **2** DEP shot.
cañonear *t* to shell.
cañonera *f* → **cañonero,-a.**
cañonería 1 *f* (*de artillería*) artillery. **2** (*de órgano*) pipes *pl.*
cañonero,-a 1 *adj* armed. **– 2 cañonero,** *m* (*barco*) gunboat. **– 3 cañonera,** *f* (*lancha*) gunboat.
caoba *f* mahogany.
caolín *m* kaolin.
caos *m* chaos.
▲ *pl caos.*
caótico,-a *adj* chaotic.
cap. *abr* (*capítulo*) chapter; (*abreviatura*) ch.
Cap. *abr* (*capitán*) captain; (*abreviatura*) Capt.
capa 1 *f* (*prenda*) cloak, cape. **2** GEOL stratum, layer. **3** (*de pintura*) coat; (*de polvo*) layer; (*de chocolate etc*) coating, layer: *una capa de pintura,* a coat of paint. **4** *fig* (*estrato social*) class, stratum. **5** (*estrato social*) stratum.
● **andar de capa caída,** *fig* to be on the decline, have seen better days. ‖ **defender algo a capa y espada,** *fig* to defend sth. to the last. ‖ **hacer de su capa un sayo,** *fam* to do whatever one feels like. ‖ **so capa de,** *fig* under the pretext of.
■ **capa freática,** water table. ‖ **capa pluvial,** REL pluvial, cope.
capacha *f* basket.
capacho *m* basket, hamper.
capacidad 1 *f* (*gen*) capacity: *hay capacidad para cinco personas,* there's room for five people; *el teatro tiene capacidad para acoger a doscientas personas,* the theatre has a seating capacity of two hundred; *una botella con dos litros de capacidad,* a two-litre bottle. **2** *fig* (*habilidad*) capability, ability: *tiene gran capacidad para las matemáticas,* she has a talent for mathematics; *es una persona de mucha capacidad,* she's a very intelligent person.
capacitación *f* training.
capacitado,-a 1 *pp* → **capacitar. – 2** *adj* qualified. **3** JUR qualified, competent.
● **estar capacitado,-a,** to be trained, be qualified: *está capacitado para enseñar inglés,* he's qualified to teach English.
capacitar 1 *t* (*instruir*) to train, qualify. **2** (*autorizar*) to qualify, entitle.
capar 1 *t* to geld, castrate. **2** *fam fig* to curtail.
caparazón 1 *m* shell. **2** *fig* cover, protection.
caparrosa *f* vitriol.
capataz,-za *m,f* (*hombre*) foreman; (*mujer*) forewoman.
capaz 1 *adj* (*competente*) capable, able: *es una persona muy capaz,* she's very capable. **2** (*cualificado*) qualified. **3** (*capable*) capable (**de,** of): *no es capaz de eso,* he's incapable of doing that, he wouldn't do that; *¡no serías capaz!,* you wouldn't dare! **4** (*grande*) spacious, roomy. **5** (*con espacio*) big enough (**para,** for): *el salón es capaz para cincuenta personas,* there's room for fifty people in the hall.
capazo 1 *m* (*cesto*) basket. **2** (*para bebé*) carry-cot.
capcioso,-a *adj pey* cunning, insidious, artful: *una pregunta capciosa,* a trick question.
capea *f* amateur bullfight.

capear 1 *t* (*tauromaquia*) to confront the bull with the cape. **2** *fam fig* (*entretener con engaños*) to stall, put off. **3** *fam fig* (*dificultades*) to dodge: *sabe capear las dificultades,* he knows how to dodge difficulties.
● **capear el temporal,** *fig* to weather the storm, ride out the storm.
capellán *m* chaplain.
capellanía *f* chaplaincy.
capelo 1 *m* (*sombrero rojo*) cardinal's hat. **2** (*dignidad de cardenal*) cardinalship.
caperuza 1 *f* (*prenda*) hood. **2** (*tapa*) cap, top: *la caperuza del bolígrafo,* the top of the biro.
capicúa 1 *adj* reversible. **– 2** *m* (*número*) reversible number; (*palabra*) palindrome: *424 es capicúa,* 424 is a reversible number.
capilar 1 *adj* (*del cabello*) hair: *tónico capilar,* hair tonic. **2** FÍS capillary. **– 3** *m* capillary.
capilaridad *f* capillarity.
capilla 1 *f* (*iglesia*) chapel. **2** MÚS choir. **3** (*capucho*) hood. **4** *fig* (*grupo de adictos*) clan.
● **estar en capilla,** (*condenado a muerte*) to be awaiting execution; (*en ascuas*) to be like a cat on hot bricks.
■ **capilla ardiente,** funeral chapel, mortuary chapel.
capillo 1 *m* (*gorrito para niño*) bonnet; (*para bautizar*) christening cape. **2** (*capucha*) hood. **3** (*refuerzo del calzado*) toe lining.
capirotazo *m* flip, flick.
capirote 1 *m* (*gen*) hood; (*de mujer*) hennin. **2** (*capirotazo*) flip, flick.
■ **tonto,-a de capirote,** *fam* silly idiot.
capisayo 1 *m* (*capotillo*) hooded cape. **2** (*vestidura de los obispos*) mantelletta.
capitación *f* capitation.
capital 1 *adj* (*principal*) capital, principal, main, chief: *es de importancia capital,* it's of capital importance. **2** (*relativo a la pérdida de la cabeza*) deadly, capital: *un pecado capital,* a deadly sin, a cardinal sin; *una pena capital,* capital punishment. **3** (*ciudad*) capital. **– 4** *m* FIN capital. **– 5** *f* capital, chief town.
■ **capital activo,** working capital. ‖ **capital inicial,** capital. ‖ **capital líquido,** net capital. ‖ **capital social,** share capital. ‖ **capital de provincia,** county town, US county seat.
capitalismo *m* capitalism.
capitalista 1 *adj* capitalist, capitalistic. **– 2** *mf* capitalist.
capitalización *f* capitalization.
capitalizar *t* to capitalize.
▲ *Conjugation model* [4], *like realizar.*
capitán,-ana 1 *m,f* MAR MIL captain. **2** (*jefe*) leader, chief. **3** DEP captain. **– 4 capitana,** *f* (*nave*) flagship.
■ **capitán de corbeta,** lieutenant commander. ‖ **capitán de fragata,** commander. ‖ **capitán general,** field marshal, US general of the army. ‖ **capitán general de la Armada,** Admiral of the Fleet.
capitana *f* → **capitán,-ana.**
capitanear 1 *t* MIL MAR to captain, command. **2** (*dirigir*) to lead. **3** DEP to captain.
capitanía *f* captaincy, captainship.
■ **capitanía general,** (*cargo*) rank of field marshal; (*edificio*) military headquarters *pl.*
capitel *m* capital, chapiter.
capitolio *m* capitol.
capitoné 1 *adj* (*acolchado*) upholstered. **– 2** *m* (*camión de mudanzas*) removal van.
capitoste *mf pey* bigwig.
capitulación 1 *f* MIL capitulation. **2** (*acuerdo*) agreement. **– 3 capitulaciones,** *fpl* JUR marriage settlement *sing.*

caracol

capitular 1 *adj* capitular, capitulary: *sala capitular,* chapter house. – **2** *m* (*individuo de alguna comunidad eclesiástica*) capitular. – **3** *i* MIL (*rendirse*) to capitulate. **4** (*pactar*) to come to an agreement, reach an agreement. – **5** *t* (*pactar*) to agree to: *capitular las condiciones,* to agree to the conditions. **6** (*hacer capítulos de cargos*) to charge.

capítulo 1 *m* (*gen*) chapter. **2** *fig* (*tema*) subject, matter. ● **llamar a algn. a capítulo,** *fig* to call sb. to account. ‖ **ser capítulo aparte,** *fig* to be another story.

capó *m* bonnet, us hood.

capón[1] *m* (*pollo*) capon.

capón[2] *m* (*golpe*) rap on the head with the knuckles.

caponera 1 *f* (*jaula*) coop. **2** *fig* (*prisión*) nick, clink. **3** *fig* (*sitio en que se encuentra buen trato*) open house.

caporal 1 *m* (*jefe*) head, leader. **2** (*en una granja*) farm manager.

capota 1 *f* (*sombrero femenino*) bonnet. **2** (*cubierta plegadiza*) folding hood, folding top.

capotar 1 *i* (*un avión*) to nosedive. **2** (*un coche*) to overturn.

capote 1 *m* (*capa con mangas*) cloak with sleeves, cape. **2** (*prenda militar*) greatcoat. **3** (*capa de torero*) cape. ● **echarle un capote a algn.,** *fam* to give sb. a hand. ‖ **pensar para su capote / decir algo para su capote,** *fam* to think to os. / to say to os.

capotear 1 *t* (*capear al toro*) to make passes using the cape. **2** *fig* (*evadir las dificultades*) to dodge. **3** *fig* (*entretener con engaños*) to stall.

capricho 1 *m* (*deseo*) caprice, whim, fancy. **2** MÚS caprice, capriccio. ● **hacer algo por/a capricho,** to do sth. because it takes one's fancy.

caprichoso,-a 1 *adj* capricious, whimsical, fanciful. – **2** *m,f* whimsical person.

caprichudo,-a *adj* → **caprichoso,-a**.

Capricornio *m* Capricorn.

caprino,-a *adj* goat: *ganado caprino,* goats *pl.*

cápsula 1 *f* (*gen*) capsule. **2** (*de arma*) cap. **3** (*de botella*) cap, top.

capsular 1 *adj* capsular. – **2** *t* to capsulate.

Capt. *abr* (*capitán*) captain; (*abreviatura*) Capt.

captación 1 *f* (*de ondas*) reception; (*de agua*) harnessing. **2** (*comprensión*) understanding, comprehension, grasping. **3** (*atracción*) winning, convincing: *captación de votos,* winning of votes.

captar 1 *t* (*ondas*) to receive, pick up; (*agua*) to harness. **2** (*entender*) to understand, grasp: *no pudo captar el significado de la palabra,* he couldn't grasp the meaning of the word. **3** (*atraer a personas*) to attract, recruit: *captó nuevos adeptos para la secta,* he recruited new followers to the sect. **4** (*atención, interés*) to hold; (*confianza*) to win, gain. – **5 captarse,** *p* to draw, attract, win over.

captura *f* capture.

capturar *t* to capture, seize.

capucha *f* hood.

capuchino,-a 1 *adj* Capuchin. – **2** *m,f* (*monje*) Capuchin monk; (*monja*) Capuchin nun. – **3 capuchino,** *m* (*café*) cappuccino, frothy white coffee.

capuchón *m* (*de estilográfica etc*) cap.

capullo 1 *m* (*de insectos*) cocoon. **2** BOT bud. **3** *tabú* (*prepucio*) foreskin. **4** *tabú* (*estúpido*) silly bugger, dickhead.

capuz 1 *m* (*capucho*) hood. – **2** *vestidura larga y con capuche* type of hooded cloak.

caquexia *f* cachexy, cachexia.

caqui[1] *m* (*árbol*) persimmon.

caqui[2] *adj* khaki.

cara 1 *f* (*rostro*) face: *tiene una cara muy bonita,* she's got a pretty face. **2** (*expresión*) face, expression: *tenía la cara muy triste,* he looked sad; *nos miró con cara de asco,* he looked at us with disgust. **3** (*lado*) side; (*de moneda*) right side: *mira la hoja por la otra cara,* look at the other side of the sheet; *¿cara o cruz?,* heads or tails? **4** (*superficie*) face. **5** *fig* (*aspecto*) look: *este pastel tiene muy buena cara,* this cake looks very good. **6** *fam fig* (*desvergüenza*) cheek, nerve: *¡vaya cara!,* what a cheek!; *¡vaya cara que tienes!,* you've got a cheek!, you've got a nerve! – **7** *mf fam* (*cadradura*) cheeky person.

● **a la cara,** to sb.'s face: *se lo dijo a la cara,* he said it to her face. ‖ **caérsele a uno la cara de vergüenza,** *fam* to die of shame. ‖ **cara a,** facing: *cara al sol,* facing the sun; *cara a la pared,* facing the wall. ‖ **cara a cara,** face to face. ‖ **dar la cara,** *fig* to face the consequences. ‖ **dar la cara por algn.,** *fig* to stand up for sb.: *el padre dio la cara por su hijo,* the father stood up for his son. ‖ **de cara,** facing: *tenemos el viento de cara,* we're facing into the wind. ‖ **echar algo a cara o cruz,** to toss for sth. ‖ **echar en cara,** *fig* to reproach for: *le echó en cara su comportamiento,* he reproached her for her behaviour. ‖ **en la cara,** in sb.'s face: *se le rió en la cara,* he laughed in her face. ‖ **jugar algo a cara o cruz,** to toss for sth. ‖ **lavar la cara a algo,** *fig* to give sth. a facelift, give sth. a once-over: *si le lavamos la cara al piso lo venderemos más caro,* if we give the flat a once-over we'll get more for it. ‖ **no saber qué cara poner,** not to know what to do with os. ‖ **no tener cara para hacer algo,** *fig* not to dare do sth.: *no tengo cara para decírselo,* I daren't tell her. ‖ **plantar cara a algn.,** *fig* to face up to sb. ‖ **poner al mal tiempo buena cara,** to put on a brave face, grin and bear it. ‖ **poner buena cara,** to look pleased. ‖ **poner mala cara,** to pull a long face. ‖ **romperle la cara a algn.,** *fam* to smash sb.'s face in. ‖ **tener buena cara,** to look well. ‖ **tener cara de,** to look: *tenía cara de asustada,* she looked frightened; *tenía cara de haber llorado,* he looked as if he had been crying. ‖ **tener mala cara,** to look bad. ‖ **tener más cara que espalda,** *fam* to have a lot of cheek. ‖ **verse las caras,** *fig* to come face to face. ‖ **volver la cara,** to look the other way.

■ **cara de circunstancias,** *fig* serious look. ‖ **cara de perro,** *fam* scowling face. ‖ **cara de pocos amigos,** *fam* unfriendly face. ‖ **cara dura,** *fig* cheek, nerve: *¡qué cara más dura!,* what a cheek!, what a nerve! ‖ **cara larga,** *fig* long face.

caraba ser la caraba, *f fam* to be the limit, be the last straw.

carabao *m* carabao.

carabela *f* caravel.

carabina 1 *f* (*arma*) carbine, rifle. **2** *fam fig* chaperon, chaperone. ● **hacer de carabina / ir de carabina,** *fam* to act as chaperone.

carabinero,-a 1 *m,f* (*oficial*) customs officer. – **2 carabinero,** *m* HIST (*soldado*) carabineer, carabinier. **3** (*crustáceo*) large prawn.

cárabo[1] *m* (*escarabajo*) carabus, carabid beetle.

cárabo[2] *m* (*ave*) tawny owl.

caracense 1 *adj* of Guadalajara, from Guadalajara. – **2** *mf* person from Guadalajara, inhabitant of Guadalajara.

caracho *interj* goodness me!, damn it!

caracol 1 *m* (*de tierra*) snail. **2** (*de mar*) winkle. **3** (*concha*) sea shell. **4** (*del oído*) cochlea. **5** (*rizo*) kiss curl. **6** (*del reloj*)

caracola snail wheel. **7** (*de caballo*) caracole. – **8 caracoles**, *interj* good heavens! ● **hacer caracoles**, to caracole.
caracola *f* conch.
caracolear *i* to caracole.
carácter **1** *m* (*personalidad*) character: *es una mujer de mucho carácter*, she's got a strong character. **2** (*condición*) nature, kind: *este proyecto es de carácter científico*, this project is of a scientific nature; *asistió en carácter de observador*, he attended as an observer. **3** (*imprenta*) letter. ● **tener buen carácter**, to be good-natured. ‖ **tener mal carácter**, to be bad-tempered. ■ **caracteres de imprenta**, type *sing*, typeface *sing*. ‖ **caracteres góticos**, Gothic type *sing*. ▲ *pl* **caracteres**.
característica *f* → **característico,-a**.
característico,-a **1** *adj* characteristic. – **2** *m,f* (*actor*) character actor; (*actriz*) character actress. – **3 característica**, *f* characteristic.
caracterización *f* characterization.
caracterizado,-a **1** *pp* → **caracterizar**. – **2** *adj* (*distinguido*) distinguished: *un caracterizado político*, a distinguished politician.
caracterizar **1** *t* (*determinar*) to characterize, portray: *caracterizó las figuras de la comedia*, he portrayed the characters in the comedy. **2** (*enaltecer*) to characterize. **3** (*representar*) to play well. – **4 caracterizarse**, *p* (*distinguirse*) to be characterized: *la vida en el campo se caracteriza por la tranquilidad*, life in the country is peaceful; *se caracteriza por su sinceridad*, she is noted for her sincerity. **5** (*vestirse, arreglarse*) to dress up (**de**, as): *se caracterizó de policía*, he dressed up as a policeman. ▲ *Conjugation model* |4|, *like* *realizar*.
caracterología *f* characterology.
caracterológico,-a *adj* character type.
caradura **1** *adj fam* cheeky. – **2** *mf fam* cheeky devil. ● **tener (mucha) caradura**, *fam* to have (a lot of) cheek.
carajillo *m fam* coffee with a dash of brandy.
carajo **1** *m tabú* (*pene*) prick. – **2** *interj tabú* shit! ● **irse algo al carajo**, *tabú* (*planes*) to fall through, go to pot; (*empresa*) to go bust. ‖ **¡vete al carajo!**, *tabú* go to hell!
caramba **1** *interj* (*extrañeza*) good heavens!, my God! **2** (*enfado*) damn it!
carámbano *m* icicle.
carambola *f* (*billar*) cannon, US carom. ● **por carambola**, *fam* by a fluke, by chance: *ganó por carambola*, she won by a fluke.
caramelo **1** *m* (*dulce*) sweet, US candy. **2** (*azúcar quemado*) caramel, caramel syrup. ● **a punto de caramelo**, syrupy; *fig* just right.
caramillo **1** *m* (*flautilla*) pipe. **2** (*montón*) heap. **3** (*chisme*) piece of gossip.
carantoña **1** *f fam pey* (*mujer*) mutton dressed as lamb. – **2 carantoñas**, *fpl* (*caricias*) caresses; (*lisonjas*) wheedling *sing*, cajolery *sing*. ● **hacer carantoñas a algn.**, (*acariciar*) to caress sb.; (*adular*) to butter sb. up.
carapacho *m* (*caparazón*) carapace.
caraqueño,-a **1** *adj* of Caracas, from Caracas. – **2** *m,f* person from Caracas, inhabitant of Caracas.
carátula **1** *f* (*máscara*) mask. **2** (*cubierta*) cover. **3** *fig* theatre (US theater).

caravana **1** *f* (*expedición*) caravan. **2** (*atasco*) traffic jam, tailback: *había mucha caravana*, there was a big tailback. **3** (*remolque*) caravan, US trailer.
caravaning *m* caravanning, (US traveling by trailer).
caravansar *m* → **caravasar**.
caravasar *m* caravanserai, caravansary.
caray *interj* good heavens!, God!: *¡caray, qué tarde es!*, good heavens, it's very late!; *¡este caray de coche ya se ha estropeado!*, this damn car has broken down again!
carbón **1** *m* (*gen*) coal. **2** (*carboncillo*) charcoal. ● **negro,-a como el carbón**, as black as coal. ‖ **¡se acabó el carbón!**, *fam* that's that! ■ **carbón de leña**, charcoal. ‖ **carbón de piedra**, coal. ‖ **carbón mineral**, coal. ‖ **carbón vegetal**, charcoal.
carbonado *m* black diamond, carbonado.
carbonar *t* to turn into charcoal.
carbonatar *t* to carbonate.
carbonato *m* carbonate.
carboncillo *m* charcoal.
carbonear *t* to turn into charcoal.
carbonería *f* coal merchant's.
carbonero,-a **1** *adj* coal. – **2** *m,f* coal dealer, coal merchant. – **3 carbonera**, *f* (*donde se guarda carbón*) coal cellar. – **4 carbonero**, *m* (*ave*) tit. ■ **barco carbonero**, collier. ‖ **carbonero común**, (*ave*) great tit.
carbónico,-a *adj* carbonic. ■ **anhídrido carbónico**, carbon dioxide. ‖ **agua carbónica**, mineral water.
carbonífero,-a **1** *adj* carboniferous. – **2 el carbonífero**, *m* (*período geológico*) the Carboniferous, the Carboniferous period.
carbonilla **1** *f* (*residuo de carbón*) coal dust. **2** (*de locomotora*) soot.
carbonización **1** *f* (*reducción a carbón*) carbonization. **2** (*combustión*) burning, charring.
carbonizar **1** *t* (*reducir a carbón*) to carbonize. **2** (*quemar*) to burn, char: *murió carbonizado*, he was burnt to death. – **3 carbonizarse**, *p* to carbonize. ▲ *Conjugation model* |4|, *like* *realizar*.
carbono *m* carbon. ■ **dióxido de carbono**, carbon dioxide.
carbunco *m* anthrax.
carburación *f* carburation.
carburador *m* carburettor (US carburetor).
carburante *m* fuel.
carburar **1** *t* (*quemar*) to carburet, carburate. – **2** *i fam fig* (*funcionar*) to work properly: *esta máquina de afeitar no carbura*, this shaver doesn't work properly; *su cabeza ya no carbura*, his brain is out to lunch.
carburo *m* carbide.
carca **1** *adj fam* square, straight. **2** POL reactionary. – **3** *mf fam* square, straight. **4** POL *fam* reactionary.
carcaj *m* quiver. ▲ *pl* **carcajes**.
carcajada *f* burst of laughter, guffaw. ● **reír(se) a carcajadas**, to laugh one's head off, roar with laughter. ‖ **soltar una carcajada**, to burst out laughing.
carcajear **1** *i* to laugh heartily. – **2 carcajearse**, *p* (*reírse*) to laugh heartily. **3** (*burlarse*) to laugh (**de**, at): *se carcajea de todo lo que digo*, he laughs at everything I say.
carcamal *m fam pey* old fogey.
carcasa *f* (*armazón*) frame, framework.

cárcava *f* (*zanja*) ditch, trench.
cárcel 1 *f* jail, gaol, prison: *en la cárcel,* in jail. 2 (*aparato para sujetar*) clamp. 3 (*ranura*) groove.
carcelario,-a *adj* prison, goal, jail: *el régimen carcelario es duro,* prison regulations are harsh.
carcelero,-a 1 *adj* prison, goal, jail. – 2 *m,f* jailer, gaoler, warder, us warden; *arg* screw.
carcinógeno,-a *adj* carcinogen.
carcinoma *m* carcinoma, cancer.
cárcola *f* pedal.
carcoma 1 *f* (*insecto*) woodworm. 2 (*polvo*) wood dust. 3 *fig* plague: *la envidia es la carcoma de la mejor amistad,* envy can sour the best of friendships.
carcomer 1 *t* (*roer*) to eat away. 2 *fig* (*salud*) to undermine, eat away at; (*envidia etc*) to eat up, consume: *aquella enfermedad fue carcomiendo su salud,* that illness undermined his health; *le carcomen los celos,* he is consumed with jealousy. – 3 **carcomerse,** *p fig* to be consumed (**de,** with), be eaten up (**de,** with).
carcomido,-a 1 *pp* → **carcomer.** – 2 *adj* (*roído*) worm-eaten, riddled with woodworm. 3 *fig* (*salud*) undermined; (*envidia etc*) consumed, eaten up.
carda 1 *f* (*acción de cardar*) carding. 2 (*instrumento*) card, teasel. 3 *fig* (*reprensión*) scolding, telling off.
cardado,-a 1 *pp* → **cardar.** – 2 cardado, *m* (*carda*) carding. 3 (*del cabello*) backcombing.
cardador,-ra 1 *m,f* (*persona*) carder. – 2 cardador, *m* (*miriápodo*) millepede.
cardamomo *m* cardamom.
cardar 1 *t* (*lana etc*) to card. 2 (*cabello*) to backcomb.
cardenal[1] *m* REL cardinal.
cardenal[2] *m* (*hematoma*) bruise.
cardenalato *m* cardinalship.
cardenalicio,-a *adj* of a cardinal, related to a cardinal, cardinal's: *colegio cardenalicio,* college of cardinals.
cardencha 1 *f* (*planta*) card thistle. 2 (*instrumento*) card, teasel.
cárdeno,-a *adj* purple, violet.
cardiaco,-a 1 *adj* cardiac, heart: *ataque cardiaco,* heart attack. – 2 *m,f* person with a heart condition, person with heart disease.
cardíaco,-a *adj-m,f* → **cardiaco.**
cardias *m* cardia.
▲ *pl* **cardias.**
cardillo *m* golden thistle.
cardinal *adj* cardinal.
■ **número cardinal,** cardinal number.
cardiografía *f* cardiography.
cardiógrafo *m* cardiograph.
cardiograma *m* cardiogram.
cardiología *f* cardiology.
cardiólogo,-a *m,f* cardiologist.
cardiopatía *f* heart condition, heart disease.
cardiovascular *adj* cardiovascular.
cardo 1 *m* BOT (*comestible*) cardoon; (*espinoso*) thistle. 2 *fam fig* (*persona arisca*) cutting person, harsh person. 3 *fam pey* (*persona fea*) ugly person: *su novio es un cardo (borriquero),* her boyfriend is as ugly as sin.
■ **cardo borriquero,** BOT milk thistle; *fam* ugly person.
cardume *m* shoal of fish.
cardumen *m* → **cardume.**
carear 1 *t* JUR to confront, bring face to face: *carearon al sospechoso con las dos víctimas,* the suspect was confronted with his victims. 2 *fig* (*comparar*) to compare: *ha careado la copia con el original,* he has compared the

copy with the original. – 3 **carearse,** *p* (*enfrentarse*) to meet face to face: *al carearse casi discutieron,* when they met face to face they almost quarrelled.
carecer *i* to lack (**de,** -): *el pueblo carecía de alumbrado público,* the village lacked street lighting, the village had no street lighting.
▲ Conjugation model [43], like *agradecer.*
carena 1 *f* (*de nave*) careening. 2 (*de vehículo*) streamlining.
carenado *m* → **carena.**
carenar 1 *t* (*un barco*) to careen. 2 (*un vehículo*) to streamline.
carencia *f* lack (**de,** of): *hay carencia de médicos,* there's a lack of doctors.
carente *adj* lacking (**de,** -): *carente de agua,* lacking water; *es una película carente de emoción,* the film lacks emotion.
careo *m* confrontation.
carero,-a 1 *adj fam* pricey, dear: *en esa charcutería son bastante careros,* that delicatessen's quite pricey. – 2 *m,f fam* (*persona*) shopkeeper who sells things at a high price; (*tienda*) pricey shop.
carestía 1 *f* (*falta*) lack, shortage. 2 (*precio alto*) high cost, high price: *la carestía de la vida,* the high cost of living.
careta *f* (*máscara*) mask.
● **quitarle la careta a algn.,** *fig* to unmask sb.
■ **careta antigás,** gas mask.
careto *m fam* face.
carey 1 *m* (*animal*) sea turtle. 2 (*concha*) tortoiseshell.
▲ *pl* **careyes.**
carezco *pres indic* → **carecer.**
carga 1 *f* (*acción*) loading: *la carga de las mulas nos ha llevado media hora,* the loading of the mules took us half an hour. 2 (*lo cargado*) load; (*de avión, barco*) cargo, freight. 3 (*peso*) weight: *las vigas aguantan una carga de varias toneladas,* the girders can hold a weight of several tons. 4 (*de pluma, bolígrafo*) refill. 5 (*de arma*) charge. 6 MIL DEP charge. 7 ELEC (*de condensador*) charge; (*de circuito*) load. 8 (*tributo*) tax, charge. 9 *fig* (*responsabilidad*) responsibility, duty: *los directores de empresas tienen muchas cargas,* managing directors have a lot of responsibilities. 10 *fig* (*molestia*) burden: *el abuelo no es una carga,* our grandfather is not a burden.
● **ser un burro de carga,** *fam* to be a dogsbody. ‖ **volver a la carga,** *fig* to go on and on about sth.
■ **andén de carga,** loading platform. ‖ **carga afectiva,** *fig* emotional content. ‖ **carga de profundidad,** depth charge. ‖ **carga eléctrica,** electric charge. ‖ **carga explosiva,** explosive charge. ‖ **carga fiscal,** tax charge. ‖ **zona de carga y descarga,** loading and unloading bay.
cargado,-a 1 *pp* → **cargar.** – 2 *adj* (*atmósfera*) heavy, dense. 3 (*bebida*) strong: *dame un café cargado,* give me a strong cup of coffee; *este combinado está un poco cargado de ron,* this drink has a bit too much rum in it. 4 *fam* (*borracho*) drunk, (us loaded). 5 *fig* burdened, weighed down: *cargado,-a de responsabilidades,* weighed down with responsibility.
● **ser cargado,-a de espaldas,** to be round-shouldered.
cargador,-ra 1 *adj* loading. – 2 *m,f* (*gen*) loader; (*de muelle*) docker, stevedore; (*de alto horno*) stocker. – 3 cargador, *m* (*de arma*) chamber. 4 TÉC charger. 5 (*de pluma etc*) filler.
cargamento *m* (*gen*) load; (*de avión, barco*) cargo, freight.
cargante *adj fam fig* boring, annoying, tedious.

cargar 1 t (*poner peso*) to load: *cargaremos los muebles en el camión,* we'll load the furniture onto the lorry; *cargaron el barco de trigo,* the boat was loaded with wheat. **2** (*arma, máquina de fotos*) to load. **3** ELEC to charge: *cargar las pilas,* to charge the batteries. **4** (*pluma etc*) to fill. **5** (*precio*) to charge; (*en cuenta*) to debit: *nos cargaron un 6% de IVA,* we were charged 6% VAT. **6** fig (*poner muchas cosas*) to fill (**de,** with), cram (**de,** with): *cargó su habitación de adornos,* she filled her room with ornaments. **7** fig (*trabajo*) to burden with, lumber with; (*responsabilidad*) to put on, lay on: *le cargó ese trabajo a Pedro,* Pedro was lumbered with that job. **8** fam fig (*molestar*) to bother, annoy: *ese tipo me carga,* that guy annoys me. **9** JUR to charge. **10** INFORM to load. **11** MIL to charge. **12** (*naipes*) to trump; (*dados*) to load. **– 13** i (*gen*) to load. **14** ARQ to rest. **15** (*atacar*) to charge (**contra/sobre,** -): *el ejército cargó contra el enemigo,* the army charged the enemy. **16** (*hacerse cargo de*) to carry (**con,** -); (*cul-*) to shoulder (**con,** with): *yo cargaré con la maleta,* I'll carry the suitcase; *su padre cargó con las deudas,* his father took on the debts. **– 17 cargarse,** p (*llenarse*) to load OS. (**de,** with)· *cargarse de trabajo,* to burden os. with work. **18** (*el cielo*) to get cloudy, become overcast. **19** ELEC to become charged. **20** EDUC fam (*suspender*) to fail, (US flunk): *el profesor se ha cargado a la mitad de los alumnos,* the teacher failed half the pupils. **21** fam (*destrozar*) to smash, ruin: *me he cargado el coche,* I've wrecked the car. **22** fam (*matar*) to knock off.
● **cargar algo en la cuenta de algn.,** COM to debit sb.'s account with sth. ‖ **cargar con algn.,** fig to take charge of sb. ‖ **cargar con el muerto,** fam to be left holding the baby; (*ser culpado*) to get the blame. ‖ **cargar con la culpa,** to take the blame. ‖ **cargar con la responsabilidad,** to take the responsibility. ‖ **cargar con las consecuencias,** to suffer the consequences. ‖ **cargar la mano de algo,** fam (*poner mucho*) to add too much (of) sth.: *cargar la mano de sal,* to add too much salt. ‖ **cargar las culpas a algn.,** to put the blame on sb. ‖ **cargar las tintas,** fam to exaggerate. ‖ **cargarse de,** fig to weigh os. down with, saddle os. with, burden os. with: *estaba cargado de deudas,* he was burdened with debt. ‖ **cargarse de paciencia,** to summon up one's patience. ‖ **cargárselas,** fam to get into trouble: *te las vas a cargar,* you'll get into trouble, you're in for it.
▲ Conjugation model [7], like *llegar.*

cargazón 1 m (*cargamento*) load. **2** (*de estómago, de cabeza*) heavy feeling. **3** (*de nubes*) heavy cloud.

cargo 1 m (*peso*) load, weight. **2** (*empleo*) post, position: *el cargo de director,* the post of director. **3** (*gobierno, custodia*) charge, responsibility: *tiene dos empleados a su cargo,* he has two employees under him. **4** FIN charge, debit. **5** JUR (*falta*) charge, accusation.
● **correr a cargo de algo,** (*ser responsable*) to be responsible for sth.; (*pagar*) to pay for sth.: *yo corro a cargo de la comida,* I'll pay for the meal. ‖ **desempeñar el cargo de / ocupar el cargo de,** to have a post as. ‖ **estar al cargo de,** to be in charge of. ‖ **hacerse cargo de,** (*responsabilizarse de*) to take charge of; (*entender*) to realize: *me hago cargo,* I realize that. ‖ **jurar el cargo,** to take an oath.
■ **alto cargo,** top job, high-ranking position. ‖ **cargo de conciencia,** fig weight on one's conscience.

carguero 1 m (*embarcación*) freighter. **2** (*avión*) transport plane.

cariacontecido,-a adj down in the mouth, crestfallen.

cariado,-a adj decayed, carious.

cariar 1 t to cause to decay. **– 2 cariarse,** p to decay.
▲ Conjugation model [12], like *cambiar.*

cariátide f caryatid.

Caribe el Caribe, m the Caribbean.

caribeño,-a adj Caribbean.

caribú m caribou.

caricato m impressionist, impersonator.

caricatura f caricature.

caricaturista mf caricaturist.

caricaturizar t to caricature.
▲ Conjugation model [4], like *realizar.*

caricia f caress, stroke: *su madre le hizo una caricia en la mejilla,* his mother stroked his cheek.

caridad f charity.
● **¡por caridad!,** for pity's sake!
■ **obra de caridad,** charitable deed.

caries f (*enfermedad*) tooth decay, caries pl; (*lesión*) cavity: *tengo una caries,* I've got a cavity.
▲ pl *caries.*

carilla f (*plana*) page, side.

carillón m carillon.

cariñena m (*vino*) sweet wine from Cariñena.

cariño 1 m (*amor*) love, affection: *los padres sienten mucho cariño por sus hijos,* the parents love their children dearly; *tenía cariño a aquella pulsera,* she was fond of that bracelet. **2** (*esmero*) loving care: *bordó sus iniciales con mucho cariño,* she embroidered his initials with loving care. **3** (*apelativo*) darling, love, (us honey): *¿pasa algo, cariño?,* what's the matter, darling? **4** fig (*expresión*) caress, hug, kiss, cuddle: *siempre le está haciendo cariños a su nieta,* he's always cuddling his granddaughter. **– 5 cariños,** mpl (*recuerdos, saludos*) love sing.
● **coger/tomar cariño a algn./algo,** to grow fond of sb./sth. ‖ **"con todo cariño",** (*en una carta*) "lots of love".
▲ In 3, also used in plural with the same meaning.

cariñosamente adv affectionately.

cariñoso,-a adj loving, affectionate: *es muy cariñoso con los niños,* he's very affectionate with the children.

carioca 1 adj of Rio de Janeiro, from Rio de Janeiro. **– 2** mf person from Rio de Janeiro, inhabitant of Rio de Janeiro.

carisma m charisma.

carismático,-a adj charismatic.

caritativo,-a adj charitable.

cariz m aspect, look: *este asunto está tomando muy mal cariz,* this affair is beginning to look bad.

carlinga f (*cabina del piloto*) cockpit; (*de pasajeros*) cabin.

carlismo m Carlism.

carlista 1 adj Carlist. **– 2** mf Carlist.

carmelita 1 adj Carmelite. **– 2** mf Carmelite.

carmesí 1 adj crimson. **– 2** m crimson.
▲ pl *carmesíes.*

carmín 1 adj (*color*) carmine. **– 2** m (*color*) carmine. **3** (*rosal*) wild rose. **4** (*pintalabios*) lipstick.
■ **carmín de labios,** lipstick.

carminativo,-a 1 adj carminative. **– 2 carminativo,** m carminative.

carnación f flesh colour (us color).

carnada f bait.

carnal 1 adj carnal: *pecados carnales,* carnal sins. **2** fig (*terrenal*) material: *no le interesa lo espiritual sino lo carnal,* he's not interested in spiritual things but material things. **3** (*pariente*) first: *es primo carnal,* he's my first cousin.

carnaval *m* carnival.

carnaza 1 *f* (*de las pieles*) derma. 2 (*carnada*) bait. 3 (*carne en abundancia y de mala calidad*) low-grade meat: *hoy no he comprado carne en el mercado porque sólo he visto carnaza*, I didn't buy any meat at the market today because it all looked bad quality.

carne 1 *f* ANAT flesh. 2 CULIN meat: *me gusta la carne*, I like meat. 3 (*de fruta*) pulp. 4 *fig* (*cuerpo*) flesh: *la carne es débil*, the flesh is weak.
● **echar toda la carne en el asador**, *fig* to go in for everything. ‖ **en carne viva**, red raw. ‖ **en carne y hueso**, *fig* in person. ‖ **estar metido,-a en carnes**, *fam* to be plump. ‖ **ser de carne y hueso**, to be only human. ‖ **ser de pocas carnes**, *fam* to be thin. ‖ **ser uña y carne**, *fig* to be hand in glove.
■ **carne asada**, roasted meat. ‖ **carne de cañón**, *fig* cannon fodder. ‖ **carne de cerdo**, pork. ‖ **carne de cordero**, lamb. ‖ **carne de gallina**, *fig* goose pimples *pl*, goose bumps, goose flesh: *se me pone la carne de gallina*, it gives me goose pimples. ‖ **carne de ternera**, veal. ‖ **carne de vaca**, beef. ‖ **carne picada**, mince, mincemeat, (US ground meat, loose meat). ‖ **carne viva**, raw flesh.

carné *m* card.
■ **carné de conducir**, driving licence. ‖ **carné de identidad**, identity card.
▲ *pl* **carnés**.

carnero 1 *m* (*animal*) ram. 2 (*carne*) mutton.

carnestolendas *fpl* Carnival *sing*.

carnet *m* → **carné**.

carnicería 1 *f* butcher's, butcher's shop. 2 *fig* carnage, slaughter: *la batalla fue una carnicería*, the battle was a bloodbath.

carnicero,-a 1 *adj* (*animal*) carnivorous. 2 *fam* (*que le gusta la carne*) fond of meat: *Juan es muy carnicero*, Juan is a real meat-lover. 3 *fig* (*cruel*) bloodthirsty, sanguinary. – 4 *m,f* (*profesión*) butcher. 5 *fig* (*persona*) butcher. – 6 *m* (*animal*) carnivore.

cárnico,-a *adj* meat: *industrias cárnicas*, meat industries.

carnívoro,-a 1 *adj* carnivorous. – 2 *m,f* carnivore.

carnosidad 1 *f* (*en una llaga*) proud flesh. 2 (*en una parte del cuerpo*) outgrowth. 3 (*michelín*) bulge.

carnoso,-a *adj* fleshy.

caro,-a 1 *adj* (*costoso*) expensive, dear. 2 (*difícil*) difficult: *los aprobados están caros en esta escuela*, it's difficult to pass in this school. – 3 *caro, adv* at a high price.
● **costar caro,-a / salir caro,-a**, (*ser costoso*) to cost a lot; (*causar daño*) to cost dear: *la cena nos salió muy cara*, the dinner turned out very expensive; *conducir borracho puede costar caro*, there's a high price to pay for drinking and driving. ‖ **pagar caro,-a**, to pay a high price (for). ‖ **vender caro,-a**, to sell at a high price.

Carolina *f* Carolina: *Carolina del Norte*, North Carolina.
■ **Carolina del Sur**, South Carolina.

carolingio,-a *adj* Carolingian, Carlovingian.

carota *mf fam* cheeky person.

carótida *f* carotid.

carotina *f* carotene.

carozo *m* cob.

carpa[1] *f* (*de uvas*) small bunch of grapes.

carpa[2] *f* (*pez*) carp.
■ **salto de la carpa**, DEP jack-knife.

carpa[3] 1 *f* (*de circo*) big top, marquee. 2 (*tenderete*) stall.

carpanta *f fam* ravenous hunger: *¡tengo una carpanta!*, I'm starving!

Cárpatos los (montes) Cárpatos, *mpl* the Carpathians.

carpe *m* hornbeam.

carpeta 1 *f* (*archivador*) folder, file. 2 (*de escritorio*) table cover. 3 (*cartera*) briefcase.

carpetazo dar carpetazo, *loc* to shelve.

carpetovetónico,-a *adj pey* over-patriotically Spanish, Spanish to the core.

carpintería 1 *f* (*establecimiento*) carpenter's shop. 2 (*obra y oficio*) carpentry.
■ **carpintería metálica**, metalwork.

carpintero,-a 1 *adj* carpenter. – 2 *m,f* carpenter.

carpo *m* carpus.

carpología *f* carpology.

carraca[1] *f* (*instrumento*) rattle.

carraca[2] *f* (*ave*) roller.

carraca[3] 1 *f pey* (*barco viejo*) old tub. 2 *fam* (*coche viejo*) banger, wreck: *tu coche está hecho una carraca*, your car is an old banger. 3 *fam* (*persona achacosa*) wreck; (*persona vieja*) old crock.

carrasca *f* (*encina*) holm oak.

carraspear *i* to clear one's throat: *carraspeó antes de hablar*, he cleared his throat before speaking.

carraspeo *m* throat-clearing.

carraspera *f fam* hoarseness.

carrasposo,-a *adj* hoarse.

carrera 1 *f* (*acción*) run. 2 (*trayecto - de desfile*) route; (- de taxi) ride, journey; (- de planeta) course. 3 (*camino*) road. 4 DEP race: *ganó la carrera*, she won the race. 5 (*estudios*) degree course, university education: *hacer la carrera de medicina*, to study medicine; *¿qué carrera hiciste?*, what did you study at University?, (us what did you major in?). 6 (*profesión*) career: *quiere una carrera en el teatro*, he wants a career in the theatre; *es una mujer de carrera*, she's a career woman. 7 (*de media*) ladder, (US run). 8 (*calle*) street, avenue.
● **a la carrera**, in a hurry. ‖ **dar carrera a algn.**, to pay for sb.'s studies. ‖ **darse una carrera**, to hurry, run as fast as one can. ‖ **de carrera**, *fig* parrot-fashion. ‖ **hacer carrera**, *fig* to get on. ‖ **hacer carrera en la vida**, *fig* to succeed in life. ‖ **hacer la carrera**, *euf* to walk the streets. ‖ **no poder hacer carrera con/de algn.**, not to be able to do a thing with sb.: *Mariano es muy cabezota y no se puede hacer carrera de él*, Mariano is so stubborn that you can't get anywhere with him. ‖ **tomar carrera**, to take a run.
■ **carrera contra reloj**, race against the clock. ‖ **carrera de armamentos / carrera armamentística**, arms race. ‖ **carrera de caballos**, horse race. ‖ **carrera de coches / carrera de automóviles**, car race. ‖ **carrera de relevos**, relay race. ‖ **carrera de vallas**, hurdle race. ‖ **carrera diplomática**, diplomatic career.

carrerilla *f* MÚS run.
● **coger carrerilla / tomar carrerilla**, to take a run. ‖ **saber algo de carrerilla**, to know sth. by heart.

carreta *f* cart.

carretada 1 *f* (*carga*) cartload. 2 *fam* (*montón*) heaps *pl*, loads *pl*: *había una carretada de libros*, there were loads of books.

carrete 1 *m* (*de hilo*) bobbin, reel. 2 ELEC coil. 3 (*de caña de pescar*) reel. 4 (*de película*) spool; (*de fotos*) film, roll of film. 5 (*de máquina de escribir*) cartridge.
● **dar carrete**, *fam* (*dar conversación*) to go on and on: *¡con la prisa que tenía y él, venga a darme carrete!*, I was in such a hurry and he kept going on and on! ‖ **tener carrete**, *fam* (*hablar mucho*) to go on and on.

carretera *f* road.
■ carretera comarcal, B road. ‖ carretera nacional, A road, main road. ‖ carretera de acceso, approach road. ‖ carretera de circunvalación, ring road, bypass. ‖ mapa de carreteras, road map. ‖ red de carreteras, road network.

carretería 1 *f* (*oficio*) cartwright's work. 2 (*taller*) cartwright's shop.

carretero 1 *m* (*conductor*) carter, cart driver. 2 (*constructor*) cartwright.
● fumar como un carretero, *fam* to smoke like a chimney. ‖ hablar como un carretero / jurar como un carretero, *fam* to swear like a trooper.

carretilla *f* wheelbarrow.
● decir algo de carretilla, *fig* to say sth. parrot fashion. ‖ saber algo de carretilla, *fig* to know sth. off by heart.

carretón *m* (*carro pequeño*) small cart.

carricero *m* teal.

carricoche 1 *m* (*carro cubierto*) caravan. 2 *pey* (*coche viejo*) old banger, wreck.

carril 1 *m* (*de ferrocarril*) rail. 2 (*de carretera*) lane. 3 (*surco*) furrow. 4 (*de cortina*) rail.
■ carril bus, bus lane. ‖ carril de aceleración, slip road. ‖ carril de adelantamiento, overtaking lane, fast lane. ‖ carril lateral, service road.

carrillo *m* cheek.
● comer a dos carrillos, *fam* to gobble up, devour.

carro 1 *m* (*vehículo*) cart. 2 (*de supermercado, aeropuerto*) trolley, (US cart). 3 MIL tank. 4 (*carga de un carro*) cartload. 5 (*de máquina de escribir*) carriage. 6 *fam* (*coche*) car.
● apearse del carro, *fam* to give up, quit. ‖ ¡para el carro!, *fam* hold your horses!, hold on! ‖ carros y carretas, *fam* (*ofensas*) insults, abuse; (*molestias*) setbacks, hitches, trouble, problems: *tuvo que aguantar carros y carretas,* he had to put up with a lot of abuse.
■ carro blindado, armoured (US armored) car. ‖ carro de combate, tank. ‖ carro de la compra, shopping trolley, (US shopping cart).

carrocería *f* body, bodywork.

carrocha *f* eggs *pl.*

carromato *m* covered wagon.

carroña 1 *f* carrion. 2 *fig* (*personas despreciables*) trash, riffraff.

carroñero,-a 1 *adj* carrion-eating. – 2 *m,f* scavenger.

carroza 1 *adj fam* old, old-fashioned. – 2 *f* (*tirado por caballos*) coach, carriage. 3 (*coche adornado*) float. 4 (*coche fúnebre*) hearse. – 5 *mf fam* old fogey, square: *¡estás hecho un carroza!*, you're so old-fashioned!

carruaje *m* carriage, coach.

carrusel 1 *m* (*ejercicio ecuestre*) horse tattoo. 2 (*tiovivo*) merry-go-round, US carrousel.

carta 1 *f* (*misiva*) letter. 2 (*naipe*) card. 3 (*minuta*) menu. 4 JUR GEOG chart.
● a la carta, à la carte. ‖ dar carta blanca a algn., to give sb. a free hand; POL to give sb. carte blanche. ‖ echar una carta, to post a letter, (US mail a letter). ‖ echar las cartas a algn., to tell sb.'s fortune. ‖ jugárselo todo a una carta, *fig* to put all one's eggs in one basket. ‖ no saber a qué carta quedarse, *fig* not to know what to do. ‖ poner las cartas sobre la mesa, *fig* to put one's cards on the table. ‖ tomar cartas en un asunto, *fig* to take part in an affair.
■ carta abierta, open letter. ‖ carta blanca, carte blanche. ‖ carta certificada, registered letter. ‖ carta de ajuste, TV test card. ‖ carta de naturaleza / carta de ciudadanía, naturalization papers *pl.* ‖ carta de navegación, navigation chart. ‖ carta de presentación / carta de recomendación, letter of introduction. ‖ carta de vinos, wine list. ‖ carta urgente, express letter. ‖ "cartas al director", (*de un periódico*) "letters to the editor".

cartabón *m* set square, triangle.

cartagenero,-a 1 *adj* of Cartagena, from Cartagena. – 2 *m,f* person from Cartagena, inhabitant of Cartagena.

cartaginense 1 *adj* Carthaginian. – 2 *mf* Carthaginian.

cartaginés,-esa *adj-m,f* → **cartaginense**.

Cartago *m* Carthage.

cartapacio 1 *m* (*cuaderno*) notebook. 2 (*carpeta*) folder, file.

cartearse *p* to correspond (**con**, with), exchange letters (**con**, with), write (**con**, to): *me carteo con una chica en Irlanda,* I have a pen-friend in Ireland.

cartel *m* poster, bill.
● de cartel, *fig* reputed. ‖ en cartel, running, on: *esa película lleva 6 meses en cartel,* that film has been running for 6 months. ‖ "prohibido fijar carteles", "post no bills". ‖ tener (buen) cartel, *fig* to be popular.

cártel *m* cartel, trust.

cartelera 1 *f* (*para carteles*) hoarding, US billboard. 2 (*en periódicos*) entertainment section.
● en cartelera, running, on: *esta película lleva dos años en cartelera,* this film has been running for two years.

carteo *m* correspondence, exchange of letters.

cárter 1 *m* TÉC housing. 2 (*de bicicleta*) chain guard. 3 (*de coche*) crankcase.

cartera 1 *f* (*monedero*) wallet. 2 (*de colegial*) satchel, schoolbag. 3 (*de ejecutivo*) briefcase. 4 *fig* portfolio: *ministro sin cartera,* minister without portfolio. 5 COM portfolio.
● tener algo en cartera, *fig* to be planning sth.
■ cartera de clientes, client portfolio. ‖ cartera de pedidos, order book.

cartería 1 *f* (*empleo*) job of postal worker. 2 (*oficina*) sorting office.

carterista *mf* pickpocket.

cartero,-a *m,f* (*hombre*) postman; (*mujer*) postwoman.

cartesianismo *m* Cartesianism.

cartesiano,-a 1 *adj* Cartesian. – 2 *m,f* Cartesian.

cartilaginoso,-a *adj* cartilaginous.

cartílago *m* cartilage.

cartilla 1 *f* (*para aprender*) first reader. 2 (*tratado breve*) primer. 3 (*cuaderno*) book.
● cantar la cartilla a algn. / leer la cartilla a algn., *fam* to tell sb. off.
■ cartilla de ahorros, savings book. ‖ cartilla de racionamiento, ration book. ‖ cartilla del seguro, social-security card. ‖ cartilla militar, military record.

cartografía *f* cartography.

cartográfico,-a *adj* cartographic, cartographical.

cartógrafo,-a *m,f* cartographer.

cartograma *m* cartogram.

cartomancia *f* cartomancy.

cartomancía *f* cartomancy.

cartón 1 *m* (*material*) cardboard. 2 (*de cigarrillos*) carton. 3 (*dibujo*) sketch.
■ cartón piedra, papier mâché.

cartoné en cartoné, *loc* in hardback: *este libro está encuadernado en cartoné,* this book is bound in hardback.

cartuchera *f* cartridge holder, cartridge belt.

cartuchería *f* cartridge factory.

cartucho 1 *m* (*de explosivo*) cartridge. **2** (*de monedas*) roll (of coins). **3** (*cucurucho*) paper cone. **4** (*carga*) cartridge, refill.
● **quemar el último cartucho,** *fam* to play one's last card.
■ **cartucho de fogueo,** blank cartridge.
cartuja *f* → **cartujo,-a**.
cartujano,-a 1 *adj* Carthusian. **2** (*caballo*) Andalusian breed of horse. – **3** *m,f* Carthusian.
cartujo,-a 1 *adj* Carthusian. – **2 cartujo,** *m* Carthusian. – **3 cartuja,** *f* Charterhouse.
cartulina *f* thin cardboard.
carúncula *f* caruncle.
carvajo *m* oak.
carvallo *m* oak.
casa 1 *f* (*vivienda*) house. **2** (*piso*) flat. **3** (*edificio*) building. **4** (*hogar*) home: *vete a casa,* go home; *nos quedamos en casa,* we stayed at home; *fuimos a casa de Ana,* we went to Ana's. **5** (*familia*) family. **6** (*linaje*) house: *la casa de los Austria,* the House of Hapsburg. **7** (*empresa*) firm, company.
● **buscar casa,** to go house-hunting. ‖ **caerse la casa encima,** *fig* not to be able to stand being in the house. ‖ **como Pedro por su casa,** *fig* as if he (*she, you, etc*) owned the place. ‖ **de andar por casa,** (*ropa*) for wearing around the house; (*procedimiento, arreglo*) rough, makeshift. ‖ **echar la casa por la ventana / tirar la casa por la ventana,** *fig* to spare no expense, push the boat out. ‖ **empezar la casa por el tejado,** *fig* to put the cart before the horse. ‖ **hacer la casa,** *fam* to do the housework. ‖ **jugar en casa,** DEP to play at home. ‖ **llevar la casa,** *fig* to run the house. ‖ **no parar en casa,** to never be at home. ‖ **no salir de casa,** not to go out. ‖ **pasar por casa,** to come round, come over. ‖ **poner casa,** to set up house. ‖ **ser muy de casa,** *fig* to be home-loving.
■ **casa de citas,** *euf* brothel. ‖ **casa de comidas,** eating house. ‖ **casa de huéspedes,** boarding-house. ‖ **casa de juego,** gambling house. ‖ **casa de modas,** fashion house. ‖ **casa de pisos,** block of flats. ‖ **casa de socorro,** first aid post. ‖ **casa matriz / casa principal,** COM head office, central office. ‖ **la casa de Tócame Roque,** *fam* bedlam.
casaca *f* fitted short coat.
casación *f* cassation, annulment.
casadero,-a *adj* of marrying age.
casado,-a 1 *pp* → **casar**. – **2** *adj* married: *es una mujer casada,* she's a married woman; *está casado con Elena,* he's married to Elena. – **3** *m,f* (*hombre*) married man; (*mujer*) married woman.
■ **los recién casados,** the newly-weds.
casamata *f* casemate.
casamentero,-a 1 *adj* matchmaking. – **2** *m,f* matchmaker.
casamiento 1 *m* (*contrato*) marriage. **2** (*ceremonia*) wedding.
casanova *m desus* Casanova, ladies' man.
casar[1] 1 *t* (*disponer matrimonio*) to marry: *casó a su segunda hija,* she married off her second daughter. **2** (*unir*) to join, fit. – **3** *i* (*casarse*) to marry (**con,** -), get married (**con,** to): *Pedro casó con su vecina,* Pedro married his neighbour, Pedro got married to his neighbour. **4** (*armonizar*) to match, go together, fit together: *estos colores no casan,* this colours don't match. – **5 casarse,** *p* to get married (**con,** to) marry (**con,** -).
● **casarse de penalty,** *fam* to have a shotgun wed-

ding. ‖ **casarse por la iglesia,** to get married in church, have a church wedding. ‖ **casarse por lo civil,** to get married in a registry office. ‖ **no casarse con nadie,** *fig* to keep os. to os.
casar[2] *t* JUR to annul, quash.
cascabel 1 *m* bell. **2** *fam fig* (*persona alegre*) happy person; (*poco juiciosa*) rattlebrain.
● **ponerle el cascabel al gato,** *fig* to bell the cat.
cascabelear 1 *t fig* (*infundir esperanzas*) to take in, raise the hopes of. – **2** *i fam fig* (*portarse con ligereza*) to act recklessly.
cascabelero,-a 1 *adj fig* (*poco juicioso*) scatterbrained. – **2 cascabelero,** *m* (*sonajero*) baby's rattle.
cascada *f* cascade, waterfall.
cascado,-a 1 *pp* → **cascar**. – **2** *adj* (*sonido, voz*) harsh, hoarse. **3** (*objeto*) broken-down, clapped-out: *el radiador está muy cascado,* the radiator is on its last legs. **4** *fam* (*persona*) worn-out: *mi abuelo ya está muy cascado por los años,* my grandfather is really showing his age.
cascajo 1 *m* (*guijo*) gravel, rubble. **2** (*fragmentos*) bits *pl*, fragments *pl*. **3** *fam* (*trasto viejo*) piece of junk.
● **estar hecho,-a un cascajo,** *fam* (*persona*) to be a wreck.
cascanueces *m* nutcracker.
▲ *pl* **cascanueces**.
cascapiñones *m* nutcracker.
▲ *pl* **cascapiñones**.
cascar 1 *t* (*romper*) to crack: *cascar un huevo,* to crack an egg. **2** *fam* (*pegar*) to hit, beat up. – **3** *i fam* (*morir*) to snuff it, kick the bucket. **4** *fam* (*charlar*) to chat. – **5** *t fam* (*dañar*) to harm: *la bebida casca,* drinking is bad for you. – **6 cascarse,** *p* (*romperse*) to crack. **7** (*la voz*) to become harsh, become hoarse.
● **cascarla,** *fam* (*morir*) to kick the bucket. ‖ **cascársela,** *tabú* to wank, US jerk off.
▲ *Conjugation model* [1], *like* **sacar**.
cáscara 1 *f* (*de huevo, nuez*) shell. **2** (*de fruta*) skin, peel. **3** (*de grano*) husk. – **4 cáscaras,** *interj* (*sorpresa*) good grief!; (*enfado*) damn it!
● **ser de la cáscara amarga,** *fam* (*de ideas izquierdistas*) to be a lefty, be a left-winger.
cascarilla 1 *f* (*de metal*) sheet. **2** (*de cacao*) cocoa.
cascarón *m* eggshell.
● **recién salido del cascarón,** *fam* wet behind the ears.
cascarrabias *mf fam* grumpy person, bad-tempered person.
▲ *pl* **cascarrabias**.
casco 1 *m* (*para la cabeza*) helmet. **2** (*cráneo*) skull. **3** (*fragmento*) broken piece, fragment. **4** (*de metralla*) piece of shrapnel. **5** (*de sombrero*) crown. **6** (*envase*) empty bottle. **7** MAR hull. **8** (*de caballería*) hoof. – **9 cascos,** *mpl* (*auriculares*) headphones. **10** *fam* (*cabeza*) head *sing,* brains.
● **calentarse los cascos / romperse los cascos,** *fam* to rack one's brains. ‖ **ser alegre de cascos / ser ligero,-a de cascos,** *fam* to be scatterbrained.
■ **casco protector,** crash helmet. ‖ **casco urbano,** town centre (US center).
cascote 1 *m* (*fragmento*) piece of rubble, piece of debris. **2** (*de metralla*) piece of shrapnel. – **3 cascotes,** *mpl* rubble *sing.*
caseína *f* casein.
caserío 1 *m* (*casa*) country house. **2** (*pueblo*) hamlet, small village.
casero,-a 1 *adj* (*persona*) home-loving. **2** (*productos*) home-made: *pan casero,* home-made bread. **3** (*fami-*

liar) family. **4** DEP (*árbitro, juez*) favouring (US *favoring*) *the home team*: *el equipo local ganó porque el árbitro estuvo muy casero,* the home team won because the referee was biased in their favour. – **5** *m,f* (*dueño - hombre*) landlord; (*mujer*) landlady. **6** (*guarda*) keeper.

caserón *m* big rambling house.

caseta 1 *f* (*casita*) hut, booth. **2** (*de feria*) stall, stand. **3** (*de bañistas*) bathing hut, US bath house. **4** DEP changing room. **5** (*de perro*) kennel, doghouse.

casete 1 *m* (*magnetófono*) cassette player, cassette recorder. – **2** *f* (*cinta*) cassette, cassette tape.

casi *adv* almost, nearly: *había casi cincuenta personas,* there were almost fifty people; *me tropecé y casi me caí,* I tripped and nearly fell over; *no comió casi nada,* she hardly ate anything; *casi prefiero el vestido rojo,* I think I prefer the red dress.
● **casi, casi,** *fam* just about. ‖ **¡casi nada!,** *fam* peanuts!: *le tocaron 5 millones, ¡casi nada!,* he won 5 million, peanuts! ‖ **casi no,** hardly: *casi no los vemos,* we hardly see them. ‖ **casi nunca,** hardly ever: *casi nunca llama,* he hardly ever phones.

casilla 1 *f* (*casita*) hut, lodge. **2** (*de casillero*) pigeonhole. **3** (*cuadrícula*) square.
● **sacar a algn. de sus casillas,** *fig* to drive sb. mad.

casillero *m* pigeonholes *pl*.

casino *m* casino.

casis *m* blackcurrant bush.
▲ *pl casis.*

caso 1 *m* (*ocasión*) case, occasion. **2** (*suceso*) event, happening. **3** (*asunto*) affair: *el caso Roldán,* the Roldán affair. **4** MED LING case: *es un caso clínico,* it's a clinical case.
● **cuando llegue el caso,** in due course. ‖ **dado el caso de que ...,** in the event of ... ‖ **el caso es que ...,** the fact is that ..., the thing is that ... ‖ **en caso contrario,** otherwise. ‖ **en caso de,** in case of, in the event of. ‖ **en caso de necesidad,** if need be, if necessary. ‖ **en caso de que,** if: *en caso de que te pierdas, llámame,* if you get lost, call me. ‖ **en cualquier caso,** in any case. ‖ **en el mejor de los casos,** at best. ‖ **en el peor de los casos,** at worst. ‖ **en este caso,** in such a case. ‖ **en todo caso,** anyhow, at any rate. ‖ **en último caso,** as a last resort. ‖ **en un caso extremo,** as a last resort. ‖ **¡eres (es, etc) un caso!,** *fam* you're (*he's etc*) a case! ‖ **hacer al caso / venir al caso,** to be relevant. ‖ **hacer caso de algn. / hacer caso a algn.,** to pay attention to sb., take notice of sb.: *no le hagas caso,* don't pay any attention to him. ‖ **hacer caso omiso de algo,** to take no notice of sth., ignore sth. ‖ **no venir al caso,** to be beside the point. ‖ **para el caso es igual,** it's the same, it doesn't make any difference. ‖ **pongamos por caso,** let's say, suppose. ‖ **verse en el caso de,** to be compelled to.
■ **caso de fuerza mayor,** dire necessity. ‖ **caso perdido,** hopeless case.

casona *f* large house.

casorio *m fam* wedding.

caspa *f* dandruff.

Caspio el mar Caspio, *m* the Caspian Sea.

cáspita *interj* dear me!, goodness gracious!

casquería *f* tripe shop.

casquero,-a *m,f* tripe seller.

casquete 1 *m* (*prenda*) skullcap. **2** (*peluca*) toupée. **3** *tabú* (*polvo*) shag, screw.
● **echar un casquete,** *tabú* to have a shag, have a screw.

■ **casquete esférico,** fragment of a sphere. ‖ **casquete polar,** polar cap.

casquillo 1 *m* TÉC ferrule, metal tip. **2** (*de cartucho*) case. **3** (*de flecha*) head.

casquivano,-a *adj fam* scatterbrained.

cassette *m-f* → **casete.**

casta 1 *f* (*grupo social*) caste. **2** (*linaje*) lineage, descent. **3** (*de animales*) breed. **4** *fig* (*calidad*) quality: *esta carne es de buena casta,* this meat is good quality.
● **de casta,** (*persona*) of breeding, of good stock; (*animal*) thoroughbred, purebred. ‖ **de casta le viene al galgo,** *fam* it runs in the family.

castaña *f* → **castaño,-a.**

castañal *m* chestnut grove.

castañar *m* chestnut grove.

castañazo 1 *m fam* (*golpe*) thump, whack. **2** *fam* (*de coche*) crash.
● **pegarse un castañazo,** *fam* to crash.

castañero,-a *m,f* chestnut seller.

castañeta 1 *f* (*chasquido*) snap of the fingers. **2** MÚS (*castañuela*) castanet.

castañetear 1 *t* (*tocar castañuelas*) to play castanets. – **2** *i* (*dientes*) to chatter. **3** (*los dedos*) to snap one's fingers.

castañeteo 1 *m* (*de castañuelas*) sound of castanets. **2** (*de dientes*) chattering. **3** (*de dedos*) snapping.

castaño,-a 1 *adj* chestnut-brown, chestnut; (*pelo*) brown. – **2 castaño,** *m* BOT (*árbol*) chestnut tree. **3** (*madera*) chestnut. – **4 castaña,** *f* BOT chestnut. **5** (*de pelo*) bun. **6** (*vasija*) demijohn. **7** *fam* (*bofetada*) slap; (*golpe*) blow, punch: *ayer se dio una castaña con el coche,* he crashed his car yesterday. **8** *fam* (*borrachera*) binge, skinful: *anoche cogió una buena castaña,* he got plastered last night.
● **pasar de castaño oscuro,** *fam* to be going a bit too far. ‖ **sacarle a algn. las castañas del fuego,** *fig* to bail sb. out, get sb. out of trouble.

castañuela *f* castanet.
● **alegre como unas castañuelas,** *fam* happy as a sandboy.

castellanismo *m word common to the Castilian spoken in Castile, expression common to the Castilian spoken in Castile.*

castellanizar *t* to Hispanicize.
▲ *Conjugation model* [4], *like realizar.*

castellano,-a 1 *adj* Castilian. – **2** *m,f* (*persona*) Castilian. – **3 castellano,** *m* (*idioma*) Castilian, Spanish.

castellonense 1 *adj* of Castellón, from Castellón. – **2** *mf* person from Castellón, inhabitant of Castellón.

casticismo 1 *m* (*de tradiciones*) love of tradition. **2** (*de lengua*) purity.

casticista *mf* purist.

castidad *f* chastity.

castigador,-ra *m,f fam* (*hombre*) ladies' man; (*mujer*) man-eater.

castigar 1 *t* (*aplicar una pena*) to punish: *su madre la castigó,* her mother punished her. **2** JUR DEP to penalize. **3** (*dañar*) to damage, ruin: *la sequía castigó las cosechas,* the drought ruined the crops. **4** (*una cabalgadura*) to ride hard. **5** *fam* (*seducir*) to seduce.
▲ *Conjugation model* [7], *like llegar.*

castigo 1 *m* punishment. **2** JUR DEP penalty.
● **levantar un castigo,** to withdraw a punishment.
■ **área de castigo,** DEP penalty area. ‖ **castigo ejemplar,** exemplary punishment. ‖ **castigo máximo,** DEP penalty.

Castilla *f* Castile.
● **¡ancha es Castilla!,** *fig* it's a free world!

■ **Castilla la Nueva,** New Castile. ‖ **Castilla la Vieja,** Old Castile.

castillejo *m* (*andamio*) scaffold.

castillo *m* castle.

● **hacer castillos en el aire / levantar castillos en el aire,** *fig* to build castles in the air, build castles in Spain.

■ **castillo de fuegos artificiales,** firework display. ‖ **castillo de naipes,** *fig* house of cards.

casting *m* casting, audition.

▲ *pl* **castings**.

castizo,-a *adj* pure, authentic.

casto,-a *adj* chaste.

castor *m* beaver.

castración *f* castration.

castrado,-a 1 *pp* → **castrar**. – 2 castrado, *m* eunuch.

castrar 1 *t* (*capar*) to castrate. 2 (*podar*) to prune. 3 (*las colmenas*) to uncap. 4 *fig* (*debilitar*) to mutilate.

castrense *adj* military.

castrismo *m* Castroism.

castrista 1 *adj* Castroist. – 2 *mf* Castroist.

casual *adj* accidental, chance: *muchos descubrimientos surgen de forma casual,* many discoveries are made purely by chance.

● **por un casual,** *fam* just by chance, by any chance.

casualidad 1 *f* chance, accident. 2 (*coincidencia*) coincidence.

● **dar la casualidad,** to just happen: *dio la casualidad de que ya nos conocíamos,* it just happened that we had already met. ‖ **de casualidad / por casualidad,** by chance.

casualmente *adv* by chance, by accident: *nos encontramos casualmente,* we met by chance.

casuario *m* cassowary.

casuca *f pey* hovel.

casucha *f pey* hovel.

casuística *f* → **casuístico,-a**.

casuístico,-a 1 *adj* casuistic, casuistical. – 2 casuística, *f* casuistry.

casulla *f* chasuble.

cata 1 *f* (*degustación*) tasting: *se realizó una cata de vinos,* there was a wine tasting. 2 (*porción*) sample.

catabólico,-a *adj* catabolic.

catabolismo *m* catabolism.

cataclismo *m* cataclysm.

catacumbas *fpl* catacombs.

catador,-ra *m,f* taster.

■ **catador,-ra de vinos,** wine taster.

catadura *f pey* looks *pl*.

catafalco *m* catafalque.

catalán,-ana 1 *adj* Catalan, Catalonian. – 2 *m,f* (*persona*) Catalan. – 3 catalán, *m* (*idioma*) Catalan.

catalanismo 1 *m* LING Catalan word, Catalan expression. 2 POL Catalan nationalism.

catalanista 1 *adj* POL relating to Catalan nationalism. – 2 *mf* POL Catalan nationalist.

catalejo *m* telescope.

catalepsia *f* catalepsy.

cataléptico,-a 1 *adj* cataleptic. – 2 *m,f* cataleptic.

catalicores *m* sampling tube.

catálisis *f* catalysis.

▲ *pl* **catálisis**.

catalizador,-ra 1 *adj* catalytic. – 2 **catalizador,** *m* catalyst. 3 AUTO cataliser (US catalyzer), catalytic converter.

catalizador *m* → **catalizador,-ra**.

catalizar 1 *t* QUÍM to catalyse (US catalyze). 2 *fig* to act as a catalyst for.

▲ *Conjugation model* [4], *like* **realizar**.

catalogación *f* cataloguing (US cataloging).

catalogar 1 *t* to catalogue (US catalog). 2 *fig* to classify, class.

▲ *Conjugation model* [7], *like* **llegar**.

catálogo *m* catalogue (US catalog).

catalpa *f* catalpa, Indian bean tree.

Cataluña *f* Catalonia.

catamarán *m* catamaran.

cataplasma 1 *f* poultice, cataplasm. 2 *fam fig* (*pelma*) bore.

cataplines *mpl fam* nuts, balls.

catapulta *f* catapult.

catapultar *t* to catapult.

catar 1 *t* (*probar*) to taste. 2 (*examinar*) to examine, inspect.

catarata 1 *f* waterfall. 2 MED cataract.

● **operar de cataratas,** MED to perform a cataract operation on.

■ **las cataratas del Niágara,** the Niagara Falls.

cátaro,-a *adj* Cathar, Catharist.

catarral *adj* catarrhal, cold.

catarro *m* cold, catarrh: *cogí un catarro,* I caught a cold.

catarsis *f* catharsis, katharsis.

▲ *pl* **catarsis**.

catártico,-a *adj* cathartic, kathartic.

catastral *adj* cadastral.

catastro *m* cadastre, cadaster, official register.

catástrofe *f* catastrophe.

catastrófico,-a *adj* catastrophic.

catastrofismo 1 *m* (*teoría*) catastrophism. 2 (*pesimismo*) pessimism.

catatonía *f* catatonia.

catavino 1 *m* (*recipiente*) wine taster. – 2 catavinos, *mf* (*persona*) wine taster.

▲ *In* 2, *pl* **catavinos**.

catchup *m* ketchup.

cate 1 *m* EDUC *fam* failed subject, fail: *he tenido tres cates,* I failed three subjects. 2 *fam* (*golpe*) thump, whack.

catear *t* EDUC *fam* to fail, US flunk.

catecismo *m* catechism.

catecúmeno,-a *m,f* catechumen.

cátedra 1 *f* (*cargo de universidad*) professorship; (*de instituto*) post of head of department. 2 (*departamento*) department: *la cátedra de latín,* the Latin department. 3 (*aula*) lecture room.

● **ex cátedra,** ex cathedra. ‖ **sentar cátedra,** *fig* to give a lesson.

■ **cátedra de San Pedro,** Holy See.

catedral 1 *adj* cathedral. – 2 *f* cathedral.

● **como una catedral,** *fam* huge, massive.

catedralicio,-a *adj* cathedral.

catedrático,-a *m,f* (*de universidad*) professor; (*de instituto*) head of department.

cátedro,-a *m,f fam* → **catedrático,-a**.

categoría *f* category, class; (*social*) class: *un restaurante de primera categoría,* a first-class restaurant.

● **de categoría,** important, prominent: *Mozart fue un músico de categoría,* Mozart was a prominent musician; *se han comprado una casa de categoría,* they have bought a luxury house.

categórico,-a *adj* categoric, categorical.

■ **un no categórico,** a flat refusal.

categorizar t to categorize.
▲ *Conjugation model* [4], *like realizar.*
catenaria f → **catenario,-a.**
catenario,-a 1 *adj* catenary. – **2 catenaria,** f catenary.
catequesis f catechesis.
▲ *pl catechesis.*
catequismo m catechism.
catequista mf catechist, catechizer.
catequizar 1 t REL to catechize. **2** *(persuadir)* to persuade.
▲ *Conjugation model* [4], *like realizar.*
catering m catering, catering service.
caterva f *pey* throng, crowd.
catéter m catheter.
cateto[1] m *(de triángulo)* side of a right-angled triangle forming the right angle.
cateto,-a[2] m,f *pey (palurdo)* dimwit, yokel.
catión m cation.
catiusca f wellington, wellington boot, (US rubber boot).
cátodo m cathode.
catolicismo m Catholicism.
católico,-a 1 *adj* Catholic. – **2** m,f Catholic.
● **no estar muy católico,-a,** *fam (persona)* not to feel well, be under the weather; *(alimento)* to be a bit off: *no estoy muy católico, me duele la cabeza,* I don't feel very well, I've got a headache.
catolizar t to Catholicize.
▲ *Conjugation model* [4], *like realizar.*
catón[1] m *fig (censor)* harsh critic.
catón[2] m *(libro)* primer, first reading book.
catorce 1 *adj (cardinal)* fourteen; *(ordinal)* fourteenth. – **2** m *(número)* fourteen. **3** *fam (quiniela)* jackpot: *ha sacado un catorce,* he hit the jackpot.
▲ *See also* **seis.**
catorceavo,-a 1 *adj* fourteenth. – **2** m,f fourteenth.
▲ *See also* **sexto,-a.**
catre 1 m *(plegable)* folding bed; *(de campaña)* camp bed. **2** *fam* bed, sack: *se fue al catre,* he hit the sack.
● **llevarse a algn. al catre,** *arg* to lay sb.
catrecillo m small folding chair.
catsup m → **catchup.**
caucásico,-a *adj* Caucasian.
Cáucaso el Cáucaso, m the Caucasus.
■ **las montañas del Cáucaso,** the Caucasus mountains.
cauce 1 m *(de río)* bed. **2** *(conducto descubierto)* ditch, trench. **3** *fig (canal)* channel, way: *el cauce reglamentario,* the official channels.
caucho m rubber.
caución 1 f guarantee. **2** JUR bail.
caudal[1] *adj (de la cola)* caudal: *aleta caudal,* caudal fin.
caudal[2] 1 m *(de río)* flow. **2** *(bienes)* wealth, riches *pl.* **3** *fig (abundancia)* abundance, wealth: *un caudal de recuerdos,* a wealth of memories.
caudaloso,-a 1 *adj (río)* deep, plentiful. **2** *fig (persona)* wealthy.
caudillaje m leadership.
caudillo m leader, head.
causa 1 f *(gen)* cause: *murió por la causa,* he died for the cause; *estamos aquí por tu causa,* we are here for your sake. **2** *(motivo)* cause, reason, motive: *el niño lloraba sin causa,* the child was crying for no reason. **3** JUR *(caso)* case, lawsuit; *(juicio)* trial.
● **a causa de,** because of, on account of. ‖ **hacer cau-**sa común con,** to make common cause with. ‖ **instruir una causa,** JUR to take legal proceedings. ‖ **por causa de,** because of, on account of.
■ **causa mayor,** good reason: *no se puede faltar al trabajo si no es por causa mayor,* you can't stay off work unless it's for a very good reason. ‖ **causa pública,** JUR public good.
causal *adj* causal.
causalidad f causality.
causante 1 *adj* causal, causing: *el coche causante del accidente fue el amarillo,* the car which caused the accident was the yellow one. – **2** mf *(persona)* person who is the cause, causer.
causar 1 t *(provocar)* to cause, bring about: *las inundaciones causaron daños cuantiosos,* the floods caused a great deal of damage. **2** *(proporcionar)* to make, give: *su visita me causó un gran placer,* her visit gave me great pleasure; *el nuevo portero me ha causado muy mala impresión,* the new porter made a bad impression on me.
causticidad f causticity.
cáustico,-a *adj* caustic.
cautela f caution, cautiousness: *tuvo la cautela de cerrar la puerta,* he took the precaution of locking the door.
● **con cautela,** cautiously.
cautelosamente *adv* cautiously.
cauteloso,-a *adj* cautious, wary.
cauterización f cauterization.
cauterizador,-ra 1 *adj* cauterizing, cauterant. – **2** cauterizador, m cautery, cauterant.
cauterizante *adj* cauterizing.
cauterizar 1 t to cauterize, fire. **2** *fig* to apply drastic measures to.
▲ *Conjugation model* [4], *like realizar.*
cautivador,-ra 1 *adj* captivating. **2** *(encantador)* charming.
cautivar 1 t to take prisoner, capture. **2** *fig (atraer)* to captivate, charm: *su sonrisa me cautivó,* I was captivated by his smile.
cautiverio m captivity.
cautividad f captivity.
cautivo,-a 1 *adj* captive. – **2** m,f captive.
cauto,-a *adj* cautious, wary.
cava 1 m *(bebida)* cava, champagne. – **2** f *(bodega)* wine cellar.
cavar 1 t to dig. – **2** i *(ahondar)* to go deep: *la herida cava para adentro,* the wound is quite deep. **3** *fig (meditar)* to meditate (**en,** on).
● **cavar su propia tumba,** *fig* to dig one's own grave.
caverna 1 f cavern, cave. **2** MED cavity.
■ **hombre de las cavernas,** caveman.
cavernario,-a *adj* cave, cavern.
cavernícola 1 *adj* cave dwelling. **2** *fam fig (reaccionario)* reactionary. – **3** mf cave dweller, caveman. **4** *fam fig (reaccionario)* reactionary.
cavernoso,-a 1 *adj* cavernous. **2** *(voz etc)* hollow, deep: *una voz cavernosa,* a deep voice.
caviar m caviar.
cavidad f cavity.
cavilación f pondering, musing.
cavilar i to ponder, think about, brood over: *cavilar sobre un problema,* to ponder (over) a problem.
cavitación f cavitation.
cayado 1 m *(de pastor)* shepherd's crook. **2** *(de obispo)* crozier.
■ **cayado de la aorta,** MED arch of the aorta.

cayo *m* key.

caz *m* irrigation canal.
▲ *pl caces*.

caza 1 *f (acción)* hunting. **2** *(de animales)* game. **3** *fig (persecución)* pursuit, chase. – **4** *m* AV fighter, fighter plane.
● andar a la caza de algo / ir a la caza de algo, *fig* to hunt for sth., be in search of sth.: *el periodista va a la caza de la mejor foto,* the reporter hunts for the best photograph. ‖ dar caza, to give chase. ‖ ir de caza, to go hunting. ‖ levantar la caza, to give the game away. ■ caza de brujas, witch-hunt. ‖ caza mayor, big game. ‖ caza menor, small game.

cazabombardero *m* fighter bomber.

cazador,-ra 1 *adj* hunting. – **2** *m,f* hunter. – **3** cazadora, *f (chaqueta)* (waist-length) jacket.
■ cazador de dotes, fortune hunter. ‖ cazador de pieles, trapper.

cazadora *f* → **cazador,-ra**.

cazadotes *m* fortune hunter.
▲ *pl cazadotes*.

cazalla *f* aniseed spirit.

cazar 1 *t* to hunt: *Oscar salió a cazar liebres,* Oscar went out hunting hares. **2** *fam (conseguir)* to catch, land: *cazó una fortuna,* she landed a fortune; *cazó un buen marido,* she landed a good husband. **3** *fam (descubrir)* to find out, discover: *las mentiras siempre se cazan,* lies always catch up with you. **4** *fam (entender)* to understand, catch: *este chico no caza ni una,* this boy doesn't understand a thing.
● cazar furtivamente, to poach. ‖ cazarlas al vuelo, *fam* to be quick on the uptake.
▲ *Conjugation model* [4], *like realizar*.

cazasubmarinos *m* submarine chaser.
▲ *pl cazasubmarinos*.

cazatalentos *m,f* head-hunter, talent scout.
▲ *pl cazatalentos*.

cazatorpedero *m* torpedo-boat destroyer, destroyer.

cazcarria *f* splash of mud.

cazo 1 *m (cucharón)* ladle. **2** *(cacerola)* saucepan.

cazoleta 1 *f (de espada)* hand guard. **2** TÉC housing. **3** *(de pipa)* bowl.

cazón *m* dogfish.

cazuela 1 *f (utensilio)* casserole, saucepan. **2** *(guiso)* casserole, stew. **3** *(de sostén)* cup.
● a la cazuela, CULIN stewed: *fideos a la cazuela,* stewed noodles.

cazurrería *f* sullenness, surliness.

cazurro,-a *adj* sullen, surly.

CC¹ *abr (Cuerpo Consular)* consular corps.

CC² *abr (Código de Circulación)* highway code.

CC³ *abr (Código Civil)* civil code.

c/c *abr (cuenta corriente)* current account; *(abreviatura)* c/a.

c.c. *abr (centímetros cúbicos)* cubic centimetres; *(abreviatura)* cc.

CC.OO. *abr (Comisiones Obreras)* Workers' Commission (Spanish Communist-run labour union).

CD *abr (Cuerpo Diplomático)* diplomatic corps (Corps Diplomatique); *(abreviatura)* CD.

CDC *abr (Convergència Democràtica de Catalunya)* Catalan centre party.

CDS *abr* POL *(Centro Democrático y Social)* Spanish centre party.

ce *f* name of the letter *c*.
● ce por ce / ce por be, *fig* in great detail. ‖ por ce o por be, *fig* for one reason or another.

CE *abr (Comunidad Europea)* European Community; *(abreviatura)* EC.

cebada *f* barley.

cebadera 1 *f (morral)* nosebag. **2** *(cajón)* barley hopper.

cebadilla *f* wild barley.

cebador *m* primer.

cebar 1 *t (animal)* to fatten, fatten up. **2** *(poner cebo)* to bait: *cebó el anzuelo con una lombriz,* he baited the hook with an earthworm. **3** TÉC *fig* to prime. **4** *fig (pasiones etc)* to nourish: *cebar el alma con esperanza,* to nourish one's soul with hope. – **5** cebarse, *p fig (dedicarse)* to devote os. (en, to): *se ha cebado en el estudio,* she devoted herself to study. **6** *fig (ensañarse)* to show no mercy (en/con, towards), take it out (en/con, on), vent one's anger (en/con, on): *el asesino se cebó en su víctima,* the killer showed no mercy towards his victim; *la peste se cebó con toda la población,* the plague ravaged the whole town.

cebo 1 *m (para animales)* food. **2** *(para pescar)* bait. **3** *fig (de arma)* primer. **4** *fig (señuelo)* bait, lure.

cebolla 1 *f* onion. **2** *(bulbo)* bulb. **3** *(de ducha)* rose, nozzle.

cebolleta 1 *f (especia)* chives *pl.* **2** *(cebolla)* spring onion.

cebollino 1 *m (especia)* chives *pl.* **2** *(cebolla)* spring onion. **3** *fam fig (persona)* idiot, nitwit.

cebollón *m* sweet onion.

cebón,-ona 1 *adj* fattened. – **2** *m,f* fattened animal. – **3** cebón, *m (cerdo)* pig.

cebra *f* zebra.
■ paso cebra, zebra crossing, US crosswalk.

cebrado,-a *adj* striped.

cebú *m* zebu.

ceca *f* Royal Mint.
● ir de la ceca a la Meca, *fam* to go from pillar to post.

cecear *i* to lisp.

ceceo *m* lisp.

cecidia *f* cecidium.

cecina *f* cured meat.

ceda *f* zed.

cedacillo *m* quaking grass.

cedazo *m* sieve.

ceder 1 *t (dar)* to cede, give: *deberías ceder tu asiento a esa señora anciana,* you ought to give up your seat to that old lady; *cedió sus tierras al Ayuntamiento,* he gave his land to the city council. **2** DEP *(balón)* to pass. – **3** *i (rendirse)* to yield (a, to), give way (a, to): *cedió a sus deseos,* he yielded to her wishes; *no cedas,* don't make any concessions, don't give in. **4** *(caerse)* to fall, give way: *cedieron las paredes,* the walls caved in. **5** *(disminuir)* to diminish, slacken, go down: *la fiebre ha cedido,* his temperature has gone down.
● ceder el paso, AUTO to give way, US yield.

cedilla *f* cedilla.

cedro *m* cedar.

cédula 1 *f* document, certificate. **2** COM FIN bond, warrant.
■ cédula de citación, JUR summons. ‖ cédula hipotecaria, mortgage bond.

CEE *abr (Comunidad Económica Europea)* European Economic Community; *(abreviatura)* EEC.

cefalalgia *f* cephalalgia, headache.

cefalea *f* migraine.

cefálico,-a *adj* cephalic.

cefalópodo,-a 1 *adj* cephalopod. – **2** cefalópodo, *m* cephalopod.

cefalotórax *m* cephalothorax.

céfiro *m* zephyr.

cegador,-ra *adj* blinding.

cegar 1 *t* (*gen*) to blind: *el sol me cegó,* the sun blinded me; *le ciega la ambición,* he's blind with ambition. 2 (*tapar*) to block up; (*puerta, ventana*) to wall up: *cegaron el pozo con cemento,* the well was blocked up with concrete. – 3 *i* (*volverse ciego*) to go blind. – 4 **cegarse,** *p fig* to become blind, be blinded.
▲ Conjugation model [48], *like regar.*

cegato,-a 1 *adj fam* short-sighted. – 2 *m,f fam* short-sighted person.

ceguedad *f →* **ceguera.**

ceguera 1 *f* blindness. 2 *fig* shortsightedness, blindness.

Ceilán *m* Ceylon.

ceilanés,-esa 1 *adj* Ceylonese. – 2 *m,f* Ceylonese.

ceja 1 *f* eyebrow. 2 *fig* (*parte saliente*) projecting edge; (*de un libro*) joint. 3 MÚS bridge.
● **estar hasta las cejas de algo,** *fam* to be fed up to the back teeth with sth. ‖ **fruncir las cejas,** to frown. ‖ **quemarse las cejas,** *fam* to burn the midnight oil. ‖ **tener algo entre ceja y ceja,** *fig* to have sth. in one's head.

cejar 1 *i* (*retroceder*) to back up. 2 *fig* (*aflojar*) to give up, let up: *los trabajadores no cejaron hasta que consiguieron un aumento de sueldo,* the workers didn't give up until they got a pay rise.

cejijunto,-a 1 *adj* with bushy eyebrows too close together. 2 *fig* (*ceñudo*) frowning.

cejilla *f* capo.

celada[1] *f* (*de armadura*) sallet, helmet.

celada[2] *f* (*emboscada*) ambush, trap.

celador,-ra 1 *m,f* (*gen*) attendant. 2 (*de colegio*) monitor; (*de cárcel*) warden.

celar[1] *t* (*la ley*) to observe closely, abide strictly by. 2 (*vigilar*) to watch over: *celo la conducta de mi hijo,* I watch over my son's behaviour. – 3 *i* to watch (**por/sobre,** over).

celar[2] *t fml* (*encubrir, ocultar*) to hide, conceal: *pienso que me ha celado algo,* I think he's hiding something from me.

celda *f* cell.
■ **celda de castigo,** punishment cell.

celdilla *f* cell.

celebérrimo,-a *adj* most famous, well-known.

celebración 1 *f* (*fiesta*) celebration. 2 (*de una reunión etc*) holding: *la celebración del debate será esta tarde,* the debate will be held this afternoon. 3 (*aplauso*) praise, applause.

celebrante 1 *adj* celebrant. – 2 *m* celebrant.

celebrar 1 *t* (*festejar*) to celebrate: *celebrar una boda,* to celebrate a wedding. 2 (*organizar*) to hold: *celebraron el debate ayer,* the debate was held yesterday. 3 (*alabar*) to praise: *celebrar virtudes,* to praise virtues. 4 (*estar contento*) to be happy about: *celebro lo de tu ascenso,* I congratulate you on your promotion. 5 REL (*misa*) to say, celebrate. – 6 *i* (*misa*) to say Mass. – 7 **celebrarse,** *p* (*tener lugar*) to take place, be held: *el congreso se celebró en Granada,* the conference was held in Granada; *mi cumpleaños se celebra en julio,* my birthday is in July.

célebre *adj* well-known, famous, celebrated.

celebridad *f* celebrity, fame.

celeridad *f* celerity, speed.
● **con celeridad,** quickly.

celeste 1 *adj* celestial. 2 (*color*) sky-blue. – 3 *m* (*color*) sky blue.

celestial 1 *adj* celestial, heavenly. 2 *fig* (*delicioso*) heavenly, delightful.

celestina *f* procuress, bawd.

celíaco,-a *adj* coeliac (US celiac).

celibato *m* celibacy.

célibe 1 *adj* celibate. – 2 *mf* celibate.

cellisca *f* sleetstorm.

celo[1] *m fam* sellotape, US Scotch tape.

celo[2] 1 *m* (*cuidado*) zeal, fervour (US fervor). 2 BIOL (*macho*) rut; (*hembra*) heat. – 3 **celos,** *mpl* jealousy *sing:* *Pedro tiene celos de su hermana,* Pedro is jealous of his sister.
● **dar celos,** to make jealous: *así le dará más celos,* he'll only make her more jealous. ‖ **estar en celo,** (*macho*) to be in rut; (*hembra*) to be on heat.

celofán *m* cellophane.

celosamente 1 *adv* (*con cuidado*) zealously. 2 (*con envidia*) jealously.

celosía 1 *f* (*reja*) lattice. 2 (*ventana*) lattice window.

celoso,-a 1 *adj* (*cuidadoso*) zealous, conscientious. 2 (*envidioso*) jealous. 3 (*receloso*) suspicious.

celta 1 *adj* Celtic. – 2 *mf* (*persona*) Celt. – 3 *m* (*idioma*) Celtic.

celtibérico,-a *adj →* **celtíbero.**

celtibero,-a *adj →* **celtíbero.**

celtíbero,-a 1 *adj* Celtiberian. – 2 *m,f* Celtiberian.

céltico,-a *adj* Celtic.

célula *f* cell.

celular *adj* cell, cellular.
■ **coche celular,** Black Maria, US police wagon.

celulitis *f* cellulitis.
▲ *pl* celulitis.

celuloide 1 *m* celluloid. 2 *fig* (*cine*) screen: *las estrellas del celuloide,* screen stars; *llevaron esta novela al celuloide,* they made a film of this novel.

celulosa *f* cellulose.

cembro *m* arolla pine.

cementación *f* case-hardening.

cementar *t* to case-harden.

cementerio *m* cemetery, graveyard.
■ **cementerio de coches,** scrapyard.

cemento 1 *m* (*gen*) concrete, cement. 2 (*de los dientes*) cement.
● **tener la cara de cemento (armado),** *fam* to have a lot of cheek.
■ **cemento armado,** reinforced concrete.

cena *f* (*gen*) supper; (*formal*) dinner.
■ **la Santa Cena,** the Last Supper.

cenacho *m* basket.

cenáculo 1 *m* HIST cenacle. 2 *fig* (*reunión*) coterie.

cenador *m* bower, arbour (US arbor).

cenagal 1 *m* marsh, swamp. 2 *fig* jam, tight spot.

cenagoso,-a *adj* muddy.

cenar 1 *i* to have supper, have dinner: *vamos a cenar,* we're going to have supper; *me gusta salir a cenar,* I like going out to dinner. – 2 *t* to have for supper, have for dinner: *hemos cenado sopa,* we had soup for dinner.

cenceño,-a *adj* thin, lean.

cencerrada *f fam* tin-pan serenade *given to a widow or to a widower who remarries.*

cencerrear 1 *i* (*cencerros*) to ring persistently. 2 *fig* (*un instrumento*) to scrape. 3 *fig* (*puertas, máquinas*) to rattle.

cencerro *m* cowbell.
● **estar como un cencerro,** to be nuts, be crackers.

cendal *m* (*tela*) silk stuff, sendal.

cenefa 1 *f* (*sobre tejido*) edging, trimming. 2 (*sobre muro, pavimento, etc*) ornamental border, frieze.

cenetista 1 *adj* of the CNT, related to the CNT. **– 2** *mf* member of the CNT.

cenicero *m* ashtray.

cenicienta *f* → **ceniciento,-a**.

ceniciento,-a 1 *adj* ashen, ash-grey. **– 2 cenicienta,** *f* dogsbody, skivvy. **3 la Cenicienta,** Cinderella.

cenit *m* zenith.

cenital *adj* zenithal.

ceniza *f* → **cenizo,-a**.

cenizo,-a 1 *adj* (*de color gris*) ashen, ash-grey. **– 2** *m,f fam fig* (*aguafiestas*) wet blanket, killjoy. **3** *fam fig* (*gafe*) jinx. **– 4 ceniza,** *f* ash, ashes *pl.* **– 5 cenizas,** *fpl* (*restos*) ashes.

cenobio *m* monastery.

cenobita *m* coenobite.

cenotafio *m* cenotaph.

censar 1 *t* (*hacer el censo*) to take a census of. **2** (*registrar en el censo*) to register (in a census). **– 3** *i* (*hacer el censo*) to take a census.

censo 1 *m* (*padrón*) census. **2** JUR tax.
■ **censo electoral,** electoral roll.

censor 1 *m* censor. **2** *fig* (*crítico*) critic.
■ **censor jurado de cuentas,** auditor.

censura 1 *f* censorship: *la película pasó por la censura,* the film went through the censors. **2** (*crítica*) censure, criticism, condemnation: *su comportamiento es digno de censura,* his behaviour should be condemned.
■ **censura de cuentas,** COM FIN audit, auditing.

censurable *adj* censurable.

censurar 1 *t* to censor: *el libro fue censurado,* the book was censored. **2** (*criticar*) to censure, criticize.

cent. *abr* (*centavo*) cent; (*abreviatura*) c.

cént. *abr* (*céntimo*) cent, centime; (*abreviatura*) c.

centaura *f* centaury.

centauro *m* centaur.

centavo,-a 1 *adj* hundredth. **– 2 centavo,** *m* (*parte*) hundredth, hundredth part. **3** (*moneda*) cent, centavo.
▲ *See also* **sexto,-a**.

centella 1 *f* (*rayo*) lightning. **2** (*chispa*) spark, flash. **3** *fig* spark.
● **ser rápido,-a como una centella,** *fig* to be as quick as a flash.

centelleante *adj* sparkling, flashing.

centellear 1 *i* (*gen*) to sparkle, flash. **2** (*estrellas*) to twinkle.

centelleo *m* sparkling, flashing.

centena *f* hundred.

centenar *m* hundred.
● **a centenares / por centenares,** in hundreds.

centenario,-a 1 *adj* (*persona*) hundred-year-old, centenarian: *su abuela es centenaria,* his grandmother is over a hundred years old. **2** (*periodo, fecha*) centenary, centennial. **3** (*cifra, cantidad*) three-figure: *una cantidad centenaria,* a three-figure amount. **– 4** *m,f* (*persona*) centenarian. **– 5 centenario,** *m* (*aniversario*) centenary, centennial, hundredth anniversary.

centeno[1] *m* rye.

centeno,-a[2] *adj* hundredth.
▲ *See also* **sexto,-a**.

centesimal *adj* centesimal.

centésimo,-a 1 *adj* hundredth. **– 2** *m,f* hundredth. **– 3** **centésimo,** *m* (*moneda*) cent, centesimo.
▲ *See also* **sexto,-a**.

centiárea *f* square metre (US meter).

centígrado,-a *adj* centigrade.

centigramo *m* centigram, centigramme.

centilitro *m* centilitre (US centiliter).

centímetro *m* centimetre (US centimeter).

céntimo *m* cent, centime.
● **estar sin un céntimo,** *fam* to be penniless.

centinela 1 *m & f* MIL sentry. **2** (*guardián*) watch, lookout.
● **estar de centinela,** to stand sentry.

centinodia *f* knotgrass.

centolla *f* spider crab.

centollo *m* spider crab.

centón 1 *m* (*manta*) patchwork quilt. **2** LIT *fig* cento.

centrado,-a 1 *pp* → **centrar.** **– 2** *adj* centred (US centered) (**en,** on). **3** *fig* (*equilibrado*) balanced. **4** *fig* (*atento*) devoted (**en,** to).

central 1 *adj* central. **– 2** *f* (*oficina principal*) head office, headquarters *pl.* **3** (*eléctrica*) power station.
■ **central de correos,** central post office, main post office. || **central nuclear,** nuclear power station. || **central telefónica,** telephone exchange. || **central térmica,** thermal power station.

centralismo *m* centralism.

centralista 1 *adj* centralist, centralistic. **– 2** *mf* centralist, centralistic.

centralita *f* switchboard.

centralización *f* centralization.

centralizador,-ra *adj* centralizing.

centralizar 1 *t* to centralize. **– 2 centralizarse,** *p* to be centralized.
▲ *Conjugation model* [4], *like* **realizar**.

centrar 1 *t* (*gen*) to centre (US center). **2** *fig* (*atención etc*) to centre (US center), focus. **3** *fig* (*basar*) to centre (US center) around, base on. **– 4** *i* DEP to centre (US center). **– 5 centrarse,** *p* to centre (US center) (**en,** on), focus (**en,** on): *se centró en el tema principal,* he focused on the main topic. **6** (*concentrarse*) to concentrate (**en,** on).

céntrico,-a *adj* central, US downtown: *una calle céntrica,* a street in the city centre.

centrifugado *m* spin.

centrifugador,-ra 1 *adj* centrifugal. **– 2 centrifugadora,** *f* centrifugal machine, spinning machine; (*para ropa*) spin-dryer.

centrifugadora *f* → **centrifugador,-ra**.

centrifugar 1 *t* to centrifuge. **2** (*ropa*) to spin-dry.
▲ *Conjugation model* [7], *like* **llegar**.

centrífugo,-a *adj* centrifugal.

centrípeto,-a *adj* centripetal.

centrismo *m* centrism.

centrista 1 *adj* centre (US center): *es un partido centrista,* it's a centre party. **– 2** *m,f* centrist.

centro 1 *m* centre (US center), middle: *el centro de la habitación,* the centre of the room. **2** (*de ciudad*) town centre, city centre, (US downtown area): *me voy al centro,* I'm going into town, US I'm going downtown. **3** (*asociación*) centre (US center), association, institution. **4** DEP cross, centre (US center). **5** POL centre (US center).
■ **centro benéfico,** charitable organization. || **centro ciudad,** city centre, US downtown area. || **centro comercial,** shopping centre, US mall. || **centro cultural,** cultural centre (US center). || **centro de atracción,** centre (US center) of attraction. || **centro de interés,** centre (US center) of interest. || **centro de mesa,** centrepiece (US centerpiece). || **centro docente / centro de enseñanza,** educational institution. || **centro sanitario,** hospital, clinic. || **medio centro,** DEP centre (US center) half. || **partido de centro,** POL centre (US center) party.

centroafricano,-a 1 *adj* Central African. **– 2** *m,f* Central African.

■ **República Centroafricana,** Central-African Republic.

Centroamérica f Central America.

centroamericano,-a 1 adj Central American. – 2 m,f Central American.

centrocampista mf midfield player.

centroeuropeo,-a 1 adj Central European. – 2 m,f Central European.

centuplicar 1 t to centuple, multiply a hundredfold. – 2 centuplicarse, p to be multiplied a hundredfold.
▲ Conjugation model [1], like sacar.

céntuplo,-a 1 adj centuple, hundredfold. – 2 céntuplo, m centuple, hundredfold.

centuria f century.

centurión m centurion.

cénzalo m mosquito.

ceñido,-a 1 pp → ceñir. – 2 adj (ropa) close-fitting, tight-fitting, clinging. 3 (curva) tight. 4 fig (moderado) tight: el presupuesto era muy ceñido, the budget was very tight.

ceñir 1 t (estrechar) to cling to, be tight on: el vestido le ciñe mucho el pecho, her dress is too tight round the bust. 2 (rodear) to surround, encircle: las murallas ciñen la ciudad de Avila, the walls encircle the city of Avila. 3 (abrazar) to embrace. 4 (la espada) to gird. – 5 ceñirse, p (atenerse) to keep (a, to), limit os. (a, to): ceñirse al tema, to keep to the subject. 6 (adaptarse) to adhere (a, to), stick (a, to), abide (a, by): se ciñe a la normativa, she sticks to the rules. 7 (ajustarse una prenda) to cling.
▲ Conjugation model [36].

ceño m frown.
● arrugar el ceño / fruncir el ceño, to frown.

ceñudo,-a adj frowning.

CEOE abr (Confederación Española de Organizaciones Empresariales) ≈ Confederation of British Industry; (abreviatura) CBI.

cepa 1 f (de vid) vine. 2 (tronco) stump; (de vid) rootstalk. 3 fig (origen) origin.
● de buena cepa, of good stock. ‖ de pura cepa, fig authentic, pure.

cepillado 1 m brushing. 2 (de carpintería) planing.

cepillar 1 t (gen) to brush. 2 (madera) to plane. 3 fam (adular) to butter up. – 4 cepillarse, p (gen) to brush: está cepillándose el pelo, she's brushing her hair. 5 fam (matar) to do in, wipe out. 6 fam (suspender) to fail, us flunk: se ha cepillado a cuatro, he failed four students. 7 fam (acabarse) to polish off, finish up: se cepilló todo el pastel, he polished off the whole cake. 8 tabú (tirarse a) to lay.

cepillo 1 m brush. 2 (de carpintería) plane. 3 (para limosnas) collection box.
■ cepillo de dientes, toothbrush. ‖ cepillo de ropa, clothes brush. ‖ cepillo de uñas, nailbrush. ‖ cepillo del pelo, hairbrush.

cepo 1 m (rama) bough, branch. 2 (de yunque) stock. 3 (de reo) pillory, stocks pl. 4 (trampa) trap. 5 (para auto) clamp.

ceporro 1 m (cepo) log. 2 fig dimwit, blockhead.
● dormir como un ceporro, fig to sleep like a log.

cera 1 f wax; (de abeja) beeswax. 2 (de la oreja) earwax, cerumen. 3 (pulimento) wax, polish.
● blanco,-a como la cera, as white as snow.

cerámica f → cerámico,-a.

cerámico,-a 1 adj ceramic. – 2 cerámica, f (arte) ceramics, pottery. 3 (objeto) piece of pottery.

ceramista mf ceramist, potter.

cerbatana f blowpipe.

cerca[1] f (vallado) fence, wall.

cerca[2] adv (lugar y tiempo) near, close: el museo está muy cerca, the museum is nearby; vente más cerca, come closer; aquí cerca, near here.
● cerca de, (cercano a) near, close; (aproximadamente) nearly, about, around: cerca de la estación, near the station, close to the station; cerca de un año, nearly a year; cerca de dos mil, about two thousand. ‖ de cerca, closely: lo vi de cerca, I saw it close up.

cercado 1 m (lugar) enclosure. 2 (cerca) fence, wall.

cercanía 1 f proximity, nearness. – 2 cercanías, fpl outskirts, suburbs.

cercano,-a 1 adj (inmediato) near, close: el fin está cercano, the end is near. 2 (vecino) nearby, neighbouring (us neighboring). 3 (pariente) close.
■ el Cercano Oriente, the Near East.

cercar 1 t (poner una cerca) to fence in, enclose: cercaron la hacienda, they fenced in the property. 2 (rodear) to surround, encircle: unos árboles cercan la plaza, several trees encircle the square. 3 MIL to besiege, surround.
▲ Conjugation model [1], like sacar.

cercenar 1 t (cortar) to cut, trim; (amputar) to amputate, cut off. 2 (reducir) to cut, reduce: tuvieron que reducir el presupuesto, they had to cut the budget.

cerceta f teal.

cerciorar 1 t to assure, affirm. – 2 cerciorarse, p to make sure (de, of): se cercioró de que las ventanas estaban bien cerradas, she made sure (that) the windows were closed tight.

cerco 1 m (lo que rodea) circle, ring. 2 (aureola) halo. 3 (marco) frame. 4 (asedio) siege.
● alzar el cerco, to raise the siege. ‖ poner el cerco, to besiege (a, -).
■ cerco policíaco, police cordon.

cerda f → cerdo,-a.

cerdada f fam dirty trick.
● hacerle una cerdada a algn., to do the dirty on sb.

cerdamen m tuft of bristle.

Cerdeña f Sardinia.

cerdo,-a 1 m,f (macho) pig; (hembra) sow. 2 fam pey (persona sucia) pig, slob; (persona despreciable) pig, swine, bastard. – 3 cerdo, m (carne) pork. – 4 cerda, f (pelo - de cerdo) bristle; (- de caballo) horsehair.
■ cepillo de cerda, bristle brush.

cereal 1 adj cereal. – 2 m cereal. – 3 cereales, mpl (desayuno) breakfast cereal sing.

cerealista adj cereal, cereal-producing.

cerebelo m cerebellum.

cerebral 1 adj cerebral, brain. 2 fig calculating.

cerebro 1 m ANAT brain. 2 fig brains pl: es el cerebro de la banda, he's the brains behind the gang.

ceremonia 1 f ceremony. 2 (cumplido) deference, ceremony.
● con mucha ceremonia / con gran ceremonia, with great pomp.

ceremonial 1 adj ceremonial. – 2 m ceremonial.

ceremonioso,-a 1 adj (que observa las ceremonias) ceremonious, formal. 2 pey (que gusta de cumplimientos) pompous, stiff.

céreo,-a adj wax, waxen.

cerería f chandler's shop, candle shop.

cereza f cherry.

cerezo m cherry tree.

cerilla 1 f (fósforo) match. 2 (de los oídos) earwax.

cerillero,-a m,f match seller.

cerina 1 *f* (*del alcornoque*) cerin. 2 (*silicato*) cerium silicate.
cerio *m* cerium.
cerne *m* heart of the tree.
cerneja *f* fetlock.
  ▲ *Also used in plural with the same meaning.*
cerner 1 *t* (*harina*) to sift. 2 *fig* to observe. – 3 *i* (*plantas*) to bud, blossom. 4 (*llover*) to drizzle. – 5 **cernerse,** *p* (*pájaro*) to hover. 6 (*amenazar*) to threaten, loom, hang: *el miedo se cernía sobre la población,* fear hung over the population.
  ▲ *Conjugation model* [28], *like* **entender**.
cernícalo 1 *m* (*ave*) kestrel. 2 *fig* blockhead, dolt, dimwit.
cernidillo 1 *m* (*lluvia menuda*) drizzle. 2 *fig* (*paso*) wiggle.
cernir *t-p* → **cerner**.
  ▲ *Conjugation model* [29], *like* **discernir**.
cero 1 *m* MAT zero: *diez grados bajo cero,* ten degrees below zero. 2 (*cifra*) nought, zero: *saqué un cero en mates,* I got nought out of ten in maths. 3 DEP nil: *ganamos tres a cero,* we won three nil.
  ● **partir de cero,** *fig* to start from scratch. ‖ **ser un cero a la izquierda,** *fig* to be useless, be a good-for-nothing.
cerote *m* cobbler's wax.
cerrado,-a 1 *pp* → **cerrar**. – 2 *adj* shut, closed: *la ventana está cerrada,* the window is closed. 3 LING close, closed: *vocal cerrada,* close vowel. 4 (*acento*) broad, thick: *hablar un gallego cerrado,* to speak with a broad Galician accent. 5 (*curva*) tight, sharp. 6 (*ovación*) thunderous. 7 (*barba*) bushy, thick. 8 (*noche*) black, dark; (*cielo*) overcast, dark. 9 *fig* (*oculto*) obscure, hidden. 10 *fig* (*persona introvertida*) uncommunicative, reserved. 11 *fig* (*intransigente*) intransigent, unyielding. 12 *fam fig* (*torpe*) thick, dim.
  ● **a ojos cerrados,** *fig* with one's eyes closed. ‖ **ser cerrado,-a de mollera,** *fam* to be thick-headed.
cerradura *f* lock.
  ■ **cerradura de seguridad,** security lock.
cerrajería 1 *f* (*oficio*) locksmith's trade. 2 (*negocio*) locksmith's shop.
cerrajero,-a *m,f* locksmith.
cerrar 1 *t* to close, shut: *cierra la puerta,* close the door; *cerró los ojos,* she closed her eyes. 2 (*grifo, gas*) to turn off; (*luz*) to turn off, switch off. 3 (*cuenta*) to close. 4 (*cremallera*) to zip (up). 5 (*un negocio*) to close; (- *definitivamente*) to close down. 6 (*carta*) to seal. 7 (*discusión*) to end, finish. 8 (*compra*) to close, conclude. 9 (*agujero*) to plug; (*grieta*) to fill. 10 (*paraguas*) to close, shut, put down. 11 (*los puños*) to clench, close. 12 (*frontera, puerto*) to close; (*camino*) to block. 13 (*en dominó*) to block. – 14 *i* to close, shut: *no cierra bien,* it doesn't close properly. 15 (*punto*) to cast off. 16 (*una herida*) to close up, heal. – 17 **cerrarse,** *p* to close, shut. 18 (*una herida*) to close up, heal. 19 AUTO (*meterse*) to cut in. 20 METEOR to cloud over. 21 *fig* (*obstinarse*) to dig one's heel in, stand fast; (*ponerse en actitud intransigente*) to close one's mind (**a,** to): *se cerró en sus ideas,* he stuck fast to his ideas.
  ● **cerrar con cerrojo,** to bolt. ‖ **cerrar con llave,** to lock. ‖ **cerrar con siete llaves,** *fig* to lock and double-lock. ‖ **cerrar el paso a algn.,** to block sb.'s way, bar sb.'s way. ‖ **cerrar el pico,** *fam* to shut one's trap. ‖ **cerrar la boca,** to shut up. ‖ **cerrar la puerta en las narices,** *fig* to shut the door in sb.'s face. ‖ **cerrar las filas,** *fig* to close ranks. ‖ **cerrarse de golpe,** to slam shut.
  ▲ *Conjugation model* [27], *like* **acertar**.
cerrazón 1 *f* (*del cielo*) stormy sky, black sky. 2 *fig* (*estupidez*) dimness, denseness. 3 *fig* (*obstinación*) obstinacy.

■ **cerrazón mental,** narrow-mindedness.
cerril 1 *adj* (*terreno*) rough, uneven. 2 (*animal*) wild, untamed. 3 (*obstinado*) pigheaded, stubborn.
cerro *m* hill.
  ● **irse por los cerros de Úbeda,** *fig* to beat around the bush.
cerrojazo *m* sharp bolting.
  ● **dar cerrojazo a algo/algn.,** *fig* to cut sth./sb. short.
cerrojo 1 *m* bolt. 2 (*en fútbol*) blanket defence (US defense).
  ● **echar el cerrojo / correr el cerrojo,** to bolt.
certamen *m* competition, contest.
certero,-a 1 *adj* (*disparo*) accurate, good. 2 (*seguro*) certain, sure.
certeza *f* certainty.
  ● **saber algo con certeza,** to be certain of sth. ‖ **tener la certeza de que ...,** to be sure that ..., be certain that ...
certidumbre *f* certainty.
certificación 1 *f* (*documento*) certificate. 2 (*confirmación*) certification. 3 (*de envío etc*) registration.
certificado,-a 1 *pp* → **certificar**. – 2 *adj* (*envío*) registered. – 3 **certificado,** *m* (*documento*) certificate. 4 (*carta*) registered letter; (*paquete*) registered package.
  ■ **certificado médico,** medical certificate.
certificar 1 *t* (*gen*) to certify. 2 (*carta, paquete*) to register.
  ▲ *Conjugation model* [1], *like* **sacar**.
cerúleo,-a *adj* cerulean, deep-blue.
cerumen *m* earwax, cerumen.
cerusa *f* ceruse.
cerval *adj* cervine, deer.
  ● **tener un miedo cerval,** *fig* to be scared stiff.
cervantino,-a *adj* of Cervantes, relating to Cervantes, Cervantine.
cervato *m* fawn.
cervecería 1 *f* (*bar*) pub, bar. 2 (*destilería*) brewery.
cervecero,-a 1 *adj* beer. – 2 **cervecero,** *m* (*fabricante*) brewer.
cerveza *f* beer, ale.
  ■ **cerveza de barril,** draught (US draft) beer. ‖ **cerveza dorada,** lager. ‖ **cerveza ligera,** lager. ‖ **cerveza negra,** stout.
cervical *adj* cervical, neck.
cérvido,-a 1 *adj* cervid. – 2 **cérvido,** *m* cervid.
cerviz *f* cervix, nape of the neck.
  ● **doblar la cerviz,** *fig* to humble os. ‖ **ser duro,-a de cerviz,** *fig* to be pigheaded, be stubborn.
cervuno,-a *adj* cervine.
CES *abr* (*Consejo Económico y Social*) Economic and Social Council.
cesación *f* cessation, suspension.
cesante 1 *adj* (*gen*) dismissed; (*ministro*) removed from office; (*embajador*) recalled. – 2 *mf* suspended official.
cesar 1 *i* to cease, stop: *cesó de llover,* it stopped raining. 2 (*en un empleo*) to leave, quit: *cesó en su cargo de ministro,* he ceased his functions as minister.
  ● **sin cesar,** incessantly.
césar *m* Caesar.
cesárea *f* → **cesáreo,-a.**
cesáreo,-a 1 *adj* Caesarean. – 2 **cesárea,** *f* Caesarean (US Cesarean), Caesarean (US Cesarean) section.
cese 1 *m* cessation. 2 (*despido*) dismissal.
  ● **dar el cese a algn.,** to dismiss sb.
CESID *abr* (*Centro Superior de Información de la Defensa*) Spanish military intelligence agency.

cesio *m* caesium, cesium.
cesión 1 *f* cession. 2 JUR assignment, transfer.
cesionario,-a *m,f* cessionary, assignee.
cesionista *mf* grantor, assignee.
césped *m* lawn, grass.
cesta 1 *f* basket. 2 DEP (*baloncesto*) basket; (*pelota*) pelota basket, jai-alai basket.
■ **cesta de la compra,** shopping basket. ‖ **cesta de Navidad,** Christmas hamper.
cestería 1 *f* (*arte*) wickerwork, basketwork. 2 (*establecimiento*) basket shop.
cestero,-a *m,f* basketmaker.
cesto *m* basket.
■ **cesto de los papeles,** wastepaper basket.
cestodo *m* cestode.
cesura *f* caesura.
ceta *f* → **zeta.**
cetáceo *m* cetacean.
cetme *m* Spanish gun used in the military service.
cetrería *f* falconry.
cetrino,-a 1 *adj* (*color*) sallow, greenish yellow. 2 *fig* melancholic.
cetro *m* sceptre (US scepter).
● **empuñar el cetro,** to ascend the throne. ‖ **ostentar el cetro,** *fig* to hold the lead.
ceutí 1 *adj* of Ceuta, from Ceuta. – 2 *mf* person from Ceuta, inhabitant of Ceuta.
▲ *pl* **ceutíes.**
Cf. *abr* (*confer*) confer; (*abreviatura*) Cf.
C.F. *abr* (*Club de Fútbol*) Football Club; (*abreviatura*) FC.
▲ Also written CF.
CFC *abr* (*chloro-fluorocarbono*) chloro-fluorocarbon; (*abreviatura*) CFC.
cfr. *abr* (*confer*) confer; (*abreviatura*) Cf.
cg *sím* (*centigramo*) centigram, centigramme; (*símbolo*) cg.
CGPJ *abr* (*Consejo General del Poder Judicial*) general council of the judiciary.
ch/. *abr* (*cheque*) cheque (US check).
cha *m* shah.
chabacanada 1 *f* (*vulgaridad*) vulgarity, bad taste. 2 (*grosería*) rude remark, coarse remark.
chabacanería *f* → **chabacanada.**
chabacano,-a *adj* coarse, vulgar.
chabola *f* shack: *un barrio de chabolas,* a shanty town.
chabolismo *m* shanty towns *pl,* slums *pl.*
chabolista *mf* shanty dweller.
chacal *m* jackal.
chacha 1 *f fam* (*niñera*) nanny, nursemaid. 2 *fam* (*sirvienta*) maid.
chachachá *m* → **cha-cha-chá.**
cha-cha-chá *m* cha-cha, cha-cha-cha.
cháchara 1 *f fam* (*conversación*) small talk, chatter. – 2 **chácharas,** *fpl* (*baratijas*) trinkets, junk *sing.*
● **estar de cháchara,** to have a yap.
chacharear *i fam* (*hablar*) to chatter, gossip.
chachi *adj fam* → **chanchi.**
chacho,-a *m,f fam* (*muchacho*) boy, lad; (*muchacha*) girl, lass.
chacina 1 *f* (*carne*) seasoned pork. 2 (*embutido*) cold cut.
chacinería *f* pork butcher's shop.
chacinero,-a *m,f* pork butcher.
chacó *m* shako.
▲ *pl* **chacós.**
chacolí *m* dry Basque wine.
▲ *pl* **chacolíes.**

chacolotear *i* to clatter.
chacoloteo *m* clattering.
chacota *f* joking, banter.
● **hacer chacota de algo,** to make a joke of sth. ‖ **tomar algo a chacota,** to take sth. as a joke.
chacotear 1 *i* (*burlarse*) to poke fun, make fun. – 2 **chacotearse,** *p* to poke fun (**de,** at), make fun (**de,** of).
Chad *m* Chad.
chadiano,-a 1 *adj* Chadian. – 2 *m,f* Chadian.
chador *m* chuddar, chador, chadar.
chafaldete *m* clew line.
chafallar *t fam* to botch (up).
chafallo 1 *m fam* (*chapuza*) botched job, botch up. 2 (*borrón*) crossing out.
chafar 1 *t* (*aplastar*) to squash, crush, flatten. 2 (*arrugar*) to crumple, crease. 3 *fam* (*interrumpir*) to butt in on. 4 *fam* (*estropear*) to ruin, spoil: *este frío me ha chafado los planes,* this cold weather has ruined my plans. 5 *fam fig* (*abatir*) to crush; (*desengañar*) to disappoint: *hoy está algo chafado,* he's feeling a bit down today. – 6 **chafarse,** *p* (*aplastarse*) to be squashed, be crushed, be flattened; (*arrugarse*) to become creased, become crumpled.
chafarote *m* *type of* scimitar.
chafarrinada *f* mark, stain.
chafarrinar *t* to stain, mark.
chafarrinón *m* spot, stain, mark.
chaflán 1 *m* (*bisel*) chamfer. 2 (*esquina*) corner: *la casa del chaflán,* the corner house.
chaira 1 *f* (*cuchillo*) shoemaker's knife. 2 (*cilindro de afilar*) steel, sharpening steel. 3 *fam* (*navaja*) jack-knife, clasp-knife.
chal *m* shawl.
chalado,-a 1 *pp* → **chalar.** – 2 *adj* (*loco*) mad, crazy, nuts.
● **estar chalado,-a por algo/algn.,** to be mad about sth./sb., be crazy about sth./sb.
chaladura 1 *f fam* (*chifladura*) crazy idea. 2 *fam* (*manía*) craze. 3 *fam* (*enamoramiento*) crazy infatuation.
chalán,-ana 1 *m,f* horse-dealer. 2 (*timador*) wheeler-dealer, shark.
chalana *f* barge, lighter.
chalanear *t pey* to wheel and deal.
chalar 1 *t fam* (*enloquecer*) to drive crazy: *me chalan los bombones,* I'm mad about chocolates, I'm crazy about chocolates, I simply adore chocolates. – 2 **chalarse,** *p fam* to go mad, go crazy, go nuts.
● **chalarse por algo/algn.,** to be mad about sth./sb.
chalaza *f* chalaza.
chalé *m* → **chalet.**
▲ *pl* **chalés.**
chaleco *m* waistcoat, US vest; (*de punto*) sleeveless pullover, tank top.
■ **chaleco antibalas,** bullet-proof vest. ‖ **chaleco salvavidas,** life jacket.
chalet 1 *m* (*casa individual*) house, detached house. 2 (*en el campo*) country house, cottage; (*en la montaña*) mountain chalet. 3 (*de lujo*) villa. 4 (*adosado*) semi-detached house.
▲ *pl* **chalets.**
chalina *f* (*corbata*) cravat.
chalote *m* shallot.
chalupa 1 *f* (*embarcación*) boat, launch. – 2 *adj fam fig* (*chalado*) nuts, crazy; (*muy enamorado*) crazy, mad.
● **volverse chalupa,** to go crazy.
chamán *m* sorcerer, wizard, shaman.

chamar *t* to swap, exchange.
chámara 1 *f* (*leña*) brushwood. **2** (*llama*) blaze.
chamarasca *f* → **chámara**.
chamarilear *t* to swap, exchange.
chamarileo *m* trading in second-hand goods.
chamarilero,-a *m,f* second-hand dealer, junk dealer.
chamarillero,-a *m,f* → **chamarilero**.
chamariz *m* greenfinch.
chamarra *f* (*zamarra*) sheepskin jacket.
chamba *f fam* → **chiripa**.
chambelán *m* chamberlain.
chambergo *m* broad-brimmed hat.
chambón,-ona 1 *adj fam* (*torpe*) clumsy. **2** *fam* (*con suerte*) lucky, flukey. **– 3** *m,f fam* clumsy person.
chambonada 1 *f fam* (*torpeza*) clumsiness. **2** *fam* (*patinazo*) blunder. **3** *fam* (*suerte*) fluke, piece of luck.
chambonear *i* to botch, bungle.
chambra *f* housecoat.
chamicera *f* patch of burnt mountain.
chamiza 1 *f* (*hierba*) chamiso. **2** (*leña*) brushwood.
chamizo 1 *m* (*árbol chamuscado*) half-burnt tree. **2** (*leño quemado*) half-burnt log. **3** (*choza*) thatched hut. **4** *pey* (*tugurio*) hovel, shack.
chamorro,-a *adj* shaved, shorn.
champán[1] *m* (*vino*) champagne.
champán[2] *m* (*embarcación*) sampan.
champaña *m* champagne.
champiñón *m* mushroom.
champú *m* shampoo.
■ **champú anticaspa**, dandruff shampoo.
▲ *pl* **champúes** *or* **champús**.
champurrar *t* to mix.
chamullar 1 *i fam* (*hablar*) to speak, talk. **2** *fam* (*chapurrear*) to speak a little: *chamulla un poco el francés,* she speaks a little French.
chamuscar 1 *t* to singe, scorch. **– 2 chamuscarse**, *p* to be singed, get scorched.
▲ *Conjugation model* [1], *like* **sacar**.
chamusquina 1 *f* scorching, singeing. **2** *fam fig* quarrel, fight.
● **esto huele a chamusquina**, *fam* there's something fishy going on.
chanada *f fam* trick, ruse.
chance *m* chance.
chancear 1 *i* to joke, jest. **– 2 chancearse**, *p* to joke (**de**, about), make fun (**de**, of): *se chancea de todo,* he makes fun of everything.
chancero,-a *adj* fond of joking.
chanchi 1 *adj fam* great, terrific, brilliant. **– 2** *adv fam* great: *lo pasamos chanchi,* we had a great time.
chancho *m* AM (*animal*) pig; (*carne*) pork.
chanchullero,-a 1 *adj fam* crooked, bent, underhand. **– 2** *m,f fam* crook, racketeer.
chanchullo *m fam* fiddle, wangle, racket.
● **tener chanchullos**, *fam* to be on the fiddle.
chancillería *f* chancery.
chancla 1 *f* (*zapato viejo*) old shoe. **2** (*chancleta*) flip-flop.
chancleta *f* flip-flop.
● **en chancletas**, with the back(s) trodden down: *has estropeado las zapatillas por llevarlas siempre en chancletas,* you've ruined your slippers by wearing them with the backs trodden down.
chancletear *i* to shuffle.
chanclo 1 *m* (*zueco*) clog. **2** (*elástico*) galosh, overshoe.
chancro *m* chancre.

chándal *m* track suit, jogging suit.
chanfaina 1 *f* (*vegetal*) ≈ ratatouille. **2** (*de carne*) offal stew.
changüí 1 *m fam* (*engaño*) trick, hoax. **2** *fam* (*novato*) beginner.
● **dar changüí a algn.**, *fam* (*engañar*) to play a trick on sb.; (*hacer una broma*) to tease sb.
▲ *pl* **changüíes**.
chanquete *m* transparent goby.
chantaje *m* blackmail.
● **hacer chantaje a algn.**, to blackmail sb.
chantajear *t* to blackmail.
chantajista *mf* blackmailer.
chantillí *m* whipped cream.
▲ *pl* **chantillíes**.
chantre *m* precentor, cantor.
chanza *f* joke.
● **en chanza**, jokingly, as a joke. ‖ **estar de chanza**, to be joking.
chao *interj fam* bye-bye!, cheerio!, so long!, ciao!
chapa 1 *f* (*de metal*) sheet, plate. **2** (*de madera*) panel, sheet; (*enchapado*) veneer; (*contrachapado*) plywood. **3** (*tapón*) bottle top, cap. **4** (*ficha metálica*) metal tag, tally, token. **5** (*medalla*) badge, disc. **6** *fam fig* (*sentido común*) common sense. **7** AUTO bodywork. **– 8 chapas**, *fpl* game *sing* of tossing up coins.
● **estar sin chapa**, *fam* to be penniless.
■ **chapa de identificación**, MIL identity disc. ‖ **chapa ondulada**, corrugated iron.
chapado,-a 1 *pp* → **chapar**. **– 2** *adj* (*metal*) plated: *chapado,-a en plata,* silver-plated. **3** (*madera*) veneered, finished.
● **estar chapado,-a a la antigua**, *fig* to be old-fashioned.
chapalear *i* to splash about.
chapaleo *m* splash, splashing.
chapaleta *f* flap valve.
chapar 1 *t* (*metal*) to plate. **2** (*madera*) to veneer, finish. **3** *fig* (*encajar*) to come out with. **4** *fam fig* (*estudiar*) to study.
chaparrada *f* downpour, heavy shower.
chaparral *m* thicket, chaparral.
chaparrear *i* to pour down, rain heavily.
chaparro,-a 1 *adj fig* tubby, chubby. **– 2** *m,f fig* tubby person, chubby person.
chaparrón 1 *m* (*lluvia*) downpour, heavy shower: *cayó un buen chaparrón,* there was a downpour. **2** *fig* shower, bombardment.
● **aguantar el chaparrón**, *fig* to weather the storm.
chapear 1 *t* (*metal*) to plate. **2** (*madera*) to veneer, finish.
chapero *m arg* male prostitute, rent boy, arse peddlar.
chapín *m* (*chanclo*) chopine, chopin.
chapista 1 *mf* sheet metal worker. **2** AUTO panel beater.
chapistería 1 *f* sheet metal work. **2** AUTO panel beating.
■ **taller de chapistería**, body repair shop, US body shop.
chapitel 1 *m* (*de torre*) spire. **2** (*de columna*) capital.
chapó[1] *m* (*de billar*) type of billiards.
▲ *pl* **chapós**.
chapó[2] *interj fam* well done!, bravo!
chapodar *t* to prune, trim.
chapón *m* ink blot.
chapotear 1 *i* (*agitar en el agua*) to splash about. **– 2** *t* (*humedecer*) to moisten, dampen, sponge.
chapoteo 1 *m* (*agitación en el agua*) splashing, paddling. **2** (*humidificación*) moistening, sponging.

chapucear *t* to botch, bungle.
chapucería **1** *f* (*tosquedad*) shoddiness. **2** (*chapuza*) botched job, shoddy piece of work.
chapucero,-a **1** *adj* (*trabajo*) botched, slapdash, shoddy; (*persona*) bungling, clumsy. – **2** *m,f* (*que trabaja mal*) bungler, botcher, shoddy worker. **3** (*embustero*) con artist, trickster; (*mentiroso*) liar.
chapurrar *t* → **chapurrear**.
chapurrear **1** *t* to speak a little, have a smattering of: *chapurreo el inglés*, I have a smattering of English, I speak a little English. **2** *fam* (*mezclar*) to mix.
chapurreo *m* jabbering.
chapuz **1** *m* (*chapuzón*) duck, ducking. **2** (*chapuza*) botched job, shoddy piece of work.
chapuza **1** *f* (*trabajo sin importancia*) odd job. **2** (*trabajo mal hecho*) botched job, shoddy piece of work.
● **hacer una chapuza,** to botch up.
chapuzar **1** *t* to duck. – **2 chapuzarse,** *p* (*zambullirse*) to dive in. **3** (*bañarse*) to have a dip.
▲ Conjugation model [4], like *realizar*.
chapuzas *mf* bungler, botcher, shoddy worker.
▲ *pl chapuzas*.
chapuzón **1** *m* (*zambullida*) duck, dive. **2** (*baño*) dip.
● **darse un chapuzón,** to have a dip.
chaqué *m* morning coat.
▲ *pl chaqués*.
chaqueta *f* jacket.
● **cambiar de chaqueta,** *fam* to change sides, be a turncoat. ‖ **ser más vago,-a que la chaqueta de un guardia,** *fam* to be bone idle.
■ **chaqueta de punto,** cardigan. ‖ **chaqueta de smoking,** dinner jacket. ‖ **traje de chaqueta,** ladies' suit.
chaquete *m type of backgammon.*
chaquetear *i fam* to change sides, be a turncoat.
chaqueteo *m fam* changing sides, turncoat tactics *pl.*
chaquetero,-a *m,f fam* turncoat.
chaquetilla *f* short jacket.
chaquetón *m* winter jacket.
■ **chaquetón tres cuartos,** three-quarter length coat.
charada *f* charade.
charanga **1** *f* brass band. **2** *fam* (*bulla*) din, racket.
charca *f* pool, pond.
charco *m* puddle, pond.
● **cruzar el charco / pasar el charco,** (*ir a América*) to cross the pond.
charcutería *f* pork butcher's shop, delicatessen.
charcutero,-a *m,f* pork butcher.
charla **1** *f* (*conversación*) talk, chat. **2** (*conferencia*) talk, informal lecture.
charlador,-ra **1** *adj fam* talkative, chatty. – **2** *m,f fam* chatterbox, us motormouth.
charlar *i* to chat, talk.
● **charlar por los codos,** *fam* to be a real chatterbox.
charlatán,-ana **1** *adj* (*hablador*) talkative. **2** (*chismoso*) gossipy. – **3** *m,f* (*parlanchín*) chatterbox. **4** (*chismoso*) gossip; (*bocazas*) bigmouth. **5** (*embaucador*) trickster.
charlatanería **1** *f* (*palabrería*) verbosity, talkativeness. **2** (*de vendedor*) spiel, patter.
charlestón *m* charleston.
charlotada **1** *f* (*festejo taurino bufo*) comic bullfight. **2** *fam* (*payasada*) clowning around, buffoonery.
charlotear *i fam* to chatter, prattle.
charloteo *m fam* chatter, prattle.
charnego,-a *m,f pey person from another region of Spain who has settled in Catalonia.*

charnela *f* hinge.
charol **1** *m* (*barniz*) varnish. **2** (*cuero*) patent leather: *zapatos de charol*, patent leather shoes.
● **darse charol,** *fam* to blow one's trumpet, brag.
charolar *t* to varnish.
charrán[1] *m* (*pillo*) rogue, rascal, scoundrel.
charrán[2] *m* (*ave*) tern.
charranada *f* dirty trick.
charrancito *m* little tern.
charretera *f* epaulette.
charro,-a **1** *adj fig* (*persona*) coarse, uncouth. **2** *fig* (*cosa*) gaudy, flashy, loud. **3** (*de Salamanca*) from Salamanca. – **4** *m,f* person from Salamanca.
chárter **1** *adj* charter. – **2** *m* charter.
■ **vuelo chárter,** charter flight.
▲ *pl chárter.*
chas *interj* wham!, crash!
chasca *f* (*leña menuda*) brushwood.
chascar **1** *t* (*lengua*) to click; (*dedos*) to snap. **2** (*látigo*) to crack. **3** (*un manjar quebradizo*) to crunch. – **4** *i* (*madera*) to crack.
▲ Conjugation model [1], like *sacar*.
chascarrillo *m fam* (*chiste*) crack, joke; (*anécdota*) witty anecdote.
chasco **1** *m* (*engaño*) trick; (*broma*) joke. **2** *fig* (*decepción*) disappointment.
● **dar un chasco a algn.,** to play a trick on sb. ‖ **llevarse un chasco,** to be disappointed.
chasis **1** *m* (*del coche*) chassis. **2** (*en fotografía*) plate holder.
● **quedarse en el chasis,** *fam* to be all skin and bone.
chasquear[1] **1** *t* (*bromear*) to play a trick on. **2** (*engañar*) to deceive. **3** (*decepcionar*) to disappoint, let down. **4** (*faltar a lo prometido*) to break, fail to keep. – **5** *i* (*decepcionarse*) to be disappointed. – **6 chasquearse,** *p* to be disappointed.
chasquear[2] **1** *i* (*lengua*) to click; (*dedos*) to snap. **2** (*látigo, madera*) to crack. **3** (*un manjar*) to crunch.
chasquido **1** *m* (*de la lengua*) click; (*de los dedos*) snap. **2** (*de látigo, madera*) crack. **3** (*de manjar*) crunch.
chatarra **1** *f* (*escoria*) slag. **2** (*hierro viejo*) scrap iron, scrap. **3** *fam pey* (*calderilla*) small change. **4** *fam pey* (*joyas*) junk jewellery (us jewelry). **5** *fam fig* (*trasto*) piece of junk: *este máquina es una chatarra,* this machine is a piece of junk.
■ **parque de chatarra,** scrap yard.
chatarrería *f* scrap metal dealer's.
chatarrero,-a *m,f* scrap dealer.
chatear *i fam* to go out drinking.
chateo **ir de chateo,** *loc fam* to go on a pub crawl, go out drinking.
chati *adj fam* duckie, love, us honey.
chato,-a **1** *adj* (*nariz*) snub; (*persona*) snub-nosed. **2** (*objeto*) flat, flattened; (*barco*) flat, shallow; (*torre*) low, squat. – **3** *m,f* (*persona*) snub-nosed person. **4** *fam* (*cariño*) love, dear, duckie: *¡adiós, chata!,* bye, love! – **5** chato, *m fam* (*vaso de vino*) (small) glass of wine: *tomamos unos chatos,* we had a few glasses of wine.
● **dejar chato,-a a algn.,** (*vencer*) to crush sb., defeat sb.; (*engañar*) to trick sb., deceive sb. ‖ **quedarse chato,-a,** *fig* to be left dumbfounded.
chatungo,-a *adj fam* snub-nosed.
chauvinismo *m* chauvinism.
chauvinista **1** *adj* chauvinist. – **2** *mf* chauvinist.
chaval,-la **1** *adj fam* young. – **2** *m,f* (*joven*) kid, youngster; (*chico*) lad, boy; (*chica*) lass, girl. **3** (*apelativo*) mate.

● estar hecho un chaval, *fam* to look very young.
chavea *m fam* kid, lad.
chaveta *f* TÉC cotter, cotter pin, key.
● estar mal de la chaveta, *fam* to have a screw loose. ‖ perder la chaveta, *fam* to go off one's rocker. ‖ perder la chaveta por algo/algn., *fam* to be crazy about sth./sb.
chavo 1 *m fam* brass farthing. − 2 **chavos,** *mpl* (*dinero*) money *sing*, cash *sing*.
● estar sin un chavo, *fam* to be penniless, be broke. ‖ no tener un chavo, *fam* to be skint, be broke.
chayote *m* chayote.
chayotera *f* chayote plant.
che¹ 1 *interj* AM *fam* hey!, listen! 2 AM (*muletilla*) you know, I mean, man, mate: *no sé dónde está, che,* I don't know where it is, mate.
che² *f name of the digraph ch.*
▲ *pl* **ches**.
checa 1 *f* (*policía secreta soviética*) Soviet secret police organization. 2 (*lugar*) unofficial political court or prison.
checo,-a 1 *adj* Czech. − 2 *m,f* (*persona*) Czech. − 3 **checo,** *m* (*idioma*) Czech.
■ **República Checa,** Czech Republic.
checoslovaco,-a 1 *adj* Czechoslovak, Czechoslovakian. − 2 *m,f* Czechoslovak, Czechoslovakian.
Checoslovaquia *f* Czechoslovakia.
chef *m* chef.
▲ *pl* **chefs**.
cheli *m arg* Madrid slang.
chelín *m* shilling.
chelo *m* → **violonchelo**.
chepa *f fam* hump.
cheque *m* cheque (US check).
● cobrar un cheque, to cash a cheque (US check). ‖ extender un cheque, to write a cheque (US check). ‖ extender un cheque a nombre de / hacer un cheque a nombre de, to make a cheque (US check) out to, make a cheque (US check) payable to.
■ **cheque abierto,** open cheque (US check). ‖ **cheque al portador,** cheque (US check) payable to bearer. ‖ **cheque cruzado,** crossed cheque (US check). ‖ **cheque de viaje / cheque de viajero,** traveller's cheque (US traveler's check). ‖ **cheque en blanco,** blank cheque (US check). ‖ **cheque nominal,** cheque (US check) to order, order cheque (US check). ‖ **cheque sin fondos,** dud cheque (US check), bad cheque (US check). ‖ **talonario de cheques,** cheque book, US checkbook.
chequear 1 *t* (*controlar*) to check. 2 (*comprobar*) to check up on. 3 MED to give a check-up to.
chequeo *m* MED check-up.
chéster *m* Cheshire cheese.
▲ *pl* **chéster** or **chésteres**.
chevió *m* cheviot.
cheviot *m* cheviot.
▲ *pl* **cheviots**.
chic *adj* chic.
▲ *pl* **chic**.
chica *f* → **chico,-a**.
chicana 1 *f* (*artimaña*) chicanery, trickery. 2 (*broma*) joke. − 3 *adj* → **chicano,-a**.
chicane *f* AUTO chicane.
▲ *pl* **chicanes**.
chicanero,-a *adj* trickster.
chicano,-a 1 *adj* chicano, Chicano. − 2 *m,f* (*hombre*) chicano; (*mujer*) chicana.
chicarrón,-ona *m,f fam* (*chico*) strapping lad; (*chica*) strapping lass.

chicha *f fam* (*carne en lenguaje infantil*) meat.
● no ser ni chicha ni limonada, *fam* to be neither fish nor fowl. ‖ tener muchas chichas, *fam* to be chubby.
chícharo *m* AM (*guisante*) pea.
chicharra 1 *f* (*cigarra*) cicada. 2 (*timbre*) buzzer. 3 *fig* (*persona habladora*) chatterbox.
● cantaba la chicharra, *fig* it was boiling hot.
chicharrero,-a 1 *m,f fam* (*tinerfeño*) person from Tenerife, inhabitant of Tenerife. − 2 **chicharrero,** *m fig* (*lugar caluroso*) oven, hothouse.
chicharro 1 *m* (*chicharrón*) pork crackling, fried pork rind. 2 (*pez*) scad, horse mackerel.
chicharrón 1 *m* (*de cerdo*) pork crackling, fried pork rind. 2 *fig* (*persona*) sunburnt person.
● estar/quedar hecho,-a un chicharrón, *fig* to be burnt to a cinder.
chichear 1 *t* to hiss. − 2 *i* to hiss.
chicheo *m* hissing.
chichisbeo 1 *m* (*galantería*) flattery, gallantry. 2 (*hombre*) gallant.
chichón *m* bump, lump: *ayer me pegué un buen chichón en la cabeza,* I got a nasty bump on the head yesterday.
chichonera *f* helmet.
chicle *m* chewing gum.
chiclear *i* to chew gum.
chico,-a 1 *adj* (*pequeño*) small, little. − 2 *m,f* (*gen*) kid, youngster; (*muchacho*) boy, lad; (*muchacha*) girl, lass: *es buen chico,* he's a good boy. − 3 **chico,** *m* (*aprendiz*) errand boy; (*de oficina*) office boy. − 4 **chica,** *f* (*criada*) maid.
● como chico con zapatos nuevos, *fam* like a kid with a new toy. ‖ dejar chico,-a a algn., *fig* to make sb. look small.
chicolear *i fam* to pay compliments, say nice things.
chicoleo *m fam* compliment.
chicoria *f* chicory.
chicote,-a 1 *m,f fam* (*hombre*) fine lad; (*mujer*) fine lass. − 2 *m fig* (*cigarro puro*) cigar. 3 (*extremo de cuerda*) rope end.
chifla¹ *f* (*silbato*) whistle.
chifla² *f* (*cuchilla*) skiver, parer.
chiflado,-a 1 *pp* → **chiflar**. − 2 *adj fam* mad, crazy, barmy, nuts, bonkers. − 3 *m,f fam* nut, loony, headcase.
● estar chiflado,-a con/por algo, *fam* to be crazy about sth., be mad about sth. ‖ estar chiflado,-a por algn., *fam* (*enamorado*) to be madly in love with sb.
chifladura 1 *f fam* (*locura*) craziness, madness. 2 *fam* (*afición*) craze, mania.
chiflar¹ 1 *i* (*silbar*) to hiss, whistle. − 2 *t* (*silbar*) to hiss, boo. 3 *fam* (*gustar*) to fascinate, enchant: *le chifla el patinaje,* he's mad about skating; *me chifla Lola,* I'm crazy about Lola. − 4 **chiflarse,** *p fam* (*enloquecer*) to go mad, go crazy, go round the bend.
● chiflarse por algn./algo, *fam* to be crazy about sb./sth., be mad about sb./sth.
chiflar² *t* (*raspar las pieles*) to skive, pare.
chifle *m* (*reclamo*) decoy.
chiflido *m* whistle, whistling.
chihuahua *m* (*perro*) chihuahua.
chií 1 *adj* Shiite. − 2 *mf* Shiite.
▲ *pl* **chiíes**.
chiíta *adj-mf* → **chií**.
chilaba *f* jellabah, jellaba.
chile *m* (*pimiento*) chili, chili pepper.
Chile *m* Chile.

chileno,-a 1 *adj* Chilean. – 2 *m,f* Chilean.
chilindrina 1 *f fam* (*cosa sin importancia*) trifle. 2 *fam* (*anécdota*) anecdote, story. 3 *fam* (*chiste*) joke.
chilindrón 1 *m* (*juego de naipes*) type of card game. 2 (*salsa*) sauce made from tomatoes, red peppers and onions.
chilla *m* (*reclamo*) decoy.
chillar 1 *i* (*persona*) to scream, shriek, shout: *¡no chilles!*, stop shouting!; *chilla más que no te oigo,* speak up, I can't hear you. 2 (*cerdo*) to squeal; (*ratón*) to squeak; (*pájaro*) to squawk, screech. 3 (*radio*) to blare; (*frenos*) to screech, squeal; (*puerta, ventana*) to creak, squeak. 4 (*colores*) to be loud, be gaudy, clash. 5 *fam* (*reñir*) to tell off. 6 *fig* (*protestar*) to protest, complain.
chillería 1 *f* (*chillidos*) screaming, yelling, howling. 2 (*regaño*) dressing-down, telling-off, reprimand.
chillido 1 *m* (*de persona*) shriek, scream, cry. 2 (*de cerdo*) squeal; (*de ratón*) squeak; (*de pájaro*) squawk, screech. 3 (*de puerta, ventana*) creak, creaking, squeaking.
chillón,-ona 1 *adj* (*que chilla mucho*) screaming, loud. 2 (*voz*) shrill, high-pitched; (*sonido*) harsh, strident. 3 *fig* (*color*) loud, gaudy. – 4 *m,f* loudmouth.
chimenea 1 *f* chimney. 2 (*hogar*) fireplace, hearth. 3 (*de barco*) funnel, stack. 4 *fam* (*cabeza*) nut, block.
● **no andar bien de la chimenea,** *fam* to be off one's rocker.
■ **chimenea de campana,** canopy fireplace. ‖ **chimenea de ventilación,** air shaft. ‖ **chimenea francesa,** fireplace with a mantelpiece.
chimpancé *m* chimpanzee.
▲ *pl chimpancés.*
china[1] 1 *f* (*piedra*) pebble. 2 *arg* (*droga*) small piece.
● **tocarle a uno la china,** *fam* to lose out, be left carrying the can.
china[2] *f* → **chino,-a.**
China *f* China.
chinarro *m* stone.
chinazo 1 *m* (*piedra*) stone. 2 (*golpe*) blow with a stone.
chinchar 1 *t fam* to annoy, pester, bug: *deja de chinchar a la niña,* stop pestering the little girl. – 2 **chincharse,** *p fam* to grin and bear it, put up with it, lump it.
● **¡chínchate!,** *fam* hard luck!, tough luck! ‖ **¡para que te chinches!,** *fam* so there!
chincharrero *m* flea pit, bug-infested place.
chinche 1 *m & f* zool bedbug, bug. – 2 *mf fam fig* (*persona*) bore, nuisance, pest.
● **caer como chinches / morir como chinches,** *fam* to go down like flies.
chincheta *f* drawing pin, us thumbtack.
chinchilla *f* chinchilla.
chinchín 1 *m* (*ruido*) chink, chink, tinkle. 2 (*brindis*) toast: *¡chinchín!,* cheers!, good health!
● **hacer chinchín con las copas,** to clink glasses.
chinchón *m* aniseed liquor.
▲ Registered trademark.
chinchona *f* quinine.
chinchorrería 1 *f* (*impertinencia*) insolence, disrespect. 2 (*exigencia*) fussiness. 3 (*chisme*) piece of gossip.
chinchorrero,-a 1 *adj* (*impertinente*) insolent. 2 (*quisquilloso*) fussy. 3 (*chismoso*) gossipy.
chinchorro 1 *m* (*red*) dragnet. 2 (*embarcación*) dinghy.
chinchoso,-a *adj fam fig* wearisome, tiresome.
chiné 1 *adj* chiné. – 2 *m* chiné fabric.
▲ *pl chinés.*
chinela *f* slipper, mule.
chinero *m* china cupboard.

chinesco,-a *adj* Chinese.
chingada *f fam* bother.
chingar 1 *t* tabú to fuck, screw. 2 tabú (*robar*) to pinch: *me han chingado la cartera,* my wallet has been pinched.
▲ Conjugation model [7], like **llegar.**
chino[1] 1 *m* (*piedrecita*) pebble. – 2 **chinos,** *mpl* guessing game sing.
chino,-a[2] 1 *adj* Chinese. – 2 *m,f* (*persona*) Chinese person. – 3 **chino,** *m* (*idioma*) Chinese. 4 (*colador*) sieve. – 5 **china,** *f* (*seda*) china silk. 6 (*porcelana*) china. 7 (*vajilla*) china, chinaware.
● **engañar a algn. como a un chino,** *fam* to take sb. for a ride. ‖ **eso me suena a chino,** *fam* it's all Greek to me. ‖ **ser un trabajo de chinos,** *fam* to be a fiddly piece of work. ‖ **trabajar como un chino,** *fam* to work like a slave.
chip 1 *m* INFORM chip. – 2 **chips,** *mpl fam* crisps, us potato chips.
▲ *pl chips.*
chipén 1 *adj fam* terrific, marvellous (us marvelous), smashing. – 2 *adv fam* great, super: *lo pasamos chipén,* we had a great time.
chipirón *m* baby squid.
Chipre *m* Cyprus.
chipriota 1 *adj* Cypriot. – 2 *mf* Cypriot.
chips *mpl* → **chip.**
chiquero 1 *m* (*pocilga*) pigsty. 2 (*toril*) bullpen.
chiquilicuatro *m fam* whippersnapper.
chiquillada 1 *f* (*travesura*) childish prank. 2 (*niñería*) childish thing.
● **hacer chiquilladas,** to behave childishly.
chiquillería *f fam* kids *pl*, children *pl*.
chiquillo,-a *m,f* kid, youngster.
chiquitear *i* to have a few drinks.
chiquitín,-ina 1 *adj fam* tiny, weeny. – 2 *m,f* tiny tot.
chiquito,-a 1 *adj* tiny, very small, weeny. – 2 *m,f* tot, kid. – 3 **chiquito,** *m* small glass of wine.
● **no andarse con chiquitas,** *fam* not to beat about the bush.
chiribita 1 *f* (*chispa*) spark. – 2 **chiribitas,** *fpl fam* spots before the eyes.
● **echar chiribitas,** *fam* to be livid.
chiribitil 1 *m* (*desván*) attic, garret. 2 (*cuarto pequeño*) tiny room, cubbyhole, den.
chirigota *f fam* joke.
● **estar de chirigota,** *fam* to be joking. ‖ **tomarse algo a chirigota,** *fam* to take sth. as a joke.
chirigotero,-a *adj fam* fond of joking.
chirimbolo *m fam* thing, thingummyjig, whatsit.
chirimía *f* chirimia, chirimilla.
chirimiri *m* drizzle, fine misty rain.
chirimoya *f* custard apple, cherimoya, cherimoyer.
chirimoyo *m* custard apple tree, cherimoya tree.
chiringuito *m fam* (*en playa*) refreshment stall, refreshment stand; (*en carretera*) roadside snack bar, hot food stand.
● **montarse un chiringuito,** *fam* to set up a small business.
chirinola 1 *f* (*juego*) skittles *pl*. 2 (*conversación*) conversation. 3 *fig* (*fruslería*) trifle. 4 (*riña*) quarrel, row.
● **estar de chirinola,** to be in good spirits.
chiripa 1 *f* (*en el billar*) fluke, lucky stroke, scratch. 2 *fig* (*suerte*) fluke.
● **de chiripa / por chiripa,** *fam* by a fluke, by sheer

luck: *ganó por chiripa,* he won by sheer luck, he won by a fluke.

chirivía 1 *f (planta)* parsnip. 2 *(ave)* wagtail.

chirla *f* small clam.

chirle *adj fam* insipid, wishy-washy.

chirlo 1 *m (herida)* wound in the face. 2 *(cicatriz)* scar on the face.

chirona *f arg* clink, nick.
● **estar en chirona,** *arg* to be in the nick, be inside.

chirrear *i* → **chirriar.**

chirriar 1 *i (al freír comida etc)* to sizzle. 2 *(rueda, frenos)* to screech, squeal; *(puerta)* to creak. 3 *(aves)* to squawk. 4 *fig (persona)* to sing out of tune.
▲ *Conjugation model* [13], *like desviar.*

chirrido 1 *m (de rueda, frenos)* screech; *(de puerta)* creak, creaking. 2 *(de aves)* squawk, squawking.

chirrión *m (carro)* cart.

chirucas *fpl* canvas boots.

chirumen *m fam* brains *pl,* grey matter.

chis *interj* sh!, ssh!, hush!

chischás *m* clash, clashing.

chiscón *m* hut, hovel.

chisgarabís *m fam* busybody, meddler.
▲ *pl* chisgarabises.

chisguete 1 *m fam (trago)* swig. 2 *fam (chorrillo)* jet, spurt.

chisme 1 *m (comentario)* piece of gossip. 2 *(trasto)* knickknack; *(de cocina etc)* gadget; *(cosa)* thing, thingumajig: *¿cómo funciona este chisme?,* how does this thing work?
● **andar con chismes,** *fam* to gossip.

chismear *i* to gossip.

chismería *f* gossip, piece of gossip.

chismero,-a *adj* gossipy, gossiping.

chismografía *f irón* gossip, gossiping.

chismorrear *i fam* to gossip.

chismorreo *m fam* gossip, gossiping.

chismoso,-a 1 *adj* gossipy, gossiping. – 2 *m,f* gossip.

chispa 1 *f (de lumbre, eléctrica, etc)* spark. 2 *(brillo)* sparkle, glitter. 3 *(brillante pequeño)* small diamond. 4 *fam fig (un poco)* bit: *bebió una chispa de licor,* she had a drop of liqueur; *no me gustó ni chispa,* I didn't like it one bit; *no hay ni una chispa de azúcar,* there isn't a bit of sugar left; *no corre ni chispa de aire,* there's not a breath of wind. 5 *(de lluvia)* drop, droplet: *caen chispas,* it's spitting. 6 *fig (ingenio, gracia)* wit, sparkle; *(inteligencia)* intelligence; *(viveza)* liveliness. 7 *fam (borrachera)* drunkenness. 8 *(mentira)* lie.
● **coger una chispa / pillar una chispa,** *fam* to get sloshed. ‖ **echar chispas,** *fig* to be raging. ‖ **no tiene ni chispa de gracia,** *fig* it's not funny at all, it's not a bit funny. ‖ **ser una chispa,** *fig* to be very bright. ‖ **tener chispa,** *fig* to be witty, be funny.
■ **chispa eléctrica,** spark.

chisparse *p fam* to get tipsy, get drunk.

chispazo 1 *m (chispa)* spark. 2 *(quemadura)* burn. 3 *(chisme)* piece of gossip: *dar el chispazo,* to gossip. – 4 *f fig* spark, flash: *los últimos chispazos de la guerra,* the last flickers of war; *tuvo un chispazo de ingenio,* she had a flash of inspiration.

chispeante 1 *adj* sparkling. 2 *fig* brilliant, scintillating.

chispear 1 *i (echar chispas)* to spark, throw out sparks. 2 METEOR to drizzle, spit. 3 *fig (relucir)* to sparkle, shine: *sus ojos chispeaban de ilusión,* her eyes shone with hope.
▲ *In 2 used only in the 3rd pers; it does not take a subject.*

chispitina 1 *f fam* → **chispa** 4. 2 *fam (espacio de tiempo muy corto)* sec, mo: *espera una chispitina,* wait a sec.

chispoleto,-a *adj* bright, sharp.

chisporrotear 1 *i fam (el fuego)* to spark; *(la leña)* to crackle. 2 *fam (el aceite)* to spit.

chisporroteo 1 *m fam (del fuego)* sparking; *(de la leña)* crackling. 2 *fam (del aceite)* spitting.

chisquero *m* pocket lighter.

chist 1 *interj (silencio)* sh!, ssh!, hush! 2 *(para llamar)* psst!

chistar *i* to speak.
● **no chistar,** not to say a word. ‖ **sin chistar,** without saying a word: *se fueron sin chistar,* they left without saying a word.

chiste 1 *m (dicho)* joke, funny story. 2 *(dibujo)* cartoon.
● **caer en el chiste,** to get the joke. ‖ **contar un chiste / explicar un chiste,** to tell a joke. ‖ **tener chiste,** *irón* to be funny. ‖ **tomar algo a chiste,** to take sth. as a joke.
■ **chiste verde,** blue joke, dirty joke.

chistera 1 *f (de pescador)* fish basket, angler's basket. 2 *fig (sombrero)* top hat. 3 DEP pelota basket.

chistorra *f* thin spicy pork sausage.

chistoso,-a 1 *adj (persona)* witty, funny, fond of joking. 2 *(suceso)* funny, amusing. – 3 *m,f (persona)* joker, comic, comedian.

chistu *m* Basque flute.

chistulari *m* Basque flute player.

chita 1 *f* ANAT anklebone. 2 *(juego)* jacks *pl,* quoits *pl.*
● **a la chita callando,** *fam (en silencio)* quietly; *(con disimulo)* on the quiet, secretly. ‖ **dar en la chita,** to hit the nail on the head.

chiticalla *mf fam (persona)* clam.

chiticallando 1 *adv fam (en silencio)* quietly. 2 *fam fig (en secreto)* secretly, on the quiet.

chito *interj* → **chitón.**

chitón *interj fam* sh!, ssh!, hush!, silence!

chivar 1 *t fam (molestar)* to annoy, pester. 2 *fam (delatar)* to squeal on, tell on. – 3 **chivarse,** *p fam* to tell, squeal, split: *se chivó al profe,* he told the teacher.

chivatazo *m fam* tip-off.
● **dar el chivatazo,** to inform, squeal, give a tip-off.

chivatear *i fam* to inform, split, squeal.

chivato,-a 1 *m,f fam (delator)* informer, squealer, grass; *(acusica)* telltale. – 2 **chivato,** *m (dispositivo)* gadget. 3 ZOOL kid, young goat.

chivo,-a *m,f (cría macho)* kid, young goat; *(cría hembra)* kid, young she-goat.
● **estar como un,-a chivo,-a,** *fam* to be crazy, be mad.
■ **chivo expiatorio,** *fig* scapegoat.

choc *m* shock.
● **choc nervioso,** nervous shock.
▲ *pl* chocs.

chocante 1 *adj (divertido)* funny. 2 *(sorprendente)* surprising, striking, startling. 3 *(raro)* strange, odd. 4 *(escandaloso)* shocking, offensive.

chocar 1 *i (colisionar con algo)* to collide (**contra/con,** with), crash (**contra/con,** into), run (**contra/con,** into): *el coche chocó con la pared,* the car crashed into the wall. 2 *(colisionar entre sí)* to collide (with each other), crash (into each other): *dos coches chocaron,* two cars collided with each other. 3 *(una pelota)* to hit (**contra,** -), strike (**contra,** -). 4 *fig (pelear)* to fight, clash. 5 *fig (en una discusión)* to clash, fall out. – 6 *t fig (sorprender)* to surprise; *(extrañar)* to shock: *me choca que no haya llegado todavía,* I'm surprised he hasn't arrived yet, it's strange that he hasn't arrived yet; *me chocó lo que dijo,* I was shocked at what he said, what he said shocked me. 7 *(las manos)* to shake. 8 *(copas)* to clink.

● **¡choca esos cinco! / ¡chócala!,** put it there!, give me five!
▲ Conjugation model [1], *like sacar.*
chocarrería *f* coarse joke, dirty joke.
chocarrero,-a *adj* coarse, vulgar.
chocha *f* woodcock.
chochear 1 *i* to dodder, be senile. 2 *fig (de cariño)* to be tender, be soft: *chochea por su nieto,* her grandson makes her soft.
chochera 1 *f (senilidad)* dotage, senility. 2 *(cariño)* tenderness, sentimentality.
chochez *f →* **chochera**.
chochín *m* wren.
chocho[1] 1 *m (altramuz)* lupin. 2 *(dulce)* cinnamon candy stick. 3 *tabú* cunt, pussy. – 4 **chochos,** *mpl (chucherías)* sweets, us candies.
chocho,-a[2] 1 *adj* doddering, senile. 2 *fig (de cariño)* tender, soft.
● **estar chocho,-a por algn.,** *fig* to be soft about sb.
choco *m* small cuttlefish.
chocolate 1 *m (sólido)* chocolate. 2 *(líquido)* drinking chocolate, cocoa. 3 *arg (hachís)* dope, hash.
● **las cosas claras y el chocolate espeso,** *fam* let's get things clear.
■ **chocolate a la taza,** drinking chocolate. ‖ **chocolate con leche,** milk chocolate. ‖ **pastilla de chocolate,** bar of chocolate. ‖ **tableta de chocolate,** bar of chocolate.
chocolatera *f →* **chocolatero,-a**.
chocolatería 1 *f (fábrica)* chocolate factory. 2 *(tienda)* chocolate shop. 3 *(donde se toma)* café specializing in drinking chocolate.
chocolatero,-a 1 *adj (aficionado al chocolate)* fond of chocolate, chocolate-loving. – 2 *m,f (aficionado al chocolate)* chocolate lover. 3 *(fabricante)* chocolate maker. 4 *(vendedor)* chocolate seller. – 5 **chocolatera,** *f (vasija)* chocolate pot. 6 *fam fig (coche viejo)* old banger.
chocolatín 1 *m (tableta)* bar of chocolate, chocolate bar. 2 *(bombón)* chocolate.
chocolatina *f →* **chocolatín**.
chofer *m →* **chófer**.
chófer 1 *m (particular)* chauffeur. 2 *(de autocar etc)* driver.
▲ *pl* **chóferes**.
chola *f →* **cholla**.
cholla 1 *f fam (cabeza)* nut, block, head. 2 *fam (inteligencia)* brains *pl*, grey matter.
chollo 1 *m fam (ganga)* bargain, snip, gift. 2 *(trabajo)* cushy job: *¡qué chollo!,* what luck!
chopera *f* poplar grove.
chopo[1] *m (árbol)* poplar.
■ **chopo blanco,** white poplar. ‖ **chopo negro,** black poplar.
chopo[2] *m fam (fusil)* gun.
● **cargar con el chopo,** *fig* to join up.
chopped *m (embutido, fiambre)* chopped ham.
choque 1 *m (gen)* collision, impact. 2 *fig (enfrentamiento)* clash. 3 MIL skirmish. 4 *(discusión)* dispute, quarrel. 5 MED shock.
■ **choque de frente,** head-on collision. ‖ **choque múltiple,** pile-up. ‖ **fuerzas de choque,** shock troops. ‖ **policía de choque,** riot police.
choquezuela *f* kneecap.
chorbo,-a 1 *m,f fam* fellow. 2 *fam (novio)* boyfriend; *(novia)* girlfriend.
choricero,-a 1 *m,f (fabricante)* sausage maker. 2 *(vendedor)* sausage seller. 3 *fam (persona vulgar)* coarse person.

4 *fam (ratero)* pickpocket. 5 *irón* person from Extremadura, inhabitant of Extremadura.
chorizada *f fam* coarse saying, vulgar saying.
chorizar *t fam* to pinch, nick.
chorizo,-a 1 *m,f fam (carterista)* thief, pickpocket; *(delincuente)* yob. – 2 **chorizo,** *m* highly-seasoned pork sausage, chorizo. 3 *(balancín)* balancing pole.
chorlitejo *m* plover.
■ **chorlitejo chico,** little ringed plover. ‖ **chorlitejo grande,** ringed plover. ‖ **chorlitejo patingro,** Kentish plover.
chorlito *m* plover.
■ **cabeza de chorlito,** *fam fig* scatterbrain.
chorra 1 *adj tabú* stupid, foolish. – 2 *mf tabú* idiot, fool. – 3 *f fam (suerte)* luck: *tiene mucha chorra,* he's very lucky. 4 *tabú (pene)* prick, dick.
chorrada 1 *f (de líquido)* extra drop. 2 *fam (necedad)* piece of nonsense: *decir chorradas,* to talk rubbish. 3 *(regalito)* little something. 4 *fam (adorno superfluo)* frill. 5 *fam (fruslería)* trinket, knick-knack.
chorrear 1 *i (caer a chorro)* to spout, gush, spurt. 2 *(gotear)* to drip: *le chorrea el pelo,* her hair is dripping wet. 3 *fam (ir sin interrupción)* to flow: *los escándalos chorrean,* scandals are pouring out one after the other. – 4 *t (echar)* to drip: *la herida chorreaba sangre,* blood was pouring from the wound; *la brocha chorrea pintura,* the brush is dripping with paint. 5 *fam (abroncar)* to tick off, give a dressing-down to.
● **estar chorreando,** *fam* to be dripping wet, be soaking; *(de sudor)* to pour with sweat, be dripping with sweat.
chorreo 1 *m (en chorro)* gush, gushing, spurting, spouting. 2 *(goteo)* dripping, trickle. 3 *fam (bronca)* dressing-down, ticking-off. 4 *fam fig (gasto)* drain. 5 *fam fig (flujo)* flow, flood, torrent: *un chorreo de quejas,* a flood of complaints.
chorrera 1 *f (paraje)* channel. 2 *(señal del agua)* water mark. 3 *(de un río)* rapids *pl*. 4 *(de camisa)* shirt frill.
chorretada 1 *f (chorro)* gush, spurt, jet. 2 *(cantidad)* extra drop.
● **hablar a chorretadas,** to gabble.
chorrillo *m fig (cantidad pequeña)* trickle, steady flow.
chorro 1 *m (de líquido)* jet, spout, spurt, gush. 2 *(de gas)* jet, blast. 3 *(de poca cantidad)* trickle. 4 *(de luz)* flood. 5 *fig (de cosas)* stream, flood, torrent: *un chorro de insultos,* a torrent of abuse.
● **a chorros,** in abundance: *tiene dinero a chorros,* he's got plenty of money, he's loaded (with money). ‖ **beber a chorro,** *to drink by directing a stream of liquid into the mouth.* ‖ **estar como los chorros del oro,** *fam* to be as clean as a whistle. ‖ **de propulsión a chorro,** jet-propelled. ‖ **hablar a chorros,** to gabble, jabber. ‖ **llover a chorros,** to pour down. ‖ **salir a chorros,** to gush forth, gush out.
■ **avión a chorro,** jet plane. ‖ **chorro de arena,** sandblast. ‖ **chorro de vapor,** steam jet. ‖ **chorro de voz,** loud voice.
chotacabras *m & f* nightjar.
▲ *pl* **chotacabras**.
chotearse *p fam* to make fun (**de**, of).
choteo *m fam* fun, joking: *¡ya basta de choteo!,* stop joking!
● **tomarse algo a choteo,** to take sth. as a joke.
chotis *m* schottische.
● **ser más agarrado,-a que un chotis,** to be a skinflint.

choto,-a 1 *m,f* (*cabrito*) kid, young goat; (*cabrita*) female kid, young she-goat. **2** (*ternero*) sucking calf.
● **estar como una chota,** *fam* to be nuts, be round the bend.

chova *f* chough.

chovinismo *m* excessive patriotism, chauvinism.

chovinista 1 *adj* excessively patriotic, chauvinist. – **2** *mf* excessively patriotic person, chauvinist.

choza *f* hut, shack.

chozno,-a *m,f* great-great-great-grandchild.

chozo *m* small hut.

christmas *m* Christmas card.
▲ *pl christmas*.

chubascada *f* heavy shower.

chubasco 1 *m* (*chaparrón*) heavy shower, downpour. **2** *fig* (*adversidad*) setback, adversity.
■ **chubasco de nieve,** brief snowstorm.

chubasquero *m* raincoat.

chubesqui *m* stove.

chucha *f* → **chucho,-a**.

chuchear 1 *i* (*cuchichear*) to whisper. **2** (*cazar*) to hunt with traps.

chuchería 1 *f fam* (*fruslería*) trinket, knick-knack. **2** *fam* (*bocado*) tidbit, delicacy. **3** *fam* (*golosina*) sweet, US candy.

chuchirrido,-a 1 *adj fam* (*ajado*) wrinkled, wizened. **2** *fam* (*marchito*) faded.

chucho,-a 1 *m,f fam* (*perro*) mutt, US pooch. – **2 chucha,** *f fam* (*peseta*) peseta. – **3 chucho,** *interj fam* shoo!, scat!

chucrut *m* sauerkraut.

chucruta *f* sauerkraut.

chueca[1] 1 *f* (*del tronco*) stump. **2** (*juego*) *game resembling hockey*. **3** *fig* (*burla*) joke.

chueca[2] *f* (*hueso*) ball of socket joint.

chueta *mf* Balearic Jew.

chufa 1 *f* (*planta*) chufa; (*fruto*) tiger nut. **2** *fam fig* (*bofetada*) slap.

chufla *f fam* (*broma*) joke; (*burla*) taunt, jeer.
● **hacer chufla de algo/algn.,** *fam* to make fun of sth./sb.

chufleta *f* → **chufla**.

chufletear *i fam* to joke, jest, banter.

chulada 1 *f fam* (*acto grosero*) coarse act, vulgar act; (*dicho grosero*) coarse remark, vulgar remark: *no digas chuladas,* don't say such vulgar things. **2** *fam* (*acto insolente*) cheeky act; (*dicho insolente*) cheeky remark. **3** *fam* (*bravuconada*) brag, boast, swagger. **4** *fam* (*algo bonito*) lovely thing: *tu vestido nuevo es una chulada,* your new dress is gorgeous.

chulapo,-a 1 *m,f fam* (*hombre chulo*) spiv, flash Harry, show-off. **2** (*de Madrid*) working-class person from Madrid.

chulapón,-ona *m,f* → **chulapo,-a**.

chulear 1 *t fam* (*burlar*) to make fun of. **2** *fam* (*hacer de chulo*) to pimp for: *ese hombre chulea a varias mujeres del barrio,* that bloke pimps for several women in the area. **3** *fam* (*robar*) to pinch, nick. – **4** *i fam* (*presumir*) to brag, show off: *mira a Felipe cómo chulea con su coche nuevo,* look at Felipe showing off his new car. – **5 chulearse,** *p fam* (*burlarse*) to make fun (**de,** of): *no te chulees más de ella,* stop making fun of her. **6** *fam* (*presumir*) to brag, boast.

chulería 1 *f fam* (*jactancia*) bragging, swaggering. **2** *fam* (*gracia*) wit, charm, sparkle. **3** *fam* (*descaro*) cheek, insolence. **4** *fam* (*acto grosero*) coarse act, vulgar act; (*dicho grosero*) coarse remark, vulgar remark.

chulesco,-a 1 *adj fam* (*descarado*) cheeky, cocky. **2** *fam* (*vulgar*) flashy, loud, brassy.

chuleta 1 *f* (*costilla*) chop, cutlet. **2** *fam fig* (*entre estudiantes*) crib, crib note, US trot. **3** *fam fig* (*bofetada*) slap. – **4** *adj fam* (*chulo*) cheeky, cocky. – **5** *mf fam* (*chulo*) cheeky person.
■ **chuleta de cerdo,** pork chop.

chulo,-a 1 *adj fam* (*descarado*) cocky, cheeky. **2** *fam* (*vistoso*) showy, flashy. **3** *fam* (*bonito*) nice, pretty: *¡qué vestido tan chulo!,* what a nice dress! – **4** *m,f fam* (*presuntuoso*) show-off, swank. **5** *fam* (*castizo*) working-class person from Madrid. – **6 chulo,** *m fam* (*proxeneta*) pimp.
● **ponerse chulo,-a,** *fam* to get cocky, get cheeky.

chumacera 1 *f* TÉC bearing. **2** (*de bote*) rowlock, US oarlock.

chumbera *f* prickly pear.

chuminada *f fam* silly thing, stupid thing.

chunga *f fam* → **chungo,-a**.

chungarse *i fam* → **chunguearse**.
▲ *Conjugation model* [7], *like llegar*.

chungo,-a 1 *adj fam* (*malo*) bad, dud, naff: *es una peli muy chunga,* it's a naff film; *lo tenemos chungo,* we've got problems. **2** *arg* (*estropeado*) broken down, on the blink. **3** *arg* (*divertido*) funny. – **4 chunga,** *f fam* joke, fun.
● **estar de chunga,** *fam* to be joking. ‖ **tomar a chunga / tomar en chunga,** to take as a joke.

chungón,-ona *adj fam* fond of joking.

chunguearse 1 *p fam* (*hacer broma*) to joke. **2** *fam* (*burlarse*) to take the piss (**de,** out of).

chunguero,-a *adj fam* fond of joking.

chupa *f fam* (*chaqueta*) short jacket, bomber jacket.
● **poner a algn. como chupa de dómine,** *fam* to give sb. a dressing-down, haul sb. over the coals.

chupachups *m fam* lollipop.
▲ *Registered trademark; pl chupachups*.

chupacirios *m fam pey* Holy Joe.
▲ *pl chupacirios*.

chupada *f* → **chupado,-a**.

chupado,-a 1 *pp* → **chupado,-a**. – **2** *adj fig* (*muy flaco*) skinny, thin; (*mejillas, cara*) hollow. **3** *fig* (*ajustado*) tight. **4** *arg fig* (*muy fácil*) dead easy: *el examen estaba chupado,* the exam was dead easy, the exam was a cinch. – **5** *chupada,* *f* (*a caramelo*) suck; (*a cigarro*) puff: *le dio una chupada a la piruleta,* he sucked the lollipop; *le dio una chupada al cigarro,* he puffed at the cigar.

chupador,-ra 1 *adj* (*animal*) suctorial. – **2 chupador,** *m* (*para bebé*) teething ring.

chupalámparas *m fam* altar boy.
▲ *pl chupalámparas*.

chupar 1 *t* to suck. **2** (*absorber*) to absorb, soak up, suck up: *esta planta chupa mucha agua,* this plant absorbs a lot of water. **3** (*hacienda*) to drain, sponge on. **4** *fam* (*aprovecharse*) to milk. – **5** *i* to suck. – **6 chuparse,** *p* (*consumirse*) to grow thin, waste away. **7** *fam* (*aguantar*) to put up with: *me chupé toda la conferencia,* I sat through the whole lecture; *nos chupamos tres horas de cola,* we had to queue up for three hours.
● **chuparle la sangre a algn.,** to bleed sb. dry. ‖ **chuparse los dedos,** to lick one's fingers. ‖ **¡chúpate ésa!,** *fam* stick that in your pipe and smoke it! ‖ **está para chuparse los dedos,** *fam* it's really mouthwatering, it's fingerlicking good.

chupatintas *mf fam pey* penpusher.
▲ *pl chupatintas*.

chupete 1 *m* dummy, soother, US pacifier. **2** (*tetina*) teat.

chupetear 1 *t* to suck at. – **2** *i* to suck.

chupeteo *m* sucking.
chupi 1 *adj fam* great, terrific, fantastic. – **2** *adv fam* great: *lo pasamos chupi,* we had a great time.
chupinazo 1 *m* (*disparo*) loud bang. **2** *fam* (*en fútbol*) hard kick.
chupito *m* nip, snifter.
chupón,-ona 1 *adj* (*que chupa*) sucking. **2** *fam fig* (*gorrón*) sponging, scrouging. **3** *fam fig* (*en deporte, que retiene mucho tiempo el balón*) selfish. – **4** *m,f fam fig* (*gorrón*) sponger, scrounger. **5** *fam fig* (*en deporte, que retiene mucho tiempo el balón*) player who hogs the ball. – **6 chupón,** *m* BOT sucker. **7** (*pirulí*) lollipop. **8** TÉC sucker, piston.
chupóptero *m fam* irón sponger, scrounger.
churdón *m* raspberry.
churra *f fam* fluke, good luck.
churrascado,-a *adj* scorched.
churrasco *m* barbecued meat, barbecued steak.
churre *m fam* (*pringue*) filth, grease.
churrería *f* fritter shop.
churrero,-a 1 *m,f* fritter maker, fritter seller. **2** *arg* (*con suerte*) lucky devil.
churrete *m fam* dirty mark, grease spot.
churretón *m fam* → **churrete**.
churretoso,-a *adj fam* dirty, filthy.
churriento,-a *adj fam* dirty, filthy.
churrigueresco,-a 1 *adj* ARQ Churrigueresque, Spanish baroque. **2** *fig* excessively ornate, loud, flashy, tawdry.
churro[1] 1 *m* (*dulce*) fritter, US cruller. **2** *fam* (*chapuza*) botch, slapdash job. **3** *fam* (*malo*) rubbish, mess: *este programa de televisión es un churro,* this TV programme is lousy, US this TV programme sucks; *el examen me ha salido un churro,* I made a hash of the exam, I mucked up the exam. **4** *fam* (*suerte*) fluke: *¡qué churro de gol!,* what a jammy goal!
● **de churro,** by a fluke, by a stroke of luck: *consiguió el trabajo de churro,* he was really lucky to get the job.
churro,-a[2] *adj* (*res*) coarse-woolled (US coarse-wooled).
churrullero,-a 1 *adj* (*charlatán*) talkative; (*chismoso*) gossipy. – **2** *m,f* (*charlatán*) talkative; (*chistoso*) gossip.
churruscar 1 *t* to burn. – **2 churruscarse,** *p* to be burnt: *el arroz se ha churruscado,* the rice got burnt.
▲ *Conjugation model* [1], *like* **sacar.**
churrusco *m* piece of burnt toast.
churumbel *m fam* kid, nipper.
churumbela *f* MÚS hornpipe.
chus *interj* (*al perro*) here, boy!
● **no decir ni chus ni mus,** *fam* not to say a word.
chuscada *f* funny remark, joke.
chusco[1] *m* (*de pan*) chunk of stale bread, stale crust.
chusco,-a[2] *adj* (*divertido*) funny, witty.
chusma *f* riffraff, rabble, mob.
chusquero *m* MIL *fam* ranker.
chut *m* DEP shot, kick.
chutar 1 *i* DEP to shoot, kick. – **2 chutarse,** *p arg* (*droga*) to shoot up, mainline.
● **ir algn. que chuta,** *fam* to be plenty, be more than enough: *toma 500 pesetas, ¡y vas que chutas!,* here, take 500 pesetas, and that's your lot!
chute *m arg* fix.
chuzo *m* short pike.
● **caer chuzos de punta,** *fam* to rain cats and dogs, pour down. ‖ **llover chuzos,** *fam* to come down in sheets, bucket down.
chuzón,-ona 1 *adj* (*astuto*) crafty, sly. **2** (*ingenioso*) witty, sharp, clever.

chuzonada *f* piece of clowning around, prank.
CI *abr* (*coeficiente intelectual*) intelligence quotient; (*abreviatura*) IQ.
cía *f* hipbone.
Cía. *abr* (*compañía*) Company - Co.; (*abreviatura*) Co.
ciaboga *f* turn.
cianhídrico,-a *adj* hydrocyanic.
cianita *f* cyanite.
cianuro *m* cyanide.
■ **cianuro potásico,** potassium cyanide.
ciar 1 *i* (*remar hacia atrás*) to back water. **2** (*andar hacia atrás*) to walk backwards. **3** *fig* (*aflojar*) to give up.
▲ *Conjugation model* [13], *like* **desviar.**
ciática *f* → **ciático,-a.**
ciático,-a 1 *adj* sciatic. – **2 ciática,** *f* sciatica.
cibernética *f* → **cibernético,-a.**
cibernético,-a 1 *adj* cybernetic. – **2 cibernética,** *f* cybernetics.
ciborio *m* ciborium.
cicatería *f* stinginess, meanness.
cicatero,-a 1 *adj* stingy, mean. – **2** *m,f* miser.
cicatriz *f* scar.
cicatrización *f* healing, cicatrization.
cicatrizar 1 *t* to heal, cicatrize. – **2** *i* to heal, cicatrize. – **3 cicatrizarse,** *p* to heal, cicatrize.
▲ *Conjugation model* [4], *like* **realizar.**
cícero *m* pica.
cicerone *mf* guide, cicerone.
ciclamen *m* cyclamen.
cíclico,-a *adj* cyclic, cyclical.
ciclismo *m* cycling.
ciclista 1 *adj* cycle, cycling. – **2** *mf* cyclist.
ciclo 1 *m* (*gen*) cycle. **2** (*de conferencias etc*) course, series.
ciclocross *m* cyclo-cross.
▲ *pl* ciclocross.
ciclocróss *m* cyclo-cross.
▲ *pl* ciclocróss.
cicloide *f* cycloid.
ciclomotor *m* moped.
ciclón *m* cyclone.
● **como un ciclón,** *fig* like a whirlwind.
ciclónico,-a *adj* cyclonic.
cíclope *m* Cyclops.
ciclópeo,-a *adj* Cyclopean, gigantic, huge, massive.
ciclorama *m* cyclorama.
ciclostil *m* cyclostyle, mimeograph.
ciclostilar *t* to cyclostyle, mimeograph.
ciclostilo *m* → **ciclostil.**
cicloturismo *m* touring by bicycle.
cicunferir *t* to circumscribe.
▲ *Conjugation model* [35], *like* **hervir.**
cicunstancialmente *adv* temporarily.
cicunvolución *f* circumvolution.
cicuta *f* hemlock.
cidra *f* citron.
cidro *m* citron tree.
ciegamente *adv* blindly: *creía ciegamente en él,* she had blind faith in him.
ciego,-a 1 *adj* (*persona*) blind. **2** (*conducto*) blocked up. – **3** *m,f* (*persona*) blind person. – **4 ciego,** *m* ANAT caecum (US cecum), blind gut. – **5 los ciegos,** *mpl* the blind.
● **a ciegas,** (*sin ver*) blindly; (*sin pensar*) without thinking: *no digas las cosas a ciegas,* don't say things off the top of your head. ‖ **estar ciego,-a de ira,** to be blind

with anger. ‖ **ponerse ciego,-a,** *fam* (*bebiendo*) to get blind drunk; (*de drogas*) to get stoned. ‖ **quedarse ciego,-a,** to go blind. ‖ **ser ciego,-a de nacimiento,** to be born blind.

cielo 1 *m* (*gen*) sky. 2 (*clima*) weather, climate. 3 REL heaven. 4 *fig* (*Dios*) God. 5 *fig* (*techo*) ceiling; (*de cama*) canopy. 6 *fig* (*de boca*) roof. – 7 **cielos,** *interj* good heavens! ● **a cielo abierto,** opencast, US opencut. ‖ **a cielo raso,** in the open (air). ‖ **bajado,-a del cielo / caído,-a del cielo / llovido,-a del cielo,** *fig* heaven-sent. ‖ **¡cielo santo!,** good heavens! ‖ **clamar al cielo,** *fig* to be crying out for a solution. ‖ **despejarse el cielo,** to clear up. ‖ **estar en el séptimo cielo,** *fig* to be in seventh heaven. ‖ **mover cielo y tierra / remover cielo y tierra,** *fig* to move heaven and earth. ‖ **poner a algo/ algn. por los cielos,** to praise sth./sb. to the skies. ‖ **poner el grito en el cielo,** to hit the ceiling. ‖ **ser un cielo (de persona),** *fam* to be an angel. ‖ **venirse el cielo abajo,** (*llover*) to pour down; (*desmoralizarse*) to lose heart. ‖ **ver el cielo abierto,** *fig* to see a way out. ■ **cielo raso,** ceiling. ‖ **El reino de los cielos,** the kingdom of heaven.

ciempiés *m* centipede.
▲ *pl* **ciempiés**.

cien 1 *adj* one hundred, a hundred: *cien libras,* one hundred pounds. – 2 *m* one hundred, a hundred. ● **cien por cien,** one hundred per cent: *si estás segura al cien por cien,* if you're one hundred per cent sure. ‖ **ponerse a cien,** *fam* to blow one's top, get all worked up.
▲ *Used only before plural nouns; see also* **ciento** *and* **seis**.

ciénaga *f* marsh, bog.

ciencia 1 *f* (*disciplina*) science. 2 (*saber*) knowledge, learning. ● **saber algo a ciencia cierta,** *fig* to know sth. for certain. ‖ **ser un pozo de ciencia,** to be a well of knowledge. ■ **ciencia ficción,** science fiction. ‖ **ciencia infusa,** intuition. ‖ **ciencias empresariales,** business studies. ‖ **ciencias exactas,** mathematics *sing*. ‖ **ciencias naturales,** natural sciences. ‖ **ciencias ocultas,** the occult *sing*.

cienmilésimo,-a 1 *adj* hundred thousandth. – 2 *m,f* hundred thousandth.
▲ See also **sexto,-a**.

cienmillonésimo,-a 1 *adj* hundred millionth. – 2 *m,f* hundred millionth.
▲ See also **sexto,-a**.

cieno *m* mud, mire.

científico,-a 1 *adj* scientific. – 2 *m,f* scientist.

ciento 1 *adj* one hundred, a hundred: *ciento ocho,* one hundred and eight. – 2 *m* (*número*) hundred. 3 **un ciento,** (*centena*) about a hundred: *he comprado un ciento de caramelos,* I have bought about a hundred sweets. ● **por ciento,** per cent: *cuarenta por ciento,* forty per cent. ‖ **por cientos,** in hundreds, by the hundred.
▲ See also **cien**; see also **seis**.

cierne *m* blossoming, blooming.
● **en cierne / en ciernes,** *fig* in embryo, potential, budding: *la política urbanística está en cierne,* the town-planning policy is in its early stages.

cierre 1 *m* (*acción*) closing, shutting; (*de fábrica*) shutdown; (*de radio etc*) close-down. 2 (*de prenda*) fastener; (*de bolso*) clasp; (*de cinturón*) buckle, clasp. 3 (*de tienda*) shutter, blind; (*de puerta*) catch; (*de automóvil*) choke. ■ **cierre centralizado,** centralized locking system. ‖ **cierre de seguridad,** safety lock. ‖ **cierre patronal,** lock-out.

ciertamente *adv* certainly.

cierto,-a 1 *adj* (*seguro*) certain, sure. 2 (*verdadero*) true: *no es cierto,* that's not true. 3 (*algún*) certain, some: *ciertos libros,* some books; *cierto tiempo,* a certain time; *cierto día,* one day. – 4 **cierto,** *adv* certainly. ● **en ciertos casos,** in certain cases, in some cases. ‖ **estar en lo cierto,** to be right. ‖ **lo cierto es que ...,** the fact is that ... ‖ **por cierto,** by the way.

ciervo,-a *m,f* (*gen*) deer; (*macho*) stag, hart; (*hembra*) doe, hind.

cierzo *m* north wind.

cifra 1 *f* (*número*) figure, number: *un número de cuatro cifras,* a four-figure number. 2 (*cantidad*) amount, number. 3 (*código*) cipher, code. ● **en cifra,** (*codificado*) in code; *fig* mysteriously. ■ **cifra global,** lump sum.

cifrado,-a 1 *pp* → **cifrar**. – 2 *adj* (*codificado*) coded, in code: *un mensaje cifrado,* a coded message. 3 *fig* (*ilusiones*) placed.

cifrar 1 *t* (*codificar*) to encode. 2 (*compendiar*) to summarize. 3 *fig* (*poner*) to place (**en,** in), pin (**en,** on): *cifró todas sus esperanzas en su hijo,* he placed all his hopes on his son. – 4 **cifrarse,** *p* (*valorar*) to come (**en,** to).

cigala *f* Dublin Bay prawn.

cigarra *f* cicada.

cigarral *m* country house *in* Toledo.

cigarrera *f* → **cigarrero,-a**.

cigarrero,-a 1 *m,f* street tobacco seller. – 2 **cigarrera,** *f* (*caja*) cigar case.

cigarrillo *m* cigarette.
■ **cigarrillo con filtro,** filter-tip cigarette, filter cigarette.

cigarro 1 *m* (*puro*) cigar. 2 (*cigarrillo*) cigarette.

cigarrón *m* grasshopper.

cigoñal *m* shadoof, shaduf.

cigoñino *m* young stork.

cigoto *m* zygote.

cigüeña 1 *f* (*ave*) stork. 2 TÉC crank.

cigüeñal *m* TÉC crankshaft.

cilantro *m* coriander.

ciliado,-a *adj* ciliated.

ciliar *adj* ciliary.

cilicio *m* hair shirt.

cilindrada *f* cylinder capacity: *¿qué cilindrada tiene?,* what size is the engine?

cilindrar *t* to roll.

cilíndrico,-a *adj* cylindric, cylindrical.

cilindro *m* cylinder.

cilindroeje *m* axis cylinder, axon.

cilio *m* cilium.

cima 1 *f* (*de montaña*) summit, top; (*de árbol*) top. 2 *fig* (*cumbre*) summit, peak. ● **dar cima a algo,** *fig* to complete sth., crown sth.

címbalo *m* cymbal.

cimborio *m* dome.

cimborrio *m* dome.

cimbra 1 *f* (*armazón*) centring (US centering). 2 (*curvatura*) soffit.

cimbrar *t* → **cimbrear**.

cimbreante 1 *adj* (*flexible*) flexible, supple. 2 (*garboso*) swaying.

cimbrear 1 *t* (*hacer vibrar*) to make quiver; (*caña*) to waggle. 2 (*contonear*) to sway. – 3 **cimbrearse,** *p* (*contonearse*) to sway.

cimbreo 1 *m* (*movimiento*) quiver, waggle. 2 (*contoneo*) sway, swaying.

cimentación 1 *f* (*acción*) laying of foundations. **2** (*cimientos*) foundation, foundations *pl*.

cimentar 1 *t* ARQ to lay the foundations of. **2** *fig* (*afianzar*) to strengthen, consolidate. **3** *fig* (*establecer*) to found, establish: *cimentó su fe en la lectura de la Biblia,* his faith was founded on his reading of the Bible.
▲ *Conjugation model* [27], *like* **acertar.**

cimero,-a 1 *adj* (*que remata*) highest, top. **2** *fig* (*insigne, ilustre*) famous, distinguished.

cimiento 1 *m* ARQ foundation, foundations *pl*. **2** *fig* basis, origin.
● **desde los cimientos,** *fig* from the very start. ‖ **echar los cimientos / poner los cimientos,** to lay the foundations.
▲ *Also used in plural with the same meaning.*

cimitarra *f* scimitar.

cinabrio *m* cinnabar.

cinamomo *m* cinnamon, cinnamon tree.

cinc *m* zinc.
▲ *pl* **cines.**

cincel *m* chisel.

cincelado *m* chiselling (US chiseling).

cincelar *t* to chisel, engrave.

cincha 1 *f* (*de caballo*) girth, saddle-strap, US cinch. **2** (*de silla etc*) webbing.

cinchar 1 *t* (*la silla*) to girth. **2** (*barril, rueda, etc*) to hoop.

cinchera *f* belly.

cincho 1 *m* (*cinturón*) belt. **2** (*aro*) hoop.

cinco 1 *adj* (*cardinal*) five; (*ordinal*) fifth. **– 2** *m* (*número*) five.
● **¡choca esos cinco! / ¡venga esos cinco!,** *fam,* put it there!, give me five!
▲ *See also* **seis.**

cincoenrama *f* cinquefoil.

cincografía *f* zincography.

cincuenta 1 *adj* (*cardinal*) fifty; (*ordinal*) fiftieth. **– 2** *m* (*número*) fifty.
▲ *See also* **seis.**

cincuentavo,-a 1 *adj* fiftieth. **– 2** *m,f* fiftieth.
▲ *See also* **sexto,-a.**

cincuentena *f* (*exacto*) fifty; (*aproximado*) about fifty.

cincuentenario *m* fiftieth anniversary.

cincuentón,-ona 1 *adj fam* fifty-year-old. **– 2** *m,f* fifty-year-old.

cine 1 *m* (*local*) cinema, US movie theater: *ir al cine,* to go to the cinema, US go to the movies. **2** (*arte*) cinema.
● **hacer cine,** to make films, US make movies. ‖ **ser de cine,** *fam* to be fabulous.
■ **cine de estreno,** first-run cinema. ‖ **cine mudo,** silent films *pl*, US silent movies. ‖ **cine negro,** film noir. ‖ **cine sonoro,** talkies *pl*, talking films *pl*, US talking movies.

cineasta *mf* film director, film-maker.

cineclub 1 *m* (*organización*) film society, film club. **2** (*local*) cinema, US movie theater.
▲ *pl* **cineclubs.**

cinéfilo,-a *m,f* film buff, US movie buff.

cinegética *f* → **cinegético,-a.**

cinegético,-a 1 *adj* of hunting, related to hunting, cynegetic. **– 2** cinegética, *f* hunting.

cinema *m* → **cine.**

cinemascope *m* Cinemascope.
▲ *Registered trademark.*

cinemateca 1 *f* (*archivo*) film library. **2** (*sala*) film institute.

cinemática *f* kinematics.

cinematografiar *t* to film.
▲ *Conjugation model* [13], *like* **desviar.**

cinematografía *f* film-making, cinematography, US movie-making.

cinematográfico,-a *adj* cinematographic: *la industria cinematográfica,* the film industry, US the movie industry.

cinematógrafo *m* film projector, US movie projector.

cinerama *m* cinerama.

cinerario,-a *adj* cinerary.

cinestesia *f* kinaesthesis.

cinética *f* → **cinético,-a.**

cinético,-a 1 *adj* kinetic. **– 2** cinética, *f* kinetics.

cingalés,-esa 1 *adj* Sinhalese. **– 2** *m,f* (*persona*) Sinhalese. **– 3** cingalés, *m* (*idioma*) Sinhalese.

cíngaro,-a 1 *adj* gypsy, Tzigane. **– 2** *m,f* gypsy, Tzigane.

cinglar[1] *t* (*un bote*) to scull.

cinglar[2] *t* (*forjar*) to puddle.

cíngulo *m* REL cord.

cínico,-a 1 *adj* cynical. **– 2** *m,f* cynic.

cinismo *m* cynicism.

cinquillo *m* card game.

cinta 1 *f* (*gen*) band, strip; (*decorativa*) ribbon. **2** COST braid, edging. **3** (*para el pelo*) headband. **4** TÉC tape. **5** (*de máquina de escribir*) ribbon. **6** CINEM film. **7** (*casete*) tape.
■ **cinta adhesiva,** adhesive tape. ‖ **cinta aislante,** insulating tape. ‖ **cinta de video,** videotape. ‖ **cinta magnética,** magnetic tape. ‖ **cinta magnetofónica,** recording tape. ‖ **cinta métrica,** tape measure. ‖ **cinta transportadora,** conveyor belt.

cinto *m* (*cinturón*) belt; (*de sable*) swordbelt.

cintra *f* curvature, arch.

cintura *f* waist.
● **coger a algn. por la cintura,** to hold sb. round the waist. ‖ **meter a algn. en cintura,** *fam* to bring sb. into line.

cinturilla *f* waistband.

cinturón *m* belt.
● **apretarse el cinturón,** *fig* to tighten one's belt.
■ **cinturón de castidad,** chastity belt. ‖ **cinturón de seguridad,** safety belt, seat belt.

cipayo *m* sepoy.

cipo *m* cippus.

cipote 1 *adj* (*bobo*) stupid. **2** (*rechoncho*) chubby, tubby. **– 3** *m tabú* (*pene*) prick, cock.

ciprés *m* cypress.

CIR *abr* MIL (*Centro de Instrucción de Reclutas*) ≈ Recruits Training Unit.

circense *adj* circus.

circo 1 *m* (*gen*) circus. **2** GEOG cirque.

circón *m* zircon.

circonio *m* zirconium.

circonita *f* zirconite.

circuito 1 *m* (*eléctrico*) circuit. **2** (*contorno*) circumference. **3** (*recorrido*) tour, circuit. **4** (*de carreras*) track, circuit.
■ **circuito cerrado de televisión,** closed-circuit television. ‖ **corto circuito,** short circuit.

circulación 1 *f* (*gen*) circulation. **2** (*de vehículos*) traffic: *esta autopista tiene mucha circulación,* this is a busy motorway.
● **estar fuera de circulación,** to be out of circulation. ‖ **poner en circulación,** to put into circulation. ‖ **quitar de la circulación / retirar de la circulación,** to withdraw from circulation.

■ **circulación sanguínea / circulación de la sangre,** blood circulation. ‖ **circulación rodada,** vehicular traffic, traffic. ‖ **código de (la) circulación,** highway code.

circular 1 *adj* circular. – 2 *f (carta)* circular, circular letter. – 3 *i (gen)* to circulate, move, go round: *los billetes falsos todavía circulan,* the false notes are still going around. 4 *(líquido, electricidad)* to circulate, flow: *la sangre no puede circular,* the blood can't flow. 5 *(coche)* to drive; *(trenes, autobuses)* to run; *(peatón)* to walk: *circular por la izquierda,* to drive on the left. 6 *fig (rumor etc)* to spread, get round.
● "circule por la derecha", "keep to the right". ‖ ¡circulen!, move along!

circulatorio,-a *adj* circulatory.

círculo 1 *m (gen)* circle. 2 *(asociación)* club, circle. – 3 **círculos,** *mpl (ambientes)* circles.
■ **círculo familiar,** family circle. ‖ **círculo polar antártico,** Antarctic Circle. ‖ **círculo polar ártico,** Arctic Circle. ‖ **círculo vicioso,** *fig* vicious circle.

circuncidar *t* to circumcise.

circuncisión *f* circumcision.

circunciso,-a 1 *adj* circumcised. – 2 **cicunciso,** *m* circumcised man.

circundante *adj* surrounding.

circundar *t* to surround.

circunferencia *f* circumference.

circunflejo,-a 1 *adj* circumflex. – 2 **circunflejo,** *m* circumflex.

circunlocución *f* circumlocution.

circunloquio *m* circumlocution.

circunnavegar *t* to circumnavigate.
▲ *Conjugation model* [7], *like* **llegar**.

circunscribir 1 *t* to circumscribe. – 2 **circunscribirse,** *p (ceñirse)* to confine os. **(a,** to), limit os. **(a,** to): *el director se circunscribe a organizar el trabajo,* the director limits himself to organizing the work.
▲ *pp* **circunscrito,-a.**

circunscripción *f* district, area.
■ **circunscripción electoral,** constituency.

circunscrito,-a *pp* → **circunscribir.**

circunspección *f* circumspection.

circunspecto,-a *adj* circumspect, serious, grave.

circunstancia *f* circumstance.
● **en estas circunstancias,** under the circumstances. ‖ **poner cara de circunstancias,** *fam* to look grave.

circunstancial *adj* circumstantial.

circunvalación *f* circumvallation.
■ **línea de circunvalación,** *(de autobús)* circular route; *(de tren)* circular line.

circunvalar *t* to surround, circumvallate.

circunvolar *t* to fly around.
▲ *Conjugation model* [31], *like* **contar.**

cirial *m* candlestick.

cirílico,-a *adj* Cyrillic.

cirio *m* long wax candle.
● **armar un cirio,** *fam* to kick up a rumpus.

cirro¹ *m (tumor)* scirrhus.

cirro² *m (nube)* cirrus.

cirrópodo *m* cirriped.

cirrosis *f* cirrhosis.
▲ *pl* **cirrosis.**

cirroso,-a *adj* cirrhotic.

cirrótico,-a *adj* cirrhotic.

ciruela *f* plum.
■ **ciruela claudia,** greengage. ‖ **ciruela pasa,** prune.

ciruelo *m* plum tree.

cirugía *f* surgery.
■ **cirugía estética / cirugía plástica,** plastic surgery.

cirujano,-a *m,f* surgeon.

ciscar 1 *t fam (ensuciar)* to dirty. – 2 **ciscarse,** *p euf (cagarse)* to soil os.
▲ *Conjugation model* [1], *like* **sacar.**

cisco 1 *m (carbón)* coal dust, slack. 2 *fam (reyerta)* row, rumpus.
● **estar hecho,-a un cisco,** *fam* to be all in, be a wreck. ‖ **hacer cisco algo,** to shatter sth., smash sth. to pieces. ‖ **meter cisco,** *fam* to kick up a stink.

ciscón *m* clinker.

cisma 1 *m* REL schism. 2 *(desacuerdo)* discord, split. 3 POL split.

cismático,-a 1 *adj* schismatic. – 2 *m,f* schismatic.

cisne *m* swan.
■ **canto del cisne,** swan song.

cisterciense 1 *adj* Cistercian. – 2 *m* Cistercian.

cisterna *f* cistern, tank.
■ **buque cisterna / camión cisterna,** tanker.

cistitis *f* cystitis.
▲ *pl* **cistitis.**

cisura *f* incision.

cita 1 *f (para negocios, médico, etc)* appointment: *tengo una cita con mi abogado,* I have an appointment with my lawyer. 2 *(amorosa)* date. 3 *(mención)* quotation.
● **darse cita,** to meet; *fig* fig: *se dieron cita en el cine,* they met at the cinema; *estos aspectos se dan cita en el ensayo,* these aspects come together in the essay. ‖ **tener una cita,** to have an appointment, have an engagement.
■ **cita a ciegas,** blind date.

citación 1 *f (mención)* quotation. 2 JUR citation, summons.

citado,-a 1 *pp* → **citar.** – 2 *adj* aforementioned, said: *la cantidad citada,* the said amount.

citar 1 *t (dar cita)* to make an appointment with, arrange to meet. 2 *(mencionar)* to quote. 3 JUR to summon. – 4 **citarse,** *p* to arrange to meet **(con,** -).
● **citar a algn. a juicio,** to call sb. as a witness. ‖ **citar de memoria,** to quote from memory.

citara *f* brick partition.

cítara *f* zither.

citerior *adj* hithermost.

citología *f* cytology.

citoplasma *m* cytoplasm.

cítrico,-a 1 *adj* citric. – 2 **cítricos,** *mpl* citrus fruits.

citrina *f* → **citrino,-a.**

citrino,-a 1 *adj* sallow. – 2 **citrina,** *f* lemon oil.

CiU *abr* POL *(Convergència i Unió) conservative Catalan nationalist coalition.*

ciudad *f* city, town: *fuimos a la ciudad,* we went into town, we went to town.
■ **ciudad dormitorio,** dormitory suburb, dormitory town, commuter suburb. ‖ **ciudad jardín,** garden city. ‖ **ciudad universitaria,** university campus.

ciudadanía *f* citizenship.

ciudadano,-a 1 *adj* civic. – 2 *m,f* citizen. – 3 **los ciudadanos,** *mpl* townspeople, city dwellers.

ciudadela *f* citadel, fortress.

ciudad-realeño,-a 1 *adj* of Ciudad Real, from Ciudad Real. – 2 *m,f* person from Ciudad Real, inhabitant of Ciudad Real.

civet *m* game stew.

civeta f civet.
cívico,-a adj civic.
civil 1 adj civil: *derecho civil,* civil law. **2** (*no militar*) civilian. **3** (*no eclesiástico*) lay, secular. **– 4** m (*de la Guardia Civil*) civil guard, member of the Guardia Civil.
civilista mf expert in civil law.
civilización f civilization.
civilizado,-a 1 pp → **civilizar**. **– 2** adj civilized.
civilizador,-ra 1 adj civilizing. **– 2** m,f civilizer.
civilizar 1 t to civilize. **– 2 civilizarse,** p to become civilized.
▲ Conjugation model [4], like *realizar*.
civismo 1 m good citizenship, community spirit. **2** (*al servicio de los demás*) civility.
cizalla 1 f (*tijeras*) metal shears pl, wire cutters pl. **2** (*fragmento de metal*) metal clippings pl, metal cuttings pl.
▲ Also used in plural with the same meaning.
cizaña f BOT bearded darnel.
● **meter cizaña / sembrar cizaña,** fig to cause trouble, stir up trouble.
cizañero,-a m,f troublemaker.
cl sím (*centilitro*) centilitre (US centiliter); (*símbolo*) cl.
clac 1 m (*de copa alta*) opera hat. **2** (*de tres picos*) cocked hat, three-cornered hat.
▲ pl *claques*.
clamar 1 i to clamour (US clamor) (**por,** for), cry out (**por,** for): *clamar por la justicia,* to cry out for justice. **– 2** t to cry out for: *clamar ayuda,* to cry out for help.
● **esto clama al cielo,** fig this is crying out for a solution.
clamor 1 m (*griterío*) shouting, din, noise. **2** (*voces de protesta o queja*) clamour (US clamor), outcry: *hubo un clamor popular contra esa ley,* there was a public outcry against the law. **3** (*toque de campanas*) knell, toll.
clamoroso,-a 1 adj (*de voces*) clamorous, loud. **2** (*de quejas*) complaining. **3** (*éxito*) overwhelming.
clan m clan.
▲ pl *clanes*.
clandestinidad f secrecy.
● **en la clandestinidad,** in secret, underground.
clandestino,-a adj clandestine, underground, secret.
claque f fig claque.
claqué m tap dancing.
claqueta f clapperboard.
clara f → **claro,-a**.
claraboya f skylight.
claramente adv clearly.
clarear 1 t (*dar claridad*) to light up, illuminate. **2** (*aclarar un color*) to make lighter: *tienes que clarear ese azul,* you have to make that blue lighter. **– 3** i (*amanecer*) to dawn. **4** (*despejar el cielo*) to clear up. **– 5 clarearse,** p (*transparentarse*) to let the light through, be transparent. **6** fig (*delatarse*) to give os. away.
▲ In 3 and 4, used only in the 3rd pers; it does not take a subject.
clarete 1 adj dark rosé. **– 2** m dark rosé.
claridad 1 f (*luminosidad*) light, brightness. **2** (*del agua, voz, etc*) clearness. **3** (*inteligibilidad*) clearness, clarity.
● **con claridad,** clearly: *lo pudimos ver con claridad,* we could see it clearly.
clarificación 1 f clarification. **2** fig explanation.
clarificador,-ra 1 adj clarifying. **– 2 clarificador,** m clarifier.
clarificar 1 t to clarify, clear up. **– 2 clarificarse,** p to become clear, be cleared up.
▲ Conjugation model [1], like *sacar*.

clarín 1 m (*instrumento*) bugle. **– 2** mf (*músico*) bugler.
clarinete 1 m (*instrumento*) clarinet. **– 2** mf (*músico*) clarinettist, clarinetist.
clarinetista mf clarinettist, clarinetist.
clarión m chalk.
clarisa f nun of the order of Saint Clare, Poor Clare, Clare.
clarividencia 1 f (*percepción paranormal*) clairvoyance. **2** (*comprensión*) lucidity.
clarividente 1 adj (*adivino*) clairvoyant. **2** (*perspicaz*) lucid. **– 3** mf clairvoyant.
claro,-a 1 adj (*gen*) clear: *no está nada claro,* it's not clear at all. **2** (*iluminado*) bright, well-lit. **3** (*color*) light: *azul claro,* light blue. **4** (*salsa etc*) thin; (*café, chocolate, etc*) weak. **5** (*evidente*) clear. **– 6** adv clearly. **– 7 claro;** m (*gen*) gap, space; (*de bosque*) clearing. **8** (*en el pelo*) bald patch. **– 9** interj of course!: *¡claro que no puedes!,* of course you can't!
● **a las claras,** openly. ‖ **dejar algo claro,** to make sth. clear. ‖ **estar claro,** to be clear. ‖ **¡lo llevas claro! / ¡lo tienes claro!,** fam you've got it coming to you! ‖ **más claro,-a que el agua,** fam as clear as daylight. ‖ **poner en claro,** to make plain, clear up. ‖ **sacar en claro,** to get out: *no sacamos nada en claro del informe,* we didn't get anything out of the report.
■ **claro de luna,** moonlight. ‖ **mente clara,** fig clear mind.
claroscuro m chiaroscuro, clair-obscure.
clase 1 f (*grupo, categoría*) class. **2** (*aula*) classroom; (*de universidad*) lecture hall. **3** (*tipo*) type, sort.
● **asistir a clase,** to attend class. ‖ **dar clase,** to teach. ‖ **de buena clase,** good quality. ‖ **de todas clases,** of all kinds, of all sorts. ‖ **tener clase,** to have class. ‖ **toda clase de,** all sorts of.
■ **clase alta,** upper class. ‖ **clase baja,** lower class. ‖ **clase de conducir,** driving lesson. ‖ **clase dirigente,** ruling class. ‖ **clase media,** middle class. ‖ **clase obrera,** working class. ‖ **clase particular,** private class, private lesson. ‖ **clase preferente,** business class. ‖ **clases de recuperación,** remedial classes. ‖ **clases pasivas,** pensioners. ‖ **primera clase,** first class. ‖ **segunda clase,** second class.
clásicas fpl → **clásico,-a**.
clasicismo m classicism.
clasicista 1 adj classicistic. **– 2** mf classicist.
clásico,-a 1 adj (*de los clásicos*) classical: *literatura clásica,* classical literature. **2** (*típico*) classic, typical: *la clásica pregunta,* the typical question. **3** (*tradicional*) classic: *es un vestido clásico,* it's a classic dress. **– 4 clásico,** m classic: *este libro es un clásico de la ciencia ficción,* this book is a science-fiction classic. **– 5 clásicas,** fpl LING the classics.
clasificación 1 f (*gen*) classification. **2** (*distribución*) sorting, filing. **3** DEP league, table. **4** (*de discos*) top twenty, hit parade.
clasificador,-ra 1 adj classifying. **– 2** m,f classifier. **– 3 clasificador,** m (*mueble*) filing cabinet. **4** (*carpeta*) box file.
clasificar 1 t to class, classify. **2** (*distribuir*) to sort, file. **– 3 clasificarse,** p DEP to qualify: *Pedro no se clasificó para la final,* Pedro didn't qualify for the final. **4** (*llegar*) to come: *se clasificó en primera posición,* she came first.
▲ Conjugation model [1], like *sacar*.
clasismo m class-consciousness.
clasista 1 adj class-conscious. **– 2** mf class-conscious person.

claudicación f submission, yielding.
claudicar i to yield, give in.
   ▲ Conjugation model [1], like **sacar**.
claustral adj claustral, cloistral.
claustro 1 m ARQ cloister. 2 (estado monástico) monastic life. 3 (conjunto de profesores) staff. 4 (junta de profesores) staff meeting; (de universidad) senate.
claustrofobia f claustrophobia.
cláusula f clause.
clausura 1 f (cierre) closure: la policía procedió a la clausura de los bares nocturnos, the police closed down the late-night bars. 2 (acto) closing ceremony, closing session: la clausura de los Juegos Olímpicos tendrá lugar a las siete de la tarde, the closing ceremony of the Olympic Games will be held at seven p.m. 3 REL enclosure: es una monja de clausura, she's an enclosed nun.
clausurar 1 t (poner fin) to close, conclude. 2 (cerrar) to close (down).
clavado,-a 1 pp → **clavar**. - 2 adj (con clavos) nailed, nail-studded. 3 fam (preciso) exact, precise: llegó a las seis clavadas, he arrived at six o'clock on the dot. 4 (fijo) firmly fixed: tenía los ojos clavados en el suelo, he was staring at the floor.
   ● dejar clavado,-a a algn., to leave sb. dumbfounded. ‖ ser clavado,-a a algn., fam to be the spitting image of sb.
clavadura f prick with a nail.
clavar 1 t (con clavos) to nail. 2 (un clavo) to bang, hammer in; (estaca) to drive: la víctima tenía una navaja clavada en el pecho, the victim had a knife stuck in his chest. 3 fig (atención) to fix; (ojos) to rivet. 4 fam (cobrar caro) to sting, fleece: me clavaron veinte mil pesetas, I got stung for twenty thousand pesetas. - 5 clavarse, p (gen) to stick: se clavó un cuchillo en el pie, she stuck a knife in her foot; me clavé una astilla en el dedo, I got a splinter in my finger.
clave 1 f (de un enigma etc) key, clue: la clave del éxito, the key to success. 2 (de signos) code, key, cipher: un mensaje en clave, a coded message. 3 MÚS key: en clave de sol, in the key of G. 4 ARQ key-stone. - 5 m (instrumento) harpsichord. - 6 adj (importante) key: el hombre clave es el ministro de Hacienda, the key man is the Chancellor of the Exchequer.
clavel m carnation.
clavelito m pink.
clavellina f carnation.
clavero m clove tree.
clavetear t to stud with nails.
clavicémbalo m clavicembalo, harpsichord.
clavicordio m clavichord.
clavícula f clavicle, collarbone.
clavija 1 f TÉC peg. 2 ELEC (de enchufe) pin.
   ● apretarle las clavijas a algn., fam to tighten the screws on sb.
clavijero m MÚS pegbox.
clavillo 1 m (de abanico, tijeras) pivot, pin. 2 (de piano) wrest pin.
clavo 1 m nail. 2 BOT clove. 3 (callo) corn. 4 tabú (polvo) screw: echar un clavo, to have a screw.
   ● como un clavo, fam very punctual, on the dot: llegó como un clavo, she arrived on the dot. ‖ dar en el clavo, fig to hit the nail on the head. ‖ estar sin un clavo, fam to be flat broke. ‖ no dar ni clavo, fam not to lift a finger. ‖ ¡por los clavos de Cristo!, for Christ's sake! ‖ remachar el clavo, fig to make matters worse.
claxon m horn, hooter.
   ▲ pl **cláxones**.

clemencia f clemency, mercy.
clemente adj forgiving, merciful.
clementina f clementine.
clepsidra f clepsydra.
cleptomanía f kleptomania.
cleptómano,-a 1 adj kleptomaniac. - 2 m,f kleptomaniac.
clerecía f clergy.
clergyman m (traje) clericals pl, clergyman's suit.
   ▲ pl **clergymans**.
clerical 1 adj clerical. - 2 mf clericalist.
clericalismo m clericalism.
clérigo m priest.
clero m clergy.
cliché 1 m (imprenta) plate. 2 (fotografía) negative. 3 fig (lugar común) cliché.
clienta f client, customer.
cliente mf client, customer.
clientela f customers pl, clients pl, clientele.
clima 1 m climate. 2 fig atmosphere, climate.
climatérico,-a adj climacteric, climacterical.
climaterio m climacteric.
climático,-a adj climatic, climatical: un cambio climático, a change in the climate, a change in the weather.
climatización f air-conditioning.
climatizado,-a 1 pp → **climatizar**. - 2 adj air-conditioned.
climatizar t to air-condition.
   ▲ Conjugation model [4], like **realizar**.
climatología f climatology.
climatológico,-a adj climatological.
clímax m climax.
   ▲ pl **clímax**.
clínica f → **clínico,-a**.
clínico,-a 1 adj clinical: muerte clínica, clinical death. - 2 m,f (médico) clinician, physician. - 3 clínica, f (departamento) clinic. 4 (hospital) clinic, private hospital.
clip 1 m (para papel) paper clip. 2 (para pelo) hair-grip, US bobby pin. 3 (pendiente) clip-on earring.
   ▲ pl **clips**.
clíper m clipper.
   ▲ pl **clíperes**.
clisar t to stereotype.
clisé m → **cliché**.
clítoris m clitoris.
   ▲ pl **clítoris**.
cloaca f sewer, drain.
clon m clone.
clonar t to clone.
cloquear i to cluck.
cloqueo m cluck, clucking.
cloral m chloral.
clorato m chlorate.
clorhídrico,-a adj hydrochloric.
   ■ ácido clorhídrico, hydrochloric acid.
clórico,-a adj chloric.
cloro m chlorine.
clorofila f chlorophyll.
clorofílico,-a adj chlorophyllous.
cloroformizar t to chloroform.
cloroformo m chloroform.
cloroplasto m chloroplast.
clorosis f chlorosis.
   ▲ pl **clorosis**.

cloruro *m* chloride.
∎ **cloruro sódico,** sodium chloride.
clown *m* clown.
▲ *pl clowns.*
club *m* club, society.
∎ **club náutico,** yacht club. ‖ **club nocturno,** night club.
▲ *pl clubs or clubes.*
clueca 1 *adj* broody. – 2 *f* broody hen.
cluniacense 1 *adj* Cluniac. – 2 *m* Cluniac.
cm *sím* (*centímetro*) centimetre (US centimeter); (*símbolo*) cm.
Cnel. *abr* (*Coronel*) Colonel; (*abreviatura*) Col.
CNT *abr* (*Confederación Nacional del Trabajo*) National Confederation of Workers (*Spanish anarcho-syndicalist labour union*).
coacción *f* coercion, compulsion.
coaccionar *t* to coerce, compel.
coactivo,-a *adj* coercive, compelling.
coadjutor,-ra 1 *m,f* coadjutant. – 2 coadjutor, *m* REL coadjutor.
coadyuvante *adj fml* coadjutant.
coadyuvar *t fml* to contribute, help.
coagulación *f* coagulation, clotting.
coagulante 1 *adj* coagulative. – 2 *m* coagulant.
coagular 1 *t* (*gen*) to coagulate, clot; (*leche*) to curdle. – 2 **coagularse,** *p* to coagulate, clot; (*leche*) to curdle.
coágulo *m* coagulum, clot.
coala *m* koala, koala bear.
coalición *f* coalition.
coaligarse *p* to ally.
coartada *f* alibi.
coartar *t* to limit, restrict.
coautor,-ra *m,f* coauthor.
coaxial *adj* coaxial.
coba *f fam* soft soap.
● **dar coba a algn.,** *fam* to soft-soap sb.
cobalto *m* cobalt.
∎ **bomba de cobalto,** cobalt bomb.
cobarde 1 *adj* cowardly. – 2 *mf* coward.
cobardía *f* cowardice.
cobaya *m* guinea pig.
cobayo *m* guinea pig.
cobertizo *m* shed, shack.
cobertor 1 *m* (*colcha*) bedspread. 2 (*manta*) blanket.
cobertura *f* cover.
∎ **cobertura de chocolate,** chocolate coating. ‖ **cobertura de seguros,** insurance cover.
cobijar 1 *t* (*cubrir*) to cover. 2 *fig* to shelter. 3 *fig* (*a un criminal*) to harbour (US harbor). – 4 **cobijarse,** *p* to take shelter.
cobijo 1 *m* (*hospedaje*) lodging. 2 (*refugio*) shelter. 3 *fig* protection, refuge.
cobista 1 *adj fam* soapy. – 2 *mf* crawler, toady.
cobla *f* brass band.
cobol *m* INFORM Cobol, COBOL.
cobra[1] *f* (*coyunda*) rope for yoking oxen.
cobra[2] *f* (*serpiente*) cobra.
cobrador,-ra 1 *m,f* (*de luz etc*) collector. 2 (*de transporte - hombre*) conductor; (*- mujer*) conductress.
cobrar 1 *t* (*fijar precio por*) to charge; (*cheques*) to cash; (*salario*) to earn: *¿cuánto te ha cobrado?,* how much did he charge you?; *¿cuánto cobras?,* how much do you earn?; *cobro cada lunes,* I get paid every Monday. 2 (*caza*) to retrieve. 3 to get: *si no te estás quieto vas a cobrar una*

torta, if you don't keep still you'll get a smack. **4** *fig* (*adquirir*) to gain, get: *le he cobrado cariño a ese lugar,* I've taken a liking to this place, I've grown fond of this place; *cobrar fuerzas,* to gather strength. – **5** *i* to be in for it. – **6 cobrarse,** *p* (*dinero*) to take, collect: *cóbrate el café,* can you take for the coffee? **7** (*víctimas*) to claim. **8** (*recuperar*) to recover (**de,** from); (*volver en sí*) to come round.
● **cobrarse venganza,** to take revenge.
cobre 1 *m* (*metal*) copper. 2 (*batería de cocina*) copper pans *pl.*
● **batir el cobre,** *fam* to go hard at it.
cobrizo,-a *adj* copper, copper-coloured (US copper-colored), coppery.
cobro 1 *m* (*pago*) payment. 2 (*cobranza*) collection; (*de cheque*) cashing. 3 (*en caza*) retrieval.
● **llamar a cobro revertido,** to reverse the charges, US call collect.
∎ **cobro revertido,** reverse-charge, US collect.
coca[1] 1 *f* (*arbusto*) coca. 2 *arg* coke. 3 *fam* (*bebida*) Coke R.
coca[2] *f* (*baya*) berry.
coca[3] 1 *f* (*moño*) bun. 2 (*cabeza*) head.
coca[4] *f* (*dulce*) type of flat sponge cake; (*salada*) flat pizzalike tart.
cocaína *f* cocaine.
cocainómano,-a *m,f* cocaine addict.
cocción *f* (*gen*) cooking; (*en agua*) boiling; (*en horno*) baking.
cóccix *m* coccyx.
▲ *pl cóccix.*
cocear *i* to kick.
cocer 1 *t* (*gen*) to cook; (*hervir*) to boil; (*al horno*) to bake. – 2 *i* (*hervir*) to boil: *el café cuece,* the coffee is boiling. – 3 **cocerse,** *p* (*gen*) to cook; (*hervir*) to boil; (*al horno*) to bake. **4** *fam* (*de calor*) to be roasting, be boiling: *me cuezo,* I'm boiling. **5** *fam* (*tramarse*) to be cooking, be afoot, be going on: *se está cociendo algo a nuestras espaldas,* there's something fishy (going on) behind our backs.
▲ *Conjugation model* [54].
cochambre 1 *m & f fam* (*porquería*) filth, muck. 2 *fam* (*objeto*) filthy object.
cochambroso,-a *adj fam* filthy, dirty.
coche 1 *m* (*automóvil*) car, automobile, motorcar: *fuimos en coche,* we went by car. 2 (*de tren, de caballos*) carriage, coach. 3 (*de niño*) pram, US baby carriage.
∎ **coche bomba,** car bomb. ‖ **coche cama,** sleeping car. ‖ **coche de alquiler,** hired car, US rented car. ‖ **coche de bomberos,** fire engine. ‖ **coche de carreras,** racing car. ‖ **coche de época,** vintage car. ‖ **coche deportivo,** sports car. ‖ **coche familiar,** estate (car), US station wagon. ‖ **coche fúnebre,** hearse. ‖ **coches de choque,** dodgems, bumper cars.
cochera *f* depot.
cochero *m* coachman.
cochifrito *m* (*cordero*) mutton stew; (*cabrito*) goat stew.
cochinada 1 *f fam* (*porquería*) dirty thing, filthy thing. 2 *fam* (*obscenidad*) obscenity. 3 *fam fig* dirty trick.
● **decir cochinadas,** *fam* to say filthy words, say obscene things. ‖ **hacer una cochinada a algn.,** *fam* to play a dirty trick on sb.
cochinería *f* → **cochinada.**
cochinilla 1 *f* (*crustáceo*) woodlouse. 2 (*insecto*) cochineal.
cochinillo *m* sucking pig.
cochino,-a 1 *adj* (*sucio*) filthy, disgusting. 2 (*miserable*) damn, bloody, lousy: *¡cochino trabajo!,* bloody work! –

3 *m,f* ZOOL (*gen*) pig; (*macho*) swine; (*hembra*) sow. **4** *fam* (*persona*) dirty person, filthy person, pig.

cochiquera *f fam* pigsty.

cocido,-a **1** *pp* → **cocer**. – **2** *adj* cooked; (*en agua*) boiled; (*al horno*) baked. – **3 cocido,** *m* CULIN stew.
● estar cocido,-a, *fam* to be sloshed.

cociente *m* quotient.

cocina **1** *f* (*lugar*) kitchen. **2** (*gastronomía*) cooking: *cocina española,* Spanish cooking, Spanish cuisine. **3** (*aparato*) cooker, US stove.
■ cocina casera, home cooking. ‖ cocina de gas, gas cooker, US gas stove. ‖ cocina de mercado, food in season, seasonal produce. ‖ cocina económica, cooking range. ‖ cocina eléctrica, electric cooker, US electric stove. ‖ libro de cocina, cookery book, US cookbook.

cocinar **1** *t* to cook. – **2** *i* to cook.

cocinero,-a *m,f* cook.
■ primer cocinero, chef.

cocinilla *f* (small portable) cooker, US stove.

cocker *m* cocker, cocker spaniel.
▲ *pl cockers*.

cocktail *m* → **cóctel**.

coco[1] **1** *m* BOT (*árbol*) coconut palm. **2** (*fruta*) coconut.
■ coco rallado, desiccated coconut.

coco[2] *m* (*bacteria*) coccus.

coco[3] *m* (*larva*) larva, worm, grub.

coco[4] **1** *m fam* (*fantasma*) bogeyman. **2** *arg* (*cabeza*) noddle, noggin, nut.
● comer el coco a algn., *fam* to brainwash sb. ‖ comerse el coco, *fam* to get worked up, worry about it. ‖ ser un coco, *fam* (*feo*) to be ugly; (*dar miedo*) to be frightening.

cocodrilo *m* crocodile.

cocorota *f fam* head, nut.

cocotal *m* coconut grove.

cocotero *m* coconut palm.

cóctel **1** *m* (*bebida*) cocktail. **2** (*fiesta*) cocktail party.
■ cóctel molotov, Molotov cocktail.

coctelera *f* cocktail shaker.

Cód. *abr* (*código*) code.

coda[1] *f* MÚS coda.

coda[2] *f* (*cuña*) wedge.

codadura *f* layer.

codaste *m* sternpost.

codazo **1** *m* (*golpe*) poke with one's elbow, blow with one's elbow: *le pegó un codazo,* she poked him with her elbow. **2** (*señal*) nudge with one's elbow.
● abrirse paso a codazos / abrirse camino a codazos, to elbow one's way through.

codear **1** *i* (*empujar*) to elbow. – **2 codearse,** *p* to rub shoulders (**con,** with), hobnob (**con,** with).

codeína *f* codeine.

codera *f* elbow patch.

códice *m* codex.

codicia *f* greed, covetousness, coveting.

codiciable *adj* desirable, covetable.

codiciado,-a **1** *pp* → **codiciar**. – **2** *adj* coveted, much desired.

codiciar *t* to covet, desire, crave for.
▲ *Conjugation model* |12|, *like* **cambiar**.

codicilo *m* codicil.

codicioso,-a **1** *adj* covetous, greedy. – **2** *m,f* covetous person, greedy person.

codificación **1** *f* (*de leyes*) codification. **2** (*de mensajes*) encoding. **3** INFORM coding, code.

codificador,-ra **1** *adj* JUR codifying. **2** (*de mensajes*) encoding. – **3** *m,f* JUR codifier. **4** (*de mensajes*) encoder. – **5 codificador,** *m* INFORM encoder.

codificar **1** *t* (*leyes*) to codify. **2** (*mensajes*) to encode. **3** INFORM to code.

código *m* code.
■ código de barras, bar code. ‖ código de la circulación, highway code. ‖ código del honor, code of honour (US honor). ‖ código de señales, MAR flag signals. ‖ código Morse, Morse code.

codillo **1** *m* (*del brazo*) elbow. **2** (*en cocina*) shoulder. **3** (*de tubería*) elbow.

codo **1** *m* ANAT elbow. **2** TÉC bend.
● alzar el codo / empinar el codo, *fam* to have a few drinks, knock them back. ‖ codo a codo / codo con codo, *fig* side by side, closely. ‖ de codos, on one's elbows. ‖ hablar por los codos, *fam* to talk nineteen to the dozen, talk nonstop. ‖ romperse los codos, *fig* to study a lot, swot, cram.

codoñate *m* quince marmalade.

codorniz *f* quail.

COE[1] *abr* (*Comité Olímpico Español*) Spanish Olympic Committee.
▲ Used as masculine.

COE[2] *abr* MIL (*Compañías de Operaciones Especiales*) special operations group.
▲ Used as feminine plural.

coeducación *f* coeducation.

coeficiente **1** *m* MAT coefficient. **2** (*grado*) degree, rate.
■ coeficiente de crecimiento, growth rate. ‖ coeficiente de inteligencia, intelligence quotient, IQ.

coercer *t* to coerce.
▲ *Conjugation model* |2|, *like* **mecer**.

coerción *f* coercion, restraint.

coercitivo,-a *adj* coercive.

coetáneo,-a **1** *adj* contemporary. – **2** *m,f* contemporary.

coexistencia *f* coexistence.
■ coexistencia pacífica, peaceful coexistence.

coexistir *i* to coexist.

cofa *f* top.
■ cofa mayor, maintop.

cofederado,-a **1** *pp* → **confederar**. – **2** *adj* confederate. – **3** *m,f* confederate.

cofia *f* bonnet.

cofrade *mf* (*gen*) member; (*hombre*) brother; (*mujer*) sister.

cofradía **1** *f* (*hermandad*) brotherhood. **2** (*asociación*) association. **3** (*gremio*) guild.

cofre *m* (*grande*) trunk, chest; (*pequeño*) box, casket.

cogedor *m* dustpan.

coger **1** *t* (*asir*) to seize, take hold of: *coge al bebé,* hold the baby. **2** (*apresar*) to capture, catch. **3** (*tomar*) to take: *coger un empleo,* to take a job; *coger algo para beber,* take a drink. **4** (*contratar*) to take on: *cogimos a una secretaria,* we took on a secretary. **5** (*tren etc*) to catch. **6** (*tomar prestado*) to borrow: *te he cogido el libro,* I've borrowed your book. **7** (*recolectar frutos etc*) to pick; (*del suelo*) to gather. **8** (*enfermedad, balón*) to catch: *cogí un resfriado,* I caught a cold. **9** (*acento, costumbres*) to pick up. **10** (*velocidad, fuerza*) to gather. **11** (*atropellar*) to run over, knock down. **12** (*emisora, canal*) to pick up, get: *coger la BBC,* to get the BBC. **13** (*notas*) to take, take down. **14** (*oír*) to catch: *no he cogido lo que ha dicho,* I didn't catch what she said. **15** (*entender*) to understand, get: *no cogí el final,* I didn't get the end. **16** AM tabú to fuck. – **17** *i* (*plantas, colores*) to take: *el limonero no ha cogido,* the lemon tree didn't take. **18** (*ir*) to turn, take, go: *coge a la izquierda,* turn left; *coge todo recto,* go straight on. **19** *fam* (*caber*) to fit: *coge allí,* it fits there; *no cogemos todos,* there isn't room for all of us. **– 20 cogerse,** *p* (*pillarse*) to catch. **21** (*agarrarse*) to hold on: *cógete fuerte,* hold on tight.

● **coger algo por los pelos,** *fig* to just make sth.; **cogimos el tren por los pelo,** we just made the train. ‖ **coger del brazo a algn.,** to take sb. by the arm, grab sb. by the arm. ‖ **coger cariño a algo/algn.,** to become fond of sth./sb., take a liking to sth./sb. ‖ **coger desprevenido,-a,** *fig* to catch unawares. ‖ **coger miedo a algo,** to become afraid of sth. ‖ **coger por sorpresa,** to catch by surprise. ‖ **coger puntos,** (*de media etc*) to pick up stitches. ‖ **coger una borrachera,** *fam* to get drunk. ‖ **coger una manía a algn.,** *fam* to take a dislike to sb. ‖ **coger y ...,** *fam* to up and ..., go and ...: *cogió y se fue,* she upped and left; *y entonces coge y lo insulta,* so then she goes and insults him. ‖ **cogerse un cabreo,** *fam* to get very angry. ‖ **no hay por dónde cogerlo,** he hasn't got a leg to stand on.
▲ *Conjugation model* |5|, *like* ***proteger.***

cogestión *f* copartnership.
cogida *f* → **cogido,-a.**
cogido,-a 1 *pp* → **coger. – 2** *adj* (*sujeto*) fixed. **3** (*atrapado*) trapped, caught. **– 4 cogido,** *m* (*pliegue*) gather, pleat; (*de cortina*) tie. **– 5 cogida,** *f* (*de toro*) gore, goring.
● **cogidos del brazo,** arm in arm.
cognación *f* cognation, kinship.
cognición *f* cognition.
cognoscitivo,-a *adj* cognitive.
cogollo 1 *m* (*de lechuga etc*) heart. **2** (*brote*) shoot. **3** *fig* heart, centre (*us* center). **4 el cogollo,** *fig* the cream, the best.
● **hasta el cogollo,** *fam* to the core.
cogorza agarrar una cogorza / pillar una cogorza, *loc fam* to get plastered, get drunk.
cogotazo *m fam* blow on the back of the neck.
cogote *m* back of the neck, nape of the neck.
cogujada *f* crested lark.
cogulla 1 *f* (*hábito*) habit. **2** (*capucha*) cowl.
cohabitación *f* cohabitation.
cohabitar *i* to cohabit, live together.
cohechar[1] *t* JUR to bribe, suborn.
cohechar[2] *t* AGR to plough for the last time before sowing.
cohecho *m* JUR bribery.
coherencia *f* coherence, coherency.
coherente *adj* coherent, connected.
cohesión *f* cohesion.
cohesivo,-a *adj* cohesive.
cohete *m* rocket.
● **como un cohete,** *fam* like a rocket.
■ **cohete espacial,** space rocket.
cohibición *f* inhibition, restraint.
cohibido,-a 1 *pp* → **cohibir. – 2** *adj* inhibited, restrained.
cohibir 1 *t* to inhibit, restrain. **– 2 cohibirse,** *p* to feel inhibited, feel embarrassed.
▲ *Conjugation model* |21|, *like* ***prohibir.***
cohombro *m* cucumber.
cohorte 1 *f* MIL cohort. **2** *fig* collection, group.
COI *abr* (*Comité Olímpico Internacional*) International Olympic Committee; (*abreviatura*) IOC.
coincidencia 1 *f* (*gen*) coincidence. **– 2** *m* (*acuerdo*) agreement.

● **dio la coincidencia de que ...,** it just happened that ... ‖ **en coincidencia con ...,** in agreement with ...
coincidente *adj* coincident, coinciding.
coincidir 1 *i* (*estar de acuerdo*) to agree (**en,** on), coincide (**en,** in): *siempre coincidimos en gustos,* we always have the same tastes. **2** (*ajustarse*) to coincide. **3** (*ocurrir al mismo tiempo*) to be at the same time (**con,** as), coincide (**con,** with); (*en el mismo lugar*) to meet: *la muerte del rey coincidió con la victoria,* the king's death coincided with the victory; *coincidimos en Barcelona,* we met in Barcelona.
coito *m* coitus, intercourse.
cojear 1 *i* (*persona*) to limp, hobble. **2** (*muebles*) to wobble. **3** *fam fig* (*adolecer*) to falter.
● **cojear del mismo pie,** *fam* to have the same faults.
cojera *f* limp, lameness.
cojín *m* cushion.
cojinete *m* TÉC bearing.
■ **cojinete de agujas,** needle bearing. ‖ **cojinete de bolas,** ball bearing.
cojitranco,-a 1 *adj fam pey* lame. **– 2** *m,f fam pey* cripple.
cojo,-a 1 *adj* (*persona*) lame, crippled. **2** (*mueble*) wobbly. **3** *fig* (*defectuoso*) faulty, incomplete. **– 4** *m,f* lame person, cripple.
● **andar a la pata coja,** to hop, hop along.
cojón 1 *m* ANAT *tabú* ball, bollock. **– 2 cojones,** *interj tabú* fuck it!
● **de cojones,** *tabú* (*estupendo*) fucking brilliant, fucking good; (*malo*) fucking awful, fucking bad. ‖ **ponérsele a uno los cojones de corbata,** *tabú* to shit bricks. ‖ **por cojones,** *tabú* like it or not. ‖ **tener cojones,** *tabú* to have balls.
cojonudo,-a *adj tabú* fucking great.
col *f* cabbage.
■ **col de Bruselas,** Brussels sprout. ‖ **col lombarda,** red cabbage. ‖ **col rizada,** curly kale.
col.[1] *abr* (*colección*) collection.
col.[2] *abr* (*columna*) column; (*abreviatura*) col.
cola[1] **1** *f* (*gen*) tail. **2** (*de vestido*) train; (*de chaqueta*) tail. **3** (*fila*) queue, *us* line.
● **a la cola,** at the back, at the rear. ‖ **estar en la cola,** *fig* to be the last. ‖ **hacer cola,** to queue up, *us* stand in line. ‖ **ponerse en la cola,** to get into the queue, *us* get in line. ‖ **traer cola,** *fam* to have serious consequences.
■ **cola de caballo,** BOT horsetail; (*peinado*) ponytail. ‖ **vagón de cola,** rear coach.
cola[2] *f* (*pegamento*) glue.
● **no pega ni con cola,** *fam* it doesn't match at all.
cola[3] *f* (*árbol*) kola, cola.
colaboración 1 *f* collaboration. **2** (*prensa*) contribution.
colaboracionista 1 *adj* collaborating. **– 2** *mf* collaborator.
colaboracionismo *m* collaboration.
colaborador,-ra 1 *adj* collaborating. **– 2** *m,f* collaborator. **3** (*prensa*) contributor.
colaborar 1 *i* to collaborate (**con,** with). **2** (*prensa*) to contribute (**en,** to).
colación 1 *f* (*comparación*) collation. **2** (*refrigerio*) light meal, snack, collation.
● **sacar a colación / traer a colación,** to mention, bring up.
colacionar *t fml* (*comparar*) to compare, collate.
colactáneo,-a *m,f* (*niño*) foster brother; (*niña*) foster sister.
colada *f* → **colado,-a.**

coladero 1 *m* (*colador*) strainer, sieve. **2** (*paso estrecho*) narrow pass. **3** *fam* (*lugar por el que es fácil colarse*) easy place to get into. **4** *fam* (*examen fácil*) cinch, doddle; (*centro que aprueba mucho*) *school where it is easy to pass exams.*

colado,-a 1 *pp* → **colar**. – **2** *adj fam fig* (*enamorado*) madly in love, head over heels in love. **3** (*metal*) cast. – **4 colada**, *f* (*lavado*) washing, laundry; (*con lejía*) bleaching. **5** (*ropa*) washing, wash. **6** (*de metal*) tapping. **7** (*volcánica*) outflow.

● **hacer la colada,** to do the washing, do the laundry.
colador 1 *m* (*de té, café*) strainer. **2** (*de caldo, alimentos*) colander, sieve.

● **como un colador,** *fam* full of holes, like a sieve. ‖ **dejar como un colador,** *fam* to riddle with bullets.
coladura *f fam* clanger, slip-up.
colágeno *m* collagen.
colapsar 1 *t* to cause to collapse, make collapse. – **2** *i* to collapse. – **3 colapsarse,** *p* to collapse.
colapso 1 *m* MED collapse. **2** *fig* breakdown.
colar 1 *t* (*líquido*) to strain, filter. **2** (*lavar*) to wash; (*con lejía*) to bleach. **3** (*metales*) to cast. **4** *fam* (*hacer pasar*) to pass, slip; (*moneda*) to pass off; (*historia*) to give: *quería colar la cámara,* he wanted to sneak the camera in. – **5** *i fam* to wash: *veremos si cuela,* we'll see if it washes. – **6 colarse,** *p* (*escabullirse*) to slip in, gatecrash. **7** (*en una cola*) to push in, jump the queue, US jump the line. **8** *fam* (*equivocarse*) to slip up, make a mistake. **9** (*enamorarse*) to fall (**por,** for): *se coló por Ana,* he fell for Ana.

▲ *Conjugation model* [31], *like* **contar**.
colateral *adj* collateral.
colcha *f* bedspread.
colchón *m* mattress.

■ **colchón de aire,** air cushion. ‖ **colchón neumático,** air mattress.
colchonería *f* mattress maker's (shop).
colchonero,-a 1 *m,f* mattress maker. **2** *fam* Atlético de Madrid supporter. – **3** *adj fam relating to Atlético de Madrid football club.*
colchoneta *f* small mattress.
colcrén *m* cold cream.
coleada *f* → **coletazo**.
colear 1 *i* (*perro etc*) to wag its tail; (*vaca, caballo, etc*) to swisch its tail. **2** *fam* to drag on: *aunque ya está casi solucionado, aún hay algún aspecto que colea,* although almost everything has been sorted out, there are still some sticky points.
colección *f* collection.
coleccionar *t* to collect.
coleccionista *mf* collector.
colect. *abr* (*colectivo*) association.
colecta *f* collection.
colectar *t* to collect.
colectividad *f* community.

● **en colectividad,** communally.
colectivismo *m* collectivism.
colectivización *f* collectivization.
colectivizar *t* to collectivize.

▲ *Conjugation model* [4], *like* **realizar**.
colectivo,-a 1 *adj* collective, group. – **2 colectivo,** *m* (*asociación*) association, guild. **3** LING collective noun.
colector,-ra 1 *adj* collecting. – **2 colector,** *m* (*caño*) water pipe. **3** (*cloaca*) main sewer.

■ **colector de admisión,** inlet manifold. ‖ **colector de escape,** exhaust manifold.
colega 1 *mf* colleague. **2** *arg* (*amigo*) chum, mate, US buddy.

colegatario,-a *m,f* co-legatee.
colegiación *f* membership of a college.
colegiado,-a 1 *pp* → **colegiarse**. – **2** *adj* collegiate. – **3** *m,f* collegian. – **4 colegiado,** *m* DEP referee.
colegial,-la 1 *adj* collegial, collegiate. **2** (*escolar*) school. – **3** *m,f* (*gen*) schoolchild; (*chico*) schoolboy; (*chica*) schoolgirl.
colegiarse *p* to join a professional association.

▲ *Conjugation model* [12], *like* **cambiar**.
colegiata *f* collegiate church.
colegio 1 *m* (*escuela*) school: *van al colegio en autobús,* they go to school by bus. **2** (*asociación*) college, association. **3** (*residencia*) hall of residence, US dormitory.

■ **colegio de abogados,** the Bar. ‖ **colegio de monjas,** convent school. ‖ **colegio electoral,** (*votantes*) electoral college; (*lugar*) polling station. ‖ **colegio mayor / colegio universitario,** hall of residence, US dormitory. ‖ **colegio privado / colegio de pago,** public school, US private school. ‖ **colegio público,** state school.
colegir *t* to infer, conclude.

▲ *Conjugation model* [55], *like* **elegir**.
coleóptero *m* coleopteron.
cólera[1] *f* (*bilis*) bile. **2** *fig* (*ira*) anger, rage.
cólera[2] *m* MED cholera.
colérico,-a *adj* furious, irascible: *es colérico,* he's bad-tempered.
colesterina *f* cholesterin.
colesterol *m* cholesterol.
coleta *f* pigtail, ponytail.

● **cortarse la coleta,** (*los toreros*) to retire from bull-fighting; *fig* to retire.
coletazo 1 *m* (*de la cola-perro*) wag of the tail, (*-vaca, caballo, etc*) swisch of the tail. **2** *fig* death throes *pl*, final tremor, stir.

● **dar coletazos,** (*un coche*) to sway about.
coletilla *f* postscript, addition.

■ **coletilla interrogativa,** question tag.
coleto *m* (*casaca*) doublet, jerkin.

● **decir para su coleto,** *fam* to say to os. ‖ **echarse algo al coleto,** *fam* (*comer*) to put sth. away; (*beber*) to knock sth. back; (*leer*) to devour sth.
colgadero,-a 1 *adj* hangable. – **2 colgadero,** *m* (*garfio*) hook.
colgado,-a 1 *pp* → **colgar**. – **2** *adj* hanging (**de,** from): *colgado del techo,* hanging from the ceiling; *siempre está colgada del teléfono,* she's always on the phone. **3** (*ahorcado*) hanged. **4** *fam* (*pendiente de resolución*) pending: *le ha quedado una asignatura colgada,* she has to resit one exam, she has to do one retake. **5** *fam* (*totalmente pendiente*) dependent (**de,** on): *estábamos colgados de sus palabras,* we were hanging on to his every word. **6** *arg* (*drogado*) stoned, high; (*loco*) crazy, off one's head. – **7** *m,f arg* (*drogado*) drug addict.

● **dejar a algn. colgado,-a,** *fam* to leave sb. in the lurch, leave sb. high and dry, leave sb. stranded: *mi amiga me dejó colgada,* my friend didn't turn up. ‖ **estar colgado,-a,** (*en apuros*) to be in a fix, be in a tight spot.
colgador *m* (*coat*) hanger.
colgadura *f* hangings *pl*, US drapes *pl*, drapery.
colgajo 1 *m* (*de ropa*) rag, torn piece. **2** (*de piel*) flap, graft. **3** (*de uva*) bunch.
colgante 1 *adj* hanging: *puente colgante,* suspension bridge. – **2** *m* ARQ festoon. **3** (*joya*) pendant.
colgar 1 *t* (*gen*) to hang (up): *colgó el abrigo en el perchero,* he hung his coat on the coat stand. **2** (*la colada*)

to hang out. **3** (*ahorcar*) to hang. **4** (*atribuir*) to pin: *le han colgado el delito a él*, they've pinned the crime on him. **5** (*el teléfono*) to put down. **6** *fam* (*suspender*) to fail: *me han colgado cuatro*, I've failed four. **7** (*abandonar*) to give up: *colgar los libros*, to give up studying; *el futbolista colgó sus botas*, the footballer hung up his boots. **– 8** *i* (*estar colgado*) to hang (**de**, from): *cuelga del techo*, it hangs from the ceiling. **9** (*una prenda*) to hang down, be crooked: *esa falda te cuelga de un lado*, that skirt's crooked on one side. **10** (*teléfono*) to hang up, ring off: *¡no cuelgue!*, please hold!, hold the line, please!; *me colgó*, he hung up on me. **– 11 colgarse**, *p* (*ahorcarse*) to hang os.
● **colgar de un hilo**, *fig* to hang by a thread.
▲ *Conjugation model* [52].
colibrí *m* humming bird.
cólico *m* colic.
coliflor *f* cauliflower.
coligarse *p* to associate (**con**, with), ally (**con**, with).
colijo *pres indic* → **colegir**.
colilla *f* cigarette end, cigarette butt, butt.
colimbo *m* diver.
colín 1 *adj* (*caballo*) bobtail. **– 2** *m* (*de pan*) bread stick.
colina *f* hill, slope.
colinabo *m* kohlrabi.
colindante *adj* adjacent, adjoining.
colindar *i* to be adjacent (**con**, to).
colirio *m* eye drops *pl*.
colirrojo *m* redstart.
coliseo *m* coliseum, colosseum.
colisión 1 *f* (*de vehículos*) collision, crash: *se produjo una colisión entre un autobús y un camión*, there was a collision between a bus and a lorry. **2** *fig* (*conflicto*) clash, conflict.
colisionar 1 *i* (*chocar*) to collide (**con/contra**, with), crash (**con/contra**, into). **2** (*enfrentarse*) to clash.
colista 1 *adj* DEP last. **– 2** *m* DEP (*equipo*) bottom team.
● **ser el colista**, to be last, be in last place.
colitis *f* colitis.
▲ *pl* **colitis**.
colla¹ *f* (*de pesca*) fish trap.
colla² *f* (*descargadores*) team of dockers.
collado 1 *m* (*colina*) hill. **2** (*paso entre montañas*) mountain pass.
collage *m* collage.
▲ *pl* **collages**.
collalba *f* wheatear.
collar 1 *m* (*adorno*) necklace. **2** (*de animal*) collar. **3** TÉC collar, ring.
collarín 1 *m* (*alzacuello*) bands *pl*. **2** (*aparato ortopédico*) surgical collar. **3** (*de botella*) label.
collarino *m* gorgerin.
collera 1 *f* (*de caballerías*) collar. **2** *fig* (*de presidiario*) chain gang.
colmado,-a 1 *pp* → **colmar**. **– 2** *adj* full, filled: *una cuchara colmada*, a heaped spoonful. **– 3 colmado**, *m* grocer's (shop), grocery store.
colmar 1 *t* (*gen*) to fill (**de**, with); (*vaso, copa*) to fill to the brim. **2** *fig* to shower (**de**, with), overwhelm (**de**, with).
colmena *f* beehive.
colmenar *m* apiary.
colmenero,-a *m,f* beekeeper.
colmenilla *f* morel.
colmillo 1 *m* eye tooth, canine tooth. **2** (*de carnívoro*) fang; (*de jabalí, elefante, morsa*) tusk.

● **enseñar los colmillos**, (*animal*) to bare its teeth; (*persona*) to show one's teeth.
colmo¹ *m* height, summit: *el colmo de la hipocresía*, the height of hypocrisy.
● **¡esto es el colmo!**, this is the last straw!, this is the limit! ‖ **para colmo**, to top it all, to make matters worse.
colmo,-a² *adj* (*que está colmado*) full, filled to the top.
colocación 1 *f* (*situación*) positioning, collocation. **2** (*de una alfombra, moqueta*) laying; (*de un cuadro*) hanging. **3** (*de dinero*) investment. **4** (*empleo*) employment, job: *tiene una buena colocación*, she has a good job.
colocado,-a 1 *pp* → **colocar**. **– 2** *adj* (*empleado*) employed: *está bien colocada*, she has a good job. **3** *arg* (*embriagado*) sozzled; (*drogado*) stoned, high.
colocar 1 *t* (*gen*) to place, put; (*alfombra*) to lay; (*cuadro*) to hang. **2** (*dar empleo*) to get a job for. **3** (*casar*) to marry off: *ha colocado a su hija*, he has married off his daughter. **4** MIL to position. **5** FIN to invest: *colocar dinero*, to invest money. **6** (*mercancías*) to sell well. **7** *fam* (*artículos defectuosos*) to fob off. **8** *fam* (*explicar*) to give: *me colocó el mismo rollo*, he gave me the same old story. **9** *arg* (*drogas*) to get stoned. **– 10 colocarse**, *p* (*situarse*) to place os., put os., find os. a place: *el gato se colocó allí*, the cat settled down there. **11** (*trabajar*) to find a job (**de**, as), get a job (**de**, as): *se ha colocado de enfermera*, she has got a job as a nurse. **12** DEP (*clasificarse*) to be: *se han colocado segundos*, they are in second place. **13** *arg* (*embriagarse*) to get sozzled; (*drogarse*) to get stoned.
▲ *Conjugation model* [1], *like* **sacar**.
colocón *m* *arg* high.
colodrillo *m* back of the neck.
colofón 1 *m* (*apéndice*) colophon. **2** *fig* (*remate*) crowning, climax, culmination: *el director dijo unas palabras de agradecimiento como colofón del acto*, the director said a few words of thanks to round off the ceremony.
colofonía *f* colophony.
coloidal *adj* colloidal.
coloide *m* colloid.
Colombia *f* Colombia.
colombiano,-a 1 *adj* Colombian. **– 2** *m,f* Colombian.
colombino,-a *adj* of Christopher Columbus, Columbian.
colombofilia *f* pigeon fancying, pigeon breeding.
colombófilo,-a 1 *adj* pigeon-breeding. **– 2** *m,f* pigeon fancier.
colon *m* ANAT colon.
colón *m* colón (*monetary unit of Costa Rica and El Salvador*).
colonato *m* tenant farming.
colonia¹ 1 *f* (*grupo*) colony. **2** (*vacaciones infantiles*) summer camp.
▲ *In 2, also used in plural with the same meaning.*
colonia² *f* (*perfume*) cologne.
Colonia *f* Cologne.
colonial 1 *adj* POL colonial. **2** (*importado*) imported. **– 3 coloniales**, *mpl* imported foodstuffs.
colonialismo *m* colonialism.
colonialista 1 *adj* colonialist. **– 2** *mf* colonialist.
colonización *f* colonization.
colonizador,-ra 1 *adj* colonizing. **– 2** *m,f* colonizer, colonist.
colonizar *t* to colonize, settle.
▲ *Conjugation model* [4], *like* **realizar**.
colono 1 *m* (*habitante*) colonist, settler. **2** AGR tenant farmer.

coloquial *adj* colloquial.
coloquialismo *m* colloquialism.
coloquio *m* talk, discussion, colloquium.
color **1** *m* colour (US color): *es de color verde,* it's green. **2** *fml fig (carácter)* character. **3** *fig (tendencia)* tendency. – **4** *m & f (del rostro)* colour (US color), complexion. – **5 colores,** *mpl (bandera)* colours (US colors), flag *sing*; *(equipo)* team *sing*.
● **dar color,** *(colorear)* to colour (US color); *fig* to liven up. ‖ **de color,** *(en color)* in colour (US color), coloured (US colored); *(persona)* coloured (US colored). ‖ **en color / en colores,** *(cine, foto)* in colour (US color). ‖ **coger color,** *(cebolla)* to turn brown; *(hojas etc)* to turn yellow, turn brown. ‖ **no haber color,** to be no comparison: *entre tu coche y el mío no hay color, porque el mío es mucho mejor,* your car isn't a patch on mine. ‖ **sacarle a algn. los colores,** *fam* to make sb. blush. ‖ **subido,- a de color,** *fig* risqué. ‖ **tener color,** to be lively. ‖ **verlo todo de color de rosa,** *fig* to see life through rose-coloured (US rose-colored) spectacles.
■ **color local,** *fig* local colour (US color). ‖ **color sólido,** fast colour (US color).
coloración *f* coloration, colouring (US coloring).
colorado,-a **1** *adj* coloured (US colored). **2** *(rojo)* red. – **3 colorado,** *m* red.
● **ponerse colorado,-a,** to blush, go red.
colorante **1** *adj* colouring (US coloring). – **2** *m* colouring (US coloring), dye.
colorar *t* to colour (US color).
colorear *t* to colour (US color): *coloreó el dibujo,* she coloured in the drawing.
colorete *m* rouge, blusher.
colorido *m* colour (US color).
colorín **1** *m* bright colour (US color), vivid colour (US color). **2** *(jilguero)* goldfinch.
● **... y colorín colorado este cuento se ha acabado,** ... and that's the end of the story.
colorir **1** *t (dar color)* to colour (US color). – **2** *i (tomar color)* to colour (US color).
▲ In 2, *used only in the 3rd pers; it does not take a subject.*
colorismo *m* predominant use of colour (US color).
colorista **1** *adj* colouristic (US coloristic). – **2** *mf* colourist (US colorist).
colosal **1** *adj* colossal, giant, huge. **2** *fig* splendid, excellent.
coloso *m* colossus.
colt *m* colt.
▲ *pl* **colts.**
columbario *m* columbarium.
columbino,-a *adj* columbine, dovelike.
columbrar **1** *t (vislumbrar)* to see, make out. **2** *fig (conjeturar)* to guess, conjecture.
columna **1** *f (gen)* column. **2** ANAT spine. **3** *(elemento central)* backbone.
■ **columna de dirección,** steering column. ‖ **columna miliar,** milestone. ‖ **columna vertebral,** *(de un cuerpo)* vertebral column, spinal column; *(de un sistema)* backbone.
columnata *f* colonnade.
columnista *mf* columnist.
columpiar **1** *t* to swing. – **2 columpiarse,** *p* to swing **(de,** on). **3** *(al caminar)* to swing one's hips.
▲ *Conjugation model* |12|, *like* **cambiar.**
columpio *m* swing.
colutorio *m* mouthwash.
colza *f* colza, rape.
■ **aceite de colza,** rape-seed oil, colza oil.

coma[1] **1** *f* GRAM MÚS comma. **2** MAT point: *cuatro coma cinco,* four point five.
● **sin faltar ni una coma,** *fig* down to the last detail.
■ **punto y coma,** semicolon.
coma[2] *m* MED coma.
● **entrar en coma,** to go into a coma.
■ **coma profundo,** deep coma.
comadre **1** *f (partera)* midwife. **2** *(madrina)* godmother. **3** *fam (vecina)* neighbour (US neighbor); *(amiga)* friend. **4** *pey (chismosa)* gossip, gossipmonger. **5** *fam (alcahueta)* go-between.
comadrear *i* to gossip, chat.
comadreja *f* weasel.
comadreo *m* gossip, gossiping, chit-chat, tittle-tattle.
comadrería *f* piece of gossip.
comadrero,-a **1** *adj* gossipy. – **2** *m,f* gossip, gossip-monger.
comadrón,-ona *m,f (hombre)* male midwife; *(mujer)* midwife.
comandancia **1** *f (grado)* command. **2** *(edificio)* headquarters *pl*. **3** *(zona)* area under a commander's jurisdiction.
comandante **1** *m (oficial)* commander, commanding officer. **2** *(graduación)* major. **3** *(piloto)* pilot.
■ **comandante en jefe,** commander-in-chief.
comandar *t* to command.
comandita *f* COM limited partnership, US silent partnership.
● **ir en comandita,** *fam* to go en masse.
■ **sociedad en comandita,** limited partnership, US silent partnership.
comanditar *t* to enter as a sleeping partner, US enter as a silent partner.
comanditario,-a *adj* sleeping, US silent: *sociedad comanditaria,* limited partnership, US silent partnership.
comando **1** *m* MIL commando. **2** INFORM command.
comarca *f* area, region.
comarcal *adj* regional, local.
comatoso,-a *adj* comatose.
● **estar en estado comatoso,** to be in a coma.
comba *f* → **combo,-a.**
combadura **1** *f (de cuerda, cable)* bend, curve. **2** *(de viga, pared)* sag, bulge. **3** *(de carretera)* camber.
combar **1** *t* to bend. – **2 combarse,** *p (una cuerda)* to bend; *(viga, pared)* to sag, bulge.
combate **1** *m (gen)* combat, battle. **2** MIL battle. **3** *(boxeo)* fight, contest.
● **fuera de combate,** *(gen)* out of action; *(en boxeo)* knocked out. ‖ **librar combate,** to wage battle.
■ **combate nulo,** draw.
combatiente **1** *adj* fighting. – **2** *mf* fighter, combatant. – **3** *m (ave)* ruff.
combatir **1** *i* to fight **(contra,** against /-), struggle **(contra,** against): *combatir contra el enemigo,* to fight (against) the enemy. – **2** *t (luchar contra)* to fight: *combatir el cáncer,* to fight cancer. **3** *fig* to combat, fight. **4** *fig (batir, golpear)* to beat, lash: *las olas combaten el acantilado,* the waves beat against the cliff.
combatividad *f* fighting spirit, aggressiveness.
combativo,-a *adj* spirited, aggressive.
combinación **1** *f* combination. **2** *(prenda)* slip. **3** *(cóctel)* cocktail. **4** *(lotería, quiniela)* permutation, numbers *pl*: *la combinación ganadora es la siguiente,* the winning numbers are as follows. **5** *fig (artimaña)* fiddle, wangle.
combinado,-a **1** *pp* → **combinar.** – **2** *adj* MIL combined. – **3 combinado,** *m (cóctel)* cocktail. **4** DEP all-star team. **5** QUÍM compound, combination.

combinar 1 t (gen) to combine. **2** (disponer) to arrange, plan. **3** QUÍM to combine. **4** (colores) to match (**con**, -), go (**con**, with). – **5 combinarse**, p (ponerse de acuerdo) to get together.

combo,-a 1 adj bent, curved. **2** (pared) sagging. – **3 comba**, f (de cuerda, cable) bend, curve. **4** (de viga, pared) sag, bulge. **5** (de carretera) camber. **6** (cuerda), skipping rope. **7** (juego) skipping.
● **no perder comba,** fam not to miss a chance. ‖ **saltar a la comba,** to skip, US skip rope.

combustible 1 adj combustible. – **2** m fuel.

combustión f combustion, burning.

comecocos 1 m arg (juego) Pacman. **2** (asunto, libro, etc) soul-destroyer.
▲ pl comecocos.

comedero m feeding trough, manger.

comedia 1 f TEAT comedy, play. **2** fig farce, pretence (US pretense).
● **hacer comedia,** fam to put on an act.
■ **comedia de costumbres,** comedy of manners. ‖ comedia de enredo, farce. ‖ **comedia musical,** musical, musical comedy.

comediante,-a 1 m,f (hombre) actor; (mujer) actress. **2** fig hypocrite, comedian.

comedido,-a 1 pp → **comedirse**. – **2** adj (cortés) courteous, polite. **3** (moderado) moderate, self-restrained, reserved.

comedimiento m restraint, moderation.

comediógrafo,-a m,f playwright, dramatist.

comedirse p to restrain os.
▲ Conjugation model [34], like **servir**.

comedón m blackhead.

comedor,-ra 1 adj with a huge appetite. – **2** m,f (persona) big-eater. – **3 comedor,** m (sala) dining room; (en una fábrica) canteen; (en universidad) refectory, dining hall. **4** (muebles) dining-room suite.

comendador m commander.

comensal mf person at the table, diner: había cuatro comensales, there were four people dining together.

comentar 1 t (texto) to comment on. **2** (expresar una opinión) to talk about, discuss.

comentario 1 m (observación) remark, comment. **2** LIT RAD TV commentary. – **3 comentarios,** mpl (murmuración) gossip sing.
● **dar lugar a comentarios,** to cause gossip. ‖ **sin comentario,** no comment.

comentarista mf commentator.

comenzar 1 t to begin, start. – **2** i to begin, start: comenzó a reír, he began to laugh, he began laughing.
● **comenzar con,** to begin with. ‖ **comenzar +** ger, to start by + ger: comenzó explicando ..., he started by explaining ... ‖ comenzar por + inf, to begin by +-ing: comenzó por decir que ..., he began by saying that ... ‖ **comenzar por el principio,** to begin at the beginning, start at the beginning.
▲ Conjugation model [47], like **empezar**.

comer 1 t to eat: comer pescado, to eat fish. **2** (tomar) to have: para cenar comimos sopa, we had soup for dinner. **3** (color) to fade. **4** (corroer) to corrode. **5** fig (gastar) to eat away; (combustible) to use, use up. **6** (en ajedrez) to take, capture. – **7** i (gen) to eat; (a mediodía) to have lunch, lunch; (por la noche) to have dinner, dine: ayer comimos a las dos, yesterday we had lunch at two; mañana vamos a comer fuera, tomorrow we're going to eat out; David me ha invitado a comer, David's invited me to lunch. – **8 comerse,** p to eat: se comió el cocido, he

ate the stew. **9** fig (saltarse) to omit; (párrafo) to skip; (palabra) to swallow: se come las palabras, she doesn't pronounce her words very clearly. **10** (color) to fade. **11** (el mar, la tierra) to swallow. – **12 comer,** m eating.
● **comer como un pajarito,** fam not to eat enough to feed a sparrow. ‖ **comer como una lima / comer como un regimiento / comer por cuatro,** fam to eat like a horse. ‖ **come con los ojos,** his (her, your, etc) eyes are bigger than his (her, your, etc) belly. ‖ **comerse a algn. a besos,** fig to smother sb. with kisses. ‖ **comerse a algn. con los ojos,** fig to look at sb. lovingly. ‖ **comerse algo con los ojos,** fam to devour sth. with one's eyes. ‖ **comerse las uñas,** to bite one's nails. ‖ **¿con qué se come eso?,** fam what the heck is that? ‖ **dar de comer,** to feed. ‖ **echar de comer (a los animales),** to feed (the animals). ‖ **está para comérsela,** fam (mujer) she's really tasty. ‖ **me come la envidia,** fig I'm green with envy. ‖ **no tener qué comer,** not to have enough to live on. ‖ **ser de buen comer,** to be a good eater. ‖ **sin comerlo ni beberlo,** fam without having had anything to do with it.

comercial 1 adj (del comercio) commercial. **2** (de tiendas) shopping. – **3** mf (vendedor) seller; (hombre) salesman; (mujer) saleswoman.
■ **banco comercial,** commercial bank. ‖ **tratado comercial,** commercial treaty.

comercialización f commercialization, marketing.

comercializar t to commercialize, market.
▲ Conjugation model [4], like realizar.

comerciante 1 adj business-minded. – **2** mf merchant. **3** (interesado) moneymaker.

comerciar i (comprar y vender) to trade, deal, buy and sell. **2** (hacer negocios) to do business (**con**, with).
▲ Conjugation model [12], like cambiar.

comercio 1 m (ocupación) commerce, trade. **2** (tienda) shop, store. **3** fig (trato sexual) dealings pl, intercourse.
● **comercio al por mayor,** wholesale trade. ‖ **comercio al por menor,** retail trade.
■ **comercio exterior,** foreign trade. ‖ **libre comercio,** free trade.

comestible 1 adj edible, eatable. – **2 comestibles,** mpl groceries, food sing, foodstuffs pl.
■ **tienda de comestibles,** grocer's shop, US grocery store.

cometa 1 m ASTRON comet. – **2** f kite.

cometer t (crimen) to commit; (falta, error) to make.

cometido 1 m (encargo) task, assignment: desempeñó su cometido, she carried out her task. **2** (deber) duty: cumplió su cometido, he did his duty.

comezón f itch, itching.
● **sentir comezón,** (tener picor) to have an itch. ‖ **sentir comezón por + inf,** fig to be itching to +inf.

cómic m comic.

comicial adj election, relating to elections.

comicidad f comicalness, funniness.

comicios mpl POL elections.

cómico,-a 1 adj (divertido) comic, comical, funny. **2** (de comedia) comedy. – **3** m,f (actor) comedian, comic.
■ **actor cómico,** comedian. ‖ **cómico,-a de la legua,** strolling player.

comida f → **comido,-a**.

comidilla f fam fig gossip, talk: su embarazo es la comidilla del barrio, her pregnancy is the talk of the town.

comido,-a 1 pp → **comer**. – **2** adj eaten. **3** fam (fig) having eaten: saldré comido, I'll have something to eat before leaving. – **4 comida**, f (alimento) food. **5** (desayuno

etc) meal: *la primera comida del día,* the first meal of the day. **6** (*almuerzo*) lunch.
● **lo comido por lo servido,** *fam* fair do's.
■ **comida campestre,** picnic.
comience *pres subj-imperat* → **comenzar.**
comienzo *m* start, beginning.
● **a comienzos de,** at the beginning of. ‖ **dar comienzo,** to begin, start. ‖ **estar en sus comienzos,** to be in its early stages.
comillas *fpl* inverted commas, quotation marks.
● **abrir las comillas,** to open quotation marks. ‖ **cerrar las comillas,** to close quotation marks. ‖ **entre comillas,** in inverted commas.
comilón,-ona 1 *adj* greedy, gluttonous. – **2** *m,f* big eater, glutton. – **3** comilona, *f fam* big meal, blow-out.
comilona *f* → **comilón,-ona.**
comino *m* BOT cumin, cummin.
● **me importa un comino,** *fam* I don't give a damn. ‖ **no valer un comino,** *fam* not to be worth tuppence.
comisaría 1 *f* commissariat. **2** (*de policía*) police station.
comisario 1 *m* commissioner, delegate. **2** (*de policía*) police inspector.
comiscar 1 *t fam* to nibble. – **2** *i fam* to nibble.
▲ Conjugation model [1], like *sacar.*
comisión 1 *f* (*retribución*) commission. **2** (*comité*) committee. **3** (*encargo*) assignment, commission. **4** JUR perpetration, committing.
● **a comisión / con comisión,** on a commission basis: *trabajar a comisión,* to work on a commission basis. ‖ **cobrar una comisión por algo,** to get a commission on sth.
■ **comisión bancaria,** service charge, bank commission. ‖ **comisión permanente,** standing committee.
comisionado,-a 1 *pp* → **comisionar.** – **3** *adj* commissioned. – **3** *m,f* commissioner.
comisionar *t* to commission.
comiso *m* confiscation, seizure.
comisura *f* corner, angle.
comité *m* committee.
■ **comité de empresa,** works committee.
comitiva *f* suite, retinue.
■ **comitiva fúnebre,** funeral procession.
como 1 *adv* (*modo*) how: *así fue como nos encontramos,* this is how we met; *lo hizo como quiso,* he did it the way he wanted to. **2** (*comparación*) as, like: *negro como la noche,* as dark as night; *camina como su madre,* he walks like his mother; *hablas como un político,* you talk like a politician. **3** (*en calidad de*): *como director,* as director; *como invitado,* as a guest. **4** (*según*) as: *como dice tu amigo,* as your friend says. **5** *fam* (*aproximadamente*) about: *había como unos cien,* there were about a hundred. – **6** *conj* (*así que*) as: *como llegaban se presentaban,* they introduced themselves as they arrived. **7** (*si*) if: *como lo vuelvas a hacer...,* if you do it again... **8** (*porque*) as, since: *como llegamos tarde no pudimos entrar,* since we arrived late we couldn't get in.
● **como quiera que,** (*no importa cómo*) however; (*ya que*) since, as, inasmuch as. ‖ **como no sea que,** unless. ‖ **como sea,** whatever happens, no matter what. ‖ **como si lo viera,** *fam* I can imagine perfectly well. ‖ **como si nada / como si tal cosa,** as if nothing had happened. ‖ **hacer como quien,** to pretend to +*inf: hizo como quien estaba enfermo,* he pretended to be ill. ‖ **hacer como si,** to pretend to +*inf: hace como si no viese nada,* he's pretending not to see anything. ‖ **tanto como eso no,** *fam* not as much as that.

cómo 1 *adv* (*interrogativo*) how: *¿cómo está usted?,* how do you do?; *¿cómo lo supo?,* how did he know?; *¿cómo ha dicho?,* I beg your pardon?; *¿cómo te llamas?,* what's your name? **2** (*por qué*) why: *¿cómo no viniste?,* why didn't you come? **3** (*admiración*) how: *¡cómo corre el tiempo!,* how time flies!
● **¿a cómo están ... ?,** how much are ... ?: *¿a cómo están las peras?,* how much are the pears? ‖ **¿cómo?,** *fam* what? ‖ **¿cómo es eso?,** how come? ‖ **¿cómo es que ...?,** how is it that ...? ‖ **¡cómo no!,** but of course!, certainly!
■ **el cómo y el porqué,** the whys and wherefores.
cómoda *f* chest of drawers, commode.
cómodamente *adv* comfortably.
comodidad 1 *f* (*confort*) comfort. **2** (*facilidad*) convenience.
● **con comodidad,** comfortably.
comodín 1 *m* (*mono*) joker; (*otra carta*) wild card. **2** *fig* (*persona*) factotum, man Friday, girl Friday; (*cosa*) multipurpose tool. **3** *fig* (*excusa*) excuse.
■ **palabra comodín,** word applicable to anything.
cómodo,-a 1 *adj* comfortable, cosy. **2** (*útil*) convenient, handy. **3** (*carácter*) easy-going.
● **ponerse cómodo,-a,** to make os. comfortable.
comodón,-ona 1 *adj fam* comfort-loving. – **2** *m,f fam* comfort lover.
comodoro *m* commodore.
comoquiera. 1 comoquiera que, *adv* anyway, anyhow: *comoquiera que sea,* whatever way, one way or another. – **2** *conj* (*causal*) since, as: *comoquiera que llegará tarde, no lo esperaremos,* as he'll be late, we won't wait for him.
compactar *t* to compact, compress.
compacto *adj* compact, dense.
compadecer 1 *t* to pity, feel sorry for: *compadecer a los pobres,* to pity the poor. – **2** compadecerse, *p* to take pity (**de**, on), pity (**de**, -), feel sorry (**de**, for): *se compadeció de la viuda,* he took pity on the widow.
▲ Conjugation model [43], like *agradecer.*
compadraje *m* conspiracy, plot.
compadre 1 *m* (*padrino*) godfather. **2** (*padre*) father. **3** *fam* (*amigo*) mate, pal, friend.
compaginar 1 *t* (*combinar*) to combine, make compatible: *compagina el trabajo con los estudios,* he can combine his job with his studies. **2** (*en impresión*) to make up. – **3** compaginarse, *p* to go together, be compatible.
compaña *f* company, friends *pl.*
compañerismo *m* companionship, fellowship, comradeship.
compañero,-a 1 *m,f* companion, fellow, mate; POL comrade. **2** *fig* (*guante, zapato, etc*) other one.
■ **compañero,-a de armas,** comrade-in-arms. ‖ **compañero,-a de colegio,** schoolmate. ‖ **compañero,-a de equipo,** team-mate. ‖ **compañero.-a de fatigas,** fellow sufferer. ‖ **compañero,-a de habitación,** roommate.
compañía *f* company.
● **en compañía de,** in the company of. ‖ **hacer compañía a algn.,** to keep sb. company.
■ **compañía de seguros,** insurance company. ‖ **compañía de teatro,** theatre (US theater) company. ‖ **malas compañías,** bad company *sing.*
comparable *adj* comparable.
comparación *f* comparison.
● **en comparación con,** compared to, in comparison

to. ‖ **no tienen ni punto de comparación,** there is no comparison. ‖ **sin comparación,** beyond compare.
comparado,-a 1 *pp* → **comparar**. – **2** *adj* compared (**con,** to). **3** (*gramática, lingüística*) comparative.
comparar *t* to compare: *compara este vino con aquél,* compare this wine to that one.
● **¡no compares!,** *fam* far from it!
comparativo,-a 1 *adj* comparative. – **2** comparativo, *m* comparative.
comparecencia *f* appearance.
■ **no comparecencia,** non-appearance. ‖ **orden de comparecencia,** summons.
comparecer 1 *i* JUR to appear (**ante,** before). **2** (*presentarse*) to show up.
▲ *Conjugation model* [43], *like* **agradecer.**
comparsa 1 *f* (*de teatro*) extras *pl.* **2** (*de carnaval*) masquerade, group of people in fancy dress. – **3** *mf* walkon, extra.
compartimentado,-a *adj* partitioned.
compartimento *m* compartment: *compartimento de primera clase,* first-class compartment.
■ **compartimento estanco,** watertight compartment.
compartimiento *m* → **compartimento.**
compartir 1 *t* (*dividir*) to divide (up), split, share (out). **2** (*poseer en común*) to share: *compartimos la misma habitación,* we share the same room; *no comparto su opinión,* I don't share his opinion.
compás 1 *m* (*instrumento*) compass, compasses *pl.* **2** (*brújula*) compass. **3** MÚS (*división*) time; (*intervalo*) beat; (*ritmo*) rhythm.
● **al compás de,** in time to. ‖ **llevar el compás,** (*con la mano*) to beat time; (*al bailar*) to keep time. ‖ **perder el compás,** to lose the beat.
■ **compás de espera,** MÚS bar rest; *fig* delay.
compasado,-a 1 *pp* → **compasar.** – **2** *adj* moderate, measured.
compasar 1 *t* (*medir con compás*) to measure with compasses. **2** *fig* to settle. **3** MÚS to divide into bars.
compasión *f* compassion, pity.
● **sin compasión,** merciless. ‖ **tener compasión de algn.,** to feel sorry for sb.
compasivo,-a *adj* compassionate, sympathetic.
compatibilidad *f* compatibility.
compatibilizar *t* to make compatible.
▲ *Conjugation model* [4], *like* **realizar.**
compatible *adj* compatible.
compatiblemente *adv* compatibly.
compatriota *mf* compatriot; (*hombre*) fellow countryman; (*mujer*) fellow countrywoman.
compeler *t fml* to compel, force.
compendiar *t* to summarize, abridge, sum up.
▲ *Conjugation model* [12], *like* **cambiar.**
compendio *m* summary, digest, précis, synopsis.
compenetración 1 *f fig* mutual understanding. **2** FÍS interpenetration.
compenetrarse 1 *p* (*uso recíproco*) to understand each other: *se compenetran muy bien,* they understand each other very well. **2** FÍS to interpenetrate.
● **compenetrarse con un papel,** (*actor*) to get into one's role.
compensación *f* compensation, indemnity.
● **en compensación,** (*en pago*) in payment, as compensation; (*a cambio*) in exchange.
■ **cámara de compensación,** clearing house. ‖ **compensación bancaria,** clearing.
compensador,-ra 1 *adj* compensating. – **2** compensador, *m* compensator.

compensar 1 *t* (*pérdida, error*) to make up for. **2** (*indemnizar*) to compensate, indemnify: *nos compensó con veinte mil pesetas,* he gave us twenty thousand pesetas in compensation. **3** TÉC to balance, compensate. **4** *fam* (*merecer la pena*) to be worth one's while: *este trabajo no me compensa,* this job's not worth my while.
competencia 1 *f* (*rivalidad*) competition, rivalry: *hay una gran competencia entre los dos tenistas,* there's great competition between the two tennis players. **2** (*competidores*) competitors *pl,* rival company: *Emilio trabaja ahora para la competencia,* Emilio is now working for our competitors. **3** (*habilidad*) competence, ability, proficiency. **4** (*incumbencia*) responsibility; (*jurisdicción*) jurisdiction: *este asunto no es de su competencia,* this matter is outside his jurisdiction, this matter is outside his area of responsibility.
● **en competencia con,** in competition with. ‖ **hacer la competencia a,** to compete with, compete against.
competente 1 *adj* (*capaz*) competent, capable, proficient. **2** (*adecuado*) adequate. **3** JUR competent.
competer 1 *i* (*corresponder*) to be incumbent (**a,** on), be the responsibility (**de,** of). **2** (*incumbir*) to come under the jurisdiction (**a,** of).
competición *f* competition, contest.
■ **espíritu de competición,** competitive spirit.
competido,-a 1 *pp* → **competer.** – **2** *adj* hard-fought.
competidor,-ra 1 *adj* (*que compite*) competing. **2** (*rival*) rival. – **3** *m,f* COM DEP competitor. **4** (*participante*) contestant, candidate. **5** (*rival*) rival, opponent.
competir *i* to compete: *los corredores compiten por el primer premio,* the runners are competing for the first prize.
▲ *Conjugation model* [34], *like* **servir.**
competitividad *f* competitiveness.
competitivo,-a *adj* competitive.
compilación 1 *f* (*acción*) compiling. **2** (*obra*) compilation.
compilador,-ra *m,f* compiler.
compilar *t* to compile.
compincharse *p fam* to conspire, plot, get together.
● **estar compinchado con algn.,** to be in cahoots with sb.
compinche 1 *mf fam* (*amigo*) chum, pal, mate, US buddy. **2** *fam pey* (*cómplice*) accomplice, sidekick.
complacencia 1 *f* (*placer*) pleasure, satisfaction. **2** (*indulgencia*) indulgence.
● **tener excesivas complacencias con algn.,** to be over-indulgent towards sb.
complacer 1 *t* (*satisfacer*) to satisfy, gratify, oblige: *Juan me complace en todos mis deseos,* Juan satisfies all my desires; *¿en qué puedo complacerle?,* what can I do for you? **2** (*agradar*) to please: *siempre intenta complacerla,* he always tries to please her. **3** *fml* to please, give pleasure: *me complace anunciar ...,* it gives me great pleasure to announce... – **4 complacerse,** *p* to take pleasure (**en,** in): *los señores Solano se complacen en invitarle al enlace matrimonial de su hijo,* Mr and Mrs Solano have great pleasure in inviting you to their son's wedding.
▲ *Conjugation model* [76], *like* **placer.**
complacido,-a 1 *pp* → **complacer.** – **2** *adj* pleased, satisfied.
complaciente 1 *adj* obliging, helpful. **2** (*marido*) complaisant.
complejidad *f* complexity.
complejo,-a 1 *adj* complex. – **2 complejo,** *m* complex.
■ **complejo industrial,** industrial complex. ‖ **complejo turístico,** tourist resort.

complementar I *t* to complement. – **2 complementarse,** *p* to complement each other, be complementary to each other.

complementario,-a *adj* complementary.

complemento I *m* (*gen*) complement. **2** GRAM object, complement. **3** (*perfección*) perfection, culmination.

■ complemento circunstancial, adverbial complement. ‖ complemento directo, direct object. ‖ complemento indirecto, indirect object.

completamente *adv* completely.

completar I *t* (*gen*) to complete. **2** (*acabar*) to finish; (*perfeccionar*) to round off.

completivo,-a *adj* LING object.

completo,-a I *adj* (*terminado*) finished, completed. **2** (*lleno*) full.

● al completo, full up, filled to capacity. ‖ por completo, completely.

complexión *f* constitution, build: *su hermano es de complexión fuerte,* his brother is well-built.

complicación *f* complication.

● buscarse complicaciones, to make life difficult for os.

complicado,-a I *pp* → **complicar.** – **2** *adj* (*gen*) complicated, complex. **3** (*carácter*) complex. **4** (*implicado*) involved: *estaba complicado en la estafa,* he was involved in the fraud.

complicar I *t* (*gen*) to complicate, make complicated. **2** (*implicar*) to involve (**en,** in). – **3 complicarse,** *p* (*gen*) to make difficult for os. **4** (*implicarse*) to get involved (**en,** in).

● complicarse la vida, to make life difficult for os., make things hard for os.

▲ *Conjugation model* [1]*, like* **sacar.**

cómplice *mf* accomplice.

complicidad *f* complicity.

complot *m* plot, conspiracy.

▲ *pl* complots.

componenda *f* shady deal, trick.

● hacer componendas, to scheme.

componente I *adj* component, constituent. – **2** *m* (*pieza*) component, constituent; (*ingrediente*) ingredient. **3** (*miembro*) member.

● de componente norte, METEOR northerly. ‖ de componente sur, METEOR southerly.

componer I *t* (*formar*) to compose, make up, form: *componer una medicina,* to make up a medicine. **2** (*reparar*) to fix, repair, mend. **3** (*adornar*) to adorn, decorate. **4** (*ataviar*) to dress up, make up. **5** (*riña*) to settle; (*ánimos*) to soothe. **6** (*música, versos*) to compose. **7** (*en impresión*) to set. **8** *fam* (*restablecer*) to settle: *la sopa me ha compuesto el estómago,* the soup settled my stomach. – **9 componerse,** *p* (*consistir*) to consist (**de,** of), be made up (**de,** of): *las palabras se componen de sílabas,* words are made up of syllables. **10** (*arreglarse*) to get ready; (*vestirse*) to get dressed: *la novia se está componiendo,* the bride is getting ready.

● componérselas, *fam* to manage, make do: *si hay algún problema que se las componga como pueda,* if there's any problem he'll have to manage as best he can.

▲ *Conjugation model* [78]*, like* **poner***; pp* **compuesto,-a.**

comportamiento *m* behaviour (US behavior), conduct.

comportar I *t* (*implica*) to involve, entail: *eso comporta un cambio de planes,* that involves a change of plan. – **2 comportarse,** *p* (*portarse*) to behave: *se comportó mal,* she misbehaved.

composición I *f* (*gen*) composition. **2** (*acuerdo*) agreement. **3** (*arreglo*) arrangement. **4** (*en impresión*) setting, composition.

● hacer composición de lugar, (*decidirse*) to make a plan of action; (*formarse una idea*) to get a picture of a situation.

compositor,-ra *m,f* composer.

compostelano,-a I *adj* of Santiago de Compostela, from Santiago de Compostela. – **2** *m,f* person from Santiago de Compostela, inhabitant of Santiago de Compostela.

compostura I *f* (*composición*) composition. **2** (*reparación*) repair, mending. **3** (*dignidad*) composure, dignity; (*moderación*) restraint, moderation: *perdió la compostura,* she lost her composure. **4** (*ajuste*) settlement, adjustment. **5** (*convenio*) agreement. **6** (*aseo*) neatness, tidiness.

compota *f* compote.

compra *f* purchase, buy.

● hacer la compra, to do the shopping, go shopping. ‖ ir a la compra, to go shopping. ‖ ir de compras, to go shopping.

■ compra a crédito, credit purchase. ‖ compra a plazos, hire purchase, US instalment buying. ‖ compra al contado, cash purchase.

comprador,-ra *m,f* purchaser, buyer, shopper.

comprar I *t* to buy. **2** *fig* (*sobornar*) to bribe, buy off.

● comprar al contado, to pay cash: *lo compré al contado,* I paid cash for it.

compraventa *f* buying and selling, dealing.

■ contrato de compraventa, contract of sale.

comprender I *t* (*entender*) to understand: *lo comprendiste mal,* you misunderstood it. **2** (*contener*) to comprise, include.

● ¿comprendes?, (*en conversación*) you see? ‖ hacerse comprender, to make os. understood. ‖ todo comprendido, (*excursión etc*) all-in, inclusive.

comprensible *adj* understandable.

comprensión *f* understanding.

comprensivo,-a I *adj* (*tolerante*) understanding. **2** (*que comprende o incluye*) comprehensive.

● comprensivo,-a de, comprising, made up of.

compresa I *f* (*higiénica*) sanitary towel. **2** (*vendaje*) compress.

compresibilidad *f* compressibility.

compresible *adj* compressible.

compresión *f* compression.

compresor,-ra I *adj* compressing. – **2 compresor,** *m* compressor.

comprimible *adj* compressible.

comprimido,-a I *pp* → **comprimir.** – **2** *adj* compressed. – **3 comprimido,** *m* tablet.

comprimir I *t* (*apretar*) to compress; (*gente*) to cram together. **2** (*reprimir*) to restrain. – **3 comprimirse,** *p* (*apretarse*) to get compressed; (*gente*) to squeeze. **4** (*contenerse*) to restrain os.: *me comprimí las ganas de llorar,* I fought back the tears.

comprobable *adj* verifiable, provable.

comprobación *f* verification, check, checking.

comprobante I *m* (*recibo*) receipt, voucher. **2** JUR document in proof.

comprobar I *t* (*verificar*) to verify, check. **2** (*demostrar*) to prove. **3** (*observar*) to see, observe: *como podrán ustedes comprobar,* as you can see for yourselves. **4** (*confirmar*) to confirm.

▲ *Conjugation model* [31]*, like* **contar.**

comprometedor,-ra 1 *adj* (*situación etc*) compromising. **2** (*persona*) troublemaking.

comprometer 1 *t* (*exponer a riesgo*) to endanger, jeopardize, risk; (*a una persona*) to compromise: *el general comprometió a los soldados,* the general put the soldiers at visk. **2** (*implicar*) to involve, implicate: *esta carta compromete al alcalde en el asunto,* this letter implicates the mayor in the affair. **3** (*obligar*) to commit. **4** (*poner en un aprieto*) to embarrass. **5** (*juzgar un tercero*) to submit to arbitration. – **6 comprometerse,** *p* (*contraer una obligación*) to commit os., pledge: *se comprometió a pagar,* she promised to pay. **7** (*involucrarse*) to get involved. **8** (*establecer relaciones formales*) to get engaged.
● **comprometerse a hacer algo,** to undertake to do sth.

comprometido,-a 1 *pp →* **comprometer.** – **2** *adj* (*difícil, arriesgado*) difficult, in jeopardy. **3** (*escritor, artista, etc*) committed. **4** (*involucrado*) involved. **5** (*para casarse*) engaged.

compromisario,-a 1 *adj* representative. – **2** *m,f* representative.

compromiso 1 *m* (*obligación*) commitment, obligation: *cumplió sus compromisos,* she fulfilled her obligations. **2** (*acuerdo*) agreement. **3** (*cita*) appointment; (*amorosa*) date. **4** (*dificultad*) difficult situation, bind. **5** (*matrimonial*) engagement.
● **libre de compromiso,** without obligation. ‖ **poner a algn. en un compromiso,** to put sb. in a tight spot, put sb. in a difficult situation. ‖ **por compromiso,** out of a sense of duty. ‖ **soltero,-a y sin compromiso,** free and single, footloose and fancy-free.
■ **compromiso matrimonial,** engagement. ‖ **compromiso verbal,** verbal agreement.

compuerta *f* sluice, floodgate.

compuesto,-a 1 *pp →* **componer.** – **2** *adj* (*gen*) compound. **3** (*reparado*) repaired, mended. **4** (*elegante*) dressed up; (*arreglado*) tidy. **5** *fig* (*comedido*) composed. – **6 compuesto,** *m* (*químico, farmacéutico, etc*) compound.
● **quedarse compuesta y sin novio,** to be left in the lurch.

compulsa 1 *f* (*cotejo*) collation, comparison. **2** JUR certified true copy.

compulsar 1 *t* (*cotejar*) to collate. **2** JUR to make a certified true copy of.

compulsión *f* compulsion.

compulsivo,-a *adj* compelling, compulsive.

compunción 1 *f* (*arrepentimiento*) compunction. **2** *fig* (*tristeza*) sorrow, sadness.

compungido,-a 1 *pp →* **compungir.** – **2** *adj* (*arrepentido*) remorseful. **3** *fig* (*triste*) sorrowful, sad.

compungir 1 *t* *fml* (*entristecer*) to sadden, make sad. – **2 compungirse,** *p* (*entristecerse*) to be saddened, feel sad.
▲ *Conjugation model* [6], *like* **dirigir.**

compuse *pt indef →* **componer.**

computable *adj* computable.

computación *f* computing.

computador *m* computer.

computadora *f* computer.

computadorizar *t* to computerize.
▲ *Conjugation model* [4], *like* **realizar.**

computar 1 *t* (*calcular*) to compute, calculate. **2** *fml* (*tomar en cuenta*) to take into account, count.

computarizar *t* to computerize.
▲ *Conjugation model* [4], *like* **realizar.**

computerizar *t* to computerize.

cómputo *m* computation, calculation.

comulgante 1 *adj* communicant. – **2** *mf* communicant.

comulgar 1 *i* REL to receive Holy Communion. **2** *fig* (*compartir ideas etc*) to share (**con,** -), agree (**con,** with): *no comulgo con sus ideas,* I don't share his ideas. – **3** *t* (*administrar comunión*) to administer Holy Communion to.
● **comulgar con ruedas de molino,** *fam* to believe anything: *¡no me hagas comulgar con ruedas de molino!,* don't expect me to believe that!
▲ *Conjugation model* [7], *like* **llegar.**

comulgatorio *m* communion rail, altar rail.

común 1 *adj* (*gen*) common: *eso es poco común,* that's unusual. **2** (*compartido*) shared, communal. **3** (*amigos*) mutual. – **4 el común,** *m* the community. – **5 los Comunes,** *mpl* POL the Commons.
● **fuera de lo común,** out of the ordinary. ‖ **hacer algo en común,** to do sth. jointly. ‖ **por lo común,** generally. ‖ **tener en común,** (*parecerse*) to have in common; (*compartir*) to share: *las dos hermanas no tienen nada en común,* the two sisters have nothing in common; *tenemos el despacho en común,* we share the same office.
■ **bien común,** common good. ‖ **el común de la gente,** the majority of people.

comuna *f* commune.

comunal *adj* communal.

comunicable 1 *adj* communicable. **2** (*persona*) sociable.

comunicación 1 *f* (*gen*) communication. **2** (*comunicado*) communication; (*oficial*) communiqué. **3** (*telefónica*) connection. **4** (*unión*) link, connection. – **5 comunicaciones,** *fpl* communications.
● **estar en comunicación con algn.,** to be in touch with sb. ‖ **poner a algn. en comunicación con algn.,** to put sb. in touch with sb.; (*por teléfono*) to put sb. through to sb. ‖ **ponerse en comunicación con algn.,** to get in touch with sb.; (*por teléfono*) to get through to sb.
■ **vía de comunicación,** thoroughfare.

comunicado,-a 1 *pp →* **comunicar.** – **2** *adj* served: *el área está bien comunicada,* the area is easily accessible by rail and road; *dos países bien comunicados,* two countries with good (rail and road) communications. – **3 comunicado,** *m* communiqué.
■ **comunicado de prensa,** press release.

comunicador,-ra 1 *adj* transmitting. – **2** *m,f* RAD TV (*persona*) communicator.

comunicante 1 *adj* communicating. – **2** *mf* informer.

comunicar 1 *t* (*hacer partícipe*) to communicate, convey, transmit: *Celia comunica a todos su alegría,* Celia conveys her joy to everybody. **2** (*hacer saber*) to communicate, make known, tell. **3** (*conectar*) to connect. – **4** *i* (*ponerse en comunicación*) to communicate; (*por carta*) to correspond: *comunicaremos con usted,* we'll get in touch with you. **5** (*teléfono*) to be engaged, US be busy. **6** (*estar conectado*) to communicate, be connected: *las habitaciones comunican,* the rooms are connected. – **7 comunicarse,** *p* (*tener relación*) to communicate; (*ponerse en contacto*) to get in touch, get in contact (**con,** with): *hace mucho que no me comunico con mi familia,* I haven't been in contact with my family for ages. **8** (*extenderse*) to spread: *el fuego se comunicó al bosque,* the fire spread to the wood. **9** (*estar conectado*) to be connected (**con,** to).
▲ *Conjugation model* [1], *like* **sacar.**

comunicativo,-a 1 *adj* (*actitud, sentimiento*) catching, infectious. **2** (*persona*) communicative, sociable, open.

comunidad f community.
● **en comunidad,** together.
■ **comunidad autónoma,** autonomous region. ‖ **comunidad de bienes,** JUR co-ownership. ‖ **comunidad de propietarios,** owners' association. ‖ **Comunidad Económica Europea,** European Economic Community.

comunión 1 f communion, fellowship. **2** REL Holy Communion.
● **hacer la primera comunión,** to make one's First Communion.

comunismo m communism.

comunista 1 adj communist. – **2** mf communist.

comunitario,-a 1 adj (gen) of the community, relating to the community: *centro comunitario,* community centre (US center). **2** (de la Unión Europea) Community, of the EC, relating to the EC: *España es un país comunitario,* Spain is a member of the EC, Spain is an EC country.

comúnmente adv (normalmente) commonly, usually, generally; (frecuentemente) often.

comuña f mixture of wheat and rye.

con 1 prep (instrumento, medio) with: *se defendió con un puñal,* she defended herself with a knife; *hay que comerlo con una cuchara,* you have to eat it with a spoon; *me divirtió con sus chistes,* I really enjoyed his jokes. **2** (modo, circunstancia) in, with: *¿vas a salir con este frío?,* are you going out in this cold?; *me gustas con ese vestido,* you look nice in that dress, I like that dress on you. **3** (juntamente, en compañía) with: *se encerró con su prima en la habitación,* she shut herself up in the room with her cousin; *Juan se quedó con las maletas,* Juan was left with the suitcases. **4** (contenido) with: *encontré una cartera con dinero,* I found a wallet with some money in it. **5** (relación) to: *yo hablo con todos,* I speak to everybody; *fui amable con él,* I was nice to him. **6** (reciprocidad): *ámense unos con otros,* love one another. **7** (comparación) compared to: *su fuerza no es nada con la mía,* his strength is nothing compared to mine. **8** (a pesar de) in spite of, despite: *con la nota que tenía no fue aceptado,* he wasn't accepted in spite of his grade. – **9** con + inf, loc by + ger: *con disculparte no solucionas nada,* you won't solve anything just by apologizing. **10** (aunque) in spite of: *con ser tan fuerte ...,* in spite of being so strong ...
● **con que / con tal de que / con tal que,** provided, as long as. ‖ **con todo (y eso),** nevertheless, even so.

conato 1 m (intento) attempt: *hizo un conato de hablar,* she made an attempt to speak. **2** (principio) beginnings pl, start: *hubo un conato de incendio,* a fire was started (and put out).

concadenar t → **concatenar**.

concatenación f concatenation.

concatenar 1 t to concatenate, link together. – **2** concatenarse, p to concatenate, link together.

concavidad f concavity.

cóncavo,-a adj concave.

concavoconvexo,-a adj concavo-convex.

concebible adj conceivable, imaginable.

concebir 1 t (engendrar) to conceive. **2** fig (comprender) to understand: *no concibo tanta crueldad,* I can't understand so much cruelty. **3** fig (comenzar a sentir) to experience, have: *concebir esperanzas,* to build up one's hopes. – **4** i (quedarse embarazada) to become pregnant, conceive.
▲ Conjugation model [34], like *servir.*

conceder 1 t (otorgar) to grant, concede; (premio) to award: *le concedieron el primer premio,* he was awarded the first prize. **2** (atribuir) to give, attach: *no le concedí importancia a aquel asunto,* I didn't attach importance to that affair. **3** (oportunidad, tiempo) to give. **4** (admitir) to concede, admit: *le concedo que no tengo razón,* I admit I'm not right.

concejal,-la m,f (hombre) town councillor, US town councilman; (mujer) town councillor, US town councilwoman.

concejalía f councillorship.

concejo m town council, council.

concelebrar t to concelebrate.

concentración 1 f (gen) concentration. **2** (de gente) gathering, rally.
■ **concentración parcelaria,** land consolidation, consolidation.

concentrado,-a 1 pp → **concentrate**. – **2** adj concentrated. **3** fig (persona) absorbed. – **4** concentrado, m concentrate, extract.

concentrar 1 t to concentrate. – **2** concentrarse, p (reunirse) to concentrate. **3** (fijar la atención) to concentrate (en, on): *no conseguí concentrarme,* I couldn't concentrate.

concéntrico,-a adj concentric.

concepción f conception.

conceptismo m conceptism.

concepto 1 m (idea) concept, conception, idea. **2** (opinión) opinion, view. **3** FIN heading, section.
● **bajo ningún concepto,** under no circumstances. ‖ **en concepto de,** by way of. ‖ **formarse un concepto de algo/algn.,** to form an opinion of sth./sb. ‖ **tener a algn. en buen concepto,** to have a high opinion of sb. ‖ **tener buen concepto de algo/algn.,** to have a high opinion of sth./sb. ‖ **tener mal concepto de algo/algn.,** to have a low opinion of sth./sb.

conceptual adj conceptual.

conceptualismo m conceptualism.

conceptualizar t to conceptualize.
▲ Conjugation model [4], like *realizar.*

conceptuar t to deem, think, consider: *siempre te he conceptuado de inteligente,* I have always considered you to be intelligent.
● **estar bien/mal conceptuado,-a,** to be well/badly considered.
▲ Conjugation model [11], like *actuar.*

conceptuoso,-a adj high-sounding, affected.

concerniente adj concerning, relating.
● **en lo concerniente a,** fml with regard to.

concernir 1 i (afectar) to concern, touch. **2** (corresponder) to be up to.
● **en lo que a mí (ti, él, etc) concierne,** as far as I am (you are, he is, etc) concerned. ‖ **en lo que concierne a,** with regard to, with respect to. ‖ **por lo que a mí (ti, él, etc) concierne,** as far as I am (you are, he is, etc) concerned.
▲ Conjugation model [29], like *discernir,* used only in the third persons of pres indic, imperf indic and pres subj; and non-personal forms.

concertación f agreement, reconciliation.

concertadamente 1 adv (de acuerdo) of a common accord. **2** (en orden) systematically.

concertado,-a 1 pp → **concertar**. – **2** adj concerted.

concertar 1 t (planear) to plan, coordinate. **2** (entrevista) to arrange; (acuerdo) to reach; (tratado, negocio) to conclude, settle: *concertar una cita,* to arrange a meeting.

3 (*precio*) to agree on. **4** MÚS to harmonize. – **5** *i* (*concordar*) to agree, match up; (*números*) to tally. **6** LING to agree. **7** MÚS to harmonize, be in tune. – **8 concertarse**, *p* (*ponerse de acuerdo*) to reach an agreement, get together.
▲ *Conjugation model* |27|, *like* **acertar**.

concertina *f* concertina.

concertino *m* first violin.

concertista *mf* soloist.

concesión l *f* concession, granting. **2** (*de premio*) awarding.
● **hacer concesiones**, to make concessions.

concesionario,-a l *adj* concessionary. – **2** *m,f* concessionaire, licence holder, licensee. **3** (*de coches*) dealer.

concesivo,-a *adj* LING concessive.

concha l *f* (*caparazón*) shell. **2** (*carey*) tortoiseshell. **3** (*ostra*) oyster. **4** TEAT prompt box.
● **meterse en su concha**, *fig* to withdraw into one's shell. ‖ **tener muchas conchas**, *fam* to be a sly one.
■ **concha de peregrino**, scallop shell.

conchabar l *t* (*unir*) to blend. – **2 conchabarse**, *p fam* (*confabularse*) to plot, scheme.

conciencia l *f* (*moral*) conscience. **2** (*conocimiento*) consciousness, awareness.
● **a conciencia**, conscienciously. ‖ **con la conciencia tranquila**, with a clear conscience. ‖ **en conciencia**, in truth. ‖ **remorderle a algn. la conciencia**, to weigh on sb.'s conscience. ‖ **tener conciencia de algo**, to be aware of sth. ‖ **tomar conciencia de algo**, to become aware of sth.
■ **conciencia de clase**, class-consciousness.

concienciado,-a l *pp* → **concienciar**. – **2** *adj* aware.

concienciar l *t* to make aware (**de**, of). – **2 concienciarse**, *p* to become aware (**de**, of).
▲ *Conjugation model* |12|, *like* **cambiar**.

concienzudo,-a *adj* conscientious.

concierto l *m* MÚS (*sesión*) concert; (*composición*) concerto. **2** (*acuerdo*) agreement. **3** (*armonía*) concert, concord.
■ **concierto económico**, flat rate.

conciliábulo *m* secret meeting.

conciliación *f* conciliation, reconciliation.

conciliador,-ra *adj* conciliatory, conciliating.

conciliar l *adj* conciliar. – **2** *t* (*gen*) to conciliate, bring together. **3** (*enemigos*) to reconcile. – **4 conciliarse**, *p* to win.
▲ *Conjugation model* |12|, *like* **cambiar**.

conciliatorio,-a *adj* conciliatory.

concilio *m* council.
■ **el Concilio de Trento**, el Council of Trent. ‖ **el Concilio Vaticano Segundo**, the Second Vatican Council.

concisión *f* concision, conciseness.

conciso,-a *adj* concise, brief.

concitar *t* to excite, incite, stir up, raise.

conciudadano,-a *m,f* fellow citizen.

conclave l *m* REL conclave. **2** *fig* (*reunión*) private meeting.
● **tener un conclave**, to sit in conclave.

cónclave *m* → **conclave**.

concluir l *t* (*terminar*) to finish. **2** (*trato, negocio*) to close. **3** (*inferir*) to conclude, infer. **4** (*dar remate*) to put the finishing touches to. – **5** *i* (*finalizar*) to finish, come to an end, conclude.
▲ *Conjugation model* |62|, *like* **huir**.

conclusión l *f* (*final*) conclusion, end. **2** (*deducción*) conclusion.
● **en conclusión**, in conclusion. ‖ **llegar a una conclusión**, to come to a conclusion.

concluso,-a *adj* adjourned pending sentence.

concluyente *adj* conclusive, decisive.

concomerse *p* to be consumed (**de**, with), itch (**de**, with): *concomerse de impaciencia*, to itch with impatience; *concomerse de envidia*, to be green with envy.

concomitancia *f* concomitance.

concomitante *adj* concomitant.

concordancia l *f* concordance, agreement. **2** LING agreement.

concordante *adj* concordant.

concordar l *t* (*poner de acuerdo*) to bring into agreement, reconcile. **2** LING to make agree. – **3** *i* (*convenir*) to agree, coincide, match; (*números*) to tally: *yo no concuerdo contigo en este asunto*, I don't agree with you on this matter; *la copia concuerda con el original*, the copy matches the original. **4** LING to agree: *el adjetivo concuerda con el sustantivo*, the adjective agrees with the noun.
▲ *Conjugation model* |31|, *like* **contar**.

concordato *m* concordat.

concorde *adj* in agreement.

concordia *f* concord, harmony.

concreción l *f* (*concisión*) concision, conciseness. **2** MED GEOL concretion.

concretamente l *adv* (*exactamente*) exactly: *no entiendo concretamente lo que quieres decir*, I don't understand exactly what you mean. **2** (*en particular*) specifically, in particular: *me ofreció ese libro concretamente*, he specifically offered me that book.

concretar l *t* (*precisar*) to specify, state explicitly: *concretar los planes*, to specify the plans. **2** (*hora, precio*) to fix, set: *aún no puedo concretar una fecha*, i can't set a date yet. **3** (*resumir*) to sum up: *concretemos*, let's sum up. **4** (*limitar*) to limit, confine: *concretó su actuación a cantar los éxitos*, he limited his performance to just singing the hits. – **5 concretarse**, *p* (*limitarse*) to limit os. (**a**, to), confine os. (**a**, to), keep (**a**, to): *me concreté a decir lo que sabía*, I confined myself to just saying what I knew. **6** (*materializarse*) to materialize; (*tomar forma*) to take shape; (*realizarse*) to become realized, come true.

concreto,-a l *adj* (*real*) concrete, real. **2** (*particular*) particular, specific: *quiero ese libro concreto*, I want that particular book.
● **en concreto**, (*en particular*) in particular, specifically; (*exactamente*) exactly. ‖ **en el caso concreto de ...,** in the particular case of ...

concubina *f* concubine.

concubinato *m* concubinage.

conculcar *t* to infringe, break, violate: *conculcó la ley*, he broke the law.
▲ *Conjugation model* |1|, *like* **sacar**.

concuñado,-a *m,f* (*hombre*) wife's brother-in-law, sister-in-law's husband; (*mujer*) husband's sister-in-law, brother-in-law's wife.

concupiscencia *f* concupiscence, lustfulness.

concupiscente *adj* concupiscent, lustful.

concurrencia l *f* (*confluencia*) combination, concurrence. **2** (*público*) audience. **3** (*participación*) participation.

concurrente l *adj* concurrent. **2** (*competidores*) competing, contending. – **3** *mf* (*persona presente*) person present. **4** (*público*) member of the audience. **5** (*competidor*) competitor, contestant. – **6 los concurrentes**, *mpl* the audience *sing*, those present.

concurrido,-a l *pp* → **concurrir**. – **2** *adj* (*lugar público*) busy, crowded. **3** (*espectáculo*) well-attended, popular.

concurrir I *i (juntarse en un lugar - gente)* to gather, come together, meet: *los fieles concurren en la iglesia,* the faithful gather at church; *hoy concurren en las urnas 20 millones de alemanes,* 20 million Germans go to the polls today. **2** *(asistir)* to attend, be present: *muchos ciudadanos concurrieron al acto,* many citizens attended the ceremony. **3** *(tomar parte - concurso etc)* to compete, take part; *(- elección)* to stand, to run; *(- examen)* to be a candidate: *varios candidatos concurrieron al certamen,* several candidates took part in the contest. **4** *(factores, circunstancias, etc)* to come together, combine: *las causas que concurren hacen inviable su venta,* the combination of causes make its sale unviable; *esto sólo será posible si concurren circunstancias especiales,* this will only be possible if there are special circumstances; *es raro que concurran tantas cualidades en una sola persona,* it's strange to find so many qualities in a single person. **5** *(coincidir en el tiempo)* to coincide, concur, be at the same time. **6** *(contribuir)* to contribute **(a/ en,** to). **7** *(estar de acuerdo)* to agree **(en,** on): *concurrieron todos en el mismo sentir,* they all shared the same opinion. **8** *(calles etc)* to meet, converge; *(en geometría)* to cross, intersect.

concursante *mf (a concurso)* contestant, participant, competitor. **2** *(a empleo)* candidate.

concursar I *i (competir)* to compete, take part. **2** *(para un empleo)* to be a candidate.

concurso I *m (gen)* competition; *(de belleza, deportivo)* contest; *(en televisión)* quiz. **2** *(para puestos)* public examination: *las tres plazas de profesor saldrán a concurso,* applications are invited for the three teaching positions. **3** *fml (concurrencia)* gathering; *(de factores, circunstancias)* combination. **4** *(ayuda)* help, aid, collaboration. **5** *(licitación)* tender.
● **estar fuera de concurso,** to be out of the running.
■ **concurso hípico,** horse show. ‖ **concurso literario,** literary competition. ‖ **concurso radiofónico,** radio quiz, radio quiz programme (us program).

condado *m* county.

condal *adj* of a count, relating to a count.
■ **la Ciudad Condal,** Barcelona.

conde *m* count.

condecoración *f* decoration, medal.

condecorar *t* to decorate.

condena I *f* JUR sentence, conviction. **2** *(desaprobación)* condemnation, disapproval.
● **cumplir una condena,** to serve a sentence.
■ **condena a perpetuidad,** life sentence. ‖ **condena condicional,** suspended sentence.

condenable *adj* condemnable, blameworthy.

condenación I *f* condemnation. **2** REL damnation.

condenadamente *adv fam* darned, damned.

condenado,-a I *pp* → **condenar.** – **2** *adj* JUR convicted. **3** REL damned. **4** *(cegado)* condemned. **5** *(sin remedio)* hopeless. **6** *fig (maldito)* damn, damned: *ese condenado perro vuelve a ladrar,* that damned dog is barking again. – **7** *m,f* JUR convict; *(a muerte)* condemned prisoner. **8** *fig (malvado)* wretch. – **9** **los condenados,** *mpl* REL the damned.
● **trabajar como un condenado,** *fam* to slog one's guts out, work like one possessed.

condenar I *t* JUR *(declarar culpable)* to convict, find guilty. **2** JUR *(decretar condena)* to sentence, condemn: *lo condenaron a muerte,* he was sentenced to death. **3** *(desaprobar)* to condemn. **4** *(forzar)* to condemn, doom. **5** *(tabicar)* to wall up, brick up. – **6** **condenarse,** *p* to be damned, condemn os.

condenatorio,-a *adj* condemnatory.

condensable *adj* condensable.

condensación I *f (acción)* condensing. **2** *(efecto)* condensation.

condensado,-a I *pp* → **condensar.** – **2** *adj* condensed.

condensador,-ra I *adj* condensing. – **2** **condensador,** *m* ELEC condenser.

condensar I *t* to condense. – **2** **condensarse,** *p* to condense.

condesa *f* countess.

condescendencia I *f (deferencia)* condescension. **2** *(amabilidad)* affability.

condescender I *i (adaptarse)* to comply **(a,** with), consent **(a,** to): *no estaba de acuerdo pero tuvo que condescender a la voluntad de los demás,* he didn't agree but he had to comply with all of the others. **2** *(dignarse)* to condescend.
▲ *Conjugation model* [28], *like* **entender.**

condescendiente I *adj (transigente)* condescending. **2** *(complaciente)* obliging, helpful.

condestable *m* High Constable.

condición I *f (naturaleza)* nature, condition. **2** *(carácter)* nature, character: *es de condición apacible,* he is a gentle person. **3** *(circunstancia)* circumstance, condition. **4** *(estado social)* status, position: *de condición humilde,* of humble origins. **5** *(calidad)* capacity: *en su condición de profesor,* as a teacher. **6** *(exigencia)* condition: *nos puso la condición de que llegáramos pronto,* he made it a condition that we should arrive early. – **7 condiciones,** *fpl (estado)* condition *sing,* state *sing: condiciones de salud,* state of health. **8** *(aptitud)* aptitude *sing,* talent *sing: tiene condiciones para el canto,* she has a talent for singing.
● **a condición de que ...,** provided (that) ... ‖ **con la condición de que ...,** on the condition that ... ‖ **en estas condiciones,** under these circumstances. ‖ **estar en condiciones de hacer algo,** *(físicas)* to be fit to do sth.; *(posición, autoridad)* to be in a position to do sth. ‖ **estar en malas condiciones,** *(gen)* to be in a bad state, be in bad condition; *(comida)* to be off. ‖ **poner en condiciones,** to get ready.
■ **condiciones de pago,** conditions of payment. ‖ **condiciones de trabajo,** working conditions. ‖ **condiciones requeridas,** requirements. ‖ **persona de condición,** high-class person.

condicionado,-a I *pp* → **condicionar.** – **2** *adj* conditioned.

condicional I *adj* conditional. – **2** *m* conditional.

condicionamiento *m* conditioning.

condicionar I *t (influir en)* to condition, determine. **2** *(supeditar)* to make conditional.

cóndilo *m* condyle.

condimentación *f* seasoning, flavouring (us flavoring).

condimentar *t* to season, flavour (us flavor).

condimento *m* seasoning, flavouring (us flavoring).

condiscípulo,-a *m,f* fellow pupil, fellow student, schoolmate.

condolencia *f* condolence, sympathy.

condolerse *p* to sympathize **(de,** with), feel sorry **(de,** for), feel pity **(de,** for).
▲ *Conjugation model* [32], *like* **mover.**

condominio I *m (copropiedad)* joint ownership. **2** *(de un territorio)* condominium.

condón *m* condom.

condonación *f* condonation, remission.
condonar 1 *t* (*perdonar*) to condone. **2** (*una deuda*) to cancel, remit.
cóndor *m* condor.
conducción 1 *f* FÍS conduction. **2** (*transporte*) transportation. **3** (*por tubería*) piping; (*eléctrica*) wiring. **4** AUTO driving. **5** (*cañería*) pipe, intake.
conducir 1 *t* (*guiar*) to lead, take, show: *un amigo nos condujo al lugar de los hechos,* a friend led us to the scene of the crime. **2** (*coche, animales*) to drive: *conducir un camión,* to drive a lorry. **3** (*negocio*) to manage. **4** (*transportar*) to transport. **5** (*líquido*) to convey; (*electricidad*) to carry, conduct. − **6** *i* (*un coche*) to drive: *conduce muy bien,* she drives very well. **7** (*llevar*) to lead (**a**, -): *esto no conduce a nada,* this leads nowhere. − **8** **conducirse,** *p* (*comportarse*) to behave, conduct os.
▲ Conjugation model [46].
conducta *f* conduct, behaviour (US behavior).
■ **mala conducta,** misconduct, misbehaviour (US misbehavior).
conductancia *f* conductance.
conductibilidad *f* conductivity.
conductismo *m* behaviourism (US behaviorism).
conductividad *f* conductivity.
conducto 1 *m* (*tubería*) pipe, conduit. **2** (*eléctrico*) cable, lead. **3** ANAT duct, canal: *conducto auditivo,* auditory duct; *conducto alimenticio,* alimentary canal. **4** *fig* channel: *lo supimos por conductos oficiales,* we found out through official channels.
● **por conducto de,** through.
conductor,-ra 1 *adj* FÍS conductive. − **2** *m,f* AUTO driver. − **3 conductor,** *m* FÍS conductor.
condumio *m fam* grub, nosh, food.
conectar 1 *t* (*gen*) to connect (up). **2** (*aparato eléctrico*) to switch on, plug in. − **3** *i* RAD TV (*coger*) to tune in (**con**, to); (*dar conexión*) to tune in (**con**, with): *conectar con la BBC,* to tune in to the BBC. **4** *fam* (*llevarse bien*) to hit it off, get on well: *Juan y yo conectamos enseguida,* Juan and I hit it off immediately.
conector *m* connector.
coneja *f →* **conejo,-a.**
conejar *m* rabbit hutch.
conejera *f →* **conejero,-a.**
conejero,-a 1 *adj* rabbit-hunting. − **2** *m,f* rabbit breeder. − **3 conejera,** *f* (*conejal*) rabbit hutch. **4** (*madriguera*) rabbit warren, rabbit burrow. **5** *fig* (*cueva*) cave. **6** *fig* (*tugurio*) den, dive.
conejillo *m* young rabbit.
■ **conejillo de Indias,** guinea pig.
conejo,-a 1 *m,f* (*gen*) rabbit; (*macho*) buck; (*hembra*) doe. − **2 conejo,** *m tabú* (*coño*) cunt, pussy.
● **ser una coneja,** *fam* to breed like a rabbit.
■ **conejo de Indias,** guinea pig.
conexión 1 *f* TÉC connection. **2** *fig* relationship, connection.
● **estar en conexión con,** to be connected to.
conexionar *t* to connect.
conexo,-a *adj* connected, related.
confabulación *f* conspiracy, plot.
confabulador,-ra *m,f* conspirator, plotter.
confabular 1 *i* to confabulate, discuss. − **2 confabularse,** *p* to conspire, plot.
confección 1 *f* (*acción*) dressmaking, tailoring; (*ropa*) off-the-peg clothes *pl*, ready-to-wear clothes *pl*: *la industria de la confección,* the clothing industry. **2** (*realización*) making, making up: *la confección de una lista,* the drawing up of a list.

confeccionador,-ra 1 *m,f* COST outfitter. **2** (*realizador*) maker; (*de un escrito*) writer, author.
confeccionar *t* (*vestido*) to make, make up; (*list*) to draw up; (*plato*) to prepare.
confeccionista *mf* outfitter.
confederación *f* confederation, confederacy.
confederal *adj* confederative.
confederar 1 *t* to confederate. − **2 confederarse,** *p* to confederate, become a confederation.
conferencia 1 *f* (*charla*) talk, lecture. **2** POL conference, meeting. **3** (*teléfono*) long-distance call.
● **dar una conferencia sobre algo,** to lecture on sth., give a lecture on sth. ‖ **poner una conferencia con,** to make a call to, place a call to.
■ **conferencia a cobro revertido,** reverse-charge call, US collect call. ‖ **conferencia de prensa,** press conference. ‖ **conferencia interurbana,** long-distance call.
conferenciante *mf* lecturer.
conferenciar *i* to confer: *el embajador conferenció con el primer ministro sobre la crisis,* the ambassador conferred with the Prime Minister on the crisis.
▲ Conjugation model [12], like *cambiar.*
conferir 1 *t* (*conceder*) to confer, bestow, award. **2** (*dar*) to give.
▲ Conjugation model [35], like *hervir.*
confesar 1 *t* (*reconocer*) to confess, admit. **2** (*un crimen*) to own up to. **3** (*pecados*) to confess. **4** REL to confess, hear in confession. − **5** *i* JUR to own up. − **6 confesarse,** *p* to go to confession, confess.
● **confesarse culpable,** to admit one's guilt, plead guilty. ‖ **confesar de plano,** *fam* to admit everything.
▲ Conjugation model [27], like *acertar.*
confesión 1 *f* (*expresión*) confession, admission. **2** REL confession. **3** (*credo*) confession, faith.
confesional *adj* denominational.
confesionario *m* confessional.
confeso,-a 1 *adj* JUR self-confessed. **2** (*judío*) converted. − **3** *m,f* (*judío*) converted Jew.
confesonario *m* confessional.
confesor *m* confessor.
confeti *m* confetti.
▲ *pl* **confetis.**
confiadamente 1 *adv* (*con confianza*) confidently. **2** (*con engreimiento*) conceitedly.
confiado,-a 1 *pp →* **confiar.** − **2** *adj* (*crédulo*) unsuspecting, gullible. **3** (*seguro*) confident, self-confident. **4** (*engreído*) self-satisfied; (*presumido*) conceited.
confianza 1 *f* (*seguridad*) confidence. **2** (*fe*) trust. **3** (*familiaridad*) familiarity, intimacy. **4** (*presunción*) conceit.
● **con toda confianza,** in all confidence. ‖ **de confianza,** (*fiable*) reliable; (*de responsabilidad*) trustworthy: *María es de confianza,* María is trustworthy. ‖ **en confianza,** confidentially, in confidence. ‖ **estar en confianza,** to be among friends. ‖ **tener confianza en uno mismo,** to be self-confident. ‖ **tener mucha confianza con algn.,** to be on intimate terms with sb. ‖ **tomarse (muchas) confianzas,** to take liberties. ‖ **tratar a algn. con confianza,** to treat sb. like a friend.
confiar 1 *i* (*tener fe*) to trust (**en**, -), confide (**en**, in): *no confiamos en él,* we don't trust him. **2** (*estar seguro*) to be confident, trust: *confío en que no llegarán tarde,* I am confident that they won't be late. **3** (*contar*) to count (**en**, on), rely (**en**, on): *confío en mi inteligencia para resolver el problema,* I am counting on my intelligence to solve the problem. − **4** *t* (*depositar*) to entrust. **5** (*secretos,*

problemas, etc) to confide. – **6 confiarse,** *p (entregarse)* to entrust os.: *se confió a los médicos,* she put herself in the hands of the doctors. **7** *(confesarse)* to confide (**a,** in): *me confiaré a mi mejor amiga,* I'll confide in my best friend. **8** *(estar seguro)* to be overconfident: *se confió demasiado y suspendió el examen,* he got overconfident and failed the exam.
▲ *Conjugation model* |13|, *like desviar.*
confidencia *f* confidence, secret.
confidencial *adj* confidential.
confidencialmente *adv* confidentially.
confidente,-a 1 *adj* trustworthy, reliable. – **2** *m,f (hombre)* confidant; *(mujer)* confidante. **3** *euf (de la policía)* informer.
configuración 1 *f* configuration, shape. **2** INFORM configuration.
■ **la configuración del terreno,** the lie of the land.
configurar 1 *t* to form, shape. **2** INFORM to configure.
confín 1 *adj* bordering. – **2** *m* limit, boundary: *los confines de la tierra,* the ends of the earth.
▲ In 2, *often used in plural.*
confinación *f* → **confinamiento.**
confinamiento 1 *m (encarcelamiento)* confinement. **2** *(exilio)* exile, banishment.
confinar 1 *i (limitar)* to border: *España confina con Francia y Portugal,* Spain borders on France and Portugal. – **2** *t (recluir)* to confine: *confinaron al preso en una celda,* the prisoner was locked up in a cell. – **3** confinarse, *p* to shut os. away.
confirmación *f* confirmation.
confirmar 1 *t* to confirm. – **2 confirmarse,** *p* to be confirmed.
confirmatorio,-a *adj* confirmatory.
confiscación *f* confiscation.
confiscar *t* to confiscate.
▲ *Conjugation model* |1|, *like sacar.*
confitado,-a 1 *pp* → **confitar.** – **2** *adj (fruta)* candied, glacé.
■ **frutas confitadas,** candied fruit *sing.*
confitar *t (frutas)* to candy; *(carne)* to preserve.
confite *m* sweet, US candy.
confitería *f* confectioner's, sweet shop, US candy shop.
confitero,-a *m,f* confectioner.
confitura *f* preserve, jam.
conflagración 1 *f (incendio)* conflagration. **2** *(de guerra)* flare-up.
conflictividad *f* disputes *pl.*
■ **conflictividad laboral,** industrial disputes *pl,* US labor disputes *pl.*
conflictivo,-a *adj (situación)* difficult; *(tema)* controversial: *zona conflictiva,* area of conflict.
conflicto 1 *m (choque)* conflict. **2** *fig (apuro)* dilemma.
■ **conflicto laboral,** industrial dispute.
confluencia *f* confluence.
■ **punto de confluencia,** *fig* meeting point.
confluente 1 *adj* confluent. – **2** *m* confluence.
confluir *i (personas)* to converge, come together; *(ríos, caminos, etc)* to meet, converge.
▲ *Conjugation model* |62|, *like huir.*
conformación *f* shape, structure.
conformar 1 *t (dar forma)* to shape. **2** *(adaptar)* to conform, adjust: *habrá que conformar los gastos a los beneficios,* we'll have to adjust the expenses to the profits. – **3** *i (concordar)* to agree (**con,** with). – **4 conformarse,** *p (contentarse)* to resign os. (**con,** to), be content (**con,** with), make do (**con,** with): *tendré que*

conformarme con este sueldo, I'll have to be content with this salary.
● **ser de buen conformar,** to be easy-going.
conforme 1 *adj (satisfecho)* satisfied: *estaba conforme con la nota,* he was satisfied with his mark. **2** *(de acuerdo)* in accordance with, in keeping with: *eso está conforme con nuestras expectativas,* that meets our expectations. **3** *(resignado)* resigned. – **4** *adv (según, como)* as: *todo salió conforme habíamos planeado,* everything turned out as we'd planned. **5** *(en cuanto)* as soon as: *telefoneó conforme llegó,* as soon as she arrived she phoned. **6** *(a medida que)* as: *se presentaba conforme entraban los invitados,* she introduced herself as the guests came in. – **7** *m* approval, agreement. – **8** *interj* all right!
● **conforme a,** in accordance with, according to: *conforme a lo que dijo,* according to what he said. ‖ **estar conforme,** to agree. ‖ **quedar conforme,** to agree: *quedamos conformes con el precio,* we agreed on the price.
conformemente *adv* in accordance.
conformidad 1 *f (acuerdo)* agreement. **2** *(aprobación)* approval, consent: *nos dio su conformidad,* she gave us her consent. **3** *(resignación)* patience, resignation. **4** *(afinidad)* conformity.
● **en conformidad con algo,** in conformity with sth., in agreement with.
■ **no conformidad,** non-conformity.
conformismo *m* conformism.
conformista 1 *adj* conformist. – **2** *mf* conformist.
confort *m* comfort.
● **"todo confort",** *(en anuncio)* "all mod cons", "fully equipped".
▲ *pl conforts.*
confortable *adj* comfortable.
confortablemente *adv* comfortably.
confortador,-ra *adj* → **confortante.**
confortante 1 *adj (que fortalece)* invigorating. **2** *fig (consolador)* comforting, cheering.
confortar 1 *t (dar vigor)* to invigorate. **2** *fig (consolar)* to comfort. **3** *fig (animar)* to cheer.
confraternal *adj* fraternal, brotherly.
confraternar *i* to fraternize.
confraternidad *f* confraternity, brotherhood.
confraternizar *i* to fraternize.
▲ *Conjugation model* |4|, *like realizar.*
confrontación 1 *f (enfrentamiento)* confrontation. **2** *(comparación)* comparison, collation.
confrontar 1 *t (gen)* to confront; *(carear)* to bring face to face. **2** *(cotejar)* to compare (**con,** with), collate (**con,** with). – **3** *i (lindar)* to border (**con,** on). – **4 confrontarse,** *p* to face (**con,** -), confront (**con,** -): *confrontarse con un competidor,* to face a competitor.
confundible *adj* easily confused.
confundir 1 *t (mezclar)* to mix up. **2** *(equivocar)* to confuse (**con,** with), mistake (**con,** for): *confundí un libro con otro,* I confused one book with another. **3** *(no reconocer)* to mistake (**con,** for): *la confundí con su hermana,* I mistook her for her sister. **4** *(turbar)* to confound, embarrass. – **5 confundirse,** *p (mezclarse)* to mingle; *(colores, formas)* to blend: *los ladrones se confundieron con la multitud,* the thieves mingled with the crowd; *la figura se confunde con los árboles,* the figure blends into the trees. **6** *(equivocarse)* to get mixed up, make a mistake: *me he confundido,* I have made a mistake *me confundí de calle,* I got the wrong street; *se ha confundido de número,* you've got the wrong number. **7** *(turbarse)* to be confused, be embarrassed.

confusión 1 *f* (*desorden*) confusion, chaos. **2** (*equivocación*) mistake, confusion. **3** (*turbación*) confusion, embarrassment.
confusionismo *m* confusion.
confuso,-a 1 *adj* (*ideas*) confused. **2** (*estilo etc*) obscure, confused. **3** (*recuerdos, formas*) vague, blurred. **4** (*mezclado*) mixed up. **5** *fig* (*turbado*) confused, embarrassed.
confutar *t* to refute, confute.
conga *f* conga.
congelación 1 *f* (*gen*) freezing. **2** (*precios, salarios, etc*) freeze. **3** MED (*gen*) exposure; (*extremidades*) frostbite.
congelado,-a 1 *pp* → **congelar**. – **2** *adj* (*gen*) frozen. **3** MED frostbitten. – **4 congelados,** *mpl* frozen food *sing*.
congelador *m* freezer.
congelar 1 *t* (*gen*) to freeze: *congelar salarios,* to freeze salaries. **2** MED to cause frostbite on. – **3 congelarse,** *p* to freeze. **4** MED to get frostbite.
congénere 1 *adj* congeneric, congenerous. – **2** *mf* BOT ZOOL congener. **3** *pey* sort, kind: *las prostitutas y sus congéneres,* prostitutes and their kind.
congeniar *i* to get on: *no congenia con mis amigos,* she doesn't get on with my friends.
▲ *Conjugation model* |12|, *like* **cambiar**.
congénito,-a 1 *adj* congenital. **2** *fig* innate.
congestión *f* congestion.
■ **congestión cerebral,** stroke.
congestionar 1 *t* to congest. – **2 congestionarse,** *p* to become congested. **3** (*la cara*) to go red, blush.
conglobar *t* to conglobate.
conglomeración *f* conglomeration.
conglomerado 1 *m* TÉC conglomerate. **2** *fig* conglomeration, collection.
conglomerar 1 *t* to conglomerate. – **2 conglomerarse,** *p* to conglomerate.
Congo *m* Congo.
congoja 1 *f* (*angustia*) anguish, distress. **2** (*pena*) grief, sorrow.
congoleño,-a 1 *adj* Congolese. – **2** *m,f* Congolese.
congolés,-esa *adj-m,f* → **congoleño,-a**.
congraciar 1 *t* to win over. – **2 congraciarse,** *p* to ingratiate os. (**con,** with).
▲ *Conjugation model* |12|, *like* **cambiar**.
congratulación *f fml* congratulation.
congratular 1 *t fml* to congratulate on. – **2 congratularse,** *p fml* to congratulate os. (**de/por,** on).
congregación 1 *f* (*reunión*) assembly. **2** REL congregation.
congregante *mf* member of a congregation.
congregar 1 *t* to congregate, assemble. – **2 congregarse,** *p* to congregate, assemble.
▲ *Conjugation model* |7|, *like* **llegar**.
congresista *mf* member of a congress; (*hombre*) congressman; (*mujer*) congresswoman.
congreso *m* congress.
■ **congreso de los Diputados,** Parliament, US Congress.
congrio *m* conger, conger eel.
congruencia 1 *f* (*conveniencia*) congruity. **2** MAT congruence.
congruente 1 *adj* (*coherente*) coherent, suitable. **2** MAT congruent.
congruo,-a *adj* → **congruente**.
cónico,-a 1 *adj* conical. **2** (*en geometría*) conic.
conífera *f* → **conífero,-a**.
conífero,-a 1 *adj* coniferous. – **2 conífera,** *f* conifer.

conjetura *f* conjecture.
● **hacer conjeturas,** to make conjectures. ‖ **por conjetura,** by guesswork.
conjeturar *t* to conjecture.
conjugable *adj* conjugable.
conjugación *f* conjugation.
conjugado,-a 1 *pp* → **conjugar**. – **2** *adj* (*enlazado*) combined.
conjugar 1 *t* to conjugate. **2** *fig* to join, combine, bring together. – **3 conjugarse,** *p* to conjugate, be conjugated. **4** *fig* to fit together.
▲ *Conjugation model* |7|, *like* **llegar**.
conjunción *f* conjunction.
conjuntado,-a 1 *pp* → **conjuntar**. – **2** *adj* coordinated.
conjuntamente *adv* jointly, together.
conjuntar *t* to coordinate.
conjuntiva *f* conjunctiva.
conjuntivitis *f* conjunctivitis.
▲ *pl* **conjunctivitis**.
conjuntivo,-a *adj* conjunctive.
conjunto,-a 1 *adj* (*compartido*) joint: *misión conjunta,* joint mission. **2** (*combinado*) combined. – **3 conjunto,** *m* (*grupo*) group, collection: *un conjunto de libros,* a collection of books. **4** (*todo*) whole: *el conjunto de los actores no convence,* the actors as a whole are not convincing. **5** (*prenda*) outfit, ensemble; (*jersey y chaqueta*) twinset. **6** MÚS (*clásico*) ensemble; (*pop*) band, group. **7** MAT set. **8** DEP team.
● **de conjunto,** overall. ‖ **en conjunto,** altogether, on the whole. ‖ **en su conjunto,** as a whole.
■ **base conjunta,** joint base. ‖ **conjunto residencial,** housing estate. ‖ **conjunto urbanístico,** housing estate.
conjura *f* plot, conspiracy.
conjuración *f* plot, conspiracy.
conjurado,-a 1 *pp* → **conjurar**. – **2** *adj* conspiring, plotting. – **3** *m,f* conspirator, plotter.
conjurar 1 *t* (*gen*) to exorcise; (*peligro*) to avert, stave off, ward off. **2** *lit* (*rogar*) to beseech. – **3** *i* (*conspirar*) to conspire (**contra,** against). – **4 conjurarse,** *p* to conspire (**contra,** against).
conjuro 1 *m* (*exorcismo*) exorcism. **2** (*encantamiento*) spell, incantation.
conllevar 1 *t* (*implicar*) to involve, entail; (*acarrear*) to imply, bring in its wake. **2** (*enfermedad*) to put up with; (*dolor*) to bear. **3** (*ayudar*) to help.
conmemoración *f* commemoration.
conmemorar *t* to commemorate.
conmemorativo,-a *adj* commemorative.
conmensurable *adj* commensurable.
conmigo *pron* with me, to me: *vino conmigo,* she came with me; *hablaba conmigo,* he was talking to me.
conminación *f* threat, commination.
conminador,-ra *adj* threatening, menacing.
conminar *t* to threaten, menace.
conminativo,-a 1 *adj* threatening, menacing. **2** (*sentencia*) coercive.
conminatorio,-a *adj* → **conminativo,-a**.
conmiseración *f fml* commiseration, pity.
conmoción 1 *f* commotion, shock: *causar conmoción,* to cause a commotion. **2** MED concussion. **3** (*levantamiento*) riot.
■ **conmoción cerebral,** concussion.
conmocionar 1 *t* to shock. **2** MED to concuss. **3** *fig* to trouble, disturb.

conmovedor,-ra *adj* moving, touching.

conmover 1 *t* (*persona*) to move, touch. 2 (*cosa*) to shake. – 3 **conmoverse,** *p* (*persona*) to be moved, be touched. 4 (*cosa*) to be shaken.
  ▲ *Conjugation model* [32], *like mover.*

conmutabilidad *f* commutability.

conmutable *adj* commutable.

conmutación *f* commutation.
  ■ **conmutación de pena,** commutation of sentence.

conmutador *m* switch.

conmutar 1 *t* (*cambiar*) to exchange. 2 JUR to commute. 3 ELEC to commutate.

conmutativo,-a *adj* commutative.

connatural *adj* connatural, inherent.

connaturalizarse *p* to become accustomed (**con,** to).
  ▲ *Conjugation model* [4], *like realizar.*

connivencia *f* connivance, collusion.

connotación *f* connotation.

connotar *t* to connote.

connubio *m lit* matrimony, marriage.

cono *m* cone.

conocedor,-ra 1 *adj* expert. – 2 *m,f* expert (**de,** on), connoisseur (**de,** of): *es un conocedor de mariposas,* he's an expert on butterflies.

conocer 1 *t* (*gen*) to know; (*noticia*) to hear. 2 (*persona*) to meet, get to know: *la conocí ayer,* I met her for the first time yesterday. 3 (*reconocer*) to recognize: *me conoció enseguida,* she recognized me at once. 4 (*país, lugar*) to have been to: *no conozco Inglaterra,* I've never been to England. – 5 *i* (*saber*) to know (**de,** about): *conocer de pinturas,* to know about painting. 6 JUR to hear (**de,** -). – 7 **conocerse,** *p* (*a sí mismo*) to know os.; (*dos o más personas*) to know each other; (*por primera vez*) to meet, get to know: *conócete a ti mismo,* know yourself; *nos conocemos desde hace un año,* we've known each other for a year; *nos conocimos en Berlín,* we first met in Berlín.
  ● **conocer al dedillo / conocer palmo a palmo,** to know like the back of one's hand, know backwards. ‖ **conocer de vista,** to know by sight. ‖ **dar a conocer,** to make known: *la emisora dio a conocer la noticia por la tarde,* the radio station broadcast the news in the afternoon. ‖ **darse a conocer,** to make os. known. ‖ **se conoce que ...,** *fam* apparently: *se conoce que no supo qué decir,* apparently he didn't know what to say.
  ▲ *Conjugation model* [44].

conocido,-a 1 *pp* → **conocer.** – 2 *adj* known: *ese nombre me es conocido,* I've heard that name before. 3 (*famoso*) well-known. – 4 *m,f* acquaintance: *un conocido mío,* an acquaintance of mine.

conocimiento 1 *m* (*saber*) knowledge: *tiene pocos conocimientos de pintura,* she knows little about painting. 2 (*sensatez*) good sense. 3 (*conciencia*) consciousness.
  ● **con conocimiento de causa,** with full knowledge of the facts. ‖ **perder el conocimiento,** to lose consciousness. ‖ **poner algo en conocimiento de algn.,** to make sth. known to sb., inform sb. of sth. ‖ **recobrar el conocimiento,** to regain consciousness, come round. ‖ **tener conocimiento de algo,** to know about sth.
  ▲ In *1, also used in plural with the same meaning.*

conoide *adj* conoid.

conopeo *m* canopy.

conque *conj* so: *ya hemos acabado, conque ya te puedes ir,* we've finished now, so you can go.

conquense 1 *adj* of Cuenca, from Cuenca. – 2 *mf* person from Cuenca, inhabitant of Cuenca.

conquista *f* conquest.
  ● **hacer una conquista,** (*amorosa*) to make a conquest.

conquistador,-ra 1 *adj* conquering. – 2 *m,f* conqueror. – 3 **conquistador,** *m* (*de América*) conquistador. 4 *fam fig* (*galán*) lady-killer.

conquistar 1 *t* (*con las armas*) to conquer. 2 *fig* (*título etc*) to win. 3 *fig* (*ganarse*) to win, win over: *nos conquistó con su amabilidad,* she won us over with her kindness. 4 *fig* (*enamorar*) to win.

consabido,-a 1 *adj fml* (*usual*) usual, familiar. 2 (*ya sabido*) well-known.

consagración 1 *f* REL consecration. 2 (*artista etc*) recognition. 3 (*de una costumbre*) establishment. 4 (*dedicación*) dedication.

consagrado,-a 1 *pp* → **consagrar.** – 2 *adj* REL consecrated. 3 (*reconocido*) recognized, established. 4 (*frase, costumbre*) time-honoured (US time-honored). 5 (*dedicado*) dedicated.

consagrar 1 *t* REL to consecrate. 2 (*palabra, expresión*) to establish. 3 (*dedicar*) to dedicate: *consagró su vida a los pobres,* he dedicated his life to the poor. 4 (*artista etc*) to confirm, establish: *su última novela lo consagró como escritor,* his last novel established him as a writer. – 5 **consagrarse,** *p* (*dedicarse*) to devote os. (**a,** to), dedicate os. (**a,** to). 6 (*hacerse reconocido*) to establish os.

consanguíneo,-a 1 *adj* consanguineous: *hermana consanguínea,* half-sister. – 2 *m,f* blood relation.

consanguinidad *f* consanguinity, blood relationship.

consciencia *f* → **conciencia.**

consciente 1 *adj* conscious, aware. 2 MED conscious. 3 (*responsable*) reliable, responsible.
  ● **estar consciente,** to be conscious. ‖ **ser consciente de algo,** to be aware of sth.: *es muy consciente de sus limitaciones,* he's well aware of his own limitations.

conscientemente *adv* consciously.

consecución 1 *f* (*objetivo*) attainment, achievement; (*deseo*) realization. 2 (*obtención*) obtaining, obtainment.

consecuencia 1 *f* consequence, result. 2 (*coherencia*) consistency.
  ● **a consecuencia de,** as a consequence of, as a result of. ‖ **atenerse a las consecuencias,** to suffer the consequences. ‖ **como consecuencia de,** as a consequence of, as a result of. ‖ **en consecuencia,** consequently, therefore, thus. ‖ **por consecuencia,** consequently, therefore. ‖ **sacar en consecuencia,** to conclude. ‖ **tener buenas consecuencias / traer buenas consecuencias,** to do good. ‖ **tener malas consecuencias / traer malas consecuencias,** to have ill effects.

consecuente 1 *adj* (*siguiente*) consequent. 2 (*resultante*) resulting. 3 (*coherente*) consistent.

consecuentemente 1 *adv* (*coherentemente*) consistently. 2 (*seguidamente*) consequently, therefore.

consecutivamente *adv* consecutively.

consecutivo,-a *adj* consecutive.

conseguir 1 *t* (*cosa*) to obtain, get; (*objetivo*) to attain, achieve. 2 (*lograr*) to manage, succeed in: *conseguí abrirlo,* I managed to open it; *¡lo conseguí!,* I did it!
  ▲ *Conjugation model* [56], *like seguir.*

conseja *f lit* fable, legend.

consejería 1 *f* (*lugar*) Council. 2 (*cargo*) councillor.

consejero,-a 1 *m,f* (*asesor*) adviser, advisor, counsellor. 2 POL councillor. 3 (*de un consejo de administración*) member of a board of directors).
  ● **ser buen,-na consejero,-a,** *fam* to give sound advice.

■ **consejero delegado,** managing director. ‖ **consejero técnico,** technical adviser.

consejo 1 m (*recomendación*) advice: *nos dio un consejo,* she gave us a piece of advice; *procura seguir sus consejos,* try to follow her advice. **2** (*junta*) council, board. ● **celebrar consejo,** to hold council. ‖ **pedir consejo a algn.,** to ask sb. for advice. ■ **consejo de administración,** (*grupo*) board of directors; (*reunión*) board meeting. ‖ **consejo de disciplina,** disciplinary council. ‖ Consejo de Europa, European Council. ‖ **consejo de guerra,** court martial. ‖ **consejo de ministros,** (*grupo*) cabinet; (*reunión*) cabinet meeting.

consenso 1 m (*acuerdo*) consensus. **2** (*consentimiento*) consent, assent.

consensual adj consensual.

consensuar t to reach a consensus on.
▲ *Conjugation model* [11], *like* **actuar**.

consentido,-a 1 pp → **consentir**. – **2** adj (*mimado*) spoiled, spoilt. – **3** m,f (*persona*) spoiled person, spoilt person; (*niño*) spoiled child, spoilt child.

consentimiento m consent.

consentir 1 t (*tolerar*) to allow, permit, tolerate: *no consentiré que se marche así,* I won't allow him to leave that way. **2** (*mimar*) to spoil. **3** (*admitir*) to take, withstand: *el ascensor consiente hasta quinientos kilos,* the lift can take up to five hundred kilos. – **4** i (*admitir*) to consent (**en,** to), agree (**en,** to): *el niño no consiente en comer,* the child refuses to eat. **5** (*ceder*) to weaken. – **6 consentirse,** p (*rajarse*) to crack, break.
▲ *Conjugation model* [35], *like* **hervir**.

conserje 1 m (*portero*) porter; (*de hotel*) hall porter. **2** (*encargado*) caretaker.

conserjería 1 f (*lugar*) porter's lodge, reception. **2** (*oficio*) job of porter.

conserva 1 f (*en lata*) tinned food, canned food. **2** (*dulces*) preserves pl.
▲ *Also used in plural with the same meaning.*

conservación 1 f (*de alimentos*) preservation. **2** (*calor etc*) conservation. **3** (*mantenimiento*) maintenance, upkeep. ■ **instinto de conservación,** instinct of self-preservation.

conservador,-ra 1 adj POL conservative. – **2** m,f POL conservative. **3** (*de museos*) curator.

conservadurismo m conservatism.

conservante m preservative.

conservar 1 t (*alimentos*) to preserve. **2** (*mantener*) to keep in, maintain. **3** (*guardar*) to keep, save: *aún conservo las entradas,* I still have the tickets. **4** (*enlatar*) to tin, can. – **5 conservarse,** p (*tradición etc*) to survive. **6** fig (*mantenerse*) to keep well: *tu padre se conserva muy bien,* your father looks good for his age. ● **conservarse con salud / conservarse en salud,** to keep fit and well.

conservatorio m conservatory, conservatoire, school of music.

conservería 1 f (*industria*) canning industry. **2** (*fábrica*) cannery.

conservero,-a 1 adj canning: *industria conservera,* canning industry. – **2** m,f canner.

considerable adj considerable.

consideración 1 f (*reflexión*) consideration, attention: *este tema merece nuestra consideración,* this subject deserves our attention. **2** (*respeto*) regard. ● **con consideración,** (*respeto*) respectfully; (*cuidado*) carefully. ‖ **de consideración,** important, serious: *es-*taba herido de consideración, he was seriously injured. ‖ **en consideración a,** considering. ‖ **por consideración a,** out of consideration for: *lo hizo por consideración a su hijo,* he did it out of consideration for his son. ‖ **tomar algo en consideración,** to take sth. into account, take sth. into consideration. ‖ **tratar con consideración,** to treat with care. ‖ **tratar sin consideración,** to treat carelessly. ■ **falta de consideración,** lack of consideration.

considerado,-a 1 pp → **considerar**. – **2** adj (*atento*) considerate, thoughtful. **3** (*apreciado*) respected. ● **estar bien considerado,-a,** to be well thought of, be highly regarded. ‖ **estar mal considerado,-a,** to be badly thought of.

considerar 1 t (*reflexionar*) to consider, think over, think about: *debes considerar seriamente mi petición,* you should consider my request seriously. **2** (*tomar en consideración*) to take into account: *considera todas las ventajas,* take all the advantages into account. **3** (*respetar*) to treat with consideration, respect. **4** (*juzgar*) to judge, regard, deem. – **5 considerarse,** p to consider os. ● **considerando que,** considering that, considering.

consigna 1 f (*en estación etc*) left-luggage office, US checkroom. **2** (*señal, lema*) watchword. **3** MIL orders pl, instructions pl.

consignación 1 f (*asignación*) allocation. **2** (*de mercancías*) consignment.

consignar 1 t (*mercancías*) to consign, ship, dispatch. **2** (*destinar - dinero etc*) to allocate; (*- cantidad*) to assign. **3** (*anotar*) to note down, take down.

consignatario,-a 1 m,f (*depositario*) trustee, mortgagee. **2** COM consignee. ■ **consignatario,-a de buques,** shipbroker.

consigo¹ pres indic → **conseguir**.

consigo² 1 pron (3ª *persona singular - hombre*) with him; (*- mujer*) with her; (*- cosa, animal*) with it: *lo trajo consigo,* she brought it with her; *hablaba consigo mismo,* he was talking to himself. **2** (*usted*) with you: *¿lo lleva consigo?,* have you got it with you? **3** (3ª *persona plural*) with them: *las azafatas llevaban las maletas consigo,* the hostesses carried their suitcases with them. **4** (*ustedes*) with you: *¿ustedes llevan toda la documentación consigo?,* have you got all your papers with you? ● **no tenerlas todas consigo,** fam not to rate one's chances highly.

consiguiente adj consequent, resulting, resultant. ● **por consiguiente,** therefore, consequently.

consiguientemente adv therefore, consequently.

consintiente adj consenting, agreeing.

consistencia 1 f (*dureza*) consistency, firmness, solidness. **2** (*coherencia*) coherence, soundness. ● **sin consistencia,** (*sin coherencia*) insubstantial; CULIN too thin, too runny. ‖ **tomar consistencia,** (*tomar forma*) to take form, materialize; CULIN to thicken.

consistente 1 adj (*firme*) firm, solid. **2** fig sound, solid: *un argumento consistente,* a sound argument. **3** CULIN thick. ● **consistente en,** consisting of.

consistir 1 i (*estribar*) to lie (**en,** in), consist (**en,** in): *la solución consiste en crear un nuevo archivo,* the solution lies in creating a new file. **2** (*estar formado*) to consist (**en,** of).

consistorial adj REL consistorial. ■ **casa consistorial,** town hall.

consistorio 1 m (*ayuntamiento*) town council. **2** REL consistory.

consocio,-a *m,f* partner, associate.

consola 1 *f* (*mueble*) console table. 2 (*de ordenador etc*) console.

consolación *f* consolation, comfort.
■ **premio de consolación,** consolation prize.

consolador,-ra 1 *adj* consoling, comforting. – 2 **consolador,** *m* dildo.

consolar 1 *t* to console, comfort. – 2 **consolarse,** *p* to take comfort (**con,** from).
▲ *Conjugation model* |31|, *like contar.*

consólida *f* comfrey.

consolidación *f* consolidation.

consolidar 1 *t* to consolidate. – 2 **consolidarse,** *p* to consolidate.

consolidativo,-a *adj* consolidating, consolidatory.

consomé *m* clear soup, consommé.

consonancia 1 *f* LIT consonance, rhyme. 2 *fig* harmony.
● **en consonancia con,** in harmony with.

consonante 1 *adj* consonant. – 2 *f* consonant.

consonántico,-a *adj* consonantal, consonant.

consonantismo *m* consonantism.

consonar 1 *i* (*rimar*) to rhyme. 2 MÚS to harmonize. 3 *fig* to agree (**con,** with), fit (**con,** -), be in harmony (**con,** -).
▲ *Conjugation model* |31|, *like contar.*

consorcio *m* consortium, partnership, association.

consorte 1 *mf* (*cónyuge*) spouse. – 2 **consortes,** *mpl* JUR accomplices, joint partners.
■ **príncipe consorte,** prince consort.

conspicuo,-a *adj* conspicuous, outstanding.

conspiración *f* conspiracy, plot.

conspirador,-ra *m,f* conspirator, plotter.

conspirar *i* to conspire, plot.

constancia 1 *f* (*perseverancia*) constancy, perseverance. 2 (*evidencia*) evidence, proof: *no había constancia de delito,* there wasn't any proof of crime.
● **dejar constancia de algo,** (*registrar*) to put sth. on record; (*probar*) to prove sth.

constante 1 *adj* (*invariable*) constant. 2 (*persona*) steadfast. – 3 *f* MAT constant.
■ **constantes vitales,** vital signs.

constantemente *adv* constantly: *la gente entraba y salía constantemente,* people were constantly going in and out, people kept going in and out all the time.

Constantinopla *f* Constantinople.

constar 1 *i* (*consistir en*) to consist (**de,** of), be made up (**de,** of), comprise (**de,** -): *el libro consta de cuatro capítulos,* the book has four chapters. 2 (*figurar*) to figure, be included, appear: *su nombre consta en todas partes,* his name appears everywhere. 3 (*ser cierto*) to be a fact: *me consta que ha llegado,* I am certain that she has arrived, I know for a fact that she has arrived. 4 (*quedar claro*) to be clear, to be known: *pero que conste que yo no se lo dije,* but I'd like it to be quite clear that I didn't tell her; *que conste que ...,* and let it be clearly understood that ...
● **hacer constar,** (*señalar*) to point out, state; (*escribir*) to put down, include. ‖ **para que así conste,** *fml* for the record.

constatación *f* verification.

constatar *t* to verify, confirm.

constelación *f* constellation.

constelado,-a 1 *adj* (*estrellado*) starry. 2 *fig* strewn (**de,** with).

consternación *f* consternation, dismay.

consternar 1 *t* to dismay, shatter. – 2 **consternarse,** *p* to be dismayed, be aghast: *se consternó con la enfermedad,* she was dismayed by her illness.

constipación *f* cold.

constipado,-a 1 *pp* → **constiparse.** – 2 **constipado,** *m* MED cold.
● **estar constipado,-a,** to have a cold.

constiparse *p* to catch a cold.

constitución *f* constitution.

constitucionalidad *f* constitutionality.

constitucional 1 *adj* constitutional. – 2 *mf* constitutionalist.

constituir 1 *t* (*formar*) to comprise, make up, constitute: *el sol y los planetas constituyen el sistema solar,* the solar system is made up of the sun and the planets. 2 (*ser*) to be, constitute: *eso constituye un inconveniente,* that's a drawback. 3 (*crear*) to create, set up, establish: *Carlos V constituyó un imperio,* Charles V built an empire. – 4 **constituirse,** *p* to set os. up as, become: *el general se constituyó en jefe del Estado,* the general became Head of State.
▲ *Conjugation model* |62|, *like huir.*

constitutivo,-a *adj* constituent, component.

constituyente 1 *adj* constituent. – 2 *mf* (*componente*) constituent.

constreñimiento 1 *m* (*obligación*) constraint, imposition. 2 (*opresión*) restriction.

constreñir 1 *t* (*forzar*) to constrain, compel, force. 2 (*limitar*) to limit, restrict. 3 MED (*cerrar*) to constrict.
▲ *Conjugation model* |36|, *like ceñir.*

constricción *f* constriction.

constrictor 1 *adj* constricting, constrictive. – 2 **constrictor,** *m* constrictor.

construcción 1 *f* construction: *la industria de la construcción,* the construction industry. 2 (*edificio*) building.
● **en construcción / en vías de construcción,** under construction.

constructivo,-a *adj* constructive.

constructor,-ra 1 *adj* construction, building. – 2 *m,f* (*de edificios*) builder; (*de barcos*) shipbuilder.
■ **empresa constructora,** construction company, builders *pl.*

construir *t* to construct, build.
▲ *Conjugation model* |62|, *like huir.*

consubstanciación *f* consubstantiation.

consubstancial *adj* → **consustantial.**

consuegro,-a *m,f* (*padre - del yerno*) son-in-law's father; (*- de la nuera*) daughter-in-law's father; (*madre - del yerno*) son-in-law's mother; (*- de la nuera*) daughter-in-law's mother.

consuelo *m* consolation, comfort.
● **sin consuelo,** inconsolably.

consuetudinario,-a *adj* habitual, customary.

cónsul *mf* consul.

consulado 1 *m* (*oficina*) consulate. 2 (*cargo*) consulship.

consular *adj* consular.

consulta 1 *f* (*acción*) consultation. 2 (*consejo*) advice, opinion: *¿te puedo hace una consulta?,* can I ask you something? 3 MED surgery, US doctor's office; (*consultorio*) consulting room: *horas de consulta,* surgery hours, US office hours.
● **pasar consulta,** to see patients, hold surgery.
■ **obra de consulta,** reference book.

consultar 1 *t* (*pedir opinión*) to consult (**con,** with/-), seek advice (**con,** from): *consulté con mis padres,* I consulted with my parents. 2 (*buscar en un libro*) to look up: *con-*

sulté la palabra en el diccionario, I looked up the word in the dictionary. ● consultar con un abogado, to consult a lawyer, take legal advice. ‖ consultar con un médico, to consult a doctor, take medical advice. ‖ consultarlo con la almohada, *fig* to sleep on it.

consultivo,-a *adj* consultative, advisory.

consultor,-ra 1 *adj* consulting. – 2 *m,f* consultant.

consultoría *f* (*servicio*) consultancy; (*empresa*) consultancy firm.

consultorio 1 *m* MED (*consulta*) surgery, US doctor's office; (*habitación*) consulting room. 2 (*ambulatorio*) outpatients' (department). 3 (*de información*) office; (*consultoría*) consultancy. 4 (*en periódicos*) problem page, advice column, agony column; (*en radio*) phone-in.

consumación *f* consummation, completion; (*de un crimen*) perpetration.

consumado,-a 1 *pp* → **consumar.** – 2 *adj* (*perfecto*) consummate, accomplished. 3 *fam* complete, perfect: *un tonto consumado,* a complete and utter fool.

consumar 1 *t* (*terminar*) to complete, carry out. 2 (*crimen*) to commit. 3 (*matrimonio*) to consummate.

consumición 1 *f* consumption. 2 (*bebida*) drink.
■ consumición mínima, basic charge.

consumido,-a 1 *pp* → **consumir.** – 2 *adj fig* (*muy flaco*) thin, emaciated. 3 *fig* (*afligido*) consumed.
● estar consumido,-a por algo, *fig* to be consumed with sth., be eaten up with sth.

consumidor,-ra 1 *adj* consuming. – 2 *m,f* consumer.

consumir 1 *t* (*gastar, usar*) to consume, use. 2 (*destruir*) to destroy, consume: *el fuego consume la madera,* fire destroys wood. 3 (*tomar*) to take, consume: *en España se consume más aceite de oliva que en otros países de Europa,* more olive oil is consumed in Spain than in other European countries; *no consumimos alcohol,* we don't drink alcohol. 4 *fig* (*carcomer, afligir*) to consume; (*poner nervioso*) to get on one's nerves, infuriate: *la envidia lo consumía,* he was consumed with envy. – 5 consumirse, *p* (*extinguirse*) to burn out. 6 (*secarse*) to boil away. 7 (*destruirse*) to be destroyed. 8 *fig* (*afligirse*) to waste away. 9 *fig* (*carcomerse*) to be consumed, be devoured.

consumismo *m* consumerism.

consumista 1 *adj* consumerist. – 2 *mf* consumerist.

consumo *m* consumption.
■ artículos de consumo, staple commodities.

consunción *f* consumption.

consuno de consuno, *adv* together, with one accord.

consustancial *adj* innate (**a**, in), inherent (**a**, in).
● ser consustancial con, to be inseparable from.

contabilidad 1 *f* (*profesión*) accountancy; (*carrera*) accounting. 2 (*de empresa etc*) accounting, book-keeping.
● llevar la contabilidad, to keep the books.

contabilizar *t* to enter in the books.
▲ *Conjugation model* [4], *like realizar.*

contable 1 *adj* countable. – 2 *mf* book-keeper, accountant.

contactar *t* to contact, get in touch (**con**, with).

contacto 1 *m* contact. 2 AUTO ignition.
● entrar en contacto con / ponerse en contact con, to get in touch with, get in contact with. ‖ establecer contacto con, to make contact with, get in contact with. ‖ mantenerse en contacto con, to keep in touch with, keep in contact with. ‖ perder el contacto, to lose touch.
■ contacto sexual, sexual contact.

contactología *f* contact-lens manufacturing.

contactólogo,-a *m,f* contact-lens specialist.

contadero,-a *adj* countable.

contado,-a 1 *pp* → **contar.** – 2 *adj* few: *son contados los alumnos que aprobaron,* the pupils who passed are few and far between.
● en contadas ocasiones, seldom, rarely. ‖ tiene los días contados, *fig* his days are numbered.

contador,-ra 1 *adj* counting. – 2 *m,f* (*contable*) accountant, book-keeper. – 3 contador, *m* meter: *contador de gas,* gas meter.

contaduría 1 *f* (*oficio*) accountancy. 2 (*oficina*) accountant's office.

contagiar 1 *t* (*enfermedad*) to transmit, pass on. 2 *fig* to infect, pass on, give: *me has contagiado tu resfriado,* you've given me your cold; *me contagió la risa,* her laugh was infectious. – 3 contagiarse, *p* (*enfermar*) to get infected: *se contagió de malaria,* he caught malaria. 4 (*transmitirse*) to be contagious: *esta enfermedad no se contagia,* this disease is not contagious.
▲ *Conjugation model* [17], *like descafeinar.*

contagio 1 *m* MED contagion, infection. 2 *fig* (*perversión*) perversion, corruption. 3 *fig* (*transmisión*) contagion.

contagioso,-a *adj* infectious, contagious: *enfermedad contagiosa,* infectious disease, contagious disease; *risa contagiosa,* infectious laugh.

contáiner *m* container.
▲ *pl* contáiners.

contaminación *f* contamination; (*de agua, aire*) pollution.

contaminador,-ra *adj* contaminating; (*de agua, aire*) polluting.

contaminante 1 *adj* polluting. – 2 *m* polluting agent.

contaminar 1 *t* to contaminate; (*agua, aire*) to pollute. 2 *fig* to contaminate, corrupt. – 3 contaminarse, *p* to become contaminated; (*agua, aire*) to become polluted. 4 *fig* to be infected, be corrupted.

contante *adj* (*dinero*) cash: *dinero contante y sonante,* ready cash, hard cash.

contar 1 *t* (*calcular*) to count: *cuenta los días,* count the days. 2 (*considerar*) to count, consider: *la cuenta entre sus amigas,* he considers her one of his friends. 3 (*incluir*) to count, include: *éramos veinte contando a los niños,* there were twenty of us including the children. 4 (*tener*) to have: *cuenta cuarenta años,* she's forty. 5 (*explicar*) to tell: *me contó un cuento,* she told me a story. – 6 *i* to count: *los niños saben contar,* the children know how to count. 7 contar con, (*confiar en*) to rely on, count on: *cuento contigo,* I'm relying on you; *contamos con tu ayuda,* we're relying on your help. 8 (*incluir*) to count in: *cuenta conmigo para la fiesta,* you can count me in for the party. 9 (*tener presente*) to take into account. 10 (*estar provisto de*) to have, be provided with: *el coche cuenta con aire acondicionado,* the car is equipped with air-conditioning. – 11 contarse, *p* (*incluirse*) to be included.
● a contar desde, starting from. ‖ contar con los dedos, to count on one's fingers. ‖ contarse que, to be said (that): *se cuenta que huyó,* it is said he ran away. ‖ ¡cuéntamelo a mí!, *fam* you're telling me!, tell me about it! ‖ ¡cuéntaselo a tu abuela!, *fam* come off it!, pull the other one! ‖ ¡habría mucho que contar!, it's a long story! ‖ ¿qué cuentas? / ¿qué te cuentas?, *fam* how's it going?, how's things?
▲ *Conjugation model* [31].

contemplación 1 *f* (*acción*) contemplation. – 2 contemplaciones, *fpl* (*miramientos*) indulgence *sing.*

● **no andarse con contemplaciones,** *fam* to make no bones about it, come straight to the point.
contemplar 1 *t* (*mirar*) to contemplate, look at. **2** (*pensar*) to contemplate, consider. **3** (*tener en cuenta*) to provide for. **4** (*tratar bien*) to spoil. **– 5** *i* to contemplate.
contemplativo,-a *adj* contemplative.
contemporaneidad *f* contemporaneousness, contemporaneity.
contemporáneo,-a 1 *adj* contemporary. **– 2** *m,f* contemporary.
contemporizador,-ra 1 *adj* compliant, compromising. **– 2** *m,f* conformist.
contemporizar *i* to compromise, be compliant.
▲ *Conjugation model* |4|, *like* **realizar.**
contención 1 *f* (*moderación*) moderation, control. **2** JUR lawsuit.
■ **muro de contención,** retaining wall.
contencioso,-a 1 *adj* contentious. **2** JUR litigious. **– 3** contencioso, *m* legal action, case.
■ **asunto contencioso,** judicial matter.
contendedor,-ra *m,f* contender, antagonist.
contender 1 *i* (*pelear*) to contend, fight. **2** (*competir*) to contest.
▲ *Conjugation model* |28|, *like* **entender.**
contendiente 1 *adj* contending, competing. **– 2** *mf* contender, contestant.
contenedor,-ra 1 *adj* containing. **– 2 contenedor,** *m* container.
■ **contenedor de basura,** rubbish skip.
contener 1 *t* (*incluir*) to contain, hold: *este paquete contiene treinta galletas,* this packet contains thirty biscuits. **2** (*detener*) to hold back, restrain: *la presa contiene el cauce del río,* the dam holds back the flow of the river. **3** (*reprimir*) to restrain, hold back, contain; (*respiración*) to hold: *contuvo su alegría,* he held back his joy; *contuve mis lágrimas,* I held back the tears. **– 4 contenerse,** *p* to control os., contain os., keep a hold on os.
▲ *Conjugation model* |87|, *like* **tener.**
contenido,-a 1 *pp* → **contener.** **– 2** *adj* (*moderado*) moderate, reserved. **– 3 contenido,** *m* content, contents *pl.*
contentadizo,-a *adj* easy to please.
contentar 1 *t* (*satisfacer*) to please, content. **– 2 contentarse,** *p* (*conformarse*) to make do (**con,** with), be satisfied (**con,** with).
● **ser de buen contentar,** *fam* to be easy to please. ‖ **ser de mal contentar,** *fam* to be hard to please.
contento,-a 1 *adj* happy, pleased: *estoy contento de conocerle,* I'm pleased to meet you. **– 2 contento,** *m* happiness, joy, contentment.
● **darse por contento,-a,** to consider os. lucky. ‖ **estar más contento,-a que unas Pascuas,** *fam* to be as happy as a lark. ‖ **sentir gran contento,** to feel great joy.
conteo *m* calculation.
contera 1 *f* (*de bastón etc*) tip; (*de espada*) chape. **2** *fig* (*remate*) end, finish.
● **echar la contera,** *fig* to finish, end. ‖ **por contera,** *fig* to cap it all.
contertulio,-a *m,f* fellow guest.
contestable *adj* debatable.
contestación 1 *f* (*respuesta*) answer, reply. **2** (*oposición*) opposition. **3** JUR plea.
● **dar contestación a,** to answer. ‖ **en contestación a su carta ...,** (*en correspondencia*) in reply to your letter ...

■ **mala contestación,** (*errónea*) wrong answer; (*con mala educación*) retort.
contestador *m* answering machine.
■ **contestador automático,** answering machine.
contestar 1 *t* (*responder*) to answer: *contestó bien,* she gave the right answer. **2** JUR to confirm. **– 3** *i* (*responder*) to answer; (*replicar*) to answer back: *¡no contestes!,* don't answer back! **4** (*oponer*) to contest, question.
contestatario,-a 1 *adj* argumentative; *fam* bolshie. **– 2** *m,f* attacker, dissenter.
contexto 1 *m* context. **2** *fig* environment.
contextualizar *t* to put into context, contextualize.
▲ *Conjugation model* |4|, *like* **realizar.**
contextuar *t* to prove with texts.
▲ *Conjugation model* |1|, *like* **sacar.**
contextura 1 *f* (*de materiales*) contexture. **2** (*de persona*) build.
contienda *f* contest, dispute, struggle.
contigo *pron* with you: *iré contigo,* I'll go with you.
contigüidad *f* contiguity, closeness, nearness.
contiguo,-a *adj* contiguous (**a,** to), adjoining, adjacent (**a,** to): *la puerta contigua,* the adjoining door; *la casa contigua,* the house next door.
continencia *f* continence.
continental *adj* continental.
continente 1 *m* GEOG continent. **2** (*recipiente*) container. **3** (*compostura*) countenance.
contingencia 1 *f* (*probabilidad*) contingency, eventuality. **2** (*riesgo*) risk, hazard.
contingente 1 *adj* (*posible*) contingent,. **– 2** *m* MIL contingent. **3** (*cuota*) quota, share.
continuación *f* continuation, follow-up.
● **a continuación,** next. ‖ **tener continuación,** to be continued.
continuadamente *adv* continuously.
continuador,-ra 1 *adj* continuing. **– 2** *m,f* continuator.
continuamente *adv* continuously.
continuar 1 *t* (*proseguir*) to continue, carry on: *continuó su camino,* she continued on her way, *continuaron su viaje,* the continued their journey. **– 2** *i* (*permanecer, durar*) to continue, go on: *el espectáculo continúa,* the show continues; *continúa lloviendo,* it's still raining; *Pablo continúa en Praga,* Pablo is still in Prague. **– 3 continuarse,** *p* (*extenderse*) to extend, run.
● **"continuará",** (*capítulos, episodios, etc*) "to be continued".
▲ *Conjugation model* |11|, *like* **actuar.**
continuativo,-a *adj* continuative.
continuidad *f* continuity.
continuo,-a 1 *adj* (*seguido*) continuous. **2** (*continuado*) continual, constant. **– 3 continuo,** *m* (*todo*) continuum. **4** (*de gente*) flow.
■ **corriente continua,** direct current; (*en dibujo*) unbroken line. ‖ **movimiento continuo,** perpetual motion.
contonearse *p* (*mujer*) to swing one's hips, wiggle; (*hombre*) to swagger.
contoneo *m* (*de mujer*) swinging of the hips, wiggle; (*de hombre*) swaggering, swagger.
contornar 1 *t* (*dar vueltas*) to skirt. **2** (*hacer los perfiles*) to trace the outline of.
contornear *t* → **contornar.**
contorno 1 *m* (*perfil*) outline; (*perímetro*) perimeter. **2** (*canto*) rim, edge. **3** (*afueras*) surroundings *pl,* environment.
■ **contorno de pecho/cintura,** bust/waist measurement.

▲ In *2, usually used in plural.*
contorsión *f* contortion.
contorsionarse *p* to contort os., twist os.
contorsionista *mf* contortionist.
contra 1 *prep* against: *juegan contra nosotros,* they're playing against us; *lucharon contra los cartagineses,* they fought against the Carthaginians; *tres contra uno,* three against one. **2** for: *un producto contra las picaduras de mosquitos,* a product for mosquito bites. **3** *(enfrente)* facing, opposite. **– 4** *f fam* drawback, snag. **– 5** *interj* gosh!, good grief! **– 6** la Contra, *f (grupo contrarevolucionario)* the Contras *pl.*
● en contra, against: *estaba en contra,* he was against it; *los tienes en contra de ti,* they're against you. ‖ en contra de lo que..., contrary to...: *en contra de lo que decían,* contrary to what they said. ‖ llevar la contra a algn., to contradict sb., disagree with sb. ‖ opinar en contra, to disagree.
contraalmirante *m* rear admiral.
contraatacar *t* to counterattack.
▲ *Conjugation model* |1|, *like sacar.*
contraataque *m* counterattack.
contrabajo 1 *m (instrumento)* double bass. **2** *(voz)* low bass.
contrabalancear *t* to counterbalance.
contrabandista *mf* smuggler; *(de armas)* gun runner.
contrabando 1 *m* smuggling, contraband; *(de armas)* gunrunning. **2** *(mercancías)* smuggled goods *pl,* contraband.
● de contrabando, contraband: *tabaco de contrabando,* contraband tobacco. ‖ pasar algo de contrabando, to smuggle sth. in.
contrabarrera *f* second row of seats.
contracción *f* contraction.
contracepción *f* contraception.
contraceptivo,-a 1 *adj* contraceptive. **– 2** contraceptivo, *m* contraceptive.
contrachapado *m* plywood.
contracorriente *f* crosscurrent.
● ir contracorriente, to go against the tide.
contráctil *adj* contractile.
contractilidad *f* contractility.
contractual *adj* contractual.
contractura *f* contracture.
contracultura *f* counterculture.
contradanza *f* contredanse, contradance.
contradecir 1 *t (decir lo contrario)* to contradict: *no me contradigas,* don't contradict me. **2** *(obrar en contradicción)* to be inconsistent with, be at variance with: *su comportamiento contradice lo que dijo,* his behaviour is inconsistent with what he said. **– 3** contradecirse, *p (decir lo contrario)* to contradict os.: *supimos que mentía porque se contradijo,* we knew he was lying because he contradicted himself. **4** *(decir contradicciones)* to be inconsistent.
▲ *Conjugation model* |69|, *like decir, pp* contradicho,-a.
contradicción *f* contradiction.
● estar en contradicción con, to be inconsistent with, contradictory to.
■ espíritu de la contradicción, contrariness.
contradicho,-a *pp →* contradecir.
contradictorio,-a *adj* contradictory.
contraer 1 *t (encoger)* to contract: *contraer un músculo,* to contract a muscle. **2** *(enfermedad)* to catch. **3** *(deuda)* to contract, incur; *(hábito)* to pick up. **4** LING to contract. **– 5** contraerse, *p (encogerse)* to contract.

● contraer matrimonio con algn., to marry sb. ‖ contraer obligaciones, to enter into obligations.
▲ *Conjugation model* |88|, *like traer.*
contraespionaje *m* counterespionage.
contrafaz *f* reverse.
contrafuego *m* backfire.
contrafuerte 1 *m (de zapato)* stiffener. **2** *(de montaña)* spur. **3** ARQ buttress.
contragolpe 1 *m* MED *(efecto)* counterstroke. **2** *(golpe)* counterblow. **3** *(contraataque)* counterattack.
contrahacer 1 *t (falsificar)* to fake; *(moneda)* to counterfeit. **2** *(imitar)* to imitate.
▲ *Conjugation model* |72|, *like haber, pp* contrahecho,-a.
contrahecho,-a 1 *pp →* contrahacer. **– 2** *adj* deformed, hunchbacked. **– 3** *m,f* deformed person, hunchback.
contrahechura *f (falsificación)* fake; *(de moneda)* counterfeit.
contrahuella *f* riser.
contraigo *pres indic →* contraer.
contraindicación *f* contraindication, counterindication.
● "contraindicaciones, ninguna", MED "may be used safely by anyone".
contraindicar *t* to contraindicate.
contraje *pt indef →* contraer.
contralmirante *m* rear admiral.
contralto *mf* contralto.
contraluz *mf* view against the light, back light.
● a contraluz, against the light.
contramaestre 1 *m (capataz)* foreman. **2** MAR boatswain.
contramano a contramano, *loc adv* the wrong way: *circulaba a contramano,* he was driving on the wrong side of the road.
contraofensiva *f* counteroffensive.
contraorden *f* countermand.
contrapartida 1 *f* COM balancing entry. **2** *fig* compensation.
contrapelo a contrapelo, *loc adv (contra la inclinación del pelo)* the wrong way; *fig* unwillingly, reluctantly.
contrapesar 1 *t* to counterbalance, counterpoise. **2** *fig* to balance, offset.
contrapeso 1 *m* counterweight. **2** *fig* counterbalance.
contraponer 1 *t (oponer)* to set in opposition (a, to). **2** *fig (contrastar)* to contrast (a, with). **– 3** contraponerse, *p (oponerse)* to be opposed.
▲ *Conjugation model* |78|, *like poner, pp* contrapuesto,-a.
contraportada *f* back page.
contraposición 1 *f (contraste)* contrast. **2** *(oposición)* conflict, clash: *contraposición de intereses,* conflict of interests.
● estar en contraposición, to clash.
contraprestación *f* contractual obligation.
contraproducente *adj* counterproductive.
contraproposición *f* counterproposal.
contrapropuesta *f* counterproposal.
contrapuerta *f* storm door, double door.
contrapuesto,-a 1 *pp →* contraponer. **– 2** *adj* opposed.
contrapunto *m* counterpoint.
contrariado,-a 1 *pp →* contrariar. **– 2** *adj (disgustado)* upset, cross.
contrariamente *adv* contrary (a, to).
contrariar 1 *i (oponerse)* to oppose, go against. **2** *(disgustar)* to annoy, upset: *no quería contrariarte,* I didn't want to upset you. **3** *(dificultar)* to obstruct, hinder.

▲ *Conjugation model* |13|, *like desviar.*
contrariedad I *f* (*oposición*) opposition. **2** (*disgusto*) annoyance. **3** (*dificultad*) setback, obstacle.
contrario,-a I *adj* (*opuesto*) contrary, opposite: *iba en sentido contrario,* he was going in the opposite direction; *puntos de vista contrarios,* contrary points of view. **2** (*perjudicial*) harmful (**a**, to), bad (**a**, for): *el fumar es contrario a la salud,* smoking is bad for your health. – **3** *m,f* opponent, adversary, rival.
● **al contrario,** on the contrary. ‖ **de lo contrario,** otherwise. ‖ **en dirección contraria,** in the wrong direction. ‖ **llevar la contraria a algn.,** to oppose sb. ‖ **por el contrario,** on the contrary. ‖ **todo lo contrario,** quite the opposite.
■ **la parte contraria,** JUR the opponent; DEP the opposing team.
contrarreforma *f* Counter Reformation.
contrarreloj I *adj* against the clock. – **2** *f* race against the clock.
■ (**etapa**) **contrarreloj,** time trial.
contrarrestar I *t* (*hacer frente*) to resist, oppose. **2** (*neutralizar*) counteract, neutralize. **3** (*pelota*) to return.
contrarrevolucionario,-a I *adj* counter-revolutionary. – **2** *m,f* counter-revolutionary.
contrarrevolución *f* counter-revolution.
contrasentido I *m* (*contradicción*) contradiction. **2** (*disparate*) piece of nonsense: *eso es un contrasentido,* that's nonsense. **3** (*mala interpretación*) misinterpretation.
contraseña I *f* (*seña*) secret sign; (*palabra*) password. **2** MIL password, watchword, countersign.
■ **contraseña de salida,** (*en teatros etc*) pass.
contrastar I *t* (*hacer frente*) to resist, repel: *contrastar al enemigo,* to resist the enemy. **2** (*comprobar*) to check, verify. **3** (*pesos y medidas*) to check. **4** (*oro o plata*) to hallmark. – **5** *i* (*oponerse*) to contrast (**con**, with): *la vegetación de los jardines contrasta con la sequedad del campo,* the vegetation of the gardens contrasts with the dryness of the countryside.
contraste I *m* (*oposición*) contrast. **2** (*pesos y medidas*) verification. **3** (*oro y plata*) hallmark.
contrata *f* contract.
contratación I *f* (*contrato - obrero*) hiring; (- *empleado*) engagement. **2** (*pedido*) total orders *pl,* volume of business.
contratar I *t* (*servicio etc*) to sign a contract for. **2** (*obrero*) to hire; (*empleado*) to engage; (*deportista*) to sign up. **3** (*un arriendo*) to take on.
contraterrorista *adj* anti-terrorist.
contratiempo *m* (*contrariedad*) setback, hitch; (*accidente*) mishap.
● **a contratiempo,** MÚS on the offbeat.
contratista *mf* contractor.
■ **contratista de obras,** building contractor.
contrato *m* contract.
■ **contrato de alquiler / contrato de arrendamiento,** lease, leasing agreement. ‖ **contrato de compraventa,** contract of sale. ‖ **contrato de trabajo,** work contract. ‖ **contrato temporal,** temporary contract.
contravención *f* contravention, infringement, violation.
contravenir *t* to contravene, infringe, violate: *contravenir las leyes,* to infringe the law.
▲ *Conjugation model* |90|, *like venir.*
contraventana *f* shutter.
contrayente I *adj* contracting. – **2** *mf* (*en matrimonio*) contracting party.

contrecho,-a *adj* crippled.
contribución I *f* contribution. **2** (*impuesto*) tax.
● **poner a contribución,** to use, draw on.
■ **contribución territorial,** land tax. ‖ **contribución urbana,** rates *pl.*
contribuir I *t* (*pagar*) to pay: *los propietarios contribuyen el 20%,* the owners pay 20%. – **2** *i* (*aportar*) to contribute: *el rey contribuyó con cuantiosas cantidades,* the king contributed a considerable amount; *contribuir a los gastos,* to contribute to the expenses; *varios factores contribuyen al crecimiento del paro,* several factors contribute to the rise in unemployment. **3** (*pagar impuestos*) to pay taxes.
▲ *Conjugation model* |62|, *like huir.*
contributivo,-a *adj* contributive.
contribuyente I *adj* taxpaying. – **2** *mf* taxpayer.
contrición *f* contrition.
● **hacer un acto de contrición,** to repent.
■ **acto de contrición,** act of contrition.
contrincante *m* opponent, rival.
contristar I *t* to make sad. – **2 contristarse,** *p* to become sad.
contrito,-a *adj* contrite, repentant.
control I *m* (*gen*) control. **2** (*comprobación*) check. **3** (*sitio*) checkpoint.
● **bajo el control de,** under the supervision of. ‖ **estar bajo control,** to be under control. ‖ **estar fuera de control,** to be out of control. ‖ **llevar el control,** to be in control. ‖ **perder el control,** to lose control.
■ **control a distancia,** remote control. ‖ **control de calidad,** quality control. ‖ **control de natalidad,** birth control. ‖ **control de pasaportes,** passport control: *pasaron por el control de pasaportes,* they went through passport control. ‖ **control de sí mismo,** self-control. ‖ **control policial,** road-block. ‖ **torre de control,** control tower.
controlador,-ra I *adj* control. – **2** *m,f* (*aéreo*) air-traffic controller.
controlar I *t* (*gen*) to control. **2** (*comprobar*) to check. – **3 controlarse,** *p* (*moderarse*) to control os.
controversia *f* controversy, argument.
controvertido,-a I *pp* → **controvertir.** – **2** *adj* controversial.
controvertir I *t* to dispute, argue about. – *i* to argue.
contubernio I *m* (*cohabitación*) cohabitation. **2** *fig* (*confabulación*) conspiracy, collusion.
contumacia I *f* (*obstinación*) obstinacy; (*rebeldía*) insubordination. **2** JUR contumacy.
contumaz I *adj* (*obstinado*) obstinate, stubborn. **2** (*rebelde*) insubordinate. **3** JUR contumacious.
contundencia I *f* (*de arma*) contusive properties *pl.* **2** *fig* (*convicción*) weight: *la contundencia de un argumento,* the weight of an argument.
contundente I *adj* (*arma*) blunt. **2** *fig* (*categórico*) convincing, overwhelming, weighty: *un "no" contundente,* a firm "no".
contundir *t* to bruise, contuse.
conturbación *f* anxiety, dismay, perturbation.
conturbado,-a I *pp* → **conturbar.** – **2** *adj* anxious, dismayed, perturbed.
conturbar I *t* to trouble, dismay, perturb. – **2 conturbarse,** *p* to be troubled, be dismayed, become perturbed.
contusión *f* contusion, bruise.
contusionar *t* to contuse, bruise.
conurbación *f* conurbation.

convalecencia *f* convalescence.
convalecer *i* to convalesce (**de,** after), recover (**de,** from).
▲ *Conjugation model* |43|, *like* **agradecer.**
convaleciente 1 *adj* convalescent. – 2 *mf* convalescent.
convalidación 1 *f* EDUC validation. 2 (*documentos*) ratification, authentication.
convalidar 1 *t* EDUC to validate. 2 (*documentos*) to ratify, authenticate.
convección *f* convection.
convecino,-a 1 *adj* neighbouring (US neighboring). – 2 *m,f* neighbour (US neighbor).
convector *m* convector.
convencer 1 *t* (*de algo*) to convince; (*para hacer algo*) to persuade: *lo convencieron de su error,* they convinced him of his mistake; *me han convencido para ir a un restaurante japonés,* they've persuaded me to go to a Japanese restaurant. 2 *fam* (*en frases negativas*) to like, be keen on: *la película no me convenció,* I didn't like the film very much; *ese color no me acaba de convencer,* I'm not sure about that colour. – 3 *i* to be convincing: *el equipo local no convenció con su actuación,* the local team's performance was not very convincing. – 4 **convencerse,** *p* to become convinced, be convinced, convince os.: *se convenció de que era guapo,* he convinced himself that he was good-looking.
▲ *Conjugation model* |2|, *like* **mecer.**
convencimiento *m* conviction.
● **llegar al convencimiento de que ...,** to be convinced that ...
convención 1 *f* (*congreso*) convention, congress. 2 (*acuerdo*) convention, treaty. 3 (*costumbre*) convention.
convencional *adj* conventional.
convencionalismo *m* conventionalism, conventionality.
convenible 1 *adj* (*conveniente*) suitable, fitting. 2 (*precio*) fair, reasonable. 3 (*persona*) accommodating.
convenido,-a 1 *pp* → **convenir.** – 2 *adj* agreed, set, arranged.
conveniencia 1 *f* (*utilidad*) usefulness: *ya veo la conveniencia de tener aire acondicionado,* I can see the usefulness of having air-conditioning. 2 (*oportunidad*) suitability, advisability: *la conveniencia de estas medidas,* the advisability of these measures. 3 (*provecho*) interest, benefit: *sólo se preocupa de su propia conveniencia,* he only looks out for his own interests. 4 (*convenio*) agreement.
● **faltar a las conveniencias,** not to keep social conventions.
■ **conveniencias sociales,** social conventions. ‖ **matrimonio de conveniencia,** marriage of convenience.
conveniente 1 *adj* (*útil*) useful. 2 (*oportuno*) suitable, convenient. 3 (*ventajoso*) advantageous. 4 (*aconsejable*) advisable: *es conveniente llegar pronto,* it's advisable to arrive early. 5 (*precio*) good, fair.
● **creer conveniente,** to think advisable, be better: *creo conveniente decirle la verdad,* I think it's better to tell him the truth. ‖ **en el momento conveniente,** at the right time.
convenio *m* agreement, treaty.
■ **convenio colectivo / convenio laboral,** collective agreement.
convenir 1 *t* (*acordar*) to agree, arrange: *convenimos el precio,* we agreed the price. – 2 *i* (*acordar*) to agree: *convinimos en la fecha,* we agreed on the date; *convinieron en que se repartirían el trabajo,* they agreed on sharing

the work; *"sueldo a convenir",* "salary negotiable". **3** (*ser oportuno o conveniente*) to be good for: *no te conviene hacer esfuerzos,* it's not good for you to exert yourself; *nos conviene llevarnos bien,* it's in our interest to get on well with each other. **4** (*ser adecuado o propio*) to suit: *ese chico no te conviene,* that boy is not right for you; *a un cura esas palabras no convienen,* a priest shouldn't use that sort of language.
● **conviene + inf,** it is as well to + *inf: conviene mencionar que ...,* it's as well to mention that ... ‖ **conviene que + subj,** it is better that, it is advisable + *inf: conviene que te vayas,* it is better that you go.
▲ *Conjugation model* |90|, *like* **venir.**
convento *m* (*de monjas*) convent; (*de monjes*) monastery.
conventual *adj* conventual.
convergencia *f* convergence.
convergente *adj* convergent, converging, concurring.
converger *i* to converge, come together.
▲ *Conjugation model* |5|, *like* **proteger.**
convergir *i* to converge, come together.
▲ *Conjugation model* |6|, *like* **dirigir.**
conversación *f* conversation, talk.
● **dar conversación a algn.,** to talk to sb., keep sb. chatting. ‖ **dejar caer algo en la conversación,** *fig* to bring sth. up in conversation. ‖ **entablar conversación con algn.,** to get into conversation with sb., engage sb. in conversation. ‖ **tener mucha conversación,** to have plenty to say. ‖ **tener poca conversación,** not to be very talkative. ‖ **trabar conversación con algn.,** to strike up a conversation with sb., get into conversation with sb.
conversador,-ra 1 *adj* talkative. – 2 *m,f* conversationalist, talker.
conversar *i* to converse (**con,** with), talk (**con,** to).
conversión *f* conversion.
converso,-a 1 *adj* converted. – 2 *m,f* convert.
convertibilidad *f* convertibility.
convertible *adj* convertible.
convertidor *m* converter.
convertir 1 *t* (*transformar*) to change, turn, transform, convert: *el calor convierte el agua en vapor,* heat transforms water into steam. 2 (*valores, monedas*) to change, exchange: *convirtió sus pesetas en libras,* he changed his pesetas into pounds. 3 REL to convert: *la convirtió al cristianismo,* he converted her to Christianity. – 4 **convertirse,** *p* (*transformarse*) to turn (**en,** into), change (**en,** into). 5 (*volverse*) to become (**en,** -), turn (**en,** into): *se convirtió en una joven preciosa,* she turned into a beautiful young woman; *su sueño se convirtió en realidad,* his dream came true. 6 REL to be converted (**a,** to).
▲ *Conjugation model* |29|, *like* **discernir.**
convexidad *f* convexity.
convexo,-a *adj* convex.
convicción *f* conviction: *tengo la convicción de que vendrán,* I firmly believe that they'll come.
convicto,-a *adj* guilty, convicted.
convidado,-a 1 *pp* → **convidar.** – 2 *adj* invited. – 3 *m,f* guest.
● **como un convidado de piedra,** *fig* silent as a grave.
convidar 1 *t* (*invitar*) to invite: *me convidó a una fiesta,* he invited me to a party; *nos ha convidado a comer,* she's invited us to lunch. 2 (*ofrecer*) to offer: *nos convidó a pastel,* he offered us some cake. 3 *fig* (*incitar, mover, animar*) to prompt, inspire, move: *este tiempo convida*

a pasear, this weather makes you want to go for a walk. – **4 convidarse,** *p fam* (*invitarse*) to invite os.

convincente *adj* convincing.

convite 1 *m* (*invitación*) invitation. **2** (*comida*) meal; (*fiesta*) party.

convivencia 1 *f* living together. **2** *fig* coexistence.

convivir 1 *i* to live together. **2** *fig* to coexist.
● **saber convivir,** to give and take.

convocar *t* to convoke, summon, call together.
● **convocar oposiciones,** to hold competitive examinations. ‖ **convocar una reunión,** to call a meeting.
▲ Conjugation model [1], like *sacar.*

convocatoria 1 *f* (*citación*) convocation, summons *sing,* call to a meeting. **2** EDUC examination: *convocatoria de septiembre,* (September) resits *pl.*

convoy 1 *m* (*escolta*) convoy. **2** (*tren*) train.
▲ *pl* **convoyes.**

convoyar *t* to convoy, guard, escort.

convulsión 1 *f* MED convulsion. **2** *fig* upheaval.

convulsionar 1 *t* MED to convulse. **2** *fig* to throw into confusion: *los atentados han convulsionado el país,* the bombings have thrown the country into confusion.

convulsivo,-a *adj* convulsive.

convulso,-a *adj* convulsed (**de,** with): *convulso de dolor,* convulsed with pain.

conyugal *adj* conjugal.
■ **vida conyugal,** married life.

cónyuge 1 *mf* (*gen*) spouse, partner; (*marido*) husband; (*mujer*) wife. – **2 cónyuges,** *mpl* husband and wife, married couple *sing.*

coña 1 *f tabú* (*broma*) joke. **2** *tabú* (*molestia*) nuisance, pain, drag, pain in the neck: *es una coña tener que levantarse tan temprano,* it's a pain having to get up so early.
● **dar la coña,** *tabú* to pester. ‖ **decir algo de coña,** *tabú* to be joking, be kidding. ‖ **estar de coña,** *tabú* (*estar de broma*) to be joking, be kidding; (*estar muy bien*) to be terrific, be brilliant. ‖ **¡ni de coña!,** no way! ‖ **ser la coña,** *tabú* to be the limit. ‖ **tomar algo a coña,** *tabú* to take sth. as a joke, treat sth. as a joke.

coñac *m* cognac, brandy.
▲ *pl* **coñacs.**

coñazo *m tabú* pain, drag.
● **dar el coñazo,** *tabú* to be a real pain, pester, hassle.

coñearse *p tabú* to take the piss (**de,** out of).

coño 1 *m tabú* cunt. – **2** *interj tabú* (*sorpresa*) bloody hell, bugger me!, fuck me!; (*disgusto*) for God's sake, for fuck's sake!
● **estar en el quinto coño,** *tabú* to be in the back of beyond. ‖ **¿qué coño quieres?,** *tabú* what the hell do you want?

coop. *abr* (*cooperativa*) cooperative; (*abreviatura*) coop, co-op.

cooperación *f* cooperation.

cooperador,-ra 1 *adj* cooperative, collaborating, participating. – **2** *m,f* collaborator, cooperator.

cooperar *i* to cooperate: *cooperó con la policía en la detención,* he cooperated with the police in the arrest.

cooperativa *f →* **cooperativo,-a.**

cooperativista 1 *adj* cooperative. – **2** *mf* (*socio*) member of a cooperative.

cooperativo-a 1 *adj* cooperative. – **2 cooperativa,** *f* cooperative.
■ **cooperativa agrícola,** farmer's cooperative.

coordenada *f* coordinate.

coordinación *f* coordination.

coordinado,-a 1 *pp →* **coordinar.** – **2** *adj* coordinated. – **3 coordinado,** *m* (*conjunto de ropa*) outfit, ensemble.

coordinador,-ra 1 *adj* coordinating. – **2** *m,f* coordinator. – **3 coordinadora,** *f* (*comité*) coordinating committee.
■ **coordinadora general,** joint committee.

coordinadora *f →* **coordinador,-ra.**

coordinar *t* to coordinate: *coordinaron la compaña,* they coordinated the campaign.

copa 1 *f* (*vaso*) glass; (*bebida*) drink: *¿quieres una copa de vino?,* do you want a glass of wine?; *¿te apetece una copa?,* do you fancy a drink? **2** (*de árbol*) top. **3** (*trofeo*) cup. **4** (*de sujetador*) cup. – **5 copas,** *fpl* (*naipes*) hearts.
● **convidar a una copa,** to treat to a drink. ‖ **ir con una copa de más,** to have had one too many. ‖ **ir de copas,** to go out drinking, go on a pub crawl. ‖ **llevar una copa de más,** to have had one too many. ‖ **tomar una copa,** to have a drink.

copal *m* copal.

copar 1 *t* (*acaparar*) to win, take: *el equipo sueco copó el primer puesto,* the Swedish team took the first place; *los mejores asientos están copados,* the best seats are taken. **2** (*llenar*) to fill. **3** (*en juegos de azar*) to go banco. **4** *fig* (*en una elección*) to win all the seats. **5** MIL to capture, take.

copartícipe *mf* (*socio*) partner; (*colaborador*) collaborator; (*copropietario*) joint owner.

COPE *abr* RAD (*Cadena de Ondas Populares Españolas*) *Spanish private broadcasting company.*

copear *i* to drink, go drinking.

copec *m* kopek, kopeck.
▲ *pl* **copecs.**

copeck *m* kopek, kopek.
▲ *pl* **copecks.**

copela *f* cupel.

Copenhague *m* Copenhagen.

copeo *m* pub crawl.
● **ir de copeo,** to go on a pub crawl, go out drinking.

copete 1 *m* (*cabello*) tuft. **2** (*penacho*) crest. **3** (*de caballo*) forelock. **4** (*de mueble*) ornamental top, ornamentation; (*de montaña, helado*) top. **5** *fig* (*atrevimiento*) arrogance.
● **de alto copete,** *fam* high-class.

copia 1 *f* (*gen*) copy. **2** (*de fotografía*) print. **3** *fig* (*persona*) image: *es la copia de su padre,* he's the image of his father. **4** *lit* (*abundancia*) abundance.
● **sacar una copia,** to make a copy.
■ **copia legalizada,** certified true copy. ‖ **papel de copia,** copy paper.

copiador,-ra 1 *adj* copying. – **2 copiadora,** *f* photocopier.

copiadora *f →* **copiador,-ra.**

copiar 1 *t* (*gen*) to copy: *lo copió del libro,* he copied it from the book. **2** EDUC to cheat, copy. **3** (*escribir*) to take down.
● **copiar al pie de la letra,** to copy word for word.
▲ Conjugation model [12], like *cambiar.*

copiloto 1 *m* AV copilot. **2** AUTO co-driver.

copión,-ona 1 *m,f* EDUC *fam* cheat, copier. **2** *fam* (*imitador*) copycat.

copiosidad *f* abundance.

copioso,-a 1 *adj fml* (*abundante*) plentiful, abundant, copious. **2** *fml* (*lluvia*) heavy; (*cabello*) long.

copista *mf* copyist.

copla 1 *f* (*verso, estrofa*) verse, stanza. **2** (*canción*) popular folk song. **3** *fam* (*monserga*) story, tale: *no te lo voy a re-*

galar, así que deja ya esa copla, I'm not going to give it to you, so stop going on about it.
● **andar en coplas,** *fam* to be the talk of the town, be common knowledge.
copo[1] *m* (*gen*) flake; (*de nieve*) snowflake; (*de algodón*) ball (of cotton).
■ **copos de avena,** rolled oats.
copo[2] *m* (*de red*) bottom of a seine.
copón *m* REL ciborium.
● **del copón,** *tabú* a hell of a: *me has dado un susto del copón,* you gave me one hell of a shock; *tiene una moto del copón,* he's got this great big motorbike.
coproducción *f* co-production, joint production.
coproductor,-ra *m,f* co-producer.
copropiedad *f* joint ownership.
copropietario,-a *m,f* joint owner, co-owner, co-proprietor.
copto,-a 1 *adj* Coptic. – 2 *m,f* Copt. – 3 copto, *m* (*lengua*) Coptic.
copudo,-a *adj* bushy, thick.
cópula 1 *f* (*nexo*) link. 2 (*coito*) copulation, intercourse. 3 LING conjunction.
copular *i* to copulate (**con,** with).
copulativo,-a *adj* copulative.
copyright *m* copyright.
coque *m* coke.
coqueta *f* → **coqueto,-a.**
coquetear *i* to flirt.
coquetería *f* coquetry, flirting, flirtation.
coqueto,-a 1 *adj* flirtatious. – 2 *m,f* (*mujer*) coquette, flirt; (*hombre*) flirt. – 3 coqueta, *f* dressing table.
coquetón,-ona 1 *adj* (*persona*) coquettish. 2 *fam* (*habitación etc*) cute, charming.
coquina *f* small cockle.
coquito *m* (*gesto*) face.
coracha *f* leather bag.
coraje 1 *m* (*valor*) courage, toughness. 2 (*ira*) anger.
● **dar coraje,** *fam* to infuriate, make furious: *me da coraje que haya ganado él,* it makes me furious that he won. ‖ **echarle coraje a algo,** to put some spirit into sth.
corajudo,-a 1 *adj* (*valiente*) tough, brave. 2 (*irritable*) quick-tempered.
coral[1] 1 *adj* MÚS choral. – 2 *f* MÚS (*grupo*) choir, choral society. – 3 *m* MÚS (*composición*) choral, chorale.
coral[2] 1 *m* ZOOL coral. – 2 corales, *mpl* coral beads.
coralina *f* → **coralino,-a.**
coralino,-a 1 *adj* coral. – 2 coralina, *f* coralline.
corambre *f* hides *pl*, skins *pl*.
Corán *m* Koran.
coránico,-a *adj* Koranic.
coraza 1 *f* (*armadura*) armour (US armor), cuirass. 2 (*caparazón*) shell, carapace. 3 *fig* (*protección*) armour (US armor), protection.
corazón 1 *m* ANAT heart. 2 *fig* (*parte central*) heart, core: *en el corazón de la ciudad,* in the heart of the city. 3 (*de fruta*) core. 4 (*apelativo*) darling, dear, sweetheart: *¿qué quieres, corazón?,* what do you want, darling? – 5 corazones, *mpl* (*naipes*) hearts.
● **abrir el corazón a algn.,** *fig* to open one's heart to sb. ‖ **de corazón / de todo corazón,** *fig* sincerely, in all sincerity. ‖ **estar con el corazón en un puño,** *fig* to have one's heart in one's mouth. ‖ **estar enfermo del corazón,** to have heart trouble. ‖ **hablar con el corazón en la mano,** *fig* to speak from the heart. ‖

llegar al corazón de algn., to touch sb.'s heart. ‖ **llevar el corazón en la mano,** to wear one's heart on one's sleeve. ‖ **me dice el corazón que ...,** I have a feeling that ... ‖ **padecer del corazón,** to have heart trouble. ‖ **romper el corazón a algn.,** *fig* to break sb.'s heart. ‖ **ser duro de corazón,** to be hard-hearted. ‖ **ser todo corazón,** *fig* to be all heart, be kindness itself. ‖ **tener buen corazón,** *fig* to be kind-hearted.
corazonada 1 *f* (*sentimiento*) hunch, feeling, inkling: *tuve la corazonada de que él no estaba,* I had a hunch that he wasn't there. 2 (*impulso*) impulse.
corbata 1 *f* tie, us necktie: *iba con corbata,* he was wearing a tie. 2 (*de bandera*) sash, tassel.
● **tenerlos por corbata,** *tabú* to be scared shitless.
corbatín *m* bow tie.
corbeta *f* corvette.
Córcega *f* Corsica.
corcel *m* lit steed, charger.
corchea *f* quaver.
corchero,-a *adj* cork.
corcheta *f* eye.
corchete 1 *m* COST hook and eye, snap fastener. 2 (*signo impreso*) square bracket.
corcho 1 *m* cork; (*corteza*) cork bark. 2 (*tapón*) cork. 3 (*para pescar, nadar*) float. 4 (*tabla*) cork mat. 5 (*tablón para anuncios, notas*) cork board.
córcholis *interj fam* goodness me!, us gee!
corcova *f* hunchback, hump.
corcovado,-a 1 *pp* → **corcovar.** – 2 *adj* hunchbacked. – 3 *m,f* hunchback.
corcovar *t* to bend, curve.
corcovo *m* prance.
cordada *f* rope.
cordaje 1 *m* (*cuerdas*) ropes *pl*, cordage. 2 MAR rigging.
cordal *m* tailpiece.
cordel *m* rope, cord.
● **a cordel,** in a straight line.
cordelería 1 *f* (*oficio*) ropemaking. 2 (*cuerdas*) ropes *pl*. 3 MAR rigging.
cordelero,-a 1 *adj* ropemaking. – 2 *m,f* ropemaker.
cordero,-a 1 *m,f* lamb. 2 *fig* (*persona dócil*) lamb, angel: *este chico es un corderito,* this boy is a little angel. – 3 cordero, *m* (*piel*) lambskin. 4 (*carne - joven*) lamb; (*- crecido*) mutton.
● **ser manso como un cordero,** to be as gentle as a lamb.
■ **Cordero de Dios,** Lamb of God. ‖ **cordero lechal,** sucking lamb. ‖ **cordero pascual,** paschal lamb. ‖ **la madre del cordero,** *fam fig* the crux of the matter.
cordial 1 *adj* (*afectuoso*) cordial, friendly, warm: *una bienvenida cordial,* a warm welcome. 2 (*que fortalece*) cordial, stimulating. – 3 *m* (*bebida*) cordial.
cordialidad *f* cordiality, warmth, friendliness.
cordialmente 1 *adv* cordially, warmly. 2 (*despedida en carta*) sincerely.
cordillera *f* mountain range, mountain chain.
Córdoba *f* Córdoba.
cordobán *m* (*piel*) cordovan.
cordobés,-esa 1 *adj* of Córdoba, from Córdoba. – 2 *m,f* person from Córdoba.
cordón 1 *m* (*cuerda*) string. 2 (*de zapatos*) shoelace, shoestring. 3 (*de adorno*) braid, cord. 4 ELEC flex. 5 REL cord. 6 (*cadena humana*) cordon.
■ **cordón umbilical,** umbilical cord.
cordoncillo 1 *m* (*en tejido*) rib, ribbing. 2 (*bordado*) braid, piping. 3 (*de moneda*) milling.

cordura f good sense.
● **con cordura,** sensibly, prudently, wisely.
corea f MED Saint Vitus's dance, chorea.
Corea f Korea.
■ **Corea del Norte,** North Korea. ‖ **Corea del Sur,** South Korea.
coreano,-a 1 adj Korean. – **2** m,f (persona) Korean. – **3** coreano, m (idioma) Korean.
corear 1 t (cantar) to chorus, sing in chorus. **2** (hablar) to chorus, speak in chorus. **3** fig (aclamar) to applaud.
coreografía f choreography.
coreográfico,-a adj choreographic.
coreógrafo,-a m,f choreographer.
coriambo m choriamb, choriambus.
corifeo 1 m coryphaeus. **2** fig leader.
corimbo m corymb.
corindón m corundum.
corintio,-a 1 adj Corinthian. – **2** m,f Corinthian.
corinto,-a 1 adj maroon. – **2** corinto, m (color) maroon.
corion m chorion.
corista f chorus girl.
coriza f coryza.
cormorán m cormorant.
■ **cormorán moñudo,** shag.
cornada f goring.
● **dar cornadas,** to gore. ‖ **sufrir una cornada,** to be gored.
cornadura f → **cornamenta**.
cornalina f cornelian, carnelian.
cornamenta f (gen) horns pl; (del ciervo) antlers pl.
● **poner la cornamenta a algn.,** to cuckold sb., be unfaithful to sb.
cornamusa f bagpipe.
córnea f → **córneo,-a**.
cornear t to gore.
corneja f crow.
cornejo m dogwood.
córneo,-a 1 adj hornlike, corneous. – **2** córnea, f cornea.
córner m DEP (lugar) corner; (golpe) corner, corner kick.
● **lanzar un córner / sacar un córner / tirar un córner,** to take a corner.
corneta 1 f (instrumento) bugle. – **2** mf MIL (persona) bugler.
● **a toque de corneta,** under the bugle call.
■ **corneta de llaves,** cornet.
cornete 1 m (de nariz) turbinate, turbinate bone. **2** (de helado) cornet, cone.
cornetín 1 m (instrumento) cornet. – **2** mf (persona) cornet player.
cornijal m corner.
cornisa f ARQ cornice.
■ **la Cornisa Cantábrica,** the Cantabrian Coast.
cornisamento m entablature.
cornisamiento m entablature.
corno 1 m BOT (cornejo) dogwood. **2** MÚS horn.
■ **corno inglés,** MÚS cor anglais, English horn.
cornucopia 1 f (vaso) cornucopia, horn of plenty. **2** (espejo) small mirror.
cornudo,-a 1 adj (animal) horned, antlered. **2** fam pey (marido) cuckolded. – **3** cornudo, m fam pey cuckold.
coro 1 m MÚS choir. **2** TEAT chorus.
● **a coro,** fig all together. ‖ **hacer coro,** fig to join in the chorus.
corografía f chorography.

coroides f choroid.
▲ pl coroides.
corola f corolla.
corolario m corollary.
corona 1 f (aro, cerco) crown. **2** (de flores etc) wreath, garland, crown. **3** fig (dignidad real) King's, Queen's: **el discurso de la corona,** the King's speech. **4** fig (reino) crown, kingdom. **5** (coronilla) crown, crown of the head. **6** (aureola) halo. **7** (de diente, moneda) crown. **8** (en geometría) annulus, ring.
■ **corona funeraria,** funeral wreath. ‖ **corona solar,** solar corona.
coronación 1 f coronation. **2** fig (culminación) crowning.
coronamento m → **coronamiento**.
coronamiento 1 m fig (culminación) crowning. **2** ARQ fig crown.
coronar 1 t to crown. – **2** i to crown.
coronario,-a adj coronary.
■ **insuficiencia coronaria,** cardiac arrest.
coronel m colonel.
coronilla 1 f (parte de la cabeza) crown of the head. **2** (tonsura) tonsure.
● **andar de coronilla,** fam to run around in circles. ‖ **estar hasta la coronilla,** fam to be fed up (de, with).
corpachón 1 m (de ave) carcass of a fowl. **2** fam big body, carcass.
corpanchón m → **corpachón**.
corpiño m bodice.
corporación f corporation.
■ **corporación metropolitana,** city corporation.
corporal 1 adj corporal, body. – **2** m REL corporal, corporale.
corporativismo m corporativism.
corporativo,-a adj corporative, corporate.
■ **asociación corporativa,** syndicate. ‖ **imagen corporativa,** corporate image.
corpore misa de corpore insepulto, loc funeral mass said in the presence of the deceased.
corporeidad f corporeity.
corpóreo,-a adj corporeal, bodily.
corpulencia f corpulence, stoutness.
corpulento,-a adj corpulent, stocky, stout.
corpus m (conjunto) corpus.
■ **Corpus (Christi),** REL Corpus Christi.
corpuscular adj corpuscular.
corpúsculo m corpuscle.
corral 1 m (de casa) yard, courtyard. **2** (de granja) farmyard, US corral. **3** (para niños) playpen. **4** TEAT playhouse.
correa 1 f (tira de piel) strap, leather strip. **2** (de perro) lead, leash. **3** (de reloj) watchstrap. **4** (cinturón) belt. **5** TÉC belt. **6** (elasticidad) elasticity, stretch.
● **tener mucha correa,** fam to have a lot of patience.
■ **correa del ventilador,** fan belt. ‖ **correa sin fin,** conveyor belt.
correaje m straps pl.
correazo m lash with a belt.
corrección 1 f (rectificación) correction. **2** (educación) courtesy, correctness, politeness, good manners pl. **3** (represión) rebuke. **4** (en impresión) proof-reading.
● **tratar con corrección,** to be polite.
■ **corrección de pruebas,** proofreading.
correccional 1 adj correctional. – **2** m detention centre, reformatory.
correctamente 1 adv (sin errores) correctly, accurately. **2** (con educación) correctly, politely, properly.

correctivo,-a 1 *adj* corrective. – **2** *m* corrective.
correcto,-a 1 *adj* (*sin errores*) correct, accurate. **2** (*adecuado*) suitable. **3** (*educado*) polite, courteous. **4** (*conducta*) proper.
corrector,-ra 1 *adj* corrective. – **2** *m,f* (*de pruebas impresas*) proofreader.
corredera *f* → **corredero,-a**.
corredero,-a 1 *adj* sliding: *ventana corredera,* sliding window. – **2 corredera,** *f* TÉC runner, groove, track.
● **de corredera,** sliding.
corredizo,-a *adj* sliding.
corredor,-ra 1 *adj* running. **2** (*ave*) flightless: *ave corredora,* flightless bird. – **3** *m,f* DEP runner; (*de coches*) driver. **4** FIN broker. – **5 corredor,** *m* (*pasillo*) corridor, gallery.
■ **corredor,-ra de bolsa,** stockbroker. ‖ **corredor,-ra de coches,** racing driver. ‖ **corredor,-ra de fincas,** estate agent. ‖ **corredor,-ra de seguros,** insurance broker.
corredura *f* overflow.
correduría *f* brokerage.
■ **correduría de seguros,** insurance brokerage.
corregible *adj* rectifiable, which can be corrected.
corregidor 1 *m* HIST (*magistrado*) corregidor. **2** HIST (*alcalde*) mayor.
corregir 1 *t* (*amendar*) to correct, rectify. **2** (*reprender*) to reprimand, scold, tell off. **3** EDUC to mark. **4** (*en impresión*) to read, proofread. – **5 corregirse,** *p* (*persona*) to mend one's ways. **6** (*defecto*) to right itself.
▲ Conjugation model [55], like *elegir*.
correlación *f* correlation.
correlacionar 1 *t* to correlate. – **2 correlacionarse,** *p* to be correlated.
correlativo,-a 1 *adj* correlative. – **2 correlativo,** *m* correlative.
correligionario,-a *m,f* co-religionist (US coreligionist).
correlimos *m* dunlin.
▲ *pl* **correlimos.**
correntío *adj* flowing, running.
correo 1 *m* (*servicio, correspondencia*) post, US mail. **2** (*persona*) courier. **3** MIL dispatch rider. – **4 correos,** *mpl* (*oficina*) post office *sing*.
● **echar al correo,** to post, US mail. ‖ **por correo,** by post, US by mail.
■ **apartado de correos,** (post office) box. ‖ **correo aéreo,** airmail. ‖ **correo certificado,** registered post, US registered mail. ‖ **correo electrónico,** electronic mail, E-mail. ‖ **correo urgente,** special delivery.
correoso,-a 1 *adj* (*flexible*) flexible. **2** *fig* (*alimento*) tough, leathery.
correr 1 *i* (*gen*) to run: *se marchó corriendo,* she ran off. **2** (*darse prisa*) to rush, hurry: *¡corre, es tarde!,* hurry up, it's late! **3** (*viento*) to blow. **4** (*agua*) to flow, run. **5** (*tiempo*) to pass, fly. **6** (*noticias*) to spread, circulate: *el rumor corría por la ciudad,* the rumour spread throughout the city. **7** (*conductor*) to drive fast: *Juan corre mucho,* Juan drives very fast. **8** (*coche*) to go fast. **9** (*sueldo, interés*) to be payable. **10** (*puerta, ventana*) to slide. **11** (*moneda*) to be legal tender. – **12** *t* (*distancia*) to cover; (*país*) to travel through. **13** (*carrera*) to run; (*caballo*) to race, run. **14** (*echar*) to close; (*cortina*) to draw; (*cerrojo*) to bolt. **15** (*mover*) to pull up, move, draw up: *corre la mesa,* move the table. **16** (*estar expuesto*) to run: *correr un peligro,* to run a risk. **17** (*aventura*) to have. **18** (*avergonzar*) to make ashamed. **19** (*turbar*) to make embarrassed. – **20 correrse,** *p* (*persona*) to move over; (*objeto*) to shift, slide. **21** (*color, tinta*) to run. **22** (*media*) to ladder. **23** (*avergonzarse*) to blush, go red. **24** *tabú* (*tener orgasmo*) to come.

● **a todo correr,** at full speed. ‖ **correr a cargo de algn.,** (*ocuparse*) to take care of sth.; (*pagar*) to pay for sth.: *la cena corre a mi cargo,* I'll pay for the dinner. ‖ **correr con algo,** to be responsible for sth. ‖ **correr con los gastos,** to foot the bill. ‖ **corre la voz de que ...,** rumour has it that ... ‖ **correr mundo,** to be a globetrotter. ‖ **correr un peligro,** to be in danger. ‖ **correrla,** *fam* to live it up. ‖ **dejar correr algo,** to let sth. drop, let sth. ride. ‖ **deprisa y corriendo,** in a hurry. ‖ **el mes que corre,** the current month.
correría 1 *f* MIL (*incursión*) raid, foray. **2** (*viaje*) trip, journey. – **3 correrías,** *fpl fam* (*aventuras*) adventures; (*viajes*) travels.
correspondencia 1 *f* (*gen*) correspondence. **2** (*cartas*) post, US mail. **3** (*de trenes etc*) connection.
● **mantener correspondencia con algn.,** to correspond with sb.
■ **curso por correspondencia,** correspondence course.
corresponder 1 *i* (*ser adecuado*) to become, befit; (*color, aspecto*) to match, go with: *este comportamiento es el que corresponde a su educación,* this behaviour befits his education; *los zapatos no corresponden al vestido,* the shoes don't go with the dress. **2** (*encajar*) to correspond (**a**, to), tally (**a**, with); (*descripción*) to fit. **3** (*pertenecer*) to belong, pertain: *esta mesa corresponde a mi habitación,* this table belongs in my bedroom. – **4** *t* (*ser el turno*) to be one's turn: *me corresponde a mí,* it's my turn. – **5** *i* (*en un reparto*) to get: *me correspondió un coche,* I got a car. **6** (*incumbir*) to be the job of, be the responsibility of: *eso te corresponde a ti,* that's your job. **7** (*devolver*) to return; (*amabilidad*) to repay: *ella le correspondió con otro regalo,* she repaid him with another gift. – **8 corresponderse,** *p* (*ajustarse*) to correspond; (*cifras*) to tally: *la dirección que te dio no se corresponde con la que yo tengo,* the address he gave you doesn't correspond to the one I have. **9** (*armonizar*) to be in harmony, go with. **10** (*cartearse*) to correspond. **11** (*amarse*) to love each other.
correspondiente 1 *adj* (*que corresponde*) corresponding (**a**, to). **2** (*apropiado*) suitable, appropriate. **3** (*respectivo*) own. **4** (*miembro*) correspondent.
corresponsal *mf* correspondent.
corresponsalía *f* post of correspondent.
corretaje *m* brokerage.
corretear 1 *i* *fam* (*correr*) to run about. **2** *fam* (*vagar*) to hang about.
correteo *m* running about, hustle and bustle.
correvedile 1 *mf fam fig* (*chismoso*) tell-tale, gossip. **2** *fam fig* (*alcahuete*) go-between.
▲ *pl* **correvediles.**
correveidile *mf* → **correvedile.**
▲ *pl* **correveidiles.**
corrida *f* → **corrido,-a.**
corrido,-a 1 *adj* (*peso*) good: *una tonelada corrida,* a good ton. **2** (*seguido*) full, continuous: *balcón corrido,* continuous balcony. **3** *fig* (*avergonzado*) abashed. **4** *fig* (*experimentado*) experienced. **5** (*tiempo*) running: *tres semanas corridas,* three weeks running. – **6 corrida,** *f* (*carrera*) run, race. **7** (*de toros*) bullfight.
● **de corrida,** (*rápidamente*) hastily, in a flash; (*de memoria*) by heart. ‖ **de corrido,** (*sin parar*) without stopping; (*con fluidez*) fluently: *hablar un idioma de corrido,* to speak a language fluently; *recitar de corrido,* to reel off; *traducir de corrido,* to translate at sight. ‖ **dejar corrido,-a a algn.,** *fig* to embarrass sb. ‖ **quedarse corrido,-a,** *fig* to feel embarrassed.

corriente 1 *adj* (*común*) ordinary, average: *personas corrientes,* ordinary people; *una familia corriente,* an average family; *lo corriente es hablarlo primero,* the usual thing is to talk it over first. **2** (*agua*) running. **3** (*fecha*) current, present: *el cinco del corriente mes,* the fifth of the current month, the fifth of this month. **4** (*cuenta*) current. – **5** *m* (*mes*) current month, this month. – **6** *f* (*masa de agua*) current, stream, flow. **7** (*de aire*) draught (US draft). **8** ELEC current. **9** (*de arte etc*) trend, current, school.

● **al corriente,** (*actualizado*) up to date; (*enterado*) aware; (*informado*) informed, in the know: *¿estás al corriente de los pagos?,* are you up to date with the payments?; *¿estás al corriente de lo que ha pasado?,* do you know what's happened? ‖ **corriente y moliente,** *fam* ordinary, run-of-the-mill. ‖ **dejarse llevar por la corriente,** *fig* to follow the herd, go with the flow. ‖ **ir contra corriente / navegar contra corriente,** *fig* to go against the tide. ‖ **llevarle la corriente a algn. / seguirle la corriente a algn.,** to humour (US humor) sb. ‖ **poner al corriente,** to bring up to date, put in the picture. ‖ **ponerse al corriente,** to get up to date, catch up. ‖ **salirse de lo corriente,** to be out of the ordinary. ‖ **tener al corriente,** to keep informed.
■ **corriente abajo,** downstream. ‖ **corriente alterna,** alternating current. ‖ **corriente arriba,** upstream. ‖ **Corriente del Golfo,** Gulf Stream. ‖ **corriente sanguínea,** bloodstream.

corrientemente *adv* usually, normally.

corrijo *pres indic* → **corregir.**

corrillo 1 *m* (*corro*) small group of people talking, clique. **2** (*en la bolsa*) round enclosure.

corrimiento 1 *m* (*acción*) slipping, sliding. **2** MED discharge. **3** *fig* (*vergüenza*) embarrassment.
■ **corrimiento de tierras,** landslide.

corro 1 *m* (*cerco*) circle, ring. **2** (*juego*) ring-a-ring o'roses. **3** (*en la bolsa*) round enclosure.
● **entrar en el corro,** to join in the circle. ‖ **hacerle corro a algn.,** *fig* to gather round sb. ‖ **hacer corro aparte,** *fig* to form a small circle.

corroboración *f* corroboration.

corroborar *t* to corroborate: *corroborar con pruebas,* to corroborate with proof.

corroborativo,-a *adj* corroborative.

corroer 1 *t* (*desgastar*) to corrode: **2** GEOL to erode. **3** *fig* (*perturbar*) to corrode, eat away, eat up: *los celos lo corroen,* he's eaten up with jealousy. – **4 corroerse,** *p* (*desgastarse*) to become corroded. **5** *fig* to be eaten up (**de,** with).
▲ Conjugation model [82], like *roer.*

corromper 1 *t* (*pudrir*) to turn bad. **2** (*pervertir*) to corrupt, pervert. **3** (*sobornar*) to bribe. – **4 corromperse,** *p* (*pudrirse*) to go bad, rot. **5** (*pervertirse*) to become corrupted.

corrosión 1 *f* corrosion, rust. **2** GEOL erosion.

corrosivo,-a 1 *adj* corrosive. **2** *fig* caustic. – **3 corrosivo,** *m* corrosive.

corrupción 1 *f* (*putrefacción*) rot, decay. **2** *fig* corruption, degradation. **3** *fig* (*soborno*) bribery.
■ **corrupción de menores,** corruption of minors.

corruptela *f* corruption, sharp practice.

corrupto,-a *adj* corrupt.

corruptor,-ra 1 *adj* corrupting. – **2** *m,f* corrupter, perverter.

corrusco *m fam* crust of stale bread.

corsario 1 *adj* privateer. – **2** *m* corsair, privateer.

corsé *m* corset.

corsetería *f* ladies' underwear shop.

corso,-a 1 *adj* Corsican. – **2** *m,f* Corsican.

corta *f* tree felling.

cortaalambres *m* wire cutters *pl.*
▲ *pl* **cortaalambres.**

cortacésped *m & f* lawnmower.

cortacircuitos *m* circuit breaker.
▲ *pl* **cortacircuitos.**

cortado,-a 1 *pp* → **cortar.** – **2** *adj* (*troceado*) cut; (*en lonchas*) sliced. **3** (*leche*) sour. **4** *fig* (*estilo*) concise, clipped. **5** *fam* (*aturdido*) dumbfounded. – **6 cortado,** *m* (*café*) coffee with a dash of milk.
● **quedarse cortado,-a,** *fam* (*sin palabras*) to be speechless, be lost for words; (*avergonzado*) to become embarrassed.

cortador,-ra 1 *adj* cutting. – **2** *m,f* (*sastre, zapatero*) cutter. – **3 cortadora,** *f* (*máquina*) cutting machine.

cortadora *f* → **cortador,-ra.**

cortadura 1 *f* (*corte*) cut. **2** (*paso*) gorge. – **3 cortaduras,** *fpl* (*recortes*) cuttings, clippings.

cortafrío *m* cold chisel.

cortafuego 1 *m* (*en el campo*) firebreak. **2** (*en un edificio*) fire wall.

cortahuevos *m* egg-slicer.
▲ *pl* **cortahuevos.**

cortalápices *m* pencil sharpener.
▲ *pl* **cortalápices.**

cortante 1 *adj* (*que corta*) cutting, sharp. **2** *fig* (*aire*) biting. **3** *fig* (*persona, estilo*) sharp, brusque.

cortapapeles 1 *m* paper knife. **2** TÉC guillotine.

cortapastas *m* pastry-cutter.
▲ *pl* **cortapastas.**

cortapisa 1 *f* (*condición*) condition, restriction. **2** (*dificultad*) difficulty, obstacle.
● **poner cortapisas,** to impose conditions. ‖ **sin cortapisas,** with no strings attached.

cortaplumas *m* penknife.
▲ *pl* **cortaplumas.**

cortapuros *m* cigar-cutter.
▲ *pl* **cortapuros.**

cortar 1 *t* (*gen*) to cut: *cortar una cinta,* to cut a ribbon; *cortar una película,* to cut a film. **2** (*pelo*) to cut, trim. **3** (*árbol*) to cut down. **4** (*carne*) to carve. **5** (*pastel*) to cut up. **6** (*cabeza, teléfono, gas*) to cut off. **7** (*mayonesa, leche*) to curdle. **8** (*piel*) to chap, crack. **9** (*viento, frío*) to chill, bite. **10** COST to cut out. **11** (*interrumpir*) to cut off, interrupt. **12** (*bloquear*) to block: *cortaron la carretera,* the road was blocked. **13** (*suprimir*) to cut out. **14** *fig* (*separar*) to divide, split, cut. – **15** *i* to cut. – **16 cortarse,** *p* to cut: *este metal se corta fácilmente,* this metal cuts easily. **17** (*herirse*) to cut, cut os.: *me he cortado,* I've cut myself; *se cortó el dedo,* he cut his finger. **18** (*el pelo - por otro*) to have one's hair cut; (*- uno mismo*) to cut one's hair: *¿te has cortado el pelo?,* have you had your hair cut? **19** (*piel*) to become chapped. **20** (*leche*) to go off, curdle; (*mayonesa*) to curdle. **21** (*comunicación*) to be cut off. **22** *fam* (*aturdirse*) to get embarrassed, get tongue-tied, go all shy: *no te cortes,* don't be shy.
● **¡corta el rollo!,** knock it off! ‖ **cortar con algn.,** *fam* to split up with sb. ‖ **cortar el apetito,** to ruin one's appetite. ‖ **cortar el bacalao,** *fam* to be the boss. ‖ **cortar en seco,** *fig* to cut short. ‖ **cortar la digestión,** to give one indigestion, upset one's stomach. ‖ **cortar la palabra,** to interrupt. ‖ **cortar por la mitad,** to split down the middle. ‖ **cortar por lo sano,** *fam* to take drastic measures.

cortaúñas *m* nail clippers.
▲ *pl* cortaúñas.
corte[1] 1 *f* (*del rey etc*) court. **2** (*séquito*) retinue. **3** AM JUR court. – **4 las Cortes**, *fpl* Spanish Parliament *sing*.
● **hacer la corte a,** to court, pay court to.
corte[2] **1** *m* (*gen*) cut: *me he hecho un corte en el dedo,* I've cut my finger. **2** (*filo*) edge. **3** (*sección*) section: *corte horizontal,* horizontal section. **4** (*de un libro*) edge. **5** (*de pelo*) cut, haircut. **6** (*de helado*) wafer, US ice-cream sandwich. **7** COST (*cantidad de tela*) length. **8** *fam fig* (*réplica*) rebuff. **9** *fam fig* (*vergüenza*) embarrassment: *le daba corte entrar y se quedó fuera,* he was too embarrassed to go in so he stayed outside.
● **dar un corte a algn.,** *fam* to cut sb. dead. ‖ **¡qué corte!,** *fam* what a blow!
■ **corte de mangas,** *tabú* V-sign. ‖ **corte y confección,** dressmaking.
cortedad 1 *f* (*pequeñez*) shortness, smallness. **2** *fig* (*falta*) lack: *cortedad de instrucción,* lack of education. **3** *fig* (*timidez*) shyness, timidity.
cortejar *t* to court.
cortejo 1 *m* (*acompañantes*) entourage, retinue. **2** (*galanteo*) courting.
■ **cortejo fúnebre,** funeral cortège. ‖ **cortejo nupcial,** wedding party.
cortés *adj* courteous, polite.
● **lo cortés no quita lo valiente,** *fam* you can be polite but brave at the same time.
cortesana *f* → **cortesano,-a.**
cortesano,-a 1 *adj* (*de la corte*) court. **2** (*cortés*) courteous, courtly. – **3** *m,f* (*de la corte*) courtier. – **4 cortesana,** *f* (*prostituta*) courtesan, courtezan.
cortesía 1 *f* (*educación*) courtesy, politeness: *ha sido una cortesía de tu parte acompañarnos hasta el aeropuerto,* it was very kind of you to come with us to the airport. **2** (*en cartas*) formal ending. **3** (*tratamiento*) title. **4** (*reverencia*) bow, curtsy. **5** (*regalo*) present: *esta bolsa es una cortesía de la empresa,* this bag is courtesy of the company.
■ **visita de cortesía,** courtesy call.
cortésmente *adv* courteously, politely.
corteza 1 *f* (*de árbol*) bark. **2** (*de pan*) crust. **3** (*de fruta*) peel, skin. **4** (*de queso*) rind. **5** *fig* (*apariencia*) outside appearance, outward appearance.
■ **corteza cerebral,** cerebral cortex. ‖ **la corteza terrestre,** the earth's crust.
cortical *adj* cortical.
cortijero,-a *m,f* Andalusian farmer.
cortijo *m* Andalusian farm, Andalusian farmhouse.
cortina 1 *f* curtain. **2** *fig* curtain, screen.
● **correr las cortinas,** to draw the curtains.
■ **cortina de fuego,** MIL *fig* barrage. ‖ **cortina de humo,** *fig* smoke screen.
cortinaje *m* drapery.
cortinilla *f* small lace curtain.
cortisona *f* cortisone.
corto,-a 1 *adj* (*extensión*) short: *distancia corta,* short distance. **2** (*duración*) short, brief: *una película corta,* a short film. **3** (*escaso*) scant, meagre (US meager). **4** *fig* (*tonto*) thick, dim. **5** *fig* (*tímido*) shy, timid. – **6 corto,** *m* short film, short.
● **a la corta o a la larga,** *fig* sooner or later, in the long run. ‖ **corto,-a de alcances,** *fam* thick, dim. ‖ **corto,-a de medios,** of scant means. ‖ **corto,-a de miras,** *fam* narrow-minded. ‖ **corto,-a de vista,** short-sighted. ‖ **ni corto,-a ni perezoso,-a,** *fam* without thinking twice. ‖

quedarse corto,-a, (*ropa*) to become too short; (*calcular mal*) to underestimate, miscalculate; (*un tiro*) to fall short; (*no decir todo*) to hold something back, not say enough: *el pantalón se me ha quedado corto,* my trousers have become too short for me.
cortocircuito *m* short circuit.
cortometraje *m* short film, short.
Coruña La Coruña, *f* Corunna.
coruñés,-esa 1 *adj* of Corunna, from Corunna. – **2** *m,f* person from Corunna, inhabitant of Corunna.
corva *f* back of the knee.
corvadura *f* curvature, curve.
corvejón 1 *m* (*de caballo*) hock. **2** (*de gallo*) spur. **3** (*ave*) cormorant.
corveta *f* curvet.
corvina *f* corvina.
corvo,-a 1 *adj* arched, curved. **2** (*nariz*) hooked.
corzo,-a *m,f* (*macho*) roe buck; (*hembra*) roe deer.
cosa 1 *f* (*gen*) thing: *coge tus cosas,* take your things, take your stuff; *me dijo una cosa,* she told me something; *¿alguna cosa más?,* anything else? **2** (*asunto*) matter, business: *es cosa tuya,* it's your business; *eso es otra cosa,* that's something different. **3** (*nada*) nothing, not anything: *no hay cosa igual,* there's nothing like it. – **4 cosas,** *fpl fam* (*manías*) hang-ups; (*comportamiento*) : *todos tenemos nuestras cosas,* we've got all our hang-ups; *son cosas de niños,* kids do that kind of thing.
● **así están las cosas,** that's the way things are, that's how things stand. ‖ **como cosa tuya,** as if it were your idea. ‖ **como están las cosas,** as things stand. ‖ **como si tal cosa,** just like that. ‖ **cosa de,** about: *es cosa de unos minutos,* it'll just take a few minutes. ‖ **cosa nunca vista,** something surprising. ‖ **cosas de la vida,** that's life. ‖ **decir cuatro cosas,** to tell a few home truths. ‖ **es cosa de ...,** (*tiempo*) it's time to ...; (*cuestión*) it's a matter of ... ‖ **lo que son las cosas,** much to my surprise. ‖ **no sea cosa que ...,** in case ... ‖ **no ser gran cosa,** not to be important. ‖ **no valer gran cosa,** not to be worth much. ‖ **ser cosa hecha,** *fam* to be no sooner said than done. ‖ **ser poquita cosa,** *fam* not to be much, not to amount to too much.
■ **cosas de negocios,** business matters.
cosaco,-a 1 *adj* Cossack. – **2 cosaco,** *m* Cossack.
● **beber como un cosaco,** *fam* to drink like a fish.
coscorrón *m* blow on the head, knock on the head.
coscurro *m fam* crust of stale bread.
cosecante *f* cosecant.
cosecha 1 *f* harvest, crop. **2** (*tiempo*) harvest time. **3** (*año del vino*) vintage.
● **de cosecha propia,** home-grown; *fig* of one's own invention.
cosechador,-ra 1 *m,f* harvester. – **2 cosechadora,** *f* combine harvester.
cosechadora *f* → **cosechador,-ra.**
cosechar 1 *i* to harvest, reap. – **2** *t* (*recoger*) to harvest. **3** (*cultivar*) to grow. **4** *fig* to reap, harvest, win: *cosechar éxitos,* to achieve success.
cosechero,-a *m,f* harvester, grower.
coseno *m* cosine.
coser 1 *t* (*unir*) to sew; (*un botón*) to sew on; (*pespuntes etc*) to stitch: *le cosí los pantalones,* I sewed up her trousers. **2** MED to stitch up. **3** (*grapar*) to staple together. **4** *fig* (*unir*) to join. **5** *fig* (*atravesar*) to pierce: *coser a balazos,* to riddle with bullets.
● **coser a puñaladas,** *fam* to cut to pieces. ‖ **eso es coser y cantar,** *fam* it's plain sailing, it's a piece of cake, it's child's play.

■ **máquina de coser,** sewing machine.
cosido 1 *m* sewing. **2** MED stitching.
cosificar *t* to trivialize, belittle.
▲ *Conjugation model* [1], *like* **sacar**.
cosmética *f* → **cosmético,-a**.
cosmético,-a 1 *adj* cosmetic. – **2 cosmético,** *m* cosmetic. – **3 cosmética,** *f* cosmetics *pl: línea de cosmética,* range of cosmetics.
cósmico,-a *adj* cosmic.
cosmogonía *f* cosmogony.
cosmografía *f* cosmography.
cosmográfico,-a *adj* cosmographic, cosmographical.
cosmología *f* cosmology.
cosmológico,-a *adj* cosmologic, cosmological.
cosmonauta *mf* cosmonaut.
cosmonave *f* spaceship, spacecraft.
cosmopolita 1 *adj* cosmopolitan. – **2** *mf* cosmopolitan.
cosmopolitismo *m* cosmopolitanism.
cosmorama *m* cosmorama.
cosmos *m* cosmos.
▲ *pl* **cosmos**.
coso[1] 1 *m (lugar cercado)* arena, enclosure. **2** *(calle)* main street. **3** lit *(plaza de toros)* bullring.
coso[2] *m (carcoma)* woodworm.
cospel *m* blank.
cosquillas *fpl* tickling *sing.*
● **hacer cosquillas a algn.,** to tickle sb. ‖ **tener cosquillas,** to be ticklish. ‖ **buscarle las cosquillas a algn.,** *fam* to needle sb., annoy sb.
cosquillear *t* to tickle.
● **me cosquillea la idea de ...,** I've been toying with the idea of ...
cosquilleo *m* tickling.
cosquilloso,-a *adj* ticklish.
costa[1] *f (litoral)* coast, coastline; *(playa)* beach, seaside, US shore: *tenemos una casa en la costa,* we have a house at the seaside, US we have a house on the shore.
costa[2] 1 *f* FIN cost, price. – **2 costas,** *fpl* JUR costs.
● **a costa de,** *(aprovechándose)* at the expense of; *(a base de)* by, by dint of, by means of: *vive a costa de su padre,* he lives at his father's expense; *lo consiguió a costa de muchos sacrificios,* he managed it by making a lot of sacrifices. ‖ **a toda costa,** at all costs, at any price. ‖ **condenar a costas,** to order to cover the costs. ‖ **pagar las costas,** to pay costs.
Costa de Marfil *f* Ivory Coast.
costado 1 *m* side. **2** MIL flank. – **3 costados,** *mpl* lineage *sing.*
● **por los cuatro costados,** through and through.
costal *m* sack.
● **ser harina de otro costal,** *fig* to be another kettle of fish. ‖ **vaciar el costal,** *fig* to relieve os. of the burden.
costalada *f* fall.
● **darse una costalada,** to fall flat on one's face.
costalazo *m* → **costalada**.
costalero 1 *m (mozo)* porter. **2** *(de un paso)* bearer.
costanero,-a 1 *adj (inclinado)* sloping. **2** *(costero)* coastal.
costanilla *f* steep street.
costar 1 *i (valer)* to cost: *¿cuánto costó?,* how much was it? **2** *(ser difícil)* to be hard, be difficult; *(resultar difícil)* to be difficult for: *cuesta encontrar trabajo,* it's hard to find a job; *me cuesta el italiano,* I find Italian difficult. **3** *(tiempo)* to take: *me costó cuatro horas,* it took me four hours.

● **costar barato,-a,** to be cheap: *me costaron baratas las cortinas,* I got the curtains cheap. ‖ **costar caro,-a,** to be expensive, cost a lot; *fig* to pay dearly for sth.: *esa afirmación le costará cara,* he'll pay dearly for that statement. ‖ **costar mucho / costar trabajo,** to be hard. ‖ **costar un ojo de la cara,** *fam* to cost an arm and a leg. ‖ **cueste lo que cueste,** at any cost, whatever it costs.
▲ *Conjugation model* [31], *like* **contar**.
Costa Rica *f* Costa Rica.
costarricense 1 *adj* Costa Rican. – **2** *mf* Costa Rican.
costarriqueño,-a *adj-m,f* → **costarricense**.
coste *m* cost, price, expense.
■ **coste de la vida,** cost of living. ‖ **precio de coste,** cost price.
costear[1] *t* MAR to coast, sail along.
costear[2] 1 *t (pagar)* to pay for, afford: *su padre le costeó el viaje,* his father paid for his journey. – **2 costearse,** *p* to pay one's way.
costera *f* → **costero,-a**.
costero,-a 1 *adj* coastal, coast. – **2 costero,** *m (barco)* coasting vessel, coaster. – **3 costera,** *f (costado)* side. **4** *(tiempo de pesca)* fishing season.
costilla 1 *f* ANAT rib. **2** CULIN cutlet. **3** *fam fig (mujer)* wife, better half. – **4 costillas,** *fpl fam (espalda)* back *sing.*
● **medirle las costillas a algn.,** to give sb. a good hiding.
costillar *m* ribs *pl.*
costo[1] *m* cost, price.
costo[2] *m* arg *(hachís)* dope.
costoso,-a 1 *adj (caro)* costly, expensive. **2** *(difícil)* hard, difficult.
costra 1 *f* crust. **2** MED scab.
costumbre 1 *f (hábito)* habit: *tengo la costumbre de comer temprano,* I'm in the habit of having lunch early. **2** *(tradición)* custom: *es una costumbre rusa,* it's a Russian custom. **3** JUR usage. – **4 costumbres,** *fpl (personales)* ways, manner *sing; (de un pueblo)* customs.
● **como de costumbre,** as usual. ‖ **perder la costumbre,** to lose the habit. ‖ **tener por costumbre + inf,** to be in the habit of + *ger.*
■ **la fuerza de la costumbre,** the force of habit. ‖ **persona de buenas costumbres,** respectable person.
costumbrismo *m* folk literature.
costumbrista 1 *adj* about local customs. – **2** *mf* writer of folk literature.
costura 1 *f (cosido)* sewing. **2** *(línea de puntadas)* seam: *medias sin costura,* seamless stockings. **3** *(confección)* dressmaking.
● **meter a algn. en costura,** *fig* to bring sb. to reason. ‖ **sentar las costuras a algn.,** *fig* to give sb. a dressing-down.
■ **alta costura,** haute couture. ‖ **cesto de la costura,** sewing basket.
costurera *f* seamstress.
costurero 1 *m (estuche)* sewing basket, sewing kit. **2** *(mueble)* workbox.
costurón 1 *m (cosido)* untidy seam. **2** *(cicatriz)* noticeable scar.
cota[1] *f (traje)* tabard.
■ **cota de malla,** coat of mail.
cota[2] 1 *f (altura)* height above sea level: *la cota mil,* one thousand metres above sea level. **2** *(número en mapa)* spot height. **3** *fig (nivel)* level: *la xenofobia está llegando a cotas muy altas,* xenophobia is showing an alarming increase.

cotangente f cotangent.
cotarro m fam fig noisy gathering.
● dirigir el cotarro / ser el amo del cotarro, fam to be the boss, run the show.
cotejable adj comparable.
cotejar t (gen) to compare; (textos) to collate, compare.
cotejo m (gen) comparison; (textos) collation, comparison.
coterráneo,-a 1 adj compatriot, from the same country, from the same region. – 2 m,f (hombre) fellow countryman; (mujer) fellow countrywoman.
cotidianamente adv daily, everyday.
cotidiano,-a adj daily, everyday: la vida cotidiana, everyday life.
cotila f socket.
cotiledón m cotyledon.
cotilla 1 f (faja) corset. – 2 mf fam busybody, gossip.
cotillear i fam to gossip, tittle-tattle.
cotilleo m fam gossip, gossiping, tittle-tattle.
cotillo m hammerhead.
cotillón 1 m (danza) cotillion, cotillon. 2 (fiesta) party, celebration especially on New Year's Eve.
cotizable adj quotable.
■ acciones cotizables en bolsa, stock market shares.
cotización 1 f FIN quotation, market price. 2 (cuota) membership fee, subscription.
■ cotización de cierre, closing price. ‖ cotización del día, current price. ‖ cotización máxima, high.
cotizar 1 t FIN to quote, price. – 2 i (pagar cuota) to pay a subscription. – 3 cotizarse, p (acciones) to sell (a, at): estas acciones se cotizan a diez mil pesetas, these shares are selling at ten thousand pesetas. 4 fig (valorarse) to be valued, be in demand: este pintor se cotiza mucho, this painter is in great demand.
▲ Conjugation model [4], like realizar.
coto¹ 1 m (terreno) enclosure, reserve. 2 (poste) boundary mark. 3 (límite) restriction.
● poner coto a algo, to put a stop to sth.
■ coto de caza, game preserve.
coto² m (pez) miller's thumb.
cotonificio m cotton industry.
cotorra 1 f (ave) parrot. 2 fam fig chatterbox.
● hablar como una cotorra, to be a chatterbox.
cotorrear i fam fig to chatter, prattle (on).
cotorreo m fam fig chatter, prattle.
cotudo,-a adj fluffy, cottony.
coturno m cothurnus.
COU abr EDUC (Curso de Orientación Universitaria) ≈ GCE A level studies, sixth-form studies.
coulomb m coulomb.
covacha f small cave.
covachuela f small cellar, small cave.
cowboy m cowboy.
▲ pl cowboys.
coxis m coccyx.
▲ pl coxis.
coy m hammock.
▲ pl coyes.
coyote m coyote.
coyuntura 1 f ANAT joint, articulation. 2 fig (circunstancia) moment, juncture.
■ coyuntura económica, economic situation. ‖ coyuntura política, political situation. ‖ coyuntura social, social situation.
coz f kick.
● dar coces / dar una coz, to kick. ‖ tratar a algn. a coces, fig to treat sb. like dirt.

C.P. abr (código postal) postcode, US zip code.
crac 1 m (quiebra) crash, bankruptcy: el crac de la bolsa de Nueva York, the Wall Street crash. 2 (onomatopeya) crack, snap: el brazo me hizo crac, my arm gave a crack.
crack 1 m (droga) crack. 2 (persona) star, ace: es un auténtico crack del fútbol, he's a crack football player.
crampón m crampon.
▲ pl crampones.
craneal adj cranial.
craneano,-a adj cranial.
cráneo m cranium, skull.
● ir de cráneo, fam to have a lot on one's plate, have one's work cut out. ‖ romperle el cráneo a algn., fam to smash sb.'s head in.
crápula 1 f (borrachera) drunkenness. 2 fig (disipación) dissipation, debauchery. – 3 m (hombre) reprobate, rake.
crascitar i to caw, croak.
craso,-a 1 adj (gordo) fat, gross. 2 fig (error) gross, crass.
cráter m crater.
crawl m crawl.
creación 1 f (gen) creation. 2 (fundación) foundation, establishment, setting up.
creador,-ra 1 adj creative. – 2 m,f creator, maker.
crear 1 t (gen) to create: crear problemas, to create problems. 2 (fundar) to found, establish; (partido) to set up. 3 (inventar) to invent. – 4 crearse, p to make, make for os.: crearse enemigos, to make enemies for os. 5 (imaginarse) to imagine.
creatividad f creativity.
creativo,-a adj creative.
crecendo in crecendo, loc adv in crescendo.
● ir en crecendo, to be increasing.
crecepelo m hair restorer.
crecer 1 i (persona, planta) to grow: has crecido mucho, you've grown a lot; se dejó crecer la barba, he grew a beard. 2 (incrementar) to increase, grow, get bigger: la población ha crecido en un uno por ciento, the population has grown by one percent. 3 (corriente, marea) to rise. 4 (luna) to wax. 5 (días) to get longer: los días crecen, the days are getting longer. 6 (en labor de punto) to add, increase. – 7 crecerse, p (tomar mayor fuerza) to grow in confidence: se crece ante las dificultades, he comes into his own when faced with problems.
▲ Conjugation model [43], like agradecer.
creces fpl increase sing in volume.
● con creces, fully: el dinero recaudado superó con creces lo que se necesitaba, the money collected far exceeded what was needed; nos devolvió el dinero con creces, she returned the money with interest; pagó su error con creces, he paid dearly for his mistake.
crecida f → crecido,-a.
crecido,-a 1 adj (persona) grown, grown-up. 2 (cantidad) big, large. 3 (río) in flood, in spate. 4 fig (engreído) vain, conceited. – 5 crecida, f flood, spate.
creciente 1 adj (que crece) growing; (que aumenta) increasing: un interés creciente, an increasing interest. 2 (precios) rising. 3 (luna) crescent (in the first quarter). – 4 f (de agua) flood, spate.
crecimiento 1 m (desarrollo) growth, increase. 2 (subida) rise. 3 (de un río) flooding, rising.
credencial 1 adj credential. – 2 credenciales, fpl credentials.
■ cartas credenciales, credentials.
credibilidad f credibility.
crediticio,-a adj credit.
crédito 1 m COM credit. 2 (confianza) credit, belief, credence. 3 (fama) reputation, standing.

● **a crédito,** on credit. ‖ **dar crédito a,** (*creer*) to believe (in): *no doy crédito a mis oídos,* I can't believe what I'm hearing. ‖ **ser digno,-a de crédito,** to be reliable. ‖ **tener crédito,** to have a good reputation.
■ **crédito hipotecario,** debt secured by a mortgage.
credo 1 *m* REL creed. **2** MÚS Credo. **3** *fig* (*creencias*) credo, creed.
credulidad *f* credulity, gullibility.
crédulo,-a *adj* credulous, gullible.
creencia *f* belief.
■ **creencia religiosa,** religious belief.
creer 1 *t* (*dar por cierto*) to believe: *si no lo veo no lo creo,* I've got to see it to believe it. **2** (*suponer, opinar*) to think, suppose: *¿y tú que crees?,* what do you think?; *creo que sí,* I think so; *creo que no,* I don't think so. **3** (*tener fe*) to believe. – **4** *i* (*tener fe*) to believe: *creo en Dios,* I believe in God. – **5** *creerse,* *p* (*aceptar*) to believe: *no me lo creo,* I don't believe it, I can't believe it; *no puedo creerme que sea tan barato,* I can't believe it's so cheap. **6** (*considerarse*) to think: *se cree un gran cantante,* he thinks he's a great singer; *¿quién te has creído que eres?,* who do you think you are?
● **creer a ciencia cierta,** to be convinced. ‖ **creer a ojos cerrados,** to believe blindly. ‖ **creer a pies juntillas,** to firmly believe. ‖ **¡no creas!,** do you really think so?, I'm not so sure. ‖ **no vayas a creer que ...,** don't go thinking that ... ‖ **¡que te crees tú eso!,** that's what you think! ‖ **¡ya lo creo!,** of course!
▲ *Conjugation model* |61|, *like leer.*
creíble *adj* credible, believable.
creído,-a 1 *pp* → **creer.** – **2** *adj* arrogant, vain, conceited.
● **ser un creído,-a,** to be full of os.
crema 1 *f* (*de leche, licor, ungüento*) cream. **2** (*natillas*) custard. **3** (*betún*) shoe polish. **4** *fig* (*lo mejor*) cream. – **5** *adj* cream, cream coloured (US cream colored).
■ **crema bronceadora,** suntan cream. ‖ **crema catalana,** *type of crème brûlée.* ‖ **crema de afeitar,** shaving cream. ‖ **crema de belleza,** beauty cream. ‖ **crema de champiñones,** cream of mushroom soup. ‖ **crema hidratante,** moisturizing cream.
cremación *f* cremation.
cremallera 1 *f* (*de vestido*) zip, zip fastener (US zipper). **2** TÉC rack.
● **echar la cremallera,** *fam* to shut one's mouth, zip up.
■ **ferrocarril de cremallera,** rack-railway, cog railway.
cremática *f* → **cremático,-a.**
cremático,-a 1 *adj* chrematistic. – **2 cremática,** *f* (*economía política*) chrematistics. **3** *fam* money matters *pl.*
crematorio *m* crematorium.
cremoso,-a *adj* creamy: *queso cremoso,* full-fat cheese.
crencha 1 *f* (*raya*) parting. **2** (*parte*) side of the hair.
crepe *f* (*torta*) pancake, crêpe.
crepé 1 *m* (*postizo*) hairpiece. **2** (*tejido, caucho*) crepe, crêpe.
crepería *f* creperie, crêperie.
crepitar *i* to crackle.
crepuscular *adj* twilight.
crepúsculo *m* twilight.
crescendo in crescendo, *loc adv* → **crecendo.**
crespo,-a 1 *adj* (*pelo*) frizzy. **2** (*estilo*) obscure. **3** *fig* (*irritado*) angry.
crespón *m* crepe, crêpe.
cresta 1 *f* (*de ave*) crest; (*de gallo*) comb. **2** (*de pelo*) toupée. **3** (*de montaña, ola*) crest.

● **dar a algn. en la cresta,** *fam* to deflate sb., bring sb. down to earth. ‖ **estar en la cresta de la ola,** *fam* to be on the crest of a wave. ‖ **levantar la cresta / alzar la cresta,** *fam* to give os. airs, get on one's high horse.
crestomatía *f* chrestomathy, anthology.
crestón *m* outcrop.
creta *f* chalk.
Creta *f* Crete.
cretense 1 *adj* Cretan. – **2** *mf* Cretan.
cretinismo 1 *m* (*enfermedad*) cretinism. **2** *fam fig* cretinism, stupidity.
cretino,-a 1 *adj* stupid, cretinous. – **2** *m,f* cretin, idiot.
cretona *f* cretonne.
creyente 1 *adj* believing. – **2** *mf* believer.
crezco *pres indic* → **crecer.**
cría *f* → **crío,-a.**
criada *f* → **criado,-a.**
criadero 1 *m* (*de plantas*) nursery; (*de animales*) breeding ground, breeding farm; (*de peces*) hatchery. **2** (*mina*) seam.
■ **criadero de ostras,** oyster bed.
criadilla 1 *f* CULIN bull's testicle. **2** (*patata*) potato. **3** (*panecillo*) small roll.
■ **criadilla de tierra,** truffle.
criado,-a 1 *pp* → **criar.** – **2** *adj* (*animal*) reared, raised; (*persona*) bred, brought up. – **3** *m,f* servant. – **4 criada,** *f* maid.
● **bien criado,-a,** well-bred. ‖ **mal criado,-a,** ill-bred, spolit, spoiled.
criador *m,f* breeder.
crianza 1 *f* (*de animales*) breeding. **2** (*lactancia*) nursing. **3** (*educación*) upbringing.
■ **vino de crianza,** mature wine.
criar 1 *t* (*educar niños*) to bring up, rear, care for: *lo crió una tía,* his aunt brought him up. **2** (*nutrir*) to feed (**con,** -); (*con pecho*) to suckle, nurse, breast-feed. **3** (*animales*) to breed, raise, rear. **4** (*producir*) to have, grow; (*vinos*) to make, mature. – **5** *i* (*engendrar*) to give birth. – **6 criarse,** *p* (*crecer*) to grow; (*formarse*) to be brought up. **7** (*producirse*) to grow.
▲ *Conjugation model* |13|, *like desviar.*
criatura 1 *f* creature. **2** (*niño*) baby, child. **3** *fig* baby.
criba 1 *f* (*tamiz*) sieve. **2** *fig* (*selección*) screening.
● **estar como una criba,** *fam* to be riddled with holes. ‖ **hacer una criba,** to screen; (*en examen*) to fail many students. ‖ **pasar por la criba,** *fig* to screen.
cribar 1 *t* (*colar*) to sift, sieve. **2** *fig* (*seleccionar*) to screen.
cric *m* jack.
▲ *pl* **crics.**
cricoides 1 *adj* cricoid. – **2** *m* cricoid.
▲ *pl* **cricoides.**
cricquet *m* cricket.
▲ *pl* **cricquets.**
crimen 1 *m* (*delito*) crime. **2** (*asesinato*) murder.
■ **crimen pasional,** crime of passion.
▲ *pl* **crímenes.**
criminal 1 *adj* criminal. **2** *fam* (*muy malo*) awful, criminal, appalling. – **3** *mf* criminal.
■ **criminal de guerra,** war criminal.
criminalidad *f* criminality.
■ **índice de criminalidad,** crime rate.
criminalista 1 *mf* (*abogado*) criminal lawyer. **2** (*estudioso*) criminologist.
criminología *f* criminology.
crin *f* mane.
▲ *Also used in plural with the same meaning.*

crío,-a 1 *m,f fam* kid, child. – **2** *adj fam* young: *todavía eres muy crío,* you're still too young. – **3 cría,** *f (acto de criar)* nursing; *(de animal)* breeding, raising. **4** *(cachorro)* young. **5** *(camada - ovíparos)* brood; *(- mamíferos)* litter.
● **ser un crío,-a,** *fam* to be childish.
criollo,-a 1 *adj* Creole. – **2** *m,f (persona)* Creole. – **3** *m (idioma)* Creole.
cripta *f* crypt.
críptico,-a *adj* cryptic.
criptografía *f* cryptography.
criptograma *m* cryptogram.
criptón *m* krypton.
críquet *m* cricket.
▲ *pl* **críquets**.
crisálida *f* chrysalis.
crisantemo *m* chrysanthemum.
crisis 1 *f (dificultad)* crisis. **2** *(ataque)* fit, attack: *crisis de asma,* asthma attack; *crisis de llanto,* fit of tears. **3** *(escasez)* shortage: *crisis de alimentos,* food shortage.
▲ *pl* **crisis**.
● **estar en crisis,** to be in crisis, reach crisis point.
■ **crisis de gobierno,** cabinet crisis. ‖ **crisis financiera,** financial crisis. ‖ **crisis nerviosa,** nervous breakdown.
crisma 1 *m* & *f* REL chrism. **2** *fam (cabeza)* head, nut.
● **romperle la crisma a algn.,** to knock sb.'s block off.
crisol 1 *m* crucible. **2** *fig* melting pot.
crisólito *m* chrysolite.
crispación *f fig* tension: *un clima de crispación,* a tense atmosphere.
crispado,-a 1 *pp →* **crispar**. – **2** *adj* on edge, touchy, tense: *tengo los nervios crispados,* my nerves are shot.
crispar 1 *t* ANAT to contract, tense. **2** *fig (irritar)* to irritate, annoy, infuriate: *ese tipo me crispa,* that guy infuriates me. – **3 crisparse,** *p* ANAT to contract, tense. **4** *fig (irritarse)* to get annoyed, get angry.
● **crispar los nervios a algn.,** *fig* to get on sb.'s nerves.
cristal 1 *m (mineral)* crystal. **2** *(vidrio)* glass. **3** *(de ventana)* window pane, pane. **4** *(de lente)* lens. **5** *(de coche)* window. – **6 cristales,** *mpl (trozos)* glass *sing*: *ten cuidado, hay cristales por el suelo,* be careful, there's some broken glass on the floor. **7** *(ventanas)* windows.
■ **botella de cristal,** glass bottle. ‖ **copa de cristal,** wine glass. ‖ **cristal de aumento,** magnifying glass. ‖ **cristal de cuarzo,** quartz crystal. ‖ **cristal de roca,** rock crystal. ‖ **cristal tallado,** cut glass. ‖ **vaso de cristal,** drinking glass.
cristalería 1 *f (fábrica)* glassworks. **2** *(tienda)* glassware shop. **3** *(conjunto)* glassware; *(vasos)* glasses *pl*.
cristalero,-a *m,f* glazier.
cristalino,-a 1 *adj* transparent, crystal-clear. – **2 cristalino,** *m* crystalline lens.
cristalización 1 *f* crystallization. **2** *fig* consolidation.
cristalizar 1 *t* to crystallize. – **2** *i* to crystallize. **3** *fig* to crystallize (**en**, into). – **4 cristalizarse,** *p* to crystallize.
▲ *Conjugation model* [4], *like* **realizar**.
cristalografía *f* crystallography.
cristaloide *m* crystalloid.
cristianar *t fam* to christen, baptize.
cristiandad *f* Christendom.
cristianismo *m* Christianity.
cristianizar *t* to convert to Christianity.
▲ *Conjugation model* [4], *like* **realizar**.
cristiano,-a 1 *adj* REL Christian. **2** *fam (vino)* watered-down. – **3** *m,f* REL Christian. – **4 cristiano,** *m fam* per-

son, soul: *cualquier cristiano lo entendería,* anybody would understand it.
● **hablar en cristiano,** *fam (claro)* to speak plainly; *(en español)* to speak Spanish.
■ **cristiano,-a nuevo,-a,** HIST Moor or Jew converted to Christianity. ‖ **cristiano,-a viejo.-a,** HIST Christian without Moorish or Jewish ancestors.
Cristo 1 *m* REL Christ. **2** *(crucifijo)* crucifix.
● **antes de Cristo,** before Christ. ‖ **armar un Cristo,** *fam* to kick up a big fuss. ‖ **después de Cristo,** anno domini. ‖ **donde Cristo dio las tres voces / donde Cristo perdió el gorro,** *fam* in the middle of nowhere. ‖ **estar hecho un Cristo,** *fam* to be a sorry sight, look a right state. ‖ **ni Cristo,** *fam* nobody: *no había ni Cristo,* nobody was there, there wasn't a soul. ‖ **poner a algn. hecho un Cristo,** *fam* to have a real go at sb.
criterio 1 *m (en lógica)* criterion. **2** *(juicio)* judgement, discernment. **3** *(opinión)* opinion, point of view: *en mi criterio,* in my opinion; *muchos comparten ese criterio,* many others share that opinion.
● **cambiar de criterio,** to change one's mind. ‖ **dejar a criterio de algn.,** to leave to sb.'s discretion. ‖ **ser de amplios criterios,** to be broad-minded.
crítica *f →* **crítico,-a**.
criticar 1 *t* to criticize. – **2** *i (murmurar)* to gossip.
▲ *Conjugation model* [1], *like* **sacar**.
crítico,-a 1 *adj* critical. – **2** *m,f* critic. – **3 crítica,** *f (juicio, censura)* criticism. **4** *(prensa)* review, write-up. **5** *(conjunto de críticos)* critics *pl*.
● **hacer críticas,** to criticize. ‖ **ser dado,-a a las críticas,** to be very critical. ‖ **tener buena crítica,** to get good reviews.
■ **crítica teatral,** theatre (US theater) column.
criticón,-ona 1 *adj fam* faultfinding, nit-picking, hypercritical. – **2** *m,f fam* faultfinder, nit-picker.
Croacia *f* Croatia.
croar *i* to croak.
croata 1 *adj* Croatian, Croat. – **2** *mf (persona)* Croat, Croatian. – **3** *m (idioma)* Croat, Croatian.
crocante *m* almond brittle.
crocanti *m* almond brittle.
croché *m* crochet.
croissant *m* croissant.
▲ *pl* **croissants**.
croissantería *f* croissant shop.
crol *m* crawl.
cromado,-a 1 *pp →* **cromar**. – **2** *adj* chrome. – **3 cromado,** *m* chroming.
cromar *t* to chrome.
cromático,-a *adj* chromatic.
cromatina *f* chromatin.
cromatismo *m* chromatism.
crómico,-a *adj* chromic.
crómlech *m* cromlech.
cromo 1 *m (metal)* chromium, chrome. **2** *(cromolitografía)* chromolithograph, chromo. **3** *(estampa)* picture card, sticker: *un álbum de cromos,* a picture-card album.
● **ir hecho,-a un cromo,** *fam* to look a picture.
cromosoma *m* chromosome.
crónica 1 *f (gen)* account, chronicle. **2** *(en periódico)* article, column, feature. **3** RAD TV *(programa)* programme (US program); *(reportaje)* feature, report. **4** HIST chronicle.
■ **crónica de sociedad,** society column, social column. ‖ **crónica de sucesos,** news in brief, news headlines *pl*.
crónico,-a 1 *adj* chronic. **2** *fig* deeply rooted.

169

cronicón *m* short chronicle.
cronista 1 *mf* HIST chronicler. 2 (*de prensa*) columnist, feature writer. 3 RAD TV commentator.
crono 1 *m* (*cronómetro*) chronometer. 2 DEP (*tiempo*) time.
cronógrafo,-a 1 *m,f* chronographer. – 2 **cronógrafo**, *m* chronograph.
cronología *f* chronology.
cronológicamente *adv* chronologically.
cronológico,-a *adj* chronological.
cronometraje *m* timing.
cronometrar *t* to time.
cronómetro 1 *m* chronometer. 2 DEP stopwatch.
croquet *m* croquet.
croqueta *f* croquette.
croquis *m* sketch, outline.
  ▲ *pl croquis.*
cros *m* (*a pie*) cross-country race; (*en moto*) motorcross race.
  ▲ *pl cros.*
cruasán *m* croissant.
  ▲ *pl cruasanes.*
cruce 1 *m* cross, crossing. 2 AUTO crossroads. 3 (*de razas*) crossbreeding. 4 (*interferencia telefónica etc*) crossed line: *hay un cruce*, there's a crossed line. 5 ELEC short circuit.
crucería *f* ARQ ogives *pl*, ribs *pl.*
crucero 1 *m* (*buque*) cruiser. 2 (*viaje*) cruise. 3 ARQ transept.
  ● **hacer un crucero**, to go on a cruise.
crucial 1 *adj* crucial. 2 *fig* crucial, critical.
crucificado,-a 1 *pp* → **crucificar**. – 2 *adj* crucified.
crucificar 1 *t* to crucify. 2 *fam fig* to torture.
  ▲ *Conjugation model* |1|, *like sacar.*
crucifijo *m* crucifix.
crucifixión *f* crucifixion.
cruciforme *adj* cruciform, cross-shaped.
crucigrama *m* crossword (puzzle).
crudeza 1 *f* (*sin cocer*) rawness; (*sin madurar*) unripeness. 2 (*rudeza*) crudeness, rudeness, coarseness. 3 (*del clima*) harshness. – 4 **crudezas**, *fpl* undigested food *sing.*
crudo,-a 1 *adj* (*sin cocer*) raw; (*poco hecho*) underdone: *la carne está cruda*, the meat is underdone, the meat isn't cooked enough. 2 *fig* (*duro*) crude, coarse. 3 (*color*) natural, unbleached. 4 (*clima*) harsh. – 5 **crudo**, *m* (*petróleo*) crude oil, crude.
  ● **verlo muy crudo**, *fam* not to hold out much hope.
  ■ **seda cruda**, raw silk.
cruel 1 *adj* (*persona*) cruel (**con/para**, to). 2 (*clima*) harsh, severe.
crueldad 1 *f* cruelty. 2 (*dureza*) harshness, severity.
cruentamente *adv* bloodily.
cruento,-a *adj* bloody.
crujido 1 *m* (*de puerta*) creak, creaking. 2 (*de patatas fritas*) crunching. 3 (*seda, papel*) rustle, rustling. 4 (*de dientes*) grinding.
crujiente 1 *adj* (*alimentos*) crunchy. 2 (*seda*) rustling.
crujir 1 *i* (*puerta*) to creak. 2 (*patatas fritas*) to crunch. 3 (*seda, hojas*) to rustle. 4 (*dientes*) to grind.
crupié *mf* croupier.
crupier *mf* croupier.
crustáceo *m* crustacean.
cruz 1 *f* (*gen*) cross. 2 (*de moneda*) tails *pl*: *¿cara o cruz?*, heads or tails? 3 *fig* (*carga*) burden, cross.
  ● **con los brazos en cruz**, with outstretched arms. ‖ **hacer cruz y raya**, *fig* to swear never again. ‖ **hacerse cruces de algo**, *fig* to be astonished at sth.

■ **cruz gamada**, swastika. ‖ **Cruz Roja**, Red Cross. ‖ **la señal de la cruz**, the sign of the cross.
cruzada *f* → **cruzado,-a**.
cruzado,-a 1 *pp* → **cruzar**. – 2 *adj* (*gen*) crossed. 3 (*animal, planta*) crossbred. 4 (*prenda*) double-breasted. 5 (*brazos*) folded. – 6 **cruzada**, *f* HIST crusade. 7 (*campaña*) campaign. – 8 **cruzado**, *m* HIST crusader.
cruzamiento 1 *m* crossing. 2 (*de animales*) cross-breeding.
cruzar 1 *t* (*gen*) to cross: *cruzar los dedos*, to cross one's fingers; *cruzar una calle*, to cross a street. 2 (*poner atravesado*) to lay across; (*estar atravesado*) to lie across: *cruzar la carretera con un tronco*, to lay a tree trunk across the road. 3 (*en geometría*) to intersect. 4 (*animales*) to cross. 5 (*miradas, palabras*) to exchange. – 6 **cruzarse**, *p* (*encontrarse*) to cross, pass each other. 7 (*intercambiarse*) to exchange.
  ● **cruzar a nado**, to swim across. ‖ **cruzar apuestas**, to make bets. ‖ **cruzar con una raya**, to draw a line across. ‖ **cruzar los brazos**, to fold one's arms. ‖ **cruzarle la cara a algn.**, *fig* to slap sb.'s face. ‖ **cruzarse en el camino de algn.**, *fig* to cross sb.'s path.
  ▲ *Conjugation model* |4|, *like realizar.*
CSD *abr* (*Consejo Superior de Deportes*) ≈ Sports Council.
c.s.f. *abr* (*coste, seguro y flete*) cost, insurance and freight; (*abreviatura*) cif.
CSIC *abr* (*Consejo Superior de Investigaciones Científicas*) Council for Scientific Research (*state body responsible for allocating grants for higher education and research*).
cta. *abr* (*cuenta*) account; (*abreviatura*) a/c, acc, acct.
cta. cte. *abr* (*cuenta corriente*) current account; (*abreviatura*) c/a.
cte. *abr* (*corriente*) of the present month, of the present year.
Cte. *abr* (*comandante*) commander; (*abreviatura*) Cmdr.
CTNE *abr* (*Compañía Telefónica Nacional de España*) ≈ British Telecom.
ctra. *abr* (*carretera*) road; (*abreviatura*) Rd.
cts. *abr* (*céntimos*) cents.
cu 1 *f* name of the letter *q*. 2 (*naipes*) queen.
c/u *abr* COM (*cada uno*) each; (*abreviatura*) ea.
cuaderna *f* frame.
cuadernillo *m* booklet.
cuaderno *m* (*libreta*) notebook, journal; (*escolar*) exercise book.
  ■ **cuaderno de bitácora**, logbook.
cuadra 1 *f* (*establo*) stable. 2 AM (*manzana*) block, block of houses.
cuadradillo 1 *m* (*azúcar*) lump. 2 (*barra de hierro*) square iron bar. 3 (*regla*) square ruler.
cuadrado,-a 1 *pp* → **cuadrar**. – 2 *adj* (*forma*) square. 3 *fam* (*persona*) broad, stocky. 4 *fig* (*mente*) rigid, one-track. – 5 **cuadrado**, *m* square.
  ● **elevar al cuadrado**, to square: *tres al cuadrado son nueve*, three squared is nine. ‖ **tenerlos cuadrados**, *tabú* to have balls.
cuadrafonía *f* quadraphony.
cuadrafónico,-a *adj* quadraphonic.
cuadragenario,-a 1 *adj* quadragenarian. – 2 *m,f* quadragenarian.
cuadragésimo,-a 1 *adj* fortieth. – 2 *m,f* fortieth.
  ▲ *See also* *sexto,-a*.
cuadrangular *adj* quadrangular.
cuadrante 1 *m* (*reloj*) sundial. 2 (*instrumento*) quadrant. 3 (*cojín*) square pillow.

cuadrante

cuadrar 1 *t* (*dar figura cuadrada*) to square, make square. 2 (*geometría, matemáticas*) to square. 3 COM to balance. − 4 *i* (*coincidir*) to square, agree. 5 COM to tally, add up: *las cuentas de este mes no cuadran,* the accounts don't add up this month. 6 *fig* (*ir bien*) to suit: *el estilo no cuadra con el tema,* the style doesn't suit the subject. − 7 **cuadrarse,** *p* MIL to stand to attention. 8 *fig* to stand firm, stick to one's guns, dig one's heels in: *su madre se cuadró y él no pudo salir,* his mother stuck to her guns and he couldn't go out.

cuadratura *f* quadrature.
● **la cuadratura del círculo,** *fig* squaring the circle.

cuádriceps *m* quadriceps.
▲ *pl cuádriceps.*

cuadrícula *f* squares *pl,* grid: *papel cuadriculado,* squared paper.

cuadriculado,-a 1 *adj* squared. − 2 **cuadriculado,** *m* squares *pl,* grid.

cuadricular 1 *t* to square, divide into squares. − 2 *adj* squared.

cuadrienio *m* quadrennium.

cuadriga *f* quadriga.

cuadrilátero,-a 1 *adj* quadrilateral, four-sided. − 2 **cuadrilátero,** *m* (*boxeo*) ring.

cuadrilla 1 *f* (*grupo*) party, gang. 2 (*de bandidos etc*) gang, band. 3 (*de obreros*) gang, team. 4 MIL squad. 5 (*de toreros*) bullfighter's team.

cuadrilongo,-a *adj* rectangular.

cuadripartito,-a *adj* quadripartite.

cuadriplicar 1 *t* to quadruple. − 2 *i* to quadruple.
▲ Conjugation model [1], like *sacar.*

cuadro 1 *m* (*cuadrado*) square. 2 (*pintura*) painting, picture. 3 TEAT scene. 4 (*descripción*) description, picture: *un cuadro de la vida estudiantil,* a description of student life. 5 MIL cadre. 6 (*dirigentes*) leaders *pl;* (*personal*) staff. 7 (*conjunto de datos*) chart, graph. 8 (*tablero de control*) panel. 9 (*de un jardín etc*) bed, patch, plot. 10 *fig* (*escena*) scene, sight: *desde la cima se ofrecía un cuadro maravilloso,* there was a wonderful view from the summit. 11 (*de bicicleta*) frame. 12 (*armazón*) frame.
● **a cuadros,** checked, US checkered: *tela a cuadros,* checked (US checkered) cloth. ‖ **en cuadro,** in a square. ‖ **estar en cuadro / quedarse en cuadro,** *fig* to be greatly reduced in numbers.
■ **cuadro clínico,** clinical pattern. ‖ **cuadro de costumbres,** study of manners. ‖ **cuadro de distribución,** switchboard. ‖ **cuadro de mandos,** control panel. ‖ **cuadro facultativo,** medical staff. ‖ **cuadro sinóptico,** diagram, chart.

cuadrumano,-a 1 *adj* quadrumanous. − 2 **cuadrumano,** *m* quadrumane.

cuadrúmano *m* → **cuadrumano,-a.**

cuadrúpedo,-a 1 *adj* quadruped. − 2 **cuadrúpedo,** *m* quadruped.

cuádruple *adj* quadruple, fourfold.

cuadruplicar 1 *t* to quadruple. − 2 *i* to quadruple.

cuajada *f* → **cuajado,-a.**

cuajado,-a 1 *pp* → **cuajar.** − 2 *adj* (*leche*) curdled; (*sangre*) clotted; (*huevo*) set. 3 (*lleno*) full, filled: *el mar está cuajado de algas,* the sea is full of seaweed; *tenía los ojos cuajados de lágrimas,* his eyes were brimming with tears. 4 *fig* (*asombrado*) dumbfounded, astonished. − 5 **cuajada,** *f* (*leche*) curd; (*requesón*) cottage cheese.

cuajar 1 *t* (*gen*) to coagulate; (*leche*) to curdle; (*sangre*) to clot. 2 (*huevo*) to set. 3 *fig* (*recargar de adornos*) to fill with, cover. − 4 *i* (*nieve*) to lie. 5 *fig* (*tener éxito*) to be a success,

come off: *la minifalda cuajó,* the miniskirt was a success; *la cosa no cuajó,* it didn't come off. 6 *fig* (*gustar*) to fit in, hit it off with: *Iván ha cuajado muy bien entre sus compañeros,* Iván has really hit it off with his workmates. − 7 **cuajarse,** *p* to coagulate; (*leche*) to curdle; (*sangre*) clot. 8 (*huevo*) to set. 9 *fig* (*llenarse*) to fill up.

cuajarón *m* clot.

cuajo 1 *m* (*cuajadura*) rennet. 2 *fam fig* phlegm, calmness.
● **arrancar algo de cuajo,** to tear sth. out by the roots. ‖ **tener cuajo,** *fam* to be cool, be laid-back.

cuákero,-a *adj-m,f* → **cuáquero,-a.**

cual 1 *pron* (*precedido de artículo - persona*) who, whom: *entrevistamos a los obreros, los cuales nos informaron adecuadamente,* we interviewed the workers, who duly informed us; *la gente a la cual preguntamos, the people whom we asked.* 2 (*precedido de artículo - cosa*) which: *la casa tiene un mirador desde el cual se ve el mar,* the house has a balcony with a view of the sea; *la ciudad en la cual nací,* the city where I was born. 3 (*correlativo*) such as: *descubrimientos cuales los del Renacimiento,* discoveries such as those made in the Renaissance. − 4 *adv fml* as, like: *se enamoró cual si tuviese quince años,* he fell in love like a teenager.
● **cada cual,** everyone, everybody.
▲ *pl cuales.*

cuál 1 *pron* (*interrogativo*) which, which one, what: *¿cuál es el más alto?,* which one is the tallest?; *¿cuáles son tus maletas?,* which suitcases are yours? 2 (*valor distributivo*) some: *tiene muchos libros, cuáles de historia, cuáles de arte,* he's got a lot of books, some on history, some on art. 3 (*exclamativo*) how, what: *¡cuál no sería mi asombro!,* imagine my amazement! − 4 *adj* (*interrogativo*) which.
● **a cuál más,** equally: *a cuál más listo,* each as clever as the other. ‖ **cuál más, cuál menos,** some more than others, to a greater or lesser degree.
▲ *pl cuáles.*

cualidad 1 *f* (*de persona*) quality, attribute. 2 (*de cosa*) quality, property.

cualificado,-a 1 *pp* → **cualificar.** − 2 *adj* qualifed, skilled.

cualificar 1 *t* to qualify. − 2 **cualificarse,** *p* to become qualified, complete one's training.
▲ Conjugation model [1], like *sacar.*

cualitativo,-a *adj* qualitative.

cualquier *adj* (*indefinido*) any: *cualquier otro día,* any other day; *cualquier cosa,* anything; *cualquier persona,* anyone.
▲ Used only *before* a noun (*but it may be separated from the noun by an adjective*); *pl* **cualesquier;** *see also* **cualquiera.**

cualquiera 1 *adj* (*indefinido*) any: *un día cualquiera,* any day; *una página cualquiera,* any page. 2 (*ordinario*) ordinary: *no es una corbata cualquiera,* it's not an ordinary tie. − 3 *pron* (*persona indeterminada*) anybody, anyone; (*cosa indeterminada*) any, any one: *cualquiera lo compraría,* anybody would buy it; *coge cualquiera,* take any one you want. 4 (*nadie*) nobody: *¡cualquiera lo coge!,* nobody would take it! − 5 *mf pey* nobody: *ser un cualquiera,* to be a nobody. − 6 *f pey* (*prostituta*) hussy, floozy, tart. − 7 **cualquiera que,** *pron* (*persona*) whoever; (*cosa*) whatever, whichever: *cualquiera que diga eso, miente,* whoever says that is lying; *cualquiera que sea,* whatever it is.
▲ *pl* **cualesquiera.**

cuan *adv fml* as: *hizo el discurso cuan corto supo,* he made the speech as short as he could; *cayó cuan largo era,* he fell flat on the floor.

▲ Used only *before adjectives and adverbs; see also* **cuanto**.
cuán *adv* (*interrogativo*) how: *¡cuán idiota!*, how stupid!
▲ Used only *before adjectives and adverbs; see also* **cuanto**.
cuando I *adv* (*tiempo*) when: *cuando tenía diez años*, when he was ten. − **2** *conj* (*temporal*) when, whenever: *ven a verme cuando quieras*, come and see me whenever you want; *iba conduciendo cuando vi una extraña luz*, I was driving along when I saw a strange light. **3** (*condicional*) if: *cuando él lo dice*, if he says so. **4** (*causal*) since. − **5** *prep* during, at the time of: *cuando la guerra*, during the war.
● **cuando más**, at the most. ‖ **cuando menos**, at least. ‖ **cuando mucho**, at the most. ‖ **cuando quiera que**, whenever. ‖ **de cuando en cuando / de vez en cuando**, now and then, from time to time. ‖ **hasta cuando**, until.
cuándo I *adv* (*interrogativo*) when: *¿cuándo es tu cumpleaños?*, when is your birthday? − **2** *m* when: *no sé el cómo ni el cuándo*, I don't know how or when.
● **¿de cuándo acá?**, since when?
cuantía I *f* (*cantidad*) quantity; (*importe*) amount: *la cuantía de una factura*, the amount of a bill. **2** (*dimensión*) extent: *la cuantía del desastre ecológico*, the extent of the ecological disaster.
● **de mayor cuantía**, important. ‖ **de menor cuantía**, insignificant, lesser.
cuantificar *t* to quantify, measure.
▲ Conjugation model |1|, *like* **sacar**.
cuantioso,-a *adj* (*grande - en cantidad*) substancial, considerable; (*- en número*) numerous.
cuantitativo,-a *adj* quantitative.
cuanto¹ *m* FÍS quantum: *la teoría de los cuantos*, the quantum theory.
cuanto,-a² I *adj* (*singular*) as much as; (*plural*) as many as: *puedes beber cuanta agua quieras*, you can drink as much water as you want; *puedes coger cuantos libros quieras*, you can take as many books as you want. − **2** *pron* (*singular*) everything, all: *vendió cuanto tenía*, he sold everything he had; *escribe cuanto quieras*, write as much as you want. **3** (*plural*) all who, everybody who: *cuantos entraron se asustaron*, everybody who came in was frightened.
● **cuanto a**, with respect to, regarding, as for. ‖ **cuanto antes**, as soon as possible. ‖ **cuanto más**, (*máximo*) all the more. ‖ **cuanto más ... más**, the more ... the more: *cuanto más habla más me asusta*, the more he talks the more he frightens me. ‖ **cuantos,-as más, mejor**, the more, the merrier. ‖ **cuanto menos ... menos**, the less ... the less: *cuanto menos comas, menos engordarás*, the less you eat, the less weight you'll put on. ‖ **cuantos,-as ... tantos,-as**, as many ... as: *cuantas cabezas, tantos sombreros*, as many heads as hats. ‖ **en cuanto**, as soon as, when: *en cuanto llegue dile ...*, as soon as he arrives tell him ... ‖ **en cuanto a**, with respect to, regarding, as for: *en cuanto a mí*, as for me, as far as I'm concerned. ‖ **por cuanto**, given that, since. ‖ **unos,-as cuantos,-as**, some, a few.
▲ *pl* **cuantos,-as**.
cuánto,-a I *adj* (*pregunta - singular*) how much; (*- plural*) how many: *¿cuánto dinero cuesta?*, how much does it cost?; *¿cuántos coches hay?*, how many cars are there?; *¿cuántos años tienes?*, how old are you? **2** (*exclamación*) what a lot of, so many, so much: *¡cuánta gente!*, there are so many people!, what a lot of people!; *¡cuánto tiempo!*, it's been a long time! − **3** *pron* (*singular*) how much; (*plural*) how many: *¿cuánto es?*, how much is it?; *¿cuánto pesas?*, how much do you weigh?; *¿cuántos*

érais?, how many of you were there?; *¿a cuánto están los aguacates?*, how much are the avocados? − **4** *adv* how, how much: *¡cuánto me alegro!*, I'm so glad!; *no sabes cuánto lo odio*, you don't know how much I hate him.
▲ *pl* **cuántos,-as**.
cuaquerismo *m* Quakerism.
cuáquero,-ra I *adj* Quaker. − **2** *m,f* Quaker.
cuarcita *f* quartzite.
cuarenta I *adj* (*cardinal*) forty; (*ordinal*) fortieth. − **2** *m* (*número*) forty.
● **cantarle las cuarenta a algn.**, to give sb. a piece of one's mind.
▲ See also **seis**.
cuarentavo,-a I *adj* fortieth. − **2** *m,f* fortieth.
▲ See also **sexto,-a**.
cuarentena I *f* (*exacto*) forty; (*aproximado*) about forty. **2** MED quarantine.
● **poner a algn. en cuarentena**, MED to quarantine sb., put sb. in quarantine; *fig* to send sb. to Coventry.
cuarentón,-ona I *adj* forty-year-old. − **2** *m,f* (*hombre*) forty-year-old man, man in his forties; (*mujer*) forty-year-old woman, woman in her forties.
cuaresma *f* Lent.
cuarta *f* → **cuarto,-a**.
cuartear I *t* (*dividir en cuatro*) to quarter, divide into four. **2** (*descuartizar*) to quarter. **3** (*rajar*) to crack. − **4** **cuartearse**, *p* (*rajarse*) to crack, split.
cuartel I *m* MIL barracks *pl*. **2** (*cuarta parte*) quarter.
● **no dar cuartel**, *fig* to show no mercy.
■ **cuartel de invierno**, winter quarters *pl*. ‖ **cuartel general**, headquarters *sing*. ‖ **lucha sin cuartel**, merciless fight, fight to the end. ‖ **vida de cuartel**, army life.
cuartelada *f* putsch, military uprising.
cuartelazo *m* putsch, military uprising.
cuartelero,-a *adj* barrack, barracks.
cuartelillo *m* post, station.
■ **dar cuartelillo a algn.**, *fam* to bail sb. out.
cuarterón,-ona I *m,f* (*mestizo*) quadroon. − **2** cuarterón, *m* (*de puerta*) panel.
cuarteta *f* quatrain.
cuarteto *m* quartet.
cuartilla *f* sheet of paper.
cuartillo *m* liquid measure equivalent to 0.504 litres (US liters).
cuarto,-a I *adj* (*ordinal*) fourth: *llegó cuarto*, he arrived in fourth place, he came fourth. − **2** *m,f* fourth. − **3** cuarto, *m* (*parte*) quarter: *un cuarto de hora*, a quarter of an hour. **4** (*de animal*) quarter. **5** (*de ropa*) quarter: *un chaquetón tres cuartos*, a three-quarter length jacket. **6** (*habitación*) room. − **7** cuarta, *f* (*palmo*) span. **8** ASTRON quadrant. − **9** cuartos, *mpl fam* (*dinero*) money *sing*, dough *sing*.
● **de tres al cuarto**, *fam* worthless, third-rate. ‖ **estar sin un cuarto**, *fam* to be broke. ‖ **no levantar una cuarta del suelo**, *fam* to be a shorty. ‖ **tres cuartos de lo mismo**, *fam* exactly the same.
■ **cuarto creciente**, first quarter. ‖ **cuarto de baño**, bathroom. ‖ **cuarto de estar**, living room. ‖ **cuarto delantero**, (*carne*) shoulder. ‖ **cuarto menguante**, last quarter. ‖ **cuarto oscuro**, (*fotografía*) darkroom. ‖ **cuarto trasero**, (*carne*) hindquarter. ‖ **cuarto trastero**, junk room. ‖ **cuartos de final**, DEP quarter finals. ‖ **cuatro cuartos**, *fam* very little money *sing*.
▲ In *1* and *2*, *see also* **sexto,-a**.
cuartucho *m fam* hovel, cramped room.

cuarzo m quartz.
cuaternario,-a 1 adj Quaternary. – 2 **cuaternario,** m Quaternary.
cuatralbo,-a adj with four white feet.
cuatreño,-a adj four-year-old.
cuatrero m cattle thief, rustler.
cuatrienio m quadrennium, four-year-period.
cuatrillizo,-a 1 adj quadruplet. – 2 m,f quadruplet.
cuatrillón m quadrillion, us septillion.
cuatrimestral adj (en frecuencia) four-monthly; (en duración) four-month.
cuatrimestre m four-month period: en el primer cuatrimestre de 1996, in the first four months of 1996.
cuatrimotor m four-engined plane.
cuatrisílabo,-a 1 adj quadrisyllabic. – 2 **cuatrisílabo,** m quadrisyllable.
cuatro 1 adj (cardinal) four; (ordinal) fourth. – 2 m (número) four.
● caer cuatro gotas, fam to rain very lightly, spit. ‖ decirle cuatro cosas a algn., to tell sb. off. ‖ más de cuatro, fam several, a fair few.
■ cuatro gatos, fam just a few people, hardly anyone.
▲ See also seis.
cuatrocientos,-as 1 adj four hundred. – 2 **cuatrocientos,** m (número) four hundred.
▲ See also seis.
cuatrojos mf fam four-eyes.
▲ pl cuatrojos.
cuba f cask, barrel.
● estar como una cuba, fam to be (as) drunk as a lord.
Cuba f Cuba.
cubalibre m rum and coke.
cubano,-a 1 adj Cuban. – 2 m,f Cuban.
cubata m fam rum and coke.
cubertería f cutlery.
cubeta 1 f (rectangular) tray, tank, dish. 2 (cubo) bucket. 3 (de barómetro) bulb.
cubicar t to cube.
cúbico,-a adj cubic: raíz cúbica, cube root.
cubículo m cubicle.
cubierta f → **cubierto,-a.**
cubierto,-a 1 pp → **cubrir.** – 2 adj (gen) covered. 3 (cielo) overcast. 4 (plaza) filled. – 5 **cubierto,** m (techumbre) cover. 6 (en la mesa) place setting. 7 (menú) meal at a fixed price: el cubierto costó dos mil pesetas, it was two thousand pesetas a head. – 8 cubiertos, mpl cutlery sing. – 9 cubierta, f (gen) cover, covering. 10 (de libro) jacket. 11 ARQ roof. 12 (de neumático) tyre (us tire). 13 (capó) bonnet, us hood. 14 AV MAR deck.
● a cubierto de, safe from. ‖ en cubierta, on deck. ‖ estar a cubierto, to be under cover. ‖ ponerse a cubierto, to take cover. ‖ tener las espaldas cubiertas, fam to be well-heeled.
■ cubierta de lona, tarpaulin, canvas. ‖ juego de cubiertos, canteen of cutlery, set of cutlery. ‖ precio del cubierto, cover charge.
cubil m den, lair.
cubilete 1 m (molde) mould (us mold). 2 (de dados) dice cup, dice shaker; (juego) cup.
cubiletear i (dados) to shake. 2 fig to cheat, fiddle.
cubiletero m CULIN (molde) pastry mould (us mold).
cubilote m cupola.
cubismo m cubism.
cubista 1 adj cubist. – 2 mf cubist.

cubito 1 m little cube. 2 (de hielo) ice cube.
cúbito m cubitus.
cubo[1] 1 m (recipiente) bucket. 2 (de rueda) hub.
■ cubo de la basura, rubbish bin, us garbage can.
cubo[2] m MAT cube.
● elevar al cubo, to cube.
cubrecama m bedspread.
cubrerradiador m radiator muff.
cubrir 1 t (gen) to cover: cubre la silla con una sábana, cover the chair with a sheet. 2 CULIN to coat (de, with). 3 (poner tejado) to put a roof on. 4 (niebla etc) to shroud (de, in), cloak. 5 (ocultar) to hide: cubrir un sentimiento, to hide a feeling. 6 (llenar) to fill (de, with), cover (de, with): cubrir de agua, to fill with water; cubrir una plaza, to fill a vacancy. 7 (alcanzar) to come up: el agua le cubría hasta los tobillos, the water came up to his ankles. 8 (gastos, necesidades) to cover; (deuda) to meet, repay. 9 (recorrer) to cover; (distancia) to travel. 10 (prensa) to cover: Juan cubrió el accidente, Juan covered the accident. 11 (animales) to pair, cover. – 12 **cubrirse,** p (abrigarse) to cover os. 13 (la cabeza) to put one's hat on. 14 fig (protegerse) to protect os. 15 (cielo) to become overcast. 16 (llenarse) to be filled.
● cubrir de besos, to smother with kisses. ‖ cubrir las apariencias, to keep up appearances.
▲ pp cubierto,-a.
cuca 1 f tabú penis. – 2 **cucas,** fpl fam (chucherías) sweets. 3 fam (dinero) pesetas.
cucamonas fpl fam caresses.
cucaña 1 f (palo, juego) greasy pole. 2 fam (bicoca) easy-pickings pl.
cucar 1 t (guiñar) to wink (-, at). 2 (hacer burla) to mock.
▲ Conjugation model [1], like sacar.
cucaracha f cockroach.
cuchara f spoon.
● meter algo con cuchara a algn., fam to drum sth. into sb. ‖ meter cuchara, fam to butt in.
cucharada f spoonful.
■ cucharada colmada, heaped spoonful. ‖ cucharada rasa, level spoonful. ‖ cucharada sopera, tablespoonful.
cucharadita f teaspoonful.
cucharilla f teaspoon.
■ cucharilla de café, coffee spoon.
cucharón m ladle.
cuché adj coated: papel cuché, coated paper.
cuchichear i to whisper.
cuchicheo m whispering.
cuchilla f (hoja) blade.
■ cuchilla de afeitar, razor blade.
cuchillada f (golpe) stab, slash; (herida) stab wound, knife wound.
● dar una cuchillada, to stab. ‖ matar a cuchilladas, to stab to death.
cuchillazo m → **cuchillada.**
cuchillería f cutler's shop.
cuchillo 1 m knife. 2 ARQ support.
● pasar a algn. a cuchillo, to put sb. to the sword.
■ cuchillo de monte, hunting knife. ‖ cuchillo de pan, breadknife. ‖ cuchillo de trinchar, carving knife. ‖ cuchillo eléctrico, electric carving knife.
cuchipanda f fam (juerga) spree; (comilona) feast.
● salir de cuchipanda, fam (de juerga) to go on a spree; (de comilona) to have a good feed.
cuchitril 1 m (establo) pigsty. 2 fam (cuartucho) hovel.
cuchufleta f fam joke.

cuclillas en cuclillas, *loc adv* crouching.
● ponerse en cuclillas, to crouch down.
cuclillo *m* cuckoo.
cuco[1] *m* (*insecto*) caterpillar.
cuco,-a[2] **1** *adj fam* (*coquetón*) cute. **2** (*taimado*) shrewd, crafty. – **3** cuco, *m* (*ave*) cuckoo.
cucú 1 *m* (*canto*) cuckoo. **2** (*reloj*) cuckoo clock.
▲ *pl* cucúes.
cucurucho 1 *m* (*de papel*) paper cone. **2** (*helado*) cornet, cone. **3** (*capirote*) pointed hood.
cuelgaplatos *m* plate rack.
▲ *pl* cuelgaplatos.
cuellicorto,-a *adj* short-necked.
cuellilargo,-a *adj* long-necked.
cuello 1 *m* ANAT neck. **2** (*de camisa, vestido, abrigo*) collar; (*de jersey*) neck: *un jersey de cuello alto,* a polo neck jumper, US a turtleneck jumper. **3** (*de botella*) bottleneck.
● apostar el cuello por algo, *fam* to put one's shirt on sth. ‖ cortar el cuello a algn., to slit sb.'s throat. ‖ estar con el agua al cuello, *fig* to be in a tight spot. ‖ estar metido,-a hasta el cuello, *fam* to be up to one's neck in it. ‖ hablar para el cuello de su camisa, *fam* to mutter to os.
■ cuello cisne, polo neck, US turtle neck, cuello de pajarita, bow tie. ‖ cuello de pico, V-neck. ‖ cuello redondo, crew neck. ‖ cuello vuelto, roll neck.
cuenca 1 *f* (*escudilla*) wooden bowl. **2** ANAT socket. **3** GEOG basin. **4** (*minera*) coalfield.
cuenco *m* (*vasija*) earthenware bowl.
cuenta 1 *f* (*bancaria*) account. **2** (*factura*) bill. **3** (*cálculo*) count, counting. **4** (*de collar etc*) bead.
● caer en la cuenta, to realize: *y entonces caí en la cuenta de que ...,* and then I realized that ..., and then it dawned on me that ... ‖ cargar algo en cuenta de algn., to charge sth. to sb.'s account. ‖ dar a cuenta, to give on account. ‖ dar cuenta de algo, (*comunicar*) to report sth.; (*acabar*) to polish sth. off: *dio cuenta del jamón,* he polished off the ham. ‖ en resumidas cuentas, in short. ‖ habida cuenta de, taking into account. ‖ hacer cuentas, to do sums. ‖ la cuenta de la vieja, *fam* counting on one's fingers: *aún lo hace a la cuenta de la vieja,* she still counts on her fingers. ‖ las cuentas del Gran Capitán, *fam* fictitious accounts. ‖ más de la cuenta, too much, too many: *comió más de la cuenta,* she ate too much. ‖ pasar la cuenta, to send the bill. ‖ pedir cuentas, to ask for an explanation. ‖ por cuenta de la casa, on the house. ‖ por la cuenta que le trae, in one's own interest. ‖ sacar cuentas, to work out. ‖ tener en cuenta, to take into account. ‖ trabajar por cuenta propia, to be self-employed. ‖ traer cuenta, to be worthwhile.
■ cuenta al descubierto, overdrawn account. ‖ cuenta atrás, countdown. ‖ cuenta corriente, current account. ‖ cuenta bancaria, bank account.
cuentagotas *m* dropper.
▲ *pl* cuentagotas.
cuentakilómetros *m* (*de velocidad*) speedometer; (*de distancia*) milometer.
▲ *pl* cuentakilómetros.
cuentarrevoluciones *m* rev counter.
▲ *pl* cuentarrevoluciones.
cuentavueltas *m* rev counter.
▲ *pl* cuentavueltas.
cuentista 1 *adj fam* over-dramatic. – **2** *mf* (*autor*) story story writer; (*narrador*) storyteller. **3** *fam* (*que exagera*) over-dramatic person; (*que miente*) fibber, liar.

cuentitis *f* pretending to be ill to get out of something.
cuento[1] **1** *m* (*relato*) story, tale. **2** LIT short story. **3** *fam* (*chisme*) gossip. **4** *fam* (*embuste*) fib, story.
● ¿a cuento de qué?, *fam* why?, what for? ‖ dejarse de cuentos, *fam* (*ir al grano*) to get to the point; (*decir mentiras*) to stop telling fibs. ‖ ir con el cuento a algn., to go and tell sb. ‖ no hagas como el cuento de la lechera, *fig* don't count your chickens before they are hatched. ‖ tener mucho cuento, *fam* to make a lot of fuss. ‖ traer algo a cuento, *fig* to bring sth. up. ‖ venir a cuento, to be pertinent.
■ cuento chino, tall story. ‖ cuento de hadas, fairy tale.
cuerda 1 *f* (*cordel*) rope, string. **2** MÚS (*instrumento*) string, cord; (*voz*) voice. **3** (*de reloj*) spring: *dar cuerda a un reloj,* to wind up a watch. **4** (*en geometría*) chord. **5** DEP (*interior*) interior. – **6** cuerdas, *fpl* (*boxeo*) ropes. **7** MÚS strings.
● aflojar la cuerda, *fig* to ease up. ‖ apretar la cuerda, *fig* to tighten up. ‖ bailar en la cuerda floja, *fig* to be hanging from a thread. ‖ bajo cuerda, *fig* dishonestly, under the counter. ‖ contra las cuerdas, on the ropes. ‖ dar cuerda a algn., *fam* to encourage sb. (to speak). ‖ rompérsele uno la cuerda, to be at the end of one's tether.
■ cuerda de la ropa, clothes-line. ‖ cuerda de presos, chain gang. ‖ cuerda floja, tightrope. ‖ cuerdas vocales, vocal chords.
cuerdamente *adv* wisely.
cuerdo,-a 1 *adj* (*persona*) sane. **2** (*acción*) prudent, sensible. – **3** *m,f* (*persona*) sane person, person in one's right mind.
cuerna 1 *f* (*cornamenta*) antlers *pl*, horns pl. **2** (*caza*) hunting horn.
cuerno 1 *m* horn; (*de ciervo*) antlers pl. **2** (*de antena*) antlers *pl*. **3** MIL wing. **4** MÚS horn. – **5** *interj* golly!, gosh!
● oler a cuerno quemado, *fam* to be fishy; *esto huele a cuerno quemado,* there's something fishy going on. ‖ mandar a algn. al cuerno, *fam* to send sb. packing, tell sb. to get lost. ‖ mandar algo al cuerno, *fam* to pack sth. in. ‖ romperse los cuernos, *fam* to break one's back. ‖ poner cuernos a algn., *fam* to cheat on sb., be unfaithful to sb. ‖ ¡vete al cuerno!, *fam* get lost!
cuero 1 *m* (*de animal*) skin, hide. **2** (*curtido*) leather: *pantalón de cuero,* leather trousers. **3** (*odre*) wineskin. **4** DEP (*balón*) ball.
● en cueros, *fam* naked. ‖ en cueros vivos, *fam* stark naked, starkers. ‖ quedarse en cueros, *fam* to strip off.
cuerpo 1 *m* ANAT body. **2** (*constitución*) build. **3** (*figura*) figure; (*tronco*) trunk. **4** (*tronco*) trunk. **5** (*grupo*) body, force, corps: *el cuerpo de bomberos,* the fire brigade (US the fire department). **6** (*cadáver*) corpse, body. **7** (*parte*) section, part; (*parte principal*) main part, main body: *el cuerpo del libro,* the main body of the book; *un armario de dos cuerpos,* a wardrobe in two sections. **8** QUÍM substance; FÍS body. **9** (*vino, tela, etc*) body. **10** DEP length.
● a cuerpo descubierto, defenceless (US defenseless). ‖ cuerpo a cuerpo, hand-to-hand. ‖ de cuerpo entero, full-length. ‖ en cuerpo y alma, *fig* heart and soul, body and soul. ‖ estar de cuerpo presente, to lie in state. ‖ hacer de cuerpo, *euf* to relieve os. ‖ no tener nada en el cuerpo, to have an empty stomach. ‖ tener buen cuerpo, to have a good figure. ‖ tomar cuerpo, *fig* to take shape.
■ cuerpo de baile, corps de ballet. ‖ cuerpo del delito, IUR evidence, corpus delicti. ‖ cuerpo diplomá-

tico, diplomatic corps. ‖ **cuerpo legislativo,** legislative body. ‖ **cuerpo geométrico,** regular solid. ‖ **cuerpos celestes,** heavenly bodies.

cuervo m (ave) raven.
● **cría cuervos y te sacarán los ojos,** don't bite the hand that feeds you.
■ **cuervo marino,** cormorant.

cuesco 1 m (hueso) stone. **2** fam (pedo) fart.

cuesta f (pendiente) slope.
● **a cuestas,** on one's back, on one's shoulders. ‖ **cuesta abajo,** downhill. ‖ **cuesta arriba,** uphill. ‖ **hacérsele a uno algo cuesta arriba,** fig to find sth. an uphill struggle, find sth. very difficult. ‖ **ir cuesta abajo,** fig to go downhill.
■ **la cuesta de enero,** fig the January squeeze.

cuestación f charity collection.
● **hacer una cuestación,** to raise money for charity.

cuestión 1 f (pregunta) question. **2** (asunto) business, matter, question. **3** (discusión) dispute, quarrel, argument.
● **en cuestión,** in question. ‖ **en cuestión de ...,** (tiempo) in just a few ..., in a matter of ...: *lo acabaré en cuestión de minutos,* I'll finish it in a few minutes. ‖ **eso es otra cuestión,** that's a whole different matter. ‖ **la cuestión es que ...,** the thing is that ... ‖ **ser cuestión de vida o muerte,** fig to be a matter of life or death.
■ **cuestión candente,** burning question.

cuestionable adj questionable.

cuestionar t to question.

cuestionario m questionnaire.

cuestor 1 m (magistrado) quaestor. **2** (el que pide) collector.

cueto 1 m (sitio elevado) protected peak. **2** (colina peñascosa) rocky peak.

cueva f cave.
■ **cueva de ladrones,** fig den of thieves.

cuévano m pannier.

cuezo[1] pres indic → **cocer.**

cuezo[2] m trough.
● **meter el cuezo,** fam to put one's foot in it.

cuidado 1 m (atención) care, carefulness. **2** (recelo) worry. **– 3** interj look out!, watch out!: *¡cuidado con la moto!,* mind the motorbike!
● **andarse con cuidado / ir con cuidado,** to go carefully. ‖ **"cuidado con el perro",** "beware of the dog". ‖ **con cuidado,** carefully. ‖ **de cuidado,** (enfermo) very ill; (peligroso) dangerous. ‖ **estar al cuidado de,** (cosa) to be in charge of; (persona) to look after. ‖ **tener cuidado,** to be careful. ‖ **traer sin cuidado,** not to care.
■ **cuidados intensivos,** intensive care sing.

cuidadosamente adv carefully.

cuidadoso,-a 1 adj (atento) careful. **2** (celoso) cautious.

cuidar 1 t to look after, take care of, care for. **– 2** cuidarse, p to take care of os., look after os.: *¡cuídate mucho!,* take good care of yourself!
● **cuidar(se) de que,** to make sure that: *cuida de que no llegue tarde,* make sure he doesn't arrive late. ‖ **cuidar los detalles,** to pay attention to details. ‖ **cuidar una herida,** to dress a wound. ‖ **cuidarse de,** (preocuparse) to worry about, mind: *no se cuida de lo que dicen,* she doesn't care what they say.

cuita f trouble, sorrow, worry.

cuitado,-a adj worried, troubled.

culada f fall on one's backside.

culamen m fam fat arse, us fat ass.

culata 1 f (de arma) butt. **2** AUTO cylinder head. **3** (carne) haunch, hindquarters pl.

culatazo m kick, recoil.

culé 1 adj fam relating to Barcelona football club. **– 2** mf fam Barcelona supporter.

culear i fam (mover el culo) to wiggle one's bottom.

culebra f snake.

culebrear 1 i (persona) to zigzag. **2** (río) to meander, wind.

culebrilla 1 f MED ringworm. **2** (de cometa) zigzag.

culebrina f forked lightning.

culebrón m television serial, soap opera.

culero,-a adj (perezoso) lazy.

culín m fam (de recipiente) tiny bit, drop: *quedaba un culín de vino,* there was a drop of wine left.

culinario,-a adj culinary, cooking: *arte culinario,* cuisine.

culminación f culmination, climax.

culminante adj (momento) culminating, climatic; (punto) highest.

culminar 1 i to reach a peak. **2** fig (acabar) to finish, end.

culo 1 m fam bottom, bum, arse (us ass). **2** fam (ano) arse (us ass). **3** (de recipiente) bottom: *queda un culo,* there's a bit left in the bottom.
● **caer de culo,** fam to fall flat on one's bottom. ‖ **con el culo al aire,** fig in a fix, in a tight spot. ‖ **ir de culo,** fam to be rushed off one's feet. ‖ **lamer el culo a algn.,** tabú to lick sb.'s arse (us ass). ‖ **mojarse el culo,** fig to come down off the fence, make up one's mind. ‖ **ser culo de mal asiento,** fig to be a fidget, not to be able to sit still. ‖ **¡vete a tomar por el culo!,** tabú fuck off!, up yours!

culombio m coulomb.

culón,-ona adj fam big-bottomed.

culpa 1 f (culpabilidad) guilt, blame. **2** (falta) fault: *esto es culpa mía,* it's my fault.
● **echar la culpa a algn.,** to put the blame on sb. ‖ **tener la culpa,** to be to blame (de, for): *yo no tengo la culpa,* I'm not to blame, it's not my fault.

culpabilidad f guilt, culpability.

culpable 1 adj guilty. **– 2** mf offender, culprit: *él no es el culpable,* he's not to blame.
● **declararse culpable,** to plead guilty.

culpar 1 t (gen) to blame (de, for): *la culpó de todo,* he blamed her for everything. **2** (de un delito) to accuse (de, of).

cultamente adv in a refined manner.

culteranismo m gongorism.

cultismo m cultism.

cultivado,-a 1 pp → **cultivar. – 2** adj cultivated. **3** fig (con cultura) cultured, refined.

cultivar 1 t to cultivate, farm. **2** (ejercitar facultades) to work at, practise (us practice), improve: *cultivar la memoria,* to improve one's memory. **3** (en biología) to produce.
● **cultivar las amistades,** fig to cultivate friendships.

cultivo 1 m (acción) cultivation, farming. **2** (cosecha) crop. **3** BIOL culture. **4** fig (desarrollo) development, growth.
● **dedicarse al cultivo de,** to grow. ‖ **poner en cultivo,** to cultivate.

culto,-a 1 adj (persona) cultured, educated. **2** (estilo) refined. **– 3** culto, m worship.
● **rendir culto a,** to pay homage to, worship.
■ **culto dominical,** Sunday worship.

cultura f culture.
● **de cultura,** educated.

cultural adj cultural.

culturismo m body-building.

culturista *mf* body-builder.
cumbia *f* Columbian dance.
cumbre 1 *f* (*de montaña*) summit, top. 2 *fig* (*culminación*) pinnacle. 3 (*reunión*) summit conference, summit meeting.
cumpleaños *m* birthday.
▲ *pl cumpleaños*.
cumplidamente 1 *adv* (*ampliamente*) sufficiently. 2 (*totalmente*) completely.
cumplido,-a 1 *pp* → **cumplir**. – 2 *adj* (*completo*) complete, full: *el pago está cumplido*, the payment has been made in full. 3 (*abundante*) large, ample: *esa camisa te va demasiado cumplida*, that shirt is too big for you. 4 (*perfecto*) perfect: *es un cumplido caballero*, he's a perfect gentleman. 5 (*educado*) polite, courteous. – 6 cumplido, *m* compliment.
● **cambiar cumplidos con algn.**, to exchange pleasantries with sb. ‖ **de cumplido**, courtesy: *una visita de cumplido*, a courtesy visit. ‖ **deshacerse en cumplidos**, to be profuse in attentions. ‖ **devolverle el cumplido a algn.**, to return sb.'s compliment. ‖ **hacer cumplidos**, to stand on ceremony. ‖ **por cumplido**, out of courtesy. ‖ **sin cumplidos**, informally.
cumplidor,-ra 1 *adj* (*que cumple*) who delivers the goods: *es una chica muy cumplidora*, she always delivers the goods, she always fulfils her promises. 2 (*fiable*) reliable, dependable.
cumplimentar 1 *t* (*felicitar*) to congratulate. 2 (*ejecutar*) to carry out, execute.
cumplimiento 1 *m* (*orden*) carrying out, execution; (*deber, deseo*) fulfilment (*us* fulfillment)). 2 (*cumplido*) compliment.
■ **cumplimiento de la ley**, observance of the law.
cumplir 1 *t* (*orden*) to carry out; (*deseo*) to fulfil (*us* fulfill); (*deber*) to do. 2 (*promesa*) to keep. 3 JUR (*ley*) to observe, abide by; (*pena*) to serve. 4 (*años*) to be, turn: *mañana cumplo treinta años*, I'll be thirty tomorrow; *ha cumplido cuarenta años*, she has turned forty; *¡que cumplas muchos más!*, many happy returns! 5 (*satisfacer*) to do, carry out, fulfil (*us* fulfill). – 6 *i* (*plazo*) to expire, end. 7 (*deuda, pago*) to fall due. – 8 cumplirse, *p* (*realizarse*) to be fulfilled, come true: *se cumplió la profecía*, the prophecy came true. 9 (*fecha*) to be: *hoy se cumplen cinco años de nuestra boda*, it's our fifth wedding anniversay today; *se cumple una semana del comienzo del curso*, it's a week since the course began.
● **cumplir con algn.**, to keep one's promise to sb. ‖ **cumplir con el deber**, to do one's duty. ‖ **cumplir con la Iglesia**, to fulfil (*us* fulfill) one's religious obligations. ‖ **cumplir con la ley**, to abide by the law. ‖ **cumplir con las obligaciones**, to fulfil (*us* fulfill) one's obligations. ‖ **cumplir con su palabra**, to keep one's word. ‖ **para cumplir / por cumplir**, as a formality.
cúmulo 1 *m* (*montón*) load, pile, heap; (*cantidad*) series, host, string: *un cúmulo de desgracias*, a series of misfortunes. 2 METEOR cumulus.
cumulonimbo *m* cumulonimbus.
cuna 1 *f* (*cama*) cradle. 2 (*linaje*) birth, lineage, stock. 3 *fig* (*origen*) cradle, beginning: *la cuna de la filosofía*, the cradle of philosophy. 4 (*lugar de nacimiento*) birthplace.
■ **canción de cuna**, lullaby.
cundir 1 *i* (*extenderse*) to spread: *cundió el pánico*, panic spread. 2 (*dar de sí*) to go a long way, go far: *una hora cunde muy poco*, you can't do much in an hour; *si me cunde el trabajo, te ayudaré con el tuyo*, if I get a lot of work done, I'll help you with yours. 3 (*aumentar de vo-*

lumen) to swell, expand: *los fideos cunden al cocerse*, noodles expand when cooked.
● **cundió la voz que ...**, rumour (*us* rumor) had it that ...
cuneiforme *adj* cuneiform.
cunero,-a 1 *adj* (*expósito*) foundling. 2 *fig* (*toro*) unpedigreed. – 3 *m,f* (*expósito*) foundling.
cuneta 1 *f* (*de carretera*) verge. 2 (*zanja*) ditch.
cuña 1 *f* (*pieza*) wedge. 2 *fig* (*influencia*) influence. 3 (*anuncio*) jingle. 4 (*para el enfermo*) bedpan.
● **hacer cuña**, to be wedged in. ‖ **meter cuña**, *fig* to stir up trouble. ‖ **tener cuña**, *fig* to have influence.
cuñado,-a *m,f* (*hombre*) brother-in-law; (*mujer*) sister-in-law.
cuño 1 *m* (*troquel*) die, stamp. 2 (*sello*) stamp, mark.
● **de nuevo cuño**, *fig* newly-coined. ‖ **tener el cuño**, to bear the mark.
cuota 1 *f* (*pago*) membership fee, dues *pl*. 2 (*porción*) quota, share.
■ **cuota de mercado**, FIN market share.
cuotidiano,-a *adj* daily.
cupe *pt indef* → **caber**.
cupé *m* coupé.
cupido *m* Cupid.
cupiera *imperf subj* → **caber**.
cuplé *m* popular lyrical song.
cupletista *f* music-hall singer.
cupo 1 *m* (*cuota*) quota. 2 MIL contingent.
● **ser excedente de cupo**, MIL to be exempt from military service.
cupón 1 *m* (*vale*) coupon, voucher. 2 COM trading stamp. 3 (*de lotería*) ticket.
■ **cupón de los ciegos**, *fam* lottery ticket for the blind.
cúprico,-a *adj* cupric.
cúpula *f* cupola, dome.
cuquería 1 *f* (*astucia*) craftiness. 2 *fam* (*monada*) pretty little thing.
cura 1 *m* REL priest. – 2 *f* cure, healing. 3 (*tratamiento*) treatment: *cura de adelgazamiento*, slimming treatment.
● **hacer las primeras curas**, to give first aid. ‖ **no tiene cura**, *fam* (*situación*) it's hopeless, there's no way out; (*persona*) he/she is incorrigible.
■ **cura párroco**, parish priest. ‖ **primeras curas**, first aid *sing*.
curación 1 *f* (*gen*) cure. 2 (*de herida*) healing. 3 (*recuperación*) recovery.
curado,-a 1 *pp* → **curar**. – 2 *adj* (*carne, pescado*) cured, salted; (*piel*) tanned. 3 *fig* (*persona*) hardened.
curador,-ra *m,f* healer.
curanderismo 1 *m* (*charlatanismo*) quackery. 2 (*de curador*) folk healing.
curandero,-a *m,f* 1 *m* (*charlatán*) quack. 2 (*curador*) folk healer.
curar 1 *t* (*sanar*) to cure. 2 (*herida*) to dress; (*enfermedad*) to treat. 3 (*carne, pescado*) to cure; (*piel*) to tan; (*madera*) to season. – 4 *i* (*cuidar*) to take care (**de**, of). 5 (*recuperarse*) to recover, get well. 6 (*herida*) to heal (up). – 7 curarse, *p* (*recuperarse*) to recover (**de**, from), get well. 8 (*herida*) to heal up.
● **curar un mal**, *fig* to right a wrong. ‖ **curarse en salud**, *fig* to take precautions.
curare *m* curare.
curasao *m* curaçao.
curativo,-a *adj* curative: *poder curativo*, healing power.
curato 1 *m* (*cargo*) curacy. 2 (*parroquia*) parish.

curda *f fam* drunkenness.
● **agarrar una curda / coger una curda,** *fam* to get plastered.
curdo,-a 1 *adj* Kurdish. – 2 *m,f* Kurd.
curia 1 *f* REL curia. 2 JUR Bar.
curiana *f* blackbeetle.
curiosamente 1 *adv* (*con curiosidad*) curiously, strangely. 2 (*limpiamente*) cleanly.
curiosear 1 *i* (*fisgar*) to pry, nose around. 2 (*mirar*) to look around. – 3 *t* (*fisgar*) to pry into.
curiosidad 1 *f* (*gen*) curiosity. 2 (*aseo*) cleanliness, tidiness. 3 (*cuidado*) care.
● **despertar la curiosidad de algn.,** to arouse sb.'s curiosity. ‖ **tener curiosidad de algo,** to be curious about sth.
curioso,-a 1 *adj* curious. 2 (*indiscreto*) inquisitive. 3 (*aseado*) clean, tidy, neat. 4 (*extraño*) strange, odd. – 5 *m.f* (*mirón*) onlooker. 6 *pey* (*indiscreto*) nosey-parker, busybody.
currante *mf arg* worker.
currar *i arg* to grind, slave, graft.
curre *m arg* job, meal ticket.
currelar *i arg* → **currar**.
currelo *m arg* job, meal ticket.
currículo *m* curriculum, curriculum vitae.
▲ *pl* **currículos** *or* **currícula**.
currículum *m* curriculum, curriculum vitae.
▲ *pl* **currículums** *or* **currícula**.
curro *m arg* job, meal ticket.
curry *m* curry.
cursado,-a 1 *pp* → **cursar**. – 2 *adj* (*versado*) experienced. 3 (*cartas*) dispatch.
cursante *mf* student.
cursar 1 *t* (*estudiar*) to study, attend. 2 (*enviar*) to send, dispatch; (*orden*) to give. 3 (*tramitar*) to make an application.
cursi 1 *adj fam* (*afectado*) pretentious, affected, twee. – 2 *mf fam* pretentious person, affected person.
cursilada 1 *f* (*cualidad*) affectation, pretentiousness. 2 (*hecho*) pretentious thing to do. 3 (*obra, cosa*) pretentious thing: *las películas románticas me parecen una cursilada,* for me romantic films are just sentimental slush.
cursilería *f* → **cursilada**.
cursillista *m,f* person on a course.
cursillo *m* short course, training course.
■ **cursillo de conferencias,** course of lectures. ‖ **cursillo de reciclaje,** refresher course.
cursiva *f* → **cursivo,-a**.
cursivo,-a 1 *adj* cursive: *letra cursiva,* italics *pl*. – 2 **cursiva,** *f* (*escritura*) cursive; (*tipografía*) italics *pl*.
curso 1 *m* (*dirección*) course, direction: *el curso de los acontecimientos,* the course of events. 2 EDUC (*nivel*) year, class; (*materia*) course; (*escolar*) school year: *vamos al mismo curso,* we are in the same class; *un curso de historia,* a history course; *¿cuándo empieza el curso?,* when do classes start? 3 (*río*) flow, current.
● **dar curso a algo,** (*tramitar*) to deal with sth.; (*dar libertad*) to give free rein to sth. ‖ **dejar que las cosas sigan su curso,** *fig* to let things take their course. ‖ **en**

el curso de ..., *fig* during the course of ... ‖ **estar en curso,** *fig* to be under way.
■ **año en curso,** current year. ‖ **curso acelerado,** crash course. ‖ **mes en curso,** current month. ‖ **moneda de curso legal,** legal tender.
cursor 1 *m* INFORM cursor. 2 TÉC slide.
curtido,-a 1 *pp* → **curtir**. – 2 *adj* (*por el sol*) tanned, sunburnt. 3 (*cuero*) tanned. 4 *fig* (*endurecido*) hardened. – 5 **curtido,** *m* (*operación*) tanning. – 6 **curtidos,** *mpl* tanned leather *sing*.
curtidor,-ra *m.f* tanner.
curtidos *mpl* → **curtido,-a**.
curtiduría *f* tannery.
curtir 1 *t* (*piel*) to tan. 2 *fig* (*acostumbrar*) to harden, toughen. – 3 **curtirse,** *p* (*por el sol*) to get tanned. 4 *fig* (*acostumbrarse*) to become hardened.
curva 1 *f* (*gen*) curve. 2 (*de carretera*) bend. 3 (*gráfico*) curve, graph. – 4 **curvas,** *fpl fam* (*cuerpo de mujer*) curves, curvy figure *sing*.
● **coger una curva / tomar una curva,** to take a bend. ‖ **trazar una curva,** to draw a curve.
■ **curva cerrada,** sharp bend. ‖ **curva peligrosa,** dangerous bend.
curvar 1 *t* (*gen*) to curve, bend. 2 (*espalda*) to arch.
curvatura *f* curvature.
curvilíneo,-a 1 *adj* curvilinear, curvilineal. 2 *fam* (*del cuerpo*) curvaceous, shapely.
curvo,-a *adj* curved, bent.
cuscurrear *i* to crunch.
cuscurro *m* crust of bread.
cuscús *m* couscous.
cúspide 1 *f* (*cumbre*) summit, peak. 2 (*en geometría*) apex. 3 *fig* peak.
cusqui **hacer la cusqui,** *loc fam* (*molestar*) to annoy; (*perjudicar*) to do the dirty on.
custodia 1 *f* custody, care. 2 REL monstrance.
● **bajo custodia,** in custody.
custodiar 1 *t* (*proteger*) to keep, take care of. 2 (*vigilar*) to guard, watch over.
▲ *Conjugation model* [12], *like* ***cambiar***.
custodio *m* custodian, guard, keeper.
cutáneo,-a *adj* cutaneous, skin: *enfermedad cutánea,* skin disease.
cúter *m* MAR cutter.
cutícula *f* cuticle.
cutis *m* skin, complexion.
▲ *pl* **cutis**.
cutre 1 *adj* (*tacaño*) mean, stingy. 2 *fam* (*sórdido*) grotty, seedy.
cuyo,-a 1 *pron* (*personas*) whose, of whom: *el hombre cuya casa vimos,* the man whose house we saw; *esta mujer, cuya hermana trabaja en Alemania...,* this woman, whose sister works in Germany, this woman, the sister of whom works in Germany. 2 (*cosas*) whose, of which: *un árbol cuyas hojas presentan esta enfermedad,* a tree with leaves that show signs of this disease.
● **a cuyo efecto / con cuyo objeto,** to which end. ‖ **en cuyo caso,** in which case.
CV *sím* (*caballos de vapor*) horse power; (*símbolo*) HP

D

D, d f (*la letra*) D, d.

D. *abr* (*don*) Mister; (*abreviatura*) Mr.

Dª *abr* (*doña*) Mrs, Miss, Ms.

Da. *abr* (*doña*) Mrs, Miss, Ms.

dable *adj* feasible, possible.

dabute 1 *adj arg* great, terrific, fantastic. − 2 *adv arg* great, terrifically.

dabuten *adj-adv arg* → **dabute**.

dactilar *adj* digital.

■ **huellas dactilares,** fingerprints.

dactilografía f typing, typewriting.

dactilógrafo,-a *m,f* typist.

dadá *adj* → **dadaísta**.

dadaísmo *m* Dadaism.

dadaísta 1 *adj* Dadaist. − 2 *mf* Dadaist.

dádiva 1 f (*regalo*) gift, present. 2 (*donación*) donation.

dadivoso,-a *adj* generous.

dado[1] 1 *m* (*para jugar*) die. 2 TÉC block. 3 ARQ dado.

● **cargar los dados,** to load the dice. ‖ **echar los dados,** to throw the dice.

dado,-a[2] 1 *pp* → **dar**. − 2 *adj* given: *en un momento dado,* at a given moment, at a certain point; *dada la base y la altura, hallar la superficie,* given the base and the height, find the area. 3 (*en vista de*) in view of: *dada su experiencia,* in view of his experience. 4 (*hora*) past: *son las cinco dadas,* it's past five o'clock.

● **dado que,** since, as, given that: *dado que llueve no saldremos,* as it's raining we won't go out. ‖ **ir dado,-a,** to be in for trouble: *vas dado si crees que te esperaré,* if you think I'm going to wait for you, you've got another think coming. ‖ **ser dado,-a a,** to be keen on, be fond of: *mi tío es muy dado a las hierbas medicinales,* my uncle is very fond of medicinal herbs.

dador,-ra 1 *m,f* (*que da*) giver. 2 (*una carta*) bearer. 3 COM drawer.

daga f dagger.

daguerrotipo 1 *m* (*arte*) daguerreotypy. 2 (*aparato, retrato*) daguerreotype.

daiquiri *m* daiquiri.

Dakota f Dakota.

■ **Dakota del Norte,** North Dakota. ‖ **Dakota del Sur,** South Dakota.

dalai lama *m* Dalai Lama.

dalia f dahlia.

dálmata 1 *adj* Dalmatian. − 2 *m* Dalmatian.

daltoniano,-a 1 *adj* colour-blind (US color-blind), daltonic. − 2 *m,f* person who is colour-blind (US colorblind).

daltonismo *m* colour (US color) blindness, daltonism.

dama 1 f (*señora*) lady. 2 (*en el juego de damas*) king; (*en ajedrez*) queen. − 3 **damas,** fpl draughts, (US checkers).

● **¡damas y caballeros!,** ladies and gentlemen!

■ **dama de honor,** (*de novia*) bridesmaid; (*de reina*) lady-in-waiting. ‖ **primera dama,** (*actriz*) leading lady;

(*en política*) first lady. ‖ **tablero de damas,** draughtboard, (US checkerboard).

damajuana f demijohn.

damán *m* marmot.

damasco 1 *m* (*tejido*) damask. 2 (*árbol, fruto*) damson.

Damasco *m* Damascus.

damasquina f French marigold.

damasquinado,-a *adj* damascene.

damasquinar t to damascene, damask.

damisela f *irón* young lady, damsel.

damnificado,-a 1 *pp* → **damnificar**. − 2 *adj* (*persona*) injured, harmed. 3 (*cosa*) damaged. − 4 *m,f* victim: *él era uno de los damnificados por las inundaciones,* he was one of the flood victims.

damnificar 1 *t* (*a una persona*) to injure, harm. 2 (*cosa*) to damage.

▲ *Conjugation model* [1], *like sacar*.

Damocles *m* Damocles.

■ **espada de Damocles,** *fig* Sword of Damocles.

dandi *m* dandy.

▲ *pl* dandis.

dandy *m* dandy.

▲ *pl* dandys.

danés,-esa 1 *adj* Danish. − 2 *m,f* (*persona*) Dane. − 3 **danés,** *m* (*idioma*) Danish.

dantesco,-a *adj* Dantesque.

Danubio el Danubio, *m* the Danube.

danza 1 f (*baile*) dance. 2 *fig* (*negocio sucio*) shady business, shady deal; (*lío*) mess: *no te metas en esa danza,* don't get mixed up in a deal like that. 3 *fam fig* (*riña*) row.

● **armar una danza,** *fig* to make a scene. ‖ **estar siempre en danza,** *fig* to be always on the go.

■ **la danza de la muerte,** the dance of death.

danzante 1 *adj* dancing. − 2 *m,f* dancer. 3 *fam fig* (*intrigante*) busybody, meddler. 4 *fam fig* (*botarate*) scatterbrain.

danzar 1 *t* (*bailar*) to dance. − 2 *i* (*bailar*) to dance (**con,** with). 3 (*zascandilear*) to wander: *se pasó la mañana danzando y no hizo los deberes,* he spent the morning milling about and he didn't do his homework. 4 (*estar tirado*) to lie around: *tienes todas las hojas danzando por la mesa,* your papers are lying all over the table. 5 (*entrometerse*) to meddle, interfere (**en,** with/in).

▲ *Conjugation model* [4], *like realizar*.

danzarín,-ina *m,f* dancer.

dañado,-a 1 *pp* → **dañar**. − 2 *adj* damaged, spoiled.

dañar 1 *t* (*causar dolor*) to hurt, harm. 2 (*estropear*) to damage, spoil. 3 *fig* to damage, stain: *ese asunto dañará su reputación,* that affair will damage his reputation. − 4 **dañarse,** *p* (*estropearse*) to get damaged, spoil; (*alimentos*) to go bad, go off.

dañino,-a *adj* harmful (**para,** to), damaging (**para,** to).

■ **animales dañinos,** pests, vermin *sing*.

daño *m* (*a persona*) harm, injury; (*a cosa*) damage; (*perjuicio*) wrong.
● **hacer daño,** (*doler*) to hurt; (*causar dolor a alguien*) to hurt; (*ser malo para algo*) to damage, harm; (*ser malo para alguien*) to do sb. harm: *me hace daño la pierna,* my leg hurts; *me hizo daño con sus palabras,* her words hurt me; *aquellas fotografías hicieron daño a su reputación,* those photographs damaged her reputation; *una copa de vino no te hará ningún daño,* a glass of wine won't do you any harm. ‖ **hacerse daño,** to hurt os.: *se hizo daño en la mano,* she hurt her hand.
■ **daños materiales,** material damage *sing.* ‖ **daños y perjuicios,** JUR damages.

dañoso,-a *adj* harmful (**para,** to).

dar **1** *t* (*gen*) to give: *te daré un libro,* I'll give you a book. **2** (*poner en las manos, entregar*) to deliver, hand over; (*poner al alcance*) to pass, hand: *dar un paquete,* to deliver a parcel; *dame la sal,* pass me the salt. **3** (*proporcionar, ofrecer, procurar algo no material a una persona - noticia*) to tell, announce, report; (*consejo*) to give; (*recuerdos, recado*) to pass on, give: *dales recuerdos a tus padres,* give your parents my regards; *este amuleto me da suerte,* this lucky charm brings me good luck; *espero que los niños no te den problemas,* I hope the children don't give you much trouble. **4** (*permitir tener algo, conceder*) to give: *dale tiempo,* give him time; *dales permiso,* give them permission. **5** (*pagar a cambio*) to give, pay: *¿cuánto me daría por esto?,* how much would you give me for it? **6** (*realizar una acción*) *dimos un paseo,* we went for a walk; *dame un beso,* give me a kiss; *le dio un golpe,* he hit him; *dar palmadas,* to clap; *dar un grito,* to let out a cry; *dar un paso,* to take a step; *dar una puñalada,* to stab; *dar brillo,* to polish. **7** (*producir - cosecha*) to produce, yield; (*fruto, flores*) to bear, produce; (*beneficio, interés*) to produce, yield: *la higuera da higos,* the fig tree bears figs; *el sol da luz,* the sun shines. **8** (*celebrar, tener lugar - película*) to show, screen; (*obra de teatro*) to perform, put on; (*musical*) to play, perform; (*concierto*) to give, perform, put on; (*fiesta*) to give, throw: *dio una conferencia,* he gave a talk; *daremos una fiesta,* we'll have a party; *en la tele dan una película estupenda,* there's a wonderful film on the telly. **9** (*pegar*) to hit: *le dieron bien fuerte,* they hit him hard. **10** (*comunicar felicitaciones, pésames, etc*) to say: *nos ha dado la enhorabuena por la boda,* she congratulated us on our marriage; *dar los buenos días,* to say good morning; *nos dio las gracias por el regalo,* he thanked us for our present. **11** (*afectar, causar*) to hit, make: *me da el frío,* I'm cold; *me da un dolor,* I feel a pain; *el sol me daba en los ojos,* the sun was shining in my eyes. **12** (*expeler, desprender*) to give off: *eso da humo,* it gives off smoke. **13** (*sonar el reloj las horas*) to strike: *el reloj dio las 6,* the clock struck six. **14** (*untar, recubrir una superficie*) to apply, give: *dio dos manos de pintura,* he gave it two coats of paint. **15** (*abrir el paso de conductos*) to turn on: *he dado el gas,* I've turned the gas on. **16** (*en naipes*) to deal. – **17** *i* (*pegar, golpear*) to hit. **18** (*en naipes*) to deal. **19 dar a,** (*accionar*) to start: *dale al botón,* press the button. **20** (*mirar una cosa hacia una parte*) to look out onto, overlook; (*ir a parar a una parte*) to lead to, open onto: *la ventana da a la playa,* the window looks out onto the beach; *esa puerta da a la cocina,* this door leads to the kitchen. **21 dar con,** (*encontrar algo*) to find, discover; (*encontrar a alguien*) to meet, come across, bump into; (*acertar*) to find: *dio con la calle,* she found the street; *al salir de casa dio con mi primo,* as he was leaving the house, he bumped into my cousin;

dio con la solución, he found a solution. **22 dar con/contra,** (*chocar*) to bump into: *el coche dio contra el árbol,* the car hit the tree. **23 dar de,** (*caer*) to fall: *dio de narices en el suelo,* he fell flat on his face. **24** (*suministrar*) to give: *les dio de comer/beber,* he gave them something to eat/drink; *dar de palos/bofetadas/tortas a algn.,* to beat sb. up. **25 dar en,** (*acertar*) to find, hit on. **26 dar para,** (*ser suficiente*) to be enough for, be sufficient for: *la sopa da para cuatro,* the soup serves four. **27 dar sobre,** (*golpear*) to hit: *dar sobre el yunque,* to hit the anvil. – **28 darse,** *p* (*entregarse*) to give in, surrender. **29** (*suceder, existir*) to happen, occur: *a veces se da este caso,* this sometimes happens; *se da el caso que ...,* the thing is that ... **30** (*crecer*) to grow; (*cultivarse*) to be found, grow: *aquí se dan bien las patatas,* potatoes grow well here. **31 darse a,** (*consagrarse*) to devote os. to; (*a un vicio*) to take to, abandon os. to: *se dio al estudio,* she devoted herself to study; *se ha dado a la bebida,* he has taken to drink. **32 darse con/contra,** (*chocar*) to crash (**contra/con,** into). **33 darse por,** (*considerarse*) to consider os.: *date por pagado,* consider yourself paid.

● **¡dale!,** *fam* (*seguir*) go on!; (*venga*) come on! ‖ **dale que dale,** *fam* on and on. ‖ **dale que te pego,** *fam* on and on: *y siguió dale que te pego contando batallitas,* and he kept on and on telling stories. ‖ **dar a algn. por,** to assume, consider: *la dieron por muerta,* they presumed she was dead. ‖ **dar a entender que ...,** to give to understand that ..., imply that ...: *dio a entender que no vendría,* she implied she wouldn't come. ‖ **dar a luz,** to give birth (**a,** to). ‖ **dar a uno (mucho) gusto + infinitivo,** to be very pleased + to: *nos da mucho gusto verla,* we are very pleased to see her. ‖ **dar a uno no sé qué,** *fam* to give one a strange feeling: *me da no sé qué que te vayas,* I feel funny about you leaving. ‖ **dar a uno + sentimiento,** to make one + *adjective*: *me da asco,* it makes me sick. ‖ **dar algo por,** to assume, consider. ‖ **dar con los huesos en,** *fam* to end up: *dio con sus huesos en la cárcel,* he ended up in jail. ‖ **dar de lado,** (*una cosa*) to discard; (*una persona*) to cold-shoulder. ‖ **dar de sí,** (*ropa*) to stretch, give; (*dinero, comida*) to go a long way. ‖ **dar igual,** to be all the same, not matter: *le daba igual,* it didn't matter to him, he didn't care. ‖ **dar la mano a algn.,** to shake hands with sb. ‖ **dar lo mismo,** to be all the same, not matter: *me da lo mismo,* I don't mind. ‖ **dar gusto + infinitivo,** to be nice + *to* + *inf*: *da gusto verla jugar,* it's nice to see her playing. ‖ **dar muerte a,** to kill. ‖ **dar muestras de algo,** to look: *daba muestras de cansancio,* she looked tired. ‖ **dar parte de algo,** to report sth. ‖ **dar razón de algn.,** to give sb.'s whereabouts: *no nos supo dar razón de José,* he couldn't tell us where José was. ‖ **dar razón de algo,** to give an account of sth.; (*correr la voz*) to let it be known. ‖ **darle a algo,** *fam* to be too fond of sth.: *¡cómo le da a la cerveza!,* he certainly knocks the beer back! ‖ **darle a uno algo,** (*sobrevenirle*) to have: *le dio un ataque de tos,* he had a coughing fit; *si sigue así le dará algo,* if she goes on like that she'll do herself a mischief. ‖ **darle a uno por hacer algo,** to take it into one's head to do sth.: *le ha dado por cantar,* she's taken up singing, she's got into singing. ‖ **dar(se) a conocer,** (*persona*) to introduce; (*noticia*) to release. ‖ **darse de narices con, dar de narices con,** to bump into. ‖ **darse por aludido,-a,** (*entender una indirecta*) to take the hint; (*ofenderse*) to take it personally. ‖ **darse por ofendido,-a,** to take offence. ‖ **darse por satisfecho,-a,** to feel sat-

isfied. ‖ **darse por vencido,** to give in, surrender. ‖ **dárselas de,** *fam* to pose as, fancy os. as: *se las da de presidente,* he fancies himself as president. ‖ **dársele a uno bien/mal algo,** to be good/bad at: *se le dan bien los idiomas,* he's good at languages. ‖ **no dar una,** *fam* not to get anything right. ‖ **¿qué se me da?,** why should I care? ‖ **¡y dale!,** *fam* there he (*you, they, etc*) goes (*go*) again!
▲ *Conjugation model* |68|.

dardo 1 *m* (*arma*) dart, arrow. **2** *fig* (*dicho*) cutting remark, caustic remark.

dársena *f* dock, basin.

darvinismo *m* Darwinism.

darvinista 1 *adj* Darwinist. – **2** *mf* Darwinist.

data 1 *f* (*fecha*) date. **2** COM item.

datar 1 *t* (*poner la data*) to date, put a date on. **2** COM to credit, enter. – **3** *i* (*tener origen*) to date (**de,** from), date back (**de,** to): *esa iglesia data del siglo XI,* that church dates from the eleventh century.

dátil 1 *m* date. **2** *fam* (*dedo*) finger.
■ **dátil de mar,** date shell.

datilera *f* date palm.

dativo,-a 1 *adj* dative. – **2 dativo,** *m* dative.
● **en dativo,** in the dative.

dato *m* (*información*) fact, piece of information, datum: *no pudimos resolver el problema por falta de datos,* we couldn't solve the problem due to lack of information.
■ **base de datos,** data base. ‖ **datos personales,** personal details. ‖ **procesamiento/proceso de datos,** data processing.

dB *sím* (*decibelio*) decibel; (*símbolo*) dB.

d.C. *abr* (*después de Cristo*) Anno Domini; (*abreviatura*) AD.

dcha. *abr* (*derecha*) right.

DDT *abr* (*diclorodifeniltricloroetano*) dichlorodiphenyltrichloroethane; (*abreviatura*) DDT.

de¹ *f name of the letter d.*

de² 1 *prep* (*posesión, pertenencia*) of: *el libro de Juan,* Juan's book; *el coche de mis padres,* my parents' car; *el hermano de mi padre,* my father's brother; *la mesa de mi habitación,* the table in my bedroom. **2** (*procedencia, origen*) from: *soy de Córdoba,* I'm from Córdoba; *viene de Barcelona,* she comes from Barcelona. **3** (*descripción*) with: *la niña de ojos castaños,* the girl with dark eyes, the dark-eyed girl; *el señor del abrigo azul,* the man in the blue coat. **4** (*tema*) of, on, about: *hablaron del tiempo,* they talked about the weather. **5** (*materia*) made of, of: *una mesa de madera,* a wooden table; *un anillo de oro,* a gold ring; *lo hicieron de plástico,* they made it out of plastic. **6** (*contenido*) of: *un vaso de agua,* a glass of water. **7** (*uso*) for: *aguja de calcetar,* knitting needle; *gallo de pelea,* fighting cock. **8** (*oficio*) by, as: *trabaja de profesor,* he works as a teacher; *es médico de profesión,* he's a doctor by profession. **9** (*modo*) on, in, as: *de pie,* standing up; *estar de moda,* to be in fashion. **10** (*tiempo*) at, by, in: *de día,* by day, during the day; *de noche,* at night; *a las diez de la mañana,* at ten in the morning. **11** (*lugar*) *varias traducciones:* *la vecina de arriba,* our upstairs neighbour; *el lavabo de abajo,* the downstairs toilet; *la ventana de la derecha,* the window on the right; *la puerta de la calle,* the street door. **12** (*precio*) at: *manzanas de doscientas pesetas el kilo,* apples at two hundred pesetas a kilo. **13** (*medida*) measuring: *una botella de dos litros,* a two litre bottle; *una mesa de un metro de ancho,* a metre-wide table. **14** (*causa*) with, because of, of: *llorar de alegría,* to cry with joy; *morir de*

frío, to die of cold. **15** (*agente*) by: *es una obra de Lope,* a play by Lope. **16** (*con superlativo*) in, of: *el mejor de España,* the best in Spain; *el mayor de los tres,* the eldest of the three. **17** (*suposición*) if: *de haberlo dicho,* if he had told us. **18** (*en una aposición*) of: *la ciudad de Barcelona,* the city of Barcelona.
▲ See also *del.*

dé *pt indef →* **dar.**

deambular *i* to saunter, stroll.

deambulatorio *m* ambulatory.

debacle *f* disaster, downfall.

debajo *adv* below, underneath: *el libro verde está debajo,* the green book is underneath; *dame el de debajo,* give me the one underneath.
● **debajo de,** under, below, underneath: *el brasero está debajo de la mesa,* the brazier is under the table. ‖ **por debajo,** underneath: *tuvieron que pasar por debajo,* they had to go underneath. ‖ **por debajo de,** below, under: *eso es por debajo del nivel del mar,* that's below sea level; *jugaron por debajo de sus posibilidades,* they played below form; *el gato salió por debajo de la mesa,* the cat came out from under the table.

debate *m* debate, discussion.

debatir 1 *t* to debate, discuss. – **2 debatirse,** *p* (*forcejear*) to struggle: *el enfermo se debatía entre la vida y la muerte,* the patient fought for his life.

debe *m* debit side.
■ **el debe y el haber,** the debit and credit.

deber 1 *t* (*estar obligado a algo*) to owe: *debemos respeto a nuestros padres,* we owe respect to our parents. **2** (*dinero, cosa*) to owe: *te debo cinco mil pesetas,* I owe you five thousand pesetas. – **3** *aux* (*obligación presente*) must, have to, have got to: *debo ir a comprar,* I must go shopping; *debes acabar antes de que lleguen,* you have to finish before they arrive. **4** (*obligación pasada*) should, ought to: *debía haberlo comprado ayer,* I should have bought it yesterday. **5** (*obligación futura*) must, have to, have got to: *deberás tenerlo a las cinco,* you must have it ready by five o'clock. **6** (*obligación moral*) should, ought to: *no deberías haberlo hecho,* you shouldn't have done it. **7 deber de,** (*probabilidad*) must; (*negativa*) can't: *deben de ser las seis,* it must be six o'clock; *debes de haberlo oído,* you must have heard it; *no sé cuántas veces he debido de decírtelo,* I don't know how many times I must have told you; *no deben de haber llegado,* they can't have arrived. – **8 deberse,** *p* (*ser consecuencia*) to be due (**a,** to): *esto se debe a su falta de interés,* this is due to his lack of interest. **9** (*tener una obligación*) to have a duty (**a,** to): *un soldado se debe a su patria,* a soldier has a duty to his country. – **10 deber,** *m* (*obligación*) duty, obligation. – **11 deberes,** *mpl* (*escolares*) homework *sing.*
● **cumplir con su deber,** to do one's duty. ‖ **hacer los deberes,** to do one's homework.

debidamente *adv* duly, properly: *entrega este impreso debidamente rellenado,* hand in this form duly filled in; *los niños no se portaron debidamente,* children didn't behave properly.

debido,-a 1 *pp →* **deber.** – **2** *adj* (*merecido*) due: *con el debido respeto, ...,* with all due respect, ... **3** (*conveniente*) right: *no pongas a la verdura más sal de la debida,* don't put more salt than necessary on the vegetables. **4** (*adecuado*) proper, necessary: *tomaremos las debidas precauciones,* we'll take the necessary precautions.
● **como es debido,** (*correctamente*) right, properly; (*como es merecido*) deservedly: *siéntate en la silla como es debido,* sit properly on the chair; *lo recibieron con todos*

los honores, como era debido, he was received with full honours, as was his due. ‖ **debido,-a a,** due to, owing to, because of: *las carreteras están cortadas debido al mal tiempo,* the roads have been closed due to bad weather. ‖ **debido a que,** because: *no pudieron venir debido a que tenían el coche averiado,* they couldn't come because their car had broken down. ‖ **en debida forma,** in due form. ‖ **más de lo debido,** too much.

débil 1 *adj* (*persona*) weak, feeble: *está aún muy débil para caminar,* he's still too weak to walk. **2** (*ruido*) faint; (*luz*) dim, feeble. **3** LING weak. **– 4** *mf* weak person. **– 5 los débiles,** *mpl* the weak.
■ **débil mental,** mentally retarded person, mentally deficient person.

debilidad 1 *f* (*de una persona*) weakness, feebleness; (*de un sonido*) faintness. **2** *fig* weakness: *los coches de carreras son su debilidad,* he has a weakness for racing cars.
● **tener debilidad por,** (*algo*) to have a weakness for; (*alguien*) to have a soft spot for: *tengo debilidad por mi sobrina,* I have a soft spot for my niece.

debilitación *f* weakening, debilitation.

debilitador,-ra *adj* weakening, debilitating.

debilitamiento *m* weakening.

debilitar 1 *t* to weaken, debilitate. **– 2 debilitarse,** *p* to weaken, get weak, become weak.

debilucho,-a 1 *adj pey* weak, frail, delicate. **– 2** *m,f* weakling.

débito 1 *m* (*deuda*) debt. **2** (*debe*) debit.

debut *m* debut, début.

debutante 1 *mf* (*actor*) first-time actor; (*actriz*) first-time actress. **– 2** *f* (*en sociedad*) debutante, débutante.

debutar *i* to make one's debut, make one's début.

década *f* decade.

decadencia *f* decadence, decline, decay.
● **estar en (franca) decadencia,** to be in (full) decline.

decadente 1 *adj* decadent. **– 2** *mf* decadent.

decaedro *m* decahedron.

decaer 1 *i* (*perder fuerzas*) to weaken; (- *entusiasmo, interés*) to flag; (- *salud*) to go down, deteriorate, decay; (- *belleza etc*) to lose: *su interés está decayendo,* his interest is flagging; *Elena ha decaído en belleza,* Elena has lost her beauty. **2** (*imperio, costumbre*) to decay. **3** (*fiebre*) to go down. **4** (*negocio*) to fall off, decline. **5** (*ánimo*) to lose heart: *su ánimo no decae,* she doesn't lose heart.
▲ Conjugation model |67|, like *caer.*

decagonal *adj* decagonal.

decágono *m* decagon.

decagramo *m* decagram, decagramme.

decaído,-a 1 *pp →* **decaer.** **– 2** *adj* (*débil*) weak. **3** (*triste*) sad, depressed, low.

decaimiento 1 *m* (*debilidad*) weakness, weakening. **2** (*tristeza*) sadness.

decalcificación *f →* **descalcificación.**

decalcificar *t →* **descalcificar.**

decalitro *m* decalitre (US decaliter).

decálogo *m* decalogue.

decámetro *m* decametre (US decameter).

decanato 1 *m* (*cargo, tiempo*) deanship: *la facultad fue reformada durante su decanato,* the faculty was reformed during his deanship. **2** (*lugar*) deanery.

decano,-a 1 *m,f* (*cargo*) dean. **2** (*miembro más antiguo*) senior member; (*hombre*) doyen; (*mujer*) doyenne.

decantación *f* decanting.

decantar¹ *t* (*verter*) to decant, pour off.

decantar² 1 *t* (*alabar*) to praise, laud. **– 2 decantarse,** *p* (*preferir*) to prefer (**hacia/por,** -): *el público se decantó por el equipo local,* the spectators were on the side of the local team.

decapar 1 *t* (*óxido, cal*) to descale. **2** (*pintura*) to strip (off).

decapitación *f* beheading, decapitation.

decapitar *t* to behead, decapitate.

decápodo *m* decapod.

decasílabo,-a 1 *adj* decasyllabic. **– 2 decasílabo,** *m* decasyllable.

decatlón *m* decathlon.

deceleración *f* deceleration.

decelerar *i* to decelerate.

decena 1 *f* (*exacto*) ten. **2** (*aproximado*) about ten: *he invitado a una decena de personas,* I have invited ten or so people.
● **por decenas,** in tens.

decenal *adj* decennial.

decencia 1 *f* (*decoro*) decency, propriety. **2** (*honestidad*) honesty.
● **con decencia,** decently.

decenio *m* decade.

decentar 1 *t* (*empezar a cortar*) to start: *decentamos el queso,* we started the cheese. **2** *fig* (*empezar a destruir*) erode: *esa vida le decentaba la salud,* that lifestyle eroded his health. **– 3 decentarse,** *p* (*ulcerarse*) to ulcerate.
▲ Conjugation model |27|, like *acertar.*

decente 1 *adj* (*decoroso*) decent, proper. **2** (*honesto*) honest, upright; (*respetable*) decent, respectable. **3** (*limpio*) tidy, clean. **4** (*adecuado*) suitable, right: *ponte ropa decente para salir a cenar,* put on some suitable clothes to go out for dinner.

decepción *f* disappointment, disenchantment: *se llevó una gran decepción,* she was terribly disappointed.

decepcionante *adj* disappointing.

decepcionar *t* to disappoint, let down: *no nos decepciones,* don't disappoint us.

deceso *m fml* decease.

dechado *m* model, example: *ese hombre es un dechado de virtudes,* that man is a paragon of virtue.

decibel *m* decibel.

decibelio *m* decibel.

decididamente 1 *adv* (*con determinación*) resolutely, with determination: *solicitó el trabajo decididamente,* he applied for the job with determination. **2** (*definitivamente*) definitely: *decididamente no compraremos esa casa,* we definitely won't buy that house.

decidido,-a 1 *pp →* **decidir.** **– 2** *adj* determined, resolute: *está decidido a acabar el trabajo,* he's determined to finish the job; *ya lo tengo decidido,* I've made up my mind.

decidir 1 *t* (*gen*) to decide; (*asunto*) to settle: *decidieron responder las preguntas,* they decided to answer the questions; *aún no hay nada decidido,* nothing is settled yet. **2** (*convencer*) to persuade, convince: *aquellas circunstancias la decidieron a marchar,* those circumstances persuaded her to leave. **3** (*resolver*) to resolve, decide: *decidió dejar de fumar,* he resolved to stop smoking. **– 4** *i* to decide, choose: *tuvo que decidir entre los dos,* she had to decide between the two. **– 5 decidirse,** *p* to make up one's mind: *tienes que decidirte lo antes posible,* you have to make up your mind as soon as possible.
● **decidirse por,** to decide on: *se decidió por la falda roja,* she decided on the red skirt.

decidor,-ra 1 *adj* eloquent, silver-tongued, witty. – 2 *m,f* wit.

decigramo *m* decigram, decigramme.

decilitro *m* decilitre (US deciliter).

décima *f* → **décimo,-a**.

decimal 1 *adj* decimal. – 2 *m* decimal.

decímetro *m* decimetre (US decimeter).

décimo,-a 1 *adj* tenth. – 2 *m,f* tenth. – 3 **décimo,** *m* tenth part of a lottery ticket. – 4 **décima,** *f* LIT stanza of ten octosyllabic lines.
● **tener (unas) décimas,** *fam* to have a slight temperature.
▲ See also **sexto,-a**.

decimoctavo,-a 1 *adj* eighteenth. – 2 *m,f* eighteenth.
▲ See also **sexto,-a**.

décimocuarto,-a 1 *adj* fourteenth. – 2 *m,f* fourteenth.
▲ See also **sexto,-a**.

decimonónico,-a *adj* nineteenth-century: *un escritor decimonónico,* a nineteenth-century writer.

decimonono,-a 1 *adj* nineteenth. – 2 *m,f* nineteenth.
▲ See also **sexto,-a**.

decimonoveno,-a *adj-m,f* → **decimonono,-a**.
▲ See also **sexto,-a**.

decimoquinto,-a 1 *adj* fifteenth. – 2 *m,f* fifteenth.
▲ See also **sexto,-a**.

decimoséptimo,-a 1 *adj* seventeenth. – 2 *m,f* seventeenth.
▲ See also **sexto,-a**.

decimosexto,-a 1 *adj* sixteenth. – 2 *m,f* sixteenth.
▲ See also **sexto,-a**.

decimotercero,-a 1 *adj* thirteenth. – 2 *m,f* thirteenth.
▲ See also **sexto,-a**.

decimotercio,-a *adj-m,f* → **decimotercero,-a**.

decir 1 *t* (*gen*) to say: *dice que llegarán tarde,* she says they'll be late; *dijo algo interesante,* he said something interesting. 2 (*contar, revelar*) to tell: *me dijo una mentira,* he told me a lie; *dijo la verdad,* she told the truth. 3 (*nombrar, llamar*) to call: *le dicen Cuca,* she's called Cuca; *le dicen la casa encantada,* it's known as the haunted house. 4 (*opinar*) to have to say: *¿qué me dices de la película?,* what did you think of the film? 5 (*denotar*) to tell, show: *su cara dice que está contento,* you can tell from his face that he's happy. 6 (*sugerir*) to mean: *¿te dice algo esa palabra?,* does this word mean anything to you? 7 (*recitar*) to recite: *dijo un poema,* he recited a poem. 8 (*un texto*) to read, say: *el texto dice lo siguiente,* the text reads as follows. – 9 **decirse,** *p* (*reflexionar*) to say to os.: *y yo me digo, ¿para qué sirve esto?,* and I wonder, what is this for? 10 (*llamarse*) to say: *¿cómo se dice mesa en alemán?,* how do you say table in German?, what's the German word for table? – 11 **decir,** *m* saying.
● **¿cómo diría yo?,** how shall I put it? ‖ **como quien dice,** so to speak, as it were. ‖ **como si dijéramos,** so to speak, as it were. ‖ **decir bien/mal,** to look good/bad (**a,** on): *el amarillo dice mal a una morena,* yellow doesn't suit a dark-haired woman. ‖ **decir para sí,** to say to os. ‖ **decir por decir,** to speak for the sake of speaking: *no lo digo por decir,* I'm not just saying that. ‖ **digamos que ...,** let's say that ... ‖ **digan lo que digan,** whatever they say. ‖ **digo yo,** in my opinion, I think. ‖ **¡dímelo a mí!,** you're telling me! ‖ **el qué dirán,** what people say. ‖ **es decir,** that is (to say). ‖ **es un decir,** *fam* it's just a saying. ‖ **ni que decir tiene,** needless to say. ‖ **¡no me digas!,** really! ‖ **querer decir,** to mean: *¿qué quieres decir?,* what do you mean?;

no quería decir eso, I didn't mean to say that; *quiero decir, ...,* I mean, ... ‖ **se dice ...,** they say ..., it is said ... ‖ **y no digamos ...,** not to mention ... ‖ **¡y que lo digas!,** you bet!
▲ Conjugation model [69], *pp* **dicho,-a**.

decisión 1 *f* (*resolución*) decision: *sus padres tuvieron que tomar una decisión,* his parents had to make a decision. 2 (*determinación*) determination, resolution: *se levantó con decisión y la invitó a bailar,* he stood up resolutely and asked her to dance.

decisivo,-a 1 *adj* (*importante*) decisive. 2 (*concluyente*) decisive, final: *un argumento decisivo,* a decisive argument.
● **de forma decisiva,** definitely.

decisorio,-a *adj* → **decisivo,-a**.

declamación 1 *f* (*acción*) recitation. 2 (*arte*) declamation.

declamar 1 *i* to declaim, recite. – 2 *t* to declaim, recite.

declamatorio,-a *adj* declamatory.

declaración 1 *f* (*gen*) declaration: *declaración de renta,* income tax return; *declaración de guerra,* declaration of war. 2 (*explicación pública*) statement, comment: *el ministro hizo una declaración sorprendente,* the minister made a surprising statement; *la artista se negó a hacer declaraciones sobre su divorcio,* the star refused to comment on her divorce. 3 JUR evidence. 4 (*en bridge*) bid.
● **prestar declaración,** JUR to give evidence.
▲ In *2*, also used in plural with the same meaning.

declaradamente *adv* openly.

declarado,-a *adj* open, professed.

declarante 1 *adj* declaring, who declares. 2 JUR who gives evidence. – 3 *m,f* declarer, declarant. 4 JUR witness.

declarar 1 *t* (*gen*) to declare; (*manifestar*) to state: *el inspector nos preguntó si teníamos algo que declarar,* the inspector asked us whether we had anything to declare; *lo declararon vencedor,* he was declared the winner; *el presidente declaró que no se devaluaría la peseta,* the President stated that the peseta wouldn't be devaluated. 2 JUR to find: *lo declararon culpable,* he was found guilty. 3 (*en bridge*) to bid, declare. – 4 *i* to declare. 5 JUR to testify. – 6 **declararse,** *p* (*amor*) to declare one's love (**a,** for): *le declaró su amor durante la fiesta,* he declared his love for her during the party. 7 (*fuego, guerra, etc*) to break out, start: *se declaró un incendio en el monte,* a fire broke out on the mountain.
● **declarar la guerra a un país,** to declare war on a country. ‖ **declararse a favor de,** to declare os. in favour (US in favor) of: *se declaró a favor del aborto,* she declared herself in favour of abortion. ‖ **declararse en contra,** to declare os. against. ‖ **declararse en huelga,** to go on strike. ‖ **declararse en quiebra,** to go into bankruptcy, declare os. bankrupt.

declarativo,-a *adj* declarative.

declaratorio,-a *adj* declaratory.

declinable *adj* declinable.

declinación 1 *f* GRAM declension. 2 ASTRON declination, deviation.

declinar 1 *i* (*brújula*) to decline. 2 (*disminuir*) to decline, come down: *la fiebre ha empezado a declinar,* her fever has started to come down; *la salud del enfermo declinó en otoño,* the patient's health declined in autumn. 3 (*acercarse al fin*) to end, draw to an end: *salimos cuando declinaba la tarde,* we went out as evening fell. – 4 *t* (*rechazar*) to decline, refuse. 5 GRAM to decline.

declive 1 *m* (*inclinación*) slope, incline. **2** *fig* (*decadencia*) decline.
● **en declive,** *fig* on the decline.
decodificación *f* decoding.
decodificador *m* decoder.
decodificar *t* to decode.
decoloración *f* (*pérdida del color*) fading, discolouring (US discoloring); (*blanqueo*) bleaching.
decolorante *adj* bleaching agent.
decolorar 1 *t* (*perder el color*) to discolour (US discolor). **2** (*blanquear*) to bleach. – **3 decolorarse,** *p* (*perder el color*) to fade, become discoloured (US discolored). **4** (*blanquearse*) to be bleached.
decomisar *t* to confiscate, seize.
decomiso 1 *m* (*acción*) confiscation, seizure. **2** (*lo confiscado*) confiscated article, confiscated goods *pl.*
decoración 1 *f* (*gen*) decoration. **2** TEAT scenery, set.
■ **decoración de escaparate,** window dressing.
decorado 1 *m* (*efecto*) decoration. **2** TEAT scenery, set.
decorador,-ra 1 *adj* decorating. – **2** *m,f* decorator. **3** TEAT set designer.
■ **decorador,-ra de escaparates,** window dresser. || **pintor,-ra decorador,-ra,** painter and decorator.
decorar *t* (*gen*) to decorate, adorn, embellish; (*una casa*) to decorate.
decorativo,-a *adj* decorative, ornamental.
● **estar de figura decorativa,** *fam fig* to be mere decoration. || **ser una figura decorativa,** *fam fig* to be mere decoration.
decorazonar 1 *t* to dishearten, discourage. – **2 decorazonarse,** *p* to lose heart, become discouraged.
decoro 1 *m* (*honor*) decorum; (*respeto*) respect. **2** (*pudor*) modesty, decency.
● **guardar el decoro a algn.,** to show respect for sb. || **con/sin decoro,** (*adj*) decent/indecent; (*adv*) decently/indecently; **vivir con decoro,** to live decently.
decorosamente 1 *adv* (*como se debe*) with decorum. **2** (*con dignidad*) with dignity. **3** (*con decencia*) decently.
decoroso,-a 1 *adj* (*apropiado*) decorous, proper. **2** (*digno*) decent, respectable: *un sueldo decoroso,* a decent salary. **3** (*respetable*) respectable, honourable (US honorable): *un trabajo decoroso,* an honourable job. **4** (*decente*) decent: *una muchacha decorosa,* a decent girl.
decrecer *i* (*gen*) to decrease, diminish; (*aguas*) to subside, go down; (*días*) to get shorter, draw in; (*interés*) to decline: *los días ya decrecen,* the days are drawing in now.
▲ *Conjugation model* |43|, *like* **agradecer.**
decreciente *adj* decreasing, diminishing.
decrecimiento *m* decrease, drop.
decrepitar *i* to decrepitate.
decrépito,-a *adj* decrepit.
decrepitud *f* decrepitude.
decrescendo 1 *adj* decrescendo. – **2** *adv* decrescendo. – **3** *m* decrescendo.
decretar 1 *t* (*con decreto*) to decree. **2** (*ordenar*) to ordain, order.
decreto *m* decree, order.
■ **decreto ley,** decree.
decúbito *m* decubitus.
■ **decúbito prono/supino,** supine/prone decubitus.
decuplicar *t* to decuple.
décuplo,-a 1 *adj* decuple, tenfold. – **2 décuplo,** *m* decuple.
decurrente *adj* decurrent.

decurso *m* course: *en el decurso de la historia,* in the course of history.
dedada 1 *f* (*cantidad*) pinch. **2** (*mancha*) finger-mark.
dedal *m* thimble.
dédalo *m* labyrinth.
dedicación 1 *f* dedication, devotion. **2** REL dedication, consacration.
● **de dedicación exclusiva,** full-time: *este trabajo es de dedicación exclusiva,* this is a full-time job. || **de plena dedicación,** full-time.
dedicar 1 *t* (*una dedicatoria*) to dedicate, inscribe. **2** (*tiempo, dinero*) to devote (**a,** to). **3** (*palabras*) to address: *dedicó unas palabras al público,* she addressed a few comments to the audience. **4** (*tener admiración, atenciones, etc*) to show, have: *le dedica muchas atenciones,* she devotes a lot of attention to him. **5** REL to dedicate, consecrate. – **6 dedicarse,** *p* to devote os. (**a,** to), dedicate os. (**a,** to): *se dedica a la enseñanza,* she's a teacher, she teaches; *en verano se dedica a pasear,* in summer he spends his time walking; *¿a qué te dedicas?,* what do you do for a living?
▲ *Conjugation model* |1|, *like* **sacar.**
dedicatoria *f* → **dedicatorio,-a.**
dedicatorio,-a 1 *adj* dedicatory. – **2 dedicatoria,** *f* dedication, inscription.
dedil *m* fingerstall.
dedillo al dedillo, *loc adv* perfectly: *se conoce la legislación al dedillo,* she knows the law inside out; *se conoce la zona al dedillo,* he knows the area like the back of his hand.
dedo 1 *m* (*de la mano*) finger; (*del pie*) toe. **2** (*medida*) finger, digit.
● **a dos dedos de,** *fig* only an inch away from. || **chuparse el dedo,** (*un niño*) to suck one's thumb; *fig* to have been born yesterday: *a mí no me engañas, que yo no me chupo el dedo,* you can't fool me, I wasn't born yesterday. || **elegir a algn. a dedo,** *fig* to hand-pick sb. || **estar para chuparse los dedos,** *fam* to be finger-licking good, be mouthwatering. || **hacer dedo,** *fam* to hitchhike. || **ir a dedo,** *fam* to hitchhike. || **meterse los dedos en la nariz,** to pick one's nose. || **no mover un dedo,** *fig* not to lift a finger. || **no tener dos dedos de frente,** *fig* to be as thick as two short planks. || **pillarse/cogerse los dedos,** *fig* to get caught, get one's fingers burnt. || **poner el dedo en la llaga,** *fig* to touch on a sore spot.
■ **dedo anular,** ring finger, third finger. || **dedo del corazón,** middle finger. || **dedo gordo,** (*de la mano*) thumb; (*del pie*) big toe. || **dedo índice,** forefinger, index finger. || **dedo meñique,** little finger. || **dedo pulgar,** thumb. || **yema del dedo,** fingertip.
deducción *f* deduction.
deducible 1 *adj* deducible, inferable. **2** COM deductible.
deducir 1 *t* to deduce, infer: *de ahí dedujimos que no había podido jugar,* from that we deduced that he hadn't been able to play. **2** (*dinero*) to deduct, subtract. – **3 deducirse,** *p* to follow: *de aquí se deduce que ...,* from this it follows that ...
▲ *Conjugation model* |46|, *like* **conducir.**
deductivo,-a *adj* deductive.
defecación *f* defecation.
defecar *i* to defecate.
▲ *Conjugation model* |1|, *like* **sacar.**
defección *f* defection, desertion.
defectivo,-a *adj* defective.
defecto 1 *m* (*gen*) defect, fault; (*de una joya*) imperfection, flaw. **2** (*de persona - moral*) fault, shortcoming; (-

física) handicap: *nació con un defecto físico,* she was born handicapped.
● **en defecto de,** for lack of. ‖ **pecar por defecto,** to be too conservative: *al hacer la comida, pecó por defecto,* when she made lunch, she didn't do enough. ‖ **por defecto,** INFORM default: *la impresora por defecto,* the default printer.
■ **defecto de pronunciación,** speech defect. ‖ **defecto de fábrica,** manufacturing fault.
defectuoso,-a *adj* defective, faulty.
defender 1 *t* (*gen*) to defend (**contra/de,** against): *defendió el castillo de sus enemigos,* he defended the castle against his enemies. **2** (*mantener una opinión, afirmación*) to defend, uphold; (*respaldar a algn.*) to stand up for, support. **3** (*proteger*) to protect (**contra/de,** against/from). **4** JUR (*algo*) to argue, plead; (*a alguien*) to defend. – **5 defenderse,** *p* (*espabilarse*) to manage, get by, get along: *¿qué tal se defiende en inglés?,* how does she get by in English?, what's her English like?
● **defender una causa,** JUR to argue a case.
▲ *Conjugation model* |28|, *like entender.*
defendible 1 *adj* (*que se puede defender*) defensible. **2** (*que se puede justificar*) justifiable.
defendido,-a 1 *pp* → **defender.** – **2** *adj* JUR defendant. – **3** *m,f* JUR defendant.
defenestración *f* defenestration.
defenestrar *t* to throw out the window.
defensa 1 *f* defence (US defense). – **2** *mf* DEP (*jugador*) back, defender; (*conjunto de jugadores*) defence (US defense), defenders *pl.* – **3 defensas,** *fpl* (*colmillos de un animal*) tusks.
● **en defensa propia,** in self-defence (US in self-defense). ‖ **en legítima defensa,** in self-defence (US in self-defense).
defensiva *f* → **defensivo,-a.**
defensivo,-a 1 *adj* defensive. – **2 defensiva,** *f* defensive.
● **estar/ponerse a la defensiva,** to be/go on the defensive. ‖ **jugar a la defensiva,** DEP to play a defensive game.
defensor,-ra 1 *adj* defending. – **2** *m,f* defender. **3** JUR counsel for the defence (US defense).
■ **abogado,-a defensor,-ra,** counsel for the defence (US defense). ‖ **defensor del pueblo,** ombudsman.
deferencia *f* deference.
● **en/por deferencia a,** in deference to: *por deferencia a su padre no mencionó aquel asunto,* in deference to his father he didn't mention that affair.
deferente *adj* deferential.
deferir 1 *i* to defer (**a,** to). – **2** *t* JUR to delegate (**a,** to), transfer (**a,** to).
▲ *Conjugation model* |35|, *like hervir.*
deficiencia 1 *f* (*defecto*) deficiency, defect, shortcoming. **2** (*insuficiencia*) lack: *fue debido a la deficiencia de medios,* it was due to the lack of means.
■ **deficiencia mental,** mental deficiency.
deficiente 1 *adj* (*defectuoso*) deficient, faulty: *el resultado es deficiente,* the result is poor. **2** (*insuficiente*) lacking, insufficient. – **3** *mf* mentally retarded person.
■ **deficiente mental,** mentally retarded person.
déficit 1 *m* COM deficit. **2** *fig* shortage.
▲ *pl* **déficit.**
deficitario,-a *adj* showing a deficit.
■ **balance deficitario,** balance showing a deficit.
definible *adj* definable.
definición *f* definition.
● **por definición,** by definition.

definido,-a 1 *pp* → **definir.** – **2** *adj* defined, definite.
definir 1 *t* to define. – **2 definirse,** *p* to be defined. **3** (*explicarse*) to make os. clear, define one's position: *se definió a favor de la medida,* he came out in favour of the measure.
definitivamente 1 *adv* (*para siempre*) for good, once and for all: *se marchó definitivamente,* she left for good. **2** (*finalmente*) finally: *definitivamente llegaremos el veinte,* we'll finally get there on the twentieth.
definitivo,-a *adj* definitive, final.
● **en definitiva,** finally, in short, all in all: *en definitiva, no lo compro porque no tengo dinero,* in short, I'm not buying it because I haven't got enough money.
deflación *f* deflation.
deflacionista *adj* deflationary.
deflagrar *i* to deflagrate.
deflector *m* baffle, deflector.
defoliación *f* defoliation.
deforestación *f* deforestation.
deforestar *t* to deforest.
deformación *f* deformation, distortion.
deformado,-a 1 *pp* → **deformar.** – **2** *adj* → **deforme.**
deformar 1 *t* (*gen*) to deform, put out of shape; (*cara*) to disfigure; (*realidad, imagen, etc*) to distort. – **2 deformarse,** *p* to become distorted, go out of shape.
deforme *adj* (*persona*) deformed; (*cosa*) misshapen, out of shape; (*imagen, cara*) distorted.
deformidad 1 *f* deformity, malformation. **2** *fig* fault, shortcoming.
defraudación 1 *f* (*estafa*) fraud, cheating. **2** (*decepción*) disappointment.
■ **defraudación fiscal,** tax evasion.
defraudado,-a 1 *pp* → **defraudar.** – **2** *adj* (*decepcionado*) disappointed.
defraudador,-ra 1 *adj* (*decepcionante*) disappointing. **2** (*engañoso*) deceiving, cheating. – **3** *m,f* person who commits fraud.
■ **defraudador,-ra fiscal,** tax evader.
defraudar 1 *t* (*estafar*) to defraud, cheat: *defraudó a Hacienda,* he evaded taxes. **2** (*decepcionar*) to disappoint, deceive: *su actitud me ha defraudado,* I'm disappointed with her attitude. **3** *fig* (*frustrar*) to betray: *defraudar las esperanzas,* to dash one's hopes.
defunción *f fml* death, decease.
degeneración *f* degeneration.
degenerado,-a 1 *pp* → **degenerar.** – **2** *adj* degenerate. – **3** *m,f* degenerate.
degenerar *i* to degenerate.
degenerativo,-a *adj* degenerative.
deglución *f* swallow, swallowing.
deglutir 1 *t* to swallow. – **2** *i* to swallow.
degollación 1 *f* (*degüello*) throat cutting. **2** (*decapitación*) beheading, decapitation. **3** (*matanza*) slaughter, massacre.
degolladero *m* slaughterhouse.
degolladura *f* cut in the throat.
degollar 1 *t* (*cortar la garganta*) to slit the throat of. **2** (*decapitar*) to behead, decapitate. **3** *fig* (*arruinar*) to ruin, spoil.
▲ *Conjugation model* |31|, *like contar.*
degollina *f fam* slaughter, massacre.
degradación 1 *f* degradation, debasement. **2** MIL demotion. **3** ART gradation.
degradante *adj* degrading, humiliating.
degradar 1 *t* to degrade, debase. **2** MIL to demote. – **3 degradarse,** *p* to demean os., degrade os.

degüello 1 *m* (*degolladura*) throat cutting. 2 (*decapitación*) beheading, decapitation.
degustación *f* tasting.
■ degustación de vinos, wine tasting.
degustar *t* to taste, sample, try.
dehesa *f* pasture, meadow.
dehiscente *adj* dehiscent.
deidad *f* deity, divinity.
deificación *f* deification.
deificar 1 *t* to deify. 2 *fig* to glorify.
▲ Conjugation model [1], like *sacar*.
deísmo *m* deism.
deísta 1 *adj* deistic. – 2 *mf* deist.
dejadez 1 *f* (*negligencia de sí mismo*) neglect, slovenliness. 2 (*negligencia*) negligence, carelessness. 3 (*pereza*) laziness, apathy.
dejado,-a 1 *pp* → **dejar**. – 2 *adj* (*descuidado*) untidy, slovenly. 3 (*negligente*) negligent. 4 (*perezoso*) lazy. – 5 *m,f* untidy person, slovenly person.
● dejado,-a de la mano de Dios, *fam* godforsaken.
dejar 1 *t* (*colocar*) to leave, put: *dejó unos tomates en la mesa,* he left some tomatoes on the table. 2 (*abandonar - persona, lugar*) to leave; (*- hábito, cosa, actividad*) to give up: *dejó el despacho a las ocho,* she left the office at eight o'clock; *ha dejado a su mujer,* he has left his wife; *dejó el tabaco,* he gave up smoking. 3 (*permitir*) to allow, let: *déjale jugar,* let him play; *no nos dejaron ir allí,* we were not allowed go there. 4 (*prestar*) to lend: *me dejó su abrigo,* she lent me her coat. 5 (*ceder*) to give. 6 (*producir dinero*) to bring in, make: *esta tienda deja un buen dinero,* this shop makes a lot of money. 7 (*producir humo, ceniza*) to produce, leave. 8 (*esperar*) to wait: *deja que llegue,* wait till he arrives. 9 (*aplazar*) to put off: *dejémoslo hasta mañana,* let's leave it till tomorrow. 10 (*omitir*) to leave out, omit. 11 (*causar un efecto*) to make: *me ha dejado nuevo,* I feel like a new man; *le película me ha dejado triste,* the film made me sad. 12 (*legar*) to bequeath, leave. – 13 dejar de + *inf*, *aux* (*cesar - voluntariamente*) to stop + *ger*, give up + *ger*; (*- involuntariamente*) to stop + *ger*: *ha dejado de llover,* it's stopped raining; *dejó de fumar,* he gave up smoking. 14 no dejar de + *inf*, not to fail *to* + *inf*: *no deja de sorprenderme,* she never fails to surprise me; *no dejes de hacerlo,* don't forget to do it; *no deja de molestarme,* she's always annoying me. 15 dejar + *pp*,: *dejó dicho que vendría mañana,* he left a message that he would come tomorrow; *lo dejó escrito en su agenda,* he wrote it down in his diary. – 16 dejarse, *p* (*abandonarse*) to neglect os., let os. go. 17 (*olvidar*) to forget, leave behind: *me he dejado las llaves en casa,* I've left my keys at home. 18 (*permitir*) to let os., allow os. to: *se dejó pegar,* he let himself be hit. 19 dejarse de, (*cesar*) to stop: *déjate de llorar,* stop crying; *déjate de tonterías,* don't be silly.
● dejar algo por imposible, to give up on sth. ‖ dejar caer, to drop. ‖ dejar en paz, to leave alone. ‖ dejar frío,-a, *fig* to leave cold. ‖ dejar mal a algn., to make sb. look bad. ‖ dejar plantado,-a a algn., to stand sb. up. ‖ dejar preocupado,-a, to worry. ‖ dejarse caer, to drop, fall; (*en casa de alguien*) to drop in: *déjate caer por mi casa cuando puedas,* drop in whenever you can. ‖ dejarse llevar por algn., to be influenced by sb. ‖ dejarse llevar por algo, to get carried away with sth. ‖ dejarse oír, (*gen*) to be heard; (*gritar*) to make os. heard. ‖ dejarse sentir el frío/verano/invierno, to feel the cold/summer/winter; *se deja sentir el invierno,* one can feel that winter's here.

deje 1 *m* slight accent: *tienes un deje andaluz,* you've got a slight Andalusian accent. 2 (*regusto*) aftertaste.
dejo *m* → **deje**.
del *contr* (*de* + *el*) → **de**.
delación *f* denunciation, accusation.
delagatorio,-a *adj* delegating, that delegates.
delantal *m* apron, pinafore.
delante 1 *adv* (*enfrente*) in front; (*adelantado*) in front, ahead: *él iba delante,* he was ahead. 2 de delante, in front: *los de delante,* the ones in front; *el asiento de delante,* the front seat. 3 delante de, in front of, ahead of, before: *delante de mis ojos,* before my eyes; *estaba delante de nosotros,* she was in front of us; *se encontraron delante del teatro,* they met outside the theatre. 4 por delante, in front, ahead: *tenemos mucho tiempo por delante,* we've got plenty of time ahead.
● llevarse todo por delante, *fig* to destroy everything.
delantera *f* → **delantero,-a**.
delantero,-a 1 *adj* front, front part: *el asiento delantero,* the front seat. – 3 delantero, *m* DEP forward. 4 COST front. – 5 delantera, *f* (*frente*) front (part). 6 DEP forward line, forwards *pl.* 7 (*ventaja*) lead, advantage. – 8 delanteras, *fpl fam* (*tetas*) tits, boobs.
● coger/tomar la delantera, to get ahead, take the lead. ‖ coger/tomar a algn. la delantera, (*en una carrera*) to take over the lead from sb.; *fig* to beat sb. to it: *quiso sentarse en el asiento libre, pero alguien le tomó la delantera,* he was about to sit in the free seat when someone beat him to it. ‖ llevar la delantera, to be in the lead, be ahead.
■ delantero centro, centre (US center) forward.
delatar 1 *t* to inform on. 2 (*revelar*) to give away, reveal: *el humo lo delató,* the smoke gave it away. – 3 delatarse, *p* to give os. away.
delator,-ra 1 *adj* accusing, denouncing. 2 (*reveladora*) which gives away. – 3 *m,f* accuser, denouncer.
delco *m* distributor.
deleble *adj* which can be erased easily, which can be rubbed out easily.
delectación *f* delight, delectation.
delegación 1 *f* (*gen*) delegation. 2 (*cargo*) office. 3 (*oficina*) branch, local office.
delegado,-a 1 *pp* → **delegar**. – 2 *adj* delegated. – 3 *m,f* delegate. 4 COM representative.
■ delegado,-a de Hacienda, chief tax inspector. ‖ delegado,-a del gobierno, government representative.
delegar *t* to delegate: *delegó sus poderes en Jaime,* he delegated powers to Jaime.
▲ Conjugation model [7], like *llegar*.
deleitar 1 *t* to delight, please. – 2 deleitarse, *p* to delight (**con/en**, in), take delight (**con/en**, in): *se deleita con la música clásica,* he takes delight in classical music.
deleite *m* pleasure, delight.
deleitoso,-a *adj* delightful, enjoyable.
deletéreo,-a *adj* poisonous, deadly.
deletrear 1 *t* to spell, spell out. 2 *fig* (*descifrar*) to decipher.
deletreo 1 *m* spelling (out). 2 *fig* (*desciframiento*) deciphering.
deleznable 1 *adj* (*que se rompe fácilmente*) fragile, crumbly. 2 (*resbaladizo*) slippery. 3 *fig* (*inconsistente*) weak. 4 *fig* (*despreciable*) despicable, contemptible.
delfín[1] *m* HIST dauphin.
delfín[2] *m* (*animal*) dolphin.

delga f (varilla) segment; (conmutador) comutator bar.
delgadez 1 f (esbeltez) slenderness, slimness. 2 (flacura) thinness.
delgado,-a 1 adj (poco ancho) thin. 2 (esbelto) slim, slender. 3 (flaco) thin. 4 fig (voz) soft.
● ponerse delgado,-a, to slim, get thin.
delgaducho,-a adj pey skinny, scrawny.
deliberación f deliberation.
deliberado,-a 1 pp → **deliberar**. – 2 adj deliberate, intentional.
deliberante adj deliberative.
deliberar 1 t to decide. – 2 i to deliberate (sobre, on).
deliberativo,-a adj deliberative.
delicadeza 1 f (finura) delicacy, daintiness. 2 (tacto) thoughtfulness; (refinamiento) refinement. 3 (de salud) frailty, delicacy.
● con delicadeza, (con tacto) tactfully; (con suavidad) delicately, gently. ‖ tener la delicadeza de, to be kind enough to.
■ falta de delicadeza, (falta de tacto) tactlessness; (de modales) bad manners pl.
delicado,-a 1 adj (fino) delicate; (exquisito) exquisite; (refinado) refined: un color delicado, a delicate colour. 2 (difícil) delicate, difficult: una situación delicada, a delicate situation. 3 (enfermizo) frail, delicate. 4 (frágil) fragile. 5 (exigente) fussy, fastidious, hard to please. 6 (cortés) refined, polite. 7 (muy sensible) hypersensitive, extremely sensitive.
■ manjar delicado, delicacy.
delicaducho,-a adj pey frail, sickly.
delicia f delight, pleasure: este libro es una delicia, this book is delightful.
● hacer las delicias de algn., to delight sb.
delicioso,-a adj delightful, charming; (una comida) delicious.
delictivo,-a adj criminal, punishable.
■ hecho delictivo, crime.
delimitación f delimitation, demarcation.
delimitar 1 t (terreno) to delimit, mark off. 2 (definir) to define, specify.
delincuencia f delinquency.
delincuente 1 adj delinquent. – 2 mf delinquent.
■ delincuente habitual, offender. ‖ delincuente sin antecedentes penales, first offender.
delineación f delineation, outlining.
delineante mf (hombre) draughtsman; (mujer) draughtswoman.
delinear t to delineate, outline, sketch.
delinquir i to break the law, commit an offence (US offense).
▲ Conjugation model [9].
delirante adj delirious, frenzied.
delirar 1 i to be delirious. 2 fig (decir despropósitos) to talk nonsense.
delirio 1 m (desvarío) delirium: ¡fue el delirio!, it was great! 2 fig (disparate) nonsense.
● con delirio, madly. ‖ tener delirio por algo, to be crazy about sth.
■ delirios de grandeza, delusions of grandeur.
delirium tremens m delirium tremens.
delito m offence (US offense), crime.
● ser cogido,-a en flagrante delito, to be caught red-handed.
■ el cuerpo del delito, the corpus delicti. ‖ delito común, common offence.
delta 1 f (letra) delta. 2 (ala delta) hang-gliding. – 3 m GEOG delta.

deltoides 1 adj deltoid, deltoidal. – 2 m deltoid.
▲ pl deltoides.
demacrado,-a 1 pp → **demacrar**. – 2 adj (gen) emaciated; (cara) haggard, drawn.
demacrarse p to waste away, become emaciated.
demagogia f demagogy.
demagógico,-a adj demagogic, demagogical.
demagogo,-a m,f demagogue.
demanda 1 f (petición) petition, request. 2 (pregunta) inquiry. 3 COM (pedido de mercancías) demand: este verano la demanda de ventiladores ha aumentado, this summer the demand for fans has increased. 4 JUR lawsuit.
● en demanda de, asking for. ‖ estimar una demanda, to allow a claim. ‖ presentar una demanda contra algn., to take legal action against sb.
■ la ley de la oferta y la demanda, the law of supply and demand.
demandado,-a 1 pp → **demandar**. – 2 m,f defendant.
■ parte demandada, defendant.
demandante 1 mf JUR plaintiff. 2 (persona que busca) seeker, hunter; (persona que compra) buyer: demandantes de asilo político procedentes del este de Europa, eastern European asylum seekers; la mayoría de los demandantes de piso prefieren una vivienda nueva, most flat hunters prefer a brand new home. – 3 adj pleading, begging: una mirada demandante, a pleading look.
■ parte demandante, plaintiff. ‖ demandante de divorcio, person suing for divorce. ‖ demandante de empleo, job hunter.
demandar 1 t (pedir) to request, ask for; (desear) to desire: los lectores demandaban nuevas aventuras, the readers asked for new adventures. 2 JUR to sue.
demarcación 1 f (separación) demarcation. 2 (territorio) district, zone.
■ línea de demarcación, demarcation line.
demarcar t to demarcate.
▲ Conjugation model [1], like sacar.
demás 1 adj other, rest of: las demás cosas, the other things; los demás niños, the rest of the children. – 2 pron the other, the rest: los demás llegaron tarde, the others arrived late; lo demás ya lo conoces, you already know the rest. – 3 adv besides, moreover.
● por demás, (inútil) in vain, useless; (muy, demasiado) too: es por demás que vayas, there's no point in going; su marido es por demás tacaño, her husband is too mean. ‖ por lo demás, apart from that, otherwise: es una película larga, pero por lo demás es interesante, it's a long film, but otherwise it's interesting. ‖ todo lo demás, everything else: me gustó el principio y todo lo demás, I liked the beginning and everything else. ‖ y demás, fam and so on: compramos claveles, rosas y demás flores, we bought some carnations, some roses and so on.
demasía 1 f (exceso) excess, surplus. 2 (abuso) abuse, outrage. 3 (descaro) insolence, impudence.
● en demasía, excessively, in excess: fuma en demasía, he smokes too much.
demasiado,-a 1 adj (singular) too much; (plural) too many: tienes demasiados discos, you've got too many records; hay demasiado pan, there's too much bread. – 2 adv (modificador de adjetivo) too; (modificador de verbo) too much: es demasiado gordo, he's too fat; bebes demasiado, you drink too much.
demencia 1 f insanity, madness, dementia. 2 fig (disparate) silly thing.
■ demencia precoz, dementia praecox. ‖ demencia senil, senile dementia.

demencial *adj* chaotic.
demente 1 *adj* mad, insane. – 2 *mf* mental patient; *ofens* lunatic.
demérito *m* demerit, fault.
demiurgo *m* demiurge.
democracia *f* democracy.
demócrata 1 *adj* democratic. – 2 *mf* democrat.
democratacristiano,-a 1 *adj* Christian Democratic. – 2 *m,f* Christian Democrat.
democráticamente *adv* democratically.
democrático,-a *adj* democratic.
democratización *f* democratization.
democratizar 1 *t* to democratize. – 2 **democratizarse**, *p* to democratize.
▲ Conjugation model [4], like *realizar*.
democristiano,-a *adj-m,f* → **democratacristiano,-a**.
demografía *f* demography.
demográfico,-a *adj* demographic: *crecimiento demográfico,* population increase/growth; *explosión demográfica,* population explosion.
demoledor,-ra 1 *adj* demolishing. 2 *fig* devastating: *fue una crítica demoledora,* that was a devastating criticism.
demoler 1 *t* to demolish, pull down, tear down. 2 *fig* to demolish, tear to pieces: *demolieron su argumentación,* they tore her argument to pieces.
▲ Conjugation model [32], like *mover*.
demolición *f* demolition.
demoniaco,-a *adj* demoniacal, demonic, possessed by the devil.
demoníaco,-a *adj* → **demoniaco**.
demonio *m* demon, devil.
● *¿cómo/dónde/quién/qué demonios ...?, fam* how/where/who/what the hell ...? ‖ *¿qué demonios haces aquí?, fam* what the hell are you doing here? ‖ **darse a (todos) los demonios,** *fam* to fly off the handle. ‖ **de mil demonios,** *fam* a hell of a: *un examen de mil demonios,* a hell of an exam. ‖ **de todos los demonios,** *fam* → **de mil demonios**. ‖ *¡demonio!, fam* hell!, damn! ‖ *¡demonio con ...!, fam* to hell with ...!: *¡demonio con el niño!,* to hell with the child! ‖ *¡demonios!, fam* hell!, damn! ‖ *¡demonio de niño!, fam* you little devil! ‖ **llevarse a algn. el demonio/los demonios,** *fam* to get really angry, go spare. ‖ **ponerse como un demonio,** *fam* to get really angry. ‖ *¡que me lleve el demonio si ...!, fam* I'll be blowed if ...!: *¡que me lleve el demonio si te entiendo!,* I'll be blowed if I can understand you! ‖ *¡qué demonio!, fam* damn it! ‖ **oler a demonios,** *fam* to smell horrible. ‖ **saber a demonios,** *fam* to taste horrible. ‖ **ser el mismo demonio,** *fam* (*muy malo*) to be a real devil; (*muy travieso*) to be the devil himself; (*muy hábil*) to be a sly devil, be a crafty devil. ‖ **ser un demonio,** *fam* to be a real devil. ‖ **tener el demonio en el cuerpo,** *fam* to have the devil in one, be always on the go.
demontre *interj* damn it!
demora *f* delay.
● **sin demora,** without delay.
demorar 1 *t* (*retrasar*) to delay, hold up: *demoramos la fecha de publicación hasta la primavera,* we delayed the date of publication till springtime. – 2 *i* (*detenerse*) to stop: *nos demoramos allí poco tiempo,* we stopped there for a short time. – 3 **demorarse**, *p* (*retrasarse*) to be delayed, be held up: *me he demorado a causa de la lluvia,* I was delayed by the rain. 4 (*detenerse en alguna parte*) to stop, linger.

demóstenes *m fig* eloquent man.
demostrable *adj* demonstrable.
demostración 1 *f* (*gen*) demonstration: *hizo una demostración de su funcionamiento,* she demonstrated how it worked. 2 (*manifestación*) show, display: *una demostración deportiva,* a sports display; *una demostración de cariño,* a show of love. 3 MAT proof.
demostrar 1 *t* (*probar*) to prove, show: *eso demuestra que no es nada inteligente,* that proves he's not clever at all. 2 (*hacer una demostración*) to demonstrate, show. 3 (*manifestar*) to show: *demostró buena voluntad,* she showed goodwill. 4 MAT to prove.
▲ Conjugation model [31], like *contar*.
demostrativo,-a 1 *adj* demonstrative. – 2 *m* demonstrative.
demudado,-a 1 *pp* → **demudar**. – 2 *adj* (*pálido*) pale. 3 (*alterado*) changed, distorted.
demudar 1 *t* (*gen*) to change, alter: *el susto le demudó el color de la cara,* her face turned pale with fright. – 2 **demudarse**, *p* (*palidecer*) to turn pale. 3 (*alterarse*) to change one's expression.
denario *m* denarius.
dendrita *f* dendrite.
denegación *f* (*rechazo*) refusal; (*negación*) denial.
■ **denegación de demanda,** JUR dismissal.
denegar *t* (*desestimar*) to refuse; (*negar*) to deny.
● **denegar una demanda,** JUR to dismiss a claim.
▲ Conjugation model [48], like *regar*.
denegrido,-a *adj* blackened, darkened.
dengue 1 *m* (*melindre*) affectation, fussiness. 2 (*enfermedad*) dengue fever.
● **hacer dengues,** to be fussy, be finicky.
denigración *f* denigration, disparagement.
denigrante *adj* denigrating, disparaging.
denigrar 1 *t* to denigrate, disparage, run down. 2 (*insultar*) to insult, revile.
denodadamente *adv* (*con valentía*) bravely, courageously; (*con resolución*) determinedly, resolutely.
denodado,-a 1 *adj* (*valiente*) bold, brave. 2 (*decidido*) determined, resolute.
denominación 1 *f* (*acción*) denomination, naming. 2 (*nombre*) denomination, name.
■ **denominación de origen,** (*vinos*) guarantee of origin, ≈ appellation d'origine contrôlée.
denominado,-a número denominado, *m* MAT compound number.
denominador,-ra 1 *adj* denominative. – 2 **denominador,** *m* MAT denominator.
■ **mínimo común denominador,** lowest common denominator.
denominar *t* to denominate, name.
denominativo,-a *adj* denominative.
denostar *t* to insult.
▲ Conjugation model [31], like *contar*.
denotar *t* to denote, indicate, show: *su rostro denotaba cierto disgusto,* his face showed displeasure.
densidad 1 *f* (*gen*) density. 2 *fig* (*espesura*) thickness, denseness: *la densidad de la niebla,* the thickness of the fog. 3 *fig* (*oscuridad*) darkness.
■ **densidad de población,** population density. ‖ **doble densidad,** INFORM double density. ‖ **high density,** INFORM high density.
densificar 1 *t* to make dense, densify. 2 (*espesar*) to thicken.
▲ Conjugation model [1], like *sacar*.
denso,-a 1 *adj* (*gen*) dense; (*espeso*) dense, thick. 2 *fig* (*oscuro*) dark.

dentado,-a 1 *pp* → **dentar**. – **2** *adj* (*con dientes*) toothed. **3** (*cuchillo*) serrated. **4** BOT dentate. – **5 dentado,** *m* perforation.
■ **rueda dentada,** cogwheel, gearwheel.
dentadura *f* teeth *pl*, set of teeth.
■ **dentadura postiza,** false teeth *pl*, dentures *pl*.
dental 1 *adj* dental. – **2** *m* LING dental.
■ **cepillo dental,** toothbrush. ‖ **crema dental,** toothpaste.
dentar 1 *i* (*echar los dientes*) to teethe. – **2** *t* (*formar dientes a una sierra*) to provide with teeth; (*a un cuchillo*) to serrate; (*a una rueda*) to provide with cogs.
dentario,-a *adj* dental.
dente al dente, *loc* al dente.
dentellada 1 *f* (*movimiento*) snap of the jaws. **2** (*mordisco*) bite. **3** (*señal*) toothmark.
dentellar *i* to chatter: *dentellaba de miedo,* her teeth were chattering with fear.
dentellear *t* to nibble (at).
dentera *f fig* (*envidia*) envy.
● **dar dentera a algn.,** (*dar grima*) to set sb.'s teeth on edge; (*dar envidia*) to make sb. green with envy: *ese ruido le da dentera,* that noise sets his teeth on edge.
dentición 1 *f* (*acción de dentar*) teething, dentition, cutting of the teeth. **2** (*época en que dentan los niños*) dentition. **3** (*serie de dientes*) set of teeth.
dentículo *m* dentil, denticle.
dentífrico,-a 1 *adj* tooth. – **2 dentífrico,** *m* toothpaste.
■ **pasta dentífrica,** toothpaste.
dentina *f* dentine (US dentin).
dentista *mf* dentist.
● **ir al dentista,** to go to the dentist's.
dentón,-ona 1 *adj* toothy, buck-toothed, goofy. – **2** *m,f* toothy person. – **3 dentón,** *m* (*pez*) dentex.
dentro *adv* inside; (*de edificio*) indoors, inside: *lo puse dentro,* I put it inside; *vayamos a tomar una copa dentro,* let's have a drink indoors; *está ahí dentro,* it's in there.
● **dentro de,** (*lugar*) in, inside; (*tiempo*) in: *dentro de la casa,* in the house; *dentro de una semana,* in a week, in a week's time. ‖ **dentro de lo posible,** as far as possible. ‖ **dentro de lo que cabe,** under the circumstances. ‖ **dentro de poco,** soon, shortly. ‖ **entrar/estar dentro de lo posible,** to be possible. ‖ **muy dentro,** deep down, deep inside: *sentía amor muy dentro,* he felt love deep inside. ‖ **por dentro,** (*de una cosa*) (on the) inside; (*de una persona*) deep down, inside, inwardly: *está podrido por dentro,* it's rotten inside; *se siente muy solo por dentro,* he feels lonely inside.
dentudo,-a *adj-m,f* → **dentón,-ona**.
denuedo *m* bravery, courage.
denuesto *m* insult, affront.
denuncia 1 *f* (*acusación*) accusation, formal complaint, report; (*delación*) denunciation. **2** JUR (*acción*) reporting; (*documento*) report.
● **presentar una denuncia contra algn.,** to lodge a complaint against sb., bring an action against sb., report sb.
denunciable *adj* which may be reported.
denunciador,-ra *m,f* person who reports a crime.
denunciante *m,f* person who reports a crime.
denunciar 1 *t* JUR (*poner una denuncia*) to report. **2** (*dar noticia*) to denounce: *denunció la falta de interés,* he denounced the lack of interest. **3** (*indicar*) to indicate: *ese humo denuncia la presencia de un fuego,* that smoke indicates there's a fire.
▲ *Conjugation model* [12], *like cambiar*.

deontología *f* deontology.
D.E.P. *abr* (*descanse en paz*) rest in peace; (*abreviatura*) R.I.P.
Dep. *abr* (*departamento*) department; (*abreviatura*) Dept.
deparar 1 *t* (*presentar*) to bring, hold in store: *nadie sabe lo que el destino nos deparará,* nobody knows what fate holds in store for us. **2** (*proporcionar*) to give, afford: *su victoria me deparó una gran alegría,* his triumph made me very happy.
departamental *adj* departmental.
departamento 1 *m* (*sección*) department, section: *Departamento de Química,* Chemistry Department. **2** (*provincia*) district, province. **3** (*de tren*) compartment. **4** (*de un objeto*) compartment, section.
departir *i* *fml* to talk, converse.
depauperación 1 *f fml* (*empobrecimiento*) impoverishment. **2** MED (*debilitamiento*) weakening.
depauperar 1 *t fml* (*empobrecer*) to impoverish. **2** MED (*debilitar*) to weaken. – **3 depauperarse,** *p* (*empobrecerse*) to impoverish. **4** MED (*debilitarse*) to weaken.
dependencia 1 *f* (*hecho de depender*) dependence. **2** (*política*) dependency. **3** (*departamento*) department, section. **4** (*habitación*) room, outbuilding: *el castillo tenía muchas dependencias,* the castle had several outbuildings. **5** (*sucursal*) branch. **6** (*conjunto de dependientes*) sales staff.
● **estar bajo la dependencia de,** to be dependent on.
depender 1 *i* to depend (**de,** on): *depende de ti,* it's up to you; *depende de lo que quieras,* it depends on what you want. **2** (*estar bajo el mando o autoridad*) to be under, be answerable to; (*necesitar*) to be dependent on: *los vendedores dependen de Juan,* the salesmen are answerable to Juan, Juan is in charge of the salesmen; *aún depende de sus padres,* she's still dependent on her parents.
● **en lo que de mí** (*ti, él, etc*) **depende ...,** as far as I (*you, he,* etc) am (*are, is*) concerned ...
dependienta *f* shop assistant, salesgirl, saleswoman.
dependiente 1 *adj* dependent (**de,** on). – **2** *m* shop assistant, salesman.
depilación *f* depilation, hair removal.
● **depilación a la cera,** waxing.
depilar *t* to depilate, remove the hair from; (*cejas*) to pluck.
depilatorio,-a 1 *adj* depilatory. – **2 depilatorio,** *m* depilatory.
■ **crema depilatoria,** hair-removing cream.
deplorable *adj* deplorable, regrettable.
deplorar *t* to deplore, lament, regret deeply.
deponente 1 *adj* JUR testifying. **2** LING deponent. – **3** *mf* JUR deponent, witness. – **4** *m* LING deponent verb.
deponer 1 *t* (*dejar*) to lay down, set aside; (*las armas*) to lay down: *depuso su cólera tras la explicación que le dieron,* he set aside his anger when he was given an explanation. **2** (*destituir*) to remove from office; (*a un rey*) to depose. **3** JUR (*exponer*) to declare, testify, give evidence about. – **4** *i* (*defecar*) to defecate.
▲ *Conjugation model* [78], *like poner, pp depuesto,-a.*
deportación *f* deportation.
deportado,-a 1 *pp* → **deportar**. – **2** *adj* deported. – **3** *m,f* deportee, deported person.
deportar *t* to deport.
deporte *m* sport: *¿practicas algún deporte?,* do you do any sport?, do you play any sport?
● **hacer algo por deporte,** to do sth. as a hobby. ‖ **hacer deporte,** to do some sport.

■ **campo de deportes,** sports ground. ‖ **deportes de invierno,** winter sports.
deportista 1 *adj* sporty, keen on sport. – **2** *mf* (*hombre*) sportsman; (*mujer*) sportswoman.
deportividad *f* sportsmanship.
deportivo,-a 1 *adj* (*aficionado al deporte*) sporting, sporty. **2** (*relacionado con el deporte*) sports: *coche deportivo,* sports car; *club deportivo,* sports club. **3** (*informal*) casual: *ropa deportiva,* casual clothes. **4** *fig* (*correcto*) sportsmanlike, sporting. – **5** deportivo, *m* (*coche*) sports car.
deposición 1 *f* (*destitución*) removal from office; (*de un rey*) deposition, deposal. **2** JUR testimony, deposition, evidence. **3** *fml* (*defecación*) defecation.
depositador,-ra *m,f* depositor.
depositante 1 *adj* who deposits. – **2** *m,f* depositor.
depositar 1 *t* (*dinero, joyas*) to deposit: *depositó los valores en el banco,* he deposited the bonds in the bank. **2** (*colocar*) to place, put: *depositó el maletín en el asiento de atrás,* he placed the briefcase on the back seat. **3** *fig* (*dar, conceder*) to place: *depositó en ella su confianza,* he placed his trust in her. **4** (*almacenar*) to store. **5** (*sedimentar*) to deposit. – **6** depositarse, *p* (*caer en el fondo*) to settle.
depositaría *f* depository.
depositario,-a 1 *m,f* (*de algo material*) depositary, trustee; (*de algo inmaterial*) repository. **2** (*tesorero*) treasurer. – **3** depositario, *m* (*cajero*) cashier; (*tesorero*) treasurer.
depósito 1 *m* (*recipiente*) tank. **2** (*almacén*) store, warehouse, depot. **3** (*financiero*) deposit. **4** (*sedimento*) deposit, sediment.
● **en depósito,** in bond.
■ **depósito de cadáveres,** mortuary, morgue. ‖ **depósito de gasolina,** petrol tank. ‖ **depósito de municiones,** dump. ‖ **depósito de objetos perdidos,** lost property office, US lost-and-found department. ‖ **depósito legal,** copyright.
depravación *f* depravity, depravation.
depravado,-a 1 *pp* → **depravar**. – **2** *adj* depraved. – **3** *m,f* depraved person, degenerate.
depravar 1 *t* to deprave. – **2** depravarse, *p* to become depraved.
depre 1 *f fam* depression, downer. – **2** *adj fam* low, down, depressed.
deprecación *f* deprecation.
deprecar *t* to beg, implore.
▲ *Conjugation model* [1], *like sacar*.
depreciación *f* depreciation.
depreciar 1 *t* to depreciate. – **2** depreciarse, *p* to depreciate.
▲ *Conjugation model* [12], *like cambiar*.
depredación 1 *f* (*saqueo*) pillaging, plundering. **2** (*malversación*) misappropriation (of funds), embezzlement.
depredador,-ra 1 *adj* depredatory. – **2** *m,f* depredator, pillager.
depredar *t* to depredate, pillage.
depresión *f* depression: *depresión atmosférica,* atmospheric depression; *depresión económica,* economic depression, slump.
■ **depresión nerviosa,** nervous breakdown.
depresivo,-a 1 *adj* (*deprimente*) depressing. **2** MED depressive.
depresor,-ra 1 *adj* depressing. – **2** depresor, *m* MED depressor.
deprimente *adj* depressing.
deprimido,-a 1 *pp* → **deprimir**. – **2** *adj* depressed.
deprimir 1 *t* to depress. – **2** deprimirse, *p* to get depressed.

deprisa *adv* quickly.
depto. *abr* (*departamento*) department; (*abreviatura*) Dept.
depuesto,-a *pp* → **deponer**.
depuracion 1 *f* (*del agua*) purification, depuration; (*de la sangre*) cleansing. **2** *fig* (*purga*) purge, purging.
depurado,-a 1 *pp* → **depurar**. – **2** *adj* (*pulido*) elaborate, carefully worked: *un estilo depurado,* a carefully worked style.
depurador,-ra 1 *adj* purifying. – **2** depurador, *m* (*sustancia*) depurative; (*aparato*) purifier.
depurar 1 *t* (*purificar agua*) to purify, depurate; (*sangre*) to cleanse. **2** POL to purge. **3** *fig* (*perfeccionar*) to purify, refine.
depurativo,-a 1 *adj* depurative. – **2** depurativo, *m* MED depurative.
derby *m* derby.
derecha *f* → **derecho,-a**.
derechamente 1 *adv* (*directamente*) directly, straight. **2** (*con discreción*) properly.
derechazo 1 *m* (*bofetada*) right-hander. **2** (*en tauromaquia*) right-handed pass with the cape.
derechismo *m* right-wing ideas *pl*.
derechista 1 *adj* right-wing, rightist. – **2** *m,f* right-winger, rightist.
derecho,-a 1 *adj* right: *la mano derecha,* the right hand. **2** (*recto*) straight, upright: *el cuadro no está derecho,* the picture isn't straight. – **3** derecho, *adv* straight: *se fue derecho a la cama,* he went straight to bed; *siga derecho,* go straight on. – **4** *m* (*leyes*) law: *ha estudiado derecho,* he studied law. **5** (*privilegio*) right: *los derechos de las minorías,* the rights of minority groups. **6** (*de una tela, calcetín, etc*) right side. – **7** derechos, *mpl* (*impuestos*) duties, taxes; (*tarifa*) fees. – **8** derecha, *f* (*mano*) right hand. **9** (*lugar*) right: *dame el de la derecha,* give me the one on the right. **10** la derecha, POL the right, the right wing. – **11** derecha, *interj* MIL right turn!
● **con derecho a,** with the right to. ‖ *¿con qué derecho ...?,* what right ...?: *¿con qué derecho te marchaste?,* what right did you have to leave? ‖ **dar derecho,** to entitle to: *el billete te da derecho a jugar media hora,* the ticket entitles you to play for half an hour. ‖ **de derecho,** by right. ‖ **estar en su derecho,** to be within one's rights. ‖ **no hacer nada a derechas,** *fig* to do nothing right. ‖ *¡no hay derecho!,* it's not fair! ‖ *"reservados todos los derechos",* "all rights reserved", "copyright". ‖ *"se reserva el derecho de admisión",* "the management reserves the right to refuse admission". ‖ **ser de derechas,** to be right-wing. ‖ **ser un hombre hecho y derecho,** *fig* to be a real man. ‖ **tener derecho a,** to be entitled to, have the right to: *nadie tiene derecho a quejarse,* nobody is entitled to complain.
■ **derecho civil,** civil law. ‖ **derecho de admisión,** right *sing* to refuse admission. ‖ **derecho mercantil,** commercial law, mercantile law. ‖ **derecho penal,** criminal law. ‖ **derecho político,** constitutional law. ‖ **derechos civiles,** civil rights. ‖ **derechos de aduana,** customs duties. ‖ **derechos de autor,** royalties. ‖ **derechos de matrícula,** registration fees. ‖ **derechos de sucesión,** death duties. ‖ **derechos humanos,** human rights. ‖ **el derecho al voto,** the right to vote.
deriva *f* drift.
● **a la deriva,** adrift. ‖ **ir a la deriva,** to drift.
derivación 1 *f* LING derivation. **2** (*en electricidad*) shunt. **3** (*de una carretera*) turn-off, diversion.

derivada *f* → **derivado,-a**.
derivado,-a 1 *pp* → **derivar**. – 2 *adj* derived, derivative. – 3 **derivado**, *m* LING derivative. 4 (*subproducto*) derivative, byproduct. – 5 **derivada**, *f* MAT derivative.
derivar 1 *i* (*proceder*) to spring, arise, come, stem: *este respeto deriva de su autoridad,* this respect stems from his authority. 2 MAR to drift. 3 LING to be derived (**de**, from), derive (**de**, from): *"pequeñito" deriva de "pequeño",* "pequeñito" is derived from "pequeño". 4 (*conducir*) to drift: *la conversación derivó hacia otro tema,* the conversation drifted onto a different subject. – 5 *t* (*dirigir*) to direct, divert. 6 LING to derive. 7 (*en electricidad*) to shunt. 8 MAT to derive. – 9 **derivarse**, *p* (*proceder*) to result (**de**, from), stem (**de**, from). 10 LING to be derived (**de**, from).
derivativo,-a 1 *adj* derivative. – 2 **derivativo**, *m* derivative.
dermatitis *f* dermatitis.
▲ *pl dermatitis.*
dermatoesqueleto *m* exoskeleton, dermoskeleton.
dermatología *f* dermatology.
dermatólogo,-a *m,f* dermatologist.
dermatosis *f* dermatosis.
▲ *pl dermatosis.*
dérmico,-a *adj* dermal, dermic, skin.
dermis *f* dermis.
▲ *pl dermis.*
dermoprotector,-ra *adj* which is kind to the skin: *gel dermoprotector,* shower gel which is kind to the skin.
derogable *adj* repealable.
derogación *f* abolition, repeal.
derogar 1 *t* JUR to abolish, repeal. 2 (*contrato*) to rescind, cancel.
▲ *Conjugation model* |7|, *like llegar.*
derogatorio,-a *adj* repealing, abolishing, annulling.
derrama 1 *f* (*repartimiento*) apportionment of taxes. 2 (*contribución*) special levy.
derramamiento 1 *m* spilling; (*rebosamiento*) overflowing. 2 (*dispersión de gente*) scattering.
■ **derramamiento de sangre**, bloodshed.
derramar 1 *t* to pour out, spill: *derramó el agua,* he spilt the water. 2 (*sangre, lágrimas*) to shed. 3 (*impuestos, etc*) to share out, distribute. 4 *fig* (*divulgar*) to spread: *derramar una noticia,* to spread a piece of news. – 5 **derramarse**, *p* to spill, pour out. 6 (*divulgarse*) to spread. 7 (*desembocar*) to flow (**en**, into): *el Tajo se derrama en el Atlántico,* the Tagus flows into the Atlantic.
derrame 1 *m* pouring out, spilling. 2 (*de sangre, lágrimas*) shedding. 3 (*pérdida*) leak, leakage. 4 MED discharge. 5 ARQ splay.
■ **derrame cerebral**, MED brain haemorrhage.
derrapar *i* to skid.
derrape *m* skid.
derredor *m* surroundings *pl.*
● **al/en derredor**, round, around: *miró en derredor y no pudo ver a nadie,* he looked round and couldn't see anybody.
▲ *See also alrededor.*
derrengar 1 *t* (*lastimar la espalda*) to sprain the back of. 2 (*torcer*) to twist. 3 *fig* (*cansarse*) to wear out, exhaust, shatter: *estoy derrengada,* I'm shattered. – 4 **derrengarse**, *p* (*lastimarse la espalda*) to sprain one's back. 5 (*cansarse*) to wear os. out.
derretido,-a 1 *pp* → **derretir**. – 2 *adj* (*gen*) melted; (*metales*) molten: *nieve derretida,* melted snow.
● **estar derretido,-a por algn.**, *fig* to be madly in love with sb.

derretimiento 1 *m* melting; (*de la nieve*) thawing. 2 *fig* (*dilapidación*) wasting, squandering. 3 *fam* (*amor*) intense love, passion.
derretir 1 *t* (*gen*) to melt; (*hielo, nieve*) to melt, thaw; (*metal*) to melt down. 2 (*dilapidar*) to waste, squander: *derritió su fortuna en un año,* he wasted his fortune in a year. – 3 **derretirse**, *p* (*fundirse*) to melt; (*hielo, nieve*) to melt, thaw. 4 *fig* (*de amor*) to burn (**de**, with). 5 (*inquietarse*) to worry, fret.
▲ *Conjugation model* |34|, *like servir.*
derribar 1 *t* (*demoler*) to pull down, demolish, knock down: *derribar un edificio,* to demolish a building, knock down a building. 2 (*hacer caer a una persona*) to knock over; (*de un caballo*) to throw: *el viento derribó a cuatro transeúntes,* four people were blown over by the wind; *el caballo lo derribó,* the horse threw him. 3 (*avión, enemigo*) to shoot down, bring down. 4 (*una puerta*) to batter down. 5 *fig* (*gobierno*) to overthrow; (*ministro*) to topple.
derribo *m* (*demolición*) demolition, knocking down, pulling down.
■ **materiales de derribo**, rubble *sing.*
derrocamiento 1 *m* (*demolición*) demolition, knocking down, pulling down. 2 *fig* (*gobierno*) overthrow; (*ministro*) toppling.
derrocar 1 *t* (*demoler*) to pull down, demolish, knock down. 2 (*gobierno*) to overthrow, bring down; (*ministro*) to oust from office, topple.
▲ *Conjugation model* |1|, *like sacar.*
derrochador,-ra 1 *adj* wasteful, squandering, spendthrift. – 2 *m,f* squanderer, wasteful person, spendthrift.
derrochar 1 *t* (*dilapidar*) to waste, squander. 2 *fig* (*rebosar*) to be full of: *esta chica derrocha salud,* this girl is full of health.
derroche 1 *m* (*despilfarro*) waste, squandering. 2 (*abundancia*) profusion, abundance: *un derroche de energía,* a burst of energy.
● **hacer un derroche de energía**, *fig* to put a lot of energy (**en**, into).
derrochón,-ona *adj-m,f* → **derrochador,-ra**.
derrota[1] 1 *f* (*camino*) path, road. 2 MAR course.
derrota[2] 1 *m* (*de un ejército*) defeat. 2 (*fracaso*) failure, setback.
● **sufrir una derrota**, to suffer a defeat.
derrotado,-a 1 *pp* → **derrotar**. – 2 *adj* defeated. 3 (*ropa*) worn out. 4 (*andrajoso*) in tatters, ragged. 5 *fam* (*cansado*) tired, bushed, whacked; (*deprimido*) depressed.
derrotar *t* to defeat, beat: *me derrotó al tenis,* he beat me at tennis.
derrote *m* butt.
derrotero 1 *m* MAR (*rumbo*) course; (*dirección*) direction. 2 MAR (*libro*) book of charts. 3 *fig* (*camino, medio*) path, course of action.
derrotismo *m* defeatism.
derrotista 1 *adj* defeatist. – 2 *mf* defeatist.
derrubiar *t* to erode, wash away.
▲ *Conjugation model* |12|, *like cambiar.*
derrubio 1 *m* (*acción*) erosion, washing away. 2 (*material*) alluvium.
derruido,-a 1 *pp* → **derruir**. – 2 *adj* in ruins.
derruir *t* to pull down, demolish, knock down.
▲ *Conjugation model* |62|, *like huir.*
derrumbadero *m* precipice, cliff.
derrumbamiento 1 *m* falling down, collapse. 2 (*techo*) caving in. 3 (*de tierras*) landslide.

derrumbar 1 *t* (*demoler*) to pull down, demolish, knock down. 2 (*despeñar*) to throw down, hurl down. – 3 derrumbarse, *p* (*un edificio*) to collapse, fall down; (*un techo*) to fall in, cave in. 4 *fig* to collapse: *después de tanta tensión se derrumbó y rompió a llorar,* with all the tension she collapsed and burst into tears.

derrumbe *m →* **derrumbadero, derrumbamiento.**

derviche *m* dervish.

desabastecido,-a *adj* out of: *las tiendas se encuentran desabastecidas de alimentos,* there's no food in the shops, the shops are out of food.

desaborido,-a 1 *adj* (*comida*) tasteless, insipid. 2 *fig* (*persona*) dull. – 3 *m,f fig* dull person.

desabotonar 1 *t* (*desabrochar*) to unbutton, undo. – 2 *i* (*abrirse las flores*) to open out, bloom, blossom.

desabrido,-a 1 *adj* (*comida*) tasteless, insipid. 2 *fig* (*persona*) surly; (*tono*) harsh, sharp. 3 (*tiempo*) unpleasant.

desabrigado,-a 1 *pp →* **desabrigar.** – 2 *adj* (*lugar*) open, exposed. 3 *fig* (*sin protección*) unprotected, defenceless.
● ir desabrigado,-a, not to be well wrapped up: *hace frío, no puedes salir desabrigado,* it's cold, you have to wrap up warm to go out.

desabrigar 1 *t* (*ropa*) to take someone's coat off. 2 desabrigarse, (*uso reflexivo*) to take off one's coat; (*en la cama*) to throw off the bedclothes.
▲ *Conjugation model* [7], *like* llegar.

desabrimiento 1 *m* (*falta de sazón*) insipidness, insipidity. 2 *fig* (*desazón interior*) uneasiness. 3 *fig* (*aspereza en el trato*) harshness, sharpness.

desabrochar 1 *t* to undo, unfasten. – 2 desabrocharse, *p* (*una prenda*) to come undone, come unfastened: *la camisa se me desabrochó,* my shirt came undone.

desacatar 1 *t* (*faltar al respeto*) to show no respect towards, be disrespectful. 2 (*desobedecer*) to disobey, not observe, defy.

desacato 1 *m* (*falta de respeto*) lack of respect (**a**, for), disrespect (**a**, for). 2 JUR contempt (**a**, for).
● desacato a la autoridad, contempt. || desacato al tribunal, contempt of court.

desacerbar *t* to temper.

desacertadamente *adv* (*erróneamente*) wrongly, mistakenly. 2 (*inadecuadamente*) unfortunately, unwisely; (*sin tacto*) tactlessly.

desacertado,-a 1 *pp →* **desacertar.** – 2 *adj* (*erróneo*) wrong, mistaken. 3 (*inadecuado*) unfortunate, unwise, inappropiate; (*sin tacto*) tactless: *un comentario desacertado,* a tactless remark, an unfortunate remark.

desacertar 1 *i* (*fallar*) to be wrong, be mistaken. 2 (*faltar de tacto*) to lack tact, be tactless.
▲ *Conjugation model* [27], *like* acertar.

desacierto 1 *m* (*error*) mistake: *fue un desacierto creer que lo entenderían,* it was a mistake thinking they could understand it. 2 (*falta de tacto*) lack of tact.

desacomodado,-a 1 *pp →* **desacomodar.** – 2 *adj* (*sin empleo*) unemployed. 3 (*falto de medios económicos*) badly off, poor.

desacomodar 1 *t* (*privar de comodidad*) to inconvenience. 2 (*dejar sin empleo*) to dismiss. – 3 desacomodarse, *p* (*perder el trabajo*) to lose one's job.

desacompañado,-a *adj* alone, lonely.

desaconsejado,-a 1 *pp →* **desaconsejar.** – 2 *adj* unwise: *está desaconsejado comer demasiada sal,* it's unwise to eat too much salt.

desaconsejar *t* to advise against.

desacoplar 1 *t* TÉC to uncouple, remove. 2 ELEC to disconnect.

desacorde 1 *m* MÚS discordant. 2 *fig* clashing, discordant, conflicting; (*colores*) clashing: *opiniones desacordes,* conflicting opinions.

desacostumbrado,-a 1 *pp →* **desacostumbrar.** – 2 *adj* unusual, strange.

desacostumbrar 1 *t* (*hacer perder un uso*) to break of a habit, get out of a habit: *cuando un niño empieza a hacer eso hay que desacostumbrarlo en seguida,* when a child starts to do that you have to get him out of the habit straightaway. – 2 desacostumbrarse, *p* (*perder la costumbre*) to get out of the habit (**de**, of), lose the habit (**de**, of), give up (**de**, -): *me he desacostumbrado de beber,* I've given up drinking. 3 (*perder la tolerancia*) to be no longer used (**a**, to): *me he desacostumbrado al calor,* I'm no longer used to the heat, I can't take the heat any more.

desacreditar *t* to discredit, bring discredit on, bring into discredit: *tal comportamiento lo desacredita,* such behaviour brings discredit on him.

desactivar *t* to defuse.

desacuerdo *m* disagreement.
● estar en desacuerdo con, to be in disagreement with.

desafecto,-a 1 *adj* disaffected, opposed. – 2 desafecto, *m* lack of affection, coldness.

desaferrar 1 *t* (*soltar*) to let go, release. 2 *fig* (*disuadir*) to dissuade. 3 MAR to weigh.

desafiante *adj* challenging, defiant.

desafiar 1 *t* (*gen*) to defy: *explicaciones que desafían el entendimiento,* explanations which defy understanding. 2 (*no hacer caso a*) to flout; (*no obedecer*) to defy: *rocas que parecen desafiar las leyes de la gravedad,* rocks which appear to defy the laws of gravity; *desafiaron el bloqueo naval,* they flouted the naval blockade. 3 (*plantar cara a - persona*) to defy, stand up to; (- *dificultad*) to brave: *poca gente había que desafiara la tormenta y saliese a la calle,* few were prepared to brave the storm and go out onto the streets.
● desafiar a algn. a hacer algo, to challenge sb. to do sth., dare sb. to do sth.: *lo desafió a comerse todo el pastel,* she dared him to eat the whole cake.
▲ *Conjugation model* [13], *like* desviar.

desafición *f* lack of affection, coldness.

desafinadamente *adv* out of tune.

desafinado,-a 1 *pp →* **desafinar.** – 2 *adj* out of tune.

desafinar 1 *i* (*gen*) to be out of tune; (*cantar*) to sing out of tune; (*tocar*) to play out of tune: *esta guitarra desafina,* this guitar is out of tune. – 2 *t* to put out of tune. – 3 desafinarse, *p* to go out of tune.

desafío 1 *m* (*reto*) challenge. 2 (*duelo*) duel. 3 (*provocación*) provocation, defiance.

desaforadamente 1 *adv* (*con exceso*) excessively. 2 (*de forma escandalosa*) outrageously. 3 (*con atropello*) lawlessly.

desaforado,-a 1 *adj* (*exagerado*) huge, enormous, terrible: *hizo un esfuerzo desaforado,* he made a great effort. 2 (*escandaloso*) outrageous. 3 (*fuera de la ley*) lawless.

desaforar 1 *t* (*quebrantar los fueros*) to encroach on the rights of. 2 (*privar del fuero*) to deprive of one's rights. – 3 desaforarse, *p* (*descomedirse*) to be disrespectful, be rude.
▲ *Conjugation model* [31], *like* contar.

desafortunadamente *adv* unfortunately.

desafortunado,-a 1 *adj* (*sin suerte*) unlucky, unfortunate. 2 (*sin tino*) unfortunate.

desafuero 1 *m* JUR infringement of the law. 2 (*abuso*) outrage, excess.
● **cometer un desafuero,** JUR to break the law; (*abusar*) to commit an outrage.

desagradable *adj* disagreeable, unpleasant.

desagradar *i* to displease: *me desagrada su música,* I don't like her music.

desagradecer *t* to be ungrateful for, show ingratitude for.
▲ *Conjugation model* [43], *like agradecer.*

desagradecido,-a 1 *pp* → **desagradecer.** − 2 *adj* ungrateful. − 3 *m,f* ungrateful person.
● **mostrarse desagradecido,-a,** to be ungrateful, show ingratitude.

desagradecimiento *m* ingratitude, ungratefulness.

desagrado *m* displeasure, discontent.
● **con desagrado,** reluctantly.

desagraviar 1 *t* (*reparar el agravio*) to make amends for, make up for: *lo desagravió pidiendo disculpas en público,* he made amends by making a public apology. 2 (*compensar el agravio*) to indemnify, compensate.
▲ *Conjugation model* [12], *like cambiar.*

desagravio *m* ammends *pl,* compensation.

desaguadero *m* drain.

desaguar 1 *t* (*extraer el agua*) to drain. − 2 *i* (*un líquido*) to drain, drain off/away; (*un contenedor*) to drain. 3 (*desembocar*) to flow (**en,** into), drain (**en,** into): *el Duero desagua en el Atlántico,* the Douro flows into the Atlantic.
▲ *Conjugation model* [22], *like averiguar.*

desagüe 1 *m* (*acción*) draining, drainage. 2 (*agujero*) drain, outlet. 3 (*cañería*) waste pipe, drainpipe.
■ **desague del radiador,** AUTO radiator overflow pipe.

desaguisado,-a 1 *adj* (*contra la ley*) illegal, unlawful. 2 (*contra la razón*) outrageous. − 3 **desaguisado,** *m* (*delito*) offence (US offense); (*atropello*) outrage. 4 *fig* (*destrozo*) damage; (*fechoría*) mischief.

desahogadamente 1 *adv* (*con holgura*) comfortable, with room to spare: *aquí cabemos cuatro desahogadamente,* the four of us can fit in here comfortably. 2 (*con dinero*) comfortably. 3 (*con descaro*) insolently.

desahogado,-a 1 *pp* → **desahogar.** − 2 *adj* (*espacioso*) roomy, spacious. 3 (*con dinero*) well-off, well-to-do, comfortable: *una posición desahogada,* comfortable circumstances. 4 *fig* (*descarado*) cheeky, shameless, insolent.

desahogar 1 *t* (*consolar*) to comfort; (*aliviar*) to relieve. 2 *fig* (*mostrar*) to vent, pour out: *desahogó sus penas,* he vented his grief. − 3 **desahogarse,** *p* (*desfogarse*) to let off steam: *¡desahógate!,* don't bottle it up! 4 (*confiarse*) to open one's heart (**con,** to): *se desahogó con su madre,* she poured her heart out to her mother. 5 (*descargar un problema*) to get off one's chest: *necesitas desahogarte,* you need to get it off your chest.
▲ *Conjugation model* [7], *like llegar.*

desahogo 1 *m* (*alivio*) relief. 2 (*esparcimiento*) amusement, relaxation: *el fútbol le sirve de desahogo,* football helps him let off steam. 3 (*descaro*) impudence, nerve. 4 *fig* (*económico*) comfort, ease: *viven con desahogo,* they live comfortably.

desahuciado,-a 1 *pp* → **desahuciar.** − 2 *adj* (*enfermo*) hopeless. 3 (*inquilino*) evicted.

desahuciar 1 *t* to deprive of all hope: *los médicos desahuciaron al paciente,* doctors abandoned all hope of saving the patient. 2 JUR (*inquilino*) to evict.
▲ *Conjugation model* [12], *like cambiar.*

desahucio *m* eviction.

desairadamente 1 *adv* (*sin gracia*) ungracefully. 2 (*con rudeza*) rudely.

desairado,-a 1 *pp* → **desairar.** − 2 *adj* (*sin gracia*) ungraceful; (*sin éxito*) unsuccessful; (*desagradable*) awkward: *fue una situación desairada,* it was an awkward situation. 3 (*humillante*) humiliating.
● **quedar desairado,-a,** to come off badly.

desairar 1 *t* (*desatender*) to slight, snub: *lo desairó durante el cóctel de la embajada,* she snubbed him during the cocktail party at the embassy. 2 (*desestimar*) to reject.

desaire 1 *m* (*menosprecio*) slight, rebuff. 2 (*falta de gracia*) lack of charm.
● **hacerle un desaire a algn.,** to snub sb.

desajustar 1 *t* (*máquina*) to put out of order. 2 *fig* (*planes etc*) to upset, spoil. − 3 **desajustarse,** *p* (*máquina*) to go wrong, break down; (*piezas*) to come apart, pull apart; (*tornillo*) to come loose.

desajuste 1 *m* (*mal funcionamiento*) maladjustment; (*avería*) breakdown. 2 *fig* (*planes etc*) upsetting.
■ **desajuste de horarios,** clashing timetables *pl.* ‖ **desajuste económico,** economic imbalance.

desalado,-a¹ 1 *pp* → **desalar ¹.** − 2 *adj* CULIN desalted.

desalado,-a² 1 *pp* → **desalar ².** − 2 *adj* (*sin alas*) wingless. 3 *fig* (*acelerado*) hasty; (*ansioso*) anxious.
● **ir desalado,-a,** to rush, hurry, dash.

desalar¹ *t* to desalt, remove the salt from.

desalar² 1 *t* (*quitar las alas*) to clip the wings of. − 2 **desalarse,** *p* (*darse prisa*) to rush, hurry. 3 *fig* (*sentir anhelo*) to long (**por,** for).

desalentador,-ra *adj* discouraging, disheartening.

desalentar 1 *t* (*dificultar el aliento*) to leave breathless, make get out of breath. 2 *fig* (*quitar el ánimo*) to discourage, dishearten. − 3 **desalentarse,** *p* to lose heart, get discouraged.
▲ *Conjugation model* [27], *like acertar.*

desaliento *m* discouragement.

desalinear *t* to put out of line.

desaliñadamente *adv* untidily, scruffily.

desaliñado,-a 1 *pp* → **desaliñar.** − 2 *adj* untidy, unkempt, scruffy.

desaliñar *t* to make untidy, make scruffy.

desaliño *m* untidiness, scruffiness.

desalmado,-a 1 *adj* (*malvado*) wicked. 2 (*cruel*) cruel, heartless. − 3 *m,f* (*malvado*) wicked person. 4 (*cruel*) cruel person, heartless person.

desalojamiento 1 *m* (*expulsión*) eviction, ejection. 2 (*marcha de un lugar*) evacuation, clearing.

desalojar 1 *t* (*marcharse*) to evacuate, clear, move out of: *¡desalojen el edificio!,* evacuate the building! 2 (*inquilino*) to evict (**de,** from). 3 MAR to displace. − 4 *i* (*mudarse*) to move house, move out.

desalojo *m* → **desalojamiento.**

desalquilado,-a 1 *pp* → **desalquilar.** − 2 *adj* vacant, unrented.

desalquilar 1 *t* to vacate. − 2 **desalquilarse,** *p* to become vacant.

desamarrar 1 *t* (*desatar*) to untie. 2 MAR to unmoor, cast off.

desambientado,-a 1 *adj* (*persona*) out of place. 2 (*lugar*) lacking in atmosphere.

desambiguar *t* to clear up, clarify.

desamor 1 *m* (*desafecto*) lack of affection. 2 (*frialdad*) coldness, indifference. 3 (*antipatía*) dislike.

desamortizable *adj* alienable.
■ **bienes desamortizables,** alienable property *sing.*

desamortización *f* alienation, disentailment.
desamortizar *t* to alienate, disentail.
　▲ *Conjugation model* [4], *like realizar.*
desamparadamente *adv* helplessly.
desamparado,-a 1 *pp* → **desamparar**. – 2 *adj* (*persona*) helpless, unprotected. 3 (*lugar*) abandoned, forsaken.
desamparar 1 *t* to abandon, desert, leave helpless. 2 JUR to renounce, relinquish.
desamparo 1 *m* (*abandono*) abandonment, desertion. 2 (*falta de ayuda*) helplessness.
　● **en desamparo,** abandoned, helpless.
desamueblado,-a 1 *pp* → **desamueblar**. – 2 *adj* unfurnished.
desamueblar *t* to remove the furniture from, clear the furniture from.
desanclar *i* to weigh anchor.
desancorar *i* to weigh anchor.
desandar *t* to go back over, retrace.
　● **desandar lo andado,** to retrace one's steps.
　▲ *Conjugation model* [64], *like andar.*
desandrajado,-a *adj* ragged, tattered.
desangelado,-a *adj* insipid, lacking in charm.
desangrado,-a *pp* → **desangrar**.
　● **morir desangrado,-a,** to bleed to death. ‖ **estar desangrado,-a,** to have lost blood.
desangramiento *m* bleeding.
desangrar 1 *t* (*sangrar*) to bleed: *los médicos lo desangraron,* the doctors bled him. 2 (*desaguar*) to drain. 3 *fig* (*empobrecer*) to bleed dry: *el hijo mayor está desangrando a sus padres,* the eldest son is bleeding his parents dry. – 4 **desangrarse,** *p* to bleed heavily, lose blood.
desanidar 1 *i* (*dejar el nido*) to leave the nest. – 2 *t fig* (*desalojar*) to oust (**de,** from).
desanimación *adj* discouragement.
desanimado,-a 1 *pp* → **desanimar**. – 2 *adj* (*decaído*) dejected, downhearted. 3 (*espectáculo etc*) dull, lifeless.
desanimar 1 *t* to discourage, dishearten. – 2 **desanimarse,** *p* to be discouraged, be disheartened, lose heart.
desánimo *m* despondency, discouragement, dejection.
desanudar 1 *t* (*nudo*) to untie; (*corbata, paquete*) to undo. 2 *fig* (*desenmarañar*) to straighten out, sort out.
desapacible *adj* (*gen*) unpleasant, disagreeable; (*tiempo*) nasty, unpleasant; (*sonido, tono*) harsh, unpleasant.
desaparecer *i* (*dejar de estar*) to disappear.
　● **desaparecer del mapa,** *fig* to vanish off the face of the earth. ‖ **hacer desaparecer,** to cause to disappear, hide; (*quitar*) to get rid of.
　▲ *Conjugation model* [43], *like agradecer.*
desaparecido,-a 1 *pp* → **desaparecer**. – 2 *adj* missing. – 3 *m,f* missing person: *había diez desaparecidos,* there were ten missing.
desaparejar 1 *t* (*quitar los arreos*) to unharness. 2 MAR to unrig.
desaparición *f* disappearance: *ya han pasado tres días desde su desaparición,* she's been missing for three days.
desapasionadamente *adv* dispassionately, objectively, impartially.
desapasionado,-a 1 *pp* → **desapasionar**. – 2 *adj* dispassionate, objective, impartial.
desapasionar 1 *t* to make lose interest. – 2 **desapasionarse,** *p* to lose interest.
desapegar *t* to estrange.
　▲ *Conjugation model* [7], *like llegar.*

desapego *m* aloofness, indifference, lack of affection.
desapercibido,-a 1 *adj* (*inadvertido*) unnoticed. 2 (*desprevenido*) unprepared, unready.
　● **pasar desapercibido,-a,** to go unnoticed.
desaplicado,-a 1 *adj* lazy, slack. – 2 *m,f* lazybones, slacker.
desapoderado,-a 1 *adj* (*precipitado*) rash. 2 *fig* (*furioso*) violent, furious.
desapolillarse *p fam fig* to shake off the cobwebs.
desaprensión *f* unscrupulousness.
desaprensivo,-a 1 *adj* unscrupulous. – 2 *m,f* unscrupulous person.
desaprobación *f* disapproval.
desaprobador,-ra *adj* disapproving.
desaprobar *t* to disapprove of: *sus padres desaprueban esa relación,* his parents disapprove of the relationship.
　▲ *Conjugation model* [31], *like contar.*
desapropiar 1 *t* to deprive (**de,** of). – 2 **desapropiarse,** *p* to give up, surrender, cede.
　▲ *Conjugation model* [12], *like cambiar.*
desaprovechado,-a 1 *pp* → **desaprovechar**. – 2 *adj* (*falto de rendimiento*) unused: *sus capacidades están totalmente desperdiciadas,* his abilities are not being put to good use. 3 (*desperdiciado*) wasted.
desaprovechamiento *m* misuse.
desaprovechar 1 *t* (*no sacar suficiente provecho*) not to take advantage of. 2 (*desperdiciar*) to waste.
　● **desaprovechar una ocasión,** to miss an opportunity, waste an opportunity.
desapuntalar *t* to remove the props from.
desarbolar *t* to dismast, unmast.
desarmable *adj* that can be taken to pieces.
desarmado,-a 1 *pp* → **desarmar**. – 2 *adj* (*sin armas*) unarmed. 3 (*desmontado*) dismantled, taken to pieces.
desarmar 1 *t* (*quitar las armas*) to disarm. 2 (*desmontar*) to dismantle, take apart, take to pieces: *el mecánico desmontó el motor,* the mechanic stripped the engine down.
desarme 1 *m* disarmament. 2 (*de una máquina*) dismantling.
　■ **desarme nuclear,** nuclear disarmament.
desarraigado,-a 1 *pp* → **desarraigar**. – 2 *adj* (*árbol*) uprooted. 3 *fig* (*persona*) rootless, without roots, uprooted. 4 *fig* (*eliminado*) eradicated.
desarraigar 1 *t* (*árbol, persona*) to uproot. 2 *fig* (*eliminar*) to eradicate, wipe out. – 3 **desarraigarse,** *p* (*árbol*) to become uprooted. 4 *fig* (*persona*) to pull up one's roots.
　▲ *Conjugation model* [7], *like llegar.*
desarraigo 1 *m* (*de árbol, persona*) uprooting. 2 *fig* (*de hábito etc*) eradication.
desarrapado,-a *adj-m,f* → **desharrapado,-a**.
desarrebujar 1 *t* (*desenmarañar*) to untangle. 2 *fig* (*poner en claro*) to clarify, explain.
desarreglado,-a 1 *pp* → **desarreglar**. – 2 *adj* (*lugar*) untidy, messy. 3 (*persona*) untidy, slovenly, unkempt. 4 (*vida, costumbres*) disorderly, irregular, disorganized.
desarreglar 1 *t* (*desordenar*) make untidy, mess up, untidy. 2 (*estropear*) to spoil, upset: *su indiscreción desarregló los planes,* his tactless remark upset our plans.
desarreglo *m* mess, untidiness, disorder, confusion.
desarrendar 1 *t* (*dejar una finca*) to vacate. 2 (*hacer dejar una finca*) to evict.
desarrimar *t* to move away.
desarrollado,-a 1 *pp* → **desarrollar**. – 2 *adj* developed: *es un país desarrollado,* it's a developed country;

este niño está muy desarrollado para su edad, this boy is quite grown up for his age.

desarrollar 1 *t (gen)* to develop: *desarrolló una gran inteligencia,* he showed great intelligence; *desarrollar el cuerpo,* to develop one's body. **2** *(deshacer un rollo)* to unroll, unfold. **3** *(exponer)* to expound, explain. **4** *(llevar a cabo)* to carry out: *desarrollar un proyecto,* to carry out a project. **5** MAT to expand, develop. – **6 desarrollarse,** *p (crecer)* to develop. **7** *(transcurrir)* to take place: *la novela se desarrolla en el siglo XIX,* the novel is set in the 19th century; *la representación se desarrolló perfectamente,* the performance went off without a hitch.

desarrollo 1 *m (gen)* development: *es una industria en pleno desarrollo,* it's a flourishing industry; *el desarrollo de las ideas,* the development of ideas. **2** MAT expansion. **3** DEP run, course.
■ **índice de desarrollo,** growth rate. ‖ **país en vías de desarrollo,** developing country.

desarropar 1 *t (ropa)* to take some clothes off. **2** *(destapar)* to uncover. – **3 desarroparse,** *p (en la cama)* to throw off one's bedclothes.

desarrugar 1 *t (alisar)* to smooth out. **2** *(quitar las arrugas)* to get the creases out of.
● **desarrugar el entrecejo,** to stop frowning. ‖ **desarrugar la frente,** to stop frowning.
▲ *Conjugation model* |7|, *like llegar.*

desarticulación 1 *f* MED dislocation. **2** *fig* breaking up, dismantling: *la desarticulación de un grupo,* the breaking up of a group.

desarticulado,-a 1 *pp* → **desarticular.** – **2** *adj* disjointed: *un discurso desarticulado,* a disjointed speech.

desarticular 1 *t* MED to disarticulate, put out of joint, dislocate. **2** *(un mecanismo)* to take to pieces. **3** *fig (organización, banda, plan, etc)* to break up, dismantle.

desaseado,-a 1 *adj (sucio)* untidy, dirty. **2** *(dejado)* untidy, slovenly, unkempt, scruffy. – **3** *m,f* untidy person, scruff.

desasear 1 *t (ensuciar)* to dirty. **2** *(desordenar)* to mess up.

desaseo *m* untidiness, scruffiness, dirtiness, slovenliness.

desasimiento *m fig* unselfishness.

desasir 1 *t* to release, let go of. – **2 desasirse,** *p fig (desprenderse)* to rid os. **(de,** of), get rid **(de,** of): *desasirse de malos hábitos,* to give up bad habits.
▲ *Conjugation model* |65|, *like asir.*

desasistencia *f* desertion, abandonment.

desasistido,-a 1 *pp* → **desasistir.** – **2** *adj* neglected.

desasistir *t* to abandon, desert, forsake.

desasnar *t fam* to civilize, refine, teach good manners to.

desasosegadamente *adv* restlessly, anxiously.

desasosegado,-a 1 *pp* → **desasosegar.** – **2** *adj* restless, anxious.

desasosegar 1 *t* to make restless, make uneasy. – **2 desasosegarse,** *p* to become restless, become uneasy.
▲ *Conjugation model* |48|, *like regar.*

desasosiego *m* uneasiness, anxiety, restlessness.

desastrado,-a 1 *adj (desgraciado)* unfortunate. **2** *(deseado)* untidy, slovenly, unkempt, scruffy. – **3** *m,f* untidy person, scruff.

desastre 1 *m (catástrofe)* disaster, catastrophe. **2** *fam (calamidad)* disaster, flop: *la excursión fue un desastre,* the trip was a washout; *ese tío es un desastre,* that guy is absolutely hopeless; *es un desastre de mujer,* she's a dead loss, she's a hopeless case.

desastrosamente *adv* disastrously.

desastroso,-a *adj* disastrous.

desatado,-a 1 *pp* → **desatar.** – **2** *adj* loose, undone. **3** *fig* wild, uncontrolled.

desatar 1 *t (soltar - gen)* to untie, undo, unfasten; *(- perro etc)* to let loose: *desató un paquete,* she undid a parcel; *desata al perro,* let the dog loose. **2** *fig (desencadenar)* to spark off, give rise to; *(pasiones)* to unleash: *su dimisión desató la polémica en el seno del partido,* his resignation sparked off a dispute within the party. – **3 desatarse,** *p (soltarse)* to come untied, come undone, come unfastened. **4** *fig (desencadenarse)* to break, explode: *se desató una gran tormenta,* a great storm broke; *se desató su alegría,* she exploded with happiness.
● **desatarse en,** to lash out with: *se desató en insultos,* he lashed out with a stream of insults. ‖ **desatarse la lengua,** to loosen one's tongue.

desatascador *m* plunger.

desatascar *t* to unblock, clear.
▲ *Conjugation model* |1|, *like sacar.*

desatavío *m* untidiness, scruffiness.

desatención 1 *f (falta de atención)* lack of attention. **2** *(descortesía)* impoliteness, discourtesy, disrespect.

desatender 1 *t (no prestar atención)* to pay no attention to. **2** *(no hacer caso)* to neglect, disregard: *desatendió las órdenes,* he disregarded the orders; *tuve que dejar el puesto desatendido,* I had to leave the stall unattended.
▲ *Conjugation model* |28|, *like entender.*

desatentamente 1 *adv* inattentively. **2** *(con descortesía)* impolitely, rudely.

desatento,-a 1 *adj (distraído)* inattentive: *está muy desatento,* he doesn't pay attention. **2** *(descortés)* discourteous, impolite. – **3** *m.f (descortés)* impolite person, discourteous person.

desatinadamente 1 *adv (con imprudencia)* rashly, recklessly. **2** *(tontamente)* foolishly, stupidly.

desatinado,-a 1 *pp* → **desatinar.** – **2** *adj (imprudente)* rash, reckless. **3** *(tonto)* foolish, silly.

desatinar 1 *i (hacer)* to act foolishly; *(decir)* to talk nonsense. – **2** *t* to make act foolishly.

desatino 1 *m (error)* mistake, blunder. **2** *(locura)* foolishness; *(tontería)* nonsense, silly thing: *decir desatinos,* to talk nonsense. **3** *(falta de tacto)* clumsiness, heavy-handedness.

desatornillador *m* screwdriver.

desatornillar *t* to unscrew.

desatracar 1 *t* MAR to cast off, unmoor. – **2** *i* MAR to shove off.
▲ *Conjugation model* |1|, *like sacar.*

desatrancar 1 *t (una puerta - con tranca)* to unbar; *(- con cerrojo)* to unbolt. **2** *(un conducto)* to unblock, clear.

desautorización 1 *f* disapproval. **2** *(mentís)* denial. **3** *(descrédito)* discredit.

desautorizadamente *adv* without authorization.

desautorizado,-a 1 *pp* → **desautorizar.** – **2** *adj* unauthorized. **3** *(prohibido)* banned, forbidden. **4** *(desmentido)* denied. **5** *(desacreditado)* discredited.

desautorizar 1 *t (desaprobar)* to disapprove. **2** *(prohibir)* to ban, forbid: *el gobierno desautorizó la manifestación,* the Government banned the demonstration. **3** *(desmentir)* to deny. **4** *(desacreditar)* to discredit.
▲ *Conjugation model* |4|, *like realizar.*

desavenencia 1 *f (desacuerdo)* disagreement, discord. **2** *(riña)* quarrel, row.

desavenido,-a 1 *pp* → **desavenir.** – **2** *adj (en desacuerdo)* in disagreement. **3** *(reñido)* on bad terms: *her-*

manas desavenidas, sisters who are on bad terms, sisters who have fallen out.

desavenir 1 *t* to cause to quarrel: *esa mujer los desavino,* that woman made them quarrel. – 2 **desavenirse,** *p* to quarrel.
● **desavenirse con algn.,** to fall out with sb., have a difference of opinion with sb.
▲ Conjugation model [90], like *venir.*

desaventajado,-a 1 *adj* (*persona*) at a disadvantage, underpriviledged. 2 (*situación*) disadvantageous, unfavourable (us unfavorable).

desavío 1 *m* (*desorden*) mess, disorder. 2 (*incomodidad*) inconvenience.

desayunar 1 *i* to have breakfast, breakfast. – 2 *t* to have for breakfast: *he desayunado un café,* I had coffee for breakfast. – 3 **desayunarse,** *p* to have breakfast: *se desayuna con tostadas todos los días,* he has toast for breakfast every day.
● **ahora me desayuno,** (*enterarse*) that's the first I've heard of it.

desayuno *m* breakfast.

desazón 1 *f* (*desabrimiento*) lack of flavour (us flavor), tastelessness. 2 *fig* (*disgusto*) grief, affliction, worry: *esa respuesta le causó una intensa desazón,* that answer upset her.

desazonado,-a 1 *pp* → **desazonar.** – 2 *adj fig* (*disgustado*) upset. 3 *fig* (*inquieto*) anxious, uneasy. 4 (*soso*) tasteless, insipid.

desazonar 1 *t* (*quitar el sabor*) to make tasteless. 2 *fig* (*disgustar*) to annoy, upset. 3 *fig* (*inquietar*) to make uneasy, worry. – 4 **desazonarse,** *p fig* (*disgustarse*) to get upset. 5 *fig* (*inquietarse*) to worry. 6 *fig* (*sentirse indispuesto*) to feel unwell, feel off-colour (us off-color).

desbancar 1 *t* (*en el juego*) to clean out. 2 *fig* (*suplantar*) to supplant, replace, take the place of.
▲ Conjugation model [1], like *sacar.*

desbandada *f* scattering: *hubo una desbandada general,* everybody scattered.
● **a la desbandada,** helter-skelter, in all directions.

desbandarse *p* to scatter, disperse: *el rebaño se desbandó,* the flock ran off in all directions.

desbarajustar 1 *t* (*desordenar*) to mess up, turn upside down: *llegó él y lo desbarajustó todo,* he arrived and turned everything upside down. 2 (*trastornar*) to upset.

desbarajuste *m* disorder, confusion, mess: *¡qué desbarajuste!,* what a mess!

desbaratado,-a *adj fig* debauched, dissolute.

desbaratamiento 1 *m* (*desarreglo*) wrecking, destruction. 2 (*frustración*) frustration. 3 (*derroche*) waste, squandering. 4 MIL rout.

desbaratar 1 *t* (*desarreglar*) to spoil, ruin, wreck. 2 (*frustrar*) to spoil, ruin: *nos desbarató los planes,* she spoilt our plans. 3 (*malgastar*) to waste, squander. 4 MIL to rout, throw into confusion. – 5 *i* (*disparatar*) to talk nonsense. – 6 **desbaratarse,** *p* (*actuar*) to act foolishly; (*hablar*) to talk nonsense.

desbarrar 1 *i fig* (*hablar*) to talk nonsense. 2 *fig* (*actuar*) to act foolishly, do silly things.

desbastar 1 *t* (*madera*) to rough plane; (*piedra*) to smooth down; (*metal*) to rough down. 2 *fig* to refine, polish.

desbloquear 1 *t* TÉC to free. 2 FIN to unfreeze. 3 (*un sitio*) to lift the blockade on.

desbloqueo *m* TÉC freeing. 2 FIN unfreezing. 3 (*de un sitio*) lifting of the blockade.

desbocadamente *adv* impudently, cheekily.

desbocado,-a 1 *pp* → **desbocar.** – 2 *adj* (*arma*) widemouthed, bell-mouthed. 3 (*jarra*) with a chipped mouth. 4 (*caballo*) runaway. 5 (*una prenda*) loose-fitting. 6 (*río*) overflowing. 7 *fig* (*imaginación*) wild. 8 *fig* (*mal hablado*) foul-mouthed. – 9 *m,f fig* foul-mouthed person.

desbocar 1 *t* (*jarra*) to break the mouth of. 2 (*una prenda*) to tear open, rip open. – 3 *i* (*desembocar*) to flow (**en,** into). – 4 **desbocarse,** *p* (*caballo*) to run away, bolt. 5 (*una prenda*) to tear open. 6 *fig* (*persona*) to blow up, let out a stream of abuse.
▲ Conjugation model [1], like *sacar.*

desbordamiento 1 *m* overflowing. 2 *fig* outbreak, outburst, explosion.

desbordante 1 *adj* overflowing, bursting: *llegó desbordante de ilusión,* she arrived bursting with excitement. 2 (*sin límite*) unrestrained, unbounded.

desbordar 1 *t* (*sobrepasar*) to overflow: *el río desbordó su cauce,* the river burst its banks. 2 *fig* (*exceder*) to surpass, exceed: *eso desborda mis conocimientos,* that's way over my head. – 3 *i* (*salirse*) to overflow: *el río desbordó,* the river overflowed. – 4 **desbordarse,** *p* (*salirse*) to overflow, flood. 5 *fig* to burst.

desborrar 1 *t* to burl.

desbravar 1 *t* (*animal*) to tame; (*caballo*) to break in. – 2 *i* (*perder braveza*) to become less wild, become less fierce. 3 (*calmarse*) to calm down. 4 (*licor*) to lose its strength. – 5 **desbravarse,** *p* (*perder braveza*) to become less wild, become less fierce. 6 (*calmarse*) to calm down. 7 (*un licor*) to lose its strength.

desbroce *m* → **desbrozo.**

desbrozar 1 *t* (*terreno*) to clear of weeds, clear of undergrowth; (*paso*) to clear.
▲ Conjugation model [4], like *realizar.*

desbrozo 1 *m* (*acción*) clearing, clearing of weeds, clearing of undergrowth. 2 (*broza*) twigs *pl,* cuttings *pl,* undergrowth.

desbullar *t* to shell.

descabalar 1 *t* (*dejar incompleto*) to leave incomplete. 2 (*desnivelar*) to make uneven.

descabalgar *i* to dismount.
▲ Conjugation model [7], like *llegar.*

descabellado,-a 1 *pp* → **descabellar.** – 2 *adj fig* wild, crazy: *eso es totalmente descabellado,* that's absolutely crazy; *una idea descabellada,* a crackpot idea.

descabellar 1 *t* (*despeinar*) to ruffle. 2 (*en tauromaquia*) *to kill with the point of a sword on the cervix.*

descabezado,-a 1 *pp* → **descabezar.** – 2 *adj fig* wild, reckless, crazy. – 3 *m,f fig* wild person, reckless person.

descabezar 1 *t* (*quitar la cabeza*) to behead, decapitate. 2 (*planta*) to top; (*árbol*) to cut the top off. – 3 **descabezarse,** *p* (*desgranarse*) to shed grain. 4 *fam fig* to rack one's brains.
● **descabezar un sueño,** *fam fig* to take a nap.
▲ Conjugation model [4], like *realizar.*

descabullirse *p fig* to slip away.
▲ Conjugation model [41], like *mullir.*

descacharrante *adj fam* hilarious.

descacharrar *t fam* (*romper*) to break; (*estropear*) to ruin, mess up, spoil.

descafeinado,-a 1 *adj* decaffeinated. 2 *fam fig* watered-down. – 3 **descafeinado,** *m* decaffeinated coffee.
■ **café descafeinado,** decaffeinated coffee.

descafeinar *t* to decaffeinate.
▲ Conjugation model [17].

descalabazarse *p fam fig* to rack one's brains.

descalabrado,-a 1 *pp* → **descalabrar.** – 2 *adj* (*herido*) wounded, injured; (*en la cabeza*) wounded in the head, injured in the head. **3** *fig* damaged, ruined: *dejamos su negocio descalabrado,* we left his business in ruins.

descalabradura **1** *f* (*herida*) head wound. **2** (*cicatriz*) scar.

descalabrar **1** *t* (*herir*) to injure; (*en la cabeza*) to injure in the head. **2** *fig* (*causar daño*) to ruin, damage: *la pérdida de las acciones ha descalabrado mi negocio,* the fall in share prices has ruined my business. – **3** descalabrarse, *p* to injure one's head.

descalabro *m* misfortune, damage, loss: *sufrir un descalabro,* to suffer a misfortune.

descalcificación *f* decalcification.

descalcificar **1** *t* to decalcify. – **2** descalcificarse, *p* to become decalcified.

▲ *Conjugation model* [1], *like* **sacar**.

descalificación **1** *f* disqualification. **2** (*descrédito*) discredit.

descalificar **1** *t* to disqualify. **2** (*desacreditar*) to discredit.

▲ *Conjugation model* [1], *like* **sacar**.

descalzar **1** *t* (*zapatos*) to take off sb.'s shoes: *le descalzó a toda prisa,* she tore off his shoes. **2** (*calzos*) to remove the chocks from. – **3** descalzarse, *p* (*person*) to take off one's shoes. **4** (*caballo*) to lose a shoe.

▲ *Conjugation model* [4], *like* **realizar**.

descalzo,-a **1** *adj* barefoot, barefooted. **2** REL barefoot. **3** *fig* (*pobre*) poor. – **4** *m,f* REL (*hombre*) barefoot monk; (*mujer*) barefoot nun.

descamación *f* desquamation, flaking, flakiness.

descamarse *p* to desquamate, flake off.

descambiar *t* to change back.

▲ *Conjugation model* [12], *like* **cambiar**.

descaminado,-a *pp* → **descaminar**.

● andar/ir/estar descaminado,-a, to be on the wrong track, be on the wrong road.

descaminar **1** *t* (*desviar del camino*) to mislead, send in the wrong direction. **2** *fig* (*corromper*) to lead astray, mislead.

descamisado,-a **1** *adj* shirtless, without a shirt. **2** *fig* (*pobre*) poor, wretched. – **3** *m,f fig* wretch, poor person. – **4** descamisados, *mpl* HIST (*en España*) liberals *who* took part in the 1820 *revolution*; (*en Argentina*) supporters of Perón.

descampado,-a **1** *adj* open. – **2** descampado, *m* open space, open field.

● al/en descampado, in the open country.

descansadamente *adv* without effort, comfortably, easily.

descansado,-a **1** *pp* → **descansar**. – **2** *adj* rested, refreshed. **3** (*tranquilo*) easy, effortless: *vida descansada,* easy life; *trabajo descansado,* easy job.

descansar **1** *i* (*gen*) to rest, have a rest; (*un momento*) to take a break. **2** (*dormir*) to sleep: *¡que descanses!,* sleep well! **3** (*confiar*) to rely (**en**, on): *se puede descansar en él,* you can rely on him. **4** (*apoyarse*) to rest (**sobre**, on), be supported (**sobre**, by). **5** (*basarse*) to be based (**en**, on): *la felicidad descansa en la libertad,* happiness is based on freedom. **6** (*estar enterrado*) to lie, rest. **7** (*un terreno*) to lie fallow. – **8** *t* (*aliviar*) to rest: *descansa la cabeza,* rest your head. **9** MIL to order.

● descansar en paz, to rest in peace: *que en paz descanse,* may he rest in peace. ‖ ¡descansen armas!, order arms!

descansillo *m* landing.

descanso **1** *m* rest, break. **2** (*en un espectáculo*) interval; (*en un partido*) interval, half-time. **3** (*alivio*) relief, comfort: *¡qué descanso!,* what a relief! **4** (*rellano*) landing.

● ¡descanso!, MIL at ease! ‖ sin descanso, without a break.

■ descanso eterno, eternal rest. ‖ día de descanso, day off.

descantillar **1** *t* (*romper los cantos*) to chip. **2** *fig* (*rebajar*) to deduct. – **3** descantillarse, *p* to get chipped.

descapitalizar *t* (*perder el capital*) to undercapitalize.

▲ *Conjugation model* [4], *like* **realizar**.

descapotable **1** *adj* convertible. – **2** *m* convertible.

descapsulador *m* bottle opener.

descaradamente *adv* impudently, cheekily.

descarado,-a **1** *adj* (*actitud*) shameless, brazen, insolent; (*persona*) cheeky. **2** (*patente*) blatant: *es una copia descarada de mi novela,* it's a blatant copy of my novel. – **3** *m,f* shameless person, cheeky person.

descararse *p* to behave insolently, be cheeky: *se descaró a pedir un aumento,* he had the nerve to ask for a rise.

descarbonatar *t* to decarbonate.

descarburar *t* to decarburize.

descarga **1** *f* (*acción*) unloading. **2** (*eléctrica*) discharge. **3** (*de fuego*) discharge, firing.

■ descarga cerrada, volley.

descargadero *m* wharf, unloading dock.

descargador **1** *m* (*gen*) unloader. **2** (*estibador*) docker, stevedore.

descargar **1** *t* (*quitar una carga*) to unload. **2** (*disparar una arma*) to fire, discharge, shoot; (*vaciar una arma*) to unload: *descargaron salvas en su honor,* they fired a salute in his honour. **3** (*dar un golpe*) to deal: *le descargó un puñetazo,* he dealt him a blow. **4** *fig* (*de obligaciones, preocupaciones*) to free, relieve, release: *descargó sus preocupaciones contándole todo a su madre,* he got everything off his chest by telling his mother all about it. **5** *fig* (*enfado*) to vent, give vent to. **6** ELEC to discharge; (*batería*) to run down. **7** JUR to absolve (**de**, of), acquit (**de**, of). – **8** *i* ELEC to discharge. **9** (*tormenta*) to break; (*nubes*) to burst. **10** (*desembocar*) to flow. – **11** descargarse, *p* (*pilas, baterías*) to discharge. **12** (*desahogarse*) to blow up. **13** JUR to clear os.

▲ *Conjugation model* [7], *like* **llegar**.

descargo **1** *m* (*descarga*) unloading. **2** COM credit. **3** JUR discharge, acquittal. **4** *fig* (*excusa*) excuse; (*alivio*) relief.

● en/para su descargo, in his defence (US defense).

■ pliego de descargo, evidence for the defence (US defense).

descarnado,-a **1** *pp* → **descarnar**. – **2** *adj fig* straightforward, plain.

descarnador *m* scraper.

descarnar **1** *t* (*quitar la carne*) to strip the flesh from. **2** (*poner al descubierto*) to lay bare: *el agua descarnó las rocas de algas,* the sea scoured the algae from the rocks.

descaro *m* impudence, cheek, nerve: *tuvo el descaro de hacer algunas preguntas,* she had the nerve to ask some questions.

● ¡qué descaro!, what a cheek!, what a nerve!, of all the cheek!

descarriado **1** *pp* → **descarriar**. – **2** *adj fig* lost.

● ser la oveja descarriada, *fig* to be the lost sheep.

descarriar **1** *t* (*apartar del camino*) to send the wrong way, put on the wrong road, misdirect. **2** *fig* to lead astray. – **3** descarriarse, *p* (*perderse*) to lose one's way, get lost, go the wrong way. **4** *fig* to go astray.

▲ *Conjugation model* [13], *like* **desviar**.

descarrilamiento *m* derailment.

descarrilar *i* to be derailed, run off the rails, go off the rails.

descarrío *m fig* deviation.

descartar 1 *t* to discard, reject, rule out: *descartamos esa posibilidad,* we ruled out that possibility. – 2 descartarse de, *p (cartas)* to discard, throw away.
● quedar descartado,-a, to be left out, be ruled out.

descarte *m* discard, discarded cards *pl.*

descasar 1 *t (un matrimonio)* to annul the marriage of. 2 *fig (alterar)* to alter, upset.

descascarar *t* to shell.

descascarillar 1 *t* to husk. – 2 descascarillarse, *p* to chip, peel, flake off.

descastado,-a 1 *adj (poco cariñoso)* unaffectionate, cold. 2 *(desagradecido)* ungrateful. – 3 *m,f (poco cariñoso)* unaffectionate person. 4 *(desagradecido)* ungrateful person.

descendencia *f* offspring, descendants *pl.*
● morir sin descendencia, to die without issue, leave no children.

descendente *adj* descending, downward.

descender 1 *i* to descend, go down, come down. 2 *(temperatura, nivel, etc)* to drop, fall, go down. 3 *(ser descendiente)* to descend (**de,** from), issue (**de,** from). 4 *(provenir)* to come (**de,** from). – 5 *t (llevar más bajo)* to take down, bring down, lower. 6 *(bajar)* to go down: *descendió la escalera muy rápidamente,* he went down the stairs very quickly.
▲ *Conjugation model* |28|, *like entender.*

descendiente *mf* descendant; *(hijos)* offspring.
● ser descendiente de, to be a descendant of.

descendimiento *m* descent, lowering.

descenso 1 *m (acción)* descent, lowering. 2 *(de temperatura)* drop, fall. 3 *fig (declive)* decline, fall. 4 DEP *(de división)* relegation; *(en esquí)* downhill race.

descentrado,-a 1 *pp →* **descentrar.** – 2 *adj* off-centre (US off-center). 3 *fig (desorientado)* disoriented, all-at-sea.

descentralización *f* decentralization.

descentralizar *t* to decentralize.
▲ *Conjugation model* |4|, *like realizar.*

descentrar 1 *t* to put off-centre (US off-center). 2 *fig* to disorientate, throw, put off. – 3 descentrarse, *p* to go off-centre (US off-center). 4 *fig* to become disorientated.

desceñir 1 *t* to loosen. – 2 desceñirse, *p* to come loose.
▲ *Conjugation model* |36|, *like ceñir.*

descepar 1 *t* to uproot. 2 *fig (exterminar)* to erradicate.

descerebrar *t* to decerebrate.

descerrajar 1 *t* to force, break open. 2 *fam fig (un tiro)* to fire.

descifrable 1 *adj* decipherable. 2 *(letra)* legible.

desciframiento *m* deciphering, decoding.

descifrar 1 *t* to decipher, decode. 2 *fig (llegar a comprender)* to solve, figure out.

desclavar 1 *t (quitar los clavos)* to remove the nails from. 2 *(desprender)* to take off.

descoagulación *f* decoagulation.

descoagulante *adj* dissolving, liquefying.

descoagular *t* to dissolve, liquefy.

descocado,-a 1 *pp →* **descocarse.** – 2 *adj fam* bold, brazen, cheeky, barefaced.

descocarse *p* to be brazen, be cheeky.
▲ *Conjugation model* |1|, *like sacar.*

descoco *m* boldness, cheek.

descodificar *t* to decode.
▲ *Conjugation model* |1|, *like sacar.*

descojonante *adj arg* bloody hilarious.

descojonarse *p arg* to piss os. laughing.

descolgado,-a 1 *pp →* **descolgar.** – 2 *adj* cut off from one's friends. – 3 *m,f* loner.

descolgar 1 *t (cuadro etc)* to take down. 2 *(bajar)* to lower, let down. 3 *(el teléfono)* to pick up, lift: *dejó el teléfono descolgado,* she left the telephone off the hook. – 4 descolgarse, *p (escurrirse)* to slip down, slide down: *se descolgó por la pared,* he slid down the wall. 5 *fam fig (dejarse caer)* to drop in, turn up: *se descolgó a cenar con dos amigos,* he dropped in for dinner with two friends. 6 *fam fig (separarse)* to break away; *(quedarse rezagado)* to fall behind. 7 *fam fig (decir)* to come out (**con,** with); *(hacer)* to do unexpectedly, surprise: *se descolgó con una tontería,* he made a stupid remark.
▲ *Conjugation model* |52|, *like colgar.*

descollante *adj* outstanding.

descollar *i* to stand out, excel: *descollaba en ingenio entre todos sus compañeros,* her talent set her apart from her friends.
▲ *Conjugation model* |31|, *like contar.*

descolocado,-a *adj* unemployed, out of a job, out of work.

descolonización *f* decolonization.

descolonizar *t* to decolonize.
▲ *Conjugation model* |4|, *like realizar.*

descoloramiento *m* discolouration (US discoloration); *(del pelo)* bleaching.

descolorar 1 *t* to discolour (US discolor), fade; *(pelo)* to bleach. – 2 descolorarse, *p* to lose colour (US color), fade.

descolorido,-a 1 *pp →* **descolorir.** – 2 *adj* discoloured (US discolored), faded. 3 *fig* dull, lifeless.

descolorimiento *m →* **descoloramiento.**

descolorir *t →* **descolorar.**

descombrar *t* to clear.

descombro *m* clearing.

descomedido,-a 1 *pp →* **descomedirse.** – 2 *adj (excesivo)* excessive, immoderate. 3 *(descortés)* rude, impolite. – 4 *m,f* rude person, impolite person.

descomedimiento *m* rudeness, insolence.

descomedirse *p* to be rude, be disrespectful.
▲ *Conjugation model* |34|, *like servir.*

descompaginar *t* to mess up, upset.

descompasar 1 *t (hacer perder el compás)* to make lose the beat. – 2 descompasarse, *p* to be rude.

descompensado,-a *adj* unbalanced.

descompensar *t* to unbalance, upset, throw out of kilter.

descomponer 1 *t (separar)* to break down, split up. 2 *(estropear)* to break. 3 *(desorganizar)* to mess up, upset. 4 *(desordenar)* to mess up: *me ha descompuesto toda la habitación,* he messed up my bedroom. 5 FÍS to resolve. 6 QUÍM to decompose. 7 MAT to split up. 8 *fig (molestar)* to disturb, upset; *(irritar)* irritate. 9 *(pudrir)* to rot. – 10 descomponerse, *p (pudrirse)* to decompose, rot. 11 *(estropearse)* to break down. 12 *(enfermar)* to feel ill. 13 *(enfadarse)* to lose one's temper, get angry: *me descompongo cuando dices tantas tonterías,* it makes me angry when you say such rubbish. 14 FÍS to resolve. 15 QUÍM to decompose. 16 MAT to split.
▲ *Conjugation model* |78|, *like poner,* pp descompuesto,-a.

descomponible *adj* which can be broken down.

descomposición 1 *f (pudrimiento)* decomposition, decay. 2 *fig (decadencia)* decline, decadence. 3 *fam (diarrea)* diarrhoea (US diarrhea).

descompostura 1 *f* (*desaliño*) untidiness, slovenliness. **2** *fig* (*descaro*) insolence, cheek.

descompresión *f* decompression.

descompresor *m* decompressor.

descomprimir *t* to decompress, depressurize.

descompuesto,-a 1 *pp*→ **descomponer**. – **2** *adj* (*podrido*) decomposed, decayed, rotten. **3** (*estropeado*) out of order, broken down. **4** *fig* (*alterado*) upset. **5** *fig* (*atrevido*) insolent, impudent.
● **estar descompuesto,-a**, to have diarrhoea (US diarrhea).

descompuse *pt indef* → **descomponer**.

descomunal *adj* huge, enormous.

desconceptuar *t* to discredit.
▲ *Conjugation model* [11], *like* **actuar**.

desconcertado,-a *adj* disconcerted, confused, upset.

desconcertante *adj* disconcerting, upsetting.

desconcertar 1 *t* (*perturbar*) to disconcert, upset, disturb. **2** (*desorientar*) to confuse. **3** MED to dislocate. – **4** **desconcertarse**, *p* (*perturbarse*) to be disconcerted. **5** (*desorientarse*) to be bewildered, be confused. **6** MED to be dislocated.
▲ *Conjugation model* [27], *like* **acertar**.

desconchado,-a 1 *pp* → **desconchar**. – **2** **desconchado**, *m* (*pared*) flaking, peeling; (*loza*) chipping.

desconchar 1 *t* (*pared*) to peel off, flake; (*loza*) to chip. – **2** **desconcharse**, *p* to peel off, flake off; (*loza*) to chip.

desconchón *m* (*en pared*) bare patch; (*en loza*) chip.

desconcierto *m* disorder, confusion, chaos: *tales preguntas sembraron el desconcierto,* such questions sowed the seeds of doubt.

desconcordia *f* discord, disagreement.

desconectado,-a 1 *pp* → **desconectar**. – **2** *adj fig* cut off (**de**, from): *estoy desconectado de mi familia política,* I have no contact with my in-laws.

desconectar 1 *t* ELEC to disconnect. **2** (*un aparato*) to switch off, turn off. **3** (*desenchufar*) to unplug. **4** *fam fig* to turn off, switch off: *como no le interesaba el tema desconectó,* as she wasn't interested in the subject she switched off. – **5** **desconectarse**, *p fam fig* (*separarse*) to cut os. off (**de**, from): *me desconecté de mis amigos del colegio,* I lost touch with my school friends.

desconexión *f* disconnection.

desconfiado,-a 1 *pp* → **desconfiar**. – **2** *adj* distrustful, suspicious, wary. – **3** *m,f* distrustful person, suspicious person, wary person.

desconfianza *f* distrust, mistrust, suspicion.

desconfiar 1 *i* (*faltar la confianza*) to distrust (**de**, -), mistrust (**de**, -), be suspicious (**de**, of). **2** (*dudar*) to doubt (**de**, -). **3** (*tener cuidado*) to beware (**de**, of): *"desconfíe de las imitaciones",* "beware of imitations".
▲ *Conjugation model* [13], *like* **desviar**.

descongelar 1 *t* (*comida*) to thaw, thaw out. **2** (*nevera*) to defrost. **3** FIN to unfreeze.

descongestión *f* (*nasal*) decongestion, clearing; (*del tráfico*) easing of congestion.

descongestionar *t* to clear.

desconocer 1 *t* not to know, be unaware of: *desconozco su nombre,* I don't know her name. **2** (*no reconocer*) not to recognize: *me lo encontré pero lo desconocí,* I met him but I didn't recognize him. **3** (*rechazar*) to disown: *desconoce a sus amistades,* he disowns his friends. **4** (*no prestar atención*) not to pay attention to, ignore.
▲ *Conjugation model* [44], *like* **conocer**.

desconocido,-a 1 *pp* → **desconocer**. – **2** *adj* (*no conocido*) unknown. **3** (*no reconocido*) unrecognized. **4** (*extraño*) strange, unfamiliar. – **5** *m,f* stranger, unknown person. – **6 lo desconocido**, *m* the unknown.
● **estar desconocido,-a**, to be unrecognizable.

desconocimiento *m* ignorance (**de**, of).

desconsideración *f* lack of consideration, inconsiderateness, thoughtlessness.

desconsiderado,-a 1 *pp* → **desconsiderar**. – **2** *adj* inconsiderate, thoughtless. – **3** *m,f* inconsiderate person, thoughtless person.

desconsiderar *t* to lack consideration for.

desconsolado,-a 1 *pp* → **desconsolar**. – **2** *adj* disconsolate, grief-stricken, inconsolable.

desconsolador,-ra *adj* heartbreaking, distressing.

desconsolar 1 *t* to distress, grieve. – **2** **desconsolarse**, *p* to be distressed.
▲ *Conjugation model* [31], *like* **contar**.

desconsuelo *m* affliction, grief, sorrow.

descontado,-a 1 *pp* → **descontar**.
● **dar por descontado**, *fam* to take for granted: *dimos por descontado que aprobaría,* we took it for granted he would pass. ‖ **por descontado**, needless to say, of course.

descontaminación *f* decontamination.

descontaminar *t* to decontaminate.

descontar 1 *t* (*restar*) to deduct, take off, knock off: *me han descontado el 12%,* they gave me a 12% discount. **2** (*excluir*) to leave out, exclude: *si descontamos esa partida todavía quedan cuatro,* leaving out that consignment there are still four left. **3** *fig* to discount: *su comportamiento descuenta credibilidad a la empresa,* his behaviour adversely affects the credibility of the firm. **4** DEP to add on.
▲ *Conjugation model* [31], *like* **contar**.

descontentadizo,-a *adj* hard to please.

descontentar 1 *t* to make dissatisfied, make discontent, displease. – **2** **descontentarse**, *p* to be displeased (**con**, with).

descontento,-a 1 *adj* displeased, unhappy, dissatisfied, discontented. – **2** *m,f* malcontent. – **3** **descontento**, *m* discontent, dissatisfaction.

descontrol *m fam* lack of control, chaos.

descontrolado,-a 1 *pp* → **descontrolarse**. – **2** *adj* uncontrolled, out of control. **3** *fam fig* out of control, wild.

descontrolarse *p* (*persona*) to lose control; (*avión etc*) to go out of control.

desconvenir *i* to disagree.
▲ *Conjugation model* [90], *like* **venir**.

desconvocar *t* to cancel, call off.
▲ *Conjugation model* [1], *like* **sacar**.

descorazonador,-ra *adj* disheartening, discouraging.

descorazonar 1 *t* to dishearten, discourage. – **2** **descorazonarse**, *p* to lose heart, get discouraged.

descorchador *m* corkscrew.

descorchar *t* to uncork.

descorche *m* uncorking.

descornar 1 *t* to dehorn, remove the horns of. – **2** **descornarse**, *p fam fig* (*pensar*) to rack one's brains; (*trabajar*) to slave away, slog one's guts out.
▲ *Conjugation model* [31], *like* **contar**.

descorrer 1 *t* (*cortinas*) to draw; (*cerrojo*) to unbolt. **2** (*volver atrás*) to retrace, go back over. – **3** *i* (*escurrirse*) to drip, trickle. – **4** **descorrerse**, *p* to drip, trickle.

descorrimiento *m* dripping, trickling.

descortés *adj* impolite, rude, discourteous.

descortesía *f* impoliteness, rudeness, discourtesy.

descortezar 1 *t* (*árbol*) to bark, remove the bark from.
2 (*pan*) to remove the crust from; (*fruta*) to peel. 3 *fig*
(*desbastar*) to refine, polish.
▲ *Conjugation model* |4|, *like realizar.*
descoser 1 *t* to unpick. – 2 **descoserse**, *p* to come un-
stitched.
descosido,-a 1 *pp* → **descoser**. – 2 *adj fig* (*hablador*)
talkative. 3 *fig* (*incoherente*) disconnected. – 4 **descosido**, *m* open seam.
● **como un descosido**, *fam* (*con exceso*) like wild, too
much: *hablar como un descosido*, to talk nineteen to
the dozen; *beber como un descosido*, to drink like a fish;
comer como un descosido, to eat like a horse.
descoyuntar 1 *t* (*hueso*) to dislocate, disjoint. 2 *fig* (*cansar*) to exhaust, tire out. – 3 **descoyuntarse**, *p* to become dislocated.
● **descoyuntarse de risa**, *fam fig* to split one's sides
laughing.
descrédito *m* discredit, disrepute: *el gobierno cayó en
descrédito*, the government was discredited.
● **ir en descrédito de**, to be to the discredit of.
descreer *t* to disbelieve.
▲ *Conjugation model* |61|, *like leer.*
descreído,-a 1 *adj* disbelieving, unbelieving. – 2 *m,f*
disbeliever, unbeliever.
descreimiento *m* disbelief, unbelief.
descremado,-a 1 *pp* → **descremar**. – 2 *adj* skimmed.
■ **yogur descremado**, low-fat yoghurt.
descremar *t* to skim.
describir 1 *t* to describe. 2 (*trazar*) to trace, describe.
▲ *pp descrito,-a.*
descripción 1 *f* description. 2 (*acción de trazar*) tracing,
describing, description.
descriptible *adj* describable.
descriptivo,-a *adj* descriptive.
descrito,-a 1 *pp* → **describir**. – 2 *adj* described. 3 (*trazado*) traced, described.
descruzar *t* to uncross.
▲ *Conjugation model* |4|, *like realizar.*
descuadernar *t* → **desencuadernar**.
descuajar 1 *t* (*liquidar*) to liquefy. 2 (*arrancar de raíz*) to
uproot. 3 *fig* (*desesperanzar*) to dishearten.
descuajaringar 1 *t* (*desvencijar*) to pull to pieces, take
to pieces. – 2 **descuajaringarse**, *p fam fig* (*cansarse*) to
be exhausted, be worn out. 3 *fam fig* (*reírse*) to fall about
laughing.
▲ *Conjugation model* |7|, *like llegar.*
descuaje *m* → **descuajo**.
descuajo *m* uprooting.
descuartizamiento *m* (*de persona*) quartering; (*de animal*) quartering, cutting up.
descuartizar 1 *t* (*persona*) to quarter; (*animal*) to quarter, cut up. 2 *fam fig* to pull to pieces, tear apart.
▲ *Conjugation model* |4|, *like realizar.*
descubierta *f* → **descubierto,-a**.
descubierto,-a 1 *pp* → **descubrir**. – 2 *adj* open, uncovered: *el cielo está descubierto*, the sky is clear. 3 (*sin
sombrero*) bareheaded. – 4 **descubierto**, *m* FIN overdraft. – 5 **descubierta**, *f* MIL reconnaissance, recon-
noitring, scouting.
● **a cielo descubierto**, in the open. ‖ **al descubierto**,
in the open. ‖ **estar en descubierto**, COM to be overdrawn, be in the red. ‖ **poner al descubierto**, to expose, bring out into the open. ‖ **quedar al
descubierto**, to be exposed, come out into the open,
come to light.

descubridor,-ra *m,f* discoverer.
descubrimiento *m* discovery.
descubrir 1 *t* (*gen*) to discover; (*petróleo, oro, minas*) to
find; (*conspiración*) to uncover; (*crimen*) to bring to light:
Colón descubrió América, Columbus discovered America. 2 (*revelar*) to reveal. 3 (*averiguar*) to find out, discover: *descubrimos sus intenciones*, we found out his
intentions. 4 (*delatar*) to give away. 5 (*divisar*) to make
out, see. 6 (*destapar*) to uncover: *el ministro descubrió la
estatua*, the minister unveiled the statue. – 7 **descubrirse**, *p* (*la cabeza*) to take off one's hat. 8 *fig* (*abrirse*)
to open one's heart (**a/con**, to). 9 (*en boxeo*) to lower
one's guard.
▲ *pp descubierto,-a.*
descuello 1 *m* protrusion. 2 *fig* (*altanería*) haughtiness,
arrogance.
descuento 1 *m* discount, reduction, deduction. 2 DEP
injury time.
● **con descuento**, at a discount, on offer: *el precio con
descuento es de mil pesetas*, the discount price is one
thousand pesetas. ‖ **descuento por pronto pago**,
cash discount.
descuidado,-a 1 *pp* → **descuidar**. – 2 *adj* (*negligente*)
careless, negligent. 3 (*desaseado*) slovenly, untidy, neglected. 4 (*desprevenido*) unprepared.
descuidar 1 *t* to neglect, overlook: *ha descuidado su higiene*, he has neglected his personal hygiene. 2 (*distraer*) to distract. 3 (*liberar*) to free, release. – 4
descuidarse, *p* (*no tener cuidado*) to be careless: *se des-
cuidó y se perdió*, he was careless and got lost; *como
te descuides, te vas a mojar los pies*, if you don't look
out, you're going to get your feet wet. 5 (*no arreglarse*)
to neglect os., let os. go.
● **¡descuida / descuidad / descuiden!**, don't worry!
descuidero *m* pickpocket.
descuido 1 *m* (*negligencia*) negligence, carelessness,
neglect. 2 (*distracción*) oversight, slip, mistake. 3 (*desaliño*) slovenliness, untidiness.
● **al descuido**, casually, nonchalantly. ‖ **con descuido**, without thinking. ‖ **por descuido**, inadvertently,
by mistake.
descurtir *t* to bleach, whiten.
desde 1 *prep* (*tiempo*) since: *desde 1992*, since 1992; *¿desde cuándo?*, since when?; *desde entonces*, since then,
from then on; *no hemos ido al cine desde hace un mes*,
we haven't been to the cinema for a month. 2 (*lugar*)
from: *desde allí*, from there; *desde lo alto*, from the top
of.
● **desde ahora**, from now on. ‖ **desde hace mucho
tiempo**, for a long time. ‖ **desde ... hasta**, from ... to:
desde la una hasta las cuatro, from one o'clock to four;
desde Barcelona hasta Tarragona, from Barcelona to
Tarragona. ‖ **desde luego**, (*en realidad*) really; (*como respuesta*) of course, certainly. ‖ **desde que**, since: *desde
que nos encontramos llama cada día*, since we met he
phones me every day.
desdecir 1 *i* (*no ser igual*) not to be equal (**de**, to), not
live up (**de**, to): *ese libro desdice mucho del anterior*,
that book doesn't measure up to the previous one. 2
(*no armonizar*) not to match (**de**, -), not to go (**de**, with):
ese tocado desdice del vestido, that headdress doesn't
go with that dress. 3 (*orígenes, familia, raza*) to be unworthy (**de**, of): *desdice de sus orígenes*, he is unworthy
of his origins. – 4 **desdecirse**, *p* to go back on one's
word, recant.
▲ *Conjugation model* |79|, *like predecir, pp desdicho,-a.*
desdén *m* disdain, scorn, contempt.
● **con desdén**, scornfully, disdainfully.

desdentado,-a 1 *pp* → **desdentar**. – 2 *adj* toothless. – 3 **desdentado,** *m* ZOOL edentate.
desdentar *t* to remove the teeth of.
desdeñable 1 *adj* (*despreciable*) contemptible, despicable. 2 (*insignificante*) negligible, insignificant: *ha alcanzado la cifra nada desdeñable de cinco millones,* it has reached the not insignificant figure of five million.
desdeñar 1 *t* (*despreciar*) to disdain, scorn. 2 (*rechazar*) to turn down. – 3 **desdeñarse,** *p* not to deign (**de,** to): *desdeñarse de hacer algo,* not to deign to do sth.
desdeñoso,-a *adj* disdainful, contemptuous, scornful.
desdibujado,-a 1 *pp* → **desdibujar**. – 2 *adj* blurred, faint.
desdibujar 1 *t* to blur. – 2 **desdibujarse,** *p* to become blurred, become faint.
desdicha *f* misfortune, misery, adversity.
● **para colmo de desdichas,** to top it all. ‖ **por desdicha,** unfortunately.
desdichadamente *adv* unfortunately.
desdichado,-a 1 *adj* unfortunate, wretched, unlucky. – 2 *m,f* poor devil, wretch.
desdicho,-a *pp* → **desdecir**.
desdigo *pres indic* → **desdecir**.
desdinerar 1 *t* to impoverish. – 2 **desdinerarse,** *p* (*quedarse sin dinero*) to run out of money.
desdiré *fut* → **desdecir**.
desdoblamiento 1 *m* unfolding. 2 (*duplicación*) splitting.
■ **desdoblamiento de personalidad,** split personality.
desdoblar 1 *t* to unfold. 2 *fig* (*duplicar*) to split.
desdorar *t* to tarnish.
desdoro *m* tarnishing.
desdramatizar *t* to make less traumatic, play down.
▲ *Conjugation model* [4], *like* ***realizar***.
deseable *adj* desirable.
deseado,-a 1 *pp* → **desear**. – 2 *adj* desired: *en el momento deseado,* at the right time.
desear 1 *t* (*querer*) to want: *deseo que venga,* I want him to come. 2 (*anhelar*) to long for, wish for, desire; (*para alguien*) to wish: *estoy deseando que lleguen las vacaciones de Navidad,* I can't wait for the Christmas holidays; *desearía tener un coche,* I wish I had a car; *le deseó la mejor suerte,* she wished him good luck; *¿qué desea?,* can I help you?, what can I do for you? 3 (*sexualmente*) to desire.
● **dejar mucho/bastante que desear,** to leave a lot to be desired. ‖ **es de desear que,** it is to be hoped that.
desecación 1 *f* (*gen*) drying; (*plantas*) withering; (*pantano*) draining, drainage. 2 QUÍM desiccation.
desecar 1 *t* (*gen*) to dry up. 2 (*pantano, laguna, etc*) to drain. – 3 **desecarse,** *p* to dry up.
▲ *Conjugation model* [1], *like* ***sacar***.
desechable *adj* disposable, throw-away.
desechar 1 *t* (*tirar*) to discard, throw out, throw away: *desecharon los libros que no les interesaban,* they threw away the books they weren't interested in. 2 (*rechazar*) to refuse, reject; (*proyecto, idea*) to drop, discard: *desechó el proyecto,* she turned down the job. 3 (*apartar de sí*) to put aside, cast aside: *deberías desechar esa idea,* you should give up that idea.
desecho 1 *m* (*residuo después de haber escogido lo mejor*) reject. 2 (*ropa*) castoff. – 3 **desechos,** *mpl* waste *sing,* rubbish: *desechos radioactivos,* radioactive waste.
● **de desecho,** (*ropa*) cast-off; (*material*) waste. ‖ **ser un desecho de la sociedad,** *fig* to be a social outcast.

deselectrizar *t* to discharge.
▲ *Conjugation model* [4], *like* ***realizar***.
desembalaje *m* unpacking.
desembalar *t* to unpack.
desembaldosar *t* to remove the tiles from.
desembarazado,-a 1 *pp* → **desembarazar**. – 2 *adj* free and easy, uninhibited.
desembarazar 1 *t* (*dejar libre*) to free. 2 (*desocupar*) to empty, clear. – 3 **desembarazarse,** *p* (*librarse*) to rid os. (**de,** of), get rid (**de,** of): *no conseguía desembarazarse de sus perseguidores,* he wasn't able to shake off his pursuers.
▲ *Conjugation model* [4], *like* ***realizar***.
desembarazo *m* confidence, assurance, ease.
desembarcadero *m* landing stage, quay, pier.
desembarcar 1 *i* to disembark, land, go ashore. – 2 *t* (*mercancías*) to unload; (*personas*) to disembark, put ashore. – 3 **desembarcarse,** *p* to disembark, land, go ashore.
▲ *Conjugation model* [1], *like* ***sacar***.
desembarco *m* (*mercancías*) landing, unloading; (*personas*) disembarkation, landing; (*tropas*) landing.
desembargar *t* JUR to raise an embargo, lift an embargo.
▲ *Conjugation model* [7], *like* ***llegar***.
desembargo *m* JUR raising of an embargo, lifting of an embargo.
desembarque *m* → **desembarco**.
desembarrancar *t* to refloat.
▲ *Conjugation model* [1], *like* ***sacar***.
desembocadura 1 *f* (*de río*) mouth, outlet. 2 (*salida*) way out, exit.
desembocar 1 *i* (*río*) to flow (**en,** into). 2 (*calle*) to end (**en,** at), lead (**en,** into). 3 *fig* to lead (**en,** to), end (**en,** in): *todo desembocó en un final feliz,* it all ended well.
▲ *Conjugation model* [1], *like* ***sacar***.
desembolsar *t* to pay out.
desembolso 1 *m* (*entrega de dinero*) payment; (*plazo*) instalment (US installment). 2 (*gasto*) expense, outlay, expenditure.
■ **desembolso inicial,** down payment.
desemborrachar *t* to sober up.
desembotar *t* *fig* to liven up.
● **desembotar el entendimiento,** to sharpen one's understanding.
desembozar 1 *t* (*quitar el embozo*) to unmask, uncover. 2 *fig* to uncover, bring out into the open.
▲ *Conjugation model* [4], *like* ***realizar***.
desembragar 1 *t* TÉC to disengage. 2 AUTO to release. – 3 *i* AUTO to release the clutch, declutch.
▲ *Conjugation model* [7], *like* ***llegar***.
desembrague 1 *m* TÉC disengaging. 2 AUTO declutching.
desembravecer *t* to tame.
▲ *Conjugation model* [43], *like* ***agradecer***.
desembriagar *t* to sober up.
▲ *Conjugation model* [7], *like* ***llegar***.
desembridar *t* to unbridle.
desembrollar *t* to clarify, clear up.
desembrujar *t* to remove a spell from.
desembuchar 1 *t* (*aves*) to disgorge. 2 *fam fig* to let out, come clean about. – 3 *i* to come clean, spill the beans: *¡desembucha de una vez!,* come out with it once and for all!
desemejante *adj* dissimilar, different.
desemejanza *f* dissimilarity, difference.

desemejar 1 *i* to differ, be dissimilar. – 2 *t* to change.
desempacar *t* to unpack.
▲ *Conjugation model* [1], *like sacar.*
desempachar 1 *t* to relieve from indigestion. – 2 desempacharse, *p* to be relieved from indigestion.
desempacho *m fig* assurance, self-confidence.
desempadronar 1 *t* (*dar de baja en el padrón*) to remove from the register. 2 *fig* (*matar*) to kill. – 3 desempadronarse, *p* to remove os. from the register.
desempalmar *t* to disconnect.
desempañar *t* to wipe the steam from, demist.
desempapelar *t* to strip.
desempaquetar *t* to unpack, unwrap.
desemparejado,-a 1 *pp* → **desemparejar**. – 2 *adj* (*sin pareja*) without a partner. 3 (*suelto*) odd: *un calcetín desemparejado,* an odd sock.
desemparejar *t* to separate.
desempatar 1 *t* to break a tie between: *no pudieron desempatar los votos,* they couldn't break the tie between the votes. – 2 *i* DEP (*desempatar un resultado*) to break the deadlock; (*jugar un partido de desempate*) to play a deciding match, play off.
desempate 1 *m* tie-break, tiebreaker: *los miembros del jurado tuvieron que hacer una votación de desempate,* the members of the jury had to take a deciding vote. 2 DEP play-off, tie-break.
■ **gol de desempate,** deciding goal. ‖ **partido de desempate,** play off, deciding match.
desempedrar 1 *t* (*arrancar las piedras*) to remove the paving from. 2 *fig* (*correr*) to run; (*pasear*) to take a walk.
▲ *Conjugation model* [3], *like zurcir.*
desempeñar 1 *t* (*sacar lo empeñado*) to redeem, take out of pawn. 2 (*liberar a una persona de deudas*) to pay the debts of. 3 (*cumplir una obligación*) to discharge, fulfil (us fulfill), carry out; (*un cargo*) to fill, hold, occupy: *desempeña el mismo cargo desde hace veinte años,* he's held the same post for twenty years. 4 (*papel*) to play: *desempeñó el papel de Don Juan,* he played the part of Don Juan; *desempeña un papel vital,* she plays a vital role.
desempeño 1 *m* (*de algo empeñado*) redeeming; (*deuda*) payment. 2 (*obligaciones, cargo*) carrying out, fulfilment (us fulfillment). 3 TEAT performance, acting.
desempleado,-a 1 *adj* unemployed, out of work. – 2 *m,f* unemployed person. – 3 los desempleados, *mpl* the unemployed.
desempleo *m* unemployment.
● cobrar el desempleo, to be on the dole, (us be on welfare).
desempolvar 1 *t* (*quitar el polvo*) to dust. 2 *fig* (*volver a usar*) to unearth.
● desempolvar recuerdos, *fig* to revive memories.
desemponzoñar *t* (*persona*) to detoxicate; (*cosa*) to remove the poison from.
desenamorar 1 *t* to make fall out of love (**de**, with). – 2 desenamorarse, *p* to fall out of love.
desencadenamiento 1 *m* (*de algo encadenado*) unchaining. 2 *fig* outbreak, outburst.
desencadenar 1 *t* (*quitar la cadena*) to unchain. 2 (*pasiones*) to unleash. 3 *fig* (*producir*) to spark off, give rise to: *la detención desencadenó la revuelta,* the arrest sparked off the riot. – 4 desencadenarse, *p* (*desatarse*) to break loose. 5 (*guerra*) to break out: *se desencadenó una tormenta,* a storm broke. 6 (*acontecimientos*) to start.
desencajado,-a 1 *pp* → **desencajar**. – 2 *adj* (*desunido*) out of place, out of joint. 3 *fig* (*rostro*) distorted; (*ojos*) wild.

desencajar 1 *t* (*desunir*) to take apart, disjoint. – 2 desencajarse, *p* (*desunirse*) to come apart, come loose. 3 *fig* (*rostro*) to become distorted, become twisted; (*ojos*) to look wild.
desencajonar *t* to unpack, take out of a box.
desencallar *t* to refloat.
desencaminar *t* → **descaminar**.
desencantamiento *m* disenchantment.
desencantar 1 *t* (*deshacer el encantamiento*) to disenchant. 2 (*desilusionar*) to disillusion, disappoint. – 3 desencantarse, *p* to be disappointed, be disillusioned.
desencanto 1 *m* (*pérdida del encantamiento*) disenchantment. 2 (*desilusión*) disillusionment, disappointment.
desencapotar 1 *t* desus (*quitar el capote*) to uncloak. 2 *fig* (*descubrir*) to uncover. – 3 desencapotarse, *p fig* (*despejar el cielo*) to clear.
desencapricharse *p* to go off (**de**, -), lose interest (**de**, in).
desencarcelar *t* to release from prison, free.
desencargar *t* to cancel an order for.
▲ *Conjugation model* [7], *like llegar.*
desenchufar *t* to unplug, disconnect.
desencofrar *t* to remove the shuttering from.
desencoger 1 *t* (*estirar*) to stretch out; (*desdoblar*) to unfold. – 2 desencogerse, *p* (*extenderse*) to stretch, give. 3 *fig* (*perder el encogimiento*) to come out of one's shell, become more confident.
▲ *Conjugation model* [5], *like proteger.*
desencogimiento *m fig* self-confidence, ease.
desencolar 1 *t* to unglue, unstick. – 2 desencolarse, *p* to come unglued, come unstuck.
desenconar 1 *t* (*quitar la inflamación*) to relieve the inflammation. 2 *fig* (*desahogar*) to calm. – 3 desenconarse, *p fig* to cool off, calm down.
desencordar *t* to unstring.
▲ *Conjugation model* [31], *like contar.*
desencorvar *t* to straighten.
desencuadernar 1 *t* to unbind. – 2 desencuadernarse, *p* to come unbound.
desendemoniar *t* to exorcise.
▲ *Conjugation model* [12], *like cambiar.*
desendiosar *t fig* to humble, bring down to earth.
desenfadadamente 1 *adv* (*con desenvoltura*) casually, with ease, confidently. 2 (*con humor*) light-heartedly.
desenfadado,-a 1 *pp* → **desenfadar**. – 2 *adj* (*despreocupado*) free and easy, carefree. 3 (*cómico*) light-hearted. 4 (*ropa*) casual.
desenfadar 1 *t* to calm down. – 2 desenfadarse, *p* to calm down.
desenfado 1 *m* (*soltura*) self-confidence, assurance. 2 (*franqueza*) frankness, openness. 3 (*facilidad*) ease.
desenfocado,-a 1 *pp* → **desenfocar**. – 2 *adj* out of focus. 3 *fig* wrongly approached.
desenfocar 1 *t* to take out of focus. 2 *fig* to approach wrong.
▲ *Conjugation model* [1], *like sacar.*
desenfoque 1 *m* incorrect focusing. 2 *fig* wrong approach (**de**, to).
desenfrenado,-a 1 *pp* → **desenfrenar**. – 2 *adj* (*gen*) frantic, uncontrolled, wild. 3 (*pasiones, vicios*) unbridled, uncontrolled.
desenfrenar 1 *t* to unbridle. – 2 desenfrenarse, *p fig* to let loose, go wild.
desenfreno *m* (*vicio*) licentiousness, debauchery; (*falta de control*) lack of control, wild abandon.

desenfundar 1 *t* (*quitar*) to draw out, pull out. 2 (*destapar*) to uncover.

desenganchar 1 *t* (*gen*) to unhook, unfasten; (*despegar*) to unstick. 2 (*caballerías*) to uncouple, unhitch.

desengañado,-a 1 *pp* → **desengañar**. – 2 *adj* (*desilusionado*) disillusioned. 3 (*decepcionado*) disappointed, let down.

desengañar 1 *t* (*hacer conocer la verdad*) to open the eyes of, put in the know. 2 (*decepcionar*) to disappoint. 3 (*desilusionar*) to disillusion. – 4 **desengañarse**, *p* (*ver la verdad*) to have one's eyes opened (**de**, about): *cuando vio a sus oponentes se desengañó de ganar la carrera,* when he saw his opponents he realized he wouldn't win the race. 5 (*tener una decepción*) to be disappointed. 6 (*tener una desilusión*) to become disillusioned, be let down.

● **¡desengáñate!**, face facts!, don't delude yourself!, stop kidding yourself!

desengaño 1 *m* (*conocimiento de la verdad*) eye-opener. 2 (*desilusión*) disillusion; (*decepción*) disappointment.

● **llevarse/sufrir un desengaño**, to be disappointed.

desengarzar *t* to unravel.

▲ *Conjugation model* |4|, *like realizar.*

desengastar *t* to remove from its setting.

desengrasar *t* to remove the grease from.

desenguantarse *p* to take off one's gloves.

desenhebrar 1 *t* to unthread. – 2 **desenhebrarse**, *p* to come unthreaded.

desenjaular *t* to let out of a cage, release.

desenlace 1 *m* (*resultado*) outcome, result. 2 (*de una obra*) ending, dénouement. 3 (*final*) end.

desenlazar 1 *t* (*desatar*) to untie, undo. 2 *fig* to unravel, solve. – 3 **desenlazarse**, *p* (*desatarse*) to come undone. 4 *fig* (*resolverse una acción*) to unfold, turn out: *todo se desenlaza como el espectador espera,* everything turns out as the viewer expects.

▲ *Conjugation model* |4|, *like realizar.*

desenmarañar 1 *t* (*desenredar*) to untangle, unravel. 2 *fig* (*poner en claro*) to unravel, clear up; (*un asunto*) to sort out.

desenmascarar *t* to unmask.

desenmohecer 1 *t* to remove the mould from. – 2 **desenmohecerse**, *p* *fig* (*recuperar un buen estado*) to recover, get back to normal, get back into the swing of things.

▲ *Conjugation model* |43|, *like agradecer.*

desenmudecer 1 *t* to give back the power of speech to. – 2 *i* to recover one's power of speech. 3 *fig* (*romper el silencio*) to break one's silence.

▲ *Conjugation model* |43|, *like agradecer.*

desenredar 1 *t* to untangle, disentangle. – 2 **desenredarse**, *p* to get out (**de**, of), extricate os. (**de**, from).

desenrollar *t* to unroll, unwind.

desenroscar 1 *t* to unscrew, uncoil. – 2 **desenroscarse**, *p* to unscrew, uncoil.

▲ *Conjugation model* |1|, *like sacar.*

desensamblar *t* to separate.

desensillar *t* to unsaddle.

desensortijado,-a *adj* straightened.

desentenderse 1 *p* (*afectar ignorancia*) to pretend not to know (**de**, -/about), ignore (**de**, -), feign ignorance (**de**, of): *cuando ve la tele, se desentiende del teléfono,* when he's watching the telly, he pretends not to hear the telephone; *se desentiende de mí,* she ignores me. 2 (*no tomar parte en algo*) to take no part (**de**, in), have nothing to do (**de**, with).

▲ *Conjugation model* |28|, *like entender.*

desenterrar 1 *t* (*un objeto*) to unearth, dig up; (*cadáver*) to disinter, exhume. 2 *fig* (*recuerdos*) to recall, revive.

▲ *Conjugation model* |27|, *like acertar.*

desentoldar *t* to remove the awnings from.

desentonar 1 *i* MÚS (*instrumento*) to be out of tune; (*cantante*) to sing out of tune. 2 *fig* (*combinar*) not to match (**con**, -): *esos calcetines desentonan con tus zapatos,* those socks don't match your shoes. 3 *fig* (*estar fuera de lugar*) to be out of place, not to fit in (**con**, with).

desentrañar 1 *t* (*sacar las entrañas*) to disembowel. 2 *fig* to find out, solve, unravel. – 3 **desentrañarse**, *p* *fig* (*darlo todo*) to give one's all.

desentrenado,-a *adj* out of training.

desentrenarse *p* to be out of training, get out of training.

desentumecer *t* (*gen*) to loosen up; ; (*piernas*) to stretch.

▲ *Conjugation model* |43|, *like agradecer.*

desenvainar *t* to unsheathe, draw.

desenvoltura 1 *f* *fig* (*soltura*) confidence, assurance. 2 *fig* (*gracia*) grace, ease. 3 *fig* (*atrevimiento*) boldness, forwardness.

desenvolver 1 *t* (*quitar lo que envuelve*) to unwrap. 2 (*aclarar*) to clear up. – 3 **desenvolverse**, *p* (*desembalarse*) to come unwrapped. 4 (*transcurrir*) to develop, go. 5 (*manejarse*) to manage, cope: *se desenvuelve muy bien en los negocios,* he manages very well in business.

▲ *Conjugation model* |32|, *like mover*, *pp* **desenvuelto,-a**.

desenvuelto,-a 1 *pp* → **desenvolver**. – 2 *adj* (*seguro*) confident, self-assured. 3 (*natural*) easy-going, natural, relaxed. 4 (*hábil*) graceful, natural. 5 (*descarado*) bold, forward.

desenzarzar 1 *t* (*sacar de las zarzas*) to disentangle from brambles. 2 *fig* (*separar*) to separate (**de**, from).

▲ *Conjugation model* |4|, *like realizar.*

deseo *m* wish, desire.

● **formular un deseo**, to make a wish. ‖ **tener deseo de algo**, to wish sth.: *tengo muchos deseos de que llegue el verano,* I wish summer would come, I'm longing for the summer.

■ **buenos deseos**, good intentions.

deseoso,-a *adj* desirous, eager, anxious.

● **estar deseoso,-a de algo**, to long for sth., yearn for sth. ‖ **estar deseoso,-a de hacer algo**, to be eager to do sth.

desequilibrado,-a 1 *pp* → **desequilibrar**. – 2 *adj* unbalanced, off-balance. 3 (*persona*) mentally unbalanced. – 4 *m,f* unbalanced person: *es un desequilibrado mental,* he's mentally unbalanced.

desequilibrar 1 *t* to unbalance, throw off balance. 2 *fig* to unbalance. – 3 **desequilibrarse**, *p* *fig* to become unbalanced, become mentally disturbed.

desequilibrio 1 *m* lack of balance, imbalance. 2 *fig* (*mental*) unbalanced state of mind.

■ **desequilibrio mental**, mental imbalance.

deserción 1 *f* MIL desertion. 2 *fig* (*abandono*) abandonment, desertion.

desertar 1 *i* MIL to desert. 2 *fig* (*abandonar*) to abandon, desert.

desértico,-a *adj* desert.

desertización *f* desertification.

desertor,-ra *m,f* deserter.

desespañolizar 1 *t* to take away the Spanish qualities from, make un-Spanish. – 2 **desespañolizarse**, *p* to lose one's Spanish qualities.

▲ Conjugation model |4|, like *realizar.*
desesperación 1 *f* despair, desperation. 2 (*irritación*) exasperation.
● **ser una desesperación,** to be exasperating, be unbearable.
desesperado,-a 1 *pp* → **desesperar.** – 2 *adj* (*sin esperanza*) hopeless, desperate. 3 (*irritado*) exasperated, infuriated. – 4 *m,f* desperate person.
● **a la desesperada,** *fig* as a last hope, in desperation.
‖ **como un,-a desesperado,-a,** *fig* like a mad person: *corría como un desesperado,* he ran about like a madman.
desesperante *adj* exasperating, infuriating.
desesperanza *f* despair, desperation, hopelessness.
desesperanzar 1 *t* to drive to despair. – 2 **desesperanzarse,** *p* to despair, lose hope, give up hope (**de,** of).
▲ Conjugation model |4|, like *realizar.*
desesperar 1 *t* (*hacer perder la paciencia*) to drive to despair, make lose one's patience. 2 (*exasperar*) to exasperate. – 3 *i* (*desesperanzar*) to lose hope, despair: *desespero de volverla a ver,* I've lost hope of ever seeing her again. – 4 **desesperarse,** *p* (*desesperanzar*) to lose hope, despair. 5 (*irritarse*) to get irritated, become exasperated: *se desespera por todo,* everything exasperates her.
desestabilización *f* destabilization.
desestabilizar *t* to destabilize.
▲ Conjugation model |4|, like *realizar.*
desestima *f* disrespect, lack of respect.
desestimación 1 *f* disrespect, lack of respect. 2 JUR refusal, rejection.
desestimar 1 *t* to disregard, underestimate. 2 JUR to reject, refuse.
desfachatado,-a *adj fam* insolent, cheeky.
desfachatez *f* cheek, nerve.
desfalcar *t* FIN to embezzle.
▲ Conjugation model |1|, like *sacar.*
desfalco *m* embezzlement, defalcation.
desfallecer 1 *t* (*disminuir las fuerzas*) to weaken. – 2 *i* (*debilitar*) to weaken, lose strength. 3 (*decaer*) to lose heart.
▲ Conjugation model |43|, like *agradecer.*
desfallecido,-a 1 *pp* → **desfallecer.** – 2 *adj* weak, faint.
desfallecimiento *m* faintness.
desfasado,-a 1 *pp* → **desfasar.** – 2 *adj* out-dated, out of date; (*persona*) old-fashioned, behind the times: *¡eres un desfasado!,* you're just not with it!
desfasar 1 *t* TÉC to phase out. – 2 **desfasarse,** *p* TÉC to change phase. 3 (*persona*) to be out of synch.
desfase 1 *m* (*diferencia*) imbalance, gap: *hay un gran desfase entre la demanda y la oferta,* there's great imbalance between supply and demand. 2 TÉC phase difference.
■ **desfase horario,** (*entre países*) time difference; (*al volar en avión*) jet lag.
desfavorable *adj* unfavourable (US unfavorable).
desfavorecer 1 *t* (*perjudicar*) to disadvantage, put at a disadvantage. 2 (*afear*) not to suit, not flatter: *ese traje te desfavorece,* that dress doesn't suit you.
desfibrar *t* to shred.
desfigurado,-a 1 *pp* → **desfigurar.** – 2 *adj* (*persona*) disfigured. 3 (*estatua etc*) defaced. 4 *fig* (*hecho*) distorted.
desfigurar 1 *t* (*cara*) to disfigure. 2 (*estatua etc*) to deface. 3 *fig* (*realidad, hechos, etc*) to distort. – 4 **desfigurarse,** *p* (*descomponerse*) to become distorted.

desfiladero *m* defile, gorge, narrow pass.
desfilar 1 *i* (*gen*) to march. 2 MIL to march, march past, parade. 3 (*moda*) to parade, walk up and down. 4 *fam* (*dejarse caer*) to pass, drop in: *por este restaurante desfilan muchas estrellas de cine,* many film stars drop in at this restaurant. 5 *fam* (*irse*) to file out, leave.
desfile 1 *m* (*gen*) parade, procession. 2 MIL parade. 3 (*moda*) fashion show.
desfloración *f* deflowering.
desflorar 1 *t* (*ajar*) to spoil, ruin. 2 (*desvirgar*) to deflower. 3 (*un tema*) to touch on, skim over.
desflorecer *i* to lose its bloom.
▲ Conjugation model |43|, like *agradecer.*
desfogar 1 *t* (*descargar*) to give vent to, vent: *no pudo resistirlo más y desfogó su ira,* he couldn't cope anymore and vented his anger. 2 (*la cal*) to slake. 3 (*dar salida al fuego*) to vent. – 4 *i* MAR (*tormenta*) to burst, break. – 5 **desfogarse,** *p* to let off steam, vent one's anger.
▲ Conjugation model |7|, like *llegar.*
desfondar 1 *t* (*romper el fondo*) to break the bottom of. 2 MAR to damage the bottom of. 3 *fig* (*perder fuerza*) to wear out, tire out. 4 (*la tierra*) to plough deeply. – 5 **desfondarse,** *p* (*romperse el fondo*) to cave in, collapse, give way: *la butaca se ha desfondado,* the bottom has come out of the chair. 6 *fig* (*perder fuerzas*) to get exhausted, run out of steam: *no ganó porque se desfondó en el último kilómetro,* he didn't win because he ran out of steam in the last kilometre.
desfonde 1 *m* (*rotura del fondo*) collapsing. 2 *fig* (*cansancio*) exhaustion.
desgabilado,-a *adj* ungraceful, clumsy.
desgaire 1 *m* (*desaliño*) nonchalance, carelessness. 2 (*ademán de desprecio*) scornful gesture.
● **al desgaire,** nonchalantly, carelessly.
desgajar 1 *t* (*rama*) to tear off; (*página*) to rip out, tear out. 2 (*romper*) to break. 3 (*despedazar*) to tear to pieces. – 4 **desgajarse,** *p* to break off, come off.
desgalichado,-a *adj fam* gawky, ungainly.
desgana 1 *f* (*inapetencia*) lack of appetite. 2 (*tedio*) boredom, weariness.
● **con desgana,** reluctantly.
desganado,-a 1 *pp* → **desganar.** – 2 *adj* (*sin gana*) not hungry: *está desganado,* he has no appetite. 3 (*apático*) apathetic, half-hearted.
desganar 1 *t* (*quitar el apetito*) to spoil the appetite of. 2 (*quitar las ganas*) to turn off. – 3 **desganarse,** *p* (*perder el apetito*) to lose one's appetite. 4 (*perder el interés*) to lose interest (**de,** in), go off (**de,** -).
desgañitarse *p fam* to shout os. hoarse, shout one's head off.
desgarbado,-a *adj* ungainly, ungraceful, clumsy.
desgarrador,-ra 1 *adj* heart-breaking, heart-rending. 2 (*aterrador*) blood-curdling.
desgarramiento *m* ripping, tearing.
desgarrar 1 *t* (*rasgar*) to tear, rip. 2 *fig* (*herir los sentimientos*) to break, rend. – 3 **desgarrarse,** *p* (*rasgarse*) to tear, rip.
desgarro 1 *m* (*rompimiento*) tear, rip. 2 *fig* (*desvergüenza*) effrontery, insolence. 3 *fig* (*fanfarronada*) brag, boast.
desgarrón 1 *m* tear, rip. 2 (*jirón*) tatter.
desgastar 1 *t* (*ropa*) to wear out, wear away; (*tacones*) to wear down. 2 (*erosionar*) to erode. 3 *fig* (*debilitar*) to weaken. – 4 **desgastarse,** *p* (*gastarse*) to wear out, get worn. 5 *fig* (*debilitarse*) to weaken. 6 *fig* (*persona*) to wear os. out.

desgaste 1 *m* (*gen*) wear; (*metal*) corrosion; (*cuerda*) fraying; (*piedra*) erosion. 2 (*deterioro*) damage, deterioration. 3 *fig* (*debilitamiento*) weakening.
■ desgaste natural, wear and tear.
desglosar 1 *t* (*escrito*) to detach. 2 (*gastos*) to break down.
desglose *m* breakdown, separation.
desgobernar 1 *t* (*perturbar el gobierno*) to disturb; (*gobernar sin tino*) to misgovern, misrule. 2 MAR to steer badly. 3 (*perturbar*) to disturb, upset.
▲ Conjugation model |27|, like **acertar**.
desgobierno *m* misgovernment, mishandling, mismanagement.
desgracia 1 *f* (*desdicha*) misfortune. 2 (*mala suerte*) bad luck, mischance. 3 (*pérdida de favor*) disfavour (us disfavor). 4 (*accidente*) mishap, accident.
● caer en desgracia, to lose favour (us favor), fall from grace. ‖ para colmo de desgracias / para mayor desgracia, to top it all, to top everything. ‖ por desgracia, unfortunately. ‖ ¡qué desgracia!, how awful!
desgraciadamente *adv* unfortunately.
desgraciado,-a 1 *pp* → **desgraciar**. – 2 *adj* (*sin suerte*) unfortunate, unlucky. 3 (*infeliz*) unhappy. – 4 *m,f* wretch, unfortunate person.
● ser un,-a pobre desgraciado,-a, to be a poor devil.
desgraciar 1 *t* (*echar a perder*) to spoil. 2 (*herir*) to injure. 3 *fam* (*deshonrar a una mujer*) to dishonour (us dishonor), disgrace. – 4 **desgraciarse**, *p* (*malograrse*) to fail, be spoiled; (*plan, proyecto*) to fall through.
▲ Conjugation model |12|, like **cambiar**.
desgranadora *f* threshing machine.
desgranamiento *m* (*guisantes, maíz*) shelling; (*trigo*) threshing.
desgranar 1 *t* (*guisante, maíz*) to shell; (*trigo*) to thresh; (*un racimo de uvas*) to pick the grapes from. 2 (*soltar*) to reel off. – 3 **desgranarse**, *p* (*soltarse*) to come apart, come unstrung: *se desgranó el collar,* the beads on the necklace came unstrung.
desgravable *adj* tax-deductible.
desgravación *f* deduction.
■ desgravación fiscal, tax deduction.
desgravar *t* to deduct.
desgreñado,-a 1 *pp* → **desgreñar**. – 2 *adj* dishevelled, ruffled, tousled.
desgreñar *t* to dishevel, ruffle, tousle.
desguace 1 *m* (*de barco*) breaking up; (*coche*) car breaking, scrapping. 2 (*lugar*) breaker's yard, scrapyard.
desguarnecer 1 *t* (*quitar los adornos*) to remove the trimmings from. 2 MIL to dismantle. 3 (*animales de tiro*) to unharness, unhitch.
▲ Conjugation model |43|, like **agradecer**.
desguazar 1 *t* (*barco*) to break up; (*coche*) to scrap. 2 (*madera*) to rough-hew.
▲ Conjugation model |4|, like **realizar**.
deshabillé *m* negligé (us negligee).
deshabitado,-a 1 *pp* → **deshabitar**. – 2 *adj* (*pueblo, lugar*) uninhabited; (*casa, piso*) unoccupied.
deshabitar *t* to leave, abandon, vacate.
deshabituar 1 *t* (*hacer perder el hábito*) to break from the habit. – 2 **deshabituarse**, *p* to get out of the habit (**a**, of), give up (**a**, -).
▲ Conjugation model |11|, like **actuar**.
deshacer 1 *t* (*destruir*) to destroy. 2 (*estropear*) to ruin, damage; (*romper*) to break; (*desordenar*) to upset. 3

(*nudo*) to untie, loosen; (*paquete*) to undo, unwrap; (*cama*) to strip; (*equipaje*) to unpack; (*puntadas*) to unpick. 4 MIL (*poner en fuga*) to rout, put to flight. 5 (*romper un acuerdo*) to break off. 6 (*disolver*) to dissolve; (*derretir*) to melt. 7 (*desandar*) to retrace. 8 (*desmontar*) to take apart, take to pieces. 9 (*planes, proyectos*) to spoil, ruin. – 10 **deshacerse**, *p* (*nudo*) to come undone, come untied; (*puntada*) to come unsewn. 11 (*disolverse*) to dissolve; (*derretirse*) to melt. 12 (*desaparecer*) to disappear, fade away: *la nube se deshizo y salió el sol,* the cloud disappeared and the sun came out. 13 (*afligirse*) to go to pieces, be shattered: *cuando fue despedido se deshizo,* when he was fired he went to pieces. 14 (*librarse*) to get rid (**de,** of): *se deshizo del cadáver,* he got rid of the corpse. 15 (*agotarse*) to break one's back, wear os. out. 16 (*desvivirse*) to go out of one's way (**por,** to), bend over backwards. 17 (*chiflarse*) to be crazy (**por,** about), be mad (**por,** about): *se deshace por las películas del oeste,* he's crazy about westerns.
● deshacerse en atenciones, to be extremely kind. ‖ deshacerse en elogios/cumplidos, to be full of praise. ‖ deshacerse en excusas, to apologize profusely. ‖ deshacerse en llanto/lágrimas, to cry one's eyes out.
▲ Conjugation model |73|, like **hacer**, pp **deshecho,-a**.
desharrapado,-a 1 *adj* ragged, in tatters. – 2 *m,f* person dressed in rags.
deshebrar 1 *t* (*sacar las hebras*) to ravel out, undo. 2 *fig* (*deshacer en partes delgadas*) to tear into shreds.
deshecho,-a 1 *pp* → **deshacer**. – 2 *adj* (*destruido*) destroyed. 3 (*estropeado*) damaged, ruined. 4 (*nudo*) untied, undone; (*paquete*) unwrapped; (*cama*) unmade; (*equipaje*) unpacked. 5 (*disuelto*) dissolved; (*derretido*) melted. 6 *fig* (*cansado*) shattered, exhausted. 7 *fig* (*abatido*) devastated, shattered.
deshelar 1 *t* to thaw, melt. 2 (*congelador*) to defrost. 3 (*coche*) to de-ice. – 4 **deshelarse**, *p* to thaw out, melt.
▲ Conjugation model |27|, like **acertar**.
desherbar *t* to weed.
▲ Conjugation model |27|, like **acertar**.
desheredado,-a 1 *pp* → **desheredar**. – 2 *adj* disinherited. 3 *fig* deprived, underprivileged. – 4 *m,f* disinherited person. 5 *fig* deprived person, underprivileged person. – 6 los desheredados, *mpl* the deprived.
desheredar *t* to disinherit.
deshermanar 1 *t* to change, make different. – 2 **deshermanarse**, *p* to behave in an unbrotherly way.
deshidratación *f* dehydration.
deshidratado,-a 1 *pp* → **deshidratar**. – 2 *adj* dehydrated.
deshidratar 1 *t* to dehydrate. – 2 **deshidratarse**, *p* to become dehydrated.
deshidrogenar *t* to dehydrogenate, dehydrogenize.
deshielo 1 *m* thaw; (*de congelador*) defrosting; (*de parabrisas*) de-icing. 2 *fig* thaw.
deshilachado,-a 1 *pp* → **deshilachar**. – 2 *adj* frayed.
deshilachar *t* to fray.
deshilado *m* openwork.
deshilar *t* → **deshilachar**.
deshilvanado,-a 1 *pp* → **deshilvanar**. – 2 *adj* untacked. 3 *fig* disconnected, incoherent, disjointed.
deshilvanar *t* to untack.
deshinchado,-a 1 *pp* → **deshinchar**. – 2 *adj* (*neumático etc*) flat, deflated. 3 (*sin hinchazón*) not swollen: *la rodilla ya la tienes deshinchada,* the swelling in your knee has gone down.

deshinchar 1 *t* (*neumático etc*) to deflate, let down. **2** (*reducir la hinchazón*) to reduce the swelling of. **3** *fig* (*quitar importancia*) to play down. **4** *fig* (*hacer perder el orgullo*) to bring down a peg or two. **5** *fig* (*enfado*) to give vent to. – **6 deshincharse,** *p* to deflate, go down. **7** (*reducirse la hinchazón*) to go down: *se me ha deshinchado el grano,* my spot has gone down. **8** *fam fig* (*perder el orgullo*) to get off one's high horse. **9** *fam fig* (*perder fuerzas*) to flag, run out of steam. **10** *fam fig* (*desanimarse*) to lose interest, become discouraged.

deshipotecar *t* to free from mortgage.
▲ *Conjugation model* |1|, *like* ***sacar***.

deshojar 1 *t* (*flor*) to strip the petals off; (*árbol*) to strip the leaves off. **2** (*libro*) to tear the pages out of. – **3 deshojarse,** *p* (*flor*) to lose its petals; (*árbol*) to lose its leaves.

deshollinador *m* chimney sweep.

deshollinar *t* to sweep.

deshonestidad 1 *f* (*sin honestidad*) dishonesty. **2** (*impudor*) indecency, immodesty.

deshonesto,-a 1 *adj* (*sin honestidad*) dishonest. **2** (*inmoral*) immodest, indecent.

deshonor *m* dishonour (us dishonor), disgrace.

deshonra *f* dishonour (us dishonor), disgrace.

deshonrar 1 *t* (*gen*) to dishonour (us dishonor), disgrace. **2** (*injuriar*) to insult, defame. **3** (*a una mujer*) to dishonour (us dishonor).

deshonroso,-a *adj* dishonourable (us dishonorable), shameful, disgraceful.

deshora *f* inconvenient time.
● **a deshora,** (*inoportuno*) at an inconvenient time; (*muy tarde*) very late.

deshuesadora *f* (*de fruta*) stoning machine; (*de carne*) boning machine.

deshuesar *t* (*fruta*) to stone; (*carne*) to bone.

deshumanización *f* dehumanization.

deshumanizado,-a 1 *pp* → **deshumanizar**. – **2** *adj* dehumanized.

deshumanizar *t* to dehumanize.
▲ *Conjugation model* |4|, *like* ***realizar***.

desiderata *f* desiderata *pl*.

desiderativo,-a *adj* desiderative.

desiderátum *m* desideratum.

desidia *f* negligence, idleness, slovenliness.

desidioso,-a *adj* negligent, lazy, slovenly.

desierto,-a 1 *adj* (*sin habitantes*) uninhabited, deserted: *una isla desierta,* a desert island. **2** (*vacío*) deserted, empty: *la habitación estaba desierta,* the room was empty. **3** (*no adjudicado*) void: *el primer premio ha sido declarado desierto,* there was no first prize awarded. – **4 desierto,** *m* desert.
● **clamar en el desierto,** *fig* to cry in the desert. ‖ **predicar en el desierto,** *fig* to preach in the desert.

designación 1 *f* (*nombre*) name, designation. **2** (*nombramiento*) designation, appointment.

designar 1 *t* (*denominar*) to designate: *ese término se ha usado para designar diversos conceptos,* that term has been used to designate several concepts. **2** (*nombrar para un cargo*) to appoint, name, assign: *designaron a cuatro hombres para la misión,* four men were assigned to the mission. **3** (*fijar*) to set, arrange, fix: *hay que designar el punto de encuentro,* we have to arrange a meeting place.

designio *m* intention, plan.
■ **los designios del Señor,** God's will *sing*.

desigual 1 *adj* (*gen*) unequal, uneven. **2** (*diferente*) different, unequal. **3** (*irregular*) uneven, irregular: *constru-* yeron la casa en un terreno desigual, the house was built on uneven ground. **4** (*no liso*) uneven, rough. **5** (*variable*) changeable: *tiene un carácter muy desigual,* she is very changeable.

desigualar 1 *t* (*hacer diferente*) to make unequal, make different; (*tratar de modo distinto*) to treat unequally. **2** (*un terreno*) to make uneven, make rough. – **3 desigualarse,** *p* (*adelantarse*) to get ahead (**a,** of).

desigualdad 1 *f* (*gen*) inequality, difference. **2** (*irregularidad*) unevenness. **3** (*terreno*) unevenness, roughness. **4** (*inconstancia*) changeability.

desilusión *f* disappointment, disillusion, disillusionment.

desilusionado,-a 1 *pp* → **desilusionar**. – **2** *adj* disappointed, disillusioned, disheartened.

desilusionar 1 *t* to disappoint, disillusion, dishearten. – **2 desilusionarse,** *p* to be disappointed, become disillusioned.

desimanar *t* to demagnetize.

desimantar *t* to demagnetize.

desincrustar *t* to descale, unscale.

desinencia *f* ending, desinence.

desinfección *f* disinfection.

desinfectante 1 *adj* disinfectant. – **2** *m* disinfectant.

desinfectar *t* to disinfect.

desinflamación *f* reduction of inflammation.

desinflamar 1 *t* to reduce the inflammation in, reduce the swelling in. – **2 desinflamarse,** *p* to go down, become less swollen.

desinflar 1 *t* (*gen*) to deflate; (*una rueda*) to let down. – **2 desinflarse,** *p* to go down, deflate. **3** *fam fig* (*desanimarse*) to lose heart, become disheartened.

desinformación *f* disinformation.

desinformar *i* to misinform.

desinsectación *f* fumigation.

desinsectar *t* to fumigate.

desintegración 1 *f* disintegration. **2** *fig* disintegration, break-up.
■ **desintegración atómica,** atomic disintegration. ‖ **desintegración nuclear,** nuclear fission.

desintegrar 1 *t* to disintegrate. **2** *fig* to disintegrate, break up. **3** FÍS to split. – **4 desintegrarse,** *p* to disintegrate. **5** *fig* to break up. **6** FÍS to split.

desinterés 1 *m* (*generosidad*) unselfishness, generosity. **2** (*falta de interés*) lack of interest, indifference.

desinteresadamente *adv* unselfishly, generously.

desinteresado,-a 1 *pp* → **desinteresarse**. – **2** *adj* disinterested, unselfish.

desinteresarse 1 *p* (*perder el interés*) to lose interest (**de,** in), go off (**de,** -). **2** (*desentenderse*) to have nothing to do with (**de,** with).

desintoxicación *f* detoxication, detoxification: *cura de desintoxicación alcohólica,* drying-out treatment.

desintoxicar 1 *t* to detoxicate, detoxify. **2** (*alcohol*) to dry out.
▲ *Conjugation model* |1|, *like* ***sacar***.

desistir 1 *i* to desist, give up: *finalmente desistieron de su propósito,* they finally gave up on their idea. **2** JUR to waive.

desjuntar 1 *t* to divide, separate. – **2 desjuntarse,** *p* to come off.

deslabonar *t* to unlink.

deslavado,-a 1 *pp* → **deslavar**. – **2** *adj* (*desteñido*) washed out, faded.

deslavar *t* to half-wash.

deslavazado,-a I *adj* (*insulso*) insipid. 2 (*mal compuesto*) disjointed. 3 (*falto de vigor*) limp.

desleal *adj* disloyal.

deslealtad *f* disloyalty.

desleír I *t* (*sólido*) to dissolve; (*líquido*) to dilute. 2 *fig* to dilute. – 3 **desleírse,** *p* (*sólido*) to dissolve; (*líquido*) to be diluted.

▲ Conjugation model [37], like *reír*.

deslenguado,-a I *pp* → **deslenguarse.** – 2 *adj fig* (*descarado*) insolent, cheeky; (*grosero*) coarse, foul-mouthed.

deslenguarse *p* to be rude.

▲ Conjugation model [22], like *averiguar*.

desliar I *t* (*desatar*) to undo, untie. 2 (*un paquete*) to unwrap, open. – 3 **desliarse,** *p* (*desatarse*) to come undone, come untied.

▲ Conjugation model [13], like *desviar*.

desligar I *t* (*desatar*) to untie, unfasten. 2 *fig* (*separar*) to separate (**de,** from). 3 *fig* (*librar de una obligación*) to release (**de,** from), free (**de,** from): *lo desligó del compromiso que había contraído,* he released him from the commitment he had entered into. – 4 **desligarse,** *p* (*desatarse*) to break away (**de,** from). 5 (*librarse*) to release os. (**de,** from), free os. (**de,** from).

▲ Conjugation model [7], like *llegar*.

deslindar I *t* to delimit, mark the boundaries of. 2 *fig* to clarify, define, outline.

deslinde I *m* delimitation, demarcation. 2 *fig* definition.

deslío¹ *pres indic* → **desleír**.

deslío² *pres indic* → **desliar**.

desliz I *m* (*resbalón*) slide, slip. 2 *fig* (*error*) slip, mistake error.

● cometer/tener un desliz, *fig* to slip up, make a slip.

deslizamiento *m* slipping, slip.

■ deslizamiento de tierra, landslide.

deslizante *adj* sliding.

deslizar I *t* (*pasar*) to slide, slip: *le deslizó un billete en la mano,* she slipped a note into his hand. 2 (*decir o hacer por descuido*) to slip: *deslizó los datos en la conversación,* she slipped the information into the conversation. – 3 *i* (*resbalar*) to slide, slip. – 4 **deslizarse,** *p* (*gen*) to slide; (*sobre agua*) to glide. 5 (*salir*) to slip out (**de,** of); (*entrar*) to slip (**en,** into): *se deslizó en la habitación,* he slipped into the room. 6 (*fluir*) to flow, run: *el riachuelo se desliza por el valle,* the stream flows through the valley. 7 (*transcurrir*) to go by, fly.

▲ Conjugation model [4], like *realizar*.

deslomar I *t* (*dañar la espalda*) to break the back of. 2 (*agotar*) to wear out. – 3 **deslomarse,** *p* (*trabajar mucho*) to wear os. out, break one's back.

deslucido,-a I *pp* → **deslucir.** – 2 *adj* (*sin brillantez*) faded, dull. 3 (*sin gracia*) unimpressive, unexciting, dull, lacklustre (us lackluster).

deslucir I *t* (*quitar la brillantez*) to tarnish, take the shine off; (*descolorar*) to fade. 2 *fig* (*quitar la gracia*) to mar, spoil; (*desacreditar*) to discredit.

▲ Conjugation model [45], like *lucir*.

deslumbrador,-ra I *adj* dazzling. 2 (*que impresiona*) dazzling, impressive.

deslumbramiento *m* dazzle, dazzling.

deslumbrante *adj* → **deslumbrador,-ra**.

deslumbrar *t* to dazzle.

deslustrar I *t* (*telas*) to take the shine off, dull. 2 (*vidrio*) to grind, frost. 3 (*metal*) to tarnish. 4 *fig* (*desacreditar*) to tarnish. – 5 **deslustrarse,** *p* (*metal*) to become dull.

deslustre I *m* (*falta de lustre*) lack of shine. 2 *fig* (*descrédito*) discredit.

desluzco *pres indic* → **deslucir**.

desmadejado,-a I *pp* → **desmadejar**. – 2 *adj fig* tired out, exhausted.

desmadejamiento *m fig* exhaustion.

desmadejar *t fig* to tire out, exhaust.

desmadrado,-a I *pp* → **desmadrar**. – 2 *adj fam fig* wild, unruly.

desmadrar I *t* to take from its mother. – 2 **desmadrarse,** *p fam fig* to go wild.

desmadre *m fam* chaos: *la fiesta fue un desmadre total,* the party was really wild.

desmagnetizar *t* to demagnetize.

▲ Conjugation model [4], like *realizar*.

desmán¹ *m* (*animal*) desman.

desmán² I *m* (*exceso*) outrage, excess, abuse. 2 (*desgracia*) misfortune.

desmanarse *p* to stray from the herd.

desmandado,-a I *pp* → **desmandar**. – 2 *adj* (*persona*) rebellious, unruly. 3 (*animal*) stray; (*caballo*) runaway.

desmandar I *t* (*revocar*) to revoke. – 2 **desmandarse,** *p* (*descomedirse*) to rebel, misbehave, get out of hand. 3 (*animal*) to stray from the herd; (*caballo*) to bolt.

desmano a desmano, *loc adv* out of the way: *eso me coge a desmano,* that's out of my way.

desmantelado,-a I *pp* → **desmantelar**. – 2 *adj* dismantled. 3 MAR dismasted, unrigged.

desmantelamiento I *m* dismantling. 2 MAR dismasting, unrigging.

desmantelar I *t* to dismantle. 2 MAR to dismast, unrig.

desmañado,-a *adj* clumsy, awkward.

desmaquillador,-ra I *adj* cleansing. – 2 **desmaquillador,** *m* make-up remover.

■ crema/leche desmaquilladora, cleansing cream/milk.

desmaquillar I *t* to remove make-up from. – 2 **desmaquillarse,** *p* to remove one's make-up.

desmarcarse I *p* DEP to get into an unmarked position. 2 (*distanciarse*) to distance os. (**de,** from), disassociate os. (**de,** from). 3 *fig* (*escabullirse*) to skive off, slip away.

▲ Conjugation model [1], like *sacar*.

desmarrido,-a *adj* dejected, downhearted.

desmayado,-a I *pp* → **desmayar**. – 2 *adj* (*color*) dull, washed-out. 3 (*inconsciente*) unconscious. 4 (*cansado*) exhausted, worn-out.

● caer desmayado,-a, to faint.

desmayar I *t* (*causar desmayo*) to make faint. – 2 *i fig* (*acobardarse*) to lose heart. – 3 **desmayarse,** *p* (*perder el sentido*) to faint, lose consciousness.

desmayo I *m* (*desaliento*) discouragement. 2 (*pérdida del conocimiento*) faint, fainting fit.

● sin desmayo, unfaltering. ‖ sufrir/tener un desmayo, to faint.

desmedido,-a I *pp* → **desmedirse**. – 2 *adj* (*desproporcionado*) excessive, disproportionate, out of all proportion. 3 (*sin límite*) boundless, unbounded.

desmedirse *p* to go too far.

▲ Conjugation model [34], like *servir*.

desmedrado,-a I *pp* → **desmedrar**. – 2 *adj* puny, emaciated, tiny.

desmedrar I *t* (*deteriorar*) to deteriorate. – 2 *i* (*decaer*) to decline, deteriorate, go down.

desmejora *f* decline, deterioration.

desmejorar I *t* to spoil, make worse, damage. – 2 *i* to deteriorate, get worse, go downhill. – 3 **desmejorarse,** *p* to deteriorate, get worse, go downhill.

● **estar desmejorado,-a,** to look unwell, look worse.
desmelenado,-a 1 *pp* → **desmelenarse**. – 2 *adj* tousled, dishevelled (us disheveled), ruffled.
desmelenar 1 *t* (*desgreñar*) to tousle, dishevel. – 2 desmelenarse, *p fam* (*desmadrarse*) to let one's hair down.
desmembración 1 *f* dismemberment. 2 *fig* separation, division.
desmembramiento *m* → **desmembración**.
desmembrar 1 *t* to dismember. 2 *fig* to split up, break up, divide.
▲ *Conjugation model* [3], *like zurcir*.
desmemoriado,-a 1 *adj* forgetful, absent-minded. – 2 *m,f* forgetful person, absent-minded person.
desmemoriarse *p* to lose one's memory.
▲ *Conjugation model* [12], *like cambiar*.
desmentir 1 *t* (*negar*) to deny. 2 (*contradecir*) to contradict, belie. 3 (*desmerecer*) not to live up to.
▲ *Conjugation model* [35], *like hervir*.
desmenuzar 1 *t* (*gen*) to break into little pieces; (*carne*) to chop up; (*pan*) to crumble; (*pescado*) to flake. 2 *fig* (*examinar*) to examine, look into, analyse (us analyze).
▲ *Conjugation model* [4], *like realizar*.
desmerecer 1 *t* (*quitar mérito a*) to mar, detract from: *la actuación del árbitro desmereció el partido,* the game was marred by the referee's performance. – 2 *i* (*perder valor*) to lose value, deteriorate: *la victoria desmereció por la caída de su rival,* his triumph was marred by the fact that his rival fell over. 3 (*ser inferior*) to compare unfavourably (us unfavorably) (**de,** with), be inferior (**de,** to): *el nuevo presidente no desmerece de su predecesor,* the new president doesn't compare unfavourably with his predecessor.
● **no desmerecer algo/a algn.,** to give sth. it's due/ sb. their due: *ganó Shaw, pero no hay que desmerecer a Wilson que es muy buena jugadora,* Shaw won, but one must give Wilson her due, she's a very good player.
▲ *Conjugation model* [43], *like agradecer*.
desmerecimiento *m* demerit.
desmesura *f* immoderation, disproportion.
desmesuradamente *adv* extremely, excessively, disproportionately.
desmesurado,-a 1 *pp* → **desmesurarse**. – 2 *adj* (*excesivo*) excessive, disproportionate. 3 (*descortés*) insolent, discourteous, rude.
desmesurarse *p* to go too far.
desmigajar *t* to crumble.
desmigar *t* to crumble.
▲ *Conjugation model* [7], *like llegar*.
desmilitarización *f* demilitarization.
desmilitarizar *t* to demilitarize.
▲ *Conjugation model* [4], *like realizar*.
desmineralización *f* demineralization.
desmineralizar *t* to demineralize.
▲ *Conjugation model* [4], *like realizar*.
desmirriado,-a *adj fam* weedy, puny.
desmitificar *t* to demystify.
▲ *Conjugation model* [1], *like sacar*.
desmochar 1 *t* (*árbol*) to pollard, lop. 2 *fig* (*eliminar una parte*) to edit.
desmoldar *t* to remove from a mould, turn out.
desmontable *adj* that can be taken to pieces.
desmontar 1 *t* (*desarmar*) to take to pieces, take down, dismantle. 2 (*edificio*) to knock down. 3 (*arma*) to uncock. 4 (*cortar en un bosque*) to clear. 5 (*allanar*) to level. 6 (*quitar de la montura*) to unset, unmount. 7 (*motor*) to strip. – 8 *i* (*del caballo*) to dismount (**de, -**).

desmonte 1 *m* (*tala*) clearing of trees. 2 (*terreno allanado*) levelled (us leveled) ground.
desmoralización *f* demoralization.
desmoralizador,-ra *adj* demoralizing.
desmoralizar 1 *t* to demoralize. – 2 desmoralizarse, *p* to become demoralized.
▲ *Conjugation model* [4], *like realizar*.
desmoronamiento *m* crumbling, disintegration, fall.
desmoronar 1 *t* to crumble, destroy. – 2 desmoronarse, *p* to crumble, collapse, fall to pieces. 3 (*venir a menos*) to crumble, collapse. 4 *fig* (*decaer el ánimo*) to lose heart, fall apart.
desmovilización *f* demobilization.
desmovilizar *t* to demobilize.
▲ *Conjugation model* [4], *like realizar*.
desnacionalización *f* denationalization, privatization.
desnacionalizar *t* to denationalize, privatize.
▲ *Conjugation model* [4], *like realizar*.
desnarigado,-a 1 *adj* (*sin nariz*) noseless; (*de nariz pequeña*) snub-nosed. – 2 *m,f* (*sin nariz*) person without a nose; (*de nariz pequeña*) snub-nosed person.
desnatado,-a 1 *pp* → **desnatar**. – 2 *adj* (*leche*) skimmed; (*yogur*) low-fat.
desnatar *t* to skim.
desnaturalización 1 *f* QUÍM denaturalization. 2 (*destierro*) banishment. 3 (*adulteración*) adulteration.
desnaturalizado,-a 1 *pp* → **desnaturalizar**. – 2 *adj* QUÍM denatured. 3 (*adulterado*) adulterated, distorted. 4 (*persona*) unnatural.
desnaturalizar 1 *t* (*adulterar*) to adulterate. 2 QUÍM to denature. 3 (*desterrar*) to banish.
▲ *Conjugation model* [4], *like realizar*.
desnivel 1 *m* unevenness. 2 (*cuesta*) slope, drop. 3 *fig* difference.
desnivelación *f* unevenness, unlevelling (us unleveling).
desnivelado,-a 1 *pp* → **desnivelar**. – 2 *adj* (*desigual*) uneven, not level, unequal. 3 (*desequilibrado*) out of balance.
desnivelar 1 *t* (*sacar de nivel*) to make uneven, put on a different level. 2 (*desequilibrar*) to throw out of balance; (*balanza*) to tip. – 3 desnivelarse, *p* to become uneven.
desnucar 1 *t* to break the neck of. – 2 desnucarse, *p* to break one's neck.
▲ *Conjugation model* [1], *like sacar*.
desnuclearizar *t* to denuclearize.
desnudar 1 *t* to undress. 2 *fig* (*despojar*) to strip. 3 *fig* (*desenvainar*) to unsheathe. – 4 desnudarse, *p* (*persona*) to get undressed, take one's clothes off: *el niño se desnudó,* the boy got undressed. 5 *fig* (*rechazar*) to cast aside (**de, -**): *se desnudó de las pasiones,* he cast aside his passions.
desnudez *f* nudity, nakedness.
desnudismo *m* nudism.
desnudista 1 *adj* nudist. – 2 *m,f* nudist.
desnudo,-a 1 *adj* (*persona*) naked, nude; (*parte del cuerpo*) bare: *estaba totalmente desnuda,* she was totally naked; *con los brazos desnudos,* with bare arms. 2 *fig* (*falto de lo que cubre o adorna*) plain, bare. 3 *fig* (*falto de fortuna*) destitute. 4 *fig* (*falto de algo no material*) devoid: *este científico está desnudo de méritos,* this scientist is devoid of merit. 5 *fig* (*patente, claro*) plain: *la verdad desnuda,* the plain truth. – 6 desnudo, *m* ART nude.
● **al desnudo,** (*sin ropa*) naked; (*sin protección*) unprotected, exposed. ‖ **poner al desnudo,** to lay bare, expose.

desnutrición f malnutrition, undernourishment.
desnutrido,-a 1 pp → **desnutrir**. – 2 adj undernourished.
desnutrirse p to become undernourished.
desobedecer t to disobey.
▲ Conjugation model |43|, like **agradecer**.
desobediencia f disobedience.
desobediente 1 adj disobedient. – 2 mf disobedient person.
desobligar 1 t (librar de una obligación) to free from an obligation. 2 fig (disgustar) to disoblige.
▲ Conjugation model |7|, like **llegar**.
desobstruir t to clear.
▲ Conjugation model |62|, like **huir**.
desocupación 1 f (ociosidad) leisure. 2 (desempleo) unemployment.
desocupado,-a 1 pp → **desocupar**. – 2 adj (libre) free, vacant: **esta mesa está desocupada,** this table is free. 3 (ocioso) free, not busy. 4 (desempleado) unemployed, out of work.
desocupar 1 t to vacate, leave, empty. 2 MIL to evacuate. – 3 **desocuparse,** p (casa, habitación, etc) to become empty, become vacant. 4 (perder el empleo) to become unemployed; (quedarse libre) to be free.
desodorante 1 adj deodorant. – 2 m deodorant.
desodorar t to deodorize.
desoír t to ignore, take no notice of, turn a deaf ear to.
▲ Conjugation model |75|, like **oír**.
desojar 1 t (una aguja) to break the eye of. – 2 **desojarse,** p fig (estropearse la vista) to strain one's eyes.
desolación 1 f desolation. 2 (tristeza) affliction, grief.
desolado,-a 1 pp → **desolar**. – 2 adj (devastado) desolated, devastated. 3 (triste) distressed, heartbroken.
desolador,-ra 1 adj (devastador) devastating, ravaging. 2 (desconsolador) heartbreaking, devastating.
desolar 1 t (devastar) to devastate. 2 (desconsolar) to desolate, distress. – 3 **desolarse,** p to be grieved.
▲ Conjugation model |31|, like **contar**.
desollar 1 t to skin, flay. 2 fig (persona) to injure.
● **desollar vivo,-a,** fig to skin alive.
▲ Conjugation model |31|, like **contar**.
desorbitado,-a 1 pp → **desorbitar**. – 2 adj exhorbitant, exaggerated, disproportionate: **un precio desorbitado,** an exhorbitant price.
● **tener los ojos desorbitados,** to be wide-eyed.
desorbitar t to exaggerate, blow out of proportion.
desorden 1 m disorder, disarray, mess, untidiness: **¡vaya desorden!,** what a mess! 2 (irregularidad) irregularity. – 3 **desórdenes,** mpl (disturbios) riots, disturbances, disorder sing. 4 (excesos) excesses. 5 (malestar) disorders: **desórdenes gástricos,** stomach disorders.
desordenado,-a 1 pp → **desordenar**. – 2 adj (habitación etc) untidy, messy: **tienes la habitación desordenada,** your room is a mess. 3 (persona) slovenly. 4 (ideas) confused. 5 fig (vida) licentious.
desordenar 1 t to untidy, disarrange, mess up; (alterar) to disturb. – 2 **desordenarse,** p to get untidy, become untidy, get messed up.
desorejar t to cut the ears off.
desorganización f disorganization.
desorganizar t to disorganize, disrupt.
▲ Conjugation model |4|, like **realizar**.
desorientación 1 f disorientation. 2 fig confusion.
desorientado,-a 1 pp → **desorientar**. – 2 adj disorientated. 3 fig confused.
desorientar 1 t to disorientate. 2 fig (confundir) to confuse. – 3 **desorientarse,** p to lose one's bearings, lose

one's sense of direction, get lost. 4 fig (confundirse) to get confused.
desosar t (fruta) to stone; (carne) to bone.
▲ Conjugation model |59|.
desovar i (insectos) to lay eggs; (peces) to spawn.
desove m (insectos) egg-laying; (peces) spawning.
desovillar 1 t to unwind, unravel. 2 fig to clear up.
desoxidación f deoxidization.
desoxidante 1 adj deoxidizing. – 2 m deoxidizer.
desoxidar t to deoxidize.
desoxirribonucleico,-a adj deoxyribonucleic.
desoye pres indic → **desoír**.
despabilado,-a 1 pp → **despabilar**. – 2 adj (desvelado) wide-awake. 3 fig (listo) smart, sharp, quick.
● **ser despabilado,-a,** fig to be quick on the uptake, have one's wits about one.
despabilar 1 t (quitar el pábilo) to snuff. 2 fig (despertar) to wake up. 3 fig (despertar el ingenio) to make get one's act together. 4 fig (despachar con presteza) to rush off. – 5 i (darse prisa) to hurry up: **despabila que tenemos que marcharnos,** hurry up, we have to go. – 6 **despabilarse,** p (despertarse) to wake up: **despabílate, que es tarde,** wake up, it's late. 7 (avivarse) to get one's act together, buck one's ideas up, wise up: **ya se despabilará en el colegio,** he'll get his act together when he gets to school.
despachaderas 1 fpl (insolencia) insolence, cheek. 2 (habilidad) skill, ability.
● **tener buenas despachaderas,** fig to be on the ball.
despachado,-a 1 pp → **despachar**. – 2 adj (desfachatado) insolent, cheeky. 3 (hábil) skilful (us skillful).
despachar 1 t (terminar) to finish, dispatch. 2 (resolver) to resolve, get through; (tratar un asunto) to deal with, attend: **despachar la correspondencia,** to deal with the mail; **despachamos varios asuntos en una hora,** we attended to several matters in an hour. 3 (enviar) to send, dispatch. 4 (despedir) to dismiss, sack, fire: **hemos despachado al portero,** we dismissed the doorman. 5 (en tienda) to serve; (vender) to sell: **¿ya le despachan?,** are you being served?; **¿quién despachaba las entradas?,** who was selling the tickets? 6 fam fig (comer o beber) to polish off, get through. 7 fam fig (matar) to kill. – 8 **despacharse,** p (desembarazarse) to get rid (**de,** of). 9 fam fig (comer o beber) to put away, polish off. 10 fam (decir a uno lo que viene en gana) to speak one's mind: **se despachó ante todos antes de presentar su dimisión,** he gave them all a piece of his mind before handing in his resignation.
● **despacharse a gusto con algn.,** to give sb. a piece of one's mind.
despacho 1 m (envío) sending, dispatch. 2 (oficina) office; (estudio) study. 3 (venta) sale, selling. 4 (lugar de venta) office. 5 (comunicación) message, dispatch: **despacho telefónico,** telephone message; **despacho telegráfico,** telegram.
■ **despacho de billetes/localidades,** ticket/box office. ‖ **despacho de vino,** wine merchant's.
despachurrar 1 t fam to crush, squash. – 2 **despachurrarse,** p fam to get crushed, get squashed: **se despachurraron los higos,** the figs got all squashed.
despacio 1 adv (gen) slowly: **entró despacio,** she came in slowly. 2 (silenciosamente) quietly. – 3 interj slow down!, take it easy!
despacioso,-a adj slow, sluggish.
despajar 1 t (separar la paja) to winnow. 2 fig (cribar la tierra) to sieve, riddle.

despaldillar *t* to break the shoulder of.
despalillar 1 *t* (*la uva*) to remove the stalks from. 2 (*el tabaco*) to strip.
despampanante *adj fam* stunning.
despanzurrar *t fam* to squash, crush.
desparejado,-a 1 *pp* → **desparejar**. – 2 *adj* (*persona*) without a partner; (*objeto*) odd: *un calcetín desparejado*, an odd sock.
desparejar *t* to separate.
desparejo,-a *adj* unlike, different.
desparpajo 1 *m* (*desenvoltura*) ease, self-assurance. 2 (*descaro*) nerve, impudence.
● **con desparpajo**, in a carefree way, confidently.
desparramar 1 *t* to spread, scatter; (*un líquido*) to spill. 2 (*divulgar*) to spread. – 3 **desparramarse**, *p* to spread, scatter; (*líquido*) to spill. 4 (*divulgar*) to spread.
desparvar *t* to pile up.
despatarrado,-a 1 *pp* → **despatarrar**. – 2 *adj* with one's legs wide open, with one's legs wide apart.
despatarrar 1 *t* (*asombrar*) to astonish, amaze. 2 *fam* (*abrir las piernas*) to send sprawling. – 3 **despatarrarse**, *p* (*asombrarse*) to be astonished. 4 (*abrirse de piernas*) to open one's legs wide: *se despatarró*, he opened his legs wide. 5 (*caer*) to go sprawling. 6 (*mueble*) to collapse.
despatillar 1 *t* (*madera*) to tenon. 2 (*cortar las patillas*) to shave the sideboards off.
despavesar 1 *t* (*quitar el pábilo*) to snuff. 2 (*quitar la ceniza*) to blow the ashes off.
despavorido,-a *adj* terrified.
despavorirse *p* to be terrified.
▲ *Used only in the infinitive and pp.*
despechado,-a 1 *pp* → **despechar** [1]. – 2 *adj* bearing a grudge, spiteful.
despechar[1] 1 *t* to vex. – 2 **despecharse**, *p* to become vexed.
despechar[2] *t fam* (*destetar*) to wean.
despecho *m* spite.
● **a despecho de**, in spite of, despite. ‖ **por despecho**, out of spite.
despechugado,-a 1 *pp* → **despechugar**. – 2 *adj fam* bare-breasted.
despechugar 1 *t* to cut the breast off. – 2 **despechugarse**, *p fam* fig to show one's breast, bare one's breast.
▲ *Conjugation model* [7], *like llegar.*
despectivamente *adv* contemptuously, disparagingly.
despectivo,-a 1 *adj* contemptuous, disparaging. 2 GRAM pejorative, derogatory.
despedazar 1 *t* to tear to pieces, cut to pieces. 2 fig (*maltratar*) to break: *le despedazó el alma*, she broke his heart.
▲ *Conjugation model* [4], *like realizar.*
despedida *f* → **despedido,-a**.
despedido,-a 1 *pp* → **despedir**. - 2 *adj* (*sin empleo*) dismissed, sacked, fired. – 3 **despedida**, *f* farewell, goodbye. 4 (*en una carta*) closing formula. 5 MÚS last verse.
■ **despedida de soltero/soltera**, stag/hen party.
despedir 1 *t* (*lanzar*) to shoot, fire: *la catapulta despedía piedras contra el muro*, the catapult fired stones against the wall. 2 (*echar*) to throw out. 3 (*emitir*) to emit, give off: *las flores despedían buen olor*, the flowers gave off a nice smell. 4 (*del trabajo*) to dismiss, fire, sack. 5 (*decir adiós*) to see off, say goodbye to: *me despidió en la puerta*, she saw me off at the door. – 6 **despedirse**, *p* (*decirse adiós*) to say goodbye (**de**, to): *se despidió de todos*,

she said goodbye to everyone. 7 (*de un empleo*) to leave (**de**, -). 8 fig (*olvidarse, renunciar*) to forget (**de**, -), give up (**de**, -): *puedes despedirte de volverla a ver*, you can forget the idea of ever seeing her again.
● **despedirse a la francesa**, to take French leave. ‖ **salir despedido,-a**, to shoot off.
▲ *Conjugation model* [34], *like servir.*
despegado,-a 1 *pp* → **despegar**. – 2 *adj* detached, unstuck: *el sobre está despegado*, the envelope has come unstuck. 3 fig cool, indifferent, distant.
despegar 1 *t* (*desenganchar*) to unstick, take off, detach. – 2 *i* (*avión*) to take off; (*nave espacial*) to lift off, blast off. 3 (*comenzar el desarrollo*) to take off: *la industria ha despegado con fuerza*, the industry has really taken off. – 4 **despegarse**, *p* (*separarse*) to come unstuck. 5 fig (*perder afecto*) to lose affection (**de**, for).
● **no despegar los labios**, fig not to say a word.
▲ *Conjugation model* [7], *like llegar.*
despego *m* coolness, indifference.
● **con despego**, with indifference.
despegue 1 *m* (*avión*) takeoff; (*nave espacial*) liftoff, blast-off. 2 fig (*desarrollo*) takeoff, launching: *despegue económico*, economic boom.
■ **pista de despegue**, runway.
despeinado,-a 1 *pp* → **despeinar**. – 2 *adj* dishevelled (us disheveled), unkempt, tousled.
despeinar 1 *t* to dishevel, ruffle: *el viento la despeinó*, the wind messed her hair up. – 2 **despeinarse**, *p* to mess up one's hair.
despejado,-a 1 *pp* → **despejar**. – 2 *adj* (*seguro*) assured, self-confident. 3 (*sin sueño*) wide awake; (*listo*) bright, smart clever; (*lúcido*) clear-headed. 4 (*espacioso, ancho*) wide, spacious: *tiene una frente despejada*, she's got a broad forehead. 5 (*sin nubes*) cloudless, clear.
despejar 1 *t* (*desalojar*) to clear. 2 (*espabilar*) to wake up, clear the head of. 3 fig (*aclarar*) to clarify, clear up. 4 DEP to clear. 5 MAT to find. 6 INFORM to clear. – 7 **despejarse**, *p* METEOR to clear up. 8 (*espabilarse*) to wake os. up, clear one's head: *voy a tomar el aire para despejarme*, I'm going to get some fresh air to wake myself up. 9 (*aclararse*) to become clear.
despeje *m* clearance.
despellejar 1 *t* (*quitar la piel*) to skin. 2 fig (*criticar*) to pull to pieces: *en cuanto tiene ocasión nos despelleja ante los jefes*, he runs us down in front of the bosses whenever he gets the chance. – 3 **despellejarse**, *p* to peel.
despelotado,-a 1 *pp* → **despelotarse**. – 2 *adj fam* naked, starkers.
despelotarse 1 *p fam* (*desnudarse*) to strip off. 2 *fam* (*reírse*) to laugh one's head off, split one's sides.
despelote 1 *m fam* (*desnudo*) strip. 2 *fam* (*de risa*) laugh.
despeluchar 1 *i* (*cambiar el pelo un animal*) to moult, shed. – 2 **despelucharse**, *p* (*perder pelo*) to shed: *esta alfombra debe ser de mala calidad porque se despelucha*, it must be a poor quality rug because it's shedding.
despeluzar 1 *t* (*desordenar el pelo*) to ruffle the hair of. 2 (*erizar el cabello*) to make one's hair stand on end: *la noticia le despeluzó*, the news made his hair stand on end.
▲ *Conjugation model* [4], *like realizar.*
despeluznante *adj* horrible, dreadful.
despenalización *f* legalization, decriminalization.
despenalizar *t* to legalize, decriminalize.
▲ *Conjugation model* [4], *like realizar.*
despender 1 *t* (*gastar*) to spend. 2 (*malgastar*) to waste, squander.
despensa 1 *f* (*lugar*) pantry, larder. 2 (*víveres*) provisions *pl*, stock of food.

despeñadero *m* cliff, precipice.

despeñar 1 *t* to throw over a cliff. – 2 **despeñarse,** *p* (*caer*) to fall over a cliff. 3 *fig* (*perderse*) to go off the straight and narrow.

despepitar *t* to remove the pips from.

despepitarse 1 *p* (*gritar*) to shout. 2 *fig* (*hablar, proceder descomedidamente*) to be rash.
● **despepitarse por algo,** (*chiflarse*) to be mad about sth.

desperdiciar *t* to waste, squander; (*oportunidad*) to throw away.
▲ *Conjugation model* |12|, *like* **cambiar.**

desperdicio 1 *m* waste. – 2 **desperdicios,** *mpl* (*basura*) rubbish *sing*; (*desechos*) scraps, leftovers.
● **no tener desperdicio,** *fig* to be good from start to finish: *este libro no tiene desperdicio,* that's an excellent book from start to finish.

desperdigamiento *m* scattering.

desperdigar 1 *t* to scatter, disperse. – 2 **desperdigarse,** *p* to scatter, disperse.
▲ *Conjugation model* |7|, *like* **llegar.**

desperezarse *p* to stretch.
▲ *Conjugation model* |4|, *like* **realizar.**

desperfecto 1 *m* (*daño*) damage. 2 (*defecto*) flaw, defect.
● **causar desperfectos,** to damage, cause damage: *el terremoto causó desperfectos,* the earthquake caused some damage. ‖ **sufrir desperfectos,** to get damaged.

despersonalizar *t* to depersonalize.
▲ *Conjugation model* |4|, *like* **realizar.**

despertador 1 *adj* awakening. – 2 **despertador,** *m* alarm clock.

despertar 1 *t* to wake, wake up, awaken. 2 (*apetito*) to whet. 3 *fig* (*pasiones, deseos, etc*) to arouse; (*interés*) to awake; (*recuerdos*) to bring back: *su actitud despertó la duda,* his attitude raised doubts. – 4 *i* to wake up, awake. – 5 **despertarse,** *p* to wake up, awake: *me desperté a las siete,* I woke up at seven.
▲ *Conjugation model* |27|, *like* **acertar.**

despestañar 1 *t* (*quitar las pestañas*) to pluck the eyelashes of. – 2 **despestañarse,** *p fig* (*mirar con ahínco*) to strain one's eyes; (*estudiar mucho*) to burn the midnight oil.

despiadado,-a *adj* ruthless, merciless.

despicar 1 *t* (*satisfacer*) to satisfy. – 2 **despicarse,** *p* (*vengarse*) to take one's revenge.
▲ *Conjugation model* |1|, *like* **sacar.**

despido *m* dismissal, sacking.
■ **despido improcedente,** wrongful dismissal, unfair dismissal.

despiece *m* quartering.

despierto,-a 1 *adj* awake. 2 (*espabilado*) lively, smart, sharp, bright.

despiezo *m* bevelling.

despilfarrador,-ra 1 *adj* spendthrift, wasteful. – 2 *m,f* spendthrift, waster, squanderer.

despilfarrar *t* to waste, squander.

despilfarro *m* waste.

despintar 1 *t* to take the paint off. 2 *fig* (*desfigurar*) to distort. – 3 **despintarse,** *p* (*borrarse los colores*) to fade. 4 (*olvidar*) to forget: *lo he visto sólo una vez, pero no se me despinta,* I've only seen him once, but I'll never forget him.

despiojar 1 *t* (*quitar los piojos*) to delouse. 2 *fig* (*sacar de la miseria*) to pull out of the gutter.

despique *m* revenge, satisfaction.

despistado,-a 1 *pp →* **despistar.** – 2 *adj* (*distraído*) absent-minded. 3 (*confundido*) confused. 4 (*desorientado*) lost: *estoy despistado, ya no sé dónde estamos,* I'm lost, I don't know where we are. – 5 *m,f* absent-minded person, scatterbrain.
● **hacerse el/la despistado,-a,** to pretend not to understand.

despistar 1 *t* (*hacer perder la pista*) to lose, give the slip. 2 *fig* (*desorientar*) to mislead, confuse: *aquella casa me despistó y casi me pierdo,* that house confused me and I almost got lost. 3 *fig* (*distraer la atención*) to distract. – 4 *i* (*disimular*) to mess about, play-act: *no despistes y contesta a lo que te pregunto,* stop messing about and answer my question. – 5 **despistarse,** *p* (*perderse*) to get lost, lose one's way. 6 (*distraerse*) to get confused, get muddled: *se despistó y se equivocó de calle,* he wasn't thinking and took the wrong turning.

despiste 1 *m* (*distracción*) absent-mindedness. 2 (*error*) mistake, slip.
● **tener un despiste,** to be absent-minded: *tiene un despiste tan grande que no sabe qué hora es,* he's so absent-minded he doesn't know what time of day it is.

desplacer *m* displeasure.

desplantador,-ra 1 *adj* uprooting. – 2 **desplantador,** *m* trowel.

desplantar *t* to uproot, pull up.

desplante *m fig* impudent remark, impudent act.

desplazado,-a 1 *pp →* **desplazar.** – 2 *adj* out of place.

desplazamiento 1 *m* (*traslado*) moving, removal. 2 (*viaje*) trip, journey: *el empleo require mucho desplazamiento,* the job involves a lot of travelling. 3 MAR displacement.

desplazar 1 *t* (*mover*) to move, shift. 2 MAR to displace. 3 *fig* (*sustituir*) to replace, take over from: *el compact-disc ha desplazado al disco de vinilo,* compact discs have taken over from records. – 4 **desplazarse,** *p* to travel: *tiene que desplazarse a Barcelona cada día,* he has to commute to Barcelona every day.
▲ *Conjugation model* |4|, *like* **realizar.**

desplegar 1 *t* (*extender*) to unfold, spread (out), open (out); (*alas*) to spread. 2 MIL to deploy. 3 *fig* (*aclarar*) to clarify: *desplegar el significado de una palabra,* to clarify the meaning of a word. 4 *fig* (*ejercitar*) to show, display: *desplegar prudencia,* to show prudence. – 5 **desplegarse,** *p* MIL to deploy.
▲ *Conjugation model* |48|, *like* **regar.**

despliegue 1 *m* MIL deployment. 2 *fig* (*exhibición*) display, show, manifestation.

desplomar 1 *t* (*hacer perder la verticalidad*) to put out of plumb. – 2 **desplomarse,** *p* (*caer una pared*) to tumble down. 3 (*caer algo de peso*) to fall down, collapse, topple over. 4 (*persona*) to collapse. 5 (*precios*) to slump, fall sharply.

desplome 1 *m* ARQ overhang. 2 (*caída*) collapse.

desplumar 1 *t* (*quitar las plumas*) to pluck. 2 *fig* (*estafar*) to fleece, swindle. – 3 **desplumarse,** *p* to moult.

despoblación *f* depopulation.
■ **despoblación forestal,** deforestation.

despoblado *m* deserted place.

despoblar 1 *t* to depopulate. 2 *fig* (*despojar*) to clear; (*de árboles*) to deforest. – 3 **despoblarse,** *p* to become depopulated, become deserted.
▲ *Conjugation model* |31|, *like* **contar.**

despojar 1 *t* (*quitar*) to deprive (**de,** of), strip: *la despojaron de todas sus joyas,* she was stripped of all her jewels. 2 JUR to dispossess. 3 (*quitar lo que acompaña o cubre*) to strip. 4 *fam fig* (*quitar el dinero*) to fleece. – 5 **despojarse,** *p* (*quitarse ropa*) to take off (**de,** -). 6 (*des-*

poseerse voluntariamente) to forsake (**de**, -), give up (**de**,-): *se despojó de su hacienda,* she gave up her property. **7** *fig* to free os. (**de**, of).

despojo 1 *m* (*botín*) plunder, booty. – **2 despojos,** *mpl* (*sobras*) leavings, scraps, leftovers. **3** (*de un animal*) offal *sing.* **4** (*restos mortales*) mortal remains.

despolitización *f* depoliticization.

despolitizar *t* depoliticize.
▲ Conjugation model |4|, *like realizar.*

desportilladura *f* chip.

desportillar 1 *t* to chip. – **2 desportillarse,** *p* to chip.

desposado,-a 1 *pp* → **desposar**. – **2** *adj fml* newly-wed. – **3** *m,f* newly-wed. – **4 los desposados,** *mpl fml* the newly-weds.

desposar 1 *t fml* to marry. – **2 desposarse,** *p fml* (*prometerse*) to get engaged (**con**, to). **3** *fml* (*casarse*) to get married (**con**, to).

desposeer 1 *t* (*gen*) to dispossess: *lo desposeyó de sus bienes,* he was dispossessed of his properties. **2** (*autoridad*) to remove. – **3 desposeerse,** *p* (*renunciar*) to give up (**de**, -).
▲ Conjugation model |61|, *like leer.*

desposeído,-a 1 *pp* → **desposeer**. – **2 los desposeídos,** *mpl* the have-nots, the dispossessed.

desposorios 1 *mpl fml* (*boda*) marriage *sing.* **2** (*compromiso*) betrothal *sing,* engagement *sing.*

déspota *mf* despot, tyrant.

despótico,-a *adj* despotic.

despotismo *m* despotism.
■ despotismo ilustrado, enlightened despotism.

despotricar *i* to rave, rant on (**contra**, about).
▲ Conjugation model |1|, *like sacar.*

despreciable 1 *adj* despicable, contemptible: *es un hombre despreciable,* he's a despicable man. **2** (*sin importancia*) negligible.

despreciar 1 *t* (*desdeñar*) to despise, scorn, look down on: *desprecia a sus vecinos,* he looks down on his neighbours. **2** (*desestimar*) to reject; (*ignorar*) to disregard, ignore: *no debemos despreciar ningún dato,* we mustn't reject any piece of information: *los conductores borrachos desprecian el peligro,* drunk drivers ignore danger.
▲ Conjugation model |12|, *like cambiar.*

despreciativo,-a *adj* scornful, contemptuous.

desprecio 1 *m* (*desestima*) contempt, scorn, disdain. **2** (*desaire*) slight, snub.

desprender 1 *t* (*separar*) to detach, remove. **2** (*soltar*) to release. – **4 desprenderse,** *p* (*soltarse*) to come off, come away. **5** (*emanar*) to emanate, be given off. **6** (*renunciar*) to part with, give away: *se desprendió de todo,* she gave everything away. **7** *fig* (*liberarse*) to rid os. (**de**, of), free os. (**de**, from): *se desprendió de la ira,* he rid himself of his wrath. **8** (*deducirse*) to follow, be inferred, be implied: *de aquí se desprende que no quiere volver a verte,* from this it follows that she doesn't want to see you again.

desprendido,-a 1 *pp* → **desprender**. – **2** *adj fig* generous, disinterested, unselfish.

desprendimiento 1 *m* (*acción de desprenderse*) detachment, loosening. **2** *fig* (*desinterés*) generosity, unselfishness.
■ desprendimiento de retina, detachment of the retina. ‖ desprendimiento de tierras, landslide.

despreocupación 1 *f* (*tranquilidad*) nonchalance, unconcern. **2** (*negligencia*) negligence, carelessness. **3** (*indiferencia*) indifference.

despreocupado,-a 1 *pp* → **despreocuparse**. – **2** *adj* (*tranquilo*) unconcerned, unworried. **3** (*negligente*) negligent, careless, sloppy. **4** (*indiferente*) indifferent.

despreocuparse 1 *p* (*dejar de preocuparse*) to stop worrying: *puedes despreocuparte de eso, yo me ocuparé,* you can stop worrying about that, I'll deal with it. **2** (*desentenderse*) to be unconcerned (**de**, about), be indifferent (**de**, to): *mi hermana se ha despreocupado de él,* my sister wants nothing to do with him.

desprestigiar 1 *t* to discredit, ruin the reputation of: *aquella actitud lo desprestigió,* that attitude ruined his reputation. – **2 desprestigiarse,** *p* to lose one's prestige, lose one's good reputation.
▲ Conjugation model |12|, *like cambiar.*

desprestigio *m* discredit, loss of prestige, loss of reputation.
■ campaña de desprestigio, smear campaign.

despresurizar *t* to depressurize.
▲ Conjugation model |4|, *like realizar.*

desprevenido,-a *adj* unprepared, unready.
● coger/pillar a algn. desprevenido,-a, to catch sb. unawares, take sb. by surprise.

desproporción *f* disproportion, lack of proportion.

desproporcionado,-a 1 *pp* → **desproporcionar**. – **2** *adj* disproportionate, disproportioned, out of proportion.

desproporcionar *t* to disproportion.

despropósito *m* absurdity, nonsense.
● decir despropósitos, to talk nonsense.

desproveer *t* to deprive.
▲ Conjugation model |61|, *like leer,* *pp* desproveído,-a and desprovisto,-a.

desprovisto,-a 1 *pp* → **desproveer**. – **2** *adj* lacking (**de**, -), devoid (**de**, of), without (**de**, -).
● estar desprovisto,-a de, to be lacking, lack: *estaba desprovisto de experiencia,* he lacked experience.

después 1 *adv* afterwards, later: *iremos después,* we'll go later. **2** (*entonces*) then: *y después dijo que sí,* and then he said yes. **3** (*luego*) next.
● después de, (*tiempo*) after; (*desde*) since; (+ *pp*) after, once: *después de la cena,* after supper; *después de 1992 se ha dedicado a la pintura,* he's been a painter since 1992; *después de recogida la habitación se fue a dormir,* he went to bed after tidying up his room. ‖ después de todo, after all: *después de todo no está tan mal,* it's not that bad after all. ‖ después que, after, when: *después que saliera empezó a llover,* it started to rain just after he'd left.

despulpar *t* to pulp.

despumar *t* to skim.

despuntado,-a 1 *pp* → **despuntar**. – **2** *adj* blunt.

despuntar 1 *t* (*quitar la punta*) to blunt, make blunt. **2** MAR to round. – **3** *i* (*planta*) to sprout; (*flor*) to bud. **4** (*destacar*) to excel, stand out: *este autor despunta en poesía,* this writer's poetry is outstanding; *despuntaba por su destreza,* she was renowned for her cleverness.
● al despuntar el alba/día, at dawn, at daybreak.

desquiciar 1 *t* (*desencajar*) to unhinge, take off its hinges. **2** *fig* (*descomponer una cosa*) to upset, unsettle. **3** *fig* (*trastornar a una persona*) to unsettle, unhinge. – **4 desquiciarse,** *p* (*desencajarse*) to come off its hinges. **5** *fig* (*volverse loco*) to go crazy, to become unhinged.
▲ Conjugation model |12|, *like cambiar.*

desquitar 1 *t* (*compensar un mal*) to compensate. **2** (*vengar*) to avenge. – **3 desquitarse,** *p* (*compensar de un mal*) to make good: *se desquitó de la pérdida comprando otro,* he made good the loss by buying another one. **4** (*vengarse*) to take one's revenge (**de**, on), get even (**de**, with): *el equipo se desquitó venciendo a los campeones,* the team got their own back by beating the champions.

desquite 1 *m* (*compensación*) compensation. **2** (*venganza*) revenge, retaliation. **3** DEP return match.
● **tomarse el desquite,** to have one's revenge.

desratizar *t* to rid of rats.
▲ *Conjugation model* |4|, *like realizar.*

desriñonar 1 *t* to break the back of. **2** (*agotar*) to wear out. – **3 desriñonarse,** *p* to break one's back. **4** (*agotarse*) to wear os. out.

destacado,-a 1 *pp* → **destacar.** – **2** *adj* (*persona*) outstanding, distinguished, prominent, leading; (*actuación*) outstanding.

destacamento *m* detachment.

destacar 1 *i* (*despuntar*) to stand out: *destaca por su sabiduría,* he stands out because of his wisdom. – **2** *t* MIL to detach. **3** (*en pintura*) to highlight, make stand out. **4** *fig* (*dar énfasis*) to point out, emphasize: *quiero destacar las dificultades,* I want to point out the difficulties. – **5 destacarse,** *p* to stand out.
▲ *Conjugation model* |1|, *like sacar.*

destajador *m* blacksmith's hammer.

destajar 1 *t* (*ajustar las condiciones*) to settle the conditions for. **2** (*en los naipes*) to cut.

destajo *m* piecework.
● **a destajo,** by the piece. ‖ **hablar a destajo,** *fig* to talk nineteen to the dozen. ‖ **trabajar a destajo,** to do piecework.

destalonar 1 *t* (*gastar el talón*) to wear down the heel of. **2** (*quitar un talón de un talonario*) to detach.

destapar 1 *t* (*gen*) to open: *destapé la caja y vi que estaba vacía,* I opened the box and saw it was empty. **2** (*tapón*) to uncork; (*tapa*) to take the lid off. **3** (*en la cama*) to uncover. **4** *fig* (*descubrir*) to reveal, uncover. – **5 destaparse,** *p* (*en la cama*) to take the bedclothes off, take the covers off. **6** *fig* (*darse a conocer*) to open up: *cuando se destapó resultó ser encantador,* when he opened up he turned out to be charming.

destape *m fam* striptease.
● **película de destape,** *fam* blue movie.

destapiar *t* to pull down the walls of.

destaponar 1 *t* (*de botella*) to uncork. **2** (*algo que obstruye*) to clear, unblock.

destarar *t* to deduct the tare from.

destartalado,-a *adj* (*casa etc*) tumbledown, ramshackle; (*coche etc*) clapped-out, rickety; (*mueble*) dilapidated, shabby.

destejar 1 *t* (*quitar las tejas*) to remove the tiles from. **2** *fig* (*dejar sin defensa*) to leave unprotected.

destejer 1 *t* (*deshacer lo tejido*) to unweave; (*punto*) to undo. **2** *fig* (*desbaratar*) to mess up, take apart.

destellar *i* (*gen*) to sparkle, glitter; (*estrella*) to twinkle.

destello 1 *m* (*resplandor*) sparkle, flash; (*brillo*) gleam, shine. **2** *fig* (*atisbo*) glimmer, flash: *a pesar de su enfermedad tiene destellos de lucidez,* despite his illness he can be lucid at times.

destemplado,-a 1 *pp* → **destemplar.** – **2** *adj* MÚS out of tune. **3** (*voz, gesto*) sharp, snappy. **4** (*carácter*) irritable, tetchy. **5** (*tiempo*) unpleasant. **6** MED off colour, unwell. **7** (*acero*) untempered.
● **con cajas destempladas,** rudely, brusquely. ‖ **sentirse destemplado,-a,** not to feel well.

destemplanza 1 *f* (*falta de sobriedad*) intemperance. **2** (*del clima*) unsettledness. **3** (*malestar general*) indisposi-

tion. **4** (*de un instrumento*) dissonance. **5** *fig* (*falta de moderación*) lack of moderation.

destemplar 1 *t* (*alterar*) to disturb, upset: *los nervios destemplaron al equipo,* the team lost concentration due to nerves. **2** (*poner en infusión*) to infuse. **3** MÚS to make go out of tune. **4** (*un metal*) to untemper. – **5 destemplarse,** *p* MED to feel indisposed, feel unwell. **6** (*un instrumento*) to go out of tune. **7** (*perder la moderación*) to become upset, get agitated. **8** (*un metal*) to lose its temper.

desteñir 1 *t* to discolour (US discolor), fade: *tus pantalones han desteñido mi camisa blanca,* your trousers have discoloured my white shirt; *el sol destiñó la ropa del escaparate,* the sun faded the clothes in the shop window. – **2** *i* to lose colour (US color), fade, run: *si lavas esa camiseta en agua caliente desteñirá,* if you wash that T-shirt in hot water it will run. – **3 desteñirse,** *p* to lose colour (US color), fade: *la camiseta se destiñó,* the T-shirt faded.
▲ *Conjugation model* |36|, *like ceñir.*

desternillarse *p fam.*
● **desternillarse de risa,** to split one's sides laughing, be in stitches.

desterrado,-a 1 *pp* → **desterrar.** – **2** *adj* exiled, banished. – **3** *m,f* exile, outcast.

desterrar 1 *t* to exile, banish. **2** *fig* to banish: *destierra el enfado y alégrate,* bury your anger and cheer up.
▲ *Conjugation model* |27|, *like acertar.*

desterronar *t* to break up the clods in.

destetar *t* to wean.

destete *m* weaning.

destiempo a destiempo, *loc adv* inopportunely, at the wrong time, at the wrong moment: *llegó a destiempo,* he arrived at the wrong moment.

destierro 1 *m* (*pena*) banishment, exile. **2** (*lugar*) place of exile. **3** *fig* (*lugar muy apartado*) back of beyond.

destilación *f* distillation.

destiladera *f* still.

destilado,-a 1 *pp* → **destilado.** – **2** *adj* distilled. – **3** destilado, *m* distillate.

destilador,-ra 1 *adj* distilling. – **2** *m,f* (*persona*) distiller. – **3** destilador, *m* (*alambique*) still.

destilar 1 *t* to distil (US distill). **2** (*pus, sangre*) to exude: *la herida destilaba pus,* pus oozed from the wound. **3** (*filtrar*) to filter. **4** *fig* to exude, reveal: *su poesía destila tristeza,* his poems exude sorrow. – **5** *i* (*gotear*) to drip.

destilería *f* distillery.

destinado,-a 1 *pp* → **destinar.** – **2** *adj* destined (**a**, to), bound (**a**, for).
● **estar destinado,-a al fracaso,** to be doomed to failure.

destinar 1 *t* (*asignar*) to assign, set aside, destine; (*dinero*) to allocate, set aside: *destinó la ambulancia a casos de urgencia,* he kept the ambulance for emergencies. **2** (*persona*) to appoint, assign, send, post: *lo han destinado a Madrid,* he has been posted to Madrid. – **3** MIL to post.

destinatario,-a 1 *m,f* (*de carta*) addressee. **2** (*de mercancías*) consignee.

destino 1 *m* (*sino*) destiny, fate. **2** (*uso*) purpose, use. **3** (*lugar*) destination. **4** (*empleo*) post.
● **con destino a,** bound for, going to: *un avión con destino a Madrid,* a plane bound for Madrid; *el vuelo 977 con destino a París,* flight 977 to Paris. ‖ **salir con destino a,** to leave for.

destitución *f* dismissal, removal.

destituir t to dismiss, remove from office.
▲ *Conjugation model* |62|, *like huir*.
destocar 1 t (*deshacer el tocado*) to mess up the hair of. –
2 **destocarse,** p (*descubrirse la cabeza*) to take off one's hat.
▲ *Conjugation model* |1|, *like sacar*.
destorcer 1 t (*deshacer lo retorcido*) to untwist. 2 *fig* (*enderezar*) to straighten. – 3 **destorcerse,** p MAR (*perder el rumbo*) to drift.
destornillador m screwdriver.
destornillar 1 t to unscrew. – 2 **destornillarse,** p to come unscrewed. 3 *fig* to go crazy.
destrabar 1 t (*quitar las trabas*) to unfetter. 2 (*desprender*) to remove, detach.
destral m hatchet, small axe.
destrenzar t to unplait, (US unbraid).
▲ *Conjugation model* |4|, *like realizar*.
destreza f skill, dexterity: *tiene destreza,* she's skilful.
destripar 1 t (*quitar las tripas*) to disembowel; (*pescado*) to gut. 2 (*cosa*) to tear open, cut open: *destripó el colchón,* she ripped the mattress open. 3 *fig* (*despachurrar*) to crush, squash: *la rueda le destripó el pie,* the wheel crushed her foot. 4 *fam fig* (*un relato*) to ruin: *me destripó el chiste cuando iba por la mitad,* he ruined my joke when I was only halfway through it.
destripaterrones m *fam pey* clodhopper.
▲ *pl* **destripaterrones**.
destronamiento 1 m dethronement. 2 *fig* overthrow.
destronar 1 t to dethrone. 2 *fig* to overthrow, unseat.
destroncar 1 t (*tronchar un árbol*) to chop down. 2 (*interrumpir*) to interrupt. 3 (*cortar*) to cut.
▲ *Conjugation model* |1|, *like sacar*.
destrozado,-a 1 *pp* → **destrozar**. – 2 *adj* (*objeto*) smashed, broken, ruined: *el coche quedó destrozado,* the car was a write-off. 3 (*persona - moralmente*) devastated, shattered; (- *físicamente*) exhausted, done in, worn out.
destrozar 1 t (*romper*) to destroy, shatter, wreck; (*despedazar*) to tear to pieces, tear to shreds: *la explosión destrozó el puente,* the explosion wrecked the bridge. 2 *fig* (*gastar*) to wear out: *destroza los zapatos,* she wears her shoes out. 3 *fig* (*estropear*) to ruin, spoil; (*corazón*) to break: *destrozó sus sueños,* she shattered her dreams. 4 *fig* (*causar daño moral*) to crush, shatter, devastate.
▲ *Conjugation model* |4|, *like realizar*.
destrozo 1 m (*acción*) destruction. 2 (*daño*) damage: *la lluvia causó grandes destrozos en el huerto,* the rain caused terrible damage in the orchard.
▲ In 2, also used in plural with the same meaning.
destrozón,-ona 1 *adj* destructive. – 2 *m,f* destroyer, destructive person.
destrucción f destruction.
destructivo,-a *adj* destructive.
destructor,-ra 1 *adj* destructive. – 2 **destructor,** m MAR destroyer.
destruir 1 t to destroy. 2 *fig* to destroy, ruin, wreck: *han destruido sus esperanzas,* they've shattered her hopes.
▲ *Conjugation model* |62|, *like huir*.
desuerar t to drain the whey from.
desuncir t to unyoke.
▲ *Conjugation model* |3|, *like zurcir*.
desunión 1 f (*separación*) separation, division. 2 *fig* (*discordia*) discord, feud, dissension.
desunir 1 t (*separar*) to divide, separate. 2 *fig* to cause discord, disunite.
desusado,-a 1 *pp* → **desusar**. – 2 *adj* (*insólito*) unusual, strange. 3 (*anticuado*) old-fashioned, out of date.

desuso m disuse: *eso está en desuso,* that's obsolete, that's outdated.
● caer en desuso, to fall into disuse.
desvaído,-a 1 *adj* (*color disipado*) faded, pale; (*borroso*) blurred. 2 (*persona*) tall and lanky.
desvainar t to shell.
desvalido,-a 1 *adj* needy, destitute. – 2 *m,f* needy person, destitute person. – 3 **los desvalidos,** *mpl* the needy, the destitute.
desvalijamiento m theft, robbery.
desvalijar 1 t (*a alguien*) to rob: *me desvalijaron,* I was robbed. 2 (*un lugar*) to burgle: *desvalijaron la tienda,* the shop was burgled. 3 *fig* to strip (bare), clean out: *tu amigo me desvalija la nevera cada vez que viene,* your friend cleans out my fridge every time he comes.
desvalimiento m helplessness, lack of protection.
desvalorización f devaluation, depreciation.
desvalorizar t to devalue, depreciate.
▲ *Conjugation model* |4|, *like realizar*.
desván m loft, attic.
desvanecer 1 t (*hacer desaparecer*) to clear, dispel, disperse: *el viento desvaneció la niebla,* the wind cleared the fog. 2 (*color*) to fade; (*contorno*) to blur. 3 *fig* (*recuerdo etc*) to dispel, banish: *aquella respuesta desvaneció nuestras dudas,* that answer dispelled our doubts. – 4 **desvanecerse,** p (*disiparse*) to disperse, clear. 5 *fig* (*desaparecer*) to vanish, disappear; (*recuerdos*) to fade. 6 *fig* (*demayarse*) to faint.
▲ *Conjugation model* |43|, *like agradecer*.
desvanecimiento 1 m (*desaparición*) disappearance, dispelling. 2 (*desmayo*) faint, fainting fit.
desvariar i to be delirious, rave, talk nonsense.
▲ *Conjugation model* |13|, *like desviar*.
desvarío 1 m (*delirio*) delirium, raving. 2 (*disparate*) nonsense, act of madness. 3 (*capricho*) fancy, whim.
desvelado,-a 1 *pp* → **desvelar**. – 2 *adj* awake, wide awake.
desvelar 1 t (*quitar el sueño*) to keep awake: *las películas de miedo me desvelan,* horror films keep me awake. 2 *fig* (*revelar*) to reveal, disclose: *nos desveló el secreto,* she revealed the secret to us. – 3 **desvelarse,** p to be unable to sleep. 4 *fig* (*dedicarse*) to devote os. (**por,** to): *siempre se ha desvelado por su familia,* she has always devoted herself to her family.
desvelo 1 m (*insomnio*) sleeplessness, insomnia. 2 (*dedicación*) devotion, dedication: *cuidaba a sus hijos con desvelo,* she doted on her children. – 3 **desvelos,** *mpl* (*esfuerzos*) efforts, pains.
desvenar 1 t (*quitar las venas a la carne, los nervios de las hojas del tabaco*) to remove the veins from. 2 (*sacar del filón*) to extract from a vein.
desvencijado,-a 1 *pp* → **desvencijar**. – 2 *adj* rickety, broken-down, dilapidated.
desvencijar 1 t to break, ruin. – 2 **desvencijarse,** p to fall apart, fall to pieces.
desvendar t to remove the bandage from.
desventaja 1 f disadvantage, drawback. 2 (*problema*) problem.
● estar en desventaja, to be at a disadvantage.
desventajoso,-a *adj* disadvantageous, unfavourable (US unfavorable).
desventura f misfortune, bad luck.
desventuradamente *adv* unfortunately.
desventurado,-a 1 *adj* unfortunate, unlucky. – 2 *m,f* unfortunate person, wretch. – 3 **los desventurados,** *mpl* the unfortunate.

desvergonzadamente 1 *adv* (*sin vergüenza*) shamelessly. 2 (*con descaro*) impudently, cheekily.
desvergonzado,-a 1 *adj* (*sinvergüenza*) shameless, brazen. 2 (*descarado*) cheeky, rude, impudent. – 3 *m,f* (*sinvergüenza*) shameless person. 4 (*descarado*) cheeky person.
desvergüenza 1 *f* (*falta de decoro*) shamelessness. 2 (*descaro*) cheek, nerve, impudence. 3 (*impertinencia*) insolent remark, rude remark.
desvestir 1 *t* to undress. – 2 desvestirse, *p* to undress, get undressed: *se desvistió,* he got undressed.
▲ Conjugation model [34], like *servir.*
desviación 1 *f* deviation. 2 (*de carretera*) diversion, detour.
■ desviación de columna, MED slipped disc.
desviacionismo *m* deviationism.
desviacionista 1 *adj* deviationist. – 2 *mf* deviationist.
desviar 1 *t* (*gen*) to deviate, change the course of: *desvió la mirada,* she looked away. 2 (*golpe, balón*) to deflect. 3 (*carretera, río, barco, avión*) to divert. 4 *fig* (*tema*) to change. 5 *fig* (*disuadir*) to dissuade, put off: *sólo su madre conseguirá desviarlo de esa idea,* only his mother will be able to put him off that idea. – 6 desviarse, *p* (*avión, barco*) to go off course; (*coche*) to make a detour. 7 (*golpe, balón*) to be deflected. 8 (*persona, camino*) to leave: *tenemos que desviarnos de la carretera en el kilómetro cinco,* we have to turn off at the five-kilometre mark. 9 *fig* (*tema*) to stray (**de,** from), go (**de,** off).
▲ Conjugation model [13].
desvinculación *f* releasing, freeing.
desvincular 1 *t* (*gen*) to separate, detach, dissociate. 2 (*de la familia*) to cut off (**de,** from). – 3 desvincularse, *p* to cut os. off (**de,** from), break away (**de,** from), dissociate os. (**de,** from).
desvío 1 *m* diversion, detour. 2 *fig* (*desagrado*) displeasure, indifference: *lo trataron con desvío,* they treated him coldly.
desvirgar *t* to deflower.
▲ Conjugation model [7], like *llegar.*
desvirtuar 1 *t* to impair, spoil, distort. 2 *fig* to contradict, belie: *desvirtuó sus palabras con sus actos,* his behaviour belied his words.
▲ Conjugation model [11], like *actuar.*
desvitrificar *t* to devitrify.
▲ Conjugation model [1], like *sacar.*
desvivirse 1 *p* (*desvelarse*) to do one's utmost (**por,** for), be devoted (**por,** to). 2 (*desear*) to be mad (**por,** about).
desyemar 1 *t* (*quitar las yemas a las plantas*) to disbud. 2 (*sacar la yema al huevo*) to remove the yolk from.
detall al detall, *loc adv* retail: *vender algo al detall,* to sell something retail.
detalladamente *adv* in detail.
detallado,-a 1 *pp* → **detallar.** – 2 *adj* detailed, thorough.
detallar 1 *t* to detail, give the details of, tell in detail. 2 (*especificar*) to specify. 3 COM to retail, sell retail.
detalle 1 *m* (*pormenor*) detail, particular. 2 (*delicadeza*) nice gesture, nice thought. 3 (*toque decorativo*) touch.
● al detalle, COM retail. ‖ contar algo con detalle, to tell sth. in (great) detail. ‖ ¡qué detalle!, how nice!, how sweet! ‖ sin entrar en detalles, without going into details. ‖ tener un detalle, to be considerate, be thoughtful: *tuvo el detalle de comprar unos bombones,* she was thoughtful enough to buy some chocolates.
detallista 1 *adj* (*perfeccionista*) perfectionist. 2 (*que piensa en los demás*) thoughtful, considerate. – 3 *mf* COM retailer, retail trader.

detección *f* detection.
detectar *t* to detect.
detective *mf* detective.
■ detective privado,-a, private detective, private eye.
detector,-ra 1 *adj* detecting. – 2 detector, *m* detector.
■ detector de incendios, fire detector. ‖ detector de mentiras, lie detector. ‖ detector de radar, radar scanner.
detención 1 *f* (*paro*) stopping, halting; (*interrupción*) stoppage, stop, halt. 2 JUR detention, arrest. 3 (*atención*) care.
● con detención, carefully, thoroughly: *lo explicó todo con mucha detención,* he explained it all very carefully.
detener 1 *t* (*parar*) to stop, halt; (*proceso, negociación*) to hold up. 2 (*retener*) to keep, delay, detain: *nos detuvo durante una hora,* she kept us for an hour. 3 JUR to detain, arrest. – 4 detenerse, *p* (*pararse*) to stop, halt: *el tren se detuvo,* the train stopped. 5 (*entretenerse*) to hang about, linger. 6 (*pararse a considerar algo*) to dwell: *no podemos detenernos en este asunto,* we can't dwell upon this matter.
▲ Conjugation model [87], like *tener.*
detenidamente *adv* carefully, thoroughly.
detenido,-a 1 *pp* → **detener.** – 2 *adj* (*parado*) held up. 3 (*minucioso*) detailed, thorough, careful. 4 JUR under arrest: *está detenido,* he's under arrest. – 5 *m,f* JUR prisoner.
detenimiento con detenimiento, *loc adv* carefully, thoroughly.
detentar *t* JUR to hold unlawfully.
detergente 1 *adj* detergent. – 2 *m* detergent.
deterger *t* to deterge.
deteriorado,-a 1 *pp* → **deteriorar.** – 2 *adj* damaged, worn.
deteriorar 1 *t* (*estropear*) to damage, spoil; (*gastar*) to wear out. – 2 deteriorarse, *p* (*estropearse*) to get damaged; (*gastarse*) to wear out. 3 *fig* to deteriorate, go downhill: *su relación se ha deteriorado mucho últimamente,* their relationship has got a lot worse lately.
deterioro 1 *m* (*daño*) damage, deterioration; (*desgaste*) wear and tear. 2 *fig* (*empeoramiento*) deterioration, worsening.
● ir en deterioro de, to harm.
determinable *adj* determinable.
determinación 1 *f* (*valor*) determination, resolution. 2 (*decisión*) decision. 3 (*firmeza*) firmness.
● con determinación, determinedly. ‖ tomar una determinación, to make a resolution, make a decision.
determinado,-a 1 *pp* → **determinar.** – 2 *adj* (*preciso*) definite, precise, certain, given, particular. 3 (*día, hora, etc*) fixed, set, appointed. 4 (*resuelto*) determined, decisive, resolute. 5 GRAM definite. 6 MAT determinate.
determinante 1 *adj* decisive, determinant. – 2 *m* MAT determinant.
determinar 1 *t* (*decidir*) to resolve, decide, determine: *hemos determinado empezar en septiembre,* we've decided to start in September; *"determinar la raíz cuadrada de ...",* "find the square root of ...". 2 (*señalar*) to determine. 3 (*fijar*) to fix, set, appoint. 4 (*estipular*) to stipulate, specify: *la ley determina cómo hacerlo,* the law stipulates how to do it. 5 (*causar*) to bring about, cause: *tales circunstancias determinaron la caída del Imperio,* such circumstances brought about the fall of the Empire. 6 (*hacer decidir*) to make decide, decide: *su actitud me determinó a obrar,* his attitude made me decide

to do something. – **7 determinarse,** *p (decidirse)* to make up one's mind, decide.

determinativo,-a 1 *adj* determinant. **2** LING determinative.

determinismo *m* determinism.

determinista 1 *adj* determinist. – **2** *mf* determinist.

detersión *f* detersion.

detestable *adj* detestable, hateful, repulsive.

detestación *f* detestation, hatred.

detestar *t* to detest, hate, abhor.

detonación *f* detonation.

detonador *m* detonator.

detonante 1 *adj* detonating, explosive. – **2** *m* detonator. **3** *fig* trigger.

detonar 1 *i* to detonate, explode. – **2** *t* to detonate, set off.

detractar *t* to slander, discredit.

detractor,-ra 1 *adj* slanderous, defamatory. – **2** *m,f* slanderer, defamer.

detraer 1 *t (substraer)* to withdraw. – **2** *f fig (denigrar)* to denigrate.

detrás 1 *adv* behind: *detrás de la puerta,* behind the door. **2** *(en la parte posterior)* at the back, in the back: *el jardín está detrás,* the garden is at the back. **3** *(después)* then, afterwards: *llegaron detrás de él,* they arrived after him.
● **detrás mío (tuyo, suyo, etc),** after me (you, him, etc). ‖ **ir detrás de,** to go after: *voy detrás de Pedro,* I'm after Pedro. ‖ **por detrás,** *fig* behind one's back: *se rieron de él por detrás,* they laughed at him behind his back.

detrimento 1 *m* detriment. **2** *fig (daño moral)* harm, damage.
● **en detrimento de,** to the detriment of. ‖ **sin detrimento de,** without detriment to.

detrito *m* detritus.

detritus *m* detritus.
▲ *pl detritus.*

detuve *pt indef* → **detener.**

deuda 1 *f* debt. **2** REL trespass.
● **contraer una deuda,** to get into debt. ‖ **estar en deuda con algn.,** *(de dinero)* to be in debt to sb.; *fig* to be indebted to sb.
■ **deuda del Estado,** public debt. ‖ **deuda exterior,** external debt. ‖ **deuda pública,** national debt.

deudor,-ra 1 *adj* debtor. – **2** *m,f* debtor.

devalimiento *m* destitution.

devaluación *f* devaluation.

devaluar *t* to devaluate, devalue.
▲ *Conjugation model* [11], *like actuar.*

devanado,-a 1 *pp* → **devanar.** – **2** devanado, *m* winding, coiling.

devanador,-ra 1 *adj* winding. – **2** *m,f* winder. – **3** devanador, *m* reel, spool.

devanar *t (hilo)* to wind, reel; *(alambre)* to coil.
● **devanarse los sesos,** *fam fig* to rack one's brains.

devaneo 1 *m (delirio)* delirium, nonsense. **2** *(pasatiempo vano)* waste of time, frivolity. **3** *(amorío)* fling.

devastación *f* devastation, destruction.

devastador,-ra 1 *adj* devastating. – **2** *m,f* devastator.

devastar *t* to devastate, ravage, lay waste.

devengado,-a 1 *pp* → **devengar.** – **2** *adj (sueldo)* due; *(intereses)* accrued, earned.

devengar 1 *t (sueldo)* to earn. **2** *(interés)* to earn, accrue.
▲ *Conjugation model* [7], *like llegar.*

devengo *m* amount due.

devenir¹ *i* to happen, occur.
▲ *Conjugation model* [90], *like venir.*

devenir² *m* flux.

deverbal *adj* derived from a verb.

devoción 1 *f* devotion, devoutness. **2** *(afición)* devotion, dedication.
● **con devoción,** devoutly. ‖ **no ser santo,-a de devoción,** *fam* not to be one's cup of tea: *Pedro no es santo de mi devoción,* Pedro is not my cup of tea.

devocionario *m* prayer book.

devolución 1 *f (acción)* return, giving back; *(dinero)* repayment, refund: *exigieron la devolución del importe,* they demanded a refund, they demanded their money back. **2** JUR devolution.
● **"no se admiten devoluciones",** COM "no refunds", "goods cannot be exchanged".

devolver 1 *t (volver algo a un estado anterior)* to put back, return: *devuelve la lámpara a su sitio,* put the lamp back in its place. **2** *(por correo)* to send back, return. **3** *(restituir un dinero)* to refund, return. **4** *(una visita, un cumplido, etc)* to return, pay back: *nos devolvió la visita al martes siguiente,* he returned the visit the following Tuesday. **5** *(restaurar)* to restore, give back: *la democracia devolvió las libertades,* democracy restored freedom. **6** *fam (vomitar)* to vomit, throw up, bring up. – **7** *i fam (vomitar)* to throw up, be sick.
▲ *Conjugation model* [32], *like mover,* pp *devuelto,-a.*

devorador,-ra 1 *adj* devouring: *tenía una hambre devoradora,* he was ravenously hungry. – **2** *m,f* devourer.
■ **devoradora de hombres,** man-eater.

devorar 1 *t* to devour. **2** *(engullir)* to eat up, gobble up. **3** *fig (consumir)* to devour, consume: *el fuego devoró los libros,* the fire devoured the books. **4** *fig (corroer)* to eat up: *la envidia lo devoraba,* he was eaten up with envy.

devotería *f* false piety.

devoto,-a 1 *adj (piadoso)* devout, pious. **2** *(digno de devoción)* devotional. **3** *fig (dedicado)* devoted. – **4** *m,f* REL pious person, devout person. **5** *fig (seguidor)* devoted follower, devotee, admirer.

devuelto,-a 1 *pp* → **devolver.** – **2** devuelto, *m (vómito)* vomit.

dextrina *f* dextrin, dextrine.

dextrorso,-a *adj* dextrorse, dextrorsal.

dextrosa *f* dextrose.

deyección 1 *f (de volcán)* ejecta *pl.* **2** MED *(defecación)* defecation; *(extremento)* dejecta *pl,* faeces *pl.*

DF *abr (Distrito Federal)* federal district.

dg *sím (decigramo)* decigram; *(símbolo)* dg.

Dg *sím (decagramo)* decagram; *(símbolo)* Dg.

DGS¹ *abr (Dirección General de Sanidad) government department responsible for public health.*

DGS² *abr (Dirección General de Seguridad) government department responsible for national security.*

DGT¹ *abr (Dirección General de Tráfico) government department responsible for traffic.*

DGT² *abr (Dirección General de Turismo) government department responsible for tourism.*

di 1 *pt indef* → **dar.** – **2** *imperat* → **decir.**

día 1 *m* day: *¿qué día es hoy?,* what day is it today?, what's the date today? **2** *(con luz)* daylight, daytime: *ya es de día,* it's daylight. **3** *(tiempo)* day, weather: *tuvimos un buen día,* it was a fine day. – **4** días, *mpl (vida)* days.
● **a la luz del día,** in daylight. ‖ **a los pocos días,** a few days later. ‖ **al caer el día,** at dusk. ‖ **al despuntar el día,** at dawn, at daybreak. ‖ **al día siguiente / al**

otro día, the following day. ‖ **¡buenos días!,** good morning! ‖ **cada día / todos los días,** each day, every day. ‖ **cualquier día de estos,** any day now. ‖ **dar los buenos días,** to say good morning. ‖ **de día,** during the day. ‖ **de un día para otro,** from one day to the next, overnight. ‖ **del día,** fresh. ‖ **día a día,** day by day. ‖ **el día de mañana,** *fig* in the future. ‖ **el día menos pensado,** *fig* when you least expect it. ‖ **estar al día,** *fig* to be up to date. ‖ **hacer buen/mal día,** to be a nice/horrible day. ‖ **hasta el fin de sus días,** to the end of his days. ‖ **poner al día,** to bring up to date. ‖ **ser de día,** to be daylight. ‖ **si algún día,** if ever: *si algún día lo ves ...,* if you ever see him ... ‖ **un buen día,** *fig* one fine day. ‖ **un día sí y otro no,** every other day. ‖ **vivir al día,** *fig* to live from hand to mouth, not to save a penny.
■ **día de año nuevo,** New Year's Day. ‖ **día de descanso,** day off. ‖ **día de fiesta / día festivo,** holiday, bank holiday. ‖ **día de paga,** payday. ‖ **día entre semana,** weekday. ‖ **día lectivo,** teaching day. ‖ **día libre,** day off: *mañana cogeré el día libre,* I'll take the day off tomorrow. ‖ **días alternos,** every other day *sing.*

diabetes *f* diabetes.
▲ *pl diabetes.*

diabético,-a 1 *adj* diabetic. – 2 *m,f* diabetic.

diabla *f* (*diablesa*) she-devil.
● **a la diabla,** *fig* any old how.

diablear *i* to get up to mischief.

diablesa *f* she-devil.

diablillo *m fam* little devil, little imp.

diablo 1 *m* devil, demon. 2 *fig* (*niño*) little devil. 3 (*malvado*) wicked person.
● **¡al diablo con ...!,** *fam* to hell with ...! ‖ **del diablo / de todos los diablos,** the devil of a ...: *armó un follón del diablo,* he kicked up a hell of a rumpus. ‖ **¡diablos!,** damn! ‖ **enviar al diablo,** to send to the devil. ‖ **¿qué/dónde/cuándo diablos ...?,** *fam* what/where/when the hell ...?: *¿dónde diablos se han metido?,* where the hell have they got to?
■ **el abogado del diablo,** the devil's advocate. ‖ **un pobre diablo,** a poor devil.

diablura *f* mischief, naughtiness.
● **hacer diabluras,** to get up to mischief.

diabólico,-a *adj* diabolic, devilish, diabolical.

diábolo *m* diabolo.

diaconado *m* diaconate, deaconate.

diaconal *adj* diaconal.

diaconato *m* → **diaconado**.

diácono *m* deacon.

diacrítico,-a *adj* diacritic, diacritical.

diacrónico,-a *adj* diachronic.

diadema 1 *f* (*joya*) diadem. 2 (*adorno para el pelo*) hairband.

diafanidad *f* diaphaneity, translucence; (*transparencia*) transparence.

diáfano,-a 1 *adj* diaphanous, translucent; (*transparente*) transparent. 2 (*claro*) clear, bright. 3 *fig* (*explicación*) clear; (*conducta*) impeccable.

diafragma 1 *m* ANAT diaphragm. 2 (*en fotografía*) aperture. 3 MED diaphragm, cap.

diagnosis *f* diagnosis.
▲ *pl diagnosis.*

diagnosticar *t* to diagnose: *le han diagnosticado un cáncer,* he was diagnosed as having cancer.
▲ *Conjugation model* [1], *like sacar.*

diagnóstico,-a 1 *adj* diagnostic. – 2 **diagnóstico,** *m* diagnosis.

diagonal 1 *adj* diagonal. – 2 *f* diagonal.
● **en diagonal,** diagonally.

diagrama *m* diagram.
■ **diagrama de flujo,** INFORM flowchart.

dial *m* dial.

dialectal *adj* dialectal.

dialectalismo *m* dialectalism.

dialéctica *f* → **dialéctico,-a**.

dialéctico,-a 1 *adj* dialectical. – 2 **dialéctica,** *f* dialectic, dialectics.

dialecto *m* dialect.

dialectología *f* dialectology.

diálisis *f* dialysis.
▲ *pl diálisis.*

dialogador,-ra *adj* willing to talk, willing to discuss matters.

dialogar 1 *i* (*conversar*) to talk, have a conversation. 2 *fig* (*negociar*) to negotiate, hold talks (**sobre,** on): *los ministros de ambos estados están dialogando sobre el tema,* the ministers of both countries are discussing the matter. – 3 *t* (*escribir en forma de diálogo*) to write in dialogue form.
▲ *Conjugation model* [7], *like llegar.*

diálogo *m* dialogue, conversation.

diamantar *t* to diamond.

diamante *m* diamond.
■ **diamante en bruto,** uncut diamond.

diamantino,-a *adj* diamond-like, diamantine.

diametral *adj* diametrical, diametral.

diametralmente *adv* diametrically: *son diametralmente opuestos,* they're diametrically opposed.

diámetro *m* diameter.

diana 1 *f* MIL reveille. 2 DEP (*objeto*) target; (*para dardos*) dartboard; (*blanco*) bull's eye.
● **hacer diana,** to hit the bull's eye. ‖ **tocar diana,** MIL to sound reveille.

diantre 1 *interj fam* (*sorpresa*) crikey!, crumbs!, (US geez!). 2 *fam* (*enfado*) damn it!, (US darn!).

diapasón 1 *m* MÚS (*instrumento*) diapason, tuning fork. 2 MÚS (*trozo de madera*) fingerboard. 3 MÚS (*escala*) diapason, scale, range.
● **bajar/subir el diapasón,** *fig* to lower/raise the tone of one's voice.

diapositiva *f* slide.

diariamente *adv* daily, every day.

diario,-a 1 *adj* daily, everyday: *en esta ciudad llevamos diez muertos diarios,* there are ten deaths a day in this city. – 2 **diario,** *m* (*prensa*) daily, paper, daily newspaper. 3 (*íntimo*) diary, journal.
● **a diario,** daily, every day: *eso pasa a diario,* that happens every day. ‖ **de diario,** daily, every day: *ropa de diario,* everyday clothes.
■ **diario de a bordo,** logbook. ‖ **diario matinal / diario de la mañana,** morning newspaper. ‖ **diario de la tarde,** evening newspaper. ‖ **diario de navegación,** logbook. ‖ **diario de sesiones,** parliamentary report. ‖ **diario hablado,** news, news bulletin.

diarquía *f* diarchy.

diarrea *f* diarrhoea (US diarrhea).
■ **diarrea verbal,** *fam fig* verbal diarrhoea (US diarrhea).

diáspora *f* diaspora.

diastasa *f* diastase.

diástole *f* diastole.

diátesis *f* diathesis.
▲ *pl diátesis.*

diatriba f diatribe.
● lanzar una diatriba, to launch a diatribe.
diávolo m diabolo.
dibujante 1 mf artist, drawer. 2 (de dibujos animados) cartoonist. 3 TÉC (hombre) draughtsman (US draftsman); (mujer) draughtswoman (US draftswoman).
dibujar 1 t to draw, sketch. 2 TÉC to design. 3 fig (describir) to describe. – 4 dibujarse, p (mostrarse) to appear, be outlined: a lo lejos se dibuja la silueta del castillo, there is the outline of a castle in the distance.
dibujo 1 m (arte) drawing, sketching. 2 (imagen) drawing. 3 (motivo) pattern, design: esta camisa tiene un dibujo de rombos, this shirt has a diamond pattern on it.
■ academia de dibujo, school of art, art school. ‖ dibujo artístico, artistic drawing. ‖ dibujo lineal, draughtsmanship (US draftmanship). ‖ dibujos animados, cartoons.
dicción f diction.
diccionario m dictionary.
dicha 1 f (alegría) happiness. 2 (suerte) fortune, good luck.
● nunca es tarde si la dicha es buena, better late than never.
dicharachero,-a adj talkative and funny, witty.
dicharacho m coarse expression.
dicho,-a 1 pp → **decir**. – 2 adj said, mentioned: dicha casa ..., the said house ...; dicho esto se marchó, having said this he left. – 3 dicho, m saying, proverb. – 4 dichos, mpl betrothal sing.
● del dicho al hecho hay mucho trecho, there's many a slip twixt cup and lip, it's easier said than done. ‖ dicho de otro modo, to put it another way, in other words. ‖ dicho sea de paso, let it be said in passing. ‖ dicho y hecho, no sooner said than done. ‖ lo dicho, what we (I, you, etc) said. ‖ propiamente dicho,-a, strictly speaking.
dichosamente adv fortunately, luckily, happily.
dichoso,-a 1 adj happy. 2 (con suerte) lucky, fortunate. 3 fam (molesto) damn, damned, bloody: ¡este dichoso calor!, this damn heat!
diciembre m December.
▲ See marzo.
dicotomía f dichotomy.
dicroísmo m dichroism.
dicromatismo m dichromatism.
dictado,-a 1 pp → **dictar**. – 2 dictado, m dictation. – 3 dictados, mpl fig dictates.
● escribir al dictado, to take dictation.
dictador,-ra m,f dictator.
dictadura f dictatorship.
dictáfono m Dictaphone.
▲ Registered trademark.
dictamen 1 m (opinión) opinion. 2 (informe) report.
dictaminar i to give an opinion (sobre, on): los expertos dictaminaron sobre la causa del incendio, the experts gave their opinion on the cause of the fire.
dictar 1 t to dictate. 2 JUR (ley) to enact, decree, announce; (sentencia) to pronounce, pass. 3 fig (sugerir) to suggest, say: hizo lo que le dictaba el corazón, he did what his heart told him.
dictatorial adj dictatorial.
dicterio m insult.
didáctica f → **didáctico,-a**.
didáctico,-a 1 adj didactic. – 2 didáctica, f didactics.
diecinueve 1 adj (cardinal) nineteen; (ordinal) nineteenth. – 2 m (número) nineteen. 3 (fecha) nineteenth: el diecinueve de marzo, the nineteenth of March.

▲ See also seis.
diecinueveavo,-a 1 adj nineteenth. – 2 m,f nineteenth.
▲ See also sexto,-a.
dieciochesco,-a adj eighteenth-century.
dieciochista adj eighteenth-century.
dieciocho 1 adj (cardinal) eighteen; (ordinal) eighteenth. – 2 m (número) eighteen. 3 (fecha) eighteenth.
▲ See also seis.
dieciochoavo,-a 1 adj eighteenth. – 2 m,f eighteenth.
▲ See also sexto,-a.
dieciséis 1 adj (cardinal) sixteen; (ordinal) sixteenth. – 2 m (número) sixteen. 3 (fecha) sixteenth.
▲ See also seis.
dieciseisavo,-a 1 adj sixteenth. – 2 m,f sixteenth.
▲ See also sexto,-a.
diecisiete 1 adj (cardinal) seventeen; (ordinal) seventeenth. – 2 m (número) seventeen. 3 (fecha) seventeenth.
▲ See also seis.
diecisieteavo,-a 1 adj seventeenth. – 2 m,f seventeenth.
▲ See also sexto,-a.
diente 1 m ANAT ZOOL tooth. 2 (de ajo) clove. 3 (de rueda de engranaje) cog, tooth; (de sierra) tooth; (de tenedor) prong. 4 ARQ (adaraja) toothing stone.
● apretar los dientes, to grit one's teeth. ‖ echar los dientes, to teethe. ‖ hablar entre dientes, fig to mumble, mutter. ‖ hincar el diente en, (apropiarse de) to get one's hands on; (abordar y tratar) to get to grips with, get one's teeth into; (criticar) to slate, slander, attack. ‖ poner los dientes largos a algn., fig to make sb. green with envy. ‖ tener buen diente, fam to have a good appetite.
■ diente de leche, milk tooth. ‖ diente de león, dandelion. ‖ diente picado, decayed tooth. ‖ dientes postizos, false teeth.
diera imperf subj → **dar**.
diéresis f diaeresis, dieresis.
▲ pl diéresis.
diesel 1 adj diesel. – 2 m diesel engine.
diestra f → **diestro,-a**.
diestramente adv skilfully (US skillfully).
diestro,-a 1 adj lit right. 2 (hábil) skilful (US skillful). – 3 diestra, f right hand. – 4 diestro, m bullfighter.
● a diestro y siniestro, left, right and centre (US center). ‖ a la diestra, on the right.
dieta[1] f (régimen, alimentación) diet.
● estar a dieta, to be on a diet.
dieta[2] 1 f (asamblea) diet, assembly. – 2 dietas, fpl expenses, allowance sing. 3 (de médico) doctor's fees. 4 (de diputado) emoluments.
dietario 1 m accounts book. 2 (agenda) diary.
dietética f → **dietético,-a**.
dietético,-a 1 adj dietary, dietetic. – 2 f dietetics.
■ médico dietético, dietician.
dietista mf dietician.
diez 1 adj (cardinal) ten; (ordinal) tenth. – 2 m (número) ten. 3 (fecha) tenth.
▲ See also seis.
diezmar t to decimate.
diezmilésimo,-a 1 adj ten-thousandth. – 2 m,f ten-thousandth.
▲ See also sexto,-a.
diezmo m tithe.
difamación f defamation, slander. 2 (por escrito) libel.
difamador,-ra 1 adj defamatory, slanderous. 2 (por escrito) libellous (US libelous). – 3 m,f defamer, slanderer.

difamar 1 *t* to defame, slander. 2 (*por escrito*) to libel.

difamatorio,-a 1 *adj* defamatory, slanderous. 2 (*por escrito*) libellous (us libelous).

diferencia 1 *f* difference. 2 (*de opinión*) difference, disagreement.
● **a diferencia de,** unlike: *a diferencia de ellos,* unlike them. ‖ **hacer diferencia entre,** to make a distinction between.

diferenciación *f* differentiation.

diferencial 1 *adj* distinguishing. – 2 *m* differential.

diferenciar 1 *t* (*distinguir*) to differentiate, distinguish (**entre,** between). 2 (*hacer diferente*) to make different: *diferenció la caja de mayor peso con una cruz,* he marked the heaviest box with an X. – 3 **diferenciarse,** *p* to differ, be different (**por,** because of). 4 (*destacarse*) to distinguish os., stand out (**por,** because of): *se diferencia por su acento,* she stands out because of her accent.
▲ *Conjugation model* [12], *like* **cambiar**.

diferente *adj* different: *es diferente de/a todos,* it's different to/from them all.

diferido,-a 1 *pp* → **diferir**. – 2 **en diferido** *adj* recorded.

diferir 1 *t* to defer, postpone, put off. – 2 *i* to differ, be different (**de/entre,** from).
▲ *Conjugation model* [35], *like* **hervir**.

difícil 1 *adj* difficult, hard: *es difícil de complacer,* she's hard to please; *lo que dices es difícil de entender,* what you're saying is difficult to understand. 2 (*improbable*) unlikely: *es difícil que nos encontremos allí,* it's unlikely that we'll meet there, we're unlikely to meet there.

difícilmente 1 *adv* (*apenas*) hardly: *difícilmente puede oírnos,* he can hardly hear us. 2 (*con dificultad*) with difficulty: *difícilmente ganará el torneo,* he's unlikely to win the tournament.

dificultad 1 *f* difficulty. 2 (*obstáculo*) obstacle; (*problema*) trouble, problem.

dificultar *t* to make difficult, hinder, obstruct: *el fumar le dificultó la respiración,* smoking made it difficult for him to breathe.

dificultosamente *adv* with difficulty.

dificultoso,-a *adj* difficult, hard.

difteria *f* diphtheria.

diftérico,-a *adj* diptheric.

difuminar *t* to blur, soften.

difumino *m* stump.

difundir 1 *t* (*luz, calor*) to diffuse. 2 *fig* (*noticia, enfermedad*) to spread. 3 RAD TV to broadcast. – 4 **difundirse,** *p* (*luz, calor*) to be diffused. 5 *fig* (*noticia, enfermedad*) to spread.

difunto,-a 1 *adj* deceased, late. – 2 *m,f* deceased.
■ **Día de los difuntos,** All Souls' Day, All Saints' Day.

difusible *adj* diffusible.

difusión 1 *f* (*de luz, calor*) diffusion. 2 *fig* (*de noticia, enfermedad, etc*) spreading. 3 RAD broadcast, broadcasting.
● **tener gran difusión,** to be widely known, be widespread: *esa teoría tiene gran difusión,* it's a widely-known theory.

difuso,-a 1 *adj* diffuse. 2 *fig* diffuse, wordy.

difusor,-ra 1 *adj* spreading, propagating. 2 RAD TV broadcasting. – 3 **difusor,** *m* (*de secador*) diffuser.

digerible *adj* digestible.

digerir 1 *t* to digest. 2 *fig* (*asimilar*) to assimilate, absorb, digest, take in: *no ha digerido la noticia,* the news hasn't sunk in yet. 3 *fig* (*sufrir*) to suffer.
▲ *Conjugation model* [35], *like* **hervir**.

digestión *f* digestion.
■ **corte de digestión,** stomach cranp.

digestivo,-a 1 *adj* digestive. – 2 **digestivo,** *m* after dinner drink.

digitado,-a *adj* digitate.

digital *adj* digital.
■ **huellas digitales,** fingerprints. ‖ **reloj digital,** (*de pulsera*) digital watch; (*de mesa*) digital clock.

digitalizar *t* to digitize.

dígito *m* digit.

dignamente *adv* (*con dignidad*) with dignity; (*decentemente*) decently; (*merecidamente*) worthily.

dignarse *p* to deign (**a,** to), condescend (**a,** to): *no se dignó a hablarnos,* he didn't deign to talk to us.

dignatario,-a *m,f* dignitary.

dignidad 1 *f* (*cualidad*) dignity. 2 (*cargo*) rank, office, post.

dignificante *adj* dignifying.

dignificar *t* to dignify.
▲ *Conjugation model* [1], *like* **sacar**.

digno,-a 1 *adj* (*merecedor*) worthy, deserving: *digno,-a de confianza,* trustworthy. 2 (*adecuado*) fitting, appropiate. 3 (*respetable*) worthy, honourable (us honorable). 4 (*decente*) decent: *un trabajo digno,* a decent job.
● **digno,-a de admiración,** worthy of admiration, admirable. ‖ **digno,-a de compasión,** pitiful. ‖ **digno,-a de mención,** worth mentioning. ‖ **digno,-a de verse,** worth seeing.

digo *pres indic* → **decir**.

digresión *f* digression.

dije[1] *pt indef* → **decir**.

dije[2] 1 *m* (*alhaja*) trinket, charm. 2 *fig* (*persona*) treasure, gem.

dilacerar 1 *t* to dilacerate, lacerate. 2 *fig* to hurt, harm.

dilación *f* delay.
● **sin dilación,** without delay.

dilapidación *f* wasting, squandering.

dilapidar *t* to waste, squander.

dilatación 1 *f* dilation. 2 FÍS expansion.

dilatadamente *adv* extensively, at length.

dilatado,-a 1 *pp* → **dilatar**. – 2 *adj* dilated. 3 (*vasto*) vast, extensive, large. 4 FÍS expanded.

dilatar 1 *t* to dilate. 2 FÍS to expand: *el calor dilata el hierro,* heat expands iron. 3 (*prolongar*) to prolong, extend: *dilataron la reunión más de lo esperado,* they made the meeting go on longer than expected. 4 (*retrasar*) to put off, delay, postpone. – 5 **dilatarse,** *p* to dilate. 6 FÍS to expand. 7 (*prolongarse*) to be prolonged, to drag on. 8 (*extenderse*) to go on, be a long time: *no quisiera dilatarme demasiado así que concluiré,* I don't want to go on too long so I'll finish. 9 (*retrasarse*) to be delayed, to be put off, to be postponed.

dilatoria *f* → **dilatorio,-a**.

dilatorio,-a 1 *adj* delaying. – 2 **dilatoria,** *f* delay.

dilección *f* affection, love.

dilecto,-a *adj* beloved, dearly beloved.

dilema *m* dilemma.

diletante *mf* dilettante.

diletantismo *m* dilettantism.

diligencia 1 *f* (*cuidado*) diligence, care. 2 (*rapidez*) rapidity, speed. 3 (*carreta*) stagecoach. 4 (*nota oficial*) stamp. – 5 **diligencias,** *fpl* (*trámites*) steps, measures; (*investigaciones*) investigations; (*resultados*) results of the investigations, findings; (*actuación*) proceedings: *el juez practicará las diligencias que estime oportunas,* the judge will take whatever steps he thinks fit; *el juez que instruye las diligencias del caso Paz,* the judge who

is carrying out the investigation into the Paz case; *las diligencias contra Pedro Paz han sido archivadas por falta de pruebas,* the case against Pedro Paz has been dropped due to lack of evidence. **6** (*preparativos*) preparations: *las diligencias para construir el nuevo teatro se iniciaron el año pasado,* preparations for the building of the new theatre began last year. **7** (*gestiones*) business *sing.*
● **con diligencia,** diligently.
■ **diligencias previas,** preliminary inquiries.
diligenciar 1 t (*poner los medios necesarios*) to take the necessary steps to. **2** (*tramitar*) to make a formal application for.
▲ *Conjugation model* [12], *like* **cambiar.**
diligente 1 *adj* (*cuidadoso*) diligent. **2** (*rápido*) quick.
dilucidación f elucidation.
dilucidar t to elucidate, clear up, throw light on.
dilución 1 f (*de un sólido*) dissolution, dissolving. **2** (*de un líquido*) dilution.
diluir 1 t (*un sólido*) to dissolve. **2** (*un líquido*) to dilute. **3** (*hacer más débil*) to tone down: *ese rojo es demasiado fuerte, hay que diluirlo,* that red is too bright, it needs to be toned down. **4** *fig* (*repartir*) to spread out: *para evitar abusos de poder, diluyó las competencias,* to avoid abuse of power, he shared out responsibilites. **– 5** diluirse, p (*un sólido*) to dissolve. **6** (*un líquido*) to dilute.
▲ *Conjugation model* [62], *like* **huir.**
diluvial *adj* diluvial.
diluviar i to pour with rain, pour down.
▲ *Conjugation model* [12], *like* **cambiar.** *Used only in the 3rd pers; it does not take a subject.*
diluvio 1 m flood. **2** *fig* torrent, deluge, flood: *un diluvio de preguntas,* a deluge of questions.
■ **el Diluvio (Universal),** the Flood.
diluyente *adj* diluting, solvent.
diluyo *pres indic* → **diluir.**
dimanar 1 i to emanate (**de,** from): *el arroyo dimana de esa montaña,* the stream emanates from that mountain. **2** *fig* (*proceder*) to emanate, come (**de,** from), proceed (**de,** from): *esa actitud dimana de su forma de pensar,* that attitude comes from his way of thinking.
dimensión 1 f dimension, size. **2** *fig* (*importancia*) importance.
● **de gran dimensión / de grandes dimensiones,** very large, large-scale. ‖ **tomar las dimensiones de,** to measure, take the measurements of.
▲ *In 1, also used in plural with the same meaning.*
dimensional *adj* dimensional.
dimensionar t to measure, take the measurements of.
dimes dimes y diretes, *loc fam* quibbling *sing,* bickering *sing.*
● **andar en dimes y diretes,** *fam* to quibble, bicker.
diminutivo,-a 1 *adj* diminutive. **– 2** diminutivo, m diminutive.
diminuto,-a *adj* tiny, minute.
dimisión f resignation.
● **presentar la dimisión,** to hand in one's resignation.
dimisionario,-a 1 *adj* outgoing, resigning. **– 2** m,f person who has just resigned.
dimitir 1 t to resign. **– 2** i to resign (**de,** from): *dimitió del/el cargo de presidente,* he resigned his post as president.
dimorfismo m dimorphism.
dimorfo,-a *adj* dimorphous, dimorphic.
din m *fam* money.
● **el din y el don,** money and style, money and class.

dina f dyne.
Dinamarca f Denmark.
dinamarqués,-esa *adj-m-m,f* → **danés,-esa.**
dinámica f → **dinámico,-a.**
dinámico,-a 1 *adj* dynamic. **– 2** dinámica, f dynamics.
dinamismo m dynamism.
dinamita 1 f dynamite. **2** *fig* dynamite: *esa chica es dinamita pura,* that girl is pure dynamite.
● **volar con dinamita,** to dynamite, blow up.
dinamitar t to dynamite, blow up.
dinamitero,-a 1 m,f person who blows things up with dynamite: *atentados llevados a cabo por dinamiteros del Cartel de Medellín,* bomb attacks carried out by agents of the Medellín Cartel. **– 2** *adj* dynamite: *una ola de atentados dinamiteros,* a wave of dynamite attacks.
dinamo f dynamo.
dínamo f dynamo.
dinamoeléctrico,-a *adj* dynamoelectric, dynamo-electrical.
dinamometría f dynamometry.
dinamómetro m dynamometer.
dinar m dinar.
dinastía f dynasty.
dinástico,-a *adj* dynastic.
dineral m fortune: *ese coche cuesta un dineral,* that car costs a fortune.
dinerillo m *fam* pittance, small amount of money.
dinero 1 m money. **2** (*fortuna*) wealth.
● **andar bien de dinero,** to have plenty of money. ‖ **andar mal/escaso,-a de dinero,** to be short of money. ‖ **de dinero,** wealthy, rich. ‖ **dinero llama dinero,** money makes money. ‖ **ganar dinero a espuertas,** to make a pile. ‖ **hacer dinero,** to make money. ‖ **tirar el dinero por la ventana,** to throw money down the drain.
■ **dinero contante (y sonante),** ready money, cash. ‖ **dinero (en) efectivo,** cash. ‖ **dinero en metálico,** cash. ‖ **dinero falso,** counterfeit money. ‖ **dinero negro/sucio,** dirty money. ‖ **dinero suelto,** loose change, change.
dinosaurio m dinosaur.
dintel m lintel.
diñar t *fam* to give.
● **diñarla,** *fam* to kick the bucket, snuff it.
diocesano,-a 1 *adj* diocesan. **– 2** m,f diocesan.
diócesi f → **diócesis.**
diócesis f diocese.
▲ *pl* diócesis.
diodo m diode.
dionisiaco,-a *adj* Dionysiac, Dionysian.
dionisíaco,-a *adj* Dionysiac, Dionysian.
dioptría f dioptre.
dios m god.
● **¡a Dios gracias!,** thank God! ‖ **a Dios rogando y con el mazo dando,** God helps those who help themselves. ‖ **a la buena de Dios,** at random, any old how. ‖ **¡alabado sea Dios!,** God be praised! ‖ **armar la de Dios es Cristo,** *fam* to raise hell, make an almighty racket. ‖ **¡costar algo Dios y ayuda,** to be very difficult, be a real hassle. ‖ **¡Dios dirá!,** we shall see! ‖ **Dios los cría y ellos se juntan,** birds of a feather flock together. ‖ **¡Dios le bendiga!,** God bless you! ‖ **¡Dios me libre!,** God forbid! ‖ **Dios mediante,** God willing. ‖ **¡Dios mío!,** my God!, good heavens! ‖ **¡Dios nos coja confesados!,** God help us! ‖ **hacer algo como Dios**

manda, to do sth. properly. ‖ **ni Dios,** *fam* not a soul. ‖ **¡por Dios!,** for goodness sake!, for God's sake! ‖ **que Dios me perdone, pero ...,** God forgive me, but ... ‖ **todo Dios,** *fam* everybody. ‖ **¡vaya con Dios!,** farewell!, God be with you! ‖ **¡vaya por Dios!,** good heavens!

diosa *f* goddess.

dióxido *m* dioxide.

diplejía *f* diplegia.

diplodoco *m* diplodocus.

diploma *m* diploma.

diplomacia *f* diplomacy.

diplomado,-a 1 *pp* → **diplomarse.** – 2 *adj* qualified, having a diploma. – 3 *m,f* qualified person. 4 *(universitario)* graduate.

diplomarse *p* to graduate.

diplomática *f* → **diplomático,-a.**

diplomático,-a 1 *adj* diplomatic. 2 *fig* diplomatic, tactful. – 3 *m,f* diplomat. – 4 **diplomática,** *f* diplomatics.

díptero,-a 1 *adj* ZOOL dipterous. 2 ARQ dipteral. – 3 **díptero,** *m* dipteran. – 4 **los dípteros,** *mpl* Diptera *pl.*

díptico *m* diptych.

diptongación *f* diphthongization.

diptongar *t* to diphthongize.

diptongo *m* diphthong.

diputación 1 *f (cargo de diputado)* post of deputy, *member of the Spanish Cortes.* 2 *(conjunto de diputados)* deputies *pl.*
■ **diputación provincial,** county council.

diputado,-a 1 *m,f (miembro del Congreso)* deputy, *member of the Spanish Cortes.* 2 *(miembro de una diputación)* county councillor.

dique 1 *m (muro)* dike, breakwater. 2 *fig* barrier, obstacle, check.
■ **dique de contención,** dam. ‖ **dique seco,** dry dock.

Dir. *abr (director)* director; *(abreviatura)* Dir.

dire *m fam* boss.

diré *fut* → **decir.**

dirección 1 *f (acción de dirigir)* management, running: *le han encomendado la dirección de un banco,* he has been entrusted with managing a bank. 2 *(cargo)* directorship, position of manager; *(de un partido)* leadership; *(de un colegio)* headship; *(de editorial)* position of editor. 3 *(junta)* board of directors, management. 4 *(oficina)* head office, headquarters *pl.* 5 *(sentido)* direction, way. 6 *(destino)* destination: *salió con dirección a Cádiz,* he left for Cádiz. 7 *(domicilio)* address. 8 TÉC steering. 9 *fig (orientación)* direction: *el premio que gané cambió la dirección de mi vida,* the prize I won changed my way of life.
● **llevar la dirección de algo,** to run sth., direct sth.
■ **calle de dirección única,** one-way street. ‖ **dirección asistida,** AUTO power assisted steering, power steering. ‖ **dirección general,** head office. ‖ **"dirección prohibida",** "no entry".

directa *f* → **directo,-a.**

directamente 1 *adv (en seguida)* directly, straight away. 2 *(derecho)* straight, directly: *ven directamente a casa,* come straight home. 3 *(sin intermediario)* directly: *díselo tú directamente,* tell him yourself.

directiva *f* → **directivo,-a.**

directivo,-a 1 *adj* directive, managing. – 2 *m,f* director, manager, board member. – 3 **directiva,** *f (de una empresa)* board of directors, management. 4 *(directriz)* guideline.

directo,-a 1 *adj* direct, straight. – 2 **directo,** *m* DEP straight hit. – 3 **directa,** *f* AUTO top gear.
● **en directo,** TV live.

director,-ra 1 *adj* directing, managing. – 2 *m,f* director, manager. 3 *(de colegio - hombre)* headmaster; *(mujer)* headmistress. 4 *(de universidad)* rector. 5 *(de editorial)* editor. 6 *(de cárcel)* governor. 7 *(de orquesta)* conductor.
■ **director,-ra de cine,** film director. ‖ **director,-ra de escena,** stage manager. ‖ **director espiritual,** father confessor. ‖ **director,-ra gerente,** managing director.

directorio,-a 1 *adj* directional, directive. – 2 **directorio,** *m (gobierno)* governing body. 3 *(de direcciones)* directory, guide. 4 *(normas)* instructions *pl,* directive. 5 INFORM directory.

directriz 1 *adj* guiding. – 2 *f* MAT directrix. – 3 **directrices,** *fpl* instructions.
■ **líneas directrices,** guidelines.

dirigente 1 *adj* leading, directing. – 2 *mf* leader. 3 *(de empresa)* manager.

dirigible 1 *adj* dirigible. – 2 *m* dirigible.

dirigir 1 *t (empresa)* to manage; *(negocio, escuela)* to run; *(un periódico)* to edit. 2 *(orquesta)* to conduct; *(película)* to direct; *(obra de teatro)* to direct, produce. 3 *(coche)* to drive, steer; *(barco)* to steer; *(avión)* to pilot. 4 *(un partido)* to lead; *(expedición, revuelta)* to head; *(negociaciones)* to conduct. 5 *(carta, protesta)* to address; *(consejos)* to aim; *(esfuerzos, atención)* to concentrate. 6 *(apuntar - arma, telescopio)* to direct, aim, point; *(- mirada)* to turn: *dirigió la mirada hacia abajo,* she looked down; *dirigió sus pasos hacia la puerta,* he walked towards the door. – 7 **dirigirse,** *p (ir)* to go (**a,** to), make one's way (**a,** to), make (**a,** for): *nos dirigimos al cine,* we made our way to the cinema. 8 *(hablar)* to address (**a,** -), speak (**a,** to): *se dirigió a su padre,* she addressed her father. 9 *(escribir)* to write: *si quiere más información diríjase a esta dirección,* if you want further information write to this address.
▲ *Conjugation model* [6].

dirigismo *m* state control.

dirimente 1 *adj (que anula)* nullifying. 2 *(que acaba)* decisive, final.

dirimir 1 *t (anular)* to annul, nullify, declare void. 2 *(resolver)* to solve, end.

discernimiento *m* discernment, judgement.

discernir *t* to discern, distinguish, tell: *disernir el cristal del vidrio,* to distinguish between crystal and glass.
▲ *Conjugation model* [29].

disciplina 1 *f (conjunto de reglas)* discipline. 2 *(doctrina)* doctrine. 3 *(asignatura)* subject. 4 *(azote)* scourge, discipline.

disciplinadamente *adv* with discipline.

disciplinado,-a *adj* disciplined.

disciplinar 1 *t (imponer disciplina)* to discipline. 2 *(enseñar)* to instruct, teach.

disciplinario,-a *adj* disciplinary.

discípulo,-a 1 *m,f (seguidor)* disciple, follower. 2 *(alumno)* pupil, student.

disc-jockey *mf* disc jockey, DJ.
▲ *pl* disc jockey *or* disc jockeys.

discman *m* discman.

disco 1 *m* disc. 2 DEP discus. 3 *(de música)* record. 4 INFORM disk.
■ **disco duro,** hard disk.

discóbolo *m* discus thrower, discobolus.

discografía *f (lista)* discography; *(conjunto)* records *pl.*

discográfica *f* → **discográfico,-a.**

discográfico,-a 1 *adj* record. – 2 **discográfica,** *f* record company.
■ **casa discográfica,** record company.

discoidal *adj* discoid, discoidal.
discoideo *adj* discoid, discoidal.
díscolo,-a *adj* ungovernable, disobedient, unruly.
disconforme *adj* in disagreement, not in agreement: *estoy disconforme contigo,* I disagree with you, I don't agree with you.
disconformidad *f* disagreement, disconformity.
discontinuar *t* to discontinue.
discontinuidad *f* discontinuity, lack of continuity.
discontinuo,-a *adj* discontinuous.
■ línea discontinua, *(en carretera)* broken white line.
discordancia 1 *f* *(disconformidad)* disagreement, conflict. 2 *(diversidad)* difference, divergence. 3 *(de estilo, color)* clash. 4 MÚS dissonance, discordance.
discordante 1 *adj* *(en desacuerdo)* discordant, conflicting. 2 *(diferente)* divergent, differing. 3 *(estilo, color)* clashing. 4 MÚS dissonant, discordant.
● dar la nota discordante / ser la nota discordante, *fig* to clash, hold a conflicting opinion: *a todos les pareció bien menos a él que siempre tenía que dar la nota discordante,* it seemed fine to everyone except him, who always had to be different.
discordar 1 *i* *(no convenir)* to disagree, not to agree. 2 *(diferir)* to differ. 3 MÚS to be dissonant, be discordant.
discorde 1 *adj* *(en desacuerdo)* in disagreement. 2 *(diferente)* differing. 3 MÚS dissonant.
discordia *f* discord.
● ser el tercero en discordia, to be awkward, complicate things.
■ manzana de la discordia, bone of contention.
discoteca 1 *f* *(local)* discotheque, nightclub. 2 *(colección de discos)* record collection, record library.
discotequero,-a *adj fam* disco: *es muy discotequera,* she loves going to discos.
discreción 1 *f* *(sensatez)* discretion, tact. 2 *(agudeza)* wit.
● a discreción, *(a voluntad)* at one's discretion; *(sin límite)* in great amounts: *cada uno tomará a discreción la herramienta que crea más adecuada,* it will be left to one's own discretion to choose a suitable tool; *nos dieron pasteles a discreción,* they gave us an endless supply of cakes.
discrecional *adj* optional.
■ servicio discrecional, *(autobuses)* special bus service.
discrecionalmente *adv* at one's discretion.
discrepancia 1 *f* *(diferencia)* discrepancy. 2 *(desacuerdo)* dissent, disagreement.
discrepante 1 *adj* *(diferente)* discrepant. 2 *(en desacuerdo)* differing, dissenting.
discrepar 1 *i* *(diferenciarse)* to differ *(de,* from): *esta pieza discrepa de la otra en diez gramos,* this piece differs from the other by ten grams. 2 *(disentir)* to disagree *(de,* with): *discrepó de su padre,* she disagreed with her father.
discreto,-a 1 *adj* *(prudente)* discreet, prudent, tactful. 2 *(sobrio)* sober, discreet: *llevaba un traje negro muy discreto,* she wore a very discreet black dress. 3 *(moderado)* moderate, average, reasonable: *sus resultados fueron discretos,* her results were average. – 4 *m,f* discreet person.
discriminación *f* discrimination.
■ discriminación racial, racial discrimination.
discriminar 1 *t* *(diferenciar)* to discriminate, distinguish. 2 *(por raza, religión, etc)* to discriminate against: *nos discriminaron porque éramos extranjeros,* we were discriminated against because we were foreigners.

discriminatorio,-a *adj* discriminatory.
discromía *f* dyschroa, dyschroia.
disculpa *f* excuse, apology.
● dar disculpas, to make excuses. ‖ pedir disculpas a algn., to apologize to sb.
disculpable *adj* excusable, forgivable.
disculpar 1 *t* *(descargar de culpa)* to excuse: *su enfermedad le disculpa,* his illness excuses him. 2 *(perdonar)* to excuse, forgive: *espero que ustedes sabrán comprender y disculpar a mi amigo,* I hope you will understand and forgive my friend; *¡disculpe!,* excuse me! – 3 disculparse, *p* to apologize *(por,* for), excuse os.: *se disculpó por haber mentido,* she apologized for having lied.
discurrir 1 *i* *(andar)* to walk, wander. 2 *(fluir)* to flow, run: *el río discurría despacio,* the river flowed slowly. 3 *(transcurrir)* to pass, go by: *los días discurren tranquilos,* the days go by peacefully. 4 *fig* *(reflexionar)* to think *(sobre,* about), ponder *(sobre,* on/over), meditate *(sobre,* on): *solía discurrir sobre la esencia del mundo,* she used to ponder on the essence of the world. – 5 *t* *(idear)* to invent, think up.
discursivo,-a *adj* discursive.
discurso 1 *m* *(conferencia)* speech, lecture, discourse. 2 *(razonamiento)* reasoning. 3 *(escrito, tratado)* discourse, dissertation. 4 *(expresión de lo que se piensa)* discourse: *he perdido el hilo del discurso,* I've lost my train of thought. 5 *(del tiempo)* passing, passage: *el lento discurso de las horas,* the slow passage of time.
discusión 1 *f* *(charla)* discussion. 2 *(disputa)* argument.
● tener una discusión, to argue, have an argument, quarrel.
discutible *adj* debatable, questionable.
discutido,-a 1 *pp* → discutir. – 2 *adj* controversial.
discutir 1 *t* *(examinar)* to discuss: *tenemos que discutir el modo de hacerlo,* we have to discuss how to go about it. 2 *(contender)* to dispute, question, argue: *discutieron el precio,* they argued over the price. – 3 *i* *(examinar)* to discuss *(de,* -): *discutieron de fútbol,* they talked about football. 4 *(contender)* to argue: *los niños discutieron por la bicicleta,* the boys argued over the bicycle.
disecación *f* dissection.
disecar 1 *t* *(dividir en partes)* to dissect. 2 *(rellenar animales)* to stuff. 3 *(planta)* to dry. 4 *fig* to dissect.
▲ *Conjugation model* [1], *like* sacar.
disección *f* → disecación.
diseminación *f* dissemination, spreading.
diseminar 1 *t* to disseminate, scatter, spread. – 2 diseminarse, *p* to spread.
disensión 1 *f* dissension, disagreement. 2 *fig* quarrel.
disentería *f* dysentery.
disentimiento *m* dissent, disagreement.
disentir *i* to dissent, disagree *(de,* with): *disiento de usted en las ideas fundamentales,* I disagree with you on the main points.
▲ *Conjugation model* [35], *like* hervir.
diseñador,-ra *m,f* designer.
diseñar *t* to design.
diseño 1 *m* design. 2 *(descripción con palabras)* description.
disertación *f* dissertation, discourse.
disertar *t* to discourse *(sobre,* on/upon), lecture *(sobre,* on).
diserto,-a *adj* fluent, eloquent.
disfasia *f* dysphasia.
disforme *adj* deformed.
disfraz 1 *m* *(para engañar)* disguise. 2 *(para una fiesta etc)* fancy dress outfit, fancy dress costume. 3 *fig* *(simulación)* simulation, pretence (US pretense).

● **bajo el disfraz de,** *fig* under the guise of, under the pretence of. ‖ **sin disfraz,** plainly.
■ **baile de disfraces,** fancy dress ball, (US costume ball).

disfrazar 1 *t* (*persona*) to disguise, dress up. 2 (*emoción*) hide, conceal; (*voz*) disguise. – 3 **disfrazarse,** *p* (*para engañar*) to disguise os. (**de,** as). 4 (*para una fiesta etc*) to dress up (**de,** as): *se disfrazó de payaso,* he dressed up as a clown.
▲ Conjugation model |4|, *like realizar.*

disfrutar 1 *t* (*poseer*) to own, enjoy, possess; (*pensión, renta*) to receive: *Pepe disfruta las fincas de sus padres,* Pepe owns his parents' properties. 2 (*aprovechar*) to make the most of. – 3 *i* (*poseer*) to enjoy (**de,** -), have (**de,** -), possess (**de,** -): *disfruta de buena salud,* he enjoys good health; *el caballero disfrutaba de excelente fama en la ciudad,* the gentleman had an excellent reputation in the city. 4 (*gozar*) to enjoy, enjoy os.: *disfuta con el café,* she enjoys coffee; *disfruté mucho en el cine,* I enjoyed myself very much at the cinema; *disfruta haciéndome preguntas,* she enjoys asking me questions.

disfrute 1 *m* (*aprovechamiento*) benefit. 2 (*goce*) enjoyment.

disfunción *f* dysfunction.

disgregación 1 *f* (*separación*) disintegration. 2 (*dispersión*) break-up.

disgregar 1 *t* (*separar*) to disintegrate. 2 (*dispersar*) to disperse, break up.
▲ Conjugation model |7|, *like llegar.*

disgustado,-a 1 *pp* → **disgustar**. – 2 *adj* angry, displeased, upset.

disgustar 1 *t* (*molestar*) to displease, annoy, upset: *me disgusta mucho tu actitud,* your attitude upsets me. 2 (*desagradar*) to dislike: *me disgusta ese sabor dulce,* I don't like that sweet taste. – 3 **disgustarse,** *p* (*enfadarse*) to get angry, get upset: *se disgustó con nosotros por no poder ir al teatro,* she got angry with us because she couldn't go to the theatre. 4 (*pelearse*) to quarrel (**con,** with).

disgusto 1 *m* (*enfado*) displeasure, annoyance, anger. 2 (*desgracia*) misfortune, problem: *sus padres han tenido varios disgustos,* her parents have had their share of misfortunes. 3 *fig* (*pesadumbre*) sorrow, grief, pain: *aquel accidente le produjo gran disgusto,* that road accident upset her tremendously. 4 *fig* (*pelea*) argument, quarrel. ● **a disgusto,** against one's will, reluctantly, unwillingly. ‖ **dar un disgusto,** to upset. ‖ **llevarse un disgusto,** to get upset. ‖ **sentirse/estar/hallarse a disgusto,** to feel ill at ease.

disidencia *f* dissidence, disagreement.

disidente 1 *adj* dissident. – 2 *mf* dissident.

disidir *i* to dissent.

disimétrico,-a *adj* dissymmetric, dissymmetrical.

disimilar *t* to dissimilate.

disimulación *f* pretence (US pretense), dissemblance.

disimuladamente 1 *adv* (*furtivamente*) without being seen, furtively. 2 (*astutamente*) craftily.

disimulado,-a 1 *pp* → **disimular**. – 2 *adj* (*oculto*) hidden, concealed. 3 (*persona*) sly, crafty. ● **hacerse el/la disimulado,-a,** to act dumb.

disimular 1 *t* (*ocultar*) to hide, conceal: *no sabía cómo disimular su miedo,* he couldn't hide his fear. 2 (*disculpar*) to excuse, overlook: *la madre disimulaba las travesuras del hijo,* the mother overlooked her son's naughtiness. 3 (*disfrazar*) to disguise, hide. – 4 *i* to pretend, dissemble: *no disimules,* stop pretending.

disimulo *m* pretence (US pretense), dissemblance.

disipación *f* dissipation.

disipado,-a 1 *pp* → **disipar**. – 2 *adj* dissipated, wasted, debauched. ■ **vida disipada,** life of debauchery.

disipar 1 *t* (*desvanecer*) to disperse, dissipate: *el sol disipa la niebla,* the sun disperses the fog. 2 (*derrochar*) to squander, dissipate. 3 *fig* (*dudas, temores*) to dispel; (*esperanzas*) to destroy; (*sospechas*) to allay. – 4 **disiparse,** *p* (*desvanecerse*) to clear, disperse, dissipate. 5 (*evaporarse*) to evaporate. 6 *fig* to vanish, be dispelled.

dislate *m* absurdity, nonsense.

dislexia *f* dyslexia.

disléxico,-a 1 *adj* dyslexic. – 2 *m,f* dyslexic person.

dislocación 1 *f* (*de huesos*) dislocation. 2 *fig* dismembering.

dislocar 1 *t* (*sacar de lugar*) to dislocate. 2 (*dispersar*) to disperse. 3 *fig* (*desmembrar*) to dismember.
▲ Conjugation model |1|, *like sacar.*

disloque *m fam* last straw, end.

disminución *f* decrease, reduction. ● **ir en disminución,** to diminish, decrease.

disminuido,-a 1 *pp* → **disminuir**. – 2 *adj* disabled. – 3 *m,f* disabled person. – 4 **los disminuidos,** *mpl* the disabled.

disminuir 1 *t* (*gen*) to decrease. 2 (*medidas, velocidad*) to reduce. – 3 *i* (*gen*) to diminish. 4 (*temperatura, precios*) to drop, fall.
▲ Conjugation model |62|, *like huir.*

disociable *adj* dissociable.

disociación *f* dissociation.

disociar *t* to dissociate.
▲ Conjugation model |12|, *like cambiar.*

disolubilidad *f* solubility.

disoluble *adj* soluble, dissoluble.

disolución 1 *f* (*gen*) dissolution. 2 (*anulación*) invalidation. 3 *fig* (*relajación*) looseness, dissoluteness. 4 QUÍM solution, dissolution.

disoluto,-a 1 *adj* dissolute. – 2 *m,f* dissolute person, libertine, debauchee.

disolvente 1 *adj* solvent, dissolvent. – 2 *m* solvent, dissolvent.

disolver 1 *t* (*gen*) to dissolve. 2 (*anular*) to annul. 3 (*destruir*) to destroy: *la muerte disuelve todas las cosas,* death destroys everything. 4 *fig* (*manifestación etc*) to break up. – 5 **disolverse,** *p* (*gen*) to dissolve. 6 *fig* to be dissolved.
▲ Conjugation model |32|, *like mover, pp disuelto,-a.*

disonancia 1 *f* MÚS dissonance. 2 *fig* disharmony, dissonance.

disonante 1 *adj* MÚS dissonant, discordant. 2 *fig* discordant.

disonar 1 *i* MÚS to be dissonant, be discordant. 2 *fig* (*discrepar*) to disagree.
▲ Conjugation model |31|, *like contar.*

dispar *adj* unlike, different, disparate.

disparadero *m* trigger. ● **poner a algn. en el disparadero,** *fam* to force sb. into a corner, put sb. on the spot.

disparado,-a *adj fam* in a hurry: *salió disparado de casa,* he rushed out of the house.

disparador 1 *m* (*de arma*) trigger. 2 (*de cámara*) shutter release. 3 (*de reloj*) escapement.

disparar 1 *t* (*arma*) to fire; (*bala, flecha*) to shoot: *disparar un tiro,* to fire a shot. 2 (*lanzar*) to hurl, throw: *disparar una piedra,* to throw a stone. 3 DEP to shoot. – 4 *i fig* (*disparatar*) to talk nonsense. – **5 dispararse,** *p* (*arma*) to go off, fire; (*despertador*) to go off. **6** *fig* (*correr*) to dash off, rush off. **7** *fig* (*precios*) to shoot up. **8** *fig* (*saltar fuera de razón*) to blow up, explode: *estaba tan enfadado que se disparó en cuanto le dirigieron la palabra,* he was so angry that he simply blew up when they spoke to him.

disparatado,-a 1 *pp* → **disparatar.** – **2** *adj* absurd, foolish, ridiculous.

disparatar 1 *i* (*decir*) to talk nonsense. **2** (*hacer*) to act foolishly.

disparate 1 *m* (*hecho*) foolish act, silly thing: *has cometido un disparate,* you did something foolish. **2** (*dicho*) nonsense: *no digas disparates,* don't talk nonsense. **3** (*error*) blunder, mistake: *el examen estaba lleno de disparates,* the exam was full of mistakes. **4** *fam* (*barbaridad*) ridiculous amount: *pidieron un disparate por la casa,* they asked a ridiculous amount for the house.

disparejo,-a *adj* different, unequal, uneven.

disparidad *f* disparity, difference.

disparo 1 *m* (*acción*) firing. **2** (*efecto*) shot: *en la pared se veían dos disparos,* two bullet marks could be seen in the wall. **3** DEP shot.

dispendio *m* squandering, waste.

dispensa *f* dispensation, exemption.

dispensar 1 *t* (*conceder*) to give, grant; (*elogios*) to confer. **2** (*medicamentos*) to dispense. **3** (*eximir*) to exempt, free: *lo dispensaron del servicio militar,* he was exempted from doing military service. **4** (*disculpar*) to forgive, pardon: *dispénsenos por el error,* forgive us for the mistake.
● dispense, excuse me, pardon me.

dispensario *m* dispensary, clinic.

dispersar 1 *t* (*gen*) to disperse, scatter. **2** (*manifestantes*) to break up. **3** *fig* (*esfuerzos, atención, etc*) to spread, divide. **4** MIL to disperse, rout. – **5 dispersarse,** *p* (*gen*) to disperse, scatter. **6** (*manifestantes*) to disperse, break up. **7** MIL to spread out.

dispersión *f* (*separación*) dispersion; (*esparcimiento*) scattering.

disperso,-a *adj* (*separado*) dispersed; (*esparcido*) scattered.

displasia *f* dysplasia.

display *m* display.

displicencia 1 *f* (*indiferencia en el trato*) coolness, indifference. **2** (*desaliento*) discouragement.

displicente 1 *adj* (*indiferente*) indifferent; (*que desagrada*) awkward, unpleasant. **2** (*descontento*) unhappy, discontented. – **3** *mf* discontent.

disponer 1 *t* (*colocar*) to dispose, arrange, set out. **2** (*preparar*) to prepare, get ready: *dispondremos la habitación,* we'll get the room ready. **3** (*ordenar*) to order, decree. **4** JUR to provide, stipulate: *la ley lo dispone,* the law stipulates it. – **5** *i* (*tener*) to have (**de,** -): *todas las habitaciones disponen de aire acondicionado,* all the rooms are equipped with air conditioning; *no disponemos de tiempo,* we haven't got time. **6** (*hacer uso*) to make use (**de,** of), have the use (**de,** of): *dispuso de su dinero,* he made use of his money. – **7 disponerse,** *p* (*prepararse*) to get ready (**a,** to), prepare (**a,** to): *me dispongo a salir,* I'm getting ready to go out.
▲ *Conjugation model* [78], *like* **poner,** *pp* **dispuesto,-a.**

disponibilidad 1 *f* availability. **2** (*dinero*) financial assets *pl*, available funds *pl*; (*mercancía*) available stock.
▲ *In 2, also used in plural with the same meaning.*

disponible 1 *adj* (*gen*) available: *no podrás ver a Lucía esta tarde, no está disponible,* you won't be able to see

Lucía this afternoon, she's busy. **2** (*tiempo*) spare, free. **3** (*a mano*) on hand.

disposición 1 *f* (*capacidad*) disposal. **2** (*estado de ánimo*) disposition, frame of mind. **3** (*colocación*) arrangement, layout. **4** (*aptitud*) aptitude, talent, gift. **5** JUR order, regulation.
● a la disposición de, at the disposal of. ‖ a su disposición, at your disposal, at your service. ‖ estar en disposición de, to be ready to, be in a state to: *Paco aún no está en disposición de ir a trabajar,* Paco isn't ready to go to work yet.
■ disposiciones legales, statutory provisions.

dispositivo *m* device, gadget.

dispuesto,-a 1 *pp* → **disponer.** – **2** *adj* (*decidido*) determined: *estamos dispuestos a ir,* we are determined to go. **3** (*preparado*) prepared, ready, willing. **4** (*arreglado*) arranged, settled, ready: *está todo dispuesto,* everything is set. **5** (*despabilado*) bright, clever, capable. **6** (*servicial*) helpful.

disputa 1 *f* (*discusión*) dispute, argument, quarrel. **2** (*enfrentamiento*) clash, struggle.
● sin disputa, without dispute. ‖ tener una disputa, to quarrel.

disputar 1 *i* (*discutir*) to dispute, argue: *disputaron por una tontería,* they argued over something stupid. – **2** *t* (*competir*) to compete for, contend for. **3** DEP to play: *los equipos disputaron un partido amistoso,* the teams played a friendly match. – **4 disputarse,** *p* (*competir*) to compete for, contend for: *los dos amigos se disputan la misma plaza,* both friends are contending for the same post. **5** DEP to be played: *mañana se disputa la final,* the final will be played tomorrow, tomorrow is the final.

disquete *m* diskette, floppy disk.

disquetera *f* disk drive.

disquisición 1 *f* disquisition. – **2 disquisiciones,** *fpl* digressions.

distancia 1 *f* distance: *a tres metros de distancia,* at a distance of three metres. **2** *fig* (*diferencia*) difference, gap.
● a distancia, from a distance: *lo vimos a distancia,* we saw it from a distance. ‖ acortar distancias, to bridge the gap. ‖ guardar las distancias, to keep one's distance.
■ distancia de seguridad, AUTO safety distance. ‖ distancia focal, focal length.

distanciado,-a 1 *pp* → **distanciar.** – **2** *adj* distant, separated.

distanciamiento *m* distancing, separation: *he notado cierto distanciamiento entre ellos,* I don't think they're as close as they used to be.

distanciar 1 *t* to distance, separate. – **2 distanciarse,** *p* to move away, become separated. **3** *fig* (*no tratarse*) to grow apart, drift apart: *se ha distanciado mucho de sus amigos,* he's grown apart from his friends. **4** *fig* (*desvincularse*) to distance os, disassociate os.
▲ *Conjugation model* [12], *like* **cambiar.**

distante 1 *adj* (*en el espacio*) distant, far; (*en el tiempo*) distant, remote. **2** *fig* distant.

distar 1 *i* to be distant, be away: *ambas casas distan cuatro kilómetros entre sí,* the houses are four kilometres apart. **2** (*ser diferente*) to be different: *Juan y Pedro no se entienden porque sus gustos distan mucho,* Juan and Pedro don't get on well with each other because they have very different tastes.
● distar mucho de, *fig* to be far from: *eso dista mucho de ser cierto,* that's far from being true.

distender 1 *t* (*aflojar*) to loosen. **2** MED to strain, pull. **3** *fig* to ease: *distender las relaciones entre países ene-*

migos, to ease the relations between enemy countries. **– 4 distenderse,** *p (aflojarse)* to slacken. **5** MED to be strained. **6** *fig* to ease.
▲ *Conjugation model* |28|, *like* ***entender.***

distensión I *f (acción)* slackening. **2** MED strain. **3** *fig* easing. **4** POL détente.

distinción I *f (gen)* distinction. **2** *(elegancia)* distinction, elegance, refinement. **3** *(deferencia)* deference, respect, consideration.
● **a distinción de,** unlike, in contrast to. ‖ **hacer una distinción con algn.,** to treat sb. with deference. ‖ **sin distinción de,** irrespective of: *la ley se aplicará sin distinción de razas,* the law will apply regardless of race.

distingo *m* distinction.

distinguido,-a I *pp* → ***distinguir.*** **– 2** *adj* distinguished. **3** *(elegante)* elegant.

distinguir I *t (diferenciar)* to distinguish: *no distinguió el vino bueno del malo,* he couldn't tell the difference between good wine and bad, he couldn't tell good wine from bad. **2** *(caracterizar)* to mark, distinguish. **3** *(ver)* to see, make out. **4** *(preferir)* to single out. **5** *(honrar)* to honour (US honor): *distinguieron al soldado con una cruz,* the soldier was honoured with a cross. **– 6** **distinguirse,** *p (destacar)* to stand out, distinguish os. **7** *(diferenciarse)* to differ (**por,** in), be distinguished: *se distinguen por el color,* they differ in colour. **8** *(ser visible)* to be visible; *(ser audible)* to be audible.
▲ *Conjugation model* |8|.

distintivo,-a I *adj* distinctive, distinguishing. **– 2** distintivo, *m (insignia)* badge, emblem; *(marca)* mark.
■ **rasgo distintivo,** characteristic feature.

distinto,-a I *adj (diferente)* different. **2** *(claro)* distinct. **3** distintos,-as, various, several: *hay distintas maneras de hacerlo,* there are various ways of doing it.

distorsión *f* distortion.

distorsionar *t* to distort.

distracción I *f (divertimiento)* amusement, pastime, recreation, entertainment: *su principal distracción es hacer punto,* knitting is her favourite pastime; *la ciudad tiene muchas distracciones,* the city offers many forms of entertainment. **2** *(despiste)* distraction, absent-mindedness. **3** *(error)* oversight, slip.

distraer I *t (divertir)* to amuse, entertain. **2** *(atención)* to distract; *(pena, dolor, preocupaciones)* to take one's mind off. **3** *euf (dinero)* to embezzle. **– 4 distraerse,** *p (divertirse)* to amuse os., enjoy os. **5** *(entretenerse)* to relax, pass the time: *se distrajo leyendo,* she passed the time reading. **6** *(despistarse)* to get distracted, be inattentive, be absent-minded.
▲ *Conjugation model* |88|, *like* ***traer.***

distraído,-a I *pp* → ***distraer.*** **– 2** *adj (desatento)* absent-minded. **3** *(entretenido)* entertaining, fun. **– 4** *m.f* absent-minded person.
● **hacerse el/la distraído,-a,** to pretend not to notice.

distribución I *f* distribution. **2** *(colocación)* arrangement. **3** *(reparto)* delivery. **4** *(disposición de una casa etc)* layout.

distribuidor,-ra I *adj* distributing, distributive. **– 2** *m.f* distributor. **3** COM wholesaler. **– 4 distribuidor,** *m* AUTO distributor.

distribuir I *t (repartir)* to distribute. **2** *(correo)* to deliver; *(trabajo)* to share, allot; *(agua, gas, etc)* to supply. **3** *(un piso)* to lay out. **4** *(colocar)* to arrange, place: *he distribuido todo en el armario,* I've placed everything in the cupboard.
▲ *Conjugation model* |62|, *like* ***huir.***

distributivo,-a *adj* distributive.

distrito *m* district.
■ **distrito postal,** postal district.

distrofia *f* dystrophy.

disturbar *t* to disturb.

disturbio *m* disturbance, riot.

disuadir *t* to dissuade (**de,** from).

disuasión *f* dissuasion.

disuasivo,-a *adj* dissuasive, deterrent.

disuasorio,-a *adj* dissuasive, deterrent.

disuelto,-a *pp* → ***disolver.***

disyunción *f* disjunction.

disyuntiva *f* → ***disyuntivo,-a.***

disyuntivo,-a I *adj* disjunctive. **– 2** disyuntiva, *f* alternative.

ditirambo *m* dithyramb.

DIU *abr* MED *(dispositivo intrauterino)* intrauterine device; *(abreviatura)* IUD.

diuresis *f* diuresis.
▲ *pl* diuresis.

diurético,-a I *adj* diuretic. **– 2** diurético, *m* diuretic.

diurno,-a *adj* daily, daytime.

diva *f* → ***divo,-a.***

divagación *f* digression.

divagar *i* to digress, ramble.
▲ *Conjugation model* |7|, *like* ***llegar.***

diván *m* divan, couch.

díver *adj fam* great fun.
▲ *pl* díver.

divergencia *f* divergence.
■ **divergencia de opiniones,** diverging opinions *pl.*

divergente *adj* divergent, diverging.

divergir *i* to diverge.
▲ *Conjugation model* |6|, *like* ***dirigir.***

diversidad *f* diversity, variety.

diversificación *f* diversification.

diversificar I *t* to diversify, vary. **– 2 diversificarse,** *p* to be diversified, diversify.
▲ *Conjugation model* |1|, *like* ***sacar.***

diversión *f* fun, amusement, entertainment: *en este pueblo hay pocas diversiones,* there's not much to do in this village.

diverso,-a I *adj* different. **2** diversos,-as, several, various.

divertido,-a I *pp* → ***divertir.*** **– 2** *adj (gracioso)* funny, amusing. **3** *(entretenido)* fun, entertaining, enjoyable.

divertimento *m* MÚS divertimento.

divertimiento I *m (entretenimiento)* amusement, fun, entertainment. **2** MÚS divertimento.

divertir I *t* to amuse, entertain. **– 2 divertirse,** *p* to enjoy os., have a good time: *¡diviértete!,* enjoy yourself!; *lo hice por divertirme,* I did it for fun.
▲ *Conjugation model* |35|, *like* ***hervir.***

dividendo *m* dividend.

dividir I *t* to divide: *dividir 4 entre 2,* to divide 4 by 2. **2** *(separar)* to divide, separate: *el río divide las dos comarcas,* the river separates the two counties. **3** *(repartir)* to divide, split: *el hombre dividió la herencia entre sus hijos,* the man divided the inheritance between his children. **– 4 dividirse,** *p (separarse)* to divide, split up.
● **divide y vencerás,** divide and conquer, divide and rule.

divieso *m* boil.

divinamente *adv* divinely, wonderfully.

divinidad I *f* divinity, God. **2** *(deidad pagana)* deity. **3** *(maravilla)* delight, wonderful thing.

● **¡es una divinidad!,** *fam* it's (*he's, she's*) gorgeous!
divinización *f* deification.
divinizar *t* to deify.
▲ *Conjugation model* [4], *like realizar.*
divino,-a 1 *adj* divine. 2 *fam* (*bonito*) beautiful, gorgeous; (*extraordinario*) wonderful, fantastic.
divisa 1 *f* (*emblema*) badge, emblem. 2 (*en heráldica*) device. 3 (*moneda*) currency, foreign currency: *diez mil pesetas en divisas,* ten thousand pesetas in foreign currency.
divisar *t* to discern, make out, distinguish.
divisibilidad *f* divisibility.
divisible 1 *adj* dividable. 2 MAT divisible.
división 1 *f* division. 2 *fig* division, divergence: *hay división de opiniones,* there's a divergence of opinion.
■ **división acorazada/blindada,** MIL armoured (US armored) division. ‖ **división de honor,** DEP league of honour (US honor). ‖ **primera/segunda división,** DEP first/second division.
divisor,-ra 1 *adj* dividing. – 2 **divisor,** *m* divider. 3 MAT divisor.
■ **máximo común divisor,** MAT highest common factor, (US highest common denominator). ‖ **mínimo común divisor,** MAT lowest common factor, (US lowest common denominator).
divisorio,-a *adj* dividing.
divo,-a 1 *m,f* star. – 2 **diva,** *f* MÚS prima donna, diva.
divorciado,-a 1 *pp* → **divorciar.** – 2 *adj* divorced. – 3 *m,f* (*hombre*) divorcé; (*mujer*) divorcée.
divorciar 1 *t* to divorce. – 2 **divorciarse,** *p* to get divorced (**de,** from): *se divorció de ella,* he divorced her, he got a divorce from her.
▲ *Conjugation model* [12], *like cambiar.*
divorcio 1 *m* divorce. 2 *fig* discrepancy: *cada vez es más manifiesto su divorcio de opiniones,* their discrepancy is increasingly noticeable.
divulgación 1 *f* (*difusión*) spreading. 2 (*de conocimientos*) popularization.
divulgador,-ra 1 *adj* divulging, revealing. – 2 *m,f* popularizer.
divulgar 1 *t* (*difundir*) to divulge, spread, disclose. 2 (*por radio*) to broadcast. 3 (*propagar*) to popularize. – 4 **divulgarse,** *p* to become known, spread.
▲ *Conjugation model* [7], *like llegar.*
Djibouti *m* Djibouti, Jibouti.
Djibuti *m* Djibouti, Jibouti.
dl *sím* (*decilitro*) decilitre (US deciliter); (*símbolo*) dl.
Dl *sím* (*decalitro*) decalitre (US decaliter); (*símbolo*) Dl.
D.L. *abr* (*depósito legal*) legal deposit, bond.
dm *sím* (*decímetro*) decimetre (US decimeter); (*símbolo*) dm.
Dm *sím* (*decámetro*) decametre (US decameter); (*símbolo*) Dm.
D.m. *abr* (*Dios mediante*) God willing.
DNI *abr* (*Documento Nacional de Identidad*) Identity Card; (*abreviatura*) ID card.
do *m* (*de solfa*) doh, do; (*de escala diatónica*) C.
● **dar el do de pecho,** *fam fig* to surpass os.
■ **do de pecho,** high C.
doberman *m* Doberman (pinscher).
dobladillo 1 *m* (*de vestido etc*) hem. 2 (*de pantalones*) turn-up, US cuff.
doblado,-a 1 *pp* → **doblar.** – 2 *adj* (*mediana estatura y recio*) thick-set. 3 (*curvo*) bent. 4 (*película*) dubbed. 5 *fam* (*agotado*) dead beat.
doblaje *m* dubbing.

doblar 1 *t* (*duplicar*) to double: *le doblo la edad,* I'm twice as old as she is. 2 (*plegar*) to fold: *doblar en cuatro,* to fold in four. 3 (*torcer*) to bend: *doblar un dedo,* to bend a finger. 4 (*esquina*) to turn, go round. 5 (*película*) to dub. 6 (*a un actor*) to stand in (**a,** for), double (**a,** for): *una bailarina la dobla en esa escena,* a dancer stands in for her in that scene. – 7 *i* (*girar*) to turn: *doblar a la derecha,* to turn right. 8 (*campana*) to toll. 9 CINEM to play two parts, double. – 10 **doblarse,** *p* (*plegarse*) to fold. 11 (*torcerse*) to bend. 12 (*rendirse*) to give in.
doble 1 *adj* double. 2 (*nacionalidad*) dual. 3 (*fuerte*) thick: *franela doble,* thick flannel. 4 (*fornido*) thick-set. 5 *fig* (*engañoso*) two-faced. – 6 *m* double: *tiene el doble que yo,* he's got twice as much as I have. 7 (*duplicado*) duplicate. 8 (*dobladillo*) hem. 9 (*de campana*) toll. – 10 *m,f* CINEM stand-in, double; (*hombre*) stunt man; (*mujer*) stunt woman. – 11 *adv* double. – 12 **dobles,** *mpl* (*tenis*) doubles: *dobles femeninos,* ladies' doubles.
● **ver doble,** to see double.
doblegar 1 *t* (*doblar*) to bend, fold. 2 (*vencer*) to force to yield, subdue. – 3 **doblegarse,** *p* (*inclinarse*) to bend over, stoop. 4 (*rendirse*) to give in.
▲ *Conjugation model* [7], *like llegar.*
doblemente 1 *adv* doubly: *su hermano es doblemente imbécil,* his brother is twice as stupid. 2 *fig* deceitfully.
doblete 1 *m* (*gen*) double. 2 (*serie de victorias*) series of wins, run of wins. 3 LING doublet. – 4 *adj* medium.
● **hacer doblete,** (*gen*) to do something twice; (*en espectáculo*) to come on twice, appear twice; (*en deporte*) to do the double.
doblez 1 *m* (*pliegue*) fold. – 2 *m & f fig* (*duplicidad*) duplicity, deceitfulness, two-facedness.
doblón *m* doubloon.
doc.¹ *abr* (*documento*) document; (*abreviatura*) doc.
doc.² *abr* (*docena*) dozen; (*abreviatura*) doz.
doce 1 *adj* (*cardinal*) twelve; (*ordinal*) twelfth. – 2 *m* (*número*) twelve. 3 (*fecha*) twelfth.
▲ *See also seis.*
doceavo,-a 1 *adj* twelfth. – 2 *m,f* twelfth.
▲ *See also sexto,-a.*
docena *f* dozen: *una docena de manzanas,* a dozen apples; *vinieron a docenas,* they came in dozens.
● **a docenas,** COM by the dozen.
■ **la docena del fraile,** *fig* a baker's dozen.
docencia *f* teaching.
docente 1 *adj* teaching. – 2 *mf* teacher.
■ **centro docente,** educational centre (US center). ‖ **personal docente,** teaching staff.
dócil *adj* docile, obedient.
docilidad *f* docility, obedience.
dock 1 *m* (*dársena*) dock. – 2 **docks,** *mpl* (*almacenes*) warehouse *sing.*
▲ *pl* docks.
doctamente *adv* learnedly.
docto,-a 1 *adj* learned: *es docto en matemáticas,* he's well versed in mathematics. – 2 *m,f* learned person, expert.
doctor,-ra *m,f* doctor: *es doctor en físicas,* he's a doctor of physics.
■ **doctor,-ra honoris causa,** honorary doctor.
doctorado *m* doctorate, PhD.
doctoral 1 *adj* doctoral. 2 *fam* (*pedante*) pedantic, pompous.
doctorando,-a *m,f* doctoral student, doctoral candidate, PhD student.
doctorar 1 *t* to confer a doctorate on. – 2 **doctorarse,** *p* to get one's doctorate, get one's PhD.

doctrina 1 *f* doctrine. 2 (*enseñanza*) teachings *pl.*
doctrinal *adj* doctrinal.
doctrinario,-a 1 *adj* doctrinaire. – 2 *m,f* doctrinaire.
doctrino *m* orphan.
documentación 1 *f* documentation, documents *pl.* 2 (*para identificar*) papers *pl,* identification.
documentado,-a 1 *pp* → **documentar**. – 2 *adj* documented, researched. 3 *fam* (*enterado*) informed.
documental 1 *adj* documentary. – 2 *m* documentary.
documentalista *mf* documentarist, documentary maker.
documentar 1 *t* to document. 2 (*a una persona*) to give information. – 3 **documentarse,** *p* to research (**sobre,** -), get information (**sobre,** about/on).
documento *m* document.
■ Documento Nacional de Identidad, identity card.
dodecaedro *m* dodecahedron.
dodecafónico,-a *adj* dodecaphonic.
dodecágono,-a 1 *adj* dodecagonal. – 2 **dodecágono,** *m* dodecagon.
dodecasílabo,-a 1 *adj* dodecasyllabic, alexandrine. – 2 **dodecasílabo,** *m* dodecasyllable, Alexandrine.
dogal 1 *m* (*para un animal*) halter. 2 (*soga de reo*) noose, hangman's noose.
dogma *m* dogma.
dogmático,-a 1 *adj* dogmatic. – 2 *m,f* dogmatic.
dogmatismo *m* dogmatism.
dogmatista *mf* dogmatist.
dogmatizar *i* to dogmatize.
▲ *Conjugation model* [4], *like* **realizar**.
dogo *m* bulldog.
doladera *f* cooper's axe.
dolaje *m* wine absorbed by the barrel.
dólar *m* dollar.
dolby *m* dolby.
▲ *Registered trademark*.
dolencia *f* ailment, illness.
doler 1 *i* to ache, hurt: *me duele la cabeza,* I've got a headache; *me duele la espalda,* my back hurts, my back aches. 2 (*afligir*) to distress, sadden, upset, hurt: *me duele tal pobreza,* such poverty distresses me. 3 (*sentir*) to be sorry, be sad: *me duele habérselo dicho,* I'm sorry I told her about it. – 4 **dolerse,** *p* (*arrepentirse*) to repent (**de,** of), feel sorry (**de,** for): *se duele de sus pecados,* he repents of his sins. 5 (*lamentarse*) to complain (**de,** of). 6 (*notar el efecto*) to feel the effects (**de,** of).
▲ *Conjugation model* [32], *like* **mover**.
dolido,-a 1 *pp* → **doler.** – 2 *adj fig* hurt.
doliente *mf* mourner.
dolmen *m* dolmen.
▲ *pl* **dólmenes**.
dolo *m* fraud.
Dolomitas los Dolomitas, *mpl* the Dolomites.
dolor 1 *m* pain, ache. 2 *fig* pain, sorrow, grief.
● **causar dolor,** *fig* to sadden, hurt, upset. ‖ **estar con los dolores,** (*de parto*) to be in labour (*us* labor).
■ **dolor de cabeza,** headache. ‖ **dolor de muelas,** toothache.
dolorido,-a 1 *adj* sore, aching. 2 *fig* sorrowful, sad, hurt.
dolorosa *f* → **doloroso,-a**.
doloroso,-a 1 *adj* painful. 2 *fig* painful, distressing. – 3 **dolorosa,** *f arg* bill: *tráigame la dolorosa,* what's the damage? 4 **la Dolorosa,** REL Our Lady of Sorrow.
doloso,-a *adj* fraudulent.
doma *f* taming; (*de caballos*) breaking in.

domador,-ra *m,f* tamer; (*de caballos*) horse breaker.
domar 1 *t* to tame; (*caballos*) to break in. 2 *fig* to tame, control.
domeñar *t* to subdue.
domesticable 1 *adj* (*que se puede domesticar*) tamable, domesticable. 2 (*que se puede enseñar*) trainable.
domesticación 1 *f* domestication, taming. 2 (*adiestramiento*) training.
domesticar 1 *t* to domesticate, tame. 2 (*adiestrar*) to train. 3 *fig* to subdue.
▲ *Conjugation model* [1], *like* **sacar**.
doméstico,-a 1 *adj* domestic. – 2 *m,f* domestic, servant.
■ **servicio doméstico,** domestic help.
domiciliación *f* payment by direct debit.
domiciliado,-a 1 *pp* → **domiciliar**. – 2 *adj* resident, living.
domiciliar 1 *t* (*dar domicilio*) to house, lodge. 2 FIN to pay by direct debit. – 3 **domiciliarse,** *p* (*fijar domicilio*) to take up residence.
▲ *Conjugation model* [12], *like* **cambiar**.
domiciliario,-a *adj* house.
■ **arresto domiciliario,** house arrest.
domicilio 1 *m* residence, home, abode. 2 (*dirección*) address.
● **sin domicilio fijo,** of no fixed abode. ‖ "**reparto a domicilio gratuito**", "free delivery".
■ **domicilio fiscal,** registered office.
dominación *f* domination, dominion.
dominante 1 *adj* dominant, dominating. 2 (*que prevalece*) prevailing, predominating. 3 (*que avasalla*) domineering.
dominar 1 *t* (*tener bajo dominio*) to dominate. 2 (*avasallar*) to domineer. 3 (*controlar*) to control, restrain: *dominar los nervios,* to control one's nerves. 4 (*conocer a fondo*) to master: *domina el inglés,* she has a good command of English. 5 (*ver*) to overlook, dominate: *el jardín domina toda la playa,* the garden has a commanding view of the whole beach. – 6 *i* (*ser superior*) to dominate. 7 (*destacar*) to stand out: *domina mucho el rojo,* red is the predominant colour. 8 (*predominar*) to predominate: *en esta fiesta dominan las mujeres,* there are mostly women at this party. – 9 **dominarse,** *p* (*controlarse*) to control os., restrain os.
dómine 1 *m arc* Latin teacher. 2 *pey* pedant.
domingas *fpl arg* boobs.
domingo *m* Sunday.
■ **domingo de Ramos,** Palm Sunday. ‖ **domingo de Resurrección/Pascua,** Easter Sunday. ‖ **el traje de los domingos,** one's Sunday best.
▲ *See also* **jueves**.
dominguero,-a 1 *adj* Sunday. – 2 *m,f pey* (*conductor*) Sunday driver; (*excursionista*) day-tripper.
dominguillo *m* tumbler.
Dominica *f* Dominica.
dominical 1 *adj* Sunday. – 2 *m* (*periódico*) Sunday newspaper; (*suplemento*) Sunday supplement.
dominicano,-a 1 *adj* Dominican. – 2 *m,f* Dominican.
■ **República Dominicana,** Dominican Republic.
dominico,-a 1 *adj* Dominican. – 2 *m,f* Dominican.
dominio 1 *m* (*soberanía*) dominion. 2 (*poder*) power, control. 3 (*supremacía*) supremacy. 4 (*de conocimientos*) mastery, good knowledge; (*de un idioma*) good command: *tiene un buen dominio del francés,* she has a good command of French. 5 (*territorio*) domain.
● **dominio de sí mismo,** self-control. ‖ **ejercer do-**

minio, to exert control. ‖ **ser del dominio público,** to be public knowledge.
dominó 1 *m* (*juego*) dominoes *pl.* 2 (*fichas*) set of dominoes. 3 (*disfraz*) domino.
▲ *pl* **dominós.**
don[1] 1 *m* (*regalo*) gift, present. 2 (*talento*) talent, natural gift: *tienes el don de la palabra,* you've got a way with words.
■ **don de gentes,** natural ability to get on well with people.
don[2] *m* Mr: *Señor Don Juan Pérez,* Mr Juan Pérez; *don Luis llegó tarde,* Luis was late.
■ **Don Fulano de Tal,** Mr So-and-So. ‖ **un don nadie,** a nobody.
▲ *Courtesy title placed before first names of men.*
donación *f* donation.
donaire 1 *m* (*gracia*) grace, elegance. 2 (*soltura de cuerpo*) poise. 3 (*chiste*) wisecrack, witticism.
donante *mf* donor.
■ **donante de sangre,** blood donor.
donar *t fml* to donate, give: *donar los ojos,* to donate one's eyes.
donativo *m* donation.
doncel 1 *m* (*noble*) young nobleman. 2 (*paje*) pageboy.
doncella 1 *f* (*joven*) maiden, dansel. 2 (*criada*) maid, maidservant.
doncellez *f* maidenhood.
donde *adv* where, in which: *el colegio donde estudié,* the school where I studied.
● **de donde / desde donde,** from where, whence: *ésta es la casa desde donde procedió el disparo,* this is the house where the shot came from. ‖ **donde las dan las toman,** *fam* tit for tat. ‖ **¡mira por donde! / ¡vaya por donde!,** *fam* fancy that!
dónde *pron* where: *¿dónde está?,* where is it?; *no sé dónde está,* I don't know where it is; *¿a dónde va?,* where is he going?; *¿hasta dónde?,* how far?
dondequiera *adv* (*en cualquier parte*) anywhere; (*en todas partes*) everywhere: *dondequiera que esté lo encontraremos,* wherever he is we'll find him.
dondiego *m* marvel-of-Peru, four-o'clock.
■ **dondiego de día,** morning glory. ‖ **dondiego de noche,** marvel-of-Peru, four-o'clock.
donjuán *m* Don Juan, womanizer, Casanova.
donjuanesco *adj* womanizing, fond of women.
donjuanismo *m* womanizing.
donoso,-a 1 *adj desus* (*gracioso*) graceful, elegant. 2 *desus* (*ocurrente*) witty.
donostiarra 1 *adj* of San Sebastian, from San Sebastian. – 2 *mf* person from San Sebastian, inhabitant of San Sebastian.
donosura 1 *f* (*gracia*) elegance, grace, poise. 2 (*humor*) wit.
donut *m* doughnut.
▲ *pl* **dónuts.**
doña *f* Mrs: *Doña Elena Suárez,* Mrs Elena Suárez; *Doña Elena está enferma,* Elena is ill.
▲ *Courtesy title placed before first names of women.*
dopaje *m* doping.
dopar *t* to dope, drug.
doping *m* doping, drug-taking.
doquier *adv* anywhere: *doquier que esté,* wherever he may be.
● **por doquier,** everywhere.
doquiera *adv* → **doquier.**
dorada *f* → **dorado,-a.**

dorado,-a 1 *pp* → **dorar.** – 2 *adj* golden; (*cubierto de oro*) gold-plated, gilt. – 3 **dorado,** *m* TÉC gilding. – 4 **dorada,** *f* (*pez*) gilthead bream.
dorar 1 *t* (*cubrir con oro*) to gild. 2 (*dar un baño de oro*) to goldplate. 3 CULIN to brown.
● **dorar la píldora,** *fig* to sugar the pill.
Dordoña el Dordoña, *m* the Dordogne.
dórico,-a 1 *adj* Dorian. – 2 **dórico,** *m* Doric.
■ **orden dórico,** Doric order.
dormida *f* → **dormido,-a.**
dormidero,-a *adj* soporific, sleep-inducing.
dormido,-a 1 *adj* asleep. 2 (*soñoliento*) sleepy: *tengo el brazo dormido,* my arm has gone numb, my arm has gone to sleep. – 3 **dormida,** *f* sleep.
● **quedarse dormido,-a,** (*dormir*) to fall asleep; (*dormirse más de la cuenta*) to oversleep.
dormilón,-ona 1 *adj fam* fond of sleeping: *es una chica muy dormilona,* she's a real sleepyhead. – 2 *m,f* sleepyhead.
dormir 1 *i* to sleep: *tengo ganas de dormir,* I feel sleepy. 2 (*pernoctar*) to spend the night: *dormimos en Zaragoza,* we spent the night in Zaragoza. – 3 *t* to put to sleep. – 4 **dormirse,** *p* to fall asleep, nod off. 5 *fig* to go to sleep: *se me ha dormido el pie,* my foot has gone to sleep. 6 *fig* (*dejar de esforzarse*) to let things slide.
● **¡a dormir!,** to bed! ‖ **dormir a pierna suelta,** *fam* to sleep like a log. ‖ **dormir como un lirón,** *fam* to sleep like a log. ‖ **dormir la mona,** *fam* to sleep it off. ‖ **dormir la siesta,** to have a nap. ‖ **dormirla,** *fam* to sleep it off. ‖ **dormirse en los laureles,** *fig* to rest on one's laurels.
▲ *Conjugation model* [33].
dormitar *i* to doze, snooze.
dormitorio 1 *m* (*en una casa*) bedroom. 2 (*colectivo*) dormitory. 3 (*muebles*) bedroom suite.
dorsal 1 *adj* dorsal, back. 2 LING dorsal. – 3 *m* DEP number.
dorso *m* back, reverse.
● **"instrucciones al dorso",** "instructions over". ‖ **"véase al dorso",** "see overleaf".
■ **dorso de la mano,** back of the hand.
dos 1 *adj* (*cardinal*) two; (*ordinal*) second: *entre ellas dos,* between the two of them. – 2 *m* (*número*) two; (*fecha*) second.
● **cada dos por tres,** *fam* every five minutes. ‖ **como dos y dos son cuatro,** *fam* as sure as night follows day, as sure as eggs is eggs. ‖ **de dos en dos,** in twos, in pairs. ‖ **en un dos por tres,** *fam* in a flash.
■ **dos veces,** twice: *es dos veces mayor que su hermana,* she's twice as old as her sister.
▲ *See also* **seis.**
dosalbo,-a *adj* with two white feet.
doscientos,-as 1 *adj* (*numeral*) two hundred; (*cardinal*) two-hundredth. – 2 *m,f* two hundred.
▲ *See also* **seis.**
dosel *m* canopy.
dosificación *f* dosage.
dosificar 1 *t* (*gen*) to dose. 2 (*esfuerzos etc*) to measure.
▲ *Conjugation model* [1], *like* **sacar.**
dosis *f* dose.
● **a/en pequeñas dosis,** in small doses.
▲ *pl* **dosis.**
dossier *m* dossier.
dotación 1 *f* (*con lo que se dota*) endowment. 2 (*tripulación*) complement, crew. 3 (*personal*) staff, personnel.
dotado,-a 1 *pp* → **dotar.** – 2 *adj* (*equipado*) equipped, provided: *está dotado con airbag,* it's equipped with an

airbag. **3** (con dotes) gifted: *está muy dotado para las matemáticas,* he has a talent for mathematics. **4** *arg* (*genitales*) well-hung.

dotar 1 *t* (*dar dote*) to give a dowry: *dotaron a su hija con un millón,* they gave their daughter a million-peseta dowry. **2** (*proveer de personal*) to staff (**de,** with); (*de material*) to equip (**de,** with). **3** (*bienes, dinero*) to assign. **4** *fig* (*dones y cualidades*) to endow (**de,** with), provide (**de,** with): *la naturaleza la dotó de un sexto sentido,* nature endowed her with a sixth sense.

dote 1 *m* & *f* dowry. – **2** dotes, *fpl* gift *sing,* talent *sing: tiene dotes para el violín,* he's a gifted violinist.
■ dotes de mando, leadership qualities.

dovela *f* voussoir.

dovelar *t* to make wedge-shaped.

doy *pres indic* → **dar**.

DP *abr* (*distrito postal*) postal district; (*abreviatura*) PD.

dpt. *abr* (*departamento*) department; (*abreviatura*) dept.

Dr. *abr* (*doctor*) doctor; (*abreviatura*) Dr.

Dra. *abr* (*doctora*) doctor; (*abreviatura*) Dr.

dracma *m* drachma.

draconiano,-a *adj* draconian, harsh, drastic.

draga 1 *f* (*máquina*) dredge. **2** (*barco*) dredger.

dragado *m* dredging.

dragaminas *m* minesweeper.
▲ *pl* dragaminas.

dragar *t* to dredge.
▲ Conjugation model [7], like *llegar*.

drago *m* dragon tree.

dragón 1 *m* (*reptil*) flying dragon. **2** (*animal fabuloso*) dragon. **3** (*planta*) snapdragon. **4** (*pez*) greater weever. **5** (*soldado*) dragoon.

dralón *m* dralon.
▲ Registered trademark.

drama *m* drama.

dramático,-a 1 *adj* dramatic. – **2** *m,f* dramatist.

dramatismo *m* dramatism, drama.

dramatizar *t* to dramatize.
▲ Conjugation model [4], like *realizar*.

dramaturgia *f* dramatics.

dramaturgo,-a *m,f* playwright, dramatist.

dramón *m fam* melodrama.

drapeado,-a 1 *adj* draped. – **2** drapeado, *m* drapery.

drapear *t* to drape.

drástico,-a *adj* drastic.

drenaje *m* drainage.
■ colector de drenaje, main drain. ‖ tubo de drenaje, drainpipe, drain.

drenar *t* to drain.

Dresde *f* Dresden.

driblar *i* to dribble.

dribling *m* dribbling.

dril 1 *m* (*tela*) drill, drilling. **2** (*mono*) drill.

drive *m* drive.

driza *f* halyard.

droga 1 *f* drug. **2** *fig* (*cosa desagradable*) nuisance.
■ droga blanda/dura, soft/hard drug.

drogadicción *f* drug addiction.

drogadicto,-a 1 *adj* addicted to drugs. – **2** *m,f* drug addict.

drogado,-a 1 *pp* → **drogar**. – **2** *adj* drugged (up). – **3** *m,f* drug addict.

drogar 1 *t* to drug. – **2** drogarse, *p* to take drugs.
▲ Conjugation model [7], like *llegar*.

drogata *mf arg* junkie.

drogodependencia *f* drug addiction, drug dependency.

drogodependiente *mf* drug addict.

drogota *mf arg* junkie.

droguería *f* hardware and household goods shop.

dromedario *m* dromedary.

druida,-esa *m,f* druid.

dto. *abr* (*descuento*) discount.

dual 1 *adj* dual. – **2** *m* dual.
■ emisión en dual, bilingual broadcast.

dualidad *f* duality.

dualismo *m* dualism.

dualista *adj* dualistic.

dubitativo,-a *adj* doubtful.

Dublín *m* Dublin.

dublinés,-esa 1 *adj* of Dublin, from Dublin. – **2** *m,f* Dubliner.

ducado 1 *m* dukedom, duchy. **2** (*antigua moneda*) ducat.

ducal *adj* duke's, ducal.

ducentésimo,-a 1 *adj* two-hundredth. – **2** *m,f* two-hundredth.

ducha *f* shower.
● darse/tomar una ducha, to take a shower, have a shower. ‖ una ducha de agua fría, *fam fig* a blow, a shock.

duchar 1 *t* to give a shower. – **2** ducharse, *p* to take a shower, have a shower.

ducho,-a *adj* knowledgeable.
● estar ducho,-a en la materia, to be well versed in the subject, to be an expert on the subject.

duco *m* lacquer.
● pintar al duco, to lacquer.

dúctil *adj* ductile.

ductilidad *f* ductility.

duda *f* doubt.
● no hay duda, there is no doubt. ‖ no te quepa duda, make no mistake about it. ‖ poner algo en duda, to question sth. ‖ sacar a algn. de dudas, to dispel sb.'s doubts. ‖ salir de dudas, to shed one's doubts. ‖ sin duda, no doubt, without a doubt. ‖ sin la menor duda, without the slightest doubt.

dudar 1 *i* to doubt, have doubts: *dudo de lo que dijo,* I have doubts about what he said. **2** (*titubear*) to hesitate: *dudó en ir,* he hesitated whether to go or not; *dudo entre quedarme o marcharme,* I'm not sure whether to stay or leave. – **3** *t* to doubt: *lo dudo,* I doubt it; *dudo que venga,* I doubt if he'll come.
● dudar de algn., to doubt sb., mistrust sb.

dudosamente 1 *adv* (*con incerteza*) doubtfully. **2** (*con vacilación*) hesitantly. **3** (*con sospecha*) suspiciously.

dudoso,-a 1 *adj* (*incierto*) doubtful, uncertain. **2** (*vacilante*) hesitant, undecided. **3** (*sospechoso*) suspicious, dubious. **4** (*poco seguro*) questionable.

duela *f* stave.

duelo¹ *m* (*combate*) duel.
● batirse en duelo, to fight a duel.

duelo² *m* (*dolor*) grief, affliction. **2** (*luto*) mourning; (*reunión de parientes*) wake; (*cortejo*) cortege, funeral procession.
● sin duelo, regardless.

duende 1 *m* (*espíritu travieso*) goblin, elf. **2** (*encanto*) charm, magic: *es una chica con duende,* she's got charm.

dueña *f* → **dueño,-a**.

dueño,-a 1 *m,f* (*propietario*) owner: *¿quién es la dueña?,* who is the owner? **2** (*de casa, piso - hombre*) landlord; (*mujer*) landlady.

● **hacerse dueño,-a de la situación,** *fig* to get the situation under control. ‖ **ser dueño,-a de sí mismo,-a,** to be self-possessed. ‖ **ser muy dueño,-a de,** *fig* to be entirely free to: *es muy dueña de hacer lo que quiera,* she's entirely free to do whatever she wants.
■ **dueño y señor,** lord and master.
Duero el Duero, *m* the Douro.
dueto *m* short duet.
dulce 1 *adj* (*gen*) sweet. **2** (*clima*) mild. **3** *fig* soft, gentle. **– 4** *m* CULIN (*caramelo*) sweet; (*pastel*) cake.
■ **dulce de membrillo,** quince jelly.
dulcería 1 *f* confectionery. **2** (*tienda*) confectioner's, US candy store.
dulcero,-a 1 *adj* sweet-toothed: *es muy dulcero,* he has a sweet tooth. **– 2** *m,f* confectioner.
dulcificar 1 *t* to sweeten. **2** *fig* to soften.
▲ *Conjugation model* |1|, *like* **sacar**.
dulcinea *f* sweetheart.
dulzaina *f* → **dulzaino,-a**.
dulzaino,-a 1 *adj* sweetish, sugary. **– 2 dulzaina,** *f* dulzaina, old type of pipe.
dulzarrón,-ona *adj* sickly sweet, oversweet.
dulzón,-ona *adj* sickly sweet, oversweet.
dulzor 1 *m* sweetness. **2** *fig* gentleness, sweetness, softness.
dulzura 1 *f* sweetness. **2** *fig* softness, gentleness, sweetness. **3** *fig* (*clima*) mildness.
dumdum *m* dumdum.
dumping *m* dumping.
duna *f* dune.
dúo *m* duet.
duodécimo,-a 1 *adj* twelfth. **– 2** *m,f* twelfth.
▲ *See also* **sexto,-a**.
duodenal *adj* duodenal.
duodeno *m* duodenum.
dupdo. *abr* (*duplicado*) duplicate; (*abreviatura*) dupl.
dúplex 1 *adj* duplex. **– 2** *m* (*casa*) duplex, duplex apartment. **3** TÉC duplex.
▲ *pl* **dúlpex**.
duplicación *f* duplication, doubling.
duplicado,-a 1 *pp* → **duplicar. – 2** *adj* duplicate. **– 3** duplicado, *m* duplicate, copy.
● **por duplicado,** in duplicate.
duplicar 1 *t* (*gen*) to duplicate; (*cantidad*) to double. **– 2** duplicarse, *p* to double.

▲ *Conjugation model* |1|, *like* **sacar**.
duplicidad 1 *f* duplicity. **2** *fig* duplicity, falseness.
duplo,-a 1 *adj* double. **– 2** *m,f* double.
duque *m* duke.
duquesa *f* duchess.
durabilidad *f* durability.
durable *adj* durable, lasting.
duración 1 *f* duration, length: *¿cuál es la duración de la obra?,* how long is the play? **2** (*coche, máquina, etc*) life.
● **de larga duración,** (*periodo de tiempo*) long, long-term; (*bombilla etc*) long-life; (*enfermedad*) long-term.
duradero,-a *adj* durable, lasting.
duralex *m* duralex.
▲ *Registered trademark*.
duramen *m* duramen.
▲ *pl* **durámenes**.
duramente 1 *adv* (*con dificultad*) hard. **2** (*con severidad*) harshly.
durante *adv* during, in, for: *viví allí durante un año,* I lived there for a year; *durante el verano,* during the summer; *durante todo el día,* all day long.
durar 1 *i* to last, go on for: *la película duró tres horas,* the film went on for three hours. **2** (*ropa, calzado*) to wear well, last: *ese abrigo le duró mucho,* he got a lot of wear out of that coat.
durativo,-a 1 *adj* lasting. **2** GRAM durative.
duraznero *m* peach tree.
durazno 1 *m* (*fruto*) peach. **2** (*árbol*) peach tree.
dureza 1 *f* hardness, toughness. **2** *fig* (*de carácter*) toughness, harshness, severity. **3** (*callosidad*) corn.
■ **dureza de corazón,** hardheartedness, callousness.
durmiente 1 *adj* sleeping. **– 2** *m* sleeper.
■ **la Bella Durmiente,** Sleeping Beauty.
duro,-a 1 *adj* hard. **2** (*carne*) tough; (*pan*) stale. **3** (*difícil*) hard, difficult. **4** (*cruel*) tough, hardhearted, callous. **5** (*resistente*) strong, tough. **6** (*obstinado*) obstinate, stubborn. **– 7 duro,** *m* five-peseta coin. **8** *fam* tough guy. **– 9** *adv* hard: *dale duro,* hit him hard.
● **lo que faltaba para el duro,** *fam* just what I (*we etc*) needed! ‖ **ser duro,-a de mollera,** to be thick, be as thick as two short planks.
dux *m* HIST doge.
▲ *pl* **dux**.
d/v *abr* (*días vista*): *a diez d/v,* due within ten days.

E

E, e f (la letra) E, e.

e conj and: *compramos manzanas e higos,* we bought some apples and figs.
▲ *Used instead of y before words beginning with i or hi.*

E sím (*este*) east; (*símbolo*) E.

ea 1 interj (*ánimo*) come on! 2 (*resolución*) so there!

EA abr POL (*Eusko Alkartasuna*) Basque Union (*Basque nationalist party*).

easonense 1 adj of San Sebastián, from San Sebastián. – 2 mf person from San Sebastián, inhabitant of San Sebastián.

EAU abr (*Emiratos Árabes Unidos*) United Arab Emirates; (*abreviatura*) UAE.

ebanista mf cabinet-maker.

ebanistería 1 f (*oficio*) cabinet-making. 2 (*taller*) cabinet-maker's.

ébano m ebony.

ebonita f ebonite.

ebriedad f drunkenness, intoxication, inebriation.

ebrio,-a 1 adj drunk, intoxicated, inebriated. 2 fig blind: *ebrio de ira,* blind with anger.

Ebro el Ebro, m the Ebro.

ebullición 1 f (*hervor*) boil, boiling. 2 fig (*agitación*) excitement, turmoil, ebullience.
● entrar en ebullición, to come to the boil. ‖ estar en ebullición, fig to be in turmoil.
■ punto de ebullición, boiling point.

ebúrneo,-a adj eburnean.

eccehomo m Ecce Homo.
● estar hecho,-a un eccehomo, fam to be a wreck.

eccema m eczema.

echada f → **echado,-a**.

echado,-a 1 pp → **echar**. – 2 adj (*tumbado*) lying down. – 3 echada, f throw.
● ser un,-a echado,-a p'alante, fam to be forward.

echador,-ra m,f (*de cartas*) fortune-teller.

echar 1 t (*lanzar*) to throw: *echar monedas en la fuente,* to throw coins in the fountain. 2 (*dejar caer*) to put, drop. 3 (*líquido*) to pour; (*comida*) to give; (*sal*) to add, put in. 4 (*carta*) to post, US mail. 5 (*expulsar*) to throw out: *lo han echado del cine,* he was thrown out of the cinema. 6 (*despedir de empleo*) to sack, dismiss, fire: *me han echado,* I've been sacked. 7 (*brotar, salir - plantas*) to sprout; (- *dientes*) to cut; (- *pelo*) to grow. 8 (*decir*) to tell. 9 (*emanar*) to give out, give off: *la caja de fusibles echa chispas,* sparks are coming out of the fuse box. 10 (*suponer, calcular*) to guess: *yo le echo 40,* I think she's 40. 11 (*poner, aplicar*) to put on, apply. 12 (*llave*) to lock, turn; (*cerrojo*) to bolt, fasten: *echa la llave,* lock the door, lock it; *echa el cerrojo,* bolt the door, fasten the bolt. 13 (*multas, tributos*) to give, impose. 14 (*en naipes*) to deal. 15 fam (*en el cine, teatro*) to show, put on: *echan una buena película en la tele,* there's a good film on TV. – 16 echar a + *inf,* i (*empezar*) to begin to: *echó a andar,*

he began to walk; *echó a correr,* she ran off. 17 echar de + *inf,* (*dar*): *echar de comer,* to feed. 18 echar por, (*seguir, ir*) to take, follow: *echó por la izquierda,* he went left. – 19 echarse, p (*arrojarse*) to throw os. 20 (*tenderse*) to lie down: *me voy a echar un rato,* I'm going to lie down for a bit. 21 (*ponerse*) to put on. 22 (*novio, novia*) to get os. – 23 echarse a + *inf,* i (*empezar*) to begin to: *se echó a reír,* he burst out laughing.
● echar a cara o cruz, to toss for. ‖ echar a un lado, to push aside. ‖ echar a perder, to spoil. ‖ echar a suertes, to draw lots. ‖ echar abajo, → echar por tierra. ‖ echar algo a suertes, fig to draw lots for sth. ‖ echar barriga / echar carnes, to put on weight. ‖ echar cuentas, to calculate. ‖ echar de menos / echar en falta, to miss: *la echa de menos,* he misses her. ‖ echar el freno, to put the brake on. ‖ echar en cara, to blame. ‖ echar la buenaventura, to tell sb.'s fortune. ‖ echar la casa por la ventana, fig to spare no expense, splash out. ‖ echar las bases de, to lay the foundations for. ‖ echar leña al fuego, fig to add fuel to the fire. ‖ echar maldiciones, to curse. ‖ echar mano a algo, to reach for sth. ‖ echar mano de, to make use of. ‖ echar pelillos a la mar, fig to bury the hatchet. ‖ echar por tierra, to demolish; fig to ruin. ‖ echar un cigarrillo, to smoke a cigarette. ‖ echar una mano, to give a hand. ‖ echar una mirada / echar una ojeada, to have a look, have a quick look. ‖ echar una parrafada, to have a chat. ‖ echar una partida, to play a game. ‖ echar una regañina a algn. / echar un sermón a algn., to tell sb. off. ‖ echar una siesta, to have a siesta. ‖ echarse a perder, (*alimentos*) to go bad; (*personas*) to go downhill. ‖ echarse a un lado, to move to one side. ‖ echarse atrás, (*inclinarse*) to lean back; fig to have second thoughts, get cold feet. ‖ echárselas de, fam to claim to be: *se las echa de valiente,* he claims to be brave.

echarpe m shawl, stole.

echazón f jetsam.

eclampsia f eclampsia.

eclecticismo m eclecticism.

ecléctico,-a 1 adj eclectic. – 2 m,f eclectic.

eclesial adj ecclesiastic, ecclesiastical, church.

eclesiástico,-a 1 adj ecclesiastic, ecclesiastical, church. – 2 eclesiástico, m (*clérigo*) clergyman.

eclipsar 1 t (*astro*) to eclipse. 2 fig to eclipse, outshine. – 3 eclipsarse, p (*astro*) to be eclipsed. 4 fig (*desaparecer*) to disappear, vanish.

eclipse m eclipse.

eclíptica f → **eclíptico,-a**.

eclíptico,-a 1 adj ecliptic. – 2 eclíptica, f ecliptic.

eclisa f TÉC fishplate.

eclosión 1 f ZOOL hatching, emergence. 2 BOT blossoming. 3 fig upsurge, flowering, emergence.

eclosionar i to break out, emerge, burst out.

eco 1 m echo. 2 fig echo, response.
● hacerse eco de, to echo. ■ tener eco, fig to have impact, arouse interest.

■ **ecos de sociedad,** gossip column *sing.*
ecografía *f* ultrasound scan.
ecógrafo *m* ultrasound scanner.
ecología *f* ecology.
ecológico,-a *adj* ecological.
ecologismo *m* ecology movement.
ecologista 1 *adj* ecological: *partido ecologista,* ecology party. − 2 *mf* ecologist.
ecólogo,-a *m,f* ecologist.
economato *m* company store.
econometría *f* econometrics.
economía 1 *f* (*administración*) economy. 2 (*ciencia*) economics. 3 (*ahorro*) economy, saving. 4 (*moderación*) economy, thrift, thriftiness. − 5 **economías,** *fpl* savings.
● **hacer economías,** to economize.
■ **economía de libre mercado,** free-market economy. ‖ **economía de mercado,** market economy. ‖ **economía doméstica,** housekeeping. ‖ **economía sumergida,** black economy.
económicamente 1 *adv* economically. 2 (*barato*) cheaply.
económico,-a 1 *adj* (*gen*) economic. 2 (*barato*) cheap, economical, inexpensive: *la habitación resultó económica,* the room was cheap. 3 (*persona*) thrifty, careful with money.
■ **cocina económica,** wood-fired stove. ‖ **crisis económica,** economic crisis, recession.
economista *mf* economist.
economizar 1 *t* (*ahorrar*) to economize, save. 2 (*usar con cuidado*) to use sparingly. − 3 *i* to economize, save.
▲ *Conjugation model* [4], *like* **realizar.**
ecónomo 1 *m* FIN trustee. 2 REL acting parish priest.
ecosistema *m* ecosystem.
ectoparásito,-a 1 *adj* ectoparasitic. − 2 **ectoparásito,** *m* ectoparasite.
ectoplasma *m* ectoplasm.
ecu *m* ecu.
ecuación *f* equation.
■ **ecuación de primer grado,** simple equation. ‖ **ecuación de segundo grado,** quadratic equation. ‖ **sistema de ecuaciones,** set of equations.
ecuador *m* 1 GEOG equator. 2 EDUC half-way point.
● **pasar el ecuador,** to cross the equator.
■ **paso del ecuador,** EDUC *fam* half-way point in a degree.
Ecuador *m* Ecuador.
ecualizador *m* equalizer.
ecuánime 1 *adj* (*temperamento*) calm, placid, equable, even-tempered. 2 (*juicio, opinión*) fair, impartial.
ecuanimidad 1 *f* (*temperamento*) equanimity. 2 (*juicio*) impartiality, fairness.
ecuatoguineano,-a 1 *adj* of Equatorial Guinea, from Equatorial Guinea. − 2 *m,f* person from Equatorial Guinea, inhabitant of Equatorial Guinea.
ecuatorial *adj* equatorial.
ecuatoriano,-a 1 *adj* Ecuadorian. − 2 *m,f* Ecuadorian.
ecuestre *adj* equestrian.
ecuménico,-a *adj* ecumenical, ecumenic.
ecumenismo *m* ecumenicalism, ecumenicism.
eczema *m* eczema.
ed. 1 *abr* (*edición*) edition; (*abreviatura*) ed. 2 (*editorial*) publishing house. 3 (*editor*) editor; (*abreviatura*) ed.
edad 1 *f* age: *a la edad de 20 años,* at the age of 20; *¿qué edad tiene usted?,* how old are you?; *ya tiene edad para entenderlo,* he's old enough to understand it. 2 (*tiempo, época*) time, period.

● **de cierta edad,** *euf* elderly. ‖ **de mediana edad,** middle-aged. ‖ **en edad escolar,** of school age.
■ **edad de oro,** golden age. ‖ **edad del pavo,** awkward age. ‖ **Edad Media,** Middle Ages *pl.* ‖ **Edad Moderna,** Modern Age. ‖ **la tercera edad,** *euf* old age, retirement age.
edelweiss *m* edelweiss.
edema *m* edema.
edén 1 *m* Eden. 2 *fig* paradise, heaven.
edénico,-a *adj fig* idyllic, heavenly.
edición 1 *f* (*ejemplares*) edition. 2 (*publicación*) publication; (*de sellos*) issue: *Ediciones Biblograf,* Biblograf Publications. 3 INFORM editing.
■ **edición anotada,** annotated text. ‖ **edición de bolsillo,** pocket edition. ‖ **edición en rústica,** paperback edition. ‖ **edición pirata,** pirate edition. ‖ **primera edición,** first edition.
edicto *m* edict, proclamation.
edificable *adj* which can be built on: *terreno edificable,* building land.
edificación *f* building, construction.
edificador,-ra *adj* building.
edificante *adj* edifying, uplifting.
edificar 1 *t* (*construir*) to build, construct. 2 *fig* (*crear*) to build, create. 3 *fig* (*dar ejemplo*) to edify, uplift.
▲ *Conjugation model* [1], *like* **sacar.**
edificio *m* building.
edil,-la 1 *m,f* (*concejal*) town councillor. − 2 **edil,** *m* (*magistrado romano*) aedile.
Edimburgo *m* Edinburgh.
Edipo *m* Oedipus.
■ **complejo de Edipo,** Oedipus complex.
editar 1 *t* (*libros, revistas*) to publish; (*discos*) to release. 2 INFORM to edit.
editor,-ra 1 *adj* publishing. − 2 *m,f* (*que edita*) publisher; (*que prepara*) editor. − 3 **editor,** *m* INFORM editor.
■ **editor de fichero,** file editor. ‖ **editor de textos,** text editor.
editorial 1 *adj* publishing. − 2 *m* (*artículo*) editorial, leading article, leader. − 3 *f* publishing house, publisher.
editorialista *mf* leader writer.
edredón *m* eiderdown, US comforter.
■ **edredón nórdico,** continental quilt, duvet.
educación 1 *f* (*preparación*) education. 2 (*crianza*) upbringing, breeding. 3 (*modales*) manners *pl,* politeness: *no tiene ninguna educación en la mesa,* he has no table manners at all.
■ **falta de educación,** rudeness, discourtesy. ‖ **mala educación,** bad manners *pl.*
educado,-a *adj* polite.
educador,-ra 1 *adj* educating. − 2 *m,f* educator, teacher.
educando,-a *m,f* pupil, student.
educar 1 *t* (*enseñar*) to educate, teach. 2 (*criar*) to bring up. 3 (*en la cortesía etc*) to teach manners. 4 (*sentidos*) to educate, train.
▲ *Conjugation model* [1], *like* **sacar.**
educativo,-a *adj* educational: *sistema educativo,* education system.
edulcorante *m* sweetener.
edulcorar 1 *t* to sweeten. 2 *fig* to soften, alleviate: *los amigos edulcoraban su sufrimiento,* her friends alleviated her suffering.
EE *abr* POL (*Euskadiko Ezkerra*) *left-wing Basque party.*
EE UU *abr* (*Estados Unidos*) the United States of America; (*abreviatura*) USA.

efe *f* name of the letter f.
efebo *m* ephebe.
efectismo *m* showiness, theatricality.
efectista *adj* showy, stagy.
efectivamente 1 *adv* (*realmente*) in fact, actually. 2 (*de verdad*) indeed.
efectividad *f* effectiveness.
● con efectividad desde, (*ley etc*) with effect from.
efectivo,-a 1 *adj* (*real*) real, true, actual. 2 (*que tiene efecto*) effective. 3 (*empleo*) permanent. – 4 efectivo, *m* (*dinero*) cash. 5 (*plantilla*) staff, personnel. – 6 efectivos, *mpl* MIL forces: *efectivos de la Guardia Civil desactivaron el dispositivo,* members of the Civil Guard made the device safe.
● efectivo en caja, petty cash. ‖ en efectivo, (*dinero*) in cash: *pagar en efectivo,* to pay cash, pay in cash. ‖ hacer algo efectivo,-a, to carry sth. out. ‖ hacer efectivo un cheque, to cash a cheque. ‖ hacerse efectivo,-a, JUR to come into effect.
■ dinero en efectivo, cash.
efecto 1 *m* (*resultado*) effect, result, end: *aquel jarabe no produjo ningún efecto,* that cough syrup had no effect. 2 (*impresión*) impression: *la escena le hizo un gran efecto,* the scene made a great impression on her. 3 (*fin*) aim, object. 4 DEP spin: *dio efecto a la pelota,* he put some spin on the ball. 5 COM bill, draft. – 6 efectos, *mpl* (*bienes*) effects, possessions; (*mercancías*) goods; (*personales*) effects, belongings.
● a efectos de ..., with the object of ... ‖ a tal efecto, to that end. ‖ causar efecto, to make an impression. ‖ chutar con efecto, to curl the ball, swerve the ball. ‖ en efecto, quite, yes indeed. ‖ hacer buen efecto, to be impressive, look good. ‖ hacer efecto, to make an impression, take effect, work. ‖ ser de efecto retardado, *fig* to be slow on the uptake. ‖ surtir efecto, to work, be effective. ‖ tener efecto, (*celebrarse*) to take place; (*entrar en vigor*) to take effect.
■ efecto interbancario, bank draft, bank bill. ‖ efectos de escritorio, stationery *sing*. ‖ efectos especiales, special effects. ‖ efectos personales, personal belongings. ‖ efectos públicos, public bonds. ‖ efectos secundarios, side effects.
efectuación *f* accomplishment.
efectuar 1 *t* (*gen*) to carry out, perform, make, do: *efectuaron una detención,* they carried out an arrest. 2 (*pago*) to make; (*pedido*) to place. 3 (*suma etc*) to do. 4 (*viaje, visita, etc*) to make. – 5 efectuarse, *p* (*realizarse*) to be carried out; (*acto etc*) to take place.
▲ Conjugation model [1], like *sacar*.
efeméride 1 *f* (*aniversario*) anniversary; (*conmemoración*) commemoration. 2 (*acontecimiento*) event. – 3 efemérides, *fpl* (*en periódico etc*) list of the day's anniversaries.
efervescencia 1 *f* (*gen*) effervescence. 2 (*de bebida*) fizziness. 3 *fig* (*excitación*) high spirits *pl*; (*agitación*) turmoil.
efervescente 1 *adj* (*gen*) effervescent. 2 (*bebida*) sparkling, fizzy. 3 (*pastilla*) soluble. 4 *fig* high-spirited, vivacious.
eficacia 1 *f* (*persona*) efficiency, effectiveness; (*cosas*) efficacy, effectiveness. 2 (*rendimiento*) efficiency.
eficaz 1 *adj* (*eficiente*) efficient. 2 (*cosa*) efficacious, effective. 3 (*que produce rendimiento*) efficient.
eficazmente *adv* effectively.
eficiencia *f* efficiency.
eficiente *adj* efficient.
eficientemente *adv* efficiently.
efigie *f* effigy.

efímero,-a *adj* ephemeral, brief.
eflorescencia *f* efflorescence.
efluvio 1 *m* emanation, effusion, flow. 2 *fig* surge.
efusión 1 *f* (*derramamiento*) effusion, pouring out. 2 *fig* effusiveness, warmth.
● con efusión, *fig* effusively.
efusivamente *adv* effusively, warmly.
efusividad *f* effusiveness.
efusivo,-a *adj* effusive, warm.
EGB *abr* EDUC (*Enseñanza General Básica*) ≈ Primary School Education.
egeo,-a *adj* Aegean.
■ el (mar) Egeo, the Aegean (Sea).
égida *f* aegis.
● bajo la égida de ..., under the auspices of ...
egipcio,-a 1 *adj* Egyptian. – 2 *m,f* (*persona*) Egyptian. – 3 egipcio, *m* (*idioma*) Egyptian.
Egipto *m* Egypt.
egiptología *f* Egyptology.
egiptólogo,-a *m,f* Egyptologist.
eglantina *f* eglantine.
eglefino *m* haddock.
égloga *f* eglogue, eclogue (US eclog).
ego *m* ego.
egocéntrico,-a *adj* egocentric, self-centred (US self-centered).
egocentrismo *m* egocentricity.
egoísmo *m* selfishness, egoism.
egoísta 1 *adj* selfish, egoistic, egoistical. – 2 *mf* egoist, selfish person.
ególatra 1 *adj* egomaniacal. – 2 *mf* egomaniac.
egolatría *f* egomania, self-worship.
egotismo *m* egotism.
egotista 1 *adj* egotistic, egotistical. – 2 *mf* egotist.
egregio,-a *adj* eminent, renowned, illustrious.
eh 1 *interj* *fam* (*para llamar*) hey!, hey you! 2 *fam* (*pregunta*) you what? 3 *fam* (*al final de frase*) OK?, right?: *no te quiero volver a ver, ¿eh?,* I don't want to see you again, OK?; *vendrás, ¿eh?,* you'll come, won't you?
eider *m* eider duck.
einstenio *m* einsteinium.
Eire *m* Eire.
ej. 1 *abr* (*ejemplo*) example; (*abreviatura*) e.g. 2 (*ejemplar*) copy.
eje 1 *m* MAT FÍS axis. 2 TÉC shaft, spindle. 3 AUTO axle. 4 *fig* (*zona principal*) centre (US center), main area: *el eje comercial de la ciudad,* the city's main shopping area. 5 *fig* (*parte esencial*) crux, main idea, core: *el eje de un discurso,* the core of a speech. 6 (*calle, carretera*) thoroughfare. 7 el Eje, POL the Axis.
● partir por el eje a algn., *fam* to kill sb.
■ eje de abcisas, MAT x-axis. ‖ eje de ordenadas, MAT y-axis. ‖ eje delantero, AUTO front axle. ‖ eje trasero, AUTO rear axle.
ejecución 1 *f* (*de una orden etc*) carrying out, execution. 2 MÚS performance. 3 (*ajusticiamiento*) execution. 4 JUR seizure.
ejecutante *mf* performer.
ejecutar 1 *t* (*una orden etc*) to carry out. 2 MÚS to perform, play. 3 (*ajusticiar*) to execute. 4 JUR to seize. 5 INFORM to run.
ejecutiva *f* → **ejecutivo,-a**.
ejecutivo,-a 1 *adj* executive. 2 (*rápido*) prompt. – 3 *m,f* executive. – 4 el ejecutivo, *m* (*gobierno*) the government: *las propuestas del Ejecutivo han sido rechazadas*

por los sindicatos, the Government's proposals have been rejected by the unions. **– 5 la ejecutiva,** *f* the executive, executive committee: *la ejecutiva provincial del PSOE se reunió ayer en Málaga,* the provincial executive of the Socialist Party met yesterday in Málaga. ■ **poder ejecutivo,** the executive.

ejecutor,-ra 1 *m,f* executor. **2** *(verdugo)* executioner. ■ **ejecutor,-ra testamentario,-a,** executor of a will.

ejecutoria *f* → **ejecutorio,-a**.

ejecutorio,-a 1 *adj* executory, enforceable. **– 2 ejecutoria,** *f* writ of execution.

ejem *interj* ahem, hmm.

ejemplar 1 *adj* exemplary, model: *un ciudadano ejemplar,* a model citizen. **– 2** *m (copia)* copy, number, issue: *ejemplar gratuito,* free copy. **3** *(prototipo)* specimen.

ejemplaridad *f* exemplariness.

ejemplarizar *t* to set an example to.
▲ *Conjugation model* [4], *like realizar.*

ejemplificación *f* exemplification, illustration.

ejemplificar *t* to illustrate, exemplify.
▲ *Conjugation model* [1], *like sacar.*

ejemplo 1 *m* example. **2** *(modelo)* model. ● **dar ejemplo,** to set an example. ‖ **poner de ejemplo,** to give as an example. ‖ **por ejemplo,** for example, for instance. ‖ **servir de ejemplo,** to serve as an example. ‖ **tomar ejemplo de algn.,** to follow sb.'s example.

ejercer 1 *t (profesión etc)* to practise (US practice), be in practice as: *ejerce la abogacía,* she's in practice as a lawyer. **2** *(usar)* to exercise; *(influencia)* to exert. **– 3** *i* to practise (US practice), work: *ejerce de médico,* he works as a doctor. ● **ejercer el derecho de,** to exercise one's right to.
▲ *Conjugation model* [2], *like mecer.*

ejercicio 1 *m (de profesión)* practice; *(de derecho)* use, exercise; *(de función)* performance. **2** EDUC exercise; *(examen)* test; *(pregunta de examen)* question; *(deberes)* homework. **3** DEP exercise. **4** FIN year. ● **en ejercicio,** practising (US practicing). ‖ **hacer ejercicio,** to do exercise, take exercise. ■ **ejercicio económico,** financial year, fiscal year. ‖ **ejercicios espirituales,** spiritual retreat.

ejercitar 1 *t (profesión)* to practise (US practice). **2** *(enseñar)* to train. **– 3 ejercitarse,** *p (aprender)* to train; MIL to exercise.

ejército *m* army. ■ **ejército de tierra,** army. ‖ **ejército del aire,** air force.

ejido *m* common land.

el 1 *art def* the: *el coche,* the car; *el agua,* water; *el Japón,* Japan; *la Sra. Rodríguez,* Mrs. Rodríguez; *llegó el martes,* he arrived on Tuesday. **2 el + de,** the one: *el del traje azul,* the one in the blue suit; *el de Valencia,* the one from Valencia; *el de tu hermano,* your brother's; *el de hoy,* today's. **3 el + que,** *(persona - sujeto)* the one who; *(- objeto)* the one, the one that, the one whom: *el que vino ayer,* the one who came yesterday; *el que vi,* the one I saw. **4** *(cosa)* the one, the one that, the one which: *el que me diste,* the one (that) you gave me.

él 1 *pron (sujeto - persona)* he; *(- cosa, animal)* it: *él vive aquí,* he lives here; *él ladró,* it barked. **2** *(objeto - persona)* him; *(- cosa, animal)* it: *comió con él,* she had lunch with him; *no puedo vivir sin él,* I can't live without him. ● **de él,** *(posesivo)* his: *es de él,* it's his. ‖ **él mismo,** himself.
▲ *pl ellos; feminine ella.*

elaboración 1 *f (producto)* manufacture, production. **2** *(madera, metal, etc)* working. **3** *(idea)* working out, development. ● **de elaboración casera,** home-made.

elaborar 1 *t (producto)* to make, manufacture, produce. **2** *(madera, metal, etc)* to work. **3** *(idea)* to work out, develop.

elasticidad 1 *f (gen)* elasticity. **2** *(tela)* stretch. **3** *fig* flexibility.

elástico,-a 1 *adj* elastic. **2** *(telas)* elastic, stretch. **3** *fig* flexible: *un horario elástico,* a flexible timetable. **– 4 elástico,** *m* elastic. **– 5 elásticos,** *mpl* braces, US suspenders. ● **ser algo muy elástico,-a,** *fig* to be open to a number of interpretations. ■ **cama elástica,** trampoline.

elastina *f* elastin.

ele[1] *interj* eh!

ele[2] *f name of the letter l.*

elección 1 *f (nombramiento)* election. **2** *(opción)* choice: *lo dejamos a tu elección,* we'll leave it up to you; *el color es a elección del cliente,* the choice of colour is left up to the customer. **– 3 elecciones,** *fpl* elections. ● **convocar elecciones,** to call an election. ‖ **no tener elección,** to have no choice, have no option. ■ **elecciones generales,** general election *sing.*

electivo,-a *adj* elective.

electo,-a *adj* elect.

elector,-ra *m,f* voter, elector.

electorado *m* electorate, voters *pl.*

electoral *adj* electoral. ■ **campaña electoral,** election campaign. ‖ **colegio electoral,** polling station. ‖ **distrito electoral,** constituency.

electoralismo *m pey* electioneering.

electoralista *adj pey* electioneering.

electorero,-a *m,f pey* electioneer.

electricidad *f* electricity.

electricista 1 *adj* electrical. **– 2** *mf* electrician. ■ **ingeniero electricista,** electrical engineer.

eléctrico,-a *adj* electric, electrical. ■ **manta eléctrica,** electric blanket. ‖ **silla eléctrica,** electric chair.

electrificación *f* electrification.

electrificar *t* to electrify.
▲ *Conjugation model* [1], *like sacar.*

electrizante *adj fig* electrifying.

electrizar 1 *t fig* to electrify, thrill, excite.
▲ *Conjugation model* [4], *like realizar.*

electroacústica *f* electro-acoustics.

electrobomba *f* electric pump.

electrocardiografía *f* electrocardiography.

electrocardiograma *m* electrocardiogram.

electrocardiógrafo *m* electrocardiograph.

electrochoque *m* electro-shock therapy.

electrocución *f* electrocution.

electrocutar 1 *t* to electrocute. **– 2 electrocutarse,** *p* to be electrocuted, electrocute os.

electrodinámica *f* → **electrodinámico,-a**.

electrodinámico,-a 1 *adj* electrodynamic. **– 2 electrodinámica,** *f* electrodynamics.

electrodo *m* electrode.

electrodoméstico *m* electrical appliance.

electroencefalografía *f* electroencephalography.

electroencefalógrafo *m* electroencephalograph.

electroencefalograma m electroencephalogram.
electrógeno,-a 1 adj generating, generating. – 2 electrógeno, m electricity generator.
■ equipo electrógeno, electricity generator.
electroimán m electromagnet.
electrólisis f electrolysis.
▲ pl electrólisis.
electrolito m electrolyte.
electrólito m electrolyte.
electrolizar t to electrolyse.
▲ Conjugation model [4], like realizar.
electromagnetismo m electromagnetism.
electromagnético,-a adj electromagnetic.
electromecánico,-a 1 adj electromechanical. – 2 electromecánica, f electromechanics.
electromecánica f → electromecánico,-a.
electrometalurgia f electrometallurgy.
electrometría f electrometry.
electromotor,-ra 1 adj electromotive. – 2 electromotor, m electric motor.
electromotriz adj electromotive.
electrón m electron.
electronegativo,-a adj electronegative.
electrónica f → electrónico,-a.
electrónico,-a 1 adj electronic. – 2 electrónica, f electronics.
electronvoltio m electron volt.
electropositivo,-a adj electropositive.
electroquímica f → electroquímico,-a.
electroquímico,-a 1 adj electrochemical. – 2 electroquímica, f electrochemistry.
electroscopio m electroscope.
electrostática f → electrostático,-a.
electrostático,-a 1 adj electrostatic. – 2 electrostática, f electrostatics.
electrotecnia f electrotechnics.
electroterapia f electrotherapy.
electrotermia f electrothermy, electrothermics.
electuario m electuary.
elefancía f elephantiasis.
elefante,-a m,f (macho) elephant; (hembra) cow elephant, female elephant.
■ elefante marino, elephant seal.
elefantiasis f elephantiasis.
elegancia f elegance, smartness, style.
elegante adj elegant, smart, stylish.
elegantemente adv elegantly, smartly.
elegía f elegy.
elegiaco,-a 1 adj elegiac. 2 fig elegiac, plaintive.
elegíaco,-a adj → elegiaco,-a.
elegibilidad f elegibility.
elegible adj elegible.
elegido,-a 1 pp → elegir. – 2 adj (escogido) chosen. 3 (predilecto) preferred. 4 POL elected. – 5 m,f chosen one. 6 POL elected person. – 7 los elegidos, mpl the chosen few.
elegir 1 t (escoger) to choose: puedes elegir entre cuatro destinos, you can choose from four destinations. 2 POL to elect.
▲ Conjugation model [55].
elemental 1 adj (del elemento) elemental. 2 (obvio) elementary, basic.
elemento 1 m (gen) element. 2 (parte) component, part. 3 (individuo) type, sort. – 4 elementos, mpl (atmosféricos) elements. 5 (fundamentos) rudiments, basic principles.

● estar uno en su elemento, fig to be in one's element. ‖ ¡menudo elemento! / ¡vaya elemento!, fam he's a right one!
■ elementos de juicio, facts of the case.
elenco 1 m (catálogo) index, catalogue (US catalog). 2 TEAT CINEM cast. 3 (personal) staff.
elepé m LP (record).
elevación 1 f (de terreno) elevation, rise. 2 (precios) rise, raising, increasing; (voz, tono) raising; (peso) raising, lifting. 3 MAT raising. 4 REL elevation.
elevado,-a 1 pp → elevar. – 2 adj (gen) high. 3 fig lofty, noble.
● elevado,-a a, MAT raised to: elevado a la quinta potencia, raised to the power of five; elevado al cubo, cubed; elevado al cuadrado, squared.
elevador,-ra 1 adj elevating. – 2 elevador, m AM lift, US elevator.
elevalunas m window-winding mechanism.
■ elevalunas eléctrico, electric window.
▲ pl elevalunas.
elevar 1 t (peso etc) to elevate, raise, lift. 2 (precios) to raise, increase, put up; (tono, voz) to raise. 3 (enaltecer) to promote, raise: lo elevaron a gerente, he was promoted to manager. 4 MAT to raise. – 5 elevarse, p (subir) to rise (up): el humo se elevaba, the smoke was rising up. 6 (alcanzar) to reach: se eleva hasta el techo, it reaches the ceiling. 7 (erguirse, levantarse) to stand: allí se elevaba la catedral, there stood the cathedral. 8 (sumar) to amount to, come to: los gastos se elevan a dos mil pesetas, the expenses amount to two thousand pesetas. 9 fig (engreírse) to become conceited.
elfo m elf.
elidir 1 t to elide. – 2 elidirse, p to elide, be elided.
elijo pres indic → elegir.
eliminación f elimination.
eliminador,-ra 1 adj eliminating. – 2 m,f eliminator.
eliminar 1 t (gen) to eliminate, exclude: han eliminado el equipo del campeonato, they've eliminated the team from the championship. 2 (esperanzas, miedos, etc) to get rid of, cast aside. 3 fam (matar) to kill, eliminate.
eliminatoria f → eliminatorio,-a.
eliminatorio,-a 1 adj eliminatory. – 2 eliminatoria, f heat, qualifying round.
elipse f ellipse.
elipsis f ellipsis.
▲ pl elipsis.
elipsoidal adj ellipsoidal.
elipsoide m ellipsoid.
elíptico,-a adj elliptic, elliptical.
elisión f elision.
elite f elite.
élite f elite.
elitismo m elitism.
elitista adj elitist.
élitro m elytrum.
elixir m elixir.
elíxir m elixir.
ella 1 pron (sujeto - persona) she; (- cosa, animal) it: ella vive aquí, she lives here. 2 (objeto - persona) her; (- cosa, animal) it: vino con ella, he came with her.
● de ella, (posesivo) hers: es de ella, it's hers. ‖ ella misma, herself.
elle f name of the digraph ll.
ello pron it: no me digas nada de ello, don't tell me anything about it.

● **¡a ello!,** to work! ‖ **ello es que ...,** the thing is that ..., the fact is that ... ‖ **por ello,** that's why: *por ello llegamos tarde,* that's why we arrived late.
▲ *pl ello.*

ellos,-as 1 *pron (sujeto)* they: *ellas lo dijeron,* they said so. 2 *(objeto)* them: *vino con ellos,* she came with them.
● **de ellos,-as,** theirs: *el coche es de ellos,* the car is theirs. ‖ **ellos,-as mismos,-as,** themselves.

elocución *f* elocution.

elocuencia *f* eloquence.

elocuente *adj* eloquent.

elogiable *adj* praiseworthy.

elogiar *t* to praise, eulogize.
▲ *Conjugation model* [12], *like* **cambiar.**

elogio *m* praise, eulogy.
● **digno,-a de elogio,** praiseworthy. ‖ **hacer elogios de,** to sing the praises of.

elogiosamente *adv* eulogistically, admiringly.

elogioso,-a *adj* appreciative, complimentary, eulogistic.

elongación *f* elongation.

elucidación *f* elucidation, clarification.

elucidar *t* to elucidate, explain.

elucubración *f* lucubration.

elucubrar *t* to lucubrate.

eludible *adj* avoidable.

eludir 1 *t (responsabilidad, justicia, etc)* to evade. 2 *(pregunta)* to avoid, evade; *(persona)* to avoid.

elusivo,-a *adj* evasive.

E.M. *abr* MIL (*Estado Mayor*) staff.

Em³ *abr* (*Eminencia*) Eminence.

emanación *f* emanation.

emanar 1 *i (olor etc)* to emanate. 2 *(derivar)* to derive (**de,** from), come (**de,** from).

emancipación *f* emancipation.

emancipado,-a 1 *pp* → **emancipar.** – 2 *adj* emancipated, free.

emancipador,-ra *adj* emancipating, liberating.

emancipar 1 *t* to emancipate, free. – 2 **emanciparse,** *p* to become emancipated, become free.

emasculación *f* emasculation, castration.

emascular *t* to emasculate, castrate.

embabiamiento *m fam* daydreaming, absent-mindedness.

embadurnar *t* to daub, smear: *embadurnar de/con yeso,* to daub with plaster.

embajada 1 *f (cargo)* ambassadorship, post of ambassador. 2 *(edificio)* embassy. 3 *(mensaje)* message. 4 *fam (proposición)* cheeky proposition, cheeky suggestion.

embajador,-ra *m,f* ambassador.

embalador,-ra *m,f* packer.

embalaje *m* packing, packaging.
■ **gastos de embalaje,** packing charge. ‖ **papel de embalaje,** wrapping paper.

embalar 1 *t (empaquetar)* to pack, wrap. – 2 *i (acelerar)* to speed up. – 3 **embalarse,** *p (acelerar)* to speed up. 4 *fig (al hablar)* to gabble. 5 *fig (dejarse llevar)* to get carried away.

embaldosado 1 *m (trabajo)* tiling. 2 *(suelo)* tiled floor.

embaldosar *t* to tile.

embalsadero *m* fen, marsh, swamp.

embalsamador,-ra *m,f* embalmer.

embalsamar *t* to embalm.

embalsar 1 *t (agua)* to dam up. 2 MAR to hoist, lift. – 3 **embalsarse,** *p* to be dammed up.

embalse 1 *m (acción)* damming. 2 *(presa)* dam, reservoir.

embanastar 1 *t* to put into a basket. 2 *fig (gente)* to cram into.

embancarse *p* to run aground.
▲ *Conjugation model* [1], *like* **sacar.**

embarazada *adj-f* → **embarazado,-a.**

embarazado,-a 1 *pp* → **embarazar.** – 2 *adj (mujer)* pregnant. 3 *(turbado)* embarrassed. – 4 **embarazada,** *f* pregnant woman, expectant mother.

embarazar 1 *t (mujer)* to make pregnant. 2 *(estorbar)* to hinder. 3 *(turbar)* to embarrass. – 4 **embarazarse,** *p (quedarse encinta)* to become pregnant. 5 *(turbarse)* to get embarrassed.
▲ *Conjugation model* [4], *like* **realizar.**

embarazo 1 *m (preñez)* pregnancy. 2 *(obstáculo)* obstruction, obstacle. 3 *(turbación)* embarrassment.
■ **embarazo fantasma,** phantom pregnancy.

embarazoso,-a *adj* embarrassing, awkward, troublesome.

embarcación 1 *f (nave)* boat, vessel, craft. 2 *(embarco)* embarkation. 3 *(viaje)* voyage.
■ **embarcación de pesca,** fishing boat. ‖ **embarcación de recreo,** pleasure boat.

embarcadero *m* pier, jetty, quay.

embarcador,-ra *m,f* docker.

embarcar 1 *t (personas)* to embark, put on board; *(mercancías)* to load. 2 *fig* to involve, implicate. – 3 **embarcarse,** *p (en barco)* to embark, go on board; *(en avión)* to board. 4 *fig* to embark upon, engage in: *se embarcó en una empresa peligrosa,* he embarked upon a dangerous enterprise.
● **embarcarse en un asunto,** *fig* to get involved in a matter.
▲ *Conjugation model* [1], *like* **sacar.**

embarco *m* embarkation.

embardar *t* to thatch.

embargar 1 *t* JUR to seize, sequestrate, impound. 2 *(emociones)* to overcome: *un sentimiento de pena la embargaba,* she was overcome by grief; *el dolor embargó mis sentidos,* my senses were dulled by sorrow.
▲ *Conjugation model* [7], *like* **llegar.**

embargo 1 *m* JUR seizure of property, sequestration. 2 COM POL embargo.
● **sin embargo,** nevertheless, however.

embarnizar *t* to varnish.
▲ *Conjugation model* [4], *like* **realizar.**

embarque *m (de personas)* boarding; *(de mercancías)* loading.
■ **tarjeta de embarque,** boarding card.

embarrado,-a 1 *pp* → **embarrar.** – 2 *adj* muddy.

embarrancar 1 *i* MAR to run aground. 2 *fig* to get bogged down. – 3 **embarrancarse,** *p* MAR to run aground. 4 *fig* to get bogged down.
▲ *Conjugation model* [1], *like* **sacar.**

embarrar 1 *t (untar de barro)* to cover with mud. 2 *(embadurnar)* to daub, smear. – 3 **embarrarse,** *p* to get covered in mud.

embarullador,-ra 1 *adj* bungling, muddling. – 2 *m,f* bungler, muddler.

embarullar 1 *t (mezclar)* to muddle. 2 *(hacer mal)* to bungle. 3 *fam (liar)* to confuse. – 4 **embarullarse,** *p (liarse)* to get muddled up, get confused.

embastar *t* to baste, tack.

embastecer 1 *i (engordar)* to grow fat. – 2 **embastecerse,** *p (ponerse basto)* to become coarse.
▲ *Conjugation model* [43], *like* **agradecer.**

embate 1 *m* (*de olas*) dashing, breaking. 2 (*viento*) summer sea breeze. 3 *fig* (*acometida*) outburst.

embaucador,-ra 1 *adj* deceitful. – 2 *m,f* cheat, swindler, trickster.

embaucar *t* to deceive, trick, dupe, cheat, swindle.
▲ *Conjugation model* [1], *like* ***sacar.***

embaular 1 *t* (*meter en baúl*) to pack in a trunk. 2 *fig* (*engullir*) to gorge, guzzle. 3 *fig* (*llenar*) to cram, stuff.

embebecer 1 *t* to delight, fascinate. – 2 **embebecerse,** *p* to be delighted, be fascinated.
▲ *Conjugation model* [43], *like* ***agradecer.***

embeber 1 *t* (*absorber*) to soak up. 2 (*empapar*) to soak, drench. 3 COST to take in. 4 *fig* (*incorporar*) to insert: *embeber un nuevo capítulo,* to insert a new chapter. – 5 *i* (*encogerse*) to shrink: *la lana embebe,* wool shrinks. – 6 **embeberse,** *p* to become absorbed (**en,** in).

embebido,-a 1 *pp* → **embeber.** – 2 *adj* absorbed, engrossed.

embelecar *t* to deceive, cheat.
▲ *Conjugation model* [1], *like* ***sacar.***

embeleco *m* deception, cheating.

embelesado,-a 1 *pp* → **embelesar.** – 2 *adj* fascinated, delighted.

embelesar *t* to charm, delight, fascinate.

embeleso *m* delight, fascination.

embellecedor,-ra 1 *adj* beautifying: *loción embellecedora,* beauty lotion. – 2 **embellecedor,** *m* AUTO hubcap.

embellecer 1 *t* to make beautiful, beautify. – 2 **embellecerse,** *p* to make os. beautiful, beautify os.
▲ *Conjugation model* [43], *like* ***agradecer.***

embellecimiento *m* beautification.

emberrenchinarse *p fam* to fly into a tantrum.

emberrincharse *p fam* to fly into a tantrum.

embestida 1 *f* (*gen*) onslaught, attack. 2 (*de toro*) charge.

embestir 1 *t* (*atacar*) to assault, attack. 2 (*toro*) to charge. 3 (*coche*) to smash (into).
▲ *Conjugation model* [34], *like* ***servir.***

embetunar *t* (*calzado*) to polish.

emblandecer 1 *t* to soften. – 2 **emblandecerse,** *p* to soften, go soft. 3 *fig* to relent.
▲ *Conjugation model* [43], *like* ***agradecer.***

emblanquecer 1 *t* to whiten, bleach. – 2 **emblanquecerse,** *p* to go white, bleach.
▲ *Conjugation model* [43], *like* ***agradecer.***

emblema 1 *m* emblem, badge. 2 (*de marca*) logo.

emblemático,-a *adj* emblematic.

embobado,-a 1 *pp* → **embobar.** – 2 *adj* fascinated, entranced.

embobamiento *m* fascination, amazement.

embobar 1 *t* to fascinate, amaze, entrance. – 2 **embobarse,** *p* to be fascinated, be entranced: *se embobaron con las luces,* they were fascinated by the lights.

embobecer *t* to turn silly.
▲ *Conjugation model* [43], *like* ***agradecer.***

embocadura 1 *f* (*de río*) mouth. 2 MÚS mouthpiece. 3 (*de vino*) taste, flavour (US flavor).

embocar 1 *t* (*en la boca*) to put into the mouth. 2 (*calle, canal*) to enter. 3 (*engullir*) to guzzle. 4 *fig* (*hacer creer*) to make believe: *le embocó la historia,* he made her believe the story. 5 (*en golf*) to hole.
▲ *Conjugation model* [1], *like* ***sacar.***

embolado 1 *m* TEAT minor role. 2 *fig* (*engaño*) fib, lie. 3 *fig* (*problema*) tight spot. 4 (*en toros*) bull with protective wooden balls on its horns.

embolar *t* (*toro*) to put wooden balls on the horns of a bull.

embolia *f* embolism, clot.

émbolo *m* TÉC piston; (*de cafetera*) plunger.

embolsar 1 *t* to pocket. 2 (*cobrar*) to collect. – 3 **embolsarse,** *p* (*cobrar*) to make, earn; (*ganar*) win.

emboquillado,-a *adj* filter-tipped.

emboquillar 1 *t* (*cigarrillos*) to tip. 2 (*túnel, galería*) to open up.

emborrachar 1 *t* to make drunk. – 2 **emborracharse,** *p* to get drunk: *se emborrachó con tequila,* he got drunk on tequila.

emborrascarse *p* to become stormy, become overcast.

emborregado *adj* cloudy.

emborricarse 1 *p fam* (*aturdirse*) to become confused, become bewildered. 2 *fam* (*enamorarse*) to fall in love.
▲ *Conjugation model* [1], *like* ***sacar.***

emborronar 1 *t* (*echar borrones*) to blot. 2 (*hacer garabatos*) to scribble on. 3 *fig* (*escribir mal*) to scribble. – 4 **emborronarse,** *p* (*correrse la tinta*) to smudge.

emborrullarse *p fam* to argue, quarrel.

emboscada *f* ambush.
● **tender una emboscada,** to lay an ambush.

emboscar *t* to ambush.
▲ *Conjugation model* [1], *like* ***sacar.***

embotado,-a 1 *pp* → **embotar.** – 2 *adj* (*sentidos*) dull. 3 (*desafilado*) blunt. .

embotadura 1 *f* (*de los sentidos*) dulling. 2 (*despunte*) bluntness.

embotar 1 *t* (*arma etc*) to blunt. 2 *fig* (*sentidos*) to dull; (*mente*) to numb, fuddle. 3 *fig* (*enervar*) to enervate, debilitate. – 4 **embotarse,** *p* (*arma etc*) to become blunt. 5 *fig* (*sentidos*) to be dulled; (*mente*) to become numb.

embotellado,-a 1 *pp* → **embotellar.** – 2 *adj* bottled. – 3 **embotellado,** *m* bottling.

embotellador,-ra 1 *m,f* bottler. – 2 **embotelladora,** *f* bottling machine.
■ **planta embotelladora,** bottling plant.

embotelladora *f* → **embotellador,-ra.**

embotellamiento 1 *m* (*acción de embotellar*) bottling. 2 AUTO *fig* traffic jam.

embotellar 1 *t* (*meter en botella*) to bottle. 2 AUTO *fig* to block, jam. 3 *fig* (*aprender de memoria*) to learn by heart.

embotijar 1 *t* to put in jugs. – 2 **embotijarse,** *p* (*hincharse*) to swell. 3 (*enojarse*) to become angry.

embozar 1 *t* (*el rostro*) to muffle. 2 (*animales*) to muzzle. 3 *fig* (*ocultar*) to disguise, conceal. – 4 **embozarse,** *p* (*el rostro*) to muffle os. up.

embozo 1 *m* (*prenda*) muffler, mask. 2 *fig* (*recato*) reserve, caution, wariness.

embragar *i* to engage the clutch.
▲ *Conjugation model* [7], *like* ***llegar.***

embrague *m* clutch.

embravecer 1 *t* to enrage. – 2 **embravecerse,** *p* to fly into a rage. 3 (*el mar*) to become rough.
▲ *Conjugation model* [43], *like* ***agradecer.***

embrear *t* to tar, pitch.

embriagado,-a 1 *pp* → **embriagar.** – 2 *adj* intoxicated, drunk.

embriagador,-ra *adj* intoxicating.

embriagar 1 *t* to make drunk, intoxicate. 2 *fig* to transport, enrapture. – 3 **embriagarse,** *p* to get drunk. 4 *fig* to be transported, be enraptured.
▲ *Conjugation model* [7], *like* ***llegar.***

embriaguez 1 *f* intoxication, drunkenness. 2 *fig* intoxication, rapture.

embridar *t* to bridle.
embriología *f* embryology.
embrión 1 *m* embryo. 2 *fig* (*idea etc*) beginnings *pl*, embryo; (*revolución*) seeds *pl*.
 ● en embrión, in embryo.
embrionario,-a *adj* embryonic, embryonal.
embrolladamente *adv* confusedly.
embrollado,-a 1 *pp* → **embrollar**. − 2 *adj* confused, muddled.
embrollador,-ra 1 *adj* confusing, muddling. − 2 *m,f* troublemaker.
embrollar 1 *t* to confuse, muddle. − 2 **embrollarse**, *p* to get confused, get muddled.
embrollo 1 *m* (*confusión*) muddle, mess. 2 (*mentira*) lie. 3 *fig* (*situación embarazosa*) embarrassing situation.
embromar *t* to play jokes on, play a trick on, tease.
embrujado,-a 1 *pp* → **embrujar**. − 2 *adj* (*persona*) bewitched; (*lugar*) haunted.
embrujar 1 *t* (*persona*) to bewitch; (*lugar*) to haunt. 2 *fig* (*fascinar*) to bewitch, enchant.
embrujo 1 *m* spell, charm. 2 *fig* (*fascinación*) fascination, attraction.
embrutecer 1 *t* (*facultades etc*) to dull, deaden. − 2 embrutecerse, *p* to become dull, become stupefied.
 ▲ *Conjugation model* [43], *like* **agradecer**.
embuchado 1 *m* (*embutido*) processed cold meat. 2 *fig* (*negocio*) cover-up. 3 *fig* (*fraude electoral*) rigging of elections.
embuchar 1 *t* (*embutir*) to stuff; (*aves*) to force-feed. 2 (*comer mucho*) to stuff os. with. 3 *fam fig* (*hacer creer*) to make believe.
embudo 1 *m* funnel. 2 *fig* trick.
embuste *m* (*mentira*) lie; (*engaño*) trick.
embustero,-a 1 *adj* lying, deceitful. − 2 *m,f* liar.
embutido 1 *m* (*alimento*) processed cold meat, cold cut. 2 (*incrustación*) inlay.
embutir 1 *t* (*llenar*) to stuff, cram, squeeze. 2 (*carne*) to stuff. 3 (*incrustar*) to inlay. 4 *fig* (*condensar*) to condense: *embutieron el texto en una página*, they condensed the text into one page. 5 *fig* (*hacer creer*) to make believe. 6 *fig* (*llenar de comida*) to stuff. − 7 **embutirse**, *p fig* (*atiborrarse*) to stuff os. (**de**, with).
eme *f* name of the letter *m*.
 ● esto es una eme, *fam euf* this is rubbish. ‖ ¡vete a la eme!, *fam euf* eff off!
emergencia 1 *f* (*imprevisto*) emergency. 2 (*salida*) emergence.
 ● en caso de emergencia, in an emergency, in case of emergency.
 ■ estado de emergencia, state of emergency. ‖ salida de emergencia, emergency exit.
emergente 1 *adj* emerging, emergent. 2 *fig* resulting, consequent.
emerger 1 *i* to emerge. 2 (*aparecer*) to appear, emerge, come into view. 3 *fig* to result.
 ▲ *Conjugation model* [5], *like* **proteger**.
emérito,-a *adj* emeritus.
emersión *f* emersion.
emigración 1 *f* emigration. 2 (*aves, pueblo*) migration.
emigrado,-a 1 *pp* → **emigrar**. − 2 *adj* emigrant. 3 POL émigré.
emigrante 1 *adj* emigrant. − 2 *mf* emigrant.
emigrar *i* to emigrate; (*aves, pueblo*) to migrate.
eminencia 1 *f* (*elevación*) height, elevation, hill. 2 *fig* (*mérito*) prominence. 3 *fig* (*persona*) eminence, eminency.

 ■ eminencia gris, éminence grise. ‖ Su Eminencia, REL His Eminence.
eminente 1 *adj* (*elevado*) high. 2 *fig* eminent, distinguished.
eminentemente *adv* eminently.
emir *m* emir.
emirato *m* emirate.
 ■ Emiratos Árabes Unidos, United Arab Emirates.
emisario,-a *m,f* emissary.
emisión 1 *f* (*gen*) emission. 2 (*bonos, sellos, monedas*) issue. 3 RAD TV (*programa*) broadcast; (*transmisión*) transmission.
 ■ cierre de la emisión, RAD TV close-down. ‖ emisión de bonos, FIN bond issue. ‖ emisión de obligaciones, FIN issue of debentures. ‖ emisión en directo, RAD TV live transmission. ‖ emisión pública, FIN public issue.
emisor,-ra 1 *adj* (*banco etc*) issuing. 2 RAD TV broadcasting, transmitter. − 3 *m,f* (*banco etc*) issuer. − 4 **emisor**, *m* RAD radio transmitter. − 5 **emisora**, *f* broadcasting station, radio station.
emitir 1 *t* (*sonido, luz*) to emit; (*olor*) to give off. 2 (*manifestar*) to express. 3 (*bonos, monedas, sellos*) to issue. 4 RAD TV to broadcast, transmit. − 5 *i* RAD TV to transmit.
 ● emitir un fallo, JUR to pronounce judgement. ‖ emitir un juicio, to express an opinion. ‖ emitir una sentencia, JUR to pass sentence.
Emmo. *abr* (*Eminentísimo*) Most Eminent.
emoción 1 *f* (*sentimiento*) emotion, feeling. 2 (*excitación*) excitement.
 ● ¡qué emoción!, how exciting!
emocionado,-a 1 *pp* → **emocionar**. − 2 *adj* (deeply) moved, (deeply) touched.
emocional *adj* emotional.
emocionante 1 *adj* (*conmovedor*) moving, touching. 2 (*excitante*) exciting, thrilling.
emocionar 1 *t* (*conmover*) to move, touch: *nos emocionaron sus palabras*, we were touched by her words. 2 (*excitar*) to excite, thrill. − 3 **emocionarse**, *p* (*conmoverse*) to be moved, be touched. 4 (*excitarse*) to get excited.
emoliente 1 *adj* emollient. − 2 *m* emollient.
emolumento *m* emolument.
emotividad *f* emotiveness.
emotivo,-a *adj* (*persona*) emotional; (*acto ect*) moving, touching; (*palabras*) emotive, stirring, rousing.
empacadora *f* (*de cajas etc*) packing machine; (*de pacas*) baling machine, baler.
empacar *t* (*empaquetar - cajas etc*) to pack; (*- pacas*) to bale.
 ▲ *Conjugation model* [1], *like* **sacar**.
empacarse 1 *p* (*emperrarse*) to dig one's heels in. 2 (*turbarse*) to become embarrassed.
empachado,-a 1 *pp* → **empachar**. − 2 *adj* (*apocado*) slow-witted. 3 (*ahíto*) bloated, full.
empachar 1 *t* (*comer demasiado*) to give indigestion. 2 (*impedir*) to obstruct. 3 *fig* (*aburrir*) to bore, make sick. − 4 **empacharse**, *p* (*de comer*) to have indigestion, get indigestion, get an upset stomach.
empacho 1 *m* (*indigestión*) indigestion, upset stomach. 2 *fig* (*turbación*) embarrassment.
 ● no tener empacho en decir algo, *fig* to have no qualms about saying sth. ‖ sin empacho, *fig* unashamedly. ‖ tener un empacho de algo, *fig* to have had one's fill of sth.
empachoso,-a 1 *adj* (*comida*) heavy, indigestible. 2 *fig* (*empalagoso*) sugary, cloying. 3 *fig* (*vergonzoso*) shameful.

empadrarse *p* to become too attached to one's father/parents.
empadronamiento 1 *m* (*acción*) census taking. 2 (*padrón*) census.
empadronar 1 *t* (*hacer el censo*) to take a census of. 2 (*apuntar*) to register in a census. – 3 **empadronarse**, *p* to register.
empajar *t* (*cubrir*) to cover with straw; (*rellenar*) to stuff with straw.
empalagamiento 1 *m* (*de comida*) sickliness. 2 *fig* bother, annoyance.
empalagar 1 *i* (*dulces*) to be too sweet, be sickly. 2 *fig* to be cloying, pall.
▲ *Conjugation model* [7], *like llegar.*
empalago *m* → **empalagamiento**.
empalagoso,-a 1 *adj* (*dulces*) too sweet, sickly. 2 *fig* (*persona*) sickly sweet, cloying.
empalar *t* to impale.
empalizada *f* palisade, fence.
empalizar *t* to palisade.
▲ *Conjugation model* [4], *like realizar.*
empalmar 1 *t* (*unir*) to join, connect. 2 (*cinta, cuerda, película*) to splice. 3 *fig* (*planes etc*) to combine, link up. 4 (*carpintería*) to join. 5 DEP to volley. – 6 *i* (*enlazar*) to join, connect. 7 (*seguir*) to follow on from: *esta idea empalma con la anterior,* this idea follows on from the previous one. – 8 **empalmarse**, *p tabú* to get a hard-on.
empalme 1 *m* (*gen*) connection. 2 (*cinta, cuerda, película*) splice. 3 (*carpintería*) joint. 4 DEP volley. 5 (*ferrocarril*) junction; (*carretera*) intersection, T-junction.
empanada *f* → **empanado,-a**.
empanadilla *f* pasty.
empanado,-a 1 *pp* → **empanar**. – 2 *adj* (*rebozado*) breaded, in breadcrumbs. – 3 **empanada**, *f* pasty, pie.
empanar 1 *t* (*rebozar*) to coat in breadcrumbs. 2 (*poner entre masa*) to fill.
empantanado,-a 1 *pp* → **empantanar**. – 2 *adj* (*inundado*) flooded. 3 *fig* (*atascado*) bogged down.
empantanar 1 *t* (*inundar*) to flood. 2 *fig* (*detener*) to bring to a standstill. – 3 **empantanarse**, *p* (*inundarse*) to become flooded. 4 *fig* (*detenerse*) to be bogged down.
empañado,-a 1 *pp* → **empañar**. – 2 *adj* (*cristal*) steamed up, misty. 3 (*voz*) faint. 4 *fig* (*honor*) tainted, tarnished.
empañar 1 *t* (*bebés*) to put a nappy on. 2 (*cristal*) to steam up. 3 *fig* (*honor etc*) to taint, tarnish. – 4 **empañarse**, *p* (*cristal*) to steam up. 5 *fig* (*honor etc*) to become tainted, become tarnished.
empapado,-a 1 *pp* → **empapar**. – 2 *adj* soaked.
empapar 1 *t* (*humedecer*) to soak; (*penetrar*) to soak, drench: *empapar un vestido en agua jabonosa,* to soak a dress in soapy water; *la lluvia nos empapó,* we got drenched. 2 (*absorber*) to soak up: *el algodón empapa el agua,* cotton soaks up water. – 3 **empaparse**, *p* (*humedecerse*) to get soaked. 4 (*persona*) to get soaked, get drenched, be soaked, be drenched: *se empapó en sudor,* he was drenched in sweat. 5 *fig* (*ideas etc*) to soak up. 6 *fig* (*enterarse bien*) to swot up (**de**, on).
empapelado 1 *m* (*acción*) wallpapering. 2 (*papel*) wallpaper.
empapelar 1 *t* (*envolver*) to wrap up in paper. 2 (*una pared*) to wallpaper, paper. 3 *fam fig* (*persona*) to try, prosecute.
empapuciado,-a 1 *pp* → **empapuciar**. – 2 *adj fam* full, stuffed, bloated.
empapuciar *t fam* (*personas*) to stuff with food; (*animales*) to force-feed.

▲ *Conjugation model* [12], *like cambiar.*
empapujado,-a 1 *pp* → **empapujar**. – 2 *adj fam* full, bloated.
empapujar *t fam* → **empapuciar**.
empapuzado,-a 1 *pp* → **empapuzar**. – 2 *adj fam* full, stuffed, bloated.
empapuzar *t fam* → **empapuciar**.
▲ *Conjugation model* [4], *like realizar.*
empaque¹ *m* (*de paquete*) packing.
empaque² *m* (*de una persona*) presence, bearing.
empaquetador,-ra *m,f* packer.
empaquetadura *f* packing.
empaquetar 1 *t* (*hacer paquetes*) to pack (up), wrap (up). 2 *fig* (*personas*) to pack in, squeeze in. 3 MIL (*castigar*) to punish.
emparedado *m* sandwich.
emparedar 1 *t* (*entre paredes*) wall in. 2 (*en prisión*) to imprison, confine.
emparejadura *f* matching.
emparejar 1 *t* (*cosas*) to put into pairs, match; (*personas*) to pair off: *empareja los dibujos,* put the drawings into pairs. 2 (*nivelar*) to make level; (*comparar*) to put on a par (**con**, with). 3 (*cuadrar*) to match (**con**, with): *empareja el animal con el país,* match the animal with the country. – 4 *i* (*ser parejo*) to be even (**con**, with). 5 (*alcanzar*) to catch up (**con** , with). – 6 **emparejarse**, *p* (*personas*) to pair up, pair off. 7 (*alcanzar nivel*) to catch up.
emparentado,-a 1 *pp* → **emparentar**. – 2 *adj* related (**con**, to): *estoy emparentado con su hermana,* I'm related to his sister by marriage.
emparentar *i* to become related by marriage (**con**, to).
● emparentar con una familia, to marry into a family.
▲ *Conjugation model* [31], *like contar.*
emparrado *m* vine arbour (US arbor).
emparrar *t* to train a vine.
emparrillar *t* to grill.
empastar 1 *t* (*diente*) to fill, put a filling in. 2 (*encuadernar*) to bind. 3 (*pintura*) to impaste.
empaste 1 *m* (*de diente*) filling. 2 (*encuadernación*) binding. 3 (*pintura*) impasting.
empastelar *t fig* to find a way out.
empatar *t* (*acabar igualados*) to tie, draw; (*igualar*) to equalize: *empataron a uno,* they drew one all; *Pérez acaba de empatar,* Pérez has just equalized; *estamos empatados,* we're equal.
empate *m* DEP tie, draw; POL tie.
● empate a tres, three all; (*resultado final*) three-all draw, US tie three to three.
■ el gol del empate, the equalizer.
empatía *f* empathy.
empavesada *f* hammock cloth, tarpaulin.
empavesado *m* bunting.
empavesar 1 *t* (*engalanar*) to decorate with bunting, deck out with bunting. 2 (*cubrir con empavesados*) to tarpaulin.
empecatado,-a *adj* wretched.
empecinado,-a 1 *pp* → **empecinarse**. – 2 *adj* stubborn, pigheaded.
empecinarse *p* to be stubborn (**en**, about), be pigheaded (**en**, about).
● empecinarse en hacer algo, to be set on doing sth.: *se empecinó en ganar el premio,* she was set on winning the prize.
empedernido,-a *adj* confirmed, inveterate, hardened.
● un,-a fumador,-ra/bebedor,-ra empedernido,-a, a hardened smoker/drinker.

empedrado,-a 1 *pp* → **empedrar**. – 2 *adj (calle)* cobbled. 3 *(cielo)* cloudy. – 4 **empedrado,** *m (adoquines)* cobbles *pl*, cobblestones *pl*. 5 *(acción)* cobbling, paving. 6 dish of rice with beans, lentils, etc.
empedrar *t* to cobble, pave.
▲ *Conjugation model* [27], *like* **acertar.**
empeine 1 *m (pie, zapato)* instep. 2 *(pubis)* groin.
empellar *t* to push, jostle, shove.
empeller *t* → **empellar.**
▲ *Conjugation model* [39].
empellón *m* push, shove.
● **abrirse paso a empellones,** to push one's way through.
empenachar *t* to adorn with plumes.
empeñar 1 *t (objetos)* to pawn, us hock. 2 *(palabra)* to pledge: *empeñó su palabra,* he pledged his word. – 3 **empeñarse,** *p (endeudarse)* to get into debt. 4 *(insistir)* to insist (**en,** on): *se empeñó en venir con nosotros,* he insisted on coming with us.
● **estar empeñado,-a,** to be in debt.
empeño 1 *m (insistencia)* determination. 2 *(deuda)* pawn.
● **con empeño,** eagerly. ‖ **poner empeño en,** to take pains to. ‖ **tener empeño en,** to be eager to.
■ **casa de empeños,** pawn-shop. ‖ **papeleta de empeño,** pawn ticket.
empeoramiento *m* deterioration, worsening.
empeorar 1 *i* to worsen, deteriorate. – 2 *t* to make worse: *has empeorado la situación,* you've made the situation worse. – 3 **empeorarse,** *p* to get worse: *su estado de salud se ha empeorado,* his health has got worse.
empequeñecer 1 *t* to diminish, make smaller. 2 *fig (persona)* to put in the shade, belittle. 3 *fig (edificio)* to dwarf.
▲ *Conjugation model* [43], *like* **agradecer.**
empequeñecimiento 1 *m* diminishment, reduction. 2 *fig* belittlement.
emperador 1 *m* emperor. 2 *(pez)* swordfish.
emperatriz *f* empress.
emperejilarse *p fam* to get dolled up.
emperifollarse *p fam* to get dolled up.
empero *conj lit* yet, however.
emperramiento *m* stubbornness.
emperrarse *p* to dig one's heels in, become stubborn.
empezar 1 *t* to begin, start: *el profesor empezó la clase,* the teacher began the lesson; *he empezado la botella,* I've started the bottle. – 2 *i* to begin, start: *empezó a leer,* he began to read; *empezó diciendo que ...,* she began by saying that ...
● **al empezar,** at the beginning. ‖ **empezar con buen pie,** to get off to a good start, start well. ‖ **para empezar,** to begin with.
▲ *Conjugation model* [47].
empicarse *p* to get the bug: *se ha empicado por el golf,* he's got the golf bug.
▲ *Conjugation model* [1], *like* **sacar.**
empiece *m fam* start, beginning.
empiltrarse *p fam* to hit the sack.
empinado,-a 1 *pp* → **empinar**. – 2 *adj (alto)* very high. 3 *fig (inclinado)* steep; *(vertical)* upright. 4 *fig (orgulloso)* stiff, upright, proud.
empinar 1 *t (levantar)* to raise, lift. 2 *(recipiente)* to raise, tip up. – 3 *i fam (beber mucho)* to drink a lot. – 4 **empinarse,** *p (persona)* to stand on tiptoe; *(animal)* to rear up. 5 *(alcanzar altura)* to tower.
● **empinar el codo,** *fam* to to bevvy, booze, have a few drinks.

empingorotado,-a 1 *pp* → **empingorotar**. – 2 *adj (de clase alta)* upper-class. 3 *(engreído)* stuck-up, posh.
empingorotar 1 *t (levantar)* to lift, raise. – 2 **empingorotarse,** *p (envanecerse)* to become conceited.
empiparse *p fam* to stuff os.
empíricamente *adv* empirically, by rule of thumb.
empírico,-a 1 *adj* empirical (us empiric). – 2 *m,f* empiricist.
empirismo *m* empiricism.
empitonar *t* to gore.
empizarrar *t* to put a slate roof, slate.
empizarrado *m* slate roof.
emplastar *t* to apply a poultice to, put a poultice on.
emplasto 1 *m* MED poultice. 2 *fig (componenda)* botched job, bad job. 3 *fig (cosa pegajosa)* sticky thing. 4 *fig (persona)* sickly person.
emplazamiento[1] *m* JUR summons.
emplazamiento[2] 1 *m (localización)* location, site. 2 MIL positioning.
emplazar[1] 1 *t (citar)* to call together; JUR to summons.
● **emplazar a la huelga,** to call out on strike.
▲ *Conjugation model* [4], *like* **realizar.**
emplazar[2] *t (situar)* to locate, place, situate.
▲ *Conjugation model* [4], *like* **realizar.**
empleado,-a *m,f* employee, clerk.
■ **empleado,-a de hogar,** servant.
emplear 1 *t (dar empleo)* to employ. 2 *(usar)* to use: *empleó un cuchillo,* he used a knife. 3 *(dinero)* to spend. 4 *(tiempo)* to invest, spend. – 5 **emplearse,** *p (usarse)* to be used: *este tipo de ordenador ya no se emplea,* this type of computer is no longer used. 6 *(tener trabajo)* to be employed.
● **emplear mal,** to misuse. ‖ **emplearse a fondo,** to do one's utmost. ‖ **estarle bien empleado a algn.** / **tenerlo bien empleado,** to serve sb. right: *te está bien empleado, haberlo dejado en paz,* it serves you right, you should have left it alone.
empleo 1 *m (trabajo)* occupation, job. 2 POL employment. 3 *(uso)* use.
● **sin empleo,** unemployed, out of work, jobless.
■ **empleo juvenil,** youth employment. ‖ **modo de empleo,** instructions for use. ‖ **pleno empleo,** full employment. ‖ **solicitud de empleo,** application for a job.
emplomado *m (ventana)* leading; *(tejado)* lead roof.
■ **vidrio emplomado,** leaded glass.
emplomar 1 *t (cubrir)* to cover with lead. 2 *(soldar)* to join with lead, seal with lead. 3 *(sellar)* to seal with lead.
emplumar 1 *t (poner plumas)* to put feathers on, put a feather on. 2 *fam (arrestar)* to nick; *(castigar)* to punish. – 3 *i (pájaro)* to grow feathers.
empobrecer 1 *i* to impoverish. – 2 **empobrecerse,** *p* to become poor, become impoverished.
▲ *Conjugation model* [43], *like* **agradecer.**
empobrecimiento *m* impoverishment.
empollar 1 *t (huevos)* to hatch. 2 *fam (estudiar)* to swot, swot up, us bone up on: *tendrías que empollar historia,* you'll have to swot up your history.
empollón,-ona 1 *adj fam pey* swotty. – 2 *m,f fam pey* swot.
empolvado,-a 1 *pp* → **empolvar**. – 2 *adj* dusty.
empolvar 1 *t* to cover with dust. – 2 **empolvarse,** *p (la cara)* to powder one's face.
emponzoñamiento *m* poisoning.
emponzoñar 1 *t* to poison. 2 *fig* to corrupt.

emporcar *t* to foul, dirty.
emporio 1 *m* COM trading centre (US center), commercial centre (US center). **2** (*centro artístico*) artistic centre (US center), cultural centre (US center).
emporrado,-a 1 *pp* → **emporrarse**. – **2** *adj arg* stoned, high.
emporrarse *p arg* to get high, get stoned.
empotrado,-a 1 *pp* → **empotrar**. – **2** *adj* fitted, built-in.
empotrar 1 *t* (*armario etc*) to fit, build in. **2** (*de golpe etc*) to embed: *el viento lo empotró en el árbol,* the wind embedded it in the tree. – **3 empotrarse,** *p* (*de golpe etc*) to crash: *el coche se empotró en la pared,* the car crashed into the wall.
emprendedor,-ra *adj* enterprising, resourceful.
emprender 1 *t* (*gen*) to start. **2** (*misión*) to tackle; (*viaje*) to set off on; (*tarea*) to undertake.
● **emprender el vuelo,** to take flight. ‖ **emprender la marcha,** to start out. ‖ **emprenderla con algn.,** *fam* to pick on sb.
empreñar 1 *t* (*fecundar*) to mate with. **2** *fam fig* (*molestar*) to bother, bug.
empresa 1 *f* (*compañía*) firm, company. **2** (*dirección*) management. **3** (*acción*) undertaking, venture.
■ **empresa filial,** subsidiary company. ‖ **empresa multinacional,** multinational company. ‖ **empresa naviera,** shipping company. ‖ **libre empresa,** free enterprise.
empresariado *m* employers *pl*.
empresarial *adj* managerial, management.
■ **ciencias empresariales,** business studies, management studies.
empresario,-a *m,f* (*gen*) employer, manager; (*hombre*) businessman, manager; (*mujer*) businesswoman, manageress.
■ **empresario,-a de pompas fúnebres,** undertaker. ‖ **empresario,-a de teatro,** impresario.
empréstito *m* loan.
● **lanzar un empréstito,** to float a loan.
■ **empréstito consolidado,** consolidated loan. ‖ **empréstito público/oficial,** government loan.
empujar 1 *t* to push, shove, thrust. **2** *fig* to force, urge, press: *la empujó a estudiar,* she pushed her into studying.
empuje 1 *m* push, thrust, drive. **2** (*presión*) pressure. **3** *fig* (*energía*) energy, drive.
● **necesitar empuje,** *fig* to need encouragement. ‖ **ser una persona de empuje,** *fig* to be a person with a lot of go.
empujón *m* push, shove.
● **a empujones,** (*irregularmente*) by/in fits and starts; (*violentamente*) violently, pushing, shoving. ‖ **abrirse paso a empujones,** to push one's way through. ‖ **dar empujones,** to push and shove. ‖ **dar un empujón a algo,** *fig* to give sth. a push.
empuñadura *f* (*gen*) handle; (*espada etc*) hilt.
● **hasta la empuñadura,** up to the hilt.
empuñar 1 *t* (*asir*) to grasp, seize. **2** *fig* to take up.
emú *m* emu.
emulación *f* emulation.
emulador,-ra *adj* emulating.
emular *t* to emulate.
émulo,-a 1 *adj* emulous. – **2** *m,f* emulator, rival.
emulsión *f* emulsion.
emulsionar *t* to emulsify.
emulsivo,-a *adj* emulsifying.

en 1 *prep* (*lugar - gen*) in, at: *en Valencia,* in Valencia; *en casa,* at home; *en el trabajo,* at work; *en la estación,* at the station; *en la tele,* on TV. **2** (*- en el interior*) in, inside: *en el cajón,* in the drawer. **3** (*lugar - sobre*) on: *en la mesa,* on the table. **4** (*año, mes, estación*) in; (*día*) on; (*época, momento*) at: *en 1994,* in 1994; *en septiembre,* in September; *en otoño,* in autumn; *en aquel día,* on that day; *en el día de Navidad,* on Christmas Day; *en aquel momento,* at that moment. **5** (*dirección*) into: *el helicóptero cayó en el mar,* the helicopter fell into the sea; *entró en su casa,* he went into his house. **6** (*transporte*) by: *ir en coche,* to go by car; *ir en avión,* to fly. **7** (*tema, materia*) at, in: *experto en economía,* expert in economics; *bueno en ajedrez,* good at chess; *Doctor en Medicina,* Doctor of Medicine. **8** (*modo, manera*) in: *en broma,* in fun; *en voz baja,* in a low voice; *en inglés,* in English; *lo conocí en el andar,* I recognized him by his walk. **9** (*porcentaje*) by: *los valores aumentaron en un 6%,* securities increased by 6%. **10 en + gerund,** upon: *en llegando el maestro, los niños se levantan,* upon the teacher's arrival, the children stand up.
● **de casa en casa,** from house to house. ‖ **en cuanto,** as soon as. ‖ **en camino,** on the way.
enaceitar *t* to oil, grease.
enagua *f* petticoat, underskirt.
▲ *Also used in plural with the same meaning.*
enagüillas 1 *fpl* short petticoat *sing*. **2** (*del traje griego*) fustanella *sing*.
enajenación 1 *f* (*distracción*) distraction, absent-mindedness. **2** (*transferencia*) transfer, alienation.
■ **enajenación mental,** insanity, mental derangement.
enajenador,-ra *adj* alienating.
enajenamiento *m* → **enajenación**.
enajenar 1 *t* (*propiedad*) to alienate. **2** *fig* (*sacar de sí*) to drive mad, drive to distraction. **3** *fig* (*extasiar*) to enrapture. – **4 enajenarse,** *p* (*desposeerse*) to deprive os. (**de,** of). **5** (*apartarse del trato*) to become estranged, become alienated. **6** *fig* (*enloquecer*) to go mad.
enaltecer 1 *t* (*ennoblecer*) to do credit to, ennoble. **2** (*alabar*) to praise, extol.
▲ *Conjugation model* [43], *like* ***agradecer***.
enamoradizo,-a *adj* easily infatuated.
enamorado,-a 1 *adj* in love, lovesick. – **2** *m,f* lover, sweetheart.
● **ser un,-a enamorado,-a de algo,** to love sth., be a lover of sth.
enamoramiento *m* infatuation, falling in love.
enamorar 1 *t* to win the heart of. – **2 enamorarse,** *p* to fall in love (**de,** with).
enanismo *m* dwarfism.
enano,-a 1 *adj* dwarf. – **2** *m,f* dwarf.
● **divertirse como un,-a enano,-a,** *fam* to have a whale of a time. ‖ **trabajar como un,-a enano,-a,** *fam* to work like a slave.
enarbolar 1 *t* (*bandera*) to hoist. **2** (*arma*) to brandish. **3** *fig* (*defender*) to defend. – **4 enarbolarse,** *p* (*caballo*) to rear up. **5** *fig* (*enojarse*) to get angry.
enarcar *t* (*lomo*) to arch; (*cejas*) to raise.
▲ *Conjugation model* [1], *like* ***sacar***.
enardecedor,-ra *adj* rousing, exciting.
enardecer 1 *t fig* (*excitar*) to excite, inflame, kindle. – **2 enardecerse,** *p fig* to get worked up.
▲ *Conjugation model* [43], *like* ***agradecer***.
enardecimiento *m* excitement, passion, enthusiasm.
enarenar 1 *t* to sand. – **2 enarenarse,** *p* to run aground.

enastar *t* to put a handle on.
encabalgamiento 1 *m (para artillería)* gun carriage. **2** *(armazón)* support of crossbeams. **3** LIT enjambment.
encabestrar 1 *t (poner cabestro)* to put a halter on. – **2** encabestrarse, *p (enredarse)* to get tangled in the halter.
encabezamiento 1 *m (gen)* heading. **2** *(fórmula)* form of address. **3** *(preámbulo)* preamble.
encabezar 1 *t (carta, lista)* to head. **2** *(acaudillar)* to lead. **3** DEP *(carrera)* to lead; *(clasificación)* to head, top.
▲ *Conjugation model* |4|, *like realizar.*
encabritarse 1 *p (caballo)* to rear up. **2** *(barco)* to rise; *(avión)* to zoom. **3** *fig (enojarse)* to get angry, get cross.
encabronar 1 *t* tabú to piss off. – **2** encabronarse, *p* tabú to get pissed off.
encadenado 1 *m* ARQ buttress, reinforcement. **2** CINEM dissolve and fade-in.
encadenamiento 1 *m* TÉC chaining. **2** *(unión)* connection, linking. **3** LIT concatenation, linking.
encadenar 1 *t (poner cadenas)* to chain (up). **2** *fig (enlazar)* to connect, link up. **3** *fig (atar)* to tie down: *el cuidado de su madre la encadena en casa,* looking after her mother ties her to the house.
encajar 1 *t (ajustar)* to fit. **2** *(hueso)* to set. **3** *(recibir)* to take, withstand. **4** *(soportar)* to bear; *(hacer aguantar)* to force to sit through, force to listen to: *nos encajó un discurso de dos horas,* we were forced to sit through a two hour speech. **5** *(indirecta, comentario)* to get in. **6** *(dar un golpe)* to land: *le encajó un golpe,* he landed him a blow. **7** TÉC to gear. – **8** *i (caber)* to fit: *la ventana no encaja bien,* the window doesn't fit properly. **9** *fig (corresponderse)* to fit (in), correspond, tally: *lo que dices no encaja con lo que vimos,* what you're saying doesn't tally with what we saw. **10** *fig (ir bien)* to go, match, suit. **11** *fig (adaptarse)* to fit in, settle. – **12** encajarse, *p (atascarse)* to get stuck, stick. **13** *fig (vestido)* to slip on; *(sombrero)* to put on.
encaje 1 *m (acto)* fit, fitting. **2** *(hueco)* socket; *(caja)* housing. **3** COST lace.
encajonar 1 *t (poner en cajas)* to put in a box, box up. **2** *(en un espacio)* to squeeze. **3** *(toros)* to pen. **4** ARQ to buttress. – **5** encajonarse, *p (en un sitio)* to squeeze in. **6** *(río)* to narrow.
encalabrinar 1 *t (olor, vino)* to go to one's head. **2** *(irritar)* to annoy, irritate. – **3** encalabrinarse, *p (obstinarse)* to be stubborn. **4** *fam (enamorarse)* to fall in love.
encalado *m* whitewashing.
encalar *t* to whitewash.
encalladero *m* sandbank, reef.
encallar 1 *i* MAR to run aground. **2** *fig* to flounder, fail.
encallecer 1 *i (piel)* to harden, become calloused. – **2** encallecerse, *p fig (persona)* to become hardened.
encalmarse *p (viento)* to drop; *(mar)* to become calm.
encalvecer *i* to go bald.
▲ *Conjugation model* |43|, *like agradecer.*
encamar 1 *t (echar al suelo)* to lay out, put down. – **2** encamarse, *p (meterse en cama)* to take to one's bed. **3** *(caza)* to hide. **4** *(cereales)* to be laid.
encaminar 1 *t (guiar, orientar)* to direct, guide, set on the right road, put on the right road. – **2** encaminarse, *p (dirigirse)* to head (**a**, for); (**hacia**, towards).
● encaminar esfuerzos a, to concentrate one's efforts on. ‖ estar bien encaminado,-a, to be on the right track.
encamisar 1 *t (camisa)* to put a shirt on. **2** *(funda)* to cover up. **3** *fig (encubrir)* to conceal.

encampanado,-a *adj* bell-shaped.
encanallar 1 *t* to degrade, debase. – **2** encanallarse, *p* to degrade os., debase os.
encandecer 1 *t* to make white-hot. – **2** encandecerse, *p* to get white-hot.
▲ *Conjugation model* |43|, *like agradecer.*
encandilado,-a 1 *pp* → **encandilar.** – **2** *adj (deslumbrado)* starry-eyed.
encandilar 1 *t (deslumbrar)* to dazzle. **2** *(el fuego)* to poke. **3** *fig (fascinar)* to fascinate, daze. **4** *fig (amor etc)* to kindle. – **5** encandilarse, *p (ojos, rostro)* to light up.
encanecer 1 *i (pelo)* to go grey (US gray). **2** *fig (persona)* to grow old. – **3** encanecerse, *p (pelo)* to go grey (US gray). **4** persona, *fig (persona)* to grow old.
▲ *Conjugation model* |43|, *like agradecer.*
encanijarse *p* to become weak, become puny.
encantado,-a 1 *pp* → **encantar.** – **2** *adj (contento)* pleased, delighted: *estoy encantada de conocerlo,* I'm pleased to meet you. **3** *fig (embrujado)* haunted, enchanted: *castillo encantado,* haunted castle. **4** *(distraído)* absent-minded.
encantador,-ra 1 *adj* enchanting, charming, delightful. – **2** *m,f (hombre)* charmer; *(mujer)* enchantress, charmer.
■ encantador,-ra de serpientes, snake charmer.
encantamiento *m* spell, charm, enchantment.
encantar 1 *t (hechizar)* to cast a spell on, bewitch. **2** *fam (gustar)* to delight, love: *me encanta la natación,* I love swimming.
encante 1 *m (subasta)* auction. **2** *(lugar)* auction room.
encanto 1 *m (hechizo)* spell, enchantment, charm. **2** *fig (cosa)* delight, enchantment; *(persona)* charm: *ese restaurante es un encanto,* it's a delightful restaurant; *Pepe es un encanto,* Pepe is charming. **3** *fam (apelativo)* love, darling, sweetheart: *lo que tú digas, encanto,* whatever you say, darling. – **4** encantos, *mpl (gracias)* charms.
encañada *f* gorge, ravine.
encañado 1 *m (conducción)* piping, drainage system. **2** *(para plantas)* trellis.
encañar 1 *t (agua)* to pipe. **2** *(tierras)* to drain. **3** *(plantas)* to train.
encañizada 1 *f (para peces)* crawl. **2** *(para plantas)* cane frame.
encañonar 1 *t (encauzar)* to pipe, channel. **2** *(apuntar)* to aim at, point at. **3** *(planchar)* to goffer, flute. – **4** *i (aves)* to grow feathers.
encaperuzado,-a *adj* hooded.
encapirotado,-a *adj* hooded.
encapotado,-a 1 *pp* → **encapotar.** – **2** *adj* overcast, cloudy.
encapotar 2 1 *t (cubrir)* to put a cloak on. – **2** encapotarse, *p (persona)* to frown, look grim. **3** *(cielo)* to become overcast, become cloudy.
▲ *In 3, used only in the 3rd pers; it does not take a subject.*
encaprichamiento *m* infatuation.
encapricharse 1 *p (empeñarse)* to set one's mind on (**con/en**, to). **2** *(encariñarse)* to take a fancy (**con**, to); *(enamorarse)* to get a crush (**con**, on).
encapuchado,-a *adj* hooded.
encarado,-a *adj: bien encarado,* good-looking, nice-looking; *mal encarado,* nasty-looking.
encaramar 1 *t (levantar)* to raise, lift up. **2** *fig (elogiar)* to praise, extol. **3** *fig (elevar)* to promote to a high position. – **4** encaramarse, *p (subirse)* to climb up, get high up. **5** *fig (encumbrarse)* to reach a high position.

encarar 1 *t* (*afrontar*) to face, face up to, confront. **2** (*arma*) to point, aim. **3** (*poner cara a cara*) to face, face up to, confront. – **4 encararse,** *p* (*situación, problema*) to face up (**a/con**, to). **5** (*persona*) to stand up (**a/con**, to): *se encaró con el jefe y lo despidieron,* he stood up to the boss and they fired him.

encarcelación *f* imprisonment, incarceration.

encarcelamiento *m* imprisonment, incarceration.

encarcelar *t* to imprison, jail, incarcerate.

encarecer 1 *t* (*precios*) to put up the price of. **2** *fig* (*elogiar*) to praise. **3** *fig* (*recomendar*) to urge, strongly recommend: *te encarezco que vengas,* I urge you to come. – **4 encarecerse,** *p* (*precio*) to become more expensive, go up in price.
▲ Conjugation model [43], like *agradecer.*

encarecidamente *adv* earnestly, insistently.

encarecimiento 1 *m* (*precio*) increase in price, rise in price: *el encarecimiento de la vida,* the rise in the cost of living. **2** (*insistencia*) insistence. **3** (*alabanza*) praising, extolling.
● con encarecimiento, earnestly, insistently.

encargado,-a 1 *pp* → **encargar.** – **2** *adj* in charge. – **3** *m,f* COM (*hombre*) manager; (*mujer*) manageress. **4** (*empleado*) person in charge.
■ encargado,-a de curso, EDUC tutor. ‖ encargado,-a de negocios, POL chargé d'affaires.

encargar 1 *t* (*encomendar*) to entrust, put in charge of. **2** (*recomendar*) to recommend, advise. **3** COM (*pedir*) to order, place an order for: *encargó 4 kilos de naranjas,* he ordered 4 kilos of oranges. **4** (*mandar hacer*) to have made: *se encargó un vestido,* she had a dress made. – **5** encargarse de, *p* to take charge of, look after, see to, deal with.
▲ Conjugation model [7], like *llegar.*

encargo 1 *m* (*recado*) errand. **2** (*empleo*) job, assignment. **3** (*responsabilidad*) responsibility. **4** COM order, commission.
● como hecho,-a de encargo, perfect. ‖ hacer un encargo, (*recado*) to run an errand; (*pedido*) to place an order. ‖ hecho,-a de encargo, (*a petición*) made to order; (*a la medida*) made to measure.

encariñado,-a 1 *pp* → **encariñarse.** – **2** *adj* attached (**con**, to), fond (**con**, of).

encariñarse *p* to become fond (**con**, of), get attached (**con**, to).

encarnación 1 *f* REL incarnation. **2** *fig* embodiment, incarnation: *es la encarnación de la sabiduría,* she's wisdom personified.

encarnado,-a 1 *pp* → **encarnar.** – **2** *adj* (*hecho carne*) incarnate. **3** (*color*) red. – **4** encarnado, *m* (*rojo*) red. **5** (*color de carne*) flesh colour (US color).
● ponerse encarnado,-a, to blush, go red.

encarnadura *f*: *buena encarnadura,* skin with good healing qualities; *mala encarnadura,* skin with poor healing qualities.

encarnar 1 *i* REL to become incarnate. **2** MED to heal. – **3** *t* *fig* (*personificar*) to embody, personify. **4** TEAT *fig* to play. **5** (*en anzuelo*) to bait. **6** (*dar color carne*) to give flesh colour (US color) to.

encarnecer *i* to get fat.

encarnizadamente *adv* cruelly, fiercely.

encarnizado,-a 1 *pp* → **encarnizar.** – **2** *adj* bloody, fierce.

encarnizamiento *m* fierceness, savagery, cruelty.

encarnizar 1 *t* (*perro*) to flesh, blood. **2** *fig* (*enfurecer*) to enrage. – **3** encarnizarse, *p* *fig* to be cruel (**con/en**, to), be brutal (**con/en**, to).

● encarnizarse con, to attack savagely.
▲ Conjugation model [4], like *realizar.*

encarpetar *t* to file (away).

encarrilar 1 *t* (*vehículo*) to put on the road, put on the rails. **2** *fig* (*encaminar*) to direct, guide, put on the right track.
● encarrilar bien/mal un asunto, *fig* to get off to a good/bad start.

encartar 1 *t* JUR (*proscribir*) to proscribe, outlaw, ban; (*encausar*) to indict. **2** (*incluir en libro*) to insert. **3** (*implicar*) to involve, implicate. **4** (*naipes*) to lead.

encarte 1 *m* (*naipes*) lead. **2** (*folleto*) free leaflet, booklet; (*hoja intercalada*) insert.

encartonado *m* cardboard binding.

encartonar 1 *t* (*poner cartones*) to cover with cardboard. **2** (*encuadernar*) to bind with cardboard.

encasillado,-a 1 *pp* → **encasillar.** – **2** *adj* (*actor*) typecast. – **3** encasillado, *m* (*casillero*) pigeonholes *pl.*

encasillar 1 *t* (*poner en casillas*) to pigeonhole. **2** (*clasificar*) to classify, class. **3** (*actor, actriz*) to typecast. – **4** encasillarse, *p* *fig* to limit os.

encasquetar 1 *t* (*sombrero etc*) to pull down, put on. **2** *fig* (*idea etc*) to put into sb.'s head. **3** *fam* (*colocar*) to dump on, foist on: *me encasquetaron a los niños y ellos se fueron al cine,* they dumped the kids on me and went to the cinema. – **4** encasquetarse, *p* *fam* *fig* (*empeñarse*) to get into one's head.

encasquillamiento *m* jamming.

encasquillarse *p* to jam.

encastrar 1 *t* (*encajar*) to fit in, set in. **2** (*endentar*) to mesh.

encauchar *t* to rubberize.

encausar *t* to prosecute.

encáustico *m* protective polish.

encauzamiento 1 *m* channelling. **2** *fig* orientation, guidance.

encauzar 1 *t* to channel. **2** *fig* to direct, guide.
▲ Conjugation model [4], like *realizar.*

encebollado,-a 1 *pp* → **encebollar.** – **2** *adj* with onion.

encebollar *t* to cook with onions.

encefálico,-a *adj* encephalic.

encefalitis *f* encephalitis.
▲ *pl* encefalitis.

encéfalo *m* encephalon.

encefalografía *f* encephalography.

encefalograma *m* encephalogram.

enceguecer 1 *t* (*cegar*) to blind. **2** *fig* (*ofuscar*) to blind, dazzle. – **3** *i* (*perder la vista*) to go blind. – **4** enceguecerse, *p* (*perder la vista*) to go blind, lose one's sight.
▲ Conjugation model [43], like *agradecer.*

encelado,-a 1 *pp* → **encelar.** – **2** *adj* *fam* madly in love.

encelar 1 *t* (*dar celos*) to make jealous. – **2** encelarse, *p* (*tener celos*) to be jealous. **3** (*estar en celo - ciervo*) to be in rut; (*- perro, gato*) to be on heat.

encella *f* cheese mould (US mold).

encenagado,-a 1 *pp* → **encenagar.** – **2** *adj* muddy, covered in mud. **3** *fig* (*vicioso*) depraved.

encenagarse 1 *p* to get covered in mud. **2** *fig* (*en el vicio*) to wallow.
▲ Conjugation model [7], like *llegar.*

encendedor *m* lighter.

encender 1 *t* (*hacer arder*) to light, set fire to; (*cerilla*) to strike, light; (*vela*) to light. **2** (*luz, radio, tv*) to turn on, switch on, put on; (*gas*) to turn on, light. **3** *fig* (*ocasionar*) to kindle, provoke, spark off: *la construcción de la valla encendió las disputas entre las dos familias,* the building of the fence sparked off the rows between the two families. **4** *fig (excitar)* to inflame, stir up. **– 5 encenderse,** *p (incendiarse)* to catch fire, ignite: *el edificio se encendió,* the building caught fire. **6** *(luz)* to go on, come on; *(llama)* to flare up. **7** *fig (excitarse)* to flare up. **8** *fig (ruborizarse)* to blush, go red.

▲ *Conjugation model* [28], *like* **entender**.

encendidamente *adv fig* passionately, ardently.

encendido,-a 1 *pp →* **encender**. **– 2** *adj (incendiado)* on fire, burning. **3** *(cigarrillo etc)* lit. **4** *(luz etc)* on. **5** *(color)* glowing, fiery. **6** *(rostro)* red, flushed. **– 7 encendido,** *m (gen)* lighting. **8** AUTO ignition.

encenizar *t* to cover with ashes.

▲ *Conjugation model* [4], *like* **realizar**.

encerado 1 *m (lienzo)* tarpaulin. **2** *(capa de cera)* wax coating. **3** *(pizarra)* blackboard.

encerador,-ra 1 *adj* waxing, polishing. **– 2** *m,f (persona)* floor waxer, floor polisher. **– 3 enceradora,** *f (máquina)* floor waxer, floor polisher.

enceradora *f →* **encerador,-ra**.

encerar *t* to wax, polish.

encerradero 1 *m (para rebaños)* pen, fold. **2** *(para toros)* bull pen.

encerrar 1 *t (gen)* to shut in, shut up. **2** *(con llave)* to lock in, lock up: *se ha encerrado en el baño,* she's locked herself in the bathroom. **3** *(palabras, frases, etc)* to put: *encerrar entre paréntesis,* to put in brackets. **4** *(ajedrez, damas)* to block. **5** *fig (contener)* to contain, include; *(implicar)* to involve. **– 6 encerrarse,** *p (recogerse)* to go into retreat; *(en sí mismo)* to become withdrawn.

▲ *Conjugation model* [27], *like* **acertar**.

encerrona 1 *f (retiro)* retreat, seclusion. **2** *(toros)* private bullfight. **3** *(para examen)* revision session before oral examination. **4** *fig (trampa)* trap.

● *preparar una encerrona a algn.* / *tender una encerrona a algn.,* *fig* to lay a trap for sb.

encestar *t* to score a basket.

enceste *m* basket.

enchapado 1 *m (chapería)* veneering. **2** *(chapa)* veneer.

encharcado,-a 1 *pp →* **encharcar**. **– 2** *adj* flooded, swamped.

encharcar 1 *t* to flood, swamp. **– 2 encharcarse,** *p (terreno)* to swamp, get flooded. **3** *(estómago)* to become bloated.

▲ *Conjugation model* [1], *like* **sacar**.

enchinar *t* to pave with pebbles.

enchironar *t arg* to put away, put in the slammer.

enchufado,-a 1 *pp →* **enchufar**. **– 2** *adj fam* well connected, well in, with good connections. **– 3** *m,f fam (gen)* string-puller, US wire-puller; *(en la escuela)* teacher's pet.

enchufar 1 *t* ELEC to connect, plug in. **2** *(unir)* to join, connect, fit. **3** *fam fig* to pull strings for: *no consigo trabajo porque no tengo a nadie que me enchufe,* I can't get a job because I have nobody to pull strings for me; *enchufó a su hija en su empresa,* he got his daughter a job in his company. **– 4 enchufarse,** *p fam fig* to get a job.

enchufe 1 *m* ELEC *(hembra)* socket; *(macho)* plug. **2** *fam fig (trabajo)* easy job; *(influencias)* contacts *pl,* friends *pl* in high places.

● *tener enchufe,* *fam* to have contacts.

■ *enchufe bipolar,* two-pin plug. ‖ *enchufe tripolar,* three-pin plug.

enchufismo *m fam* string-pulling.

encía *f* gum.

encíclica *f* encyclical.

enciclopedia *f* encyclopaedia, encyclopedia.

enciclopédico,-a *adj* encyclopaedic, encyclopedic.

enciclopedismo *m* encyclopaedism, encyclopedism.

encierro 1 *m (toril)* bull pen; *(recorrido)* bull-running. **2** *(prisión)* locking up, confinement. **3** *(protesta)* sit-in. **4** REL retreat.

encima 1 *adv (más arriba)* above, overhead; *(sobre)* on top: *tenían las estrellas encima,* they had the stars overhead; *está allí encima,* it's there on top. **2** *(ropa etc)* on, on top: *se puso la americana y encima el abrigo,* he put on his jacket and his coat on top; *ponte algo encima,* put something on. **3** *(consigo)* on you *(him etc)*: *¿llevas cambio encima?,* do you have any change on you? **4** *(además)* in addition, besides: *les dio un coche nuevo y muchas más cosas encima,* he gave them a new car and lots more besides. **5** *fam (por si fuera poco)* what's more, on top of that, besides: *le robaron y encima le dieron una paliza,* they robbed him and on top of that they beat him up.

● *de encima,* top, on top, above: *el piso de encima,* the floor above. ‖ **encima de,** *(a más altura)* over, above; *(sobre)* on; *(además)* besides, as well as, on top of that: *van a construir otro piso encima del nuestro,* they're going to build another flat above ours; *está encima de la mesa,* it's on the table. ‖ **estar algn. encima de otro,** *fam* to be on sb.'s back, be breathing down sb.'s neck. ‖ **por encima,** *(a más altura)* above; *(de pasada)* superficially: *lo repasó muy por encima,* he checked it through superficially. ‖ **por encima de,** *(más importante)* above; *(más allá)* beyond: *Pepe está por encima de ti,* Pepe is above you; *está por encima de sus posibilidades,* it's beyond her capabilities. ‖ **por encima de todo,** above all. ‖ **quitarse algo de encima** / **quitarse a algn. de encima,** *fig* to get rid of sth. / get rid of sb. ‖ **tener algo encima,** *fig* to be just round the corner: *tenemos el invierno encima,* winter is almost upon us.

encimera *f →* **encimero,-a**.

encimero,-a 1 *adj* top: *sábana encimera,* top sheet. **– 2 encimera,** *f (en cocina - superficie)* worktop; *(- con fogones)* hob.

encina *f* holm oak, evergreen oak, ilex.

encinta *adj* pregnant.

encintar *t* to decorate with ribbons.

encizañar 1 *t* to cause trouble between, stir things up between. **– 2** *i* to cause trouble.

enclaustrar 1 *t* to cloister, shut up in a convent, shut up in a monastery. **2** *fig* to cloister, shut up. **– 3 enclaustrarse,** *p* to shut os. up.

enclavar 1 *t (clavar)* to nail. **2** *(atravesar)* to pierce, transfix. **3** *(ubicar)* to locate, place.

enclave *m* enclave.

enclenque 1 *adj (flaco)* skinny. **2** *(débil)* weak, puny; *(enfermizo)* sickly. **– 3** *mf (flaco)* skinny person. **4** *(débil)* weak person, puny person; *(enfermizo)* sickly person.

enclítico,-a 1 *adj* enclitic. **– 2** *m,f* enclitic.

encocorar 1 *t fam* to get on one's nerves, annoy, pester. **– 2 encocorarse,** *p* to get annoyed.

encofrado 1 *m (para hormigón)* formwork, shuttering. **2** *(de mina)* timbering.

encofrar 1 *t (hormigón)* to put up shuttering for. **2** *(mina)* to timber.

encoger 1 *t (contraer)* to contract. **2** *(tejido)* to shrink. **3** *fig (asustar)* to intimidate, frighten. **– 4** *i (tejido)* to shrink. **– 5 encogerse,** *p (contraerse)* to contract. **6** *(tejido)* to

shrink. **7** *fig (amilanarse)* to be intimidated: *sé valiente y no te encojas ante los demás,* be brave and don't let others intimidate you.
● **encogerse de hombros,** to shrug one's shoulders. ‖ **se me encogió el corazón,** *fig* my heart sank.
▲ *Conjugation model* |5|, *like* **proteger**.

encogido,-a I *pp* → **encoger**. – **2** *adj fig (persona)* timid, shy, diffident. **3** *fig (corazón)* heavy; *(estómago)* in knots.

encogimiento I *m (de tejido)* shrinkage. **2** *(del cuerpo)* hunching. **3** *fig (timidez)* shyness, diffidence.
● **encogimiento de hombros,** shrug of the shoulders.

encolado I *m (vinos)* clarification. **2** *(pintura)* sizing, pasting. **3** *(con cola)* gluing. **4** *(de películas)* splicing.

encolar I *t (dar cola)* to glue. **2** *(en pintura)* to size, paste. **3** *(películas)* to splice. **4** *(vinos)* to clarify.

encolerizar I *t* to anger, irritate, infuriate, exasperate. – **2** **encolerizarse**, *p* to get angry, lose one's temper.
▲ *Conjugation model* |4|, *like* **realizar**.

encomendar I *t* to entrust, commend, put in charge: *el rey le encomendó una importante misión,* the king entrusted him with an important mission. – **2** **encomendarse**, *p* to entrust os. **(a**, to).
● **encomendarse a Dios,** to put one's trust in God, commend one's soul to God.
▲ *Conjugation model* |27|, *like* **acertar**.

encomiar *t* to extol, laud.
▲ *Conjugation model* |12|, *like* **cambiar**.

encomiástico,-a *adj* laudatory, eulogistic.

encomienda I *f (encargo)* assignment, mission. **2** HIST estate.
● **digno,-a de encomio,** praiseworthy.

encomio *m fml* praise, tribute, eulogy.
● **digno,-a de encomio,** praiseworthy.

enconado,-a I *pp* → **enconar**. – **2** *adj* MED inflamed, sore. **3** *fig (apasionado)* passionate, eager. **4** *fig (discusión, lucha)* bitter, fierce, heated.

enconar I *t* MED to inflame. **2** *fig* to anger. – **3** **enconarse,** *p* MED to become inflamed. **4** *fig (exasperarse)* to get irritated, get angry. **5** *fig (discusión)* to become heated; *(lucha)* to become fierce.

encono *m* ill feeling, rancour *(us* rancor*)*.

encontradizo,-a *adj:* *hacerse el encontradizo,* to manage to bump into sb., feign surprise at meeting sb.

encontrado,-a I *pp* → **encontrar**. – **2** *adj* conflicting, contrary, opposing: *opiniones encontradas,* conflicting opinions.

encontrar I *t (gen)* to find. **2** *(una persona sin buscar)* to come across, meet, bump into. **3** *(dificultades)* to run into, come up against. **4** *(creer)* to think, find: *no lo encuentro adecuado,* I don't think it's suitable. **5** *(notar)* to find: *lo encuentro más difícil,* I find it more difficult; *lo encuentro muy salado,* it tastes too salty; *la encontré muy cambiada,* she has changed a lot. **6** *(chocar)* to collide. – **7** **encontrarse,** *p (estar)* to be: *se encuentra enfermo,* he's ill. **8** *(persona)* to meet; *(por casualidad)* to bump into, run into, meet: *nos encontraremos allí,* we'll meet there. **9** *(dificultades)* to run into. **10** *(chocar)* to collide. **11** *fig (sentirse)* to feel, be: *me encuentro mal,* I feel bad.
● **encontrarse con ganas de hacer algo / encontrarse con fuerzas para hacer algo,** to feel like doing sth.
▲ *Conjugation model* |31|, *like* **contar**.

encontrón *m* → **encontronazo**.

encontronazo I *m (choque)* collision, crash. **2** *(riña)* quarrel. **3** *fig (ideas etc)* clash.

encoñado,-a I *pp* → **encoñarse**. – **2** *adj tabú* infatuated, besotted.

encoñarse *p tabú* to become infatuated **(de,** with), have the hots **(de,** for).

encopetado,-a I *adj fig (presumido)* conceited, haughty, stuck-up. **2** *fig (de clase alta)* upper-class.

encorajar I *t* to encourage. – **2** **encorajarse,** *p* to get furious, get angry.

encorajinar I *t fam* to make angry. – **2** **encorajinarse,** *p fam* to get angry, lose one's temper.

encorbatarse *p fam* to be dress-conscious.

encorchar *t* to cork.

encordar I *t (instrumento)* to string. **2** *(rodear)* to tie with a rope. – **3** **encordarse,** *p (alpinistas)* to rope up.

encordonar *t* to tie up with cords.

encorralar *t* to pen, put in a pen.

encorsetado,-a I *pp* → **encorsetar**. – **2** *adj fig* strict, rigorous.

encorsetar I *t* to corset. **2** *fig* to limit, restrict.

encorvado,-a I *pp* → **encorvar**. – **2** *adj (cosa)* bent, curved; *(persona)* bent, stooping.

encorvadura I *f (acción)* bending. **2** *(de persona)* stoop, curvature. **3** *(curva)* bend, curve.

encorvamiento *m* → **encorvadura**.

encorvar I *t* to bend, curve. – **2** **encorvarse,** *p* to bend, curve. **3** *(persona)* to become round-shouldered.

encrespado,-a I *pp* → **encrespar**. – **2** *adj (pelo)* curly. **3** *(mar)* rough, choppy.

encrespar I *t (pelo)* to curl, frizz. **2** *(mar)* to make choppy, make rough. **3** *fig (enfurecer)* to infuriate. – **4** **encresparse,** *p (pelo)* to stand on end. **5** *(mar)* to get rough. **6** *fig (enfurecerse)* to get cross, get irritated.

encristalar *t* to glaze, put in glass.

encrucijada I *f* crossroads, intersection. **2** *fig* crossroads.
● **estar en la encrucijada,** *fig* to be at crisis point.

encrudecer I *t fig (exasperar)* to irritate. – **2** *i (clima)* to get colder, get worse. – **3** **encrudecerse,** *p (clima)* to become colder.
▲ *Conjugation model* |43|, *like* **agradecer**.

encuadernación I *f (arte)* bookbinding. **2** *(cubierta)* binding.
■ **encuadernación en rústica,** paperback. ‖ **encuadernación en tela,** cloth binding. ‖ **taller de encuadernación,** bindery.

encuadernador,-ra *m,f* bookbinder.

encuadernar *t* to bind.

encuadramiento *m* framing.

encuadrar I *t (cuadro etc)* to frame. **2** *fig (encajar)* to fit in, insert. **3** *fig (servir de límite)* to frame: *las patillas encuadraban el rostro,* his sideboards framed his face. **4** *fig (en un grupo)* to incorporate. – **5** **encuadrarse,** *p (incorporarse)* to join.

encuadre *m* CINEM TV framing.

encubar *t* to vat.

encubierta *f* → **encubierto,-a**.

encubiertamente I *adv (secretamente)* secretly. **2** *(fraudulentamente)* fraudulently.

encubierto,-a I *pp* → **encubrir**. – **2** *adj (secreto)* secret, hidden, concealed. **3** *(fraudulento)* fraudulent, underhand. – **4** **encubierta,** *f* fraud.

encubridor,-ra *m,f* accessory, abettor.

encubrimiento I *m* concealment, hiding. **2** JUR cover-up.

encubrir I *t (ocultar)* to conceal, hide. **2** JUR *(delito)* to cover up; *(criminal)* to cover up for.

▲ *pp* **encubierto,-a**.

encuentro 1 *m* (*de personas*) meeting. **2** DEP meeting, clash; (*partido*) match, game: *un encuentro amistoso*, a friendly game. **3** (*choque*) collision. **4** (*opiniones etc*) clash. **5** MIL skirmish.
● ir al encuentro de algn., to go to meet sb. ‖ salir al encuentro de algn., to set off to meet sb.

encuesta 1 *f* (*sondeo*) poll, survey. **2** (*pesquisa*) inquiry, investigation.
● hacer una encuesta, to carry out an opinion poll.

encuestador,-ra *m,f* pollster.

encuestar *t* to poll.

encumbrado,-a 1 *pp* → **encumbrar**. – **2** *adj* (*eminente*) distinguished, eminent. **3** (*socialmente*) upper-class.

encumbramiento 1 *m* (*acción*) rise, raising. **2** (*posición*) high position, elevated status.

encumbrar 1 *t fig* to exalt, elevate. – **2 encumbrarse,** *p fig* (*envanecerse*) to grow proud, become haughty.

encurtidos *mpl* pickles.

encurtir *t* to pickle.

ende por ende, *loc adv* therefore.

endeble *adj fml* feeble, weak, puny.

endeblez *f* weakness, feebleness.

endecasílabo,-a 1 *adj* hendecasyllabic. – **2 endecasílabo,** *m* hendecasyllable.

endemia *f* endemic disease.

endémico,-a 1 *adj* MED endemic. **2** *fig* endemic, inherent.

endemoniado,-a 1 *adj* (*poseso*) possessed. **2** *fig* (*diabólico*) diabolical. **3** *fig* (*maldito*) evil, wretched.

endemoniar 1 *t* to bedevil. **2** *fig* (*irritar*) to anger. – **3 endemoniarse,** *p fig* to get angry.
▲ *Conjugation model* |12|, *like* **cambiar**.

endentar 1 *t* (*encajar*) to interlock. **2** (*poner dientes*) to tooth.
▲ *Conjugation model* [31], *like* **contar**.

endentecer *i* to teethe.
▲ *Conjugation model* [43], *like* **agradecer**.

enderezamiento *m* (*derecho*) straightening out, straightening up; (*vertical*) setting upright.

enderezar 1 *t* (*poner derecho*) to straighten out. **2** (*poner vertical*) to set upright. **3** *fig* (*situación etc*) to put right. **4** *fig* (*dirigir*) to direct, guide. **5** *fig* (*comportamiento*) to sort out, put straight, make behave: *su padre se encargará de enderezarla,* her father will see that she behaves. – **6 enderezarse,** *p* (*ponerse recto*) to straighten up. **7** (*dirigirse*) to be directed (**a**, at).
▲ *Conjugation model* [4], *like* **realizar**.

endeudamiento *m* borrowing, state of indebtedness.
■ endeudamiento **exterior,** foreign debt.

endeudarse *p* to get into debt, fall into debt.

endiabladamente 1 *adv* diabolically. **2** *fig* extremely.

endiablado,-a 1 *adj* (*poseso*) possessed. **2** *fig* (*malo*) evil, wicked. **3** *fig* (*maldito*) wretched, cursed. **4** *fig* (*travieso*) devilish, mischievous. **5** *fig* (*feo*) ugly, horrible. **6** *fig* (*frenético*) wild, frenzied.

endiablar 1 *t* to bedevil.

endibia *f* endive.

endilgar 1 *t fam* (*trabajo etc*) to palm off onto, lumber with: *me endilgó la parte más difícil,* he lumbered me with the most difficult bit. **2** *fam* (*hacer aguantar*) to make sit through, make listen to: *nos endilgó un concierto de tres horas,* he made us sit through a concert which lasted three hours. **3** *fam* (*golpe*) to land.
▲ *Conjugation model* [7], *like* **llegar**.

endiñar *t fam* → **endilgar** *2 and 3*.

endiosamiento *m* conceit, vanity.

endiosar 1 *t* to deify. – **2 endiosarse,** *p fig* to become conceited, become proud, become vain.

endocardio *m* endocardium.

endocarpio *m* endocarp.

endocarpo *m* endocarp.

endocrino,-a 1 *adj* endocrine, endocrinal. – **2** *m,f fam* endocrinologist.
■ glándula endocrina, endocrine gland.

endocrinología *f* endocrinology.

endocrinólogo,-a *m,f* endocrinologist.

endogamia *f* endogamy, inbreeding.

endomingado,-a 1 *pp* → **endomingarse**. – **2** *adj fam* in one's Sunday best.

endomingarse *p fam* to put on one's Sunday best.

endoplasma *m* endoplasm.

endosar 1 *t* to endorse: *endosó el cheque,* he endorsed the cheque. **2** *fam fig* to lumber with.

endoscopia *f* endoscopy.

endoscopio *m* endoscope.

endoso *m* endorsement.
● sin endoso, unendorsed.

endotérmico,-a *adj* endothermic.

endovenoso,-a *adj* intravenous.

endrina *f* → **endrino,-a**.

endrino,-a 1 *adj* blue-black. – **2 endrino,** *m* sloe bush, blackthorn. – **3 endrina,** *f* sloe.

endulzar 1 *t* to sweeten. **2** *fig* (*suavizar*) to alleviate, soften, ease.
▲ *Conjugation model* [4], *like* **realizar**.

endurecer 1 *t* to harden, make hard. **2** *fig* to harden, toughen. – **3 endurecerse,** *p* to become hardened, harden. **4** *fig* to become tough, become hardened.
▲ *Conjugation model* [43], *like* **agradecer**.

endurecimiento *m* hardening, toughening.

ene 1 *f name of the letter n*. – **2** *adj* (*indeterminado*) n: *ene veces,* n times.

ENE *sím* (*estenordeste*) east-northeast; (*símbolo*) ENE.

enebrina *f* juniper berry.

enebro *m* juniper.

eneldo *m* dill.

enema *m* enema.

enemigo,-a 1 *adj* enemy, hostile. – **2** *m,f* enemy, foe.
● ser enemigo,-a de algo, to be against sth.

enemistad *f* hostility, enmity, hatred.

enemistar 1 *t* to make enemies of, set at odds, cause a rift between. – **2 enemistarse,** *p* to become enemies.
● enemistarse con algn., (*enfadarse*) to fall out with sb.

energética *f* → **energético,-a**.

energético,-a 1 *adj* energy, power: *la crisis energética,* the energy crisis. – **2 energética,** *f* energetics.

energía 1 *f* energy, power. **2** *fig* vigour (us vigor).
■ energía cinética, kinetic energy. ‖ energía eléctrica, electric power. ‖ energía hidráulica, water power. ‖ energía nuclear, nuclear power. ‖ energía vital, *fig* vitality.

enérgico,-a 1 *adj* energetic, vigorous. **2** *fig* (*decisión*) firm; (*palabra*) strong.
● en tono enérgico, emphatically.

energúmeno,-a 1 *m,f* energumen. **2** *fam fig* (*hombre*) madman; (*mujer*) mad woman.
● ponerse como un,-a energúmeno,-a, to go up the wall, blow one's top.

enero *m* January.
■ **la cuesta de enero,** the post-Christmas slump.
▲ See also *marzo.*
enervación 1 *f* MED enervation. 2 *fam (irritación)* irritation, exasperation.
enervante 1 *adj* MED enervating. 2 *fam (irritante)* irritating, exasperating.
enervar 1 *t* MED to enervate. 2 *fam (irritar)* to irritate, exasperate, get on one's nerves. **– 3 enervarse,** *p fam* to get flustered, get worked up.
enésimo,-a 1 *adj* nth: *a la enésima potencia,* to the nth power. 2 *fam* umpteenth: *te lo digo por enésima vez,* this is the umpteenth time I've told you.
enfadadizo,-a *adj* irritable, touchy.
enfadado,-a 1 *pp →* **enfadar. – 2** *adj* angry, cross, annoyed, US mad: *parece enfadado,* he looks angry.
enfadar 1 *t* to make angry, make cross, annoy. **– 2 enfadarse,** *p* to get angry (**con,** with), get cross (**con,** with): *no te enfades conmigo,* don't get angry with me. 3 *(pelearse)* to fall out (**con,** with) (**por,** about).
enfado *m* anger, irritation.
● **causar enfado,** to irritate, annoy. ‖ **pasarse el enfado,** to calm down.
enfadoso,-a *adj* annoying, irritating.
enfaenado,-a *adj* hard at work.
enfaldado *adj* tied to one's mother's apron strings.
enfangar 1 *t (ropa, persona)* to cover with mud; *(camino)* to turn to mud. **– 2 enfangarse,** *p (ropa, persona)* to get muddy, get covered in mud; *(camino)* to turn to mud. 3 *fig (en negocios)* to get involved in dirty business; *(en vicios)* to wallow in vice.
▲ *Conjugation model* [7], *like* **llegar.**
enfardar 1 *t* AGR to bale. 2 *(empaquetar)* to wrap up.
énfasis *m & f* emphasis, stress.
● **dar énfasis a algo,** to emphasize sth. ‖ **poner énfasis en algo,** to place emphasis on sth., emphasize sth., stress sth.: *puso énfasis en la importancia de la solidaridad,* he stressed the importance of solidarity.
▲ *pl énfasis.*
enfático,-a *adj* emphatic.
enfatizar *t* to emphasize, stress.
▲ *Conjugation model* [4], *like* **realizar.**
enfermar *i* to fall ill, become ill, be taken ill.
● **enfermar de agotamiento,** to suffer from exhaustion. ‖ **enfermar del corazón,** to have heart trouble.
enfermedad 1 *f* illness, disease, sickness. 2 *fig* malaise, sickness.
● **estar de baja por enfermedad,** to be off sick.
■ **enfermedad contagiosa,** contagious disease. ‖ **enfermedad infantil,** children's complaint. ‖ **enfermedad mental,** mental illness. ‖ **enfermedad venérea,** venereal disease.
enfermería *f* infirmary, sick bay.
enfermero,-a *m,f (hombre)* male nurse; *(mujer)* nurse.
enfermizo,-a 1 *adj* sickly, unhealthy. 2 *fig* morbid, unhealthy.
enfermo,-a 1 *adj* sick, ill: *María está enferma,* María's ill. **– 2** *m,f* sick person. 3 *(paciente)* patient.
● **caer enfermo,-a,** to be taken ill. ‖ **poner enfermo,-a a algn.,** *fig* to make sb. sick, make sb. ill. ‖ **ponerse enfermo,-a,** to be taken ill.
enfermucho,-a *adj fam* ailing, sickly.
enfervorizar *t* to arouse fervour (US fervor) in, arouse passions, enthuse.
▲ *Conjugation model* [4], *like* **realizar.**
enfilar 1 *t (poner en fila)* to line up. 2 *(una calle)* to go along, go down; *(túnel)* to go through. 3 *(dirigir)* to di-

rect. **– 4** *i (tomar dirección)* to head for, head towards, make for: *enfilamos hacia Burgos,* we headed for Burgos.
enfisema *m* emphysema.
enflaquecer 1 *t (poner flaco)* to make thin. 2 *fig (debilitar)* to weaken. **– 3** *i (adelgazar)* to lose weight, get thin. **– 4 enflaquecerse,** *p (adelgazar)* to lose weight, grow thin.
▲ *Conjugation model* [43], *like* **agradecer.**
enflaquecido,-a 1 *pp →* **enflaquecer. – 2** *adj (delgado)* thin; *(débil)* weak, puny.
enflaquecimiento 1 *m (adelgazamiento)* loss of weight. 2 *(debilidad)* weakening.
enfocar 1 *t* to focus, focus on, get into focus. 2 *(luz)* to shine a light on. 3 *fig (problema etc)* to focus on, approach, look at.
● **bien enfocado,-a,** *(fotografía)* in focus. ‖ **mal enfocado,-a,** *(fotografía)* out of focus.
▲ *Conjugation model* [1], *like* **sacar.**
enfoque 1 *m (acción)* focus, focussing. 2 *fig* focus, approach, angle.
enfrascado,-a 1 *pp →* **enfrascarse. – 2** *adj* absorbed.
enfrascarse 1 *p fig* to become absorbed (**en,** in), become engrossed (**en,** in): *se enfrascó en su trabajo,* he became engrossed in his work. 2 *fig (en lectura)* to bury os. (**en,** in).
▲ *Conjugation model* [1], *like* **sacar.**
enfrenar *t* to brake, slow down.
enfrentamiento *m* confrontation.
enfrentar 1 *t (poner frente a frente)* to bring face to face, confront: *el debate enfrentó a los líderes,* the debate brought the leaders face to face. 2 *(encarar)* to face, confront. **– 3 enfrentarse,** *p (hacer frente)* to face (**a/con, -**), confront (**a/con, -**): *tuvo que enfrentarse con los sindicatos,* he had to confront the unions. 4 DEP to meet (**a/con, -**). 5 *(pelearse)* to have an argument (**a,** with), fall out (**a,** with); *(chocar)* to clash (**a/con,** with).
enfrente 1 *adv* opposite, in front, facing: *la iglesia está enfrente de mi casa,* the church is opposite my house. 2 *fig* opposed to, against: *Pepe se puso enfrente del proyecto,* Pepe was against the project.
enfriador,-ra 1 *adj* cooling. **– 2 enfriador,** *m* cooler.
enfriamiento 1 *m (acción)* cooling. 2 MED cold, chill.
● **pillar un enfriamiento,** to catch a cold, catch a chill.
enfriar 1 *t* to cool (down), chill. 2 *fig* to cool down. **– 3** *i (clima)* to get cold, get colder. 4 *(ponerse frío)* to cool, cool down. **– 5 enfriarse,** *p (lo demasiado caliente)* to cool down; *(ponerse demasiado frío)* to go cold, get cold: *déjalo enfriar, está muy caliente,* let it cool down, it's too hot; *se te enfría la sopa,* your soup is getting cold. 6 *(tener frío)* to get cold; *(resfriarse)* to catch a cold, get a cold. 7 *fig* to cool off.
▲ *Conjugation model* [13], *like* **desviar.**
enfundar 1 *t (espada)* to sheathe; *(pistola)* to put into one's holster. **– 2 enfundarse,** *p (ponerse)* to put on; *(abrigarse)* to wrap os. up.
enfurecer 1 *t* to infuriate, enrage. **– 2 enfurecerse,** *p* to get furious, lose one's temper. 3 *(mar)* to become rough.
▲ *Conjugation model* [43], *like* **agradecer.**
enfurecimiento *m* fury, infuriation, temper, rage.
enfurruñamiento *m fam* sulking.
enfurruñarse *p fam* to sulk, get in a huff.
engaitar *t fam* to trick, take in.
engalanado,-a 1 *pp →* **engalanar. – 2** *adj* decked out, festooned.

engalanar 1 *t* (*cosa*) to festoon, deck out. **– 2 engalanarse,** *p* (*persona*) to dress up, get dressed up.
engallado,-a 1 *pp* → **engallarse.** **– 2** *adj fig* (*erguido*) straight, upright. **3** *fig* (*altanero*) conceited, haughty.
engallarse *p fig* to be cocky, get cocky.
enganchado,-a 1 *pp* → **enganchar.** **– 2** *adj arg* (*drogas*) hooked.
enganchar 1 *t* (*agarrar con gancho*) to hook. **2** (*colgar*) to hang, hang up. **3** (*animales*) to harness. **4** (*vagones*) to couple. **5** *fig* (*atraer*) to rope in, persuade: *lo han enganchado para la obra,* he's been roped into doing the play. **6** *fig* (*coger*) to catch: *la policía lo enganchó,* the police caught him. **– 7 engancharse,** *p* to get caught (**en,** on), snag (**en,** on): *se le enganchó la camisa en un clavo,* his shirt got caught on a nail. **8** MIL to enlist, join up. **9** *arg* (*drogas*) to get hooked (**a,** on).
enganche 1 *m* (*gancho*) hook. **2** (*de animales*) hitching, harnessing. **3** (*de vagones*) coupling. **4** MIL enlistment, recruitment.
enganchón *m* snag.
engañabobos 1 *mf fam* (*persona*) con artist, trickster. **– 2** *m fam* (*trampa*) con trick, trap.
▲ *pl* **engañabobos.**
engañadizo,-a *adj* gullible.
engañar 1 *t* (*gen*) to deceive, mislead, fool, take in. **2** (*estafar*) to cheat, trick. **3** (*ser infiel*) to be unfaithful to. **– 4** *i* to be deceptive. **– 5 engañarse,** *p* (*ilusionarse*) to deceive os. **6** (*equivocarse*) to be mistaken, be wrong.
● **engañar el hambre,** *fig* to stave off hunger. ‖ **engañar el tiempo,** *fig* to kill time. ‖ **las apariencias engañan,** appearances can be deceptive.
engañifa 1 *f fam* trick, hoax. **2** *fam* (*estafa*) swindle.
engaño 1 *m* deceit, deception. **2** (*estafa*) fraud, trick, swindle. **3** (*mentira*) lie. **4** (*error*) mistake.
● **estar en un engaño,** to be mistaken.
engañoso,-a 1 *adj* (*gen*) deceptive. **2** (*palabras*) deceitful; (*consejo*) misleading.
engarce 1 *m* (*de perlas etc*) threading, stringing. **2** (*de piedra*) setting, mounting. **3** (*hilo*) string. **4** (*conexión*) connection, linking.
engarzar 1 *t* (*perlas etc*) to string, thread. **2** (*piedras*) to mount, set. **3** *fig* (*palabras, frases*) to string together.
▲ *Conjugation model* |4|, *like* **realizar.**
engastar *t* to set, mount.
engaste *m* setting, mounting.
engatusar *t fam* to get round, coax, cajole: *la engatusó para que cantara,* he coaxed her into singing.
engendrar 1 *t* to engender, beget. **2** *fig* to generate, give rise to.
engendro 1 *m* (*feto*) foetus (US fetus). **2** (*ser informe*) malformed child. **3** *fam fig* (*persona*) freak. **4** *fig* (*cosa*) monstrosity.
englobar 1 *t* (*incluir*) to include, comprise. **2** (*reunir*) to bring together, lump together.
engolado,-a 1 *adj* (*persona*) arrogant, pompous. **2** (*estilo etc*) high-flown.
engolfarse *p fam fig* to get absorbed (**en,** in).
engolletado,-a *adj fam* vain, conceited.
engolosinar 1 *t* to tempt, entice. **– 2 engolosinarse,** *p* to become fond (**con,** of), develop a taste (**con,** for): *se ha engolosinado con el buen vino,* he's developed a taste for fine wines.
engomado,-a 1 *pp* → **engomar.** **– 2** *adj* (*gomoso*) sticky. **– 3 engomado,** *m* gum, glue.
engomar *t* to gum, glue, stick.
engominarse *p* (*brillantina*) to put hair cream on; (*fijador*) to gel one's hair, put hair gel on.

engordar 1 *t* to fatten, fatten up, make fat. **– 2** *i* (*persona*) to put on weight, get fatter: *he engordado,* I've got fatter. **3** (*alimento*) to be fattening: *la nata engorda mucha,* cream is really fattening.
engorde *m* fattening (up).
engorro *m fam* bother, nuisance.
engorroso,-a *adj fam* bothersome, annoying, awkward.
engranaje 1 *m* TÉC gears *pl.* **2** (*de reloj*) cogs *pl.* **3** *fig* machinery.
engranar 1 *i* TÉC to engage, mesh. **2** *fig* (*enlazar*) to connect, link. **– 3** *t* TÉC to engage, mesh. **4** *fig* to connect, link.
engrandecer 1 *t* (*hacer grande*) to enlarge, magnify. **2** (*exaltar*) to extol, exalt. **3** *fig* (*enaltecer*) to enhance. **4** *fig* (*mente, espíritu*) to widen, broaden.
▲ *Conjugation model* |43|, *like* **agradecer.**
engrandecimiento 1 *m* (*aumento*) enlargement. **2** (*exaltación*) exaltation. **3** *fig* (*enaltecimiento*) enhancement.
engranujarse *p* to become a rogue.
engrasar 1 *t* (*dar grasa*) to grease, oil, lubricate. **2** (*manchar*) to make greasy, stain with grease. **3** *fam fig* (*sobornar*) to grease sb.'s palm.
engrase 1 *m* (*acción*) greasing, lubrication, oiling. **2** (*sustancia*) lubricant.
engreído,-a *adj* vain, conceited, stuck-up.
engreimiento *m* vanity, conceit.
engreír 1 *t* (*envanecer*) to make vain, make conceited. **– 2 engreírse,** *p* to become vain, become conceited.
▲ *Conjugation model* |37|, *like* **reír.**
engrescar *t* **1** (*incitar*) to cause trouble between; (*animar*) to whip up enthusiasm, get going: *intentó engrescar al público,* he tried to get the audience going. **– 2 engrescarse** *p* to get embroiled.
▲ *Conjugation model* |1|, *like* **sacar.**
engrosar 1 *t* (*hacer grueso*) to thicken. **2** *fig* (*aumentar*) to increase, swell: *Pepe pasó a engrosar las filas del ejército,* Pepe went on to swell the army's ranks. **– 3** *i* (*engordar*) to get fat.
▲ *Conjugation model* |31|, *like* **contar.**
engrudar *t* to paste, stick with flour and water paste.
engrudo *m* paste, flour and water paste.
engrumecerse *p* (*gen*) to go lumpy; (*sangre*) to clot; (*leche*) to curdle.
▲ *Conjugation model* |43|, *like* **agradecer.**
enguantado,-a 1 *pp* → **enguantarse.** **– 2** *adj* gloved.
enguantarse *p* to put on one's gloves.
enguatar *t* to pad.
enguijarrado *m* cobbles *pl.*
enguirnaldar *t* to garland.
engullir *t* to shallow, gobble up, gulp down.
▲ *Conjugation model* |41|, *like* **mullir.**
enharinar 1 *t* (*cubrir*) to flour; (*manchar*) to sprinkle with flour. **2** (*la cara*) to whiten.
enhebrar 1 *t* to thread. **2** *fig* to connect, link.
enhiesto,-a *adj* erect, upright.
enhilar 1 *t* (*enhebrar*) to thread. **2** *fig* (*ideas etc*) to connect, link. **3** *fig* (*dirigir*) to direct, guide.
enhorabuena 1 *f* congratulations *pl*: *enhorabuena por el resultado,* congratulations on the result. **– 2** *adv* thank God: *has llegado enhorabuena,* thank God you've arrived.
● **dar la enhorabuena a,** to congratulate. ‖ **estar de enhorabuena,** to be happy.
enhoramala *adv* inopportunely, at the wrong time.

enhornar *t* to put into the oven.
enigma *m* enigma, puzzle, mystery.
enigmático,-a *adj* enigmatic, mysterious, puzzling.
enjabonar 1 *t* to soap. 2 *fig* to soft-soap, butter-up.
enjaezar *t* to harness.
▲ *Conjugation model* [4], *like* **realizar**.
enjalbegar 1 *t* (*pared etc*) to whitewash. 2 (*la cara*) to paint.
▲ *Conjugation model* [7], *like* **llegar**.
enjambrar 1 *t* to hive. – 2 *i* to swarm.
enjambre 1 *m* swarm. 2 *fig* swarm, throng, crowd.
enjarciar *t* to rig up: *enjarciaron el barco*, they rigged up the boat.
▲ *Conjugation model* [12], *like* **cambiar**.
enjaretado *m* latticework.
enjaretar 1 *t fam fig* (*discurso etc*) to reel off. 2 *fam fig* (*trabajo etc*) to palm off.
enjaular 1 *t* to cage. 2 *fam fig* to put in jail, put inside.
enjoyar 1 *t* to adorn with jewels. 2 *fig* to adorn, decorate. 3 (*engastar*) to set. – 4 **enjoyarse**, *p fam* to put on lots of jewellery (US jewelry), be dripping with jewels.
enjuagadientes *m* mouthwash.
▲ *pl* **enjuagadientes**.
enjuagar 1 *t* to rinse: *se enjuagó las manos y las secó con la toalla*, she rinsed her hands and dried them with the towel; *la tetera debe enjuagarse con agua caliente*, the teapot should be rinsed out with hot water. – 2 **enjuagarse**, *p* to rinse one's mouth out.
▲ *Conjugation model* [7], *like* **llegar**.
enjuagatorio 1 *m* (*líquido*) mouthwash. 2 *fig* (*intriga*) scheme, plot.
enjuague 1 *m* (*acción*) rinse. 2 (*líquido*) mouthwash. 3 *fig* (*intriga*) scheme, plot.
enjugar 1 *t* (*secar*) to dry, wipe (away), mop up. 2 FIN to clear, wipe out.
enjuiciamiento 1 *m* (*opinión*) judgement, judgment. 2 JUR (*civil*) lawsuit; (*criminal*) trial, prosecution.
enjuiciar 1 *t* (*juzgar*) to judge; (*examinar*) to examine. 2 JUR (*civil*) to sue; (*criminal*) to indict, prosecute.
▲ *Conjugation model* [12], *like* **cambiar**.
enjundia 1 *f* (*grasa*) fat. 2 *fig* (*sustancia*) substance; (*importancia*) importance. 3 *fig* (*fuerza*) force, vitality. 4 *fig* (*carácter*) character.
enjundioso,-a 1 *adj* (*grasoso*) fatty. 2 *fig* meaty, substantial.
enjuto,-a *adj* thin, skinny, lean.
enlace 1 *m* (*conexión*) link, connection. 2 (*boda*) marriage. 3 (*tren etc*) connection. 4 (*intermediario*) liaison, link. 5 QUÍM bond.
● **establecer un enlace**, to forge a link. ‖ **servir de enlace**, to provide a link.
■ **enlace sindical**, shop steward, US union delegate. ‖ **estación de enlace**, junction; (*metro*) connecting station. ‖ **vía de enlace**, crossover.
enladrillado,-a 1 *pp* → **enladrillar**. – 2 *adj* brick. – 3 enladrillado, *m* brick paving.
enladrillar *t* to pave with bricks.
enlanado,-a *adj* covered with wool.
enlatado,-a 1 *pp* → **enlatar**. – 2 *adj* canned, tinned. – 3 enlatado, *m* canning, tinning.
enlatar *t* to can, tin.
enlazar 1 *t* (*unir*) to link, connect, tie (together). 2 (*ideas etc*) to link, connect, relate. 3 (*carreteras etc*) to connect. – 4 *i* (*trenes etc*) to connect (**con**, with). – 5 **enlazarse**, *p* (*unirse*) to be linked, be connected. 6 (*casarse*) to get married, marry. 7 (*familias*) to become linked by marriage.

▲ *Conjugation model* [4], *like* **realizar**.
enlodar 1 *t* to muddy, cover with mud. 2 *fig* to stain, besmirch, sully: *el escándalo ha enlodado su reputación*, the scandal has sullied his reputation. – 3 **enlodarse**, *p* to get muddy.
enloquecedor,-ra *adj* maddening.
enloquecer 1 *t* (*volver loco*) to drive mad. 2 *fam* (*gustar*) to be mad/crazy about, be wild about: *le enloquece el teatro*, she's mad about the theatre. – 3 *i* (*volverse loco*) to go mad/crazy, go out of one's mind. – 4 **enloquecerse**, *p* to go mad/crazy, go out of one's mind.
▲ *Conjugation model* [43], *like* **agradecer**.
enloquecimiento *m* insanity, madness.
enlosado *m* (*de losas*) paving; (*de baldosas*) tiling.
enlosar *t* (*losas*) to pave; (*baldosas*) to tile.
enlucido *m* plaster.
enlucir 1 *t* (*paredes etc*) to plaster. 2 (*metales*) to polish.
enlutado,-a 1 *pp* → **enlutar**. – 2 *adj* mourning, in mourning.
enlutar 1 *t* to cast a pall over, plunge into mourning. 2 *fig* (*obscurecer*) to darken. 3 *fig* (*entristecer*) to sadden. – 4 **enlutarse**, *p* to dress in mourning, go into mourning.
enmaderar *t* (*pared*) to panel; (*suelo*) to lay down floorboards.
enmadrado,-a 1 *pp* → **enmadrarse**. – 2 *adj* tied to one's mother's apron strings.
enmadrarse *p* to be tied to one's mother's apron strings.
enmarañamiento 1 *m* entanglement, tangle. 2 *fig* muddle, confusion.
enmarañar 1 *t* (*enredar*) to tangle. 2 *fig* to embroil, muddle up, confuse: *ha enmarañado el asunto*, he's confused the issue. – 3 **enmarañarse**, *p* (*enredarse*) to get tangled: *se le ha enmarañado el pelo*, her hair's got all tangled. 4 *fig* to get into a muddle, get confused. 5 METEOR to become overcast.
enmarcar 1 *t* to frame. 2 (*rodear*) to surround.
▲ *Conjugation model* [1], *like* **sacar**.
enmascarado,-a 1 *pp* → **enmascarar**. – 2 *adj* masked. – 3 *m,f* masked person.
enmascarar 1 *t* to mask. 2 *fig* to mask, disguise, conceal. – 3 **enmascararse**, *p* (*uso reflexivo*) to put on a mask.
enmasillar *t* to putty.
enmendadura *f* correction, amendment.
enmendar 1 *t* to correct, put right. 2 (*un daño*) to repair, put right. 3 JUR to amend. – 4 **enmendarse**, *p* to reform, mend one's ways.
▲ *Conjugation model* [27], *like* **acertar**.
enmienda 1 *f* correction. 2 (*de daño*) repair, indemnity, compensation. 3 JUR amendment.
● **hacer propósito de enmienda**, to turn over a new leaf. ‖ **no tener enmienda**, to be incorrigible.
enmohecer 1 *t* (*pan, queso, etc*) to make mouldy (US moldy); (*metal*) to rust. 2 *fig* to make rusty. – 3 **enmohecerse**, *p* (*pan, queso, etc*) to go mouldy (US moldy); (*metal*) to rust, go rusty. 4 *fig* to go rusty.
▲ *Conjugation model* [43], *like* **agradecer**.
enmoquetar *t* to carpet.
enmudecer 1 *t* (*hacer callar*) to silence. – 2 *i* (*quedar mudo*) to be struck dumb; (*perder la voz*) to lose one's voice. 3 (*callar*) to fall silent, keep quiet.
▲ *Conjugation model* [43], *like* **agradecer**.
ennegrecer 1 *t* to blacken, turn black. – 2 **ennegrecerse**, *p* to turn black, go black. 3 *fig* to get dark, darken.

▲ *Conjugation model* [43], *like **agradecer***.
ennoblecer 1 *t* to ennoble. **2** *fig (dignificar)* to do honour (us honor) to, be a credit to. **3** *fig (dar distinción)* to add distinction, add refinement. – **4 ennoblecerse,** *p* to become noble.
▲ *Conjugation model* [43], *like **agradecer**.*
enojadizo,-a *adj* irritable, touchy, quick-tempered.
enojado,-a 1 *pp* → **enojar.** – **2** *adj* angry, cross.
enojar 1 *t* to anger, annoy, make angry. – **2 enojarse,** *p* to get angry (**con,** with), get annoyed (**con,** with), lose one's temper (**con,** with): *se enojó con su jefe,* he got annoyed with his boss.
● **enojarse por algo,** to get angry about sth.
enojo *m* anger, annoyance, irritation.
enojosamente *adv* angrily.
enojoso,-a *adj* annoying, irritating.
enología *f* oenology, enology.
enólogo,-a *m,f* oenologist.
enorgullecer 1 *t* to fill with pride. – **2 enorgullecerse,** *p* to be proud (**de,** of), pride os. (**de,** on): *se enorgullecía de su conocimientos,* he was proud of his knowledge.
▲ *Conjugation model* [43], *like **agradecer**.*
enorgullecimiento *m* pride.
enorme 1 *adj (grande)* enormous, huge, vast. **2** *(desmedido)* tremendous, great. **3** *fam (muy bueno)* very good, excellent.
enormemente *adv* enormously, greatly, tremendously.
enormidad 1 *f (grandeza)* enormity, hugeness. **2** *(monstruosidad)* monstrous thing. **3** *(desatino)* nonsense, gross mistake. **4** *fam (mucho)* a lot, loads: *comimos una enormidad,* we ate loads.
enquiciar *t (puerta)* to put on; *(ventana)* to put in.
▲ *Conjugation model* [12], *like **cambiar**.*
enquistamiento *m* encystment.
enquistarse *p* to encyst.
enrabiar 1 *t* to enrage, infuriate. – **2 enrabiarse,** *p* to become enraged, be furious.
▲ *Conjugation model* [12], *like **cambiar**.*
enraizado,-a 1 *pp* → **enraizar.** – **2** *adj* rooted.
enraizar 1 *i* BOT to take root. **2** *fig (persona)* to put down roots. – **3 enraizarse,** *p (planta, árbol)* to take root; *(persona)* to put down roots.
▲ *Conjugation model* [24].
enramada 1 *f (ramas)* branches *pl.* **2** *(adorno)* decoration made of branches. **3** *(cobertizo)* bower, arbour.
enranciar 1 *t* to make rancid. – **2 enranciarse,** *p* to go rancid, go off.
▲ *Conjugation model* [12], *like **cambiar**.*
enrarecer 1 *t (aire)* to rarefy. – **2** *(hacer escaso)* to make scarce. **3** *fig (situación, relación, etc)* to put a strain on: *aquella discusión enrareció nuestra relación,* that argument put a strain on our relationship. – **4** *i (escasear)* to become scarce. – **5 enrarecerse,** *p (aire)* to rarefy. **6** *(escasear)* to become scarce. **7** *fig (situación, relación, etc)* to become strained.
▲ *Conjugation model* [43], *like **agradecer**.*
enrarecido,-a 1 *pp* → **enrarer.** – **2** *adj (aire)* rarefied. **3** *fig (situación, ambiente)* tense, strained.
enrasar 1 *t* to make level, make even. – **2** *i (líquido)* to become level.
enredadera *f* creeper, climbing plant.
enredador,-ra 1 *adj (entrometido)* troublemaking, meddlesome, interfering; *(chismoso)* gossipy. – **2** *m,f (entrometido)* troublemaker; *(chismoso)* busybody, gossip.

enredar 1 *t (prender con red)* to catch in a net, net. **2** *(para cazar)* to set. **3** *(engatusar)* to involve, implicate. **4** *(meter cizaña)* to sow discord, cause trouble. **5** *(enmarañar)* to tangle up, entangle. **6** *(entretener)* to hold up, delay. **7** *fig (asunto etc)* to confuse, complicate; *(trabajo)* to make a mess of. – **8** *i (travesear)* to be mischievous. – **9 enredarse,** *p (hacerse un lío)* to get tangled up, get entangled, get into a tangle. **10** *(complicarse)* to get complicated, get confused. **11** *(en discusión)* to become involved, get caught up. **12** *(amancebarse)* to have an affair.
enredo 1 *m (maraña)* tangle. **2** *(confusión)* mess, muddle, confusion, mix-up. **3** *(engaño)* deceit. **4** *(travesura)* mischief. **5** *(amoroso)* love affair. **6** LIT plot: *comedia de enredo,* comedy of intrigue. – **7 enredos,** *mpl fam (trastos)* bits and pieces.
enrejado 1 *m (reja)* railings *pl,* grating. **2** *(de celda etc)* bars *pl;* *(de jardín)* trellis; *(de ventana)* lattice; *(alambrada)* wire netting. **3** COST openwork.
enrejar 1 *t (puerta, ventana)* to put a grating on. **2** *(vallar)* to fence, put railings round.
enrevesado,-a *adj* complicated, difficult.
enriar *t* to ret.
enriquecer 1 *t (hacer rico)* to make rich. **2** *fig* to enrich. – **3 enriquecerse,** *p* to become rich, get rich.
▲ *Conjugation model* [43], *like **agradecer**.*
enriquecimiento *m* enrichment, enhancement.
enristrar[1] *t (lanza)* to couch.
enristrar[2] *t (ajos etc)* to string together.
enrocar 1 *i (ajedrez)* to castle. – **2** *t (ajedrez)* to castle.
▲ *Conjugation model* [1], *like **sacar**.*
enrojecer 1 *t (volver rojo)* to redden, turn red; *(metal)* to make red-hot. **2** *fig (ruborizar)* to make blush, make turn red. – **3** *i (ponerse rojo)* to redden, turn red. **4** *fig (ruborizarse)* to blush, turn red. – **5 enrojecerse,** *p (volverse rojo)* to turn red; *(metal)* to get red-hot. **6** *fig (ruborizarse)* to blush.
▲ *Conjugation model* [43], *like **agradecer**.*
enrojecimiento 1 *m (metal)* reddening, glowing. **2** *(rostro)* blushing.
enrolar 1 *t* to enrol (us enroll), sign on, sign up. **2** MIL to enlist. – **3 enrolarse,** *p* to enrol (us enroll), sign on. **4** MIL to enlist, join up.
enrollable *adj* that rolls up, roll-up: *persiana enrollable,* roller blind.
enrollado,-a 1 *pp* → **enrollar.** – **2** *adj (papel)* rolled up; *(cable)* coiled. **3** *fam (guay)* cool, great: *es una tía muy enrollada,* she's a great woman. **4** *(ocupado)* busy, wrapped up (**con,** in), engrossed (**con,** in).
● **estar enrollado,-a con algn.,** *fam (hablar)* to be deep in conversation with sb.; *(salir juntos)* to be going out with sb., be seeing sb.; *(tener relaciones)* to be having an affair with sb.
enrollar 1 *t (papel)* to roll up; *(hilo)* to wind up; *(cable)* to coil. **2** *(a alguien)* to involve, mix up: *su familia lo enrolló en el negocio,* his family got him involved in the business. – **3 enrollarse,** *p fam fig (hablar)* to go on and on (**con,** to), chatter (**con,** to). **4** *fam fig (tener relaciones)* to have an affair (**con,** with). **5** *fam fig (liarse)* to get involved (**con,** with).
● **enrollarse bien,** *arg fig* to get on well with people. ‖ **enrollarse como una persiana,** *fam* to rabbit on and on. ‖ **enrollarse mal,** *arg fig* to be difficult to get on with.
enronquecer 1 *t* to make hoarse. – **2** *i* to go hoarse, become hoarse. – **3 enronquecerse,** *p* to go hoarse, become hoarse.

▲ Conjugation model [43], like *agradecer.*
enronquecimiento *m* hoarseness, huskiness.
enroque *m* castling.
enroscar 1 *t* (*gen*) to wind, coil (round); (*cable*) to twist. 2 (*tornillo*) to screw in. – 3 **enroscarse,** *p* to wind, coil; (*cable*) to roll up; (*serpiente*) to coil itself (up).
▲ Conjugation model [1], like *sacar.*
ensacar *t* to pack in sacks, bag, pack in bags.
▲ Conjugation model [1], like *sacar.*
ensaimada *f spiral-shaped pastry made of light dough.*
ensalada 1 *f* salad. 2 *fig* mix-up, mess.
■ ensalada de frutas, fruit salad. ‖ ensalada rusa, Russian salad.
ensaladera *f* salad bowl.
ensaladilla *f* vegetable salad.
■ ensaladilla rusa, Russian salad.
ensalivar *t* to moisten with saliva.
ensalmo *m* spell, incantation, charm.
● como por ensalmo, as if by magic.
ensalzamiento 1 *m* (*enaltecimiento*) exaltation. 2 (*elogio*) praise.
ensalzar 1 *t* (*enaltecer*) to exalt. 2 (*elogiar*) to praise, extol (us extoll).
▲ Conjugation model [4], like *realizar.*
ensamblador 1 *m* (*carpintería*) joiner. 2 INFORM assembler.
ensambladura *f* joint.
ensamblaje *m* assembly, joining.
ensamblar *t* to join, assemble.
ensanchamiento *m* widening, broadening.
ensanchar 1 *t* (*gen*) to widen, enlarge, extend. 2 COST to let out. – 3 **ensancharse,** *p* to get wider, expand, spread, stretch. 4 *fig* (*envanecerse*) to become conceited, get big-headed.
ensanche 1 *m* (*gen*) widening, enlargement, extension. 2 (*de ciudad*) urban development.
ensangrentado,-a 1 *pp* → **ensangrentar.** – 2 *adj* bloodstained, bloody.
ensangrentar 1 *t* to stain with blood, cover in blood. – 2 **ensangrentarse,** *p* to get stained with blood, be covered with blood.
▲ Conjugation model [27], like *acertar.*
ensañamiento *m* cruelty, brutality.
ensañar 1 *t* to enrage. – 2 **ensañarse,** *p* to be cruel (**con,** to), be brutal (**con,** with).
ensartar 1 *t* (*cuentas*) to string (together), thread; (*aguja*) to thread. 2 *fig* to reel off, rattle off.
ensayar 1 *t* TEAT to rehearse; MÚS to practise (us practice). 2 (*probar*) to try out, test.
ensayismo *m* essay writing.
ensayista *mf* essayist.
ensayo 1 *m* TEAT rehearsal; MÚS practice. 2 (*prueba*) test, experiment, trial, attempt. 3 (*literario etc*) essay. 4 (*rugby*) try.
● a modo de ensayo, as an experiment.
■ ensayo general, dress rehearsal.
ensebar *t* to grease.
enseguida *adv* at once, straight away, immediately.
▲ Also written **en seguida**.
ensenada *f* cove, inlet.
enseña *f* ensign, standard.
enseñado,-a 1 *pp* → **enseñar.** – 2 *adj* (*educado*) educated, instructed; (*adiestrado*) trained: *un niño bien enseñado,* a well-educated child.
enseñante 1 *adj* teaching. – 2 *mf* teacher.

enseñanza 1 *f* (*educación*) education, teaching. 2 (*doctrina*) teaching, doctrine.
● dedicarse a la enseñanza, to be a teacher.
■ enseñanza general básica, general basic education. ‖ enseñanza laboral, vocational training. ‖ enseñanza primaria, primary education. ‖ enseñanza privada, private education. ‖ enseñanza pública, state education. ‖ enseñanza secundaria, secondary education. ‖ enseñanza secundaria obligatoria, compulsory secondary education. ‖ enseñanza superior, higher education. ‖ enseñanza universitaria, university education.
enseñar 1 *t* (*en escuela etc*) to teach, train, instruct: *nos enseñó a leer,* he taught us how to read. 2 (*educar*) to educate. 3 (*mostrar, dejar ver*) to show: *me enseñó el libro,* he showed me the book; *con ese jersey enseña el ombligo,* that sweater shows her navel. 4 (*señalar*) to point out.
● enseñar los dientes, *fig* to bare one's teeth.
enseñorearse *p* to take over (**de,** -), take possession (**de,** of).
enseres *mpl* (*bienes*) belongings, goods; (*material*) equipment *sing*; (*herramientas*) tools.
ensilar *t* to ensile, store in a silo.
ensilladura 1 *f* (*de la caballería*) back. 2 (*encorvadura*) curvature.
ensillar *t* to saddle (up), put a saddle on.
ensimismado,-a 1 *pp* → **ensimismarse.** – 2 *adj* engrossed, absorbed, lost.
ensimismamiento *m* absorption.
ensimismarse 1 *p* (*absorberse*) to become engrossed. 2 (*abstraerse*) to become lost in thought.
ensoberbecer 1 *t* to make arrogant, make conceited. – 2 **ensoberbecerse,** *p* to become arrogant. 3 MAR *fig* to get rough.
▲ Conjugation model [43], like *agradecer.*
ensombrecer 1 *t* to cast a shadow over. – 2 **ensombrecerse,** *p* to darken. 3 *fig* (*entristecerse*) to become gloomy.
▲ Conjugation model [43], like *agradecer.*
ensoñación *f* daydream, pipe dream.
ensoñador,-ra 1 *adj* dreamy. – 2 *m,f* dreamer.
ensoñar *t* to daydream about.
▲ Conjugation model [31], like *contar.*
ensopar *t* to dunk, dip, soak.
ensordecedor,-ra *adj* deafening.
ensordecer 1 *t* to deafen. – 2 *i* to go deaf.
▲ Conjugation model [43], like *agradecer.*
ensordecimiento *m* deafness.
ensortijado,-a 1 *pp* → **ensortijar.** – 2 *adj* curly.
ensortijar 1 *t* (*gen*) to wind; (*cabello*) to curl. – 2 **ensortijarse,** *p* (*cabello*) to curl. 3 (*ponerse sortijas*) to put rings on.
ensuciar 1 *t* to dirty, make dirty. 2 *fig* (*reputación etc*) to tarnish, sully. – 3 *i fam* (*evacuar*) to mess os., soil os. – 4 **ensuciarse,** *p* (*mancharse*) to get dirty. 5 *fam* (*evacuar*) to mess os., soil os.
▲ Conjugation model [12], like *cambiar.*
ensueño *m* dream, fantasy.
● de ensueño, dream: *una casa de ensueño,* a dream home.
entablado 1 *m* (*entarimado*) planking, planks *pl.* 2 (*suelo*) wooden floor.
entablar 1 *t* (*poner tablas*) to plank, board. 2 (*conversación*) to begin, start, open; (*amistad*) to strike up; (*negocio*) to start; (*relaciones*) to establish. 3 (*ajedrez etc*) to set up.

■ **entablar acción / entablar demanda,** AM to take legal action.
entablillado *m* splint.
entablillar *t* to splint, put in a splint.
entalegar 1 *t* (*en talegos*) to put in sacks. 2 (*atesorar*) to hoard. 3 *arg fig* to put inside, put in the nick.
entallar 1 *t* (*esculpir*) to carve. 2 COST to take in at the waist: *una camisa entallada,* a fitted shirt. – 3 *i* COST to fit.
entallecer *i* to shoot, sprout.
▲ *Conjugation model* [43], *like* **agradecer**.
entarimado *m* parquet floor.
entarimar *t* to cover with parquet.
entarugado *m* wooden paving blocks *pl.*
entarugar *t* to lay wooden paving blocks.
▲ *Conjugation model* [7], *like* **llegar**.
éntasis *f* entasis.
▲ *pl* **éntasis**.
ente 1 *m* (*ser*) being. 2 (*institución*) entity, body, organization. 3 *fig* oddball.
enteco,-a *adj* weak, puny, frail.
entelarañado,-a *adj* full of spider's webs.
entelequia *f* entelechy.
entendederas *mpl fam* brains, brain-box *sing.*
● **ser duro,-a de entendederas,** *fam* to be slow on the uptake. ‖ **tener buenas entendederas,** *fam* to be quick-witted.
entendedor,-ra 1 *adj* well-up: *es entendedor de la música,* he's well up on music. – 2 *m,f* expert.
entender 1 *m* (*opinión*) understanding, opinion. – 2 *t* (*comprender*) to understand: *no entendió nada,* he didn't understand anything. 3 (*darse cuenta*) to realize. 4 (*discurrir*) to think, believe: *entiendo que sería mejor ir,* I think it would be better to go. 5 (*conocer a alguien*) to know. 6 (*interpretar*) to understand, take it: *¿debo entender que ya no quieres ir?,* do I take it you don't want anymore? – 7 *i* (*tener conocimiento*) to know (**de,** about). 8 (*ser autoridad*) to be an expert (**en,** in); (*encargarse*) to deal (**en,** with). 9 *arg* (*ser homosexual*) to be gay. – 10 **entenderse,** *p* (*comprenderse*) to be understood: *esta frase no se entiende,* you can't understand this sentence, this sentence is impossible to understand. 11 *fam* (*conocerse*) to know what one is doing: *yo ya me entiendo,* I have my reasons. 12 *fam* (*llevarse bien*) to get along: *mi suegra y yo no nos entendemos,* my mother-in-law and I don't get on. 13 *fam* (*relación amorosa*) to have an affair (**con,** with): *dicen que se entiende con la vecina de al lado,* they say he's having an affair with the woman next door.
● **a mi entender ...,** to my way of thinking ... ‖ **dar a entender que ...,** to imply that ... ‖ **entender mal,** to misunderstand. ‖ **entenderse con algo,** to deal with, fathom out: *no me entiendo con estas instrucciones,* I can't fathom out these instructions. ‖ **entenderse con algn.,** (*tratar*) to deal with sb., negotiate with sb.; (*ponerse de acuerdo*) to agree with sb. ‖ **entenderse por señas,** to make os. understood by gestures. ‖ **hacerse entender,** to make os. understood. ‖ **no entiendo ni jota,** *fam* I don't understand a word of it. ‖ **tener entendido que ...,** to understand (that) ...: *tengo entendido que llegaron tarde,* I understand they were late.
▲ *Conjugation model* [28].
entendido,-a 1 *pp* → **entender**. – 2 *m,f* expert.
entendimiento 1 *m* (*comprensión*) understanding, comprehension. 2 (*sentido común*) understanding, sense, judgement. 3 (*inteligencia*) intelligence.

entenebrecer 1 *t* to darken, obscure. – 2 **entenebrecerse,** *p* to become dark, get dark.
▲ *Conjugation model* [43], *like* **agradecer**.
entente *f* agreement.
■ **entente cordial,** entente cordiale.
enterado,-a 1 *pp* → **enterar**. – 2 *adj* knowledgeable, well-informed. – 3 *m,f fam* expert, authority.
● **darse por enterado,-a de algo,** to be aware of sth. ‖ **estar enterado,-a,** to be in the know. ‖ **estar enterado,-a de algo,** to be aware of sth. ‖ **no darse por enterado,-a,** to turn a deaf ear.
enteramente *adv* completely, entirely.
enterar 1 *t* to inform (**de,** about/of); (*poner al corriente*) to acquaint (**de,** with), tell (**de,** about). – 2 **enterarse,** *p* (*averiguar*) to find out (**de,** about). 3 (*tener conocimiento*) to learn, hear: *me enteré del accidente,* I heard about the accident. 4 (*darse cuenta*) to realize.
● **para que te enteres,** *fam* for your information.
entercarse *p* to insist, persist.
▲ *Conjugation model* [1], *like* **sacar**.
entereza 1 *f* entirety, wholeness. 2 *fig* (*de carácter etc*) integrity, strength.
enterizo,-a *adj* in one piece, whole.
enternecedor,-ra *adj* moving, touching.
enternecer 1 *t* (*ablandar*) to soften. 2 (*conmover*) to move, touch. – 3 **enternecerse,** *p* to be moved, be touched.
▲ *Conjugation model* [43], *like* **agradecer**.
enternecidamente *adv* tenderly.
enternecimiento 1 *m* (*cariño*) tenderness. 2 (*compasión*) pity.
entero,-a 1 *adj* (*completo*) entire, whole, complete. 2 *fig* (*recto*) honest, upright. 3 *fig* (*firme*) firm, resolute. 4 (*robusto*) robust. – 5 **entero,** *m* FIN point. 6 MAT whole number.
● **bajar enteros,** FIN to go down points. ‖ **darse por entero a algo,** to devote os. entirely to sth. ‖ **subir enteros,** FIN to go up points.
enterrador *m* gravedigger.
enterramiento *m* burial, interment.
enterrar 1 *t* to bury, inter. 2 *fig* (*olvidar*) to forget, give up. – 3 **enterrarse,** *p fig* to bury os.
● **enterrarse en vida,** *fig* to cut os. off from the world.
▲ *Conjugation model* [27], *like* **acertar**.
entesar *t* (*dar fuerza*) to strengthen; (*dar tensión*) to tighten.
▲ *Conjugation model* [27], *like* **acertar**.
entibiar 1 *t* to cool, make lukewarm. 2 *fig* to cool down, temper. – 3 **entibiarse,** *p* to become lukewarm. 4 *fig* to cool off.
▲ *Conjugation model* [12], *like* **cambiar**.
entidad 1 *f* (*esencia*) entity. 2 (*asociación etc*) firm, company. 3 *fig* (*importancia*) importance, significance.
● **de entidad,** important, of importance.
entierro 1 *m* (*acción*) burial. 2 (*ceremonia*) funeral.
● **parecer un entierro de tercera,** *fam* to be like a funeral.
entintar 1 *t* (*manchar*) to stain with ink. 2 (*en impresión*) to ink. 3 *fig* (*teñir*) to dye.
entlo. *abr* (*entresuelo*) first floor, mezzanine, US second floor.
entoldado 1 *m* (*toldos*) awnings *pl.* 2 (*para fiestas etc*) marquee.
entoldar 1 *t* to put an awning over. – 2 **entoldarse,** *p* (*el tiempo*) to become overcast, cloud over.
entomología *f* entomology.

entomológico,-a *adj* entomologic, entomological.
entomólogo,-a *m,f* entomologist.
entonación *f* intonation.
entonado,-a 1 *pp* → **entonar**. – 2 *adj* arrogant, conceited.
entonar 1 *t* (*nota*) to pitch; (*canción*) to sing, intone. 2 (*organismo*) to tone up. 3 (*colores*) to match. – 4 *i* MÚS to intone. 5 (*colores*) to match. 6 *fig* (*armonizar*) to be in harmony (**con**, with), be in tune (**con**, with). – 7 **entonarse**, *p* (*engreírse*) to give os. airs, be conceited.
entonces 1 *adv* (*en aquel momento*) then. 2 (*en tal caso*) so, then: *entonces no lo quieres,* so you don't want it.
● **de entonces**, in those days, of that time: *los coches de entonces,* cars of that time. ‖ **desde entonces**, since then. ‖ **en aquel entonces**, at that time. ‖ **por (aquel) entonces**, at that time.
entono *m* arrogance.
entontecer 1 *i* to befuddle. – 2 **entontecerse**, *p* to become confused.
▲ *Conjugation model* [43], *like* **agradecer**.
entorchado *m* braid.
entorchar 1 *t* (*velas*) to twist together. 2 (*hilo, cuerda - seda*) to cover with silk; (- *metal*) to cover with wire.
entornado,-a 1 *pp* → **entornar**. – 2 *adj* (*ojos etc*) half-closed; (*puerta*) ajar.
entornar 1 *t* (*ojos etc*) to half-close. 2 (*puerta*) to leave ajar.
entorno 1 *m* environment, surroundings *pl*. 2 INFORM environment.
entorpecer 1 *t* to make numb, make dull. 2 *fig* (*dificultar*) to obstruct, impede, hinder; (*retardar*) to delay.
▲ *Conjugation model* [43], *like* **agradecer**.
entorpecimiento 1 *m* dullness, numbness. 2 *fig* (*obstrucción*) obstruction, hinderance; (*retraso*) delay.
entortadura *f* crookedness.
entortar *t* to make crooked.
entosigar *t* to poison.
entrada 1 *f* (*gen*) entrance, entry. 2 (*vestíbulo*) hall, entrance. 3 (*billete*) ticket, admission: *Juan fue a sacar las entradas,* Juan went to buy the tickets; *la entrada cuesta mil pesetas,* admission is a thousand pesetas. 4 (*público*) audience. 5 (*recaudación*) takings *pl*, receipts *pl*; (*ingresos*) receipts *pl*, earnings *pl*. 6 (*de libro, oración, etc*) opening; (*de año, mes*) beginning: *la entrada de la primavera,* the beginning of spring. 7 (*pago inicial*) down payment, deposit: *pagué una entrada de diez mil libras para la casa,* I made a down payment of ten thousand pounds for the house. 8 (*en libro cuentas*) entry. 9 CULIN entrée, starter. 10 INFORM input. 11 DEP tackle. 12 (*en diccionario*) entry.
● **dar entrada a**, to let in, allow in. ‖ **de entrada**, (*desde el principio*) straight away, from the outset; (*en comida*) for starters. ‖ **"prohibida la entrada"**, "no admittance". ‖ **tener entradas**, (*en la frente*) to have a receding hairline: *tiene entradas en la frente,* he's got a receding hairline.
■ **derechos de entrada**, import duty *sing*. ‖ **entrada de capital**, capital inflow. ‖ **entrada principal**, main entrance. ‖ **media-entrada**, (*aforo*) half-capacity crowd.
▲ *In 13, often used in plural.*
entramado *m* wooden framework.
entramar *t* to make a framework for.
entrambos,-as 1 *adj fml* both. – 2 *pron fml* both: *entrambos lo entendieron,* they both understood it.
entrampar 1 *t* (*animal*) to trap. 2 *fig* (*engañar*) to trick. 3 *fig* (*enredar*) to mess up, muddle. – 4 **entramparse**, *p*

(*enredarse*) to get into a mess. 5 (*endeudarse*) to get into debt.
entrante 1 *adj* entering, coming, incoming: *el año entrante,* the coming year; *el mes entrante,* next month. – 2 *m* CULIN starter.
entraña 1 *f* (*órgano*) entrails *pl*, bowels *pl*. 2 *fig* (*parte importante*) core, heart. – 3 **entrañas**, *fpl* ANAT entrails. 4 *fig* (*parte oculta*) bowels: *las entrañas de la tierra,* the bowels of the earth. 5 *fig* (*sentimiento, afecto*) feelings.
● **de buenas entrañas**, *fig* good-hearted. ‖ **de malas entrañas**, *fig* heartless. ‖ **echar las entrañas**, *fig* to puke, throw up. ‖ **no tener entrañas**, *fig* to be heartless. ‖ **sacarle a uno las entrañas**, *fig* to bleed sb. dry. ‖ **sin entrañas**, *fig* heartless.
▲ *In 1, often used in plural.*
entrañable 1 *adj* (*amistad*) intimate, close. 2 (*amigo*) dear. 3 (*recuerdo*) fond.
entrañablemente *adv* deeply, dearly.
entrañar 1 *t* (*introducir*) to bury deep. 2 (*contener*) to contain; (*implicar*) to involve, entail: *el negocio entraña ciertas dificultades,* the business involves a number of difficulties. – 3 **entrañarse**, *p* to get deeply attached (**con**, to).
entrar 1 *i* (*ir adentro*) to come in, go in: *entró por una puerta secreta,* he went in through a secret door; *entró corriendo,* she ran in; *entró en la casa,* he went into the house. 2 (*tener entrada*) to be welcome. 3 (*en una sociedad etc*) to join; (*en una profesión*) to take up, join: *ha entrado en la masonería,* he's joined the Masons; *ha entrado en la abogacía,* she's taken up law; *ha entrado en la armada,* he's joined the navy. 4 (*encajar, caber*) to fit: *las maletas no entran en el maletero,* the suitcases won't fit in the boot; *este tornillo no entra,* this screw doesn't fit. 5 (*empezar - año, estación*) to begin, start; (- *período, época*) to enter; (- *libro, carta*) to begin, open: *ya ha entrado el verano,* summer has begun; *el libro entra con un asesinato,* the book begins with a murder. 6 (*venir*) to come over, come on: *le entra fiebre,* she's got fever coming on; *me entró dolor de cabeza,* I got a headache; *me entraron ganas de llorar,* I felt like crying. 7 (*alcanzar*) to reach: *ha entrado en los cuarenta,* he has reached forty. 8 (*deberes, planes*) to come, enter: *ese no entraba en el trato,* that didn't enter into the deal. 9 (*adoptar*) to enter (into), get (into): *entrar en las modas,* to get into fashion. 10 INFORM to access. 11 AUTO to engage, change into: *no me entró la primera,* I couldn't change into first gear. 12 MÚS to come in, enter; TEAT to enter: *entró Peribáñez,* Peribáñez entered. – 13 *t* (*meter*) to put: *entra la bici en el garaje,* put your bike into the garage. 14 (*de contrabando*) to smuggle. 15 COST to take in. – 16 **entrarse**, *p* to get in.
● **bien entrado,-a ...**, well into ...: *bien entrada la tarde,* well into the evening; *bien entrado enero,* well into January. ‖ **el año que entra**, next year, the coming year. ‖ **entrado,-a en años / entrado,-a en edad,** *fig* getting on in years. ‖ **entrar a trabajar**, to begin work. ‖ **entrar con buen pie**, *fig* to get off on the right foot. ‖ **entrar en cólera**, to get angry. ‖ **entrar en contacto**, to get in touch. ‖ **entrar en detalles**, to go into details. ‖ **entrar en materia**, to give an introduction. ‖ **entrar en religión**, to enter a religious order. ‖ **ese tío no me entra**, *fam* I can't stand that guy. ‖ **hacer entrar**, to invite in. ‖ **no entrar ni salir en algo**, *fam* to be indifferent to sth. ‖ **no me entra el latín**, *fam* I can't get the hang of Latin. ‖ **no me entra en la cabeza**, *fam* I can't believe it, I can't get my head round it.
entre 1 *prep* (*dos términos*) between: *entre las cuatro y las cinco,* between four and five; *entre tú y yo,* between the

two of us. **2** (*varios*) among, amongst: *entre los periódicos,* among the newspapers. **3** (*sumando*) counting: *entre niños y adultos somos doce,* there are twelve of us counting children and adults; *entre todos éramos veinte,* there were twenty of us all together. **4** (*en*) in: *entre la lluvia,* in the rain. **5** (*entremedio*) somewhere between: *entre azul y verde,* somewhere between blue and green. ● **de entre,** from among, out of: *la mejor de entre todas,* the best out of all of them. ‖ **entre ... y ...,** what with ... and ...: *entre el frío y la lluvia ...,* what with the cold and the rain ... ‖ **entre tanto,** meanwhile, in the meantime. ‖ **por entre,** (*entre*) among, amongst; (*a través*) through: *pasó por entre la multitud,* he made his way through the crowd.

entreabierto,-a 1 *pp* → **entreabrir. – 2** *adj* (*ojos etc*) half-opened; (*puerta*) ajar.

entreabrir 1 *t* (*ojos*) to half open. **2** (*puerta etc*) to leave ajar.
▲ *pp entreabierto,-a.*

entreacto *m* interval.

entrecano,-a *adj* greying, greyish.

entrecejo *m* space between the eyebrows; (*ceño*) frown: *lo miró con entrecejo,* she frowned at him.
● **fruncir el entrecejo,** to frown.

entrecerrar *t* to half close.
▲ *Conjugation model* [27], *like acertar.*

entrechocar *t* to crash, collide.
▲ *Conjugation model* [1], *like sacar.*

entreclaro,-a *adj* fairly clear.

entrecó *m* entrecôte.

entrecomar *t* → **entrecomillar.**

entrecomillado,-a 1 *pp* → **entrecomillar. – 2** *adj* in inverted commas, in quotation marks.

entrecomillar *t* to put in inverted commas, put in quotation marks.

entrecoro *m* chancel.

entrecortado,-a 1 *pp* → **entrecortar. – 2** *adj* (*voz*) faltering, hesitant; (*respiración*) laboured (us labored), difficult. **3** (*intermitente*) intermittent.

entrecortar 1 *t* to cut partially. **2** *fig* to cut off, interrupt.

entrecot *m* entrecôte.

entrecruzar *t* to interweave.
▲ *Conjugation model* [4], *like realizar.*

entrecubiertas *fpl* between-decks.

entredicho 1 *m* (*prohibición*) prohibition, ban. **2** REL interdict. **3** (*duda*) doubt, question.
● **estar en entredicho,** to be in doubt, be in question. ‖ **poner algo en entredicho,** to have one's doubts about sth., call sth. into question, cast doubt on sth.

entredós 1 *m* COST insertion, panel. **2** (*mueble*) cabinet, dresser.
▲ *pl entredoses.*

entrefilete *m* (*en la prensa*) brief article, little piece.

entrefino,-a *adj* medium-quality, of medium quality.

entrega 1 *f* (*gen*) handing over. **2** (*de premios*) presentation. **3** COM delivery. **4** (*de posesiones*) surrender. **5** (*fascículo*) instalment (us installment), part. **6** *fig* (*devoción*) selflessness, devotion. **7** DEP pass.
● **hacer entrega de algo,** (*dar*) to hand over; (*repartir*) to deliver; (*premios*) to present.
■ **entrega a domicilio,** home delivery. ‖ **entrega contra reembolso,** cash on delivery.

entregar 1 *t* (*dar*) to hand over: *le entregó la escritura,* he handed the deeds over to him. **2** (*deberes, ejercicios*) to hand in, give in; (*premios*) to present, award. **3** COM to deliver. **4** MIL to surrender. **– 5 entregarse,** *p* (*ren-*

dirse) to give in (**a,** to), surrender: *el enemigo se entregó,* the enemy surrendered; *se entregó a las autoridades,* he gave himself up to the authorities. **6** (*dedicarse*) to devote os. (**a,** to), be devoted (**a,** to): *se entrega plenamente a su trabajo,* she's totally devoted to her work. **7** *pey* (*caer en*) to give os. over (**a,** to), take (**a,** to): *se entregó a la bebida,* he took to the bottle.
▲ *Conjugation model* [7], *like llegar.*

entreguerras de entreguerras, *loc* between the wars, interwar: *el periodo de entreguerras,* the period between the wars.

entrelargo,-a *adj* medium-length, of medium length.

entrelazar *t* to entwine, interweave, interlace.
● **entrelazar las manos,** to join one's hands, hold hands.
▲ *Conjugation model* [4], *like realizar.*

entrelínea *f* interlineation.

entrelinear *t* to interline, write between lines, insert between lines.

entrelistado,-a *adj* striped.

entrelucir *i* to show through.
▲ *Conjugation model* [45], *like lucir.*

entremedias 1 *adv* in between. **2** (*mientras tanto*) meanwhile, in the meantime.
● **entremedias de,** between, among.

entremés 1 *m* CULIN hors d'oeuvre. **2** TEAT interlude, short play, short farce.
▲ *In 1, often used in plural with the same meaning.*

entremeter 1 *t* to insert, place between. **– 2 entremeterse,** *p* → **entrometerse.**

entremezclar 1 *t* to intermingle. **– 2 entremezclarse,** *p* to intermingle.

entrenador,-ra *m,f* trainer, coach.

entrenamiento *m* training.

entrenar 1 *t* to train, coach. **– 2 entrenarse,** *p* to train.

entreno *m* training.

entrenzar *t* to plait, braid.
▲ *Conjugation model* [4], *like realizar.*

entreoír *t* to hear vaguely.
▲ *Conjugation model* [75], *like oír.*

entrepaño 1 *m* (*de puerta etc*) panel. **2** (*entre columnas etc*) alcove, bay. **3** (*de estante*) shelf.

entrepierna 1 *f* crotch, crutch.
● **pasarse algo por la entrepierna,** not to give a toss about sth.: *se lo pasó por la entrepierna,* she didn't give a toss about it.

entreponer *t* to interpose, place between.
▲ *Conjugation model* [78], *like poner. pp entrepuesto,-a.*

entrepuesto,-a *pp* → **entreponer.**

entresacar 1 *t* (*elegir*) to select, pick out. **2** (*pelo, plantas*) to thin out.
▲ *Conjugation model* [1], *like sacar.*

entresijo *m* *fig* secret, mystery.
● **conocer todos los entresijos,** *fig* to know all the ins and outs. ‖ **tener algo muchos entresijos,** *fig* to be very complicated.

entresuelo *m* mezzanine, GB first floor, US second floor.

entretallar 1 *t* (*labrar*) to carve. **2** (*calados*) to do openwork on. **3** *fig* (*detener*) to stop. **– 4 entretallarse,** *p* to fit in.

entretanto *adv* meanwhile, for the time being.
● **en el entretanto,** in the meantime.

entretejer *t* to interweave, intertwine.

entretela 1 *f* COST interfacing, interlining. **– 2 entretelas,** *fpl fam fig* heart *sing*: *amor de mis entretelas,* my darling, my beloved.

entretenedor,-ra *adj* entertaining.

entretener 1 *t (detener)* to hold up, detain; *(retrasar)* to delay: *no quiero entreteneros más,* I don't want to hold you up any longer. **2** *(ocupar)* to keep busy: *ese asunto me ha entretenido todo el día,* that business has kept me busy all day. **3** *(distraer)* to occupy, keep occupied. **4** *(divertir)* to entertain, amuse, distract. **5** *(hambre)* to kill, stave off; *(tiempo)* to while away. – **6 entretenerse,** *p (retrasarse)* to be delayed, be held up. **7** *(distraerse)* to keep os. occupied. **8** *(divertirse)* to amuse os.
● **sólo para entretenerse,** just for fun.
▲ *Conjugation model* |87|, *like tener.*

entretenida *f* → **entretenido,-a.**

entretenido,-a 1 *pp* → **entretener.** – **2** *adj (divertido)* entertaining, amusing. **3** *(complicado)* time-consuming: *un trabajo entretenido,* a time-consuming job. – **4 entretenida,** *f* mistress, kept woman.
● **dar a algn. la entretenida,** to try to put sb. off.

entretenimiento 1 *m (distracción)* entertainment, distraction, amusement. **2** *(mantenimiento)* maintenance, upkeep.

entretiempo *m* period between seasons; *(primavera)* spring; *(otoño)* autumn.
● **un traje de entretiempo,** a lightweight suit.

entreventana *f* pier.

entrever 1 *t* to glimpse, catch sight of, make out: *entrevimos unas casas a lo lejos,* we could make out some houses in the distance. **2** *fig (conjeturar)* to guess, suspect: *entreveo lo que pretende,* I can guess what he wants.
● **dejar entrever,** to hint.
▲ *Conjugation model* |91|, *like ver. pp entrevisto,-a.*

entreverado,-a 1 *pp* → **entreverar.** – **2** *adj* mixed, patchy. **3** CULIN streaky.

entreverar *t* to mix, mix up.

entrevés *pres indic* → **entrever.**

entreví *pt indef* → **entrever.**

entrevía *f* gauge.

entrevista 1 *f (prensa)* interview. **2** *(reunión)* meeting.
● **hacer una entrevista a algn.,** to interview sb.

entrevistador,-ra *m,f* interviewer.

entrevistar 1 *t* to interview. – **2 entrevistarse,** *p (prensa)* to have an interview (**con,** with). **3** *(reunirse)* to have a meeting (**con,** with): *el presidente se entrevistó con el rey,* the president had a meeting with the king.

entrevisto,-a *pp* → **entrever.**

entristecedor,-ra *adj* saddening.

entristecer 1 *t* to sadden, make sad. – **2 entristecerse,** *p* to be sad (**por,** about).
▲ *Conjugation model* |43|, *like agradecer.*

entrometerse *p* to meddle, interfere: *se entrometió en nuestros asuntos,* he interfered in our affairs.

entrometido,-a 1 *pp* → **entrometerse.** – **2** *adj* interfering, nosy. – **3** *m,f* meddler, busybody, nosey-parker.

entromparse *p fam* to get sloshed.

entroncamiento 1 *m (relación)* relationship; *(por matrimonio)* relationship by marriage. **2** *(ferroviario)* junction.

entroncar 1 *t* to relate, link, connect: *la historia entronca las dinastías,* history links the dinasties. – **2** *i (parentesco)* to be related; *(por matrimonio)* to be related by marriage: *la familia de mi mujer entronca con la vuestra,* my wife's family is related to yours.
● **entroncar con una familia,** to marry into a family.
▲ *Conjugation model* |1|, *like sacar.*

entronización *f* enthronement.

entronizar 1 *t* to enthrone, put on the throne. **2** *fig* to worship, put on a pedestal.
▲ *Conjugation model* |4|, *like realizar.*

entronque *m* → **entroncamiento.**

entropía *f* entropy.

entruchar *t fam* to trick, dupe.

entubar 1 *t* to tube, put in a tube. **2** MIL *arg* to punish.

entuerto 1 *m (agravio)* wrong, injustice. – **2 entuertos,** *mpl* afterpains.
● **deshacer entuertos,** to right wrongs.

entumecer 1 *t* to numb, make numb: *el frío le entumeció los dedos,* the cold made his fingers numb. – **2 entumecerse,** *p* to go numb, go to sleep. **3** *fig (mar, río)* to swell.
▲ *Conjugation model* |43|, *like agradecer.*

entumecido,-a 1 *pp* → **entumecer.** – **2** *adj* numb. **3** *fig (mar, río)* swollen.

entumecimiento 1 *m* numbness. **2** *(mar, río)* swelling.

entumido,-a *adj* numb.

entumirse *p* to go numb.

enturbiar 1 *t* to make muddy, make cloudy, cloud. **2** *fig* to cloud, muddle, obscure. – **3 enturbiarse,** *p* to get muddy, become cloudy. **4** *fig* to get confused, get muddled.
▲ *Conjugation model* |12|, *like cambiar.*

entusiasmar 1 *t (causar entusiasmo)* to fill with enthusiasm, excite. **2** *(gustar)* to like, love: *me entusiasma la ópera,* I love opera. – **3 entusiasmarse,** *p* to get enthusiastic (**con,** about), get excited (**con,** about). **4** *(gustar)* to love (**con,** -), like (**con,** -).

entusiasmo *m* enthusiasm.
● **con entusiasmo,** keenly, enthusiastically.

entusiasta 1 *adj* enthusiastic. – **2** *mf* lover, fan.

entusiástico,-a *adj* enthusiastic.

enumeración *f (cómputo)* enumeration, count, reckoning; *(relación)* listing, enumeration.

enumerar *t* to enumerate.

enunciación *f* → **enunciado.**

enunciado 1 *m (teoría etc)* enunciation. **2** LING statement. **3** *(problema etc)* wording.

enunciar 1 *t (teoría)* to enunciate. **2** *(expresar)* to express, state, word.
▲ *Conjugation model* |12|, *like cambiar.*

enunciativo,-a 1 *adj* enunciative. **2** LING declarative.

envainar *t* to sheathe.

envalentonamiento *m* arrogance, boldness.

envalentonar 1 *t* to make bold, make daring. – **2 envalentonarse,** *p (volverse valiente)* to become bold, become daring. **3** *(insolentarse)* to become arrogant, become aggressive.

envanecer 1 *t* to make vain, make proud. – **2 envanecerse,** *p* to become conceited (**de/por,** about), become vain (**de/por,** about): *se envaneció de/por sus éxitos,* he got conceited about his success, his success went to his head.
▲ *Conjugation model* |43|, *like agradecer.*

envanecimiento *m* vanity, conceit.

envarado,-a 1 *pp* → **envarar.** – **2** *adj (tieso)* stiff. **3** *(orgulloso)* conceited, proud.

envaramiento *m* stiffness.

envarar 1 *t (entumecer)* to numb, make numb. – **2 envararse,** *p (entumecerse)* to go numb. **3** *fam fig (engreírse)* to become vain, become conceited.

envasado,-a 1 *pp* → **envasar.** – **2** *adj (bebidas)* bottled; *(conservas)* canned, tinned; *(paquetes)* packed. – **3 en-**

vasado, *m* (*bebidas*) bottling; (*conservas*) canning; (*paquetes*) packing.
■ **envasado al vacío,** vacuum-packed.
envasar *t* (*botellas*) to bottle; (*latas*) to can, tin; (*paquetes*) to pack.
envase 1 *m* (*acción - paquetes*) packing; (- *botellas*) bottling; (- *latas*) canning. 2 (*recipiente*) container. 3 (*botella vacía*) empty.
■ **envase de cartón,** carton. ‖ **envase de plástico,** plastic container. ‖ **envase sin retorno,** non-returnable bottle.
envedijarse 1 *p* to get tangled. 2 *fig* to quarrel.
envejecer 1 *t* to age, make look old: *este peinado te envejece,* that hairstyle makes you look old. – 2 *i* to get old, grow old. – 3 *i* to get old, grow old.
▲ *Conjugation model* |43|, *like* **agradecer**.
envejecido,-a 1 *pp* → **envejecer**. – 2 *adj* aged, old, old-looking: *Pablo está muy envejecido,* Pablo looks very old.
envejecimiento *m* ageing, growing old.
envenenamiento *m* poisoning.
envenenar 1 *t* to poison. 2 *fig* (*palabras, acciones*) to interpret wrongly. 3 *fig* (*corromper*) to corrupt, poison.
enverar *i* to begin to ripen.
enverdecer *i* to become green.
envergadura 1 *f* (*de pájaro*) spread, span, wingspan. 2 MAR breadth (of sail). 3 *fig* (*de avión*) span, wingspan. 4 *fig* (*importancia*) importance, scope.
● **de gran envergadura / de mucha envergadura,** very important, consequential, far-reaching. ‖ **de poca envergadura,** unimportant, inconsequential.
envergar *t* to fasten.
▲ *Conjugation model* |7|, *like* **llegar**.
enverjado *m* → **enrejado**.
envés 1 *m* (*de página*) back, reverse. 2 (*de tela*) wrong side. 3 BOT reverse.
▲ *pl* **envés**.
envestidura *f* investiture, inauguration.
enviado,-a 1 *pp* → **enviar**. – 2 *m,f* messenger, envoy.
■ **enviado,-a especial,** special correspondent.
enviar 1 *t* (*gen*) to send: *nos enviaron un telegrama,* they sent us a telegram. 2 COM to dispatch, remit; (*por barco*) to ship.
● **enviar a algn. de paseo,** *fam* (*fig*) to send sb. packing.
▲ *Conjugation model* |13|, *like* **desviar**.
enviciar 1 *t* (*pervertir*) to corrupt, pervert. – 2 *i* BOT to produce too many leaves and not enough fruit. 3 *fig* (*deformarse*) to become distorted. – 4 **enviciarse,** *p* (*pervertirse*) to become corrupted, fall into bad habits; (*aficionarse demasiado*) to become addicted (**en,** to).
▲ *Conjugation model* |12|, *like* **cambiar**.
envidar *i* to bid, bet.
envidia *f* envy.
● **dar envidia,** to make envious. ‖ **morirse de envidia,** *fig* to be green with envy. ‖ **tener envidia de algo/algn.,** to envy sth./sb.
envidiable *adj* enviable.
envidiar *t* to envy, be envious of: *le envidia su éxito,* he envies her success.
▲ *Conjugation model* |12|, *like* **cambiar**.
envidiosamente *adv* with envy, enviously.
envidioso,-a *adj* envious.
envigar *t* to put the beams in.
▲ *Conjugation model* |7|, *like* **llegar**.
envilecer 1 *t* to debase, degrade. – 2 *i* to lose value, be debased. – 3 **envilecerse,** *p* to debase os., degrade

os.: *bebió tanto que se envileció,* he debased himself by drinking so much.
▲ *Conjugation model* |43|, *like* **agradecer**.
envilecimiento *m* degradation, debasement.
envinagrar *t* to put vinegar on.
envío 1 *m* (*acción*) sending, dispatch. 2 COM dispatch, shipment. 3 (*remesa*) consignment; (*paquete*) parcel.
● **hacer un envío,** COM to dispatch an order.
■ **envío contra reembolso,** cash on delivery. ‖ **gastos de envío,** postage and packing.
envite 1 *m* (*apuesta*) bet. 2 *fig* (*ofrecimiento*) offer, bid. 3 (*empujón*) push.
● **al primer envite,** staightaway, right away.
enviudar *i* (*hombre*) to become a widower, lose one's wife; (*mujer*) to become a widow, lose one's husband.
envoltorio 1 *m* (*de caramelo etc*) wrapper. 2 (*lío*) bundle.
envoltura *f* wrapping, wrapper.
envolver 1 *t* (*con papel*) to wrap, wrap up: *no hace falta que me lo envuelva,* there's no need to wrap it. 2 (*con ropa*) to wrap, wrap up: *estaba envuelta en una manta,* she was wrapped in a blanket. 3 (*hilo, cinta*) to wind: *envuelva el hilo en la bobina,* wind the thread onto the bobbin. 4 (*pasteles etc*) to coat, cover: *galletas envueltas en chocolate,* chocolate-coated biscuits. 5 *fig* (*rodear*) to envelop, shroud: *la niebla envolvía el campanario,* the fog enveloped the bell tower. 6 *fig* (*implicar*) to involve (**en,** in), implicate (**en,** in): *lo envolvieron en aquel asunto,* they involved him in that affair. 7 *fig* (*confundir*) to confound. 8 MIL to surround, encircle. – 9 **envolverse,** *p* (*uso reflexivo*) to wrap os. up (**en,** in). 10 *fig* (*implicarse*) to become involved (**en,** in).
▲ *Conjugation model* |32|, *like* **mover**; *pp* **envuelto,-a**.
envuelto,-a *pp* → **envolver**.
enyesado 1 *m* plastering. 2 MED plaster cast.
enyesar 1 *t* to plaster. 2 MED to put in plaster.
enzarzar 1 *t* (*de zarzas*) to cover with brambles. 2 *fig* (*engrescar*) to sow discord among, set at odds. – 3 **enzarzarse,** *p* (*enredarse en zarzas*) to get entangled in brambles. 4 *fig* (*discusión, asunto*) to get involved (**en,** in).
▲ *Conjugation model* |4|, *like* **realizar**.
enzima *m* & *f* enzyme.
eñe *f* name of the letter ñ.
eoceno,-a 1 *adj* Eocene. – 2 **eoceno,** *m* Eocene.
eólico,-a *adj* wind: *energía eólica,* wind power.
eolito *m* eolith.
eón *m* aeon (US eon).
epatar *t* *arg* to knock dead.
E.P.D. *abr* (*en paz descanse*) rest in peace; (*abreviatura*) R.I.P.
epéntesis *f* epenthesis.
▲ *pl* **epéntesis**.
épica *f* → **épico,-a**.
epicarpio *m* epicarp.
epicarpo *m* epicarp.
epiceno *adj* epicene.
epicentro *m* epicentre (US epicenter).
épico,-a 1 *adj* epic, heroic. – 2 **épica,** *f* epic poetry.
epicureísmo *m* Epicureanism.
epicúreo,-a *adj* Epicurean.
epidemia *f* epidemic.
epidémico,-a *adj* epidemic.
epidérmico,-a *adj* epidermic, skin: *enfermedad epidérmica,* skin disease.
epidermis *f* epidermis, skin.
▲ *pl* **epidermis**.

epifanía f Epiphany, Twelfth Night.
epiglotis f epiglottis.
▲ pl *epiglotis.*
epígono m epigone.
epígrafe 1 m (cita) epigraph. 2 (título) title, heading.
epigrafía f epigraphy.
epigrama m epigram, satirical poem.
epilepsia f epilepsy.
epiléptico,-a 1 adj epileptic. – 2 m,f epileptic.
epílogo 1 m (parte final) epilogue (US epilog). 2 (resumen) summary.
episcopado 1 m (obispos) episcopacy. 2 (lugar) bishopric. 3 (época) episcopate.
episcopal adj episcopal.
episiotomía f episiotomy.
episódico,-a adj episodic.
episodio 1 m (literario) episode. 2 (suceso) incident, event.
epístola f fml epistle, letter.
epistolario m collection of letters.
epitafio m epitaph.
epitalamio m epithalamium.
epitelio m epithelium.
epíteto m epithet.
epítome m epitome, abstract, summary.
E.P.M. abr (en propia mano) in person, personally.
época 1 f time, age: *en la época de Enrique VIII,* in the time of Henry VIII; *en la época de los romanos,* in Roman times. 2 HIST period, epoch: *muebles de época,* period furniture. 3 AGR season, time: *la época de la recolección,* harvest time.
● hacer época, to be a landmark, make history: *un descubrimiento que hizo época,* a discovery which had a huge impact; *un acuerdo que hizo época,* an agreement which made history. ‖ por aquella época, about that time. ‖ ser de su época, to be with the times.
epodo m epode.
epónimo,-a 1 adj eponymous. – 2 epónimo, m eponym.
epopeya 1 f LIT epic poem. 2 (hecho) heroic deed.
épsilon f epsilon.
epsomita f Epsom salts pl.
equidad 1 f JUR equity. 2 (moderación) fairness, reasonableness.
equidistancia f equidistance.
equidistante adj equidistant.
equidistar i to be equidistant (de, from).
équido,-a 1 adj equine. – 2 équido, m equine, equid.
equilátero,-a adj equilateral.
equilibrado,-a 1 pp → equilibrar. – 2 adj balanced. 3 (persona) sensible, well-balanced.
equilibrar 1 t to balance, poise: *equilibrar los platillos de una balanza,* to balance the trays on a set of scales. 2 fig to balance, adjust: *tenemos que equilibrar el presupuesto,* we have to balance the budget. – 3 equilibrarse, p to balance (en, on). 4 fig to recover one's balance.
equilibrio 1 m (estabilidad) balance: *perdió el equilibrio,* he lost his balance. 2 FÍS equilibrium. 3 fig (armonía) balance, harmony. 4 fig (serenidad) poise, composure.
● hacer equilibrios, fig to perform a balancing act: *tuvo que hacer equilibrios para llegar a fin de mes,* he had to pinch pennies to get to the end of the month. ‖ mantener el equilibrio, to keep one's balance. ‖ perder el equilibrio, to lose one's balance.

■ equilibrio de poderes, balance of power.
equilibrismo m (gen) balancing act; (de funámbulo) tightrope walking.
equilibrista mf (funámbulo) tightrope walker.
equino[1] m (erizo marino) sea urchin.
equino,-a[2] adj equine, horse.
equinoccio m equinox.
equinodermo m echinoderm.
equipaje 1 m luggage, baggage. 2 (instrumental) equipment, outfit. 3 (tripulación) crew.
● hacer el equipaje, to pack, do the packing.
■ equipaje de mano, hand luggage.
equipar 1 t to equip, furnish. 2 (barco) to fit out. – 3 equiparse, p (uso reflexivo) to kit os. out (con/de, with), equip os. (con/de, with).
equiparable adj comparable (a/con, to/with).
equiparación f comparison.
equiparar t to compare (a/con, with), liken (a/con, to).
equipo 1 m (prestaciones) equipment. 2 (ropas, utensilios) outfit, kit. 3 (de personas) team.
■ bienes de equipo, capital goods. ‖ equipo de alta fidelidad, hi-fi system. ‖ equipo de fútbol, football team. ‖ equipo de música, music centre, stereo system. ‖ equipo de novia, trousseau. ‖ equipo de salvamento, rescue team. ‖ gastos de equipo, capital expenditure sing.
equis 1 f name of the letter x. 2 MAT x, unknown quantity.
▲ pl *equis.*
equitación f horsemanship, horse-riding, US horseback riding.
equitativo,-a adj equitable, fair.
equivalencia 1 f (igualdad) equivalence. 2 (sustitución) compensation.
equivalente 1 adj (igual) equivalent. 2 (que sustituye) compensatory. – 3 m equivalent.
equivaler 1 i (ser igual) to be equivalent (a, to), be equal (a, to). 2 (significar) to be tantamount (a, to), amount (a, to), mean (a, -): *eso equivale a una declaración de guerra,* this amounts to a declaration of war.
▲ Conjugation model [89], like valer.
equivocación 1 f (error) mistake, error. 2 (malentendido) misunderstanding.
● cometer una equivocación, to make a mistake.
equivocadamente adv by mistake.
equivocado,-a 1 pp → equivocar. – 2 adj mistaken, wrong.
equivocar 1 t to mistake, get wrong: *equivoqué el precio,* I got the price wrong. 2 (cambiar) to get mixed up: *equivoqué vuestros regalos,* I got your presents mixed up. – 3 equivocarse, p to make a mistake, be mistaken, be wrong; (de dirección, camino etc) to go wrong, get wrong: *lo siento pero me he equivocado,* I'm sorry but I've made a mistake; *quedamos el miércoles si no me equivoco,* we had an appointment on Wednesday if I'm not mistaken; *te has equivocado de fecha,* you got the date wrong; *me equivoqué de calle,* I got the wrong street.
▲ Conjugation model [1], like sacar.
equívoco,-a 1 adj equivocal, misleading, ambiguous. – 2 equívoco, m ambiguity, double meaning. 3 (malentendido) misunderstanding.
era[1] f (tiempo) era, age.
■ era cristiana, Christian era.
era[2] 1 f AGR threshing floor. 2 (cuadro de jardín) bed, plot.
era[3] imperf indic → ser.
eral m bullock.

erario *m* exchequer, treasury.
erasmismo *m* Erasmianism.
erbio *m* erbium.
ERC *abr* POL (*Esquerra Republicana de Catalunya*) pro-independence Catalan party.
ere *f name of the letter* r.
ERE *abr* (*Expediente de regulación de empleo*) job rationalization scheme.
erección 1 *f* (*levantamiento*) erection, raising. 2 (*órgano*) erection. 3 (*institución*) foundation, establishment.
eréctil *adj* erectile.
erecto,-a *adj* erect.
eremita *m* hermit, eremite.
erensano,-a 1 *adj* of Orense, from Orense. – 2 *m,f* person from Orense, inhabitant of Orense.
eres *pres indic* → **ser**.
eretismo *m* erethism.
erg *m* erg.
ergio *m* erg.
ergonomía *f* ergonomics.
ergonómico,-a *adj* ergonomic.
erguido,-a 1 *pp* → **erguir**. – 2 *adj* erect, upright, straight. 3 *fig* proud.
erguir 1 *t* to raise (up straight), erect, lift up. – 2 **erguirse**, *p* (*ponerse derecho*) to straighten up, stand up straight. 3 (*alzarse*) to rise. 4 *fig* (*engreírse*) to swell with pride.
▲ *Conjugation model* [70].
erial 1 *adj* uncultivated, untilled. – 2 *m* uncultivated land.
erica *f* erica.
erigir 1 *t* (*alzar*) to erect, build. 2 (*instituir*) to establish, found. 3 (*convertir*) to convert: *erigieron el edificio en embajada*, they converted the building into the embassy. 4 (*elevar de categoría*) to make: *le erigieron jefe de la pandilla*, they made him gang leader. – 5 *i* (*elevar de categoría*) to promote (**en**, to). – 6 **erigirse**, *p* (*atribuirse*) to set os. up (**en**, as): *se erigió en presidente*, he set himself up as president.
▲ *Conjugation model* [6], *like* **dirigir**.
eritema *m* erythema.
erizado,-a 1 *pp* → **erizar**. – 2 *adj* bristly, prickly. 3 *fig* fraught (**de**, with), full (**de**, of): *una situación erizada de dificultades,* a situation fraught with difficulties.
erizar 1 *t* (*pelo - animal*) to bristle; (- *persona*) make stand on end: *lo que vio le erizó el pelo,* what he saw made his hair stand on end. – 2 **erizarse**, *p* (*pelo - animal*) to bristle; (- *persona*) to stand on end: *el pelo se le erizó,* his hair stood on end.
▲ *Conjugation model* [4], *like* **realizar**.
erizo 1 *m* (*animal*) hedgehog. 2 (*planta*) burr. 3 *fig* (*persona*) surly person, prickly character.
■ **erizo de mar** / **erizo marino,** sea urchin.
ermita *f* hermitage, shrine.
ermitaño,-a 1 *adj* recluse: *lleva la vida de una persona ermitaña,* she lives the life of a recluse. – 2 *m,f* (*persona solitaria*) hermit. – 3 **ermitaño,** *m* ZOOL hermit crab.
erogación *f* distribution, division, apportionment.
erogar *t* to distribute, divide, apportion.
▲ *Conjugation model* [7], *like* **llegar**.
erógeno,-a *adj* erogenous, erogenic.
erosión 1 *f* erosion, wearing away. 2 *fig* wear and tear.
erosionar 1 *t* to erode. 2 (*gastar*) to wear away.
erótico,-a *adj* erotic.
erotismo *m* eroticism.

erotizar *t* to eroticize.
▲ *Conjugation model* [4], *like* **realizar**.
errabundo,-a 1 *adj* wandering, vagrant. 2 *fig* aimless.
erradamente *adv* mistakenly.
erradicación 1 *f* eradication. 2 (*de enfermedad*) stamping out.
erradicar 1 *t* to eradicate. 2 (*enfermedad*) to stamp out.
▲ *Conjugation model* [1], *like* **sacar**.
errado,-a 1 *pp* → **errar**. – 2 *adj* mistaken, wrong, erroneous.
errante *adj* wandering, vagrant, errant.
errar 1 *t* (*objetivo*) to miss, get wrong. – 2 *i* (*vagar*) to wander, rove, roam. 3 (*equivocarse*) to be mistaken, be wrong.
● **errar el camino,** to take the wrong road; *fig* to fail in one's duties. ‖ **errar la respuesta,** to give the wrong answer. ‖ **errar el tiro,** to miss the mark. ‖ **errar y porfiar,** to persist in error.
▲ *Conjugation model* [57].
errata *f* erratum, misprint.
■ **fe de erratas,** errata *pl*.
errático,-a *adj* erratic.
erre *f name of the digraph* rr.
● **erre que erre,** *fam* stubbornly, pigheadedly.
erróneamente *adv* wrongly, erroneously.
erróneo,-a *adj* erroneous, wrong, mistaken, unsound: *juicio erróneo,* unsound judgement; *explicación errónea,* wrong explanation; *identificación errónea,* mistaken identity.
error *m* error, mistake: *cometió varios errores,* he made a number of mistakes; *el artículo estaba lleno de errores,* the article was full of mistakes.
● **caer en un error,** to make a mistake. ‖ **estar en un error,** to be mistaken. ‖ **por error,** by mistake, in error.
■ **error de imprenta,** misprint. ‖ **error judicial,** miscarriage of justice.
eructar *i* to belch, burp.
eructo *m* belch, burp.
erudición *f* erudition, learning, scholarship.
eruditamente *adv* eruditely.
erudito,-a 1 *adj* erudite, learned, scholarly: *una mujer erudita,* an erudite woman; *erudito en historia,* learned in history. – 2 *m,f* scholar, expert.
■ **erudito,-a a la violeta,** *fam* pseudo-intellectual.
erupción 1 *f* (*volcánica*) eruption. 2 (*cutánea*) rash.
● **entrar en erupción,** to erupt.
eruptivo,-a *adj* eruptive.
es *pres indic* → **ser**.
esa *adj* → **ese**.
ésa *pron* → **ése**.
esbeltez 1 *f* slenderness, slimness. 2 (*elegancia*) gracefulness.
esbelto,-a 1 *adj* slim, slender, willowy. 2 (*elegante*) graceful.
esbirro 1 *m* HIST bailiff. 2 (*ayudante*) henchman.
esbozar *t* to sketch, outline.
● **esbozar una sonrisa,** *fig* to force a smile, smile weakly.
▲ *Conjugation model* [4], *like* **realizar**.
esbozo *m* sketch, outline, rough draft.
escabechado,-a 1 *pp* → **escabechar**. – 2 *adj* pickled, in brine; (*arenque*) pickled, soused.
escabechar 1 *t* to pickle, preserve in brine; (*arenque*) to souse, pickle. 2 *fam fig* (*matar*) to do in, bump off. 3 *fam fig* (*suspender*) to fail.

escabeche *m* brine, pickle: *atún en escabeche,* tuna in brine; *arenques en escabeche,* soused herrings.

escabechina *f fam* massacre.

● **hacer una escabechina,** EDUC *fam* to fail a lot of students.

escabel *m* low stool, footstool.

escabrosamente 1 *adv fig* (*con dificultad*) with difficulty. 2 *fig* (*con crudeza*) crudely, coarsely.

escabrosidad 1 *f* (*desigualdad*) unevenness, roughness. 2 *fig* (*de carácter*) harshness. 3 *fig* (*dificultad*) toughness, difficulty. 4 *fig* (*indecencia*) coarseness, crudeness.

escabroso,-a 1 *adj* (*desigual*) uneven, rough: *terreno escabroso,* rough terrain. 2 *fig* (*carácter*) harsh, rude. 3 *fig* (*difícil*) tough, difficult. 4 *fig* (*indecente*) indecent, coarse, crude.

escabullirse 1 *p* (*entre las manos*) to slip through. 2 *fig* (*persona*) to slip away, sneak off, disappear.

▲ *Conjugation model* |41|, *like mullir.*

escachar *t fam* (*espachurrar*) to squash; (*romper*) to break.

escacharrar 1 *t fam* (*romper*) to break. 2 *fam* (*estropear*) to ruin, spoil. 3 *fam* (*coche*) to smash up. – 4 **escacharrarse,** *p fam* (*estropearse*) to be ruined, be spoilt.

escafandra *f* diving suit.

■ **escafandra autónoma,** scuba.

escafandrista *mf* diver.

escafandro *m* → **escafandra**.

escagarruzarse *p fam* to crap os.

▲ *Conjugation model* |4|, *like realizar.*

escala 1 *f* (*escalera - de mano*) ladder; (- *de tijera*) stepladder. 2 (*graduación*) scale; (*de colores*) range. 3 (*mapa, plano, etc*) scale: *lo dibujó a escala,* he drew it to scale. 4 MAR port of call; AV stopover. 5 MÚS scale. 6 MIL promotion list.

● **a gran escala / en gran escala,** on a large scale. ‖ **en pequeña escala,** on a small scale. ‖ **hacer escala,** to stop over (**en,** in).

■ **escala de gato,** rope ladder. ‖ **escala móvil,** sliding scale. ‖ **escala musical,** scale.

escalada 1 *f* (*montaña*) climb, climbing; (*pendiente*) scaling. 2 *fig* (*precios etc*) rise, increase; (*armas*) escalation: *la escalada del terrorismo,* the increase in terrorism; *la escalada de las armas nucleares,* the escalation in nuclear weapons.

escalador,-ra *m,f* climber, mountaineer.

escalafón 1 *m* (*de personas*) roll, promotion list. 2 (*graduación*) ladder; (*de salarios*) salary scale, wage scale.

escalar 1 *t* (*montaña*) to climb; (*pendiente*) to scale. 2 (*asaltar*) to burgle. 3 *fig* (*subir*) to climb; (*armas, guerra*) to escalate.

escaldado,-a 1 *pp* → **escaldar**. – 2 *adj* scalded. 3 *fig* wary, cautious.

● **salir escaldado,-a,** *fig* to get one's fingers burnt.

escaldadura *f* scald, scalding.

escaldar 1 *t* to scald. – 2 **escaldarse,** *p* to get scalded.

escaleno 1 *adj* scalene. – 2 MAT scalene.

escalera 1 *f* stairs *pl,* staircase. 2 (*escala*) ladder. 3 (*naipes*) run, sequence.

■ **escalera de caracol,** spiral staircase. ‖ **escalera de incendios,** fire escape. ‖ **escalera de servicio,** back stairs *pl,* servant's staircase. ‖ **escalera doble / escalera de tijera,** stepladder. ‖ **escalera mecánica / escalera automática,** escalator.

escalerilla 1 *f* MAR gangway; AV steps *pl.* 2 (*en naipes*) run of three cards.

escalfar *t* to poach: *huevos escalfados,* poached eggs.

escalinata *f* outside steps *pl.*

escalofriante *adj* chilling, blood-curdling, hair-raising.

escalofriar 1 *t* to give the shivers to. – 2 **escalofriarse,** *p* to get the shivers.

▲ *Conjugation model* |13|, *like desviar.*

escalofrío *m* (*de frío*) shiver; (*de miedo*) shudder, shiver; (*de fiebre*) chill, shiver: *me da escalofríos nada más pensar en ello,* just thinking about it gives me the shivers.

● **tener escalofríos,** to shiver.

escalón 1 *m* (*peldaño*) step, stair; (*de escala*) rung. 2 *fig* (*grado*) degree, level, grade. 3 *fig* (*paso, medio*) stepping stone. 4 MIL echelon.

escalonado,-a 1 *pp* → **escalonar**. – 2 *adj* (*espaciado*) spaced out, at regular intervals. 3 (*graduado*) graded. 4 (*corte de pelo*) in layers, layered.

escalonar 1 *t* (*espaciar*) to place at intervals, space out. 2 (*graduar*) to grade. 3 (*cabello*) to layer, cut in layers.

escalopar *t* to slice at an angle.

escalope *m* escalope.

escalpelo *m* scalpel.

escama 1 *f* scale. 2 *fig* (*de piel, de jabón*) flake: *jabón en escamas,* soap flakes. 3 *fig* (*recelo*) suspicion, resentment.

escamado,-a 1 *pp* → **escamar**. – 2 *adj fam fig* wary, suspicious.

escamar 1 *t* (*quitar escamas*) to scale, remove the scales from. 2 *fam fig* to make suspicious, make wary. – 3 **escamarse,** *p fam fig* to become suspicious, become wary, smell a rat.

escamón,-ona 1 *adj* suspicious. – 2 **escamón,** *m fam* telling-off.

escamoso,-a 1 *adj* scaly. 2 (*piel*) dry, flaky.

escamotear 1 *t* (*hacer desaparecer*) to make vanish, make disappear. 2 *fam* (*robar*) to pinch, lift; (*quitar*) to take, withold, keep back. 3 *fam* (*problema, dificultad*) to skip, skirt round. 4 (*ocultar*) to keep secret.

escamoteo 1 *m* (*prestidigitación*) sleight of hand, conjuring. 2 *fam* (*robo*) pilfering, pinching, lifting.

escampar 1 *t* to clear out. – 2 *i* METEOR to stop raining, clear up.

▲ *In 2, used only in the 3rd person; it does not take a subject.*

escanciador *m* wine waiter.

escanciar 1 *t* (*servir*) to pour, serve. – 2 *i* (*beber*) to drink.

▲ *Conjugation model* |12|, *like cambiar.*

escandalera *f* racket, fuss, din, uproar.

escandalizar 1 *t* to scandalize, shock: *el crimen escandalizó al público,* the crime scandalized the public. – 2 *i* to make a racket, make a fuss, make a din. – 3 **escandalizarse,** *p* to be shocked (**de/por,** at), be scandalized (**de/por,** by): *se escandalizaron por la película,* they were scandalized by the film.

▲ *Conjugation model* |4|, *like realizar.*

escandallar 1 *t* (*sondar*) to sound. 2 COM to fix the price of.

escandallo 1 *m* (*del mar*) sounding lead. 2 COM price fixing, cost accounting.

escándalo 1 *m* scandal: *su comportamiento es un escándalo,* his behaviour is scandalous. 2 (*alboroto*) racket, fuss, din, uproar. 3 *fig* (*asombro*) astonishment, shock.

● **armar un escándalo,** to kick up a fuss. ‖ **causar escándalo,** to cause a scandal.

escandalosamente *adv* scandalously, shockingly, outrageously.

escandaloso,-a 1 *adj* scandalous, shocking, outrageous. 2 (*alborotado*) noisy, rowdy. 3 (*color*) loud; (*risa*) uproarious.

Escandinavia *f* Scandinavia.
escandinavo,-a 1 *adj* Scandinavian. – 2 *m,f* Scandinavian.
escandio *m* scandium.
escandir *t* to scan.
escáner *m* scanner.
escantillón *m* template.
escaño 1 *m* (*banco*) bench. 2 POL seat.
escapada 1 *f fam* (*salida*) quick trip. 2 DEP breakaway. 3 (*huida*) escape.
● **en una escapada,** in a jiffy. ‖ **hacer una escapada,** to make a quick trip, nip off, escape: *hicieron una escapada a la costa este fin de semana,* they nipped off to the coast this weekend.
escapar 1 *i* (*huir*) to escape, get away, run away: *escapó del campamento,* he escaped from the camp. 2 (*librarse*) to escape. 3 (*quedar fuera del alcance*) to be beyond. – 4 **escaparse,** *p* (*huir*) to escape, run away, get away. 5 (*librarse*) to escape, avoid. 6 (*gas etc*) to leak. 7 (*autobús etc*) to miss: *se me escapó el autobús,* I missed the bus.
● **dejar escapar un suspiro,** to let out a sigh. ‖ **dejar escapar una oportunidad,** to let an opportunity slip. ‖ **escapar a algn.,** to run away from sb. ‖ **escapar con vida,** to get out alive. ‖ **escapar de las manos,** to slip out of one's hands: *el pez le escapó de las manos,* the fish slipped out of his hands. ‖ **escaparse con algo,** to make off with sth. ‖ **escaparse por un pelo,** *fam* to have a narrow escape, have a close shave. ‖ **escapársele a uno algo,** *fig: su visita se me escapó,* her visit slipped my mind. *se me escapó la cometa,* I let go of the kite; *se me escapó la risa,* I burst out laughing; *se le escapó el secreto,* he let the secret slip out.
escaparate *m* shop window.
escaparatismo *m* window-dressing.
escaparatista *mf* window-dresser.
escapatoria 1 *f* (*huida*) escape, flight. 2 (*excusa*) excuse, way out. 3 *fam* (*escapada*) quick trip.
● **no hay escapatoria,** there is no way out.
escape 1 *m* (*huida*) escape, flight, getaway. 2 (*de gas etc*) leak. 3 TÉC exhaust.
● **a escape,** at full tilt. ‖ **salir a escape,** *fig* to rush out. ■ **tubo de escape,** exhaust pipe.
escápula *f* scapula, shoulder-blade.
escapulario *m* scapulary, scapular.
escaque *m* square.
escaqueado,-a 1 *pp* → **escaquearse**. – 2 *adj* chequered (US checkered).
escaquearse *p fam* to shirk, skive off, wriggle out of: *¡no te escaquees!,* don't try and wriggle out of it!
escara *f* eschar.
escarabajo 1 *m* beetle. 2 *fam fig* (*persona*) little squirt. 3 (*de tejido*) flaw. – 4 **escarabajos,** *mpl* scribble *sing.*
escaramujo 1 *m* (*rosal*) wild rose, dog rose. 2 (*fruto*) rose-hip. 3 (*crustáceo*) barnacle.
escaramuza 1 *f* MIL skirmish. 2 (*riña*) run-in, squabble.
escaramuzar *i* to skirmish.
▲ *Conjugation model* [4], *like* **realizar.**
escarapela *f* cockade, rosette.
escarbar 1 *t* (*suelo*) to scratch. 2 (*dientes, orejas*) to pick. 3 (*fuego*) to poke. 4 (*bolsillo, papeles*) to rummage in. 5 *fig* (*inquirir*) to inquire into, delve into.
escarceo 1 *m* small wave, ripple. 2 (*prueba*) attempt, foray. 3 (*aventura amorosa*) flirtation, start of a love affair. – 4 **escarceos,** *mpl* (*del caballo*) prancing *sing.*
■ **escarceos amorosos,** affairs.
escarcha *f* frost, hoarfrost.

escarchado,-a 1 *pp* → **escarchar.** – 2 *adj* METEOR frosty, frost-covered. 3 CULIN crystallized, candied: *frutas escarchadas,* crystallized fruit.
escarchar 1 *i* METEOR to be frosty, be freezing. – 2 *t* CULIN to crystallize.
▲ In *1,* used only in the 3rd person; it does not take a subject.
escarda *f* weeding hoe.
escardar 1 *t* to weed. 2 *fig* to weed out.
escardilla *f* weeding hoe.
escardillo *m* weeding hoe.
escariar *t* to ream.
▲ *Conjugation model* [12], *like* **cambiar.**
escarificar *t* to scarify.
▲ *Conjugation model* [1], *like* **sacar.**
escarlata 1 *adj* scarlet. – 2 *m* (*color*) scarlet. – 3 *f* (*tela*) scarlet. 4 MED scarlet fever.
escarlatina *f* scarlet fever.
escarmentar 1 *t* to punish severely, teach a lesson to. – 2 *i* to learn one's lesson: *a ver si escarmientas,* that'll teach you (a lesson).
● **escarmentar en cabeza ajena,** to learn from sb. else's mistakes.
▲ *Conjugation model* [27], *like* **acertar.**
escarmiento *m* punishment, lesson.
escarnecer *t* to scoff at, mock, ridicule.
▲ *Conjugation model* [43], *like* **agradecer.**
escarnecimiento *m* mockery, derision, ridicule.
escarnio *m* derision, mockery, ridicule.
escarola *f* curly endive, us escarole.
escarpa 1 *f* (*declive*) escarpment, scarp, slope. 2 MIL escarpment, scarp.
escarpado,-a 1 *adj* (*inclinado*) steep, sheer. 2 (*abrupto*) craggy.
escarpadura *f* → **escarpa**.
escarpia *f* spike, hook.
escarpidor *m* large-toothed comb.
escarpín 1 *m* (*zapato*) pump. 2 (*calzado interior*) slipper.
escasamente 1 *adv* (*insuficientemente*) scantly, sparingly, meagrely (US meagerly). 2 (*raramente*) scarcely, hardly, barely.
escasear 1 *i* (*faltar*) to be scarce, get scarce: *escasea la leche,* milk is scarce. – 2 *t* (*dar poco*) to be sparing with, skimp on.
escasez 1 *f* (*carencia*) scarcity, lack, shortage. 2 (*mezquindad*) meanness, stinginess.
escaso,-a 1 *adj* (*insuficiente*) scarce, scant, very little, small. 2 (*recursos*) slender; (*dinero*) tight; (*público*) small; (*lluvias*) low; (*tiempo*) very little; (*salario*) poor. 3 (*poco de algo*) few: *escasos días,* few days. 4 (*que le falta poco*) hardly, scarcely, barely: *un kilo escaso,* barely a kilo. 5 (*mezquino*) miserly, mean.
● **andar escaso,-a de algo,** to be short of sth.
escatimar 1 *t* (*escasear*) to stint, skimp on. 2 (*ahorrar*) to save, spare.
● **no escatimar esfuerzos,** to spare no efforts.
escatimoso,-a 1 *adj* (*mezquino*) sparing, stingy, mean. 2 (*malicioso*) malicious, cunning, sly.
escatología[1] *f* REL eschatology.
escatología[2] *f* (*de excrementos*) scatology.
escatológico,-a[1] *adj* REL eschatological.
escatológico,-a[2] *adj* (*de excrementos*) scatological.
escayola 1 *f* (*yeso*) plaster of Paris; (*estuco*) stucco. 2 MED plaster.
escayolar *t* to put in plaster, plaster.
escena 1 *f* TEAT (*parte*) scene; (*lugar*) stage. 2 *fig* scene.
● **desaparecer de escena,** *fam* to vanish. ‖ **entrar en**

escena, to go on stage. ‖ **hacer una escena / montar una escena,** *fam* to make a scene. ‖ **poner en escena,** to stage.

escenario 1 *m* TEAT stage. 2 CINEM scenario. 3 *fig* scene, setting.

escénico,-a *adj* scenic.

escenificar 1 *t* (*dar forma*) to dramatize. 2 (*poner en escena*) to stage.

escenografía 1 *m* CINEM set design. 2 TEAT stage design.

escenógrafo,-a 1 *m,f* CINEM set designer. 2 TEAT stage designer.

escepticismo *m* scepticism (US skepticism).

escéptico,-a 1 *adj* sceptic (US skeptic). – 2 *m,f* sceptic (US skeptic).

escindible *adj* divisible.

escindir 1 *t* to split, divide. – 2 **escindirse,** *p* to split (off) (**en**, into).

escisión 1 *f* split, division. 2 FÍS fission. 3 MED excision.

esclarecer 1 *t* (*iluminar*) to light up, illuminate. 2 *fig* (*poner en claro*) to clear up, make clear, shed light on. 3 *fig* (*entendimiento*) to enlighten. 4 *fig* (*ennoblecer*) to ennoble. – 5 *i* (*amanecer*) to dawn.

▲ *Conjugation model* [43], *like* *agradecer*.

esclarecidamente *adv* illustriously.

esclarecido,-a 1 *pp* → **esclarecer.** – 2 *adj* illustrious, distinguished.

esclarecimiento 1 *m* (*explicación*) explanation, clarification. 2 (*entendimiento*) enlightenment. 3 *fig* (*ennoblecimiento*) ennoblement.

esclava *f* → **esclavo,-a.**

esclavina *f* short cape.

esclavista 1 *adj* pro-slavery. – 2 *mf* slavery supporter.

esclavitud *f* slavery, servitude.

esclavizar *t* to enslave.

▲ *Conjugation model* [4], *like* *realizar*.

esclavo,-a 1 *adj* enslaved; *fig* tied: *es esclavo de su familia,* he's tied to his family. – 2 *m,f* slave. – 3 **esclava,** *f* (*brazalete*) bangle.

● **ser esclavo,-a del tabaco / ser esclavo,-a de la bebida,** to be addicted to cigarettes / be addicted to drink. ‖ **trabajar como un,-a esclavo,-a,** to work like a slave.

esclerosis *f* sclerosis.

■ **esclerosis múltiple,** multiple sclerosis.

▲ *pl* *esclerosis*.

esclusa *f* lock, sluicegate, floodgate.

escoba *f* brush, broom.

● **estar como una escoba,** *fam* to be as thin as a rake. ‖ **pasar la escoba,** to sweep up. ‖ **no vender una escoba,** *fam* not to sell a thing.

escobajo 1 *m* (*escoba*) old broom. 2 (*raspa*) stalk.

escobazo 1 *m* (*golpe*) blow with a brush, blow with a broom. 2 (*barredura*) quick sweep (round): *voy a dar un escobazo en la cocina,* I'm going to give the kitchen a quick sweep.

● **echar a algn. a escobazos,** *fam* to boot sb. out.

escobilla 1 *f* small brush. 2 AUTO windscreen-wiper blade.

escobillón *m* swab.

escobón *m* large brush, large broom.

escocedura 1 *f* (*herida*) sore. 2 (*dolor*) soreness, smarting.

escocer 1 *i* to smart, sting: *le escuecen sus heridas,* his cuts sting. 2 *fig* to hurt. – 3 **escocerse,** *p* (*irritarse*) to become sore, become chapped; (*estar irritado*) to be sore, be chapped: *se le ha escocido el culito,* his bottom's chapped.

▲ *Conjugation model* [54], *like* *cocer*.

escocés,-a 1 *adj* Scottish. – 2 *m,f* (*persona*) Scot; (*hombre*) Scotsman; (*mujer*) Scotswoman. – 3 **escocés,** *m* (*idioma*) Scottish, Scottish Gaelic.

■ **falda escocesa,** kilt. ‖ **whisky escocés,** Scotch, Scotch whisky.

Escocia *f* Scotland.

■ **Nueva Escocia,** Nova Scotia.

escofina *f* rasp.

escoger *t* to choose, pick out, select: *escogió un libro del montón,* she chose a book from the pile; *escogió entre cuatro libros,* he chose between four books; *lo escogió para/por marido,* she chose him as her husband.

● **a escoger,** to choose from: *hay cuatro premios a escoger,* there are four prizes to choose from. ‖ **no hay donde escoger,** they are all just as bad. ‖ **tener donde escoger,** to have a good choice.

▲ *Conjugation model* [5], *like* *proteger*.

escogidamente *adv* discerningly.

escogido,-a 1 *pp* → **escoger.** – 2 *adj* chosen, selected; (*selecto*) choice, select: *obras escogidas,* selected works; *productos escogidos,* select products.

escogimiento *m* choice, selection.

escolanía *f* (church) choir.

escolano *m* choirboy.

escolar 1 *adj* school, scholastic. – 2 *mf* (*chico*) schoolboy; (*chica*) schoolgirl.

■ **año escolar / curso escolar,** school year. ‖ **edad escolar,** school age.

escolaridad *f* schooling.

■ **escolaridad obligatoria,** compulsory schooling. ‖ **libro de escolaridad,** school-report book.

escolarizar *t* to school.

▲ *Conjugation model* [4], *like* *realizar*.

escolasticismo *m* scholasticism.

escolástico,-a *adj* scholastic.

escolio *m* scholium.

escoliosis *f* scoliosis.

▲ *pl* *escoliosis*.

escollera *f* breakwater, jetty.

escollo 1 *m* MAR reef, rock. 2 *fig* difficulty, pitfall, snag.

escolopendra *f* centipede.

escolta 1 *f* escort. 2 MAR convoy.

● **dar escolta,** to escort, accompany.

■ **escolta personal,** bodyguard.

escoltar 1 *t* to escort. 2 MAR to convoy.

escombrar *t* to clear (out): *escombraron el barrio de indeseables,* they cleared out all the undesirables from the district.

escombrera *f* dump, rubbish heap, GB tip.

escombros *mpl* rubble *sing*, debris *sing*.

esconder 1 *t* to hide, conceal: *escondió el dinero debajo de la cama,* he hid the money under the bed. – 2 **esconderse,** *p* to hide: *se esconde de nosotros,* she is hiding from us.

escondidas a **escondidas,** *loc adv* secretly, in secret.

● **hacer algo a escondidas de algn.,** to do sth. behind sb.'s back.

escondite 1 *m* (*lugar*) hiding place. 2 (*juego*) hide-and-seek.

● **jugar al escondite,** to play hide-and-seek.

escondrijo *m* hiding place.

escoñado,-a 1 *pp* → **escoñar.** – 2 *adj tabú* knackered, kaput: *tengo el coche escoñado,* my car's kaput.

escoñar 1 *t tabú* to knacker. – 2 **escoñarse,** *p tabú* to be knackered.

escopeta *f* shotgun.
- **escopeta de aire comprimido,** air gun. ‖ **escopeta de cañones recortados,** sawn-off shotgun.
escopetazo 1 *m* (*tiro*) gunshot. 2 (*herida*) gunshot wound. 3 *fig* (*noticia*) bombshell.
escopeteado,-a *pp* → **escopetear**.
- **ir escopeteado,-a / salir escopeteado,-a,** *fam* to be off like a shot.
escopetear 1 *t* to shoot at with a shotgun. – 2 **escopetearse,** *p fig* (*lisonjas*) to shower each other with compliments; (*insultos*) to shower each other with insults.
escoplear *t* to chisel.
escoplo *m* chisel.
escora 1 *f* (*línea*) load line. 2 (*puntal*) stanchion. 3 (*inclinación*) list.
escorar *i* to list, heel (over): *el barco está escorado,* the ship is listing.
- **escorar a babor,** to list to port. ‖ **escorar a estribor,** to list to starboard.
escorbuto *m* scurvy.
escoria 1 *f* (*metal*) slag, dross; (*carbón*) slag. 2 (*de volcán*) scoria. 3 *fig* dregs *pl*, scum: *la escoria de la sociedad,* the dregs of society.
escoriación *f* scraping.
escorial *m* slag heap.
escoriar 1 *t* (*rozar*) to chafe, scrape; (*raspar*) to graze. – 2 **escoriarse,** *p* (*roce*) to be chafed; (*raspadura*) to be grazed.
▲ *Conjugation model* [17], *like* ***descafeinar***.
escorificar *t* to scorify.
▲ *Conjugation model* [1], *like* ***sacar***.
Escorpio *m* Scorpio.
escorpión 1 *m* scorpion. 2 **Escorpión,** ASTROL ASTRON Scorpio.
escórpora *f* rascasse.
escorzar *t* to foreshorten.
▲ *Conjugation model* [4], *like* ***realizar***.
escorzo *m* foreshortening.
escota *f* sheet.
- **escotas mayores,** main sheets.
escotado,-a 1 *pp* → **escotar**[1]. – 2 *adj* COST low-necked, low-cut: *va muy escotada,* she's wearing a low-necked dress. – 3 **escotado,** *m* low neckline.
escotadura *f* low neckline.
escotar[1] *t* COST to cut a low neckline in, cut out the neck of.
escotar[2] 1 *t* (*pagar*) to share the cost of; (*pareja*) to go Dutch on. 2 (*río*) to draw water from.
escote[1] *m* COST low neckline.
escote[2] *m* (*parte*) share.
- **pagar a escote,** to share the cost of; (*pareja*) to go Dutch on: *pagamos la cuenta a escote,* we went Dutch on the bill.
escotilla *f* hatchway, hatch.
escotillón 1 *m* TEAT trapdoor. 2 MAR small hatch, scuttle.
escoto,-a 1 *adj* HIST Scottish. – 2 *m,f* HIST Scot.
escozor 1 *m* stinging, smarting. 2 *fig* pain, grief.
escriba *m* scribe.
escribanía 1 *f* (*oficio*) job of clerk, clerkship. 2 (*oficina*) clerk's office. 3 (*mueble*) writing desk. 4 (*material*) writing set.
escribano,-a 1 *m* clerk; JUR clerk of court. 2 (*ave*) bunting.
- **escribano cerillero,** yellowhammer. ‖ **escribano hortelano,** ortolan bunting. ‖ **escribano palustre,** reed bunting. ‖ **escribano soteño,** cirl bunting.

escribidor *m* hack, scribbler.
escribiente *m* (office) clerk.
escribir 1 *t* (*gen*) to write: *escribe novelas en sus ratos libres,* he writes novels in his spare time. 2 (*deletrear*) to spell, write: *ni siquiera sabe escribir su nombre,* he can't even write his name. – 3 *i* to write. – 4 **escribirse,** *p* (*deletrear*) to spell, be spelt: *¿cómo se escribe?,* how do you spell it? 5 (*uso recíproco*) to write to each other: *se escriben cada quince días,* they write to each other every fortnight.
- **escribir a mano,** to write in longhand, write by hand. ‖ **escribir a máquina,** to type.
- **papel de escribir,** notepaper, writing-paper.
▲ *pp escrito,-a*.
escrito,-a 1 *pp* → **escribir**. – 2 *adj* written; (*mencionado*) stated: *un examen escrito,* a written exam; *lo que viene escrito arriba,* what is stated above. – 3 **escrito,** *m* (*documento*) writing, document, text. 4 (*obra*) work, writing: *los escritos de Orwell,* Orwell's writings. 5 JUR writ.
- **escrito,-a a máquina,** typewritten, typed. ‖ **poner por escrito,** to write down. ‖ **por escrito,** in writing, in black and white: *se lo mandé por escrito,* I sent it to him in writing.
escritor,-ra *m,f* writer.
escritorio 1 *m* (*mueble*) writing desk, bureau. 2 (*oficina*) office.
- **objetos de escritorio,** stationery *sing*.
escritura 1 *f* (*gen*) writing: *escritura fonética,* phonetic script. 2 (*caligrafía*) handwriting, writing. 3 JUR deed, document.
- **escritura de propiedad,** title deed. ‖ **escritura de venta,** bill of sale. ‖ **escritura notarial,** notarial deed. ‖ **Sagradas Escrituras,** Holy Scriptures.
escriturar 1 *t* (*hacer constar*) to formalize legally; (*una propiedad*) to register. 2 (*contratar*) to engage.
escrotal *adj* scrotal.
escroto *m* scrotum.
escrúpulo 1 *m* (*recelo*) scruple, doubt, qualm: *no tuvo escrúpulos en decírselo,* he had no qualms about telling her. 2 (*aprensión*) fussiness: *eso me da escrúpulos,* I'm finicky about it, I'm fussy about it. 3 *fig* (*cuidado*) extreme care: *lo hizo con escrúpulo,* he did it with extreme care. 4 (*china*) pebble, stone.
- **sin escrúpulos,** unscrupulous.
▲ *In* 1 *and* 2, *often used in plural with the same meaning.*
escrupulosamente *adv* scrupulously.
escrupulosidad *f* scrupulousness, extreme care.
escrupuloso,-a 1 *adj* scrupulous. 2 (*aprensivo*) finicky, fussy. 3 *fig* (*exacto*) scrupulous, meticulous.
escrutador,-ra *adj* scrutinizing, searching, penetrating.
escrutar 1 *t* (*examinar*) to scrutinize, examine carefully. 2 (*votos*) to count.
escrutinio 1 *m* (*examen*) scrutiny, examination. 2 (*de votos*) count.
escuadra 1 *f* (*instrumento -de dibujo*) set square; (*-de carpintería*) square; (*pieza de metal*) bracket. 2 MIL squad; MAR squadron, fleet. 3 (*fútbol*) angle.
- **a escuadra,** at right angles.
escuadrar *t* to square.
escuadrilla *f* squadron.
escuadrón *m* squadron.
escualidez 1 *f* (*delgadez*) extreme thinness, emaciation. 2 (*suciedad*) squalor.
escuálido,-a 1 *adj* (*delgado*) emaciated, extremely thin, skinny. 2 (*sucio*) squalid, filthy.

escualo *m* (spiny) shark.

escucha 1 *f* (*acción*) listening: *dedica poco tiempo a la escucha de la radio,* she spends little time listening to the radio; *para entender la música, la escucha es insustituible,* to understand music, there's no substitute for listening to it. − 2 *m* MIL scout. 3 (*aparato*) monitor. − 4 *m,f* (*persona*) programme monitor.
● **estar a la escucha de,** to be listening out for. ‖ **estar en escucha,** to be listening out.
■ **escuchas telefónicas,** phone tapping *sing.*

escuchar 1 *t* to listen to; (*oír*) to hear: *escuchar ópera,* to listen to opera. 2 (*atender*) to listen to, pay attention to: *no escuchaba mis consejos,* he didn't listen to my advice. − 3 **escucharse,** *p* to speak in an affected way.

escuchimizado,-a 1 *pp* → **escuchimizarse.** − 2 *adj fam* puny, scrawny.

escuchimizarse *p fam* to get thin, become scrawny.
▲ *Conjugation model* [4], *like realizar.*

escudar 1 *t* to shield. 2 *fig* to shield, protect, defend. − 3 **escudarse,** *p fig* (*ampararse*) to hide behind, use as an excuse: *se escuda en su enfermedad para no ir,* he uses his illness as an excuse for not going.

escudería *f* racing team.

escudero *m* (*hidalgo*) knight; (*paje*) page.

escudilla *f* bowl.

escudo 1 *m* (*arma*) shield. 2 (*de armas*) coat of arms. 3 (*moneda*) escudo. 4 *fig* (*amparo*) protection, shield.
■ **escudo de armas,** coat of arms. ‖ **escudo humano,** human shield.

escudriñar *t* (*examinar*) to scrutinize, examine; (*inquirir*) to inquire into, investigate.

escuela 1 *f* (*gen*) school. 2 (*experiencia*) experience, instruction.
● **ser de la vieja escuela,** to be of the old school. ‖ **tener buena escuela,** to be well trained.
■ **escuela de artes y oficios,** Technical College. ‖ **escuela de Bellas Artes,** Art School. ‖ **escuela de conducir,** driving school. ‖ **escuela de idiomas,** language school. ‖ **escuela nocturna,** night school. ‖ **escuela privada,** private school, GB public school. ‖ **escuela pública,** state school.

escuetamente *adv* simply, succincttly.

escueto,-a 1 *adj* (*sin adornos*) bare, plain, unadorned. 2 (*conciso*) concise, brief, succinct

escuezo *pres indic* → **escocer.**

esculcar *t* (*espiar*) to spy on.
▲ *Conjugation model* [1], *like sacar.*

esculpir *t* (*gen*) to sculpt, sculpture; (*madera*) to carve; (*metal*) to engrave.

escultismo *m* scouting; (*organización*) scout movement.

escultor,-ra 1 *m,f* (*hombre*) sculptor; (*mujer*) sculptress. 2 (*en madera*) carver; (*en metal*) engraver.

escultórico,-a *adj* sculptural.

escultura *f* (*gen*) sculpture; (*en madera*) carving; (*en metal*) engraving.

escultural 1 *adj* sculptural. 2 *fig* (*mujer*) statuesque.

escupidera *f* spittoon, US cuspidor.

escupidura 1 *f* (*escupitajo*) spit, spittle. 2 (*en labios*) cracking.

escupiña *f* warty venus.

escupir 1 *i* to spit: *le escupió en la cara,* he spat in his face. − 2 *t* to spit out: *escupió la papilla,* he spat out his food. 3 *fig* (*despedir*) to belch out: *la fábrica escupía humo,* the factory belched out smoke. 4 *fam fig* (*confesar*) to come clean, confess.

escupitajo *m fam* gob, spit.

escurreplatos *m* plate rack.
▲ *pl* escurreplatos.

escurridero *m* draining board.

escurridizo,-a 1 *adj* slippery. 2 *fig* slippery, elusive.
■ **lazo escurridizo,** slipknot.

escurrido,-a 1 *pp* → **escurrir.** − 2 *adj* (*seco*) drained. 3 (*persona*) thin, slim; (*mujer*) slim-hipped.

escurridor 1 *m* (*colador*) strainer, colander. 2 (*de platos*) plate rack. 3 (*para ropa*) wringer, mangle.

escurriduras *fpl* dregs: *las escurriduras del vino,* the dregs of the wine.

escurrir 1 *t* (*platos etc*) to drain; (*ropa*) to wring out; (*comida*) to strain. − 2 *i* (*destilar*) to drip, trickle. 3 (*deslizar*) to slip, slide. − 4 **escurrirse,** *p* (*platos etc*) to drain. 5 (*líquido*) to drip, trickle. 6 (*deslizarse*) to slip, slide. 7 *fam* (*escapar*) to run away, slip away. 8 *fam* (*decir demasiado*) to let slip.
● **escurrir el bulto,** *fam* to dodge the issue.

escúter *m* scooter.

esdrújulo,-a 1 *adj* proparoxytone, stressed on the antepenultima syllable. − 2 **esdrújulo,** *m* proparoxytone, word stressed on the antepenultimate syllable.

ese 1 *f name of the letter* s. − 2 **eses,** *fpl* zigzags.
● **hacer eses,** (*gen*) to zigzag; (*por borrachera*) to stagger about.

ESE *sím* (*estesudeste*) east-southeast; (*símbolo*) ESE.

ese,-a 1 *adj* that; (*plural*) those: *ese coche,* that car; *esas casas,* those houses; *¿te acuerdas del tío ese?,* do you remember that bloke?; *¡qué idiota es el tipo ese!,* what a stupid guy!
▲ *pl* esos,-as.

ése,-a 1 *pron* (*cosa*) that one: *dame ése,* give me that one; *tiene una casa como ésa,* she's got a house like that one. 2 (*hombre - sujeto*) he; (*mujer - sujeto*) she: *ése me lo dijo,* he told me. 3 (*hombre - complemento*) him; (*mujer - complemento*) her: *se lo dio a ésa,* he gave it to her; *lo compré a ése del bigote,* I bought it from the one with the moustache; *hablé con ése que llegó anoche,* I talked to the one who arrived last night. 4 (*anterior*) the former: *Juan y Pepe fueron al bar; éste pidió dos cañas y ése buscó una mesa,* Juan and Pepe went to the bar; the latter ordered two beers and the former looked for a table.
● **¡conque ésas tenemos!,** so that's the way things are! ‖ **¡ni por ésas!,** *fam* no way! ‖ **¡no me vengas con ésas!,** *fam* come off it!
▲ *pl* ésos,-as; *the written accent may be omitted when no confusion with adjectives is possible.*

esencia 1 *f* essence. 2 (*perfume*) essence, perfume, scent.
● **en esencia,** (*brevemente*) briefly; (*esencialmente*) in essence.
■ **quinta esencia,** quintessence.

esencial *adj* essential.
● **en lo esencial,** in the main. ‖ **lo esencial,** the main thing.

esencialmente *adv* essentially.

esfera 1 *f* sphere, globe. 2 (*de reloj*) dial, face. 3 *fig* (*campo*) field, sphere; (*ambiente*) sphere, circle.

esférico,-a 1 *adj* spherical. − 2 **esférico,** *m* (*balón*) ball.

esferoidal *adj* spheroidal.

esferoide *m* spheroid.

esfinge *f* sphinx.
● **parecer una esfinge,** *fig* to be enigmatic, be inscrutable.

esfínter *m* sphincter.

esforzado,-a 1 *pp* → **esforzar**. - 2 *adj* (*animoso*) energetic, vigorous; (*valiente*) bold.
esforzar 1 *t* (*forzar*) to strain: *esforzar la vista/voz*, to strain one's eyes/voice. 2 (*animar*) to encourage, spur on. - 3 **esforzarse**, *p* (*físicamente*) to make an effort, exert os.; (*moralmente*) to try hard, strive: *se esfuerza en ser educado*, he tries hard to be polite; *debes esforzarte si quieres aprobar*, you'll have to work hard if you want to pass; *se ha esforzado para llegar a la cumbre*, she has striven to get to the top.
▲ *Conjugation model* [50], *like forzar*.
esfuerzo 1 *m* effort, endeavour (US endeavor). 2 (*valor*) courage, spirit.
● *hacer un esfuerzo*, (*físico*) to make an effort, exert os.; (*moral*) to try hard, strive. ‖ *sin esfuerzo*, effortlessly.
esfumar 1 *t* (*esfuminar*) to stump, blend. 2 (*colores*) to tone down. - 3 **esfumarse**, *p fam* (*largarse*) to disappear, fade away.
esfuminar *t* to stump.
esfumino 1 *m* (*utensilio*) stump, soft pencil. 2 (*dibujo*) stump drawing.
esgrima *f* fencing.
esgrimidor,-ra *m,f* fencer.
esgrimir 1 *t* (*arma*) to wield, brandish. 2 *fig* (*argumento*) to put forward. - 3 *i* to fence.
esguince 1 *m* MED sprain: *se hizo un esguince en el tobillo*, she sprained her ankle. 2 (*gesto*) swerve, dodge. 3 (*gesto de disgusto*) frown.
eslabón 1 *m* link. 2 (*para sacar fuego*) steel. 3 (*alacrán*) scorpion.
■ *el eslabón perdido*, the missing link.
eslabonamiento *m* linking.
eslabonar 1 *t* to link together, join. 2 *fig* to link, connect. - 3 **eslabonarse**, *p fig* to link together.
eslalon *m* slalom.
eslavo,-a 1 *adj* Slavonic. - 2 *m,f* (*persona*) Slav. - 3 **eslavo**, *m* (*idioma*) Slavonic.
eslinga *f* sling.
eslip 1 *m* (*ropa interior*) men's briefs *pl*, underpants *pl*. 2 (*bañador*) trunks *pl*.
▲ *pl* **eslips**.
eslogan *m* slogan.
■ *eslogan publicitario*, advertising slogan.
▲ *pl* **eslóganes**.
eslora 1 *f* length. - 2 **esloras**, *fpl* binding strakes.
eslovaco,-a 1 *adj* Slovak. - 2 *m,f* (*persona*) Slovak. - 3 **eslovaco**, *m* (*idioma*) Slovak.
Eslovaquia *f* Slovakia.
esmaltado,-a 1 *pp* → **esmaltar**. - 2 *adj* enamelled (US enameled). - 3 **esmaltado**, *m* enamelling (US enameling).
esmaltar 1 *t* to enamel. 2 (*uñas*) to varnish. 3 *fig* (*adornar*) to decorate, adorn.
esmalte 1 *m* (*gen*) enamel. 2 (*de uñas*) nail varnish, nail polish. 3 (*objeto esmaltado*) enamelled object. 4 (*color*) smalt. 5 *fig* (*adorno*) adornment, decoration; (*esplendor*) splendour (US splendor).
■ *esmalte de uñas*, nail polish, nail varnish.
esmeradamente *adv* carefully, neatly.
esmerado,-a 1 *pp* → **esmerar**. - 2 *adj* (*trabajo*) careful, neat. 3 (*persona*) careful, painstaking, conscientious.
esmeralda *f* emerald.
esmerar 1 *t* (*pulir*) to polish. - 2 **esmerarse**, *p* to do one's best (**en/por**, to), take great pains (**en/por**, over).
esmerejón *m* merlin.

esmeril *m* emery.
■ *papel de esmeril*, emery paper.
esmerilar *t* to polish with emery paper.
esmero *m* great care, neatness.
● *poner esmero en algo*, to take great pains over sth.
esmirriado,-a *adj fam* puny, scraggy.
esmoquin *f* dinner jacket, US tuxedo.
▲ *pl* **esmóquines**.
esnifada *f arg* sniff, snort.
esnifar *t arg* to sniff, snort.
esnob 1 *adj* (*persona*) snobbish; (*lugar etc*) posh. - 2 *mf* snob.
▲ *pl* **esnobs**.
esnobismo *m* snobbery, snobbishness.
eso *pron* that: *eso es lo que dijo*, that's what she said.
● *a eso de las ...*, *fam* (*hora*) at about ..., around ...: *llegaron a eso de las tres*, they arrived around three. ‖ *¿cómo es eso?*, how come? ‖ *en eso*, at that moment. ‖ *eso de ...*, all that: *eso de tu hermana es una mentira*, all that about your sister is a lie. ‖ *¡eso es!*, that's it! ‖ *eso mismo ...*, that's just ...: *eso mismo pienso yo*, that's just what I think. ‖ *¡eso sí que no!*, certainly not! ‖ *¡nada de eso!*, none of that! ‖ *por eso ...*, that's why: *por eso no vinieron*, that's why they didn't come. ‖ *y eso que ...*, *fam* ever though: *no se acuerda, y eso que se lo acaban de decir*, he can't remember, even though he has just been told.
ESO *abr* EDUC (*Enseñanza Secundaria Obligatoria*) compulsory secondary education up to 16.
esofágico,-a *adj* oesophageal (US esophageal).
esófago *m* oesophagus (US esophagus), gullet.
esos,-as *adj* those.
▲ *See also ese,-a*.
ésos,-as *pron* those (ones).
▲ *See also ése,-a*.
esotérico,-a *adj* esoteric.
esoterismo *m* esotericism.
espabilado,-a 1 *pp* → **espabilar**. - 2 *adj* → **despabilado,-a**.
espabilar *t-i-p* → **despabilar**.
espachurrar *t* to squash.
espaciador *m* space-bar.
espacial 1 *adj* MAT spatial, spacial. 2 ASTRON space: *estación espacial*, space station; *misión espacial*, space mission.
espaciar 1 *t* to space out. - 2 **espaciarse**, *p* to spread os. out, stretch out.
▲ *Conjugation model* [12], *like cambiar*.
espacio 1 *m* (*gen*) space: *queda un espacio entre el armario y la pared*, there's a space between the wardrobe and the wall; *la exploración del espacio*, the exploration of space. 2 (*que se ocupa*) space, room: *necesitamos más espacio*, we need more room. 3 (*de tiempo*) period, space. 4 (*programa*) programme (US program).
● *a doble espacio*, double-spaced. ‖ *por espacio de ...*, for ...: *se interrumpió el programa por espacio de veinte minutos*, the programme was interrupted for twenty minutes.
■ *doble espacio*, double spacing. ‖ *espacio aéreo*, air space. ‖ *espacio radiofónico*, radio programme (US program). ‖ *espacio televisivo*, TV programme (US program). ‖ *espacio verde*, open space, green space. ‖ *espacio vital*, living space.
espacioso,-a 1 *adj* (*ancho*) spacious, roomy. 2 (*lento*) slow.

espada 1 f (arma) sword. 2 (naipe) spade. – 3 m (torero) matador. – 4 espadas, fpl (palo de baraja) spades.
● desnudar la espada, to draw one's sword. ‖ entrar con espada en mano, fig to come in looking for trouble. ‖ estar entre la espada y la pared, fig to be between the devil and the deep blue sea.
■ espada de dos filos, fig double-edged sword. ‖ pez espada, swordfish.
espadachín 1 m swordsman. 2 pey (presuntuoso) bully.
espadaña 1 f ARQ bell gable. 2 BOT bulrush.
espadista mf arg burglar.
espaguetis mpl spaghetti sing.
espalda 1 f (gen) back. 2 (natación) backstroke.
● a espaldas de algn., fig behind sb.'s back. ‖ a las espaldas, on one's back. ‖ ancho,-a de espaldas, broad-shouldered. ‖ caerse de espaldas, fig to fall flat on one's back. ‖ cargado,-a de espaldas, round-shouldered, stooping. ‖ dar la espalda, fig to turn one's back on. ‖ de espaldas, from behind: lo vimos de espaldas, we saw him from behind. ‖ echarse algo a la espalda, fig to take sth. on. ‖ echarse entre pecho y espalda / meterse entre pecho y espalda, fam to tuck away. ‖ por la espalda, from behind. ‖ tener las espaldas anchas, fig to be easy-going. ‖ tener las espaldas guardadas, fig to have friends in high places, have contacts. ‖ volver la espalda a algn., to turn one's back on sb.
■ espalda mojada, fam fig wetback.
▲ In 1, often used in plural with the same meaning.
espaldar 1 m (de silla) back. 2 (para plantas) trellis.
espaldarazo 1 m (golpe) slap on the back. 2 fig accolade.
espaldera 1 f (para plantas) trellis. – 2 espalderas, fpl DEP wall bars.
espaldilla 1 f ANAT shoulder-blade. 2 CULIN shoulder.
espantada 1 f (animales) stampede. 2 (personas) withdrawal.
● dar la espantada, to stampede, run away. ‖ pegar una estampada, to withdraw, pull out.
espantadizo,-a adj easily frightened.
espantajo 1 m (muñeco) scarecrow. 2 fig (cosa) sight, fright. 3 fig (persona) sight, fright; (coco) bogeyman.
espantalobos m bladder senna.
▲ pl espantalobos.
espantapájaros m scarecrow.
▲ pl espantapájaros.
espantar 1 t (asustar) to frighten, scare, scare off. 2 (ahuyentar) to frighten away. – 3 espantarse, p (asustarse) to be frightened, be scared: el perro se espantó con el ruido, the dog was scared by the noise; se espantó de sus amenazas, their threats frightened him. 4 (asombrarse) to be amazed, be astonished.
espanto 1 m (miedo) fright, dread, terror. 2 (asombro) astonishment, amazement.
● de espanto, (miedo) frightening, terrifying; (feo) horrible; (intensidad) dreadful, shocking: nos llovió de espanto, the rain was dreadful, it was pouring down. ‖ ¡qué espanto!, how awful!
espantoso,-a 1 adj (terrible) frightful, dreadful. 2 (asombroso) astonishing, amazing. 3 (desmesurado) dreadful, terrible: hizo un frío espantoso, the cold was awful, it was absolutely freezing.
España f Spain.
español,-la 1 adj Spanish. – 2 m,f (persona) Spaniard. – 3 español, m (idioma) Spanish, Castilian.
Española f Hispaniola.

españolada f pey something pseudo-Spanish.
españolear i to give exaggerated publicity to Spain or Spanish things.
españolismo 1 m (giro, expresión) Spanish word, Spanish expression. 2 (carácter) Spanishness, Spanish quality. 3 (amor) love of Spain, love of Spanish things.
españolista 1 adj pro-Spanish, Hispanophile. 2 DEP relating to Español football club. – 3 mf Hispanophile. 4 DEP Español supporter.
españolizar 1 t to hispanicize, make Spanish. – 2 españolizarse, p to adopt Spanish ways.
esparadrapo m sticking plaster.
esparaván m sparrowhawk.
esparavel 1 m (red) casting net. 2 (albañilería) mortarboard.
esparcido,-a 1 pp → esparcir. – 2 adj (desparramado) scattered. 3 (rumor) widespread. 4 (divertido) cheerful, gay; (franco) frank, open.
esparcimiento 1 m (franqueza) frankness, openness; (alegría) cheerfulness, gaiety. 2 (recreo) amusement, diversion.
esparcir 1 t (desparramar) to scatter. 2 fig (divulgar) to spread. 3 fig (divertir) to amuse. – 4 esparcirse, p (desparramarse) to scatter, be scattered. 5 fig (divulgarse) to spread out. 6 fig (divertirse) to amuse os.
▲ Conjugation model [3], like zurcir.
espárrago m asparagus.
● ¡vete a freír espárragos!, fam get lost!
■ espárrago triguero, wild asparagus.
esparraguera 1 f BOT asparagus plant. 2 CULIN asparagus dish.
esparrancado,-a 1 pp → esparrancarse. – 2 adj (abierto de piernas) with one's legs wide apart. 3 (cosa) too far apart.
esparrancarse p fam to open one's legs.
▲ Conjugation model [1], like sacar.
Esparta f Sparta.
espartano,-a 1 adj Spartan. 2 fig Spartan, austere. – 3 m,f Spartan.
espartero,-a m,f esparto worker.
esparto m esparto grass.
espasmo m spasm.
espasmódico,-a adj spasmodic, jerky.
espástico,-a adj spastic.
espata f spathe.
espatarrarse 1 p fam (abrir) to open one's legs wide, sprawl. 2 fam (al caer) to go sprawling.
espato m spar.
■ espato flúor, fluorspar.
espátula 1 f (gen) spatula. 2 (de pintor) palette knife; (de cristalero) putty knife. 3 TÉC stripping knife. 4 (ave) spoonbill.
especia f spice.
especial 1 adj (gen) special. 2 (remilgado) fussy (para, about), finicky (para, about): es un poco especial para la comida, she's a bit finicky about food.
● en especial, especially. ‖ especial para ..., suitable for ...
especialidad 1 f (gen) speciality (us specialty). 2 EDUC main subject, specialized field.
especialista 1 adj specialist. – 2 mf specialist. 3 CINEM stand-in; (hombre) stuntman; (mujer) stuntwoman.
especialización f specialization.
especializado,-a 1 pp → especializar. – 2 adj specialized.

● **estar especializado,-a en algo,** to be a specialist in sth., be specialized in sth.

especializar 1 *i* to specialize. – **2** *t* to specialize. – **3** especializarse, *p* to specialize (**en**, in).

▲ *Conjugation model* [4], *like realizar.*

especialmente 1 *adv* (*exclusivamente*) specially. **2** (*particularmente*) especially.

especie 1 *f* (*de animales, plantas*) species. **2** (*tipo*) kind, sort. **3** (*tema*) matter, notion, idea; (*noticia*) piece of news.

● **en especie,** in kind: *pagar en especie,* to pay in kind.

especiería 1 *f* (*tienda*) grocer's shop. **2** (*especias*) spices *pl.*

especiero,-a 1 *m,f* grocer. – **2 especiero,** *m* spice rack.

especificación *f* specification.

específicamente *adv* specifically.

especificar *t* to specify.

▲ *Conjugation model* [1], *like sacar.*

especificativo,-a *adj* specificative.

específico,-a 1 *adj* specific. – **2 específico,** *m* (*medicamento*) specific; (*especialidad*) patent medicine.

■ **peso específico,** specific gravity.

espécimen *m* specimen.

▲ *pl* **especímenes.**

especioso,-a 1 *adj* beautiful. **2** *fig* specious, deceitful.

espectacular *adj* spectacular.

espectacularidad *f* spectacular nature.

espectacularmente *adv* spectacularly.

espectáculo 1 *m* spectacle, sight. **2** (*diversión*) entertainment. **3** (TV, *radio, etc*) performance, show. **4** (*escándalo*) scandal.

● **dar un espectáculo,** *irón* to make a scene, make a spectacle of os. ‖ **montar un espectáculo,** to put on a show; *irón* to make a scene, make a spectacle of os.

espectador,-ra 1 *m,f* DEP spectator. **2** TEAT CINEM member of the audience; TV viewer. **3** (*de accidente etc*) onlooker. – **4 espectadores,** *mpl* TEAT CINEM audience *sing*; TV viewers.

espectral *adj* spectral, ghostly.

espectro 1 *m* FÍS spectrum. **2** (*fantasma*) spectre (US specter), ghost, apparition. **3** *fig* (*persona*) ghost. **4** (*conjunto, serie*) range.

espectrografía *f* spectrography.

espectrógrafo *m* spectrograph.

espectrograma *m* spectrogram.

espectroscopia *f* spectroscopy.

espectroscopio *m* spectroscope.

especulación *f* speculation.

■ **especulación del suelo,** land speculation.

especulador,-ra 1 *adj* speculating. – **2** *m,f* speculator.

especular 1 *t* *fig* (*reflexionar*) to speculate about. – **2** *i* (*comerciar*) to speculate (**en**, in); (*en bolsa*) to speculate (**en**, on). **3** (*conjeturar*) to speculate (**sobre**, about).

especulativo,-a *adj* speculative, theoretical.

espejear *i* to shine, gleam.

espejismo 1 *m* mirage. **2** *fig* mirage, illusion.

espejo 1 *m* mirror. **2** *fig* (*imagen*) mirror, reflection. **3** *fig* (*modelo*) model.

● **la cara es el espejo del alma,** *fig* the eyes are the window of the soul.

■ **espejo retrovisor,** rear-view mirror.

espejuelo 1 *m* (*yeso*) selenite. **2** (*señuelo*) lark mirror. – **3 espejuelos,** *mpl* (*anteojos*) spectacles, glasses.

espeleología *f* potholing, speleology.

espeleólogo,-a *m,f* potholer, speleologist.

espeluznante *adj* hair-raising, terrifying, horrifying.

espeluznar *t* to horrify, terrify, make one's hair stand on end.

espeluzno *m* shiver, shudder.

espera 1 *f* wait, waiting. **2** (*paciencia*) patience. **3** JUR respite.

● **en espera de ...,** waiting for ... ‖ **estar a la espera,** to be waiting, be expecting. ‖ **tener espera,** to have patience.

■ **sala de espera,** waiting room.

esperanto *m* esperanto.

esperanza *f* hope, expectance.

● **abrigar esperanzas,** to foster hopes. ‖ **con la esperanza de ...,** in the hope of ... ‖ **con la esperanza de que ...,** in the hope that ... ‖ **dar esperanzas a algn.,** to give sb. hope. ‖ **estar en estado de buena esperanza,** to be pregnant, be expecting. ‖ **tener la esperanza puesta en algo,** to have one's hopes pinned on sth. ‖ **tener muchas esperanzas,** to have high hopes. ‖ **tener pocas esperanzas,** to have little hope.

■ **esperanza de vida,** life expectancy.

esperanzador,-ra *adj* encouraging.

esperanzar 1 *t* to give hope to. – **2** *i* to have hope. – **3** esperanzarse, *p* to have hope.

▲ *Conjugation model* [4], *like realizar.*

esperar 1 *t* (*tener esperanza*) to hope for, expect: *esperan un milagro,* they're hoping for a miracle; *esperar la gloria,* to hope for glory. **2** (*contar, creer*) to expect: *no te esperábamos hasta mañana,* we didn't expect you till tomorrow; *llegaron tarde como era de esperar,* they arrived late as expected. **3** (*aguardar*) to wait for, await: *espera un momento,* wait a moment; *espero a mi padre,* I'm waiting for my father. **4** (*desear*) to hope: *espero que cantes,* I hope you'll sing; *espero verlo,* I hope to see him. **5** (*ser inevitable*) to await, be ahead: *mala noche nos espera,* there's a bad night ahead. **6** *fig* (*bebé*) to expect. – **7** *i* to wait: *esperaré hasta que lleguen,* I'll wait until they get here. – **8 esperarse,** *p* (*aguardar*) to wait: *espérense en recepción,* please wait in reception. **9** (*creer, contar*) to expect: *se espera que seas puntual,* you're expected to be punctual. **10** (*desear*) to hope: *se espera que lo hayan pasado bien,* we hope you've had a good time.

● **en espera de noticias tuyas,** we hope to hear from you soon. ‖ **¡espérate sentado!,** don't hold your breath!, you'll be waiting till the cows come home! ‖ **espero que no,** I hope not. ‖ **espero que sí,** I hope so. ‖ **hacer esperar a algn.,** to keep sb. waiting. ‖ **hacerse esperar,** to keep people waiting. ‖ **quien espera desespera,** a watched pot never boils.

esperma *m* sperm.

■ **esperma de ballena,** spermaceti.

espermaticida 1 *adj* spermicide. – **2** *m* spermicide.

espermatozoide *m* spermatozoid.

esperpéntico,-a 1 *adj fam* (*grotesco*) grotesque, macabre. **2** *fam* (*ridículo*) ridiculous, absurd.

esperpento 1 *m fam* (*cosa, persona*) fright, sight. **2** *fam* (*absurdo*) absurdity, piece of nonsense.

espesante *m* thickener.

espesar 1 *t* (*salsa etc*) to thicken; (*tejido etc*) to make thicker. – **2 espesarse,** *p* (*gen*) to get thicker. **3** (*salsa etc*) to thicken.

espeso,-a 1 *adj* (*líquido, sustancia, objeto*) thick. **2** (*bosque, niebla*) thick, dense. **3** (*pasta, masa*) stiff. **4** *fig* (*libro*) dense, difficult.

● **estar espeso,-a,** *fam* not to be able to think straight.

espesor *m* thickness: *cuatro centímetros de espesor,* four centimetres thick.

espesura 1 *f* (*líquido, objeto*) thickness. – **2** *adj* (*niebla etc*) denseness. – **3** *f fig* (*bosque*) thicket, dense wood.

espetar 1 *t* (*carne etc*) to skewer. **2** (*clavar*) to stab. **3** *fig* (*decir*) to blurt out.

espeto *m* spit, skewer.

espetón *m* spit, skewer.

espía *mf* spy.

espiar *t* to spy on, watch.
▲ *Conjugation model* [13], *like* **desviar**.

espichar 1 *t* (*pinchar*) to stab. – **2** *i fam* (*morir*) to snuff it, kick the bucket.

● **espicharla,** *fam* to snuff it, kick the bucket.

espiga 1 *f* (*gen*) spike; (*de trigo*) ear. **2** (*de tejido*) herringbone. **3** (*clavija*) peg, pin. **4** (*de cuchillo*) tang; (*de tornillo*) bolt; (*de clavo*) shank. **5** (*de campana*) clapper.

espigado,-a 1 *pp* → **espigar**. – **2** *adj* BOT ripe. **3** (*en forma de espiga*) ear-shaped. **4** *fig* (*persona*) tall, lanky.

espigar 1 *t* AGR to glean. **2** *fig* (*datos*) to glean, collect. – **3** *i* AGR to ear. – **4 espigarse,** *p* (*persona*) to shoot up.
▲ *Conjugation model* [7], *like* **llegar**.

espigón 1 *m* MAR breakwater, jetty. **2** (*punta*) sharp point, spike. **3** (*cerro*) peak.

espiguilla 1 *f* (*espiga*) spikelet. **2** (*dibujo*) herring-bone.

espín *m* spin.

espina 1 *f* (*de planta*) thorn. **2** (*de pez*) fishbone. **3** (*columna vertebral*) spine, backbone. **4** *fig* (*pesar*) sadness, sorrow, grief. **5** *fig* (*duda*) suspicion, doubt. **6** *fig* (*dificultad*) difficulty, problem.

● **dar mala espina,** *fig* to arouse one's suspicions, not to like the look of sth.: *eso me da mala espina,* I don't like the look of it. ‖ **estar en espinas,** to be on edge. ‖ **no hay rosa sin espinas,** *fig* you have to take the rough with the smooth. ‖ **sacarse la espina,** *fig* to get even, get one's own back. ‖ **tener clavada una espina,** to be suffering, be smarting.

■ **espina dorsal,** spinal column, spine, backbone.

espinaca *f* spinach.

espinal *adj* spinal: *médula espinal,* spinal marrow.

espinapez *m* herring-bone.

espinar 1 *t* (*punzar*) to prick. **2** *fig* (*herir*) to offend, hurt. – **3 espinarse,** *p* (*punzarse*) to prick.

espinazo *m* spine, backbone.

● **doblar el espinazo,** *fam* to bow and scrape.

espingarda *f fig* beanpole.

espinilla 1 *f* (*de la pierna*) shinbone. **2** (*grano*) blackhead.

espinillera *f* shin-pad.

espino 1 *m* (*árbol*) hawthorn. **2** (*alambre*) barbed wire.

■ **espino albar,** common hawthorn. ‖ **espino negro,** blackthorn.

espinosillo *m* stickleback.

espinoso,-a 1 *adj* (*planta*) thorny. **2** (*pez*) spiny. **3** *fig* thorny, prickly, difficult, tricky.

espionaje *m* spying, espionage: *película de espionaje,* spy film.

■ **espionaje industrial,** industrial espionage.

espira *f* (*vuelta de espiral*) spire.

espiración *f* breathing out, exhalation, expiration.

espiral 1 *adj* spiral: *escalera espiral,* spiral staircase. – **2** *f* spiral. **3** (*de reloj*) hairspring.

espirar 1 *t* to exhale, breathe out. – **2** *i* to breathe.

espiritismo *m* spiritualism.

espiritista 1 *adj* spiritualistic. – **2** *mf* spiritualist.

espiritoso 1 *adj* (*animoso*) spirited. **2** (*licor etc*) spirituous.

espíritu 1 *m* (*gen*) spirit. **2** (*alma*) soul, spirit. **3** (*fantasma*) ghost, spirit. **4** (*licores*) spirits *pl.* **5** *fig* (*idea central*) spirit, essence, soul.

● **exhalar el espíritu,** to give up the ghost. ‖ **levantar el espíritu,** to cheer up. ‖ **ser pobre de espíritu,** to be poor in spirit.

■ **el espíritu de la ley,** the spirit of the law. ‖ **el Espíritu Santo,** the Holy Ghost. ‖ **espíritu de contradicción,** contrariness. ‖ **espíritu de cuerpo,** esprit de corps. ‖ **espíritu de vino,** purified alcohol. ‖ **espíritu deportivo,** sportsmanship. ‖ **grandeza de espíritu,** noble-heartedness.

espiritual *adj* spiritual.

espiritualidad *f* spirituality.

espiritualismo *m* spiritualism.

espiritualista *adj* spiritualist.

espiritualizar *t* to spiritualize.
▲ *Conjugation model* [4], *like* **realizar**.

espiritualmente *adv* spiritually.

espirómetro *m* spirometer.

espita *f* tap, US spigot.

espitoso,-a *adj* spaced out, high.

espléndidamente 1 *adv* (*con magnificencia*) splendidly, magnificently. **2** (*con generosidad*) generously, lavishly.

esplendidez 1 *f* (*magnificencia*) magnificence, splendour (US splendor). **2** (*generosidad*) generosity.

espléndido,-a 1 *adj* (*magnífico*) splendid, magnificent. **2** (*generoso*) generous, lavish.

esplendor 1 *m* (*resplandor*) brilliance, shining. **2** *fig* (*magnificencia*) magnificence, splendour (US splendor). **3** (*auge*) glory.

esplendoroso,-a 1 *adj* (*resplandeciente*) brilliant, radiant, shining. **2** (*grandioso*) magnificent, lavish.

espliego *m* lavender.

esplín *m* melancholy, spleen.
▲ *pl* **esplines**.

espolada 1 *f* (*golpe*) prick with a spur. **2** (*trago*) swig.

espoleadura *f* spur wound.

espolear 1 *t* to spur on. **2** *fig* to spur on, encourage.

espoleta[1] *f* (*de bomba etc*) fuse.

● **quitar la espoleta,** to defuse.

espoleta[2] *f* (*de ave*) wishbone.

espolio *m* → **expolio**.

espolón 1 *m* (*de ave*) spur. **2** (*de caballería*) fetlock. **3** (*de nave*) ram. **4** (*malecón*) sea wall. **5** *fam* (*sabañón*) chilblain.

● **embestir con el espolón,** MAR to ram.

espolvorear 1 *t* (*despolvorear*) to dust. **2** (*esparcir*) to powder, sprinkle.

espondeo *m* spondee.

esponja 1 *f* sponge. **2** *fig* (*gorrón*) sponger. **3** *fig* (*bebedor*) hard drinker. **4** (*tejido*) towelling.

● **beber como una esponja,** *fig* to drink like a fish. ‖ **pasar la esponja,** *fam* to let it drop, forget about it.

esponjar 1 *t* (*ahuecar*) to fluff up; (*tierra*) to loosen. – **2 esponjarse,** *p* (*envanecerse*) to swell with pride. **3** *fig* (*físicamente*) to glow with health.

esponjoso,-a *adj* (*gen*) spongy; (*bizcocho*) light.

esponsales *mpl fml* betrothal *sing,* engagement *sing.*

espontáneamente *adv* spontaneously.

espontanearse *p* to confide (**con,** in).

espontaneidad *f* spontaneity.

● **con espontaneidad,** naturally.

espontáneo,-a 1 *adj* (*cosa*) spontaneous; (*discurso*) impromptu, unprepared. **2** (*persona*) natural, unaffected. – **3** *m,f* spectator who spontaneously joins in the bullfight.

espora *f* spore.
esporádicamente *adv* sporadically.
esporádico,-a *adj* sporadic.
esportear *t* to carry in baskets.
esportillo *m* esparto basket.
esposado,-a 1 *pp* → **esposar**. – 2 *adj* (*casado*) married. 3 (*con esposas*) handcuffed.
esposar *t* to handcuff, put handcuffs on.
esposas *fpl* → **esposo,-a**.
esposo,-a 1 *m,f* spouse; (*hombre*) husband; (*mujer*) wife. – 2 esposos, *mpl* husband and wife. – 3 esposas, *fpl* handcuffs.
● poner las esposas, to put handcuffs on.
esprint *m* sprint.
esprintar *i* to sprint.
esprínter *mf* sprinter.
espuela 1 *f* spur. 2 *fig* spur, stimulus.
● poner espuelas a algn., *fig* to spur sb. on.
espuerta *f* two-handled rush basket.
● a espuertas, *fig* in abundance.
espulgar 1 *t* (*limpiar - de pulgas*) to deflea; (- *de piojos*) to delouse. 2 *fig* (*examinar*) to examine, scrutinize.
▲ Conjugation model [7], like *llegar*.
espuma 1 *f* (*gen*) foam; (*de jabón*) lather; (*de cerveza*) froth, head; (*olas*) surf. 2 (*impurezas*) scum. 3 (*tejido*) foam.
● crecer como la espuma, *fig* to shoot up. ‖ hacer espuma, (*jabón*) to lather; (*cerveza*) to froth; (*olas*) to foam.
■ espuma de afeitar, shaving foam.
espumadera *f* skimmer.
espumante *m* foaming agent.
espumar 1 *t* (*quitar espuma*) to skim. – 2 *i* (*hacer espuma - jabón*) to lather; (- *cerveza*) to froth; (- *vino*) to sparkle; (- *olas*) to foam.
espumarajo *m* foam, froth.
● echar espumarajos, *fig* to foam at the mouth.
espumear *i-t* → **espumar**.
espumillón *m* tinsel.
espumosidad *f* frothiness.
espumoso,-a *adj* (*ola*) foamy, frothy; (*jabón*) lathery; (*vino*) sparkling.
espurio,-a 1 *adj* (*bastardo*) illegitimate. 2 *fig* (*falso*) spurious, adulterated.
▲ The form *espúreo,-a* is incorrect.
espurrear *t* to sprinkle.
espurriar *t* to sprinkle.
esputar *t* to spit (out).
esputo *m* sputum, spit.
esqueje *m* cutting.
esquela 1 *f* (*carta*) short letter. 2 (*mortuoria*) obituary notice.
■ esquela de defunción, obituary notice.
esquelético,-a 1 *adj* (*del esqueleto*) skeletal: *estructura esquelética*, bone structure. 2 *fam* (*delgado*) skinny, bony.
● estar esquelético,-a, *fam* to be skin and bones.
esqueleto 1 *m* ANAT skeleton. 2 ARQ framework.
● mover el esqueleto, *fam* to boogie, party on down.
esquema 1 *m* (*gráfica*) diagram. 2 (*plan*) outline, plan.
esquemático,-a *adj* schematic, diagrammatic.
● corte esquemático, cross-section.
esquematizar 1 *t* (*plan, idea*) to outline. 2 (*plano etc*) to sketch.
▲ Conjugation model [4], like *realizar*.
esquí 1 *m* (*tabla*) ski. 2 DEP skiing.
■ esquí acuático / esquí náutico, water-skiing. ‖ es-

quí alpino, Alpine skiing. ‖ esquí de fondo, cross-country skiing. ‖ esquí nórdico, Nordic skiing.
▲ *pl esquís.*
esquiador,-ra *m,f* skier.
esquiar *i* to ski.
▲ Conjugation model [13], like *desviar*.
esquife *m* skiff.
esquila[1] *f* (*campanilla*) small bell, handbell, cow-bell.
esquila[2] 1 *f* (*camarón*) squilla. 2 (*cebolla*) squill.
esquila[3] *f* (*esquileo*) sheep-shearing.
esquilador,-ra 1 *m,f* sheep-shearer. – 2 esquiladora, *f* shears *pl*.
esquiladora *f* → **esquilador,-ra**.
esquilar 1 *t* (*pelo*) to clip. 2 (*ovejas*) to shear.
esquileo 1 *m* (*acción*) sheep-shearing. 2 (*época*) shearing time.
esquilmar 1 *t* (*cosecha etc*) to harvest. 2 *fig* (*agotar*) to exhaust. 3 *fig* (*abusar*) to fleece.
esquilón *m* large cowbell.
esquimal 1 *adj* Eskimo. – 2 *mf* Eskimo. – 3 *m* (*idioma*) Eskimo.
esquina *f* corner.
● a la vuelta de la esquina, just round the corner. ‖ doblar la esquina, to turn the corner. ‖ hacer esquina con, to be on the corner of.
esquinado,-a 1 *pp* → **esquinar**. – 2 *adj fig* (*persona*) difficult, irritable.
esquinar 1 *t* (*hacer esquina*) to form a corner with, be on the corner of: *la tienda esquina la Calle Mayor,* the shop's on the corner of the High Street. 2 (*poner en esquina*) to put in a corner: *hay que esquinar el armario,* we have to put the wardrobe in the corner. 3 (*madero*) to square. 4 *fig* (*enemistar*) to set against. – 5 *i* (*hacer esquina*) to form a corner with. – 6 esquinarse, *p fig* (*enemistarse*) to fall out.
esquinazo *m* corner.
● dar el esquinazo a algn., *fam* to give sb. the slip.
esquirla *f* splinter.
esquirol *m* blackleg, scab.
esquivar 1 *t* (*persona*) to avoid, shun. 2 (*golpe*) to dodge, elude.
esquivez *f* coldness, aloofness.
esquivo,-a *adj* cold, aloof.
esquizofrenia *f* schizophrenia.
esquizofrénico,-a 1 *adj* schizophrenic. – 2 *m,f* schizophrenic.
esquizoide 1 *adj* schizoid. – 2 *mf* schizoid.
esta *adj* → **este,-a**.
está *pres indic* → **estar**.
ésta *pron* → **éste,-a**.
estabilidad *f* stability.
estabilización *f* stabilization.
estabilizador,-ra 1 *adj* stabilizing. – 2 estabilizador, *m* stabilizer.
estabilizar 1 *t* to stabilize, make stable. – 2 estabilizarse, *p* to become stable, become stabilized.
▲ Conjugation model [4], like *realizar*.
estable *adj* stable, steady.
establecer 1 *t* (*gen*) to establish; (*fundar*) to found, set up. 2 (*récord*) to set. 3 (*ordenar*) to state, lay down, establish: *tal como establece la ley,* as the law states. – 4 establecerse, *p* (*en un lugar*) to settle; (*en un negocio*) to set up in business.
▲ Conjugation model [43], like *agradecer*.
establecimiento 1 *m* (*acto*) establishment, founding, setting-up. 2 (*de gente*) settlement. 3 (*local*) establishment, shop, store. 4 JUR statute, ordinance.

establo 1 *m* stable, cowshed, stall. **2** *fig* filthy place, pigsty.

estabulación *f* stabling.

estabular *t* to stable.

estaca 1 *f* (*palo con punta*) stake, post; (*para tienda de campaña*) peg. **2** (*garrote*) stick, cudgel. **3** (*rama*) cutting. **4** (*clavo*) spike.

estacada 1 *f* (*obra*) fence, fencing. **2** MIL stockade.
● **dejar a algn. en la estacada,** *fig* to leave sb. in the lurch. ‖ **estar en la estacada,** *fig* to be in a fix.

estacazo *m* blow with a stick.

estación 1 *f* (*del año, temporada*) season: *la estación de las nieves,* the snowy season. **2** (*de tren, radio*) station. **3** REL station.
● **hacer estación,** to make a stop.
■ **estación balnearia,** spa. ‖ **estación de esquí,** ski resort. ‖ **estación de servicio,** service station. ‖ **estación de trabajo,** INFORM workstation. ‖ **estación meteorológica,** weather station.

estacional *adj* seasonal.

estacionamiento 1 *m* AUTO (*acción*) parking; (*lugar*) car park, US parking lot. **2** MIL stationing. **3** *fig* (*estancamiento*) impasse.

estacionar 1 *t* (*colocar*) to position, place. **2** AUTO to park. – **3 estacionarse,** *p* (*estancarse*) to be stationary, remain in the same place. **4** AUTO to park.

estacionario,-a *adj* stationary, stable.

estadía 1 *f* (*estancia*) stay. **2** (*indemnización*) demurrage. **3** (*del modelo*) sitting.

estadio 1 *m* (*lugar*) stadium. **2** (*fase*) stage, phase. **3** *arc* (*medida*) stadium, furlong.

estadista 1 *mf* POL (*hombre*) statesman; (*mujer*) stateswoman. **2** MAT statistician.

estadística *f →* **estadístico,-a**.

estadístico,-a 1 *adj* statistical. – **2** *m,f* statistician. – **3 estadística,** *f* (*ciencia*) statistics. **4** (*dato*) statistic, figure.

estado 1 *m* (*situación*) state, condition: *su estado es delicado,* his condition is delicate; *ahora les informamos del estado de las carreteras,* and now for some traffic news. **2** (*en orden social*) status. **3** HIST estate. **4** POL state: *varios jefes de estado asistieron al congreso,* various heads of state attended the congress.
● **estar en buen estado,** to be in good condition. ‖ **estar en estado,** to be pregnant. ‖ **estar en estado de funcionamiento,** to be in working order. ‖ **estar en mal estado,** to be in bad condition.
■ **estado civil,** marital status. ‖ **estado de ánimo,** state of mind. ‖ **estado de bienestar,** welfare state. ‖ **estado de cuentas,** statement of accounts. ‖ **estado de excepción,** state of emergency. ‖ **estado de guerra,** state of war. ‖ **estado de salud,** state of health. ‖ **estado mayor,** MIL staff. ‖ **estado noble,** noble estate. ‖ **estado sólido,** solid state. ‖ **hombre de estado,** statesman.

Estados Unidos *mpl* The United States.

estadounidense 1 *adj* American, from the United States. – **2** *mf* American, person from the United States.

estafa *f* fraud, swindle.

estafador,-ra *m,f* racketeer, swindler, trickster.

estafar *t* to swindle, trick, cheat, defraud.
● **me han estafado,** *fam* I've been done, I've been had.

estafermo 1 *m* *fig* (*parado*) slow person, dummy. **2** *fig* (*de mal aspecto*) sight, mess.

estafeta *f* sub-post office, US branch post office.

estafilococo *m* staphylococcus.

estalactita *f* stalactite.

estalagmita *m* stalagmite.

estalinismo *m* Stalinism.

estalinista 1 *adj* Stalinist. – **2** *mf* Stalinist.

estallar 1 *i* (*reventar*) to explode, blow up. **2** (*neumático*) to burst; (*bomba*) to explode, go off; (*cristal*) to shatter. **3** (*volcán*) to erupt. **4** (*látigo*) to crack. **5** *fig* (*rebelión, epidemia*) to break out. **6** *fig* (*pasión, sentimientos*) to burst: *estallar en lágrimas,* to burst into tears.

estallido 1 *m* (*explosión*) explosion. **2** (*de trueno*) crash; (*de látigo*) crack. **3** *fig* outbreak.

estambre 1 *m* COST worsted, woollen yarn (US woolen yarn). **2** BOT stamen.

Estambul *m* Istanbul.

estamento *m* class, stratum.

estameña *f* serge.

estaminífero,-a *adj* staminiferous.

estampa 1 *f* (*imagen*) picture. **2** (*escena*) scene: *una estampa conmovedora,* a moving scene. **3** (*impresión*) print; (*proceso*) printing. **4** (*marca*) hallmark: *la estampa del éxito,* the hallmark of success. **5** *fig* (*aspecto*) appearance, look, aspect: *tiene estampa de delincuente,* he looks like a criminal. **6** *fig* (*parecido*) image.
● **dar a la estampa,** to publish. ‖ **tener buena estampa,** *fig* to be good-looking. ‖ **ser la viva estampa de ...,** to be the spitting image of ...: *es la viva estampa de su madre,* she's the spitting image of her mother.

estampación *f* printing.

estampado,-a 1 *pp →* **estampar**. – **2** *adj* (*gen*) patterned, print; (*tela*) printed; (*metal*) stamped. – **3 estampado,** *m* (*tela*) print. **4** (*proceso - tela*) printing; (*- metal*) stamping.

estampar 1 *t* (*imprimir*) to print. **2** (*metales*) to stamp. **3** (*dejar huella*) to stamp. **4** *fam* (*arrojar*) to hurl: *estampó el jarrón contra la puerta,* he hurled the vase against the door. **5** *fam* (*dar -beso*) to plant; *-golpe*) to land, deal: *le estampó un puñetazo,* he punched him. – **6 estamparse,** *p fam* (*estrellarse*) to crash: *el coche se estampó contra la pared,* the car crashed into the wall.
● **estampar la firma,** to sign.

estampida 1 *f* (*ruido*) bang. **2** (*de animales*) stampede.
● **de estampida,** suddenly: *salir de estampida,* to be off like a shot.

estampido *m* bang.
● **dar un estampido,** to go bang.

estampilla *f* stamp, rubber stamp.

estampillado *m* rubber stamping.

estampillar *t* (*gen*) to stamp; (*documento*) to rubber-stamp.

estampita *f* religious print.
■ **el timo de la estampita,** *con trick involving a supposedly winning lottery ticket.*

estancado,-a 1 *pp →* **estancar**. – **2** *adj* (*agua*) stagnant. **3** *fig* (*asunto, negocio*) at a standstill; (*negociaciones*) deadlocked; (*persona*) stuck, bogged down.

estancamiento 1 *m* stagnancy, stagnation. **2** *fig* deadlock, standstill.

estancar 1 *t* (*aguas*) to hold up, hold back, dam; (*flujo*) to check. **2** *fig* (*progreso*) to check, block, hold up; (*negociaciones*) to bring to a standstill. **3** *fig* (*monopolizar*) to have a state monopoly on. – **4 estancarse,** *p* (*líquido*) to stagnate, become stagnant. **5** *fig* to stagnate, get bogged down; (*negociaciones*) to be deadlocked, make no headway.
▲ *Conjugation model* [1], *like **sacar.***

estancia 1 *f* (*permanencia*) stay. **2** (*aposento*) room. **3** (*estrofa*) stanza.

estanco,-a 1 *adj* watertight: *compartimento estanco*, watertight compartment. **– 2 estanco**, *m* (*monopolio*) state monopoly. **3** (*tienda*) tobacconist's.

estándar 1 *adj* standard, standardized: *modelo estándar*, standard model; *reglas estándar*, set rules. **– 2** *m* standard.

▲ *pl estándares*.

estandarización *f* standardization.

estandarizar *t* to standardize.

▲ *Conjugation model* [4], *like realizar*.

estandarte *m* standard, banner.

estanque 1 *m* (*de peces etc*) pool, pond. **2** (*para proveer agua*) reservoir, tank.

estanquero,-a *m,f* tobacconist.

estanquidad *f* watertightness.

estante 1 *m* (*anaquel*) shelf; (*para libros*) bookcase. **2** (*de máquina*) stand.

estantería *f* shelving, shelves *pl*.

estantigua *f fig* sight, scarecrow.

estañado *m* tin plating.

estañar 1 *t* (*con estaño*) to tin-plate. **2** (*soldar*) to solder.

estaño *m* tin.

estaquilla 1 *f* (*de madera*) peg, pin; (*de tienda de campaña*) tent peg. **2** (*clavo*) tack, spike.

estaquillar *t* to peg down, fasten with pegs.

estar 1 *i* (*lugar, posición*) to be: *estaba sobre la mesa*, it was on the table; *allí está*, there it is; *estamos en casa*, we are at home; *los precios están altos*, prices are high. **2** (*permanecer*) to be, stay: *estuvimos allí diez días*, we stayed there for ten days. **3** (*cualidades transitorias*) to be: *está cansado*, he's tired; *está mal*, he's ill. **4** (*una prenda*) to suit, be: *el vestido negro te está bien*, the black dress suits you; *te está grande*, it's too big for you. **– 5 estar + gerundio**, *aux* to be: *estaban cantando*, they were singing. **– 6 estar a**, *i* (*precio*) to be, sell at; (*fecha*) to be: *están a 200 pesetas*, they're 200 pesetas; *estamos a 15 de marzo*, it's the 15th of March. **7 estar con**, (*tener*) to have; (*estar de acuerdo*) to agree with: *estoy con gripe*, I have the flu; *estoy con Ana*, I agree with Ana. **8 estar de**, (*gen*) to be; (*trabajar*) to be, be working as; (*ir vestido*) to be, be dressed in: *estar de vacaciones*, to be on holiday; *estar de exámenes*, to be doing exams; *está de mal humor*, she's in a bad mood; *está de profesor*, he works as a teacher; *está de defensa*, he plays in defence; *está de uniforme*, he's in uniform. **9 estar en**, (*consistir*) to be, lie; (*entender*) to understand; (*creer*) to think, believe; (*depender de uno*) to be up to: *el motivo está en el dinero*, money is the reason; *su fracaso está en su falta de motivación*, his failure lies in his lack of motivation; *estoy en lo que quieres decir*, I understand what you mean; *estoy en que no vendrán*, I don't think they'll come; *está en él decírselo*, it's up to him to tell her. **10 estar para**, (*estar a punto*) to be about to; (*estar acabado*) to be finished, be ready; (*estar de humor*) to feel like, be in the mood for: *está para marchar*, she's about to leave; *no estoy para bromas*, I'm in no mood for jokes; *estará para las cuatro*, it'll be finished by four. **11 estar por**, (*no haberse ejecutado*) to remain to be; (*estar determinado*) to be for; (*ir a*) to be going to; (*a favor*) to be for: *está por escribir*, it still has to be written; *estoy por quedarme*, I'm for staying; *está por salir*, she's going to go out; *estamos por este partido*, we're for this party. **12 estar que**, *fam* to be nearly, be really, be practically: *está que se hunde*, it's practically ruined. **13 estar sin** + *inf*, not

to have been + *pp*: *el coche está sin lavar*, the car hasn't been washed, the car still needs washing. **– 14 estarse**, *p* (*permanecer*) to spend, stay: *se estuvo todo el día leyendo*, she spent all day reading.

● **en seguida está**, it'll be ready in a moment. ‖ **está bien**, it's all right. ‖ **está mal**, it's wrong. ‖ **está que rabia**, *fam* he/she is hopping mad. ‖ **estar a la que salta**, *fam* to be ready to seize any opportunity. ‖ **estar a matar**, *fam* to be at daggers drawn. ‖ **estar a punto de**, to be about to. ‖ **estar a tiempo de**, to be in time to. ‖ **estar al caer**, to be here any minute. ‖ **estar de más**, not to be needed. ‖ **estar de miedo**, *fam* to be a real cracker. ‖ **estar en lo cierto**, to be right. ‖ **estar en todo**, not to miss a trick. ‖ **¡estáte quieto,-a!**, keep still!, stop fidgeting! ‖ **estoy que no puedo más**, *fam* I can't take anymore.

▲ *Conjugation model* [71]. *If it is followed by a noun it always takes a preposition. When followed by an adjective it expresses a quality which is neither permanent nor inherent.*

estarcido *m* stencil.

estarcir *t* to stencil.

▲ *Conjugation model* [3], *like zurcir*.

estás *pres indic* → **estar**.

estasis *f* stasis.

▲ *pl estasis*.

estatal *adj* state.

estática *f* → **estático,-a**.

estático,-a 1 *adj* static. **– 2 estática**, *f* statics.

estatificar *t* to nationalize.

▲ *Conjugation model* [1], *like sacar*.

estatismo 1 *m* (*inmovilidad*) immobility. **2** (*poder del estado*) statism.

estator *m* stator.

estatoscopio *m* statoscope.

estatua *f* statue.

● **quedarse hecho,-a una estatua**, *fig* to be transfixed.

estatuaria *f* → **estatuario,-a**.

estatuario,-a 1 *adj* statuary. **2** *fig* statuesque. **– 3 estatuaria**, *f* statuary.

estatuilla *f* statuette, figurine.

estatuir *t* to establish, state.

▲ *Conjugation model* [62], *like huir*.

estatura *f* height, stature: *¿qué estatura tiene?*, how tall is he?

estatutario,-a *adj* statutory.

estatuto *m* statute.

■ **estatuto de autonomía**, statute of autonomy.

estay *m* stay.

este[1] 1 *adj* east, eastern. **2** (*dirección*) easterly; (*viento*) east, easterly: *dirección este*, easterly direction. **– 3** *m* east. **4** (*viento*) east wind.

este,-a[2] 1 *adj* this; (*plural*) these: *este libro*, this book; *estas manzanas*, these apples; *la película esta no vale nada*, this film's not any good.

▲ *pl estos,-as*.

esté *pres subj* → **estar**.

éste,-a 1 *pron* (*cosa*) this one: *dame éste*, give me this one; *coge éstas*, take these. **2** (*hombre - sujeto*) he; (*mujer - sujeto*) she: *ésta me lo dijo*, she told me. **3** (*hombre - complemento*) him; (*mujer - complemento*) her: *se lo dio a éste*, she gave it to him. **4** (*este último*) the latter: *Pepe y Luis fueron al bar; éste pidió dos cañas y ése buscó una mesa*, Pepe and Luis went to the bar; the latter ordered two beers and the former looked for a table. **5** *pey* this one.

● **y en éstas** ..., *fam* and then ..., and suddenly ...
▲ *pl **éstos,-as**; the written accent may be omitted when no confusion with adjectives is possible.*
estearina *f* stearin.
estela[1] 1 *f* (*de barco*) wake, wash; (*de avión*) vapour (US vapor) trail; (*de cometa*) tail. 2 *fig* trail.
estela[2] *f* (*monumento*) stela.
estelar 1 *adj* (*sideral*) stellar. 2 *fig* star: **figura estelar,** star.
■ **luz estelar,** starlight.
estenocardia *f* stenocardia.
estenografía *f* shorthand, stenography.
estenografiar *t* to take down in shorthand, stenograph.
▲ *Conjugation model* |13|, *like desviar.*
estenográfico,-a *adj* (in) shorthand, stenographic.
estenógrafo,-a *m,f* shorthand writer, shorthand typist, stenographer.
estenordeste 1 *m* east-northeast. 2 (*viento*) east-northeast wind.
▲ **En 2 es marca registrada.**
estenotipia 1 *f* (*arte*) stenotypy. 2 TÉC Stenotype.
estenotipista *mf* stenotypist.
estentóreo,-a *adj* stentorian, thundering, booming.
estepa[1] *f* (*llanura*) steppe.
estepa[2] *f* (*planta*) rockrose.
estepario,-a *adj* steppe, from the steppes.
éster *m* ester.
estera *f* rush mat.
esterar *t* to cover with rush matting.
estercolar 1 *t* (*abonar*) to manure. – 2 *i* (*excremento*) to dung.
estercolero 1 *m* dunghill, dung heap. 2 *fig* pigsty.
estéreo *m* stereo.
estereóbato *m* stereobate.
estereofonía *f* stereo, stereophony, stereophonic sound.
estereofónico,-a *adj* stereo, stereophonic.
estereografía *f* stereography.
estereográfico,-a *adj* stereographic.
estereógrafo,-a *m,f* stereographer.
estereograma *m* stereogram.
estereometría *f* stereometry.
estereoscopia *f* stereoscopy.
estereoscopio *m* stereoscope.
estereotipado,-a 1 *pp* → **estereotipar.** – 2 *adj fig* stereotyped, standard, set.
■ **frase estereotipada,** hackneyed phrase, cliché.
estereotipar *t* to stereotype.
estereotipia 1 *f* (*arte*) stereotypy. 2 (*máquina*) stereotype. 3 *fig* (*de un gesto*) stereotypy.
estereotipo *m* stereotype.
estereotomía *f* stereotomy.
estéril 1 *adj* (*tierra*) sterile, barren. 2 (*hombre*) sterile; (*mujer*) sterile, infertile. 3 (*aséptico*) sterile. 4 *fig* futile, useless.
esterilete *m* coil, IUD.
esterilidad 1 *f* (*de terreno*) sterility, barrenness. 2 (*de hombre*) sterility; (*de mujer*) sterility, infertility. 3 *fig* futility, uselessness.
esterilización *f* sterilization.
esterilizador,-ra 1 *adj* sterilizing. – 2 **esterilizador,** *m* sterilizer.
esterilizar *t* to sterilize.
▲ *Conjugation model* |4|, *like realizar.*
esterilla 1 *f* (*felpudo*) small mat. 2 (*de cañamazo*) rush matting, wickerwork. 3 (*trencilla*) gold braid, silver braid.

■ **esterilla de playa,** beach mat.
esterlina 1 *adj* sterling. – 2 *f* sterling.
■ **libra esterlina,** pound (sterling).
esternocleidomastoideo 1 *adj* sternocleidomastoid. – 2 *m* sternocleidomastoid.
esternón *m* sternum, breastbone.
estero *m* estuary, inlet.
esteroide *m* steroid.
estertor *m* death-rattle.
estesudeste 1 *m* east-southeast. 2 (*viento*) east-southeast wind.
esteta *mf* aesthete (US esthete).
estética *f* → **estético,-a.**
esteticismo *m* aestheticism (US estheticism).
esteticista *mf* beautician.
estético,-a 1 *adj* aesthetic (US esthetic). – 2 **estética,** *f* aesthetics (US esthetics).
■ **cirugía estética,** plastic surgery.
estetoscopia *f* stethoscopy.
estetoscopio *m* stethoscope.
esteva *f* plough-handle (US plow-handle).
estevado,-a 1 *adj* bow-legged, bandy-legged. – 2 *m,f* bow-legged person.
estiaje *m* low water level.
estiba *f* MAR stowing, loading.
estibador *m* docker, stevedore.
estibar 1 *t* (*apretar*) to compress. 2 MAR (*distribuir los pesos*) to trim; (*colocar*) to stow.
estiércol *m* dung, manure.
estigma 1 *m* (*gen*) stigma. 2 (*marca*) brand, mark; (*de nacimiento*) birthmark. 3 REL stigma.
estigmatizar 1 *t* (*marcar con hierro*) to brand. 2 REL to stigmatize. 3 *fig* (*afrentar*) to stigmatize, brand.
▲ *Conjugation model* |4|, *like realizar.*
estilar 1 *t* JUR to draw up. – 2 *i* (*acostumbrar*) to be in the habit of: *estila levantarse pronto,* she usually gets up early. – 3 **estilarse,** *p* (*ser costumbre*) to be customary; (*estar de moda*) to be fashionable, be in vogue, be in fashion.
estilete 1 *m* (*punzón*) stylus. 2 (*puñal*) stiletto. 3 MED probe.
estilismo *m* stylism.
estilista 1 *mf* (*escritor*) stylist. 2 (*diseñador*) stylist, designer.
estilística *f* → **estilístico,-a.**
estilístico,-a 1 *adj* stylistic. – 2 **estilística,** *f* stylistics.
estilización *f* stylization.
estilizar 1 *t* to stylize. 2 (*hacer delgado*) to make thinner: *ese vestido te estiliza,* that dress makes you look thinner.
▲ *Conjugation model* |4|, *like realizar.*
estilo 1 *m* (*gen*) style. 2 (*modo*) manner, fashion. 3 GRAM speech. 4 (*natación*) stroke.
● **al estilo de** ..., in the style of ... ‖ **algo por el estilo,** something like that.
■ **estilo de vida,** way of life. ‖ **estilo braza,** breaststroke. ‖ **estilo directo,** LING direct speech. ‖ **estilo indirecto,** LING indirect speech. ‖ **estilo libre,** freestyle. ‖ **estilo mariposa,** butterfly.
estilográfica *f* → **estilográfico,-a.**
estilográfico,-a 1 *adj* stylographic. – 2 **estilográfica,** *f* fountain pen.
estima 1 *f* esteem, respect. 2 MAR dead reckoning.
● **tener a algn. en gran estima,** to hold sb. in great esteem.

estimable 1 *adj* esteemed, reputable, worthy. 2 (*cantidad*) considerable.
estimación 1 *f* (*afecto*) esteem, respect. 2 (*valoración*) estimation, evaluation. 3 (*cálculo*) estimate.
■ estima propia, self-esteem.
estimado,-a 1 *pp* → **estimar**. – 2 *adj* (*apreciado*) esteemed, respected. 3 (*valorado*) valued, estimated: *el precio estimado,* the estimated price.
● estimado señor / estimada señora, (*en carta*) Dear Sir / Dear Madam.
estimar 1 *t* (*apreciar*) to esteem, respect, hold in esteem, admire. 2 (*valorar*) to value: *estimaron el cuadro en dos millones,* the picture was valued at two million. 3 (*juzgar, creer*) to consider, think, reckon. 4 (*calcular*) to estimate: *estimamos el costo en diez mil pesetas,* we estimated the cost at ten thousand pesetas. 5 JUR (*una demanda*) to admit.
estimativo,-a *adj* estimated, approximate.
estimulante 1 *adj* stimulating, encouraging. – 2 *m* stimulant.
estimular 1 *t* (*animar*) to encourage, stimulate. 2 (*apetito, pasiones*) to whet.
estímulo 1 *m* stimulus, stimulation. 2 *fig* encouragement. 3 COM incentive.
estío *m* summer.
estipendiar *t* to remunerate.
▲ Conjugation model [12], *like cambiar.*
estipendio *m* stipend, fee, remuneration.
estipulación 1 *f* JUR stipulation, condition, proviso. 2 (*acuerdo*) agreement.
estipular *t* to stipulate.
estirada *f* → **estirado,-a**.
estiradamente *adv* scarcely, hardly.
estirado,-a 1 *pp* → **estirar**. – 2 *adj fig* (*en el vestir*) stiff, formal, starchy. 3 *fig* (*orgulloso*) stiff, conceited, haughty. – 4 estirado, *m* (*textil*) drawing. 5 (*del pelo*) straightening; (*de la piel*) lift. – 6 estirada, *f* DEP dive.
estirar 1 *t* (*gen*) to stretch. 2 (*cuello*) to crane. 3 (*medias*) to pull up; (*falda*) to pull down. 4 (*planchar ligeramente*) to iron out the creases, give a quick iron; (*alisar*) to smooth out. 5 *fig* (*escrito, opinión, etc*) to spin out, stretch out. 6 *fig* (*dinero*) to spin out, make go further. – 7 *i* (*crecer*) to shoot up. – 8 estirarse, *p* (*crecer*) to shoot up. 9 (*desperezarse*) to stretch.
● estirar las piernas, *fam* to stretch one's legs. ‖ estirar la pata, *fam* to kick the bucket, snuff it.
estirón *m* pull, jerk, tug.
● dar un estirón / pegar un estirón, *fam* to shoot up, grow up quickly.
estirpe *f* stock, lineage, race.
estival *adj* summer.
■ época estival, summertime.
esto *pron* this: *esto es lo que me dio,* this is what she gave me; *esto me gusta,* I like this.
● a todo esto, by the way: *a todo esto, ¿cómo te llamas?,* by the way, what's your name? ‖ en esto ..., just then, when: *me estaba hablando y en esto rompió a llorar,* she was talking to me when she burst out crying. ‖ esto ..., (*vacilación*) er ... ‖ esto es, that is, ie: *vendrán pasado mañana, esto es, el miércoles,* they're coming day after tomorrow, that is, on Wednesday. ‖ esto de ..., the business about ..., all that about ...
estocada *f* stab, thrust.
■ estocada final, *fig* coup de grâce.
Estocolmo *m* Stockholm.
■ síndrome de Estocolmo, Stockholm syndrome.

estofa *f fig* class, type: *gente de baja estofa,* low-class people.
estofado¹ *m* CULIN stew.
estofado² *m* COST quilting.
estofar¹ *t* CULIN to stew.
estofar² *t* (*acolchar*) to quilt.
estoicismo *m* stoicism.
estoico,-a 1 *adj* stoic, stoical. – 2 *m,f* stoic.
estola *f* stole.
estolidez *f fml* stupidity, denseness.
estólido,-a *adj fml* stupid, thick, dense.
estoma *m* stoma.
estomacal 1 *adj* (*del estómago*) stomach, of the stomach. 2 (*digestivo*) digestive. – 3 *m* (*bebida*) digestive liqueur.
estómago *m* stomach.
● revolver el estómago, *fam* to turn one's stomach. ‖ tener buen estómago, to have strong stomach; *fig* to be thick-skinned.
■ dolor de estómago, stomachache.
estomatología *f* stomatology.
estomatólogo,-a *m,f* stomatologist.
Estonia *f* Estonia.
estonio,-a 1 *adj* Estonian. – 2 *m,f* (*persona*) Estonian. – 3 estonio, *m* (*idioma*) Estonian.
estopa 1 *f* (*fibra*) tow. 2 (*tela*) burlap.
■ estopa de acero, steel wool.
estopilla *f* cheesecloth.
estoque 1 *m* (*espada*) sword. 2 BOT gladiolus.
estoquear *t* to stab, thrust at.
estor *m* roller blind.
estorbar 1 *t* (*dificultar*) to hinder, get in the way; (*obstruir*) to obstruct, block, hold up: *esa mesa estorba el paso,* that table is blocking the way. 2 *fig* (*molestar*) to annoy, bother, disturb. – 3 *i* (*ser obstáculo*) to be in the way. 4 *fig* (*molestar*) to be a nuisance.
estorbo 1 *m* (*obstáculo*) obstruction, obstacle. 2 (*molestia*) hindrance, encumbrance; (*persona*) nuisance.
estornino *m* starling.
estornudar *i* to sneeze.
estornudo *m* sneeze.
estos,-as *adj* these.
▲ See also este,-a.
éstos,-as *pron* these (ones).
▲ See also éste,-a.
estoy *pres indic* → **estar**.
estrabismo *m* strabismus, squint: *tengo estrabismo,* I have a squint.
estrado 1 *m* stage, platform; (*tarima*) dais. – 2 estrados, *mpl* JUR courtrooms.
estrafalario,-a 1 *adj fam* (*desaliñado*) slovenly. 2 *fam fig* (*extravagante*) eccentric, weird, outlandish.
estragar 1 *t* (*dañar*) to devastate, ruin, ravage. 2 (*viciar*) to corrupt, deprave.
estrago *m* havoc, ruin, ravage.
● causar estragos en / hacer estragos en, to play havoc with, badly damage.
estragón *m* tarragon.
estrambote *m* additional verses *pl*.
estrambótico,-a *adj fam* outlandish, eccentric, weird.
estramonio *m* thorn-apple.
estrangulación 1 *f* strangling. 2 MED strangulation.
estrangulador,-ra 1 *adj* strangling. 2 MED strangulating. – 3 *m,f* strangler. – 4 estrangulador, *m* AUTO choke.
estrangulamiento *m* → **estrangulación**.

estrangular 1 *t* (*ahogar*) to strangle. **2** MED to strangulate. **3** AUTO to throttle.

estraperlear *i* to deal in black-market goods.

estraperlista *mf* black marketeer.

estraperlo *m* black market.

estrás *m* strass.

Estrasburgo *m* Strasbourg.

estratagema 1 *f* MIL stratagem. **2** *fam fig* trick.

estratega *mf* strategist.

estrategia *f* strategy.

estratégico,-a *adj* strategic.

estratificación *f* stratification.

estratificar 1 *t* to stratify. − **2 estratificarse,** *p* to be stratified.
▲ *Conjugation model* [1]*, like* **sacar**.

estrato 1 *m* GEOL stratum. **2** (*capa*) stratum. **3** (*nivel social*) stratum, class. **4** (*nube*) stratus.
■ **estratos sociales,** social strata.

estratocúmulo *m* stratocumulus.

estratosfera *f* stratosphere.

estrave *m* stern.

estraza *f* rag, piece of cloth.
■ **papel de estraza,** brown paper.

estrechamente 1 *adv* (*con estrechez*) narrowly, tightly. **2** *fig* (*con exactitud*) exactly. **3** *fig* (*con rigor*) rigorously, strictly. **4** *fig* (*con intimidad*) closely, intimately: *están estrechamente unidos,* they're very close.

estrechamiento 1 *m* (*de valle, carretera, etc*) narrowing. **2** (*de prenda*) taking in. **3** (*lugar estrecho*) narrow point. **4** *fig* coming closer together, rapprochement: *estrechamiento de relaciones diplomáticas,* rapprochement in diplomatic relations.
● *"estrechamiento de calzada",* AUTO *"road narrows".*

estrechar 1 *t* (*carretera*) to make narrower. **2** (*prenda*) to take in. **3** (*abrazar*) to squeeze, hug; (*mano*) to shake: *nos estrechamos las manos,* we shook hands. **4** *fig* (*obligar*) to compel, constrain. **5** *fig* (*relaciones, lazos*) to strengthen. **6** *fig* (*unir*) to bring closer, bring together: *aquellas penalidades nos estrecharon,* that hardship brought us together. − **7 estrecharse,** *p* (*valle etc*) to narrow, become narrower. **8** (*apretarse*) to squeeze together, squeeze up. **9** *fig* (*relaciones etc*) to strengthen, get stronger. **10** *fig* (*gastos etc*) to economize, tighten one's belt.
● **estrechar la mano de algn.,** to shake hands with sb., shake sb.'s hand. ‖ **estrechar los lazos de amistad,** *fig* to strengthen the bonds of friendship.

estrechez 1 *f* (*poco ancho*) narrowness. **2** (*falta espacio*) lack of space. **3** (*prendas*) tightness. **4** *fig* (*económica*) want, need. **5** *fig* (*de tiempo*) lack of time. **6** *fig* (*amistad*) closeness, intimacy. **7** *fig* (*rigidez*) strictness. **8** *fig* (*apuro*) tight spot.
● **pasar estrecheces,** *fig* to be hard up. ‖ **vivir en la estrechez / vivir con estrecheces,** *fig* to live from hand to mouth.
■ **estrechez de miras / estrechez de ideas,** *fig* narrow-mindedness.

estrecho,-a 1 *adj* (*poco ancho*) narrow. **2** (*ropa*) tight; (*calzado*) tight, small. **3** (*habitación*) cramped, pokey, small. **4** (*sin espacio*) packed, jam-packed. **5** *fig* (*amistad etc*) close, intimate. **6** *fig* (*mezquino*) mean. **7** *fig* (*estricto*) narrow, rigid. **8** *fam fig* (*conservador con el sexo*) prudish, straitlaced. − **9 estrecho,** *m* GEOG strait, straits *pl*.
● **ser estrecho,-a de miras,** *fig* to be narrow-minded.
■ **el Estrecho de Gibraltar,** the Straits of Gibraltar.

estrechura 1 *f* (*de paso*) narrowness, narrow point. **2** *fig* (*de amistad*) closeness, intimacy.

estregadera 1 *f* (*cepillo*) scrubbing-brush. **2** (*para los pies*) scraper.

estregar *t* (*con paño*) to rub; (*con cepillo*) to scrub.
▲ *Conjugation model* [48]*, like* **regar**.

estrella 1 *f* (*gen*) star: *hotel de cuatro estrellas,* four-star hotel. **2** *fig* (*destino*) destiny, fate.
● **haber nacido con buena estrella,** *fig* to be born under a lucky star. ‖ **tener buena estrella / tener mala estrella,** *fig* to be lucky / be unlucky. ‖ **ver las estrellas,** *fig* to see stars.
■ **estrella de cine,** film star. ‖ **estrella de mar,** starfish. ‖ **estrella errante / estrella fugaz,** shooting star.

estrellado,-a 1 *pp* → **estrellar**. − **2** *adj* (*cielo*) starry, star-spangled, full of stars. **3** (*forma*) star-shaped. **4** (*hecho pedazos*) smashed, shattered. **5** (*huevo*) fried.

estrellar 1 *t* (*llenar de estrellas*) to cover with stars. **2** *fam* (*hacer pedazos*) to smash (to pieces), shatter. **3** (*freír*) to fry. − **4 estrellarse,** *p* (*llenarse de estrellas*) to be full of stars. **5** (*hacerse pedazos*) to smash, shatter: *el vaso se estrelló contra el suelo,* the glass smashed against the floor. **6** (*chocar*) to crash: *el camión se estrelló contra el muro,* the lorry crashed into the wall. **7** *fig* (*problema, dificultad*) to come up against, run into.

estrellato *m* stardom.

estremecedor,-ra 1 *adj* startling. **2** (*grito*) blood-curdling.

estremecer 1 *t* (*gen*) to shake. **2** *fig* (*asustar*) to startle, frighten. − **3 estremecerse,** *p* (*temblar*) to shake. **4** (*de miedo*) to tremble, shudder; (*de frío*) to shiver, tremble. **5** *fig* to shudder.
▲ *Conjugation model* [43]*, like* **agradecer**.

estremecido,-a 1 *pp* → **estremecer**. − **2** *adj* shaking, trembling: *estaba estremecida de frío,* she was trembling with cold.

estremecimiento 1 *m* (*movimiento*) tremor, vibration. **2** (*de miedo*) trembling, shuddering; (*de frío*) shiver, trembling.

estrena *f* gift, present.

estrenar 1 *t* (*gen*) to use for the first time; (*ropa*) to wear for the first time. **2** TEAT to perform for the first time, give the first performance of; CINEM to release, put on release. − **3 estrenarse,** *p* to make one's début.
● **estrenar piso,** to move into a new flat.

estreno 1 *m* (*de algo*) first use. **2** (*persona*) début, first appearance. **3** TEAT first performance; CINEM new release, premiere.
■ **riguroso estreno,** world premiere.

estreñido,-a 1 *pp* → **estreñir**. − **2** *adj* constipated. **3** *fig* mean, stingy.

estreñimiento *m* constipation.

estreñir 1 *t* to constipate, make constipated. − **2 estreñirse,** *p* to become constipated.
▲ *Conjugation model* [36]*, like* **ceñir**.

estrépito 1 *m* din, racket, clatter. **2** *fig* ostentation, fuss.

estrepitosamente *adv* noisily.

estrepitoso,-a 1 *adj* noisy, clamorous. **2** (*ruido*) deafening. **3** *fig* (*éxito*) resounding; (*fracaso*) spectacular.

estreptococo *m* streptococcus.

estreptomicina *f* streptomycin.

estrés *m* stress.
▲ *pl* **estreses**.

estresado,-a *adj* under stress.

estresante *adj* stressful.

estría 1 *f* (*ranura*) groove. **2** ARQ flute. **3** (*en la piel*) stretch mark.

estriar 1 *t* (*hacer ranuras*) to groove. **2** ARQ to flute. **3** (*piel*) to give stretch marks. – **4 estriarse,** *p* (*piel*) to get stretch marks.
▲ *Conjugation model* [13], *like* ***desviar.***
estribación 1 *f* spur. – **2 estribaciones,** *fpl* foothills.
estribar 1 *i* (*apoyarse*) to rest (**en,** on). **2** *fig* (*basarse*) to lie (**en,** in).
estribillo 1 *m* (*de poesía*) refrain; (*de canción*) chorus. **2** (*muletilla*) pet phrase, pet saying.
estribo 1 *m* (*de jinete*) stirrup. **2** (*de carruaje, tren*) step. **3** AUTO running board; (*de moto*) footrest. **4** ARQ buttress; (*de puente*) pier, support. **5** (*del oído*) stirrup bone. **6** (*de alpinista*) rope ladder. **7** *fig* (*apoyo*) support.
● **perder los estribos,** *fig* to lose one's head, lose one's temper.
estribor *m* starboard.
estricnina *f* strychnine.
estrictamente *adv* strictly.
estricto,-a *adj* strict, rigorous.
estridencia 1 *f* (*ruido*) stridency, shrillness. **2** (*color etc*) loudness, garishness, gaudiness.
estridente 1 *adj* (*ruido*) strident, shrill. **2** (*color etc*) loud, garish, gaudy.
estro 1 *m* (*inspiración*) inspiration. **2** (*mosca*) bot-fly, oestrus (US estrus).
estrofa *f* strophe, stanza, verse.
estrógeno,-a 1 *adj* oestrogenic (US estrogenic). – **2 estrógeno,** *m* oestrogen (US estrogen).
estroncio *m* strontium.
estropajo 1 *m* (*para fregar*) scourer. **2** (*planta*) loofah. **3** *fig* (*desecho*) useless thing.
estropajoso,-a 1 *adj* (*lengua*) furry. **2** (*forma de hablar*) stammering. **3** (*desaseado*) slovenly; (*andrajoso*) ragged. **4** (*carne etc*) gristly, tough. **5** (*pelo*) straw-like.
estropear 1 *t* (*máquina*) to damage, break, ruin. **2** (*cosecha*) to spoil, ruin. **3** (*plan etc*) to spoil, ruin. **4** (*salud*) to be bad for. **5** (*envejecer*) to age. **6** (*manos, pelo*) to ruin. – **7 estropearse,** *p* (*máquina*) to break down. **8** (*cosecha*) to be spoiled, get damaged. **9** (*plan etc*) to fail, fall through, go wrong. **10** (*comida*) to go bad.
estropicio 1 *m fam* (*rotura*) breakage, damage; (*ruido producido*) crash, clatter, smash. **2** *fam* (*desorden*) mess; (*jaleo*) fuss, rumpus.
estructura 1 *f* (*gen*) structure. **2** (*armazón*) frame, framework.
estructuración *f* structure, organization.
estructurado,-a 1 *pp* → **estructurar.** – **2** *adj* structured, organized.
estructural *adj* structural.
estructuralismo *m* structuralism.
estructurar 1 *t* to structure, organize. – **2 estructurarse,** *p* to be structured, be organized.
estruendo 1 *m* (*ruido*) great noise, din. **2** (*confusión*) uproar, tumult. **3** *fig* (*pompa*) pomp, ostentation.
estruendoso,-a *adj* (*ruido*) noisy, deafening; (*aplauso*) thunderous.
estrujar 1 *t* (*exprimir*) to squeeze. **2** (*apretar - alguien*) to crush; (*- algo*) to screw up: *casi le estrujaron en el ascensor,* they almost crushed him in the lift; *estrujó el papel,* she screwed the paper up. **3** (*ropa*) to wring. **4** *fig* (*sacar partido*) to drain, bleed dry. – **5 estrujarse,** *p* (*apretujarse*) to crowd, throng.
● **estrujarse los sesos / estrujarse el cerebro,** *fam* to rack one's brains.
estrujón *m* tight squeeze, big hug.
estuario *m* estuary.

estucado *m* stucco, stucco work.
estucar *t* to stucco.
▲ *Conjugation model* [1], *like* ***sacar.***
estuche 1 *m* (*caja*) case, box. **2** (*vaina*) sheath. **3** (*conjunto*) set.
■ **estuche de aseo,** toilet bag.
estuco *m* stucco.
estudiado,-a 1 *pp* → **estudiar.** – **2** *adj* (*afectado*) affected, studied; (*rebuscado*) elaborate, recherché.
estudiantado *m* students *pl*, student body.
estudiante *mf* student.
estudiantil *adj* student, of students.
estudiantina *f* student band.
estudiar 1 *t* (*gen*) to study, learn: *estudia francés en el colegio,* she's learning French at school. **2** (*en universidad*) to read, study: *estudia medicina en Barcelona,* he's studying medicine at Barcelona. **3** (*trabajar*) to work, study: *tienes que estudiar más,* you have to work harder. **4** (*observar*) to examine, observe. – **5** *i* to study: *estudia para maestro,* he's training to be a teacher. – **6 estudiarse,** *p* to consider: *se está estudiando la posibilidad,* the possibility is being considered.
● **estudiar de memoria,** to learn by heart.
▲ *Conjugation model* [12], *like* ***cambiar.***
estudio 1 *m* (*gen*) study. **2** (*encuesta*) survey, study; (*investigación*) research. **3** (*apartamento*) studio flat (US apartment), bedsit. **4** (*sala*) studio. – **5 estudios,** *mpl* (*conocimientos*) studies, education *sing*.
● **cursar estudios,** to study. ‖ **dar estudios a algn.,** to pay for sb.'s education. ‖ **dedicarse al estudio de algo,** to study sth. ‖ **estar algo en estudio,** to be under consideration. ‖ **hacer estudios,** to study. ‖ **tener estudios,** to be well-educated.
■ **estudio cinematográfico,** film studio. ‖ **estudio de grabación,** recording studio. ‖ **estudio de mercado,** market research. ‖ **estudio de televisión,** television studio.
estudioso,-a 1 *adj* studious. – **2** *m,f* student, scholar.
estufa 1 *f* (*calentador*) heater, stove; (*de gas, eléctrica*) fire. **2** (*invernadero*) greenhouse, hothouse.
estufilla 1 *f* (*brasero*) brazier, foot-warmer. **2** (*manguito*) muff.
estulticia *f lit* stupidity, foolishness.
estulto,-a *adj lit* stupid, foolish.
estupa 1 *f arg* (*grupo*) drug squad. – **2** *mf* (*oficial*) drug-squad officer.
estupefacción *f* stupefaction, astonishment, amazement.
estupefaciente 1 *adj* stupefying. – **2** *m* drug, narcotic.
estupefacto,-a *adj* astounded, dumbfounded, flabbergasted.
estupendamente *adv* marvellously (US marvelously), wonderfully.
estupendo,-a *adj* marvellous (US marvelous), wonderful, super.
● **¡estupendo!,** *fam* great!
estupidez *f* stupidity, stupid thing.
● **cometer una estupidez,** to do something stupid, do something silly. ‖ **¡qué estupidez!,** (*dicho*) what a stupid thing to say!; (*hecho*) what a stupid thing to do!
estúpido,-a 1 *adj* stupid, silly. – **2** *m,f* berk, idiot.
estupor *m* stupor, amazement, astonishment.
● **causar estupor,** to astonish.
estuprar *t* to rape.
estupro *m* rape.
estuquista *mf* stucco worker.

esturión *m* sturgeon.

estuve *pt indef* → **estar**.

esvástica *f* swastika.

ETA *abr* (*Euzkadi Ta Askatasuna*) Basque Land and Liberty (*radical Basque separatist movement*).

etano *m* ethane.

etapa 1 *f* period, stage. 2 (*parada*) stop, stage: *la primera etapa es Zaragoza,* the first stop is Zaragoza. 3 DEP leg, stage.
● **por etapas,** in stages. ‖ **quemar etapas,** *fig* to get on in leaps and bounds.

etarra 1 *adj* ETA, of ETA, from ETA. – 2 *mf* member of ETA.

etc. *abr* (*etcétera*) etcetera; (*abreviatura*) etc.

etcétera *f* etcetera, and so on.
● **y un largo etcétera,** and much/many more besides.

éter 1 *m* QUÍM ether. 2 (*celestial*) ether, heavens *pl*, sky.
▲ *pl éteres.*

etéreo,-a *adj* ethereal.

eternidad 1 *f* eternity. 2 *fam* ages *pl*: *te esperé una eternidad,* I waited for you for ages.

eternizar 1 *t* to eternize, eternalize. 2 *fam* to prolong endlessly. – 3 **eternizarse,** *p fam* (*ser interminable*) to be interminable, be endless; (*discusión*) to drag on. 4 *fam* (*tardar mucho*) to take ages.
▲ *Conjugation model* [4], *like realizar.*

eterno,-a *adj* eternal, everlasting, endless.

ética *f* → **ético,-a**.

ético,-a 1 *adj* ethical. – 2 *m,f* ethicist. – 3 **ética,** *f* ethics *pl*, ethic: *ética del trabajo,* work ethic.

etileno *m* ethylene.

etílico,-a *adj* ethylic.
● **en estado etílico,** intoxicated.
■ **alcohol etílico,** ethyl alcohol. ‖ **intoxicación etílica,** alcohol poisoning.

etilo *m* ethyl.

etimología *f* etymology.

etimológico,-a *adj* etymological.

etimologizar *t* to etymologize.
▲ *Conjugation model* [4], *like realizar.*

etiología *f* aetiology (US etiology).

etiope *adj* → **etíope**.

etíope 1 *adj* Ethiopian. – 2 *mf* (*persona*) Ethiopian. – 3 etíope, *m* (*idioma*) Ethiopian, Ethiopic.

Etiopía *f* Ethiopia.

etiópico,-a 1 *adj* Ethiopian. – 2 *m,f* (*persona*) Ethiopian. – 3 etiópico, *m* (*idioma*) Ethiopian, Ethiopic.

etiqueta 1 *f* (*rótulo*) label, tag. 2 (*formalidad*) etiquette, formality, ceremony.
● **de etiqueta,** formal: *traje de etiqueta,* formal dress, evening dress. ‖ **vestirse de etiqueta,** to wear formal dress.

etiquetar *t* to label, put a label on.

etiquetero,-a *adj* formal, ceremonious.

etmoides *m* ethmoid bone.
▲ *pl etmoides.*

etnia *f* ethnic group.

étnico,-a *adj* ethnic.
■ **limpieza étnica,** ethnic cleansing.

etnografía *f* ethnography.

etnográfico,-a *adj* ethnographic, ethnographical.

etnología *f* ethnology.

etnológico,-a *adj* ethnologic, ethnological.

etnólogo,-a *m,f* ethnologist.

etrusco,-a 1 *adj* Etruscan. – 2 *m,f* (*persona*) Etruscan. – 3 etrusco, *m* (*idioma*) Etruscan.

ETS *abr* (*Escuela Técnica Superior*) technical college.

eucalipto *m* eucalyptus.

eucaristía *f* Eucharist.

eucarístico,-a *adj* eucharistic, eucharistical.

eufemismo *m* euphemism.

eufemístico,-a *adj* euphemistic.

eufonía *f* euphony.

eufónico,-a *adj* euphonic, euphonious.

euforia *f* euphoria, elation.

eufórico,-a *adj* euphoric, elated.

Eufrates el Eufrates, *m* the Euphrates.

eunuco *m* eunuch.

eureka *interj* eureka!

euritmia *f* eurythmics.

euroafricano,-a 1 *adj* Eurafrican. – 2 *m,f* Eurafrican.

euroasiático,-a 1 *adj* Eurasian. – 2 *m,f* Eurasian.

eurocomunismo *m* Eurocommunism.

eurocomunista 1 *adj* Eurocommunist. – 2 *mf* Eurocommunist.

eurodiputado,-a *m,f* Member of the European Parliament, MEP.

eurodivisa *f* Eurocurrency.

euromisil *f* Euromissile.

Europa *f* Europe.

europeidad *f* Europeanity.

europeísmo *m* Europeanism.

europeísta 1 *adj* pro-European. – 2 *mf* pro-European.

europeización *f* Europeanization.

europeizar *t* to europeanize.
▲ *Conjugation model* [26], *like homogeneizar.*

europeo,-a 1 *adj* European. – 2 *m,f* European.
■ **Comunidad Europea,** European Community. ‖ **Unión Europea,** European Union.

eurovisión *f* Eurovision.

euscalduna 1 *adj* Basque. 2 (*que habla vasco*) Basque-speaking. – 3 *mf* Basque speaker.

Euskadi *m* the Basque Country.

euskera *m* (*idioma*) Basque.

eusquera *m* → **euskera**.

Eustaquio *m* Eustachian.
■ **trompa de Eustaquio,** Eustachian tube.

eutanasia *f* euthanasia.

evacuación *f* evacuation.

evacuado,-a 1 *pp* → **evacuar**. – 2 *m,f* evacuee.

evacuar 1 *t* (*lugar*) to evacuate. 2 JUR to issue. 3 ANAT to empty. 4 (*llevar a cabo*) to carry out.
● **evacuar el vientre,** to have a bowel movement.
▲ *Conjugation model* [10], *like adecuar.*

evadido,-a 1 *pp* → **evadir**. – 2 *adj* escaped. – 3 *m,f* escapee, fugitive.

evadir 1 *t* (*peligro, respuesta*) to avoid; (*responsabilidad*) to shirk. 2 (*capital, impuestos*) to evade. – 3 **evadirse,** *p* (*escaparse*) to escape.

evaluación 1 *f* evaluation, assessment. 2 EDUC (*acción*) assessment; (*examen*) exam.

evaluar *t* to evaluate, assess.
▲ *Conjugation model* [11], *like actuar.*

evanescente *adj* evanescent.

evangélico,-a *adj* evangelic, evangelical.

evangelio *m* gospel: *el Evangelio según San Mateo,* the Gospel according to Saint Matthew.

evangelismo *m* evangelism.

evangelista *m* evangelist.

evangelización *f* evangelization, evangelizing.

evangelizador,-ra 1 *adj* evangelizing. – 2 *m,f* evangelist.

evangelizar *t* to evangelize, preach the gospel to.
▲ *Conjugation model* [4], *like realizar.*

evaporable *adj* evaporable.

evaporación *f* evaporation.

evaporar 1 *t* to evaporate. – 2 **evaporarse,** *p* to evaporate. 3 *fig* to vanish, disappear.

evasión 1 *f* (*fuga*) escape, flight. 2 *fig* escape, escapism.
■ **evasión fiscal / evasión de impuestos,** tax evasion. ‖ **novela de evasión,** escapist novel.

evasiva *f* → **evasivo,-a.**

evasivo,-a 1 *adj* evasive. – 2 **evasiva,** *f* evasive answer.
● **contestar con una evasiva,** not to give a straight answer, avoid the issue.

evección *f* evection.

evento 1 *m* (*acontecimiento*) event. 2 (*imprevisto*) eventuality, contingency.
● **a todo evento,** in any event.

eventual 1 *adj* (*casual*) chance; (*probable*) possible. 2 (*trabajo*) casual, temporary, provisional. 3 (*ingresos, gastos*) incidental. – 4 *mf* casual worker, temporary worker.

eventualidad *f* eventuality, contingency.

eventualmente 1 *adv* (*casualmente*) by chance; (*posiblemente*) possibly. 2 (*temporalmente*) provisionally.

evicción *f* eviction.

evidencia *f* (*claridad*) obviousness, clearness; (*certeza*) certainty.
● **poner algo en evidencia,** to demonstrate sth. ‖ **poner a algn. en evidencia,** to make a fool of sb., show sb. up. ‖ **ponerse en evidencia,** to show os. up.

evidenciar *t* to show, make evident, prove, make obvious.
▲ *Conjugation model* [12], *like cambiar.*

evidente *adj* evident, obvious.

evidentemente *adv* evidently, obviously.

evitable *adj* avoidable, preventable.

evitación *f* avoidance, prevention.

evitar 1 *t* (*gen*) to avoid: *evitó una confrontación,* he avoided a confrontation. 2 (*impedir*) to prevent, avoid: *no pudo evitar que lo hiciera,* he couldn't prevent him (from) doing it. 3 (*ahorrar*) to spare, save: *intenté evitarle la molestia,* I tried to save him the trouble.

evocación *f* evocation, recollection, recalling.

evocador,-ra *adj* evocative.

evocar 1 *t* (*recuerdo*) to evoke, call up; (*pasado*) to recall. 2 (*recordar*) to evoke, bring to mind: *aquel paisaje evocaba el de su pueblo natal,* the landscape evoked that of her home town. 3 (*a espíritu*) to invoke.
▲ *Conjugation model* [1], *like sacar.*

evolución 1 *f* (*cambio*) evolution; (*desarrollo*) development. 2 (*vuelta*) turn. 3 MIL manoeuvre (US maneuver).

evolucionar 1 *i* (*gen*) to evolve, develop. 2 (*dar vueltas*) to turn. 3 MIL to manoeuvre (US maneuver).
● **evolucionar a pasos agigantados,** to take giant strides.

evolucionismo *m* evolutionism.

evolucionista 1 *adj* evolutionist. – 2 *mf* evolutionist.

evolutivo,-a *adj* evolutionary, evolving.

ex- *pref* ex-, former: *el ex primer ministro,* the former prime minister.
■ **ex alumno,** (*colegio - chico*) old boy; (*- chica*) old girl; (*universidad*) former student, ex-student. ‖ **ex combatiente,** ex-serviceman, ex veteran.

exabrupto *m* sharp comment, sudden outburst.
● **contestar con un exabrupto,** to snap back.

exacción 1 *f* (*impuestos*) exaction. 2 (*extorsión*) extortion.

exacerbación 1 *f* (*agravamiento*) exacerbation, aggravation. 2 (*irritación*) exacerbation, exasperation.

exacerbante 1 *adj* (*agravante*) aggravating. 2 (*irritante*) irritating, exasperating.

exacerbar 1 *t* (*agravar*) to exacerbate, aggravate, make worse. 2 (*irritar*) to exacerbate, exasperate, irritate. – 3 **exacerbarse,** *p* (*agravarse*) to be exacerbated, worsen. 4 (*irritarse*) to become exasperated.

exactamente *adv* exactly, precisely.

exactitud *f* (*fidelidad*) exactness; (*precisión*) accuracy.
● **con exactitud,** accurately.

exacto,-a 1 *adj* (*fiel*) faithful, true; (*preciso*) accurate, exact. 2 (*verdad*) true: *eso no es exacto,* that's not true.
● **¡exacto!,** precisely! ‖ **para ser exacto ...,** to be precise ...

exageración *f* exaggeration.
● **¡qué exageración!,** come off it!

exageradamente 1 *adv* (*con exageración*) exaggeratedly. 2 (*excesivamente*) exaggeratedly, extremely, exceedingly.

exagerado,-a 1 *pp* → **exagerar.** – 2 *adj* (*gen*) exaggerated; (*historia*) far-fetched. 3 (*excesivo*) excessive. 4 (*precio*) exorbitant. 5 (*gesto*) flamboyant.
● **ser exagerado,-a,** (*persona*) to exaggerate.

exagerar 1 *t* to exaggerate. – 2 *i* to exaggerate. 3 (*abusar*) to overdo it, do too much: *exagera con el trabajo,* he's doing too much work.

exaltación 1 *f* (*gloria*) exaltation, praise. 2 (*júbilo*) exaltation, elation. 3 (*excitación*) overexcitement. 4 POL *fam* fanaticism.

exaltado,-a 1 *pp* → **exaltar.** – 2 *adj* (*discusión etc*) heated, impassioned. 3 (*persona*) hot-headed, worked up. – 4 *m,f fam* fanatic, extremist. 5 POL *fam* fanatic, extremist.

exaltar 1 *t* (*elevar*) to raise, promote. 2 *fig* (*alabar*) to exalt, praise, extol. – 3 **exaltarse,** *p* (*excitarse*) to get overexcited, get worked up, get carried away.

examen 1 *m* examination, exam. 2 (*estudio*) consideration, examination, study.
● **aprobar un examen,** to pass an exam. ‖ **hacer un examen,** to do an exam. ‖ **presentarse a un examen,** to take an exam, sit an exam.
■ **examen de conciencia,** soul-searching. ‖ **examen de conducir,** driving test. ‖ **examen de ingreso,** entrance examination. ‖ **examen final,** final examination. ‖ **examen médico,** check-up. ‖ **examen oral,** oral examination.
▲ *pl* **exámenes.**

examinador,-ra 1 *adj* examining. – 2 *m,f* examiner.

examinando,-a *m,f* candidate, examinee.

examinar 1 *t* (*gen*) to examine. 2 (*investigar*) to consider, inspect, go over. – 3 **examinarse,** *p* to take an examination, sit an examination.

exangüe 1 *adj* (*desangrado*) bloodless. 2 *fig* (*débil*) weak, lifeless.

exánime 1 *adj* (*muerto*) dead. 2 *fig* (*débil*) worn-out, exhausted; (*desmayado*) lifeless.

exantema *m* exanthema.

exasperación *f* exasperation.

exasperante *adj* exasperating.

exasperar 1 *t* to exasperate. – 2 **exasperarse,** *p* to get exasperated.

Excª *abr* (*Excelencia*) Excellency; (*abreviatura*) Exc.

Exca. *abr* (*Excelencia*) Excellency; (*abreviatura*) Exc.

excarcelación *f* release (from prison).

excarcelar *t* to release (from prison).

excavación 1 *f* excavation, digging. 2 (*arqueológica*) dig.

excavador,-ra 1 *adj* excavating, digging. – 2 *m,f* excavator, digger. – 3 **excavadora,** *f* digger.
excavadora *f* → **excavador,-ra**.
excavar *t* to excavate, dig.
excedencia 1 *f* (*de funcionario etc*) leave: *excedencia por maternidad,* maternity leave. 2 (*sueldo*) paid leave. 3 (*de profesor*) sabbatical leave.
excedente 1 *adj* (*excesivo*) excessive. 2 (*sobrante*) excess, surplus. 3 (*funcionario*) on leave; (*profesor*) on sabbatical leave. – 4 *m* COM surplus, excess.
■ **excedente de cupo,** MIL person who is exempted from military service.
exceder 1 *t* (*superar*) to excel, surpass: *éste excede al tuyo en calidad,* this one surpasses yours in quality. 2 (*sobrepasar*) to exceed, be in excess of: *las ventas han excedido nuestras previsiones,* sales have exceeded our predictions. – 3 *i* (*sobrar*) to be surplus, be left over: *los agricultores venderán a bajo precio los productos que exceden,* the farmers will sell the surplus products at a low price. 4 (*ser demasiado*) to be beyond, be outside: *esto excede su competencia,* this is outside his jurisdiction. – 5 **excederse,** *p* (*pasarse*) to overdo it, go too far. 6 (*en atenciones etc*) to be extremely kind.
● **exceder de,** to exceed, be over. ‖ **excederse a sí mismo,-a,** to surpass os., excel os. ‖ **excederse en sus funciones,** to exceed one's duty.
excelencia *f* excellence.
● **por excelencia,** par excellence. ‖ **Su Excelencia / Vuestra Excelencia,** (*hombre*) His Excellency; (*mujer*) Her Excellency.
excelente *adj* excellent, first-rate.
excelentísimo,-a *adj* (*alcalde*) Your Worship; (*juez*) Your Honour (US Honor); (*embajador*) Your Excellency.
excelso,-a *adj* lofty, sublime.
excentricidad *f* eccentricity.
excéntrico,-a *adj* eccentric.
excepción *f* exception.
● **a excepción de / con excepción de,** with the exception of, except for. ‖ **de excepción,** exceptional. ‖ **hacer una excepción,** to make an exception. ‖ **la excepción confirma la regla,** the exception proves the rule.
■ **estado de excepción,** POL state of emergency.
excepcional 1 *adj* (*extraordinario*) exceptional, outstanding. 2 (*raro*) exceptional, unusual.
excepto *adv* except (for), apart from, excepting.
exceptuación *f* exception, exclusion.
exceptuar 1 *t* to except, leave out, exclude. – 2 **exceptuarse,** *p* to be excepted, be excluded.
▲ *Conjugation model* |11|, *like* **actuar.**
excesivo,-a *adj* excessive.
exceso *m* excess; COM surplus.
● **en exceso,** too much, in excess, excessively: *fuma en exceso,* he smokes too much.
■ **exceso de equipaje,** excess baggage. ‖ **exceso de peso,** excess weight. ‖ **exceso de velocidad,** speeding.
excipiente *m* excipient.
excisión *f* excision.
excitabilidad *f* excitability.
excitable *adj* excitable, easily worked up.
excitación 1 *f* (*acción*) excitation. 2 (*sentimiento*) excitement.
excitante 1 *adj* exciting. 2 MED stimulating. – 3 *m* stimulant.
excitar 1 *t* to excite. 2 (*emociones*) to stimulate, arouse. – 3 **excitarse,** *p* to get excited, get worked up, get carried away.

exclamación 1 *f* exclamation; (*grito*) cry. 2 (*signo*) exclamation mark.
● **exhalar una exclamación / lanzar una exclamación,** to cry out.
■ **signo de exclamación,** exclamation mark.
exclamar 1 *t* to exclaim, cry out. – 2 *i* to exclaim, cry out.
exclamativo,-a *adj* exclamatory.
exclamatorio,-a *adj* exclamatory.
exclaustrado,-a 1 *pp* → **exclaustrar.** – 2 *m,f* (*monje*) secularized monk; (*monja*) secularized nun.
exclaustrar 1 *t* to secularize. – 2 **exclaustrarse,** *p* to secularize.
excluir 1 *t* to exclude, shut out. 2 (*rechazar*) to reject; (*descartar*) to rule out; (*expulsar*) to throw out.
▲ *Conjugation model* |62|, *like* **huir.**
exclusión *f* exclusion, shutting out.
● **a exclusión de / con exclusión de,** with the exclusion of, excluding, not counting.
exclusiva *f* → **exclusivo,-a.**
exclusivamente *adv* exclusively.
exclusive 1 *adv* (*exclusivamente*) exclusively. 2 (*sin contar*) exclusive: *del cinco al diez de enero exclusive,* from the fifth to the tenth of January exclusive.
exclusividad *f* exclusiveness, exclusivity.
exclusivismo *m* exclusivism.
exclusivista 1 *adj* exclusivist. – 2 *mf* exclusivist.
exclusivo,-a 1 *adj* exclusive. – 2 **exclusiva,** *f* COM sole right. 3 (*prensa*) exclusive, scoop.
● **en exclusiva,** exclusively. ‖ **tener la exclusiva de algo,** to have the sole rights to sth.
excluyente *adj* exclusive.
Excmo.,-a. *abr* (*Excelentísimo*) Most Excellent.
excombatiente *m* ex-serviceman, US veteran.
excomulgar *t* to excommunicate.
▲ *Conjugation model* |7|, *like* **llegar.**
excomunión *f* excommunication.
excoriación 1 *f* excoriation, chafing. 2 (*raspadura*) graze.
excoriar 1 *t* (*rozar*) to chafe. 2 (*raspar*) to graze. – 3 **excoriarse,** *p* (*roce*) to be chafed. 4 (*raspadura*) to be grazed.
▲ *Conjugation model* |12|, *like* **cambiar.**
excrecencia *f* excrescence.
excreción *f* excretion.
excrementar *i* to defecate.
excremento *f* excrement.
excretar *i* to excrete.
excretor,-ra *adj* excretory.
excretorio,-a *adj* excretory.
exculpación 1 *f* exoneration. 2 JUR acquittal.
exculpar 1 *t* to exonerate. 2 JUR to acquit.
excursión *f* excursion, trip.
● **hacer una excursión / ir de excursión,** to go on an excursion, go on a trip.
excursionismo *m* hiking, rambling.
excursionista *mf* tripper; (*a pie*) hiker, rambler.
excusa 1 *f* (*pretexto*) excuse. 2 (*disculpa*) excuse, apology.
● **dar excusas,** to make excuses. ‖ **ofrecer sus excusas / presentar sus excusas,** to apologize.
excusable *adj* excusable, forgivable, pardonable.
excusado[1] *m* toilet.
excusado,-a[2] 1 *pp* → **excusar.** – 2 *adj* (*perdonado*) excused, forgiven, pardoned. 3 (*exento*) excused, exempt: *excusado de pagar,* exempt from paying. 4 (*reservado*) private. 5 (*superfluo*) unnecessary, superfluous.

● **excusado es decir que ...,** needless to say (that) ..., it goes without saying (that)...

excusar 1 *t* (*justificar*) to excuse. **2** (*disculpar*) to pardon, forgive, excuse. **3** (*evitar*) to avoid, prevent; (*ahorrar*) to save, spare. **4** (*eximir*) to exempt (**de,** from). **5 excusar** + *inf,* to have no need: *excusas comprarlo,* you don't need to buy it. – **6 excusarse,** *p* (*justificarse*) to excuse os.; (*disculparse*) to apologize: *se excusó por llegar tarde,* he apologized for being late.

execrable *adj* execrable, abominable.

execración *f* execration.

execrar *t* to execrate, abhor, deplore.

exégesis *f* exegesis.

▲ *pl exégesis.*

exegeta *m* exegete.

exención *f* exemption.

■ **exención de impuestos,** tax exemption.

exento,-a 1 *pp* → **eximir.** – **2** *adj* free (**de,** from), exempt (**de,** from). **3** JUR exempt. **4** (*descubierto*) open.

● **exento,-a de aduanas,** duty-free. ‖ **exento,-a de peligro,** without danger. ‖ **exento,-a de preocupaciones,** carefree.

exequias *fpl* obsequies, funeral rites.

exergo *m* exergue.

exfoliación *f* exfoliation.

exfoliar 1 *t* to exfoliate. – **2 exfoliarse,** *p* to exfoliate.

▲ *Conjugation model* [12], *like cambiar.*

exhalación 1 *f* exhalation. **2** (*estrella*) shooting star; (*rayo*) flash of lightning.

● **pasar como una exhalación,** *fig* to flash past.

exhalar 1 *t* (*gases, vapores, etc*) to give off; (*aire*) to exhale, breathe out. **2** *fig* (*suspiros etc*) to heave, let out; (*quejas*) to utter. – **3 exhalarse,** *p fig* (*persona*) to rush.

exhaustivamente *adv* exhaustively, thoroughly, comprehensively.

exhaustivo,-a *adj* exhaustive, thorough, comprehensive.

● **de modo exhaustivo,** thoroughly.

exhausto,-a *adj* exhausted.

exheredación *f* disinheritance.

exheredar *t* to disinherit.

exhibición 1 *f* (*exposición*) exhibition, show. **2** CINEM showing.

exhibicionismo *m* exhibitionism.

exhibicionista *mf* exhibitionist.

exhibir 1 *t* to exhibit, show, display. **2** (*ostentar*) to show off. **3** JUR to produce. – **4 exhibirse,** *p* (*ostentar*) to show off, make an exhibition of os.

exhortación *f* exhortation.

exhortar *t* to exhort.

exhortativo,-a *adj* exhortative.

exhumación *f* exhumation.

exhumar 1 *t* to exhume. **2** *fig* to revive, recall.

exigencia 1 *f* demand, exigency. **2** (*requisito*) requirement.

exigente *adj* demanding, exacting.

exigir 1 *t* (*pedir por derecho*) to demand. **2** (*pedir con energía*) to insist on, demand. **3** *fig* (*necesitar*) to require, call for: *esta planta exige muchos cuidados,* this plant requires a lot of care.

● **exigir demasiado,** to be very demanding.

▲ *Conjugation model* [6], *like dirigir.*

exigüidad 1 *f* (*de tamaño*) smallness, slightness. **2** (*de cantidad*) scantiness, meagreness, scarcity.

■ **exigüidad de recursos,** lack of funds.

exiguo,-a 1 *adj* (*pequeño*) small, tiny, slight. **2** (*escaso*) scanty, meagre (US meager).

exilado,-a 1 *pp* → **exilar.** – **2** *adj* exiled, in exile. – **3** *m,f* exile.

exilar 1 *t* to exile, send into exile. – **2 exilarse,** *p* to go into exile.

exiliado,-a 1 *pp* → **exiliar.** – **2** *adj-m,f* → **exilado,-a.**

exiliar *t-p* → **exilar.**

▲ *Conjugation model* [12], *like cambiar.*

exilio 1 *m* (*acción*) exile, banishment. **2** (*lugar*) exile, place of exile.

● **enviar al exilio,** to send into exile.

eximio,-a *adj* distinguished, renowned, eminent.

eximir 1 *t* to exempt (**de,** from), free (**de,** from), excuse (**de,** from): *le eximieron de sus responsabilidades,* they freed him from his responsibilities. – **2 eximirse,** *p* to free os. (**de,** from).

▲ *pp exento,-a or eximido,-a.*

exinanido,-a *adj* debilitated, very weak.

existencia 1 *f* (*vida*) existence, life. – **2 existencias,** *fpl* stock *sing,* stocks.

● **en existencia,** in stock. ‖ **liquidación de existencias,** clearance sale. ‖ **renovar las existencias,** to restock.

existencial *adj* existential.

existencialismo *m* existentialism.

existencialista 1 *adj* existentialist. – **2** *mf* existentialist.

existente 1 *adj* existing, existent. **2** COM in stock.

existir *i* to exist, be: *existe un problema,* there's a problem; *la tienda existe desde hace cincuenta años,* the shop has been in existence for fifty years.

● **dejar de existir,** (*empresa*) to fold.

exitazo *m fam* terrific success, smash hit.

éxito *m* success: *la obra fue un éxito rotundo,* the play was a huge success.

● **con éxito,** successfully. ‖ **no tener éxito,** to fail, not succeed. ‖ **sin éxito,** unsuccessfully, without success. ‖ **tener éxito,** to be successful: *ha tenido éxito en el mundo del espectáculo,* he's been successful in showbusiness.

■ **éxito de taquilla,** box-office success.

exocrino,-a *adj* exocrine.

éxodo *m* exodus.

exogamia *f* exogamy.

exógamo,-a *adj* exogamic.

exógeno,-a *adj* exogenous.

exoneración *f* exoneration.

exonerar 1 *t* to exonerate. **2** (*despedir*) to dismiss.

exorable *adj* exorable.

exorbitancia *f* exorbitance, excessiveness.

exorbitante *adj* exorbitant, excessive.

exorbitar *t* to exaggerate.

exorcismo *m* exorcism.

exorcista *mf* exorcist.

exorcizar *t* to exorcise.

▲ *Conjugation model* [4], *like realizar.*

exordio *m* foreword, exordium.

exornar *t* to adorn, embellish.

exotérico,-a *adj* exoteric.

exotérmico,-a *adj* exothermic.

exótico,-a *adj* exotic.

exotismo *m* exoticism.

expandir 1 *t* (*dilatar*) to expand. **2** *fig* (*divulgar*) to spread. – **3 expandirse,** *p* (*dilatarse*) to expand. **4** *fig* (*divulgarse*) to spread.

expansión I f (*dilatación*) expansion. **2** (*difusión*) spreading. **3** (*aumento*) expansion, increase, growth: *la expansión industrial,* industrial growth. **4** *fig* (*manifestación efusiva*) expansiveness. **5** *fig* (*recreo*) relaxation, recreation.

expansionarse I p (*dilatarse*) to expand. **2** *fig* (*divertirse*) to amuse os., relax. **3** *fig* (*espontanearse*) to open one's heart.

expansionismo m expansionism.

expansionista adj expansionist.

expansivo,-a I adj (*gas etc*) expansive. **2** *fig* (*franco*) expansive, open, frank.

expatriación f (*exilio*) expatriation; (*emigración*) emigration.

expatriado,-a I pp → **expatriar**. – **2** m,f expatriate.

expatriar I t to expatriate, banish. – **2 expatriarse,** p (*emigrar*) to emigrate, become an expatriate; (*exilarse*) to go into exile.
▲ *Conjugation model* [14], *like* **auxiliar**.

expectación I f (*esperanza*) expectation, expectancy, anticipation. **2** (*emoción*) excitement: *su visita fue motivo de una gran expectación,* her visit caused a lot of excitement.

expectante adj expectant.

expectativa I f (*esperanza*) expectation, hope. **2** (*posibilidad*) prospect.
■ estar a la expectativa de algo, to be waiting for sth.
■ expectativa de vida, life expectancy.

expectoración I f (*acción*) expectoration. **2** (*flema*) sputum, phlegm.

expectorante I adj expectorant. – **2** m expectorant.

expectorar I t to expectorate. – **2** i to expectorate.

expedición I f (*gen*) expedition. **2** (*grupo de personas*) expedition, party. **3** (*acción de expedir*) dispatch, shipping; (*remesa*) shipment.

expedicionario,-a I adj expeditionary. – **2** m,f member of an expedition.
■ cuerpo expedicionario / grupo expedicionario, MIL expeditionary force.

expedidor,-ra m,f sender, dispatcher, shipper.

expedientar t to take disciplinary action against, open a file on.

expediente I m JUR proceedings pl, action: *expediente judicial,* legal proceedings. **2** (*informe*) dossier, record; (*ficha*) file. **3** (*recurso*) expedient.
● cubrir el expediente, *fam* to keep up appearances. ‖ formar expediente a algn., to take proceedings against sb. ‖ incoar expediente, to start proceedings.
■ expediente académico, school record. ‖ expediente de regulación de empleo, job adjustment plan.

expedienteo m *pey* red tape.

expedir I t (*mercancías*) to send, dispatch, ship; (*correo*) to send, dispatch. **2** (*pasaporte, título*) to issue. **3** (*contrato, documento*) to draw up.
▲ *Conjugation model* [34], *like* **servir**.

expeditivo,-a adj expeditious.

expedito,-a I adj (*libre*) free, clear. **2** (*rápido*) expeditious, speedy, prompt.

expelente adj expelling.

expeler t to expel, eject, throw out.
▲ pp **expulso,-a** or **expelido,-a**.

expendeduría f tobacconist's (shop).

expendedor,-ra I adj selling, retailing, retail. – **2** m,f dealer, retailer, seller.

■ expendedor,-ra de tabaco, tobacconist. ‖ expendedor automático, vending machine. ‖ máquina expendedora, vending machine.

expender I t (*gastar*) to spend. **2** (*vender*) to sell. **3** (*vender al menudeo*) to retail, sell.

expensas fpl expenses, charges, costs.
● a expensas de, at the expense of.

experiencia I f (*gen*) experience. **2** (*experimento*) experiment.
● por experiencia, from experience.

experimentación f experimentation, experimenting, testing.

experimentado,-a I pp → **experimentar**. – **2** adj (*persona*) experienced. **3** (*método*) tested, tried.

experimental adj experimental.

experimentar I t (*hacer experimentos*) to experiment, test. **2** (*probar*) to test, try out. **3** (*sentir, notar*) to experience, feel; (*- cambio*) to undergo; (*- aumento*) to show; (*- pérdida, derrota*) to suffer.
● experimentar una mejoría, to improve, make progress.

experimento m experiment, test.
● hacer experimentos de, to perform experiments on.

expertamente adv expertly, skilfully (us skillfully).

experto,-a I adj expert. – **2** m,f expert.

expiación f expiation, atonement.

expiar t to expiate, atone for.
▲ *Conjugation model* [13], *like* **desviar**.

expiración f expiration; (*mes, plazo*) expiry.
■ fecha de expiración, expiry date.

expirar i to expire.

explanada f esplanade.

explanar I t (*allanar*) to level, grade. **2** *fig* (*explicar*) to explain, elucidate; (*aclarar*) to clear up.

explayar I t *fml* (*extender*) to extend, spread out. – **2 explayarse,** p (*dilatarse al hablar*) to dwell (**en,** on), talk at length (**en,** about). **3** (*confiarse*) to confide (**con,** in), open one's heart (**con,** to). **4** *fig* (*divertirse*) to amuse os., enjoy os.

explicable adj explicable, explainable.

explicación I f explanation. **2** (*motivo*) reason.
● sin dar explicaciones, without giving any reason.

explicaderas fpl *fam* way *sing* of explaining.
● tener buenas explicaderas, *fam* to be good at explaining things.

explicar I t (*gen*) to explain, expound, tell: *¿puedes explicar cómo desmontarlo?,* can you explain how to dismantle it?; *explícame por qué no viniste,* tell me why you didn't come. **2** (*justificar*) to justify: *no pudo explicar su presencia,* he couldn't justify his presence. – **3 explicarse,** p (*expresarse*) to explain os., make os. understood, make os. clear. **4** (*comprender*) to understand, make out: *no me lo explico,* I can't understand it.
● ¿me explico?, do you understand?
▲ *Conjugation model* [1], *like* **sacar**.

explicativo,-a adj explanatory.

explicitar t to state explicitly.

explícito,-a adj explicit.

exploración I f (*gen*) exploration. **2** TÉC scanning. **3** MIL reconnaissance.

explorador,-ra I adj exploring, exploratory. **2** MIL scouting. – **3** m,f (*persona*) explorer. **4** (*niño*) boy scout; (*niña*) girl guide, us girl scout. – **5 explorador,** m MED probe. **6** TÉC scanner. **7** MIL scout.

explorar I t (*gen*) to explore. **2** MED to probe. **3** MIL to reconnoitre. **4** TÉC to scan. **5** (*de mina*) to drill, prospect.

● **explorar el terreno,** *fig* to see how the land lies.
exploratorio,-a 1 *adj* exploratory. 2 MED exploratory, probing.
explosión 1 *f* explosion, blast, blowing up. 2 *fig* outburst.
● **hacer explosión,** to explode.
■ **explosión demográfica,** population explosion. ‖ **motor de explosión,** internal-combustion engine.
explosionar 1 *t* to explode. – 2 *i* to explode, blow up.
explosivo,-a 1 *adj* explosive. 2 LING plosive. – 3 explosivo, *m* explosive. – 4 explosiva, *f* LING plosive.
explotable 1 *adj* (*mina*) exploitable, workable. 2 (*terreno*) which can be farmed, which can be cultivated.
explotación 1 *f* (*gen*) exploitation. 2 (*de terreno*) cultivation, farming. 3 (*de industria*) running, operating. 4 (*de recursos*) tapping, exploitation. 5 *pey* (*abuso*) exploitation.
■ **explotación agrícola,** farm. ‖ **explotación forestal,** forestry. ‖ **explotación minera,** mine.
explotador,-ra *m,f pey* exploiter.
explotar 1 *t* (*sacar provecho*) to exploit; (*mina*) to work; (*tierra*) to cultivate; (*industria*) to operate, run; (*recursos*) to tap, exploit. 2 *pey* (*personas*) to exploit. 3 (*bomba*) to explode. – 4 *i* (*explosionar*) to explode, blow up.
expoliación *f* plundering, pillaging, despoiling.
expoliar *t* to plunder, pillage, despoil.
▲ *Conjugation model* [12], *like* **cambiar**.
expolio 1 *m* (*acción*) plundering, pillaging, despoiling. 2 (*botín*) loot, booty. 3 *fam* (*alboroto*) din, racket, row.
exponente 1 *adj* exponent, expounding. – 2 *m* MAT index, exponent. 3 (*prototipo*) exponent: *Gandhi fue el máximo exponente del pacifismo,* Gandhi was the greatest exponent of pacifism.
exponer 1 *t* (*explicar*) to expound, explain; (*propuesta*) to put forward; (*hechos*) to state, set out. 2 (*mostrar*) to show, exhibit; (*mercancías*) to display. 3 (*arriesgar*) to expose, risk, endanger. 4 (*al sol etc*) to expose. 5 (*un recién nacido*) to abandon. – 6 exponerse, *p* (*arriesgarse*) to expose os. (**a,** to), run the risk (**a,** of): *se ha expuesto a muchos peligros,* he has exposed himself to many dangers.
● **exponer mucho,** to take great risks, run a lot of risks.
▲ *Conjugation model* [78], *like* **poner**. *pp* **expuesto,-a**.
exportable *adj* exportable, for exportation.
exportación *f* export, exportation.
■ **artículos de exportación,** export items. ‖ **derechos de exportación,** export duties. ‖ **licencia de exportación,** export licence.
exportador,-ra 1 *adj* exporting. – 2 *m,f* exporter.
exportar *t* to export.
exposición 1 *f* (*de arte*) exhibition, show; (*de mercancías*) display. 2 (*explicación*) account, explanation; (*hechos, ideas*) exposé. 3 (*al sol etc*) exposure. 4 (*fotografía*) exposure. 5 (*riesgo*) risk.
■ **exposición universal,** world fair. ‖ **sala de exposiciones,** art gallery, gallery.
expositivo,-a *adj* explanatory.
expósito,-a 1 *adj* abandoned. – 2 *m,f* foundling.
expositor,-ra 1 *adj* exponent. – 2 *m,f* (*de teoría*) exponent; (*de arte*) exhibitor. – 3 expositor, *m* (*objeto*) display stand.
exprés 1 *adj* (*tren*) express. 2 (*café*) expresso, espresso. 3 (*olla*) pressure.
expresado,-a 1 *pp* → **expresar**. – 2 *adj* (*mencionado*) aforesaid, above-mentioned.

expresamente 1 *adv* (*específicamente*) specifically, expressly. 2 (*deliberadamente*) on purpose, deliberately.
expresar 1 *t* (*gen*) to express: *expresó los sentimientos del pueblo,* he expressed the feelings of the people. 2 (*manifestar*) to state; (*comunicar*) to convey. – 3 expresarse, *p* to express os.: *se expresa bien,* he expresses himself well.
expresión 1 *f* expression. – 2 expresiones, *fpl* greetings, regards.
● **perdone la expresión,** pardon the expression. ‖ **reducir algo a la mínima expresión,** to reduce sth. to the bare minimum.
■ **expresión corporal,** free expression.
expresionismo *m* expressionism.
expresionista 1 *adj* expressionist. – 2 *mf* expressionist.
expresivamente 1 *adv* (*con expresividad*) expressively. 2 (*con cariño*) affectionately.
expresivo,-a 1 *adj* (*elocuente*) expressive. 2 (*mirada*) meaningful; (*silencio*) eloquent. 3 (*afectuoso*) affectionate, warm.
● **ser poco expresivo,-a,** not to show one's feelings.
expreso,-a 1 *adj* (*especificado*) express. – 2 expreso, *m* (*tren*) express, express train. – 3 *adv* (*expresamente*) on purpose, deliberately.
● **con el fin expreso de,** with the express purpose of.
exprimidera *f* squeezer, US juicer.
exprimidor *m* squeezer, US juicer.
exprimir 1 *t* (*fruto*) to squeeze; (*zumo*) to squeeze out. 2 *fig* (*persona*) to exploit, bleed dry.
expropiación *f* expropriation.
expropiar *t* to expropriate.
▲ *Conjugation model* [12], *like* **cambiar**.
expuesto,-a 1 *pp* → **exponer**. – 2 *adj* (*peligroso*) dangerous, risky; (*sin protección*) exposed.
● **estar expuesto a algo,** to be exposed to sth.
expugnar *t* to take by storm.
expulsar 1 *t* (*expeler*) to expel, eject, throw out; (*humo etc*) to belch out. 2 DEP to send off. 3 (*alumno*) to expel; (*de universidad*) to send down, US expel.
expulsión 1 *f* expulsion, ejection. 2 (*dep*) sending off. 3 (*alumno*) expulsion; (*de universidad*) sending down, US expulsion.
expulso,-a *pp* → **expeler**.
expulsor,-ra 1 *adj* ejecting: *mecanismo expulsor,* ejector mechanism. – 2 expulsor, *m* TÉC ejector.
expurgación 1 *f* expurgation. 2 *fig* purge, purging.
expurgar 1 *t* to expurgate. 2 *fig* to purge.
▲ *Conjugation model* [7], *like* **llegar**.
expuse *pt indef* → **exponer**.
exquisitamente *adv* exquisitely.
exquisitez 1 *f* exquisiteness. 2 (*manjar*) delicacy.
exquisito,-a 1 *adj* (*gen*) exquisite. 2 (*gusto*) refined; (*sabor*) delicious, exquisite; (*lugar*) delightful, exquisite.
extasiado,-a 1 *pp* → **extasiar**. – 2 *adj* ecstatic.
● **quedarse extasiado,-a,** to go into ecstasies, go into raptures.
extasiar 1 *t* to enrapture. – 2 extasiarse, *p* to go into ecstasies, go into raptures.
▲ *Conjugation model* [13], *like* **desviar**.
éxtasis *m* ecstasy, rapture.
▲ *pl* **éxtasis**.
extemporáneo,-a 1 *adj* (*lluvia etc*) unseasonable. 2 (*inconveniente*) inappropriate, untimely, unfortunate.
extender 1 *t* (*mapa, papel*) to spread (out), open (out). 2 (*brazo etc*) to stretch (out); (*alas*) to spread. 3 (*mantequilla etc*) to spread. 4 (*documento*) to draw up; (*cheque*)

to make out; (*pasaporte, certificado*) to issue. **5** *fig* (*hacer mayor*) to extend, enlarge. **6** *fig* (*idea, creencia, noticia*) to spread. **– 7 extenderse,** *p* (*durar*) to extend, last: *el periodo que estudiaremos se extiende entre los siglos XVIII y XIX,* the period we're going to study goes from the 18th century to the 19th century. **8** (*terreno*) to stretch. **9** *fig* (*difundirse*) to spread, extend. **10** *fig* (*al hablar*) to enlarge, expand, go into detail.
▲ *Conjugation model* [28], *like* ***entender.***

extendido,-a **1** *pp* → **extender.** **– 2** *adj* (*difundido*) widespread. **3** (*mano etc*) outstretched.

extensamente **1** *adv* at length, extensively. **2** (*ampliamente*) widely.

extensible *adj* extendable: *mesa extensible,* extendable table.

extensión **1** *f* (*gen*) extension. **2** (*dimensión*) extent, size; (*superficie*) area, expanse. **3** (*duración*) duration, length. **4** (*de un escrito, discurso*) length. **5** MÚS range.
● **en toda la extensión de la palabra,** in every sense of the word. ‖ **por extensión,** by extension.

extensivo,-a *adj* extendable, extensive.
● **hacer algo extensivo,-a a algn.,** to extend sth. to sb. ‖ **ser extensivo,-a a,** to extend to, to apply to.

extenso,-a **1** *adj* (*amplio*) extensive, vast; (*grande*) large. **2** (*largo*) lengthy, long: *una carta extensa,* a long letter.
● **por extenso,** at length, in detail.

extensor,-ra **1** *adj* extending: *músculo extensor,* extensor muscle. **– 2 extensor,** *m* DEP chest expander.

extenuación **1** *f* (*agotamiento*) exhaustion. **2** (*debilidad*) weakening. **3** (*enflaquecimiento*) emaciation.

extenuado,-a **1** *pp* → **extenuar.** **– 2** *adj* (*agotado*) exhausted. **3** (*débil*) weak. **4** (*flaco*) emaciated.

extenuante *adj* exhausting.

extenuar **1** *t* (*agotar*) to exhaust. **2** (*debilitar*) to weaken. **– 3 extenuarse,** *p* (*agotarse*) to exhaust os., wear os. out.
▲ *Conjugation model* [11], *like* ***actuar.***

exterior **1** *adj* (*gen*) exterior, outer, external. **2** (*ventana, puerta*) outside; (*pared*) outer. **3** (*aspecto*) outward. **4** (*extranjero*) foreign: *política exterior,* foreign policy. **– 5** *m* (*superficie externa*) exterior, outside. **6** (*extranjero*) abroad, overseas. **7** (*de una persona*) appearance. **8** DEP outside. **– 9 exteriores,** *mpl* CINEM location shots.
■ **Ministerio de Asuntos Exteriores,** Ministry of Foreign Affairs, GB Foreign Office, US State Department.

exterioridad *f* outward appearance, external appearance.

exteriorización *f* manifestation, externalization.

exteriorizar *t* to show, reveal, express outwardly.
▲ *Conjugation model* [4], *like* ***realizar.***

exteriormente *adv* outwardly, externally.

exterminación *f* (*supresión*) extermination, wiping out; (*destrucción*) destruction.

exterminador,-ra **1** *adj* exterminating. **– 2** *m,f* exterminator.

exterminar *t* (*suprimir*) to exterminate, wipe out; (*destruir*) to destroy.

exterminio *m* extermination, wiping out; (*destrucción*) destruction.

externado *m* day school.

externamente *adv* externally, outwardly.

externo,-a **1** *adj* external, outward: *parte externa,* outside. **2** (*alumno*) day. **– 3** *m,f* (*alumno*) day pupil.
● **"de uso externo",** (*medicamentos*) "external use only".

extinción *f* extinction.

extinguir **1** *t* (*fuego etc*) to extinguish, put out. **2** (*especie, deuda, epidemia*) to wipe out. **– 3 extinguirse,** *p* (*fuego etc*) to go out. **4** (*especie etc*) to become extinct, die out. **5** (*amor*) to die away. **6** (*plazo*) to expire, run out.
▲ *Conjugation model* [8], *like* ***distinguir.***

extinto,-a **1** *adj* (*fuego etc*) extinguished, out. **2** (*raza etc*) extinct.

extintor *m* fire extinguisher.

extirpable **1** *adj* MED removable. **2** *fig* eradicable.

extirpación **1** *f* MED removal, extraction. **2** *fig* eradication, wiping out, stamping out.

extirpar **1** *t* MED to remove, extract. **2** *fig* to eradicate, wipe out, stamp out.

extorsión **1** *f* (*usurpación*) extortion. **2** *fig* (*molestia*) inconvenience, trouble.
● **causar extorsión a algn.,** to cause great inconvenience to sb., put sb. out.

extorsionar **1** *t* (*usurpar*) to extort, exact. **2** *fig* (*molestar*) to inconvenience, cause inconvenience to.

extra **1** *adj fam* extra. **2** *fam* (*superior*) top-quality, best-quality. **3** (*paga*) bonus. **– 4** *m* CINEM extra. **– 5** *m fam* (*gasto*) additional expense. **6** *fam* (*plus*) bonus. **– 7 la extra,** *f fam* (*paga*) bonus payment.
● **hacer un extra,** *fam* to give os. a treat, treat os.: *aunque estoy a régimen hoy he hecho un extra y me he comido un trozo de pastel,* although I'm on a diet I've given myself a treat today and had a piece of cake.
■ **horas extras,** overtime. ‖ **paga extra,** bonus.

extra- *pref* extra-.

extracción **1** *f* (*gen*) extraction; (*de lotería*) draw. **2** (*origen*) descent, extraction.
■ **extracción de datos,** INFORM data retrieval.

extractar *t* to summarize.

extracto **1** *m* (*substancia*) extract. **2** (*trozo*) extract, excerpt. **3** (*resumen*) summary.
■ **extracto de cuenta,** statement of account, bank statement.

extractor *m* extractor.

extracurricular *adj* extracurricular.

extradición *f* extradition.
● **otorgar la extradición de algn.,** to extradite sb.

extradir *t* to extradite.

extraditar *t* to extradite.

extradós *m* extrados.

extraer **1** *t* to extract, take out: *le han extraído las muelas del juicio,* they've taken his wisdom teeth out. **2** QUÍM MAT to extract. **3** (*conclusión*) to draw, reach.
▲ *Conjugation model* [88], *like* ***traer.***

extraescolar *adj* out of school, extracurricular.
■ **actividades extraescolares,** out-of-school activities.

extrafino,-a *adj* superfine, best quality.
■ **azucar extrafino,** castor sugar. ‖ **chocolate extrafino,** superfine chocolate.

extrajudicial *adj* extrajudicial.

extralimitación *f* abuse.

extralimitarse *p fig* to go too far, overstep.
● **extralimitarse en sus funciones,** *fig* to exceed one's authority.

extramuros *adv* outside the city.

extranjería *f* status of foreigners.
■ **ley de extranjería,** immigration law.

extranjerismo *m* foreign expression.

extranjerizar *t* to introduce foreign customs into, foreignize.
▲ *Conjugation model* [4], *like* ***realizar.***

extranjero,-a 1 *adj* foreign, alien. – 2 *m,f* foreigner. – 3 extranjero, *m* foreign countries *pl*, abroad: *ir al extranjero,* to go abroad.
● **del extranjero,** from abroad. ‖ **en el extranjero,** abroad.

extranjis de extranjis, *loc adv fam* secretly, on the sly.

extrañamente *adv* strangely, oddly.

extrañamiento 1 *m* (*destierro*) banishment, exile. 2 (*sorpresa*) surprise, astonishment.

extrañar 1 *t* (*sorprender*) to surprise: *me extraña que no lo hayas visto,* I'm surprised you haven't seen it. 2 (*notar extraño*) to find strange, not to be used to: *extraño esta cama,* I'm not used to this bed. 3 (*desterrar*) to banish, exile. – 4 extrañarse, *p* (*desterrarse*) to go into exile. 5 (*sorprenderse*) to be surprised (**de/por,** at).
● **no es de extrañar,** it's hardly surprising, (it's) no wonder: *no es de extrañar que te echaran,* no wonder they threw you out.

extrañeza 1 *f* strangeness. 2 (*sorpresa*) surprise, wonder, astonishment.
● **causar extrañeza,** to surprise.

extraño,-a 1 *adj* (*no conocido*) alien, foreign: *cuerpo extraño,* foreign body. 2 (*particular*) strange, peculiar, odd, funny: *vimos una cosa extraña anoche,* we saw something strange last night. – 3 *m,f* stranger: *es un extraño en su familia,* he's a stranger to his family.
● **no es extraño que ...,** it is not surprising that ... ‖ **ser extraño,-a a algo,** to have nothing to do with sth.

extraoficial 1 *adj* unofficial, informal. 2 (*declaración etc*) off-the-record.

extraordinariamente *adv* extraordinarily, unusually.

extraordinario,-a 1 *adj* (*fuera de lo común*) extraordinary, unusual; (*sorprendente*) surprising; (*admirable*) outstanding, exceptional. 2 (*raro*) queer, odd. 3 (*gastos etc*) additional, extra; (*paga*) bonus. 4 (*revista etc*) special. – 5 extraordinario, *m* (*correo*) special delivery. – 6 (*revista etc*) special issue. 7 (*manjar*) extra dish. – 8 extraordinaria, *f* (*paga*) bonus payment.
■ **horas extraordinarias,** overtime.

extraplano,-a *adj* slimline.

extrapolar *t* to extrapolate.

extrarradio *m* outskirts *pl*, suburbs *pl*.

extrasensorial *adj* extrasensory.

extraterreno,-a *adj* extraterrestrial, extramundane.

extraterrestre 1 *adj* extramundane, extraterrestrial. – 2 *mf* alien.

extraterritorialidad *f* extraterritoriality.

extraterritorial *adj* extraterritorial.

extrauterino,-a *adj* extra-uterine: *embarazo extrauterino,* ectopic pregnancy.

extravagancia *f* extravagance, eccentricity.

extravagante 1 *adj* (*comportamiento*) extravagant outrageous; (*persona, ropa*) flamboyant. – 2 *mf* flamboyant person.

extravasar 1 *t* to extravasate. – 2 extravasarse, *p* to extravasate.

extravenarse *p* to extravasate.

extraversión *f* extraversion.

extravertido,-a *adj-m,f* → **extrovertido,-a**.

extraviado,-a 1 *pp* → **extraviar.** – 2 *adj* (*disoluto*) dissolute. 3 (*perdido - persona, objeto*) missing, lost; (*- perro, niño*) stray. 4 (*lugar*) out-of-the-way. 5 (*vista*) vacant.

extraviar 1 *t* (*persona*) to mislead. 2 (*objeto*) to mislay, lose. 3 (*desorientar*) to make get lost. 4 (*pervertir*) to lead astray. – 5 extraviarse, *p* (*persona*) to get lost, lose one's way. 6 (*objeto*) to get mislaid. 7 *fig* (*descarriarse*) to go astray. 8 *fig* (*errar*) to be mistaken.

▲ *Conjugation model* [13], *like* **desviar**.

extravío 1 *m* (*persona*) misleading; (*cosa*) loss, mislaying. 2 *fig* (*perversión*) deviation, leading astray. 3 *fig* (*error*) mistake, error.

extremadamente *adv* extremely.

extremado,-a 1 *pp* → **extremar.** – 2 *adj* extreme.

Extremadura *f* Estremadura.

extremar 1 *t* to carry to extremes, carry to the limit, overdo: *han extremado los preparativos,* they've overdone the preparations. – 2 extremarse, *p* to do one's best, do one's utmost, take great pains: *se ha extremado en acabarlo,* she's done her utmost to finish it.
● **extremar la prudencia,** to be extremely careful.

extremaunción *f* extreme unction.

extremeño,-a 1 *adj* Estremaduran. – 2 *m,f* Estremaduran.

extremidad 1 *f* (*parte extrema*) extremity; (*punta*) end, tip. 2 ANAT limb, extremity.

extremis in extremis, *loc adv* as a last resort: *un intento in extremis de evitar la huelga,* a last-ditch attempt to stop the strike; *un gol in extremis fue anulado por el colegiado,* a last-minute goal was disallowed by the referee.

extremismo *m* extremism.

extremista 1 *adj* extremist. – 2 *mf* extremist.

extremo,-a 1 *adj* (*exagerado*) extreme: *calor extremo,* extreme heat; *extrema vejez,* extreme old age. 2 (*distante*) further. 3 *fig* (*intenso*) utmost. – 4 extremo, *m* (*punta*) extreme, end: *el extremo de la calle,* the end of the street. 5 (*punto último*) point, extreme: *pasar de un extremo a otro,* to go from one extreme to another; *llegó al extremo de mendigar por la calle,* she got to the point of begging in the street. 6 (*asunto, materia*) matter, question. 7 DEP wing.
● **en caso extremo,** as a last resort. ‖ **en extremo,** extremely, very much. ‖ **en último extremo,** as a last resort. ‖ **hasta tal extremo,** to such a point. ‖ **los extremos se tocan,** *fig* extremes meet. ‖ **pasar de un extremo a otro,** to go from one extreme to another. ■ **Extremo Oriente,** Far East. ‖ **extremo-derecha,** (*fútbol*) outside-right. ‖ **extremo-izquierda,** (*fútbol*) outside-left.

extremoso,-a 1 *adj* effusive, demonstrative. 2 (*vehemente*) extreme, excessive.

extrínseco,-a *adj* extrinsic.

extroversión *f* extroversion.

extrovertido,-a 1 *adj* extroverted, extraverted. – 2 *m,f* extrovert, extravert.

extrudir *t* to extrude.

extrusión *f* extrusion.

exuberancia *f* exuberance.

exuberante 1 *adj* exuberant. 2 (*vegetación*) lush, abundant.

exudar 1 *i* to exude, ooze (out). – 2 *t* to exude, ooze (out).

exultación *f* exultation.

exultar *i* to rejoice, exult.
● **exultar de alegría,** to jump for joy.

exvoto *m* votive offering.

eyaculación *f* ejaculation.
■ **eyaculación precoz,** premature ejaculation.

eyacular *i* to ejaculate.

eyección *f* ejection.

eyectable *adj* ejectable: *asiento eyectable,* ejector seat.

eyectar *t* to eject.

eyector *m* ejector.

F

F, f *f* (*la letra*) F, f.
F *sím* (*Fahrenheit*) Fahrenheit; (*símbolo*) F.
f^a *abr* (*franco a bordo*) free on board; (*abreviatura*) FOB.
f.ª *abr* (*factura*) invoice.
f° *abr* (*folio*) folio; (*abreviatura*) fo.
fa *m* F.
fa. *abr* (*franco a bordo*) free on board; (*abreviatura*) FOB.
fabada *f* bean stew *including pork sausage and bacon.*
fábrica 1 *f* (*industria*) factory, plant. 2 (*fabricación*) manufacture. 3 ARQ masonry: *las paredes son de fábrica,* the walls are made of stone.
■ **fábrica de cerveza,** brewery. ‖ **fábrica de conservas,** cannery, canning factory. ‖ **fábrica de gas,** gasworks. ‖ **fábrica de harina,** flour mill. ‖ **fábrica de montaje,** assembly plant. ‖ **fábrica de papel,** paper mill. ‖ **precio de fábrica,** factory price, ex-works price.
fabricación *f* manufacture, production, making.
● **de fabricación casera,** home-made. ‖ **de fabricación propia,** our own make.
■ **defecto de fabricación,** manufacturing fault. ‖ **fabricación en cadena,** mass production. ‖ **productos de fabricación defectuosa,** seconds.
fabricante *mf* manufacturer, maker.
fabricar 1 *t* (*producir*) to make, manufacture, produce. 2 *fig* (*inventar*) to fabricate, invent.
● **fabricado,-a en España,** made in Spain. ‖ **fabricar en serie,** to mass-produce.
▲ *Conjugation model* [1], *like* **sacar.**
fabril *adj* manufacturing.
fábula 1 *f* LIT fable. 2 (*mito*) myth, legend. 3 (*mentira*) invention.
● **de fábula,** *fam* smashing, fabulous: *el examen me ha ido de fábula,* the exam went really well.
fabular 1 *t* (*contar fábulas*) to fable. 2 (*imaginar*) to imagine.
fabulista *mf* writer of fables.
fabuloso,-a 1 *adj* (*fantástico*) fabulous, fantastic. 2 LIT fabulous, mythical.
faca *f* large *curved* knife.
facción 1 *f* POL faction. – 2 **facciones,** *fpl* (*rasgos*) facial features, features.
faccioso,-a 1 *adj* factious, seditious. – 2 *m,f* rebel.
faceta *f* facet.
facha[1] 1 *f* *fam* (*aspecto*) appearance, look: *ese chico tiene muy buena facha,* that boy's really good-looking. 2 (*mamarracho*) mess, sight.
● **estar hecho,-a una facha,** to look a mess, look a sight.
facha[2] 1 *adj* *pey* fascist. – 2 *mf* *pey* fascist, extreme rightwinger.
fachada 1 *f* ARQ façade, front. 2 *fam* (*apariencia*) outward show.
● **con fachada a,** facing, overlooking.
fachado,-a 1 **bien fachado,-a,** *adj* *fam* good-looking. 2 **mal fachado,-a,** *fam* ugly.

fachenda 1 *f* (*actitud*) swankiness, conceit. – 2 *mf* (*persona*) swank, show-off.
fachendear *i* *fam* to swank, show-off.
fachendoso,-a *adj* *fam* swanky.
fachoso,-a *adj* *fam* odd-looking.
facial *adj* facial.
fácil 1 *adj* easy. 2 (*probable*) probable, likely: *no es muy fácil que vengan,* they're not likely to come. 3 *pey* (*mujer*) loose.
facilidad 1 *f* (*simplicidad*) ease, facility: *ya puede caminar con gran facilidad,* he can already walk well. 2 (*aptitud*) talent, gift: *tiene facilidad para la música,* he has a gift for music. 3 **facilidades,** (*medios que facilitan*) facilities: *nos dieron facilidades de financiación,* we were given favourable terms.
■ **facilidad de palabra,** fluency. ‖ "**facilidades de pago**", "easy terms".
facilitación 1 *f* (*simplificación*) facilitation. 2 (*abastecimiento*) provision, supply.
facilitar 1 *t* (*simplificar*) to make easy, make easier, facilitate. 2 (*proporcionar*) to provide with, supply with: *nos facilitaron información muy útil,* they provided us with some very useful information. 3 (*concertar entrevista etc*) to arrange: *nos facilitó una entrevista para el martes,* she arranged a meeting for us on Tuesday.
fácilmente *adv* easily.
facilón,-ona 1 *adj* *fam* (*muy fácil*) dead easy. 2 (*trivial*) hackneyed, lacking originality.
facineroso,-a *m,f* criminal.
facistol *m* (*atril*) lectern.
facsímil *m* facsimile.
facsímile *m* facsimile.
factible *adj* feasible, practicable, workable.
facticio,-a *adj* factitious, artificial.
fáctico,-a 1 *adj* (*relativo a hechos*) factual, of fact: *es una simple cuestión fáctica,* it's a simple question of fact. 2 (*basado en hechos*) factual, real, actual.
■ **poderes fácticos,** extraparlamentary political powers.
factor 1 *m* (*gen*) factor. 2 (*empleado de ferrocarriles*) luggage clerk.
factoría 1 *f* COM trading post. 2 (*fábrica*) factory, mill.
factótum 1 *m* (*empleado*) factotum. 2 (*persona entremetida*) busybody. 3 (*persona de confianza*) right-hand man.
▲ *pl* **factotums.**
factura *f* invoice, bill.
● **pasar factura a, presentar factura a,** to invoice, send a bill to. ‖ **pasar factura,** *fig* to make sb. pay; (*traer consecuencias*) to take its toll: *me ayudó mucho pero después me pasó factura,* I paid dearly for his help; *beber mucho acaba pasando factura,* heavy drinking takes its toll.
■ **factura pro forma,** pro forma invoice.
facturación 1 *f* COM invoicing. 2 (*de equipajes*) registration, check-in.

facturar 1 *t* COM to invoice, charge for. 2 (*equipaje*) to register, check in.

facultad 1 *f* (*capacidad*) faculty, ability. 2 (*poder*) faculty, power. 3 (*universitaria*) faculty, school.
● **tener facultad para hacer algo,** to be authorized to do sth.
■ **facultades mentales,** mental powers.

facultar *t* to empower, authorize.

facultativo,-a 1 *adj* (*opcional*) optional. 2 (*profesional*) professional. – 3 *m,f* doctor, physician.

facundia *f* verbosity, wordiness, long-windedness.

facundo,-a *adj* (*locuaz*) verbose, wordy, long-winded; (*parlanchín*) talkative.

fado *m* fado (*type of Portuguese folk song*).

faena 1 *f* (*tarea*) task, job. 2 *fam* (*mala pasada*) dirty trick. 3 (*tauromaquia*) performance.
● **estar metido,-a en faena,** *fam* to be hard at work.
■ **faenas agrícolas,** agricultural work. ‖ **faenas de la casa,** housework *sing*, household chores. ‖ **mujer de la faena,** cleaning lady, home help.

faenar 1 *i* (*pescar*) to fish. 2 (*laborar*) to work. – 3 *t* (*matar reses*) to slaughter.

faetón *m* phaeton.

fagocito *m* phagocyte.

fagot 1 *m* (*instrumento*) bassoon. – 2 *mf* (*músico*) bassoonist.

FAI *abr* POL (*Federación Anarquista Ibérica*) Spanish anarchist federation.

fair play *m* fair play.

faisán *m* pheasant.

faja 1 *f* (*cinturón*) band, belt. 2 (*ropa interior*) corset, girdle. 3 (*banda*) sash. 4 (*correo*) wrapper. 5 (*franja de terreno*) strip.

fajar *t* to bind, wrap.

fajín *m* sash.

fajina 1 *f* (*haces de mies*) rick. 2 (*haz de leña*) brushwood, kindling.

fajo *m* bundle; (*de billetes*) wad.

fakir *m* fakir.

falacia 1 *f* (*error*) fallacy. 2 (*engaño*) deceit, trick. 3 (*hábito de engañar*) deceitfulness.

falange 1 *f* ANAT phalange, phalanx. 2 MIL phalanx. 3 (*movimiento político*) the Spanish Falangist Movement.

falangismo *m* Falangist Movement.

falangista 1 *adj* Falangist. – 2 *mf* Falangist.

falaz 1 *adj* (*erróneo*) fallacious. 2 (*engañoso*) deceitful, false.

falca *f* wedge.

falda 1 *f* (*prenda*) skirt. 2 (*regazo*) lap. 3 (*ladera*) slope. 4 (*corte de carne*) brisket. 5 (*de mesa camilla*) tablecloth. – 6 **faldas,** *fpl fam fig* (*mujeres*) women, girls: *dimitió porque le descubrieron un lío de faldas,* he resigned after being caught having an affair.
● **andar siempre entre faldas,** to be always with women. ‖ **andar pegado,-a a las faldas de la madre,** to be tied to one's mother's apron strings.
■ **falda escocesa,** kilt. ‖ **falda pantalón,** culottes *pl*.
▲ In 5 *also used in plural with the same meaning.*

faldero,-a *adj* (*mujeriego*) fond of women.

faldillas *fpl* tails.

faldón 1 *m* (*de traje*) coat-tail; (*de camisa*) shirt-tail. 2 (*prenda de bebé*) wrap-around skirt. 3 (*de tejado*) gable.

faldriquera *f* → **faltriquera.**

falibilidad *f* fallibility.

falible *adj* fallible.

fálico,-a *adj* phallic.

falla[1] 1 *f* (*defecto*) defect, fault. 2 GEOG fault.

falla[2] 1 *f* (*figura*) cardboard figure burnt on Saint Joseph's Day in Valencia. – 2 **las fallas,** *fpl* firework celebrations held in Valencia on Saint Joseph's Day.

fallar[1] 1 *i* JUR to pass sentence, pass judgement. 2 (*premio*) to award a prize. – 3 *t* JUR to pass, pronounce. 4 (*premio*) to award.

fallar[2] 1 *i* (*fracasar, no funcionar*) to fail. 2 (*puntería*) to miss; (*plan*) to go wrong. 3 (*ceder*) to give way, collapse. – 4 *t* (*en naipes*) to trump.

falleba *f* espagnolette.

fallecer *i fml* to pass away, die.
▲ Conjugation model [43], *like* **agradecer.**

fallecido,-a *adj* deceased.

fallecimiento *m* decease, demise.

fallido,-a *adj* unsuccessful, frustrated.
■ **deuda fallida,** COM bad debt.

fallo[1] 1 *m* JUR judgement, ruling. 2 (*en concurso*) decision.

fallo[2] 1 *m* (*error*) mistake, blunder; (*fracaso*) failure. 2 (*defecto*) fault, defect.

fallo,-a *adj* (*naipes*) void.

falo *m* phallus.

falocracia *f* male chauvinism.

falócrata *m* male chauvinist, male chauvinist pig.

falsario,-a 1 *m,f* (*mentiroso*) liar. 2 (*falsificador*) forger, counterfeiter.

falseamiento *m* falsification.

falsear 1 *t* (*deformar un informe etc*) to falsify; (*unos hechos, la verdad*) to distort. 2 (*falsificar*) to counterfeit, forge. 3 (*en construcción*) to bevel. – 4 *i* (*perder consistencia*) to sag. 5 MÚS to be dissonant, be out of tune.

falsedad 1 *f* (*hipocresía*) falseness, hypocrisy; (*doblez*) duplicity. 2 (*mentira*) falsehood, lie.

falsete *m* falsetto.

falsía *f* (*hipocresía*) falseness, hypocrisy; (*doblez*) duplicity.

falsificación 1 *f* (*acto*) falsification; (*de firma, cuadro*) forging, forgery; (*de dinero*) counterfeiting. 2 (*objeto*) forgery.

falsificador,-ra 1 *adj* (*de firma, cuadro*) forging; (*de dinero*) counterfeiting. – 2 *m,f* (*de firma, cuadro*) forger; (*de dinero*) counterfeiter.

falsificar 1 *t* (*gen*) to falsify. 2 (*firma, cuadro*) to forge; (*dinero*) to counterfeit, forge.
▲ Conjugation model [1], *like* **sacar.**

falsilla *f* writing guide, guide sheet.

falso,-a 1 *adj* (*no verdadero*) false, untrue. 2 (*moneda*) false, counterfeit; (*cuadro, sello*) forged. 3 (*persona*) insincere, false; (*sonrisa*) false. – 4 *m,f* (*persona*) insincere person.
● **dar un paso en falso,** (*tropezar*) to trip, stumble; (*cometer un error*) to make a mistake, make a wrong move. ‖ **en falso,** (*con falsedad*) falsely; (*sin apoyo*) without proper support. ‖ **jurar en falso,** to commit perjury.

falta 1 *f* (*carencia*) lack: *falta de sensibilidad,* lack of sensitivity. 2 (*escasez*) shortage: *existe una falta de agua,* there is a water shortage. 3 (*ausencia*) absence. 4 (*error*) mistake: *has hecho una falta de ortografía,* you've made a spelling mistake. 5 (*defecto*) fault, defect. 6 (*mala acción*) misdeed. 7 MED missed period. 8 JUR misdemeanour (*us* misdemeanor). 9 DEP (*fútbol*) foul; (*tenis*) fault.
● **a falta de ...,** for want of ..., for lack of ... ‖ **coger a algn. en falta,** to catch sb. out. ‖ **echar en falta,** to miss. ‖ **hacer falta,** to be necessary: *hizo falta un martillo,* we needed a hammer. ‖ **no hace falta que ...,** there is no need for ... ‖ **pillar a algn. en falta,** to catch sb. out. ‖ **poner falta a algn.,** to mark sb. absent. ‖ **por**

falta de ..., → **a falta de**. ‖ sacar faltas a, to find fault with. ‖ sacar una falta, DEP to take a free kick. ‖ **sin falta,** without fail. ‖ **tirar una falta,** DEP to take a free kick. ‖ ¡falta hacía!, and about time too!
■ **falta de educación,** bad manners *pl.* ‖ **falta de pago,** nonpayment.

faltar 1 *i (no estar una cosa)* to be missing; *(una persona)* to be absent: *me falta un zapato,* one of my shoes is missing; *¿quién falta?,* who's missing?; *ha faltado mucho a clase,* he has missed a lot of classes; *mañana a las tres, ¡no faltes!,* tomorrow at three, be sure to come! **2** *(haber poco)* to be lacking, be needed: *falta (más) leche,* we need (more) milk, there isn't enough milk. **3** *(no tener)* to lack, not have (enough): *le falta genio,* she's got no character. **4** *(quedar)* to remain, be left: *¿cuánto falta para Alicante?,* how much further is it to Alicante?; *falta poco para que ...,* it won't be long till ...; *falta mucho por hacer,* there's still a lot to be done. **5** *(no respetar)* to insult, be rude to: *no la perdonaré que me faltara,* I'll never forgive her for being rude to me.
● faltar a la verdad, not to tell the truth, lie. ‖ faltar a su deber, to fail in one's duty. ‖ faltar a su palabra, to break one's word. ‖ faltar a su promesa, not to keep one's promise. ‖ faltar al respeto a algn., to be rude to sb., insult sb. ‖ faltar en los pagos, not to keep up with the payments. ‖ ¡lo que me *(te, le, etc)* faltaba!, that's all I *(you, he, etc)* needed! ‖ ¡no faltaba más!, *(por supuesto)* of course!, but of course!; *(por supuesto que no)* absolutely not! ‖ ¡sólo me *(te, le, etc)* faltaba eso!, that's all I *(you, he, etc)* needed!

falto,-a falto,-a de, *adj* lacking, without, short of: *estamos faltos de dinero,* we're short of money; *el país está falto de recursos,* the country lacks resources.

faltón,-ona 1 *adj (informal)* unreliable. **2** *(grosero)* rude, disrespectful.

faltriquera *f* fob.
● rascarse la faltriquera, *fam* to dig into one's pocket.

falúa *f* launch.

falucho *m* felucca.

fama 1 *f (renombre)* fame, renown. **2** *(reputación)* reputation.
● de fama, famous. ‖ de fama mundial, world-famous. ‖ tener buena fama, to have a good name. ‖ tener mala fama, to have a bad name.

famélico,-a *adj* starving, famished.

familia 1 *f* family. **2** *(prole)* children *pl,* family.
● acordarse de la familia de algn., *fam* to insult sb. ‖ en familia, *(con la familia)* with the family; *(con muy poca gente)* in private. ‖ estar en familia, to be among friends. ‖ sentirse como en familia, to feel at home, feel like one of the family. ‖ ser como de la familia, to be like one of the family. ‖ ser de buena familia, to come from a good family. ‖ ser de familia humilde, to be of humble origin. ‖ venir algo de familia, to run in the family.
■ familia numerosa, large family. ‖ familia política, in-laws *pl.* ‖ la Sagrada Familia, the Holy Family.

familiar 1 *adj (de la familia)* family, of the family. **2** *(conocido)* familiar, well-known. **3** *(tamaño)* family. **4** LING colloquial. – **5** *mf* relation, relative.

familiaridad *f* familiarity, informality.

familiarizar 1 *t* to familiarize (con, with), make familiar (con, with): *ha familiarizado a todo el mundo con la música clásica,* he has familiarized everyone with classical music. **2 familiarizarse,** *p* to get to know, familiarize os.: *familiarízate con el teclado,* get to know the keyboard, get used to the keyboard.

▲ Conjugation model [4], *like realizar*.

familiarmente *adv* familiarly.

famoso,-a 1 *adj* famous, well-known. – **2** los famosos, *mpl* the famous.

fan *mf* fan, admirer.
● ser un,-a fan de algo, to be mad about sth.

fanal 1 *m (farol grande)* beacon. **2** *(campana)* bell glass.

fanático,-a 1 *adj* fanatic, fanatical. – **2** *m,f* fanatic.

fanatismo *m* fanaticism.

fanatizar *t* to make a fanatic.

▲ Conjugation model [4], *like realizar*.

fandango 1 *m* MÚS fandango. **2** *fam (jaleo)* row, rumpus.

fandanguero,-a *m,f fam* reveller (US reveler).

fandanguillo *m type of* fandango.

fanega 1 *f (medida de grano - en Castilla)* unit of dry measure equivalent to 55.5 litres or 1.58 bushels; *(- en Aragón)* unit of dry measure equivalent to 22.4 litres or 0.64 bushels. **2** *(medida de superficie)* unit of area equivalent to 6,460 square metres or 1.59 acres.

fanerógamo,-a 1 *adj* phanerogam, phanerogamous. – **2** fanerógamo, *m* phanerogam.

fanfarria 1 *f* MÚS fanfare. **2** *fam (bravata)* boasting, bragging, showing-off.

fanfarrón,-ona 1 *adj fam* swanky, boastful. – **2** *m,f* show-off, swank, braggart.

fanfarronada 1 *f fam (chulería)* showing off, swanking. **2** *fam (bravata)* brag, boast.

fanfarronear 1 *i fam (chulear)* to show off, swank. **2** *(bravear)* to brag, boast.

fanfarronería *f →* fanfarronada.

fangal *m* mire, quagmire, bog.

fango 1 *m (barro)* mud, mire. **2** *fig* degradation.

fangoso,-a *adj* muddy, miry.

fantasear 1 *i (forjar en la imaginación)* to daydream, dream. **2** *(presumir)* to boast, show off. – **3** *t (imaginar)* dream.

fantasía 1 *f (imaginación)* fantasy. **2** *(irrealidad)* fancy.
● de fantasía, *(gen)* fancy; *(joya)* imitation. ‖ tener mucha fantasía, to be too full of imagination.

▲ In **2** also used in plural with the same meaning.

fantasioso,-a *adj* imaginative.

fantasma 1 *m (espectro)* phantom, ghost. **2** *fam (fanfarrón)* braggart, show-off.

fantasmagoría *f* phantasmagoria.

fantasmal *adj* ghostly.

fantásticamente 1 *adv (con fantasía)* fantastically. **2** *(estupendamente)* wonderfully.

fantástico,-a 1 *adj* fantastic. **2** *(estupendo)* wonderful.

fantochada *f fam* foolish act, silly thing.

fantoche 1 *m (títere)* puppet, marionette. **2** *pey (fanfarrón)* braggart, show-off. **3** *pey (mamarracho)* nincompoop, ninny: *iba hecho un fantoche con aquel sombrero,* he looked ridiculous with that hat on.

faquir *m* fakir.

farad *m* farad.

faradio *m* farad.

faralá *m* flounce, frill.

▲ Often used in plural faralaes.

farallón *m* crag, rock.

faramalla 1 *f (charla)* blarney, patter. **2** *(farfolla)* bauble.

farándula 1 *f (compañía de teatro)* group of strolling players. **2** *(profesión, mundo del teatro)* acting, the theatre (US theater), the stage. **3** *fam fig (charla embrollada)* blarney.

farandulero,-a 1 *m,f (actor)* strolling player. **2** *(hablador y engañador)* confidence trickster, con man.

faraón *m* Pharaoh.

faraónico,-a *adj* Pharaonic.

fardada 1 *f arg* (*acción*) show, display: *se pegó una fardada, dijo que había aprobado sin estudiar,* he boasted that he'd passed the exam without working. **2** *arg* (*objeto*) flash thing: *esa moto es una fardada,* that motorbike's really flash.

fardar 1 *i arg* (*presumir*) to show off, swank: *siempre anda fardando de coche,* he's always showing off his car. **2** (*lucir*) to be classy, be flash: *ese coche farda mucho,* it's a really flash car.

fardo *m* (*paquete*) bundle, pack.
● estar hecho,-a un fardo, *fam* to be really fat.

fardón,-ona *adj arg* classy, flash.

farero,-a *m,f* lighthouse keeper.

farfolla 1 *f* BOT husk. **2** (*cosa sin importancia*) worthless thing.

farfulla *f* gabble.

farfullador,-ra *m,f* gabbler, jabberer.

farfullar *t* to gabble, jabber.

farfullero,-a 1 *adj* (*tartamudo*) gabbling, jabbering. **2** (*chapucero*) slapdash, shoddy.

faria *f* kind of cigar.
▲ *Registered trademark.*

farináceo,-a *adj* starchy, farinaceous.

faringe *f* pharynx.

faríngeo,-a *adj* pharyngeal.

faringitis *f* pharyngitis.
▲ *pl faringitis.*

farisaico,-a 1 *adj* Pharisaic, Pharisaical. **2** *fig* (*falso*) hypocritical.

fariseísmo 1 *m* Phariseeism. **2** *fig* (*falsedad*) hypocrisy.

fariseo,-a 1 *m,f* Pharisee. **2** *fig* (*falso*) hypocrite.

farmacéutico,-a 1 *adj* pharmaceutical. **– 2** *m,f* (*licenciado*) pharmacist. **3** (*en una farmacia*) chemist, US druggist, pharmacist.

farmacia 1 *f* (*estudios*) pharmacology. **2** (*tienda*) chemist's (shop), US drugstore, pharmacy.

fármaco *m* medicine, medication.

farmacología *f* pharmacology.

farmacológico,-a *adj* pharmacological.

farmacólogo,-a *m,f* pharmacologist, pharmacist.

faro 1 *m* (*torre*) lighthouse, beacon. **2** (*coche*) headlight. **3** *fig* (*guía*) guiding light, guide.

farol 1 *m* (*luz*) lantern; (*farola*) streetlamp, streetlight. **2** *arg* (*fardada*) bragging, swank; (*engaño*) bluff. **3** *arg* (*en juegos de naipes*) bluff.
● ¡adelante con los faroles!, come on then!, keep it up! ‖ marcarse un farol, *fam* to brag, boast, swank. ‖ tirarse un farol, *fam* to brag, boast, swank.
■ farol de situación, navigation lights *pl.*

farola *f* streetlight, streetlamp; (*de gas*) gas lamp.

farolear *i fam* to brag, boast, swank.

farolero,-a 1 *adj fam* (*que fanfarronea*) boastful. **– 2** *m,f fam* (*fanfarrón*) show-off. **– 3 farolero,** *m* (*de profesión*) lamplighter.

farolillo 1 *m* (*farol de papel*) Chinese lantern. **2** BOT Canterbury bell.
■ el farolillo rojo, the last one.

farra *f fam* binge, spree.
● ir de farra, to go out on the town.

fárrago *m* hotch-potch, jumble.

farragoso,-a *adj* confused, rambling.

farruco,-a *adj fam* conceited, cocky.

farsa 1 *f* TEAT farce. **2** (*enredo*) sham, farce.

farsante 1 *adj* lying, deceitful. **– 2** *mf* fake, impostor.

fas por fas o por nefas, *loc adv* by hook or by crook, by any means.

fascículo *m* fascicle, instalment (US installment): *esta enciclopedia se vende en fascículos semanales,* this encyclopaedia is sold in weekly instalments.

fascinación *f* fascination.

fascinador,-ra *adj* fascinating.

fascinante *adj* fascinating.

fascinar *t* to fascinate, captivate.

fascismo *m* fascism.

fascista 1 *adj* fascist. **– 2** *mf* fascist.

fase 1 *f* (*etapa*) phase, stage. **2** (*en electricidad*) phase.

fastidiado,-a 1 *adj* (*hastiado*) sickened, disgusted. **2** (*molesto*) annoyed. **3** (*dañado*) damaged, in bad condition. **4** *fam* (*estropeado*) ruined, spoilt. **5** *fam* (*mal de salud*) ill, sick, in a bad way; (*órgano, miembro*) bad: *su madre está bastante fastidiada,* his mother is in a bad way; *tenía el estómago fastidiado,* she had a bad stomach.
● estar fastidiado,-a de, andar fastidiado,-a de ..., *fam* to have a bad ...: *anda fastidiado del corazón,* he has a bad heart.

fastidiar 1 *t* (*hastiar*) to sicken, disgust. **2** (*molestar*) to annoy, bother: *me fastidia tener que salir,* it's a nuisance having to go out. **3** (*partes del cuerpo*) to hurt: *le fastidia el estómago,* he's got a bad stomach. **4** *fam* (*estropear*) to damage, ruin; (*planes*) to spoil, upset, mess up: *la lluvia nos fastidió los planes,* the rain spoilt our plans. **– 5 fastidiarse,** *p* (*aguantarse*) to put up with, grin and bear it: *si no le gusta el plan que se fastidie,* if he doesn't like the plan he can lump it. **6** *fam* (*estropearse*) to go wrong, break down: *se ha fastidiado la tele,* the telly has gone wrong. **7** (*lastimarse*) to hurt os., injure os.: *me he fastidiado los dedos,* I've hurt my fingers.
● ¡a fastidiarse tocan!, we'll have to grin and bear it! ‖ ¡no fastidies!, *fam* you're kidding! ‖ ¡que se fastidie!, *fam* that's his (*her*) tough luck!
▲ *Conjugation model* [12], *like cambiar.*

fastidio 1 *m* (*molestia*) bother, nuisance. **2** (*aburrimiento*) boredom. **3** (*repugnancia*) repugnance, revulsion.
● ¡qué fastidio!, what a nuisance!

fastidioso,-a 1 *adj* (*molesto*) annoying, irksome. **2** (*aburrido*) boring, tedious.

fasto *m* pomp, display.

fastos *mpl* annals, archives.

fastuosamente *adv* magnificently, pompously.

fastuosidad *f* pomp, lavishness.

fastuoso,-a 1 *adj* (*cosa*) splendid, lavish. **2** (*persona*) lavish, ostentatious.

fatal 1 *adj* (*inexorable*) fateful. **2** (*mortal*) deadly, fatal: *el accidente fue fatal,* the accident was fatal. **3** *fam* (*muy malo*) awful, horrible, terrible: *su redacción estaba fatal,* his composition was awful; *nos lo pasamos fatal,* we had a rotten time. **– 4** *adv fam* awfully, terribly.

fatalidad 1 *f* (*destino*) fate. **2** (*desgracia*) misfortune.

fatalismo *m* fatalism.

fatalista 1 *adj* fatalistic. **– 2** *mf* fatalist.

fatalmente 1 *adv* (*inevitablemente*) inevitably. **2** (*muy mal*) awfully, terribly.

fatídicamente *adv* fatefully.

fatídico,-a 1 *adj* (*desastroso*) disastrous, calamitous. **2** *fml* (*profético*) fateful, ominous.

fatiga 1 *f* (*cansancio*) fatigue. **– 2 fatigas,** *fpl* (*penalidades*) troubles, difficulties.

fatigar 1 *t* (*cansar*) to wear out, tire: *jugar con niños fatiga a cualquiera,* playing with children is enough to tire any-

one out. **2** (*molestar*) to annoy. – **3 fatigarse,** *p* to tire, get tired: *se fatigó de tanto subir y bajar escaleras,* she got tired of going up and down the stairs all the time.
▲ *Conjugation model* |7|, *like* **llegar.**

fatigosamente *adv* with (great) difficulty, painfully.

fatigoso,-a **1** *adj* (*cansado*) tiring, exhausting. **2** (*respiración*) laboured (us labored).

fatuidad *f* fatuity, fatuousness.

fatuo,-a **1** *adj* (*necio*) fatuous. **2** (*vano*) vain, conceited.

fauces **1** *fpl* (*en anatomía*) fauces, gullet *sing.* **2** *fig* jaws.

fauna *f* fauna.

fauno *m* faun.

fausto[1] *m* pomp, splendour (us splendor).

fausto,-a[2] *adj fml* fortunate, auspicious.

fauvismo *m* fauvism.

fauvista *mf* fauvist.

favor *m* favour (us favor).
● **a favor de,** in favour (us favor) of. ‖ **a mi** *(tu, su, etc)* **favor,** in my (*your, his, etc*) favour (us favor): *al final quedamos 2 a 1 a nuestro favor,* we finally won 2 to 1. ‖ **en favor de,** in favour (us favor). ‖ **haga** *(hagan, etc)* **el favor de + inf,** *fml* please + *inf.* ‖ *¿me harías (harían, haríais, etc)* **el favor de + inf?,** could you + *inf?* ‖ **por favor,** please. ‖ **tener a algn. a su favor,** to have sb. on one's side. ‖ **tener algo a su favor,** to have sth. in one's favour (us favor).

favorable *adj* favourable (us favorable); (*condiciones*) suitable.
● **mostrarse favorable a algo,** to be in favour (us favor) of sth.

favorablemente *adv* favourably (us favorably).

favorecedor,-ra **1** *adj* (*gen*) favouring (us favoring), favourable (us favorable). **2** (*que embellece*) becoming: *un vestido favorecedor,* a becoming dress. **3** (*retrato*) flattering.

favorecer **1** *t* (*ayudar*) to favour (us favor), help: *su política ha favorecido la economía,* his policies have benefitted the economy. **2** (*agraciar*) to flatter, suit: *el azul no me favorece,* blue doesn't suit me.
▲ *Conjugation model* |43|, *like* **agradecer.**

favorecido,-a **1** *adj* (*atractivo*) well-favoured (us well-favored): *está muy favorecida con ese vestido,* that dress really suits her. **2** (*afortunado*) lucky, fortunate: *resultó poco favorecido por la suerte,* fortune did not smile on him.

favoritismo *m* favouritism (us favoritism).

favorito,-a **1** *adj* favourite (us favorite). – **2** *m,f* favourite (us favorite).

fax **1** *m* (*sistema, documento*) fax. **2** (*aparato*) fax machine, fax.
● **enviar por fax,** to fax.

faz **1** *f lit* (*cara*) face: *su faz estaba perfectamente rasurada,* his face was perfectly shaven; *fueron borrados de la faz de la tierra,* they were wiped off the face of the earth. **2** (*de moneda, medalla*) obverse.
■ **la Santa Faz, la Sacra Faz,** the Holy Face.
▲ *pl* **faces.**

F.C.[1] *abr* (*Fútbol Club*) football club; (*abreviatura*) F.C.

F.C.[2] *abr* (*Ferrocarril*) railway; (*abreviatura*) rly.

f.c. *abr* (*ferrocarril*) railway; (*abreviatura*) rly.

F. de T. *abr* (*Fulano de Tal*) Mr. So-and-So.

fdo. *abr* (*firmado*) signed.

fe **1** *f* faith. **2** *JUR* (*certificado*) certificate.
● **de buena fe,** in good faith, with good intentions: *lo hizo de buena fe, pensando que nos ayudaría,* he did it

in good faith thinking it would help us. ‖ **de mala fe,** dishonestly, with dishonest intentions. ‖ **tener una fe ciega,** to have blind faith (**en,** in).
■ **fe de bautismo,** baptism certificate. ‖ **fe de matrimonio,** marriage certificate. ‖ **fe de erratas,** errata *pl.* ‖ **fe de vida,** *document proving that sb. is still alive.* ‖ **la fe cristiana,** the Christian faith.

fealdad *f* ugliness.

febrero *m* February.
▲ *See also* **marzo.**

febrífugo,-a **1** *adj* febrifuge. – **2 febrífugo,** *m* febrifuge.

febril **1** *adj* MED feverish. **2** (*muy intenso*) hectic, restless.

febrilidad *f* feverishness.

febrilmente *adv* feverishly, hectically.

fecal *adj* faecal.

fecha **1** *f* date: *¿qué fecha es hoy?,* what's the date today? **2** (*día*) day: *la carta tardó tres fechas en llegar,* the letter took three days to get here; *en unas fechas debutará en el Teatro Nacional,* in a few days he'll be making his debut at the National Theatre. – **3 fechas,** *fpl* (*época*) time *sing: por esas fechas,* at that time; *en estas fechas,* at this time of year; *el año pasado por estas fechas,* this time last year.
● **a seis** *(cuatro, diez, etc)* **días fecha,** COM six (*four, ten, etc*) days after sight. ‖ **con fecha ...,** dated ... ‖ **de fecha ...,** dated ... ‖ **en fecha próxima,** at an early date. ‖ **fijar la fecha,** to fix a date. ‖ **hasta la fecha,** so far, until now. ‖ **poner fecha a,** to date. ‖ **sin fecha,** undated.
■ **fecha de caducidad,** expiry date. ‖ **fecha de nacimiento,** date of birth. ‖ **fecha límite,** deadline, closing date. ‖ **fecha tope,** deadline, closing date.

fechador *m* date stamp.

fechar *t* to date, put the date on.

fechoría *f* misdeed, misdemeanour (us misdemeanor); (*de niño*) mischief.

fécula *f* starch.

feculento,-a *adj* starchy.

fecundable *adj* fertilizable.

fecundación *f* fertilization.

fecundar *t* to fertilize.

fecundidad **1** *f* (*fertilidad*) fertility. **2** (*productividad*) productivity, fruitfulness.

fecundizar *t* to make fertile.
▲ *Conjugation model* |4|, *like* **realizar.**

fecundo,-a *adj* fertile, fecund.

FED *abr* (*Fondo Europeo de Desarrollo*) European Development Fund.

federación *f* federation.

federado,-a *adj* federated.

federal **1** *adj* federal. – **2** *mf* federal.

federalismo *m* federalism.

federalista **1** *adj* federalist. – **2** *mf* federalist.

federar *t* to federate.

federativo,-a **1** *adj* federative. – **2 federativo,** *m* federation member.

fehaciente *adj fml* (*irrefutable*) incontrovertible, irrefutable; (*fiable*) reliable: *tenemos pruebas fehacientes,* we have irrefutable proof.
■ **copia fehaciente,** certified true copy.

fehacientemente *adv* for certain.

felación *f* fellatio.

feldespato *m* feldspar, felspar.

felicidad *f* happiness.
● **¡(muchas) felicidades!,** (*éxitos*) congratulations!;

(*cumpleaños*) happy birthday!; (*Navidad*) Merry Christmas!

felicitación 1 *f* (*acción*) congratulation. 2 (*tarjeta*) greetings card. – 3 **felicitaciones,** *fpl* congratulations.

felicitar 1 *t* to congratulate (**por,** on): *nos felicitó por el acuerdo,* he congratulated us on the agreement. 2 (*Navidades, Santo, cumpleaños*) to wish sb....: *felicitar a algn. las Navidades,* to wish sb. a Merry Christmas; *felicitar a algn. por su Santo,* to wish sb. a happy Saint's Day. – 3 **felicitarse,** *p* to be glad, be pleased: *me felicito de que hayas aprobado el examen,* I'm pleased you passed the exam.
● ¡*te (le, os, etc)* felicito!, congratulations!

félido,-a *m,f* cat, felid.

feligrés,-esa *m,f* parishioner.

feligresía *f* parish, parishioners *pl*.

felino,-a 1 *adj* feline. – 2 **felino,** *m* feline.

feliz 1 *adj* happy. 2 (*acertado*) fortunate.
● ¡feliz Navidad!, ¡felices Navidades!, Happy Christmas, Merry Christmas!

felizmente 1 *adv* (*con felicidad*) happily. 2 (*por suerte*) fortunately.

felón,-ona 1 *adj* treacherous, villainous, wicked. – 2 *m,f* traitor, villain.

felonía *f* treachery, villainy.

felpa *f* plush.
■ osito de felpa, teddy bear.

felpudo,-a 1 *adj* (*textil*) plushy, velvety. – 2 **felpudo,** *m* (*alfombrilla*) mat, doormat.

femenino,-a 1 *adj* feminine. 2 (*sexo*) female; (*equipo, asociación*) women's: *la asociación femenina de tenis,* the women's tennis association.

femineidad *f* femininity.

feminidad *f* femininity.

feminismo *m* feminism.

feminista 1 *adj* feminist. – 2 *mf* feminist.

femoral *adj* femoral.

fémur *m* femur.

fenecer 1 *i arc* (*terminar*) to come to an end, expire. 2 *euf* (*morir*) to pass away, die.
▲ *Conjugation model* |43|, *like agradecer.*

fenecimiento 1 *m arc* (*fin*) close, end. 2 *euf* (*muerte*) decease, death.

Fenicia *f* Phoenicia.

fenicio,-a 1 *adj* Phoenician. – 2 *m,f* (*persona*) Phoenician. – 3 **fenicio,** *m* (*idioma*) Phoenician.

fénix 1 *m* (*mitología*) phoenix. 2 (*genio*) genius, prodigy.
▲ *pl* **fénix**.

fenol *m* phenol.

fenomenal 1 *adj* (*relativo al fenómeno*) phenomenal. 2 *fam* (*fantástico*) great, terrific. 3 *fam* (*enorme*) colossal, huge. – 4 *adv* wonderfully, marvellously: *lo pasamos fenomenal jugando al tenis,* we had a fantastic time playing tennis.

fenómeno 1 *m* (*manifestación*) phenomenon. 2 (*prodigio*) genius. 3 (*monstruo*) freak. – 4 *adj fam* (*fantástico*) fantastic, terrific. – 5 *interj* terrific!, fantastic!
■ fenómeno atmosférico, atmospheric phenomenon.

fenotipo *m* phenotype.

feo,-a 1 *adj* (*persona - nada atractiva*) ugly; (*- poco atractiva*) plain. 2 (*aspecto, situación, tiempo, etc*) nasty, horrible, unpleasant, awful: *hizo un tiempo feísimo,* the weather was really awful; *al asunto se está poniendo feo,* things are turning nasty. 3 (*acción*) horrible, awful: *robar a un amigo es una acción muy fea,* stealing from a friend is a

horrible thing to do. 4 (*indigno*) rude, not nice, improper: *insultar es feo,* it's rude to insult people. – 5 *m,f* ugly person. – 6 **feo,** *m* (*ofensa*) slight, snub.
● hacerle un feo a algn., to slight sb., snub sb. ‖ ser más feo que Picio, to be as ugly as sin. ‖ siempre me (*te, etc*) toca bailar con la más fea, I (*you, etc*) always get the short end of the stick.

feracidad *f* fertility.

feraz *adj* fertile.

féretro *m* coffin.

feria 1 *f* COM fair. 2 (*fiesta*) fair, festival.
■ feria de ganado, livestock fair. ‖ feria de muestras, trade fair, trade exhibition. ‖ la Feria de Sevilla, the Seville Festival.

feriado,-a día feriado, *m* holiday.

ferial 1 *adj* fair. – 2 *m* fair.

feriante 1 *mf* (*vendedor*) stallholder, trader. 2 (*comprador*) fair-goer.

feriar *t* to trade at a fair.
▲ *Conjugation model* |12|, *like cambiar.*

ferina tos ferina, *f* whooping cough.

fermentación *f* fermentation.

fermentar *i* to ferment.

fermento *m* ferment.

fermio *m* fermium.

ferocidad *f* ferocity, fierceness.

ferodo *m* brake lining.
▲ *Registered trademark.*

feroz *adj* fierce, ferocious.
■ el lobo feroz, the big bad wolf.

ferozmente *adv* fiercely, ferociously.

férreo,-a 1 *adj* ferreous. 2 *fig* (*tenaz*) iron: *voluntad férrea,* iron will.

ferrería *f* ironworks, foundry.

ferretería 1 *f* (*tienda*) ironmonger's (shop), hardware store. 2 (*género*) ironmongery, hardware. 3 (*ferrería*) forge.

ferretero,-a *m,f* ironmonger, hardware dealer.

férrico,-a *adj* ferric.

ferrita *f* ferrite.

ferrocarril *m* railway, US railroad.

ferrohormigón *m* ferroconcrete.

ferroso,-a *adj* ferrous.

ferrovial *adj* railway, rail, US railroad.

ferroviario,-a 1 *adj* railway, rail, US railroad. – 2 *m,f* (*trabajador*) railway worker, US railroad worker.

ferruginoso,-a *adj* ferruginous.

ferry *m* ferry.

fértil *adj* fertile, rich.

fertilidad *f* fertility, fecundity.

fertilización *f* fertilization.

fertilizante 1 *adj* fertilizing. – 2 *m* (*abono*) fertilizer.

fertilizar *t* to fertilize.
▲ *Conjugation model* |4|, *like realizar.*

férula *f* ferule, rod.
● bajo la férula de algn., *fig* under the rule of sb.

férvido,-a *adj* fervid, ardent.

ferviente *adj* fervent, passionate.

fervientemente *adv* fervently, passionately.

fervor *m* fervour (US fervor).

fervoroso,-a *adj* fervent, passionate.

festejar 1 *t* (*celebrar*) to celebrate: *festejaron su victoria con cava,* they celebrated his victory with cava. 2 (*agasajar*) to wine and dine, entertain: *festejaron al campeón en su pueblo natal,* the champion was given a very warm welcome in his hometown. 3 (*cortejar*) to court, woo.

festejo 1 *m* feast, entertainment. **2** (*galanteo*) courting, courtship. – **3 festejos,** *mpl* festivities.
festín *m* feast, banquet.
festival *m* festival.
festividad 1 *f* (*fiesta*) festivity, celebration. **2** (*día*) feast day, holiday.
festivo,-a 1 *adj* (*alegre*) festive, merry. **2** (*humorístico*) witty.
■ **día festivo,** holiday.
festón 1 *m* COST festoon. **2** (*adorno floral*) garland.
festonear *t* to festoon.
fetal *adj* foetal (us fetal).
■ **posición fetal,** foetal position.
fetén 1 *adj fam* (*formidable*) terrific, smashing, great. **2** *fam* (*auténtico*) genuine. – **3** *adv fam* (*muy bien*) great: *ambos equipos jugaron fetén,* both teams played great. – **4 la fetén,** *f fam* (*la verdad*) the truth.
fetiche *m* fetish.
fetichismo *m* fetishism.
fetichista 1 *adj* fetishist. – **2** *mf* fetishist.
fetidez *f* stink, stench, fetidness.
fétido,-a *adj* stinking, fetid.
■ **bomba fétida,** stink bomb.
feto 1 *m* foetus (us fetus). **2** *fam* (*feo*) monster, ugly sod.
feúcho,-a *adj fam* plain, unattractive.
feudal *adj* feudal.
feudalismo *m* feudalism.
feudo *m* fief, feud.
FEVE *abr* (*Ferrocarriles Españoles de Vía Estrecha*) Spanish narrow railway line company.
fez *m* fez.
FF.A. *abr* (*Fuerzas Armadas*) Armed Forces.
FF.CC. *abr* (*ferrocarriles*) railways; (*abreviatura*) rly.
FF.NN. *abr* MIL (*Fuerzas Navales*) Navy.
fiabilidad *f* reliability, trustworthiness.
fiable *adj* reliable, trustworthy.
fiado,-a 1 *adj* COM on credit. **2** (*confiado*) trusting.
● **comprar al fiado,** to buy on credit. ‖ **vender al fiado,** to sell on credit.
fiador,-ra 1 *m,f* person who sells on credit. – **2** fiador, *m* (*de escopeta*) safety catch. **3** (*cerrojo*) bolt.
● **ser fiador,-ra de algn.,** (*pagar fianza*) to stand bail for sb.; (*avalar*) to vouch for sb.
fiambre 1 *adj* served cold, cold. **2** *irón* (*noticia etc*) stale, old. – **3** *m* CULIN cold meat, cold cut: *nos sirvieron toda clase de fiambres y patés,* we were served all kinds of cold meats and pâtés. **4** *fam* (*cadáver*) stiff, corpse.
● **dejar fiambre a algn.,** to do sb. in, bump sb. off.
fiambrera *f* lunch box.
fianza 1 *f* (*depósito*) deposit, security. **2** JUR bail.
● **bajo fianza,** on bail.
fiar 1 *t* (*asegurar*) to vouch for: *hará lo que promete, yo lo fío,* he'll do what he promises, I can vouch for him. **2** (*vender*) to sell on credit: *el lechero me fía,* the milkman lets me owe him, the milkman lets me pay him later. **3** (*confiar*) to confide, entrust: *fió a su nieto toda su fortuna,* he entrusted his entire fortune to his grandson. – **4** fiarse, *p* (*confiarse*) to trust (**de,** -): *no me fío de él,* I don't trust him; *no te fíes, la apariencias engañan,* watch out, appearances can be deceptive.
● **de fiar,** (*persona*) trustworthy, reliable; (*cosa*) reliable. ‖ **"no se fía",** "no credit given".
▲ *Conjugation model* [13], *like* desviar.
fiasco *m* fiasco, failure.
FIBA *abr* (*Federación Internacional de Baloncesto Amateur*) International Amateur Basketball Association.

fibra 1 *f* (*filamento*) fibre (us fiber); (*de madera*) grain. **2** *fig* (*carácter*) push, go.
■ **fibra de carbono,** carbon fibreglass (us fiber). ‖ **fibra de vidrio,** fibreglass (us fiberglass). ‖ **fibra óptica,** optical fibre (us fiber).
fibroma *m* fibroma.
fibrosis *f* fibrosis.
▲ *pl* fibrosis.
fibroso,-a *adj* fibrous.
fíbula *f* fibula.
ficción *f* fiction.
ficha 1 *f* (*tarjeta*) index card, file card. **2** (*de teléfono*) token. **3** (*en juegos*) counter; (*naipes*) chip; (*ajedrez*) piece, man; (*dominó*) domino. **4** (*de un deportista*) signing-on fee.
■ **ficha artística,** cast. ‖ **ficha policíaca,** police record. ‖ **ficha técnica,** technical specifications *pl*; CINEM credits *pl*.
fichaje *m* signing (up).
fichar 1 *t* (*anotar*) to put on an index card; (*registrar*) to open a file on. **2** *fam* (*conocer*) to size up: *ya lo tienen bien fichado,* they've got him sized up. **3** DEP to sign up, sign on: *el entrenador fichó a varios jugadores,* the manager signed up some players. – **4** *i* (*al entrar*) to clock in; (*al salir*) to clock out. **5** DEP to sign up (**por,** with): *finalmente fichó por el Barcelona,* he finally signed up with Barcelona F.C.
● **estar fichado,-a (por la policía),** to have a police record.
fichero 1 *m* (*archivo*) card index. **2** (*mueble*) filing cabinet, file. **3** INFORM file.
ficticio,-a *adj* fictitious.
ficus *m* rubber plant.
▲ *pl* ficus.
fidedigno,-a *adj* trustworthy, reliable.
fideicomisario,-a *m,f* trustee.
fideicomiso *m* trusteeship.
● **bajo fideicomiso / en fideicomiso,** in trusteeship.
fidelidad 1 *f* (*lealtad*) fidelity, faithfulness. **2** (*exactitud*) accuracy.
■ **alta fidelidad,** high fidelity, hi-fi.
fideo *m* noodle.
● **estar como un fideo,** *fam* to be as thin as a rake.
Fidji *m* Fiji.
fidjiano,-a 1 *adj* Fijian. – **2** *m,f* (*persona*) Fijian. – **3** fidjiano, *m* (*idioma*) Fijian.
fiduciario,-a 1 *adj* fiduciary. – **2** *m,f* fiduciary.
fiebre 1 *f* (*enfermedad*) fever, temperature: *tiene la fiebre muy alta,* she has a very high temperature. **2** (*agitación*) fever, excitement: *la fiebre del oro,* gold fever, the gold rush; *una fiebre religiosa sacudió al país,* religious fever shook the country.
● **tener fiebre,** to have a temperature.
■ **fiebre amarilla,** yellow fever. ‖ **fiebre de Malta,** brucellosis. ‖ **fiebre del heno,** hay fever. ‖ **fiebre puerperal,** puerperal fever. ‖ **fiebre reumática,** rheumatic fever.
fiel 1 *adj* (*leal*) faithful, loyal. **2** (*exacto*) accurate; (*memoria*) reliable. – **3** *m* (*de balanza*) needle, pointer. – **4 los fieles,** *mpl* the faithful.
● **ser fiel a,** to be faithful to.
fielmente 1 *adv* (*con lealtad*) faithfully, loyally. **2** (*con exactitud*) accurately, exactly.
fieltro *m* felt.
fiera *f* → fiero,-a.
fieramente *adv* wildly.
fiereza *f* (*ferocidad*) ferocity, ferociousness; (*crueldad*) cruelty.

fiero,-a 1 *adj* (*animal salvaje*) wild; (*feroz*) fierce, ferocious. **2** (*persona*) cruel. – **3 fiera,** *f* (*animal*) wild animal, wild beast. **4** *fig* (*persona*) beast, brute. **5** *fig* (*genio*) wizard. **6** (*toro*) bull.
● **estar hecho,-a una fiera,** *fam* to be in a rage. ‖ **ser una fiera para algo,** to be brilliant at sth.
■ **casa de fieras,** menagerie.

fiesta 1 *f* (*día no laborable*) holiday: *el viernes es fiesta,* Friday's a holiday. **2** (*reunión*) party: *celebraron una fiesta en mi honor,* they held a party in my honour. **3** REL feast: *es la fiesta de San Crispín,* it's the feast of St Crispin. **4 fiestas,** (*festividades*) festivity, fiesta: *el pueblo está en fiestas,* it's the local festivities. – **5** *fpl* (*navidad*) Christmas: *a ver si nos vemos estas fiestas,* maybe we'll see each other this Christmas.
● **aguar la fiesta,** to be a wet blanket, be a killjoy. ‖ **estar de fiesta,** *fig* to be in a festive mood. ‖ **¡felices fiestas!,** Merry Christmas! ‖ **hacer fiesta un día,** to take a day off. ‖ **no estar para fiestas,** to be in no mood for jokes. ‖ **¡tengamos la fiesta en paz!,** let's not argue!
■ **fiesta de cumpleaños,** birthday party. ‖ **fiesta de disfraces,** fancy-dress party. ‖ **fiesta de guardar,** day of obligation. ‖ **fiesta de la cerveza,** beer festival. ‖ **Fiesta de la Hispanidad,** Columbus Day. ‖ **fiesta de precepto,** day of obligation. ‖ **Fiesta del Trabajo,** Labour (US Labor) Day. ‖ **fiesta fija,** immovable feast. ‖ **fiesta móvil,** movable feast. ‖ **la fiesta de los toros,** bullfighting. ‖ **fiesta nacional,** (*día festivo*) public holiday; (*tauromaquia*) bullfighting. ‖ **las fiestas de Navidad,** Christmas *sing*.

FIFA *abr* (*Federación Internacional de Fútbol Asociación*) Fédération International de Football Association; (*abreviatura*) FIFA.

fig. *abr* (*figura*) figure; (*abreviatura*) fig.

figle *m* ophicleide.

figón *m arc* cheap restaurant, greasy spoon.

figura 1 *f* (*gen*) figure. **2** (*forma*) shape. **3** CINEM TEAT character.
● **tener buena figura,** to have a good figure. ‖ **tener mala figura,** to have a bad figure.
■ **figura decorativa,** figurehead. ‖ **figura geométrica,** geometrical figure. ‖ **figura retórica,** figure of speech.

figuración *f* imagination.
● **son figuraciones mías** (*tuyas, suyas, etc*), it's just my (*your, his, etc*) imagination.

figurado,-a *adj* figurative.
● **en sentido figurado,** figuratively.

figurante 1 *mf* (*comparsa*) extra. **2** (*figurón*) figurehead.

figurar 1 *t* (*representar*) to represent: *estas líneas figuran una casa,* these lines represent a house. **2** (*simular*) to simulate, feign: *figuró un desmayo,* she pretended to faint. – **3** *i* (*encontrarse*) to appear, be, figure: *su nombre no figura en la lista,* his name isn't on the list; *figura como director,* he appears as director. **4** (*destacar*) to stand out, be important: *le gusta mucho figurar,* he likes to be noticed. – **5 figurarse,** *p* (*imaginarse*) to imagine, suppose: *me figuro que quieres más dinero,* I suppose you want some more money.
● **¡figúrate!,** just imagine! ‖ **ya me lo figuraba,** I thought as much.

figurativo,-a *adj* figurative.

figurín 1 *m* (*dibujo*) sketch. **2** (*revista*) fashion magazine.
● **ir hecho,-a un figurín,** to be dressed up to the nines.

figurinista *mf* costume designer.

figurón *m pey* show-off, swank.
■ **figurón de proa,** figurehead.

fijacarteles *mf* billposter.
▲ *pl* **fijacarteles**.

fijación 1 *f* (*colocación*) setting, fixing. **2** (*sujeción*) fastening. **3** (*obsesión*) obsession. – **4 fijaciones,** *fpl* (*esquí*) bindings.

fijado *m* fixing.

fijador,-ra 1 *adj* fixing. – **2 fijador,** *m* (*para pelo*) hairspray, hair gel. **3** (*para dibujo etc*) fixative; (*para foto*) fixer.

fijamente *adv* fixedly.

fijapelo *m* hair spray, styling gel.

fijar 1 *t* (*sujetar*) to fix, fasten; (*puerta*) to hang; (*ventana*) to put in. **2** (*pegar*) to stick. **3** (*establecer*) to set, determine, fix: *fijamos un precio,* we fixed a price. **4** (*en fotografía, química*) to fix. – **5 fijarse,** *p* (*hacerse fijo*) to settle: *el dolor se fijó en la cabeza,* the pain settled in his head. **6** (*darse cuenta*) to notice: *¿te fijaste en el color de sus ojos?,* did you notice the colour of his eyes? **7** (*poner atención*) to pay attention, watch: *fíjate cómo se hace,* watch how it's done.
● **fijar la vista,** to stare (**en**, at). ‖ **fijar los ojos,** to stare (**en**, at). ‖ **fijar residencia,** to take up residence. ‖ **¡fíjate!,** (just) fancy that! ‖ **"prohibido fijar carteles",** "post no bills".

fijasello *m* stamp hinge.

fijativo *m* fixative.

fijeza 1 *f* (*persistencia*) insistence, firmness. **2** (*seguridad*) certainty.
● **mirar algo con fijeza,** to stare at sth. ‖ **saber algo con fijeza,** to know sth. for certain.

fijo,-a 1 *adj* (*sujeto*) fixed, fastened. **2** (*establecido*) set, definite, firm: *fecha fija,* set date. **3** (*firme*) steady, stable, firm. **4** (*permanente*) permanent: *empleo fijo,* permanent job; *residencia fija,* fixed address. **5** (*fotografía*) fast.
● **de fijo,** for certain, for sure. ‖ **estar fijo,-a en,** to be settled in.

fila 1 *f* (*línea*) file, line. **2** (*de local*) row. – **3 filas,** *fpl* MIL & POL ranks.
● **cerrar filas,** MIL to close ranks. ‖ **en fila de uno,** en fila india, in single file. ‖ **en primera fila,** in the front row. ‖ **estar en filas,** MIL to be doing one's military service. ‖ **llamar a algn. a filas,** MIL to call sb. up. ‖ **poner en fila,** to line up. ‖ **¡rompan filas!,** MIL fall out!, dismiss! ‖ **salirse de la fila,** to step out of line.

Filadelfia *f* Philadelphia.

filamento *m* filament.

filantropía *f* philanthropy.

filantrópico,-a *adj* philanthropic.

filántropo,-a *m,f* philanthropist.

filarmónico,-a *adj* philharmonic.

filatelia *f* philately, stamp collecting.

filatélico,-a *adj* philatelic.

filatelista *mf* philatelist, stamp collector.

filete 1 *m* (*de carne, pescado*) fillet (US filet); (*solomillo*) sirloin steak. **2** (*encuadernación, moldura*) fillet. **3** (*de tornillo*) thread.

filfa *f fam* hoax.

filiación 1 *f* (*datos personales*) particulars *pl*. **2** POL affiliation.

filial 1 *adj* (*del hijo*) filial. **2** COM subsidiary. – **3** *f* COM subsidiary, branch.

filiforme *adj* thread-like.

filigrana 1 *f* (*orfebrería*) filigree. **2** (*papel*) watermark. **3** (*cosa delicada*) delicate piece of work.

filípica *f* philippic, tirade.

Filipinas las Filipinas, *fpl* the Philippines.
filipino,-a 1 *adj* Filipino. – 2 *m,f* (*persona*) Filipino. – 3 filipino, *m* (*idioma*) Filipino.
filisteo,-a 1 *adj* Philistine. – 2 *m,f* Philistine.
film *m* film, us movie.
▲ *pl* *films*.
filmación *f* filming, shooting.
filmar *t* to film, shoot.
filme *m* → **film**.
fílmico,-a *adj* film, cinema.
filmina *f* slide, transparency.
filmografía *f* filmography, films *pl*.
filmoteca 1 *f* (*archivo*) film library. 2 (*sala de proyección*) film institute. 3 (*colección*) film collection.
filo *m* cutting edge, edge.
● sacar filo a algo, to sharpen sth. ‖ al filo de, *fig* on the stroke of. ‖ arma de doble filo, *fig* double-edged sword. ‖ como el filo de un cuchillo, (*aire, viento*) biting.
filo- *pref* philo-.
filología *f* philology.
filológico,-a *adj* philological.
filólogo,-a *m,f* philologist.
filón 1 *m* (*mineral*) seam, vein. 2 (*buen negocio*) gold mine.
filosofal piedra filosofal, *adj* philosopher's stone.
filosofar *i* to philosophize.
filosofía *f* philosophy.
● tomarse algo con filosofía, to take sth. philosophically.
filosófico,-a *adj* philosophical.
filósofo,-a *m,f* philosopher.
filoxera *f* phylloxera.
filtración 1 *f* filtration. 2 (*de información*) leak.
filtrador,-ra 1 *adj* filtering. – 2 filtrador, *m* filter.
filtrar 1 *t* (*hacer pasar*) to filter: *filtra el café para que no queden posos,* filter the coffee to remove the grounds. 2 (*seleccionar*) to filter: *la secretaria filtra las llamadas,* the secretary filters his phone calls. 3 (*divulgar*) to leak: *filtró al enemigo información reservada,* he leaked confidential information to the enemy. – 4 filtrarse, *p* (*pasar a través*) to filter: *la luz se filtraba a través de la cortina,* the light filtered through the curtain.
filtro¹ *m* (*material*) filter.
filtro² *m* (*poción*) philtre, love potion.
fimbria 1 *f* (*borde*) hem. 2 (*orla*) edging, border.
fimosis *f* phimosis.
▲ *pl* *fimosis*.
fin 1 *m* (*final*) end. 2 (*objetivo*) purpose, aim.
● a fin de, in order to, so as to. ‖ a fin de que, so that. ‖ a fines de, at the end of. ‖ al fin y al cabo, when all's said and done. ‖ ¡al fin!, at last! ‖ con buen fin, with good intentions. ‖ con el fin de, with the intention of. ‖ con este fin, with this aim. ‖ dar fin a, to put an end to. ‖ en fin, anyway. ‖ llegar a su fin, to come to an end. ‖ no tener fin, to be endless. ‖ poner fin a, to put an end to. ‖ ¡por fin!, at last! ‖ sin fin, endless. ‖ tocar a su fin, to come to an end.
■ fin de fiesta, grand finale. ‖ fin de semana, weekend. ‖ (noche de) Fin de Año, New Year's Eve.
finado,-a *m,f* deceased.
final 1 *adj* (*último*) final, last. – 2 *m* end. 3 MÚS finale. – 4 *f* DEP final.
● al final, in the end. ‖ al final del día, at the end of the day. ‖ hasta el final, until the end.
■ final de línea, terminus. ‖ final feliz, happy ending.

finalidad *f* purpose, aim.
finalista 1 *adj* in the final: *Brasil es uno de los equipos finalistas,* Brazil is one of the teams in the final. – 2 *mf* finalist.
finalizar 1 *t* to end, finish. – 2 *i* to end, finish.
▲ Conjugation model [4], like *realizar*.
finalmente *adv* finally.
finamente 1 *adv* (*con delicadeza*) delicately, elegantly. 2 (*con agudeza*) shrewdly. 3 (*con sutileza*) subtly.
financiación *f* financing.
financiamiento *m* financing.
financiar *t* to finance.
▲ Conjugation model [12], like *cambiar*.
financiero,-a 1 *adj* financial. – 2 *m,f* financier.
finanzas *fpl* finances.
finar 1 *i* *fml* (*morir*) to pass away, die. – 2 finarse, *p* (*desear*) to yearn (**por**, for).
finca *f* property, estate.
■ finca rústica, country property. ‖ finca urbana, building.
fineza 1 *f* delicacy, daintiness. 2 (*cumplido*) courtesy, compliment.
fingido,-a 1 *pp* → **fingir**. – 2 *adj* feigned, false. 3 (*hipócrita*) hypocritical.
■ nombre fingido, false name.
fingimiento *m* pretence (us pretense), simulation.
fingir 1 *t* to feign, pretend: *fingió indiferencia,* he feigned indifference; *fingía no conocerme,* she pretended not to know me; *fingió la voz de su madre,* she imitated her mother's voice. – 2 fingirse, *p* to pretend to be: *se finge cojo,* he pretends to be lame.
▲ Conjugation model [6], like *dirigir*.
finiquitar 1 *t* (*saldar una cuenta*) to settle; (*saldar una deuda*) to discharge. 2 *fam* (*acabar*) to finish, end.
finiquito 1 *m* (*acción*) settlement. 2 (*documento*) final discharge.
finisecular *adj* turn-of-the-century.
finito,-a *adj* finite.
finlandés,-esa 1 *adj* Finnish. – 2 *m,f* (*persona*) Finn. – 3 finlandés, *m* (*idioma*) Finnish.
Finlandia *f* Finland.
fino,-a 1 *adj* (*delicado*) fine, delicate. 2 (*alimentos*) choice, select. 3 (*sentidos*) sharp, acute. 4 (*delgado*) thin. 5 (*educado*) refined, polite. 6 (*sutil*) subtle. – 7 fino, *m* (*vino*) dry sherry.
● estar fino,-a, *fam* to be witty. ‖ ir fino,-a, *fam* irón to have had a few.
■ oro fino, pure gold.
finolis 1 *adj* *fam* (*remilgado*) fussy, finicky. 2 *fam* (*cursi*) affected.
▲ *pl* *finolis*.
finta *f* feint.
fintar *i* to feint.
finura 1 *f* (*calidad*) fineness. 2 (*agudeza*) sharpness, acuteness. 3 (*refinamiento*) refinement. 4 (*sutileza*) finesse.
■ finura de espíritu, sensitivity.
fiordo *m* fiord, fjord.
firma 1 *f* (*autógrafo*) signature. 2 (*acto*) signing. 3 (*empresa*) firm.
firmamento *m* firmament.
firmante 1 *adj* signatory. – 2 *mf* signatory.
● el (la) abajo firmante, the undersigned.
firmar *t* to sign.
firme 1 *adj* (*estable*) firm, steady. 2 (*color*) fast. – 3 *m* (*pavimento*) road surface. – 4 *adv* hard.

● **de firme,** hard. ‖ **en firme,** firm: *nos hizo una propuesta en firme,* he made us a firm proposal. ‖ **estar en lo firme,** to be in the right. ‖ **¡firmes!,** MIL attention! ‖ **mantenerse firme,** *fig* to hold one's ground. ■ **sentencia firme,** final judgement. ‖ **tierra firme,** terra firma.

firmemente *adv* firmly.

firmeza *f* firmness, steadiness.

fiscal 1 *adj* fiscal, tax. – 2 *mf* JUR public prosecutor, US district attorney. 3 *fig* snooper, informer.

fiscalía *f* public prosecutor's office, US district attorney's office.

fiscalización *f* supervision, inspection.

fiscalizar *t* to supervise, inspect.
▲ *Conjugation model* [4], *like realizar.*

fisco *m* exchequer, US treasury.

fisgar *t fam* to pry, snoop.
▲ *Conjugation model* [7], *like llegar.*

fisgón,-ona *adj* (*espía*) snooper; (*curioso*) busybody.

fisgonear *t* to pry, snoop.

física *f* → **físico,-a.**

físicamente *adv* physically.

físico,-a 1 *adj* physical. – 2 *m,f* (*profesión*) physicist. – 3 físico, *m* (*aspecto*) physique. – 4 física, *f* physics.

fisiología *f* physiology.

fisiológico,-a *adj* physiological.

fisiólogo,-a *m,f* physiologist.

fisión *f* fission.

fisioterapeuta *mf* physiotherapist.

fisioterapia *f* physiotherapy.

fisonomía *f* physiognomy, appearance.

fisonómico,-a *adj* physiognomical, physiognomic.

fisonomista *mf* physiognomist.
● **ser buen fisonomista,** to be good good at remembering faces. ‖ **ser mal fisonomista,** to be no good at remembering faces.

fístula *f* fistula.

fisura *f* fissure.

fito- *pref* phyto-.

FIV *abr* MED (*fecundación in vitro*) in vitro fertilization; (*abreviatura*) IVF.

flaccidez *f* flaccidity, flabbiness, flaccidness.

fláccido,-a *adj* flaccid, flabby.

flacidez *f* → **flaccidez.**

flácido,-a *adj* → **fláccido.**

flaco,-a 1 *adj* (*delgado*) thin, skinny. 2 (*débil*) weak, frail. – 3 flaco, *m* (*debilidad*) weak point, weak spot; (*vicio*) bad habit.

flacucho,-a *adj pey* skinny.

flacura *f* thinness, skinniness.

flagelación *f* flagellation, whipping.

flagelar 1 *t* (*azotar*) to flagellate, whip. 2 *fig* (*censurar*) to flay, criticize.

flagelo 1 *m* (*objeto*) whip. 2 (*calamidad*) calamity. 3 BIOL flagellum.

flagrante *adj* flagrant.
● **en flagrante delito,** red-handed.

flamante 1 *adj* (*vistoso*) splendid, brilliant. 2 (*nuevo*) brand-new.

flameado,-a *adj* flambé.

flameante *adj* flamboyant.

flamear 1 *i* (*llamear*) to flame, blaze. 2 (*ondear*) to flutter, flap. – 3 *t* CULIN to flambé.

flamenco,-a 1 *adj* (*de Flandes*) Flemish. 2 (*gitano*) Andalusian gypsy. 3 (*música*) flamenco. 4 (*robusto*) sturdy;

(*saludable*) healthy. – 5 *m,f* (*persona*) Fleming. – 6 flamenco, *m* (*idioma*) Flemish. 7 (*música*) flamenco music, flamenco. 8 (*ave*) flamingo.

flámula *f* streamer, pennant.

flan 1 *m* (*dulce*) crème caramel. 2 (*de arena, arroz, etc*) pie.
● **estar como un flan,** to be shaking like a leaf. ‖ **estar hecho,-a un flan,** → **estar como un flan.**

flanco *m* flank, side.

Flandes *m* Flanders.

flanera *f* mould (US mold).

flanquear *t* to flank.

flaquear 1 *i* (*ceder*) to weaken, give in. 2 (*fallar*) to fail: *su memoria ya flaquea,* his memory is already failing. 3 (*desalentarse*) to lose heart. 4 (*disminuir*) to decrease.

flaqueza *f* weakness, frailty.

flash 1 *m* (*fotografía*) flash, flashlight. 2 (*noticia breve*) newsflash.
▲ *pl* **flashes.**

flato *m* (*dolor*) stitch: *le dio flato,* he got a stitch.

flatulencia *f* flatulence, wind.

flatulento,-a *adj* flatulent.

flauta 1 *f* (*instrumento*) flute. – 2 *mf* (*músico*) flautist (US flutist), flute player.
● **sonar la flauta,** to happen by chance, be a lucky fluke.
■ **flauta de Pan,** pipes *pl* of Pan. ‖ **flauta dulce,** recorder. ‖ **flauta travesera,** flute, transverse flute, cross flute.

flautín 1 *m* (*instrumento*) piccolo. – 2 *mf* (*músico*) piccolo player.

flautista *mf* flute player, flautist (US flutist).
■ **el Flautista de Hamelín,** the Pied Piper of Hamelin.

flebitis *f* phlebitis.
▲ *pl* **flebitis.**

flecha 1 *f* (*arma*) arrow; (*dardo*) dart. 2 ARQ spire, flèche. 3 (*indicación*) arrow.
● **salir como una flecha,** to go off like a shot. ‖ **"siga la flecha",** "follow the arrow".

flechar *t* to sweep off one's feet.

flechazo 1 *m* (*disparo*) arrow shot. 2 (*herida*) arrow wound. 3 *fig* (*enamoramiento*) love at first sight.

fleco 1 *m* (*adorno*) fringe. 2 (*borde deshilachado*) frayed edge. 3 (*asunto pendiente menor*) minor point, final detail: *quedan por resolver unos pocos flecos,* just a few minor points remain to be solved.

fleje 1 *m* TÉC metal strip, metal band. 2 (*de tonel*) hoop.

flema *f* phlegm.

flemático,-a *adj* phlegmatic.

flemón *m* (*en la encía*) gumboil; (*en el cuerpo*) abscess.

flequillo *m* fringe, US bangs *pl.*

fletador,-ra *m,f* charterer, freighter.

fletamiento *m* chartering.

fletar *t* to charter, freight.

flete 1 *m* (*alquiler*) freightage. 2 (*carga*) cargo.

flexibilidad *f* flexibility.

flexible *adj* flexible.

flexión 1 *f* (*doblegamiento*) flexion, bending. 2 LING inflection. 3 DEP press-up, US push-up.
▲ *In 3 also used in plural with the same meaning.*

flexionar *t* (*músculo*) to flex; (*cuerpo*) to bend.

flexo *m* adjustable table lamp, anglepoise lamp.

flipado,-a 1 *pp* → **flipar.** – 2 *adj arg* (*drogado*) stoned.

flipante *adj arg* incredible, unbelievable, amazing.

flipar 1 *t arg* (*gustar mucho*) to drive wild: *le flipan los coches de carreras,* he's crazy about racing cars; *me flipa* *este disco,* I really love this record. **– 2** *i (asombrarse)* to be amazed, be stunned: *era increíble, yo flipaba con lo que decía,* it was incredible, I couldn't believe what he was saying. **3** *(pasárselo bomba)* to freak out: *la música era una caña, la gente flipaba,* the music was brilliant, everyone was freaking out. **– 4 fliparse,** *p arg (drogarse)* to get high.

flipe *m arg* trip.

flirtear *i* to flirt.

flirteo *m* flirtation, flirting.

flojear **1** *i (disminuir)* to fall off, go down. **2** *(debilitarse)* to weaken, grow weak.

flojedad **1** *f (debilidad)* weakness, slackness. **2** *(atonía)* flabbiness, limpness.

flojera *f fam* weakness, faintness.

flojo,-a **1** *adj (suelto)* loose; *(no tensado)* slack. **2** *(débil)* weak: *soplarán vientos flojos del nordeste,* there will be light northeasterly winds. **3** *(perezoso)* lazy, idle. **4** *(mediocre)* poor: *es un estudiante flojo,* he's a poor student; *una colecta floja,* a poor collection. **5** *(poco activo)* slack, slow: *por la mañana trabajamos pero la tarde fue muy floja,* we worked hard in the morning, but the afternoon was very slack. **– 6** *m,f* lazybones, idler.
● **estar flojo,-a en algo,** to be weak at sth. ‖ **me la trae floja,** *arg* I couldn't give a toss.

flor **1** *f* BOT flower. **2** *(piropo)* compliment.
● **a flor de piel,** skin-deep. ‖ **a flor de tierra,** at ground level. ‖ **echar flores a algn.,** to pay sb. compliments. ‖ **en flor,** in flower, in bloom, in blossom. ‖ **en la flor de la vida,** *fig* in the prime of life.
■ **flor de azahar,** orange blossom. ‖ **flor de harina,** pure wheat flour. ‖ **flor de lis,** fleur-de-lis. ‖ **la flor de la canela,** the best. ‖ **la flor y nata,** *fig* the cream, the crème de la crème.

flora *f* flora.

floración *f (plantas)* flowering, blooming; *(árboles)* blossoming.

floral *adj* floral.

florar *i (plantas)* to flower, bloom; *(árboles)* to blossom.

florear **1** *t (adornar)* to adorn with flowers. **2** *fam (piropear)* to pay compliments to. **– 3** *i (guitarra)* to play in arpeggio. **4** *(esgrima)* to flourish.

florecer **1** *i (plantas)* to flower, bloom; *(árboles)* to blossom. **2** *(prosperar)* to flourish, thrive. **– 3 florecerse,** *p (enmohecerse)* to go mouldy (us moldy).
▲ *Conjugation model* |43|, *like* **agradecer**.

floreciente *adj* flourishing, prosperous.

florecimiento **1** *m (plantas)* flowering, blooming; *(árboles)* blossoming. **2** *(auge)* flourishing.

Florencia *f* Florence.

florentino,-a **1** *adj* Florentine. **– 2** *m,f* Florentine.

floreo *m* flourish.

florería *f* florist's (shop).

florero *m* vase.

florescencia *f* florescence.

floresta *f* wood, thicket.

florete *m* foil.

florezco *pres indic* → **florecer**.

floricultor,-ra *m,f* flower grower.

floricultura *f* flower growing, floriculture.

florido,-a **1** *adj (con flores)* flowery. **2** *(selecto)* choice, select. **3** *(lenguaje, estilo)* florid.
● **lo más florido,** the cream.

florilegio *m* anthology.

florín *m* florin.

floripondio **1** *m pey (flor grande)* great big gaudy flower. **2** *(adorno exagerado)* heavy ornamentation.

florista *mf* florist.

floristería *f* florist's (shop).

floritura *f pey* heavy ornamentation.

florón **1** *m* ARQ rosette. **2** *(heráldica)* fleuron.

flota *f* fleet.
■ **flota de guerra,** war fleet. ‖ **flota pesquera,** fishing fleet.

flotación *f* flotation, floating.

flotador **1** *m* float. **2** *(de niño)* rubber ring. **3** *(de cisterna)* float, ballcock.

flotante *adj* floating.

flotar **1** *i* to float. **2** *(ondear)* to wave, flutter.

flote **a flote,** *loc adv* afloat.
● **sacar a flote un negocio,** to put a business on a sound footing. ‖ **salir a flote,** *(superar dificultades)* to get back on one's feet, get out of difficulty; *(surgir)* to come to the surface, resurface: *durante la reunión salieron a flote antiguas rencillas,* old quarrels resurfaced during the meeting.

flotilla *f* flotilla.

fluctuación *f* fluctuation.

fluctuante *adj* fluctuating, subject to fluctuation.

fluctuar **1** *i (variar)* to fluctuate. **2** *(vacilar)* to hesitate.
▲ *Conjugation model* |11|, *like* **actuar**.

fluente *adj* flowing, fluid.

fluidez **1** *f (facilidad de paso)* fluidity. **2** *(facilidad de expresión)* fluency.
■ **fluidez verbal,** fluency.

fluido,-a **1** *adj (sin obstáculos)* fluid. **2** *(lenguaje, estilo)* fluent. **– 3 fluido,** *m* Fís fluid.
■ **fluido eléctrico,** current, power.

fluir *i* to flow.
▲ *Conjugation model* |62|, *like* **huir**.

flujo **1** *m (brote)* flow. **2** *(marea)* rising tide. **3** Fís flux. **4** MED discharge. **5** INFORM discharge.

flúor *m* fluorine.

fluorescencia *f* fluorescence.

fluorescente **1** *adj* fluorescent. **– 2** *m* fluorescent light.

fluorización *f* fluoridation.

fluoruro *m* fluoride.

fluvial *adj* fluvial, river.

flux *m* flush.

fluyo *pres indic* → **fluir**.

FM *abr* RAD *(modulación de frecuencia, frecuencia modulada)* frequency modulation; *(abreviatura)* FM.

FMI *abr (Fondo Monetario Internacional)* International Monetary Fund; *(abreviatura)* IMF.

fo. *abr (folio)* folio; *(abreviatura)* fo.

fobia *f* phobia.

foca **1** *f* seal. **2** *fam (persona)* fat lump.
■ **piel de foca,** sealskin.

focal *adj* focal.

focha *f* coot.

foco **1** *m (centro)* centre (us center), focal point. **2** Fís & MAT focus. **3** *(lámpara)* spotlight, floodlight. **4** *fig (lugar)* centre (us center).
■ **foco de atención,** focus of attention.

fofo,-a **1** *adj (material)* soft, spongy. **2** *(persona)* flabby.

fogarada *f* bonfire.

fogata *f* bonfire.

fogón **1** *m (de cocina)* kitchen range, stove. **2** *(de máquina de vapor)* firebox.

fogonazo *m* flash.

fogonero *m* stoker.
fogosamente *adv* fierily.
fogosidad *f* (*persona*) ardour (us ardor) fire.
fogoso,-a *adj* fiery, spirited.
foguear 1 *t* MIL to accustom to gunfire. **2** *fig* to harden.
fogueo de fogueo, *adj* blank: *un cartucho de fogueo*, a blank, a blank cartridge.
foie-gras *m* foie-gras.
foja *f* coot.
fol. *abr* (*folio*) folio; (*abreviatura*) fol.
folclor *m* → **folclore**.
folclore 1 *m* folklore. **2** (*juerga, jaleo*) binge.
folclórica *f* → **folclórico,-a**.
folclórico,-a 1 *adj* (*popular*) folkloric, popular, traditional. **2** *fam pey* quaint. – **3** folclórica, *f* (*cantante*) flamenco singer.
folclorista *mf* folklorist.
folía *f* popular song and dance of the Canary Islands.
foliación *f* foliation.
foliar *t* to foliate, folio, number.
▲ *Conjugation model* |12|, *like* **cambiar**.
folicular *adj* follicular.
folículo *m* follicle.
folio *m* folio, leaf.
● *en folio*, in folio, folio.
foliolo *m* foliole.
folíolo *m* foliole.
folk *m* folk music.
folklore *m* → **folclore**.
folklórico,-a *adj* → **folclórico,-a**.
folklorista *mf* → **folclorista**.
folla mala folla, *f* tabú (*mala pata*) bad luck.
● *tener mala folla*, *tabú* (*hombre*) to be a bastard; (*mujer*) to be a bitch.
follada *f* tabú screw, fuck.
follaje 1 *m* BOT foliage, leaves *pl*. **2** (*palabrería*) verbiage, verbosity.
follar 1 *i* tabú (*copular*) to fuck (**con**, with), screw (**con**, -). – **2** *t* tabú (*suspender*) to fail: *me han follado en mates*, I've failed maths. – **3** follarse, *p* tabú (*copular*) to fuck (**a**, -), screw (**a**, -): *se folló a aquel tío*, she screwed that guy.
folletín 1 *m* (*relato*) newspaper serial. **2** *fig* (*melodrama*) melodrama, saga.
● ¡*menudo folletín!*, what a saga!
folletinesco,-a *adj* melodramatic.
folletinista *mf* serial writer.
folleto *m* (*prospecto*) pamphlet, leaflet, brochure; (*explicativo*) instruction leaflet; (*turístico*) brochure.
follón 1 *m* fam (*alboroto*) rumpus, shindy. **2** *fam* (*enredo, confusión*) mess, trouble.
● *armar (un) follón*, *fam* to kick up a rumpus. || *meterse en un follón*, to get into a mess, get into trouble.
follonero,-a 1 *adj* troublemaking. – **2** *m,f* troublemaker.
fomentar *t* to promote, encourage, foster.
fomento 1 *m* (*promoción*) promotion, encouragement. **2** MED fomentation.
fonación *f* phonation.
fonda *f* (*mesón*) inn.
fondeadero *m* anchorage.
fondeado,-a 1 *adj* (*anclado*) anchored. **2** (*rico*) well-off, wealthy.
fondear 1 *t* (*sondear*) to sound. **2** (*registrar*) to search. **3** *fig* (*examinar*) to get to the bottom of, delve into. – **4** *i* to anchor.

fondeo 1 *m* (*sondeo*) sounding. **2** (*registro*) searching. **3** (*acto de anclar*) anchoring.
fondillos *mpl* seat *sing* (*of trousers*).
fondista 1 *mf* (*de mesón*) innkeeper. **2** DEP long-distance runner.
fondo 1 *m* (*parte más baja*) bottom: *en el fondo del pozo*, at the bottom of the well; *hay un fondo de verdad en lo que dice*, there is an element of truth in what he says. **2** (*parte más lejana*) end, back: *al fondo de la sala*, at the back of the hall; *al fondo del pasillo*, at the end of the corridor. **3** (*segundo término*) background. **4** (*profundidad*) depth: *tiene poco fondo*, it's not very deep. **5** (*aguante*) stamina: *estoy entrenando para coger fondo*, I'm training to build up my stamina. **6** FIN fund. **7** (*de libros etc*) stock. **8** (*motivo*) reason; (*raíz*) root: *el fondo de nuestra protesta*, the reason for our protest; *esto no toca el fondo de la cuestión*, this does not get to the root of the question. – **9** fondos, *mpl* (*dinero*) funds, money *sing*: *recaudamos fondos a beneficio de los necesitados*, we raise funds for the needy.
● *a fondo*, (*adjetival*) thorough; (*adverbial*) thoroughly. || *a fondo perdido*, non-recoverable, non-returnable: *les concedieron una subvención a fondo perdido*, they were given a grant. || *de ... en fondo*, ... abreast. || *en el fondo*, *fig* deep down, at heart. || *reunir fondos*, to raise funds. || *tocar fondo*, MAR to touch bottom; *fig* to reach rock bottom.
■ *artículo de fondo*, leading article. || *carrera de fondo*, long-distance race. || *carrera de medio fondo*, middle-distance race. || *corredor,-ra de fondo*, long-distance runner. || *corredor,-ra de medio fondo*, middle-distance runner. || *doble fondo*, false bottom. || *esquiador,-ra de fondo*, cross-country skier. || *fondo común*, kitty. || *fondo de inversión*, investment fund. || *fondo de pensiones*, pension fund. || *Fondo Monetario Internacional*, International Monetary Fund. || *fondo del mar*, sea bed. || *fondo y forma*, form and substance. || *fondos bloqueados*, frozen assets. || *fondos disponibles*, available funds, liquid assets. || *fondos públicos*, public funds. || *música de fondo*, background music.
fondón,-ona *adj fam* big-bottomed, fat.
fonducha *f* pey (*restaurante*) cheap restaurant; (*pensión*) cheap boarding house.
fonducho *m* pey → **fonducha**.
fondue *f* fondue.
fonema *m* phoneme.
fonémico,-a *adj* phonemic.
fonendoscopio *m* stethoscope.
fonética *f* → **fonético,-a**.
fonético,-a 1 *adj* phonetic. – **2** fonética, *f* phonetics *sing*.
foniatra *mf* phoniatrician.
foniatría *f* phoniatrics *sing*.
fónico,-a *adj* phonic.
fono- *pref* phono-.
fonocaptor *m* pick-up.
fonográfico,-a *adj* phonographic.
fonógrafo *m* gramophone, us phonograph.
fonología *f* phonology.
fonológico,-a *adj* phonological.
fonólogo,-a *m,f* phonologist.
fonoteca *f* record library.
fontana *f* lit fountain, spring.
fontanería *f* plumbing.
fontanero,-a *m,f* plumber.

footing *m* jogging.
● **hacer footing,** to go jogging.
FOP *abr (Fuerzas del Orden Público)* Spanish police.
foque *m* jib.
forajido,-a *m,f* outlaw, desperado.
foral *adj of the fueros, relating to the fueros.*
foráneo,-a *adj* alien, foreign.
forastero,-a 1 *adj* foreign, alien. – 2 *m,f* stranger, outsider.
forcejear *i* to wrestle, struggle.
forcejeo *m* struggle, struggling.
fórceps *m* forceps *pl.*
▲ *pl* fórceps.
forense 1 *adj* forensic, legal. – 2 *mf* forensic surgeon.
■ **médico forense,** forensic surgeon.
forestal *adj* forest.
forfait *m* ski pass.
▲ *pl* forfaits.
forja 1 *f (fragua)* forge. 2 *(forjado)* forging. 3 *(ferrería)* ironworks, foundry. 4 *fig (formación)* formation: *la forja del carácter,* the formation of character.
forjado,-a 1 *adj* forging. – 2 **forjado,** *m* ARQ *(entramado)* framework.
forjar 1 *t (metales)* to forge. 2 *fig (crear)* to create, make. 3 *fig (imaginar)* to imagine: *forjar sueños,* to dream. – 4 **forjarse,** *p (crearse)* to forge for os.: *forjarse un buen futuro,* to forge a fine future for os. 5 *(imaginarse)* to dream up: *forjarse ilusiones,* to build up false hopes.
forma 1 *f (gen)* form, shape: *en forma de X,* X-shaped. 2 *(manera)* way. 3 DEP form. – 4 **formas,** *fpl (modales)* manners, social conventions. 5 *fam (de mujer)* curves.
● **de esta forma,** in this way. ‖ **de forma que,** so that. ‖ **de todas formas,** anyway, in any case. ‖ **estar en baja forma,** to be off form. ‖ **estar en forma,** to be in shape, be fit. ‖ **ponerse en forma,** to get fit.
■ **buenas formas,** good manners. ‖ **forma de pago,** method of payment. ‖ **forma física,** physical fitness. ‖ **la Sagrada Forma,** the Host.
formación 1 *f (gen)* formation. 2 *(educación)* upbringing. 3 *(enseñanza)* education, training.
● **en formación,** MIL in formation.
■ **formación musical,** musical training. ‖ **formación profesional,** vocational training. ‖ **formación universitaria,** university education.
formal 1 *adj (con los requisitos necesarios)* formal: *noviazgo formal,* formal engagement; *promesa formal,* formal promise. 2 *(serio)* serious, serious-minded. 3 *(cumplidor)* reliable, dependable. 4 *(cortés)* polite.
● **sed formales,** behave yourselves.
formaldehído *m* formaldehyde.
formalidad 1 *f (norma de comportamiento)* formality. 2 *(seriedad)* seriousness. 3 *(fiabilidad)* reliability. 4 *(trámite)* formality, requisite.
● **¡un poco de formalidad!,** please behave yourselves!
■ **una mera formalidad,** a mere formality.
formalina *f* formalin.
formalismo *m* formalism.
formalista 1 *adj* formalistic. – 2 *mf* formalist.
formalizar 1 *t (hacer formal)* to make formal: *formalizaron su noviazgo,* they made their engagement formal. 2 *(legalizar)* to formalize, legalize: *formalizaron la venta del terreno,* they formalized the sale of the land. – 3 **formalizarse,** *p (hacerse serio)* to become serious, grow serious.
▲ *Conjugation model* [4], *like* realizar.

formalmente 1 *adv (con formalidad)* formally. 2 *(con seriedad)* seriously. 3 *(con cortesía)* politely. 4 *(respecto a la forma)* formally.
formar 1 *t (gen)* to form. 2 *(integrar, constituir)* to form, constitute: *formar parte de algo,* to be a part of sth. 3 *(educar)* to bring up. 4 *(enseñar)* to educate. – 5 *i* MIL *(colocarse)* to form up. – 6 **formarse,** *p (desarrollarse)* to grow, develop. 7 *(educarse)* to be educated, be trained.
● **¡a formar!,** MIL fall in!
formatear *t* to format.
formativo,-a 1 *adj (que forma)* formative. 2 *(que educa)* educational.
formato 1 *m (gen)* format. 2 *(del papel)* size.
formica *f* Formica.
▲ *Registered trademark.*
fórmico,-a *adj* formic.
formidable 1 *adj (tremendo)* tremendous, formidable. 2 *(maravilloso)* wonderful, terrific. – 3 *interj* great!
formol *m* formol.
formón *m* firmer chisel.
Formosa *f* Formosa.
fórmula 1 *f (gen)* formula. 2 *(receta)* recipe. 3 AUTO *(categoría)* formula: *fórmula uno,* formula one.
● **por pura fórmula,** for form's sake.
formulación *f* formulation.
formular 1 *t (una teoría)* to formulate. 2 *(quejas, peticiones)* to express, make; *(deseo)* to make; *(pregunta)* to ask. – 3 *i* QUÍM to write formulae.
formulario,-a 1 *adj (rutinario)* routine: *una visita formularia,* a formal visit. – 2 **formulario,** *m (documento)* form: *formulario de solicitud,* application form. 3 *(recetario)* formulary, collection of formulae.
formulismo *m* formulism.
fornicación *f fml* fornication.
fornicador,-ra 1 *adj fml* fornicating. – 2 *m,f fml* fornicator.
fornicar *i fml* to fornicate.
▲ *Conjugation model* [1], *like* sacar.
fornido,-a *adj* strapping, hefty.
fornitura 1 *f* MIL *(correaje y cartuchera)* belts *pl* and cartridge belt. 2 COST *(accesorios)* accessories *pl.* 3 *(de un reloj)* spare parts *pl.*
▲ *In 1 also used in plural with the same meaning.*
foro 1 *m* HIST forum. 2 *(tribunal)* law court, court of justice. 3 *(abogacía)* bar, legal profession: *se dedicó al foro,* he joined the bar. 4 TEAT back (of the stage). 5 *(reunión)* meeting.
forofo,-a *m,f fam* fan, supporter.
forrado,-a 1 *adj* COST lined. 2 *(tapizado)* upholstered. 3 *fam (rico)* well-heeled, well-off.
forraje 1 *m (pienso)* fodder, forage. 2 *fam (mezcla)* hotchpotch.
forrajear 1 *t* to get in the fodder. 2 MIL to forage.
forrajero,-a *adj* fodder.
■ **plantas forrajeras,** fodder crops.
forrar 1 *t (por dentro)* to line. 2 *(por fuera)* to cover. 3 *(tapizar)* to upholster. – 4 **forrarse,** *p fam (de dinero)* to make a fortune, make a packet.
forro 1 *m (interior)* lining. 2 *(funda)* cover, case. 3 *(tapizado)* upholstery.
● **ni por el forro,** *fam* not in the slightest.
fortachón,-ona *adj fam* strong, strapping.
fortalecedor,-ra *adj* fortifying.
fortalecer 1 *t* to fortify, strengthen. – 2 **fortalecerse,** *p* to strengthen, become stronger.

▲ *Conjugation model* |43|, *like **agradecer***.
fortalecimiento *m* fortification, strengthening.
fortaleza 1 *f* (*vigor*) strength, vigour (US vigor). 2 (*de espíritu*) fortitude. 3 (*recinto fortificado*) fortress, stronghold.
forte *m* forte.
fortificación *f* fortification, fortifying.
fortificante 1 *adj* fortifying. – 2 *m* fortifier, tonic.
fortificar *t* to fortify, strengthen.
▲ *Conjugation model* |1|, *like **sacar***.
fortín *m* small fort, bunker.
fortísimo,-a 1 *adj* (*muy fuerte*) very strong. 2 MÚS fortissimo.
fortuito,-a *adj* chance, fortuitous.
fortuna 1 *f* (*destino*) fortune, fate. 2 (*suerte*) luck. 3 (*capital*) fortune. 4 (*éxito, aceptación*) success.
● **por fortuna**, fortunately. ‖ **probar fortuna**, to try one's luck.
■ **buena fortuna**, good luck. ‖ **la rueda de la fortuna**, the wheel of fortune. ‖ **mala fortuna**, misfortune.
forum *m* discussion.
forúnculo *m* boil, furuncle.
forzado,-a 1 *adj* (*obligado*) forced. 2 (*rebuscado*) forced, strained.
■ **risa forzada**, forced laugh. ‖ **trabajos forzados**, hard labour (US labor) *sing*.
forzar 1 *t* (*persona*) to force, compel. 2 (*cosa*) to force open, break open. 3 (*violar*) to rape.
▲ *Conjugation model* |50|.
forzosamente *adv* necessarily.
forzoso,-a 1 *adj* (*inevitable*) inevitable, unavoidable. 2 (*obligatorio*) obligatory, compulsory.
forzudo,-a *adj* strong, brawny.
fosa 1 *f* (*sepultura*) grave. 2 (*hoyo*) pit, hollow. 3 ANAT fossa.
■ **fosa común**, common grave. ‖ **fosas nasales**, nostrils.
fosfato *m* phosphate.
■ **fosfato de cal**, calcium phosphate.
fosforecer *i* to phosphoresce, glow.
▲ *Conjugation model* |43|, *like **agradecer***.
fosforero,-a 1 *m,f* match seller. – 2 **fosforera**, *f* (*caja*) matchbox. 3 (*fábrica*) match factory.
fosforescencia *f* phosphorescence.
fosforescente *adj* phosphorescent.
fosfórico,-a *adj* phosphoric.
fósforo 1 *m* QUÍM phosphorus. 2 (*cerilla*) match.
fósil 1 *adj* fossil. – 2 *m* fossil.
fosilización *f* fossilization.
fosilizado,-a *adj* fossilized.
fosilizarse *p* to fossilize, become fossilized.
▲ *Conjugation model* |4|, *like **realizar***.
foso 1 *m* (*hoyo*) hole, pit. 2 (*de fortaleza*) moat. 3 (*en teatro, deportes*) pit. 4 (*en un garaje*) inspection pit.
■ **foso de la orquesta**, orchestra pit.
foto *f fam* photo, picture.
● **sacar fotos**, to take photos.
foto- *pref* photo-.
fotocalco *m* photoprint.
fotocomposición *f* typesetting, US photosetting.
fotocopia *f* photocopy.
● **hacer una fotocopia de algo / sacar una fotocopia de algo**, to photocopy sth.
fotocopiadora *f* photocopier, photocopying machine.
fotocopiar *t* to photocopy.
▲ *Conjugation model* |12|, *like **cambiar***.
fotoeléctrico,-a *adj* photoelectric.
■ **célula fotoeléctrica**, photoelectric cell.

fotogénico,-a *adj* photogenic.
fotograbado *m* photogravure, photoengraving.
fotograbar *t* to photoengrave.
fotografía 1 *f* (*proceso*) photography. 2 (*retrato*) photograph.
● **hacer fotografías / sacar fotografías**, to take photographs.
fotografiar 1 *t* to photograph, take a photograph of. – 2 **fotografiarse**, *p* to have one's photograph taken.
▲ *Conjugation model* |13|, *like **desviar***.
fotográfico,-a *adj* photographic.
fotógrafo,-a *m,f* photographer.
■ **fotógrafo de prensa**, press photographer.
fotograma *m* shot.
fotólisis *f* photolysis.
▲ *pl* **fotólisis**.
fotolito *m* photolith, film.
fotomatón *m* photo booth.
fotomecánica *f* process engraving.
fotómetro *m* light meter, exposure meter.
fotomontaje *m* photomontage.
fotón *m* photon.
fotonovela *f* photo romance.
fotosíntesis *f* photosynthesis.
▲ *pl* **fotosíntesis**.
fotostato *m* photostat.
fototeca *f* photograph library.
foxterrier 1 *adj* fox-terrier. – 2 *mf* fox-terrier.
fox-trot *m* foxtrot.
FP *abr* EDUC (*Formación Profesional*) Professional Formation (*vocational training*).
Fr. *abr* (*Fray*) friar, frater, brother; (*abreviatura*) Fr.
frac *m* dress coat, tails *pl*.
▲ *pl* **fracs** *or* **fraques**.
fracasado,-a 1 *adj* (*fallido*) unsuccessful. – 2 *m,f* (*persona*) failure.
fracasar *i* to fail, be unsuccessful, fall through.
fracaso *m* failure.
fracción 1 *f* (*gen*) fraction. 2 POL faction.
fraccionamiento *m* breaking up, splitting up, division; (*de petróleo*) cracking.
fraccionar 1 *t* to divide, break up, split up. – 2 **fraccionarse**, *p* to break up, split up.
fraccionario,-a *adj* fractional.
■ **moneda fraccionaria**, small change.
fractura *f* fracture.
fracturar *t* to fracture, break.
fragancia *f* fragrance.
fragante *adj* fragrant, scented.
fraganti in fraganti, *loc adv* in flagrante, red-handed.
fragata *f* frigate.
frágil 1 *adj* (*quebradizo*) fragile, breakable. 2 (*débil*) frail, weak.
fragilidad 1 *f* (*cualidad*) fragility. 2 (*debilidad*) frailty, weakness.
fragmentación *f* fragmentation.
fragmentar 1 *t* (*partir*) to fragment. 2 (*dividir*) to divide up. – 3 **fragmentarse**, *p* to break up, break into pieces.
fragmentario,-a *adj* fragmentary.
fragmento 1 *m* (*pedazo*) fragment, piece. 2 (*literario*) passage.
fragor *m* din, roar; (*de trueno*) crash.
fragoroso,-a *adj* thunderous, deafening.
fragosidad 1 *f* (*del terreno*) roughness, unevenness. 2 (*de la vegetación*) thickness, denseness.

fragoso,-a *adj* (*abrupto*) rough, uneven.
fragua *f* forge.
fraguado *m* setting, hardening.
fraguar 1 *t* (*metal*) to forge. 2 *fig* (*plan*) to dream up, fabricate; (*conspiración*) to hatch. – 3 *i* (*endurecerse*) to set, harden.
▲ Conjugation model [10], *like adecuar.*
fraile *m* friar, monk.
frailecillo *m* puffin.
frailesco,-a *adj* monkish.
frailuno,-a *adj* monkish.
frambuesa *f* raspberry.
francachela *f fam* feast.
francamente 1 *adv* (*con franqueza*) frankly. 2 (*claramente*) clearly.
francés,-esa 1 *adj* French. – 2 *m,f* (*persona*) French person; (*hombre*) Frenchman; (*mujer*) Frenchwoman. – 3 francés, *m* (*idioma*) French. 4 *tabú* (*felación*) blow job.
● hacer un francés al algn., *tabú* to give sb. a blow job. ‖ marcharse a la francesa, to take French leave.
■ tortilla francesa, plain omelette.
francesilla *f* buttercup.
Francfort *m* Frankfurt.
franchute *m,f pey* Frog.
Francia *f* France.
francio *m* francium.
franciscano,-a 1 *adj* Franciscan. – 2 *m,f* Franciscan.
francmasón,-ona *m,f* freemason.
francmasonería *f* freemasonry.
franco³ *m* franc.
franco,-a¹ 1 *adj* HIST Frankish. – 2 *m,f* HIST (*persona*) Frank. – 3 franco, *m* HIST (*idioma*) Frankish.
franco,-a² 1 *adj* (*persona*) frank, open. 2 (*cosa*) clear, obvious. 3 COM free.
● franco,-a a bordo, free on board. ‖ franco de aduana, duty-free. ‖ franco,-a de porte y embalaje, post and packaging free. ‖ franco fábrica, ex-works.
francófilo,-a 1 *adj* francophile. – 2 *m,f* francophile.
francófono,-a 1 *adj* French-speaking, francophone. – 2 *m,f* French speaker, francophone.
francote,-a *adj fam* outspoken, forthright.
francotirador,-ra *m,f* sniper.
franela *f* flannel.
frangollón,-ona *adj* bungling.
franja 1 *f* (*banda*) band, strip. 2 (*de tierra*) strip. 3 COST fringe, border.
■ la franja de Gaza, the Gaza strip.
franqueable 1 *adj* crossable, which can be crossed. 2 (*obstáculo*) surmountable.
franquear 1 *t* (*dejar libre*) to free, clear. 2 (*atravesar*) to cross; *fig* to overcome: *franquear un problema*, to overcome a problem. 3 (*carta*) to frank. – 4 franquearse, *p* to unbosom os., open up one's heart.
● a franquear en destino, postage paid.
■ máquina de franquear, franking machine.
franqueo *m* postage.
franqueza 1 *f* (*sinceridad*) frankness, openness. 2 (*confianza*) familiarity, intimacy.
franquicia 1 *f* exemption. 2 COM franchise.
■ franquicia arancelaria, exemption from customs duty.
franquismo 1 *m* (*movimiento*) Francoism. 2 (*régimen*) the Franco regime.
franquista 1 *adj* Francoist, pro-Franco. – 2 *mf* Francoist, Franco supporter.

frasco *m* flask.
frase 1 *f* (*oración*) sentence. 2 (*expresión*) phrase.
■ frase hecha, set phrase, set expression, idiom.
fraseología 1 *f* LING phraseology. 2 (*palabrería*) verbosity.
fraternal *adj* fraternal, brotherly.
fraternalmente *adv* fraternally.
fraternidad *f* fraternity, brotherhood.
fraternización *f* fraternization.
fraternizar *i* to fraternize.
▲ Conjugation model [4], *like realizar.*
fraterno,-a *adj* fraternal, brotherly.
fratricida 1 *adj* fratricidal. – 2 *mf* fratricide.
fratricidio *m* fratricide.
fraude *m* fraud.
■ fraude fiscal, tax evasion.
fraudulencia *f* fraudulence.
fraudulento,-a *adj* fraudulent.
fray *m* Brother.
frecuencia *f* frequency.
● con frecuencia, frequently, often.
■ alta frecuencia, high frequency. ‖ baja frecuencia, low frequency. ‖ frecuencia modulada, frequency modulation.
frecuentado,-a 1 *pp* → **frecuentar**. – 2 *adj* frequented, popular: *un bar frecuentado por soldados*, a bar popular with soldiers, a bar frequented by soldiers.
frecuentar *t* to frequent, visit.
frecuente 1 *adj* (*repetido*) frequent. 2 (*usual*) common.
frecuentemente *adv* frequently, often.
fregadero *m* kitchen sink.
fregado 1 *m* (*lavado*) washing; (*frotado*) scrubbing. 2 *fam* (*riña*) fight, quarrel; (*lío*) mess, muddle.
fregar 1 *t* (*lavar*) to wash. 2 (*frotar*) to scrub. 3 (*el suelo*) to mop.
● fregar los platos, to wash the dishes, GB do the washing up, wash up.
▲ Conjugation model [48], *like regar.*
fregona 1 *f pey* (*sirvienta*) drudge, GB skivvy. 2 (*utensilio*) mop. 3 (*mujer ordinaria*) common woman.
fregotear *t fam* to give a quick wipe.
fregoteo *m fam* quick wipe.
freidora *f* fryer, deep fryer.
freiduría *f* bar or shop specializing in fried fish.
freír 1 *t* (*guisar*) to fry. 2 *fig* to annoy, exasperate. – 3 freírse, *p* (*comida*) to fry. 4 (*pasar mucho calor*) to be roasting, be boiling hot.
● freír a preguntas, to bombard with questions.
▲ Conjugation model [37], *like reír; pp frito,-a.*
frenado *m* braking.
frenar 1 *t* to brake. 2 *fig* to restrain, check. – 3 *i* to brake: *frenó de golpe*, he jammed on the brakes.
frenazo *m* sudden braking.
● dar un frenazo, to jam on the brakes.
frenesí *m* frenzy.
▲ *pl* frenesíes.
frenéticamente 1 *adv* (*exaltadamente*) frantically. 2 (*con cólera*) wildly.
frenético,-a 1 *adj* (*exaltado*) frenzied, frantic. 2 (*colérico*) wild, mad.
frenillo *m* fraenum (US frenum).
freno 1 *m* (*de auto*) brake. 2 (*de caballería*) bit. 3 *fig* (*contención*) curb, check.
● morder el freno, *fig* to champ at the bit. ‖ poner freno a algo, *fig* to curb sth. ‖ poner el freno, to put on the brake. ‖ soltar el freno, to release the brake.

■ **freno de disco,** disc brake. ‖ **freno de mano,** handbrake. ‖ **freno de tambor,** drum brake. ‖ **líquido de frenos,** brake fluid.
frente 1 *m* (*gen*) front. **2** MIL front, front line. – **3** *f* ANAT forehead.
● **al frente de,** (*delante*) at the head of; (*hacia delante*) ahead. ‖ **arrugar la frente,** to frown. ‖ **chocar de frente,** to crash head on. ‖ **con la frente muy alta,** with one's head up high. ‖ **de frente,** (*hacia adelante*) straight ahead; (*sin rodeos*) straight. ‖ **frente a,** (*enfrente de*) in front of, opposite; (*en contra de*) against; (*en presencia de*) in the presence of. ‖ **frente a frente,** face to face. ‖ **hacer frente a algn.,** to challenge sb., face up to sb. ‖ **hacer frente a algo,** to face sth., face up to sth. ‖ **no tener dos dedos de frente,** to be as thick as two short planks. ‖ **ponerse al frente de algo,** to take command of sth.
fresa 1 *f* (*planta*) strawberry plant. **2** (*fruto*) strawberry. **3** TÉC milling cutter. **4** (*del dentista*) drill. – **5** *adj* strawberry.
fresado 1 *m* TÉC milling. **2** (*del dentista*) drilling.
fresadora 1 *f* TÉC milling machine. **2** (*del dentista*) drill.
fresar 1 *t* TÉC to mill. **2** (*dentista*) to drill.
fresca *f* → **fresco,-a**.
frescachón,-ona *adj fam* healthy, sturdy.
frescales *mf* cheeky devil.
▲ *pl* **frescales.**
fresco,-a 1 *adj* (*temperatura*) cool, cold: *viento fresco,* cool wind; *agua fresca,* cold water. **2** (*tela, vestido*) light, cool. **3** (*aspecto*) healthy, fresh. **4** (*comida*) fresh. **5** (*reciente*) fresh, new: *noticias frescas,* latest news *sing.* **6** *fig* (*impasible*) cool, calm, unworried. **7** (*desvergonzado*) cheeky, shameless. – **8 fresco,** *m* (*frescor*) fresh air, cool air. **9** ART fresco. – **10 fresca,** *f* (*aire fresco*) fresh air, cool air. **11** *fam* (*impertinencia*) cheeky remark.
● **al fresco,** in the cool. ‖ **decirle cuatro frescas a algn.,** to tell sb. a few home truths. ‖ **hacer fresco,** to be chilly. ‖ **¡qué fresco,-a!,** what a nerve! ‖ **quedarse tan fresco,-a,** not to bat an eyelid. ‖ **¡sí que estamos frescos!,** now we're in a fine mess! ‖ **tomar el fresco, tomar la fresca,** to get some fresh air.
frescor *m* coolness, freshness.
frescura 1 *f* (*frescor*) freshness, coolness. **2** (*desvergüenza*) cheek, nerve. **3** (*calma*) coolness, calmness.
● **¡qué frescura!,** what a nerve!
fresno *m* ash tree.
fresón 1 *m* (*planta*) strawberry plant. **2** (*fruto*) (large) strawberry.
fresquera *f* meat safe.
freudiano,-a 1 *adj* Freudian. – **2** *m,f* Freudian.
frialdad 1 *f* (*frío*) coldness. **2** (*indiferencia*) coldness, indifference: *fue recibido con frialdad,* he was given a cool reception. **3** (*frigidez*) frigidity.
fríamente *adv* coldly, coolly.
fricandó *m* fricandeau.
fricasé *m* fricassee.
fricativo,-a *adj* fricative.
fricción 1 *f* (*roce*) friction. **2** (*friega*) rub, rubbing. **3** (*desacuerdo*) friction, discord.
friccionar *t* to rub, massage.
friega *f* rub, rubbing.
friegaplatos *mf* dishwasher.
▲ *pl* **friegaplatos.**
Frigia *f* Phrygia.
frigidez *f* frigidity.
frígido,-a 1 *adj* frigid. – **2** *m,f* frigid person.
frigio,-a 1 *adj* Phrygian. – **2** *m,f* (*persona*) Phrygian. – **3** **frigio,** *m* (*idioma*) Phrygian.

frigorífico,-a 1 *adj* refrigerating. – **2 frigorífico,** *m* (*electrodoméstico*) refrigerator, fridge. **3** (*cámara frigorífica*) cold store.
frijol *m* bean, kidney bean.
frijol *m* bean, kidney bean.
frío,-a 1 *adj* (*gen*) cold. **2** (*indiferente*) cold, cool, indifferent; (*pasmado*) stunned: *la película me dejó frío,* the film left me cold. – **3 frío,** *m* cold.
● **coger a algn. en frío,** *fig* to catch sb. on the hop. ‖ **coger frío,** to catch (a) cold. ‖ **hace un frío que pela,** *fam* it's freezing cold. ‖ **hacer frío,** to be cold. ‖ **pillar frío,** to catch a cold. ‖ **tener frío / pasar frío,** to be cold.
friolera *f* → **friolero,-a**.
friolero,-a 1 *adj* sensitive to the cold: *es muy friolero,* he really feels the cold. – **2 friolera,** *f* (*chuchería*) trifle, trinket. **3** *fam* (*gran cantidad*) fortune: *se gastó la friolera de 30.000 pesetas en unos zapatos,* he spent a mere 30,000 pesetas on a pair of shoes.
frisar¹ *i* (*acercarse*) to approach, border (**con/en**, on).
● **frisar con ... / frisar en ...,** to be getting on for ..., be going on ...: *frisa en los cincuenta,* she's getting on for fifty.
frisar² *t* (*refregar*) to rub.
Frisia *f* Friesland.
frisio,-a 1 *adj* Friesian. – **2** *m,f* (*persona*) Friesian. – **3 frisio,** *m* (*idioma*) Friesian.
friso 1 *m* ARQ frieze. **2** (*zócalo*) skirting board.
frisón,-ona 1 *adj* Friesian. – **2** *m,f* (*persona*) Friesian. – **3 frisón,** *m* (*idioma*) Friesian.
fritada *f* fried dish.
■ **fritada de pescado,** dish of fried fish.
fritanga *f pey* greasy food, greasy dish.
frito,-a 1 *adj* CULIN fried. **2** *fam* fed up, sick: *este niño me tiene frita,* I'm sick and tired of this kid. – **3 frito,** *m* piece of fried food.
● **quedarse frito,-a,** *fam* (*dormido*) to fall fast asleep; (*muerto*) to snuff it.
fritura *f* fried dish.
■ **fritura de pescado,** dish of fried fish.
frivolidad *f* frivolity.
frívolo,-a *adj* frivolous.
fronda *f* foliage.
frondosidad *f* foliage, luxuriance.
frondoso,-a *adj* leafy, luxuriant.
frontal 1 *adj* ANAT frontal. **2** (*choque etc*) head-on. **3** (*delantero*) front. – **4** *m* ANAT frontal bone.
frontera *f* → **frontero,-a**.
fronterizo,-a 1 *adj* border, frontier. **2** *fig* borderline.
frontero,-a 1 *adj* opposite. – **2 frontera,** *f* frontier, border. **3** *fig* limit, bounds *pl*, borderline.
frontis 1 *m* (*fachada*) façade, front. **2** (*frontón*) pediment. **3** (*en artes gráficas*) frontispiece.
▲ *pl* **frontis.**
frontispicio *m* → **frontis**.
frontón 1 *m* (*juego*) pelota. **2** (*edificio*) pelota court. **3** ARQ pediment.
frotación *f* rubbing.
frotamiento *m* rubbing.
frotar *t* to rub.
● **frotarse las manos,** to rub one's hands together.
frote *m* rubbing.
fructífero,-a 1 *adj* BOT fruit-bearing. **2** *fig* fruitful.
fructificar 1 *i* (*dar fruto*) to bear fruit, produce a crop. **2** *fig* (*ser provechoso*) to be fruitful.

▲ Conjugation model [1], like *sacar.*

fructuoso,-a *adj* fruitful.

frugal *adj* frugal.

frugalidad *f* frugality, frugalness.

frugívoro,-a *adj* frugivorous.

fruición *f* pleasure, delight, enjoyment.

frunce *m* gather, gathering.
● con frunces, gathered.

fruncido,-a 1 *pp* → **fruncir.** − 2 *adj* gathered. − 3 fruncido, *m (frunces)* gathers; *(acción)* gathering.

fruncir 1 *t* cost to gather. 2 *(los labios)* to purse, pucker.
● fruncir el ceño, to frown, knit one's brow.
▲ Conjugation model [3], like *zurcir.*

fruslería 1 *f (chuchería)* trinket. 2 *fam (tontería)* trifle.

frustración *f* frustration.

frustrado,-a 1 *adj (persona)* frustrated. 2 *(hechos)* frustrated, unsuccessful.

frustrar 1 *t (cosa)* to frustrate, thwart. 2 *(persona)* to disappoint. − 3 **frustrarse**, *p (proyectos, planes)* to fail, come to nothing. 4 *(persona)* to get frustrated, get disappointed.

frustre *m fam* frustration.

fruta *f* fruit.
■ fruta de sartén, fritter. ‖ fruta del tiempo, fresh fruit. ‖ fruta escarchada, candied fruit. ‖ fruta seca, dried fruit.

frutal 1 *adj* fruit. − 2 *m* fruit tree.

frutería *f* fruit shop.

frutero,-a 1 *adj* fruit. − 2 *m,f* fruit seller, fruiterer. − 3 frutero, *m* fruit dish, fruit bowl.

fruticultura *f* fruit farming.

fruto 1 *m (fruta)* fruit. 2 *(resultado)* fruit, result, product.
● dar fruto, to bear fruit; *fig* to be fruitful. ‖ sacar fruto de algo, to profit from sth.
■ frutos secos, *(almendras etc)* nuts; *(pasas etc)* dried fruit *sing.*

fu ni fu ni fa, *loc* so-so, average.

fucsia 1 *f* fuchsia. − 2 *adj* fuchsia.

fuego 1 *m* fire. 2 *(lumbre)* light. 3 *(cocina)* burner, ring. 4 *(ardor)* ardour (us ardor), zeal.
● a fuego lento, on a low flame; *(al horno)* in a slow oven. ‖ estar entre dos fuegos, to be caught between the Devil and the deep blue sea. ‖ hacer fuego, mil to open fire. ‖ ¿me da fuego?, have you got a light? ‖ poner las manos en el fuego por algo/algn., to stake one's life on sth./sb. ‖ prender fuego a algo, to set fire to sth. ‖ romper fuego, mil to open fire.
■ fuego cruzado, crossfire. ‖ fuego de Santelmo, Saint Elmo's fire. ‖ fuego fatuo, will-o'-the-wisp, Jack-o'-lantern. ‖ fuego graneado, sustained fire. ‖ fuego nutrido, heavy fire. ‖ fuegos artificiales, fireworks. ‖ prueba de fuego, acid test.

fuel *m* fuel oil.

fuelle 1 *m (aparato)* bellows *pl.* 2 *(de flauta)* bag. 3 *(de bolso)* accordion pleats *pl.* 4 *(de cámara fotográfica)* bellows *pl.*

fuel-oil *m* fuel oil.

fuente 1 *f (manantial)* spring. 2 *(artificial)* fountain. 3 *(recipiente)* serving dish, dish. 4 *fig* source.
● de buena fuente, from reliable sources. ‖ de fuente fidedigna, from reliable sources.

fuer a fuer de, *loc fml* as a: *a fuer de amiga,* as a friend.

fuera¹ 1 *adv (exterior)* out, outside: *por fuera,* on the outside; *gente de fuera,* people from other places; *salimos fuera,* we went out, we went outside. 2 *(alejado)* away; *(en el extranjero)* abroad. − 3 *interj* get out! − 4 fuera de, *prep (un lugar)* out of; *(más allá de)* outside, beyond; *(excepto)* except for, apart from.

● estar fuera de sí, to be beside os. ‖ fuera de combate, knocked out. ‖ fuera de duda, beyond doubt. ‖ fuera de lo normal, extraordinary, very unusual. ‖ fuera de peligro, out of danger. ‖ fuera de serie, extraordinary. ‖ jugar fuera, dep to play away.
■ el equipo de fuera, dep the away team. ‖ fuera de juego, offside.

fuera² 1 *imperf subj* → **ser**. 2 → **ir.**

fueraborda 1 *m (motor)* outboard engine, outboard motor. − 2 *f (embarcación)* dinghy with an outboard motor.

fuero 1 *m (ley)* code of laws. 2 *(privilegio)* privilege; *(exención)* exemption. 3 *(jurisdicción)* jurisdiction. − 4 fueros, *mpl (presunción)* arrogance: *no tengas tantos fueros,* don't be so arrogant.
● en el fuero interno de algn., deep down, in one's heart of hearts.

fuerte 1 *adj (gen)* strong: *un café bien fuerte,* a good strong coffee; *un fuerte olor a gas,* a strong smell of gas; *tiene un sabor fuerte,* it has a strong taste; *una cuerda fuerte,* a strong rope; *un acento vasco fuerte,* a strong Basque accent; *la peseta está muy fuerte,* the peseta is very strong; *hay una fuerte conexión betweeen ellos,* there is a strong connection betweeen them. 2 *(en asignatura)* strong, good: *está muy fuerte en historia,* she's very strong on history. 3 *(viento)* strong; *(lluvia, nevada)* heavy; *(tormenta, seísmo)* severe; *(calor)* intense: *vientos fuertes del norte,* strong northerly winds; *los fuertes calores del verano,* the intense summer heat. 4 *(escena - violento)* violent; *(- escandaloso)* shocking; *(- inquietante)* disturbing. 5 *(dolor, enfermedad)* severe, bad: *una fuerte colitis,* a severe stomach infection; *una jaqueca fuerte,* a splitting headache. 6 *(golpe)* hard, heavy. 7 *(sonido)* loud. 8 *(subida)* steep, sharp; *(bajada)* sharp: *el fuerte aumento del paro,* the steep rise in unemployment; *un fuerte descenso en el precio del petróleo,* a sharp fall in the price of oil. 9 *(discusión)* heated, violent; *(protesta)* violent, vigorous; *(polémica)* bitter; *(aplauso)* loud, thunderous. 10 *(presión)* intense; *(influencia)* powerful, strong. 11 *(suma de dinero)* large: *pagaron una fuerte suma de dinero,* they paid a large sum of money; *tuvo que hacer un fuerte desembolso,* he had to spend a great deal of money; *esto requiere una fuerte inversión,* this requires large-scale investment. 12 *(comida - pesado)* heavy; *(- cargado)* rich: *no le gustan las cenas muy fuertes,* he doesn't like heavy suppers; *este guiso lo encuentro un poco fuerte,* I find this stew a little rich. 13 *(color)* intense. 14 *(contraste)* marked, sharp; *(tendency)* strong, marked. 15 *(cosa fija)* stiff, tight. 16 *fam (terrible)* awful. − 17 *m (fortificación)* fort. 18 *(punto fuerte)* strong point. − 19 *adv (mucho)* a lot: *comer fuerte,* to eat a lot. 20 *(con fuerza)* hard: *empuja fuerte,* push hard; *llovía fuerte,* it was raining hard; *le pegó fuerte,* she hit him hard. 21 *(volumen)* loud: *la música sonaba fuerte,* the music was loud.
● ¡abrázame fuerte!, hold me tight! ‖ estar fuerte en algo, to be good at something. ‖ ¡habla más fuerte!, speak up!

fuertemente *adv (con fuerza)* strongly; *(mucho)* heavily: *iban fuertemente armados,* they were heavily armed; *fuertemente subvencionado,* heavily subsidised.

fuerza 1 *f (gen)* strength. 2 *(violencia)* force: *recurrió a la fuerza,* he resorted to violence. 3 fís & mil force. 4 *(electricidad)* power, electric power. 5 *(poder)* power. − 6 fuerzas, *fpl (el poder)* authorities: *las fuerzas vivas de la localidad,* the local authorities.
● a fuerza de, by dint of, by force of. ‖ a la fuerza, by

force. ‖ **con fuerza,** (*gen*) strongly; (*llover*) heavily; (*apretar, agarrar*) tightly; (*pegar, empujar*) hard. ‖ **írsele a algn. la fuerza por la boca,** to be all talk. ‖ **por fuerza,** by force. ‖ **por la fuerza,** against one's will. ‖ **por la fuerza de la costumbre,** by force of habit. ■ **fuerza bruta,** brute force. ‖ **fuerza de voluntad,** willpower. ‖ **fuerza mayor, force majeure.** ‖ **fuerza de gravedad,** force of gravity. ‖ **Fuerzas Aéreas,** Royal Air Force. ‖ **Fuerzas Armadas,** Armed Forces. ‖ **fuerzas del orden público,** police force *sing.*

fuese 1 *imperf subj* → **ser.** 2 → **ir.**

fuga 1 *f* (*huida*) flight, escape. 2 (*escape*) leak. 3 MÚS fugue. ● **darse a la fuga,** to take flight. ‖ **poner en fuga,** to put to flight. ■ **fuga de cerebros,** brain drain. ‖ **fuga de divisas,** flight of capital.

fugacidad *f* fleetingness.

fugarse *p* (*gen*) to flee, escape; (*de casa*) to run away from home; (*de casa y con amante*) to elope (**con,** with). ▲ *Conjugation model* [7], *like* **llegar.**

fugaz *adj* fleeting, brief.

fugazmente *adv* fleetingly.

fugitivo,-a 1 *adj* (*en fuga*) fleeing. 2 *fig* (*efímero*) ephemeral, fleeting. – 3 *m,f* fugitive, runaway.

fui 1 *pt indef* → **ser.** 2 → **ir.**

ful 1 *adj* (*falso*) bogus, phoney. – 2 *f* arg (*mierda*) shit.

fulana *f* → **fulano,-a.**

fulano,-a 1 *m,f* so-and-so; (*hombre*) what's his name; (*mujer*) what's her name. – 2 **fulano,** *m* fam pey guy, GB bloke. – 3 **fulana,** *f* pey whore, tart. ● **Don Fulano de tal,** Mr So-and-so. ‖ **Doña Fulana de tal,** Mrs So-and-So.

fular *m* foulard, scarf.

fulcro *m* fulcrum.

fulero,-a 1 *adj* cheating, crooked. – 2 *m,f* cheater.

fúlgido,-a *adj* lit shining, glowing, bright.

fulgor 1 *m* (*resplandor*) brilliance, glow. 2 *fig* (*esplendor*) splendour (US splendor).

fulgurante 1 *adj* (*brillante*) brilliant, shining. 2 *fig* (*rápido*) rapid.

fulgurar *i* to shine, glow.

fullería 1 *f* (*trampa*) cheating. 2 (*en los naipes*) cardsharping. ● **hacer fullerías,** to cheat.

fullero,-a 1 *adj* (*tramposo*) cheating. – 2 *m,f* (*en los naipes*) cheat, cardsharp, cardsharper.

fulmar *m* fulmar.

fulminación *f* fulmination.

fulminado,-a *adj* struck by lightning.

fulminante 1 *adj* (*que arroja rayos*) fulminating. 2 *fig* (*instantáneo*) instantaneous; (*rápido*) swift; (*súbito*) sudden: *su destitución fue fulminante,* he was dismissed on the spot, he was summarily dismissed. 3 (*enfermedad*) sudden. – 4 *m* (*materia explosiva*) fuse, detonator. ■ **cápsula fulminante,** percussion cap. ‖ **mirada fulminante,** withering look.

fulminar 1 *t* to strike with lightning. 2 *fig* to strike dead. ● **fulminar a algn. (con la mirada),** to look daggers at sb.

fumada *f* puff (of smoke).

fumadero *m* pey smoking den.

fumado,-a *adj* arg stoned.

fumador,-ra 1 *adj* smoking. – 2 *m,f* smoker. ● **los no fumadores,** nonsmokers.

fumar 1 *t* to smoke. – 2 *i* to smoke. – 3 **fumarse,** *p* to smoke: *se fumó diez cigarrillos,* he smoked ten ciga-

rettes. 4 (*malgastar*) to waste: *se fumó su fortuna en dos años,* he wasted his fortune in two years. ● **fumarse las clases,** fam to play truant, US play hooky. ‖ **"no fumar",** "no smoking".

fumarel *m* tern. ■ **fumarel cariblanco,** whiskered tern. ‖ **fumarel común,** black tern.

fumeta *mf* arg dope fiend, pot-head.

fumigación *f* fumigation.

fumigar *t* to fumigate. ▲ *Conjugation model* [7], *like* **llegar.**

funámbulo,-a *m,f* tightrope walker.

función 1 *f* (*gen*) function. 2 (*cargo*) duty. 3 (*espectáculo*) performance, show. ● **en función de,** according to. ‖ **en funciones,** acting: *el presidente en funciones cerró la reunión,* the acting president closed the meeting. ‖ **entrar en función,** (*persona*) to take up one's post. ‖ **estar en funciones,** to be in office. ■ **función de noche,** evening performance. ‖ **función de tarde,** matinée.

funcional *adj* functional.

funcionamiento *m* operation, working. ● **poner en funcionamiento,** to put into operation.

funcionar *i* (*desempeñar una función*) to work, function: *funciona con gasolina/diesel,* it runs on petrol/diesel. ● **hacer funcionar algo,** to operate sth. ‖ **"no funciona",** "out of order".

funcionario,-a *m,f* functionary, employee. ■ **funcionario,-a público,-a,** civil servant, government employee.

funda 1 *f* (*flexible*) cover. 2 (*rígida*) case. 3 (*de arma blanca*) sheath. 4 (*de disco*) sleeve. ■ **funda de almohada,** pillowcase. ‖ **funda de colchón,** mattress cover.

fundación *f* foundation.

fundado,-a *adj* firm, well-founded, justified. ● **mal fundado,-a,** ill-founded.

fundador,-ra *m,f* founder.

fundamental *adj* fundamental.

fundamentalismo *m* fundamentalism.

fundamentalista 1 *adj* fundamentalist. – 2 *mf* fundamentalist.

fundamentalmente *adv* fundamentally, basically.

fundamentar 1 *t* fig to base (**en,** on). 2 (*construcción*) to lay the foundations of.

fundamento 1 *m* (*base*) basis, grounds *pl.* 2 (*seriedad*) seriousness; (*confianza*) reliability: *Cecilia es persona de fundamento,* Cecilia is reliable. – 3 **fundamentos,** *mpl* (*construcción*) foundations. ● **sin fundamento,** unfounded.

fundar 1 *t* (*crear*) to found; (*erigir*) to raise: *su padre fundó la empresa,* her father founded the company. 2 (*basar*) to base, found: *funda su teoría en falsos argumentos,* he bases his theory on false arguments. – 3 **fundarse,** *p* (*crearse*) to be founded: *la empresa se fundó en 1845,* the company was founded in 1845. 4 (*teoría, afirmación*) to be based (**en,** on); (*persona*) to base os. (**en,** on): *la teoría se funda en falsos argumentos,* the theory is based on false arguments.

fundición 1 *f* (*derretimiento*) melting. 2 (*de metales*) smelting. 3 (*acción de dar forma*) casting. 4 (*lugar*) foundry, smelting works. ■ **fundición de acero,** steelworks. ‖ **hierro de fundición,** cast iron.

fundido *m* (*entrando*) fade-in; (*saliendo*) fade-out.

fundidor m smelter, caster.
fundir 1 t (derretir) to melt: *el sol funde la nieve,* the sun melts the snow. **2** (separar mena y metal) to smelt. **3** (dar forma) to cast: *fundir una figura en bronce,* to cast a figure in bronze. **4** (bombilla, plomos) to blow. **5** (unir) to unite, join. **6** fam (despilfarrar) to waste, blow: *fundió todo el dinero en aquel regalo,* he blew all his money on that present. – **7 fundirse,** p (derretirse) to melt: *la nieve se funde,* snow melts. **8** (bombilla, plomos) to fuse, go, blow, burn out: *se han fundido los plomos,* the fuses have gone. **9** (unirse) to merge.
fúnebre 1 adj (mortuorio) funeral. **2** (lúgubre) mournful, lugubrious.
funeral 1 adj funeral. – **2** m (entierro) funeral. **3** (conmemoración) memorial service.
▲ In 2 and 3 also used in plural with the same meaning.
funerala a la funerala, loc adv MIL with reversed arms.
■ ojo a la funerala, fam black eye.
funeraria f → **funerario,-a**.
funerario,-a 1 adj funerary, funeral. – **2 funeraria,** f undertaker's, US funeral parlor.
funesto,-a adj ill-fated, fatal: *el accidente tuvo consecuencias funestas,* the accident had fatal consequences.
fungicida 1 adj fungicidal. – **2** m fungicide.
funicular m funicular, funicular railway.
furcia f pey whore, tart.
furgón 1 m AUTO van, truck. **2** (de tren) (goods) wagon, US boxcar.
■ furgón de cola, guard's van.
furgoneta f van.
furia f fury, rage.
● ponerse hecho,-a una furia, to get furious, fly into a rage.
furibundo,-a adj furious, enraged.
furiosamente adv furiously.
furioso,-a 1 adj (colérico) furious. **2** (tempestad, vendaval) raging.
● ponerse furioso,-a, to get angry.
furor m fury, rage.
● hacer furor, fig to be all the rage.
furriel m quartermaster.
furtivamente adv furtively.
furtivo,-a adj furtive.
■ caza furtiva, poaching. ‖ cazador furtivo, poacher. ‖ pesca furtiva, poaching. ‖ pescador furtivo, poacher.
furúnculo m boil.
fusa f demisemiquaver, US thirty-second note.
fuseaux m ski pants pl.
fuselaje m fuselage.
fusible 1 adj fusible. – **2** m fuse.

fusil m rifle, gun.
● echarse el fusil a la cara, to aim one's rifle.
■ fusil ametrallador, automatic rifle. ‖ fusil de juguete, popgun, toy gun. ‖ fusil de repetición, repeater, magazine rifle.
fusilamiento m shooting, execution.
fusilar 1 t (ejecutar) to shoot, execute. **2** (plagiar) to plagiarize.
fusilería 1 f (fusiles) rifles pl. **2** (soldados fusileros) fusiliers pl. **3** (descarga) rifle fire, rifle shots pl.
■ descarga de fusilería / fuego de fusilería, fusillade.
fusilero m fusilier, rifleman.
fusión 1 f (de metales) fusion, melting; (de hielo) thawing, melting. **2** (de intereses, partidos, ideas) fusion. **3** (de empresas) merger, amalgamation.
■ punto de fusión, melting point.
fusionar 1 t (fundir) to fuse. **2** (unir) to join, unite. **3** COM to merge: *proponen fusionar ambas empresas,* they propose to merge the two companies. – **4 fusionarse,** p (unir) to join, unite; (empresas) to merge.
fusta f riding whip.
fuste 1 m (palo) stick. **2** (de columna) shaft. **3** (importancia) importance: *una empresa de fuste,* an important firm; *un hombre de fuste,* a man of consequence.
fustigar 1 t (al caballo) to whip, lash. **2** (censurar, criticar) to criticize severely.
▲ Conjugation model [7], like llegar.
futbol m → **fútbol**.
fútbol m football, soccer.
■ fútbol americano, American football.
futbolero,-a 1 m,f fam football fan, soccer fan. – **2** adj football-crazy, soccer-crazy.
futbolín m table football.
futbolista mf footballer, football player, soccer player.
futbolístico,-a adj football.
futesa f fam trifle.
fútil adj unimportant, trivial.
futilidad f triviality.
● hablar de futilidades, to talk about trivialities.
futón m futon.
futura f → **futuro,-a**.
futurismo m futurism.
futurista 1 adj futuristic. – **2** mf futurist.
futuro,-a 1 adj future. – **2 futuro,** m future. **3** (prometido) fiancé, intended. – **4 futura,** f (prometida) fiancée, intended. – **5 futuros,** mpl ECON futures.
● en un futuro próximo, in the near future.
■ futuro imperfecto, future. ‖ futuro perfecto, future perfect.
futurología f futurology.
futurólogo,-a m,f futurologist

G

G, g[1] *f (la letra)* G, g.
g[2] *sím (gramo)* gram, gramme; *(símbolo)* g.
g/ *abr* FIN *(giro)* giro.
gabacho,-a I *adj pey* frog. – **2** *m,f pey* frog.
gabán *m* overcoat.
gabardina I *f (impermeable)* raincoat. **2** *(tela)* gabardine.
● **en gabardina / con gabardina,** fried in batter: *tomamos gambas en gabardina,* we had prawns in batter.
gabarra *f* barge, lighter.
gabela *f* tax, duty.
gabinete I *m (habitación)* study. **2** POL cabinet. **3** *(despacho)* office. **4** *(en museo)* section, room. **5** *(departamento)* department: *el Gabinete de Industria aprobó algunas medidas,* the Industry Department passed some measures.
■ **gabinete de consulta,** MED surgery. ‖ **gabinete de crisis,** emergency cabinet. ‖ **gabinete de lectura,** reading room. ‖ **gabinete en la sombra,** Shadow Cabinet.
gablete *m* gable, gable end.
Gabón *m* Gabon.
gabonés,-esa I *adj* Gabonese. – **2** *m,f* Gabonese.
gacela *f* gazelle.
gaceta I *f (publicación)* gazette. **2** *fam (persona)* gossip.
● **ser una gaceta,** *fam* to be the local newspaper.
gacetilla *f* "news in brief" section.
gacetillero,-a I *m,f (editor)* editor of "news in brief" section. **2** *(periodista)* journalist.
gacha I *f (masa)* paste. – **2 gachas,** *fpl (papilla)* porridge *sing.*
● **hacerse unas gachas,** *fig* to turn sentimental.
gachí *f arg* bird, chick.
gachó *m arg* bloke, guy, geezer.
gacho,-a *adj* drooping, bent.
● **a gachas,** on all fours. ‖ **con la cabeza gacha,** with one's head bowed. ‖ **con las orejas gachas,** *fig* with one's tail between one's legs.
gachón,-ona *adj fam* amusing, charming.
gaditano,-a I *adj* of Cádiz, from Cádiz. – **2** *m,f* person from Cádiz, inhabitant of Cádiz.
gafa I *f (agarrar)* clamp. – **2 gafas,** *fpl* spectacles, glasses. **3** *(de motorista, esquí, natación)* goggles.
■ **gafas de bucear,** diving mask *sing.* ‖ **gafas de sol,** sunglasses.
gafar I *t (agarrar)* to hook. **2** *fam (traer mala suerte)* to put a jinx on, bring bad luck to.
gafe I *adj fam* jinx. – **2** *mf fam* jinx.
gafete *m* hook and eye.
gafotas *mf fam* four-eyes.
gafudo,-a I *adj fam* four-eyed. – **2** *m,f fam* four-eyes.
gag *m* gag, sketch.
▲ *pl* **gags.**
gaita I *f* bagpipes *pl,* pipes *pl.* **2** *fam* bother, drag, pain.
● **¡menuda gaita! / ¡qué gaita!,** *fam* what a drag! ‖ **templar gaitas,** *fam* to smooth things out.

gaitero,-a I *m,f* MÚS piper, bagpipe player. – **2** *adj (chillón)* gaudy, flashy. **3** *(bufo)* buffoonish, clownish.
gajes *mpl (dietas)* allowance *sing,* expenses.
■ **gajes del oficio,** *irón* occupational hazards.
gajo I *m (de fruta)* segment. **2** *(racimo)* bunch. **3** *(rama)* torn-off branch.
GAL *abr* POL *(Grupos Antiterroristas de Liberación)* Anti-Terrorist Liberation Squads *(counter-terror unit).*
gala I *f (espectáculo)* gala. **2** *(vestido)* best dress. – **3 galas,** *fpl (adorno)* finery *sing: se pusieron sus mejores galas para la fiesta,* they dressed up in their best clothes for the party.
● **de gala,** *(gen)* dressed up; *(militar)* in full uniform. ‖ **hacer gala de,** to make a show of. ‖ **lucir sus mejores galas,** to be dressed in all one's finery. ‖ **tener algo a gala,** to be proud of sth.
■ **cena de gala,** gala dinner. ‖ **galas de novia,** bridal attire. ‖ **noche de gala,** gala night.
galáctico,-a *adj* galactic.
galán I *m (atractivo)* handsome young man; *(mujeriego)* ladies' man. **2** *(pretendiente)* suitor. **3** TEAT hero. – **4** *adj* smart, handsome.
■ **galán de noche,** *(flor)* night jasmine; *(mueble)* valet.
galancete I *m pey* foppish young man. **2** TEAT young male lead.
galano,-a *adj* smart, elegant.
galante *adj* courteous, gallant, chivalrous.
galanteador,-ra *adj* flirtatious.
galantear *t* to court, woo.
galantemente *adv* gallantly, politely.
galanteo *m* flirtation, wooing.
galantería I *f (caballerosidad)* gallantry, chivalry. **2** *(piropo)* compliment.
galanura *f* gracefulness, elegance.
galápago I *m (animal)* turtle. **2** *(lingote)* ingot. **3** *(silla de montar)* light saddle.
Galápagos las (islas) Galápagos, *fpl* the Galápagos Islands.
galardón *m* prize.
galardonado,-a I *pp* → **galardonar.** – **2** *adj* prizewinning: *no me gustó la novela galardonada,* I didn't like the prizewinning novel. – **3** *m,f* prizewinner.
galardonar *t (premio)* to award a prize to; *(medalla)* to award a medal to: *lo galardonaron con varios premios literarios,* he was awarded several literary prizes.
galaxia *f* galaxy.
galbana *f fam* sluggishness, laziness, apathy.
● **tener galbana,** to feel lazy, feel sluggish.
galena *f* lead sulphide.
galeno *m fam* doctor.
galeón *m* galleon.
galera I *f (mar)* galley. **2** *(crustáceo)* squilla. **3** *(imprenta)* galley.
● **condenar a algn. a galeras,** to send sb. to the galleys.

galerada *f* galley proof.
galería 1 *f* (*gen*) gallery. 2 (*corredor descubierto*) balcony, verandah. 3 TEAT gallery, balcony. 4 (*para cortinas*) pelmet, US cornice.
● **hacer algo de cara a la galería,** to play to the gallery. ‖ **hacer algo para la galería,** to play to the gallery.
■ **galería comercial / galerías comerciales,** shopping centre *sing.*
galerín *f* small galley.
galerna *f* strong northwest wind.
galerno *m* → **galerna.**
Gales *m* Wales.
■ **País de Gales,** Wales.
galés,-a 1 *adj* Welsh. − 2 *m,f* (*persona*) Welsh person; (*hombre*) Welshman; (*mujer*) Welshwoman. − 3 **galés,** *m* (*idioma*) Welsh.
galga *f* boulder, large stone.
galgo,-a *m,f* greyhound.
● **¡échale un galgo!,** *fam* don't count on it. ‖ **salir como un galgo,** *fam* to shoot out, shoot off.
Galia *f* Gaul.
gálibo *m* loading gauge.
■ **luces de gálibo,** clearance lights.
Galicia *f* Galicia.
galicismo *m* gallicism.
Galilea *f* Galilee.
■ **Mar de Galilea,** Sea of Galilee.
galileo,-a 1 *adj* Galilean. − 2 *m,f* Galilean.
galimatías *m fam* gibberish, double Dutch.
▲ *pl* **galimatías.**
gallardear *i* to strut.
gallardete *m* pennant.
gallardía 1 *f* (*elegancia*) elegance, poise. 2 (*arresto*) gallantry, bravery.
gallardo,-a 1 *adj* (*apuesto*) elegant, handsome. 2 (*valeroso*) brave, gallant.
gallear *i* to swank, show off.
gallego,-a 1 *adj* Galician. − 2 *m,f* (*persona*) Galician. − 3 **gallego,** *m* (*idioma*) Galician.
gallera *f* coop.
galleta 1 *f* CULIN biscuit, US cookie. 2 *fam* (*cachete*) slap, smack: *le dio una galleta al niño sin motivo,* he smacked the child for no reason at all. 3 *fam* (*golpe*) crash: *¡menuda galleta se dio contra el muro!,* he crashed into the wall! 4 (*mineral*) *type of* anthracite.
■ **galleta maría,** Marie biscuit, rich tea biscuit.
gallina 1 *f* hen. − 2 *mf fam* chicken, coward.
● **acostarse con las gallinas,** to go to bed very early. ‖ **como gallina en corral ajeno,** *fam* like a fish out of water. ‖ **jugar a la gallina ciega,** to play blind man's buff. ‖ **matar la gallina de los huevos de oro,** *fam* to kill the goose that lays the golden eggs.
■ **carne de gallina,** gooseflesh, goose pimples *pl.* ‖ **gallina clueca,** broody hen. ‖ **gallina de agua,** coot. ‖ **gallina de Guinea,** guinea fowl. ‖ **gallina de mar,** stargazer. ‖ **piel de gallina,** gooseflesh, goose pimples *pl.*
gallinero 1 *m* henhouse. 2 *fam* bedlam, madhouse: *aquello era un gallinero, todos hablaban a la vez,* it was a madhouse, everyone was talking at the same time. 3 *el* **gallinero,** TEAT the gods *pl.*
gallinita **la gallinita ciega,** *f* blind man's buff.
gallito 1 *m fam* (*presumido*) cock of the walk, show-off. 2 *fam* (*bravucón*) bully, troublemaker.
gallo 1 *m* cock, rooster. 2 (*pez*) John Dory. 3 *fig* (*al cantar*) false note; (*al hablar*) squeak. 4 *fam fig* (*mandón*) cock of

the walk. 5 *fam* (*presumido, bravucón*) cocky person, tough guy.
● **alzar el gallo,** *fam* to get on one's high horse. ‖ **bajar el gallo,** *fam* to get off one's high horse. ‖ **en menos que canta un gallo,** in a flash. ‖ **estar como gallo en gallinero,** *fam* to strut about like a cock. ‖ **otro gallo me** *(te, le, etc)* **cantara,** *fam* things would have turned out differently. ‖ **tener mucho gallo,** *fam* to be very cocky.
■ **gallo de pelea,** fighting cock, gamecock. ‖ **gallo silvestre,** capercaillie, woodgrouse.
galo,-a 1 *adj* HIST Gaulish. 2 *irón* French: *el país galo,* France. − 3 *m,f* HIST (*persona*) Gaul. − 4 **galo,** *m* HIST (*idioma*) Gaulish.
galocha *f type of* clog.
galón¹ 1 *m* (*cinta*) braid. 2 MIL stripe, chevron.
galón² *m* (*medida*) gallon.
galopada *f* gallop.
galopante 1 *adj* (*equitación*) galloping. 2 *fig* galloping: *una gangrena galopante se lo llevó de la noche a la mañana,* galloping gangrene did away with him overnight.
galopar *i* to gallop.
galope *m* gallop.
● **a galope / al galope,** at a gallop; *fig* in a rush. ‖ **a galope tendido,** at full gallop. ‖ **a medio galope,** at a canter.
galopín 1 *m* (*golfillo*) urchin, ragamuffin. 2 (*bribón*) rogue.
galvánico,-a *adj* galvanic.
galvanismo *m* galvanism.
galvanización *f* galvanization.
galvanizado,-a 1 *pp* → **galvanizar.** − 2 *adj* galvanized. − 3 **galvanizado,** *m* FÍS galvanization.
galvanizar *t* to galvanize.
▲ *Conjugation model* |4|, *like* **realizar.**
galvanómetro *m* galvanometer.
gama¹ 1 *f* MÚS scale. 2 (*gradación, variedad*) range: *el cuadro tenía toda la gama de verdes,* there was every shade of green in the painting.
gama² *f* ZOOL doe.
gamba¹ *f* ZOOL prawn; (*pequeña*) shrimp.
gamba² *f arg* (*pierna*) leg.
● **meter la gamba,** *fam* to put one's foot in it.
gamberrada *f* act of hooliganism, act of vandalism: *su última gamberrada ha sido romper todos los cristales,* his latest act of vandalism was to break all the windows.
● **hacer una gamberrada,** to cause trouble.
gamberrismo *m* hooliganism, vandalism.
gamberro,-a 1 *adj* loutish, rowdy. − 2 *m,f* vandal, hooligan, lout.
gambeta 1 *f* (*en danza*) cross-step. 2 (*equitación*) curvet, prance.
gambetear 1 *i* (*danzar*) to cross-step. 2 (*equitación*) to curvet, prance.
Gambia *f* Gambia.
gambiano,-a 1 *adj* Gambian. − 2 *m,f* Gambian.
gambito *m* gambit.
gamella *f* feeding trough.
gameto *m* gamete.
gamma *f* gamma.
■ **rayos gamma,** gamma rays.
gamo *m* fallow deer.
gamuza 1 *f* ZOOL chamois. 2 (*piel*) chamois leather. 3 (*paño*) duster.
gana 1 *f* (*deseo*) wish (*de,* for), desire. 2 (*apetito*) appetite; (*hambre*) hunger.

● **dar a algn. la gana de hacer algo,** *fam* to feel like doing sth.: *no me da la real gana,* I don't damn well feel like it. ‖ **de buena gana,** willingly. ‖ **de mala gana,** reluctantly. ‖ **entrarle a uno ganas de (hacer) algo,** to really feel like (doing) sth. ‖ **hacer algo con ganas,** *fam* to really enjoy doing sth.: *después del viaje durmió con ganas,* after the journey she had a good long sleep. ‖ **quedarse con las ganas de hacer algo,** *fam* not to get to do sth., not get a chance to do sth.: *se quedó con las ganas de explicarnos su viaje,* she didn't get to tell us about her journey. ‖ **tener gana,** *(hambre)* to be hungry. ‖ **tener ganas de (hacer) algo,** to feel like (doing) sth. ‖ **tenerle ganas a algn.,** *fam* to have it in for sb. ‖ **venir a uno en gana,** *fam* to feel like: *no me viene en gana,* I don't feel like it.

ganadería 1 *f (crianza)* cattle-raising, stock-breeding. **2** *(ganado)* cattle, livestock. **3** *(raza particular)* herd: *el toro era de la ganadería Domecq,* the bull was from the Domecq herds. **4** *(rancho)* stock farm, cattle ranch.

ganadero,-a 1 *adj* cattle. – **2** *m,f (propietario)* cattle breeder, stockbreeder. **3** *(cuidador de ganado)* herdsman, us herder.

ganado 1 *m* livestock, stock; *(vacas)* cattle. **2** *fam (gente)* crowd: *¡menudo ganado había en la fiesta!,* there was a real odd crowd at the party!
■ **ganado bovino,** cattle *pl.* ‖ **ganado caballar,** horses *pl.* ‖ **ganado caprino,** goats *pl.* ‖ **ganado de cerda,** pigs *pl.* ‖ **ganado equino,** horses *pl.* ‖ **ganado lanar,** sheep *pl.* ‖ **ganado mayor,** *(bovino)* cattle *pl*; *(caballar)* horses *pl.* ‖ **ganado menor,** *(ovino)* sheep *pl*; *(caprino)* goats *pl*; *(porcino)* pigs *pl.* ‖ **ganado ovino,** sheep *pl.* ‖ **ganado vacuno,** cattle *pl.*

ganador,-ra 1 *adj* winning. – **2** *m,f* winner.

ganancia 1 *f* gain, profit: *tuvieron buenas ganancias gracias a la ampliación,* they made a lot of money thanks to the extension.
● **no *(te, le, etc)* arriendo la ganancia,** I wouldn't like to swap places with *(you, him, etc)*.
■ **ganancia líquida,** COM net profit. ‖ **margen de ganancia,** COM profit margin.

ganancial *adj* relating to profit, relating to earnings.
■ **bienes gananciales,** community property *sing.*

ganancioso,-a *adj* profitable, lucrative.
● **salir ganancioso,-a de algo,** to gain from sth., benefit from sth., do well out of sth.

ganapán 1 *m (recadero, botones)* odd-jobber, dogsbody. **2** *(hombre tosco)* lout.

ganar 1 *t (partido, concurso, premio)* to win: *ganaron el partido,* they won the match. **2** *(dinero)* to earn: *¿cuánto ganas al año?,* how much do you earn a year? **3** *(conquistar)* to capture: *ganaron la ciudad a los árabes,* they captured the city from the Arabs. **4** *(alcanzar)* to reach: *ganaron la cima,* they reached the summit. **5** *(lograr)* to win: *finalmente ganaron la amistad de sus vecinos,* they finally won the friendship of their neighbours. – **6** *i (mejorar)* to improve: *ha ganado mucho con los años,* it has improved greatly with age. **7** *(cambiar favorablemente)* to gain: *ganamos con el cambio,* we gained with the change. – **8** **ganarse,** *p* to earn: *me gano cien mil al mes,* I earn a hundred thousand pesetas a month; *se gana bien la vida,* he makes a good living. **9** *(ser merecedor)* to deserve: *se lo han ganado,* they deserve it.
● **ganar a algn. en algo,** to be better than sb. at sth.: *me ganas en inglés,* you're better at English than I am; *ella le gana en inteligencia,* she's much more intelligent than he is. ‖ **ganar terreno,** to gain ground. ‖ **llevar las de ganar,** *fig* to hold the winning card, hold all the

cards. ‖ **no ganar para disgustos,** *fig* to be one thing after another. ‖ **salir ganando,** to gain, benefit,do well out of it. ‖ **ganarse la vida,** to earn a living, earn one's living. ‖ **ganarse el pan,** *fam* to earn one's bread and butter. ‖ **¡te la vas a ganar!,** *fam* you're going to get it!

ganchillo 1 *m (aguja)* crochet hook. **2** *(labor)* crochet work.
● **hacer ganchillo,** to crochet.

gancho 1 *m* hook. **2** *(para ropa)* peg. **3** *(cayado)* shepherd's crook. **4** *fam (atractivo)* attractiveness, charm. **5** *fam (compinche de un estafador)* bait, decoy. **6** *(en boxeo)* hook. **7** *(en baloncesto)* hook shot.
● **echar el gancho a algn.,** *fam* to hook sb. ‖ **tener gancho,** *fam* to be attractive, have charm.

ganchudo,-a *adj* hook-shaped.

gandul,-la 1 *adj* lazy, idle. – **2** *m,f* idler, loafer, lazybones, slacker.

gandulear *i* to idle, loaf around, laze around, slack.

gandulería *f* idleness, laziness.

ganga[1] 1 *f (algo barato)* bargain, good buy. **2** *fam (algo fácil)* gift, cinch, piece of cake. **3** *(ave)* sand-grouse.
■ **precio de ganga,** bargain price.

ganga[2] *f (en minería)* gang, gangue.

Ganges el Ganges, *m* the Ganges.

ganglio *m* ganglion.

gangoso,-a *adj* nasal, twanging.

gangrena *f* gangrene.

gangrenarse *p* to become gangrenous.

gángster *m* gangster.
▲ *pl* gángsteres.

ganguear *i* to speak with a twang.

gangueo *m* nasal accent, twang.

gansada *f fam* silly thing to say, silly thing to do: *estoy harto de tus gansadas,* I'm fed up with your fooling about.

gansear *i* to do silly things, to say silly things.

ganso,-a 1 *m,f* ZOOL goose; *(macho)* gander. **2** *(gandul)* lazy oaf. **3** *(torpe)* dimwit, fool, idiot. **4** *(bromista)* clown, prankster. – **5** *adj (gandul)* slow, lazy. **6** *(torpe)* dim. **7** *(bromista)* fond of joking.
● **hacer el ganso,** *fam* to play the fool. ‖ **¡no seas ganso!,** don't be an idiot!
■ **ganso bravo / ganso salvaje,** wild goose. ‖ **paso de ganso,** MIL goose-step.

ganzúa 1 *f (garfio)* picklock. **2** *(ladrón)* burglar. **3** *(sonsacador)* coaxer, wheedler.

gañán 1 *m (mozo de labranza)* farmhand. **2** *(hombre tosco)* big brute.

gañido *m* yelp.

gañir 1 *i (aullar)* to yelp; *(aves)* to caw, croak. **2** *fig (resollar)* to scream, shriek. **3** *fam (estar ronco)* to croak, wheeze.
▲ *Conjugation model* [40], *like muñir.*

gañote *m fam* throat, gullet.
● **de gañote,** free.

garabatear 1 *t (escribir)* to scribble, scrawl; *(dibujar)* to doodle. – **2** *i (escribir)* to scribble, scrawl; *(dibujar)* to doodle.

garabato 1 *m (gancho)* hook. **2** *(dibujo)* doodle; *(escritura)* scrawl, scribble.

garaje *m* garage.

garambaina 1 *f* cheap finery, frippery. – **2 garambainas,** *fpl fam* fooling about *sing,* messing about *sing,* nonsense *sing*: *déjate de garambainas y haz los deberes,* stop messing about and do your homework.

garante 1 *adj* responsible, acting as guarantor. – **2** *mf* guarantor.

garantía 1 *f* (*seguridad*) guarantee, security. **2** COM guarantee, warranty: *la televisión tiene garantía por seis meses,* the television has a six-month guarantee. **3** JUR bond, warranty, security.
● **bajo garantía,** under guarantee.
■ **certificado de garantía,** guarantee. ‖ **garantías constitucionales,** constitutional guarantees.
garantizado,-a 1 *pp* → **garantizar.** − **2** *adj* guaranteed. **3** JUR secured.
garantizar 1 *t* to guarantee. **2** COM to warrant. **3** (*responder por*) to vouch for, stand as guarantor for: *su padre le garantizó para la compra de la moto,* his father stood as guarantor for him when he bought the motorbike.
▲ *Conjugation model* [4], *like realizar.*
garañón *m* stud donkey.
garapiña *f* sugar coating.
garapiñar 1 *t* (*gen*) to coat with sugar. **2** (*fruta*) to candy.
■ **almendra garapiñada,** sugared almond.
garbanzo *m* chickpea.
● **en toda tierra de garbanzos,** everywhere. ‖ **ganarse los garbanzos,** *fam* to earn one's bread and butter.
■ **garbanzo negro,** *fam* black sheep.
garbearse *p fam* to take a stroll.
garbeo 1 *m fam* walk, stroll. **2** (*viaje*) trip.
● **dar un garbeo / darse un garbeo,** to go for a walk.
garbo 1 *m* (*airosidad al andar*) gracefulness, poise. **2** (*gracia*) grace, stylishness. **3** (*generosidad*) generosity, unselfishness.
garboso,-a 1 *adj* (*airoso*) graceful, stylish. **2** (*generoso*) generous.
gardenia *f* gardenia.
garduña *f* marten.
garduño,-a 1 *adj* thieving. − **2** *m,f* sneak thief.
garete ir(se) al garete, *loc* to collapse, fail.
garfio *m* hook, grapple.
gargajear *i* to clear one's throat noisily, spit.
gargajo *m* spit, phlegm.
garganta 1 *f* (*cuello*) throat. **2** (*desfiladero*) gorge, narrow pass. **3** (*voz*) voice. **4** (*empeine*) instep.
● **tener buena garganta,** to have a good voice. ‖ **tener a algn. atravesado en la garganta,** *fam* not to be able to stand sb. ‖ **tener un nudo en la garganta,** *fig* to have a lump in one's throat.
■ **dolor de garganta,** sore throat.
gargantilla *f* short necklace, choker.
gárgaras *mpl* gargles *pl,* gargling *sing.*
● **hacer gárgaras,** to gargle. ‖ **mandar a hacer gárgaras,** *fam* to tell sb. to get lost: *¡vete a hacer gárgaras!,* get lost!
gargarismo 1 *m* (*gárgaras*) gargles *pl,* gargling. **2** (*líquido*) gargling solution.
gargarizar *i* to gargle.
▲ *Conjugation model* [4], *like realizar.*
gárgola *f* gargoyle.
garguero *m fam* throat.
gargüero *m fam* throat.
garita 1 *f* (*caseta*) box, cabin, hut; (*de centinela*) sentry box. **2** (*portería*) porter's lodge.
garito 1 *m* (*casa de juego*) gambling den, gaming house. **2** (*antro de diversión*) dive, joint: *este garito abre hasta la 6 de la madrugada,* this joint is open till 6 a.m.
garlar *i fam* to chatter, prattle.
garlito 1 *m* (*red*) net. **2** *fig* (*trampa*) trap.
● **caer en el garlito,** *fam* to fall into the trap. ‖ **coger a algn. en el garlito,** *fig* to catch sb. in the act, catch sb. red-handed.

garlopa *f* jack plane.
garnacha 1 *f* (*uva*) sweet reddish-black grape. **2** (*vino*) wine made from this grape.
Garona el Garona, *m* the Garonne.
garra 1 *f* (*de mamífero*) paw, claw; (*de ave*) talon. **2** *fig* (*fuerza*) personality, character: *es una persona con mucha garra,* she has a lot of character. **3** *fam pey* (*de persona*) hand, paw: *¡quita tus sucias garras de aquí!,* get your dirty hands off that! − **4** garras, *fpl* (*poder*) clutches. **5** (*piel poco apreciada*) poor pelt: *su abrigo ha sido más barato porque es de garras,* her coat was cheaper as it's made of poor pelt.
● **caer en las garras de algn.,** *fig* to fall into sb.'s clutches. ‖ **echar la garra a algn.,** *fig* to lay one's hands on sb. ‖ **tener garra,** (*relato etc*) to be compelling; (*persona*) to have character.
garrafa *f* carafe.
● **de garrafa,** *fam* cheap, bad quality: *en aquel bar el whisky es de garrafa,* the whisky's cheap and nasty in that bar.
garrafal *adj* monumental, huge, terrible: *cometieron un error garrafal,* they made a terrible mistake.
garrafón *m* demijohn, large carafe.
garrapata *f* tick.
garrapatear *i* (*escribir*) to scribble, scrawl; (*dibujar*) to doodle.
garrapato *m* (*escritura*) scribble, scrawl; (*dibujo*) doodle.
garrapatoso,-a *adj* scrawled, scribbled.
garrapiñar *t* → **garapiñar.**
garrido,-a 1 *adj* (*hombre*) handsome; (*mujer*) pretty. **2** (*elegante*) smart.
garrocha 1 *f* (*gen*) goad stick. **2** (*en tauromaquia*) pike, lance.
garrochazo *m* jab from a goad stick, pike thrust.
garrota *f* thick stick, cudgel.
garrotazo *m* blow with a stick.
● **dar un garrotazo a,** to hit with a stick.
garrote 1 *m* thick stick, cudgel, club. **2** (*pena capital*) garrotte.
● **dar garrote a algn.,** to garrotte sb.
■ **garrote vil,** garrotte.
garrotillo *m* croup.
garrucha *f* pulley.
garrulería *f* garrulity.
garrulo,-a 1 *adj* uncouth. − **2** *m,f* uncouth person.
gárrulo,-a 1 *adj* (*ave*) twittering. **2** (*persona*) garrulous.
garulo,-a *adj* → **garrulo,-a.**
garza *f* heron.
■ **garza real,** grey heron.
garzo,-a 1 *adj* lit (*ojos*) forget-me-not blue. **2** lit (*persona*) blue-eyed.
gas 1 *m* (*gen*) gas. − **2** gases, *mpl* (*flatulencias*) wind *sing,* flatulence *sing,* US gas *sing.*
● **a todo gas,** *fam* flat out, at full tilt. ‖ **tener gases,** to have wind.
■ **agua con gas,** carbonated water, fizzy water. ‖ **gas butano,** butane gas. ‖ **gas ciudad,** town gas. ‖ **gas de escape,** exhaust fumes *pl.* ‖ **gas hilarante,** laughing gas. ‖ **gas mostaza,** mustard gas. ‖ **gas natural,** natural gas. ‖ **gas noble,** inert gas. ‖ **gas pobre,** producer gas.
gasa 1 *f* gauze. **2** (*pañal*) gauze nappy, US gauze diaper.
■ **gasa hidrófila,** surgical gauze.
gascón,-ona 1 *adj* Gascon. − **2** *m,f* Gascon.
Gascuña *f* Gascony.
gaseosa *f* → **gaseoso,-a.**

gaseoso,-a 1 *adj* gaseous, gassy. **2** (*bebida*) carbonated, fizzy. – **3 gaseosa,** *f* GB lemonade, US soda, US pop.
gasificación *f* gasification.
gasificar *t* to gasify.
▲ *Conjugation model* [1], *like* **sacar**.
gasoducto *m* gas pipeline.
gasógeno *m* gazogene.
gasoil *m* diesel oil.
gasóleo *m* diesel oil.
gasolina *f* petrol, US gasoline, gas.
● **poner gasolina,** to get some petrol.
■ **gasolina normal,** three-star petrol. ‖ **gasolina super,** four-star petrol. ‖ **gasolina sin plomo,** unleaded petrol.
gasolinera 1 *f* petrol station, US gas station. **2** (*lancha*) motorboat.
gasómetro *m* gasometer.
gastado,-a 1 *pp* → **gastar**. – **2** *adj* (*desgastado*) worn-out. **3** (*acabado*) finished, empty, used up. **4** (*manido*) hackneyed, well-worn: *ese tema está ya muy gastado,* that's a very well-worn topic. **5** (*abatido*) worn-out, drained; (*aviejado*) old. **6** (*debilitado*) weak, spent, finished: *este gobierno ya está gastado,* this government is finished.
gastador,-ra 1 *adj* (*derrochador*) spendthrift. – **2** *m,f* (*derrochador*) spendthrift, spender. – **3 gastador,** *m* (*zapador*) sapper.
gastar 1 *t* (*consumir dinero, tiempo*) to spend; (*gasolina, electricidad*) to use (up), consume: *este coche gasta mucha gasolina,* this car uses a lot of petrol. **2** (*malgastar*) to waste: *gastó la fortuna en cuatro días,* he squandered all the money in four days. **3** (*usar perfume, jabón*) to use; (*ropa*) to wear: *¿qué número gastas?,* what size do you take? **4** (*tener*) to have: *gastar mal genio,* to have a bad temper. – **5 gastarse,** *p* (*desgastarse*) to wear out: *se le han gastado los zapatos,* his shoes are worn out. **6** (*consumirse*) to run out: *se nos ha gastado toda la gasolina,* we've run out of petrol.
● **gastarlas,** *fam* to behave: *ya sé cómo las gastas,* I know what you get up to.
gasterópodo *m* gasteropod.
gasto *m* expenditure, expense: *este mes el gasto de agua se ha disparado,* expenditure on water has shot up this month.
■ **gastos de mantenimiento,** running costs, maintenance costs. ‖ **gastos de representación,** entertainment allowance *sing.* ‖ **gastos diarios,** daily expenses.
gástrico,-a *adj* gastric.
gastritis *f* gastritis.
▲ *pl* **gastritis.**
gastroenteritis *f* gastroenteritis.
▲ *pl* **gastroenteritis.**
gastronomía *f* gastronomy.
gastronómico,-a *adj* gastronomic, gastronomical.
gastrónomo,-a 1 *m,f* (*especialista*) gastronome: *el cocinero de ese restaurante es un gastrónomo reconocido,* the chef at that restaurant is a well-known gastronome. **2** (*aficionado a comer bien*) gourmet.
gata *f* → **gato,-a.**
gatas a gatas, *loc adv* on all fours.
● **andar a gatas,** to crawl.
gatear 1 *i* (*andar a gatas*) to crawl. **2** (*trepar*) to climb.
gatera 1 *f* cat door, cat flap. **2** MAR cathole.
gatillazo *m* click of the trigger.
gatillo *m* trigger.
● **apretar el gatillo,** to pull the trigger.

gato,-a 1 gato, *m* cat, tomcat. **2** (*de coche*) jack. – **3 gata,** *f* she-cat, cat. – **4 gato,-a,** *m,f fam* person from Madrid, inhabitant of Madrid.
● **buscarle tres/cinco pies al gato,** *fam* to split hairs, complicate things. ‖ **dar gato por liebre,** *fam* to take sb. in, con sb. ‖ **hay gato encerrado,** *fam* there's something fishy going on. ‖ **llevar el gato al agua / llevarse el gato al agua,** *fam* to pull it off, succeed. ‖ **ser cuatro gatos,** *fam* to be a handful of people: *eran cuatro gatos,* there was hardly a soul there. ‖ **ser gato viejo,** *fam* to be an old hand.
■ **gato de algalia,** civet cat. ‖ **gato de Angora,** Angora cat. ‖ **gato montés,** wildcat. ‖ **gato siamés,** Siamese cat.
gatuno,-a *adj* catlike, feline.
gatuperio 1 *m* (*mezcla*) hotch-potch, mess, jumble. **2** (*chanchullo*) web of intrigue, tangle.
gaudeamus *m fml* party.
▲ *pl* **gaudeamus.**
gaveta 1 *f* (*cajón*) drawer. **2** (*mueble*) chest of drawers.
gavia *f* topsail.
gavilán *m* sparrowhawk.
gavilla 1 *f* (*de ramas etc*) sheaf. **2** *pey* (*de gente*) gang, band.
gaviota *f* seagull, gull.
■ **gaviota argéntea,** herring gull. ‖ **gaviota cana,** common gull. ‖ **gaviota enana,** little gull. ‖ **gaviota reidora,** black-headed gull. ‖ **gaviota tridáctila,** kittiwake.
gay 1 *adj* gay, homosexual. – **2** *m* gay, homosexual.
■ **el movimiento gay,** the Gay Liberation Movement.
▲ *pl* **gays.**
gayo,-a *adj lit* gay, cheerful.
■ **la gaya ciencia,** poetry, the art of poetry.
gazapo[1] *m* ZOOL young rabbit.
gazapo[2] 1 *m* (*mentira*) lie. **2** (*error*) blunder, slip.
gazmoñada *f* prudishness, prudery.
gazmoñería *f* prudishness, prudery.
gazmoñero,-a *adj* prudish.
gazmoño,-a *adj* prudish.
gaznápiro,-a 1 *adj fam* dim, thick. – **2** *m,f fam* dolt, dimwit.
gaznate *m* gullet.
gazpacho *m* cold soup made of tomatoes and other vegetables.
gazuza *f fam* hunger.
● **tener gazuza,** *fam* to be famished.
ge *f name of the letter g.*
géiser *m* geyser.
geisha *f* geisha.
gel *m* gel.
■ **gel de baño / gel de ducha,** shower gel.
gelatina 1 *f* (*sustancia*) gelatine. **2** (*preparado alimenticio*) jelly.
gelatinoso,-a *adj* gelatinous, jelly-like.
gélido,-a *adj* icy, icy cold.
gema 1 *f* BOT bud. **2** (*piedra*) gem.
gemación *f* gemation.
gemebundo,-a *adj* grumbling, complaining.
gemelo,-a 1 *adj* twin. – **2** *m,f* twin. – **3 gemelo,** *m* (*músculo*) calf muscle. – **4 gemelos,** *mpl* (*botones*) cufflinks. **5** (*anteojos*) binoculars. **6 Gemelos,** (*zodiaco*) Gemini *sing.*
■ **gemelo idéntico,** identical twin. ‖ **hermano gemelo,** twin. ‖ **alma gemela,** *fig* kindred spirit.
gemido 1 *m* (*quejido*) groan, moan. **2** (*gimoteo*) whimper.
geminado,-a *adj* geminate.

Géminis *m* Gemini.
▲ *pl Géminis.*
gemir 1 *i* (*quejarse*) to moan, groan: *estuvo toda la noche gimiendo de dolor,* she was moaning with pain all night. **2** *fig* (*aullar*) to whimper.
▲ *Conjugation model* [34], *like servir.*
gemología *f* gemology.
gen *m* gene.
genciana *f* gentian.
gendarme *m* gendarme.
gendarmería *f* gendarmerie.
gene *m* gene.
genealogía *f* genealogy.
genealógico,-a *adj* genealogical.
■ **árbol genealógico,** family tree.
genealogista *mf* genealogist.
generación *f* generation.
generacional *adj* generation, generational.
■ **la barrera generacional,** the generation gap.
generador,-ra 1 *adj* generating. – **2 generador,** *m* (*máquina*) generator.
general 1 *adj* general. **2** (*común*) common, usual, widespread: *es un comportamiento muy general,* it is a very common sort of behaviour. – **3** *m* MIL & REL general.
● **en general,** in general, generally. ‖ **por lo general,** in general, generally.
generala *f* general's wife.
● **tocar a generala,** to call to arms.
generalato 1 *m* (*grado*) generalship. **2** (*conjunto de generales*) generals *pl.*
generalidad 1 *f* (*gen*) generality. **2** (*mayoría*) majority: *la generalidad de los comerciantes se opuso a la ley,* the majority of traders were against the law. **3** (*generalización*) general statement. – **4 generalidades,** *fpl* (*nociones*) basic knowledge *sing: no está muy informado de este tema, sólo sabe generalidades,* he's not well informed on the subject, his knowledge is very general.
generalísimo *m* generalissimo, supreme commander.
Generalitat *f autonomous government of Catalonia and Valencia.*
generalización 1 *f* (*gen*) generalization. **2** (*extensión*) spread, spreading: *la generalización de las tarjetas de crédito es evidente,* it is evident that credit cards are now widely used.
generalizado,-a 1 *pp* → **generalizar.** – **2** *adj* widespread, common.
generalizador,-ra *adj* generalizing.
generalizar 1 *t* (*gen*) to generalize. **2** (*extender*) to spread, popularize: *la televisión ha generalizado ciertas costumbres,* television has popularized certain habits. – **3 generalizarse,** *p* to spread, become widespread, become common: *el uso de cascos se ha generalizado últimamente,* the use of helmets has recently become widespread.
▲ *Conjugation model* [4], *like realizar.*
generalmente *adv* generally, usually.
generar *t* to generate.
generativo,-a *adj* generative.
generatriz *f* generatrix.
genéricamente *adv* generically.
genérico,-a *adj* generic.
género 1 *m* (*clase*) kind, sort: *no me gustó ese género de vida,* I didn't like that sort of life. **2** (*tela*) cloth. **3** (*mercancía*) article, piece of merchandise. **4** GRAM gender. **5** BIOL genus. **6** ART & LIT genre. **7 géneros,** *mpl* (*mercancías*) goods.

■ **género chico,** light opera. ‖ **género dramático,** drama. ‖ **género lírico,** opera. ‖ **género de punto,** knitwear. ‖ **géneros de punto,** knitted goods.
generosamente *adv* generously.
generosidad *f* generosity, unselfishness.
generoso,-a *adj* generous (**con/para,** to).
génesis 1 *f* genesis. – **2 el Génesis,** *m* Genesis.
▲ *pl génesis.*
genética *f* → **genético,-a.**
genético,-a 1 *adj* genetic. – **2 genética,** *f* genetics *sing.*
genial 1 *adj* brilliant, inspired. **2** *fam* terrific, great, smashing: *eso me parece genial,* that sounds terrific. – **3** *adv fam* great: *ese tío toca el saxo genial,* that guy's a great sax player.
genialidad 1 *f* (*idea*) brilliant idea, stroke of genius. **2** (*acción*) peculiarity: *una de sus genialidades es llevar un calcetín de cada color,* he has the peculiar habit of wearing odd socks. **3** (*cualidad*) genius.
genio 1 *m* (*carácter*) temper, disposition. **2** (*facultad*) genius: *Einstein fue un genio,* Einstein was a genius. **3** (*espíritu*) spirit: *el genio del Renacimiento,* the Renaissance spirit. **4** (*ser fantástico*) genie.
● **estar de mal genio,** to be in a bad mood. ‖ **tener mal genio,** to have a bad temper.
genital 1 *adj* genital. – **2 genitales,** *mpl* genitals.
genitivo *m* genitive.
geniudo,-a *adj* bad-tempered.
Genl. *abr* (*General*) general; (*abreviatura*) Gen.
genocidio *m* genocide.
genoma *m* genome, genom.
genotipo *m* genotype.
Génova *f* Genoa.
genovés,-esa 1 *adj* Genoese. – **2** *m,f* Genoese.
gente 1 *f* people *pl: había mucha gente,* there were a lot of people. **2** (*familia*) family, folks *pl,* people *pl: me gusta estar con mi gente,* I like being with my family. **3** (*personal*) staff. **4** MIL troops *pl.*
■ **gente baja,** low-class people. ‖ **la gente bien,** *pey* the well-to-do, the well-off: *son gente bien,* they're well-to-do. ‖ **gente de bien,** honest people. ‖ **gente gorda,** *fam* bigwigs *pl.* ‖ **gente menuda,** *fam* nippers *pl,* kids *pl.*
gentil 1 *adj* (*amable*) kind. **2** (*apuesto*) charming. **3** (*pagano*) heathen, pagan; (*no judío*) gentile. – **4** *mf* Gentile.
gentileza 1 *f* (*gracia*) grace, elegance, poise: *caminaba con gran gentileza,* she walked very gracefully. **2** (*cortesía*) politeness, kindness: *tuvo la gentileza de dedicarnos la última canción,* he was kind enough to dedicate the last song to us.
● **es una gentileza de la casa,** it's on the house. ‖ **por gentileza de,** *fml* by courtesy of.
gentilhombre *m arc* gentleman.
gentilicio 1 *adj* gentile. – **2** *m* gentile.
gentilmente *adv* gracefully.
gentío *m* crowd.
● **¡qué gentío!,** what a crowd!
gentuza *f pey* mob, rabble, riffraff.
genuflexión *f* genuflexion.
genuinamente *adv* genuinely.
genuino,-a *adj* genuine, authentic.
GEO *abr* MIL (*Grupos Especiales de Operaciones*) ≈ Special Air Service; (*abreviatura*) SAS.
geocéntrico,-a *adj* geocentric.
geodesia *f* geodesy.
geofísica *f* → **geofísico,-a.**

geofísico,-a 1 *adj* geophysical. – 2 *m,f* geophysicist. – 3 **geofísica,** *f* geophysics *sing.*
geografía *f* geography.
■ **geografía física,** physical geography. ‖ **geografía política,** political geography. ‖ **geografía social,** social geography.
geográfico,-a *adj* geographic, geographical.
geógrafo,-a *m,f* geographer.
geología *f* geology.
geológico,-a *adj* geologic, geological.
geólogo,-a *m,f* geologist.
geomagnético,-a *adj* geomagnetic.
geomagnetismo *m* geomagnetism.
geómetra *mf* geometer, geometrician.
geometría *f* geometry.
■ **geometría del espacio,** solid geometry. ‖ **geometría descriptiva,** descriptive geometry.
geométrico,-a *adj* geometric, geometrical.
geomorfología *f* geomorphology.
geopolítica *f* geopolitics.
geoquímico,-a 1 *adj* geochemical. – 2 **geoquímica,** *f* geochemistry.
Georgia *f* Georgia.
■ **Georgia del Sur,** South Georgia.
georgiano,-a 1 *adj* Georgian. – 2 *m,f* (*persona*) Georgian. – 3 **georgiano,** *m* (*idioma*) Georgian.
geotectónico,-a *adj* geotectonic.
geranio *f* geranium.
gerencia 1 *f* (*actividad*) management, administration. 2 (*oficina*) manager's office: *hay que pasar por gerencia para cobrar,* you have to go to the manager's office to get paid.
gerente *mf* (*hombre*) manager; (*mujer*) manageress.
geriatra *mf* geriatrician.
geriatría *f* geriatrics *sing.*
geriátrico,-a 1 *adj* geriatric. – 2 **geriátrico,** *m* (*sanatorio*) geriatric hospital; (*residencia*) old people's home.
■ **residencia geriátrica,** old people's home.
gerifalte 1 *m* (*ave*) gerfalcon, gyrfalcon. 2 *fam* (*persona sobresaliente*) bigwig.
● **estar como un gerifalte / vivir como un gerifalte,** to live like a lord.
germanía *f* thieves' cant.
germanio *m* germanium.
germanismo *m* Germanism.
germanista *mf* Germanist, German specialist.
germanooccidental 1 *adj* West German. – 2 *mf* West German.
germanooriental 1 *adj* East German. – 2 *mf* East German.
germen *m* germ.
■ **germen de trigo,** wheatgerm.
▲ *pl* **gérmenes.**
germicida 1 *adj* germicidal. – 2 *m* germicide.
germinación *f* germination.
germinal *adj* germinal.
germinar *i* to germinate.
gerontocracia *f* gerontocracy.
gerontología *f* gerontology.
gerontólogo,-a *m,f* gerontologist.
gerundense 1 *adj* of Gerona, from Gerona. – 2 *mf* person from Gerona, inhabitant of Gerona.
gerundio *m* gerund.
gesta *f arc* heroic deed, exploit.
■ **cantar de gesta / canción de gesta,** chanson de geste.

gestación 1 *f* gestation. 2 (*período*) gestation period.
● **en gestación,** *fig* in preparation, in the pipeline. ‖ **estado de gestación,** state of pregnancy.
gestante 1 *adj* gestating. – 2 *f* expectant mother.
gestar 1 *t* to gestate. – 2 **gestarse,** *p fig* (*sentimiento*) to grow; (*idea*) to develop; (*plan*) to be under way, be in the pipeline: *un sentimiento de ira se gestó en la población,* a feeling of anger spread among the population; *el plan de recuperación se gestó en varias reuniones,* the recovery plan was the product of several meetings; *este movimiento se gestó en Europa en el siglo quince,* this movement developed in Europe in the fifteenth century; *se está gestando cambios importantes,* important changes are on the way.
gestatorio,-a *adj* gestatorial.
■ **silla gestatoria,** gestatorial chair.
gesticulación *f* gesticulation, gestures *pl.*
gesticular *i* to gesticulate.
gestión 1 *f* (*trámite*) step, measure, move: *tengo que realizar varias gestiones, después nos veremos,* I have a few errands to do, so I'll see you later. 2 (*comercial*) administration, management: *la gestión de la empresa corre a cargo del hijo del dueño,* the owner's son is in charge of managing the company. 3 (*negociación*) negotiation: *su gestión para liberar a los rehenes fracasó,* his efforts to free the hostages failed.
▲ In 1 and 3, also used in plural with the same meaning.
gestionar 1 *t* (*negociar*) to negotiate. 2 (*administrar*) to manage, run. 3 (*hacer diligencias*) to take steps to, arrange.
gesto 1 *m* (*movimiento*) gesture: *hizo un gesto con la mano y todos callaron inmediatamente,* she waved her hand and everyone fell silent. 2 (*mueca*) grimace. 3 (*rostro*) face: *vimos que habían perdido porque traían el gesto triste,* we could tell they'd lost by the sad look on their faces. 4 (*acción*) gesture, sign: *dar la mano al vencedor es un gesto de educación,* shaking the winner's hand is a sign of politeness.
● **estar de buen gesto,** to be in a good mood. ‖ **estar de mal gesto,** to be in a bad mood. ‖ **hacer gestos a,** *fam* to make gestures at. ‖ **torcer el gesto,** *fam* to look disappointed.
gestor,-ra 1 *adj* managing. – 2 *m,f* (*administrador*) manager, director. 3 *person who transacts official business on his clients' behalf,* ≈ solicitor.
■ **gestor administrativo,** agent, business agent.
gestoría *f agency which transacts official business on its clients' behalf,* ≈ solicitor's.
gestual *adj* using gestures.
Ghana *f* Ghana.
ghanés,-a 1 *adj* Ghanaian. – 2 *m,f* Ghanaian.
Ghates los Ghates, *mpl* the Ghats.
GIA *abr* (*Grupo Islámico Armado*) armed islamic group.
giba *f* hump, hunch.
gibar *t fam* to annoy: *¡no te giba, ahora resulta que no quiere ir!,* get this - now he's decided not to go!
gibón *m* gibbon.
giboso,-a 1 *adj* humpbacked, hunchbacked. – 2 *m,f* humpback, hunchback.
Gibraltar *m* Gibraltar.
gibraltareño,-a 1 *adj* Gibraltarian. – 2 *m,f* Gibraltarian.
gigante *adj* giant, gigantic, huge.
gigante,-a *m,f* (*hombre*) giant; (*mujer*) giantess.
gigantesco,-a *adj* giant, gigantic, giant-size.
gigantismo *m* gigantism, giantism.
gigoló *m* gigolo.

gijonense 1 *adj* of Gijón, from Gijón. – 2 *mf* person from Gijón, inhabitant of Gijón.

gili *adj-mf arg pey* → **gilipolla**.
▲ *pl gilis*.

gilí *adj-mf arg pey* → **gilipolla**.
▲ *pl gilís*.

gilipolla 1 *adj tabú* stupid. – 2 *mf tabú* jerk, arsehole (US asshole), GB prat.

gilipollada 1 *f (dicho)* bullshit, rubbish: *eso es una gilipollada,* that's bullshit. 2 *tabú (hecho)* stupid thing to do.

gilipollas 1 *adj tabú* stupid. – 2 *mf* jerk, arsehole (US asshole), GB prat.

gilipollez *f tabú* → **gilipollada**.

gillette *f* razor blade.
▲ *Registered trademark.*

gimiente *adj* whimpering.

gimnasia *f* gymnastics *sing.*
● confundir la gimnasia con la magnesia, *fam* to confuse two totally different things. ‖ hacer gimnasia, to do gymnastics.
■ gimnasia deportiva, gymnastics. ‖ gimnasia rítmica, rythmic gymnastics. ‖ gimnasia sueca, callisthenics.

gimnasio *m* gymnasium, gym.

gimnasta *mf* gymnast.

gimnástico,-a *adj* gymnastic.

gimnospermo,-a 1 *adj* gymnospermous. – 2 gimnosperma, *f* gymnosperm.

gimotear *i* to whine, whimper.

gimoteo *m* whining, whimpering.

gincana *f* gymkhana.

ginebra *f* gin.

Ginebra *f* Geneva.

gineceo 1 *m* BOT gynoecium. 2 *(lugar)* gynaecium.

ginecología *f* gynaecology (US gynecology).

ginecológico,-a *adj* gynaecological (US gynecological).

ginecólogo,-a *m,f* gynaecologist (US gynecologist).

gineta *f* genet.

gingival *adj* gingival, gum.

gingivitis *f* gingivitis.
▲ *pl gingivitis.*

gingko *m* ginkgo, ginkgo, maidenhair tree.

gira 1 *f (artística)* tour: *la compañía de teatro realizó una gira de dos meses,* the theatre company went on a two-month tour. 2 *(excursión)* trip, excursion.
● estar de gira, to be on tour.

girado,-a *m,f* drawee.

girador,-ra *m,f* drawer.

giralda *f* weathercock.
■ La Giralda, The Tower of Seville Cathedral.

girar 1 *i (dar vueltas)* to rotate, whirl, spin: *el dinero hace girar al mundo,* money makes the world go round. 2 *(torcer)* to turn: *girar a la izquierda,* to turn left. 3 *fig (versar)* to deal with: *la conversación giró en torno al teatro,* the conversation evolved around theatre. 4 COM to have a turnover: *esta empresa gira mucho,* this company has a big turnover; *giran por valor de cien millones al mes,* they have a monthly turnover of a hundred million. – 5 *t* COM to issue: *girar una letra,* to issue a draft. 6 *(cambiar de sentido)* to turn, turn around: *girar el cuerpo,* to turn one's body.
● girar en descubierto, COM to overdraw.

girasol *m* sunflower.

giratorio,-a *adj* rotating, gyratory.
■ silla giratoria, swivel chair.

giro 1 *m (vuelta)* turn, turning. 2 *(dirección)* course, direction. 3 COM draft. 4 *(frase)* turn of phrase, expression.
● dar un nuevo giro a, to give a new twist to, put in a new light. ‖ tomar un nuevo giro, to take a new turn.
■ giro en descubierto, overdraft. ‖ giro postal, money order. ‖ giro telegráfico, money order.

girola *f* ambulatory.

gitanada *f* wheedling, cajolement.

gitanear *t* to wheedle, cajole.

gitanería 1 *f (gitanos)* gypsies *pl,* gipsies *pl.* 2 *fig (engaño)* wheedling, cajolement.

gitanesco,-a *adj* gypsy-like, gipsy-like.

gitanismo 1 *m* gypsy customs *pl.* 2 LING gipsy word, gipsy phrase, gipsy expression.

gitano,-a 1 *adj* gypsy, gipsy. 2 *fig (zalamero)* flattering. – 3 *m,f* gypsy, gipsy. 4 *fig (zalamero)* flatterer. 5 *fam (estafador)* fiddler, swindler. 6 *fam (vagabundo)* vagrant.

glaciación *f* glaciation.

glacial 1 *adj* glacial. 2 *fig* glacial, icy: *tuvo un recibimiento glacial,* he had an icy reception.

glaciar *m* glacier.

gladiador *m* gladiator.

gladiolo *m* gladiolus.

gladíolo *m* gladiolus.

glamour *m* charm, glamour.

glande *m* glans penis.

glándula *f* gland.
■ glándula pineal, pineal body, pineal gland. ‖ glándula pituitaria, pituitary gland. ‖ glándula sudorípara, sweat gland. ‖ glándula tiroides, thyroid gland.

glandular *adj* glandular.

glasé 1 *adj* glacé. – 2 *m (tafetán)* glacé silk.

glaseado *m* glacé.

glasear *t* to glaze.

glauco,-a *adj fml* bluish-green, glaucous.

glaucoma *m* glaucoma.

gleba *f* land.
■ siervo de la gleba, serf.

glicerina *f* glycerin, glycerine.

global *adj* global, comprehensive, overall.

globalmente *adv* globally, as a whole.

globo 1 *m (esfera)* globe, sphere. 2 *(tierra)* globe. 3 *(de aire)* balloon. 4 *(pantalla de lámpara)* globe, glass lampshade. 5 *arg (condón)* rubber, johnny. 6 *(de tebeo)* speech balloon. 6 *(en tenis)* lob.
■ globo aerostático, hot air balloon, hydrogen balloon. ‖ globo celeste, globe. ‖ globo dirigible, airship. ‖ globo ocular, eyeball. ‖ globo terráqueo / globo terrestre, globe.

globoso,-a *adj* globular.

globular *adj* globular.

globulina *f* globulin.

glóbulo *m* globule.
■ glóbulo blanco, white corpuscle. ‖ glóbulo rojo, red corpuscle.

gloria 1 *f (bienaventuranza)* glory. 2 *(fama)* fame, honour (US honor). 3 *(cielo)* heaven. 4 *(esplendor)* boast. 5 *(cántico)* gloria. 6 *fam (placer)* bliss, delight: *es una gloria verlos crecer tan felices,* it's delightful to watch them grow up so happy. 7 *fam (héroe)* hero.
● cubrirse de gloria, *irón* to make a fool of os. ‖ dar gloria, to be a delight. ‖ estar en la gloria, *fam* to be in seventh heaven. ‖ oler a gloria, *fam* to smell divine. ‖ saber a gloria, *fam* to taste divine.

gloriar 308

gloriar I *t* to glorify. – **2 gloriarse,** *p (jactarse)* to boast **(de,** about), show off: *se gloria de ser el alumno predilecto,* he boasts that he's her favourite pupil. **3** *(complacerse)* to take pride **(de,** in).

glorieta I *f (en un jardín)* arbour (US arbor). **2** *(plazoleta)* small square. **3** *(cruce de calles)* roundabout, US traffic circle.

glorificación *f* glorification.

glorificar *t* to glorify.
▲ *Conjugation model* |1|, *like sacar.*

gloriosamente *adv* gloriously.

glorioso,-a *adj* glorious.

glosa I *f (explicación, comentario)* gloss, comment note. **2** *(poema)* gloss.

glosar I *t (explicar)* to gloss. **2** *(interpretar)* to interpret. **3** *(comentar)* to comment on, speak about: *la prensa glosó extensamente el discurso del presidente,* the press gave the president's speech wide coverage.

glosario *m* glossary.

glotis *f* glottis.
▲ *pl glotis.*

glotón,-ona I *adj* greedy, gluttonous. – **2** *m,f* glutton. – **3** glotón, *m* ZOOL wolverine, glutton.

glotonear *i* to eat greedily.

glotonería *f* gluttony, greed.

glucemia *f* glycemia.

glúcido *m* glucide.

glucosa *f* glucose.

gluten *m* gluten.

glúteo,-a I *adj* gluteal. – **2** glúteo, *m* gluteus.

gneis *m* gneiss.
▲ *pl gneis.*

gnomo *m* gnome.

gnosis *f* gnosis.
▲ *pl gnosis.*

gnosticismo *m* gnosticism.

gnóstico,-a I *adj* gnostic. – **2** *m,f* gnostic.

gobernable *adj* governable.

gobernación *f* government.
■ **Ministerio de la Gobernación,** Home Office, US Department of the Interior.

gobernador,-ra I *adj* governing. – **2** *m,f* governor.
■ **gobernador civil,** provincial governor. ‖ **la junta gobernadora,** the governing board.

gobernanta I *f (en un hotel)* staff manageress. **2** *(en una casa)* housekeeper.

gobernante I *adj* ruling, governing. – **2** *mf* ruler, leader.
■ **la clase gobernante,** the ruling class.

gobernar I *t (gen)* to govern. **2** *(un país)* to rule. **3** *(una familia)* to run. **4** *(un negocio)* to run, handle. **5** *(un barco)* to steer. **6** *(guiar)* to guide. **7** *(dominar)* to dominate, boss about: *lo gobierna su mujer,* his wife bosses him about. – **8** *i (un barco)* to steer. – **9 gobernarse,** *p* to manage one's own affairs, manage by oneself, look after oneself: *desde que vive sola ha aprendido a gobernarse,* living alone has taught her to look after herself.
▲ *Conjugation model* |27|, *like acertar.*

gobierno I *m* POL government. **2** *(mando)* command, running, handling: *ambos comparten el gobierno de la casa,* they share the running of the household; *no le compete el gobierno de tales asuntos,* he is not entitled to handle such affairs. **3** *(conducción)* direction, control; *(de un barco)* steering; *(de timón)* rudder.
● **para tu** *(su)* **gobierno,** for your own information. ‖ **servir de gobierno,** to serve as a guideline.

gobio *m* gudgeon.

goce *m* pleasure, enjoyment.

godo,-a I *adj* Gothic. – **2** *m,f (persona)* Goth. – **3** godo, *m (idioma)* Gothic.

gol *m* goal.
● **marcar un gol / meter un gol,** to score a goal. ‖ **meter un gol a algn.,** *fam fig* to pull a fast one on sb.
■ **gol cantado,** open goal. ‖ **gol fantasma,** controversial goal. ‖ **tiro a gol,** shot at goal.

gola I *f (garganta)* throat, gullet. **2** *(gorguera)* ruff.

goleada *f* feast of goals.
● **ganar por goleada,** to hammer the opposition.

goleador,-ra *m,f* scorer.
■ **el máximo goleador,** the top scorer.

golear *t* to hammer.

goleta *f* schooner.

golf I *m (deporte)* golf. **2** *(terreno)* golf course.
■ **campo de golf,** golf course. ‖ **club de golf,** golf club. ‖ **palo de golf,** golf club.

golfa *f* → **golfo,-a.**

golfante I *adj* rascally. **2** *fam* rascal, scoundrel.

golfear I *i (vagabundear)* to loaf around. **2** *(hacer gamberradas)* to get up to no good.

golfería I *f (golfos)* layabouts *pl,* good-for-nothings *pl,* louts *pl.* **2** *(acción)* loutish act, act of vandalism: *andar rompiendo cristales es una golfería,* going about breaking windows is vandalism.

golfillo,-a *m,f* street urchin.

golfista *mf* golfer.

golfo[1] *m* gulf, large bay.

golfo,-a[2] I *adj (niño)* naughty; *(joven)* idle, lazy. – **2** *m,f (holgazán)* good-for-nothing, layabout; *(niño)* rascal, little devil. – **3** golfa, *f fam (prostituta)* slut, tart, hussy.
■ **sesión golfa,** late-night showing.

gollete I *m (de persona)* throat, gullet. **2** *(de botella)* neck.

golondrina I *f (ave)* swallow. **2** *(embarcación)* motorboat.

golondrino I *m (ave)* young swallow. **2** *(vagabundo)* tramp. **3** *(forúnculo)* boil in the armpit. **4** *(desertor)* deserter.

golosear *i* to eat sweets, US eat candy.

golosina *f* sweet, US candy.

golosinear *i* to eat sweets, US eat candy.

goloso,-a I *adj* sweet-toothed. **2** *fig (apetecible)* mouthwatering, inviting: *le hicieron una oferta tan golosa que no se pudo resistir,* the offer was so tempting that she couldn't resist. – **3** *m,f* sweet lover, US candy lover.
● **ser un,-a goloso,-a,** to have a sweet tooth; *pey* to be greedy.

golpazo *m* heavy blow, bang.

golpe I *m* blow, knock; *(puñetazo)* punch: *le dio un golpe,* he hit him. **2** *(de coche)* collision; *(fuerte)* bang; *(ligero)* bump. **3** *fig (desgracia)* blow, misfortune: *su muerte fue un duro golpe para nosotros,* his death was a great blow to us. **4** *(gracia)* witticism, sally: *aunque parece serio tiene golpes muy buenos,* he may seem rather serious, but he's really good crack. **5** *fam (robo)* hold-up, robbery. **6** *(militar)* coup.
● **a golpes,** by force. ‖ **al primer golpe de vista,** at first glance. ‖ **de golpe / de golpe y porrazo,** suddenly, all of a sudden. ‖ **de un golpe,** all at once, in one go. ‖ **errar el golpe,** to miss. ‖ **no dar golpe / no pegar ni golpe,** fam not to lift a finger, not do a blessed thing. ‖ **parar el golpe,** to soften the blow.
■ **golpe bajo,** *fig* punch below the belt. ‖ **golpe de efecto,** dramatic move. ‖ **golpe de Estado,** coup, coup d'état. ‖ **golpe de fortuna,** stroke of luck. ‖ **golpe de gracia,** coup de grâce. ‖ **golpe de mano,** surprise

attack. ‖ **golpe de vista,** quick glance. ‖ **golpe franco,** (*fútbol*) free kick.

golpear *t* (*gen*) to hit, strike; (*personas*) to thump, hit, punch; (*puerta*) to knock on.

golpetazo *m* heavy blow.

golpetear 1 *t* to bang. – 2 *i* to bang: *la ventana golpeteaba con el viento,* the window was banging in the wind.

golpeteo *m* banging, hammering.

golpismo *m* tendency towards coups d'état.

golpista 1 *mf* person involved in a coup d'état: *los golpistas asaltaron el parlamento,* the rebels attacked the parliament building. – 2 *adj* relating to coups d'état.

goma 1 *f* (*material*) gum, rubber. 2 (*de borrar*) rubber, us eraser. 3 (*de pegar*) glue, gum. 4 (*banda elástica*) rubber band. 5 *arg* (*preservativo*) rubber.
- ■ **goma arábiga,** gum arabic. ‖ **goma de mascar,** chewing gum. ‖ **suela de goma,** rubber sole.

gomaespuma *f* foam rubber.

gomina *f* hair cream.

gomoso,-a 1 *adj* sticky. – 2 gomoso, *m pey* fop.

gónada *f* gonad.

góndola 1 *f* (*embarcación*) gondola. 2 (*carruaje*) carriage.

gondolero,-a *m,f* gondolier.

gong *m* gong.
- ▲ *pl* gongs.

gongo *m* gong.

gongorino,-a *adj* Gongoristic.

gongorismo *m* Gongorism.

gongorista *mf* Gongorist.

goniómetro *m* goniometer.

gonococo *m* gonococcus.

gonorrea *f* gonorrhoea (us gonorrhea).

gordiano nudo gordiano, *m* Gordian knot.

gordinflón,-ona 1 *adj* chubby, fat. – 2 *m,f* chubby person, fatty.

gordo,-a 1 *adj* (*carnoso*) fat: *se puso gordo,* he got fat. 2 (*grueso*) thick. 3 (*grave*) serious. 4 (*importante*) big: *¡qué mentira tan gorda!,* what a big lie! – 5 *m,f* fat person; *fam* fatty. – 6 gordo, *m fam* (*grasa*) fat. 7 el gordo, the first prize *in the lottery.*
- ● armarse la gorda, *fam* to be hell to pay. ‖ caer gordo,-a, *fam* not to stand sb: *el vecino me cae gordo,* I can't stand my neighbour. ‖ estar sin gorda, *fam* to be broke. ‖ hacer la vista gorda, *fam* to turn a blind eye. ‖ ni gorda, *fam* not a thing, nothing: *sin gafas no veo ni gorda,* I can't see a thing without glasses. ‖ quedarse sin gorda, *fam* to be broke.

gordura *f* fatness.

gorgojo 1 *m* (*insecto*) weevil. 2 *fam fig* dwarf, small person.

gorgorito *m* trill.

gorgotear *i* to gurgle.

gorgoteo *m* gurgle, gurgling.

gorguera 1 *f* (*de adorno*) ruff. 2 (*de armadura*) gorget.

gorigori *m fam* dirge, funeral chant.
- ● cantar el gorigori a algn., *fam* to bury sb.

gorila 1 *m* (*animal*) gorilla. 2 *fam* (*guardaespaldas*) bodyguard; (*en club*) bouncer.

gorjear 1 *i* to chirp, twitter. – 2 gorjearse, *p* to gurgle, burble.

gorjeo 1 *m* (*ave*) chirping, twittering. 2 (*bebé*) gurgling.

gorra 1 *f* (*gen*) cap. 2 (*con visera*) peaked cap.
- ● de gorra, *fam* free, for nothing.
- ■ gorra con orejeras, cap with earflaps.

gorrear *i* to scrounge, be a parasite.

gorrero,-a *m,f* sponger, scrounger.

gorrinada 1 *f fam* something dirty, disgusting thing. 2 *fam* (*mala pasada*) dirty trick: *aquello fue una gorrinada y no una broma,* that was a dirty trick, not a joke.

gorrinería 1 *f fam* something dirty, disgusting thing. 2 *fam* (*mala pasada*) dirty trick.

gorrino,-a 1 *adj* dirty, piglike. – 2 *m,f* pig.

gorrión,-ona *m,f* sparrow.
- ■ gorrión común, house sparrow. ‖ gorrión chillón, rock sparrow. ‖ gorrión molinero, tree sparrow. ‖ gorrión moruno, Spanish sparrow.

gorro 1 *m* cap. 2 (*de bebé*) bonnet. 3 (*de cocinero*) chef's hat.
- ● estar hasta el gorro, *fam* to have had enough (de, of), to be fed up (de, with). ‖ ponerle el gorro a algn., (*irritar*) to annoy sb., get on sb.'s nerves; (*ridiculizar*) to make fun of sb.
- ■ gorro de dormir, nightcap. ‖ gorro frigio, Phrygian cap.

gorrón,-ona 1 *adj fam* scrounging, sponging. – 2 *m,f* sponger, scrounger.

gorronear *i* to scrounge, be a parasite.

gota 1 *f* drop. 2 (*de sudor*) bead. 3 (*de aire*) breath. 4 MED gout. 5 ARQ gutta.
- ● caer cuatro gotas / caer unas gotas, to be spitting with rain. ‖ gota a gota, drop by drop. ‖ ni gota, not a bit, nothing at all: *con tanta gente no vimos ni gota,* there were so many people we couldn't see a thing. ‖ ser la gota que colma el vaso, to be the straw that broke the camel's back. ‖ ser la última gota, to be the last straw. ‖ sudar la gota gorda, to sweat blood.
- ■ gota fría, *stationary cold front which can cause prolonged torrential rain.* ‖ gota a gota / transfusión gota a gota, drip, drip feed.

gotear 1 *i* (*grifo*) to drip; (*tejado*) to leak. 2 (*lluvia*) to drizzle.
- ▲ In 2, 3rd person only; it does not take a subject.

goteo *m* dripping.

gotera 1 *f* (*agujero*) leak. 2 (*agua*) drip. 3 (*mancha*) drip mark. 4 *fam fig* (*achaque*) chronic ailment.
- ● estar lleno,-a de goteras, *fam fig* to be full of aches and pains.

goterón *m* large drop.

gótico,-a 1 *adj* Gothic. – 2 gótico, *m* (*idioma*) Gothic.

gourmet *mf* gourmet.
- ▲ *pl* gourmets.

goyesco,-a *adj* in the style of Goya.

gozada *f fam* delight: *¡qué gozada de película!,* what a great film!

gozar 1 *t* (*poseer, disfrutar*) to enjoy: *gozaron una gran fortuna,* they possessed a great fortune. 2 (*trato carnal*) take advantage of: *después de gozarla la abandonó,* after taking advantage of her, he abandoned her. – 3 *i* (*poseer, disfrutar*) to enjoy (de, -): *goza de extensas propiedades,* it has many properties; *goza de muy buena salud,* he enjoys very good health. 4 (*sentir placer*) to enjoy os.: *gozamos con su presencia,* we really enjoy her company.
- ▲ Conjugation model [4], *like realizar.*

gozne *m* hinge.

gozo 1 *m* joy, delight, pleasure. – 2 gozos, *mpl* (*composición poética*) poem *sing* in honour of the Virgin.

gozoso,-a 1 *adj* (*contento*) delighted. 2 (*que produce alegría*) joyful, happy.

g/p *abr* (*giro postal*) postal order; (*abreviatura*) p.o.

g.p. *abr* → **g/p**.
grabación *f* recording.
grabado,-a 1 *pp* → **grabar**. – 2 *adj* engraved. – 3 grabado, *m* (*arte*) engraving. 4 (*dibujo*) picture, drawing.
■ **grabado al agua fuerte,** etching.
grabador,-ra 1 *adj* recording. – 2 *m,f* engraver. – 3 grabadora, *f* (*aparato*) tape recorder.
grabadora *f* → **grabador,-ra**.
grabar 1 *t* ART to engrave. 2 (*registrar*) to record. 3 INFORM to save.
● **grabarse en la memoria,** *fig* to be engraved on one's memory. ‖ **quedarse algo muy grabado,** *fig* to stick in one's mind.
gracejo *m* charm, winsomeness.
● **con mucho gracejo,** most engagingly.
gracia 1 *f* REL grace. 2 (*favor*) favour (US favor). 3 (*clemencia*) pardon: *el condenado esperó la gracia del rey,* the prisoner awaited the king's pardon. 4 (*buen trato*) graciousness. 5 (*atractivo*) grace, charm. 6 (*garbo*) grace. 7 (*chiste*) joke. 8 *irón* (*algo molesto*) nuisance, pain: *¡vaya gracia tener que esperar tanto!,* what a nuisance to have to wait so long! 9 *fml* (*nombre*) name: *dígame su gracia,* tell me your name. – 10 **gracias,** *fpl* thank you, thanks. 11 **las gracias,** (*mitología*) the Graces.
● **caer en gracia a algn.,** to make a hit with sb.: *le has caído en gracia,* he's taken a liking to you. ‖ **dar gracias a algn.,** to thank sb. ‖ **estar en gracia,** to be in a state of grace. ‖ **gracias a,** thanks to. ‖ **gracias a Dios,** thank God, thank goodness. ‖ **hacer gracia, tener gracia,** (*diversión*) to be funny; (*desprecio*) to be ridiculous: *me hace gracia, se cree que lo invitaré,* isn't it funny, he thinks I'm inviting him! ‖ **por la gracia de Dios,** by the grace of God. ‖ **¡qué gracia!,** how funny! ‖ **reírle las gracias a algn.,** to laugh at sb.'s jokes. ‖ **¡vaya gracia! / ¡vaya una gracia!,** well, that's great that is!, that's just great! ‖ **y gracias,** *irón* you should be so lucky: *nada de comida fina, te darán un bocadillo y gracias,* there'll be no posh food, with a bit of luck you'll get a sandwich.
■ **petición de gracia,** appeal for clemency. ‖ **tiro de gracia,** coup de grâce.
grácil *adj* lissom, gracile.
gracilidad *f* lissomness.
grácilmente *adv* lissomly.
gracioso,-a 1 *adj* (*atractivo*) graceful, charming. 2 (*bromista*) witty, facetious. 3 (*divertido*) funny, amusing. 4 (*tratamiento*) Gracious: *Su Graciosa Majestad,* Her Gracious Majesty. – 5 *m,f* TEAT jester, clown, fool.
● **hacerse el gracioso,** to try to be funny.
grada 1 *f* (*peldaño*) step, stair. 2 (*gradería*) tier. 3 (*tarima*) stand. 4 MAR slipway, building berth. – 5 **gradas,** *fpl* stands, terraces.
gradación 1 *f* gradation. 2 MÚS scale. 3 (*retórica*) climax.
gradería *f* stands *pl,* terraces *pl.*
graderío *m* → **gradería**.
gradiente *m* gradient, US grade.
grado 1 *m* (*gen*) degree: *estábamos a 27 grados,* it was 27 degrees. 2 (*estado*) stage. 3 EDUC (*curso*) class, year, US grade. 4 EDUC (*título*) degree. 5 (*peldaño*) step. 6 MIL rank. 7 LING degree.
● **de buen grado,** willingly, with good grace. ‖ **de mal grado,** unwillingly, with bad grace. ‖ **en sumo grado,** to the highest degree. ‖ **en tal grado,** so much so.
graduable *adj* adjustable.
graduación 1 *f* (*gen*) graduation. 2 (*de alcohol*) strength: *ese vino tiene mucha graduación,* that wine is very

strong. 3 MIL rank, degree of rank. 4 EDUC graduation: *todos los alumnos celebraron su graduación,* all the students celebrated their graduation.
graduado,-a 1 *pp* → **graduar**. – 2 *adj* graduated. – 3 *m,f* EDUC graduate.
■ **gafas graduadas,** prescription glasses. ‖ **graduado escolar,** *certificate of elementary school studies.*
gradual *adj* gradual.
gradualmente *adv* gradually.
graduar 1 *t* (*termómetro*) to graduate, calibrate. 2 (*regular*) to adjust, regulate. 3 (*conceder un diploma*) to confer a degree on, US graduate; (*conceder un grado*) to confer a rank. 4 (*medir*) to gauge, measure; (*la vista*) to test, check. – 5 **graduarse,** *p* to graduate, get one's degree.
● **graduarse la vista,** to have one's eyes tested.
▲ *Conjugation model* |11|, *like* **actuar**.
grafema *m* grapheme.
graffiti *mpl* → **grafiti**.
grafía 1 *f* (*signo*) graphic symbol. 2 (*escritura*) writing. 3 (*ortografía*) spelling.
gráfico,-a 1 *adj* graphic. 2 *fig* (*vívido*) vivid, graphic. – 3 gráfica, *f* graph, diagram. – 4 **gráfico,** *m* (*dibujo*) sketch, chart.
■ **artes gráficas,** graphic arts.
grafismo 1 *m* (*diseño gráfico*) graphic design, graphics *pl.* 2 (*grafía*) graphic symbol. 3 *fig* (*fuerza descriptiva*) vividness, graphicness.
grafista *mf* graphic designer.
grafiti *mpl* graffiti.
grafito *m* graphite.
grafología *f* graphology.
grafólogo,-a *m,f* graphologist.
gragea *f* pill, tablet.
grajilla *f* jackdaw.
grajo,-a *m,f* rook.
gral. *abr* (*general*) general; (*abreviatura*) gen.
grama *f* Bermuda grass.
gramática *f* → **gramático,-a**.
gramatical *adj* grammatical.
gramaticalidad *f* grammaticality.
gramático,-a 1 *m,f* grammarian. – 2 **gramática,** *f* grammar.
■ **gramática generativa,** transformational grammar. ‖ **gramática tradicional,** traditional grammar. ‖ **gramática parda,** *fig* cunning, astuteness.
gramináceo,-a *adj* gramineous.
gramíneo,-a 1 *adj* gramineous, graminaceous. – 2 gramíneas, *fpl* grasses, the grass family *sing.*
gramo *m* gram, gramme.
gramófono *m* gramophone.
gramola *f* gramophone.
Grampianos los montes Grampianos, *mpl* the Grampians.
gran 1 *adj* (*fuerte, intenso*) great: *el coche tomó la curva a gran velocidad,* the car went into the bend at high speed; *se llevaron un gran susto,* they were terribly shocked. 2 (*excelente*) great: *aquél era un gran libro,* that was a great book. 3 (*principal*) grand: *el gran maestre de la orden,* the grand master of the order.
▲ *Used before singular noun; see also* **grande**.
grana¹ 1 *f* (*semilla*) seed. 2 (*acción*) seeding.
grana² 1 *f* (*insecto*) cochineal. 2 (*sustancia*) cochineal. 3 (*color*) maroon, claret. – 4 *adj* maroon, claret.
■ **grana del paraíso,** cardamom.
granada *f* → **granado,-a**.

Granada *f* Granada.

granadero *m* grenadier.

granadina *f* → **granadino,-a**.

granadino,-a 1 *adj* of Granada, from Granada. – **2** *m,f* person from Granada, inhabitant of Granada. – **3** granadina, *f (refresco)* grenadine. **4** *(cante)* flamenco song from Granada.

granado,-a 1 *pp* → **granar**. – **2** *adj (maduro)* mature, ripened, of a certain age: *es un muchacho ya granado,* he's a fine young man now. **3** *(ilustre)* illustrious. – **4** granado, *m* pomegranate tree. – **5** granada, *f* BOT pomegranate. **6** MIL grenade, shell.
● el más granado / lo más granado, the finest.
■ granada de mano, hand grenade.

granar *i* to seed.

granate 1 *adj* maroon, claret. – **2** *m (color)* maroon, claret. **3** *(mineral)* garnet.

granazón *f* seeding, ripening.

grande 1 *adj (tamaño)* large, big: *esta casa es demasiado grande para ellos dos,* this house is too big for the two of them. **2** *(fuerte, intenso)* great: *su partida les produjo una pena muy grande,* his departure caused them great sorrow. **3** *(mayor)* grown-up, old, big. – **4** *m (de elevada jerarquía)* great.
● a lo grande, on a grand scale, in a big way. ‖ estar grande una cosa a algn., to be too big on sb. ‖ pasarlo en grande, *fam* to have a great time. ‖ vivir a lo grande, *fig* to live in style.
■ Grande de España, grandee.
▲ See also gran.

grandeza 1 *f (tamaño)* size. **2** *(importancia)* greatness. **3** *(generosidad)* generosity. **4** *(dignidad nobiliaria)* nobility.
■ grandeza de alma, magnanimity. ‖ grandeza de ánimo, moral courage.

grandilocuencia *f* grandiloquence, pomp.

grandilocuente *adj* grandiloquent, pompous.

grandiosidad *f* grandeur, magnificence, splendour (us splendor).
■ gesto de grandiosidad, grand gesture.

grandioso,-a *adj* grandiose, grand, magnificent.

grandote *adj fam* huge, great big.

grandullón,-ona 1 *adj fam pey* great big. – **2** *m,f fam pey (chico)* oversized boy; *(chica)* oversized girl.

granel. 1 a granel, *loc adv (sin envase)* in bulk: *compramos el aceite a granel,* we buy oil in bulk. **2** *(en abundancia)* tons of, lots of: *whisky a granel,* whisky galore.

granero *m* granary, barn.

granítico,-a *adj* granitic, granite.

granito *m* granite.

granívoro,-a *adj* granivorous.

granizada *f* → **granizar**.

granizado,-a 1 *pp* → **granizar**. – **2** granizado, *m* iced drink. – **3** granizada, *f* hailstorm. **4** *fig (lluvia)* hail, shower: *lanzaron una granizada de flechas,* they fired a hail of arrows.
■ granizado de limón, iced lemon drink.

granizar *i* to hail.
▲ *Conjugation model* |4|, *like* realizar; *3rd person only; it does not take a subject.*

granizo *m* hail, hailstone.

granja *f* farm.

granjearse *p* to win, obtain, earn: *se ha granjeado la amistad de todos,* he has won the friendship of everyone.

granjero,-a *m,f* farmer.

grano 1 *m* grain; *(de café)* bean. **2** MED pimple, spot: *me ha salido un grano en la nariz,* I've got a spot on my nose. – **3** granos, *mpl* cereals.

● grano de arena, *fig* small contribution, bit: *nosotros también pusimos nuestro grano de arena,* we did our bit too. ‖ ir al grano, *fam* to come to the point, get to the point. ‖ ni un grano, not a bit. ‖ no es grano de anís, *fam* it's not to be sniffed at.

granuja 1 *f (uva)* grapes *pl.* – **2** *m (pilluelo)* ragamuffin, urchin. **3** *(estafador)* crook, trickster.

granujada *f* nasty trick.

granujería *f* gang of rogues, gang of urchins.

granulación *f* granulation.

granulado,-a 1 *pp* → **granular**. – **2** *adj* granulated. – **3** granulado, *m (en farmacia)* powder.

granular 1 *adj* granular. – **2** *t* to granulate.

gránulo 1 *m* granule. **2** *(en farmacia)* small pill.

granuloso,-a 1 *adj (superficie)* granular. **2** *(piel)* pimply.

grao *m* landing beach, shore.

grapa 1 *f (para papel)* staple. **2** *(en construcción)* cramp iron. **3** *(de uvas)* bunch, bunch of grapes.

grapadora *f* stapler.

grapar *t* to staple.

GRAPO *abr (Grupos de Resistencia Antifascista Primero de Octubre)* radical left-wing group employing direct action methods.

grasa *f* → **graso,-a**.

grasiento,-a *adj* greasy, oily.

graso,-a 1 *adj* greasy, oily, fatty: *tiene la piel grasa y el pelo graso,* he's got oily skin and greasy hair. – **2** grasa, *f* grease, fat.

grasoso,-a *adj* greasy, oily.

gratamente *adv* pleasantly.

gratén *m* gratin.
● al gratén, au gratin.

gratificación 1 *f (satisfacción)* gratification. **2** *(recompensa)* reward. **3** *(extra)* bonus.

gratificador,-ra *adj* gratifying, rewarding.

gratificante *adj* gratifying, rewarding.

gratificar 1 *t (satisfacer)* to gratify. **2** *(recompensar)* to reward, tip: *"se gratificará",* "reward offered".
▲ *Conjugation model* |1|, *like* sacar.

gratinar *t* to cook au gratin.

gratis *adv* free: *el segundo paquete te sale gratis,* you get the second packet free.

gratitud *f* gratitude.

grato,-a *adj* pleasant, pleasing (**para,** to): *me es grato anunciarles que ...,* I am pleased to inform you that ...

gratuidad 1 *f:* *en algunos países la gratuidad de la enseñanza es un hecho,* in some countries free education is a fact. **2** *(arbitrariedad)* gratuitousness.

gratuitamente 1 *adv (de balde)* free of charge, free. **2** *(sin fundamento)* unfoundedly.

gratuito,-a 1 *adj (de balde)* free: *muestra gratuita,* free sample. **2** *(sin fundamento)* arbitrary, gratuitous.

grava 1 *f (guijas)* gravel. **2** *(piedra machacada)* crushed stone.

gravamen 1 *m (carga)* burden, obligation. **2** *(impuesto)* tax, duty.
▲ *pl* gravámenes.

gravar *t* to tax: *el gobierno ha decidido gravar el tabaco,* the Government has decided to tax tobacco; *esta finca está gravada con una hipoteca,* there is a mortgage on this property.

grave 1 *adj (pesado)* heavy. **2** *(serio)* grave, serious: *los últimos acontecimientos suponen un grave empeoramiento de la situación,* recent events pose a grave threat to the situation; *fue acusado de grave negligencia,* he was

charged with gross negligence. **3** (*difícil*) difficult. **4** (*solemne*) solemn. **5** (*voz, nota*) deep, low. **6** LING (*acento*) grave; (*palabra*) paroxytone.
● **estar grave,** to be seriously ill.
gravedad 1 *f* FÍS gravity. **2** (*importancia*) gravity, seriousness: *fue herido de gravedad,* he was seriously injured. **3** (*seriedad*) solemnity, gravity. **4** (*de sonido*) depth.
■ **centro de gravedad,** centre of gravity. ‖ **fuerza de gravedad,** force of gravity.
gravemente 1 *adv* (*seriamente*) seriously. **2** (*solemnemente*) solemnly, gravely.
gravidez *f* pregnancy.
● **en estado de gravidez,** pregnant.
grávido,-a 1 *adj fml* (*lleno*) full. **2** (*embarazada*) pregnant, gravid.
gravilla *f* fine gravel.
gravitación *f* gravitation.
gravitacional *adj* gravitational.
gravitar 1 *i* FÍS to gravitate. **2** (*apoyarse en*) to rest (**sobre,** on). **3** *fig* (*amenazar*) to loom (**sobre,** over).
gravitatorio,-a *adj* gravitational.
gravoso,-a 1 *adj* (*costoso*) costly, expensive. **2** (*molesto*) burdensome.
graznar 1 *i* (*cuervo*) to caw, croak. **2** (*oca*) to honk. **3** (*pato*) to quack.
graznido 1 *m* (*de cuervo*) caw, croak. **2** (*de oca*) honk. **3** (*de pato*) quack.
greba *f* greave.
greca *f* fret, fretwork.
Grecia *f* Greece.
grecolatino,-a *adj* Graeco-Latin.
grecorromano,-a *adj* Graeco-Roman.
greda *f* fuller's earth, clay.
gregario,-a 1 *adj* gregarious. **– 2 gregario,** *m* (*en ciclismo*) *cyclist who rides so as to help a teammate.*
■ **instinto gregario,** herd instinct.
gregoriano,-a *adj* Gregorian.
■ **canto gregoriano,** Gregorian chant.
greguería 1 *f* (*algarabía*) hubbub. **2** LIT *type of* aphorism.
grelo *m* turnip top.
gremial 1 *adj* trade union, union. **2** HIST guild.
gremio 1 *m* HIST guild, corporation. **2** (*sindicato*) union. **3** (*profesión*) profession.
Grenada *f* Grenada.
greña 1 *f* lock of entangled hair. **– 2 greñas,** *pl* untidy mop of hair.
● **andar a la greña,** *fam* to squabble.
greñudo,-a 1 *adj* (*pelo*) tangled. **2** (*persona*) unkempt, dishevelled (us disheveled).
gres *m* stoneware.
■ **gres flameado,** glazed earthenware.
gresca 1 *f* (*bulla*) racket. **2** (*riña*) row.
● **armar gresca,** to kick up a racket.
grey 1 *f* (*rebaño*) flock, herd. **2** (*de personas*) group, bunch; (*en religión*) flock.
grial *m* grail.
■ **el Santo Grial,** the Holy Grail.
griego,-a 1 *adj* Greek. **– 2** *m,f* (*persona*) Greek. **– 3 griego,** *m* (*idioma*) Greek.
grieta 1 *f* crack, crevice. **2** (*en la piel*) chap, crack.
grifa *f arg* marijuana.
grifería *f* taps *pl,* us faucets *pl.*
grifo 1 *m* (*llave*) tap, us faucet. **2** (*animal*) griffin, gryphon, griffon.
● **abrir el grifo,** to turn the tap on. ‖ **cerrar el grifo,** to turn the tap off.

grill *m* grill: *pollo al grill,* grilled chicken.
▲ *pl* **grills.**
grilla *f* female cricket.
grillado,-a *adj fam* barmy.
grillete *m* shackle.
grillo[1] *m* ZOOL cricket.
● **andar a grillos,** *fam* to potter about.
grillo[2] *m* (*tallo*) sprout.
grillos *mpl* fetters, shackles.
grima *f* displeasure, disgust, annoyance.
● **dar grima,** (*dar dentera*) to set one's teeth on edge.
grímpola *f* pennant.
gringo,-a 1 *adj fam* yankee. **– 2** *m,f fam* Yankee.
gripal *adj* related to flu: *síntomas gripales,* flu symptoms.
■ **afección gripal,** flu.
gripe *f* flu, influenza.
● **coger la gripe,** to catch (the) flu. ‖ **estar con gripe,** to have (the) flu. ‖ **tener la gripe,** to have (the) flu.
griposo,-a *adj* flu.
● **estar griposo,** to have (the) flu.
gris 1 *adj* grey (us gray). **2** *fig* (*mediocre*) mediocre, third-rate. **3** *fig* (*triste*) grey (us gray), gloomy. **– 4** *m* (*color*) grey (us gray). **5** *arg* (*policía*) cop. **– 6 los grises,** *mpl arg* the cops, the police *sing.*
■ **gris marengo,** charcoal grey. ‖ **gris perla,** pearl-grey.
grisáceo,-a *adj* greyish.
grisalla *f* chiaroscuro, grisaille.
grisú *m* firedamp.
gritar *i* (*gen*) to shout; (*chillar*) cry out, scream: *¡no me grites!,* don't shout at me!
griterío *m* shouting, uproar.
grito *m* shout; (*chillido*) cry, scream.
● **a grito limpio / a grito pelado,** at the top of one's voice. ‖ **a voz en grito,** at the top of one's voice. ‖ **dar un grito,** to shout; (*chillar*) to scream. ‖ **el último grito,** *fig* the latest thing, the last word. ‖ **pedir algo a gritos,** *fig* to be crying out for sth., be badly in need of sth. ‖ **pegar un grito,** to shout; (*chillar*) to scream. ‖ **poner el grito en el cielo,** *fig* to hit the ceiling, hit the roof.
gritón,-ona 1 *adj* noisy, loud-mouthed. **– 2** *m,f* loud-mouth.
groenlandés,-esa 1 *adj* Greenlandic. **– 2** *m,f* (*persona*) Greenlander. **– 3 groenlandés,** *m* (*idioma*) Greenlandic.
Groenlandia *f* Greenland.
grog *m* grog, punch.
grogui 1 *adj* DEP punch-drunk, groggy. **2** *fig* groggy, half-asleep.
grosella *f* redcurrant.
■ **grosella espinosa,** gooseberry. ‖ **grosella negra,** blackcurrant. ‖ **grosella roja,** redcurrant. ‖ **grosella silvestre,** gooseberry.
grosellero *m* redcurrant bush.
■ **grosellero negro,** blackcurrant bush. ‖ **grosellero espinoso,** gooseberry bush.
grosería 1 *f* (*ordinariez*) rude word, rude expression. **2** (*rusticidad*) rudeness, coarseness.
● **decir una grosería,** to say something rude.
grosero,-a 1 *adj* (*tosco*) coarse, crude. **2** (*maleducado*) rude. **– 3** *m,f* rude person.
grosor *m* thickness.
grosso **grosso modo,** *loc adv* roughly, approximately.
grosura *f* fat, suet.
grotesco,-a *adj* grotesque, ridiculous.

grúa 1 *f* (*construcción*) crane, derrick. **2** AUTO breakdown van, US towtruck.
grueso,-a 1 *adj* (*objeto*) thick. **2** (*persona*) fat, stout. – **3** **grueso,** *m* (*grosor*) thickness. **4** (*parte principal*) bulk. – **5** **gruesa,** *f* (*doce docenas*) gross.
grulla *f* crane.
grullo,-a *adj* scrounging.
grumete *m* cabin boy.
grumo *m* lump; (*de sangre*) clot; (*de leche*) curd.
grumoso,-a *adj* lumpy, clotted.
gruñido *m* grunt, growl.
gruñir *i* to grunt.
▲ *Conjugation model* [40], *like muñir*.
gruñón,-ona 1 *adj* grumbling, grumpy. – **2** *m,f* grumbler, grouch.
grupa *f* croup, hindquarters *pl*.
● **montar a la grupa,** to ride pillion.‖ **volver grupas,** *fig* to turn back, retrace one's steps.
grupo 1 *m* group. **2** TÉC unit, set.
● **en grupo,** together, en masse: *todos bajaron en grupo a quejarse,* they all went down together to complain.
■ **grupo electrógeno,** power plant.‖ **grupo sanguíneo,** blood group.
grupúsculo *m* small group.
gruta *f* cavern, grotto, cave.
gruyere *m* gruyère.
gua 1 *m* (*juego*) marbles *pl*. **2** (*hoyo*) hole for the marbles.
guacamayo *m* macaw.
guache *m* gouache.
guadalajareño,-a 1 *adj* of Guadalajara, from Guadalajara. – **2** *m,f* person from Guadalajara, inhabitant of Guadalajara.
Guadalupe *f* Guadeloupe.
guadamecí *m* embossed leather.
▲ *pl* **guadamecíes**.
guadaña *f* scythe.
guadañador,-ra 1 *m,f* (*persona*) mower. – **2** **guadañadora,** *f* (*máquina*) mowing machine.
guadañadora *f* → **guadañador,-ra**.
guadañar *t* to mow, scythe.
guadarnés,-esa 1 *m,f* (*hombre*) stable boy; (*mujer*) stable girl. – **2** **guadarnés,** *m* tack room.
guagua *f* worthless thing.
gualdo,-a *adj* yellow.
■ **la bandera roja y gualda,** the Spanish flag.
gualdrapa *f* horse blanket.
guanaco *m* guanaco.
guano 1 *m* (*abono natural*) guano. **2** (*abono artificial*) manure, fertilizer.
guantada *f* slap.
guantazo *m* slap.
guante *m* glove.
● **arrojar el guante a algn.,** *fig* to throw down the gauntlet to sb.‖ **colgar los guantes,** (*en boxeo*) to give up boxing.‖ **echar el guante a algn.,** *fam* to catch sb.‖ **echar el guante a algo,** *fam* to nick sth.‖ **recoger el guante,** *fig* to take up the gauntlet.‖ **sentar como un guante,** *fig* to fit like a glove.‖ **suave como un guante,** *fig* as meek as a lamb.
guantelete *m* gauntlet.
guantera *f* glove compartment.
guaperas 1 *adj fam* good-looking, US cute. – **2** *mf* good looker, looker, US cutie.
▲ *pl* **guaperas**.

guapetón,-ona *adj fam* good-looking.
guapo,-a 1 *adj* good-looking, US cute; (*hombre*) handsome; (*mujer*) beautiful, pretty: *este chico es muy guapo,* this boy is very handsome; *estás muy guapa,* you look very pretty. **2** *arg* (*bonito*) nice, smart. – **3** *m,f* good-looking person, good-looker. **4** *fam* (*decidido*) daredevil: *a ver quién es el guapo que se atreve a ir,* I wonder who'll be brave enough to go. – **5** **guapo,** *m* (*galán*) ladies' man.
● **hacerse el guapo,** *fam* to act the tough guy.
guapote,-a *adj fam* good-looking.
guapura *f fam* good looks *pl*.
guarda 1 *mf* (*persona*) guard, keeper. – **2** *f* (*custodia*) custody, care. **3** (*de la ley etc*) observance. **4** (*de libro*) flyleaf.
■ **Angel de la Guarda,** Guardian Angel.‖ **guarda forestal,** forester.‖ **guarda jurado,** security guard.
guardabarrera *mf* gatekeeper.
guardabarros *m* mudguard, US fender.
▲ *pl* **guardabarros**.
guardabosque *m* forester.
guardacoches *mf* parking attendant.
▲ *pl* **guardacoches**.
guardacostas 1 *mf* (*persona*) coastguard. **2** *m* coastguard vessel.
▲ *pl* **guardacostas**.
guardaespaldas *mf* bodyguard.
▲ *pl* **guardaespaldas**.
guardafrenos *mf* guard; US (*hombre*) brakeman.
▲ *pl* **guardafrenos**.
guardagujas *mf* (*hombre*) pointsman; US switchman; (*mujer*) pointswoman; US switchwoman.
▲ *pl* **guardagujas**.
guardameta *mf* goalkeeper.
guardamuebles *m* furniture warehouse.
▲ *pl* **guardamuebles**.
guardapelo *m* locket.
guardapolvo 1 *m* (*cubierta*) dust cover. **2** (*mono*) overalls *pl*.
guardar 1 *t* (*cuidar*) to keep, watch over, keep an eye on: *el pastor guarda su rebaño,* the shepherd watches over his flock. **2** (*conservar*) to keep, hold: *guardo muy buenos recuerdos de la infancia,* I have very fond memories of my childhood; *guardo pocas esperanzas de que vuelva,* I hold out little hope that he will return. **3** (*la ley*) to observe, obey; (*un secreto*) to keep. **4** (*poner en un sitio*) to put away: *guárdate el dinero,* put your money away; *guárdatelo en el bolsillo,* put it in your pocket. **5** (*reservar*) to save, keep: *le guardaron el mejor sitio,* they saved the best seat for him. **6** (*proteger*) to protect, save: *¡Dios salve al rey!,* God save the King! INFORM to save. – **8** **guardarse de,** *p* (*precaverse, evitar*) to guard against, avoid, be careful not to: *te guardarás muy bien de revelar nuestro secreto,* be very careful not to reveal our secret.
● **guardar cola,** to queue up, US wait in line.‖ **guardar conexión con,** to be connected with.‖ **guardar la derecha,** to keep to the right.‖ **guardar las formas,** to be polite.‖ **guardar parecido con,** to be similar to.‖ **guardar relación con,** to be related to.‖ **guardar rencor,** to harbour resentment (**a,** against).‖ **guardársela a algn.,** *fig* to have it in for sb.
guardarropa 1 *m* (*armario*) wardrobe. **2** (*cuarto*) cloakroom. – **3** *mf* cloakroom attendant.
guardarropía *f* wardrobe for props.
guardavía *m* (*hombre*) signalman.
guardería 1 *f* crèche, nursery. **2** (*oficio de guarda*) keeping.

■ **guardería infantil,** nursery, nursery school.
guardia I f (*vigilancia*) watch, lookout. **2** (*servicio*) duty, call: *dos veces al mes le toca guardia en el hospital,* she's on call at the hospital twice a month. **3** (*tropa*) guard. – **4** mf (*hombre*) policeman; (*mujer*) policewoman.
● **bajar la guardia,** to lower one's guard. ‖ **estar de guardia,** (*doctor*) to be on duty, be on call; (*soldado*) to be on guard duty; (*marino*) to be on watch. ‖ **estar en guardia,** to be on guard. ‖ **mantener la guardia,** to keep watch. ‖ **montar la guardia,** to mount guard. ‖ **ponerse en guardia,** to put os. on one's guard.
■ **farmacia de guardia,** duty chemist's. ‖ **guardia civil,** Civil Guard. ‖ **guardia de asalto,** assault guard. ‖ **guardia de corps,** Royal Guard. ‖ **guardia de tráfico,** (*hombre*) traffic policeman; (*mujer*) traffic policewoman. ‖ **guardia urbano,-a,** (*hombre*) policeman; (*mujer*) policewoman. ‖ **médico de guardia,** doctor on duty.
guardián,-ana m,f guardian, keeper, custodian.
guardilla f attic, garret.
guarecer t to take shelter (**de**, from), shelter (**de**, from): *nos guarecimos de la lluvia bajo un árbol,* we sheltered from the rain under a tree.
▲ *Conjugation model* |43|, *like agradecer.*
guarida I f ZOOL haunt, den, lair. **2** pey (*refugio*) hide-out.
guarismo m cipher, figure.
guarnecer I t (*decorar*) to adorn, decorate; (*en cocina*) to garnish. **2** (*proveer*) to provide (**de**, with). **3** MIL to garrison. **4** (*en construcción*) to plaster. **5** (*joya*) to set. **6** (*caballo*) to harness.
▲ *Conjugation model* |43|, *like agradecer.*
guarnecido,-a I pp → **guarnecer.** – **2** adj (*gen*) decorated, trimmed; (*en cocina*) garnished (**de**, with). **3** (*dotado*) equipped. **4** MIL garrisoned. – **5** guarnecido, m (*en construcción*) plaster.
guarnición I f (*gen*) decoration, trimmings pl. **2** (*de joya*) setting. **3** CULIN accompaniment to a main dish: *bistec con guarnición,* steak with vegetables/chips/salad etc. **4** MIL garrison. **5** (*en arma blanca*) guard. – **6 guarniciones,** fpl (*en equitación*) harness sing.
guarnicionería f saddlery.
guarnicionero,-a m,f saddler.
guarrada I f fam something dirty, disgusting thing: *¡no hagas guarradas!,* don't do such filthy things! **2** fam (*mala pasada*) dirty trick: *¡vaya guarrada me ha hecho!,* he really did the dirty on me!
● **decir guarradas,** to have a foul mouth.
guarrería f → **guarrada.**
guarro,-a I adj dirty, filthy. – **2** m,f pig, dirty pig.
guasa f jest, fun, mockery.
● **con guasa,** jokingly: *le dijo con guasa que era muy simpático,* she jokingly told him that he was very nice. ‖ **estar de guasa,** to be joking.
guasearse p to tease (**de**, -), make fun (**de**, of): *se guasearon tanto de él que ya no volvió,* they teased him so much that he never went back.
guasón,-ona I adj funny, joking. – **2** m,f jester, joker.
guata I f (*algodón*) raw cotton. **2** (*relleno*) padding.
guateado,-a I pp → **guatear.** – **2** adj padded, quilted.
guatear t to wad, pad.
Guatemala f Guatemala.
guatemalteco,-a I adj Guatemalan. – **2** m,f Guatemalan.
guateque m party.
guau I interj (*perro*) woof!, bow-wow! **2** (*asombro*) wow!
guay adj fam great, cool.
guayaba f guava.

guayabera f summer shirt *for men.*
guayabo m guava tree.
Guayana f Guiana.
guayanés,-esa I adj Guianese. – **2** m,f Guianese.
guayaquileño,-a I adj of Guayaquil, from Guayaquil. – **2** m,f person from Guayaquil, inhabitant of Guayaquil.
gubernamental adj government, governmental: *la política gubernamental,* government policy.
gubernativo,-a adj government, governmental.
gubia f gouge.
guedeja I f (*cabellera*) long hair. **2** (*de león*) mane.
güelfo,-a m,f Guelph, Guelf.
guepardo m cheetah.
guerra f war.
● **dar guerra,** fam to cause problems, cause trouble: *cuando era niño nos daba mucha guerra,* when he was a child he was a real handful. ‖ **declarar la guerra a,** to declare war on. ‖ **en guerra,** at war. ‖ **ser de antes de la guerra,** fam to be donkey's years old. ‖ **tenerle la guerra declarada a algn.,** fam to have it in for sb.
■ **guerra bacteriológica / guerra biológica,** germ warfare. ‖ **guerra civil,** civil war. ‖ **guerra comercial,** trade war. ‖ **guerra de Cuba,** Spanish-American War. ‖ **guerra de la Independencia,** Spanish War of Independence. ‖ **guerra de las galaxias,** star wars. ‖ **guerra de los Seis Días,** Six Day War. ‖ **guerra de los Treinta Años,** Thirty Years' War. ‖ **guerra de nervios,** war of nerves. ‖ **guerra del Golfo,** Gulf War. ‖ **guerra fría,** cold war. ‖ **guerra mundial,** world war. ‖ **guerra nuclear,** nuclear war. ‖ **guerra psicológica,** psychological warfare. ‖ **guerra química,** chemical warfare. ‖ **guerra santa,** holy war. ‖ **guerra total,** all-out war. ‖ **la Primer Guerra Mundial,** World War I, the First World War, World War I. ‖ **la Segunda Guerra Mundial,** World War II, the Second World War.
guerrear i to war.
guerrera f → **guerrero,-a.**
guerrero,-a I adj warlike. **2** fam (*niño*) difficult: *de pequeño era muy guerrero,* he was quite a handful when he was a boy. – **3** m,f warrior, soldier. – **4 guerrera,** f (*chaqueta*) army jacket.
guerrilla I f (*guerra*) guerrilla warfare. **2** (*banda*) guerrilla band.
guerrillero,-a m,f guerrilla.
gueto m ghetto.
guía I mf (*persona*) guide, leader. – **2** f (*norma*) guidance, guideline. **3** (*libro*) guidebook. **4** (*de bicicleta*) handlebar. **5** (*de bigote*) end, tip. **6** (*carril*) rail, guide. **7** BOT main stem.
■ **guía de teléfonos,** telephone directory, phone book.
guiar I t to guide, lead. **2** (*conducir automóvil*) to drive; (*barco*) to steer; (*avión*) to pilot; (*caballo, bici*) to ride. **3** (*plantas*) to train. – **4 guiarse,** p to be guided: *nos guiamos por tu consejo,* we are guided by your advice.
▲ *Conjugation model* |13|, *like desviar.*
guija[1] f (*legumbre*) vetch.
guija[2] f (*piedra*) pebble.
guijarral m pebbly place.
guijarro m pebble, stone.
guijo m gravel.
guillado,-a I pp → **guillarse.** – **2** adj fam nutty, loony.
guilladura f fam madness, craziness.
guillarse I p fam (*chiflarse*) to become a real loony, go bonkers. **2** fam (*escabullirse*) to get away.

● **guillárselas,** *fam* to clear out.
guillotina *f* guillotine.
guillotinar *t* to guillotine.
guinda I *f* (*fruta*) sour cherry, morello cherry. **2** (*remate*) finishing touch, final touch: *la última aria fue la guinda de un recital extraordinario,* the final aria made a fitting finale to an extraordinary recital.
guindaleza *f* hawser.
guindar I *t* (*izar*) to hoist, raise. **2** *fam* (*colgar*) to hang. **3** (*conseguir*) to snatch: *les guindó la única plaza vacante,* she snatched the only vacancy. **4** *arg* (*robar*) to nick, lift. – **5 guindarse,** *p* to let os. down (**de/por,** -), slide down (**de/por,** -): *se guindó por la cuerda hasta el suelo,* he slid down the rope to the ground.
guindilla I *f* red pepper, chilli. **2** *fam* (*policía*) cop.
guindo *m* morello cherry tree.
● **caerse algn. del guindo,** *fam* to cotton on, twig.
Guinea *f* Guinea.
■ **Guinea Ecuatorial,** Equatorial Guinea. ‖ **Guinea-Bissau,** Guinea-Bissau. ‖ **Nueva Guinea,** New Guinea.
guineano,-a I *adj* Guinean. – **2** *m,f* Guinean.
guiñapo I *m* (*andrajo*) rag, tatter. **2** *fig* (*persona*) wreck.
● **poner a algn. como un guiñapo,** to pull sb. to pieces.
guiñar I *t* to wink: *me guiñó un ojo,* he winked at me. **2** MAR to yaw.
guiño *m* wink.
guiñol *m* puppet theatre.
guiñolesco,-a *adj* like a puppet show.
guión I *m* (*esquema*) notes *pl*, sketch, outline. **2** GRAM hyphen, dash. **3** CINEM script. **4** (*estandarte*) standard, banner.
■ **guión de codornices,** corncrake.
guionista *mf* scriptwriter.
guipar I *t fam* (*ver*) to see, spot. **2** *fam* (*descubrir*) to see through.
guipure *m* guipure.
guiri *mf arg* foreigner.
▲ *pl* **guiris.**
guirigay I *m* (*lenguaje*) gibberish. **2** (*griterío*) racket, noise, din.
guirlache *m* almond brittle.
guirnalda *f* garland, wreath.
guiropa *f* meat and potato stew.
guisa *f* manner, way.
● **a guisa de,** by way of, as, like: *se puso la caja a guisa de sombrero,* he put the box on his head like a hat; *sólo a ti se te ocurre presentarse de esa guisa,* only you could turn up like that.
guisado,-a I *pp →* **guisar.** – **2** *adj* cooked, stewed. – **3** guisado, *m* stew.
guisante *m* pea.
guisar I *t* to cook, stew. – **2 guisarse,** *p* to cook, stew: *el pollo se guisó en muy poco tiempo,* the chicken cooked very quickly.
● **tú te lo guisas, tú te lo comes,** as you make your bed so you must lie on it.
guiso *m* stew.
güisqui *m* whisky.
■ **güisqui escocés,** Scotch whisky, Scotch.
guita *f arg* dough, bread.
● **quedarse sin guita,** *arg* to be broke.
guitarra I *f* guitar. – **2** *mf* guitarrist.
guitarreo *m* strumming on the guitar.

guitarrería I *f* (*tienda*) guitar shop. **2** (*fábrica*) guitar factory.
guitarrero,-a I *m,f* (*vendedor*) guitar seller. **2** (*fabricante*) guitar maker.
guitarrillo *m* small four-string guitar.
guitarrista *mf* guitarist.
guitarro *m →* **guitarrillo.**
gula *f* gluttony.
gumía *f* Moorish dagger.
guripa I *m fam* (*soldado*) soldier. **2** *fam* (*policía*) cop. **3** *fam* (*granuja*) scoundrel.
gurmet *mf* gourmet.
▲ *pl* **gurmets.**
gurriato I *m* (*ave*) young sparrow. **2** *fam* (*niño*) kid, nipper.
gurrumino,-a *adj* weak.
gurú *m* guru.
gusanillo I *m* little worm. **2** (*espiral*) spiral binding. **3** (*intranquilidad*) niggling doubt: *me quedo con el gusanillo de saber si estará bien,* I can't help wondering if she'll be all right.
● **matar el gusanillo,** *fam* to have a snack. ‖ **entrarle a algn. el gusanillo de algo,** *fam* to get the bug: *ya de pequeña le entró el gusanillo del teatro,* she got the theatre bug while she was still young.
gusano I *m* worm; (*oruga*) caterpillar. **2** *fig* (*persona*) worm.
■ **gusano de seda,** silkworm.
gusarapo *m* tiny creature.
gustar I *t* (*agradar*) to like: *me gusta el vino,* I like wine. **2** (*probar*) to taste, try: *gusté una pizca para ver si estaba salado,* I tasted a little bit to see if it was too salty. – **3** *i* (*tener complacencia*) to enjoy (**de,** -): *gusta del buen comer,* she enjoys good food.
● **cuando guste / cuando gustes,** *fml* whenever you want. ‖ **¿gustas?,** *fml* would you like some? ‖ **¿Ud. gusta?,** *fml* would you like some?
gustativo,-a *adj* gustative.
■ **papila gustativa,** taste bud.
gustazo *m* (*fam*) great pleasure.
● **darse el gustazo de algo,** *fam* to take great pleasure in sth., take great delight in sth. ‖ **darse un gustazo,** to treat os.
gustillo I *m fam* (*regusto*) aftertaste: *ese gustillo ácido es desagradable,* that sharp aftertaste is unpleasant. **2** *fam* (*satisfacción*) satisfaction, pleasure: *verlo tan enfadado me dio cierto gustillo,* I got a kick out of seeing him so angry.
gusto I *m* (*sentido, sabor*) taste. **2** (*inclinación*) liking, taste: *es una persona de gustos sencillos,* she's a person of simple tastes. **3** (*placer*) pleasure: *tengo el gusto de presentarle a mi marido,* may I introduce you to my husband? **4** (*capricho*) whim, fancy.
● **cogerle el gusto a algo,** to take a liking to sth. ‖ **con mucho gusto,** with pleasure. ‖ **dar gusto,** to please, delight: *me da gusto verla comer,* I enjoy watching her eat. ‖ **darse el gusto de,** to treat os. to. ‖ **de buen gusto,** in good taste. ‖ **de mal gusto,** in bad taste. ‖ **el gusto es mío,** the pleasure is mine. ‖ **estar a gusto,** to feel comfortable, feel at ease. ‖ **hacer algo a gusto,** to enjoy doing sth. ‖ **hacer algo por gusto,** to do sth. for fun. ‖ **ir algo a gustos,** to be a matter of taste. ‖ **por gusto,** for the sake of it. ‖ **¡qué gusto!,** how lovely! ‖ **tanto gusto,** pleased to meet you. ‖ **tener buen gusto,** to have good taste. ‖ **tener mal gusto,** to have bad taste. ‖ **tener el gusto de +** *inf,* to

have the pleasure of + *ger.* ‖ **tener mucho gusto en** + *inf,* to be delighted to + *inf.*

gustosamente *adv* with pleasure, gladly, willingly.

gustoso,-a 1 *adj (sabroso)* tasty, savoury, palatable. **2** *(agradable)* agreeable, pleasant. **3** *(con gusto)* glad, willing, ready: *aceptó gustosa,* she accepted willingly.

gutapercha *f* gutta-percha.

gutural *adj* guttural.

Guyana *f* Guyana.

■ **Guyana Francesa,** French Guyana.

guyanés,-esa 1 *adj* Guyanese. – **2** *m,f* Guyanese

H

H, h *f* (*la letra*) H, h.

h[1] *abr* (*hora*) hour; (*abreviatura*) h.

h[2] *abr* (*habitante*) inhabitant.

ha[1] *sím* (*hectárea*) hectare; (*símbolo*) ha.

ha *pres indic* → **haber.**

haba 1 *f* (*legumbre*) broad bean. **2** (*café, cacao*) bean. **3** (*para votación*) voting ball. **4** (*roncha*) swelling.
● **en todas partes cuecen habas,** *fig* it's the same the whole world over. ‖ **son habas contadas,** *fam* it's for sure, it's a cert.
■ **haba de las Indias,** sweet pea.

Habana La Habana, *f* Havana.

habanera *f* → **habanero,-a.**

habanero,-a 1 *adj* of Havana, from Havana. – **2** *m,f* person from Havana, inhabitant of Havana. – **3** **habanera,** *f* music and dance from Havana.

habano,-a 1 *adj* of Havana, from Havana. – **2 habano,** *m* Havana cigar.

hábeas hábeas corpus, *m* JUR habeas corpus.
▲ *pl* **hábeas corpus.**

haber 1 *aux* (*en tiempos compuestos*) to have: *lo has hecho,* you have done it; *la había visto,* I had seen her. – **2** *t arc* (*poseer*) to have: *los hijos habidos en el matrimonio,* the children of the marriage. – **3** *i* (*impersonal*) to be: *hay un coche,* there's a car; *había cuatro libros,* there were four books; *hubo una fiesta,* there was a party; *habrá pasteles,* there will be some cakes; *¿cuántos había?,* how many were there? – **4** *m* COM credit, assets *pl.* – **5 haber de** + *infin, aux* (*obligación*) to have to, must, should: *has de pedirlo,* you have to ask for it; *han de venir hoy,* they must come today. **6 haber que** + *infin,* (*obligación*) must, have to: *hay que decírselo,* we have to tell her; *no hay que reír,* you mustn't laugh; *habrá que hacerlo,* we'll have to do it. – **7 haberes,** *mpl* (*posesiones*) property *sing,* assets. **8** (*sueldo*) salary *sing,* pay *sing,* wages.
● **algo habrá,** there must be something in it. ‖ **años ha,** years ago: *dos años ha,* two years ago. ‖ **¡de haberlo sabido!,** if only I had known! ‖ **¡haberlo dicho!,** why didn't you say so! ‖ **habérselas con algn.,** *fam* to be up against sb. ‖ **había una vez ...,** once upon a time there was ..., there was once ... ‖ **¡habráse visto!,** what a cheek! ‖ **has de saber que ...,** you should know that ... ‖ **¡hay que ver!,** well, really!, well, I never! ‖ **¡he dicho!,** and that's that! ‖ **no hay de qué,** you're welcome, don't mention it. ‖ **no hay (nada) como ...,** there's nothing like ... ‖ **no hay quien ...,** it's impossible ...: *no hay quien lo beba,* it's impossible to drink; *no hay quien pueda con esa gente,* those people are impossible to deal with. ‖ **no hay por donde cogerlo,** *fam* he's impossible. ‖ **no hay tal,** it isn't true. ‖ **¿qué hay?,** hello!, hi!, how are you doing? ‖ **ser de lo que no hay,** *fam* to be impossible. ‖ **tener en su haber,** *fig* to be to one's credit. ‖ **todos los habidos y por haber,** *fam* every single one of them.

■ **debe y haber,** debit and credit.
▲ Conjugation model [72; in **3** and **5**], used only in the 3rd person and does not take a subject.

haberes *mpl* → **haber.**

habichuela *f* (*gen*) bean; (*judía blanca*) haricot bean; (*judía verde*) French bean, green bean.

hábil 1 *adj* (*diestro*) skilful (us skillful). **2** (*despabilado*) clever, smart. **3** (*acto*) clever. **4** (*apto, adecuado*) good, suitable: *un local hábil para restaurante,* a suitable place for a restaurant.
● **en tiempo hábil,** at the proper time. ‖ **ser hábil en algo / ser hábil para algo,** (*persona*) to be good at sth. ■ **día hábil,** working day.

habilidad 1 *f* (*aptitud*) skill. **2** (*astucia*) cleverness, smartness. **3** JUR capacity, competence. **4** (*gracia*) talent.
● **con gran habilidad,** very skilfully. ‖ **tener habilidad manual,** to be good with one's hands. ‖ **tener habilidad para algo,** to be good at sth.

habilidoso,-a *adj* skilful (us skillful), clever.

habilitación 1 *f* (*empleo del habilitado*) paymastership; (*oficina*) paymaster's office. **2** (*de un espacio*) fitting out. **3** (*capacitación*) qualification; (*autorización*) authorization.

habilitado,-a 1 *pp* → **habilitar.** – **2** *m,f* (*hombre*) paymaster; (*mujer*) paymistress.

habilitar 1 *t* (*espacio*) to fit out; (*tiempo*) to set aside: *habilitó una habitación para consulta,* he fitted a bedroom out as a consulting room; *habilitó algún tiempo para preguntas,* she set some time aside for questions. **2** (*capacitar*) to entitle, qualify; (*autorizar*) to empower, authorize. **3** FIN to finance.

hábilmente *adv* skilfully (us skillfully).

habitable *adj* habitable, livable, liveable.

habitación 1 *f* (*gen*) room. **2** (*dormitorio*) bedroom. **3** BIOL habitat.
■ **habitación doble,** double room. ‖ **habitación individual,** single room.

habitáculo 1 *m* (*vivienda*) dwelling. **2** BIOL habitat. **3** (*cabina*) cabin.

habitante *mf* inhabitant.

habitar 1 *t* to live in, inhabit. – **2** *i* to live.

hábitat *m* habitat.
▲ *pl* **hábitats.**

hábito 1 *m* (*costumbre*) habit, custom. **2** (*vestido*) habit.
● **adquirir el hábito de ...,** to get into the habit of ... ‖ **colgar los hábitos,** to give up the cloth. ‖ **crear hábito,** to be habit-forming. ‖ **el hábito no hace al monje,** *fig* clothes don't make the man. ‖ **tener el hábito de ...,** to be in the habit of ... ‖ **tener malos hábitos,** to have bad habits. ‖ **tomar el hábito,** (*hombre*) to take holy orders; (*mujer*) to take the veil.

habituación *f* habituation.

habitual 1 *adj* usual, habitual, customary. **2** (*asiduo*) regular.

habitualmente adv (repetidamente) usually; (regularmente) regularly.

habituar 1 t to accustom (**a**, to). – **2 habituarse,** p to become accustomed (**a**, to), get used (**a**, to).

▲ Conjugation model [11], like **actuar.**

habla 1 f (facultad) speech. 2 (idioma) language; (dialecto) dialect.

● ¡al habla!, (al teléfono) speaking! ‖ de habla española / de habla hispana, Spanish-speaking. ‖ estar al habla con algn., to be in touch with sb. ‖ perder el habla, to lose one's power of speech. ‖ ponerse al habla con algn., to get in touch with sb. ‖ quedarse sin habla, to be left speechless.

■ habla regional, regional dialect.

▲ Takes **el** in singular.

hablado,-a 1 pp→ **hablar.** – **2** adj spoken, oral: **francés hablado,** spoken French.

● bien hablado,-a, well-spoken. ‖ ser un,-a mal hablado,-a, to be foul-mouthed, be coarse.

■ cine hablado, talkies pl.

hablador,-ra 1 adj (parlanchín) talkative. **2** (chismoso) gossipy. – **3** m,f (parlanchín) talker, chatterbox. **4** (chismoso) gossip.

habladuría f (chisme) piece of gossip; (rumor) rumour (us rumor).

▲ Also used in plural with the same meaning.

hablante 1 adj speaking. – **2** mf speaker.

hablar 1 i (gen) to speak, talk: **habló conmigo,** he spoke to me. 2 (mencionar) to talk, mention: **no me habló de eso,** she didn't mention that. 3 (murmurar) to talk: **eso dará que hablar,** that will set people talking. 4 (dar un tratamiento) to call (**de,** -): **háblame de tú,** call me by my first name. 5 fig (salir) to go out: **habló tres años con Luis,** she went out with Luis for three years. – **6** t (idioma) to speak: **habla francés,** he speaks French. 7 (tratar) to talk over, discuss: **ya lo hablaremos después,** we'll discuss it later. – **8 hablarse,** p (uso recíproco) to speak, talk: **ayer nos hablamos por teléfono,** we spoke on the 'phone yesterday.

● es como hablar a la pared, fig it's like talking to a brick wall. ‖ eso es hablar, now you're talking. ‖ estar hablando, (cuadro etc) to be almost alive. ‖ hablar a solas, to talk to os. ‖ hablar alto, to speak loud: **¿puedes hablar más alto?,** can you speak up, please? ‖ hablar bajo, to speak softly. ‖ hablar bien de algn., to speak well of sb. ‖ hablar claro, to speak plainly. ‖ hablar como un libro, (expresarse muy bien) to speak very well, express os. very clearly; (hablar con afectación) to speak affectedly. ‖ hablar con el corazón, to speak from the heart. ‖ hablar en broma, to be joking. ‖ hablar en cristiano, fam to talk plainly. ‖ hablar en nombre de algn., to speak on sb.'s behalf. ‖ hablar mal de algn., to speak badly of sb. ‖ hablar por hablar, to talk for the sake of talking. ‖ hablar por los codos, fam to be a chatterbox. ‖ no hablarse con algn., not to be on speaking terms with sb. ‖ no hay más que hablar, there's nothing more to be said. ‖ no se hable más de ello, and that's that. ‖ ¡quién fue a hablar!, look who's talking! ‖ se habla de que ..., it is said that ... ‖ "se habla inglés", "English spoken". ‖ sin hablar de, not to mention. ‖ sin hablar palabra, without saying a word.

hablilla f (rumor) rumour (us rumor); (chisme) piece of gossip.

habón m bump, swelling, lump.

habré fut → **haber.**

hacedero,-a adj feasible, practicable, possible.

hacedor,-ra m,f maker.

■ el Sumo Hacedor / el Supremo Hacedor, the Maker.

hacendado,-a 1 pp → **hacendar.** – **2** adj landed. – **3** m,f landowner.

hacendar 1 t to give property to. – **2 hacendarse,** p to settle.

hacendista mf financial expert, tax consultant.

hacendoso,-a adj house-proud, hard-working.

hacer 1 t (producir, fabricar, crear) to make: **hacer ruido,** to make noise; **hacer un pastel,** to make a cake; **hacer un esfuerzo,** to make an effort; **hacer un error,** to make a mistake; **hacer un poema,** to write a poem; **hacer una casa,** to build a house; **hacer los deberes,** to do one's homework. 2 (arreglar, disponer - uñas) to do; (- barba) to trim; (- cama) to make; (- maleta) to pack. 3 (obrar, ejecutar) to do: **haz lo que quieras,** do what you want; **hazme un favor,** do me a favour; **hacer recados,** to run errands. 4 (conseguir amigos, dinero) to make. 5 (obligar) to make: **hazla callar,** make her shut up; **nos hizo leer,** she made us read. 6 (creer, suponer) to think: **la hacía en Roma,** I thought she was in Rome; **me hacía más alta,** he thought I was taller. 7 (recorrer) to do: **hice Barcelona-Bruselas en dos días,** I did Barcelona to Brussels in two days; **hacer cincuenta kilómetros por hora,** to do fifty kilometres per hour. 8 (en suma) to make: **con esta hacen ochenta,** that makes eighty. 9 (ocupar un lugar) to be: **él hace el número cuatro,** he's the fourth on the list. 10 (hacer parecer) to make look: **ese vestido te hace mayor,** that dress makes you look older. 11 (acostumbrar) to accustom. 12 (practicar) to practise (us practise): **hacer abdominales,** to do sit-ups; **hacer dedos,** to limber up (on the piano); **hacer piernas,** to limber up. 13 (sustituyendo a otro verbo) to do: **su hermano no quiso ir y ella hizo lo mismo,** her brother didn't want to go and neither did she. – **14** i (actuar) to play (**de,** -); (representar) to act: **hizo de Peribáñez,** he played Peribáñez; **hizo de abuela,** she played the grandmother. 15 (comportarse) to pretend to be, act: **hacer el tonto,** to act the fool. 16 (clima) to be: **hace buen día,** it's a fine day; **hacía frío,** it was cold. 17 (tiempo pasado) ago: **hace tres años,** three years ago. – **18 hacerse,** p (volverse) to become, get: **hacerse viejo,** to grow old; **hacerse rico,** to get rich. 19 (crecer) to grow: **se ha hecho mucho,** he's grown a lot. 20 (acostumbrarse) to get used (**a,** to), become accustomed (**a,** to): **se hizo al colegio nuevo,** he got used to his new school. 21 (resultar) to become, go on, seem: **la película se hizo muy larga,** the film went on too long, I found the film too long; **los días se hacían eternos,** the days seemed endless. 22 (simular) to pretend: **se hizo la elegante,** she pretended to be elegant. 23 (mandar hacer) to have made, have done: **me hice un vestido en la modista,** I had a dress made at the dressmaker's; **me hice la permanente en la peluquería,** I had a perm at the hairdresser's.

● a medio hacer, half-done, half-finished. ‖ ¡así se hace!, that's it!, that's the way! ‖ ¡buena la has hecho!, fam you've done it now! ‖ eso no hace al caso, that has nothing to do with it. ‖ ¿hace? / ¿te hace?, OK? ‖ hace mucho, a long time ago. ‖ hacer a todo, to turn one's hand to anything. ‖ hacer bien, to do the right thing. ‖ hacer bien en ..., to be right to ...: **hice bien en ir,** I was right to go. ‖ hacer burla de, to make fun of. ‖ hacer como que + ind, to pretend, act as if: **hizo como que no sabía nada,** he acted as if he knew nothing. ‖ hacer como si + subj, to pretend, act as if: **hizo como si supiera la verdad,** she acted as if she

knew the truth. ‖ **hacer conocer,** to make known. ‖ **hacer saber,** (*noticia*) to make known; (*a una persona*) to inform, let know: *si tienes algún problema, házmelo saber,* if you have any problems, let me know. ‖ **hacer de vientre / hacer del cuerpo,** *euf* to move one's bowels. ‖ **hacer el amor,** to make love. ‖ **hacer el cuerpo a algo,** *fig* to get used to sth.: *necesita hacer el cuerpo al calor,* she needs to get her body used to the heat. ‖ **hacer el indio,** *fam* to fool around. ‖ **hacer el ridículo,** to make a fool of os. ‖ **hacer gracia,** to amuse: *a mí no me hace ninguna gracia,* I don't find that at all funny. ‖ **hacer mal,** to do the wrong thing: *hice mal en invitarlo,* I was wrong to invite him. ‖ **hacer para + infin,** → **hacer por.** ‖ **hacer por + infin,** to try to, do one's best to: *haz por llegar pronto,* try to arrive early. ‖ **hacer algo por hacer,** to do sth. for the sake of it. ‖ **hacer tiempo,** to kill time. ‖ **hacer de las suyas,** *fam* to do it again, be back to one's old tricks. ‖ **hacerse a la mar,** to put to sea. ‖ **hacerse a un lado,** to step aside. ‖ **hacerse a uno mismo,** (*hombre*) to be a self-made man; (*mujer*) to be a self-made woman. ‖ **hacerse con,** to get hold of: *me hice con el disco,* I managed to get the record. ‖ **hacerse el/la sordo,-a,** *fig* to turn a deaf ear. ‖ **hacerse una idea de algo,** to imagine sth. ‖ **ser el que hace y deshace,** *fig* to call the shots. ‖ **tener mucho que hacer,** to have a lot to do.
▲ *Conjugation model* |73; *pp* hecho],-a; *in* 16 *and* 17, *used only in the* 3rd *person and does not take a subject.*

hacha¹ *f* (*instrumento*) axe (us ax).
● **ser una hacha en algo,** to be an ace at sth., be a wizard at sth.
▲ *Takes el in singular.*

hacha² 1 *f* (*vela*) large candle. 2 (*antorcha*) torch.

hachazo *m* blow with an axe (us ax), hack.

hache *f* (*la letra*) aitch.
● **¡llámalo hache!,** *fam* it's all the same!, call it what you like! ‖ **por hache o por be,** *fam* for one reason or another.

hachear 1 *t* to chop. – 2 *i* to chop.

hachís *m* hashish.

hachón 1 *m* (*vela*) large candle. 2 (*brasero*) type of brazier.

hacia 1 *prep* (*dirección*) towards, to: *hacia la inmortalidad,* towards immortality. 2 (*tiempo*) at about, at around: *estaremos ahí hacia las dos,* we'll be there at about two.
● **hacia abajo,** downward(s), down: *empújalo hacia abajo,* push it downwards. ‖ **hacia acá,** this way. ‖ **hacia adelante,** forward(s): *inclínate hacia delante,* lean forward. ‖ **hacia allá,** that way. ‖ **hacia atrás,** backward(s), back. ‖ **hacia casa,** home, homeward, towards home.

hacienda 1 *f* (*bienes*) property, wealth, possessions *pl.* 2 (*finca*) estate, property, us ranch. 3 FIN Treasury.
■ **Delegación de Hacienda,** local Inland Revenue office. ‖ **hacienda pública,** public funds *pl,* public finances *pl.* ‖ **Ministerio de Hacienda,** Finance Ministry, GB Exchequer, us Treasury. ‖ **Ministro de Hacienda,** Minister of Finance, GB Chancellor of the Exchequer, us Secretary of the Treasury.

hacina *f* stack.

hacinamiento *m* (*de cosas*) piling, heaping; (*de personas*) overcrowding.

hacinar 1 *t* AGR to stack. 2 *fig* (*amontonar*) to pile up, heap up. – 3 **hacinarse,** *p fig* (*personas*) to be packed, be crowded.

hada *f* fairy.
■ **hada madrina,** fairy godmother.

▲ *Takes el in singular.*

hadado,-a 1 *adj* related to fate. 2 (*mágico*) magic, prodigious.

hado *m* destiny, fate.

hagiografía *f* hagiography.

hagiógrafo,-a *m,f* hagiographer, hagiographist.

hago *pres indic* → **hacer.**

haiga *f fam* luxurious limousine.
▲ *Takes el in singular.*

Haití *m* Haiti.

haitiano,-a 1 *adj* Haitian. – 2 *m,f* Haitian.

hala 1 *interj* (*dar prisa*) go on!, get moving! 2 (*infundir ánimo*) come on! 3 (*sorpresa*) oh dear! 4 (*fuera*) clear off!, get out! 5 (*exageración*) come off it!

halagador,-ra *adj* flattering.

halagar 1 *t* (*lisonjear*) to flatter. 2 (*satisfacer*) to please.
▲ *Conjugation model* |7|, *like* llegar.

halago *m* compliment, flattery.

halagüeño,-a 1 *adj* (*adulador*) flattering. 2 (*promesa, futuro*) promising.
● **en tono halagüeño,** flatteringly.

halar *t* to haul, pull.

halcón *m* falcon.
■ **halcón común,** (peregrine) falcon.

halconería *f* falconry.

halconero,-a *m,f* falconer.

halda 1 *f* (*falda*) skirt. 2 (*arpillera*) sackcloth, sacking.

hale 1 *interj* (*dar prisa*) get going!, get a move on! 2 (*sorpresa*) oh dear!

haleche *m* anchovy.

halibut *m* halibut.

hálito 1 *m* (*aliento*) breath. 2 (*vapor*) vapour (us vapor). 3 *lit* gentle breeze.

halitosis *f* halitosis, bad breath.
▲ *pl* halitosis.

hallado,-a 1 *pp* → **hallar.** – 2 *adj:* bien hallado,-a, at ease, in one's element; mal hallado,-a, uneasy, uncomfortable.

hallar 1 *t* (*encontrar*) to find. 2 (*averiguar*) to find out; (*descubrir*) to discover. 3 (*ver, notar*) to see, observe. – 4 **hallarse,** *p* (*estar*) to be: *se hallaba en Manresa,* she was in Manresa; *se hallaba enfermo,* he was ill.

hallazgo 1 *m* (*descubrimiento*) finding, discovery: *"hallazgo de un cadáver",* "body found". 2 (*cosa descubierta*) find.

halo *m* halo, aura.

halógeno,-a 1 *adj* halogenous. – 2 **halógeno,** *m* halogen.

haloideo *m* haloid.

haltera *f* dumbbell.

halterofilia *f* weightlifting.

hamaca 1 *f* (*de red*) hammock. 2 (*tumbona*) deck chair.

hámago 1 *m* bee glue. 2 *fig* repugnance.

hambre *f* hunger, starvation, famine.
● **entretener el hambre,** *fig* to stave off hunger: *eso te entretendrá el hambre hasta la cena,* that'll tide you over until dinner. ‖ **hambre y sed de justicia,** *fig* hunger and thirst for justice. ‖ **matar de hambre a algn.,** to starve sb. to death. ‖ **matar el hambre,** *fig* to stave off hunger. ‖ **morirse de hambre,** to die of starvation, to be starving. ‖ **pasar hambre,** go hungry, be starving. ‖ **ser más listo,-a que el hambre,** *fig* to be a cunning devil. ‖ **ser un,-a muerto,-a de hambre,** *pey* to be a good-for-nothing. ‖ **tener hambre,** to be hungry.
■ **huelga de hambre,** hunger strike. ‖ **salario de hambre,** starvation wages *pl.*

▲ Takes *el* in singular.

hambriento,-a 1 *adj* hungry, starving. 2 *fig* hungry, longing: *hambriento de justicia,* longing for justice. – 3 *m,f* hungry person, starving person. – 4 **los hambrientos,** *mpl* the hungry.

hambrón,-ona *adj pey* famished.

Hamburgo *m* Hamburg.

hamburgués,-esa 1 *adj* of Hamburg, from Hamburg. – 2 *m,f* person from Hamburg, inhabitant of Hamburg. – 3 hamburguesa, *f* hamburger, beefburger.

hamburguesa *f* → **hamburgués,-esa**.

hamburguesería *f* hamburger restaurant.

hampa *f* underworld.

▲ Takes *el* in singular.

hampesco,-a *adj* underworld, criminal.

hampón,-ona 1 *adj* tough, rowdy. – 2 *m,f* thug, criminal.

hámster *m* hamster.

▲ *pl* hámsters.

hándicap *m* handicap.

▲ *pl* hándicaps.

hangar *m* hangar.

hápax *m* hapax legomenon.

haragán,-ana 1 *adj* lazy, idle. – 2 *m,f* lazybones, idler.

haraganear *i* to idle, loaf around.

harakiri *m* hara-kiri.

harapiento,-a *adj* ragged, tattered, in rags.

harapo *m* rag, tatter.

● hecho,-a un harapo, in tatters.

haraquiri *m* hara-kiri.

harem *m* harem.

harén *m* harem.

▲ *pl* harenes.

harina *f* flour.

● eso es harina de otro costal, *fam fig* that's another kettle of fish.

■ harina de avena, oatmeal. ‖ harina de maíz, cornflour, US cornstarch. ‖ harina de pescado, fish meal. ‖ harina de trigo, wheat flour. ‖ harina lacteada, malted milk.

harinoso,-a *adj* floury.

harnero *m* sieve.

hartar 1 *t* (*atiborrar*) to satiate, fill up: *los pasteles de chocolate hartan mucho,* chocolate cakes are very filling. 2 *fig* (*deseo etc*) to satisfy. 3 (*fastidiar*) to annoy, irritate: *me harta con sus tonterías,* his silly remarks get on muy nerves. 4 (*cansar*) to tire, bore. 5 (*causar, dar*) to overwhelm (de, with): *lo hartó de regalos,* she showered him with presents; *lo hartaron a golpes,* they beat him up. – 6 hartarse, *p* (*atiborrarse*) to eat one's fill, stuff os. 7 (*cansarse*) to get fed up (de, with), get tired (de, of): *me harté de esperarla,* I got tired of waiting for her. 8 *fam* (*hacer algo*) to do nothing but: *me harté de leer,* I did nothing but read.

● hasta hartarse, to repletion: *dormir hasta hartarse,* to have one's fill of sleep; *comer hasta hartarse,* to eat os. sick.

hartazgo *m* bellyful.

● darse un hartazgo de ..., to stuff os. with ..., have one's fill of ...

hartazón *m* → **hartazgo**.

harto,-a 1 *adj* (*repleto*) full, satiated. 2 *fam* (*cansado*) tired (de, of), fed up (de, with): *estoy harto de leer,* I'm tired of reading. 3 *desus* (*bastante*) enough: *hartas dificultades,* enough difficulties. – 4 harto, *adv desus* (*muy*) quite, very: *harto bueno,* very good.

● ¡me tienes harto,-a!, I'm fed up with you! ‖ ¡ya estoy harto,-a!, I'm fed up!, I'm sick and tired of it!

hartura 1 *f* (*hartazgo*) bellyful. 2 (*abundancia*) abundance, plenty, glut. 3 *fig* (*deseo etc*) fulfilment (US fulfillment).

● ¡qué hartura!, what a drag! ‖ tener una hartura de algo, to be fed up with sth.

has *pres indic* → **haber**.

hasta 1 *prep* (*tiempo*) until, till, up to: *hasta enero,* until January; *hasta el sábado,* until Saturday; *desde las diez hasta las dos,* from ten to two; *sabe contar hasta 20,* he can count (up) to 20. 2 (*lugar*) as far as, up to, down to: *hasta allí,* up to there. 3 (*cantidad*) up to, as many as: *había hasta seis coches,* there were up to six cars. 4 (*incluso*) even: *hasta sabe escribir,* she even knows how to write. 5 (*como despedida*) see you: ¡hasta el lunes!, see you on Monday!; ¡hasta mañana!, see you tomorrow!

● desde ... hasta ..., from ... to ...: *de Berga hasta Sabadell,* from Berga to Sabadell. ‖ ¿hasta cuándo?, until when?, how long?: ¿hasta cuándo tendremos que aguantar este gobierno?, how long are we going to have to put up with this government? ‖ ¿hasta dónde?, how far? ‖ hasta el punto que ..., to such a point that ... ‖ ¡hasta la vista!, see you!, cheerio!, us so long! ‖ ¡hasta luego!, see you later! ‖ hasta más no poder, as much as possible: *bebió hasta más no poder,* he drank as much as he could take. ‖ hasta que, until: *estaré aquí hasta que volváis,* I'll be here until you come back.

hastiado,-a 1 *pp* → **hastiar**. – 2 *adj* disgusted (de, with), sick (de, of).

hastial *m* gable (end).

hastiar 1 *t* to bore. – 2 hastiarse, *p* to get sick (de, of), get tired (de, of).

▲ *Conjugation model* [13], *like* desviar.

hastío 1 *m* (*repugnancia*) disgust, loathing. 2 *fig* (*aburrimiento*) boredom, weariness.

hatajo 1 *m* small herd, small flock. 2 *fig* heap, lot, bunch: *un hatajo de disparates,* a load of nonsense; *un hatajo de ladrones,* a gang of thieves; *un hatajo de mentiras,* a pack of lies.

hatillo *m* small bundle.

hato 1 *m* (*rebaño*) herd, flock. 2 (*de ropa etc*) bundle.

● liar el hato, *fig* to pack one's bags, get ready to go.

Hawai *m* Hawaii.

hawaiano,-a 1 *adj* Hawaian. – 2 *m,f* Hawaian.

hay *pres indic* → **haber**.

haya[1] 1 *f* BOT beech. 2 (*madera*) beech, beech wood.

■ haya cobriza, copper beech.

haya[2] *pres subj* → **haber**.

Haya La Haya, *f* The Hague.

hayal *m* beech grove.

hayedo *m* beech grove.

hayo 1 *m* (*arbusto*) coca. 2 (*mezcla*) coca leaves and lime salts.

hayuco *m* beechnut.

haz[1] 1 *m* (*de cosas*) bundle. 2 (*de mieses etc*) sheaf. 3 (*de luz*) shaft, beam.

▲ *pl* haces.

haz[2] *m* (*cara*) face.

haz[3] *imperat* → **hacer**.

haza *f* piece of arable land.

hazaña *f* deed, exploit, heroic feat.

hazmerreír *m* laughing stock.

HB *abr* POL (*Herri Batasuna*) Popular Union (*pro-independence Basque party*).

he[1] *adv: he aquí un ejemplo,* here is an example; *he aquí los papeles,* here are the papers; *hete aquí,* here you are; *heme aquí,* here I am.
● he ahí la cuestión, that's the question. ‖ he aquí el problema, that's the problem.
he[2] *interj* hey!
he[3] *pres indic* → **haber**.
hebdomadario,-a *adj* weekly.
hebijón *m* pin of a buckle, prong of a buckle.
hebilla *f* buckle.
hebra 1 *f (de hilo)* thread, piece of thread. 2 *(de carne)* sinew; *(de legumbre)* string; *(de madera)* grain; *(de planta)* strand. 3 *(veta)* vein. 4 *fig* thread.
● pegar la hebra, *fam* to get chatting, chew the fat.
hebraico,-a *adj* Hebraic, Hebraical, Hebrew.
hebraísmo *m* Hebraism.
hebraísta *mf* Hebraist.
hebreo,-a 1 *adj* Hebrew. – 2 *m,f (persona)* Hebrew. – 3 hebreo, *m (idioma)* Hebrew.
● jurar en hebreo, *fam* to curse and swear.
Hébridas (Islas) Hébridas, *fpl* Hebrides.
hecatombe 1 *f* HIST hecatomb. 2 *(desgracia)* disaster, catastrophe.
hechicería 1 *f (arte)* sorcery, witchcraft. 2 *(hechizo)* spell, charm.
hechicero,-a 1 *adj* bewitching, charming. – 2 *m,f (hombre)* sorcerer, wizard; *(mujer)* sorceress, witch.
hechizar 1 *t (embrujar)* to bewitch, cast a spell on. 2 *fig (cautivar)* to charm, bewitch.
▲ Conjugation model [4], *like realizar.*
hechizo 1 *m (embrujo)* charm, spell. 2 *fig (embelesamiento)* fascination, charm.
hecho,-a 1 *pp* → **hacer**. – 2 *adj (carne)* done. 3 *(persona)* mature. 4 *(frase, expresión)* set. 5 *(ropa)* ready-made. – 6 hecho, *m (realidad)* fact. 7 *(suceso)* event, incident. – 8 ¡hecho!, *interj* done!, agreed!
● a lo hecho pecho, it's no use crying over spilt milk. ‖ ¡bien hecho!, well done! ‖ de hecho, in fact. ‖ el hecho es que ..., the fact is that ... ‖ eso está hecho, *fig* that won't take long, that'll only take a minute. ‖ estar hecho,-a un,-a ..., to be ...: *esta habitación está hecha un asco,* this room is in a right mess; *está hecho un vago,* he's a real waster, he's a real layabout. ‖ hecho,-a a mano, hand-made. ‖ hecho,-a a máquina, machine-made. ‖ hecho,-a en casa, home-made. ‖ hechos son amores, actions speak louder than words. ‖ lo hecho hecho está, what's done is done. ‖ muy hecho,-a, *(carne)* well-cooked; *(pasada)* overdone. ‖ poco,-a hecho,-a, *(carne)* rare; *(insuficientemente)* underdone. ‖ ser un hombre hecho y derecho, to be a real man.
■ hecho consumado, fait accompli. ‖ hecho de armas, feat of arms. ‖ Hechos de los Apóstoles, REL Acts of the Apostles.
hechura 1 *f (forma)* shape. 2 COST cut. 3 *(elaboración)* making. 4 *fml (obra)* creation, product.
■ hechura de Dios, God's creature.
hectárea *f* hectare.
hectogramo *m* hectogramme (us hectogram).
hectolitro *m* hectolitre (us hectoliter).
hectómetro *m* hectometre (us hectometer).
hectovatio *m* hectowatt.
hedentina 1 *f (olor)* stink. 2 *(lugar)* stinking place, stinking hole.
heder 1 *i (apestar)* to stink (**a**, of): *hedía a muerto,* it stank of death. 2 *fig (cansar)* to annoy, pester.

▲ Conjugation model [28], *like* **entender**.
hediondez *f* stink, stench.
hediondo,-a 1 *adj (apestoso)* stinking, foul-smelling, smelly. 2 *fig (asqueroso)* filthy, repulsive. 3 *fig (molesto)* annoying.
hedonismo *m* hedonism.
hedonista 1 *adj* hedonistic, hedonic. – 2 *mf* hedonist.
hedor *m* stink, stench.
hegeliano,-a 1 *adj* Hegelian. – 2 *m,f* Hegelian.
hegemonía *f* hegemony.
hégira *f* Hegira, Hejira.
héjira *f* Hegira, Hejira.
helada *f* → **helado,-a**.
heladera *f* → **heladero,-a**.
heladería *f* ice-cream parlour (us parlor).
heladero,-a 1 *m,f (hombre)* ice-cream man; *(mujer)* ice-cream woman. – 2 heladera, *f (nevera)* refrigerator. 3 *(máquina de helados)* ice-cream maker.
helado,-a 1 *pp* → **helar**. – 2 *adj (gen)* frozen; MED frostbitten: *estoy helado,* I'm frozen. 3 *(muy frío)* icy, freezing cold. 4 *(café, té)* iced. 5 *fig (pasmado)* dumbfounded. – 6 helado, *m* ice-cream. – 7 helada, *f* METEOR frost, freeze.
● caer una helada, to freeze. ‖ dejar a algn. helado,-a, to stun sb. ‖ quedarse helado,-a, *fam fig* to be flabbergasted, be stunned.
■ helada blanca, hoarfrost, white frost. ‖ helado de corte, wafer.
helador,-ra 1 *adj* icy, freezing. – 2 heladora, *f* ice-cream maker.
heladora *f* → **helador,-ra**.
helar 1 *t (congelar)* to freeze. 2 *(plantas)* to kill, freeze: *el frío ha helado los geranios,* the frost has killed the geraniums. – 3 *i* METEOR to freeze: *anoche heló,* it froze last night. – 4 helarse, *p (congelarse)* to freeze: *el estanque se ha helado,* the pond has frozen over. 5 *(planta)* to be killed by frost. 6 *(persona)* to freeze, freeze to death: *me estoy helando,* I'm freezing.
● se me heló la sangre, *fig* my blood ran cold.
▲ Conjugation model [27], *like* **acertar**; in 4 used only in the 3rd person; it does not take a subject.
helechal *m* fern-covered place.
helecho *m* fern.
helénico,-a *adj* Hellenic, Greek.
helenio *m* elecampane.
helenismo *m* Hellenism.
helenista 1 *adj* Hellenistic. – 2 *mf* Hellenist.
helenístico,-a *adj* Hellenistic, Hellenistical.
helenizar *t* to Hellenize.
heleno,-a 1 *adj* Hellene, Hellenian, Greek. – 2 *m,f* Hellene, Greek.
helero *m (masa)* ice sheet. 2 *(capa)* snow cap.
helgadura *f* gap.
heliaco,-a *adj* heliacal.
helíaco,-a *adj* heliacal.
hélice 1 *f* ANAT MAT ARQ helix. 2 AV MAR propeller.
helicoidal *adj* helicoidal.
helicón *m* helicon.
helicóptero *m* helicopter.
● en helicóptero, by helicopter.
helio *m* helium.
heliocéntrico,-a *adj* heliocentric.
heliograbado *m* photogravure.
heliografía *f* heliography.
heliógrafo *m* heliograph.
heliosis *f* heliosis.
▲ *pl* heliosis.

heliotropo *m* heliotrope.
helipuerto *m* heliport.
helitransportado,-a *adj* transported by helicopter.
helminto *m* helminth.
Helsinki *m* Helsinki.
Helvecia *f* Helvetia.
helvético,-a 1 *adj* Helvetian, Swiss. – 2 *m,f* Helvetian, Swiss.
hematíe *m* red blood corpuscle.
hematites *f* haematite (US hematite).
  ▲ *pl* **hematites**.
hematología *f* haematology (US hematology).
hematólogo,-a *m,f* haematologist (US hematologist).
hematoma *m* haematoma (US hematoma), bruise.
hematosis *f* haematosis (US hematosis).
  ▲ *pl* **hematosis**.
hembra 1 *f* (*animal*) female: *la mula hembra,* the she-ass. 2 (*mujer*) woman: *es una real hembra,* she's a good-looking woman. 3 TÉC female. 4 (*de tornillo*) nut. 5 (*de enchufe*) socket. 6 (*corchete*) eye.
hembrilla 1 *f* (*piececita*) female. 2 (*armella*) eyebolt.
hemeroteca *f* newspaper library.
hemiciclo 1 *m* (*semicírculo*) hemicycle. 2 (*parlamento*) floor.
hemiplejia *f* hemiplegia.
hemiplejía *f* hemiplegia.
hemipléjico,-a *adj* hemiplegic.
hemíptero *m* hemipteran.
hemisférico,-a *adj* hemispheric, hemispherical.
hemisferio *m* hemisphere.
  ■ **hemisferio cerebral**, cerebral hemisphere. ‖ **hemisferio norte**, northern hemisphere. ‖ **hemisferio sur**, southern hemisphere.
hemistiquio *m* hemistich.
hemodiálisis *f* haemodialysis (US hemodialysis).
  ▲ *pl* **hemodiálisis**.
hemofilia *f* haemophilia (US hemophilia).
hemofílico,-a 1 *adj* haemophilic (US hemophilic). – 2 *m,f* haemophiliac (US hemophiliac).
hemoglobina *f* haemoglobin (US hemoglobin).
hemorragia *f* haemorrhage (US hemorrhage).
hemorroide *f* haemorrhoid (US hemorrhoid).
hemos *pres indic* → **haber**.
henar 1 *m* (*henil*) hayloft. 2 (*terreno*) hayfield, hay meadow.
henchidura *f* filling.
henchir 1 *t* (*llenar*) to fill (**de**, with), stuff (**de**, with), cram (**de**, with): *henchir de aire,* to fill with air. – 2 **henchirse**, *p* (*atiborrarse*) to stuff os. (**de**, with).
  ● **henchirse de orgullo**, *fig* to swell with pride.
  ▲ *Conjugation model* [34], *like* **servir**.
hendedura *f* → **hendidura**.
hender 1 *t* (*cortar*) to cleave, split, crack. 2 *fig* (*agua, olas*) to cut: *el buque hiende las aguas,* the ship cuts through the water. 3 *fig* (*abrirse paso*) to make one's way through. – 4 **henderse**, *p* to split, crack.
  ▲ *Conjugation model* [28], *like* **entender**.
hendidura *f* cleft, crack.
hendir *t-p* → **hender**.
  ▲ *Conjugation model* [29], *like* **discernir**.
henificar *t* to ted.
henil *m* hayloft.
heno *m* hay.
hepático,-a *adj* hepatic, liver.
hepatitis *f* hepatitis.
  ▲ *pl* **hepatitis**.

hepatología *f* hepatology.
heptaedro *m* heptahedron.
heptagonal *adj* heptagonal.
heptágono,-a 1 *adj* heptagonal. – 2 **heptágono**, *m* heptagon.
heptasílabo,-a 1 *adj* heptasyllabic. – 2 **heptasílabo**, *m* heptasyllable.
heráldica *f* → **heráldico,-a**.
heráldico,-a 1 *adj* heraldic. – 2 **heráldica**, *f* heraldry.
heraldo *m* herald.
herbáceo,-a *adj* herbaceous.
herbaje *m* grass, pasture.
herbario,-a 1 *adj* herbal. – 2 *m,f* (*botánico*) botanist. – 3 **herbario**, *m* (*colección*) herbarium.
herbecer *i* to begin to grow.
  ▲ *Conjugation model* [43], *like* **agradecer**.
herbicida *m* weedkiller, herbicide.
herbívoro,-a 1 *adj* herbivorous, grass-eating. – 2 *m,f* herbivore.
herbolario,-a 1 *m,f* (*persona*) herbalist. – 2 *adj fig* (*botarate*) crazy, foolish. – 3 **herbolario**, *m* (*tienda*) herbalist's (shop).
herboristería *f* herbalist's (shop).
herborizar *i* to herborize.
  ▲ *Conjugation model* [4], *like* **realizar**.
herboso,-a *adj* grassy.
hercio *m* hertz.
hercúleo,-a *adj* Herculean.
hércules *m fig* Hercules.
heredable *adj* inheritable.
heredad 1 *f* (*terreno*) country estate. 2 (*bienes*) private estate, property.
heredado,-a 1 *pp* → **heredar**. – 2 *adj* inherited.
heredar 1 *t* to inherit: *heredó una fortuna de sus padres,* she inherited a fortune from her parents. 2 *fig* to inherit: *ha heredado los ojos de su padre,* he's got his father's eyes.
heredero,-a *m,f* (*hombre*) heir; (*mujer*) heiress.
  ● **nombrar heredero,-a a algn.**, to make sb. one's heir/heiress.
  ■ **príncipe heredero / princesa heredera**, crown prince / crown princess. ‖ **único heredero,-a**, (*hombre*) sole heir; (*mujer*) sole heiress.
hereditario,-a *adj* hereditary.
hereje 1 *mf* heretic. 2 *fig* (*descarado*) rascal.
herejía 1 *f* heresy. 2 *fam fig* (*disparate*) nonsense.
herencia 1 *f* inheritance, legacy. 2 (*genética*) heredity.
heresiarca *mf* heresiarch.
herético,-a *adj* heretical.
herida *f* → **herido,-a**.
herido,-a 1 *pp* → **herir**. – 2 *adj* (*físicamente*) wounded, injured, hurt: *el niño resultó herido,* the boy was injured. 3 *fig* (*emocionalmente*) hurt, wounded. – 4 *m,f* wounded person, injured person. – 5 **los heridos**, *mpl* the wounded. – 6 **herida**, *f* wound. 7 *fig* wound, outrage.
  ● **caer herido,-a**, to be wounded. ‖ **herido,-a de gravedad**, badly injured. ‖ **herido,-a de muerte**, mortally wounded. ‖ **hurgar en la herida**, *fig* to turn the knife in the wound. ‖ **lamerse las heridas**, *fig* to lick one's wounds. ‖ **sentirse herido,-a**, *fig* to feel hurt. ‖ **tocar a algn. en la herida**, *fig* to touch sb.'s sore spot.
herir 1 *t* (*dañar*) to wound, injure, hurt: *lo hirieron en la pierna,* they wounded him in the leg. 2 (*golpear*) to beat, hit. 3 (*un instrumento*) to play, pluck. 4 (*la vista*) to offend, hurt; (*el oído*) to hurt, offend: *este color hiere la*

vista, this colour hurts your eyes. **5** *(luz)* to dazzle. **6** *fig (ofender)* to hurt, offend. **– 7** **herirse,** *p (uso reflexivo)* to injure os., hurt os.: *se hirió en la mano,* he injured his hand.
● **herir a algn. en lo vivo,** *fig* to cut sb. to the quick. ‖ **herir a algn. en su amor propio,** *fig* to wound sb.'s pride. ‖ **herir de muerte,** to mortally wound.
▲ *Conjugation model* [35], *like hervir.*

hermafrodita **1** *adj* hermaphrodite. **– 2** *mf* hermaphrodite.

hermanable **1** *adj (compatible)* compatible. **2** *(a juego)* matching **(con, -).**

hermanado,-a **1** *pp →* **hermanar. – 2** *adj fig (semejante)* similar, alike. **3** *(a juego)* matched. **4** *(ciudad, pueblo)* twinned.

hermanar **1** *t (unir)* to unite, join. **2** *(combinar)* to combine. **3** *(personas)* to unite spiritually. **4** *(ciudades)* to twin. **– 5** **hermanarse,** *p (combinarse)* to combine. **6** *(hombres)* to become brothers in spirit; *(mujeres)* to become sisters in spirit. **7** *(ciudades)* to become twinned.

hermanastro,-a *m,f (hombre)* stepbrother; *(mujer)* stepsister.

hermandad **1** *f (de hermanos)* fraternity, brotherhood; *(de hermanas)* fraternity, sisterhood. **2** *fig (cofradía)* brotherhood; *(grupo)* association. **3** *fig (amistad íntima)* close relationship.

hermano,-a **1** *adj (gen)* related, similar. **2** *(ciudades)* twin; *(lenguas, países)* sister. **– 3** *m,f (hombre)* brother; *(mujer)* sister: *¿cuántos hermanos tienes?,* how many brothers and sisters have you got?
■ **hermano gemelo / hermana gemela,** twin brother / twin sister. ‖ **hermano político / hermana política,** brother-in-law / sister-in-law. ‖ **primo,-a hermano,-a,** first cousin.

hermenéutica *f* hermeneutics.

herméticamente *adv* hermetically: *cerrado herméticamente,* hermetically sealed.

hermético,-a **1** *adj* hermetic, hermetical, airtight: *un envase hermético,* an airtight container. **2** *fig* impenetrable, secretive.

hermetismo **1** *m* hermetism. **2** *fig* impenetrability, secrecy, secretiveness.

hermosear *t* to beautify, make beautiful.

hermoso,-a **1** *adj (gen)* beautiful, lovely: *una mujer hermosa,* a beautiful woman; *hace un día hermoso,* it's a lovely day. **2** *(hombre)* handsome.

hermosura **1** *adj (cualidad - de mujer, lugar)* beauty, loveliness; *(- de hombre)* handsomeness. **– 2** *f (mujer hermosa)* beautiful woman, beauty. **3** *(persona, cosa):* *¡qué hermosura de ojos!,* what beautiful eyes!; *¡qué hermosura de niño!,* what a beatiful child!

hernia *f* hernia, rupture.

herniado,-a **1** *pp →* **herniarse. – 2** *adj* ruptured.

herniarse *p* to rupture os.
▲ *Conjugation model* [12], *like cambiar.*

Herodes *m* Herod.
● **ir de Herodes a Pilatos,** *fig* to go from pillar to post.

héroe *m* hero.

heroicamente *adv* heroically.

heroico,-a *adj* heroic.

heroína **1** *f (mujer)* heroine. **2** *(droga)* heroin.

heroinómano,-a *m,f* heroin addict.

heroísmo *m* heroism.

herpe *m* herpes, shingles.

herpes *m* herpes, shingles.
▲ *pl herpes.*

herpético,-a *adj* herpetic.

herrada *f* wooden bucket.

herradero **1** *m (acción)* branding.

herrador *m* blacksmith.

herradura *f* horseshoe.
● **en forma de herradura,** horseshoe-shaped.

herraje *m* iron fittings *pl,* ironwork.

herramienta *f* tool.
■ **caja de herramientas,** toolbox.

herrar **1** *t (caballo)* to shoe. **2** *(ganado)* to brand.
▲ *Conjugation model* [27], *like acertar.*

herreño,-a **1** *adj* of Hierro, from Hierro. **– 2** *m,f* person from Hierro, inhabitant of Hierro.

herrería **1** *f (fábrica)* ironworks *pl.* **2** *(taller)* forge, smithy, blacksmith's. **3** *(oficio)* smithery. **4** *fig (alboroto)* racket.

herrerillo *m* great tit.
■ **herrerillo capuchino,** crested tit.

herrero *m* blacksmith, smith.

herrete *m* tag, metal tip.

herrumbre **1** *f (óxido)* rust. **2** *(sabor)* rusty taste.

herrumbroso,-a *adj* rusty.

hertz *m* hertz.
▲ *pl hertz.*

hertziano,-a *adj* Hertzian.

hervidero **1** *m (ebullición)* boiling, bubbling. **2** *(manantial)* hot spring. **3** *fig (multitud)* swarm, throng: *el metro era un hervidero de gente,* the underground was seething with people. **4** *fig (sitio)* hotbed: *el país era un hervidero de rebelión,* the country was a hotbed of rebellion.

hervir **1** *t* to boil. **– 2** *i* to boil: *el agua ya hierve,* the water is boiling. **3** *fig (el mar)* to surge. **4** *fig (excitarse)* to boil, seethe: *está que hierve de ira,* he's seething with anger. **5** *fig (abundar)* to swarm **(de/en,** with), seethe **(de/en,** with): *aquel lugar hervía de gente,* that place was swarming with people.
● **hervir en deseos de,** *fig* to be consumed with. ‖ **romper a hervir,** to come to the boil.
▲ *Conjugation model* [35].

hervor **1** *m* boiling, bubbling. **2** *fig* fire, ardour (us ardor).
● **dar un hervor a algo,** to blanch sth.

hetaira *f* hetaera.

hetera *f* hetaera.

heteróclito,-a **1** *adj* heteroclite. **2** *fml fig* heterogeneous, irregular.

heterodoxia *f* heterodoxy.

heterodoxo,-a **1** *adj* heterodox, unorthodox. **– 2** *m,f* heterodox person.

heterogamia *f* heterogamy.

heterogeneidad *f* heterogeneity, heterogeneousness.

heterogéneo,-a *adj* heterogeneous.

heteronimia *f* heteronymy.

heterónomo,-a *adj* heteronomous.

heterosexual **1** *adj* heterosexual. **– 2** *mf* heterosexual.

heterosexualidad *f* heterosexuality.

heurística *f →* **heurístico,-a.**

heurístico,-a **1** *adj* heuristic. **– 2** **heurística,** *f* heuristics.

hexaedro *m* hexahedron.

hexagonal *adj* hexagonal.

hexágono *m* hexagon.

hexámetro *m* hexameter.

hez **1** *f (poso)* sediment, dregs *pl.* **2** *fig (lo más vil)* scum, dregs *pl.* **– 3** **heces,** *fpl* faeces (us feces). excrement.

▲ *pl* **heces**.
Hg *sím* (*hectogramo*) hectogramme; (*símbolo*) Hg.
hialino,-a *adj* hyaline.
hiato *m* hiatus.
hibernación *f* hibernation.
hibernar *i* to hibernate.
hibisco *m* hibiscus.
híbrido,-a 1 *adj* hybrid. – 2 *m,f* hybrid.
hice *pt indef* → **hacer**.
hiciste *pt indef* → **hacer**.
hidalgo,-a 1 *adj desus* noble. 2 *fig* (*noble*) noble, generous. 3 *fig* (*caballeroso*) gentlemanly. – 4 **hidalgo**, *m* nobleman, gentleman.
hidalguía 1 *f desus* nobility. 2 *fig* (*generosidad*) generosity, nobleness. 3 *fig* (*caballerosidad*) chivalry, gentlemanliness.
hidra 1 *f* (*culebra*) sea snake. 2 (*pólipo*) hydra.
hidrácido *m* hydracid.
hidratación 1 *f* hydration. 2 (*de la piel*) moisturizing.
hidratante 1 *adj* moisturizing. – 2 *f* moisturizing cream.
hidratar 1 *t* to hydrate. 2 (*piel*) to moisturize.
hidrato *m* hydrate.
■ hidrato de carbono, carbohydrate.
hidráulica *f* → **hidráulico,-a**.
hidráulico,-a 1 *adj* hydraulic. – 2 **hidráulica**, *f* hydraulics.
hídrico,-a *adj* hydric.
hidroavión *m* seaplane, us hydroplane.
hidrocarburo *m* hydrocarbon.
hidrocefalia *f* hydrocephalus, hydrocephaly.
hidrodinámica *f* → **hidrodinámico,-a**.
hidrodinámico,-a 1 *adj* hydrodynamic. – 2 **hidrodinámica**, *f* hydrodynamics.
hidroelectricidad *f* hydroelectricity.
hidroeléctrico,-a *adj* hydroelectric.
hidrófilo,-a 1 *adj* (*organismo*) hydrophilous. 2 (*absorbente*) absorbent: *algodón hidrófilo,* cotton wool, us absorbent cotton.
hidrofobia *f* hydrophobia, rabies.
hidrófobo,-a 1 *adj* hydrophobic. – 2 *m,f* hydrophobic person.
hidrófugo,-a *adj* water-repellent.
hidrogenar *t* to hydrogenate.
hidrógeno *m* hydrogen.
hidrografía *f* hydrography.
hidrográfico,-a *adj* hydrographic.
hidrólisis *f* hydrolysis.
▲ *pl* **hidrólisis**.
hidrolizar *t* to hydrolize.
▲ *Conjugation model* |4|, *like* **realizar**.
hidrología *f* hydrology.
hidrometría *f* hydrometry.
hidropesía *f* dropsy.
hidrópico,-a *adj* dropsical, dropsied.
hidroplano 1 *m* (*hidroavión*) seaplane, us hydroplane. 2 (*embarcación*) hydroplane.
hidrosfera *f* hydrosphere.
hidrosoluble *adj* soluble in water.
hidrostática *f* → **hidrostático,-a**.
hidrostático,-a 1 *adj* hydrostatic. – 2 **hidrostática**, *f* hydrostatics.
hidroterapia *f* hydrotherapy.
hidróxido *m* hydroxide.
hiedra *f* ivy.

hiel 1 *f* bile. 2 *fig* bitterness, gall.
hielo 1 *m* ice. 2 *fig* (*frialdad*) coldness.
● romper el hielo, *fig* to break the ice.
■ cubito de hielo, ice cube.
hiena *f* hyaena, hyena.
hierático,-a 1 *adj* REL hieratic, hieratical. 2 (*rígido*) rigid.
hierba 1 *f* grass. 2 CULIN herb. 3 *arg* (*marihuana*) grass. – 4 **hierbas**, *fpl* (*veneno*) poison *sing*, potion *sing*. 5 (*pastos*) grass *sing*, pastureland *sing*.
● mala hierba nunca muere, the Devil looks after his own. || ... y otras hierbas, *fam* irón among others.
■ finas hierbas, mixed herbs. || hierba luisa, lemon verbena. || hierba mate, maté. || mala hierba, weed; *fig* bad lot.
hierbabuena *f* mint.
hierbajo *m* weed.
hierro 1 *m* (*metal*) iron. 2 (*punta*) head, point. 3 (*marca*) brand. 4 *fig* (*arma*) steel, weapon. – 5 **hierros**, *mpl* (*prisiones*) chains, shackles.
● machacar en hierro frío, *fig* to bang one's head against a brick wall. || quien a hierro mata a hierro muere, *fig* he who lives by the sword, shall die by the sword. || quitarle hierro a algo, *fam fig* to play sth. down. || ser de hierro, *fig* to be as strong as an ox.
■ hierro colado / hierro fundido, cast iron. || hierro forjado, wrought iron. || voluntad de hierro, *fig* will of iron, iron will.
higa 1 *f* (*amuleto*) fist-shaped amulet. 2 (*gesto*) obscene gesture. 3 *fig* (*burla*) mockery; (*desprecio*) scorn.
● no me importa una higa, *fam* I don't give a fig.
higadilla *f* → **higadillo**.
higadillo *m* liver.
● echar los higadillos, *fam fig* to go flat out.
hígado 1 *m* liver. – 2 **hígados**, *mpl euf* guts.
● tener hígados, *fam* to have guts.
higiene *f* hygiene.
higiénico,-a *adj* hygienic.
higienista *mf* hygienist.
higienizar *t* to make hygienic.
▲ *Conjugation model* |4|, *like* **realizar**.
higo *m* fig.
● de higos a brevas, *fig* once in a blue moon. || estar hecho,-a un higo, *fam fig* (*persona*) to be wizened; (*cosa*) be screwed up, be crumpled. || me importa un higo, *fam* I couldn't care less. || ¡y un higo!, *fam* not on your life!, nothing doing!
■ higo chumbo, prickly pear.
higrometría *f* hygrometry.
higroscopio *m* hygroscope.
higuera *f* fig tree.
● caer de la higuera, *fig* to come back to earth. || estar en la higuera, *fig* to have one's head in the clouds.
■ higuera chumba, prickly pear.
hijastro,-a *m,f* (*niño, niña*) stepchild; (*hijo*) stepson; (*hija*) stepdaughter.
hijo,-a 1 *m,f* (*niño, niña*) child; (*chico*) son; (*chica*) daughter: *¿dónde está mi hijo?,* where's my son?; *tiene dos hijos y dos hijas,* he has two sons and two daughters. 2 (*aposición*) junior: *Juan Rodríguez, hijo,* Juan Rodríguez junior. – 3 **hijos**, *mpl* children: *tiene cuatro hijos,* she has four children. 4 (*descendientes*) descendants.
● ¡hijo,-a de mi alma!, *fam* my dear child! || hijo,-a mío,-a, (*chico*) my boy, my son, my child; (*chica*) my girl, my daughter, my child; (*hombre, mujer*) my dear. || todo hijo de vecino, *fam* everyone, everyone else. || un hijo de tal, *fam* a real so-and-so.

■ hijo,-a adoptivo,-a, (*niño, niña*) adopted child; (*chico*) adopted son; (*chica*) adopted daughter. ‖ hijo,-a de papá, (*chico*) daddy's boy; (*chica*) daddy's girl. ‖ hijo,-a de puta, *tabú* bastard, son of a bitch. ‖ hijo político / hija política, son-in-law / daughter-in-law. ‖ hijo,-a único,-a, (*niño, niña*) only child; (*chico*) only son; (*chica*) only daughter.

hijoputa *m tabú* bastard, motherfucker.

hijos *mpl →* hijo.

hijuelo *m* shoot.

hila[1] *f* (*acción de hilar*) spinning. – 2 hilas, *fpl* (*hebras*) lint *sing*.

hila[2] 1 *f* (*hilera*) line, row. 2 (*tripa*) thin gut.
● a la hila, in a row.

hilacha 1 *f* (*hilacho*) loose thread. 2 (*resto*) rest.

hilacho *m* loose thread.

hilada *f →* hilado,-a.

hiladillo *m* braid.

hilado,-a 1 *pp →* hilar. – 2 *adj* spun. – 3 hilado, *m* (*operación*) spinning. 4 (*hilo*) thread. – 5 hilada, *f* (*hilacho*) loose thread. 6 (*de ladrillos*) course.
■ fábrica de hilados, spinning mill. ‖ tejidos de hilado, spun textiles.

hilador,-ra *m,f* spinner.

hilandería 1 *f* (*arte*) spinning. 2 (*fábrica*) spinning mill; (*de algodón*) cotton mill.

hilandero,-a *m,f* spinner.

hilar 1 *t* to spin. 2 *fig* to work out.
● hilar muy fino / hilar muy delgado, *fig* to split hairs.

hilarante *adj* hilarious: *gas hilarante,* laughing gas.

hilaridad *f fml* hilarity, mirth.

hilas *fpl →* hila[1].

hilatura 1 *f* (*arte*) spinning. 2 (*industria*) spinning mill.

hilaza 1 *f* (*hilado*) thread, yarn. 2 (*hilo gordo*) thick thread. 3 (*hilo basto*) coarse thread.

hilera 1 *f* (*línea*) line, row. 2 (*hilo*) thread. 3 (*viga*) ridgepiece.
● en hilera, in line.

hilo 1 *m* thread; (*grueso*) yarn. 2 (*lino*) linen. 3 (*alambre, cable*) wire. 4 *fig* (*de luz*) thread, thin beam; (*de líquido*) trickle, thin stream. 5 *fig* (*de historia, discurso*) thread; (*de pensamiento*) train. 6 *fig* (*de la vida*) course.
● al hilo, on the grain: *cortar al hilo,* to cut on the grain. ‖ coger el hilo, *fig* to catch the drift, get the drift. ‖ con un hilo de voz, in a tiny voice, in a faint voice. ‖ estar colgando de un hilo, *fig* to be hanging by a thread. ‖ estar pendiente de un hilo, *fig* to be hanging by a thread. ‖ mover los hilos, *fig* to pull the strings. ‖ perder el hilo, *fig* to lose the thread. ‖ seguir el hilo, *fig* to follow.
■ hilo musical, piped music, Musak.

hilván 1 *m* (*costura*) tacking, basting. 2 (*punto*) tack, tacking stitch, basting stitch.

hilvanar 1 *t* to tack, baste. 2 *fig* to put together, outline.

Himalaya *m →* himalayo,-a.

himalayo,-a 1 *adj* Himalayan. – 2 el Himalaya, *m* the Himalayas *pl*.

himen *m* hymen.

himeneo 1 *m lit* (*casamiento*) wedding, marriage. 2 (*epitalamio*) epithalamium.

himenóptero,-a *adj* hymenopterus.

himno *m* hymn.
■ himno nacional, national anthem.

hincapié hacer hincapié, *loc* (*insistir*) to insist on; (*subrayar*) to emphasize (**en, -**), put emphasis (**en, on**), stress (**en, -**).

hincar 1 *t* (*clavar*) to drive (in). 2 (*apoyar*) to set firmly.
● hincar el diente en algo, to sink one's teeth into sth.; *fig* to get one's teeth into sth. ‖ hincarla, *fig* to work. ‖ hincarse de rodillas, to kneel (down).
▲ *Conjugation model* [1], *like* **sacar**.

hincha 1 *f* (*antipatía*) dislike, grudge. – 2 *mf* DEP fan, supporter.
● tener hincha a algn., to have it in for sb., bear a grudge against sb.: *le tiene hincha,* she's got it in for him.

hinchada *f →* hinchado,-a.

hinchado,-a 1 *pp →* hinchar. – 2 *adj* (*inflado*) inflated, blown up. 3 (*piel*) swollen, puffed up; (*estómago*) bloated. 4 *fig* (*persona*) vain, conceited. 5 *fig* (*estilo, lenguaje*) pompous, bombastic. – 6 hinchada, *f* DEP *fam* fans *pl*, supporters *pl*.

hinchar 1 *t* (*inflar*) to inflate, blow up; (*con bomba*) to pump up: *hinchar una pelota,* to pump up a ball; *hinchar un globo,* to blow up a balloon. 2 (*exagerar*) to inflate, blow up, exaggerate. – 3 hincharse, *p* MED to swell (up): *se me ha hinchado el pie,* my foot has swollen up. 4 (*engreírse*) to become conceited, become bigheaded. 5 *fam* (*comer*) to stuff os. 6 *fam* (*hacer dinero*) to make a packet, line one's pockets.
● hinchar a golpes / hinchar a palos, *fam* to beat, thrash. ‖ hincharle a algn. la cabeza con algo, *fig* to stuff sb.'s head with sth. ‖ hincharse de algo, to do sth. a lot: *hincharse de llorar,* to cry one's eyes out; *hincharse de correr,* to run around a lot. ‖ hinchársele a uno las narices, *fam fig* to get sick and tired.

hinchazón 1 *f* swelling, inflation. 2 *fig* (*presunción*) vanity, conceit; (*pomposidad*) pomposity, pompousness.

hindi *m* Hindi.

hindú 1 *adj* Hindu. – 2 *mf* Hindu.

hinduismo *m* Hinduism.

hiniesta *f* broom.

hinojo[1] *m* arc knee.
● de hinojos, on one's knees. ‖ postrarse de hinojos, to kneel down.

hinojo[2] *m* BOT fennel.

hioides *m* hyoid.
▲ *pl* hioides.

hipar 1 *i* (*tener hipo*) to hiccup, hiccough, have the hiccups, have the hiccoughs. 2 (*gimotear*) to whine, whimper.
● hipar por algo, *fam* to long for sth., yearn for sth.

hipérbaton *m* hyperbaton.

hipérbola *f* hyperbola.

hipérbole *f* hyperbole.

hiperbólico,-a *adj* hyperbolic, hyperbolical.

hiperbóreo,-a *adj* hyperborean.

hipercrítico,-a *adj* hypercritical.

hiperespacio *m* hyperspace.

hiperglucemia *f* hyperglycaemia (us hyperglycemia).

hipermercado *m* hypermarket, superstore.

hipermétrope 1 *adj* long-sighted. – 2 *mf* long-sighted person.

hipermetropía *f* long-sightedness.

hipernervioso,-a *adj* highly strung.

hiperónimo *m* superordinate.

hipersensible *adj* hypersensitive.

hipertensión *f* high blood pressure, hypertension.

hipertenso,-a 1 *adj* hypertensive. – 2 *m,f* hypertensive.

hipertrofia *f* hypertrophy.

hipertrofiar 1 *t* to hypertrophy. – 2 hipertrofiarse, *p* to hypertrophy.

hípico,-a 1 *adj* horse, equestrian. – 2 **hípica,** *f* horse riding.
■ **club hípico,** riding club.
hipido *m* whimper, sob.
hipnosis *f* hypnosis.
▲ *pl hipnosis.*
hipnótico,-a *adj* hypnotic.
hipnotismo *m* hypnotism.
hipnotizador,-ra 1 *adj* hypnotizing. – 2 *m,f* hypnotist.
hipnotizar *t* to hypnotize.
▲ *Conjugation model* [4], *like realizar.*
hipo *m* hiccup, hiccough: *tengo hipo,* I've got the hiccups.
● **quitar el hipo,** to cure hiccups; *fig* to take one's breath away. ‖ **tener hipo por algo,** *fig* to be longing for sth. ‖ **tener hipo contra algn.,** *fig* to bear a grudge against sb.
hipoalergénico,-a *adj* hypoallergic.
hipocalórico,-a *adj* low-calorie.
hipocampo *m* sea horse.
hipocentro *m* hypocentre (us hypocenter).
hipocondría *f* hypochondria.
hipocondríaco,-a 1 *adj* hypochondriac. – 2 *m,f* hypochondriac.
hipocondrio *m* hypochondrium.
hipocorístico *m* pet name, nickname.
hipocrático,-a *adj* Hippocratic.
hipocresía *f* hypocrisy.
hipócrita 1 *adj* hypocritical. – 2 *mf* hypocrite.
hipodérmico,-a *adj* hypodermic.
hipodermis *f* hypodermis.
▲ *pl hipodermis.*
hipódromo *m* racetrack, racecourse.
hipófisis *f* hypophysis.
▲ *pl hipófisis.*
hipogrifo *m* hippogriff, hippogryph.
hipomóvil *adj* horse-drawn.
hipónimo *m* hyponym.
hipopótamo *m* hippopotamus.
hipotálamo *m* hypothalamus.
hipotaxis *f* hypotaxis, subordination.
▲ *pl hipotaxis.*
hipoteca 1 *f* mortgage. 2 *fig* drawback.
hipotecar 1 *t* to mortgage. 2 *fig* to jeopardize.
▲ *Conjugation model* [1], *like sacar.*
hipotecario,-a *adj* mortgage.
hipotensión *f* low blood pressure, hypotension.
hipotenso,-a *adj* hypotensive.
hipotenusa *f* hypotenuse.
hipótesis *f* hypothesis.
■ **hipótesis de trabajo,** working thesis.
▲ *pl hipótesis.*
hipotético,-a *adj* hypothetic, hypothetical.
hippie 1 *adj* hippy. – 2 *mf* hippy.
hiriente 1 *adj* wounding. 2 *fig* hurtful, cutting, wounding.
hirsuto,-a 1 *adj* hirsute, hairy; (*cerdoso*) bristly. 2 *fig* (*persona*) rough, brusque, surly.
hirviente *adj* boiling, seething.
hisopear *t* to sprinkle.
hisopo 1 *m* BOT hyssop. 2 REL aspergillum, sprinkler.
hispalense 1 *adj fml* of Seville, from Seville. – 2 *mf fml* person from Seville, inhabitant of Seville.
hispánico,-a *adj* hispanic, Spanish.
■ **filología hispánica,** (*carrera*) Spanish language and literature.

hispanidad 1 *f* (*carácter*) Spanishness. 2 (*mundo hispánico*) Spanish world, Hispanic world.
■ **Día de la Hispanidad,** Columbus Day.
hispanismo 1 *m* (*cultural*) Hispanism, Hispanic studies *pl.* 2 (*lingüístico*) hispanicism.
hispanista *mf* Hispanist.
hispanizar *t* to hispanicize.
▲ *Conjugation model* [4], *like realizar.*
hispano,-a 1 *adj* (*de España*) Spanish, Hispanic. 2 (*de América*) Spanish-American. – 3 *m,f* (*de España*) Spaniard. 4 (*de América*) Spanish American, us Hispanic.
hispanoamericanismo *m* Latin Americanism.
hispanoamericano,-a *adj* Spanish American, Latin American.
Hispanoamérica *f* Spanish America, Latin America.
hispanoárabe 1 *adj* Hispano-Arabic. – 2 *mf* Spanish Arab.
hispanofilia *f* love of Spain.
hispanófilo,-a 1 *adj* Hispanophile. – 2 *m,f* Hispanophile.
hispanófobo,-a 1 *adj* hispanophobic. – 2 *m,f* hispanophobe.
hispanófono,-a *adj-m,f* → **hispanohablante**.
hispanohablante 1 *adj* Spanish-speaking. – 2 *mf* Spanish speaker: *los hispanohablantes,* native Spanish speakers.
híspido,-a *adj* hispid.
histamina *f* histamine.
histeria *f* hysteria.
■ **ataque de histeria,** hysterics *pl.* ‖ **histeria colectiva,** *fam fig* mass hysteria.
histérico,-a 1 *adj* hysterical. 2 *m,f* hysteric.
● **poner histérico,-a a algn.,** *fam fig* to drive sb. mad, wind sb. up.
histerismo 1 *m* hysteria. 2 *fig* hysterics *pl.*
histología *f* histology.
histológico,-a *adj* histological.
historia 1 *f* (*estudio*) history. 2 (*narración*) story, tale. 3 *fig* (*cuento*) story, take, excuse.
● **¡déjate de historias!,** get to the point!, stop beating about the bush! ‖ **la historia de siempre,** it's the same old story. ‖ **ir con historias,** to tell stories. ‖ **pasar a la historia,** to go down in history. ‖ **tener una historia con algn.,** (*lío*) to have some trouble with sb.; (*aventura*) to have a fling with sb.
■ **historia antigua,** ancient history. ‖ **historia natural,** natural history. ‖ **historia universal,** world history.
historiado,-a 1 *pp* → **historiar**. – 2 *adj fig* overelaborate, florid.
historiador,-ra *m,f* historian.
historial 1 *m* MED medical record, case history. 2 (*currículo*) curriculum vitae. 3 (*antecedentes*) background.
historiar 1 *t* (*contar*) to tell the story of; (*acontecimientos*) to recount. 2 (*escribir*) to write the history of; (*acontecimientos*) to chronicle. 3 (*en pintura*) to depict.
▲ *Conjugation model* [13], *like desviar.*
historicidad *f* historicity.
historicismo *m* historicism.
histórico,-a 1 *adj* (*relativo a la historia*) historical. 2 (*importante*) historic, memorable. 3 (*cierto*) factual, true: *el libro se basa en hechos históricos,* the book is based on historical facts. 4 LING historical.
historieta 1 *f* (*cuento*) short story, tale, anecdote. 2 (*viñetas*) comic strip, cartoon.
historiografía *f* historiography.

historiógrafo,-a 1 *m,f* (*historiador*) historian. **2** (*cronista*) chronicler.
histrión 1 *m* (*actor*) player, actor. **2** *fig* clown, buffoon.
histriónico,-a *adj* histrionic.
histrionismo *m* histrionics *pl*, theatrical behaviour (US behavior).
hita *f* sprig.
hitita 1 *adj* Hittite. – **2** *m,f* (*persona*) Hittite. – **3** *m* (*idioma*) Hittite.
hitleriano,-a *adj* Hitler, Hitlerite.
hitlerismo *m* Hitlerism.
hito 1 *m* (*mojón - para distancias*) milestone; (*- para límites*) boundary stone. **2** (*juego*) quoits *pl*. **3** (*blanco*) bull's eye. **4** *fig* (*objetivo*) target, aim, goal. **5** *fig* (*hecho importante*) milestone, landmark.
● **dar en el hito,** to hit the nail on the head. ‖ **mirar de hito en hito,** to stare at.
hizo *pt indef* → **hacer.**
Hl *sím* (*hectolitro*) hectolitre (US hectoliter); (*símbolo*) Hl.
Hm *sím* (*hectómetro*) hectometre (US hectometer); (*símbolo*) Hm.
hnos. *abr* (*hermanos*) brothers; (*abreviatura*) bros.
hobby *m* hobby.
▲ *pl* **hobbys.**
hocicar 1 *t* (*hozar*) to root in, root among. – **2** *i* (*dar con los hocicos*) to hit one's face (**con/contra/en,** against). **3** *fig* (*con un obstáculo*) to run (**con/contra/en,** into).
hocico 1 *m* (*de animal*) snout, muzzle. **2** *pey* (*de persona*) nose, snout.
● **caer de hocicos / darse de hocicos,** to fall flat on one's face. ‖ **dar de hocicos contra,** to bump into. ‖ **estar de hocico / poner hocico,** to be in a bad mood. ‖ **meter los hocicos en algo,** *fam* to stick one's nose into sth., poke one's nose into sth.
hocicón,-ona 1 *adj* (*animal*) big-snouted. **2** (*persona*) big-mouthed.
hocicudo,-a *adj* → **hocicón,-ona.**
hocino¹ *m* (*hoz*) billhook.
hocino² 1 *m* (*terreno*) valley floor. **2** (*angostura*) narrows *pl*.
hociquear *t-i* → **hocicar.**
hockey *m* hockey.
■ **hockey sobre hielo,** ice hockey. ‖ **hockey sobre hierba,** (field) hockey.
hodierno,-a *adj* present-day.
hogaño 1 *adv* this present year. **2** *lit* these days, in this day and age.
hogar 1 *m* (*de chimenea*) hearth, fireplace. **2** *fig* (*casa*) home. **3** *fig* (*familia*) family.
● **crear un hogar / formar un hogar,** to start a family. ‖ **hogar dulce hogar,** *fam* home sweet home. ‖ **sin hogar,** homeless.
■ **la vida del hogar,** family life, home life.
hogareño,-a 1 *adj* (*vida*) home, family. **2** (*persona*) home-loving, stay-at-home.
hogaza *f* large loaf (of bread).
hoguera 1 *f* bonfire. **2** *fig* blaze.
● **morir en la hoguera,** *euf* to be burnt at the stake.
hoja 1 *f* (*gen*) leaf. **2** (*pétalo*) petal. **3** (*de papel*) sheet; (*impreso*) handout, printed sheet. **4** (*de libro*) leaf, page. **5** (*de metal*) sheet. **6** (*de cuchillo etc*) blade. **7** (*de puerta, ventana*) leaf; (*de mesa*) leaf, flap: *una ventana de dos hojas,* a double-leaf window. **8** (*porción de tierra*) fallow land.
● **batir hoja,** to beat metal. ‖ **de hoja caduca,** BOT deciduous. ‖ **de hoja perenne,** BOT evergreen. ‖ **no tiene vuelta de hoja,** *fig* there's no doubt about it. ‖ **tem-**

blar como una hoja, to shake like a leaf. ‖ **volver la hoja,** *fig* to change the subject.
■ **hoja de afeitar,** razor blade. ‖ **hoja de cálculo,** spreadsheet. ‖ **hoja de parra,** *fig* cover, alibi. ‖ **hoja de ruta,** waybill. ‖ **hoja de servicios,** service record. ‖ **hoja en blanco,** blank sheet of paper. ‖ **hoja seca,** dead leaf. ‖ **hoja suelta,** loose leaf, loose sheet.
hojalata *f* tin, tin plate.
hojalatería 1 *f* (*oficio*) tinwork. **2** (*objetos*) tinware. **3** (*taller, tienda*) tinsmith's.
hojalatero *m* tinsmith.
hojaldrado,-a 1 *pp* → **hojaldrar.** – **2** *adj* puff: *pasta hojaldrada,* puff pastry.
hojaldrar *t* to make into puff pastry.
hojaldre *m* & *f* puff pastry.
▲ *Often used as masculine.*
hojarasca 1 *f* (*hojas caídas*) fallen leaves *pl*, dead leaves *pl*. **2** (*frondosidad*) foliage. **3** *fig* (*cosa inútil*) rubbish; (*palabras*) waffle, padding: *tu libro está lleno de hojarasca,* your book is rubbish.
hojear *t* to leaf through, flick through.
hojoso,-a *adj* leafy.
hojuela 1 *f* CULIN pancake. **2** (*de la aceituna*) pressed olive skins *pl*. **3** (*hoja de metal*) foil.
hola *interj fam* hello!, hullo!, US hi!
Holanda *f* Holland.
holandés,-esa 1 *adj* Dutch. – **2** *m,f* (*persona*) Dutch person; (*hombre*) Dutchman; (*mujer*) Dutchwoman. – **3** holandés, *m* (*idioma*) Dutch. – **4** holandesa, *f* (*papel*) quarto sheet.
holandesa *f* → **holandés,-esa.**
holding *m* holding company.
▲ *pl* **holdings.**
holgadamente 1 *adv* (*con amplio margen*) easily: *caben cuatro niños holgadamente,* four children fit in easily; *ganaron holgadamente,* they won easily. **2** (*con comodidad*) comfortably: *viven holgadamente,* they are well off, they are comfortably off.
holgado,-a 1 *pp* → **holgar.** – **2** *adj* (*desocupado*) idle. **3** (*ropa*) loose, baggy: *un jersey holgado,* a loose-fitting jumper. **4** (*espacio*) roomy. **5** (*victoria*) easy, comfortable; (*mayoría*) comfortable. **6** (*posición*) comfortable, well-off.
● **andar/estar holgado,-a de tiempo,** to have plenty of time. ‖ **ir holgado,-a,** to have plenty of room.
holganza 1 *f* (*ocio*) leisure, idleness. **2** (*diversión*) pleasure.
holgar 1 *i* (*descansar*) to rest. **2** (*estar ocioso*) to be idle. – **3 holgarse,** *p* (*alegrarse*) to be pleased (**con/de,** with). **4** (*divertirse*) to enjoy os.
● **huelga decir que ...,** needless to say (that) ... ‖ **huelgan las palabras,** no comment.
▲ *Conjugation model* [52]*, like* **colgar.**
holgazán,-ana 1 *adj* idle, lazy. – **2** *m,f* lazybones, layabout.
holgazanear *i* to laze around, loaf around, idle.
holgazanería *f* idleness, laziness.
holgorio *m* revelry, merriment.
holgura 1 *f* (*ropa*) looseness. **2** (*espacio*) roominess, space: *cabíamos con holgura,* there was plenty of room for us. **3** TÉC play. **4** *fig* (*bienestar*) affluence, comfort: *viven con holgura,* they live comfortably, they are well-off.
holladura 1 *f* (*huella*) footprint. **2** (*pisoteo*) trampling.
hollar 1 *t* (*comprimir*) to tread (on), set foot on. **2** (*pisar*) to trample on. **3** *fig* (*humillar*) to humiliate.
▲ *Conjugation model* [31]*, like* **contar.**

hollejo *m* skin, peel.
hollín *m* soot.
holmio *m* holmium.
holocausto *m* holocaust.
● ofrecer algo en holocausto, *fig* to offer sth. as a sacrifice.
holografía *f* holography.
holograma *m* hologram.
hombrada *f* manly action.
hombre 1 *m* (*individuo*) man: *el hombre y la mujer,* man and woman. 2 (*especie*) man, mankind. 3 *fam* (*marido*) husband. – 4 *interj* (*asombro*) hey!, hey there!, well!: *¡hombre, Pedro, no te esperaba!,* hey, Pedro, I didn't expect you! 5 (*enfático*) sure!: *¡sí hombre!,* you bet!, yeah sure!; *¡hombre claro!,* of course!, you bet! 6 (*enfado*) but really!: *¡pero hombre!,* but really!; *¡anda hombre!,* come on!
● de hombre a hombre, man-to-man. ‖ hacer un hombre, to make a man of: *te hará un hombre,* it'll make a man of you. ‖ hacerse un hombre, to become a man. ‖ ¡hombre al agua!, man overboard! ‖ ¡pobre hombre!, poor chap!, poor bloke! (*us* poor guy!). ‖ portarse como un hombre, to act like a man. ‖ ser muy hombre, to be every inch a man. ‖ ser otro hombre, to be a changed man.
■ buen hombre, good fellow. ‖ el hombre de la calle, the man in the street. ‖ el hombre medio, the average man. ‖ hombre anuncio, sandwich man. ‖ hombre de bien, good man, upstanding man. ‖ hombre de estado, statesman. ‖ hombre de letras, man of letters. ‖ hombre de mundo, man of the world. ‖ hombre de negocios, businessman. ‖ hombre de paja, *fig* front man. ‖ hombre de palabra, man of his word. ‖ hombre de peso, important figure. ‖ hombre de pro, honest man. ‖ hombre del tiempo, weatherman. ‖ hombre del saco, *fam* bogey man. ‖ hombre lobo, werewolf. ‖ hombre orquesta, one-man band. ‖ hombre rana, frogman.
hombrear[1] *i* (*dárselas de hombre*) to act the man; (*parecerse al hombre*) to be turning into a man.
hombrear[2] 1 *i* (*con hombros*) to push with one's shoulders. 2 *fig* (*querer igualarse*) to try to act (**con**, like): *hombrear con los mayores,* to try to act like an adult.
hombrera 1 *f* (*almohadilla*) shoulder pad. 2 (*tirante*) shoulder strap. 3 *mil* epaulette.
hombretón *m* big fellow, well-built fellow.
hombría *m* manliness, virility.
hombro *m* shoulder.
● a hombros, on one's shoulders. ‖ arrimar el hombro, to help out, lend a hand. ‖ echarse algo al hombro, to shoulder sth. ‖ estar hombro a hombro con algn., *fig* to rub shoulders with sb. ‖ tener la cabeza sobre los hombros, *fig* to have one's head squarely on one's shoulders.
hombruno,-a *adj* mannish, manly.
homenaje *m* homage, tribute.
● en homenaje a, in honour (*us* honor) of. ‖ rendir homenaje a algn., to pay homage to sb., pay tribute to sb.
homenajear *t* to pay tribute to.
homeópata 1 *adj* homeopathic. – 2 *mf* homeopath.
homeopatía *f* homeopathy.
homeopático,-a *adj* homeopathic.
homérico,-a *adj* Homeric.
homicida 1 *adj* homicidal, murder: *el arma homicida,* the murder weapon. – 2 *mf* (*hombre*) murderer; (*mujer*) murderess.

homicidio *m* (*voluntario*) homicide, murder; (*involuntario*) manslaughter.
homilía *f* homily, sermon.
homínido 1 *adj* hominoid. – 2 *m* hominid, hominoid.
homofonía *f* homophony.
homófono,-a 1 *adj* homophonous, homophonic. – 2 homófono, *m* homophone.
homogeneidad *f* homogeneity, uniformity.
homogeneización *f* homogenization.
homogeneizar *t* to homogenize, make homogeneous.
▲ *Conjugation model* [26].
homogéneo,-a *adj* homogeneous, uniform.
homógrafo,-a 1 *adj* homographic. – 2 homógrafo, *m* homograph.
homologable *adj* equivalent.
homologación 1 *f* (*registro*) official approval, official recognition. 2 *dep* ratification. 3 (*equiparación*) parity.
homologado,-a 1 *pp* → **homologar**. – 2 *adj* (*centro, estudios*) officially approved, officially recognized: *centro de estudios homologado,* officially recognized school. 3 (*productos*) authorized.
homologar 1 *t* (*comprobar*) to approve, recognize, authorize. 2 *dep* to ratify.
▲ *Conjugation model* [7], *like llegar.*
homólogo,-a 1 *adj* equivalent, homologous. – 2 *m,f* opposite number, counterpart.
homónimo,-a 1 *adj* homonymous. – 2 homónimo, *m* homonym.
homosexual 1 *adj* homosexual. – 2 *mf* homosexual.
homosexualidad *f* homosexuality.
honda *f* sling.
hondear 1 *t* (*reconocer el fondo*) to sound. 2 (*descargar*) to unload.
hondo,-a 1 *adj* deep. 2 *fig* profound, deep. – 3 hondo, *m* (*fondo*) bottom, depths *pl*: *en lo hondo de la caja,* at the bottom of the box. 4 (*medida*) depth: *tiene dos metros de hondo,* it's two metres deep.
■ cante hondo, flamenco song.
hondonada *f* hollow, depression.
hondura *f* depth.
● meterse en honduras, (*profundizar*) to go into too much detail; (*tratar sin conocimiento*) to get out of one's depth, get in over one's head.
Honduras *m* Honduras.
hondureño,-a 1 *adj* Honduran. – 2 *m,f* Honduran.
honestamente 1 *adv* (*con honestidad*) honestly. 2 (*con decencia*) decently, properly. 3 (*con recato*) modestly.
honestidad 1 *f* (*honradez*) honesty, uprightness. 2 (*decencia*) decency. 3 (*recato*) modesty.
honesto,-a 1 *adj* (*honrado*) honest, upright. 2 (*decente*) decent. 3 (*recatado*) modest.
hongo 1 *m* (*gen*) fungus; (*comestible*) mushroom; (*venenoso*) toadstool. 2 (*sombrero*) bowler, bowler hat.
■ hongo atómico / hongo nuclear, mushroom cloud.
honor 1 *m* (*virtud*) honour (*us* honor). 2 (*reputación*) reputation, honour (*us* honor), good name. 3 (*de la mujer*) virtue. – 4 honores, *mpl* (*título*) title *sing*, distinction *sing*. 5 (*agasajo*) honours (*us* honors).
● con honores militares, with military honours (*us* honors). ‖ en honor a la verdad, to be fair, in all fairness. ‖ es un honor para mí, it's an honour (*us* honor) for me. ‖ hacer honor a, to live up to: *hace honor a su reputación,* he lives up to his reputation. ‖ hacer los honores, to do the honours (*us* honors). ‖ jurar por su honor, to swear on one's honour (*us* honor). ‖ per-

der su honor, (*una mujer*) to lose one's honour (US honor). ‖ **por mi honor,** upon my honour (US honor). ‖ **rendir los honores a,** to pay honour (US honor) to. ‖ **ser cuestión de honor,** to be a point of honour (US honor).
■ **hombre de honor,** man of honour (US honor).
honorabilidad *f* honourableness (US honorableness).
honorable *adj* honourable (US honorable).
honorablemente *adv* honourably (US honorably).
honorario,-a **1** *adj* honorary, honorific. – **2** **honorarios,** *mpl* fee *sing*, fees, emoluments.
honorífico,-a *adj* honorific.
■ **cargo honorífico,** unpaid post.
honoris honoris causa, *loc* honoris causa.
honra **1** *f* (*dignidad propia*) dignity. **2** (*honor*) honour (US honor). **3** (*buena reputación*) reputation, good name. **4** (*de la mujer*) virtue. – **5 honras,** *fpl* (*fúnebres*) last honours (US honors).
● **¡a mucha honra!,** and (I'm) proud of it! ‖ **me cabe la honra de ...,** I have the honour (US honor) of ... ‖ **tener a mucha honra algo,** to be very proud of sth.
honradez *f* honesty, integrity.
honrado,-a **1** *pp* → **honrar.** – **2** *adj* (*honesto*) honest. **3** (*decente*) upright, respectable. **4** (*honorable*) honourable (US honorable).
honrar **1** *t* (*gen*) to honour (US honor): *nos honró con su presencia,* he honoured us with his presence. **2** (*enaltecer*) to do credit to: *ese gesto te honra,* that gesture does you credit. – **3 honrarse,** *p* to be honoured (US honored).
honrilla *f* self-respect, pride.
● **por la negra honrilla,** for the sake of appearances.
honroso,-a **1** *adj* (*que honra*) honourable (US honorable). **2** (*decoroso*) respectable, reputable.
hontanar *m* spring.
hopear **1** *i* (*la cola*) to wag its tail. **2** *fig* (*corretear*) to run about.
hopo¹ **1** *m* (*cola*) bushy tail. **2** (*mechón*) shock of hair.
hopo² *interj* (*fuera*) out!
hora **1** *f* (*unidad de tiempo*) hour: *media hora,* half an hour. **2** (*tiempo*) time: *¿qué hora es?,* what time is it?; *es hora de marchar,* it's time to go; *no es hora de ...,* this is no time to ... **3** (*cita*) appointment: *tengo hora para las cuatro y media,* I have an appointment at half past four.
● **a altas horas,** in the small hours. ‖ **a buena hora,** (*oportunamente*) at the right time; (*afortunadamente*) fortunately. ‖ **¡a buenas horas!,** and about time too! ‖ **a estas horas,** (*ahora*) by now; (*indicando sorpresa*) at this time (of the day): *a estas horas la tienda estará cerrada,* the shop will be closed by now; *¿qué haces aquí a estas horas?,* what are you doing here at this time? ‖ **a la hora,** at the proper time, on time. ‖ **a la hora de la verdad,** at the moment of truth, when it comes to it. ‖ **a primera hora,** first thing in the morning. ‖ **a su hora,** at the proper time, in time. ‖ **a última hora,** at the last moment. ‖ **comer entre horas,** to eat between meals, snack. ‖ **dar la hora,** to give an appointment. ‖ **dar la hora,** to strike the hour. ‖ **de última hora,** last-minute: *una noticia de última hora,* some last-minute news. ‖ **en mala hora,** (*inoportunamente*) at the wrong time; (*desafortunadamente*) unfortunately. ‖ **ir con la hora pegada al culo,** *tabú* to run around like a blue-arsed fly. ‖ **pedir hora,** to make an appointment. ‖ **poner en hora,** to set. ‖ **por horas,** by the hour: *cobro por horas,* I get paid by the hour. ‖ **tener horas de vuelo,** *fig* to be an old hand. ‖ **¡ya era hora!,** and about time too!

■ **hora oficial,** standard time. ‖ **hora de acostarse,** bedtime. ‖ **hora de cenar,** dinner time. ‖ **hora de comer,** lunch time, dinner time. ‖ **hora peninsular,** time in mainland Spain. ‖ **hora punta,** rush hour. ‖ **horas extras,** overtime: *no quiere hacer horas extras,* he doesn't want to work overtime. ‖ **horas muertas,** spare time. ‖ **libro de horas,** LIT Book of Hours.
horadar **1** *t* (*perforar*) to pierce. **2** (*taladrar*) to drill (through), bore (through).
horario,-a **1** *adj* time: *cambio horario,* time change. – **2 horario,** *m* timetable, US schedule. **3** (*jornada laboral*) hours *pl*, timetable: *tengo horario de mañana,* I work mornings. **4** (*de reloj*) hour hand.
■ **horario comercial,** (*tienda*) opening hours *pl*; (*empresa*) business hours *pl*. ‖ **horario laboral,** working hours *pl*.
horca **1** *f* (*patíbulo*) gallows *pl*, gibbet. **2** AGR hayfork, pitchfork. **3** (*de ajos, cebollas*) string.
horcadura *f* fork.
horcajadas a horcajadas, *loc adv* astride.
horcajadura *f* crotch.
horchata *f* sweet milky drink made from tiger nuts or almonds.
● **tener sangre de horchata,** *fam fig* to have water in one's veins, be gutless.
horchatería *f* bar where *horchata* is sold.
horchatero,-a *m,f* horchata seller.
horcón *m* pitchfork.
horda **1** *f* horde, mob. **2** *fig* gang.
horizontal *adj* horizontal.
horizontalidad *f* horizontality.
horizontalmente *adv* horizontally.
horizonte *m* horizon.
horma **1** *f* mould (US mold), form. **2** (*de zapato*) last.
● **encontrar uno la horma de su zapato,** *fig* to meet one's match.
hormiga *f* ant.
■ **hormiga blanca,** white ant. ‖ **hormiga obrera,** worker ant.
hormigón *m* concrete.
■ **hormigón armado,** reinforced concrete.
hormigonera *f* concrete mixer.
hormiguear **1** *i* to itch, tingle: *me hormigueaba la mano,* I had pins and needles in my hand. **2** (*bullir*) to swarm, teem.
hormigueo **1** *m* pins and needles *pl*, tingling sensation, itching sensation. **2** *fig* anxiety, uneasiness.
hormiguero *m* anthill, ant's nest.
● **ser un hormiguero,** *fig* to be swarming with people, be crawling with people: *el centro era un hormiguero,* the city centre was crawling with people.
hormiguilla **1** *f* (*cosquilleo*) pins and needles *pl*, tingling sensation, itching sensation. **2** *fam fig* (*remordimiento*) remorse.
hormiguillo **1** *m* (*cosquilleo*) pins and needles *pl*, tingling sensation, itching sensation. **2** (*línea de obreros*) line.
hormiguita *f fam* small ant.
● **ser una hormiguita,** *fam fig* to be hardworking and thrifty.
hormona *f* hormone.
hormonal *adj* hormonal.
hornacho *m* excavation.
hornacina *f* niche.
hornada **1** *f* batch. **2** *fig* set, batch.
hornaza **1** *f* (*horno*) silversmith's crucible. **2** (*color amarillo*) light yellow glazing.

hornazo *m* (*rosca*) sausage and ham pie decorated with hard-boiled eggs.
hornear 1 *i* to bake. – 2 *t* to bake.
hornillo 1 *m* TÉC small furnace. 2 (*para cocinar*) stove. 3 (*en las minas*) blast hole.
■ **hornillo eléctrico,** hotplate.
horno 1 *m* (*de cocina*) oven. 2 TÉC furnace. 3 (*cerámica, ladrillos*) kiln. 4 (*panadería*) bakery.
● **no estar el horno para bollos,** *fam* not to be the right time. ‖ **ser un horno,** *fam fig* to be boiling hot, be roasting.
■ **horno crematorio,** crematorium. ‖ **horno de fundición,** smelting furnace. ‖ **horno (de) microondas,** microwave oven. ‖ **horno eléctrico,** electric oven.
horóscopo *m* horoscope.
horquilla 1 *f* (*de pelo*) hairgrip, hairclip, US bobby pin. 2 AGR pitchfork. 3 (*de bicicleta*) fork.
horrendo,-a *adj* horrible, horrifying, awful, frightful.
hórreo *m* granary.
horrible *adj* horrible, dreadful, awful.
horripilación *f* horripilation.
horripilante *adj* hair-raising, horrifying, terrifying.
horripilar *t* to horrify, scare stiff, give the creeps: *los detalles del asesinato los horripilaron,* the details of the murder made their hair stand on end.
horrísono,-a *adj* terrible.
horro,-a 1 *adj* (*esclavo*) free. 2 *fig* (*carente*) lacking.
horror 1 *m* (*repulsión*) horror, terror. 2 (*temor*) hate. 3 *fig* (*atrocidad*) atrocity. 4 *fam fig* (*gran cantidad*) an awful lot: *me gusta un horror,* I'm crazy about him; *bebió horrores,* he drank a tremendous amount.
● **¡qué horror!,** how awful!
horrorizar 1 *t* (*causar horror*) to horrify, terrify. 2 *fam* (*disgustar*) to disgust, turn off: *me horroriza ese tipo de película,* that kind of film really turns me off. – 3 **horrorizarse,** *p* to be horrified.
▲ *Conjugation model* [4], *like realizar.*
horrorosamente 1 *adv* horribly. 2 *fam* terribly, awfully.
horroroso,-a 1 *adj* (*que causa miedo*) horrifying, terrifying. 2 *fam* (*feo*) ghastly, hideous. 3 *fam* (*malísimo*) dreadful, awful. 4 *fam* (*muy grande*) awful: *tenía una hambre horrorosa,* I was terribly hungry.
hortaliza *f* vegetable.
hortelano,-a 1 *adj* market-gardening, US truck-farming. – 2 *m,f* market gardener, US truck gardener.
● **como el perro del hortelano,** *fig* a dog in the manger.
hortense *adj* vegetable.
hortensia *f* hydrangea.
hortera 1 *adj fam* (*grosero*) common, vulgar, tasteless; (*cursi*) corny, tacky; (*ostentoso*) flashy. – 2 *mf* vulgar person, person with no taste: *tu amiga es una hortera,* your friend has no taste.
horterada *f fam* (*cosa*) tacky thing; (*acto*) tacky thing to do.
hortícola *adj* horticultural.
horticultor,-ra *m,f* horticulturist.
horticultura *f* horticulture.
hosco,-a 1 *adj* (*insociable*) sullen, surly. 2 (*lugar*) gloomy, dark.
hospedaje 1 *m* (*acción*) lodging; (*precio*) cost of lodging. 2 (*lugar*) lodgings *pl*, accomodation.
hospedar 1 *t* to lodge, put up. – 2 **hospedarse,** *p* to stay (**en,** at).
hospedería *f* inn, hostelry.

hospiciano,-a 1 *m,f* (*huérfano*) orphan, child living in an orphanage. 2 (*peregrino*) person staying in a hospice. 3 (*pobre*) person living in a poorhouse.
hospicio 1 *m* (*de huérfanos*) orphanage. 2 (*de peregrinos*) hospice. 3 (*de pobres*) poorhouse.
hospital *m* hospital, infirmary: *Marta está en el hospital,* Marta is in hospital, (US Marta is in the hospital).
■ **hospital de (primera) sangre,** MIL field hospital.
hospitalario,-a 1 *adj* (*acogedor*) hospitable. 2 MED hospital.
hospitalidad *f* hospitality.
hospitalización *f* hospitalization.
hospitalizar *t* to send into hospital, hospitalize.
▲ *Conjugation model* [4], *like realizar.*
hosquedad 1 *f* surliness, sullenness. 2 (*de un lugar*) darkness.
hostal *m* hostel, hotel.
hostelería 1 *f* (*actividad*) catering business. 2 (*estudios*) hotel management.
hostelero,-a 1 *m,f* hotel manager. – 2 *adj* hotel: *la industria hostelera,* the hotel industry.
hostería *f* inn, lodging house.
hosti *interj* tabú → **hostia.**
hostia 1 *f* REL host, Eucharistic wafer. 2 tabú (*choque*) bump, bash; (*torta*) slap, smack, punch. – 3 *interj* tabú damn it!, Jesus!, bloody hell!, fuck!
● **darse de hostias,** tabú to fight. ‖ **darle una hostia a algn.** / **pegarle una hostia a algn.,** tabú to give sb. a hiding, give sb. a smack in the face. ‖ **darse una hostia / pegarse una hostia,** tabú to give os. a real bash, come a cropper. ‖ **darse/pegarse una hostia con el coche,** to have a car crash. ‖ **de la hostia,** tremendous, a hell of a: *tienen una casa de la hostia,* they've got one hell of a house; *hacían un ruido de la hostia,* they were making one hell of a racket. ‖ **estar de mala hostia,** tabú to be in a shitty mood. ‖ **ir a toda hostia,** tabú to go flat out. ‖ **ser la hostia,** tabú (*fantástico*) to be bloody amazing, be bloody fantastic; (*penoso*) to be bloody useless.
hostiar *t* tabú to thump, whack.
hostiario 1 *m* (*caja*) wafer box. 2 (*molde*) wafer mould (US mold).
hostigamiento *m* harassment.
hostigar 1 *t* (*azotar*) to whip. 2 *fig* (*perseguir*) to plague, persecute; (*al enemigo*) to harass. 3 *fig* (*molestar*) to pester.
▲ *Conjugation model* [7], *like llegar.*
hostil *adj* hostile.
hostilidad 1 *f* hostility. – 2 **hostilidades,** *fpl* hostilities.
hostilizar *t* to harrass.
hotel 1 *m* (*establecimiento*) hotel. 2 (*casa*) villa, mansion. 3 *arg* (*cárcel*) clink, nick.
hotelero,-a 1 *adj* hotel. – 2 *m,f* hotel manager, hotelier.
hotentote,-a 1 *adj* Hottentot. – 2 **hotentote,** *m* Hottentot.
hoy 1 *adv* (*día*) today. 2 *fig* (*actualmente*) now, nowadays.
● **de hoy a mañana,** very soon, overnight. ‖ **de hoy en adelante,** from now on. ‖ **en el día de hoy,** today. ‖ **hasta hoy,** up till now. ‖ **hoy (en) día,** nowadays, today, these days. ‖ **hoy por hoy,** at the present time, right now. ‖ **por hoy,** for the present.
hoya 1 *f* (*hoyo*) hole, pit. 2 (*sepultura*) grave. 3 GEOG valley, dale.
hoyanca *f* common grave.
hoyo 1 *m* (*agujero*) hole, pit. 2 (*sepultura*) grave. 3 (*hoyuelo*) dimple. 4 (*golf*) hole.

hoyuelo *m* dimple.

hoz[1] *f* AGR sickle.
● **la hoz y el martillo,** POL the hammer and the sickle.

hoz[2] *f* GEOG ravine, gorge.

hozar *t* to root in, root among, dig up.
▲ Conjugation model [4], *like realizar.*

HR *abr* (*Hotel Residencia*) guesthouse, boarding house.

hube *pt indef* → **haber**.

hubiera *imperf subj* → **haber**.

hucha 1 *f* moneybox, piggy-bank. 2 *fig* savings *pl,* nest egg.

hueco,-a 1 *adj* hollow: *pared hueca,* hollow wall, stud wall. 2 (*vacío*) empty. 3 (*cóncavo*) concave. 4 (*sonido*) hollow; (*voz*) deep. 5 (*mullido*) spongy, soft. 6 *fig* (*presumido*) vain, conceited. 7 (*estilo etc*) affected, empty. – 8 *hueco, m* (*cavidad*) hollow, hole. 9 (*de tiempo*) slot, free time; (*de espacio*) empty space: *sólo tengo un hueco después de comer,* I'm only free after lunch. 10 *fig* (*vacante*) vacancy. 11 ARQ opening.
● **dejar un hueco,** to leave a gap. ‖ **hacer un hueco a algn.,** to make room for sb. ‖ **llenar un hueco,** *fig* to fill a need, fill a gap.
■ **hueco de la escalera,** stairwell. ‖ **hueco de la ventana,** window recess. ‖ **hueco del ascensor,** lift shaft, (US elevator shaft).

huecograbado *m* photogravure.

huele *pres indic* → **oler**.

huelga *f* strike.
● **estar en huelga / estar de huelga,** to be on strike. ‖ **hacer huelga,** to go on strike. ‖ **ir a la huelga,** to go on strike.
■ **huelga a la japonesa,** work-in. ‖ **huelga de brazos caídos,** go-slow. ‖ **huelga de celo,** work-to-rule. ‖ **huelga general,** general strike. ‖ **huelga de hambre,** hunger strike. ‖ **huelga salvaje,** wildcat strike.
▲ See also *holgar.*

huelgo 1 *m* (*aliento*) breath. 2 TÉC play.

huelguista *mf* striker.

huella 1 *f* (*de pie*) footprint; (*de ruedas*) track. 2 *fig* (*vestigio*) trace, sign: *las huellas del tiempo,* the traces of time.
● **dejar huella,** to leave one's mark (**en,** on). ‖ **no quedar ni huella,** not to be a trace. ‖ **seguir las huellas de algn.,** *fig* to follow in sb.'s footsteps.
■ **huella dactilar,** fingerprint.

huelveño,-a 1 *adj* of Huelva, from Huelva. – 2 *m,f* person from Huelva, inhabitant of Huelva.

huérfano,-a 1 *adj* orphan, orphaned. 2 *fig* (*carente*) lacking, devoid of: *huérfano de afecto,* devoid of affection. – 3 *m,f* orphan.
■ **huérfano,-a de guerra,** war orphan. ‖ **huérfano,-a de madre,** motherless. ‖ **huérfano,-a de padre,** fatherless.

huero,-a *adj fig* empty.

huerta 1 *f* (*terreno*) market garden, US truck garden. 2 (*zona*) irrigated agricultural and market-gardening region.

huerto *m* (*de verduras*) vegetable garden, kitchen garden; (*de frutas*) orchard.
● **llevarse a algn. al huerto,** *fam fig* (*engañar*) to lead sb. up the garden path; (*llevarse a la cama*) to have one's way with sb.

huesa *f fml* grave.

hueso 1 *m* ANAT bone. 2 (*de fruta*) stone, US pit. 3 *fam fig* (*cosa difícil*) struggle, problem: *las mates son un hueso para mí,* I find maths really hard. 4 *fam fig* (*persona desagradable*) pain in the neck, jerk. 5 *fam fig* (*profesor*) strict teacher, stickler.
● **dar con los huesos en,** *fig* to end up in. ‖ **dar con los huesos en el suelo,** to end up on the floor. ‖ **darle a la sin hueso,** to talk one's head off. ‖ **estar en los huesos,** *fig* to be all skin and bone. ‖ **no poder con sus huesos,** *fig* to be all in. ‖ **romperle los huesos a algn.,** *fig* to beat sb. up. ‖ **ser un hueso duro de roer,** *fig* to be a hard nut to crack. ‖ **tener los huesos molidos,** to be exhausted, be dead beat.

huesoso,-a *adj* bony.

huésped,-da 1 *m,f* (*invitado*) guest. 2 (*en hotel*) lodger, boarder. 3 (*anfitrión*) host; (*anfitriona*) hostess.
■ **casa de huéspedes,** guesthouse.

hueste 1 *f* MIL army, host. – 2 **huestes,** *fpl fig* (*seguidores*) followers, supporters, fans.
▲ In *1,* also used in plural with the same meaning.

huesudo,-a *adj* bony.

hueva *f* roe, spawn.
■ **huevas de esturión,** caviar *sing.*

huevar *i* to begin to lay.

huevazos *m tabú* wanker (US asshole).
▲ *pl* huevazos.

huevera *f* → **huevero,-a**.

huevería *f* egg shop.

huevero,-a 1 *m,f* (*persona*) egg dealer. – 2 **huevera,** *f* (*copa*) egg cup. 3 (*cartón*) egg box.

huevo 1 *m* egg. 2 COST darning egg. – 3 **huevos,** *mpl fam* balls *pl.*
● **costar un huevo,** *fam* to cost an arm and a leg. ‖ **estar hasta los huevos,** *fam* to be pissed off (**de,** with). ‖ **hacer algo por huevos,** *fam* to do sth. even if it kills one. ‖ **parecerse como un huevo a una castaña,** *fig* to be as different as chalk and cheese. ‖ **poner a huevo,** *fam* to hand on a plate: *se lo pusieron a huevo,* they handed it to him on a plate. ‖ **ser el huevo de Colón,** *fig* to be easier than it seems. ‖ **tener huevos,** *fam* to have balls. ‖ **¡y un huevo!,** *fam* like hell!
■ **huevo duro,** hard-boiled egg. ‖ **huevo escalfado,** poached egg. ‖ **huevo estrellado / huevo frito,** fried egg. ‖ **huevo pasado por agua,** soft-boiled egg. ‖ **huevos revueltos,** scrambled eggs.

huevón,-ona *adj* sluggish.

huevos *mpl* → **huevo**.

hugonote 1 *adj* Huguenot. – 2 *mf* Huguenot.

huida 1 *f* flight, escape. 2 (*de caballo*) shying, bolting.

huidero,-a 1 *adj* → **huidizo,-a**. – 2 **huidero,** *m* shelter, cover.

huidizo,-a 1 *adj* (*esquivo*) fleeting, elusive. 2 (*tímido*) shy.

huir 1 *i* (*escapar*) to flee, run away: *huir de la policía,* to get away from the police. 2 (*evitar*) to avoid (**de,** -), keep away (**de,** from), shun (**de,** -): *huir del pecado,* to shun sin. 3 (*el tiempo*) to fly. – 4 *t* (*evitar*) to avoid: *huye la tentación, hijo mío,* avoid temptation, my son.
▲ Conjugation model [62].

hule *m* oilcloth, oilskin.

hulla *f* coal.
■ **hulla blanca,** white coal.

hullero,-a *adj* coal.
■ **explotación hullera,** (*industria*) mining; (*mina*) mine.

humanamente 1 *adv* (*como humano*) humanly. 2 (*con humanidad*) humanely.

humanidad 1 *f* (*género humano*) humanity, mankind. 2 (*cualidad*) humanity, humaneness. 3 (*benignidad*) compassion, benevolence, kindness. 4 (*corpulencia*) corpulence. – 5 **humanidades,** *fpl* EDUC humanities.

humanismo *m* humanism.

humanista *mf* humanist.

humanístico 332

humanístico,-a *adj* humanistic.
humanitario,-a *adj* humanitarian.
humanitarismo *m* humanitarianism.
humanización *f* humanization.
humanizar 1 *t* to humanize. − 2 **humanizarse,** *p* to become more human.
▲ *Conjugation model* |4|, *like realizar.*
humano,-a 1 *adj* human. 2 *(benigno)* humane. − 3 humano, *m* human (being).
humanoide 1 *adj* humanoid. − 2 *mf* humanoid.
humarada *f* cloud of smoke.
humareda *f* cloud of smoke.
humazo *m* dense smoke.
humeante 1 *adj (de humo)* smoky, smoking. 2 *(de vaho)* steaming.
humear 1 *i (humo)* to smoke, give off smoke. 2 *(vaho)* to steam, give off steam. 3 *fig (presumir)* to be conceited. 4 *fig (estar vivo - enemistad etc)* to smoulder (US smolder).
humectador *m* humidifier.
humectante *adj* moistening.
humedad 1 *f* humidity. 2 *(de vapor)* moisture. 3 *(sensación)* dampness: *la habitación tiene humedad,* the room is damp.
humedecer 1 *t* to moisten, dampen. − 2 **humedecerse,** *p* to become damp, become wet, become moist.
▲ *Conjugation model* |43|, *like agradecer.*
húmedo,-a 1 *adj (clima)* humid, damp. 2 *(impregnado)* damp, moist, wet.
humeral *adj* humeral.
humero *m* chimney.
húmero *m* humerus.
humidificador *m* humidifier.
humidificar *t* to humidify.
humildad *f* humility, humbleness.
humilde *adj* humble, modest.
● **de humilde cuna,** of humble birth.
humildemente *adv* humbly.
humillación *f* humiliation, humbling.
humilladero *m* calvary.
humillante *adj* humiliating, humbling.
humillar 1 *t* to humiliate, humble. 2 *(bajar - la cabeza)* to bow; *(- la rodilla)* to bend. − 3 **humillarse,** *p* to humble os., lower os.: *se humilló ante el jefe,* he humbled himself before his boss.
humo 1 *m* smoke. 2 *(gas)* fumes *pl.* 3 *(vapor)* steam, vapour (US vapor). − 4 **humos,** *mpl fig (vanidad)* conceit *sing,* airs.
● **a humo de pajas,** *fig* thoughtlessly. ‖ **bajarle los humos a algn.,** *fig* to put sb. in his/her place. ‖ **echar humo,** to smoke. ‖ **subírsele los humos a uno,** *fig* to become conceited, get on one's high horse. ‖ **tener muchos humos,** *fig* to put on airs.
humor 1 *m (ánimo)* mood. 2 *(carácter)* temper. 3 *(gracia)* humour (US humor). 4 *(líquido)* humour (US humor).
● **estar de buen humor / estar de mal humor,** to be in a good mood / to be in a bad mood. ‖ **estar de humor para algo / tener humor para algo,** to feel like (doing) sth., feel in the mood for (doing) sth.: *no estoy de humor para cotilleos,* I'm not in the mood for gossiping. ‖ **tener un humor de perros,** *fam* to be in a foul mood.
■ **humor acuoso,** aqueous humour (US humor). ‖ **humor negro,** black comedy. ‖ **humor vítreo,** vitreous humour (US humor).
humorada *f →* **humorado,-a**.

humorado,-a 1 *adj: bien humorado,* good-humoured (US good-humored); *mal humorado,* bad-humoured (US bad-humored). − 2 **humorada,** *f (gracia)* joke, witticism. 3 *(extravagancia)* caprice, whim.
humorismo *m* humour (US humor).
humorista 1 *adj* humorous. − 2 *mf (autor)* humorist; *(cómico)* comedian.
humorístico,-a *adj* humorous, funny, amusing.
humoso,-a *adj* smoky.
humus *m* humus.
▲ *pl humus.*
hundible *adj* sinkable.
hundido,-a 1 *pp →* **hundir.** − 2 *adj (barco etc)* sunken. 3 *(ojos)* deep-set; *(mejillas)* hollow. 4 *fig (abrumado)* demoralized.
hundimiento 1 *m (barco)* sinking. 2 *(tierra)* subsidence. 3 *(edificio)* collapse. 4 FIN *fig* crash, slump.
hundir 1 *t (sumir)* to submerge, plunge: *hundió la mano en la arena,* she plunged her hand into the sand. 2 *(barco)* to sink. 3 *(cuchillo etc)* to drive, thrust. 4 *(derrumbar)* to demolish, ruin: *el terremoto hundió el edificio,* the earthquake caused the building to collapse. 5 *fig (abatir)* to demoralize; *(al enemigo)* to defeat. 6 *fig (arruinar)* to ruin, destroy: *su indiscreción hundió el proyecto,* his remark ruined the project. − 7 **hundirse,** *p (barco)* to sink. 8 *(derrumbarse)* to collapse, fall down. 9 *(arruinarse)* to be ruined, collapse. 10 *fig (sucumbir)* to go to pieces: *se hundió en el dolor,* she was grief-stricken.
● **hundir a algn. en la miseria,** *fig* to plunge sb. into misery.
húngaro,-a 1 *adj* Hungarian. − 2 *m,f (persona)* Hungarian. − 3 **húngaro,** *m (idioma)* Hungarian.
Hungría *f* Hungary.
huno,-a 1 *adj* Hunnic, Hunnish. − 2 *m,f* Hun.
huracán *m* hurricane.
huracanado,-a *adj* hurricane: *vientos huracanados,* hurricane winds.
huraño,-a *adj* sullen, unsociable.
hurgar 1 *t (remover)* to poke, rake. 2 *(bolsillo, bolso, etc)* to rummage in, go through. 3 *fig (fisgar)* to stir up. 4 *fig (incitar)* to poke at. − 5 **hurgarse,** *p* to pick.
● **hurgar en el pasado,** to dig up the past. ‖ **hurgar en la herida,** *fig* to turn the knife (in the wound), rub salt in the wound. ‖ **hurgarse las narices,** to pick one's nose.
▲ *Conjugation model* |7|, *like llegar.*
hurgón *m* poker; *(de fuego)* rake.
hurgonear *t* to poke, rake.
hurguillas *mf* busybody.
▲ *pl hurguillas.*
hurí *f* houri.
hurón,-ona 1 *m,f fam fig (fisgón)* busybody, nosey-parker. 2 *fam fig (huraño)* unsociable person. − 3 **hurón,** *m (animal)* ferret.
huronear 1 *i (cazar con hurón)* to ferret. 2 *fig (escudriñar)* to pry, snoop, ferret.
hurra *interj* hurray!, hurrah!
hurraca *f* magpie.
hurtadillas a hurtadillas, *adv* stealthily, on the sly.
hurtar 1 *t (robar)* to steal, pilfer. 2 *(no dar el peso)* to cheat on the weight. 3 *fig (desviar)* to dodge. 4 *fig (plagiar)* to plagiarize.
hurto *m* petty theft, pilfering.
húsar *m* hussar.
husillo[1] *m (tornillo)* screw.
husillo[2] *m (desagüe)* drain.

husmeador,-ra 1 *adj (con la nariz)* sniffing. **2** *fig (fisgón)* prying, snooping. – **3** *m,f fig (fisgón)* snooper.

husmear 1 *t (con el olfato)* to sniff, scent. **2** *fig (indagar)* to pry (**en,** into), snoop (**en,** into). – **3** *i* to sniff. **4** *fig* to snoop around.

husmeo 1 *m* sniffing. **2** *fig* prying, snooping.

huso *m (para hilar)* spindle, bobbin.
■ **huso horario,** time zone.

huy 1 *interj (sorpresa)* well!, wow!: *¡huy qué grande!,* wow! it's huge! **2** *(dolor)* ouch!, ow! **3** *(miedo)* argh!, aah!

huyo *pres indic* → **huir**.

huyuyuy *interj (reproche)* tut, tut, tut!

Hz *sím (hertzio)* hertz; *(símbolo)* Hz

I, i *f (la letra)* I, i.
■ **i griega,** *name of the letter* y. ‖ **i latina,** *name of the letter i.*
▲ *pl íes.*
IAE *abr (Impuesto de/sobre actividades económicas)* tax paid by businesses and self-employed people in order to operate legally).
ib. *abr (ibidem)* ibidem; *(abreviatura)* ibid., ib.
Iberia *f* Iberia.
ibérico,-a *adj* Iberian.
■ **Península Ibérica,** Iberian Peninsula.
ibero,-a *adj-m,f →* **íbero,-a.**
íbero,-a 1 *adj* Iberian. − **2** *m,f (persona)* Iberian. − **3** íbero, *m (idioma)* Iberian.
Iberoamérica *f* Latin America.
iberoamericano,-a 1 *adj* Latin American. − **2** *m,f* Latin American.
IBI *abr (Impuesto de Bienes e Inmuebles)* tax on property.
íbice *m* ibex.
ibicenco,-a 1 *adj* Ibizan. − **2** *m,f* Ibizan.
ibid. *abr (ibidem)* ibidem; *(abreviatura)* ibid., ib.
ibis *m* ibis.
▲ *pl ibis.*
Ibiza *f* Ibiza.
iceberg *m* iceberg.
▲ *pl icebergs.*
ICONA *abr (Instituto para la Conservación de la Naturaleza)* Spanish institute for the conservation of nature.
icono *m* icon.
iconoclasía *f* iconoclasm.
iconoclasta 1 *adj* iconoclastic. − **2** *mf* iconoclast.
iconografía *f* iconography.
ictericia *f* jaundice.
ictiófago,-a 1 *adj* ichthyophagous, fish-eating. − **2** *m,f* fish eater.
íd. *abr (ídem)* idem; *(abreviatura)* id.
ida *f (acción)* going; *(salida)* departure.
● **de ida sola,** single, US one-way. ‖ **de ida y vuelta,** *(billete)* return, US round-trip. ‖ **idas y venidas,** comings and goings.
IDE *abr (Iniciativa de Defensa Estratégica)* Strategic Defense Initiative; *(abreviatura)* SDI.
idea 1 *f* idea. **2** *(noción)* notion. **3** *(ingenio)* imagination.
● **cambiar de idea,** to change one's mind. ‖ **darle ideas a algn.,** to put ideas in sb.'s head. ‖ **hacer algo a mala idea,** to do sth. on purpose, do sth. deliberately. ‖ **hacerse a la idea de algo,** to get used to the idea of sth., accept sth. ‖ **llevar idea de,** to intend to, have the intention of. ‖ **¡ni idea!,** no idea!, not a clue! ‖ **no te puedes hacer una idea,** you have no idea. ‖ **no tener ni idea,** *fam* to have no idea, not have a clue. ‖ **ser de ideas fijas,** to be narrow-minded, have very fixed ideas. ‖ **tener ideas de bombero,** to have funny ideas, have madcap ideas. ‖ **tener mala idea,** *fam* to be a nasty piece of work.

■ **idea fija,** fixed idea. ‖ **ligera idea,** vague idea. ‖ **mala idea,** evil intention.
ideal 1 *adj* ideal. **2** *fam (perfecto)* marvellous. − **3** *m* ideal.
idealismo *m* idealism.
idealista 1 *adj* idealistic. − **2** *mf* idealist.
idealización *f* idealization.
idealizar *t* to idealize.
▲ *Conjugation model* [4], *like realizar.*
idear 1 *t (concebir)* to conceive. **2** *(inventar)* to design.
ideario *m* ideology.
ídem *adv* ditto, idem.
● **ídem de ídem,** *fam* as well, too: *yo quiero una cerveza −y yo ídem de ídem,* I'd like a beer −me too.
idénticamente *adv* identically.
idéntico,-a *adj* identical: *es idéntico a su padre,* he's the (spitting) image of his father.
identidad *f* identity.
■ **carnet de identidad,** identity card.
identificable *adj* identifiable.
identificación *f* identification.
identificar 1 *t* to identify. − **2** identificarse, *p (mostrar la documentación)* to identify os. **3** *(solidarizarse)* to identify (**con,** with).
▲ *Conjugation model* [1], *like sacar.*
ideograma *m* ideogram.
ideología *f* ideology.
ideológico,-a *adj* ideological.
ideólogo,-a *m,f* ideologist.
idílico,-a *adj* idyllic.
idilio 1 *m lit* idyll. **2** *fam* romance.
idiocia *f* idiocy.
idiolecto *m* idiolect.
idioma *m* language: *es imprescindible saber idiomas,* it's essential to have languages.
idiomático,-a *adj* idiomatic.
■ **expresión idiomática,** idiom.
idiosincrasia *f* idiosyncrasy.
idiosincrásico,-a *adj* idiosyncratic.
idiota 1 *adj* MED idiotic. **2** *fam (tonto)* stupid: *es idiota perdido el pobre,* he's such an idiot. − **3** *mf* idiot.
● **hacer el idiota,** *(hacer payasadas)* to be silly, fool about; *(perder una oportunidad)* to be stupid.
idiotez 1 *f* MED idiocy. **2** *(estupidez)* stupid thing to say, stupid thing to do: *deja ya de hacer idioteces,* stop being silly.
● **decir idioteces,** to talk rubbish. ‖ **ser una idiotez,** to be absurd.
idiotizar *t* to turn into an idiot: *el dinero lo está idiotizando,* money's making him lose his head; *los críos de hoy día están idiotizados por los videojuegos,* kids today are turning into zombies because of video games.
▲ *Conjugation model* [4], *like realizar.*
ido,-a 1 *adj (loco)* mad. **2** *(despistado)* absent-minded.
● **estar ido,-a,** *fam (loco)* to be mad; *(despistado)* to be miles away.

335

iluminar

idólatra 1 *adj* idolatrous. **- 2** *mf* (*hombre*) idolater; (*mujer*) idolatress.
idolatrar 1 *t* to worship. **2** *fig* to idolize.
idolatría *f* idolatry.
ídolo *m* idol.
idoneidad *f* suitability.
idóneo,-a *adj* suitable.
idus *mpl* HIST ides.
i.e. *abr* (*id est, esto es*) that is to say; (*abreviatura*) i.e.
iglesia 1 *f* (*edificio*) church. **2** (*institución*) Church.
● **casarse por la iglesia,** to have a church wedding. ‖ **con la iglesia hemos topado,** we're really up against it now.
■ **iglesia parroquial,** parish church. ‖ **la Iglesia Católica,** the Catholic Church. ‖ **la Iglesia Protestante,** the Protestant Church.
iglú *m* igloo.
▲ *pl* **iglúes.**
ígneo,-a *adj* igneous.
ignición *f* ignition.
ignominia *f* ignominy, public shame.
ignominioso,-a *adj* ignominious.
ignorancia *f* ignorance.
ignorante 1 *adj* ignorant. **- 2** *mf* ignoramus.
● **ser un pobre ignorante,** to be a poor fool.
ignorar 1 *t* (*desconocer*) not to know, not be aware of, be unaware of: *ignoraba que fueran vecinos,* I didn't know they were neighbours; *se ignora el paradero del delincuente,* the criminal's whereabouts are unknown. **2** (*no hacer caso*) to ignore.
ignoto,-a *adj* unknown.
igual 1 *adj* (*parte*) equal. **2** (*lo mismo*) the same: *estas dos copias son iguales,* these two copies are the same; *es igual de alto que tú,* he is as tall as you; *son de igual tamaño,* they are equal in size; *tengo dos vestidos iguales,* I've two identical dresses. **3** (*muy parecido*) just like: *es igual que su hermano,* he's just like his brother. **4** MAT equal: *A es igual a B,* A equals B, A is equal to B; *dos más dos es igual a cuatro,* two plus two makes four. **- 5** *m* (*persona*) equal: *sólo habla con sus iguales,* he only talks to his equals. **6** MAT (*signo*) equals sign: *no te dejes el igual,* don't leave the equals sign out. **- 7** *adv* (*en comparativas*) the same: *he comido igual que tú,* I've eaten as much as you; *cobra igual que yo,* she earns the same as I do. **8** *fam* maybe, perhaps: *igual no vienen,* they may well not come. **- 9 iguales,** *adj* (*en tenis*) all: *iguales a treinta,* thirty all; *iguales a cuarenta,* deuce.
● **a partes iguales,** into equal parts. ‖ **al igual que,** like. ‖ **da igual,** it doesn't matter. ‖ **de igual a igual,** as an equal. ‖ **es igual,** it doesn't matter. ‖ **ir iguales,** (*al mismo nivel*) to be at the same level; (*en deportes*) to be even; (*en el vestir*) to be dressed the same. ‖ **por igual,** (*uniformemente*) evenly. ‖ **siempre igual,** always the same. ‖ **sin igual,** (*hallazgo*) unparalleled; (*persona*) unrivalled; (*belleza*) unique. ‖ **¡habráse visto cosa igual!,** I've never seen anything like it.
iguala 1 *f* (*contrato*) agreement. **2** (*cuota*) agreed fee.
igualación 1 *f* (*de cantidades*) equalization; (*del marcador*) levelling. **2** (*de un terreno*) levelling. **3** (*igualdad*) equality: *la mujer aspira a la igualación de su capacidad laboral a la de los varones,* women aspire to equality of opportunities with men in the labour market.
igualado,-a 1 *pp →* **igualar. - 2** *adj* (*allanado*) level; (*pulido*) smooth. **3** DEP evenly matched, closely fought: *tras un primer tiempo muy igualado,* after a very evenly matched first half.

igualar 1 *t* to make equal: *ambas delegaciones han logrado finalmente igualar sus posturas,* the two delegations have managed to iron out their differences; *tendremos que igualar los precios a los de la competencia,* we'll have to bring our prices into line with those of our competitors; *se ha llegado a un nivel de progreso nunca antes igualado,* progress has reached previously unattained levels. **2** (*allanar*) to level; (*pulir*) to smooth. **3** (*comparar*) to match: *no hay nadie que lo iguale,* nobody can match him, he has no equal. **4** DEP (*partido*) to draw; (*tanteo*) to equalize. **- 5 igualarse,** *p* (*ser iguales*) to be equal. **6** (*compararse*) to be compared.
igualdad 1 *f* equality. **2** (*de superficie*) levelness.
● **en igualdad de condiciones, ...,** all things being equal, ... ‖ **estar en igualdad de condiciones,** to be on equal terms.
■ **igualdad de derechos,** equal rights. ‖ **igualdad de oportunidades,** equal opportunities.
igualitario,-a *adj* egalitarian.
igualmente 1 *adv* (*del mismo modo*) equally: *es igualmente usual que ...,* it is just as usual that ... **2** (*también*) likewise; (*a pesar de ello*) all the same, still: *se refirió igualmente a ...,* he also referred to ...; *aunque no te hayan invitado puedes venir igualmente,* even though you haven't been invited you can still come. **3** (*como respuesta*): *¡que haya suerte! –¡igualmente!,* good luck! –the same to you!
iguana *f* iguana.
ijada *f* flank.
ikastola *f* Basque school.
ikurriña *f* Basque flag.
ilación *f* cohesion.
ilegal *adj* illegal.
ilegalidad *f* illegality.
ilegalmente *adv* illegally.
ilegibilidad *f* illegibility.
ilegible *adj* unreadable, illegible.
ilegitimidad *f* illegitimacy.
ilegítimo,-a *adj* illegitimate.
íleon *m* ileum.
ilerdense 1 *adj* of Lérida, from Lérida. **- 2** *mf* person from Lérida, inhabitant of Lérida.
ileso,-a *adj* unharmed, unhurt.
● **resultar ileso,-a,** to be unhurt, be unharmed. ‖ **salir ileso,-a,** to escape unhurt, escape unharmed.
iletrado,-a *adj* illiterate.
ilícitamente *adv* illicitly.
ilícito,-a *adj* unlawful, illicit.
ilimitado,-a *adj* unlimited.
ilion *m* ilium.
Ilmo.,-a. *abr* (*ilustrísimo*) Your Excellence, Your Excellency.
ilógicamente *adv* illogically.
ilógico,-a *adj* illogical.
Iltre. *abr* (*ilustre*) eminent, distinguished.
iluminación 1 *f* (*de una sala*) lighting; (*de una feria*) illumination; (*de una película, un espectáculo*) lighting. **2** (*de manuscritos*) illumination.
■ **iluminación artificial,** artificial lighting. ‖ **iluminación indirecta,** indirect lighting.
iluminado,-a 1 *pp →* **iluminar. - 2** *adj* (*habitación*) lit; (*calles*) lit, lit up. **- 3** *m,f* illuminate.
iluminador,-ra 1 *adj* illuminating. **- 2** *m,f* (*de manuscritos*) illuminator.
iluminar 1 *t* to light, light up. **2** (*manuscrito*) to illuminate. **3** *fig* to enlighten.

iluminaria f → **luminaria**.
ilusión 1 f (no real) illusion, illusory hope. 2 (esperanza) hope. 3 (sueño) dream. 4 (emoción) excitement.
● **hacerle ilusión algo a algn.**, to be excited about sth., look forward to sth.: *me hizo mucha ilusión que me llamaras,* I was really pleased you phoned; *me hace mucha ilusión que vengáis,* I'm really looking forward to your visit. ‖ **hacerse ilusiones,** to raise one's hopes, expect too much.
■ **ilusión óptica,** optical illusion.
ilusionado,-a 1 pp → **iluminar**. – 2 adj excited.
● **estar ilusionado,-a con algo,** to be excited about sth.
ilusionar 1 t (crear ilusiones) to raise hopes. 2 (entusiasmar) to excite. – 3 **ilusionarse,** p (esperanzarse) to build up one's hopes. 4 (entusiasmarse) to be excited (**con,** about).
ilusionismo m conjuring.
ilusionista 1 adj illusionistic. – 2 mf conjurer, illusionist.
iluso,-a 1 adj naive, gullible. – 2 m,f naive person, gullible person.
ilusorio,-a adj illusory.
ilustración 1 f (de un texto) illustration. 2 (erudición) learning, erudition. 3 **la Ilustración,** HIST the Enlightenment.
● **como ilustración,** by way of illustration.
ilustrado,-a 1 adj (texto) illustrated. 2 (culto) learned, erudite. 3 HIST of the Enlightenment.
ilustrador,-ra 1 adj illustrative. – 2 m,f illustrator.
ilustrar 1 t (texto) to illustrate. 2 (aclarar) to explain. 3 (instruir) to enlighten. – 4 **ilustrarse,** p to learn.
ilustrativo,-a adj illustrative.
ilustre 1 adj (célebre) renowned, illustrious. 2 (distinguido) distinguished.
ilustrísimo,-a 1 adj (superlativo) most illustrious. 2 (forma de tratamiento) honourable.
● **Ilustrísimo Sr Alcalde,** (en una carta) Dear Sir. ‖ **Su Ilustrísima,** (al mencionarlo) His Grace, His Lordship; (dirigiéndose a él) Your Grace, My Lord.
imagen 1 f image. 2 TV picture.
● **ser la viva imagen de algn.,** to be the spitting image of sb.
imaginable adj imaginable.
imaginación f imagination, fantasy.
● **son imaginaciones tuyas,** you're imagining things.
imaginar 1 t (gen) to imagine: *imagina un mundo sin fronteras,* imagine a world without frontiers; *imaginemos que estamos en la selva,* let's imagine we're all in the jungle. 2 (pensar) to think, imagine: *¡imagina que todos estamos a su entera disposición!,* she thinks we're all at her beck and call! 3 (idear) to devise, think up: *imaginó una estrategia para despistar al vigilante,* he thought up a way to distract the guard's attention.
▲ *The form imaginarse is also used in all senses, especially in colloquial speech.*
imaginario,-a 1 adj imaginary. – 2 **imaginaria,** f MIL (guardia) reserve guard; (guardia nocturna) night guard.
imaginativo,-a adj imaginative.
imaginería f religious images pl.
imaginero m maker of religious images.
imán¹ m magnet.
imán² m REL imam.
imanación f → **imantación**.
imanar t → **imantar**.

imantación f magnetization.
imantar t to magnetize.
imbatible adj unbeatable.
imbatido,-a adj unbeaten.
imbécil 1 adj MED (retrasado) imbecile. 2 fam stupid, imbecile. – 3 mf MED imbecile. 4 fam idiot, imbecile.
imbecilidad 1 f MED imbecility. 2 fam stupidity, imbecility.
imberbe adj beardless.
imbornal 1 m (de una terraza) drain. 2 (de un barco) scupper.
imborrable adj indelible.
imbricación f interweaving.
imbricar 1 t to interweave. – 2 **imbricarse,** p to be interwoven.
imbuir 1 t to imbue. – 2 **imbuirse,** p to become imbued (**de,** with).
imitable adj imitable.
imitación 1 f (copia) imitation. 2 (parodia) impression.
● **de imitación,** imitation.
imitador,-ra 1 adj imitative. – 2 m,f imitator. 3 (cómico) impressionist.
imitamonas mf fam copycat.
▲ pl **imitamonas**.
imitar t to copy, imitate; (gestos) to mimic; (persona) to mimic, do an impression of.
impaciencia f impatience.
impacientar 1 t to make lose one's patience, exasperate. – 2 **impacientarse,** p to lose one's patience, get impatient.
impaciente adj impatient, anxious: *ya estoy impaciente por llegar,* I can't wait to get there.
impacto 1 m (choque) impact. 2 (marca) mark; (agujero) hole.
● **causar impacto,** to cause a stir.
■ **impacto de bala,** bullet hole: *recibió tres impactos de bala,* he was hit by three bullets.
impagable 1 adj unpayable. 2 fig (de mucho valor) invaluable.
impagado,-a 1 adj unpaid. – 2 **impagado,** m (cosa) unpaid item; (deuda) unpaid debt.
impago m non-payment.
impala m impala.
impalpable adj impalpable.
impar 1 adj odd. – 2 m odd number.
imparable adj unstoppable.
imparcial adj impartial, fair.
imparcialidad f impartiality.
imparcialmente adv impartially.
impartir t (justicia) to administer; (lección) to give.
● **impartir clases,** (en colegio) to teach; (en universidad) to lecture. ‖ **impartir la bendición,** to bless.
impasibilidad f impassiveness.
impasible adj impassive.
● **quedarse impasible,** to remain impassive.
impasse m impasse.
impavidez f dauntlessness.
impávido,-a adj dauntless.
impecable adj impeccable, faultless.
● **ir impecable,** to be impeccably dressed.
impedido,-a 1 pp → **impedir**. – 2 adj disabled, handicapped. – 3 m,f disabled person, handicapped person. – 4 **los impedidos,** mpl the disabled, the handicapped.
impedimento 1 m (gen) impediment; (obstáculo) hindrance, obstacle; (problema) hitch: *no hay ningún impe-*

dimento para que salga del país, there is no reason why he should not leave the country; *hicimos el viaje hasta Sigüenza sin ningún impedimento,* we reached Sigüenza without a hitch. **2** JUR *(a un matrimonio)* impediment.
impedir 1 *t (hacer imposible)* to prevent, stop: *¿hay algo que te lo impida?,* is there anything stopping you?; *su enfermedad le impide desplazarse,* her illness makes it impossible for her to get about. **2** *(obstaculizar)* to hinder, impede.
● **impedir el paso,** to block the way.
▲ *Conjugation model* |34|, *like servir.*
impelente *adj* driving.
impeler 1 *t* to drive forward, propel. **2** *fig (incitar)* to impel, incite.
impenetrabilidad *f* impenetrability.
impenetrable 1 *adj (bosque)* impenetrable. **2** *fig (misterio)* impenetrable, unfathomable. **3** *(persona, actitud)* inscrutable.
impenitencia *f* impenitence.
impenitente 1 *adj (pecador)* impenitent, unrepentant. **2** *fig (lector, bebedor)* inveterate.
impensable *adj* unthinkable.
impensado,-a 1 *adj (espontáneo)* spontaneous, impromptu. **2** *(inesperado)* unexpected.
impepinable *adj fam* unavoidable, certain, inevitable.
impepinablemente *adj fam* unavoidably, for sure, for certain.
imperar *i* to rule, prevail.
imperativamente *adv* imperatively.
imperativo,-a 1 *adj* imperative. – **2** imperativo, *m* LING imperative.
imperceptibilidad *f* imperceptibility.
imperceptible *adj* imperceptible.
imperdible *m* safety pin.
imperdonable *adj* unforgivable, inexcusable.
imperecedero,-a 1 *adj (producto)* imperishable. **2** *fig* everlasting.
imperfección 1 *f* imperfection. **2** *(defecto)* defect, fault.
imperfecto,-a 1 *adj* imperfect. **2** LING imperfect. – **3** imperfecto, *m* imperfect, imperfect tense.
imperial *adj* imperial.
imperialismo *m* imperialism.
imperialista 1 *adj* imperialist. – **2** *mf* imperialist.
impericia *f* inexperience.
imperio *m* empire.
● **valer un imperio,** *fam* to be priceless, be worth a fortune.
imperiosamente 1 *adv (con autoridad)* imperiously. **2** *(con urgencia)* imperatively.
imperioso,-a 1 *adj (autoritario)* imperious. **2** *(necesario)* urgent, pressing.
● **tener una necesidad imperiosa,** *fam euf* to be dying to go.
● **necesidad imperiosa,** pressing need.
impermeabilidad *f* impermeability.
impermeabilizar *t* to waterproof.
▲ *Conjugation model* |4|, *like realizar.*
impermeabilización 1 *f (de un tejido)* waterproofing. **2** *(de un suelo)* sealing. **3** *fig (de una frontera)* sealing.
impermeable 1 *adj (gen)* impermeable, impervious; *(tejido, ropa)* waterproof. **2** *fig* impervious. – **3** *m* raincoat.
impersonal *adj* impersonal.
impersonalidad *f* impersonality.
impertérrito,-a *adj* imperturbable, undaunted.

impertinencia 1 *f* impertinence. **2** *(palabras)* impertinent remark.
● **decir impertinencias,** to be impertinent.
impertinente 1 *adj* impertinent. – **2 impertinentes,** *mpl* lorgnette *sing.*
imperturbable *adj* imperturbable.
impétigo *m* impetigo.
ímpetu 1 *m (fuerza)* vigour (US vigor); *(entusiasmo)* enthusiasm; *(energía)* energy: *entró con ímpetu en la sala,* he burst into the room; *empezaron con mucho ímpetu,* they started off eagerly, they started off with great gusto. **2** *(impulso)* impetus; *(fuerza)* force.
impetuosidad *f* impetuosity.
impetuoso,-a 1 *adj (persona)* impetuous. **2** *(viento)* violent.
impiedad *f* impiety.
impío,-a 1 *adj* impious. – **2** *m,f* infidel.
implacable *adj* implacable, relentless.
implantación 1 *f (de modas, costumbres)* introduction. **2** MED implant.
implantar 1 *t* to introduce. **2** MED to implant.
implicación *f* implication.
implicar 1 *t (conllevar)* to imply. **2** *(involucrar)* to implicate, involve (**en,** in): *lo implicaron en la huida,* they implicated him in the escape.
▲ *Conjugation model* |1|, *like sacar.*
implícitamente *adv* implicitly.
implícito,-a *adj* implicit.
● **llevar implícito,-a algo,** to imply sth.
implorante *adj* imploring.
implorar *t* to implore, entreat, beg.
implosión *f* implosion.
implosivo,-a 1 *adj* implosive. – **2 implosiva,** *f* implosive.
impolítico,-a *adj* impolitic.
impoluto,-a *adj* immaculate, spotless.
imponderabilidad *f* imponderability.
imponderable 1 *adj (factor)* imponderable; *(valor)* incalculable. – **2** *m* imponderable.
■ **factores imponderables,** imponderables, imponderabilia.
imponente 1 *adj* impressive. – **2** *adv fam (buenísimo)* terrific.
imponer 1 *t (ley, límite, sanción)* to impose. **2** *(obediencia)* to exact. **3** *(respeto)* to inspire. **4** FIN *(cantidad)* to deposit. – **5** *i (asustar)* to be frightening. – **6 imponerse,** *p* to impose one's authority (**a,** on). **7** *(obligarse)* to force os. to. **8** *(prevalecer)* to prevail. **9** *(predominar)* to become fashionable.
▲ *Conjugation model* |78|, *like poner; pp impuesto,-a.*
imponible *adj* taxable, subject to taxation.
impopular *adj* unpopular.
impopularidad *f* unpopularity.
importación 1 *f (acción)* importation, import. **2** *(productos)* imports *pl: la importación ha crecido este trimestre,* imports have risen this quarter.
■ **artículo de importación,** imported item. || **artículos de importación,** imported goods.
importador,-ra 1 *adj* importing. – **2** *m,f* importer.
importancia *f* importance.
● **dar importancia a algo,** to take sth. seriously. || **darse importancia,** to give os. airs. || **de importancia,** *(gen)* important; *(herida, lesión)* serious. || **no tiene importancia,** it's nothing, it doesn't matter, it's not important. || **quitar importancia a algo,** restar im-

portancia a algo, to play sth. down. ‖ sin importancia, unimportant. ‖ tener importancia, to be important.
importante 1 *adj* (*gen*) important; (*por su gravedad*) serious; (*por su cantidad*) considerable: *es importante que aprenda a nadar*, it is important that he (should) learn to swim. 2 (*influyente*) important.
importar 1 *t* COM (*traer de fuera*) to import. 2 (*valer*) to amount to: *¿a cuánto importa la factura?*, how much does the bill amount to? – 3 *i* (*tener importancia*) to matter: *me importa mucho tu opinión*, your opinion matters a lot to me. 4 (*molestar*) to mind: *¿te importaría cerrar la ventana?*, would you mind closing the window?; *no me importa el qué dirán*, I don't mind what people say.
● **¡a ti qué te importa!**, *fam* mind your own business! ‖ **lo que importa es que ...**, the important thing is that ... ‖ **me importa un bledo/pito/comino**, *fam* I couldn't care less. ‖ **no importa**, it doesn't matter.
importe *m* (*gen*) price, cost; (*cantidad*) amount; (*tarifa*) fare.
importunar *t* (*molestar*) to pester; (*uso formal*) to importune.
importuno,-a *adj* importunate.
imposibilidad *f* impossibility.
imposibilitado,-a 1 *adj* (*inválido*) disabled: *ha quedado imposibilitado de las dos piernas*, he has lost the use of both legs; *está imposibilitada en la cama*, she's bedridden. 2 (*incapaz*) unable.
● **verse imposibilitado,-a para hacer algo**, to be unable to do sth.
imposibilitar *t* (*impedir*) to make impossible, prevent.
imposible *adj* impossible.
● **estar imposible**, to be impossible. ‖ **hacer lo imposible**, to do the impossible, do one's utmost. ‖ **hacerle la vida imposible a algn.**, to make life impossible for sb. ‖ **parece imposible que ...**, I can't believe that ... ‖ **ponerse imposible**, *fam* to become impossible.
imposición 1 *f* (*gen*) imposition. 2 FIN (*cantidad*) deposit; (*impuesto*) tax.
● **hacer una imposición**, to make a deposit.
■ **imposición de manos**, laying on of hands.
impositivo,-a *adj* tax.
■ **tipo impositivo**, tax rate.
impositor,-ra *m,f* depositor.
impostor,-ra 1 *m,f* (*farsante*) impostor. 2 (*difamador*) slanderer.
impostura 1 *f* (*trampa*) imposture, fraud. 2 (*calumnia*) slander.
impotencia *f* impotence.
impotente *adj* impotent.
● **sentirse impotente**, to feel powerless, feel helpless: *me sentí impotente ante tanta injusticia*, I felt powerless against so much injustice.
impracticable 1 *adj* (*irrealizable*) unfeasible. 2 (*camino etc*) impassable. 3 (*puerta, ventana*) which doesn't open or shut.
imprecación *f* imprecation, curse.
● **proferir imprecaciones**, to curse.
imprecar *t* to imprecate.
imprecisión *f* imprecision, lack of precision.
impreciso,-a *adj* imprecise, vague.
impredecible *adj* (*persona*) unpredictable; (*circunstancia*) unforeseeable.
impregnación *f* impregnation.
impregnar 1 *t* to impregnate (**de**, with). – 2 **impregnarse**, *p* to become impregnated.

imprenta 1 *f* (*arte*) printing: *la invención de la imprenta*, the invention of printing. 2 (*taller*) printer's, printing house.
■ **letra de imprenta**, print. ‖ **libertad de imprenta**, freedom of the press.
imprescindible *adj* essential, indispensable.
impresentable 1 *adj* (*gen*) unpresentable. 2 *fig* (*vergonzoso*) shameful.
● **ser un,-a impresentable**, *fam* to be an embarrassment.
impresión 1 *f* (*en imprenta*) printing. 2 (*huella*) impression, imprint. 3 *fig* (*efecto*) impression; (*negativo*) shock: *en una entrevista es importante causar buena impresión*, in an interview it's important to create a good impression; *no me ha causado buena impresión el conferenciante*, I wasn't very impressed with the speaker; *el día en que lo conocí me llevé muy mala impresión*, my first impression of him was not very favourable; *me da la impresión de que no va a volver*, I get the impression she's not coming back; *una ducha fría de buena mañana da impresión*, a cold shower in the morning is a shock to the system. 4 (*opinión*) impression.
● **cambiar impresiones**, to compare notes. ‖ **de impresión**, *fam* amazing.
impresionabilidad *f* impressionability.
impresionable *adj* impressionable.
impresionante 1 *adj* (*admirable*) impressive: *una actuación impresionante*, an impressive performance. 2 (*impactante*) powerful; (*inquietante*) disturbing: *un impresionante documental sobre los crímenes de guerra*, a powerful documentary on war crimes. 3 (*sorprendente*) astonishing, amazing: *me ocurrió algo realmente impresionante*, something really astonishing happened to me. 4 *fam* (*gen*) incredible; (*negativamente*) terrible; (*enorme*) tremendous: *había unas olas impresionantes*, there were some tremendous waves; *hace un calor impresionante*, it's terribly hot; *tiene una fuerza impresionante*, he's incredibly strong; *la vista desde arriba era impresionante*, the view from the top was breathtaking.
impresionar 1 *t* (*causar admiración*) to impress: *nos impresionó su facilidad de palabra*, we were impressed by her articulateness; *me impresionó mucho el libro cuando lo leí por primera vez*, the first time I read the book it made a great impression on me; *sus hazañas bélicas no me impresionan ni lo más mínimo*, his war exploits don't impress me in the slightest; (*afectar*) to affect; (*inquietar*) to disturb: *su muerte me impresionó mucho*, I was greatly affected by his death; *la escena de la ejecución nos dejó impresionados*, we found the execution scene very disturbing. 3 (*película*) to expose.
impresionismo *m* impressionism.
impresionista 1 *adj* impressionist. – 2 *mf* impressionist.
impreso,-a 1 *pp* → **imprimir**. – 2 *adj* printed. – 3 **impreso,-a** *m* (*formulario*) form. – 4 **impresos**, *mpl* (*en carta etc*) printed matter *sing*.
■ **impreso postal**, printed matter.
impresor,-ra 1 *adj* printing. – 2 *m,f* (*persona*) printer. – 3 **impresora**, *f* (*máquina*) printer.
imprevisible *adj* (*hecho*) unforeseeable; (*persona*) unpredictable.
imprevisión *f* lack of foresight.
imprevisor,-ra *adj* improvident.
imprevisto,-a 1 *adj* (*circunstancia*) unforeseen; (*visita*) unexpected. – 2 *m* (*incidente*) unforeseen event: *diles que ha surgido un imprevisto*, tell them something

unexpected has cropped up. **– 3 imprevistos**, *mpl* (*gastos*) incidental expenses.
imprimación *f* priming.
imprimar *t* to prime.
imprimátur *m* imprimatur.
▲ *pl* **imprimátur.**
imprimible *adj* printable.
imprimir 1 *t* (*gen*) to print. **2** (*dejar huella*) to stamp. **3** *fig* (*grabar*) to fix. **4** (*dar*) to give: *éstas son circunstancias que imprimen carácter,* these are character-building experiences.
● **imprimir estilo,** to leave one's mark. ‖ **imprimir un ritmo,** to set the pace.
■ **máquina de imprimir,** printing machine.
▲ *pp* **imprimido,-a** or **impreso,-a.**
improbabilidad *f* improbability.
improbable *adj* improbable, unlikely.
ímprobo,-a 1 *adj* (*trabajo*) arduous, laborious: *tuve que hacer un esfuerzo ímprobo para acabar a tiempo,* I had to make a super-human effort to finish on time. **2** (*deshonesto*) dishonest.
improcedencia 1 *f* inappropriateness. **2** JUR inadmissibility.
improcedente 1 *adj* inappropriate. **2** JUR inadmissible.
improductivo,-a *adj* unproductive.
impronta *f* mark.
impronunciable *adj* unpronounceable.
improperio *m* insult.
impropiamente *adv* improperly.
impropiedad *f* (*gen*) unsuitableness, inappropriateness; (*del lenguaje*) impropriety.
impropio,-a 1 *adj* (*inadecuado*) unsuitable, inappropriate. **2** (*incorrecto*) improper.
● **ser impropio,-a de algn.,** not to be worthy of sb., be beneath sb. ‖ **ser impropio,-a para algo,** to be unsuitable for sth.
improrrogable *adj* (*gen*) that can not be extended; (*plazo*) final.
improvisación *f* improvisation.
improvisado,-a *adj* (*gen*) improvised; (*discurso*) impromptu.
improvisador,-ra 1 *adj* improvising. **– 2** *m,f* improviser.
improvisar 1 *t* to improvise. **– 2** *i* to improvise.
improviso de improviso, *adv* (*repentinamente*) suddenly, all of a sudden; (*inesperadamente*) unexpectedly.
imprudencia 1 *f* (*falta de prudencia*) imprudence, carelessness; (*en la carretera*) dangerous driving. **2** (*acción imprudente*) rash move, reckless move; (*indiscreción*) indiscretion: *fue una imprudencia dejarle que llevara el coche,* it was unwise to let him drive the car; *cometió una imprudencia con decírselo,* it was unwise to tell him.
● **las imprudencias se pagan,** carelessness costs lives.
■ **imprudencia temeraria,** (*gen*) criminal negligence; (*en carretera*) reckless driving.
imprudente 1 *adj* imprudent, careless: *es imprudente conducir a esa velocidad,* it is dangerous to drive at that speed. **– 2** *mf* (*imprudente*) imprudent person, careless person; (*indiscreto*) indiscreet person.
impúber 1 *adj* pre-pubescent. **– 2** *mf* pre-pubescent child.
impublicable *adj* unpublishable.
impudicia *f* immodesty.
impúdico,-a 1 *adj* (*indecente*) immodest, indecent. **2** (*desvergonzado*) shameless.

impudor *m* immodesty.
impuesto,-a *pp* → **imponer. – 2** impuesto, *m* tax, duty.
■ **impuesto revolucionario,** protection money (*paid to a terrorist organization*). ‖ **impuesto sobre el valor añadido (IVA),** value added tax (VAT). ‖ **impuesto sobre la renta,** income tax. ‖ **tienda libre de impuestos,** duty-free shop.
impugnable 1 *adj* (*decisión, resultado*) contestable. **– 2** *m* (*opinión, teoría*) refutable.
impugnación 1 *f* (*de lo reglamentado*) contestation. **2** (*de una teoría*) refutation.
impugnar 1 *t* (*resultado*) to contest. **2** (*teoría*) to refute.
impulsar 1 *t* to impel. **2** TÉC to drive forward. **3** (*potenciar*) to promote. **4** (*incitar*) to drive.
● **impulsar a algn. a hacer algo,** to drive sb. to do sth.
impulsión *f* impulsion.
impulsivo,-a 1 *adj* impulsive. **– 2** *m,f* impulsive person.
impulso 1 *m* impulse. **2** (*fuerza, velocidad*) momentum.
● **actuar por impulso,** to act on an impulse. ‖ **tomar impulso,** to take a run-up.
impulsor,-ra 1 *adj* driving. **– 2** *m,f* promoter, driving force: *los impulsores del proceso de paz,* those behind the peace process.
impune *adj* unpunished.
● **quedar impune,** to go unpunished. ‖ **salir impune,** to go unpunished.
impunemente *adv* with impunity.
impunidad *f* impunity.
impuntualidad *f* unpunctuality.
impureza *f* impurity.
impuro,-a *adj* impure.
imputable *adj* attributable (**a**, to).
imputación *f* imputation, accusation.
imputar *t* to impute.
● **imputar algo a algn.,** to impute sth. to sb.
inabarcable *adj* huge, vast.
inabordable *adj* unapproachable.
inacabable *adj* interminable, endless.
inacabado,-a *adj* unfinished.
inaccesibilidad *f* inaccessibility.
inaccesible *adj* inaccessible.
inacción *f* inaction, inactivity.
inaceptable *adj* unacceptable.
inactividad *f* inactivity.
inactivo,-a *adj* inactive.
inadaptable *adj* unadaptable.
inadaptación *f* maladjustment.
inadaptado,-a 1 *adj* maladjusted. **– 2** *m,f* misfit.
inadecuación *f* inadequacy.
inadecuado,-a 1 *adj* unsuitable. **2** (*inapropiado*) inappropriate.
inadmisible *adj* unacceptable, inadmissible.
inadvertencia *f* inadvertence.
inadvertido,-a 1 *adj* (*no visto*) unseen, unnoticed. **2** (*distraído*) inattentive.
● **pasar inadvertido,-a,** to go unnoticed.
inagotable 1 *adj* (*cantidad*) inexhaustible. **2** (*persona*) tireless.
inaguantable *adj* unbearable.
inalámbrico,-a 1 *adj* cordless. **– 2** inalámbrico, *m* (*teléfono*) cordless phone.
inalcanzable *adj* unattainable, unreachable.
inalienable *adj* inalienable.
■ **derecho inalienable,** inalienable right.

inalterable 1 *adj* (*propiedad*) unchanging. **2** (*color*) fast. **3** (*persona, vida*) impassive, imperturbable.

inalterado,-a *adj* (*marcador*) unaltered, unchanged.

inamovible 1 *adj* (*gen*) immovable; (*permanente*) permanent; (*no cambiable*) unchangeable. **2** (*tradición, máxima*) unchanging. **3** (*certeza*) unwavering, unshakeable; (*oferta*) final, non-negotiable; (*desicion*) final, irrevocable.

inane *adj* pointless, futile.

inanición *f* starvation.

inanidad *f* pointlessness.

inanimado,-a *adj* inanimate, lifeless.

inánime *adj* lifeless.

inapagable *adj* unextinguishable.

inapelable *adj* (*sentencia*) unappealable.

inapetencia *f* lack of appetite, loss of appetite.

inapetente *adj* lacking in appetite.

inaplazable *adj* which cannot be postponed.

inaplicable *adj* inapplicable.

inapreciable 1 *adj* (*insignificante*) imperceptible, insignificant. **2** (*valioso*) invaluable, priceless.

inaprensible 1 *adj* (*inasible*) which cannot be held. **2** (*incomprensible*) impossible to grasp.

inapropiado *adj* inappropriate.

inarmónico,-a *adj* unharmonious.

inarrugable *adj* crease-resistant.

inarticulable *adj* unpronounceable.

inarticulado,-a *adj* inarticulate.

inasequible 1 *adj* (*objetivo*) unattainable. **2** (*precio*) prohibitive. **3** (*persona*) unapproachable.

inasistencia *f* non-attendance, absence.

inastillable *adj* (*vidrio*) shatterproof.

inatacable 1 *adj* (*posición, fortaleza*) unassailable. **2** (*idea, postura*) irrefutable.

inatento,-a *adj* inattentive.

inaudible *adj* inaudible.

inaudito,-a 1 *adj* (*nunca oído*) unheard-of. **2** (*monstruoso*) outrageous.

inauguración *f* opening, inauguration.

inaugural *adj* inaugural, opening.

inaugurar *t* to inaugurate, open.

INB *abr* EDUC (*Instituto Nacional de Bachillerato*) ≈ state secondary school.

inca 1 *adj* Inca. **– 2** *mf* Inca.

incaico,-a *adj* Inca.

incalculable *adj* incalculable.

incalificable *adj* (*intolerable*) unspeakable.

incandescencia *f* incandescence.

incandescente *adj* incandescent.

incansable *adj* tireless.

incapacidad 1 *f* (*gen*) incapacity, inability: *su incapacidad para el trabajo queda patente,* his inability to do the job is obvious. **2** (*insuficiencia*) disability. **3** JUR incapacity.
■ **incapacidad física,** physical disability. ‖ **incapacidad laboral,** invalidity. ‖ **incapacidad laboral transitoria,** temporary disability. ‖ **incapacidad parcial,** partial disability. ‖ **incapacidad psíquica,** mental handicap. ‖ **incapacidad total,** total disability.

incapacitado,-a *adj* (*físicamente*) incapacitated, handicapped, disabled; (*mentalmente*) incapacitated, unfit.

incapacitar 1 *t* (*impedir*) to incapacitate. **2** JUR to disqualify.

incapaz 1 *adj* incapable (**de,** of): *es incapaz de decir que no,* he's incapable of saying no, he can't say no. **2** (*incompetente*) incompetent: *para los trabajos duros es totalmente incapaz,* he's totally incapable of doing heavy work.

incautación *f* seizure.

incautarse. 1 incautarse de, *p* JUR (*confiscar*) to seize, confiscate. **2** (*apropiarse de*) to appropriate.

incauto,-a 1 *adj* (*crédulo*) gullible. **– 2** *m,f* gullible person.

incendiar 1 *t* to set on fire, set fire to. **– 2** incendiarse, *p* to catch fire.
▲ *Conjugation model* [12], *like* **cambiar.**

incendiario,-a 1 *adj* (*bomba*) incendiary. **2** *fig* (*escrito*) inflammatory. **– 3** *m,f* arsonist.

incendio *m* fire.
■ **incendio intencionado / incendio provocado,** arson.

incensario *m* censer, thurible.

incensurable *adj* irreproachable.

incentivar 1 *t* (*persona*) to motivate, encourage. **2** (*producción*) to boost, encourage.

incentivo *m* incentive.

incertidumbre *f* uncertainty.

incesante *adj* incessant, unceasing.

incesantemente *adv* incessantly.

incesto *m* incest.

incestuoso,-a *adj* incestuous.

incidencia 1 *f* (*repercusión*) repercussion, consequence; (*efecto*) effect, impact: *la crisis ha tenido incidencia directa en el transporte,* the crisis has had a direct impact on transport; *son reformas legislativas sin incidencia histórica alguna,* they are legislative reforms with no historical repercussions whatever. **2** (*frecuencia*) incidence.

incidental *adj* incidental.

incidente 1 *adj* incidental. **– 2** *m* incident, event.

incidir. 1 incidir en, *i* (*repercutir en*) to have an effect on, affect: *la crisis ha incidido notablemente en el turismo,* the crisis has had a considerable effect on tourism. **2** (*incurrir en*) to fall into: *su retórica incide en lamentables lugares comunes,* his rhetoric is plagued with silly clichés. **3** (*tratar*) to touch upon; (*insistir en*) to stress: *el ministro volvió a incidir en el tema del racismo,* the minister again touched upon the subject of racism. **4** (*luz, rayo*) to fall on. **5** MED to incise in, incise into.
● **incidir en un error,** to make a mistake.

incienso *m* incense.

incierto,-a 1 *adj* (*poco seguro*) uncertain, doubtful. **2** (*desconocido*) unknown.

incineración *f* (*de basuras*) incineration; (*de cadáveres*) cremation.

incinerador *m* (*de basuras*) incinerator.

incinerar *t* (*basura*) to incinerate; (*cadáveres*) to cremate.

incipiente *adj* incipient.

incisión *f* incision.

incisivo,-a 1 *adj* (*instrumento*) cutting, sharp. **2** *fig* (*persona, humor*) incisive, mordant. **– 3** *m* (*diente*) incisor.

inciso,-a 1 *adj* (*estilo*) jerky. **– 2** inciso, *m* (*comentario*) comment, passing remark; (*de un artículo*) subsection. **3** LING interpolated clause.
● **a modo de inciso,** in passing.

incitación *f* incitement (**a,** to).

incitador,-ra 1 *adj* inciting. **– 2** *m,f* inciter.

incitante 1 *adj* (*estimulante*) inciting. **2** (*provocativo*) provocative.

incitar *t* to incite (**a,** to): *incitó a la tropa a la rebelión,* he incited the troops to mutiny; *sus escritos incitan al racismo,* his writings encourage racism.

incivil 1 *adj* (*sin civismo*) uncivil. **2** (*grosero*) uncivil, rude.

incivilidad *f* incivility.

incivilizado,-a *adj* uncivilized.

inclasificable *adj* unclassifiable.

inclemencia *f* inclemency, harshness: *las inclemencias del tiempo,* the inclement weather.

inclemente *adj* inclement, harsh.

inclinación 1 *f* (*desviación*) slant. **2** (*tendencia*) leaning. **3** (*afición, cariño*) penchant. **4** (*saludo*) bow; (*asentimiento*) nod: *me saludó con una inclinación de la cabeza,* he nodded to me.

● sentir inclinación por ..., to have a penchant for ...: *siente inclinación por la música,* he has a musical bent.

inclinado,-a *adj* (*terreno*) sloping; (*edificio*) leaning, tilting.

■ la torre inclinada de Pisa, the Leaning Tower of Pisa.

inclinar 1 *t* (*ladear*) to tilt: *inclina un poco más la jarra,* tilt the jug a bit more; *con el plato inclinado hacia ti,* with the plate tilted towards you. **2** *fig* (*persuadir*) to dispose, move. – **3 inclinarse,** *p* (*doblarse*) to bend, lean; (*como saludo*) to bow: *este árbol se inclina hacia la derecha,* this tree leans towards the right; *se inclinó ante la primera dama,* she bowed to the First Lady; *inclinado sobre el cadáver,* leaning over the body. **4 inclinarse a,** *fig* (*propender a*) to incline to, incline towards: *me inclino a pensar que nos ha engañado,* I am inclined to think that he has cheated us. **5 inclinarse por,** (*escoger*) to choose, opt for: *se inclinaron por el candidato más joven,* they opted for the youngest candidate.

● inclinar la cabeza, to bow.

ínclito,-a *adj lit* illustrious.

incluido,-a *adj* (*gen*) included; (*adjunto*) enclosed.

incluir 1 *t* to include. **2** (*contener*) to contain, comprise: *este precio incluye todos los gastos,* this is an all-inclusive price. **3** (*adjuntar - en carta etc*) to enclose.

▲ *Conjugation model* |62|, *like huir.*

inclusa *f* foundling home.

inclusero,-a 1 *adj* foundling. – **2** *m,f* foundling.

inclusión *f* inclusion.

inclusive *adv* inclusive: *"cerrado del 1 al 8, ambos inclusive",* "closed from 1st to 8th inclusive".

inclusivo,-a *adj* inclusive.

incluso 1 *adv* even. – **2** *prep* even.

incoar *t* to initiate.

● incoar expediente contra, to initiate proceedings against.

incoativo,-a *adj* LING inchoative.

incógnito,-a 1 *adj* unknown. – **2** *f* MAT unknown quantity. **3** incógnita, *fig* (*misterio*) mystery.

● de incógnito, incognito.

incoherencia *f* (*falta de coherencia*) incoherence: *esta tesis está plagada de incoherencias,* this thesis is full of inconsistencies.

incoherente *adj* incoherent, disconnected.

incoloro,-a *adj* colourless.

incólume *adj* unscathed, unharmed.

incombustible *adj* incombustible, fireproof.

incomestible *adj* uneatable, inedible.

incomible *adj* uneatable, inedible.

incomodar 1 *t* (*causar molestia*) to inconvenience. **2** (*fastidiar*) to annoy, bother. **3** (*enojar*) to anger. – **4 incomodarse,** *p* (*tomarse la molestia*) to put os. out. **5** (*enfadarse*) to get annoyed, get angry.

incomodidad 1 *f* discomfort. **2** (*molestia*) inconvenience. **3** (*malestar*) unrest, uneasiness.

incómodo,-a *adj* uncomfortable.

● sentirse incómodo,-a, to feel uncomfortable, feel awkward.

incomparable *adj* incomparable.

incomparecencia *f* non-attendance, failure to attend, non-appearance.

incompatibilidad *f* incompatibility.

● incompatibilidad de caracteres, mutual incompatibility.

incompatible *adj* incompatible.

incompetencia *f* incompetence.

incompetente *adj* incompetent.

incompleto,-a 1 *adj* incomplete. **2** (*inacabado*) unfinished.

incomprendido,-a *adj* misunderstood.

● ser un,-a incomprendido,-a, to be misunderstood.

incomprensibilidad *f* incomprehensibility.

incomprensible *adj* incomprehensible.

incomprensión *f* lack of understanding.

incomunicación 1 *f* (*de un lugar*) isolation. **2** (*de un preso*) solitary confinement. **3** (*entre dos personas*) lack of communication.

incomunicado,-a 1 *adj* (*aislado*) isolated. **2** (*por la nieve*) cut off: *nos hemos quedado incomunicados,* we are cut off. **3** (*preso*) in solitary confinement.

incomunicar 1 *t* (*lugar*) to isolate, cut off. **2** (*habitación*) to shut off. **3** (*preso*) to hold in solitary confinement.

▲ *Conjugation model* |1|, *like sacar.*

inconcebible *adj* inconceivable, unthinkable.

inconciliable *adj* irreconcilable.

inconcluso,-a *adj* unfinished.

inconcreto,-a *adj* vague.

incondicional 1 *adj* (*rendición*) unconditional. **2** (*amistad, admiración*) unquestioning. – **3** *mf* staunch supporter.

inconexión *f* lack of connection.

inconexo,-a *adj* disconnected.

inconfesable *adj* shameful.

inconfeso,-a *adj* JUR unconfessed.

inconformismo *m* nonconformism.

inconformista 1 *adj* nonconformist. – **2** *mf* nonconformist.

inconfundible *adj* unmistakable.

incongruencia *f* incongruity.

incongruente *adj* incongruous.

inconmensurable *adj* immensurable.

inconmovible 1 *adj* (*decisión*) unshakable, firm. **2** (*personas*) immovable.

inconquistable *adj* invincible, unconquerable.

inconsciencia 1 *f* MED unconsciousness. **2** (*irreflexión*) thoughtlessness.

inconsciente 1 *adj* MED unconscious. **2** (*irreflexivo*) thoughtless. – **3** *mf* (*persona*) thoughtless person. – **4** el inconsciente, *m* (*en psicoanálisis*) the unconscious.

inconsecuencia *f* inconsistency, inconsequence.

inconsecuente 1 *adj* inconsistent. – **2** *mf* inconsistent person.

inconsideración *f* inconsiderateness, lack of consideration.

inconsiderado,-a *adj* inconsiderate.

inconsistencia 1 *f* (*de un terreno*) softness. **2** (*de una teoría*) insubstantiality, lack of substance; (*de una investigación*) lack of substantial evidence.

inconsistente 1 *adj* (*sin firmeza*) flimsy. **2** (*sin rigor*) weak.

inconsolable *adj* inconsolable, disconsolate.
inconstancia 1 *f* (*indolencia*) lack of discipline. 2 (*variabilidad*) inconstancy, changeability.
inconstante 1 *adj* (*indolente*) lacking in discipline. 2 (*variable*) inconstant, changeable.
inconstitucionalidad *f* unconstitutionality.
inconstitucional *adj* unconstitutional.
incontable *adj* countless, uncountable.
incontaminado,-a *adj* unpolluted.
incontenible *adj* uncontrollable.
incontestable *adj* indisputable.
incontinencia *f* incontinence.
incontinente *adj* incontinent.
incontrolable *adj* uncontrollable.
incontrolado,-a *adj* uncontrolled.
incontrovertible *adj* incontrovertible, indisputable.
inconveniencia 1 *f* (*gen*) inconvenience. 2 (*imprudencia*) tactless remark.
● **decir una inconveniencia,** to be tactless.
inconveniente 1 *adj* (*gen*) inconvenient; (*inapropiado*) inappropriate. – 2 *m* (*desventaja*) drawback; (*dificultad*) problem.
● **no tener inconveniente en hacer algo,** to have no objection to doing sth.: *por mí no hay ningún inconveniente,* that's fine by me; *si no tienen inconveniente, se aplazará la reunión,* if there is no objection, the meeting will be postponed.
incordiar *t* to pester, bother.
▲ *Conjugation model* [12], *like* **cambiar**.
incordio *m fam* nuisance.
incorporación 1 *f* (*llegada*) arrival; (*inclusión*) inclusion; (*unión*) joining: *han anunciado la incorporación de tres nuevas secretarias a la plantilla,* they have announced that three new secretaries are joining the staff; *la incorporación de la mujer al mundo del trabajo,* women entering the job market; *fue el año de la plena incorporación de España a la CEE,* it was the year Spain became a full member of the EEC; *la incorporación del sonido al cine,* the coming of sound to the cinema; *espera su incorporación a filas,* he's waiting to be called up; *la incorporación de Nadal ha reforzado notablemente el equipo,* Nadal's joining the team has strengthened it considerably. 2 (*del cuerpo*) sitting-up.
incorporado,-a 1 *pp* → **incorporar**. – 2 *adj* (*elemento*) built-in: *con radio-casete incorporado,* with a built-in radiocassette.
incorporar 1 *t* (*añadir*) to incorporate, include: *habrá que incorporar el documento al acta,* the document will have to be included in the minutes. 2 CULIN (*añadir*) to add; (*salsa*) to blend in. 3 (*enfermo*) to help to sit up: *incorporado en la cama,* sitting up in bed. – 4 **incorporarse,** *p* (*levantarse*) to sit up. 5 (*a un trabajo*) to start; (*a una empresa, equipo, etc*) to join: *acaba de incorporarse a la plantilla,* he has recently joined the company.
● **incorporarse a filas,** to join up. ‖ **incorporarse a su destino,** to take up one's post.
incorpóreo,-a *adj* incorporeal.
incorrección 1 *f* (*falta de corrección*) incorrectness. 2 (*error*) mistake. 3 (*descortesía*) impoliteness; (*palabra descortés*) impolite remark.
incorrecto,-a 1 *adj* (*inexacto*) incorrect. 2 (*descortés*) impolite.
incorregible *adj* incorrigible.
incorruptible *adj* incorruptible.
incorrupto,-a *adj* uncorrupted.
incrédulo,-a 1 *adj* incredulous. 2 REL unbelieving. – 3 *m,f* disbeliever, incredulous person. 4 REL unbeliever.

increíble *adj* incredible, unbelievable.
incrementar *t* to increase.
incremento *m* increase, rise.
■ **incremento salarial,** wage rise, US raise.
increpar 1 *t* (*reprender*) to rebuke. 2 (*insultar*) to abuse.
incriminación *f* incrimination.
incriminar *t* to incriminate.
incriminatorio,-a *adj* (*testimonio*) incriminatory.
incruento,-a *adj* bloodless.
incrustación 1 *f* incrustation, encrustation. 2 (*artística*) inlaying, inlay.
incrustar 1 *t* to incrust, encrust. 2 (*arte*) to inlay. – 3 **incrustarse,** *p* to become embedded (**en**, in): *la bala se incrustó en el muro,* the bullet embedded itself in the wall.
incubación *f* incubation.
incubadora *f* incubator.
incubar *t* to incubate.
íncubo *m* incubus.
incuestionable *adj* unquestionable.
inculcación *f* inculcation.
inculcar *t* to inculcate, instil: *les inculcaron la necesidad de tener estudios,* they instilled in them the need to study.
▲ *Conjugation model* [1], *like* **sacar**.
inculpación *f* accusation.
inculpado,-a 1 *adj* accused. – 2 *m,f* accused: *la inculpada ha presentado recurso contra su procesamiento,* the accused has appealed against her prosecution; *son cuatro los inculpados en el caso Alfesa,* four people have been charged in connection with the Alfesa case.
inculpar *t* to accuse (**de,** of).
inculto,-a 1 *adj* (*persona*) uneducated. 2 (*terreno*) uncultivated, untilled. – 3 *m,f* (*persona*) ignorant person, ignoramus.
incultura *f* ignorance, lack of education.
incumbencia *f* duty, concern: *eso es incumbencia del estado,* that is the government's concern; *no es asunto de tu incumbencia,* it is none of your business; *no es mi incumbencia,* it is not my responsibility.
incumbir *i* to be incumbent (**a,** upon), be the responsibility (**a,** of): *la decisión incumbe al director,* the decision is up to the manager.
incumplido,-a *adj* (*promesa*) broken.
incumplimiento *m* (*de una promesa*) failure to keep; (*de una orden*) non-compliance, failure to obey; (*de un deber*) negligence.
■ **incumplimiento de contrato,** breach of contract.
incumplir *t* (*promesa*) to break; (*deber*) to fail to fulfil; (*contrato*) to break; (*orden*) to disobey, fail to comply with.
incunable 1 *adj* incunabular. – 2 *m* incunabulum.
incurabilidad *f* incurability.
incurable *adj* incurable.
incurrir 1 incurrir en, *i* (*error*) to fall into; (*delito*) to commit. 2 (*ira etc*) to incur.
incursión *f* incursion.
indagación *f* investigation, inquiry.
indagar *t* to investigate, inquire into.
▲ *Conjugation model* [7], *like* **llegar**.
indebido,-a 1 *adj* (*injusto*) unfair; (*injustificado*) unjustified; (*ilegal*) wrongful, unlawful, illegal: *el uso indebido de hábitos religiosos es castigado por la ley,* unlawful wearing of religious habits is punishable by law; *lo multaron por estacionamiento indebido,* he was fined for

illegal parking. **2** (*excesivo*) excessive; (*inapropiado*) inappropriate; (*impropio*) improper: *hizo uso indebido del claxon*, he made improper use of the horn.
indecencia 1 *f* indecency. **2** (*acción indecente*) scandal, outrage.
indecente 1 *adj* (*impúdico*) indecent; (*indecoroso*) improper. **2** (*indigno*) miserable; (*cochambroso*) filthy. **3** (*vil*) wretched.
indecible *adj* indescribable.
● *sufrir lo indecible*, to suffer unspeakably.
indecisión *f* indecision.
indeciso,-a 1 *adj* (*persona - por naturaleza*) indecisive; (*-puntualmente*) undecided. **2** (*asunto - no resuelto*) undecided; (*- que no resuelve*) inconclusive. – **3** *m,f* (*persona*) ditherer.
indeclinable 1 *adj* LING (*sin declinación*) indeclinable. **2** (*ineludible*) unavoidable.
indecoroso,-a *adj* indecorous.
indefectible *adj* inevitable, unavoidable.
indefectiblemente *adv* (*inevitablemente*) inevitably, unavoidably; (*invariablemente*) invariably.
indefendible *adj* indefensible.
indefensión *f* defencelessness.
indefenso,-a *adj* defenceless, helpless.
indefinible *adj* indefinable, vague.
indefinido,-a 1 *adj* (*periodo de tiempo*) indefinite; (*contrato*) open-ended. **2** (*impreciso*) indefinite, indefinable. **3** LING indefinite.
indeformable *adj* which will not lose its shape.
indeleble *adj* indelible.
indelicadeza 1 *f* lack of tact. **2** (*acto indelicado*) tactless act.
indemne *adj* (*persona*) unharmed, unhurt; (*cosa*) undamaged.
indemnidad *f* indemnity.
indemnización 1 *f* (*compensación*) compensation, indemnity. **2** (*acción*) indemnification.
■ *indemnización por daños y perjuicios*, damages *pl*. ‖ *indemnización por despido*, severance pay.
indemnizar *t* to compensate (**de/por**, for), indemnify (**de/por**, for).
▲ *Conjugation model* [4], *like realizar*.
indemostrable *adj* unprovable.
independencia *f* independence.
● *con independencia de*, independently of.
independentismo *m* independence movement.
independentista 1 *adj* (*movimiento*) independence. – **2** *mf* supporter of independence.
independiente 1 *adj* independent. **2** (*individualista*) self-sufficient: *el garaje tiene entrada independiente*, the garage has its own separate entrance.
independientemente 1 *adv* independently (**de**, of): *los dos sistemas de seguridad funcionan independientemente*, both security systems work independently. **2** (*sin tener en cuenta*) regardless (**de**, of), irrespective (**de**, of); (*aparte de*) leaving aside.
independizar 1 *t* to make independent. – **2** *independizarse*, *p* to become independent (**de**, of).
▲ *Conjugation model* [4], *like realizar*.
indescifrable *adj* indecipherable.
indescriptible *adj* indescribable.
indeseable *adj* undesirable.
indesmallable *adj* ladderproof.
indestructible *adj* indestructible.
indeterminable *adj* indeterminable.

indeterminación 1 *f* (*de una persona*) indecisiveness, irresolution. **2** (*de una fecha, un asunto*) unfixed nature: *la indeterminación de la cantidad no plantea problema alguno*, the fact that the quantity has not been fixed presents no problem.
indeterminado,-a 1 *adj* (*gen*) indeterminate; (*en tiempo, número*) indefinite. **2** (*impreciso*) vague. **3** LING (*artículo*) indefinite.
● *por tiempo indeterminado*, indefinitely.
indexación *f* indexing.
indexar *t* to index.
India *f* India.
indiano,-a 1 *adj* HIST (*de Las Indias*) from the Americas. – **2** *m,f* Spanish emigrant who returned to Spain after making his fortune in the Americas.
indicación 1 *f* (*indicio*) indication, mention: *no hay indicación del nombre del autor*, there is no indication as to the name of the author. **2** (*gesto, señal*) sign: *el policía nos hizo una indicación de que paráramos*, the policeman signalled us to stop; *no vimos la indicación de prohibido aparcar*, we didn't see the "No Parking" sign; *para ir a Córdoba se siguen las indicaciones Granada-Sevilla*, for Córdoba, you follow the signs for Granada and Seville. **3** (*instrucción*) instruction; (*recomendación*) recommendation; (*sugerencia*) suggestion.
● "*Indicaciones*", (*en prospecto médico*) "Recommended uses". ‖ *por indicación de*, (*instrucciones*) on the orders of; (*sugerencia*) at the suggestion of; (*recomendación*) on the recommendation of.
indicado,-a *adj* appropriate, suitable.
indicador,-ra 1 *adj* (*gen*) which indicates, indicating. – **2** *m* (*gen*) indicator; (*señal de tráfico*) sign, roadsign; (*con aguja, escala*) gauge: *el indicador de la gasolina no funciona*, the petrol gauge doesn't work.
■ *indicador económico*, economic indicator.
indicar 1 *t* to indicate, point out: *¿cuánto indica la aguja?*, what does the gauge read? **2** (*aconsejar*) to advise.
● *indicarle el camino a algn.*, to show sb. the way.
▲ *Conjugation model* [1], *like sacar*.
indicativo,-a 1 *adj* indicative. – **2** indicativo, *m* LING indicative.
índice 1 *m* (*gen*) index; (*indicio*) sign, indicator. **2** (*de un libro*) index, table of contents; (*catálogo*) catalogue. **3** (*dedo*) index finger, forefinger.
■ *índice de mortalidad*, death rate. ‖ *índice de natalidad*, birth rate. ‖ *índice de precios al consumo*, retail price index.
indicio 1 *m* (*señal*) sign. **2** (*resto*) trace.
índico,-a *adj* East Indian, Indian.
■ *el (océano) Índico*, the Indian Ocean.
indiferencia *f* indifference.
indiferenciación *f* lack of differentiation.
indiferente *adj* indifferent.
● *me es indiferente*, I don't care.
indígena 1 *adj* indigenous, native. – **2** *mf* native.
indigencia *f* extreme poverty, indigence.
indigenismo 1 *m* (*movimiento*) indigenous movement. **2** (*vocablo*) native language borrowing.
indigente 1 *adj* indigent, poverty-stricken. – **2** *mf* poor person: *los indigentes*, the needy.
indigerible 1 *adj* (*comida*) indigestible. **2** *fig* (*persona*) hard to stomach.
indigestarse 1 *p* (*comida*) to give indigestion: *se me ha indigestado la comida*, I haven't digested my food. **2** *fam fig* (*no agradar*) to be hard to stomach.

indigestión f indigestion.
indigesto,-a adj (alimento) hard to digest, indigestible.
● **estar indigesto,-a,** to have indigestion.
indignación f indignation.
indignado,-a adj indignant (**por,** at/about).
indignante adj outrageous.
indignar 1 t to infuriate. – **2 indignarse,** p to become indignant (**por,** at/about).
indignidad f indignity.
indigno,-a 1 adj unworthy (**de,** of). 2 (vil) low, contemptible.
indio,-a 1 adj Indian. – **2** m,f Indian.
● **en fila india,** in single file. ‖ **hablar como los indios,** to speak pidgin English (Spanish etc). ‖ **hacer el indio,** fam to muck about, act the goat, play the fool.
indirecta f hint, insinuation.
● **lanzar una indirecta / tirar una indirecta,** to drop a hint.
indirecto,-a adj indirect.
indiscernible adj indiscernible.
indisciplina f indiscipline, lack of discipline.
indisciplinado,-a 1 adj undisciplined. – **2** m,f undisciplined person.
indisciplinarse p to become undisciplined.
indiscreción f indiscretion.
indiscreto,-a 1 adj indiscreet. – **2** m,f indiscreet person.
indiscriminadamente adv indiscriminately.
indiscriminado,-a adj indiscriminate.
indiscutible adj indisputable, unquestionable.
indisolubilidad f indissolubility.
indisoluble adj (sustancia) indissoluble.
indispensable adj indispensable, essential.
indisponer 1 t (enemistar) to set (**contra,** against): los rumores lo han indispuesto contra mí, the rumours have set him against me. 2 MED to upset, make unwell. 3 (plan, proyecto) to upset, spoil. – **4 indisponerse,** p (enemistarse) to fall out (**con,** with). 5 (enfermarse) to be unwell.
▲ Conjugation model [78], like poner; pp indispuesto,-a.
indisposición 1 f MED indisposition. 2 (reticencia) indisposition, unwillingness.
indispuesto,-a 1 pp → **indisponer.** – **2** adj MED indisposed, unwell. 3 (enemistado) on bad terms (**con,** with).
indistinguible adj indistinguishable.
indistintamente 1 adv (por igual) equally: las normas se aplican a hombres y mujeres indistintamente, the rules apply equally to both men and women. 2 (con imprecisión) indistinctly.
indistinto,-a 1 adj (indiferente) immaterial: es indistinto, it makes no difference. 2 (difuso, impreciso) indistinct. 3 (indiferenciado) non-differentiated. 4 FIN (cuenta) joint.
individual 1 adj individual. – **2** (mantelito) individual, m table mat. – **3 individuales,** mpl DEP singles.
individualidad f individuality.
individualismo m individualism.
individualista 1 adj individualistic. – **2** mf individualist.
individualización f individualization.
individualizar 1 t (hacer individual) to individualize. 2 (diferenciar) to single out.
▲ Conjugation model [4], like realizar.
individualmente adv individually.
individuo,-a. 1 individuo, m person. – **2** individuo,-a, m,f pey (gen) character, individual; (hombre) bloke, guy, chap; (mujer) woman.

indivisible adj indivisible.
indiviso,-a adj undivided.
Indo el Indo, m the Indus.
indócil adj unmanageable.
indocumentado,-a 1 adj (sin documentación) without means of identification. 2 pey (ignorante) ignorant. – **3** m,f (sin documentación) person not carrying identity papers. 4 pey ignoramus.
indoeuropeo,-a 1 adj Indo-European. – **2** m,f (persona) Indo-European. – **3 indoeuropeo,** m (idioma) Indo-European.
índole 1 f (carácter) disposition, nature. 2 (tipo) type, kind.
indolencia f indolence.
indolente adj indolent.
indoloro,-a adj painless.
indomable 1 adj (animal) untamable. 2 fig (valor, heroísmo) indomitable; (carácter) unruly.
indomesticable adj untamable.
indomesticado,-a adj untamed.
indómito,-a adj indomitable.
Indonesia f Indonesia.
indonesio,-a 1 adj Indonesian. – **2** m,f Indonesian.
indubitable adj indubitable.
inducción f induction.
inducir 1 t (incitar) to induce. 2 (inferir) to infer, deduce. 3 ELEC to induce.
● **inducir a error,** to mislead.
▲ Conjugation model [46], like conducir.
inductivo,-a adj inductive.
inductor,-ra 1 adj (instigador) instigating. 2 FÍS inductive. – **3** m,f instigator. – **4 inductor,** m inductor.
indudable adj unquestionable.
● **es indudable que ...,** there is no doubt that ...
indudablemente adv doubtlessly, undoubtedly.
indulgencia f indulgence, leniency.
■ **indulgencia plenaria,** REL plenary indulgence.
indulgente adj indulgent, lenient.
indultar 1 t JUR to pardon. 2 (eximir) to exempt.
indulto m pardon, amnesty.
indumentaria f clothing, clothes pl.
industria 1 f (gen) industry. 2 (fábrica) factory.
industrial 1 adj industrial. – **2** mf industrialist, manufacturer.
industrialismo m industrialism.
industrialización f industrialization.
industrializar 1 t to industrialize. – **2 industrializarse,** p to become industrialized.
▲ Conjugation model [4], like realizar.
industrioso,-a adj industrious.
inédito,-a 1 adj (libro) unpublished. 2 (nuevo) new, unheard of. 3 (desconocido) unknown.
INEF abr EDUC (Instituto Nacional de Educación Física) physical education college.
inefable adj ineffable.
inefectivo,-a adj (irreal) unreal.
ineficacia 1 f (falta de eficacia) inefficiency. 2 (falta de efectividad) ineffectiveness.
ineficaz 1 adj (incompetente) inefficient. 2 (improductivo) ineffective.
ineficiencia f inefficiency.
ineficiente adj inefficient.
ineluctable adj inescapable.
ineludible adj unavoidable, inevitable.
INEM abr (Instituto Nacional de Empleo) ≈ Unemployment Benefit Office; (abreviatura) UBO.

inenarrable *adj* indescribable.
ineptitud *f* incompetence, ineptitude.
inepto,-a 1 *adj* (*persona*) incompetent, inept. – **2** *m,f* incompetent person: *es un inepto,* he's incompetent.
inequívoco,-a *adj* unmistakable.
inercia 1 *f* inertia. **2** (*pasividad*) apathy.
 ● **hacer algo por inercia,** to do sth. out of habit.
inerme 1 *adj* (*desarmado*) unarmed. **2** (*indefenso*) defenceless.
inerte 1 *adj* (*materia, gas*) inert. **2** (*cadáver*) lifeless.
inesperadamente *adv* unexpectedly.
inesperado,-a *adj* unexpected.
inestabilidad *f* instability, unsteadiness.
 ■ **inestabilidad atmosférica,** changeable weather.
inestable *adj* unstable, unsteady.
inestimable *adj* inestimable, invaluable.
inevitable *adj* inevitable, unavoidable.
inexactitud 1 *f* inaccuracy, incorrectness. **2** (*error*) error.
inexacto,-a *adj* inexact, inaccurate.
inexcusable 1 *adj* (*imperdonable*) inexcusable. **2** (*obligatorio*) unavoidable.
inexistencia *f* non-existence.
inexistente *adj* non-existent.
inexorabilidad *f* inexorability.
inexorable *adj* inexorable.
inexperiencia *f* inexperience.
inexperto,-a *adj* inexperienced.
inexplicable *adj* inexplicable.
inexplorado,-a *adj* unexplored.
inexpresable *adj* inexpressible.
inexpresivo,-a *adj* (*cara, persona*) inexpressive, expressionless.
inexpugnable 1 *adj* (*fortaleza*) unassailable, impregnable. **2** (*persona*) hard-headed, stubborn.
inextinguible *adj* inextinguishable.
inextricable *adj* inextricable.
infalibilidad *f* infallibility.
infalible *adj* infallible.
infamar *t* to defame.
infame 1 *adj* (*vil*) despicable, vile. **2** (*muy malo*) awful, terrible.
infamia *f* (*deshonra*) disgrace; (*hecho vil*) disgraceful thing to do, despicable thing to do.
infancia 1 *f* (*de una persona - gen*) childhood; (- *primera parte*) infancy. **2** (*de un proyecto etc*) infancy. **3** (*los niños*) children *pl*.
 ■ **primera infancia,** infancy.
infantado *m* title and territory of the *infante* or *infanta*.
infantazgo *m* → **infantado**.
infante,-a 1 *m,f* (*hombre*) infante, prince; (*mujer*) infanta, princess. – **2** infante, *m lit* (*niño*) infant. **3** (*soldado*) infantryman.
infantería *f* infantry.
 ■ **infantería ligera,** light infantry. ‖ **infantería de marina,** marines *pl*.
infanticida 1 *adj* infanticidal. – **2** *mf* infanticide, child-murderer.
infanticidio *m* infanticide.
infantil 1 *adj* (*literatura, juego*) children's; (*equipo*) junior; (*parálisis*) infantile. **2** (*aniñado*) childlike. **3** (*inmaduro*) childish.
infantilismo *m* infantilism.
infarto 1 *m* (*de miocardio*) heart attack. **2** (*de otros órganos*) infarction, infarct.

■ **infarto de miocardio,** heart attack.
infatigable *adj* indefatigable, tireless.
infausto,-a *adj lit* ill-starred.
infección *f* infection.
infeccioso,-a *adj* infectious.
infectar 1 *t* to infect (**de,** with). – **2** infectarse, *p* to become infected (**de,** with).
infecto,-a 1 *adj* (*gen*) infected. **2** *fig* (*olor*) putrid; (*lugar*) foul; (*mente*) filthy.
infecundidad *f* infertility.
infecundo,-a *adj* infertile.
infelicidad *f* unhappiness.
infeliz 1 *adj* (*desdichado*) unhappy. **2** (*ingenuo*) ingenuous. – **3** *mf* (*ingenuo*) poor soul.
inferencia *f* inference.
inferior 1 *adj* (*situado debajo*) lower. **2** (*cantidad*) less, lower: *un número inferior a diez,* a number below ten. **3** (*en calidad*) inferior (**a,** to). – **4** *mf* (*en rango*) subordinate; (*en calidad*) inferior.
inferioridad *f* inferiority.
 ● **estar en inferioridad de condiciones,** to be at a disadvantage.
inferir 1 *t* (*deducir*) to infer (**de,** from), conclude. **2** (*daño físico*) to inflict; (*daño moral*) to cause.
 ▲ *Conjugation model* [35], *like* hervir.
infernal 1 *adj* (*del infierno*) infernal. **2** *fam fig* hellish: *hace un calor infernal,* it's hellishly hot.
infernillo *m* → **infiernillo**.
infestar *t* (*invadir*) to infest: *los turistas han infestado la costa,* the coast is swarming with tourists; *el perro ha infestado la casa de pulgas,* the dog has filled the house with fleas.
infidelidad 1 *f* (*sexual*) infidelity, unfaithfulness. **2** (*de un amigo*) disloyalty. **3** (*inexactitud*) inaccuracy.
infiel 1 *adj* (*esposo*) unfaithful (**a/con/para,** to); (*amigo*) disloyal (**a,** to): *le fue infiel con su mejor amigo,* she was unfaithful to him with her best friend. **2** (*inexacto*) inaccurate. **3** REL unbelieving, infidel. – **4** *mf* REL unbeliever, non-believer, infidel.
infiernillo *m* portable stove.
infierno *m* hell.
 ● **estar en el quinto infierno,** to be in the back of beyond. ‖ **ir al infierno,** to go to hell. ‖ **mandar a algn. al infierno,** to tell sb. to get lost. ‖ **¡vete al infieno!,** go to hell!, get lost!
infijo *m* infix.
infiltración 1 *f* (*de un espía, una idea*) infiltration. **2** (*de un líquido*) seepage.
infiltrado,-a 1 *adj* infiltrated. – **2** *m,f* infiltrator.
infiltrar 1 *t* to infiltrate. – **2** infiltrarse, *p* to infiltrate (**en,** -): *el topo se infiltró en el servicio de inteligencia,* the mole infiltrated the intelligence service. **3** (*líquido*) to seep (**en,** into); (*luz*) to filter (**en,** into).
ínfimo,-a *adj* (*en calidad*) lowest, poorest; (*precio*) ridiculous: *es de ínfima calidad,* it's of the poorest quality.
infinidad 1 *f* (*infinito*) infinity. **2** (*gran cantidad*) great number, infinite number: *una infinidad de problemas,* an infinite number problems; *en infinidad de ocasiones,* on countless occasions.
infinitamente *adv* infinitely.
infinitesimal *adj* infinitesimal.
infinitivo,-a 1 *adj* infinitive. – **2** infinitivo, *m* infinitive.
infinito,-a 1 *adj* infinite. – **2** el infinito, *m* the infinite, infinity. – **3** infinito, *adv* (*muchísimo*) infinitely.
inflación *f* inflation.

inflacionario,-a *adj* inflationary.
inflacionismo *m* inflationism.
inflacionista 1 *adj* inflationist. 2 (*inflacionario*) inflationary.
inflamable *adj* inflammable.
inflamación 1 *f* MED inflammation. 2 (*combustión*) combustion, ignition.
inflamar 1 *t* (*encender*) to ignite, set on fire. 2 *fig* (*pasiones etc*) to excite, arouse, stir. 3 MED to inflame. – 4 inflamarse, *p* MED to become inflamed.
inflamatorio,-a *adj* inflammatory.
inflar 1 *t* (*balón*) to blow up, inflate. 2 *fig* (*hechos, noticias*) to exaggerate. 3 (*precios*) to inflate. – 4 inflarse, *p* to inflate one's opinion of os. 5 *fam* (*hartarse de comer*) to stuff os. (**de**, with): *nos inflamos de salchichas*, we stuffed ourselves with sausages; *este fin de semana me he inflado a leer*, I read non-stop all weekend.
inflexibilidad *f* inflexibility.
inflexible *adj* inflexible.
inflexión *f* inflection.
infligir *t* (*castigo*) to inflict, impose; (*pena*) to cause.
  ● infligir daños, to cause damage. ‖ infligir una derrota a, to defeat.
  ▲ *Conjugation model* [6], *like dirigir.*
inflorescencia *f* inflorescence.
influencia *f* influence.
  ● tener influencia sobre algn., to have an influence on sb. ‖ tener influencias, to be influential.
influenciable *adj* easily influenced, easily led.
influenciar *t* to influence.
  ▲ *Conjugation model* [12], *like cambiar.*
influir 1 *t* to influence. – 2 *i* to have influence.
  ● influir en algo, to have influence on sth.
  ▲ *Conjugation model* [62], *like huir.*
influjo *m* influence.
influyente *adj* influential.
información 1 *f* (*conocimiento*) information. 2 (*noticia*) piece of news; (*conjunto de noticias*) news. 3 (*oficina*) information department; (*mesa*) information desk. 4 (*en telefónica*) directory enquiries *pl*, US information.
  ■ información deportiva, (*en televisión*) sports news; (*en prensa*) sports pages *pl*. ‖ oficina de información, information bureau.
informador,-ra 1 *adj* informing. – 2 *m,f* (*que facilita información*) informant; (*de la policía*) informer. 3 (*periodista*) reporter.
informal 1 *adj* (*desenfadado*) informal. 2 (*persona*) unreliable.
informalidad 1 *f* (*desenfado*) informality. 2 (*en persona*) unreliability: *¡qué informalidad!, dijo que venía a las tres y todavía sin aparecer*, she's so unreliable!, she said she'd be here at three and she still hasn't shown up.
informalmente 1 *adv* (*con desenfado*) informally. 2 (*con irresponsabilidad*) unreliably.
informante 1 *adj* providing information, informing. – 2 *mf* (*en encuesta*) informant.
informar 1 *t* (*dar noticia*) to inform (**de**, about). – 2 *i* to inform (**de**, about), tell (**de**, about). – 3 informarse, *p* to find out (**de**, about).
informática *f* → **informático,-a**.
informático,-a 1 *adj* computer, computing. – 2 *m,f* computer expert. – 3 informática, *f* computer science, computing.
informativo,-a 1 *adj* (*ilustrativo*) informative: *una campaña con carácter informativo*, a public awareness campaign. 2 (*programa*) news. – 3 informativo, *m* news programme, news.

  ● abrir expediente informativo a algn., to investigate sb.
  ■ espacio informativo, news programme. ‖ folleto informativo, information leaflet. ‖ programa informativo, news programme.
informatización *f* computerization.
informatizar *t* to computerize.
  ▲ *Conjugation model* [4], *like realizar.*
informe 1 *adj* (*sin forma*) shapeless, formless. – 2 *m* report. – 3 informes, *mpl* references.
  ● dar informes sobre algn., (*referencias*) to provide references for sb.; (*datos*) to give information about sb.
infortunado,-a *adj* unfortunate.
infortunio *f* misfortune.
infracción *f* infraction, infringement.
  ■ infracción de tráfico, driving offence.
infractor,-ra 1 *adj* offending. – 2 *m,f* offender.
infraestructura 1 *f* (*de una organización*) infrastructure: *infraestructura hotelera*, hotel infrastructure; *la infraestructura sanitaria de la zona es excelente*, health services in the area are excellent. 2 (*de una edificación*) foundations *pl*.
in fraganti *loc adv* in the act, red-handed.
  ● pillar a algn. in fraganti, *fam* to catch sb. red-handed.
infrahumano,-a *adj* subhuman.
infranqueable 1 *adj* impassable. 2 *fig* insurmountable.
infrarrojo,-a *adj* infrared.
infrautilizar *t* to underuse.
infravalorar *t* to underestimate.
infrecuente *adj* infrequent.
infringir *t* (*gen*) to infringe; (*ley*) to break.
  ▲ *Conjugation model* [6], *like dirigir.*
infructuosamente *adv* unsuccessfully.
infructuoso,-a *adj* fruitless, unsuccessful.
ínfulas *fpl* pretensions.
  ● darse ínfulas, to put on airs.
infumable *adj* (*tabaco*) unsmokable.
infundado,-a *adj* unfounded, groundless.
infundio *m* untruth: *¡eso no son más que infundios!*, that is nothing but a pack of lies!
infundir *t* (*respeto*) to command; (*miedo*) to fill with; (*valor*) to instil; (*deseo*) to infuse with.
  ▲ *pp infundido,-a or infuso,-a.*
infusión *f* (*acción*) infusion; (*bebida*) herbal tea, infusion: *infusión de manzanilla/menta*, camomile/mint tea.
infuso,-a 1 *pp* → **infundir**. – 2 *adj* inspired.
  ● saber algo por ciencia infusa, *fam* to intuit sth.
ingeniar 1 *t* to devise. – 2 ingeniárselas, *p* to manage, find a way, contrive: *habrá que ingeniárselas para que nos dejen pasar gratis*, we'll have to find some way of getting in free; *se las ingenió para que le subieran el sueldo*, he wangled a salary increase.
  ▲ *Conjugation model* [12], *like cambiar.*
ingeniería *f* engineering.
ingeniero,-a *m,f* engineer.
  ■ ingeniero,-a agrónomo, agronomist. ‖ ingeniero,-a de caminos, canales y puertos, civil engineer. ‖ ingeniero,-a forestal, forestry expert. ‖ ingeniero,-a industrial, industrial engineer. ‖ ingeniero,-a de minas, mining engineer. ‖ ingeniero,-a técnico, technical engineer.
ingenio 1 *m* (*talento*) talent; (*chispa*) wit. 2 (*habilidad*) ingenuity. 3 (*individuo*) genius. 4 (*aparato*) device.
  ● aguzar el ingenio, to sharpen one's wits.
ingenioso,-a *adj* (*inteligente*) ingenious, clever; (*con chispa*) witty.

ingente *adj* enormous.
ingenuidad *f* ingenuousness, naivety.
ingenuo,-a 1 *adj* naive, ingenuous. – 2 *m,f* naive person.
ingerir *t* (*alimentos*) to eat; (*bebida*) to drink.
● **ingerir alimentos,** to eat. ‖ **ingerir bebidas alcohólicas,** to drink alcohol.
▲ Conjugation model |35|, *like hervir.*
ingesta *f* → **ingestión.**
ingestión *f* ingestion, consumption, swallowing: *en caso de ingestión accidental ...,* if swallowed by accident ...; *su muerte fue provocada por la ingestión de setas venenosas,* her death was caused by eating poisonous toadstools.
Inglaterra *f* England.
ingle *f* groin.
inglés,-esa 1 *adj* English. – 2 *m,f* (*persona*) English person; (*hombre*) Englishman; (*mujer*) Englishwoman. – 3 inglés, *m* (*idioma*) English.
● **los ingleses,** the English.
ingobernable 1 *adj* (*nación*) ungovernable. 2 (*nave*) unsteerable.
ingratitud *f* ingratitude, ungratefulness.
ingrato,-a 1 *adj* (*persona*) ungrateful. 2 (*trabajo, tarea*) thankless. 3 (*tiempo*) unpleasant.
ingravidez *f* weightlessness.
ingrávido,-a *adj* weightless.
ingrediente *m* ingredient.
ingresar 1 *t* (*dinero*) to pay in, deposit: *quiero ingresar este dinero en mi cuenta,* I would like to pay this money into my account. – 2 **ingresar en,** *i* (*entrar*) to join. 3 (*hospital*) to be admitted to.
● **ingresar cadáver,** to be dead on arrival.
ingreso 1 *m* (*en club, ejército*) joining; (*en hospital*) admission; (*en prisión*) entrance; (*en universidad*) entrance: *el juez ordenó su ingreso en prisión,* the judge ordered that he be remanded in custody. 2 (*entrada*) entry. 3 FIN deposit: *quiero hacer un ingreso de un millón de pesetas,* I want to make a deposit of a million pesetas. – 4 **ingresos,** *mpl* (*sueldo, renta*) income *sing;* (*beneficios*) revenue *sing.*
inguinal *adj* inguinal.
inhábil 1 *adj* (*poco habilidoso*) unskilful (US unskillful). 2 (*día*) non-working.
inhabilitación *f* JUR disqualification.
inhabilitar *t* JUR to disqualify: *lo han inhabilitado para el ejercicio de la medicina,* he has been debarred from practising medicine, he has been struck off as a doctor.
inhabitable *adj* uninhabitable.
inhabitado,-a *adj* uninhabited.
inhalación *f* inhalation.
inhalador *m* inhaler.
inhalar *t* to inhale, breathe in.
inherente *adj* inherent (**a,** in).
inhibición *f* inhibition.
inhibir 1 *t* (*reprimir*) to inhibit. 2 MED to inhibit. – 3 **inhibirse,** *p* (*reprimirse*) to be inhibited. 4 (*abstenerse*) to refrain (**de,** from); (*negarse*) to refuse (**de,** to). 5 JUR to disqualify os.: *el juez se inhibió a favor del tribunal supremo,* the judge referred the case to the supreme court.
● **inhibirse de una decisión,** to avoid making a decision. ‖ **inhibirse de un problema,** to refuse to acknowledge a problem.
inhóspito,-a *adj* inhospitable.
inhumación *f* burial.

inhumano,-a 1 *adj* (*persona*) inhuman, cruel. 2 (*dolor, sufrimiento*) inhuman.
inhumar *t* to bury.
INI *abr* (*Instituto Nacional de Industria*) ≈ National Enterprise Board; (*abreviatura*) NEB.
iniciación 1 *f* (*comienzo*) start, beginning. 2 (*de una persona*) initiation, introduction (**a,** to).
iniciado,-a 1 *adj* (*persona*) initiated. – 2 *m,f* initiate.
iniciador,-ra 1 *adj* initiatory. – 2 *m,f* initiator.
inicial 1 *adj* initial. – 2 *f* initial.
iniciar 1 *t* (*empezar*) to start, begin. 2 (*introducir*) to initiate (**en,** in). – 3 **iniciarse,** *p* (*empezar*) to start, begin.
● **iniciarse en,** to start to learn about.
▲ Conjugation model |12|, *like cambiar.*
iniciativa *f* initiative.
● **por propia iniciativa,** on one's own initiative. ‖ **tomar la iniciativa,** to take the initiative.
■ **iniciativa privada,** private enterprise.
inicio *m* beginning, start.
inicuo,-a *adj* iniquitous.
inigualable *adj* unrivalled.
inigualado,-a *adj* unequalled.
inimaginable *adj* unimaginable.
inimitable *adj* inimitable.
ininteligible *adj* unintelligible.
ininterrumpido,-a *adj* uninterrupted.
iniquidad *f* iniquity.
injerencia *f* interference.
injerirse *p* to interfere (**en,** in).
injertar *t* to graft.
injerto *m* graft.
injuria 1 *f* insult, affront. 2 JUR slander.
injuriar 1 *t* (*insultar*) to insult. 2 JUR to slander.
▲ Conjugation model |12|, *like cambiar.*
injurioso,-a 1 *adj* offensive. 2 JUR slanderous.
injustamente *adv* unjustly, unfairly.
injusticia *f* injustice, unfairness.
injustificado,-a *adj* unjustified.
injusto,-a *adj* unfair, unjust.
● **ser injusto,-a con algn.,** to do sb. an injustice.
inmaculado,-a *adj* immaculate.
■ **la Inmaculada,** the Virgin Mary.
inmadurez *f* immaturity.
inmaduro,-a *adj* immature.
inmanencia *f* immanency.
inmanente *adj* immanent.
inmarcesible *adj* lit unfading.
inmediaciones *fpl* (*de una zona*) surrounding area *sing;* (*de una casa*) vicinity *sing: las inmediaciones de Nápoles,* the area surrounding Naples; *registraron las inmediaciones de la zona,* they searched the immediate area.
inmediatamente *adv* immediately.
inmediatez *f* immediacy, immediateness.
inmediato,-a 1 *adj* (*poco después*) immediate. 2 (*contiguo*) next (**a,** to), adjoining (**a,** -).
● **de inmediato,** immediately.
inmejorable *adj* (*gen*) unbeatable, unsurpassable; (*calidad*) excellent.
inmemorial *adj* immemorial.
● **desde tiempos inmemoriales,** from time immemorial.
inmensamente *adv* immensely.
inmensidad 1 *f* immensity: *la inmensidad del océano,* the vast expanse of the ocean. 2 (*gran cantidad*) great number.

inmenso,-a *adj* immense, vast.
inmerecido,-a *adj* undeserved.
inmersión *f* (*gen*) immersion; (*de un buceador, submarino*) dive.
inmerso,-a *adj* immersed (**en**, in).
inmigración *f* immigration.
inmigrante 1 *adj* immigrant. **– 2** *mf* immigrant.
inmigrar *i* to immigrate.
inminencia *f* imminence.
inminente *adj* imminent.
inmiscuirse *p* to interfere, meddle (**en**, in).
▲ *Conjugation model* [62], *like huir.*
inmobiliario,-a 1 *adj* property, US real estate. **– 2** (*agencia*) **inmobiliaria,** *f* (*dedicada a la compraventa*) estate agency, US real estate company; (*dedicada a la construcción*) construction company.
■ **agente de la propiedad inmobiliaria,** estate agent, US realtor. ‖ **mercado inmobiliario,** property market.
inmoderado,-a *adj* immoderate.
inmodestia *f* arrogance, immodesty, lack of modesty.
inmolación *f* immolation.
inmolar *t* to immolate, sacrifice.
inmoral *adj* immoral.
inmoralidad *f* immorality.
inmortal 1 *adj* immortal. **– 2** *mf* immortal.
inmortalidad *f* immortality.
inmortalizar *t* to immortalize.
▲ *Conjugation model* [4], *like realizar.*
inmotivado,-a 1 *adj* (*sin motivo*) uncalled for. **2** (*sin motivación*) unmotivated.
inmóvil 1 *adj* still, motionless. **2** *fig* (*constante*) determined, steadfast.
● **estar inmóvil,** to stand still. ‖ **quedarse inmóvil,** to remain still, keep still.
inmovilidad *f* immobility.
inmovilismo *m* immobilism.
inmovilista 1 *adj* reactionary. **– 2** *mf* reactionary.
inmovilización *f* immobilization.
inmovilizar *t* to immobilize.
▲ *Conjugation model* [4], *like realizar.*
inmueble 1 *m* building. **– 2 bienes inmuebles,** *adj* real estate *sing.*
inmundicia 1 *f* (*suciedad*) dirt. **2** (*basura*) rubbish.
inmundo,-a 1 *adj* (*sucio*) dirty, filthy; (*asqueroso*) disgusting: *es un lugar inmundo,* it's a pigsty. **2** *fig* dirty.
inmune 1 *adj* MED immune (**a**, to). **2** (*exento*) exempt (**de**, from).
inmunidad *f* immunity.
■ **inmunidad diplomática,** diplomatic immunity. ‖ **inmunidad parlamentaria,** parliamentary immunity.
inmunitario,-a *adj* immnune.
inmunizar *t* to immunize.
▲ *Conjugation model* [4], *like realizar.*
inmunodeficiente 1 *adj* immunodeficient. **– 2** *mf* immnunodeficient.
inmunodeficiencia *f* immunodeficiency.
inmunodepresor,-ra *adj* immunodepressant.
inmunología *f* immunology.
inmunoterapia *f* immunotherapy.
inmutabilidad *f* immutability.
inmutable *adj* unchangeable, immutable.
inmutar 1 *t* to affect. **– 2 inmutarse,** *p* to react.
● **no inmutarse,** not to bat an eyelid. ‖ **sin inmutarse,** without batting an eyelid.

innato,-a *adj* innate, inborn.
innecesario,-a *adj* unnecessary.
innegable *adj* undeniable.
innoble *adj* ignoble.
innombrable *adj* unmentionable.
innominado,-a *adj* nameless.
innovación *f* innovation.
innovador,-ra 1 *adj* innovatory. **– 2** *m,f* innovator.
innovar *i* to innovate.
innumerable *adj* innumerable, countless.
inobservancia *f* non-observance (**de**, of).
inocencia 1 *f* innocence. **2** (*ingenuidad*) naivety, innocence.
inocentada *f* practical joke.
● **gastarle la inocentada a algn.,** to play a practical joke on sb., play a trick on sb.
inocente 1 *adj* innocent. **2** (*ingenuo*) naive, innocent. **– 3** *mf* innocent person. **4** naive person, innocent person.
● **hacerse el inocente / la inocente,** to play the innocent.
■ **día de los Inocentes,** 28th December, (≈ *April Fools' Day*). ‖ **los Santos Inocentes,** the Holy Innocents.
inocentemente *adv* innocently.
inocentón,-ona 1 *adj fam* naive. **– 2** *m,f fam* naive person, gullible person.
inocuidad *f* harmlessness, innocuousness.
inoculación *f* inoculation.
inocular *t* to inoculate.
inocuo,-a *adj* innocuous, harmless.
inodoro,-a 1 *adj* odourless. **– 2 inodoro,** *m* toilet.
inofensivo,-a *adj* harmless, inoffensive.
inolvidable *adj* unforgettable.
inoperancia *f* ineffectiveness.
inoperante *adj* ineffective, inoperative.
inopia estar en la inopia, *loc fam* (*distraído*) to have one's head in the clouds; (*ignorante*) to be in the dark.
inopinado,-a *adj* unexpected.
inoportuno,-a *adj* (*visita etc*) inopportune, untimely; (*comentario etc*) inopportune, ill-timed.
inorgánico,-a *adj* inorganic.
inoxidable *adj* rustproof.
inquebrantable *adj* (*promesa*) unbreakable; (*fe*) unshakeable, unwavering; (*fidelidad*) unswerving.
inquietante *adj* disturbing.
inquietar 1 *t* to worry. **– 2 inquietarse,** *p* to worry (**por**, about).
inquieto,-a 1 *adj* (*agitado*) restless. **2** (*preocupado*) worried, anxious. **3** (*interesado*) eager, interested.
inquietud 1 *f* (*agitación*) restlessness. **2** (*preocupación*) worry, anxiety. **3** (*interés*) interest.
● **tener inquietudes,** to have many interests.
inquilino,-a *m,f* tenant.
inquina *f* animosity, antipathy.
● **tener inquina a algn.,** to feel animosity towards sb.
inquirir *t* to inquire, investigate.
▲ *Conjugation model* [30], *like adquirir.*
inquisición 1 *f* inquiry. **2 la (Santa) Inquisición,** HIST the Inquisition.
inquisidor,-ra 1 *adj* inquisitive, inquiring. **– 2 inquisidor,** *m* inquisitor.
inquisitivo,-a *adj* inquisitive.
inri para más inri, *loc fam* to make things even worse, to cap it all, on top of that.
INRI *abr* (*Iesus Nazarenus Rex Iudaeorum*) INRI.

insaciable *adj* insatiable.

insalubre *adj* insalubrious, unhealthy.

insalubridad *f* insalubrity.

Insalud *abr* (*Instituto Nacional de la Salud*) Spanish national health service.

insano,-a 1 *adj* (*no sano*) unhealthy. 2 (*loco*) insane.

insatisfacción *f* dissatisfaction.

insatisfecho,-a *adj* dissatisfied, unsatisfied.

inscribir 1 *t* (*grabar*) to inscribe. 2 (*apuntar*) to register (*en un concurso*) to enter; (*en un curso*) to enrol (us enroll): ¿con qué fecha lo inscribieron en el Registro Civil?, on what date was his birth registered? – 3 **inscribirse**, *p* (*gen*) to register; (*para un concurso*) to enter; (*para un curso*) to enrol (us enroll): *me inscribí para el concurso*, I entered the competition.
  ▲ *pp* **inscrito,-a**.

inscripción 1 *f* (*grabado*) inscription. 2 (*registro*) registration; (*en un concurso*) entry; (*en un curso*) enrolment (us enrollment).

inscrito,-a *pp* → **inscribir**.

insecticida 1 *adj* insecticidal. – 2 *m* insecticide.

insectívoro,-a 1 *adj* insectivorous. – 2 **insectívoro,** *m* insectivore.

insecto *m* insect.

inseguridad 1 *f* (*falta de confianza*) insecurity. 2 (*duda*) uncertainty. 3 (*peligro*) lack of safety.
  ■ **inseguridad ciudadana,** lack of safety on the streets: *hay que solucionar el problema de la inseguridad ciudadana,* we have to make our streets safer.

inseguro,-a 1 *adj* (*sin confianza*) insecure. 2 (*que duda*) uncertain. 3 (*peligroso*) unsafe.

inseminación *f* insemination.
  ■ **inseminación artificial,** artificial insemination.

inseminar *t* to inseminate.

insensatez *f* foolishness.
  ● **decir insensateces,** to talk nonsense. ‖ **hacer insensateces,** to be foolish.

insensato,-a 1 *adj* foolish. – 2 *m,f* fool.

insensibilidad *f* insensitivity.

insensibilizar 1 *t* MED to desensitize. 2 to make insensitive.

insensible 1 *adj* insensitive (**a**, to). 2 MED numb, without feeling.
  ● **insensible al dolor,** insensitive to pain.

inseparable *adj* inseparable.

insepulto,-a *adj* unburied.

inserción *f* insertion.

Inserso *abr* (*Instituto Nacional de Servicios Sociales*) national institute for social services.

insertar *t* to insert (**en**, into).

inserto,-a *adj* inserted.

inservible *adj* useless.

insidia 1 *f* (*palabra*) malicious remark; (*acto*) act of malice, malicious deed: *fue víctima de las insidias de sus compañeros,* he was a victim of his colleagues' malicious talk. 2 (*maldad*) maliciousness.

insidioso,-a *adj* malicious.

insigne *adj* distinguished, eminent.

insignia 1 *f* (*distintivo*) badge. 2 (*bandera*) flag; (*estandarte*) banner.

insignificancia 1 *f* (*cualidad*) insignificance. 2 (*pequeñez*) trifle.

insignificante *adj* insignificant.

insinuación 1 *f* (*indicación*) insinuation, hint. 2 *fam* (*amorosa*) overture.

● **hacerle insinuaciones a algn.,** (*insinuarse*) to make a pass at sb.

insinuante 1 *adj* (*gen*) insinuating. 2 (*provocativo*) suggestive.

insinuar 1 *t* to insinuate, hint: *¿qué insinúas?,* what are you insinuating?; *me insinuó que no tenía intención de contratarme,* he hinted that he had no intention of taking me on. – 2 **insinuarse**, *p* (*amorosamente*) to a pass (**a**, at).
  ▲ *Conjugation model* [11], *like* **actuar**.

insipidez *f* insipidity.

insípido,-a 1 *adj* (*comida*) tasteless, insipid. 2 *fig* insipid.

insistencia *f* (*acción*) insistence, persistence; (*cualidad*) insistency: *perdóneme la insistencia, pero ...,* forgive me for being so insistent but ...; *llamé a su puerta con insistencia,* I knocked at her door repeatedly.

insistente *adj* insistent.

insistir 1 *i* to insist (**en**, on): *insistió en que acudiera a su fiesta,* he insisted that I should go to his party; *no insistas,* stop going on about it. 2 (*enfatizar*) to stress (**en**, -), emphasize (**en**, -).

in situ *loc adv* in situ.

insobornable *adj* incorruptible.

insociable *adj* unsociable.

insolación 1 *f* MED sunstroke. 2 (*en meteorología*) sunshine, sunlight.

insolencia 1 *f* (*atrevimiento*) insolence. 2 (*palabra*) cheeky remark; (*acción*) cheeky thing to do.
  ● **decir insolencias,** to be insolent, be cheeky.

insolente 1 *adj* (*descarado*) insolent. 2 (*soberbio*) haughty. – 3 *m,f* (*descarado*) insolent person. 4 (*soberbio*) haughty person.

insolidaridad *f* lack of solidarity.

insolidario,-a *adj* unsupportive, selfish.

insólito,-a *adj* extremely unusual.

insoluble *adj* insoluble.

insolvencia *f* insolvency.

insolvente *adj* insolvent.
  ● **declararse insolvente,** to declare os. bankrupt.

insomne 1 *adj* sleepless: *una noche insomne,* a sleepless night; *hizo un estudio de las personas insomnes,* she carried out a study on insomniacs. – 2 *mf* insomniac.

insomnio *m* insomnia.
  ● **tener insomnio,** to suffer from insomnia.
  ■ **noches de insomnio,** sleepless nights.

insondable *adj* unfathomable.

insonorización *f* soundproofing.

insonorizado,-a *adj* soundproof.

insonorizar *t* to soundproof.
  ▲ *Conjugation model* [4], *like* **realizar**.

insoportable *adj* unbearable.

insoslayable *adj* unavoidable.

insospechable 1 *adj* (*inimaginable*) unforeseeable. 2 (*sorprendente*) amazing, outlandish.

insospechado,-a 1 *adj* (*no sospechado*) unsuspected. 2 (*inesperado*) unexpected.

insostenible *adj* untenable.

inspección *f* (*gen*) examination, inspection; (*policial*) search.
  ■ **inspección sanitaria,** health inspection. ‖ **inspección tributaria,** tax inspection.

inspeccionar *t* (*gen*) to inspect; (*zona, lugar del crimen*) to search.

inspector,-ra *m,f* inspector.
  ■ **inspector,-ra de hacienda,** tax inspector. ‖ **inspec-**

tor,-ra de policía, police inspector. ‖ **inspector,-ra de trabajo,** factory inspector. ‖ **inspector,-ra de sanidad,** health inspector. ‖ **inspector,-ra jefe,** chief inspector.

inspiración 1 *f* inspiration. **2** (*inhalación*) inhalation.

inspirado,-a *adj* inspired.

inspirar 1 *t* (*aspirar*) to inhale, breathe in. **2** (*infundir*) to inspire. – **3 inspirarse,** *p* to be inspired (**en,** by).

INSS *abr* (*Instituto Nacional de la Seguridad Social*) *national institute for social security.*

instalación 1 *f* (*de un aparato*) installation: *¿quién le hizo la instalación del gas?* who did the gas installation?, who installed the gas? **2** (*de personas*) settling in; (*de empresas*) establishment, setting up: *ha aumentado la instalación en nuestro suelo de empresas extranjeras,* more foreign companies have set up here. – **3 instalaciones,** *fpl* (*de un servicio*) facilities *pl*: *el nuevo complejo deportivo tiene unas instalaciones fabulosas,* the new sports complex has fabulous facilities. ■ **instalación deportiva,** sports centre. ‖ **instalación eléctrica,** electrical system, electrics *pl*.

instalador,-ra *m,f* installer, fitter.

instalar 1 *t* (*colocar*) to install: *aún no han instalado la alarma,* they haven't installed the alarm yet. **2** (*equipar*) to fit out. **3** (*acomodar*) to put, put up, house: *nos instalaron en el ala derecha de la mansión,* they put us in the right wing of the mansion. – **4 instalarse,** *p* (*persona*) to settle; (*empresa*) to set up.

instancia 1 *f* (*petición*) request; (*solicitud*) form. **2** JUR instance. ● **a instancia de / a instancias de,** at the request of. ‖ **en última instancia,** as a last resort.

instantánea *f →* **instantáneo,-a**.

instantáneo,-a 1 *adj* (*inmediato*) instantaneous, immediate. **2** (*momentáneo*) brief, fleeting. – **3 instantánea,** *f* (*foto*) snapshot. ■ **café instantáneo,** instant coffee. ‖ **muerte instantánea,** instantaneous death.

instante *m* moment, instant. ● **a cada instante,** all the time. ‖ **al instante,** instantly, immediately. ‖ **en un instante,** in a minute.

instar *i* (*insistir*) to press, urge. ● **instar a algn. a que haga algo,** to urge sb. to do sth.

instauración *f* establishment.

instaurar *t* to establish.

instigador,-ra 1 *adj* instigating. – **2** *m,f* instigator.

instigar *t* (*a una persona*) to instigate; (*a una acción*) to incite: *la rebelión fue instigada por los nobles,* the uprising was instigated by the nobles; *fue su amante quien la instigó a cometer el asesinato,* it was her lover who incited her to commit the murder.
▲ *Conjugation model* [7], *like* **llegar**.

instintivo,-a *adj* instinctive.

instinto *m* instinct. ● **por instinto,** instinctively.

institución 1 *f* (*organismo*) institution. **2** (*creación*) establishment, institution; (*introducción*) introduction. ● **ser una institución,** to be an institution. ■ **institución benéfica,** charitable organization.

institucional *adj* institutional.

institucionalizar *t* to institutionalize.

institucionalización *f* institutionalization.

instituir 1 *t* (*crear*) to institute, establish. **2** (*nombrar*) to appoint.
▲ *Conjugation model* [62], *like* **huir**.

instituto 1 *m* (*asociación*) institute. **2** EDUC state secondary school, US high school. ■ **instituto de bachillerato,** state secondary school, US high school. ‖ **instituto de belleza,** beauty salon. ‖ **instituto de enseñanza media,** state secondary school, US high school. ‖ **instituto de formación profesional,** ≈ technical college. ‖ **Instituto Nacional de la Vivienda,** ≈ Ministry of Housing.

institutriz *f* governess.

instrucción 1 *f* (*enseñanza*) instruction; (*cultura*) education: *una persona de vasta instrucción,* a highly educated person. **2** MIL military training. **3** JUR (*de un expediente*) preliminary investigation: *¿quién llevó a cabo la instrucción del sumario?,* who carried out the preliminary investigation into the case? **4** (*orden*) instruction: *tengo instrucciones de no dejar entrar a nadie,* I have instructions not to let anyone in. – **5 instrucciones,** *fpl* (*indicaciones*) instructions: *siga las instrucciones de montaje,* follow the assembly instructions. ■ **instrucción militar,** military training. ‖ **juez,-za de instrucción,** examining magistrate. ‖ **manual de instrucciones,** instruction manual.

instructivo,-a *adj* (*conferencia*) instructive; (*juguete*) educational.

instructor,-ra 1 *adj* (*gen*) instructing. **2** JUR (*juez*) examining, investigating. – **3** *m,f* instructor. ■ **instructor,-ra de vuelo,** flying instructor. ‖ **juez,-za instructor,-ra,** examining magistrate.

instruido,-a *adj* well-educated.

instruir 1 *t* (*enseñar*) to instruct. **2** MIL to train. **3** JUR to examine, investigate: *el juez Murriñas instruyó la causa,* judge Murriñas investigated the case.
▲ *Conjugation model* [62], *like* **huir**.

instrumentación *f* instrumentation.

instrumental 1 *adj* (*música*) instrumental. – **2** *m* instruments *pl*, instrumentation. ■ **instrumental quirúrgico,** surgical instruments *pl*.

instrumentar *t* (*gen*) to arrange; (*para orquesta*) to orchestrate.

instrumentista 1 *mf* (*músico*) instrumentalist. **2** (*fabricante*) instrument maker.

instrumento *m* instrument. ■ **instrumento de cuerda,** stringed instrument. ‖ **instrumento de percusión,** percussion instrument. ‖ **instrumento de viento,** wind instrument.

insubordinación *f* insubordination.

insubordinado,-a 1 *adj* insubordinate. – **2** *m,f* insubordinate person.

insubordinar 1 *t* to stir up. – **2 insubordinarse,** *p* to rebel.

insubstancial *adj* insubstantial.

insubstancialidad *f* insubstantiality.

insubstituible *adj* irreplaceable.

insuficiencia 1 *f* (*escasez*) shortage, insuffiency. **2** MED failure, insufficiency. ■ **insuficiencia cardiaca,** heart failure.

insuficiente 1 *adj* insufficient. – **2** *m* EDUC fail: *saqué un insuficiente en inglés,* I failed the English exam.

insufrible *adj* insufferable.

ínsula *f* LIT island.

insular 1 *adj* insular. – **2** *mf* islander.

insulina *f* insuline.

insulso,-a 1 *adj* (*comida*) insipid, tasteless. **2** (*persona*) dull.

insultante *adj* insulting.

insultar *t* to insult.

insulto *m* insult.

insumisión l *f* (*gen*) rebelliousness. **2** MIL refusal to do military service.

insumiso,-a l *adj* rebellious. – **2** *m,f* MIL *person who refuses to do military service or community service in lieu.*

insuperable *adj* (*calidad, capacidad*) unbeatable; (*obstáculo, miedo, complejo*) unsurmountable, insuperable; (*maestro*) unparalelled, unrivalled.

insurgente l *adj* insurgent. – **2** *mf* insurgent.

insurrección *f* insurrection, uprising.

insurrecto,-a l *adj* insurgent. – **2** *m,f* insurgent.

insustancial *adj* → **insubstancial**.

insustancialidad *f* → **insubstancialidad**.

insustituible *adj* → **insubstituible**.

intachable *adj* irreproachable.

intacto,-a *adj* intact.

intangible *adj* intangible.

integración *f* integration.

integral l *adj* (*intrínseco*) integral; (*completo*) full. **2** (*pan, pasta*) wholemeal; (*arroz*) brown. – **3** *f* MAT integral.

integralmente *adv* completely.

íntegramente *adv* entirely.

integrante l *adj* integral. – **2** *mf* member: *han apresado a un tercer integrante de la banda,* they've captured a third member of the gang.

■ **parte integrante,** integral part.

integrar l *t* (*formar*) to make up: *¿qué países integran las Naciones Unidas?,* which countries make up the United Nations? **2** (*ayudar a la integración*) to integrate, fit in: *es un grupo difícil de integrar en nuestra sociedad,* it's a group which is to integrate into our society. – **3** integrarse, *p* to integrate.

● **integrarse en un país,** to become integrated into a country.

integridad *f* integrity.

integrismo *m* (*gen*) reaction; (*religioso*) fundamentalism.

integrista l *adj* (*gen*) reactionary; (*religioso*) fundamentalist. – **2** *mf* (*gen*) reactionary; (*en religión*) fundamentalist.

íntegro,-a l *adj* (*completo*) whole, entire; (*versión*) unabridged. **2** (*honrado*) honest, upright.

intelecto *m* intellect.

intelectual l *adj* intellectual. – **2** *mf* intellectual.

intelectualidad *f* intellectuals *pl*, intelligentsia.

intelectualizar *t* to intellectualize.

inteligencia *f* intelligence.

■ **inteligencia artificial,** artificial intelligence.

inteligente l *adj* intelligent. **2** (*edificio*) smart.

inteligibilidad *f* intelligibility.

inteligible *adj* intelligible.

intemperante *adj* intolerant.

intemperie *f* bad weather.

● **a la intemperie,** in the open (air), outdoors.

intempestivo,-a *adj* untimely, inopportune.

intemporal *adj* timeless.

intención l *f* (*propósito*) intention. **2** (*malicia*) maliciousness.

● **con doble intención,** with double meaning. ‖ **con intención,** deliberately, intentionally. ‖ **con intención de,** in order to, with the intention of. ‖ **con la mejor intención,** with the best of intentions. ‖ **con mala intención,** deliberately, intentionally. ‖ **con segunda intención,** with double meaning. ‖ **tener buenas intenciones,** to mean well, be well-intentioned. ‖ **tener intención de,** to intend to.

■ **buena intención,** good will. ‖ **mala intención,** ill will, malice.

intencionadamente *adv* intentionally, deliberately.

intencionado,-a *adj* deliberate, intentional.

■ **bien intencionado,-a,** (*acción*) well-meant; (*persona*) well-meaning. ‖ **mal intencionado,-a,** (*acción*) ill-meant; (*persona*) malicious.

intencional *adj* intentional.

intencionalidad *f* intent, intention.

intendencia *f* MIL (*cuerpo*) ≈ service corps, US quartermaster corps.

intendente l *m* supervisor. **2** MIL quartermaster general.

intensidad l *f* (*gen*) intensity: *está nevando con mucha intensidad,* it's snowing heavily. **2** (*del viento*) force; (*de un ruido*) loudness, high volume. **3** (*de una enfermedad*) severity; (*del dolor*) acuteness. **4** (*de la luz, del color*) brightness, intensity; (*del amor, de la fe*) strength.

intensificación *f* intensification.

intensificar *t* to intensify.

▲ *Conjugation model* [1], *like* ***sacar***.

intensivo,-a *adj* intensive.

■ **curso intensivo,** crash course.

intenso,-a l *adj* (*gen*) intense. **2** (*dolor*) acute. **3** (*luz, color*) bright, intense. **4** (*amor*) passionate.

intentar *t* to try.

intento *m* attempt, try.

● **al primer intento,** at the first attempt. ‖ **intento de asesinato,** attempted murder.

intentona *f* frustrated attempt.

■ **intentona golpista,** attempted coup.

interacción *f* interaction.

interactivo,-a *adj* interactive.

interbancario,-a *adj* interbank.

intercalar *t* to insert.

intercambiable *adj* interchangeable.

intercambiar *t* to exchange.

▲ *Conjugation model* |12|, *like* ***cambiar***.

intercambio *m* exchange, interchange.

interceder *i* to intercede.

● **interceder ante algn. por algn.,** to intercede with sb. on sb.'s behalf.

interceptar l *t* (*mensaje, correspondencia*) to intercept. **2** (*obstruir*) to block; (*tráfico*) to hold up.

interceptor l *adj* intercepting. – **2** *m* interceptor.

intercesión *f* intercession, mediation.

intercesor,-ra l *adj* interceding. – **2** *m,f* intercessor.

intercomunicación *f* intercommunication.

interconexión *f* interconnection.

intercontinental *adj* intercontinental.

intercostal *adj* intercostal.

intercultural *adj* cross-cultural.

interdental *adj* interdental.

interdependencia *f* interdependence.

interdicción *f* interdiction.

interés l *m* (*gen*) interest; (*propio*) self-interest: *ha mostrado mucho interés por el piso,* he has shown great interest in the flat; *lo hace sólo por interés,* he's only doing it for what he can get out of it; *cuando crezcas verás que era por tu interés,* when you're older you'll realize it was for your own good. **2** FIN interest.

● **de gran interés,** very interesting. ‖ **ir en interés de,** to be in the interests of. ‖ **poner interés en algo,** to take an interest in sth., put effort into sth.: *debes poner más interés en tu trabajo,* you should take more interest in your work. ‖ **tener interés en,** to be interested in.

■ interés compuesto, compound interest. ‖ **interés simple,** simple interest. ‖ **intereses creados,** vested interests.
interesado,-a 1 *adj* (*gen*) interested. **2** (*egoísta*) selfish, self-interested. **– 3** *m,f* (*gen*) interested party. **4** (*egoísta*) selfish person.
● **estar interesado,-a en algo,** to be interested in sth. ‖ **estar interesado,-a por algn.,** to take an interest in sb. ‖ **ser un,-a interesado,-a,** to be selfish, act out of self-interest.
■ parte interesada, interested party.
interesante *adj* interesting.
● **estar en estado interesante,** to be expecting. ‖ **hacerse el/la interesante,** to try to attract attention.
interesar 1 *t* to interest: *la política no me interesa,* politics doesn't interest me. **2** (*despertar interés*) to interest: *quiero interesarlos en mi proyecto,* I want to interest them in my project. **3** (*afectar*) to concern: *todos tus problemas me interesan,* all of your problems concern me. **4** (*ser útil*) to be in sb.'s interest: *la construcción del pantano nos interesa a todos,* the construction of the reservoir is in everyone's interest; *no te interesa vender el coche ahora,* it wouldn't be a good idea to sell the car now. **– 5 interesarse,** *p* to take an interest (**por,** in).
● **interesarse por la salud de algn.,** to ask after sb.'s health.
interfaz *f* interface.
interfecto,-a 1 *m,f* JUR victim. **2** *fam* person in question.
interferencia 1 *f* (*gen*) interference; (*intencionada*) jamming. **2** *fig* interference.
interferir 1 *t* (*transmisión, programa*) to jam. **2** (*obstaculizar*) to interfere in. **– 3** *i* to meddle, interfere.
▲ Conjugation model [35], like *hervir.*
interfono *m* intercom.
intergubernamental *adj* intergovernmental.
ínterin en el ínterin, *loc adv* meanwhile.
interina *f →* **interino,-a.**
interinidad 1 *f* (*gen*) temporariness. **2** (*trabajo*) temporary post; (*en la enseñanza*) temporary teaching post (*in state education*).
interino,-a 1 *adj* temporary, provisional. **2** (*director, presidente*) acting. **– 3** *m,f* (*sustituto*) stand-in. **– 4 interina,** *f* (*asistenta*) cleaning lady.
interior 1 *adj* (*bolsillo*) inside; (*habitación*) without a view, interior; (*jardín*) interior: *es un piso muy oscuro porque es todo interior,* it's a very dark flat as none of the rooms has an outside window. **2** (*del país*) domestic, internal. **3** GEOG inland. **– 4** *m* (*en una vivienda*) inside: *pasemos al interior,* let's go inside. **5** (*conciencia*) inside: *en mi interior pienso que me he equivocado,* deep down I think I made a mistake. **6** GEOG interior. **7 Interior,** Ministry of the Interior, ≈ GB Home Office, ≈ US Department of the Interior. **– 8 interiores,** *mpl* (*en cine*) interiors, interior shots: *rodaron los interiores en el palacio,* they shot the interiors in the palace.
■ patio interior, inner courtyard.
interioridad 1 *f* inside, heart of hearts: *en su interioridad siente desasosiego por la decisión tomada,* deep down inside he regrets the decision he took. **– 2 interioridades,** *fpl* private affairs.
interiorismo *m* interior design.
interiorista *mf* interior designer.
interiorización 1 *f* (*de una creencia*) internalization. **2** (*de sentimientos*) suppression, repression.
interiorizar 1 *t* (*creencia, principio*) to internalize. **2** (*sentimiento*) to suppress, repress.

▲ Conjugation model [4], like *realizar.*
interiormente *adv* inside.
interjección *f* interjection.
interlocutor,-ra *m,f* speaker, interlocutor: *mi interlocutor,* the person I was speaking to.
interludio *m* interlude.
intermediar *i* to mediate.
intermediario,-a 1 *adj* intermediary. **– 2** *m,f* (*gen*) intermediary; (*en disputas*) mediator. **– 3 intermediario,** *m* (*en negocios*) middleman: *es mucho mejor comprar sin intermediarios,* it's much better to cut out the middleman.
● **servir de intermediario,-a,** to act as an intermediary.
intermedio,-a 1 *adj* (*gen*) intermediate; (*tamaño*) medium; (*calidad*) average, medium; (*tiempo*) transitional, intervening; (*espacio*) between. **– 2 intermedio,** *m* (*de un espectáculo*) interval, intermission.
interminable *adj* endless, interminable.
interministerial *adj* interministerial.
intermitencia *f* intermittence.
● **con intermitencia,** intermittently.
intermitente 1 *adj* (*gen*) intermittent; (*luz, destello*) flashing. **– 2** *m* AUTO indicator, US blinker.
internacional 1 *adj* international. **– 2 La Internacional,** *f* POL the Internationale.
internacionalizar 1 *t* to internationalize. **– 2 internacionalizarse,** *p* to become international.
internacionalismo *m* internationalism.
internacionalidad *f* internationality.
internacionalmente *adv* internationally.
internado,-a 1 *pp →* **internar. – 2 internado,** *m* boarding school.
internamiento *m* (*en un hospital*) confinement.
internar 1 *t* (*en un colegio*) to send to boarding school; (*en un hospital*) to confine (**en,** to). **– 2 internarse,** *p* (*penetrar*) to penetrate: *se internaron en la selva,* they went deep into the jungle.
internista *mf* US internist.
interno,-a 1 *adj* (*órgano*) internal. **2** (*política*) domestic, home. **3** (*alumno*) boarding. **– 4** *m,f* (*alumno*) boarder. **5** (*médico*) intern. **6** (*preso*) prisoner.
■ medicina interna, internal medicine.
interparlamentario,-a *adj* interparliamentary.
interpelación 1 *f* POL interpellation. **2** (*gen*) question.
interpelar *t* POL to interpellate.
interpersonal *adj* interpersonal.
interplanetario,-a *adj* interplanetary.
Interpol *f* Interpol.
interpolación *f* interpolation.
interpolar *t* to interpolate.
interponer 1 *t* to interpose. **2** JUR to lodge: *su intención es interponer recurso contra la sentencia,* they intend to lodge an appeal against the sentence. **– 3 interponerse,** *p* (*físicamente*) to interpose os. **4** *fig* to intervene.
● **interponerse en el camino de algn.,** to stand in sb.'s way.
▲ Conjugation model [78], like *poner*; pp *interpuesto,-a.*
interposición 1 *f* interposition. **2** JUR lodging: *estudian la interposición de un recurso,* they are considering lodging an appeal.
interpretación 1 *f* interpretation. **2** MÚS TEAT performance. **3** (*de idiomas*) interpreting.
interpretar 1 *t* to interpret. **2** (*obra, pieza*) to perform; (*papel*) to play; (*canción*) to sing.

interpretativo,-a *adj* interpretative.
intérprete 1 *mf* (*traductor*) interpreter. 2 (*actor, músico*) performer.
interpuesto,-a *pp* → **interponer**.
interracial *adj* interracial.
interregno *m* interregnum.
interrelación *f* interrelation.
interrelacionar *t* to interrelate.
interrogación 1 *f* (*acción*) interrogation, questioning. 2 (*signo*) question mark, interrogation mark. 3 (*pregunta*) question.
■ **signo de interrogación,** question mark, interrogation mark.
interrogante 1 *adj* (*mirada, gesto*) interrogating, questioning. – 2 *m* (*incógnita*) question mark.
interrogar 1 *t* to question. 2 (*a testigo etc*) to interrogate.
▲ *Conjugation model* [7], *like llegar.*
interrogativo,-a *adj* interrogative.
interrogatorio *m* interrogation.
● **someter a algn. a un interrogatorio,** to interrogate sb.
interrumpir 1 *t* (*gen*) to interrupt: *no me interrumpas,* don't interrupt me. 2 (*obras*) to stop, halt. 3 (*discurso*) to break off. 4 (*vacaciones*) to cut short. 5 (*tráfico*) to block.
● **interrumpir el paso,** to block the way.
interrupción *f* interruption.
● **sin interrupción,** uninterruptedly.
■ **interrupción del embarazo,** termination of pregnancy.
interruptor *m* switch.
intersección *f* intersection.
intersticio *m* interstice.
interurbano,-a *adj* intercity.
■ **conferencia interurbana / llamada interurbana,** trunk call, long-distance call.
intervalo 1 *m* (*de tiempo*) interval. 2 (*de espacio*) gap.
intervención 1 *f* (*gen*) intervention. 2 (*discurso*) speech. 3 MED operation. 4 (*de una empresa*) auditing. 5 (*de un teléfono*) tapping.
■ **intervención quirúrgica,** surgical operation.
intervencionista 1 *adj* interventionist. – 2 *mf* interventionist.
intervencionismo *m* interventionism.
intervenir 1 *i* (*tomar parte*) to take part (**en,** in); (*mediar*) to intervene. 2 (*interrumpir*) to intervene. 3 (*hablar*) to speak (**en,** at). – 4 *t* MED to operate on. 5 (*alijo, mercancía*) to seize. 6 (*teléfono*) to tap. 7 (*cuentas*) to audit.
▲ *Conjugation model* [90], *like venir.*
interventor,-ra 1 *m,f* (*gen*) inspector, auditor; (*de ayuntamiento*) treasurer. 2 (*en elecciones*) scrutineer.
■ **interventor,-ra de cuentas,** auditor.
interviú *m* interview.
intervocálico,-a *adj* intervocalic.
intestado,-a *adj* intestate.
intestinal *adj* intestinal.
intestino,-a 1 *adj* (*lucha*) internecine. – 2 intestino, *m* intestine.
■ **intestino delgado,** small intestine. ‖ **intestino grueso,** large intestine.
intimar *i* to become close (**con,** to).
intimidación *f* intimidation.
intimidad 1 *f* (*amistad*) intimacy. 2 (*vida privada*) privacy, private life. – 3 **intimidades,** *fpl* (*asuntos privados*) private matters, personal affairs: *no pienso contar mis intimidades en público,* I'm not going to discuss my personal affairs in public.

● **en la intimidad,** in private: *la boda se celebró en la intimidad,* it was a private wedding.
intimidar *t* to intimidate.
intimismo *m* intimism.
intimista *adj* intimist.
íntimo,-a 1 *adj* (*vida*) private. 2 (*amigo, relación*) close. 3 (*sentimiento, emoción*) most intimate. 4 (*higiene*) personal. 5 (*ambiente, decoración*) intimate. – 6 *m,f* (*amigo*) close friend.
intocable *adj* untouchable.
intolerable *adj* intolerable, unbearable.
intolerancia *f* intolerance: *intolerancia a la lactosa,* intolerance of lactose.
intolerante 1 *adj* intolerant. – 2 *mf* intolerant person.
intoxicación *f* poisoning.
■ **intoxicación alimenticia,** food poisoning.
intoxicar 1 *t* to poison. – 2 intoxicarse, *p* to poison os.
▲ *Conjugation model* [1], *like sacar.*
intraducible *adj* untranslatable.
intramuros *adj* within the city walls.
intranquilidad *f* worry, uneasiness.
intranquilizar 1 *t* to worry. – 2 intranquilizarse, *p* to worry, get worried.
▲ *Conjugation model* [4], *like realizar.*
intranquilo,-a *adj* worried, uneasy.
intransferible *adj* nontransferable.
intransigencia *f* intransigence.
intransigente *adj* intransigent.
intransitable *adj* impassable.
intransitivo,-a *adj* intransitive.
intrascendencia *f* unimportance, insignificance.
intrascendente *adj* unimportant, insignificant.
intratable 1 *adj* (*persona*) bad-tempered, unsociable. 2 (*asunto*) intractable.
intrauterino,-a *adj* intrauterine.
intravenoso,-a *adj* intravenous.
intrepidez *f* fearlessness, courage.
intrépido,-a *adj* intrepid.
intriga 1 *f* (*maquinación secreta*) intrigue: *las intrigas palaciegas han existido en todas las épocas,* court intrigues have always existed. 2 (*curiosidad*) curiosity. 3 (*de una narración, película*) intrigue.
intrigado,-a *adj* intrigued.
intrigante 1 *adj* (*curioso, interesante*) intriguing. 2 *pey* scheming. – 3 *mf* (*persona*) intriguer, schemer.
intrigar 1 *t* (*interesar*) to intrigue. – 2 *i* (*maquinar*) to intrigue, plot, scheme.
▲ *Conjugation model* [7], *like llegar.*
intrincado,-a 1 *adj* (*asunto*) intricate, complicate. 2 (*camino*) winding, roundabout.
intríngulis *m fam* (*dificultad*) snag, catch.
● **tener intríngulis,** to be tricky, be difficult.
▲ *pl intríngulis.*
intrínseco,-a *adj* intrinsic.
introducción *f* introduction.
introducir 1 *t* (*gen*) to introduce; (*legislación*) to introduce, bring in; (*cambios*) to make (**en,** to): *quieren introducir un nuevo impuesto,* they want to bring in a new tax; *el sistema se introdujo en el año 1984,* the system was introduced in 1984. 2 (*meter*) to put, place; (*insertar*) insert: *el domador introduce su cabeza en las fauces del león,* the lion tamer puts his head in the lion's mouth; *introduce la llave en la cerradura,* insert the key in the lock; *la introdujeron violentamente en un coche,* they bundled her into a car. 3 (*importar*) to bring in, import;

(*clandestinamente*) to smuggle in: *logró introducir en el penal una lima,* he managed to smuggle a file into the prison; *introducía la droga en cajetillas de tabaco,* he smuggled the drugs in in cigarette packets. – **4** introducirse, *p* (*entrar*) to go in, get in, enter: *el balón se introdujo en la portería,* the ball went into the net; *los vemos introducirse en el ascensor,* we see them get into the lift.
● introducir modificaciones/novedades/cambios en algo, to modify sth., make changes to sth.
▲ *Conjugation model* |46|, *like conducir.*
introductor,-ra 1 *adj* introductory. – **2** *m,f* introducer.
introductorio,-a *adj* introductory.
intromisión *f* interference, meddling.
introspección *f* introspection.
introspectivo,-a *adj* introspective.
introversión *f* introversion.
introvertido,-a 1 *adj* introverted. – **2** *m,f* introvert.
intrusión *f* intrusion.
intrusismo *m* quackery.
intruso,-a 1 *adj* intrusive. – **2** *m,f* intruder.
intubación *f* intubation.
intubar *t* to intubate.
intuición *f* intuition.
intuir *t* to sense, feel.
▲ *Conjugation model* |62|, *like huir.*
intuitivamente *adv* intuitively.
intuitivo,-a *adj* intuitive.
inundación *f* flood, flooding.
inundar 1 *t* to flood. **2** *fig* to inundate.
inusitado,-a *adj* uncommon, rare.
inusual *adj* unusual.
inútil 1 *adj* (*gen*) useless. **2** (*intento*) vain, futile. **3** MED disabled. **4** MIL unfit: *lo declararon inútil para el servicio,* he was declared unfit for military service. – **5** *mf fam* (*persona*) hopeless case.
● es inútil que + *subj,* there is no point in + *ger*: *es inútil que le digas nada,* there's no point in saying anything to her.
inutilidad *f* uselessness.
inutilizar 1 *t* to render useless. **2** (*máquina*) to put out of action.
▲ *Conjugation model* |4|, *like realizar.*
invadir *t* to invade: *le invadió la nostalgia,* he was overcome by nostalgia.
invalidación *f* invalidation.
invalidar *t* to invalidate.
invalidez 1 *f* JUR (*nulidad*) invalidity. **2** MED (*incapacidad*) disablement, disability.
inválido,-a 1 *adj* JUR (*nulo*) invalid. **2** (*persona*) disabled, handicapped. – **3** *m,f* disabled person, handicapped person.
invariabilidad *f* invariability.
invariable *adj* invariable.
invasión *f* invasion.
invasor,-ra 1 *adj* invading. – **2** *m,f* invader.
invectiva *f* invective.
invencible *adj* (*ejército*) invincible; (*obstáculo*) unsurmountable.
invención 1 *f* (*invento*) invention. **2** (*mentira*) fabrication.
invendible *adj* unsaleable.
inventar 1 *t* (*crear*) to invent. **2** (*imaginar*) to imagine. **3** (*mentir*) to make up, fabricate.
● inventar excusas, to make up excuses.
inventariar *t* to make an inventory of.

inventario *m* inventory.
● hacer inventario, to do the stocktaking.
inventiva *f* inventiveness.
invento *m* invention.
inventor,-ra *m,f* inventor.
invernáculo *m* greenhouse, hothouse.
invernadero *m* greenhouse, hothouse.
■ efecto invernadero, greenhouse effect.
invernal *adj* winter, wintry.
invernar 1 *i* to (spend the) winter (**en,** in). **2** (*animales*) to hibernate.
▲ *Conjugation model* |27|, *like acertar.*
inverosímil *adj* unlikely.
inverosimilitud *f* unlikeliness.
inversión 1 *f* (*gen*) inversion. **2** FIN investment.
inversionista *mf* investor.
inverso,-a *adj* inverse, opposite.
● a la inversa, (*al contrario*) on the contrary; (*en el otro sentido*) the other way round. ‖ y a la inversa, and vice versa. ‖ en orden inverso, in reverse order. ‖ en sentido inverso, in the opposite direction.
inversor,-ra *m,f* investor.
invertebrado,-a 1 *adj* invertebrate. – **2** invertebrado, *m* invertebrate.
invertido,-a 1 *pp* → **invertir.** – **2** *adj* reversed, inverted. **3** homosexual. – **4** *m,f* homosexual.
invertir 1 *t* (*orden*) to invert, reverse. **2** (*dirección*) to reverse. **3** (*tiempo*) to spend (**en,** on). **4** FIN to invest (**en,** in).
▲ *Conjugation model* |35|, *like hervir.*
investidura *f* investiture.
investigación 1 *f* (*indagación*) investigation, enquiry. **2** (*estudio*) research.
investigador,-ra 1 *adj* (*que indaga*) investigating. **2** (*que estudia*) research. – **3** *m,f* (*científico*) researcher. **4** (*detective*) investigator.
■ investigador,-ra privado,-a, private investigator.
investigar 1 *t* (*indagar*) to investigate. **2** (*campo*) to do research on.
▲ *Conjugation model* |7|, *like llegar.*
investir *t* to invest.
▲ *Conjugation model* |34|, *like servir.*
inveterado,-a *adj* inveterate, deep-rooted.
inviable *adj* non-viable, unfeasible.
invicto,-a *adj* unconquered.
invidente 1 *adj* blind. – **2** *mf* blind person.
invierno *m* winter.
inviolabilidad *f* inviolability.
inviolable *adj* inviolable.
invisible *adj* invisible.
invitación *f* invitation.
invitado,-a 1 *adj* invited. – **2** *m,f* guest.
invitar 1 *t* to invite: *a esta ronda invito yo,* this round is on me; *invita la casa,* it's on the house; *me invitó a una cerveza,* she bought me a beer; *nos han invitado a cenar en un restaurante,* they are taking us out to dinner; *me invitó a que pasara,* she invited me in. – **2** *i* (*incitar*) to encourage; (*a la violencia*) to incite: *esta piscina invita a bañarse,* the water is tempting.
in vitro *loc adv* in vitro.
invocación *f* invocation.
invocar *t* to invoke.
▲ *Conjugation model* |1|, *like sacar.*
involución 1 *f* BIOL involution. **2** POL regression, reaction.

involucionista 1 *adj* POL reactionary. – **2** *mf* POL reactionary.
involucrar *t* to involve (**en**, in).
involuntario,-a *adj* (*reflejo, movimiento*) involuntary; (*error*) unintentional.
involutivo,-a 1 *adj* BIOL involutional. **2** POL regressive.
invulnerable *adj* invulnerable.
inyección *f* injection.
● **poner una inyección**, to give an injection.
inyectable 1 *adj* injectable. – **2** *m* injection.
inyectar *t* to inject (**en**, into): *le inyectaron morfina*, he was injected with morphine.
inyector *m* injector.
ión *m* ion.
iónico,-a *adj* ionic.
ionizador *m* ionizer.
ionizar *t* to ionize.
ionosfera *f* ionosphere.
IPC *abr* (*Índice de Precios al Consumo*) retail price index; (*abreviatura*) RPI.
ir 1 *i* (*gen*) to go; (*acudir*) to come: *fuimos a Grecia*, we went to Greece; *¿adónde vas?*, where are you going?, *¿dónde van estos platos?*, where do these plates go?, *este tren va muy lento*, this train is very slow, *ella siempre va a la última*, she's very trendy, *¡ya voy!*, I'm coming! **2** (*camino etc*) to lead: *este camino va a la aldea*, this road leads to the village. **3** (*funcionar*) to work, go: *el ascensor no va*, the lift isn't working; *¿cómo te fue en la entrevista?* how did your interview go? **4** (*sentar bien*) to suit; (*agradar*) to like: *el rojo no te va*, red doesn't suit you, *no me va la música tecno*, I don't like techno music. **5** (*tratar*) to be about: *¿de qué va la película?*, what's the film about? – **6** ir + *a* + *infin*, aux going to: *voy a venderlo*, I'm going to sell it. **7** ir + *gerundio*,: *fuimos andando*, we walked, we went on foot; *fue corriendo al pueblo*, he ran to the village. **8** ir + *pp*, to be: *ir cansado,-a*, to be tired. – **9** *irse*, *p* (*marcharse*) to go away, leave: *se ha ido al cine*, he's gone to the cinema, *me voy a la piscina*, I'm going to the swimming pool; *¡vete!*, go away!, *se fueron a las nueve*, they left at nine. **10** (*deslizarse*) to slip. **11** (*gastarse*) to go, disappear.
● **ir a pie/en tren/en coche**, to go on foot/by train/by car. ‖ **ir de compras**, to go shopping. ‖ **ir de culo**, *fam* to be rushed off one's feet. ‖ **ir tirando**, to get by. ‖ **irse a pique**, to sink; *fig* to fall through. ‖ **irse de vacaciones**, to go on holiday. ‖ **irse por las ramas**, to get sidetracked, beat about the bush. ‖ **¡qué va!**, not at all!, no way! rubbish! ‖ **vas que chutas**, *fam* you're set. ‖ **¡vete a saber!**, who knows!
▲ *Conjugation model* |74|.
ira *f* wrath, rage.
iracundo,-a *adj* irritable, irate.
Irak *m* Iraq.
Irán *m* Iran.
iraní 1 *adj* Iranian. – **2** *mf* Iranian.
▲ *pl iraníes*.
iranio,-a 1 *adj* Iranian. – **2** *m,f* (*persona*) Iranian. – **3** iranio, *m* (*idioma*) Iranian.
iraquí 1 *adj* Iraqi. – **2** *mf* (*persona*) Iraqi. – **3** *m* (*idioma*) Iraqi.
▲ *pl iraquíes*.
irascibilidad *f* irascibility.
irascible *adj* irascible, irritable.
iris *m* iris.
▲ *pl iris*.
irisación *f* iridescence.

irisado,-a *adj* iridescent.
Irlanda *f* Ireland.
■ **Irlanda del Norte**, Northern Ireland.
irlandés,-esa 1 *adj* Irish. – **2** *m,f* (*persona - hombre*) Irishman; (*- mujer*) Irish woman. – **3** irlandés, *m* (*idioma*) Irish.
ironía *f* irony.
● **con ironía**, ironically.
■ **ironías del destino**, quirks of fate.
irónico,-a *adj* ironic.
ironizar *t* to be ironical about.
▲ *Conjugation model* |4|, *like realizar*.
IRPF *abr* (*Impuesto sobre la Renta de las Personas Físicas*) income tax.
irracional *adj* irrational.
irracionalidad *f* irrationality.
irradiación *f* irradiation.
irradiar *t* to irradiate, radiate.
▲ *Conjugation model* |12|, *like cambiar*.
irrazonable *adj* unreasonable.
irreal *adj* unreal.
irrealidad *f* unreality.
irrealizable *adj* unfeasible.
irrebatible *adj* irrefutable.
irreconciliable *adj* irreconcilable.
irreconocible *adj* unrecognizable.
irrecuperable *adj* irretrievable.
irreemplazable *adj* irreplaceable.
irreflexión *f* rashness.
irreflexivo,-a *adj* (*acto*) rash; (*persona*) impetuous.
irrefrenable *adj* uncontrollable.
irrefutable *adj* irrefutable.
irregular *adj* irregular.
irregularidad *f* irregularity.
irrelevante *adj* irrelevant.
irremediable *adj* (*daño*) irremediable; (*pérdida*) irreplaceable; (*vicio*) incurable.
irremisible *adj* unpardonable, unforgivable.
irreparable *adj* irreparable.
irreprimible *adj* irrepressible.
irreprochable *adj* irreproachable.
irresistible 1 *adj* irresistible. **2** *pey* (*insoportable*) unbearable.
irresponsable 1 *adj* irresponsible. – **2** *mf* irresponsible person.
irreverencia *f* irreverence.
irreverente *adj* irreverent.
irreversible *adj* irreversible.
irrevocable *adj* irrevocable.
irrigación *f* irrigation.
irrigar *t* to irrigate.
irrisorio,-a 1 *adj* derisory, ridiculous. **2** (*insignificante*) insignificant.
irritabilidad *f* irritability.
irritable *adj* irritable.
irritación *f* irritation.
irritar 1 *t* to irritate. – **2** irritarse, *p* to lose one's temper, get annoyed.
irrompible *adj* unbreakable.
irrumpir *i* to burst (**en**, into).
irrupción *f* irruption.
isabelino,-a 1 *adj* (*en España*) Isabelline. **2** (*en Inglaterra*) Elizabethan.
isla *f* island.

islam *m* Islam.
islámico,-a *adj* Islamic.
islamismo *m* Islamism.
islamita *adj* Islamic.
islamizar *t* to Islamize.
islandés,-esa 1 *adj* Icelandic. – 2 *m,f* (*persona*) Icelander. – 3 **islandés,** *m* (*idioma*) Icelandic.
Islandia *f* Iceland.
isleño,-a 1 *adj* island. – 2 *m,f* islander.
isleta 1 *f* GEOG islet. 2 (*de una calzada*) traffic island.
islote *m* small unhinhabited island.
ismo *m* ism.
isobara *f* isobar.
isósceles *adj* isosceles.
isotérmico,-a *adj* isothermal: *pon los congelados en una bolsa isotérmica,* put the frozen food in a freezer bag; *un camión isotérmico,* a refrigerated lorry.
isótopo *m* isotope.
Israel *m* Israel.
israelí 1 *adj* Israeli. – 2 *mf* Israeli.
israelita 1 *adj* HIST Israelite. – 2 *mf* HIST Israelite.
istmo *m* isthmus.
ít. *abr* (*ítem*) item, likewise.
Italia *f* Italy.

italiano,-a 1 *adj* Italian. – 2 *m,f* (*persona*) Italian. – 3 **italiano,** *m* (*idioma*) Italian.
itálica *f* → **itálico,-a.**
itálico,-a 1 *adj* Italic. – 2 **itálica,** *f* (*letra*) italics.
itinerante *adj* itinerant.
itinerario *m* itinerary.
ITV *abr* AUTO (*Inspección Técnica de Vehículos*) ≈ Ministry of Transport test; (*abreviatura*) MOT test.
IU *abr* POL (*Izquierda Unida*) United Left (*left-wing political coalition whose nucleus is formed by the Communist Party*).
IVA *abr* (*impuesto sobre el valor añadido*) value-added tax; (*abreviatura*) VAT.
izar *t* to hoist.
▲ Conjugation model |4|, *like realizar.*
izqd° *abr* (*izquierdo*) left.
izqdª *abr* (*izquierda*) left.
izqdo.,-a. *abr* (*izquierdo*) left.
izquierdista 1 *adj* left-wing. – 2 *mf* left-winger.
izquierdo,-a 1 *adj* left. – 2 **la izquierda,** *f* (*mano*) left hand; (*pierna*) left leg. 3 POL the left.
● **girar a la izquierda,** to turn left. ‖ **ser de izquierdas,** to be left-wing.
izquierdoso,-a *adj fam* leftish.

J

J, j f (la letra) J, j.

ja ¡ja, ja!, *interj* (risa) ha, ha!; (con sarcasmo) tee hee!, ho ho!; (con incredulidad) ha ha!, ho ho!

jabalí m wild boar.
  ▲ pl *jabalíes*.

jabalina[1] f ZOOL female wild boar.

jabalina[2] f DEP javelin.
  ■ lanzamiento de jabalina, the javelin.

jabato 1 m ZOOL young wild boar. 2 (hombre valiente) daredevil.

jabón m soap.
  ● darle jabón a algn., *fam fig* to butter sb. up.
  ■ jabón de olor, toilet soap. ‖ jabón de sastre, French chalk. ‖ jabón de tocador, toilet soap.

jabonada f soaping.

jabonar t → enjabonar.

jaboncillo 1 m (pastilla) small bar of toilet soap. 2 (de sastre) French chalk. 3 BOT soapberry.

jabonera 1 f soapdish. 2 BOT soapwort.

jabonero,-a 1 adj (industria) soap. 2 (toro) dirty white.

jabonoso,-a adj soapy.

jabugo m → jamón.

jaca f cob, small horse.

jacaranda f jacaranda.

jacarandoso,-a adj jolly, merry.

jacinto m hyacinth.

jacobeo,-a adj of Saint James.
  ■ la ruta jacobea, the pilgrim's route to Santiago de Compostela.

jacobino,-a 1 adj HIST Jacobin. – 2 m,f HIST Jacobin.

jacobita 1 adj HIST REL Jacobite. – 2 mf HIST REL Jacobite.

jactancia f boastfulness, boasting, bragging.

jactancioso,-a 1 adj boastful. – 2 m,f braggart.

jactarse p to boast, brag (de, about).

jaculatoria f short prayer.

jade m jade.

jadeante adj panting, breathless.

jadear i to pant.

jadeo m panting.

jaez 1 m fig gente de ese jaez, people of that ilk. – 2 jaeces, mpl trappings.

jaguar m jaguar.

jai f arg bird, US broad, chick.

jalar 1 t (tirar de) to pull, heave. 2 fam (comer) to wolf down.

jalbegar t (pared) to whitewash.

jalea f jelly.
  ■ jalea real, royal jelly.

jalear 1 t (animar) to cheer (on), clap and shout at. 2 (caza) to urge on.

jaleo 1 m (alboroto) din, racket: no se oye nada con este jaleo, I can't hear a thing with all this racket. 2 (escándalo) fuss, commotion: cuando se enteren se va montar un jaleo tremendo, there'll be a terrible fuss when they find out. 3 (riña) row. 4 (confusión) muddle: me he armado tal jaleo que no sé ni dónde estoy, I'm so mixed up I don't know whether I'm coming or going; menudo jaleo de cuentas tenéis montado, you've made a right mess of the accounts. 5 MÚS Andalusian dance and music.

jaleoso,-a adj (enredoso) complicated, mixed-up.

jalón[1] 1 m (estaca) stake, post. 2 fig milestone, landmark.
  ● marcar un jalón, to mark a watershed.

jalón[2] m (tirón) pull.

jalonar 1 t (con estacas) to stake out. 2 fig to mark: el viaje estuvo jalonado de incidentes, it was an eventful journey.

Jamaica f Jamaica.

jamaicano,-a 1 adj Jamaican. – 2 m,f Jamaican.

jamás adv (+ indic) never; (+ subj) ever: jamás volveré, I shall never return; el mejor presidente que jamás haya existido, the best president ever.
  ● jamás de los jamases, never ever. ‖ por siempre jamás, for ever (and ever).

jamba f jamb.

jamelgo m pey nag, hack.

jamón 1 m (curado) cured ham; (pata del cerdo) leg of ham. 2 fam (muslo) thigh.
  ● estar jamón, fam to be a hunk. ‖ ¡y un jamón (con chorreras)!, fam you should be so lucky!, you must be joking!
  ■ jamón de jabugo, cured ham. ‖ jamón de York, boiled ham. ‖ jamón en dulce, boiled ham. ‖ jamón serrano, cured ham.

jamona 1 adj fam buxom. – 2 f fam buxom woman.

Japón m Japan.

japonés,-esa 1 adj Japanese. – 2 m,f (persona) Japanese. – 3 japonés, m (idioma) Japanese.

japuta f Ray's bream.

jaque m check.
  ● dar jaque a, to put in check. ‖ tener en jaque a algn., to have sb. on the rack.
  ■ jaque al rey, check. ‖ jaque mate, checkmate.

jaquear 1 t (en ajedrez) to check. 2 fig (hostigar) to harass.

jaqueca f migraine, headache.

jara f rockrose.

jarabe 1 m CULIN syrup. 2 MED syrup, mixture, medicine.
  ● darle a algn. jarabe de palo, to give sb. a good hiding.
  ■ jarabe para la tos, cough syrup.

jarana 1 f fam (juerga) wild party, spree. 2 (jaleo) racket, din.
  ● armar jarana, to make a racket. ‖ irse de jarana, to go out on the town.

jaranero,-a adj party-loving.

jarcha f LIT Mozarabic stanza.

jarcia 1 f (náutica) rigging, ropes pl. 2 (pesca) fishing tackle.

jardín *m* garden.
■ jardín botánico, botanical garden. ‖ jardín de infancia, nursery school.
jardinera 1 *f* (*mujer*) gardener. 2 (*mueble para tiestos*) plant stand; (*en ventana*) window box.
jardinería *f* gardening.
jardinero,-a *m,f* gardener.
jareta *f* (*de adorno*) tuck; (*dobladillo hueco*) casing.
jaro,-a *adj* red-haired.
jarra 1 *f* (*para servir*) jug, US pitcher. 2 (*para beber*) tankard, beer mug: *dos jarras de cerveza y unas patatas fritas, por favor,* two pints of beer and a packet of crisps, please.
● con los brazos en jarras, arms akimbo, hands on hips.
jarrete *m* (*de una res*) hock.
jarretera *f arc* garter.
■ la Orden de la Jarretera, the Order of the Garter.
jarro 1 *m* (*recipiente*) jug. 2 (*contenido*) jugful.
● caer como un jarro de agua fría, to come as a shock. ‖ echar un jarro de agua fría a algn., to dash sb.'s hopes.
jarrón 1 *m* vase. 2 ART urn.
jaspe *m* jasper.
jaspeado,-a 1 *pp* → **jaspear**. – 2 *adj* mottled, speckled.
jaspear *t* to speckle.
Jauja *f* (*sitio*) promised land; (*situación*) the good life.
● esto es Jauja, this is the life!: *éste se cree que esto es Jauja,* he thinks the world owes him a living.
jaula 1 *f* (*para animales*) cage. 2 (*embalaje*) crate. 3 (*niños*) playpen.
jauría 1 *f* pack of hounds. 2 *fig* gang.
Java *f* Java.
javanés,-esa 1 *adj* Javanese. – 2 *m,f* Javanese.
jazmín *m* jasmine.
jazz *m* jazz.
jazzístico,-a *adj* jazz.
J.C. *abr* (*Jesucristo*) Jesus Christ; (*abreviatura*) J.C.
je *interj* ha!
jeep *m* jeep.
▲ *pl jeeps.*
jefa *f fam* → **jefe,-a**.
jefatura 1 *f* (*sede*) central office; MIL headquarters. 2 (*cargo, dirección*) leadership.
jefe,-a 1 *m,f* boss, head, chief. 2 COM (*hombre*) manager; (*mujer*) manageress. 3 POL leader. 4 MIL officer in command. 5 (*de una tribu*) chief. – 6 ¡jefe!, *interj fam* waiter! – 7 la jefa, *f fam* the old lady, the wife.
■ jefe de cocina, chef. ‖ jefe de estación, station master. ‖ jefe de Estado, Head of State. ‖ jefe de Estado Mayor, Chief of Staff. ‖ jefe de redacción, editor-in-chief. ‖ jefe de taller, foreman. ‖ jefe de ventas, sales manager. ‖ jefe supremo, commmander-in-chief.
Jehová *m* Jehovah.
■ testigos de Jehová, Jehovah's Witnesses.
jengibre *m* ginger.
jeque *m* sheik, sheikh.
jerarca *m* hierarch.
jerarquía 1 *f* hierarchy. 2 (*grado*) scale. 3 (*categoría*) rank. 4 (*persona*) high-ranking person.
jerárquico,-a *adj* hierarchical, hierarchic.
jerarquizado,-a 1 *pp* → **jerarquizar**. – 2 *adj* hierarchical.

jerarquizar *t* to organize into hierarchies.
jeremiada *f* jeremiad.
jeremías *mf* whinger, whiner.
▲ *pl jeremías.*
jerez *m* sherry.
jerga¹ 1 *f* (*lenguaje*) jargon. 2 *pey* (*jerigonza*) gibberish, jargon.
jerga² *f* (*tela*) serge.
jergal *adj* jargon.
jergón *m* (*colchón*) pallet.
jerigonza 1 *f pey* gibberish, jargon. 2 (*argot*) slang.
jeringa *f* syringe.
■ jeringa de engrase, grease gun.
jeringar 1 *t* MED *desus* to syringe. 2 *fam* to pester. – 3 jeringarse, *p fam euf* → **joderse**.
jeringuilla *f* syringe, hypodermic syringe.
jeroglífico,-a 1 *adj* hieroglyphic. – 2 jeroglífico, *m* hieroglyph, hieroglyphic. 3 (*juego*) rebus.
jersey *m* sweater, pullover, jumper.
▲ *pl jerséis.*
Jerusalén *m* Jerusalem.
jesuita 1 *adj* Jesuit. – 2 *mf* Jesuit.
jesuítico,-a 1 *adj* Jesuitic. 2 *fig* cautious.
Jesús 1 *m* Jesus. – 2 *interj* (*al estornudar*) bless you! 3 ¡Jesús, (por Dios)!, *fam* (*como queja*) for God's sake!, for goodness' sake!; (*con sorpresa*) oh my God!
■ el Niño Jesús, Baby Jesus.
jet 1 *m* jet. – 2 la jet, *f* (*famosos*) the jet set.
■ la jet set, the jet set.
jeta 1 *f fam* (*cara*) mug, face. 2 (*hocico*) snout. 3 (*descaro*) cheek. – 4 *mf fam* cheeky monkey, cheeky bugger.
● tener jeta, *fam* to be cheeky, have a nerve.
jetudo,-a 1 *adj fam* (*trompudo*) big-nosed. 2 *fam* (*descarado*) cheeky.
ji *interj* hee!
jíbaro,-a 1 *adj* (*indígena*) Jivaro. – 2 *m,f* peasant.
jibia *f* cuttlefish.
jiddish *m* → **yiddish**.
jihad *f* → **yihad**.
jijona *m* type of soft nougat.
jilguero *m* goldfinch.
jilipollas *mf tabú* → **gilipollas**.
jineta¹ *f* ZOOL genet.
jineta² a la jineta, *loc* with short stirrups.
jinete *m* rider, horseman.
jiñar 1 *i tabú* to shit os. – 2 jiñarse, *p tabú* to shit os.
jipi *mf* → **hippy**.
jipiar 1 *i* (*gemir*) to groan. 2 (*cantar*) to wail.
jipido *m* → **jipío**.
jipijapa *m* Panama hat.
jipío *m fam* (*en el cante*) wailing.
jipioso,-a 1 *adj fam pey* scruffy-looking, hippyish. – 2 *m,f fam pey* scruff.
jira *f desus* (*merienda*) picnic.
jirafa 1 *f* giraffe. 2 *fam* (*persona*) beanpole. 3 (*de micrófono*) boom.
jirón 1 *m* shred: *una camisa hecha jirones,* a tattered shirt. 2 LIT fragment: *jirones de frases,* unfinished sentences.
● hacer algo jirones, to tear sth. to shreds.
jitomate *m* tomato.
jiu-jitsu *m* jujitsu, jiujitsu.
JJ.OO. *abr* (*Juegos Olímpicos*) Olimpic Games.
jo *interj fam* (*para indicar - sorpresa*) wow!, blimey!; (- admiración) wow!; (- disgusto) damn!, blast!

jobar *interj fam* → **jo.**

jockey *m* jockey.

jocosamente *adv* jocularly, humorously.

jocoserio,-a *adj* tragicomic.

jocosidad **1** *f* (*humor*) jocularity. **2** (*broma*) joke.

jocoso,-a *adj* (*persona*) jocular; (*tono*) humorous, jokey.

jocundo,-a *adj lit* jolly, jovial.

joder 1 *t tabú* (*copular*) to fuck, screw. **2** *tabú* (*fastidiar*) to pester, annoy, piss off. **3** *tabú* (*estropear*) to fuck up. **4** *tabú* (*lastimar*) to do in, bugger up: *se jodió la rodilla,* he did his knee in. – **5** *interj tabú* (*con enfado, fastidio*) damn it!, shit!, bloody hell!, fuck!; (*con asombro*) Christ!, Jesus!: *¡joder, qué frío hace!,* Christ, it's freezing! – **6** *joderse, p tabú* (*aguantarse*) to lump it, put up with it. **7** *tabú* (*echarse a perder*) to get fucked up. **8** *tabú* (*estropearse*) to go bust.

● **¡hay que joderse!,** *tabú* tough shit! ‖ **¡la jodiste!,** *tabú* you screwed it up! ‖ **¡no me jodas!,** *tabú* (*con asombro*) bugger me!; fuck me!; (*con fastidio*) bugger off!; fuck off! ‖ **¡que se joda(n)!,** *tabú* bugger him/her/them!; fuck him/her/them!

jodido,-a 1 *pp* → **joder.** – **2** *adj tabú* (*enfermo*) in a bad way; (*cansado*) knackered, fucked. **3** *tabú* (*maldito, molesto*) bloody, fucking, sodding. **4** *tabú* (*estropeado, roto*) bust, fucked up, buggered. **5** *tabú* (*difícil*) fucking difficult.

jodienda 1 *f tabú* screwing. **2** *tabú* (*fastidio*) bugger, pain in the arse.

jofaina *f* washbasin.

jogging *m* jogging: *practican el jogging,* they go jogging.

jolgorio 1 *m* (*juerga*) binge. **2** (*algazara*) party: *menudo jolgorio tienen montado los vecinos,* the neighbours are really living it up.

jolín 1 *interj fam* (*asombro*) wow!, good grief! **2** (*enfado*) blast!, damn!

jolines *interj fam* → **jolín.**

jónico,-a 1 *adj* (*mar*) Ionian; (*pueblo, dialecto*) Ionian, Ionic. **2** (*orden, capitel*) Ionic. – **3** *m,f* Ionian. – **4** *jónico, m* (*dialecto*) Ionian.

■ **el (mar) Jónico,** the Ionian Sea.

Jordán el río Jordán, *f* the river Jordan.

Jordania *f* Jordan.

jordano,-a 1 *adj* Jordanian. – **2** *m,f* Jordanian.

jornada 1 *f* (*día de trabajo*) working day: *una jornada de ocho horas,* an eight-hour day; *ha sido una jornada intensiva,* it's been a hard day's work. **2** (*camino recorrido*) day's journey: *estamos a dos jornadas de camino,* we've got another two days' travelling to do. **3** (*en periodismo*) day: *las noticias de la jornada,* today's news; *la jornada deportiva del sábado,* Saturday's sport. – **4** *jornadas, fpl* conference *sing.*

■ **jornada completa,** full-time. ‖ **jornada intensiva,** *eight-to-three working day without a lunch break.* ‖ **jornada laboral,** working day. ‖ **jornada partida,** working day with a lunch break. ‖ **media jornada,** half-day.

jornal *m* day's wage.

● **trabajar a jornal,** to be paid by the day.

jornalero,-a *m,f* day labourer.

joroba 1 *f* (*deformidad*) hump. **2** *fam* (*fastidio*) nuisance, drag. – **3** *interj fam* (*sorpresa, admiración*) wow!; (*disgusto*) damn!, blast!

jorobado,-a 1 *adj* hunchbacked, humpbacked. – **2** *m,f* hunchback, humpback.

jorobar 1 *t fam* (*fastidiar*) to bother, pester, annoy. **2** *fam* (*romper*) to smash up, break. **3** *fam* (*estropear*) to ruin, wreck. – **4** **jorobarse,** *p fam* (*aguantarse*) to put up with it.

● **¡no jorobes!,** (*fastidio*) stop pestering me!; (*incredulidad*) pull the other one!

jota¹ 1 *f name of the letter j.* **2** (*cantidad mínima*) jot, scrap. **3** (*naipe*) jack.

● **ni jota,** *fam* not a thing: *no se ve ni jota,* you can't see a thing; *no entendí ni jota de lo que me dijo,* I didn't understand a word he said.

jota² *f popular Spanish dance and music.*

joule *m* joule.

joven 1 *adj* young: *yo de joven no hacía esas cosas,* I didn't do things like that when I was young. – **2** *mf* (*hombre*) youth, young man; (*mujer*) young lady, girl: *los jóvenes de hoy día,* the youth of today.

jovial *adj* jovial, cheerful, good-humoured.

jovialidad *f* joviality, cheerfulness.

joya 1 *f* jewel, piece of jewellery (*us* jewelry): *le robaron las joyas,* they stole her jewellery. **2** *fig* treasure.

joyería 1 *f* (*tienda*) jewellery (*us* jewelry) shop, jeweller's shop, *us* jeweler's store. **2** (*comercio*) jewellery (*us* jewelry) trade.

joyero,-a 1 *m,f* jeweller (*us* jeweler). – **2** **joyero,** *m* jewellery (*us* jewelry) case.

Juan *m* John.

● **Juan Palomo, yo me lo guiso, yo me lo como,** I'm all right Jack. ‖ **ser un Don Juan,** to be a flirt, be a philanderer.

■ **Juan Lanas,** (*endeble*) wimp; (*marido dominado*) henpecked husband.

juanete 1 *m* (*en el pie*) bunion. **2** (*en un barco*) topgallant.

jubilación 1 *f* (*acción*) retirement. **2** (*dinero*) pension.

■ **jubilación anticipada,** early retirement.

jubilado,-a 1 *pp* → **jubilar.** – **2** *adj* retired. – **3** *mf* pensioner, retired person, *us* retiree.

jubilar 1 *t* (*retirar*) to retire. **2** (*persona*) to pension off; (*objeto*) to get rid of, ditch. – **3** **jubilarse,** *p* (*retirarse*) to retire.

jubileo *m* (*perdón*) indulgence.

júbilo *m* jubilation, joy.

jubiloso,-a *adj* jubilant, joyful.

jubón *m arc* doublet.

Judá *f* Judah.

judaico,-a *adj* Judaic.

judaísmo *m* Judaism.

judas *m* traitor, Judas.

▲ *pl* **judas.**

Judea *f* Judaea.

judeocristiano,-a *adj* Judaeo-Christian.

judeoespañol,-la *adj* Judaeo-Spanish.

judería *f* Jewish quarter.

judía *f* (*planta*) bean.

■ **judía blanca,** haricot bean. ‖ **judía pinta,** kidney bean. ‖ **judía verde,** French bean, green bean.

judiada *f fam* dirty trick.

judicatura 1 *f* (*profesión*) judgeship. **2** (*cuerpo*) judiciary, judicature. **3** (*duración del cargo*) term of office *as a judge.*

judicial *adj* judicial.

judío,-a 1 *adj* (*gen*) Jewish. **2** HIST (*de Judá*) Judaean. **3** *fam* pey miserly. – **4** *m,f* (*persona*) Jew. **5** HIST (*de Judá*) Judaean. **6** *fam* pey miser, scrooge.

judión *m* large bean.

judo *m* judo.

judoca *mf* judoka.

juego 1 *m* (*actividad recreativa*) game; (*actividad deportiva*) sport. **2** (*con dinero*) gambling. **3** (*acción de jugar*) playing. **4** (*en tenis*) game; (*en naipes*) round, game. **5** (*conjunto de* *piezas*) set: *un juego de llaves,* a set of keys. **6** (*movimiento*) play: *este eje tiene demasiado juego,* there's too much play on this axle; *el tobillo ha perdido todo el juego,* my ankle has gone stiff. **7** (*combinación de elementos*) coordination: *con cortinas a juego,* with matching curtains. ● **descubrirle el juego a algn.,** to see through sb.'s game. ‖ **entrar en juego,** (*persona*) to come on; (*factor*) to come into play. ‖ **andar en juego / estar en juego,** to be at stake. ‖ **hacer juego,** (*combinar*) to match. ‖ **hacerle el juego a algn.,** (*apoyar*) to back sb. up; (*seguir el juego*) to play along with sb.; (*dejarse engañar*) to play into sb.'s hands. ‖ **¡hagan juego!,** place your bets! ‖ **ir a juego con algo,** to match sth. ‖ **poner en juego,** (*usar*) to use; (*arriesgar*) to risk, stake. ‖ **seguirle el juego a algn.,** to play along with sb. ■ **juego de azar,** game of chance. ‖ **juego de café/té,** coffee/tea service. ‖ **juego de ingenio,** guessing game. ‖ **juego de manos,** sleight of hand. ‖ **juego de mesa,** board game. ‖ **juego de niños,** *fig* piece of cake. ‖ **juego de palabras,** play on words, pun. ‖ **juego limpio/sucio,** fair/foul play. ‖ **juegos florales,** poetry competition *sing.* ‖ **juegos malabares,** juggling *sing.* ‖ **Juegos Olímpicos,** Olympic Games.

juerga *f fam* rave-up, bash: *está siempre de juerga,* he's always out having a good time, he's always out partying. ● **correrse una juerga,** to have a ball. ‖ **irse de juerga,** to go out on the town.

juerguearse *p fam* to have a good time.

juerguista 1 *adj* fun-loving. **– 2** *mf* raver.

jueves *m* Thursday: *todos los jueves,* every Thursday; *el jueves que viene,* next Thursday; *el jueves de la semana que viene,* next Thursday; *este jueves no, el otro,* next Thursday; *del jueves en ocho,* a week on Thursday; *el jueves pasado,* last Thursday; *el otro jueves,* last Thursday; *el jueves por la mañana/noche,* on Thursday morning/night; *viene a verme los jueves,* she comes to see me on Thursdays; *el partido del jueves,* Thursday's match. ● **no ser nada del otro jueves,** to be nothing to write home about. ■ **Jueves Santo,** Maundy Thursday. ▲ *pl jueves.*

juez,-za *m,f* judge. ● **ser juez y parte,** to be biased. ■ **juez de banda,** linesman. ‖ **juez de campo,** field judge. ‖ **juez de instrucción,** examining magistrate. ‖ **juez de línea,** linesman. ‖ **juez de paz,** justice of the peace. ‖ **juez de primera instancia,** examining magistrate. ‖ **juez de salida,** starter. ‖ **juez de silla,** umpire.

jugada 1 *f* (*en ajedrez*) move; (*en billar*) shot; (*en dardos*) throw. **2** (*momento del juego*) move, piece of play: *la jugada del gol,* the move which lead to the goal. **3** *fam* dirty trick. **4** FIN speculation. ● **hacerle una mala jugada a algn.,** to play a dirty trick on sb.

jugador,-ra 1 *m,f* player. **2** (*apostador*) gambler. ■ **jugador,-ra de Bolsa,** speculator.

jugar 1 *i* to play: *unos jugaron a cartas, otros a fútbol,* some played cards, others football. **2** (*burlarse*) to play: *estás jugando con mis sentimientos,* you're playing with my feelings. **– 3** *t* (*intervenir*) to play, go: *juega tú primero,* you go first; *¿quién juega?,* whose go is it? **4** (*hacer uso - una pieza*) to move; (*- una carta*) to play. **5** (*apostar*) to bet, stake. **– 6 jugarse,** *p* (*arriesgar*) to risk: *se jugó la vida por mí,* he risked his life for me. **7** (*apostarse*) to

bet: *¿cuánto te juegas a que no viene?,* what's the bet he won't come?
● **jugar con fuego,** to play with fire. ‖ **jugar fuerte,** to play hard. ‖ **jugar limpio,** to play fair. ‖ **jugar sucio,** to play dirty. ‖ **jugarse el todo por el todo,** to stake everything one has. ‖ **jugársela a algn.,** (*engañar*) to take sb. for a ride; (*al cónyuge*) to do the dirty on sb., cheat on sb.
▲ *Conjugation model* [53].

jugarreta *f fam* dirty trick.

juglar *m* minstrel.

juglaresa *f female* minstrel.

juglaresco,-a *adj* minstrel.

juglaría *f* minstrelsy.

jugo 1 *m* (*gen*) juice. **2** (*interés*) substance: *una novela con mucho jugo,* it's a meaty novel. ● **sacar el jugo a algo,** *fig* to make the most of sth. ‖ **sacarle el jugo a algn.,** to exploit sb. ■ **jugos gástricos,** gastric juices.

jugosidad *f* juiciness.

jugoslavo,-a 1 *adj* Yugoslav, Yugoslavian. **– 2** *m,f* Yugoslav, Yugoslavian.

jugoso,-a 1 *adj* (*fruta, carne*) juicy. **2** (*negocio*) substantial, lucrative. **3** (*comentario, novela*) meaty.

juguete 1 *m* toy. **2** *fig* plaything. ● **ser el juguete de algn.,** to be sb.'s plaything: *somos juguetes del destino,* we are the playthings of fate.

juguetear *i* to play (**con,** with).

jugueteo *m* playing.

juguetería 1 *f* (*tienda*) toy shop. **2** (*industria*) toy business.

juguetón,-ona *adj* playful, frolicsome.

juicio 1 *m* (*gen*) judgement: *a mi juicio,* in my opinion. **2** (*sensatez*) reason, common sense. **3** JUR trial, lawsuit. **4** REL judgement. ● **a juicio de algn.,** in sb.'s opinion. ‖ **dejar algo a juicio de algn.,** to leave sth. to sb.'s discretion. ‖ **emitir un juicio sobre algo,** to express an opinion about sth. ‖ **en su sano juicio,** in one's right mind. ‖ **llevar a algn. a juicio,** to take legal action against sb., sue sb. ‖ **perder el juicio,** to go mad. ■ **Juicio Final / Juicio Universal,** Final Judgement.

juicioso,-a *adj* (*persona*) sensible, wise; (*decisión*) judicious.

julandrón,-ona *m arg* sucker, mug.

julay *m arg* sucker, mug.

julepe 1 *m* (*juego*) type of card game. **2** *fam* (*esfuerzo*) hard work. **3** (*bebida*) julep.

juliana *f* damewort.

julio¹ *m* July. ▲ *See also marzo.*

julio² *m* FÍS joule.

jumento *m* ass, donkey.

jumera *f fam* bender. ● **agarrar una jumera / pillar una jumera,** *fam* to get plastered, go on a bender.

jumilla *m* wine from Jumilla, Murcia.

juncal 1 *adj* BOT rushlike. **2** *lit* graceful. **– 3** *m* BOT reedbed.

juncia *f* sedge.

junco¹ 1 *m* BOT rush, reed. **2** (*bastón*) walking stick, cane.

junco² *m* MAR junk.

jungla *f* jungle. ■ **la jungla del asfalto,** the concrete jungle.

junio *m* June. ▲ *See also marzo.*

júnior 1 *adj* DEP junior. – **2** *mf* REL junior novice. **3** DEP junior.
▲ *pl* **júniors**.
junípero *m* juniper.
junquillo 1 *m* BOT jonquil. **2** (*moldura*) beading.
junta 1 *f* (*reunión*) meeting, assembly, conference. **2** (*conjunto de personas*) board, council, committee. **3** (*sesión*) session, sitting. **4** MIL junta. **5** TÉC ARQ joint.
■ **junta administrativa**, administrative board. ‖ **junta de accionistas**, shareholders' meeting. ‖ **junta de empresa**, works council. ‖ **junta directiva**, board of directors. ‖ **junta militar**, military junta. ‖ **junta de culata**, gasket.
juntar 1 *t* (*unir*) to join together, put together; (*piezas*) to assemble: *junta las mesas,* put the tables together. **2** *fam* (*coleccionar*) to collect. **3** (*reunir - dinero*) to raise; (*gente*) to gather together. – **4 juntarse**, *p* (*unirse*) to join, get together; (*ríos, caminos*) to meet: *nos juntamos todos los domingos,* we get together every Sunday. **5** (*acercarse*) to squeeze up: *juntaos un poco que no quepo,* squeeze up, I can't get in. **6** (*relacionarse*) to go out (**con**, with), mix (**con**, with): *últimamente no se junta con nadie,* she is being remarkably antisocial lately. **7** (*amancebarse*) to move in (**con**, with), to start living together.
juntillas a pies juntillas, *loc fam* → **pie**.
junto,-a 1 *adj* together: *colocó dos sillas juntas,* he put two chairs next to each other; *es la primera vez que veo tanto dinero junto,* it's the first time I've seen so much money in one place. – **2 junto a**, *loc* next to: *vive junto a mí,* he lives next door to me; *un hotel junto al lago,* a hotel by the lake. **3 junto con**, along with, together with: *me lo mandó junto con el paquete,* he sent it along with the parcel.
juntura *f* joint.
jura *f* (*acción*) oath; (*ceremonia*) swearing-in, pledge.
■ **jura de bandera**, oath of allegiance to the flag.
jurado,-a 1 *pp* → **jurar**. – **2** *adj* sworn. – **3 jurado**, *m* JUR (*tribunal*) jury; (*miembro del tribunal*) juror, member of the jury. **4** (*en un concurso*) panel of judges, jury.
juramentar 1 *t* to swear in. – **2 juramentarse**, *p* to take the oath.
juramento 1 *m* JUR oath. **2** (*blasfemia*) swearword.
● **tomar juramento a algn.**, to swear sb. in.
■ **juramento de fidelidad**, oath of allegiance. ‖ **juramento falso**, perjury.
jurar 1 *t* to swear, take an oath. – **2** *i* (*blasfemar*) to curse, swear.
● **jurar en falso**, to commit perjury. ‖ **jurar en vano**, to take the name of the Lord in vain. ‖ **jurar fidelidad**, to pledge allegiance. ‖ **jurársela(s) a algn.**, to have it in for sb. ‖ **¡(te) lo juro por Dios!**, I swear to God!
jurásico,-a 1 *adj* Jurassic. – **2 el jurásico**, *m* the Jurassic.
jurel *m* scad, horse mackerel.
jurídico,-a *adj* legal, juridical.
● **por la vía jurídica**, in court.
■ **sistema jurídico**, legal system.
jurisconsulto *m* jurist, legal expert.
jurisdicción *f* jurisdiction.
jurisdiccional *adj* jurisdictional.
jurispericia *f* jurisprudence.
jurisperito,-a *m,f* jurist, legal expert.
jurisprudencia *f* jurisprudence.
jurista *mf* jurist, lawyer.
justa 1 *f* HIST joust. **2** (*certamen*) competition.
justamente 1 *adv* (*con justicia*) justly, fairly. **2** (*exactamente*) exactly. **3** (*precisamente*) precisely.

justeza *f* fairness.
justicia 1 *f* (*equidad, derecho*) justice, fairness. **2 la justicia**, (*organismo*) the law.
● **administrar justicia**, to administer justice. ‖ **en justicia**, in all fairness. ‖ **hacer justicia**, to do justice. ‖ **hacer justicia a algo/algn.**, to do justice to sb./sth. ‖ **ser de justicia**, to be only fair. ‖ **tomarse la justicia por su mano**, to take the law into one's own hands.
justiciero,-a *adj* avenging.
justificable *adj* justifiable.
justificación *f* justification: *no tiene justificación subir los precios,* there is no justification for putting prices up.
justificante 1 *adj* justifying. – **2** *m* (*prueba*) written proof.
justificar 1 *t* (*acción*) to justify. **2** (*persona*) to excuse. – **3 justificarse**, *p* (*persona*) to justify os.; (*acción*) to be justified.
● **justificarse con algn.**, to apologize to sb.
▲ Conjugation model [1], like *sacar*.
justipreciación *f* valuation.
justipreciar *t* to value.
justiprecio *m* valuation.
justo,-a 1 *adj* (*persona, decisión*) just, fair; (*sentencia*) just: *es justo que te den el premio a ti,* it is only fair that you should get the prize. **2** (*ropa*) tight: *esta falda me queda muy justa,* this skirt is too tight for me. **3** (*exacto*) exact: *tengo el dinero justo para el autobús,* I have the exact money for the bus; *en el lugar justo donde lo enterraron,* in the exact place where he was buried. **4** (*escaso*) just enough: *me queda lo justo para llegar a fin de mes,* I have just enough money to get by. **5** (*preciso*) exact, precise: *estamos los justos para jugar una partida,* there are just the right number of us to play. – **6** *m,f* just person, fair person. – **7 justo**, *adv* (*en el preciso momento*) just; (*en el preciso lugar*) right: *me ascendieron justo cuando menos lo esperaba,* I got a promotion just when I was least expecting it; *justo en este momento iba para allí,* I was just on my way there; *vivo justo en el centro de la ciudad,* I live right in the centre of town. – **8 los justos**, *mpl* REL the just.
● **ir justo,-a de dinero**, to be short of money. ‖ **ir justo,-a de tiempo**, to be pressed for time. ‖ **justo en ese momento**, just at that moment. ‖ **no es justo**, it isn't fair.
juvenil 1 *adj* young, youthful: *estás muy juvenil con ese vestido,* you look very young in that dress. **2** DEP junior, youth. – **3** *mf* DEP junior, youth: *los juveniles,* the juniors, the youth team.
■ **moda juvenil**, teenage fashion.
juventud 1 *f* (*período*) youth. **2** (*aspecto joven*) youthfulness. **3** (*los jóvenes*) young people *pl*, youth *pl*: *la juventud actual,* the youth of today, young people today.
● **conservar la juventud**, to keep one's youthful looks.
■ **las Juventudes Socialistas**, the Young Socialists.
juzgado *m* (*local*) court.
● **ser de juzgado de guardia**, *fam fig* to be outrageous, be scandalous.
■ **juzgado de guardia**, court, police court. ‖ **juzgado de instrucción**, court of first instance. ‖ **juzgado de primera instancia**, court of first instance. ‖ **juzgado municipal**, town court, city court.
juzgar 1 *t* (*formar juicio*) to judge: *mañana lo juzgan,* he will appear in court tomorrow; *no me juzgues mal, pero ...,* don't get me wrong, but ... **2** (*considerar*) to consider, think: *juzgo conveniente que se le traslade a otra oficina,* I consider it appropriate that he be moved to a different office.
● **a juzgar por**, judging by. ‖ **juzgar como válido,-a**, to deem valid.
▲ Conjugation model [7], like *llegar*

K

K, k *f* (*la letra*) K, k.
ka 1 *f name of the letter k.* 2 (*naipes*) king.
kafkiano,-a *adj* Kafkaesque.
káiser *m* kaiser.
kaki 1 *m* (*árbol*) persimmon tree. 2 (*fruta*) persimmon.
Kampuchea *f* Kampuchea.
karaoke 1 *m* (*práctica*) karaoke. 2 (*aparato*) karaoke machine. 3 (*local*) karaoke bar.
kárate *m* karate.
karateca *mf* karateist.
karateka *mf* karateist.
karst *m* karst.
kárstico,-a *adj* karstic.
kart *m* go-kart, kart.
    ▲ *pl* karts.
karting *m* go-kart racing, karting.
Kathmandu *m* Katmandu, Kathmandu.
katiuska *f* Wellington boot, rubber boot.
kéfir *m* kefir.
kendo *m* kendo.
Kenia *f* Kenya.
keniano,-a 1 *adj* Kenyan. – 2 *m,f* Kenyan.
keroseno *m* kerosene.
kg *sím* (*kilogramo*) kilogram; (*símbolo*) kg.
Khartum *m* Khartoum.
kilo 1 *m* kilogram. 2 *arg* million pesetas.
kilocaloría *f* kilocalorie.
kilogramo *m* kilogram.
kilohercio *m* → **kilohertz**.
kilohertz *m* kilohertz.
kilolitro *m* kilolitre, US kiloliter.
kilometraje *m* ≈ mileage.
kilometrar *t* to measure the distance of (*in kilometres*).

kilométrico,-a 1 *adj* kilometric: *este mapa indica la distancia kilométrica entre las ciudades,* this map shows the distance in kilometres between towns. 2 *fam* (*larguísimo*) endless. – 3 *m* runabout ticket.
kilómetro *m* kilometre, US kilometer.
kilovatio *m* → **kilowatt**.
kilowatt *m* kilowatt.
kimono *m* → **quimono**.
kiolobyte *m* kilobyte.
kiosko *m* → **quiosco**.
Kirguizistán *m* Kirghizstan.
Kiribati *m* Kiribati.
kit *m* kit.
    ▲ *pl* kits.
kiwi 1 *m* (*ave*) kiwi. 2 (*fruta*) kiwi, kiwi fruit.
Kl *sím* (*kilolitro*) kilolitre (US kiloliter); (*símbolo*) Kl.
kleenex *m* Kleenex, tissue.
    ▲ *Registered trademark.*
km *sím* (*kilómetro, kilómetros*) kilometre, (US kilometer); (*símbolo*) km.
km/h *abr* (*kilómetros hora*) kilometres per hour (US kilometers per hour); (*abreviatura*) kmph.
KO *abr* (*knock-out*) knock-out; (*abreviatura*) KO.
    ● **dejar a algn. KO,** *fam fig* to knock sb. out.
koala *m* koala.
kurdo,-a 1 *adj* Kurdish. – 2 *m,f* (*persona*) Kurd. – 3 kurdo, *m* (*idioma*) Kurdish.
Kuwait *m* Kuwait.
kuwaití 1 *adj* Kuwaiti. – 2 *m,f* Kuwaiti.
kw *sím* (*kilovatio*) kilowatt; (*símbolo*) kw.
kw/h *abr* (*kilovatios hora*) kilowatts per hour; (*abreviatura*) kwph

L

L, l *f* (*la letra*) L, l.

l *sím* (*litro*) litre (US liter); (*símbolo*) l.

la¹ *art def f sing* the: *la casa*, the house.
● **la de,** the amount of, the number of: *¡la de coches que había!*, the number of cars there were!

la² *pron pers f sing* (*persona*) her; (*cosa*) it: *la invité a cenar,* I invited her to supper; *no la he leído,* I haven't read it.
▲ *See also* **las.**

la³ *m* MÚS la, lah, A.

LAB *abr* (*Langile Abertzaleen Batzordea*) Assembly of Nationalist Workers (*Basque nationalist labour union*).

laberíntico,-a *adj* labyrinthic, labyrinthine.

laberinto *m* labyrinth, maze.

labia *f fam* loquacity.
● **tener labia,** *fam* to have the gift of the gab.

labiado,-a *adj* labiate.

labial 1 *adj* (*gen*) labial. – **2** *f* LING labial.

lábil 1 *adj* (*no estable*) unstable; (*frágil*) fragile. **2** QUÍM labile.

labio *m* lip.
■ **labio leporino,** harelip.

labiodental 1 *adj* labiodental. – **2** *f* labiodental.

labor 1 *f* (*gen*) work. **2** (*costura*) embroidery, needlework; (*punto*) knitting.
● **estar por la labor,** to be willing to help. ‖ "profesión: sus labores", "occupation: housewife".
■ **labores del campo,** farm work. ‖ **labores del hogar,** housework.
▲ In 2 also **labores.**

laborable 1 *adj* (*de trabajo*) working. **2** AGR arable.
■ **día laborable,** working day, workday.

laboral *adj* labour.
■ **accidente laboral,** industrial accident, accident in the workplace.

laboralista *adj* (*abogado*) labour relations.

laboratorio *m* laboratory.

laboriosamente *adv* painstakingly.

laboriosidad *f* laboriousness.

laborioso,-a 1 *adj* (*trabajador*) industrious, diligent. **2** (*trabajoso*) laborious.

laborismo *m* Labour Movement.

laborista 1 *adj* Labour. – **2** *mf* Labour (Party) member.

labrado,-a 1 *pp* → **labrar.** – **2** labrado, *m* (*de piedra, mármol*) carving.

labrador,-ra *m,f* farmer.

labranza *f* farming.

labrar 1 *t* AGR (*campo*) to work; (*con arado*) to plough (US plow). **2** (*metal*) to work; (*madera*) to carve; (*piedra*) to cut.
● **labrarse un futuro,** to make a future for os.

labriego,-a *m,f* farm worker.

laburno *m* laburnum.

laca 1 *f* (*en arte*) lacquer; (*resina*) shellac. **2** (*para pelo*) hair spray.

■ **laca de uñas,** nail varnish, nail polish.

lacar *t* to lacquer.

lacayo *m* lackey, footman.

laceración *f* laceration.

lacerante *adj lit* (*dolor*) searing.

lacerar 1 *t* to lacerate, tear. **2** *fig* to harm, damage.

lacería *f* ornamental bows *pl.*

lacero,-a 1 *m,f* (*de ganado*) lassoer. **2** (*furtivo*) poacher. **3** (*de perros*) dog-catcher.

lacio,-a 1 *adj* (*cabello*) straight. **2** (*marchito*) withered. **3** (*sin vigor*) limp.

lacón *m* ham.
■ **lacón con grelos,** hock of pork with turnip tops.

lacónico,-a *adj* laconic.

laconismo *m* laconicism.

lacra 1 *f* (*señal*) mark, scar. **2** (*mal*) evil, scourge. **3** (*defecto*) fault.

lacrado,-a 1 *pp* → **lacrar.** – **2** *adj* (*sobre*) sealed with wax.

lacrar *t* to seal (with sealing wax).

lacre *m* sealing wax.

lacrimal *adj* tear, lachrymal.

lacrimógeno,-a *adj* tearful: *una historia lacrimógena,* a tear jerker.
■ **gas lacrimógeno,** tear-gas.

lacrimoso,-a *adj* tearful, lachrymose.

lactancia *f* (*acción*) lactation; (*periodo*) breast-feeding: *durante la lactancia, la madre ...,* while she is breast-feeding, the mother ...

lactante 1 *adj* lactational. – **2** *mf* unweaned baby.

lacteado,-a *adj* with milk.

lácteo,-a *adj* milk, milky.
■ **productos lácteos,** dairy products.

láctico,-a *adj* lactic.

lactosa *f* lactose.

lacustre *adj* lake.

ladear 1 *t* to tilt. – **2 ladearse,** *p* (*inclinarse*) to lean, lean over. **3** *fam* (*apartarse*) to move.

ladeo *m* tilt.

ladera *f* hillside.

ladilla *f* crab louse.

ladino,-a 1 *adj* sly. – **2 ladino,** *m* (*lengua*) Ladino.

lado *m* (*gen*) side.
● **al lado de algn.,** next to sb.: *me puse a su lado,* I sat next to her; *a su lado no vale nada,* he's nothing compared to her; *no se movió de su lado en toda la enfermedad,* he stood by him all through his illness. ‖ **al lado de algo,** beside sth.: *lo he dejado al lado del teléfono,* I've left it beside the phone; *la casa de al lado,* next door. ‖ **dar de lado a algn.,** to ignore sb. ‖ **de medio lado,** tilted, on the tilt. ‖ **de un lado para otro,** about, all over the place, to and fro, backwards and forwards. ‖ **dejar a algn. de lado,** to leave sb. out.

‖ **dejar algo a un lado,** to leave sth. aside. ‖ **dejar algo de lado,** to leave sth. aside. ‖ **estar al lado,** (*muy cerca*) to be very near. ‖ **hacerse a un lado,** to get out of the way. ‖ **poner a un lado,** to set aside. ‖ **poner algo de lado,** to put sth. sideways. ‖ **por un lado ... por otro ...,** on the one hand ... on the other hand ...
ladrador,-ra *adj* barking.
ladrar *i* to bark.
ladrido *m* bark: *con tanto ladrido no se oye nada,* you can't hear a thing with all that barking.
● **dar ladridos,** to bark.
ladrillazo *m* blow with a brick.
ladrillo 1 *m* (*en construcción*) brick. 2 *fam* pain, bore.
ladrón,-ona 1 *adj* thieving. – 2 *m,f* (*persona - que roba*) thief; (- *que tima, engaña*) crook. – 3 **ladrón,** *m* (*enchufe*) adaptor.
● **¡al ladrón!,** stop thief!
ladronzuelo,-a *m,f* petty thief.
lagar *m* press.
lagarta *f* → **lagarto,-a.**
lagartija *f* small lizard.
lagarto,-a 1 *m,f* (*animal*) lizard. 2 *fam* (*pícaro*) sly devil.
● **¡lagarto, lagarto!,** *fam* God preserve us!, Heaven help us!
lagartón,-ona *m,f fam* sly devil.
lago *m* lake.
lágrima 1 *f* (*ocular*) tear. 2 (*de lámpara, pendiente*) teardrop.
● **llorar a lágrima viva,** *fam* to cry one's eyes out. ‖ **saltársele las lágrimas a algn.,** to bring tears to one's eyes: *se me saltaron las lágrimas,* tears came to my eyes, it brought tears to my eyes.
■ **lágrimas de cocodrilo,** crocodile tears.
lagrimal 1 *adj* tear, lachrymal. – 2 *m* corner of the eye.
lagrimear *i* (*ojos*) to run, water. 2 (*persona*) to cry easily.
lagrimeo 1 *m* (*del ojo*) watering. 2 (*llanto*) weeping, shedding of tears.
lagrimón *m* large teardrop, large tear.
lagrimoso,-a *adj* tearful.
laguna 1 *f* small lake, lagoon. 2 *fig* (*de conocimiento*) gap; (*de la memoria*) memory lapse.
laicado *m* laity.
laicismo *m* laicism, secularism.
laico,-a 1 *adj* lay, secular. – 2 *m,f* (*hombre*) layman; (*mujer*) laywoman.
laísmo *m incorrect use of la, las as indirect objects instead of le, les.*
laísta 1 *adj* given to *laísmo.* – 2 *mf person who is given to laísmo.*
laja *f* slab.
lama[1] *m* REL lama.
lama[2] 1 *f* (*lámina*) slat. 2 (*barro*) slime.
lamé *m* lamé.
lameculos *mf tabú* arse licker, US ass licker.
▲ *pl* **lameculos.**
lamedura *f* licking.
lamentable *adj* (*injusticia*) regrettable, deplorable; (*estado*) sorry, pitiful.
lamentablemente *adv* regrettably.
lamentación *f* wail, wailing, lamentation.
lamentar 1 *t* to regret. – 2 **lamentarse,** *p* to complain.
lamento *m* moan, cry.
lamer *t* to lick.
lametazo *m* lick.
lametón *m* lick.

lamido,-a 1 *adj* (*relamido*) prissy. 2 (*flaco*) scrawny. 3 (*desgastado*) worn.
lámina 1 *f* (*gen*) sheet, plate. 2 (*ilustración*) illustration; (*grabado*) engraving.
laminación *f* lamination.
laminado,-a 1 *pp* → **laminar.** – 2 *adj* laminated. – 3 **laminado,** *m* lamination.
laminar 1 *adj* laminar. – 2 *t* to laminate.
lampar *i fam* to beg.
lámpara 1 *f* lamp. 2 RAD valve.
■ **lámpara de mesa,** table lamp. ‖ **lámpara de pie,** standard lamp.
lamparilla 1 *f* (*lámpara*) small lamp. 2 (*vela*) candle.
lamparón *m fam* stain.
lampiño,-a *adj* hairless.
lampista *mf fam* (*gen*) handyman; (*fontanero*) plumber; (*electricista*) electrician.
lamprea *f* lamprey.
lana 1 *f* wool. – 2 **lanas,** *fpl fam* (*pelo*) long hair *sing:* **¡córtate esas lanas!,** get your hair cut!
● **de lana,** woollen (US woolen). ‖ **cardarle la lana a algn.,** *fam* to tick sb. off, tell sb. off. ‖ **ir por lana y salir trasquilado,-a,** *fam* to go for wool and come home shorn.
lanar *adj* wool-bearing.
lance 1 *m* (*suceso*) event. 2 (*infortunio*) incident. 3 (*pelea*) quarrel. 4 DEP move.
● **de lance,** second-hand.
■ **lance de fortuna,** stroke of luck. ‖ **lance de honor,** duel.
lanceado,-a *adj* → **lanceolado,-a.**
lanceolado,-a *adj* lanceolate.
lancero *m* lancer.
lancha *f* (*bote*) launch, boat; (*a motor*) speedboat, motorboat.
■ **lancha motora,** speedboat, motorboat. ‖ **lancha neumática,** rubber dinghy. ‖ **lancha salvavidas,** lifeboat.
lanchero *m* boatman.
lanchón *m* barge.
landa *f* moor.
landó *m* landau.
lanero,-a *adj* wool.
langosta 1 *f* (*crustáceo*) crawfish, spiny lobster. 2 (*insecto*) locust.
langostino *m type of prawn.*
languidecer *i* to languish.
▲ Conjugation model |43|, like **agradecer.**
languidez 1 *f* (*falta de vigor*) languor. 2 (*flaqueza*) listlessness.
lánguido,-a 1 *adj* (*falto de vigor*) languid, languorous. 2 (*débil*) listless.
lanilla 1 *f* (*tejido*) flannel. 2 (*pelusilla*) fluff.
lanolina *f* lanolin, lanoline.
lanoso,-a *adj* (*gen*) furry, woolly (US wooly).
lanudo,-a *adj* woolly (US wooly).
lanza 1 *f* lance, spear. 2 (*de carro*) shaft.
● **lanza en ristre,** *fam* ready for action. ‖ **romper una lanza por,** to stick up for, defend.
lanzacohetes *m* rocket launcher.
▲ *pl* **lanzacohetes.**
lanzadera *f* shuttle.
lanzado,-a 1 *pp* → **lanzar.** – 2 *adj* (*impetuoso*) impetuous; (*decidido*) determined.
● **ir lanzado,-a,** to be zooming along. ‖ **salir lanzado,-**

a, to zoom out. ‖ **ser un,-a lanzado,-a,** *fam* to be very forward.

lanzador,-ra *m,f* (*de jabalina*) thrower; (*de béisbol*) pitcher; (*de cricket*) bowler.

lanzagranadas *m* grenade launcher.
▲ *pl lanzagranadas.*

lanzallamas *m* flame-thrower.
▲ *pl lanzallamas.*

lanzamiento 1 *m* (*acción de lanzar*) throwing. 2 AER (*de cohete*) launching; (*de proyectil*) firing; (*de bomba*) dropping.
■ **lanzamiento de disco,** discus throwing. ‖ **lanzamiento de jabalina,** javelin throwing. ‖ **lanzamiento de peso,** shot put.

lanzaminas *m* minelayer.
▲ *pl lanzaminas.*

lanzar 1 *t* (*gen*) to throw: *lanzó una piedra al arroyo,* he threw a stone into the stream; *se lanzó al vacío de un rascacielos,* he threw himself off a skyscraper. 2 (*cohete*) to launch. 3 *fig* (*grito*) to let out; (*insulto*) to fire: *me lanzó una mirada furtiva,* she gave me a furtive look. 4 (*producto*) to launch. – 5 **lanzarse,** *p* (*actuar decididamente*) to throw os., launch os. into: *se lanzaron al ataque sin pensarlo dos veces,* they threw themselves straight into the attack; *se lanzaron a la calle en protesta por la nueva ley,* they went out onto the streets to protest against the new law.
● **lanzarse contra algn.,** to attack sb.
▲ Conjugation model [4], *like realizar.*

laña *f* clamp.

Laos *m* Laos.

laosiano,-a 1 *adj* Laotian. – 2 *m,f* (*persona*) Laotian. – 3 **laosiano,** *m* (*idioma*) Laotian.

lapa 1 *f* (*molusco*) limpet. 2 *pey* (*persona*) bore.
● **pegarse como una lapa,** *fam* to cling like a leech.

lapicero *m* pencil.

lápida *f* (*sepulcral*) tombstone, slab; (*conmemorativa*) plaque.

lapidación *f* lapidation, stoning.

lapidar *t* to stone.

lapidario,-a 1 *adj* (*frase - concisa*) terse, concise; (*- contundente*) categorical. – 2 *m,f* (*de piedras preciosas*) lapidary. 3 (*de lápidas*) monumental mason.

lapislázuli *m* lapis lazuli.

lápiz *m* pencil.
■ **lápices de colores,** coloured (us colored) pencils, crayons. ‖ **lápiz de labios,** lipstick. ‖ **lápiz de ojos,** eyeliner. ‖ **lápiz óptico,** light pen.

lapo *m fam* gob.

lapón,-ona 1 *adj* Lapp. – 2 *m,f* Laplander, Lapp.

Laponia *f* Lapland.

lapso 1 *m* (*de tiempo*) period of time, lapse: *en el lapso de un mes,* in the space of a month. 2 (*error*) → **lapsus.**

lapsus *m* (*error*) slip; (*de memoria*) memory lapse, lapse of memory.
■ **lapsus linguae,** slip of the tongue.

laquear *t* to lacquer.

lar 1 *m* (*deidad*) lar. 2 (*de lumbre*) hearth. – 3 **lares,** *mpl* (*dioses*) lares. 4 *lit* (*casa*) home *sing.*

larga *f* → **largo,-a.**

largamente *adv* at length, for a long time.

largar 1 *t fam* (*dar*) to give: *le largó un discurso de media hora,* he gave him a half-hour speech; *le largó un sopapo en toda la cara,* she slapped him in the face. 2 *fam* (*despedir*) to sack, fire, give the push: *creo que me van a largar,* I think I'm going to get the sack. 3 *fam* (*contar*)

to tell: *si la presionan un poco más lo largará todo,* if they push her a bit more she'll tell them everything; *esa lo larga todo,* she can't keep anything to herself. – 4 *i fam* (*hablar*) to chatter, natter. – 5 **largarse,** *p fam* (*irse*) to go, leave: *me largo,* I'm off, US I'm out of here.
● **largar amarras,** to cast off. ‖ **¡lárgate!,** *fam* get lost!, clear off!, get out!
▲ Conjugation model [7], *like llegar.*

largo,-a 1 *adj* (*en longitud*) long: *me he comprado un vestido largo,* I've bought myself a long dress. 2 (*en extensión*) long: *esta redacción es demasiado larga,* this composition is too long; *se me hizo muy larga la película,* I thought the film dragged on; *hace largo tiempo de eso,* it's a long time now. 3 (*alto*) tall: *¡qué largo está tu hijo!,* hasn't your son grown!; *se cayó cuan larga era,* she fell flat on her face. 4 (*en cantidad*) good: *llevo una hora larga esperándote,* I've been waiting for you for over an hour. – 5 **largo,** *m* length: *¿qué mide de largo?,* how long is it?, what length is it? 6 (*de tela*) length: *con dos largos te basta para una falda,* two lengths will be enough for a skirt. 7 (*de piscina*) length, US lap. 8 MÚS largo. – 9 **largas,** *fpl* (*de vehículo*) full beam, full headlights: *llevas las largas puestas,* you've got full beam on. – 10 **¡largo!,** *interj fam* get out!: *¡largo de aquí!,* get out of here!
● **a la larga,** in the long run. ‖ **a lo largo,** lengthwise: *mídelo a lo largo,* measure it lengthwise. ‖ **a lo largo de,** along, throughout: *a lo largo del año,* throughout the year; *he aprendido mucho a lo largo de los años,* I've learned a lot over the years. ‖ **dar largas a algn.,** to put sb. off. ‖ **dar largas a algo,** to put off doing sth. ‖ **esto va para largo,** this is going to take a long time. ‖ **ir de largo,** to wear a long dress. ‖ **largo y tendido,** at length. ‖ **ser más largo,-a que un día sin pan,** *fam* to take ages, take forever. ‖ **pasar de largo,** to pass by. ‖ **tener para largo,** to be busy for a long time: *¿tienes para largo?,* will you be long? ‖ **venir de largo,** to go back a long way. ‖ **vestir de largo,** to wear a long dress.

largometraje *m* feature film, full-length film.

larguero 1 *m* (*en fútbol*) crossbar. 2 (*en construcción*) crossbeam; (*de puerta*) jamb; (*de cama*) side.

largueza *f* largesse, US largess, generosity.

larguirucho,-a *adj fam* lanky.

largura *f* length.

laringe *f* larynx.

laríngeo,-a *adj* laryngeal.

laringitis *f* laryngitis.
▲ *pl laringitis.*

laringología *f* laryngology.

laringólogo,-a *m,f* laryngologist.

larva *f* larva.

larvado,-a *adj* (*enfermedad*) dormant.

larvario,-a *adj* larval.

las 1 *art def fpl* the: *las casas,* the houses. – 2 *pron fpl* (*objeto directo*) them: *las vi,* I saw them.
▲ See also *la.*

lasaña *f* lasagne.

lasca *f* chip.

lascivia *f* lasciviousness, lewdness.

lascivo,-a *adj* lascivious, lewd.

láser *m* laser.
▲ *pl láser.*

lasitud *f* lassitude, weariness.

lástima *f* pity.
● **por lástima,** out of pity. ‖ **¡qué lástima!,** what a pity! ‖ **tener lástima a algn.,** to feel sorry for sb.

lastimar 1 t (*herir*) to hurt, injure. 2 (*ofender*) to offend. – 3 **lastimarse,** p to hurt os.
lastimero,-a adj pitiful.
lastimoso,-a adj pitiful, sorry.
lastrar 1 t MAR to ballast. 2 *fig* to hinder.
lastre 1 m MAR ballast. 2 *fig* dead weight, burden.
lata 1 f (*hojalata*) tinplate. 2 (*envase*) tin, can: *una lata de atún,* a tin of tuna; *una lata de cerveza,* a can of beer. 3 (*fastidio*) bore, drag: *es una lata tener que rellenar estos formularios,* it's a drag having to fill in all these forms. ● **dar la lata,** *fam* to annoy, be a nuisance (**a,** to). ‖ **en lata,** canned, tinned: *sardinas en lata,* tinned sardines.
latencia f latency.
latente adj latent.
lateral 1 adj (*gen*) side. 2 (*parentesco*) lateral. – 3 m (*de carretera*) service lane; (*de avenida*) side lane.
lateralmente adv sideways, laterally.
látex m latex.
latido m beat.
latifundio 1 m (*finca*) latifundium (*large estate*). 2 (*sistema*) → **latifundismo**.
latifundismo m distribution of land in large estates.
latifundista 1 adj relating to latifundismo. – 2 mf estate owner, large land owner.
latigazo 1 m (*golpe de látigo*) lash; (*herida*) whiplash injury. 2 (*sonido*) crack. 3 *arg* (*trago*) swig. ● **dar latigazos a,** to whip.
látigo m whip.
latiguillo m fam (*muletilla*) verbal tic.
latín m Latin. ● **saber (mucho) latín,** *fam* to be too clever by half.
latinajo m fam Latin phrase.
latinismo m Latinism.
latinizar t to latinize.
latino,-a 1 adj Latin. – 2 m,f Latin.
Latinoamérica f Latin America.
latinoamericano,-a 1 adj Latin American. – 2 m,f Latin American.
latir i to beat.
latitud 1 f latitude. – 2 **latitudes,** *fpl fig* (*zona, región*) area *sing*: *¿qué haces tú por estas latitudes?,* what are you doing around here?
latitudinal adj latitudinal.
lato,-a adj broad, wide.
latón m brass.
latoso,-a 1 adj fam annoying, boring. – 2 m,f fam bore.
latrocinio m fml theft, robbery.
LAU¹ abr (*Ley de Arrendamientos Urbanos*) law on urban leasing.
LAU² abr (*Ley de Autonomía Universitaria*) University Autonomy Law.
laúd m lute.
laudable adj laudable, praiseworthy.
láudano m laudanum.
laudatorio,-a adj laudatory.
laureado,-a 1 adj prize-winning: *el artista laureado,* the prize-winning artist; *es el tenista más laureado del circuito,* he's won more trophies than anyone else on the circuit. – 2 **laureada,** f MIL (*insignia*) decoration.
laurear 1 t to award a prize to: *lo laurearon con varios premios,* he was awarded several prizes. 2 (*militar*) to decorate: *fue laureado por su valor,* he was decorated for his bravery.
laurel m (*árbol*) bay. ■ **hoja de laurel,** bay leaf.

Lausana f Lausanne.
lava f lava.
lavable adj washable.
lavabo 1 m (*pila*) washbasin. 2 (*cuarto de baño*) washroom. 3 (*público*) toilet: *¿dónde están los lavabos de señoras?,* where's the ladies' toilet?
lavada f → **lavado,-a**.
lavadero 1 m (*en casa*) laundry room. 2 (*público*) public washing place. 3 (*pila*) sink. 4 (*de una mina*) washery.
lavado,-a 1 pp → **lavar**. – 2 adj washed. – 3 **lavado,** m wash: *a esas cortinas les hace falta un buen lavado,* those curtains need a good wash. – 4 **lavada,** f big wash: *con quince hijos, imagínate las lavadas que hacía mi madre,* with fifteen children, imagine the washes my mother used to do.
● **hacerle un lavado de cerebro a algn.,** to brainwash sb. ‖ **hacer un lavado de estómago a algn.,** to pump sb.'s stomach out.
■ **lavado a mano,** handwashing. ‖ **lavado de cara,** facelift. ‖ **lavado de cerebro,** brainwashing. ‖ **lavado en seco,** dry-cleaning.
lavadora f washing machine.
lavafrutas m finger bowl.
▲ pl *lavafrutas*.
lavamanos m washbasin.
▲ pl *lavamanos*.
lavanda f lavender.
lavandera 1 f (*mujer*) washerwoman, laundress. 2 (*pájaro*) wagtail.
lavandería f (*automática*) launderette, US laundromat; (*con servicio completo*) laundry.
■ **servicio de lavandería,** laundry service.
lavaojos m eyebath.
▲ pl *lavaojos*.
lavaplatos m dishwasher.
▲ pl *lavaplatos*.
lavar 1 t (*ropa, cuerpo, etc*) to wash: *¿me has lavado los calcetines?,* have you washed my socks? 2 (*platos*) to wash up. 3 *fig* (*conciencia, honor*) to clean. – 4 **lavarse,** p to wash os., have a wash.
● **lavar a mano,** to hand-wash. ‖ **lavar en seco,** to dry-clean. ‖ **lavar los platos,** to wash the dishes, GB do the washing-up, wash up.
lavativa f enema.
lavatorio 1 m (*ceremonia de Jueves Santo*) maundy. 2 (*de la misa*) lavabo.
lavavajillas m dishwasher.
▲ pl *lavavajillas*.
lavotear i to wash hurriedly.
lavoteo m quick wash.
laxante 1 adj laxative. – 2 m laxative.
laxar t to loosen.
laxitud f laxity, laxness.
laxo,-a 1 adj (*sin tensión*) slack. 2 (*poco estricto*) lax.
laya f kind.
● **de toda laya,** of all kinds.
lazada 1 f (*nudo*) knot. 2 (*lazo*) bow.
lazareto 1 m (*hospital de leprosos*) lazaretto. 2 (*para cuarentenas*) quarantine station.
lazarillo m guide.
■ **perro lazarillo,** guide dog.
lazo 1 m (*cinta*) ribbon; (*de adorno*) bow. 2 *fig* (*vínculo*) tie, bond. 3 (*trampa*) snare, trap.
■ **lazo corredizo,** slipknot.
lb sím (*libra*) pound; (*símbolo*) lb.

Lda. *abr* (*licenciada*) woman graduate, graduate.
Ldo. *abr* (*licenciado*) man graduate, graduate.
le 1 *pron m sing* (*objeto directo*) him; (*usted*) you: *unos atra-cadores le mataron,* some muggers killed him; *¿quién le sirvió?,* who served you? – 2 *pron mf sing* (*objeto indirecto - a él*) him; (*- a ella*) her; (*- a usted*) you: *le regalaron un perrito,* they gave him a puppy; *le repito la pregunta,* I'll repeat the question for you.
▲ *See also* **les** *and* **leísmo.**
leal 1 *adj* loyal, faithful. 2 (*justo*) fair.
lealmente *adv* loyally, faithfully.
lealtad *f* loyalty, faithfulness.
leandra *f arg* peseta.
lebrato *m* leveret.
lebrel *m* greyhound.
lebrillo *m* bowl.
lección *f* lesson.
● **dar una lección a algn.,** *fig* to teach sb. a lesson. ‖ **tomarle la lección a algn.,** to test sb.
■ **lección inaugural,** inaugural lecture. ‖ **lección magistral,** master class.
lechada *f* whitewash.
lechal *adj* sucking.
lechazo *m* (*cordero*) sucking lamb.
leche 1 *f* milk. 2 *fam* (*golpe*) knock; (*accidente*) crash: *te voy a dar una leche como no te estés quieto,* I'll wallop you if you don't keep still; *se pegó una leche bajando las escaleras,* she crashed down the stairs; *no corras tanto que nos vamos a dar una leche,* don't drive so fast, we're going to crash. 3 *tabú* (*fastidio*) drag, bastard, bummer: *vaya una leche tener que levantarse tan temprano,* what a bastard having to get up so early. 4 *fam* (*suerte*) luck: *¡qué mala leche, mira que perder el avión!,* what rotten luck, fancy missing the plane!; *¡qué leche tienes hijo!,* you jammy bugger! 5 *tabú* (*semen*) spunk, US scum.
● **a toda leche,** *fam* at full belt, flat out. ‖ **de la leche,** *arg* bloody, bleeding, frigging. ‖ **estar de mala leche,** *fam* to be in a foul mood. ‖ **más blanco,-a que la leche,** as white as a sheet. ‖ **ser la leche,** *tabú* to be bloody incredible. ‖ **tener mala leche,** *fam* (*mal carácter*) to have a foul temper; (*malicia - hombre*) to be a bastard; (*- mujer*) to be a bitch.
■ **leche condensada,** condensed milk. ‖ **leche descremada,** skimmed milk. ‖ **leche desnatada,** skimmed milk. ‖ **leche entera,** whole milk. ‖ **leche en polvo,** powdered milk. ‖ **leche frita,** *dessert made of fried milk and flour batter.* ‖ **leche merengada,** *iced drink made from milk, eggwhites and sugar, flavoured with cinnamon.*
lechecillas *fpl* sweetbreads.
lechera *f* → **lechero,-a.**
lechería *f* dairy.
lechero,-a 1 *adj* milk. – 2 *m,f* (*hombre*) milkman, dairyman; (*mujer*) milkmaid, dairymaid. – 3 **lechera,** *f* (*recipiente - de mesa*) milk jug; (*- para llevar leche*) milk churn.
■ **central lechera,** dairy, dairies *pl*. ‖ **el cuento de la lechera,** counting one's chickens before they're hatched.
lecho *m* (*gen*) bed; (*de un río*) river bed.
lechón *m* (*animal*) piglet; (*en cocina*) sucking pig.
lechoso,-a *adj* (*de la leche*) milky; (*color*) pasty white.
lechuga *f* lettuce.
● **fresco,-a como una lechuga,** *fam* as fresh as a daisy.
lechuguino *m* fop.
lechuza *f* owl.
■ **lechuza común,** barn owl.

lecitina *f* lecithin.
lectivo,-a *adj* school: *mañana es día lectivo,* tomorrow's a school day, there are classes tomorrow.
■ **horas lectivas,** (*gen*) hours of classes; (*de profesor*) teaching hours.
lector,-ra 1 *adj* reading. – 2 *m,f* reader. 3 EDUC foreign language assistant. – 4 **lector,** *m* TÉC scanner.
■ **lector óptico,** optical scanner.
lectorado *m* language assistantship.
lectura 1 *f* reading. 2 (*material de lectura*) reading matter. 3 (*interpretación*) interpretation, reading.
leer 1 *t* (*gen*) to read. 2 (*tesis*) to defend. – 3 *i* to read.
● **leer entre líneas,** to read between the lines.
▲ *Conjugation model* [61].
legación *f* legation.
legado,-a 1 *pp* → **legar.** – 2 **legado,** *m* (*herencia*) legacy, bequest. 3 (*persona*) legate, representative.
legajo *m* dossier.
legal 1 *adj* (*gen*) legal. 2 *arg* (*persona*) aboveboard, upfront.
legalidad 1 *f* (*de una acción etc*) legality, lawfulness. 2 (*sistema de leyes*) law.
■ **la legalidad vigente,** the law as it stands.
legalista 1 *adj* legalistic. – 2 *mf* legalist.
legalización 1 *f* (*de una situación, unión*) legalization. 2 (*de documento, firma*) to authenticate.
legalizar 1 *t* (*situación, unión*) to legalize. 2 (*documento, firma*) to authenticate. – 3 **legalizarse,** *p* to become legal.
▲ *Conjugation model* [4], *like* **realizar.**
legalmente *adv* legally, lawfully.
légamo *m* slime.
legaña *f* sleep.
legañoso,-a *adj* bleary-eyed.
legar 1 *t* to bequeath. 2 *fig* to hand down, pass on.
▲ *Conjugation model* [7], *like* **llegar.**
legatario,-a *m,f* legatee.
legendario,-a *adj* legendary.
legibilidad *f* legibility.
legible *adj* legible.
legión 1 *f* MIL legion. 2 *fig* crowd: *una legión de seguidores,* a crowd of followers.
■ **Legión Extranjera,** Foreign Legion.
legionario,-a 1 *adj* legionary. – 2 **legionario,** *m* legionary, legionnaire.
■ **enfermedad del legionario,** Legionnaire's disease.
legionella 1 *f* (*enfermedad*) Legionnaire's disease. 2 (*bacteria*) legionella bacterium.
legislación *f* legislation.
legislador,-ra 1 *adj* legislative. – 2 *m,f* legislator.
legislar *i* to legislate.
legislativo,-a *adj* legislative.
legislatura 1 *f* (*período*) term of office. 2 (*cuerpo*) legislative body.
legitimación *f* legitimization.
legitimar *t* to legitimate.
legitimidad *f* legitimacy.
legítimo,-a *adj* JUR legitimate. 2 (*genuino*) real, authentic.
lego,-a 1 *adj* lay, secular. 2 (*ignorante*) ignorant: *soy lego en la materia,* I know nothing about the subject. – 3 *m,f* REL (*hermano*) lay brother; (*hermana*) lay sister.
legrado 1 *m* (*de matriz*) curettage. 2 (*de huesos*) scraping.
legrar *t* (*matriz*) to curette; (*hueso*) to scrape.

legua *f* (*medida*) league.
● notarse a la legua, *fam* to stick out a mile.
■ legua marina, marine league.
leguleyo,-a *m,f pey* pettifogging solicitor.
legumbre 1 *f* (*planta*) legume. 2 (*fruto*) pulse.
leguminoso,-a 1 *adj* leguminous. – 2 leguminosas, *fpl* leguminous plants.
lehendakari *m* President of the Basque autonomous government.
leída *f* → **leído,-a**.
leído,-a 1 *pp* → **leer**. – 2 *adj* well-read. – 3 leída, *f* (*lectura*) reading.
leísmo *m* incorrect use of *le*, *les* as direct object instead of *lo,los*.
leísta 1 *adj* given to leísmo. – 2 *mf* person who is given to leísmo.
leitmotiv *m* leitmotiv.
lejanía *f* distance.
lejano,-a *adj* (*tierra, país*) distant, far-off, far-away; (*pariente, familia*) distant.
lejía *f* bleach.
lejísimo,-a *adj* far away, far off, distant: *en un país lejísimo,* in a country far far away.
lejísimos *adv* very far.
lejos *adv* far, far away, far off.
● a lo lejos, in the distance, far away. ‖ de lejos, from a distance. ‖ desde lejos, from a distance. ‖ lejos de, far from: *lejos de reponerse, empeoró y al final murió,* far from recovering, he got worse and eventually died. ‖ quedar lejos, to be far. ‖ sin ir más lejos, (*por ejemplo*) for example, to take a case in point; (*por cierto*) as a matter of fact, as it happens.
lelo,-a *adj fam* gormless, stupid.
lema *m* (*gen*) motto; (*en publicidad*) slogan.
lempira *m* lempira.
lencería 1 *f* (*ropa interior*) lingerie. 2 (*ropa blanca*) linen. 3 (*tienda - de ropa interior*) lingerie shop; (*- de ropa blanca*) linen shop.
lencero,-a *m,f* draper.
lendakari *m* → **lehendakari**.
lengua 1 *f* ANAT tongue. 2 (*idioma*) language. 3 (*de tierra*) strip.
● con la lengua fuera, *fam* with one's tongue hanging out. ‖ darle a la lengua, *fam* to chat. ‖ dicen las malas lenguas que ..., gossip has it that ... ‖ hacerse lenguas de algo, to rave about sth. ‖ irse de la lengua, *fam* to let the cat out of the bag; (*uso figurado*) to hold one's tongue. ‖ no tener pelos en la lengua, *fig* not to mince one's words. ‖ tener algo en la punta de la lengua, *fig* to have sth. on the tip of one's tongue. ‖ tener la lengua muy larga, *fam* to have a loose tongue. ‖ tener una lengua viperina, to have a vicious tongue. ‖ tirar de la lengua a algn., *fam* to pump sb. for information. ‖ trabarse la lengua, to get tongue-tied.
■ lengua de gato, langue de chat. ‖ lengua d'oc, langue d'oc. ‖ lengua d'oïl, langue d'oïl. ‖ lengua de trapo, babbling. ‖ lengua madre, parent language. ‖ lengua materna, mother tongue.
lenguado *m* sole.
lenguaje 1 *m* (*gen*) language. 2 (*habla*) speech.
lenguaraz *adj* (*hablador*) garrulous; (*descarado*) insolent.
lengüeta 1 *f* MÚS reed. 2 (*de zapato*) tongue.
lengüetada *f* lick.
lengüetazo *m* lick.
lenidad *f* leniency.
Leningrado *m* Leningrad.

leninismo *m* Leninism.
leninista 1 *adj* Leninist. – 2 *mf* Leninist.
lenitivo,-a 1 *adj* soothing, lenitive. – 2 lenitivo, *m* lenitive.
lenocinio *m* procuring.
■ casa de lenocinio, brothel.
lentamente *adv* slowly.
lente 1 *m & f* lens. – 2 lentes, *mpl* glasses, spectacles.
■ lente de aumento, magnifying glass. ‖ lentes de contacto, contact lenses.
lenteja *f* lentil.
lentejuela *f* sequin.
lentilla *f* contact lense.
lentitud *f* slowness.
● con lentitud, slowly.
lento,-a 1 *adj* slow. – 2 lento, *adv* slowly.
leña 1 *f* wood, firewood. 2 *fam fig* (*paliza*) hiding; (*violencia*) trouble.
● dar leña a algn., *fam* to give sb. a hiding.
leñador,-ra *m,f* woodcutter, lumberjack.
leñazo *m fam* (*golpe*) whack, thwack; (*accidente*) crash.
leñe *interj fam* bloody hell!, damn it! US dammit!
leñera *f* woodshed.
leño 1 *m* log. 2 *fig* (*tonto*) blockhead, thickhead.
● dormir como un leño, to sleep like a log.
leñoso,-a *adj* ligneous, woody.
Leo 1 *adj* Leo. – 2 *m* (*signo*) Leo. – 3 *mf* (*persona*) Leo.
León *m* León.
■ golfo de León, Gulf of Lions.
león,-ona 1 *m,f* (*animal - macho*) lion; (*- hembra*) lioness. 2 (*persona*) lion-hearted person.
● no es tan fiero el león como lo pintan, he's not as bad as he's made out to be.
■ león marino, sea lion.
leonado,-a *adj* tawny.
leonera 1 *f* lion's den. 2 *fig* (*habitación*) tip.
leonés,-esa 1 *adj* of León, from León. – 2 *m,f* person from León, inhabitant of León.
leonino,-a 1 *adj* (*de león*) lion-like, leonine. 2 (*contrato*) unfair.
leontina *f desus* watch chain.
leopardo *m* leopard.
leotardos *mpl* thick woollen tights.
Lepe saber más que Lepe, *loc fam* to be smart, be sharp: *ese chaval sabe más que Lepe,* there are no flies on that lad.
lepidóptero,-a 1 *adj* lepidopterous. – 2 lepidóptero, *m* lepidopteran.
lepra *f* leprosy.
leprosería *f* leper hospital.
leproso,-a 1 *adj* leprous. – 2 *m,f* leper.
lerdo,-a *adj fam* slow-witted.
leridano,-a 1 *adj* of Lérida, from Lérida. – 2 *m,f* person from Lérida, inhabitant of Lérida.
les 1 *pron mpl* (*objeto directo*) them; (*ustedes*) you: *dice que les vió ayer,* she says she saw them yesterday; *no les entiendo,* I don't understand you. – 2 *pron mf pl* (*objeto indirecto*) them; (*a ustedes*) you: *entraron en casa ladrones y les robaron,* burglars broke in and robbed them; *les doy una oportunidad más,* I'll give you one more chance.
▲ See also *le*.
lesa majestad *f* lese majesty.
lesbianismo *m* lesbianism.
lesbiano,-a 1 *adj* lesbian. – 2 lesbiana, *f* lesbian.
lésbico,-a *adj* lesbian.

lesión 1 *f* (*daño físico*) wound, injury. **2** (*perjuicio*) harm.
lesionado,-a 1 *pp* → **lesionar**. – **2** *adj* injured. – **3** *m,f* injured person.
lesionar 1 *t* (*herir*) to injure. **2** (*perjudicar*) to harm. – **3 lesionarse,** *p* to get injured.
lesivo,-a *adj* damaging, injurious.
Lesotho *m* Lesotho.
letal *adj* lethal, deadly.
letanía 1 *f* REL litany. **2** *fam* (*lista*) long list; (*sermón*) spiel.
letárgico,-a *adj* lethargic.
letargo *m* lethargy.
letra 1 *f* (*del alfabeto*) letter. **2** (*de imprenta*) character. **3** (*escritura*) handwriting: *tiene muy buena letra,* she has very nice handwriting. **4** (*de canción*) lyrics *pl,* words *pl.* **5** (*de cambio*) bill of exchange. – **6 letras,** *fpl* EDUC arts; (*literatura*) letters.
● **a la letra,** to the letter. ‖ **al pie de la letra,** to the letter. ‖ **aprender las primeras letras,** to learn to read and write. ‖ **con la letra clara,** clearly, neatly. ‖ **la letra con sangre entra,** spare the rod and spoil the child. ‖ **letra por letra,** word for word. ‖ **ponerle a algn. unas letras,** to write to sb., drop a line to sb.
■ **letra de cambio,** bill of exchange, draft. ‖ **letra de imprenta,** block capitals *pl.* ‖ **letra de molde,** print. ‖ **letra del tesoro,** treasury bond. ‖ **letra gótica,** Gothic script. ‖ **letra mayúscula,** capital letter. ‖ **letra menuda,** small print. ‖ **letra pequeña,** small print. ‖ **letra minúscula,** small letter.
letrado,-a 1 *adj* learned, erudite. – **2** *m,f* lawyer.
letrero *m* sign, notice.
letrina *f* latrine.
letrista *mf* lyricist.
leucemia *f* leukaemia, US leukemia.
leucocito *m* leucocyte, US leukocyte, white blood cell.
leucoma *m* leukoma.
leva 1 *f* MIL levy. **2** MAR weighing anchor.
levadizo,-a *adj* which can be raised.
levadura *f* yeast.
levantador,-ra levantador,-ra de pesas, *m,f* weight-lifter.
levantamiento 1 *m* (*de objeto, peso*) lifting. **2** (*de una sanción*) lifting, raising. **3** (*de un ejército etc*) uprising, revolt. **4** (*de un edificio*) erection, raising. **5** (*de terreno*) uplifting.
■ **levantamiento de pesas,** weightlifting. ‖ **levantamiento del cadáver,** removal of the body.
levantar 1 *t* (*alzar*) to raise, lift: *no lo puedo levantar, pesa mucho,* I can't lift it, it's heavy; *la levantó con una sola mano,* he lifted her up with just one hand; *levanta la tapa,* lift the lid up; *que levanten la mano los que quieran venir,* all those who want to come, raise their hands. **2** (*construir*) to erect, build. **3** (*empresa - hacer rentable*) to get off the ground; (*- establecer*) to set up. **4** (*despegar*) to loosen, unstick: *la humedad ha levantado el papel,* the damp has made the wallpaper come off; *el agua ha levantado el parqué,* the water lifted the parquet floor. **5** (*suprimir*) to lift: *levantaron la prohibición de fumar,* they lifted the ban on smoking. **6** (*cadáver*) to remove. **7** (*causar*) to cause: *el ruido me ha levantado dolor de cabeza,* the noise has given me a headache; *procura no levantar sospechas,* try not to arouse suspicion. **8** (*trazar, dibujar*) to draw. **9** (*animal de caza*) to flush out. – **10** *i* (*día*) to brighten up; (*nubes*) to clear: *si el día levanta, iremos a la playa,* if the weather brightens up, we'll go to the beach. – **11 levantarse,** *p* (*alzarse*) to rise: *el rascacielos se levantaba ante nosotros,* the skyscraper rose up in front of us. **12** (*ponerse de pie*) to stand up. **13** (*dejar la cama*) to get up, get out of bed. **14** (*sublevarse*) to rebel, rise up. **15** (*viento, oleaje*) to get up: *se levantó una tormenta violentísima,* a violent storm got up.
● **levantar el campamento,** to strike camp. ‖ **levantar falsos testimonios contra algn.,** to bear false witness against sb. ‖ **levantar la moral a algn.,** to cheer sb. up, raise sb.'s spirits. ‖ **levantar la vista,** to look up. ‖ **levantar la voz,** to raise one's voice. ‖ **levantarse con el pie izquierdo,** *fig* to get out of bed on the wrong side. ‖ **se levanta la sesión,** court adjourned.
levante 1 *m* (*este*) East. **2** (*viento*) east wind. **3 Levante,** (*región española*) the regions of Valencia and Murcia. **4 el Levante,** (*oriente medio*) the Levant.
levantino,-a 1 *adj* (*valenciano*) Valencian; (*murciano*) of Murcia, from Murcia. – **2** *m,f* (*valenciano*) Valencian; (*murciano*) person from Murcia.
levantisco,-a *adj* (*persona*) rebellious; (*momento*) turbulent.
levar *t* (*ancla*) to weigh.
● **levar anclas,** (*acción*) to weigh anchor, set sail; (*orden*) anchors aweigh!
leve 1 *adj* (*ligero, suave*) slight; (*de poco peso*) light. **2** (*poco importante*) slight, trifling; (*poco grave*) minor.
levedad 1 *f* (*ligereza*) lightness. **2** (*poca importancia*) insignificance.
levemente *adv* lightly, slightly.
leviatán *m* leviathan.
levita 1 *f* (*abrigo*) frock coat. – **2** *mf* (*de Leví*) Levite.
levitación *f* levitation.
levitar *i* to levitate.
levítico,-a 1 *adj* (*valenciano*) Levitical. – **2 el Levítico,** *m* Leviticus.
lexema *m* lexeme.
léxico,-a 1 *adj* lexical. – **2 léxico** *m* (*diccionario*) lexicon. **3** (*vocabulario*) vocabulary.
lexicografía *f* lexicography.
lexicográfico,-a *adj* lexicographical, lexicographic.
lexicógrafo,-a *m,f* lexicographer.
lexicología *f* lexicology.
lexicológico,-a *adj* lexicological.
lexicólogo,-a *m,f* lexicologist.
lexicón *m* lexicon.
ley 1 *f* (*gen*) law; (*proyecto de ley*) bill, act; (*regla*) rule. **2** (*de metal*) purity.
● **aprobar una ley,** to pass a bill. ‖ **con todas las de la ley,** proper. ‖ **de ley,** (*oro*) pure; (*plata*) sterling; (*persona*) genuine. ‖ **¡es ley de vida!,** that's life!, that's the way the cookie crumbles! ‖ **estar fuera de la ley,** to be outside the law. ‖ **hecha la ley, hecha la trampa,** whatever the law, there's always a loophole, laws are made to be broken. ‖ **por ley,** by law.
■ **la ley del más fuerte,** the law of the jungle. ‖ **ley del embudo,** double standards *pl.* ‖ **ley marcial,** martial law. ‖ **ley orgánica,** constitutional law. ‖ **ley sálica,** Salic law. ‖ **ley seca,** prohibition law.
leyenda 1 *f* (*narración*) legend. **2** (*inscripción*) inscription.
■ **leyenda negra,** black legend.
LGE *abr* (*Ley General de Educación*) general education law.
lía *f* (*cuerda*) thick rope.
liado,-a 1 *pp* → **liar**. – **2** *adj* (*ocupado*) busy. **3** (*confuso*) mixed up.
● **estar liado,-a,** to be busy. ‖ **estar liado,-a con algn.,** to be involved with sb., be having an affair with sb.: *¿crees que están liados?,* do you think they're involved with each other?

liana f liana.
liar 1 t (atar) to tie up, bind; (envolver) to wrap up. 2 (cigarrillo) to roll. 3 (lana) to wind. 4 fam (complicar) to mix up, make a mess of; (confundir) to confuse: *con tus inventos lo has liado todo,* you've messed everything up with your silly ideas; *cuéntale la verdad y no lo líes más,* tell him the truth and stop messing him about; *vete por pasos que así no te lías,* take it slowly, that way you won't get all mixed up. 5 fam (engatusar) to involve: *me han liado para que me meta en el negocio,* they managed to get me involved in the deal. – 6 **liarse** a + *sustantivo, p* to start + *ger: se liaron a patadas/golpes,* they started kicking/hitting each other.
● **liarse con algn.,** to have an affair with sb.
▲ Conjugation model [13], like **desviar.**
libación f libation.
libanés,-esa 1 adj Lebanese. – 2 m,f Lebanese.
Líbano el Líbano, m the Lebanon.
libar 1 t (néctar) to suck. 2 lit (bebida) to imbibe.
libelo m libel.
libélula f dragonfly.
liberación 1 f (de una dependencia) liberation; (de una persona) freeing, release: *la liberación de la mujer,* Women's Lib. 2 (de hipoteca) redemption.
liberado,-a 1 pp → **liberar.** – 2 adj liberated.
liberador,-ra 1 adj liberating. – 2 m,f liberator.
liberal 1 adj liberal. – 2 mf liberal. 3 (del partido liberal) Liberal.
liberalidad f (generosidad) generosity, liberality.
liberalismo m liberalism.
liberalista 1 adj liberalist. – 2 mf liberal.
liberalización f (en política) liberalization; (en economía) relaxation of restrictions: *la liberalización del comercio internacional generará riqueza,* the relaxation of international trade restrictions will generate wealth.
liberalizar 1 t (país, política) to liberalize; (mercado) to relax restrictions on. – 2 **liberalizarse,** p to become more liberal.
liberar 1 t (persona, animal) to free; (país, ciudad) to liberate. 2 (energía) to release.
● **liberar a algn. de algo,** to free sb. from sth.
liberatorio,-a adj liberating.
Liberia f Liberia.
liberiano,-a 1 adj Liberian. – 2 m,f Liberian.
libérrimo,-a adj lit free, totally free.
libertad 1 f (gen) freedom, liberty. 2 (confianza) freedom: *puede disponer de él con toda libertad,* he may use it with complete freedom. – 3 **libertades,** fpl liberties.
● **dejar en libertad,** to free, release. ‖ **poner en libertad,** to free, release. ‖ **tomarse la libertad de** + inf, to take the liberty of + ger. ‖ **tomarse libertades con algn.,** to take liberties with sb.
■ **libertad bajo fianza,** bail. ‖ **libertad bajo palabra,** parole. ‖ **libertad condicional,** parole. ‖ **libertad de expresión,** freedom of expression. ‖ **libertad provisional,** bail.
libertador,-ra 1 adj liberating. – 2 m,f liberator.
libertar 1 t to liberate.
libertario,-a 1 adj libertarian. – 2 m,f libertarian.
libertinaje m licentiousness.
libertino,-a 1 adj licentious. – 2 m,f libertine.
liberto,-a m,f (hombre) freedman; (mujer) freedwoman.
Libia f Libya.
libidinoso,-a adj libidinous, lustful.
libido f libido.

líbido f libido.
libio,-a 1 adj Libyan. – 2 m,f Libyan.
libra 1 f (moneda, medida) pound. 2 arg (cien pesetas) a hundred pesetas. 3 **Libra,** ASTROL ASTRON Libra.
■ **libra esterlina,** pound sterling. ‖ **libra irlandesa,** Irish pound, punt.
libraco m pey big fat book, great big thick book.
librado,-a 1 pp → **librar.** – 2 m,f drawee.
librador,-ra m,f drawer.
libramiento m order of payment.
libranza f order of payment.
librar 1 t to save (de, from): *lo hemos librado del castigo,* we have saved him from punishment; *la nevada nos libró de ir al colegio,* the snow stopped us from having to go to school; *me libraron de toda responsabilidad,* they absolved me of all responsibility; *el Señor os librará del mal,* the Lord will deliver you from evil. 2 (batalla) to fight, wage: *libraron una larga batalla,* they fought a long battle. 3 (letra) to issue. – 4 i fam (tener libre) to be off, not to work: *libro todos los lunes,* I've got Mondays off, I'm off on Mondays. – 5 **librarse,** p to escape (de, from): *intentaron librarse de sus perseguidores,* they tried to throw off their pursuers; *siempre se libra de hacer los trabajos sucios,* he always gets out of doing the dirty work.
● **¡Dios me (nos etc) libre!,** Heaven forbid!, God forbid! ‖ **librarse de una buena,** fam to have a close shave.
libre 1 adj (gen) free. 2 (asiento) free, vacant: *¿está libre?,* is this seat free? 3 (sin ocupación) free: *mañana tenemos el día libre,* we've got the day off tomorrow; *si tengo un rato libre ya me pasaré,* if I've a spare moment I'll call round. 4 (exento) free: *el que esté libre de pecado que tire la primera piedra,* let he who is without sin cast the first stone; *es una inversión libre de impuestos,* it's a tax-free investment. 5 (alumno) external. 6 (en natación) free-style.
● **dejar libre a algn.,** to set sb. free. ‖ **ir por libre,** fam to do one's own thing.
■ **entrada libre,** free admittance.
librea f livery.
● **de librea,** liveried.
librecambio m free trade.
librecambismo m free trade.
librecambista 1 adj free-trade. – 2 mf free-trader.
librepensador,-ra 1 adj freethinking. – 2 m,f freethinker.
librepensamiento m freethinking.
librería 1 f (tienda) bookshop, bookstore. 2 (mueble) bookcase; (estantería) bookshelf.
librero,-a m,f bookseller.
libresco,-a adj bookish.
libreta 1 f (para anotar) notebook. 2 (de ahorros) savings book.
■ **libreta de ahorros,** savings book.
libretista mf librettist.
libreto m libretto.
librillo 1 m (libro) small book. 2 (estómago) third stomach.
librito m small book.
■ **librito de lomo,** escalope cordon bleu.
libro 1 m (gen) book. 2 ZOOL third stomach. – 3 **libros,** mpl accounts.
● **llevar los libros,** to do the bookkeeping. ‖ **como un libro abierto,** (con claridad) clearly.
■ **libro blanco,** POL white paper. ‖ **libro de bolsillo,** paperback. ‖ **libro de cabecera,** (favorito) favourite

book; (*guía*) bible. ‖ **libro de caja,** cash-book. ‖ **libro de cocina,** cookery book, recipe book. ‖ **libro de consulta,** reference book. ‖ **libro de coro,** hymn book. ‖ **libro de familia,** *book recording details of births, marriages, etc. in a family.* ‖ **libro de horas,** book of hours. ‖ **libro de reclamaciones,** complaints book. ‖ **libro de texto,** textbook. ‖ **libro de visitas,** visitors' book.

Lic. *abr* (*licenciado,-a*) licenciate, graduate.

licantropía *f* lycanthropy.

licántropo *m* lycanthrope.

licencia 1 *f* (*permiso*) licence (US license), permission. **2** (*documento*) licence (US license), permit. **3** MIL discharge.
● **tomarse la licencia de,** to take the licence (US license) to.
■ **licencia fiscal,** *tax paid by businesses and the self-employed in order to operate legally.* ‖ **licencia poética,** poetic licence (US license).

licenciado,-a 1 *pp* → **licenciar.** – **2** *m,f* EDUC graduate: *es licenciada en Matemáticas,* she's a Maths graduate. **3** (*abogado*) lawyer. – **4 licenciado,** *m* MIL discharged soldier.

licenciar 1 *t* EDUC to award a degree to. **2** MIL to discharge. – **3 licenciarse,** *p* to graduate.

licenciatura *f* (*five year*) university degree.

licencioso,-a *adj* licentious, dissolute.

liceo 1 *m* (*colegio*) secondary school. **2** (*sociedad*) literary society, recreational society.

licitación *f* bid.

licitar *t* to bid.

lícito,-a 1 *adj* (*legal*) licit, lawful. **2** (*justo*) fair.

licitud 1 *f* (*legalidad*) lawfulness. **2** (*justicia*) fairness.

licor *m* (*dulce*) liqueur; (*bebida alcohólica*) liquor, spirits *pl*.

licorera 1 *f* (*botella*) decanter. **2** (*mueble*) drinks cabinet.

licuación *f* liquefaction.

licuadora *f* juice extractor.

licuar *t* to liquefy.
▲ *Conjugation model* [10], *like* **adecuar.**

licuefacción *f* liquefaction.

lid 1 *f* contest, fight. **2** *fig* (*controversia*) dispute.
● **en buena lid,** fair and square. ‖ **experto,-a en estas lides,** experienced in these matters.

líder *mf* leader.

liderar *t* to lead.

liderato *m* leadership.

liderazgo *m* leadership.

lidia 1 *f* (*de toros*) bullfight. **2** (*lucha*) fight, struggle.

lidiar 1 *t* (*toro*) to fight. – **2 lidiar con,** *i fig* (*luchar con*) to battle with, struggle against.
▲ *Conjugation model* [12], *like* **cambiar.**

liebre 1 *f* (*animal*) hare. **2** DEP pacemaker.
● **levantar la liebre,** to let the cat out of the bag.

Liechtenstein *m* Liechtenstein.

liendre *f* nit.

lienzo 1 *m* ART (*tela*) canvas; (*cuadro*) painting. **2** (*tejido*) linen.

lifting *m* facelift.
▲ *pl* **liftings.**

liga 1 *f* (*para media*) garter. **2** (*asociación*) league, alliance. **3** DEP league.

ligado,-a 1 *pp* → **ligar.** – **2** *adj* linked. – **3 ligado,** *m* (*al escribir*) ligature.

ligadura 1 *f* (*atadura*) tie, bond. **2** MED ligature.
■ **ligadura de trompas,** sterilization.

ligamento *m* ligament.

ligar 1 *t* (*atar*) to tie, bind: *lo ligaron de manos y pies,* they bound him hand and foot. **2** (*unir*) to link, connect: *un*

hombre estrechamente ligado a la historia española, a man closely linked with Spanish history. **3** (*metales*) to alloy: *ligan cinc y cobre para hacer latón,* they alloy zinc and copper to make brass. **4** CULIN to bind: *liga la carne picada con huevo,* bind the mince with egg. – **5** *i fam* (*conquistar*) to score: *con esa pinta no me sorprende que no ligues,* I'm not surprised you never score looking like that; *ligó con una italiana,* he picked up an Italian girl, he got off with an Italian girl.
● **estar ligado,-a a,** to be linked to, be connected. ‖ **ir ligado,-a a,** → **estar ligado,-a.** ‖ **ligarse a algn.,** *fam* to pick sb. up, get off with sb.

ligazón *f* link, bond.

ligeramente *adv* (*por encima*) lightly; (*un poco*) slightly; (*con ligereza*) superficially.

ligereza 1 *f* (*poco peso*) lightness. **2** (*prontitud*) swiftness. **3** (*agilidad*) agility. **4** *fig* (*frivolidad*) flippancy, frivolity.
● **con ligereza,** (*con rapidez, agilidad*) swiftly; (*a la ligera*) flippantly.

ligero,-a 1 *adj* (*liviano*) light. **2** (*sin importancia*) minor, light. **3** (*rápido*) swift. **4** (*ágil*) agile. **5** (*frívolo*) flippant.
● **a la ligera,** lightly, flippantly. ‖ **ser ligero,-a de cascos,** to be irresponsible. ‖ **tomarse las cosas a la ligera,** to make light of things, not take things seriously. ‖ **viajar ligero,-a de peso,** to travel light.

lignito *m* lignite.

ligón,-ona *m,f fam* flirt.

ligoteo *m fam* flirting.
● **ir de ligoteo,** *fam* to go out on the pick-up.

ligue *m fam* pick-up, date: *su último ligue es poli,* her latest boyfriend's a cop; *no busca una relación estable, prefiere los ligues de fin de semana,* he doesn't want a steady girlfriend, he prefers one-night stands; *los sábados van de ligue,* on Saturday they go out looking for talent.

liguero,-a 1 *adj* (*de la liga*) league. – **2 liguero,** *m* (*de las medias*) suspender belt.

liguilla *f* round-robin tournament, mini-league.

ligur 1 *adj* Ligurian. – **2** *m,f* Ligurian.
■ **Mar Ligur,** Ligurian Sea.

Liguria *f* Liguria.

ligurino,-a *adj-m,f* → **ligur.**

lija 1 *f* (*papel*) sandpaper. **2** (*pez*) dogfish.
■ **papel de lija,** sandpaper.

lijado *m* sanding.

lijadora *f* sanding machine.

lijar *t* to sand.

lila[1] 1 *adj* (*color*) lilac. – **2** *f* (*flor*) lilac.

lila[2] 1 *adj fam* (*tonto*) dim. – **2** *mf fam* nitwit.

liliputiense 1 *adj* Lilliputian. **2** *fig* lilliputian. – **3** *mf* Lilliputian.

lima[1] 1 *f* (*herramienta*) file; (*para uñas*) nail file. **2** (*acabado*) final polish.
● **comer como una lima,** *fam* to eat like a horse.

lima[2] *f* (*fruta*) lime; (*árbol*) lime tree.

limadura *f* filing.

limar 1 *t* (*pulir*) to file. **2** *fig* (*perfeccionar*) to polish up.
● **limar asperezas,** *fig* to smooth things off.

limbo 1 *m* REL limbo. **2** BOT limb.
● **estar en el limbo,** *fam* to be miles away.

limeño,-a 1 *adj* of Lima, from Lima. – **2** *m,f* person from Lima, inhabitant of Lima.

limero *m* lime tree.

limitación *f* limitation.

limitado,-a 1 *pp* → **limitar.** – **2** *adj* limited.

limitar 1 *t* (*gen*) to limit. – **2 limitar con,** *i* to border with.

● **limitarse a** + *inf,* to restrict os. to + *ger,* to do no more than + *inf: una persona inteligente no se limita a ver la televisión,* an intelligent person does not restrict himself to watching television; *limítate a cumplir ordenes,* just obey orders.
límite I *m* (*extremo*) limit; (*en un terreno*) boundary. **2** (*frontera*) boundary.
● **sin límites,** boundless. ‖ **todo tiene un límite,** there's a limit to everything.
■ **límite de velocidad,** speed limit.
limítrofe *adj* bordering.
limo *m* slime.
limón *m* lemon.
limonada *f* lemonade.
limonar *m* lemon grove.
limonero,-a I *adj* (*del limón*) lemon. – **2** limonero, *m* lemon tree.
limonita *f* limonite.
limosna *f* alms *pl,* charity.
● **dar limosna,** to give money to the poor: *le di una limosna,* I gave him some money. ‖ **pedir limosna,** to beg.
limoso,-a *adj* slimy.
limousine *f →* **limusina.**
limpia *f →* **limpio,-a.**
limpiabotas *m* bootblack.
▲ *pl* **limpiabotas.**
limpiacristales I *m* (*producto*) window cleaning fluid. – **2** *mf* (*persona*) window cleaner.
▲ *pl* **limpiacristales.**
limpiada *f* clean.
limpiador,-ra I *adj* cleaning. – **2** *m,f* (*persona*) cleaner. – **3** limpiador, *m* (*producto*) cleaning product.
limpiaparabrisas *m* windscreen wiper, us windshield wiper.
▲ *pl* **limpiaparabrisas.**
limpiar I *t* (*gen*) to clean, cleanse. **2** (*con paño*) to wipe. **3** *fig* (*purificar*) to purify. **4** *fam* (*robar*) to pinch, nick.
▲ Conjugation model [12], like *cambiar.*
limpidez *f* limpidity.
límpido,-a *adj* limpid.
limpieza I *f* (*ausencia de suciedad*) cleanliness. **2** (*acción de limpiar*) cleaning. **3** (*pureza*) purity. **4** (*honradez*) honesty, fairness. **5** (*precisión*) precision, accuracy.
● **hacer limpieza general,** to have a spring clean, have a general clean-up, us do a spring-cleaning.
■ **limpieza de sangre,** purity of blood. ‖ **limpieza en seco,** dry-cleaning. ‖ **limpieza étnica,** ethnic cleansing. ‖ **señor de la limpieza,** cleaner. ‖ **señora de la limpieza,** cleaner, cleaning lady.
limpio,-a I *adj* (*sin suciedad*) clean: *este detergente lo deja todo muy limpio,* this detergent gets everything beautifully clean. **2** (*claro*) neat, tidy. **3** (*puro*) pure. **4** (*honesto*) honest, fair. **5** (*juego*) fair. **6** com (*neto*) net: *al mes vendré a salir por las 70.000 limpias,* I make roughly 70,000 a month after tax; *ganó 40.000 limpias,* she made 40,000 clear profit. – **7** *f fam* (*eliminación*) clearing-out. – **8** *adv* fairly: *no juegan limpio, hacen trampa,* they don't play fair, they cheat.
● **dejar limpio,-a a algn.,** *fam* to clean sb. out. ‖ **pasar algo a limpio,** to make a fair copy of sth., write sth. out neatly. ‖ **sacar en limpio,** to conclude, infer.
limusina *f* limousine.
linaje I *m* (*ascendencia*) lineage. **2** *fig* (*clase*) kind, sort.
linaza *f* linseed.
lince I *m* zool lynx. **2** *fig* (*persona*) sharp-eyed person.

linchamiento *m* lynching.
linchar *t* to lynch.
lindante *adj* adjoining, bordering.
lindar *i* to border (**con,** on), adjoin (**con,** -).
linde *m* & *f* boundary.
lindero,-a I *adj* bordering, adjoining. – **2** lindero, *m →* **linde.**
lindeza I *f* (*belleza*) prettiness. **2** (*piropo*) flattering remark. – **3** lindezas, *fpl* irón (*insultos*) insults.
lindo,-a *adj* pretty, nice, lovely.
● **de lo lindo,** *fam* a great deal.
línea I *f* (*gen*) line. **2** (*tipo*) figure.
● **de primera línea,** first-class, first-rate. ‖ **en líneas generales,** in general. ‖ **guardar la línea,** to keep one's figure.
■ **línea aérea,** airline. ‖ **línea continua,** solid line, unbroken line. ‖ **línea de meta,** finishing line. ‖ **línea de puntos,** dotted line. ‖ **línea de salida,** starting line.
lineal *adj* linear.
linealidad *f* linearity.
linfa *f* lymph.
linfático,-a *adj* lymphatic.
lingotazo *m fam* swig.
lingote *m* ingot.
lingual *adj* lingual.
lingüista *mf* linguist.
lingüística *f →* **lingüístico,-a.**
lingüístico,-a I *adj* linguistic. – **2** lingüística, *f* linguistics.
linimento *m* liniment.
lino I *m* (*tela*) linen. **2** bot flax.
linóleo *m* linoleum.
linotipia *f* linotype.
linotipista *mf* typesetter.
linotipo *m* linotype.
linterna I *f* (*de pilas*) torch. **2** (*farol*) lantern, lamp. **3** arq lantern.
■ **linterna (eléctrica),** flashlight, torch.
lío I *m* (*embrollo*) mess. **2** (*aventura amorosa*) affair. **3** (*fardo*) bundle.
● **armar un lío,** to make a fuss. ‖ **hacerse un lío,** (*uso literal*) to get tangled up; (*uso figurado*) to get muddled up. ‖ **meterse en un lío,** to get os. into a mess. ‖ **¡qué lío!,** what a mess! ‖ **tener un lío con algn.,** to be having an affair with sb.
liofilizado,-a *adj* freeze-dried.
liofilizar *t* to freeze-dry.
lioso,-a *adj* confusing.
lípido *m* lipid.
liposoluble *adj* fat-soluble.
liposoma *m* liposome.
lipotimia *f* blackout.
liquen *m* lichen.
liquidación I *f* (*venta*) sale. **2** (*pago*) settlement. **3** (*de activos*) liquidation. **4** (*fin*) end.
■ **liquidación total,** clearance sale.
liquidar I *t* (*deuda*) to settle, liquidate. **2** (*mercancías*) to sell off. **3** *fam* (*dinero*) to spend, blow. **4** *fam* (*matar*) to knock off.
liquidez *f* liquidity.
líquido,-a I *adj* (*gen*) liquid. **2** (*neto*) net. **3** (*en metálico*) in cash. – **4** líquido, *m* liquid.
lira¹ *f* mús lyre.
lira² *f* (*moneda*) lira.
lírica *f →* **lírico,-a.**

lírico,-a 1 *adj* lyric, lyrical. – 2 *m,f* lyric poet. – 3 **lírica,** *f* poetry, lyric poetry.
lirio *m* lily.
■ lirio de agua, calla lily.
lirismo *m* lyricism.
lirón *m* dormouse.
● dormir como un lirón, to sleep like a log.
lis *f* (*planta*) lily.
■ flor de lis, fleur-de-lis.
lisa *f* grey mullet.
Lisboa *f* Lisbon.
lisiado,-a 1 *adj* crippled. – 2 *m,f* cripple.
lisiar *t* to cripple.
liso,-a 1 *adj* (*sin desigualdades*) smooth, even. 2 (*sin desniveles*) flat. 3 (*sin arrugas*) smooth. 4 (*pelo*) straight. 5 (*color*) plain.
● lisa y llanamente, purely and simply.
lisonja *f* flattering remark.
lisonjear *t* to flatter.
lisonjero,-a *adj* flattering.
lista 1 *f* (*relación*) list: *mira la lista de precios,* look at the price list. 2 (*raya*) stripe: *me he comprado una camisa a listas,* I've bought myself a striped shirt. 3 (*tira*) strip, slip.
● pasar lista, to call the roll. ‖ tachar de la lista, to cross out, cross off the list.
■ lista de bodas, wedding list. ‖ lista de correos, poste restante, us general delivery. ‖ lista de espera, waiting list. ‖ lista negra, blacklist.
listado,-a 1 *pp* → **listar**. – 2 *adj* (*a rayas*) striped. – 3 **listado,** *m* (*lista*) list.
listeza *f* smartness, sharpness.
listillo,-a *m,f fam* smart aleck, GB clever cloggs.
listo,-a 1 *adj* (*inteligente*) clever, smart. 2 (*preparado*) ready: *¿estás lista?,* are you ready? 3 (*acabado*) finished: *lo quiero listo para el lunes,* I want it finished by Monday. 4 (*diligente*) quick, prompt. – 5 *m,f* clever person.
● ir listo,-a, *fam* to have another thing coming: *va listo si se cree que el premio es suyo,* if he thinks he's going to get the prize he's got another thing coming. ‖ pasarse de listo,-a, *fam* to be too clever by half.
listón 1 *m* (*de madera*) lath, strip. 2 DEP bar.
listura *f* cleverness.
lisura *f* smoothness.
litera *f* bunk bed; (*en barco*) bunk; (*tren*) couchette.
literal *adj* literal.
literalmente *adv* literally.
literario,-a *adj* literary.
literato,-a *m,f* (*gen*) writer; (*hombre*) man of letters; (*mujer*) woman of letters.
literatura *f* literature.
litigación *f* litigation.
litigante 1 *adj* litigant. – 2 *mf* litigant.
litigar 1 *i* JUR to litigate. 2 (*disputar*) to argue, dispute.
▲ Conjugation model [7], like **llegar**.
litigio 1 *m* JUR litigation, lawsuit. 2 (*disputa*) dispute.
litio *m* lithium.
litografía 1 *f* (*arte*) lithography. 2 (*reproducción*) lithograph.
litografiar *t* to lithograph.
litográfico,-a *adj* lithographic.
litoral 1 *adj* coastal. – 2 *m* coast.
litosfera *f* lithosphere.
litro *m* litre, us liter.
litrona *f arg* litre bottle of beer.

liturgia *f* liturgy.
litúrgico,-a *adj* liturgical.
liviandad *f* lightness.
liviano,-a 1 *adj* (*ligero*) light. 2 *fig* (*inconstante*) frivolous. 3 *fig* (*lascivo*) lewd.
lividecer *i* to become livid.
lívido,-a *adj* livid.
living *m* living room, sitting room.
▲ *pl* livings.
liza 1 *f* HIST lists *pl.* 2 *fig* (*lucha*) struggle, combat.
● entrar en liza, to enter the arena.
llaga *f* (*gen*) sore; (*en la boca*) ulcer.
● poner el dedo en la llaga, to touch a sore spot.
llagar 1 *t* to cover with ulcers. – 2 **llagarse,** *p* to get sores: *se le ha llagado el cuerpo de tanto estar en la cama,* he has got bedsores after such a long time in bed.
llama¹ *f* (*de fuego*) flame.
● en llamas, ablaze, in flames.
llama² *f* ZOOL llama.
llamada 1 *f* (*gen*) call. 2 (*a la puerta*) knock, ring. 3 (*en texto*) reference mark.
■ llamada interurbana, long-distance call. ‖ llamada urbana, local call.
llamado,-a 1 *pp* → **llamar**. – 2 *adj* called, named.
llamador 1 *m* (*de una puerta*) door knocker. 2 (*timbre*) bell.
llamamiento 1 *m* (*petición*) appeal. 2 (*convocatoria*) call.
llamar 1 *t* (*gen*) to call: *llámalo, creo que no te ha visto,* call him, I don't think he's seen you; *tu madre te llama,* your mum's calling you. 2 (*convocar*) to summon: *habrá que llamar al médico,* we'll have to call the doctor; *llueve, mejor que llamemos un taxi,* it's raining, we'd better call a taxi. 3 (*dar nombre*) to name: *¿cómo vais a llamar al niño?,* what are you going to call the baby? 4 (*atraer*) to appeal to: *a mí viajar no me llama mucho,* travelling doesn't really appeal to me. – 5 *i* (*a la puerta*) to knock; (*al timbre*) to ring; (*al teléfono*) to ring, call, phone: *¿quién llama?,* who's there?; *han llamado a la puerta,* there's somebody at the door; *te llaman por la otra línea,* there's a call for you on the other line. – 6 **llamarse,** *p* (*tener nombre*) to be called: *me llamo Juan,* my name is Juan, I'm called Juan.
● llamar a algn. por señas, to wave at sb. ‖ llamar a filas, to call up. ‖ llamar a algn. de todo, *fam* to call sb. everything under the sun. ‖ llamar a la huelga, to call out on strike. ‖ llamar por teléfono, to call, phone, GB ring, ring up.
llamarada 1 *f* (*de fuego*) sudden blaze. 2 *fig* (*de vergüenza*) sudden flush, blush. 3 *fig* (*de ira, cólera*) outburst.
llamativo,-a *adj* showy, flashy.
llamear *i* to blaze.
llanero,-a *adj* (*hombre*) plainsman; (*mujer*) plainswoman.
■ el Llanero Solitario, the Lone Ranger.
llaneza 1 *f* (*sencillez*) simplicity. 2 (*franqueza*) frankness.
llanito,-a 1 *adj* Gibraltarian. – 2 *m,f* Gibraltarian.
llano,-a 1 *adj* (*plano*) flat, even, level. 2 (*franco*) open, frank. 3 (*sencillo*) simple. – 4 **llano,** *m* (*llanura*) plain.
● en llano,-a, plainly.
llanote,-a *adj fam* down-to-earth.
llanta *f* wheel rim, rim.
■ llantas de aleación, alloy wheels.
llantera *f fam* → **llantina**.
llantina *f fam* sobbing: *agarró una llantina porque no le quise comprar el juguete,* he started sobbing because I wouldn't buy him the toy.

llanto *m* crying, weeping.
llanura 1 *f* (*llano*) plain. **2** (*igualdad*) plainness.
llave 1 *f* (*de puerta etc*) key. **2** TÉC wrench. **3** (*en judo*) lock. **4** (*en texto*) bracket. **5** MÚS key.
● **bajo llave,** under lock and key. ‖ **cerrar con llave,** to lock. ‖ **echar la llave,** to lock the door. ‖ **llave en mano,** ready for immediate occupancy.
■ **llave de contacto,** ignition key. ‖ **llave de paso,** (*del gas*) mains tap; (*del agua*) stopcock. ‖ **llave falsa,** skeleton key. ‖ **llave inglesa,** monkey wrench. ‖ **llave maestra,** master key.
llavero *m* key ring.
llavín *m* latchkey.
llegada 1 *f* (*entrada*) arrival. **2** DEP finishing line.
llegar 1 *i* to arrive (**a,** at/in), get (**a,** at), reach (**a,** -): *cuando llegues a París, llámanos,* call us when you arrive in Paris; *el tren ha llegado tarde,* the train arrived late; *¿a qué hora llegaste al trabajo?,* what time did you get to work?; *llegó a casa cansado,* he was tired when he got home; *llegó el primero,* he arrived first. **2** (*alcanzar*) to reach: *¿llegas a ese estante?,* can you reach that shelf?; *llegó a los noventa,* he reached the age of ninety; *llegamos a los objetivos previstos,* we reached our target. **3** (*ser suficiente*) to be enough, suffice: *una sola tarta no llegará para todos,* one cake won't be enough for all of us; *¿te llega con mil pesetas?,* is a thousand pesetas enough? **4** (*conseguir*) to manage: *no llego a entender lo que quiere decir,* I can't quite understand what he's trying to say. **5** (*cantidad*) to amount (**a,** to): *su sueldo no llega a cinco millones,* his salary is less than five million. **6** (*suceder*) to come, arrive: *llegó el momento,* the moment arrived. – **7 llegar a + inf,** *loc* (*uso enfático*): *llegó a llamarme ladrón,* he went so far as to call me a thief, he even called me a thief; *si llego a saber que hay huelga, no me levanto,* if I'd known there was a strike, I wouldn't have got out of bed; *si lo llega a pillar lo mata,* if he'd caught him he'd have killed him. – **8 llegarse a,** *p fam* (*ir a*) to go over to, nip over to, slip over to, hop over to: *llégate al súper y trae jabón,* nip over to the supermarket and get some soap.
● **¡hasta ahí podíamos llegar!,** that's about the limit! ‖ **llegar lejos,** to go far. ‖ **llegar a más,** (*persona*) to better os.; (*cosa - empeorar*) to worsen; (- *mejorar*) to improve.
▲ *Conjugation model* [7].
llenado,-a 1 *pp* → **llenar.** – **2 llenado,** *m* (*de un recipiente*) filling.
llenar 1 *t* (*espacio, recipiente*) to fill. **2** (*formulario*) to fill in. **3** (*tiempo*) to fill, occupy. **4** (*satisfacer*) to fulfil, please: *el trabajo que hago no me llena,* I don't find my job very fulfilling. – **5** *i* (*comida*) to be very filling. – **6 llenarse,** *p* (*gen*) to fill. **7** (*de gente*) to fill up: *el estadio se llena todos los domingos,* the stadium fills up every Sunday. **8** (*de comida*) to get full, overeat: *me he llenado tanto que no puedo ni respirar,* I've eaten so much I can't breathe; *se llena con nada que come,* he gets full up very quickly. – **9 llenar de,** (*alegría*) to fill with; (*favores, regalos*) to shower with; (*insultos*) to heap on.
llenito,-a *adj fam* chubby.
lleno,-a 1 *adj* full (**de,** of): *dame un vaso lleno de agua,* give me a glass full of water; *está lleno de gente,* it's full of people. **2** (*cubierto*) covered (**de,** with). – **3 lleno,** *m* TEAT full house: *hoy hay lleno total,* it's a full house today.
● **de lleno,** smack, right: *le dio de lleno en el ojo,* it hit him smack in the eye. ‖ **lleno,-a hasta el borde,** brimful.

llevadero,-a *adj* bearable.
llevar 1 *t* (*gen*) to take: *llévale esto a tu abuela,* take this to your granny; *llévate los libros a tu habitación,* take these books to your bedroom; *lleva a tu hermanita al colegio,* take your little sister to school; *te llevo en coche,* I'll take you in the car, I'll give you a lift. **2** (*tener*) to have; (*tener encima*) to have, carry: *¿qué llevas ahí?,* what's that you've got there?; *¿cuánto dinero llevas?,* how much money have you got on you?; *llevaba un bate de béisbol,* she was carrying a baseball bat; *llevaba las luces de posición encendidas,* his sidelights were on; *llevo la calefacción puesta,* I've got the heating on; *llevas los pantalones sucios,* your trousers are dirty. **3** (*prenda*) to wear, have on: *no me gusta llevar sombrero,* I don't like wearing a hat; *no llevaba nada,* she had nothing on; *llevaré un clavel en el ojal,* I shall be wearing a carnation in my buttonhole. **4** (*aguantar*) to cope with: *¿cómo lleva lo de quedarse sin trabajo?,* how's he coping with losing his job? **5** (*dirigir*) to be in charge of: *¿quién lleva el tema de los pedidos?,* who's in charge of orders?; *lleva la empresa ella solita,* she runs the company all by herself. **6** (*conducir - coche*) to drive; (*moto*) - to ride: *lleva un Seat azul,* he drives a blue Seat. **7** (*pasar tiempo*) to be: *llevo un mes aquí,* I have been here for a month; *lleva tres días sin venir a trabajar,* he hasn't been to work for three days. **8** (*libros, cuentas*) to keep. **9** (*años*) to be older: *te llevo tres años,* I'm three years older than you. **10** (*vida*) to lead: *lleva una vida muy ajetreada,* she leads a hectic life. **11** (*tiempo, esfuerzo*) to take: *este trabajo nos llevará más de un mes,* this job will take us over a month. **12** (*compás, paso, ritmo*) to keep: *contigo no bailo, no sabes llevar el paso,* I'm not dancing with you, you can't keep in step. **13** *fam* (*cobrar*) to charge: *¿cuánto te llevaron por la reparación?,* how much did they charge you for the repairs? – **14 llevar a,** *i* (*conducir*) to take, lead: *esta senda lleva a la cima,* this path takes you to the summit; *y esto, ¿adónde nos lleva?,* and where will this lead us? **15 llevar a + inf,** (*inducir*) to lead to, make: *esto me lleva a pensar que ...,* this leads me to think that ...; *¿qué lo llevó a actuar así?,* what made him act like that? – **16 llevar + participio,** *aux* to have: *llevo escritas cuatro cartas,* I've written four letters. – **17 llevarse,** *p* (*obtener*) (*ganar*) to win: *los rusos se llevaron todas las medallas,* the Russians won all the medals. **18** (*recibir*) to get: *se llevó un buen susto,* he got quite a shock; *me llevé una agradable sorpresa,* I had a pleasant surprise. **19** (*estar de moda*) to be fashionable: *este color ya no se lleva,* this colour is not fashionable any more. **20** (*entenderse*) to get on (**con,** with), get along (**con,** with): *se lleva bien con sus padres,* he gets on well with his parents; *se llevan muy mal,* they don't get on at all. **21** MAT to carry over.
● **dejarse llevar por ...,** to be influenced by ..., get carried away with ... ‖ **llevar a la práctica,** to put into practice. ‖ **llevar adelante,** to carry out. ‖ **llevar la cuenta de,** to keep track of. ‖ **llevar las de + inf,** to be likely to + *inf*: *las llevas de perder,* you'll lose. ‖ **llevarse a matar,** to be at daggers drawn. ‖ **llevarse por delante,** (*gen*) to carry away, sweep away; (*viento*) to blow away; (*coche*) to run over.
llorar 1 *i* to cry, weep. **2** *fam* (*quejarse*) to moan. – **3** *t* to mourn.
● **echarse a llorar,** to start crying. ‖ **el que no llora no mama,** *fam* if you don't ask you never get. ‖ **llorar a lágrima viva,** *fam* to cry one's heart out. ‖ **llorar a moco tendido,** *fam* to cry one's heart out.
llorera *f fam* sobbing, crying: *al decir adiós nos entró la llorera,* we started sobbing when we said goodbye.

llorica *mf fam* → **llorón,-ona**.
lloriquear *i* to whimper, weep.
lloriqueo *m* whimpering.
lloro *m* tears *pl*, weeping.
llorón,-ona 1 *adj* weeping. – 2 *m,f fam* crybaby. – 3 la llorona, *f*: *en cuanto se emborracha le da la llorona*, when she gets drunk she comes over all weepy.
lloroso,-a *adj* tearful, weeping.
llover *i* to rain: *llueve*, it's raining; *no llueve desde hace meses*, it hasn't rained for months; *parece que va a llover*, it looks like rain.
● **como llovido del cielo**, out of the blue. ‖ **como quien oye llover**, like water off a duck's back. ‖ **ha llovido mucho desde entonces**, a lot of water's passed under the bridge since then. ‖ **llover a cántaros**, to pour down, rain cats and dogs. ‖ **siempre llueve sobre mojado**, it never rains but it pours. ‖ **nunca llueve a gusto de todos**, you can't please everyone.
▲ *Conjugation model* [32], *like* **mover**; *used only in the 3rd pers; it does not take a subject.*
llovizna *f* drizzle.
lloviznar *i* to drizzle.
▲ *Used only in the 3rd pers; it does not take a subject.*
lluvia 1 *f* rain. 2 *fig* shower, barrage.
■ **lluvia ácida**, acid rain. ‖ **lluvia de estrellas**, meteor shower.
lluvioso,-a *adj* rainy, wet.
lo 1 *art neut* the: *lo mismo me pasó a mí*, the same thing happened to me; *lo mejor de la película es la música*, the best part of the film is the music; *lo difícil es encontrar respuestas*, what's difficult is finding answers; *le gusta todo lo francés*, she likes anything French. – 2 *pron m & neut (objeto directo)* him; *(cosa, animal)* it; *(usted)* you: *no lo conozco de nada*, I don't know him from Adam; *¿lo has probado?*, have you tried it?; *a usted no lo quiero ver más por aquí*, I don't want to see you here again.
● **con lo cual**, so. ‖ **lo cual**, which. ‖ **lo que**, what.
loa *f* praise.
loable *adj* laudable, praiseworthy.
LOAPA *abr* (*Ley Orgánica de Armonización del Proceso Autonómico*) *institutional law for the harmonization of the devolution process.*
loar *t* to praise, extol.
lobanillo *m* wen.
lobato 1 *m* ZOOL wolf cub. 2 *(en los Scouts)* Cub.
lobezno,-a *m,f* wolf cub.
lobo,-a *m,f (macho)* wolf; *(hembra)* she-wolf.
● **menos lobos Caperucita**, *fam* come off it! ‖ **oscuro,-a como la boca del lobo**, pitch-dark.
■ **lobo de mar**, *(persona)* sea dog. ‖ **lobo marino**, sea lion.
lobotomía *f* lobotomy.
lóbrego,-a *adj* bleak, gloomy.
lobreguez *f* gloominess, bleakness.
lobulado,-a *adj* lobulated.
lóbulo *m* lobe.
lobuno,-a *adj* wolfish.
loca *f* → **loco,-a**.
local 1 *adj* local. – 2 *m (para negocio)* premises *pl*.
■ **local comercial**, business premises *pl*.
localidad 1 *f (ciudad)* town. 2 TEAT *(asiento)* seat; *(billete)* ticket.
● **"agotadas las localidades"**, "sold out".
localismo 1 *m (al hablar)* localism. 2 *pey* parochialism.

localista *adj pey* parochial.
localizable *adj* traceable: *no está localizable*, he cannot be contacted.
localización 1 *f (determinación del lugar)* localization: *la localización de un donante llevó varias horas*, it took several hours to find a donor. 2 *(limitación)* restriction: *la localización del brote será difícil*, it will be difficult to restrict the spread of the outbreak.
localizar 1 *t (encontrar)* to locate, find. 2 *(infección, incendio)* to localize.
locatis 1 *adj fam* loopy, loony. – 2 *mf fam* loony, nutter, nutcase.
locativo,-a 1 *adj* locative. – 2 **locativo**, *m* locative.
locato,-a *m,f* loony, crackpot.
loc. cit. *abr (loco citato)* loco citato; *(abreviatura)* loc. cit., lc.
loción *f* lotion.
■ **loción para después del afeitado**, after-shave.
loco,-a 1 *adj (gen)* mad, crazy, insane. 2 *(muy ocupado)* terribly busy. 3 *fam (asombroso)* amazing: *tiene unas ganas locas de casarse*, she's dying to get married. – 4 *m,f* lunatic, insane person. – 5 **loca**, *f arg (homosexual afeminado)* queen.
● **a lo loco**, any old how. ‖ **como un,-a loco,-a**, like mad. ‖ **estar loco,-a de alegría**, to be over the moon. ‖ **estar loco,-a por algn.**, to be mad about sb. ‖ **hacer el loco**, to act wild. ‖ **hacerse el/la loco,-a**, to pretend to know nothing, act dumb. ‖ **¡ni loco,-a!**, no way! ‖ **volver loco,-a a algn.**, to drive sb. crazy, drive sb. mad: *este ruido me vuelve loco*, this noise is driving me mad; *esa chica me vuelve loco*, I'm crazy about that girl. ‖ **volverse loco,-a**, to go mad.
■ **loco,-a de remate**, stark raving mad.
locomoción *f* locomotion.
locomotor,-ra 1 *adj* locomotive. – 2 **locomotora**, *f* locomotive.
locomotora *f* → **locomotor,-ra**.
locomotriz *adj* locomotive.
locuacidad *f* loquacity.
locuaz *adj* loquacious, talkative.
locución *f* phrase, locution.
locuelo,-a *adj fam* clown, goon.
locura 1 *f (perturbación)* madness, insanity. 2 *(insensatez)* folly.
● **con locura**, madly. ‖ **de locura**, *fam* amazing. ‖ **hacer una locura**, to do something silly. ‖ **¡qué locura!**, it's mad!
locutor,-ra *m,f (gen)* announcer; *(de noticias)* news reader.
locutorio 1 *m (de cárcel)* visiting room; *(de convento)* parlour, us parlor. 2 *(de teléfonos)* telephone booth. 3 *(de radio)* studio.
lodazal *m* mire.
LODE *abr (Ley Orgánica del Derecho a la Educación)* *institutional law on the right to education.*
lodo *m* mud.
lodoso,-a *adj* muddy.
logarítmico,-a *adj* logarithmic.
logaritmo *m* logarithm.
logia 1 *f (masónica)* lodge. 2 ARQ loggia.
lógica *f* → **lógico,-a**.
lógicamente *adv* logically.
lógico,-a 1 *adj (de la lógica)* logical. 2 *(natural)* normal, to be expected: *es lógico que lo niegue*, it's to be expected that he should deny it. – 3 *m,f* logician. – 4 **lógica**, *f* logic.

■ **lógica matemática,** mathematical logic.
logística f → **logístico,-a**.
logístico,-a I adj logistic. – **2 logística,** f logistics.
logopeda mf speech therapist.
logopedia f speech therapy.
logotipo m logo, logotype.
logrado,-a I pp → **lograr**. – **2** adj (conseguido) successful.
lograr t (conseguir) to manage to get, achieve; (sueño) to fulfil; (victoria, premio) to win: **logré hacerlo,** I managed to do it.
logro I m (éxito) success, achievement. **2** (beneficio) gain, profit.
logroñés,-esa I adj of Logroño, from Logroño. – **2** m,f person from Logroño, inhabitant of Logroño.
LOGSE abr (Ley de Ordenación General del Sistema Educativo) institutional law on the overall structuring of the education system.
Loira el Loira, m the Loire.
loísmo m incorrect use of lo, los as indirect objects instead of le, les.
loma f hill.
lombriz f (de tierra) earthworm; (intestinal) worm.
lomo I m CULIN (de cerdo) loin; (de ternera) sirloin. **2** ANAT back. **3** (de libro) spine.
● **ir a lomos de,** to ride.
■ **lomo de cerdo,** loin of pork.
lona f canvas.
loncha f (de jamón, queso, etc) slice; (de tocino, bacon) rasher.
londinense I adj of London, from London. – **2** mf Londoner.
Londres m London.
loneta f sailcloth.
longaniza f cured pork sausage.
longevidad f longevity.
longevo,-a adj long-lived.
longitud I f length: **tiene cinco metros de longitud,** it's five metres long. **2** GEOG longitude.
■ **longitud de onda,** wavelength.
longitudinal adj longitudinal, lengthwise.
longui **hacerse el longui,** loc fam to act dumb, pretend not to have heard, pretend not to have noticed.
longuis m fam → **longui**.
lonja I f (mercado) exchange, market. **2** ARQ raised porch. **3** (loncha) slice, rasher.
lontananza f (fondo) background.
● **en lontananza,** in the distance.
loor m lit praise.
loquero,-a m,f fam (enfermero) nurse in a mental hospital.
lor m → **lord**.
▲ pl **lores**.
lord m lord.
loriga f HIST cuirass.
loro I m (pájaro) parrot. **2** arg (mujer fea) bag. **3** arg (charlatán) windbag. **4** arg (radio) radio cassette.
● **estar al loro,** arg (atento) to be on the ball, keep one's wits about one; (informado) to know the score.
los I art def mpl the: **los niños,** the boys. – **2** pron mpl (objeto directo) them; (ustedes) you: **los vi,** I saw them; **a ustedes dos no los quiero volver a ver,** I don't want to see you two again.
▲ See also **lo, el**.
losa I f flagstone, slab. **2** (de sepulcro) gravestone.
loseta f floor tile.

lote I m (parte) share, portion. **2** COM lot, batch.
● **darse el lote,** fam to pet. ‖ **pegarse el lote,** fam to pet.
lotería f lottery.
● **tocarle la lotería a uno,** (uso literal) to win a prize in the lottery; (uso figurado) to strike it lucky.
■ **lotería primitiva,** ≈ National Lottery.
loto m (flor) lotus.
loza I f (cerámica) china. **2** (de cocina) crockery.
lozanía I f (de persona) healthiness, lustiness. **2** (de planta) freshness. **3** (de vegetación) lushness, luxuriance.
lozano,-a I adj (persona) healthy, lusty. **2** (planta) fresh. **3** (vegetación) lush, luxuriant.
ltda. abr (limitada) limited; (abreviatura) ltd.
lubina f bass.
lubricación f lubrication.
lubricante I adj lubricating. – **2** m lubricant.
lubricar t to lubricate.
▲ Conjugation model [1], like **sacar**.
lubricidad I f (lujuria) lubricity, lewdness. **2** (calidad de resbaladizo) resbaladizo) slipperiness.
lúbrico,-a I adj (lujurioso) lubricious, lewd. **2** (resbaladizo) slippery.
lucense I adj of Lugo, from Lugo. – **2** mf person from Lugo, inhabitant of Lugo.
lucerna f skylight.
lucero m bright star.
■ **lucero del alba,** morning star, Venus.
lucha I f (gen) fight, struggle. **2** DEP wrestling.
■ **lucha de clases,** class struggle. ‖ **lucha libre,** freestyle wrestling.
luchador,-ra I m,f (gen) fighter. **2** DEP wrestler.
luchar I i (gen) to fight. **2** DEP to wrestle.
lucidez f lucidity.
lucido,-a I pp → **lucir**. – **2** adj beautiful.
lúcido,-a adj lucid, clear-headed.
luciérnaga f glow-worm.
lucífero,-a adj lit resplendent.
lucimiento I m (oportunidad de lucirse) showing off. **2** (brillo) brilliance.
lucio m pike.
lucir I t (mostrar) to show, display; (ropa) to wear, sport: **lucía un modelo precioso,** she was sporting a beautiful outfit. **2** (presumir de) to show off: **luce su cartera como si fuera un trofeo,** she flashes her wallet about as if it were a trophy. – **3** i (tener buen aspecto) to look good: **esas cortinas no lucen en esta sala tan oscura,** those curtains don't look their best in such a dark room. **4** (rendir resultado) to pay off, do good: **va mucho a la peluquería pero no le luce nada,** she goes to the hairdresser's, but it doesn't seem to make any difference; **hay que ver que poco le lucen tantos años de estudio,** all those years of study have done him no good at all. **5** (sobresalir) to excel: **lucía más que nadie con su traje nuevo,** he stood out from the rest in his new suit. **6** (brillar las estrelllas) to shine, glow. – **7 lucirse,** p (sobresalir) to be brilliant: **realmente se lució con su interpretación de Otelo,** his interpretation of Othello was brilliant. **8** (presumir) to show off: **sacó el coche nuevo para lucirse ante los amigos,** he got out his new car to show off to his friends.
▲ Conjugation model [45].
lucrarse p to make a profit.
lucrativo,-a adj lucrative, profitable.
lucro m gain, profit.
■ **afán de lucro,** profit motive: **lo hizo sin afán de lucro,** he did it with no profit motive in mind.

luctuoso,-a *adj lit* mournful, sorrowful.
ludibrio *m lit* scoff.
lúdico,-a *adj* playful, ludic.
ludópata *mf* compulsive gambler.
ludopatía *f* compulsive gambling.
lúdrico,-a *adj* → **lúdico,-a**.
luego 1 *adv* (*después*) then, afterwards, next: *primero cómete la sopa y luego ya traeré la carne,* first eat your soup and then I'll bring the meat. 2 (*más tarde*) later: *luego te llamo, que ahora estoy ocupada,* I'm busy now, I'll call you later. 3 (*prontamente*) presently, immediately. – 4 *conj* so, therefore: *no han llamado, luego no creo que vengan,* they haven't called so I don't think they'll come.
● **hasta luego,** see you, see you later, so long.
lugar 1 *m* (*sitio, ciudad*) place: *tiene que aparecer por algún lugar,* it has to be somewhere; *he descubierto el lugar más idílico del mundo,* I've discovered the most idyllic place in the world; *la iglesia no es lugar para bailar,* the church is no place to dance. 2 (*posición, situación*) place, position: *tú ponte en mi lugar y lo entenderás,* put yourself in my position and you'll understand; *¿qué lugar ocupa en la empresa?,* what's her position in the company? 3 (*espacio*) room, space: *ya no hay lugar para más muebles,* there's no room for any more furniture.
● **dar lugar a,** to give rise to. ‖ **dejar a algn. en mal lugar,** to make sb. look foolish, show sb. up. ‖ **en lugar de,** instead of. ‖ **en primer lugar,** firstly. ‖ **fuera de lugar,** (*descolocado*) out of place; (*inoportuno*) inappropriate. ‖ **hacer lugar,** to make room. ‖ **no ha lugar la protesta,** objection overruled. ‖ **sin lugar a dudas,** undoubtedly. ‖ **tener lugar,** to take place.
■ **lugar común,** commonplace.
lugareño,-a 1 *adj* local. – 2 *m,f* local.
lugarteniente *m* deputy.
lúgubre *adj* (*triste*) bleak, lugubrious; (*fúnebre*) sombre (*us* somber), mournful.
Luisiana *f* Louisiana.
lujo *m* luxury.
● **con todo lujo de detalles,** in great detail. ‖ **de lujo,** luxury, luxurious. ‖ **vivir con mucho lujo,** to live in luxury.
lujosamente *adv* luxuriously.
lujoso,-a *adj* luxurious.
lujuria *f* lewdness, lust, lechery.
lujurioso,-a 1 *adj* lustful, lecherous. – 2 *m,f* lecher.
lumbago *m* lumbago.
lumbar *adj* lumbar.
lumbre 1 *f* (*fuego*) fire; (*candela*) light. 2 (*para cigarrillo*) light: *¿me das lumbre?,* could you give me a light please?
● **a la luz de la lumbre,** by the light of the fire.
lumbrera *f fam* (*persona*) genius, whizz kid.
luminaria 1 *f* (*en iglesia*) altar lamp. 2 (*en fiestas*) light.
lumínico,-a *adj* light.
luminiscencia *f* luminiscence.
luminiscente *adj* luminiscent.
luminosidad *f* brightness, luminosity.
luminoso,-a *adj* bright, luminous.
luminotecnia *f* lighting.
luminotécnico,-a *adj* lighting.
lumpen *m* lumpenproletariat.
luna 1 *f* ASTRON moon. 2 (*cristal*) window pane; (*de coche*) window; (*de ventana*) glass. 3 (*espejo*) mirror. 4 (*de uña*) half-moon.

● **dejar a la luna de Valencia,** to thwart, disappoint. ‖ **estar en la luna,** *fam* to be miles away. ‖ **pedir la luna,** *fam* to ask for the moon. ‖ **quedarse a la luna de Valencia,** *fam* to be thwarted, be disappointed.
■ **luna creciente,** waxing moon. ‖ **luna llena,** full moon. ‖ **luna menguante,** waning moon. ‖ **luna nueva,** new moon. ‖ **luna de miel,** honey moon.
lunación *f* lunation.
lunar 1 *adj* lunar, moon: *las fases lunares,* the phases of the moon. – 2 *m* (*en la piel*) beauty spot.
● **de lunares,** spotted.
lunático,-a 1 *adj* lunatic. – 2 *m,f* lunatic.
lunes *m* Monday.
▲ *pl* **lunes**; *see also* **jueves**.
luneta *f car* window.
■ **luneta térmica,** heated rear windscreen. ‖ **luneta trasera,** rear windscreen, rear window.
lunfardo *m* Buenos Aires slang.
lúnula *f* lunule.
lupa *f* magnifying glass.
● **con lupa,** meticulously.
lupanar *m* brothel.
lúpulo *m* hop.
lustrar *t* to polish.
lustre 1 *m* (*brillo*) polish, shine, lustre, *us* luster. 2 *fig* (*esplendor*) glory.
lustro *m* five years *pl*: *tras casi un lustro de ausencia,* after almost five years' absence.
lustroso,-a *adj* shiny.
luteranismo *m* Lutheranism.
luterano,-a 1 *adj* Lutheran. – 2 *m,f* Lutheran.
luto 1 *m* mourning. 2 *fig* grief.
● **estar de luto,** to mourn. ‖ **ir de luto,** to be in mourning.
■ **luto oficial,** official mourning. ‖ **medio luto,** half-mourning.
lux *m* lux.
luxación *f* dislocation.
Luxemburgo *m* Luxembourg.
luxemburgués,-esa 1 *adj* of Luxembourg, from Luxembourg. – 2 *m,f* Luxembourger, person from Luxembourg.
luz 1 *f* (*gen*) light: *en esta sala entra mucha luz,* this room gets plenty of light; *ya no queda luz para leer,* there's not enough light to read. 2 *fam* (*electricidad*) electricity: *nos han cortado la luz,* we've had the electricity cut off; *nos hemos quedado sin luz,* the power has gone off; *da la luz,* turn the light on. 3 (*iluminación*) lighting. 4 ARQ span. 5 (*modelo*) torch: *Dios es mi luz y mi guía,* God is my torch and my guide. – 6 **luces,** *fpl fam* intelligence *sing*: *es un hombre de pocas luces,* he's not very bright.
● **a la luz del día,** in daylight. ‖ **a plena luz del día,** in broad daylight. ‖ **a todas luces,** obviously, clearly. ‖ **dar a luz,** to give birth. ‖ **dar luz verde a,** to give the green light to. ‖ **sacar a la luz,** to bring to light. ‖ **salir a la luz,** to come out. ‖ **ver la luz,** (*persona*) to come into the world; (*libro etc*) to come out.
■ **luces de cruce,** dipped headlights. ‖ **luces de posición,** sidelights. ‖ **luces cortas,** dipped headlights. ‖ **luces de carretera,** full beam. ‖ **luz del día,** daylight. ‖ **luz del sol,** sunlight. ‖ **luces largas,** full beam. ‖ **traje de luces,** bullfighter's costume.
luzco *indic pres* → **lucir**

M

M, m f (la letra) M, m.
m¹ sím (metro) metre (us meter); (símbolo) m.
m² sím (milla) mile; (símbolo) m.
m³ abr (minuto) minute; (abreviatura) min.
m/¹ abr (mes) month.
m/² abr (mi) my.
maca 1 f (en fruta) bruise. 2 (señal) flaw, blemish.
macabeo rollo macabeo, m → **rollo**.
macabro,-a adj macabre.
macaco,-a 1 m,f ZOOL macaque. 2 fam (niño) little monkey. 3 fam pey squirt.
macadán m macadam.
▲ Also written macadam.
macanudo,-a adj fam great, terrific.
macarra 1 adj fam (de mal gusto) tacky. 2 fam (propio de matones) thuggish. – 3 m (hortera) flash Harry. 4 fam (matón) thug. 5 fam (proxeneta) pimp.
macarrilla mf → **macarra**.
macarrón 1 m (pasta italiana) piece of macaroni. 2 (dulce) macaroon. 3 TÉC (de cable) sheath, sheathing. – 4 macarrones, mpl macaroni.
macarrónico,-a adj fam broken: habla un español macarrónico, his Spanish is absolutely awful.
macarse p to go bad.
macedonia f fruit salad.
■ macedonia de frutas, fruit salad. ‖ macedonia de verduras, mixed vegetables.
Macedonia f Macedonia.
macedonio,-a 1 adj Macedonian. – 2 m,f (persona) Macedonian. – 3 macedonio, m (idioma) Macedonian.
maceración 1 f (remojo - de fruta) maceration, soaking; (- de carne, pescado) marinading. 2 (a golpes) pounding, tenderizing.
maceramiento m → **maceración**.
macerar 1 t (poner en remojo - fruta) to macerate, soak; (- carne, pescado) to marinade. 2 (golpeando) to pound, tenderize.
maceta¹ f flowerpot.
● regar las macetas, to water the plants.
maceta² f (herramienta) mallet.
macetero m flowerpot holder.
macferlán m inverness.
macha adj (almeja) type of clam.
machaca 1 mf arg (persona) dogsbody. – 2 m arg (soldado) squaddie.
machacante m fam five-peseta coin.
machacar 1 t (triturar) to crush. 2 fam (vencer) to hammer, thrash. 3 fam (dañar) to kill; (cansar, agotar) to wear out, kill. 4 fam (estudiar) to swot up on, us grind away at. 5 fam (insistir en) to harp on about, go on about. – 6 i (estudiar) to swot up, cram, us grind. 7 (insistir en) to go on (con, about), harp on (con, about).
● machacársela, tabú to wank, us jerk off. ‖ por mí como si se la machaca, tabú I couldn't give a toss.

▲ Conjugation model [1], like sacar.
machacón,-ona 1 adj fam insistent, repetitive. – 2 m,f fam pain.
machaconería f fam insistence, repetition.
machada 1 f fam pey (fanfarronada) bragging, swanking. 2 fam (acto de valentía) brave act, stunt.
machamartillo a machamartillo, loc adv firmly, staunchly.
machaque 1 m (golpes repetidos) beating. 2 (trituración) crushing, pounding. 3 fam (derrota) hammering. 4 (insistencia) dogged insistence.
machaqueo m → **machaque**.
machetazo m blow with a machete: se abrieron el paso a machetazos, they cut their way through with a machete.
machete m machete.
machihembrado,-a m (ranura y lengüeta) tongue and groove joint; (caja y espiga) mortise and tenon joint.
machihembrar t (ranura y lengüeta) to join with a tongue and groove; (caja y espiga) to mortise, join with a mortise and tenon.
machismo m male chauvinism.
machista 1 adj male chauvinist. – 2 mf male chauvinist.
macho 1 adj (animal, planta) male. 2 (persona) macho, tough. – 3 m (animal, planta) male. 4 (del enchufe) plug; (del corchete) hook. 5 (mula) mule. 6 fam (hombre) macho man, tough guy. 7 fam (como apelativo) mate, pal, man; ¡qué tal, macho!, hello, mate!
■ macho cabrío, billy goat.
machón m ARQ buttress.
machorra f tabú (lesbiana) dyke.
machote,-a 1 adj (valiente) tough. 2 fam (hombre) manly, tough; (mujer) tomboyish. – 3 machote, m fam he-man, tough guy. – 4 machota, f fam tomboy.
machucar t → **machacar**.
macilento,-a adj wan, pallid.
macillo m hammer.
macizo,-a 1 adj (plata) solid. 2 (fuerte) solid, well-built: se ha puesto maciza con tanto deporte, she's developed a strong body with so much sport. 3 fam (persona) good-looking: el profe está macizo, the teacher is a hunk; la protagonista está maciza, the actress who plays the lead is gorgeous. – 4 macizo, m (montañoso) massif, mountain mass. 5 (de flores) bed. 6 (de una pared) section.
macramé m macramé.
macro f INFORM macro.
macrobiótica f macrobiotics.
macrobiótico,-a 1 adj macrobiotic. – 2 m,f macrobiotic.
macrocefalia f macrocephaly, macrocephalia.
macrocosmo m macrocosm.
macrocosmos m macrocosm.
▲ pl macrocosmos.

macroeconomía *f* macroeconomics.
macroscópico,-a *adj* macroscopic.
mácula *f lit* blemish.
● **sin mácula,** unblemished, flawless.
macuto *m* knapsack, rucksack.
■ **radio macuto,** *fam* bush telegraph, the grapevine.
Madagascar *m* Madagascar.
madama *f fam* brothel keeper.
madeja *f (de lana)* skein, hank.
● **enredar la madeja,** to complicate matters. ‖ **ser una madeja de nervios,** to be a bundle of nerves.
madera l *f (en el árbol)* wood; *(cortada)* timber, us lumber: *es de madera,* it's made of wood, it's wooden. **2** *fig (aptitudes)* talent.
● **tener madera de ...,** to have the makings of a ...: *tiene madera de artista,* she has the makings of an artist; *no tiene madera de gerente,* he's not management material. ‖ **tocar madera,** to touch wood.
maderable *adj* timber-yielding.
maderaje *m* timbering.
maderamen *m* → **maderaje**.
maderero,-a *adj (industria)* timber.
madero l *m* piece of timber. **2** *arg (policía)* cop.
madrastra *f* stepmother.
madraza *f fam* doting mother.
madre l *f* mother: *es madre de seis hijos,* she's a mother of six; *pronto será madre,* she'll soon be a mother; *ha sido como una madre para mí,* she's been like a mother to me. **2** *(causa)* root: *la madre de todos los vicios,* the root of all evil. **3** *(monja)* sister. **4** *(del río)* bed.
● **ahí está la madre del cordero,** *fam* that's where the trouble lies. ‖ **ciento y la madre,** *fam* the world and his wife, us everyone and his brother. ‖ **de puta madre,** *tabú* brilliant, fucking brilliant. ‖ **¡la madre que te parió!,** *tabú (hombre)* you bastard!; *(mujer)* you bitch! ‖ **¡madre mía!,** *fam* good heavens! ‖ **salirse de madre,** *fam (río)* to burst its banks; *(persona)* to lose control. ‖ **¡tu madre!,** *tabú* up yours!
■ **futura madre,** mother-to-be. ‖ **madre adoptiva,** adoptive mother. ‖ **madre alquilada / madre de alquiler,** surrogate mother. ‖ **madre de familia,** mother. ‖ **madre de leche,** wet nurse. ‖ **madre patria,** one's motherland. ‖ **madre política,** mother-in-law. ‖ **madre soltera,** single mother. ‖ **madre superiora,** mother superior. ‖ **reina madre,** queen mother.
madreperla l *f (molusco)* pearl oyster. **2** *(concha)* mother-of-pearl.
madrépora *f* madrepore.
madrero,-a *adj* very tied to one's mother: *es muy madrero,* he's a mummy's boy.
madreselva *f* honeysuckle.
Madrid *f* Madrid.
madridista l *adj* relating to Real Madrid football club. **– 2** *mf* Real Madrid supporter.
madrigal *m* madrigal.
madriguera l *f (de conejo)* burrow, warren; *(de zorro)* den, lair; *(de tejón)* set. **2** *(de gente)* den, lair, hideout.
madrileño,-a l *adj* of Madrid, from Madrid. **– 2** *m,f* person from Madrid, inhabitant of Madrid.
Madriles Los Madriles, *mpl fam* Madrid *sing.*
madrina l *f (de bautizo)* godmother. **2** *(de boda)* ≈ matron of honour *(usually the bridegroom's mother)*. **3** *(de una asociación)* patroness, patron. **4** *(de un acto oficial)* lady president. **5** *(de barco)* woman who launches a ship.
madroño l *m (árbol)* strawberry tree. **2** *(fruto)* fruit of the strawberry tree. **3** *(borla)* tassel.

■ **el oso y el madroño,** *symbol of the city of Madrid.*
madrugada l *f (alba)* dawn, daybreak. **2** *(después de medianoche)* early morning: *a las cinco de la madrugada,* at five o'clock in the morning.
● **de madrugada,** *(al amanecer)* at dawn; *(muy temprano)* very early (in the morning).
madrugador,-ra l *m,f* early riser. **– 2** *adj*: *es una mujer madrugadora,* she's an early riser, she gets up very early.
madrugar l *i (levantarse pronto)* to get up early. **2** *(adelantarse)* to get there first. **3** *(ocurrir pronto)* to come out early.
● **a quien madruga Dios le ayuda,** the early bird catches the worm. ‖ **no por mucho madrugar amanece más temprano,** time must take its course.
▲ *Conjugation model* |7|, *like* **llegar**.
madrugón darse un madrugón / pegarse un madrugón, *loc fam* to get up at the crack of dawn.
maduración l *f (de un fruto)* ripening. **2** *(de una persona)* maturing. **3** *(de un plan)* fruition.
madurar l *i (fruto)* to ripen. **2** *(persona)* to mature. **– 3** *t (fruto)* to ripen. **4** *(plan, proyecto)* to think about carefully, develop fully.
madurez l *f (de la persona)* maturity. **2** *(de la fruta)* ripeness.
maduro,-a l *adj (persona)* mature. **2** *(fruta)* ripe.
● **de edad madura,** of mature years.
maese *m arc* master: *maese Pérez,* Master Pérez.
maestranza l *f (instalaciones - de ejército)* arsenal; *(- de armada)* dockyard. **2** *(personal - de ejército)* arsenal workers *pl*; *(- de armada)* dockyard workers *pl*.
maestrazgo l *m (cargo)* mastership. **2** *(territorio)* territory under a master's jurisdiction.
maestre *m* HIST master: *fue maestre de la Orden de Alcántara,* he was Master of the Order of Alcántara.
maestresala *m arc* butler.
maestría l *f (destreza)* mastery, skill. **2** *(título)* mastership.
maestrillo,-a *m,f pey.*
● **cada maestrillo tiene su librillo,** to each his own.
maestro,-a l *adj (principal)* master; *(pared, viga)* main, supporting. **– 2** *m,f (de primaria - hombre)* schoolmaster; *(- mujer)* schoolmistress. **3** *(instructor)* teacher: *fue mi maestro en todo,* he taught me everything I know. **4** *(experto)* master: *es un maestro en el arte de mentir,* he is a master in the art of lying, he is a consummate liar. **5** *(que alecciona)* teacher: *la vida es la mejor maestra,* life is the best teacher. **– 6 maestro,** *m (compositor)* composer; *(director)* conductor: *el maestro Falla,* Falla; *¡música, maestro!,* music, maestro! **7** *(de un oficio)* master: *maestro albañil/carpintero,* master bricklayer/carpenter. **8** *(en toros)* matador.
■ **golpe maestro,** masterstroke. ‖ **grandes maestros,** great masters. ‖ **llave maestra,** master key. ‖ **obra maestra,** masterpiece. ‖ **maestro de ceremonias,** master of ceremonies. ‖ **maestro de escuela,** schoolteacher. ‖ **maestro de esgrima,** fencing master. ‖ **maestro de obras,** foreman. ‖ **pared maestra,** structural wall.
mafia *f* mafia.
mafioso,-a l *adj* mafia. **– 2** *m,f (de la mafia siciliana)* mafioso; *(criminal)* gangster.
magacín l *m (revista)* magazine. **2** *(programa)* chatshow.
magazine *m* → **magacín**.
magdalena *f* small sponge cake.
Magdalena *f* Magdalene.
● **llorar como una Magdalena,** to cry one's eyes out.

magia f magic.
● **como por arte de magia,** as if by magic.
■ **magia blanca,** white magic. ‖ **magia negra,** black magic. ‖ **número de magia / truco de magia,** magic trick.
magiar 1 adj Magyar. – **2** mf Magyar.
mágico,-a 1 adj (pócima, palabra) magic; (ritual) magical. **2** (maravilloso) magical, wonderful.
magisterio 1 m (estudios) teacher training: *estudia magisterio,* she's training to be a teacher. **2** (profesión) teaching profession. **3** (profesores) teachers pl. **4** fig (gravedad) seriousness.
magistrado,-a 1 m,f (juez) judge. **2** (miembro del Tribunal Supremo) High Court judge, us Supreme Court judge.
magistral 1 adj EDUC magisterial. **2** (interpretación) masterly, masterful. **3** (tono, lenguaje) magisterial, bombastic.
magistralmente adv masterfully.
magistratura 1 f (cuerpo) judges pl. **2** (profesión) judgeship. **3** (tiempo) judgeship.
■ **Magistratura de Trabajo,** Industrial Tribunal.
magma f magma.
magnanimidad f magnanimity.
magnánimo,-a adj magnanimous.
magnate m tycoon, magnate.
magnesia f magnesia.
magnésico,-a adj magnesic.
magnesio m magnesium.
magnético,-a adj magnetic.
magnetismo m magnetism.
magnetización f magnetization.
magnetizar 1 t (cuerpo) to magnetize. **2** fig (persona) to hypnotize, captivate.
▲ Conjugation model |4|, like *realizar.*
magneto m magneto.
magnetofón m → **magnetófono.**
magnetofónico,-a adj sound recording.
■ **cinta magnetofónica,** sound recording tape.
magnetófono m tape recorder.
magnicida mf assassin.
magnicidio m assassination.
magnificar 1 t (ensalzar) to praise, extol. **2** (exagerar) to exaggerate, magnify.
▲ Conjugation model |1|, like *sacar.*
magníficat m REL Magníficat.
magnificencia 1 f (grandiosidad) magnificence, splendour. **2** (generosidad) lavishness, generosity.
magnificente adj lavish, generous.
magnífico,-a adj magnificent, splendid.
magnitud 1 f FÍS magnitude. **2** fig (importancia) magnitude, extent, size.
magno,-a adj great.
■ **Alejandro Magno,** Alexander the Great.
magnolia f (árbol, flor) magnolia.
magnolio m magnolia.
mago,-a m,f (gen) magician, conjurer; (de los cuentos) wizard.
■ **los Reyes Magos,** the Magi, the Three Wise Men, the Three Kings.
magrear t tabú to grope.
magreo m tabú groping.
magrez f leanness.
magro,-a 1 adj lean. – **2** magro, m (de carne de cerdo) loin of pork.
■ **carne magra,** lean meat.

magulladura f bruise, contusion.
magullar 1 t to bruise. – **2 magullarse,** p (fruta) to bruise; (person) to bruise os., be bruised.
mahatma m mahatma.
mahometano,-a 1 adj Mohammedan. – **2** m,f Mohammedan.
mahometismo m Mohamedanism.
mahonesa f → **mayonesa.**
maillot 1 m (de ciclista) jersey. **2** (de baile) leotard. **3** (de natación) swimsuit.
maitines mpl REL matins.
maître mf maître d'hôtel, maitre d'.
maíz 1 m (planta) maize, us corn. **2** (grano) sweetcorn, us corn.
maizal m maize field, us corn field.
majada 1 f (redil) sheepfold. **2** (excremento) cowpat.
majadería f nonsense, balderdash: *eso son majaderías,* that's nonsense.
majadero,-a 1 adj stupid, dim-witted. – **2** m,f idiot, dimwit.
majar t to crush.
majara 1 adj fam loony, nuts, crazy: *está majara perdido,* he's off his rocker; *se ha vuelto majara,* he's gone crackers. – **2** mf loony, nutter.
majareta adj fam → **majara.**
majestad 1 f (distinción) majesty. **2** (tratamiento) Majesty: *Su Majestad el Rey,* His Majesty the King.
majestuosidad f majesty.
majestuoso,-a adj majestic.
majeza f (simpatía) niceness, charm.
majo,-a 1 adj (persona - simpático) nice; (- bonito) nice, good-looking; (cosa) nice, lovely. **2** (tratamiento) love, us honey. – **3** m,f member of the XVIII-XIXth century Madrid populace.
majoleta f hawthorn berry, haw.
majoleto m hawthorn.
majuelo¹ m (majoleto) hawthorn.
majuelo² m (viña) young vine.
mal 1 m evil: *el bien y el mal,* good and evil; *luchar contra el mal,* to fight against evil. **2** (daño) harm. **3** (enfermedad) sickness. – **4** adj (forma apocopada de malo) bad: *este ha sido mal año de fresas,* this has been a bad year for strawberries. – **5** adv (no adecuadamente) badly: *se portó mal con nosotros,* he treated us badly. **6** (enfermo) ill, sick: *me encuentro mal,* I feel ill, I don't feel well. **7** (incorrectamente) wrong: *lo has hecho mal,* you've done it wrong. **8** (difícilmente) hardly, scarcely: *veo muy mal desde aquí,* I can hardly see from here. **9** (desagradablemente) bad: *aquí huele mal,* it smells bad in here; *como sigas así, acabarás mal,* if you keep on like that, you'll end up in trouble. **10** (en frases negativas) bad, badly: *la película no está mal,* the film's not bad.
● **a grandes males, grandes remedios,** desperate situations call for desperate measures. ‖ **de mal en peor,** from bad to worse. ‖ **estar a mal con algn.,** to be on bad terms with sb. ‖ **mal que bien,** one way or another. ‖ **mal que les (te, etc) pese,** whether they (you, etc) like it or not. ‖ **menos mal que ...,** it's a good job that ... , thank God that ... ‖ **no hay mal que cien años dure,** nothing goes on forever. ‖ **no hay mal que por bien no venga,** every cloud has a silver lining.
■ **mal de altura,** altitude sickness. ‖ **mal de ojo,** evil eye. ‖ **mal de la rosa,** pellagra. ‖ **mal de la tierra,** homesickness. ‖ **mal francés,** syphilis.
malabar adj → **juego.**

malabarismo *m* juggling.
● **hacer malabarismos,** to juggle.
malabarista *mf* juggler.
malacostumbrado,-a *adj* spoilt.
malacostumbrar 1 *t* (*malcriar*) to spoil. **2** (*viciar*) to get into bad habits.
málaga *m* sweet Malaga wine.
malagueño,-a 1 *adj* of Málaga, from Málaga. – **2** *m,f* person from Málaga, inhabitant of Málaga. – **3** malagüeña, *f popular music and dance originally from Malaga.*
malagueta *f* (*especia*) allspice.
malaje 1 *adj fam* (*malvado*) wicked, mean, nasty. **2** *fam* (*soso*) dull, boring. – **3** *mf fam* (*malvado*) villain, baddie, nasty person. **4** *fam* (*soso*) bore, killjoy, wet blanket.
malandanza *f arc* misfortune.
malandrín,-ina 1 *adj* roguish. – **2** *m,f* rogue.
malapata 1 *f fam* bad luck. – **2** *mf fam* clumsy idiot.
malaquita *f* malachite.
malar *adj* malar.
malaria *f* malaria.
malasio,-a 1 *adj* Malaysian. – **2** *m,f* Malaysian.
malasombra 1 *adj* dreary, dull, boring. – **2** *mf fam* clod, clumsy idiot. – **3** *f* (*aburrimiento*) dreariness.
malaúva *f* → **uva.**
malavenido,-a *adj* → **avenido,-a.**
malaventura *f* misfortune.
malaventurado,-a 1 *adj* ill-fated, unfortunate. – **2** *m,f* unfortunate person.
Malawi *m* Malawi.
malawiano,-a 1 *adj* Malawian. – **2** *m,f* Malawian.
Malaya *f* Malaya.
malayo,-a 1 *adj* Malay. – **2** *m,f* (*persona*) Malay. – **3** malayo, *m* (*idioma*) Malay.
Malaysia *f* Malaysia.
malbaratar 1 *t* (*derrochar*) to waste, squander. **2** (*malvender*) to undersell.
malcarado,-a 1 *adj* (*enfadado*) grim-faced, annoyed. **2** (*de poco fiar*) suspicious-looking.
malcasado,-a 1 *adj* (*no feliz*) unhappily married. **2** (*separado*) separated; (*divorciado*) divorced.
malcasarse *p* to make an unhappy marriage.
malcomer *i* not to eat enough.
malcriado,-a 1 *adj* (*maleducado*) ill-mannered; (*mimado*) spoilt. – **2** *m,f* spoilt child.
malcriar *t* to spoil.
▲ *Conjugation model* [13], *like* **desviar.**
maldad 1 *f* (*cualidad*) evil, wickedness. **2** (*acto*) evil thing, wicked thing.
maldecir 1 *t* to curse, damn. – **2** *i* to curse.
● **maldecir de,** to speak ill of.
▲ *Conjugation model* [79], *like* **predecir.**
maldiciente 1 *adj* (*que difama*) slanderous, defamatory. **2** (*que blasfema*) foul-mouthed. – **3** *mf* (*difamador*) slanderer. **4** (*blasfemo*) foul-mouthed person.
maldición 1 *f* curse. – **2** *interj* damnation!, damn it!
maldito,-a 1 *pp* → **maldecir.** – **2** *adj* (*no bendito*) damned. **3** *fam* (*que causa molestia*) damned, wretched, bloody, damn: *ese maldito niño acabará conmigo,* that wretched boy will be the death of me; *malditas las ganas que tengo de verlo,* I'm not looking forward to seeing to him one bit.
● **¡maldita sea!,** *fam* damn it!
Maldivas *m* Maldives.
maldivo,-a 1 *adj* Maldivian. – **2** *m,f* Maldivian.
maleabilidad *f* malleability.

maleable *adj* malleable.
maleante *mf* delinquent, criminal.
malear 1 *t* (*dañar*) to spoil, damage. **2** (*pervertir*) to corrupt, lead astray. – **3** malearse, *p* (*cosecha, producto*) to go bad. **4** (*pervertirse*) to go astray: *se ha maleado desde que va con esa gente,* those people have led her astray.
malecón 1 *m* (*muro - en el mar*) sea wall; (- *en la vía férrea*) embankment. **2** (*dique, rompeolas*) mole, breakwater; (*embarcadero*) jetty.
maledicencia 1 *f* (*en la vida política*) slander. **2** (*en la vida civil*) evil talk, gossip.
maleducado,-a 1 *adj* bad mannered, rude. – **2** *m,f* bad-mannered person, rude person: *es una maleducada,* she's really rude.
maleducar *t* (*niño*) to spoil.
maleficio *m* curse, evil spell.
maléfico,-a *adj* evil, harmful.
malentendido *m* misunderstanding.
malestar 1 *m* (*incomodidad*) discomfort. **2** *fig* (*inquietud*) unease, unrest.
● **sentir un malestar general,** to feel generally unwell.
maleta 1 *f* suitcase, case. – **2** *mf fam* useless person.
● **hacer la maleta,** (*empacar*) to pack; (*irse*) to pack up.
maletero 1 *m* AUTO boot, US trunk. **2** (*mozo*) porter.
maletilla *m* novice bullfighter.
maletín 1 *m* (*de ejecutivo*) briefcase. **2** (*maleta*) small case.
malevolencia *f* malevolence.
malévolo,-a *adj* malevolent.
maleza 1 *f* (*malas hierbas*) weeds *pl.* **2** (*arbustos*) undergrowth, scrub.
malformación *f* malformation.
malgache 1 *adj* Madagascan, Malagsy. – **2** *mf* Madagascan.
■ **República Malgache,** Malagasy Republic.
malgastador,-ra *m,f* spendthrift, squanderer.
malgastar *t* to waste, squander.
malhablado,-a 1 *adj* foul-mouthed. – **2** *m,f* foul-mouthed person: *es un malhablado,* he's always swearing.
malhadado,-a *adj lit* ill-fated.
malhecho,-a *adj* (*cuerpo, persona*) deformed.
malhechor,-ra 1 *adj* criminal. – **2** *m,f* wrongdoer, criminal.
malherir *t* to wound badly: *fue malherido en la refriega,* he was badly wounded in the scuffle.
▲ *Conjugation model* [35], *like* **hervir.**
malhumor *m* bad temper.
● **estar de malhumor,** to be in a bad mood. ‖ **tener malhumor,** to be bad-tempered.
malhumorado,-a *adj* bad-tempered.
● **estar malhumorado,-a,** to be in a bad mood.
Mali *m* Mali.
malicia 1 *f* (*mala intención*) malice. **2** (*maldad*) evil, maliciousness. **3** (*astucia*) slyness, craftiness, cunning: *para triunfar hay que tener un poco de malicia,* to get ahead you have to be a bit crafty. **4** (*sospecha*) suspicion.
● **decir algo con malicia,** to say sth. maliciously. ‖ **hacer algo con malicia,** to do sth. with malice.
maliciar 1 *t* to suspect. – **2** maliciarse, *p* to suspect.
malicioso,-a 1 *adj* (*malintencionado*) malicious, spiteful. **2** (*malpensado*) suspicious-minded. – **3** *m,f* (*malicioso*) malicious person. **4** (*malpensado*) person with a suspicious mind.
maliense 1 *adj* Malian. – **2** *mf* Malian.

malignidad 1 *f* (*de un tumor*) malignancy. **2** (*de una persona*) malignity, evil nature.

maligno,-a 1 *adj* (*tumor*) malignant. **2** (*persona, intención*) evil, malicious. – **3 el Maligno**, *m* the Evil One.

malillo,-a 1 *adj* (*diminutivo de malo*) → **malo,-a**. **2** *fam* (*mediocre*) poor, second-rate.

malintencionado,-a 1 *adj* malicious, spiteful. – **2** *m,f* malicious person.

malinterpretar *t* to misinterpret.

malísimo,-a *adj* really bad, terrible, awful.

malito,-a 1 *adj* (*diminutivo de malo*) → **malo,-a**. **2** (*enfermo*) poorly: *como comas tantos caramelos, te vas a poner malito,* if you eat so many sweets, you'll make yourself ill.

malla 1 *f* (*red*) mesh. **2** (*prenda*) leotard. – **3 mallas,** *fpl* (*medias sin pie*) leggings.
■ **cota de mallas,** coat of mail.

Mallorca *f* Majorca.

mallorquino,-a 1 *adj* Majorcan. – **2** *m,f* (*persona*) Majorcan. – **3 mallorquino,** *m* (*dialecto*) Majorcan.

malmirado,-a *adj* inconsiderate.
● **estar malmirado,-a,** (*comportamiento*) to be frowned upon; (*persona*) to be disliked.

malnacido,-a 1 *adj* despicable. – **2** *m,f* despicable person: *hacer eso es de malnacidos,* that is despicable.

malnutrición *f* malnutrition.

malnutrido,-a *adj* malnourished.

malo,-a 1 *adj* bad: *¡qué día tan malo hace!,* what dreadful weather!; *este vino es muy malo,* this wine is very bad; *es mala señal que no hayan llamado todavía,* it's a bad sign that they haven't phoned yet. **2** (*malvado*) wicked, evil: *es muy mala persona,* he's a nasty piece of work. **3** (*travieso*) naughty: *¡qué niño más malo!,* what a naughty child! **4** (*nocivo*) harmful: *el tabaco es malo para la salud,* smoking is bad for you. **5** (*enfermo*) ill, sick: *no ha venido a trabajar porque está malo con gripe,* he's off sick with flu. **6** (*estropeado*) off: *este pescado ya está malo,* this fish has gone off already. **7** (*falso*) false: *este rubí es malo,* this ruby is false. **8** (*difícil*) difficult: *el tobillo es malo de curar,* ankles take a long time to heal. – **9** *m,f* (*en la ficción*) baddy, villain: *¿quién es el malo?,* who's the baddy?
● **de mala manera,** badly, rudely. ‖ **estar a malas con algn.,** to be on bad terms with sb. ‖ **estar de malas,** (*malhumorado*) to be in a bad mood; (*desafortunado*) to be unlucky. ‖ **estar mala,** *fam* to have one's period. ‖ **estar malo,-a,** *fam* to be ill, us be sick. ‖ **lo malo es que ...,** the trouble is that ... ‖ **¡malo!,** bad news!: *cuando no mira a los ojos ¡malo!,* if he doesn't look you in the eye it's bad news. ‖ **poner malo,-a a algn.,** *fam* to drive sb. mad. ‖ **ponerse malo,-a,** *fam* to get ill, us get sick. ‖ **por las buenas o por las malas,** whether one likes it or not. ‖ **por las malas,** by force. ‖ **ser el malo de la película,** to be the baddy.
■ **mala hierba,** weed. ‖ **mala jugada / mala pasada,** dirty trick. ‖ **mala pata,** bad luck. ‖ **malos tratos,** ill-treatment. ‖ **mala voluntad,** ill will.

malogrado,-a 1 *adj* (*desaprovechado*) wasted. **2** (*frustrado*) abortive, failed. **3** (*difunto*) ill-fated.

malograr 1 *t* (*desaprovechar*) to waste. **2** (*estropear*) to spoil, ruin. – **3 malograrse,** *p* (*plan, proyecto*) to fail, fall through; (*cosecha*) to fail, be ruined. **4** (*persona*) to die before one's time.

maloliente *adj* foul-smelling, stinking.

malparado,-a salir malparado,-a, *loc* to come off badly.

● **dejar malparado,-a a algn.,** (*en una situación*) to make sb. look bad; (*en una pelea*) to leave sb. in a bad way.

malpensado,-a 1 *adj* nasty-minded. – **2** *m,f* nasty-minded person: *es una malpensada,* she thinks the worst of people.

malquerencia *f* aversion, ill will.

malsano,-a *adj* (*ambiente, vida*) unhealthy; (*curiosidad*) morbid, unhealthy; (*mente*) sick.

malsonante 1 *adj* ill-sounding. **2** (*grosero*) offensive, rude.
■ **palabras malsonantes,** swearwords.

malta *f* malt.

Malta *f* Malta.

maltés 1 *adj* Maltese. – **2** *m,f* (*persona*) Maltese. – **3 maltés,** *m* (*idioma*) Maltese.

maltraer *t* to ill-treat.
● **llevar a algn. a maltraer,** *fam* to give sb. a hard time.

maltratar *t* (*tratar mal*) to ill-treat, mistreat; (*pegar*) to batter.

maltrato *m* mistreatment, ill-treatment.

maltrecho,-a 1 *adj* (*persona*) battered, wrecked. **2** (*cosa*) damaged, destroyed.

maltusianismo *m* Malthusianism.

maltusiano,-a 1 *adj* Malthusian. – **2** *m,f* Malthusian.

malucho,-a 1 *adj fam* (*de baja calidad*) poor, bad. **2** *fam* (*enfermo*) under the weather, poorly.

malva 1 *adj* (*color*) mauve. – **2** *f* BOT mallow.
● **estar criando malvas,** *fam* to be pushing up the daisies. ‖ **estar como una malva,** to be as meek as a lamb.
■ **malva loca,** hollyhock, rose mallow.

malvado,-a 1 *adj* wicked, evil. – **2** *m,f* villain, evil person.

malvasía *f* (*uva*) malvasia; (*vino*) malmsey, malvasia.

malvavisco *m* marshmallow.

malvender *t* to sell at a loss.

malversación *f* misappropriation, embezzlement.
■ **malversación de fondos,** embezzlement.

malversador,-ra 1 *adj* embezzling. – **2** *m,f* embezzler.

malversar *t* to embezzle, misappropriate.

Malvinas Islas Malvinas, *fpl* Falkland Islands, Falklands.

malvinense 1 *adj* of the Falklands, from the Falklands. – **2** *mf* Falklander, Falkland islander.

malvinero,-a *adj-m,f* → **malvinense**.

malvivir *i* to live very badly, eke out a living, get by: *no tenemos más que para malvivir,* we've only just got enough to get by on.
● **de malvivir,** (*persona*) shady, unsavoury.

mama 1 *f* (*pecho*) breast; (*de animal*) mammary gland. **2** *fam* (*madre*) mum.

mamá *f fam* mum, mummy, us mom.

mamada *f* → **mamado,-a**.

mamado,-a 1 *adj* tabú (*borracho*) pissed, plastered. – **2** mamada, *f* (*acción*) sucking; (*toma de bebé*) feed.

mamar 1 *t* (*succionar*) to suck. **2** *fig* (*aprender de pequeño*) to grow up with. – **3** *i* (*bebé*) to feed; (*animal*) to suckle. – **4 mamarse,** *p* tabú (*emborracharse*) to get pissed, get plastered.
● **dar de mamar,** to breast-feed.

mamario,-a *adj* mammary.

mamarrachada *f fam* (*acción*) ridiculous thing to do; (*ropa*) ridiculous thing to wear.

mamarracho 1 *m fam* (*ridículo - persona*) sight; (*- vestido, cuadro*) monstrosity. **2** *fam* (*tonto*) moron, idiot.

mambo *m* mambo.

mamella 1 *f* (*de un animal*) mammary gland. – 2 **mamellas,** *fpl tabú* knockers.

mameluco 1 *m* HIST Mameluke. **2** *fam* idiot, moron.

mamífero,-a 1 *adj* mammalian, mammal. – 2 **mamífero** *m* mammal.

mamografía *f* (*técnica*) mammography; (*radiografía*) mammogram, mammograph.

mamola hacerle la mamola a algn., *loc fam* (*para hacer reír*) to chuck sb. under the chin; (*para engatusar*) to make a fool out of sb.

mamón,-ona *adj tabú* (*hombre*) pillock, prick; (*mujer*) bitch.

mamotreto 1 *m* (*libro*) great big thick book, weighty tome. **2** (*armatoste*) monstrosity, massive thing.

mampara *f* screen.
■ mampara de baño, shower screen.

mamporro 1 *m fam* (*golpe que se da*) punch, thump, thwack. **2** *fam* (*golpe que se recibe involuntariamente*) bump, bang.

mampostería *f* masonry, stone work.
■ mampostería en seco, dry-stone work. ‖ muro de mampostería, stone wall.

mamut *m* mammoth.

maná *m* manna.

manada 1 *f* (*vacas, elefantes*) herd; (*ovejas*) flock; (*lobos, perros*) pack. **2** *fam* (*personas*) horde.
● a manadas / en manada, en masse.

manager *mf* (*hombre*) manager; (*mujer*) manageress.

managüense 1 *adj* of Managua, from Managua. – 2 *mf* person from Managua, inhabitant of Managua.

manantial *m* spring.
■ agua de manantial, spring water.

manar 1 *i* (*salir*) to flow (**de,** from), pour (**de,** from), well (**de,** from): *el agua manaba de la roca,* water welled from the rock. **2** *fig* (*abundar*) to abound in, be rich in. – 3 *t* to drip with: *la herida mana sangre,* blood is flowing from the wound, the wound is bleeding.

manatí *m* manatee.

manazas 1 *adj* clumsy. – 2 *mf inv fam* clumsy person.

manceba *f* → **manabo,-a.**

mancebía *f arc* brothel.

mancebo,-a 1 *m,f arc* (*joven - hombre*) young man; (*- mujer*) young woman. **2** (*dependiente*) assistant. – 3 **manceba,** *f* concubine.

mancha 1 *f* stain, spot. **2** *fig* blemish.
● sin mancha, flawless, spotless.
■ mancha solar, sunspot.

manchado,-a 1 *pp* → **manchar.** – 2 *adj* stained. **3** (*café*) with a spot of milk. **4** (*animal*) spotted.

manchar 1 *t* to stain, dirty. **2** *fig* to tarnish. – 3 *i* to stain. – 4 **mancharse,** *p* to get dirty: *me he manchado la camisa de aceite,* I've got oil on my shirt.

manchego,-a 1 *adj* of La Mancha , from La Mancha. – 2 *m,f* native of La Mancha. – 3 **manchego,** *m cheese from La Mancha.*

manchú 1 *adj* Manchu. – 2 *mf* (*persona*) Manchu. – 3 **manchú,** *m* (*idioma*) Manchu.

Manchuria *f* Manchuria.

mancilla *f arc* blemish, stain.

mancillar *t arc* to sully: *mancilló el honor de la familia,* he sullied the family's reputation.

manco,-a 1 *adj* (*sin un brazo*) one-armed; (*sin brazos*) armless; (*sin una mano*) one-handed; (*sin manos*) handless:

quedó manco del brazo derecho, he lost his right arm. – 2 *m,f* (*sin brazo*) one-armed person; (*sin brazos*) armless person; (*sin mano*) one-handed person; (*sin manos*) person with no hands.
● no ser manco,-a / no quedarse manco,-a, *fam* (*bueno*) to be pretty useful; (*lanzado*) not to be backward.

mancomunar 1 *t* to bring together, join. – 2 **mancomunarse,** *p* to join forces, unite.

mancomunidad 1 *f* (*asociación*) community, association. **2** (*de municipios*) association.

mandado,-a 1 *pp* → **mandar.** – 2 *m,f* dogsbody, minion: *a mí me da igual, yo sólo soy un mandado,* I don't mind, I'm just doing my job. – 3 **mandado,** *m* (*recado*) errand.
● hacer un mandado, *fam* to run an errand.

mandamás *mf fam* bigwig, boss.
▲ *pl* mandamases.

mandamiento 1 *m* REL commandment. **2** JUR warrant, order.
■ los Diez Mandamientos, the Ten Commandments. ‖ mandamiento judicial, court order.

mandanga 1 *f fam* (*calma*) sluggishness, slowness. – 2 **mandangas,** *fpl fam* nonsense *sing.*
● ¡no me vengas con mandangas!, don't give me that!

mandar 1 *t* (*ordenar*) to order, tell: *nos mandó que fuéramos puntuales,* he told us to be on time. **2** (*enviar*) to send: *mi madre me mandó por pan,* my mother sent me out to get some bread; *lo mandé por correo,* I sent it by post; *hoy mismo he mandado la carta,* I posted the letter today. – 3 *i* (*dirigir - un grupo*) to be in charge; (*- un país*) to be in power: *¿quién manda aquí?,* who's in charge here?
● ¡a mandar!, you're in charge! ‖ lo que usted mande, as you wish, as you say. ‖ mandar a algn. a paseo/hacer gárgaras/freír espárragos, *fam* to tell sb. to get lost, tell sb. to take a running jump. ‖ ¿mande?, *fam* pardon?

mandarín 1 *m* (*persona*) mandarin. **2** (*idioma*) Mandarin, Mandarin Chinese.

mandarina *f* mandarin, tangerine.

mandarino *m* mandarin, mandarin orange tree.

mandatario,-a 1 *m,f* JUR agent. **2** POL leader: *el primer mandatario,* the leader, the head of state.

mandato 1 *m* (*orden*) order, command. **2** JUR mandate. **3** POL term of office.
■ mandato judicial, court order.

mandíbula *f* jaw.

mandil *m* apron.

mandioca *f* manioc, cassava.

mando 1 *m* (*autoridad*) command: *le han relevado en el mando,* he's been dismissed. **2** (*período*) term of office. **3** (*persona*) person in charge; (*oficial*) officer. **4** (*botón*) control.
● ejercer el mando, to be in charge. ‖ estar al mando de, to be in charge of.
■ alto mando, high-ranking officer. ‖ cuadro de mandos, instrument panel. ‖ mandos intermedios, middle management. ‖ mandos militares, military officers. ‖ mandos policiales, police officers. ‖ mando a distancia, (*sistema*) remote control; (*aparato*) remote control unit.

mandoble 1 *m fam* (*con la mano*) blow. **2** (*con espada*) blow with a sword, swordstroke. **3** *fam* (*espada*) large sword.

mandolina *f* mandolin.

mandón,-ona 1 *adj fam* bossy. – 2 *m,f fam* bossy-boots.
mandrágora *f* mandrake.
mandril 1 *m* ZOOL mandril. 2 TÉC mandrel.
manduca *f fam* grub, nosh, food.
manducar *t fam* to eat, stuff os.
manecilla *f* (*de reloj*) hand.
manejable *adj* manageable, easy-to-handle.
manejar 1 *t* (*manipular*) to handle, operate, use: *maneja muy bien el bisturí,* he's an expert with the scalpel. 2 (*dirigir*) to run, mange. 3 (*manipular*) to manipulate. 4 AM to drive. – 5 *i* AM to drive. – 6 **manejarse,** *p* to manage, get by: *se las maneja muy bien sola,* she manages very well by herself.
manejo 1 *m* (*uso*) handling, use: *ya le ha cogido el manejo al ordenador,* she's got the hang of the computer now. 2 (*funcionamiento*) running. 3 (*de un negocio*) management. 4 (*ardid*) trick, scheme. 5 AM (*de coche*) driving.
manera 1 *f* (*gen*) way, manner. – 2 **maneras,** *pl* (*educación*) manners.
● **a manera de,** by way of. ‖ **a la manera de,** in the style of. ‖ **a mi** *(tu etc)* **manera,** my (*your etc*) way. ‖ **de cualquier manera,** (*en cualquier caso*) in any case; (*sin cuidado, consideración, interés*) carelessly. ‖ **de manera que,** so that. ‖ **de ninguna manera,** certainly not. ‖ **de todas maneras,** in any case, anyhow. ‖ **de mala manera,** *fam* (*groseramente*) rudely; (*con violencia*) roughly. ‖ **¡de una manera!,** in such a way! ‖ **de una manera o de otra,** whatever way. ‖ **en cierta manera,** in a way. ‖ **en gran manera,** enormously. ‖ **no hay manera,** it's impossible. ‖ **¡qué manera de ... !,** what a way to ... !
■ **manera de ser,** character.
manga 1 *f* sleeve: *de manga corta/larga,* short/long-sleeved; *en mangas de camisa,* in shirt sleeves; *sin mangas,* sleeveless. 2 (*manguera*) hose (pipe). 3 (*de pescar*) casting net. 4 CULIN (*de pastelero*) icing bag; (*de filtrar*) muslin strainer. 5 DEP round.
● **estar algo manga por hombro,** *fam* to be in a mess, be topsy-turvy. ‖ **hacerle un corte de mangas a algn.,** *tabú* to put two fingers up at sb., US give sb. the finger. ‖ **sacarse algo de la manga,** to pull sth. out of one's hat. ‖ **ser de manga ancha,** to be very lenient. ‖ **tener algo en la manga,** to keep sth. up one's sleeve. ‖ **tener manga ancha,** to be very lenient.
■ **manga abombada / manga abullonada,** puffed sleeve. ‖ **manga camisera,** shirt sleeve. ‖ **manga corta,** short sleeve. ‖ **manga japonesa,** seamless sleeve. ‖ **manga larga,** long sleeve. ‖ **manga raglán,** raglan sleeve. ‖ **manga tres cuartos,** three-quarter sleeve. ‖ **manga de riego,** hosepipe. ‖ **media manga,** elbow-length sleeve.
manganeso *m* manganese.
mangante 1 *mf fam pey* (*ladrón*) thief. 2 *fam pey* (*estafador*) crook, con man.
mangar *t fam* to pinch, nick, swipe.
▲ Conjugation model [7], like *llegar.*
manglar *m* mangrove swamp.
mango[1] *m* handle.
mango[2] *m* BOT mango.
mangoneador,-ra 1 *m,f fam* (*entrometido*) busybody. 2 (*mandón*) bossy-boots.
mangonear 1 *t fam* (*dominar*) to boss around, boss about. – 2 *i fam* (*entrometerse*) to be a busybody; (*dominar*) to be bossy.
mangoneo *m fam* (*entrometimiento*) meddling.
mangosta *f* mongoose.

manguera 1 *f* (*de riego*) hose, hosepipe. 2 (*de bombero*) hose, fire hose.
mangui 1 *mf arg* (*ladrón*) thief. 2 *arg* (*sinvergüenza*) crook.
manguito 1 *m* (*de manos*) muff. 2 (*de manga*) oversleeve. 3 TÉC sleeve.
mani *f arg* demo.
maní *m* peanut.
▲ *pl* **manises.**
manía 1 *f* MED mania. 2 (*ojeriza*) dislike, grudge: *le tiene manía,* he's got it in for her; *tengo manía a ese cantante,* I can't stand that singer. 3 (*costumbre*) habit; (*rareza*) quirk, peculiar habit; (*obsesión*) obsession, mania: *tiene la manía de morderse las uñas,* she has a habit of biting her nails. 4 (*pasión*) craze, fad, mania: *ahora le ha dado la manía por las antigüedades,* she's really into antiques at the moment.
● **cogerle/tomarle manía a algn.,** *fam* to take a dislike to sb.
■ **mania persecutoria,** persecution mania.
maníaco,-a *m,f* → **maníaco,-a.**
maníaco,-a 1 *adj* MED manic. – 2 *m,f fam* maniac.
■ **maníaco,-a depresivo,-a,** manic depressive. ‖ **maníaco,-a sexual,** sex maniac.
maniatar *t* to tie up: *lo maniataron,* they tied his hands.
maniático,-a 1 *adj* (*raro*) cranky; (*quisquilloso*) fussy, finicky; (*fanático*) obsessive. – 2 *m,f* (*quisquilloso*) fusspot: *es un maniático del orden,* he's a stickler for tidiness. 3 (*loco*) crackpot, crank.
manicomio *m* mental hospital.
manicura *f* → **manicuro, -a.**
manicuro,-a 1 *m,f* manicurist. – 2 **manicura,** *f* manicure.
● **hacerse la manicura,** to have a manicure.
manido,-a 1 *adj* (*frase*) hackneyed; (*tema*) stale. 2 (*objeto*) well-worn.
manierismo *m* mannerism.
manierista 1 *adj* manneristic. – 2 *mf* mannerist.
manifestación 1 *f* (*de protesta etc*) demonstration. 2 (*expresión - gen*) sign; (*- artística*) example. – 3 **maifestaciones,** *fpl* (*declaración*) statement *sing,* declaration *sing,* comments *pl.*
manifestante *mf* demonstrator.
manifestar 1 *t* (*declarar*) to state; (*expresar*) to express: *el ministro manifestó que no asistiría a la cumbre,* the minister stated that he would not attend the summit; *manifestaron su desacuerdo con la decisión,* they expressed their disagreement with the decision; *queremos manifestar nuestro apoyo a los huelguistas,* we want to express our support for the strikers. 2 (*mostrar*) to show: *cuando abre la boca manifiesta su ignorancia,* as soon as he opens his mouth he shows his ignorance. – 3 **manifestarse,** *p* (*hacerse evidente*) to become apparent. 4 to demonstrate: *se manifestaron a favor del desarme nuclear,* they demonstrated in favour of nuclear disarmament. 5 to declare os., express: *se manifiesta contrario a la monarquía,* he is against the monarchy.
▲ Conjugation model [27], like *acertar.*
manifiesto,-a 1 *adj* obvious, evident. – 2 **manifiesto,** *m* manifesto.
● **poner de manifiesto,** to make evident. ‖ **ser un hecho manifiesto,** to be blatantly obvious.
manija *f* handle.
manilla 1 *f* (*grillete*) handcuff. 2 (*de reloj*) hand. 3 → **manija.**
manillar *m* handlebars *pl.*

maniobra 1 *f* (*con un coche*) manoeuvre, US maneuvre: *tuve que hacer muchas maniobras para meter el coche en el hueco,* it took me a lot of manoeuvring to get the car into the space. **2** (*táctica*) manoeuvre, US maneuvre, ploy. – **3 maniobras,** *fpl* MIL manoeuvres, US maneuvres.
● **estar de maniobras,** to me on manoeuvres (US maneuvers).

maniobrable *adj* manoeuvrable, US maneuverable.

maniobrar *i* to manoeuvre, US maneuver.

manipulación 1 *f* (*ilícita*) manipulation. **2** (*de alimentos*) handling. **3** (*de una máquina*) use, operation. **4** TÉC manipulation.
■ **manipulación de alimentos,** food handling.

manipulador,-ra 1 *adj* manipulative. – **2** *m,f* manipulator.

manipular 1 *t* (*persona*) to manipulate. **2** (*mercancías, alimentos*) to handle. **3** (*aparato, máquina*) to use, operate. **4** *fig* to interfere with.

maniqueísmo *m* (*doctrina*) Manichaeism.

maniqueo,-a 1 *adj* HIST Manichaean. – **2** *m,f* HIST Manichaean.

maniquí 1 *m* (*muñeco*) dummy, mannequin. – **2** *mf* (*modelo*) model.
▲ *pl* **maniquíes.**

manirroto,-a 1 *adj fam* spendthrift, extravagant. – **2** *m,f fam* spendthrift.

manitas 1 *adj fam* handy. – **2** *mf* (*hombre*) handyman; (*mujer*) handywoman.
● **hacer manitas,** to hold hands. ‖ **ser un/una manitas,** to be very good with one's hands.
▲ *pl* **manitas.**

manivela *f* crank, handle.

manjar *m* delicious dish, delicacy.
■ **manjar de dioses,** delicacy.

mano 1 *f* ANAT hand. **2** ZOOL (*de caballo*) forefoot; (*de gato, perro, etc*) paw. **3** (*lado*) side: *el lavabo está a mano derecha,* the toilet is on the right. **4** (*de reloj*) hand. **5** (*de pintura*) coat. **6** (*de jabón*) soaping. **7** (*habilidad*) skill: *tienes muy buena mano con los niños,* you're very good with children. **8** (*influencia*) influence. **9** (*ayuda*) hand. **10** (*de mortero*) pestle. **11** (*de naipes - jugada, conjunto de cartas*) hand; (*- jugador*) leader: *en esta jugada soy mano yo,* it's my lead this time. **12** DEP (*en fútbol*) handball. – **13 manos,** *fpl* (*poder*) hands *sing*, power *sing.*
● **a mano,** (*escrito*) handwritten; by hand; (*hecho*) handmade, by hand; (*lavado*) by hand; (*cerca*) to hand, handy, near. ‖ **abrir la mano,** to become more flexible, become more lenient. ‖ **a mano armada,** armed. ‖ **a manos llenas,** generously. ‖ **alzar/levantar la mano a algn.,** to raise one's hand to sb. ‖ **bajo mano,** underhandedly. ‖ **cogidos,-as de la mano,** hand-in-hand. ‖ **con el corazón en la mano,** sincerely, with one's heart on one's sleeve. ‖ **con las manos en la masa,** red-handed. ‖ **con las manos vacías,** empty-handed. ‖ **con una mano detrás y otra delante,** *fam* without a penny to one's name. ‖ **dar la mano a / tender la mano a,** (*saludar*) to shake hands with; (*ayudar*) to offer one's hand to. ‖ **darse la mano,** (*dos personas*) to shake hands; (*dos cosas*) to be very similar. ‖ **de primera mano,** (*objeto*) brand-new; (*noticia*) first-hand. ‖ **dejar de la mano,** to abandon. ‖ **echar mano de algo,** to resort to sth., draw on sth. ‖ **echar una mano,** to give a hand, lend a hand. ‖ **en buenas manos,** in good hands. ‖ **estar en las manos de algn.,** to be in sb.'s hands. ‖ **hecho,-a a mano,** handmade. ‖ **írsele la mano a algn.,** (*no contenerse*) to lose control; (*exagerar*)

to go over the top: *se le fue la mano al echarle sal al pescado,* he put too much salt on the fish. ‖ **¡las manos quietas!,** *fam* hands off! ‖ **lavarse las manos,** *fig* to wash one's hands. ‖ **llegar a las manos,** to come to blows. ‖ **llevarse las manos a la cabeza,** to be horrified. ‖ **mano sobre mano,** idle, twiddling one's thumbs. ‖ **¡manos arriba!,** hands up! ‖ **meter la mano en algo,** to get involved in sth., intervene in sth. ‖ **meter mano,** *fam* (*toquetear*) to grope, touch up; (*intervenir*) to do sth., take action. ‖ **pedir la mano de algn.,** to ask for sb.'s hand. ‖ **ponerle la mano encima a algn.,** to lay a hand on sb. ‖ **poner la mano en el fuego por algn.,** to risk one's neck for sb. ‖ **poner manos a la obra,** to get down to work, get cracking. ‖ **quedar algo muy a mano,** to be very near. ‖ **ser la mano derecha de algn.,** to be sb.'s right hand. ‖ **ser mano de santo,** to work wonders. ‖ **tener algo a mano,** to have sth. handy. ‖ **tener buena mano para algo,** to have a knack for sth., be a dab hand at sth. ‖ **tener buenas manos,** to be good with one's hands. ‖ **tener la mano (muy) larga,** (*para pegar*) to be quick to lift a hand; (*para robar*) to be light-fingered, have sticky fingers. ‖ **tener las manos limpias,** to be clean. ‖ **tener mano dura,** to be strict. ‖ **tener mano de hierro,** to rule with an iron fist. ‖ **tener mano izquierda,** to have a lot of tact. ‖ **traerse algo entre manos,** to be planning sth., to be up to sth.
■ **apretón de manos,** handshake. ‖ **mano a mano,** (*entre dos*) two-sided contest; (*conversación*) tête-a-tête. ‖ **equipaje de mano,** hand luggage. ‖ **mano de cerdo,** pig's trotter. ‖ **mano de obra,** labour.

manojo *m* bunch.
● **ser un manojo de nervios,** to be a bundle of nerves.

manoletina 1 *f* (*en toros*) *type of pass.* **2** (*calzado*) open, low-heeled shoe, *similar to those used by bullfighters.*

manómetro *m* pressure gauge.

manopla 1 *f* (*guante*) mitten. **2** (*de armadura*) gauntlet.

manoseado,-a 1 *adj* (*objeto*) worn; (*book*) well-thumbed; (*fruit etc*) handled. **2** (*idea, tema*) well-worn, hackneyed.

manosear *t* (*objeto*) to handle; (*persona*) to feel up, grope.

manoseo *m* (*de una cosa*) handling; (*de una persona*) touching, groping.

manotada *f →* **manotazo.**

manotazo *m* slap, smack, swipe.
● **quitar algo a algn. de un manotazo,** to swipe sth. away from sb.

manotear *i* (*gesticular*) to wave one's hands about.

manoteo *m* (*gesticulación*) waving.

mansalva 1 **a mansalva,** *loc* (*en gran cantidad*) loads, stacks, tons: *repartieron premios a mansalva,* they handed out prizes left, right and centre. **2** (*disparar*) at point-blank range, at close range.

mansarda *f* attic.

mansedumbre 1 *f* (*de una persona*) meekness, docility. **2** (*de un animal*) tameness.

mansión *f* mansion.

manso,-a 1 *adj* (*animal*) tame. **2** (*persona*) docile, meek.

mansurrón,-ona *adj fam* very gentle, very tame.

manta 1 *f* (*gen*) blanket. – **2** *mf fam* (*perezoso*) lazybones.
● **a manta,** *fam* by the dozen: *en esta zona hay conejos a manta,* there are loads of rabbits in this area. ‖ **liarse la manta a la cabeza,** to take the plunge, throw caution to the wind. ‖ **tirar de la manta,** to let the cat out of the bag.

■ **manta de palos,** *fam* thrashing. ‖ **manta de viaje,** travelling rug. ‖ **manta eléctrica,** electric blanket.

mantear *t* to toss in a blanket.

manteca *f* (*de animal*) fat; (*elaborado*) lard; (*de leche*) cream.
■ **manteca de cacahuete,** peanut butter. ‖ **manteca de cacao,** cocoa butter. ‖ **manteca de cerdo,** lard. ‖ **manteca de vaca,** butter.

mantecada *f* small spongecake.

mantecado 1 *m* (*dulce*) very crumbly shortbread (*eaten particularly at Christmas*). **2** (*helado*) dairy ice cream.

mantecoso,-a *adj* greasy.

mantel *m* (*de mesa*) tablecloth; (*del altar*) altar cloth.

mantelería *f* table linen.

mantención *f* maintenance.

mantener 1 *t* (*conservar*) to keep: *la policía mantiene el orden público,* the police keep law and order; *la nevera mantiene los alimentos en buenas condiciones,* the fridge keeps food fresh; *"Mantenga Zamora limpia",* "Keep Zamora tidy". **2** (*tener*) to keep: *"mantener en posición vertical",* "keep vertical"; *"mantener fuera del alcance de los niños",* "keep out of the reach of children". **3** (*sostener*) to support, hold up, hold: *estos pilares mantienen el techo,* these pillars support the roof; *no sé como se mantiene en pie con lo que ha bebido,* I don't know how he can stand up after having drunk so much. **4** (*sustentar*) to support, maintain: *ella sola mantiene a toda la familia,* she supports the whole family by herself. **5** (*afirmación etc*) to maintain: *pues yo mantengo que no es verdad,* well, I maintain that it is not true. **6** (*conversación, relaciones*) to have; (*reunión*) to hold, have; (*correspondencia*) to keep up; (*promesa, palabra*) to keep: *afirma que no mantuvieron relaciones sexuales,* he states that they did not have sexual intercourse; *mantuvieron una larga correspondencia,* they kept up a lengthy correspondence; *mantuvimos una reunión en su despacho,* we held a meeting in her office. – **7** **mantenerse,** *p* (*sostenerse*) to remain, stand. **8** (*continuar en un estado, una posición*) to keep: *se mantuvo a distancia,* she kept her distance; *se mantiene firme en sus creencias,* he remains firm in his beliefs. **9** (*sustenerse*) to manage, maintain os., support os. **10** (*alimentarse*) to eat, live: *se mantiene a base de fruta,* she lives on fruit, she eats only fruit; *no nos mantenemos del aire,* we can't live on air.
● **mantener algo en secreto,** to keep sth. secret. ‖ **mantenerse aparte,** to stay out of it, not get involved. ‖ **mantenerse en contacto con,** to stay in contact with. ‖ **mantenerse en forma,** to keep in shape, keep in trim, keep fit. ‖ **mantenerse en pie,** to stand, remain standing. ‖ **mantenerse en sus trece,** to stick to one's guns. ‖ **mantenerse vivo,-a,** to stay alive.
▲ *Conjugation model* [87], *like* tener.

mantenido,-a 1 *pp* → **mantener.** – **2** *adj* continuous. – **3 mantenida,** *f pey* kept woman.

mantenimiento 1 *m* (*gen*) maintenance. **2** (*alimento*) sustenance.
■ **clase de mantenimiento,** keep-fit class. ‖ **servicio de mantenimiento,** maintenance service. ‖ **técnico de mantenimiento,** maintenance engineer.

manteo *m* tossing in a blanket.

mantequería 1 *f* (*tienda*) delicatessen. **2** (*fábrica*) dairy.

mantequilla *f* butter.
● **de mantequilla,** *fam* weak.

mantilla 1 *f* (*de mujer*) mantilla. **2** (*de niño*) shawl.
● **estar en mantillas,** to be in its early stages, be in its infancy.

mantillo 1 *m* (*abono del suelo*) humus. **2** (*abono del estiércol*) manure.

mantis *f* mantis.
■ **mantis religiosa,** praying mantis.

manto 1 *m* (*capa*) cloak. **2** (*de la Tierra*) layer, stratum. **3** *fig lit* veil, cloak.

mantón *m* large shawl.
■ **mantón de Manila,** embroidered silk shawl.

manual 1 *adj* manual. – **2** *m* manual, handbook.
■ **trabajos manuales,** handicrafts.

manualidad 1 *f* handicraft. – **2 manualidades,** *fpl* arts and crafts.

manubrio *m* crank, crankhandle.

manufactura 1 *f* (*acción*) manufacture. **2** (*producto*) product, manufactured article. **3** (*fábrica*) factory.

manufacturar *t* to manufacture.

manufacturero,-a *adj* manufacturing.

manumisión *f* manumission, freedom.

manumiso,-a *adj* free from slavery.
■ **esclavo manumiso,** freed slave.

manumitir *t* to manumit, set free.

manuscrito,-a 1 *adj* handwritten, manuscript. – **2 manuscrito,** *m* manuscript.

manutención 1 *f* (*gen*) maintenance. **2** (*alimenticia*) food, board.

manzana 1 *f* BOT apple. **2** (*de casas*) block.
● **ser la manzana de la discordia,** to be a bone of contention.

manzanilla 1 *f* (*planta*) camomile. **2** (*infusión*) camomile tea.

manzanillo *m* manzanilla.

manzano *m* apple tree.

maña 1 *f* (*habilidad*) skill, knack. **2** (*astucia*) trick.
● **más vale maña que fuerza,** brain is better than brawn. ‖ **tener maña para algo,** to be skilful (US skillful) at sth., be good at sth.

mañana 1 *f* morning: *hace una mañana preciosa,* it's a beautiful morning; *me levanté a las seis de la mañana,* I got up at six in the morning. – **2** *m* tomorrow, future: *tienes que pensar en el mañana,* you have to think of the future. – **3** *adv* tomorrow: *mañana no tengo que ir a trabajar,* I don't have to go to work tomorrow.
● **de mañana,** in the morning. ‖ **¡hasta mañana!,** see you tomorrow! ‖ **mañana por la mañana,** tomorrow morning. ‖ **mañana será otro día,** tomorrow is another day. ‖ **pasado mañana,** the day after tomorrow. ‖ **por la mañana,** in the morning.

mañanero,-a 1 *adj* (*de la mañana*) morning. **2** (*madrugador*) early-rising: *es muy mañanero,* he's an early riser.

mañanita *f* bed shawl.

maño,-a 1 *adj fam* Aragonese. – **2** *m,f fam* Aragonese person.

mañoso,-a 1 *adj* (*habilidoso*) handy, skilful, US skillful. **2** (*astuto*) crafty.

maoísmo *m* maoism.

maoísta 1 *adj* Maoist. – **2** *mf* Maoist.

maorí 1 *adj* Maori. – **2** *m,f* (*persona*) Maori. – **3** *m* (*idioma*) Maori.

mapa *m* map.
● **borrar algo del mapa,** *fam* to wipe sth. off, to get rid of sth. ‖ **hecho,-a un mapa,** *fam* disfigured. ‖ **mapa de carreteras,** road map. ‖ **mapa del tiempo,** weather map.

mapache *m* racoon.

mapamundi *m* map of the world.

maqueta 1 *f* (*de edificio, monumento, etc*) scale model. **2** (*de libro*) dummy. **3** (*de disco*) demo.

maqueto,-a *m,f fam pey name used by Basque people to refer to immigrants from the rest of Spain.*

maqui *mf* → **maquis**.

maquiavélico,-a *adj* Machiavellian.

maquiavelismo *m* Machiavellism.

maquillador,-ra *m,f* make-up assistant.

maquillaje *m* make-up.

maquillar 1 *t* to make up. – **2 maquillarse,** *p* (*ponerse maquillaje*) to make os. up, put one's make-up on; (*llevar maquillaje*) to wear make-up.

máquina 1 *f* (*gen*) machine. **2** (*de un tren*) engine. **3** *fig* machinery: *la máquina del Estado,* the State machinery. **4** (*expendedora*) vending machine.

● **a máquina,** (*cosido*) machine-sewn; (*escrito*) typewritten. ‖ **a toda máquina,** at full blast. ‖ **coser a máquina,** to use a sewing machine, sew on a sewing machine. ‖ **escribir a máquina,** to type, typewrite. ■ **máquina de afeitar,** shaver, electric razor. ‖ **máquina de coser,** sewing machine. ‖ **máquina de escribir,** typewriter. ‖ **máquina de fotos / máquina fotográfica,** camera. ‖ **máquina de lavar,** washing machine. ‖ **máquina de tabaco,** cigarette machine. ‖ **máquina de tricotar,** knitting machine. ‖ **máquina de vapor,** steam engine. ‖ **máquina tragaperras,** slot machine.

maquinación *f* plot, scheme, machination.

maquinador,-ra 1 *adj* scheming, machinating. – **2** *m,f* plotter, schemer, machinator.

maquinal *adj* mechanical.

maquinar *t* to scheme, plot.

maquinaria 1 *f* (*conjunto de máquinas*) machinery. **2** (*mecanismo*) mechanism.

maquinilla *f* razor.

■ **maquinilla eléctrica / maquinilla de afeitar,** razor.

maquinismo *m* mechanization.

maquinista 1 *mf* (*operador*) machinist. **2** (*de tren*) engine driver, US engineer. **3** CINEM camera assistant.

maquinización *f* mechanization.

maquinizar *t* to mechanize.

▲ *Conjugation model* |4|, *like* **realizar**.

maquis 1 *m* underground resistance movement. – **2** *mf* resistance fighter.

▲ *pl* **maquis**.

mar 1 *m & f* (*gen*) sea. **2** (*marejada*) swell. – **3 la mar de,** *f loc fam* (*mucha cantidad*): *fue la mar de divertido,* it was great fun; *vino la mar de gente,* loads of people came; *estás la mar de guapa,* you look really lovely.

● **en alta mar,** on the high sea, on the open sea. ‖ **estar hecho,-a un mar de lágrimas,** to be crying his/her eyes out, be in floods of tears. ‖ **hacerse a la mar,** to put (out) to sea, set sail. ‖ **llover a mares,** to rain cats and dogs, bucket down. ‖ **¡pelillos a la mar!,** *fam* let bygones be bygones! ‖ **por mar,** by sea. ■ **mar adentro,** out to sea. ‖ **mar de fondo,** (*corriente*) ground swell; (*agitación*) undercurrent. ‖ **mar gruesa,** heavy sea. ‖ **mar picada,** rough sea. ‖ **mar rizada,** slightly choppy sea.

marabino,-a 1 *adj* of Maracaibo, from Maracaibo. – **2** *m,f* person from Maracaibo, inhabitant of Maracaibo.

marabú *m* marabou.

marabunta 1 *f* swarm of ants. **2** *fam fig* mob, crowd.

maraca *f* maraca.

maracaibero,-a 1 *adj* of Maracaibo, from Maracaibo. – **2** *m,f* person from Maracaibo, inhabitant of Maracaibo.

maracuyá *f* passion fruit.

marajá *m* maharajah.

maraña 1 *f* (*espesura*) thicket. **2** (*enredo*) tangle. **3** (*asunto confuso*) muddle, mess.

marasmo 1 *m* MED marasmus. **2** *fig* apathy, stagnation.

maratón *m* marathon.

maratoniano,-a *adj* marathon.

maravedí *m* maravedi.

maravilla 1 *f* wonder, marvel: *las maravillas de la ciencia,* the wonders of science; *¡qué maravilla de reloj!,* what a wonderful watch! **2** (*pasta*) semolina.

● **a las mil maravillas,** wonderfully well. ‖ **de maravilla,** wonderfully: *el examen me salió de maravilla,* the exam went wonderfully. ‖ **decir maravillas de algo/algn.,** to sing the praises of sth./sb. ‖ **hacer maravillas,** to do wonders. ‖ **venir de maravilla,** to be just the thing, be perfect.

maravillar 1 *t* to astonish, amaze. – **2 maravillarse,** *p* to marvel (**de,** at).

maravilloso,-a *adj* wonderful, marvellous.

marbete *m* (*etiqueta*) label.

marca 1 *f* (*señal*) mark, sign. **2** (*en comestibles, productos del hogar*) brand; (*en otros productos*) make. **3** DEP record. **4** (*acción*) marking.

● **de marca,** named-brand. ‖ **de marca mayor,** *fam* terrible, tremendous. ■ **marca de fábrica,** trademark. ‖ **marca registrada,** registered trademark.

marcadamente *adv* markedly.

marcado,-a 1 *pp* → **marcar**. – **2** *adj* (*señalado*) marked. **3** (*evidente*) distinct, definite; (*acento*) marked, pronounced.

marcador *m* DEP scoreboard.

marcaje *m* marking.

marcapasos *m* pacemaker.

▲ *pl* **marcapasos**.

marcar 1 *t* (*señalar*) to mark; (*ganado*) to brand. **2** (*herir físicamente*) to slash; (*traumatizar*) to mark: *le marcaron la cara de un navajazo,* they slashed his face with a knife; *la muerte de su hijo la marcó para siempre,* the death of her son marked her for life. **3** DEP (*gol, canasta*) to score. **4** DEP (*al contrario*) to mark. **5** (*pelo*) to set. **6** (*cantidad*) to indicate, show: *el termómetro marca 20 grados,* the thermometer shows 20 degrees; *¿qué precio marca la etiqueta?,* what's the price on the tag? **7** (*en teléfono*) to dial. **8** (*resaltar*) to show.

● **marcar el compás,** to mark the rhythm. ‖ **marcar el paso,** to mark time. ‖ **marcarse un farol,** to show off. ‖ **marcarse un tanto, marcarse un triunfo,** to score points.

▲ *Conjugation model* |1|, *like* **sacar**.

marcha 1 *f* (*de protesta, soldados*) march. **2** (*progreso*) course, progress: *la marcha de las negociaciones,* the progress of the negotiations. **3** (*partida*) departure; (*abandono*) leaving: *lamentaremos su marcha,* we'll be sorry when he leaves. **4** (*velocidad*) speed. **5** AUTO gear. **6** MÚS march. **7** DEP walk. **8** *fam* (*de persona*) go, energy; (*de lugar, ambiente*) life: *esta mujer tiene una marcha increíble,* she's full of life, she's full of energy; *aquí no hay marcha,* this place is dead.

● **a marchas forzadas,** against the clock. ‖ **a toda marcha,** at full speed. ‖ **abrir la marcha,** to head the march. ‖ **cerrar la marcha,** to bring up the rear. ‖ **dar marcha atrás,** (*coche*) to reverse; (*proyecto*) to fall through. ‖ **estar en marcha,** (*máquina*) to be on, be working; (*cambio, proyecto*) to be underway. ‖ **ir de mar-**

cha, (*en el ejército*) to go on a march; (*por la noche*) to go out on the razzle, go out on the town. ‖ **irle la marcha a algn.**, *fam* to be a real raver. ‖ **poner en marcha,** (*coche*) to start; (*proyecto*) to start up. ‖ **sobre la marcha,** as we (I, *you, etc*) go along, as we (I, *you, etc*) go. ‖ **¡en marcha!**, off we go!
■ **cambio de marchas,** AUTO gearshift. ‖ **marcha atlética,** DEP walk. ‖ **marcha atrás,** AUTO reverse (gear). ‖ **marcha fúnebre,** funeral march. ‖ **marcha nupcial,** wedding march.

marchamo *m* seal.

marchante *mf* dealer.
■ **marchante de arte,** art dealer.

marchar 1 *i* (*ir*) to go, walk. 2 (*funcionar*) to work, run. 3 MIL to march. – 4 **marcharse,** *p* to leave.
● **¡marchando!**, *fam* coming up!: *¡marchando una de patatas!*, one portion of chips coming up! ‖ **marchar sobre ruedas,** to go smoothly.

marchitar 1 *t* to wither. – 2 **marchitarse,** *p* to wither.

marchito,-a *adj* (*planta*) withered; (*belleza*) faded.

marchoso,-a 1 *adj fam* (*persona*) fun-loving, wild; (*música, sitio*) lively. – 2 *m,f* raver, fun-lover.

marcial *adj* martial.

marcianitos los marcianitos, *mpl fam* space invaders.

marciano,-a 1 *adj* Martian. – 2 *m,f* Martian.

marco 1 *m* (*de cuadro, ventana*) frame. 2 *fig* framework, setting. 3 (*moneda*) mark. 4 DEP goalpost.
■ **acuerdo marco,** framework agreement. ‖ **marco jurídico,** legal framework.

marea 1 *f* tide. 2 (*multitud*) sea: *una marea de gente,* a sea of people.
■ **marea alta,** high tide. ‖ **marea baja,** low tide. ‖ **marea negra,** oil slick. ‖ **marea roja,** red tide. ‖ **marea viva,** spring tide.

mareado,-a 1 *adj* (*en general*) sick; (*en el coche*) carsick; (*en el mar*) seasick; (*en avión*) airsick: *estoy mareado,* I feel sick. 2 (*aturdido*) dizzy, giddy; (*a punto de desmayarse*) faint: *estoy como mareada,* I feel a bit dizzy. 3 (*bebido*) tipsy.

mareaje *m* (*rumbo*) ship's course.

mareante 1 *adj* (*que marea*) sickening. 2 (*pesado*) tedious.

marear 1 *t* (*producir malestar*) to make sick: *el coche me marea mucho,* I get carsick easily. 2 (*aturdir*) to make dizzy: *este ruido marea,* this noise makes your head spin. 3 *fam* (*molestar*) to annoy: *deja ya de marear, niño,* stop being a nuisance. – 4 **marearse,** *p* (*en general*) to get sick; (*en el coche*) to get carsick; (*en el mar*) to get seasick; (*en avión*) to get airsick. 5 (*sentir vértigo*) to get dizzy; (*a punto de desmayarse*) to feel faint. 6 (*emborracharse*) to get tipsy.

marejada *f* swell.

marejadilla *f* slight swell.

maremagno *m* → **mare mágnum.**

maremágnum *m* → **mare magnum.**

mare mágnum 1 *m* (*abundancia*) wealth. 2 (*confusión*) confusion, chaos, mayhem: *un mare mágnum de gente,* a sea of people; *un mare mágnum de papeles,* masses of papers.

maremoto *m* (*seísmo*) seaquake; (*ola*) tidal wave.

marengo gris marengo, *m* dark grey.

mareo 1 *m* (*en general*) sickness; (*en el mar*) seasickness; (*en el coche*) carsickness; (*en avión*) airsickness. 2 (*aturdimiento*) dizziness. 3 (*confusión*) muddle, mess.

marfil *m* ivory.

marfileño,-a 1 *adj* (*color, piel*) ivory. 2 (*de Costa de Marfil*) of the Ivory Coast, from the Ivory Coast. – 3 *m,f* native of the Ivory Coast, inhabitant of the Ivory Coast.

marga *f* marl, loam.

margarina *f* margarine.

margarita 1 *f* BOT daisy. 2 (*de máquina*) daisywheel. – 3 *m* (*cóctel*) margarita.
● **deshojar la margarita,** to play "he/she loves me, he/she loves me not". ‖ **echarle margaritas a los cerdos,** to cast pearls before swine.

margen 1 *m & f* (*extremidad*) border, edge. 2 (*de río*) bank; (*de camino*) edge. – 3 *m* (*del papel*) margin. 4 (*oportunidad*) chance. 5 COM margin.
● **al margen de ...,** apart from ..., out of ... ‖ **al margen de la ley,** outside the law. ‖ **dar margen para,** to give scope for. ‖ **dejar algo al margen,** to leave sth. aside. ‖ **dejar a algn. al margen,** to leave sb. out. ‖ **mantenerse al margen,** not to get involved.
■ **margen de beneficios,** profit margin. ‖ **margen de error,** margin of error.

marginación 1 *f* (*rechazo social*) ostracism, marginalization. 2 (*exclusión*) exclusion.

marginado,-a 1 *pp* → **marginar.** – 2 *adj* (*proyecto*) pushed aside, excluded. 3 (*persona*) marginalized, alienated. – 4 *m,f* social outcast, social misfit.
● **sentirse marginado,-a,** to feel like an outsider, to feel rejected.

marginal 1 *adj* (*ilustración, nota*) marginal, in the margin. 2 (*tema, asunto*) marginal, minor. 3 (*persona*) marginalized; (*grupo*) on the margins of society. 4 (*teatro, música*) fringe.

marginar 1 *t* (*persona*) to leave out, exclude; (*grupo social*) to ostracize, marginalize. 2 (*asunto*) to push aside.

maría 1 *f fam* (*asignatura fácil*) easy subject. 2 *fam* (*ama de casa*) housewife. 3 *arg* (*marihuana*) pot, grass.

mariachi *m* (*persona, música*) mariachi; (*orquesta*) mariachi band.

marianista 1 *adj* Marianist. – 2 *mf* Marianist.

mariano,-a *adj* Marian.

marica *m fam pey* poof, queer.
● **¡marica el último!,** *fam* last one's a sissy!

maricastaña del tiempo de Maricastaña, *loc fam* as old as the hills.

maricón 1 *m fam pey* (*homosexual*) poofter, poof, queer. 2 *fam* (*indeseable*) bastard.

mariconada 1 *f fam* (*faena*) rotten thing to do. 2 *fam* (*acción, gesto*) poofy thing to do; (*ropa etc*) poofy thing to wear.

mariconear *i fam* to ponce about, camp it up.

mariconeo *m fam* campness.

mariconera *f fam* man's clutch bag.

mariconería 1 *f fam* (*homosexualidad*) queerness. 2 *fam* (*acción, gesto*) poofy thing to do; (*ropa etc*) poofy thing to wear.

maridaje 1 *m* (*entre parejas*) married life, marriage. 2 (*entre empresas*) close cooperation.

maridar 1 *t* (*personas*) to marry. 2 (*empresas, proyectos*) to interlink.

marido *m* husband.

marihuana *f* marijuana.

marijuana *f* → **marihuana.**

marimacho 1 *m fam* (*niña, joven*) tomboy; (*mujer*) butch woman. 2 *fam* (*lesbiana*) dyke.

marimandón,-ona *m,f fam* bossy-boots.

marimba *f* marimba.

marimorena *f fam* rumpus, row: *cuando se enteraron se armó la marimonera,* when they found out all hell broke loose.
● **armar la marimorena,** *fam* to kick up a row.

marina *f* → **marino,-a**.
marinar *t* to marinate.
marine *m* marine.
marinería I *f* (*profesión*) navy. **2** (*marinos*) sailors *pl*, crew.
marinero,-a I *adj* (*embarcación*) seaworthy; (*nación*) seafaring: *un pueblo marinero*, a fishing village. **2** (*blusa, cuello*) sailor. **- 3 marinero**, *m* sailor.
● **a la marinera**, CULIN (cooked) in garlic, onions and parsley. ‖ **marinero de agua dulce**, *fam* landlubber.
■ **traje de marinero**, sailor suit.
marino,-a I *adj* (*corriente, animal*) marine. **- 2 marino**, *m* (*profesional*) seaman, sailor. **- 3 marina**, *f* (*flota*) navy. **4** (*zona*) seacoast. **5** (*pintura*) seascape. **6** (*navegación*) seamanship.
■ **azul marino**, navy blue. ‖ **comandancia de marina**, naval command. ‖ **marina de guerra**, navy. ‖ **marina mercante**, merchant navy, merchant marine. ‖ **marino mercante**, merchant sailor.
mariología *f* Mariology, Maryology.
marioneta I *f* (*muñeco*) puppet, marionette. **2** *fig pey* (*persona*) puppet.
■ **(teatro de) marionetas**, puppet show.
mariposa I *f* (*insecto*) butterfly. **2** (*natación*) butterfly. **3** (*lamparilla*) oil lamp. **4** (*tuerca*) wing nut. **5** *fam pey* (*afeminado*) pansy.
● **a otra cosa mariposa**, *fam* and now for something completely different. ‖ **nadar mariposa**, to swim butterfly style, do the butterfly.
■ **mariposa nocturna**, moth.
mariposear I *i* (*ser inconstante*) to be fickle; (*en el amor*) to flirt; (*en el trabajo*) to flit. **2** (*andar alrededor*) to buzz around.
mariposón I *m fam* (*ligón*) flirt. **2** *fam* (*afeminado*) pansy.
mariquita I *f* ZOOL ladybird. **- 2** *m fam* (*marica*) sissy.
marisabidilla *f fam* know-all.
mariscada *f* (*comida*) seafood dish; (*en menú*) seafood platter.
mariscal *m* marshal.
■ **mariscal de campo**, field marshal.
mariscar *i* to fish for shellfish.
marisco *m* seafood, shellfish.
marisma *f* salt marsh.
marismeño,-a *adj* (*cultivo*) marshy.
marisquería *f* seafood restaurant.
marista I *adj* Marist. **- 2** *mf* Marist.
marital *adj* marital.
marítimo,-a *adj* (*legislación*) maritime; (*ciudad*) coastal; (*ruta, transporte*) sea; (*seguro*) marine; (*agente*) shipping.
■ **paseo marítimo**, promenade.
marjal *m* marsh.
marketing *m* marketing.
Mármara Mar de Mármara, *m* Sea of Marmara.
marmita *f* casserole, cooking pot.
marmitako *m* (*Basque*) tuna and potato stew.
mármol *m* marble.
marmolería I *f* (*taller*) marble cutter's workshop. **2** (*de un edificio*) marblework.
marmolista *mf* marblecutter.
marmóreo,-a *adj* marmoreal, marble.
marmota I *f* ZOOL marmot. **2** *fam* (*dormilón*) sleepyhead. **3** *fam* scullery maid.
● **dormir como una marmota**, *fam* to sleep like a log.
■ **marmota de América**, groundhog.
maroma *f* thick rope.
maromo *m fam* guy, bloke.

marqués,-esa *m,f* (*hombre*) marquis, marquess; (*mujer*) marchioness.
marquesado *m* marquisate.
marquesina *f* (*de un hotel*) canopy; (*de una parada de autobús*) bus-shelter.
marquetería *f* marquetry, inlaid work.
marrajo,-a I *adj* (*persona*) sly. **- 2 marrajo**, *m* (*pez marino*) mako.
marranada I *f fam* (*cosa sucia*) filthy thing: *esta camiseta está hecha una marranada*, this T-shirt is filthy. **2** *fam* (*indecencia*) filthy thing: *esta película es una marranada*, this film's filthy, this film's pure filth. **3** *fam* (*vileza*) dirty trick: *me ha hecho una marranada en toda regla*, he really did the dirty on me.
marranería *f fam* → **marranada**.
marrano,-a I *adj fam* (*sucio*) filthy, dirty. **2** *fam* (*sinvergüenza*) swine. **- 3** *m,f fam* (*sucio*) filthy pig, dirty pig. **4** *fam* (*sinvergüenza*) swine. **- 5 marrano**, *m* ZOOL pig.
marrar I *t* to miss. **- 2** *i* to go wrong, fail.
marras de marras, *loc adj fam* in question.
marrasquino *m* maraschino.
marron glacé *m* marron glacé.
marrón I *adj* brown. **- 2** *m* (*color*) brown. **3** *arg* (*condena*) sentence. **4** *arg* (*fastidio*) pain, drag.
● **comerse un marrón**, *arg* to own up.
marroquí,-ina I *adj* Moroccan. **- 2** *m,f* Moroccan.
marroquinería I *f* (*fabricación*) leather industry. **2** (*artículos*) leather goods *pl*.
Marruecos *m* Morocco.
marrullería *f fam* (*engaño*) craftiness.
marrullero,-a *adj fam* (*gen*) crafty, devious; (*jugador*) dirty.
Marsella *f* Marseilles.
marsopa *f* porpoise.
marsupial I *adj* marsupial. **- 2** *m* marsupial.
marsupio *m* marsupium.
marta *f* marten.
■ **marta cebellina**, sable.
Marte *m* Mars.
martes *m* Tuesday.
■ **martes y trece**, ≈ Friday the thirteenth. ‖ **martes de carnaval**, Shrove Tuesday, Pancake Tuesday.
▲ *See also jueves*.
martillar *t* to hammer.
martillazo *m* blow with a hammer.
martillear *t* to hammer.
martilleo *m* hammering.
martillo *m* hammer.
■ **lanzamiento de martillo**, throwing the hammer. ‖ **martillo neumático**, pneumatic drill. ‖ **pez martillo**, hammerhead shark.
martín pescador *m* kingfisher.
martinete[1] I *m* (*ave*) heron. **2** (*penacho*) plume.
martinete[2] I *m* (*mazo*) drop hammer. **2** (*de piano*) hammer.
martingala I *f fam* (*artimaña*) ruse, trick. **2** *fam* (*asunto pesado*) pain, drag.
Martinica *f* Martinique.
mártir *mf* martyr.
martirio I *m* martyrdom. **2** *fig* torture, torment.
martirizar I *t* to martyr. **2** *fig* to torment, torture.
▲ *Conjugation model* |4|, *like realizar*.
maruja *f fam* housewife.
marxismo *m* Marxism.
marxista I *adj* Marxist. **- 2** *mf* Marxist.

marzo *m* March: *el día 16 de marzo,* March the sixteenth, the sixteenth of March; *el 1 de marzo cae en Sábado,* the first of March is a Saturday; *mi cumpleaños es el 2 de marzo,* my birthday is on the 2nd of March; *nací el 6 de marzo de 1961,* I was born on March 6th 1961; *durante el mes de marzo,* in March; *en marzo del año que viene,* next March; *en marzo del año pasado,* last March; *a finales de marzo,* at the end of March; *a mediados de marzo,* in mid-March; *a principios de marzo,* at the beginning of March.

mas *conj* but.

más 1 *adv* (*comparativo*) more: *éste es más alto que aquél,* this one is taller than that one; *este año ha llovido más,* it has rained more this year; *no te lo puedo dar porque no tengo más,* I can't give it to you because I haven't got any more; *hay más niñas que niños,* there are more girls than boys; *es más listo de lo que tú te crees,* he's cleverer than you think. 2 (*con números o cantidades*) more: *más de tres,* more than three. 3 (*superlativo*) most: *el más caro,* the most expensive; *es la más guapa,* she's the prettiest. 4 (*después de pron interrog e indef*) else: *¿algo más?,* anything else?; *¿dónde/qué/quién más?,* where/what/who else?; *nada/nadie más,* nothing/nobody else. 5 (*exclamativo*) so: *¡está más despistado!,* he's so absent-minded!; *¡qué película más buena!,* what a wonderful film! – 6 *prep* MAT plus: *dos más dos igual a cuatro,* two plus two is four. – 7 *m* (*signo*) plus sign. – 8 los/las **más,** *m,f pl* (*la mayoría*): *los más opinan que ...,* the majority think that ...

● **a lo más,** at the most. ‖ **a lo más tardar,** at the latest. ‖ **cada vez más,** more and more. ‖ **como el que más,** as well as anyone. ‖ **cuanto más, mejor,** the more the better. ‖ **cuanto más ... menos ...,** the more ... the less ...: *cuanto más lo digo, menos caso me hacen,* the more I insist, the less anyone listens to me. ‖ **de más,** spare, extra. ‖ **de más está decir,** needless to say. ‖ **el que más y el que menos,** every single one. ‖ **es más,** what's more. ‖ **estar de más,** to be unwanted, not be needed. ‖ **no estaría de más,** it wouldn't be a bad idea. ‖ **más bien,** rather. ‖ **más o menos,** more or less. ‖ **ni más ni menos,** exactly. ‖ **por más (que),** however much. ‖ **¿qué más da?,** what difference does it make?, what does it matter? ‖ **sin más ni más,** just like that, without reason. ‖ **tener sus más y sus menos,** (*personas*) to have some problems, have diffences; (*cosas*) to have good points and bad points.

■ **el más allá,** the beyond.

masa 1 *f* (*en general*) mass. 2 FÍS mass: *unidad de masa,* unit of mass; *masa de agua,* mass of water. 3 CULIN (*para pan*) dough; (*para tartas*) pastry; (*para pasteles*) mixture. 4 (*de gente*) mass, crowd: *atraer a las masas,* to draw the crowds; *en masa,* en masse. 5 (*mortero*) mortar. 6 ELEC earth, US ground.

■ **masa atómica,** atomic mass. ‖ **masa encefálica,** brain. ‖ **masa específica,** specific mass.

masacrar *t* to massacre.

masacre *f* massacre.

masaje *m* massage.

● **darle a algn. un masaje,** to give sb. a massage.

masajista 1 *mf* (*hombre*) masseur; (*mujer*) masseuse. – 2 *m,f* DEP (*en fútbol*) physiotherapist, physio.

mascar *t* to chew.

▲ Conjugation model [1], like *sacar*.

máscara 1 *f* (*careta*) mask. 2 *fig* (*disfraz, pretexto*) mask, front. 3 (*traje*) fancy dress. 4 (*persona*) masked person. – 5 máscaras, *pl* (*fiesta*) masquerade *sing.*

● **quitarle la máscara a algn.,** to unmask sb. ‖ **quitarse la máscara,** to reveal os.

■ **máscara antigas / máscara de gas,** gas mask. ‖ **máscara de oxígeno,** oxygen mask. ‖ **traje de máscara,** fancy dress.

mascarada 1 *f* (*fiesta*) masquerade, masked ball. 2 (*enredo*) farce.

mascarilla 1 *f* mask. 2 (*cosmética - de belleza*) face mask; (*- de barro*) face pack. 3 MED face mask.

■ **mascarilla de oxígeno,** oxygen mask.

mascarón 1 *m* (*máscara*) large mask. 2 MAR figurehead.

■ **mascarón de proa,** figurehead.

mascarse *p fam* to be in the air: *ya se masca la tragedia,* there's a feeling of tragedy in the air.

Mascate *m* Muscat.

mascota 1 *f* (*figura*) mascot. 2 (*animal doméstico*) pet.

masculinidad *f* masculinity.

masculinizar *t* to make masculine.

masculino,-a 1 *adj* male: *la población masculina,* male population. 2 (*para hombres*) men's; (*propio de hombres*) maculine, manly: *ropa masculina,* men's clothes. 3 GRAM masculine. – 4 **masculino,** *m* masculine.

mascullar *t* to mumble, mutter.

masía *f* Catalan farmhouse.

masificación 1 *f* (*ocupación masiva*) overcrowding. 2 (*indiferenciación*) lumping together.

masificado,-a 1 *pp* → **masificar.** – 2 *adj* overcrowded.

masificar 1 *t* (*llenar*) to overcrowd. 2 (*igualar*) to lump together.

masilla *f* putty.

masivo,-a *adj* mass, massive, on a mass scale.

masoca *mf fam* masochist.

masón,-ona 1 *adj* masonic. – 2 *m,f* Mason, Freemason.

masonería *f* Masonry, Freemasonry.

masónico,-a *adj* masonic.

masoquismo *m* masochism.

masoquista 1 *adj* masochistic. – 2 *mf* masochist.

mastaba *f* mastaba.

mastectomía *f* mastectomy.

master *m* EDUC Master's degree.

masticación *f* chewing, mastication.

masticar *t* to chew, masticate.

▲ Conjugation model [1], like *sacar.*

mástil 1 *m* (*asta*) mast, pole. 2 MAR mast. 3 MÚS neck.

mastín *m* mastiff.

mastitis *f* mastitis.

▲ *pl mastitis.*

mastodonte 1 *m* (*animal*) mastodon. 2 *fam* (*cosa*) huge thing, enormous thing; (*persona*) giant.

mastodóntico,-a *adj fam* huge, enormous.

mastoides *m* mastoid.

▲ *pl mastoides.*

mastuerzo 1 *m* (*berro*) cress. 2 *fam pey* dolt, moron, oaf.

masturbación *f* masturbation.

masturbar 1 *t* to masturbate. – 2 **masturbarse,** *p* to masturbate.

mata 1 *f* (*arbusto*) shrub, bush. 2 (*ramita*) sprig: *una mata de tomillo,* a sprig of thyme. 3 AM (*bosque*) forest.

■ **mata de pelo,** head of hair.

matachín 1 *m* (*matarife*) slaughterman. 2 *fam* (*camorrista*) thug.

matadero *m* slaughterhouse, abattoir.

matador,-ra 1 *adj fam* (*agotador*) exhausting, killing. 2 *fam* (*de mal gusto*) dreadful, appalling. – 3 **matador,** *m* matador, bullfighter.

matadura *f* harness sore, sore.
matalahúga *f*→ **matalahúva**.
matalahúva 1 *f* (*planta*) anise. 2 (*semilla*) aniseed.
matamoscas 1 *m* (*insecticida*) fly spray. 2 (*pala*) fly swat.
matanza 1 *f* (*gen*) slaughter. 2 (*del cerdo*) pig killing. 3 (*carne*) pork products *pl*.
matar 1 *t* (*persona - gen*) to kill; (- *asesinar*) to murder. 2 (*animal - gen*) to kill; (- *para alimentación*) to slaughter. 3 *fam* (*sorprender*) to have on, kid: *¿que se ha fugado? ¡no me mates!*, he ran away? you're having me on! 4 *fam* (*incomodar, causar dolor*) to kill; (*volver loco*) to drive mad: *estos zapatos me están matando*, this shoes are killing me. 5 (*dejar pasmado*) to amaze, stun: *me han matado con el cambio de jefe*, the change of boss really knocked me sideways. 6 (*pasar*) to kill: *mientras, voy a matar el tiempo dando una vuelta*, meanwhile, I'll go for a walk just to kill time. 7 (*satisfacer - sed*) to quench; (- *hambre*) to stay, stave off. 8 (*inutilizar - sello*) to frank. 9 (*destruir - ilusanos*) to kill. 10 (*limar - arista, esquina*) to round. 11 (*suavizar - color*) to tone down. 12 *arg fam* (*porro, cigarrillo*) to stub out. – 13 **matarse**, *p* (*involuntariamente*) to die; (*voluntariamente*) to kill os.: *se mató en un accidente de tráfico*, she was killed in a car crash.
● **llevarse a matar con algn.**, to be at daggers drawn with sb. ‖ **matarlas callando**, to be a wolf in a sheep's clothing. ‖ **matarse a trabajar**, to work os. to death. ‖ **que me maten si ...**, I'll be damned if ...
matarife *m* slaughterman.
matarratas 1 *m* (*raticida*) rat poison. 2 *fam* (*aguardiente*) rotgut.
▲ *pl* **matarratas**.
matasanos *mf fam* quack.
▲ *pl* **matasanos**.
matasellos 1 *m* (*marca*) postmark. 2 (*instrumento*) stamp, date stamp.
▲ *pl* **matasellos**.
matasuegras *m* blower, party blower.
▲ *pl* **matasuegras**.
mate[1] *adj* (*sin brillo*) matt.
mate[2] *m* (*ajedrez*) mate.
■ **jaque mate**, checkmate.
mate[3] *m* (*hierba*) maté.
matemáticamente *adv* mathematically.
matemáticas *fpl* mathematics *sing*.
▲ *pl* **matemáticas**.
matemático,-a 1 *adj* mathematical. – 2 *m,f* mathematician. 3 **matemática**, *f* (*ciencia*) mathematics.
materia 1 *f* (*sustancia*) matter. 2 (*material*) material, substance. 3 (*asignatura*) subject. 4 (*asunto*) subject, matter: *ésta es la materia objeto de discusión*, this is the subject in question.
● **en materia de ...**, on the subject of ... ‖ **entrar en materia**, to get to the point.
■ **índice de materias**, table of contents. ‖ **materia gris**, grey matter. ‖ **materia prima**, raw material.
material 1 *adj* (*en general*) material; (*físico*) physical. 2 (*real*) real: *el autor material del asesinato*, the murderer. – 3 *m* (*sustancia*) material. 4 (*conjunto de cosas*) material, materials *pl*, equipment. 5 (*datos, información*) material.
■ **daños materiales**, damage. ‖ **material escolar**, teaching material(s). ‖ **material de guerra**, war material. ‖ **material de oficina**, office stationery. ‖ **materiales de construcción**, building materials. ‖ **materiales de desecho**, waste material *sing*.
materialidad *f* material nature.
materialismo *m* materialism.

materialista 1 *adj* materialistic. – 2 *mf* materialist.
materialización *f* materialization.
materializar 1 *t* to put into practice (us practise), carry out. – 2 **materializarse**, *p* to materialize.
▲ *Conjugation model* [4], *like* **realizar**.
materialmente 1 *adv* materially, physically: *es materialmente imposible*, it is physically impossible. 2 (*realmente*) absolutely, utterly.
maternal *adj* maternal, motherly.
maternidad 1 *f* maternity, motherhood. 2 (*hospital*) maternity hospital.
materno,-a *adj* (*abuelo etc*) maternal.
● **por parte materna**, on my (*his, her, etc*) mother's side.
■ **leche materna**, mother's milk. ‖ **lengua materna**, mother tongue.
mates *fpl fam* maths (us math).
matinal 1 *adj* morning. – 2 *f* matinée.
matinée *f* matinée.
matiz 1 *m* (*color*) shade, tint. 2 (*variación*) nuance. 3 (*rasgo*) hint.
matización 1 *f* ART (*combinación*) blending; (*con otro tono*) shading. 2 (*variación*) nuances *pl*. 3 (*aclaración*) clarification.
matizar 1 *t* ART (*colores*) to blend. 2 (*sonido*) to modulate. 3 (*añadir un matiz*) to tinge (**de**, with). 4 (*añadir*) to add (by way of clarification): *el presidente madridista matizó que ...*, the Madrid chairman added that ... 5 (*aclarar*) to qualify, clarify: *el portavoz del gobierno matizó posteriormente las declaraciones del ministro*, a government spokesman later clarified the minister's statements; *esta cuestión habría que matizarla*, let's examine this question more closely. 6 (*revisar*) to revise: *recientes investigaciones podrían obligarnos a matizar este juicio*, recent investigations may oblige us to revise this judgement.
▲ *Conjugation model* [4], *like* **realizar**.
matojo *m* small shrub, bush.
matón,-ona 1 *m,f fam* bully, thug. 2 *fam* (*guardaespaldas*) bodyguard.
matorral 1 *m* (*maleza*) bushes *pl*, thicket. 2 (*terreno*) scrubland.
matraca 1 *f* (*instrumento*) wooden rattle. 2 *fam* (*molestia*) pest, nuisance.
● **dar la matraca**, *fam* to be a nuisance.
matraquear 1 *i* to rattle. 2 *fig* to be a nuisance.
matraz *m* flask.
matriarcado *m* matriarchy.
matriarcal *adj* matriarchal.
matricida *f* matricide.
matricidio *m* matricide.
matrícula 1 *f* (*lista*) list, roll. 2 (*registro - de personas*) registration, enrollment; (*de vehículos*) registration: *plazo de matrícula*, registration period. 3 (*tasa*) registration fee(s), tuition fee(s). 4 AUTO (*número*) registration number, us license number. 5 AUTO (*placa*) number plate, us license plate.
■ **matrícula de honor**, distinction.
matriculación *f* (*de personas*) registration, enrollment; (*de vehículos*) registration.
matricular 1 *t* (*persona*) to register, enroll; (*vehículo*) to register. – 2 **matricularse**, *p* to register, enroll: *me he matriculado en Filosofía*, I've registered as a Philosophy student.
matrimonial *adj* (*derecho*) matrimonial; (*problema*) marital.

■ **agencia matrimonial,** marriage bureau. ‖ **enlace matrimonial,** wedding. ‖ **vida matrimonial,** married life.

matrimonialista *adj (abogado)* divorce.

matrimonio 1 *m (estado)* marriage, matrimony. 2 *(pareja)* married couple.

● **consumar el matrimonio,** to consummate one's marriage.

■ **matrimonio civil,** civil marriage.

matritense *adj* of/from Madrid.

matriz 1 *adj* principal. – 2 *f* ANAT womb. 3 TÉC mould (US mold). 4 *(original)* original, master copy. 5 *(de talonario)* stub, counterfoil. 6 MAT matrix.

■ **empresa/casa/sociedad matriz,** parent company.

matrona 1 *f (madre)* matron. 2 *(comadrona)* midwife. 3 *(en cárceles)* female prison warden.

matusalén más viejo que matusalén, *loc* as old as Methuselah.

matute 1 *m (acción)* smuggling. 2 *(género)* smuggled goods. – 3 de matute, *loc adv* illegally, smuggled.

matutino,-a 1 *adj* morning. – 2 **matutino,** *m (periódico)* morning paper.

maula *mf fam* dead loss.

maullar *i* to mew, miaow, US meow.

▲ Conjugation model [16], like **aunar.**

maullido *m* mewing, miaow, US meow.

Mauricio *m* Mauritius.

Mauritania *f* Mauritania.

mauritano,-a 1 *adj* Mauritanian. – 2 *m,f* Mauritanian.

máuser *m* mauser.

▲ Registered trademark.

mausoleo *m* mausoleum.

maxilar 1 *adj* maxillary. – 2 *m* jaw, jawbone.

maxilofacial *adj* maxillofacial.

máxima *f →* **máximo,-a.**

maximalismo *m* maximalism.

maximalista 1 *adj* maximalist. – 2 *mf* maximalist.

máxime *adv fml* especially.

máximo,-a 1 *adj (velocidad)* maximum; *(puntuación, condecoración)* highest: *el máximo dirigente del país,* the leader of the country. – 2 **máximo,** *m* maximum: *tenéis una hora como máximo para acabar,* you must be finished in an hour; *llegó a casa como máximo a las dos,* he was home by two o'clock at the latest; *me tomé (como) máximo tres cervezas,* I had three beers at the most; *pon la calefacción al máximo,* turn the heating up to the maximum. – 3 **máxima** *f (frase breve)* maxim, saying. 4 *(regla)* rule, maxim. 5 *(temperatura)* maximum temperature.

máximum *m* maximum.

maxisingle *m* twelve inch single.

▲ pl **maxisingles.**

maya 1 *adj* Mayan. – 2 *mf (persona)* Mayan. – 3 **maya,** *m (idioma)* Mayan.

mayar *i* to miaow, mew, US meow.

mayestático,-a 1 *adj* majestic. – 2 **el plural mayestático,** *m* the royal "we".

mayido *m* miaowing.

mayo 1 *m* May. 2 *(palo)* maypole.

● **hasta el cuarenta de mayo, no te quites el sayo,** never cast a clout till May be out.

■ **el primer de mayo,** May Day.

▲ See also **marzo.**

mayólica *f* majolica.

mayonesa *f* mayonnaise.

mayor 1 *adj (comparativo)* bigger, greater, larger; *(persona)* older; *(hermanos, hijos)* elder, older: *necesito una talla mayor,* I need a larger size; *tengo dos hermanos mayores,* I have two older brothers; *mi hermano mayor vendrá a la fiesta,* my elder brother will come to the party. 2 *(superlativo)* biggest, greatest, largest; *(persona)* eldest; *(hermanos, hijos)* eldest, oldest: *el mayor gato que jamás he visto,* the biggest cat I've ever seen; *su mayor preocupación,* her biggest worry; *este es mi hijo mayor,* this is my eldest son. 3 *(de edad)* mature, elderly: *la gente mayor,* elderly people; *mi padre está ya muy mayor,* my father is very old now. 4 *(adulto)* grown-up: *ya eres mayor, así que defiéndete tú solo,* you are old enough to stand up for yourself now; *siéntate como una persona mayor,* sit up properly. 5 *(principal)* main. 6 MÚS major. – 7 *m* MIL major. 8 **mayor que,** MAT *(signo)* more than. – 9 **los mayores,** *mpl (adultos)* grown-ups, adults; *(antepasados)* ancestors. – 10 **el/la mayor,** *m,f (entre varios)* the oldest; *(entre hermanos, hijos)* the eldest, the oldest.

● **al por mayor,** wholesale. ‖ **hacerse mayor,** to grow up. ‖ **no ir/pasar a mayores,** not to come to anything, not to be anything serious. ‖ **ser mayor de edad,** to be of age.

■ **calle mayor,** high street, US main street. ‖ **colegio mayor,** hall of residence, US dormitory. ‖ **plaza mayor,** main square.

mayoral 1 *m (pastor)* head shepherd. 2 *(cochero)* coachman. 3 *(capataz)* foreman.

mayorazgo 1 *m (institución)* primogeniture. 2 *(bienes)* entailed estate. 3 *(persona)* heir. 4 *fig (primogénito)* eldest son.

mayordomo *m* butler.

mayoría *f* majority: *la mayoría de los hombres ...,* most men ...

● **alcanzar la mayoría de edad,** to come of age. ‖ **estar en mayoría,** to be in the majority. ‖ **tener mayoría de edad,** to be of age.

■ **mayoría absoluta,** absolute majority. ‖ **mayoría de edad,** age of majority. ‖ **mayoría relativa,** relative majority. ‖ **mayoría silenciosa,** silent majority.

mayorista 1 *adj* wholesale. – 2 *mf* wholesaler.

mayoritario,-a 1 *adj (de la mayoría)* majority. 2 FIN principal.

mayormente *adv* mainly.

mayúscula *f →* **mayúsculo,-a.**

mayúsculo,-a 1 *adj (enorme)* enormous, gigantic; *(terrible)* terrible. 2 *(letra)* capital. – 3 **mayúscula,** *f* capital letter, capital.

maza 1 *f* HIST *(arma)* mace. 2 *(utensilio)* sledgehammer. 3 MÚS drumstick. – 4 *n* DEP club.

mazacote *m* CULIN *(masa)* stodge.

mazapán *m* marzipan.

mazazo 1 *m (golpe)* heavy blow *(with a mace).* 2 *fam fig* blow: *su ascenso ha caído como un mazazo en la oficina,* her promotion came as a blow to everyone in the office.

mazmorra *f* dungeon.

mazo 1 *m (martillo)* mallet. 2 *(del mortero)* pestle. 3 *(de naipes)* pack, deck; *(de billetes, papeles)* wad.

mazorca *f* cob.

■ **mazorca de maíz,** corncob.

mazurca *f* mazurka.

m/c *abr (mi cuenta)* my account.

m/cta. *abr (mi cuenta)* my account.

me 1 *pron pers sing* me: *no me lo dijo,* she didn't tell me; *dámelo,* give it to me; *me envió una postal desde Me-*

norca, he sent me a postcard from Minorca; *me han robado la cartera,* I've had my wallet stolen. **2** *(reflexivo)* myself: *me veo en el espejo,* I can see myself in the mirror; *me he comprado unos zapatos,* I bought myself some shoes; *me levanto a las ocho,* I get up at eight o'clock.

meada 1 *f fam* piss, slash. **2** *fam (mancha)* piss stain.
● echar una meada, *fam* to have a piss, go for a pee.
meadero *m fam* bog.
meado *m fam* piss, pee: *meados de gato,* cat piss.
meandro *m* meander.
mear 1 *i fam* to have a piss, have a wee, have a pee, piss. – **2 mearse,** *p fam* to wet os.: *me estoy meando,* I'm dying for a pee.
MEC *abr (Ministerio de Educación y Ciencia)* ≈ Department of Education and Science; *(abreviatura)* DES.
meca 1 *f* mecca. **2 la Meca,** *(ciudad)* Mecca.
● andar de la ceca a la meca, *fam* to rush around.
mecachis *interj fam* damn!, us darn!
mecánica 1 *f (ciencia)* mechanics. **2** *(mecanismo)* mechanism.
■ mecánica cuántica, quantum mechanics.
mecanicismo *m* mechanism.
mecanicista 1 *adj* mechanistic. – **2** *mf* mechanist.
mecánico,-a 1 *adj* mechanical. – **2** *m,f* mechanic.
■ mecánico dentista, dental technician.
mecanismo 1 *m* mechanism. **2** *fig (funcionamiento)* working, mechanism.
■ mecanismo de dirección, steering mechanism.
mecanización *f* mechanization.
mecanizado,-a *adj* mechanized.
mecanizar *t* to mechanize.
▲ *Conjugation model* [4], *like realizar.*
mecano *m* Meccano.
▲ *Registered trademark.*
mecanografía *f* typing.
mecanografiar *t* to type.
▲ *Conjugation model* [13], *like desviar.*
mecanógrafo,-a *m,f* typist.
mecedora *f* rocking chair.
mecenas *mf* patron.
mecenazgo *m* patronage.
mecer 1 *t* to rock. – **2 mecerse,** *p (en una silla)* to rock; *(en un columpio)* to swing. **3** *(bambolearse)* to sway.
▲ *Conjugation model* [2].
mecha 1 *f (de vela)* wick. **2** MIL fuse. **3** CULIN lardoon, lardon. – **4 mechas,** *fpl (de pelo)* highlights.
● a toda mecha, *fam* at full pelt. ‖ aguantar mecha, *fam* to grin and bear it. ‖ ponerse mechas, to have highlights put in (one's hair).
mechado,-a *adj* larded.
■ carne mechada, larded meat.
mechar *t (carne)* to lard.
mechero *m* (cigarette) lighter.
mechón 1 *m (de pelo)* lock, strand. **2** *(de hilos)* tuft.
medalla 1 *f (deportiva)* medal; *(religiosa)* holy medal; *(medallón)* small medallion. – **2** *mf* DEP medallist (us medalist), medal winner.
medallero *m* DEP medals table.
medallista *mf* DEP medallist (us medalist), medal winner.
medallón 1 *m (joya - medalla)* medallion; *(- cajita colgante)* locket. **2** ART medallion. **3** *(de carne, pescado)* médaillon, medallion, slice.
■ medallones de merluza, slices of hake.

médano *m (duna)* sand dune; *(banco)* sandbank.
medellinense 1 *adj* of Medellín, from Medellín. – **2** *mf* person from Medellín, inhabitant of Medellín.
media *f* → **medio,-a.**
mediación *f* mediation.
● por mediación de, through.
mediado,-a 1 *adj (recipiente)* half-full, half-empty; *(sesión, representación)* halfway through. – **2 a mediados de,** *loc* halfway through: *llegaré a mediados de mes,* I'll be there around the middle of the month; *lo quiero para mediados de semana,* I need it mid-week, I'd like it sometime in the middle of the week; *a mediados de año ya me quedé sin dinero,* I'd run out of money halfway through the year.
mediador,-ra 1 *adj* mediating. – **2** *m,f* mediator.
medialuna 1 *f (símbolo)* crescent. **2** CULIN croissant.
mediana 1 *f* MAT median. **2** *(de la carretera)* central reservation. **3** *(cerveza en Cataluña)* bottle of beer containing a third of a litre.
medianero,-a *adj* dividing.
■ pared medianera, party wall.
medianía 1 *f (mediocridad)* mediocrity. **2** *(persona)* mediocre person.
mediano,-a 1 *adj (de calidad)* average; *(de tamaño)* medium, medium-sized. **2** *(mediocre)* ordinary, mediocre.
medianoche 1 *f* midnight. **2** CULIN sweet bun.
mediante *adj* by means of.
mediar 1 *i (interceder)* to intercede (**en favor de,** on behalf of). **2** *(interponerse)* to mediate (**en,** in), intervene (**en,** in). **3** *(estar en medio): entre las dos calles media un parque,* in between the two streeets there is a park; *medió una semana entre sus visitas,* a week went by in between his visits; *de una casa a otra media un abismo,* there's a world of difference between one house and the other. **4** *(llegar a la mitad): mediaba la primavera cuando nos fuimos,* it was halfway through spring when we left. **5** *(ocurrir): media el hecho de que ...,* it so happens that ...
▲ *Conjugation model* [12], *like cambiar.*
mediatización *f* influence.
mediatizar *t* to influence.
medicación 1 *f (tratamiento)* medication, medical treatment. **2** *(medicamentos)* medication, medicines *pl.*
medicamento *m* medicine, drug.
medicamentoso,-a *adj* medicinal.
medicar 1 *t (administrar medicamentos)* to medicate; *(recetar)* to prescribe. – **2 medicarse,** *p* to take medicine.
medicastro *m pey* quack.
medicina *f* medicine.
■ estudiante de medicina, medical student. ‖ medicina preventiva, preventive medicine.
medicinal *adj* medicinal.
medición 1 *f (acción)* measuring. **2** *(número)* measurement.
● hacer mediciones, to take measurements.
médico,-a 1 *adj* medical. – **2** *m,f* doctor, physician.
■ médico,-a de cabecera, general practitioner, GP. ‖ médico,-a de familia, family doctor. ‖ médico,-a forense, forensic scientist. ‖ médico interno, houseman, us intern.
medida 1 *f (acción)* measuring; *(dato, número)* measurement: *¿qué medidas tienes?,* what are your measurements? **2** *(disposición)* measure: *habrá que tomar medidas cuanto antes,* measures will have to be taken as soon as possible. **3** *(grado)* extent: *en cierta medida,* to a certain extent; *en mayor medida,* to a greater extent. **4** *(prudencia)* moderation. **5** LIT measure, metre.

● **a (la) medida,** (*traje*) made-to-measure. ‖ **a medida que,** as. ‖ **en la medida de lo posible,** as far as possible. ‖ **tomar/adoptar medidas,** to take steps, take measures. ‖ **tomarle las medidas a algn.,** to take sb.'s measurements.

■ **medida de capacidad,** measure of capacity. ‖ **medida de longitud,** measure of length. ‖ **medida de volumen,** measure of volume.

medidor,-ra 1 *adj* measuring. – 2 **medidor,** *m* AM (*contador*) meter.

medieval *adj* medieval, mediaeval.

medievalismo *m* medievalism, mediaevalism.

medievalista 1 *adj* medievalist, mediaevalist. – 2 *mf* medievalist, mediaevalist.

medievo *m* Middle Ages *pl*.

medina *f* medina.

medio,-a 1 *adj* (*mitad*) half: *las dos y media,* half past two; *media docena de huevos,* half a dozen eggs; *un año y medio,* a year and a half. 2 (*intermedio*) middle: *a media tarde,* in the middle of the afternoon. 3 (*de promedio*) average: *una velocidad media de ...,* an average speed of ... – 4 *adv* half: *medio terminado,-a,* half-finished; *he dejado los platos a medio lavar,* I've left the washing-up half-done. – 5 **medio,** *m* (*mitad*) half. 6 (*centro*) middle: *en el medio de la plaza,* in the middle of the square. 7 (*contexto - físico*) environment: *tiene problemas de adaptación al medio,* she has problems adapting to her environment. 8 (*social*) circle: *se mueve en un medio muy poco estimulante,* he moves in rather boring circles. – 9 **medios,** *mpl* (*recursos*) means. – 10 **media,** *f* (*media calza*) stocking; (*calcetín*) sock. 11 (*promedio*) average. 12 MAT mean. 13 **la media,** (*hora*) half past, half past the hour: *llegó a la media en punto,* he arrived at exactly half past; *al dar la media,* at half past the hour. – 14 **medias,** *fpl* (*enteras*) tights, US panty hose; (*no enteras*) stockings.

● **a medias,** (*sin terminar*) not finished, half done; (*compartido*) half each: *ha dejado ese cuadro a medias,* he's left that painting half finished; *compramos el ordenador a medias,* we went halves on the computer. ‖ **equivocarse de medio a medio,** to get it all wrong. ‖ **estar (todo) por el medio,** to be in the way. ‖ **hacer media,** to knit. ‖ **ir/pagar a medias,** to go halves. ‖ **ponerse en medio,** to get in the way. ‖ **por medio de,** through, by means of. ‖ **por todos los medios,** by all means. ‖ **quitar algo/algn. de en medio,** to get sth./sb. out of the way.

■ **media aritmética,** arithmetic mean. ‖ **media naranja,** better half. ‖ **media pensión,** half board. ‖ **medias enteras,** tights. ‖ **medio ambiente,** environment. ‖ **medios de comunicación,** (mass) media. ‖ **medios de transporte,** means of transport. ‖ **término medio,** average: *como término medio,* on average.

medioambiental *adj* environmental.

mediocampista *mf* midfield player.

mediocre *adj* mediocre.

mediocridad *f* mediocrity.

mediodía 1 *m* (*las doce*) noon, midday. 2 (*hora del almuerzo*) lunchtime. 3 (*orientación*) South.

medioevo *m* → **medievo**.

mediofondista *mf* middle-distance runner.

mediopensionista *mf* day student.

medir 1 *t* (*dimensiones*) to measure. 2 (*riesgos*) to gauge, weigh up. 3 (*palabras*) to weigh, choose carefully. 4 (*versos*) to scan. – 5 *i* (*tener una dimensión*) to measure, be:

¿cuánto mides?, how tall are you?; *mide dos metros de alto por uno de ancho,* it's two metres high by one metre wide. – 6 **medirse,** *p* to measure os.

● **medirse con algn.,** to measure os. against sb.

▲ Conjugation model |34|, like *servir.*

meditabundo,-a *adj* pensive, thoughtful.

meditación *f* meditation.

meditar 1 *t* to meditate, think. – 2 *i* to meditate (**sobre,** over), ponder.

meditativo,-a *adj* meditative.

mediterráneo,-a 1 *adj* Mediterranean. – 2 *m,f* Mediterranean.

■ **el (mar) Mediterráneo,** the Mediterranean (Sea).

médium *mf* medium.

▲ *pl* **médiums.**

medo,-a 1 *adj* Median. – 2 *m,f* (*persona*) Mede. – 3 **medo,** *m* (*idioma*) Median.

medrar 1 *i* (*planta, animal*) to thrive, grow. 2 (*mejorar socialmente*) to get rich, prosper.

medro 1 *m* (*crecimiento*) growth. 2 (*mejora*) progress, achievements *pl*.

medroso,-a 1 *adj* fearful. – 2 *m,f* fearful person.

médula 1 *f* ANAT marrow. 2 BOT pith. 3 *fig* (*esencia*) core, heart.

● **hasta la médula,** to the marrow, through and through.

■ **médula espinal,** spinal cord. ‖ **médula ósea,** bone marrow.

medular 1 *adj* ANAT marrow. 2 *fig* essential, fundamental.

■ **trasplante medular,** bone marrow transplant.

medusa *f* jellyfish.

mefistofélico,-a *adj* Mephistophelian.

mefítico,-a *adj* mephitic, poisonous.

megabyte *m* megabyte.

megaciclo *m* megacycle.

megafonía 1 *f* (*técnica*) sound amplification. 2 (*aparato*) PA system, public-address system: *avisaron por megafonía,* they gave it out over the PA.

megáfono *m* megaphone.

megalítico,-a *adj* megalithic.

megalito *m* megalith.

megalomanía *f* megalomania.

megalómano,-a 1 *adj* megalomaniac. – 2 *m,f* megalomaniac.

megalópolis *f* megalopolis.

▲ *pl* **megalópolis.**

megatón *m* megaton.

megavatio *m* megawatt.

megavoltio *m* megavolt.

meiosis *f* meiosis.

▲ *pl* **meiosis.**

mejicanismo *m* Mexicanism.

mejicano,-a 1 *adj* Mexican. – 2 *m,f* Mexican.

Méjico *m* Mexico.

mejilla *f* cheek.

● **poner la otra mejilla,** to turn the other cheek.

mejillón *m* mussel.

mejillonero,-a 1 *adj* mussel. – 2 *f* (*instalación*) mussel farm.

mejor 1 *adj* (*comparativo*) better: *este libro es mejor que aquél,* this book is better than that one; *es mejor no hablar de eso,* it's better not talk about that. 2 (*superlativo*) best: *la mejor película que he visto jamás,* the best film I've ever seen; *mi mejor amigo,-a,* my best friend. –

3 *adv* (*comparativo*) better: *cada vez mejor,* better and better every day. **4** (*superlativo*) best: *es el que mejor canta,* he's the one who sings the best. – **5** **el/la mejor,** *m,f* the best (one).
● **a lo mejor,** perhaps, maybe. ‖ **en el mejor de los casos,** at the very best. ‖ **mejor dicho,** or rather. ‖ **mejor o peor,** one way or another. ‖ **mejor que mejor,** so much the better. ‖ **tanto mejor,** so much the better.
mejora 1 *f* (*progreso*) improvement. – **2 mejoras,** *fpl* (*obras*) alterations, improvements.
mejorable *adj* which could be improved.
mejoramiento *m* improvement.
mejorana *f* marjoram.
mejorar 1 *t* to improve. – **2** *i* to improve, get better. – **3 mejorarse,** *p* to get better: *¡que te mejores!,* I hope you get better.
mejoría *f* improvement.
mejunje *m* concoction.
melancolía *f* melancholy, sadness.
melancólico,-a 1 *adj* melancholic, melancholy. – **2** *m,f* melancholic person.
melanina *f* melanine.
melaza *f* molasses.
melcocha *f* honey toffee.
melé *m* scrum.
melena 1 *f* (*de persona*) long hair. **2** (*de león, caballo*) mane. – **3 melenas,** *fpl* unruly mop of hair *sing.*
● **soltarse la melena,** *fam* to let one's hair down.
melenudo,-a 1 *adj pey* long-haired. – **2 melenudo,** *m pey* long-haired layabout.
melifluo,-a *adj* mellifluous.
melindre 1 *m* CULIN honey fritter. **2** *fig* affectation.
● **andarse con melindres,** (*en los modales*) to be fussy; (*al hablar*) to mince one's words.
melindroso,-a *adj* finicky, affected.
melisa *f* lemon balm.
mella 1 *f* (*hendedura*) nick, notch. **2** (*hueco*) hollow, gap; (*en los dientes*) gap.
● **hacer mella en,** (*en objeto*) to dent; (*en persona*) to make an impression on; (*en honor, reputación*) to damage.
mellado,-a 1 *adj* (*persona*) gap-toothed. **2** (*objeto*) notched, chipped. **3** (*honor, orgullo*) damaged.
mellar 1 *t* (*objeto*) to chip, nick. **2** *fig* to dent, damage.
mellizo,-a 1 *adj* twin. – **2** *m,f* twin.
melocotón *m* peach.
■ **melocotón en almíbar,** tinned peach, peach in syrup, US canned peach.
melocotonar *m* peach orchard.
melocotonero *m* peach tree.
melodía *f* melody.
melódico,-a *adj* melodic.
melodioso,-a *adj* melodious.
melodrama *m* melodrama.
melodramático,-a *adj* melodramatic.
melomanía *f* love of music.
melómano,-a *adj* music lover.
melón 1 *m* (*fruto*) melon. **2** *fam* (*cabeza*) head, nut, noggin. **3** *fam* (*persona*) bonehead, dummy.
● **estrujarse el melón,** *fam* to rack one's brains.
melonar *m* melon patch.
melopea *f fam* booze-up.
● **agarrar una melopea / pillar una melopea,** *fam* to get sloshed.
melosidad *f* (*dulzura*) sweetness; (*en exceso*) sickliness.

meloso,-a *adj* (*dulce*) sweet, honeyed; (*empalagoso*) sickly.
membrana *f* membrane.
■ **membrana mucosa,** mucous membrane.
membranoso,-a *adj* membranous.
membrete *m* letterhead.
membrillo 1 *m* (*árbol*) quince tree. **2** (*fruta*) quince. **3** (*dulce*) quince jelly.
■ **carne de membrillo,** quince jelly.
membrudo,-a *adj* burly.
memento *m* REL (*oración*) memento.
memez 1 *f* (*falta de juicio*) stupidity. **2** (*tontería*) stupid thing to do/say etc: *¡eso son memeces!,* that's balderdash!
memo,-a 1 *adj fam* stupid, dim. – **2** *m,f fam* dummy, moron.
memorable *adj* memorable.
memorando *m* → **memorándum**.
memorándum 1 *m* (*cuaderno*) notebook. **2** (*informe diplomático*) memorandum.
▲ *pl* **memorándums**.
memoria 1 *f* (*gen*) memory: *me falla la memoria,* my memory is playing tricks on me. **2** (*informe*) report. **3** (*inventario*) inventory. – **4 memorias,** *fpl* (*biografía*) memoirs.
● **a la memoria de,** in memory of. ‖ **de memoria,** (off) by heart, by memory. ‖ **hacer memoria,** to try to remember. ‖ **si no me falla la memoria...,** if my memory serves me well/right... ‖ **tener buena/mala memoria,** to have a good/bad memory. ‖ **traer a la memoria,** to call to mind.
■ **memoria de acceso aleatorio,** random access memory. ‖ **memoria de elefante,** a memory like an elephant. ‖ **memoria RAM,** RAM memory.
memorial 1 *m* (*acto*) memorial, conmemoration. **2** (*escrito*) request.
memorión,-ona 1 *adj fam* with a brilliant memory. – **2** *m,f fam* (*persona*) person with a brilliant memory. – **3 memorión,** *m fam* brilliant memory.
memorístico,-a *adj* memory.
memorización *f* memorizing.
memorizar *t* to memorize.
mena *f* ore.
menaje *m* household goods.
■ **menaje de cocina,** kitchen equipment.
mención *f* mention.
● **digno de mención,** worth mentioning. ‖ **hacer mención de algo,** to mention sth.
■ **mención honorífica,** honourable mention.
mencionar *t* to mention, cite.
menda. 1 el menda / la menda / mi menda, *pron fam* yours truly: *mi menda se va a dar un paseo ahora mismo,* yours truly is going out for a walk now. – **2** *mf fam* (*hombre*) bloke, guy; (*mujer*) woman.
mendacidad *f lit* mendacity.
mendaz *adj lit* mendacious.
mendelevio *m* mendelevium.
mendelismo *m* Mendelism, Mendelianism.
mendicante *adj* mendicant.
mendicidad *f* begging.
mendigar *i* to beg.
mendigo,-a *m,f* beggar.
mendrugo 1 *m* hard crust (of bread). **2** *fam* (*tonto*) blockhead.
menear 1 *t* (*cabeza*) to shake; (*cola*) to wag; (*cuerpo, caderas*) to wiggle. – **2 menearse,** *p* (*moverse*) to move. **3** (*darse prisa*) to hurry (up), get a move on.

● **de no te menees,** *fam* a hell of a: *se armó un follón de no te menees,* there was a hell of a fuss. ‖ **meneársela,** *tabú* to wank, US jerk off.

meneo 1 *m (de cola)* wagging; *(de caderas)* wiggling. 2 *(sacudida)* shake: *le dio un meneo para que se despertara,* he shook her to wake her up. 3 *fam (golpe)* bang, bump; *(paliza)* hiding.

menester 1 *m (necesidad)* need. – 2 **menesteres,** *mpl fam (actividades)* business *sing;* (*necesidades)* call of nature *sing.*

● **es menester que ...,** it is necessary that ...

menesteroso,-a 1 *adj* needy. – 2 *m,f* needy person.

menestra *f (plato)* vegetable stew; *(ingrediente)* mixed vegetables *pl.*

mengano,-a *m,f* so-and-so.

mengua 1 *f (disminución)* decrease, decline. 2 *(descrédito)* discredit.

● **sin mengua de,** without detriment to.

menguado,-a *adj* diminished.

menguante *adj (luna)* waning.

■ **cuarto menguante,** last quarter. ‖ **luna menguante,** waning moon.

menguar 1 *i (número, cantidad)* to diminish, decrease; *(temperatura, nivel)* to fall, drop. 2 *(salud)* decline. 3 *(luna)* to wane. 4 *(labor)* to decrease. – 5 *t (disminuir)* to diminish, reduce. 6 *(en labor)* to decrease.

▲ *Conjugation model* [22], *like averiguar.*

menhir *m* menhir.

meninge *m* meninx.

meningitis *m* meningitis.

▲ *pl meningitis.*

menisco *m* meniscus.

menopausia *f* menopause.

menor 1 *adj (comparativo - en tamaño)* smaller; (- *en calidad, importancia)* lesser; (- *en edad)* younger: *necesito una talla menor,* I need a smaller size; *se corre menor peligro,* it's less dangerous; *mi hermano menor,* my younger brother. 2 *(superlativo - en tamaño)* smallest; (- *en calidad, importancia)* least; (- *en edad)* youngest: *cogió el trozo de menos tamaño,* she took the smallest piece; *no tiene la menor importancia,* it's not at all important; *su hermano menor se quedará en casa,* his youngest brother is going to stay at home. 3 *(inferior)* minor. 4 MÚS minor. – 5 *mf* JUR minor.

● **al por menor,** retail. ‖ **apto,-a para menores,** *(gen)* suitable for all ages; *(película)* U-certificate, US rated G. ‖ **ser menor de edad,** to be under age.

■ **menor de edad,** minor. ‖ **tribunal de menores,** juvenile court.

Menorca *f* Minorca.

menorquino,-a 1 *adj* Minorcan. – 2 *m,f* Minorcan.

menos 1 *adj (comparativo - en cantidad)* less; (- *en número)* fewer: *hoy hay menos gente,* there are fewer people today; *viajar en tren cuesta menos dinero,* going by train costs less money; *hay menos mesas que en el otro restaurante,* there are fewer tables than in the other restaurant; *yo tengo menos años que tú,* I'm younger than you. 2 *(superlativo - de cantidad)* least; (- *de número)* fewest: *yo soy la que menos culpa tiene,* I'm the least guilty. – 3 *adv (comparativo - de cantidad)* less; (- *de número)* fewer: *voy al gimnasio menos que antes,* I go to the gym less than before; *vinieron menos de viente personas,* fewer than twenty people came; *deberías ir menos deprisa,* you shouldn't go so fast; *hay que conducir a menos de 100km/h,* one cannot drive over 100 km/h. 4 *(superlativo)* least: *es el menos guapo de toda la familia,* he's the least

good-looking member of the family. 5 *(con horas)* to: *las tres menos cuarto,* a quarter to three. 6 MAT minus: *cuatro menos dos, dos,* four minus two is two. – 7 *prep* but, except: *todo menos eso,* anything but that; *todos fueron al cine menos Alberto,* everyone went to the cinema except Alberto. – 8 *pron (cantidad)* less; *(número)* fewer: *me pagó menos,* he paid me less; *esperaban a más de mil personas pero vinieron menos,* they were expecting over a thousand people but fewer came. – 9 *m* MAT minus sign.

● **a menos que,** unless. ‖ **al menos / a lo menos,** at least. ‖ **aún menos,** much less. ‖ **cada vez menos,** less and less. ‖ **dar (dinero) menos,** to shortchange. ‖ **en menos de nada,** in no time at all. ‖ **eso es lo de menos,** that's the least of my worries. ‖ **ir a menos,** to go down in the world. ‖ **lo menos,** at least: *lo menos que puedes hacer,* the least you can do. ‖ **menos da una piedra,** something's better than nothing. ‖ **¡menos mal!,** thank God! ‖ **¡ni mucho menos!,** far from it! ‖ **no ser para menos,** to be no wonder. ‖ **para no ser menos,** so as not to be outdone. ‖ **por lo menos,** at least. ‖ **por menos de nada,** for no reason at all. ‖ **qué menos que ...,** ... is the least sb. could do/could have done. ‖ **si al menos ...,** if only ... ‖ **venirse a menos,** to come down in the world. ‖ **¡ya será menos!,** come off it!

menoscabar 1 *t (mermar)* to reduce, lessen, diminish. 2 *(dañar)* to impair, spoil. 3 *(desprestigiar)* to discredit.

menoscabo 1 *m (mengua)* reduction, lessening. 2 *(daño)* damage. 3 *(perjuicio)* impairment.

● **con menoscabo de,** to the detriment of. ‖ **sin menoscabo de,** without detriment to.

menospreciable *adj* contemptible.

menospreciar 1 *t (despreciar)* to despise, scorn: *toda su familia lo menospreciaba,* he was despised by his entire family. 2 *(no valorar)* to undervalue, underrate: *le empresa menospreciaba su importancia,* the company undervalued his importance.

▲ *Conjugation model* [12], *like cambiar.*

menosprecio 1 *m (desprecio)* scorn, contempt. 2 *(poco aprecio)* underestimation, lack of appreciation.

mensáfono *m* pager.

mensaje 1 *m* message: *deje su mensaje después de oír la señal,* please leave your message after the tone. 2 *(de la Corona)* speech.

mensajería *f* courier service.

mensajero,-a 1 *adj* message-carrying. – 2 *m,f (profesional)* courier; *(que trae un mensaje)* messenger.

■ **paloma mensajera,** carrier pigeon.

menstruación *f* menstruation.

menstrual *adj* menstrual.

menstruar *i* to menstruate.

▲ *Conjugation model* [11], *like actuar.*

menstruo *m* menstruation.

mensual *adj* monthly: *gana 170.000 pesetas mensuales,* he earns 170,000 pesetas a/per month.

mensualidad *f (que se cobra)* monthly salary; *(que se paga)* monthly instalment.

mensurable *adj* measurable.

menta 1 *f (hierba)* mint. 2 *(infusión)* mint tea. 3 *(licor)* crème de menthe.

mentado,-a 1 *adj fml (mencionado)* aforementioned. 2 *fml (famoso)* famous.

mental *adj* mental.

mentalidad *f* mentality.

mentalización *f* awareness: *es una cuestión de mentalización,* it's a question of getting into the right frame of mind.

mentalizar 1 *t* to make aware, make realize: *hay que mentalizar a la gente para que sepa lo que pasa,* the people must be made aware of what's happening. **– 2** **mentalizarse,** *p* (*tomar conciencia*) to become aware. **3** (*hacerse a la idea*) to get used to the idea, come to terms with the idea: *tendremos que mentalizarnos todos,* we'll all have to get used to the idea.
▲ Conjugation model [4], like *realizar.*
mentar *t* to mention.
▲ Conjugation model [27], like *acertar.*
mente 1 *f* (*pensamiento*) mind. **2** (*facultades*) mind, intelligence, intellect.
● tener algo en mente, to bear sth. in mind.
mentecato,-a 1 *adj* idiot. **– 2** *m,f* fool.
mentir *i* to lie: *eso me ha dicho, pero sé que miente,* that's what he said, but I know he's lying.
● miente más que habla, he's lying through his teeth.
▲ Conjugation model [35], like *hervir.*
mentira *f* lie.
● aunque parezca mentira, strange though it may seem. ‖ de mentira, (*en broma*) for a laugh, as a joke; (*artificial*) false. ‖ decir mentiras, to tell lies. ‖ parece mentira, it's unbelievable.
■ mentira piadosa, white lie. ‖ una mentira como una casa, *fam* a whopper.
mentirijilla 1 *f fam* fib. **– 2 de mentirijillas,** *loc adv* (*en broma*) as a joke, for a laugh; (*artificial*) false, make-believe.
mentiroso,-a 1 *adj* lying. **– 2** *m,f* liar.
mentís *m* denial.
● dar un mentís a un rumor, to deny a rumour.
▲ *pl* mentís.
mentol *m* menthol.
mentolado,-a *adj* mentholated.
mentón *m* chin.
mentor *m* mentor.
menú 1 *m* CULIN menu. **2** INFORM menu.
■ menú del día, set menu.
▲ *pl* menús.
menudear 1 *t* to repeat frequently. **– 2** *i* to happen frequently.
menudencia 1 *f* (*bagatela*) trifle. **2** (*exactitud*) exactness, accuracy, precision. **3** (*esmero*) meticulousness.
menudillos *mpl* giblets.
menudo,-a 1 *adj* (*pequeño*) small, tiny. **2** (*enfático*) fine, some, what a...: *¡menudo lío!,* what a mess! **– 3** me-**nudos,** *mpl* (*moneda*) change *sing.* **4** (*de res*) offal *sing;* (*de ave*) giblets.
● a menudo, often, frequently: *nos vemos a menudo,* we often meet up.
meñique *adj* little.
■ (*dedo*) meñique, little finger.
meódromo *m tabú* bog, us john.
meollo 1 *m* ANAT (*sesos*) brains *pl;* (*médula*) marrow. **2** (*lo esencial*) core, heart, crux.
● el meollo de la cuestión, the crux of the matter.
meón,-ona 1 *m,f fam* person who wets himself/herself. **2** *fam fig* (*cobarde*) wimp, wet, yellow-belly: *¡eres un meón!,* what a wimp! **3** *fam fig* (*recién nacido*) baby.
mequetrefe *mf* whippersnapper.
mercachifle 1 *mf pey* (*comerciante*) pedlar. **2** (*interesado*) money-grubber.
mercadear *i* to trade.
mercader *m arc* merchant.
mercadería *f* merchandise.

mercadillo *m* flea market, bazaar.
mercado *m* market.
■ estudio de mercado, market survey. ‖ mercado bursátil, stock market. ‖ Mercado Común, Common Market. ‖ mercado de abastos, wholesale food market. ‖ mercado de trabajo, job market. ‖ mercado de valores, stock market. ‖ mercado negro, black market.
mercadotecnia *f* marketing.
mercancía 1 *f* (*gen*) goods. **– 2** (*tren*) mercancías, *m* goods train.
mercante *adj* merchant.
■ buque mercante, merchant ship. ‖ marina mercante, merchant navy.
mercantil *adj* mercantile, commercial.
■ derecho mercantil, mercantile law.
mercantilismo *m* mercantilism.
mercantilista 1 *adj* mercantilist. **– 2** *mf* mercantilist.
mercantilizar *t* to commercialize.
merced *f* favour.
● a merced de, at the mercy of. ‖ merced a, thanks to.
■ Vuestra Merced, Your Worship.
mercedario,-a 1 *adj* belonging to the order of Our Lady of Mercy. **– 2** *m,f* member of the order of Our Lady of Mercy.
mercenario,-a 1 *adj* mercenary. **– 2** *m,f* mercenary.
mercería 1 *f* (*artículos*) haberdashery, us notions store. **2** (*tienda*) haberdasher's shop, us notions store.
mercero,-a *m,f* haberdasher, us notions dealer.
mercurio *m* QUÍM mercury, quicksilver.
Mercurio *m* Mercury.
merecedor,-ra *adj* worthy.
● ser merecedor,-ra de, to be worthy of.
merecer 1 *t* to deserve, be worth: *mereció el premio,* he deserved the prize; *merece la pena verlo,* it's worth a visit. **2** (*tener necesidad*) to need to be + *pp,* need + *ger: la información merece ser comprobada,* the information needs checking. **3** (*valer*) to earn, get: *su comportamiento le mereció una reprimenda,* his behaviour earned him a severe telling off.
● merecer la pena, to be worth it. ‖ lo tiene bien me-**recido,** (*premio, etc*) he (*she, etc*) really deserved it; (*castigo*) he (*she, etc.*) asked for it, it serves him (*her, etc,*) right.
▲ Conjugation model [43], like *agradecer.*
merecido,-a 1 *pp →* **merecer. – 2** *adj* fully deserved, well deserved. **– 3 merecido,** *m* (just) deserts *pl,* come-uppance.
● llevar su merecido, to get one's come-uppance. ‖ bien merecido lo tiene, he (*she, etc*) had it coming to him (*her, etc*).
merecimiento 1 *m* (*mérito*) merit, worthiness. **2** (*esfuerzo*) effort.
● hacer merecimientos para algo, to bend over backwards to do sth.
merendar 1 *i* to have an afternoon snack, have tea. **– 2** *t* to have for tea. **– 3 merendarse,** *p fam* (*vencer*) to thrash (**a, -**), beat (**a, -**). **4** (*acabar rápidamente*) to knock off.
▲ Conjugation model [27], like *acertar.*
merendero 1 *m* (*instalación*) open-air snack bar. **2** (*en el campo*) picnic spot; (*en la playa*) beachfront snack bar.
merendola *f fam* slap-up meal.
merengado,-a *adj →* **leche.**
merengar *t fam* to ruin.

merengue 1 *m* CULIN meringue. 2 *fam* (*persona*) weakling, weed. 3 MÚS merengue. – 4 *mf fam* Real Madrid supporter. – 5 *adj fam related to Real Madrid football club.*
meretriz *f* prostitute.
meridiano,-a 1 *adj* (*de mediodía*) midday. 2 *fig* (*claro*) obvious. – 3 *m* meridian.
meridional 1 *adj* southern. – 2 *mf* southerner.
merienda 1 *f* (*a media tarde*) afternoon snack, tea. 2 (*en el campo*) picnic.
● **ir de merienda,** to go for a picnic. ‖ **ser una merienda de negros,** *fam* to be pandemonium, be in an uproar.
merina *f* → **merino,-a.**
merino,-a 1 *adj* merino. – 2 **merina,** *f* merino sheep.
■ **lana merina,** merino wool.
mérito 1 *m* (*de alguien*) merit: *le han dado el premio por sus méritos,* she was awarded the prize on her merits. 2 (*de algo*) merit, worth: *tiene mucho mérito lo que has hecho,* what you have done is quite an achievement.
● **hacer mérito de algo,** to mention sth.: *hicieron mérito de su generosidad,* they mentioned his generosity. ‖ **hacer méritos para algo,** to strive to be deserving of sth.
meritorio,-a 1 *adj* praiseworthy, meritorious. – 2 *m,f* unpaid trainee.
merluza *f* hake.
● **agarrar una merluza,** *fam* to get plastered.
merluzo,-a 1 *adj fam* foolish, silly. – 2 *m,f* fool, twit, twerp.
merma *f* decrease, reduction.
mermar 1 *t* to reduce. – 2 *i* to decrease, diminish.
mermelada *f* jam; (*de cítricos*) marmalade.
mero *m* (*pez*) grouper.
mero,-a *adj* mere.
merodeador,-ra 1 *adj* prowling. 2 MIL marauding. – 3 *m,f* prowler. 4 MIL marauder.
merodear 1 *i* (*curiosear*) to prowl about. 2 MIL to maraud.
merodeo 1 *m* prowling. 2 MIL marauding.
merovingio,-a 1 *adj* Merovingian. – 2 *m,f* Merovingian.
mes 1 *m* month: *en el mes de abril,* in (the month of) April; *dentro de un mes,* in a month's time; *¿cuánto ganas al mes?,* how much do you earn a month? 2 (*mensualidad - que cobrar*) monthly salary; (*- que pagar*) monthly instalment (us installment).
● **estar con el mes,** *fam* to have one's period.
■ **el mes pasado/que viene,** last/next month. ‖ **mes civil,** calendar month.
mesa 1 *f* (*gen*) table; (*de oficina*) desk: *mis llaves están encima de la mesa,* my keys are on the table; *se sentaron todos a la mesa,* they all sat at the table. 2 (*comida*) food. 3 (*personas*) board, committee.
● **a mesa puesta,** with one's every need catered for. ‖ **de mesa,** (*vino*) table. ‖ **levantarse de la mesa,** to leave the table. ‖ **poner la mesa,** to set the table, lay the table. ‖ **quitar/recoger la mesa,** to clear the table. ‖ **ser amante de la buena mesa,** to be a gourmet. ‖ **servir la mesa,** to wait at table.
■ **mesa camilla,** *round table under which a heater is usually placed.* ‖ **mesa de despacho,** desk. ‖ **mesa de mezclas,** mixing desk. ‖ **mesa de noche,** bedside table. ‖ **mesa de operaciones,** operating table. ‖ **mesa electoral,** electoral college. ‖ **mesa nido,** nest of tables. ‖ **mesa plegable,** folding table. ‖ **mesa redonda,** (*coloquio*) round table.
mesana 1 *f* (*palo*) mizen, mizzen. 2 (*vela*) mizen-sail.
■ **palo de mesana,** mizen-mast.

mesar 1 *t* to tear. – 2 **mesarse la barba/el pelo,** *loc* to tear at one's beard/hair.
mescalina *f* mescaline.
mescolanza *f* → **mezcolanza.**
mesenterio *m* mesentery.
meseta 1 *f* GEOG plateau, tableland, plain. 2 (*descansillo*) staircase landing.
mesiánico,-a *adj* Messianic.
mesianismo *m* Messianism.
mesías *m* Messiah.
▲ *pl* mesías.
Mesías el Mesías, *m* the Messiah.
mesilla *f* small table.
■ **mesilla de noche,** bedside table.
mesnada 1 *f* HIST armed retinue. 2 *fig* followers *pl*.
mesocarpio *m* mesocarp.
mesocracia 1 *f* (*forma de gobierno*) mesocracy, middle-class government. 2 (*clase media*) mesocracy, middle-class society.
mesocrático,-a *adj* middle-class, pertaining to the middle classes.
mesolítico,-a 1 *adj* mesolithic. – 2 *m* mesolithic.
mesón 1 *m* (*antiguamente*) inn, tavern. 2 (*actualmente*) old-style restaurant.
mesonero,-a *m,f* inn-keeper.
Mesopotamia *f* HIST Mesopotamia.
mesopotamio,-a 1 *adj* HIST Mesopotamian. – 2 *m,f* HIST Mesopotamian.
mesta *f* HIST farmers' guild.
mestizaje *m* crossbreeding.
mestizo,-a 1 *adj* of mixed race, mestizo. 2 *pey* half-breed. – 3 *m,f* person of mixed race, mestizo. 4 *pey* half-breed.
mesura *f* restraint, moderation.
mesurar 1 *t* to moderate. – 2 **mesurarse,** *p* to restrain os.
meta 1 *f* (*en atletismo, motociclismo*) finishing line; (*en carreras de caballos*) winning post. 2 (*portería*) goal. 3 *fig* goal, aim, purpose.
metabólico,-a *adj* metabolic.
metabolismo *m* metabolism.
metacrilato 1 *m* QUÍM methacrylate. 2 (*material*) Perspex.
▲ *In 2 registered trademark.*
metadona *f* methadone, methadon.
metafísica *f* metaphysics.
metafísico,-a 1 *adj* metaphysical. – 2 *m,f* metaphysician.
metáfora *f* metaphor.
metafórico,-a *adj* metaphorical, metaphoric.
metal 1 *m* metal. 2 MÚS brass.
■ **el vil metal,** filthy lucre, money. ‖ **metal noble,** noble metal. ‖ **metal precioso,** precious metal.
metalenguaje *m* metalanguage.
metálico,-a 1 *adj* metallic. – 2 *m* cash.
metalingüística *f* metalinguistics.
metalingüístico,-a *adj* metalinguistic.
metalización *f* metallization (us metalization).
metalizar *t* to metallize (us metalize).
metaloide *m* metalloid.
metalurgia *f* metallurgy.
metalúrgico,-a 1 *adj* metallurgical. – 2 *m,f* metallurgist.
metamórfico,-a *adj* metamorphic.
metamorfismo *m* metamorphism.

metamorfosear *t* to metamorphose.
metamorfosis *f* metamorphosis.
▲ *pl metamorfosis.*
metano *m* methane.
metanol *m* methanol.
metástasis *f* metastasis.
▲ *pl metástasis.*
metatarso *m* metatarsus.
metátesis *f* metathesis.
▲ *pl metátesis.*
metedura metedura de pata, *f fam* faux pas, blunder, booboo.
metempsicosis *f* metempsychosis.
▲ *pl metempsicosis.*
meteórico,-a *adj* meteoric.
meteorito *m* meteorite.
meteoro *m* meteor.
meteorología *f* meteorology.
meteorológico,-a *adj* meteorological.
■ parte meteorológico, weather report.
meteorólogo,-a *m,f* meteorologist.
metepatas *mf fam* bigmouth.
meter 1 *t* (*introducir*) to put: *mete esto en el armario,* put this in the wardrobe; *lo metieron en la cárcel,* they put him in prison; *mete el dinero en el banco,* put your money in the bank. 2 (*implicar*) to put into (**en**, -), get into (**en**, -), involve in (**en**, -): *en buen lío nos has metido,* you've got us into a real mess; *tú me metiste en este asunto,* you got me involved in this business. 3 *fam* (*dar*) to give: *menudo susto que nos metió,* he gave us a real fright; *nos metió una bofetada por hablar,* he gave us a slap for talking; *ya le has metido miedo al niño,* now you've frightened the baby; *nos metió un rollo insoportable,* he bored us to death; *métele prisa o no llegamos,* hurry him up or we won't get there on time. 4 (*hacer*) to make: *no metáis tanto ruido,* don't be so noisy. 5 (*ropa - acortar*) to take up; (*- estrechar*) to take in. 6 AUT (*marcha*) to put into: *mete primera,* put it into first. 7 DEP to score: *metieron dos goles,* they scored two goals. – 8 **meterse,** *p* (*introducirse en*) to get in: *métete dentro,* get in; *se metió en el coche rápidamente,* he got quickly into the car, he jumped into the car; *se metió en la cama,* he got into bed. 9 (*tomar parte - negocio*) to go into (**en**, -); (*involucrarse en*) to get involved (**en**, in/with), get mixed up (**en**, in/with): *se ha metido en un negocio de compraventa,* she's gone into buying and selling; *se ha metido en una secta,* she's got mixed up with a sect. 10 (*introducirse*) to get involved (**en**, in): *se ha metido en la especulación del terreno,* he's got involved in property speculation; *se ha metido en el Ayuntamiento,* now he's on the council; *siempre te estás metiendo donde no te llaman,* you're always sticking your nose in where you're not wanted; *me metí totalmente en el papel,* I got completely into the role; *se mete a fondo en todo lo que hace,* he throws himself into everything he does; *nos vamos a meter en la compra de un piso,* we're going to take the plunge and buy a flat. 11 (*ir*) to go: *¿dónde se habrá metido?,* where can he have got to? 12 (*provocar*) to pick (**con**, on): *no te metas con él que es más fuerte que tú,* don't pick on him, he's stronger than you. 13 (*dedicarse*) to go (**en**, into): *quiere meterse en política,* he wants to go into politics.
● a todo meter, at full blast. ‖ meterse algn. donde no le llaman, to poke one's nose into others' affairs. ‖ meterse algn. en lo que no le importa, to stick one's nose into others' business. ‖ meterse en todo, to be a meddler, stick one's nose into everything. ‖ no meterse en nada, not to get involved. ‖ ¡métetelo donde te quepa!, *tabú* you can stuff it!
meticulosidad *f* meticulousness.
meticuloso,-a 1 *adj* (*cuidadoso*) meticulous. 2 *pey* (*escrupuloso*) fussy, finicky.
metida metida de pata, *f* → **metedura.**
metidito,-a. 1 metidito,-a en años, *loc fam euf* getting on a bit, a bit long in the tooth. 2 metidito,-a en carnes, *fam euf* on the plump side,.
metido,-a 1 *pp* → **meter.** – 2 *adj* (*envuelto, implicado*) involved (**en**, in). – 3 metido, *m* (*empujón*) shove. 4 *fam* dressing-down, telling-off.
● darle/pegarle un metido a algn., *fam* to have a go at sb., give sb. a dressing down. ‖ estar metido,-a en años, *fam* to be getting on. ‖ estar metido,-a en carnes, *fam* to be a bit on the plump side.
metijón,-ona *m,f fam* busybody, nosy parker.
metileno *m* methylene.
metílico,-a *adj* methylic.
metódico,-a *adj* methodical.
metodismo *m* Methodism.
metodista 1 *adj* Methodist. – 2 *mf* Methodist.
método 1 *m* method. 2 (*en pedagogía*) course.
metodología *f* methodology.
metodológico,-a *adj* methodological.
metomentodo *mf fam* busybody.
metonímia *f* metonymy.
metraje *m* (*longitud*) length; (*película rodada*) footage.
■ corto metraje, short (film). ‖ largo metraje, (full-length) feature film.
metralla *f* shrapnel.
metralleta *f* submachine gun.
métrica *f* metrics *pl.*
métrico,-a 1 *adj* (*sistema, unidad*) metric. 2 (*del verso*) metrical, metric.
■ sistema métrico, metric system.
metro 1 *m* metre (US meter). 2 (*cinta*) tape measure. 3 (*transporte*) underground, tube, US subway.
■ metro cuadrado, square metre. ‖ metro cúbico, cubic metre.
metrónomo *m* metronome.
metrópoli *f* metropolis.
metrópolis *f* → **metrópoli.**
metropolitano,-a 1 *adj* metropolitan. – 2 metropolitano, *m fml* underground, tube, US subway.
■ área metropolitana, metropolitan area.
meublé *m* (*casa de citas*) brothel.
mexicanismo *m* Mexicanism.
mexicano,-a 1 *adj* Mexican. – 2 *m,f* Mexican.
México *m* Mexico.
mezcla 1 *f* (*acción*) mixing, blending. 2 (*producto*) mixture, blend. 3 CINEM TV mixing. 4 TEX mixed fibres: *una falda de mezcla,* a skirt made from mixed fibres. 5 (*argamasa*) mortar.
■ mezcla de razas, mixture of races.
mezclador,-ra 1 *adj* mixing. – 2 *m,f* mixer.
mezclar 1 *t* (*incorporar, unir*) to mix, blend: *hay que mezclar el huevo con la harina,* you have to mix the egg with the flour. 2 (*desordenar*) to mix up. 3 (*persona*) to involve (**en**, in): *le han mezclado en negocios turbios,* they've involved him in shady dealings. – 4 mezclarse, *p* (*personas*) to mix (**con**, with): *a mí no me gusta la gente con quien te mezclas,* I don't like the people you're mixing with. 5 (*cosas*) to get mixed up: *se me han mezclado to-*

dos los papeles, my papers have got all mixed up. **6** *(entremeterse)* to interfere (**en,** in).

mezclilla *f (tela)* lightweight mixed fibre.

mezcolanza *f* mixture, hotchpotch.

mezquindad 1 *f* meanness, stinginess. **2** *(acción)* mean thing.

mezquino,-a 1 *adj (avaro)* stingy, niggardly. **2** *(bajo)* low, base. **3** *(pobre)* miserable, poor.

mezquita *f* mosque.

m/f *abr (mi favor)* my favour.

mg *sím (miligramo)* milligramme (US milligram); *(símbolo)* mg.

mi ¹ *adj* my: *éste es mi hermano,* this is my brother; *son mis libros,* they're my books.

mi² *m* MÚS E.

mí *pron* me: *éste es para mí,* this one is for me; *a mí no me gusta,* I don't like it.
● **en cuanto a mí...,** as far as I'm concerned... ‖ **para mí que ...,** I think that ... ‖ **¡por mí!,** I don't mind.

miaja *f fam* → **migaja**.

miasma *m* miasma.

miau *m* miaow, meow, mew.

mica¹ *f* GEOL mica.

mica² *f* ZOOL female (long-tailed) monkey.

micción *f* micturition.

micénico,-a *adj* Mycenaean.

michelín *m fam* spare tyre.

mico 1 *m (animal)* (long-tailed) monkey. **2** *fam fig (niño)* little monkey. **3** *fam fig (feo)* sight.
● **ir hecho,-a un mico,** *fam* to look a sight. ‖ **quedarse hecho,-a un mico,** to be shown up. ‖ **ser el último mico,** *fam* to be the lowest of the low, be last in the pecking order.

micología *f* mycology.

micosis *f* mycosis.
▲ *pl micosis.*

micra *f* micron.

micro *m fam* mike, microphone.

microbio 1 *m* microbe. **2** *fam (enano)* little squirt.

microbiología *f* microbiology.

microbus *m* minibus.

microchip *m* microchip.

microclima *m* microclimate.

microcosmo *m* microcosm.

microcosmos *m* microcosm.
▲ *pl microcosmos.*

microelectrónica *f* micro-electronics.

microficha *f* microfiche.

microfilm *m* microfilm.

microfilme *m* microfilm.

micrófono *m* microphone.

microondas *m* microwave.
■ **horno microondas,** microwave oven.

microordenador *m* microcomputer.

microprocesador *m* microprocessor.

microscópico,-a *adj* microscopic.

microscopio *m* microscope.

microsurco *m* microgroove.

miedica *mf fam* scaredy cat.

miedo 1 *m* fear: *no dijo nada por miedo a las represalias,* he said nothing for fear of reprisals; *me da miedo el avión,* I'm scared of flying; *¡qué miedo!,* how frightening!
● **dar/meter miedo a algn.,** to frighten sb., scare sb. ‖ **morirse de miedo,** to be scared stiff. ‖ **tener miedo,**

to be scared, be frightened, be afraid: *tiene miedo a la oscuridad,* he's afraid of the dark. ‖ **de miedo,** *fam (fabuloso)* great, terrific.
■ **miedo al escenario,** stage fright. ‖ **película de miedo,** horror film.

miedoso,-a 1 *adj* easily frightened. **2** *(cobarde)* cowardly: *¡no seas tan miedoso, que no duele nada!,* be brave, it doesn't hurt at all!

miel *f* honey.
● **dejar a algn. con la miel en los labios,** to leave sb. wanting more. ‖ **miel sobre hojuelas,** it just gets better and better, it's even better than it sounded. ‖ **no hay miel sin hiel,** you've got to take the rough with the smooth. ‖ **ser todo miel,** *fig* to be all sweetness and light.

mielina *f* myelin.

miembro 1 *m (extremidad)* limb. **2** *(viril)* member. **3** *(socio)* member. **4** MAT member.
■ **estado miembro,** member state. ‖ **miembro viril,** male member, penis.

miente *f arc* mind.
● **parar en mientes,** to notice.

mientras 1 *adv* in the meantime, meanwhile: *voy por unas toallas, mientras (tanto), vete calentando el agua,* I'm going to get some towels, in the meantime you can start heating the water. – **2** *conj (temporal)* while, whilst: *mientras estés de vacaciones no pienses en el trabajo,* while you're on holiday, don't think about work; *mientras estaba fuera tuvo un accidente,* he had an accident while he was away. **3** *(adversativa)* whereas: *yo al menos he estudiado, mientras que tú no,* at least I have studied, whereas you haven't. **4** *(hasta que)* until: *no sabremos quién lo hizo mientras no tengamos las pruebas necesarias,* we won't know who did it until we have the necessary evidence.

miércoles *m* Wednesday.
■ **Miércoles de Ceniza,** Ash Wednesday.
▲ *See also* **jueves**.

mierda 1 *f tabú (excremento)* shit: *he pisado una mierda de perro,* I've stepped in some dog shit. **2** *tabú fig* crap: *esta película es una mierda,* this film is crap. **3** *tabú (borrachera)* drunken state: *¡vaya mierda lleva encima!,* he's pissed as a fart! – **4** *interj (tabú)* shit!
● **una mierda de...,** a crappy..., a shitty...: *es una mierda de coche,* it's a crappy old car. ‖ **¡(y) una mierda!,** up yours! ‖ **mandar a algn. a la mierda,** to tell sb. to get lost: *si no te deja en paz mándalo a la mierda,* if he doesn't leave you alone tell him to get lost; *¡vete a la mierda!,* piss off!

mies 1 *f* corn, grain. **2** *(cosecha)* harvest time. – **3 mieses,** *fpl* cornfields.
▲ *pl mieses.*

miga 1 *f (parte blanda del pan)* crumb, soft part; *(pan desmenuzado)* breadcrumbs. **2** *(trocito)* bit, small piece. **3** *fig (sustancia)* substance: *un hombre de miga,* a man of substance. – **4 migas,** *fpl* CULIN fried breadcrumbs.
● **estar hecho,-a migas,** *fam (persona - agotado)* to be exhausted, be worn out; *(- destrozado moralmente)* to be a wreck. ‖ **hacer algo migas,** to smash sth. to smithereens. ‖ **hacer buenas/malas migas con,** to get along well/badly with. ‖ **tener algo miga,** to be no easy matter.
■ **migas de pan,** breadcrumbs *pl.*

migaja 1 *f (gen)* crumb; *(de pan)* breadcrumb. **2** *fam fig* bit, scrap: *no tiene ni una migaja de inteligencia,* he hasn't got a scrap of intelligence.

migar *t* to crumble.

migración f migration.
migraña f migraine.
migrar i to migrate.
migratorio,-a adj migratory.
mijo m millet.
mil 1 adj thousand. 2 (milésimo) thousandth. – 3 m a thousand, one thousand.
■ **el año dos mil**, the year two thousand. ‖ **las Mil y Una Noches**, the Arabian Nights. ‖ **mil millones**, a thousand million, us billion.
▲ See also **seis** and **sexto,-a**.
milagrería f belief in miracles.
milagrero,-a 1 adj (que cree) who believes in miracles. 2 fam (que hace milagros) who works miracles.
milagro m miracle: no se ha caído de milagro, it's a miracle it hasn't fallen over.
● **contar su vida y milagros**, to tell one's life story. ‖ **hacer milagros**, to work miracles.
milagroso,-a 1 adj miraculous. 2 (asombroso) marvellous.
milanesa a la milanesa, loc adv done in breadcrumbs.
milano m kite.
milenario,-a 1 adj millenial. – 2 milenario, m millenium.
milenio m millenium.
milésimo,-a 1 adj thousandth. – 2 m,f thousandth.
▲ See also **sexto,-a**.
milhojas m CULIN mille-feuille, puff pastry.
▲ pl **milhojas**.
mili f fam military service.
● **hacer la mili**, fam to do one's military service.
milicia 1 f (disciplina) art of warfare. 2 (militares) military. 3 (gente armada) militia.
■ **milicias (universitarias)**, military service for University students.
miliciano,-a 1 adj of the militia. – 2 m,f (hombre) militiaman; (mujer) militiawoman.
miligramo m milligram, milligramme.
mililitro m millilitre (us milliliter).
milímetro m millimetre (us millimeter).
militancia f militancy.
militante 1 adj militant. – 2 mf (de una asociación) active member; (de un partido político) active party member; (activista) militant.
militar 1 adj military. – 2 m military man, soldier: los militares, the armed forces. – 3 i MIL to serve. 4 POL (ser miembro) to be an active member; (ser activista) to be a militant, be an activist.
■ **tribunal militar**, military court.
militarismo m militarism.
militarista 1 adj militarist. – 2 mf militarist.
militarización f militarization.
militarizar t to militarize.
milla f mile.
■ **milla náutica**, nautical mile.
millar m thousand.
● **a millares**, by the thousands.
millón m million: un millón de pesetas, a million pesetas; ha pagado millones por ese cuadro, the picture cost him a fortune.
● **millones de veces**, thousands of times. ‖ **un millón de gracias**, thanks a million.
millonada f fam bomb, fortune, packet: el piso les costó una millonada, the flat cost them a packet.
millonario,-a 1 adj millionaire. – 2 m,f (hombre) millionaire; (mujer) millionairess.

millonésimo,-a 1 adj millionth. – 2 m,f millionth.
▲ See also **sexto,-a**.
milonga f milonga, (Argentinian song and dance).
milrayas m (tejido) candy stripe.
mimar t (consentir) to spoil; (mimar con exceso) to pamper, mollycoddle: se comporta como un niño mimado, he behaves like a spoilt child; lo miman demasiado, he's too pampered, he's spoilt.
mimbre m wicker.
mimesis f mimesis.
▲ pl **mimesis**.
mimético,-a adj mimetic.
mimetismo m mimicry.
mímico,-a 1 adj mimic. – 2 mímica, f mimicry.
mimo 1 m (actor) mime artist. 2 (cariño) pampering. 3 (cuidado) care: trátame el cachorro con mucho mimo, treat the puppy with tender loving care.
● **hacerle mimos a algn.**, to pamper sb. ‖ **tener mucho mimo**, to be spoilt.
mimosa f BOT mimosa.
mimoso,-a 1 adj (mimado) spoilt. 2 (cariñoso) affectionate, loving; (meloso) over-affectionate, clingy.
mina 1 f mine: trabaja en una mina, he works down a mine. 2 fig (cosa) gold mine: este negocio es una mina, this business is a gold mine. 3 (explosivo) mine. 4 (de lápiz) lead; (de bolígrafo) refill.
● **ser una mina de información**, to be a mine of information.
■ **campo de minas**, minefield. ‖ **detector de minas**, mine detector. ‖ **mina de carbón**, coalmine. ‖ **mina de oro**, gold-mine. ‖ **mina de plata**, silver-mine.
minar 1 t (terreno) to mine. 2 fig (salud, resistencia) to undermine, weaken.
minarete m minaret.
mineral 1 adj mineral. – 2 m mineral.
■ **agua mineral**, mineral water. ‖ **mineral de hierro**, iron ore.
mineralización f mineralization.
mineralizar t to mineralize.
mineralogía f mineralogy.
mineralógico,-a adj mineralogical.
minería 1 f (técnica) mining. 2 (mineros) miners pl. 3 (industria) mining industry.
minero,-a 1 adj mining. – 2 m,f miner.
mineromedicinal aguas mineromedicinales, fpl medicinal waters.
minga f tabú dick.
mingitorio m public toilet.
mini f fam miniskirt.
miniar t ART to illuminate.
miniatura 1 f (reproducción) miniature. 2 ART (pintura) miniature; (de manuscritos) illumination, miniature. 3 ART (técnica - en retrato) miniaturization; (- en manuscritos) illumination. 4 fig tiny thing: ¡qué miniatura de perro!, what a tiny little dog!
● **en miniatura**, in miniature.
miniaturista mf ART (de manuscritos) illuminator; (de retratos) miniaturist.
miniaturizar 1 t to miniaturize. 2 (manuscritos) to illuminate.
minifalda f mini skirt.
minifundio m smallholding.
minifundista mf smallholder.
minigolf m crazy golf.
mínima f → **mínimo,-a**.

minimizar *t* to minimize.

mínimo,-a I *adj* minimum, lowest: *con un esfuerzo mínimo ya habremos llegado,* if we try just a bit harder we'll get there; *hemos llegado a temperaturas mínimas,* we've reached minimum temperatures; *no me importa lo más mínimo,* I couldn't care less. – **2 mínimo,** *m* minimum: *pon el gas en el mínimo,* turn the gas right down. – **3 mínima** *f (temperatura)* minimum temperature: *ayer la mínima la dio Burgos,* Burgos had the lowest temperature yesterday.
● **como mínimo,** at least. ‖ **ni la más mínima idea,** not the faintest (idea).
■ **mínimo común múltiplo,** lowest common multiple.

minina *f tabú* willie.

minino *m fam* pussy, kitty.

minio *m* red lead, minium.

minipimer *mf* hand blender.
▲ *Registered trademark.*

ministerial *adj* ministerial.

ministerio I *m* POL ministry, US department. **2** REL ministry.
■ **Ministerio de Defensa,** Ministry of Defense. ‖ **ministerio fiscal,** ≈Department of Public Prosecution. ‖ **Ministerio de Asuntos Exteriores,** Ministry of Foreign Affairs, GB ≈ Foreign Office, US ≈ State Department. ‖ **Ministerio de Economía y Hacienda,** Ministry of Finance, GB ≈ Exchequer, Treasury, US Treasury Department. ‖ **Ministerio del Interior,** Ministry of the Interior, GB ≈ Home Office, US ≈ Department of the Interior. ‖ **Ministerio de Obras Públicas,** Ministry of Public Works, US Department of Public Works.

ministrable *adj* who is in the running for ministry, who may become a minister.

ministro,-a I *m,f* POL minister, US secretary. **2** REL minister.
■ **Ministro,-a de Asuntos Exteriores,** Minister for Foreign Affairs, GB ≈ Foreign Secretary, US ≈ Secretary of State. ‖ **Ministro,-a de Defensa,** Minister of Defence, US Defense Secretary. ‖ **ministro de Dios,** minister of God. ‖ **Ministro,-a de Economía y Hacienda,** Minister of Finance, GB ≈ Chancellor of the Exchequer, US ≈ Secretary of the Treasury. ‖ **Ministro,-a del Interior,** Minister of the Interior, GB ≈ Home Secretary, US ≈ Secretary of the Interior. ‖ **Ministro,-a de Justicia,** Minister of Justice, GB ≈ Lord Chancellor. ‖ **ministro,-a sin cartera,** minister without portfolio. ‖ **primer,-ra ministro,-a,** prime minister.

minoico,-a *adj* Minoan.

minoría *f* minority.

minorista I *adj* retail. – **2** *mf* retailer.

minoritario,-a *adj* minority: *un grupo minoritario,* a minority group.

minucia *f* trifle.

minuciosidad *f* meticulousness, thoroughness.

minucioso,-a *adj* meticulous, thorough, painstaking.

minué *m* minuet.

minuendo *m* minuend.

minueto *m* minuet.

minúsculo,-a I *adj (letra)* small; *(persona, objeto)* minute, miniscule; *(detalle)* insignificant. – **2 minúscula,** *f (letra)* small letter; *(en imprenta)* lower-case letter.
● **con minúscula,** in small letters.

minusvalía I *f* ECON decrease in value. **2** *(de una persona)* handicap, disability.

minusválido,-a I *adj* disabled, handicapped. – **2** *m,f* disabled person.

minusvalorar *t* to underestimate.

minuta I *f (factura)* bill; *(de un abogado)* solicitor's fees *pl.* **2** *(borrador)* draft. **3** CULIN menu.

minutero *m* minute hand.

minuto *m* minute.
● **al minuto,** at once.

mío,-a I *adj* my, of mine: *no es vecino mío,* he's not my neighbour; *un pariente mío,* a relative of mine; *es muy amiga mía,* she's a good friend of mine. – **2** *pron* mine: *este abrigo es mío,* this coat is mine; *dámelo, es mío,* give it to me, it's mine; *esto no es lo mío,* I don't think this is my scene; *lo mío es el fútbol,* football is what I really like; *¿tú no eras de los míos?,* weren't you on my side?; *este chico es de los míos,* this guy is just like me.
● **ésta es la mía,** this is what I've been waiting for. ‖ **los míos,** *fam* my family *sing,* my folks.

miocardio *m* myocardium.

miope I *adj* short-sighted, myopic. – **2** *mf* short-sighted person.

miopía *f* short-sightedness.

MIR *abr* MED *(Médico Interno Residente)* houseman, US intern.

mira I *f (dispositivo)* sight. **2** *fig* intention: *no sé cuáles son sus miras en este asunto,* I don't know what his intentions are.
● **con miras a,** with a view to: *lo hizo con miras a montar un negocio,* he did it with a view to setting up a business. ‖ **estrecho,-a de miras,** narrow-minded. ‖ **tener sus miras en algo/algn.,** to have one's eye on sth./sb.
■ **mira telescópica,** telescopic sights *pl.* ‖ **punto de mira,** *(de fusil)* front sight; *(punto de vista)* viewpoint.

mirada *f →* **mirado,-a.**

miradero *m →* **mirador.**

mirado,-a I *pp →* **mirar.** – **2** *adj (cauto)* cautious. **3** *(cuidadoso)* careful. **4** *(considerado)* considerate. – **5 mirada,** *f (gen)* look; *(vistazo)* glance: *una mirada de odio,* a look of hate; *échale una mirada a esto,* have a glance at this.
● **estar muy bien mirado,-a,** to be highly respected. ‖ **estar muy mal mirado,-a,** to be looked down on. ‖ **bien mirado,** after all. ‖ **aguantar la mirada a algn.,** to stare sb. out. ‖ **apartar la mirada,** to look away. ‖ **clavar la mirada en algo/algn.,** to stare at sth./sb., fix one's eye on sth./sb. ‖ **devorar con la mirada,** to leer at. ‖ **echar una mirada a algo/algn.,** to take a look at sth./sb. ‖ **fulminar a algn. con la mirada,** to look daggers at sb. ‖ **levantar la mirada,** to look up.
■ **mirada asesina,** evil look. ‖ **mirada fija,** gaze. ‖ **mirada perdida/vaga,** far-away look. ‖ **mirada de soslayo,** sideways glance.

mirador I *m (balcón)* glassed-in balcony. **2** *(lugar)* viewing point.

miraguano I *m (palmera)* kapok tree. **2** *(material)* kapok.

miramiento *m* consideration.
● **andarse con miramientos,** to be over-polite. ‖ **sin miramientos,** with total disregard.

mirar I *t (observar)* to look at; *(con atención)* to watch: *mira lo que dice este letrero,* look at this sign; *mírame a los ojos,* look me in the eye; *pasa todo el día mirándose en el espejo,* he spends all day looking at himself in the mirror; *se miraron sorprendidos,* they looked at each other in surprise. **2** *(buscar)* to look; *(registrar)* to search: *ya he mirado por todas partes y no lo encuentro,* I've looked everywhere and I can't find it; *me miraron todo al pasar por la aduana,* they went through everything at customs. **3** *(tener cuidado con)* to watch: *mira bien lo que*

haces, watch what you do. **4** (*averiguar*) to see, find out: *mira (a ver) si lo han vendido ya,* see whether they have sold it yet. **5** (*dar*) to face: *el dormitorio mira a poniente,* the bedroom faces west. **6** (*tener cuidado con*) to watch, mind, be careful: *mira bien lo que dices,* watch what you say. **7** (*tener en cuenta*) to consider: *cuando le apetece algo no mira nada,* when he wants something he just goes for it; *los jóvenes de hoy no miran nada,* young people today have no consideration. – **8** *i* (*gen*) to look; (*con atención*) to stare. **9** (*buscar*) to look: *mira debajo de la cama,* look under the bed. **10** (*tener cuidado*) to mind, watch, be careful: *mira que no te engañen,* mind they don't cheat you.
● **de mírame y no me toques,** very fragile, delicate. ‖ **mira que si ...,** what if ... ‖ **¡mira!,** (*gen*) look!; (*con asombro*) well I never!, fancy that!; (*como aviso*) look here! ‖ **mira que te lo dije,** I did tell you, didn't I? ‖ **mira quién habla,** look who's talking. ‖ **mira, yo no digo nada,** look, I'm not saying a thing. ‖ **mirándolo bien ...,** thinking about it ... ‖ **mirar a algn. por encima del hombro,** to look down one's nose at sb. ‖ **mirar algo/a algn. con buenos/malos ojos,** to have a good/bad opinion of sth./sb. ‖ **mirar algo por encima,** to have a quick look at sth. ‖ **mirar atrás,** to look back. ‖ **mirar de arriba a abajo a algn.,** to look sb. up and down. ‖ **mirar por algn.,** to think of sb. ‖ **mirarse en algn.,** to look up to sb. ‖ **¡mira por donde!,** would you believe it! ‖ **¡mira que!:** *¡mira que es tonto!,* he's so stupid!
miríada *f* myriad.
mirilla *f* peep-hole, spyhole.
miriñaque *m* crinoline.
miriópodo *m* myriapod.
mirlo *m* blackbird.
● **ser un mirlo blanco,** to be one in a million.
mirón,-ona **1** *adj fam pey* nosey. **2** (*espectador*) onlooking. – **3** *m,f fam pey* (*curioso*) noseyparker. **4** (*espectador*) onlooker. **5** *pey* (*voyeur*) voyeur, Peeping Tom.
mirra *f* myrrh.
mirto *m* myrtle.
misa *f* mass.
● **cantar misa,** to celebrate one's first mass. ‖ **decir misa,** to say mass. ‖ **por mí como si dice misa,** *fig* I couldn't care less. ‖ **ir a misa,** (*asistir*) to go to mass; (*ser cierto*) to be gospel: *esto va a misa,* you can take it from me. ‖ **no saber de la misa la media,** not to have a clue. ‖ **oír misa,** to hear mass.
■ **misa cantada,** sung mass. ‖ **misa de campaña,** open-air mass. ‖ **misa de difuntos,** requiem mass. ‖ **misa del gallo,** Midnight Mass on Christmas Eve.
misal *m* missal.
misantropía *f* misanthropy.
misántropo,-a **1** *adj* misanthropic. – **2** *m,f* misanthrope, misanthropist.
misceláneo,-a **1** *adj* miscellaneous. – **2** miscelánea, *f* miscellany.
miserable **1** *adj* (*desdichado*) miserable. **2** (*insignificante*) miserly; (*tacaño*) mean. **3** (*malvado*) wretched. – **4** *mf* (*malvado*) wretch. **5** (*tacaño*) miser.
miseria **1** *f* (*pobreza*) extreme poverty: *viven en la miseria,* they live in extreme poverty. **2** (*desgracia*) misery, wretchedness. **3** (*tacañería*) meanness. **4** *fam* (*dinero*) pittance: *pagan una miseria,* the pay is dreadful.
misericordia *f* mercy.
misericordioso,-a **1** *adj* merciful. – **2** los misericordiosos, *mpl* the merciful.

mísero,-a **1** *adj* miserable: *no nos dieron ni una mísera peseta,* we weren't paid one peseta for it; *¡oh, mísero de mí!,* woe is me! – **2** *m,f* miser.
misil *m* missile.
■ **misil balístico,** ballistic missile.
misión **1** *f* (*tarea*) mission, task. **2** REL mission.
● **irse a las misiones,** to become a missionary.
■ **misión de buena voluntad,** goodwill mission. ‖ **misión diplomática,** diplomatic mission.
misionero,-a **1** *adj* mission. – **2** *m,f* missionary.
Misisipí. **1** el Misisipí, *m* (*río*) the Mississippi. **2** (*estado*) Mississippi.
misiva *f* missive.
mismamente *adv fam* precisely.
mismísimo,-a *adj* (very) same: *nació el mismísimo día que yo,* he was born on the very same day as me; *llegaré hasta el mismísimo presidente si hace falta,* I'll talk to the President himself if it's necessary; *este niño es el mismísimo demonio,* this child is the devil himself.
mismito ahora mismito, *loc adv* right now.
mismo,-a **1** *adj* (*idéntico*) same: *el mismo color,* the same colour; *tiene la misma cara que su padre,* he looks just like his dad. **2** (*enfático*) same: *en esta misma casa nací yo,* I was born in this very house; *ni sus mismos amigos lo entienden,* even his own friends don't understand him. – **3** *pron* same: *es el mismo del año pasado,* it's the same one as last year. – **4** mismo, *adv* same: *piensa lo mismo que tu,* he thinks the same as you; *ahora mismo viene,* he'll be here in a second; *parece que fue ayer mismo,* it seems like only yesterday; *para mañana mismo lo tengo acabado,* I'll have it done by tomorrow; *vamos a sentarnos aquí mismo,* let's sit right here.
● **yo** *(ti, etc)* **mismo,-a,** myself (*yourself, etc*): *lo hice yo mismo,* I did it myself; *te estás perjudicando a ti mismo,* you're not doing yourself any favours; *con el sr. Suárez por favor –yo mismo,* may I speak to Mr Suárez please? –speaking. ‖ **es lo mismo,** (*la misma cosa*) it amounts to the same thing; (*no importa*) it doesn't matter. ‖ **lo mismo da,** it doesn't matter. ‖ **o lo que es lo mismo,** that is to say. ‖ **¡por eso mismo!,** precisely: *por eso mismo no fui,* that's why I didn't go. ‖ **volver a las mismas / estar en las mismas,** to be back at square one.
misoginia *f* misogyny.
misógino,-a **1** *adj* misogynous. – **2** *m,f* misogynist.
miss *f* miss.
mistela *f* sweet wine.
míster *m* (*en fútbol*) manager, coach.
▲ *pl* místers.
misterio *m* mystery: *no han podido resolver el misterio,* they haven't been able to solve the mystery.
● **hacer algo con mucho misterio,** to do sth. in secret.
misterioso,-a *adj* mysterious.
mística *f →* **místico,-a.**
misticismo *m* mysticism.
místico,-a **1** *adj* mystic, mystical. – **2** *m,f* (*persona*) mystic. – **3** mística, *f* (*misticismo*) mysticism. **4** (*teología*) mystic theology.
mistral *m* mistral.
MIT *abr* (*Ministerio de Información y Turismo*) Ministry of Information and Tourism.
mitad **1** *f* half: *me llevo la mitad,* I'll take half; *estamos a mitad de camino,* we're halfway there; *a mitad de precio,* half-price; *llegó en mitad de la película,* he arrived halfway through the film. **2** (*medio*) middle: *en mitad de la plaza,* in the middle of the square.

● partir algo por la mitad, to cut/split sth. in half.
mítico,-a *adj* mythical.
mitificación I *f* (*conversión en mito*) making into a myth. 2 (*adoración*) hero-worship; (*de políticos*) personality cult.
mitificar 1 *t* (*convertir en mito*) to make a myth of, mythicize. 2 (*adorar*) to hero-worship.
mitigación *f* mitigation.
mitigador,-ra *adj* mitigating.
mitigar *t* to mitigate, relieve.
▲ *Conjugation model* [7], *like* **llegar**.
mitin *m* meeting, rally.
▲ *pl* **mítines**.
mito *m* myth.
mitología *f* mythology.
mitológico,-a *adj* mythological.
mitomanía I *f* mythomania, tendency to embroider the truth. 2 (*idolatría*) hero-worship.
mitómano,-a 1 *adj* mythomaniac. – 2 *m,f* mythomaniac. 3 (*idólatra*) hero-worshipper.
mitón *m* mitten.
mitosis *f* mitosis.
▲ *pl* **mitosis**.
mitra 1 *f* (*tocado*) mitre. 2 (*cargo*) bishopric.
mitral 1 *adj* mitral, mitre-shaped. 2 MED (*válvula*) mitral.
mixomatosis *f* myxomatosis.
▲ *pl* **mixomatosis**.
mixteca 1 *adj* Mixtec. – 2 *mf* Mixtec.
mixteco,-a *adj-m,f* → **mixteca**.
mixto,-a 1 *adj* mixed: *una ensalada mixta,* a mixed salad. – 2 mixto, *m* (*sandwich*) toasted ham and cheese sandwich.
■ colegio mixto, coeducational school, co-ed school.
mixtura *f* mixture.
ml *sím* (*mililitro*) millilitre (US milliliter); (*símbolo*) ml.
m/L *abr* (*mi letra, mi letra de crédito*) my credit bill.
mm *sím* (*milímetro*) millimetre (US millimeter); (*símbolo*) mm.
Mm *sím* (*miriámetro*) myriametre (US myriameter); (*símbolo*) Mm.
m.n. *abr* (*moneda nacional*) national currency.
mnemotecnia *f* mnemonics.
mnemotécnico,-a *adj* mnemonic.
moabita 1 *adj* HIST Moabite. – 2 *mf* HIST Moabite.
moaré *m* moiré.
mobiliario *m* furniture.
MOC *abr* (*Movimiento de Objetores de Conciencia*) conscientious objectors' movement.
moca *f* (*café*) mocha.
mocasín *m* moccasin.
mocedad *f* youth: *en mis mocedades,* in my youth.
mocerío *m* young people *pl.*
mocetón,-ona *m,f* (*hombre*) strapping young lad; (*mujer*) strapping young woman.
mochales *adj fam* round the bend.
mochila *f* rucksack, backpack.
mochilero,a *m,f* backpacker.
mocho,-a 1 *adj* (*torre*) flat-topped; (*árbol*) lopped, pollarded. – 2 mocho, *m* (*de la escopeta*) butt.
mochuelo 1 *m* ZOOL little owl. 2 *fam fig* (*fastidio*) bore.
● cada mochuelo a su olivo, each to his own. ‖ cargar con el mochuelo, to be lumbered with it. ‖ cargarle el mochuelo a algn., to pass the buck.
moción 1 *f* motion. 2 (*movimiento*) motion, movement.
● aprobar una moción, to pass a motion.
■ moción de censura, vote of no confidence.

moco 1 *m* (*mucosidad*) mucus; *fam* snot. 2 (*de vela*) drips *pl.* 3 (*de pavo*) wattle.
● limpiarse los mocos, *fam* to blow one's nose. ‖ llorar a moco tendido, to cry one's eyes out. ‖ no es moco de pavo, *fam* it's not to be sneezed at. ‖ tener mocos, *fam* to have a runny nose. ‖ tirarse el moco, *fam* to show off.
mocoso,-a 1 *adj* snotty. – 2 *m,f fam* brat.
moda 1 *f* fashion: *me gusta ir a la moda,* I like to keep up with fashion. 2 (*locura*) craze.
● de moda, fashionable, popular. ‖ estar de moda, to be in fashion. ‖ la última moda, the latest fashion. ‖ pasado,-a de moda, old-fashioned. ‖ pasar de moda, to go out of fashion. ‖ ser un,-a esclavo,-a de la moda, to be a slave to fashion.
■ casa de modas, fashion house.
modal *adj* modal.
modales *mpl* manners.
● tener buenos/malos modales, to have good/bad manners.
modalidad 1 *f* form, method, means, way. 2 (*deporte*) sport; (*en atletismo, esquí*) event; (*en vela*) class: *ganó la modalidad de 400 metros vallas,* he won the 400 metres hurdles.
■ modalidad de pago, method of payment. ‖ modalidad deportiva, sport.
modelado *m* modelling (US modeling).
modelador,-ra *m,f* modeller (US modeler).
modelar *t* to model, shape.
modélico,-a *adj* model.
modelismo *m* (*de arcilla etc*) modelling; (*de piezas*) model-making.
modelo 1 *adj* model: *un estudiante modelo,* a model student. – 2 *mf* (*persona*) (fashion) model. – 3 *m* (*patrón*) model: *esto te puede servir de modelo,* you can use this as a model. 4 (*diseño*) model: *este modelo es más económico,* this is a more economical model. 5 (*traje*) number.
■ desfile de modelos, fashion show.
módem *m* modem.
▲ *pl* **módems**.
moderación *f* moderation: *beber con moderación,* to drink in moderation; *conducir con moderación,* to drive carefully.
moderado,-a 1 *adj* moderate. – 2 *m,f* moderate.
moderador,-ra 1 *adj* moderating. – 2 *m,f* (*de reunión*) chairperson; (- *hombre*) chairman; (- *mujer*) chairwoman; (*de debate*) moderator.
moderar 1 *t* (*gen*) to moderate; (*velocidad*) to reduce. – 2 moderarse, *p* to control os.
● moderarse en las palabras, to measure one's words, mind what one says.
modernamente 1 *adv* (*actualmente*) nowadays, at present, currently. 2 (*recientemente*) recently.
modernidad 1 *f* modernity. 2 *fam* in-crowd.
modernismo 1 *m* ART, LIT modernism. 2 ART (*en España*) Spanish Art Nouveau, Modernismo.
modernista 1 *adj* ART, LIT modernist. 2 ART (*en España*) Spanish Art Nouveau, Modernista. – 3 *mf* ART, LIT modernist. 4 ART (*en España*) Modernista.
modernización *f* modernization.
modernizar 1 *t* to modernize. – 2 modernizarse, *p* to be modernized.
▲ *Conjugation model* [4], *like* **realizar**.
moderno,-a *adj* modern.
modestia *f* modesty.
● con modestia, modestly. ‖ modestia aparte, in all modesty.

modesto,-a 1 adj modest. – **2** m,f modest person.
módico,-a 1 adj modest. **2** (precio) reasonable.
modificable adj modifiable.
modificación f alteration, modification.
modificador,-ra 1 adj modifying. – **2 modificador,** m modifier.
modificar t to alter, modify.
  ▲ Conjugation model [1], like **sacar.**
modismo m idiom.
modistilla f dressmaker's assistant.
modisto,-a 1 m,f (diseñador) fashion designer. **2** (sastre) dressmaker.
modo 1 m way, manner: no me convence su modo de trabajar, I'm not sure about the way he does his job. **2** LING mood: el modo subjuntivo, the subjunctive mood; adverbios de modo, adverbs of manner. – **3 modos,** pl manners.
  ● **a modo de,** as a, like a: lo utilizaron a modo de un jarrón, they used it as a vase. ‖ **de cualquier modo,** (como conector de frases) in any case, anyway; (despreocupadamente) any old how. ‖ **de modo que,** so: de modo que ya lo sabes, so now you know. ‖ **de todos modos,** anyhow, at any rate. ‖ **en cierto modo,** in a way.
  ■ **modo de empleo,** instructions pl. ‖ **modo de ser,** character: es su modo de ser, that's the way he is.
modorra f fam drowsiness, sleepiness: me ha entrado la modorra, I feel sleepy.
modoso,-a adj quiet, well-behaved.
modulación f modulation.
modulador,-ra 1 adj modulating. – **2** m,f modulator.
modular 1 t to modulate. – **2** adj modular.
módulo 1 m (gen) module. **2** (mueble) unit: muebles por módulos, modular furniture, furniture in units.
mofa 1 f mockery, derision. – **2 mofarse,** p to scoff (**de,** at).
  ● **hacer mofa de algo/algn.,** to mock sth./sb. ‖ **mofarse de algo/algn.,** to mock sth./sb., scoff (**de,** at) sth./sb.
mofeta f skunk.
moflete m fam chubby cheek.
mofletudo,-a adj fam chubby-cheeked.
Mogadiscio m Mogadishu, Mogadiscio.
mogol,-la adj-m,f → **mongol,-la.**
  ■ **el Gran Mogol,** the Great Mogul.
mogollón 1 m fam heaps pl, stacks pl, loads pl: había mogollón de gente, there were loads of people. **2** fam (alboroto) racket. – **3** adv fam a lot: nos gustó mogollón, it was dead brilliant.
mohair m mohair.
mohicano,-a 1 adj Mohican. – **2** m,f Mohican.
mohín m grimace, face, look: hizo un mohín de enfado, he gave an angry look.
  ● **hacer mohínes,** to pull faces.
mohíno,-a adj sulky.
  ● **estar mohíno,-a,** to sulk, be sulking.
moho 1 m mould, (US mold). **2** (de metales - hierro) rust; (- cobre) verdigris.
  ● **criar moho,** to go mouldy (US moldy). ‖ **no criar moho,** fig to be always on the move: no cría moho, he never sits still.
mohoso,-a 1 adj mouldy (US moldy). **2** (oxidado) rusty.
moisés m wicker carrycot, Moses basket.
  ▲ pl moisés.
mojado,-a adj (húmedo) wet, moist; (empapado) drenched, soaked, wet through.

mojama f dried salted tuna.
mojar 1 t (gen) to wet. **2** (humedecer) to dampen. **3** (alimento) to dip, dunk: moja el pan en la salsa, dip your bread in the sauce. **4** (cama) to wet. – **5 mojarse,** p to get wet. **6** fam (comprometerse) to commit os., get involved.
mojarra f two-banded bream.
moje m sauce.
mojicón 1 m (bollo) sponge bun. **2** (golpe) punch.
mojiganga 1 f TEAT short farce. **2** mockery.
mojigatería 1 f (gazmoñería) prudishness. **2** (falsa humildad) sanctimoniousness.
mojigato,-a 1 adj (gazmoño) prudish; (falso) sanctimonious. – **2** m,f (gazmoño) prude; (falso) sanctimonious person.
mojón m (poste - de distancia) milepost; (piedra) milestone; (- de camino) landmark.
  ■ **mojón kilométrico,** ≈ milestone.
moka f → **moca.**
molar[1] 1 adj molar. – **2** m (diente) molar.
molar[2] 1 i arg (gustar) to be cool; (estar de moda) to be hip, be in: esta música mola cantidad, this music's really cool. **2** arg (presumir) to show off, be flash.
Moldavia f Moldavia.
moldavo,-a 1 adj Moldavian. – **2** m,f Moldavian.
molde m mould (US mold).
  ● **romper el molde,** to break the mould (US mold).
  ■ **pan de molde,** soft loaf, soft bread.
moldeable adj mouldable (US moldable).
moldeado,-a 1 adj moulded (US molded). – **2 moldeado,** m ART moulding (US molding). **3** (de pelo) soft perm.
moldeador,-ra 1 adj ART moulding (US molding). – **2 moldeador,** m (de pelo) curling tongs pl.
moldear 1 t ART (dar forma) to mould (US mold); (- en un molde) to cast. **2** (pelo) to give a soft perm.
Moldova f Moldova.
moldura f moulding (US molding).
mole f mass, bulk, hulk: ese edificio es una mole de cemento, the building is a mass of cement; este tío es una mole, he's a hulking great bloke.
molécula f molecule.
molecular adj molecular.
moler 1 t (gen) to grind, mill; (machacar) to pound. **2** (cansar) to wear out.
  ● **moler a palos,** to beat up.
  ▲ Conjugation model [32], like **mover.**
molestar 1 t (interrumpir) to disturb: no lo molestes, que está durmiendo, don't disturb him, he's asleep. **2** (perturbar) to bother, annoy, upset: me molestan los ruidos, noise bothers me; todo le molesta, everything upsets him; sus comentarios empiezan a molestarme, his comments are starting to get on my nerves. **3** (importunar) to pester: ¡deja de molestarme ya!, stop pestering me! **4** (hacer daño - apretar) to hurt, be too tight; (- picar) to irritate: estos zapatos me molestan, these shoes hurt my feet. **5** (ofender) to upset: me molesta que no me lo dijeran, I'm upset I wasn't told. – **6 molestarse,** p (tomarse la molestia) to bother: no se moleste en venir, que se lo mandaremos a casa, don't bother coming, we'll send it round to you; ni se molestó en decir adiós, he didn't even bother to say goodbye; perdone que le moleste, I'm sorry to bother you. **7** (ofenderse) to take offence: se ha molestado con tu comentario, he was offended by your comment.
molestia 1 f (incomodidad) bother, trouble; (fastidio) nuisance. **2** MED trouble, slight pain.

● **no es molestia,** it's no trouble. ‖ **perdonen las molestias,** please excuse the inconvenience. ‖ **ser una molestia,** to be a nuisance. ‖ **si no es molestia,** if you don't mind. ‖ **tomarse la molestia de hacer algo,** to take the trouble to do sth.

molesto,-a 1 *adj* annoying, troublesome. 2 (*enfadado*) annoyed. 3 (*incómodo*) uncomfortable. 4 MED sore: *los puntos ya han cicatrizado, pero todavía está molesto,* the stitches have healed, but he's still sore.
● **estar molesto,-a con algn.,** to be upset with sb. ‖ **ser molesto,** to be a nuisance.

molido,-a 1 *adj* (*café*) ground; (*trigo*) milled. 2 *fam* (*cansado*) worn-out.
● **estar molido,-a,** *fam* to be worn-out.

molienda *f* (*de café*) grinding; (*de trigo*) milling.

moliente corriente y moliente, *loc* run of the mill, common or garden.

molinero,-a *m,f* miller.

molinete 1 *m* (*ventilador*) fan. 2 (*juguete*) toy windmill. 3 (*de puerta*) turnstile.

molinillo *m* grinder, mill.
■ **molinillo de café,** coffee grinder.

molino *m* mill.
■ **molino de viento,** windmill.

molla 1 *f* (*parte magra de la carne*) lean (meat). 2 (*pulpa*) flesh. – 3 **mollas,** *fpl fam* flab *sing,* spare tyres.

mollar 1 *adj* (*carnoso*) fleshy. 2 *fam* (*cosa*) good quality; (*persona*) good-looking.

molleja 1 *f* (*de ave*) gizzard. 2 (*de res*) sweetbread.

mollera *f fam* (*inteligencia*) brains *pl,* sense; (*cabeza*) loaf, bonce.
● **duro,-a de mollera,** *fam* (*tonto*) dense, thick; (*testarudo*) pig-headed.

molón,-na *adj arg* cool, brill, fab.

molusco *m* mollusc (us mollusk).

momentáneo,-a *adj* (*que dura poco tiempo*) momentary; (*provisional*) temporary.

momento 1 *m* moment: *¡espera un momento!,* hang on a moment!; *en un momento estoy contigo,* I'll be with you in a moment; *llegamos en un momento,* it took us no time at all to get there. 2 (*período*) time: *fueron momentos difíciles,* they were difficult times; *has escogido mal momento para venir,* you've chosen a bad time to call. 3 (*oportunidad*) time, moment: *ya llegará tu momento,* your time will come.
● **a cada momento,** every second, all the time. ‖ **al momento,** immediately. ‖ **de momento,** for the moment. ‖ **de un momento a otro,** any minute now. ‖ **del momento,** (*en el pasado*) of the time, of that time; (*de ahora*) current, present-day. ‖ **desde el momento en que ...,** (*en cuanto*) from the moment ..., as soon as ...: *desde el momento en que te vi...,* from the moment I saw you... ‖ **en cualquier momento,** at any moment, at any time. ‖ **en este momento,** at the moment. ‖ **por el momento,** for the time being. ‖ **por momentos,** by the minute.

momia *f* mummy.

momificación *f* mummification.

momificar *t* to mummify.

momio *m fam* cushy number.

mona *f →* **mono,-a.**

monacal *adj* monastic.

monacato 1 *m* (*profesión*) monkhood. 2 (*institución*) monastic community.

Mónaco *m* Monaco.

monada 1 *f* (*cosa bonita*) beauty, lovely thing; (*persona*) gorgeous person, sweet thing, delight: *¡este niño es una monada!,* what a gorgeous baby!; *¡qué monada de jersey!,* what a lovely jumper! 2 (*gracia*) funny little ways *pl;* (*jugada*) trick: *hace las mismas monadas que su hermano,* he has his brother's funny little ways; *deja ya de hacer monadas,* stop fooling around. 3 (*zalamería*) winning ways *pl.*

monaguillo *m* altar boy.

monarca *m* monarch.

monarquía *f* monarchy.
■ **monarquía absoluta,** absolute monarchy.

monárquico,-a 1 *adj* monarchic, monarchical. – 2 *m,f* monarchist.

monarquismo *m* monarchism.

monasterio *m* monastery.

monástico,-a *adj* monastic.

monda *f →* **mondo,-a.**

mondadientes *m* toothpick.
▲ *pl* **mondadientes.**

mondadura 1 *f* (*piel - de fruta*) peel; (*- de patata*) peelings *pl.* 2 (*acción*) peeling.

mondar 1 *t* (*pelar*) to peel. 2 (*podar*) to prune.
● **mondarse de risa,** to laugh one's head off.

mondo,-a 1 *adj* (*limpio*) bare; (*sencillo*) plain. – 2 **monda,** *f* (*piel*) peel, skin. 3 (*acción*) peeling.
● **mondo,-a y lirondo,-a,** *fam* pure and simple. ‖ **ser la monda (lironda),** *fam* (*divertido*) to be a scream; (*indignante*) to be just too much.

mondongo *m* innards *pl.*

moneda 1 *f* (*pieza*) coin: *una moneda de diez pesetas,* a ten peseta coin. 2 (*divisa*) currency.
● **pagar a algn. con la misma moneda,** to pay sb. back in kind. ‖ **ser moneda corriente,** *fig* to be commonplace.
■ **moneda corriente,** legal tender. ‖ **moneda divisionaria/fraccionaria,** small change. ‖ **moneda falsa,** counterfeit money. ‖ **moneda fuerte,** strong currency. ‖ **moneda suelta,** small change.

monedero *m* purse.

monegasco,-a 1 *adj* Monegasque. – 2 *m,f* Monegasque.

monería *f →* **monada.**

monetario,-a 1 *adj* monetary. – 2 **monetario,** *m* collection of coins and medals.
■ **sistema monetario,** monetary system. ‖ **crisis monetaria,** monetary crisis.

monetarismo *m* monetarism.

monetarista 1 *adj* monetarist. – 2 *mf* monetarist.

mongol,-la 1 *adj* Mongolian, Mongol. – 2 *mf* (*habitante*) Mongolian, Mongol. – 3 *m* (*idioma*) Mongolian.

Mongolia *f* Mongolia.
■ **Mongolia Interior/Exterior,** Inner/Outer Mongolia.

mongólico,-a 1 *adj* affected by Down's syndrome. – 2 Mongolian. – 3 *m,f* person affected by Down's syndrome. 4 Mongolian.

mongolismo *m* Down's syndrome, mongolism.

monicaco *m fam* (*hombre*) dodgy geezer.

monigote 1 *m* (*figura*) rag doll, paper doll. 2 *fig pey* stooge, puppet. 3 (*dibujo*) matchstick man, doodle. 4 (*de convento*) lay brother.

monismo *m* monism.

monista 1 *adj* monistic. – 2 *mf* monist.

monitor,-ra 1 *m,f* (*profesor*) instructor. – 2 *m* monitor, (*pantalla*) monitor, screen.

monja *f* nun.
● **meterse a monja,** to take the veil, become a nun.

monje *m* monk.

monjil *adj* of a nun, nun-like.

mono,-a 1 *adj* (*bonito*) nice, lovely, cute: *¡qué vestido más mono!,* what a lovely dress!; *su novia es muy mona,* his girlfriend's really cute. – 2 *m,f* ZOOL monkey. 3 *fam pey* (*joven*) little brat. – 4 mono, *m pey* (*persona fea*) ugly devil. 5 (*prenda - de trabajo*) overalls *pl*; (- *de calle*) jumpsuit, dungarees *pl*; (- *de niños*) romper suit, rompers *pl*. 6 *arg* (*síndrome abstinencia - drogas*) cold turkey; (- *tabaco, alcohol*) withdrawal symptoms: *lleva tres días sin fumar y está con el mono,* he hasn't smoked for three days and he's suffering from withdrawal symptoms; *tengo mono de cine,* I've got a craving to go to the cinema. – 7 mona, *f fam* (*borrachera*) drunken state: *lleva una mona que no se tiene,* he's absolutely legless. 8 *fam* (*imitador*) copycat.

● aunque la mona se vista de seda, mona se queda, you can't make a silk purse out of a sow's ear. ‖ mandar a freír monas a algn., *fam* to tell sb. to get stuffed. ‖ ser el último mono, *fam* to be a nobody. ‖ ¡tengo monos en la cara, o qué!, *fam* do you want a photo?

■ mona (de Pascua), Easter cake. ‖ mono de imitación, copycat.

monocarril *m* monorail.

monocolor *adj* monochrome.

monocorde 1 *adj* (*canto*) single-stringed. 2 *fig* (*monótono*) dull, monotonous.

monocotiledóneo,-a 1 *adj* monocotyledonous. – 2 monocotiledónea, *f* monocotyledon.

monocromático,-a *adj* monochromatic.

monocular *adj* monocular.

monóculo *m* monocle.

monocultivo *m* monoculture.

monódico,-a *adj* monodic.

monofásico,-a *adj* single-phase.

monogamia *f* monogamy.

monógamo,-a 1 *adj* monogamous. – 2 *m,f* monogamist.

monografía *f* monograph.

monográfico,-a *adj* monographic, single-theme.

monograma *m* monogram.

monokini *m* monokini.

monolingüe *adj* monolingual.

monolítico,-a *adj* monolithic.

monolito *m* monolith.

monologar *i* to soliloquize.

monólogo *m* (*reflexión*) monologue; (*en teatro*) soliloquy.

monomanía 1 *f* MED monomania. 2 *fam* obsession, fixation.

monomaníaco,-a *adj* MED monomaniac.

monopatín *m* skateboard.

monoplano *m* monoplane.

monoplaza 1 *adj* single-seat. – 2 *m* single-seater.

monopolio *m* monopoly.

monopolista 1 *adj* monopolistic. – 2 *mf* monopolist.

monopolización *f* monopolization.

monopolizador,-ra 1 *adj* monopolizing. – 2 *m,f* monopolizer.

monopolizar *t* to monopolize.

▲ Conjugation model [4], like *realizar.*

monorraíl *m* monorail.

monosabio *m* picador's assistant.

monosilábico,-a *adj* monosyllabic.

monosílabo,-a 1 *adj* monosyllabic. – 2 monosílabo, *m* monosyllable.

monoteísmo *m* monotheism.

monoteísta 1 *adj* monotheistic. – 2 *mf* monotheist.

monotonía *f* monotony.

monótono,-a *adj* monotonous.

monóxido *m* monoxide.

■ monóxido de carbono, carbon monoxide.

Mons *abr* (*monseñor*) monsignor; (*abreviatura*) mgr.

monseñor *m* monsignor.

monserga *f fam* (*lección*) nagging, preaching; (*despropósito*) drivel, rubbish: *déjame de monsergas que ya sé lo que tengo que hacer,* stop nagging me, I know what I've got to do; *tú a lo tuyo y no me vengas con monsergas,* you get on with your own job and stop lecturing me.

monstruo 1 *adj fam* (*extraordinario*) fantastic, terrific: *una película monstruo,* a terrific film. – 2 *m* monster. 3 (*en fealdad*) monstrosity. 4 *fam* (*genio*) genius, prodigy.

monstruosidad *f* (*cosa*) monstrosity; (*fealdad*) hideousness: *este edifico es una monstruosidad,* this building is absolutely monstrous.

monstruoso,-a 1 *adj* (*por tamaño, crueldad*) monstrous. 2 (*por fealdad*) hideous.

monta 1 *f* (*importancia*) value, account, importance. 2 (*de un caballo*) riding. 3 (*apareamiento*) mating season.

● de poca monta, insignificant.

montacargas *m* goods lift, service lift, US freight elevator.

montador,-ra 1 *m,f* (*operario*) fitter. 2 (*de joyas*) setter. 3 (*de cine*) film editor.

montaje 1 *m* (*de piezas*) assembly. 2 (*de una película*) editing. 3 (*de un espectáculo*) staging. 4 (*en foto*) montage. 5 *fam* (*farsa*) set-up.

■ cadena de montaje, assembly line. ‖ montaje fotográfico, montage.

montaña *f* mountain.

● hacer una montaña de algo, to blow sth. out of all proportion. ‖ hacer una montaña de un grano de arena, to make a mountain out of a molehill.

■ montaña rusa, roller coaster, big dipper. ‖ las Montañas Rocosas, the Rocky Mountains.

montañero,-a 1 *adj* mountaineering. – 2 *m,f* mountaineer.

montañés,-esa 1 *adj* (*de montaña*) mountain, highland. 2 (*de Santander*) from Santander. – 3 *m,f* (*de la montaña*) highlander, mountain person. 4 (*santanderino*) person from Santander.

montañismo *m* mountaineering, mountain climbing.

montañoso,-a *adj* mountainous.

montaplatos *m* dumb waiter.

▲ *pl* montaplatos.

montar 1 *i* (*subir - caballo, bicicleta*) to mount, get on; (- *coche*) to get in; (- *avión*) to get on, board. 2 (*viajar*) to travel; (*cabalgar, ir en bicicleta*) to ride: *está acostumbrado a montar en avión,* he's used to travelling by plane; *¿sabes montar a caballo/en bicicleta?,* can you ride a horse/bicycle? – 3 *t* (*subir - caballo*) to mount, get on: *montó el caballo y salió al galope,* he mounted his horse and galloped away. 4 (*subir - persona*) to put on: *monté al niño en la bicicleta,* I lifted the kid onto his bike; *la monté atrás y le di una vuelta en la moto,* I took her for a ride on the back of my bike. 5 (*ensamblar*) to assemble, put together; (*tienda de campaña*) to put up: *ya he montado la librería,* I've assembled the bookcase. 6 (*fusil*) to cock. 7 (*sobreponer*) to overlap. 8 (*nata*) to whip; (*claras*) to whisk. 9 (*joyas*) to set. 10 (*negocio, consulta*) to set up, start. 11 (*casa*) to set up: *han montado el piso en poco*

tiempo, they've decorated and furnished the flat in no time. **12** CINEM to edit, mount. **13** TEAT to stage. **14** COM to amount to, come to: *el total monta diez mil pesetas,* the total amounts to ten thousand pesetas. – **15** mon- tarse, *p (subirse)* to get on; (*- en un coche*) to get in; (*- en un caballo*) to mount, get on. **16** *fam (armarse)* to break out: *se montó un buen jaleo,* there was a real to-do.
● montar a pelo, to ride bareback. ‖ montar en có- lera, to fly into a rage. ‖ montar guardia, to stand guard; *(escándalo)* to kick up a fuss. ‖ montárselo, *fam* to set os. up, get things nicely worked out: *hay que ver cómo te lo montas,* you've got things nicely worked out, you certainly do all right for yourself. ‖ tanto monta, it makes no difference.

montaraz **1** *adj (de montaña)* mountain. **2** *(tosco)* rough, coarse. **3** *(arisco)* unsociable, unapproachable.

monte **1** *m* mountain, mount. **2** *(bosque)* wild, woodland. ● de monte, wild. ‖ echarse/tirarse al monte, to take to the hills.
■ monte alto, woodland, forest. ‖ monte bajo, scrub. ‖ Monte Olimpo, Mount Olimpus. ‖ monte de pie- dad, pawnbroker's, pawnshop. ‖ monte de Venus, *(del pubis)* mons Veneris; *(de la mano)* Mount of Venus.

Monte Carlo *m* Monte Carlo.

montenegrino,-a **1** *adj* Montenegrin. – **2** *m,f* Monte- negrin.

Montenegro *m* Montenegro.

montepío **1** *m (sociedad)* friendly society, benefit socie- ty. **2** *(depósito)* welfare fund.

montera *f* → **montero,-a**.

montería *f (caza)* hunt; *(arte de cazar)* hunting.

montero,-a **1** *m,f* hunter. – **2** montera, *f* bullfighter's hat.

montés *adj* wild.
■ gato montés, wild cat, US bobcat.

montevideano,-a **1** *adj* of Montevideo, from Montevi- deo. – **2** *m,f* person from Montevideo, inhabitant of Montevideo.

montículo *m* mound, hillock.

montilla *m* montilla wine, *dry sherry from Montilla, Cór- doba.*

monto *m* total, total amount.

montón **1** *m* heap, pile: *un montón de revistas,* a pile of magazines. **2** *fam (gran cantidad)* stacks *pl,* loads *pl,* heaps *pl: vino un montón de gente,* loads of people came; *los tienen a montones,* they've got stacks of them.
● ser del montón, to be nothing special, be one of the crowd: *es del montón,* he's just an ordinary bloke.

montura **1** *f (cabalgadura)* mount. **2** *(silla)* saddle; *(arreos)* harness. **3** *(armazón - de gafas)* frame; *(- de joyas)* setting. **4** *(armadura)* mounting.

monumental **1** *adj* monumental: *Paris es una ciudad monumental,* Paris is famous for its monuments. **2** *fam (enorme)* phenomenal.

monumento **1** *m* ART monument. **2** *fam (mujer)* statu- esque woman.

monzón *m* monsoon.

monzónico,-a *adj* monsoon.

moña **1** *f (lazo)* ribbon. **2** *fam (borrachera)* bender.
● coger una moña, *fam* to get plastered.

moño *m* bun.
● estar hasta el moño, *fam* to be fed up to the back teeth.

MOPTMA *abr (Ministerio de Obras Públicas, Transportes y Medio Ambiente) ministry of public works, transport and the environment.*

MOPU *abr (Ministerio de Obras Públicas y Urbanismo) ministry of public works and town planning.*

moquear *i* to have a runny nose.

moqueo *m* runny nose.

moqueta **1** *f* fitted carpet. **2** *(material)* moquette.
● de moqueta, moquette.

moquillo *m (de perro)* distemper; *(de ave)* pip.

mor *por mor de, prep* for the sake of.

mora **1** *f (de moral)* mulberry. **2** *(zarzamora)* blackberry.

morada *f* adobe, dwelling.

morado,-a **1** *adj (color)* purple; *(ojo)* black. – **2** morado, *m (color)* purple. **3** *(hematoma)* bruise.
● pasarlas moradas, *fam* to have a tough time. ‖ po- nerse morado,-a, *fam (de comida)* to stuff os.; *(de vino, placer etc)* to get one's fill.

morador,-ra *m,f* dweller, inhabitant.

moradura *f* bruise.

moral¹ **1** *adj* moral. – **2** *f (reglas)* morals *pl.* **3** *(ánimo)* mo- rale, spirits *pl.*
● levantar la moral a algn., to boost sb.'s morale, raise sb.'s spirits. ‖ estar bajo,-a de moral, to be in low spirits. ‖ estar con la moral por los suelos, to be down in the dumps. ‖ tener más moral que el Al- coyano, to be a born optimist.
■ obligación moral, moral duty.

moral² *m* BOT mulberry tree.

moraleja *f* moral.

moralidad *f* morality.

moralina *f* false morals *pl.*

moralista **1** *adj* moralistic. – **2** *mf* moralist.

moralizar **1** *i* to moralize. – **2** *t* to moralize.
▲ *Conjugation model* [4], *like* **realizar.**

moralmente *adv* morally.

morapio *m* red plonk.

morar *i* to reside, dwell.

moratón *m fam* bruise.

moratoria *f* moratorium.

morbidez *f* softness, tenderness.

mórbido,-a **1** *adj (suave)* soft, delicate. **2** MED *(malsano)* morbid.

morbilidad *f* morbidity (rate).

morbo **1** *m (enfermedad)* sickness. **2** *fam (excitación)* thrill; *(interés)* morbid curiosity.
● producir morbo a, *fam* to turn on. ‖ tener morbo, *fam (persona)* to be sexy, be a turn-on; *(cosa)* to be a turn- on.

morbosidad **1** *f (enfermedad)* morbidity. **2** *(excitación)* morbid pleasure; *(interés)* morbid curiosity.

morboso,-a **1** *adj* MED *(enfermo)* morbid. **2** *fam (obsesión, placer)* morbid; *(persona)* kinky.
● ser un,-a morboso,-a, *fam* to be a pervert.
■ placer morboso, morbid pleasure.

morcilla **1** *f* black pudding. **2** TEAT ad lib.
● meter morcilla, to ad lib. ‖ que le *(les, etc)* den morcilla, *fam* he *(she, etc)* can drop dead for all I care, stuff him *(her, etc)*!: *que te den morcilla,* stuff you!

mordacidad *f* mordacity, sharpness.

mordaz *adj* mordant, sarcastic.

mordaza *f* gag.

mordedor,-ra *adj* biting.
● perro mordedor, poco ladrador, his/her bark is worse than his/her bite.

mordedura *f* bite.

morder **1** *t* to bite: *le ha mordido mi perro,* my dog's bit- ten him. – **2** *i* to bite: *ten cuidado que muerde,* be care- ful, it bites. – **3** morderse, *p* to bite.

● **está que muerde,** *fam* he's/she's fuming. ‖ **morder el anzuelo,** to take the bait. ‖ **morder el polvo,** to bite the dust. ‖ **morderse la lengua,** (*por accidente*) to bite one's tongue; (*callarse*) to hold one's tongue. ‖ **morderse las uñas,** to bite one's nails.
▲ *Conjugation model* [32]*, like* **mover.**

mordida 1 *f fam* (*mordisco*) bite. **2** *fam* (*soborno*) bribe.
mordiente *m* mordant.
mordisco *m* bite.
mordisquear *t* to nibble.
morena¹ *f* → **moreno,-a.**
morena² *f* (*pez*) morray eel.
morenez *f* brownness.
moreno,-a 1 *adj* (*pelo*) dark, dark-haired. **2** (*piel*) dark, dark-skinned: *de piel morena,* dark-skinned. **3** (*de raza negra*) black. **4** (*bronceado*) brown, suntanned, tanned. **5** (*pan, azúcar*) brown. – **6** *m,f* (*de pelo*) dark-haired person. **7** (*de piel*) dark-skinned person. **8** (*de raza negra*) black person. – **9** moreno, *m* suntan.
● **estar moreno,-a,** to be brown, suntanned. ‖ **ponerse moreno,-a,** to get brown, get tanned, get a suntan. ‖ **ser moreno,-a,** (*de pelo*) to have dark hair; (*de piel*) to have dark skin.
morera *f* white mulberry.
morería *f* (*barrio*) Moorish Quarter.
moretón *m* bruise.
morfema *m* morpheme.
morfina *f* morphine.
morfinomanía *f* morphine addiction, morphinism.
morfinómano,-a 1 *adj* addicted to morphine. – **2** *m,f* morphine addict.
morfología *f* morphology.
morfológico,-a *adj* morphological.
morganático,-a *adj* morganatic.
morgue *f* morgue.
moribundo,-a 1 *adj* moribund. – **2** *m,f* moribund.
morigerar *t* to moderate.
moriles *m* wine from Moriles, Córdoba.
morir 1 *i* (*ser vivo*) to die: *murieron de hipotermia,* they died of hypothermia; *murió joven,* he died young; *murió de vejez,* she died of old age. **2** (*día*) to finish, come to an end. **3** (*fuego*) to die down. **4** (*sendero, río*) to end. – **5** morirse, *p* to die: *se murió a pocas horas del accidente,* he died shortly after the accident; *se le murieron los padres cuando era niño,* his parents died when he was a child.
● **morir ahogado,** to drown. ‖ **morir con las botas puestas,** to die with one's boots on. ‖ **morirse de aburrimiento,** to be bored to death. ‖ **morirse de frío,** (*fallecer*) to die of cold; (*tener frío*) to be freezing. ‖ **morirse de ganas de ...,** to be dying to ... ‖ **morirse de hambre,** to starve; *fig* to be starving. ‖ **morirse de miedo,** to be scared stiff. ‖ **morirse de pena,** to die of a broken heart. ‖ **morirse de risa,** to kill os. laughing: *es para morirse de risa,* it's a scream. ‖ **morirse del susto,** to die of shock. ‖ **morirse de vergüenza,** to die of embarrassment. ‖ **morirse por + inf** algo, to be dying to + *inf* sth.: *se muere por verla,* he's dying to see her. ‖ **morirse por algn.,** to be mad about sb. ‖ *¡muera...!/¡mueran...!,* death to...!, down with...!: *¡mueran los dictadores!,* down with the dictators!
▲ *Conjugation model* [33]*, like* **dormir**; *pp* **muerto,-a.**
morisco,-a 1 *adj* Moorish, Morisco. – **2** *m,f* Morisco (*Spanish Moor converted to Christianity*).
morisqueta 1 *f* (*mueca*) grimace. **2** (*engaño*) dirty trick.
● **hacer morisquetas,** to pull faces.

morlaco *m* bull.
mormón,-ona 1 *adj* Mormon. – **2** *m,f* Mormon.
mormónico,-a *adj* Mormon.
mormonismo *m* Mormonism.
moro,-a 1 *adj* Moorish. **2** *fam* (*árabe*) Arab. – **3** *m,f* Moor. **4** (*árabe*) Arab. – **5** moro, *m fam pey* male chauvinist.
● **bajar al moro,** *arg* to travel down to Morocco to buy hash. ‖ **hay moros en la costa,** the coast isn't clear.
morosidad 1 *f* (*tardanza*) delay; (*- en un pago*) arrears *pl.* **2** (*lentitud*) sluggishness.
moroso,-a 1 *adj* FIN (*cliente*) defaulting, slow in paying, in arrears. **2** (*lento*) slow, sluggish. – **3** *m,f* defaulter.
morrada *f* → **morrazo.**
morral 1 *m* hunter's bag. **2** MIL knapsack, haversack.
morralla 1 *f pey* (*gente*) riff-raff. **2** *pey* (*cosas*) junk. **3** *pey* (*cambio*) small change, worthless coins.
morrazo pegarse un morrazo, *loc fam* to bash os., give os. a bash.
morrear 1 *t fam* to snog. – **2** morrearse, *p fam* to snog, have a snog.
morrena *f* moraine.
morreo *m fam* snog.
morrillo *m* (*de animal*) back of the neck.
morriña *f* homesickness.
morrión *m* helmet.
morro *m fam* (*de persona - boca*) lips *pl,* mouth; (*cara*) face: *le pegó una bofetada en los morros,* he smacked him in the face. **2** *fam* (*cara dura*) cheek: *tiene un morro que se lo pisa,* he's got an incredible nerve! **3** (*de animal*) snout, nose. **4** (*de coche*) nose.
● **beber a morro,** *fam* to drink straight from the bottle. ‖ **estar de morros,** *fam* to be in a foul mood. ‖ **poner morros,** *fam* to pout. ‖ **torcer el morro,** *fam* to pout.
morrocotudo,-a *adj fam* terrific, fantastic, brilliant.
morrón 1 pimiento morrón, *m* sweet red pepper. **2** *fam* → **morrazo.**
morrudo,-a *adj fam* thick-lipped.
morsa *f* walrus.
Morse *m* Morse code.
mortadela *f* mortadella.
mortaja *f* shroud.
mortal 1 *adj* (*criatura, ser*) mortal. **2** (*veneno*) lethal, deadly; (*peligro, herida*) mortal. **3** (*propio de un muerto*) deathly. **4** (*aburrimiento, susto*) deadly. – **5** *mf* mortal. – **6** los mortales, *mpl* mortals.
■ **golpe mortal,** fatal blow, deathblow. ‖ **odio mortal,** mortal hatred. ‖ **pecado mortal,** mortal sin.
mortalidad *f* mortality.
■ **índice de mortalidad,** mortality rate, death rate.
mortandad *f* death toll.
mortecino,-a 1 *adj* (*luz*) faint, dull. **2** (*color*) lifeless, dull.
mortero *m* mortar.
mortífero,-a *adj* deadly, lethal.
mortificación *f* mortification.
mortificante *adj* mortifying.
mortificar *t* to mortify.
▲ *Conjugation model* [1]*, like* **sacar.**
mortuorio,-a *adj* mortuary.
moruno,-a *adj* Moorish.
■ **pincho moruno,** shish kebab.
Mosa el Mosa, *m* the Meuse.
mosaico *m* mosaic.
mosca 1 *f* fly. **2** (*barba*) tuft. **3** *fam* (*dinero*) dough.
● **aflojar/soltar la mosca,** *fam* to fork out money,

cough up. ‖ **caer como moscas,** to drop like flies. ‖ **estar con la mosca detrás de la oreja,** to be suspicious. ‖ **estar mosca,** *fam* (*sospechar*) to be suspicious; (*estar enfadado*) to be cross. ‖ **no se oía una mosca,** you could have heard a pin drop. ‖ **por si las moscas,** just in case. ‖ **¿qué mosca te** *(le, etc)* **ha picado?,** *fam* what's bugging you (*him, etc*)?
■ **mosca muerta,** *fig* hypocrite.

moscada nuez moscada, *f* nutmeg.
moscarda *f* blowfly, bluebottle.
moscardón 1 *m* blowfly. 2 (*persona*) pest.
moscatel 1 *adj* muscat. – 2 *m* muscat, muscatel.
moscón *m* → **moscardón.**
mosconear 1 *t fam* to pester. – 2 *i fam* to be a pest, be a pain.
moscovita 1 *adj* Muscovite. – 2 *mf* Muscovite.
moscovita,-a 1 *adj* Muscovite. – 2 *m,f* Muscovite.
Moscú *m* Moscow.
mosquear 1 *t fam* to annoy. – 2 mosquearse, *p fam* (*enfadarse*) to get cross. 3 *fam* (*sospechar*) to smell a rat.
mosquerío *m* swarm of flies.
mosquete *m* musket.
mosquetero *m* musketeer.
mosquetón 1 *m* (*arma*) short carbine. 2 (*cierre*) snap link.
mosquita hacerse la mosquita muerta, to look as if butter wouldn't melt in one's mouth.
mosquitera *f* mosquito net.
mosquitero 1 *m* mosquito net. 2 (*pájaro*) chiffchaff, warbler.
mosquito *m* mosquito.
mostacho *m* moustache.
mostachón *m* CULIN macaroon.
mostaza *f* mustard.
mosto 1 *m* (*del vino*) must. 2 (*zumo*) grape juice.
mostrador *m* (*de tienda*) counter; (*de bar*) bar.
mostrar 1 *t* to show: *nos mostró una parte de su colección,* he showed us part of his collection. 2 (*exponer*) to exhibit, display. 3 (*señalar*) to point out, explain. – 4 mostrarse, *p* to appear: *no se ha mostrado en público después del escándalo,* he hasn't appeared in public since the scandal; *no se mostró muy apenado,* he didn't seem too upset. 5 (*ser*) be; (*resultar ser*) to prove to be, turn out to be: *se mostró muy valiente cuando atracaron el banco,* he was very brave when they held up the bank; *se mostró un buen padre,* he proved to be a good father.
mostrenco,-a 1 *adj* (*tonto*) thick. 2 (*grande*) mammoth. – 3 *m,f* (*tonto*) thickhead. 4 (*grande*) fatso.
mota 1 *f* (*partícula*) speck. 2 (*mancha*) spot; (*dibujo*) dot.
■ **mota de polvo,** speck of dust.
mote *m* nickname.
moteado,-a *adj* dotted, speckled.
motejar *t* to nickname.
motel *m* motel.
motilidad *f* motility.
motín 1 *m* (*levantamiento*) riot, uprising. 2 (*de tropas*) mutiny.
motivación 1 *f* (*estímulo*) motivation. 2 (*razón*) motive.
motivar 1 *t* (*causar*) to cause, give rise to: *el despido de los trabajadores motivó la huelga,* the sacking of the workers caused the strike. 2 (*estimular*) to motivate.
motivo 1 *m* motive, reason, cause, grounds *pl*: *no tienes motivo para estar deprimido,* you have no reason to be depressed; *no pudo venir por motivos de salud,* he

couldn't come for health reasons; *no sé cuál es el motivo de su queja,* I don't know what his grounds for complaint are. 2 (*de dibujo, música*) motif, leitmotif.
● **bajo ningún motivo,** under no circumstances. ‖ **con motivo de,** (*debido a*) owing to; (*en ocasión de*) on the occasion of. ‖ **dar motivo a,** to give rise to. ‖ **sin motivo,** for no apparent reason. ‖ **tener motivos para ...,** to have reason to ...
moto *f fam* (*motocicleta*) motorbike; (*escúter*) moped.
● **como una moto,** *fam* (*inquieto*) all excited; (*loco*) off one's trolley; (*enfadado*) fuming: *cuando se enteró se puso como una moto,* he blew his top when he found out.
■ **moto acuática,** jet ski.
motocarro *m* three-wheeled van.
motocicleta *f* motorcycle, motorbike.
motociclismo *m* motorcycling.
motociclista *mf* motorcyclist.
motociclo *m* motorcycle.
motocross *m* moto-cross.
motocultivo *m* mechanised agriculture.
motonáutico,-a 1 *adj* speedboat, motorboat. – 2 motonáutica, *f* speedboat racing, motorboat racing.
motor,-ra 1 *adj* motive: *fuerza motora,* motive power. 2 BIOL motor: *función motora,* motor function. – 3 motor, *m* TÉC engine. 4 *fig* driving force: *él es el motor de la empresa,* he is the driving force behind the company. – 5 motora, *f* small motorboat.
■ **motor de arranque,** starter motor. ‖ **motor de explosión,** internal-combustion engine. ‖ **motor de inyección,** fuel-injection engine. ‖ **motor de reacción,** jet engine. ‖ **motor fuera bordo,** outboard motor.
motorismo *m* motorcycling.
motorista *mf* motorcyclist.
motorizado,-a *adj* motorized.
motorizar 1 *t* to motorize. – 2 motorizarse, *p* to get wheels, be mobile.
▲ Conjugation model [4], like *realizar.*
motosierra *f* power saw.
motriz *adj* motive.
■ **fuerza motriz,** motive power.
▲ Used only with feminine nouns.
motu de motu propio, *adv* of one's own accord.
mousse *f* CULIN mousse.
mouton 1 *m* (*piel*) sheepskin. 2 (*abrigo*) sheepskin coat.
mover 1 *t* (*gen*) to move; (*de un sitio a otro*) to move, shift: *movió el pie,* he moved his foot; *¿quieres que te mueva la mesa?,* do you want me to shift the table? 2 (*hacer funcionar*) to drive, make work: *esta manivela mueve la máquina,* this crank makes the machine work. 3 (*suscitar*) to incite, cause, provoke: *la declaración movió guerra,* the statement provoked a war; *actuó movido por los celos,* he was driven by jealousy. 4 (*hacer gestiones*) to deal with: *él movía todo el asunto,* he dealt with the whole business. – 5 moverse, *p* (*gen*) to move: *no te muevas de aquí hasta que yo vuelva,* don't move till I get back. 6 *fam* (*darse prisa*) to get a move on: *¡muévete, que llegaremos tarde!,* get a move on or we'll be late! 7 *fam* (*espabilarse*) to get a move on: *como no te muevas, no encuentras piso,* if you don't get a move on you won't find a flat; *hay que saber moverse en este mundo,* you've got to be able to find you way around in this world. 8 (*relacionarse*) to move: *se mueve en ambientes muy selectos,* he moves in very high circles.
▲ Conjugation model [32].
movible *adj* movable.

movida f → **movido,-a**.

movido,-a 1 pp → **mover**. – 2 adj (día, temporada) busy, hectic: he tenido una mañana muy movida, I've had a really hectic morning. **3** (persona) active. **4** (fiesta, concurso) lively. **5** (foto) blurred. – **6 movida**, f fam (animación) action. **7** fam (agitación) to-do, stir, commotion. **8 la movida** (madrileña), the Madrid nightclub and music scene in the early 80's.

móvil 1 adj movable, mobile. – **2** m FÍS moving body. **3** (motivo) motive. **4** (decoración, juguete) mobile.

movilidad f mobility.

movilización f mobilization.

movilizar t to mobilize.
▲ Conjugation model |4|, like realizar.

movimiento 1 m (gen) movement; TÉC motion. **2** (de gente, ideas) activity; (de vehículos) traffic: en esta ciudad hay mucho movimiento, this is a very lively town. **3** ART LIT POL movement. **4** FIN operations pl: un extracto de los movimientos de la cuenta, a bank statement. **5** MÚS (parte de la composición) movement; (velocidad de una composición) tempo. **6** POL uprising, movement. **7 el Movimiento**, the Falangist Movement.
● **en movimiento**, in motion.
■ **movimiento de caja**, turnover. ‖ **movimiento sísmico**, earth tremor.

moviola f (máquina) editing projector, movieola.

moza f → **mozo,-a**.

mozalbete m young lad.

Mozambique m Mozambique.

mozambiqueño,-a 1 adj Mozambiquean. – **2** m,f Mozambiquean.

mozárabe 1 adj Mozarab. – **2** mf Mozarab.

mozo,-a 1 adj young. **2** (soltero) unmarried, single. – **3** mozo, m (joven) young man, lad. **4** (camarero) waiter. **5** (de hotel) bellboy. **6** (de estación) porter. **7** MIL conscript. – **8** moza, f (chica) lass. **9** arc maid.
● **ser un buen mozo/una buena moza**, to be a fine young man/woman.
■ **años mozos**, youth: en mis años mozos, when I was young, in my young day.

mozuelo,-a m,f (hombre) young lad; (mujer) young lass.

m/p abr (mi pagaré) I owe you; (abreviatura) I.O.U.

ms. abr (manuscrito) manuscript; (abreviatura) ms.

MSF abr (Médicos Sin Fronteras) Doctors Without Frontiers.

Mtro. abr (maestro) master.

mu interj (mugido) moo.
● **no decir ni mu**, fam not to say a word.

muaré m moiré.

muchachada 1 f (acción) childish prank, childish antics pl: a su edad todavía intenta hacer muchachadas, he still larks about around as if he were a boy. **2** (grupo) youngsters pl.

muchacho,-a 1 m,f (chico) boy; (chica) girl. – **2** f (sirvienta) maid, girl.

muchedumbre 1 f (de personas) crowd. **2** (de cosas) pile.

mucho,-a 1 adj (singular - en afirmativas) a lot of; (- en negativas, interrogativas) a lot of, much: hicieron mucho ruido, they made a lot of noise; no tiene mucho dinero, he hasn't got a lot of/much money; ¿nos queda mucha gasolina?, have we got a lot of/much petrol left? **2** (plural - en afirmativas) a lot of, lots of; (- en negativas, interrogativas) a lot of, many: son muchos socios en ese club, the club has a lot of members; hay mucha gente esperando, there are a lot of people waiting; tiene muchos discos, he's got lots of records; no hay muchas copas,

there aren't a lot of/many glasses; ¿tienes muchos libros?, have you got a lot of/many books?; hace mucho calor/frío, it's very hot/cold; tengo mucha hambre/sed, I'm very hungry/thirsty. **3** (demasiado - singular) too much; (- plural) too many: es mucho trabajo para una sola persona, it's too much work for just one person; el proyecto supone demasiados problemas, the project involves too many problems; ya son muchas preguntas, that's far too many questions. – **4** pron (singular) a lot, much; (plural) a lot, many: no me queda mucho por hacer, I haven't got much left to do; muchos de ellos acudieron, many of them came; muchos de mis amigos viven en el extranjero, a lot of my friends live abroad; muchos dicen que no es apto para el trabajo, a lot of people say he's not suitable for the job. – **5** adv (de cantidad) a lot, much: mucho mejor/peor, much better/worse; era mucho más peligroso de lo que pensábamos, it was much more dangerous than we thought; se preocupa mucho por ellos, he worries a lot about them; me gusta mucho, I like it a lot; lo siento mucho, I'm really sorry; me alegro mucho de verte, I'm very pleased to see you; ¿te ha gustado la película? –sí, mucho, did you like the film? –yes, very much; ¿estaba buena la comida? –sí, mucho, was the food good? –yes, very good. **6** (de tiempo): mucho antes/después, much earlier/later; hace mucho que no nos vemos, we haven't seen each other for a long time. **7** (de frecuencia) often: no vienen mucho por aquí, they don't come here often.
● **como mucho**, at the most: te pagarán como mucho cinco mil pesetas, they'll pay you five thousand pesetas at the most. ‖ **con mucho**, by far: es con mucho el mejor concursante, he's the best competitor by far. ‖ **muy mucho**, fam very much so. ‖ **ni con mucho**, nowhere near as: no es ni con mucho tan inteligente, he's nowhere near as clever. ‖ **ni mucho menos**, far from: no es ni mucho menos tonto, he's far from stupid. ‖ **por mucho que**, however much: por mucho que lo intentes no lo conseguirás, you won't get it however much you try.

mucosa f → **mucoso,-a**.

mucosidad f mucus.

mucoso,-a 1 adj mucous. – **2** (membrana) mucosa, f mucous membrane.

muda 1 f (de ropa) change of clothes, particularly underwear. **2** (de plumas) moulting (us molting). **3** (de la voz) breaking.

mudable 1 adj changeable. **2** (carácter) fickle.

mudanza 1 f (de residencia) moving. **2** (cambio) change. **3** (de ideas) changeability. – **4 mudanzas**, fpl removals pl, removal firm: Mudanzas Gimeno, Gimeno Removals.
● **estar de mudanza**, to be moving: los González están de mudanza, the González's are moving.

mudar 1 t to change, alter. **2** (trasladar) to change, move: nos van a mudar a otro edificio, they're going to move us to another building. **3** (plumas) to moult (us molt). **4** (voz) to break: le está mudando la voz, his voice is breaking. **5** (piel) to shed. – **6 mudarse**, p to change. **7** (de residencia) to move.
● **mudarse de casa**, to move, move house. ‖ **mudarse de ropa**, to change clothes.

mudéjar 1 adj Mudejar. – **2** mf Mudejar.

mudez f dumbness, muteness.

mudo,-a 1 adj (por defecto) dumb; (por voluntad) silent, quiet. **2** CINE silent. **3** (vocal, consonante) mute. – **4** m,f dumb person.
● **estar mudo,-a**, to be dumb. ‖ **mudo,-a de asombro**, dumbfounded. ‖ **quedarse mudo,-a**, to be left speechless.

■ **cine mudo,** silent films, US silent movies. ‖ **mapa mudo,** blank map.

mueble 1 *m* piece of furniture. – 2 *adj* movable. – 3 **muebles** *pl* furniture *sing*: *no tienen muchos muebles,* they haven't got a lot of furniture.
● **con muebles,** furnished. ‖ **sin muebles,** unfurnished.
■ **bienes muebles,** movables, chattels. ‖ **mueble bar,** cocktail cabinet.

mueblista *mf* (*que fabrica*) furniture maker; (*que vende*) furniture dealer.

mueca 1 *f* (*de burla*) mocking gesture, face. 2 (*de dolor*) grimace.
● **hacer muecas,** (*de burla*) to pull faces; (*de dolor*) to wince.

muela 1 *f* (*diente*) tooth, molar. 2 (*de molino*) millstone. 3 (*para afilar*) grindstone.
■ **dolor de muelas,** toothache. ‖ **muela del juicio,** wisdom tooth.

muelle¹ 1 *adj* (*vida*) cushy. 2 (*blando*) soft, springy. – 3 *m* (*elástico*) spring.
■ **colchón de muelles,** spring mattress.

muelle² *m* MAR dock, wharf; (*malecón*) pier, jetty.

muérdago *m* mistletoe.

muerdo *m fam* bite.

muermo *m fam* (*situación, fiesta*) drag, pain, bore; (*persona pesada*) pain in the neck, bore, drag; (- *sosa*) drip, wet: *¡tengo un muermo!,* I can't be bothered to move!

muerte 1 *f* death: *una muerte natural,* a natural death. 2 (*asesinato*) murder. 3 **la muerte,** death.
● **a vida o muerte,** life-and-death. ‖ **dar muerte a algn.,** to kill sb. ‖ **de mala muerte,** *fam* grotty, crummy, rotten: *nos alojamos en una pensión de mala muerte,* we stayed in this grotty old guest house. ‖ **estar de muerte,** *fam* (*comida*) to be scrumptious; (*persona*) to be gorgeous. ‖ **a muerte,** to the death: *un duelo a muerte,* a duel to the death. ‖ **hasta que la muerte nos separe,** till death do us part. ‖ **odiar a muerte,** to detest, loathe.
■ **muerte cerebral,** brain death.

muerto,-a *pp* → **morir.** – 2 *adj* (*sin vida*) dead; (*sin actividad*) lifeless: *este pueblo está muerto,* there's nothing going on in this village. 3 *fam* (*cansado*) tired, worn out: *estoy muerto,* I'm beat; *la mudanza me ha dejado muerto,* moving house has finished me off. 4 (*marchito*) faded, withered. – 5 *m,f* dead person; (*cadáver*) corpse. 6 (*víctima*) victim. – 7 **muerto,** *m fam* drag, bore.
● **dejar muerto,-a a algn.,** *fam* (*de cansancio*) to finish sb. off; (*de asombro*) to leave sb. dumbfounded. ‖ **caer muerto,-a,** to drop dead. ‖ **cargar con el muerto,** to be left holding the baby. ‖ **cargarle el muerto a algn.,** to pass the buck to sb. ‖ **hacer el muerto,** (*en el agua*) to float on one's back. ‖ **hacerse el muerto,** to pretend to be dead. ‖ **"muerto en combate",** "killed in action". ‖ **no tener dónde caerse muerto,-a,** not to have a penny to one's name. ‖ **ser un/una muerto,-a de hambre,** to be a good-for-nothing. ‖ **¡tus muertos!,** *tabú* up yours! ‖ **medio muerto,-a,** half-dead.
■ **horas muertas,** spare time *sing*. ‖ **punto muerto,** AUTO neutral.

muesca 1 *f* (*corte*) nick, notch. 2 (*concavidad*) mortise, mortice.

muestra 1 *f* (*ejemplar*) sample: *¿me da una muestra de esta tela?,* could I have a sample of this fabric? 2 (*modelo*) pattern: *usa este patrón como muestra,* use this pattern as a sample. 3 (*señal*) proof, sign: *a mitad de la carrera ya daba muestras de cansancio,* he was showing signs of tiredness halfway through the race. 4 (*rótulo*) sign. 5 (*exposición*) show, display: *había una muestra de algunos de sus productos,* they had some of their products on display.
● **como muestra un botón,** as a sample.
■ **feria de muestras,** trade fair. ‖ **muestra gratuita,** free sample.

muestrario *m* collection of samples.

muestreo *m* (*gen*) sampling; (*aleatorio*) random sample, cross-section.

muflón *m* mouflon, moufflon.

mugido 1 *m* (*de vaca - uno*) moo; (- *varios*) mooing. 2 (*de toro - uno*) bellow; (- *varios*) bellowing.

mugir 1 *i* (*vaca*) to moo. 2 (*toro*) to bellow.
▲ *Conjugation model* [6], *like* **dirigir.**

mugre *f* grime, filth.

mugriento,-a *adj* grimy, filthy.

muguet *m* → **muguete.**

muguete *m* lily of the valley.

mujer 1 *f* woman: *sale con dos mujeres a la vez,* he's going out with two women at the same time. 2 (*esposa*) wife.
● **ser muy mujer de su casa,** to be very houseproud. ‖ **ya es mujer,** she's become a woman. ‖ **ser muy mujer,** to be very womanly.
■ **mujer fatal,** femme fatale. ‖ **mujer de la calle/vida,** street-walker. ‖ **mujer de la limpieza,** cleaning lady. ‖ **mujer de mundo,** woman of the world. ‖ **mujer de negocios,** businesswoman. ‖ **mujer de vida alegre,** floozy, hussy. ‖ **mujer objeto,** sex object. ‖ **mujer pública,** prostitute.

mujeriego,-a 1 *adj pey* fond of the ladies. – 2 **mujeriego,** *m* womanizer.
● **ser mujeriego,** to be a womanizer, be a ladies' man.

mujeril *adj* womanly, woman's, femenine.

mujerío *m* group of women: *el mujerío del pueblo,* the women of the village.

mujerona *f fam* big woman.

mujerzuela *f pey* harlot, loose woman.

mújol *m* grey mullet.

mula *f* → **mulo,-a.**

muladar *m* dump.

muladí *mf* Spanish Christian converted to Islam.

mular *adj* ganado mular, *m* mules *pl.*

mulato,-a 1 *adj* mulatto. – 2 *m,f* mulatto.

mulero *m* muleteer, mule-driver.

muleta 1 *f* (*para andar*) crutch. 2 *fig* (*apoyo*) prop, support. 3 (*en toros*) muleta red cape.

muletilla 1 *f* (*bastón*) cross-handled cane. 2 (*frase repetida*; (- *de persona famosa*) catch-phrase; (*palabra*) pet word.

muletón *m* flannelette.

mulillas *fpl* team *sing* of mules (*which drag the dead bull from the ring*).

mullido,-a *adj* soft, springy.

mullir 1 *t* (*lana*) to soften; (*almohada, colchón*) to fluff up. 2 (*tierra*) to break up.
▲ *Conjugation model* [41].

mulo,-a *m,f* (*macho*) mule; (*hembra*) she-mule.
● **estar hecho,-a un/una mulo,-a,** to be as strong as an ox. ‖ **ser más terco,-a que una mula,** to be as stubborn as a mule.

multa *f* (*gen*) fine; (*de tráfico*) ticket: *me pusieron una multa por aparcar en la acera,* I got a ticket for parking on the pavement.
● **poner una multa a algn.,** to fine sb., give sb. a fine:

me pusieron una multa de diez mil pesetas, I was fined ten thousand pesetas.

multar *t* to fine: *¿cuánto te multaron?,* how much did they fine you?

multicines *mpl* multiplex *sing,* multi-screen cinema *sing.*

multicolor *adj* multicoloured, us multicolored.

multicopista *f* duplicator.

multidimensional *adj* multidimensional.

multidireccional *adj* multidirectional.

multidisciplinar *adj* multidisciplinary.

multiforme *adj* multiform.

multigrado *adj* multigrade.

multilateral *adj* multilateral.

multimedia *adj* multi-media.

multimillonario,-a **1** *adj* (*de libras, dólares*) multimillion-pound, multimillion-dollar: *un contrato multimillonario,* a multimillion-dollar contract; *una operación multimillonaria,* a six-figure operation. – **2** *m,f* multimillionaire.

multinacional **1** *adj* multinational. – **2** *f* multinational.

multípara *f* multiparous.

múltiple **1** *adj* multiple: *un efecto múltiple,* a multiple effect; *sistema múltiple,* multiple system. **2** (*muchos*) many, a number of, numerous: *opiniones múltiples,* a number of opinions.

multiplicable *adj* multipliable.

multiplicación *f* multiplication.

multiplicador,-ra **1** *adj* multiplying. – **2** multiplicador, *m* multiplier.

multiplicar **1** *t* to multiply (**por,** by). – **2 multiplicarse,** *p* (*reproducirse*) to multiply. **3** *fig* (*atender a todo*) to be everywhere at the same time.

▲ *Conjugation model* |1|, *like* **sacar.**

multiplicidad *f* multiplicity.

múltiplo **1** *adj* multiple. – **2** *m* multiple.

■ **mínimo común múltiplo,** lowest common multiple.

multipropiedad *f* time-share.

multirriesgo *adj* fully comprehensive.

■ **seguro/póliza multirriesgo,** fully-comprehensive insurance policy.

multitud **1** *f* (*de personas*) crowd. **2** (*de cosas, ideas*) multitude.

■ **baño de multitud,** walkabout.

multitudinario,-a *adj* multitudinous.

multiuso *adj* multipurpose.

mundanal *adj* of the world, mundane.

● **huir del mundanal ruido,** to get away from it all.

mundano,-a *adj* of the world, mundane.

mundial **1** *adj* worldwide, world. – **2** *m* world championship.

● **de fama mundial,** world-famous.

■ **guerra mundial,** world war: *la Primera/Segunda Guerra Mundial,* the First/Second World War. ‖ **mundial de fútbol,** World Cup.

mundialmente *adv* worldwide, all over the world.

● **mundialmente conocido,-a,** world-famous.

mundillo *m* world, circles *pl: el mundillo teatral,* theatrical circles.

mundo **1** *m* world: *ha dado la vuelta al mundo dos veces,* he's been around the world twice; *se cree que hay otros mundos habitados,* people believe that there are other inhabited worlds; *vive aislado en su propio mundo,* he's isolated himself in his own little world; *el mundo de la* aristocracia, the world of the aristocracy; *el mundo del cine,* the cinema, the world of cinema. **2** *fig* (*abismo*): *entre su forma de vivir y la mía hay un mundo,* our ways of life are worlds apart. **3** (*baúl*) trunk.

● **caérsele/venírsele a algn. el mundo encima,** to see one's world turned upside down. ‖ **correr/ver mundo,** to see places. ‖ **desde que el mundo es mundo,** since the beginning of time. ‖ **el mundo es un pañuelo,** it's a small world. ‖ **hacer un mundo de algo,** to make a big fuss over sth. ‖ **medio mundo,** *fig* absolutely everybody. ‖ **no ser nada del otro mundo,** to be nothing to write home about. ‖ **ponerse el mundo por montera,** not to care what people think. ‖ **por nada del mundo,** not for all the world. ‖ **ser una mujer/un hombre de mundo,** to be a woman/man of the world. ‖ **tener mundo,** to know the ways of the world. ‖ **traer al mundo,** to bring into the world. ‖ **venir al mundo,** to come into the world.

■ **el fin del mundo,** the end of the world. ‖ **el Nuevo Mundo,** the New World. ‖ **el otro mundo,** the hereafter. ‖ **el Tercer Mundo,** the Third World.

mundología *f fam* worldliness.

● **tener mundología,** (*tener experiencia*) to know the ways of the world; (*haber viajado*) to have travelled (us traveled) the world, be a seasoned traveller (us traveler).

munición *f* ammunition, munitions *pl.*

municipal **1** *adj* (*gobierno*) town, municipal; (*instalaciones*) council. – **2** *mf* (*hombre*) policeman; (*mujer*) policewoman. – **3 las municipales,** *fpl* local elections.

municipio **1** *m* municipality. **2** (*ayuntamiento*) town council.

munificencia *f* munificence.

muñeca *f →* **muñeco,-a.**

muñeco,-a **1** *m,f* (*juguete*) doll. **2** *fam fig* beauty. – **3** muñeco, *m fig* (*títere*) puppet: *un juguete en manos del destino,* a puppet in the hands of fate. – **4 muñeca,** *f* ANAT wrist.

■ **muñeca de trapo,** rag doll. ‖ **muñeco de nieve,** snowman.

muñeira *f* popular Galician dance.

muñequera *f* wristband.

muñir *t* (*amañar*) to fix.

muñón *m* ANAT stump.

mural **1** *adj* mural. – **2** *m* mural.

muralla *f* city wall.

murciano,-a **1** *adj* of Murcia, from Murcia. – **2** *m,f* person from Murcia, inhabitant of Murcia.

murciélago *m* bat.

murga *f fam* nuisance.

● **dar la murga,** *fam* to be a pain in the neck.

murmullo *m* (*susurro*) whisper, whispering; (*voz baja*) murmur, murmuring; (*de arroyo*) babbling, burbling; (*de hojas*) rustle, rustling; (*del viento*) sighing, murmur.

murmuración *f* gossip, backbiting.

murmurador,-ra **1** *adj* gossipy. – **2** *m,f* gossip.

murmurar **1** *t* (*susurrar*) to murmur, whisper. – **2** *i* (*criticar*) to gossip. **3** (*persona - susurrar*) to whisper; (- *decir en voz baja*) to murmur; (*agua*) to murmur, babble; (*hojas*) to rustle; (*viento*) to sigh, murmur.

muro *m* wall.

■ **el muro de las lamentaciones,** the Wailing Wall.

murrio,-a **1** *adj* down, sad. – **2 murria,** *f* sadness, melancholy.

mus *m card game in which players use signs to communicate.*

musa **1** *f* muse. – **2 las musas,** *fpl* the Arts.

musaraña f ZOOL shrew.
● **estar pensando en las musarañas,** to daydream.
musculación f body-building.
muscular adj muscular.
musculatura f muscles pl, musculature.
músculo m muscle.
musculoso,-a adj muscular.
muselina f muslin.
museo m museum.
■ **museo de arte,** art museum. ‖ **museo de cera,** wax museum.
musgo m moss.
● **cubierto,-a de musgo,** mossy, moss-covered.
musgoso,-a adj mossy.
música f → **músico,-a.**
musical 1 adj musical. – **2** m musical.
musicalidad f musicality.
musicar t to write the music for, set to music.
músico,-a 1 adj musical: *composición música,* musical composition. – **2** m,f musician. – **3** música, f music.
● **irse con la música a otra parte,** fam to clear off.
■ **instrumento músico,** musical instrument. ‖ **música ambiental,** muzak. ‖ **música de fondo,** background music. ‖ **música clásica,** classical music. ‖ **música de cámara,** chamber music. ‖ **música ligera,** easy listening.
musicología f musicology.
musicólogo,-a m,f musicologist.
musiquero,-a m,f fam music lover, music buff.
musiquilla f fam pey tacky music.
musitar i (*susurrar*) to whisper; (*hablar entre dientes*) to mumble, mutter.
muslamen m fam thighs, good pair of thighs.
muslo 1 m thigh. **2** CULIN (*de ave*) drumstick.
mustango m mustang.
mustiarse i to wilt, wither.

mustio,-a 1 adj (*plantas*) withered, faded. **2** (*persona*) down, downcast, sad.
musulmán,-ana 1 adj Muslim, Moslem. – **2** m,f Muslim, Moslem.
mutabilidad f mutability, changeability.
mutable adj mutable.
mutación 1 f change. **2** BIOL mutation.
mutante 1 adj mutant. – **2** mf mutant.
mutilación f mutilation.
mutilado,-a 1 adj (*persona*) crippled, disabled; (*objeto*) mutilated. – **2** m,f cripple.
■ **mutilado de guerra,** war cripple.
mutilar t (*persona*) to cripple; (*objeto*) to mutilate.
mutis m TEAT exit.
● **hacer mutis,** (*salir*) to make os. scarce; (*callar*) to say nothing; (*en teatro*) to exit.
mutismo m silence.
mutualidad 1 f (*asociación*) mutual benefit society. **2** (*reciprocidad*) mutuality.
mutualista 1 adj of a mutual benefit society. – **2** mf member of a mutual benefit society.
mutuo,-a 1 adj mutual, reciprocal: *por mutuo acuerdo,* by mutual agreement. – **2** mutua, f mutual benefit society.
■ **mutua de seguros,** mutual insurance company.
muy adv very: *es muy difícil,* it's very difficult; *se levantó muy temprano,* he got up very early; *lo has hecho muy bien,* you've done it very well; *es un trabajador muy bueno,* he'a very good worker; *el muy tonto se cree que no lo he visto,* the idiot thinks I haven't seen him.
● **muy de mañana,** very early in the morning. ‖ **muy señor mío,** (*en carta*) Dear Sir. ‖ **ser muy hombre/mujer,** fam to be a real man/woman. ‖ **por muy...,** no matter how..., however...: *por muy astuto que sea no nos podrá engañar,* now matter how crafty he is he won't be able to con us.

N

N, n f (la letra) N, n.
n.[1] abr (nacido,-a) born; (abreviatura) b.
n.[2] abr (nombre) name; (abreviatura) n.
N sím (norte) north; (símbolo) N.
n/ abr (nuestro,-a) our.
n° abr (número) number; (abreviatura) n.
nabo 1 m (planta) turnip. **2** (raíz) root vegetable. **3** tabú prick, cock.
nácar m mother-of-pearl.
nacarado,-a adj mother-of-pearl, nacred.
nacarino,-a adj nacreous, mother-of-pearl.
nacer 1 i (persona) to be born; (ave) to hatch out; (semilla, planta) to sprout: *nació con muchos problemas de salud*, she was born with a lot of health problems; *nació en una buena familia*, he was born into a good family; *no ha nacido para sufrir*, he wasn't born to suffer. **2** (río) to rise; (agua) to spring; (camino) to start, begin. **3** (sol) to rise. **4** (pelo) to start to grow: *ya le ha nacido la barba*, his beard has started to grow. **5** (idea, sentimiento) to originate (de, from), spring (de, from), stem (de, from): *el miedo nace de la ignorancia*, fear stems from ignorance.
● *al nacer*, at birth. ‖ *nacer a algo*, (persona) to take one's first steps in; (cosa) to give birth to: *nacieron a la democracia el día que se firmó la constitución*, democracy was born the day the constitution was signed. ‖ *nacer ayer*, to be born yesterday: *no nací ayer*, I wasn't born yesterday. ‖ *nacer con suerte / nacer de pie*, to be born under a lucky star. ‖ *nacer para algo*, to be born to be sth.: *nació para ser estrella*, she was born to be a star. ‖ *nadie nace enseñado*, we all have to learn. ‖ *volver a nacer*, to have a lucky escape.
▲ Conjugation model [42].
nacido,-a adj born.
● *bien nacido,-a*, (de buena cuna) of noble birth; (de buen corazón) kind-hearted. ‖ *mal nacido,-a*, despicable.
naciente 1 adj (nuevo) new. **2** (creciente) growing. – **3** m (este) East.
nacimiento 1 m birth. **2** (de río) source: *vamos a visitar el nacimiento del río Segura*, we're going to see the source of the river Segura. **3** fig origin, beginning. **4** (pesebre) crib, Nativity scene.
● *de nacimiento*, from birth: *es ciega de nacimiento*, she was born blind; *es una mancha de nacimiento*, it's a birthmark; *éste es tonto de nacimiento*, what a stupid idiot!
nación f nation.
■ *Naciones Unidas*, United Nations.
nacional 1 adj national. **2** (producto, mercado) domestic. **3** (vuelo) domestic; (noticias) national. – **4 los Nacionales**, mpl HIST the Nationalists supporters of Franco during the Spanish Civil War.
nacionalidad f nationality: *ser de nacionalidad española*, to have Spanish nationality.

● *tener doble nacionalidad*, to have dual nationality.
nacionalismo m nationalism.
nacionalista 1 adj nationalist. – **2** mf nationalist.
nacionalización 1 f (de una persona) naturalization. **2** (de una empresa) nationalization.
nacionalizar 1 t (persona) to naturalize. **2** ECON (empresa) to nationalize. – **3 nacionalizarse**, p (persona) to become naturalized: *nacionalizarse español (británico etc)*, to take up Spanish (British etc) citizenship.
▲ Conjugation model [4], like realizar.
nacionalsocialismo m National Socialism.
nacionalsocialista 1 adj National Socialist. – **2** mf National Socialist.
nada 1 pron nothing: *no quiero nada*, I don't want anything; *(no hay) nada como ...*, there's nothing like ...; *no hace nada que lo vi por aquí*, I saw him round here just a minute ago; *¿te has hecho daño? –no, no ha sido nada*, did you hurt yourself? –no, I'm all right thank you. – **2** adv (not) at all: *no me gusta nada*, I don't like it at all; *no la veo nada cambiada*, she hasn't changed at all. – **3** f nothingness.
● *antes de nada*, first of all. ‖ *como si nada*, just like that. ‖ *de nada*, (no hay de qué) don't mention it, think nothing of it, (US you're welcome); (insignificante) insignificant: *gracias, –de nada*, thanks, –don't mention it; *es una tontería de nada*, it's nothing much. ‖ *dentro de nada*, in a moment. ‖ *nada de eso*, not at all, nothing of the kind: *¿se casa Maribel? –¡nada de eso!*, is Maribel getting married? –absolutely not!, no way!; *no quiero llantos ni nada de eso*, I don't want any crying or anything of that sort. ‖ *nada más ...*, as soon as ..., no sooner ...: *nada más verlo quiso comprarlo*, as soon as he saw it he wanted to buy it; *nada más llegar se puso a llover*, no sooner had we arrived than it started to rain. ‖ *nada menos que*, no less than: *está aquí nada menos que el presidente*, the president himself is here no less. ‖ *por nada*, for no reason at all. ‖ *por nada del mundo*, (not) for anything in the world. ‖ *¡y nada de ...!*, and don't ...!: *¡y nada de bañarse en el río!*, and don't go bathing in the river!
nadador,-ra m,f swimmer.
nadar i to swim.
● *nadar contra corriente*, fig to go against the tide. ‖ *nadar en la abundancia*, to be rolling in it, live in the lap of luxury. ‖ *nadar entre dos aguas*, to sit on the fence. ‖ *nadar y guardar la ropa*, to have one's cake and eat it, have it both ways.
nadería f trifle.
nadie pron nobody, not ... anybody: *aquí no hay nadie*, there's nobody here; *no vino nadie de su familia*, none of his relatives came; *¿nadie quiere más pastel?*, doesn't anybody want any more cake?
● *ser un don nadie*, to be a nobody.
nadir m nadir.

nado a nado, *loc adv* swimming: *cruzaron el río a nado,* they swam across the river.

nafta *f* naphtha.

naftalina *f* naphtalene.

■ bola de naftalina, mothball.

náhuatl *m* (*lengua*) Nahuatl.

naif 1 *adj* naïf, naive. – 2 *m* naïf art.

nailon *m* nylon.

naipe *m* playing card.

nal. *abr* (*nacional*) national; (*abreviatura*) nat.

nalga *f* buttock.

Namibia *f* Namibia.

namibio,-a 1 *adj* Namibian. – 2 *m,f* Namibian.

nana *f* lullaby.

● del año de la nana, *fam* as old as the hills.

nanay *interj fam* no way!

nao *f lit* vessel.

napa *f* napa, nappa.

napalm *m* napalm.

napias *fpl fam* snout *sing*, conk *sing*.

napoleónico,-a *adj* Napoleonic.

Nápoles *m* Naples.

napolitano,-a 1 *adj* Neapolitan. – 2 *m,f* Neapolitan.

naranja 1 *f* (*fruto*) orange. – 2 *adj* (*color*) orange.

● encontrar su media naranja, to find the man/woman of one's dreams. ‖ mi media naranja, my better half. ‖ ¡naranjas de la China!, *fam* no way!

■ naranja sanguina, blood orange.

naranjada *f* orangeade, orange drink.

naranjal *m* orange grove.

naranjo *m* orange tree.

narcisismo *m* narcissim.

narcisista 1 *adj* narcissistic. – 2 *mf* narcissist.

narciso 1 *m* (*flor*) daffodil, narcissus. 2 (*hombre*) narcissist.

narco *mf arg* drug trafficker.

narcosis *f* narcosis.

▲ *pl narcosis.*

narcótico,-a 1 *adj* narcotic. – 2 narcótico, *m* (*medicamento*) narcotic; (*droga*) drug.

narcotizar *t* (*medicar*) to narcotize; (*drogar*) to drug.

narcotraficante 1 *adj* drug trafficking. – 2 *mf* drug trafficker.

narcotráfico *m* drug trafficking.

nardo *m* nard, spikenard.

narguile *m* hookah, water pipe.

narices *interj fam* → **nariz**.

narigón,-ona 1 *adj fam* big-nosed. – 2 narigón, *m fam* huge conk, big nose.

narigudo,-a *adj* → **narigón,-ona**.

nariz 1 *f* ANAT nose. 2 *fig* (*sentido*) sense of smell. – 3 ¡narices!, *interj fam* not on your life!

● asomar las narices, to nose about, nose around. ‖ dar en la nariz algo a algn., to get the feeling (that) ...: *me da en la nariz que nos oculta algo,* I get the feeling he's hiding something. ‖ darle a algn. con la puerta en las narices, to slam a door in sb.'s face. ‖ darse de narices con algo/algn., to bump into sth./sb. ‖ dejar a algn. con tantas narices / dejar a algn. con un palmo de narices, to let sb. down. ‖ ¡de narices!, *fam* brilliant! ‖ en las narices de algn., right under sb.'s nose. ‖ estar hasta las narices de, *fam* to be fed up (to the back teeth) with. ‖ hacer lo que le sale a uno de las narices, *fam* to do whatever one likes, do whatever one feels like. ‖ meter las narices en algo, to

poke one's nose into sth. ‖ no ver uno más allá de sus narices, to see no further than the end of one's nose. ‖ pasar algo por las narices a algn., to keep going on about sth. to sb., harp on about sth. to sb. ‖ romper las narices a algn., to smash sb.'s face in. ‖ romperse las narices, to fall flat on one's face. ‖ salirle algo a uno de las narices, to feel like doing sth.: *no voy porque no me sale de las narices,* I'm not going because I don't bloody well feel like it. ‖ tener narices, *fam* (*ser abusivo*) to be beyond a joke, be too much; (*tener valor*) to have guts. ‖ ¡tiene narices (la cosa)!, *fam* it's a bit much! ‖ tocar las narices, *fam* to be a nuisance, be a pest: ¡quieres dejar de tocarme las narices!, will you get off my back! ‖ tocarse las narices, *fam* to do sod all. ‖ ¡tócate las narices!, *fam* (*con asombro*) would you believe it?; (*con enfado*) (isn't it) bloody marvellous!

■ nariz aguileña, aquiline nose. ‖ nariz griega, straight nose. ‖ nariz respingona, turned-up nose.

narizotas *mf fam* big-nose.

▲ *pl narizotas.*

narración 1 *f* (*exposición*) narration, account. 2 (*historia*) story.

narrador,-ra *m,f* storyteller, narrator.

narrar *t* (*gen*) to tell, relate, narrate; (*partido*) to commentate.

narrativa *f* → **narrativo,-a**.

narrativo,-a 1 *adj* narrative. – 2 narrativa, *f* (*género*) fiction.

nártex *m* narthex.

▲ *pl nártex.*

nasa *f* (*aparejo*) keepnet; (*cesta*) creel.

nasal 1 *adj* nasal. – 2 *f* (*letra*) nasal.

nasalización *f* nasalization.

nasalizar *t* to nasalize.

nata 1 *f* cream. 2 (*de leche hervida*) skin.

■ nata líquida, single cream. ‖ nata montada, whipped cream.

natación *f* swimming.

■ natación sincronizada, synchronized swimming.

natal *adj* native.

■ ciudad natal, home town: *murió en su ciudad natal,* he died in his home town, he died in the town where he was born. ‖ país natal, native country. ‖ pueblo natal, home town.

natalicio,-a 1 *adj* birthday. – 2 natalicio, *m* birthday.

natalidad *f* birth rate.

natillas *fpl* custard *sing*.

natividad *f* nativity.

nativo,-a 1 *adj* native. – 2 *m,f* native.

■ (profesor,-ra) nativo,-a, native teacher.

nato,-a *adj* born.

natura *f* nature.

● contra natura, against nature.

natural 1 *adj* (*no artificial*) natural. 2 (*fruta, flor*) fresh. 3 (*sin elaboración*) plain; (*sin alteración*) additive-free: *yogur natural,* plain yoghurt. 4 (*espontáneo*) unaffected, natural: *en esta foto has quedado más natural,* you look more natural in this photo. 5 (*lógico*) natural, to be expected. 6 (*ilegítimo*) natural, illegitimate. – 7 *m* (*temperamento*) nature, disposition: *es de natural irritable,* he is irritable by nature. 8 (*nativo*) native, inhabitant. 9 (*en toreo*) type of pass.

● al natural, (*en la realidad*) in real life; CULIN in its own juice. ‖ de tamaño natural, life-size. ‖ del natural, (*pintado, sacado*) from life. ‖ ser natural de, to be a native of, come from.

naturaleza I *f* nature. **2** (*temperamento*) nature, character. **3** (*complexión*) physical constitution. **4** (*clase, tipo*) nature, kind.
● **en plena naturaleza,** in the wild. ‖ **por naturaleza,** by nature.
■ **naturaleza humana,** human nature, human condition. ‖ **naturaleza muerta,** ART still life. ‖ **protección de la naturaleza,** nature conservation.

naturalidad I *f* (*sencillez*) naturalness. **2** (*espontaneidad*) ease, spontaneity: *actúa con mucha naturalidad,* acting seems to come naturally to him, he acts very naturally.
● **con la mayor naturalidad del mundo,** as if it were the most natural thing in the world.

naturalismo *m* naturalism.

naturalista I *adj* naturalist. – **2** *mf* naturalist.

naturalización *f* naturalization.

naturalizar I *t* to naturalize. – **2 naturalizarse,** *p* to become naturalized: *se ha naturalizado español,* he has taken up Spanish citizenship.
▲ *Conjugation model* [4], *like realizar.*

naturalmente I *adv* naturally. – **2** *interj* naturally!, of course!: *sí, naturalmente,* yes, of course!; *naturalmente que no,* of course not.

naturismo *m* naturism.

naturista I *adj* naturist. – **2** *mf* naturist.

naturópata I *adj* naturopathic. – **2** *mf* naturopath.

naturopatía *f* naturopathy.

naufragar I *i* (*barco*) to sink, be wrecked; (*persona*) to be shipwrecked. **2** *fig* to fail.
▲ *Conjugation model* [7], *like llegar.*

naufragio I *m* shipwreck. **2** *fig* failure.

náufrago,-a I *adj* wrecked, shipwrecked. – **2** *m,f* shipwrecked person, castaway.

Nauru *m* Nauru.

nauruano,-a I *adj* Nauruan. – **2** *m,f* Nauruan.

náusea I *f* nausea, sickness: *¿sintió usted náuseas en su anterior embarazo?,* did you experience any nausea in your previous pregnancy? **2** *fig* (*repugnancia*) repulsion.
● **dar náusea(s),** to make sick: *me da náuseas,* it makes me sick.
▲ *Often used in plural with the same meaning.*

nauseabundo,-a *adj* nauseating, sickening.

náutica *f* → **náutico,-a.**

náutico,-a I *adj* nautical. – **2 náutica,** *f* navigation, seamanship. – **3 náuticos,** *mpl* (*calzado*) deck shoes.
■ **deportes náuticos,** water sports.

navaja I *f* (*cuchillo*) penknife, pocketknife. **2** (*molusco*) razor-shell.
■ **navaja de afeitar,** razor. ‖ **navaja de monte,** hunting knife.

navajazo I *m* (*acción*) stab. **2** (*herida*) stab wound, knife wound.

navajero,-a *m,f* thug (*armed with a knife*).

navajo,-a I *adj* Navajo. – **2** *m,f* Navajo.

naval *adj* naval.

Navarra *f* Navarre.

navarro,-a I *adj* Navarrese. – **2** *m,f* Navarrese.

nave I *f* (*náutica*) ship, vessel. **2** (*espacial*) spaceship, spacecraft. **3** ARQ (*central*) nave; (*lateral*) aisle. **4** (*almacén*) industrial warehouse; (*fábrica*) plant.
● **quemar las naves,** to burn one's boats, burn one's bridges.
■ **nave espacial,** spaceship. ‖ **nave central,** nave. ‖ **nave lateral,** aisle. ‖ **nave industrial,** industrial unit.

navegabilidad I *f* (*de las aguas*) navigability. **2** (*de un barco*) seaworthiness; (*de un avión*) airworthiness.

navegable I *adj* (*río*) navigable. **2** (*barco*) seaworthy.

navegación I *f* (*arte*) navigation. **2** (*tráfico*) shipping. **3** (*viaje por mar*) sea journey, voyage.
■ **instrumento de navegación,** instrument of navigation. ‖ **navegación aérea,** air navigation, flying. ‖ **navegación fluvial,** river navigation.

navegante I *adj* seafaring. – **2** *mf* navigator, seafarer.

navegar I *i* (*persona*) to sail, navigate. **2** (*barco*) to sail. **3** (*avión*) to fly.
● **navegar a la deriva,** to drift. ‖ **navegar contra corriente,** to go against the tide.
▲ *Conjugation model* [7], *like llegar.*

Navidad *f* Christmas.
● **felicitar las Navidades a algn.,** to wish sb. a merry Christmas.
■ **árbol de Navidad,** Christmas tree. ‖ **tarjeta de Navidad,** Christmas card.

navideño,-a *adj* Christmas: *había un ambiente navideño,* there was a Christmassy feeling.

naviera *f* → **naviero,-a.**

naviero,-a I *adj* shipping. – **2** *m,f* (*propietario*) shipowner. – **3 naviera,** *f* (*empresa*) shipping company.

navío *m* vessel, ship.
■ **navío de guerra,** war vessel, warship.

náyade *f* naiad.

nazareno,a I *adj* HIST Nazarene, Nazarite. – **2** *m,f* HIST Nazarene, Nazarite. – **3 nazareno,** *m* (*penitente*) penitent *in Holy Week processions.*
■ **Jesús el Nazareno,** Jesus of Nazareth.

nazarí I *adj* HIST Nazarite. – **2** *mf* HIST Nazarite.
▲ *pl* **nazaríes.**

nazarita *adj* → **nazarí.**

nazi I *adj* Nazi. – **2** *mf* Nazi.

nazismo *m* Nazism.

N.B. *abr* (*nota bene*) note well; (*abreviatura*) N.B, n.b.

n/c *abr* (*nuestra cuenta*) our account.

n/cta *abr* (*nuestra cuenta*) our account.

NE² *sím* (*nordeste*) northeast; (*símbolo*) NE.

Neandertal *adj* Neanderthal.

neblina *f* mist.

neblinoso,-a *adj* misty.

nebulizador *m* nebulizer.

nebulosa *f* → **nebuloso,-a.**

nebuloso,-a I *adj* cloudy, hazy. **2** *fig* vague, nebulous. – **3 nebulosa,** *f* ASTRON nebula.

necedad I *f* (*ignorancia*) stupidity, foolishness. **2** (*acción*) stupid thing to do; (*comentario*) stupid thing to say.
● **decir necedades,** to talk nonsense, talk rubbish.

necesariamente *adv* necessarily.

necesario,-a *adj* necessary: *fue necesario hacerlo,* it had to be done; *es necesario que acudas a la reunión,* you must attend the meeting.
● **hacerse necesario,-a,** (*algo*) to be required; (*persona*) to become vital, become essential. ‖ **si fuera necesario,** if need be, if necessary.

neceser I *m* (*bolsa de aseo*) toilet bag. **2** (*de maquillaje*) make-up bag, make-up kit. **3** (*de viaje*) vanity case. **4** (*de costura*) sewing kit.
■ **neceser de viaje,** vanity case.

necesidad I *f* necessity, need. **2** (*hambre*) hunger. **3** (*pobreza*) poverty, want.
● **de necesidad,** essential. ‖ **hacer sus necesidades,** *fam* to relieve os. ‖ **no hay necesidad de ...,** there's no need to ... ‖ **pasar necesidades,** to be in need, suffer hardship.
■ **artículos de primera necesidad,** essentials.

necesitado 418

necesitado,-a *adj* needy, poor.
necesitar *t* to need.
● "se necesita chico", "boy wanted".
necio,-a 1 *adj* stupid. – 2 *m,f* imbecile, idiot.
nécora *f* fiddler crab.
necrofilia *f* necrophilia.
necrófilo,-a 1 *adj* necrophiliac. – 2 *m,f* necrophiliac.
necrología 1 *f (biografía)* obituary. 2 *(lista)* obituaries *pl.*
necrológico,-a 1 *adj* obituary, necrological. – 2 necrológicas, *fpl (sección prensa)* obituaries *pl.*
■ nota necrológica, obituary.
necrópolis *f* necropolis.
▲ *pl necrópolis.*
necrosis *f* necrosis.
▲ *pl necrosis.*
néctar *m* nectar.
nectarina *f* nectarine.
neerlandés,-esa 1 *adj* Dutch. – 2 *m,f (persona - hombre)* Dutchman; *(- mujer)* Dutch woman. 3 *(idioma)* Dutch.
nefando,-a *adj* nefarious, unspeakable.
nefasto,-a 1 *adj (desgraciado)* unlucky, ill-fated, bad. 2 *(perjudicial)* harmful, fatal.
nefrítico,-a *adj* nephritic.
■ cólico nefrítico, nephrocolic.
nefritis *f* nephritis.
▲ *pl nefritis.*
negación 1 *f (de un ideal, derecho)* negation. 2 *(de una acusación)* denial. 3 *(negativa)* refusal. 4 *(en gramática)* negative.
negado,-a 1 *adj (inepto)* hopeless, useless. – 2 *m,f* no-hoper, total loss.
● ser negado,-a para algo, to be hopeless at sth., be useless at sth., be a total loss at sth.
negar 1 *t (rechazar)* to deny: *lo negó rotundamente,* she denied it categorically. 2 *(no conceder)* to refuse. – 3 negarse, *p* to refuse (a, to): *se negó a devolverme el dinero,* he refused to give me my money back.
● negar con la cabeza, to shake one's head. ‖ negar la entrada a algn., to refuse entrance to sb., not let sb. in. ‖ negarse a sí mismo,-a, to deny os.
▲ *Conjugation model* [48], *like regar.*
negativa *f* → **negativo,-a.**
negativismo *m* negativism.
negativo,-a 1 *adj* negative: *su respuesta ha sido negativa,* his answer was no. – 2 negativa, *f (negación)* negative answer; *(de una acusación)* denial; *(rechazo)* refusal. – 3 negativo, *m (en fotografía)* negative.
negligé *m* negligée, negligee, negligé.
negligencia *f* negligence, carelessness.
negligente 1 *adj* negligent. – 2 *mf* negligent person.
negociable *adj* negotiable.
negociación *f* negotiation.
■ negociación colectiva, collective bargaining.
negociado *m (sección)* department.
negociador,-ra 1 *adj* negotiating. – 2 *m,f* negotiator.
negociante 1 *adj* negotiating. 2 *fam* money-grubbing. – 3 *mf* dealer, merchant. 4 *fam* money-grubber.
negociar 1 *i (comerciar)* to do business, deal (con, in): *negocian con trigo,* they deal in wheat. – 2 *t* POL to negotiate.
▲ *Conjugation model* [12], *like cambiar.*
negocio 1 *m (actividad)* business. 2 *(gestión)* deal, transaction. 3 *(asunto)* affair. 4 *(local)* shop, US store: *hemos abierto un negocio en pleno centro,* we've opened up a new shop right in the centre of town.

● ¡bonito negocio hemos hecho!, *(con ironía)* some deal that was!, some deal that turned out to be! ‖ hablar de negocios, to talk business. ‖ hacer negocio, to make a profit. ‖ hacer un buen negocio, *(comercialmente)* to do a good deal; *(gen)* to do well.
■ hombre de negocios, businessman. ‖ mujer de negocios, businesswoman.
negra *f* → **negro,-a.**
negrear *i* to turn black.
negrero,-a 1 *adj* HIST slave. – 2 *m,f* HIST slave trader. 3 *fam fig* slave driver.
■ barco negrero, slave ship.
negrilla *f* → **negrillo,-a.**
negrillo,-a 1 *adj (color)* blackish. – 2 (letra) negrilla, *f* bold, bold type, boldface.
negrita *f* → **negrilla** [2].
negro,-a 1 *adj (gen)* black. 2 *(oscuro)* dark: *el cielo está negro completamente,* the sky is very dark. 3 *(bronceado)* brown, tanned, suntanned: *me he puesto negra estas vacaciones,* I got really brown on holiday this year. 4 *(poco favorable)* awful, terrible: *llevamos una semana negra,* we've had a terrible week. 5 *(cine, novela)* detective. 6 *(tabaco)* black. – 7 *m,f (hombre)* black (man); *(mujer)* black (woman). – 8 negro, *m (color)* black. 9 *(escritor)* ghostwriter. 10 *(tabaco)* black tobacco. – 11 negra, *f* MÚS crotchet, US quarter note.
● estar negro,-a, *fam (enfadado)* to be cross; *(bronceado)* to be really brown, be really tanned. ‖ negro,-a como la boca de lobo, pitch-black. ‖ negro,-a como un tizón, as black as coal. ‖ pasarlas negras, *fam* to have a rough time of it. ‖ poner negro,-a a algn., to drive sb. up the wall. ‖ ponerse negro,-a, *(persona)* to get angry, get mad; *(ambiente, situación)* to look bad. ‖ tener la negra, *fam* to be unlucky. ‖ trabajar como un negro, to work like a dog, work like a slave. ‖ verlo todo negro, to be very pessimistic. ‖ verse negro,-a para hacer algo, to have a tough time doing sth.: *se veían negros para arreglarlo todo en una tarde,* they had their work cut out to get it all done in one afternoon. ‖ vérselas negras, *fam* to have a tough time.
■ novela negra, detective novel. ‖ peste negra, Black Death.
negroide 1 *adj* Negroid. – 2 *mf* Negro, Negroid.
negror *m* blackness.
negrura *f* blackness.
negruzco,-a *adj* blackish.
nemotecnia *f* → **mnemotecnia.**
nemotécnico,-a *adj* → **mnemotécnico,-a.**
nene,-a 1 *m,f (niño)* baby boy; *(niña)* baby girl. 2 *(apelativo)* baby.
nenúfar *m* water lily.
neoclasicismo *m* neoclassicism.
neoclásico,-a 1 *adj* neoclassic. – 2 *m,f* neoclassicist.
neófito,-a *m,f* neophyte.
neolítico,-a 1 *adj* neolithic. – 2 neolítico, *m* Neolithic.
neologismo *m* neologism.
neón *m* neon.
neonatal *adj* neonatal.
neonato,-a *m,f* neonate.
neonatología *f* neonatology.
neorrealismo *m* neorealism.
Nepal *m* Nepal.
nepalés,-esa 1 *adj* Nepalese, Nepali. – 2 *m,f (persona)* Nepalese, Nepali. – 3 nepalés, *m (idioma)* Nepalese, Nepali.
nepalí *adj-mf-m* → **nepalés,-esa.**

nepotismo *m* nepotism.
Neptuno *m* Neptune.
nereida *f* nereid.
nervadura 1 *f* ARQ ribs *pl.* 2 BOT nervures *pl.*
nervio 1 *m* ANAT nerve. 2 BOT nervure, vein. 3 (*tendón de la carne*) sinew. 4 ARQ rib. 5 (*de un libro*) rib. 6 (*vigor*) energy, vitality. – 7 nervios, *mpl* nerves.
● ataque de nervios, fit of panic, attack of nerves. ‖ estar mal de los nervios, *fam* to suffer with one's nerves. ‖ ponerle los nervios de punta a algn., to get on sb.'s nerves. ‖ ser puro nervio, to be a real live wire. ‖ tener los nervios de punta, to be on edge.
■ nervio óptico, optical nerve.
nerviosidad *f* → **nerviosismo**.
nerviosismo 1 *m* (*excitación*) nervousness. 2 (*inquietud*) disquiet.
nervioso,-a 1 *adj* (*gen*) nervous. 2 (*excitable*) excitable. 3 (*intranquilo*) nervous, uptight, edgy.
● poner nervioso,-a a algn., to get on sb.'s nerves. ‖ ponerse nervioso,-a, (*intranquilizarse*) to get nervous; (*impacientarse*) to get all excited; (*aturullarse*) to get flustered.
nervudo,-a *adj* ANAT sinewy, wiry.
neto,-a 1 *adj* (*peso, cantidad*) net. 2 (*claro*) neat, clear.
neumático,-a 1 *adj* pneumatic. – 2 neumático, *m* tyre (us tire).
neumonía *f* pneumonia.
neumotórax *m* pneumothorax.
neura 1 *f fam* obsession: *ahora le ha dado la neura de que no quiere ir a clase,* now he's got it into his head that he doesn't want to go to school. – 2 *adj fam* neurotic. – 3 *mf* neurotic.
neuralgia *f* neuralgia.
neurálgico,-a 1 *adj* MED neuralgic. 2 *fig* (*fundamental*) key, main: *el centro neurálgico de la organización,* the nerve centre of the organization.
neurastenia *f* neurasthenia.
neurasténico,-a 1 *adj* neurasthenic. – 2 *m,f* neurasthenic person.
neurocirujano,-a *m,f* neurosurgeon.
neurología *f* neurology.
neurólogo,-a *m,f* neurologist.
neurona *f* neuron, neurone.
neurosis *f* neurosis.
▲ *pl* neurosis.
neurótico,-a 1 *adj* neurotic. – 2 *m,f* neurotic.
neurovegetativo,-a *adj* neurovegetative.
neutral *adj* neutral.
neutralidad *f* neutrality.
neutralización *f* neutralization.
neutralizar *t* to neutralize.
neutro,-a 1 *adj* neutral. 2 LING neuter. – 3 neutro, *m* neuter.
neutrón *m* neutron.
nevada *f* → **nevado,-a**.
nevado,-a 1 *adj* (*gen*) covered with snow; (*montaña*) snow-capped. – 2 nevada, *f* snowfall.
nevar *i* to snow.
▲ *Conjugation model* [27], *like* **acertar***; used only in the 3rd person; it does not take a subject subject.*
nevera 1 *f* (*eléctrica*) fridge, refrigerator. 2 (*para excursiones*) cool box. 3 *fam fig* freezing cold place: *esta casa es una nevera,* this house is freezing.
nevero *m* snowfield, ice field.
nevisca *f* light snowfall.

newton *m* newton.
▲ *pl* newtons.
nexo 1 *m* (*union*) connection, link. 2 LING connective.
■ nexo de unión, nexus.
n/f *abr* (*nuestro favor*) our favour (us favor); (*abreviatura*) our fav.
n/g *abr* (*nuestro giro*) our order; (*abreviatura*) our o.
ni 1 *conj* neither, nor: *no tengo tiempo ni ganas,* I don't have the time or the inclination. 2 (*ni siquiera*) not even: *no lo quiero ni regalado,* I wouldn't want it even if they were giving it away; *no tengo tiempo ni para comer,* I don't even have time to eat.
● ¡ni hablar!, no way! ‖ ni que, it's not as if: *ni que fuera tonta,* it's not as if I were stupid!; *ni que hubiera sido millonario,* anyone would think he were a millonaire!
Nicaragua *f* Nicaragua.
nicaragüeño,-a 1 *adj* Nicaraguan. – 2 *m,f* Nicaraguan.
nicho 1 *m* (*funerario*) wall tomb. 2 (*para escultura*) niche.
■ nicho ecológico, niche.
nicotina *f* nicotine.
nidada *f* (*huevos*) clutch; (*polluelos*) brood.
nidal *m* nest.
nidificar *i* to nest.
nido *m* nest.
● caerse del nido, *fig* to be born yesterday: *¿qué crees, que me acabo de caer del nido o qué?,* what do you take me for? I wasn't born yesterday you know!
■ nido de abeja, smocking. ‖ nido de amor, love nest. ‖ nido de ladrones, den of thieves.
niebla 1 *f* (*nubes*) fog. 2 *fig* mist.
■ niebla tóxica, smog.
nieto,-a *m,f* grandchild; (*niño*) grandson; (*niña*) granddaughter: *tiene muchos nietos,* he has many grandchildren.
nieve *f* snow.
NIF *abr* (*Número de Identificación Fiscal*) *tax identification number.*
Níger *m* Niger.
Nigeria *f* Nigeria.
nigeriano,-a 1 *adj* Nigerian. – 2 *m,f* Nigerian.
nigromancia *f* necromancy.
nigromante *mf* necromancer.
nigromántico,-a 1 *adj* necromantic. – 2 *m,f* necromancer.
nihilismo *m* nihilism.
nihilista 1 *adj* nihilistic. – 2 *mf* nihilist.
Nilo el Nilo, *m* the Nile.
nilón *m* nylon.
nimbado,-a *adj* nimbused.
nimbo *m* nimbus.
nimiedad 1 *f* (*cualidad*) smallness, triviality. 2 (*cosa nimia*) trifle.
nimio,-a *adj* insignificant, trivial.
ninfa *f* nymph.
ninfómana *f* nymphomaniac.
ninfomanía *f* nymphomania.
ningún *adj* → **ninguno,-a**.
● de ningún modo, in no way.
▲ *Used before a masculine singular noun.*
ninguno,-a 1 *adj* no, not any: *aquí no veo ningún bolígrafo azul,* I can't see any blue biro here; *no lo encuentro por ningún sitio,* I can't find it anywhere; *no tengo ningunas ganas de salir,* I don't feel like going out at all. – 2 *pron* (*persona*) nobody, no one: *ninguno lo vio,* no one

saw it. **3** (*objeto*) not any, none: *ninguno me gusta,* I don't like any of them; *de ese color no me queda ninguna,* I don't have any left in that colour.
● **en ninguna parte,** nowhere. ‖ **ninguna cosa,** nothing. ‖ **ninguno,-a de nosotros** *(ellos etc),* none of us (*them etc*).
▲ *See also* **ningún**.

niña *f* → **niño,-a.**

niñada *f* → **niñería.**

niñato,-a *m,f fam* brat.

niñera *f* → **niñero,-a.**

niñería 1 *f* (*chiquillada*) childishness, childish behaviour (us behavior). **2** (*nimiedad*) trifle.
● **hacer niñerías,** to be childish.

niñero,-a 1 *adj* fond of children: *el abuelo es muy niñero,* granddad loves children. – **2 niñera,** *f* nanny.

niñez *f* (*de una persona*) childhood; (*de una idea, proyecto*) infancy.

niño,-a 1 *m,f* (*gen*) child; (*chico*) boy, little boy; (*chica*) girl, little girl: *tienen dos niños y una niña,* they've got two boys and a girl. **2** (*bebé*) baby: *¿para cuándo es el niño?,* when is the baby due?; *ha tenido una niña preciosa,* she's had a beautiful baby girl. **3** *pey* (*en comportamiento*) baby; (*en experiencia*) child: *no seas niño y acábate la cena,* don't be such a baby, eat up your dinner!; *en cuestiones de dinero es un niño aún,* in money matters he's still very naive. – **4 niños,** *mpl* children, kids.
● **de niño,-a,** as a child. ‖ **desde niño,-a,** from childhood: *vivo en esta casa desde muy niña,* I've lived in this house since I was a little girl. ‖ **la niña bonita,** *the number* 15. ‖ *... **ni que niño muerto,** fam* my foot!: *¡qué moto ni qué niño muerto!,* motorbike, my foot! ‖ **querer a algn. como a la niña de sus ojos,** to adore sb., have a soft spot for sb. ‖ **ser como la niña de sus ojos para algn.,** to be the apple of sb.'s eye.
■ **niña del ojo,** pupil. ‖ **niño,-a bien,** rich kid. ‖ **niño,-a bonito,-a,** (*de los padres*) spoilt child; (*de otros*) pet: *es el niño bonito del profe,* he's the teacher's pet. ‖ **niño,-a probeta,** test-tube baby. ‖ **niño de papá,** rich kid.

nipón,-ona 1 *adj* Nipponese. – **2** *m,f* Nipponese.

niquel *m* nickel.

niquelado,-a 1 *adj* nickel-plated. – **2 niquelado,** *m* nickelling.

niquelar *t* to nickel.

niqui *m* T-shirt.

nirvana *m* nirvana.

níscalo *m* milk cap.

níspero 1 *m* (*fruto*) medlar. **2** (*árbol*) medlar tree.

nitidez 1 *f* (*transparencia*) clearness, transparency. **2** (*claridad*) accuracy, precision. **3** (*de imagen*) sharpness.

nítido,-a 1 *adj* (*transparente*) clear, transparent. **2** (*claro*) accurate, precise. **3** (*imagen*) sharp.

nitrato *m* nitrate.

nítrico,-a *adj* nitric.

nitrito *m* nitrite.

nitrogenado,-a *adj* nitrogenous.

nitrógeno *m* nitrogen.

nitroglicerina *f* nitroglycerine.

nitroso,-a *adj* nitrous.

nivel 1 *m* (*altura*) level, height: *el nivel de las aguas de un río,* the water level of a river; *el sofa está al nivel de la ventana,* the sofa is level with the window. **2** (*categoría*) level, standard, degree: *no están al mismo nivel intelectual,* they are not at the same intellectual level; *mis alumnos tienen muy buen nivel de inglés,* my students' English is very good. **3** (*instrumento*) level.

● **a nivel de,** as for: *a nivel de gastos,* as far as expenses are concerned, regarding expenses. ‖ **al más alto nivel,** at the highest level.
■ **nivel de producción,** production level. ‖ **nivel de vida,** standard of living. ‖ **nivel del mar,** sea level.

nivelación 1 *f* (*de un tereno*) levelling (us leveling). **2** (*de diferencias, posturas*) reconciliation.

nivelador,-ra 1 *adj* levelling (us leveling). – **2** *m,f* leveller (us leveler).

nivelar 1 *t* (*gen*) to level out, level off. **2** (*diferencias etc*) to reconcile.

níveo,-a *adj lit* snow-white.

Niza *f* Nice.

n/L *abr* (*nuestra letra, nuestra letra de crédito*) our letter of credit; (*abreviatura*) our L/C.

NNE *sím* (*nordnoreste*) north-northeast; (*abreviatura*) NNE.

NNO *sím* (*nordnoroeste*) north-northwest; (*abreviatura*) NNW.

NO² *sím* (*nordoeste*) northwest; (*símbolo*) NW.

no 1 *adv* no, not: *no, no quiero agua,* no, I don't want any water; *tú no,* not you. **2** (*en frases negativas*) not: *no lo compres,* don't buy it; *ella no es alemana, es belga,* she's not german, she's Belgian; *no me gusta el arroz,* I don't like rice; *no vendrá,* he won't come; *no vinieron,* they didn't come. **3** (*en frases interrogativas*): *¿te gusta, no?,* you like it, don't you?; *¿a que no me pillas?,* I bet you can't catch me; *¿no se habrá apuntado él también, no?,* he wouldn't have signed up as well, would he? **4** (*en comparativas*): *mejor gastarse el dinero ahora que no guardarlo para después,* it's better to spend the money now than to save it for later. **5** (*prefijo*) non-: *la no violencia,* non-violence. – **6** *m* no: *un no rotundo,* a definite no.
● **¡a que no!,** do you want a bet?, what's the bet? ‖ **no bien,** the moment, as soon as: *no bien entró por la puerta vio que faltaba el dinero,* he noticed the moment was missing the moment he came in the door. ‖ **no más,** (*sólo*) only; (*basta de*) no more. ‖ **no obstante,** notwithstanding. ‖ **no sin,** not without: *se marchó, no sin antes expresar su disconformidad,* he left, but not without first expressing his disagreement. ‖ **o, si no,** (*rectificación*) or rather; (*hipótesis*) or otherwise, or if not. ‖ **¡que no!,** I said no!

n/o *abr* (*nuestra orden*) our order; (*abreviatura*) our o.

nobel *m* Nobel prize.
■ **premio Nobel,** Nobel prize.

nobiliario,-a *adj* nobiliary.
■ **título nobiliario,** noble title.

noble 1 *adj* (*gen*) noble; (*madera*) fine. – **2** *mf* (*hombre*) nobleman; (*mujer*) noblewoman. – **3 los nobles,** *mpl* the nobility *sing*.

nobleza 1 *f* (*cualidad*) nobility, honesty, uprightness. **2** (*los nobles*) nobility.

noblote,-a *adj fam* sincere, open.

noche *f* (*gen*) night; (*al atardecer*) evening: *esta noche salimos,* we are going out tonight; *hasta mañana por la noche,* see you tomorrow night; *¡pero, si son las 10 de la noche!,* look at the time, it's ten o'clock!; *llegaremos de noche,* it'll be dark when we arrive.
● **ayer (por la) noche,** last night. ‖ **buenas noches,** (*saludo*) good evening; (*despedida*) good night. ‖ **de noche todos los gatos son pardos,** all cats are grey in the dark. ‖ **hacer noche en,** to spend the night in: *hicimos noche en Belfast,* we stayed overnight in Belfast. ‖ **hacer turno de noche,** to work nights. ‖ **hacerse de noche,** to grow dark. ‖ **la noche de los tiempos,** the

dawn of time. ‖ **noche y día**, day and night. ‖ **pasar mala noche**, to sleep badly, have a bad night. ‖ **pasar la noche en blanco**, not to sleep a wink all night. ‖ **por la noche**, at night, after dark: *llegamos por la noche*, we arrived after dark; *por la noche no abren*, it is not open at night. ‖ **ser de noche**, to be dark. ‖ **ser noche cerrada**, to be pitch dark. ‖ **ser la noche y el día**, to be like chalk and cheese. ‖ **de la noche a la mañana**, *fig* overnight.
■ **media noche**, midnight. ‖ **noche toledana**, *fam* sleepless night.

Nochebuena *f* Christmas Eve.

Nochevieja *f* New Year's Eve.

noción 1 *f* notion, idea. – 2 **nociones**, *fpl* smattering *sing*, basic knowledge *sing*.
● **perder la noción del tiempo**, to lose track of time.

nocividad *f* noxiousness.

nocivo,-a *adj* noxious, harmful.

noctambulismo *m* nocturnality.

noctámbulo,-a 1 *adj* nocturnal. – 2 *m,f fam* (*trasnochador*) night owl, US night hawk.

noctívago,-a *adj lit* nocturnal.

nocturnidad 1 *f* (*noche*) night-time. 2 JUR *the aggravating circumstance of a crime having been committed at night.*

nocturno,-a 1 *adj* (*gen*) nocturnal; (*vida*) night; (*clase*) evening. 2 ZOOL nocturnal. – 3 **nocturno**, *m* night school. 4 MÚS nocturne.

NODO *abr* CINEM (*Noticiarios y Documentales Cinematográficos*) *Spanish cinema newsreels* (*shown from 1942 to 1976*).

nodriza 1 *f* (*mujer*) wet nurse. 2 (*vehículo*) supply.
■ **avión nodriza**, supply plane.

nogal *m* walnut tree.

nogalina *f* walnut dye.

nogueral *m* walnut grove.

nómada 1 *adj* nomadic. – 2 *mf* nomad.

nomadismo *m* nomadism.

nombradía *f* fame.

nombrado,-a *adj* well-known.

nombramiento *m* appointment.

nombrar 1 *t* (*dar nombre, mencionar*) to name. 2 (*llamar*) to call. 3 (*designar*) to name, appoint: *lo han nombrado director*, he has been appointed director.

nombre 1 *m* name: *se le conoce más por el nombre de Pepe*, he's better known as Pepe; *¿este cheque va a su nombre?*, is this cheque in your name? 2 LING noun. 3 (*fama*) reputation: *es un cirujano de nombre*, he is a well-known surgeon.
● **a nombre de**, in the name of: *mándalo a nombre del director*, address it to the manager; *va a nombre de todos nosotros*, it's addressed to all of us; *abrimos una cuenta a nombre de los dos*, we opened a joint account. ‖ **conocer a algn. de nombre**, to know sb. by name. ‖ **en el nombre del Padre, del Hijo ...**, in the name of the Father, the Son ... ‖ **en nombre de**, on behalf of. ‖ **llamar a las cosas por su nombre**, *fig* to call a spade a spade. ‖ **no tener nombre**, *fig* to be unspeakable.
■ **nombre artístico**, stage name. ‖ **nombre comercial**, trade name. ‖ **nombre de guerra**, nom de guerre. ‖ **nombre de pila**, first name, Christian name. ‖ **nombre propio**, proper noun. ‖ **nombre y apellidos**, full name *sing*.

nomenclador *m* → **nomenclatura**.

nomenclátor *m* → **nomenclatura**.

nomenclatura *f* nomenclature.

nomeolvides 1 *m* (*flor*) forget-me-not. 2 (*pulsera*) identity bracelet.
▲ *pl* **nomeolvides**.

nómina 1 *f* (*plantilla*) payroll. 2 (*sueldo*) pay cheque (US check); (*papel*) pay slip. 3 (*lista*) list.
● **estar en nómina**, to be on the staff.

nominación *f* nomination.

nominal *adj* nominal.

nominalismo *m* nominalism.

nominalista 1 *adj* nominalist, nominalistic. – 2 *mf* nominalist.

nominalización *f* substantivization.

nominalizar *t* to substantivize.

nominar *t* to nominate.

nominativo,-a 1 *adj* (*cheque*) personal: *un talón nominativo a favor de ...*, a cheque made out to ..., a cheque payable to ... 2 LING nominative. – 3 **nominativo**, *m* nominative.

non 1 *adj* (*número*) odd. – 2 *m* odd number.
● **pares y nones**, odds and evens.

nonagenario,-a 1 *adj* nonagenarian. – 2 *m,f* nonagenarian.

nonagésimo,-a 1 *adj* ninetieth. – 2 *m,f* ninetieth.

nones *interj* no way!: *me ha dicho que nones*, the answer is no.

nono,-a *adj* → **noveno,-a**.

noquear *t* to knock out.

norcoreano,-a 1 *adj* North Korean. – 2 *m,f* North Korean.

nordeste 1 *m* northeast. 2 (*viento*) northeasterly.

nórdico,-a 1 *adj* (*del norte*) northern. 2 (*de los países del norte*) Nordic. – 3 *m,f* (*persona*) Scandinavian. – 4 **nórdico**, *m* (*idioma*) Norse.
■ **funda nórdica**, duvet cover.

noreste *m* → **nordeste**.

noria 1 *f* (*para agua*) water-wheel. 2 (*de feria*) big wheel.

norirlandés,-esa 1 *adj* Northern Irish. – 2 *m,f* (*hombre*) Northern Irishman; (*mujer*) Northern Irishwoman.

norma *f* norm, rule.
■ **norma de conducta**, rule of conduct.

normal 1 *adj* (*corriente, habitual*) normal, usual, average; (*lógico*) normal, natural. – 2 *f* (*escuela*) teacher training college. 3 (*gasolina*) two-star petrol, US regular gasoline. 4 (*en geometría*) perpendicular, normal.

normalidad *f* normality: *las elecciones transcurrieron en la más absoluta normalidad*, the elections went off without incident; *normalidad absoluta en las carreteras españolas*, traffic is completely normal on Spanish roads.
● **con normalidad**, normally, as normal. ‖ **volver a la normalidad**, to return to normal.

normalización *f* normalization.

normalizar *t* to normalize, restore to normal.
▲ *Conjugation model* [4], *like realizar*.

Normandía *f* Normandy.
■ **el desembarco en Normandía**, the Normandy Landings *pl*, D-Day.

normando,-a 1 *adj* (*de Normandía*) Norman. 2 HIST (*germánico*) Norse. – 3 *m,f* (*de Normandía*) Norman.

normativa *f* → **normativo,-a**.

normativo,-a 1 *adj* normative. – 2 **normativa**, *f* rules *pl*, regulations *pl*.

noroeste 1 *m* northwest: *navegamos en dirección noroeste*, we're sailing in a northwestwardly direction. 2 (*viento*) northwesterly.

norte 1 *m* north: *la estrella polar señala el norte,* the Pole Star shows where north is; *vive al norte de la región,* he lives to the north of the region; *los países del norte,* the Northern countries; *nos dirigimos hacia el norte,* we're heading North. **2** *(viento)* northerly wind. **3** *fig (dirección, sentido)* direction; *(objetivo)* aim.
● **perder el norte,** to lose sight of one's objectives, lose one's way. ‖ **sin norte,** aimless.
■ **norte magnético,** magnetic North.

Norteamérica *f* (*América del Norte*) North America; (*Estados Unidos*) America.

norteamericano,-a 1 *adj* (*de América del Norte*) North American; (*de Estados Unidos*) American. **– 2** *m,f* (*de América del Norte*) North American; (*de Estados Unidos*) American.

Noruega *f* Norway.

noruego,-a 1 *adj* Norwegian. **– 2** *m,f* (*persona*) Norwegian. **– 3 noruego,** *m* (*idioma*) Norwegian.

nos 1 *pron* (*complemento*) us: *nos van a pillar,* they're going to catch us; *nos dijo que no nos moviéramos,* he told us not to move. **2** (*uso reflexivo*) ourselves: *nos lavamos,* we wash ourselves. **3** (*uso recíproco*) each other: *nos vemos mucho,* we see each other often.

nosotros,-as 1 *pron* (*sujeto*) we: *nosotros no fuimos,* we didn't go; *¿quién viene? –¡nosotros!,* who's coming? –we are! **2** (*complemento*) us: *con nosotros,-as,* with us.

nostalgia 1 *f* nostalgia. **2** (*añoranza*) homesickness.

nostálgico,-a *adj* nostalgic.

nota 1 *f* (*anotación*) note: *déjale una nota diciendo que nos hemos ido,* leave him a note telling him that we've left. **2** (*calificación*) mark, grade; (*calificación alta*) high mark: *me han puesto muy mala nota en inglés,* I got a very bad mark in English; *mi examen estaba para nota,* my paper deserved a high mark; *si quieres nota tendrás que presentarte al oral,* if you want a higher mark you'll have to go for a viva. **3** (*cuenta*) bill: *¿nos trae la nota por favor?,* could you bring us the bill please? **4** *fig (detalle)* touch: *las velas le daban una nota de distinción a la cena,* the candles gave the dinner a touch of class. **5** MÚS note. **– 6** *m arg (tipo)* bloke.
● **dar la nota,** *fam* to draw attention to os. ‖ **sacar buenas notas,** to get good marks. ‖ **tomar nota de algo,** (*apuntar*) to note sth. down; (*fijarse*) to take note of sth.

notable 1 *adj* (*apreciable*) noticeable; (*considerable, marcado*) considerable, remarkable: *la diferencia entre un coche y otro es notable,* there's a considerable difference between one car and another. **2** (*digno de mención*) noteworthy, notable. **3** (*ilustre*) well-known. **– 4** *m* (*persona*) dignitary, notable. **5** (*calificación*) mark equivalent to between 70% and 80% in the Spanish marking system.

notación *f* notation.

notar 1 *t* (*percibir*) to notice: *he notado que han subido los precios,* I've noticed they've put their prices up. **2** (*sentir*) to feel: *noto un poco de calor,* I feel a bit hot; *la noto un poco triste últimamente,* she looks a bit down lately. **– 3 notarse,** *p* (*percibirse*) to be noticeable, be evident, show: *apenas se le nota la cicatriz,* you can hardly see his scar; *¿se nota que no me he peinado?,* can you tell I haven't combed my hair? **4** (*sentirse*) to feel.
● **hacer notar,** to point out. ‖ **hacerse notar,** to draw attention to os. ‖ **se nota que ...,** one can see that ...

notaría 1 *f* (*profesión*) profession of notary. **2** (*despacho*) notary's office.

notariado 1 *m* (*profesión*) profession of notary. **2** (*conjunto de notarios*) notaries *pl.*

notarial *adj* notarial.

notario,-a *m,f* notary, notary public.

noticia 1 *f* (*información*) news *pl*: *una noticia,* a piece of news; *acaba de llegarnos la noticia de que ...,* news is just coming in of ...; *eso no es noticia,* that's nothing new; *¿has tenido noticias de Laura?,* have you had any news from Laura?, have you heard anything from Laura?; *tengo noticias para ti,* I've got news for you. **2** (*conocimiento*) idea: *no tenía noticia de que hubieran quebrado,* I had no idea they had gone bankrupt. **– 3 las noticias,** *fpl* the news.
● **dar la noticia,** to break the news. ‖ **¡primera noticia!,** that's news to me! ‖ **ser noticia,** to be in the news.
■ **noticia bomba,** bombshell.

noticiario *m* news.

notición *m fam* bombshell.

notificación *f* notification.
■ **notificación judicial,** summons *sing.*

notificar *t* to notify, inform.
▲ *Conjugation model* [1], *like* sacar.

notoriedad 1 *f* (*fama*) fame, prestige. **2** (*evidencia*) obviousness.

notorio,-a *adj* well-known.

novatada 1 *f* (*broma*) practical joke (*played on a new student, recruit, etc*). **2** (*fallo*) beginner's mistake.
● **pagar la novatada,** to learn the hard way.

novato,-a 1 *adj* (*persona*) inexperienced, green. **– 2** *m,f* (*principiante*) novice, beginner. **3** (*universidad*) fresher (US freshman).

novecentismo *m* Spanish literary movement of the 1900s; spirit of the 20th century.

novecientos,-as 1 *adj* nine hundred; (*ordinal*) ninehundredth. **– 2 novecientos,** *mpl* nine hundred.
▲ *See also* seis.

novedad 1 *f* (*cualidad*) newness. **2** (*cosa nueva*) novelty. **3** (*cambio*) change, innovation: *está introduciendo muchas novedades en el departamento,* he's making a lot of changes in the department; *no ha habido ninguna novedad desde que te fuiste,* nothing has changed since you left. **4** (*noticia*) news: *¡vaya una novedad, hace tiempo que lo sabíamos!,* that's nothing new - we've known for quite a while!
● **sin novedad,** without incident. ‖ **sin novedad en el frente,** all's quiet on the Western front.
■ **últimas novedades,** (*en ropa*) latest fashion *sing*; (*en libros, discos*) latest releases.

novedoso,-a *adj* novel.

novel 1 *adj* (*escritor, escultor*) novice. **– 2** *m* beginner.

novela 1 *f* novel. **2** (*en TV, radio*) serial.
■ **novela corta,** novella. ‖ **novela de caballerías,** romance of chivalry. ‖ **novela negra / novela policíaca,** detective story. ‖ **novela por entregas,** serial. ‖ **novela rosa,** romance, novelette.

novelar 1 *t* to novelize, convert into a novel. **– 2** *i* to write novels.

novelero,-a 1 *adj* (*aficionado a leer novelas*) fond of reading novels. **2** (*fantasioso*) highly imaginative. **3** (*chismoso*) gossipy.

novelesco,-a 1 *adj* (*de la novela*) fictional, novelistic. **2** (*de novela*) fiction-like.

novelista *mf* novelist.

novelística *f →* **novelístico,-a.**

novelístico,-a 1 *adj* novelistic. **– 2 novelística,** *f* novel, fiction.

novena *f* REL novena.

noveno,-a 1 *adj* ninth. – **2** *m,f* ninth.
  ▲ *See also* **sexto**.
noventa 1 *adj* ninety. – **2** *m* ninety.
  ▲ *See also* **sesenta**.
noventayochista *mf* member *of the* **Generación del 98** *generation of Spanish writers.*
novia *f* → **novio,-a**.
noviazgo *m* engagement.
noviciado *m* noviciate, novitiate.
novicio,-a 1 *m,f* (*principiante*) beginner. **2** REL novice.
noviembre *m* November.
  ▲ *See also* **marzo**.
noviero,-a *adj fam* (*chico*) girl-mad; (*chica*) boy-mad: *ella es muy noviera,* she's totally boy-mad.
novilla *f* → **novillo,-a**.
novillada 1 *f* (*corrida*) bullfight with young bulls. **2** (*novillos*) herd of young bulls.
novillero,-a 1 *m,f* (*torero*) novice bullfighter. **2** (*estudiante*) truant.
novillo,-a. 1 novillo, *m* young bull. – **2** novilla, *f* heifer.
  ● hacer novillos, *fam* to play truant, skip school, us play hooky.
novilunio *m* new moon.
novio,-a. 1 novio, *m* (*amigo*) boyfriend; (*prometido*) fiancé; (*en boda*) bridegroom. – **2** novia, *f* (*amiga*) girlfriend; (*prometida*) fiancée; (*en boda*) bride.
  ● quedarse compuesto y sin novio, *fam* to be left in the lurch, be left high and dry. ‖ los novios, the bride and groom. ‖ ser novios, (*estar prometidos*) to be engaged; (*salir juntos*) to be going out.
  ■ viaje de novios, honeymoon.
novísimo,-a *adj* very new.
Nª. Sª. *abr* Our Lady.
N.S. *abr* (**Nuestro Señor**) Our Lord.
nto. *abr* (**neto**) net; (*abreviatura*) n.
nubarrón 1 *m* (*nube*) storm cloud. **2** *fam fig* cloud on the horizon.
nube 1 *f* cloud. **2** *fig* (*multitud - de personas*) swarm, crowd; (*- de insectos*) cloud.
  ● caído,-a de las nubes, out of the blue. ‖ estar por las nubes, (*precio*) to be sky-high. ‖ estar en las nubes / vivir en las nubes, to have one's head in the clouds. ‖ poner a algn. por las nubes, *fig* to praise sb. to the skies.
  ■ nube de verano, (*nube*) sudden summer storm; (*enfado*) storm in a teacup.
núbil *adj* nubile.
nublado,-a 1 *adj* cloudy, overcast. – **2** nublado, *m* storm cloud.
nublar 1 *t* (*cielo*) to cloud. – **2** nublarse, *p* to cloud over.
nublo *adj* cloudy.
nubosidad *f* cloudiness.
  ■ nubosidad variable, variable cloud cover.
nuboso,-a *adj* cloudy.
nuca *f* nape (of the neck): *con las manos en la nuca,* hands behind one's neck.
nuclear 1 *adj* nuclear. – **2** *f* nuclear power station.
núcleo 1 *m* nucleus. **2** (*parte central*) core. **3** (*grupo de gente*) circle, group.
  ■ núcleo urbano, city centre (us center).
nudillo *m* knuckle.
nudismo *m* nudism.
nudista 1 *adj* nudist. – **2** *mf* nudist.
nudo 1 *m* knot: *hazme un nudo en este hilo,* tie a knot in this thread for me; *¿me haces el nudo de la corbata?,*

can you tie my tie for me? **2** *fig* (*vínculo*) link, tie. **3** (*de un argumento*) climax. **4** (*en madera*) knot. **5** (*unidad de velocidad*) knot.
  ● el nudo de la cuestión, the heart of the matter. ‖ hacer un nudo, to tie a knot. ‖ hacérsele a uno un nudo en la garganta, *fig* to get a lump in one's throat.
  ■ nudo corredizo, slip-knot. ‖ nudo ferroviario, junction. ‖ nudo gordiano, Gordian knot. ‖ nudo de carreteras, spaghetti junction. ‖ nudo marinero, sailor's knot.
nudosidad *f* knottiness.
nudoso,-a *adj* (*madera*) knotty, knobbly; (*manos, vara*) gnarled.
nuera *f* daughter-in-law.
nuestro,-a 1 *adj* our, of ours: *éste es nuestro colegio,* this is our school; *un amigo nuestro,* a friend of ours. – **2** *pron* ours: *este libro es nuestro,* this book is ours.
  ● la nuestra, *fam* our chance. ‖ lo nuestro, (*relación*) our relationship, us; (*asunto*) our business; (*actividad*) our thing. ‖ los nuestros, *fam* our side *sing,* our people.
nueva *f* → **nuevo,-a**.
nuevamente *adv* again.
nueve 1 *adj* nine; (*noveno*) ninth. – **2** *m* nine.
  ▲ *See also* **seis**.
nuevo,-a 1 *adj* new. **2** (*adicional*) further. – **3** *m,f* newcomer; (*principiante*) beginner; (*universidad*) fresher (us freshman). – **4** nueva, *f* tidings *pl.*
  ● de nuevo, again. ‖ coger a algn. de nuevas, to take sb. by surprise. ‖ estar (como) nuevo,-a, (*objeto*) to be as good as new; (*persona*) to feel like new, feel as good as new. ‖ hacerse de nuevas, to pretend not to know. ‖ ¿qué hay de nuevo?, *fam* what's new?
  ■ la buena nueva, glad tidings *pl.*
nuez *f* BOT walnut.
  ● rebanar la nuez a algn., *fam* to slit sb.'s throat.
  ■ nuez (de Adán), Adam's apple. ‖ nuez moscada, nutmeg.
nulidad 1 *f* (*ineptitud*) incompetence. **2** (*persona*) hopeless person. **3** JUR nullity.
  ● conceder la nulidad de un matrimonio, to have a marriage annulled. ‖ ser una nulidad (para algo), to be useless (at sth.).
nulo,-a 1 *adj* (*persona*) useless, totally inept. **2** (*sin valor*) null and void, invalid.
  ● ser nulo,-a para algo, to be useless at sth.
  ■ voto nulo, invalid vote.
núm. *abr* (*número*) number; (*abreviatura*) n.
numantino,-a 1 *adj* HIST Numantian. **2** *fig* (*resistencia*) heroic. – **3** *m,f* Numantian.
numen *m* lit muse.
  ■ numen poético, poetic inspiration.
numeración 1 *f* (*proceso*) numbering. **2** (*conjunto*) numbers *pl* **3** (*sistema*) numbers *pl,* numerals *pl.*
  ■ numeración arábiga, Arabic numerals *pl.* ‖ numeración decimal, decimal system. ‖ numeración romana, Roman numerals *pl.*
numerador *m* numerator.
numeral 1 *adj* numeral. – **2** *m* numeral.
numerar 1 *t* to number. – **2** numerarse, *p* MIL to number off.
  ● sin numerar, unnumbered.
numerario,-a *adj* with tenure, permanent.
  ■ profesor,-ra numerario,-a, *lecturer who has tenure, lecturer who has a permanent contract.* ‖ profesor,-ra no numerario,-a, *lecturer without tenure.*
numerarse *p* → **numerar**.

numérico,-a *adj* numerical.
número 1 *m* (*gen*) number. 2 (*de una publicación*) number, issue. 3 (*de zapatos*) size: *¿qué número calzas?*, what's your shoe size?, what size shoe do you take? 4 (*de un espectáculo*) act. 5 (*de lotería*) lottery ticket number. 6 (*cargo sin graduación*) officer. 7 LING number. 8 *fam* scene. 9 *fam* (*persona*) case: *tenemos un profesor que es un número*, we have a teacher who's a real case.
● **en números redondos**, in round figures. ‖ **en números rojos**, in the red. ‖ **hacer números**, to do the figures. ‖ **montar un número**, *fam* to make a scene. ‖ **pedir número**, to take a numbered ticket. ‖ **ser el número uno**, to be the number one. ‖ **ser miembro de número**, to be a full member. ‖ **sin número**, (*edificio*) unnumbered; (*en abundancia*) countless.
■ **número arábigo**, Arabic numeral. ‖ **número atrasado**, back number. ‖ **número de matrícula**, registration number, US license number. ‖ **número de serie**, serial number. ‖ **número entero**, whole number. ‖ **número extraordinario**, (*en prensa*) special edition, special issue. ‖ **número fraccionario**, fraction. ‖ **número impar**, odd number. ‖ **número ordinal**, ordinal number. ‖ **número par**, even number. ‖ **número primo**, prime number. ‖ **número quebrado**, fraction. ‖ **número romano**, Roman numeral.
numeroso,-a *adj* numerous: *son familia numerosa*, they're a large family.
numerus clausus *mpl* numerus clausus, quota.
numismática *f* → **numismático,-a**.
numismático,-a 1 *adj* numismatic. – 2 *m,f* numismatist. – 3 **numismática**, *f* numismatics.

nunca 1 *adv* never. 2 (*en interrogativa*) ever: *¿has visto nunca cosa igual?*, have you ever seen anything like it?
● **más que nunca**, more than ever. ‖ **nunca jamás**, never ever. ‖ **nunca más**, never again. ‖ **ser lo nunca visto**, to be unheard of.
nunciatura *f* nunciature.
nuncio *m* nuncio.
■ **nuncio apostólico**, papal nuncio.
nupcial *adj* (*marcha, tarta*) wedding; (*misa*) nuptial; (*lecho*) marriage.
nupcialidad *f* number of weddings.
nupcias *fpl fml* wedding *sing*, nuptials.
● **casarse en segundas nupcias**, to remarry, marry for the second time.
nurse *f* nanny.
nutria *f* otter.
nutrición *f* nutrition.
nutrido,-a 1 *adj* (*alimentado*) nourished. 2 *fig* (*abundante*) large: *nutridos aplausos*, enthusiastic applause.
● **nutrido,-a de**, filled with, abounding in.
■ **bien nutrido,-a**, well-nourished. ‖ **mal nutrido,-a**, undernourished.
nutriente 1 *adj* nutrient. – 2 *m* nutrient.
nutrir 1 *t* (*alimentar*) to feed, nourish. 2 *fig* to encourage. 3 (*abastecer*) to supply (**de**, with). – 4 **nutrirse**, *p* (*alimentarse*) to receive nourishment (**de**, from). 5 *fig* (*abastecerse*) to draw (**de**, on).
nutritivo,-a *adj* nutritious, nourishing.
■ **sustancia nutritiva**, nutrient. ‖ **valor nutritivo**, nutritional value

Ñ

Ñ, ñ *f the fifteenth letter of the Spanish alphabet.*
ñame *m* AM yam.
ñam ñam *interj* yum yum.
ñandú *m* AM rhea.
ñoñería *f (tontería)* inanity, nonsense.
ñoñez 1 *f (sosera)* insipidness, dullness. 2 *(falta de seguridad)* wetness, wimpishness. 3 *(tontería)* inanity, nonsense.

ñoño,-a 1 *adj (soso)* insipid, dull. 2 *(tímido)* shy. 3 *(remilgado)* fussy. 4 *(poco seguro)* wet, drippy, wimpish: *no seas ñoño, no es más que un rasguño,* don't be such a wimp, it's no more than a scratch; *es tan ñoña, no tiene iniciativa,* she's such a drip, she's got no initiative. 5 AM old. – 6 *m,f* drip.
ñoqui *m* gnocchi *pl.*
ñora *f type of* red pepper.
ñu *m* gnu

O, o *f* (la letra) O, o.
● **no saber hacer la o con un canuto,** *fam* to be as thick as two short planks.

o **1** *conj* or: *¿té o café?,* tea or coffee? **2** *(concesiva)* whether ... or: *estudie o no, tiene que aprobar,* whether he studies or not, he has to pass.
● **o ... o ...,** either ... or ...: *o vamos hoy o mañana,* we'll either go today or tomorrow. ‖ **o sea que,** so: *o sea que no vienes,* so you're not coming then; *o sea, que no voy,* in other words, I am not going.
▲ *Often written* **ó** *between numbers.*

O *sím* (*oeste*) west; *(símbolo)* W.

OAA *abr* (*Organización para la Agricultura y la Alimentación*) Food and Agriculture Organisation; *(abreviatura)* FAO.

oasis *m* oasis.
▲ *pl oasis.*

obcecación *f* (*empeño*) obstinacy; (*ofuscación*) blindness.

obcecado,-a *adj* blind: *está obcecado con ella,* he is infatuated with her.

obcecar **1** *t* to blind: *lo obcecan los celos,* he is blinded by jealousy. **– 2 obcecarse,** *p* to be obstinate: *se obcecó en venderlo,* he got it into his head that he wanted to sell it.
▲ *Conjugation model* [1], *like* **sacar.**

ob. cit. *abr* (*obra citada*) in the work cited; (*abreviatura*) op. cit.

obedecer **1** *t* (*autoridad, regla, ley*) to obey: *tú a callar y a obedecer,* shut up and do as you are told; *este niño no obedece,* this child is disobedient. **– 2** *i* (*persona*) to obey. **3** (*responder*) to respond (**a,** to). **4** (*tener por causa*) to be due (**a,** to): *¿a qué obedece su visita?,* what is the reason for your visit?
▲ *Conjugation model* [43], *like* **agradecer.**

obediencia *f* obedience.

obediente *adj* obedient.

obelisco *m* obelisk.

obertura *f* MÚS overture.

obesidad *f* obesity.

obeso,-a *adj* obese.

óbice *m fml* impediment: *eso no es óbice para que dejes de asistir,* that is no reason for you not to attend.

obispado **1** *m* (*diócesis, cargo*) bishopric. **2** (*residencia*) episcopal residence.

obispal *adj* episcopal.

obispo *m* bishop.

óbito *m fml* demise.

obituario **1** *m* (*de una parroquia*) register of deaths. **2** (*de un periódico*) obituary.

objeción *f* objection.
● **poner objeción a algo,** to object to sth. ‖ **poner una objeción,** to raise an objection.
■ **objeción de conciencia,** conscientious objection.

objetante *adj* objecting.

objetar *t* to object: *no tengo nada que objetar,* I have no objections.

objetivar *t* to objectify, present objectively.

objetividad *f* objectivity.

objetivismo *m* objectivism.

objetivo,-a **1** *adj* objective. **– 2 objetivo,** *m* (*fin*) aim, objective. **3** MIL target. **4** (*lente*) lens.

objeto **1** *m* (*cosa*) object. **2** (*fin*) aim, purpose, object: *el objeto de la campaña es recaudar fondos,* the object of the campaign is to raise funds. **3** (*finalidad*) intention: *¿con qué objeto acudió Vd. al domicilio de la acusada?,* with what intention did you visit the home of the accused? **4** (*blanco*) object: *era objeto de gran admiración,* she was an object of great admiration; *fui objeto de grandes muestras de cariño,* I was showered with affection. **5** (*tema*) subject: *el objeto de esta charla es la acupuntura,* the subject of this talk is acupuncture.
● **sin objeto,** pointlessly. ‖ **con objeto de,** in order to. ‖ **no tiene objeto que + subj,** there's no point in + ger: *no tiene objeto que vengas,* there's no point in you coming. ‖ **tener por objeto + inf,** to be designed to + inf.
■ **objetos de regalo,** gifts. ‖ **objetos de valor,** valuables. ‖ **objetos perdidos,** lost property *sing.*

objetor,-ra **1** *adj* objecting, dissenting. **– 2** *m,f* objector.
■ **objetor de conciencia,** conscientious objector.

oblación *f* oblation.

oblea *f* wafer.

oblicuidad *f* obliquity.

oblicuo,-a *adj* oblique.

obligación **1** *f* (*deber*) duty, obligation: *no tengo ninguna obligación de ir,* I am under no obligation to go; *cumplió con su obligación,* he did his duty. **2** FIN bond.
● **antes la obligación que la devoción,** business before pleasure.
■ **obligaciones familiares,** family obligations.

obligacionista *mf* bondholder.

obligado,-a **1** *pp* → **obligar. – 2** *adj* (*forzoso*) required; (*normal*) customary: *la Acrópolis es visita obligada,* visiting the Acropolis is a must; *es cortesía obligada regalar un ramo de flores a la anfitriona,* it is customary to give the hostess a bunch of flowers.
● **estar obligado,-a a algn.,** to be obliged to sb. ‖ **estar obligado,-a a hacer algo,** to be obliged to do sth.

obligar **1** *t* to force, oblige, make. **– 2 obligarse,** *p* to undertake, promise.
● **obligar a algn. a hacer algo,** to force sb. to do sth., make sb. do sth.
▲ *Conjugation model* [7], *like* **llegar.**

obligatoriedad *f* obligatory nature.

obligatorio,-a *adj* compulsory, obligatory.

oblongo,-a *adj* oblong.

obnubilación **1** *f* (*de la vista*) blurring; (*de la mente*) confusion. **2** (*fascinación*) fascination.

obnubilado,-a adj (ofuscado) blinded, dazzled: desde que la conoció está obnubilado, he's been obsessed ever since he met her.

obnubilar 1 t to cloud, blind. 2 (fascinar) to fascinate. – 3 obnubilarse, p to become confused. 4 (quedarse fascinado) to be fascinated, be amazed.

oboe m oboe.

obpo. abr (obispo) bishop.

obra 1 f (trabajo) work. 2 LIT (obras completas) work; (libro) book. 3 (acto) deed: esto seguro que es obra suya, I'm sure it's his work. 4 (institución) institution, foundation. 5 (construcción) building site. – 6 fpl (en casa) alterations, repairs; (en carretera) roadworks: no quiero meterme en obras, I don't want to start having alterations done; esta semana estamos de obras, we've got the workmen in this week; había retenciones a causa de las obras, there were delays because of the roadworks; "carretera cortada por obras", "road closed for repairs".
● "en obras", "building works". ‖ ¡manos a la obra!, let's get cracking! ‖ obras son amores, que no buenas razones, actions speak louder than words. ‖ por obra y gracia de, thanks to. ‖ por obra y gracia del Espíritu Santo, by the power of the Holy Spirit; fam as if by magic.
■ maestro de obras, (arquitecto) master builder; (capataz) foreman; (aparejador) clerk of works. ‖ obra benéfica, charity. ‖ obra de arte, work of art. ‖ obra de caridad, good deed. ‖ obra de teatro, play. ‖ obra maestra, masterpiece. ‖ obra musical, musical. ‖ obras completas, collected works. ‖ obras públicas, public works.

obrador m workshop: obrador de pastelería, baker's, cake maker's.

obraje m manufacturing.

obrar 1 i (proceder) to act, behave: obró de buena fe, he acted in good faith. 2 (encontrarse) to be: la carta obra en mi poder, the letter is in my hands. – 3 t (hacer) to work: obrar milagros, to work miracles.

obrero,-a 1 adj working. – 2 m,f worker, labourer.

obscenidad f obscenity.

obsceno,-a adj obscene.

obscurantismo m obscurantism.

obscurantista 1 adj obscurantist. – 2 mf obscurantist.

obscurecer 1 i to get dark: está obscureciendo, it's getting dark. – 2 t (ensombrecer) to darken. 3 fig (ofuscar) to cloud, obscure. 4 ART to shade. – 5 obscurecerse, p (día, tiempo) to get cloudy.
▲ Conjugation model [43], like agradecer.

obscurecimiento m darkening.

obscuridad 1 f darkness. 2 fig obscurity.

obscuro,-a 1 adj (cielo, color) dark. 2 (idea, razonamiento) obscure. 3 (futuro, porvenir) uncertain, gloomy. 4 (intención) dubious, unclear.
● a obscuras, in the dark.

obsequiar t (regalar) to give, offer: la obsequió con unas flores, he gave her some flowers.
▲ Conjugation model [12], like cambiar.

obsequio m gift, present.

obsequioso,-a 1 adj (amable, complaciente) obliging. 2 pey obsequious.

observable adj noticeable, observable.

observación 1 f (acción) observation. 2 (comentario) observation, comment, remark.
● estar en observación, to be under observation.

observador,-ra 1 adj observant. – 2 m,f observer.

observancia f observance.

observar 1 t (mirar) to observe, watch. 2 (notar) to notice: hemos observado que llega usted tarde con frecuencia, we have noticed that you often arrive late; me he observado un bulto extraño, I've noticed that I have a strange lump. 3 (mostrar) to display, show: observa buen comportamiento, he is well behaved. 4 (cumplir) to observe, obey.

observatorio m observatory.
■ observatorio meteorológico, weather station.

obsesión f obsession.

obsesionar t to obsess: el trabajo lo tiene obsesionado, he is a workaholic.
● estar obsesionado,-a con algn., to be obsessed with sb. 2 obsesionarse, p to get obsessed: se obsesiona con todo, he has an obsessive personality.

obsesivo,-a adj obsessive.

obseso,-a 1 m,f maniac. – 2 adj obsessed.
■ obseso,-a sexual, sex maniac.

obsidiana f obsidian.

obsoleto,-a adj obsolete.

obstaculizar t to obstruct, hinder.
▲ Conjugation model [4], like realizar.

obstáculo 1 m (barrera) obstacle: las escaleras pueden ser un insuperable obstáculo para el minusválido, stairs can be an unsurmountable obstacle for a disabled person. 2 (inconveniente) objection: no vamos a avanzar si sigues poniendo obstáculos, we won't get anywhere if you keep raising objections. 3 (valla) fence, jump.
● salvar un obstáculo, to overcome an obstacle.
■ carrera de obstáculos, (para niños) obstacle race; (de caballos, atletas) steeplechase.

obstante no obstante, 1 adv nevertheless, however. – 2 prep in spite of, despite.

obstar no obstar para, loc not to prevent from: esto no obsta para que cumpla el servicio militar, this will not prevent him from doing his military service.

obstetricia f obstetrics.

obstétrico,-a adj obstetric.

obstinación f obstinacy, stubbornness.

obstinado,-a adj obstinate, stubborn.

obstinarse p to persist (en, in), insist (en, on).

obstrucción f obstruction.

obstruccionismo m obstructionism.

obstruccionista mf obstructionist.

obstruir 1 t to obstruct, block. – 2 obstruirse, p to get blocked up.
▲ Conjugation model [62], like huir.

obtención f obtaining.

obtener 1 t (beca, resultados) to get, obtain; (premio) to win; (ganancias) to make: obtener el perdón, to be pardoned. – 2 obtenerse, p to get, be obtained: con este detergente se obtienen resultados sorprendentes, with this detergent you get surprising results; la energía se obtiene de la descomposición del átomo, energy is obtained by splitting the atom.
▲ Conjugation model [87], like tener.

obturación f blockage, obstruction.

obturador 1 m stopper. 2 (de cámara fotográfica) shutter.

obturar t to block up, plug up.

obtuso,-a adj obtuse.

obús 1 m MIL (proyectil) shell; (cañón) howitzer. 2 AUTO valve core.

obviar t fml to obviate, remove.

obvio,-a adj obvious.

oca f goose.
■ el juego de la oca, ≈ snakes and ladders.

ocarina *f* ocarina.

ocasión 1 *f* (*momento*) occasion: *la conocí con ocasión de un congreso,* I met her at a conference; *fuimos con ocasión de su aniversario,* we went on the occasion of her anniversary. **2** (*oportunidad*) opportunity, chance: *cómpralo, aprovecha la ocasión,* buy it while you've got the chance; *puedes aprovechar la ocasión para ir a verla,* while you are there you could call in on her. **3** COM bargain. **4** (*motivo*) reason: *no me ha dado ocasión para enfadarme con él,* I have never had reason to get annoyed with him.
● **de ocasión,** (*de segunda mano*) secondhand; (*barato*) cut-price, at bargain prices. ‖ **en cierta ocasión,** once, on one occasion. ‖ **la ocasión hace al ladrón,** opportunity makes the thief. ‖ **a la ocasión la pintan calva,** strike while the iron is hot.

ocasional 1 *adj* (*gen*) occasional. **2** (*trabajo*) temporary, casual. **3** (*encuentro*) chance. **4** (*ingreso*) irregular.

ocasionar *t* (*causar*) to cause, bring about.

ocaso 1 *m* (*anochecer*) sunset. **2** *fig* (*declive*) fall, decline. **3** (*occidente*) west.

occidental 1 *adj* western, occidental. – **2** *mf* (*persona*) westerner.

occidente *m* the West.

occipital 1 *adj* occipital. – **2** *m* occipital, occipital bone.

occitano,-a 1 *adj* Occitan. – **2** *m,f* Occitan.

OCDE *abr* (*Organización de Cooperación y Desarrollo Económicos*) Organization for Economic Cooperation and Development; (*abreviatura*) OECD.

Oceanía *f* Oceania.

Oceanía *f* Oceania.

oceánico,-a *adj* (*corriente*) oceanic: *la inmensidad oceánica,* the inmensity of the ocean.

océano *m* ocean.
▲ *In poetry also written* oceano.

oceanografía *f* oceanography.

oceanográfico, -a *adj* oceanographic.

oceanógrafo, -a *m,f* oceanographer.

ocelote *m* ocelot.

ochavado,-a *adj* octagonal, eight-sided.

ochavo *m desus* old copper coin.
● **no tener un ochavo,** *fam* to be penniless. ‖ **no vale un ochavo,** it's not worth a farthing.

ochenta 1 *adj* eighty; (*octagésimo*) eightieth. – **2** *m* eighty.
▲ *See also* sesenta.

ochentón,-ona 1 *adj* eighty-year-old. – **2** *m,f* eighty-year-old, octogenarian.

ocho 1 *adj* eight; (*octavo*) eighth. – **2** *m* eight.
● **a los ocho días,** in a week's time. ‖ **darle igual a uno ocho que ochenta,** *fam* not to mind either way. ‖ **más chulo,-a que un ocho,** *fam* (*engreído*) full of os.; (*guapo*) smart.
▲ *See also* seis.

ochocientos,-as 1 *adj* eight hundred; (*ordinal*) eight hundreth. – **2** *m,f* eight hundred.

ocio 1 *m* (*tiempo libre*) leisure. **2** (*desocupación*) idleness.
● **ratos de ocio,** spare time *sing,* leisure time *sing.*

ociosidad *f* idleness.
● **la ociosidad es madre de todos los vicios,** the devil finds work for idle hands to do.

ocioso,-a 1 *adj* (*desocupado*) idle. **2** (*innecesario*) pointless, useless. – **3** *m,f* idler.

ocluir 1 *t* to occlude. – **2** **ocluirse,** *p* to become obstructed.
▲ *Conjugation model* [62], *like* huir.

oclusión *f* occlusion.

oclusiva *f* → oclusivo,-a.

oclusivo,-a 1 *adj* occlusive. – **2** **oclusiva,** *f* LING occlusive.

ocre 1 *adj* ochre. – **2** *m* ochre.

octaédrico,-a *adj* octahedronal.

octaedro *m* octahedron.

octagonal *adj* octagonal.

octágono,-a 1 *adj* octagonal. – **2** **octágono,** *m* octagon.

octanaje *m* number of octanes.

octano *m* octane.

octava *f* → octavo,-a.

octaviano, -a *adj* Octavian.

octavilla 1 *f* (*impreso*) pamphlet. **2** *arc* (*pliego*) octavo.

octavo,-a 1 *adj* eighth: *llegó en octavo lugar,* he came eighth. – **2** *m,f* eighth: *era la octava en la lista,* she was the eighth on the list. – **3** **octavo,** *m* (*parte*) eighth. – **4** **octava,** *f* LIT MÚS octave.
■ **octavos de final,** round before the quarter finals.
▲ *See also* sexto.

octogenario,-a 1 *adj* octogenarian. – **2** *m,f* octogenarian.

octogésimo,-a *adj* eightieth.

octogonal *adj* octagonal.

octógono *m* octagon.

octosílabo,-a 1 *adj* octosyllabic. – **2** **octosílabo,** *m* octosyllable.

octubre *m* October.
▲ *See also* marzo.

OCU *abr* (*Organización de Consumidores y Usuarios*) consumers's organization.

ocular 1 *adj* eye, ocular: *problema ocular,* eye problem; *inspección ocular,* visual inspection. – **2** *m* eyepiece.
■ **testigo ocular,** eyewitness.

oculista *mf* eye specialist, ophthalmologist.
■ **médico,-a oculista,** eye specialist.

ocultación 1 *f* concealment: *ocultación de bienes,* nondeclaration of assets; *ocultación de los hechos,* concealment of evidence. **2** ASTRON occultation.

ocultar *t* (*gen*) to hide, conceal: *se ocultó en un árbol,* he hid in a tree; *me ocultó la verdad,* he hid the truth from me.

ocultismo *m* occultism.
■ **el ocultismo,** the occult.

ocultista 1 *adj* occult, occultist. – **2** *mf* occultist.

oculto,-a 1 *adj* (*escondido*) hidden: *quedaba oculto tras las ramas,* it was hidden behind the branches. **2** (*misterioso*) cryptic; (*esotérico*) occult.

ocupación 1 *f* (*llenado*) occupation: *la ocupación hotelera en agosto superó el 82%,* hotels were 82% full in August. **2** MIL occupation. **3** (*empleo*) occupation, employment, job. **4** (*actividad*) activity, duty, job.
● **ocupación ilegal de viviendas,** squatting.

ocupado,-a 1 *pp* → ocupar. – **2** *adj* (*persona*) busy. **3** (*asiento*) taken; (*teléfono*) engaged, US busy; (*puesto de trabajo*) filled: *¿está ocupado el baño?,* is there anyone in the bathroom? **4** MIL occupied.

ocupante 1 *mf* occupant. **2** (*de una vivienda*) occupier, occupant; (*ilegal*) squatter.

ocupar 1 *t* to occupy, take: *él siempre ocupa este asiento,* he always occupies this seat, he always sits here. **2** (*adueñarse de*) to occupy, take: *el ejército invasor ocupó la ciudad,* the invading army occupied the city. **3** (*llenar*) to take up: *la mesa ocupa casi toda la habitación,* the table takes up most of the room. **4** (*dedicar*) to do: *¿en qué ocupa sus ratos libres?,* what do you do in your spare time? **5** (*habitar*) to live in, occupy: *los García ocu-*

pan el piso de arriba, the Garcías live in the flat upstairs; *la delegación japonesa ocupa las habitaciones superiores,* the Japanese delegation occupies the upper rooms. **6** (*estar - en un cargo*) to hold, fill; (*- en posición*) to occupy, be in: *ahora ocupa la cartera de Trabajo,* he is now Minister of Labour; *no tiene intención de ocupar el cargo,* he has no intention of taking up the position; *nuestro equipo ocupa la cuarta posición,* our team is in fourth place. **7** (*dar trabajo*) to employ: *el calzado ocupa a casi toda la población,* most of the town works in the shoe industry; *mis hijos me ocupan demasiado,* my children take up too much of my time. – **8 ocuparse de,** *p* (*encargarse de*) to take care of; (*tratar*) to deal with.

● **ocuparse de lo suyo,** to mind one's own business.

ocurrencia **1** *f* (*idea*) idea; (*disparatada*) absurd idea. **2** (*agudeza*) witty remark.

● **¡qué ocurrencia!,** that's ridiculous!

ocurrente *adj* witty, amusing.

ocurrir **1** *i* to happen: *¿qué fue lo que ocurrió?,* what happened?; *¿qué ocurre?,* what's wrong?; *¿te ocurre algo?,* are you alright? – **2 ocurrirse,** *p* to occur to: *no se me ocurre nada,* nothing occurs to me, I can't think of anything; *a nadie se le ocurrió nada,* nobody came up with any ideas; *se me ocurrió pensar que ...,* it crossed my mind that ..., it occurred to me that; *¡se te ocurre cada cosa!,* you come out with some funny ideas!

● **lo que ocurre es que ...,** the thing is that ... ‖ **por lo que pueda ocurrir,** just in case.

oda *f* ode.

odalisca *f* odalisque.

odeón *m* odeum, odeon.

odiar *t* to hate, loathe: *la odio a muerte,* I hate her guts.

● **odio tener que ...,** I hate having to ...

▲ *Conjugation model* [12], *like cambiar.*

odio *m* hatred, loathing.

● **tenerle odio a algn.,** to hate sb.

■ **mirada de odio,** glare. ‖ **odio mortal,** hatred.

odioso,-a *adj* hateful, despicable, odious.

odisea **1** *f* odyssey. **2** *fam* ordeal.

odontología *f* dentistry, odontology.

odontológico,-a *adj* dental, odontological.

odontólogo,-a *m,f* dental surgeon, odontologist.

odorífero,-a *adj* odoriferous.

odorífico,-a *adj* odoriferous.

OEA *abr* (*Organización de Estados Americanos*) Organization of American States; (*abreviatura*) OAS.

oeste **1** *m* west. – **2** *adj* (*ala, viento*) west; (*rumbo*) westerly.

● **en dirección oeste,** westward.

■ **el lejano Oeste,** the Far West. ‖ **el Oeste americano,** the American West. ‖ **películas del oeste,** westerns. ‖ **viento oeste,** west wind, westerly.

ofender **1** *t* (*herir*) to offend: *lo he dicho sin ánimo de ofender,* I didn't mean to offend you; *no quisiera ofenderte, pero ...,* no offence, but ... **2** (*disgustar*) to hurt: *esta decoración ofende a la vista,* this decoration is an eyesore. – **3 ofenderse,** *p* to get offended: *se ofendió conmigo por lo que le dije,* what I said offended him.

● **ofenderse por nada,** to be quick to take offence.

ofendido,-a **1** *pp* → **ofender.** – **2** *adj* offended.

● **darse por ofendido,-a,** to take offence.

ofensa *f* offence.

ofensiva *f* → **ofensivo,-a.**

ofensivo,-a **1** *adj* offensive. – **2 ofensiva,** *f* MIL offensive.

● **tomar la ofensiva,** to take the offensive.

ofensor,-ra **1** *adj* offending. – **2** *m,f* offender.

oferta **1** *f* offer. **2** COM bid, tender. **3** (*suministro*) supply.

● **estar de oferta,** to be on (special) offer. ‖ **la ley de la oferta y la demanda,** the law of supply and demand.

■ **oferta pública de adquisición (OPA),** takeover bid.

ofertar **1** *t* (*vender en oferta*) to offer at reduced prices. **2** (*ofrecer*) to offer.

ofertorio *m* offertory.

off **1** *adj* (*apagado*) off. **2** TEAT offstage; CINEM offscreen.

■ **voz en off,** voice offstage.

office *m* pantry.

■ **cocina-office,** kitchen-diner.

offset *m* offset.

oficial **1** *adj* official. – **2** *mf* (*en oficina*) office worker, clerk; (*en oficio*) assistant. **3** MIL officer. **4** (*en la Administración*) official, officer. **5** (*en albañilería*) skilled labourer.

oficiala *f* (*operaria*) assistant: *oficiala de peluquería,* hairdresser's assistant.

oficialidad **1** *f* official nature, officiality. **2** MIL officers *pl,* officialdom.

oficializar *t* to make official.

▲ *Conjugation model* [4], *like realizar.*

oficiante *mf* officiant.

oficiar **1** *t* (*misa*) to say. – **2** *i* (*sacerdote*) to officiate. **3** (*ejercer*) to act (**de,** as): *oficiar de intermediario,* to act as a go-between; *oficiar de maestro de ceremonias,* to act as master of ceremonies.

oficina *f* office.

■ **horas de oficina,** business hours. ‖ **oficina de empleo,** job centre, US job office. ‖ **oficina pública,** government office. ‖ **oficina de turismo,** tourist information office.

oficinista *mf* office worker, clerk.

oficio **1** *m* (*ocupación*) job, occupation; (*especializado*) trade: *aprender un oficio,* to learn a trade. **2** (*función*) role, function. **3** (*comunicado oficial*) official letter, official note. **4** REL service.

● **de oficio,** by trade. ‖ **ser del oficio,** to be in the trade. ‖ **no tener ni oficio ni beneficio,** to be idle.

■ **oficio de difuntos,** funeral mass. ‖ **oficio divino,** divine office. ‖ **el Santo Oficio,** the Inquisition, the Holy Office.

oficioso,-a **1** *adj* (*noticia, fuente*) unofficial. **2** (*persona*) officious.

ofidio *m* snake.

ofrecer **1** *t* (*dar - premio, amistad*) to offer; (*- banquete, fiesta*) to hold; (*- regalo*) to give. **2** (*presentar*) to present: *la montaña ofrecía un panorama desolador,* the mountain looked desolate; *ofrecer resistencia,* to offer resistance. – **3** *ofrecerse,* *p* (*prestarse*) to offer, volunteer: *se ofreció a llevarme,* he offered to give me a lift; *se ofreció voluntario,* he volunteered. **4** (*disponer*) to want: *¿qué se le ofrece?,* what can I do for you?

▲ *Conjugation model* [43], *like agradecer.*

ofrecimiento *m* offer, offering.

ofrenda *f* offering.

ofrendar *t* to make an offering of.

oftálmico,-a *adj* ophthalmic.

oftalmología *f* ophthalmology.

oftalmólogo,-a *m,f* eye specialist, ophthalmologist.

ofuscación *f* blinding, dazzling.

ofuscar **1** *t* (*confundir*) to muddle, befuddle. **2** (*deslumbrar*) to dazzle. – **3 ofuscarse,** *p* to get muddled: *de pronto se ofuscó y no pudo continuar con el examen,* his mind suddenly went blank and he couldn't go on with the exam.

▲ *Conjugation model* |1|, *like* sacar.

ogaño *adv* → **hogaño**.

ogro *m* ogre.

oh *interj* oh!

ohm *m* ohm.

▲ *pl* ohms.

ohmio *m* ohm.

oídas de oídas, *loc* by hearsay: *yo sólo lo sé de oídas,* it's just hearsay; *lo conozco de oídas,* I've heard of him.

oído 1 *m* (*sentido*) hearing. 2 (*órgano*) ear.
● aguzar el oído, to prick up one's ears. ‖ aprender de oído, to learn by ear. ‖ decirle algo a algn. al oído, to whisper sth. in sb.'s ear. ‖ entrarle algo a algn. por un oído y salirle por el otro, to go in one ear and out the other. ‖ hacer oídos sordos, to turn a deaf ear. ‖ llegar algo a oídos de algn., to come to sb.'s notice. ‖ regalarle a algn. el oído, to flatter sb. ‖ ser duro,-a de oído, to be hard of hearing. ‖ ser todo oídos, to be all ears. ‖ tener buen oído, to have a good ear. ‖ tocar de oído, to play by ear.

oiga 1 *pres subj* → **oír**. – 2 *interj* (*para llamar la atención*) excuse me!; (*en bar etc*) waiter!; (*por teléfono*) hello?; (*con enfado*) listen!, look here!

oír 1 *t* (*percibir sonidos*) to hear: *no oigo nada,* I can't hear a thing; *no se oye ni una mosca,* you could hear a pin drop. 2 (*atender*) to answer: *¡Dios te oiga!,* if only! 3 JUR to hear.
● como lo oyes, *fam* believe it or not. ‖ ¡lo que hay que oír!, what next! ‖ oír, ver y callar, hear no evil, see no evil, speak no evil.

▲ *Conjugation model* |75|.

OIRT *abr* TV (*Organización Internacional de Radiodifusión y Televisión*) International Radio and Television Organization; (*abreviatura*) IRTO.

OIT *abr* (*Organización Internacional del Trabajo*) International Labour Organization; (*abreviatura*) ILO.

ojal *m* buttonhole.

ojalá *interj* I hope so: *ojalá que llueva,* I wish it would rain; *¡ojalá sea verdad!,* I hope it's true!

ojeada *f* glance, quick look.
● echar una ojeada, (*mirar*) to take a quick look (**a**, at); (*vigilar*) to keep an eye (**a**, on).

ojeador,-ra *m,f* beater.

ojear[1] *t* (*mirar*) to have a quick look at.

ojear[2] *t* (*caza*) to beat.

ojeo *m* beating.

ojeras *fpl* dark rings under the eyes.

ojeriza *f fam* dislike.
● tenerle ojeriza a algn., to have it in for sb.

ojeroso,-a *adj* haggard.
● estar ojeroso,-a, to have rings under one's eyes.

ojete 1 *m* (*en zapato*) eyelet. 2 *tabú* arsehole.

ojiva 1 *f* ARQ ogive. 2 MIL warhead.

ojival *adj* (*arte*) ogival.
■ arco ojival, lancet arch, gothic arch, ogive.

ojo 1 *m* eye. 2 (*agujero*) hole; (*de aguja*) eye. 3 (*cuidado, precaución*) care: *¡ojo!,* careful!, watch out!; *ojo con lo que hacéis,* behave yourselves! 4 (*perspicacia*) insight, eye: *tiene buen ojo para vestirse,* he has a good eye for fashion; *tiene mucho ojo para los negocios,* she's got a head for business. 5 (*enjabonado*) wash: *hay que darle un ojo (de jabón),* it just needs a quick wash.
● a ojo (de buen cubero), (*aproximadamente*) at a rough guess; (*a primera vista*) at a glance. ‖ a ojos vis-

tas, visibly. ‖ andar con cien ojos, to keep one's wits about one. ‖ andarse con ojo, to be very careful. ‖ costar un ojo de la cara, to cost an arm and a leg. ‖ cuatro ojos ven más que dos, two heads are better than one. ‖ echar el ojo a algo, to lay eyes on sth. ‖ en un abrir y cerrar de ojos, in the twinkling of an eye. ‖ estar con cien ojos, to keep one's wits about one. ‖ mirar con buenos ojos, to look favourably on, approve of. ‖ no pegar ojo, *fam* not to sleep a wink. ‖ ojos que no ven, corazón que no siente, out of sight, out of mind. ‖ poner los ojos en blanco, to swoon. ‖ saltar a los ojos, to be evident. ‖ saltarle un ojo a algn., to poke sb.'s eye out. ‖ tener buen ojo (para algo), to have a good eye (for sth.). ‖ tenerle el ojo echado a algo, to have one's eye on sth. ‖ ¡dichosos los ojos que te ven!, it's so great to see you!
■ cuatro ojos, *fam* four-eyes. ‖ ojo a la funerala, *fam* black eye. ‖ ojo a la virulé, *fam* black eye. ‖ ojo de buey, MAR porthole. ‖ ojo de la cerradura, keyhole. ‖ ojo morado, black eye. ‖ ojos saltones, bulging eyes.

okapi *m* okapi.

okupa *mf arg* squatter.

ola *f* wave.
● la nueva ola, the new wave.
■ ola de calor, heat wave. ‖ ola de frío, cold spell.

ole *interj* (*en los toros*) olé!; (*en espectáculo*) bravo!; (*como enhorabuena*) hoorah!, hurray!

▲ *Also written* olé.

oleáceo,-a 1 *adj* oleaceous. – 2 **oleáceas,** *fpl* oleaceae.

oleada 1 *f* big wave. 2 *fig* wave: *una oleada de atentados,* a wave of terrorist attacks.

oleaginoso,-a *adj* oleaginous.

oleaje *m* swell: *se ha levantado mucho oleaje,* the sea has got very choppy.

oleicultura 1 *f* (*cultivo*) olive-growing. 2 (*fabricación*) olive oil industry.

óleo 1 *m* (*material*) oil; (*obra*) oil painting. 2 REL chrism, oil.
● pintar al óleo, to paint in oils.
■ pintura al óleo, oil painting. ‖ santos óleos, holy oils.

oleoducto *m* pipeline.

oleoso,-a *adj* oily.

oler 1 *t* to smell: *huele esta sopa,* smell this soup. – 2 *i* to smell: *huele a gas,* it smells of gas in here. – 3 **olerse,** *p* to feel, sense: *se ha olido que nos vamos,* she has sensed that we are leaving; *me huelo que esto no va a ir bien,* I have a hunch this is not going to work out.
● oler mal, (*pescado etc*) to smell bad; (*asunto*) to be fishy: *este negocio me huele mal,* this business sounds a bit fishy to me. ‖ huele que apesta, it stinks. ‖ oler a chamusquina, *fam* to smell fishy. ‖ oler a cuerno quemado, *fam* to smell fishy.

▲ *Conjugation model* |60|.

olfatear 1 *t* (*oler*) to sniff, smell. 2 *fig* (*indagar*) to nose into, pry into. 3 (*sospechar*) to suspect.

olfateo 1 *m* sniffing. 2 *fig* snooping.

olfativo,-a *adj* olfactory.

olfato 1 *m* sense of smell: *con la gripe he perdido el olfato,* the flu has left me with no sense of smell. 2 *fig* (*intuición*) good nose; (*cualidades*) flair: *tiene olfato para la noticia,* he's got a nose for news; *tiene olfato para los negocios,* she has a flair for business.

olfatorio,-a *adj* olfactory.

oligarca *mf* oligarch.

oligarquía f oligarchy.
oligárquico,-a adj oligarchic, oligarchical.
oligofrenia 1 f (enfermedad) mental handicap. 2 pey imbecility.
oligofrénico,-a 1 adj mentally retarded. 2 fam pey moronic. – 3 m,f mentally retarded person. 4 fam pey moron.
olimpiada f HIST Olympiad.
■ **las Olimpiadas,** the Olympic Games.
▲ Also written **olimpíada.**
olímpicamente pasar olímpicamente, loc fam not to give a damn (**de,** about): paso olímpicamente de ir a clase, I can't be bothered to go to my class.
olímpico,-a 1 adj Olympic. 2 (grandioso) monumental.
■ **los Juegos Olímpicos,** the Olympic Games.
Olimpo el Olimpo, m Mount Olympus.
■ **los dioses del Olimpo,** the Olympian Gods, the Olympians.
oliscar t → **olisquear.**
olisquear 1 t (olfatear) to sniff. – 2 i fig (curiosear) to nose around.
oliva f olive.
■ **aceite de oliva,** olive oil. ‖ **verde oliva,** olive green.
oliváceo,-a adj olive green.
olivar m olive grove.
olivarero,-a 1 adj (industria) olive; (región) olive-growing. – 2 m,f olive grower.
olivicultura f olive-growing.
olivo m olive tree.
olla 1 f (utensilio) pan. 2 (comida) type of stew.
■ **olla a presión,** pressure cooker. ‖ **olla de grillos,** fam bedlam. ‖ **olla exprés,** pressure cooker. ‖ **olla gitana,** type of vegetable stew. ‖ **olla podrida,** type of meat stew.
olmedo m elm grove.
olmo m elm tree.
ológrafo,-a adj → **hológrafo.**
olor m smell: hay olor a quemado, it smells as if something's burning.
● **al olor de,** attracted by. ‖ **en olor de santidad,** like a saint.
● **olor corporal,** body odour.
oloroso,-a 1 adj fragrant, sweet-smelling. – 2 m (vino) full-bodied sherry.
OLP abr (Organización para la Liberación de Palestina) Palestine Liberation Organization; (abreviatura) PLO.
olvidadizo,-a adj forgetful: no te hagas el olvidadizo, don't pretend you've forgotten.
olvidado,-a 1 pp → **olvidar.** – 2 adj forgotten.
● **olvidado,-a de Dios,** godforsaken.
olvidar 1 t to forget: no te olvidaré nunca, I'll never forget you; he olvidado el paraguas en casa, I've left my umbrella at home. – 2 olvidarse, p to forget (**de,** -): se me ha olvidado tu número de teléfono, I've forgotten your telephone number; se olvidó de cerrar la puerta, he forgot to close the door; me olvidé de que venías hoy, I forgot you were coming today.
● **¡olvídame!,** fam get lost!
olvido 1 m (desmemoria) oblivion. 2 (descuido) forgetfulness, absentmindedness. 3 (lapsus) oversight, lapse (of memory): fue un olvido imperdonable, it was an unforgivable oversight.
● **relegar al olvido,** to cast into oblivion.
OM abr RAD (onda media) medium wave; (abreviatura) MW.
O.M. abr (Orden Ministerial) ministerial order.
Omán m Oman.

omaní 1 adj Omani. – 2 mf Omani.
ombligo m navel.
● **el ombligo del mundo,** the centre of the world.
omega f (letra) omega.
omeya 1 adj HIST Ommiad. – 2 mf HIST Ommiad.
ominoso,-a adj fml abominable.
omisión f omission.
omiso,-a hacer caso omiso de, loc to ignore, pay no attention to.
omitir 1 t (no decir) to omit, leave out. 2 (dejar de hacer) to neglect, overlook.
ómnibus m bus.
▲ pl **ómnibus.**
omnímodo,-a adj fml all-embracing.
omnipotencia f omnipotence.
omnipotente adj omnipotent, almighty.
omnipresencia f omnipresence.
omnipresente adj omnipresent.
omnisapiente adj all-knowing, omniscient.
omnisciencia f omniscience.
omnisciente adj omniscient.
omnívoro,-a 1 adj omnivorous. – 2 m,f omnivore.
omóplato m shoulder blade.
▲ Also written **omoplato.**
OMS abr (Organización Mundial de la Salud) World Health Organization; (abreviatura) WHO.
onagra f evening primrose.
■ **aceite de onagra,** evening primrose oil.
onanismo m onanism.
once 1 adj eleven; (undécimo) eleventh. – 2 m eleven.
▲ See also **seis.**
ONCE abr (Organización Nacional de Ciegos Españoles) ≈ Royal National Institute for the Blind; (abreviatura) RNIB.
onceavo,-a 1 adj (parte) eleventh: la onceava parte de ..., an eleventh of ... – 2 m eleventh: tres onceavos, three elevenths.
▲ See also **sexto.**
onceno,-a adj → **undécimo,-a.**
oncología f oncology.
oncológico,-a adj oncological.
oncólogo,-a m,f oncologist.
onda 1 f wave. 2 (en el agua) ripple. 3 (en el pelo) wave. 4 fam wavelength.
● **coger la onda,** to understand, get it. ‖ **estar en la misma onda que algn.,** fam to be on the same wavelength as sb. ‖ **estar en la onda,** arg to know what it's all about, be up to date.
■ **onda expansiva,** shock wave. ‖ **onda larga,** long wave. ‖ **onda media,** medium wave.
ondear 1 i (bandera) to fly, flutter. 2 (agua) to ripple. 3 (pelo) to blow about.
● **ondear a media asta,** to be flying at half mast.
ondina f Nereid.
ondulación 1 f undulation, wave. 2 (agua) ripple.
ondulado,-a 1 pp → **ondular.** – 2 adj (pelo) wavy.
ondulante adj (paisaje, terreno) undulating, rolling; (serpiente) sinuous; (movimiento, melodía) rolling.
ondular 1 i (pelo) to wave. – 2 i lit (agua) to undulate.
ondulatorio,-a adj undulatory.
■ **mecánica ondulatoria,** wave mechanics.
oneroso,-a adj onerous.
● **resultar oneroso,-a,** to be a financial burden.
ONG abr (Organización no Gubernamental) nongovernmental organization; (abreviatura) NGO.

ónice *m* onyx.

onírico,-a *adj* dream, of dreams.

ónix *m* onyx.

ONO *sím* (*oesnoroeste*) west-northwest; (*símbolo*) WNW.

onomástica *f* → **onomástico,-a.**

onomástico,-a 1 *adj* onomastic: *fiesta onomástica,* saint's day; *lista onomástica,* list of names. − 2 onomástica, *f* saint's day.

onomatopeya *f* onomatopoeia.

onomatopéyico,-a *adj* onomatopoeic.

ontogénesis *f* ontogenesis.
▲ *pl ontogénesis.*

ontología *f* ontology.

ontológico,-a *adj* ontological.

ONU *abr* (*Organización de las Naciones Unidas*) United Nations Organization; (*abreviatura*) UNO.

onubense 1 *adj* of Huelva, from Huelva. − 2 *mf* person from Huelva, inhabitant of Huelva.

onza[1] *f* (*peso*) ounce.

onza[2] *f* ZOOL ounce, snow leopard.

Órcadas las Islas Órcadas, *fpl* the Orkneys, the Orkney Islands, Orkney.

OPA *abr* (*Oferta Pública de Adquisición*) take-over bid.

opacidad *f* opaqueness, opacity.

opaco,-a 1 *adj* (*ventana, pantalla*) opaque. 2 *lit* (*persona, día*) dull.

opalescencia *f* opalescence.

opalescente *adj* opalescent.

opalino,-a *adj* (*de ópalo*) opal; (*opalescente*) opal-like, opaline.

ópalo *m* opal.

opción 1 *f* (*en general*) option: *esta opción es la mejor,* this is the best option. 2 (*alternativa*) option, choice: *no tienes otra opción,* you have no choice; *España tiene opción a dos medallas,* Spain is in the running for two medals. 3 (*derecho*) right: *esto te da opción a participar otra vez,* this gives you the right to take part again.
■ opción de compra, option to buy.

opcional *adj* optional.

op. cit. *abr* → **ob. cit..**

open *m* DEP open.
▲ *pl open.*

OPEP *abr* (*Organización de los Países Exportadores de Petróleo*) Organization of Petroleum Exporting Countries; (*abreviatura*) OPEC.

ópera *f* opera.

operable *adj* operable.

operación 1 *f* (*gen*) operation. 2 FIN transaction, deal.
■ operación quirúrgica, operation.

operacional *adj* operational.

operador,-ra 1 *m,f* (*telefónico*) operator. 2 CINEM (*de cámara* - *hombre*) cameraman; (- *mujer*) camerawoman; (- *de proyector*) projectionist. 3 TÉC operator. 4 FIN trader. − 5 operador, *m* MAT (*signo*) operator.
▲ operador turístico, tour operator.

operando *m* operand.

operante *adj* operative.

operar 1 *t* MED to operate (**a**, on): *¿quién te operó?,* who operated on you? 2 (*producir*) to bring about. − 3 *i* (*actuar*) to operate. 4 (*negociar*) to deal (**con**, with). − 5 operarse, *p* MED to have an operation: *se ha operado del corazón,* he has had a heart operation. 6 (*producirse*) to come about: *se han operado grandes cambios en el país,* the country has undergone many changes.

operario,-a *m,f* operator, worker.

operativo,-a *adj* operative.

operatorio,-a *adj* MED operative.

opereta *f* operetta.

operístico,-a *adj* operatic: *la temporada operística,* the opera season.

opiáceo,-a *adj* opiate.

opinable *adj* debatable.

opinar *i* to think (**de**, about): *¿qué opinas de esta cuestión?,* what do you think about this matter?; *aquí todos tenemos derecho a opinar,* we all have the right to give our opinion here.

opinión *f* (*juicio*) opinion, view: *en mi opinión,* in my opinion, in my view; *este colegio no me merece muy buena opinión,* I have a poor opinion of that school.
● cambiar de opinión, to change one's mind.
■ la opinión pública, public opinion.

opio *m* opium.

opiómano,-a 1 *adj* opium-addicted. − 2 *m,f* opium addict.

opíparo,-a *adj fml* lavish: *una cena opípara,* a feast.

oponente 1 *adj* opposing. − 2 *mf* opponent.

oponer 1 *t* to reply with, counter with: *él opuso sus razones para no aceptar el cargo,* he gave his reasons for not accepting the post; *no tienen nada que oponer a nuestras razones,* they cannot reply to our arguments. − 2 oponerse, *p* (*estar en contra*) to oppose (**a**, -), be against (**a**, -): *se opusieron a nuestra boda,* they were against our wedding. 3 (*ser contrario*) to be in opposition (**a**, to), contradict (**a**, -).
● oponer resistencia, to offer resistance.
▲ Conjugation model [78], like *poner;* *pp opuesto,-a.*

oporto *m* port.

Oporto *m* Oporto.

oportunidad 1 *f* opportunity, chance. 2 (*ganga*) bargain.

oportunismo *m* opportunism.

oportunista 1 *adj* (*persona*) opportunist; (*política*) opportunistic. − 2 *mf* opportunist.

oportuno,-a 1 *adj* (*a tiempo*) opportune, timely: *la oferta llegó en el momento oportuno,* the offer came at the right time. 2 (*conveniente*) appropriate: *habrá que tomar las medidas oportunas,* the appropriate measures will have to be taken. 3 (*ingenioso*) witty: *estás hoy muy oportuno,* you're really sharp today.

oposición 1 *f* (*antagonismo*) opposition. 2 (*examen*) competitive examination.
● preparar las oposiciones, to study for a competitive exam.

opositar *i* (*presentarse a examen*) to sit for a competitive exam; (*prepararse*) to study for a competitive exam.

opositor,-ra *m,f* candidate *preparing for an official exam.*

opresión *f* oppression.
● opresión en el pecho, tightness of the chest.

opresivo,-a *adj* oppressive.

opresor,-ra 1 *adj* oppressive, oppressing. − 2 *m,f* oppressor.

oprimido,-a 1 *pp* → **oprimir.** − 2 *adj* oppressed. − 3 *m,f* oppressed person. − 4 los oprimidos, *mpl* the oppressed.

oprimir 1 *t* (*botón*) to press: *oprima el botón verde,* press the green button; *me oprime el cinturón,* this belt is too tight for me. 2 *fig* to oppress.

oprobio *m* opprobrium.

optar 1 *i* (*elegir*) to choose (**entre**, from): *puede optar entre tres modelos diferentes,* you have three different models to choose from; *opté por no decir nada,* I decided not to say anything. 2 (*aspirar*) to apply (**a**, for).

optativa $f \rightarrow$ **optativo,-a.**
optativo,-a 1 *adj* optional. 2 LING (*oración, modo*) optative. – 3 **optativa,** *f* EDUC (*asignatura*) optional subject. 4 LING optative.
óptica $f \rightarrow$ **óptico,-a.**
óptico,-a 1 *adj* (*nervio, ángulo*) optic; (*ilusión, instrumento, efecto*) optical. – 2 *m,f* optician. – 3 **óptica,** *f* (*tienda*) optician's. 4 FÍS optics. 5 (*enfoque*) viewpoint.
optimismo *m* optimism.
optimista 1 *adj* optimistic. – 2 *mf* optimist.
óptimo,-a *adj* very best, optimum.
opuesto,-a 1 *pp* → **oponer.** – 2 *adj* (*contrario*) contrary, opposed: *versiones opuestas de los hechos,* contrasting versions of the facts; *en sentido opuesto,* in the opposite direction. 3 (*de enfrente*) opposite.
opugnar *t fml* to oppose.
opulencia *f* opulence.
● **vivir en la opulencia,** to live in opulence.
opulento,-a *adj* opulent.
opus *m* MÚS opus.
■ Opus Dei, Opus Dei.
opúsculo *m fml* opuscule, short work.
oquedad 1 *f* (*hueco*) cavity. 2 *fig* vacuity, emptiness.
ora *conj arc* now.
● **ora ... ora ...,** be it ... or ...
oración 1 *f* REL (*plegaria*) prayer; (*acción*) praying. 2 LING clause, sentence.
■ **oración compuesta,** complex sentence. ‖ **oración principal,** main clause. ‖ **oración simple,** simple sentence. ‖ **oración subordinada,** subordinate clause. ‖ **partes de la oración,** parts of speech.
oráculo *m* oracle.
orador,-ra *m,f* speaker, orator: *es muy buen orador,* he is a very good speaker.
oral 1 *adj* oral. – 2 *m* EDUC (*examen*) oral, oral exam; UNIV viva, viva voce.
● **por vía oral,** MED to be taken orally.
orangután *m* ZOOL orang-utan, orang-outang.
orante *adj* praying, at prayer: *estatua orante,* statue of a person kneeling in prayer.
orar *i* to pray.
orate *mf lit* lunatic.
oratoria $f \rightarrow$ **oratorio,-a.**
oratorio,-a 1 *adj* (*estilo, arte*) oratorical. – 2 **oratorio,** *m* MÚS oratorio. 3 REL oratory. – 4 **oratoria,** *f* oratory.
orbe *m* (*esfera*) orb; (*mundo*) world: *por todo el orbe,* around the world.
órbita 1 *f* (*de un astro*) orbit. 2 (*del ojo*) socket: *se le salían los ojos de las órbitas,* his eyes were popping out of his head. 3 (*ámbito*) field.
■ **órbita de actuación,** field of activity.
orbital *adj* orbital.
orca *f* killer whale, orc.
órdago *m* bet *in the card game of mus.*
● **de órdago,** *fam* amazing: *hace un frío de órdago,* it's freezing cold.
orden 1 *m* (*ordenación*) order: *es un amante del orden,* he loves order; *clasificados por orden alfabético,* classified in alphabetical order. 2 BIOL order. 3 ARQ order: *el orden jónico,* the Ionic order. 4 field, sphere: *cuestiones de orden internacional,* international matters. – 5 *f* (*mandato*) order: *¡es una orden!,* that's an order!; *¡a la orden mi comandante!,* right away sir!; *siempre está dando órdenes,* he's always ordering people about. 6 REL order: *la orden franciscana,* the Franciscan order.

● **del orden de,** of the order of, US on the order of. ‖ **de primer orden,** first-rate. ‖ **estar algo a la orden del día,** to be the done thing. ‖ **por orden de aparición,** in order of appearance. ‖ **por orden de,** by order of. ‖ **sin orden ni concierto,** any old how.
■ **el orden del día,** the agenda. ‖ **la orden del día,** MIL the order of the day. ‖ **las fuerzas del orden,** the security forces. ‖ **orden de búsqueda y captura,** → **orden de detención.** ‖ **orden de caballería,** order of knighthood. ‖ **orden de detención,** arrest warrant: *se ha dictado una orden de detención contra Juan Gómez,* an order has been issued for the arrest of Juan Gómez. ‖ **orden de pago,** order of payment. ‖ **orden de registro,** search warrant. ‖ **orden judicial,** court order. ‖ **orden público,** public order, the peace, law and order: *una alteración del orden público,* a breach of the peace.
ordenación 1 *f* (*disposición*) arrangement, organizing. 2 REL ordination.
ordenada *f* MAT ordinate.
ordenado,-a 1 *pp* → **ordenar.** – 2 *adj* (*habitación*) tidy, in order; (*persona*) tidy, well-organized. 3 REL ordained.
ordenador,-ra 1 *adj* ordering. 2 REL ordaining. – 3 **ordenador,** *m* INFORM computer.
■ **ordenador personal,** personal computer.
ordenamiento 1 *m* JUR ordinance. 2 (*ordenación*) ordering, arranging.
ordenanza 1 *m* (*soldado*) orderly. 2 (*empleado*) office boy. – 3 *f* (*norma*) ordinance.
■ **ordenanza municipal,** bylaw.
ordenar 1 *t* (*arreglar*) to put in order; (*habitación*) to tidy up: *ordenó a los alumnos en filas,* she lined up the students; *los libros estaban ordenados por materias,* the books were classified by subject matter. 2 (*mandar*) to order: *me ordenó que saliera de la habitación,* he ordered me to leave the room. 3 REL to ordain. 4 (*encaminar*) to direct.
● **ordenar las ideas,** *fig* to collect one's thoughts.
ordeñadora *f* milking machine.
ordeñar *t* to milk.
ordeño *m* milking.
ordinal 1 *adj* ordinal. – 2 *m* ordinal.
ordinariez 1 *f* (*defecto*) vulgarity. 2 (*expresión*) vulgar remark: *¡qué ordinariez!,* how vulgar!
● **decir ordinarieces,** to be vulgar.
ordinario,-a 1 *adj* (*corriente*) ordinary, common. 2 (*grosero*) vulgar, common.
● **de ordinario,** usually.
orear 1 *t* to air. – 2 **orearse,** *p* to get some fresh air.
orégano *m* oregano.
● **no todo el monte es orégano,** life's not all beer and skittles.
oreja 1 *f* ear. 2 (*de sillón*) wing.
● **poner/tener una sonrisa de oreja a oreja,** to grin like a Cheshire cat, grin from ear to ear. ‖ **verle las orejas al lobo,** to see the red light, wake up to a danger, realize things could go wrong.
■ **sillón de orejas,** wing chair.
orejera *f* (*de gorro*) earflap; (*de sillón*) wing.
orejero *m* (*sillón*) wing chair.
orejón 1 *m* dried apricot or peach. 2 *fam* big-ears.
orejudo,-a 1 *adj* big-eared. – 2 *m* long-eared bat.
oremus *m* REL let us pray.
● **perder el oremus,** (*ir desorientado*) to be all at sixes and sevens; (*perder la paciencia*) to lose one's cool.
orfanato *m* orphanage.

orfandad f orphanage.
orfebre m goldsmith, silversmith.
orfebrería f (en oro) gold work; (en plata) silver work.
orfelinato m orphanage.
orfeón m choral society.
orfeonista mf member of a choral society.
órfico,-a adj lit orphic.
organdí m organdie.
orgánico,-a adj organic.
organigrama m (de empresa) organization chart; (de informática) flow chart.
organillero,-a m,f organ-grinder.
organillo m barrel organ.
organismo 1 m (humano) organism. 2 (institucional) organization, body.
organista mf organist.
organización f organization.
organizado,-a 1 pp → **organizar**. – 2 adj organized.
organizador,-ra 1 adj organizing. – 2 m,f organizer.
organizar 1 t to organize: van a organizar una fiesta, they're going to have a party. – 2 **organizarse**, p (ordenarse) to get organized: no sabe organizarse, he is very badly organized. 3 (crearse) to be organized: se ha organizado una colecta, a collection has been organized. 4 (armarse) to be, occur: se organizó un escándalo tremendo, there was a terrible to-do.
▲ Conjugation model [4], like **realizar**.
órgano m organ.
orgasmo m orgasm.
orgía f orgy.
orgiástico,-a adj orgiastic.
orgullo 1 m (propia estima) pride. 2 (arrogancia) arrogance, haughtiness.
orgulloso,-a 1 adj (satisfecho) proud. 2 (arrogante) arrogant, haughty.
● estar orgulloso,-a de ..., to be proud of ... ‖ ser orgulloso,-a, to be arrogant.
orientación 1 f (capacidad) sense of direction. 2 (de un edificio) aspect: la casa tiene orientación sur, the house faces south. 3 (dirección) orientation, direction; (tendencia) leanings pl, tendency. 4 (guía) guidance, orientation.
■ orientación profesional, career guidance, vocational guidance.
orientador,-ra 1 adj (función) advisory, guiding. – 2 m,f guide, adviser, counsellor.
oriental 1 adj eastern, oriental. – 2 mf Oriental.
orientalismo m Orientalism.
orientalista 1 adj Orientalistic. – 2 mf Orientalist.
orientar 1 t (casa) to face; (antena, barco) to point; (velas) to trim: la casa está orientada al mar, the house faces the sea; orientaron la barca hacia la costa, they pointed the boat towards the coast. 2 (esfuerzos, investigaciones) to direct. 3 (guiar) to guide; (aconsejar) to advise: el examen nos orientó de cómo íbamos, the exam gave us an idea of how we were getting on. – 4 **orientarse**, p to find one's bearings: nos orientamos por las estrellas, we were guided by the stars; yo me oriento muy mal, I have an appalling sense of direction; todavía no me he orientado en este trabajo, I haven't learnt the ropes yet.
oriente m East.
■ el Extremo Oriente, the Far East. ‖ el Lejano Oriente, the Far East. ‖ el Oriente Medio, the Middle East. ‖ el Oriente Próximo, the Near East.
orificio m (agujero) hole; (abertura) opening; (en el cuerpo) orifice.

origen 1 m (causa) cause, origin: el origen del problema del paro, the cause of the unemployment problem. 2 procedencia - gen) origin; (- de persona) extraction: de origen español, of Spanish extraction; de origen modesto, of humble origins; Zamora es mi ciudad de origen, I am originally from Zamora.
● dar origen a, to give rise to. ‖ en su origen, originally. ‖ tener su origen en, to originate in.
■ idioma de origen, source language. ‖ país de origen, country of origin.
▲ pl orígenes.
original 1 adj (gen) original. – 2 m original.
● en el original, in the original. ‖ ser original de, (procedente de, nacido en) from: productos originales de Cuba, products from Cuba; mi familia es original de América, my family is originally from America.
originalidad f originality.
originar 1 t to cause, give rise to. – 2 **originarse**, p to originate.
originario,-a adj original.
● ser originario,-a de, (persona) to come from; (costumbre) to originate in.
orilla 1 f (borde) edge. 2 (del río) bank; (del mar) shore.
● a la orilla del mar, by the sea.
orillar 1 t (resolver) to solve. 2 (sortear) to get round.
orín[1] m rust.
orín[2] m urine.
▲ pl orines.
orina f urine.
orinal m chamber pot; (para niños) potty.
orinar 1 i to urinate. – 2 t (sangre) to pass. – 3 **orinarse**, p fam to wet os.: todavía se orina en la cama, he still wets the bed.
oriundo,-a 1 adj native of. – 2 m,f DEP foreign player of Spanish parentage playing for a Spanish team.
● ser oriundo,-a de, to come from.
orla 1 f (adorno) edging. 2 (foto) class graduation photo.
ornamentación f ornamentation.
ornamental adj ornamental.
ornamentar t to adorn, decorate.
ornamento m ornament.
ornar t to adorn.
ornato m ornateness.
ornitología f ornithology.
ornitológico,-a adj ornithological.
ornitólogo,-a m,f ornithologist.
ornitorrinco m platypus.
oro 1 m gold: un reloj de oro, a gold watch. – 2 adj (color) golden. – 3 **oros** mpl (baraja española) ≈ diamonds.
● guardar algo como oro en paño, to cherish sth. ‖ hacerse de oro, to make a fortune. ‖ no es oro todo lo que reluce, all that glitters is not gold. ‖ prometer el oro y el moro, to promise the earth. ‖ tener un corazón de oro, to have a heart of gold.
■ oro de ley, pure gold. ‖ oro negro, oil.
orografía f orography.
orográfico,-a adj orographic.
orondo,-a 1 adj (gordo) hearty, plump. 2 (satisfecho) smug, self-satisfied.
oropel 1 m (material) tinsel. 2 (ostentosidad) glitter.
● de oropel, glittery.
orquesta 1 f (clásica) orchestra; (popular) dance band. 2 (lugar) orchestra pit.
orquestación f orchestration.
orquestal adj orchestral.

orquestar *t* to orchestrate.
orquídea *f* orchid.
orsay *m fam* offside.
ortiga *f* nettle.
ortodoncia *f* orthodontics, dental orthopaedics.
ortodoxia *f* orthodoxy.
ortodoxo,-a 1 *adj* orthodox. – 2 *m,f* orthodox.
ortografía *f* spelling; (*uso formal*) orthography: *se me da muy mal la ortografía,* I can't spell.
■ falta de ortografía, spelling mistake.
ortográfico,-a *adj* spelling; (*uso formal*) orthographic: *regla ortográfica,* spelling rule.
● signo ortográfico, punctuation mark; (*tilde*) written accent. ‖ signos ortográficos, punctuation and accents.
ortopedia *f* orthopaedics.
ortopédico,-a 1 *adj* orthopaedic. – 2 *m,f* orthopaedist.
oruga *f* caterpillar.
orujo 1 *m* (*bebida*) eau-de-vie, spirit. 2 marc, pomace: *el aceite de orujo de oliva es de inferior calidad,* olive oil from a second pressing is of inferior quality.
orza[1] *f* earthenware jar.
orza[2] *f* MAR luff.
orzuelo *m* sty.
os 1 *pron pl* (*complemento directo*) you: *os escucho,* I am listening to you. 2 (*complemento indirecto*) you: *os traje un libro,* I brought you a book; *os he dicho que no os mováis,* I told you not to move. 3 (*reflexivo*) yourselves: *¿ya os estáis vistiendo?,* are you getting dressed already? 4 (*recíproco*) each other: *os parecéis mucho,* you look very much alike.
osa *f* → oso,-a.
osadía 1 *f* (*audacia*) audacity, daring. 2 (*desvergüenza*) effrontery, nerve.
osado,-a 1 *adj* (*audaz*) audacious, daring. 2 (*desvergonzado*) shameless.
osamenta *f* (*esqueleto*) skeleton; (*huesos*) bones *pl.*
osar *i lit* to dare, have the audacity to.
osario 1 *m* (*parte del cementerio*) ossuary. 2 (*cementerio*) burial ground.
oscar *m* CINEM Oscar.
▲ *pl oscar.*
oscense 1 *adj* of Huesca, from Huesca. – 2 *mf* person from Huesca, inhabitant of Huesca.
oscilación 1 *f* (*de precios*) fluctuation. 2 FÍS oscillation.
oscilador *m* oscillator.
oscilante 1 *adj* (*precios etc*) fluctuating. 2 FÍS oscillating.
oscilar 1 *i* (*variar*) to vary, fluctuate. 2 FÍS to oscillate.
oscilatorio,-a *adj* oscillating.
oscilógrafo *m* oscillograph.
ósculo *m lit* kiss.
oscurantismo *m* obscurantism.
oscurantista *adj & mf* → obscurantista.
oscuras a oscuras, *loc* in the dark.
oscurecer *t-i* → obscurecer.
oscuridad *f* → obscuridad.
oscuro,-a *adj* → obscuro.
óseo,-a *adj* (*tejido, estructura*) bone.
osera *f* bear's den.
osezno *m* bear cub.
osificación *f* ossification.
osificar *t* to ossify.
osito *m* (*cachorro*) bear cub.
■ osito de peluche, teddy bear.
Oslo *m* Oslo.

osmio *m* osmium.
ósmosis *f* osmosis.
oso,-a 1 oso, *m* bear. – 2 osa, *f* she-bear.
● ¡anda la osa!, *fam* crikey! ‖ hacer el oso, *fam* to fool around. ‖ como un oso, *fam* (*muy peludo*) as hairy as an ape.
■ Osa Mayor, Great Bear, US Big Dipper. ‖ Osa Menor, Little Bear. ‖ oso hormiguero, anteater. ‖ oso panda, panda. ‖ oso pardo, brown bear. ‖ oso polar, polar bear.
OSO *sím* (*oessudoeste*) west-southwest; (*símbolo*) WSW.
ostensible *adj* obvious, visible.
ostentación *f* ostentation: *vive sin ostentación alguna,* she lives totally without ostentation.
● con ostentación, ostentatiously. ‖ hacer ostentación, to be ostentatious. ‖ hacer ostentación de algo, to flaunt sth.
ostentar 1 *t* (*jactarse de*) to show off, flaunt. 2 (*poseer*) to hold.
● ostentar el cargo de, to hold the position of.
ostentoso,-a *adj* ostentatious.
osteomielitis *f* osteomyelitis.
▲ *pl osteomyelitis.*
osteópata *mf* osteopath.
osteopatía *f* osteopathy.
osteopático,-a *adj* osteophatic.
ostión *m* large oyster.
ostra *f* oyster.
● ¡ostras!, crikey!, wow!, US gee!
ostracismo *m* ostracism.
ostrero,-a 1 *adj* oyster. – 2 ostrero, *m* ORN oystercatcher.
ostrogodo,-a 1 *adj* Ostrogothic. – 2 *m,f* Ostrogoth.
osuno,-a *adj* bear-like.
OTAN *abr* (*Organización del Tratado del Atlántico Norte*) North Atlantic Treaty Organization; (*abreviatura*) NATO.
oteador,-ra *m,f* lookout.
otear *t* (*horizonte*) to scan.
otero *m* hillock.
OTI *abr* TV (*Organización de la Televisión Iberoamericana*) Latin-American television organization.
otitis *f* ear infection, otitis.
▲ *pl otitis.*
otología *f* otology.
otomán *m* (*tela*) ottoman.
otomana *f* → otomano,-a.
otomano,-a 1 *adj* Ottoman. – 2 *m,f* (*persona*) Ottoman. – 3 otomana, *f* (*cama turca*) ottoman.
otoñal *adj* autumnal, autumn, US fall.
otoño *m* autumn, US fall.
otorgante *adj* (*de un premio*) awarding.
otorgar 1 *t* (*conceder*) to grant, give (a, to); (*premio*) to award (a, to). 2 JUR to execute, draw up.
▲ *Conjugation model* [7], *like* llegar.
otorrino *mf fam* → otorrinolaringólogo,-a.
otorrinolaringología *f* ear, nose and throat, ENT.
otorrinolaringólogo,-a *m,f* ear, nose and throat specialist, ENT specialist.
otro,-a 1 *adj indef* other, another: *quiero otro pastel,* I want another cake; *eso ya es otra cosa,* that's different; *otra vez será,* some other time; *el otro día ...,* the other day ...; *otro día venís todos juntos,* next time you could all come. – 2 *pron* other, another: *otros,* others; *unos te dicen que sí y otros que no,* you get a different opinion

from everyone; *no hay otro como él,* he's something else; *otro que te busca,* somebody else looking for you; *otro no lo hubiera hecho,* not everyone is like that.
● **otro de tantos,** nothing exceptional. ‖ **otro que tal baila,** he (*she*) is just as bad. ‖ **¡otra! ¡otra!,** encore!, more!

otrora *adv arc* formerly.
OUA *abr* (*Organización de la Unidad Africana*) Organization of African Unity; (*abreviatura*) OAU.
ovación *f* ovation, cheering, applause.
ovacionar *t* to give an ovation (**a,** to), applaud (**a,** -).
oval *adj* oval.
ovalado,-a *adj* oval.
óvalo *m* oval.
ovario *m* ovary.
oveja *f* sheep, ewe.
● **cada oveja con su pareja,** like should stick to like.
■ **la oveja negra de la familia,** the black sheep of the family.
overtura *f* MÚS overture.
ovetense 1 *adj* of Oviedo, from Oviedo. **– 2** *mf* person from Oviedo, inhabitant of Oviedo.
ovillar *t* to roll into a ball.
ovillo *m* ball of wool.
● **hacerse un ovillo,** *fig* to curl up into a ball.
ovino,-a *adj* ovine, sheep.
ovíparo,-a *adj* oviparous.
OVNI *abr* (*Objeto Volador no Indentificado*) Unidentified Flying Object; (*abreviatura*) UFO.

ovulación *f* ovulation.
ovular 1 *adj* ovular. **– 2** *i* to ovulate.
óvulo *m* ovule.
oxidable *adj* oxidizable.
oxidación 1 *f* QUÍM oxidation. **2** (*proceso*) rusting; (*capa*) rust.
oxidado,-a 1 *adj* rusty. **2** QUÍM oxidized.
oxidante 1 *adj* oxidizing. **– 2** *m* oxidizer.
oxidar 1 *t* QUÍM to oxidize. **2** (*enmohecer*) to rust. **– 3** **oxidarse,** *p* QUÍM to oxidize. **4** (*enmohecerse*) to rust, go rusty.
óxido 1 *m* (*herrumbre*) rust. **2** QUÍM oxide.
oxigenación 1 *f* *fig* airing. **2** QUÍM oxygenation.
oxigenado,-a 1 *adj* QUÍM oxygenated. **2** (*pelo*) bleached.
■ **agua oxigenada,** hydrogen peroxide. ‖ **rubia oxigenada,** peroxide blonde.
oxigenar 1 *t* QUÍM to oxygenate. **2** (*blanquear*) to bleach. **3** (*pulmones*) to get some fresh air in: *hay que oxigenar el cuerpo,* you must get some fresh air. **– 4** **oxigenarse,** *p* (*persona*) to get some fresh air.
oxígeno *m* oxygen.
oye 1 *pres indic* → **oír. – 2** *interj fam* (*para llamar la atención*) hey!; (*con enfado*) listen!, look here!: *oye, guapo,* look here, sunshine!
oyente 1 *mf* RAD listener. **2** (*alumno*) unregistered student. **– 3** *adj* listening.
ozono *m* ozone.
■ **capa de ozono,** ozone layer

P

P, p f (la letra) P, p.
P abr (parking) car park, US parking lot.
p. abr (página) page; (abreviatura) p.
P. abr REL (padre) Father; (abreviatura) Fr.
p.a. abr (por autorización) on behalf of; (abreviatura) pp.
pabellón 1 m ARQ pavilion. **2** (en una feria) stand. **3** (bandera) flag. **4** ANAT (external) ear.
pabilo m wick.
pábilo m wick.
pábulo m fuel.
  ● dar pábulo a, to fuel, encourage.
pacato,-a adj fam prudish.
pacense 1 adj of Badajoz, from Badajoz. – **2** mf person from Badajoz, inhabitant of Badajoz.
paceño,-a 1 adj of La Paz, from La Paz. – **2** m,f person from La Paz, inhabitant of La Paz.
pacer i to graze.
  ▲ Conjugation model |42|, like *nacer*.
pachá m pasha, pacha.
  ● vivir como un pachá, to live like a king.
pachanga f (bullicio) party atmosphere; (música) party music.
pachanguero,-a adj (música) rowdy and catchy.
pacharán m sloe liqueur.
pachón,-ona 1 adj (perro) pointer. **2** fam (persona) laid-back.
  ■ perro pachón, pointer.
pachorra f fam phlegm.
  ● tener pachorra, fam to be laid-back.
pachucho,-a 1 adj fam (persona) poorly. **2** fam (fruta) overripe.
  ● estar pachucho,-a, to feel under the weather.
pachulí m patchouli.
paciencia f patience.
  ● agotar la paciencia a algn., to try sb.'s patience. ‖ armarse de paciencia, to grin and bear it. ‖ tener paciencia, to be patient.
paciente 1 adj patient. – **2** mf patient.
pacientemente adv patiently.
pacificación f pacification.
pacificador,-ra 1 adj pacifying. – **2** m,f peacemaker.
pacíficamente adv peacefully.
pacificar 1 t to pacify. **2** (calmar) to appease.
  ▲ Conjugation model |1|, like *sacar*.
pacífico,-a adj peaceful.
  ■ el (océano) Pacífico, the Pacific (Ocean).
pacifismo m pacifism.
pacifista 1 adj pacifist. – **2** mf pacifist.
pacotilla de pacotilla, loc fam second-rate.
pactar 1 t to agree (to). – **2** i to come to an agreement.
pacto m pact, agreement.
padecer 1 t to suffer: *padece una enfermedad incurable,* he suffers from an incurable disease. – **2** i (sufrir) to suffer (de, from).

▲ Conjugation model |43|, like *agradecer*.
padecimiento m suffering.
padrastro 1 m (padre) stepfather. **2** (en las uñas) hangnail.
padrazo m fam loving father.
padre 1 m father. **2** REL (sacerdote) father. – **3** adj fam (fenomenal) terrific. – **4** Padre, m REL Father. – **5** padres, mpl parents.
  ● de padre y muy señor mío, fam almighty. ‖ no tener ni padre, ni madre, ni perrito que le ladre, to be all alone in the world. ‖ ser cada uno de su padre y su madre, to be an odd mixture. ‖ ¡su *(tu etc)* padre!, fam and the same to you!
  ■ padre de familia, head of the family. ‖ padre espiritual, confessor. ‖ padre político, father-in-law. ‖ el Santo Padre, the Holy Father, the Pope.
padrenuestro m Lord's Prayer.
  ● rezar un padrenuestro, to say the Lord's Prayer.
padrinazgo 1 m (protección) patronage. **2** (de un niño) godfathership.
padrino 1 m (de bautizo) godfather. **2** (de boda) bride's father who acts as best man. **3** (patrocinador) sponsor. – **4** padrinos, mpl godparents.
  ● tener buenos padrinos, fig to have good contacts.
padrón m (censo) census; (para votar) electoral roll.
paella 1 f (comida) paella. **2** → **paellera**.
paellera f paella pan.
paf interj splat.
pág abr (página) page; (abreviatura) p.
pag. abr (pagaré) I owe you; (abreviatura) IOU.
paga 1 f (sueldo) pay. **2** (de los niños) pocket money.
  ■ paga extra, bonus. ‖ paga y señal, down payment.
pagadero,-a adj payable.
pagado,-a pp → **pagar**.
  ● pagado,-a de sí mismo,-a, smug, self-satisfied.
pagador,-ra 1 adj paying. – **2** m,f (gen) payer. **3** (en banco) cashier.
pagaduría f pay office.
paganismo m paganism.
pagano,-a[1] 1 adj REL pagan. – **2** m,f REL pagan.
pagano,-a[2] m,f fam one who pays.
pagar 1 t to pay: *ya he pagado lo que debía,* I've already paid what I owed. – **2** i to pay: *en esta empresa pagan muy bien,* this company pays very well.
  ● pagar al contado, to pay cash. ‖ pagar en metálico, to pay cash. ‖ ¡me las pagarás!, fam you'll pay for this! ‖ pagarlas todas juntas, fam to pay for one's sins: *las pagarás todas juntas,* your sins will catch up with you in the end.
  ▲ Conjugation model |7|, like *llegar*.
pagaré m promissory note.
  ■ pagaré del Tesoro, government bond.
página f page.
  ■ páginas amarillas, yellow pages.

paginación f pagination.
paginar t to paginate.
pago[1] **1** m payment. **2** (recompensa) reward.
● **en pago por,** in return for.
■ **pago a cuenta,** payment on account. ‖ **pago por adelantado,** advance payment.
pago[2] m area.
● **por estos pagos,** around here.
pagoda f pagoda.
paipái m fan.
país m country.
● **del país,** local.
paisaje m landscape.
paisajista mf (pintor) landscape artist.
paisajístico,-a adj landscape.
paisano,-a 1 m,f (compatriota - hombre) fellow countryman; (- mujer) fellow countrywoman: es paisana mía, she comes from the same part of the country as me. **2** (campesino - hombre) countryman; (- mujer) countrywoman.
● **de paisano,** (policía) in plain clothes; (soldado) in civilian clothes.
paja 1 f straw. **2** fig (relleno) waffle. **3** tabú (masturbación) wank.
● **hacerse una paja,** tabú to wank, us jerk off. ‖ **meter paja,** to waffle. ‖ **por un quítame allá esas pajas,** for no reason at all.
pajar 1 m (lugar) hayloft. **2** (almiar) haystack.
pájara f → **pájaro,-a.**
pajarera f aviary.
pajarería f (tienda) caged-bird shop.
pajarero,-a adj of birds.
pajarito,-a 1 m,f little bird, birdie. – **2 pajarito,** m fam (pene) willy, willie. – **3 pajarita,** f (de cuello) bow tie. **4** (de papel) paper bird.
● **me lo ha dicho un pajarito,** a little bird told me. ‖ **quedarse como un pajarito,** (morir) to snuff it.
pájaro,-a 1 m zool bird. – **2** m,f fam fig (persona astuta) slyboots; (malintencionada) nasty piece of work. – **3 pájara,** f DEP fam collapse, sudden loss of physical energy.
● **más vale pájaro en mano que ciento volando,** a bird in the hand is worth two in the bush. ‖ **matar dos pájaros de un tiro,** to kill two birds with one stone. ‖ **tener la cabeza llena de pájaros,** to be scatterbrained.
■ **pájaro bobo,** penguin. ‖ **pájaro carpintero,** woodpecker. ‖ **pájaro de cuenta,** fam slyboots. ‖ **pájaro de mal agüero,** bird of ill omen.
pajarraco,-a 1 m,f (pájaro) big ugly bird. **2** pey (persona - taimada) slyboots; (- mala) swine. – **3 pajarraca,** f fam brawl.
paje m page.
● **a lo paje,** (corte de pelo) pageboy style.
pajita f (para beber) straw.
pajizo,-a adj straw-like.
pajolero,-a adj fam bloody.
pala 1 f (herramienta) shovel; (de jardinería) spade. **2** (de cocina) slice. **3** DEP (de ping-pong) bat; (de remo) blade; (de frontón) bat. **4** (de hélice) blade. **5** (de zapato) upper.
palabra f word.
● **dar su palabra,** to give one's word, promise: te doy mi palabra de que estaré allí, I promise you I'll be there. ‖ **decir la última palabra,** to have the last word. ‖ **dejar a algn. con la palabra en la boca,** to cut sb. off. ‖ **dirigirle la palabra a algn.,** to address sb. ‖ **en una palabra,** in a word. ‖ **no decir ni media palabra a**

nadie, not to breath a word to anyone. ‖ **medir las palabras,** to weigh one's words. ‖ **no dirigirle la palabra a algn.,** not to be speaking to sb. ‖ **palabra por palabra,** word for word. ‖ **quitarle a algn. la palabra,** to cut sb. short, interrupt sb. ‖ **ser hombre/mujer de palabra,** to be a man of his word/a woman of her word. ‖ **ser hombre/mujer de pocas palabras,** to be a man/woman of few words. ‖ **tener la palabra,** to have the floor. ‖ **tener palabra,** to keep one's word. ‖ **tener unas palabras con algn.,** to have words with sb. ‖ **tomarle a algn. la palabra,** to take sb. at their word.
■ **juego de palabras,** pun, play on words. ‖ **palabra clave,** key word. ‖ **palabra de honor,** word of honour. ‖ **palabras mayores,** (palabrotas) swearwords; (cosa importante) serious talk.
palabreja f difficult word.
palabrería f pey hot air, talk.
palabrota f swearword.
● **decir palabrotas,** to swear.
palacete m mansion.
palaciego,-a adj palatial.
palacio m palace.
■ **palacio de congresos,** conference hall. ‖ **Palacio de Justicia,** Law Courts pl.
palada 1 f (gen) shovelful; (de jardinería) spadeful. **2** (de remo) stroke.
paladar 1 m palate. **2** fig taste.
● **tener buen paladar,** (persona) to have a discerning palate; (vino) to be smooth.
paladear t to savour, relish.
paladín 1 m HIST paladin. **2** fig champion.
paladino,-a adj open, public.
palafito m house-on-stilts.
palafrén m palfrey.
palafrenero m groom.
palanca 1 f (gen) lever. **2** (manecilla) handle. **3** DEP diving board. **4** fig (influencia) contacts pl.
● **hacer palanca,** to lever. ‖ **tener palanca,** to have contacts, know people in the right places.
■ **palanca de cambio,** gearstick.
palangana f bowl, washbasin (us washbowl).
palangre 1 m (arte de pesca) boulter (a long stout line with many hooks). **2** (merluza) hake caught using a boulter.
palangrero 1 m (barco) fishing boat which fishes with boulters. **2** (pescador) fisherman who fishes with boulters.
palanqueta 1 f (para forzar algo) crowbar. **2** (palanca) small lever.
palanquín m (asiento) palanquin.
palatal 1 adj palatal. – **2** f palatal.
palatino,-a[1] adj (del paladar) palatal.
palatino,-a[2] adj palatine.
palco m (en el teatro) box.
■ **palco escénico,** stage.
palenque 1 m (valla) wooden palisade. **2** (área) arena.
palentino,-a 1 adj of Palencia, from Palencia. – **2** m,f person from Palencia, inhabitant of Palencia.
paleografía f palaeography (us paleography).
paleógrafo,-a m,f palaeographer (us paleographer).
paleolítico,-a 1 adj palaeolithic (us paleolithic). – **2 el paleolítico,-a,** m the Palaeolithic (us Paleolithic).
paleontología f palaeontology (us paleontology).
paleontólogo,-a m,f palaeontologist (us paleontologist).
Palestina f Palestine.

palestino,-a 1 adj Palestinian. – 2 m,f Palestinian.
palestra f arena, forum.
● salir a la palestra, to come forward. ‖ saltar a la palestra, to come to the fore.
paleta 1 f (de pintor) palette. 2 (de albañil) trowel. 3 (de cocina) slice. 4 (de hélice etc) blade. 5 fam (diente) front tooth. 6 DEP bat. 7 (pala) small shovel. 8 fam (mujer) → paleto,-a.
paletada 1 f (de albañil) going over with a trowel. 2 fam oafish thing to do or say.
paletilla 1 f ANAT shoulder blade. 2 CULIN shoulder.
paletó m HIST long fitted coat.
paleto,-a 1 m,f fam pey oaf, country bumpkin, yokel. – 2 adj fam pey oafish.
paliar t to palliate, alleviate.
▲ Conjugation model [12], like cambiar.
paliativo,-a 1 adj palliative. – 2 paliativo, m palliative.
palidecer 1 i to turn pale. 2 fig to fade.
▲ Conjugation model |43|, like agradecer.
palidez f paleness, pallor.
pálido,-a adj pale.
palillero m toothpick holder.
palillo 1 m (mondadientes) toothpick. 2 MÚS drumstick.
● estar como un palillo, fam to be as thin as a rake.
■ palillos chinos, chopsticks.
palio m canopy.
● recibir a algn. bajo palio, to give sb. a royal welcome.
palique m fam chat, small talk.
● estar de palique, fam to chat.
palisandro m rosewood.
palitroque 1 m (palo) stick. 2 (en toreo) banderilla.
paliza 1 f beating, thrashing. 2 fam (derrota) thrashing. 3 fam (pesadez) pain.
● dar una paliza a algn. / pegar una paliza a algn., to beat sb. up. ‖ dar la paliza, fam to be a pain. ‖ darse la paliza, fam to slog one's guts out. ‖ ser un paliza / ser un palizas, fam to be a pain, be a pain in the neck.
palizada f palisade, stockade.
palma 1 f BOT palm (tree). 2 (de la mano) palm. – 3 palmas, fpl (aplausos) clapping sing, applause sing.
● batir palmas / dar palmas, to clap. ‖ como la palma de la mano, like the back of one's hand. ‖ llevarse la palma, to take the biscuit.
palmada 1 f (aplauso) clapping. 2 (golpe) slap, pat: me dio una palmada en el hombro, he gave me a slap on the back.
● dar palmadas, to clap.
palmar[1] m palm grove.
palmar[2] palmarla, loc fam to snuff it, kick the bucket.
palmarés 1 m (lista) list of winners. 2 (historial) list of achievements; (de deportista) record, track record: tiene en su palmarés tres campionatos de España, he has won three Spanish championships.
palmario,-a adj obvious, evident.
palmatoria f candlestick.
palmeado,-a 1 adj BOT palmate. 2 ZOOL (dedos) webbed.
palmear i to clap.
palmense 1 adj of Las Palmas, from Las Palmas. – 2 mf person from Las Palmas, inhabitant of Las Palmas.
palmeo m clapping.
palmera 1 f BOT palm tree, palm. 2 (pasta) heart-shaped pastry.
palmeral m palm grove.
palmero,-a 1 adj (de la Palma) from La Palma, of La Palma. – 2 m,f person from La Palma, inhabitant of La Palma.

palmeta f cane.
palmetazo m stroke of the cane.
● dar un palmetazo a algn., fig to haul sb. over the coals.
palmípedo,-a 1 adj web-footed. – 2 palmípedas, fpl ZOOL (género) web-footed birds.
palmitas llevar en palmitas, loc adv to cosset sb.
palmito 1 m CULIN palm heart. 2 BOT palmetto. 3 fam (tipo) figure.
palmo m (medida) span.
● conocer algo palmo a palmo, to know sth. like the back of one's hand. ‖ dejar a algn. con un palmo de narices, fam to let sb. down badly.
palmotear i to clap.
palmoteo m clapping.
palo 1 m (estaca) stick; (de valla) post; (de telégrafos) pole. 2 (golpe) blow: le pegaron un palo que casi lo matan, they almost beat him to death; ha sido un palo que se las supendieran todas, what a drag that he's failed every subject! 3 (madera) wood. 4 (de la letra) stroke: haz el palo de la "p" más largo, make the stroke of the "p" longer. 5 (de baraja) suit. 6 MAR mast. 7 DEP (de una portería) goal post. 8 (de golf) club.
● a palo seco, (comida) on its own; (bebida) neat. ‖ dar palos, to beat. ‖ dar palos de ciego, to grope about in the dark. ‖ de tal palo tal astilla, like father like son. ‖ echar a palos, to kick out. ‖ estar hecho,-a un palo, fam to be as thin as a rake. ‖ no dar un palo al agua, fam not to do a stroke.
■ palo de escoba, bromstick. ‖ palo dulce, liquorice. ‖ palo mayor, mainmast.
paloma f (gen) pigeon; (blanca) dove.
■ paloma blanca, dove. ‖ paloma de la paz, dove of peace. ‖ paloma mensajera, carrier pigeon. ‖ paloma torcaz, wood-pigeon.
palomar m dovecote.
palometa f Ray's bream.
palomilla 1 f (de la luz) moth. 2 (tuerca) wing nut. 3 (armazón) bracket.
palomino 1 m young pigeon. 2 fam droppings pl.
palomita 1 f aniseed and water. – 2 palomitas (de maíz), fpl popcorn sing.
palomo m cock pigeon.
palote 1 m (palo) stick. 2 (dibujo) stroke.
palpable 1 adj palpable. 2 fig (evidente) obvious, evident.
palpación f palpation.
palpar 1 t MED to palpate. 2 to feel. 3 fig (percibir) to sense, feel: se palpa cierto descontento en el ambiente, there's discontent in the air.
palpitación f palpitation.
palpitante 1 adj MED palpitating, throbbing. 2 (tema, cuestión) burning. 3 (luz, reflejo) flashing.
● de palpitante actualidad, burning.
palpitar i to palpitate, throb.
pálpito m hunch, feeling.
palúdico,-a adj malarial.
■ fiebres palúdicas, malaria sing.
paludismo m malaria.
palurdo,-a 1 adj pey uncouth. – 2 m,f country bumpkin.
palustre adj (de las lagunas) lake; (de los pantanos) marshy.
pamela f wide-brimmed straw hat.
pamema f (tontería) piece of nonsense: no digas pamemas, stop talking nonsense.
pampa f pampas pl.
pámpano m vine shoot.

pamplina *f* (*tontería*) daft thing: *no me vengas con pamplinas,* don't be so daft!
pamplinero,-a *adj* sweet-talking.
pamplinoso,-a *adj* → **pamplinero,-a**.
pamplonés,-esa 1 *adj* of Pamplona, from Pamplona. – 2 *m,f* person from Pamplona, inhabitant of Pamplona.
pamplonica *adj-mf* → **pamplonés,-esa**.
pan 1 *m* (*masa*) bread; (*hogaza*) loaf of bread. 2 (*alimento*) food, bread. 3 (*de metal*) leaf, foil.
● **a falta de pan, buenas son tortas,** beggars can't be choosers. ‖ **con su pan se lo coma,** I don't give a damn. ‖ **contigo pan y cebolla,** you're all that matters to me. ‖ **estar a pan y agua,** to be on a strict diet. ‖ **ganarse el pan,** to earn one's living. ‖ **llamar al pan, pan y al vino, vino,** to call a spade a spade. ‖ **ser el pan nuestro de cada día,** to be an everyday occurrence, be par for the course. ‖ **ser más bueno que el pan,** to be very good. ‖ **ser pan comido,** *fam* to be a piece of cake.
■ **barra de pan,** loaf of bread. ‖ **pan ácimo,** unleavened bread. ‖ **pan candeal,** white bread. ‖ **pan de molde,** packet sliced bread. ‖ **pan de oro,** gold leaf. ‖ **pan de Viena,** bridge roll. ‖ **pan integral,** wholemeal bread. ‖ **pan rallado,** breadcrumbs *pl*.
pana *f* corduroy.
panacea *f* panacea.
panadería *f* bakery, baker's.
panadero,-a *m,f* baker.
panadizo *m* whitlow.
panal *m* honeycomb.
Panamá *m* Panama.
■ **sombrero panamá,** Panama hat.
panameño,-a 1 *adj* Panamanian. – 2 *m,f* Panamanian.
panamericano,-a *adj* Pan-American.
■ **la Panamericana,** the Pan-American Highway.
panavisión *f* Panavision.
pancarta *f* placard.
panceta *f* bacon.
panchito *m* roasted peanut.
pancho,-a *adj fam* calm, laid-back.
● **quedarse tan pancho,-a,** to behave as if nothing had happened, not be the least bit bothered.
páncreas *m* pancreas.
▲ *pl* **páncreas**.
pancreático,-a *adj* pancreatic.
■ **jugo pancreático,** pancreatic juice.
panda[1] *m* ZOOL panda.
panda[2] *f* (*de amigos*) group; (*de gamberros*) gang.
pandemónium *m* pandemonium.
pandereta *f* small tambourine.
pandero 1 *m* tambourine. 2 *fam* bottom, behind.
pandilla *f* group of friends.
panecillo *m* bread roll.
panegírico,-a 1 *adj* panegyrical, panegyric. – 2 **panegírico,** *m* panegyric.
panel 1 *m* (*gen*) panel. 2 (*tablero*) noticeboard; (*en la carretera*) hoarding, US billboard.
■ **panel de expertos,** a panel of experts. ‖ **panel de mando,** control panel. ‖ **panel solar,** solar panel.
panera *f* → **panero,-a**.
panero,-a 1 *adj* bread-loving: *en muy panera,* she loves bread. – 2 **panera,** *f* (*para la mesa*) breadbasket; (*de cocina*) bread bin, US bread box.
pánfilo,-a 1 *adj* (*tonto*) moronic. 2 (*lento*) slow. – 3 *m,f* moron.

panfletario,-a *adj* (*estilo*) propagandist.
panfletista *mf* pamphleteer.
panfleto 1 *m* political pamphlet. 2 *fig* propaganda.
pánico *m* panic: *tengo pánico a las serpientes,* I have a horror of snakes; *a mí el avión me da pánico,* flying absolutely terrifies me; *¡que no cunda el pánico!,* don't panic!; *nada más aparecer el tiburón, cundió el pánico entre los bañistas,* the bathers were thrown into a panic the moment the shark appeared.
● **de pánico,** (*bueno*) terrific; (*malo*) terrible. ‖ **ser presa del pánico,** to be panic-stricken.
panificadora *f* industrial bakery.
panificar *i* to manufacture bread.
panizo *m* millet.
panocha *f* (*de maíz*) corncob; (*de trigo*) ear.
panoja *f* → **panocha**.
panoli 1 *adj fam* simple. – 2 *mf fam* simpleton.
panoplia 1 *f* (*armadura*) suit of armour. 2 (*colección*) arms collection. 3 (*escudo con armas*) shield.
panorama 1 *m* (*paisaje*) panorama, view. 2 (*aspecto*) situation, outlook: *el panorama político actual,* the present political situation.
panorámico,-a 1 *adj* panoramic. – 2 **panorámica,** *f* panorama.
■ **vista panorámica,** scenic view, panoramic view.
panqueque *m* AM pancake.
pantagruélico,-a *adj* Pantagruelian.
pantalla 1 *f* screen. 2 (*de lámpara*) lampshade. 3 *fig* (*tapadera*) cover.
■ **la pequeña pantalla,** television. ‖ **pantalla de humo,** smokescreen.
pantalón *m* trousers *pl*, US pants.
● **bajarse los pantalones,** to take one's trousers down; *fig* to climb down, give in. ‖ **llevar los pantalones,** to wear the trousers.
■ **pantalón bombacho,** (*corto*) knickerbockers *pl*, breeches *pl*; (*largo*) long breeches (*tied at the ankle*). ‖ **pantalón corto,** (*gen*) shorts *pl*; (*infantil*) short trousers *pl*. ‖ **pantalón de pinzas,** pleated trousers *pl*. ‖ **pantalón tejano,** jeans *pl*. ‖ **pantalón vaquero,** jeans *pl*.
▲ Often used in plural with the same meaning.
pantano 1 *m* (*artificial*) reservoir. 2 (*cenagoso*) marsh.
pantanoso,-a *adj* marshy.
panteísmo *m* pantheism.
panteísta 1 *adj* pantheist. – 2 *mf* pantheist.
panteístico,-a *adj* pantheistic.
panteón *m* pantheon.
■ **panteón familiar,** family vault.
pantera *f* panther.
panties *mpl* tights.
pantomima 1 *f* (*representación*) pantomime, mime. 2 *fig* farce, pretence.
pantorrilla *f* calf.
pantufla *f* slipper.
panty *m* tights *pl*.
▲ Often used in plural *pantys* with the same meaning.
panza *f* belly.
panzada 1 *f fam* (*atracón - de comer*) binge, blow-out; (*de beber*) binge: *anoche me pegué una panzada de fumar,* I smoked myself silly last night. 2 (*en el agua*) belly flop.
panzazo *m* belly flop.
panzudo,-a *adj* paunchy, potbellied.
pañal *m* nappy, US diaper.
● **estar en pañales,** (*estar verde - persona*) to be very green; (*proyecto*) to be in its infancy. ‖ **ser un niño de pañales,** to be a baby.

paño I *m* (*gen*) cloth; (*de lana*) woollen cloth: *un abrigo de paño,* a woollen coat. **2** (*para polvo*) duster; (*de cocina*) dishcloth. **3** (*de pared*) panel, stretch.
● **con paños calientes,** gently: *dímelo sin paños calientes,* tell it to me straight. ‖ **conocerse el paño,** to know what's what. ‖ **en paños menores,** (*con la ropa interior*) in one's underwear; (*desnudo*) stark naked. ‖ **ser el paño de lágrimas de algn.,** to be sb.'s shoulder to cry on.
■ **paño de cocina,** dishcloth.
pañol *m* storeroom.
pañoleta I *f* (*de señora*) shawl. **2** (*de torero*) bullfighter's tie.
pañuelo I *m* handkerchief. **2** (*chal*) shawl.
papa¹ I *m fam* dad. **2 el Papa,** the Pope.
papa² *f* (*patata*) potato.
● **ni papa,** not a thing. ‖ **no saber ni papa,** *fam* not to have a clue.
▲ **papas fritas,** (*calientes*) chips, US French fries; (*de bolsa*) crisps, US chips.
papá *m fam* dad, daddy.
papada *f* double chin.
papado *m* papacy.
papagayo I *m* parrot. **2** *fig* chatterbox.
● **como un papagayo,** parrot-fashion.
papal *adj* papal.
papamoscas *m* flycatcher.
▲ *pl* papamoscas.
papamóvil *m fam* Pope-mobile.
papanatas *mf* simpleton.
▲ *pl* papanatas.
papar *t fam* → **papear.**
paparrucha I *f fam* (*mentira*) fib. **2** (*tontería*) nonsense.
paparruchada *f fam* → **paparrucha.**
papaya *f* papaya.
papayo *m* papaya tree.
papear *i fam* to eat, have something to eat.
papel I *m* (*gen*) paper; (*hoja*) piece of paper: *lo apuntó en un papel,* he wrote it down on a piece of paper. **2** CINEM TEAT role, part: *¿qué papel te ha tocado en la obra?,* what's your role in the play?; *hizo el papel de Hamlet,* he played Hamlet. **3** (*función*) role: *¿qué papel desempeñas en la empresa?,* what's your role in the company? – **4 papeles,** *mpl fam* (*documentación*) papers: *¿tienes los papeles en regla?,* are your papers in order?
● **hacer el papel,** to pretend. ‖ **hacer el papel de algn.,** (*en teatro, cine*) to play the part of sb. ‖ **hacer mal papel,** to do badly. ‖ **hacer buen papel,** to do well. ‖ **aprenderse el papel,** to learn one's lines. ‖ **saberse el papel,** to know one's lines. ‖ **perder los papeles,** to lose control. ‖ **ser papel mojado,** to be worthless, not be worth the paper it's printed on. ‖ **sobre el papel,** on paper.
■ **papel de aluminio,** aluminium foil. ‖ **papel de arroz,** rice paper. ‖ **papel de barbas,** bloom. ‖ **papel de calcar,** tracing-paper. ‖ **papel de carta,** writing paper. ‖ **papel de estaño,** tin foil. ‖ **papel de estraza,** brown paper. ‖ **papel de fumar,** cigarette paper. ‖ **papel de lija,** sandpaper. ‖ **papel de pagos al Estado,** *certificate of payment to a government department.* ‖ **papel de plata,** silver foil, tinfoil. ‖ **papel de seda,** tissue paper. ‖ **papel carbón,** carbon paper. ‖ **papel cebolla,** onionskin. ‖ **papel celo,** Sellotape. ‖ **papel charol,** glazed paper. ‖ **papel cuadriculado,** squared paper. ‖ **papel guarro,** artist's paper. ‖ **papel higiénico,** toilet paper. ‖ **papel maché,** papier-maché. ‖ **papel moneda,** paper money. ‖ **papel pintado,** wallpaper. ‖ **pa-**

pel satinado, glossy paper. ‖ **papel secante,** blotting paper. ‖ **papel vegetal,** film.
papeleo *m fam* red tape, paperwork.
papelera I *f* wastepaper basket. **2** (*en la calle*) litter bin.
papelería *f* stationer's.
papelero,-a *adj* (*del papel*) paper: *la industria papelera,* the paper industry.
papeleta I *f* (*de empeño*) ticket. **2** (*de voto*) ballot paper. **3** (*de examen*) results slip. **4** *fam* (*problema*) tricky problem: *¡vaya papeleta!,* what an awful situation!
■ **papeleta de voto,** ballot paper.
papelina *f arg* paper, bindle.
papelón I *m fam* ridiculous situation: *¡vaya papelón que hemos hecho delante de todo el mundo!,* we made right fools of ourselves in front of everybody! **2** *fam* (*actuación*) brilliant acting: *en esa película hizo un papelón,* he acted brilliantly in that film.
papelote *m* worthless piece of paper.
papeo *m arg* grub.
paperas *fpl* mumps.
papi *m fam* dad, daddy.
papila *f* papilla.
papilla I *f* (*infantil*) baby food. **2** (*masa espesa*) pap, mush.
● **echar la (primera) papilla,** *fam* to be as sick as a dog. ‖ **estar hecho,-a papilla,** *fam* (*persona*) to be shattered; (*objeto*) to be falling to bits. ‖ **hacer papilla a algn.,** *fam* to make mincemeat of sb.
papiro *m* papyrus.
papiroflexia *f* origami.
papirotazo *m* flick.
papirote *m* flick.
papista *adj* papist.
● **ser más papista que el papa,** to out-Herod Herod.
papo I *m* (*de ave*) crop; (*de animal*) dewlap. **2** *fam* (*de persona*) double chin.
Papua *f* Papua.
■ **Papua Nueva Guinea,** Papua New Guinea.
paquebote *m* packet boat.
paquete I *m* (*cajita*) packet, pack; (*bulto*) package; (*postal*) parcel: *un paquete de cigarrillos,* a packet of cigarettes. **2** (*conjunto*) set, packet: *un paquete de medidas,* a package, a package of measures. **3** *fam* (*inútil*) useless person, wally. **4** *fam* (*genitales masculinos*) bulge, packet.
● **ir de paquete,** to ride pillion. ‖ **marcar paquete,** *fam* to have a bulge in one's trousers. ‖ **meter un paquete a algn.,** *arg* to come down on sb. like a ton of bricks.
■ **paquete postal,** parcel.
paquetería *f* packaging.
paquidermo *m* pachyderm.
Paquistán *m* Pakistan.
paquistaní I *adj* Pakistani. – **2** *mf* Pakistani.
par I *adj* equal. **2** MAT even. – **3** *m* (*dos*) couple; (*pareja*) pair: *un par de naranjas,* a couple of oranges; *un par de veces,* a couple of times; *un par de pantalones,* a pair of trousers. **4** (*título*) peer.
● **a la par,** (*al mismo tiempo*) at the same time; (*juntos*) together. ‖ **a pares,** in twos, two by two. ‖ **de par en par,** wide open. ‖ **sin par,** matchless.
■ **pares y nones,** odds and evens.
PAR *abr* POL (*Partido Aragonés Regionalista*) Aragonese regionalist party.
para I *prep* (*finalidad*) for: *he comprado un regalo para mi abuela,* I've bought a present for my grandmother; *es para su cumpleaños,* it's for her birthday. **2** (*uso, utilidad*) for: *los cuchillos son para cortar, no para jugar con ellos,*

knives are for cutting, not for playing with; *¿tienes algo para el dolor de cabeza?,* have you got anything for a headache? **3** (*destino, dirección*) for, to: *salimos para Lugo el domingo,* we leave for Lugo on Sunday; *el tren para Toledo sale a las 18.00,* the train to Toledo leaves at 18.00; *¿para dónde vas?,* where are you going?; *voy para allá inmediatamente,* I'll be there in a minute. **4** (*tiempo, fechas límites*) by, before: *lo necesito para el viernes,* I need it by Friday; *la carretera estará acabada para antes del verano,* the road will be finished before the summer. **5** (*comparación*) for: *para los años que tiene está muy activa,* she's very active for her age; *pesa poquísimo para lo grande que es,* it's very light for its size. − **6** *conj* (*finalidad*) to, in order to: *lo hice para ahorrar tiempo,* I did it to save time; *para estar sano es preciso comer bien,* in order to be healthy one must eat properly. **7** (*suficiente*) enough: *tal como nos han tratado es para no volver nunca más,* the way they treated us is enough to make you never go back there again.

● **para entonces,** by then. ‖ **para con,** towards, to: *han sido muy injustos para con los empleados,* they have been very unfair to their employees; *cumplió con sus obligaciones para con la iglesia,* he fulfilled his obligations to the church. ‖ **para que,** so that: *déjale una nota a tu madre para que sepa dónde estás,* leave your mother a note so that she knows where you are; *cierra la puerta para que no entre el perro,* shut the door so that the dog doesn't get in; *aún es pronto para que vuelvan,* it's still too early for them to be back. ‖ **¿para qué?,** what for?: *¿para qué has comprado eso?,* what did you buy that for? ‖ **¡que para qué!,** *fam* very, really, terribly: *¡hace un frío que para qué!,* it's freezing; *¡es más torpe que para qué!,* she's so clumsy!

parabién *m* congratulations *pl.*

parábola **1** *f* REL parable. **2** MAT parabola.

parabólico,-a **1** *adj* parabolic. − **2 parabólica,** *f* satellite dish.

parabrisas *m* windscreen.

▲ *pl* *parabrisas.*

paracaídas *m* parachute.

● tirarse en paracaídas, to parachute.

▲ *pl* *paracaídas.*

paracaidismo *m* parachuting.

paracaidista **1** *mf* DEP parachutist. **2** MIL paratrooper.

parachoques **1** *m* AUTO bumper, US fender. **2** (*de tren*) buffer.

▲ *pl* *parachoques.*

parada[1] **1** *f* (*gen*) stop, halt. **2** (*de autobús etc*) stop. **3** (*pausa*) pause. **4** DEP save, catch.

● hacer parada en, to stop at, stop in.

■ parada de autobús, bus stop. ‖ parada de taxis, taxi rank, US cab stand. ‖ parada discrecional, request stop.

parada[2] *f* MIL parade.

■ parada militar, parade.

paradero *m* whereabouts *pl.*

● estar en paradero desconocido, to be missing. ‖ paradero desconocido, whereabouts unknown.

paradigma *m* paradigm.

paradigmático,-a *adj* paradigmatic.

paradisíaco,-a *adj* heavenly.

parado,-a **1** *pp* → **parar.** − **2** *adj* (*quieto*) still, motionless. **3** *fig* (*lento*) slow, awkward. **4** (*sin trabajo*) unemployed. − **5** *m,f* unemployed person: *los parados,* the unemployed.

● estar parado,-a, to be unemployed. ‖ salir bien pa-

rado,-a, to come off well. ‖ salir mal parado,-a, to come off badly.

paradoja *f* paradox.

paradójico,-a *adj* paradoxical.

parador **1** *m* (*hotel*) state-run hotel. **2** *arc* (*posada*) inn.

■ parador nacional de turismo, state-run hotel *usually of historic or monumental value.*

paraestatal *adj* public-sector.

parafernalia *f* paraphernalia.

parafina *f* paraffin.

parafrasear *t* to paraphrase.

paráfrasis *f* paraphrase.

▲ *pl* *paráfrasis.*

parágrafo *m* paragraph.

paraguas *m* umbrella.

▲ *pl* *paraguas.*

Paraguay *m* Paraguay.

paraguaya *f* → **paraguayo,-a.**

paraguayo,-a **1** *adj* Paraguayan. − **2** *m,f* Paraguayan. − **3 paraguaya,** *f type of flattened peach.*

paragüero *m* umbrella stand.

paraíso **1** *m* paradise. **2** TEAT (*gallinero*) gods *pl.*

■ paraíso terrenal, heaven on earth. ‖ **paraíso fiscal,** tax haven.

paraje *m* spot.

paralela *f* → **paralelo,-a.**

paralelismo **1** *m* parallelism. **2** *fig* similarity.

paralelo,-a **1** *adj* parallel. − **2 paralelo,** *m* parallel. − **3 paralela,** *f* (*línea*) parallel (line). − **4 paralelas,** *fpl* DEP parallel bars.

paralelogramo *m* parallelogram.

paralimpiada *f* Special Olympics *pl.*

paralímpico,-a **1** *adj* of or relating to the Special Olympics. − **2** *m,f* athlete competing in the Special Olympics.

■ los Juegos Paralímpicos, Special Olympic Games.

parálisis *f* paralysis.

■ parálisis infantil, poliomyelitis.

▲ *pl* *parálisis.*

paralítico,-a **1** *adj* paralytic. − **2** *m,f* paralytic.

paralización **1** *f* paralysis. **2** COM stagnation.

paralizar **1** *t* MED to paralyse. **2** (*circulación*) to bring to a standstill; (*obras, actividad*) to bring to a halt; (*negociaciones, proyecto*) to freeze.

▲ Conjugation model |4|, like *realizar.*

paramento **1** *m* (*adorno*) ornament, decoration. **2** (*de una pared*) face.

parámetro *m* parameter.

paramilitar *adj* paramilitary.

páramo *m* moor.

parangón *m* comparison.

parangonar *t fml* to compare.

paraninfo *m* assembly hall of a university.

paranoia *f* paranoia.

paranoico,-a **1** *adj* paranoic, paranoid. − **2** *m,f* paranoiac, paranoic.

paranormal *adj* paranormal.

■ fenómeno paranormal, paranormal phenomenon.

parapente **1** *m* (*deporte*) paragliding. **2** (*paracaídas*) paraglider.

parapetarse **1** *p* to take shelter, take cover. **2** *fig* to take refuge.

parapeto *m* parapet.

paraplejia *f* paraplegia.

▲ Also written *paraplejía.*

parapléjico,-a 1 *adj* paraplegic. – **2** *m,f* paraplegic.

parapsicología *f* parapsychology.

parapsicológico,-a *adj* parapsychological.

parapsicólogo,-a *m,f* parapsychologist.

parar 1 *t* to stop: *nos paró la policía,* the police stopped us. **2** DEP to save, catch: *ha parado tres pelotas,* he's made three saves. – **3** *i* to stop: *aquí no para el tren,* the train doesn't stop here; *¡para de gritar!,* stop shouting! **4** (*alojarse*) to stay: *¿dónde estás parando?,* where are you staying? **5** (*hallarse*) to be: *no para en casa,* she's never at home. **6** (*llegar*) to lead; (*acabar*) to end up: *no se sabe en qué parará esta aventura,* who knows how this adventure will end; *fue a parar a la cárcel,* he ended up in prison. – **7** pararse, *p* to stop.

● **no parar (quieto,-a),** (*ser activo, viajar*) to be always be on the go; (*ser inquieto*) not to stop moving. ‖ **pararse a,** to stop to. ‖ **pararse en seco,** to stop dead. ‖ **sin parar,** nonstop. ‖ **¿dónde vamos a parar?,** what's the world coming to?

pararrayos *m* lightning conductor.

▲ *pl* pararrayos.

parasicología *f* → **parapsicología.**

parasicológico,-a *adj* → **parapsicológico,-a.**

parasicólogo,-a *m,f* → **parapsicólogo,-a.**

parasitario,-a *adj* parasitic.

parasitismo *m* parasitism.

parásito,-a 1 *adj* parasitic. – **2** parásito, *m* BIOL parasite. **3** *pey* (*persona*) parasite, hanger-on. – **4** parásitos, *mpl* RAD interference *sing.*

parasol *m* parasol, sunshade.

parca la parca, *f fig* death.

parcela 1 *f* (*de tierra*) plot (of land). **2** *fig* share, portion.

parcelación *f* (*de un terreno*) division into plots.

parcelar *t* (*finca*) to divide into plots.

parche 1 *m* patch. **2** *fig* (*chapuza*) botch job.

● **poner un parche a algo,** to patch sth. up.

parchear *t* to patch up.

parchís *m* ludo.

▲ *pl* parchís.

parcial 1 *adj* (*gen*) partial; (*examen*) *covering part of the course.* **2** (*tendencioso*) partial, biased. – **3** *m* (*examen*) *examination covering part of the course and counting towards the final mark.*

parcialidad *f* (*injusticia*) bias, partiality.

parcialmente *adv* partially, partly.

parco,-a 1 *adj* (*escaso*) frugal, sparing. **2** (*moderado*) moderate, sober.

● **ser parco,-a en palabras/ideas,** to be a person of few words/ideas.

pardiez *interj arc* gadzooks!

pardillo,-a 1 *adj fam* (*persona*) gormless. – **2** *m,f fam* mug. – **3** pardillo, *m* (*pájaro*) linnet.

pardo,-a 1 *adj* (*color tierra*) brown. **2** (*sin luz*) dark, dim.

parduzco,-a *adj* dull brown.

pareado,-a 1 *adj* (*poesía*) rhyming. **2** (*casa*) semi-detached. – **3** pareado, *m* couplet.

■ **versos pareados,** rhyming couplets.

parecer 1 *m* (*opinión*) opinion, mind: *¿has cambiado de parecer?,* have you changed your mind? – **2** *i* to seem, look (like): *parece fácil,* it seems easy, it looks easy; *parece de verdad,* it looks real; *parece un oso,* it looks like a bear. **3** (*opinar*) to think: *me parece que sí,* I think so; *¿qué te parece?,* what do you think? **4** (*aparentar*) to look as if: *parece que va a llover,* it looks as if it's going to rain. – **5** parecerse, *p* to be alike, look like: *se parecen mucho,* they're very much alike; *el pequeño se pa-*

rece mucho a su padre, the little one looks just like his father.

● **a lo que parece,** apparently. ‖ **al parecer,** apparently. ‖ **parecer bien,** to seem right. ‖ **parecer mal,** to seem wrong. ‖ **¡parece mentira!,** I can't believe it! ‖ **según parece,** apparently.

▲ *Conjugation model* [43], *like* agradecer; *in* 4 *used only in the 3rd pers, it does not take a subject.*

parecido,-a 1 *adj* similar. – **2** parecido, *m* resemblance, likeness.

● **tener parecido con algn.,** to bear a resemblance to sb.

■ **bien parecido,-a,** good-looking. ‖ **mal parecido,-a,** ugly.

pared 1 *f* wall. **2** (*de una montaña*) side.

● **las paredes oyen,** walls have ears. ‖ **poner a algn. contra la pared,** to put sb. in a tight spot.

■ **pared maestra,** main wall. ‖ **pared medianera,** party wall.

paredón 1 *m* (*como defensa*) wall. **2** (*de fusilamiento*) execution wall.

● **llevar a algn. al paredón,** to put sb. before a firing squad.

■ **paredón de fusilamiento,** execution wall.

pareja *f* → **parejo,-a.**

parejo,-a 1 *adj* (*sin diferencia*) the same; (*por igual*) even. – **2** pareja, *f* (*gen*) pair: *he perdido la pareja de este gemelo,* I've lost the other cufflink. **3** (*de personas*) couple; (*de baile*) partner: *no hay más que parejas en esta fiesta,* everybody at this party is paired off; *¿vendrás con pareja?,* will you come with a partner?; *¡pareja, venir aquí!,* you two, come over here!; *una pareja de la Guardia Civil,* two civil guards. **4** (*de cartas*) pair.

● **hacer buena pareja,** to make a good couple. ‖ **hacer pareja,** to be two of a kind. ‖ **por parejas,** in pairs. ‖ **vivir en pareja,** to live with sb.: *están viviendo en pareja,* they're living together.

parentela *f* relatives *pl,* relations *pl.*

parentesco *m* kinship, relationship: *¿qué parentesco tenéis?,* how are you related?

paréntesis 1 *m* (*gen*) parenthesis; (*signo*) brackets *pl.* **2** *fig* (*interrupción*) break, interruption.

● **abrir paréntesis,** to open brackets. ‖ **cerrar paréntesis,** to close brackets. ‖ **entre paréntesis,** in brackets, in parentheses. ‖ **hacer un paréntesis,** *fig* to take a break.

▲ *pl* paréntesis.

pareo *m* sarong.

paria *mf* pariah.

parida *f tabú* → **parido,-a.**

paridad 1 *f* (*gen*) parity, equality. **2** FIN parity of exchange.

parido,-a 1 *pp* → **parir.** – **2** parida, *f fam* piece of nonsense: *no dices más que paridas,* you talk a load of rubbish.

pariente,-a 1 *m,f* relative. – **2 la parienta,** *f fam* (*esposa*) the missus.

parietal 1 *adj* parietal. – **2** *m* parietal.

parihuelas 1 *fpl* (*camilla*) stretcher *sing.* **2** (*para mercancías*) handbarrow *sing.*

paripé hacer el paripé, *i* to put on an act.

parir 1 *t fam* to give birth to. **2** *fig* (*producir*) to produce. – **3** *i* to give birth.

● **parirla,** *fam* to cock it up. ‖ **poner a algn. a parir,** *fam* to slag sb. off.

París *m* Paris.

parisino,-a 1 adj Parisian. − **2** m,f Parisian.
paritario,-a adj joint.
■ **comité paritario,** joint committee.
paritorio m delivery room.
parka f parka.
parking m car park, us parking lot.
■ **plaza de parking,** parking space.
párkinson m Parkinson's disease.
parlamentar i to parley.
parlamentario,-a 1 adj parliamentary. − **2** m,f member of parliament.
parlamento 1 m parliament. **2** (discurso) speech.
parlanchín,-ina 1 adj talkative. − **2** m,f fam chatterbox.
parlante adj talking.
parlar i → **parlotear.**
parlotear i fam to chatter, prattle on.
parloteo m chattering.
● **estar de parloteo,** to be chatting.
parmesano,-a 1 adj Parmesan. − **2 parmesano,** m (queso) Parmesan cheese.
parné m arg dough.
paro 1 m stop. **2** (desempleo) unemployment; (subsidio) unemployment benefit, us unemployement compensation. **3** (interrupción) stoppage, strike: **han convocado paros durante todo el mes,** they've called strikes throughout the month.
● **cobrar el paro,** to be on unemployment benefit, be on the dole. ‖ **estar en el paro,** to be unemployed.
■ **paro cardiaco,** cardiac arrest. ‖ **paro indefinido,** indefinite strike.
parodia f parody.
parodiar t to parody.
▲ Conjugation model [12], like **cambiar.**
paródico,-a adj parodic.
paroxismo m paroxysm.
paroxístico,-a adj paroxysmic.
parpadear 1 i (ojos) to blink, wink. **2** (luz) to flicker, twinkle.
parpadeo 1 m (de los párpados) blinking. **2** (de la luz, las estrellas) flickering, twinkling.
párpado m eyelid.
parque 1 m (jardines) park. **2** (coches - de un país) total number; (- de un propietario) fleet: **el parque automovilístico español,** the total number of cars in Spain. **3** (de niños) playpen.
■ **parque acuático,** waterpark. ‖ **parque de atracciones,** amusement park, funfair. ‖ **parque de bomberos,** fire station. ‖ **parque móvil,** official car pool. ‖ **parque nacional,** national park. ‖ **parque natural,** natural park. ‖ **parque temático,** theme park. ‖ **parque zoológico,** zoo, zoological gardens pl.
parqué m parquet.
parquedad 1 f (moderación) moderation. **2** (de ideas, palabras) sparseness.
parquet m → **parqué.**
parquímetro m parking meter.
párr. abr (párrafo) paragraph; (abreviatura) para.
parra f grapevine.
● **subirse a la parra,** fam (mostrarse insolente) to get cocky; (ponerse furioso) to blow one's top, hit the roof.
parrafada 1 f fam (conversación) chat. **2** fam (discurso) spiel, speech.
● **echar una parrafada con algn.,** to have a chat with sb. ‖ **soltar la parrafada,** to go on and on.
párrafo m paragraph.

parranda f fam spree.
● **ir(se) de parranda,** to go out on the town.
parrandear i fam to go out.
parricida mf parricide.
parricidio m parricide.
parrilla 1 f grill, us broiler, barbecue. **2** (restaurante) grillroom, rotisserie. **3** TÉC grate. **4** (en carrera de coches) starting grid, grid.
● **a la parrilla,** CULIN grilled.
■ **parrilla de salida,** starting grid.
parrillada f mixed grill (of meat or fish).
párroco m parish priest.
parroquia 1 f (area) parish. **2** (iglesia) parish church. **3** (feligreses) parishioners pl, congregation. **4** fam (clientela) customers pl, clientele.
parroquial adj parish, parochial.
parroquiano,-a 1 m,f (fiel) parishioner. **2** fam (cliente) customer, client.
parsimonia 1 f (lentitud) slowness. **2** (calma) calmness. **3** (moderación) parsimony.
parsimonioso,-a adj slow, unhurried.
parte 1 f (gen) part; (en una partición) portion: **divide el pastel en tres partes,** cut the cake into three (slices). **2** (en negocio) share: **yo quiero la parte que me toca de los beneficios,** I want my share of the profits. **3** (lugar) place: **no lo venden en ninguna parte,** they don't sell it anywhere; **no sabemos en qué parte del país está,** we don't know whereabouts in the country it is; **en esta parte de la ciudad hay muchos bares,** there are lots of bars in this area. **4** (en un conflicto) side: **las dos partes quieren llevar la razón,** both sides believe they are right. **5** JUR party. − **6** m (comunicado) official report: **han dicho en el parte que iba a llover,** the weather report said it was going to rain. − **7 partes,** fpl fam privates, private parts.
● **dar parte,** to report. ‖ **de parte a parte,** through. ‖ **de parte de,** on behalf of, from: **vengo de parte de mi padre,** my father sent me; **llaman de parte de la central,** I have a call from head office. ‖ **¿de parte de quien?,** who's calling please? ‖ **de un tiempo a esta parte,** until now. ‖ **en parte,** partly: **en parte tienes razón,** you have a point there. ‖ **estar de parte de,** to support. ‖ **formar parte de,** to be part of: **para formar parte del comité hay que ser socio,** you have to be a member to sit on the committee. ‖ **llevar la mejor/peor parte,** to have the best/worst of it. ‖ **no llevar a ninguna parte,** not to lead anywhere. ‖ **por todas partes,** everywhere. ‖ **por una parte, ... por otra ...,** on the one hand ..., on the other hand ... ‖ **tomar parte,** to take sides. ‖ **tomar parte en algo,** to take part in sth. ‖ **vamos/vayamos por partes,** one step at a time.
■ **parte de la oración,** part of speech. ‖ **parte médico,** medical report. ‖ **parte meteorológico,** weather report. ‖ **partes pudendas,** private parts. ‖ **partes vergonzosas,** private parts.
parteluz m mullion.
partenaire m partner.
partera f midwife.
parterre m flowerbed.
partición f (de una herencia) partition, division.
participación 1 f (intervención) participation, involvement. **2** (comunicado) announcement: **¿te han mandado la participación de boda?,** have they notified you of their wedding? **3** FIN (acción) share. **4** (en lotería) (part of a) lottery ticket.
participante 1 adj participating: **las obras participantes en el premio,** the works in contention for the prize. − **2** mf participant.

participar 1 *i* (*tomar parte - en una conversación*) to partic- ipate, take part; (- *en un proyecto*) to take part; (- *en un torneo*) to enter, take part. **2** (*compartir*) to share (**de**, -): *yo no participo de tu opinión*, I don't share your view. **3** FIN to have a share. – **4** *t* (*notificar*) to notify, inform.

partícipe 1 *adj* participating. – **2** *mf* participant.
● **hacer partícipe a algn. de** algo, (*notificar*) to inform sb. about sth.; (*compartir*) to share sth. with sb. ‖ **ser partícipe de** algo, to contribute to sth., play a part in sth.

participio *m* participle.

partícula *f* particle.
■ **partícula elemental**, elementary particle.

particular 1 *adj* (*concreto*) particular. **2** (*privado*) private: *doy clases particulares*, I give private tuition; *no pienso hablar de mi vida particular*, I will not discuss my private life; *en mi domicilio particular*, at my home address. **3** (*privativo*) peculiar, particular, special: *el olor particular del azahar*, the peculiar smell of orange blossom. **4** (*ex-traordinario*) noteworthy, extraordinary: *tiene un carác-ter muy particular*, he's very much his own man. – **5** *m* (*individuo*) private individual: *compré el coche a un par-ticular*, I bought the car from a private owner. **6** (*asunto*) matter, subject.
● **en particular**, in particular, particularly. ‖ **no tener nada de particular**, (*no ser nada especial*) to be nothing special; (*no ser nada extraño*) to be completely normal. ‖ **sin otro particular, le saluda ...**, Yours sincerely, ...

particularidad 1 *f* (*gen*) peculiarity. **2** (*singularidad*) sin-gularity, peculiarity. **3** (*detalle*) detail.

particularización 1 *f* (*gen*) particularization. **2** (*distin-ción*) difference.

particularizar 1 *t* (*distinguir*) to distinguish, make dif-ferent, differentiate. **2** (*detallar*) to detail.

particularmente 1 *adv* (*especialmente*) particularly. **2** (*personalmente*) personally.

partida *f* → **partido,-a**.

partidario,-a 1 *adj* supporting. – **2** *m,f* supporter.
● **mostrarse partidario,-a de** algo, to be in favour of sth. ‖ **ser/no ser partidario,-a de** algo, to be in favour of sth./be against sth.: *yo no soy partidario de cambiarlo de colegio*, I am not in favour of him changing schools.

partidismo *m* political bias, partisanship.
● **ser acusado,-a de partidismo**, to be accused of political bias.

partidista *adj* biased, partisan.

partido,-a 1 *pp* → **partir**. – **2** *adj* (*dividido*) divided. **3** (*roto*) broken, split. – **4 partido**, *m* (*grupo político*) party, group. **5** (*provecho*) profit, advantage. **6** DEP (*equipo*) team; (*juego*) game, match: *un partido de rugby*, a rugby match. – **7 partida**, *f* (*remesa*) consignment, lot. **8** (*do-cumento*) certificate. **9** FIN entry, item. **10** (*juego*) game: *una partida de naipes*, a game of cards. **11** (*grupo - de soldados*) squad, gang; (- *de cazadores*) party.
● **jugar una partida**, to play a game. ‖ **jugarle una mala partida a algn.**, to play a dirty trick on sb. ‖ **por partida doble**, twice over. ‖ **sacar partido de**, to prof-it from. ‖ **ser un buen partido**, *fam* to be a good catch. ‖ **tomar partido**, to take sides. ‖ **tomar partido por algn.**, to side with sb.
■ **partida de caza**, (*de caza mayor*) hunting party; (*de caza menor*) shooting party. ‖ **partida de nacimiento**, birth certificate. ‖ **partida doble**, double entry. ‖ **par-tido amistoso**, friendly game. ‖ **partido de exhibi-ción**, exhibition match. ‖ **partido de ida**, first leg. ‖ **partido de vuelta**, second leg. ‖ **partido judicial**, ad-ministrative area. ‖ **partido político**, political party. ‖ **sistema de partidos**, party system.

partir 1 *t* (*dividir*) to divide, split: *prefiero que me lo parta en lonchas*, I'd prefer it cut into slices; *voy a partir pan*, I'll cut some bread; *partió el pastel en dos mitades*, he cut the cake in two. **2** (*romper*) to break; (*nueces, almen-dras*) to crack. **3** *fam* (*fastidiar*) to mess up. – **4** *i* (*irse*) to leave, set out, set off. **5** (*proceder*) to originate from: *¿de quién partió la idea?*, whose idea was it? – **6 partirse**, *p* to break: *se ha partido la pierna*, he's broken his leg.
● **a partir de hoy**, from now on. ‖ **para partirse**, *fam* hilarious. ‖ **partir a algn. por la mitad**, to ruin sb.'s plans, mess sb. up. ‖ **partir la cara a algn.**, *fam* to smash sb.'s face in. ‖ **partirse de risa**, *fam* to split one's sides laughing.

partisano,-a *m,f* partisan.

partitivo,-a 1 *adj* partitive. – **2 partitivo**, *m* partitive.

partitura *f* score.

parto *m* (*proceso*) delivery, labour (US labor); (*efecto*) child-birth: *fue un parto difícil*, it was a difficult birth.
● **ser el parto de los montes**, *fam* (*chasco*) to be a big let-down; (*fracaso*) to be a flop. ‖ **estar de parto**, to be in labour (US labor).
■ **dolores de parto**, labour (US labor) pains. ‖ **parto múltiple**, multiple birth. ‖ **parto sin dolor**, painless birth.

parturienta *f* (*de parto*) woman in labour (US labor): (*des-pués del parto*) woman who has just given birth.

parvedad *f* paucity.

parvo,-a *adj* sparse.

parvulario *m* nursery school.

párvulo,-a *m,f* infant.

pasa *f* raisin.
■ **pasa de Corinto**, currant.

pasable *adj* passable.

pasacalle *m* lively music played in the street by bands in fiestas.

pasada *f* → **pasado,-a**.

pasadizo *m* passage.

pasado,-a 1 *pp* → **pasar**. – **2** *adj* past, gone by. **3** (*año, semana, etc*) last: *la semana pasada*, last week. **4** (*después*) after: *pasadas las once*, after eleven. **5** (*estropeado*) bad. – **6 pasado**, *m* (*tiempo*) past. **7** LING past, past tense. – **8 pasada**, *f* (*con un trapo etc*) wipe; (*con la plancha*) iron: *ya le he dado una pasada a la estantería*, I've given the shelves a quick dusting; *estas sábanas no necesitan más que una pasada*, these sheets just need a quick iron. **9** (*en costura*) stitch, tacking stitch; (*en punto*) row, row of stitches: *dale unas pasadas al dobladillo que lo tengo descosido*, just tack up my hem, it's come un-stitched. **10** (*de pintura*) coat, lick. **11** (*repaso*) check, going over: *le daré otra pasada al informe antes de en-tregarlo*, I'll just check the report again before I hand it in. **12** *fam* (*exageración*): *esa tienda es una pasada de caro*, that shop's incredibly expensive. **13** (*abuso*) rip off: *¡10.000 pesetas la hora?, ¡qué pasada!*, 10,000 pe-setas an hour?, what a rip off! **14** (*maravilla*) something else: *es una pasada de película*, that film's too much, that film's something else.
● **de pasada**, (*de paso*) in passing; (*rápidamente*) hastily. ‖ **estar muy pasado,-a**, *arg* to be really out of it.
■ **mala pasada**, dirty trick. ‖ **pasado mañana**, the day after tomorrow. ‖ **pasado,-a de moda**, out of date, out of fashion, old-fashioned.

pasador 1 *m* (*de pelo*) hair slide, slide. **2** (*de corbata*) tie-pin. **3** (*de puerta etc*) bolt, fastener. **4** (*colador*) strainer, colander.

pasaje 1 *m* (*paso*) passage. **2** (*viaje*) passage. – **3** *f* (*tarifa*) fare, ticket. – **4** *m* (*pasajeros*) passengers *pl*. **5** (*fragmento*) passage.

pasajero,-a 1 *adj* passing. – **2** *m,f* passenger.
pasamanería *f* braids *pl*.
pasamano *m* handrail.
pasamanos *m* handrail.
▲ *pl pasamanos*.
pasamontañas *m* balaclava.
▲ *pl pasamontañas*.
pasante *m* assistant.
pasaporte *m* passport.
● dar el pasaporte a algn., *fam* to chuck sb. out.
pasapurés *m* vegetable mill.
▲ *pl pasapurés*.
pasar 1 i (*ir*) to pass, pass by, go: *pasaba por ahí cuando sucedió el accidente*, I was just passing by when the accident happened; *todos los cables y tuberías pasan por debajo del suelo*, all the wires and pipes go under the floor; *pasa de un idioma a otro sin darse cuenta*, he goes from one language to another without realizing. **2** (*tiempo*) to pass, go by: *¡cómo pasa el tiempo!*, doesn't time fly!; *yo lo hago por pasar el tiempo*, I do it to pass the time. **3** (*entrar*) to come in, go in: *pasa, está abierto*, come in, it's not locked; *me dijeron que pasara sin llamar*, they told me to go in without knocking. **4** (*cesar*) to pass, cease: *en cuanto pase la tormenta salimos*, we'll go out when the storm has passed; *si no se te pasa el dolor, llámame*, if the pain doesn't go away, call me; *tranquila, que ya ha pasado todo*, don't worry, it's all over now. **5** (*límite*) to exceed (**de**, -). **6** (*ocurrir*) to happen. **7** (*sufrir*) to suffer. – **8** t (*trasladar*) to move, transfer: *pasa este documento al otro disquete*, move this file to the other diskette; *lo han pasado al departamento de ventas*, he has been transferred to the sales department. **9** (*comunicar, dar*) to give: *pásale el informe al jefe*, give this report to the boss; *mi hijo me ha pasado la gripe*, my son has given me the flu. **10** (*cruzar*) to cross: *pasamos la frontera ayer*, we crossed the border yesterday. **11** (*alcanzar*) to pass, reach: *pásame la sal, por favor*, pass me the salt, please. **12** (*aventajar*) to surpass, be better than: *tu hermano ya te pasa en matemáticas*, your brother is better than you at maths. **13** (*adelantar*) to overtake: *me pasó un deportivo rojo en una curva*, a red sports car overtook me on a bend. **14** (*deslizar*) to run: *pasó el dedo por el estante*, he ran his finger along the shelf; *la etiqueta se pasa por aquí y el precio sale en la pantalla*, you run the tag through here and the price comes up on the screen. **15** (*tolerar*) to overlook: *esta vez te la paso, pero que no se repita*, I'll overlook it this time, but don't let it happen again. **16** (*aprobar*) to pass: *pasé el examen a la primera*, I passed my test first time. **17** (*proyectar*) to show: *pasaron unas diapositivas y luego una película*, they showed some slides and then a film. **18** (*tiempo - estar*) to spend; (-*disfrutar, padecer*) to have: *pasaremos el verano en Sada*, we're spending the summer in Sada; *he pasado una noche fatal*, I've had a terrible night; *pasamos unas vacaciones estupendas*, we had a wonderful holiday. – **19** pasarse, *p* (*desertar*) to pass over (**a**, to): *se ha pasado al otro bando*, she's gone over to the other side. **20** (*pudrirse*) to go off. **21** (*olvidarse*) to forget: *se me pasó la fecha de entrega*, I forgot about the deadline. **22** (*ir*) to go by (**por**, -), call in (**por**, at): *pásate por casa cuando quieras*, pop in any time. **23** *fam* (*excederse*) to overdo it; (*ir demasiado lejos*) to go too far (**de**, -): *te has pasado de sincero*, you were too honest.
● pasar de algo, *fam* not to be bothered about sth.: *paso de hacer cola*, I can't be bothered to queue up; *pasa de todo*, he couldn't care less about anything, he

doesn't give a damn about anything. ∥ **pasar de largo**, to go past. ∥ **pasar la página**, to turn the page. ∥ **pasar por**, to pass for. ∥ **pasar por alto**, to ignore. ∥ **pasar por encima de algn.**, to go over sb.'s head. ∥ **pasarlo bien**, to have a good time. ∥ **¿qué pasa?**, what's the matter?, what's wrong? ∥ **pasar sin**, to do without. ∥ **pasarse de la raya**, to go too far, overstep the mark.
pasarela 1 *f* (*puente*) footbridge; (*de un barco*) gangway. **2** (*de modelos*) catwalk.
pasatiempo 1 *m* pastime, hobby. – **2** pasatiempos, *mpl* puzzles.
pascua 1 *f* (*cristiana*) Easter; (*judía*) Passover. – **2** pascuas, *fpl* Christmas *sing*.
● de Pascuas a Ramos, once in a blue moon. ∥ contento,-a como unas pascuas, as happy as a sandboy. ∥ hacerle la pascua a algn., to mess things up for sb. ∥ ... y santas pascuas, ... and that's that.
■ pascua de Pentecostés, Whitsun. ∥ pascua de Resurrección, Easter.
pascual *adj* Easter, Paschal.
pase 1 *m* (*permiso*) pass. **2** (*cambio*) move. **3** (*desfile*) show. **4** CINEM showing. **5** DEP pass.
■ pase de modelos, fashion show. ∥ pase de pernocta, overnight pass.
pasear 1 i to stroll, go for a walk. – **2** t to take for a walk. **3** *fig* (*exhibir*) to show off.
paseíllo *m* (*en toros*) opening procession.
paseo 1 *m* (*a pie*) walk, stroll; (*a caballo*) ride. **2** (*en coche*) drive; (*en bicicleta, moto*) ride. **3** (*calle*) avenue, promenade.
● dar el paseo a algn., to bump sb. off. ∥ dar un paseo, to go for a walk. ∥ mandar a paseo a algn., *fam* to send sb. packing. ∥ ¡vete a paseo!, *fam* go away!, get lost!
■ paseo marítimo, promenade, esplanade, seafront.
pasillo *m* corridor.
pasión *f* passion.
pasional *adj* (*gen*) passionate.
pasionaria *f* passion flower.
pasividad *f* passiveness, passivity.
pasivo,-a 1 *adj* passive. – **2** pasivo, *m* COM liabilities *pl*.
■ voz pasiva, passive voice, passive.
pasma la pasma, *f arg* the cops *pl*, the (old) bill.
pasmado,-a *adj* flabbergasted, open-mouthed: *¿qué haces ahí pasmado?*, what are you gaping at?
● dejar pasmado,-a a algn., to stun sb., amaze sb. ∥ quedarse pasmado,-a, to be flabbergasted, be stunned.
pasmar 1 t to astonish, amaze. – **2** pasmarse, *p fam* (*asombrarse*) to be astonished, be amazed. **3** *fam* (*enfriarse*) to freeze, get cold.
● pasmarse de frío, to be frozen to the marrow.
pasmarote *m fam* twit.
pasmo 1 *m* (*asombro*) amazement, astonishment: *cuando se enteren, les va a dar un pasmo*, when they find out, they'll get a right shock. **2** (*resfriado*) chill: *con el frío que hace nos va a dar un pasmo*, we'll freeze to death in this cold.
pasmoso,-a *adj* astonishing, amazing.
paso 1 *m* (*movimiento*) step, footstep: *¡no des ni un paso más!*, don't move another step!; *he oído pasos*, I heard footsteps. **2** (*distancia*) pace. **3** (*camino*) passage, way. **4** (*avance*) progress, advance. **5** (*trámite*) step, move. **6** (*de montaña*) mountain pass; (*de mar*) strait. **7** REL float (*used in Holy Week processions*).
● a cada paso, at every turn. ∥ a paso de tortuga, at

a snail's pace. ‖ **abrirse paso,** to force one's way through. ‖ **apretar el paso,** to hurry. ‖ **cerrarle el paso a algn.,** to block sb.' s way. ‖ **dar paso a,** *(hacer posible)* to pave the way for; *(provocar)* to give rise to; *(dejar pasar)* to let through, make way for; *(pasar a)* to move on to. ‖ **dar sus primeros pasos,** to start walking. ‖ **dar un paso en falso,** *(al andar)* to lose one's footing; *(equivocarse)* to make a false move. ‖ **estar a un paso/a dos pasos,** to be very close: *estamos a un paso de encontrar la solución,* the solution is just around the corner. ‖ **estar de paso,** to be passing through. ‖ **hacer algo de paso,** to do sth. as well: *de paso, tráeme tabaco,* while you're there, get me some cigarettes. ‖ **no dar un paso sin ...,** not to do a thing without ... ‖ **paso a paso,** step by step. ‖ **"prohibido el paso",** "no entry". ‖ **salir al paso de algn.,** to waylay sb. ‖ **salir al paso de algo,** to forestall sth. ‖ **seguirle los pasos a algn.,** to follow sb. close behind; *fig* to follow in sb.'s footsteps.

■ **ceda el paso,** *(señal)* give way sign, us yield sign. ‖ **paso a nivel,** level crossing, us grade crossing. ‖ **paso de cebra,** zebra crossing. ‖ **paso de peatones,** pedestrian crossing. ‖ **paso del ecuador,** half-way point *(in university studies).* ‖ **paso elevado,** flyover. ‖ **paso subterráneo,** *(de peatones)* subway.
pasodoble *m* paso doble.
pasota 1 *mf fam (joven apático)* drop-out. **2** *fam (persona despreocupada)* laidback person: *es un pasota,* he doesn't care about anything. – **3** *adj fam (jerga, joven) belonging to the late 70's-early 80's Spanish drop-out phenomenon.* **4** *fam (despreocupado)* laid-back: *es muy pasota,* he doesn't care about anything.
pasotismo *m* couldn't-care-less attitude.
paspartú *m* passe-partout.
  ▲ *pl* **paspartús.**
pasquín *m* satirical poster.
pasta 1 *f (masa)* paste. **2** CULIN *(italiana)* pasta; *(de bizcocho, crepes)* mixture; *(para pasteles)* pastry. **3** *(croissant, ensaimada, etc)* pastry; *(de té)* petit four, biscuit, us cookie. **4** *fam (dinero)* dosh, dough, money. **5** *(de encuadernación)* boards *pl.*
  ● **ser de buena pasta,** *fam* to be good-natured. ‖ **soltar la pasta,** to hand over the dosh.
  ■ **pasta choux,** choux pastry. ‖ **pasta de dientes,** toothpaste. ‖ **pasta de hojaldre,** puff pastry. ‖ **pasta gansa,** a packet, a fortune.
pastaflora *f* sweeet shortcrust pastry.
pastar 1 *t* to pasture, graze. – **2** *i* to pasture, graze.
pastel 1 *adj (color)* pastel. – **2** *m* CULIN *(tipo bizcocho)* cake; *(tipo empanada)* pie: *tenemos pastel de manzana y de chocolate,* we've got apple pie and chocolate cake. **3** ART *(material, obra)* pastel; *(técnica)* pastel drawing. **4** *fam (conspiración)* plot.
  ● **al pastel,** pastel: *dibujo al pastel,* pastel drawing. ‖ **descubrir el pastel,** to let the cat out of the bag.
  ■ **pastel de boda,** wedding cake. ‖ **pastel de carne,** meat pie, meatloaf. ‖ **pastel de pescado,** fish pie.
pastelería 1 *f (tienda)* cake shop, pastisserie. **2** *(pasteles)* cakes and pastries. **3** *(técnica)* baking.
pastelero,-a 1 *adj (industria)* baking. – **2** *m,f (cocinero)* pastrycook; *(vendedor)* cake seller.
pasterización *f* → **pasteurización.**
pasterizado,-a *adj* → **pasteurizado,-a.**
pasterizar *t* → **pasteurizar.**
pasteurización *f* pasteurization.
pasteurizado,-a *adj* pasteurized.

pasteurizar *t* to pasteurize.
pastiche *m* pastiche.
pastilla 1 *f (medicina)* tablet, pill. **2** *(de chocolate, jabón)* bar. **3 la pastilla,** *(anticonceptivo)* the pill.
  ● **a toda pastilla,** *fam (velocidad)* at full speed, at full tilt; *(volumen)* at full blast.
  ■ **pastilla para la garganta,** throat lozenge, throat pastille. ‖ **pastilla de freno,** brake shoe.
pastizal *m* pastureland, pasture.
pasto 1 *m (pastizal)* pasture. **2** *(acción)* grazing.
  ● **a todo pasto,** in large quantities: *gasta el dinero a todo pasto,* he spends money like water; *comimos a todo pasto,* we stuffed ourselves with food. ‖ **ser pasto de las llamas,** to go up in flames.
pastón *m fam* packet, bomb, fortune.
pastor,-ra 1 *m,f (del campo - hombre)* shepherd; *(- mujer)* shepherdess. – **2 pastor,** *m* REL pastor.
  ■ **pastor alemán,** German shepherd, Alsatian.
pastoral 1 *adj* pastoral. – **2** *f* LIT pastoral. **3** MÚS pastorale, pastoral.
  ■ **carta pastoral,** pastoral letter.
pastorear *i* to graze, pasture.
pastoreo *m* pasture.
pastoril *adj* pastoral.
pastosidad 1 *f (de masa)* pastiness, stickiness. **2** *(de la lengua)* furriness. **3** *(de la voz)* mellowness.
pastoso,-a 1 *adj (sustancia)* pasty, doughy. **2** *(lengua)* furry. **3** *(voz)* mellow.
Pat. *abr (patente)* patent.
pata¹ 1 *f (gen)* leg. **2** *(garra)* paw. **3** *(pezuña)* hoof.
  ● **a cuatro patas,** on all fours. ‖ **a la pata coja,** hopping, on one leg. ‖ **a la pata la llana,** *fam* down to earth. ‖ **a pata,** *fam* on foot. ‖ **meter la pata,** *fam* to put one's foot in it. ‖ **patas arriba,** upside down. ‖ **tener mala pata,** *fam* to have bad luck.
  ■ **pata de gallo,** *(dibujo, motivo)* hound's-tooth check, dog's-tooth check. ‖ **patas de gallo,** *(arrugas)* crow's feet.
pata² *f (ave)* → **pato,-a.**
patada *f* kick.
  ● **dar una patada,** to kick. ‖ **echar a algn. a patadas,** to kick sb. out. ‖ **me da cien patadas,** *fam* I can't bear it. ‖ **sentar como una patada en el estómago,** *fam* to be like a kick in the teeth. ‖ **tener de algo a patadas,** *fam* to have lots of sth. ‖ **tratar a patadas,** *fam* to treat like dirt.
patalear 1 *i (con enfado)* to stamp one's feet. **2** *(protestar)* to kick up a fuss.
pataleo 1 *m (con los pies)* stamping. **2** *(protesta)* complaining.
  ■ **derecho al pataleo,** *fam* the right to complain.
pataleta *f fam* tantrum.
patán *m* boor.
patata *f* potato.
  ● **no saber ni patata,** *fam* not to have a clue. ‖ **ser una patata,** *fam* to be useless.
  ■ **patatas bravas,** *sautéed potatoes with a spicy sauce.* ‖ **patatas fritas,** *(de bolsa)* crisps, us chips; *(de sartén)* chips, us French fries.
patatero,-a *adj (de patata)* potato.
  ● **ser un rollo patatero,** *fam* to be a real drag.
patatín **que si patatín que si patatán,** *loc adv fam* and so on and so forth.
patatús *m fam (ataque)* fit; *(susto)* shock: *como se lo cuentes le da un patatús,* he'll have a fit if you tell him.
patchuli *m* patchouli.

paté m pâté.
patear 1 t to kick. 2 (*andar*) to walk. – 3 i (*con enfado*) to stamp one's feet. – 4 **patearse**, p (*lugar*) to traipse round: *esta mañana nos hemos pateado la ciudad entera*, we've traipsed round the whole city this morning. 5 (*dinero*) to blow.
patena f paten.
● limpio,-a **como una patena**, spotless, as clean as a new pin.
patentado,-a adj patented.
patentar t to patent.
patente 1 adj (*evidente*) obvious, patent. – 2 f patent.
■ **patente de corso**, HIST letter of marque; *fig* free rein, carte blanche.
patentizar t to make evident.
pateo m stamping.
patera f boat.
paternal adj paternal.
paternalismo m paternalism.
paternalista 1 adj paternalistic. 2 *pey* patronizing.
paternidad 1 f paternity. 2 (*autoría*) authorship.
paterno,-a adj paternal.
patético,-a adj pathetic.
patetismo 1 m LIT pathos. 2 (*dramatismo*) poignancy: *imágenes de gran patetismo*, poignant scenes, moving scenes.
patibulario,-a adj sinister.
patíbulo m gallows *sing*.
paticojo,-a adj lame, gammy-legged.
paticorto,-a adj short-legged.
patidifuso,-a adj *fam* gob-smacked, flabbergasted.
● quedarse **patidifuso,-a**, *fam* to be gob-smacked.
patilla 1 f (*pata*) leg. 2 (*de las gafas*) arm. – 3 *fpl* sideboards, US sideburns.
patín 1 m (*de ruedas*) roller-skate, skate; (*de hielo*) ice skate. 2 (*tabla*) skateboard. 3 (*patinete*) scooter. 4 (*en el mar*) pedalo.
pátina f patina.
patinador,-ra m,f skater.
■ **patinador,-ra artístico,-a**, figure skater.
patinaje m skating.
■ **patinaje artístico**, figure skating. ‖ **patinaje sobre hielo**, ice-skating. ‖ **patinaje sobre ruedas**, rollerskating.
patinar 1 i (*como diversión*) to skate. 2 (*por accidente*) to slip. 3 (*vehículo*) to skid. 4 (*meter la pata*) to put one's foot in it; (*equivocarse*) to boob, make a boob.
● **patinar sobre hielo**, to ice-skate.
patinazo 1 m skid. 2 *fam* (*error*) boob, blunder.
● pegar un **patinazo**, (*resbalar - persona*) to slip; (- *coche*) to skid; (*meter la pata*) to make a boob, drop a clanger.
patinete m scooter.
patio 1 m (*de una casa*) courtyard; (*de un colegio*) playground. 2 TEAT pit.
● ¡cómo está el **patio**!, *fam* what a state things are in!
■ **patio de butacas**, stalls *pl*, US orchestra.
patitieso,-a adj *fam* (*sorprendido*) flabbergasted; (*inmóvil por el frío*) frozen-stiff.
patituerto,-a adj *fam* bandy-legged.
patizambo,-a adj (*de rodillas abajo*) knock-kneed; (*con las piernas arqueadas*) bandy-legged.
pato,-a 1 m,f (*ave - en general*) duck; (- *macho*) drake; (- *hembra*) duck. – 2 **pato**, m *fam* (*persona*) clumsy person.

● pagar el **pato**, *fam* to carry the can. ‖ **ser un pato mareado**, *fam* to be really clumsy.
patochada f *fam* nonsense.
● decir **patochadas**, to talk rubbish.
patógeno,-a adj pathogenic.
patología f pathology.
patológico,-a adj pathological.
patoso,-a adj clumsy.
patraña f story: *no cuenta más que patrañas*, he lies through his teeth.
patriarca m patriarch.
patriarcado m patriarchy.
patriarcal adj patriarchal.
patricio,-a 1 adj patrician. – 2 **patricio**, m patrician.
patrimonio 1 m (*gen*) patrimony; (*riqueza*) wealth. 2 (*histórico, cultural*) heritage.
■ impuesto sobre el **patrimonio**, capital gains tax. ‖ **patrimonio artístico**, artistic heritage. ‖ **patrimonio cultural**, cultural heritage. ‖ **patrimonio nacional**, wealth of the nation.
patrio,-a 1 adj of one's homeland. – 2 **patria**, f homeland.
■ orgullo **patrio**, national pride. ‖ **patria celestial**, heaven. ‖ **patria chica**, hometown. ‖ **patria potestad**, custody.
patriota mf patriot.
patriotería f jingoism.
patriotero,-a adj chauvinistic.
patriótico,-a adj patriotic.
patriotismo m patriotism.
patrocinador,-ra 1 adj sponsoring. – 2 m,f sponsor.
patrocinar t to sponsor.
patrocinio m sponsorship.
patrón,-ona 1 m,f (*dueño de una casa*) landlord; (*dueña*) landlady. 2 (*jefe*) employer, boss; (*hombre*) master; (*mujer*) mistress. 3 REL patron saint. – 4 **patrón**, m (*en costura*) pattern. 5 (*de barco*) skipper. 6 (*modelo*) standard.
● cortado,-a por el mismo **patrón**, cast in the same mould. ‖ donde hay **patrón** no manda marinero, what the boss says goes.
■ **patrón oro**, gold standard.
patronal 1 adj (*fiesta*) of one's patron saint. 2 (*organización, oferta*) management. – 3 f (*institución*) employers' association; (*de una empresa*) management.
patronato 1 m (*consejo*) board, council; (*benéfico*) trust. 2 (*patronal*) employers' association. 3 REL patronage.
patronazgo m patronage.
patronear t to skipper.
patronímico,-a 1 adj patronymic. – 2 **patronímico**, m patronymic.
patrono,-a m,f → **patrón,-ona**.
patrulla 1 f (*de vigilancia*) patrol. 2 (*de rescate*) party.
● estar de **patrulla**, to be on patrol.
■ **patrulla de rescate**, rescue party.
patrullar 1 t to patrol. – 2 i to be out on patrol.
patrullera f (*barco*) patrol boat; (*avión*) patrol plane.
patuco m (*de niños*) bootee; (*de adultos*) bedsock.
patulea f *fam* mob.
paulatinamente adv gradually.
paulatino,-a adj gradual.
● de modo **paulatino**, gradually.
paupérrimo,-a adj extremely poor, impoverished.
pausa 1 f pause. 2 MÚS rest.
● con **pausa**, slowly. ‖ hacer una **pausa**, to pause, take a break. ‖ sin **pausa**, uninterruptedly.

pausado,-a *adj* unhurried, slow.

pauta 1 *f* (*norma*) rule, guideline; (*modelo*) model, pattern. 2 (*en el papel*) lines *pl.* 3 MÚS staff.
● **marcar la pauta,** to set the standard, establish the guidelines.
■ **pauta de comportamiento,** standard of behaviour.

pautado,-a *adj* (*papel*) ruled.

pava 1 *f* (*de un cigarrillo*) cigarette butt. 2 (*hervidora*) kettle. 3 (*animal*) → **pavo,-a.**

pavada *f fam* silly thing to say or do.

pavesa *f* spark.

pavía *f* clingstone peach.

pavimentación *f* (*con losas*) paving; (*con asfalto*) surfacing.

pavimentar *t* (*con losas*) to pave; (*con asfalto*) to surface.

pavimento *m* (*de losas*) pavement; (*de asfalto*) road surface.

pavisoso,-a *adj fam* silly.

pavo,-a 1 *adj fam* (*soso*) wet; (*tímido*) shy. – 2 *m,f* (*ave - macho*) turkey; (- *hembra*) turkey hen. 3 *m,f fam* (*persona*) drip. – 4 *pavo, m fam* (*timidez*) shyness: *tiene un pavo horroroso,* he's incredibly shy. 5 *fam* (*dinero*) *five peseta coin.*
● **estar en la edad del pavo,** to be at that silly age. ‖ **pelar la pava,** *fam* to court. ‖ **subírsele el pavo a algn.,** *fam* to go red, blush.
■ **pava real,** peahen. ‖ **pavo real,** peacock.

pavonearse *p* to brag, swagger.

pavor *m* terror: *me da pavor,* it terrifies me.

pavoroso,-a *adj* frightful.

payasada 1 *f* buffoonery, clowning: *siempre está haciendo payasadas,* he's always clowning around. 2 *fam* silly thing, stupid thing.

payaso,-a 1 *m,f* (*artista de circo*) clown. 2 *fam* joker.
● **hacer el payaso,** *fam* to clown around.

payés,-esa *m,f* Catalan farmer or country person.

payo,-a *m,f* non-Gypsy (*in Gypsy jargon*).

paz *f* peace.
● **aquí paz y después gloria,** and there's an end to it, and that's that. ‖ **dejar en paz,** to leave alone. ‖ **estar en paz,** to be even, be quits. ‖ **firmar la paz,** to sign a peace treaty. ‖ **hacer las paces,** to make up. ‖ **poner paz,** to make peace. ‖ **que en paz descanse,** rest his (*her*) soul. ‖ **y en paz,** *fam* and that's it.

pazguatería 1 *f* prudishness. 2 (*acción*) prudish thing to say or do.

pazguato,-a 1 *adj* (*gazmoño*) prudish. – 2 *m,f* (*gazmoño*) prude; (*tonto*) nincompoop.

pazo *m* Galician country house.

pbro. *abr* (*presbítero*) presbyte.

PC *abr* (*ordenador personal*) personal computer; (*abreviatura*) PC.

p.c. *abr* (*por ciento*) per cent; (*abreviatura*) pc.

PCE *abr* POL (*Partido Comunista de España*) Spanish Communist Party.

PCUS *abr* POL (*Partido Comunista de la Unión Soviética*) Communist Party of the Soviet Union; (*abreviatura*) CPSU.

P.D. *abr* (*posdata*) postscript; (*abreviatura*) PS, ps.

pe *f name of the letter p.*
● **de pe a pa,** *fam* from A to Z, from beginning to end.

PE *abr* (*Parlamento Europeo*) European Parliament; (*abreviatura*) EP.

peaje 1 *m* (*dinero*) toll. 2 (*lugar*) tollbooth.

peana *f* pedestal, stand.

peatón *m* pedestrian.

peatonal *adj* (*calle, zona*) pedestrian.

peca *f* freckle.

pecado *m* sin.
● **cometer/hacer un pecado,** to commit a sin. ‖ **estar en pecado,** to have committed a sin.
■ **pecado capital,** deadly sin. ‖ **pecado mortal,** mortal sin. ‖ **pecado original,** original sin. ‖ **pecado venial,** venial sin.

pecador,-ra 1 *adj* sinful, sinning. – 2 *m,f* sinner.

pecaminoso,-a *adj* sinful, wicked.

pecar *i* to sin.
● **pecar de ...,** to be too ..., be over-.... *pequé de meticulosa,* I was over-meticulous.
▲ *Conjugation model* [1], *like sacar.*

peccata minuta *f* peccadillo.

pecera *f* (*redonda*) fishbowl; (*rectangular*) fish tank.

pechera 1 *f* (*de camisa*) shirt front; (*de delantal*) bib. 2 *fam* (*pecho*) bosom.

pechina *f* scallop.

pecho 1 *m* (*gen*) chest. 2 (*seno*) breast.
● **a lo hecho pecho,** what's done is done. ‖ **dar el pecho,** to breastfeed. ‖ **partirse el pecho,** *fam* to break one's back. ‖ **sacar pecho,** to stick one's chest out. ‖ **tomar a pecho algo,** (*ofenderse*) to take sth. to heart; (*mostrar mucho interés*) to take sth. very seriously.

pechuga 1 *f* (*de un ave*) breast. 2 *fam* (*de mujer*) bust.

pechugón,-ona 1 *adj fam* big-breasted. – 2 **pechugona,** *f* big-breasted woman.

peciolo *m* petiole.

pécora ser una mala pécora, *loc adv fam* to be a bitch.

pecoso,-a *adj* (*persona*) freckly; (*cara*) freckled.

pectoral 1 *adj* (*músculo*) pectoral. 2 (*pastilla, jarabe*) cough. – 3 *m* (*músculo*) pectoral muscle. 4 (*jarabe*) cough mixture. 5 (*de obispo*) pectoral cross.

pecuario, -a *adj* cattle.

peculiar 1 *adj* (*raro*) peculiar. 2 (*característico*) particular, personal.

peculiaridad *f* peculiarity.

peculio *m* savings *pl.*

pecuniario,-a *adj* pecuniary.

pedagogía *f* pedagogy.

pedagógico,-a *adj* pedagogic(al).

pedagógo,-a *m,f* pedagogue, educator.

pedal 1 *m* pedal. 2 *fam* bender.
● **agarrar/coger un pedal,** *fam* to get plastered.
■ **pedal del acelerador,** accelerator pedal, US gas pedal. ‖ **pedal del embrague,** clutch pedal. ‖ **pedal del freno,** brake pedal.

pedalada *f*: *unas cuantas pedaladas más y estaremos arriba,* a bit more pedalling and we'll be at the top.

pedalear *i* to pedal.

pedaleo *m* pedalling.

pedáneo,-a *adj* municipal.

pedanía *f* hamlet.

pedante 1 *adj* pedantic, pompous. – 2 *mf* pedant.

pedantería *f* pedantry, pomposity.

pedazo 1 *m* piece, bit. 2 *fam* (*con insultos*): *¡pedazo de animal!,* stupid idiot!
● **estar hecho,-a pedazos,** *fam* (*materialmente*) to be falling apart; (*psíquicamente*) to be going to pieces. ‖ **hacer pedazos,** to smash to pieces: *me ha hecho pedazos el cenicero,* he's smashed my ashtray. ‖ **ser un pedazo de pan,** to be a real sweetie, be a real pet.

pederasta *m* pederast.

pedernal 1 *m* (*sílex*) flint. 2 *fig* rock.
pedestal *m* pedestal.
● poner/tener a algn. en un pedestal, to put/hold sb. on a pedestal.
pedestre 1 *adj* (*a pie*) on foot. 2 (*vulgar*) pedestrian.
pediatra *mf* paediatrician (US pediatrician).
■ médico pediatra, paediatrician (US pediatrician).
pediatría *f* paediatrics (US pediatrics).
pedicuro,-a *m,f* chiropodist.
pedida *f* (*compromiso*) engagement; (*fiesta*) engagement party.
pedido 1 *m* (*de mercancías*) order. 2 (*petición*) request, petition.
● hacer un pedido, to place an order.
pedigrí *m* pedigree.
pedigüeño,-a 1 *adj* pestering. – 2 *m,f* pest.
pedir 1 *t* (*gen*) to ask for: *me pidió el teléfono,* he asked me for my phone number; *me pidió que la acompañara,* she asked me to go with her. 2 *t* (*mercancías, en restaurante*) to order: *lo pedí por teléfono,* I ordered it over the phone; *¿qué has pedido de postre?,* what did you order for dessert? 3 (*necesitar*) to need, cry out for: *este suelo está pidiendo a gritos un fregado,* this floor is crying out to be washed. – 4 *i* (*por la calle*) to beg: *siempre hay gente pidiendo,* there are always people begging.
● a pedir de boca, just right, perfectly. ‖ pedir la cuenta, to ask for the bill. ‖ pedir la mano de algn., to ask for sb's hand in marriage.
▲ Conjugation model [34], like *servir*.
pedo 1 *m fam* fart. 2 *fam* (*borrachera*) drunkenness.
● estar pedo/ir pedo, *fam* (*por el alcohol*) to be pissed; (*por drogas*) to be stoned. ‖ tirarse un pedo, *fam* to fart, drop one.
pedofilia *f* paedophilia, pedophilia.
pedorrear *i fam* to fart (*repeatedly*).
pedorrera *f fam* wind.
pedorreta *f fam* raspberry.
● hacer una pedorreta a algn., *fam* to blow a raspberry at sb.
pedorro,-a 1 *m,f fam person who farts a lot.* 2 *fam* (*tonto*) stupid fart. – 3 *adj* farting. 4 *fam* (*tonto*) stupid.
pedrada *f* blow with a stone.
● matar a algn. a pedradas, to stone sb. to death. ‖ pegarle una pedrada a algn., to hit sb. with a stone.
pedrea 1 *f* (*de la lotería*) small prizes in the Spanish national lottery: *le tocó la pedrea,* he won one of the small prizes, he had a small win. 2 (*de granizo*) hailstorm.
pedregal *m* rocky ground.
pedregoso,-a *adj* stony, rocky.
pedrera *f* stone quarry.
pedrería *f* precious stones *pl.*
pedrisco *m* (*granizo*) hail; (*tormenta*) hailstorm.
pedrusco *m* rough stone.
peerse *p tabú* to fart.
pega *f fam* (*dificultad*) snag: *me pusieron muchas pegas para ver si así desistía,* they made it difficult for me to see if I would give up.
● de pega, fake, phoney: *una pistola de pega,* a toy gun. ‖ poner pegas a todo, to find fault with everything.
pegada *f* → **pegado,-a**.
pegadizo,-a 1 *adj* (*canción, música*) catchy. 2 (*sustancia*) sticky, adhesive.
pegado,-a 1 *pp* → **pegar**. – 2 *adj* clueless: *está más pegado que un sello,* she hasn't got a clue. – 3 pegada, *f* DEP (*de boxeador*) punch.

pegajoso,-a 1 *adj* (*mano, dedo*) sticky: *hace un calor pegajoso,* it's really hot and sticky. 2 *pey* (*persona*) clingy.
pegamento *m* glue.
pegar¹ 1 *t* (*gen*) to stick; (*con pegamento*) to glue, stick with glue; (*con cola*) to paste, stick with paste: *pega estos sellos en el álbum,* stick these stamps in your album; *han pegado un póster en la puerta,* they've stuck up a poster on the door. 2 (*coser*) to sew on: *pégame este botón,* sew this button on for me. 3 (*contagiar*) to give: *me has pegado la gripe,* you've given me your flu. 4 (*acercar*) to move close to: *pega la estantería a la pared,* move the bookcase against the wall. 5 INFORM to paste. – 6 *i* (*combinar*) to match: *esta blusa no pega con la falda,* this blouse doesn't go with the skirt. – 7 pegarse, *p* (*quemarse*) to stick: *se me ha vuelto a pegar el arroz,* the rice has stuck again. 8 (*persona*) to latch onto: *a mí siempre se me pegan los chiflados,* I always seem to attract loonies; *se me pegó un tío en el pub y no hubo forma de deshacerme de él,* a bloke latched onto me in the pub and I couldn't get rid of him.
● no pegar ni con cola, (*no entonar*) to be totally wrong, look totally out of place; (*ser increíble*) to be impossible to believe.
pegar² 1 *t* (*golpear*) to hit: *mamá, Pablo me ha pegado,* mum, Pablo hit me; *pega a su mujer,* he beats his wife; *estos niños siempre se están pegando,* these kids are always fighting. 2 (*dar*) to give: *¡vaya susto me has pegado!,* you didn't half scare me!; *deja ya de pegar gritos,* stop shouting; *lleva toda la mañana pegando saltos de alegría,* she's been jumping for joy all morning. – 3 *i* (*tener fuerza*) to beat down: *¡cómo pega el sol hoy!,* it's a real scorcher today! 4 (*beber*) to knock back: *le gusta pegarle al whisky ¿eh?,* he likes knocking back the whisky, doesn't he. – 5 pegarse, *p* (*tropezar*) to bump (con, into).
● dále que te pego, over and over again, on and on. ‖ no pegar golpe, not to do a blessed thing. ‖ no pegar ojo, not to sleep a wink. ‖ pegar fuerte, (*golpear*) to hit hard; (*tener éxito*) to be all the rage. ‖ pegarle fuego a algo, to set fire to sth. ‖ pegarle un tiro a algn., to shoot sb. ‖ pegarle una paliza a algn., to beat sb. up. ‖ pegarse la vida padre, *fam* to live the life of Riley. ‖ pegarse un tiro, to shoot os. ‖ pegársela, (*caerse*) to fall over, fall down; (*tener un accidente*) to have an accident. ‖ pegársela a algn., (*engañar*) to do the dirty on sb.; (*ser infiel*) to be unfaithful to sb.
pegatina *f* sticker.
pego dar el pego, *loc fam* to look like the real thing.
pegón,-ona *m,f fam* fond of hitting people: *es un chaval muy pegón,* he's always hitting people.
pegote 1 *m fam* (*masa*) sticky dollop, blob. 2 *fam* (*chapuza*) botch-up, botched job: *ese cuadro ahí queda como un pegote,* that painting sticks out like a sore thumb. 3 *fam* (*fanfarronada*) brag, boast.
● tirarse pegotes, *fam* to show off.
peinada *f* combing.
● darse una peinada, to comb one's hair.
peinado 1 *m* (*tocado*) hairdo; (*acción*) combing: *te han hecho un peinado precioso,* they've done your hair really nicely; *¡qué pelos!, te hace falta un buen peinado,* your hair really needs combing. 2 (*registro policial*) police search.
peinado,-a 1 *pp* → **peinar**. – 2 *adj* combed.
● ir bien peinado,-a, to be well groomed. ‖ ir mal peinado,-a, to have one's hair in a mess.
peinador,-ra 1 *m,f* (*peluquero*) hairdresser. – 2 peinador, *m* (*de tela*) peignoir.

peinar I *t* (*gen*) to comb; (*con cepillo*) to brush. **2** (*registrar*) to comb, search.

peine *m* comb.

● ¡te vas a enterar de lo que vale un peine!, *fam* you're going to get what's coming to you, you're going to cop it.

peineta *f* ornamental comb.

p. ej. *abr* (*por ejemplo*) for example; (*abreviatura*) eg.

pejiguera *f fam* bother.

Pekín *m* Peking.

pela I *f fam* (*peseta*) peseta. **2** (*dinero*) money.

pelada *f* → **pelado,-a**.

peladilla *f* sugared almond.

pelado,-a I *pp* → **pelar**. **- 2** *adj* bald, bare. **3** (*cabeza*) hairless, bald. **4** (*terreno*) barren, treeless. **5** *fam* (*sin dinero*) broke. **- 6 pelado,** *m fam* short haircut. **- 7 pelada,** *f fam* short haircut.

pelagatos *mf fam* nobody.

▲ *pl* *pelagatos*.

pelaje I *m* (*de animal*) coat, fur. **2** *fam* looks *pl*.

pelambre *m* hair.

pelambrera *f fam* hair.

pelanas *mf fam* nobody.

▲ *pl* *pelanas*.

pelandusca *f fam* floozy.

pelapatatas *m* potato peeler.

▲ *pl* *pelapatatas*.

pelar I *t* (*persona*) to cut sb.'s hair. **2** (*animal - quitar las plumas*) to pluck; (*- quitar la piel*) to skin. **3** (*fruta, patata, etc*) to peel. **- 4 pelarse,** *p* (*cortarse el pelo*) to get one's hair cut. **5** (*piel*) to be peeling.

● correr que se las pela, *fam* to run like mad. ‖ pelarse de frío, *fam* to freeze. ‖ ser duro,-a de pelar, *fam* to be a tough nut to crack.

peldaño *m* step.

pelea I *f* (*física*) fight; (*verbal*) quarrel, row. **2** (*esfuerzo*) struggle.

● buscar pelea, to look for trouble.

pelear I *i* (*físicamente*) to fight; (*verbalmente*) to quarrel, argue. **2** (*hacer un esfuerzo*) to work hard, struggle. **- 3 pelearse,** *p* (*físicamente*) to fight; (*verbalmente*) to quarrel, argue.

● pelear por algo, to fight for sth.

pelele I *m* (*muñeco de paja*) straw puppet. **2** (*persona*) puppet. **3** (*de bebé*) sleepsuit.

peleón,-ona *m,f* (*persona*) quarrelsome.

● vino peleón, plonk.

peletería I *f* (*establecimiento*) fur shop, furrier's. **2** (*industria*) fur industry.

peletero,-a I *adj* (*industria*) fur. **- 2** *m,f* furrier.

peliagudo,-a *adj* tricky.

pelícano *m* pelican.

película *f* film.

● allá películas, *fam* too bad. ‖ de película, fantastic. ‖ echar/poner una película, to show a film: ¿qué película echan hoy en la tele?, what film's on the telly today? ‖ no saber de qué va la película, *fam* to have no idea, not have a clue.

■ película de miedo, horror film. ‖ película de suspense, thriller. ‖ película en blanco y negro, black-and-white film. ‖ película en color, colour film. ‖ película del oeste, western. ‖ película muda, silent movie.

peliculero,-a I *m,f* (*aficionado al cine*) cinema fan: es una peliculera tremenda, she spends her life watching films. **2** *fam* (*fantasioso, exagerado*) prone to fantasizing: es muy peliculero, he's always fantasizing.

peliculón *m fam* blockbuster.

peligrar *i* to be in danger.

peligro I *m* danger. **2** *fam* (*persona*) menace.

● correr peligro de, to be in danger of. ‖ estar en peligro, to be in danger. ‖ estar fuera de peligro, to be out of danger. ‖ poner algo en peligro, to endanger sth., put sth. at risk. ‖ poner en peligro la vida de algn., to put sb.'s life at risk.

■ "peligro de muerte", danger.

peligrosamente *adv* dangerously.

peligrosidad *f* danger, dangerousness.

peligroso,-a *adj* dangerous.

pelillo *m fam* hair.

● pelillos a la mar, let's let bygones be bygones.

pelín *m fam* teeny bit.

pelirrojo,-a I *adj* red-haired. **- 2** *m,f* redhead.

pella I *f* (*de una coliflor*) head. **2** (*masa*) lump.

pellejo I *m* (*piel*) skin. **2** (*odre*) wineskin.

● jugarse el pellejo, to risk one's neck. ‖ ponerse en el pellejo de algn., to put os. in sb.'s shoes. ‖ salvar el pellejo, to save one's skin.

pelliza *f* (*adornada con piel*) fur-trimmed coat; (*forrada de piel*) fur-lined coat.

pellizcar *t* to pinch, nip.

▲ *Conjugation model* |1|, *like* **sacar**.

pellizco *m* pinch, nip.

pelma *mf fam* bore.

pelmazo,-a *m,f fam* → **pelma**.

pelo I *m* hair: tiene un pelo muy bonito, she has beautiful hair; siempre he llevado el pelo corto, I've always had short hair. **2** (*de animal*) coat, fur. **3** *fam* bit: faltó un pelo para que lo pegara, I came to within an inch of hitting him; perdí el tren por un pelo, I missed the train by seconds.

● a pelo, (*sin montura*) bareback; (*sin ayuda*) without help; (*sin nada*) without anything. ‖ caérsele el pelo a algn., *fam* to cop it, be for it. ‖ con pelos y señales, in great detail, down to the last detail. ‖ de medio pelo, second-rate. ‖ estar hasta los pelos, *fam* to be fed up (de, with). ‖ no tener pelos en la lengua, to speak one's mind, not mince words. ‖ no tener un pelo de tonto,-a, *fam* to be nobody's fool. ‖ no verle el pelo a algn., to see neither hide nor hair of sb. ‖ poner los pelos de punta, to make one's hair stand on end. ‖ por los pelos, by the skin of one's teeth. ‖ ser un hombre de pelo en pecho, *fam* to be a real man. ‖ soltarse el pelo, to let one's hair down. ‖ tirarse de los pelos, (*estar furioso*) to be furious; (*arrepentirse*) to kick os. ‖ tocarle un pelo a algn., to lay a finger on sb. ‖ tomar el pelo a algn., to pull sb.'s leg. ‖ venir al pelo, *fam* to be just the thing.

■ pelo de camello, camelhair.

pelón,-ona I *adj* bald. **- 2** *m,f* bald person.

pelota I *f* ball. **- 2** *mf fam* creep. **- 3 pelotas,** *fpl tabú* balls.

● devolverle la pelota a algn., to pass the ball back into sb.'s court. ‖ en pelotas, *fam* starkers. ‖ estar hasta las pelotas, *tabú* to be pissed off. ‖ hacer la pelota a algn., *fam* to butter sb. up, suck up to sb. ‖ pasarse la pelota, *fam* to pass the buck.

■ pelota de fútbol, football. ‖ pelota vasca, pelota, jai alai.

pelotari *m* pelota player.

pelotazo I *m* blow with a ball: le rompieron las gafas de un pelotazo, they broke his glasses with a ball. **2** *arg* (*de bebida*) slug, swig; (*de droga*) shot.

pelotear *i* (*entrenarse - fútbol*) to kick a ball around; (*- tenis*) to knock up; (*jugar con la pelota*) to throw a ball round.
peloteo 1 *m* (*fútbol*) kickabout; (*tenis*) knock-up. **2** *fam* → **pelotilleo**.
pelotera *f fam* row.
pelotilla *f* small ball.
● **hacer la pelotilla a algn.**, *fam* to butter sb. up. ‖ **hacer pelotillas**, *fam* to pick one's nose.
pelotilleo *m fam* creeping.
pelotillero,-a 1 *adj* crawling. – **2** *m,f fam* creep, crawler.
pelotón 1 *m* MIL squad. **2** *fig* (*grupo*) bunch.
peltre *m* pewter.
peluca *f* wig.
peluche 1 *m* (*tejido*) plush. **2** (*muñeco*) teddy bear, cuddly toy.
peludo,-a *adj* hairy.
peluquería *f* hairdresser's.
peluquero,-a *m,f* hairdresser.
peluquín *m* hairpiece.
● **¡ni hablar del peluquín!**, *fam* no way!
pelusa 1 *f* (*pelo*) fluff. **2** *fam* (*celos*) jealousy.
pelusilla *f* → **pelusa**.
pelvis *f* pelvis.
▲ *pl pelvis*.
pena 1 *f* (*castigo*) sentence, punishment: *lo han condenado a una pena de seis meses de cárcel*, he was sentenced to six months' imprisonment. **2** (*tristeza*) grief, sorrow: *me da pena verlo tan solo*, it makes me sad to see him so lonely. **3** (*lástima*) pity: *¡qué pena que no podáis venir!*, it's a shame you can't make it! **4** (*dificultad*) hardship, trouble.
● **a duras penas**, with great difficulty. ‖ **de pena**, *fam* awful, terrible, pathetic. ‖ **hecho,-a una pena**, *fam* in a bad way. ‖ **merecer la pena / valer la pena**, to be worth while, be worth it. ‖ **sin pena ni gloria**, undistinguished.
■ **pena capital**, capital punishment. ‖ **pena de muerte**, death penalty.
penacho 1 *m* (*de un ave*) tuft. **2** (*adorno*) plume.
penado,-a *m,f* convict.
penal 1 *adj* (*código*) penal; (*derecho, antecedentes*) criminal. – **2** *m* (*prisión*) prison, US penitentiary.
penalidad *f* trouble, hardship.
penalista *mf* criminal lawyer.
penalización 1 *f* (*acción*) penalization; (*castigo*) penalty, punishment. **2** DEP penalty.
penalizar *t* to penalize.
▲ *Conjugation model* [4], *like realizar*.
penalti *m* penalty.
● **casarse de penalti**, *fam* to have a shotgun wedding. ‖ **marcar un gol de penalti**, to score a penalty.
penar 1 *t* (*castigar*) to punish, penalize. – **2** *i* (*padecer*) to suffer, grieve.
penca *f* fleshy leaf.
penco *m* (*caballo*) nag.
pendejo,-a *adj fam* nincompoop.
pendencia *f* brawl.
pendenciero,-a *adj* quarrelsome.
pender *i* to hang (**de**, from).
pendiente 1 *adj* hanging. **2** (*asunto*) pending, outstanding. – **3** *f* (*cuesta*) slope; (*inclinación*) gradient. – **4** *m* (*joya*) earring.
● **estar pendiente de algo**, (*a la espera*) to be waiting for sth.; (*atento*) to follow sth. closely. ‖ **estar pendien-**

te **de algn.**, (*atento*) to be watching sb.; (*dispuesto*) to be at sb.'s beck and call.
pendón 1 *m* (*bandera*) banner, standard. **2** *fam pey* (*mujer*) slut; (*hombre*) rascal.
pendular *adj* pendular.
péndulo *m* pendulum.
pene *m* penis.
penene *mf* → **PNN**.
penetración 1 *f* penetration. **2** (*perspicacia*) insight.
penetrante *adj* penetrating.
penetrar 1 *i* (*introducirse - en un territorio*) to penetrate (**en**, -); (*- en una casa, propiedad*) to enter: *no nos atrevimos a penetrar en la selva*, we didn't dare go into the jungle. **2** (*atravesar*) to penetrate, seep through: *la humedad ha penetrado por el suelo*, damp has seeped through the floor; *el frío penetra por las finas paredes*, the cold comes in through the thin walls. **3** *fig* (*entender*) to comprehend (**en**, -); (*analizar*) to look (**en**, into). – **4** *t* (*atravesar*) to penetrate; (*ruido*) to pierce: *el olor era tan fuerte que penetró la ropa*, the smell was so strong that it got right into our clothes. **5** (*descifrar - misterio*) to get to the bottom of; (*- secreto*) to fathom (out).
penicilina *f* penicillin.
Peninos los (montes) Peninos, *mpl* the Pennines.
península 1 *f* peninsula. **2** (*ibérica*) mainland Spain.
■ **la Península Ibérica**, the Iberian Peninsula.
peninsular 1 *adj* peninsular. **2** of from mainland Spain, from mainland Spain. – **3** *mf* person from mainland Spain.
penique *m* penny.
penitencia 1 *f* REL (*virtud*) penitence; (*castigo, sacramento*) penance. **2** (*pesadez*) punishment.
penitenciaría *f* penitentiary.
penitenciario,-a *adj* (*institución, sistema*) prison.
penitente 1 *adj* penitent. – **2** *mf* penitent.
penoso,-a 1 *adj* (*doloroso*) painful; (*triste*) sad. **2** (*trabajoso*) laborious, hard. **3** (*desastroso*) terrible, awful, dreadful.
pensado,-a 1 *pp* → **pensar**. – **2** *adj* (*considerado*) thought-out; (*diseñado*) designed.
● **el día menos pensado ...**, when you least expect it ... ‖ **ser mal pensado,-a**, to think the worst of people. ‖ **tener algo pensado**, to have sth. planned, have sth. in mind.
pensador,-ra 1 *adj* thinking. – **2** *m,f* thinker.
pensamiento 1 *m* (*idea*) thought. **2** (*mente*) mind. **3** BOT pansy.
pensante *adj* thinking.
pensar 1 *i* (*gen*) to think (**en**, of/about): *estuvo pensando en sus amigos*, he was thinking about his friends. **2** (*considerar*) to consider, think (**en**, about). – **3** *t* (*creer*) to think, think about. **4** (*opinar*) to think (**de**, about). **5** (*decidir*) to decide. **6** (*tener la intención*) to intend to, plan, think of. – **7** **pensarse**, *p* to think about.
● **¡ni pensarlo!**, no way! don't even think about it!. ‖ **pensar bien/mal de algn.**, to think well/badly of sb. ‖ **sin pensar**, without thinking.
▲ *Conjugation model* [27], *like acertar*.
pensativo,-a *adj* pensive.
Pensilvania *f* Pennsylvania.
pensión 1 *f* (*para jubilados*) pension; (*para ex cónyuge*) maintenance. **2** (*casa de huéspedes*) hostel, boarding house, guesthouse, lodgings *pl*. **3** (*cantidad que se paga*) board and lodging, bed and board.
■ **media pensión**, half board. ‖ **pensión completa**, full board.
pensionado,-a 1 *adj* pensioned. – **2** *m,f* pensioner. – **3** **pensionado**, *m* (*colegio*) boarding school.

pensionista I *mf (jubilado)* pensioner. **2** *(residente - en un internado)* boarder; *(- en una pensión)* lodger.
■ **medio pensionista,** person with half-board.
pentagonal *adj* pentagonal.
pentágono *m* pentagon.
pentagrama *m* MÚS stave, staff.
Pentecostés *m (cristiano)* Pentecost, Whitsunday; *(judío)* Pentecost.
penúltimo,-a I *adj* penultimate. **– 2** *m,f* last but one, next to last: *quedé la penúltima en la carrera,* I was last but one in the race. **– 3 penúltima,** *f fam* last drink: *hay que tomarse la penúltima,* let's have one for the road.
penumbra *f (gen)* semi-darkness; *(de un eclipse)* penumbra: *la habitación estaba en penumbra,* the room was in semi-darkness.
penuria I *f (escasez)* shortage. **2** *(pobreza)* extreme poverty, penury.
peña¹ *f (piedra)* rock; *(monte)* crag.
peña² *f (grupo)* group of friends; *(asociación)* club.
peñasco *m* crag.
peñazo *m fam* pain.
peñón *m* craggy rock.
▲ **el Peñón de Gibraltar,** the Rock of Gibraltar.
peón I *m (trabajador)* unskilled labourer (US laborer). **2** *(agrícola)* farm hand, farm worker. **3** *(en el ajedrez)* pawn. **4** *(peonza)* spinning-top.
■ **peón caminero,** roadmender. ‖ **peón de albañil,** building labourer (US laborer).
peonada *f* day's work.
peonía *f* BOT peony.
peonza *f* spinning-top.
peor I *adj (comparativo)* worse: *tu coche es peor que el mío,* your car is worse than mine. **2** *(superlativo)* worst.
● **en el peor de los casos,** at worst. ‖ **peor es nada,** it's better than nothing.
Pepa ¡viva la Pepa!, *interj fam* hurray!, hurrah!
pepinazo I *m (estallido)* blast. **2** *(disparo)* cannonball shot.
pepinillo *m* gherkin.
pepino *m* cucumber.
● **me importa un pepino,** *fam* I don't give a damn.
pepita I *f (de fruta)* seed, pip. **2** *(de oro)* nugget.
pepito *m* grilled meat sandwich.
pepitoria *f* stew *containing egg yolk.*
pepona *f* doll.
peque *m* kid.
pequeñez I *f (de tamaño)* smallness. **2** *(insignificancia)* trifle.
pequeño,-a I *adj (de tamaño)* little, small: *este jersey me está pequeño,* this jumper is too small for me. **2** *(de edad)* young. **3** *(en tiempo)* short: *nos hemos tomado unas pequeñas vacaciones,* we've taken a short holiday. **– 4** *m,f (niño)* little one: *a esta hora los pequeños tienen que estar en la cama,* kids should be in bed by now; *a la pequeña le encanta la tele,* the little one loves watching telly.
● **de pequeño,-a,** as a child. ‖ **ser el pequeño/la pequeña,** to be the youngest.
Pequín *m* Peking.
pera I *f (fruta)* pear. **2** *(interruptor) pear-shaped* switch: *dale a la pera de la luz,* switch the light on/off.
● **pedir peras al olmo,** *fam* to ask the impossible. ‖ **ponerle a algn. las peras al cuarto,** *fam* to tear sb. off a strip. ‖ **ser la pera,** *fam (persona divertida)* to be a

real laugh; *(situación indignante)* to be unbelievable, be incredible.
■ **niño pera,** *fam* Daddy's boy.
peral *m* pear tree.
peraltar *t (carretera)* to camber.
peralte *m (de una carretera)* camber.
perca *f* perch.
percal *m* percale.
● **conocerse el percal,** *fam* to know the score, know what's what.
percance *m* mishap.
per cápita *loc* per capita.
percatarse *p* to notice **(de, -),** realize **(de, -).**
percebe I *m* goose barnacle. **2** *fam (persona)* dimwit.
percepción *f* perception.
perceptible *adj* perceptible, noticeable.
perceptivo,-a *adj* perceptive.
percha I *f (de ropa)* hanger. **2** *(perchero de pie)* coat stand; *(perchero de pared)* rack; *(gancho)* hook. **3** *fam* body, figure: *el traje está bien, pero me gusta más la percha,* the suit's nice, but I prefer what's inside it; *con la percha que tienes seguro que te queda precioso,* you have such a nice figure I'm sure it will look lovely.
perchero *m (de pared)* clothes rack; *(de pie)* coat stand.
percherón, -ona *adj (caballo)* Percheron.
percibir I *t (notar)* to perceive, notice. **2** *(dinero)* to receive.
percusión *f* percussion.
percusionista *mf* percussionist.
percutor *m* hammer.
percutor *m →* **percusor.**
perder I *t (gen)* to lose: *he perdido el bolígrafo,* I've lost my pen. **2** *(malgastar, desperdiciar)* to waste: *se pasa el día perdiendo el tiempo,* he's always wasting time. **3** *(tren etc)* to miss. **4** *(ser causa de daños)* to be the ruin of: *le perdió su afición al juego,* gambling was his downfall. **– 5** *i (gen)* to lose; *(salir perdiendo)* to lose out. **6** *(empeorar)* to get worse: *esta ciudad ha perdido mucho, ya no es lo que era,* this city has gone downhill, it isn't what it used to be. **– 7 perderse,** *p (extraviarse - persona)* to get lost; *(- animal)* to go missing: *se me ha perdido un pendiente,* I've lost an earring. **8** *(confundirse)* to get confused, get mixed up: *en cuanto hablan de política me pierdo,* when they talk about politics I get lost. **9** *(desaparecer)* to disappear, take off: *en cuanto ve problemas, se pierde,* as soon as there's a problem, he disappears. **10** *(dejar escapar)* to miss: *¡no te lo pierdas!,* don't miss it!
● **echar a perder,** to spoil. ‖ **perder agua,** to leak. ‖ **perder color,** to fade. ‖ **perder de vista,** to lose sight of. ‖ **perderse por algo/algn.,** *fam* to give up everything for sb./sth. ‖ **perdérselo,** *fam: tú te lo pierdes,* it's your loss. ‖ **salir perdiendo,** to come off worse, lose out. ‖ **tener buen perder,** to be a good loser. ‖ **tener mal perder,** to be a bad loser. ‖ **¡piérdete!,** *fam* get lost!
▲ *Conjugation model* [28], *like* **entender.**
perdición I *f (moral)* undoing, ruin: *estas amistades lo van a llevar a la perdición,* those friends will be the ruin of him. **2** *(daño)* harm, ruin: *el tabaco es mi perdición,* smoking will be the end of me.
pérdida I *f (daño)* loss: *las tormentas han originado muchas pérdidas materiales,* the storms have caused serious damage; *no hay que lamentar pérdidas humanas,* fortunately, nobody has been killed. **2** *(desperdicio)* waste. **3** *(acción de perder)* loss: *la pérdida del billete fue*

un desastre, losing the ticket was a disaster. **4** *(escape)* leak.
● **llorar la pérdida de algn.,** to mourn for sb. ‖ **no tiene pérdida,** you can't miss it. ‖ **ser una pérdida de tiempo,** to be a waste of time.
perdidamente *adv* madly.
perdido,-a 1 *pp* → **perder.** – **2** *adj (extraviado)* lost. **3** *(desperdiciado)* wasted. **4** *(bala)* stray. **5** *(aislado)* isolated, cut-off. **6** *fam (como enfatizador)* complete, utter, total: *es idiota perdido,* he's a complete idiot. – **7** *m,f (person)* degenerate.
● **estar perdido,-a,** *(extraviado)* to be lost; *(no tener salida)* to have had it, be for it: *como hagan una inspección estamos perdidos,* if there's an inspection we've had it. ‖ **ponerse perdido,-a,** *fam* to get filthy, get dirty.
perdigón 1 *m* pellet. **2** ZOOL young partridge.
perdigonada *f (disparo)* shot; *(herida)* pellet wound.
perdiguero *m* gundog.
perdiz *f* partridge.
● **fueron felices y comieron perdices,** and they all lived happily ever after.
■ **perdiz común,** red-legged partridge. ‖ **perdiz nival,** ptarmigan. ‖ **perdiz pardilla,** common partridge.
perdón *m* pardon, forgiveness.
● **con perdón,** if you pardon the expression. ‖ **no tener perdón,** to be unforgivable. ‖ **pedir perdón,** to apologize, say sorry. ‖ **¡perdón!,** *(para excusarse)* sorry!; *(para preguntar, hacerse paso)* excuse me.
perdonar 1 *t (gen)* to forgive; *(acusado)* to pardon: *Dios te perdone,* may God forgive you. **2** *(excusar)* to excuse: *perdona que te interrumpa,* excuse me for interrupting, sorry to bother you; *"perdonen las molestias",* "we apologize for any inconvenience". **3** *(deuda)* to write off. **4** *fam (prescindir de)* to do without, go without: *las vacaciones no las perdono,* I won't go without my holidays.
● **no perdonar ni una,** *fam* to be unrelenting, not let sb. get away with anything. ‖ **perdonarle la vida a algn.,** to spare sb.'s life.
perdonavidas *mf fam* bully.
perdulario,-a *m,f* ne'er-do-well.
perdurable 1 *adj (perpetuo)* everlasting. **2** *(duradero)* long-lasting.
perdurar *i* to last, continue to exist, live on.
perecedero,-a *adj* perishable.
perecer *i* to perish, die.
▲ Conjugation model |43|, like *agradecer.*
peregrinación *f* pilgrimage.
peregrinaje *m* pilgrimage.
peregrinar 1 *i* to go on a pilgrimage. **2** *fig* to traipse, trail.
peregrino,-a 1 *adj (en peregrinaje)* travelling. **2** *(ave)* migratory. **3** *fig (idea, ocurrencia)* strange, peculiar. – **4** *m,f* REL pilgrim.
perejil *m* parsley.
perengano *m,f* → **fulano.**
perenne *adj* perennial.
perentorio,-a *adj* peremptory, urgent.
pereza *f* laziness: *¡qué pereza lavar los platos!,* I don't feel like doing the washing up; *me da pereza,* I can't be bothered.
● **tener pereza,** to feel lazy.
perezoso,-a 1 *adj* lazy. – **2** *m,f* lazy person, idler, lazybones. – **3** perezoso, *m* ZOOL sloth.
perfección *f* perfection.
● **a la perfección,** perfectly: *habla inglés a la perfección,* he speaks perfect English.

perfeccionamiento *m* improvement.
perfeccionar 1 *t (mejorar)* to improve. **2** *(hacer perfecto)* to perfect.
perfeccionismo *m* perfectionism.
perfeccionista 1 *adj* perfectionist. – **2** *mf* perfectionist.
perfectamente 1 *adv (completamente)* perfectly. **2** *(como asentimiento)* all right!, great!, fine!
perfecto,-a *adj* perfect.
perfidia *f* perfidy.
pérfido,-a 1 *adj* perfidious. – **2** *m,f* traitor.
perfil 1 *m (gen)* profile. **2** *(silueta)* outline. **3** *(para un trabajo)* outline.
● **de perfil,** in profile: *ponte de perfil,* show me your profile.
perfilar 1 *t (dar forma)* to outline. **2** *(perfeccionar)* to perfect. – **3 perfilarse,** *p* to take shape: *Torres se perfila como ganador,* Torres is beginning to look like the winner.
perforación 1 *f (gen)* perforation. **2** *(en una mina)* drilling, boring. **3** *(de papel)* punching.
perforadora 1 *f (en una mina)* drill. **2** *(de papeles)* punch.
perforar 1 *t (gen)* to perforate. **2** *(terreno)* to drill, bore. **3** *(papel)* to punch.
perfumar *t* to perfume, scent: *se perfuma antes de salir,* she puts perfume on before going out.
perfume *m* perfume.
perfumería 1 *f (tienda)* perfumery. **2** *(industria)* perfume industry.
perfumista *mf* perfumer.
pergamino *m* parchment.
pergeñar *t* to prepare.
pérgola *f* pergola.
pericardio *m* pericardium.
pericarpio *m* pericarp.
pericia *f* skill.
pericial *adj (informe)* done by an expert.
periferia 1 *f (gen)* periphery. **2** *(de una ciudad)* outskirts *pl.*
periférico,-a 1 *adj (gen)* peripheral. **2** *(barrio, zona)* outlying. – **3 periférico,** *m* INFORM peripheral unit.
perifollo 1 *m* BOT common chervil. – **2 perifollos,** *mpl fam (adornos)* frills.
perífrasis *f* periphrasis.
perifrástico,-a *adj* periphrastic.
perilla *f* goatee.
● **ir de perilla / venir de perilla,** *fam* to come in really handy.
perímetro *m* perimeter.
perindola *f* small top.
periné *m* perineum.
perineo *m* perineum.
periodicidad *f* periodicity.
periódico,-a 1 *adj* periodical. – **2 periódico,** *m* newspaper.
periodismo *m* journalism.
periodista *mf* journalist.
periodístico,-a *adj* journalistic.
periodo *m* period.
período *m* period.
peripatético,-a *adj (ridículo)* absurd, pathetic.
peripecia *f* incident.
periplo 1 *m* long journey. **2** *(por mar)* voyage.
peripuesto,-a *adj fam* all dressed up.
periquete *m fam* jiffy.
● **en un periquete,** in a jiffy, in two shakes, in a sec.

periquito,-a. 1 periquito, *mf* (*gen*) parakeet; (*australiano*) budgerigar. – 2 periquito,-a, *m,f fam* (*mujer*) girl; (*hombre*) boy, lad. 3 DEP *fam supporter of the Real Club Deportivo Español.*

periscopio *m* periscope.

perista *mf* fence.

peristáltico,-a *adj* peristaltic.

peristilo *m* peristyle.

peritaje 1 *m* (*informe*) expert's report; (*para el seguro*) loss adjuster's report. 2 (*investigación*) inspection, survey. 3 (*estudios*) technical studies *pl.*
■ peritaje mercantil, accountancy.

perito,-a 1 *adj* expert. – 2 *m,f* (*experto*) expert; (*en seguros*) loss adjuster. 3 (*en ingeniería*) technician.
■ perito,-a agrónomo,-a, agricultural technician. ‖ perito,-a industrial, engineer. ‖ perito,-a mercantil, accountant.

peritoneo *m* peritoneum.

peritonitis *f* peritonitis.
▲ *pl peritonitis.*

perjudicado,-a 1 *pp* → **perjudicar.** – 2 *m,f* person who loses out, person affected: *los más perjudicados han sido los campesinos,* farmers have been worst affected.

perjudicar *t* to adversely affect, be bad for, be detrimental to: *sabes que beber te perjudica,* you know that drinking is bad for you; *esta sequía perjudica a la agricultura,* the drought is hitting the farmers.
▲ *Conjugation model* |1|, *like sacar.*

perjudicial *adj* harmful.

perjuicio *m* (*material*) damage; (*económico*) loss.
● causar perjuicio a algn., to damage sb.'s interests. ‖ con perjuicio para, resulting in damage to. ‖ en perjuicio de, adversely affecting, to the detriment of, against. ‖ sin perjuicio de, without adversely affecting, without detriment to; JUR without prejudice to.

perjurar 1 *i* to commit perjury. – 2 *t* to swear: *juró y perjuró que él no había sido,* he swore blind he hadn't done it.

perjurio *m* perjury.

perjuro,-a 1 *adj* perjured. – 2 *m,f* perjurer.

perla 1 *f* pearl. 2 *fig* gem.
● de perlas, *fam* perfect: *tu regalo me vino de perlas,* your present was just what I needed; *la fiesta salió de perlas,* the party was a real success.
■ collar de perlas, pearl necklace. ‖ perla cultivada, cultured pearl.

perlado,-a *adj* pearled.
● perlado,-a de sudor, beaded with sweat.

permanecer *i* to stay, remain.
▲ *Conjugation model* |43|, *like agradecer.*

permanencia 1 *f* (*estancia*) stay. 2 (*continuidad*) continuance.

permanente 1 *adj* permanent, lasting. – 2 *f* (*del pelo*) permanent wave: *se ha hecho la permanente,* she's had her hair permed.
■ servicio permanente, 24-hour service.

permanentemente *adv* permanently.

permanganato *m* permanganate.

permeabilidad *f* permeability.

permeable *adj* permeable.

permisible *adj* permissible.

permisividad *f* permissiveness.

permisivo,-a *adj* permissive.

permiso 1 *m* permission. 2 (*documento*) permit. 3 MIL leave.

● con permiso, excuse me. ‖ con su permiso, if you'll excuse me. ‖ estar de permiso, to be on leave. ‖ pedir permiso, to ask permission.
■ permiso de conducir, driving licence, US driver's licence. ‖ permiso de residencia, residence permit.

permitir 1 *t* to allow, let: *permitió que sus hijas fueran al concierto,* he let his daughters go to the concert; *no te permito que hables así,* I won't allow you to talk to me like that; *no se permite fumar,* no smoking; *el sol me da en los ojos y no me permite ver,* I can't see because the sun's in my eyes. – 2 permitirse, *p* to allow os., afford: *no me puedo permitir comprarme un coche,* I can't afford to buy a car.
● ¿me permite?, may I? ‖ si el tiempo lo permite, weather permitting.

permuta *f* exchange.

permutable *adj* exchangeable.

permutar 1 *t* to exchange. 2 MAT to permute.

pernicioso,-a *adj* pernicious, harmful.

pernil *m* (*pata de animal*) haunch; (*del cerdo*) ham; (*del pantalón*) leg.

pernio *m* hinge.

perno *m* bolt.

pernocta pase de pernocta, *m* overnight pass.

pernoctar *i* to spend the night, stay overnight.

pero 1 *conj* but: *eramos pobres, pero felices,* we were poor, but happy; *era un examen difícil, pero que muy difícil, ¿sabes?,* it was a difficult exam, and I mean really difficult. – 2 *m* objection, fault.
● no hay pero que valga, I don't want any arguments. ‖ poner peros, to find fault (a, with).

perogrullada *f* platitude, truism.

perogrullo verdad de perogrullo, *loc* truism.

perol *m* cooking pot.

perola *f* saucepan, pan.

peroné *m* fibula.

peronismo *m* Peronism.

peronista 1 *adj* Peronist. – 2 *mf* Peronist.

perorar 1 *i* (*dar un discurso*) to deliver a speech. 2 *pey* to blabber on (sobre, about).

perorata *f* spiel.

perpendicular 1 *adj* perpendicular. – 2 *f* perpendicular.

perpendicularidad *f* perpendicularity.

perpetrar *t* to perpetrate, commit.

perpetuación *f* perpetuation.

perpetuar 1 *t* to perpetuate. – 2 perpetuarse, *p* to be perpetuated.
▲ *Conjugation model* |11|, *like actuar.*

perpetuidad *f* perpetuity.
● a perpetuidad, for ever and ever.

perpetuo,-a *adj* (*gen*) perpetual; (*cargo*) permanent.
■ nieves perpetuas, perpetual snows.

perplejidad *f* perplexity: *me miró con perplejidad,* he looked at me perplexed.

perplejo,-a *adj* perplexed.

perra *f* → **perro,-a.**

perrera 1 *f* (*lugar*) dog pound. 2 (*vehículo*) dog-catcher's van.
■ perrera municipal, dog pound.

perrería *f fam* dirty trick.

perrito 1 *m* (*animal*) small dog. 2 perrito (caliente), (*salchicha*) hotdog.

perro,-a 1 *adj* rotten. – 2 perro *m* ZOOL dog. – 3 perra, *f* ZOOL bitch. 4 *fam* (*pataleta*) tantrum. 5 (*deseo fuerte*) obsession: *¡vaya perra tiene con mudarse de casa!,* he's obsessed about moving house! – **6 perras,** *fpl fam* readies.

● "cuidado con el perro", "beware of the dog". ‖ a otro perro con ese hueso, pull the other one. ‖ atar los perros con longaniza, *fam* to have money to burn. ‖ coger una perra, *fam* to have a tantrum. ‖ de perros, *fam* rotten, lousy. ‖ llevar una vida de perros, *fam* to lead a dog's life. ‖ llevarse como el perro y el gato, *fam* to fight like cat and dog. ‖ no valer ni tres perras gordas, *fam* not to be worth a penny. ‖ perro ladrador, poco mordedor, his (*her etc*) bark is worse than his (*her etc*) bite. ‖ ser perro viejo, *fam* to be long in the tooth. ‖ ¡para ti la perra gorda!, *fam* OK, you win!

■ perra chica, *five-centimo coin.* ‖ perra gorda, *ten-centimo coin.* ‖ perro caliente, hotdog. ‖ perro callejero, stray dog. ‖ perro de caza, hunting dog. ‖ perro de compañía, pet dog. ‖ perro de muestra, pointer. ‖ perro de rastro, tracker dog. ‖ perro faldero, lapdog. ‖ perro pastor, sheepdog. ‖ perro perdiguero, gundog. ‖ perro policía, police dog. ‖ perro rastrero, tracker dog.

perruno,-a **1** *adj* (*del perro*) dog's. **2** *fam* (*tos*) chesty, thick.

persa **1** *adj* Persian. – **2** *mf* (*persona*) Persian. – **3** persa, *m* (*idioma*) Persian.

per se *loc adv* per se.

persecución **1** *f* pursuit. **2** (*represión*) persecution.

persecutorio,-a *adj* persecutory.

perseguidor, -ora **1** *m,f* pursuer. **2** (*represor*) persecutor.

perseguir **1** *t* to pursue, chase: *nos persiguió un coche de policía,* a police car chased us. **2** *fig* (*seguir*) to follow: *este perro me persigue,* this dog follows me everywhere. **3** (*reprimir*) to persecute. **4** *fig* (*pretender*) to be after, be looking for: *lo que persigue es que la invite a la fiesta,* she's after an invite to the party. **5** JUR to prosecute.

▲ *Conjugation model* [56], *like seguir.*

perseverancia *f* perseverance.

perseverante *adj* persevering.

perseverar *i* to persevere.

Persia *f* Persia.

persiana *f* blind.

pérsico,-a *adj* → **persa.**

■ golfo Pérsico, Persian Gulf.

persignarse *p* to cross os.

persistencia *f* persistence.

persistente *adj* persistent.

persistir **1** *i* (*mantenerse firme*) to persist, persevere. **2** (*durar*) to continue, persist.

persona *f* person: *tu tío es muy buena persona,* your uncle is a nice man; *faltan dos personas,* there are two people missing.

● en persona, in person.

■ persona física, individual. ‖ persona jurídica, legal entity.

personaje **1** *m* (*famoso*) celebrity. **2** CINEM TEAT character.

personal **1** *adj* personal. – **2** *m* (*de una empresa*) personnel, staff. **3** *fam* (*gente*) everyone, everybody: *hoy está el personal un poco apagado,* everyone's a bit down today. – **4** *f* DEP (*falta*) personal foul.

personalidad **1** *f* (*carácter*) personality. **2** (*personaje*) celebrity.

personalismo **1** *m* (*ofensa personal*) personal attack: *dejemos a un lado los personalismos,* let's not get personal. **2** (*partidismo*) partiality.

personalista **1** *adj* (*parcial*) partial, biased. **2** (*egoísta*) selfish.

personalizado,-a *adj* personalized.

personalizar **1** *t* to personalize. – **2** *i* to get personal.

personalmente *adv* personally.

personarse *p* to appear in person, present os.

personificación *f* personification.

personificar *t* to personify.

▲ *Conjugation model* [1], *like sacar.*

perspectiva **1** *f* ART perspective. **2** (*posibilidad*) prospect: *este negocio presenta muy buenas perspectivas,* this business has good prospects. **3** (*vista*) view, perspective: *desde aquí se divisa una buena perspectiva de la ciudad,* you get a really good view of the city from here. **4** (*punto de vista*) point of view.

perspicacia *f* sharpness, perspicacity.

perspicaz *adj* sharp, perspicacious.

persuadir **1** *t* to persuade, convince. – **2** persuadirse, *p* to be convinced.

persuasión *f* persuasion.

persuasivo,-a *adj* persuasive.

pertenecer *i* to belong (**a,** to).

▲ *Conjugation model* [43], *like agradecer.*

perteneciente *adj* belonging (**a,** to).

pertenencia **1** *f* (*propiedad*) property: *esto es de mi pertenencia,* this belongs to me. **2** (*afiliación*) membership. – **3** pertenencias, *fpl* (*bienes*) belongings.

pértiga *f* pole.

■ salto de pértiga, pole vault.

pertinaz **1** *adj* (*sequía, frío*) prolongued, persistent. **2** (*persona*) obstinate.

pertinencia **1** *f* (*conveniencia*) appropriateness. **2** (*relevancia*) relevance, pertinence.

pertinente **1** *adj* (*oportuno*) appropriate. **2** (*relevante*) pertinent, relevant.

pertrechar **1** *t* to supply (**de,** with). – **2** pertrecharse, *p* to equip os.

pertrechos **1** *mpl* equipment *sing.* **2** MIL military equipment *sing.*

perturbación **1** *f* disruption, disturbance. **2** (*mental*) disorder.

■ perturbación del orden público, public disorder, breach of the peace.

perturbado,-a **1** *adj* (*trastornado*) mentally disturbed. **2** (*intranquilo*) perturbed. – **3** *m,f* mentally disturbed person.

perturbador,-ra *adj* disturbing.

perturbar **1** *t* (*alterar*) to disturb, perturb. **2** (*inquietar*) to perturb.

● perturbar el orden, to disturb the peace.

Perú *m* Peru.

peruano,-a **1** *adj* Peruvian. – **2** *m,f* Peruvian.

perversidad *f* (*maldad*) wickedness.

perversión **1** *f* (*maldad*) wickedness. **2** (*sexual*) perversion.

perverso,-a **1** *adj* (*malvado*) evil, wicked. – **2** *m,f* evil person.

pervertido,-a **1** *pp* → **pervertir.** – **2** *adj* (*gen*) corrupt; (*sexualmente*) perverted. – **3** *m,f* (*sexual*) pervert.

pervertidor,-ra **1** *adj* corrupting. – **2** *m,f* (*gen*) corruptor.

pervertir *t* (*gen*) to corrupt; (*sexualmente*) to pervert.

▲ *Conjugation model* [35], *like hervir.*

pervivencia *f* survival.

pervivir *i* to live on, persist, survive.

pesa f weight.
pesabebés m baby scales pl.
▲ pl pesabebés.
pesadamente adv sluggishly.
pesadez 1 f (lentitud) sluggishness. 2 (molestia) bore: ¡menuda pesadez tener que repetirlo!, what a nuisance to have to do it all again! 3 (de un objeto) heaviness.
● tener pesadez de estómago, to have indigestion.
pesadilla f nightmare.
pesado,-a I pp→ **pesar**. – 2 adj (gen) heavy. 3 (molesto) tiresome; (aburrido) boring. 4 (trabajoso) tough, hard. 5 (sueño) deep. – 6 m,f (persona) bore, pain.
● ponerse pesado,-a, to get boring, be a pain.
pesadumbre f sorrow, grief.
pésame m condolences pl.
● darle el pésame a algn., to offer sb. one's condolences. ‖ mi más sentido pésame, my deepest sympathy.
pesar 1 i to weigh: ¿cuánto pesas?, how much do you weigh?; no pesas nada, you are really light. 2 (tener mucho peso) to be heavy: ¡cómo pesa esta maleta!, this suitcase is really heavy! 3 (sentir) to be sorry, regret: me pesa mucho no haberle invitado, I really regret not having invited him. 4 (influir) to carry weight: su opinión pesa más que la nuestra, her opinion carries more weight than ours. – 5 t to weigh. – 6 m (pena) sorrow, grief. 7 (arrepentimiento) regret.
● a mi (nuestro etc) pesar, to my (our etc) regret. ‖ a pesar de, despite, in spite of. ‖ a pesar de los pesares, in spite of everything. ‖ mal que me (le etc) pese, to my (his etc) great regret. ‖ pese a que ..., despite the fact that..., although ...
pesario m pessary.
pesaroso,-a adj sorry, regretful.
pesca 1 f (actividad) fishing. 2 (peces) fish.
■ pesca con caña, angling. ‖ pesca de altura, deep-sea fishing. ‖ pesca de arrastre, trawling. ‖ pesca de bajura, coastal fishing.
pescada f hake.
pescadería f fishmonger's, fish shop.
pescadero,-a m,f fishmonger.
pescadilla f young hake.
pescado m fish.
■ pescado azul, blue fish. ‖ pescado blanco, white fish.
pescador,-ra 1 adj fishing. – 2 m,f (hombre) fisherman; (mujer) fisherwoman.
pescante m (asiento) coachman's seat.
pescar 1 i (ir a pescar) to fish, go fishing. – 2 t (sacar del agua) to get, catch. 3 fam (agarrar) catch: he pescado un resfriado de aquí te espero, I've caught a really nasty cold. 4 (conseguir) to get, catch: lleva años intentando pescar novio, she's been trying to get a boyfriend for years. 5 fam (comprender) to understand, get: éste no pesca una, el pobre, he's a bit slow, poor thing. 6 fam (coger por sorpresa) to catch.
● ir a pescar, to go fishing.
▲ Conjugation model [1], like sacar.
pescozón m slap on the neck.
pescuezo m neck.
● retorcerle el pescuezo a algn., fam to wring sb.'s neck.
pesebre 1 m (de Navidad) crib. 2 (para animales) manger, stall.
peseta f peseta.
● mirar la peseta, to be careful with one's money.

pesetero,-a 1 adj money-grubbing. – 2 m,f money-grubber.
pésimamente adv dreadfully.
pesimismo m pessimism.
pesimista 1 adj pessimistic. – 2 mf pessimist.
pésimo,-a adj dreadful, awful.
peso 1 m (gen) weight. 2 (balanza) scales pl. 3 (carga) load, burden.
● de peso, (pesado) heavy; (importante) important; (influyente) influential; (convincente) strong, powerful. ‖ caerse por su propio peso, to be self-evident, be obvious. ‖ hacer el peso, fam to convince: no me acaba de hacer el peso, I'm not sure about it. ‖ ganar peso, to put on weight, gain weight. ‖ perder peso, to lose weight. ‖ quitar un peso de encima de algn., to take a weight off sb.'s mind.
■ peso bruto, gross weight. ‖ peso gallo, bantamweight. ‖ peso ligero, lightweight. ‖ peso neto, net weight. ‖ peso pesado, heavyweight. ‖ peso pluma, featherweight.
pespunte m backstitch.
pesquero,-a 1 adj fishing. – 2 pesquero, m fishing boat.
pesquis m fam gumption, common sense.
pesquisa f inquiry.
pestaña 1 f (del ojo) eyelash. 2 TÉC flange.
pestañear i to blink.
● sin pestañear, without batting an eyelid.
pestañeo m blinking.
peste 1 f (epidemia) plague. 2 (mal olor) stink, stench: ¡qué peste a tabaco hay aquí!, it stinks of tobacco smoke in here! 3 (cosa molesta) pest.
● decir/echar pestes de algn., to slag sb. off.
■ peste bubónica, bubonic plague.
pesticida m pesticide.
pestilencia 1 f (mal olor) stink, stench. 2 desus (epidemia) pestilence.
pestilente adj (apestoso) stinking.
pestillo 1 m (de puerta) bolt; (de ventana) catch. 2 (de una cerradura) bolt.
● cerrar con pestillo, to bolt.
pestiño 1 m CULIN honey-coated sweet fritter. 2 fam (persona) bore; (cosa) drag.
petaca 1 f (de bebida) hip flask. 2 (de cigarros) cigarette case; (de tabaco picado) tobacco pouch. 3 fam (en una cama) apple-pie bed.
pétalo m petal.
petanca f petanque.
petardo 1 m (de verbena) firecracker, banger. 2 MIL petard. 3 fam (persona - aburrido) boring fart, pain in the neck; (- feo) ugly person; (- inútil) good-for-nothing. 4 arg (de hachís) spliff.
petate 1 m (de soldado, marinero) kit bag. 2 fam (equipaje) bags pl: como sigáis así cojo el petate y me voy, if you behave like this, I'll pack up and go. 3 (para dormir) mat.
● liar el petate, fam (irse) to pack up and go.
petenera f MÚS Andalusian song.
● salirse por peteneras, fam to go off at a tangent, change the subject.
petición 1 f (gen) request. 2 JUR plea, petition.
● a petición de, at the request of.
petimetre m fop.
petirrojo m robin.
petisú m éclair.
peto 1 m (pantalón) pair of dungarees; (pieza del pantalón) bib. 2 HIST breastplate.

pétreo,-a *adj* stony.
petrificar 1 *t* (*fosilizar*) to petrify. 2 (*sorprender*) to astound; (*aterrorizar*) to petrify.
▲ *Conjugation model* |1|, *like* **sacar.**
petrodólar *m* petrodollar.
petróleo *m* oil.
petrolero,-a 1 *adj* oil. – 2 **petrolero,** *m* oil tanker.
petrolífero,-a *adj* oil-bearing.
petroquímico,-a 1 *adj* petrochemical. – 2 **petroquímica,** *f* petrochemistry.
petulancia *f* vanity.
petulante *adj* vain.
petunia *f* petunia.
peúco *m* → **patuco.**
peyorativo,-a *adj* pejorative.
pez[1] *m* fish.
● **estar/sentirse como pez en el agua,** to be in one's element. ‖ **estar pez en algo,** *fam* to be useless at sth., know nothing about sth.
■ **pez espada,** swordfish. ‖ **pez gordo,** *fig* big shot. ‖ **pez martillo,** hammerhead shark.
pez[2] *f* pitch.
● **negro,-a como la pez,** pitch-black.
pezón *m* nipple.
pezuña *f* hoof.
piadoso,-a 1 *adj* pious, devout. 2 (*clemente*) merciful, compassionate.
pianista *mf* pianist.
pianístico,-a *adj* pianistic.
piano 1 *m* piano. – 2 *adv* piano, quietly.
● **piano de cola,** grand piano. ‖ **piano vertical,** upright piano.
pianoforte *m* pianoforte.
pianola *f* Pianola.
▲ *Registered trademark.*
piar *i* to chirp, tweet.
▲ *Conjugation model* |13|, *like* **desviar.**
piara *f* herd of pigs.
piastra *f* piastre.
PIB *abr* (*producto interior bruto*) gross domestic product; (*abreviatura*) GDP.
pibe,-a *m,f* kid.
pica 1 *f* (*lanza*) pike. 2 (*de picador*) goad. 3 (*de la baraja*) spade.
● **poner una pica en Flandes,** to bring off a coup.
picacho *m* mountain peak.
picada *f* → **picado,-a.**
picadero 1 *m* (*escuela*) riding school. 2 *fam* bachelor pad.
picadillo *m* (*de carne*) minced meat, mince; (*de verduras*) chopped vegetables.
● **hacer picadillo a algn.,** *fam* to make mincemeat of sb.
picado,-a 1 *pp* → **picar.** – 2 *adj* CULIN (*cortado - verdura*) finely chopped; (*- carne*) minced. 3 (*vino*) vinegary, sour, off. 4 (*metal*) pitted. 5 (*piel, cara*) pockmarked. 6 (*tabaco*) cut. 7 (*mar*) choppy. 8 (*diente*) decayed. 9 *fam* (*ofendido*) offended. – 10 **picado,** *m* AER dive. – 11 **picada,** *f* (*picadura - de avispa*) sting; (*- de mosquito*) bite. 12 (*de pez*) bite.
● **caer en picado,** to plummet. ‖ **estar picado,-a,** *fam* to be upset, be miffed.
picador 1 *m* (*tauromaquia*) picador. 2 (*minero*) faceworker.
picadora *f* mincer.
picadura 1 *f* (*de insecto, serpiente*) bite; (*de abeja, avispa*) sting. 2 (*tabaco*) cut tobacco. 3 (*en los dientes*) decay.

picaflor *m* ORN hummingbird.
picajoso,-a *adj fam* touchy.
picante 1 *adj* (*comida*) hot. 2 *fig* (*chiste, película*) spicy. – 3 *m* (*comida*) hot food. 4 (*sabor*) hot flavour.
picapedrero *m* stonecutter.
picapica *m* (*que hace estornudar*) sneezing powder; (*que causa picor*) itching powder.
■ **polvos picapica,** itching powder.
picapleitos *mf* second-rate lawyer.
picaporte 1 *m* (*para llamar*) door knocker. 2 (*para abrir*) door handle.
picar 1 *t* (*morder - insecto*) to bite; (*- abeja, avispa*) to sting. 2 (*corroer*) to eat away, rot: **tengo el coche picado de la humedad,** my car's all rusty from the damp; **tengo las muelas picadas de comer tantos caramelos,** my teeth are bad from eating so many sweets; **la polilla me ha picado el baúl,** moths have eaten away the trunk. 3 (*perforar - papel, tarjeta*) to punch. 4 (*dar con un pico*) to jab, goad. 5 CULIN (*cortar*) to chop finely; (*carne*) to mince. 6 (*comida*) to nibble: **vamos a salir a picar algo,** we're going to get a bite to eat. 7 (*incitar*) to arouse: **me picó la curiosidad,** it aroused my curiosity. 8 (*herir*) to wound: **le ha picado el orgullo,** it has wounded his pride. 9 (*toro*) to goad. 10 (*cebo*) to bite. – 11 *i* (*sentir escozor*) to itch: **me pica todo el cuerpo,** I'm itching all over. 12 (*calentar*) to be hot, be strong: **hoy pica el sol en cantidad,** the sun's really strong today. 13 (*estar picante*) to be hot: **estos pimientos pican muchísimo,** these peppers are really hot. 14 (*pez*) to bite; (*persona*) to fall for it. 15 (*caer en la cuenta*) to cotton on, twig. 16 (*comer*) to have a nibble. – 17 **picarse,** *p* (*muela*) to decay, go bad: **se me ha picado una muela,** one of my teeth has gone bad. 18 (*fruta*) to begin to rot. 19 (*tela*) to be moth-eaten. 20 (*mar*) to get choppy. 21 (*vino*) to go vinegary, go sour, go off. 22 (*metal*) to pit. 23 (*ofenderse*) to take offence. 24 *fam* (*picar el orgullo*) to get annoyed. 25 *arg* (*pincharse droga*) to shoot up.
● **picar alto,** to aim high. ‖ **quien se pica, ajos come,** *fam* if the cap fits, wear it.
▲ *Conjugation model* |1|, *like* **sacar.**
picardía 1 *f* (*astucia*) craftiness. 2 (*atrevimiento*) naughtiness. 3 (*dicho atrevido*) risqué comment.
● **tener picardía,** to be crafty.
picardías *m sexy* negligée.
▲ *pl* **picardías.**
picaresca *f* → **picaresco,-a.**
picaresco,-a 1 *adj lit* picaresque. – 2 *f* picaresque genre.
pícaro,-a 1 *adj* (*astuto*) crafty, sly. 2 (*atrevido*) wicked. – 3 *m,f* (*persona astuta*) slyboots, crafty devil.
picatoste *m* small crouton.
picazón *f* (*picor*) itch.
picha *f tabú* prick.
pichi *m* pinafore dress, US jumper.
pichichi 1 *m* (*goleador*) top goal scorer. 2 (*trofeo*) top goal scorer's trophy.
pichón,-ona 1 *m,f* pigeon. 2 (*apelativo*) darling.
picnic *m* picnic.
● **ir de picnic,** to go for a picnic.
pico[1] 1 *m* (*de ave*) beak. 2 (*herramienta*) pickaxe, pick. 3 (*de montaña*) peak. 4 (*punta*) corner. 5 *fam* (*boca*) mouth, gob, trap: **cierra el pico,** shut your trap; **en cuanto abre el pico, mete la pata,** as soon as he opens his trap, he puts his foot in it. 6 *arg* (*de heroína*) fix. – 7 **y pico,** *loc* (*cantidad*): **tres mil y pico,** three thousand odd; **llegaremos sobre las seis y pico,** we'll be there just after six.

● **callar el pico,** *fam* to keep one's mouth shut. ‖ **costar un pico,** *fam* to cost an arm and a leg. ‖ **irse de picos pardos,** *fam* to go out on the town. ‖ **tener un pico de oro,** *fam* to have the gift of the gab.

pico² *m* woodpecker.

■ **pico menor,** lesser-spotted woodpecker. ‖ **pico picapinos,** great-spotted woodpecker.

picor 1 *m* (*gen*) itch. 2 (*de comida*) burning sensation.

● **tener picores,** to feel itchy.

picota 1 *f* HIST pillory. 2 (*fruta*) bigarreau cherry.

● **poner a algn. en la picota,** (*criticar*) to pillory sb.; (*exponer*) to put sb. on the spot.

picotazo 1 *m* (*de ave*) peck. 2 (*de insecto, reptil*) bite; (*de abeja, avispa*) sting.

picotear 1 *t* (*ave*) to peck, peck at. 2 (*persona*) to nibble, snack.

picoteo 1 *m* (*de ave*) pecking. 2 (*acción de comer*) nibbling, snacking.

picto,-a 1 *adj* Pictish. – 2 *m,f* Pict. – 3 picto, *m* Pictish.

pictórico,-a *adj* pictorial.

picudo,-a *adj* pointed.

pie 1 *m* ANAT foot: *llevo de pie todo el día,* I've been on my feet all day; *me duelen los pies,* my feet ache. 2 (*base - de una lámpara*) base; (*- de una escultura*) plinth. 3 (*de un verso*) foot. 4 (*medida de longitud*) foot. 5 (*de un documento*) foot; (*de una fotografía, dibujo*) caption.

● **a los pies de la cama,** at the foot of the bed. ‖ **a pie,** on foot. ‖ **al pie de,** (*cerca*) close by. ‖ **al pie de la letra,** word for word. ‖ **al pie del cañón,** *fam* hard at it, working. ‖ **buscarle los tres pies al gato,** *fam* to split hairs. ‖ **creer algo a pies juntillas,** *fam* to believe sth. implicitly. ‖ **dar pie a,** to give occasion for. ‖ **de los pies a la cabeza,** from head to toe. ‖ **empezar con buen/mal pie,** to start off on the right/wrong foot. ‖ **estar en pie de guerra,** to be on a war footing; *fig* to be on the war path. ‖ **hacer pie,** to touch the bottom. ‖ **ir con pies de plomo,** to tread very carefully. ‖ **nacer de pie,** to be born with a silver spoon in one's mouth. ‖ **no dar pie con bola,** to mess everything up, not get anything right. ‖ **no tener ni pies ni cabeza,** to be ludicrous, be absurd. ‖ **pararle los pies a algn.,** to put sb. in their place. ‖ **poner los pies en,** to set foot in. ‖ **ponerse de/en pie,** to get to one's feet, stand up. ‖ **saber de qué pie cojea algn.,** to know what sb.'s weakness is. ‖ **tenerse de pie,** to keep on one's feet.

■ **pie de atleta,** athlete's foot. ‖ **pie de imprenta,** imprint. ‖ **pies planos,** flat feet.

piedad 1 *f* (*misericordia*) pity, mercy. 2 (*devoción religiosa*) piety.

● **¡por piedad!,** for pity's sake! ‖ **tener piedad de algn.,** to have mercy on sb.

piedra 1 *f* stone. 2 (*granizo*) hailstone. 3 (*en el riñón*) stone. 4 (*de un encendedor*) flint. 5 (*de afilar*) grindstone.

● **no ser de piedra,** *fam* to be human, not be made of stone. ‖ **pasar a algn. por la piedra,** *tabú* to lay sb. ‖ **quedarse de piedra,** *fam* to be stunned.

■ **piedra angular,** corner-stone. ‖ **piedra filosofal,** philosopher's stone. ‖ **piedra pómez,** pumice stone. ‖ **piedra preciosa,** gem, precious stone.

piel 1 *f* (*de persona*) skin. 2 (*de animal - sin curtir*) hide; (*- curtida*) leather; (*- con pelo*) fur: *un bolso de piel,* a leather bag; *un abrigo de piel,* a fur coat. 3 (*de la fruta, patatas*) peel.

● **dejarse la piel,** *fam* to give all one's got, sweat blood. ‖ **tener la piel de gallina,** to have goose pimples.

■ **piel roja,** redskin.

piélago *m lit* ocean.

pienso *m* fodder.

pierna *f* leg.

pieza 1 *f* (*gen*) piece; (*de un aparato*) part. 2 MÚS piece, piece of music. 3 TEAT play. 4 (*de un juego de tablero*) piece. 5 (*en caza*) piece. 6 (*habitación*) room. 7 (*de tela*) roll; (*remiendo*) patch.

● **dejar de una pieza,** to dumbfound. ‖ **quedarse de una pieza,** to be dumbfounded.

■ **pieza de recambio,** spare part.

pifia *f fam* blunder.

● **hacer una pifia,** *fam* to make a blunder.

pifiar **pifiarla,** *loc fam* to put one's foot in it, make a blunder.

pigmentación *f* pigmentation.

pigmento *m* pigment.

pigmeo,-a 1 *adj* (*raza*) Pygmy. 2 *fig* pygmy. – 3 *m,f* (*raza*) Pygmy. 4 *fig* pygmy.

pignorar *t* to pawn.

pijada 1 *f fam* (*menudencia*) trifle. 2 *fam* (*tontería*) stupid thing to say: *no dice más que pijadas el pobre,* he just talks absolute rubbish.

pijama *m* pyjamas (US pajamas) *pl.*

pijería *f fam* → **pijotería**.

pijo,-a 1 *adj fam* posh. – 2 *m,f fam* (*chico*) rich boy; (*chica*) rich girl. – 3 pijo, *m tabú* prick. – 4 pija, *f tabú* prick.

pijotería 1 *f fam* (*pijos*) rich kids *pl.* 2 (*cosa insignificante*) trifle. 3 (*comentario*) stupid comment.

pijotero,-a 1 *adj* annoying. – 2 *m,f fam* pain in the neck.

pila 1 *f* ELÉC battery. 2 (*de fregar*) sink. 3 (*de bautismo*) font. 4 *fam* (*montón*) pile, heap: *tengo una pila de cosas que hacer,* I've got piles of work to do; *hace ya una pila de años que no voy,* I haven't been there for yonks.

● **ponerse las pilas,** *fam* to get one's act together.

■ **pila bautismal,** font.

pilar *m* pillar.

pilastra *f* pilaster.

píldora 1 *f* pill, tablet. 2 **la píldora,** (*anticonceptivo*) the pill.

● **tragarse la píldora,** *fam* to fall for it.

pileta *f* AM swimming pool.

pilila *f fam* willy.

pillaje *m* looting.

pillar 1 *t* (*coger*) to catch. 2 *fam* (*robar*) to nick. 3 *fam* (*atropellar*) to run over. 4 *fam* (*entender*) to catch, get, grasp. – 5 *i fam* (*encontrarse*) to be: *me pilla muy cerca de casa,* it's very near home; *te pilla un poco lejos,* it's a long way for you to go; *te pilla de camino,* it's on your way.

pillastre *m fam* rascal.

pillería *f fam* (*travesura*) mischief: *siempre está haciendo pillerías,* he's always up to no good.

pillín,-ina *m,f fam* crafty little devil.

pillo,-a 1 *adj* (*travieso*) naughty. 2 (*astuto*) crafty. – 3 *m,f* (*niño*) little monkey, little devil. 4 (*adulto*) rogue, rascal.

pilón 1 *m* (*de una fuente*) basin. 2 (*abrevadero*) trough; (*lavadero*) sink.

pilonga *adj* shrivelled.

■ **castaña pilonga,** dried chestnut.

píloro *m* pylorus.

piloso,-a *adj* hair.

pilotaje *m* (*de un avión*) piloting; (*de un barco*) steering; (*de un coche*) driving.

pilote *m* pile.

piloto 1 *m* (*conductor - de avión*) pilot; (*- de coche*) driver; (*- de barco*) pilot; (*- de moto*) rider. 2 (*luz - de un aparato*) pilot

light; (- *de un vehículo*) rear light. – **3** *adj* (*proyecto, programa*) pilot, test.
■ **piloto automático,** automatic pilot. ‖ **piloto de aviación,** air pilot. ‖ **piloto de carreras,** racing driver. ‖ **piso piloto,** show flat.

piltra *f fam* bed.

piltrafa *f* scrap.
● **estar hecho,-a una piltrafa,** (*persona*) to be just skin and bones; (*ropa*) to be tatty.

pimentero 1 *m* (*recipiente*) pepper pot. **2** (*planta*) pepper plant.

pimentón *m* paprika.
■ **pimentón picante,** cayenne pepper.

pimienta *f* (*especia*) pepper.
■ **pimienta blanca,** white pepper. ‖ **pimienta negra,** black pepper.

pimiento *m* (*gen*) pepper; (*rojo*) red pepper; (*verde*) green pepper.
● **no importar un pimiento,** *fam* not to give a damn: *le importa un pimiento lo que opine la gente,* he couldn't give a damn what people think. ‖ **no valer un pimiento,** *fam* (*cosa*) not to be worth twopence; (*persona*) to be nothing to look at. ‖ **¡y un pimiento!,** *fam* like hell!
■ **pimiento morrón,** sweet pepper. ‖ **pimiento de Padrón,** small green pepper (*either sweet or very hot*). ‖ **pimiento del piquillo,** *slightly hot* red pepper.

pimpante *adj fam* unconcerned: *tan pimpante,* as if nothing had happened.

pimpinela *f* pimpernel.

pimplar 1 *i fam* to booze. – **2 pimplarse,** *p fam* to knock back.

pimpollo 1 *m* (*brote*) shoot; (*árbol joven*) sapling; (*capullo*) bud. **2** *fam* (*persona*) dish, good-looker.
● **estar hecho,-a un pimpollo,** *fam* to look good for one's age.

pimpón *m* → **ping-pong.**

pinacoteca *f* art gallery.

pináculo *m* pinnacle.

pinar *m* pine grove.

pincel *m* paintbrush.

pincelada *f* brush stroke: *describió la situación con apenas dos pinceladas,* she briefly described the situation.
● **dar las últimas pinceladas a algo,** to put the finishing touches to sth.

pincha *mf fam* DJ, disc jockey.

pinchadiscos *mf fam* disc jockey, DJ.

pinchar 1 *t* (*punzar*) to prick: *se ha pinchado el dedo en el rosal,* he pricked his finger on the rosebush; *se nos ha pinchado un neumático,* we have had a puncture; *me han pinchado el globo, mamá,* Mum, they've burst my balloon. **2** MED (*poner inyección*) to give a injection, give a jab, US give a shot: *me pincharon tres veces porque no encontraban la vena,* they stuck the needle in me three times because they couldn't find the vein. **3** (*sujetar*) to spear, jab. **4** (*enfadar*) to needle: *como siga pinchándola van a acabar peleándose,* if he keeps needling her they'll end up fighting. **5** (*estimular*) to push: *en casa me pinchan para que me apunte al gimnasio,* the family are trying to persuade me to go to the gym. **6** *fam* (*intervenir*) to tap: *sospechan que les han pinchado el teléfono,* they suspect their phone's been tapped. **7** *fam* (*poner disco*) to play: *enróllate y pínchanos algo más movido,* get with it and put on something more lively. – **8 pincharse,** *p fam* (*droga*) to shoot up.
● **ni pinchar ni cortar,** *fam* to have nothing to do with it, have do say in something.

pinchazo 1 *m* (*de neumático*) puncture. **2** (*con aguja etc*) prick: *me he dado un pinchazo con la aguja mientras cosía,* I pricked my finger with the needle while I was sewing. **3** (*inyección*) injection, jab, US shot. **4** (*de dolor*) sharp pain.

pinche *m,f* (*de cocina*) kitchen assistant.

pinchito 1 *m* (*de carne*) shish kebab. **2** (*aperitivo*) snack.
■ **pinchito moruno,** shish kebab.

pincho 1 *m* (*de una planta*) thorn. **2** (*de un erizo*) spine, prickle. **3** (*de aperitivo*) snack. **4** (*de carne*) shish kebab. **5** (*brocheta*) skewer.
■ **pincho moruno,** shish kebab.

pineal *adj* pineal.

pineda *f* pine grove.

pingajo *m pey* (*de ropa*) rag.

pingo *m fam* (*de ropa*) rag.
● **ir hecho,-a un pingo,** *fam* to look a right mess. ‖ **ser un pingo,** *fam* to be out all the time.

ping-pong *m* table tennis, ping-pong.

pingüe *adj* substantial.

pingüino *m* penguin.

pinitos **hacer pinitos,** *loc adv* (*de un niño*) to toddle, start to walk; (*en una materia*) to try one's hand at sth.

pino *m* (*árbol*) pine tree; (*madera*) pinewood.
● **estar en el quinto pino,** *fam* to be in the back of beyond. ‖ **hacer el pino,** to do a handstand.

pinrel *m fam* foot.

pinsapo *m* Spanish fir.

pinta 1 *f* (*mancha*) dot. **2** (*medida*) pint. **3** *fam* (*aspecto*) look: *¡vaya una pinta que llevas con ese traje!,* you look dreadful in that suit!; *tu vecino tiene muy mala pinta,* I don't like the look of your neighbour; *esta película tiene pinta de estar bien,* this film looks as if it could be good. – **4** *m fam pey* (*persona*) dodgy character.

pintada *f* graffiti.

pintado,-a 1 *pp* → **pintar.** – **2** *adj* (*parecido*) identical. **3** (*maquillado*) made-up.
● **el más pintado,** *fam* anyone, anybody, any of us. ‖ **venir que ni pintado,-a,** *fam* to be just the ticket.

pintalabios *m* lipstick.
▲ *pl* pintalabios.

pintamonas 1 *mf fam* nobody. **2** *fam* (*pintor*) dauber.
▲ *pl* pintamonas.

pintar 1 *t* (*gen*) to paint; (*dibujar*) to draw. **2** (*maquillar*) to make up. **3** *fig* (*describir*) to paint a picture: *me lo pintaron todo tan bonito que firmé,* they painted such a rosy picture that I signed. **4** (*gen*) to paint. **5** (*marcar*) to write: *este boli no pinta,* this biro doesn't write. **6** *fam* (*tener que ver*) to do, have to do: *él, ¿qué pintaba allí?,* what was he doing there?; *aquí no pinto nada yo,* there's no place for me here. **7** (*en la baraja*) to be trumps. – **8 pintarse** (*maquillarse*) to put one's make up on.
● **pintarse los labios,** to put lipstick on. ‖ **pintarse los uñas,** to paint one's nails. ‖ **pintárselas,** to be an expert.

pintarrajear 1 *t fam* to daub. – **2 pintarrajearse,** *p* to doll os. up.

pintarrajo *m fam* daub.

pintaúñas *m* nail varnish, nail polish.
▲ *pl* pintaúñas.

pintiparado,-a **venir pintiparado,-a,** *loc fam* to be just perfect.

pintor,-ra *m,f* (*de cuadros*) artist, painter; (*de paredes*) painter and decorator.
■ **pintor,-ra de brocha gorda,** (*de paredes*) painter and decorator; *pey* dauber.

pintoresco,-a I *adj* (*lugar*) picturesque. **2** (*persona*) bizarre, colourful (us colorful).

pintura I *f* (*arte*) painting. **2** (*cuadro*) picture. **3** (*producto*) paint: *un bote de pintura*, a tin of paint; *esta casa necesita una buena mano de pintura*, this house really needs painting.
● **no poder ver ni en pintura**, *fam* not to be able to stand the sight of.

pinza I *f* (*de cangrejo*) pincer. **2** (*de la ropa*) clothes peg. **3** (*en pantalón, falda*) pleat. **– 4 pinzas**, *fpl* (*herramienta*) pincers. **5** (*de depilar*) tweezers. **6** (*de servir hielo*) tongs.

pinzamiento *m* trapped nerve.

pinzón *m* finch.
■ **pinzón vulgar**, chaffinch. ‖ **pinzón real**, brambling.

piña I *f* (*fruta*) pineapple. **2** (*del pino*) pine cone. **3** (*golpe*) bang; (*fuerte*) crash: *dieron una piña contra un muro*, they crashed into a wall. **4** *fam* (*de personas*) clique.
● **hacer piña / formar piña**, to close ranks, pull together.

piñata *f* hollow figure filled with sweets (which children try to break open at parties).

piño *m arg* tooth.

piñón I *m* (*del pino - semilla*) pine seed; (- *comestible*) pine nut kernel. **2** TÉC pinion.
● **estar a partir un piñón con algn.**, *fam* to be as thick as thieves with sb.

pío,-a[1] *adj* pious.

pío[2] *m* chirp.
● **no decir ni pío**, *fam* not to say a word, not open one's mouth.

piojo *m* louse.

piojoso,-a I *adj* (*lleno de piojos*) lousy, louse-infested. **2** *fam* (*sucio*) lousy, filthy. **3** (*miserable*) despicable.

piolet *m* ice axe (us ax).

pionero,-a I *adj* pioneering. **– 2** *m,f* pioneer.

piorrea *f* pyorrhoea.

pipa[1] *f* (*de tabaco*) pipe.
● **fumar en pipa**, to smoke a pipe.

pipa[2] *f* (*de girasol*) sunflower seed.
● **no tener ni para pipas**, *fam* to be broke, be skint. ‖ **pasario pipa**, *fam* to have a brilliant time, have a ball.

pipermín *m* (*licor*) crème de menthe.

pipeta *f* pipette.

pipí *m fam* pee, wee-wee.
● **hacer pipí**, to go for a pee. ‖ **hacerse pipí**, to wet os.

pipiolo,-a I *m,f fam* (*novato*) novice. **2** *fam* (*demasiado joven*) kid, baby.

pique I *m* (*resentimiento*) pique, grudge. **2** (*rivalidad*) rivalry, needle: *tiene un pique increíble con el vecino*, there's a lot of needle between him and his neighbour.
● **a pique de**, about to. ‖ **irse a pique**, (*barco*) to sink; (*plan, proyecto*) to go under, fall through.

piqué *m* piqué.

piqueta *f* pickaxe.

piquete I *m* (*de huelga*) picket. **2** (*de soldados*) squad.

pira *f* pyre.

pirado,-a I *pp* → **pirarse**. **– 2** *adj fam* (*loco*) loony, wacky. **– 3** *m,f fam* loony.

piragua *f* canoe.

piragüismo *m* canoeing.

piragüista *mf* canoeist.

piramidal *adj* pyramidal.

pirámide *f* pyramid.

piraña *f* piranha.

pirarse *p fam* to split, sling one's hook, make os. scarce: *se las ha pirado*, he has slung his hook.

pirata I *adj* pirate. **–** *m* HIST pirate. **– 3** *mf* (*de la informática*) hacker.
■ **pirata aéreo**, hijacker.

piratear I *t* (*gen*) to pirate. **2** (*avión*) to hijack.

piratería *f* (*gen*) piracy.
■ **piratería aérea**, hijacking.

pirenaico,-a I *adj* Pyrenean. **– 2** *m,f* Pyrenean.

pirindolo *m fam* thingummy.

Pirineos los Pirineos, *mpl* the Pyrenees.

piripi *adj fam* tipsy.

pirita *f* pyrite.

piro darse el piro, *loc fam* to make os. scarce.

piromanía *f* pyromania.

pirómano,-a I *adj* pyromaniacal. **– 2** *m,f* pyromaniac.

piropear *t* to make flirtatious comments to.

piropo *m* compliment, flirtatious comment.
● **echar un piropo a**, to pay a compliment to.

pirotecnia *f* fireworks *pl*, pyrotechnics.

pirotécnico,-a I *adj* pyrotechnical. **– 2** *m,f* pyrotechnist.

pirrar I *i fam* to be mad about: *me pirran los coches de carreras*, I'm mad about racing cars. **– 2 pirrarse**, *p* to be mad (**por**, about).

pirueta *f* pirouette.
● **hacer piruetas**, (*en danza*) to pirouette; (*ante una dificultad*) to work miracles.

piruleta *f* lollipop.

pirulí I *m fam* (*de caramelo*) lollipop. **2** *fam* (*de telecomunicaciones*) telecommunications tower.

pis *m fam* wee, pee.
● **hacer pis**, to wee, pee.

pisada I *f* footstep. **2** (*huella*) footprint.

pisapapeles *m* paperweight.
▲ *pl* **pisapapeles**.

pisar I *t* (*gen*) to tread on, step on: *me ha pisado al salir*, he trod on my foot as he was going out. **2** (*acelerador, embrague*) to put one's foot on. **3** *fig* (*entrar*) to set foot in: *hace años que no piso ese bar*, I haven't set foot in that bar for years. **4** *fam* (*idea, proyecto*) to steal; (*noticia*) to scoop. **5** *fig* (*rebajar*) to walk all over: *no se deja pisar por nadie*, nobody walks all over him. **– 6** *i* to tread, walk, step: *no pises muy fuerte que nos oyen los vecinos*, tread more quietly, the neighbours will hear us.
● **pisar fuerte**, *fig* to go all out, make a big impact. ‖ **pisar la uva**, to tread grapes.

pisaverde *m desus* fop.

piscifactoría *f* fish farm.

piscina *f* swimming-pool.

Piscis I *m* (*constelación*) Pisces. **– 2** *mf* (*persona*) Pisces.

piscolabis *m* snack.
▲ *pl* **piscolabis**.

piso I *m* (*para vivir*) flat. **2** (*planta*) floor: *¿a qué piso va?*, what floor do you want? **3** (*suelo*) floor. **4** (*suela del zapato*) sole. **5** (*de una tarta*) tier.

pisotear I *t* (*pisar*) to trample. **2** *fig* (*persona*) to walk all over.

pisotón *m* stamp: *me han pegado un pisotón*, somebody stepped on my foot.

pista I *f* (*rastro*) trail, track. **2** (*indicio*) clue. **3** (*de baile*) dance floor. **4** (*camino*) track. **5** (*de tenis*) court. **6** (*de circo*) ring. **7** AER runway.
● **seguirle la pista a algn.**, to be on sb.'s trail.
■ **pista de aterizaje**, landing strip. ‖ **pista de baile**,

dance floor. ‖ **pista de esquí,** ski slope. ‖ **pista de te-nis,** tennis court.

pistacho m pistachio (nut).

pistilo m pistil.

pisto m type of ratatouille.

● **darse pisto,** fam to give os. airs.

pistola 1 f gun. 2 (para pintar) spray gun. 3 (de pan) loaf of bread.

■ **pistola de juguete,** toy gun.

pistolera f holster.

pistolero m gunman.

pistoletazo m gunshot.

■ **pistoletazo de salida,** starting signal.

pistón 1 m (de un motor) piston. 2 (de un arma) cap. 3 MÚS (corneta) cornet; (llave) key.

pistonudo,-a adj fam marvellous.

pita[1] f BOT pita.

pita[2] f fam (gallina) cluck-cluck; ¡pitas, pitas!, here - chick, chick, chick!

pitada 1 f (bocinazo) hoot, honk. 2 (pitido) whistle. 3 (del público) booing.

pitanza f arc food.

pitar 1 i (silbar) to blow a whistle. 2 (tocar la bocina) to hoot, honk. 3 (abuchear) to boo and hiss. 4 (funcionar) to work: este mechero no pita, this lighter doesn't work. – 5 t DEP (falta) to whistle.

● **ir/irse pitando,** fam to rush out, dash off.

pitido 1 m (silbido) whistle. 2 (bocinazo) hoot, honk.

pitillera f cigarette case.

pitillo m cigarette.

● **de pitillo,** (pantalón) drainpipe.

pitiminí de pitiminí, loc fam small and delicate.

■ **rosal de pitiminí,** miniature rose.

pito[1] 1 m (silbato) whistle. 2 (de coche) horn. 3 (de voz) high pitch. 4 fam (pitillo) fag. 5 fam (pene) willy. 6 (abucheo) booing. 7 (con los dedos) click.

● **me importa un pito,** fam I don't give a hoot/damn. ‖ **por pitos o por flautas,** fam for one reason or another. ‖ **tocar el pito,** to hoot. ‖ **tomar a algn. por el pito de un sereno,** fam to mess sb. around.

pito[2] m (pájaro) woodpecker.

pitón[1] f ZOOL python.

pitón[2] 1 m (del toro) horn. 2 (de un botijo) spout.

pitonisa f fortune teller.

pitorrearse p fam to make fun (**de,** of).

pitorreo m fam (burla) mocking; (broma) joking: ¡vaya un pitorreo que se traen conmigo estos niños!, these kids are taking the mickey out of me.

● **tomarse las cosas a pitorreo,** fam not to take things seriously.

pitorro m spout.

pitote m fam (lío) mess; (barullo) racket.

pitufo,-a m,f fam little one.

pituitaria f pituitary (gland).

pituso,-a m,f cute child.

pivot mf centre.

pivotar i to pivot.

pivote m pivot.

pizarra 1 f (mineral) slate. 2 (para escribir) blackboard.

pizca f fam (gen) bit; (de sal) pinch.

● **no tener ni pizca de gracia,** fam not to be the slightest bit funny.

pizpireta adj lively.

pizza f pizza.

pizzería f pizzeria, pizza parlour.

placa 1 f (de metal) sheet. 2 GEOL plate. 3 (con el nombre - conmemorativa) plaque; (- insignia) badge; (- letrero) sign. 4 (de matrícula) number plate, US license plate. 5 (de cocina) ring. 6 (de hielo) sheet. 7 (radiografía) plate. 8 (dental) plaque.

placaje m tackle.

placebo m placebo.

placenta f placenta.

placentero,-a adj pleasant.

placer 1 m pleasure. – 2 i to please: haz lo que te plazca, do as you please.

■ **viaje de placer,** pleasure trip.

placidez f placidity.

plácido,-a adj placid, calm.

plafón m (lámpara - de techo) ceiling light; (- de pared) wall light.

plaga 1 f (epidemia) plague. 2 (de insectos) plague, pest. 3 fig invasion.

plagar t to plague, infest: este verano el país se ha plagado de turistas, the country was invaded by tourists this summer.

▲ Conjugation model [7], like llegar.

plagiar t to plagiarize.

▲ Conjugation model [12], like cambiar.

plagio m plagiarism.

plaguicida m pesticide.

plan 1 m (intención) plan. 2 (programa) project. 3 (régimen) diet. 4 fam (aventura amorosa) fling; (amante) bit on the side. 5 fam (para salir) plans pl: ¿tienes plan para el fin de semana?, are you doing anything this weekend? 6 fam (actitud) mood: hoy está en plan tonto, he's in a stupid mood today; me lo dijo en plan de broma, he said it as a joke.

● **a todo plan,** fam in luxury. ‖ **estar a plan,** fam to be on a diet. ‖ **no ser plan,** fam not to be on.

■ **plan de adelgazamiento,** diet. ‖ **plan de desarrollo,** development plan. ‖ **plan de estudios,** syllabus. ‖ **plan de inversiones,** investment plan.

plana f (página) page: la noticia viene en primera plana, the news is on the front page.

● **a toda plana,** full page: lo han publicado a toda plana, they did a full-page report on it.

■ **plana mayor,** (de ejército) staff; (de empresa) top management; (de partido político) caucus.

plancha 1 f (de metal) plate, sheet. 2 (electrodoméstico) iron; (acción de planchar) ironing; (ropa que planchar) clothes to be ironed: tengo un montón de plancha acumulada, I've got a mountain of clothes to iron. 3 (placa de cocina) griddle, hotplate. 4 fam (error) boob, faux pas. 5 (al saltar al agua) belly flop; (en fútbol) diving header. 6 (de imprenta) plate.

● **a la plancha,** grilled. ‖ **hacer una plancha,** fam to boob, make a boob.

planchado,-a 1 pp → **planchar.** – 2 adj fam (sorprendido) lost for words. – 3 planchado, m (acción) ironing; (acto) iron, press: con un planchado se te queda como nueva la falda, a quick press will leave your skirt like new.

planchar t to iron, press.

planchazo 1 m fam (error) boob. 2 (al tirarse al agua) belly flop.

plancton m plankton.

planeador m glider.

planear 1 t (futuro, idea) to plan. – 2 i (en el aire) to glide.

planeta m planet.

planetario,-a 1 adj planetary. – 2 planetario, m planetarium.

planicie f plain.
planificación f planning.
planificar t to plan.
planilla f application form.
plano,-a 1 adj (superficie) flat. – 2 plano, m (de una ciudad) street-plan, map. 3 (de una casa) plan. 4 (nivel) level. 5 CINEM shot. 6 MAT plane. 7 fig (perspectiva) point of view: *desde un plano particular,* from a personal point of view.
● **de plano,** (rechazar) flatly, point blank. ‖ **en primer plano,** in the foreground, close-up. ‖ **en segundo plano,** in the background.
■ **plano inclinado,** inclined plane. ‖ **primer plano,** (foto, cine) close-up.
planta 1 f BOT plant. 2 (del pie) sole. 3 (de un edificio - piso) floor; (- sección horizontal) plan. 4 (industrial) plant.
● **de nueva planta,** brand-new. ‖ **tener buena planta,** to be good-looking.
■ **planta baja,** ground floor, US first floor.
plantación 1 f (terreno) plantation. 2 (acción) planting.
plantado,-a 1 pp → **plantar**. – 2 adj planted.
● **bien plantado,-a,** good-looking. ‖ **dejar a algn. plantado,-a,** to stand sb. up.
plantar 1 t AGR to plant. 2 (colocar - gen) to put, place; (- tienda de campaña) to pitch, put up. 3 fam (persona) to leave, dump: *lo plantó dos semanas antes de la boda,* she dumped him two weeks before the wedding. 4 (dar) to give: *le plantó un beso en la mejilla,* she gave him a kiss on the cheek. – 5 plantarse, p fam (colocarse) to place os., position os.: *se plantó en la esquina,* she positioned herself on the corner. 6 fam (resistirse) to dig one's heels in: *se ha plantado en tres millones y no se mueve,* he's holding out for three million and he won't budge. 7 (en la baraja) to stick: *¡me planto!,* I stick. 8 fam (llegar) to get there, be there, arrive: *nos plantamos en casa en quince minutos,* we were home in fifteen minutes.
● **plantarle cara a algn.,** fam to stand up to sb.
plante m (laboral) stand, protest action.
● **dar un plante a algn.,** to stand sb. up.
planteamiento 1 m MAT (formulación - de un problema) formulation; (- de una teoría) exposition. 2 (enfoque) approach.
plantear 1 t (pregunta) to pose, raise; (cuestión) to raise; (acuerdo) to suggest. 2 (problema, dificultad) to cause, give rise to. 3 (trazar un plan) to plan, outline. 4 MAT (problema) to formulate. – 5 plantearse, p to consider.
plantel m cadre.
plantificar 1 t fam (colocar) to put, place. 2 fam (dar) to give. – 3 plantificarse, p fam (llegar) to get to, arrive at.
plantilla 1 f (patrón) model, pattern. 2 (para dibujo lineal) French curve; (para rotulación) stencil; (para siluetas) template. 3 (de zapato) insole. 4 (personal) staff.
● **estar en plantilla,** to be on the payroll.
plantío m field.
plantón darle plantón a algn., loc fam (no presentarse) to stand sb. up; (llegar con retraso) to keep sb. waiting.
plañidero,-a 1 adj plaintive, mournful. – 2 plañidera, f hired mourner.
plañido m mourning, lament.
plañir i to mourn.
▲ Conjugation model [40], like muñir.
plaqueta 1 f (de sangre) platelet. 2 (de gres) small tile.
plasma m plasma.
plasmar t fig to give expression to, give shape to, capture.

plasta 1 f fam (sustancia) mess. – 2 mf fam (persona) pain in the neck, nuisance.
plastelina f Plasticine.
plástica f → **plástico,-a**.
plasticidad f plasticity.
plástico,-a 1 adj plastic. 2 (lenguaje) colourful (US colorful), vivid. – 3 plástico, m (material) plastic. 4 arg record. – 5 plástica, f plastic arts pl.
plastificado,-a adj laminated.
plastificar t to laminate.
plastilina f Plasticine.
plata 1 f silver. 2 AM money.
● **hablar en plata,** fam to be frank, put in bluntly.
■ **plata de ley,** sterling silver.
plataforma 1 f platform. 2 fig (trampolín) springboard. 3 (conjunto de personas) group, grouping.
■ **plataforma continental,** continental shelf. ‖ **plataforma petrolífera,** oil rig. ‖ **plataforma sindical,** union representatives pl.
platanero,-a 1 adj banana. – 2 platanero, m banana tree.
plátano 1 m banana. 2 (árbol) plane tree.
platea f stalls pl.
plateado,-a 1 pp → **platear**. – 2 adj (color) silvery.
platear t to silver-plate.
plateresco,-a adj plateresque.
platería f (taller) silversmith's.
platero,-a m,f silversmith.
plática f talk.
platicar i to chat, talk.
▲ Conjugation model [1], like sacar.
platija f plaice.
platillo 1 m (de postre) dessert plate; (de café) saucer. 2 (de balanza) pan. – 3 platillos, mpl MÚS cymbals.
■ **platillo volante/volador,** flying saucer.
platina 1 f (de microscopio) slide. 2 MÚS → **pletina**.
platino 1 m platinum. – 2 adj (rubio) platinum, peroxide. – 3 platinos, mpl (de un motor) contact points.
plato 1 m (recipiente) plate, dish. 2 CULIN dish: *hace unos platos buenísimos,* he's a wonderful cook. 3 (en comida) course: *de primer plato hay sopa y de segundo pescado,* we've got soup for starters and fish for the main course. 4 (de una balanza) pan. 5 (de un tocadiscos) turntable.
● **fregar/lavar los platos,** to do the dishes, do the washing-up. ‖ **pagar los platos rotos,** fam to take the blame, carry the can. ‖ **tener cara de no haber roto un plato (en la vida),** fam to look as if butter wouldn't melt in one's mouth.
■ **plato combinado,** single-course meal with different things together on one plate. ‖ **plato de postre,** dessert plate. ‖ **plato fuerte,** (de una comida) main course; (de un acto) main attraction; (de un espectáculo) star attraction. ‖ **plato hondo,** soup plate, soup dish. ‖ **plato llano,** dinner plate. ‖ **plato sopero,** soup plate, soup dish. ‖ **tiro al plato,** trapshooting.
plató m (de cine) set, film set; (de televisión) floor.
platónico,-a adj platonic.
platonismo m Platonism.
plausible 1 adj (admirable) commendable. 2 (recomendable) advisable. 3 (probable) plausible.
playa f beach.
playeras fpl canvas shoes.
playero,-a adj beach.
plaza 1 f (de una población) square. 2 (mercado) marketplace. 3 (en un vehículo) seat: *se ha comprado un depor-*

tivo de dos plazas, she's bought a two-seater sports car. **4** (*puesto de trabajo*) position, vacancy: *se presentaron cien personas para tan sólo dos plazas,* there were a hundred applicants for only two vacancies. **5** (*fortaleza*) stronghold.
■ **plaza de armas,** parade ground. ‖ **plaza de toros,** bullring.

plazo 1 *m* (*periodo de tiempo*) time: *tiene tres días de plazo para presentar la documentación,* you have three days in which to hand in the papers; *se me pasó el plazo para echar la solicitud,* I missed the deadline to send the application form. **2** (*de compra*) instalment, US installment.
● **comprar algo a plazos,** to buy sth. on hire-purchase, US buy sth. on an installment plan.

plazoleta *f* small square.
pleamar *f* high tide.
plebe 1 *f* (*gen*) common people. **2** HIST masses *pl.*
plebeyo,-a 1 *adj* plebeian. – 2 *m,f* plebeian.
plebiscito *m* plebiscite.
plegable *adj* folding, collapsible.
plegamiento *m* folding.
plegar 1 *t* to fold. – 2 **plegarse,** *p* to yield, give in.
▲ *Conjugation model* [48], *like regar.*
plegaria *f* prayer.
pleitear *i* to sue.
pleitesía *f* tribute.
● **rendir pleitesía a algn.,** to pay homage to.
pleito *m* litigation, lawsuit.
● **poner un pleito a algn.,** to sue sb.
plenario,-a *adj* plenary.
plenilunio *m* full moon.
plenipotenciario,-a *adj* plenipotentiary.
plenitud 1 *f* (*cúspide*) peak: *está en la plenitud de la vida,* she's in the prime of life; *está en la plenitud de su carrera como bailarina,* she's at the peak of her career as a ballet dancer. **2** (*sensación física*) fullness.
pleno,-a 1 *adj* (*gen*) full, complete: *les robaron en pleno día,* they were mugged in broad daylight; *estamos en plena selva amazónica,* we are in the heart of the Amazonian jungle; *en pleno centro de la ciudad,* right in the centre of the city. – 2 **pleno,** *m* (*reunión*) plenary meeting.
pleonasmo *m* pleonasm.
pletina *f* deck, cassette deck.
■ **doble pletina,** twin cassette deck.
plétora *f* plethora, wealth.
pletórico,-a *adj* full.
● **pletórico de alegría/dicha,** jubilant, euphoric.
pleura *f* pleura.
pleuresía *f* pleurisy.
plexo *m* plexus.
pléyade *f* cluster.
plica *f* sealed envelope.
pliego 1 *m* (*papel*) sheet of paper. **2** (*documento*) document.
■ **pliego de cargos,** list of charges. ‖ **pliego de condiciones,** specifications *pl.* ‖ **pliego de descargos,** evidence for the defence.
pliegue 1 *m* fold. **2** (*en la ropa*) pleat.
plinto 1 *m* ARQ plinth. **2** (*en gimnasia*) vaulting horse, box.
plisado,-a *adj* pleated.
plisar *t* to pleat.
plomada 1 *f* (*de albañil*) plumb line. **2** (*sonda*) lead. **3** (*para pescar*) weights *pl.*

plomazo *mf fam* bore.
plomizo,-a *adj* (*color*) lead-coloured.
plomo 1 *m* lead. **2** (*pesa*) lead weight. **3** ELÉC fuse. **4** *fam fig* bore: *¡vaya un plomo de profe!,* this teacher is such a pain! **5** *fam* (*balas*) lead: *les llenaron el cuerpo de plomo,* they filled them full of lead.
● **a plomo,** vertically. ‖ **andar con pies de plomo,** *fam* to tread very carefully. ‖ **caer a plomo,** (*cortinas*) to hang straight; (*personas*) to collapse. ‖ **sin plomo,** (*gasolina*) unleaded, lead-free.
pluma 1 *f* (*de ave*) feather. **2** (*de relleno*) feather, down. **3** (*de escribir - estilográfica*) fountain pen; (- *usada antiguamente*) quill pen.
● **a vuela pluma,** off the top of one's head. ‖ **tener pluma,** *fam* to be really camp.
■ **pluma estilográfica,** fountain pen.
plumaje *m* (*de ave*) plumage.
plumazo *m* stroke of the pen.
● **de un plumazo,** at/in one fell swoop, at a stroke.
plumcake *m* fruitcake.
plumero 1 *m* (*para el polvo*) feather duster. **2** (*de adorno*) plume.
● **vérsele el plumero a algn.,** *fam* to see through sb., have sb.'s number.
plumier *m* pencil case, pencil box.
plumilla *f* nib.
plumín *m* nib.
plumón 1 *m* (*de un ave*) down. **2** (*anorak*) down-filled anorak.
plural 1 *adj* plural. – 2 *m* plural.
■ **plural mayestático,** royal 'we'.
pluralidad *f* (*gen*) multiplicity; (*diversidad*) diversity: *hay que aceptar la pluralidad lingüística de nuestra sociedad,* one must recognize the multilingual reality of our society.
pluralista *adj* pluralist.
pluralizar 1 *t* LING to pluralize. – 2 *i* (*generalizar*) to generalize.
pluriempleado,-a 1 *adj* who has more than one job. – 2 *m,f* *person who has more than one job.*
pluriempleo *m* having more than one job.
plus *m* bonus.
pluscuamperfecto *m* pluperfect.
plusmarca *f* record.
plusmarquista *mf* record holder.
plusvalía 1 *f* (*aumento*) appreciation. **2** (*impuesto*) capital gains tax. **3** (*en teoría marxista*) surplus value.
plutocracia *f* plutocracy.
plutócrata *mf* plutocrat.
plutonio *m* plutonium.
pluvial *adj* rain, pluvial.
pluviómetro *m* rain gauge.
pluviosidad *f* rainfall.
Plza. *abr* (*plaza*) square; (*abreviatura*) Sq.
PM *abr* (*Policía Militar*) military police; (*abreviatura*) MP.
p.m. *abr* (*post meridiem (después del mediodía)*) post meridian; (*abreviatura*) p.m.
PNB *abr* (*Producto Nacional Bruto*) gross national product; (*abreviatura*) GNP.
PNN *abr* EDUC (*Profesor No Numerario*) *university lecturer without tenure.*
▲ *Used as masculine and feminine.*
PNV *abr* POL (*Partido Nacionalista Vasco*) *conservative Basque nationalist party.*
P.O. *abr* (*por orden*) on behalf of; (*abreviatura*) pp.

población 1 *f* (*número de habitantes*) population. 2 (*lugar - ciudad*) town; (*- pueblo*) village.
■ **población activa,** working population. ‖ **población pasiva,** non-working population.
poblado,-a 1 *pp →* **poblar.** – 2 *adj* (*zona*) populated. 3 (*barba, cejas*) bushy. – 4 **poblado,** *m* (*zona habitada*) settlement.
poblador,-ra *m,f* settler.
poblamiento *m* settlement.
poblar 1 *t* (*ocupar territorio*) to settle. 2 (*habitar*) to inhabit: *muchas especies diferentes pueblan el parque,* many different species inhabit the park. 3 (*llenar*) to fill: *la casa estaba poblada de telarañas,* the house was full of cobwebs; *han poblado de árboles el campo,* they've planted the field with trees.
pobre 1 *adj* (*gen*) poor. 2 (*infeliz*) poor: *¡ojalá estuviera aquí tu pobre padre!,* if only your dear father were here now!; *pobre de ti si te acercas a ella otra vez,* don't go near her again or you'll be sorry; *¡ay, pobre de mí, que vieja estoy ya!,* poor old me, I'm getting old! – 3 *mf* (*con poco dinero*) poor person; (*mendigo*) beggar: *siempre les da dinero a los pobres,* she always gives money to the poor. 4 (*infeliz*) poor thing: *la pobre se cree que le van a devolver el dinero,* the poor thing thinks she is going to get her money back.
● **no salir de pobres,** *fam* to be condemned to eternal poverty.
pobreza 1 *f* (*escasez de dinero*) poverty. 2 (*falta*) lack, scarcity.
pocha *f →* **pocho,-a.**
pocho,-a 1 *adj fam* (*planta*) faded. 2 *fam* (*alimento*) bad. 3 *fam* (*persona*) off-colour (us off-color), poorly: *estoy pocha,* I feel poorly. – 4 **pocha,** *f* (*alubia*) white bean.
pocholada *f fam →* **monada.**
pocholo,-a 1 *adj fam* (*bonito*) cute. – 2 *m,f fam* cutie.
pocilga *f* pigsty.
pócima 1 *f* (*preparado*) potion. 2 *fam* (*brebaje*) concoction.
poción *f* potion.
poco,-a 1 *adj* little; (*plural*) few, not many: *hago muy poco ejercicio últimamente,* I do very little exercise these days; *somos pocos para tanto trabajo,* there are too few of us for so much work; *pocas Navidades salimos de viaje,* we don't often travel at Christmas. – 2 *poco, pron* little; (*en plural*) not many: *lo poco que aprendí se me ha olvidado,* what little I learned I've forgotten; *pocos conocen la importancia del descubrimiento,* not many people realize the importance of the discovery. – 3 *adv* little, not much: *voy poco por allí,* I rarely go there, I go there very little; *bebí muy poco,* I didn't drink much. – 4 **un poco,** *m* a little, a bit: *¿me das un poco?,* could you give me a little?; *échale un poco de sal,* add a bit of salt; *espera un poco,* wait a bit.
● **a poco de,** shortly after. ‖ **dentro de poco,** soon, presently. ‖ **hace poco,** not long ago. ‖ **pocas veces,** rarely, not often, seldom. ‖ **poco a poco,** slowly, gradually, bit by bit. ‖ **poco antes,** shortly before. ‖ **poco después,** shortly afterwards. ‖ **poco después de,** shortly after. ‖ **poco más o menos,** more or less. ‖ **poco menos que,** almost, nearly. ‖ **por poco,** nearly. ‖ **por si fuera poco,** as if that weren't enough, to top it all, on top of everything.
podadera *f* pruning shears *pl.*
podar *t* to prune.
podenco *m* hound.
poder 1 *t* (*de facultad*) can, be able to: *¿puedes echarme una mano?,* can you lend me a hand?; *no pude abrirlo,*

I couldn't open it, I was unable to open it; *se puede ver Mallorca desde aquí,* you can see Majorca from here; *esto no se puede comer,* you can't eat this, this is uneatable. 2 (*de permiso*) may, can: *pueden pagar en efectivo o con tarjeta,* you can pay in cash or by credit card; *¿puedo fumar?,* may I smoke?; *puede retirarse,* you may leave; *no se puede fumar aquí,* smoking is not allowed here. 3 (*conjetura*) may, might: *podría estar enfermo,* he may be ill, he might be ill, he could be ill; *podría haberlo dejado sobre la mesa,* I may have left it on the table. 4 (*juicio*) can: *¡podrías habérmelo dicho!,* you could have told me!; *no se puede ir por ahí diciendo cosas así,* you can't go around saying things like that. 5 (*sugerencias*) can: *podrías ponerte el pantalón azul con la blusa roja,* you could wear the blue trousers with the red blouse; *podríamos ir a esquiar,* we could go skiing. – 6 *i* (*superar*) to be stronger than: *la curiosidad pudo más que el miedo,* his curiosity proved stronger than his fear; *tú puedes a todos,* you can beat all of them. – 7 *m* (*gen*) power: *el poder ha quedado en manos de la emperatriz,* power has fallen into the hands of the empress. 8 (*posesión*) possession, hands *pl*: *el documento está ahora en mi poder,* the document is now in my hands.
● **a más no poder,** to one's utmost, as ... as possible: *corría a más no poder,* he was running as fast as he could go; *le gusta el helado a más no poder,* he's crazy about ice-cream; *es feo a más no poder,* he's really ugly, he's as ugly as sin. ‖ **en el poder,** (*partido*) in power, in office. ‖ **en poder de,** in the hands of. ‖ **no poder con algn.,** not to be able to stand sb. ‖ **no poder más,** (*comer*) not to be able to manage any more; (*continuar*) not to be able to go on any more: *estaba buenísimo, pero no puedo más,* it was wonderful, but I couldn't eat another thing; *se ha dormido, el pobre no podía más,* he's fallen asleep, the poor mite was tired out. ‖ **no poder menos que,** not to be able to resist, not be able to help: *no pude menos que sonreírme,* I couldn't help smiling. ‖ **no poder ser,** to be impossible: *eso no puede ser,* that's impossible, it can't be. ‖ **poder con,** to manage, cope: *¿puedes con tantas bolsas?,* can you manage all those bags?, can you carry all those bags?; *no puedo con tanta comida,* I can't eat all that food. ‖ **por poderes,** by proxy. ‖ **puede que,** maybe, perhaps: *puede que no lo sepas, pero ...,* maybe you don't know, but ...; *puede que venga más tarde,* she may come later. ‖ **¿se puede?,** can I come in?
■ **poder notarial,** power of attorney.
▲ *Conjugation model* [77].
poderío 1 *m* (*autoridad*) power. 2 (*fuerza*) strength.
poderoso,-a *adj* powerful.
podio *m* podium.
podium *m →* **podio.**
podología *f* chiropody.
podólogo,-a *m,f* chiropodist.
podómetro *m* pedometer.
podredumbre 1 *f* (*de un cuerpo*) rottenness. 2 (*lo podrido*) rot. 3 *fig* (*moral*) corruption.
podrido,-a 1 *adj* rotten. 2 *fig* corrupt.
● **estar podrido,-a de millones,** *fam* to be stinking rich.
poema 1 *m* poem. 2 *fam*: *su reencuentro fue todo un poema,* their reunion was quite something; *le han puesto la cara hecha un poema,* they've made a right mess of his face.
poesía 1 *f* poetry. 2 (*poema*) poem.
poeta *mf* poet.

poetastro *m* second-rate poet, writer of doggerel.
poético,-a *adj* poetic.
poetisa *f* poetess.
poetizar *t* to poeticize.
pointer *m* pointer.
póker *m* → **póquer**.
polaco,-a 1 *adj* Polish. – 2 *m,f* (*persona*) Pole. 3 *fam pey* (*catalán*) Catalan. – 4 **polaco,** *m* (*idioma*) Polish.
polaina 1 *f* HIST (*calza*) gaiter. – 2 **polainas,** *fpl* (*pantalón*) pantaloons.
polar *adj* polar.
▪ **estrella polar,** Pole Star, Polaris.
polaridad *f* polarity.
polarización *f* polarization.
polarizar 1 *t* FÍS to polarize. 2 (*atención*) to focus. – 3 **polarizarse,** *p* to become polarized.
polca *f* polka.
polea *f* pulley.
polémico,-a 1 *adj* controversial. – 2 **polémica,** *f* controversy.
polemizar *i* to debate.
polen *m* pollen.
poleo 1 *m* (*planta*) pennyroyal. 2 (*infusión*) mint tea.
poli 1 *mf fam* (*individuo*) cop. – 2 **la poli,** *f fam* (*cuerpo*) the (old) bill, the cops *pl*.
polichinela *m* (*personaje*) Punch.
policía 1 *f* police, police force. – 2 *mf* (*gen*) police officer; (*hombre*) policeman; (*mujer*) policewoman.
▪ **policía de tráfico,** (*cuerpo*) traffic police. ‖ **policía judicial,** (*cuerpo*) judicial police. ‖ **policía militar,** (*cuerpo*) military police. ‖ **policía nacional,** (*cuerpo*) national police force; (*agente*) member of the national police force. ‖ **policía secreta,** (*cuerpo*) secret police. ‖ **policía urbana,** (*cuerpo*) local police force; (*agente*) member of the local police force.
policíaco,-a *adj* police.
▪ **novela policíaca,** detective story.
policial *adj* police.
policlínica *f* general hospital.
policromía *f* polychromy.
policromo,-a *adj* polychrome.
polideportivo *m* sports centre.
poliedro *m* polyhedron.
poliéster *m* polyester.
▲ *pl* **poliésteres.**
polietileno *m* polythene.
polifacético,-a *adj* versatile.
polifásico,-a *adj* multiphase.
polifonía *f* polyphony.
polifónico,-a *adj* polyphonic.
poligamia *f* polygamy.
polígamo,-a 1 *adj* polygamous. – 2 *m,f* polygamist.
políglota,-a 1 *adj* polyglot. – 2 *m,f* polyglot.
poligonal *adj* polygonal.
polígono 1 *m* (*figura*) polygon. 2 (*gen*) area; (*de viviendas*) development, housing estate.
▪ **polígono de tiro,** firing range. ‖ **polígono comercial,** trading estate. ‖ **polígono industrial,** industrial estate.
polígrafo,-a *m,f* polygraph.
polilla *f* moth.
polimorfismo *m* polymorphism.
polimorfo,-a *adj* polymorphic.
polinización *f* pollination.
polinizar *t* to pollinate.

polinomio *m* polynomial.
polio *f* polio.
poliomielitis *f* poliomyelitis.
▲ *pl* **poliomielitis.**
pólipo *m* polyp.
polisemia *f* polysemy.
polisémico,-a *adj* polysemous.
polisílabo,-a 1 *adj* polysyllabic. – 2 **polisílabo,** *m* polysyllable.
polisón *m* bustle.
politécnico,-a 1 *adj* (*gen*) polytechnic. – 2 **politécnico,** *m* (*instituto*) technical college.
▪ **universidad politécnica,** polytechnic.
politeísmo *m* polytheism.
politeísta 1 *adj* polytheistic. – 2 *mf* polytheist.
política *f* → **político,-a.**
político,-a 1 *adj* political. 2 (*cortés*) tactful. 3 (*por matrimonio*) -in-law: *madre política,* mother-in-law; *padre político,* father-in-law. – 4 *m,f* politician. – 5 **política,** *f* politics. 6 (*dirección*) policy.
politiqueo *m fam* politicking.
politizar *t* to politicize.
poliuretano *m* polyurethane.
polivalente 1 *adj* MAT QUÍM polyvalent. 2 *fig* versatile, multipurpose.
póliza 1 *f* (*de seguros*) policy. 2 (*sello*) official tax stamp.
▪ **póliza de seguros,** insurance policy.
polizón *m* stowaway.
polizonte *m fam* cop.
polla 1 *f* ZOOL young hen. 2 *tabú* (*órgano sexual*) prick, cock.
▪ **polla de agua,** moorhen.
pollada *f* brood.
pollera *f* AM skirt.
pollería *f* (*tienda*) poultry shop; (*sección de supermercado*) poultry section.
pollero,-a *m,f* poulterer.
pollino,-a 1 *m,f* ZOOL donkey. 2 *fam* ignoramus.
pollito *m* chick.
pollo 1 *m* chicken. 2 *fam* (*joven*) young man.
polluelo *m* chick.
polo 1 *m* TÉC pole. 2 (*caramelo*) ice lolly. 3 DEP polo. 4 (*camiseta*) polo shirt.
● **ser polos opuestos,** to be poles apart.
▪ **polo de atracción,** *fig* centre of attraction. ‖ **polo magnético,** magnetic pole. ‖ **Polo Norte,** North Pole. ‖ **Polo Sur,** South Pole.
polonesa *f* MÚS polonaise.
Polonia *f* Poland.
poltrón,-ona 1 *adj* lazy. – 2 **poltrona,** *f* easy chair.
poltronería *f* laziness.
polución 1 *f* (*atmosférica*) pollution. 2 (*eyaculación*) emission.
▪ **polución nocturna,** nocturnal emission, wet dream.
polucionar *t* to pollute.
polvareda 1 *f* (*de polvo*) cloud of dust. 2 (*escándalo*) uproar.
● **levantar una polvareda,** to raise a cloud of dust; *fig* to cause an uproar.
polvera 1 *f* (*estuche*) (powder) compact. 2 (*borla*) powder puff.
polvo 1 *m* (*suciedad*) dust. 2 (*medicamento etc*) powder. 3 *tabú* screw, fuck. – 4 **polvos,** *mpl* (*para maquillar*) face powder.
● **echar un polvo,** *tabú* to screw. ‖ **en polvo,** (*leche, ca-*

cao) powdered; (*nieve*) powdery. ‖ **estar hecho,-a polvo,** *fam* (*persona*) to be shattered; (*coche*) to be a write-off. ‖ **hacer polvo a algn.,** *fam* to shatter sb. ‖ **limpiar el polvo / quitar el polvo,** to dust; (*ser humillado*) to eat humble pie. ‖ **polvo eres y en polvo te convertirás,** dust thou art and unto dust shalt thou return. ■ **polvos de talco,** talcum powder *sing*.
pólvora *f* gunpowder.
● **correr como la pólvora,** *fam* to spread like wildfire.
polvoriento,-a *adj* dusty.
polvorilla *f fam* (*persona inquieta*) fidget.
polvorín 1 *m* (*arsenal*) gunpowder magazine. 2 *fig* (*lugar*) powder keg.
polvorón *m* very crumbly shortcake made with flour, almonds and lard which is eaten particularly at Christmas.
polvoroso,-a *adj* dusty.
● **poner pies en polvorosa,** *fam* to beat it.
pomada *f* cream.
pomelo *m* (*fruto*) grapefruit; (*árbol*) grapefruit tree.
pómez piedra pómez, *f* pumice stone.
pomo 1 *m* (*de puerta*) knob. 2 (*de espada*) pommel.
pompa 1 *f* (*de jabón, chicle*) bubble. 2 (*ostentación*) pomp.
■ **pompas de jabón,** soap bubbles. ‖ **pompas fúnebres,** (*funeral*) funeral *sing*; (*funeraria*) funeral parlour *sing*, undertaker's *sing*.
pompis *m fam* behind, backside.
▲ *pl* **pompis**.
pompón *m* pompom.
pomposidad *f* pomposity.
pomposo,-a *adj* pompous.
pómulo 1 *m* (*hueso*) cheekbone. 2 (*mejilla*) cheek.
ponche *m* punch.
■ **ponche de huevo,** eggnog.
poncho *m* poncho.
ponderación 1 *f* (*cuidado*) deliberation, careful consideration. 2 (*admiración*) high esteem.
● **hablar con ponderación,** to weigh one's words.
ponderado,-a 1 *pp* → **ponderar**. – 2 *adj* (*prudente*) measured.
ponderar 1 *t* (*sopesar*) to ponder, consider, think over, weigh up. 2 (*alabar*) to praise highly.
ponedero *m* nest box.
ponedora 1 *adj* (*gallina*) laying. – 2 *f* layer.
ponencia *f* (*académica*) paper; (*parlamentaria*) address, speech.
ponente *mf* speaker.
poner 1 *t* (*gen*) to place, put, set: *pon el jarrón en la mesa,* put the vase on the table. 2 (*prenda*) to put on: *ponle los zapatos a Alberto,* put Alberto's shoes on; *me pondré el pantalón negro,* I'll put my black trousers on, I'll wear my black trousers. 3 (*encender*) to turn on, put on: *puso la radio,* she put the radio on; *¿has puesto la alarma?,* have you turned the alarm on? 4 (*programar*) to set: *he puesto el despertador a las siete,* I've set the alarm clock for seven. 5 (*instalar*) to install, put in: *¿habéis puesto calefacción?,* have you had central heating put in? 6 (*establecer*) to open: *han puesto un bar en la esquina,* they've opened a bar on the corner. 7 (*escribir*) to put, write: *pon tu nombre aquí,* put your name here; *¿qué has puesto aquí?,* what's this you've written here? 8 (*decir*) to say: *¿qué pone ese letrero?,* what does that sign say? 9 (*en cine, televisión*) to show: *esa película ya la han puesto cuatro veces,* they've shown that film four times already; *lo ponen mañana a las tres,* it's on tomorrow at three o'clock. 10 (*dar nombre*) to name, call: *le pusieron Laura,* they called her Laura. 11 (*huevos*) to lay. 12 (*di-*

nero) to put in: *pusimos mil pesetas cada uno,* we put in a thousand pesetas each. 13 (*telegrama, fax*) to send; (*nota*) to leave. 14 (*deber, multa*) to give: *nos han puesto deberes para las vacaciones,* they've given us homework for the holidays; *me han puesto una multa por exceso de velocidad,* I've been fined for speeding. 15 **poner** + *adj,* to make, turn, render: *la has puesto triste,* you've made her sad. – 16 **ponerse,** *p* (*sol*) to set. 17 (*volverse*) to become, get, turn: *se pone colorado por cualquier cosa,* he blushes at the slightest thing; *se puso muy contenta con la noticia,* the news made her very happy. 18 (*contestar al teléfono*) to answer the phone; (*hablar por teléfono*) to come to the phone: *llamé a tu casa y se puso un hombre,* I rang your home number and a man answered the phone; *en este momento no se puede poner,* he can't come to the phone right now; *a mí no me hace caso, ponte tú,* he won't listen to me, you speak to him. 19 **ponerse a** + *inf,* to start + *to* + *inf/* + *-ing: se puso a cantar,* he started to sing, he started singing.
● **poner a algn. de algo,** to call sb. sth.: *lo puso de ladrón y de mentiroso,* she called him a thief and a liar. ‖ **poner al corriente,** to inform, bring up to date. ‖ **poner al día,** to bring up to date. ‖ **poner bien algo/a algn.,** to speak well of sth./sb. ‖ **poner de manifiesto,** to make evident. ‖ **poner de relieve,** to emphasize. ‖ **poner en libertad,** to set free. ‖ **poner en práctica,** to carry out. ‖ **poner por las nubes,** to praise to the skies. ‖ **ponerse a malas con algn.,** to fall out with sb. ‖ **ponerse de acuerdo,** to agree. ‖ **ponerse de pie,** to stand up. ‖ **ponerse en pie,** to stand up. ‖ **pongamos que ...,** let's suppose ...
▲ *Conjugation model* [78], *pp* **puesto,-a**.
póney *m* pony.
poniente 1 *m* (*dirección*) west. 2 (*viento*) west wind, westerly wind.
pontificado *m* pontificate.
pontificar *i* to pontificate.
pontífice *m* Pope, Pontiff.
■ **el Sumo Pontífice,** the Pope, the Pontiff.
pontificio,-a *adj* pontifical.
ponzoña *f* venom.
ponzoñoso,-a *adj* venomous.
popa *f* stern.
pope *m* pope.
popelín *m* poplin.
populachero,-a *adj* common.
populacho *m* mob, masses *pl*.
popular 1 *adj* (*del pueblo*) traditional. 2 (*muy conocido*) popular.
popularidad *f* popularity.
popularización *f* popularization.
popularizar *t* to popularize.
▲ *Conjugation model* [4], *like* **realizar**.
populista *adj* populist.
populoso,-a *adj* populous.
popurri *m* potpourri.
poquedad *f* (*timidez*) timidity.
póquer *m* poker.
● **cara de póquer,** poker-faced.
por 1 *prep* (*gen*) for: *lo hice por ti,* I did it for you; *lo compré por cien pesetas,* I bought it for a hundred pesetas. 2 (*a través de*) through, by: *entra por la puerta trasera,* come in by the back door; *pasamos por Valladolid,* we went through Valladolid; *iremos por la autopista,* we'll go on the motorway. 3 (*calle, carretera*) along, down, up:

íbamos por la calle cuando ..., we were walking along the street when ...; *subí por la Calle Jovellanos*, I went up Jovellanos Street. **4** (*lugar aproximado*) in, near, round: *anda por el edificio*, he's somewhere in the building; *está por la Plaza Mayor*, it's somewhere near the Plaza Mayor; *está por aquí*, it's somewhere round here. **5** (*causa*) because of: *las plantas han muerto por el frío*, the plants have died because of the cold; *suspendieron el concierto por la lluvia*, they cancelled the concert because of the rain. **6** (*tiempo*) at, for: *nos veremos por vacaciones*, I'll see you during the holidays. **7** (*medio*) by: *lo enviaré por avión*, I'll send it by air; *está hablando por teléfono*, he's on the phone; *llegó por correo*, it arrived by post. **8** (*autoría*) by: *fue escrito por Azorín*, it was written by Azorín. **9** (*distribución*) per: *cinco por ciento*, five per cent; *tocamos a dos mil pesetas por persona*, it works out at two thousand pesetas per person; *iba a veinte kilómetros por hora*, it was going at twenty kilometers an hour. **10** (*tras*) by: *registraron la cárcel celda por celda*, they searched the prison cell by cell; *les interrogó uno por uno*, he interrogated each one in turn. **11** (*con pasiva*) by: *fue comprado por la reina*, it was bought by the queen. **12** (*a favor de*) for, in favour of, us in favor of: *estoy por una amnistía general*, I'm in favour of a general amnesty. **13** (*en calidad de*) as: *la tomó por esposa*, he took her as his wife. **14** (*en lugar de*) instead of, in the place of: *ve tú por mi*, you go in my place. **15** (*multiplicado por*) times, multiplied by: *tres por cuatro, doce*, three fours are twelve, three times four is twelve. – **16 por** *adj* **que**, *loc* no matter how *adj*: *por caro que sea, lo voy a comprar*, no matter how expensive it is I'm going to buy it; *por viejo que parezca funciona*, even though it looks old, it still works.
● **estar por** + *inf*, (*a punto de*) to be on the point of + *-ing*. ‖ **estar por hacer**, to remain to be done, not to have been done yet. ‖ **por aquí**, around here. ‖ **por lo tanto**, therefore. ‖ **por lo visto**, apparently. ‖ **por más que** + *subj*, however much, no matter how much. ‖ **por mucho que** + *subj*, however much, no matter how much. ‖ **por mí**, as far as I am concerned. ‖ **¿por qué?**, why? ‖ **por supuesto**, of course. ‖ **por tanto**, therefore, so.
porcelana *f* china, porcelain: *una porcelana*, a piece of china.
porcentaje *m* percentage.
porcentual *adj* percentage.
porche *m* veranda(h), us porch.
porcino,-a *adj* porcine.
■ **ganado porcino**, pigs *pl*, us hogs *pl*.
porción **1** *f* (*gen*) portion, part. **2** (*cuota*) share.
pordiosero,-a *m,f* beggar.
porfía 1 *f* (*insistencia*) insistence, obstinacy. **2** (*discusión*) squabble.
porfiar 1 *i* (*insistir*) to insist (**en**, on). **2** (*discutir*) to squabble.
▲ *Conjugation model* [13], *like* **desviar**.
pormenor *m* detail.
● **al pormenor**, retail.
pormenorizar *t* to detail.
porno 1 *adj fam* porno. – **2** *m* porn.
pornografía *f* pornography.
pornográfico,-a *adj* pornographic.
poro *m* pore.
porosidad *f* porosity.
poroso,-a *adj* porous.
porque 1 *conj* (*de causa*) because: *no voy porque no quiero*, I'm not going because I don't want to. **2** (*de finalidad*) in order that, so that.

porqué *m* cause, reason: *nunca sabremos el porqué*, we'll never know why.
porquería 1 *f* (*suciedad*) dirt, filth: *esta cocina está hecha una porquería*, this kitchen is filthy. **2** (*mala calidad*) rubbish: *el último libro que ha sacado es una porquería*, his latest book is rubbish; *el postre era una porquería*, the dessert was disgusting; *¡vaya una porquería de coche se ha comprado!*, what a pathetic car she's bought!; *le pagan una porquería de sueldo*, he gets paid a pittance. – **3 porquerías**, *fpl fam* (*chucherías*) rubbish, junk food: *este niño no come más que porquerías*, this kid is always eating rubbish. **4** *fam* (*obscenidades - palabrotas*) swearwords; (*- actos*) disgusting behaviour: *¡no digas esas porquerías!*, don't use such filthy language!; *esas porquerías no deberían verlas los niños*, kids shouldn't watch such filthy programmes.
porqueriza *f* pigsty.
porquero,-a *m,f* swineherd.
porra 1 *f* (*palo*) club; (*de policía*) truncheon. **2** CULIN *kind of* fritter. **3** (*juego*) sweepstake.
● **irse a la porra**, *fam* (*proyecto, objetivo*) to go up in smoke, go down the drain. ‖ **mandar a la porra a algn.**, *fam* to tell sb. to get lost, send sb. packing: *¡vete a la porra!*, get lost! ‖ **¡y una porra!**, *fam* (*incredulidad*) come off it!; (*negación*) get lost!, like hell!
porrada *f fam* (*gran cantidad*) pile.
● **una porrada de**, *fam* tons of, loads of.
porrazo *m* (*con bastón*) blow; (*al caer*) bump, knock.
● **darle/pegarle un porrazo a algn.**, to hit sb. ‖ **darse/pegarse un porrazo**, (*caerse*) to fall over; (*tener un accidente*) to have a crash. ‖ **darse/pegarse un porrazo contra algo**, to crash into sth. ‖ **de golpe y porrazo**, all of a sudden.
porreta en porreta / en porretas, *loc* starkers.
porrillo a porrillo, *loc adv fam* galore.
porro *m fam* joint, spliff.
porrón *m typical Catalan glass drinking vessel with a thin spout used for pouring wine into the mouth.*
portaaviones *m* aircraft carrier.
▲ *pl* **portaaviones**.
portada 1 *f* (*de revista, periódico*) front page; (*de libro*) title page. **2** (*tapa de libro*) cover. **3** ARQ façade.
portador,-ra 1 *adj* carrying. – **2** *m,f* (*de un virus*) carrier; (*de un cheque*) bearer.
● **páguese al portador**, pay the bearer.
portaequipajes 1 *m* (*de un coche - maletero*) boot, us trunk; (*- en el techo*) roof rack. **2** (*de un tren*) luggage rack.
▲ *pl* **portaequipajes**.
portafolios 1 *m* (*carpeta - de piel*) portfolio; (*- de cartón*) folder. **2** (*maletín*) briefcase.
▲ *pl* **portafolios**.
portal 1 *m* (*entrada de edificio*) hallway: *los buzones están en el portal*, the letterboxes are in the hallway; *nos cruzamos en el portal*, we met in the entrance hall. **2** (*de un belén*) crib, manger.
portalón *m* gateway.
portamaletas *m* → **portaequipajes**.
▲ *pl* **portamaletas**.
portaminas *m* propelling pencil.
▲ *pl* **portaminas**.
portamonedas *m* purse, us change purse.
▲ *pl* **portamonedas**.
portante *m* amble.
● **coger/tomar el portante**, *fam* to clear off, do a bunk.
portar 1 *t* to carry. – **2 portarse**, *p* to behave.
● **portarse bien**, to be good, behave os. ‖ **portarse mal**, to be naughty.

portátil *adj* portable.

portavoz *mf* (*gen*) spokesperson; (*hombre*) spokesman; (*mujer*) spokeswoman.

portazo *m* bang, slam (*of a door*): *dio un portazo y se fue*, she slammed the door and left; *no des portazos*, don't slam the door; *la puerta se cerró de un portazo*, the door slammed shut.

porte 1 *m* (*aspecto - de una persona*) bearing; (*- de un edificio etc*) appearance. 2 (*transporte*) carriage, freight: *¿quién va a pagar los portes?*, who will pay the cost of freight? ■ **portes debidos**, carriage due. ‖ **portes pagados**, carriage paid.

porteador,-ra *m,f* porter.

portear *i* to carry.

portento *m* wonder.

portentoso,-a *adj* prodigious.

portería 1 *f* (*de un edificio*) porter's lodge. 2 (*vivienda del portero*) porter's flat. 3 DEP goal.

portero,-a 1 *m,f* (*de un edificio*) porter. 2 DEP goalkeeper. ■ **portero automático**, entryphone.

pórtico *m* portico.

portillo *m* breach.

portorriqueño,-a *adj* → **puertorriqueño,-a**.

portuario,-a *adj* port, dock: *las autoridades portuarias*, the port authorities; *los trabajadores portuarios están en huelga*, the dock workers are on strike. ■ **recinto portuario**, port. ‖ **zona portuaria**, port.

Portugal *m* Portugal.

portugués,-esa 1 *adj* Portuguese. - 2 *m,f* (*persona*) Portuguese. - 3 **portugués**, *m* (*idioma*) Portuguese.

porvenir *m* future.

pos en pos de, *adv* after, in pursuit of.

posada *f* inn. ● **dar posada a algn.**, to take sb. in, give sb. shelter.

posaderas *fpl fam* buttocks.

posadero,-a *m,f* innkeeper.

posar 1 *i* (*para foto etc*) to pose. - 2 *t* (*colocar*) to rest. - 3 **posarse**, *p* (*pájaro*) to alight, perch, sit. 4 (*sedimento*) to settle.

posavasos *m* coaster. ▲ *pl* *posavasos*.

posdata *f* postscriptum, postscript.

pose 1 *f* (*postura*) pose. 2 *pey* (*actitud*) pose, air.

poseedor,-ra *m,f* owner.

poseer 1 *t* (*propiedad*) to own, possess. 2 (*conocimientos, talento, etc*) to have. ▲ *Conjugation model* |61|, *like leer*.

poseído,-a 1 *pp* → **poseer**. - 2 *adj* → **poseso,-a**.

posesión *f* possession: *lo han detenido por posesión de drogas*, he was arrested for possession of drugs. ● **estar en posesión de algn.**, to be in sb.'s hands. ‖ **estar en posesión de**, to be in possession of, have: *está en posesión del título de arquitecto*, he has an architect's degree; *se cree que está en posesión de la verdad*, she thinks she has a monopoly on the truth. ‖ **tomar posesión**, (*de un cargo*) to take up; (*de un territorio*) to occupy: *el nuevo director tomará hoy posesión de su cargo*, the new manager will take up his post today.

posesivo,-a 1 *adj* possessive. - 2 *m,f* possessive person.

poseso,-a 1 *adj* possessed. - 2 *m,f* possessed person: *actuó como un poseso*, he acted like a man possessed.

posguerra *f* postwar period.

posibilidad 1 *f* possibility: *¿hay alguna posibilidad de que salga elegida?*, is there any chance of her being elected? - 2 **posibilidades**, *fpl* (*económicas*) means *pl*: *un coche no está dentro de mis posibilidades*, I can't afford a car.

posible 1 *adj* possible. - 2 **posibles**, *mpl* (*dinero*) means. ● **de ser posible**, if possible. ‖ **hacer todo lo posible**, to do one's best.

posiblemente *adv* possibly.

posición 1 *f* (*postura, situación*) position. 2 (*condición - económica*) situation; (*- social*) status.

positivamente *adv* positively: *sé positivamente que no van a aceptar nuestra oferta*, I know for certain they won't accept our offer.

positivismo *m* positivism.

positivo,-a 1 *adj* positive. - 2 **positivo**, *m* positive.

poso 1 *m* (*del café*) dregs *pl*. 2 *fig* trace.

posponer *t* (*en el tiempo*) to postpone, delay, put off; (*en el espacio*) to put back, put in the background. ▲ *Conjugation model* |78|, *like poner, pp pospuesto,-a*.

posta 1 *f* (*de caballos*) change of horses. 2 (*lugar*) staging post. 3 (*bala*) pellet. ● **a posta**, on purpose.

postal 1 *adj* postal. - 2 *f* postcard. ■ **servicio postal**, postal service.

poste *m* post. ■ **poste indicador**, signpost. ‖ **poste telefónico**, telegraph pole.

póster *m* poster. ▲ *pl* *pósters*.

postergación 1 *f* (*aplazamiento*) deferment, delay. 2 (*de una persona*) relegation.

postergar 1 *t* (*retrasar*) to postpone, delay. 2 (*perjudicar*) to relegate, put back. ▲ *Conjugation model* |7|, *like llegar*.

posteridad *f* posterity.

posterior 1 *adj* (*en el espacio*) back, rear: *en la parte posterior del edificio*, at the back of the building. 2 (*en el tiempo*) later: *su ascenso fue posterior*, his promotion came later.

posteriori a posteriori, *loc adv* a posteriori.

posteriormente *adv* later.

postgrado *m* postgraduate course. ■ **curso de postgrado**, postgraduate course.

postgraduado,-a *m,f* postgraduate student.

postigo *m* (*de ventana*) shutter; (*de puerta*) wicket gate.

postilla *f* scab.

postín *m fam* airs *pl*, importance. ● **darse postín**, *fam* to put on airs. ‖ **de postín**, *fam* posh.

postizo,-a 1 *adj* false. - 2 **postizo**, *m* hairpiece.

postor,-ra *m,f* bidder.

postración *f* prostration.

postrado,-a *pp* → **postrar**.

postrar 1 *t* to prostrate. - 2 **postrarse**, *p* to prostrate os.

postre *m* dessert: *¿qué quieres de postre?*, what would you like for dessert? ● **a la postre**, finally.

postrero,-a *adj* last.

postrimerías *fpl* last years *pl*. ● **en las postrimerías de**, at the end of.

postulación *f* charity collection.

postulado,-a 1 *pp* → **postular**. - 2 **postulado**, *m* (*verdad*) postulate. 3 (*principio, idea*) principle.

postulante 1 *mf* (*para obras benéficas*) person who collects money for charity. 2 REL postulant.

postular 1 t (*defender*) to postulate. – **2** i (*pedir*) to collect (**para,** for).

póstumo,-a adj posthumous.

postura 1 f (*de un cuerpo*) posture, position. **2** (*actitud*) attitude. **3** (*en una subasta*) bid.

potable 1 adj drinkable. **2** (*aceptable*) acceptable.

potaje 1 m CULIN hotpot. **2** fam (*mezcla*) hotchpotch.

potasa f potash.

potasio m potassium.

pote m (*vasija*) pot.
● **ir de potes,** to go on a pub-crawl.
■ **pote gallego,** (*type of*) hotpot.

potencia 1 f (*capacidad*) power: **este coche tiene mucha potencia,** this car is very powerful. **2** (*país*) power: **una reunión de las primeras potencias mundiales,** a meeting of the world superpowers. **3** FÍS MAT power: **elevamos seis a la tercera potencia,** we raise six to the power of three.
● **en potencia,** potential, budding.

potenciación f (*impulso*) strengthening.

potencial 1 adj potential. – **2** m potential: **la región ha aumentado su potencial económico,** the region's economic potential has increased; **nuestro potencial investigador está abandonando el país,** our best researchers are leaving the country. **3** LING conditional tense.
■ **potencial humano,** human resources pl.

potenciar t to strengthen.

potentado,-a m tycoon, potentate.

potente adj powerful.

potestad f power.

potestativo,-a adj optional.

potingue 1 m fam (*crema*) face cream. **2** fam (*comida*) concoction.

potito m jar of baby food.

poto m (*planta*) scindapsus, devil's eye.

potosí valer un potosí, loc fam (*objeto*) to be worth a fortune; (*persona*) to be a treasure.

potro,-a 1 m,f ZOOL (*macho*) colt; (*hembra*) filly. – **2** potro, m (*de tortura*) rack. **3** (*en gimnasia*) horse. – **4** potra, f fam (*suerte*) luck: **¡qué potra tienes!,** you're really jammy!

poyo m stone bench.

poza 1 f (*charco*) large puddle. **2** (*en un río*) pool. **3** (*foso séptico*) cesspit.

pozo 1 m (*de agua, petróleo*) well. **2** (*de una mina*) shaft.
● **ser un pozo de sabiduría,** to be a fount of wisdom. ‖ **ser un pozo sin fondo,** to be a bottomless pit.
■ **pozo ciego/negro,** cesspit. ‖ **pozo petrolífero,** oil well.

PP abr POL (*Partido Popular*) Popular Party (*national conservative party*).

P.P. abr (*por poder*) on behalf of; (*abreviatura*) pp.

práctica f→ **práctico,-a.**

practicable 1 adj (*realizable*) feasible. **2** (*transitable*) passable.

prácticamente adv practically.

practicante 1 adj REL practising (US practicing). – **2** mf (*persona*) nurse.

practicar 1 t (*gen*) to practise (US practice). **2** (*hacer*) to make; (*deporte*) to play: **se le practicará la intervención el mes entrante,** he'll be operated on next month. – **3** i to practise (US practice).
▲ Conjugation model [1], like **sacar.**

práctico,-a 1 adj (*gen*) practical. **2** (*hábil*) skilful (US skillful). **3** (*pragmático*) practical. – **4** práctico, m MAR pilot. – **5** práctica, f practice. **6** (*habilidad*) skill. – **7** prácticas, fpl practical sing: **ahora que he aprobado la teórica puedo pasar a las prácticas,** now that I've passed the theory I can move on to the practical.
● **en la práctica,** in practice. ‖ **llevar a la práctica,** to put into practice.

pradera f prairie, grassland.

prado f meadow.

Praga f Prague.

pragmático,-a adj pragmatic.

pragmatismo m pragmatism.

pral. abr (*principal*) first floor, US second floor.

praliné m praline.

praxis f praxis.
▲ pl praxis.

preámbulo m preamble.
● **sin más preámbulos,** without further ado.

preaviso m notice.

prebenda 1 f REL prebend. **2** (*beneficio*) perk. **3** (*trabajo fácil*) cushy job.

preboste 1 m HIST provost. **2** fam leader.

precalentamiento m DEP warming up.

precariedad f precariousness.

precario,-a adj precarious.

precaución f precaution.
● **conducir con precaución,** to drive carefully. ‖ **tomar precauciones,** to take precautions.

precautorio,-a adj precautionary.

precaverse p to take precautions (**de/contra,** against).

precavido,-a adj cautious.
● **hombre precavido/mujer precavida vale por dos,** forewarned is forearmed.

precedencia f precedence.
● **dar precedencia a,** to give precedence to.
■ **orden de precedencia,** order of precedence.

precedente 1 adj preceding. – **2** m precedent.
● **sentar precedente,** to set a precedent. ‖ **servir de precedente,** to set a precedent: **hoy puedes salir, pero que no sirva de precedente,** you can go out today, but don't make a habit of it. ‖ **sin precedente,** without precedent, unprecedented.

preceder t to precede.

preceptivo,-a 1 adj compulsory. – **2** preceptiva, f precepts pl.

precepto m precept.
■ **día de precepto,** day of obligation.

preceptor,-ra m,f EDUC tutor.

preceptuar t to establish.
▲ Conjugation model [11], like **actuar.**

preces fpl prayers.

preciado,-a adj precious.

preciarse p to be proud (**de,** of).
▲ Conjugation model [12], like **cambiar.**

precintar t to seal.

precinto m seal.

precio 1 m (*coste*) price: **¿a qué precio está?,** how much is it? **2** fig (*valor*) value.
● **a cualquier precio,** at any cost. ‖ **a precio de coste,** at cost price. ‖ **no tener precio,** fig to be priceless.

preciosidad 1 f (*belleza*) loveliness. **2** (*cosa bella*) beautiful thing: **¡qué preciosidad de hija tienes!,** what a lovely daughter you have!; **me he comprado un sombrero que es una preciosidad,** I've bought myself a beautiful hat.

precioso,-a 1 adj (*bello*) beautiful. **2** (*valioso*) precious.

preciosura f fam → **preciosidad.**

precipicio *m* cliff, precipice.
● **al borde del precipicio,** on the edge of the cliff; *fig* on the edge of disaster.
precipitación 1 *f (prisa)* rush, haste, hurry. **2** METEOR precipitation, rainfall.
● **con precipitación,** hastily.
precipitadamente *adv* hastily.
precipitado,-a 1 *pp* → **precipitar. – 2** *adj (apresurado)* hasty, rash.
precipitar 1 *t (apresurar)* to rush; *(adelantar)* to bring forward. **2** QUÍM to precipitate. **3** *(lanzar)* to push, throw. –
4 precipitarse, *p (apresurarse)* to rush, be hasty. **5** *(caer)* to fall; *(arrojarse)* to throw os.
precisamente *adv (exactamente)* precisely: *precisamente por eso me gusta,* that's precisely why I like it; *no fue precisamente muy buen resultado,* it wasn't exactly a good result; *pero si fue él precisamente quien nos lo dijo,* but it was he himself who told us.
precisar 1 *t* to say exactly: *no sabría precisar cuántos entraron,* I couldn't say exactly how many came in. **2** *(necesitar)* to need: *"se precisa cocinero",* "cook wanted". **– 3** *i* to be necessary.
precisión *f* precision, accuracy.
preciso,-a 1 *adj* precise, exact, accurate. **2** *(necesario)* necessary.
● **en el preciso momento que,** at the precise moment that, just as. ‖ **ser preciso,** to be necessary, be essential: *es preciso que acabes ya,* you must finish now.
preclaro,-ra *adj* illustrious.
precocidad 1 *f (de persona)* precociousness. **2** *(de un fenómeno)* earliness.
precocinado,-a *adj* precooked.
preconcebido,-a *adj* preconceived.
preconizar *t* to advocate.
precoz 1 *adj (persona)* precocious. **2** *(cosecha)* early. **3** *(diagnóstico)* early.
precursor,-ra 1 *adj* precursory. – **2** *m,f* precursor.
predador,-ra *adj* predatory.
predecesor,-ra *m,f* predecessor.
predecir *t* to predict.
▲ *Conjugation model [79], pp predicho,-a.*
predestinación *f* predestination.
predestinado,-a 1 *pp* → **predestinar. – 2** *adj* predestined.
predestinar *t* to predestine.
predeterminación *f* predetermination.
predeterminar *t* to predetermine.
prédica *f* sermon.
predicación *f* preaching.
predicado *m* predicate.
predicador,-ra *m,f* preacher.
predicamento *m* prestige.
predicar *t* to preach.
● **predicar con el ejemplo,** to practise (us practice) what one preaches.
▲ *Conjugation model [1], like sacar.*
predicativo,-a *adj* predicative.
predicción *f* prediction.
predilección *f* predilection.
● **sentir predilección por,** to prefer: *siente predilección por su hija pequeña,* he has a soft spot for his youngest daughter.
predilecto,-a *adj* favourite.
predio *m* property.

predisponer *t* to predispose.
▲ *Conjugation model [78], like poner, pp predispuesto,-a.*
predisposición *f* predisposition.
predispuesto,-a *pp* → **predisponer.**
predominante *adj* predominant.
predominar *t* to predominate.
predominio *m* predominance.
preeminencia *f* preeminence.
preeminente *adj* preeminent.
preescolar *adj (enseñanza, edad, etapa)* pre-school, nursery-school.
preestablecer *t* to preestablish.
preestablecido,-a 1 *pp* → **preestablecer. – 2** *adj* preestablished.
prefabricado,-a *adj* prefabricated.
prefacio *m* preface.
prefecto 1 *m* REL prefect, prefect apostolic. **2** HIST prefect.
prefectura *f* prefecture.
preferencia *f* preference.
● **mostrar preferencia por algn.,** to show preference to sb. ‖ **tener preferencia,** AUTO *(de paso)* to have right of way.
■ **trato de preferencia,** preferential treatment.
preferente *adj* preferential.
preferible *adj* preferable: *es preferible que no salga del país,* he'd better not leave the country.
preferiblemente *adv* preferably.
preferido,-a 1 *adj* favourite (us favorite). – **2** *pp* → **preferir.**
preferir *t* to prefer: *prefiero el campo a la ciudad,* I prefer the country to the city; *yo preferiría que se lo dijeras tú,* I'd rather you told him.
▲ *Conjugation model [35], like hervir.*
prefijar 1 *t* LING to prefix. **2** *(determinar)* to fix in advance.
prefijo 1 *m* LING prefix. **2** *(telefónico)* dialling code, us area code.
pregón 1 *m (anuncio)* public announcement. **2** *(discurso)* speech; *(de fiestas)* opening address, opening speech.
pregonar 1 *t (noticia)* to announce, make public; *(secreto)* to tell everybody, broadcast: *se lo dije en secreto, pero lo ha estado pregonando por ahí,* I told him in confidence, but he's been broadcasting it. **2** *(mercancia)* to cry. **3** *(bando municipal)* to proclaim.
pregonero *m* town crier.
pregunta *f* question.
● **hacer una pregunta a algn.,** to ask sb. a question.
preguntar 1 *t* to ask. – **2 preguntarse,** *p* to wonder: *me pregunto si vendrá,* I wonder if he'll come.
● **preguntar por algn.,** to ask after sb., ask about sb.
preguntón,-ona *adj fam* inquisitive, nosy.
● **ser un preguntón/una preguntona,** to ask too many questions.
prehistoria *f* prehistory.
prehistórico,-a *adj* prehistoric.
prejuicio *m* prejudice: *yo no tengo prejuicios,* I'm not prejudiced.
● **sin prejuicios,** unprejudiced, unbiased.
prejuzgar *t* to prejudge.
prelación *f* priority.
prelado *m* prelate.
preliminar 1 *adj* preliminary. – **2** *m* preliminary.
preludiar 1 *t* MÚS to prelude. **2** *(iniciar)* to announce.
preludio *m* prelude.
premamá *adj (ropa)* maternity.

prematrimonial *adj* premarital.
■ **relaciones prematrimoniales,** premarital sex *sing*.
prematuro,-a 1 *adj* premature. – 2 *m,f* premature baby.
premeditación *f* premeditation.
● **con premeditación y alevosía,** with malice aforethought.
premeditado,-a *adj* premeditated.
premiar 1 *t* (*otorgar premio*) to award a prize to. 2 (*recompensar*) to reward.
▲ Conjugation model [12], like *cambiar*.
premio 1 *m* prize: *me han tocado dos premios,* I've won two prizes. 2 (*recompensa*) reward.
premiosidad *f* awkwardness.
premioso,-a *adj* (*movimiento, estilo*) awkward, laboured.
premisa *f* premise.
premonición *f* premonition.
premonitorio,-a *adj* premonitory.
premura 1 *f* (*prisa*) urgency. 2 (*escasez - de tiempo*) pressure; (- *de espacio*) shortage.
prenatal *adj* antenatal.
prenda 1 *f* (*de vestir*) garment. 2 (*prueba*) token, pledge: *te dejo este collar en prenda,* I'll leave you this necklace as a pledge. 3 (*cualidad*) talent. 4 (*persona*) darling, love. 5 (*en juego*) forfeit.
● **no soltar prenda,** not to say a word.
prendarse *p* to fall in love (**de,** with): *se quedó prendado de la camisa en cuanto la vio,* he fell in love with the shirt the minute he saw it; *la actuación los ha dejado prendados,* the performance stole their hearts.
prendedor *m* (*broche*) brooch; (*alfiler*) pin.
■ **prendedor de corbata,** tie pin.
prender 1 *t* (*agarrar*) to catch; (*arrestar*) to arrest. 2 (*sujetar*) to attach; (*con agujas*) to pin. 3 (*encender - fuego*) to light; (- *luz*) to turn on. – 4 *i* (*arraigar - planta, costumbre*) to take root. 5 (*fuego, madera, etc*) to catch light, catch fire. – 6 **prenderse,** *p* to catch fire.
● **prender fuego a,** to set fire to, set light to.
prendimiento *m* arrest.
prensa 1 *f* (*máquina*) press; (*de imprimir*) printing press. 2 (*periodistas*) press; (*periódicos*) papers *pl*: *¿lees la prensa todos los días?,* do you read the paper every day?
● **estar en prensa,** (*libro*) to be in the press. ‖ **tener buena/mala prensa,** to have a good/bad press.
■ **libertad de prensa,** freedom of the press.
prensado,-a 1 *pp* → **prensar**. – 2 *adj* pressed. – 3 prensado, *m* pressing.
prensar *t* to press.
prensil *adj* prehensile.
preñado,-a *adj* pregnant.
preñar *t* (*mujer*) to make pregnant; (*animal*) to impregnate.
preñez *f* pregnancy.
preocupación *f* worry.
preocupado,-a 1 *pp* → **preocupar**. – 2 *adj* worried.
preocupar 1 *t* to worry. – 2 preocuparse, *p* (*sentir preocupación*) to worry (**por,** about), get worried (**por,** about). 3 (*ocuparse*) to mind (**de,** -): *tú preocúpate de lo tuyo,* mind your own business.
preparación 1 *f* (*gen*) preparation: *la preparación del viaje fue muy laboriosa,* organizing the trip was a laborious task. 2 (*física, deportiva*) training. 3 (*conocimientos*) knowledge: *la candidata tiene una excelente preparación en informática,* the candidate is fully trained in computer science; *necesitamos personal con la preparación suficiente,* we need competent staff.
preparado,-a 1 *pp* → **preparar**. – 2 *adj* ready, prepared. – 3 preparado, *m* (*sustancia*) preparation.

preparador,-ra 1 *m,f* EDUC private tutor *who coaches students for competitive exams.* 2 DEP coach.
preparar 1 *t* to prepare, get ready: *voy a preparar el desayuno,* I'll get breakfast ready; *¿habéis preparado el viaje?,* have you arranged the trip?; *prepárate para recibir una buena reprimenda,* get ready for a good telling-off. 2 (*enseñar*) to teach: *en esta academia los preparan muy bien,* the standards of teaching are very high in this school. 3 DEP (*entrenar*) to train, coach: *le está preparando su padre,* his father's coaching him; *se está preparando para el maratón,* she's training for the marathon. 4 (*estudiar*) to revise for, work for: *¿has preparado el examen de inglés?,* have you studied for the English exam?
● **preparar oposiciones,** to study for competitive exams.
preparativos *mpl* arrangements, preparations.
preparatorio,-a *adj* preparatory.
preponderancia *f* preponderance.
preponderante *adj* preponderant.
preponderar *i* to prevail.
preposición *f* preposition.
preposicional *adj* prepositional.
prepotencia 1 *f* (*poder*) dominance. 2 (*arrogancia*) arrogance.
prepotente *adj* arrogant, domineering.
prepucio *m* foreskin.
prerrogativa *f* prerogative.
Pres. *abr* (*presidente,-a*) President; (*abreviatura*) Pres.
presa 1 *f* (*cosa prendida*) prey. 2 (*embalse*) dam. 3 (*acción*) capture.
● **hacer presa en,** to take hold of, seize. ‖ **presa de algo,** seized by: *la víctima gritaba presa del terror,* the victim screamed, terror-stricken. ‖ **ser fácil presa de algn.,** to be easy prey for sb.
■ **ave de presa,** bird of prey.
presagiar *t* to be a warning of, foretell.
▲ Conjugation model [12], like *cambiar*.
presagio 1 *m* (*señal*) omen. 2 (*adivinación*) premonition.
■ **mal presagio,** ill omen.
presbicia *f* long-sightedness.
presbiterianismo *m* Presbyterianism.
presbiteriano,-a 1 *adj* Presbyterian. – 2 *m,f* Presbyterian.
presbiterio *m* presbytery.
presbítero *m* priest.
prescindir prescindir de, *i* (*pasar sin*) to do without; (*no contar con*) to leave out: *prescindamos de formalismos,* let's cut out the formalities; *prescindieron de él para la organización del viaje,* they left him out of the arrangements for the trip.
prescribir 1 *t* (*recetar*) to prescribe. 2 JUR (*ordenar*) to prescribe, state. – 3 *i* (*extinguirse*) to expire, lapse.
▲ *pp prescrito,-a*.
prescripción *f* prescription.
● **por prescripción facultativa,** on doctor's orders.
prescrito,-a *pp* → **prescribir**.
presencia 1 *f* (*gen*) presence. 2 (*aspecto*) appearance: *vino un señor de muy buena presencia,* a very smart man came.
● **hacer acto de presencia,** to appear, put in an appearance.
■ **presencia de ánimo,** presence of mind.
presencial *adj*.
■ **testigo presencial,** eyewitness.
presenciar *t* (*acontecimiento*) to be present at; (*accidente, atraco*) to witness.

▲ *Conjugation model* [12], *like* **cambiar**.

presentable 1 *adj* (*arreglado*) presentable; (*a medio vestir*) decent: *no pases que no estoy presentable,* don't come in, I'm not decent. **2** (*en condiciones*) reasonable, presentable: *he hecho un dibujo que está más o menos presentable,* I've done a sketch which is more or less presentable.

presentación 1 *f* (*de un objeto, documento, etc*) presentation, showing: *la presentación del carné es imprescindible para entrar,* passes must be shown to allow access; *¿para cuándo es la presentación de la traducción?,* when do we have to hand in the translation? **2** (*de personas*) introduction: *nuestro invitado de hoy no requiere presentación alguna,* our guest today needs no introduction. **3** (*de producto - lanzamiento*) launching; (- *exposición*) presentation. **4** POL (*a elecciones*) candidature, candidacy. **5** (*aspecto*) presentation: *la presentación del curriculum tiene que ser excelente,* your CV must be extremely well presented. **6** (*de un programa*) presentation.
● **hacer las presentaciones,** to do the introductions.
■ **presentación en sociedad,** début.

presentador,-ra *m,f* presenter.

presentar 1 *t* (*gen*) to show: *hay que presentar la identificación,* you have to show your identification; *me ha presentado sus disculpas,* he has apologized; *presentó a concurso su primera novela,* she entered her first novel in a competition. **2** (*entregar*) to hand in. **3** (*sacar al mercado*) to launch. **4** (*personas*) to introduce: *¿te han presentado ya?,* have you been introduced yet?; *os presento a mi novia,* this is my girlfriend. **5** TV to present. **6** (*ofrecer*) to offer, show: *esta cicatriz no presenta buen aspecto,* that scar doesn't look good. – **7 presentarse,** *p* (*comparecer*) to turn up: *nos presentamos en su casa sin previo aviso,* we turned up at her house without prior warning; *se presentó a la policía inmediatamente,* he went straight to the police. **8** (*para elección*) to stand; (*en un concurso*) to enter.
● **presentar una denuncia,** to lodge a complaint. ‖ **presentar una ponencia,** to present a paper.

presente 1 *adj* present. – **2** *m* (*tiempo*) present. **3** LING present tense. **4** (*obsequio*) gift. – **5 presentes,** *mpl* those present: *los aquí presentes damos por válido el presupuesto,* those of us present approve the budget.
● **mejorando lo presente,** present company excepted. ‖ **por el presente,** for the moment. ‖ **por la presente ...,** (*en cartas*) hereby. ‖ **tener presente,** to bear in mind.
■ **presente histórico,** present historic.

presentimiento *m* premonition, presentiment: *tengo el presentimiento de que les ha pasado algo,* I've got the feeling something has happened to them.

presentir *t* to have a feeling (**que,** that).
▲ *Conjugation model* [35], *like* **hervir**.

preservación *f* preservation.

preservar *t* to preserve.

preservativo *m* condom.

presidencia 1 *f* POL presidency. **2** (*de una empresa*) chairmanship, US presidency. **3** (*de un club, sociedad*) presidency. **4** (*de una reunión*) chairmanship.

presidencial *adj* presidential.

presidente,-ta 1 *m,f* POL president. **2** (*de una empresa - hombre*) chairman, US president; (- *mujer*) chairwoman, US president. **3** (*de un club, sociedad*) president. **4** (*de una reunión - hombre*) chairman; (- *mujer*) chairwoman.

presidiario,-a *m,f* convict, prisoner.

presidio *m* prison, penitentiary.

presidir 1 *t* (*reunión*) to chair, preside over. **2** (*país*) to be president of. **3** (*predominar*) to prevail.

presilla *f* fastener.

presión *f* pressure.
■ **grupo de presión,** pressure group. ‖ **presión arterial,** blood pressure. ‖ **presión atmosférica,** atmospheric pressure. ‖ **presión sanguínea,** blood pressure.

presionar 1 *t* (*objeto*) to press. **2** (*persona*) to pressure, put pressure on.

preso,-a 1 *adj* imprisoned: *lo han metido preso,* he's been put in prison. – **2** *m,f* prisoner.
● **estar preso,-a,** to be in prison.

prestación 1 *f* (*servicio*) service. **2** (*de la Seguridad Social*) benefit, allowance. **3** (*características - de una cuenta bancaria*) yield; (- *de un coche, electrodoméstico*) performance.
■ **prestación por desempleo,** unemployment benefit.

prestado,-a 1 *pp* → **prestar**. – **2** *adj* lent, on loan.
● **dejar algo prestado,-a,** to lend sth. ‖ **pedir prestado,-a,** to borrow. ‖ **por servicios prestados,** for services rendered.

prestamista *mf* moneylender.

préstamo 1 *m* (*crédito*) loan. **2** (*acción de prestar*) lending; (*acción de pedir prestado*) borrowing. **3** LING loanword.
● **pedir un préstamo,** to ask for a loan.
■ **préstamo hipotecario,** home loan, mortgage.

prestancia *f* (*elegancia*) elegance.

prestar 1 *t* (*dejar prestado*) to lend, loan. **2** (*pedir prestado*) to borrow. **3** (*servicio*) to do, render. **4** (*ayuda*) to give. – **5 prestarse,** *p* (*ofrecerse*) to lend os.: *se prestó para ayudar en la operación de rescate,* he offered to help in the rescue operation. **6** (*ser motivo*) to lend itself: *estas indicaciones se prestan a malas interpretaciones,* these instructions are open misinterpretation. **7** (*acceder*) to agree, give in.
● **prestar juramento,** to swear.

presteza *f* promptness.
● **con presteza,** promptly.

prestidigitación *f* conjuring, magic.

prestidigitador,-ra *m,f* conjuror, magician.

prestigio *m* prestige.

prestigioso,-a *adj* prestigious.

presto,-a 1 *adj* (*preparado*) ready. **2** (*rápido*) quick. – **3** *presto, adv arc* swiftly.

presumible *adj* likely: *un más que presumible aumento de la inflación,* a more than likely rise in inflation; *se abalanzó sobre él con el presumible intento de robarle,* he jumped on him presumably to rob him.

presumido,-a 1 *adj* (*arrogante*) conceited; (*en el vestir*) vain. – **2** *m,f* (*arrogante*) conceited person; (*en el vestir*) vain person.

presumir 1 *i* (*vanagloriarse*) to boast (**de,** about), show off (**de,** about): *siempre está presumiendo de sus hijos,* she's always boasting about her children; *presume de habilidoso,* he likes to think he is a handyman. **2** (*ser presumido*) to be vain: *le gusta mucho presumir,* he's really vain. – **3** *t* (*suponer*) to suppose, assume: *por sus andares presumo que está borracho,* from the way he's walking I assume he's drunk.
● **como era de presumir,** as was to be expected.

presunción 1 *f* (*vanidad*) conceit. **2** (*suposición*) presumption.
■ **presunción de inocencia,** presumption of innocence.

presuntamente *adv* allegedly.

presunto,-a adj presumed, alleged: *el presunto autor del delito,* the alleged criminal.
presuntuosidad f presumptuousness.
presuntuoso,-a adj *(presumido)* conceited, vain; *(arrogante)* presumptuous.
presuponer t to presuppose.
▲ Conjugation model [78], *like poner, pp presupuesto,-a.*
presupuestar t *(proyecto)* to budget for; *(construcción, obra)* to estimate.
presupuestario,-a adj budget.
presupuesto,-a 1 pp → **presuponer.** – 2 presupuesto, m *(en finanzas, política)* budget; *(de una obra, reparación)* estimate. 3 *(supuesto)* assumption.
■ los presupuestos generales del Estado, the national budget *sing.*
presuroso,-a adj hurried, hasty.
pretencioso,-a 1 adj pretentious. – 2 m,f pretentious person.
pretender 1 t *(querer)* to want to: *pretende ganar el concurso,* he wants to win the contest. 2 *(intentar)* to try to: *no sé qué pretende hacer,* I don't know what he's trying to do. 3 *(cortejar)* to court.
pretendiente 1 m *(enamorado)* suitor. – 2 mf *(a un puesto)* applicant. 3 *(al trono)* pretender.
pretensión 1 f *(intención)* aim; *(ambición)* ambition: *no tengo pretensiones de escritor,* I don't aspire to being a writer. 2 *(derecho)* claim.
● sin pretensiones, unpretentious, of modest pretensions.
pretérito,-a 1 adj past: *en tiempos pretéritos,* in the past. – 2 pretérito, m simple past, preterite.
■ pretérito anterior, past anterior. ‖ pretérito imperfecto, imperfect. ‖ pretérito indefinido, simple past. ‖ pretérito perfecto, present perfect. ‖ pretérito pluscuamperfecto, past perfect.
pretextar t to allege.
pretexto m pretext.
● con el pretexto de, on the pretext of.
pretil m *(muro)* parapet.
pretor m HIST praetor, pretor.
pretoriano,-a adj HIST Pretorian.
■ Guarda pretoriana, Pretorian Guard.
prevalecer i to prevail.
▲ Conjugation model [43], *like agradecer.*
prevalerse p to take advantage (**de,** of).
▲ Conjugation model [89], *like valer.*
prevaricación f deliberate neglect of duty.
prevaricar i to fail deliberately to do one's duty.
prevención 1 f *(precaución)* prevention: *se tomarán medidas para la prevención de incendios,* fire prevention measures will be taken. 2 *(medida)* measure, preventive measure: *las prevenciones contra el ruido han surtido efecto,* anti-noise measures have proved effective. 3 *(prejuicio)* prejudice: *al principio le tenía cierta prevención,* at first she was somewhat prejudiced against him.
● en prevención de, as a precaution against.
■ prevención del embarazo, family planning.
prevenir 1 t *(evitar)* to avoid, prevent. 2 *(advertir)* to warn: *me previnieron contra su mal humor,* they warned me about his bad mood.
● más vale prevenir que curar, prevention is better than cure.
▲ Conjugation model [90], *like venir.*
preventivo,-a adj *(medicina, medida)* preventive, preventative.

prever 1 t *(anticipar)* to foresee, forecast. 2 *(preparar)* to plan.
▲ Conjugation model [91], *like ver, pp previsto,-a.*
previamente adv previously.
previo,-a adj previous.
previsible adj foreseeable.
previsiblemente adv forseeably, most likely: *su valor aumentará previsiblemente,* it's value is most likely to increase.
previsión 1 f *(anticipación)* forecast. 2 *(precaución)* precaution.
● en previsión de, as a precaution against.
■ previsión meteorológica, weather forecast.
previsor,-ra adj farsighted.
previsto,-a pp → **prever.**
● tener previsto,-a, to plan: *no tenía previsto salir esta tarde,* I hadn't planned to go out this afternoon.
prieto,-a adj tight.
prima → **primo,-a.**
primacía f primacy.
primado m primate.
primar 1 t *(recompensar)* to reward. 2 *(poner en primer lugar)* to put first, give precedence to. – 3 i *(predominar)* to be important; *(sobresalir)* to stand out.
● primar sobre, to be more important than.
primario,-a 1 adj primary. – 2 primaria, f primary education.
primate m primate.
primavera 1 f spring. 2 lit *(año)* year: *tiene sólo veinte primaveras,* she's is just twenty; *una chica de quince primaveras,* a girl of fifteen summers. 3 BOT primrose.
primaveral adj spring, spring-like.
primer adj → **primero,-a.**
primera f → **primero,-a.**
primerizo,-a 1 adj *(gen)* novice; *(madre)* first-time. – 2 m,f beginner. – 3 primeriza, f *(madre)* first-time mother.
primero,-a 1 adj first: *el primer día del año,* the first day of the year; *la primera calle a la derecha,* the first street on the right. – 2 m,f first: *es la primera de la clase,* she's top of the class. – 3 primero, adv *(en primer lugar)* first: *primero vamos a mirarlo en el diccionario,* let's look it up in the dictionary. – 4 primera, f AUTO first gear: *mete primera y vámonos,* put it into first and let's go. 5 *(en transportes)* first class: *viajan siempre en primera,* they always travel first-class.
● a primeros de mes/año, at the beginning of the month/year. ‖ de primera, first-rate, first-class. ‖ lo primero es lo primero, first things first.
▲ Before singular masculine nouns the form primer is used.
primicia 1 f BOT first fruit. 2 *(noticia)* scoop: *¿quién dio la primicia del asesinato?,* who carried the scoop on the murder.
primigenio,-a adj original.
primípara adj primipara, first-time mother.
primitivismo m primitivism.
primitivista 1 adj primitivist. – 2 mf primitivist.
primitivo,-a 1 adj HIST primitive. 2 *(original)* original. 3 *(rudimentario)* basic. – 4 primitiva, f *(lotería)* ≈ National Lottery.
primo,-a 1 adj *(materia)* raw. 2 MAT *(número)* prime. – 3 m,f *(familiar)* cousin. – 4 primo, m fam fool, sucker. – 5 prima, f *(gratificación)* bonus. 6 *(del seguro)* insurance premium.
● hacer el primo, fam to be taken for a ride.
■ primo,-a hermano,-a, first cousin. ‖ primo,-a segundo,-a, second cousin.

primogénito,-a 1 *adj* first-born, eldest. – 2 *m,f* first-born, eldest.

primor 1 *m* (*delicadeza*) delicateness, delicacy. 2 (*hermosura*) beauty: *tiene un niño que es un primor,* her son is lovely.
● **con primor,** delicately.

primordial *adj* essential.

primoroso,-a *adj* delicate.

prímula *f* primula.

princesa *f* princess.

principado *m* principality.

principal 1 *adj* main, chief: *lo principal es que duerma bien,* the main thing is that he sleeps well. – 2 *m* (*piso*) first floor, US second floor.

príncipe *m* prince.
■ **edición príncipe,** first edition. ‖ **príncipe azul,** Prince Charming. ‖ **príncipe de las tinieblas,** Prince of Darkness.

principesco,-a *adj* princely.

principiante,-a *m,f* beginner.

principio 1 *m* (*inicio*) beginning, start: *me voy de vacaciones a principios de mes,* I'm going on holiday at the beginning of the month. 2 (*base*) principle. 3 (*moral*) principle: *no tiene principios,* he has no principles. – 4 **principios,** *mpl* rudiments.
● **al principio,** at first, at the beginning. ‖ **en principio,** in principle.

pringado,-a 1 *pp* → **pringar.** – 2 *m,f fam pey* mug.

pringar 1 *t* (*ensuciar*) to make greasy: *me he puesto las manos pringando de grasa,* I've got my hands covered in grease. 2 (*untar*) to soak in oil. – 3 *i fam* (*trabajar*) to work hard. 4 *fam* (*meter*) to involve, mix up in: *media empresa está pringada en el asunto,* half the company are mixed up in the affair.
● **pringarla,** *arg* (*morir*) to kick the bucket; (*meter la pata*) to screw up.
▲ *Conjugation model* [7], *like* **llegar.**

pringoso,-a *adj* greasy.

pringue *m* grease.

prior,-ra *m,f* (*hombre*) prior; (*mujer*) prioress.

priorato 1 *m* REL (*cargo*) priorate; (*residencia*) priory. 2 (*vino*) wine from Priorat, Tarragona.

priori a priori, *adv* a priori.

prioridad *f* priority.

prioritario,-a *adj* priority.

prisa *f* hurry: *con tantas prisas me he olvidado la llave,* I was in such a rush that I forgot the key; *salimos del cine a toda prisa,* we dashed out of the cinema; *¡date prisa que no llegamos!,* hurry up or we'll never make it!
● **correr prisa,** to be urgent. ‖ **darse prisa,** to hurry. ‖ **de prisa,** → **deprisa.** ‖ **de prisa y corriendo,** in a mad rush. ‖ **meterle prisa a algn.,** to rush sb. ‖ **sin prisa pero sin pausa,** slowly but surely. ‖ **tener prisa,** to be in a hurry.

prisión *f* prison: *lo han condenado a tres años de prisión,* he's been sentenced to three years imprisonment.
● **estar en prisión preventiva,** to be remanded in custody, be on remand.

prisionero,-a *m,f* prisoner.

prisma 1 *m* prism. 2 *fig* (*perspectiva*) angle.

prismático,-a 1 *adj* prismatic. – 2 **prismáticos,** *mpl* binoculars.

prístino,-a 1 *adj* (*primitivo*) original. 2 (*puro*) pristine.

priva *f arg* booze.

privación *f* deprivation, privation.
● **pasar privaciones,** to suffer hardship.

privado,-a 1 *pp* → **privar.** – 2 *adj* private.
● **en privado,** in private.

privar 1 *t* (*despojar*) to deprive (**de,** of). – 2 *i fam* (*gustar*) to adore: *me priva el chocolate,* I'm crazy about chocolate. 3 *fam* (*estar de moda*) to be in fashion: *hoy día lo que priva es la bici,* bikes are all the rage these days. 4 *fam* (*beber*) to booze.
● **no privarse de nada,** *fam* to pamper os., want for nothing.

privativo,-a *adj* (*propio, exclusivo*) exclusive.
● **ser privativo,-a de,** to be the exclusive right of: *el desempleo no es privativo de nuestro país,* unemployment is not restricted to our country.

privatización *f* privatization.

privatizar *t* to privatize.

privilegiado,-a 1 *adj* privileged. – 2 *m,f* privileged person.

privilegiar *t* to privilege.

privilegio *m* privilege.

pro 1 *m* advantage. – 2 *prep* pro-, in favour of: *una campaña pro amnistía,* a pro-amnesty campaign.
● **ser un hombre/una mujer de pro,** to be a fine upstanding man/woman.
■ **los pros y los contras,** the pros and cons.

proa *f* bow, prow.

probabilidad *f* probability: *tengo muchas probabilidades de conseguir la beca,* I've a good chance of getting the grant; *las probabilidades de que ganen son mínimas,* they have a very slim chance of winning.

probable 1 *adj* (*posible*) probable, likely: *lo más probable es que haya huido,* it's very likely that he has run away; *es probable que no hayan recibido el paquete,* they probably haven't received the parcel. 2 (*demostrable*) provable.

probado,-a 1 *pp* → **probar.** – 2 *adj* proven.

probador *m* changing room, fitting room.

probar 1 *t* (*demostrar*) to prove: *esto prueba la veracidad de su testimonio,* this proves the truth of his testimony. 2 (*comprobar*) to test, check: *prueba el coche a ver cómo responde,* check the car to see how it performs. 3 (*vino, comida*) to taste, try: *prueba el estofado a ver si está bien de sal,* taste the stew for salt; *¿has probado alguna vez las judías con almejas?,* have you ever tried beans with clams?; *nunca pruebo el cava porque me da sueño,* I never drink cava because it makes me sleepy. 4 (*prenda, zapato*) to try on: *pruébatelo antes de llevártelo,* try it on before buying it. – 5 *i* to try: *prueba a cambiarle la pila,* try changing the battery.
▲ *Conjugation model* [31], *like* **contar.**

probeta *f* test-tube.

probidad *f* honesty, integrity.

problema *m* problem: *el dinero no trae más que problemas,* money brings nothing but problems.
● **dar problemas,** to cause problems. ‖ **tener problemas con,** to have trouble with.

problemático,-a 1 *adj* (*cuestión*) problematic; (*joven*) difficult. – 2 **problemática,** *f* problems *pl,* questions *pl.*

probo,-a *adj* honest.

probóscide *f* proboscis.

procacidad *f* (*atrevimiento*) impudence; (*insolencia*) insolence: *no hizo más que soltar procacidades,* he was being really obscene.

procaz *adj* indecent, vulgar.

procedencia 1 *f* (*de lugar, persona*) origin: *¿conoce la procedencia de este dinero?,* do you know where this

money came from?; *se ignora la procedencia de los detenidos,* the origin of the detainees is unknown. **2** *(de barco, tren etc)* origin. **3** *(de comportamiento)* appropriateness.
■ **país de procedencia,** country of origin.
procedente **1** *adj* coming **(de,** from): *el tren procedente de Sevilla,* the train arriving from Seville. **2** *(adecuado)* appropriate, correct.
proceder **1** *i (pasar a ejecutar)* to proceed: *ahora procedemos a la entrega de premios,* we now move on to the presentation of prizes. **2** *(actuar)* to act: *en estas situaciones uno no sabe cómo proceder,* one doesn't know what to do in these situations. **3** *(ser adecuado)* to be appropriate: *se les avisará cuando proceda,* you will be informed in due course. **4** JUR to start proceedings **(contra,** against). **- 5** *m* behaviour (US behavior): *su extraño proceder confundió a todos,* his strange behaviour confused everybody. **- 6** **proceder de,** *i (venir de)* to come from: *¿de dónde procede su familia?,* where is her family from?
procedimiento **1** *m (método)* procedure. **2** JUR proceedings *pl.*
proceloso,-a *adj* lit stormy.
prócer *m* great man.
▲ *pl* **próceres.**
procesado,-a **1** *pp* → **procesar. - 2** *adj* INFORM processed. **3** JUR tried. **- 4** **el/la procesado,-a,** *m,f* the accused.
procesador *m* processor.
■ **procesador de textos,** word processor.
procesal *adj* procedural.
■ **derecho procesal,** procedural law.
procesamiento **1** *m* JUR trial. **2** INFORM processing.
● **dictar auto de procesamiento contra algn.,** to commit sb. for trial, prosecute sb.
■ **auto de procesamiento,** prosecution. ‖ **procesamiento de datos,** INFORM data processing. ‖ **procesamiento de textos,** INFORM word processing.
procesar **1** *t (gen)* to process. **2** JUR to try.
procesión *f* procession.
● **la procesión va por dentro,** *fam* he *(she etc)* is putting on a brave face.
procesionario,-a **1** *adj* processionary. **- 2** **procesionaria,** *f* processionary caterpillar.
proceso **1** *m (gen)* process. **2** *(en el tiempo)* time. **3** JUR trial.
proclama **1** *f* MIL POL proclamation. **2** *(anuncio público)* public announcement; *(de matrimonio)* banns *pl.*
■ **proclamas matrimoniales,** banns.
proclamación *f* proclamation.
proclamar **1** *t (declarar públicamente)* to proclaim. **2** *(revelar)* to broadcast: *se lo conté ayer y ya lo ha proclamado a voz en grito,* I told him yesterday and now he's broadcast it to the whole world. **- 3** **proclamarse,** *p* to proclaim os.
proclítico,-a *adj* proclitic.
proclive *adj* prone.
● **mostrarse/ser proclive a algo,** to be prone to sth.
proclividad *f* proclivity.
procónsul *m* proconsul.
procreación *f* procreation.
procrear *i* to procreate.
procurador,-ra *m,f* JUR procurator.
procurar **1** *t* to try: *procura no enfadarte,* try not to get angry. **2** *(proporcionar)* to get: *nos han procurado billetes para el partido,* they've managed to get us some tickets for the match.

prodigar **1** *t* to be lavish with. **- 2** **prodigarse,** *p (dejarse ver)* to overexpose os.
▲ *Conjugation model* |7|, *like* **llegar.**
prodigio *m* prodigy, miracle.
■ **niño,-a prodigio,** child prodigy.
prodigioso,-a *adj* prodigious.
pródigo,-a **1** *adj (generoso - persona)* lavish; *(- naturaleza)* bountiful. **2** *(derrochador)* wasteful.
● **ser pródigo,-a en,** *(generoso)* to be generous with; *(derrochador)* to be extravagant with.
■ **el Hijo Pródigo,** the Prodigal Son.
producción *f* production.
■ **producción en cadena,** mass production.
producir **1** *t (gen)* to produce. **2** *(causar)* to cause. **3** *(cosecha, fruto)* to yield. **- 4** **producirse,** *p* to happen: *se ha producido un accidente en la autopista,* there has been an accident on the motorway.
● **producir en cadena,** to mass-produce.
▲ *Conjugation model* |46|, *like* **conducir.**
productividad *f* productivity.
productivo,-a *adj (reunión, tierra)* productive; *(inversión)* profitable.
producto *m* product.
productor,-ra **1** *adj* producing. **- 2** *m,f* producer. **- 3** **productora,** *f* CINEM production company.
proeza *f* feat, heroic deed.
profª. *abr (profesora - de instituto)* teacher; *(- de universidad)* lecturer.
prof. *abr (profesor - de instituto)* teacher; *(- de universidad)* lecturer.
profanación *f* desecration.
profanamiento *m* desecration.
profanar *t* to desecrate, profane.
profano,-a **1** *adj (no sagrado)* profane, secular. **2** *(no experto)* lay. **- 3** *m,f (hombre)* layman; *(mujer)* laywoman.
● **ser profano,-a en la materia,** to know nothing about the subject.
profecía *f* prophecy.
proferir *t (palabra, sonido)* to utter; *(insulto)* to hurl.
▲ *Conjugation model* |35|, *like* **hervir.**
profesar **1** *t (creencia, religión)* to profess. **2** *(sentimiento)* to have: *profeso una gran admiración por ella,* I have great admiration for her. **3** *(profesión)* to practise (US practice). **- 4** *i* REL to profess.
profesión **1** *f* profession. **2** REL taking of vows.
● **de profesión,** by profession: *es químico de profesión,* he's a chemist by profession.
■ **profesión de fe,** profession of faith. ‖ **profesión liberal,** profession.
profesional **1** *adj (gen)* professional: *es futbolista profesional,* he's a professional footballer. **- 2** *mf* professional: *en este barrio viven mayormente profesionales,* mostly professional people live in this neighbourhood; *trabaja el cuero de maravilla, es todo un profesional,* he does wonders with leather, he's a real professional; *los profesionales de la enseñanza están en huelga,* the teachers are on strike.
profesionalidad *f* professionalism.
profesionalizar **1** *t* to make professional: *quieren profesionalizar el ejército,* they want to make the army professional. **- 2** **profesionalizarse,** *p* to turn professional.
profesionalmente *adv* professionally.
profeso **ex profeso,** *loc* on purpose.
profesor,-ra *m,f (de enseñanza media)* teacher; *(de universidad)* lecturer.

■ **profesor,-ra particular,** private tutor.
profesorado 1 *m* (*conjunto de profesores*) teaching staff. **2** (*cargo*) teaching post; (*actividad*) teaching profession.
profeta *m* prophet.
● **nadie es profeta en su tierra,** no one is a prophet in his own land.
profético,-a *adj* prophetic.
profetisa *f* prophetess.
profetizar *t* to prophesy.
▲ *Conjugation model* [4], *like realizar.*
profiláctico,-a 1 *adj* (*medida*) prophylactic. – **2** profiláctico, *m fml* (*preservativo*) condom.
profilaxis *f* prophylaxis.
▲ *pl profilaxis.*
prófugo,-a 1 *adj* on the run, fugitive. – **2** *m,f* fugitive. – **3** prófugo, *m* MIL deserter.
● **ser prófugo,-a de la justicia,** to be a fugitive.
profundamente *adv* profoundly, deeply: *estaba profundamente dormida,* she was sound sleep; *le estoy profundamente agradecida,* I am profoundly grateful to you; *lo lamento profundamente,* I'm deeply sorry; *respirad profundamente,* take a deep breath.
profundidad 1 *f* depth: *en las profundidades del océano,* in the depths of the ocean; *tiene cuatro metros de profundidad,* it's four metres deep. **2** (*de persona, pensamiento*) depth, profundity.
● **en profundidad,** in depth.
■ **profundidad de campo,** depth of field.
profundizar 1 *t* (*agujero, hoyo*) to deepen. – **2** profundizar en, *i* (*tema, cuestión*) to look deeply into, analyse (US analyze) in depth.
▲ *Conjugation model* [4], *like realizar.*
profundo,-a 1 *adj* (*gen*) deep: *el agua es muy profunda,* the water's very deep; *se encuentra sumida en una profunda crisis,* she is going through a deep crisis; *es una quemadura profunda,* it's a serious burn; *posee un conocimiento profundo de la materia,* she has a thorough knowledge of the subject. **2** (*tristeza, dolor*) intense. **3** (*cambio, transformación*) profound, total. **4** (*pensamiento, persona*) profound, deep.
profusamente *adv* profusely.
profusión *f* profusion: *estaba ilustrado con profusión de dibujos,* it was profusely illustrated.
profuso,-a *adj* profuse.
progenie 1 *f fml* (*familia*) progeny. **2** (*linaje*) lineage.
progenitor,-ra 1 *m,f* (*padre*) father; (*madre*) mother. – **2** progenitores, *mpl* parents.
progesterona *f* progesterone.
prognosis *f* prognosis.
▲ *pl prognosis.*
programa 1 *m* (*gen*) programme (US program). **2** INFORM program. **3** EDUC (*de un curso*) syllabus. **4** (*plan*) plan.
■ **programa electoral,** election manifesto, US election program.
programable *adj* programmable (US programable).
programación 1 *f* (*de televisión, radio*) programming (US programing): *¿qué cadena tiene mejor programación?,* which channel has the best programmes? **2** (*de teatro*) billing. **3** (*de vídeo*) programming. **4** INFORM programming.
programador,-ra *m,f* INFORM programmer, programer.
programar 1 *t* (*gen*) to programme (US program). **2** INFORM to program. **3** (*organizar, planear*) to plan.
progre 1 *adj fam* lefty. – **2** *mf fam* lefty.
progresar *i* to progress, make progress: *no has progresado mucho en ortografía,* you haven't made much progress with your spelling; *desde que volvió del hospital ha progresado muchísimo,* since he came home from hospital he's made rapid progress.
progresía *f fam* lefties *pl.*
progresión *f* progression.
■ **progresión aritmética,** arithmetic progression. ‖ **progresión geométrica,** geometric progression.
progresismo *m* progressionism.
progresista 1 *adj* progressive. – **2** *mf* progressive.
progresivamente *adv* progressively.
progresivo,-a *adj* progressive.
progreso *m* progress.
● **hacer progresos,** to make good progress.
prohibición *f* prohibition, ban.
● **levantar la prohibición,** to lift the ban.
prohibicionista *adj* prohibitionist.
prohibido,-a 1 *pp →* **prohibir.** – **2** *adj* forbidden.
● **"prohibido fumar",** "no smoking".
prohibir *t* to forbid.
▲ *Conjugation model* [21].
prohibitivo,-a *adj* prohibitive.
prohijamiento *m* adoption.
prohijar *t* to adopt.
▲ *Conjugation model* [20], *like amohinar.*
prohombre *m* great man.
prójima → **prójimo,-a.**
prójimo,-a 1 *m,f fam pey* character, individual. – **2** prójimo, *m* fellow man, neighbour (US neighbor): *lo que opine el prójimo le da lo mismo,* he doesn't care what other people think. – **3** prójima, *f fam pey* floozy.
● **amarás a tu prójimo como a ti mismo,** love thy neighbour as thyself.
pról. *abr* (*prólogo*) prologue (US prolog).
prolapso *m* prolapse.
prole *f* offspring.
prolegómeno *m* (*de un texto*) introduction: *¡déjate de prolegómenos!,* stop beating about the bush!
proletariado *m* proletariat.
proletario,-a 1 *adj* proletarian. – **2** *m,f* proletarian.
proliferación *f* proliferation.
proliferar *i* to proliferate.
prolífico,-a *adj* prolific.
prolijidad 1 *f* (*extensión excesiva*) long-windedness, verbosity. **2** (*meticulosidad*) meticulousness.
prolijo,-a 1 *adj* (*largo en exceso*) long-winded, verbose. **2** (*meticuloso*) meticulous.
prologar *t* to prologue, US prolog.
prólogo *m* prologue, US prolog.
prolongación 1 *f* (*gen*) prolongation. **2** (*aplazamiento*) extension.
prolongado,-a 1 *pp →* **prolongar.** – **2** *adj* (*largo*) prolonged, lengthy.
prolongar 1 *t* (*en el tiempo*) to prolong. **2** (*en el espacio*) to extend. – **3** prolongarse, *p* to go on.
▲ *Conjugation model* [7], *like llegar.*
promediar 1 *t* to average out. – **2** *i* to mediate.
▲ *Conjugation model* [12], *like cambiar.*
promedio *m* average.
promesa 1 *f* promise. **2** (*persona*) budding talent: *la joven promesa de las letras españolas,* the promising young Spanish writer.
● **faltar a una promesa,** to break a promise. ‖ **hacer una promesa,** to make a promise.
prometedor,-ra *adj* promising.
prometer 1 *t* to promise: *¿lo prometes?,* promise?; *te prometo que no lo volveré a hacer,* I promise I won't do

it again. – **2** *i* to be promising: *esta chica es una pintora que promete,* this girl is a promising artist. – **3** prometerse, *p (pareja)* to get engaged.
● prometer el oro y el moro, to promise the Earth. ‖ prometerse en matrimonio, to get engaged. ‖ prometérselas muy felices, *fam* to have high hopes.
prometido,-a **1** *pp →* **prometer**. – **2** *m,f (hombre)* fiancé; *(mujer)* fiancée.
● lo prometido es deuda, promises are meant to be kept.
prominencia **1** *f (montículo)* hillock, mound; *(elevación)* rise. **2** *(protuberancia)* protuberance. **3** *(de partido, teoría, etc)* prominence.
prominente *adj* prominent.
promiscuidad *f* promiscuousness, promiscuity.
promiscuo,-a *adj* promiscuous.
promoción **1** *f (gen)* promotion. **2** EDUC year, US class: *esa chica era compañera mía de promoción,* that girl was in the same year as me.
■ campaña de promoción, promotion campaign. ‖ promoción interna, internal promotion.
promocionar **1** *t (gen)* to promote. **2** *(ideas, relations)* to foster.
promontorio *m* promontory, headland.
promotor,-ra **1** *m,f (inmobiliario)* developer. **2** *(de una idea, plan, etc)* promoter. **3** *(de ventas)* representative. – **4** promotora, *f* property developer.
promotora *f →* **promotor,-ra**.
promover *t* to promote.
▲ Conjugation model [32], *like* **mover**.
promulgación *f* enactment, promulgation.
promulgar *t* to enact, promulgate.
▲ Conjugation model [7], *like* **llegar**.
pronombre *m* pronoun.
■ pronombre demostrativo, demonstrative pronoun. ‖ pronombre personal, personal pronoun. ‖ pronombre relativo, relative pronoun.
pronominal *adj* pronominal.
pronosticar *t* to predict.
▲ Conjugation model [1], *like* **sacar**.
pronóstico **1** *m (del tiempo)* forecast. **2** MED prognosis.
● de pronóstico grave, serious: *ha sufrido heridas de pronóstico grave,* she sustained serious injuries. ‖ de pronóstico reservado: *el estado del paciente es de pronóstico reservado,* the patient is being kept in for observation.
■ pronóstico metereológico, weather forecast.
prontitud *f* promptness.
● con prontitud, promptly, quickly.
pronto,-a **1** *adj* quick, fast: *la pronta reacción del conductor evitó un desastre,* the driver's quick reaction prevented a disaster. – **2** pronto, *m fam (gen)* sudden urge, sudden impulse; *(de ira)* fit: *le dio un pronto de los suyos y se puso a pintar el piso,* he was overcome by a sudden urge and started to paint the flat. – **3** *adv (rápido)* soon: *no llores que pronto vendrá tu mamá,* don't cry, your mummy will be here soon. **4** *(temprano)* early: *has llegado demasiado pronto,* you've arrived too early.
● de pronto, suddenly: *de pronto se acordó de la consigna,* he suddenly remembered the watchword. ‖ ¡hasta pronto!, see you soon! ‖ lo más pronto posible, as soon as possible. ‖ por lo/de pronto, *(para empezar)* for a start; *(por el momento)* for the moment.
pronunciación **1** *f* pronunciation. **2** JUR pronouncement.
pronunciado,-a **1** *pp →* **pronunciar**. – **2** *adj (marcado)* marked, pronounced.

pronunciamiento **1** *m* MIL uprising. **2** JUR pronouncement.
pronunciar **1** *t* JUR LING to pronounce. **2** *(discurso)* to make. – **3** **pronunciarse**, *p (expresarse)* to declare os.: *se pronunció en contra de la ley,* he declared himself against the law; *aún no se ha pronunciado sobre el traslado,* he still hasn't expressed an opinion about the move. **4** *(intensificarse)* to become more pronounced.
▲ Conjugation model [12], *like* **cambiar**.
propagación *f* propagation, spreading.
propaganda **1** *f (publicidad)* advertising: *reparte propaganda por las casas,* he delivers advertising material door to door; *les han hecho mucha propaganda por televisión,* they've been advertised a lot on television. **2** *(electoral)* propaganda.
propagar *t* to propagate, spread.
propalar *t* to spread.
propano *m* propane.
propasarse *p* to go too far: *se propasó bebiendo,* he drank too much; *se propasó con ella y ella lo denunció,* he tried it on with her and she reported him to the police.
propender *i* to be inclined **(a**, to).
propensión *f* inclination, tendency.
propenso,-a *adj* inclined.
● ser propenso,-a a algo, to be prone to sth.
propiamente *adv* exactly.
propiciar **1** *t (favorecer)* to pave the way for, contribute to; *(causar)* to cause, lead to, bring about: *la muerte del dictador propició el cambio político,* the death of the dictator paved the way for political change. **2** *(ganar)* to earn, win: *se propició el respeto de todos,* he won the respect of everyone.
▲ Conjugation model [12], *like* **cambiar**.
propiciatorio,-a *adj* propitiatory.
propicio,-a *adj (gen)* suitable; *(uso formal)* propitious.
propiedad **1** *f (derecho)* ownership: *¿a quién corresponde la propiedad de esta finca?,* to whom does this property belong?; *este campo es de mi propiedad,* I own this field, this field is my property. **2** *(bien inmueble)* property: *tiene propiedades por toda la costa,* he has properties all along the coast. **3** *(corrección)* propriety: *compórtate con propiedad,* behave properly; *hay que aprender a hablar con propiedad,* one must learn to speak correctly. **4** *(cualidad)* property: *el apio tiene muy buenas propiedades,* celery has excellent properties.
■ propiedad intelectual, copyright. ‖ propiedad particular, private property. ‖ propiedad privada, private property.
propietario,-a *m,f* owner.
propina *f* tip.
● dar propina a algn., to tip sb., give sb. a tip. ‖ de propina, *fam (además)* for good measure.
propinar *t* to give.
propio,-a **1** *adj (de nuestra propiedad)* own: *lo pagué de mi propio bolsillo,* I paid for it out of my own pocket; *me lo quitaron ante mis propias narices,* they took it from right under my nose. **2** *(indicado)* proper, appropriate: *lo propio sería mandar una carta de agradecimiento,* the proper thing to do would be to send a thank-you letter. **3** *(característico)* typical: *es muy propio de él,* it's very typical of him. **4** *(mismo - él)* himself; *(- ella)* herself; *(- cosa, animal)* itself; *(- en plural)* themselves: *el propio profesor no sabía la respuesta,* the teacher himself didn't know the answer.
proponer **1** *t (persona, plan)* to propose: *les propuso irse de vacaciones juntos,* he suggested going on holiday

together; *propongo un brindis,* I propose a toast. **– 2 proponerse,** *p* to intend: *me he propuesto dejar el tabaco,* I intend to give up smoking; *se propuso ser actriz y lo consiguió,* she was determined to become an actress and she succeeded.
▲ *Conjugation model* |78|, *like* **poner,** *pp* **propuesto,-a.**

proporción *f* proportion: *se ha levantado un escándalo de grandes proporciones,* there has been a tremendous scandal.
● **en proporciones iguales,** in equal proportions.

proporcionadamente *adv* proportionately.

proporcionado,-a 1 *pp* → **proporcionar. – 2** *adj* in proportion.
● **estar bien/mal proporcionado,-a,** *(dibujo)* to be in/out of proportion; *(físico)* to be well/badly proportioned.

proporcional *adj* proportionate, proportional.

proporcionar 1 *t* *(ayuda, dinero)* to supply; *(consejo)* to give. **2** *(dibujo)* to proportion.

proposición 1 *f* *(idea)* proposal, proposition; *(sugerencia)* suggestion: *tengo una proposición que hacerte,* I have a proposition to put to you. **2** LING clause.
● **hacerle a algn. proposiciones deshonestas,** to make an indecent proposal to sb.
■ **proposición de matrimonio,** proposal of marriage.

propósito 1 *m* *(intención)* intention: *me he hecho el firme propósito de acabar el libro hoy,* it is my firm intention to finish the book today. **2** *(objetivo)* aim: *su único propósito es mantenerse en la presidencia,* his only aim is to continue in the presidency.
● **a propósito,** *(por cierto)* by the way; *(adrede)* on purpose.

propuesta *f* → **propuesto,-a.**

propuesto,-a 1 *pp* → **proponer. – 2** propuesta, *f* proposal.

propugnación *f* advocacy.

propugnar *t* to advocate.

propulsar 1 *t* *(medida, idea)* to promote. **2** *(cohete, nave)* to propel.

propulsión *f* propulsion.
■ **propulsión a chorro,** jet propulsion.

propulsor,-ra 1 *adj* propelling. **– 2** *m,f* *(de idea, medida)* promoter. **– 3 propulsor,** *m* propellent.

prorrata *f* share.
● **a prorrata,** pro rata.

prorratear *t* to apportion, us prorate.

prórroga 1 *f* *(de un plazo)* extension. **2** DEP extra time, us overtime. **3** MIL deferment.

prorrogar 1 *t* *(aplazar)* to postpone; *(alargar)* to extend: *han prorrogado el plazo de matrícula por la fuerte demanda,* the registration period has been extended due to heavy demand. **2** DEP *(partido)* to postpone.
▲ *Conjugation model* |7|, *like* **llegar.**

prorrumpir *i* to burst.
● **prorrumpir en sollozos,** to burst into tears.

prosa *f* prose.

prosaico,-a *adj* prosaic.

prosapia *f* ancestry, lineage.

proscenio *m* HIST proscenium.

proscribir 1 *t* *(prohibir)* to proscribe, ban. **2** *(exiliar)* to exile.
▲ *pp* **proscrito,-a.**

proscripción 1 *f* *(prohibición)* proscription. **2** *(exilio)* exile.

proscrito,-a 1 *pp* → **proscribir. – 2** *m,f* *(exiliado)* exile; *(criminal)* outlaw.

proseguir *t* to continue, carry on.
▲ *Conjugation model* |56|, *like* **seguir.**

proselitismo *m* proselitism.
● **hacer proselitismo,** to proselytize.

proselitista 1 *adj* proselytic. **– 2** *mf* proselytizer.

prosélito *m* proselyte.

prosista *mf* prose writer.

prosístico,-a *adj* prose: *una obra prosística,* a prose work.

prosodia *f* prosody.

prosódico,-a *adj* prosodic.

prosopopeya 1 *f* *(figura retórica)* prosopopoeia. **2** *(solemnidad)* pomposity.

prospección 1 *f* *(minera)* prospect; *(petrolífera)* prospection. **2** *(de mercado)* survey.

prospectar *t* to prospect.

prospecto *m* leaflet, prospectus.

prosperar *i* to prosper, thrive.

prosperidad *f* prosperity.

próspero,-a *adj* prosperous.
● **próspero Año Nuevo,** Prosperous New Year.

próstata *f* prostate, prostate gland.

prosternación *f* prostration.

prosternarse *p* to prostrate os.

prostíbulo *m* brothel.

prostitución *f* prostitution.

prostituir 1 *t* to prostitute. **– 2 prostituirse,** *p* to prostitute os.
▲ *Conjugation model* |62|, *like* **huir.**

prostituta *f* prostitute.

prota ir de prota, *loc fam* to want to be the centre of attention.

protagonismo *m* leading role: *el protagonismo político de la mujer es todavía escaso,* women continue to play a minor role in politics; *una tendencia con marcado protagonismo en el mundo del arte,* a prominent trend in the art world.
● **restar protagonismo a algn.,** to steal sb.'s limelight. ‖ **tener afán de protagonismo,** to want to be the centre of attention.

protagonista 1 *adj* main, leading: *el grupo protagonista del escándalo,* the group at the centre of the scandal; *con Richard James en el papel protagonista,* with Richard James in the leading role. **– 2** *mf* *(de película - actor)* leading man; *(- actriz)* leading lady: *la famosa actriz encarnará el papel de protagonista,* the famous actress will play the leading role. **3** *(de novela, obra de teatro)* main character, protagonist. **4** *(de un hecho)* main protagonist: *el protagonista del escándalo financiero del año,* the central character in the financial scandal of the year; *el humor fue el principal protagonista,* humour was the main feature; *cuando te casas te toca hacer de protagonista,* on your wedding day you are the centre of attention.
■ **protagonista principal,** star.

protagonizar 1 *t* CINEM TEAT TV to star in. **2** *(suceso, acontecimiento)* to play a leading part in.
▲ *Conjugation model* |4|, *like* **realizar.**

protección *f* protection.

proteccionismo *m* protectionism.

proteccionista 1 *adj* protectionist. **– 2** *mf* protectionist.

protector,-ra 1 *adj* protective. **– 2** *m,f* *(persona)* protector. **– 3 protector,** *m* DEP *(de boca)* gumshield; *(conquilla)* box.
■ **protector labial,** lip salve.

protectorado 1 *m* (*territorio*) protectorate. 2 (*periodo*) protectorate, protectorship.

proteger *t* to protect: *ropa de abrigo para protegerse del frío,* warm clothes to protect oneself against the cold. ▲ *Conjugation model* [5].

protegido,-a 1 *pp* → **proteger.** – 2 *m,f* (*hombre*) protégé; (*mujer*) protégée.

proteico,-a 1 *adj lit* (*cambiante*) protean. 2 QUÍM proteinous.

proteína *f* protein: *una dieta rica en proteínas,* a high-protein diet.

proteínico,-a *adj* proteinic: *es de gran contenido proteínico,* it's rich in protein.

protésico,-a dental *m,f* dental technician.

prótesis 1 *f* MED (*uso formal*) prosthesis: *lleva una prótesis de pierna,* he has an artificial leg; *lleva una prótesis de cadera,* she's had a hip replacement. 2 LING prothesis, prosthesis.
■ **prótesis dental,** denture.

protesta 1 *f* protest: *han elevado su protesta al ministerio,* they have registered their protest with the ministry. 2 JUR objection: *protesta admitida,* objection sustained; *no se admite la protesta,* objection overruled.
● **en protesta por,** in protest against, as a protest against.
■ **movimiento de protesta,** protest movement.

protestante 1 *adj* Protestant. – 2 *mf* Protestant.

protestantismo *m* Protestantism.

protestar 1 *i* (*mostrar disconformidad*) to protest (**contra,** against). 2 JUR to raise an objection: *¡protesto, su señoría!,* objection, Your Honour! 3 (*refunfuñar*) to moan: *te pasas la vida protestando,* you're always moaning.
● **sin protestar,** without protest.

protestón,-ona 1 *adj fam* moaning. – 2 *m,f fam* moaner.

protocolario,-a *adj* formal.

protocolo 1 *m* (*gen*) protocol. 2 *fig* (*formalismo*) etiquette, formality: *no me gustan las cenas con tanto protocolo,* I don't like very formal dinners.
● **de protocolo,** (*visita*) formal.

protón *m* proton.

protoplasma *m* protoplasm.

prototípico,-a *adj* archetypal.

prototipo *m* prototype.

protozoo *m* protozoan.

protráctil *adj* protractile.

protuberancia *f* protuberance.

protuberante *adj* protuberant.

prov. *abr* (*provincia*) province; (*abreviatura*) prov.

provecho 1 *m* (*beneficio*) benefit: *tanto dinero le ha hecho más daño que provecho,* so much money has done him more harm than good; *le ha sacado el máximo provecho a la herencia,* he has made the most of his inheritance. 2 (*aprovechamiento*) use: *es lamentable que no se le saque provecho a estos campos,* it's a shame that these fields aren't put to better use; *ha estudiado con provecho,* he has benefitted from his studies.
● **¡buen provecho!,** enjoy your meal! ‖ **de provecho,** (*persona*) likely; (*experiencia*) worthwhile. ‖ **en provecho de algn.,** for sb.'s benefit. ‖ **en provecho propio,** for one's own benefit.

provechoso,-a 1 *adj* (*beneficioso*) beneficial; (*lucrativo*) profitable. 2 (*de utilidad*) useful, worthwhile.

provecto,-a *adj lit* advanced.

proveedor,-ra *m,f* supplier, purveyor.

proveer 1 *t* (*suministrar*) to provide (**de,** with). 2 (*cubrir*) to fill. 3 JUR to give an interim ruling on.

● **Dios proveerá,** the Lord will provide.
▲ *Conjugation model* [61], *like* **leer,** *pp* **provisto,-a.**

proveniencia *f* origin, provenance.

proveniente de *loc* from, coming from, arriving from.

provenir *i* to come (**de,** from).
▲ *Conjugation model* [90], *like* **venir.**

Provenza *f* Provence.

provenzal 1 *adj* Provençal. – 2 *mf* (*persona*) Provençal. – 3 *m* (*idioma*) Provençal.

proverbial *adj* proverbial.

proverbio *m* proverb, saying.
■ **los proverbios de Salomón,** the Proverbs.

providencia 1 *f* REL providence. 2 JUR ruling.
● **dictar una providencia,** to issue a ruling.
■ **Providencia Divina,** Divine Providence.

providencial *adj* providential.

providencialmente *adv* providentially.

próvido,-a *adj* provident.

provincia *f* province.
● **de provincias,** provincial.

provincial 1 *adj* provincial. – 2 provincial,-la, *m,f* provincial.

provinciala *f* → **provincial.**

provincianismo *m* provincialism.

provinciano,-a 1 *adj pey* provincial. – 2 *m,f* provincial.

provisión 1 *f* (*suministro*) provision, supply: *se quedaron sin provisiones a mitad de camino,* halfway through the journey they ran out of supplies. 2 (*de un empleo*) filling. 3 JUR provision.
● **hacer provisión de,** to make provision for.

provisional *adj* provisional, temporary.
● **de forma provisional,** provisionally.

provisionalmente *adv* provisionally.

provisto,-a 1 *pp* → **proveer.** – 2 *adj* provided (**de,** with), equipped (**de,** with).

provocación 1 *f* (*gen*) provocation. 2 (*del parto*) induction.

provocador,-ra 1 *adj* provocative. – 2 *m,f* instigator.

provocar *t* to provoke.
● **provocar el parto,** to induce birth. ‖ **provocar un incendio,** (*con intención*) to commit arson; (*sin intención*) to cause a fire.
▲ *Conjugation model* [1], *like* **sacar.**

provocativo,-a *adj* provocative.

proxeneta *mf* (*hombre*) procurer; (*mujer*) procuress.

proxenetismo *m* procurement.

próximamente *adv* shortly, soon.

proximidad 1 *f* proximity. – 2 proximidades, *fpl* (*vecindad*) vicinity *sing.*
● **en las proximidades de,** in the vicinity of.

próximo,-a 1 *adj* (*cerca*) near. 2 (*siguiente*) next: *el mes próximo,* next month; *en los próximos días,* in the next few days.

proyección 1 *f* (*gen*) projection. 2 CINEM screening, showing. 3 (*alcance*) scope; (*fama*) renown; (*implicaciones*) implications *pl.*

proyectar 1 *t* (*viaje, escapada*) to plan. 2 (*luz*) to project. 3 (*película*) to show. 4 (*sentimientos*) to project. 5 ARQ to design. 6 (*cosa lanzada*) to throw, fling.

proyectil *m* projectile, missile.

proyecto 1 *m* (*propósito*) plan: *¿qué proyectos tenéis para el año próximo?,* what are your plans for next year?; *tenemos en proyecto la ampliación de la empresa,* we are planning to expand the company. 2 (*plan*) project: *el proyecto del ayuntamiento no satisface al vecindario,* the council's project doesn't satisfy the residents. **3** ARQ designs *pl.*

■ **proyecto de ley,** bill.

proyector 1 *m* (*de cine*) film projector; (*de diapositivas*) slide projector. **2** (*foco*) spotlight.

prudencia 1 *f* (*cuidado*) care, caution; (*moderación*) moderation: *hay que conducir con prudencia,* you must drive carefully. **2** (*sensatez*) prudence. **3** REL (*virtud*) prudence.

prudencial *adj* sensible, prudent.

● **a una distancia prudencial,** at a safe distance.

prudente *adj* sensible, prudent.

prueba 1 *f* (*demostración*) proof: *ahí está la prueba de que no decía la verdad,* there's the proof that he wasn't telling the truth. **2** (*experimento*) experiment, trial: *hemos hecho la prueba de no regañarla a ver qué pasa,* we've tried not telling her off to see what happens; *haz la prueba,* try it. **3** (*examen*) test. **4** TÉC trial. **5** MED test. **6** DEP event. **7** JUR evidence: *lo absolvieron por falta de pruebas,* he was acquitted due to lack of evidence. **8** (*en imprenta*) proof: *necesitamos un corrector de pruebas,* we need a proofreader. **9** (*en costura*) fitting.

● **a prueba de,** proof against: *a prueba de balas,* bulletproof; *a prueba de golpes,* shockproof. ‖ **en prueba de,** as a sign of: *toma este anillo en prueba de mi amor,* take this ring as a sign of my love. ‖ **poner a prueba,** to put to the test.

■ **prueba de fuego,** acid test. ‖ **prueba del embarazo,** pregnancy test. ‖ **prueba nuclear,** nuclear test.

prurito 1 *m* MED itching. **2** *fig* obsession.

Prusia *f* Prussia.

pruso,-a 1 *adj* Prussian. **– 2** *m,f* Prussian.

P.S. *abr* (*post scriptum*) post scriptum; (*abreviatura*) PS, ps.

PSA *abr* POL (*Partido Socialista Andaluz*) Andalusian socialist party.

PSC *abr* POL (*Partit dels Socialistes de Catalunya*) Catalan socialist party.

PSE *m* POL (*Partido Socialista de Euzkadi*) Basque socialist party.

psicoanálisis *m* psychoanalysis.

▲ *pl psicoanálisis.*

psicoanalista *mf* psychoanalyst.

psicoanalítico,-a *adj* psychoanalytic, psychoanalytical.

psicoanalizar *t* to psychoanalyse (US psychoanalyze).

psicodélico,-a *adj* psychedelic, psychodelic.

psicodrama *m* psychodrama.

psicofármaco *m* psychoactive drug.

psicología *f* psychology.

psicológicamente *adv* psychologically.

psicológico,-a *adj* psychological.

psicólogo,-a *m,f* psychologist.

psicomotriz *adj* psychomotor.

psicópata *mf* psychopath.

psicopatía *f* psychopathy.

psicopático,-a *adj* psychopathic.

psicopatología *f* psychopathology.

psicosis *f* psychosis.

▲ *pl psicosis.*

psicosomático,-a *adj* psychosomatic.

psicoterapeuta *mf* psychotherapist.

psicoterapia *f* psychotherapy.

psicótico,-a *adj* psychotic.

psique *f* psyche.

psiquiatra *mf* psychiatrist.

psiquiatría *f* psychiatry.

psiquiátrico,-a 1 *adj* psychiatric. **– 2** psiquiátrico, *m* mental hospital, psychiatric hospital.

psíquico,-a *adj* psychic, psychical.

PSOE *abr* POL (*Partido Socialista Obrero Español*) Spanish socialist party.

psoriasis *f* psoriasis.

▲ *pl psoriasis.*

PSUC *abr* POL (*Partit Socialista Unificat de Catalunya*) Catalan socialist party.

pta. *abr* (*peseta*) peseta.

pterodáctilo *m* pterodactyl.

púa 1 *f* (*de peine, cepillo*) tooth. **2** (*de erizo*) quill. **3** MÚS plectrum. **4** (*de alambre*) barb. **5** arg (*peseta*) peseta.

pub *m* pub.

▲ *pl pubs or pubes.*

púber 1 *adj* pubescent, adolescent. **– 2** *mf* adolescent.

▲ *pl púberes.*

pubertad *f* puberty.

púbico,-a *adj* pubic.

pubis 1 *m* pubes *pl.* **2** (*hueso*) pubis.

▲ *pl pubis.*

publicable *adj* publishable.

publicación *f* publication.

públicamente *adv* publicly.

publicar 1 *t* (*libro, noticia*) to publish. **2** (*secreto*) to broadcast, spread.

▲ *Conjugation model* [1], *like* sacar.

publicidad 1 *f* (*comercial*) advertising: *ahora pasemos a la publicidad,* and now for a commercial break; *tanta publicidad estropea las películas,* commercial breaks ruin films. **2** (*divulgación*) publicity: *le han dado mucha publicidad a la boda real,* the royal wedding has been given a lot of publicity.

publicista *mf* advertising executive.

publicitario,-a 1 *adj* advertising. **– 2** *m,f* advertising executive.

■ **anuncio publicitario,** (*gen*) advertisement, advert; (*de televisión, radio*) advert, commercial. ‖ **corte publicitario,** commercial break.

público,-a 1 *adj* public. **– 2** público, *m* (*de un espectáculo*) audience; (*de televisión*) audience, viewers *pl*: *el público aplaudió entusiasmado,* the audience applauded warmly; *no es autor de mucho público,* he is not a very popular author; *no hay mucho público hoy,* there aren't many people today; *su público la sigue incondicionalmente,* her fans follow her everywhere.

● **en público,** in public. ‖ **hacer público,-a,** (*comunicado*) to announce (publicly). ‖ **ser del dominio público,** to be common knowledge. ‖ **ser un peligro público,** to be a public nuisance.

■ **el gran público,** the general public. ‖ **opinión pública,** public opinion.

publirreportaje *m* (*documentary style*) television advertisement.

pucherazo *m* fam electoral rigging: *se sospecha que hubo pucherazo,* it is suspected that the election was rigged.

puchero 1 *m* (*olla*) cooking pot. **2** CULIN meat and vegetable stew. **3** (*gesto*) pout.

● **hacer pucheros,** to pout.

pudding *m* → **budín.**

pudendo,-a *adj* (*feo*) ugly; (*indecente*) indecent.

pudibundez *f* prudishness.

pudibundo,-a *adj* prudish.

púdico,-a *adj* chaste, decent.
pudiente *adj* wealthy, rich.
pudín *m* → **budín**.
pudor 1 *m* (*decencia*) decency: *se desnudó sin ningún tipo de pudor*, he undressed with no sign of embarrassment. 2 (*modestia*) modesty.
pudoroso,-a *adj* decent, chaste.
pudridero *m* (*para cadáveres*) temporary vault.
pudrir 1 *t* to rot. – 2 **pudrirse**, *p* to rot.
pueblerino,-a 1 *adj* (*de pueblo*) village. 2 *pey* countrified. – 3 *m,f* villager. 4 *pey* country bumpkin.
pueblo 1 *m* (*población*) village: *en mi pueblo no tenemos esas costumbres*, we don't do that where I come from; *es de pueblo*, he's a bit of a yokel. 2 (*gente*) people.
puente 1 *m* (*sobre un río etc*) bridge. 2 (*fiesta*) day taken off between a public holiday and the weekend or another holiday: *el Pilar cae en jueves y el viernes hacemos puente*, Columbus Day is on a Thursday and we're taking Friday off as well; *el martes es fiesta, pero el lunes no tengo puente*, Tuesday's a holiday, but I haven't got Monday off. 3 (*en dentadura, gafas*) bridge. 4 (*en un coche*) bridge circuit. 5 (*en gimnasia*) backbend.
● **hacer el puente**, *fam* (*en vehículo*) to hot-wire; (*en gimnasia*) to do a backbend.
■ **puente aéreo**, (*pasajeros*) shuttle service; (*emergencia*) airlift. ‖ **puente colgante**, suspension bridge. ‖ **puente de mando**, MAR bridge. ‖ **puente levadizo**, drawbridge.
puerco,-a 1 *adj fam* (*sucio*) filthy. 2 (*canalla*) rotten. – 3 *m,f* (*animal - macho*) pig; (*- hembra*) sow. 4 *fam* (*persona sucia*) pig. 5 *fam* (*sinvergüenza*) swine, rotter.
■ **puerco espín / puerco espino**, porcupine.
puericultor,-ora *m,f* childcare specialist.
puericultura *f* childcare.
pueril 1 *adj* (*infantil*) puerile, childish. 2 (*iluso*) naive. 3 (*insignificante*) trivial.
puerilidad 1 *f* (*infantilismo*) puerility, childishness. 2 (*ingenuidad*) naivety.
puerperal *adj* puerperal.
puerperio *m* puerperium.
puerro *m* leek.
puerta 1 *f* door: *cierrra la puerta*, shut the door. 2 (*verja*) gate: *las puertas de la ciudad*, the gates of the city; *la puerta del jardín*, the garden gate. 3 DEP (*portería*) goal.
● **a las puertas de**, on the threshold of, close to. ‖ **a las puertas de la muerte**, at death's door. ‖ **a puerta cerrada**, in private, behind closed doors. ‖ **dar a algn. con la puerta en las narices**, *fam* to slam the door in sb.'s face. ‖ **de puerta a puerta**, (from) door to door. ‖ **de puertas adentro**, in private. ‖ **en puertas**, very close. ‖ **entrar por la puerta grande**, to make a grand entrance. ‖ **escuchar detrás de la puerta**, to eavesdrop. ‖ **salir por la puerta grande**, to make a grand exit.
■ **puerta corredera**, sliding door. ‖ **puerta de embarque**, gate. ‖ **puerta de la calle**, main door, front door. ‖ **puerta de servicio**, service entrance. ‖ **puerta giratoria**, revolving door. ‖ **tiro a puerta**, shot at goal.
puerto 1 *m* MAR port, harbour. 2 (*de montaña*) (mountain) pass.
■ **puerto deportivo**, marina. ‖ **puerto franco**, free port. ‖ **puerto pesquero**, fishing port.
Puerto Príncipe *m* Port-au-Prince.
Puerto Rico *m* Puerto Rico.
puertorriqueño,-a 1 *adj* Puerto Rican. – 2 *m,f* Puerto Rican.

pues 1 *conj* (*ya que*) since, as. 2 (*por lo tanto*) therefore, so. 3 (*repetitivo*) then. 4 (*enfático*) well: *pues bien*, well then; *¡pues claro!*, of course!; *pues no*, well no.
puesta *f* → **puesto,-a**.
puesto,-a 1 *pp* → **poner**. – 2 **puesto**, *m* (*sitio*) place: *ya han llegado al primer puesto de la liga*, they've made it to the top of the league. 3 (*de mercado*) stall; (*de feria etc*) stand. 4 (*empleo*) position, post. 5 MIL post. – 6 **puesta**, *f* (*colocación*) setting. 7 (*de huevos*) laying.
● **estar muy puesto,-a en algo**, to be well up in sth. ‖ **ir (muy) puesto,-a**, to be very smart. ‖ **puesto que**, since, as.
■ **puesta a punto**, (*de vehículo*) tuning, tune-up. ‖ **puesta al día**, updating. ‖ **puesta de largo**, coming out. ‖ **puesta de sol**, sunset. ‖ **puesta en escena**, staging. ‖ **puesta en marcha**, (*de vehículo*) starting; (*de proyecto, empresa etc*) starting-up. ‖ **puesto de la Guardia Civil**, Civil Guard post. ‖ **puesto de mando**, command post. ‖ **puesto de socorro**, first-aid post. ‖ **puesto de vigilancia**, lookout post.
puf[1] *m* pouf, pouffe.
▲ *pl pufs.*
puf[2] *interj* (*por calor, cansancio*) phew!; (*con asco*) pooh!, yuck!
pufo *m fam* trick, dirty trick.
● **meterle un pufo a algn.**, *fam* to pull a fast one on sb.
púgil 1 *m* (*boxeador*) boxer. 2 HIST gladiator (*who fought bare-fisted*).
pugilato 1 *m* (*boxeo*) boxing. 2 *fig* (*disputa*) battle.
pugilista *m* boxer.
pugilístico,-a *adj* boxing.
pugna *f* battle, struggle.
pugnar *i* to fight, struggle.
pugnaz *adj* pugnatious.
puja[1] 1 *f* (*acción*) bidding. 2 (*cantidad*) bid.
puja[2] *f* (*pugna*) battle, struggle.
pujante *adj* thriving.
pujanza *f* strength.
pujar[1] *t* (*en subasta*) to bid higher.
pujar[2] *i* (*pugnar*) to struggle.
pujo *m* MED tenesmus.
pulcritud *f* neatness.
pulcro,-a *adj* neat.
pulga *f* flea.
● **buscarle las pulgas a algn.**, *fam* to wind sb. up. ‖ **tener malas pulgas**, *fam* to have a rotten temper.
pulgada *f* inch.
pulgar *m* thumb.
Pulgarcito *m* Tom Thumb.
pulgón *m* aphid.
pulgoso,-a *adj* (*perro*) flea-ridden.
pulguillas *mf fam* touchy type.
▲ *pl pulguillas.*
pulido,-a 1 *adj* (*pulimentado*) polished. 2 (*pulcro*) neat, clean. – 3 **pulido**, *m* polishing.
pulimentar *t* to polish.
pulimento *m* polishing.
pulir 1 *t* (*superficie*) to polish. 2 (*estilo*) to polish; (*maneras, modales*) to refine. 3 *fam* (*cartera, dinero*) to pinch. – 4 **pulirse**, *p fam* (*dilapidar*) to polish off.
pulla *f* gibe.
pullover *m* pullover.
▲ *pl pullovers.*
pulmón *m* lung.
● **gritar a pleno pulmón**, to scream at the top of one's voice.

■ **pulmón artificial / pulmón de acero,** iron lung.
pulmonar *adj* lung, pulmonary.
pulmonía *f* pneumonia.
pulpa *f* pulp.
pulpejo *m* fleshy part.
púlpito *m* pulpit.
pulpo 1 *m* ZOOL octopus. **2** *fam (persona)* groper. **3** *(correa)* bungee cord.
pulquérrimo,-a *adj* immaculate, spotless.
pulsación 1 *f* pulsation. **2** *(de corazón)* beat. **3** *(en mecanografía)* stroke: *¿cuántas pulsaciones tienes por minuto?,* how many words a minute can you type?
pulsador *m (gen)* push-button, button; *(de la luz)* switch.
pulsar 1 *t (botón, timbre)* to press. **2** *(tecla - de máquina de escribir)* to tap; *(- de piano)* to play. **3** *fig (opinión)* to sound out. **– 4** *i (corazón etc)* to beat, throb.
púlsar *m* pulsar.
  ▲ *pl* púlsares.
pulsátil *adj* pulsatile.
pulsera 1 *f* bracelet. **2** *(de reloj)* watch strap.
■ **reloj de pulsera,** wristwatch.
pulso 1 *m (presión sanguínea)* pulse: *déjame que te tome el pulso,* let me take your pulse. **2** *(firmeza en la mano)* steady hand: *para dibujar hay que tener buen pulso,* to be able to draw you need a steady hand; *tengo el pulso fatal,* my hand won't stop shaking. **3** *fig (prudencia)* care, tact.
  ● **echar un pulso,** to arm-wrestle. ∥ **echarse un pulso con algn.,** to have an arm-wrestle with sb. ∥ **ganarse algo a pulso,** to work hard for sth. ∥ **levantar algo a pulso,** to lift sth. with one's bare hands. ∥ **tomarle el pulso a la opinión pública,** to sound out public opinion.
pulular *i* to swarm.
pulverización 1 *f (de un sólido)* pulverization. **2** *(de un líquido)* spraying. **3** *fig* destruction.
pulverizador *m* spray, atomizer.
pulverizar 1 *t (líquido)* to atomize, spray. **2** *(sólido)* to pulverize. **3** *(enemigo)* to crush, wipe out.
  ▲ *Conjugation model* [4], *like realizar.*
pulverulento,-a *adj* powdery.
pum *interj* bang!
puma *m* puma, mountain lion, cougar.
pumba *interj fam* crash, bang, wallop!
pun *interj* bang!
  ● **ni pun,** *fam* not a thing, nothing at all: *no hace ni pun,* he doesn't do a thing.
puna 1 *f (páramo andino)* puna. **2** *(soroche)* mountain sickness, puna.
punción *f* puncture.
puncionar *t* to puncture.
pundonor *m* pride.
punible *adj* punishable.
púnico,-a *adj* Punic.
punitivo,-a *adj* punitive.
punk 1 *adj* punk. **– 2** *m* punk.
punki 1 *adj* punk. **– 2** *mf* punk.
punta 1 *f (extremo)* tip; *(extremo afilado)* point. **2** *(clavo)* nail. **3** CULIN *(pizca)* pinch. **4** GEOG point. **– 5** **puntas,** *fpl (del pelo)* ends: *sólo quiero que me corte un poco las puntas,* I just want a trim. **6** *(zapatillas de ballet)* pointe shoes, toe shoes.
  ● **a punta de pistola,** at gunpoint. ∥ **a punta pala,** *fam* by the hundreds: *había niños a punta pala,* there were hordes of kids. ∥ **de punta a punta,** from one end to

the other: *nos recorrimos la ciudad de punta a punta,* we went all round the town. ∥ **de punta en blanco,** dressed up to the nines. ∥ **en hora punta,** at peak time. ∥ **estar de punta con algn.,** to be at odds with sb. ∥ **sacar punta a,** *(lápiz)* to sharpen; *(palabras)* to read too much into. ∥ **ser la punta del iceberg,** to be the tip of the iceberg. ∥ **tener algo en la punta de la lengua,** to have sth. on the tip of one's tongue.
puntada *f* stitch.
puntal 1 *m* prop. **2** *fig* support.
puntapié *m* kick.
punteado,-a 1 *adj* dotted. **– 2** **punteado,** *m (puntos)* dotting. **3** MÚS plucking.
puntear 1 *t (dibujar)* to dot. **2** MÚS to pluck.
punteo *m* MÚS plucking, US picking.
puntera *f (de zapato, calcetín)* toe; *(protector)* toecap.
puntería *f* aim: *¡qué buena puntería!,* what a good shot!; *tiene muy buena puntería,* he's a very good shot.
puntero,-a 1 *adj* leading. **– 2** **puntero,** *m (para señalar)* pointer. **3** *(para agujerear)* chisel.
puntiagudo,-a *adj* pointed.
puntilla 1 *f* COST lace. **2** *(puñal)* dagger.
  ● **andar de puntillas,** to tiptoe, walk on tiptoe. ∥ **de puntillas,** on tiptoe: *si te pones de puntillas a lo mejor alcanzas,* if you stand on tiptoe you might reach it. ∥ **dar la puntilla,** *fam* to finish off.
puntillismo *m* pointillism.
puntillista *adj* pointillist.
puntilloso,-a 1 *adj (susceptible)* touchy. **2** *(exigente)* punctilious.
punto 1 *m (gen)* point. **2** *(marca)* dot. **3** *(tanto)* point: *nos llevan cinco puntos de ventaja,* they're five points ahead of us. **4** *(detrás de abreviatura)* dot; *(al final de la oración)* full stop, US period. **5** *(lugar)* spot: *¿en qué punto de la carretera se encuentran?,* exactly where on the road are they? **6** *(tema)* point. **7** *(tejido)* knitwear: *me he comprado una falda de punto,* I bought a knitted skirt. **8** *(en costura, sutura)* stitch: *me caí y me dieron tres puntos en la barbilla,* I fell and needed three stitches on my chin. **9** *(de libro)* bookmark. **10** *(en la media)* ladder, US run.
  ● **a punto de caramelo,** *(en repostería)* caramelized; *(en su punto)* just right, perfect: *pídele el aumento ahora que está a punto de caramelo,* ask him for a rise now that he's in the mood. ∥ **a punto de nieve,** stiff: *tienes que batir las claras a punto de nieve,* you have to beat the egg whites stiff. ∥ **al punto,** *(rápidamente)* immediately. ∥ **coger un punto,** *fam* to get tipsy, get merry. ∥ **con puntos y comas,** in detail. ∥ **dar en el punto,** to hit the nail on the head. ∥ **de todo punto,** absolutely. ∥ **en punto,** sharp, on the dot: *son las tres en punto,* it's exactly three o'clock. ∥ **estar a punto,** to be ready. ∥ **estar a punto de,** to be about to, be on the point of: *ese jarrón está a punto de caerse,* that vase is about to fall; *estuvimos a punto de matarnos,* we nearly got killed. ∥ **estar en su punto,** *(comida)* to be cooked to perfection: *la pasta está en su punto,* the pasta is just right; *este pastel te ha quedado en su punto,* this cake has turned out perfect. ∥ **ganar puntos,** to win points. ∥ **ganar por puntos,** to win on points. ∥ **hacer punto,** to knit. ∥ **hasta cierto punto,** up to a certain point. ∥ **hasta tal punto que ...,** to such an extent that ... ∥ **llegar a punto,** to arrive on time. ∥ **perder puntos,** *(gen)* to lose points; *(alumno)* to lose marks: *perdió puntos porque su letra era mala,* he lost marks because of his bad handwriting. ∥ **poner los puntos sobre las íes,** to dot one's i's and cross one's t's. ∥ **poner punto**

final a algo, to put an end to sth. ‖ ¡punto en boca!, mum's the word! ‖ punto por punto, in detail. ■ dos puntos, colon. ‖ punto cadena, chain stitch. ‖ punto cardinal, cardinal point. ‖ punto culminante, climax. ‖ punto de apoyo, (en palanca) fulcrum; (base) cornerstone. ‖ punto de break, break point. ‖ punto de congelación, freezing point. ‖ punto de contacto, point of contact. ‖ punto de cruz, cross-stitch. ‖ punto de ebullición, boiling point. ‖ punto de encuentro, meeting point. ‖ punto de fusión, melting point. ‖ punto de libro, bookmark. ‖ punto de media, stocking stitch. ‖ punto de mira, (objetivo) target; (en rifle) sight, front sight. ‖ punto de partida, starting point. ‖ punto de partido, match point. ‖ punto de referencia, point of reference. ‖ punto de ruptura, break point. ‖ punto de servicio, service point. ‖ punto de set, set point. ‖ punto de sutura, stitch. ‖ punto de venta, sales outlet. ‖ punto de vista, point of view. ‖ punto débil, weak point. ‖ punto decimal, decimal point. ‖ punto del revés, purl stitch. ‖ punto final, (en dictado) full stop, us period. ‖ punto flaco, weak point. ‖ punto fuerte, strong point. ‖ punto muerto, (en un coche) neutral; (en una negociación) standstill, stalemate, deadlock: deja el coche en punto muerto, leave the car in neutral; las negociaciones ha entrado en punto muerto, the negotiations have reached a stalemate. ‖ punto negro, (en la piel) blackhead; (en la carretera) black spot. ‖ punto neurálgico, nerve centre. ‖ punto y aparte, (en ortografía) full stop, new paragraph, us period, new paragraph. ‖ punto y coma, semicolon. ‖ punto y seguido, full stop, new sentence, us period, new sentence. ‖ puntos suspensivos, suspension points, ellipsis.

puntuable adj valid: este torneo no es puntuable para el campionato nacional, this tournament does not count towards the national championship.

puntuación 1 f (en ortografía) punctuation. 2 (acción de puntuar) scoring; (total de puntos) score: obtuvo una puntuación muy alta, she got a very high score. 3 EDUC (acción) marking; (nota) mark: obtuvo una puntuación muy alta, she got a very high mark.

puntual 1 adj (que llega a su hora) punctual: han llegado muy puntuales, they've arrived right on time. 2 (detallado) detailed. 3 (aislado) specific.

puntualidad f punctuality.
● con puntualidad, punctually.

puntualización f remark.

puntualizar 1 t (detallar) to give full details of. 2 (especificar) to point out.
▲ Conjugation model [4], like realizar.

puntualmente adv punctually, on time.

puntuar 1 t LING to punctuate. 2 EDUC to mark. – 3 i DEP to score.
▲ Conjugation model [11], like actuar.

punzada f sharp pain, stab of pain.

punzar 1 t to prick. 2 fig to torment.
▲ Conjugation model [4], like realizar.

punzón m punch.

puñado m handful.
● a puñados, fam galore.

puñal m dagger.
● poner un puñal en el pecho a algn., to hold a knife to sb.'s throat.

puñalada 1 f (acción) stab; (herida) stab wound: lo mataron a puñaladas, he was stabbed to death. 2 (disgusto) blow.
■ puñalada trapera, fam stab in the back.

puñeta 1 f fam nuisance. – 2 interj fam bloody hell!
● en la quinta puñeta, fam in the back of beyond. ‖ hacer la puñeta a algn., fam to make life difficult for sb., cause problems for sb. ‖ irse a hacer puñetas, fam (plan) to go down the drain, fall through; (persona) to go to hell, get lost: ¡vete a hacer puñetas!, go to hell! ‖ mandar a algn. a hacer puñetas, fam to tell sb. to get lost.

puñetazo m punch.
● dar/pegar un puñetazo a algn., to punch sb.

puñetero,-a 1 adj fam (fastidioso) damned. 2 fam (difícil) tricky. 3 fam (persona - molesta) annoying; (- malintencionada) bloody-minded. – 4 m.f fam (persona molesta) pain in the neck; (persona malintencionada) nasty piece of work.

puño 1 m (mano) fist. 2 (de arma) handle. 3 (de camisa, abrigo etc) cuff.
● de puño y letra de algn., written by sb.'s own hand. ‖ decir mentiras como puños, fam to lie through one's teeth. ‖ decir verdades como puños, fam to be a straight talker.

pupa 1 f (en el labio) cold sore. 2 fam (en lenguaje infantil) pain: mamá, me he hecho pupa, mummy, I've hurt myself. 3 (insecto) pupa. – 4 pupas, mf (persona) walking disaster.

pupila f pupil.

pupilaje 1 f (de huérfano) tutelage; (de alumno) pupillage. – 2 m (de coche) garaging: "se admiten coches a pupilaje", "garaging facilities available".

pupilo,-a m.f (de un tutor) pupil.

pupitre m school desk.

puramente adv purely, simply.

purasangre 1 adj thoroughbred. – 2 m (caballo) thoroughbred.

puré 1 m (espeso) purée; (sopa) thick soup: hoy tenemos puré de zanahoria, today we've got thick carrot soup.
● hacer a algn. puré, fam (físicamente) to make mincemeat of sb.; (moralmente) to shatter sb. ‖ hecho,-a puré, fam shattered.
■ puré de patatas, mashed potatoes.

pureta 1 adj arg square, fuddy-duddy. – 2 mf arg square, fuddy-duddy.

pureza 1 f (gen) purity. 2 (castidad) chastity.

purga f purge.

purgación 1 f (acción) purging. – 2 purgaciones, fpl fam blenorrhoea (us blenorrhea).

purgante 1 adj purgative. – 2 m purgative, laxative.

purgar t to purge (de, of).
▲ Conjugation model [7], like llegar.

purgatorio m purgatory.

puridad en puridad, loc in effect.

purificación f purification.

purificador,-ra 1 adj purifying. – 2 purificador, m purifier.

purificante adj purifying.

purificar t to purify.

purismo m purism.

purista 1 adj purist. – 2 mf purist.

puritano,-a 1 adj puritan, puritanic. – 2 m.f puritan.

puro,-a 1 adj (sin mezcla) pure: me voy al campo a respirar aire puro, I'm going to the country to breathe some clean air; tiene un perro de pura raza, he has a purebred dog. 2 (mero) sheer, mere, pure: me enteré por pura casualidad, I found out by pure chance. 3 (casto) chaste, pure. – 4 puro, m cigar.
● caerle a algn. un puro, to be for the high-jump, be

in big trouble, be for it: *si se entera el jefe, te caerá un puro,* if the boss finds out, you're for it. ‖ **meterle un puro a algn.,** *tabú* to throw the book at sb.

púrpura 1 *adj* purple. – **2** *m* purple.

purpúreo,-a *adj* purple.

purpurina *f* glitter.

purrusalda *f dish of leeks, potato and cod.*

purulento,-a *adj* purulent.

pus *m* pus.

pusilánime *adj* faint-hearted, pusillanimous.

pusilanimidad *f* faint-heartedness, pusillanimity.

pústula *f* pustule.

puta *f tabú* → **puto,-a.**

putada *f tabú* (*mala pasada*) dirty trick, rotten trick; (*mala suerte*) rotten luck: *me han hecho una putada gordísima,* they've really done the dirty on me; *¡qué putada, ya han cerado!,* oh bugger, it's closed already!

putañero,-a *adj tabú* whoring.

putativo,-a *adj* putative.

putear 1 *t tabú* to fuck about. – **2** *i tabú* to go whoring.

puteo *m tabú* fucking about.

putero,-a *adj tabú* whoring.

puticlub *m tabú* pick-up joint.

▲ *pl* **puticlubs** or **puticlubes.**

puto,-a 1 *adj tabú* (*miserable*) bloody, fucking: *no tengo ni un puto duro,* I haven't got any fucking money. – **2** *puto, m tabú* (*prostituto*) male prostitute, rent boy. **3** *tabú* (*sinvergüenza*) bastard, fucker. – **4** *puta, f tabú* prostitute, whore.

● **de puta madre,** great, brilliant, bloody fantastic. ‖ **de puta pena,** *tabú* dreadful, bloody awful. ‖ **ir de putas,** *tabú* to go whoring. ‖ **ni puta idea,** *tabú* not a bloody clue. ‖ **pasarlas putas,** *tabú* to go through hell.

■ **hijo,-a de puta,** *tabú* (*hombre*) son of a bitch; (*mujer*) fucking cow.

putrefacción *f* putrefaction, rotting.

putrefacto,-a *adj* putrefied, rotten.

pútrido,-a *adj* putrefied, rotten.

puya 1 *f* (*punta de lanza*) tip, point. **2** (*comentario*) gibe.

puyazo 1 *m* jab with a lance. **2** (*comentario*) gibe.

puzzle *m* puzzle.

PVP *abr* (*precio de venta al público*) recommended retail price; (*abreviatura*) RRP.

Pza. *abr* → **Plza.**

Q

Q, q f (la letra) Q, q.

Qatar m Qatar.

q.b.s.m. abr fml (que besa sus manos) formal Spanish courtesy formula.

q.b.s.p. abr fml (que besa sus pies) formal Spanish courtesy formula.

Q.D.G. abr fml (que Dios guarde) formal Spanish courtesy formula.

▲ Also written q.D.g.

q.e.g.e. abr (que en gloria esté) God rest his (her etc) soul.

q.e.p.d. abr (que en paz descanse) rest in peace; (abreviatura) RIP.

q.e.s.m. abr fml (que estrecha su mano) formal Spanish courtesy formula.

Qm sím (quintal métrico) quintal.

q.s.g.h. abr fml (que santa gloria haya) rest in peace; (abreviatura) RIP.

quantum m quantum.

▲ pl quanta.

quásar m quasar.

que[1] **1** pron (sujeto, persona) who, that; (cosa) that, which: *la chica que vino ayer está enferma,* the girl who came yesterday is ill; *el árbol que se quemó está en el jardín,* the tree that got burnt is in the garden; *este árbol, que parecía muerto en invierno, está rebrotando,* this tree, which looked dead in winter, is sprouting. **2** (complemento, persona) whom, who; (cosa) that, which: *el coche que me prestaste está ahí,* the car (that) you lent me is there; *el niño que viste ayer es mi hijo,* the boy you saw yesterday is my son. **3** prep + que, (complemento circunstancial) which; (lugar) where; (tiempo) when: *la pistola con que le hirieron era nuestra,* the gun with which he was wounded was ours, the gun he was wounded with was ours; *la casa en que vivía estaba lejos,* the house where he lived was far away. **4** def art + que, the one which, the one that: *ese libro es el que me gusta,* that's the book I like; *ésa es la que quiero,* that's the one I want.

que[2] **1** conj that: *dice que no vendrá,* he says (that) he won't come; *quiero que lo hagas,* I want you to do it. **2** (en comparaciones) than: *es más alto que su padre,* he is taller than his father. **3** (deseo, mandato): *¡que esperes un momento!,* wait a moment!; *¡que te diviertas!,* enjoy yourself! **4** (duda, extrañeza): *¿que no te hicieron pagar nada?,* (you say) they didn't make you pay anything? **5** (causal, consecutiva): *¡arriba, que ya son las ocho!,* get up, it's eight o'clock! **6** (tanto si ... como si ...) whether ... or not ...: *que llueva que no llueva, iremos de excursión,* whether it rains or not, we're going on a trip. **7** (reiterativo) and: *charla que charla se nos pasó la hora,* we were so busy talking that the hour just flew by. **8** (final) so that: *ven aquí que te vea bien,* come here so that I can see you properly. **9** fam (condicional) if: *que te gusta, te lo quedas; que no te gusta, lo cambias,* if you like it, keep it; if you don't, you can change it. **10** que no,

(adversativa) not: *justicia pido, que no gracia,* I want justice, not mercy.

● ¿a que no? / ¿a que sí?, right?, isn't that right? ‖ ¿a que no ...?, I bet you can't ...!: *a que no sabes la respuesta,* I bet you don't know the answer. ‖ ¡con lo que ...!, you know how much ...: *¡con lo que le gusta el queso y se lo han prohibido!,* you know how much he likes cheese, and now he's not allowed to have any! ‖ que si esto que si lo otro, what with one thing and the other: *que si esto, que si lo otro, total que no lo ha traído,* what with one thing and another, in the end he didn't bring it. ‖ que para qué, (para énfasis): *hace un frío que para qué,* it's really cold, it's so cold, it's freezing cold; *se da unos aires que para qué,* he puts on these ridiculous airs. ‖ que yo sepa, as far as I know. ‖ yo que tú ..., if I were you ...

qué 1 pron what: *no sé qué hacer,* I don't know what to do; *¿qué querías?,* what did you want? – **2** adj (cuál) which: *no sé qué libro quiere,* I don't know which book he wants. **3** (en frases interrogativas) how, what: *¿qué años tienes?,* how old are you?, *¿qué has dicho?,* what did you say? **4** (en frases exclamativas) how, what: *¡qué bonito!,* how nice!; *¡qué contenta estoy!,* I'm so happy!; *¡qué flor más bonita!,* what a lovely flower!; *¡qué pena!,* what a pity! **5** (cantidad) what: *¡qué de gente!,* what a crowd!

● no hay de qué, don't mention it. ‖ ¿qué hay?/¿qué tal?, fam how are things? ‖ ¡y qué!, fam so what!

quebrada f → **quebrado,-a**.

quebradero quebradero de cabeza, m fig worry, headache.

quebradizo,-a 1 adj (frágil) fragile, brittle; (pastel) short. **2** fig (enfermizo) unhealthy, sickly. **3** fig (débil moralmente) weak, frail.

quebrado,-a 1 pp → **quebrar**. – **2** adj (terreno) rugged, rough, uneven; (camino) tortuous. **3** FIN bankrupt: *este negocio está quebrado,* this business is bankrupt. **4** (pálido) pale, pallid. **5** (herniado) ruptured. **6** (número) fractional. – **7** m,f FIN bankrupt. – **8** quebrado, m MAT fraction. – **9** quebrada, f GEOL (depresión) depression; (paso) gorge, ravine.

quebradura 1 f (grieta) fissure, crack. **2** GEOL (depresión) depression; (paso) gorge, ravine. **3** (hernia) rupture.

quebrantado,-a 1 pp → **quebrantar**. – **2** adj (debilitado) feeble, weak.

quebrantador,-ra adj crushing.

quebrantahuesos 1 m (ave) lammergeier. **2** fig (persona pesada) bore, pest.

▲ pl quebrantahuesos.

quebrantamiento 1 m (rotura) breaking. **2** (debilitamiento) weakening. **3** (de una ley) violation, infringement.

quebrantaolas m breakwater.

▲ pl quebrantaolas.

quebrantar 1 t (cascar) to crack. **2** (romper) to break, shatter; (machacar) to grind. **3** (debilitar) to weaken. **4** fig (*salud, posición, fortuna*) to undermine, shatter. **5** *fig* (*incumplir*) to break, violate: *es la primera vez que quebranta la ley,* it's the first time he has broken the law. **6** *fig* (*suavizar*) to take the edge off, temper; (*ablandar*) to soften: *el sol ha quebrantado el frío,* the sun has taken the edge off the cold; *quebrantó su furor con una sonrisa,* he tempered his anger with a smile. **7** *fig* (*causar lástima*) to wound, shatter: *aquello me quebrantó el corazón,* that broke my heart. – **8 quebrantarse,** *p* (*cascarse*) to crack. **9** (*romperse*) to break. **10** (*la salud*) to be shattered: *se quebrantó con tantos esfuerzos,* he felt shattered after such hard work.

quebranto 1 *m fig* (*desaliento*) discouragement. **2** *fig* (*lástima*) pity. **3** *fig* (*pérdida*) severe loss; (*daño*) damage, harm. **4** *fig* (*aflicción*) grief, pain, sorrow.

quebrar 1 *t* (*romper, incumplir*) to break. **2** (*doblar el cuerpo*) to bend. **3** *fig* (*interrumpir*) to alter the course of, interrupt: *ese incidente quebró el curso de la discusión,* that incident altered the course of the discussion. **4** *fig* (*suavizar*) to soften; (*un color*) to fade. – **5** *i* FIN to go bankrupt. **6** *fig* (*flaquear*) to weaken. – **7 quebrarse,** *p* (*romperse*) to break. **8** (*herniarse*) to rupture os. **9** (*interrumpirse*) to be broken, open up: *la cordillera se quiebra a pocos kilómetros,* there is a break in the mountain range in a few kilometres. **10** *fig* (*ánimo*) to break, crack.
▲ *Conjugation model* |27|, *like acertar.*

queche *m* ketch.

quechemarín *m* ketch, yawl.

quechua 1 *adj* Quechua. – **2** *mf* (*persona*) Quechua. – **3** quechua, *m* (*idioma*) Quechua.

queda *f →* **quedo,-a.**

quedada *f →* **quedado,-a.**

quedado,-a 1 *pp →* **quedar.** – **2** *adj* lacking initiative. – **3** quedada, *f arg* trick.

quedamente *adv* (*suavemente*) softly; (*calladamente*) quietly.

quedar 1 *i* (*permanecer*) to remain, stay: *quedó quieto,* he remained still; *la carta quedó abierta,* the letter was left open. **2** *fig* (*terminar*) to end: *la discusión quedó aquí,* the discussion ended here. **3** (*cita*) to arrange to meet: *quedamos en el aeropuerto a las diez,* we arranged to meet at the airport at ten o'clock. **4** (*resultado de algo*) to be: *al morir sus padres quedó solo en la vida,* when his parents died he was left all alone in the world; *quedó ciego por culpa del accidente,* he went blind as a result of the accident; *te ha quedado muy bien la tarta,* your cake has turned out really well. **5** (*favorecer*) to look, fit: *el abrigo me queda grande,* the coat is too big for me; *esta falda no me queda bien,* this skirt doesn't fit me; *allí quedaría bien un cuadro,* a picture would look nice there; *¿qué tal me queda?,* does it suit me?, how does it look on me? **6** (*estar situado*) to be: *¿por dónde queda?,* whereabouts is it?; *eso queda por detrás del cine,* that's somewhere behind the cinema. **7** (*restar*) to be left, remain: *quedan tres pesetas,* there are three pesetas left; *después del incendio sólo quedan las cenizas,* after the fire only ashes remain. **8** (*faltar*) to be, be still: *queda mucho que hacer,* there's a lot to be done; *quedan cuatro kilómetros para llegar,* there are still four kilometres to go. **9** quedar en, (*convenir*) to agree to: *quedamos en volver más tarde,* we agreed to come back later; *quedamos en que la película no era buena,* we agreed that it wasn't a good film. **10** quedar por + *inf,* not to have been + *pp*: *la cama quedó por hacer,* the bed had not been made, the bed was left unmade; *quedan esos platos por lavar,* there are still those dishes to be washed up; *queda por ver si llegarán a algún acuerdo,* it remains

to be seen whether they will come to some agreement. **11** quedar + *gerundio,* to be, remain: *cuando me fui el niño quedaba durmiendo,* when I left the child was sleeping. – **12 quedarse,** *p* (*permanecer*) to remain, stay, be: *se quedaron una semana,* they stayed for a week; *Juan se ha quedado en casa,* Juan stayed at home. **13** (*resultado de algo*) to be, remain: *se quedó sin trabajo,* she lost her job; *nos quedamos sin dinero,* we ran out of money; *quedó entusiasmado,* he was delighted. **14** *euf* (*morirse*) to die. **15** (*mar, viento*) to become calm; (*viento*) to drop. **16 quedarse con,** (*retener algo*) to keep: *quédese con el cambio,* keep the change.
● **ahí quedó la cosa,** that's the way it was left. ‖ *¿en qué quedamos?,* so what's it to be? ‖ **no quedar títere con cabeza,** *fam* to leave nothing intact. ‖ "queda de usted atentamente ...", (*en cartas*) "Yours faithfully ...". ‖ **quedar a deber algo,** to owe sth. ‖ **quedar algn. bien/mal,** to make a good/bad impression. ‖ **quedar como un señor/una señora,** *fam* to create a very good impression. ‖ **quedarse atrás,** *fig* to be left behind. ‖ **quedarse con algn.,** *fam* to make a fool of sb., have sb. on. ‖ **quedarse con la boca abierta,** *fig* to be dumbfounded, be stunned. ‖ **quedarse con las ganas de algo,** *fig* to go without sth. ‖ **quedarse en blanco,** to go blank. ‖ **quedarse sin algo,** to run out of sth. ‖ **quedarse sin blanca,** *fam* to be broke. ‖ **quedarse tan tranquilo,-a,** *fam* not to bat an eyelid. ‖ **quedar en nada,** to come to nothing.

quedo,-a 1 *adj* quiet, still. **2** (*voz*) low. – **3 queda,** *f desus* curfew. – **4** quedo, *adv* (*calladamente*) quietly; (*suavemente*) softly.
● **de quedo,** slowly. ‖ **quedo a quedo,** slowly.

quehacer *m* task, chore, job.
■ **quehaceres domésticos,** housework *sing,* household chores.
▲ *Also used in pl with the same meaning.*

queimada *f hot punch made with grape spirit, typical of Galicia.*

queja 1 *f* (*descontento*) complaint. **2** (*de dolor*) moan, groan.
● **dar queja de algo/algn.,** to complaint about sth./sb. ‖ **presentar una queja,** JUR to lodge a complaint. ‖ **no tener queja de algn.,** to have no complaints about sb.

quejarse 1 *p* (*de descontento*) to complain (**de**, about): *¡no te quejes!,* stop complaining! **2** (*de dolor*) to moan, groan.

quejica 1 *adj fam* complaining, grumpy, querulous. – **2** *mf* moaner, grouse.

quejicoso,-a *adj* grumpy, querulous.

quejido *m* groan, moan.
● **dar quejidos,** to groan, moan.

quejigo *m* gall oak.

quejo *m* jaw, jawbone.

quejoso,-a *adj* complaining: *no tiene por qué estar quejoso,* he has nothing to complain about.

quejumbroso,-a 1 *adj* (*persona*) whining, plaintive. **2** (*tono*) querulous: *lo dijo con tono quejumbroso,* he said it in a querulous tone.

quelonio *adj* chelonian.

quema 1 *f* (*acción, efecto*) burning. **2** (*fuego*) fire.
● **huir de la quema,** to beat it, flee.

quemadero *m* incinerator.

quemado,-a 1 *pp →* **quemar.** – **2** *adj* burnt; (*por el sol*) sunburnt. **3** *fig* (*resentido*) embittered. **4** *fam* (*acabado*) spent, burnt-out: *este humorista está muy quemado,* this comedian is burnt-out. **5** *arg* (*sexualmente*) hot.

quemador 488

● ir quemado,-a, *arg* to be dying for it. ‖ oler a quemado, to have a burnt smell: *aquí huele a quemado*, there's a smell of burning in here; *¿hueles a quemado?*, can you smell burning? ‖ saber a quemado, to taste burnt, have a burnt taste.

quemador,-ra 1 *adj* (*que quema*) burning. 2 (*incendiario*) incendiary. – 3 *m,f* (*que quema*) burner. 4 (*incendiario*) arsonist, fire-raiser. – 5 quemador, *m* burner.

quemadura 1 *f* (*acción*) burning. 2 (*herida*) burn; (*de sol*) sunburn; (*escaldadura*) scald. 3 (*de plantas*) scorch.

quemar 1 *t* (*gen*) to burn; (*plants*) to scorch: *quemó un leño*, she burnt a log; *la lejía quemó su ropa*, the bleach burnt his clothes. 2 (*incendiar*) to set on fire. 3 (*destilar*) to distil. 4 *fig* (*dinero*) to throw away, squander. 5 *fam* (*acabar*) to burn out: *tanta popularidad lo ha quemado*, so much popularity burnt him out; *dar clase quema mucho*, teaching burns you out. – 6 *i* (*estar muy caliente*) to be burning hot: *esta sopa quema*, this soup is burning hot. – 7 quemarse, *p* (*persona*) to burn os.; (*cosa*) to be burnt: *se ha quemado la carne*, the meat got burnt; *el niño se quemó los dedos*, the boy burnt his fingers. 8 *fig* (*deteriorarse el prestigio*) to burn os. out; (*en política*) to be a has-been. 9 *fig* (*ir a acertar*) to get warm: *¡que te quemas!*, you're getting warm!

quemarropa a quemarropa, *loc adv* at close range, at point-blank range: *le dispararon a quemarropa*, he was shot at point-blank range.

quemazón 1 *f* (*calor*) intense heat. 2 *fig* (*ardor*) burning sensation; (*picor*) itch. 3 *fig* (*dicho picante*) cutting remark.

quena *f* Indian flute.

quepis *m* kepi.
▲ *pl* quepis.

quepo *pres indic* → caber.

queratina *f* keratin.

querella 1 *f* JUR action, lawsuit. 2 (*queja*) complaint. 3 (*enfrentamiento*) dispute, quarrel.
● presentar una querella contra algn., to bring an action against sb., take legal action against sb., take sb. to court.

querellante *mf* plaintiff.

querellarse *p* JUR to take legal action (**contra**, against): *se querelló contra su ex marido*, she took her ex-husband to court.

querencia 1 *f* (*acción*) love. 2 (*inclinación del animal*) homing instinct; (*inclinación del hombre*) homesickness. 3 (*lugar del animal*) lair, haunt; (*lugar del hombre*) home ground.
● buscar la querencia, to home, head for home.

querendón,-ona *m,f* lover.

querer 1 *t* (*amar*) to love: *Juan y Elena se quieren*, Juan and Elena love each other. 2 (*desear*) to want: *quiero que vengas*, I want you to come; *quiere ser ingeniera*, she wants to be an engineer; *¿cuánto quieres por la falda?*, how much do you want for the skirt?; *como tú quieras*, as you wish; *lo hizo sin querer*, he didn't mean to do it; *quieras o no, iremos*, (whether you) like it or not, we're going; *quiere ser un hombre y aún es un niño*, he's trying to be a man, but he's still a child. 3 (*buscar*) to be asking for, be looking for: *este chico quiere pelea*, this boy is asking for trouble. 4 (*petición*) would: *¿quieres venir?*, would you like to come?; *¿quiere cerrar la puerta?*, would you mind closing the door?, could you close the door? 5 (*requerir*) to need: *este traje quiere un buen planchado*, this suit needs ironing. 6 (*verificarse*) may, might: *parece que quiere llover*, it looks like it might rain. – 7 *m* love, affection.

● está como quiere, *fam* he/she is gorgeous. ‖ hacer algo queriendo, to do sth. deliberately, do sth. on purpose. ‖ hacerse querer, to have winning ways. ‖ ¡por lo que más quieras!, for heaven's sake! ‖ querer es poder, where there's a will there's a way. ‖ quien bien te quiere te hará llorar, you've got to be cruel to be kind. ‖ quien quiera que, whoever. ‖ quiero y no puedo, *fig* I would if I could, but I can't: *es de quiero y no puedo*, it doesn't quite make it, it's not quite right, it falls short. ‖ sí, quiero, (*en una boda*) I do.
▲ *Conjugation model* [80]. *In* 6 *only used in the 3rd person. It does not take a subject.*

querido,-a 1 *pp* → querer. – 2 *adj* (*amado*) dear, beloved; (*en carta*) dear. – 3 *m,f* (*amante*) lover; (*mujer*) mistress. 4 *fam* (*apelativo*) darling.

quermes *m* kermes.
▲ *pl* quermes.

quermés *f* kermis.

queroseno *m* kerosene.

querré *fut* → querer.

querube *m* cherub.

querubín *m* cherub.

quesadilla 1 *f* (*pastel de queso y masa*) cheesecake. 2 (*pastel dulce*) sweet pie.

quesera *f* → quesero,-a.

quesería *f* dairy.

quesero,-a 1 *adj* cheese. 2 (*que le gusta*) cheese-loving. – 3 *m,f* (*que lo hace*) cheese maker. 4 (*que lo vende*) cheese seller. 5 (*que le gusta*) cheese-lover. – 6 quesera, *f* (*fábrica*) cheese factory. 7 (*para servirlo*) cheese dish and cover.

quesito *m* cheese portion.

queso *m* cheese.
● darla con queso, *fam* to cheat, trick.
■ queso de bola, Edam cheese. ‖ queso de cabra, goat's cheese. ‖ queso de cerdo, brawn, US headcheese. ‖ queso en lonchas, cheese slices *pl*. ‖ queso rallado, grated cheese.

quetzal *m* quetzal.

quevedos *mpl* pince-nez *sing*.

quiá *interj* no!, surely not!, never!

quianti *m* Chianti.

quiasma *m* chiasma.

quiché 1 *adj* Quiché. – 2 *m,f* Quiché.

quichua *adj-m,f* → quechua.

quicial *m* hinging post.

quicio *m* pivot hole.
● estar fuera de quicio, *fam* to be beside os. ‖ sacar a algn. de quicio, *fam* to get on sb.'s nerves.

quico *m* roasted salted corn.

Quico ponerse como el Quico, *loc* to stuff os.

quid *m* crux: *éste es el quid de la cuestión*, this is the crux of the matter.
● dar en el quid, to hit the nail on the head.
▲ *Only used in singular.*

quídam 1 *m fam pey* (*sujeto cualquiera*) so-and-so. 2 *fam pey* (*sujeto insignificante*) nobody, nonentity.
▲ *Only used in singular.*

quiebra 1 *f* (*rotura*) break, crack. 2 (*bancarrota*) failure, bankruptcy; (*crack*) crash, collapse: *el último director llevó la empresa a la quiebra*, the last manager led the company into bankruptcy. 3 (*pérdida*) loss. 4 GEOG gorge. 5 *fig* (*fracaso*) failure.

quiebro 1 *m* (*en tauromaquia*) dodge. 2 MÚS trill.
● hacer un quiebro, to dodge, avoid.

quien 1 *pron* (*sujeto*) who: *me encontré a Toni, quien me dijo que estabas enfermo*, I met Toni, who told me you

were ill. **2** (*complemento*) who, whom: *las personas a quienes me encontré ayer están aquí,* the people (whom) I met yesterday are here; *se lo das a quien quieras,* you can give it to whoever you want. **3** (*indefinido*) whoever, anyone who: *quien sepa la respuesta que me lo diga,* anyone who knows the answer tell me.
● **como quien,** as if: *hace como quien no ve,* she acts as if she can't see. ‖ **quien más quien menos,** *fig* everybody.
▲ *pl* **quienes.**

quién I *pron* (*sujeto*) who: *¿quién te lo dijo?,* who told you? **2** (*complemento*) who, whom: *¿con quién hablas?,* who are you talking to?; *¿para quién es?,* who is it for? **3 de quién,** (*posesivo*) whose: *¿de quién es esto?,* whose is this?; *¿de quién es ese coche?,* whose car is that?
▲ *pl* **quiénes.**

quienquiera *pron* whoever: *entre, quienquiera que sea,* come in, whoever you may be.
▲ *pl* **quienesquiera.**

quiescente *adj* still.

quietismo I *m* (*inercia*) inertia, stagnation. **2** REL quietism.

quieto,-a I *adj* (*sin movimiento*) still, motionless: *¡estáte quieta!,* keep still!, don't move! **2** *fig* (*sosegado*) quiet, calm: *el mar estaba quieto,* the sea was calm.

quietud I *f* (*sin movimiento*) stillness. **2** *fig* (*sosiego*) calmness, calm.

quif *m arg* hashish, hash.

quijada *f* jaw, jawbone.

quijera *f* cheek strap.

quijotada *f* quixotic act.

quijote I *adj fig* quixotic. – **2** *m fig* quixotic man.
■ **Don Quijote,** Don Quixote.

quijotería *f* quixotic act.

quijotescamente *adv* quixotically.

quijotesco,-a *adj* quixotic.

quijotismo *m* quixotism.

quilate I *m* (*unidad de peso*) carat. **2** (*unidad del oro*) carat (US karat).
● **de muchos quilates,** *fig* of great value.

quilla *f* keel.

quilo[1] *m* (*líquido*) chyle.
● **sudar el quilo,** *fam fig* to sweat blood.

quilo[2] *m* → **kilo.**

quilogramo *m* → **kilogramo.**

quilométrico,-a *adj* → **kilométrico,-a.**

quimbambas **las quimbambas,** *fpl fam* the back of beyond, the middle of nowhere: *se fue a vivir a las quimbambas,* he went to live in the back of beyond.

quimera I *f* (*mitología*) chimera. **2** *fig* (*ilusión*) wild fancy, fantasy, pipe dream. **3** *fig* (*preocupación*) worry; (*sospecha infundada*) unfounded suspicion.

quimérico,-a *adj* unrealistic, fantastic.

química *f* → **químico,-a.**

químico,-a I *adj* chemical. – **2** *m,f* chemist. – **3** química, *f* chemistry.

quimioterapia *f* chemotherapy.

quimo *m* chyme.

quimono *m* kimono.

quina I *f* (*corteza*) cinchona bark. **2** (*líquido*) quinine.
● **tragar quina,** *fig* to swallow hard, grin and bear it.

quincalla *f* (*objetos de metal*) cheap metalware; (*baratija*) trinket.

quincallería *f* (*tienda - de objetos de metal*) hardware shop; (*- de baratijas*) cheap jewellery shop.

quincallero,-a *m,f* (*de objetos de metal*) seller of cheap metalware; (*de baratijas*) trinket seller.

quince I *adj* (*cardinal*) fifteen; (*ordinal*) fifteenth. – **2** *m* fifteen.
■ **quince días,** fortnight *sing.*
▲ See also **seis.**

quinceañero,-a I *adj* (*de quince años*) fifteen-year-old. **2** (*adolescente*) teenage. – **3** *m,f* (*de quince años*) fifteen-year-old. **4** (*adolescente*) teenager; (*aficionado a música pop*) teenybopper: *el cine estaba lleno de quinceañeros,* the cinema was full of teenagers.

quinceavo,-a I *adj* fifth. – **2** *m,f* fifth.

quincena I *f* (*tiempo*) fortnight: *la primera quincena de mayo,* the first two weeks in May. **2** (*paga*) fortnightly pay.

quincenal *adj* fortnightly, every two weeks.

quincuagenario,-a I *adj* quinquagenarian. – **2** *m,f* quinquagenarian, person in his/her fifties.

quincuagésimo,-a I *adj* fiftieth. – **2** *m,f* fiftieth.
▲ See also **sexto,-a.**

quingentésimo,-a I *adj* five hundredth. – **2** *m,f* five hundredth.
▲ See also **sexto,-a.**

quiniela *f* football pools *pl.*
● **hacer la/una quiniela,** to do the pools.

quinielista *mf* person who does the pools.

quinielístico,-a *adj* to do with football pools: *fue una jornada quinielística excelente,* it was a great day for the football pools.

quinientista *adj* fifteenth-century.

quinientos,-as I *adj* (*cardinal*) five hundred; (*ordinal*) five-hundredth: *dos mil quinientos,* two thousand five hundred, twenty-five hundred; *quinientos tres,* five hundred and three. – **2 quinientos,** *m* (*número*) five hundred.
● **a las quinientas,** *fam* very late.
▲ See also **seis.**

quinina *f* quinine.

quino *m* cinchona.

quinqué *m* oil lamp.
▲ *pl* **quinqués.**

quinquenal *adj* quinquennial, five-year: *fue un plan quinquenal,* it was a five-year plan.

quinquenio *m* quinquennium, five-year period.

quinqui *mf fam* delinquent, petty criminal.

quinta *f* → **quinto,-a.**

quintacolumnista I *adj* fifth columnist. – **2** *mf* fifth columnist.

quintaesencia *f* quintessence.

quintaesenciar *t* to quintessence, quintessentialize.
▲ Conjugation model [12], like **cambiar.**

quintal *m* quintal (46 kilogrammes).
■ **quintal métrico,** quintal (100 *kg*).

quintar I *t* (*sacar por sorteo*) to take one in five of. **2** (*para el servicio militar*) to conscript, US draft.

quinteto *m* quintet.

quintilla *f* five-line stanza.

quintillizo,-a *m,f* quintuplet, quin.

Quintín **armarse la de San Quintín,** *loc fam* to be a hell of a ruckus: *después del concierto se armó la de San Quintín,* after the concert all hell broke loose.

quinto,-a I *adj* fifth. – **2** *m,f* fifth. – **3 quinto,** *m* MIL conscript, recruit. **4** *fam* (*de cerveza*) small bottle of beer (= 20 *cl*). – **5 quinta,** *f* (*casa*) country house. **6** (*reemplazo militar*) call-up, conscript, US draft. **7** MÚS fifth.

● entrar en quintas, to be called up, us be drafted. ‖
ser de la misma quinta, *fig* to be the same age.

▲ *See also* **sexto,-a.**

quintuplicación *f* quintupling.

quintuplicar *t* to quintuple.

▲ *Conjugation model* [1], *like* **sacar.**

quíntuplo,-a 1 *adj* quintuple. – **2 quíntuplo,** *m* quintuple.

quinzavo,-a *adj-m,f* → **quinceavo,-a.**

quiñón *m* piece of land.

quiosco *m* kiosk; (*de periódicos*) newsstand, newspaper stand; (*de música*) bandstand.

quiosquero,-a *m,f* newsagent: *su tío es quiosquero,* her uncle has a newsstand.

quiqui *m child's hairstyle in the form of a tuft.*

quiquiriquí 1 *m* cock-a-doodle-doo. **2** *fig* (*gallito*) cock of the walk. **3** (*tupé*) quiff.

▲ *pl* quiquiriquíes.

quirófano *m* operating theatre (us theater).

quiromancia *f* palmistry, chiromancy.

quiromancía *f* → **quiromancia.**

quiromántico,-a *m,f* palmist, chiromancer.

quiromasaje *m* chiropractic.

quiromasijista *m,f* chiropractor.

quirúrgico,-a *adj* surgical.

quise *pt indef* → **querer.**

quisicosa *f fam* puzzle, riddle.

quisque cada quisque / todo quisque, *pron* everybody, everyone.

quisqui *pron* → **quisque.**

quisquilla 1 *f* (*camarón*) (common) prawn. **2** (*insignificancia*) triviality, trifle.

quisquilloso,-a 1 *adj* finicky, fussy, touchy. – **2** *m,f* fusspot.

quiste *m* cyst.

quita *f* partial acquittance.

quitaesmaltes *m* nail varnish remover, nail polish remover.

▲ *pl* quitaesmaltes.

quitamanchas *m* stain remover.

▲ *pl* quitamanchas.

quitamiedos *m* handrail.

▲ *pl* quitamiedos.

quitanieves *m* snowplough (us snowplow).

▲ *pl* quitanieves.

quitapón *m* ornament (*on horse's head collar*).

● de quitapón, *fam* detachable, removable.

▲ *pl* quitapones.

quitar 1 *t* (*separar*) to remove, take off: *le quitó la piel a la pera,* he peeled the pear; *quita la tapa,* remove the lid. **2** (*sacar*) to take off, take out; (*prendas*) to take off;

(*tiempo*) to take up: *el médico quitó los puntos al enfermo,* the doctor took out the patient's stitches; *quítate los zapatos,* take your shoes off. **3** (*apartar*) to take away, take off: *quita eso de ahí,* clear that away. **4** (*hacer desaparecer*) to remove; (*dolor*) to relieve; (*sed*) to quench: *si lo comes te quitará el apetito,* if you eat it, it will spoil your appetite; *eso te quitará el hambre,* that'll stop you feeling hungry; *el café me quita el sueño,* coffee keeps me awake. **5** (*despojar*) to take; (*robar*) to steal: *me han quitado la cartera,* my wallet's been stolen; *le quitó la vida,* he killed him. **6** (*restar*) to subtract; (*descontar*) to take off. **7** (*prohibir*) to forbid, rule out: *me han quitado el alcohol,* I've been told to cut out alcohol. **8** (*impedir*) to prevent: *eso no quita para que se lo diga,* that's no reason not to tell him. **9** (*disminuir*) to take away: *eso no le quita mérito a la obra,* that doesn't take anything away from the work. **10** *fam* (*radio, agua, etc*) to turn off. – **11 quitarse,** *p* (*desaparecer*) to go away, come out: *se me han quitado las ganas,* I don't feel like it any more; *esa mancha no se quita,* that stain won't come out. **12 quitarse (de, -),** (*del juego, bebida, etc*) to give up: *se quitó de fumar,* she gave up smoking.

● de quita y pon, (*que se desprende*) removable, detachable; (*no permanente*) temporary. ‖ ¡quita/quítate de ahí!, move!, get away! ‖ quitando ..., except ... ‖ quitar de delante, to clear away. ‖ quitar el hipo, *fig* to take one's breath away. ‖ quitar el sueño, (*desvelar*) to keep awake; (*preocupar*) to worry: *eso no me quitará el sueño,* I won't lose any sleep over that. ‖ quitar importancia a algo, to play sth. down. ‖ quitar la mesa, to clear the table. ‖ quitar las ganas a algn., to put sb. off. ‖ quitarse algo/a algn. de encima, to get rid of sth./sb. ‖ quitarse años, *fig* to lie about one's age. ‖ quitarse la vida, *euf* to commit suicide; (*admirar*) to admire.

quitasol *m* parasol, sunshade.

quite 1 *m* (*acción de quitar*) removal. **2** (*en esgrima*) parry. **3** (*en tauromaquia*) *distraction of the bull to allow the escape of another bullfighter.*

● estar al quite, *fig* to be on hand, be ready and waiting.

quiteño,-a 1 *adj* of Quito, from Quito. – **2** *m,f* person from Quito, inhabitant of Quito.

quitina *f* chitin.

quitinoso,-a *adj* chitinous.

quito,-a *adj* free, exempt (**de,** from).

quivi *m* kiwi fruit.

quizá *adv* → **quizás.**

quizás *adv* perhaps, maybe: *quizás venga hoy,* maybe she'll come today, she may come today.

quórum *m* quorum.

▲ *pl* quórum.

R

R, r *f* (*la letra*) R, r.

R. *abr* (*reverendo,-a*) Reverend; (*abreviatura*) Revd.

rabadán *m* head shepherd.

rabadilla 1 *f* ANAT COCCYX. **2** (*de animal*) rump.

rabanero,-a 1 *adj fig* (*vestido*) short. **2** *fig* (*desvergonzado*) insolent, cheeky.

rabanillo *m* wild radish.

rabaniza *f* (*simiente*) radish seed.

rábano *m* radish.

● **¡me importa un rábano!**, I don't give a toss!, I couldn't care less! ‖ **tomar el rábano por las hojas,** *fam* to get the wrong end of the stick. ‖ **¡un rábano! / ¡y un rábano!,** no way!

■ **rábano blanco / rábano picante,** horseradish. ‖ **rábano silvestre,** wild horseradish.

rabel *m* rebec.

rabí *m* rabbi.

▲ *pl* **rabíes.**

rabia 1 *f* MED rabies. **2** *fig* (*enfado*) rage, fury, anger.

● **dar rabia,** to make furious: *aquella pregunta me dio mucha rabia,* that question made me absolutely furious. ‖ **¡qué rabia!,** *fam* how annoying! ‖ **tener rabia a algn.,** not to be able to stand the sight of sb.

rabiar 1 *i* MED to have rabies. **2** (*enfadarse*) to rage, be furious: *Elena está que rabia,* Elena is furious. **3** *fig* (*padecer*) to suffer (**de,** from): *rabiar de hambre,* to be dying of hunger; *rabiar de dolor,* to writhe in pain.

● **a rabiar,** *fam* a lot, very much: *el niño lloraba a rabiar,* the boy cried himself sick. ‖ **estar a rabiar con algn.,** to be furious at sb. ‖ **hacer rabiar a algn.,** to make sb. see red. ‖ **rabiar por,** to be dying for, long for: *rabiaba por tener un coche nuevo,* she was dying for a new car.

▲ *Conjugation model* [12], *like* **cambiar.**

rabiatar *t* to tie by the tail.

rábico,-a *adj* rabid.

rabieta *f fam* tantrum.

● **coger una rabieta,** *fam* to throw a tantrum.

rabilargo,-a 1 *adj* long-tailed. – **2 rabilargo,** *m* (*ave*) magpie.

rabillo 1 *m* (*pecíolo*) stalk, stem. **2** (*cizaña*) darnel. **3** COST tab, strap.

● **mirar por el rabillo del ojo,** to look out of the corner of one's eye: *me miró por el rabillo del ojo,* she looked at me out of the corner of her eye.

■ **rabillo del ojo,** corner of one's eye.

rabínico,-a *adj* rabbinical.

rabino *m* rabbi.

rabión *m* rapids *pl.*

rabiosamente *adv* furiously.

rabioso,-a 1 *adj* MED rabid. **2** *fig* (*airado*) furious, angry. **3** *fig* (*excesivo*) terrible, intense. **4** *fam* (*color*) shocking, gaudy, garish; (*sabor*) very hot.

● **ponerse rabioso,-a,** to fly into a rage.

rabo *m* tail.

● **aún falta el rabo por desollar,** *fam* the worst is yet to come. ‖ **con el rabo entre piernas,** *fam fig* with one's tail between one's legs.

rabón,-ona *adj* (*de rabo corto*) bobtail; (*sin rabo*) tailless.

rabosear *t* to spoil.

racanear 1 *i fam* (*ser tacaño*) to be mean, be stingy. **2** *fam* (*ser vago*) to idle, slack.

racaneo *m fam* → **racanería.**

racanería 1 *f fam* (*tacañería*) meanness, stinginess. **2** *fam* (*holgazanería*) idleness, laziness.

rácano,-a 1 *adj fam* (*tacaño*) mean, stingy. **2** *fam* (*holgazán*) idle, lazy.

RACE *abr* AUTO (*Real Automóvil Club de España*) Spanish automobile club.

racer 1 *m* (*caballo*) racehorse. **2** (*barco*) sailing ship.

racha 1 *f* (*ráfaga*) gust, squall. **2** *fig* (*período*) spell, patch. **3** *fig* (*serie*) string, run, series *sing: hubo una racha de incendios,* there was a series of fires.

● **a rachas,** in fits and starts, on and off. ‖ **tener una buena racha,** to have a run of good luck. ‖ **tener una mala racha,** to go through a bad patch.

racheado,-a *adj* gusty.

racial *adj* racial, race: *disturbios raciales,* race riots.

racimo *m* bunch, cluster.

raciocinio 1 *m* (*razón*) reason. **2** (*argumento*) reasoning.

ración 1 *f* (*parte*) ration, portion, share. **2** (*de comida*) portion, serving, helping: *"cuatro raciones",* "serves four". **3** (*prebenda*) prebend.

racionado,-a *adj* rationed.

racional *adj* rational.

racionalidad *f* rationality.

racionalismo *m* rationalism.

racionalista 1 *adj* rationalist. – **2** *mf* rationalist.

racionalización *f* rationalization.

racionalizar *t* to rationalize.

▲ *Conjugation model* [4], *like* **realizar.**

racionalmente *adv* rationally, reasonably.

racionamiento *m* rationing.

racionar 1 *t* (*limitar*) to ration. **2** MIL (*distribuir*) to ration out.

racismo *m* racism, racialism.

racista 1 *adj* racist, racialist. – **2** *mf* racist, racialist.

racor *m* connecter, adapter, adaptor.

rada *f* bay, inlet.

radar *m* radar.

▲ *pl* **radares.**

radiación *f* radiation.

radiactividad *f* radioactivity.

radiactivo,-a *adj* radioactive.

radiado,-a 1 *pp* → **radiar.** – **2** *adj* BOT ZOOL radiate. **3** RAD TV broadcast.

radiador *m* radiator.

radial *adj* radial.
radián *m* radian.
radiante *adj fig* radiant: *radiante de alegría,* radiant with joy.
radiar 1 *i* (*irradiar*) to radiate, irradiate. – 2 *t* (*irradiar*) to radiate, irradiate. 3 (*retransmitir*) to broadcast, transmit, radio. 4 MED to X-ray.
▲ *Conjugation model* [12], *like cambiar.*
radicación 1 *f* (*instalación*) taking root, settling down. 2 (*ubicación*) setting, location.
radical 1 *adj* radical. – 2 *m* GRAM MAT root, radical.
radicalismo *m* radicalism.
radicalizar 1 *t* to radicalize. 2 (*postura*) to harden. – 3 radicalizarse, *p* (*conflicto*) to intensify. 4 (*postura*) to harden.
▲ *Conjugation model* [4], *like realizar.*
radicalmente *adv* radically.
radicar 1 *i* (*encontrarse*) to be (**en,** in), be situated (**en,** in): *el documento radica en la notaría,* the document is in the notary's office. 2 *fig* (*consistir*) to lie (**en,** in), stem (**en,** from): *el problema radica en la falta de solidaridad,* the problem lies in the lack of solidarity. 3 (*arraigar*) to take root. – 4 radicarse, *p* (*arraigarse*) to take root. 5 (*establecerse*) to settle (down).
▲ *Conjugation model* [1], *like sacar.*
radio[1] 1 *m* GEOM radius: *en un radio de 10 metros,* within a radius of 10 metres. 2 (*de rueda*) spoke. 3 (*campo*) scope.
■ **radio de acción** *fig* field of action, scope.
radio[2] 1 *f* (*radiodifusión*) radio: *lo oí por la radio,* I heard it on the radio. 2 (*aparato*) radio, wireless. – 3 *mf fam* (*persona*) radio operator.
■ **radio galera,** crystal set. ‖ **radio pirata,** pirata radio station.
radio[3] *m* QUÍM radium.
radioactividad *f* radioactivity.
radioactivo,-a *adj* radioactive.
radioaficionado,-a *m,f* radio ham.
radiobiología *f* radiobiology.
radiocasete *m* radio-cassette, radio-cassette player.
radiocomunicación *f* radio communication.
radiocontrol *m* radiocontrol.
radiodespertador *m* radio alarm clock.
radiodifusión *f* broadcasting.
radioelectricidad *f* radioelectricity.
radioescucha *mf* listener, US auditor.
radiofonía *f* radio, radiotelephony.
radiofónico,-a *adj* radio: *concurso radiofónico,* radio quiz programme (US program).
radiófono *m* radiophone.
radiofotografía *f* radiophotograph.
radiofrecuencia *f* radio frequency.
radiografía 1 *f* (*técnica*) radiography. 2 (*imagen*) X-ray, radiograph.
● **hacerse una radiografía,** to have an X-ray taken.
radiografiar *t* to X-ray.
▲ *Conjugation model* [13], *like desviar.*
radiología *f* radiology.
radiólogo,-a *m,f* radiologist.
radiometría *f* radiometry.
radiómetro *m* radiometer.
radionovela *f* serial.
radiorreceptor *m* radio, radio set, radio receiver, wireless, wireless set.
radioscopia *f* radioscopy.

radiotaxi *m* radio taxi, radio cab.
radiotecnia *f* radiotechnology.
radiotelefonía *f* radiotelephony.
radiotelefónico,-a *adj* radiotelephonic.
radioteléfono *m* radiotelephone.
radiotelegrafista *mf* radio operator, wireless operator.
radiotelegrafía *f* radiotelegraphy.
radiotelegráfico,-a *adj* radiotelegraphic.
radiotelescopio *m* radio telescope.
radiotelevisión *f* radio and television.
radioterapia *f* radiotherapy, radium therapy.
radiotransmisión *f* radio transmission, broadcasting.
radiotransmisor *m* radio transmitter.
radiotransmitir *t* to broadcast.
radioyente *mf* listener.
radón *m* radon.
RAE *abr* (*Real Academia Española*) Spanish royal academy.
raedura *f* scrapings *pl.*
raer *t* to scrape (off).
▲ *Conjugation model* [81].
ráfaga 1 *f* (*de viento*) gust, squall. 2 (*de disparos*) burst. 3 (*de luz*) flash.
rafia *f* raffia.
raglán *adj* raglan: *mangas raglán,* raglan sleeves.
▲ *pl raglán.*
ragú *m* ragout.
raid 1 *m* (*incursión*) raid. 2 (*vuelo a gran distancia*) long-distance flight, long-haul flight.
■ **raid aéreo,** air raid.
▲ *pl raids.*
raído,-a 1 *pp* → **raer.** – 2 *adj* (*deteriorado*) threadbare, worn. 3 *fig* (*descarado*) shameless, cheeky.
raigambre 1 *f* (*raíces*) roots *pl,* root system. 2 *fig* tradition, history.
● **de honda raigambre,** deeply-rooted.
rail *m* rail.
raíl *m* rail.
raíz *f* root.
● **a raíz de,** *fig* as a result of. ‖ **arrancar de raíz,** to pull up by the roots, uproot; *fig* to eradicate. ‖ **cortar algo de raíz,** (*erradicar*) to root out sth.; (*abortar*) to nip sth. in the bud. ‖ **de raíz,** entirely. ‖ **echar raíces,** (*planta*) to take root; (*persona*) to settle, put down roots.
■ **raíz cuadrada,** square root. ‖ **raíz cúbica,** cube root.
▲ *pl raíces.*
raja 1 *f* (*corte*) cut, slit. 2 (*hendidura*) crack, split. 3 (*tajada*) slice.
rajá *m* rajah.
▲ *pl rajaes.*
rajada *f tabú* → **rajado,-a.**
rajado,-a 1 *pp* → **rajar.** – 2 *adj fam* (*que falta a su palabra*) who backs out. 3 *fam* (*cobarde*) yellow. – 4 *m,f fam* (*que falta a su palabra*) quitter. 5 *fam* (*cobarde*) chicken, coward.
rajadura *f* crack, split.
rajar 1 *t* (*hender*) to split, crack. 2 (*hacer tajadas*) to slice. 3 *arg* (*acuchillar*) to cut up. – 4 *i fam fig* (*jactarse*) to show off, boast. 5 *fam fig* (*hablar mucho*) to chatter, babble on. 6 *fam fig* (*desacreditar*) to criticize. – 7 rajarse, *p* (*partirse*) to split, crack. 8 *fam* (*desistir*) to back out, quit. 9 *fam* (*acobardarse*) to chicken out.
rajatabla *a* rajatabla, *loc adv* to the letter, strictly.
ralea *f pey* type, sort, kind: *ellas son de la misma ralea,* they're two of a kind, they're birds of a feather.

ralentí *m* CINEM slow motion.
● **al ralentí,** CINEM in slow motion; AUTO ticking over.
ralentizar *t* to slow down.
rallado,-a 1 *pp* → **rallar.** – 2 *adj (queso etc)* grated.
rallador *m* grater.
ralladura *f* grated rind: *ralladura de limón,* grated lemon rind.
rallar *t* to grate.
rally *m* rally.
▲ *pl* **rallys.**
ralo,-a 1 *adj (pelo)* sparse, thin. **2** *(dientes)* with gaps between them.
rama *f* branch.
● **andarse por las ramas / irse por las ramas,** *fam fig* to beat about the bush. ‖ **en rama,** raw: *canela en rama,* cinnamon stick.
ramadán *m* Ramadan.
ramaje *m* foliage, branches *pl.*
ramal 1 *m (de cuerda)* strand. **2** *(de camino etc)* branch.
ramalazo 1 *m fam fig (ataque)* fit. **2** *fam pey (apariencia de homosexual)* effeminacy.
● **tener un ramalazo de locura,** to be a little mad, have a streak of madness.
rambla 1 *f (lecho de agua)* watercourse, channel. **2** *(paseo)* boulevard, avenue.
ramera *f* whore, prostitute.
ramificación *f* ramification.
ramificarse *p* to ramify, branch (out).
▲ *Conjugation model* |1|, *like* **sacar.**
ramillete 1 *m* posy. **2** *fig (conjunto)* bunch, group, collection.
ramiza *f* branches *pl.*
ramo 1 *m (de flores)* bunch, bouquet. **2** *(de árbol)* branch. **3** *fig (sector)* field: *el ramo de la alimentación,* the food sector, the food industry.
ramojo *m* loose branches *pl,* sticks *pl.*
ramoso,-a *adj* with many branches.
rampa[1] *f (calambre)* cramp.
rampa[2] *f (pendiente)* ramp.
■ **rampa de lanzamiento,** launching pad.
rampante *adj* rampant, blatant.
ramplón,-ona *adj fig* coarse, vulgar.
ramplonería *f* coarseness, vulgarity.
rana *f* frog.
● **salir rana,** *fam* to be a let-down: *el hijo le salió rana,* her son was a let-down.
ranchera *f* → **ranchero,-a.**
ranchero,-a 1 *m,f (granjero)* rancher, farmer. **2** *(cocinero)* cook. – **3 ranchera,** *f* AM Mexican folk song. **4** *(coche)* station wagon.
rancho 1 *m* MIL mess. **2** AM *(granja)* ranch, farm.
● **hacer rancho aparte,** *fam* to go one's own way.
rancidez *f* rancidness, rancidity, rankness.
ranciedad *f* → **rancidez.**
rancio,-a 1 *adj (comestibles)* stale; *(mantequilla)* rancid. **2** *fig (antiguo)* old, ancient: *de rancio abolengo,* of ancient lineage.
■ **vino rancio,** old wine, mellow wine.
randa[1] *f (encaje)* lace trimming.
randa[2] *m fam (ratero)* pickpocket.
ranglán *adj* → **raglán.**
rango *m* rank: *tiene rango de general,* he holds the rank of general.
● **de alto rango / de mucho rango,** high-ranking.
Rangún *m* Rangoon.

ranking *m* ranking.
▲ *pl* **rankings.**
ranura 1 *f (canal)* groove. **2** *(para monedas, fichas)* slot.
ranurado,-a *adj* grooved.
rapacidad *f* rapacity, rapaciousness.
rapapolvo *m fam* dressing-down, ticking off, talking-to.
● **echar un rapapolvo a algn.,** *fam* to give sb. a dressing-down.
rapar 1 *t (afeitar)* to shave. **2** *(pelo)* to crop.
rapavelas *m pey (sacristán)* verger; *(monaguillo)* altar boy.
▲ *pl* **rapavelas.**
rapaz[1] 1 *adj* ZOOL predatory, of prey: *ave rapaz,* bird of prey. **2** *fig (persona)* rapacious, grasping. – **3** *f (ave)* bird of prey.
rapaz,-za[2] *m,f* youngster; *(muchacho)* lad; *(muchacha)* lass.
rape[1] *m (pez)* angler fish.
rape[2] *m fam (rasura)* quick shave.
● **al rape,** close-cropped, short.
rapé *m* snuff.
rápidamente *adv* quickly.
rapidez *f* speed, rapidity: *con rapidez,* quickly.
rápido,-a 1 *adj* quick, fast. – **2** *adv* quickly: *¡rápido!,* hurry up!, make it snappy! – **3 rápido,** *m (tren)* fast train, express train. – **4 rápidos,** *mpl (del río)* rapids.
rapiña *f fam* robbery, theft.
rapiñar *t fam* to pinch, steal.
rapónchigo *m* rampion.
raposa *f* → **raposo,-a.**
raposear *i* to be sly.
raposera *f* foxhole.
raposo,-a 1 *m,f (macho)* fox; *(hembra)* female fox, vixen. **2** *fig (persona)* sly fox.
rapsoda *m* rhapsodist.
rapsodia *f* rhapsody.
raptar *t* to kidnap, abduct.
rapto 1 *m (secuestro)* kidnapping, abduction. **2** *fig (impulso)* outburst, fit.
raptor,-ra *m,f* kidnapper, abductor.
raqueta 1 *f (de tenis)* racket; *(de ping-pong)* bat, US paddle. **2** *(para nieve)* snowshoe. **3** *(en casinos)* rake.
raquídeo,-a *adj* rachidian, rachidial.
raquis *m* rachis.
▲ *pl* **raquis.**
raquítico,-a 1 *adj* MED rachitic. **2** *fig (exiguo)* meagre (US meager), small. **3** *fig (débil)* weak. – **4** *m,f* rachitic person.
raquitismo *m* rachitis, rickets *pl.*
raramente 1 *adv (rara vez)* rarely, seldom. **2** *(con rareza)* oddly, strangely.
rareza 1 *f (poco común)* rarity, rareness. **2** *(escasez)* scarcity. **3** *(peculiaridad)* oddity. **4** *(extravagancia)* eccentricity.
rarificar *t* to rarefy.
▲ *Conjugation model* |1|, *like* **sacar.**
raro,-a 1 *adj (poco común)* rare. **2** *(escaso)* scarce, rare: *son raras las personas que saben apreciarlo,* very few people can appreciate it. **3** *(peculiar)* odd, strange, weird: *últimamente la encuentro rara,* I think she's been acting a little strange recently. **4** *(excelente)* excellent: *escribió un libro raro, una verdadera obra de arte,* she wrote a very good book, a real work of art.
● **¡qué raro!,** how odd!, that's strange! ‖ **rara vez,** seldom: *rara vez aparece por aquí,* she rarely shows her face around here.
ras *a ras de,* *loc adv* (on a) level with.
● **a ras de tierra,** at ground level. ‖ **al ras,** to the brim:

he llenado los vasos al ras, I filled the glasses to the brim. ‖ **volar a ras de tierra,** to fly low, hedgehop.

rasa *f* thin patch.

rasante 1 *adj (tiro)* grazing, close; *(vuelo)* low, skimming. – **2** *f (inclinación)* slope.

■ **cambio de rasante,** brow of a hill.

rasar 1 *t (igualar)* to level. **2** *(pasar rozando)* to graze, skim.

● **rasar el suelo,** *(avión)* to fly low, hedgehop.

rasca 1 *f fam (hambre)* hunger. **2** *fam (frío)* cold. **3** *fam (borrachera)* drunkenness.

rascacielos *m* skyscraper.

▲ *pl* **rascacielos.**

rascador 1 *m (para rascar)* scraper. **2** *(para desgranar)* sheller, husker. **3** *(para cerillas)* striking surface.

rascar 1 *t (la piel)* to scratch. **2** *(con rascador)* to scrape, rasp. **3** *(un instrumento)* to strum.

▲ Conjugation model [1], like **sacar.**

rascatripas *mf fam* scratchy violinist.

rascón,-ona 1 *adj* sharp, rough. – **2 rascón,** *m (ave)* water rail.

rasera *f* spatula, fish slice.

rasero *m* leveller.

● **por el mismo rasero,** *fig* impartially.

rasgado,-a 1 *pp →* **rasgar.** – **2** *adj (roto)* torn, ripped. **3** *(ojos)* almond-shaped. **4** *(boca)* wide. **5** *fam (desenvuelto)* confident.

rasgadura *f* tear, strip.

rasgar *t* to tear, rip.

● **rasgarse las vestiduras,** *fig* to pull one's hair out.

▲ Conjugation model [7], like **llegar.**

rasgo 1 *m (línea)* stroke; *(adorno)* flourish. **2** *(facción del rostro)* feature: *sus rasgos me son familiares,* she looks familiar to me. **3** *(peculiaridad)* characteristic, feature, trait. **4** *(acto)* act, feat: *un rasgo de heroísmo,* an act of heroism.

● **explicar a grandes rasgos,** to outline, give a general outline of.

▲ In 2, often used in plural.

rasgón *m* tear, rip.

rasguear 1 *t (instrumento)* to strum. – **2** *i (al escribir)* to write with a flourish.

rasgueo *m* strumming.

rasguñar *t* to scratch, scrape.

rasguño 1 *m (arañazo)* scratch, scrape: *me he hecho un rasguño en la mano,* I scratched my hand. **2** *(dibujo)* sketch.

rasilla 1 *f (tela)* serge. **2** *(ladrillo)* tile.

raso,-a 1 *adj (plano)* flat, level; *(liso)* smooth: *una cucharada rasa,* a level spoonful. **2** *(a poca altura)* low. **3** *(atmósfera)* clear, cloudless. – **4 raso,** *m (tejido)* satin.

● **al raso,** in the open, in the open air. ‖ **hacer tabla rasa,** *fam* to make a clean sweep.

raspa 1 *f (de pescado)* bone, backbone. **2** *(de cereal)* beard.

raspado,-a *m* scraping, scrape.

raspador *m* scraper.

raspadura 1 *f (ralladura)* scraping, scrapings *pl.* **2** *(señal)* scratch, mark.

raspar 1 *t (rascar)* to scrape (off); *(dañar)* to scratch, graze. **2** *(con lija)* to sand, sand down. **3** *(hurtar)* to nick, pinch. **4** *(rasar)* to graze, skim. – **5** *i (vino)* to be sharp. **6** *(piel)* to be rough; *(toalla etc)* to scratch.

● **raspando,** *fig* by the skin of one's teeth.

raspilla *f* forget-me-not.

rasposo,-a *adj* rough, sharp.

rastra 1 *f (rastro)* trail, track. **2** *(grada)* harrow. **3** *(sarta)* string. **4** *(para pescar)* trawl, trawl net.

● **a rastras,** *(arrastrando)* dragging; *(sin querer)* unwillingly, grudgingly: *llevar a rastras,* to drag along.

rastreador *m* tracker.

■ **rastreador de minas,** minesweeper.

rastrear 1 *t (seguir el rastro)* to trail, track, trace. **2** *(río)* to drag, dredge. **3** *(para pescar)* to trawl. **4** *(zona)* to comb, search. **5** *(averiguar)* to find out. – **6** *i* AGR to rake. **7** AV to fly very low.

rastreo 1 *m (seguimiento)* tracking, trailing, tracing. **2** *(de río)* dragging, dredging. **3** *(de pesca)* trawling. **4** *(de zona)* combing. **5** AGR raking.

rastreramente *adv* basely.

rastrero,-a 1 *adj (que arrastra)* creeping, crawling. **2** BOT creeping. **3** *(vuelo)* low. **4** *fig (bajo)* vile, base.

rastrillar 1 *t (hojas etc)* to rake. **2** *(lino, cáñamo)* to comb, hackle.

rastrillo 1 *m (rastro)* rake. **2** *(para cáñamo, lino)* comb, hackle. **3** *(compuerta)* portcullis. **4** *fam (mercadillo)* flea market.

■ **rastrillo benéfico,** jumble sale.

rastro 1 *m (instrumento)* rake. **2** *(señal)* trace, track, sign; *(olor)* scent: *ni rastro de sangre,* not a trace of blood. **3** *(vestigio)* vestige. **4** *(mercado)* flea market: *el Rastro,* the Madrid flea market.

● **perder el rastro de algn.,** to lose sb.'s trail. ‖ **seguir el rastro de algn.,** to follow sb.'s trail.

rastrojar *t* to clear of stubble.

rastrojo 1 *m (paja)* stubble. **2** *(campo)* stubble field.

rasurar *t* to shave.

rata 1 *f* ZOOL rat. – **2** *m fam (ratero)* pickpocket, thief. – **3** *mf (tacaño)* miser, skinflint.

● **ser más pobre que las ratas,** *fam* to be as poor as a church mouse.

ratafía *f* ratafia.

rataplán *m* drumbeat, rub-a-dub.

ratear[1] *t fam (hurtar)* to steal. – **2** *i (andar a rastras)* to crawl, creep.

ratear[2] *t (repartir)* to share out proportionally, give out pro rata.

rateo *m* pro rata distribution.

ratería *f* petty theft, pilfering.

ratero,-a *m,f* pickpocket.

raticida *m* rat poison.

ratificación *f* ratification.

ratificar 1 *t* to ratify. – **2 ratificarse,** *p* to be confirmed, be ratified.

▲ Conjugation model [1], like **sacar.**

ratio *f* ratio.

rato 1 *m (tiempo)* time, while, moment: *habló hace un rato,* he spoke a while ago; *hace mucho rato que se fue,* she left quite a while ago; *charlamos un rato,* we chatted for a while. **2** *(espacio)* way: *hay un buen rato hasta Vigo,* it's a long way to Vigo. **3** *fam (mucho)* very, a lot: *este libro es un rato bueno,* this is a very good book; *sabe un rato de deportes,* she's a mine of information about sports; *me gusta un rato,* I love it.

● **al poco rato,** shortly after. ‖ **a ratos,** at times. ‖ **a ratos perdidos,** at odd moments. ‖ **hacer pasar un mal rato a algn.,** to give sb. a rough time. ‖ **¡hasta otro rato!,** see you later! ‖ **hay para rato,** it'll take a while. ‖ **pasar el rato,** to kill time. ‖ **pasar un buen rato,** to have a good time. ‖ **pasar un mal rato,** to have a bad time.

■ **ratos libres,** free time *sing.*

ratón *m* mouse.

■ **ratón de biblioteca,** *fam* bookworm.

ratonera *f* → **ratonero,-a.**
ratonero,-a l *adj* mousy. – 2 ratonero, *m* (*ave*) buzzard. – 3 ratonera, *f* (*trampa*) mousetrap. 4 (*agujero*) mousehole. 5 *fam fig* trap.
● **caer en la ratonera,** *fig* to fall into the trap.
raudal l *m* (*agua*) torrent, flood. 2 *fig* (*abundancia*) flood, wave.
● **a raudales,** in torrents: *la gente entraba a raudales,* people poured in, people flooded in; *hemos recibido felicitaciones a raudales,* congratulations have been flowing in.
raudo,-a *adj lit* swift, rapid.
raviolis *mpl* ravioli.
raya[1] l *f* (*línea*) line. 2 (*de color*) stripe: *pantalón a rayas,* striped trousers. 3 (*del pantalón*) crease. 4 (*del pelo*) parting, us part: *lleva la raya a un lado,* he parts his hair on the/one side. 5 (*guión*) dash. 6 (*límite*) limit. 7 *arg* (*de droga*) line.
● **cruz y raya,** *fam* that's that. ‖ **dar ciento y raya a algn.** / **dar quince y raya a algn.,** *fam* to run rings round sb. ‖ **hacerse la raya,** to part one's hair. ‖ **tener a algn. a raya,** *fig* to keep sb. under control, keep sb. at bay.
raya[2] *f* (*pez*) skate.
rayadillo *m* striped cotton.
rayado,-a l *pp* → **rayar.** – 2 *adj* (*tejido*) striped. 3 (*papel*) ruled. 4 (*arma*) rifled. – 5 rayado, *m* stripes *pl.*
rayano,-a l *adj* bordering. 2 *fig* bordering (**en,** on): *tiene unos pensamientos rayanos en la locura,* his thoughts are bordering on madness.
rayar l *t* (*líneas*) to draw lines on, line, rule. 2 (*superficie*) to scratch: *me han rayado el coche,* someone scratched my car. 3 (*tachar*) to cross out. 4 (*subrayar*) to underline. – 5 *i* (*limitar*) to border (**con,** on): *su terreno raya con el nuestro,* his plot borders on ours. 6 *fig* (*acercarse*) to border (**en,** on): *su actitud rayaba en la histeria,* his attitude bordered on hysteria; *raya en los cincuenta,* he's nearly fifty. 7 (*día, alba, luz*) to break: *al rayar el día,* at dawn, at daybreak.
rayo l *m* ray, beam: *rayo de sol,* sunbeam; *rayo de luz,* ray of light. 2 (*relámpago*) lightning, flash of lightning. 3 *fig* (*persona*) live wire.
● **caer como un rayo,** *fam* to drop like a bombshell. ‖ **echar rayos,** *fam* to be fuming, be hopping mad. ‖ **¡mal rayo lo parta!** / **¡que lo parta un rayo!,** *fam* to hell with him! ‖ **saber a rayos,** *fam* to taste awful.
■ **rayo de luna,** moonbeam. ‖ **rayos ultravioletas/ UVA,** ultraviolet rays. ‖ **rayos X,** X-rays.
rayón *m* rayon.
rayuela *f* hopscotch.
raza[1] l *f* race. 2 (*animal*) breed.
● **de raza,** (*perro*) pedigree; (*caballo*) thoroughbred.
■ **raza humana,** human race.
raza[2] l *f* (*rayo*) ray, beam. 2 (*grieta*) crack.
razia *f* razzia, raid.
razón l *f* (*facultad*) reason. 2 (*motivo*) reason, cause. 3 (*mensaje*) message. 4 (*justicia*) justice. 5 MAT ratio, rate.
● **a razón de,** in the ratio of, at the rate of. ‖ **asistirle a uno la razón,** to be in the right. ‖ **atender a razones,** to listen to reason. ‖ **con razón,** with good reason. ‖ **con razón o sin ella,** rightly or wrongly. ‖ **dar la razón a algn.,** to agree with sb., say that sb. is right. ‖ **entrar en razón,** to listen to reason: *se lo volví a explicar pero él no entraba en razón,* I explained it all again to him but he was having nothing of it. ‖ **mandar razón,** to send a message. ‖ **no tener razón,** to be

wrong. ‖ **perder la razón,** to lose one's reason. ‖ **"razón aquí",** "enquire within", "apply within". ‖ **"razón en portería",** "inquiries to caretaker". ‖ **razón de más para ...,** all the more reason to ... ‖ **tener razón,** to be right: *tienes toda la razón,* you're quite right. ‖ **tener razones para hacer algo,** to have reason to do sth.
■ **razón de Estado,** reason of State. ‖ **razón de ser,** raison d'être. ‖ **razón social,** trade name.
razonable *adj* reasonable.
● **dentro de lo razonable,** within reason.
razonablemente *adv* reasonably, rationally.
razonado,-a l *pp* → **razonar.** – 2 *adj* reasoned, well-reasoned.
razonamiento *m* reasoning.
razonar l *i* (*discurrir*) to reason. 2 (*hablar*) to talk. – 3 *t* (*explicar*) to reason out.
razzia *f* razzia, raid.
RDA *abr* (*República Democrática de Alemania*) German Democratic Republic; (*abreviatura*) GDR.
re *m* re, ray, D.
reabastecer *t* (*alimentos*) to revictual; (*combustible*) to refuel.
reabastecimiento *m* (*alimentos*) revictualling; (*combustible*) refuelling.
reabierto,-a *pp* → **reabrir.**
reabrir *t* to reopen.
▲ *pp* reabierto,-a.
reacción *f* reaction.
● **reacción en cadena,** chain reaction.
reaccionar *i* to react: *la multitud reaccionó con violencia,* the crowd reacted violently.
reaccionario,-a l *adj* reactionary. – 2 *m,f* reactionary.
reacio,-a *adj* reluctant, unwilling: *se mostró reacio a venir con nosotros,* he was reluctant to come with us.
reacondicionar *t* to recondition.
reactancia *f* reactance.
reactivar *t* to reactivate.
reactivo,-a l *adj* reactive. – 2 reactivo, *m* reagent.
reactor l *m* reactor. 2 AV jet, jet plane.
■ **reactor nuclear,** nuclear reactor.
readaptación l *f* (*rehabilitación*) rehabilitation. 2 (*profesional*) retraining.
readaptar l *t* to readapt, readjust. – 2 readaptarse, *p* to readapt, readjust.
readmisión *f* readmission.
readmitir *t* to readmit; (*un trabajador*) to reemploy.
reafirmación *f* reaffirmation, reassertion.
reafirmar *t* to reaffirm, reassert.
reagravarse *p* to get worse, worsen.
reagrupación *f* regrouping.
reagrupamiento *m* regrouping.
reagrupar l *t* to regroup. – 2 reagruparse, *p* to regroup.
reajustar *t* to readjust.
reajuste *m* readjustment.
■ **reajuste ministerial,** cabinet reshuffle.
real[1] *adj* (*verdadero*) real: *en la vida real,* in real life; *es un hecho real,* it's a true story.
real[2] l *adj* (*regio*) royal: *familia real,* royal family; *palacio real,* royal palace. 2 *fig* grand, fine: *es una real moza,* she's a good-looking girl. – 3 *m* (*de feria*) fairground. 4 (*moneda*) old Spanish coin *worth one quarter of a peseta.*
● **estar sin un real,** to be penniless. ‖ **no me da la real gana,** *fam* I don't feel like it. ‖ **no valer un real,** to be worthless, not be worth tuppence. ‖ **por real decreto,** JUR by royal decree.

realce 1 *m* (*adorno*) relief: *bordado de realce,* relief embroidery. 2 *fig* (*lustre*) prestige, distinction.
● **dar realce a algo,** to enhance sth. ‖ **poner de realce,** to highlight.
realengo,-a *adj* of the crown.
realeza *f* royalty.
realidad *f* reality.
● **en realidad,** actually, in fact. ‖ **la realidad es que ...,** the fact of the matter is that ...
realismo[1] *m* (*de la realidad*) realism.
realismo[2] *m* (*de la monarquía*) royalism.
realista[1] 1 *adj* (*de la realidad*) realistic: *hay que ser realista,* one must be realistic. – 2 *mf* (*de la realidad*) realist.
realista[2] 1 *adj* (*de la monarquía*) royalist. – 2 *mf* (*de la monarquía*) royalist.
realizable 1 *adj* (*plan etc*) feasible. 2 (*objetivo*) attainable.
realización 1 *f* (*de un deseo*) fulfilment (*us* fulfillment). 2 (*ejecución*) execution, carrying out. 3 CINEM TV TEAT production.
realizador,-ra *m,f* producer.
realizar 1 *t* (*ambición*) to realize, fulfil (*us* fulfill), achieve; (*deseo, esperanza*) to fulfil (*us* fulfill). 2 (*llevar a cabo*) to accomplish, carry out, do, fulfil (*us* fulfill). 3 (*un viaje*) to make. 4 CINEM TV to produce. 5 COM to realize. – 6 **realizarse,** *p* (*ambición, deseo*) to be fulfilled, be achieved; (*sueño*) to come true. 7 (*llevarse a cabo*) to be executed, be carried out. 8 (*persona*) to fulfil (*us* fulfill) os.
▲ *Conjugation model* [4].
realmente 1 *adv* (*de verdad*) really, truly: *realmente no sé cómo hacerlo,* I really don't know how to do it. 2 (*en realidad*) actually, in fact: *realmente no hacía tanto frío,* in fact it wasn't too cold.
realquilado,-a 1 *pp* → **realquilar.** – 2 *adj* sublet. – 3 *m,f* person who sublets from another.
realquilar *t* to sublet, sublease.
realzar 1 *t* (*elevar*) to raise, lift. 2 *fig* (*engrandecer*) to enhance, heighten: *aquel vestido realzaba su belleza,* that dress enhanced her beauty. 3 (*pintura*) to highlight.
▲ *Conjugation model* [4], *like* **realizar.**
reanimación *f* revival.
reanimar 1 *t* (*persona*) to revive. 2 (*fiesta, conversación*) to liven up. – 3 **reanimarse,** *p* (*persona*) to revive; (*volver en sí*) to come round. 4 (*fiesta, conversación*) to liven up.
reanudación 1 *f* (*gen*) renewal, resumption, re-establishment. 2 (*conversaciones, negociaciones*) resumption (*de,* of); (*clases*) return (*de,* to); (*amistad*) renewal.
reanudar 1 *t* (*gen*) to renew, resume, re-establish. 2 (*conversaciones, negociaciones*) to resume; (*clases*) to start again; (*amistad*) to renew; (*paso, marcha*) to set off again on. – 3 **reanudarse,** *p* to start again, resume.
reaparecer 1 *i* (*gen*) to reappear. 2 (*un artista etc*) to make a comeback. 3 (*un fenómeno*) to recur.
▲ *Conjugation model* [43], *like* **agradecer.**
reaparición 1 *f* (*gen*) reappearance. 2 (*artista etc*) comeback. 3 (*fenómeno*) recurrence.
reapertura *f* reopening.
reaprovisionar *t* to replenish, restock.
rearmar 1 *t* to rearm. – 2 **rearmarse,** *p* to rearm.
rearme *m* rearmament, rearming.
reaseguro *m* reinsurance.
reasumir *t* to reassume, resume.
reasunción *f* reassumption, resumption.
reata 1 *f* (*cuerda*) rope. 2 (*hilera*) packtrain.
● **de reata,** in single file.
reatar 1 *t* (*volver a atar*) to retie. 2 (*atar apretadamente*) to tie tightly. 3 (*caballerías*) to tie up in single file.

reavivar 1 *t* (*fuego*) to stoke, stoke up. 2 (*dolor*) to intensify; (*interés*) to revive.
rebaba *f* rough edge.
rebaja 1 *f* (*reducción*) reduction, lowering. 2 (*descuento*) discount, reduction: *me hizo una rebaja,* he gave me a discount. – 3 **rebajas,** *fpl* sales.
● **"grandes rebajas",** "huge reductions"
■ **precio de rebaja,** sale price.
rebajado,-a 1 *pp* → **rebajar.** – 2 *adj* (*de nivel*) lowered; (*arco*) depressed. 3 (*precio*) reduced: *a precio rebajado,* at a reduced price. 4 (*color*) softened. 5 (*humillado*) humbled. – 6 **rebajado,** *m* MIL soldier exempted from duty.
rebajar 1 *t* (*nivel*) to lower; (*arco*) to depress. 2 (*precio*) to cut, reduce. 3 (*color*) to soften, tone down; (*intensidad*) to diminish. 4 (*bebida*) to water down. 5 (*comida - sazonamiento*) to make milder; (*- densidad*) to make thinner, thin out. 6 *fig* (*humillar*) to humiliate. – 7 **rebajarse,** *p* MIL to be exempted. 8 *fig* (*humillarse*) to humble os.
● **rebajarse a hacer algo,** to stoop to do sth., lower os. to do sth. ‖ **rebajarse ante algn.,** to humble os. before sb.
rebaje *m* exemption.
rebajo *m* groove, rabbet.
rebanada *f* slice.
rebanar 1 *t* (*hacer rebanadas*) to slice, cut into slices. 2 (*cortar*) to cut off, slice off.
rebañar 1 *t* (*recoger*) to clean out. 2 (*comida*) to finish off: *rebañó el plato con pan,* he wiped his plate clean with some bread.
rebaño 1 *m* (*gen*) herd; (*de ovejas*) flock. 2 REL flock.
rebasar 1 *t* (*gen*) to exceed, go beyond, surpass. 2 (*límite, marca*) to overstep. 3 (*náutica*) to pass. 4 AUTO to overtake.
rebatible *adj* refutable.
rebatir *t* to refute.
rebato *m* alarm.
● **tocar a rebato,** to sound the alarm.
rebautizar *t* to rechristen, rebaptize.
▲ *Conjugation model* [4], *like* **realizar.**
rebeca *f* cardigan.
rebeco *m* chamois.
rebelarse *p* to rebel, revolt.
rebelde 1 *adj* rebellious. 2 *fig* (*tos etc*) persistent. – 3 *mf* rebel.
rebeldía 1 *f* rebelliousness. 2 JUR default.
● **declararse en rebeldía,** JUR to default.
rebelión *f* rebellion, revolt.
reblandecer 1 *t* to soften. – 2 **reblandecerse,** *p* to soften, become soft.
▲ *Conjugation model* [43], *like* **agradecer.**
reblandecimiento *m* softening.
rebobinado,-a 1 *pp* → **rebobinar.** – 2 *adj* rewound. – 3 **rebobinado,** *m* rewinding.
rebobinar *t* to rewind.
reborde *m* (*de mesa*) edge; (*de taza*) (*de tela*) edging.
rebosante *adj* overflowing, brimming: *rebosante de satisfacción,* brimming with satisfaction; *rebosante de salud,* bursting sith health.
rebosar 1 *i* (*derramarse*) to overflow, brim over. 2 *fig* to brim (*de,* with), burst (*de,* with): *rebosar de alegría,* to be brimming with joy. 3 *fig* (*abundar*) to abound. – 4 *t* *fig* (*sentimiento*) to brim with; (*salud*) to exude.
rebotado,-a 1 *pp* → **rebotar.** – 2 *adj* (*persona*) reject. 3 (*sacerdote*) ex-priest.
rebotar 1 *i* (*pelota*) to bounce, rebound; (*bala*) to ricochet. – 2 *t* (*clavo*) to clinch. 3 (*ataque*) to repel. 4 (*con-*

turbar) to put off, upset: *su novio me rebota,* her boyfriend puts me off. – **5 rebotarse,** *p* (*conturbarse*) to get angry, get upset.

rebote 1 *m* (*de balón*) bounce, rebound. **2** (*de bala*) ricochet.

● **de rebote,** *fig* on the rebound.

rebotica *f* back room (*in a chemist's*).

rebozado,-a 1 *pp* → **rebozar.** – **2** *adj* coated in breadcrumbs, coated in batter: *ternera rebozada,* breaded veal, veal coated in breadcrumbs.

rebozar 1 *t* (*la cara*) to cover. **2** CULIN to coat in breadcrumbs, coat in batter. – **3 rebozarse,** *p* to cover one's face.

▲ *Conjugation model* [4], *like realizar.*

rebozo 1 *m* (*prenda*) muffler, wrap. **2** *fig* (*simulación*) dissimulation.

● **de rebozo,** secretly, in secret. ‖ **sin rebozo,** openly, frankly.

rebrotar *i* to shoot, sprout.

rebufar *i* to snort loudly.

rebufo *m* loud snort.

rebujado,-a 1 *adj* (*enredado*) tangled up. **2** (*desordenado*) untidy, messy.

rebujina *f fam* bustle.

rebujiña *f fam* bustle.

rebullir 1 *i* to stir, begin to move. – **2 rebullirse,** *p* to stir, begin to move.

▲ *Conjugation model* [41], *like mullir.*

rebuscado,-a 1 *pp* → **rebuscar.** – **2** *adj* affected, recherché; (*estilo*) elaborate, contrived.

rebuscamiento *m* affectation, elaborateness.

rebuscar *t* to search carefully for.

▲ *Conjugation model* [1], *like sacar.*

rebuznar *i* to bray.

rebuzno *m* bray, braying.

recabar 1 *t* (*solicitar*) to ask for, entreat. **2** (*obtener*) to attain, obtain, manage to get.

recadero,-a *m,f* (*gen*) messenger; (*muchacho*) messenger boy; (*muchacha*) messenger girl.

recado 1 *m* (*mensaje*) message: *te dejó un recado,* he left a message for you; *¿quiere dejar algún recado?,* would you like to leave a message? **2** (*encargo*) errand: *me hizo un recado,* she ran the errand for me. – **3 recados,** *mpl* (*compras*) shopping *sing:* *tengo que hacer unos recados,* I have to go out to buy a few things.

recaer 1 *i* (*volver a caer*) to fall again. **2** (*enfermedad*) to relapse, have a relapse. **3** (*vicios etc*) to relapse, backslide. **4** (*corresponder*) to fall (**sobre,** on): *el premio recayó sobre Teresa,* the prize went to Teresa.

▲ *Conjugation model* [67], *like caer.*

recaída 1 *f* (*enfermedad*) relapse. **2** (*vicios etc*) relapse, backslide.

● **sufrir una recaída,** to have a relapse.

recalar 1 *t* to soak. – **2** *i* MAR to put in (**en,** at). **3** *fig* (*aparecer*) to show up.

recalcar *t fig* to emphasize, stress, underline.

▲ *Conjugation model* [1], *like sacar.*

recalcitrante *adj* recalcitrant.

recalentar 1 *t* (*volver a calentar*) to reheat, warm up. **2** (*calentar demasiado*) to overheat.

▲ *Conjugation model* [27], *like acertar.*

recalzo *m* (*de cimientos*) reinforcement.

recamado *m* embroidery.

recamar *t* to embroider.

recámara 1 *f* (*cuarto*) dressing room. **2** (*de mina*) blast hole. **3** (*de arma*) chamber. **4** *fig* (*cautela*) reserve, caution.

recambiar *t* to change (over).

▲ *Conjugation model* [12], *like cambiar.*

recambio *m* spare, spare part; (*de pluma, bolígrafo*) refill.

recapacitar 1 *i* to think (**sobre,** over): *recapacita sobre ello,* think it over. – **2** *t* to think over.

recapitulación *f* recapitulation, summing up.

recapitular *t* to recapitulate, sum up.

recarga *f* refill.

recargable *adj* (*pluma, mechero*) refillable; (*pila*) rechargeable.

recargado,-a 1 *pp* → **recargar.** – **2** *adj* (*sobrecargado*) overloaded. **3** *fig* (*exagerado*) overelaborate, exaggerated, contrived.

recargar 1 *t* (*volver a cargar*) to reload; (*pilas*) to recharge. **2** (*sobrecargar*) to overload. **3** *fig* (*exagerar*) to overelaborate, exaggerate. **4** FIN to increase.

▲ *Conjugation model* [7], *like llegar.*

recargo *m* extra charge, surcharge.

recatadamente 1 *adv* (*con prudencia*) prudently, cautiously. **2** (*con modestia*) modestly. **3** (*con decencia*) decently.

recatado,-a 1 *pp* → **recatar.** – **2** *adj* (*prudente*) cautious, prudent. **3** (*modesto*) modest. **4** (*decente*) decent.

recatar 1 *t* to hide, cover up. – **2 recatarse,** *p* to be cautious.

● **sin recatar,** openly.

recato 1 *m* (*cautela*) caution. **2** (*pudor*) modesty: *sin recato,* openly, unreservedly.

recauchutado *m* retreading.

recauchutar *t* to retread, remould (us remold).

recaudación 1 *f* (*cobro*) collection. **2** (*cantidad recaudada*) takings *pl:* *hicimos una buena recaudación ayer,* the takings were good yesterday. **3** (*oficina*) tax collector's office.

recaudador,-ra *m,f* tax collector.

recaudar *t* to collect.

recaudo 1 *m* (*recaudación*) collection. **2** (*precaución*) precaution.

● **estar a buen recaudo,** to be in safekeeping. ‖ **poner algo a buen recaudo,** to put sth. in a safe place.

recelar 1 *t* (*sospechar*) to suspect, distrust. **2** (*temer*) to fear. – **3** *i* (*desconfiar*) to be suspicious (**de,** of): *recela de todos,* he is suspicious of everybody.

recelo *m* suspicion: *con recelo,* suspiciously.

receloso,-a *adj* suspicious.

recensión *f* review.

recental *adj* sucking: *cordero recental,* sucking lamb.

recepción 1 *f* (*gen*) reception. **2** (*de documento, carta etc*) receipt. **3** (*oficina etc*) reception, reception desk.

recepcionista *mf* receptionist.

receptáculo *m* receptacle.

receptividad *f* receptiveness, receptivity.

receptivo,-a *adj* receptive (**a,** to).

receptor,-ra 1 *adj* receiving. – **2** *m,f* receiver, recipient. – **3** receptor, *m* (*de radio etc*) receiver.

recesión *f* recession: *una fuerte recesión,* a deep recession.

recesivo,-a *adj* recessive.

receso *m* recess.

receta 1 *f* MED prescription. **2** CULIN recipe. **3** *fig* recipe, formula.

recetar *t* to prescribe: *el médico le recetó estas pastillas,* the doctor prescribed these tablets for him.

recetario 1 *m* MED prescription pad. **2** CULIN cookery book, us cookbook.

rechace *m* DEP point-blank save.
rechazar 1 *t* (*gen*) to reject, turn down, refuse. 2 (*ataque*) to repel, repulse, drive back. 3 MED to reject.
▲ *Conjugation model* [4], *like realizar.*
rechazo 1 *m* rejection, refusal. 2 MED rejection. 3 (*negativa*) denial, rejection.
● **de rechazo,** on the rebound; (*bala*) as it ricocheted; (*uso figurado*) indirectly, as a consequence.
rechifla 1 *f fam* (*silbido*) hissing, booing, catcalls *pl.* 2 *fam* (*burla*) mockery, jeering.
rechiflar 1 *i* (*silbar*) to hiss, boo. – 2 **rechiflarse,** *p* (*burlarse*) to mock, make fun of.
rechinante *adj* creaky, squeaky.
rechinar 1 *i* (*madera*) to creak; (*metal*) to squeak, screech; (*dientes*) to grind, grate. 2 (*aceptar con repugnancia*) to accept reluctantly.
rechistar *i* to say, reply: *hazlo sin rechistar,* do it without saying a word, do it without complaining.
rechoncho,-a *adj fam* chubby, tubby.
rechupado,-a *adj* skinny, thin.
rechupete de rechupete, *loc fam* (*muy bien*) super, brill, marvellous (us marvelous); (*comida*) delicious, scrumptious, yummy.
recibí *m* COM receipt.
recibidor *m* (*de casa*) entrance hall.
recibimiento *m* reception, welcome.
recibir 1 *t* (*gen*) to receive: *el ministro nos recibió a las diez,* the minister received us at ten o'clock. 2 (*invitados*) to entertain. 3 (*salir al encuentro*) to meet: *nos recibió en la puerta,* he met us at the door. 4 (*acoger*) to welcome, receive: *recibió su ofrecimiento con alegría,* his offer was welcomed enthusiastically.
● **recibe un abrazo de,** (*en carta*) best wishes from, lots of love from. ‖ **recibí,** (*factura*) received. ‖ **recibir una negativa,** to be refused, meet with a refusal.
recibo 1 *m* (*resguardo*) receipt. 2 (*factura*) invoice, bill. 3 (*recepción*) reception, receiving.
reciclado,-a 1 *pp* → **reciclar.** – 2 *adj* recycled.
reciclaje 1 *m* (*de materias*) recycling. 2 (*de personas*) retraining.
■ **curso de reciclaje,** refresher course.
reciclar 1 *t* (*materiales*) to recycle. 2 (*personas*) to re-train.
reciedumbre *f* strength.
recién *adv* recently, newly; (*café, pan*) freshly: *un pastel recién hecho,* a freshly baked cake; *estaba recién duchado cuando llegaron,* he was just out of the shower when they arrived.
● **recién pintado,** wet paint.
■ **recién casados,** newlyweds. ‖ **recién llegado,-a,** newcomer. ‖ **recién nacido,-a,** newborn baby. ‖
▲ *Used only before pp.*
reciente *adj* recent.
recientemente *adv* recently, lately.
recinto *m* grounds *pl,* precincts *pl,* area.
■ **recinto comercial,** shopping centre (us center). ‖ **recinto ferial,** fairground.
recio,-a 1 *adj* (*fuerte*) strong, robust, sturdy. 2 (*grueso*) thick. 3 (*duro*) hard. 4 (*voz*) loud; (*clima*) harsh, severe. – 5 **recio,** *adv* (*hablar*) loudly, loud. 6 (*con fuerza*) hard, heavily.
● **en lo más recio de,** in the thick of: *en lo más recio del combate,* in the thick of the fight.
recipiente *m* container, receptacle.
reciprocidad *f* reciprocity.
recíproco,-a *adj* reciprocal, mutual: *un sentimiento recíproco,* a mutual feeling.

● **a la recíproca,** vice versa.
recitación *f* recitation.
recitado *m* recitation.
recital 1 *m* MÚS recital, concert. 2 LIT reading: *recital de poesía,* poetry reading.
recitar *t* to recite.
recitativo *m* recitative.
reclamación 1 *f* (*demanda*) claim, demand. 2 (*queja*) complaint, protest, objection.
● **presentar una reclamación,** to lodge a complaint.
■ **libro de reclamaciones,** complaints book.
reclamar 1 *t* (*pedir*) to demand, claim. 2 (*exigir*) to require, demand. – 3 *i* (*protestar*) to protest (**contra,** against): *reclamaron contra aquella medida,* they protested against the measure. 4 JUR to appeal.
reclamo 1 *m* (*para cazar*) decoy bird, lure. 2 (*silbato*) bird call. 3 (*llamada*) call. 4 (*anuncio*) advertisement; (*eslogan*) advertising slogan. 5 *fig* inducement.
reclinar 1 *t* to lean. – 2 **reclinarse,** *p* to lean back, recline: *se reclinó sobre la almohada,* he lent back on the pillow.
reclinatorio *m* prie-dieu.
recluido,-a 1 *pp* → **recluir.** – 2 *adj* (*gen*) shut in, locked in. 3 (*en cárcel*) imprisoned, interned. 4 (*en manicomio*) confined.
recluir 1 *t* (*encerrar*) to shut in. 2 (*en cárcel*) to imprison, intern. 3 (*en manicomio*) to confine.
▲ *Conjugation model* [62], *like huir.*
reclusión 1 *f* (*encierro*) seclusion. 2 (*encarcelamiento*) imprisonment, internment. 3 (*lugar*) retreat.
■ **reclusión mayor,** JUR long prision sentence. ‖ **reclusión menor,** JUR short prison sentence. ‖ **reclusión perpetua,** JUR life imprisonment.
recluso,-a 1 *adj* imprisoned: *población reclusa,* prison population. – 2 *m,f* prisoner.
recluta 1 *mf* (*voluntario*) recruit. 2 (*obligado*) conscript. – 3 *f* (*reclutamiento*) recruitment, conscription.
reclutamiento 1 *m* (*voluntario*) recruitment. 2 (*obligatorio*) conscription. 3 (*reclutas - voluntarios*) recruits *pl*; (- *obligatorios*) conscripts *pl.*
reclutar 1 *t* (*voluntarios*) to recruit. 2 (*obligatorio*) to conscript.
recobrar 1 *t* (*gen*) to recover. 2 (*conocimiento, fuerzas, esperanzas*) to regain; (*aliento*) to get back. 3 (*tiempo*) to make up. 4 MIL to recapture. – 5 **recobrarse,** *p* (*recuperarse*) to recover (**de,** from), recuperate (**de,** from).
recocer 1 *t* (*volver a cocer*) to recook. 2 (*cocer mucho*) to overcook. 3 TÉC to anneal. – 4 **recocerse,** *p* (*cocerse mucho*) to overcook. 5 *fig* (*atormentarse*) to be consumed (**de,** with).
▲ *Conjugation model* [54], *like cocer.*
recochinearse *p fam* to make fun (**de,** of), laugh (**de,** at).
recochineo *m fam* mockery.
recodar 1 *i* to lean on one's elbows. – 2 **recodarse,** *p* to lean on one's elbows.
recodo 1 *m* (*de río*) turn, twist; (*de camino*) bend. 2 (*recoveco*) nook.
recogedor *m* dustpan.
recogepelotas *mf* (*muchacho*) ball boy; (*muchacha*) ball girl.
▲ *pl* recogepelotas.
recoger 1 *t* (*volver a coger*) to take again, take back. 2 (*coger*) to pick up, take back: *recoja el paquete,* pick the parcel up. 3 (*ir a buscar*) to pick up, collect: *me recogerá a las cuatro,* he'll pick me up at four o'clock. 4 (*cosecha*)

to harvest, gather; (*fruta*) to pick. **5** (*guardar*) to put away: *recoge la plata,* put the silverware away. **6** (*poner al abrigo*) to bring in: *recoge las toallas, va a llover,* bring those towels in, it's going to rain. **7** (*suspender*) to seize: *recoger una publicación,* to seize a publication. **8** (*juntar*) to gather, collect: *hemos recogido mucho dinero,* we have collected a lot of money. **9** (*velas*) to take in; (*cortinas*) to draw. **10** (*dar asilo*) to take in, shelter: *lo recogieron sus abuelos,* he was taken in by his grandparents. **11** (*ordenar*) to clear up, tidy up. **12** (*limpiar*) to clean; (*el polvo*) to wipe off; (*líquido*) to wipe up. **13** (*remangar - prendas*) to pick up, lift up; (- *mangas*) to roll up. **14** cost to shorten, take up: *la modista me recogió la falda,* the seamstress shortened my skirt. – **15** recogerse, *p* (*irse a casa*) to go home. **16** (*irse a dormir*) to go to bed. **17** (*para meditar*) to retire, withdraw.
● **recoger la mesa,** to clear the table. ‖ **recogerse el pelo,** to put one's hair up, tie one's hair back.
▲ *Conjugation model* [5], *like proteger.*

recogida *f* → **recogido,-a.**

recogido,-a 1 *pp* → **recoger.** – **2** *adj* (*apartado*) secluded, withdrawn. **3** (*pelo*) pinned back, tied back. **4** (*pequeño*) small. – **5** recogido, *m* (*de pelo*) hairdo; (*de vestido*) tuck, gathering: *llevaba un recogido en el pelo,* she wore her hair up. – **6** recogida, *f* (*gen*) collection. **7** (*cosecha*) harvest, harvesting.

recogimiento *m* withdrawal, recollection.
● **vivir con recogimiento,** to lead a withdrawn life, lead a secluded life.

recolección 1 *f* (*recopilación*) collection, gathering. **2** (*cosecha*) harvest, harvesting. **3** (*tiempo de cosecha*) harvest time.

recolectar 1 *t* (*reunir*) to gather, collect. **2** (*cosechar*) to harvest.

recoleto,-a 1 *adj* (*lugar*) quiet, secluded. **2** (*persona*) withdrawn, retiring.

recomendable *adj* recommendable, advisable.
● **no ser recomendable,** to be unwise: *no sería recomendable salir de casa,* it would be unwise to leave home, leaving home is not recommended.

recomendación *f* (*consejo*) recommendation, advice; (*para empleo*) recommendation, reference: *¿tienes alguna recomendación?,* have you got any recommendations?

recomendado,-a 1 *pp* → **recomendar.** – **2** *adj* recommended. – **3** *m,f* (*hombre*) protégé; (*mujer*) protégée.

recomendar *t* to recommend, advise: *te recomiendo que estudies más,* I recommend that you study harder.
▲ *Conjugation model* [27], *like acertar.*

recomenzar *t* to recommence, begin again, start again.
▲ *Conjugation model* [47], *like empezar.*

recompensa *f* reward, recompense.
● **en recompensa,** as a reward, in return: *en recompensa de sus esfuerzos,* as a reward for his efforts.

recompensar 1 *t* (*compensar*) to compensate. **2** (*remunerar*) to reward, recompense.
● **"se recompensará",** "reward offered".

recomponer 1 *t* to repair, mend. **2** *fam* (*acicalar*) to dress up.
▲ *Conjugation model* [78], *like poner; pp recompuesto,-a.*

recomposición *f* repairing, mending.

recompuesto,-a 1 *pp* → **recomponer.** – **2** *adj* (*acicalado*) dressed up.

reconcentrar 1 *t* (*concentrar*) to concentrate (**en,** to). **2** (*reunir*) to bring together. **3** *fig* (*disimular*) to conceal:

reconcentraba su odio en el corazón, he concealed his hatred in his heart. – **4 reconcentrarse,** *p* (*ensimismarse*) to become absorbed in thought, concentrate, become engrossed.

reconciliable *adj* reconcilable.

reconciliación *f* reconciliation.

reconciliar 1 *t* to reconcile. – **2 reconciliarse,** *p* (*uso recíproco*) to be reconciled.
▲ *Conjugation model* [12], *like cambiar.*

reconcomerse *p* fam to be consumed (**de,** with): *se reconcomía de envidia,* he was consumed with envy.

reconcomio 1 *m* (*deseo*) itch, desire, longing. **2** *fig* (*sospecha*) suspicion. **3** *fam* (*rencor*) grudge, resentment.

recóndito,-a *adj* hidden, secret.
● **en lo más recóndito de,** in the depths of: *en lo más recóndito del alma,* deep down (in one's heart).

reconfortante 1 *adj* comforting. – **2** *m* MED tonic.

reconfortar 1 *t* (*confortar*) to comfort. **2** (*animar*) to cheer up.

reconocer 1 *t* (*gen*) to recognize: *me reconoció enseguida,* he recognized me at once. **2** (*examinar*) to examine: *los jueces reconocieron la pista,* the judges examined the track. **3** (*agradecer*) to be grateful for. **4** (*admitir*) to recognize, admit: *reconoció su error,* she admitted her mistake. **5** (*afrontar*) to face: *reconozcámoslo,* let's face it. **6** MIL (*terreno*) to reconnoitre (us reconnoiter). **7** MED (*paciente*) to examine. – **8** reconocerse, *p* to recognize each other. **9** (*admitirse*) to admit: *se reconoció culpable,* he admitted his guilt.
▲ *Conjugation model* [44], *like conocer.*

reconocible *adj* recognizable.

reconocido,-a 1 *pp* → **reconocer.** – **2** *adj* (*agradecido*) grateful.

reconocimiento 1 *m* (*gen*) recognition. **2** (*admisión*) admission. **3** MIL reconnaissance. **4** MED examination, check-up.
● **en reconocimiento de,** in recognition of, in appreciation of.

reconquista 1 *f* reconquest. **2 la Reconquista,** the Reconquest (*of Spain*).

reconquistar *t* to reconquer, recapture, regain.

reconsiderar *t* to reconsider.

reconstituir *t* to reconstitute.
▲ *Conjugation model* [62], *like huir.*

reconstituyente *m* tonic.

reconstrucción *f* reconstruction.

reconstruir *t* to reconstruct.
▲ *Conjugation model* [62], *like huir.*

recontar 1 *t* (*volver a calcular*) to recount, count again. **2** (*volver a narrar*) to recount, retell.

reconvención *f* reproach, reprimand.

reconvenir *t* to reproach, reprimand.
▲ *Conjugation model* [90], *like venir.*

reconversión 1 *f* reconversion. **2** (*industrial*) rationalization.

reconvertir 1 *t* to reconvert. **2** (*industria*) to modernize, reorganize.
▲ *Conjugation model* [35], *like hervir.*

recopilación 1 *f* (*resumen*) summary, resumé. **2** (*colección*) compilation, collection; (*de leyes*) code.

recopilador,-ra *m,f* compiler.

recopilar *t* to compile, collect.

recórcholis *interj fam* crumbs!, us rats!

récord 1 *adj* record: *en un tiempo récord,* in record time. – **2** *m* record.
▲ *pl records.*

recordar 1 *t* (*rememorar*) to remember: *no recuerdo nada,* I can't remember anything; *¿recuerdas?,* do you remember? 2 (*traer a la memoria*) to remind (**a,** of): *me recuerda a mi hermano,* he reminds me of my brother; *recuérdale que escriba,* remind her to write. 3 (*conmemorar*) to commemorate.
● **que yo recuerde,** as far as I can remember. ‖ **si mal no recuerdo,** if I remember rightly, if my memory serves me right.
▲ *Conjugation model* |31|, *like* **contar.**

recordatorio 1 *m* (*aviso*) reminder. 2 REL (*defunción*) in memoriam card; (*comunión*) souvenir of First Communion.

recordman *m* record holder.

recordwoman *f* record holder.

recorrer 1 *t* (*distancia*) to cover, travel. 2 (*país*) to tour, travel over, travel round: *recorrimos Alemania en cuatro días,* we toured Germany in four days. 3 (*ciudad*) to visit, walk round. 4 (*registrar*) to check, go through, examine: *recorrimos toda la biblioteca y no encontramos el libro,* we checked the whole library and couldn't find the book. 5 (*un escrito*) to look over, go over, look through. 6 (*reparar*) to mend, repair.

recorrido 1 *m* (*trayecto*) journey, trip: *hizo el recorrido en dos horas,* the journey took him two hours. 2 (*distancia*) distance travelled: *un tren de largo recorrido,* a long-distance train. 3 (*itinerario*) itinerary, route. 4 DEP round.

recortable 1 *adj* cutout. – 2 *m* cutout.

recortado,-a 1 *pp* → **recortar.** – 2 *adj* (*cortado*) cut out. 3 (*borde*) jagged. 4 (*irregular*) uneven, irregular.

recortar 1 *t* (*muñecos, telas, etc*) to cut out. 2 (*lo que sobra*) to cut off. 3 (*el pelo*) to trim. 4 *fig* to cut, restrict: *han recortado las subvenciones,* subsidies have been cut. – 5 *recortarse, p* (*sobresalir*) to stand out.

recorte 1 *m* (*acción*) cutting. 2 (*trozo*) cutting, clipping. 3 (*de periódico*) press clipping, newspaper cutting. 4 (*de pelo*) trim, cut, reduction. 5 *fig* (*reducción*) cut, reduction: *recorte del presupuesto,* budget cut.

recostado,-a 1 *pp* → **recostar.** – 2 *adj* reclining, leaning, lying.

recostar 1 *t* to lean: *recuéstalo en la pared,* lean it against the wall. – 2 *recostarse, p* (*apoyarse*) to lean. 3 (*tumbarse*) to lie down. 4 (*sestear*) to take a short rest.
▲ *Conjugation model* |31|, *like* **contar.**

recoveco 1 *m* (*vuelta*) turn, bend. 2 (*rincón*) nook, corner.
● **sin recovecos,** *fig* plainly, frankly.

recreación 1 *f* recreation. 2 (*diversión*) recreation, break, amusement.

recrear[1] 1 *t* (*divertir*) to amuse, entertain. – 2 *recrearse, p* to amuse os., enjoy os.
● **recrearse con / recrearse en,** to take pleasure in, take delight in.

recrear[2] *t* (*volver a crear*) to re-create, reproduce.

recreativo,-a *adj* recreational.

recremento *m* recrement.

recreo 1 *m* (*diversión*) recreation, amusement, entertainment. 2 (*en la escuela*) playtime, break: *se lo comió en la hora de recreo,* he had it at break time.
● **de recreo,** pleasure: *barco de recreo,* pleasure boat. ‖ **ser un recreo para la vista,** to be a joy to behold.

recriar *t* to breed.
▲ *Conjugation model* |13|, *like* **desviar.**

recriminación *f* recrimination.

recriminar 1 *t* (*reprender*) to recriminate. 2 (*reprochar*) to reproach.

recriminatorio,-a *adj* recriminatory.

recrudecer 1 *i* (*empeorar*) to worsen, aggravate. 2 (*aumentar*) to be increasing: *el frío ha recrudecido,* it's getting colder. – 3 **recrudecerse,** *p* (*empeorar*) to worsen, aggravate. 4 (*aumentar*) to be increasing.
▲ *Conjugation model* |43|, *like* **agradecer.**

recrudecimiento 1 *m* (*empeoramiento*) worsening. 2 (*aumento*) rise (**de,** in), deepening, upsurge.

recta *f* → **recto,-a.**

rectal *adj* rectal.

rectamente *adv fig* honestly, uprightly.

rectangular *adj* rectangular.

rectángulo,-a 1 *adj* rectangular: *triángulo rectángulo,* right-angled triangle, US right triangle. – 2 **rectángulo,** *m* rectangle.

rectificable *adj* rectifiable.

rectificación 1 *f* rectification. 2 (*corrección*) correction, remedy.

rectificador,-ra 1 *adj* rectifying. – 2 **rectificador,** *m* rectifier.

rectificar 1 *t* to rectify. 2 (*corregir*) to correct. 3 AUTO to straighten up. – 4 **rectificarse,** *p* to correct os.
▲ *Conjugation model* |1|, *like* **sacar.**

rectilíneo,-a *adj* rectilinear.

rectitud 1 *f* straightness. 2 *fig* uprightness, honesty, rectitude.

recto,-a 1 *adj* (*derecho*) straight. 2 *fig* (*honesto*) honest, upright. 3 (*ángulo*) right. – 4 **recta,** *f* (*línea*) straight line. 5 (*en carretera*) straight. – 6 **recto,** *m* ANAT rectum. – 7 *adv* straight, straight on: *vaya todo recto,* go straight on.
■ **recta final,** home straight.

rector,-ra 1 *adj* ruling, governing. – 2 *m,f* EDUC vice-chancellor, US president. 3 REL rector.

rectorado 1 *m* EDUC (*cargo*) vice-chancellorship, US presidency; (*oficina*) vice-chancellor's office, US president's office. 2 REL (*cargo*) rectorship; (*oficina*) rector's office.

rectoral *adj* rectorial.

rectoría 1 *f* (*casa*) rectory. 2 (*cargo*) rectorship.

rectriz *f* rectrix.

recua 1 *f* (*de animales*) train. 2 *fig* string, drove, line.

recuadro 1 *m* (*cuadro*) frame. 2 (*en prensa*) box.

recubierto,-a *pp* → **recubrir.**

recubrimiento *m* covering; (*de pintura*) coating.

recubrir 1 *t* to cover (**con/de,** with); (*con pintura*) to coat (**con/de,** with).
▲ *pp* **recubierto,-a.**

recuento *m* recount, count.
● **hacer (el) recuento de,** to count, recount.

recuerdo 1 *m* (*imagen*) memory, recollection. 2 (*regalo*) souvenir, keepsake. – 3 **recuerdos,** *mpl* (*saludos*) regards, greetings; (*en carta*) best wishes: *me dio recuerdos para ti,* he sends you his regards; *¡recuerdos a tu hermana!,* say hello to your sister for me!
● **en recuerdo de,** in memory of. ‖ **tener un buen recuerdo de algo,** to have happy memories of sth.

recular 1 *i* (*retroceder*) to go back. 2 (*ejército*) to retreat. 3 *fam fig* (*ceder*) to back down.

recuperable *adj* recoverable, retrievable.

recuperación *f* recovery, recuperation, retrieval.

recuperar 1 *t* (*gen*) to recover, recuperate, retrieve. 2 (*afecto*) to win back; (*conocimiento*) to regain; (*salud*) to recover; (*tiempo, clases*) to make up. – 3 **recuperarse,** *p* (*disgusto, emoción*) to get over (**de, -**), recover (**de,** from). 4 (*enfermedad*) to recover (**de,** from), recuperate (**de,** from).

recurrente 1 *adj* recurrent. 2 JUR appealing. – 3 *mf* JUR appealer.

recurrible *adj* appealable.

recurrir 1 *i* JUR to appeal. 2 (*acogerse - a algo*) to resort (**a**, to); (*- a algn.*) to turn (**a**, to): *recurrió a la mentira,* he resorted to lies; *recurrió a sus padres,* she turned to her parents.

recursividad *f* recurrence.

recurso 1 *m* (*medio*) resort. 2 JUR appeal. – 3 **recursos,** *mpl* resources, means.
● **como último recurso,** as a last resort. ‖ **de recursos,** resourceful.
■ **recurso de apelación,** appeal. ‖ **recurso de casación,** high court appeal. ‖ **recursos naturales,** natural resources.

recusable *adj* objectionable.

recusación 1 *f* rejection. 2 JUR challenge.

recusar 1 *t* to reject, refuse. 2 JUR to challenge.

red 1 *f* (*gen*) net. 2 (*redecilla*) hairnet. 3 (*sistema*) network, system. 4 ELEC mains *pl.* 5 INFORM network. 6 (*estadística*) graph. 7 *fig* (*trampa*) trap.
● **caer en la red / caer en las redes,** *fig* to fall into the trap. ‖ **echar las redes,** to cast one's nets.
■ **red comercial,** sales network. ‖ **red de carreteras,** road network. ‖ **red de espionaje,** spy ring. ‖ **red de supermercados,** chain of supermarkets. ‖ **red ferroviaria,** rail network, railway network.

redacción 1 *f* (*escritura*) writing. 2 (*escrito*) composition, essay. 3 (*estilo*) wording. 4 (*prensa*) editing. 5 (*oficina*) editorial office. 6 (*redactores*) editorial staff.

redactar 1 *t* (*escribir*) to write, compose. 2 (*con estilo*) to word: *tienes que redactarlo mejor,* you have to word it better. 3 (*tratado, discurso, etc*) to draft, draw up. 4 (*prensa*) to edit.

redactor,-ra *m,f* editor.
■ **redactor jefe,** editor-in-chief.

redada 1 *f* (*de peces*) catch, haul. 2 *fig* (*en un sitio*) raid; (*en varios sitios a la vez*) round-up: *hicieron una redada de narcotraficantes,* they rounded up drug traffickers.

redaño 1 *m* (*mesenterio*) mesentery. – 2 **redaños,** *mpl fam* (*fuerza*) guts.

redecilla 1 *f* (*tejido*) net, netting. 2 (*de pelo*) hairnet. 3 (*estómago*) reticulum.

rededor *m* surroundings *pl.*

redención *f* redemption.

redentor,-ra 1 *adj* redeeming. – 2 *m,f* redeemer. – 3 **el Redentor,** *m* REL the Redeemer.

redentorista *mf* Redemptorist.

redicho,-a *adj fam* affected, pretentious.

rediez 1 *interj fam* (*sorpresa*) good heavens! 2 *fam* (*enfado*) damn it! 3 *fam* (*dolor*) ow!, ouch!

redil *m* fold, sheepfold.
● **volver al redil,** *fig* to return to the fold.

redimible *adj* redeemable.

redimir 1 *t* to redeem. – 2 **redimirse,** *p* to redeem os.

redingote *m* redingote.

rediós *interj* → **rediez**.

redistribución *f* redistribution.

redistribuir *t* to redistribute.
▲ *Conjugation model* |62|, *like huir.*

rédito *m* interest, yield.

redivivo,-a *adj* revived, resuscitated.

redoblar 1 *t* (*aumentar*) to redouble, intensify: *redoblar esfuerzos,* to redouble one's efforts; *redoblar la vigilancia,* to step up security. 2 (*doblar*) to bend back; (*un clavo*) to clinch. – 3 *i* (*tambores*) to roll.

redoble *m* roll.

redoma *f* flask.

redomado,-a 1 *adj* (*astuto*) sly. 2 (*consumado*) utter, out-and-out: *es un hipócrita redomado,* he's an utter hypocrite.

redonda *f* → **redondo,-a**.

redondear 1 *t* (*poner redondo*) to round, make round. 2 (*cantidad*) to round off, round up, make up to a round figure. 3 COST to level off. – 4 **redondearse,** *p* (*ponerse redondo*) to become round. 5 *fig* (*enriquecerse*) to become wealthy.

redondel 1 *m* (*círculo*) circle, ring. 2 (*en toros*) ring, arena.

redondez *f* roundness.
● **en toda la redondez de la tierra,** in the whole wide world.

redondilla 1 *f* (*poema*) quatrain. 2 (*letra*) round hand.

redondo,-a 1 *adj* (*circular*) round. 2 (*sin rodeo*) straightforward. 3 (*rotundo*) categorical: *un no redondo,* a flat refusal. 4 *fig* (*perfecto*) perfect, excellent: *un beneficio redondo,* an excellent profit. 5 *fig* (*cantidad*) round: *en números redondos,* in round figures. – 6 **redondo,** *m* (*círculo*) circle. 7 (*de carne*) topside. – 8 **redonda,** *f* (*comarca*) region. 9 MÚS semibreve, US whole note.
● **a la redonda,** around: *la explosión se oyó en varios kilómetros a la redonda,* the explosion could be heard several kilometres away. ‖ **caer redondo,-a,** (*caerse*) to collapse; (*morir*) to drop dead. ‖ **en redondo,** around. ‖ **negarse en redondo,** *fig* to flatly refuse.

reducción *f* reduction.

reducido,-a 1 *pp* → **reducir.** – 2 *adj* (*limitado*) limited; (*pequeño*) small. 3 (*precio*) low.

reducir 1 *t* (*gen*) to reduce: *reducir a cenizas,* to reduce to ashes. 2 (*disminuir*) to reduce, cut, cut down on: *reducir gastos,* to cut down on expenses. 3 (*vencer*) to subdue. 4 MED to set. 5 CULIN to boil down. 6 MAT QUÍM to reduce. – 7 *i* AUTO to change down, change to a lower gear. – 8 **reducirse,** *p* (*gen*) to be reduced; (*decrecer*) to decrease. 9 (*resultar*) to come down (**a**, to): *todo se redujo a una equivocación,* it all came down to a mistake.
▲ *Conjugation model* |46|, *like conducir.*

reductible *adj* reducible.

reducto *m* redoubt, stronghold.

reductor,-ra *adj* reducing.

redundancia *f* redundancy.

redundante *adj* redundant.

redundar 1 *i* (*rebosar*) to overflow. 2 (*abundar*) to abound. 3 (*resultar*) to redound (**en**, to): *redundó en nuestro beneficio,* it was to our advantage.

reduplicación *f* reduplication, redoubling.

reduplicar *t* to reduplicate, redouble.
▲ *Conjugation model* |1|, *like sacar.*

reedición *f* reprint, reissue.

reedificación *f* rebuilding.

reedificar *t* to rebuild.
▲ *Conjugation model* |1|, *like sacar.*

reeditar *t* to reprint, reissue.

reeducación *f* re-education.

reeducar *t* to re-educate.
▲ *Conjugation model* |1|, *like sacar.*

reelección *f* re-election.

reelecto,-a *adj* re-elected.

reelegir *t* to re-elect.
▲ *Conjugation model* |55|, *like elegir.*

reembolsable *adj* reimbursable.

reembolsar 1 *t* (*pagar*) to reimburse; (*cantidad*) to repay. 2 (*devolver*) to refund. – 3 **reembolsarse,** *p* (*cobrar*) to be paid.

reembolso 1 *m* (*pago*) reimbursement; (*cantidad*) payment. 2 (*devolución*) refund.
■ contra reembolso, cash on delivery.
reemplazable *adj* replaceable.
reemplazar *t* to replace.
▲ *Conjugation model* |4|, *like realizar*.
reemplazo 1 *m* replacement. 2 MIL call-up.
reemprender *t* to start again: *después de comer reemprendieron el viaje,* after lunch they continued on their journey.
reencarnación *f* reincarnation.
reencarnarse *p* to be reincarnated.
reencontrarse *p* to find os. again.
▲ *Conjugation model* |31|, *like contar*.
reencuentro *m* reunion.
reenganchado *m* re-enlisted soldier.
reenganchar 1 *t* to re-enlist. – 2 reengancharse, *p* to re-enlist.
reenganche *m* re-enlistment.
reestrenar *t* to rerun, show again, put on again.
reestreno *m* (*teatro*) revival; (*cine*) reshowing, rerun: *cine de reestreno,* rerun moviehouse.
reestructuración *f* restructuring, reorganization.
reestructurar *t* to restructure, reorganize.
reexpedir *t* to return, send back.
▲ *Conjugation model* |34|, *like servir*.
reexportar *t* to re-export.
ref. *abr* (*referencia*) reference; (*abreviatura*) ref.
refacción *f* refreshment, snack.
refajo *m* petticoat, underskirt.
refanfinflarse *p fam* not to matter one bit to: *eso me la refanfinfla,* I don't give a toss about it.
refectorio *m* refectory, dining hall.
referencia 1 *f* (*relación*) reference. – 2 referencias, *fpl* (*informes*) references.
● con referencia a, with reference to. ‖ hacer referencia a algo, to refer to sth.
referendo *m* referendum.
referéndum *m* referendum.
▲ *pl referéndum or referendos*.
referente *adj* concerning (**a**, -), regarding (**a**, -).
referir 1 *t* (*expresar*) to tell, relate. 2 (*remitir*) to refer. 3 (*situar*) to set. – 4 referirse, *p* to refer (**a**, to): *me refiero a lo que acordamos,* I'm referring to what we agreed.
● por lo que se refiere a eso, as for that, as far as that is concerned, with regard to that.
▲ *Conjugation model* |35|, *like hervir*.
refilón. 1 de refilón, *loc adv* (*oblicuamente*) obliquely, at a slant. 2 *fig* (*de paso*) briefly.
● mirar algo de refilón, to look at sth. out of the corner of one's eye.
refinado,-a 1 *pp* → **refinar**. – 2 *adj* (*gen*) refined. 3 *fig* (*astuto*) sly. – 4 refinado, *m* (*del azúcar etc*) refining.
refinador,-ra 1 *adj* refining. – 2 *m,f* refiner.
refinamiento 1 *m* (*esmero*) refinement. 2 (*ensañamiento*) cruelty.
refinar 1 *t* (*azúcar etc*) to refine. 2 *fig* (*escrito etc*) to polish, refine. – 3 refinarse, *p* (*pulirse*) to become refined.
refinería *f* refinery.
refino,-a *adj* very fine.
reflectante *adj* reflective.
reflectar *t* to reflect.
reflector,-ra 1 *adj* reflecting. – 2 reflector, *m* (*cuerpo*) reflector. 3 ELEC searchlight, spotlight. 4 (*telescopio*) reflector, reflecting telescope.

reflejar 1 *t* (*gen*) to reflect. 2 (*mostrar*) to show: *su rostro refleja sus sentimientos,* her face shows her feelings. – 3 reflejarse, *p* to be reflected.
reflejo,-a 1 *adj* reflected. 2 GRAM reflexive. 3 (*movimiento*) reflex. – 4 reflejo, *m* (*imagen*) reflection. 5 (*destello*) gleam, glint. 6 (*en el pelo*) tint, rinse. 7 (*movimiento*) reflex. 8 *fig* (*muestra*) sign, reflection: *sus palabras son reflejo de sus pensamientos,* his words reflect his thinking. – 9 reflejos, *mpl* (*mechas*) streaks, highlights.
● tener reflejos, to have good reflexes.
■ reflejo condicionado, conditioned reflex.
réflex 1 *m* (*sistema*) reflex. 2 (*cámara*) reflex camera.
▲ *pl réflex*.
reflexión *f* reflection.
● con reflexión, on reflection. ‖ sin reflexión, without thinking.
reflexionar *i* to reflect (**sobre**, on), think (**sobre**, about): *reflexionamos sobre el tema,* we reflected on the subject.
reflexivo,-a 1 *adj* reflective, thoughtful. 2 GRAM reflexive.
reflorecer 1 *i* to blossom again, flower again. 2 *fig* to flourish again.
▲ *Conjugation model* |43|, *like agradecer*.
reflotar *t* to refloat.
reflujo *m* ebb tide, ebb.
refocilar 1 *t* (*alegrar*) to amuse, enjoy. – 2 refocilarse, *p* to delight (**con**, in), gloat (**con**, over).
reforma 1 *f* (*gen*) reform. 2 (*mejora*) improvement. 3 la Reforma, REL the Reformation. – 4 reformas, *fpl* (*en construcción*) alterations, repairs, improvements.
● "cerrado por reformas", "closed for alterations".
■ reforma agraria, agrarian reform. ‖ reforma fiscal, tax reform.
reformador,-ra 1 *adj* reforming. – 2 *m,f* reformer.
reformar 1 *t* (*gen*) to reform. 2 ARQ to renovate, do up. 3 (*una prenda*) to alter. – 4 reformarse, *p* (*corregirse*) to reform os.
reformatorio *m* reformatory, reform school.
■ reformatorio de menores, remand home.
reformismo *m* reformism.
reformista 1 *adj* reformist. – 2 *mf* reformist.
reforzado,-a 1 *pp* → **reforzar**. – 2 *adj* reinforced, strengthened.
reforzar 1 *t* to reinforce, strengthen. – 2 reforzarse, *p* to be reinforced, be strengthened.
▲ *Conjugation model* |50|, *like forzar*.
refracción *f* refraction.
■ ángulo de refracción, angle of refraction. ‖ índice de refracción, refractive index. ‖ refracción doble, double refraction, birefringence.
refractar 1 *t* to refract. – 2 refractarse, *p* to refract.
refractario,-a 1 *adj* (*al fuego*) heat-resistant. 2 (*persona - que rehúsa*) reluctant, unwilling; (- *opuesta*) opposed: *es refractario al progreso,* he's opposed to progress.
refractivo,-a *adj* refractive.
refractor *m* refractor, refracting telescope.
refrán *m* proverb, saying.
● como dice el refrán, as the saying goes.
refranero *m* collection of proverbs, collection of sayings.
refrangible *adj* refrangible.
refregar 1 *t* to rub hard. 2 *fam fig* to rub in: *me refregó mi error,* he kept on about my mistake.
▲ *Conjugation model* |48|, *like regar*.
refregón *m* rub, rubbing.

refreír 1 *t* (*volver a freír*) to fry again. **2** (*freír demasiado*) to overdo, overfry.
▲ *Conjugation model* [37], *like* **reír**; *pp* **refrito** *or* **refreído**.
refrenar 1 *t* (*contener*) to restrain, curb, control. **2** (*al caballo*) to rein in. – **3 refrenarse,** *p* to restrain os.
refrendar 1 *t* (*firmar*) to endorse, countersign. **2** (*aprobar*) to ratify, approve.
refrendo *m* (*firma*) endorsement, countersignature.
refrescante *adj* refreshing.
refrescar 1 *t* (*poner fresco*) to cool, refresh. **2** *fig* (*la memoria*) to refresh; (*idiomas*) to brush up on: *necesito refrescar un poco el francés,* I need to brush up on my French a bit. – **3** *i* (*el tiempo*) to get cooler, cool down, turn cooler. **4** (*comida, bebida*) to be refreshing. – **5 refrescarse,** *p* (*gen*) to cool down, cool off; (*lavarse*) to freshen up; (*tomar el fresco*) to get a breath of fresh air. **6** (*beber*) to have a cold drink.
▲ *Conjugation model* [1], *like* **sacar**.
refresco 1 *m* (*bebida*) soft drink.
● **de refresco,** fresh.
refriega 1 *f* (*lucha*) scuffle, brawl. **2** (*escaramuza*) skirmish.
refrigeración 1 *f* refrigeration. **2** (*aire acondicionado*) air conditioning. **3** (*sistema*) cooling system.
refrigerado,-a 1 *pp* → **refrigerar.** – **2** *adj* (*enfriado*) refrigerated, cooled. **3** (*con aire acondicionado*) air-conditioned.
refrigerador *m* fridge, refrigerator.
refrigerante 1 *adj* refrigerating, cooling. – **2** *m* refrigerant.
refrigerar 1 *t* (*enfriar*) to refrigerate. **2** (*con aire acondicionado*) to air-condition.
refrigerio *m* refreshments *pl*, snack.
refringente *adj* refringent.
refrito,-a 1 *pp* → **refreír.** – **2 refrito,** *m fam fig* rehash.
refuerzo 1 *m* (*fortalecimiento*) reinforcement, strengthening. – **2 refuerzos,** *mpl* MIL reinforcements.
refugiado,-a 1 *pp* → **refugiar.** – **2** *adj* refugee. – **3** *m,f* refugee.
■ **refugiado político,** political refugee.
refugiar 1 *t* to shelter, give refuge to. – **2 refugiarse,** *p* (*gen*) to take refuge; (*de la lluvia*) to shelter.
▲ *Conjugation model* [12], *like* **cambiar**.
refugio 1 *m* (*gen*) shelter, refuge. **2** *fig* refuge. **3** AUTO traffic island.
■ **refugio antiaéreo,** air-raid shelter. ‖ **refugio atómico,** (nuclear) fallout shelter.
refulgencia *f* radiance, brilliance.
refulgente *adj* radiant, brilliant.
refulgir *i* (*brillar*) to shine; (*resplandecer*) to glitter, sparkle.
▲ *Conjugation model* [6], *like* **dirigir**.
refundar *t fig* to re-form.
refundición 1 *f* (*metales*) recasting. **2** *fig* (*literaria*) adaptation.
refundir 1 *t* (*metales*) to recast. **2** *fig* (*comedia etc*) to adapt.
refunfuñar *i fam* to grumble, moan, complain.
refunfuñón,-ona 1 *adj fam* grumpy, grumbling, moaning. – **2** *m,f fam* grumbler, moaner.
refutable *adj* refutable, disprovable.
refutación *f* refutation, disproof.
refutar *t* to refute, disprove.
reg. *abr* (*registro*) register; (*abreviatura*) reg.
regadera *f* watering can.
● **estar como una regadera,** *fam* to be as mad as a hatter.

regadío,-a 1 *adj* irrigable. – **2** regadío, *m* (*acción*) irrigation, watering. **3** (*tierras*) irrigated land.
● **de regadío,** irrigable, irrigated.
■ **cultivo de regadío,** irrigation farming.
regala *f* gunwale, gunnel.
regaladamente *adv fig* comfortably, pleasantly.
regalado,-a 1 *pp* → **regalar.** – **2** *adj* (*de regalo*) given as a present. **3** (*muy barato*) dirt cheap: *esta camisa está regalada,* this shirt is dirt cheap. **4** (*gratis*) free. **5** (*delicado*) delicate. **6** (*agradable*) comfortable, pleasant: *llevar una vida regalada,* to lead an easy life, lead a pleasant life, live the life of Riley.
regalar 1 *t* (*dar un regalo*) to give as a present: *le podemos regalar un libro para su cumpleaños,* we can get him a book for his birthday. **2** (*dar*) to give away: *me iba corto y lo regalé,* it was too short for me so I gave it away. **3** (*dar gratis*) to give: *con cada botella regalan un vaso,* there's a free glass with each bottle. **4** (*halagar*) to flatter. **5** (*deleitar*) to delight. – **6 regalarse,** *p* (*deleitarse*) to treat os. (**con,** to): *se regaló con una copa de champaña,* he treated himself to a glass of champagne.
● **regalar el oído a algn.,** to flatter sb. ‖ **regalar la vista,** to be a pleasure to look at.
regalía 1 *f* (*prerrogativa*) royal prerogative. **2** *fig* (*privilegio*) privilege, prerogative.
regaliz *m* liquorice (US licorice).
regalo 1 *m* (*obsequio*) gift, present. **2** (*complacencia*) pleasure, joy: *este vino es un regalo para el paladar,* this is an excellent wine. **3** (*comodidad*) comfort, pleasure: *vive con gran regalo,* she lives a life of luxury. **4** (*exquisitez*) delicacy. **5** (*ganga*) bargain, steal.
regañadientes a regañadientes, *loc adv* reluctantly, grudgingly, unwillingly.
regañar 1 *t* to scold, tell off. – **2** *i* (*reñir*) to argue, quarrel, fall out: *no hacen más que regañar,* they're always quarrelling. **3** (*refunfuñar*) to moan, grumble, complain.
regañina 1 *f* (*represión*) scolding, telling-off. **2** (*riña*) quarrel, argument.
regaño *m* scolding, telling-off.
regañón,-ona 1 *adj fam* grumpy, irritable. – **2** *m,f* grumbler, moaner.
regar 1 *t* (*plantas, tierra, río*) to water. **2** (*calle*) to wash down, hose down. **3** *fig* (*esparcir*) to sprinkle, scatter. **4** *fig* (*derramar*) to pour.
● **regar con lágrimas,** *fig* to bathe in tears.
▲ *Conjugation model* [48].
regata[1] *f* MAR regatta, boat race.
regata[2] *f* (*surco*) irrigation channel.
regate 1 *m* (*gen*) dodge. **2** DEP dribbling.
regateador,-ra *m,f* haggler.
regatear 1 *t* (*un precio*) to haggle over, barter for. **2** (*escatimar*) to be sparing with: *les regatea la fruta,* he's sparing with fruit. – **3** *i* (*comerciar*) to haggle, bargain. **4** DEP to dribble. **5** MAR to race.
● **no regatear esfuerzos,** to spare no effort.
regateo 1 *m* (*precios*) haggling, bargaining. **2** DEP dribbling.
regato 1 *m* (*charco*) pool. **2** (*arroyo*) stream.
regazo *m* lap: *en el regazo,* on my (*your, his, etc*) lap.
regencia *f* regency.
regeneración *f* regeneration.
regenerador,-ra 1 *adj* regenerative. – **2** *m,f* regenerator.
regenerar *t* to regenerate.
regenta *f* → **regente,-a.**
regentar 1 *t* POL to govern, rule. **2** (*cargo*) to hold. **3** (*dirigir*) to manage, direct.

regente,-a 1 *adj* ruling, governing. – 2 *mf* POL regent. 3 JUR magistrate. 4 (*director*) manager. – 5 **regenta**, *f* (*mujer del que manda*) manager's wife. 6 (*mujer del regente*) regent's wife.

regiamente *adv* regally, royally.

regicida 1 *adj* regicidal. – 2 *mf* regicide.

regicidio *m* regicide.

regidor,-ra 1 *adj* ruling, governing. – 2 *m,f* (*concejal*) town councillor. 3 TEAT stage manager.

régimen 1 *m* POL regime. 2 MED diet. 3 (*condiciones*) system, regime, rules *pl*; (*forma de producirse*) pattern. 4 TÉC speed. 5 LING government.
● estar a régimen, to be on a diet. ‖ poner a régimen, to put on a diet. ‖ ponerse a régimen, to go on a diet.
■ régimen de vida, way of life. ‖ régimen tormentoso, (*clima*) stormy weather.
▲ *pl regímenes.*

regimiento *m* regiment.

regio,-a 1 *adj* (*real*) royal, regal. 2 *fig* (*magnífico*) magnificent, splendid, majestic: *finca regia,* magnificent building.

región *f* region.

regional *adj* regional.

regionalismo *m* regionalism.

regionalista 1 *adj* regionalist. – 2 *mf* regionalist.

regir 1 *t* (*gobernar*) to govern, rule. 2 (*dirigir*) to manage, direct, run. 3 LING to govern. – 4 *i* (*ley etc*) to be in force, apply; (*costumbre*) to prevail: *esta ley aún rige,* this law is still in force. – 5 **regirse**, *p* (*guiarse*) to follow, abide (**por**, by), go (**por**, by): *se rige por la opinión de su padre,* he goes by his father's opinion.
● el mes que rige, the present month. ‖ no regir, *fam* to have a screw loose.
▲ *Conjugation model* [55], *like elegir.*

registrado,-a 1 *pp* → **registrar**. – 2 *adj* registered, recorded, noted, listed; (*marca*) registered.

registrador,-ra 1 *adj* registering, recording: *caja registradora,* cash register. – 2 *m,f* registrar.
■ registrador,-ra de la propiedad, land registrar.

registrar 1 *t* (*inspeccionar*) to search, inspect, look through: *me registraron el bolso,* my bag was searched. 2 (*cachear*) to frisk. 3 (*inscribir*) to register, record, note; (*matricular*) to register. 4 (*grabar*) to record. 5 *fig* (*detectar*) to notice: *hemos registrado diversos fallos,* we have noticed several faults. – 6 **registrarse**, *p* (*matricularse*) to register, enrol (US enroll). 7 (*detectarse*) to be recorded. 8 (*ocurrir*) to happen: *se ha registrado un terremoto,* there has been an earthquake.

registro 1 *m* (*inspección*) search, inspection. 2 (*inscripción*) registration, recording; (*matriculación*) enrolment (US enrollment), registration. 3 JUR (*oficina*) registry; (*libro*) register. 4 MÚS register; (*de órgano*) stop. 5 INFORM register. 6 TÉC inspection hole.
● tocar todos los registros, *fig* to pull out all the stops.
■ registro civil, births, marriages and deaths register; (*oficina*) registry office. ‖ registro de la propiedad, land registry. ‖ registro electoral, electoral roll. ‖ registro mercantil, business register.

regla 1 *f* (*norma*) rule, regulation, norm. 2 (*pauta*) pattern, rule. 3 (*instrumento*) ruler. 4 MAT rule. 5 (*menstruación*) period.
● en regla, in order: *está todo en regla,* everything's in order. ‖ obrar según las reglas, to play by the rules. ‖ por regla general, as a rule, as a general rule. ‖ saber las cuatro reglas, *fam* to know the three Rs. ‖ salir de la regla, to overstep the mark. ‖ tener la regla, to have one's period.
■ las reglas del juego, the rules of the game. ‖ regla de cálculo, slide rule. ‖ regla de oro, golden rule. ‖ regla de tres, rule of three.

reglado,-a 1 *pp* → **reglar**. – 2 *adj* (*moderado*) moderate. 3 (*regulado*) regulated. 4 (*papel*) ruled, lined.

reglaje *m* adjustment.

reglamentación 1 *f* (*reglamento*) regulations *pl*, rules *pl*. 2 (*acción*) regulation.

reglamentar *t* to regulate.

reglamentariamente *adv* in due form, statutorily.

reglamentario,-a *adj* statutory, prescribed, required; (*arma*) regulation.

reglamento *m* regulations *pl*, rules *pl*.

reglar 1 *t* (*regular*) to regulate. 2 (*ajustar*) to adjust. 3 (*hacer líneas*) to rule, draw a line. – 4 **reglarse**, *p* (*regirse*) to be guided.

regleta *f* space.

regletear *t* to space out.

regocijar 1 *t* to delight, amuse. – 2 **regocijarse**, *p* (*alegrarse*) to be delighted (**con**, by). 3 (*regodearse*) to delight (**de**, in), take pleasure (**de**, in).

regocijo 1 *m* (*placer*) delight, joy, happiness. 2 (*júbilo*) merriment, rejoicing.

regodearse *p fam* to delight (**en/con**, in), take pleasure (**en/con**, in): *se regodea con el dolor ajeno,* he takes pleasure in other's people's sorrow.

regodeo *m fam* delight, pleasure.

regoldar *i fam* to belch.
▲ *Conjugation model* [31], *like contar.*

regordete,-a *adj fam* plump, chubby, tubby.

regresar *i* to return, come back, go back.

regresión 1 *f* (*retroceso*) regression. 2 (*disminución*) drop, decrease: *una regresión de la violencia,* a decrease in violence.
● en vías de regresión, on the decline.

regresivo,-a *adj* regressive.

regreso *m* return.
● a mi (*tu, su, etc*) regreso, on my (*your, his, etc*) return. ‖ estar de regreso, to be back.
■ viaje de regreso, return journey.

regüeldo *m fam* belch, burp.

reguera *f* irrigation channel.

reguero 1 *m* (*corriente*) trickle of water. 2 (*señal*) trail, trickle. 3 (*reguera*) irrigation channel.
● como un reguero de pólvora, *fig* like wildfire.

regulable *adj* adjustable.

regulación 1 *f* (*control*) regulation, control. 2 (*ajuste*) adjustment.

regulador,-ra 1 *adj* regulating. – 2 **regulador**, *m* TÉC regulator. 3 (*de radio, televisión*) control.

regular 1 *adj* (*gen*) regular. 2 *fam* (*pasable*) so-so, average, not bad: *¿qué tal la película? - regular,* what's the film like? - nothing special. – 3 *t* (*gen*) to regulate. 4 (*ajustar*) to adjust.

regularidad *f* regularity.
● con regularidad, regularly.

regularización *f* regularization.

regularizar *t* to regularize; (*normalizar*) to standardize; (*arreglar*) to sort out.
▲ *Conjugation model* [4], *like realizar.*

regularmente 1 *adv* (*con regularidad*) regularly. 2 (*medianamente*) so-so.

regurgitar *t* to regurgitate.

regusto *m* aftertaste.

rehabilitación 1 *f* rehabilitation. **2** (*en rango*) rehabilitation, reinstatement.

rehabilitar 1 *t* to rehabilitate. – **2** *f* (*en rango*) to rehabilitate, reinstate.

rehacer 1 *t* (*volver a hacer*) to do again, redo. **2** (*reconstruir*) to remake, rebuild. **3** (*reparar*) to repair, mend. **4** (*repetir*) to repeat. – **5 rehacerse,** *p* (*recuperarse*) to recover, recuperate. **6** (*serenarse*) to pull os. together.
▲ Conjugation model [73], like *hacer;* pp *rehecho,-a.*

rehecho,-a 1 *pp →* **rehacer.** – **2** *adj* (*grueso*) thick-set.

rehén *mf* hostage.

rehilete 1 *m* (*flecha*) dart. **2** (*juguete*) shuttlecock.

rehogar *t* to fry lightly.
▲ Conjugation model [7], like *llegar.*

rehostia ser la rehostia, *loc tabú* (*de bueno*) to be brilliant; (*de malo*) to be bloody awful, be the limit.

rehoyo *m* cliff.

rehuir *t* to avoid, shun.
▲ Conjugation model [62], like *huir.*

rehusar *t* to refuse, decline, turn down: *rehusé la invitación,* I declined the invitation.
▲ Conjugation model [18].

reidor,-ra *adj* happy, laughing.

Reikiavik *m* Reykjavik.

reimplantar *t* to implant again.

reimportar *t* to reimport.

reimpresión 1 *f* (*acción*) reprinting. **2** (*ejemplar*) reprint.

reimprimir *t* to reprint.
▲ *pp reimpreso,-a* or *reimprimido,-a.*

reina 1 *f* (*gen*) queen. **2** *fam* (*apelativo*) love, darling, sweetheart: *¡hasta luego, reina!,* see you, love!
■ **reina de belleza,** beauty queen. ‖ **reina madre,** queen mother.

reinado *m* reign.
● bajo el reinado de, in the reign of.

reinante 1 *adj* (*que reina*) reigning. **2** (*existente*) prevailing, reigning: *el silencio reinante,* the reigning silence.

reinar 1 *i* to reign. **2** *fig* (*prevalecer*) to reign, prevail: *reina el desconcierto,* disorder reigns.

reincidencia 1 *f* relapse. **2** JUR recidivism.

reincidente 1 *adj* relapsing. **2** JUR reoffending, recidivist. – **3** *mf* JUR reoffender, recidivist.

reincidir 1 *i* to relapse (**en,** into), fall back (**en,** into). **2** JUR to reoffend.

reincorporación 1 *f* reincorporation. **2** (*a un cargo*) reinstatement, reemployment.

reincorporar 1 *t* to reincorporate; (*a un trabajo*) to reinstate, reemploy. – **2 reincorporarse,** *p* to rejoin (**a,** -): *se reincorporó al ejército,* he rejoined the army; *se reincorporará al trabajo el lunes,* she will go back to work on Monday.

reineta *f* pippin.

reingresar 1 *t* to readmit. – **2** *i* to return.

reingreso *m* return, re-entry.

reino *m* kingdom, reign.
■ **reino de los animales,** animal kingdom. ‖ **reino de los Cielos,** Kingdom of Heaven. ‖ **Reino Unido,** United Kingdom. ‖ **reino vegetal,** vegetable kingdom.

reinserción *f* reintegration, rehabilitation: *la reinserción social,* social rehabilitation.

reinsertar 1 *t* to reintegrate. – **2 reinsertarse,** *p* to reintegrate.

reinstalar *t* to reinstall, reinstal.

reintegrable *adj* returnable, repayable.

reintegración 1 *f* (*reincorporación*) reinstatement. **2** (*pago*) refund.

reintegrar 1 *t* (*reincorporar*) to reinstate, restore. **2** (*pagar*) to refund, reimburse; (*banco*) to credit. – **3** **reintegrarse,** *p* (*volver a ejercer*) to return (**a,** to): *se reintegró a su puesto,* he returned to his job. **4** (*recobrarse*) to recover.

reintegro 1 *m* (*reincorporación*) reinstatement. **2** FIN reimbursement, repayment, refund; (*bancario*) credit. **3** (*de lotería*) refund of the price of the ticket.

reír 1 *t* to laugh at: *reír las gracias,* to laugh at jokes. – **2** *i* to laugh. – **3 reírse,** *p* to laugh (**de,** at): *¿de qué te ríes?,* what are you laughing at? **4** (*burlarse*) to laugh (**de,** at), make fun (**de,** of).
● me río yo de ..., *fam* I couldn't care less ...: *me río yo de lo que diga ése,* I couldn't care less what he says. ‖ quien ríe el último ríe mejor, he who laughs last laughs longest. ‖ reír a carcajadas, to roar with laughter. ‖ reír a costa de algn., to make fun of sb., make a fool out of sb. ‖ reír a espaldas de algn., to laugh behind sb.'s back. ‖ reír a mandíbula batiente, *fam* to laugh one's head off. ‖ reír con ganas, to laugh heartily. ‖ reír para sus adentros, to laugh to os., chuckle.
▲ Conjugation model [37].

reiteración *f* reiteration.

reiteradamente *adv* repeatedly, reiteratively.

reiterar *t* to reiterate, repeat.

reiterativo,-a *adj* repetitive, repetitious, reiterative.

reivindicación *f* claim, demand.

reivindicar *t* to claim, demand: *los terroristas reivindicaron el atentado,* the terrorists claimed responsibility for the attack.
▲ Conjugation model [1], like *sacar.*

reivindicativo,-a *adj* protest.
■ acto reivindicativo, protest.

reja[1] *f* (*del arado*) ploughshare (US plowshare).

reja[2] *f* (*de ventana*) grill, grille, bar.
● estar entre rejas, *fam* to be behind bars.

rejilla 1 *f* (*celosía*) grill, grille. **2** (*de chimenea*) grate. **3** (*de silla*) wickerwork. **4** (*de horno*) grid iron. **5** (*de ventilador*) grill. **6** (*para equipaje*) luggage rack.
■ rejilla del radiador, AUTO radiator grille.

rejón *m* lance.

rejoneador,-ra *m,f* bullfighter on horseback.

rejonear *t* to fight on horseback.

rejoneo *m* bullfighting on horseback.

rejuntarse *p fam* to cohabit.

rejuvenecedor,-ra *adj* rejuvenating, rejuvenescent.

rejuvenecer 1 *t* to rejuvenate. – **2 rejuvenecerse,** *p* to become rejuvenated.
▲ Conjugation model [43], like *agradecer.*

rejuvenecimiento *m* rejuvenation.

relación 1 *f* (*correspondencia*) relation, relationship: *una relación amistosa,* a friendship, a friendly relationship. **2** (*conexión*) link, connection. **3** (*lista*) list, record. **4** (*relato*) account, telling. **5** MAT TÉC ratio. – **6 relaciones,** *fpl* (*conocidos*) acquaintances; (*contactos*) contacts, connections.
● con relación a / en relación a, with regard to, regarding. ‖ estar en buenas relaciones con algn., to be on good terms with sb. ‖ estar en relación con algn., to be in contact with sb. ‖ hacer relación a algo, to refer to sth. ‖ tener buenas relaciones, to be well connected. ‖ tener relaciones con algn., (*salir*) to go out with sb.

■ **relación de compresión,** TÉC compression ratio. ‖ **relaciones diplomáticas,** diplomatic relations. ‖ **relaciones públicas,** public relations: *es el relaciones públicas de Enya,* he's Enya's PR man. ‖ **relaciones sexuales,** sexual relations.
relacionado,-a 1 *pp* → **relacionar.** – **2** *adj* (*referido*) concerning, regarding. **3** (*conectado*) related, connected: *está relacionado con el libro,* it's related to the book.
● **estar bien relacionado,-a,** to be well connected.
relacionar 1 *t* (*poner en relación*) to relate, connect, associate. **2** (*relatar*) to tell, list. – **3 relacionarse,** *p* (*estar conectado*) to be related (**con,** with), be connected (**con,** with). **4** (*alternar*) to get acquainted (**con,** with), mix (**con,** with), meet (**con,** -).
relajación 1 *f* (*gen*) relaxation. **2** *fig* slackening, looseness.
relajado,-a 1 *pp* → **relajar.** – **2** *adj* (*gen*) relaxed. **3** (*inmoral*) loose, dissolute.
relajante *adj* relaxing.
relajar 1 *t* (*gen*) to relax. **2** *fig* to loosen, slacken. – **3** *i* (*ser relajante*) to be relaxing: *el masaje relaja,* massage is relaxing. – **4 relajarse,** *p* (*descansar*) to relax. **5** *fig* (*en las costumbres*) to let os. go. **6** (*dilatarse*) to slacken.
relajo 1 *m* (*descanso*) relaxation, rest; (*tranquilidad*) peace. **2** (*falta de orden*) relaxed attitude. **3** (*immoralidad*) depravity, dissoluteness.
relamer 1 *t* to lick. – **2 relamerse,** *p* to lick one's lips repeatedly. **3** *fig* (*disfrutar*) to lick one's lips with anticipation: *se relamía viendo cómo su madre hacía el pastel,* watching her mother make the cake made her mouth water.
relamido,-a 1 *pp* → **relamer.** – **2** *adj pey* (*afectado*) affected. **3** (*pulcro*) prim and proper.
relámpago *m* flash of lightning.
● **como un relámpago,** *fig* as quick as a flash: *pasar como un relámpago,* to flash past.
■ **guerra relámpago,** blitzkrieg.
relampagueante *adj* flashing.
relampaguear *i* to flash.
▲ *Used only in the 3rd pers; it does not take a subject.*
relampagueo 1 *m* (*relámpago*) lightning. **2** (*centelleo*) flashing.
relanzamiento *m* relaunch.
relanzar *t* to relaunch.
relatar 1 *t* (*una historia*) to narrate, tell. **2** (*un suceso*) to report, tell.
relatividad *f* relativity.
■ **teoría de la relatividad,** theory of relativity.
relativismo *m* relativism.
relativista 1 *adj* relativist. – **2** *mf* relativist.
relativizar *t* to lessen the importance of, play down.
▲ *Conjugation model* |4|, *like realizar.*
relativo,-a 1 *adj* relative: *problemas relativos a la economía,* problems relating to the economy, problems related to the economy. – **2 relativo,** *m* LING relative.
● **en lo relativo a,** with regard to, referring to, concerning.
relato 1 *m* (*narración*) story, tale. **2** (*informe*) report, account.
relator,-ra 1 *m,f* teller, narrator. **2** (*funcionario*) clerk.
relax 1 *m* relaxation: *necesito un poco de relax,* I need to relax a bit. **2** (*prostitución*) call-girl services *pl.*
▲ *pl relax.*
relé *m* relay.
releer *t* to reread, read again.
▲ *Conjugation model* |61|, *like leer.*

relegación *f* relegation.
relegar *t* to relegate (**a,** to), consign (**a,** to).
▲ *Conjugation model* |7|, *like llegar.*
relente *m* dew.
relevación 1 *f* (*alivio*) release. **2** JUR exemption.
relevancia 1 *f* (*significación*) relevance. **2** (*importancia*) importance.
relevante 1 *adj* (*significativo*) relevant. **2** (*importante*) excellent, outstanding.
relevar 1 *t* (*sustituir*) to relieve, take over from. **2** (*eximir*) to exempt (**de,** from). **3** (*destituir*) to dismiss, remove, relieve. **4** MIL to change, relieve. **5** *fig* (*engrandecer*) to exaggerate. – **6 relevarse,** *p* to take turns.
relevista *mf* relay runner.
relevo 1 *m* MIL relief, change of the guard. **2** DEP relay.
● **tomar el relevo de,** to relieve, take over from.
■ **carrera de relevos,** relay race.
relicario 1 *m* REL reliquary. **2** (*caja*) box; (*estuche*) locket.
relieve 1 *m* relief. **2** *fig* (*renombre*) renown, fame.
● **en relieve,** in relief. ‖ **poner de relieve,** *fig* to emphasize, highlight, underline.
religión *f* religion.
● **entrar en religión,** to take vows.
religiosamente *adv* religiously.
religiosidad *f* religiousness, religiosity.
religioso,-a 1 *adj* religious. – **2** *m,f* (*hombre*) monk; (*mujer*) nun.
relinchar *i* to neigh, whinny.
relincho *m* neigh, whinny.
reliquia *f* relic.
rellano *m* landing.
rellenar 1 *t* (*volver a llenar*) to refill, fill again. **2** (*llenar del todo*) to cram, pack, stuff. **3** (*cuestionario*) to fill in, fill out. **4** CULIN (*ave*) to stuff; (*pastel*) to fill: *rellenar de chocolate,* to fill with chocolate. **5** COST to pad. **6** (*historia, relato*) to pad out, embroider.
relleno,-a 1 *adj* (*totalmente lleno*) stuffed, crammed, packed. **2** (*cara*) full. **3** CULIN stuffed; (*pasteles*) filled. – **4 relleno,** *m* CULIN (*aves*) stuffing; (*pasteles*) filling. **5** COST padding. **6** (*de un cojín etc*) stuffing. **7** (*de un escrito*) padding; (*de un discurso*) waffle.
reló *m* → **reloj.**
reloj *m* clock; (*de pulsera*) watch.
● **como un reloj,** *fig* like clockwork. ‖ **contra reloj,** against the clock.
■ **reloj de arena,** hourglass. ‖ **reloj de caja / reloj de péndulo,** grandfather clock. ‖ **reloj de cuco,** cuckoo clock. ‖ **reloj de pared,** clock. ‖ **reloj de pulsera,** wristwatch. ‖ **reloj de sol,** sundial. ‖ **reloj despertador,** (*de mesita*) alarm clock; (*de pulsera*) alarm watch.
relojería 1 *f* (*arte*) watchmaking, clockmaking. **2** (*tienda*) watchmaker's, jeweller's.
■ **bomba de relojería,** time bomb.
relojero,-a *m,f* watchmaker, clockmaker.
reluciente *adj* bright, shining, gleaming, glittering.
relucir 1 *i* (*brillar*) to shine, gleam, glitter. **2** *fig* (*destacar*) to excel, stand out, shine.
● **sacar a relucir algo,** to bring up sth. ‖ **salir a relucir,** to come to light.
▲ *Conjugation model* |45|, *like lucir.*
reluctancia *f* reluctance, reluctancy.
reluctante *adj* reluctant.
relumbrante *adj* shining, dazzling.
relumbrar *i* to shine, dazzle, gleam.
relumbro *m* → **relumbrón.**

relumbrón l *m* (*destello*) flash, glare. **2** *fig* flashiness, ostentation.
● **de relumbrón,** flashy.
reluzco *pres indic* → **relucir.**
rem *m* rem.
▲ *pl* **rems.**
remachadora *f* riveting machine.
remachar **1** *t* (*clavo etc*) to clinch; (*metal*) to rivet. **2** *fig* (*confirmar*) to drive home, hammer home, stress.
remache *m* rivet.
remanente l *adj* (*que queda*) remaining, residual. **2** (*extra*) surplus. – **3** *m* (*restos*) remainder, remains *pl*. **4** (*extra*) surplus.
remangar l *t* (*mangas, pantalones*) to roll up; (*faldas*) to pull up, hitch up. – **2 remangarse,** *p fig* to decide quickly, make a snap decision.
remanguillé **a la remanguillé,** *loc fam* upside down, in a mess.
remansarse *p* to stop flowing.
remanso l *m* (*agua estancada*) backwater. **2** (*estanque*) pool. **3** (*lugar tranquilo*) quiet place. **4** *fig* (*pachorra*) sluggishness.
● **remanso de paz,** *fig* haven of peace.
remar *i* to row.
remarcable *adj* remarkable, outstanding.
remarcar *t* to stress, underline.
▲ *Conjugation model* [1], *like* **sacar.**
rematadamente *adv* totally, completely.
rematado,-a l *pp* → **rematar.** – **2** *adj* absolute, utter, out-and-out: *es un tonto rematado,* he's an absolute idiot. **3** JUR convicted.
rematador,-ra *m,f* DEP striker.
rematante *mf* highest bidder.
rematar l *t* (*acabar*) to finish off, round off, put the finishing touches to: *rematar un trabajo,* to finish off a job. **2** (*precios*) to knock down; (*vender más barato*) to sell off cheaply. **3** (*en subasta*) to auction. **4** (*matar*) to kill, finish off. **5** DEP to shoot. – **6** *i* (*terminar*) to end up. **7** DEP to take a shot at goal, shoot.
● **rematar de cabeza,** DEP to head the ball.
remate l *m* (*final*) end, finish. **2** (*toque final*) finishing touch. **3** DEP shot. **4** (*puja*) highest bid.
● **de remate,** *fam* utter, out-and-out, total: *es tonto de remate,* he's a total idiot. ‖ **para remate,** to crown it all. ‖ **por remate,** finally, in the end.
■ **precios de remate,** knock-down prices.
rembolsar *t* → **reembolsar.**
rembolso *m* → **reembolso.**
remedar l *t* (*imitar*) to imitate, copy. **2** (*con burla*) to ape.
remediable *adj* remediable, that can be corrected.
remediar l *t* (*poner remedio*) to remedy. **2** (*reparar*) to repair, make good. **3** (*resolver*) to solve: *con llorar no remedias nada,* crying won't do any good. **4** (*socorrer*) to help, assist. **5** (*evitar*) to avoid, prevent: *no lo puedo remediar,* I can't help it.
▲ *Conjugation model* [12], *like* **cambiar.**
remedio l *m* (*cura*) remedy, cure. **2** *fig* (*solución*) solution. **3** JUR remedy, recourse.
● **como último remedio,** as a last resort. ‖ **no tener más remedio que / no haber más remedio que,** to have no choice but to, have no option but to. ‖ **¡no tienes remedio!,** *fam* you're hopeless!, you're a case! ‖ **poner remedio a algo,** to do something about sth. ‖ **¡qué remedio!,** do I have any choice?, what choice do I have?, what else can I do? ‖ **sin remedio,** without fail.

remedo l *m* (*imitación*) imitation, copy. **2** (*parodia*) parody; (*mímica*) mimicry, mimicking. **3** (*burla*) travesty, mockery.
remembranza *f* remembrance, recollection.
rememoración *f* remembrance, recollection.
rememorar *t* to remember, recall.
remendar l *t* (*arreglar*) to mend, repair; (*corregir*) to correct. **2** COST to mend; (*ropas*) to patch; (*calcetines*) to darn.
▲ *Conjugation model* [27], *like* **acertar.**
remendón,-ona l *adj* mending. – **2** *m,f* mender.
remera *f* → **remero,-a.**
remero,-a l *m,f* DEP rower; (*hombre*) oarsman; (*mujer*) oarswoman. – **2 remera,** *f* (*pluma*) remex, quill feather.
remesa l *f* (*de dinero*) remittance. **2** (*de mercancías*) consignment, shipment.
remeter l *t* (*volver a meter*) to put back. **2** (*meter adentro*) to tuck in.
remiendo l *m* (*arreglo*) mend. **2** (*de calcetín*) darn; (*parche*) patch.
● **echar un remiendo a algo,** to patch sth. up.
rémige *f* remix.
remigio *m* crapette.
remilgado,-a l *pp* → **remilgarse.** – **2** *adj* (*afectado*) affected. **3** (*con la comida*) fussy, finicky. **4** (*mojigato*) prudish.
remilgarse *p* to put on an act.
remilgo l *m* (*afectación*) affectation. **2** (*gazmoñería*) prudishness, primness.
● **andar con remilgos,** to make a fuss, be fussy.
reminiscencia *f* reminiscence.
remirado,-a l *pp* → **remirar.** – **2** *adj* over-cautious.
remirar l *t* (*volver a mirar*) to have another look at, look at again. – **2 remirarse,** *p* (*esmerarse*) to take great care (with). **3** (*mirar con complacencia*) to browse through: *se remiró los libros,* she browsed thoughtfully through the books.
remisión l *f* (*referencia*) reference. **2** (*envío*) sending. **3** REL remission, forgiveness. **4** MED remission.
● **sin remisión,** *fig* without fail.
remisivo,-a *adj* reference.
remiso,-a *adj* (*reacio*) reluctant, unwilling: *se mostró remiso a ayudar,* he was reluctant to help.
remisorio,-a *adj* remissive.
remite *m* sender's name and address.
remitente *mf* sender.
● **"devuélvase al remitente",** "return to sender".
remitido *m* advertisement, announcement.
remitir l *t* (*enviar*) to remit, send: *han remitido aquí su carta,* you letter has been sent here. **2** (*referir*) to refer: *el texto remite a la página dos,* the text refers us to page two. **3** REL to forgive. **4** (*aplazar*) to postpone. **5** JUR to transfer. **6** (*ceder*) to subside. – **7** *i* (*ceder*) to subside: *la fiebre ha remitido,* the fever has subsided. – **8 remitirse,** *p* (*atenerse*) to refer (**a,** to): *se remitió a su propio acuerdo,* he referred to his own agreement.
remo l *m* (*pala*) oar, paddle. **2** DEP rowing. **3** ANAT (*brazo*) arm; (*pierna*) leg. **4** (*ave*) wings *pl*.
● **ir a remo,** to row.
■ **barca de remo,** rowing boat. ‖ **club de remo,** rowing club.
remodelación l *f* (*modificación*) reshaping. **2** (*reorganización*) reorganization. **3** (*ministerial*) reshuffle.
remodelar l *t* (*modificar*) to reshape. **2** (*transformar*) to transform. **3** (*mejorar*) to improve. **4** (*reorganizar*) to reorganize. **5** (*ministerio*) to reshuffle.
remojar l *t* (*empapar*) to soak (**en,** in). **2** *fam fig* (*celebrar*) to celebrate, drink to.

remojo *m* soaking.
● **dejar en remojo / poner en remojo,** to soak, leave to soak.
remojón 1 *m fam (mojadura)* soaking, drenching. 2 *fam (baño)* dip. 3 *fam (lluvia)* cloudburst, downpour.
remolacha *f* beetroot.
■ **remolacha azucarera,** sugar beet.
remolachero,-a 1 *adj* beet. – 2 *m,f* beet grower.
remolcador 1 *m* MAR tug, tugboat. 2 AUTO breakdown truck, US tow truck.
remolcar *t* to tow.
▲ *Conjugation model* [1], *like* **sacar.**
remolinar 1 *i (arremolinarse)* to swirl. 2 *fig (apiñarse)* to mill. – 3 **remolinarse,** *p (arremolinarse)* to swirl. 4 *fig (apiñarse)* to crowd, throng, crowd, mass.
remolinear *t* to stir.
remolino 1 *m (de polvo)* whirl, cloud; *(de agua)* whirlpool, eddy; *(de aire)* whirlwind. 2 *(de pelo)* tuft, US cowlick. 3 *(de gente)* throng, crowd, mass.
remolón,-ona *adj* lazy, slack.
● **hacerse el remolón,** to laze around.
remolonear *i* to shirk, slack.
remolque 1 *m (acción)* towing. 2 *(vehículo)* trailer.
● **a remolque,** in tow: *llevaban la caravana a remolque,* they towed the caravan. ‖ **hacer algo a remolque,** to do sth. unwillingly. ‖ **ir a remolque de algn.,** *fig* to live in sb.'s shadow.
remontar 1 *t (elevar)* to raise. 2 *(subir)* to go up. 3 *(río)* to sail up; *(vuelo)* to soar. 4 *(superar)* to overcome, surmount: *remontar una dificultad,* to overcome a difficulty. – 5 **remontarse,** *p (al volar)* to soar. 6 *(datar)* to go back (**a,** to): *el historiador se remonta hasta el siglo XII,* the historian goes back to the 12th century.
remoquete 1 *m fig (dicho)* quip, quibble. 2 *fam (apodo)* nickname.
rémora 1 *f (pez)* remora. 2 *fig (obstáculo)* hindrance.
remorder 1 *t fig (desasosegar)* to trouble, worry: *esta acción me remuerde la conciencia,* this action weighs on my conscience, I feel guilty about what I did. – 2 **remorderse,** *p (concomerse)* to be consumed (**de,** with).
▲ *Conjugation model* [32], *like* **mover.**
remordimiento *m* remorse.
● **tener remordimientos,** to feel remorse.
remotamente *adv* remotely, vaguely.
● **ni remotamente,** not in the slightest, far from it.
remoto,-a *adj* remote, far-off: *una posibilidad remota,* a remote chance.
remover 1 *t (trasladar)* to move. 2 *(tierra)* to turn over, dig up. 3 *(líquido)* to stir. 4 *(comida)* to stir; *(ensalada)* to toss. 5 *fig (agitar)* to get moving, stir up: *lo ha removido todo mucho conseguirlo,* he stirred things up until he got his way. 6 *fig (recuerdo)* to stir up; *(tema)* to bring up. 7 *(destituir)* to remove (from office), oust. – 8 **removerse,** to stir, shift.
▲ *Conjugation model* [32], *like* **mover.**
remozamiento 1 *m (rejuvenecimiento)* rejuvenation. 2 *(fachada)* renovation, modernization; *(decoración)* redecoration; *(limpieza)* brightening up. 3 *(ropa)* brightening up.
remozar 1 *t (fachada)* to renovate, modernize; *(decorar)* to redecorate; *(limpiar)* to brighten up. 2 *(ropa)* to brighten up.
remplazable *adj* → **reemplazable.**
remplazar *t* → **reemplazar.**
remplazo *m* → **reemplazo.**
remuneración *f* remuneration, pay.

remunerado,-a 1 *pp* → **remunerar.** – 2 *adj* paid: *bien remunerado,-a,* well-paid.
remunerar *t* to remunerate, reward, pay.
renacentista *adj* Renaissance.
renacer 1 *i (volver a nacer)* to be reborn. 2 *(plantas)* to grow again; *(flores)* to bloom again. 3 *fig (revivir)* to revive, come back to life. 4 *fig (fortalecerse)* to revive, feel renewed.
▲ *Conjugation model* [42], *like* **nacer.**
renaciente *adj* renascent, reviving.
renacimiento 1 *m (vuelta a nacer)* rebirth. 2 *fig* revival, renaissance. 3 **el Renacimiento,** HIST the Renaissance.
■ **hombre del Renacimiento,** Renaissance man.
renacuajo 1 *m* ZOOL tadpole. 2 *fam (niño)* shrimp.
renal *adj* renal, kidney: *afección renal,* kidney disease.
Renania *f* Rhineland.
renano,-a 1 *adj* of the Rhine, from the Rhine. – 2 *m,f* Rhinelander.
renazco *pres indic* → **renacer.**
rencilla *f* quarrel.
rencilloso,-a *adj* quarrelsome.
renco,-a *adj* lame.
rencor 1 *m (odio)* rancour (US rancor). 2 *(resentimiento)* resentment.
● **guardar rencor a algn.,** to have a grudge against sb., bear sb. malice.
rencoroso,-a 1 *adj (hostil)* rancorous. 2 *(resentido)* resentful.
rendibú *m* flattery.
▲ *pl* **rendibúes.**
rendición *f* surrender: *rendición incondicional,* unconditional surrender.
rendido,-a 1 *pp* → **rendir.** – 2 *adj (sumiso)* humble, submissive: *un admirador rendido,* a devoted follower. 3 *(muy cansado)* worn out, exhausted.
rendija *f* crack, split.
rendimiento 1 *m (producción - de terreno)* yield; *(- de máquina)* output; *(- de persona)* progress, performance; *(- de inversión)* yield, return. 2 *(trabajo - de motor, máquina)* efficiency, performance. 3 *(sumisión)* submissiveness. 4 *(cansancio)* exhaustion, fatigue.
rendir 1 *t (vencer)* to defeat, conquer. 2 *(cansar)* to exhaust, wear out: *vas a rendir al caballo con tanta carga,* you're going to wear out the horse with that heavy load. 3 *(restituir)* to render, give back. 4 *(producir)* to yield, produce; *(progresar)* to progress: *esta hacienda rinde mucho trigo,* this plantation produces a lot of wheat; *no rinde,* it's not productive. 5 *(homenaje)* to pay. 6 MIL *(entregar)* to surrender: *rendir la ciudad,* to surrender the city. 7 MIL *(armas)* to lay down, throw down; *(la bandera)* to lower. – 8 *i (dar fruto)* to pay: *el trabajo nos ha rendido mucho,* we did well out of that job. – 9 **rendirse,** *p (entregarse al enemigo)* to surrender, give in. 10 *(darse por vencido)* to give up: *¡me rindo!,* I give up!
● **rendir cuentas,** *fig* to account for one's actions. ‖ **rendir homenaje a,** to pay tribute to, pay homage to. ‖ **rendir honores a,** to salute. ‖ **rendir el alma,** *fig* to give up the ghost. ‖ **rendirse a la evidencia,** to bow to the evidence.
▲ *Conjugation model* [34], *like* **servir.**
renegado,-a 1 *pp* → **renegar.** – 2 *adj* renegade. – 3 *m,f* renegade.
renegar 1 *t (negar)* to deny vigorously. – 2 *i (gen)* to renounce (**de,** -); *(familia)* to disown (**de,** -): *renegar de su fe,* to renounce one's faith; *el padre renegó de él,* his

father disowned him. **3** *fam fig* (*protestar*) to grumble, complain. **4** *fam fig* (*blasfemar*) to swear, curse.
▲ *Conjugation model* |48|, *like* **regar**.

renegociar *t* to renegotiate.
▲ *Conjugation model* |12|, *like* **cambiar**.

renegón,-ona 1 *adj fam* grumpy, grouchy. – **2** *m,f* grumbler, moaner.

renegrido,-a *adj* blackened.

RENFE *abr* (*Red Nacional de Ferrocarriles Españoles*) *Spanish national railway company.*

renglón 1 *m* (*línea*) line. **2** (*parte de renta*) item. – **3** **renglones,** *mpl fam* text sing.
● **a renglón seguido,** right after, immediately afterwards. ‖ **poner cuatro renglones a algn.,** to drop sb. a line.

reniego *m* curse, oath.

reniforme *adj* kidney-shaped, reniform.

renio *m* rhenium.

reno *m* reindeer.

renombrado,-a *adj* renowned, famous, well-known.

renombre *m* renown, fame.
● **de renombre,** renowned, famous.

renovable *adj* renewable.

renovación 1 *f* (*de contrato etc*) renewal. **2** (*de casa*) renovation; (*de decoración*) redecoration. **3** (*de personal*) reorganization.

renovar 1 *t* (*gen*) to renew. **2** (*casa*) to renovate; (*de decoración*) to redecorate. **3** (*de personal*) to reorganize. – **4** **renovarse,** *p* to be renewed.
▲ *Conjugation model* |31|, *like* **contar**.

renquear 1 *i* (*de la pierna*) to limp; (*del pie*) to hobble. **2** *fig* (*vacilar*) to dither. **3** *fig* (*tener dificultades*) to hardly manage, hardly get by: *estamos renqueando en el negocio familiar,* we can hardly manage the family business.

renta 1 *f* (*ingresos*) income. **2** (*declaración de renta*) tax return. **3** (*beneficio*) interest, return. **4** (*alquiler*) rent.
● **vivir de sus rentas,** to live on one's income.
■ **impuesto sobre la renta,** income tax. ‖ **renta fija,** fixed interest security. ‖ **renta fiscal,** taxable income. ‖ **renta nacional,** national income. ‖ **renta per cápita,** per capita income. ‖ **renta pública,** government debt. ‖ **renta variable,** equity securities *pl*. ‖ **renta vitalicia,** life annuity.

rentabilidad *f* profitability.
■ **tasa de rentabilidad,** rate of return.

rentabilizar *t* to make profitable.
▲ *Conjugation model* |4|, *like* **realizar**.

rentable *adj* profitable.

rentar *t* to produce, yield.

rentero,-a *m,f* tenant farmer.

rentista 1 *mf* (*experto*) financial expert. **2** (*que vive de rentas*) rentier, person of independent means.

renuencia *f* reluctance, unwillingness.

renuente *adj* reluctant, unwilling.

renuevo 1 *m* BOT shoot, sprout. **2** (*renovación*) renewal.
● **echar renuevos,** to sprout.

renuncia 1 *f* renunciation. **2** (*dimisión*) resignation.
● **presentar la renuncia,** to hand in one's resignation.

renunciar 1 *i* (*abandonar*) to give up (**a,** -), abandon (**a,** -): *renunció a la compra,* he decided not to buy; *renunció al tabaco,* she gave up smoking. **2** (*dimitir*) to resign: *renunció a su puesto,* he resigned his post, he resigned. **3** JUR to renounce (**a,** -), relinquish (**a,** -): *renunció a su fe,* she renounced her faith; *renunció a la*

herencia, he relinquished the inheritance. **4** (*en los naipes*) to revoke, not to follow suit.
▲ *Conjugation model* |12|, *like* **cambiar**.

renuncio *m fig* lie, contradiction.
● **coger en un renuncio,** *fam* to catch out.

reñido,-a 1 *pp* → **reñir**. – **2** *adj* (*enemistado*) on bad terms, at odds. **3** (*de rivalidad*) bitter, tough, hardfought. **4** (*incompatible*) incompatible.

reñir 1 *i* (*discutir*) to quarrel, argue. **2** (*pelear*) to fight: *riñeron por la herencia,* they fought over the inheritance. **3** (*desavenirse*) to fall out: *Pedro ha reñido con Ana,* Pedro fell out with Ana. – **4** *t* (*reprender*) to scold, tell off. **5** (*ejecutar*) to fight, wage: *reñir una guerra,* to wage a war.
▲ *Conjugation model* |36|, *like* **ceñir**.

reo[1] 1 *mf* (*acusado*) defendant, accused. **2** (*culpable*) culprit; (*con cargos contra la ley*) convicted offender.

reo[2] *m* (*trucha*) salmon trout.

reo[3] *m* (*turno*) turn, go.

reoca ser la reoca, *loc fam* (*excepcional*) to be incredible; (*muy bueno*) to be brilliant, be smashing; (*muy malo*) to be the pits, be the limit.

reojo de reojo, *loc adv* out of the corner of one's eye: *la miró de reojo,* he looked at her out of the corner of his eye.

reordenar *t* to rearrange.

reorganización *f* reorganization.
■ **reorganización ministerial,** cabinet reshuffle.

reorganizador,-ra 1 *adj* reorganizing. – **2** *m,f* reorganizer.

reorganizar 1 *t* to reorganize. **2** (*ministerio*) to reshuffle.
▲ *Conjugation model* |4|, *like* **realizar**.

reorientar *t fig* to redirect: *reorientaron a los estudiantes hacia otras carreras,* they redirected students to other courses of study.

reostato *m* rheostat.

reóstato *m* rheostat.

repámpanos 1 *interj fam* (*sorpresa*) good grief! **2** *fam* (*enfado*) damn it!

repanchigarse *p fam* → **repantigarse**.
▲ *Conjugation model* |7|, *like* **llegar**.

repanocha ser la repanocha, *loc fam* → **reoca**.

repantigarse *p fam* to lounge, loll.
▲ *Conjugation model* |7|, *like* **llegar**.

repantingarse *p fam* to lounge, loll.
▲ *Conjugation model* |7|, *like* **llegar**.

reparable *adj* repairable.

reparación 1 *f* (*arreglo*) repair, repairing: *está en reparación,* it's under repair, it's being repaired. **2** *fig* (*desagravio*) reparation, redress, amends *pl*.
■ **taller de reparaciones,** repair shop.

reparar 1 *t* (*arreglar*) to repair, mend, fix. **2** (*remediar - daño*) to make good; (*- perjuicio, insulto*) to make up for. **3** (*vengarse*) to avenge: *quiso reparar la injuria con un duelo,* he wanted to avenge the insult by fighting a duel. **4** (*restablecer*) to restore, renew: *reparar el ánimo,* to renew enthusiasm. **5** (*reflexionar*) to consider. **6** (*corregir*) to correct. **7** (*advertir*) to see, notice: *reparar un barco en el horizonte,* to see a ship on the horizon. – **8** *i* (*advertir*) to notice, see: *repare usted en esto,* look at this. **9** (*darse cuenta*) to realize (**en,** -): *no reparé en lo que estaba haciendo,* I didn't realize what I was doing. **10** (*hacer caso*) to pay attention to; (*considerar*) to consider: *no reparé en lo que dijo,* I didn't pay attention to what he said. **11** (*detenerse*) to stop, stall.
● **no reparar en gastos,** to spare no expense. ‖ **reparar en detalles,** to pay attention to detail.

reparo *m* objection.
● **no tener reparos en,** not to hesitate to. ‖ **poner reparos a,** to object to, find fault with.
repartición *f* distribution, sharing out.
repartidor,-ra *m,f* (*hombre*) delivery man; (*mujer*) delivery woman; (*chico*) delivery boy; (*chica*) delivery girl.
■ **repartidor de leche,** milkman. ‖ **repartidor de periódicos,** (*chico*) paperboy.
repartimiento *m* distribution, sharing out.
repartir 1 *t* (*dividir*) to distribute, divide, share out: *repartimos el dinero,* we shared out the money. **2** (*entregar*) to give out, hand out; (*correo, leche*) to deliver; (*premios*) to give out. **3** (*comida*) to hand out. **4** (*naipes*) to deal. **5** (*distribuir*) to spread out.
● **repartir golpes,** to hit out.
reparto 1 *m* (*división*) sharing out, division; (*distribución*) distribution. **2** (*de un terreno*) parcelling up; (*de un país*) partition. **3** (*entrega*) handing out; (*de mercancías*) delivery. **4** (*naipes - acción*) dealing; (*- turno*) deal. **5** CINEM TEAT cast.
■ **camioneta de reparto,** delivery van. ‖ **furgoneta de reparto,** delivery van. ‖ **reparto de premios,** prizegiving ceremony, award cermony.
repasar 1 *t* (*volver a pasar por un lugar*) to pass by, pass through again. **2** (*volver a examinar*) to revise, go over. **3** (*máquina etc*) to check, overhaul. **4** COST to mend. **5** *fam* (*mirar*) to look over: *cuando se la presentaron la repasó de arriba abajo,* when she was introduced to him he looked her up and down.
repaso 1 *m* revision, check; (*lección*) review. **2** COST mending. **3** (*máquina etc*) checkup, overhaul.
■ **curso de repaso,** refresher course.
repatear *t fam* (*fastidiar*) to annoy, disgust, turn off: *me repatea ese tipo de música,* I hate that kind of music.
repatriación *f* repatriation.
repatriado,-a 1 *pp* → **repatriar.** – **2** *adj* repatriated. – **3** *m,f* repatriate.
repatriar *t* to repatriate.
▲ *Conjugation model* [14]*, like auxiliar.*
repecho *m* short steep slope.
● **a repecho,** uphill.
repeinado,-a *adj fig* dolled up.
repelar 1 *t* (*tirar*) to pull out. **2** *fig* (*cortar - pelo*) to crop; (*- uñas*) to clip.
repelencia *f* repulse.
repelente *adj* repellent, repulsive.
■ **niño,-a repelente,** *irón* little know-all.
repeler 1 *t* (*rechazar*) to repel, repulse. **2** (*idea*) to reject; (*ataque*) to repel. **3** (*repugnar*) to disgust, repel: *esa arrogancia me repele,* that arrogance disgusts me.
repelo 1 *m* (*lo que no va al pelo*) opposite direction to hair growth. **2** (*padrastro de la uña*) hangnail. **3** *fam fig* (*repugnancia*) disgust.
● **a repelo,** in the opposite direction to hair growth; *fig* at the wrong time.
repelús *m fam* shiver.
● **darle a algn. repelús,** *fam* to give sb. the shivers.
repeluzno *m fam* → **repelús.**
repensar *t* to think over.
▲ *Conjugation model* [27]*, like acertar.*
repente 1 *m fam* (*movimiento*) sudden movement, start. **2** *fam* (*ataque*) fit, outburst.
● **de repente,** suddenly, all of a sudden.
repentinamente *adv* suddenly.
repentino,-a *adj* sudden.
repentizar 1 *i* MÚS to sight read. **2** (*improvisar*) to improvise.

▲ *Conjugation model* [4]*, like realizar.*
repera **ser la repera,** *loc fam* to take the biscuit, be the limit.
repercusión *f* repercussion.
repercutir 1 *i* (*sonido*) to resound, echo, reverberate. **2** (*rebotar*) to rebound. **3** *fig* (*trascender*) to have repercussions (**en,** on), affect: *la subida del dólar ha repercutido en los precios,* the dollar rise badly affected prices.
repertorio 1 *m* (*resumen*) list, index. **2** TEAT repertoire, repertory.
repesca *f fam* second chance; (*examen*) resit.
● **hacer un examen de repesca,** to resit an exam.
repescar *t fam* to give a second chance to; (*examen*) to allow to resit an exam.
▲ *Conjugation model* [1]*, like sacar.*
repetición 1 *f* (*gen*) repetition. **2** (*de programa*) repeat.
■ **arma de repetición,** repeater, repeating firearm. ‖ **repetición de la jugada,** DEP action replay.
repetidamente *adv* repeatedly, over and over.
repetido,-a 1 *pp* → **repetir.** – **2** *adj* repeated.
● **repetidas veces,** repeatedly, countless times.
repetidor,-ra 1 *adj* repeating: *alumno repetidor,* repeat student. – **2** *m,f* EDUC repeat student. – **3** repetidor, *m* TÉC relay, booster station.
■ **estación repetidora,** relay station. ‖ **repetidor de televisión,** relay station.
repetir 1 *t* (*gen*) to repeat: *¿puedes repetir la pregunta?,* can you repeat the question?; *se lo repetí dos veces,* I told him twice. **2** (*volver a hacer*) to do again, do over again. – **3** *i* (*volver a servirse*) to have a second helping: *quisimos repetir de pescado,* we wanted some more fish. **4** (*venir a la boca*) to repeat (on one), come up: *el ajo repite,* garlic repeats. **5** EDUC to repeat a year. – **6** **repetirse,** *p* (*persona*) to repeat OS.: *ese escritor se repite en cada novela,* that writer repeats himself in each novel. **7** (*hecho*) to recur.
● **¡que no se repita!,** don't let it happen again! ‖ **¡que se repita!,** encore!, more!
▲ *Conjugation model* [34]*, like servir.*
repetitivo,-a *adj* repetitive.
repicar 1 *t* (*campanas*) to peal, ring out. **2** (*picar*) to chop, mince. – **3** **repicarse,** *p* (*jactarse*) to boast (**de,** about).
▲ *Conjugation model* [1]*, like sacar.*
repintar 1 *t* to repaint. – **2 repintarse,** *p* (*maquillarse mucho*) to put on layers of make-up.
repipi *adj fam* la-di-da, affected: *niño repipi,* little know-all.
repique *m* peal, ringing.
repiquetear 1 *t* (*repicar*) to peal out. **2** (*tamborilear*) to beat, tap. **3** (*lluvia*) to pitter-patter.
repiqueteo 1 *m* (*de campana*) pealing. **2** (*de tambor*) beating, tapping. **3** (*de lluvia*) pitter-patter.
repisa *f* ledge, shelf.
■ **repisa de la chimenea,** mantelpiece.
replantar 1 *t* (*volver a plantar*) to replant. **2** (*transplantar*) to transplant.
replantear 1 *t* ARQ to redesign. **2** (*asunto, problema*) to re-examine, reconsider, rethink: *se replanteó su función,* he reconsidered his duties.
replegarse *p* to withdraw, fall back, retreat.
▲ *Conjugation model* [48]*, like regar.*
repleto,-a *adj* full up, full (**de,** of), jam-packed (**de,** with): *estaba repleto de niños,* it was packed with children.
réplica 1 *f* (*respuesta*) answer, reply; (*objeción*) retort. **2** ART (*copia*) replica.

replicar 1 *t* (*contestar*) to answer, reply. **2** (*poner objeciones*) to argue, answer back. **3** JUR to answer. – **4** *i* (*contestar*) to reply, retort. **5** (*poner objeciones*) to argue, answer back: *lo haces sin replicar,* you do it without arguing. **6** JUR to answer.
▲ *Conjugation model* |1|, *like sacar.*
replicón,-ona 1 *adj fam* argumentative, cheeky, bold. – **2** *m,f fam* argumentative person.
repliegue 1 *m* (*pliegue*) fold, crease. **2** MIL withdrawal, retreat. **3** *fig* recess.
repoblación *f* repopulation.
■ **repoblación forestal,** reafforestation, reforestation.
repoblar *t* to repopulate; (*bosque*) to reafforest, reforest.
▲ *Conjugation model* |31|, *like contar.*
repollo *m* cabbage.
reponer 1 *t* (*devolver*) to put back, replace, restore. **2** (*reemplazar*) to replace. **3** (*en el teatro*) to put on again, restage; (*en el cine*) to rerun; (*en televisión*) to repeat. **4** (*replicar*) to reply, retort. – **5 reponerse,** *p* (*salud, susto*) to recover: *se repuso de la operación,* he recovered from the operation.
▲ *Conjugation model* |78|, *like poner; pp repuesto,-a.*
reportaje 1 *m* (*prensa, radio*) report. **2** (*noticias*) article, news item. **3** (*documental*) documentary.
■ **reportaje gráfico,** illustrated feature.
reportar 1 *t* (*proporcionar*) to bring: *el cine le ha reportado fama y fortuna,* the cinema has brought him fame and fortune. **2** (*refrenar*) to restrain, check. – **3 reportarse,** *p* (*refrenarse*) to restrain os., control os.: *repórtate, no llames la atención, por favor,* restrain yourself, please don't create a scene.
reporte *m* report.
repórter *mf* reporter.
reportero,-a *m,f* reporter.
reposacabezas *m* headrest.
▲ *pl reposacabezas.*
reposadamente *adv* calmly, quietly.
reposado,-a 1 *pp* → **reposar.** – **2** *adj* calm, quiet, peaceful.
reposapiés *m* footrest.
▲ *pl reposapiés.*
reposar 1 *t* (*la comida*) to leave to stand. – **2** *i* (*descansar*) to rest, take a rest. **3** (*yacer*) to rest, lie, be buried. **4** (*un líquido*) to settle. – **5 reposarse,** *p* (*un líquido*) to settle.
● **dejar reposar,** CULIN to leave to stand.
reposición 1 *f* (*restitución*) restoration. **2** (*en el teatro*) revival; (*en el cine*) rerun; (*en televisión*) repeat.
repositorio *m* repository.
reposo 1 *m* (*descanso*) rest. **2** (*tranquilidad*) peace.
● **en reposo,** (*persona*) at rest; (*masa etc*) standing. || hacer **reposo,** to get some rest: *deberás hacer reposo unos días,* you'll need to rest for a few days.
repostar 1 *t* (*provisiones*) to stock up with. **2** (*avión*) to refuel; (*coche*) to fill up.
repostería 1 *f* (*tienda - de pasteles*) cake shop, pastry shop; (*- de chocolate, caramelos*) confectioner's, confectioner's shop. **2** (*pastas*) cakes *pl*; (*chocolate, caramelos*) confectionery. **3** (*arte*) pastrymaking. **4** (*despensa*) pantry, larder.
repostero,-a *m,f* (*de pasteles*) pastrycook; (*de chocolate, caramelos*) confectioner.
reprender *t* to reprimand, scold.
reprensible *adj* reprehensible.
reprensión *f* reprimand, scolding.

represa *f* dam.
represalia *f* reprisal, retaliation.
● **tomar represalias,** to take reprisals.
▲ *Often used in plural.*
represaliado,-a 1 *pp* → **represaliar.** – **2** *adj* sanctioned.
represaliar *t* to sanction.
represar *t* to hold back.
representación 1 *f* (*gen*) representation: *tiene la representación de esta marca,* he represents this firm. **2** TEAT performance.
● **en representación de,** as a representative of, representing.
representante 1 *adj* representative. – **2** *mf* representative. **3** (*actor*) actor; (*actriz*) actress.
representar 1 *t* (*gen*) to represent: *esto representa un árbol,* this represents a tree; *esta redacción representa varias horas de trabajo,* this composition represents several hours of work. **2** (*símbolo*) to represent, stand for: *una paloma representa la paz,* a dove stands for peace. **3** TEAT (*obra*) to perform; (*papel*) to play (the part of). **4** (*aparentar*) to appear to be, look: *representa veinte años,* she looks twenty. **5** (*importar*) to mean: *la música representaba mucho para él,* music meant a lot to him. – **6 representarse,** *p* (*imaginarse*) to imagine, picture.
representatividad *f* significance, importance.
representativo,-a *adj* representative.
represión *f* repression: *represión sexual,* sexual repression.
represivo,-a *adj* repressive.
reprimenda *f* reprimand.
reprimido,-a 1 *pp* → **reprimir.** – **2** *adj* repressed. – **3** *m,f* repressed person.
reprimir 1 *t* (*gen*) to repress, suppress. **2** (*pasión*) to repress; (*llanto, risa, etc*) to suppress, hold back. – **3 reprimirse,** *p* to control os.
reprís *m* acceleration.
reprise *f* acceleration.
reprivatización *f* return to private ownership.
reprivatizar *t* to return to private ownership.
reprobable *adj* reproachable, reprehensible.
reprobación *f* reprobation, reproof.
reprobador,-ra *adj* reproachful.
reprobar *t* (*cosa*) to condemn; (*persona*) to reprove, reproach, censure.
▲ *Conjugation model* |31|, *like contar.*
réprobo,-a 1 *adj* reprobate. – **2** *m,f* reprobate.
reprochable *adj* reproachable.
reprochador,-ra *adj* reproachful.
reprochar *t* to reproach, censure: *me reprochó mi actitud,* she reproached me for my attitude.
reproche *m* reproach, criticism.
reproducción 1 *f* reproduction. **2** MED recurrence.
■ **derechos de reproducción,** copyright.
reproducir 1 *t* to reproduce, repeat. – **2 reproducirse,** *p* (*gen*) to reproduce. **3** (*volver a ocurrir*) to happen again, recur: *se ha reproducido el mismo hecho,* the same thing has happened again. **4** MED to reproduce.
▲ *Conjugation model* |46|, *like conducir.*
reproductor,-ra 1 *adj* (*gen*) reproducing. **2** ANAT reproductive. **3** (*animal*) breeding. – **4** *m,f* (*animal*) breeder.
reprografía *f* reprography.
reps *m* rep, repp.
▲ *pl reps.*

reptar 1 *i* (*arrastrarse*) to crawl, slither. **2** (*adular*) to flatter.
reptil 1 *adj* reptile, reptilian. – **2** *m* reptile.
réptil *m* → **reptil**.
república *f* republic.
■ **república bananera,** *pey* banana republic. ‖ **república de las letras,** *lit* intelligentsia.
republicanismo *m* republicanism.
republicano,-a 1 *adj* republican. – **2** *m,f* republican.
repudiar *t* to repudiate.
▲ *Conjugation model* |12|, *like cambiar.*
repudio *m* repudiation.
repuesto,-a 1 *pp* → **reponer**. – **2** *adj* (*recuperado*) recovered. – **3 repuesto,** *m* (*prevención*) store, supply, stock. **4** (*recambio*) spare, spare part.
● **de repuesto,** spare, in reserve: *rueda de repuesto,* spare wheel; *una llave de repuesto,* an extra key, a spare key.
repugnancia *f* repugnance, disgust, loathing.
repugnante *adj* repugnant, repulsive, disgusting, revolting.
repugnar 1 *i* to disgust, revolt: *me repugnan las serpientes,* I loathe snakes, I find snakes repulsive. – **2** *t* (*negar*) to deny. **3** (*contradecir*) to contradict.
repujado,-a 1 *pp* → **repujar**. – **2** *adj* embossed, repoussé.
repujar *t* to emboss.
repulir 1 *t* (*volver a pulir*) to repolish. **2** (*acicalar*) to smarten up, dress up. – **3 repulirse,** *p* (*acicalarse*) to dress up.
repulsa 1 *f* (*rechazo*) rebuff. **2** (*negativa*) refusal, rejection. **3** (*condena*) condemnation. **4** (*reprimenda*) reprimand.
repulsar 1 *t* (*despreciar*) to reject. **2** (*denegar*) to deny.
repulsión *f* repulsion, repugnance.
repulsivo,-a *adj* repulsive, revolting.
repuntar 1 *i* (*la marea*) to turn. **2** (*economía*) to recover, pick up. – **3 repuntarse,** *p* (*avinagrarse*) to turn sour. **4** *fig* (*enfadarse*) to fall out.
repuse *pt indef* → **reponer**.
reputación *f* reputation: *tiene buena reputación,* she has a good reputation.
reputado,-a 1 *pp* → **reputar**. – **2** *adj* reputed, reputable.
reputar *t* to consider, deem.
requebrar 1 *t fig* (*lisonjear*) to court. **2** (*adular*) to flatter, pay compliments to.
▲ *Conjugation model* |27|, *like acertar.*
requemado,-a 1 *pp* → **requemar**. – **2** *adj* scorched, burnt.
requemar 1 *t* (*gen*) to scorch, burn. **2** (*plantas*) to scorch. **3** (*la piel*) to tan, darken. – **4 requemarse,** *p* (*gen*) to burn. **5** (*plantas*) to become scorched. **6** *fig* (*consumirse*) to be consumed.
requerimiento 1 *m* (*súplica*) request. **2** JUR (*aviso*) summons *pl;* (*intimación*) injunction.
● **a requerimiento de algn.,** at sb.'s request.
requerir 1 *t* (*necesitar*) to require, need: *esto requiere gran paciencia,* this requires a lot of patience. **2** (*decir con autoridad*) to demand, call for. **3** (*solicitar*) to request: *requirió nuestra ayuda,* he asked for our help. **4** (*persuadir*) to persuade: *nos requirió con elocuencia,* he persuaded us eloquently. **5** JUR to summon.
● **requerir de amores,** *lit* to court, woo.
▲ *Conjugation model* |35|, *like hervir.*
requesón *m* cottage cheese.
requeté 1 *m* HIST Carlist soldier. – **2 los requetés,** *mpl* the Carlist forces.

requete- *pref fam* really, very, incredibly: *requetebueno,* really good, smashing; *requetemoderno,* ultramodern, incredibly modern.
requiebro *m* compliment, flirtatious remark.
réquiem *m* requiem.
▲ *pl réquiems.*
requisa 1 *f* (*inspección*) inspection. **2** (*embargo*) requisition.
requisar 1 *t* MIL to requisition. **2** *fam* (*apropiarse*) to grab, swipe.
requisición *f* requisition.
requisito *m* requisite, requirement.
● **cumplir todos los requisitos,** to fulfil (US fulfill) all the requirements. ‖ **ser requisito indispensable,** to be absolutely essential.
■ **requisito previo,** prerequisite.
requisitoria *f* requisition, demand.
res *f* (*gen*) beast, animal; (*cabeza de ganado*) head: *un rebaño de doscientas reses,* a herd of two hundred head of cattle.
■ **res lanar,** sheep, head of sheep. ‖ **res vacuna,** head of cattle.
resabiar 1 *t* to lead astray, make fall into bad habits. – **2 resabiarse,** *p* (*comida*) to go off.
▲ *Conjugation model* |12|, *like cambiar.*
resabido,-a 1 *adj* (*muy bien sabido*) widely known, extremely well-known. **2** *pey* (*redicho*) pretentious, pedantic, know-all.
resabio 1 *m* (*mal sabor*) bad aftertaste. **2** (*vicio*) bad habit.
resaca 1 *f* (*de las olas*) undertow, undercurrent. **2** (*de borrachera*) hangover: *tenía resaca,* she had a hangover.
resalado,-a 1 *adj fam* (*gracioso*) charming, attractive. **2** *fam* (*alegre*) lively.
resaltar 1 *i* (*sobresalir*) to project, jut out: *dos balcones resaltan de la fachada principal,* two balconies jut out from the main façade. **2** *fig* (*distinguirse*) to stand out (**de,** from). – **3** *t* to highlight, stress, emphasize.
● **hacer resaltar,** to emphasize, stress, highlight.
resalte *m* ledge.
resalto *m* ledge.
resarcir 1 *t* to compensate, indemnify. – **2 resarcirse,** *p* to make up for.
▲ *Conjugation model* |3|, *like zurcir.*
resbaladizo,-a 1 *adj* slippery. **2** *fig* slippery, tricky.
resbalar 1 *i* (*deslizarse*) to slide. **2** (*sin querer*) to slip; AUTO to skid. **3** (*gotas, lágrimas*) to trickle (down). **4** *fig* to slip up, make a slip.
resbalón *m* slip.
● **dar un resbalón,** to slip, slide; *fig* to slip up.
resbaloso,-a *adj* slippery.
rescatador,-ra *m,f* rescuer.
rescatar 1 *t* (*liberar - alguien*) to rescue, save; (- *ciudad*) to recapture. **2** (*recuperar*) to recover. **3** *fig* (*recobrar - gen*) to rescue; (- *tiempo*) to make up for: *rescatar del olvido,* to rescue from oblivion. **4** *fig* (*librar*) to rescue.
rescate 1 *m* (*salvamento*) rescue; (*de ciudad*) recapture. **2** (*dinero*) ransom. **3** (*recuperación*) recovery, recapture.
● **exigir rescate por algn.,** to hold sb. to ransom.
■ **equipo de rescate,** rescue team.
rescindible *adj* cancellable, rescindable.
rescindir *t* to rescind, cancel, terminate: *me rescindió el contrato,* she cancelled my contract.
rescisión *f* rescission, cancellation, termination.
rescoldo 1 *m* (*brasa*) embers *pl.* **2** *fig* (*recelo*) lingering doubt.
resecar[1] 1 *t* to dry up. – **2 resecarse,** *p* to dry up.
▲ *Conjugation model* |1|, *like sacar.*

resecar² *t* MED to resect.
▲ *Conjugation model* |1|, *like* **sacar**.
resección *f* resection.
reseco,-a 1 *adj* (*seco*) very dry, parched: *tiene la piel reseca*, she has very dry skin. 2 (*flaco*) thin, skinny.
reseda *f* reseda.
resentido,-a 1 *pp* → **resentir**. – 2 *adj* resentful. – 3 *m,f* resentful person.
● **estar resentido,-a con/contra algn.**, to bear resentment towards sb. ‖ **estar resentido,-a por algo**, to be resentful of sth., resent sth.
resentimiento *m* resentment.
resentirse 1 *p* (*sentirse*) to suffer (**de**, from), feel the effects (**de**, of): *me resiento del tobillo*, my ankle hurts, I have a sore ankle. 2 (*flaquear*) to be weakened. 3 *fig* (*enojarse*) to become resentful, feel resentment.
● **resentirse con/contra algn.**, *fig* to bear sb. resentment. ‖ **resentirse por algo**, *fig* to take offence (US offense) at sth.
▲ *Conjugation model* |35|, *like* **hervir**.
reseña 1 *f* (*crítica*) review; (*en prensa*) write-up. 2 (*descripción*) description. 3 (*narración*) account. 4 MIL review.
reseñar 1 *t* (*crítica*) to review. 2 (*describir*) to describe. 3 (*narrar*) to give an account of.
reserva 1 *f* (*de plazas, entradas*) booking, reservation. 2 (*provisión*) reserve; (*existencias*) stock: *reservas de carburante*, fuel reserves, fuel stocks. 3 (*cautela*) reservation. 4 (*discreción*) discretion, reserve. 5 (*vino*) vintage: *es un vino de reserva*, it's a vintage wine. 6 (*de animales*) reserve; (*de personas*) reservation: *reserva de indios*, Indian reservation. 7 MIL reserve, reserves *pl*. – 8 *mf* DEP reserve, substitute. – 9 **reservas**, *fpl* COM reserves, stock *sing*.
● **"reserva de habitaciones"**, "room reservations". ‖ **con la mayor reserva**, in the strictest confidence. ‖ **guardar algo en reserva**, to keep sth. in reserve. ‖ **hacer una reserva**, to make a reservation, make a booking, to book. ‖ **pasar a la reserva**, MIL to be put in the reserves. ‖ **sin reserva / sin reservas**, openly, without reservation. ‖ **tener reservas sobre algo**, to have reservations about sth. ‖ **tener algo en reserva**, to keep sth. in reserve.
■ **reserva de divisas**, foreign currency reserves *pl*.
reservadamente *adv* in confidence.
reservado,-a 1 *pp* → **reservar**. – 2 *adj* (*plazas*) booked, reserved. 3 (*persona*) reserved, discreet. 4 (*asunto*) confidential. – 5 **reservado**, *m* (*en local*) private room; (*en tren*) reserved compartment.
reservar 1 *t* (*plazas etc*) to book, reserve. 2 (*guardar*) to keep, save: *resérvame un baile*, save a dance for me. 3 (*ocultar*) to withhold, keep to os. – 4 **reservarse**, *p* (*conservarse*) to save os. (**para**, for): *resérvate para después*, save yourself for later. 5 (*cautelarse*) to withhold, keep to os.: *se reservó su opinión*, she kept her opinion to herself.
reservista *mf* reservist.
resfriado,-a 1 *pp* → **resfriar**. – 2 *adj* with a cold: *estoy muy resfriado*, I have a bad cold. – 3 **resfriado**, *m* cold; (*poco importante*) chill.
● **coger un resfriado / pillar un resfriado**, to catch a cold; (*poco importante*) to catch a chill.
resfriar 1 *t* (*enfriar*) to cool. – 2 *i* (*empezar a hacer frío*) to cool (down). – 3 **resfriarse**, *p* MED to catch a cold.
▲ *Conjugation model* |13|, *like* **desviar**.
resfrío *m* cold.
resguardar 1 *t* (*proteger*) to protect (**de**, from), shelter (**de**, from): *resguardar del frío*, to protect from the cold.

2 (*salvaguardar*) to safeguard (**de**, against). – 3 **resguardarse**, *p* (*protegerse*) to protect os. 4 *fig* to be careful, take precautions.
resguardo 1 *m* (*protección*) protection, shelter. 2 (*garantía*) safeguard, guarantee. 3 (*recibo*) receipt, ticket; (*vale*) voucher; (*de talonario*) counterfoil, stub, (*de un ingreso*) paying-in slip.
residencia *f* (*gen*) residence.
● **tener la residencia en**, to reside in.
■ **hotel residencia**, residential hotel. ‖ **permiso de residencia**, residence permit. ‖ **residencia de ancianos**, old people's home. ‖ **residencia de estudiantes**, hall of residence, US dormitory.
residencial *adj* residential.
residente 1 *adj* resident, residing: *médico residente*, resident doctor; *residente en Barcelona*, residing in Barcelona. – 2 *mf* resident.
● **no residente**, non-resident.
residir 1 *i* to reside (**en**, in), live (**en**, in). 2 *fig* to lie (**en**, in): *ahí reside el problema*, the problem lies there.
residual *adj* residual.
residuo 1 *m* residue. – 2 **residuos**, *mpl* waste *sing*, refuse *sing*.
■ **residuos radiactivos**, radioactive waste *sing*.
resignación *f* resignation.
resignadamente *adv* resignedly.
resignado,-a 1 *pp* → **resignar**. – 2 *adj* resigned.
resignar 1 *t* to resign, relinquish. – 2 **resignarse**, *p* to resign os. (**a**, to): *se resignó a perder el partido*, he resigned himself to losing the match.
resina *f* resin.
resinoso,-a *adj* resinous.
resistencia 1 *f* (*gen*) resistance. 2 (*aguante*) endurance, stamina. 3 (*oposición*) resistance, opposition: *la propuesta no encontró resistencia*, the proposal didn't meet any resistance. 4 ELEC resistance. 5 (*de materiales*) strength. 6 **la Resistencia**, HIST the Resistance.
■ **prueba de resistencia**, endurance test. ‖ **resistencia pasiva**, passive resistance.
resistente 1 *adj* (*que resiste*) resistant (**a**, to): *resistente al agua*, water-resistant, waterproof. 2 (*fuerte*) tough, strong. 3 (*tejido*) hard-wearing.
resistir 1 *i* (*aguantar - algo*) to hold (out); (- *alguien*) to hold out, take (it), have endurance: *la cuerda no resistirá*, the rope won't hold; *no resistes nada*, you can't take anything. 2 (*durar*) to endure, last: *mi moto aún resiste*, there's still life in my motorbike yet. 3 (*ejército*) to hold out, resist. – 4 *t* (*soportar*) to stand, tolerate: *no resisto la vagancia*, I can't stand laziness. 5 (*peso etc*) to bear, withstand, take. 6 (*tentación etc*) to resist. – 7 **resistirse**, *p* (*rechazar*) to resist. 8 (*oponerse*) to resist, put up resistance. 9 *fam* (*costar*) to be difficult, be hard: *la física se le resista*, he's struggling with physics. 10 (*negarse*) to refuse: *me resisto a opinar*, I refuse to give my opinion; *me resisto a creerlo*, I find it hard to believe.
resma *f* ream, ream of paper.
resol *m* glare, glare of the sun.
resollar 1 *i* (*respirar*) to breathe. 2 (*respirar - fuertemente*) to pant; (- *con ruido*) to wheeze. 3 (*jadear*) to puff and pant.
● **sin resollar**, *fig* without a word.
▲ *Conjugation model* |31|, *like* **contar**.
resolución 1 *f* (*decisión*) resolution, decision; (*determinación*) determination, resolve. 2 (*solución*) solution; (*de un conflicto*) settlement. 3 TÉC resolution.
● **tomar una resolución**, to decide.

resolutivo

■ **resolución fatal,** death wish. ‖ **resolución judicial,** court decision.

resolutivo,-a *adj* resolvent.

resoluto,-a *adj* resolute.

resolutorio,-a *adj* resolutive.

resolver 1 *t* (*solucionar* - *gen*) to resolve, solve; (- *asunto, conflicto*) to resolve, settle; (- *dificultad*) to overcome. **2** (*decidir*) to resolve, decide (-, to): *resolvió marchar,* she decided to leave. **3** (*deshacer*) to resolve. **4** QUÍM to dissolve. – **5 resolverse,** *p* (*solucionarse*) to be solved; (*resultar*) to work out. **6** (*reducirse*) to end up (**en,** in), turn out: *todo se resolvió en unos gritos,* it turned out to be a shouting match. **7** (*decidirse*) to resolve (**a,** -), make up one's mind (**a,** to), decide (**a,** to): *se resolvió a cantar,* he decided to sing.

▲ *Conjugation model* [32], *like* **mover**; *pp* **resuelto,-a.**

resonancia 1 *f* resonance. **2** (*eco*) echo. **3** *fig* (*importancia*) importance; (*consecuencias*) repercussions *pl.*

● **tener resonancia,** to cause a sensation, cause a stir, have an impact.

■ **caja de resonancia,** sound box; *fig* sounding board.

resonante 1 *adj* resounding. **2** *fig* important.

resonar 1 *i* (*gen*) to resound. **2** (*cristal, metales*) to ring. **3** (*tener eco*) to echo. **4** *fig* to have repercussions.

▲ *Conjugation model* [31], *like* **contar.**

resoplar 1 *i* to breathe heavily. **2** (*de cansancio*) to puff and pant.

resoplido 1 *m* (*resuello*) heavy breathing; (*silbido*) wheezing; (*por cansancio*) panting. **2** (*de enfado*) snort.

resoplo *m* → **resoplido.**

resorte 1 *m* spring. **2** *fig* means *pl.*

● **conocer todos los resortes de algo,** *fig* to know all the ins and outs of sth. ‖ **tocar todos los resortes,** *fig* to pull all the strings.

respaldar 1 *t* to support, back (up). – **2 respaldarse,** *p* to lean back (**en,** on). **3** (*apoyarse*) to lean (**en,** on).

respaldo 1 *m* back. **2** *fig* support, backing.

respectar *i* to concern, regard.

● **por lo que a mí respecta,** as far as I'm concerned.

▲ *Used only in the 3rd person singular.*

respectivamente *adv* respectively: *los dos alumnos sacaron un notable y un aprobado respectivamente,* the two students got a B and a D respectively.

respectivo,-a *adj* respective: *con sus respectivas esposas,* with their respective wives.

● **en lo respectivo a,** with regard to, regarding.

respecto *m* regard, respect.

● **a este respecto,** in this respect. ‖ **al respecto,** in this respect. ‖ **con respecto a,** with regard to, regarding. ‖ **respecto a,** with regard to, as for: *respecto a mí,* as for me, as far as I am concerned.

respetabilidad *f* respectability.

respetable 1 *adj* respectable. – **2 el respetable,** *m fam* (*público*) the audience.

respetar *t* to respect.

● **hacerse respetar,** to command respect. ‖ **respetar la prioridad,** AUTO to give way.

respeto 1 *m* (*gen*) respect. **2** *fam* (*miedo*) fear. – **3 respetos,** *mpl* respects.

● **campar por sus respetos,** to do as one pleases. ‖ **por respeto a,** out of consideration for. ‖ **presentar sus respetos a algn.,** *fml* to pay one's respects to sb. ‖ **falta de respeto,** lack of respect.

respetuoso,-a *adj* respectful.

respingar 1 *i* (*caballo*) to shy. **2** *fam* (*falda etc*) to ride up.

▲ *Conjugation model* [7], *like* **llegar.**

respingo 1 *m* (*sacudida*) start, jump. **2** *fig* (*ademán*) gesture of unwillingness.

respingón,-ona *adj* snub, upturned: *nariz respingona,* snub nose.

respiración 1 *f* (*acción*) breathing, respiration. **2** (*aliento*) breath more easily, breathe. **3** (*aire*) ventilation.

● **aguantar/contener la respiración,** to hold one's breath. ‖ **que corta la respiración,** *fig* that takes one's breath away, breathtaking. ‖ **sin respiración,** breathless, out of breath.

■ **respiración artificial,** artificial resuscitation. ‖ **respiración boca a boca,** mouth-to-mouth respiration, kiss of life.

respiradero 1 *m* TÉC air vent. **2** *fig* rest.

respirar 1 *i* to breathe. **2** (*estar vivo*) to be breathing: *aún respira,* she's still breathing. **3** *fig* (*ventilar*) to air: *abre ese cuarto para que respire,* open that room to air it. **4** *fig* (*despedir olor*) to smell (**a,** of): *su vestido respira a lavanda,* her dress smells of lavender. **5** *fig* (*relajarse*) to breathe more easily, breathe a sigh of relief: *al oír al doctor, respiramos,* when we heard what the doctor had to say we breathed a sigh of relief. – **6** *t* (*absorber*) to breathe, breathe in, inhale: *el soldado respiró gases tóxicos,* the soldier breathed in toxic fumes.

● **dejar respirar,** *fig* to give a break, give a moment's peace. ‖ **no poder respirar,** (*de trabajo*) to be up to one's eyes in work. ‖ **respirar felicidad,** *fig* to radiate happiness. ‖ **sin respirar,** (*sin descanso*) non-stop; (*atención*) attentively: *habla sin respirar,* he talks nonstop. ‖ **respirar mal,** to breathe with difficulty.

respiratorio,-a *adj* respiratory.

respiro 1 *m* (*resuello*) breathing. **2** (*descanso*) breather, break. **3** (*prórroga*) respite, grace, breathing space. **4** (*alivio*) relief, respite.

● **no dar respiro,** *fig* to give no peace, give no respite. ‖ **tomarse un respiro,** to take a breather.

resplandecer 1 *i* (*sol*) to shine; (*metal*) to gleam, glint; (*fuego*) to glow. **2** *fig* to glow (**de,** with), shine (**de,** with): *sus ojos resplandecían de alegría,* her eyes sparkled with joy. **3** *fig* (*destacar*) to shine, stand out.

▲ *Conjugation model* [43], *like* **agradecer.**

resplandeciente 1 *adj* (*brillante*) shining; (*metales*) gleaming, glittering; (*fuego*) glowing; (*ojos*) sparkling. **2** (*radiante*) resplendent, radiant.

resplandor 1 *m* (*de luz*) brightness, brilliance; (*de metales, cristales*) gleam, glitter; (*del fuego*) glow, blaze. **2** (*esplendor*) splendour (US splendor); (*brillantez*) radiance.

responder 1 *t* (*contestar*) to answer, reply. – **2** *i* (*contestar*) to answer, reply: *respondió a la pregunta,* she answered to the question. **3** (*replicar*) to answer back. **4** (*corresponder*) to answer, respond to: *tengo que responder a su amabilidad,* I have to respond to his kindness. **5** (*tener el efecto deseado*) to respond: *el motor respondió bien,* the engine responded well. **6** (*rendir*) to go well, do well: *este campo responde,* this field is very productive. **7** (*ser responsable*) to answer (**de,** for), accept responsibility (**de,** for): *responderás de sus faltas,* you'll answer for her mistakes. **8** (*garantizar*) to guarantee, vouch (**de,** for).

● **responder a un tratamiento,** to respond to a course of treatment. ‖ **responder a una descripción,** to answer a description, fit a description. ‖ **responder a una necesidad,** to answer a need, meet a need. ‖ **responder al nombre de ...,** (*animal*) to answer to the name of ...; (*persona*) to go by the name of ...: *responde al nombre de Ana,* she goes by the name of Ana. ‖ **responder de algn.,** to be responsible for sb. ‖ **respon-**

der por algn., to vouch for sb., act as a guarantor for sb.

respondón,-ona *adj fam* argumentative, cheeky.

responsabilidad *f* responsibility.

● **cargar con la responsabilidad de algo,** to take responsibility for sth.

■ **responsabilidad limitada,** limited liability.

responsabilizar 1 *t* to make responsible (**de,** for), hold responsible (**de,** for). – 2 **responsabilizarse,** *p* to take responsibility (**de,** for), claim responsibility (**de,** for).

▲ *Conjugation model* |4|, *like realizar.*

responsable 1 *adj* responsible: *es una niña muy responsable,* she's a very responsible girl; *es responsable de las provisiones,* he's responsible for supplies. – 2 *mf* (*encargado*) person in charge. 3 (*de un crimen*) perpetrator, culprit, person responsible.

● **hacerse responsable de algo,** to assume responsibility for sth.

responsablemente *adv* responsibly, with responsibility.

responso 1 *m* REL prayer for the dead. 2 *fam* (*reprimenda*) ticking-off.

responsorio *m* responsorial psalm.

respuesta 1 *f* (*gen*) answer, reply. 2 (*reacción*) response.

● **en respuesta a,** in response to.

resquebrajadizo,-a *adj* fragile, brittle.

resquebrajadura *f* crack.

resquebrajamiento *m* crack.

resquebrajar 1 *t* to crack. – 2 **resquebrajarse,** *p* to crack.

resquemor *m* resentment, ill feeling.

resquicio 1 *m* (*abertura*) crack, chink. 2 *fig* glimmer; (*oportunidad*) chance; (*posibilidad*) possibility, chance: *un resquicio de esperanza,* a glimmer of hope; *si tuviese el menor resquicio lo haría,* if I had the slightest chance I would do it.

resta *f* subtraction.

restablecer 1 *t* (*gen*) to reestablish; (*orden, monarquía*) to restore. – 2 **restablecerse,** *p* (*gen*) to be reestablished; (*orden etc*) to be restored. 3 MED to recover, get better.

▲ *Conjugation model* |43|, *like agradecer.*

restablecimiento 1 *m* (*gen*) reestablishment; (*orden etc*) restoration. 2 MED recovery.

restallar 1 *i* (*látigo*) to crack. 2 (*hacer ruido*) to crackle.

restallido *m* crack.

restante 1 *adj* remaining. – 2 **lo restante,** *m* the rest, the remainder, what is left over.

restañar *t* to staunch.

restar 1 *t* MAT to subtract, take (away): *restar cuatro de seis,* to subtract four from six. 2 *fig* (*quitar*) to reduce, deduct. 3 DEP to return. – 4 *i* (*quedar*) to be left, remain: *resta poco para las vacaciones,* it won't be long until the holiday, it isn't long until the holiday.

● **restar importancia a algo,** to play sth. down, play down the importance of sth.

restauración 1 *f* (*restablecimiento*) restoration. 2 CULIN restaurant business, catering.

restaurador,-ra 1 *adj* restoring. – 2 *m,f* (*de obras etc*) restorer. 3 CULIN restaurateur, restauranteur.

restaurante *m* restaurant.

■ **coche restaurante,** (*en tren*) restaurant car, buffet car.

restaurar 1 *t* (*obra etc*) to restore. 2 (*en un cargo*) to reinstate.

restitución *f* restitution.

restituir 1 *t* (*restablecer*) to restore. 2 (*devolver*) to return, give back.

▲ *Conjugation model* |62|, *like huir.*

restitutorio,-a *adj* restitutory.

resto 1 *m* remainder, rest. 2 MAT remainder. 3 DEP return. – 4 **restos,** *mpl* (*gen*) remains; (*ruinas*) ruins. 5 (*de comida*) leftovers.

● **echar el resto,** *fam* to give sth. all one has got, go all out.

■ **restos mortales,** mortal remains.

restregar 1 *t* (*frotar*) to rub hard. 2 (*fregar*) to scrub.

▲ *Conjugation model* |48|, *like regar.*

restricción *f* restriction.

restrictivo,-a *adj* restrictive.

restricto,-a *adj* restricted.

restringir 1 *t* (*limitar*) to restrict, limit. 2 (*astringir*) to contract. – 3 **restringirse,** *p* (*reducirse*) to reduce.

▲ *Conjugation model* |6|, *like dirigir.*

resucitar 1 *t* to resuscitate. 2 *fig* to revive. – 3 *i* to resuscitate.

resudar 1 *i* (*sudar ligeramente*) to sweat slightly. 2 (*árboles*) to exude.

resuello 1 *m* (*acción*) breathing. 2 (*aliento*) breath, gasp.

resuelto,-a 1 *pp* → **resolver.** – 2 *adj* (*decidido*) resolute, determined.

resulta *f* consequence.

● **de resultas de,** as a result of.

resultado *m* result; (*consecuencia*) outcome.

● **dar buen resultado,** to work well, turn out to be good, give results; (*prenda*) to wear well: *este abrigo me ha dado muy buen resultado,* this coat has worn really well.

resultante *adj* resultant, resulting.

resultar 1 *i* (*gen*) to result, be the result of: *esto resulta de las operaciones que se realizaron,* this is the result of the transactions which were carried out. 2 (*ser*) to be: *la casa resulta pequeña,* the house is small; *resultó vencedor,* he won. 3 (*acabar siendo*) to turn out to be: *resultó ser muy agradable,* he turned out to be very nice; *aquel plan resultó un éxito,* that plan turned out to be a success. 4 (*salir*) to come out, turn out, work out: *todo resultó como esperábamos,* it all worked out as we expected. 5 (*ocurrir*) to turn out: *resulta que está enfermo y no puede venir,* it turns out that he's ill and can't come. 6 (*ser conveniente*) to be advisable: *resulta mirar bien antes de comprar,* one should have a good look around before buying. 7 (*tener éxito*) to be a success, come off: *el negocio resultó,* the business was a success; *la actuación no resultó,* the performance didn't come off. 8 (*combinarse*) to go (**con,** with), match (**con,** -): *esos zapatos no resultan con ese vestido,* those shoes don't go with that dress. 9 (*costar*) to cost (**por,** -), come (**por,** to): *los pantalones resultan por tres mil pesetas,* the trousers cost three thousand pesetas.

● **resulta que,** it turns out that: *resulta que era médico,* it turns out that he was a doctor; *ahora resulta que no tiene adónde ir,* now it seems that she hasn't got anywhere to go. ‖ **viene a resultar lo mismo,** it amounts to the same thing.

resultón,-ona *adj* (*agradable*) nice, pleasant; (*atractivo*) attractive.

resumen *m* summary.

● **en resumen,** in short, to sum up.

resumir 1 *t* (*reducir*) to summarize. 2 (*concluir*) to sum up: *resumiendo, es una novela excelente,* in short, it's an excellent novel. – **3 resumirse,** *p* to be summarized, be summed up. **4** (*venir a ser*) to be reduced (**en,** to), boil down (**en,** to).

resurgimiento *m* resurgence, reappearance.

resurgir 1 *i* (*volver a aparecer*) to reappear. **2** (*revivir*) to revive.

▲ *Conjugation model* |6|, *like dirigir.*

resurrección 1 *f* resurrection. **2 la Resurrección,** REL the Resurrection.

■ **Domingo de Resurrección,** REL Easter Sunday.

retablo *m* altarpiece, reredos.

retacear *t* (*recortar*) to cut out.

retaco 1 *m* (*escopeta*) short shotgun. **2** *fam fig* (*persona*) twirp, shorty, squirt.

retador,-ra *adj* challenging.

retaguarda *f* rearguard.

● ir a la retaguarda, to bring up the rear.

retaguardia *f* → **retaguarda.**

retahíla *f* string, series: *una retahíla de chistes,* a series of jokes.

retal 1 *m* (*sobrante*) oddment, remnant, scrap. **2** (*de tela*) offcut, remnant.

retama *f* broom.

retamal *m* broom patch, broom thicket.

retar 1 *t* (*desafiar*) to challenge. **2** *fam* (*reprender*) to scold.

● retar a duelo, to challenge to a duel.

retardado,-a 1 *pp* → **retardar.** – **2** *adj* delayed, retarded: *de efecto retardado,* delayed-action.

retardar 1 *t* (*detener*) to slow down; (*retrasar*) to delay. **2** (*posponer*) to postpone. – **3 retardarse,** *p* to be delayed, be held up, be late.

retardo *m* delay.

retazo 1 *m* (*retal*) remnant, scrap. **2** (*fragmento*) fragment, piece.

retemblar *i* to shake, tremble.

▲ *Conjugation model* |27|, *like acertar.*

retén 1 *m* MIL reserves *pl*, reinforcements *pl*. **2** (*previsión*) stock, store.

● de retén, in reserve.

retención 1 *f* (*gen*) retention. **2** FIN withholding, deduction. **3** (*de tráfico*) traffic jam, (traffic) hold-up.

■ retención de haberes, stoppages *pl*.

retener 1 *t* (*contener*) to restrain, hold back: *tuvo que retener las ganas de llorar,* she had to hold back the tears. **2** (*no dejar marchar*) to keep, keep back: *no quiero retenerte,* I don't want to keep you. **3** (*no devolver*) to keep: *retiene todo lo que le prestan,* he keeps everything he borrows. **4** (*en la memoria*) to retain, remember. **5** (*detener*) to detain; (*arrestar*) to arrest. **6** FIN to deduct, withhold. **7** (*absorber*) to retain, hold: *el algodón retiene el agua,* cotton holds water. – **8 retenerse,** *p* to restrain os., hold os. back.

▲ *Conjugation model* |87|, *like tener.*

retentiva *f* → **retentivo,-a.**

retentivo,-a 1 *adj* retentive. – **2 retentiva,** *f* retentiveness, memory.

reticencia 1 *f* (*reserva*) reticence, reserve. **2** (*insinuación*) insinuation, innuendo.

reticente *adj* insinuating.

retícula *f* reticle.

reticular *adj* reticular.

retículo *m* reticle.

retina *f* retina.

retinte *m* → **retintín.**

retintín 1 *m* (*sonido*) tinkling, ringing. **2** *fig* innuendo, sarcastic tone.

retinto,-a *adj* dark chestnut.

retirada *f* → **retirado,-a.**

retirado,-a 1 *pp* → **retirar.** – **2** *adj* (*apartado*) remote. **3** (*tranquilo*) secluded, quiet. **4** (*jubilado*) retired. – **5** *m,f* retired person, US retiree. – **6 retirada,** *f* MIL retreat, withdrawal. **7** (*de un carnet*) withdrawal. **8** (*retiro*) retirement: *la retirada de un futbolista,* a footballer's retirement.

● batirse en retirada, MIL to beat a retreat. ‖ emprender la retirada, MIL to retreat.

retirar 1 *t* (*apartar - gen*) to take away, remove; (- *un mueble*) to move away. **2** (*un carnet*) to take away. **3** (*algo dicho*) to take back. **4** (*dinero, ley, moneda*) to withdraw. **5** (*jubilar*) to retire. – **6 retirarse,** *p* MIL to retreat, withdraw. **7** (*apartarse del mundo*) to go into seclusion. **8** (*apartarse*) to withdraw, draw back, move back: *retírate, no veo,* move back, I can't see. **9** (*alejarse*) to move away: *retírate de la ventana, te van a ver,* move away from the window, they'll see you. **10** (*marcharse*) to leave: *cuando acabó, se retiró,* when he finished, he left. **11** (*irse a descansar*) to retire: *se retiró a su habitación,* she retired to her bedroom. **12** (*jubilarse*) to retire.

● no se retire, (*al teléfono*) hold on, don't hang up.

retiro 1 *m* (*jubilación*) retirement. **2** (*pensión*) pension. **3** (*lugar, recogimiento*) retreat. **4** REL retreat.

● cobrar el retiro, to receive one's pension.

■ retiro espiritual, REL retreat.

reto *m* challenge.

● lanzar un reto a algn., to challenge sb.

retocar 1 *t* (*dibujo, fotografía*) to touch up, retouch. **2** (*perfeccionar*) to put the finishing touches to.

▲ *Conjugation model* |1|, *like sacar.*

retoñar 1 *i* (*rebrotar*) to shoot, sprout. **2** *fig* to reappear.

retoño 1 *m* BOT sprout, shoot. **2** *fig* kid.

retoque *m* finishing touch.

● dar los últimos retoques a algo, to put the finishing touches to sth.

retor *m* rough cotton fabric.

retorcer 1 *t* (*gen*) to twist. **2** (*ropa*) to wring (out). **3** *fig* (*un argumento*) to twist. **4** *fig* (*tergiversar*) to distort. – **5 retorcerse,** *p* (*gen*) to become twisted, twist. **6** (*doblarse*) to bend.

● retorcerse de dolor, *fig* to writhe in pain. ‖ retorcerse de risa, *fig* to double up with laughter, split one's sides laughing.

▲ *Conjugation model* |54|, *like cocer.*

retorcido,-a 1 *pp* → **retorcer.** – **2** *adj fig* twisted: *mente retorcida,* warped mind.

retorcimiento 1 *m* twisting. **2** *fig* twistedness.

retórica *f* → **retórico,-a.**

retoricismo *m* use of rhetoric.

retórico,-a 1 *adj* rhetorical. – **2** *m,f* rhetorician. – **3 retórica,** *f* rhetoric. – **4 retóricas,** *fpl fam* verbiage *sing*.

● usar mucha retórica, *fam* to be full of hot air.

retornable *adj* returnable.

● "envase no retornable", "non returnable".

retornar 1 *t* (*restituir*) to return, give back. – **2** *i* (*volver*) to come back, go back, return. – **3 retornarse,** *p* to come back, go back, return.

retornelo *m* ritornello.

retorno 1 *m* return. **2** (*recompensa*) reward.

retorta *f* retort.

retortero *m* turn.

● andar al retortero / ir al retortero, *fam* (*tener trabajo*) to be up to one's ears in work; (*estar ansioso*) to be going up the wall; (*estar enamorado*) to be head over heels in love. ‖ **estar al retortero,** to be in a mess, be upside down. ‖ **llevar a algn. al retortero / traer a algn. al retortero,** *fam* (*tenerle enamorado*) to win sb's heart; (*tenerle dominado*) to have sb. under one's thumb; (*baquetearle*) to keep sb. on the go.

retortijón 1 *m* (*torcimiento*) twisting. **2** (*de tripas*) stomach cramp.

retostado,-a *adj* dark-coloured (us dark-colored).

retozar *i* to frolic, gambol.

▲ *Conjugation model* |4|, *like realizar.*

retozo *m* frolic.

retozón,-ona *adj* frolicsome, playful.

retracción *f* retraction, withdrawal.

retractable *adj* retractable.

retractar 1 *t* to retract, revoke, withdraw. – **2 retractarse,** *p* to retract, take back: *se retractó de aquello,* she took that back.

retráctil 1 *adj* (*uña etc*) retractile. **2** (*tren de aterrizaje*) retractable.

retraer 1 *t* (*volver a traer*) to bring back, bring again. **2** (*reprochar*) to reproach: *le retrajo todas sus faltas,* she reproached him for all his faults. **3** (*disuadir*) to dissuade. – **4 retraerse,** *p* (*apartarse*) to be dissuaded. **5** (*refugiarse*) to take refuge. **6** (*hacer vida retirada*) to withdraw. **7** POL to give up.

▲ *Conjugation model* |88|, *like traer.*

retraído,-a 1 *pp* → **retraer.** – **2** *adj* (*tímido*) shy, reserved. **3** (*solitario*) solitary. **4** (*poco comunicativo*) unsociable, withdrawn.

retraimiento 1 *m* (*timidez*) shyness, reserve, retiring nature. **2** (*soledad*) solitude.

retranca *f fig* (*intención*) hidden intentions *pl,* ulterior motives *pl.*

● **tener mucha retranca,** *fig* to have ulterior motives.

retransmisión *f* broadcast, transmission.

■ **retransmisión en diferido,** recorded transmission. ‖ **retransmisión en directo,** live broadcast.

retransmisor *m* transmitter.

retransmitir 1 *t* (*mensaje*) to pass on. **2** RAD TV to broadcast.

● **retransmitir algo en diferido,** to broadcast a recording of sth. ‖ **retransmitir algo en directo,** to broadcast sth. live.

retrasado,-a 1 *pp* → **retrasar.** – **2** *adj* (*en conocimientos, trabajo*) behind: *está retrasada en latín,* she's behind in Latin; *tengo trabajo retrasado,* I'm behind in my work. **3** (*pagos*) late: *voy retrasado en los pagos,* I'm in arrears. **4** (*reloj*) slow. **5** (*tren, avión, etc*) delayed. **6** (*país*) backward, underdeveloped. **7** (*mental*) retarded, backward. – **8** *m,f* mentally retarded person.

retrasar 1 *t* (*atrasar*) to delay, put off, postpone: *un accidente retrasó el tren,* the train was delayed by an accident. **2** (*reloj*) to put back. **3** DEP to pass back: *el público protestaba porque los jugadores retrasaban el balón,* the crowd protested because the players were passing the ball back. – **4** *i* (*ir atrás*) to fall behind: *retrasa en física,* he's behind in physics. **5** (*llegar tarde*) to be late. **6** (*reloj*) to be slow. – **7 retrasarse,** *p* (*atrasarse*) to be late, arrive late, be delayed. **8** (*reloj*) to be slow. **9** (*trabajo, conocimientos, pagos*) to fall behind.

retraso 1 *m* (*demora*) delay: *llegó con mucho retraso,* she was very late; *el vuelo saldrá con 20 minutos de retraso,* the flight will be delayed 20 minutes. **2** (*subdesarrollo*) backwardness, underdevelopment.

● **ir con retraso,** to be running late. ‖ **llevar un año de retraso,** to be a year behind schedule.

■ **retraso mental,** mental handicap, backwardness.

retratar 1 *t* (*pintura*) to portray, paint a portrait of. **2** (*foto*) to photograph, take a photograph of. **3** *fig* to describe, portray, depict. – **4 retratarse,** *p* (*darse a conocer*) to be described, be portrayed: *con aquellas palabras se retrató,* those words give a good portrayal of his character. **5** *fam* (*pagar*) to pay up, cough up.

retratista 1 *mf* (*pintor*) portrait painter, portrait artist. **2** (*fotógrafo*) photographer.

retrato 1 *m* (*pintura*) portrait. **2** (*foto*) photograph. **3** *fig* (*descripción*) description, depiction, portrayal.

● **ser el vivo retrato de algn.,** to be the spitting image of sb.

■ **retrato robot,** identikit picture, photofit picture.

retrechar *i* to back.

retrechero,-a 1 *adj fam* (*que elude*) slippery. **2** *fam* (*atractivo*) attractive, charming.

retreparse 1 *p* (*recostarse*) to lean back. **2** (*acomodarse*) to lounge back.

retreta *f* retreat.

● **tocar retreta,** to sound the retreat.

retrete *m* toilet, lavatory.

retribución 1 *f* (*pago*) pay, payment. **2** (*recompensa*) recompense, reward.

retribuir 1 *t* (*pagar*) to pay. **2** (*recompensar*) to remunerate, reward.

▲ *Conjugation model* |62|, *like huir.*

retributivo,-a *adj* retributive.

retro 1 *adj fam* (*reaccionario*) reactionary. **2** *fam* (*del pasado*) retro: *moda retro,* retro fashion.

▲ *pl retro.*

retroacción *f* retroaction.

retroactivo,-a *adj* retroactive: *ley con efecto retroactivo,* retroactive law.

retroceder 1 *i* (*recular*) to go back, move back. **2** (*bajar de nivel*) to go down. **3** (*echarse atrás*) to back down. **4** *fig* (*mirar atrás*) to look back; (*cejar*) give up. **5** MIL to fall back, retreat. **6** (*arma*) to recoil.

● **hacer retroceder a algn.,** to force sb. back, make sb. move back.

retroceso 1 *m* (*movimiento*) backward movement. **2** MED aggravation, deterioration, worsening. **3** ECON recession. **4** (*de arma*) recoil.

retrocohete *m* retrorocket, retro.

retrocuenta *f* countdown.

retrógrado,-a 1 *adj* (*que retrocede*) retrograde. **2** *fig* (*reaccionario*) reactionary. – **3** *m,f* (*reaccionario*) reactionary.

retropropulsión *f* jet propulsion.

retrospección *f* retrospection.

retrospectiva *f* → **retrospectivo,-a.**

retrospectivo,-a 1 *adj* retrospective. – **2 retrospectiva,** *f* retrospective.

retrotraer *t* to predate.

▲ *Conjugation model* |88|, *like traer.*

retrovisor *m* rear-view mirror.

retruécano *m* play on words, pun.

retuerzo *pres indic* → **retorcer.**

retumbante 1 *adj* resounding. **2** *fig* ostentatious, pretentious.

retumbar 1 *i* (*resonar*) to resound, echo. **2** (*tronar*) to thunder, boom.

retuve *pt indef* → **retener.**

reuma *m* rheumatism.

reúma *m* rheumatism.

reumático,-a 1 *adj* rheumatic. – **2** *m,f* rheumatic.

reumatismo *m* rheumatism.
reumatología *f* rheumatology.
reunificación *f* reunification.
reunificar *t* to reunify.
▲ *Conjugation model* |1|, *like* **sacar.**
reunión 1 *f* (*gen*) meeting, gathering. **2** (*reencuentro*) reunion: *reunión de ex-combatientes,* ex-servicemen's reunion. **3** (*conjunto*) collection, gathering.
● **asistir a una reunión,** to attend a meeting. ‖ celebrar una reunión, to hold a meeting: *ayer se celebró la reunión,* the meeting was held yesterday.
■ reunión en la cumbre, POL summit meeting. ‖ reunión social, social gathering.
reunir 1 *t* (*congregar*) to assemble, get together: *reunió a todos sus amigos,* she got all her friends together. **2** (*juntar algo*) to put together: *reunimos todos nuestros libros,* we put all our books together. **3** (*recoger*) to gather (together); (*dinero*) to raise. **4** (*coleccionar*) to collect. **5** (*tener*) to have, possess: *reúne las cualidades para hacerlo,* he has the ability to do it. **6** (*requisitos*) to satisfy, meet, fulfil (US fulfill): *reúne todos los requisitos,* she fulfils all the requirements. **– 7 reunirse,** *p* to meet (**con,** **-**), get together, have a meeting with: *me reuní con Juan,* I met Juan.
▲ *Conjugation model* |19|.
reválida *f* final examination.
revalidación *f* confirmation, ratification, validation.
revalidar *t* to confirm, ratify, validate: *el boxeador revalidó su título de campeón,* the boxer retained his championship title.
revalorización *f* (*de moneda*) revaluation; (*de precio*) appreciation, increase in value.
revalorizar 1 *t* (*moneda*) to revalue; (*precio*) to increase the value of. **– 2 revalorizarse,** *p* (*moneda*) to revalue; (*precio*) to appreciate, go up in value.
▲ *Conjugation model* |4|, *like* **realizar.**
revaluación *f* revaluation.
revancha 1 *f* revenge. **2** (*en naipes*) return game. **3** DEP return match.
● **tomarse la revancha,** to take revenge.
revanchismo *m* vengefulness, vindictiveness.
revanchista 1 *adj* vengeful, vindictive. **– 2** *mf* person bent on revenge.
reveillón *m* New Year's Eve party.
revelación *f* revelation.
revelado *m* developing.
revelador,-ra 1 *adj* revealing. **– 2** *m,f* revealer. **– 3** revelador, *m* developer.
revelar 1 *t* to reveal, disclose: *reveló el secreto,* she revealed the secret. **2** (*fotos*) to develop.
revendedor,-ra 1 *m,f* (*gen*) seller. **2** (*detallista*) retailer. **3** (*de entradas*) ticket tout, US scalper.
revender 1 *t* (*gen*) to resell. **2** (*al por menor*) to retail. **3** (*entradas*) to tout.
reventa 1 *f* (*gen*) resale. **2** (*al por menor*) retail. **3** (*de entradas*) touting.
reventador,-ra *m,f fam* catcaller.
reventar 1 *t* (*gen*) to burst. **2** (*neumático*) to puncture, burst. **3** (*romper*) to break, smash. **4** (*estropear*) to spoil. **5** *fig* (*agotar*) to exhaust, tire out. **6** *fam fig* (*hacer fracasar*) to spoil, mess up, ruin: *aquel grupo reventó la función,* that group spoiled the performance. **– 7** *i fam* (*fastidiar*) to annoy: *me revientan sus preguntas,* her questions get on my nerves. **8** *fam* (*disgustar*) to disgust, make sick: *me revienta su hermana,* his sister makes me sick. **9** (*estallar*) to burst: *la cañería reventó,* the pipe

burst; *el sitio donde revientan las olas,* the place where the waves break. **10** (*rajarse*) to split. **11** *fam* (*tener un deseo*) to be dying (**por,** to): *está que revienta por hablar,* she's dying to talk. **12** *fam* (*morir*) to kick it, snuff it. **– 13 reventarse,** *p* (*estallar*) to burst. **14** *fam* (*cansarse*) to tire os. out.
● **reventar de cansancio,** to be dead tired. ‖ reventar de orgullo, to be bursting with pride. ‖ reventar de rabia, to be furious, be fuming. ‖ reventar de risa, to die laughing.
▲ *Conjugation model* |27|, *like* **acertar.**
reventón,-ona 1 *adj* bursting: *clavel reventón,* large carnation. **– 2** reventón, *m* (*de cañería*) burst. **3** (*de neumático*) blowout. **4** *fam* (*apuro*) difficulty.
● **darse un reventón de trabajar,** *fam* to work os. hard, slog one's guts out.
reverberación *f* reverberation, reflection.
reverberar *i* to reverberate, reflect.
reverbero *m* reverberation, reflection.
reverdecer 1 *i* to grow green again. **2** *fig* to revive, come to life again.
▲ *Conjugation model* |43|, *like* **agradecer.**
reverencia 1 *f* (*respeto*) reverence. **2** (*gesto*) bow, curtsy.
● **hacer una reverencia,** to bow, curtsy.
■ Su Reverencia, (Your) Reverence.
reverencial *adj* reverential.
reverenciar *t* to revere, venerate.
▲ *Conjugation model* |12|, *like* **cambiar.**
reverendo,-a 1 *adj* reverend. **2** *fam* (*enorme*) enormous, great: *es una reverenda estupidez,* it's totally stupid. **– 3** *m,f* reverend.
reverente *adj* reverent.
reversible *adj* reversible.
reversión *f* reversion.
reverso *m* reverse, back.
● **el reverso de la medalla,** *fig* the exact opposite.
revertir 1 *i* (*volver*) to revert, return, go back. **2** (*resultar*) to result (**en,** in). **3** JUR to revert.
● **revertir en beneficio de,** to be to the advantage of. ‖ revertir en perjuicio de, to be to the detriment of.
▲ *Conjugation model* |35|, *like* **hervir.**
revés 1 *m* (*reverso*) back, reverse, wrong side; (*de tela*) wrong side. **2** (*bofetada*) slap; (*golpe*) backhander. **3** (*en tenis*) backhand (stroke). **4** *fig* (*contrariedad*) misfortune, setback, reverse.
● **al revés / del revés,** (*al contrario*) the other way round; (*interior en exterior*) inside out; (*boca abajo*) upside down, the wrong way up; (*la parte de detrás delante*) back to front. ‖ al revés de, contrary to: *al revés de lo que dijo,* contrary to what she said.
■ reveses de fortuna, setbacks, blows of fate. ‖ reveses de la vida, life's misfortunes.
revesado,-a 1 *adj* (*enrevesado*) complicated, difficult. **2** *fig* (*travieso*) mischievous.
revestimiento *m* covering, coating.
revestir 1 *t* (*recubrir*) to cover (**de,** with), coat (**de,** with), line (**de,** with). **2** (*disimular*) to conceal, disguise. **3** *fig* (*presentar*) to take on: *la ceremonia revistió gran solemnidad,* the ceremony took on great solemnity; *la cogida no reviste gravedad,* the goring is not serious. **– 4** revestirse, *p* to arm os.: *revestirse de paciencia,* to arm os. with patience.
▲ *Conjugation model* |34|, *like* **servir.**
revigorizar *t* to revigorate.
▲ *Conjugation model* |4|, *like* **realizar.**
revisar 1 *t* (*gen*) to revise, go through, check. **2** (*examen etc*) to check, look over. **3** (*cuentas*) to check, audit. **4** (*billetes*) to inspect. **5** (*coche*) to service, overhaul.

revisión 1 *f* (*gen*) revision, checking. **2** (*de billetes*) inspection. **3** (*de coche*) service, overhaul.
■ **revisión de cuentas,** audit, auditing. ‖ **revisión médica,** check-up.

revisionismo *m* revisionism.

revisionista 1 *adj* revisionist. – **2** *mf* revisionist.

revisor,-ra *m,f* ticket inspector.

revista 1 *f* (*publicación*) magazine, review, journal. **2** (*inspección*) inspection. **3** MIL review. **4** TEAT revue: *chica de revista,* chorus girl.
● **pasar revista a,** (*inspeccionar*) to inspect, review; (*tratar*) to review.
■ **revista de modas,** fashion magazine. ‖ **revista del corazón,** gossip magazine. ‖ **revista juvenil,** teenage magazine. ‖ **revista semanal,** weekly review.

revistar *t* to inspect, review.

revistero *m* magazine rack.

revitalizar *t* to revitalize.
▲ *Conjugation model* [4], *like realizar.*

revival *m* revival.

revivificar *t* to revivify, revive.
▲ *Conjugation model* [1], *like sacar.*

revivir 1 *i* to revive, come to life again. **2** *fig* (*reproducirse*) to be renewed: *el conflicto revivió,* further hostilities broke out. – **3** *t* to revive, bring back to life.

revocable *adj* revocable.

revocar 1 *t* (*ley*) to revoke, repeal; (*orden*) to cancel, rescind. **2** (*disuadir*) to dissuade. **3** (*enlucir*) to plaster, stucco. **4** (*encalar*) to whitewash.
▲ *Conjugation model* [1], *like sacar.*

revolcar 1 *t* (*derribar al suelo*) to knock down, knock over. **2** *fig* (*derrotar*) to floor, defeat, crush. **3** *fam fig* (*suspender un examen*) to fail, flunk. – **4** **revolcarse,** *p* (*echarse*) to roll about.
● **revolcarse de dolor,** *fig* to double up with pain. ‖ **revolcarse de risa,** *fig* to split one's sides laughing. ‖ **revolcarse en el fango,** to wallow in the mud.
▲ *Conjugation model* [49], *like trocar.*

revolcón 1 *m fam* (*revuelco*) fall, tumble. **2** *fam* (*suspenso*) failure. **3** *fam* (*sexual*) romp.

revolotear *i* to fly about, flutter about, hover.

revoloteo *m* fluttering, hovering.

revoltijo 1 *m* (*mezcla*) mess, clutter, jumble. **2** *fig* (*confusión*) mess, chaos. **3** CULIN *fig* scrambled eggs *pl*: *revoltijo de trigueros,* scrambled eggs with wild asparagus.

revoltillo *m* → **revoltijo.**

revoltoso,-a 1 *adj* (*rebelde*) rebellious, unruly. **2** (*travieso*) mischievous, naughty. – **3** *m,f* (*rebelde*) rebel. **4** (*travieso*) mischievous child: *Pablo es un revoltoso de cuidado,* Pablo is a real handful. **5** (*sedicioso*) troublemaker.

revolución *f* revolution: *80 revoluciones por minuto,* 80 revolutions per minute.
■ **la Revolución Francesa,** the French Revolution. ‖ **la Revolución Industrial,** the Industrial Revolution.

revolucionar *t* to revolutionize.

revolucionario,-a 1 *adj* revolutionary. – **2** *m,f* revolutionary.

revolver 1 *t* (*agitar*) to stir. **2** (*mezclar*) to mix. **3** (*ensalada*) to toss. **4** (*habitación, casa, etc*) to turn upside down: *revolvimos toda la habitación pero no lo encontramos,* we turned the room upside down but couldn't find it. **5** (*papeles*) to rummage through; (*bolso, bolsillo, etc*) to rummage in: *revolvió en el bolsillo y encontró el mechero,* she rummaged in her pocket and found the lighter. **6** (*producir náuseas*) to upset, turn: *le revolvió el estómago,*

it turned his stomach. – **7** **revolverse,** *p* (*moverse*) to fidget; (*en la cama*) to toss and turn. **8** (*volverse con rapidez*) to turn around, spin round. **9** (*tiempo*) to turn stormy; (*mar*) to become rough.
● **revolverse contra algn.,** *fig* to turn against sb.
▲ *Conjugation model* [32], *like mover. pp revuelto,-a.*

revólver *m* revolver.
▲ *pl* **revólveres.**

revoque 1 *m* (*enlucido*) plastering. **2** (*encalado*) whitewashing. **3** (*material*) plaster, stucco.

revuelco *m* roll; (*en barro*) wallow.

revuelo 1 *m* (*revoloteo*) fluttering. **2** *fig* commotion, stir.
● **armar un gran revuelo / provocar un gran revuelo,** to cause a great stir.

revuelta *f* → **revuelto,-a.**

revuelto,-a 1 *pp* → **revolver.** – **2** *adj* (*desordenado*) confused, mixed up, in a mess. **3** (*intricado*) intricate, involved, complex. **4** (*gente*) agitated, restless, up in arms. **5** (*líquido*) cloudy. **6** (*tiempo*) stormy, unsettled; (*mar*) rough. **7** (*cabellos*) untidy, dishevelled. **8** (*época*) turbulent: *tiempos revueltos,* turbulent times. **9** (*noche*) bad: *pasé una noche muy revuelta,* I spent all night tossing and turning. **10** CULIN scrambled: *huevos revueltos,* scrambled eggs. – **11** **revuelta,** *f* (*revolución*) revolt, riot. **12** (*curva*) bend, turn.

revulsión *f* revulsion.

revulsivo,-a 1 *adj* revulsive. – **2** **revulsivo,** *m* revulsive.

revulsorio,-a *adj* revulsive.

rey *m* king: *el rey de picos,* the king of spades; *los Reyes de España,* the King and Queen of Spain.
● **a cuerpo de rey,** *fig* like a king. ‖ **a rey muerto, rey puesto,** off with the old, on with the new.
■ (*día de*) **Reyes,** Epiphany. ‖ **el Rey Sol,** the Sun King. ‖ **los Reyes Católicos,** the Catholic Monarchs.

reyerta *f* quarrel, row, fight.

reyezuelo 1 *m pey* (*rey*) kinglet. **2** (*ave*) goldcrest.
■ **reyezuelo listado,** firecrest.

Reykjavik *m* Reykjavik.

rezagado,-a 1 *pp* → **rezagar.** – **2** *m,f* straggler, latecomer.
● **ir rezagado,-a,** to lag behind. ‖ **quedar rezagado,-a,** to be left behind.

rezagar 1 *t* (*dejar atrás*) to leave behind. **2** (*atrasar*) to delay, put off, postpone. – **3** **rezagarse,** *p* to fall behind, lag behind.
▲ *Conjugation model* [7], *like llegar.*

rezar 1 *t* (*orar*) to say: *rezar un padrenuestro,* to say the Lord's Prayer. **2** *fam* (*decir*) to say, read: *la carta así lo reza,* the letter says so. – **3** *i* (*orar*) to pray: *rezar a Dios,* to pray to God. **4** (*decir*) to say, read. **5** (*concernir*) to concern (**con,** to), apply (**con,** to): *aquel asunto no reza conmigo,* that affair doesn't concern me.
▲ *Conjugation model* [4], *like realizar.*

rezno 1 *m* (*garrapata*) tick. **2** (*larva*) bot.

rezo 1 *m* (*acción*) praying. **2** (*oración*) prayer.

rezongar *i fam fig* to grumble, moan.
▲ *Conjugation model* [7], *like llegar.*

rezongón,-ona 1 *adj fam* grumbling, griping. – **2** *m,f fam* grumbler, griper.

rezumar 1 *t* (*transpirar*) to ooze: *el cántaro rezuma agua,* there's water seeping out of this pitcher. **2** *fig* to exude, ooze: *rezumar alegría,* to ooze happiness. – **3** *i* (*contenido*) to ooze (**por,** out), seep (**por,** through); (*recipiente*) to leak: *el agua rezuma por la cañería,* water seeps through the pipe; *la vasija rezuma,* the jar is leaking. – **4** **rezumarse,** *p* to ooze out, seep, leak.

RFA *abr* (*República Federal de Alemania*) Federal Republic of Germany; (*abreviatura*) FRG.
Rhodesia *f* Rhodesia.
rhodesiano,-a 1 *adj* Rhodesian. – 2 *m,f* Rhodesian.
ría *f* (*gen*) estuary, river mouth; (*técnicamente*) ria.
riacho *m* brook, stream.
riachuelo *m* brook, stream.
riada 1 *f* flood, flooding. 2 *fig* flood.
ribazo *m* embankment, bank.
ribeiro *m* Ribeiro wine.
ribera 1 *f* (*de río*) bank: *la ribera del Ebro*, the bank of the river Ebro. 2 (*del mar*) shore, seashore. 3 (*tierra cercana a un río*) riverside, waterfront.
ribereño,-a 1 *adj* riverside, waterfront. – 2 *m,f* riverside dweller, waterfront dweller.
ribete 1 *m* (*cinta*) border, trimming, edging. – 2 **ribetes,** *mpl* (*indicios*) touch *sing*.
● **tener ribetes de ...,** to be something of a ...: *tiene ribetes de cómico,* he's something of a comic.
ribeteado,-a 1 *pp* → **ribetear.** – 2 *adj* edged, bordered.
ribetear *t* to edge, border.
ribonucleico,-a *adj* ribonucleic.
ricacho,-a *m,f fam* moneybags.
ricachón,-ona *m,f fam* moneybags.
ricamente 1 *adv* (*con riquezas*) richly. 2 *fam* (*estupendamente*) very well: *dormimos muy ricamente,* we slept very well.
ricino *m* castor-oil plant.
● **aceite de ricino,** castor oil.
rico,-a 1 *adj* (*acaudalado*) rich, wealthy. 2 (*abundante*) rich: *rico en potasio,* rich in potassium. 3 (*sabroso*) tasty, delicious. 4 (*tierra*) rich, fertile. 5 (*excelente*) rich, excellent. 6 *fam* (*bonito*) lovely, adorable: *tiene un niño muy rico,* she's got a lovely boy. 7 *fam* (*tratamiento - hombre*) mate, us man; (*- mujer*) love, us sweetheart: *mira rico, no me tomes el pelo,* look mate, don't pull my leg; *¿qué tal, rica?,* how are you doing, love? – 8 *m,f* rich person. – 9 **los ricos,** *mpl* the rich.
● **estar muy rica,** *fam* (*chica*) to be gorgeous. ‖ **hacerse rico,-a,** to get rich.
■ **nuevo,-a rico,-a,** nouveau riche.
rictus 1 *m* rictus. 2 (*de dolor*) wince. 3 (*de mofa*) grin.
▲ *pl* **rictus.**
ricura 1 *f fam* (*de comida*) deliciousness. 2 *fam* (*chica*) smashing girl. 3 *fam* (*niño*) lovely child, sweet child: *¡esta niña es una ricura!,* what a lovely girl she is! 4 *fam* (*tratamiento*) darling, love.
ridiculez 1 *f* (*cualidad*) ridiculousness. 2 (*cosa, hecho*) ridiculous thing, ridiculous action. 3 (*nimiedad*) triviality, nothing: *la diferencia de precio es una ridiculez,* there's virtually no difference in price, there's only a slight difference in price.
● **¡qué ridiculez!,** how ridiculous!
ridiculizar *t* to ridicule, deride.
▲ *Conjugation model* [4], *like* **realizar.**
ridículo,-a 1 *adj* ridiculous, absurd. – 2 **ridículo,** *m* ridicule.
● **hacer el ridículo,** to make a fool of os. ‖ **poner a algn. en ridículo,** to make a fool of sb., ridicule sb. ‖ **quedar en ridículo,** to make a fool of os.
riego *m* irrigation, watering.
■ **boca de riego,** hydrant. ‖ **riego por aspersión,** sprinkling. ‖ **riego sanguíneo,** blood circulation.
riel *m* rail.
rielar *i lit* to shimmer, gleam.

rienda 1 *f* rein. 2 *fig* (*control*) restraint.
● **aflojar las riendas,** *fig* to let up, slacken. ‖ **dar rienda suelta a,** *fig* to give free rein to. ‖ **empuñar las riendas,** *fig* to take the reins. ‖ **llevar las riendas,** *fig* to hold the reins, be in control.
riesgo *m* risk, danger.
● **a riesgo de / con riesgo de,** at the risk of. ‖ **a todo riesgo,** (*seguro*) fully-comprehensive. ‖ **correr el riesgo de,** to run the risk of. ‖ **por su cuenta y riesgo,** at one's own risk.
rifa *f* raffle.
rifar 1 *t* to raffle (off). – 2 **rifarse,** *p MAR* to split. 3 (*solicitar, desear*) to fight over: *es tan competente que todas las empresas se lo rifan,* he's so talented that he's being headhunted by all the companies.
rifirrafe *m fam* row.
rifle *m* rifle.
rigidez 1 *f* (*dureza*) stiffness, rigidity. 2 *fig* (*rectitud*) strictness, firmness, inflexibility.
rígido,-a 1 *adj* (*duro*) rigid, stiff. 2 *fig* (*severo*) strict, firm, inflexible.
rigodón *m* rigadoon.
rigor 1 *m* (*severidad*) rigour (*us* rigor), strictness, severity. 2 (*dureza*) rigour (*us* rigor), harshness: *los rigores del invierno,* the rigours of winter. 3 (*exactitud*) precision, exactness.
● **con rigor,** rigorously. ‖ **de rigor,** essential, indispensable: *el esmoquin es de rigor,* a dinner jacket is required. ‖ **en rigor,** strictly speaking. ‖ **ser el rigor de las desdichas,** *fig* to be born under an unlucky star.
rigurosamente 1 *adv* (*con severidad*) rigorously, severely. 2 (*con exactitud*) accurately. 3 (*minuciosamente*) meticulously. 4 (*totalmente*) absolutely: *es rigurosamente cierto,* it's absolutely true.
rigurosidad *f* rigorousness, strictness.
riguroso,-a 1 *adj* (*severo*) rigorous, severe, strict. 2 (*clima*) rigorous, severe, harsh. 3 (*exacto*) exact. 4 (*minucioso*) meticulous.
rija *f* row, din.
rijo *pres indic* → **regir.**
rijoso,-a 1 *adj* (*pendenciero*) quarrelsome. 2 (*lujurioso*) lustful.
rima 1 *f* rhyme. – 2 **rimas,** *fpl* poem *sing*.
■ **rima imperfecta,** half rhyme. ‖ **rima perfecta,** full rhyme.
rimar 1 *t* to rhyme. – 2 *i* to rhyme: *"frío" rima con "albedrío",* "frío" rhymes with "albedrío".
rimbombante 1 *adj* (*gen*) ostentatious, showy. 2 (*lenguaje*) pretentious, pompous.
rímel *m* mascara.
Rin **el Rin,** *m* the Rhine.
rincón 1 *m* corner. 2 *fig* (*lugar*) spot, place; (*espacio pequeño*) little space; (*lugar apartado*) remote spot, little place.
rinconada *f* corner.
rinconera *f* corner unit.
ring *m* ring.
▲ *pl* **rings.**
ringlera *f* row, line.
ringorrango 1 *m fam* (*adorno*) frill, adornment. 2 (*en la escritura*) rambling.
rinitis *f* rhinitis.
▲ *pl* **rinitis.**
rinoceronte *m* rhinoceros.
riña 1 *f* (*pelea*) fight, brawl. 2 (*discusión*) quarrel, row, argument.

riñón 1 *m* kidney. **2** *fig* (*interior, centro*) centre (US center), heart. – **3 riñones,** *mpl* kidneys. **4** *fam* (*espalda*) small of the back *sing,* back *sing: me duelen los riñones,* my back hurts.
● **costar un riñón,** *fam* to cost a bomb, cost an arm and a leg. ‖ **tener el riñón bien forrado / tener el riñón bien cubierto,** *fam* to be well off. ‖ **tener riñones,** *fam euf* to have guts.
■ **riñón artificial,** kidney machine.

riñonada 1 *f* ANAT cortical tissue of the kidney. **2** (*de res*) loin. **3** CULIN kidney stew.
● **costar una riñonada,** *fam* to cost a bomb, cost an arm and a leg.

riñonera 1 *f* (*faja*) back brace, back support. **2** (*bolsa*) moneybelt, bum bag.

río 1 *m* river. **2** *fig* stream, river: *un río de sangre,* a river of blood.
● **a río revuelto, ganancia de pescadores,** there's good fishing in troubled waters. ‖ **cuando el río suena, agua lleva,** there's no smoke without fire. ‖ **pescar en río revuelto,** *fig* to fish in troubled waters. ‖ **río abajo,** downstream. ‖ **río arriba,** upstream.

rioja *m* Rioja wine, rioja.

riojano,-a 1 *adj* of La Rioja, from La Rioja. – **2** *m,f* person from La Rioja, inhabitant of La Rioja.

rioplatense 1 *adj* of the River Plate region, from the River Plate region. – **2** *m,f* person from the River Plate region, inhabitant of the River Plate region.

RIP *abr* (*requiescat in pace* (*descanse en paz*)) rest in peace; (*abreviatura*) RIP.

ripio 1 *m* (*residuo*) refuse, waste. **2** (*de albañilería*) rubble, debris. **3** (*palabrería*) padding, verbiage, waffle.
● **no perder ripio,** *fam* not to miss a trick.

ripioso,-a *adj* padded (out).

riqueza 1 *f* (*cualidad*) richness, wealthiness. – **2 riquezas,** *fpl* (*abundancia*) wealth *sing,* riches.

risa 1 *f* laugh. **2** (*risas*) laughter. **3** (*hazmerreír*) laughing stock: *es la risa del vecindario,* she's the laughing stock of the neighbourhood.
● **darle risa a algn.,** to make sb. laugh. ‖ **entrar la risa,** to begin to laugh: *entonces le entró la risa,* then he started laughing. ‖ **llorar de risa,** to cry with laughter, laugh till one cries. ‖ **mearse de risa,** *tabú* to piss os. laughing. ‖ **morirse de risa / mondarse de risa / desternillarse de risa / troncharse de risa,** *fig* to die laughing, fall about laughing. ‖ **ser cosa de risa,** to be laughable. ‖ **tener algo muerto de risa,** *fam* to have sth. lying there unused: *tienes el diccionario ahí muerto de risa,* your dictionary is lying there unopened. ‖ **tomarse algo a risa,** to laugh sth. off.
■ **ataque de risa,** fit of laughter. ‖ **risa burlona,** mocking laugh. ‖ **risa de conejo,** forced laugh.

risco *m* crag, cliff.

risible *adj* laughable.

risilla *f* giggle, titter; (*falsa*) false laugh.

risita *f* → **risilla**.

risorio *m* risorius.

risotada *f* guffaw.

ristra 1 *f* string: *ristra de ajos,* string of garlic. **2** *fig* (*conjunto*) string, series: *una ristra de insultos,* a string of insults.
● **en ristra,** in single file.

ristre *en ristre, loc* at the ready: *pistola en ristre,* gun at the ready.

risueño,-a 1 *adj* (*sonriente*) smiling. **2** (*animado*) cheerful. **3** (*próspero*) bright, promising.

Rita *f* Rita.
● **¡cuéntaselo a Rita!,** *fam* pull the other one! ‖ **¡que lo haga Rita!,** *fam* let someone else do it!

rítmico,-a *adj* rhythmic, rhythmical: *gimnasia rítmica,* eurhythmics (US eurythmics).

ritmo 1 *m* rhythm. **2** *fig* pace, speed: *trabajar a buen ritmo,* to work at a good pace.

rito 1 *m* REL rite. **2** *fig* (*costumbre*) ritual.
■ **ritos funerarios,** funeral rites.

ritual 1 *adj* ritual. – **2** *m* ritual.
● **ser de ritual,** to be customary.

ritualidad *f* ritualism.

ritualismo *m* ritualism.

ritualista 1 *adj* ritualistic. – **2** *mf* ritualist.

rival 1 *adj* rival. – **2** *mf* rival.

rivalidad *f* rivalry.

rivalizar *i* to rival: *su simpatía rivaliza con la de su hermana,* her kindness rivals that of her sister; *rivalizar en belleza,* to rival in beauty.
▲ Conjugation model [4], like *realizar.*

rivera *f* brook, stream.

rizado,-a 1 *pp* → **rizar.** – **2** *adj* (*pelo*) curly. **3** MAR choppy. – **4 rizado,** *m* (*de pelo*) curling.

rizador *m* curling tongs *pl,* curling iron.

rizar 1 *t* (*pelo*) to curl. **2** (*papel, tela*) to crease. **3** (*el mar*) to make ripples in. – **4 rizarse,** *p* (*pelo*) to curl, go curly. **5** (*el mar*) to ripple.
● **rizar el rizo,** AV to loop the loop; *fig* to complicate matters even further.
▲ Conjugation model [4], like *realizar.*

rizo 1 *m* (*de pelo*) curl. **2** (*en el agua*) ripple. **3** (*tejido*) towelling (US toweling), terry towelling. **4** AV loop.

rizoma *m* rhizome.

rizópodo *m* rhizopod.

rizoso,-a *adj* naturally curly.

Rmo., -a *abr* (*Reverendísimo*) Most Reverend.

RNE *abr* RAD (*Radio Nacional de España*) Spanish national broadcasting corporation.

robalo *m* bass.

róbalo *m* bass.

robar 1 *t* (*banco, persona*) to rob; (*objeto*) to steal; (*casa*) to break into, burgle: *le han robado,* he's been robbed; *me han robado el bolso,* my bag has been stolen. **2** (*raptar*) to kidnap. **3** (*en naipes*) to draw. **4** *fig* (*cobrar muy caro*) to rip off: *en aquel restaurante te roban,* that restaurant is a rip-off. **5** *fig* (*corazón, alma*) to steal. **6** DEP *fam fig* to rob: *el árbitro nos ha robado el partido,* the referee robbed us of the game.

robinia *f* robinia, false acacia.

roble *m* oak, oak tree.
● **ser fuerte como un roble,** *fig* to be as strong as an ox.
■ **roble albar,** durmast oak, sessile oak. ‖ **roble americano,** red oak. ‖ **roble cerris / roble turco,** Turkey oak.

robledal *m* oak grove, oak wood.

robledo *m* oak grove, oak wood.

roblizo,-a *adj* strong, tough.

roblón *m* rivet.

robo 1 *m* (*gen*) theft, robbery; (*en casa*) burglary; (*en banco*) robbery. **2** (*en naipes*) draw. **3** *fig* (*estafa*) robbery.
● **cometer un robo,** to commit a robbery. ‖ **ser un robo,** (*muy caro*) to be daylight robbery.
■ **robo a mano armada,** armed robbery.

robot *m* robot.
▲ *pl robots.*

robótica *f* → **robótico,-a**.
robótico,-a 1 *adj* robotic, robot-like. – **2 robótica,** *f* robotics.
robotizar *t* to robotize.
robustecer 1 *t* to strengthen. – **2 robustecerse,** *p* to grow stronger, gain strength.
▲ *Conjugation model* [43], *like agradecer.*
robustecimiento *m* strengthening.
robustez *f* robustness, strength, sturdiness.
robusto,-a *adj* robust, strong, sturdy.
roca *f* rock.
● **ser firme como una roca,** *fig* to be as solid as a rock. ‖ **tener un corazón de roca,** *fig* to have a heart of stone.
■ **roca viva,** bare rock.
rocalla *f* pebbles *pl*, stone chippings *pl*.
rocambolesco,-a *adj fam* incredible, fantastic, far-fetched.
roce 1 *m* (*fricción*) rubbing; (*en piel*) chafing. **2** (*señal - en zapatos*) scuff mark; (*- en piel*) graze; (*- en coche etc*) mark. **3** (*contacto físico*) light touch, brush. **4** *fam* (*trato*) contact. **5** *fam* (*disensión*) friction, brush: *roces entre hermanas,* friction between sisters.
rociada 1 *f* (*acción*) spraying, sprinkling. **2** (*rocío*) dew. **3** *fig* (*conjunto de cosas*) shower, hail, stream: *una rociada de piedras,* a shower of stones. **4** *fig* (*reprensión*) telling-off, dressing-down: *le echó una buena rociada,* he got a good telling-off.
rociador *m* (*para la ropa*) sprayer, spray; (*para el jardín, incendios*) sprinkler.
rociar 1 *t* (*salpicar*) to spray, sprinkle. **2** *fig* (*esparcir*) to scatter, strew. **3** CULIN *fam* to wash down. – **4** *i* to fall: *hoy ha rociado,* there was a dew this morning.
▲ *Conjugation model* [13], *like desviar; in 4 used only in the 3rd pers; it does not take a subject.*
rocín 1 *m* (*caballo*) nag, hack. **2** *fam fig* blockhead, stupid idiot.
rocinante *m fig* nag, hack.
rocío *m* dew.
rock 1 *adj* rock: *música rock,* rock music. – **2** *m* rock.
rockero,-a 1 *adj* rock. – **2** *m,f* (*cantante*) rock singer; (*músico*) rock musician; (*fan*) rock fan; (*fan de rock and roll*) rocker.
rococó 1 *adj* rococo, Rococo. – **2** *m* rococo, Rococo.
Rocosas las Montañas Rocosas, *fpl* the Rocky Mountains, the Rockies.
rocoso,-a *adj* rocky, stony.
roda *f* stem.
rodaballo *m* turbot.
rodada *f* → **rodado,-a**.
rodado,-a 1 *pp* → **rodar**. – **2** *adj* AUTO (*que tiene ruedas*) wheeled, on wheels; (*que ha pasado el rodaje*) run-in: *tráfico rodado,* road traffic, vehicular traffic. **3** (*caballo*) dappled. **4** (*piedra*) rounded, smooth. **5** *fig* (*persona*) experienced. – **6 rodada,** *f* (*señal*) tyre (US tire) mark.
rodaja *f* slice.
● **en rodajas,** sliced.
rodaje 1 *m* CINEM filming, shooting. **2** AUTO running-in.
● **"en rodaje",** AUTO "running-in".
rodamiento *m* bearing.
■ **rodamiento de bolas,** ball bearing.
Ródano el Ródano, *m* the Rhône.
rodante *adj* rolling.
rodapié *m* skirting board, US baseboard.
rodar 1 *i* (*dar vueltas*) to roll; (*rueda*) to turn. **2** (*caer rodando*) to roll down; (*de escaleras*) to fall down: *la pelota rodó calle abajo,* the ball rolled down the street. **3** *fig* (*ir de un lado a otro*) to roam, wander, drift: *rodar por el mundo,* to roam the world. **4** *fig* (*estar diseminado*) to be scattered around: *los juguetes de los niños ruedan por toda la casa,* the children's toys are scattered all over the house. **5** (*vehículos*) to run; (*velocidad*) to do: *este coche rueda bien,* this car runs well; *mi coche rueda a doscientos kilómetros por hora,* mi car does two hundred kilometres an hour. – **6** *t* (*hacer que dé vueltas*) to roll: *rodar un aro,* to roll a hoop. **7** CINEM to film, shoot. **8** AUTO to run in. **9** (*recorrer*) to travel: *rodar mundo,* to travel the world.
● **echarlo todo a rodar,** (*estropearlo*) to ruin everything; (*desistir*) to throw it all up.
▲ *Conjugation model* [31], *like contar.*
Rodas *f* Rhodes.
rodear 1 *t* (*cercar*) to surround, encircle: *las murallas rodean la ciudad,* the city is surrounded by walls. – **2** *i* (*andar alrededor*) to go around: *rodearon por el bosque y llegaron tarde,* they went round the wood and were late. – **3 rodearse,** *p* to surround os. (**de,** with): *se rodeó de sus amigos,* he surrounded himself with his friends.
rodela *f* round shield.
rodeno,-a *adj* red.
rodeo 1 *m* (*desviación*) detour. **2** (*elusión*) evasiveness. **3** (*de ganado*) roundup; (*espectáculo*) rodeo.
● **andarse con rodeos,** to beat about the bush. ‖ **dar un rodeo,** to make a detour. ‖ **no andarse con rodeos,** to get straight to the point.
rodera *f* tyre (US tire) mark, track.
Rodesia *f* Rhodesia.
rodesiano,-a 1 *adj* Rhodesian. – **2** *m,f* Rhodesian.
rodete 1 *m* (*de pelo*) bun, chignon. **2** (*para llevar peso en la cabeza*) (ring-shaped) pad.
rodilla 1 *f* ANAT knee. **2** (*paño*) cloth, floorcloth.
● **de rodillas,** (*arrodillado*) kneeling; *fig* on bended knees. ‖ **doblar la rodilla / hincar la rodilla,** (*arrodillarse*) to kneel down. ‖ **caer de rodillas,** to fall on one's knees; *fig* to humble os. ‖ **hincarse de rodillas / ponerse de rodillas,** to kneel down, go down on one's knees. ‖ **estar de rodillas,** to be kneeling down, be on one's knees.
rodillada *f* → **rodillazo**.
rodillazo *m* blow with the knee, blow to the knee.
● **dar un rodillazo a algn.,** to knee sb.
rodillera 1 *f* DEP knee pad. **2** COST knee patch.
rodillo 1 *m* roller. **2** CULIN rolling pin.
rodio *m* rhodium.
rododendro *m* rhododendron.
rodomiel *m* rose honey.
rodríguez *m fam fig* grass widower.
● **estar de rodríguez,** *fam* to be a grass widower, be alone while one's family is away on holiday.
roedor,-ra 1 *adj* rodent. – **2** *m* rodent.
roedura 1 *f* (*acción*) gnawing. **2** (*señal*) gnaw mark. **3** (*lo roído*) gnawed part.
roela *f* blank.
roentgen *m* roentgen.
roer 1 *t* (*hueso*) to gnaw; (*galleta*) to nibble at. **2** *fig* (*desgastar*) to wear away: *el agua roe las rocas,* water erodes the rocks. **3** *fig* (*atormentar*) to prick, gnaw at, niggle at: *lo que dijo le roía la conciencia,* what he had said pricked his conscience.
● **ser un hueso duro de roer,** *fig* to be a hard nut to crack.

▲ Conjugation model |82|.

rogar 1 t (pedir) to request, ask; (implorar) to beg, implore, plead: **le rogaron que se quedara,** they pleaded with him to stay. – 2 i (pedir) to request, ask; (implorar) to beg, implore, plead. **3** REL to pray: rogar a Dios, to pray to God.
● **hacerse de rogar,** to play hard to get. ‖ "se ruega silencio", (hospitales etc) "silence please".
▲ Conjugation model |52|, like *colgar*.

rogativa f rogation.
● **hacer rogativas,** to pray.
▲ Often used in plural.

roído,-a 1 pp → **roer.** – 2 adj gnawed, eaten away.

roigo pres indic → **roer.**

rojear i to redden, turn red.

rojez f redness.

rojiblanco,-a adj red-and-white.

rojizo,-a adj reddish.

rojo,-a 1 adj (color) red. **2** (caliente) red-hot. **3** POL (gen) red, Communist; (en la guerra civil) Republican. – **4** m,f POL (gen) red, Communist; (en la guerra civil) Republican. – **5** rojo, m red.
● **estar al rojo vivo,** (muy caliente) to be red-hot; fig to be very heated. ‖ **estar en números rojos,** fig to be in the red. ‖ **ponerse rojo,** (gen) to turn red; (ruborizarse) to blush. ‖ **rojo de ira,** red with anger.
■ **Mar Rojo,** Red Sea. ‖ **rojo de labios,** lipstick.

rol 1 m (lista) roll, list, catalogue. **2** (papel) role.
■ **jugar un rol,** to play a role.
■ **juego de rol,** role-play game.
▲ pl **roles.**

rollero,-a adj-m,f fam → **rollista.**

rollista 1 adj (latoso) boring, annoying. **2** (cuentista) overdramatic. – **3** mf (latoso) bore, drag. **4** (cuentista) overdramatic person.

rollizo,-a adj plump, chubby.

rollo 1 m (gen) roll; (de cable, alambre) coil. **2** fam (michelín) roll of fat. **3** fam (aburrimiento) drag, bore, pain: esta peli es un rollo, this film is a drag; este tío es un rollo, this guy is a pain in the neck; ¡menudo rollo!, how boring!; siempre estamos con el mismo rollo, it's always the same old story. **4** fam (discurso, explicación, etc) long drawn-out speech, boring lecture: ¡vaya rollo nos soltó!, he didn't half go on! **5** fam (amorío) affair: tiene un rollo con la vecina, he's having a fling with his neighbour. **6** fam (asunto) business.
● **estar en el rollo,** arg to be with it, be cool. ‖ **tener buen rollo,** arg to be chatty, be easy to get on with. ‖ **tener rollo,** fam to go on a lot.
■ **rollo de papel higiénico,** roll of toilet paper. ‖ **rollo de primavera,** CULIN spring roll. ‖ **rollo pastelero,** rolling pin. ‖ **rollo patatero,** real bore, real drag.

Roma f Rome.
● **revolver Roma con Santiago,** fig to move heaven and earth. ‖ **todos los caminos llevan a Roma,** fig all roads lead to Rome.

romana f → **romano,-a.**

romance 1 adj LING Romance. – **2** m LING (gen) Romance language; (castellano) Spanish. **3** LIT romance, ballad, narrative poem. **4** (amorío) romance.
● **hablar en romance,** fig to speak plainly.

romancero m collection of romances.

romaní mf gipsy, gypsy.
▲ pl **romaníes.**

románico,-a 1 adj ARQ ART (gen) Romanesque; (en Gran Bretaña) Norman. **2** LING Romance. – **3** románico, m ARQ ART Romanesque.

romanismo m Romanism.

romanista m,f Romanist.

romanizar t to Romanize.
▲ Conjugation model |4|, like *realizar.*

romano,-a 1 adj Roman. – **2** m,f Roman.

romanticismo m romanticism.

romántico,-a 1 adj romantic. – **2** m,f romantic.

romanza f romance.

rómbico,-a adj rhombic.

rombo 1 m rhombus. **2** (naipes) diamond.

romboedro m rhombohedron.

romboide m rhomboid.

romeo m Romeo.

romería 1 f REL pilgrimage, procession. **2** (fiesta) festivities which take place at a local shrine.

romero[1] m BOT rosemary.

romero,-a[2] m,f REL pilgrim.

romo,-a 1 adj (sin punta) blunt, dull. **2** (nariz) snub.

rompecabezas 1 m (juego) (jigsaw) puzzle. **2** (problema) riddle, puzzle, conundrum.
▲ pl **rompecabezas.**

rompecorazones mf fam heart-throb, heartbreaker.
▲ pl **rompecorazones.**

rompedera f punch.

rompehielos m icebreaker.
▲ pl **rompehielos.**

rompeolas m breakwater, jetty.
▲ pl **rompeolas.**

romper 1 t (gen) to break; (papel, tela) to tear; (cristal, loza) to smash, shatter. **2** (rajar, reventar) to split. **3** (gastar) to wear out. **4** (relaciones) to break off. **5** fig (ley) to break, violate; (contrato) to break. **6** fig (cerca, límite) to break through, break down. **7** (empezar) to initiate, begin: romper las hostilidades, to initiate hostilities. **8** fig (interrumpir) to break, interrupt: romper el silencio, to break the silence. **9** (mar, aire) to cleave. – **10** i (acabar - con algo) to break; (- con alguien) to split up, us break up: romper con el pasado, to break with one's past; rompieron hace un mes, they broke up a month ago. **11** (olas, día) to break: al romper el día, at daybreak. **12** (flores) to bloom, blossom. **13** romper a + inf, fig (empezar) to burst out: romper a reír, to burst out laughing. **14** romper en + sust, fig (prorrumpir) to burst into: romper en llanto, to burst into tears. – **15** romperse, p (gen) to break: se me ha roto esta uña, I've broken this nail. **16** (papel, tela) to tear, rip: se me han roto las medias, I've ripped my stockings. **17** (rajarse, reventarse) to split: la bolsa se ha roto, the bag has split open. **18** (desgastarse) to wear out: se me han roto los zapatos, my shoes are worn out. **19** (coche) to break down.
● **de rompe y rasga,** fam fig resolute, determined. ‖ **romper con algn.,** to quarrel with sb., fall out with sb. ‖ **romper el fuego,** MIL to open fire. ‖ **romper el hielo,** fig to break the ice. ‖ **romper una lanza por algn.,** fig to defend sb. ‖ **romperle la cara a algn.** / **romperle las narices a algn.,** fam to smash sb.'s face in. ‖ **romperse la cabeza,** (pensar) to rack one's brains; (herirse) to split one's head open. ‖ **romperse por la mitad,** to break in half, split in half.
▲ pp **roto,-a.**

rompetechos mf fam fig shorty, shrimp.
▲ pl **rompetechos.**

rompible adj breakable.

rompiente m reef, shoal.

rompimiento 1 m (rotura) breaking, breakage. **2** fig (relación) breaking-off.

ron *m* rum.

roncador,-ra 1 *adj* snoring. **- 2** *m,f* snorer.

roncal[1] *m* (*ave*) nightingale.

roncal[2] *m* (*queso*) type of cheese (*made frome ewe's milk*).

roncamente *adv* roughly, coarsely.

roncar *i* to snore.
   ▲ *Conjugation model* [1], *like* **sacar.**

roncha 1 *f* (*en la piel*) swelling, lump. **2** (*rodaja*) slice, round slice.
   ● **levantar ronchas,** *fig* to cause a stir.

ronco,-a *adj* hoarse.
   ● **quedarse ronco,-a,** to lose one's voice.

ronda 1 *f* (*patrulla*) patrol, watch. **2** (*de policía*) beat. **3** (*vuelta*) round. **4** (*de bebidas, cartas*) round. **5** (*negociaciones*) round. **6** (*músicos*) group of strolling minstrels. **7** (*carretera*) ring road; (*avenida*) avenue. **8** (*en naipes*) round, hand.
   ● **hacer la ronda,** to do one's rounds. ‖ **pagar una ronda,** to pay for a round of drinks. ‖ **salir de ronda,** to go out and sing serenades.
   ■ **camino de ronda,** rampart walk. ‖ **ronda de reconocimiento,** reconnaissance mission.

rondalla 1 *f* (*cuento*) tale, story. **2** MÚS group of strolling minstrels.

rondar 1 *t* (*vigilar*) to patrol, do the rounds of. **2** *pey* (*merodear*) to prowl around, hang about, haunt: *siempre ronda la casa,* he's always prowling around the house. **3** (*cortejar*) to woo, court. **4** *fig* (*estar cerca*) to stalk: *la muerte lo rondaba,* death was stalking him; *me ronda el hambre,* I'm feeling hungry. **5** *fig* (*años*) to be about: *ronda los cincuenta,* she's about fifty. **- 6** *i* (*vigilar*) to patrol. **7** (*merodear*) to prowl around, roam around. **8** (*tocar y cantar por las calles*) to busk, serenade. **9** (*andar de noche*) to roam at night, wander at night.

rondel *m* rondel.

rondó *m* rondo.
   ▲ *pl* **rondoes.**

rondón de rondón, *loc adv* unexpectedly, unannounced.
   ● **colarse de rondón,** to slip in unnoticed.

ronquear *i* to be hoarse.

ronquera *f* hoarseness.

ronquido *m* snore, snoring.

ronronear *i* to purr.

ronroneo *m* purring.

ronzal[1] *m* halter.

ronzar[1] *t* to crunch, munch.
   ▲ *Conjugation model* [4], *like* **realizar.**

ronzar[2] *t* MAR to lever.
   ▲ *Conjugation model* [4], *like* **realizar.**

roña 1 *f* (*suciedad*) filth, dirt. **2** (*sarna*) mange. **3** *fam* (*tacañería*) meanness, stinginess. **- 4** *mf fam* (*tacaño*) scrooge, miser.

roñería *f fam* meanness, stinginess.

roñica 1 *adj fam* mean, stingy. **- 2** *mf fam* scrooge, miser.

roñosería *f fam* → **roñería.**

roñoso,-a 1 *adj* (*sucio*) filthy, dirty. **2** (*sarnoso*) mangy. **3** *fam* (*tacaño*) mean, stingy. **- 4** *m,f fam* scrooge, miser.

ropa *f* clothing, clothes *pl*: *ropa de invierno,* winter clothes; *ropa de esquí,* skiwear.
   ● **a quema ropa,** *fig* at point-blank range. ‖ **hay ropa tendida,** *fig* watch what you say. ‖ **la ropa sucia se lava en casa,** one should not wash one's dirty linen in public.
   ■ **ropa blanca,** linen, household linen. ‖ **ropa de cama,** bed linen. ‖ **ropa hecha,** COST ready-made

clothes. ‖ **ropa interior,** underwear. ‖ **ropa vieja,** CULIN meat stew.

ropaje *m* robes *pl*, apparel.

ropavejero,-a *m,f* second-hand clothes dealer.

ropero *m* wardrobe, US closet.

roque *m* rook.
   ● **estar roque,** *fam* to be asleep. ‖ **quedarse roque,** *fam* to fall asleep, go out like a light.

roqueda *f* rocky place.

roquedal *m* rocky place.

roquedo *m* rock.

roquefort *m* roquefort.

roqueño,-a 1 *adj* (*lleno de rocas*) rockstrewn. **2** (*duro*) hard.

roquero,-a *adj-m,f* → **rockero,-a.**

rorro *m fam* baby.

rosa 1 *adj* (*color*) pink. **2** *fig* (*novela*) romantic. **- 3** *m* (*color*) pink. **- 4** *f* BOT rose. **5** (*rosetón*) rose window.
   ● **fresco,-a como una rosa,** *fig* as fresh as a daisy. ‖ **la vida no es un lecho de rosas,** *fig* life is not a bed of roses. ‖ **no hay rosa sin espinas,** *fig* there's no rose without a thorn, nothing comes easy. ‖ **verlo todo de color rosa,** *fig* to see everything through rose-tinted spectacles.
   ■ **agua de rosas,** rose water. ‖ **rosa de pitiminí,** daisy rose. ‖ **rosa de té,** tea rose. ‖ **rosa náutica /rosa de los vientos,** compass rose. ‖ **rosa silvestre,** rambling rose.
   ▲ *In 1 and 2, pl* **rosa.**

rosáceo,-a *adj* rose-coloured (US rose-colored), rosy.

rosado,-a 1 *adj* (*color*) rosy, pink. **2** (*vino*) rosé. **- 3** *m* (*vino*) rosé.

rosal *m* rosebush.

rosaleda *f* rose garden.

rosarino,-a 1 *adj* of Rosario, from Rosario. **- 2** *m,f* person from Rosario, inhabitant of Rosario.

rosario 1 *m* REL rosary, beads *pl*. **2** *fig* string, series: *rosario de mentiras,* string of lies.
   ● **acabar como el rosario de la aurora,** *fig* to come to a bad end, end in disaster. ‖ **rezar el rosario,** to say the rosary.

rosbif *m* roast beef.
   ▲ *pl* **rosbifs.**

rosca 1 *f* (*de tornillo*) thread. **2** CULIN doughnut. **3** (*carnosidad*) roll of fat. **4** (*anilla*) ring.
   ● **hacer la rosca a algn.,** *fam* to suck up to sb. ‖ **no comerse una rosca,** *fam* not to get anywhere with men / women. ‖ **pasarse de rosca,** (*tornillo*) to have a crossed thread; (*pasarse*) to go too far.
   ■ **rosca de Arquímedes,** Archimedes' screw. ‖ **tapón de rosca,** screw top.

rosco 1 *m* CULIN (*roscón*) ring-shaped pastry; (*de pan*) ring-shaped roll; (*rosquilla*) doughnut. **2** EDUC *fam* zero.
   ● **no comerse un rosco,** *arg* not to get anywhere.

roscón *m* ring-shaped pastry; (*de Pascua*) Easter ring.

róseo,-a *adj* rosy.

roséola *f* roseola.

roseta 1 *f* (*rubor*) flush. **2** (*de cintas*) rosette. **3** (*de regadera*) rose, nozzle. **- 4 rosetas,** *fpl* (*palomitas*) popcorn *sing*.

rosetón *m* rose window.

rosquilla *f* doughnut, ring-shaped pastry.
   ● **venderse como rosquillas,** *fam* to sell like hot cakes.

rostro 1 *m fml* (*cara*) face. **2** (*de ave*) beak.
   ● **echarle rostro,** *fam* to be daring, be cheeky. ‖ **tener mucho rostro,** *fam* to have a lot of nerve. ‖ **¡vaya rostro!,** *fam* what a cheek!, what a nerve!

rota¹ f REL rota.
rota² f BOT rattan.
rotación f rotation.
rotativa f → **rotativo,-a**.
rotativo,-a 1 adj rotary, revolving. – 2 rotativo, m newspaper. – 3 rotativa, f rotary press.
rotatorio,-a adj rotary, rotating, revolving.
roto,-a 1 pp → **romper**. – 2 adj (gen) broken. 3 (tela, papel) torn. 4 (gastado) worn out. 5 (andrajoso) tattered, in tatters, ragged. 6 (cansado) tired. – 7 roto, m (agujero) hole, tear.
● **con el corazón roto,** fig heart-broken. ‖ **servir igual para un roto que para un descosido,** fig to be a jack of all trades.
rotonda f rotunda.
rotor m rotor.
rótula 1 f ANAT knee-cap. 2 TÉC ball-and-socket joint.
rotulación f lettering, labelling.
rotulador m felt-tip pen.
rotular 1 t to label. – 2 adj knee-cap.
rotulista 1 mf (de letreros) sign-writer. 2 (de titulares) letterer.
rótulo 1 m (etiqueta) label. 2 (letrero) sign; (luminoso) neon sign. 3 (anuncio) poster, placard. 4 (titular) heading, title.
rotundamente 1 adv (negar) flatly, categorically. 2 (afirmar) emphatically.
rotundidad f firmness.
rotundo,-a 1 adj (redondo) round. 2 fig (frase) well-rounded; (éxito) resounding. 3 (negativa) flat, categorical; (afirmación) categorical, emphatic: un no rotundo, a flat refusal.
rotura 1 f (gen) break, breaking, crack. 2 (en tela, papel) tear, rip. 3 MED fracture.
roturación f ploughing (us plowing).
roturadora f plough (us plow).
roturar t to plough (us plow).
roulotte f caravan.
round m round.
▲ pl rounds.
roya f mildew.
royalty m royalty.
▲ pl royalties.
rozadura f scratch, abrasion.
rozagante 1 adj (vestido) showy. 2 fig splendid, magnificent.
rozamiento 1 m (roce) rubbing, friction. 2 fig (discusión) friction, disagreement.
rozar 1 t (tocar ligeramente) to touch lightly, brush. 2 (raspar) to rub against, brush against; (herir) to graze: el zapato me roza el pie, my shoe's rubbing my foot. 3 fig (tema, asunto) to touch on; (bordear) to border on, verge on. 4 (pared) to scrape. – 5 i (raspar) to rub. 6 (tener relación) to border (con, on), verge (con, on). – 7 rozarse, p (rasparse) to rub (con, against), brush (con, against). 8 (desgastarse) to wear (out). 9 fig (tratarse) to come into contact (con, with), rub shoulders (con, with).
▲ Conjugation model |4|, like realizar.
r.p.m. abr (revoluciones por minuto) revolutions per minute; (abreviatura) rpm.
rte.¹ abr (restaurante) restaurant.
rte.² abr (remite, remitente) sender.
RTVE abr TV (Radio Televisión Española) Spanish national broadcasting corporation.

rúa f street.
Ruanda f Rwanda.
ruandés,-esa 1 adj Rwandan. – 2 m,f Rwandan.
rubefacción f rubefaction.
rúbeo,-a adj reddish.
rubéola f German measles pl, rubella.
rubí m ruby.
▲ pl rubíes.
rubia f → **rubio,-a**.
rubiales mf fam blondie.
▲ pl rubiales.
rubicán,-ana adj roan.
rubicundo,-a adj rosy, rubicund, reddish.
rubidio m rubidium.
rubificar t to redden.
rubio,-a 1 adj (cabello) fair; (persona) fair-haired; (hombre) blond; (mujer) blonde. 2 (tabaco) Virginia: tabaco rubio, Virginia tobacco. – 3 m,f (hombre) blond; (mujer) blonde. – 4 rubio, m (pez) red gurnard. – 5 rubia, f fam (peseta) one-peseta coin.
■ **rubia oxigenada / rubia de frasco,** peroxide blonde. ‖ **rubio,-a platino,** (hombre) platinum blond; (mujer) platinum blonde.
rublo m rouble.
rubor m blush, flush.
ruborizarse p to blush, go red, redden.
▲ Conjugation model |4|, like realizar.
ruboroso,-a adj blushing, bashful.
rúbrica 1 f (de firma) flourish (in signature). 2 (título) title, heading.
rubricar 1 t (firmar) to sign with a flourish. 2 (respaldar) to endorse, ratify.
● **firmado y rubricado,** signed and sealed.
▲ Conjugation model |1|, like sacar.
rubro,-a 1 adj fml red. – 2 rubro, m title, heading.
rucio,-a 1 adj (pardo) grey. – 2 m,f (asno) donkey.
ruda f rue.
rudeza f roughness, coarseness.
rudimentario,-a adj rudimentary.
rudimento m rudiment.
rudo,-a adj rough, coarse.
rueca f distaff.
rueda 1 f (gen) wheel: de cuatro ruedas, four-wheeled. 2 (círculo) circle, ring. 3 (rodaja) round slice. 4 (turno) round.
● **ir sobre ruedas,** fam to go like clockwork, go very smoothly.
■ **rueda de la fortuna,** wheel of fortune. ‖ **rueda de molino,** millstone. ‖ **rueda de prensa,** press conference. ‖ **rueda de recambio,** spare wheel. ‖ **rueda delantera,** front wheel. ‖ **rueda dentada,** cog wheel. ‖ **rueda trasera,** rear wheel.
ruedo 1 m (en las plazas de toros) bullring, arena. 2 (estera) round mat. 3 (de falda etc) hem.
● **dar la vuelta al ruedo,** to walk round the bullring receiving applause. ‖ **echarse al ruedo,** fig to launch os. into it.
ruego m request, petition.
■ **ruegos y preguntas,** any other business.
rufián 1 m (proxeneta) pimp. 2 (canalla) scoundrel, villain, ruffian.
rufianesca f → **rufianesco,-a**.
rufianesco,-a 1 adj villainous. – 2 rufianesca, f underworld.
rugby m rugby.

rugido *m* roar, bellow; (*del viento*) howl; (*de tripas*) rumbling.

ruginoso,-a *adj* rusty.

rugir *i* to roar, bellow; (*viento*) to howl; (*tripas*) to rumble.
▲ *Conjugation model* |6|, *like dirigir.*

rugosidad *f* rugosity.

rugoso,-a *adj* rough, wrinkled.

ruibarbo *m* rhubarb.

ruido 1 *m* (*gen*) noise. 2 (*sonido*) sound. 3 (*jaleo*) din, row. 4 *fig* stir, commotion.
● **hacer ruido / meter ruido,** to make a noise; *fig* to cause a stir. ‖ **mucho ruido y pocas nueces,** *fam fig* much ado about nothing.
■ **ruido ambiental / ruido de fondo,** background noise.

ruidosamente *adv* noisily, loudly.

ruidoso,-a 1 *adj* noisy, loud. 2 *fig* sensational.

ruin 1 *adj pey* (*vil*) mean, base, despicable, vile. 2 (*pequeño*) petty, insignificant. 3 (*tacaño*) stingy, mean.

ruina 1 *f* ruin, collapse. 2 *fig* fall, end, downfall. – 3 **ruinas,** *fpl* ruins.
● **amenazar ruina,** to be on the point of collapsing, be on the verge of collapsing. ‖ **estar hecho,-a una ruina,** *fig* to be a wreck.

ruindad 1 *f* (*maldad*) meanness, vileness. 2 (*acto*) mean act, low trick.

ruinoso,-a 1 *adj* ruinous, disastrous. 2 *fig* tumbledown, dilapidated.

ruiseñor *m* nightingale.
■ **ruiseñor bastardo,** Cetti's warbler.

rular *t* (*funcionar*) to work.

ruleta *f* roulette.
■ **ruleta rusa,** Russian roulette.

rulo 1 *m* (*para pelo*) curler, roller. 2 (*rizo*) curl, ringlet. 3 CULIN rolling pin.

rulot *f* caravan.
▲ *pl rulots.*

Rumanía *f* Romania.

rumano,-a 1 *adj* Romanian, Rumanian. – 2 *m,f* (*persona*) Romanian, Rumanian. – 3 **rumano,** *m* (*idioma*) Romanian, Rumanian.

rumba *f* rumba, rhumba.

rumbear *i* to dance the rhumba.

rumbo 1 *m* (*dirección*) course, direction. 2 *fam fig* (*pompa*) pomp, show. 3 *fam fig* (*generosidad*) lavishness, generosity.
● **con rumbo a / rumbo a,** bound for, heading for, in the direction of. ‖ **marcar el rumbo,** to set the course. ‖ **perder el rumbo,** to go off course; *fig* to lose one's bearings. ‖ **poner rumbo a,** to head for.

rumboso,-a *adj fam* lavish, sumptuous.

rumia *f* rumination.

rumiante 1 *adj* ruminant. – 2 *m* ruminant.

rumiar 1 *i* (*animal*) to ruminate, chew the cud. – 2 *t* (*mascar*) to chew. 3 *fig* (*pensar*) to ruminate, chew over, reflect on.
▲ *Conjugation model* |12|, *like cambiar.*

rumor 1 *m* (*murmullo*) murmur. 2 (*noticia, voz*) rumour (US rumor).
● **corre el rumor de que ...,** rumour (US rumor) has it that ...

rumorearse *p* to be rumoured (US rumored): *se rumorea que está enfermo,* it is rumoured that he's ill, he's rumoured to be ill.
▲ *Used only in the 3rd pers; it does not take a subject.*

rumoroso,-a *adj* murmuring.

runfla *f fam* heap, lot.

runflada *f fam* heap, lot.

runrún 1 *m* (*ruido*) buzz, noise, murmur. 2 *fam* (*rumor*) rumour (US rumor).

runrunearse *p fam* to be rumoured (US rumored).
● **se runrunea que ...,** it is rumoured (US rumored) that ..., rumour (US rumor) has it that ...
▲ *Used only in the 3rd pers; it does not take a subject.*

runruneo *m* buzz, noise, murmur.

rupestre *adj* rock.
■ **pintura rupestre,** cave painting.

rupia *f* rupee.

ruptura 1 *f* (*rotura*) breaking, breakage, break. 2 *fig* breaking-off, break-up.

rural *adj* rural, country: *médico rural,* country doctor.

Rusia *f* Russia.

ruso,-a 1 *adj* Russian. – 2 *m,f* (*persona*) Russian. – 3 **ruso,** *m* (*idioma*) Russian.

rústico,-a 1 *adj* rustic, rural. – 2 **rústico,** *m* peasant.
● **en rústica,** paper-backed: *¿lo quiere en rústica o con tapa dura?,* do you want it in paperback or hardback?

ruta *f* route, way, road.
■ **ruta aérea,** air route, airway.

rutenio *m* ruthenium.

rutilante *adj lit* shining, sparkling, gleaming.

rutilar *i lit* to shine, sparkle, gleam.

rutina *f* routine: *la rutina diaria,* the daily routine.
● **por rutina,** as a matter of course.

rutinario,-a 1 *adj* (*gen*) routine. 2 (*persona*) unimaginative, dull.

Rvdo.,-a. *abr* (*reverendo,-a*) reverend; (*abreviatura*) Revd.

S

S, s f (la letra) S, s.
s.[1] abr (siglo) century; (abreviatura) c.
s.[2] abr (siguiente) next, following.
S sím (sur) south; (símbolo) S.
s/ 1 abr (suyo, suya) → **suyo,-a**. 2 (su, sus) → **su**.
S. abr (san, santo,-a) Saint; (abreviatura) St.
S.A.[1] abr (Sociedad Anónima) Public Limited Company; (abreviatura) PLC.
S.A.[2] abr (Su Alteza) His Highness, Her Highness; (abreviatura) HH.
sábado m Saturday.
  ▲ See also jueves.
sábalo m shad.
sabana f savanna, savannah.
sábana f sheet.
  ● pegársele a uno las sábanas, fam to oversleep, sleep in.
  ■ sábana bajera, bottom sheet. ‖ sábana encimera, top sheet.
sabandija 1 f ZOOL bug. 2 fig (persona) swine, louse.
sabañón m chilblain.
sabático,-a adj sabbatical.
  ■ año sabático, sabbatical (year).
sabatino,-a adj Saturday, relating to Saturday.
sabedor,-ra adj aware (de, of), informed (de, about/ of).
sabelotodo mf pey know-all, know-it-all.
  ▲ pl sabelotodo.
saber 1 m knowledge. – 2 t (gen) to know: no sé lo que pasó allí, I don't know what happened there. 3 (tener habilidad) to be able to, know how to: sabe coser, she knows how to sew; no sabe francés, he can't speak French. 4 (enterarse) to learn, find out: lo acabamos de saber, we've just found out. – 5 i (tener sabor) to taste (a, of). – 6 saberse, p to know: se sabe la tabla de memoria, she knows the table off by heart.
  ● a saber, fml namely. ‖ ¡lo sabré yo!, I know better than anyone! ‖ me sabe mal + inf, I'm sorry to + inf: me sabe mal tener que decírselo, I hate to have to tell her. ‖ no saber dónde meterse, fig to feel embarrassed, not to know where to put os.: no supe dónde meterme, I didn't know where to put myself. ‖ no saber ni jota de algo / no saber ni papa de algo, fam not to have a clue about sth., not to have the foggiest about sth. ‖ no saber por dónde se anda, fig not to know what one is doing. ‖ no se sabe, nobody knows. ‖ para que lo sepas..., for your information... ‖ que yo sepa..., as far as I know... ‖ ¡qué sé yo!, how should I know! ‖ ¿quién sabe?, who knows? ‖ saber a gloria, fig to taste divine. ‖ saber al dedillo / saber de carrerilla / saber de corrido, fig to know by heart. ‖ saber algo de buena tinta, fig to get sth. straight from the horse's mouth. ‖ saber bien / saber mal, to taste good / taste bad. ‖ saber de algo, to know of

sth.: sé de un lugar ..., I know of a place ... ‖ saber de algn., to have heard from sb.: ¿qué sabes de Pedro?, have you heard from Pedro? ‖ saber más de la cuenta, to know too much. ‖ saber más que Lepe, fam to be nobody's fool. ‖ sabérselas todas, fig to know all the tricks. ‖ ¿se puede saber ... ?, may I ask ... ?: ¿se puede saber qué haces aquí?, may I ask what you're doing here? ‖ sépase que ..., let it be known that... ‖ vete tú a saber, goodness knows. ‖ ¡y yo que sé!, fam how should I know!, beats me!
  ▲ Conjugation model [83].
sabiamente 1 adv (con conocimiento) expertly. 2 (con sensatez) wisely.
sabidillo,-a adj-m,f → **sabihondo,-a**.
sabido,-a 1 pp → **saber**. – 2 adj known.
  ● como es sabido..., as everyone knows... ‖ sabido es que..., it is well known that... ‖ tener sabido que..., to know for a fact that...
sabiduría 1 f (conocimientos) knowledge. 2 (prudencia) wisdom.
sabiendas a sabiendas, adv knowingly: lo hizo a sabiendas de que se equivocaba, he did it knowing full well that he was wrong.
sabihondo,-a 1 adj fam pey pedantic. – 2 m,f fam pey pedant, know-all, smart aleck.
sabio,-a 1 adj (con conocimientos) learned, knowledgeable. 2 (con prudencia) wise, sensible. – 3 m,f (instruido) learned person. 4 (prudente) sage, wise person.
sabiondo,-a adj fam → **sabihondo,-a**.
sablazo 1 m (golpe) blow with a sabre (US saber); (herida) sabre (US saber) wound. 2 fam (de dinero) scrounging.
  ● dar un sablazo a algn., fam to touch sb. for money, scrounge some money off sb.
sable m sabre (US saber).
sableador,-ra m,f fam sponger, scrounger.
sablear t fam to touch for money, scrounge money from, scrounge money off.
sablista mf fam sponger, scrounger.
sabor 1 m taste, flavour (US flavor): con sabor a menta, mint-flavoured. 2 fig feeling.
  ● dejar a algn. mal sabor de boca, fig to leave a bad taste in sb.'s mouth. ‖ sin sabor, tasteless.
saborear 1 t to taste. 2 fig to savour (US savor), relish.
saboreo m savouring (US savoring).
sabotaje m sabotage.
saboteador,-ra m,f saboteur.
sabotear t to sabotage.
sabré fut → **saber**.
sabroso,-a 1 adj (con mucho sabor) tasty, delicious. 2 (agradable) pleasant, delightful.
sabueso 1 m (perro) bloodhound. 2 fig (persona) sleuth.
saca f large sack.
  ■ saca de correos, mailbag.
sacaclavos m nail-puller, nail-remover.
  ▲ pl sacaclavos.

sacacorchos *m* corkscrew.
▲ *pl sacacorchos.*

sacacuartos 1 *m fam* (*espectáculo*) swizz, rip-off, swindle.
– 2 *mf fam* (*estafador*) rip-off artist, swindler.
▲ *pl sacacuartos.*

sacadineros 1 *m fam* (*espectáculo*) swizz, rip-off, swindler. – 2 *mf fam* (*estafador*) con artist, swindler.
▲ *pl sacadineros.*

sacafaltas *mf fam* fault-finder, nit-picker.
▲ *pl sacafaltas.*

sacamuelas *mf fam* dentist.
● hablar más que un sacamuelas, *fam* to talk the hind leg off a donkey.
▲ *pl sacamuelas.*

sacapuntas *m* pencil sharpener.
▲ *pl sacapuntas.*

sacar 1 *t* (*poner en el exterior*) to take out, pull out, get out: *sacó un libro del cajón,* she took a book out of the drawer; *saca a ese hombre de aquí,* get that man out of here. 2 (*arma*) to draw. 3 (*obtener - gen*) to get; (*- premio*) to win; (*- dinero*) to get, make, earn; (*- billete*) to get, buy. 4 (*dinero del banco*) to draw, withdraw, take out. 5 (*echar hacia adelante*) to stick out: *sacar el pecho,* to stick out one's chest. 6 (*resolver*) to work out, solve. 7 (*encontrar*) to get, find. 8 (*enseñar*) to show. 9 (*quitar*) to remove. 10 (*extraer de algo*) to extract, obtain: *sacar caucho de un árbol,* to extract rubber from a tree. 11 (*agua*) to draw. 12 (*llevar fuera*) to take out: *si no llueve podemos sacarla,* it's not raining we can take her out; *luego sacó el perro,* then he took the dog out for a walk. 13 (*fotografía*) to take; (*fotocopia, copia*) to make. 14 (*producir*) to produce. 15 (*moda*) to introduce, set; (*nuevo producto*) to bring out. 16 (*publicar*) to publish, bring out. 17 *fam* (*ir por delante*) to be ahead: *nos saca media hora,* she's half an hour ahead of us. 18 *fam* (*ser más alto*) to be taller: *te saca un palmo,* he's six inches taller than you. 19 DEP (*tenis*) to serve; (*fútbol*) to kick off. 20 MAT (*restar*) to subtract; (*raíz*) to extract, find out. 21 (*mineral*) to extract. 22 QUÍM to extract. – 23 **sacarse**, *p* (*desvestirse*) to take off. 24 (*fotografía*) to have taken.
● sacar a bailar, to ask to dance. ‖ sacar a colación, to bring up. ‖ sacar a la luz, (*gen*) to bring to light; (*libro*) to publish. ‖ sacar a la venta, to put on sale. ‖ sacar a relucir, to mention, bring up. ‖ sacar adelante, (*negocio*) to make a success of; (*hijos*) to bring up well. ‖ sacar algo en claro / sacar algo en limpio, to make sense of sth., to make head or tail of sth.: *no saqué nada en claro de las instrucciones,* I couldn't make head or tail of the instructions. ‖ sacar apuntes, to take notes. ‖ sacar brillo a algo, to make sth. shine, polish sth. ‖ sacar a algn. de quicio / sacar a algn. de sí, *fig* to infuriate sb., drive sb. mad. ‖ sacar de un apuro, to bail out. ‖ sacar faltas a algo, to find fault with sth. ‖ sacar fuerzas de flaqueza, *fig* to draw strength from nowhere. ‖ sacar la lengua, to stick one's tongue out. ‖ sacar provecho de algo, to benefit from sth. ‖ sacar punta, (*lápiz*) to sharpen; *fig* to find fault with. ‖ sacar un diente, to pull a tooth out. ‖ sacarle los colores a algn., *fig* to make sb. blush.
▲ Conjugation model [1].

sacarificar *t* to saccharify.
▲ Conjugation model [1], *like sacar.*

sacarina *f* → **sacarino,-a.**

sacarino,-a 1 *adj* saccharine. – 2 **sacarina**, *f* saccharin.

sacarosa *f* sucrose, saccharose.

sacatrapos *m* worm.
▲ *pl sacatrapos.*

sacerdocio *m* priesthood.

sacerdotal *adj* priestly.

sacerdote *m* priest.

sacerdotisa *f* priestess.

sachar *t* to weed.

saciable *adj* satiable.

saciar 1 *t* (*hambre*) to satiate; (*sed*) to quench. 2 *fig* (*deseos*) to satisfy; (*ambiciones*) to fulfil (US fulfill). – 3 **saciarse**, *p* to satiate os., be satiated.
● comer hasta saciarse, to eat one's fill.
▲ Conjugation model [12], *like cambiar.*

saciedad *f* satiety, satiation.
● comer hasta la saciedad, to cat one's fill. ‖ repetir algo hasta la saciedad, to repeat sth. over and over (again), to say sth. until one is blue in the face.

saco 1 *m* (*bolsa*) sack, bag. 2 (*contenido*) sackful, bagful. 3 ANAT sac. 4 (*saqueo*) plundering, pillaging. 5 AM (*americana*) jacket.
● caer en saco roto, *fig* to go in one ear and out of the other. ‖ entrar a saco en, (*ciudad*), to pillage; (*oficina etc*) to clear out. ‖ no echar algo en saco roto, *fig* to take good note of sth.: *espero que no eches en saco roto lo que has aprendido,* I hope you won't forget what you've learnt. ‖ ser un saco sin fondo, to be a bottomless pit.
■ saco de dormir, sleeping bag. ‖ saco de mentiras, *fig* pack of lies. ‖ saco de viaje, overnight bag.

sacralizar *t* to consecrate.
▲ Conjugation model [4], *like realizar.*

sacramentado,-a 1 *pp* → **sacramentar.** – 2 *adj* (*persona*) having received the sacrament.

sacramental *adj* sacramental.
■ auto sacramental, LIT mystery play.

sacramentar 1 *t* (*convertir el pan*) to consecrate. 2 (*últimos sacramentos*) to administer the last rites to.

sacramento *m* sacrament.
■ el Santísimo Sacramento, the Blessed Sacrament.

sacrificado,-a 1 *pp* → **sacrificar.** – 2 *adj* (*persona*) self-sacrificing.

sacrificar 1 *t* (*gen*) to sacrifice. 2 *fig* (*reses*) to slaughter; (*animal doméstico*) to destroy, put down. – 3 **sacrificarse**, *p* to sacrifice os. (*por*, for).
▲ Conjugation model [1], *like sacar.*

sacrificio *m* sacrifice.

sacrilegio *m* sacrilege.

sacrílego,-a *adj* sacrilegious.

sacristán,-ana *m,f* verger, sexton.

sacristía *f* vestry, sacristy.

sacro,-a 1 *adj* (*sagrado*) sacred. 2 ANAT sacrum. – 3 sacro, *m* (*hueso*) sacrum.

sacrosanto,-a *adj* sacrosanct.

sacudida 1 *f* (*gen*) shake. 2 (*movimiento violento*) jolt, jerk. 3 (*terremoto*) earthquake. 4 (*alteración, conmoción*) shock.
● avanzar a sacudidas, to jolt along. ‖ dar una sacudida a algo, to shake sth. out, give sth. a good shake. ‖ dar una sacudida a algn., *fam* to give sb. a good hiding.
■ sacudida eléctrica, electric shock.

sacudidor *m* carpet beater.

sacudir 1 *t* (*gen*) to shake. 2 (*alfombra etc*) to shake out; (*polvo, arena*) to shake off. 3 (*golpear*) to beat. 4 (*cabeza*) to shake. 5 (*dar una paliza*) to beat up. 6 (*moscas, mosquitos, etc*) to flick away, flick off. 7 *fig* (*emocionar, alterar*) to shake. – 8 **sacudirse**, *p* (*quitarse*) to shake off: *se sacudió la arena,* he shook the sand off. 9 (*moscas, mosquitos, etc*) to flick away, flick off. 10 *fam fig* (*desembarazarse*) to get rid of, shake off: *se lo sacudieron enseguida,* they soon got rid of him.

sádico,-a 1 *adj* sadistic. – **2** *m,f* sadist.

sadismo *m* sadism.

sadoca 1 *adj fam* sadistic. – **2** *mf fam* sadist.

sadomasoquismo *m* sado-masochism.

sadomasoquista 1 *adj* sado-masochistic. – **2** *mf* sado-masochist.

saeta 1 *f* (*arma*) arrow, dart. **2** (*del reloj*) hand; (*de brújula*) needle. **3** (*copla*) religious Flamenco song sung in Holy Week celebrations.

saetera *f* loophole.

safari 1 *m* (*expedición*) safari. **2** (*lugar*) safari park.

saga *f* saga.

sagacidad 1 *f* sagacity, cleverness. **2** (*astucia*) shrewdness, astuteness.

sagaz 1 *adj* clever, sagacious. **2** (*astuto*) shrewd, astute.

Sagitario *m* Sagittarius.

▲ *pl Sagitario.*

sagrado,-a 1 *adj* sacred, holy. – **2** sagrado, *m* sanctuary, asylum.

■ Sagrada Biblia, Holy Bible. ‖ Sagrada Familia, Holy Family. ‖ Sagradas Escrituras, Holy Scriptures. ‖ Sagrado Corazón, Sacred Heart.

sagrario *m* tabernacle.

sagú 1 *m* (*palmera*) sago palm. **2** (*fécula*) sago.

▲ *pl sagúes.*

sah *m* shah.

Sáhara *m* Sahara.

■ Sáhara Occidental, Western Sahara.

saharaui 1 *adj* Saharan. – **2** *mf* Saharan.

sahariana *f* → **sahariano,-a**.

sahariano,-a 1 *adj* Saharan. – **2** sahariana, *f* safari shirt, safari jacket.

sahumerio 1 *m* (*humo*) aromatic smoke. **2** (*substancia*) aromatic substance; (*incienso*) incense.

sahúmo *m* → **sahumerio**.

S.A.I. *abr* (*Su Alteza Imperial*) His Imperial Highness, Her Imperial Highness; (*abreviatura*) HIH.

saín 1 *m* (*grasa - animal*) animal fat; (*- pescado*) fish oil. **2** (*suciedad*) dirt, grease.

sainete 1 *m* TEAT comic sketch, one-act farce. **2** *fig* (*bocadito*) titbit (US tidbit), delicacy.

sainetero,-a *m,f* writer of *sainetes*.

sainetista *mf* writer of *sainetes*.

sajadura *f* incision.

sajar *t* to make an incision in.

sajón,-ona 1 *adj* Saxon. – **2** *m,f* (*persona*) Saxon. – **3** sajón, *m* (*idioma*) Saxon.

Sajonia *f* Saxony.

sake *m* sake, saki.

sal[1] 1 *f* salt. **2** *fig* (*agudeza*) wit; (*encanto*) charm. – **3** sales, *fpl* smelling salts.

● echar sal a algo, to add salt to sth.

■ la sal de la vida, *fig* the spice of life. ‖ sal de cocina, cooking salt. ‖ sal de frutas, fruit salts *pl*. ‖ sal fina, table salt. ‖ sal gema, rock-salt. ‖ sal gorda, coarse salt. ‖ sales de baño, bath salts.

sal[2] *imperat* → **salir**.

sala 1 *f* (*aposento*) room; (*grande*) hall. **2** (*sala de estar*) lounge, living room. **3** (*de hospital*) ward; (*de cine*) cinema; (*de teatro*) theatre: *¿en qué sala la dan?*, which screen is it on? **4** JUR (*lugar*) courtroom; (*tribunal*) court.

■ sala de espectáculos, (*teatro*) theatre (US theater); (*cine*) cinema. ‖ sala de espera, waiting room. ‖ sala de estar, lounge, living room. ‖ sala de exposiciones, exhibition hall. ‖ sala de fiestas, nightclub, dis-

cotheque. ‖ sala de lectura, reading room. ‖ sala de máquinas, (*de buque*) engine room; (*de fotocopiadoras*) photocopying room. ‖ sala de operaciones, operating theatre (US theater). ‖ sala de partos, delivery room.

salacot *m* pith helmet, topee, topi.

▲ *pl salacots.*

saladero *m* saltery.

saladillo,-a 1 *adj* (*tocino*) half-salted. **2** (*almendras etc*) slightly-salted. – **3** saladillo, *m* (*tocino*) half-salted bacon. **4** (*almendras etc*) salted nuts *pl*.

salado,-a 1 *pp* → **salar**. – **2** *adj* (*con sal*) salted; (*con demasiada sal*) salty: *agua salada*, salt water. **3** *fam fig* (*agudo*) witty; (*gracioso*) funny; (*encantador*) charming, attractive.

saladura *f* salting.

salamandra *f* salamander.

salamanqués,-esa 1 *adj* of Salamanca, from Salamanca. – **2** *m,f* person from Salamanca, inhabitant of Salamanca. – **3** salamanquesa, *f* ZOOL gecko.

salamanquesa *f* → **salamanqués,-esa**.

salamantino,-a 1 *adj* of Salamanca, from Salamanca. – **2** *m,f* person from Salamanca, inhabitant of Salamanca.

salame *m* salami.

salami *m* salami.

salar 1 *t* (*curar*) to salt. **2** (*sazonar*) to salt, add salt to.

salarial *adj* salary, wage: *un aumento salarial,* a salary increase.

salario *m* salary, wages *pl*, wage.

■ salario mínimo, minimum wage.

salaz *adj* salacious.

salazón 1 *f* (*acción*) salting. **2** (*carne*) salted meat; (*pescado*) salted fish.

salchicha *f* sausage.

salchichería *f* pork butcher's (shop).

salchichón *m* salami-type sausage.

salcochar *t* to boil in salt water.

saldar 1 *t* (*cuenta*) to settle, balance; (*deuda*) to pay off. **2** (*rebajar*) to sell off. **3** *fig* (*diferencias*) to settle, resolve.

saldo 1 *m* (*de una cuenta*) balance. **2** (*pago*) liquidation, settlement. **3** (*resto de mercancía*) remnant, leftover, remainder. **4** (*venta a bajo precio*) sale.

● a precios de saldo, at bargain prices.

■ saldo acreedor, credit balance. ‖ saldo deudor, debit balance. ‖ saldo negativo / saldo en contra, negative balance, overdraft. ‖ saldo positivo / saldo a favor, positive balance, surplus.

saldré *fut* → **salir**.

saledizo,-a 1 *adj* projecting. – **2** saledizo, *m* projection, ledge.

salero 1 *m* (*recipiente*) salt-cellar, US salt-shaker. **2** (*lugar*) salt warehouse. **3** *fig* (*gracia*) charm, wit: *tiene mucho salero,* she's very witty.

saleroso,-a *adj fig* charming, witty.

salesa *f* nun of the Order of the Visitation.

salesiano,-a 1 *adj* Salesian. – **2** *m,f* Salesian.

salgo *pres indic* → **salir**.

sálico,-a *adj* Salic.

■ ley Sálica, Salic law.

salida *f* → **salido,-a**.

salido,-a 1 *pp* → **salir**. – **2** *adj* (*que sobresale*) projecting, prominent. **3** (*ojos*) bulging. **4** (*animal en celo*) on heat, in heat. – **5** salida, *f* (*partida*) departure: *la salida del tren es a las dos,* the train leaves at two. **6** (*puerta etc*) exit, way out. **7** (*momento de salir*): *nos encontramos a la salida del cine*, we met coming out of the cinema. **8** (*viaje corto*) trip. **9** (*de un astro*) rising. **10** DEP start. **11** COM outlet, market: *estas prendas no tienen salida*, there's no market for these clothes. **12** FIN outlay, expenditure. **13** *fig* (*ocurrencia*) witty remark, witticism. **14** *fig* (*escapatoria*) solution, way out. **15** *fig* (*perspectiva*) opening. **16** TÉC outlet. **17** INFORM output. **18** (*en naipes*) lead. **19** (*parte que sobresale*) projection. ● **de salida**, from the start. ‖ **no tener otra salida**, *fig* to have no other option. ‖ **tener salida a**, to open on to, to come out at. ■ **salida de artistas**, stage door. ‖ **salida de efectivo**, cash outflow. ‖ **salida de emergencia**, emergency exit. ‖ **salida de incendios**, fire exit. ‖ **salida de tono**, unfortunate remark, improper remark. ‖ **salida del sol**, sunrise. ‖ **salida nula**, false start.

saliente **1** *adj* (*que sobresale*) projecting. **2** (*cesante*) outgoing. **3** *fig* (*sobresaliente*) outstanding. – **4** *m* projection, overhang, ledge.

salífero,-a *adj* saline.

salificar *t* to salify.
▲ *Conjugation model* |1|, *like* **sacar**.

salina *f →* **salino,-a**.

salinidad *f* salinity.

salino,-a **1** *adj* saline. – **2 salina**, *f* (*mina*) salt mine. **3** (*establecimiento*) salt works.

salir **1** *i* (*ir hacia afuera*) to go out (**de**, of): *salir de casa*, to go out of the house. **2** (*venir de dentro*) to come out: *ven, sal al jardín*, come out here into the garden. **3** (*partir*) to leave: *el autobús sale a las tres*, the bus leaves at three. **4** (*no estar*) to be out: *lo siento, ha salido*, I'm sorry, she's out. **5** (*amigos, novios*) to go out. **6** (*aparecer*) to appear, be: *salió en los periódicos*, he appeared in the newspapers. **7** (*revista, novela, etc*) to come out; (*moda*) to come in. **8** (*proceder*) to come (**de**, from): *de la aceituna sale el aceite*, olive oil comes from olives. **9** (*resultar*) to turn out, turn out to be: *salió demasiado salado*, it turned out too salty. **10** (*examen, prueba*) to go, turn out: *¿cómo te salió?*, how did it go?, how did you do? **11** (*venir a costar*) to come to, cost, work out. **12** (*sobresalir*) to project, stick out. **13** (*sol etc*) to rise, come out; (*vegetales*) to come up; (*flores*) to come out; **14** (*granos*) to get, break out in, come out in; (*pelo*) to grow; (*diente*) to cut: *le salieron granos*, he broke out in spots. **15** (*mancha*) to come out, come off. **16** (*parecerse*) to take after (**a**, -): *ha salido a su padre*, she takes after her father. **17** (*al azar*) to be drawn. **18** (*nombre, palabra*) to be able to think of: *no me sale un sinónimo*, I can't think of a synonym. **19** (*solucionar*) to work out: *no me sale*, I can't work it out; *no le salía la respuesta correcta*, he couldn't get the right answer. **20** (*decir inesperadamente*) to come out (**con**, with): *¡ahora me sales con ésa!*, now you come out with this! **21** (*librarse*) to get out (**de**, of). **22** (*trabajo, oportunidad*) to come up. **23** (*dar a*) to open (**a**, onto), come out (**a**, at): *esta calle sale a la avenida*, this street comes out at the avenue. **24** (*en naipes*) to start. **25** TEAT to enter. – **26 salirse**, *p* (*líquido, gas*) to leak, leak out; (*río*) to overflow. **27** (*al hervir*) to boil over. **28** (*tornillo etc*) to come off, come out. **29** (*de la carretera*) to go off (**de**, -). ● **salga lo que salga**, whatever happens. ‖ **salir a la pizarra**, to go to the blackboard. ‖ **salir al encuentro de**, to go to meet. ‖ **salir al paso de**, *fig* to forestall. ‖ **salir adelante**, to be successful. ‖ **salir airoso,-a de algo**, to be successful in sth., pass sth. with flying colours (US colors). ‖ **salir barato,-a / salir caro,-a**, to

work out cheap / work out expensive. ‖ **salir bien / salir mal**, to turn out well / turn out badly: *le salió mal el examen*, he did badly in his exam. ‖ **salir de dudas**, *fig* to make sure, be sure: *para salir de dudas consultaron la enciclopedia*, just to be sure they looked it up in the encyclopaedia. ‖ **salir en defensa de algn.**, *fig* to come to sb.'s defence (US defense). ‖ **salir ganando**, to come out ahead, come out well, benefit. ‖ **salir perdedor,-ra**, to be the loser, lose out. ‖ **salir pitando / salir disparado,-a**, *fam* to shoot off, rush out. ‖ **salir por peteneras**, *fam* to go off at a tangent. ‖ **salir que ni pintado,-a**, *fam* to come out beautifully. ‖ **salir vencedor,-ra**, to be the winner. ‖ **salirse de lo normal**, *fig* to be out of the ordinary. ‖ **salirse de madre**, *fig* to overflow; *fig* to lose one's self-control. ‖ **salirse de quicio**, to lose one's mind.
▲ *Conjugation model* |84|.

salitre *m* saltpetre (US saltpeter).

saliva *f* saliva. ● **gastar saliva**, *fig* to waste one's breath. ‖ **tragar saliva**, *fig* to swallow one's feelings, keep quiet.

salivación *f* salivation.

salival *adj* salivary.

salivar *i* to salivate.

salivazo *m* spit.

salmantino,-a **1** *adj* of Salamanca, from Salamanca. – **2** *m,f* person from Salamanca, inhabitant of Salamanca.

salmer *m* skewback.

salmo *m* psalm. ■ **el Libro de los Salmos**, the Book of Psalms.

salmodia **1** *f* REL psalmody. **2** *fam fig* (*canturreo*) drone.

salmodiar **1** *i* (*salmear*) to sing psalms. – **2** *t fam fig* (*canturrear*) to drone.

salmón **1** *m* (*pez*) salmon. – **2** *adj* (*color*) salmon, salmon pink.

salmonado,-a **1** *adj* (*asalmonado*) salmon, salmon-like: *trucha salmonada*, salmon trout. **2** (*color*) salmon pink.

salmonelosis *f* salmonellosis, salmonella, food poisoning.
▲ *pl* **salmonelosis**.

salmonero,-a *adj* salmon.

salmonete *m* red mullet.

salmorejo **1** *m* (*salsa*) sauce *made from vinegar, oil, water, salt and pepper*. **2** (*tipo de gazpacho*) kind of gazpacho. **3** *fig* (*reprimenda*) reprimand.

salmuera *f* brine.

salobre **1** *adj* (*agua*) brackish, slightly salty. **2** (*salado*) salty; (*muy salado*) briny.

salobreño,-a *adj* saline.

salobridad *f* brackishness.

Salomón *m* Solomon. ■ **Islas Salomón**, Solomon Islands.

salomónico,-a *adj* Solomonic, Solomonian. ■ **columna salomónica**, ARQ wreathed column.

salón **1** *m* (*en casa*) sitting room, drawing room, lounge. **2** (*en edificio público*) hall. **3** (*exposición*) show, exhibition. ■ **salón de actos**, assembly hall. ‖ **salón de baile**, ballroom. ‖ **salón de belleza**, beauty salon, beauty parlour (US parlor). ‖ **salón de té**, tearoom, teashop. ‖ **salón del automóvil**, motor show. ‖ **salón náutico**, boat show.

salpicadero *m* dashboard.

salpicadura **1** *f* (*acción*) splashing. **2** (*gotas*) splash. – **3 salpicaduras**, *fpl fig* after-effects, aftermath *sing*: *las salpicaduras de la guerra dejaron sus huellas en toda Eu-*

ropa, the after-effects of the war left their mark on the whole of Europe.

salpicar 1 *t* (*rociar*) to sprinkle. 2 (*caer gotas*) to splash. 3 *fig* (*esparcir*) to sprinkle. – 4 **salpicarse,** *p* to splash (**de,** with), spatter (**de,** with): *se salpicó la chaqueta de barro,* he spattered his jacket with mud.
▲ Conjugation model |1|, *like sacar.*

salpicón 1 *m* (*salpicadura*) splash, spatter. 2 CULIN cocktail.
■ **salpicón de mariscos,** seafood cocktail.

salpimentar 1 *t* to season, add salt and pepper to. 2 *fig* to season, spice.
▲ Conjugation model |27|, *like acertar.*

salpullido *m* rash.

salsa 1 *f* sauce. 2 *fam fig* (*gracia*) zest, spice. 3 MÚS salsa.
● **estar en su propia salsa,** *fig* to be in one's element.
■ **la salsa de la vida,** *fig* the spice of life. ‖ **salsa bechamel,** white sauce, béchamel. ‖ **salsa de tomate,** tomato sauce. ‖ **salsa mayonesa,** mayonnaise.

salsera *f* → **salsero,-a.**

salsero,-a 1 *adj fam* (*entremetido*) meddlesome. – 2 **salsera,** *f* gravy boat.

salsifí *m* salsify.
▲ *pl* **salsifíes.**

saltador,-ra 1 *adj* jumping, leaping. – 2 *m,f* jumper. – 3 **saltador,** *m* (*cuerda*) skipping rope.
■ **saltador,-ra de altura,** high jumper. ‖ **saltador,-ra de pértiga,** pole vaulter.

saltamontes *m* grasshopper.
▲ *pl* **saltamontes.**

saltaojos *m* peony.
▲ *pl* **saltaojos.**

saltar 1 *i* (*gen*) to jump, leap: *saltó de la cama,* she jumped out of bed; *saltamos del muro,* we jumped off the wall. 2 (*en paracaídas*) to parachute. 3 (*romperse*) to break; (*estallar*) to burst. 4 (*desprenderse*) to come off. 5 (*tapón, corcho*) to pop out, pop off. 6 *fig* (*enfadarse*) to blow up, explode: *salta por todo,* he flies off the handle at the slightest thing. 7 *fig* (*de una cosa a otra*) to jump, skip. 8 *fig* (*decir*) to come out (**con,** with); (*contestar*) to answer (**con,** with): *saltó con una tontería,* he came out with a silly remark. 9 *fig* (*de un cargo, empleo*) to be thrown out: *saltó de la vicepresidencia por corrupción,* he was thrown out as vice-president because of corruption. – 10 *t fig* (*salvar de un salto*) to jump (over), leap (over). 11 (*arrancar*) to pull off. 12 (*ajedrez etc*) to jump. 13 *fig* (*omitir*) to skip, miss out. – 14 **saltarse,** *p* (*ley etc*) to ignore. 15 (*omitir*) to skip, miss out. 16 (*desprenderse*) to come off; (*- lentilla*) to fall out: *se le saltó un botón,* one of her buttons came off.
● **estar a la que salta,** (*estar atento*) to be always on the look out for an opportunity; (*enfadarse por todo*) to have a short fuse. ‖ **hacer saltar,** to blow up. ‖ **hacer saltar las lágrimas a algn.,** *fig* to bring tears to sb.'s eyes. ‖ **saltar a la cuerda / saltar a la comba,** to skip. ‖ **saltar a la vista,** *fig* to be obvious, be as plain as the nose on one's face. ‖ **saltar de alegría,** *fig* to jump for joy. ‖ **saltar en pedazos,** to break into pieces, smash to bits. ‖ **saltar sobre algn.,** *fig* to pounce on sb. ‖ **saltarle a algn. la tapa de los sesos,** *fam* to blow sb.'s brains out. ‖ **saltarse el turno,** to jump the queue. ‖ **saltarse un semáforo,** to jump the lights. ‖ **saltársele a uno las lágrimas,** *fig* to have tears in one's eyes: *se me saltaron las lágrimas,* tears came to my eyes.

saltarín,-ina 1 *adj* (*que salta*) lively, bouncing. 2 (*aturdido*) scatterbrained. – 3 *m,f* (*que salta*) energetic person, bundle of energy. 4 (*aturdido*) scatterbrain.

salteado,-a 1 *pp* → **saltear.** – 2 *adj* (*espaciado*) spaced out. 3 CULIN sauté, sautéed. – 4 **salteado,** *m* CULIN sauté.

salteador,-ra *m,f* (*hombre*) highwayman; (*mujer*) female highwayman.

saltear 1 *t* (*asaltar - alguien*) to hold up; (*- banco*) to rob. 2 (*hacer con interrupciones*) to do in fits and starts. 3 (*espaciar*) to space out. 4 CULIN to sauté. 5 *fig* (*sorprender*) to take by surprise.

salterio 1 *m* (*libro*) Psalter. 2 (*instrumento*) psaltery.

saltimbanqui 1 *mf* (*artista que va de pueblo en pueblo*) member of a travelling circus. 2 (*titiritero*) puppeteer; (*malabarista*) juggler; (*acróbata*) acrobat, tumbler.

salto 1 *m* (*gen*) jump, leap. 2 DEP jump; (*natación*) dive. 3 (*de agua*) waterfall. 4 (*despeñadero*) precipice. 5 *fig* (*omisión*) gap. 6 *fig* (*ascenso*) springboard.
● **a salto de mata,** (*vivir al día*) from hand to mouth; (*de cualquier manera*) slapdash, haphazardly. ‖ **a saltos,** *fig* in leaps and bounds. ‖ **bajar de un salto / subir de un salto,** to jump down / jump up. ‖ **dar un salto / pegar un salto,** to jump, leap. ‖ **dar un salto en el vacío,** *fig* to take a leap in the dark. ‖ **el corazón me daba saltos,** *fig* my heart was pounding. ‖ **en un salto,** *fig* in a flash.
■ **salto de agua,** waterfall, falls *pl.* ‖ **salto de altura,** high jump. ‖ **salto de cama,** negligée. ‖ **salto de la carpa,** jack-knife. ‖ **salto de longitud,** long jump. ‖ **salto del ángel,** swan dive. ‖ **salto mortal,** somersault. ‖ **triple salto,** triple jump.

saltón,-ona 1 *adj* (*que salta*) jumping, hopping. 2 (*que sobresale*) prominent. 3 (*ojos*) bulging.

salubre *adj* salubrious, healthy.

salubridad *f* (*estado de salud*) healthiness; (*de lugar, clima*) salubriousness, salubrity.

salud 1 *f* health. – 2 *interj fam* cheers!
● **beber a la salud de algn.,** to drink to sb.'s health. ‖ **gozar de buena salud,** to be in good health. ‖ **rebosar salud,** to be glowing with health. ‖ **tener poca salud,** not to be very healthy.
■ **salud de hierro,** *fig* iron constitution.

saludable 1 *adj* (*sano*) healthy, wholesome. 2 *fig* (*beneficioso*) good, beneficial.
● **tener un aspecto saludable,** to look healthy.

saludar 1 *t* (*demostrar cortesía*) to greet. 2 (*decir hola*) to say hello to. 3 MIL to salute.
● **le saluda atentamente,** (*en carta*) yours faithfully. ‖ **no saludarse,** not to be on speaking terms: *no se saludan,* they're not on speaking terms. ‖ **saluda de mi parte a,** give my regards to.

saludo 1 *m* greeting. 2 MIL salute.
● **reciba un atento saludo de,** (*en carta*) yours faithfully. ‖ **un saludo de / atentos saludos de,** (*en carta*) best wishes from

salutación *f* greeting, salutation.

salva 1 *f* (*de comida*) tasting. 2 (*con arma*) salvo, volley.
■ **salva de aplausos,** *fig* round of applause.

salvable *adj* (*gen*) savable, saveable, which can be saved; (*de un desastre, de un naufragio*) salvageable.

salvación 1 *f* (*gen*) salvation, rescue. 2 REL salvation.
● **no tener salvación,** *fig* to be beyond hope: *Ana no tiene salvación,* there's no hope for Ana.

salvado *m* bran.

Salvador. 1 **El Salvador,** *m* El Salvador. 2 REL the Saviour (US Savior).

salvador,-ra 1 *adj* saving. – 2 *m,f* saviour (US savior), rescuer.

salvadoreño,-a 1 *adj* Salvadorian, Salvadoran. – 2 *m,f*
Salvadorian, Salvadoran.
salvaguarda *f* → **salvaguardia**.
salvaguardar *t* to safeguard (**de,** from), protect (**de,**
from).
salvaguardia 1 *f* (*papel*) safe-conduct. 2 *fig* (*protección*)
safeguard, protection. – 3 *m* (*guardia*) guardian.
salvajada *f* atrocity, savagery, brutal act, savage act.
salvaje 1 *adj* (*planta*) wild; (*terreno*) uncultivated. 2 (*ani-*
mal) wild. 3 (*pueblo, tribu*) savage, uncivilized. 4 *fam fig*
(*violento*) savage, wild. 5 (*bruto*) uncouth, boorish. 6 *fig*
(*incontrolado*) haphazard, uncontrolled: *edificación sal-*
vaje, uncontrolled building development; *huelga sal-*
vaje, wildcat strike. – 7 *mf* (*no civilizado*) savage. 8 *fig*
(*violento*) savage. 9 (*bruto*) brute, boor.
salvajismo *m* savagery.
salvamanteles *m* table mat.
  ▲ *pl salvamanteles.*
salvamento *m* rescue.
  ■ **equipo de salvamento,** rescue party, rescue team.
salvamiento *m* rescue.
salvar 1 *t* (*librar de peligro*) to save, rescue. 2 (*barco*) to
salvage. 3 (*honor, ruina*) to save. 4 (*obstáculo*) to clear. 5
(*dificultad*) to overcome, get round. 6 (*distancia*) to cover.
7 (*atravesar*) to cross, span. 8 (*exceptuar*) to exclude, except. – 9 **salvarse,** *p* (*sobrevivir*) to survive, come out
alive. 10 (*escaparse*) to escape (**de,** from). 11 REL to be
saved, save one's soul.
  ● **salvarse por los pelos,** *fam* to have a narrow escape, get away by the skin of one's teeth. ‖ **¡sálvese
quien pueda!,** every man for himself!
salvavidas *m* lifebelt.
  ▲ *pl salvavidas.*
salve *f* Hail Mary.
salvedad 1 *f* (*excepción*) exception. 2 (*condición*) condition, proviso. 3 (*reserva*) reservation. 4 (*distinción*) distinction.
salvia *f* sage.
salvo,-a 1 *adj* (*ileso*) unharmed, safe. – 2 **salvo,** *adv* except, except for: *todos salvo ella,* everyone except for
her.
  ● **estar a salvo (de),** to be safe (from). ‖ **poner a salvo,** to put in a safe place. ‖ **ponerse a salvo,** to reach
safety. ‖ **salva sea la parte,** *euf* rear end. ‖ **salvo que,**
unless.
salvoconducto *m* safe-conduct.
Samaria *f* Samaria.
samario *m* samarium.
samaritano,-a 1 *adj* Samaritan. – 2 *m,f* (*persona*) Samaritan. – 3 **samaritano,** *m* (*idioma*) Samaritan.
samba *f* samba.
sambenito 1 *m* HIST (*escapulario*) sanbenito. 2 *fig* (*deshonra*) disgrace; (*descrédito*) stigma.
  ● **colgarle un sambenito a algn.,** *fig* to give sb. a bad
name.
Samoa *f* Samoa.
  ■ **Samoa Occidental,** Western Samoa.
samoano,-a 1 *adj* Samoan. – 2 *m,f* (*persona*) Samoan. –
3 **samoano,** *m* (*idioma*) Samoan.
samovar *m* samovar.
sampán *m* sampan.
samurai *m* samurai.
san *adj* saint: *San Carlos,* Saint Charles.
  ▲ Used before names of male saints except for *Tomás, Tomé,*
  Toribio and *Domingo.* See also *santo,-a.*
sanable *adj* curable.

sanador,-ra 1 *adj* curative. – 2 *m,f* curer.
sanar 1 *t* to heal, cure. – 2 *i* (*enfermo*) to recover, get better. 3 (*herida*) to heal.
sanatorio *m* clinic, nursing home; (*hospital*) hospital.
sanción 1 *f* (*aprobación*) sanction, approval. 2 (*pena*)
sanction, penalty.
sancionable *adj* punishable.
sancionar 1 *t* (*aprobar*) to sanction. 2 (*penar*) to penalize.
sancochar *t* to parboil.
sancocho *m* parboiled food.
sanctasanctórum *m* sanctum sanctorum, Holy of
Holies.
  ▲ *pl sanctasanctórum.*
sandalia *f* sandal.
sándalo *m* sandalwood.
sandez *f* piece of nonsense.
  ● **decir sandeces,** to talk nonsense.
sandía *f* watermelon.
sandinismo *m* Sandinista movement.
sandinista 1 *adj* Sandinista. – 2 *mf* Sandinista.
sandio,-a 1 *adj* silly, foolish. – 2 *m,f* fool.
sandunga *f fam* charm, wit.
sandunguero,-a *adj fam* charming, witty.
sándwich *m* sandwich.
  ▲ *pl sándwiches.*
sandwichería *f* sandwich bar.
saneado,-a 1 *pp* → **sanear.** – 2 *adj* sound, healthy.
saneamiento 1 *m* (*de terreno*) drainage, draining. 2 (*de
edificio*) cleaning, disinfection. 3 (*de moneda*) stabilization.
sanear 1 *t* (*tierra*) to drain. 2 (*edificio*) to clean, disinfect.
3 ECON to compensate.
sanedrín *m* Sanhedrin.
sanfermines *mpl* festival of San Fermín (held in Pamplona).
sangradera 1 *f* (*lanceta*) lancet. 2 (*vasija*) jar for blood.
3 (*acequia*) irrigation ditch. 4 (*compuerta*) floodgate.
sangrado *m* indention, indentation, indent.
sangradura *f* MED incision, cut.
sangrante 1 *adj* bleeding. 2 *fig* flagrant, blatant.
sangrar 1 *t* (*abrir una vena*) to bleed. 2 (*dar salida a un
líquido*) to drain. 3 (*resinar*) to tap. 4 *fig* (*hurtar*) to filch.
5 *fam fig* (*dejar sin dinero*) to bleed dry. 6 (*en impresión*) to
indent. – 7 *i* to bleed.
sangre *f* blood.
  ● **a sangre fría,** *fig* in cold blood. ‖ **a sangre y fuego,**
fig by fire and sword. ‖ **chupar la sangre a algn.,** *fig*
to bleed sb. dry. ‖ **de sangre caliente / de sangre
fría,** warm-blooded / cold-blooded. ‖ **donar sangre,**
to give blood. ‖ **llevar algo en la sangre,** *fig* to run in
the family: *no lo puede remediar, lo lleva en la sangre,*
he can't help it, it runs in the family; *su padre era músico, así que lo lleva en la sangre,* her father was a musician, so it's in her blood. ‖ **no llegó la sangre al río,**
fig the worst didn't happen. ‖ **no tener sangre en las
venas,** *fig* to be a cold fish, be unemotional. ‖ **subírsele a uno la sangre a la cabeza,** *fig* to see red. ‖
sudar sangre, *fig* to sweat blood. ‖ **tener mala sangre,** *fig* to be evil.
  ■ **sangre fría,** *fig* sang froid.
sangría 1 *f* (*bebida*) sangria. 2 MED bleeding, bloodletting. 3 (*en árbol*) tap. 4 *fig* (*de dinero etc*) drain. 5 (*en impresión*) indentation.
sangriento,-a 1 *adj* (*que echa sangre*) bleeding. 2 (*con
sangre*) bloody. 3 (*sanguinario*) bloody; (*cruel*) cruel.

sanguijuela f leech, bloodsucker.

sanguina f → **sanguino,-a**.

sanguinaria f → **sanguinario,-a**.

sanguinario,-a 1 adj bloodthirsty. – 2 sanguinaria, f (piedra) bloodstone.

sanguíneo,-a adj blood.

sanguino,-a 1 adj blood. – 2 sanguina, f (lápiz, dibujo) sanguine. 3 (naranja) blood orange.

sanguinolencia f bloodiness.

sanguinolento,-a 1 adj (que echa sangre) bleeding. 2 (con sangre) bloody, bloodstained; (ojos) bloodshot.

sanidad 1 f (calidad de sano) health, healthiness. 2 (servicios) health: *sanidad pública,* public health.
■ Inspector de Sanidad, Health Inspector. ‖ Ministerio de Sanidad, Ministry of Health.

sanitario,-a 1 adj sanitary, health. – 2 m,f health officer. – 3 sanitario, m toilet. – 4 sanitarios, mpl bathroom fittings.

sano,-a 1 adj (con salud) healthy, fit. 2 (saludable) healthy, wholesome. 3 fig (sin corrupción) sound. 4 fig (entero) good. 5 fig (sincero) sincere. 6 fig (juicio) right.
● sano,-a y salvo,-a, safe and sound.

sánscrito,-a 1 adj Sanskritic. – 2 sánscrito, m Sanskrit.

sanseacabó y **sanseacabó,** interj fam and that's that!

sansón m fam he-man.
● estar hecho un sansón, fam to be as strong as an ox.

santabárbara f magazine.

santacruceño,-a 1 adj of Santa Cruz de Tenerife, from Santa Cruz de Tenerife. – 2 m,f person from Santa Cruz de Tenerife, inhabitant of Santa Cruz de Tenerife.

santanderino,-a 1 adj of Santander, from Santander. – 2 m,f person from Santander, inhabitant of Santander.

santateresa f praying mantis.

santería f sanctimoniousness.

santero,-a 1 adj sanctimonious. – 2 m,f (sacristán) verger, sexton. 3 (mendigo) alms collector.

santiagués,-esa 1 adj of Santiago de Compostela, from Santiago de Compostela. – 2 m,f person from Santiago de Compostela, inhabitant of Santiago de Compostela.

santiaguino,-a 1 adj of Santiago (de Chile), from Santiago (de Chile). – 2 m,f person from Santiago (de Chile), inhabitant of Santiago (de Chile).

santiamén en un santiamén, loc adv in the twinkling of an eye, as quick as a flash, in a flash.

santidad f saintliness, holiness.
■ Su Santidad, His Holiness.

santificación f sanctification.

santificar 1 t (hacer santo) to sanctify, make holy. 2 (fiestas etc) to keep, observe.
▲ Conjugation model |1|, like *sacar.*

santiguar 1 t to bless, make the sign of the cross over. – 2 santiguarse, p (uso reflexivo) to cross os., make the sign of the cross.
▲ Conjugation model |22|, like *averiguar.*

santísimo,-a 1 adj most holy. – 2 el Santísimo, m the Holy Sacrament.
● hacer a algn. la santísima (pascua), fam to be a nuisance to sb.

santo,-a 1 adj (gen) holy, sacred: *Padre Santo,* Holy Father. 2 (persona) holy, saintly. 3 fam (para enfatizar) hell of a, real, right: *recibió una santa bofetada,* he got a hell of a whack, he got a right whack; *todo el santo día,* the whole day long. 4 (como título) saint: *Santo Tomás,* Saint

Thomas; *Santa Elena,* Saint Helen. – 5 m,f saint. – 6 santo, m (imagen) image of a saint. 7 fam (dibujo) picture. 8 (onomástica) saint's day.
● ¿a santo de qué?, fam why on earth? ‖ desnudar a un santo para vestir a otro, fig to rob Peter to pay Paul. ‖ hacer su santa voluntad, to do as one damn well pleases. ‖ írsele a uno el santo al cielo, fam to slip one's mind. ‖ llegar y besar el santo, fam as easy as pie, a piece of cake: *se cree que es llegar y besar el santo,* she thinks it'll be a piece of cake. ‖ no es santo de mi devoción, fam I'm not too fond of him, he's not my cup of tea. ‖ ¡por todos los santos!, fam for heaven's sake! ‖ quedarse para vestir santos, fam to be left on the shelf.
■ el día de Todos los Santos, All Saints' Day. ‖ Santo Oficio, Holy Office. ‖ santo y seña, password. ‖ un santo varón, a saint of a man.
▲ See also *san.*

santón 1 m REL santon. 2 fig (hipócrita) bigot. 3 fig (persona influyente) big shot.

santoral 1 m (libro) book on the lives of saints. 2 (libro de coro) sanctorale. 3 (lista de santos) calendar of saints' feast days.

santuario m sanctuary, shrine.

santurrón,-ona 1 adj sanctimonious. – 2 m,f sanctimonious person.

santurronería f sanctimoniousness.

saña 1 f (enojo) rage, fury. 2 (crueldad) cruelty, viciousness.
● con saña, (con enojo) furiously; (con crueldad) viciously.

sañudo,-a 1 adj (cruel) cruel, vicious. 2 (enojado) enraged, furious.

Saona el Saona, m the Saône.

sapiencia 1 f fml (sabiduría) wisdom. 2 (conocimiento) knowledge.

sapiente adj fml wise.

sapo m toad.
● echar sapos y culebras, fam to rant and rave.

saponificación f saponification.

saponificar t to saponify.
▲ Conjugation model |1|, like *sacar.*

saque 1 m (tenis) service. 2 (fútbol) kick-off.
● romper el saque a algn., (tenis) to break sb.'s service. ‖ tener buen saque, fam to be a big eater.
■ saque de banda, throw-in. ‖ saque de esquina, corner kick. ‖ saque inicial, kick-off.

saqueador,-ra 1 adj (de ciudades) plundering, pillaging; (de casas, comercios) looting. – 2 m,f (de ciudades) plunderer, pillager; (de casas, comercios) looter.

saquear t (casas) to plunder, pillage; (casas, comercios) to loot.

saqueo m (de ciudades) sacking, plundering; (de casa, comercio) looting.

S.A.R. abr (Su Alteza Real) His Royal Highness, Her Royal Highness; (abreviatura) HRH.

saraceno,-a 1 adj Saracen. – 2 m,f Saracen.

sarampión m measles pl.

sarao 1 m (reunión) soirée. 2 fam (jaleo) knees-up; (lío) mess.
● ¡vaya sarao!, fam what a mess!

sarasa m fam pey queer, fairy.

sarcasmo m sarcasm.
● con sarcasmo, sarcastically.

sarcásticamente adv sarcastically.

sarcástico,-a adj sarcastic.

sarcófago m sarcophagus.
sarcoma m sarcoma.
sardana f sardana, traditional Catalan folk dance.
sardina f sardine.
sardinero,-a 1 adj sardine. – 2 m,f sardine seller.
sardo,-a 1 adj Sardinian. – 2 m,f (persona) Sardinian. – 3 sardo, m (idioma) Sardinian.
sardónico,-a adj sardonic.
sarga f serge, twill.
sargazo m sargasso.
■ mar de los Sargazos, Sargasso Sea.
sargento 1 m MIL sergeant. 2 fig tyrant.
■ sargento primero, master sergeant.
sari m sari.
sarmentoso,-a adj fig (dedos etc) bony, scrawny.
sarmiento m vine shoot.
sarna f MED (en personas) scabies; (en animales) mange.
● sarna con gusto no pica, it's his (her, their) life, so let him (her, them) get on with it.
sarnoso,-a adj (piel) itchy, scabby; (animal) mangy, scabby: un perro sarnoso, a mangy dog.
sarpullido m rash.
sarraceno,-a 1 adj Saracen. – 2 m,f Saracen.
sarracina f → **sarracino,-a**.
sarracino,-a 1 adj-m,f → **sarraceno**. – 2 sarracina, f (pelea) brawl, free-for-all. 3 (masacre) massacre. 4 fam (destrozo) damage.
sarro 1 m (en los dientes) tartar. 2 (en la lengua) fur. 3 (sedimento) deposit.
sarta f string: una sarta de perlas, a string of pearls.
■ sarta de mentiras, fam fig pack of lies.
sartén f frying pan, US fry pan.
● tener la sartén por el mango, fig to have the upper hand.
sartenada f panful.
S.A.S. abr (Su Alteza Serenísima) His Serene Highness, Her Serene Highness; (abreviatura) HSH.
sastra f → **sastre,-a**.
sastre,-a 1 m,f tailor. – 2 sastra, f CINEM TEAT wardrobe mistress.
■ sastre de señoras, dressmaker.
sastrería 1 f (tienda) tailor's (shop). 2 (oficio) tailoring.
Satán m Satan.
Satanás m Satan.
satánico,-a 1 adj satanic. – 2 m,f Satanist.
satanismo m Satanism.
satélite m satellite.
■ país satélite, fig satellite state. ‖ satélite artificial, artificial satellite.
satén m satin.
satinado,-a 1 pp → satinar. – 2 adj (gen) satiny, shiny, glossy; (pintura) satin. – 3 satinado, m gloss, shine.
satinar t to gloss, make glossy.
sátira f satire.
satírico,-a 1 adj (de la sátira) satiric, satirical. 2 (del sátiro) satyric, satyrical.
satirizar t to satirize.
▲ Conjugation model [4], like realizar.
sátiro m satyr.
satisfacción 1 f (gen) satisfaction. 2 (cumplimiento) fulfilment (US fulfillment): la satisfacción de un deseo, the fulfilment of a desire.
● a satisfacción de, to the satisfaction of.
satisfacer 1 t (gen) to satisfy. 2 (deuda) to pay. 3 (requisitos, exigencias) to meet, fulfil satisfy. 4 (agravio, ofensa)

to make amends for. – 5 i to be satisfactory. – 6 satisfacerse, p to be satisfied, satisfy os.
▲ Conjugation model [85; pp satisfecho],-a.
satisfactoriamente adv satisfactorily.
satisfactorio,-a adj satisfactory.
satisfecho,-a 1 pp → **satisfacer**. – 2 adj (contento) satisfied, pleased. 3 (pagado de sí mismo) self-satisfied.
● darse por satisfecho,-a con algo, to be satisfied with sth. ‖ estar satisfecho,-a / quedar satisfecho,-a, (de comida) to be full, have had enough.
sátrapa 1 m HIST satrap. 2 fig despot, satrap.
● vivir como un sátrapa, fig to live like a king.
saturación f saturation.
saturado,-a 1 pp → **saturar**. – 2 adj saturated. 3 fig sick, tired.
saturar t to saturate.
saturnino,-a adj saturnine.
saturnismo m saturnism, lead-poisoning.
Saturno m Saturn.
sauce m willow.
■ sauce llorón, weeping willow.
saúco m elder.
saudade f nostalgia, homesickness.
saudí 1 adj Saudi. – 2 mf Saudi.
saudita adj-mf → **saudí**.
sauna f sauna.
saurio,-a 1 adj saurian. – 2 m,f saurian.
savia 1 f BOT sap. 2 fig sap, vitality.
saxo m fam → **saxofón**.
saxofón 1 m (instrumento) saxophone, sax. – 2 mf (músico) saxophonist, sax player.
saxofonista mf saxophonist.
saxófono m → **saxofón**.
saya 1 f (falda) skirt. 2 (enagua) petticoat.
sayal m sackcloth.
sayo m cassock, smock.
● cortarle un sayo a algn., fig to run sb. down. ‖ hacer de su capa un sayo, fig to do as one pleases.
sazón 1 f (madurez) ripeness. 2 (sabor) taste, flavour (US flavor). 3 (aderezo) seasoning. 4 (tiempo, ocasión) season, time.
● a la sazón, at that time. ‖ en sazón, (fruta etc) ripe, in season; (uso figurado) at the appropriate time. ‖ fuera de sazón, inopportunely.
sazonado,-a 1 pp → **sazonar**. – 2 adj fig witty.
sazonar 1 t (madurar) to ripen, mature. 2 (comida) to season, flavour (US flavor). 3 fig (historia etc) to add spice to. – 4 sazonarse, p (madurar) to ripen, mature.
s/c abr (su cuenta) your account.
scooter m scooter.
scout m scout.
Sdad. abr (sociedad) Society; (abreviatura) S.
S.D.M. abr (Su Divina Majestad) the Divine Majesty.
se[1] 1 pron (reflexivo - él) himself; (- ella) herself; (- usted, ustedes) yourself, yourselves; (- ellos, ellas) themselves; (- esto) itself: se felicitó del éxito de la campaña, he congratulated himself on the success of the campaign; se está preparando, she's getting herself ready; se miraron en el espejo, they looked at themselves in the mirror; ella se peina, she combs her hair. 2 (recíproco) each other, one another: se quieren, they love each other; se conocieron en Málaga, they met one another in Malaga. 3 (pasiva): se han abierto las puertas, the doors have been opened. 4 (impersonal): se dice que han atrapado a los ladrones, people say the thieves have been

caught; *véase también seis,* see also six; *se ve que no,* apparently not.

se² *pron (objeto indirecto - a él)* him, to him; (*- a ella*) her, to her; (*- a ellos, ellas*) them, to them; (*- a esto*) it, to it; (*- a usted, ustedes*) you, to you: *se lo dije,* I told her; *se los dio,* she gave them to him; *se la compraré yo,* I'll buy it for them.
▲ Used *before the pronouns la, las, lo and los instead of le or les.*

sé¹ *pres indic →* **saber**.

sé² *imperat →* **ser**.

SE *sím (sureste)* southeast; *(símbolo)* SE.

S.E. *abr (Su Excelencia)* His Excellency, Her Excellency; *(abreviatura)* HE.

sea *pres subj →* **ser**.

sebáceo,-a *adj* sebaceous.

sebo 1 *m (grasa)* fat. **2** CULIN suet. **3** *(para velas)* tallow. **4** *(suciedad)* grease, filth. **5** *(gordura)* fat. **6** *fam (borrachera)* drunkenness.

seborrea *f* seborrhoea (US seborrhea).

seboso,-a *adj* greasy.

seca *f (sequía)* drought.

secadero *m* drying room.

secado *m* drying.

secador 1 *m* dryer, drier. **2** *(de pelo)* hair-dryer.

secadora *f* clothes-dryer, tumble-dryer.

secamente *adv* dryly.

secano *m* dry land.
■ cultivo de secano, dry farming.

secante¹ 1 *adj (que seca)* drying. **2** *(papel)* blotting. **– 3** *m (papel)* blotting paper. **4** DEP spoiler. **5** *(para pinturas)* siccative.

secante² 1 *adj (geometría)* secant. **– 2** *f* secant.

secar 1 *t (gen)* to dry. **2** *(lágrimas, vajilla)* to wipe; *(tinta)* to blot; *(líquido)* to wipe up, mop up. **3** *(planta)* to wither, dry up; *(río, fuente, etc)* to dry up. **– 4 secarse,** *p (gen)* to dry up: *sécate las manos,* dry your hands. **5** *(líquido, río, etc)* to dry up; *(planta)* to wither, dry up. **6** *fig (enflaquecer)* to become thin.
● secarse la frente, to mop one's brow.
▲ *Conjugation model* |1|, *like sacar.*

sección 1 *f (corte)* section, cut. **2** *(geometría)* section. **3** *(departamento)* section, department. **4** *(en periódico, revista)* page, section. **5** MIL section.
■ sección transversal, cross-section.

seccionar *t* to section, cut.

secesión *f* secession.

secesionismo *m* secessionism.

secesionista 1 *adj* secessionist. **– 2** *mf* secessionist.

seco,-a 1 *adj (gen)* dry. **2** *(frutos, flores)* dried: *compramos flores secas,* we bought some dried flowers. **3** *(marchito)* withered, dried up. **4** *fig (vino)* dry. **5** *fig (carácter)* dry; *(tono, respuesta)* curt, sharp. **6** *fig (golpe, ruido)* sharp. **7** *fig (persona - delgada)* skinny; (*- vieja*) old and wizened.
● a secas, *fig* simply, just: *Carmen a secas,* just plain Carmen. || dejar seco,-a, *fam* to bump off. || en seco, *(acción)* suddenly: *frenar en seco,* to brake suddenly; *parar en seco,* to stop dead. || estar más seco,-a que un higo, *fam (delgado)* to be as thin as a rake; *(envejecido)* to be old and wizened. || estar seco,-a, *fam* to be thirsty, be dry. || limpiar en seco, to dry-clean. || quedarse seco,-a, *fam* to snuff it, croak.

secoya *f →* **secuyoa**.

secreción *f* secretion.

secreta *f →* **secreto,-a**.

secretar *t* to secrete.

secretaría 1 *f (cargo)* secretaryship, office of secretary. **2** *(oficina)* secretary's office; *(en la administración)* secretariat.
■ Secretaría de Estado, State Department.

secretariado 1 *m (cargo)* secretaryship. **2** *(oficina)* secretariat. **3** *(estudios)* secretarial course.

secretario,-a *m,f* secretary.
■ secretario,-a de Estado, Secretary of State. || secretario,-a particular, private secretary.

secretear *i* to whisper secrets.

secreteo *m* whispering.

secreter *m* writing desk, bureau.

secreto,-a 1 *adj* secret. **– 2 secreto,** *m (lo reservado)* secret: *te diré un secreto,* I'll tell you a secret. **3** *(reserva)* secrecy. **– 4 secreta,** *f fam* secret police.
● en secreto, secretly. || guardar un secreto, to keep a secret.
■ secreto a voces, *fam* open secret. || secreto de estado, state secret. || secreto profesional, *(práctica)* professional secrecy.

secretorio,-a *adj* secretory.

secta *f* sect.

sectario,-a *adj* sectarian.

sectarismo *m* sectarianism.

sector 1 *m (gen)* sector. **2** *fig (zona)* area. **3** *fig (parte)* section: *un sector de la opinión pública,* a section of public opinion.
■ sector primario / sector secundario / sector terciario, primary industry / secondary industry / tertiary industry. || sector privado / sector público, private sector / public sector.

sectorial *adj* sectorial.

secuaz *mf* follower, supporter; *pey* underling, henchman.

secuela 1 *f* consequence, result. **– 2 secuelas,** *fpl (de enfermedad, guerra)* after-effects *pl.*

secuencia *f* sequence.

secuencial *adj* sequential.

secuenciar *t* to arrange in sequence, put in sequence.
▲ *Conjugation model* |12|, *like cambiar.*

secuestrador,-ra 1 *adj (personas)* kidnapping; *(de avión)* hijacking. **2** JUR sequestrating. **– 3** *m,f (personas)* kidnapper; *(de avión)* hijacker. **4** JUR sequestrator.

secuestrar 1 *t (personas)* to kidnap; *(avión)* to hijack. **2** JUR to sequester, seize, confiscate.

secuestro 1 *m (personas)* kidnapping; *(de avión)* hijacking. **2** JUR sequestration, seizure, confiscation.

secular 1 *adj (seglar)* secular, lay. **2** *(de cada siglo)* secular. **3** *(que tiene un siglo)* century-old. **4** *fig (antiquísimo)* ancient, age-old. **– 5** *m* REL secular.

secularidad *f* secularity.

secularización *f* secularization.

secularizar *t* to secularize.
▲ *Conjugation model* |4|, *like realizar.*

secundar *t* to support, second.

secundaria *f →* **secundario,-a**.

secundario,-a 1 *adj* secondary. **– 2 secundario,** *m* GEOL secondary. **– 3 secundaria,** *f* EDUC secondary education.

secuoya *f* sequoia, redwood.

sed *f* thirst.
● apagar la sed / matar la sed / quitar la sed, to quench one's thirst. || dar sed, to make thirsty: *la comida salada me da sed,* salty food makes me thirsty. || tener sed, to be thirsty: *tengo sed,* I'm thirsty. || tener sed de, *fig* to be thirsty for.

seda f silk.
● **como una seda**, fig smoothly.
sedal m fishing line.
sedán m sedan.
sedante 1 adj MED sedative. 2 fig soothing. – 3 m MED sedative.
sedar t to sedate.
sedativo,-a adj sedative.
sede f (oficina central) headquarters, central office. 2 (del gobierno) seat.
■ **la Santa Sede**, the Holy See. ‖ **sede social**, head office.
sedentario,-a adj sedentary.
sedente adj seated, sitting.
sedeño,-a 1 adj (sedoso) silky. 2 (que tiene cerdas) bristly.
sedería 1 f (industria) silk trade. 2 (tienda) silk shop.
sedero,-a adj silk.
sedición f sedition.
sedicioso,-a 1 adj seditious. – 2 m,f rebel.
sediento,-a 1 adj thirsty. 2 fig (poder etc) hungry (**de**, for), thirsty (**de**, for).
sedimentación f sedimentation.
sedimentar 1 t to settle, deposit. – 2 **sedimentarse**, p to settle. 3 fig to calm down, settle down.
sedimentario,-a adj sedimentary.
sedimento m sediment, deposit.
sedoso,-a adj silky, silken.
seducción f seduction.
seducir 1 t (gen) to seduce. 2 (persuadir) to tempt, seduce. 3 (cautivar) to captivate.
▲ Conjugation model [46], like conducir.
seductor,-ra 1 adj seductive. 2 (atractivo) captivating. 3 (persuasivo) tempting. – 4 m,f seducer.
sefardí 1 adj Sephardic. – 2 mf Sephardi.
▲ pl sefardíes.
sefardita adj-mf → **sefardí**.
segador,-ra 1 m,f harvester, reaper. – 2 **segadora**, f harvester, reaper; (de césped) lawnmower.
segadora f → **segador,-ra**.
segar 1 t (gen) to reap, cut; (césped) to mow. 2 fig (matar) to mow down, cut down. 3 fig (truncar) to cut off.
▲ Conjugation model [48], like regar.
seglar 1 adj secular, lay. – 2 mf lay person; (hombre) layman; (mujer) laywoman.
segmentación f segmentation.
segmentar t to segment.
segmento 1 m (gen) segment. 2 INFORM overlay.
segoviano,-a 1 adj of Segovia, from Segovia. – 2 m,f person from Segovia, inhabitant of Segovia.
segregación 1 f (separación) segregation. 2 (secreción) secretion.
■ **segregación racial**, racial segregation, apartheid.
segregacionismo m segregationism.
segregacionista 1 adj segregationist. – 2 mf segregationist.
segregar 1 t (separar) to segregate. 2 (secretar) to secrete.
▲ Conjugation model [7], like llegar.
segueta f fretsaw.
seguida f → **seguido,-a**.
seguidamente 1 adv (sin interrupción) without a break. 2 (inmediatamente) straight away, at once.
seguidilla 1 f LIT type of strophe. 2 MÚS seguidilla, type of Spanish dance and song.
seguido,-a 1 pp → **seguir**. – 2 adj (continuo) continuous. 3 (consecutivo) consecutive, successive: cuatro vic-

torias seguidas, four consecutive wins; dos días seguidos, two days running, two days in a row. 4 (en línea recta) straight, direct. – 5 seguido, adv straight: todo seguido, straight on, straight ahead. – 6 seguida, f rhythm.
● **de seguida**, (seguidamente) without a break; (enseguida) at once, immediately, right away. ‖ **en seguida**, at once, immediately, straight away: vete en seguida a casa, go home straight away.
seguidor,-ra 1 adj following. – 2 m,f follower. 3 DEP follower, supporter, fan.
seguimiento 1 m (perseguimiento) pursuit. 2 (continuación) continuation. 3 fig (de un cliente etc) follow-up.
● **en seguimiento de**, in pursuit of.
■ **estación de seguimiento espacial**, tracking station.
seguir 1 t (gen) to follow: hay alguien que nos sigue, there's somebody following us; ¡sígame!, follow me! 2 (perseguir) to pursue, chase. 3 (continuar) to continue, carry on. 4 (un camino) to continue on. 5 (curso etc) to do; (explicaciones) to follow. – 6 i (proseguir) to go on, carry on: ¡sigue, es un poco más allá!, carry on, it's a bit further ahead!; siga todo recto, go straight on. 7 (continuar) to follow on, continue: siguió leyendo, she kept on reading. 8 (permanecer, mantenerse) to continue to be, be still: sigue ocupado, he's still busy; sigue en Madrid, she's still in Madrid; sigue hablando, he's still speaking. – 9 **seguirse**, p (inferirse) to deduce. 10 (suceder a continuación) to follow.
● **como sigue**, as follows. ‖ **de esto se sigue que ...**, it follows that ... ‖ **el que la sigue la consigue**, fig if at first you don't succeed, try, try again. ‖ **seguir a algn. como un perrito**, fam to tag along after sb., follow sb. everywhere. ‖ **seguir con la mirada / seguir con los ojos**, to follow with one's eyes. ‖ **seguir con vida**, to be still alive. ‖ **seguir la carrera de**, to study. ‖ **seguir la corriente**, fig to follow the crowd. ‖ **seguir sin + inf**, to still not + inf: sigue sin entender, she still doesn't understand. ‖ **seguir su curso**, to take its course. ‖ **seguir un consejo**, to follow a piece of advice.
▲ Conjugation model [56].
según 1 prep (conforme) according to: según lo que oí, according to what I heard; según tu padre, according to your father; según su opinión, in his opinion. 2 (dependiendo) depending on: según lo que digan, tomaremos una decisión, depending on what they say, we'll make a decision; según el tiempo, depending on the weather. 3 (como) just as: todo quedó según estaba, everything stayed just as it was. 4 (a medida que) as: según me miraba me di cuenta de que ya nos habíamos visto, as I looked at her I realized we had met before. 5 (tal vez) it depends: iré o me quedaré, según, I'll either go or I'll stay, it depends.
segunda f → **segundo,-a**.
segundero m second hand.
segundo,-a 1 adj second. – 2 m,f second. – 3 segundo, m (tiempo) second. – 4 **segunda**, f (vuelta doble) double turn. 5 (tren etc) second class. 6 (marcha del auto) second, second gear. 7 fig (intención) ulterior motive.
● **de segunda mano**, fig second-hand. ‖ **decir algo con segundas (intenciones)**, fig to have an ulterior motive for saying sth. ‖ **en segundo lugar**, (en texto, explicación) secondly; (en competición) in second place.
■ **segundas nupcias**, second marriage sing.
▲ See also sexto,-a.
segundón m second son.

segur 1 *m* (*hacha*) axe (US ax). **2** (*hoz*) sickle.

seguramente 1 *adv* (*con seguridad*) securely, safely. **2** (*con certeza*) for certain, for sure. **3** (*probablemente*) probably: *seguramente no vendrá,* he isn't likely to come.

seguridad 1 *f* (*gen*) security: *Pedro deseaba seguridad,* Pedro wanted security. **2** (*física*) safety: *seguridad en carretera,* road safety. **3** (*certeza*) certainty, sureness. **4** (*confianza*) confidence. **5** (*organismo*) security. **6** (*fiabilidad*) reliability.
● **con toda seguridad,** most probably. ‖ **de seguridad,** security: *medidas de seguridad,* security measures. ‖ **en la seguridad de que ...,** in the safe knowledge that ... ‖ **hablar con seguridad,** to speak with confidence. ‖ **para mayor seguridad,** (*certeza*) to be on the safe side; (*protección*) for safety's sake. ‖ **tener la seguridad de que ...,** to be certain that ..., be sure that ...
■ **seguridad en sí mismo,-a,** self-confidence. ‖ **seguridad financiera,** financial security. ‖ **seguridad social,** ≈ National Health Service.

seguro,-a 1 *adj* (*asegurado*) secure. **2** (*a salvo*) safe. **3** (*firme*) firm, steady. **4** (*cierto*) certain, sure: *estoy segura de que fue allí,* I'm sure she went there; *lo más seguro es que llegue tarde,* I'll probably be late. **5** (*de fiar*) reliable. **6** (*confiado*) confident: *está muy seguro de sí mismo,* he's very self-confident. – **7 seguro,** *m* (*contrato, póliza*) insurance. **8** (*mecanismo*) safety device, safety catch. – **9** *adv* for sure, definitely: *seguro que no,* definitely not.
● **a buen seguro,** without any doubt. ‖ **dar algo por seguro,** to take sth. for granted. ‖ **ir sobre seguro,** *fig* to play safe. ‖ **sentirse seguro,-a,** to feel safe. ‖ **sobre seguro,** without risk.
■ **seguro a todo riesgo,** fully comprehensive insurance. ‖ **seguro contra incendios,** fire insurance. ‖ **seguro contra terceros,** third-party insurance. ‖ **seguro de vida,** life insurance.

seis 1 *adj* six: *pesa seis kilos,* it weighs six kilos; *son casi las seis,* it's almost six o'clock; *son las seis en punto,* it's exactly six o'clock; *el seis de junio,* the sixth of June; *se casan el día seis,* they're getting married on the sixth; *tiene un hijo de seis años,* she has a boy of six; *somos seis,* there are six of us; *eran seis,* there were six of them; *los vendemos de seis en seis,* we sell them in sixes. **2** (*sexto*) sixth: *soy el seis de la lista,* I'm sixth on the list. – **3** *m* six: *el seis,* number six; *seis sobre diez,* six out of ten; *seis por seis treinta y seis,* six sixes are thirty-six, six times six is thirty-six; *mide seis por seis,* it measures six by six.

seisavo,-a *adj-m,f* → **sexto,-a**.

seiscientos,-as 1 *adj* (*cardinal*) six hundred; (*ordinal*) six hundredth. – **2 seiscientos,** *m* (*número*) six hundred. **3** AUTO *fam* 600 cc SEAT car.
▲ See also **seis**.

seísmo *m* (*terremoto*) earthquake; (*temblor*) earth tremor.

selección 1 *f* (*gen*) selection. **2** DEP (*gen*) team; (*fútbol*) squad.
■ **selección nacional,** DEP national team. ‖ **selección natural,** natural selection.

seleccionador,-ra *m,f* selector.

seleccionar *t* to select.

selectividad 1 *f* selectivity. **2** EDUC university entrance examination.

selectivo,-a *adj* selective.

selecto,-a 1 *adj* select. **2** (*escogido*) exclusive.

selector *m* selector button.
■ **selector de velocidades,** gear lever, gear stick, US gear shift.

selenio *m* selenium.

selenita 1 *mf* moon dweller. – **2** *f* selenite.

self-service *m* self-service cafeteria.
▲ *pl* **self-service**.

sellar 1 *t* (*timbrar*) to stamp; (*oficial*) to seal. **2** (*monedas etc*) to hallmark, stamp. **3** *fig* (*habitación etc*) to close (up), seal up. **4** *fig* (*dejar señal*) to stamp, brand. **5** *fig* (*concluir*) to seal, settle, conclude. – **6** *i* to sign on.
● **sellar los labios,** *fig* to keep one's lips sealed, keep mum.

sello 1 *m* (*de correos*) stamp. **2** (*de estampar, precinto*) seal. **3** (*distintivo*) hallmark, mark. **4** MED capsule.
■ **sello de distinción,** hallmark of distinction. ‖ **sello discográfico,** record label.

selva 1 *f* (*bosque*) forest. **2** (*jungla*) jungle.

selvático,-a 1 *adj* forest, jungle. **2** *fig* uncouth.

semáforo *m* traffic lights *pl*.

semana 1 *f* (*tiempo*) week. **2** *fig* (*salario*) weekly wage.
● **entre semana,** during the week.
■ **fin de semana,** (*tiempo*) weekend; (*bolsa*) weekend bag. ‖ **semana laboral,** working week. ‖ **Semana Santa,** Easter, Holy Week.

semanada *f* weekly wage.

semanal *adj* weekly.

semanalmente *adv* weekly.

semanario,-a 1 *adj* weekly. – **2** *m* weekly magazine.

semántica *f* semantics.

semántico,-a 1 *adj* semantic. – **2 semántica,** *f* semantics *pl*.

semblante 1 *m* (*cara*) face. **2** (*expresión*) countenance. **3** *fig* (*apariencia*) look.
● **mudar el semblante,** to change colour (US color). ‖ **tener buen semblante / tener mal semblante,** to look good / look bad.

semblanza *f* portrait.

sembrado,-a 1 *pp* → **sembrar**. – **2** *adj fig* (*cubierto*) covered (**de**, with), full (**de**, of): *la página está sembrada de correcciones,* the page is covered with corrections. – **3 sembrado,** *m* sown field.

sembrador,-ra 1 *m,f* sower. – **2 sembradora,** *f* seed drill.

sembradora *f* → **sembrador,-ra**.

sembrar 1 *t* AGR to sow. **2** *fig* (*esparcir*) to scatter, spread.
● **sembrar el pánico,** *fig* to spread panic. ‖ **sembrar la discordia,** to sow discord.
▲ *Conjugation model* |27|, *like* **acertar**.

semejante 1 *adj* (*parecido*) similar. **2** *pey* (*tal*) such, like that: *no voy a permitir semejante insolencia,* I won't allow such insolence; *no puedo tolerar semejantes idioteces,* I won't tolerate idiotic behaviour like that. **3** (*geometría*) similar. – **4** *m* fellow being.

semejanza *f* similarity, likeness.

semejar 1 *i* to resemble, be alike. – **2 semejarse,** *p* to be similar, be alike.

semen *m* semen.

semental *m* stud.

sementera 1 *f* (*acción*) sowing, seeding. **2** (*tierra*) sown field. **3** (*tiempo*) sowing season. **4** *fig* (*origen*) source, breeding ground.

sementero *m* grain sack.

semestral *adj* half-yearly, semestral.

semestre 1 *m* six-month period, semester. **2** US EDUC semester.

semicilindro *m* semicylinder.

semicircular *adj* semicircular.

semicírculo *m* semicircle.
semicircunferencia *f* semicircumference.
semiconductor *m* semiconductor.
semiconsciente *adj* half-conscious.
semiconsonante 1 *adj* semiconsonantal. – 2 *f* semi-consonant.
semicorchea *f* semiquaver, sixteenth note.
semidesierto,-a *adj* half-deserted.
semidesnudo,-a *adj* half-naked.
semidiós,-osa *m,f* demigod.
semidirecto,-a 1 *adj* semidirect. 2 (*tren*) express. – 3 semidirecto, *m* (*tren*) express train.
semieje *m* semiaxis.
semiesférico,-a *adj* hemispheroidal.
semifinal *f* semifinal.
semifinalista *mf* semifinalist.
semifondo *m* medium-distance race.
■ carrera de semifondo / prueba de semifondo, medium-distance race.
semifusa *f* hemidemisemiquaver, sixty-fourth note.
semilla 1 *f* seed. 2 *fig* seed, seeds *pl.*
semillero 1 *m* seedbed. 2 *fig* hotbed, breeding ground.
seminal *adj* seminal.
seminario 1 *m* EDUC seminar. 2 REL seminary.
seminarista *m* seminarist.
semiología *f* semiology.
semiótica *f* semiotics.
semiprecioso,-a *adj* semiprecious.
semi-seco,-a *adj* medium-dry.
semita 1 *adj* Semitic. – 2 *mf* Semite.
semítico,-a *adj* Semitic.
semitismo *m* Semitism.
semitono *m* semitone, half-step.
semivocal 1 *adj* semivocal. – 2 *f* semivowel.
sémola *f* semolina.
sempiterno,-a 1 *adj* everlasting, eternal. 2 *lit* sempiternal.
Sena el Sena, *m* the Seine.
senado 1 *m* senate. 2 *fig* (*reunión*) assembly.
senador,-ra *m,f* senator.
senaduría *f* senatorship.
senatorial *adj* senatorial.
S. en C. *abr* (*sociedad en comandita*) limited partnership.
sencillamente *adv* simply.
sencillez 1 *f* (*gen*) simplicity. 2 (*naturalidad*) simplicity, lack of affectation, unpretentiousness. 3 (*ingenuidad*) gullibility, naïvety,.
sencillo,-a 1 *adj* (*sin adornos*) simple, plain: *es un vestido sencillo,* it's a simple dress. 2 (*fácil*) simple, easy: *es muy sencillo,* it's very easy. 3 (*no compuesto*) single. 4 *fig* (*persona - natural*) natural, unaffected, unpretentious; (- *ingenua*) naïve, gullible.
senda *f* path.
sendero *m* path.
sendos,-as *adj pl* each, either: *otorgaron un premio a sendas películas,* they awarded a prize to each film; *los dos niños llevaban sendas bufandas,* the two children were each wearing a scarf.
senectud *f* old age.
Senegal *m* Senegal.
senegalés,-esa 1 *adj* Senegalese. – 2 *m,f* Senegalese.
senescal *m* seneschal.
senil *adj* senile.

senilidad *f* senility.
sénior *adj* senior: *Juan Sánchez sénior,* Juan Sánchez Senior.
▲ *pl seniores.*
seno 1 *m* (*pecho*) breast, bosom. 2 (*hueco entre el pecho y la ropa*) bosom. 3 (*matriz*) womb. 4 (*cavidad*) cavity, hollow, hole. 5 MAT sine. 6 ANAT sinus. 7 GEOG gulf, bay. 8 *fig* bosom, heart: *en el seno de la iglesia,* in the bosom of the church.
sensación 1 *f* (*impresión*) sensation, feeling: *sensación de calor,* feeling of warmth. 2 (*emoción*) sensation.
● causar sensación, to cause a sensation. ‖ tener la sensación de que ..., to have a feeling that ...
sensacional *adj* sensational.
sensacionalismo *m* sensationalism.
sensacionalista 1 *adj* sensational, sensationalistic. – 2 *mf* sensationalist.
■ prensa sensacionalista, gutter press, tabloid press, tabloids *pl.*
sensatez *f* good sense.
● obrar con sensatez, to act sensibly.
sensato,-a *adj* sensible.
sensibilidad 1 *f* (*percepción, sentido artístico*) sensitivity, feeling. 2 (*emotividad*) sensibility. 3 (*precisión*) sensitivity.
sensibilización *f* sensitization.
sensibilizar 1 *t* (*gen*) to sensitize. 2 *fig* (*concienciar*) to sensitize, make aware.
▲ *Conjugation model* [4], *like realizar.*
sensible 1 *adj* (*capaz de sentir*) sentient. 2 (*impresionable*) sensitive. 3 (*piel, oído*) sensitive. 4 (*perceptible*) perceptible, appreciable, noticeable. 5 (*considerable*) significant, considerable, sizeable. 6 (*que causa pena*) terrible, sad. 7 TÉC (*preciso*) sensitive.
● lamentamos tan sensible pérdida, *fml euf* we regret such a sad loss.
sensiblemente *adv* noticeably, considerably.
sensiblería *f* mawkishness, over-sentimentality.
sensiblero,-a *adj* mawkish, over-sentimental.
sensitivo,-a 1 *adj* (*sensible*) sensitive. 2 (*que siente*) sentient. 3 (*de los sentidos*) sense: *órganos sensitivos,* sense organs.
sensor *m* sensor.
sensorial *adj* sensory.
sensorio,-a *adj* sensory.
sensual 1 *adj* (*de los sentidos*) sensuous, sensual. 2 (*del sexo*) sensual.
sensualidad 1 *f* (*de los sentidos*) sensuousness, sensuality. 2 (*del sexo*) sensuality.
sensualismo *m* sensualism.
sentada *f* → sentado,-a.
sentado,-a 1 *pp* → sentar. – 2 *adj* seated, sitting: *estaba sentada allí,* she was sitting there. 3 (*establecido*) established, settled. 4 *fig* (*juicioso*) sensible, wise. – 5 sentada, *f* (*acción*) sitting: *lo hicimos de una sentada,* we did it in one sitting. 6 (*protesta*) sit-in.
● dar algo por sentado,-a, to take sth. for granted. ‖ dejar sentado que ..., to make it clear that ... ‖ hacer una sentada, to hold a sit-in.
sentar 1 *t* (*en silla etc*) to sit, seat. 2 *fig* (*establecer*) to establish. 3 *fig* (*alisar*) to press. – 4 *i* (*color, ropa, etc*) to suit: *esta corbata no te sienta,* this tie doesn't suit you. 5 (*comida etc*) to do; (*comentario etc*) to take. – 6 sentarse, *p* (*en silla etc*) to sit, sit down. 7 (*líquido*) to settle. 8 (*tiempo*) to settle, settle down.
● sentar bien, (*quedar bien*) to suit; (*ser reconfortante*) to do good; (*gustar*) to please, like; (*tomar bien*) to take

well: *una sopita te sentará bien,* some soup will do you good; *un dinero extra siempra sienta bien,* a little extra money always comes in handy. ‖ **sentar cabeza,** *fig* to settle down. ‖ **sentar como un tiro,** *fam (ropa etc)* to suit; *(noticia etc)* to come as a blow, come as a bombshell: *la decisión le sentó como un tiro,* the decision came as a bombshell. ‖ **sentar las bases de algo,** *fig* to lay the foundations of sth. ‖ **sentar mal,** *(quedar mal)* not to suit; *(no gustar)* not to like, not appreciate; *(tomar a mal)* to take badly; *(comida, bebida)* to disagree with: *aquel comentario le sentó mal,* he took that remark badly; *aquellos mariscos le sentaron mal,* the seafood disagreed with him. ‖ **sentar un precedente,** *fig* to set a precedent.

▲ *Conjugation model* [27], *like* **acertar**.

sentencia 1 *f* JUR *(decisión)* judgement; *(condena)* sentence. 2 *(aforismo)* proverb, maxim, saying, motto.

● **visto para sentencia,** JUR ready for sentencing.

sentenciar *t* to sentence **(a,** to).

▲ *Conjugation model* [12], *like* **cambiar**.

sentencioso,-a *adj* sententious.

sentido,-a 1 *pp →* **sentir**. – 2 *adj (muerte etc)* deeply felt: *nuestro más sentido pésame,* our deepest sympathy. 3 *(sensible)* touchy, sensitive. – 4 **sentido,** *m (gen)* sense. 5 *(significado)* sense, meaning. 6 *(conocimiento)* consciousness. 7 *(dirección)* direction.

● **de sentido único,** AUTO one-way. ‖ **dejar a algn. sin sentido,** to knock sb. out. ‖ **en cierto sentido,** in a sense. ‖ **en sentido opuesto,** in the opposite direction. ‖ **hablar sin sentido,** to talk nonsense. ‖ **hacer algo con los cinco sentidos,** *fig* to take great pains with sth. ‖ **no tiene sentido / no tiene ningún sentido,** it doesn't make sense: *no tiene sentido salir si no tenemos dinero,* there's no point in going out if we haven't got any money. ‖ **¿qué sentido tiene +** *inf* ...?, what's the point in/of + *-ing* ...?: *¿qué sentido tiene hablarle si no te hace caso?,* what's the point of talking to him if he won't listen? ‖ **perder el sentido,** to faint. ‖ **tener sentido,** to make sense.

■ **doble sentido,** double meaning. ‖ **sentido común,** common sense. ‖ **sentido de la orientación,** sense of direction. ‖ **sentido del humor,** sense of humour (US humor). ‖ **sentido figurado,** figurative meaning.

sentimental 1 *adj* sentimental. – 2 *mf* sentimental person.

sentimentalismo *m* sentimentality.

sentimentaloide *adj fam* schmaltzy, gooey, over-sentimental.

sentimiento 1 *m (gen)* feeling: *no tiene sentimientos,* he's got no feelings. 2 *(pena)* sorrow, grief.

● **le acompaño en el sentimiento,** my deepest sympathy.

■ **buenos sentimientos,** sympathy *sing*.

sentina 1 *f (de nave)* bilge. 2 *fig (albañal)* sewer. 3 *fig (antro)* den.

sentir 1 *m (sentimiento)* feeling. 2 *(opinión)* opinion, view. – 3 *t (gen)* to feel: *sintió frío,* she felt cold; *sentir amor,* to feel love. 4 *(lamentar)* to regret, be sorry about, feel sorry: *siento que no viniera,* I'm sorry she didn't come; *lo siento mucho,* I'm very sorry. 5 *(oír)* to hear: *¿sientes algo?,* can you hear anything? 6 *(presentir)* to feel, think, have a feeling that: *siento que todo acabará bien,* I think everything will turn out all right. – 7 **sentirse,** *p* to feel: *me siento cansado,* I feel tired.

● **dejarse sentir / hacerse sentir,** *fig* to make itself felt. ‖ **en mi sentir,** in my opinion. ‖ **¡lo siento!,** I'm sorry! ‖ **sentirse como en casa,** to feel at home. ‖

sentirse con ánimos de hacer algo, to feel like doing sth., feel up to doing sth. ‖ **sentirse mal,** to feel ill. ‖ **sin sentir,** just like that.

▲ *Conjugation model* [35], *like* **hervir**.

seña 1 *f (indicio, gesto)* sign. 2 *(señal)* mark. – 3 **señas,** *fpl* address *sing*: *¿me das tus señas?,* can you give me your address?

● **hablar por señas,** to talk in sign language. ‖ **hacer señas a algn.,** to signal to sb. ‖ **por más señas,** specifically.

■ **señas personales / señas de identidad,** particulars.

señal 1 *f (signo)* sign, indication. 2 *(marca)* mark; *(en libro)* bookmark. 3 *(aviso, comunicación)* signal. 4 *(placa, letrero)* sign. 5 *(vestigio)* trace. 6 *(cicatriz)* scar. 7 *(de teléfono)* tone. 8 *(de pago)* deposit.

● **dar señales de vida,** to show signs of life. ‖ **dejar señal,** to leave a mark. ‖ **dejar una señal,** *(dinero)* to leave a deposit. ‖ **en señal de,** as a sign of, as a token of. ‖ **hacer señales a algn.,** to signal to sb. ‖ **ni señal,** not a trace. ‖ **ser buena señal / ser mala señal,** to be a good sign / be a bad sign.

■ **señal de alarma,** alarm signal. ‖ **señal de comunicar,** engaged tone, US busy signal. ‖ **señal de la cruz,** REL sign of the cross. ‖ **señal de llamada,** *(teléfono)* dialling tone, US dial tone. ‖ **señal de tráfico,** road sign.

señalado,-a 1 *pp →* **señalar**. – 2 *adj (famoso)* distinguished, famous. 3 *(fijado)* appointed, fixed: *llegamos a la hora señalada,* we arrived at the the appointed time. 4 *(significativo)* noticeable. 5 *(marcado)* marked, scarred: *tiene la espalda señalada,* his back is scarred.

■ **un día señalado,** a red-letter day.

señalar 1 *t (marcar)* to mark. 2 *(rubricar)* to sign and seal. 3 *(hacer herida)* to mark, scar. 4 *(hacer notar)* to point out: *señaló algunas contradicciones,* she pointed out some contradictions. 5 *(apuntar hacia)* to point to, show: *la manecilla pequeña señala las dos,* the little hand is pointing to two. 6 *(con el dedo)* to point at. 7 *(fijar - cita)* to arrange, make; *(fecha, lugar, precio)* to set, fix. 8 *(designar)* to appoint. 9 *(subrayar la importancia)* to stress, underline. – 10 **señalarse,** *p (distinguirse)* to distinguish os. 11 *(sobresalir)* to stand out.

señalización 1 *f (señales)* road signs *pl*; *(de aeropuerto, estación)* signposting, signs *pl*. 2 *(colocación)* signposting.

señalizar *t* to signpost.

▲ *Conjugation model* [4], *like* **realizar**.

señero,-a 1 *adj (solo)* alone. 2 *(único)* unique. 3 *(destacado)* outstanding: *figura señera,* outstanding figure. – 4 **señera,** *f* Catalan flag.

señor,-ra 1 *adj (noble)* distinguished, noble. 2 *fam* fine: *es un señor coche,* it's quite a car. – 3 *m,f (hombre)* man, gentleman; *(mujer)* woman, lady. 4 *(amo - hombre)* master; *(- mujer)* mistress. 5 HIST *(hombre)* lord; *(mujer)* lady. 6 *(tratamiento - hombre)* sir; *(- mujer)* madam, US ma'am: *buenos días, señora,* good morning, madam. 7 *(ante apellido - hombre)* Mr; *(- mujer)* Mrs: *el Sr. Rodríguez,* Mr Rodríguez. 8 *(ante título)* el *señor cura,* the priest. 9 *(en carta - hombre)* Sir; *(- mujer)* Madam: *muy señora mía,* Dear Madam; *estimados señores,* Dear Sir. – 10 **señora,** *f (esposa)* wife. – 11 **el Señor,** *m* REL the Lord. – 12 **señor,** *interj* good Lord!

● **ser todo un señor / ser toda una señora,** to be a real gentleman / be a real lady. ‖ **¡señoras y señores!,** ladies and gentlemen!

■ **el señor de la casa / la señora de la casa,** the gentleman of the house / the lady of the house. ‖

Nuestro Señor / Nuestra Señora, Our Lord / Our Lady. ‖ **señor feudal,** feudal lord. ‖ **señora de compañía,** companion.

señora *f* → **señor,-ra.**

señorear 1 *t* (*mandar*) to rule, control. 2 *fig* (*dominar - edificio*) to tower over; (- *persona*) to lord it over. 3 *fam* (*dar tratamiento*) to call sir. − 4 **señorearse,** *p* (*hacerse el señor*) to give os. airs, adopt a lofty manner.

señoría *f fml* (*para hombre*) lordship; (*para mujer*) ladyship.

señorial *adj* stately, majestic.

señorío 1 *m* (*mando*) dominion, rule. 2 (*territorio*) estate, domain. 3 (*en el porte*) elegance, distinction. 4 (*nobleza*) nobility; (*majestuosidad*) stateliness.

señorita 1 *f* (*mujer joven*) young woman; *fml* young lady. 2 (*tratamiento*) Miss: *Señorita Rodríguez,* Miss Rodríguez. 3 *fam* (*puro*) small cigar. 4 **la señorita,** EDUC the teacher, Miss.

señorito 1 *m* (*tratamiento*) master (of the house). 2 *fam pey* (*joven rico*) daddy's boy, rich kid.

señorón,-ona 1 *adj fam pey* high and mighty. − 2 *m,f fam pey* big shot.

señuelo 1 *m* decoy. 2 *fig* bait.

sepa *pres subj* → **saber.**

sépalo *m* sepal.

separable *adj* separable (**de,** from), detachable (**de,** from).

separación 1 *f* separation. 2 (*espacio*) space, gap.
■ **separación matrimonial / separación conyugal,** legal separation.

separadamente *adv* separately.

separado,-a 1 *pp* → **separar.** − 2 *adj* separate. 3 (*divorciado*) separated.
● **por separado,** separately, individually.

separador,-ra 1 *adj* separative. − 2 **separador,** *m* separator, divider.

separar 1 *t* (*gen*) to separate. 2 (*hacer grupos*) to separate, sort out: *separa las lentejas de los garbanzos,* separate the lentils from the chickpeas. 3 (*guardar aparte*) to set aside, put aside: *te he separado un trozo de pastel,* I've put aside a piece of cake for you. 4 (*apartar*) to move away (**de,** from): *separa la mesa de la pared,* move the table away from the wall. 5 (*de empleo, cargo*) to remove (**de,** from), dismiss (**de,** from). 6 *fig* (*mantener alejado*) to keep away (**de,** from). − 7 **separarse,** *p* (*tomar diferente camino*) to separate, part company. 8 (*matrimonio*) to separate. 9 (*apartarse*) to move away (**de,** from). 10 (*desprenderse*) to separate (**de,** from), come off (**de,** -). 11 (*de amigo etc*) to part company (**de,** with). 12 **separarse de,** (*dejar algo*) to part with: *no me separaré nunca de este libro,* I shall never part with this book.

separata *f* offprint.

separatismo *m* separatism.

separatista 1 *adj* separatist. − 2 *mf* separatist.

sepelio *m* burial, interment.

sepia 1 *f* (*pez*) cuttlefish. − 2 *adj* (*color*) sepia. − 3 *m* (*color*) sepia.

septenario,-a 1 *adj* septenary. − 2 **septenario,** *m* septenary.

septenio *m* septennium.

septentrión *m fml* north.

septentrional *adj* northern.

septicemia *f* septicaemia (US septicemia).

séptico,-a *adj* septic.
■ **fosa séptica,** septic tank.

septiembre *m* September.
▲ *See also* **marzo.**

séptimo,-a 1 *adj* seventh. − 2 *m,f* seventh.
▲ *See also* **sexto,-a.**

septuagenario,-a 1 *adj* septuagenarian. − 2 *m,f* septuagenarian.

septuagésimo,-a 1 *adj* seventieth. − 2 *m,f* seventieth.
▲ *See also* **sexto,-a.**

septuplicar *t* to septuple.
▲ *Conjugation model* |1|, *like* **sacar.**

sepulcral *adj* sepulchral.
■ **silencio sepulcral,** *fig* deathly silence.

sepulcro *m* tomb.
● **ser un sepulcro,** *fam* to keep mum.

sepultar *t* to bury.

sepultura 1 *f* (*lugar*) grave. 2 (*acto*) burial.
● **dar sepultura a algn.,** to bury sb.

sepulturero,-a *m,f* gravedigger.

sequedad 1 *f* dryness. 2 *fig* curtness, abruptness.

sequía *f* drought.

séquito 1 *m* (*personas*) entourage, retinue. 2 POL group of followers. 3 *fig* (*consecuencias*) aftermath.

ser 1 *i* (*gen*) to be: *Sócrates era filósofo,* Socrates was a philosopher; *mi primo es alemán,* my cousin is German; *Marta es rubia,* Marta is blonde; *la falda es azul,* the skirt is blue; *era verano,* it was summer; *fue en enero,* it was in January; *son las cuatro,* it's four o'clock; *éramos tres,* there were three of us; *es crema para las manos,* it's hand cream; *esa respuesta no es de caballero,* that isn't a gentlemanly answer. 2 (*pertenecer*) to be, belong (**de,** to): *estas sillas son nuestras,* these chairs are ours; *el coche es de Ana,* the car belongs to Ana; *¿de quién es este libro?,* whose book is this? 3 (*ser propio*) to be like (**de,** -): *es muy de Pilar,* it's just like Pilar. 4 (*costar*) to be, cost: *¿cuánto es?,* how much is it? 5 (*causar*) to cause, be. 6 (*consistir en*) to be, consist of. 7 (*suceder*) to happen (**de,** to): *¿qué fue de Iván?,* what happened to Iván? 8 (*ocurrir, tener lugar*) to take place, be held: *la reunión será en el salón de actos,* the meeting will be held in the assembly hall. − 9 *aux* (*pasiva*) to be: *fue encontrado por Raúl,* it was found by Raúl. − 10 *m* (*ente*) being. 11 (*esencia*) essence, substance. 12 (*valor*) core, heart. 13 (*vida*) life, existence. − 14 **ser de,** *i* (*proceder*) to be from, come from: *Santi es de Cáceres,* Santi is from Cáceres. 15 (*indica material*) to be made of: *la puerta es de madera,* the door is made of wood. 16 (*devenir*) to become of: *¡qué sería de nosotros sin ti!,* what would become of us without you! 17 (*estar escrito*) to be by, be written by: *es de García Márquez,* it's by García Márquez. 18 **ser de + inf,** (*ser digno*) to be worth: *es de ver,* it's worth seeing; *es de admirar,* she's to be admired.
● **a no ser por,** if it were not for, if it wasn't for. ‖ **a no ser que,** unless: *a no ser que cambie de opinión,* unless he changes his mind. ‖ **a poder ser,** if possible: *a poder ser mañana,* tomorrow if possible. ‖ **¡así sea!** / **¡sea!,** so be it!, right! ‖ **como debe ser,** as it should be. ‖ **¿cómo es eso? / ¿cómo puede ser?,** how can that be? ‖ **dar el ser,** *fml* to give life. ‖ **de no ser así,** otherwise, if not. ‖ **de no ser por ...,** had it not been for ... ‖ **érase una vez ...,** once upon a time ... ‖ **es de esperar que ... / es de desear que ...,** it's to be expected that ... / it's to be hoped that ... ‖ **es decir,** in other words, that is to say. ‖ **es más,** furthermore, what is more. ‖ **es que ...,** it's just that ... ‖ **lo que sea,** whatever, anything. ‖ **no es nada, ...,** it's all right, ... ‖ **no es para tanto,** it's not all that bad. ‖ **no será para tanto,** it won't come to that. ‖ **o sea,** that is, that is to say, I mean: *en el primer trimestre, o sea, en los primeros*

tres meses, in the first quarter, that is, in the first three months. ‖ **por si fuera poco,** to top it all, to make matters worse. ‖ **no puede ser,** it can't be true. ‖ **puede ser,** it's possible, it could be. ‖ **sea como sea,** in any case. ‖ **ser de lo que no hay,** *fam* to be a real winner. ‖ **ser muy suyo,-a,** *fam* to be quite a character. ‖ **siendo así,** that being the case. ‖ **un si es no es,** a trifle, a touch.
■ **ser humano,** human being. ‖ **Ser Supremo,** Supreme Being.
▲ *Conjugation model* [86].
SER *abr* RAD (*Sociedad Española de Radiodifusión*) Spanish private broadcasting company.
sera *f* pannier, large basket.
seráfico,-a *adj* seraphic, angelic.
serafín *m* seraph.
serbal *m* service tree.
serbio,-a 1 *adj* Serb, Serbian. − 2 *m,f* Serb, Serbian. − 3 serbio, *m* (*idioma*) Serbian.
serbocroata 1 *adj* Serbo-Croatian. − 2 *mf* Serbo-Croatian. − 3 *m* (*idioma*) Serbo-Croat.
serena *f* → **sereno,-a.**
serenar 1 *t* (*gen*) to calm. 2 *fig* (*a alguien*) to calm down. − 3 serenarse, *p* METEOR to clear up. 4 (*mar*) to grow calm. 5 *fig* (*persona*) to calm down.
serenata *f* serenade.
serenidad *f* serenity, calm.
● **conservar la serenidad,** to keep calm, remain calm.
sereno,-a 1 *adj* METEOR (*cielo*) clear; (*tiempo*) fine, good. 2 *fig* (*persona - tranquila*) calm; (- *no borracha*) sober. 3 *fig* (*ambiente etc*) calm, peaceful, quiet. − 4 sereno, *m* (*vigilante*) night watchman. 5 (*ambiente de la noche*) night air, night dew. − 6 serena, *f* serenade.
● **dormir al sereno,** to sleep out in the open.
serial *m* serial.
seriamente *adv* seriously.
seriar *t* to serialize.
▲ *Conjugation model* [12], *like cambiar.*
serie 1 *f* (*gen*) series. 2 (*conjunto*) series, string, succession: *una serie de accidentes,* a series of accidents.
● **fabricado,-a en serie,** mass-produced. ‖ **fuera de serie,** out of the ordinary, unique.
■ **fabricación en serie,** mass production. ‖ **serie mundial,** DEP world series. ‖ **asesino en serie,** serial killer.
seriedad 1 *f* (*gravedad*) seriousness, gravity: *nos lo dijo con toda seriedad,* he told us in all seriousness; *¡señores, un poco de seriedad, por favor!,* gentlemen, please be serious! 2 (*formalidad*) reliability, dependability.
● **con seriedad,** seriously.
■ **falta de seriedad,** irresponsibility.
serigrafía *f* serigraphy, silk-screen printing.
serio,-a 1 *adj* (*importante*) serious, grave. 2 (*severo*) serious. 3 (*formal*) reliable, responsible, dependable. 4 (*color*) sober; (*traje etc*) formal.
● **en serio,** seriously: *lo digo en serio,* I'm quite serious, I mean it. ‖ **¿en serio?,** are you serious?, do you really mean that?, really? ‖ **ir en serio,** to be true, be serious: *cuando nos lo dijo iba en serio,* when he told us about it he was quite serious. ‖ **tomar en serio,** to take seriously.
sermón 1 *m* REL sermon. 2 *fam* sermon, ticking-off, lecture.
● **echar un sermón a algn.,** to give sb. a lecture.

sermoneador,-ra 1 *adj fam* fault-finding, nit-picking. − 2 *m,f fam* fault-finder.
sermonear 1 *i* REL to preach. 2 *fam* (*reprender*) to lecture.
serología *f* serology.
seropositivo,-a 1 *adj* seropositive. 2 (*con el* VIH) HIV positive.
serosidad *f* serosity.
seroso,-a *adj* serous.
serpentear 1 *i* (*gen*) to crawl, wriggle. 2 (*camino*) to wind, twist; (*río*) to wind, meander.
serpenteo 1 *m* (*gen*) winding. 2 (*camino*) winding, twisting; (*río*) winding, meandering.
serpentín *m* coil.
serpentina 1 *f* (*de papel*) streamer. 2 (*piedra*) serpentine.
serpiente *f* snake.
■ **serpiente de cascabel,** rattlesnake. ‖ **serpiente pitón,** python.
serpol *m* wild thyme.
serrado,-a *pp* serrated, toothed.
serraduras *fpl* sawdust *sing.*
serrallo *m* harem.
serranía *f* mountain range, mountains *pl.*
serranilla *f* lyric composition.
serrano,-a 1 *adj* mountain, highland. − 2 *m,f* highlander.
■ **cuerpo serrano,** *fam* shapely figure.
serrar *t* to saw.
▲ *Conjugation model* [27], *like acertar.*
serrería *f* sawmill.
serrijón *m* secondary chain.
serrín *m* sawdust.
serrucho *m* handsaw.
servible *adj* usable, serviceable.
servicial *adj* obliging, helpful, accommodating.
servicio 1 *m* (*gen*) service. 2 (*criados*) servants *pl;* (*asistente*) domestic help. 3 (*juego, conjunto*) set: *servicio de té,* tea set. 4 (*favor*) service, favour (US favor). 5 DEP service, serve. 6 (*retrete*) toilet, US rest room.
● **entrar en servicio,** to come into operation. ‖ **estar al servicio de algn.,** to be at sb.'s service. ‖ **estar de servicio,** to be on duty. ‖ **hacer servicio / prestar servicio,** to do a favour (US favor). ‖ **hacer un flaco servicio,** *fam* to do more harm than good. ‖ **poner en servicio,** to put into operation. ‖ **prestar servicio,** to serve. ‖ **servicio incluido,** service charge included.
■ **servicio a domicilio,** home delivery service: *servicio a domicilio gratis,* free home delivery. ‖ **servicio de urgencias,** emergency service. ‖ **servicio militar,** military service. ‖ **servicios públicos,** public services, utilities.
▲ *In 6, also used in plural with the same meaning.*
servidor,-ra 1 *m,f* servant. 2 *euf* myself: *se lo trajo un servidor,* I brought it to you myself; *¿Francisco Reyes?, −servidor,* Francisco Reyes?, −yes? − 3 servidor, *m* MIL gunner. 4 INFORM server.
● **servidor,-ra de usted,** *fml* at your service. ‖ **su seguro,-a servidor,-ra,** *fml* (*en cartas*) Yours faithfully.
servidumbre 1 *f* (*condición*) servitude. 2 (*criados*) servants *pl,* staff of servants. 3 (*obligación*) obligation. 4 *fig* (*sujeción*) compulsion. 5 JUR servitude.
servil 1 *adj* (*humilde*) servile. 2 (*obediente*) subservient. 3 (*rastrero*) base.
servilismo 1 *m* (*humildad*) servility. 2 (*obediencia*) subservience.
servilleta *f* napkin, serviette.

servilletero *m* napkin ring, serviette ring.
servio,-a *adj-m,f-m* → **serbio,-a**.
servir 1 *t* (*gen*) to serve. 2 (*comida, bebida*) to serve, wait on. 3 (*ayudar*) to help: *¿en qué puedo servirle?*, how may I help you?, what can I do for you? 4 COM (*suministrar*) to serve, supply with; (*entregar*) to deliver. – 5 *i* (*gen*) to serve. 6 (*ser útil*) to be helpful, be a help: *aquel consejo me sirvió mucho,* that piece of advice was a great help to me. 7 (*objeto*) to be no good: *esto no sirve,* this is no good. 8 (*estar al servicio de otro*) to be a servant, be in service. 9 (*asistir a la mesa*) to serve (**en**, at), wait (**en**, at): *servir en la mesa,* to wait at table. 10 (*hacer la mili*) to do one's military service. – 11 servirse, *p* (*comida etc*) to serve os., help os.: *sírvete más patatas,* help yourself to more crisps. 12 (*usar*) to use (**de**, -), make use of (**de**, -). 13 *fml* (*en carta*) to be kind enough to: *sírvase responder lo antes posible,* please reply as soon as possible.
● **no servir para nada / no servir de nada,** to be useless, be no good: *quejarse no sirve de nada,* it's no good complaining. ‖ **para servirle,** *fml* at your service. ‖ **ponerse a servir,** to go into service. ‖ **servir a la patria,** to serve one's country. ‖ **servir de,** to serve as; (*persona*) to act as: *sirvió de mediador,* he acted as mediator; *si sirve de algo,* for what it's worth. ‖ **servir de aviso,** to serve as a warning. ‖ **servir para,** to be used for, be for: *sirve para dormir,* it's used for sleeping on; *también sirve para abrir latas,* it's also used for opening tins. ‖ **servir una causa,** to serve a cause. ‖ **servirse de algn.,** *fig* to take advantage of sb.
▲ *Conjugation model* [34].
servocroata *adj-m,f* → **serbocroata**.
servodirección *f* power steering.
servofreno *m* servo brake.
servomecanismo *m* servomechanism.
servomotor *m* servomotor.
sésamo *m* sesame.
● **¡ábrete sésamo!,** open sesame!
sesear *i* to pronounce Spanish *c* before *e* or *i*, and *z* as *s*.
sesenta 1 *adj* (*cardinal*) sixty; (*ordinal*) sixtieth. – 2 *m* (*número*) sixty.
● **los años sesenta / los sesenta,** the sixties.
▲ *See also* **seis**.
sesentavo,-a 1 *adj* sixtieth. – 2 *m,f* sixtieth.
▲ *See also* **sexto,-a**.
sesentón,-ona 1 *adj fam* sixty-year old. – 2 *m,f fam* sixty-year old.
seseo *m* pronunciation of Spanish *c*, before *e* or *i*, and *z* as *s*.
sesera *f fam* brain, brains *pl*.
sesgadura *f* cut on the bias, cut on a slant.
sesgar 1 *t* (*cortar*) to cut on the bias, cut on a slant. 2 (*torcer*) to slant.
▲ *Conjugation model* [7], *like* **llegar**.
sesgo 1 *m* (*torcimiento*) slant. 2 *fig* (*curso*) slant, turn.
● **al sesgo,** COST on the bias. ‖ **tomar un sesgo favorable / tomar un sesgo desfavorable,** *fig* to take a turn for the better / take a turn for the worse.
sesión 1 *f* (*reunión*) session, meeting. 2 CINEM showing.
● **celebrar una sesión,** to hold a meeting. ‖ **reanudar la sesión,** to resume the meeting. ‖ **se abre la sesión,** the meeting is declared open. ‖ **se cierra la sesión,** the meeting is adjourned.
■ **sesión continua,** continuous session. ‖ **sesión de noche,** late show. ‖ **sesión de tarde,** matinée. ‖ **sesión plenaria,** plenary session.

seso 1 *m* brain. 2 *fam fig* brains *pl*, grey matter, sense. – 3 sesos, *mpl* CULIN brains.
● **beber el seso / beberse el seso,** *fam* to lose one's mind. ‖ **calentarse los sesos / devanarse los sesos,** *fam* to rack one's brains. ‖ **tener sorbido el seso a algn. / tener sorbidos los sesos a algn.,** *fam* to have sb. under one's spell.
sestear *i* to have a nap.
sestercio *m* sesterce.
sesudo,-a 1 *adj* (*sensato*) sensible; (*prudente*) wise. 2 (*inteligente*) intelligent, brainy.
set *m* set.
▲ *pl* sets.
seta *f* (*comestible*) mushroom; (*no comestible*) toadstool.
setecientos,-as 1 *adj* (*cardinal*) seven hundred; (*ordinal*) seven-hundredth. – 2 setecientos, *m* (*número*) seven hundred.
▲ *See also* **seis**.
setenta 1 *adj* (*cardinal*) seventy; (*ordinal*) seventieth. – 2 *m* (*número*) seventy.
● **los años setenta / los setenta,** the seventies.
▲ *See also* **seis**.
setentavo,-a 1 *adj* seventieth. – 2 *m,f* seventieth.
▲ *See also* **sexto,-a**.
setentón,-ona 1 *adj* seventy-year-old. – 2 *m,f* seventy-year-old.
setiembre *m* → **septiembre**.
seto *m* hedge.
setter *m* setter.
seudónimo *m* (*gen*) pseudonym; (*de escritores*) pen name.
Seúl *m* Seoul.
s.e.u.o. *abr* (*salvo error u omisión*) errors and omissions excepted.
severidad 1 *f* (*gravedad*) severity, harshness. 2 (*rigurosidad*) strictness.
severo,-a 1 *adj* (*grave*) severe, harsh. 2 (*riguroso*) strict. 3 (*clima*) harsh, severe, bleak. 4 (*estilo*) stark, severe.
sevicia *f* cruelty.
Sevilla *f* Seville.
sevillano,-a 1 *adj* of Sevilla, from Sevilla. – 2 *m,f* person from Sevilla, inhabitant of Sevilla. – 3 sevillana, *f* popular song and dance from Seville.
sexagenario,-a 1 *adj* sexagenarian. – 2 *m,f* sexagenarian.
sexagesimal *adj* sexagesimal.
sexagésimo,-a 1 *adj* sixtieth. – 2 *m,f* sixtieth.
▲ *See also* **sexto,-a**.
sex-appeal *m* sex appeal.
sexenio *m* six-year period.
sexi 1 *adj* sexy. – 2 *m* sex appeal.
sexismo *m* sexism.
sexista 1 *adj* sexist. 2 (*machista*) chauvinistic. – 3 *m* sexist. 4 (*machista*) male chauvinist.
■ **discriminación sexista,** sex discrimination.
sexo 1 *m* sex. 2 (*órganos*) sexual organs *pl*, genitals *pl*.
■ **el bello sexo,** the fair sex. ‖ **el sexo débil,** the weaker sex.
sexología *f* sexology.
sexólogo,-a *m,f* sexologist.
sextante *m* sextant.
sexteto *m* sextet.
sexto,-a 1 *adj* sixth: *una sexta parte,* a sixth; *el siglo sexto,* the sixth century; *Alfonso sexto,* Alfonso the Sixth; *el capítulo sexto,* chapter six, the sixth chapter; *viven en*

el sexto piso, they live on the sixth floor; *viven en un sexto piso,* they live in a sixth-floor flat; *acabó en sexto lugar,* he finished in sixth place, he came sixth. – **2** *m,f* sixth: *le correspondió un sexto de la herencia,* he got a sixth of the inheritance.
■ **sexto sentido,** sixth sense.
sextuplicar *t* to sextuple.
▲ *Conjugation model* |1|, *like sacar.*
séxtuplo,-a 1 *adj* sextuple. – **2 séxtuplo,** *m* sextuple.
sexuado,-a *adj* sexed.
sexual *adj* (*gen*) sex; (*relaciones*) sexual: *vida sexual,* sex life.
sexualidad *f* sexuality.
sexualmente *adv* sexually.
sexy 1 *adj* sexy. – **2** *m* sex appeal.
Seychelles las (islas) Seychelles, *mpl* the Seychelles.
s/f *abr* (*su favor*) your favour (us favor).
s.f. *abr* (*sin fecha*) not dated.
SGAE *abr* (*Sociedad General de Autores de España*) Spanish writers' and composers' association.
sha *m* shah.
▲ *pl shas.*
shah *m* shah.
▲ *pl shahs.*
shérif *m* sheriff.
▲ *pl shérifs.*
sherpa *m* sherpa.
shetland *m* Shetland wool.
shock *m* shock.
short *m* shorts *pl.*
▲ *pl shorts.*
show 1 *m* (*espectáculo*) show. **2** *fam* (*numerito*) show, display.
● **montar un show,** *fam* to make a scene.
▲ *pl shows.*
si[1] 1 *conj* (*condicional*) if: *si quieres puedes venir con nosotros,* you can come with us if you want to. **2** (*disyuntiva, duda*) if, whether: *no sé si decírselo (o no),* I don't know whether to tell her (or not). **3** (*énfasis*) but: *¡si yo no quería!,* but I didn't want to!; *¡pero si es facilísimo!,* ¡but it's really easy!
● **como si,** as if. ‖ **como si nada / como si tal cosa,** as if it were nothing at all. ‖ **por si acaso,** just in case: *llévatelo por si acaso,* take it with you just in case. ‖ **si bien,** although, even though.
si[2] *m* MÚS ti, si, B.
▲ *pl sis.*
sí[1] 1 *pron* (*él*) himself; (*ella*) herself; (*cosa*) itself; (*ellos, ellas*) themselves; (*usted*) yourself; (*ustedes*) yourselves: *lo hizo por sí misma,* she did it by herself; *hablaban para sí,* they were talking to themselves. **2** (*uno mismo*) oneself. **3** (*recíproco*) each other: *hablaban entre sí,* they were talking to each other.
● **de por sí / en sí,** in itself. ‖ **estar fuera de sí,** to be beside os. ‖ **estar sobre sí,** to be on one's guard. ‖ **mirar para sí mismo,-a,** to look after os.
sí[2] 1 *adv* yes: *dijo que sí,* she said yes; *a ella no le gusta pero a mí sí,* she doesn't like it but I do. **2** (*enfático*) of course: *sí que me gusta,* of course I like it; *ése sí que me gusta,* I really like that one. – **3** *m* yes.
● **¡claro que sí!,** of course! ‖ **creo que sí,** I think so. ‖ **dar el sí,** to say yes, accept, agree. ‖ **¡eso sí que no!,** certainly not! ‖ **porque sí,** (*sin razón*) just because I (*you, etc*) say so; (*por naturaleza*) that's the way it is: *¡lo harás porque sí!,* you'll do it because I say so!; *no puedes marcharte porque sí,* you can't leave just because you feel like it. ‖ **¡que sí!,** yes, I tell you!

■ **síes y noes,** yeas and nays.
▲ *In 3, pl síes.*
sial *m* sial.
Siam *m* Siam.
siamés,-esa 1 *adj* Siamese. – **2** *m,f* (*persona*) Siamese. – **3 siamés,** *m* (*idioma*) Siamese.
■ **hermano,-a siamés,-esa,** Siamese twin.
sibarita 1 *adj* sybarite, sybaritic. – **2** *mf* sybarite, bon vivant.
sibaritismo *m* sybaritism.
siberiano,-a 1 *adj* Siberian. – **2** *m,f* Siberian.
sibila *f* sibyl.
sibilante 1 *adj* sibilant. – **2** *f* sibilant.
sibilino,-a 1 *adj* sibylline. **2** *fig* cryptic, enigmatic.
sic *adv* sic.
sicalíptico,-a *adj* suggestive, erotic, pornographic.
sicario *m* hired gunman; *fam* heavy, thug.
Sicilia *f* Sicily.
siciliano,-a 1 *adj* Sicilian. – **2** *m,f* Sicilian.
sicoanálisis *m* psychoanalysis.
▲ *pl sicoanálisis.*
sicoanalista *mf* psychoanalyst.
sicoanalítico,-a *adj* → **psicoanalítico,-a.**
sicoanalizar *t-p* → **psicoanalizar.**
sicodélico,-a *adj* → **psicodélico,-a.**
sicodrama *m* psychodrama.
sicofanta *m* imposter, fake.
sicofante *m* → **sicofanta.**
sicofármaco *m* psychoactive drug.
sicología *f* psychology.
sicológicamente *adv* psychologically.
sicológico,-a *adj* psychological.
sicólogo,-a *m,f* psychologist.
sicomoro *m* sycamore.
sicómoro *m* sycamore.
sicomotriz *f* → **psicomotriz.**
sicópata *mf* → **psicópata.**
sicopatía *f* psychopathy.
sicopático,-a *adj* psychopathic.
sicopatología *f* psychopathology.
sicosis *f* psychosis.
▲ *pl sicosis.*
sicosomático,-a *adj* psychosomatic.
sicoterapeuta *mf* psychotherapist.
sicoterapia *f* psychotherapy.
sicótico,-a *adj* → **psicótico,-a.**
SIDA *abr* MED (*síndrome de inmunodeficiencia adquirida*) acquired immune deficiency syndrome; (*abreviatura*) AIDS.
sidecar *m* sidecar.
▲ *pl sidecares.*
sideral *adj* sideral, astral.
■ **espacio sideral,** outer space.
siderita *f* siderite.
siderurgia *f* iron and steel industry.
siderúrgico,-a *adj* iron and steel.
sidra *f* cider, US hard cider.
siega 1 *f* (*acción*) harvesting, reaping. **2** (*época*) harvest, harvest time. **3** (*mieses*) harvest.
siembra 1 *f* (*acción*) sowing. **2** (*época*) sowing time. **3** (*sembrado*) sown field.
siempre *adv* always: *siempre recordaré sus palabras,* I'll always remember her words; *siempre dice eso,* that's what he always says.

● **a la hora de siempre,** at the usual time. ‖ **amigos de siempre,** old friends, lifelong friends. ‖ **como siempre,** as usual. ‖ **la historia de siempre / lo de siempre,** the same old story. ‖ **para siempre,** forever, for good. ‖ **para siempre jamás,** for ever and ever. ‖ **siempre pasa lo mismo,** it's always the same. ‖ **siempre que,** (*cada vez que*) whenever; (*a condición de que*) provided, as long as: *cógelo siempre que quieras,* take it whenever you want; *siempre que cumpla su palabra,* as long as he keeps his promise. ‖ **siempre y cuando,** provided, as long as.

siempreviva *f* everlasting flower, immortelle.

sien *f* temple.

siena *adj* sienna, dark yellow.

sierpe 1 *f* (*serpiente*) serpent. 2 *fig* (*con mal genio*) bad-tempered person; (*feo*) ugly person.

sierra 1 *f* TÉC saw. 2 GEOG mountain range.
■ **sierra circular,** circular saw. ‖ **sierra de calar,** fretsaw. ‖ **sierra mecánica,** power saw.

Sierra Leona *f* Sierra Leone.

sierraleonés,-esa 1 *adj* Sierra Leonean. − 2 *m,f* Sierra Leonean.

siervo,-a 1 *m,f* (*esclavo*) slave. 2 HIST serf.
■ **siervo,-a de Dios,** REL servant of God.

siesta *f* siesta, afternoon nap.
● **dormir la siesta / echar la siesta,** to have a siesta, have an afternoon nap.
■ **la hora de la siesta,** siesta time. ‖ **la siesta del carnero,** a nap before lunch.

siete 1 *adj* (*cardinal*) seven; (*séptimo*) seventh. − 2 *m* (*número*) seven. 3 *fam* (*rasgón*) tear.
● **hablar más que siete,** *fam* to talk nineteen to the dozen.
▲ *See also* **seis**.

sietemesino,-a 1 *adj* seven-month. − 2 *m,f* baby born two months premature. 3 *fig* (*raquítico*) weakling. 4 *fam pey* (*presumido*) little squirt.

sífilis *f* syphilis.
▲ *pl* **sífilis**.

sifilítico,-a 1 *adj* syphilitic. − 2 *m,f* syphilitic.

sifón 1 *m* (*tubo encorvado*) siphon. 2 (*tubo acodado*) U-bend, trap. 3 (*bebida*) soda, soda water. 4 (*botella*) soda siphon.

sig. *abr* (*siguiente*) following; (*abreviatura*) fol.

sigilo 1 *m* (*secreto*) secrecy. 2 (*discreción*) discretion.
● **con mucho sigilo,** in great secrecy.
■ **sigilo sacramental,** secrecy of the confessional.

sigilografía *f* sigillography.

sigilosamente 1 *adv* (*discretamente*) discreetly. 2 (*en secreto*) secretly. 3 (*silenciosamente*) quietly.

sigiloso,-a 1 *adj* (*discreto*) secretive. 2 (*secreto* - *asunto*) secret; (*- persona*) secretive. 3 (*silencioso*) quiet.

sigla *f* acronym, abbreviation.

siglo 1 *m* century. 2 *fig* (*vida mundana*) world.
● **hace un siglo que ... / hace siglos que ...,** I (*we, they, etc*) haven't ... for ages: *hace siglos que no voy al cine,* I haven't been to the cinema for ages. ‖ **por los siglos de los siglos,** for ever and ever.
■ **el Siglo de las Luces,** the Eighteenth Century. ‖ **el Siglo de Oro,** the Golden Age.

sigma *f* sigma.

signar 1 *t* (*marcar*) to mark. 2 (*firmar*) to sign. 3 REL to make the sign of the cross over. − 4 **signarse,** *p* REL to make the sign of the cross, cross os.

signatario,-a 1 *adj* signatory. − 2 *m,f* signatory.

signatura 1 *f* (*en biblioteca*) catalogue (us catalog) number. 2 (*firma*) signature. 3 (*en impresión*) signature.

significación 1 *f* (*sentido*) meaning. 2 (*trascendencia*) significance.

significado,-a 1 *pp* → **significar**. − 2 *adj* well-known, important. − 3 **significado,** *m* meaning. 4 LING signifier.

significante *m* significant.

significar 1 *t* to mean: *no sé lo que significa,* I don't know what it means. 2 (*hacer saber*) to make known, express. − 3 **significarse,** *p* to stand out.
▲ *Conjugation model* [1], *like* **sacar**.

significativamente 1 *adv* (*dando a entender*) meaningfully. 2 (*con importancia*) significantly.

significativo,-a 1 *adj* (*que da a entender*) meaningful. 2 (*importante*) significant.

signo 1 *m* (*gen*) sign: *es un signo del tiempo en que vivimos,* it's a sign of the times we're living in; *¿de qué signo eres? −soy Tauro,* ¿what sign are you? −I'm Taurus. 2 GRAM mark. 3 (*destino*) fate, destiny. 4 (*tendencia*) tendency.
■ **signo de admiración / signo de interrogación,** exclamation mark / question mark. ‖ **signo de sumar,** plus sign. ‖ **signo del zodiaco,** zodiac sign.

sigo *pres indic* → **seguir**.

siguemepollo *m* ribbon on the back of a dress.

siguiente *adj* following, next: *lo vio la semana siguiente,* she saw him the following week; *vamos a leer el capítulo siguiente,* we're going to read the next chapter.
● **¡el siguiente!,** next, please!

sij 1 *adj* Sikh. − 2 *mf* Sikh.
▲ *pl* **sijs**.

sílaba *f* syllable.

silabario *m* spelling book.

silabear *i* to divide words into syllables.

silábico,-a *adj* syllabic.

silba *f* hissing.

silbar 1 *i* to whistle. 2 (*abuchear*) to hiss, boo.

silbato *m* whistle.

silbido 1 *m* (*acción*) whistle, whistling. 2 (*abucheo*) hissing. 3 (*del teléfono*) ring, ringing.

silbo *m* whistle, whistling.

silenciador 1 *m* (*de arma*) silencer. 2 AUTO silencer, US muffler.

silenciar 1 *t* (*ocultar*) to hush up. 2 (*pasar por alto*) not to mention. 3 (*las armas*) to silence.
▲ *Conjugation model* [12], *like* **cambiar**.

silencio *m* silence.
● **en silencio,** in silence. ‖ **guardar silencio,** to keep quiet. ‖ **imponer silencio a algn.,** to make sb. be quiet. ‖ **romper el silencio,** to break the silence.

silencioso,-a *adj* (*persona*) quiet; (*objeto*) silent.

silepsis *f* syllepsis.
▲ *pl* **silepsis**.

sílex *m* flint.
▲ *pl* **sílex**.

sílfide *f* sylph.

silicato *m* silicate.

sílice *f* silica.

silícico,-a *adj* silicic.

silicio *m* silicon.

silicona *f* silicone.

silicosis *f* silicosis.
▲ *pl* **silicosis**.

silla 1 *f* chair. 2 (*de montar*) saddle. 3 (*en la Academia*) seat.
■ **silla de montar,** saddle. ‖ **silla de ruedas,** wheelchair. ‖ **silla plegable / silla de tijera,** folding chair.

sillar 1 *m* (*piedra*) ashlar. **2** (*de caballería*) horse's back.
sillería 1 *f* (*sillas*) chairs *pl*, set of chairs *pl*. **2** (*del coro*) choir stalls *pl*. **3** (*taller*) chairmaker's workshop. **4** ARQ ashlar.
sillín *m* saddle.
sillón 1 *m* armchair. **2** (*de montar*) side-saddle. **3** (*en la Academia*) seat.
silo *m* silo.
silogismo *m* syllogism.
silogizar *i* to syllogize.
▲ *Conjugation model* [4], *like* **realizar**.
silueta 1 *f* (*contorno*) silhouette. **2** (*figura*) figure, shape.
siluetear *t* to silhouette.
silva 1 *f* (*colección*) miscellany. **2** (*poema*) type of poem.
silvestre *adj* wild: *una fresa silvestre,* a wild strawberry.
silvicultor,-ra *m,f* forestry expert.
silvicultura *f* forestry.
sima *f* abyss, chasm.
simbiosis *f* symbiosis.
▲ *pl* **simbiosis**.
simbiótico,-a *adj* symbiotic.
simbólico,-a *adj* symbolic, symbolical.
simbolismo *m* symbolism.
simbolista 1 *adj* symbolist. – **2** *mf* symbolist.
simbolizar *t* to symbolize.
▲ *Conjugation model* [4], *like* **realizar**.
símbolo *m* symbol.
simetría *f* symmetry.
simétrico,-a *adj* symmetric, symmetrical.
simiente *f* seed.
simiesco,-a *adj* simian, apelike.
símil 1 *adj* (*parecido*) similar. – **2** *m* (*comparación*) comparison. **3** (*semejanza*) resemblance, similarity. **4** LIT simile.
similar *adj* similar.
similitud *f* similarity, resemblance.
similor *m* pinchbeck.
simio *m* simian, monkey.
simonía *f* simony.
simoníaco,-a 1 *adj* simoniacal. – **2** *m,f* simoniac.
simpatía 1 *f* (*cordialidad*) affection (**por,** for), liking (**por,** for). **2** (*amabilidad*) warmth, pleasantness: *la simpatía no es su punto fuerte,* pleasantness isn't one of his strong points. **3** (*afinidad*) affinity (**por,** with). **4** (*solidaridad*) sympathy (**por,** towards), solidarity (**con,** with). **5** MED sympathy.
● **cogerle simpatía a algn.,** to take a liking to sb. ‖ **ganarse las simpatías de algn.,** to win sb.'s affection. ‖ **tener simpatía a algn.,** to be very fond of sb.
■ **simpatías y antipatías,** likes and dislikes.
simpático,-a 1 *adj* (*amable*) nice, likeable; (*agradable*) kind, friendly; (*encantador*) charming: *Pepe me cae simpático,* I think Pepe's a nice guy. **2** MED sympathetic.
● **hacerse el simpático / hacerse la simpática,** to ingratiate os. (**con,** with), butter up (**con,**-): *se pasa el día haciéndose el simpático con el jefe,* he spends all day buttering up his boss.
simpatizante 1 *adj* supporting. – **2** *mf* supporter.
simpatizar *i* (*con persona*) to get on (**con,** with): *es difícil simpatizar con él,* it's difficult to get on with him; *simpatizamos enseguida,* we hit it off at once. **2** (*con idea etc*) to sympathize (**con,** with).
▲ *Conjugation model* [4], *like* **realizar**.
simple 1 *adj* (*gen*) simple. **2** (*único*) single, just one: *con una simple llamada lo hubiera arreglado,* he could have settled it with just one phone call. **3** (*mero*) mere. **4**

(*persona*) simple, simple-minded. – **5** *mf* simpleton. – **6** *m* (*tenis*) singles *pl*.
● **por simple descuido,** through sheer carelessness.
simplemente *adv* simply.
simpleza 1 *f* (*idiotez*) simple-mindedness. **2** (*tontería*) nonsense.
simplicidad 1 *f* simplicity. **2** (*ingenuidad*) naïvety, ingenuousness.
simplificación *f* simplification.
simplificar *t* to simplify.
▲ *Conjugation model* [1], *like* **sacar**.
simplismo *m* simplism, oversimplification.
simplista 1 *adj* simplistic, oversimple. – **2** *mf* simplistic person.
simplón,-ona 1 *adj* simple, naïve. – **2** *m,f* simpleton.
simposio *m* symposium.
simulación *f* simulation.
simulacro *m* sham, pretence (US pretense): *un simulacro de ataque,* a mock attack; *simulacro de incendio,* fire drill.
simulado,-a 1 *pp* → **simular**. – **2** *adj* simulated.
simulador,-ra 1 *adj* simulative. – **2** *m,f* pretender. – **3** simulador, *m* TÉC simulator.
simular 1 *t* to simulate: *los especialistas simularon un accidente espectacular,* the stuntmen simulated a spectacular accident. **2** (*fingir*) to pretend.
simultáneamente *adv* simultaneously, at the same time.
simultanear 1 *t* (*hacer dos cosas*) to do simultaneously, do at the same time. **2** (*combinar*) to combine: *simultanea los estudios y el deporte,* he combines studies and sport.
simultaneidad *f* simultaneity.
simultáneo,-a *adj* simultaneous.
simún *m* simoom.
sin 1 *prep* (*carencia*) without. **2** (*además de*) not counting.
● **estar sin algo,** to be out of sth.: *estamos sin leche,* we're out of milk. ‖ **estar sin** + *inf,* not to have been + *pp*: *está sin planchar,* it hasn't been ironed; *estaba todo sin acabar,* it was all unfinished; *estoy sin comer nada desde las ocho,* I haven't eaten anything since eight o'clock. ‖ **quedarse sin algo,** to run out of sth. ‖ **seguir sin,** to still not: *sigue sin saberlo,* she still doesn't know; *sigo sin entenderlo,* I still can't understand it. ‖ **sin casar,** unmarried. ‖ **sin lo cual,** otherwise. ‖ **sin más ni más,** without further ado. ‖ **sin que** + *subj,* without + -*ing*: *entró sin que lo oyéramos,* he came in without us hearing him. ‖ **sin querer,** accidentally, by mistake: *lo hizo sin querer,* he didn't mean to do it. ‖ **sin vergüenza,** shameless.
sinagoga *f* synagogue (US synagog).
sinalefa *f* synaloepha (US sinalepha).
sinalgia *f* synalgia.
sinapismo 1 *m* MED mustard plaster. **2** *fam fig* bore, drag.
sinceramente *adv* sincerely.
sincerarse 1 *p* (*exculparse*) to exonerate os. **2** (*abrirse*) to open one's heart (**con,** to).
sinceridad *f* sincerity.
● **con toda sinceridad,** in all sincerity.
sincero,-a *adj* sincere.
sinclinal *m* syncline.
síncopa 1 *f* MÚS syncopation. **2** LING syncope.
sincopado,-a 1 *pp* → **sincopar**. – **2** *adj* MÚS syncopated.

sincopar 1 *t* MÚS LING to syncopate. **2** *fig* to abridge.
síncope *m* syncope.
sincretismo *m* syncretism.
sincronía *f* synchrony.
sincrónico,-a *adj* synchronic.
sincronismo *m* synchronism.
sincronización *f* synchronization.
sincronizar *t* to synchronize.
▲ *Conjugation model* |4|, *like realizar.*
sindicación 1 *f* (*sindicalismo*) trade unionism. **2** (*afiliación*) joining of a trade union.
sindicado,-a 1 *pp* → **sindicar.** – **2** *adj* who belongs to a trade union.
sindical *adj* trade union, union.
sindicalismo *m* trade unionism, unionism.
sindicalista 1 *adj* trade union, union. – **2** *mf* trade unionist, unionist.
sindicar 1 *t* to unionize. – **2 sindicarse,** *p* (*unirse a un sindicato*) to join a trade union. **3** (*formar un sindicato*) to form a trade union.
▲ *Conjugation model* |1|, *like sacar.*
sindicato *m* trade union, union.
síndico 1 *m* POL elected representative. **2** (*depositario*) trustee.
síndrome *m* syndrome.
sinécdoque *f* synecdoche.
sinecura *f* sinecure.
sine die *loc adv* sine die.
sinéresis *f* synaeresis (US syneresis).
sinergia *f* synergy.
sinestesia *f* synaesthesia (US synesthesia).
sinfín *m* endless number: *tuvieron un sinfín de problemas,* they had no end of problems.
sinfonía *f* symphony.
sinfónico,-a *adj* symphonic.
Singapur *m* Singapore.
singladura 1 *f* MAR day's run. **2** *fig* path, road, course: *recordó la singladura de su vida,* he recalled the course his life had taken.
single 1 *m* (*tenis*) singles *pl.* **2** (*disco*) single.
singular 1 *adj* (*único*) singular, single. **2** (*excepcional*) extraordinary, exceptional. **3** (*raro*) peculiar, odd. – **4** *m* GRAM singular.
● **en singular,** GRAM in the singular.
singularidad 1 *f* (*unicidad*) singularity. **2** (*excepcionalidad*) strangeness, uniqueness. **3** (*rareza*) peculiarity.
singularizar 1 *t* (*distinguir*) to distinguish, single out. **2** GRAM to use in the singular. – **3 singularizarse,** *p* to distinguish os. (**por,** by/with), stand out (**por,** for).
▲ *Conjugation model* |4|, *like realizar.*
sinhueso *f fam* tongue.
● **darle a la sinhueso,** *fam* to natter.
siniestra *f* → **siniestro,-a.**
siniestrado,-a *adj* damaged.
siniestro,-a 1 *adj lit* (*izquierdo*) left, left-hand. **2** (*malo*) sinister, ominous. **3** (*funesto*) fateful, disastrous. – **4** siniestro, *m* disaster, catastrophe; (*accidente*) accident; (*incendio*) fire. – **5 siniestra,** *f* (*izquierda*) left hand.
■ siniestro total, (*coche*) write-off.
sinnúmero *m* endless number.
sino¹ 1 *conj* (*contraposición*) but: *no es blanco sino negro,* it isn't white but black. **2** (*excepción*) but, except for: *nadie lo sabe sino Antonio,* nobody knows except for Antonio.
● **no sólo ... sino ...,** not only ... but ...: *merece nuestro agradecimiento no sólo por habernos ayudado sino también por haber confiado en nosotros,* he deserves our thanks not only for helping us but also for placing his trust in us.
**sino² ** *m* (*destino*) fate, destiny.
sínodo *m* synod.
sinología *f* sinology.
sinonimia *f* synonymy.
sinónimo,-a 1 *adj* synonymous. – **2 sinónimo,** *m* synonym.
sinopsis *f* synopsis.
▲ *pl sinopsis.*
sinóptico,-a *adj* synoptic, synoptical.
sinovia *f* synovia.
sinrazón *f* wrong, injustice.
sinsabor *m fig* worry, trouble, heartache.
▲ *Often used in plural.*
sinsubstancia *mf fam* flighty person, fly-by-night.
sintáctico,-a *adj* syntactic, syntactical.
sintagma *m* phrase.
■ sintagma nominal, noun phrase.
sintaxis *f* syntax.
▲ *pl sintaxis.*
síntesis *f* synthesis.
▲ *pl síntesis.*
sintético,-a *adj* synthetic.
sintetizador *m* synthesizer.
sintetizar 1 *t* to synthesize. **2** (*resumir*) to summarize: *sintetizando diría que...,* to sum up, I'd like to say that...
▲ *Conjugation model* |4|, *like realizar.*
sintoísmo *m* Shinto, Shintoism.
sintoísta *mf* Shintoist.
síntoma *m* symptom.
sintomático,-a 1 *adj* symptomatic. **2** *fig* significant.
sintomatología *f* symptomatology.
sintonía 1 *f* ELÉC RAD tuning: *aquí en la sintonía de Radio Terrassa...,* here on Radio Terrassa... **2** (*música*) signature tune. **3** *fig* (*armonía*) harmony.
● **estar en sintonía con algn.,** to get on well with sb.
sintonización 1 *f* tuning. **2** *fig* harmony.
sintonizador 1 *m* (*botón*) tuning knob. **2** (*de cadena de sonido*) tuner.
sintonizar 1 *t* RAD to tune in to: *sintonizó una emisora local,* he tuned in to a local radio station. – **2** *i fig* (*llevarse bien*) to get on well, be on the same wavelength.
▲ *Conjugation model* |4|, *like realizar.*
sinuosidad 1 *f* (*cualidad*) sinuosity. **2** (*curva*) bend, curve. **3** *fig* (*de argumento etc*) tortuousness; (*de persona*) deviousness.
sinuoso,-a 1 *adj* (*camino*) winding. **2** *fig* (*argumento*) tortuous; (*persona*) devious.
sinusitis *f* sinusitis.
▲ *pl sinusitis.*
sinvergüencería 1 *f fam* (*defecto*) shamelessness. **2** *fam* (*acto*) dirty trick.
sinvergüenza 1 *adj* (*pícaro*) shameless. **2** (*descarado*) cheeky. – **3** *mf* (*pícaro*) rotter, swine, louse. **4** (*descarado*) cheeky devil.
sionismo *m* Zionism.
sionista 1 *adj* Zionist. – **2** *mf* Zionist.
sique *f* psyche.
siquiatra *mf* psychiatrist.
siquiatría *f* psychiatry.
siquiátrico,-a *adj-m* → **psiquiátrico,-a.**
síquico,-a *adj* → **psíquico,-a.**

siquiera 1 *conj* (*adversativa*) even though, even if: *quisiera hablar contigo, siquiera fuera un momento,* I would like to speak to you, even if it's only for a moment. 2 (*distributiva*) whether. – 3 *adv* (*por lo menos*) at least: *dame siquiera la mitad,* give me at least half of it.
● **ni siquiera,** not even: *ni siquiera recuerda su nombre,* he can't even remember his name.
sir *m* sir.
▲ *pl sires.*
sirena 1 *f* (*ninfa*) siren, mermaid. 2 (*alarma*) siren.
■ **sirena de niebla,** foghorn.
sirga *f* rope, tow-rope, tow-line.
sirgar *t* to tow.
▲ Conjugation model [7], like *llegar.*
Siria *f* Syria.
sirimiri *m* fine drizzle.
sirio,-a 1 *adj* Syrian. – 2 *m,f* Syrian.
sirla *f arg* mugging.
sirlar *t arg* to mug.
sirlero,-a *m,f arg* mugger.
siroco *m* sirocco (wind).
sirope *m* syrup.
sirte *m* sandbank.
sirviente,-a *m,f* servant.
sisa 1 *f* COST armhole. 2 (*hurto*) petty theft, pilfering, filching.
sisal *m* sisal.
sisar 1 *t* COST to dart, take in. 2 (*hurtar*) to pilfer, pinch, nick; (*estafar*) to cheat.
sisear 1 *i* to hiss. – 2 *t* to hiss.
siseo *m* hiss, hissing.
sísmico,-a *adj* seismic.
sismo *m* earthquake, tremor.
sismógrafo *m* seismograph.
sismología *f* seismology.
sismológico,-a *adj* seismological.
sisón[1] *m* (*ave*) little bustard.
sisón,-ona[2] 1 *adj fam* pilfering, pinching, filching. – 2 *m,f fam* petty thief, pilferer.
sistema *m* system.
● **por sistema,** as a rule.
■ **sistema cableado,** hard-wired system. ‖ **sistema de ecuaciones,** simultaneous equations *pl.* ‖ **sistema experto,** expert system. ‖ **sistema métrico decimal,** decimal metric system. ‖ **sistema montañoso,** mountain chain. ‖ **sistema nervioso,** nervous system. ‖ **sistema operativo,** operative system. ‖ **sistema planetario,** planetary system. ‖ **sistema solar,** solar system.
sistemáticamente *adv* systematically.
sistemático,-a *adj* systematic.
sistematizar *t* to systematize.
▲ Conjugation model [4], like *realizar.*
sístole *f* systole.
sitar *m* sitar.
sitiado,-a 1 *pp* → **sitiar.** – 2 *adj* beseiged. – 3 *m,f* beseiged.
sitial *m* seat of honour (US honor).
sitiar *t* to besiege, lay siege to.
▲ Conjugation model [12], like *cambiar.*
sitio 1 *m* (*lugar*) place. 2 (*espacio*) space, room: *hay mucho sitio,* there's plenty of room. 3 (*asiento*) seat. 4 MIL siege.
● **cambiar algo de sitio,** to move sth. ‖ **cambiar de sitio con algn.,** to change places with sb. ‖ **en cualquier sitio,** anywhere. ‖ **en estado de sitio,** MIL in a

state of siege. ‖ **en todos los sitios,** everywhere. ‖ **guardar sitio a algn.,** to keep a seat for sb. ‖ **hacer sitio,** to make room (**a,** for). ‖ **levantar el sitio,** MIL to raise the siege. ‖ **ocupar mucho sitio,** to take up a lot of space. ‖ **poner sitio,** MIL to besiege. ‖ **quedarse en el sitio,** *fig* to snuff it, kick the bucket.
sito,-a *adj fml* located, situated.
situación 1 *f* (*circunstancia*) situation: *la situación política,* the political situation. 2 (*posición*) position: *su situación social,* his social position. 3 (*emplazamiento*) situation, location.
situado,-a 1 *pp* → **situar.** – 2 *adj* situated, located.
● **estar bien situado,-a,** *fig* to be comfortably off.
situar 1 *t* to place, locate, situate, put: *no puedo situarlo en el mapa,* I can't locate it on the map. – 2 **situarse,** *p* (*colocarse*) to be placed, be located, be situated. 3 (*lograr una posición*) to get on, do well, be successful.
▲ Conjugation model [11], like *actuar.*
siux 1 *adj* Sioux. – 2 *mf* Sioux.
▲ *pl siux.*
skay *m* leatherette.
sketch *m* sketch.
▲ *pl sketchs.*
s/L *abr* (*su letra, su letra de crédito*) your letter of credit; (*abreviatura*) your L/C.
s.l. *abr* (*sus labores*) housewife.
S.L. *abr* (*Sociedad Limitada*) Limited Company; (*abreviatura*) Ltd. Co.
slálom *m* slalom.
▲ *pl sláloms.*
slip *m* → **eslip.**
slogan *m* → **eslogan.**
S.M. *abr* (*Su Majestad*) His Majesty, Her Majesty; (*abreviatura*) HM.
S.M.C. *abr* (*Su Majestad Católica*) His Catholic Majesty, Her Catholic Majesty; (*abreviatura*) HCM.
SME *abr* (*Sistema Monetario Europeo*) European Monetary System; (*abreviatura*) EMS.
S.M.I. *abr* (*Su Majestad Imperial*) His Imperial Majesty, Her Imperial Majesty; (*abreviatura*) HIM.
smoking *m* → **esmoquin.**
s/n *abr* (*sin número*) no number.
snob *adj-mf* → **esnob.**
snobismo *m* → **esnobismo.**
so[1] *prep fml* under.
● **so pena de,** under penalty of, on pain of.
so[2] *interj fam: ¡so tonto!,* you damned fool!
so[3] *interj* (*para caballerías*) whoa!
SO *sím* (*suroeste*) southwest; (*símbolo*) SW.
s/o *abr* (*su orden*) your order; (*abreviatura*) your o.
soasar *t* to roast lightly.
soba 1 *f* (*acción de sobar*) fondling, groping, pawing. 2 *fig* (*zurra*) hiding, thrashing.
sobaco *m* armpit.
sobado,-a 1 *pp* → **sobar.** – 2 *adj* (*desgastado*) worn, shabby. 3 (*manoseado*) well-thumbed, dog-eared. 4 *fig* (*manido*) well-worn.
sobajar *t* to crumple, mess up.
sobaquera *f* dress shield.
sobaquina *f fam* underarm odour (US odor).
sobar 1 *t* (*ablandar*) to knead. 2 *fig* (*manosear - objeto*) to finger; (*- persona*) to grope, paw, touch up. 3 *fig* (*pegar*) to thrash. 4 *fam* (*molestar*) to pester. 5 *arg* (*dormir*) to sleep.
sobeo *m fam* groping, fondling, fingering.

soberanamente *adv* extremely, supremely.
soberanía *f* sovereignty.
● **bajo la soberanía de,** under the rule of.
soberano,-a 1 *adj* sovereign. 2 *fig* extreme, supreme. 3 *fam* huge, great. – 4 *m,f* sovereign.
soberbia *f* → **soberbio,-a**.
soberbiamente 1 *adv* (*con arrogancia*) arrogantly, haughtily. 2 (*con suntuosidad*) magnificently, superbly.
soberbio,-a 1 *adj* (*orgulloso*) proud; (*arrogante*) arrogant, haughty. 2 (*suntuoso*) sumptuous, magnificent. 3 (*magnífico*) superb, splendid, magnificent. 4 *fam* (*enorme*) great, huge. – 5 **soberbia,** *f* (*orgullo*) pride; (*arrogancia*) arrogance, haughtiness. 6 (*magnificiencia*) sumptuousness, pomp. 7 (*cólera*) rage, anger.
sobón,-ona 1 *adj fam* groping. – 2 *m,f* groper: *es un sobón,* he can't keep his hands to himself.
sobornable *adj* bribable, venal.
sobornar *t* to bribe, suborn.
soborno 1 *m* (*acción*) bribery. 2 (*regalo etc*) bribe.
sobra 1 *f* (*exceso*) excess, surplus. – 2 **sobras,** *fpl* (*desperdicios*) leftovers.
● **de sobra,** (*sobrante*) spare; (*en cantidad*) more than enough: *aquí hay un sitio de sobra,* there's a spare seat here; *con un kilo tienes de sobra,* you'll have more than enough with a kilo. ‖ **estar de sobra,** (*persona*) to be in the way. ‖ **saber algo de sobra,** to know sth. only too well.
sobradamente 1 *adv* (*sumamente*) extremely: *era sobradamente difícil,* it was extremely difficult. 2 (*extensamente*) widely: *era sobradamente conocido que...,* it was widely known that...
sobradillo *m* penthouse.
sobrado,-a 1 *pp* → **sobrar**. – 2 *adj* (*que sobra*) ample, more than enough, plenty of. – 3 **sobrado,** *adv* (*demasiado*) too. – 4 *m* (*desván*) attic, garret.
● **andar sobrado,-a,** to have a lot to spare, have plenty to spare: *andamos sobrados de tiempo,* we've got plenty of time to spare. ‖ **estar sobrado,-a de algo,** to have plenty of: *están sobrados de dinero,* they've got plenty of money. ‖ **tener sobrada razón,** to be quite right.
sobrante 1 *adj* leftover, remaining, spare. – 2 *m* excess, surplus.
sobrar 1 *i* (*haber más de lo necesario*) to be more than enough, be too much: *sobra arroz,* there's too much rice; *sobran cuatro platos,* there are four dishes too many. 2 (*estar de más*) to be superfluous, be unnecessary: *ese comentario sobra,* that remark is unnecessary. 3 (*estorbar*) to be in the way. 4 (*quedar*) to have left over, be left over: *nos sobraron dos mil pesetas,* we had two thousand pesetas left over; *sobró pastel,* there was some cake left over.
sobrasada *f* spicy Majorcan sausage.
sobre 1 *prep* (*encima*) on, upon, on top of: *sobre de la mesa,* on the table. 2 (*por encima*) over, above: *volamos sobre la ciudad,* we're flying over the town. 3 (*acerca de*) about, on: *el primer capítulo trata sobre los derechos humanos,* chapter one is about human rights. 4 (*alrededor de*) about, around: *vendré sobre las dos,* I'll come about two. 5 (*superioridad en rango*) over. 6 *fig* (*indica reiteración*) upon, after: *mentira sobre mentira,* lie after lie. – 7 *m* (*de correo*) envelope. 8 (*de sopa etc*) packet. 9 *fam fig* (*cama*) bed.
● **irse al sobre,** *fam* to hit the sack. ‖ **sobre manera,** exceedingly. ‖ **sobre todo,** above all, especially.
sobre- *pref* super-, over-.

sobreabundancia *f* superabundance, overabundance.
sobreabundante *adj* superabundant, overabundant.
sobreabundar *i* to superabound.
sobrealimentación *f* overfeeding.
sobrealimentado,-a 1 *pp* → **sobrealimentar**. – 2 *adj* overfed.
sobrealimentar *t* to overfeed.
sobreático *m* penthouse.
sobrecalentar 1 *t* to overheat. – 2 **sobrecalentarse,** *p* to overheat.
▲ *Conjugation model* [27], *like* **acertar**.
sobrecarga 1 *f* overload. 2 *fig* additional burden, further worry.
sobrecargar 1 *t* to overload. 2 *fig* to overburden.
▲ *Conjugation model* [7], *like* **llegar**.
sobrecargo *m* supercargo.
sobreceja *f* brow.
sobrecogedor,-ra 1 *adj* (*conmovedor*) dramatic, awesome. 2 (*que da miedo*) frightening.
sobrecoger 1 *t* (*coger de repente*) to startle, take by surprise. 2 (*asustar*) to frighten, scare. – 3 **sobrecogerse,** *p* (*sorprenderse*) to be startled. 4 (*asustarse*) to be frightened, be scared.
▲ *Conjugation model* [5], *like* **proteger**.
sobrecubierta *f* jacket, dust cover.
sobredicho,-a *adj fml* aforementioned, above-mentioned, aforesaid.
sobredorar 1 *t* to gild. 2 *fig* to gloss over.
sobredosis *f* overdose.
▲ *pl* **sobredosis**.
sobreentender 1 *t* (*comprender*) to understand. 2 (*deducir*) to deduce. – 3 **sobreentenderse,** *p* to be implied, be inferred: *se sobreentendía que él había cogido el dinero,* it was inferred that he'd taken the money; *se sobreentiende que su respuesta será afirmativa,* one assumes that she will say yes.
▲ *Conjugation model* [28], *like* **entender**.
sobreexceder *t* to exceed.
sobreexcitación *f* overexcitement.
sobreexcitar 1 *t* to overexcite. – 2 **sobreexcitarse,** *p* to get overexcited.
sobreexponer *t* to overexpose.
▲ *Conjugation model* [78], *like* **poner**; *pp* **sobreexpuesto,-a**.
sobreexposición *f* overexposure.
sobreexpuesto,-a *pp* → **sobreexponer**.
sobrefalda *f* overskirt.
sobrefaz *f* surface.
sobregirar *t* to overdraw.
sobregiro *m* overdraft.
sobrehilado *m* whipstitch.
sobrehilar *t* to whipstitch.
sobrehumano,-a *adj* superhuman.
sobreimpresión *f* overprint.
sobrejuanete *m* royal mast.
sobrellenar *t* to overfill.
sobrellevar *t* to bear, endure.
sobremanera *adv* exceedingly.
sobremesa 1 *f* (*período*) afternoon: *la programación de la sobremesa,* the afternoon's television programmes. 2 (*charla*) table talk.
● **estar de sobremesa,** to stay at the table and talk after a meal.
■ **lámpara de sobremesa,** table lamp.
sobremodo *adv* exceedingly.

sobrenadar *i* to float.
sobrenatural *adj* supernatural.
sobrenombre *m* nickname.
sobrentender *t-p* → **sobreentender**.
▲ *Conjugation model* [28], *like* **entender**.
sobrepaga *f* bonus.
sobreparto *m* postnatal confinement.
■ **dolores de sobreparto**, afterpains.
sobrepasar 1 *t* to exceed, surpass, be in excess of: *el precio no sobrepasará el presupuesto*, the price won't exceed the budget; *sobrepasó los doscientos kilómetros por hora*, he went at over two-hundred kilometres an hour. **2** *(competición)* to beat.
sobrepelliz *f* surplice.
sobrepeso 1 *m* overload, excess weight. **2** *(de persona)* excess weight.
sobrepoblación *f* → **superpoblación**.
sobreponer 1 *t* to put on top (**en**, of), superimpose (**en**, on). **– 2 sobreponerse**, *p fig (al dolor etc)* to overcome (**a**, **-**). **3** *fig (animarse)* to pull os. together.
▲ *Conjugation model* [78], *like* **poner**; *pp* **sobrepuesto,-a**.
sobreprecio *m* surcharge.
sobreproducción *f* excess production, overproduction.
sobrepuesto,-a *pp* → **sobreponer**.
sobrepujar *t* to surpass, outdo.
sobrepuse *pt indef* → **sobreponer**.
sobrero,-a 1 *adj (sobrante)* surplus, spare. **2** *(toro)* reserve.
sobresaliente 1 *adj* sticking out, protruding. **2** *fig* outstanding, excellent. **– 3** *m (calificación - colegio)* A; (- universidad) first, US A. **4** *(torero suplente)* reserve bullfighter. **– 5** *m,f (actor suplente)* understudy.
sobresalir 1 *i* to stick out, protrude. **2** *fig* to stand out, excel.
▲ *Conjugation model* [84], *like* **salir**.
sobresaltar 1 *t* to startle. **– 2 sobresaltarse**, *p* to be startled.
sobresalto *m* start; *(de temor)* fright, shock.
sobresdrújulo,-a *adj* accented on the antepenultimate syllable.
sobreseer *t* to dismiss.
▲ *Conjugation model* [61], *like* **leer**.
sobreseído,-a *pp* → **sobreseer**.
sobreseimiento *m* dismissal.
sobrestante *m* foreman.
sobrestimar *t* to overestimate.
sobresueldo *m* extra pay, bonus.
sobretasa *f* surcharge.
sobretensión *f* surge.
sobretodo 1 *m (abrigo)* overcoat. **2** *(guardapolvo)* overall.
sobrevalorar *t* to overestimate.
sobrevenir 1 *i* to happen to, befall: *no sabremos nunca lo que le sobrevino*, we'll never know what happened to her.
▲ *Conjugation model* [90], *like* **venir**.
sobreviviente 1 *adj* surviving. **– 2** *mf* survivor.
sobrevivir 1 *i (gen)* to survive. **2** *(a alguien)* to outlive.
sobrevolar *t* to fly over.
▲ *Conjugation model* [31], *like* **contar**.
sobrexceder *t* to exceed.
sobrexcitación *f* overexcitement.
sobrexcitar *t-p* → **sobreexcitar**.
sobrexponer *t* to overexpose.
▲ *Conjugation model* [78], *like* **poner**; *pp* **sobrexpuesto,-a**.

sobriedad 1 *f* sobriety, moderation, restraint. **2** *(en bebida)* moderation.
sobrino,-a *m,f (hombre)* nephew; *(mujer)* niece.
sobrio,-a 1 *adj (estilo, color etc)* sober, plain. **2** *(persona)* sober, moderate, restrained. **3** *(forma de expresarse)* concise. **4** *(comida)* light.
● **ser sobrio,-a en la bebida**, to drink in moderation.
socaire *m* lee.
● **al socaire**, MAR leeward. ‖ **al socaire de**, *fig* under the protection of.
socaliña *f* cunning trick, ruse.
socapa *f* pretext, dodge.
● **a socapa**, surreptitiously, on the sly.
socarrar 1 *t* to scorch, singe. **– 2 socarrarse**, *p* to burn.
socarrón,-ona 1 *adj (astuto)* sly, cunning. **2** *(burlón)* sarcastic, ironic, wry. **– 3** *m,f (astuto)* sly fox. **4** *(burlón)* sarcastic person, wry person.
socarronería 1 *f (astucia)* slyness. **2** *(ironía)* sarcasm, wryness.
socavar 1 *t (excavar)* to dig under. **2** *fig* to undermine.
socavón 1 *m (cueva excavada)* excavation. **2** *(bache)* hollow, hole. **3** *(de una mina)* gallery, tunnel.
sochantre *m* succentor.
sociabilidad *f* sociability.
sociable *adj* sociable, friendly.
social *adj* social.
socialdemocracia *f* social democracy.
socialdemócrata 1 *adj* social democratic. **– 2** *mf* social democrat.
socialismo *m* socialism.
socialista 1 *adj* socialist. **– 2** *mf* socialist.
socialización 1 *f (gen)* socialization. **2** *(nacionalización)* nationalization.
socializar 1 *t (gen)* to socialize. **2** *(nacionalizar)* to nationalize.
▲ *Conjugation model* [4], *like* **realizar**.
socialmente *adv* socially.
sociedad 1 *f (gen)* society. **2** COM company. **3** *(asociación)* society, association.
● **presentarse en sociedad**, to make one's debut.
■ **alta sociedad / buena sociedad**, high society. ‖ **sociedad anónima**, limited company, US incorporated company. ‖ **sociedad comanditaria / sociedad en comandita**, limited partnership. ‖ **sociedad de consumo**, consumer society. ‖ **Sociedad de Jesús**, REL Society of Jesus. ‖ **sociedad limitada**, private limited company, US limited corporation. ‖ **sociedad mercantil**, company, trading company. ‖ **sociedad protectora de animales**, society for the prevention of cruelty to animals.
socio,-a 1 *m,f (miembro)* member. **2** COM partner, associate. **3** *(accionista)* shareholder, member. **4** *fam (sujeto)* mate, pal.
● **hacerse socio,-a de un club**, to join a club.
■ **socio,-a capitalista**, capitalist partner. ‖ **socio,-a comanditario,-a**, sleeping partner, US silent partner. ‖ **socio,-a fundador,-ra**, founding member.
socioeconómico,-a *adj* socioeconomic.
sociología *f* sociology.
sociológico,-a *adj* sociological.
sociólogo,-a *m,f* sociologist.
socolor *m* pretext.
socorrer *t* to help, assist, come to the aid of, go to the aid of.
socorrido,-a 1 *pp* → **socorrer**. **– 2** *adj (útil)* useful, handy. **3** *(abastecido)* well-stocked. **4** *(trillado, manido)* hackneyed, well-worn.

socorrismo *m* life-saving.
socorrista *mf* life-saver, lifeguard.
socorro 1 *m (ayuda)* help, aid, assistance. 2 *(provisiones)* supplies *pl*, provisions *pl*. – 3 *interj* help!
● acudir en socorro de algn., to go to sb.'s aid.
■ puesto de socorro, first-aid post. ‖ señal de socorro, distress signal. ‖ trabajos de socorro, rescue work *sing*.
socrático,-a 1 *adj* Socratic. – 2 *m,f* Socratic.
soda 1 *f (bebida)* soda water. 2 QUÍM soda.
sódico,-a *adj* sodium.
sodio *m* sodium.
sodomía *f* sodomy.
sodomita 1 *adj* sodomite. – 2 *mf* sodomite.
sodomizar *t* to sodomize.
▲ Conjugation model [4], *like realizar.*
soez *adj* vulgar, crude, rude.
sofá *m* sofa, settee.
■ sofá cama, sofa bed.
▲ *pl sofás.*
Sofía *f* Sofia.
sofión 1 *m (bufido)* snort, bellow. 2 *(reprensión)* scolding. 3 *(trabuco)* blunderbuss.
sofisma *m* sophism.
sofista 1 *adj* sophistic. – 2 *mf* sophist.
sofisticación *f* sophistication.
sofisticado,-a 1 *pp* → **sofisticar**. – 2 *adj* sophisticated.
sofisticar *t* to sophisticate.
▲ Conjugation model [1], *like sacar.*
soflama 1 *f (llama)* flicker, glow. 2 *(rubor)* blush. 3 *(arenga)* harangue. 4 *(marrullería)* deceit.
soflamar 1 *t (abochornar)* to make blush. 2 *(socarrar)* to scorch, singe. 3 *(engañar)* to deceive. – 4 soflamarse, *p (socarrarse)* to burn.
sofocación 1 *f (ahogo)* suffocation, stifling sensation. 2 *(rubor)* blushing. 3 *fig (de incendio)* extinction; *(de rebelión)* suppression.
sofocante *adj* suffocating, stifling.
sofocar 1 *t (ahogar)* to suffocate, stifle, smother. 2 *fig (abochornar)* to make blush. 3 *fig (incendio)* to put out, extinguish; *(rebelión)* to suppress, put down. – 4 sofocarse, *p (de calor etc)* to suffocate. 5 *fig (ruborizarse)* to blush. 6 *fam (enfadarse)* to get upset, get angry.
▲ Conjugation model [1], *like sacar.*
sofoco 1 *m (ahogo)* suffocation, stifling sensation. 2 *fig (vergüenza)* embarrassment; *(rubor)* blushing. 3 *fam (disgusto)* shock.
● le *(les, etc)* dio un sofoco, *fam* it gave him *(her, them, etc)* quite a turn.
sofocón *m fam* shock.
● llevarse un sofocón, *fam* to get into a state.
sofoquina 1 *f fam (de calor)* stifling heat. 2 *fam (disgusto)* shock.
sofreír *t* to fry lightly, brown.
▲ Conjugation model [37], *like reír; pp sofrito,-a or sofreído,-a.*
sofrito,-a 1 *pp* → **sofreír**. – 2 sofrito, *m* fried tomato and onion sauce.
software *m* software.
soga *f* rope, cord.
● dar soga a algn., *(burlarse)* to make fun of sb.; *(llevarle la corriente)* to humour *(US* humor*)* sb. ‖ estar con la soga al cuello, *fig* to be in dire straits.
soja *f* soya bean, *US* soybean.
■ salsa de soja, soy sauce.

sojuzgar *t* to subjugate.
▲ Conjugation model [7], *like llegar.*
sol[1] 1 *m (estrella)* sun. 2 *(luz)* sun, sunlight, sunshine. 3 *(en los toros)* seats *pl* in the sun. 4 *fam (persona)* darling. 5 *(moneda de Perú)* sol, standard monetary unit of Peru.
● al ponerse el sol, at sunset. ‖ al salir el sol, at sunrise. ‖ al sol / bajo el sol, in the sun. ‖ arrimarse al sol que más calienta, *fig* to know which side one's bread is buttered on. ‖ de sol a sol, from sunrise to sunset. ‖ hace sol, it's sunny, the sun's shining. ‖ no dejar a algn. ni a sol ni a sombra, *fig* to pester sb., not to give sb. a moment's peace. ‖ ¡salga el sol por Antequera!, *fam* come what may! ‖ ser un sol, *fam* to be a darling. ‖ tomar el sol, *(tendido)* to sunbathe; *(al caminar)* to get some sun.
■ sol de medianoche, midnight sun. ‖ sol naciente, rising sun. ‖ sol poniente, setting sun. ‖ sol y sombra, *(en los toros)* seats *pl* which get some sun and some shade; *(bebida)* brandy and anisette drink. ‖ un día de sol, a sunny day.
sol[2] *m* MÚS sol, G.
solado *m* flooring.
solamente *adv* → **sólo**.
solana 1 *f (lugar donde da el sol)* sunny spot, suntrap. 2 *(de una casa)* sun lounge, *US* sunporch.
solanera 1 *f (insolación)* sunstroke. 2 *(lugar al sol)* sunny place, suntrap. 3 *(de una casa)* sun lounge, *US* sunporch.
solano 1 *m (viento)* easterly wind. 2 BOT nightshade.
solapa 1 *f (de prenda)* lapel. 2 *(de sobre, libro)* flap. 3 *fig (pretexto)* pretext.
solapadamente *adv* slyly, in an underhand way.
solapado,-a 1 *pp* → **solapar**. – 2 *adj fig* sly, evasive.
solapar 1 *t* COST to put lapels on. 2 *fig (ocultar)* to conceal, cover up. – 3 *i (cubrir)* to overlap.
solar[1] *adj (del sol)* solar.
solar[2] 1 *m (terreno)* plot, lot; *(en obras)* building site. 2 *(casa solariega)* ancestral home. 3 *fig (linaje)* lineage, line.
solar[3] 1 *t (zapatos)* to sole. 2 *(suelo)* to floor.
▲ Conjugation model [31].
solariego,-a 1 *adj (noble)* noble. 2 *(de la familia)* family.
■ casa solariega, ancestral home, family seat.
solario *m* solarium.
solárium *m* solarium.
▲ *pl soláriums.*
solaz 1 *m (esparcimiento)* recreation, entertainment. 2 *(descanso)* rest, relaxation. 3 *(consuelo)* consolation, solace.
solazar 1 *t (entretener)* to amuse, entertain. 2 *(descansar)* to rest, relax. – 3 solazarse, *p (divertirse)* to enjoy os. 4 *(relajarse)* to relax.
▲ Conjugation model [4], *like realizar.*
soldada *f* salary, pay.
soldadesca *f* → **soldadesco,-a.**
soldadesco,-a 1 *adj* soldier-like, soldierly. – 2 soldadesca, *f (profesión)* military profession. 3 *(soldados)* soldiery.
soldado *m* soldier.
■ soldado de artillería, artilleryman. ‖ soldado de caballería, cavalryman, trooper. ‖ soldado de infantería, infantryman. ‖ soldado de infantería de marina, marine. ‖ soldado raso, private.
soldador,-ra 1 *m,f* welder. – 2 soldador, *m* soldering iron.
soldadura 1 *f (acción)* welding, soldering. 2 *(unión)* weld, soldered joint.
soldar 1 *t (metal)* to weld, solder. 2 *fig (enmendar)* to mend. – 3 soldarse, *p (huesos)* to knit.

● **soldar por puntos,** to spot-weld.
▲ *Conjugation model* [31], *like contar.*
soleá *f* Andalusian song and dance.
▲ *pl soleares.*
soleado,-a *adj* sunny.
solear *t* to expose to the sun, put in the sun.
solecismo *m* solecism.
soledad 1 *f* (*estado*) solitude. 2 (*sentimiento*) loneliness. 3 (*lugar*) lonely place.
solemne 1 *adj* solemn, majestic. 2 *pey* downright: *es una solemne tontería,* it's downright stupidity.
solemnemente *adv* solemnly.
solemnidad 1 *f* (*pompa*) solemnity, pomp, formality. 2 (*acto, ceremonia*) solemn ceremony, ceremonial occasion. 3 (*festividad religiosa*) religious celebration.
solemnizar *t* (*celebrar*) to solemnize, celebrate; (*conmemorar*) to commemorate.
▲ *Conjugation model* [4], *like realizar.*
solenoide *m* solenoid.
sóleo *m* soleus.
soler *i* (*acostumbrar - presente*) to be in the habit of + *-ing*; (*- pasado*) used to: *no suele quejarse,* he's not in the habit of complaining; *solía venir cada martes,* she used to come every Tuesday; *suele comer a las dos,* he usually has lunch at two; *suele llover mucho en septiembre,* it usually rains a lot in September.
▲ *Conjugation model* [32], *like mover; used only in present and past tenses.*
solera 1 *f* (*soporte*) support, prop. 2 (*de molino*) lower millstone. 3 (*de horno*) floor. 4 (*del vino*) lees *pl.* 5 *fig* (*tradición*) tradition.
● **de solera / de mucha solera,** (*familia etc*) old-established; (*vino*) vintage.
solevantar *t* to lift.
solfa 1 *f* MÚS sol-fa, musical notation. 2 *fam* (*paliza*) thrashing, beating.
● **poner en solfa,** *fam* to ridicule.
solfatara *f* solfatara.
solfear 1 *t* MÚS to sol-fa. 2 *fig* (*zurrar*) to thrash, beat. 3 *fig* (*censurar*) to criticize.
solfeo *m* solfa, solfeggio.
solicitación 1 *f* (*acción*) requesting. 2 (*solicitud*) request, application.
solicitador,-ra *m,f* applicant.
solicitante *mf* applicant.
solicitar 1 *t* (*pedir*) to request. 2 (*trabajo*) to apply for; (*permiso etc*) to ask for; (*votos*) to canvass for. 3 (*persona*) to chase after. 4 (*cortejar*) to woo, court.
● **estar muy solicitado,-a,** to be in great demand, be sought after.
solícito,-a *adj* obliging, attentive.
solicitud 1 *f* (*petición*) request; (*de trabajo*) application; (*- impreso*) application form: *rellene esta solicitud,* please fill in this application form. 2 (*instancia*) petition. 3 (*diligencia*) solicitude, care.
solidaridad *f* solidarity.
solidario,-a 1 *adj* (*ligado*) united. 2 (*responsabilidad, causa*) common. 3 JUR jointly responsible.
solidarizarse 1 *p* (*gen*) to show one's solidarity (**con,** with). 2 (*apoyar*) to support (**con,** -).
▲ *Conjugation model* [4], *like realizar.*
solideo *m* skullcap.
solidez 1 *f* (*resistencia*) solidity, strength; (*firmeza*) firmness. 2 *fig* (*de color*) fastness. 3 *fig* (*principios etc*) soundness.
solidificación *f* solidification.

solidificar 1 *t* (*líquido*) to solidify. 2 (*pasta*) to harden, set. – 3 **solidificarse,** *p* (*líquido*) to solidify. 4 (*pasta*) to harden, set.
▲ *Conjugation model* [1], *like sacar.*
sólido,-a 1 *adj* (*fuerte*) solid, strong; (*firme*) firm. 2 *fig* (*color*) fast. 3 *fig* (*principios etc*) sound. – 4 **sólido,** *m* solid.
soliloquio *m* soliloquy.
solio *m* throne.
solista *mf* soloist.
solitaria *f* → **solitario,-a.**
solitario,-a 1 *adj* (*que está solo*) solitary, lone. 2 (*que se siente solo*) lonely. 3 (*lugar*) deserted, lonely. – 4 *m,f* (*persona*) solitary person. 5 (*ermitaño*) hermit. – 6 **solitario,** *m* (*diamante, naipes*) solitaire. – 7 **solitaria,** *f* MED tapeworm.
■ **vuelo en solitario,** solo flight.
sólito,-a *adj* usual, customary.
soliviantar 1 *t* (*inducir*) to rouse, stir up. 2 (*irritar*) to irritate.
sollado *m* orlop.
sollastre 1 *m* (*pinche*) kitchen assistant. 2 *fig* (*pícaro*) rogue, rascal.
sollozar *i* to sob.
▲ *Conjugation model* [4], *like realizar.*
sollozo *m* sob.
● **estallar en sollozos / prorrumpir en sollozos,** to start sobbing.
sólo *adv* only, just: *sólo vendrá David,* only David is coming; *sólo quiero café,* I just want a coffee.
● **con sólo / sólo con,** just by: *con sólo abrir la puerta ...,* just by opening the door ... ‖ **con sólo que / sólo con que,** provided that: *sólo con que vengas ...,* provided that you come ... ‖ **no sólo ... sino (también) ...,** not only ... but (also) ... ‖ **sólo para adultos,** for adults only. ‖ **sólo que,** only, but, except: *me presentaría al examen sólo que no he estudiado,* I'd sit the exam but I haven't studied. ‖ **tan sólo,** only, just: *comió tan sólo un bistec,* he just had a steak. ‖ **tan sólo con ...,** just by ...: *no aprobarás tan sólo con asistir a clase,* you won't pass just by coming to class.
solo,-a 1 *adj* (*sin compañía*) alone, on one's own, by os.; (*sin ayuda*) (by) os., (for) os.: *vive solo,* he lives alone, he lives by himself; *lo dejaron solo,* he was left on his own; *lo haré yo sola,* I'll do it (by) myself; *se apaga solo,* it switches itself off automatically. 2 (*solitario*) lonely: *me siento sola,* I feel lonely. 3 (*único*) only, sole, single: *ni una sola palabra,* not a single word; *ni una sola vez,* not even once. 4 (*café*) black; (*bebida alcohólica*) straight. – 5 **solo,** *m* (*naipes*) solitaire. 6 *fam* (*café*) black coffee. 7 MÚS solo. – 8 *adv* → **sólo.**
● **a solas,** alone, by os. ‖ **como él solo / como ella sola,** *fam* as only he can / as only she can. ‖ **quedarse solo,-a,** *fam* to have no equal: *cuando empieza a contar chistes se queda solo,* when he starts telling jokes no one can match him.
solomillo *m* sirloin.
solsticio *m* solstice.
soltar 1 *t* (*desasir*) to let go of, release, drop: *me soltó la mano,* he let go of my hand; *suelta el botón,* release the button; *¡suelta el arma!,* drop the weapon!; *¡suéltame!,* let me go! 2 (*desatar*) to untie, unfasten, undo; (*aflojar*) to loosen. 3 (*preso*) to release, free, set free. 4 (*animal*) to let out; (*perro*) to unleash. 5 (*humo, olor*) to give off. 6 (*puntos*) to drop. 7 (*de vientre*) to loosen. 8 *fam* (*dar*) to give, deal: *le soltó una torta,* he gave him a slap. 9 *fam* (*decir*) to come out with, blurt out: *nos soltó un rollo,*

he gave us a boring lecture. – **10 soltarse,** *p (desatarse)* to come untied, come unfastened. **11** *(desprenderse)* to come off. **12** *(tornillo etc)* to come loose. **13** *(animal)* to get loose, break loose. **14** *(puntos)* to come undone. **15** *(vientre)* to loosen. **16** *fig (adquirir habilidad)* to become proficient, get the knack: *ya se suelta en inglés,* he's getting fluent in English. **17** *fig (desenvolverse)* to become self-confident, loosen up.
● **soltar amarras,** to cast off. ‖ **soltar la lengua,** to speak freely. ‖ **soltar la pasta,** *fam* to cough up. ‖ **soltar un taco,** to swear. ‖ **soltarse a** + *inf,* to begin + *inf,* start + *inf/*+ *-ing: ya se suelta a caminar,* he's beginning to walk. ‖ **soltarse a su gusto,** *fam* to let off steam. ‖ **¡suelta!,** *(dejar ir)* let go!; *(decir)* out with it!, spit it out!
▲ Conjugation model [31], like *contar.*
soltería *f (gen)* single state; *(de hombre)* bachelorhood.
soltero,-a 1 *adj* single, unmarried. – **2** *m,f (hombre)* bachelor, single man; *(mujer)* single woman.
● **la Sra. Rodríguez, de soltera Vaquero,** Mrs Rodríguez, née Vaquero.
■ **apellido de soltera,** maiden name.
solterón,-ona *m,f pey (hombre)* old unmarried man, confirmed bachelor; *(mujer)* old maid, spinster.
soltura 1 *f (agilidad)* agility. **2** *fig (seguridad)* confidence, assurance. **3** *fig (al hablar)* fluency, ease. **4** *fig (descaro)* shamelessness.
solubilidad *f* solubility.
soluble *adj* soluble.
solución *f* solution: *la solución del problema,* the solution to the problem.
solucionar 1 *t (problema)* to solve. **2** *(huelga, asunto)* to settle.
solvencia 1 *f* FIN solvency. **2** *(pago)* settlement. **3** *(fiabilidad)* reliability; *(reputación)* good reputation.
solventar 1 *t (dificultad, problema)* to solve, resolve. **2** *(deuda, asunto)* to settle.
solvente 1 *adj* FIN solvent. **2** *(fiable)* reliable. – **3** *m* QUÍM solvent.
soma *m* soma.
somalí 1 *adj* Somali. – **2** *mf* Somali.
Somalia *f* Somalia.
somanta *f fam* beating, thrashing.
somatén 1 *m* civilian militia. **2** *fig* uproar.
somático,-a *adj* somatic.
somatología *f* somatology.
sombra 1 *f (falta de sol)* shade. **2** *(silueta)* shadow. **3** *(espectro)* ghost, shade. **4** *fig (oscuridad en el alma)* darkness, obscurity. **5** *fig (persona que sigue a otra)* shadow. **6** *fig (defecto)* stain, spot. **7** *fam fig (suerte)* luck. **8** *fam fig (gracia)* wit. **9** *fig (parte pequeña)* trace, shadow, bit. **10** *fig (clandestinidad)* secrecy. **11** *(en los toros)* part of the bullring in the shade.
● **a la sombra,** in the shade; *(en la cárcel)* inside, in the nick. ‖ **dar sombra,** to shade, give shade. ‖ **en la sombra,** *fig* shadow: *gobierno en la sombra,* shadow cabinet. ‖ **hacer sombra,** to cast a shadow; *fig* to overshadow. ‖ **ni por sombra,** *fig* not in the least. ‖ **ni sombra de,** *fig* not a trace of. ‖ **no fiarse ni de su sombra,** *fig* to be very distrustful. ‖ **reírse de su propia sombra,** *fig* to laugh at everything. ‖ **tener buena sombra,** *fam (tener suerte)* to have a lucky streak; *(ser gracioso)* to be witty, be funny. ‖ **tener mala sombra,** *fam (no tener suerte)* to be unlucky; *(ser desagradable)* to be a nasty piece of work.
■ **sombra de duda,** shadow of doubt. ‖ **sombra de ojos,** eye-shadow. ‖ **sombras chinescas,** shadow theatre (US theater) *sing.*

sombraje *m* shade, shelter from the sun.
sombrajo *m* → **sombraje.**
sombreado *m* shading.
sombrear 1 *t (dar sombra)* to cast a shadow upon, shade. **2** *(en dibujo)* to shade, shade in.
sombrerera *f* hatbox.
sombrerería *f (gen)* hat shop; *(de señoras)* milliner's; *(de señores)* hatter's.
sombrerero,-a *m,f (gen)* hat maker; *(para señoras)* milliner; *(para señores)* hatter.
sombrerete 1 *m (de chimenea)* cowl. **2** *(de hongo)* cap.
sombrero 1 *m (prenda)* hat. **2** *(de hongo)* cap.
● **quitarse el sombrero,** to take one's hat off. ‖ **sin sombrero,** hatless, bareheaded.
■ **sombrero canotier,** boater, straw hat. ‖ **sombrero cordobés,** wide-brimmed Andalusian hat. ‖ **sombrero de copa,** top hat. ‖ **sombrero de jipijapa,** Panama hat. ‖ **sombrero de teja / sombrero de canal,** priest's hat. ‖ **sombrero hongo,** bowler hat.
sombrilla *f* parasol, sunshade.
sombrío,-a 1 *adj (lugar)* dark. **2** *fig (tenebroso)* gloomy, sombre (US somber). **3** *fig (persona)* gloomy, sullen.
someramente *adv* superficially, briefly.
somero,-a *adj fig (superficial)* superficial, shallow; *(breve)* brief.
someter 1 *t (rebeldes)* to subdue, put down; *(rebelión)* to quell. **2** *(hacer recibir)* to subject (a, to): *lo sometió a tortura,* he was subjected to torture. **3** *(pasiones)* to subdue. **4** *(proponer, presentar)* to submit, present. – **5 someterse,** *p (rendirse)* to surrender (a, to). **6** *(tratamiento etc)* to undergo (a, -).
● **someterse a la opinión de algn.,** to bow to sb.'s opinion. ‖ **someter a prueba,** to test, put to the test. ‖ **someter algo a la autoridad,** to refer sth. to an authority. ‖ **someter algo a votación,** to put sth. to the vote, vote on sth.
sometimiento 1 *m (dominación)* subjection, subjugation. **2** *(presentación, propuesta)* submission, presentation.
somier *m* sprung bed base.
▲ *pl somieres.*
somnambulismo *m* → **sonambulismo.**
somnámbulo,-a *adj-m,f* → **sonámbulo,-a.**
somnífero,-a 1 *adj* sleep-inducing, somniferous. – **2** *somnífero, m* sleeping pill.
somnolencia *f* sleepiness, drowsiness, somnolence.
somnoliento,-a *adj* sleepy, drowsy.
somorgujar *t* to plunge, duck.
somorgujo *m* grebe.
somormujo *m* grebe.
son 1 *m (sonido)* sound. **2** *fig (modo)* manner, way: *a mi son,* my way.
● **¿a son de qué?,** whatever for?, why? ‖ **bailar al son que tocan,** fig to toe the line. ‖ **en son de paz,** in peace. ‖ **sin ton ni son,** without rhyme or reason.
sonado,-a 1 *pp* → **sonar.** – **2** *adj (conocido)* famous. **3** *(escándalo etc)* much talked-about. **4** *fam fig (loco)* mad, crazy. **5** *fam fig (boxeador)* punch-drunk.
● **hacer una que sea sonada,** *fam* to cause a great stir.
sonaja 1 *f (discos)* jingling metal disks *pl.* – **2 sonajas,** *fpl (juguete)* rattle *sing.*
sonajero *m* baby's rattle.
sonambulismo *m* sleepwalking, somnambulism.
sonámbulo,-a 1 *adj* sleepwalking. – **2** *m,f* sleepwalker, somnambulist.

sonar[1] **1** *i* (*hacer ruido*) to sound. **2** (*timbre, teléfono, etc*) to ring. **3** (*alarma, reloj*) to go off. **4** (*instrumento*) to play. **5** (*letra*) to be pronounced: *esa letra no suena,* that letter is not pronounced. **6** (*mencionarse*) to be mentioned. **7** (*tener apariencia*) to look (**a**, like), sound (**a**, like), seem (**a**, like): *el proyecto sonaba a estafa,* the project sounded like a con. – **8** *t* (*conocer vagamente*) to sound familiar, ring a bell: *no me suena esa calle,* that street doesn't ring a bell. **9** (*nariz*) to blow. **10** (*timbre etc*) to ring; (*bocina*) to blow, sound; (*instrumento*) to play. – **11** sonarse, *p* (*nariz*) to blow.
● tal y como suena, literally, just as I'm telling you.
▲ *Conjugation model* |31|, *like contar.*

sonar[2] *m* MAR sonar.
sonata *f* sonata.
sonatina *f* sonatina.
sonda 1 *f* MED (*para intervenciones quirúrgicas*) probe; (*para evacuar líquidos*) catheter. **2** MAR sounding line. **3** (*barreno*) drill, bore. **4** (*atmósfera*) sounding-balloon; (*espacio*) probe.
■ sonda espacial, space probe.
sondar *t* → **sondear**.
sondear 1 *t* MED to sound, probe. **2** MAR to sound. **3** (*subsuelo*) to drill, bore. **4** *fig* (*encuestar*) to sound out, test.
● sondear la opinión pública, *fig* to sound out public opinion.
sondeo 1 *m* MED sounding, probing. **2** MAR sounding. **3** (*del subsuelo*) drilling, boring. **4** *fig* (*encuesta*) poll.
■ sondeo de audiencia, audience rating. ‖ sondeo de la opinión pública, public opinion poll.
sonetista *mf* sonneteer.
soneto *m* sonnet.
sónico,-a *adj* sonic.
sonido *m* sound.
soniquete *m* → **sonsonete**.
sonoridad *f* sonority.
sonorización 1 *f* (*de película*) recording of the soundtrack. **2** (*amplificación*) amplification. **3** LING voicing.
sonorizar 1 *t* (*película*) to record the soundtrack. **2** (*amplificar*) to install amplifying equipment in. **3** LING to voice.
▲ *Conjugation model* |4|, *like realizar.*
sonoro,-a 1 *adj* (*resonante*) loud, resounding. **2** LING sound.
■ efectos sonoros, sound effects. ‖ película sonora, talking picture.
sonotone *m fam* hearing aid.
▲ *Registered trademark.*
sonreír 1 *i* to smile. – **2** *t* to smile at: *le sonrió,* she smiled at him. – **3** *i fig* (*favorecer*) to smile on, smile upon: *la fortuna no le sonríe,* fortune doesn't smile upon him. – **4** sonreírse, *p* to smile.
▲ *Conjugation model* |37|, *like reír.*
sonriente *adj* smiling.
sonrisa *f* smile.
sonrojar 1 *t* to make blush. – **2** sonrojarse, *p* to blush.
● hacer sonrojar a algn., to make sb. blush.
sonrojear *t-p* → **sonrojar**.
sonrojo 1 *m* (*rubor*) blush, blushing. **2** (*vergüenza*) shame, embarrassment.
sonrosado,-a 1 *pp* → **sonrosar**. – **2** *adj* rosy, pink.
sonrosar *i* to go pink, turn pink.
sonsacar 1 *t* (*gen*) to wheedle. **2** *fig* (*secreto*) to get out of, worm out.
▲ *Conjugation model* |1|, *like sacar.*

sonsonete 1 *m* (*sonido de golpecitos*) rhythmic tapping. **2** *fig* (*tonillo irónico*) mocking tone. **3** *fig* (*cantinela*) song, tune. **4** *fig* (*voz monótona*) drone, droning voice.
soñado,-a 1 *pp* → **soñar**. – **2** *adj* of one's dreams, dreamed-of.
● que ni soñado,-a, *fam* fantastic, wonderful, wild.
soñador,-ra 1 *adj* dreamy, dreaming. – **2** *m,f* dreamer.
soñar 1 *t* (*al dormir*) to dream. **2** *fig* (*fantasear*) to daydream, dream. – **3** *i* (*al dormir*) to dream (**con**, about/of): *soñé contigo,* I dreamt about you. **4** *fig* (*fantasear*) to daydream (**con**, about), dream (**con**, about/of).
● ¡ni soñarlo!, *fig* not on your life!, no way! ‖ ¡sueña con los angelitos!, *fig* sweet dreams! ‖ soñar despierto, to daydream. ‖ soñar en voz alta, (*durmiendo*) to talk in one's sleep; (*fantasear*) to fantasize.
▲ *Conjugation model* |31|, *like contar.*
soñarrera 1 *f fam* (*ganas de dormir*) sleepiness. **2** *fam* (*sueño pesado*) slumber, deep sleep.
soñera *f fam* → **soñarrera**.
soñoliento,-a *adj* drowsy, sleepy.
sopa 1 *f* (*plato*) soup. – **2** sopas, *fpl* pieces of bread soaked in a liquid, sops.
● comer de la sopa boba / vivir de la sopa boba, *fam* to be a parasite, live off sb. ‖ dar sopas con honda a algn., *fig* to outshine sb. ‖ estar hasta en la sopa, *fam* to be everywhere. ‖ estar hecho,-a una sopa / quedar hecho,-a una sopa, *fam* to be soaked to the skin.
■ sopa boba, food served to the poor, slops *pl.* ‖ sopa de ajo, garlic soup. ‖ sopa de cebolla, onion soup. ‖ sopa de fideos, noodle soup. ‖ sopa de sobre, packet soup, instant soup. ‖ sopa juliana, vegetable soup.
sopapo *m fam* slap.
sopar *t* to dunk, dip.
sopear *t* to dunk, dip.
sopera *f* → **sopero,-a**.
sopero,-a 1 *adj* soup. – **2** *m,f* (*persona*) fond of soup. – **3** sopero, *m* (*plato*) soup dish. – **4** sopera, *f* soup tureen.
sopesar 1 *t* to try the weight of. **2** *fig* to weigh up.
sopetón 1 *m fam* (*bofetada*) slap. **2** (*trozo de pan*) toast soaked in oil.
● de sopetón, all of a sudden.
sopicaldo *m* thin soup.
sopla *interj fam* good gracious!
sopladero *m* vent.
soplado,-a 1 *pp* → **soplar**. – **2** *adj fam fig* (*demasiado compuesto*) overdressed. **3** *fam fig* (*estirado*) conceited. **4** *fam fig* (*borracho*) drunk, tipsy, tight. – **5** soplado, *m* TÉC glass-blowing.
soplador,-ra *m* glass-blower.
soplagaitas *mf fam* idiot, fool.
▲ *pl* soplagaitas.
soplamocos *m fam* slap, punch.
▲ *pl* soplamocos.
soplapollas *mf tabú* jerk, nerd, arsehole (us asshole).
▲ *pl* soplapollas.
soplar 1 *i* (*viento etc*) to blow. **2** *fam* (*denunciar*) to squeal. **3** *fam* (*beber*) to booze. – **4** *t* (*polvo etc*) to blow away, blow off; (*vela*) to blow out; (*sopa*) to blow on; (*globo*) to blow up. **5** (*vidrio*) to blow. **6** *fig* (*inspirar*) to inspire. **7** *fam fig* (*robar*) to pinch, steal. **8** *fam fig* (*delatar*) to split on, grass on. **9** *fam fig* (*en un examen etc*) to whisper the answer, tell the answer. **10** *fam fig* (*hurtar*) to nick, pinch; (*- en las damas*) to huff. – **11** soplarse, *p* (*dedos, manos*) to blow. **12** *fam fig* (*tomarse*) to down.
soplete *m* blowtorch, blowlamp.

soplido *m* blow, puff.
soplillo *m* fan.
■ orejas de soplillo, *fam* sticking out ears.
soplo 1 *m* (*con la boca*) blow, puff. 2 (*de viento*) puff. 3 *fig* (*momento*) moment, minute. 4 MED murmur. 5 *fam* (*de secreto etc*) tip-off.
● dar el soplo / dar un soplo, *fam* to squeal, spill the beans. ‖ en un soplo, *fig* in a jiffy. ‖ pasar como un soplo, *fig* to fly past.
soplón,-ona 1 *adj fam* (*niño*) tell-tale; (*adulto*) informing, who informs. − 2 *m,f fam* (*niño*) telltale, sneak; (*adulto*) informer, grass.
soponcio *m fam* swoon, fainting fit: *le dio un soponcio*, he fainted.
sopor *m* drowsiness, sleepiness.
soporífero,-a 1 *adj* soporific, sleep-inducing. 2 *fig* dull, boring.
soporífico,-a *adj* → **soporífero,-a**.
soportable *adj* bearable.
soportal 1 *m* porch. − 2 soportales, *mpl* arcade *sing*.
soportar 1 *t* (*aguantar*) to support, bear. 2 *fig* (*sufrir*) to stand, bear, endure. 3 *fig* (*lluvia, tormenta, etc*) to weather.
soporte *m* support.
■ soporte de datos, INFORM data carrier. ‖ soporte físico, INFORM hardware. ‖ soporte logístico, INFORM software.
soprano *mf* soprano.
sor *f* sister: *Sor María*, Sister María.
sorber 1 *t* (*líquido*) to sip. 2 *fig* (*absorber*) to absorb, soak up. − 3 sorberse, *p fig* to absorb, soak up.
● sorberle el seso a algn., *fam* to go to sb.'s head.
sorbete *m* sorbet, US sherbet.
sorbo 1 *m* (*acción*) sip. 2 (*trago*) gulp.
● beber a sorbos, to sip, drink in small sips. ‖ de un sorbo, in one gulp.
sordera *f* deafness.
sordidez 1 *f* (*suciedad*) squalor. 2 (*mezquindad*) meanness.
sórdido,-a 1 *adj* (*sucio*) squalid, sordid. 2 (*mezquino*) mean.
sordina *f* (*de instrumentos de viento*) mute, sordino; (*de piano*) damper.
● con sordina, *fig* silently, on the quiet.
sordino *m* fiddle.
sordo,-a 1 *adj* (*persona*) deaf. 2 (*sonido, dolor, golpe*) dull. 3 LING voiceless, unvoiced. 4 *fig* (*cólera*) pent-up. − 5 *m,f* (*persona*) deaf person.
● a lo sordo, *fam* silently, on the quiet. ‖ estar sordo,-a como una tapia, *fig* to be stone-deaf, be as deaf as a post. ‖ permanecer sordo,-a a ..., *fig* to remain deaf to ... ‖ quedarse sordo,-a, to go deaf.
sordomudez *f* deaf-mutism.
sordomudo,-a 1 *adj* deaf and dumb, deaf mute. − 2 *m,f* deaf and dumb person, deaf mute.
sorgo *m* sorghum.
soriano,-a 1 *adj* of Soria, from Soria. − 2 *m,f* person from Soria, inhabitant of Soria.
soriasis *f* psoriasis.
▲ *pl soriasis*.
sorites *m* sorites.
▲ *pl sorites*.
sorna 1 *f* (*lentitud*) coolness, calmness. 2 *fig* (*mofa*) mocking tone; (*ironía*) sarcasm.
sorprendente *adj* surprising, amazing, astonishing: *lo sorprendente del caso es que...*, the surprising thing about it is...

sorprendentemente *adv* surprisingly.
sorprender 1 *t* (*coger desprevenido*) to catch unawares, take by surprise. 2 *fig* (*descubrir*) to discover; (*conversación*) to overhear. 3 *fig* (*maravillar*) to surprise, astonish, amaze. − 4 sorprenderse, *p fig* to be surprised.
● no me sorprendería nada, I wouldn't be at all surprised.
sorpresa *f* surprise.
● coger de sorpresa / coger por sorpresa, to take by surprise. ‖ llevarse una sorpresa, to be surprised.
sorpresivo,-a *adj* AM surprising, unexpected.
sorrostrada *f* insolence.
sorteable *adj* avoidable, which can be avoided.
sortear 1 *t* (*echar a suertes*) to draw lots for, cast lots for. 2 (*rifar*) to raffle. 3 MIL to draft. 4 *fig* (*obstáculos, dificultad*) to get round, overcome; (*preguntas*) to dodge, evade, get round. 5 (*en los toros*) to dodge.
sorteo *m* draw; (*rifa*) raffle.
● por sorteo, by drawing lots.
sortija 1 *f* (*anillo*) ring. 2 (*rizo*) curl, ringlet.
sortilegio 1 *m* (*hechicería*) sorcery, witchcraft. 2 (*hechizo*) spell. 3 *fig* (*atractivo*) charm.
sosa 1 *f* QUÍM soda. 2 BOT saltwort.
■ sosa cáustica, caustic soda.
sosaina *mf fam* dull person, bore.
sosegadamente *adv* calmly, quietly.
sosegado,-a 1 *pp* → **sosegar**. − 2 *adj* calm, quiet.
sosegador,-ra *adj* calming.
sosegar 1 *t* (*aplacar*) to calm, quieten. 2 *fig* (*aquietar*) to reassure. − 3 *i* (*descansar*) to rest. − 4 sosegarse, *p* (*calmarse*) to calm down.
▲ *Conjugation model* [48], *like regar*.
sosera *f* insipidity, dullness.
soseras 1 *adj fam* dull, boring. − 2 *mf fam* dull person, bore.
▲ *pl soseras*.
sosería *f* insipidity, dullness.
sosia *m* double, lookalike.
sosiego *m* calmness, peace, tranquility: *un momento de sosiego*, a moment's peace.
soslayar 1 *t* (*ladear*) to slant, put on a slant. 2 *fig* (*evitar*) to avoid, dodge.
soslayo. 1 al soslayo, *loc adv* sideways. 2 de soslayo, sideways.
● mirar de soslayo, to look sideways (at); *fig* to give a sidelong glance (to).
soso,-a 1 *adj* (*insípido*) tasteless; (*sin sal*) unsalted. 2 *fig* dull, insipid.
sospecha *f* suspicion.
● despertar sospechas, to arouse suspicion. ‖ fuera de toda sospecha / por encima de toda sospecha, above all suspicion. ‖ tener la sospecha de que ..., to suspect that ...
■ sospecha fundada, well-founded suspicion.
sospechar 1 *t* (*imaginar*) to suspect, think, suppose. − 2 *i* (*desconfiar*) to suspect (**de, -**).
sospechosamente *adv* suspiciously.
sospechoso,-a 1 *adj* suspicious. − 2 *m,f* suspect.
sostén 1 *m* (*apoyo*) support. 2 (*sustento*) sustenance. 3 (*prenda*) bra, brassière.
▲ In *3*, *also used in plural with the same meaning*.
sostener 1 *t* (*mantener firme*) to support, hold up. 2 (*sujetar*) to hold. 3 *fig* (*apoyar*) to support, back. 4 *fig* (*soportar*) to endure, bear, put up with. 5 *fig* (*defender*) to defend, uphold. 6 *fig* (*afirmar*) to maintain, affirm. 7 *fig* (*alimentar*) to support, keep. 8 *fig* (*velocidad, corresponden*-

cia, relación, etc) to keep up, maintain. **– 9 sostenerse,**
p (*mantenerse*) to support os.; (*de pie*) to stand up. **10**
(*permanecer*) to stay, remain.
● **sostener la palabra,** *fig* to keep one's word. ‖ **sostener una conversación,** *fig* to hold a conversation.
‖ **sostener la mirada a algn.,** *fig* to stare sb. out.
▲ *Conjugation model* |87|, *like* **tener.**
sostenido,-a 1 *pp* → **sostener.** **– 2** *adj* (*continuado*) sustained; (*constante*) steady. **3** mús sharp: *fa sostenido,* F
sharp. **– 4 sostenido,** *m* mús sharp.
sostenimiento 1 *m* (*apoyo*) support. **2** (*mantenimiento*)
maintenance. **3** (*sustento*) sustenance.
sostuve *pt indef* → **sostener.**
sota 1 *f* (*cartas*) jack, knave. **2** *fam* (*mujer*) (old) bag.
sotabanco 1 *m* (*piso*) attic. **2** ARQ springer.
sotabarba 1 *f* (*barba*) Newgate frill, Newgate fringe. **2**
(*papada*) double chin.
sotana *f* cassock, soutane.
sótano *m* (*gen*) basement; (*de casa*) cellar, basement.
sotavento *m* lee, leeward.
■ **Islas de Sotavento,** Leeward Islands.
sotechado *m* shed.
soterrado,-a 1 *pp* → **soterrar.** **– 2** *adj* buried. **3** *fig* hidden, concealed.
soterrar 1 *t* to bury. **2** *fig* to hide, conceal.
▲ *Conjugation model* |27|, *like* **acertar.**
soto 1 *m* (*arboleda*) grove, copse. **2** (*matorrales*) thicket.
soufflé *m* soufflé.
souvenir *m* souvenir.
▲ *pl* **sovenirs.**
soviet *m* soviet.
▲ *pl* **soviets.**
soviético,-a 1 *adj* Soviet. **– 2** *m,f* Soviet.
■ **Unión Soviética,** Soviet Union.
sovietización *f* sovietization.
sovietizar *t* to sovietize.
▲ *Conjugation model* |4|, *like* **realizar.**
sovietólogo,-a *m,f* Sovietologist.
soy *pres indic* → **ser.**
SP *abr* (*Servicio Público*) public service.
sparring *m* sparring partner.
▲ *pl* **sparrings.**
sport de sport, *loc* sports, casual.
■ **ropa de sport,** casual clothes *pl*, casual wear, sportwear.
spot *m* commercial, advert, ad.
▲ *pl* **spots.**
spray *m* spray.
▲ *pl* **sprays.**
sprint *m* sprint.
▲ *pl* **sprints.**
sprintar *i* to sprint.
sprinter *mf* sprinter.
▲ *pl* **sprinters.**
squash *m* squash.
Sr. *abr* (*señor*) mister; (*abreviatura*) Mr.
Sra. *abr* (*señora*) Mrs.
Sras. *abr* (*señoras*) ladies.
s.r.c. *abr* (*se ruega contestación*) please reply; (*abreviatura*) R.S.V.P.
Sres. *abr* (*señores*) gentlemen; (*abreviatura*) Messrs.
Sri Lanka *f* Sri Lanka.
S.R.M. *abr* (*Su Real Majestad*) His Royal Majesty, Her
Royal Majesty; (*abreviatura*) HRM.
Srta. *abr* (*señorita*) miss.

S.S.[1] *abr* (*Su Santidad*) His Holiness; (*abreviatura*) HH.
S.S.[2] *abr* (*Su Señoría*) Your Honour.
SS *abr* (*Seguridad Social*) social security.
ss. *abr* (*siguientes*) following; (*abreviatura*) fol.
SS.AA. *abr* (*Sus Altezas*) Their Royal Highnesses.
SSE *sím* (*sudsudeste*) south-southeast; (*símbolo*) SSE.
SS.MM. *abr* (*Sus Majestades*) Their Majesties.
SSO *sím* (*sudsudoeste*) south-southwest; (*símbolo*) SSW.
s.s.s. *abr* (*su seguro servidor*) your humble servant.
Sta. *abr* (*santa*) Saint; (*abreviatura*) St.
stand *m* stand.
▲ *pl* **stands.**
standard 1 *adj* standard. **– 2** *m* standard.
▲ *pl* **standards.**
standardizar *t* to standardize.
▲ *Conjugation model* |4|, *like* **realizar.**
standing *m* standing.
■ **de alto standing,** luxury, de luxe.
stárter *m* choke.
▲ *pl* **stárters.**
statu quo *m* status quo.
status *m* status.
▲ *pl* **status.**
stick *m* stick.
▲ *pl* **sticks.**
Sto. *abr* (*Santo*) Saint; (*abreviatura*) St.
stock *m* stock.
▲ *pl* **stocks.**
stop 1 *m* (*señal*) stop sign. **2** (*parada*) stop.
strip-tease *m* striptease.
● **hacer un strip-tease,** to strip.
su *adj* (*de él*) his; (*de ella*) her; (*de usted, de ustedes*) your; (*de ellos, de ellas*) their; (*de animales, cosas*) its; (*de uno*) one's:
es su coche (de ella), it's her car; *dame sus libros,* give
me their books; *uno tiene que hacer su deber,* one must
do one's duty.
suasorio,-a *adj* persuasive.
suave 1 *adj* (*agradable al tacto*) soft, smooth. **2** (*liso, llano*)
smooth, even. **3** *fig* (*apacible*) gentle, mild. **4** *fig* (*tranquilo*) easy. **5** *fig* (*música, palabras, voz, luz, movimiento, viento*) soft, gentle. **6** *fig* (*clima*) mild, clement. **7** *fig* (*tabaco, sabor*) mild.
● **suave como el terciopelo,** (as) smooth as silk.
suavemente *adv* softly, smoothly, gently.
suavidad 1 *f* (*dulzura*) softness. **2** (*lisura*) smoothness,
evenness. **3** *fig* (*docilidad*) gentleness, mildness. **– 4** *adj*
fig (*tranquilidad*) ease. **5** *fig* (*de música, palabras, viento, etc*)
softness, gentleness. **6** *fig* (*del clima, tabaco, sabor*) mildness.
suavizante 1 *adj* (*de pelo*) conditioning. **2** (*de ropa*) softening. **– 3** *m* (*de pelo*) hair conditioner, conditioner. **4**
(*de ropa*) fabric softener, fabric conditioner.
suavizar 1 *t* (*hacer agradable*) to soften. **2** (*alisar*) to
smooth (out). **3** *fig* to soften.
▲ *Conjugation model* |4|, *like* **realizar.**
subacuático,-a *adj* underwater, subaquatic.
subafluente *m* tributary.
subalimentación *f* undernourishment.
subalimentado,-a 1 *pp* → **subalimentar.** **– 2** *adj* undernourished, underfed.
subalimentar *t* to undernourish, underfeed.
subalterno,-a 1 *adj* subordinate, subaltern. **– 2** *m,f*
subordinate, subaltern.
subarrendamiento *m* sublet, sublease.
subarrendar *t* to sublet, sublease.
▲ *Conjugation model* |27|, *like* **acertar.**

subarrendatario,-a *m,f* subtenant.
subarriendo *m* sublease.
subasta 1 *f* (*venta*) auction. 2 (*adjudicación de obra*) invitation to tender.
● **sacar a subasta,** to auction (off). ‖ **salir a subasta,** to be up for auction.
subastar *t* to auction (off), sell at auction.
subatómico,-a *adj* subatomic.
subcampeón,-ona *m,f* (*en competición*) runner-up; (*en ránking*) number two: *la actual subcampeona mundial,* the current world number two.
subclase *f* subclass.
subcomisión *f* subcommittee.
subconjunto *m* subset.
subconsciencia *f* subconscious.
subconsciente 1 *adj* subconscious. – 2 *m* subconscious.
subcontratista *mf* subcontractor.
subcontrato *m* subcontract.
subcutáneo,-a *adj* subcutaneous.
subdelegación *f* subdelegation.
subdelegado,-a 1 *pp* → **subdelegar**. – 2 *adj* subdelegate. – 3 *m,f* subdelegate.
subdelegar *t* to subdelegate.
▲ Conjugation model [7], like *llegar*.
subdesarrollado,-a *adj* underdeveloped.
subdesarrollo *m* underdevelopment.
subdirector,-ra *m,f* assistant director, assistant manager.
súbdito,-a 1 *adj* subject. – 2 *m,f* (*de un rey*) subject. 3 (*ciudadano*) citizen.
subdividir *t* to subdivide.
subdivisión *f* subdivision.
subempleo *m* underemployment.
suberoso,-a *adj* subereous.
subespecie *f* subspecies.
subestación *f* substation.
subestimar *t* to underestimate.
subexponer *t* to underexpose.
▲ Conjugation model [78], like *poner; pp* subexpuesto,-a.
subexposición *f* underexposure.
subfusil *m* sub-machine-gun.
subgénero *m* subgenus.
subida *f* → **subido,-a**.
subido,-a 1 *pp* → **subir**. – 2 *adj* (*gen*) high. 3 (*color, olor*) strong. – 4 subida, *f* (*ascenso*) ascent, climb. 5 (*pendiente*) slope, hill. 6 (*automovilismo*) hill climb. 7 *fig* (*aumento - gen*) increase; (- *de temperatura*) rise; (- *de precios, salario*) rise, increase. 8 *arg* (*drogas*) high.
● **subido,-a de tono,** *fig* daring, risqué.
subíndice *m* subscript.
subir 1 i (*ir hacia arriba - gen*) to go up, come up; (- *avión*) to climb. 2 (*en un vehículo - coche*) to get in; (*autobús, avión, barco, tren*) to get on, get onto: *¡venga, sube!,* go on, get in! 3 (*montar - bicicleta*) to get on; (- *caballo*) to get on, mount. 4 (*a un árbol*) to climb up. 5 *fig* (*elevarse, aumentar*) to rise. 6 *fig* (*categoría, puesto*) to be promoted. 7 *fig* (*cuenta*) to come (**a,** to): *la deuda sube a dos mil pesetas,* the debt comes to two thousand pesetas. – 8 *t* (*escaleras, calle*) to go up, climb; (*montaña*) to climb. 9 (*mover arriba*) to carry up, take up, bring up; (*poner arriba*) to put upstairs: *súbelo arriba,* take it upstairs. 10 (*cabeza etc*) to lift, raise. 11 (*pared*) to raise. 12 COST to take up: *subir un dobladillo,* to take up a hem. 13 *fig* (*precio, salario, etc*) to raise, put up. 14 *fig* (*subir el volumen - voz*) to raise;

(- *aparato*) to turn up. 15 *fig* (*color*) to strengthen. – 16 **subirse,** *p* (*piso, escalera*) to go up. 17 (*árbol, muro, etc*) to climb up (**a,** -). 18 (*en un vehículo - coche*) to get in (**a,** -); (*autobús*) to get on (**a,** -); (*avión, barco, tren*) to get on (**a,** -), get onto (**a,**-): *¡súbete, súbete al coche!,* get in, get into the car! 19 (*en animales, bicicleta*) to get on (**a,** -), mount. 20 (*ropa, calcetines*) to pull up; (*cremallera*) to do up, zip up; (*mangas*) to roll up.
● **subir a bordo,** to get on board. ‖ **subir al trono,** *fig* to ascend to the throne. ‖ **subir como la espuma,** *fam* to spread like wildfire. ‖ **subirse por las paredes,** *fig* to hit the roof. ‖ **subírsele a uno los humos a la cabeza,** *fig* to become conceited. ‖ **subírsele algo a la cabeza,** *fig* to go to one's head.
súbitamente *adv* suddenly, all of a sudden.
súbito,-a *adj* sudden: *muerte súbita,* sudden death.
● **de súbito,** suddenly, all of a sudden.
subjefe,-a *mf* second in command.
subjetividad *f* subjectivity, subjectiveness.
subjetivismo *m* subjectivism.
subjetivo,-a *adj* subjective.
subjuntivo,-a 1 *adj* subjunctive. – 2 subjuntivo, *m* subjunctive.
sublevación *f* uprising, revolt, rebellion.
sublevamiento *m* uprising, revolt, rebellion.
sublevar 1 *t* to incite to rebellion. 2 *fig* (*indignar*) to infuriate. – 3 sublevarse, *p* to rebel, revolt.
sublimación *f* sublimation.
sublimado *m* sublimate.
sublimar 1 *t* (*gen*) to sublimate. 2 (*ensalzar*) to praise, exalt.
sublime 1 *adj* sublime. 2 (*noble*) noble, lofty. – 3 lo sublime, *m* the sublime.
subliminal *adj* subliminal.
submarinismo *m* skin-diving.
submarinista *mf* skin-diver.
submarino,-a 1 *adj* underwater, submarine. – 2 submarino, *m* submarine.
submaxilar *adj* submaxillary.
submúltiplo,-a 1 *adj* submultiple. – 2 submúltiplo, *m* submultiple.
subnormal 1 *adj* MED mentally handicapped, subnormal. – 2 *mf* MED subnormal. 3 *fam* blockhead.
suboficial 1 *m* MIL noncommissioned officer. 2 MAR petty officer.
suborden *m* suborder.
subordinación *f* subordination.
subordinado,-a 1 *pp* → **subordinar**. – 2 *adj* subordinate. – 3 *m,f* subordinate.
subordinante *adj* subordinating.
subordinar 1 *t* to subordinate. – 2 subordinarse, *p* to subordinate os.
subproducto *m* by-product.
subrayar 1 *t* to underline. 2 *fig* to emphasize, underline, stress.
subreino *m* subkingdom.
subrepticiamente *adv* surreptitiously.
subrepticio,-a *adj* surreptitious.
subrogar *t* to subrogate, substitute.
▲ Conjugation model [7], like *llegar*.
subrutina *f* subroutine.
subsanable 1 *adj* (*remediable*) reparable, rectifiable. 2 (*solucionable*) surmountable.
subsanar 1 *t* (*remediar*) to rectify, correct. 2 (*dificutad etc*) to overcome. 3 (*compensar*) to make up for.

subscribir *t-p* → **suscribir**.
▲ *pp* *subscrito,-a*.
subscripción *f* subscription.
subscriptor,-ra *m,f* subscriber.
subscrito,-a 1 *pp* → **subscribir**. – 2 *adj-m,f* → **suscrito,-a**.
subsecretaría 1 *f* (*cargo*) under-secretaryship. 2 (*oficina*) under-secretary's office.
subsecretario,-a *m,f* under-secretary.
subseguir 1 *i* to follow, come after. – 2 **subseguirse**, *p* to follow, come after.
▲ *Conjugation model* |56|, *like* **seguir**.
subsidiar *t* to subsidize.
▲ *Conjugation model* |12|, *like* **cambiar**.
subsidiario,-a *adj* subsidiary.
subsidio *m* allowance, benefit.
■ **subsidio de paro / subsidio de desempleo**, unemployment benefit.
subsiguiente *adj* subsequent, following.
subsistencia 1 *f* (*hecho*) subsistence. 2 (*lo necesario para vivir*) sustenance. – 3 **subsistencias**, *fpl* (*provisiones*) food *sing*, provisions, supplies.
subsistente *adj* surviving, lasting.
subsistir 1 *i* (*conservarse*) to subsist, remain, last. 2 (*vivir*) to subsist, live on, survive.
subsónico,-a *adj* subsonic.
substancia *f* → **sustancia**.
substancial *adj* → **sustancial**.
substanciar *t* to condense, abridge.
▲ *Conjugation model* |12|, *like* **cambiar**.
substancioso,-a *adj* → **sustancioso,-a**.
substantivar *t* to use as a noun.
substantivo,-a *adj-m* → **sustantivo**.
substitución *f* substitution, replacement.
substituible *adj* replaceable, expendable.
substituir *t* → **sustituir**.
▲ *Conjugation model* |62|, *like* **huir**.
substitutivo,-a *adj-m* → **sustitutivo,-a**.
substituto,-a *m,f* → **sustituto,-a**.
substracción *f* → **sustracción**.
substraendo *m* subtrahend.
substraer *t-p* → **sustraer**.
▲ *Conjugation model* |88|, *like* **traer**.
substrato *m* substratum.
subsuelo *m* subsoil.
subteniente *m* second lieutenant.
subterfugio *m* (*escapatoria*) subterfuge; (*pretexto*) pretext.
subterráneo,-a 1 *adj* subterranean, underground. – 2 subterráneo, *m* underground passage, tunnel, subway.
subtipo *m* subtype.
subtitular *t* CINEM to subtitle.
subtítulo 1 *m* subtitle. 2 LIT subhead, subheading.
subtropical *adj* subtropical.
suburbano,-a 1 *adj* suburban. – 2 suburbano, *m* suburban train.
suburbial *adj* suburban.
suburbio *m* (*periferia*) suburb; (*barrio pobre*) slums *pl*.
subvalorar *t* to underrate, underestimate, undervalue.
subvención *f* subsidy, grant.
subvencionar *t* to subsidize.
subvenir *t* to meet, defray.
▲ *Conjugation model* |90|, *like* **venir**.
subversión *f* subversion.
subversivo,-a *adj* subversive.

subvertir *t* to subvert, upset, overthrow.
▲ *Conjugation model* |35|, *like* **hervir**.
subyacente *adj* underlying.
subyacer *i* to underlie (**en**, -).
▲ *Conjugation model* |92|, *like* **yacer**.
subyugación *f* subjugation.
subyugar 1 *t* to subjugate. 2 *fig* to captivate.
▲ *Conjugation model* |7|, *like* **llegar**.
succión *f* suction.
succionar *t* to suck up.
sucedáneo,-a 1 *adj* substitute. – 2 sucedáneo, *m* substitute: *sucedáneo de café,* coffee substitute.
suceder 1 *i* (*acontecer*) to happen, occur: *¿qué sucede?,* what's the matter?; *sucedió ayer,* it happened yesterday. 2 (*seguir*) to follow (**a**, -), succeed (**a**, -): *sucedió a su padre en el puesto,* he succeeded his father in the job. 3 (*heredar*) to succeed. – 4 **sucederse**, *p* to follow one another.
● **por lo que pueda suceder,** just in case. ‖ **suceda lo que suceda,** whatever happens, come what may. ‖ **lo sucedido,** what happened; *no quiso hablar de lo sucedido,* he didn't want to talk about what happened.
▲ In *1*, used only in the 3rd person; it does not take a subject.
sucedido,-a 1 *pp* → **suceder**. – 2 sucedido, *m fam* event.
sucesión 1 *f* (*herencia*) succession, inheritance. 2 (*descendencia*) issue, heirs *pl*. 3 (*al trono*) succession. 4 (*serie*) series, succession.
sucesivamente *adv* successively.
● **y así sucesivamente,** and so on.
sucesivo,-a 1 *adj* (*siguiente*) following, successive. 2 (*consecutivo*) consecutive, running: *tres días sucesivos,* three days running.
● **en lo sucesivo,** from now on.
suceso 1 *m* (*hecho*) event, happening, occurrence. 2 (*incidente*) incident. 3 (*delito*) crime.
■ **sección de sucesos,** (*en prensa*) accident and crime reports.
sucesor,-ra *m,f* successor.
súchil *m* white frangipani.
suciedad 1 *f* (*inmundicia*) dirt, filth. 2 (*calidad*) dirtiness, filthiness. 3 *fig* (*obscenidad*) obscenity.
sucintamente *adv* briefly, concisely.
sucinto,-a *adj* concise, brief, succint.
sucio,-a 1 *adj* (*con manchas*) dirty, filthy. 2 (*que se ensucia fácilmente*) which dirties easily, which shows the dirt. 3 *fig* (*deshonesto*) shady, underhand. 4 *fig* (*color*) dirty. 5 DEP *fig* foul, dirty, unfair. 6 *fig* (*trabajo, lenguaje*) dirty, filthy. – 7 sucio, *adv fig* in an underhand way, dirty: *jugar sucio,* to play dirty.
● **en sucio,** in rough. ‖ **tener una lengua sucia,** to be foul-mouthed.
sucre *m* standard monetary unit of Ecuador.
suculencia *f* succulence, juiciness.
suculento,-a *adj* juicy, succulent.
sucumbir 1 *i* (*rendirse*) to succumb (**a**, to), yield (**a**, to). 2 (*morir*) to perish. 3 *fig* (*tentación etc*) to give in (**a**, to), yield (**a**, to).
sucursal 1 *f* COM FIN branch, branch office. 2 (*delegación*) subsidiary.
sudaca *mf fam pey* South American.
sudación *f* sweating.
sudadera 1 *f* (*prenda*) sweatshirt. 2 *fam* (*acción*) sweat: *se pegó una sudadera,* he worked up a sweat.
Sudáfrica *f* South Africa.
sudafricano,-a *adj* South African.

Sudamérica *f* South America.
sudamericano,-a *adj* South American.
Sudán *m* Sudan.
sudanés,-esa 1 *adj* Sudanese. – 2 *m,f* Sudanese.
sudar 1 *i* (*transpirar*) to sweat, perspire. 2 *fig* (*paredes*) to sweat. 3 *fig* (*plantas*) to exude, ooze. 4 *fam* (*trabajar*) to slog one's guts out, work hard. – 5 *t* (*transpirar*) to sweat. 6 (*empapar en sudor*) to make sweaty. 7 *fig* (*plantas*) to exude, ooze. 8 *fam fig* (*conseguir con esfuerzo*) to work hard for.
● **hacer sudar a algn.**, to drive sb. hard. ‖ **¡me la suda!**, I couldn't give a toss! ‖ **sudar el kilo / sudar la gota gorda / sudar tinta**, *fam* to sweat blood.
sudario *m* shroud.
sudeste 1 *adj* (*del sudeste*) southeast, southeastern; (*hacia el sudeste*) southeasterly. 2 (*viento*) southeast. – 3 *m* (*punto*) southeast. 4 (*viento*) southeast wind.
sudista 1 *adj* Southern. – 2 *mf* Southerner.
sudoeste 1 *adj* (*del sudoeste*) southwest, southwestern; (*hacia el sudoeste*) southwesterly. 2 (*viento*) southwest. – 3 *m* (*punto*) southwest. 4 (*viento*) southwest wind.
sudor 1 *m* sweat, perspiration. 2 *fig* effort, hard work.
● **con el sudor de la frente**, *fig* by the sweat of one's brow. ‖ **costar algo muchos sudores**, *fig* to be an uphill struggle.
sudorífero,-a *adj* sudoriferous.
sudorífico,-a 1 *adj* sudorific. – 2 **sudorífico**, *m* sudorific.
sudoríparo,-a *adj* sudoriferous, sweat.
■ **glándulas sudoríparas**, sweat glands.
sudoroso,-a *adj* sweaty.
Suecia *f* Sweden.
sueco,-a 1 *adj* Swedish. – 2 *m,f* (*persona*) Swede. – 3 **sueco**, *m* (*idioma*) Swedish.
● **hacerse el sueco,-a**, *fam* to play dumb.
suegro,-a *m,f* (*hombre*) father-in-law; (*mujer*) mother-in-law: *mis suegros*, my in-laws.
suela 1 *f* (*del calzado*) sole. 2 (*cuero curtido*) leather. 3 (*del taco de billar*) leather tip.
● **no llegarle a la suela del zapato a algn.**, *fam* not to hold a candle to sb.
sueldo *m* salary, pay, wages *pl*.
● **estar a sueldo**, to be on a salary.
■ **aumento de sueldo**, pay rise (us raise). ‖ **sueldo base**, basic pay, us base salary. ‖ **sueldo mínimo**, minimum wage.
suelo 1 *m* (*superficie*) ground; (*de interior*) floor. 2 *fig* (*tierra*) soil, land; (*mundo*) earth. 3 (*territorio*) soil, land: *suelo extranjero*, foreign soil. 4 (*terreno*) land. 5 (*pavimento*) surface. 6 *fig* (*de vasija etc*) bottom.
● **besar el suelo**, *fam* to fall flat on one's face, hit the deck. ‖ **dar consigo en el suelo**, to fall. ‖ **echar al suelo**, to demolish, knock down. ‖ **echar por los suelos**, *fig* to ruin. ‖ **estar por los suelos**, (*persona*) to be very low; (*precios*) to be rock-bottom. ‖ **poner algo por los suelos**, *fig* to run sth. down, tear sth. to pieces. ‖ **venirse al suelo**, to fall down; *fig* to fall through.
■ **suelo cultivable**, arable land. ‖ **suelo de madera**, wooden floor. ‖ **suelo patrio**, native land.
suelta *f* → **suelto,-a**.
suelto,-a 1 *adj* (*no sujeto*) loose: *perro suelto*, loose dog; *tornillo suelto*, loose screw. 2 (*desatado*) undone, untied. 3 (*no envasado o empaquetado*) loose. 4 (*desaparejado*) odd: *un guante suelto*, an odd glove. 5 (*dinero*) in change: *¿llevas cien pesetas sueltas?*, have you got a hundred pesetas in change?; *no llevo nada suelto*, I haven't got

any change. 6 (*en libertad*) free; (*huido*) at large. 7 (*disgregado*) scattered. 8 (*con diarrea*) loose. 9 (*prenda*) loose, loose-fitting. 10 *fig* (*estilo etc*) flowing, easy. 11 *fig* (*atrevido*) daring. 12 *fig* (*ligero*) agile, nimble; (*veloz*) swift. – 13 **suelto**, *m* (*en prensa*) item, short article. 14 (*cambio*) change, small change, loose change. – 15 **suelta**, *f* (*acción*) release. 16 (*libertad*) freedom.
● **estar muy suelto,-a en algo**, *fig* to be good at sth.
sueño 1 *m* (*acto*) sleep. 2 (*ganas de dormir*) sleepiness. 3 (*lo soñado*) dream. 4 *fig* (*ilusión*) dream, illusion.
● **caerse de sueño**, *fig* not to be able to keep one's eyes open. ‖ **conciliar el sueño**, to get to sleep. ‖ **dar sueño**, to make sleepy. ‖ **en sueños**, *fig* in one's dreams. ‖ **echar un sueño**, to take a nap. ‖ **entre sueños**, while half-asleep. ‖ **¡ni en sueños!**, *fam* not on your life!: *no lo haría ni en sueños*, I wouldn't dream of doing it. ‖ **perder el sueño por algo**, to lose sleep over sth. ‖ **quitar el sueño**, to keep awake. ‖ **ser un sueño**, *fam* to be a dream: *es un sueño de piso*, it's a dream of a flat. ‖ **tener el sueño ligero**, to be a light sleeper. ‖ **tener sueño**, to feel sleepy, be sleepy: *tengo mucho sueño*, I'm feeling really sleepy.
■ **sueño dorado**, *fig* cherished dream, greatest dream.
suero 1 *m* MED serum. 2 (*de la leche*) whey.
suerte 1 *f* (*fortuna*) luck, fortune. 2 (*azar*) chance. 3 (*destino*) destiny, fate. 4 (*estado, condición*) lot, situation. 5 *fml* (*tipo*) sort, kind, type: *toda suerte de libros*, all kinds of books. 6 (*en tauromaquia*) manoeuvre (us maneuver) in a bullfight.
● **¡buena suerte! / ¡suerte!**, good luck! ‖ **de otra suerte**, otherwise. ‖ **estar de suerte / estar de mala suerte**, to be in luck / be out of luck. ‖ **la suerte está echada**, the die is cast. ‖ **por suerte**, fortunately. ‖ **probar suerte**, to try one's luck. ‖ **¡que tengas suerte!**, good luck! ‖ **tener suerte**, to be lucky: *tienes mucha suerte*, you're really lucky. ‖ **tener una suerte loca**, *fam* to have the luck of the devil. ‖ **tentar la suerte**, *fig* to tempt fate. ‖ **traer (buena) suerte / traer mala suerte**, to be lucky, bring good luck / be unlucky, bring bad luck.
suertudo,-a *adj fam* lucky.
suéter *m* sweater.
▲ *pl* **suéteres**.
suficiencia 1 *f* (*capacidad*) capacity. 2 (*engreimiento*) arrogance, smugness. 3 (*conveniencia*) suitability, competence.
suficiente 1 *adj* (*bastante*) sufficient, enough: *no tiene suficiente dinero*, she hasn't got enough money. 2 (*apto*) suitable. 3 *fig* (*engreído*) smug, complacent.
suficientemente *adv* enough: *no es suficientemente alto*, it isn't high enough; *es lo suficientemente claro como para que lo entendamos todos*, it's clear enough for us all to understand.
sufijo,-a 1 *adj* suffixal. – 2 **sufijo**, *m* suffix.
sufragar 1 *t* (*costear - gastos*) to defray, pay; (*- empresa*) to finance. 2 (*ayudar*) to aid, help, assist.
▲ *Conjugation model* [7], *like* **llegar**.
sufragio 1 *m* suffrage. 2 (*voto*) vote.
● **en sufragio de ...**, (*misa etc*) for the soul of ...
■ **sufragio universal**, universal suffrage.
sufragismo *m* suffragism, suffragist movement.
sufragista *m,f* (*hombre*) suffragist; (*mujer*) suffragette.
sufrido,-a 1 *pp* → **sufrir**. – 2 *adj* (*persona*) patient, long-suffering. 3 (*color*) practical, that does not show the dirt; (*tejido*) hardwearing.
sufrimiento *m* suffering.

sufrir l t (*padecer*) to suffer. **2** (*accidente, ataque*) to have; (*operación*) to undergo. **3** (*dificultades, cambios*) to experience; (*derrota, consecuencias*) to suffer. **4** (*aguantar*) to bear, stand, put up with: *no la puedo sufrir,* I can't stand her. **5** (*consentir*) to tolerate. – **6** i (*padecer*) to suffer.
● hacer sufrir a algn., to cause sb. pain, make sb. suffer. ‖ sufrir del corazón, to have a heart condition. ‖ sufrir hambre, to go hungry. ‖ sufrir vergüenza, to be ashamed.
sugerencia f suggestion.
sugerente adj suggestive.
sugeridor,-ra adj suggestive.
sugerir l t to suggest: *te sugiero que lo vuelvas a intentar,* I suggest you try again. **2** (*insinuar*) to hint, hint at: *no sé qué sugieres con esto,* I don't know what you're hinting at. **3** (*suscitar*) to suggest, make think: *sus cuadros no me sugieren nada,* his paintings don't do anything for me.
▲ Conjugation model [35], like *hervir*.
sugestión f suggestion.
sugestionable adj impressionable, easily influenced.
sugestionar l t to influence, persuade. – **2 sugestionarse,** p to be easily influenced.
sugestivo,-a l adj (*que sugiere*) suggestive. **2** (*que atrae*) fascinating, attractive.
suicida l adj suicidal: *misión suicida,* suicide mission. – **2** mf suicide. **3** fig madcap.
suicidarse p to commit suicide.
suicidio m suicide.
suite f suite.
▲ pl suites.
Suiza f Switzerland.
suizo,-a l adj Swiss. – **2** m,f Swiss. – **3** suizo, m (*bollo*) bun. **4** (*chocolate con nata*) hot chocolate with cream.
sujeción l f (*acción*) subjection. **2** (*unión*) fastening.
sujetador,-ra l adj fastening. – **2 sujetador,** m bra, brassière.
sujetapapeles m paper clip.
▲ pl sujetapapeles.
sujetar l t (*fijar*) to fix, secure, hold. **2** (*agarrar, sostener*) to hold, hold on to. **3** (*para que no escape*) to hold down. **4** (*papeles*) to fasten; (*pelo*) to hold in place. **5** fig (*dominar, someter*) to control, restrain. **6** fig (*atar*) to tie down. – **7 sujetarse,** p (*agarrarse*) to hold on, hold tight: *sujétate, que el autobús corre mucho,* hold tight, the bus is going really fast. **8** fig (*someterse*) to subject os. (**a,** to).
● sujetar con clavos, to nail down.
sujeto,-a l adj (*sometido*) subject (**a,** to), liable (**a,** to). **2** (*agarrado, atado*) fastened, secure. **3** fig (*atado*) tied down. – **4 sujeto,** m LING subject. **5** (*individuo*) fellow, individual, character.
sulfamida f sulphonamide (US sulfonamide).
sulfatación f sulphation (US sulfation).
sulfatar t to sulphate (US sulfate).
sulfato m sulphate (US sulfate).
sulfhídrico,-a adj sulphuretted (US sulfureted).
■ ácido sulfhídrico, hydrogen sulphide (US sulfide).
sulfito m sulphite (US sulfite).
sulfurar l t QUÍM to sulphurate (US sulfurate). **2** fam fig (*irritar*) to exasperate, infuriate. – **3 sulfurarse,** p fam fig to blow one's top, lose one's rag.
sulfúrico,-a adj sulphuric (US sulfuric).
sulfuro m sulphide (US sulfide).
sulfuroso,-a adj sulphurous (US sulfurous).
sultán,-ana m,f (*hombre*) sultan; (*mujer*) sultana.

sultanato m sultanate.
suma l f (*cantidad*) sum, amount. **2** MAT sum, addition. **3** (*resumen*) summary.
● en suma, in short.
■ suma total, sum total.
sumadora f adding machine.
sumamente adv extremely, highly.
sumando m addend.
sumar l t MAT to add, add up. **2** (*componer una cantidad*) to total, amount to, come to: *eso suma cinco mil pesetas,* it comes to five thousand pesetas. **3** (*compendiar*) to summarize, sum up. – **4 sumarse,** p (*unirse*) to join (**a,** in).
● suma y sigue, carried forward; fig and that's not all.
sumarial adj pertaining to an indictment.
sumariar t to indict.
sumario,-a l adj summary, brief. **2** JUR summary. – **3** sumario, m (*resumen*) summary. **4** JUR legal proceedings pl, indictment.
sumarísimo,-a adj swift, expeditious.
sumergible l adj submergible, submersible. – **2** m submarine.
sumergir l t (*meter bajo líquido*) to submerge, submerse, immerse. **2** fig (*hundir*) to plunge, sink. – **3 sumergirse,** p (*meterse bajo líquido*) to submerge (**en,** in), go underwater. **4** fig to become immersed (**en,** in).
▲ Conjugation model [6], like *dirigir*.
Sumeria f Sumer.
sumerio,-a l adj Sumerian. – **2** m,f (*persona*) Sumerian. – **3** sumerio, m (*idioma*) Sumerian.
sumersión f submersion.
sumidero m drain, sewer.
sumiller m chamberlain.
suministración f → suministro.
suministrador,-ra m,f supplier.
suministrar t to provide, supply: *nos suministró el café,* he supplied us with the coffee.
suministro l m provision, supply, supplying. – **2 suministros,** mpl supplies.
sumir l t (*hundir*) to sink, plunge, submerge. **2** fig to plunge. – **3 sumirse,** p (*hundirse*) to sink. **4** fig to immerse os. (**en,** in), lose os. (**en,** in).
● sumir a algn. en la duda, fig to plunge sb. into doubt. ‖ sumir a algn. en la miseria, fig to plunge sb. into poverty.
sumisamente adv submissively.
sumisión l f (*acto*) submission. **2** (*carácter*) submissiveness.
sumiso,-a adj submissive, obedient.
súmmum m summit, acme.
● ser el súmmum, (*el colmo*) to be the limit.
sumo,-a l adj (*supremo*) supreme, highest. **2** fig (*muy grande*) greatest.
● a lo sumo, at most, at the most. ‖ con sumo cuidado, with extreme care.
■ suma autoridad, supreme authority. ‖ Sumo Pontífice, Sovereign Pontiff. ‖ sumo sacerdote, high priest.
sunita m Sunnite.
sunna f Sunna.
suntuario,-a adj sumptuary.
suntuosidad f sumptuousness, magnificence.
suntuoso,-a adj sumptuous, magnificent.
supe pt indef → saber.
supeditación f subjection, subordination.

supeditar 1 *t* (*subordinar*) to subordinate (**a**, to). **2** (*condicionar*) to subject (**a**, to). **– 3 supeditarse,** *p* (*someterse*) to subject os. (**a**, to), bow (**a**, to).
● **estar supeditado,-a a,** to be subject to, be dependent on.
súper 1 *adj fam* super, great. **– 2** *m fam* (*supermercado*) supermarket. **– 3** *f fam* (*gasolina*) four-star.
superable *adj* surmountable: *nuestros problemas son superables,* our problems can be overcome.
superabundancia *f* superabundance.
superabundante *adj* superabundant.
superabundar *i* to superabound.
superación 1 *f* (*problemas etc*) overcoming. **2** (*de uno mismo*) self-improvement.
■ **afán de superación,** desire to improve os., desire to better os.
superado,-a 1 *pp* → **superar. – 2** *adj* (*anticuado*) outdated, obsolete, antiquated.
superalimentar *t* to overfeed.
superar 1 *t* (*exceder*) to surpass, exceed, excel. **2** (*obstáculo etc*) to overcome, surmount. **– 3 superarse,** *p* (*sobrepasarse*) to excel os. **4** (*mejorarse*) to improve os., better os.
superávit *m* surplus.
▲ *pl* **superávit**.
supercarburante *m* high octane fuel.
superchería *f* trick, fraud.
superciliar *adj* superciliary.
superconductividad *f* superconductivity.
superconductor *m* superconductor.
superdesarrollo *m* overdevelopment.
superdesarrollado,-a *adj* overdeveloped.
superdotado,-a 1 *adj* exceptionally gifted. **– 2** *m,f* genius.
superestrato *m* superstratum.
superestructura *f* superstructure.
superferolítico,-a *adj fam* irón affected.
superficial *adj* superficial.
superficialidad *f* superficiality, superficialness.
superficialmente *adv* superficially.
superficie 1 *f* (*parte externa*) surface: *en la superficie,* on the surface. **2** (*área*) area.
■ **superficie terrestre,** land surface.
superfino,-a *adj* extra fine.
superfluidad *f* superfluity, superfluousness.
superfluo,-a *adj* superfluous.
superhombre *m* superman.
superintendencia *f* superintendence, superintendency.
superintendente *mf* superintendent.
superior 1 *adj* (*encima de*) upper, top: *labio superior,* upper lip; *está en la planta superior,* it's on the upper floor. **2** (*por encima de*) greater (**a**, than), higher (**a**, than), above (**a**, -): *es superior a cuatro,* it's greater than four. **3** *fig* (*persona - que supera*) superior; (- *mejor*) better. **4** *fig* (*calidad etc*) superior, high, excellent. **5** EDUC higher. **– 6** *m* (*jefe*) superior. **7** REL superior.
■ **calidad superior,** top quality, high quality.
superiora *f* mother superior.
superioridad 1 *f* (*ventaja*) advantage. **2** (*persona*) superiority.
superlativo,-a 1 *adj* superlative. **– 2 superlativo,** *m* superlative.
supermercado *m* supermarket.
supermujer *f* superwoman.

supernumerario,-a 1 *adj* supernumerary. **– 2** *m,f* supernumerary.
superorden *m* superorder.
superpetrolero *m* supertanker.
superpoblación *f* overpopulation, overcrowding.
superpoblado,-a *adj* overpopulated, overcrowded.
superponer 1 *t* to superpose, superimpose. **2** *fig* to put before. **– 3 superponerse,** *p fig* to come before.
▲ *Conjugation model* |78|, *like poner; pp* **superpuesto,-a**.
superposición *f* superposition.
superpotencia *f* superpower.
superproducción 1 *f* (*industrial*) overproduction. **2** (*cinematográfica*) mammoth production.
superpuesto,-a *pp* → **superponer**.
superpuse *pt indef* → **superponer**.
superrealismo *m* surrealism.
supersecreto,-a *adj* top secret.
supersónico,-a *adj* supersonic.
superstición *f* superstition.
supersticioso,-a *adj* superstitious.
supervalorar *t* to overvalue, overrate.
supervisar *t* to supervise.
supervisión *f* supervision, control.
supervisor,-ra *m,f* supervisor.
supervivencia *f* survival.
superviviente 1 *adj* surviving. **– 2** *mf* survivor.
supervivir *i* to survive.
superyó *m* superego.
supino,-a 1 *adj* (*boca arriba*) supine, face up. **2** *fig* (*absoluto*) total, absolute: *ignorancia supina,* crass ignorance. **– 3 supino,** *m* LING supine.
suplantación 1 *f* (*falsificación*) forgery. **2** (*de una persona*) supplantation.
suplantador,-ra 1 *adj* (*falsificador*) forgery. **2** (*de una persona*) supplanting.
suplantar 1 *t* (*una persona*) to supplant, take the place of. **2** (*falsificar*) to forge.
suplementario,-a 1 *adj* supplementary, extra, additional. **2** (*geometría*) supplementary.
suplemento 1 *m* (*de revista etc*) supplement. **2** (*de dinero*) extra charge. **3** (*geometría*) supplement.
■ **suplemento dominical,** Sunday supplement.
suplencia *f* substitution.
suplente 1 *adj* (*gen*) substitute, deputy. **2** DEP reserve. **– 3** *mf* (*gen*) substitute. **4** DEP reserve player. **5** TEAT understudy. **6** EDUC supply teacher, US substitute teacher. **7** MED lucum, US covering doctor.
supletorio,-a 1 *adj* supplementary, additional, extra: *cama supletoria,* extra bed. **– 2 supletorio,** *m* (*teléfono*) extension.
súplica 1 *f* request, entreaty, plea. **2** JUR petition.
● **a súplica de,** at the request of.
suplicante 1 *adj* beseeching, entreating. **– 2** *mf* supplicant, suppliant.
suplicar 1 *t* to beseech, beg, implore. **2** JUR to appeal to.
▲ *Conjugation model* |1|, *like sacar*.
suplicatorio *m* request, petition.
suplicio 1 *m* (*castigo*) torture. **2** (*dolor*) pain; *fig* torment.
suplir 1 *t* (*reemplazar*) to replace, substitute. **2** (*compensar*) to make up for. **3** (*remediar*) to remedy.
suponer 1 *t* (*gen*) to suppose, assume: *supongamos que dice la verdad,* let's suppose he's telling the truth. **2** (*significar*) to mean. **3** (*conllevar*) to mean, entail, require. **4** (*adivinar*) to guess; (*imaginar*) to imagine, think: *lo su-*

ponía, I thought as much. **5** (*creer*) to think. **– 6** *m fam* supposition.
● **como es de suponer,** as is to be expected. ‖ **ser de suponer,** to be likely: *es de suponer que no miente,* he isn't likely to be lying.
▲ *Conjugation model* [78]*, like poner*; *pp supuesto,-a.*

suposición *f* supposition, assumption.

supositorio *m* suppository.

supranacional *adj* supranational.

suprarrenal *adj* suprarenal.

supremacía *f* supremacy.

supremo,-a **1** *adj* (*gen*) supreme. **2** (*decisivo*) decisive. **3** (*último*) last, final.
■ **hora suprema / momento supremo,** *lit* dying moments *pl.* ‖ **tribunal supremo,** supreme court.

supresión **1** *f* (*de libertad etc*) suppression; (*de ley, impuesto*) abolition; (*de dificultades*) elimination; (*de restricciones*) lifting. **2** (*de palabra*) deletion. **3** (*omisión*) omission.

suprimir **1** *t* (*libertad etc*) to suppress; (*ley, impuestos*) to abolish; (*dificultades*) to eliminate, remove; (*restricciones*) to lift. **2** (*tabaco, alcohol*) to cut out: *el médico me ha suprimido la comida con mucha grasa,* the doctor has told me to cut out fatty foods. **3** (*palabra*) to delete, take out, leave out. **4** (*omitir*) to omit.

supuesto,-a **1** *pp* → **suponer.** **– 2** *adj* (*que se supone*) supposed, assumed. **3** (*pretendido*) so-called, self-styled. **– 4 supuesto,** *m* (*suposición*) supposition, assumption. **5** (*hipótesis*) hypothesis.
● **dar algo por supuesto,-a,** to take sth. for granted. ‖ **en el supuesto de que ...,** supposing that ...
■ **nombre supuesto,** assumed name.

supuración *f* suppuration.

supurar *i* to suppurate.

supuse *pt indef* → **suponer.**

sur 1 *m* south. **2** (*viento*) south wind.
● **al sur de,** south of, to the south of.

sura *f* sura.

surá *m* surah.

Suramérica *f* South America.

suramericano,-a *adj-m,f* → **sudamericano,-a.**

surcado,-a **1** *pp* → **surcar.** **– 2** *adj fig* (*cara etc*) line, wrinkled.

surcar **1** *t* AGR to plough (US plow). **2** (*agua*) to cut through, cross; (*aire*) to fly through. **3** (*hacer rayas*) to score, furrow.
● **surcar los mares,** *fig* to ply the seas.
▲ *Conjugation model* [1]*, like sacar.*

surco 1 *m* (*en tierra*) furrow. **2** (*arruga*) wrinkle. **3** (*de rueda*) rut. **4** (*de disco*) groove.

surcoreano,-a **1** *adj* South Korean. **– 2** *m,f* South Korean.

sureño,-a **1** *adj* southern. **– 2** *m,f* southerner.

sureste *adj-m* → **sudeste.**

surf *m* surf.
■ **tabla de surf,** surfboard.

surfista 1 *adj* surf. **– 2** *mf* surfer.

surgir 1 *i* (*agua*) to spring forth, spurt up. **2** *fig* (*aparecer - gen*) to appear, emerge; (*- dificultades*) to crop up, arise, come up. **3** MAR to anchor.
▲ *Conjugation model* [6]*, like dirigir.*

Surinam *m* Surinam.

suripanta 1 *f fam* (*corista*) chorus girl. **2** *fam pey* slut.

surmenaje 1 *m* (*exceso de trabajo*) overwork. **2** (*agotamiento*) mental fatigue.

suroeste *adj-m* → **sudoeste.**

surrealismo *m* surrealism.

surrealista 1 *adj* surrealist, surrealistic. **– 2** *mf* surrealist.

sursuncorda *m fam fig* the great panjandrum.

surtido,-a 1 *pp* → **surtir. – 2** *adj* (*variado*) assorted. **3** (*bien provisto*) well stocked. **– 4 surtido,** *m* assortment, selection: *un surtido de galletas,* a biscuit assortment.

surtidor 1 *m* (*fuente*) fountain. **2** (*chorro*) jet, spout.
■ **surtidor de gasolina,** petrol pump, US gas pump.

surtir 1 *t* (*proveer*) to supply (**de,** with), provide (**de,** with): *surtir de ropa,* to supply with clothes. **– 2** *i* (*brotar*) to spout, spurt. **– 3 surtirse,** *p* to supply os., provide os.

surto,-a *adj* anchored.

susceptibilidad 1 *f* (*gen*) susceptibility. **2** (*sensibilidad*) sensitivity. **3** (*propensión a ofenderse*) touchiness.

susceptible 1 *adj* (*gen*) susceptible. **2** (*sensible*) oversensitive. **3** (*propenso a ofenderse*) touchy.
● **susceptible de,** (*con tendencia a*) liable to; (*capaz de*) capable of: *el proyecto es susceptible de mejora,* the project leaves room for improvement.

suscitar 1 *t* (*gen*) to cause, provoke. **2** (*rebelión*) to stir up, arouse; (*discusión*) to start; (*problemas*) to cause, raise; (*interés*) to arouse.

suscribir 1 *t* FIN to subscribe. **2** *fig* (*convenir con alguien*) to subscribe to, endorse. **3** (*a una revista etc*) to take out a subscription for. **4** *fml* (*firmar*) to subscribe. **– 5 suscribirse,** *p* (*abonarse*) to subscribe: *me he suscrito a Time,* I've subscribed to Time.
● **el que suscribe,** the undersigned.
▲ *pp suscrito,-a.*

suscripción *f* subscription.

suscriptor,-ra *m,f* subscriber.

suscrito,-a 1 *pp* → **subscrito,-a. – 2** *adj* (*abonado*) subscribed. **3** (*firmado*) undersigned. **– 4** *m,f* undersigned.
● **estar suscrito,-a a,** to subscribe to, have a subscription to.

susodicho,-a *adj fml* above-mentioned, aforesaid.

suspender 1 *t* (*levantar*) to hang, hang up, suspend. **2** (*aplazar - gen*) to postpone, put off, delay; (*- reunión*) to adjourn. **3** EDUC *fig* to fail. **4** *fig* (*pagos*) to suspend; (*servicio*) to discontinue. **5** *fig* (*causar admiración*) to amaze, astonish.
● **suspender de empleo y sueldo,** to suspender without pay.

suspense *m* suspense.
● **mantener a algn. en suspense,** to keep sb. in suspense, keep sb. hanging on.
■ **novela de suspense / película de suspense,** thriller.

suspensión 1 *f* (*acto de levantar*) hanging, hanging up, suspension. **2** AUTO suspension. **3** (*aplazamiento - gen*) delay, postponement; (*- de reunión*) adjournment. **4** (*supresión*) suspension, discontinuation.
■ **suspensión de pagos,** suspension of payments.

suspensivo,-a *adj* suspensive.

suspenso,-a 1 *adj* (*colgado*) hanging, suspended. **2** *fig* (*alumno*) failed. **3** *fig* (*asombrado*) bewildered, amazed. **– 4 suspenso,** *m* EDUC fail.
● **en suspenso,** pending. ‖ **tener un suspenso,** EDUC to fail, be failed.

suspensorio,-a 1 *adj* suspensory. **– 2 suspensorio,** *m* DEP jockstrap.

suspicacia 1 *f* (*desconfianza*) distrust, mistrust. **2** (*sospecha*) suspicion, suspiciousness.

suspicaz 1 *adj* (*desconfiado*) mistrustful, distrustful. **2** (*que sospecha*) suspicious.

suspirado,-a 1 *pp* → **suspirar**. – **2** *adj fig (deseado)* longed-for.

suspirar *i* to sigh.
● suspirar por, *fig* to long for.

suspiro *m* sigh.
● dar el último suspiro, to breathe one's last. ‖ **deshacerse en suspiros,** *fig* to heave great sighs.

sustancia 1 *f (gen)* substance. **2** *(esencia)* substance, essence.
● ser persona de poca sustancia, *fam* to be a characterless person. ‖ sin sustancia, lacking in substance.
■ sustancia gris, grey matter.

sustancial 1 *adj (gen)* substantial. **2** *(fundamental)* essential, fundamental. **3** *(importante)* important, substantial.

sustanciar *t* to condense, abridge.
▲ *Conjugation model* |12|, *like* **cambiar**.

sustancioso,-a 1 *adj (nutritivo)* wholesome. **2** *fig (libro etc)* meaty.

sustantivar *t* to use as a noun.

sustantivo,-a 1 *adj* substantive. – **2 sustantivo,** *m* noun, substantive.

sustentable *adj* tenable.

sustentación 1 *f (soporte)* support. **2** *(mantenimiento)* sustenance, maintenance.

sustentáculo *m* support, prop.

sustentar 1 *t (familia etc)* to maintain, support, sustain. **2** *(sostener)* to hold up, support. **3** *(teoría, opinión)* to support, defend. – **4 sustentarse,** *p (alimentarse)* to sustain os., live (**de,** on). **5** *(sostenerse)* to support os.

sustento 1 *m (alimento)* sustenance, food. **2** *(apoyo)* support.
● ganarse el sustento, to earn one's living.

sustitución *f* substitution, replacement.

sustituible *adj* replaceable, expendable.

sustituir 1 *t (reemplazar)* to substitute (**por,** with), replace (**por,** with): *sustituyeron el aparato por uno nuevo,* they replaced the appliance with a new one; *he roto dos copas y me dicen que las tendré que sustituir,* I've broke two glasses and they say I'll have to replace them. **2** *(hacer las veces de)* to stand in for: *el primer ministro sustituyó al presidente mientras estaba enfermo,* the prime minister stood in for the president while he was ill; *García sustituyó a Hierro,* García came on as a substitute for Hierro.
▲ *Conjugation model* |62|, *like* **huir**.

sustitutivo,-a 1 *adj* substitutive. – **2 sustitutivo,** *m* substitute.

sustituto,-a *m,f* substitute, stand-in, replacement.

susto *m* fright, scare, shock.
● caerse del susto, *fig* to be frightened to death. ‖ dar un susto a algn., to give sb. a fright. ‖ darse un susto / llevarse un susto, to get a fright. ‖ no pasar del susto, *fig* to be just a scare.

sustracción 1 *f (robo)* theft. **2** MAT subtraction.

sustraendo *m* subtrahend.

sustraer 1 *t (robar)* to steal. **2** *(extraer)* to remove. **3** MAT to subtract. – **4 sustraerse,** *p (faltar al cumplimiento)* to evade (**a,** -), elude (**a,** -); *(tentaciones)* to resist (**a,** -).
▲ *Conjugation model* |88|, *like* **traer**.

sustrato *m* substratum.

susurrante *adj* whispering.

susurrar 1 *i* to whisper. **2** *fig (agua)* to murmur; *(hojas)* to rustle. – **3 susurrarse,** *p (divulgarse)* to be rumoured (us rumored).

susurro 1 *m* whisper. **2** *fig (agua)* murmur; *(hojas)* rustle.

sutil 1 *adj (delgado)* thin, fine. **2** *(aroma)* delicate; *(color)* soft. **3** *(brisa)* gentle. **4** *fig* subtle.

sutileza 1 *f* thinness, fineness. **2** *fig* subtlety.

sutilizar 1 *t (adelgazar)* to make fine, thin down. **2** *fig (pulir)* to polish, refine. – **3** *i fig (ser preciso)* to quibble, split hairs.
▲ *Conjugation model* |4|, *like* **realizar**.

sutilmente *adv fig* subtly, mildly.

sutura *f* suture.

suturar *t* to stitch.

suyo,-a 1 *adj (de él)* his, of his; *(de ella)* her, of hers; *(de animales, cosas)* its; *(de usted, de ustedes)* yours, of yours; *(de ellos, de ellas)* theirs, of theirs: *este libro es suyo,* this book is hers; *esta libreta es suya,* this notebook is his; *aquel amigo suyo,* that friend of yours; *aquella tía suya,* that aunt of theirs. – **2** *pron (de él)* his; *(de ella)* hers; *(de usted, de ustedes)* yours; *(de ellos, de ellas)* theirs: *éstos son los míos, los suyos están sobre la mesa,* there are mine, hers are on the table. – **3** la suya, *f (ocasión, oportunidad)* one's chance, one's opportunity: *ésta es la suya, tiene que aprovecharla,* this is your big chance, so make the most of it. – **4** lo suyo, *m (lo que toca)* what one deserves. **5** *(habilidad)* forte, one's thing: *lo suyo es el tenis,* tennis is his thing. **6** *fam (mucho)* a lot: *comió lo suyo,* he ate a lot. – **7** los suyos, *mpl (familiares)* his *(her, your, etc)* family *sing*; *(amigos)* his *(her, your, etc)* friends, his *(her, your, etc)* people.
● hacer de las suyas, *fam* to be up to one's tricks. ‖ ir a la suya / ir a lo suyo, to mind one's own business. ‖ salirse con la suya, *fam* to get one's own way, get what one wants: *no saldrá con la suya,* you won't get your own way. ‖ ser muy suyo,-a, *la vecina de al lado es muy suya,* the lady next door keeps herself to herself; *esa respuesta es muy suya,* that answer is typical of him.

svástica *f* swastika.

Swazilandia *f* Swaziland.

swing *m* swing

T

T, t f (la letra) T, t.
t. abr (tomo) volume; (abreviatura) vol.
T. abr (tara) tare.
taba 1 f ANAT ankle-bone. **2** (juego) knuckle-bones pl.
tabacal m tobacco field, tobacco plantation.
tabacalero,-a 1 adj tobacco. – **2** m,f (cultivador) tobacco grower. **3** (comerciante) tobacco trader. **4** (vendedor) tobacconist. – **5 Tabacalera,** f Spanish state-tobacco monopoly.
tabaco 1 m (gen) tobacco. **2** (cigarrillos) cigarettes pl; (cigarro) cigar: *me he quedado sin tabaco,* I've run out of cigarettes. **3** (enfermedad) black rot.
■ **tabaco negro,** black tobacco. ‖ **tabaco picado,** shredded tobacco. ‖ **tabaco rapé,** snuff. ‖ **tabaco rubio,** Virginia tobacco.
tabal m (tambor) drum.
tabalear 1 t (menear) to swing, rock. – **2** i (golpear) to drum.
tabaleo m drumming.
tábano m horsefly.
tabaquera f → **tabaquero,-a.**
tabaquero,-a 1 adj tobacco. – **2** m,f (vendedor) tobacconist; (comerciante) tobacco dealer. – **3 tabaquera,** f (caja - para tabaco) tobacco tin; (- para rapé) snuffbox. **4** (bolsa) tobacco pouch.
tabaquismo m nicotine poisoning, nicotinism.
tabardillo 1 m fam (insolación) sunstroke. **2** fam fig (persona alocada) nutcase. **3** fam fig (persona pesada) pain, drag, pest.
tabardo m tabard.
tabarra f fam pain in the neck, bore.
● **dar la tabarra,** fam to be a pest, be a pain in the neck.
tabarro m horsefly.
tabasco m tabasco sauce.
▲ *Registered trademark.*
taberna 1 f pub, bar. **2** (antiguamente) tavern.
tabernáculo m tabernacle.
tabernario,-a 1 adj (de la taberna) tavern. **2** fam fig coarse, rude.
tabernero,-a 1 m,f (gen) publican; (hombre) landlord; (mujer) landlady. **2** (antiguamente) tavern-keeper.
tabernucha f fam dive, pit, hole.
tabernucho m fam dive, pit, hole.
tabicar 1 t (ventana, puerta) to wall up. **2** (habitación) to partition off, divide.
▲ *Conjugation model* [1], *like* **sacar.**
tabique m partition, partition wall.
■ **tabique nasal,** ANAT nasal bone.
tabla 1 f (de madera) board, plank. **2** (de piedra) slab; (de metal) sheet. **3** (estante) shelf. **4** ART panel. **5** COST pleat. **6** (tablón de anuncios) notice-board, US bulletin-board. **7** (índice) index. **8** (lista) list; (catálogo) catalogue (US catalog). **9** (parte plana de miembros) flat. **10** (faja de tierra)

strip, plot; (bancal) patch; (arriate) bed. **11** MAT table. – **12 tablas,** fpl TEAT stage sing, boards. **13** (ajedrez) stalemate sing, draw sing. **14** (de plaza de toros) barrier sing.
● **a raja tabla,** strictly, to the letter. ‖ **hacer tabla rasa de algo,** to make a clean sweep of sth. ‖ **hacer tablas,** (gen) to be deadlocked, reach stalemate; (ajedrez etc) to end in a draw. ‖ **pisar las tablas,** to tread the boards, go on the stage. ‖ **quedar en tablas,** → **hacer tablas.** ‖ **tener tablas / tener muchas tablas,** (gen) to be an old hand; (en teatro - hombre) to be an experienced actor; (- mujer) be an experienced actress.
■ **tabla de cocina,** chopping-board. ‖ **tabla de lavar,** washboard. ‖ **la Tabla Redonda,** the Round Table. ‖ **las Tablas de la Ley,** REL the Tables of the Law. ‖ **tabla de materias,** contents pl, table of contents. ‖ **tabla de multiplicar,** multiplication table. ‖ **tabla de plancha / tabla de planchar,** ironing-board. ‖ **tabla de salvación,** fig last hope, last resort. ‖ **tabla de surf,** surfboard. ‖ **tabla de windsurf,** sailboard.
tablado 1 m (suelo) wooden floor. **2** (entarimado) wooden platform. **3** (del escenario) stage.
tablaje 1 m (tablas) planks pl, boards pl. **2** (casa de juego) gambling den.
tablao m fam (local) flamenco bar.
tablazón m planking.
tableado,-a 1 pp → **tablear.** – **2** adj COST pleated. – **3** tableado, m COST pleats pl.
tablear 1 t (madera) to cut into planks. **2** (tierra) to divide into plots. **3** COST to pleat.
tablero 1 m (tablón) panel, board. **2** (en juegos) board. **3** (encerado) blackboard. **4** AUTO dashboard. **5** ELEC switchboard. **6** INFORM display board.
■ **tablero de ajedrez,** chessboard. ‖ **tablero de dibujo,** drawing-board. ‖ **tablero de instrumentos,** (avión) instrument panel, instrument board.
tableta 1 f (pastilla) tablet. **2** (de chocolate) bar.
tabletear i to rattle: *el carro tableteaba en el camino,* the cart rattled along the road.
tableteo m rattling, rattle.
tablilla 1 f small board. **2** MED splint.
tablón 1 m plank. **2** (en construcción) board. **3** fam (borrachera) drunkenness.
● **agarrar un tablón / coger un tablón,** fam to get plastered.
■ **tablón de anuncios,** notice board, US bulletin board.
tabú 1 adj taboo. – **2** m taboo.
▲ pl **tabúes.**
tabuco m pey hovel.
tabulación f tabulation.
tabulador m tabulator.
tabuladora f tabulator.
tabular 1 adj tabular. – **2** t to tabulate.
taburete m stool.

tacada 1 *f* (*golpe*) stroke. **2** (*carambolas*) break. **3** (*tacos*) plugs *pl.*

tacañear *i fam* to be stingy, be mean.

tacañería *f* stinginess, meanness.

tacaño,-a 1 *adj* mean, stingy. – **2** *m,f* skinflint, miser.

tacatá *m* baby-walker.

tacataca *m* baby-walker.

tacha[1] 1 *f* (*defecto*) flaw, blemish, defect. **2** (*descrédito*) blemish.
● **sin tacha,** flawless, without blemish.

tacha[2] *f* (*tachuela*) tack.

tachadura *f* crossing out.

tachar 1 *t* (*borrar*) to cross out. **2** (*culpar*) to accuse (**de,** of): *lo tachan de fascista,* they accuse him of being a fascist.

tachón[1] *m* (*tachadura*) crossing out.

tachón[2] *m* (*tachuela*) large stud.

tachonar 1 *t* (*con tachones*) to stud, cover with studs. **2** *fig* (*salpicar*) to stud, dot.

tachuela *f* tack, stud.

tácitamente *adv* tacitly.

tácito,-a *adj* tacit.

taciturno,-a 1 *adj* (*callado*) taciturn, silent. **2** (*triste*) sad, melancholy.

taco 1 *m* (*tarugo*) plug, stopper. **2** (*para pared*) plug, rawlplug. **3** (*bloc de notas*) notepad, writing pad; (*calendario*) tear-off calendar. **4** (*de entradas*) book; (*de billetes*) wad. **5** (*de billar*) cue. **6** CULIN (*de queso etc*) cube, piece; (*en Méjico*) taco, rolled-up tortilla. **7** *fam* (*lío*) mess, muddle. **8** *fam* (*palabrota*) swear-word. **9** *fam* (*años*) year's old: *tiene 40 tacos,* she's forty. **10** *arg* (*drogas*) lump of hash.
● **armarse un taco / hacerse un taco,** to get all mixed up. ‖ **soltar un taco / soltar tacos,** to swear.

tacógrafo *m* tachograph.

tacómetro *m* tachometer.

tacón *m* heel: *zapatos de tacón alto,* high-heeled shoes.
■ **tacones aguja,** stiletto heels.

taconazo *m* blow with the heel.
● **dar un taconazo,** to click one's heels.

taconear *i* (*pisar*) to tap one's heels, click one's heels; (*golpear*) to stamp one's heels.

taconeo *m* (*pisada*) heel-tapping, clicking of the heels; (*golpe*) stamping with the heels.

táctica *f* → **táctico,-a**.

táctico,-a 1 *adj* tactical. – **2** *m,f* tactician. – **3 táctica,** *f* tactic, tactics *pl,* strategy.

táctil *adj* tactile.

tacto 1 *m* (*sentido*) touch. **2** (*acción*) touch, touching: *el jersey es suave al tacto,* the sweater is soft to the touch. **3** *fig* (*delicadeza*) tact.
● **no tener tacto,** to be tactless. ‖ **tener tacto,** to be tactful.
■ **falta de tacto,** lack of tact, tactlessness.

taekwondo *m* tae kwon do.

tafetán *m* taffeta.

tafilete *m* Morocco leather.

tagalo,-a 1 *adj* Tagalog. – **2** *m,f* Tagalog. – **3 tagalo,** *m* (*idioma*) Tagalog.

tagarnina 1 *f* (*cardillo*) Spanish oyster plant. **2** *fam* (*cigarro*) bad-quality cigar.

tagarote 1 *m* (*ave*) small hawk formerly used in falconry. **2** *fam fig* (*hombre*) lanky person, beanpole.

taheño,-a *adj* red, ginger.

Tahití *m* Tahiti.

tahitiano,-a 1 *adj* Tahitian. – **2** *m,f* (*persona*) Tahitian. – **3 tahitiano,** *m* (*idioma*) Tahitian.

tahona 1 *f* (*molino*) flour-mill. **2** (*panadería*) bakery.

tahúr,-ura *m,f* card-sharper, card-sharp.

taifa 1 *f* (*facción*) faction. **2** *fam fig* gang of villains.
■ **reinos de taifa,** *small Spanish kingdoms after the disintegration of the Caliphate of Córdoba in 1031.*

taiga *f* taiga.

tailandés,-esa 1 *adj* Thai. – **2** *m,f* (*persona*) Thai. – **3 tailandés,** *m* (*idioma*) Thai.

Tailandia *f* Thailand.

taimado,-a 1 *adj* sly, crafty. – **2** *m,f* sly person, crafty person.

taimería *f* slyness, cunning.

Taiwan *m* Taiwan.

taiwanés,-esa 1 *adj* Taiwanese. – **2** *m,f* Taiwanese.

tajada 1 *f* (*rodaja*) slice. **2** (*corte*) cut; (*cuchillada*) stab. **3** *fam* (*borrachera*) drunkenness.
● **agarrar una tajada / coger una tajada / pillar una tajada,** *fam* to get smashed, get plastered. ‖ **dar un tajada,** to cut. ‖ **llevarse la tajada del león,** *fam* to take the lion's share. ‖ **llevarse tajada / sacar tajada,** *fam* to take one's share.

tajado,-a 1 *pp* → **tajar.** – **2** *adj fam fig* (*borracho*) plastered, canned.

tajamar 1 *m* MAR cutwater. **2** AM (*malecón*) dyke.

tajante 1 *adj* sharp, strong. **2** *fig* emphatic, categorical.

tajantemente *adv* emphatically, categorically.

tajar *t* to cut, chop, slice (off).

tajo 1 *m* (*corte*) cut, slash. **2** (*filo*) cutting edge. **3** (*para cortar carne*) chopping board, chopping block. **4** (*escarpa*) steep cliff. **5** *fam* (*tarea*) work, job: *se fue al tajo,* she went to work.

Tajo el Tajo, *m* the Tagus.

tal 1 *adj* (*semejante*) such: *nunca había oído tal cosa,* I had never heard such a thing; *en tales condiciones,* in such conditions. **2** (*tan grande*) such, so: *tal es su ignorancia que ...,* he is so ignorant that ... **3** (*cosa sin especificar*) such and such: *tal día,* such and such a day. **4** (*persona sin especificar*) someone called, a certain: *vino un tal Alberto,* someone called Alberto came. – **5** *pron* (*alguno - cosa*) such a thing, something; (*- persona*) someone, somebody: *yo no dije tal,* I didn't say such a thing; *tal habrá que lo crea,* someone is bound to believe it. – **6** *adv* (*así*) in such a way, so: *tal me contestó que no supe cómo reaccionar,* he answered in such a way that I didn't know how to react; *tal estaban de cansados que se fueron a dormir en seguida,* they were so tired that they went straight to bed.
● **como si tal cosa,** as if nothing had happened. ‖ **como tal,** as such. ‖ **de tal manera que,** in such a way that. ‖ **de tal palo tal astilla,** like father, like son. ‖ **no hay tal como ...,** there's nothing like ... ‖ **¿qué tal?,** how are things? ‖ **¿qué tal ...?,** how ... ?: *¿qué tal estuvo la fiesta?,* how was the party? ‖ **tal como,** (*ejemplos*) such as; (*de la misma manera*) just as. ‖ **tal cual,** just as it is. ‖ **tal para cual,** two of a kind. ‖ **tal vez,** perhaps, maybe. ‖ **tal y como,** just as, as: *tal y como veo las cosas ...,* as I see things ... ‖ **y tal y cual,** and so on.
■ **una tal,** *fam pey* prostitute.

tala *f* tree felling.

talabarte *m* sword belt.

taladrador,-ra 1 *adj* drilling. – **2** *m,f* driller, borer. – **3 taladradora,** *f* (*herramienta*) drill.

taladrar 1 *t* (*gen*) to drill; (*pared*) to bore through. **2** (*billetes etc*) to punch. **3** *fig* (*los oídos*) to pierce.

taladro 1 *m* (*herramienta*) drill, bore; (*barrena*) gimlet, brace. **2** (*agujero*) hole.

tálamo 1 *m* (*lecho conyugal*) nuptial bed. 2 BOT ANAT thalamus.

talán *m* ringing, ding-dong.

talanquera 1 *f* (*valla, pared*) wall, fence. 2 *fig* (*seguridad*) means of safety, safeguard.

talante 1 *m* (*disposición*) disposition, mood. 2 (*voluntad*) willingness.
● **de buen talante, willingly:** *lo hizo de buen talante,* he did it willingly. ‖ **de mal talante,** unwillingly, reluctantly. ‖ **estar de buen talante,** to be in a good mood. ‖ **estar de mal talante,** to be in a bad mood.

talar¹ *adj* (*vestidura*) full-length, long.

talar² 1 *t* (*cortar*) to fell, cut down. 2 (*destruir*) to devastate.

talasocracia *f* thalassocracy.

talasoterapia *f* thalassotherapy.

talayote *m* talayot.

talco *m* talc.

taled *m* tallith.
▲ *pl* **taledes.**

talega 1 *f* (*bolsa*) bag, sack. 2 (*contenido*) bagful, sackful. 3 (*para el pelo*) hairnet. 4 (*dinero*) money.

talego 1 *m* (*bolsa*) long bag, long sack. 2 (*contenido*) bagful, sackful. 3 *arg fig* (*cárcel*) clink, hole. 4 *arg fig* (*mil pesetas*) one-thousand peseta note.
■ **medio talego,** five-hundred pesetas.

talento 1 *m* (*entendimiento*) talent, intelligence: *tiene talento,* she's talented, she's got talent. 2 (*aptitud*) gift, talent: *tiene talento para las matemáticas,* she has a gift for mathematics.

talentoso,-a *adj* talented, gifted.

talentudo,-a *adj* talented, gifted.

TALGO *abr* (*Tren Articulado Ligero Goicoechea-Oriol*) *Spanish fast passenger train.*

talio *m* thallium.

talión *m* talion.
● **la ley del talión,** an eye for an eye, a tooth for a tooth.

talismán *m* talisman, lucky charm.

talla 1 *f* (*estatura*) height. 2 *fig* (*moral, intelectual*) stature. 3 (*de prenda*) size: *¿qué talla usa?,* what size is he? 4 (*escultura*) carving, sculpture. 5 (*tallado - piedras*) cutting; (*- metal*) engraving.
● **dar la talla para hacer algo,** *fig* to be up to doing sth.: *no da la talla para el trabajo,* he's not up to the job. ‖ **de talla / de mucha talla,** *fig* outstanding, prominent.

tallado,-a 1 *pp* → **tallar.** – 2 *adj* (*piedra*) cut; (*madera*) carved; (*metal*) engraved. – 3 **tallado,** *m* (*de piedra*) cutting; (*de madera*) carving; (*de metal*) engraving.

tallador,-ra 1 *m.f* (*grabador*) engraver. – 2 **tallador,** *m* MIL man who measures the height of conscripts.

tallar 1 *t* (*madera, piedra*) to carve, shape; (*piedras preciosas*) to cut; (*metales*) to engrave. 2 (*medir*) to measure the height of. 3 (*valorar*) to value, appraise. 4 (*en naipes*) to deal.

tallarín *m* noodle, tagliatelle *sing.*

talle 1 *m* (*cintura*) waist. 2 (*figura - de hombre*) build, physique; (*- de mujer*) figure, shape. 3 COST shoulder-to-waist measurement.

tallecer *i* to sprout, shoot.

taller 1 *m* (*obrador*) workshop, shop. 2 ART studio. 3 IND factory, mill. 4 AUTO garage, repair shop. 5 *fig* (*seminario*) workshop.
■ **taller de reparaciones,** garage, repair shop. ‖ **taller de teatro,** drama workshop.

tallerina *f* clam.

tallo *m* BOT stem, stalk; (*renuevo*) sprout, shoot.

talludo,-a 1 *adj* (*planta*) leggy, tall. 2 *fig* (*crecido*) grown, grown-up. 3 *fig* (*no joven*) middle-aged. 4 *fig* (*enviciado*) with bad habits.

talmente *adv fam* exactly like.

talmud *m* Talmud.

talo *m* thallus.

talón¹ 1 *m* (*de pie, zapato, etc*) heel. 2 (*cheque*) cheque (US check). 3 (*recibo*) receipt, voucher. 4 (*de violín*) heel. 5 (*de quilla*) heel. 6 (*de neumático*) flange.
● **pisarle los talones a algn.,** *fig* to follow close on sb.'s heels, be on sb.'s heels.
■ **talón bancario,** counter cheque (US check). ‖ **talón de Aquiles,** Achilles' heel. ‖ **talón sin fondos,** bad/dud cheque, US rubber check.

talón² *m* (*patrón monetario*) monetary standard.

talonario *m* (*de cheques*) cheque book (US check book); (*de billetes*) book of tickets; (*de recibos*) stub book.

taloneador *m* hooker.

talonear *i* (*andar con prisa*) to hurry along.

talonera *f* (*pantalones*) binding; (*medias etc*) heel-piece; (*de fijación*) heel-grip.

talud *m* slope.

tamaño,-a 1 *adj* (*semejante*) such a, so big a: *no pude aguantar tamaña impertinencia,* I couldn't tolerate such an impertinent remark. – 2 **tamaño,** *m* (*medida*) size: *no sabe de qué tamaño son,* he doesn't know what size they are. 3 (*dimensión*) dimensions *pl.*
● **de gran tamaño,** large. ‖ **del tamaño de,** as large as, the size of.
■ **tamaño natural,** life size.

tamarindo *m* tamarind.

tamarisco *m* tamarisk.

tambaleante 1 *adj* (*persona*) staggering, tottering. 2 (*mueble*) wobbly, shaky. 3 *fig* shaky, unstable.

tambalearse 1 *p* (*persona*) to stagger, totter; (*mueble*) to wobble. 2 *fig* to be shaky.

tambaleo 1 *m* (*de persona*) staggering, reeling. 2 (*de mueble*) wobble, wobbling.

también 1 *adv* (*igualmente*) also, too, as well, so: *Pedro también estaba,* Pedro was also there, Pedro was there too, Pedro was there as well; *ellos están trabajando y Juan también,* they're working and so is Juan; *llegaron tarde y yo también,* they arrived late and so did I. 2 (*además*) besides, in addition.

tambor 1 *m* (*instrumento*) drum. 2 (*para tostar café*) roaster. 3 (*para bordar*) tambour, embroidery frame. 4 ARQ drum, tambour. 5 (*para tamizar*) sieve, sifter. 6 (*de arma*) cylinder, barrel. 7 (*de lavadora*) drum. 8 (*de freno*) brake drum. 9 (*para enrollar*) capstan. 10 (*del oído*) eardrum. 11 *fam* (*de jabón*) drum, giant-size pack. – 12 *mf* (*persona*) drummer.
● **a tambor batiente,** *fig* triumphantly.
■ **tambor mayor,** drum major.

tamboril *m* small drum.

tamborilear 1 *i* (*golpear el tambor*) to play the drum. 2 (*repiquetear*) to drum.

tamborileo *m* drumming.

tamborilero,-a *m.f* drummer.

Támesis el **Támesis,** *m* the Thames.

tamiz *m* sieve, sifter.
● **pasar por el tamiz,** to sift; *fig* to scrutinize.

tamizar 1 *t* (*harina, tierra*) to sieve. 2 (*luz*) to filter. 3 *fig* (*seleccionar*) to screen.
▲ *Conjugation model* |4|, *like realizar.*

tampoco *adv* neither, nor, not ... either: *mi hermano no irá a la fiesta y yo tampoco,* my brother won't go to the party and neither will I, my brother won't go to the party and I won't either; *no quiere estudiar y tampoco quiere ir al cine,* he doesn't want to study and he doesn't want to go to the cinema either; *yo no lo hice, –yo tampoco,* I didn't do it, –nor did I.

tampón 1 *m* (*de entintar*) ink-pad. 2 MED tampon.

tam-tam *m* tom-tom.

tan 1 *adv* (*tanto*) such, such a, so: *es una niña tan buena,* she's such a nice girl; *no seas tan cruel,* don't be so cruel; *son personas tan amables,* they're such kind people. 2 (*comparativo - como*) as ... as, so ... (that); (- *que*) so ..., so ... (that): *está tan gordo como tú,* he's as fat as you (are); *estaba tan bueno que me lo comí todo,* it was so good (that) I ate it all.
● **de tan ... como,** so ... (that): *de tan duro como estaba no me lo pude comer,* it was so tough (that) I couldn't eat it. ‖ **¡qué ... tan!,** what a ...!: *¡qué peli tan divertida!,* what a funny film! ‖ **tan es así que ...,** so much so that ... ‖ **tan pronto como,** as soon as. ‖ **tan siquiera,** even, just. ‖ **tan solo,** only, just: *tan solo quiero uno,* I only want one. ‖ **tan solo con ...,** just by ..., just for ...: *tan solo con ir te daban un regalo,* you were given a present just for going there.

tanatorio *m* chapel of rest.

tanda 1 *f* (*conjunto*) batch, lot; (*serie*) series, course. 2 (*turno*) shift. 3 (*en billar*) game.
● **por tandas,** in batches.
■ **tanda de palos,** thrashing.

tándem 1 *m* (*bicicleta*) tandem. 2 *fig* (*de dos personas*) team of two, tandem.
▲ *pl* **tándemes.**

tanga *m* G-string, tanga.

tangencial *adj* tangential.
■ **efecto-tangencial,** side effect.

tangente 1 *adj* tangent. – 2 *f* tangent.
● **irse por la tangente / salirse por la tangente,** *fig* to go off at a tangent.

Tánger *m* Tangier.

tangible *adj* tangible.

tango *m* tango.

tanguista *f* cabaret girl, taxi-girl.

tanque 1 *m* (*depósito*) tank, reservoir. 2 MIL tank. 3 (*vehículo cisterna*) tanker.

tanqueta *f* light tank.

tantalio *m* tantalum.

tantán *m* tom-tom, tam-tam.

tantarán 1 *m* (*sonido*) rat-a-tat-tat. 2 *fig* (*golpe*) bang.

tantarantán *m* → **tantarán.**

tantear 1 *t* (*calcular*) to estimate, guess. 2 (*probar medidas*) to size up. 3 *fig* (*ensayar*) to try out, put to the test. 4 *fig* (*persona*) to sound out. 5 (*dibujo*) to sketch. – 6 *i* DEP to score, keep score. 7 (*andar a tientas*) to feel one's way.
● **tantear el terreno,** to see how the land lies.

tanteo 1 *m* (*cálculo aproximado*) estimate, guess. 2 (*prueba*) reckoning, rough estimate; (*de medidas*) sizing up. 3 (*sondeo*) trial, test. 4 (*de persona*) sounding out. 5 DEP score.
● **igualar el tanteo,** DEP to draw.

tanto,-a 1 *adj* (*incontables*) so much; (*contables*) so many: *no cojas tanta leche,* don't take so much milk; *no comas tantos caramelos,* don't eat so many sweets; *¡tengo tanto calor!,* I'm so hot!; *¡ha pasado tanto tiempo!,* it's been so long! 2 (*comparación - incontable*) as much; (- *contables*)

as many: *trajo tanto pan como yo,* he brought as much bread as I did; *tengo tantos libros como tú,* I've got as many books as you. – 3 *pron* (*incontable*) so much; (*contable*) so many: *no había tantos,* there weren't so many. – 4 *adv* (*cantidad*) so much: *¡te quiero tanto!,* I love you so much!; *lo siento tanto,* I'm so sorry. 5 (*tiempo*) so long: *esperamos tanto,* we waited for so long; *hace tanto que no viene,* it's a long time since he last came. 6 (*frecuencia*) so often: *no los telefonees tanto,* don't phone them so much. – 7 **tanto,** *m* (*punto*) point; (*fútbol*) goal. 8 (*cantidad imprecisa*) so much, a certain amount: *percibes un tanto al mes,* you get so much a month. 9 (*poco*) bit: *es un tanto estrecho,* it's a bit narrow.
● **a las tantas,** *fam* very late, at an unearthly hour. ‖ **a tantos de,** sometime in: *fue a tantos de enero,* it was sometime in January. ‖ **apuntar un tanto / marcar un tanto,** (*gen*) to score a point; (*fútbol*) to score a goal. ‖ **con tanto / de tanto,** with so much: *se quedó afónica de tanto gritar,* she lost her voice with shouting so much. ‖ **cuanto más ... tanto más ...,** the more ... the more ... ‖ **en tanto / entre tanto / mientras tanto,** meanwhile. ‖ **eso es tanto como ...,** that is like ... ‖ **estar al tanto,** (*informado*) to be informed; (*alerta*) to be on the alert. ‖ **ni tanto ni tan poco / ni tanto ni tan calvo,** *fam* neither one extreme nor the other. ‖ **no es para tanto / no hay para tanto,** it's not that bad. ‖ **no será tanto,** it can't be as bad as you make out. ‖ **otro tanto,** as much again, the same again. ‖ **por lo tanto,** therefore. ‖ **ser uno de tantos / ser una de tantas,** to be nothing special. ‖ **tanto cuanto,** as much as. ‖ **tanto más / tanto menos,** all the more / all the less. ‖ **tanto mejor / tanto peor,** so much the better / so much the worse. ‖ **tanto si ... como si ...,** whether ... or ...: *tanto si quieres como si no,* whether you like it or not. ‖ **uno de tantos / una de tantas,** run-of-the-mill. ‖ **... y tantos / ... y tantas,** (*cantidad*) odd; (*año*) something: *treinta y tantos libros,* thirty-odd books; *en el año cuarenta y tantos,* in nineteen forty something.
■ **tanto por ciento,** so many per cent.

Tanzania *f* Tanzania.

tanzano,-a 1 *adj* Tanzanian. – 2 *m,f* Tanzanian.

tañer 1 *t* (*instrumento*) to play. 2 (*campanas*) to ring, toll.
▲ Conjugation model [38].

tañido 1 *m* (*de instrumento*) sound. 2 (*de campanas*) ringing, toll, peal.

taoísmo *m* Taoism.

tapa 1 *f* (*cubierta*) lid, top; (*de botella*) cap, top, stopper. 2 (*de libro*) cover. 3 (*de zapato*) heel-plate. 4 AUTO head. 5 CULIN (*comida*) appetizer, savoury (US savory), tapa. 6 (*de res*) round of beef.
● **levantarse la tapa de los sesos / saltarse la tapa de los sesos,** *fam* to blow one's brain out.

tapabocas *m* scarf, muffler.
▲ *pl* **tapabocas.**

tapacubos *m* hubcap.
▲ *pl* **tapacubos.**

tapadera 1 *f* cover, lid. 2 *fig* cover, front: *el club es una tapadera de la mafia,* the club is a front for the mafia.

tapadillo 1 *m* (*acción de taparse con manto*) covering one's face with a mantle. 2 (*de órgano*) flute-stop. 3 *fam* (*disimulo*) deceit, secrecy.
● **hacer algo de tapadillo,** *fam* to do sth. secretly.

tapajuntas *m* beading, fillet.
▲ *pl* **tapajuntas.**

tapar 1 *t* (*cubrir*) to cover; (*con tapa*) to put the lid on, put the top on. 2 (*con ropas etc*) to wrap up. 3 (*obstruir*) to

obstruct; (*tubería*) to block. **4** (*ocultar*) to hide; (*a la vista*) to block. **5** *fig* (*encubrir*) to cover up. **– 6 taparse,** *p* (*abrigarse*) to wrap up. **7** (*la nariz*) to be blocked up.
● **taparse los oídos,** to put one's fingers in one's ears.

taparrabo I *m* loincloth. **2** *fam* (*bañador*) bathing trunks *pl.*
▲ *Also used in plural with the same meaning.*

tapete I *m* (*alfombra*) rug. **2** (*paño*) runner.
● **estar sobre el tapete,** (*tema*) to be under discussion, be on the table. ‖ **poner sobre el tapete,** (*plantear*) to bring up for discussion.

tapia *f* (*cerca*) garden wall; (*de adobe*) mud wall, adobe wall.
● **estar más sordo,-a que una tapia,** *fam* to be as deaf as a post.

tapiar I *t* (*área*) to wall in, wall off. **2** *fig* (*puerta, ventana*) to wall up, close up.
▲ *Conjugation model* [12], *like* **cambiar.**

tapicería I *f* ART tapestry making. **2** (*tapices*) tapestries *pl.* **3** (*de muebles etc*) upholstery. **4** (*material*) upholstery material. **5** (*tienda*) upholsterer's, upholsterer's workshop.

tapicero,-a I *m,f* (*de muebles, coche*) upholsterer. **2** ART tapestry maker.

tapioca *f* tapioca.

tapir *m* tapir.

tapiz I *m* (*de pared*) tapestry. **2** (*alfombra*) rug, carpet.

tapizado I *m* (*acción*) upholstering. **2** (*material*) upholstery material.

tapizar I *t* (*muebles*) to upholster. **2** (*una pared*) to cover. **3** (*cubrir con tapices*) to cover with tapestries.
▲ *Conjugation model* [4], *like* **realizar.**

tapón I *m* stopper, plug; (*de botella*) cap, cork. **2** (*del oído*) wax in the ear. **3** *fam fig* (*persona*) shorty, stubby person. **4** (*baloncesto*) block. **5** (*embotellamiento*) traffic jam. **6** MED tampon.
■ **tapón de rosca,** screw top.

taponamiento *m* plugging, obturation.

taponar I *t* (*orificio etc*) to plug, stop. **2** (*atascar*) to block. **3** (*poner el tapón*) to put the plug in. **4** MED to tampon, plug. **– 5 taponarse,** *p* (*atascarse*) to get clogged, get blocked. **6** (*los oídos*) to get blocked up.

taponazo I *m* (*ruido*) pop. **2** *fam* (*golpe*) hit, shot: *recibió un taponazo en la cabeza,* he was hit on the head by a flying cork.

tapujo I *m* (*embozo*) muffler. **2** *fig* (*disimulo*) deceit, secrecy.
● **andarse con tapujos,** *fig* not to come clean about sth. ‖ **sin tapujos,** openly.

taqué *m* tappet.

taquicardia *f* tachycardia.

taquigrafía *f* tachygraphy, shorthand, stenography.

taquigrafiar *t* to write in shorthand.
▲ *Conjugation model* [13], *like* **desviar.**

taquigráfico,-a *adj* written in shorthand.
■ **signos taquigráficos,** shorthand symbols.

taquígrafo,-a *m,f* tachygrapher, shorthand writer, stenographer.

taquilla I *f* (*de tren etc*) ticket office, booking-office; DE CINE, TEATRO box office: *un éxito de taquilla,* a box-office success. **2** (*recaudación*) takings *pl,* returns *pl.* **3** (*casillero*) pigeonholes *pl.* **4** (*armario*) locker.

taquillero,-a I *m,f* booking-clerk, ticket-clerk. **– 2** *adj fig* popular, big at the box office: *un actor taquillero,* an actor who is big at the box office; *una película taquillera,* a film which is a box-office hit.

taquimecanografía *f* shorthand and typing.

taquimecanógrafo,-a *m,f* shorthand typist.

taquimetría *f* tacheometry.

taquímetro *m* tacheometer, tachymeter.

tara I *f* (*peso*) tare. **2** (*defecto*) defect, blemish, fault.

tarabilla I *f* (*de puerta, ventana*) catch, latch. **2** *fig* (*tropel de palabras*) jabber, prattle. **3** (*ave*) stonechat. **– 4** *mf fam fig* (*persona*) chatterbox.
■ **tarabilla común,** stonechat. ‖ **tarabilla norteña,** whinchat.

tarabita *f* tongue.

taracea *f* marquetry.

tarado,-a I *pp →* **tarar. – 2** *adj* (*defectuoso*) defective, damaged. **3** (*persona*) handicapped. **– 4** *m,f fam fig* idiot, nitwit.

tarambana I *adj fam* nutty. **– 2** *mf fam* nutcase.

tarantela *f* tarantella.

tarántula *f* tarantula.

tarar *t* to tare.

tarara *f* tantara, tantarara.

tarará *f* tantara, tantarara.

tararear *t* to hum.

tarareo *m* humming.

tararí I *m* tantara, tantarara. **– 2** *adj fam* (*bebido*) sloshed, plastered.

tararira I *f* (*juerga*) binge. **– 2** *adj fam* (*alocado*) batty, potty; (*borracho*) drunk.

tarasca I *f* (*monstruo*) monster. **2** (*persona glotona*) glutton. **3** *fam fig* (*mujer*) hag.

tarascada *f fam fig* rude reply, cutting answer.

tarascar *t* to bite.
▲ *Conjugation model* [1], *like* **sacar.**

tardanza *f* delay.

tardar I *t* (*emplear tiempo*) to take: *tardé cuatro horas,* it took me four hours; *¿cuánto se tarda?,* how long does it take? **– 2** *i* (*demorar*) to take a long time: *tardó mucho en contestar,* he took a long time to answer; *se tarda más a pie,* it takes longer on foot.
● **a más tardar,** at the latest. ‖ **no puede tardar,** he should be here any moment now. ‖ **no tardes,** don't be long. ‖ **sin tardar,** without delay, right away.

tarde I *f* (*hasta las cinco aprox.*) afternoon: *son las 3 de la tarde,* it's 3 o'clock in the afternoon, it's 3 p.m. **2** (*después de las cinco aprox.*) evening: *lo vi ayer por la tarde,* I saw him yesterday evening. **– 3** *adv* (*hora avanzada*) late: *se está haciendo tarde,* it's getting late. **4** (*demasiado tarde*) too late: *es tarde para salir,* it's too late to go out.
● **a la caída de la tarde,** at dusk. ‖ **a última hora de la tarde,** early in the evening. ‖ **buenas tardes,** (*antes de las cinco aprox.*) good afternoon; (*después de las cinco aprox.*) good evening. ‖ **de tarde en tarde,** very rarely, not very often. ‖ **más tarde o más temprano / tarde o temprano,** sooner or later. ‖ **más vale tarde que nunca,** better late than never. ‖ **tarde o temprano,** sooner or later.

tardíamente *adv* too late.

tardío,-a *adj* late, belated.
■ **fruto tardío,** late fruit.

tardo,-a I *adj* (*lento*) slow. **2** (*retrasado*) late. **3** (*torpe*) slow.
● **tardo,-a en comprender,** slow on the uptake.

tardón,-ona I *adj fam* very slow. **– 2** *m,f fam* slowcoach.

tarea *f* task, job.
■ **las tareas de la casa,** the housework *sing,* the chores. ‖ **tareas escolares,** homework *sing.*

tarifa I *f* (*precio*) tariff, rate; (*de transporte*) fare. **2** (*lista de precios*) price list.

■ **tarifa completa,** full tariff. ‖ **tarifa reducida,** reduced rate, special deal. ‖ **tarifa turística,** tourist-class rate.
tarifar 1 *t (fijar tarifa)* to put a price to, price. **– 2** *i (reñir)* to quarrel.
tarima *f* platform, dais.
tarjeta *f* card.
■ **tarjeta amarilla,** DEP yellow card. ‖ **tarjeta de crédito,** credit card. ‖ **tarjeta de embarque,** boarding card. ‖ **tarjeta de memoria,** INFORM memory card, chip card. ‖ **tarjeta de visita,** visiting-card, US calling-card. ‖ **tarjeta inteligente,** INFORM smartcard. ‖ **tarjeta multiviaje,** travel card. ‖ **tarjeta perforada,** INFORM punch card, punched card. ‖ **tarjeta postal,** postcard. ‖ **tarjeta roja,** DEP red card.
tarjetero *m* wallet for visiting-cards.
tarlatana *f* tarlatan.
tarot *m* tarot.
tarquín *m* slime.
tarraconense 1 *adj* of Tarragona, from Tarragona. **– 2** *mf* person from Tarragona, inhabitant of Tarragona.
tarrina *f* tub: *una tarrina de margarina,* a tub of margarine.
tarro[1] 1 *m (vasija)* jar, pot, tub. **2** *fam (cabeza)* bonce.
● **comerle el tarro a algn.,** *fam* to brainwash sb. ‖ **estar mal del tarro,** *fam* to be off one's rocker.
tarro[2] *m (ave)* shelduck.
tarso *m* tarsus.
tarta *f* flan, tart, pie: *tarta de manzana,* apple pie; *tarta de frutas,* fruit flan.
tartaja 1 *adj fam* stammering, stuttering. **– 2** *mf fam* stammerer, stutterer.
tartajear *i* to stammer, stutter.
tartajeo 1 *m (acción)* stammering, stuttering. **2** *(defecto)* stammer, stutter.
tartajoso,-a 1 *adj* stammering, stuttering. **– 2** *m,f* stammerer, stutterer.
tartaleta *f (moldecillo)* small pastry case; *(pastelito)* small fruit tart.
tartamudear *i* to stammer, stutter.
tartamudeo 1 *m (acción)* stammering, stuttering. **2** *(defecto)* stammer, stutter.
tartamudez *f* stammering, stuttering.
tartamudo,-a 1 *adj* stuttering, stammering: *es tartamudo,* he's got a stammer. **– 2** *m,f* stutterer, stammerer.
tartán[1] *m (tela)* tartan.
tartán[2] 1 *m (material)* Tartan. **– 2** *f (pista)* Tartan track.
tartana 1 *f (embarcación)* tartan. **2** *(carruaje)* trap. **3** *fam fig (coche)* banger, heap.
tártaro[2] *m (depósito)* tartar.
tártaro,-a[1] 1 *adj* Tartar. **– 2** *m,f* Tartar.
tartera 1 *f (fiambrera)* lunch-box. **2** *(cazuela)* earthenware baking dish.
tartesio,-a 1 *adj* Tartessian. **– 2** *m,f* Tartessian.
tartufo *m* hypocrite, Tartuffe.
tarugo 1 *m (de madera)* lump of wood. **2** *(de pan)* hunk of stale bread. **3** *fam fig (persona)* blockhead.
tarumba *adj fam* mad, crazy, bonkers.
● **estar tarumba,** to be bonkers. ‖ **volver tarumba a algn.,** *(enloquecer)* to drive sb. bonkers; *(aturdir)* to confuse. ‖ **volverse tarumba,** *(enloquecer)* to go bonkers; *(aturdirse)* to get confused.
tas *m* anvil.
▲ *pl* **tases**.
tasa 1 *f (valoración)* valuation, appraisal. **2** *(precio)* fee, charge. **3** *(impuesto)* tax, levy. **4** *(límite)* limit; *(medida)* measure. **5** *(índice)* rate.

● **sin tasa,** limitless, without limit.
■ **tasa de crecimiento,** growth rate. ‖ **tasa de desempleo,** unemployment rate. ‖ **tasa de mortalidad,** death rate. ‖ **tasa de natalidad,** birth rate. ‖ **tasas académicas,** course fees.
tasación *f* valuation, appraisal.
tasador,-ra *m,f* valuer.
tasar 1 *t (valorar)* to value, appraise. **2** *(poner precio)* to set the price of, fix the price of. **3** *(gravar)* to tax. **4** *(regular)* to regulate: *tasar los precios,* to regulate prices. **5** *fig (limitar)* to limit, restrict; *(racionar)* to ration: *tasar la libertad,* to restrict freedom; *tasar la comida,* to ration food.
tasca *f* bar, pub.
● **ir de tascas,** *fam* to go on a pub crawl.
Tasmania *f* Tasmania.
■ **Mar de Tasmania,** Tasman Sea.
tasmano,-a 1 *adj* Tasmanian. **– 2** *m,f* Tasmanian.
tata *f fam* nanny.
tatami *m* judo mat.
tatarabuelo,-a 1 *m,f (hombre)* great-great-grandfather; *(mujer)* great-great-grandmother. **– 2 tatarabuelos,** *mpl* great-great-grandparents.
tataranieto,-a 1 *m,f (hombre)* great-great-grandson; *(mujer)* great-great-granddaughter. **– 2 tataranietos,** *mpl* great-great-grandchildren.
tate[1] 1 *interj fam (cuidado)* look out!, steady! **2** *fam (sorpresa)* good grief!, blimey! **3** *fam (ya entiendo)* I see!
tate[2] *m arg (drogas)* hashish.
tatuaje 1 *m (dibujo)* tattoo. **2** *(técnica)* tattooing.
tatuar 1 *t* to tattoo. **– 2 tatuarse,** *p* to have a tattoo: *se tatuó el brazo,* he had his arm tattooed.
▲ *Conjugation model* |11|, *like* **actuar**.
tau *f* tau, taw.
taumaturgia *f* thaumaturgy.
taumaturgo,-a *m,f* thaumaturge, miracle worker.
taurino,-a *adj (del toro)* taurine; *(de la fiesta)* bullfighting, related to bullfighting.
■ **la fiesta taurina,** bullfighting.
Tauro *m* Taurus.
tauromaquia *f* bullfighting, art of bullfighting, tauromachy.
Taurus los Montes Taurus, *mpl* the Taurus Mountains.
tautología *f* tautology.
taxativamente 1 *adv (concretamente)* precisely. **2** *(tajantemente)* categorically.
taxativo,-a 1 *adj (preciso)* precise, restricted, specific. **2** *(categórico)* categorical.
● **de forma taxativa,** in a categorical way, categorically.
taxi *m* taxi, cab.
■ **parada de taxis,** taxi rank.
taxidermia *f* taxidermy.
taxidermista *mf* taxidermist.
taxímetro *m* taximeter, clock.
taxista *mf* taxi driver.
taxonomía *f* taxonomy.
taza 1 *f (recipiente)* cup. **2** *(contenido)* cupful. **3** *(de retrete)* bowl.
■ **taza de café / taza de té,** *(para)* coffee cup / teacup; *(llena de)* cup of coffee / cup of tea.
tazón *m* bowl.
TC *abr (Tribunal Constitucional)* constitutional court.
te[1] 1 *f name of the letter* t. **2** *(regla)* T-square.
te[2] 1 *pron* you, to you, for you: *no te veo,* I can't see you; *te mandó la carta,* he sent the letter to you, he sent you

the letter; *te lo compré,* I bought one for you, I bought you one. **2** REL Thee, to Thee, for Thee. **3** (*reflexivo*) yourself: *sírvete,* help yourself; *ponte el abrigo,* put your coat on. **4** REL (*reflexivo*) Thyself. **5** (*órdenes, prohibiciones*): *vete a casa,* go home; *no te muevas,* don't move.

té *m* tea.
● dar el té, *fam* to bother.
■ la hora del té, teatime. ‖ té con limón, lemon tea.
▲ *pl tés.*

tea *f* torch.
● coger una tea / cogerse una tea, *fam* to get drunk, get plastered.

teatral 1 *adj* (*del teatro*) theatrical, dramatic. **2** *fig* (*exagerado*) stagy, stagey, theatrical.
■ grupo teatral, theatre (US theater) company. ‖ obra teatral, play.

teatralidad *f* theatricality, staginess.

teatralizar 1 *t* to stage. **2** *fig* to dramatize.

teatro 1 *m* theatre (US theater). **2** ART theatre (US theater), acting, stage: *se dedica al teatro,* he's on the stage. **3** LIT drama. **4** *fig* (*lugar*) scene, theatre (US theater): *el teatro de la guerra,* the theatre of war. **5** *fig* (*exageración*) show, play-acting.
● dejar el teatro, (*artista*) to give up the stage. ‖ echarle teatro a un asunto, to play-act, be melodramatic, exaggerate. ‖ hacer teatro, *fig* to play-act, be melodramatic, exaggerate.
■ autor de teatro, playwright. ‖ obra de teatro, play. ‖ teatro de la ópera, opera house. ‖ teatro de variedades, variety theatre, US vaudeville theater.

tebeo *m* children's comic.
● estar más visto,-a que el tebeo, to be nothing new, have been around for ages.

teca[1] *f* (*árbol, madera*) teak.

teca[2] **1** *f* (*para reliquia*) reliquary. **2** ANAT BOT theca.

techado *m* roof, covering.
● bajo techado, indoors.

techar *t* to roof.

techo 1 *m* (*interior*) ceiling; (*de coche, tejado*) roof. **2** *fig* (*casa*) roof: *viven bajo el mismo techo,* they live under the same roof. **3** (*en aviación*) ceiling. **4** *fig* (*límite*) limit, end; COM & FIN ceiling.
● tocar techo, *fig* to top out. ‖ vivir bajo el mismo techo, *fig* to live under the same roof.

techumbre *f* (*techo*) roof; (*materiales*) covering, roofing.

tecla *f* key.
● dar en la tecla, *fig* to get it right. ‖ tocar muchas teclas, *fam* to try to do too many things at once. ‖ tocar teclas, *fam* to pull strings.
■ tecla de borrado, delete key. ‖ tecla de control, control key. ‖ tecla de mayúsculas, shift key. ‖ tecla de retorno, return key. ‖ tecla de retroceso, backspacer.

teclado *m* keyboard.
■ teclado expandido, INFORM expanded keyboard.

teclear 1 *i* (*piano*) to press the keys; (*máquina de escribir, ordenador*) to type, tap the keys. **2** (*tamborilear*) to drum, tap one's fingers. **3** *fig* (*para conseguir algo*) to explore different avenues.

tecleo 1 *m* MÚS fingering. **2** (*tamborileo*) drumming. **3** (*ruido*) rattle, clatter.

teclista *mf* keyboard player.

técnica *f* → **técnico,-a.**

técnicamente *adv* technically.

tecnicidad *f* technicity, technicality.

tecnicismo 1 *m* technicality. **2** (*término*) technicism, technical word, technical expression.

técnico,-a 1 *adj* technical. – **2** *m,f* technician, technical expert. – **3 técnica,** *f* (*tecnología*) technique, technology. **4** (*habilidad*) technique, method. **5** (*ingeniería*) engineering: *técnica mecánica,* mechanical engineering.

tecnicolor *m* Technicolor.

tecnocracia *f* technocracy.

tecnócrata *mf* technocrat.

tecnocrático,-a *adj* technocratic.

tecnología *f* technology.
■ tecnología punta, state-of-the-art technology.

tecnológico,-a *adj* technological.

tecnólogo,-a *m,f* technologist.

tectónica *f* → **tectónico,-a.**

tectónico,-a 1 *adj* tectonic. – **2 tectónica,** *f* tectonics.

tedéum *m* Te Deum.
▲ *pl tedéum.*

tediar *t* to loathe, hate.
▲ Conjugation model [12], like *cambiar.*

tedio *m* tedium, boredom.

tedioso,-a *adj* tedious, boring.

tegucigalpense 1 *adj* from Tegucigalpa, of Tegucigalpa. – **2** *mf* person from Tegucigalpa, inhabitant of Tegucigalpa.

tegumento *m* integument, tegument.

Teherán *m* Tehran, Teheran.

teína *f* theine.

teísmo *m* theism.

teja 1 *f* (*de barro*) tile. **2** CULIN type of petit four.
● a toca teja, *fam* cash, on the nail.

tejadillo *m* roof.

tejado *m* roof.

tejano,-a 1 *adj* Texan. – **2** *m,f* Texan. – **3 tejanos,** *mpl* (*pantalones*) jeans.

tejar 1 *t* to tile. – **2** *m* (*fábrica*) tile-works *pl.*

Tejas *m* Texas.

tejedor,-ra 1 *adj* weaving. – **2** *m,f* weaver.

tejemaneje 1 *m fam* (*afán*) fuss, bustle. **2** *fam* (*enredos*) intrigue, scheming, funny business: *seguro que se traen algún tejemaneje,* they must be involved in some kind of funny business.

tejer 1 *t* (*en telar*) to weave. **2** (*hacer punto*) to knit. **3** (*araña*) to spin. **4** *fig* (*plan*) to weave, plot, scheme.
● tejer y destejer, *fig* to chop and change.

tejido 1 *m* (*tela*) fabric, textile. **2** (*textura*) weave. **3** ANAT tissue. **4** *fig* web, tissue.
■ tejido adiposo, fatty tissue. ‖ tejido de punto, knitted fabric. ‖ tejido muscular, muscle tissue, muscular tissue. ‖ tejido nervioso, nervous tissue. ‖ tejido óseo, bone tissue.

tejo[1] **1** *m* (*juego del chito*) quoits *pl.* **2** (*juego del caracol*) hopscotch.

tejo[2] *m* (*árbol*) yew tree.

tejoleta 1 *f* (*pedazo de teja*) piece of tile. **2** (*pedazo de barro*) piece of clay.

tejón *m* badger.

tejuelo *m* label on the spine of a book.

tel. *abr* (*teléfono*) telephone; (*abreviatura*) tel.

tela 1 *f* (*textil*) material, fabric, cloth. **2** (*de araña*) cobweb. **3** (*de la leche*) skin. **4** (*membrana*) membrane. **5** ART (*lienzo*) canvas; (*cuadro*) painting. **6** *fam* (*dinero*) dough. **7** *fam* (*asunto, tema*) subject, matter: *hay tela para rato,* they've got plenty to talk about.
● en tela, (*encuadernación*) cloth. ‖ hay tela que cortar, *fam* there's plenty to be done. ‖ poner en tela de juicio, *fig* to question. ‖ tiene mucha tela, *fam* there's more to it than meets the eye, it's no mean feat.

■ **tela marinera,** *fam* long, drawn-out business: *la venta de sus propiedades tiene tela marinera,* the sale of his property is going to be a long, drawn-out business. ‖ **tela metálica,** wire gauze.
telar 1 *m* (*para tejer*) loom. **2** (*para encuadernar*) sewing-press. **3** (*en el teatro*) gridiron.
telaraña *f* cobweb, spider's web.
tele *f fam* telly, TV: *¿qué dan en la tele?,* what's on TV?
teleadicto,-a 1 *adj* addicted to television. – **2** *m,f* telly addict.
telearrastre *m* ski-lift.
telecabina *f* cable-car.
teleclub *m* television club.
telecomunicación *f* telecommunication.
▲ *Often used in plural.*
telediario *m* television news bulletin, TV news.
teledifusión *f* television broadcast.
teledinámico,-a *adj* teledynamic.
teledirigido,-a 1 *pp* → **teledirigir**. – **2** *adj* remote-controlled.
■ **proyectil teledirigido,** guided missile.
teledirigir *t* to operate by remote control, guide by remote control.
▲ *Conjugation model* [6], *like dirigir.*
telefacsímil *m* telefacsimile.
telefax *m* telefax.
▲ *pl telefax.*
teleférico *m* cable-car, cable railway.
telefilm *m* TV film.
telefilme *m* TV film.
telefonazo *m fam* buzz, ring, bell.
● **dar un telefonazo a algn.,** *fam* to give sb. a ring.
telefonear 1 *i* to telephone, phone. – **2** *t* to telephone, phone.
telefonía *f* telephony, telephone system.
■ **telefonía móvil,** mobile telephones.
Telefónica *f* → **telefónico,-a**.
telefónicamente *adv* by telephone.
telefónico,-a 1 *adj* telephone. – **2** Telefónica, *f the Spanish national telephone company.*
■ **central telefónica / centralita telefónica,** switchboard, telephone exchange. ‖ **llamada telefónica,** telephone call, phone call.
telefonista *mf* telephone operator, operator, telephonist.
teléfono *m* telephone, phone: *Ana está al teléfono,* Ana's on the phone.
● **llamar por teléfono a algn.,** to telephone sb., phone sb.
■ **guía de teléfonos / listín de teléfonos,** telephone directory. ‖ **teléfono móvil,** mobile telephone.
telegrafía *f* telegraphy.
■ **telegrafía sin hilos,** wireless telegraphy.
telegrafiar *t* to telegraph, wire.
▲ *Conjugation model* [13], *like desviar.*
telegráficamente 1 *adv* by telegraph. **2** *fam fig* (*hablar, escribir*) telegraphically.
telegráfico,-a *adj* telegraphic.
telegrafista *mf* telegraphist, telegrapher.
telégrafo 1 *m* telegraph. – **2 telégrafos,** *mpl* post office *sing.*
■ **poste de telégrafo,** telegraph pole.
telegrama *m* telegram, cable.
teleimpresor *m* teleprinter.
telejuego *m* video game.

telele *m fam* fit, wobbly.
● **darle a uno un telele,** *fam* to have a fit, throw a wobbly.
telemando *m* remote control, remote-control unit.
telemanía *f* telly addiction.
telemática *f* → **telemático,-a**.
telemático,-a 1 *adj* telematic. – **2 telemática,** *f* telematics.
telemetría *f* telemetry.
telémetro *m* telemeter, rangefinder.
telenovela *f* soap opera.
teleobjetivo *m* telephoto lens.
teleología *f* teleology.
telepatía *f* telepathy.
telepáticamente *adv* telepathically, by telepathy.
telepático,-a *adj* telepathic.
teleprocesar *t* to teleprocess.
teleproceso *m* teleprocessing.
telequinesia *f* telekinesis.
telescópico,-a *adj* telescopic.
telescopio *m* telescope.
telesilla *m* chair-lift.
telespectador,-ra *m,f* TV viewer.
telesquí *m* ski-lift.
teletexo *m* teletext.
teletipo 1 *m* (*aparato*) teletype, teleprinter. **2** (*noticia*) news from an agency.
televidente *mf* TV viewer.
televisar *t* to televise.
televisión 1 *f* (*sistema*) television. **2** *fam* (*aparato*) television set.
● **ver la televisión,** to watch TV.
■ **televisión por cable,** cable television. ‖ **televisión vía satélite,** satellite television.
televisivo,-a *adj* televisión; (*apto para televisar*) televisual, telegenic.
televisor *m* television set.
télex *m* telex.
▲ *pl telex.*
telilla *f* film, skin.
telón *m* curtain.
■ **telón de acero,** POL iron curtain. ‖ **telón de fondo,** TEAT backdrop; *fig* background. ‖ **telón de hierro,** safety curtain.
telonero,-a *adj* first on stage, support.
■ **grupo telonero,** support band.
telúrico,-a *adj* telluric.
telurio *m* tellurium.
tema 1 *m* (*de discurso, escrito, etc*) topic, subject, theme: *el tema de su discurso,* the subject of her speech. **2** (*examen*) subject. **3** MÚS theme. **4** GRAM root, stem, theme.
● **atenerse al tema,** to keep/stick to the point. ‖ **cada loco con su tema,** *fam* everyone has his hobbyhorse. ‖ **salir(se) del tema,** to go off at a tangent, get sidetracked.
■ **tema de actualidad,** current news item, current topic of interest.
temario *m* (*de examen*) programme (US program); (*de conferencia*) agenda.
temática *f* → **temático,-a**.
temático,-a 1 *adj* thematic. **2** LING stem. – **3 temática,** *f* subject-matter.
tembladera 1 *f* (*temblor*) shaking fit. **2** (*vaso*) very thin two-handled bowl. **3** BOT quaking-grass.

temblar 1 *i* (*de frío*) to shiver (**de**, with); (*de miedo*) to tremble (**de**, with); (*con sacudidas*) to shake. **2** (*voz*) to quiver. **3** *fig* (*tener miedo*) to shake with fear, shudder, fear: *tiemblo por su vida,* I fear for his life.
▲ Conjugation model [27], like *acertar.*

tembleque *m fam* shaking fit.
● me dio el tembleque / me entró el tembleque, *fam* I got the shivers, I had a shaking fit.

temblequear 1 *i fam* (*temblar*) to shake, quiver. **2** *fam* (*afectar temblor*) to pretend to tremble.

temblón,-ona *adj fam* trembling, shaky.
■ álamo temblón, aspen.

temblor 1 *m* (*gen*) tremor, shudder; (*de frío*) shivering, shivers *pl.* **2** *fig* shiver.
■ temblor de tierra, earth tremor.

tembloroso,-a 1 *adj* (*de frío*) shivering; (*de miedo*) trembling; (*con sacudidas*) shaking, shaky: *manos temblorosas,* shaky hands. **2** (*voz*) quivering.

tembloso,-a *adj* → **tembloroso,-a**.

temer 1 *t* (*tener miedo*) to fear, be afraid of: *teme a los atracadores,* he's afraid of muggers. **2** (*sospechar*) to fear, be afraid: *temo que no vendrán,* I'm afraid they won't come. **3** REL to fear: *temer a Dios,* to fear God. – **4** *i* (*tener miedo*) to be afraid. **5** (*preocuparse*) to worry: *no temas por nada,* don't worry about anything. – **6** temerse, *p* to be afraid: *me temo que no estén allí,* I'm afraid they won't be there; *me temo que sí,* I'm afraid so.
● era de temer, it had to happen. ‖ me lo temía, I was afraid this would happen. ‖ temer por, to be afraid for, fear for, be in fear of: *teme por su vida,* he's in fear of his life.

temerario,-a *adj* reckless, rash.

temeridad 1 *f* (*actitud*) temerity, rashness. **2** (*acto temerario*) reckless act.

temerosamente *adv* fearfully.

temeroso,-a 1 *adj* fearful, timid. **2** (*medroso*) frightful, fearsome.
● temeroso,-a de, afraid of. ‖ temeroso,-a de Dios, God-fearing.

temible *adj* dreadful, fearful, frightening, frightful, fearsome.

temor 1 *m* fear. **2** (*recelo*) worry, apprehension.
● por temor a / por temor de, for fear of: *por temor a disgustarle no le dije lo que había ocurrido,* I didn't tell him what had happened in case I upset him. ‖ tener temor, to feel apprehensive.

témpano *m* ice floe.
● ser como un témpano, *fig* to be as cold as ice.

temperado,-a *adj* temperate, moderate.

temperamental *adj* temperamental.

temperamento *m* temperament, nature.
● tener buen temperamento, to be good-natured. ‖ tener temperamento, to have a strong character, be temperamental.

temperancia *f* temperance, moderation, restraint.

temperante 1 *adj* calming. **2** (*sobrio*) moderate.

temperar 1 *t* to temper, mitigate. **2** MED to calm.

temperatura *f* temperature.
● tener temperatura, to have/run a temperature.
■ temperatura absoluta, absolute temperature. ‖ temperatura ambiente, room temperature. ‖ temperatura crítica, critical temperature. ‖ temperatura máxima / temperatura mínima, maximum temperature / minimum temperature.

temperie 1 *f* (*de la atmósfera*) weather. **2** (*temperamento*) temperament.

tempestad 1 *f* storm. **2** *fig* turmoil, uproar.
● levantar tempestades, *fig* to cause a turmoil. ‖ una tempestad en un vaso de agua, *fig* a storm in a teacup.
■ tempestad de arena, sandstorm. ‖ tempestad de nieve, snowstorm.

tempestear 1 *i* to storm, rage. **2** *fig* to get angry, throw a fit of rage.

tempestivo,-a *adj* opportune.

tempestuoso,-a *adj* stormy, tempestuous, wild, violent.

templado,-a 1 *pp* → **templar**. – **2** *adj* (*agua*) warm, lukewarm; (*clima, temperatura*) mild, temperate. **3** (*moderado*) moderate; (*sereno*) composed, unruffled. **4** (*valiente*) brave. **5** MÚS tuned. **6** (*metal*) tempered.
● nervios bien templados, steady nerves.

templanza 1 *f* (*moderación*) moderation, restraint. **2** (*del clima*) mildness.

templar 1 *t* (*moderar*) to moderate, temper. **2** (*algo frío*) to warm up; (*algo caliente*) to cool down. **3** *fig* (*cólera*) to appease; (*apaciguar*) to calm down. **4** (*cuerda, tornillo*) to tighten (up). **5** *fig* (*bebida*) to dilute. **6** MÚS to tune. **7** TÉC to temper. **8** (*colores*) to match. – **9** *i* (*el tiempo*) to warm up. – **10** templarse, *p* (*contenerse*) to restrain os., control os.

templario *m* Templar, Knight Templar.

temple 1 *m* (*de metal, vidrio*) temper. **2** *fig* (*estado de ánimo*) frame of mind, mood. **3** *fig* (*valentía*) boldness, courage. **4** (*pintura*) tempera. **5** MÚS tempering, tuning. **6** *fig* (*término medio*) average.
● dar temple, to temper.

templete 1 *m* (*para imagen*) niche. **2** (*templo pequeño*) small temple. **3** (*pabellón*) pavilion, kiosk.

templo *m* temple.
● como un templo, *fam* (*cosa*) huge, enormous; (*verdad*) patent, absolute; (*mentira*) utter.

tempo *m* tempo.

temporada 1 *f* (*en artes, deportes, moda*) season. **2** (*período*) period, time.
● en plena temporada, at the height of the season. ‖ por temporadas, on and off.
■ temporada alta, high season, peak season. ‖ temporada baja, low season, off-season.

temporal[1] 1 *adj* (*transitorio*) temporary, provisional: *mano de obra temporal,* temporary labour. **2** (*seglar*) temporal: *poder temporal,* temporal power. **3** LING temporal. – **4** *m* METEOR storm.
■ bienes temporales, worldly goods.

temporal[2] 1 *adj* ANAT temporal. – **2** *m* ANAT temporal bone.

temporalidad *f* temporality.

temporalizar *t* to make temporal.
▲ Conjugation model [4], like *realizar.*

temporalmente *adv* temporarily, provisionally.

temporero,-a 1 *adj* seasonal, temporary. – **2** *m,f* seasonal worker, temporary worker.

temporizador *m* timer.

temporizar 1 *i* (*contemporizar*) to temporize, comply. **2** (*pasar el tiempo*) to pass the time.
▲ Conjugation model [4], like *realizar.*

tempranal *adj* early-yielding.

tempranamente 1 *adv* (*pronto*) early. **2** (*prematuramente*) too early.

tempranero,-a 1 *adj* (*persona*) early-riser: *es tempranero,* he's an early-riser. **2** (*cosecha*) early.

temprano,-a 1 *adj* early. – **2** *adv* early: *nunca se levanta temprano,* he never gets up early. – **3** temprano, *m* (*sembrado*) early crop.

● **más temprano,** earlier.
ten ten con ten, *loc fam* caution, moderation.
● **tener mucho ten con ten,** *fam* to be very careful/cautious.
tenacidad 1 *f (perseverancia)* tenacity, perseverance. **2** *(de metal)* tensile strength.
tenacillas 1 *fpl (para rizar el pelo)* curling tongs; *(para el vello)* tweezers. **2** *(para el azúcar)* sugar tongs.
tenaz 1 *adj (persona)* tenacious; *(perseverante)* persevering, unflagging. **2** *(dolor)* persistent, unremitting; *(mancha)* hard to remove.
tenaza *f (herramienta)* pliers *pl*, pincers *pl*; *(para el fuego)* tongs *pl*.
● **no se puede coger ni con tenazas,** *fam* I wouldn't touch it with a barge pole.
▲ *Often used in plural with the same meaning.*
tenazmente *adv* tenaciously.
tenca *f* tench.
tendal 1 *m (toldo)* awning. **2** *(tendedero)* drying place.
tendedero *m (cuerda)* clothes-line; *(lugar)* drying place.
tendencia *f (inclinación)* tendency, inclination, predisposition, leaning; *(movimiento)* trend: *es de tendencias izquierdistas,* he's got left-wing tendencies; *las últimas tendencias de la moda,* the latest fashion trends.
● **tener tendencia a hacer algo,** to tend to do sth., have a tendency to do sth.
■ **tendencia del mercado,** market trends *pl*.
tendenciosidad *f* tendentiousness, partiality, bias.
tendencioso,-a *adj* tendentious, biased.
tendente *adj* directed **(a,** at), aimed **(a,** at): *propuestas tendentes a mejorar las viviendas,* proposals aimed at improving housing.
tender 1 *t (extender - mantel etc)* to spread; *(- red)* to cast. **2** *(puente)* to throw; *(vía, cable)* to lay; *(cuerda)* to stretch. **3** *(ropa, colada)* to hang out. **4** *(mano)* to stretch out, hold out. **5** *(emboscada, trampa)* to lay, set. **6** *(tumbar)* to lay: *lo tendieron en la cama,* they laid him on the bed. **7** *(esparcir)* to scatter. **8** MAR *(velas)* to spread. **9** *(revestir paredes etc)* to plaster. **– 10** *i (tener tendencia)* to tend **(a,** to), have a tendency **(a,** to): *tiende al aburrimiento,* it tends to be boring. **– 11 tenderse,** *p (tumbarse)* to lie down, stretch out. **12** *(caballo)* to run at full gallop.
▲ *Conjugation model [28], like entender.*
tenderete 1 *m (puesto)* stall. **2** *(montón)* heap, mess.
tendero,-a *m,f* shopkeeper.
tendido,-a 1 *pp →* **tender**. **– 2** *adj (extendido)* spread out, laid out. **3** *(ropa, colada)* hung out: *no hay ropa tendida,* there isn't any washing on the line. **4** *(persona)* lying down. **– 5 tendido,** *m (de cable, vía)* laying; *(de puente)* construction. **6** *(colada)* wash, washing. **7** *(en los toros)* front tiers of seats, US bleachers *pl*.
● **dejar a algn. tendido,-a,** to floor sb. ‖ **hablar largo y tendido de algo,** to talk sth. over.
■ **tendido eléctrico,** electrical installation/cables.
tendón *m* tendon, sinew.
tenducha *f* rundown shop, grotty shop.
tenducho *m* rundown shop, poky little shop.
tenebrismo *m* tenebrism.
tenebrista *adj* tenebroso.
tenebrosidad 1 *f* darkness, gloom. **2** *fig* shadiness.
tenebroso,-a 1 *adj (sombrío)* dark, gloomy. **2** *fig (siniestro)* sinister, shady.
tenedor,-ra 1 *m,f* FIN holder, bearer. **– 2 tenedor,** *m (utensilio)* fork.
■ **tenedor,-ra de acciones,** shareholder. ‖ **tenedor,-ra de libros,** book-keeper.

teneduría *f* book-keeping.
tenencia *f* tenancy, possession.
● **tenencia ilícita de armas,** JUR illegal possession of arms.
tener 1 *t (gen)* to have, have got: *tengo un problema,* I have a problem; *tengo un examen mañana,* I've got an exam tomorrow; *tiene el pelo rubio,* he's got blond hair; *tuvimos un día estupendo,* we had a wonderful day. **2** *(poseer)* to own, possess: *tiene un piso en la Costa del Sol,* he's got a flat on the Costa del Sol. **3** *(sostener)* to hold: *¿qué tienes en la mano?,* what are you holding? **4** *(coger)* to take: *ten tu copa,* take your glass. **5** *(sensación, sentimiento)* to be, feel: *tengo hambre,* I'm hungry; *tengo frío,* I'm cold. **6** *(mantener)* to keep: *la lluvia me ha tenido despierta toda la noche,* the rain has kept me up all night. **7** *(medir)* to measure: *la habitación tiene cuatro metros cuadrados,* the room is four metres square. **8** *(contener)* to hold, contain. **9** *(edad)* to be: *tiene diez años,* he is ten. **10** *(un hijo)* to have: *tuvo un hijo,* she had a baby. **11** *(celebrar)* to hold: *tener una reunión,* to hold a meeting. **12** *(considerar)* to consider, think: *lo tienen por muy listo,* they think he's very smart. **13** *(ocuparse)* to be in charge of, keep: *tiene el archivo del museo,* she's in charge of the museum archive. **– 14 tener que,** *aux (obligación)* to have to, have got to, must: *tengo que quedarme,* I must stay; *sabe que tiene que hacerlo,* he knows he's got to do it. **– 15 tenerse,** *p (sostenerse)* to stand up: *el abuelo no puede tenerse solo,* grandad can't stand up on his own. **16** *(detenerse)* to stop. **17** *(estarse)* to keep: *tente tranquilo,* keep calm. **18** *(dominarse)* to control os.
● **¡ahí tienes! / ¡ahí lo tienes!,** so, there you are! ‖ **¿con que ésas tenemos?,** *fam* so that's how it is, that's the way things are. ‖ **no saber lo que uno tiene,** *fig* not to realize how lucky one is. ‖ **no tener más que,** to have only (got) to: *no tienes más que decírmelo,* you've only (got) to tell me. ‖ **no tener nada que ver con,** to have nothing to do with; *(tener miedo)* to be afraid. ‖ **no tenerse,** to be tired out: *estoy que no me tengo,* I'm tired out. ‖ **¿qué tienes?,** what's wrong with you? ‖ **tener a algn. contento,-a,** to make sb. happy. ‖ **tener a bien,** to think it better. ‖ **tener a la vista,** to have before one's eyes. ‖ **tener a menos,** to consider it beneath os. ‖ **tener al día,** to keep up to date. ‖ **tener ante sí,** to have before one, have in front of one. ‖ **tener cariño a,** to be fond of. ‖ **tener compasión,** to take pity **(de,** on). ‖ **tener ganas de,** to feel like: *no tiene ganas de hacerlo,* he doesn't feel like doing it. ‖ **tener ilusión,** to be enthusiastic. ‖ **tener para sí,** to think: *tengo para mí que lo lograrán,* I think they'll manage it. ‖ **tener una encima / tener una buena encima,** *fam* to be plastered. ‖ **tenerla tomada con algn.,** *fam* to have it in for sb. ‖ **tenerse en mucho / tenerse en poco,** to think highly of os. / to underestimate os. ‖ **tenerse por,** to consider os., think os.: *se tiene por guapo,* he thinks he's handsome.
▲ *Conjugation model [87].*
tenería *f* tannery.
tenga *pres subj →* **tener**.
tengo *pres indic →* **tener**.
tenguerengue en tenguerengue, *loc adv* unstable.
tenia *f* tapeworm.
teniente 1 *m* MIL lieutenant. **– 2** *m,f (de alcalde)* deputy mayor.
■ **teniente coronel,** lieutenant colonel. ‖ **teniente de alcalde,** deputy mayor. ‖ **teniente general,** lieutenant general.

tenis 1 *m* (*deporte*) tennis. **2** (*campo*) tennis court; (*club*) tennis club. – **3 tenis,** *mpl* (*calzado*) tennis shoes.
■ **tennis de mesa,** table tennis, ping-pong.
tenista *mf* tennis player.
tenor 1 *m* MÚS tenor. **2** (*conforme*) tenor, purport.
● **a este tenor,** like this. ‖ **a tenor,** likewise. ‖ **a tenor de,** according to.
tenorio *m* fig Don Juan, lady-killer, Casanova.
tensado,-a 1 *pp* → **tensar.** – **2** *adj* (*cuerda, cable*) taut, tautened, tense. **3** (*arco*) drawn.
tensar 1 *t* (*cable, cuerda*) to tauten. **2** (*arco*) to draw.
tensión 1 *f* ELEC tension, voltage. **2** (*de materiales*) stress; (*de gases*) pressure. **3** MED pressure. **4** fig (*de una situación*) tension, tenseness; (*de una persona*) stress, strain.
● **estar bajo tensión,** fig to be under strain. ‖ **tener la tensión alta,** to suffer from high blood pressure.
■ **alta tensión,** ELEC high tension. ‖ **baja tensión,** ELEC low tension. ‖ **tensión arterial,** blood pressure. ‖ **tensión nerviosa,** nervous strain.
tenso,-a 1 *adj* (*cable, cuerda*) tense, taut. **2** fig (*relaciones*) strained. **3** fig (*persona*) tense.
tensor,-ra 1 *adj* tensile, tightening. – **2 tensor,** *m* ANAT MAT tensor. **3** TÉC turn-buckle.
tentación *f* temptation.
● **caer en la tentación,** to succumb to temptation, give in to temptation.
tentáculo *m* tentacle.
tentadero *m* pen (*where young bulls are tried out*).
tentador,-ra *adj* tempting, enticing.
tentalear *t* to feel.
tentar 1 *t* (*palpar*) to feel, touch. **2** (*incitar*) to tempt, entice. **3** (*intentar*) to try, attempt. **4** (*atraer*) to attract, appeal.
● **¡no me tientes!,** fam don't tempt me!, don't say it twice! ‖ **tentar al diablo,** fig to tempt the devil.
▲ *Conjugation model* |27|, *like* **acertar.**
tentativa *f* attempt, try.
■ **tentativa de asesinato,** JUR attempted murder.
tentempié 1 *m* fam (*refrigerio*) snack, bite. **2** fam (*tentetieso*) tumbler toy, US roly-poly.
▲ *pl* **tentempiés.**
tentetieso *m* tumbler toy, US roly-poly.
tenue 1 *adj* (*delgado*) thin, light, tenuous. **2** (*tela*) flimsy, thin. **3** (*luz, sonido*) subdued, faint. **4** (*niebla*) light. **5** (*de poca importancia*) insignificant. **6** (*sencillo*) natural.
teñido,-a 1 *pp* → **teñir.** – **2** *adj* dyed; (*pelo*) tinted, dyed: *un jersey teñido de verde,* a pullover dyed green. **3** fig tinged. – **4 teñido,** *m* (*acción*) dyeing. **5** (*tinte*) dye.
teñir 1 *t* (*dar un color*) to dye: *teñir unos zapatos de negro,* to dye a pair of shoes black. **2** (*rebajar un color*) to tone down. **3** fig to tinge. – **4 teñirse,** *p* (*el pelo*) to dye one's hair.
▲ *Conjugation model* |36|, *like* **ceñir.**
teocracia *f* theocracy.
teodolito *m* theodolite.
teologal *adj* theologic, theological.
teología *f* theology.
teológico,-a *adj* theological.
teologizar *i* to theologize.
▲ *Conjugation model* |4|, *like* **realizar.**
teólogo,-a *m,f* theologian, theologist.
teorema *m* theorem.
teoría *f* theory.
● **en teoría,** theoretically.
■ **teoría atómica,** atomic theory.
teórica *f* → **teórico,-a.**

teóricamente *adv* theoretically.
teórico,-a 1 *adj* theoretic, theoretical. – **2** *m,f* theoretician, theorist. – **3 teórica,** *f* theory, theoretics.
teorizar *i* to theorize (**sobre,** on).
▲ *Conjugation model* |4|, *like* **realizar.**
teosofía *f* theosophy.
tequila *f* tequila.
TER *abr* (*Tren Español Rápido*) *Spanish fast passenger train.*
terapeuta *mf* therapist.
terapéutica *f* → **terapéutico,-a.**
terapéutico,-a 1 *adj* therapeutic. – **2 terapéutica,** *f* therapeutics, therapy.
terapia *f* therapy.
■ **terapia de grupo,** group therapy.
teratología *f* teratology.
terbio *m* terbium.
tercamente *adv* stubbornly.
tercer *adj* third: *el tercer hombre,* the third man; *el tercer mundo,* the third world.
▲ *Used before a singular masculine noun; see also* **tercero,-a.**
tercera *f* → **tercero,-a.**
tercermundista *adj* third-world: *un país tercermundista,* a third-world country.
tercero,-a 1 *adj* (*ordinal*) third. – **2** *m,f* (*parte*) third. – **3 tercero,** *m* (*mediador*) mediator. **4** (*persona ajena*) outsider; JUR third party: *seguro contra terceros,* third-party insurance. **5** (*alcahuete*) pimp, procurer. – **6 tercera,** *f* (*clase*) third class. **7** (*marcha de auto*) third gear, third. **8** MÚS third. **9** (*alcahueta*) procuress.
● **a la tercera va la vencida,** third time lucky. ‖ **ser el tercero en discordia,** to be the mediator.
▲ *See also* **sexto,-a.**
terceto 1 *m* (*poesía*) tercet. **2** MÚS trio.
terciado,-a 1 *pp* → **terciar.** – **2** *adj* (*azúcar*) brown. **3** (*intermedio*) medium-size.
terciana *f* tertian fever.
terciar 1 *i* (*mediar*) to mediate, arbitrate: *terció entre los dos contrincantes,* he mediated between the two opponents. **2** (*participar*) to take part, participate: *terciaron en el debate,* they took part in the debate. – **3** *t* (*poner en diagonal*) to place diagonally, place crosswise. **4** (*dividir en tres*) to divide into three. **5** (*equilibrar la carga*) to balance. – **6 terciarse,** *p* (*venir bien, darse*) to arise.
● **si se tercia ...,** should the occasion arise ...
▲ *Conjugation model* |12|, *like* **cambiar.**
terciario,-a *adj* tertiary.
■ **industria terciaria,** tertiary industry. ‖ **sector terciario,** service sector.
tercio,-a 1 *adj* third. – **2 tercio,** *m* (*parte*) third. **3** HIST (*regimiento de infantería*) infantry regiment. **4** MIL (*división*) division. **5** (*botella de cerveza*) medium-sized bottle of beer. **6** (*en tauromaquia*) stage, part.
terciopelo *m* velvet.
terco,-a *adj* obstinate, stubborn.
terebenteno *m* terebenthene.
teresiano,-a 1 *adj* of the order of Saint Teresa of Avila, Teresian. – **2 teresiana,** *f* Teresian.
tergal *m* type of synthetic textile fibre.
▲ *Registered trademark.*
tergiversación *f* distortion, twisting.
tergiversar *t* to twist, distort.
termal *adj* thermal: *aguas termales,* thermal springs.
termas 1 *fpl* HIST thermae. **2** (*baños*) spa *sing*, hot baths, hot springs.
termes *m* termite.
▲ *pl* **termes.**

termia *f* therm.
térmico,-a *adj* thermic, thermal.
terminación 1 *f* (*acción*) ending, termination. 2 (*conclusion*) completion. 3 (*parte final*) end. 4 GRAM ending.
terminado,-a 1 *pp* → **terminar**. – 2 *adj* finished, completed.
● dar algo por terminado, to consider sth. finished.
terminal 1 *adj* terminal. – 2 *f* (*estación*) terminus, terminal. – 3 *m* INFORM ELEC terminal.
■ estación terminal, terminus. ‖ terminal aérea, air terminal. ‖ terminal conversacional/interactivo, INFORM conversational/interactive terminal.
terminante 1 *adj* (*categórico*) categorical, final. 2 (*dato, resultado*) conclusive, definitive, definite; (*prohibición*) strict.
terminantemente 1 *adv* (*categóricamente*) categorically. 2 (*definitivamente*) conclusively, definitely; (*prohibición*) strictly: *está terminantemente prohibido fumar,* smoking is strictly forbidden.
terminar 1 *t* (*acabar*) to finish, complete: *ha terminado la novela,* he's finished the novel. 2 (*dar fin*) to end: *los resultados terminaron su mandato,* the results ended his term of office. – 3 *i* (*acabar*) to finish, end: *terminó a las cuatro,* it finished at four; *termina en dos,* it ends with a two; *he terminado de leer,* I've finished reading. 4 (*acabar de*) to have just (**de**, -): *termina de marchar,* he has just left. 5 (*final de una acción, de un estado*) to end up: *terminó marchándose,* he ended up leaving; *terminó por marcharse,* he ended up leaving; *terminó loco,* he went mad. 6 (*eliminar*) to put an end (**con**, to): *quieren terminar con la violencia,* they want to put an end to violence. 7 (*estropear*) to damage (**con**, -), ruin (**con**, -): *la lluvia terminó con la cosecha,* the rain damaged the crops. 8 (*reñir*) to break up (**con**, with): *ha terminado con su novio,* she's broken up with her boyfriend. 9 (*enfermedad*) to come to the final stage. – 10 terminarse, *p* (*acabarse*) to finish, end, be over: *la reunión se ha terminado,* the meeting is over. 11 (*agotarse*) to run out: *se ha terminado el azúcar,* the sugar has run out.
● terminar bien, to have a happy ending. ‖ terminar mal, (*historia*) to have an unhappy ending; (*personas - relación*) to end up on bad terms; (- *destino*) to come to a sticky end.
término 1 *m* (*fin*) end, finish: *el término de una carrera,* the end of a race. 2 (*estación*) terminus, terminal. 3 (*límite*) limit, boundary; (*hito*) boundary marker. 4 (*plazo*) term, time, period: *en el término de cuatro años,* within a period of four years. 5 (*palabra*) term, word: *término técnico,* technical term. 6 (*estado*) condition, state. 7 (*lugar, posición*) place. 8 GRAM MAT FIL term. – 9 términos, *mpl* (*condiciones*) conditions, terms.
● dar término a algo, to conclude sth. ‖ en otros términos, in other words. ‖ en términos de, in terms of. ‖ en términos generales, generally speaking. ‖ en último término, *fig* as a last resort. ‖ invertir los términos, to get it the wrong way round. ‖ llevar algo a buen término, to carry sth. through successfully. ‖ poner término a algo, to put an end to sth. ‖ por término medio, on average.
■ primer término, ART foreground. ‖ término mayor/medio/menor, major/middle/minor term. ‖ término medio, middle ground, area of compromise: *hallar un término medio,* to reach a compromise. ‖ término municipal, district. ‖ términos de un contrato, JUR terms of a contract.
terminología *f* terminology.
terminológico,-a *adj* terminological.

termita *f* termite.
termite *f* termite.
termitero *m* termite's nest.
termo 1 *m* (*recipiente*) flask, thermos flask. 2 (*termosifón*) boiler, water heater.
termoaislante *adj* insulating.
termodinámica *f* → **termodinámico,-a**.
termodinámico,-a 1 *adj* thermodynamic. – 2 termodinámica, *f* thermodynamics.
termoelectricidad *f* thermoelectricity.
termógrafo *m* thermograph.
termología *f* thermology.
termometría *f* thermometry.
termométrico,-a *adj* thermometric, thermometrical.
termómetro *m* thermometer.
■ termómetro clínico, clinical thermometer. ‖ termómetro de máxima y mínima, maximum and minimum thermometer.
termonuclear *adj* thermonuclear.
termoquímica *f* → **termoquímico,-a**.
termoquímico,-a 1 *adj* thermochemical. – 2 termoquímica, *f* thermochemistry.
termosifón 1 *m* (*calentador*) boiler, water heater. 2 TÉC thermo-siphon.
termostato *m* thermostat.
terna *f* list of three candidates.
ternario,-a *adj* ternary.
ternera *f* → **ternero,-a**.
ternero,-a 1 *m,f* (*animal*) calf. – 2 ternera, *f* CULIN veal, beef.
terneza 1 *f* tenderness. – 2 ternezas, *fpl fam* sweet nothings.
ternilla *f* cartilage.
ternilloso,-a *adj* cartilaginous.
terno 1 *m* (*tres cosas*) set of three, group of three. 2 (*traje*) three-piece suit. 3 *fam* (*juramento*) swearword.
● echar ternos, *fam* to swear.
ternura *f* tenderness, gentleness.
terquedad 1 *f* (*obstinación*) obstinacy, stubbornness. 2 (*dureza*) toughness, hardness.
terracota *f* terracotta.
terrado *m* flat roof, terrace.
terral 1 *adj* land. – 2 *m* land breeze, terral.
Terranova *f* Newfoundland.
terraplén *m* embankment.
terráqueo,-a *adj* earth.
● globo terráqueo, earth, globe.
terrateniente *mf* landowner.
terraza 1 *f* (*balcón*) terrace, balcony. 2 (*azotea*) roof terrace, terrace. 3 (*de un café*) terrace.
terrazo *m* terrazzo.
terremoto *m* earthquake.
terrenal *adj* earthly, worldly.
terreno,-a 1 *adj* worldly, earthly. – 2 terreno, *m* (*tierra*) land, piece of land, ground; (*solar*) plot, site. 3 GEOG terrain. 4 AGR (*de cultivo*) soil; (*campo*) field. 5 DEP field, ground. 6 *fig* (*esfera de acción*) field, sphere.
● ceder terreno, *fig* to give way. ‖ conocer el terreno, *fig* to be familiar with sth. ‖ estar en su propio terreno, *fig* to be on home ground. ‖ ganar terreno / perder terreno, to gain ground / lose ground. ‖ hacer algo sobre el terreno, to do sth. on the spot; *fig* to improvise sth. ‖ saber uno el terreno que pisa, *fig* to know what one's doing. ‖ preparar el terreno, *fig* to pave the way, prepare the ground. ‖ ser terreno abonado (para algo), *fig* to be receptive (to sth.).

■ **terreno conocido,** *fig* familiar ground. ‖ **todo terreno,** AUTO all-terrain vehicle.

térreo,-a *adj* earthen.

terrera *f* → **terrero,-a.**

terrero,-a 1 *adj* (*de la tierra*) earth. 2 (*vuelo*) skimming, low. 3 *fig* (*humilde*) humble. – 4 **terrero,** *m* (*montón de tierra*) pile of earth. 5 (*blanco*) target. 6 (*depósito de tierras*) alluvium.

terrestre 1 *adj* (*de la tierra*) terrestrial, earthly. 2 (*por tierra*) by land: *transporte terrestre,* transport by land. – 3 *mf* (*persona*) terrestrial.

terrible *adj* terrible, awful.

terriblemente *adv* terribly, awfully.

terrícola 1 *adj* land. – 2 *mf* (*habitante*) earth dweller; (*en ciencia ficción*) earthling.

terrier *m* terrier.

terrígeno,-a *adj* terrigenous.

territorial *adj* territorial.
● **código territorial,** (*de teléfonos*) area code.

territorialidad *f* territoriality.

territorio *m* territory.
● **en todo el territorio nacional,** nationwide, all over the country.

terrizo,-a 1 *adj* earthenware. – 2 **terrizo,** *m* (*barreño*) bowl. – 3 **terriza,** *f* (*barreño*) bowl.

terrón 1 *m* (*de tierra*) clod. 2 (*de azúcar etc*) lump. – 3 **terrones,** *mpl* (*hacienda*) land *sing,* property *sing.*

terror *m* terror; CINEM horror.
● **dar terror,** to terrify.

terrorífico,-a *adj* terrifying, frightening.

terrorismo *m* terrorism.

terrorista 1 *adj* terrorist. – 2 *mf* terrorist.

terroso,-a 1 *adj* (*de la tierra*) earthy. 2 (*color*) earth-coloured (US earth-colored).

terruño 1 *m* (*masa de tierra*) clod. 2 (*tierra natal*) homeland, native land. 3 (*terreno*) piece of land. 4 (*tierra que se trabaja*) land.

terso,-a 1 *adj* (*liso*) smooth. 2 (*brillante*) shiny, glossy. 3 *fig* (*estilo*) polished, fluent.

tersura 1 *f* (*lisura*) smoothness. 2 (*brillo*) shine, glossiness. 3 *fig* (*de estilo*) polish, fluency.

tertulia 1 *f* (*reunión*) get-together. 2 (*lugar en cafés*) back room.
● **estar de tertulia,** to sit around and talk. ‖ **hacer tertulia,** to have a get-together.
■ **tertulia literaria,** literary gathering.

tertuliano,-a *m,f* person who participates in a gathering.

tesina *f* degree dissertation.

tesis 1 *f* thesis. 2 (*opinión*) view, theory.
● **sostener una tesis,** to maintain a theory.
■ **tesis doctoral,** doctoral thesis.
▲ *pl* **tesis.**

tesitura 1 *f* MÚS tessitura. 2 *fig* (*actitud*) attitude; (*estado de ánimo*) mood, frame of mind.

tesón *m* tenacity, firmness.

tesorería *f* (*oficina*) treasurer's office; (*cargo*) treasurer.

tesorero,-a *m,f* treasurer.

tesoro 1 *m* (*gen*) treasure. 2 (*erario*) exchequer. 3 *fig* (*diccionario*) thesaurus. 4 *fig* treasure, gem: *eres un tesoro,* you're a treasure.
■ **bono del Tesoro,** treasury-bond. ‖ **Tesoro Público,** Treasury.

test *m* test.
▲ *pl* **tests** *or* **test.**

testa *f* head.

testado,-a 1 *pp* → **testar.** – 2 *adj* testate.

testador,-ra *m,f* (*hombre*) testator; (*mujer*) testatrix.

testaferro *m* front man.

testamentaría *f* testate proceedings *pl.*

testamentario,-a 1 *adj* testamentary. – 2 *m,f* (*hombre*) executor; (*mujer*) executrix.

testamento 1 *m* JUR will, testament. 2 REL Testament.
● **hacer testamento / otorgar testamento,** to make one's will, draw up one's will.
■ **Antiguo Testamento / Nuevo Testamento,** Old Testament / New Testament.

testar *i* to make one's will, draw up one's will.

testarada 1 *f* (*golpe*) blow to the head, butt. 2 *fam* (*obstinación*) obstinacy, pigheadedness.

testarazo *m* *fam* blow to the head, butt.

testarudez *f* stubbornness, obstinacy, pigheadedness.

testarudo,-a *adj* obstinate, stubborn, pigheaded.

testículo *m* testicle.

testifical *adj* attesting, witnessing.

testificante *adj* testifying.

testificar *t* to testify.
▲ *Conjugation model* [1], *like* **sacar.**

testigo 1 *mf* witness. – 2 *m* (*prueba*) proof, evidence, witness: *las ruinas eran testigos de los bombardeos,* the ruins bore witness to the bombings. 3 DEP baton.
● **a Dios pongo por testigo,** I swear to God. ‖ **poner a algn. por testigo,** to call sb. as witness.
■ **testigo de cargo,** witness for the prosecution. ‖ **testigo de descargo,** witness for the defence (US defense). ‖ **testigo ocular / testigo presencial,** eyewitness. ‖ **Testigos de Jehová,** Jehovah's Witnesses.

testimonial 1 *adj* testimonial. – 2 **testimoniales,** *fpl* JUR documentary evidence.

testimoniar 1 *t* JUR to bear witness to, testify to, attest to. 2 *fig* to show, prove, bear witness to. 3 *fig* (*expresar*) to show, express: *testimonió su condolencia,* he expressed his sympathies.
▲ *Conjugation model* [12], *like* **cambiar.**

testimonio 1 *m* JUR testimony, evidence. 2 (*prueba*) evidence, proof.
● **dar testimonio,** to give evidence. ‖ **levantar falsos testimonios,** to commit perjury.

testosterona *f* testosterone.

testuz 1 *m* & *f* (*frente*) forehead. 2 (*nuca*) nape.

teta 1 *f* breast; *fam* tit, titty, boob. 2 (*de animal*) udder.
● **dar la teta,** to breast-feed, nurse. ‖ **es teta de monja / es teta de novicia,** *tabú* it's delicious! ‖ **quitar la teta,** to wean.
■ **niño,-a de teta,** nursing baby.

tetamen *f* *tabú* tits *pl,* boobs *pl.*

tetánico,-a *adj* tetanic.

tétano *m* tetanus.

tétanos *m* tetanus.
▲ *pl* **tétanos.**

tetera *f* teapot.

tetilla 1 *f* ANAT man's nipple. 2 (*tetina*) teat, rubber teat.
■ **queso de tetilla,** type of Galician cheese.

tetina *f* teat, rubber teat.

tetón *m* stub.

tetona 1 *adj* *fam* buxom, busty. – 2 *f* *fam* buxom woman, busty woman.

tetrabrik *m* carton.
▲ *Registered trademark; pl* **tetrabriks.**

tetraedro *m* tetrahedron.

tetragonal *adj* tetragonal.

tetralogía *f* tetralogy.

tetrarquía *f* tetrarchy.

tetrasílabo,-a **1** *adj* tetrasyllabic. **– 2 tetrasílabo,** *m* tetrasyllable.

tétrico,-a *adj* gloomy, dull, dismal.

tetuda *adj-f fam* → **tetona**.

teutón,-ona **1** *adj* HIST Teutonic. **2** (*alemán*) German. **– 3** *m,f* HIST Teuton. **4** (*alemán*) German.

textil **1** *adj* textile. **– 2** *m* textile.
■ **industria textil,** textile industry. ‖ **obrero textil,** textile worker.

texto *m* text.
■ **libro de texto,** textbook.

textual **1** *adj* textual. **2** (*exacto*) literal, precise, exact.
● **en palabras textuales,** literally.

textualmente *adv* exactly, literally, verbatim, textually.

textura **1** *f* (*textil*) texture. **2** (*minerales*) structure.

tez *f* complexion.

ti *pron* you: *te lo doy a ti,* I'll give it to you; *un regalo para ti,* a present for you; *guárdalo para ti mismo,* keep it for yourself.
▲ *Used only after a preposition.*

tía *f fam* → **tío,-a**.

tiara *f* tiara.

tiarrón,-ona *m,f fam* (*hombre*) hulking bloke; (*mujer*) strapping woman, huge woman.

Tíber el Tíber, *m* the Tiber.

Tiberiades lago de Tiberiades, *m* Lake Tiberias.

tiberio *m fam* row, uproar.

Tibet el Tibet, *m* Tibet.

tibetano,-a **1** *adj* Tibetan. **– 2** *m,f* Tibetan. **– 3 tibetano,** *m* (*idioma*) Tibetan.

tibia *f* tibia, shin-bone.

tibieza **1** *f* tepidity, tepidness. **2** *fig* lack of enthusiasm, coolness, tepidity.

tibio,-a **1** *adj* tepid, lukewarm. **2** *fig* tepid, unenthusiastic, cool.
● **poner tibio,-a a algn.,** *fam* to pull sb. to pieces.

tibor *m* large vase.

tiburón *m* shark.

tic **1** *m* tic, twitch. **2** *fig* (*manía*) habit.
■ **tic nervioso,** nervous tic, nervous twitch.
▲ *pl* tiques.

tictac *m* tick-tock, ticking.

tiempo **1** *m* (*gen*) time: *no tuve tiempo para hablar con él,* I didn't have time to talk to him. **2** (*época*) time, period, age, days *pl*: *en tiempo de los romanos,* in Roman times. **3** METEOR weather: *¿qué tiempo hace?,* what's the weather like? **4** (*edad*) age: *¿qué tiempo tiene el niño?,* how old is your baby? **5** (*temporada*) season, time: *fruta del tiempo,* fruit in season. **6** (*momento*) moment, time: *no es tiempo de preguntarle eso,* it's not the time to ask him that. **7** MÚS tempo, movement. **8** DEP (*parte*) half. **9** GRAM tense. **10** TÉC stroke.
● **a su tiempo / a su debido tiempo,** in due course. ‖ **a tiempo,** (*en el momento oportuno*) in time; (*a la hora*) on time. ‖ **a través de los tiempos,** through the ages. ‖ **a un tiempo,** at the same time. ‖ **al mismo tiempo,** at the same time. ‖ **al poco tiempo,** soon afterwards. ‖ **antes de tiempo,** too early, too soon. ‖ **con el tiempo,** in the course of time, with time. ‖ **con tiempo,** in advance. ‖ **¿cuánto tiempo ...?,** how long ...?: *¿cuánto tiempo estuviste allí?,* how long did you stay there?;

¿cuánto tiempo llevas aquí en España?, how long have you lived in Spain? ‖ **¿cuánto tiempo hace ...?,** how long ago ...?: *¿cuánto tiempo hace que no vas al cine?,* how long ago is it since you went to the cinema? ‖ **dar tiempo,** to give time. ‖ **dar tiempo al tiempo,** *fig* to let matters take their course. ‖ **dar tiempo a uno de/para,** to have enough time to: *si salgo a las cinco me dará tiempo de hacer las compras,* if I leave at five I'll have enough time to do the shopping. ‖ **de tiempo en tiempo,** from time to time. ‖ **de tiempo inmemorial,** from time immemorial. ‖ **de un tiempo a esta parte,** for some time now. ‖ **demasiado tiempo,** too long. ‖ **desde hace tiempo / desde hace mucho tiempo,** for a long time. ‖ **el tiempo corre,** time goes by, time flies. ‖ **el tiempo es oro,** *fig* time is money. ‖ **en mis tiempos,** in my time. ‖ **en otro tiempo / en otros tiempos,** formerly. ‖ **estar a tiempo de,** to still have time to. ‖ **fuera de tiempo,** (*de temporada*) out of season; (*inoportunamente*) at the wrong moment. ‖ **ganar tiempo,** to save time. ‖ **hace tiempo,** a long time: *hace tiempo que no cantas,* you haven't sung for a long time. ‖ **hacer buen tiempo / hacer mal tiempo,** the weather is good / the weather is bad. ‖ **hacer tiempo / hacer el tiempo,** to kill time. ‖ **matar (el) tiempo / pasar (el) tiempo,** to kill time. ‖ **no hay tiempo que perder,** there's no time to lose. ‖ **perder el tiempo / perder tiempo,** to waste time. ‖ **¡qué tiempos aquellos!,** those were the days! ‖ **sin perder tiempo,** at once. ‖ **tiempo atrás,** some time ago, time ago. ‖ **tomarse tiempo,** to take one's time. ‖ **¡y si no, al tiempo!,** time will tell!
■ **tiempo de perros,** *fam fig* lousy weather. ‖ **tiempo libre,** free time. ‖ **tiempos difíciles,** hard times.

tienda **1** *f* (*establecimiento*) shop, US store. **2** (*de campaña*) tent. **3** (*de carro*) cover.
● **ir de tiendas,** to go shopping.
■ **tienda de campaña,** tent. ‖ **tienda de comestibles / tienda de ultramarinos,** grocer's, US grocery store. ‖ **tienda de modas,** boutique.

tienta **1** *f* (*de becerros*) test of bravery. **2** (*sagacidad*) sagacity, cleverness.
● **a tientas,** by touch. ‖ **andar a tientas,** to feel one's way, grope one's way. ‖ **buscar algo a tientas,** to grope for sth.

tientaguja *f* sounding rod.

tiento **1** *m* (*tacto*) tact, feel. **2** (*prudencia*) caution. **3** (*de ciego*) stick. **4** (*pulso*) steady hand. **5** *fam* (*trago*) swig. **6** MÚS preliminary notes *pl*.
● **con tiento,** tactfully. ‖ **dar un tiento a la botella / echar un tiento a la botella,** *fam* to take a swig from the bottle.

tiernamente *adv* tenderly.

tierno,-a **1** *adj* (*blando*) tender, soft. **2** *fig* (*reciente*) fresh: *pan tierno,* fresh bread. **3** *fig* (*persona*) young. **4** *fig* (*propenso al llanto*) soft. **5** *fig* (*cariñoso*) affectionate.
■ **edad tierna,** tender age.

tierra **1** *f* (*planeta*) earth. **2** (*superficie sólida*) land. **3** (*terreno cultivado*) soil, land. **4** (*país*) country, land. **5** (*suelo*) ground. **6** ELEC earth, US ground. **– 7 tierras,** *fpl* land *sing*.
● **caer por tierra,** *fig* to crumble. ‖ **dar en tierra con algo,** to drop sth. on the ground, throw sth. on the ground. ‖ **echar a tierra,** to demolish. ‖ **echar por tierra,** *fig* to crush, destroy: *echaron por tierra su argumento,* they destroyed his argument. ‖ **echar tierra encima de,** *fig* to hush up. ‖ **poner tierra por medio,** *fig* to make os. scarce. ‖ **por estas tierras,** in these

parts. ‖ **por tierra,** overland, by land. ‖ **¡tierra a la vista!,** land ahoy! ‖ **tierra adentro,** inland. ‖ **¡tierra trágame!,** *fig* I wish I was somewhere else, I could curl up and die. ‖ **tirar por tierra,** *fig* to crush, destroy. ‖ **tocar tierra,** MAR to reach harbour (US harbor); AV to touch down. ‖ **vivir de la tierra,** to make a living from the land.
■ **tierra de nadie,** no-man's-land. ‖ **Tierra del Fuego,** Tierra del Fuego. ‖ **tierra firme,** terra firma, dry land. ‖ **tierra natal,** homeland. ‖ **Tierra Santa,** the Holy Land.

tieso,-a 1 *adj* (*rígido*) stiff, rigid. **2** (*erguido*) upright, erect. **3** (*tenso*) taut, tight. **4** *fig* (*terco*) stubborn. **5** *fig* (*en forma*) in good shape. **6** *fam fig* (*envarado*) stiff, starchy, stuffy. – **7** *adv* hard, strongly: *pisó tieso,* she put her foot down hard.
● **dejar tieso,-a a algn.,** (*pasmado*) to leave sb. agape; (*muerto*) to do sb. in; (*sin dinero*) to leave sb. penniless. ‖ **poner las orejas tiesas,** to prick up one's ears. ‖ **quedarse tieso,-a de frío,** *fig* to be frozen stiff.

tiesto *m* flowerpot.

tifoideo,-a *adj* typhoid.
■ **fiebre tifoidea,** typhoid fever.

tifón 1 *m* typhoon. **2** (*en el mar*) waterspout.

tifus *m* typhus, typhus fever.
▲ *pl* **tifus.**

tigra *f* tigress.

tigre *m* tiger.
● **oler a tigre,** *fam* to stink.

tigresa *f fig* femme fatale.

tija *f* stem.

tijera 1 *f* (*instrumento*) scissors *pl,* pair of scissors. **2** *fig* (*persona*) gossip.
■ **escalera de tijera,** stepladder. ‖ **salto de tijera,** scissors *pl.* ‖ **silla de tijera,** folding chair.
▲ In 1 generally used in plural.

tijereta 1 *f* (*tijerita*) small scissors *pl.* **2** (*insecto*) earwig. **3** (*de la vid*) tendril. **4** DEP scissors *pl.*

tijeretada *f* snip.

tijeretazo *m* snip.

tijeretear 1 *t* to snip, cut, clip. **2** *fig* to meddle in.

tijereteo *m* snip, clip.

tila 1 *f* (*tilo*) lime, linden. **2** (*flor*) lime blossom, linden blossom. **3** (*infusión*) lime-blossom tea, linden-blossom tea.

tílburi *m* tilbury.

tildar 1 *t* (*poner tilde*) to put a written accent on; (*de la ñ*) to put a tilde on. **2** (*tachar*) to cross out. **3** (*a una persona*) to call, brand: *lo tildaron de mentiroso,* they branded him a liar.

tilde 1 *f* (*gen*) written accent; (*de la ñ*) tilde. **2** *fig* (*tacha*) fault, flaw.

tilín *m* ting-a-ling.
● **hacer tilín,** *fam* to fancy, like: *Elena le hace tilín,* he fancies Elena.

tilo *m* lime tree.

timador,-ra *m,f* swindler, cheat.

timar 1 *t* to swindle, cheat, trick: *le timaron quinientas mil pesetas,* he was cheated out of five hundred thousand pesetas. – **2 timarse,** *p fam* to make eyes at each other.

timba 1 *f fam* (*partida*) game, hand. **2** *fam* (*casa de juego*) gambling den.

timbal 1 *m* MÚS kettledrum; (*pequeño*) small drum. **2** CULIN timbale; (*de carne*) meat pie; (*de pescado*) fish pie.

timbalero,-a *m,f* kettledrummer.

timbrado,-a 1 *pp* → **timbrar.** – **2** *adj* stamped.
■ **papel timbrado,** (*sellado*) stamped paper; (*con membrete*) stationery with a letterhead.

timbrar *t* (*carta*) to stamp, mark; (*documento*) to seal.

timbrazo *m* loud ring, long ring.
● **dar un timbrazo,** to ring the bell.

timbre 1 *m* (*de la puerta*) bell. **2** (*sello*) stamp, seal; (*sello fiscal*) fiscal stamp, revenue stamp. **3** MÚS timbre.
● **tocar el timbre,** to ring the bell.
● **timbre nasal,** twang.

timidez *f* shyness, timidity.

tímido,-a 1 *adj* shy, timid. **2** *fig* (*intento etc*) half-hearted.

timo[1] *m* (*estafa*) swindle, fiddle, confidence trick.
● **dar un timo / dar el timo,** to swindle, cheat. ‖ **¡vaya timo!,** *fam* (*película etc*) what a rip off!

timo[2] *m* (*glándula*) thymus.

timón 1 *m* (*barco, avión*) rudder. **2** (*del arado*) beam. **3** *fig* (*negocio etc*) helm.
● **empuñar el timón / llevar el timón,** *fig* to be at the helm.

timonear *i* to steer, be at the helm.

timonel *m* steersman, helmsman.

timonera *f* rectrix.

timorato,-a 1 *adj* (*tímido*) shy, timid. **2** (*mojigato*) prudish.

tímpano 1 *m* (*del oído*) eardrum. **2** ARQ tympanum. **3** MÚS (*tamboril*) kettledrum; (*instrumento*) timpani *pl,* tympani *pl,* timps *pl.*

tina 1 *f* (*recipiente*) vat, tub. **2** (*tinaja*) large earthenware vat. **3** (*bañera*) bath, bathtub.

tinaja 1 *f* (*recipiente*) large earthenware jar. **2** (*cantidad*) jar.

tinerfeño,-a 1 *adj* of Tenerife, from Tenerife. – **2** *m,f* person from Tenerife, inhabitant of Tenerife.

tinglado 1 *m* (*cobertizo*) shed. **2** (*tablado*) platform, raised floor. **3** *fig* (*embrollo*) mess. **4** *fig* (*intriga*) intrigue. **5** *fig* (*mundillo*) setup, racket, business.
● **conocer el tinglado,** *fam* to know the setup. ‖ **manejar el tinglado,** *fam* to pull the strings.

tiniebla 1 *f* (*oscuridad*) darkness. – **2 tinieblas,** *fpl fig* (*ignorancia*) ignorance *sing,* confusion *sing.*
● **estar en tinieblas sobre algo,** to be in the dark about sth.
▲ In 1, also used in plural with the same meaning.

tino 1 *m* (*puntería*) good aim, aim. **2** *fig* (*juicio*) good judgement, sense, common sense. **3** *fig* (*moderación*) moderation.
● **a tino,** feeling one's way. ‖ **con tino,** *fig* wisely. ‖ **sacar de tino a algn.,** *fig* to make sb. lose their temper, make sb. mad. ‖ **sin tino,** (*sin sentido*) foolishly; (*sin moderación*) immoderately. ‖ **tener buen tino,** to be a good shot.

tintar *t* to dye.

tinte 1 *m* (*colorante*) dye. **2** (*proceso*) dyeing. **3** (*tintorería*) dry-cleaner's. **4** *fig* (*aspecto*) shade, colouring (US coloring), overtones *pl.*
● **llevar algo al tinte,** to have sth. dry-cleaned.

tintero *m* inkpot, ink-well.
● **quedarse en el tintero,** *fig* to be left unsaid.

tintín 1 *m* (*de campanilla*) jingle, tinkle, ting-a-ling. **2** (*de copas*) clink, clinking.

tintinar 1 *i* (*vidrio*) to clink, chink. **2** (*campanillas*) to jingle, tinkle.

tintinear *i* → **tintinar.**

tintineo 1 *m* (*de vidrio*) clink, clinking, chink. **2** (*de campanillas*) jingling, ting-a-ling.

tinto,-a 1 *adj* (*teñido*) dyed, stained: *tinto en sangre,* bloodstained. **2** (*vino*) red. – **3 tinto,** *m* (*vino*) red wine.

– 4 tinta, f (*gen*) ink. **5** (*tinte*) dyeing. **– 6 tintas,** *fpl* colours (US colors), hues.
● **cargar las tintas / recargar las tintas,** *fig* to exaggerate. ‖ **escribir con tinta,** to write in ink. ‖ **hacer correr mucha tinta,** *fig* to get a lot of coverage: *la boda hizo correr mucha tinta,* there was a lot written about the wedding. ‖ **saber algo de buena tinta,** *fig* to get sth. straight from the horse's mouth. ‖ **sudar tinta,** *fig* to sweat blood.
■ **medias tintas,** *fig* vague words. ‖ **tinta china,** Indian ink. ‖ **tinta simpática,** invisible ink.
tintóreo,-a *adj* tinctorial.
tintorera f blue shark.
tintorería f dry-cleaner's.
tintorero,-a *m,f* dry-cleaner.
tintorro *m fam* plonk, cheap red wine.
tintura 1 f (*colorante*) dye. **2** (*proceso*) dyeing. **3** (*disolución*) tincture. **4** *fig* (*noción*) notion.
■ **tintura de yodo,** iodine.
tiña 1 f (*larva*) honeycomb moth. **2** MED tinea, ringworm. **3** *fig* (*miseria*) misery, poverty; (*mezquindad*) meanness, stinginess.
tiñoso,-a 1 *adj* MED scabby, mangey, mangy. **2** *fam* (*mezquino*) mean, stingy.
tío,-a 1 *m,f* (*pariente - hombre*) uncle; (- *mujer*) aunt. **2** *fam* (*persona - hombre*) fellow, bloke, US guy; (- *mujer*) girl, woman, bird: *¡eres un tío grande!,* you're a great guy! – **3** tía, f *fam* (*prostituta*) whore.
■ **tío abuelo / tía abuela,** great-uncle / great-aunt. ‖ **tío bueno / tía buena,** *fam* a bit of all right.
tiovivo *m* merry-go-round, roundabout, US carrousel.
tiparraco,-a *m fam* twerp, idiot.
tipazo *m fam* good figure.
tipejo,-a *m,f fam* twerp, idiot.
típico,-a 1 *adj* (*característico*) typical, characteristic. **2** (*pintoresco*) picturesque; (*tradicional*) traditional: *un plato típico,* a traditional dish, a local dish.
● **eso es típico de ...,** that's just like .... *eso es típico de Pedro,* that's just like Pedro. ‖ **¡lo típico!,** the same old thing!
tipificación 1 f (*normalización*) standardization. **2** (*caracterización*) typification.
tipificar 1 *t* (*normalizar*) to standardize. **2** (*caracterizar*) to typify.
▲ *Conjugation model* [1], *like* **sacar**.
tipismo *m* picturequeness, local colour (US color).
tiple 1 *m* (*voz*) treble, soprano. **2** (*guitarrita*) treble guitar. – **3** *mf* (*cantante*) soprano, soprano singer.
tipo 1 *m* (*clase*) type, kind. **2** FIN rate. **3** ANAT (*de hombre*) build, physique; (*de mujer*) figure. **4** *fam* (*persona*) guy, fellow, bloke. **5** (*en impresión*) type.
● **aguantar el tipo,** *fig* to keep cool, keep calm. ‖ **dar el tipo,** *fig* to fit a description, fit the bill. ‖ **jugarse el tipo,** *fig* to risk one's neck. ‖ **tener buen tipo,** (*hombre*) to be well-built; (*mujer*) to have a good figure. ‖ **todo tipo de,** all kind of, all kinds of.
■ **tipo bancario,** FIN bank rate. ‖ **tipo de cambio,** FIN rate of exchange. ‖ **tipo de descuento,** FIN bank rate. ‖ **tipo de interés,** FIN rate of interest. ‖ **tipo raro,** weirdo, oddball.
tipografía f typography.
tipográfico,-a *adj* typographic, typographical.
■ **error tipográfico,** printing error.
tipógrafo,-a *m,f* typographer.
tipología f typology.
tique *m* (*billete*) ticket; (*recibo*) receipt.

tíquet *m* → **tique**.
▲ *pl tíquets.*
tiquete *m* → **tique**.
tiquismiquis 1 *mpl* (*escrúpulos*) fussing *sing.* **2** (*riñas*) bickering *sing.* – **3** *mf fam* (*persona*) fusspot.
● **andarse con tiquismiquis,** *fam* to be fussy.
▲ In 3, *pl tiquismiquis.*
tira 1 f (*cinta, banda*) strip. **2** (*de zapatos*) strap. **3** (*de dibujos*) comic strip. – **4 la tira,** *loc* (*cantidad*) a lot, loads; (*mucho tiempo*) for yonks, for ages: *comimos la tira,* we ate loads; *tardamos la tira en llegar,* it took us ages to get there.
● **quitar la piel a tiras a algn.,** *fig* to tear sb. to pieces.
tirabeque *m* tender pea, mange-tout, sugar snap pea.
tirabotas *m* boot hook.
▲ *pl tirabotas.*
tirabuzón 1 *m* (*rizo*) ringlet. **2** (*sacacorchos*) corkscrew.
tirachinas *m* catapult, US slingshot.
▲ *pl tirachinas.*
tirada f → **tirado,-a**.
tirado,-a 1 *pp* → **tirar**. – **2** *adj fam* (*precio*) dirt cheap. **3** *fam* (*problema, asunto*) dead easy. **4** *fam* (*abandonado*) let down. – **5 tirada,** f (*acción*) throw: *en la segunda tirada le salieron dos seises,* he got two sixes on the second throw. **6** (*impresión*) printing; (*edición*) edition: *una tirada de cinco mil ejemplares,* a five-thousand - copy edition. **7** (*distancia*) stretch: *hay una buena tirada hasta allí,* it's a good few miles away. **8** (*serie*) series, long series.
● **de una tirada / en una tirada,** in one go. ‖ **dejar tirado,-a a algn.,** to let sb. down.
■ **tirada reducida,** limited edition.
tirador,-ra 1 *m,f* (*persona*) shooter, marksman. – **2** *m* (*de puerta, cajón*) knob, handle; (*cordón*) bell-pull. **3** (*tirachinas*) catapult, US slingshot.
tiragomas *m* catapult, US slingshot.
▲ *pl tiragomas.*
tiraje 1 *m* (*impresión*) printing. **2** (*distribución*) circulation.
▲ *pl tiralevitas.*
tiralevitas *mf fam* bootlicker.
tiralíneas *m* tracer, drawing-pen, ruling-pen.
▲ *pl tiralíneas.*
Tirana f Tirana.
tiranía f tyranny.
tiránico,-a *adj* tyrannic, tyrannical.
tiranización f tyrannizing.
tiranizar *t* to tyrannize.
▲ *Conjugation model* [4], *like* **realizar**.
tirano,-a *m,f* tyrant.
tirante 1 *adj* taut, tight. **2** *fig* (*relación, situación*) tense, strained. – **3** *m* (*de ropa en general*) strap. **4** (*de caballería*) trace. **5** TÉC brace, stay. **6** ARQ beam. – **7 tirantes,** *mpl* (*de pantalón*) braces, US suspenders.
tirantez 1 f (*tensión*) tautness, tightness. **2** *fig* (*de relación etc*) tension, strain.
tirar 1 *t* (*echar*) to throw, fling. **2** (*dejar caer*) to drop. **3** (*desechar*) to throw away. **4** (*derribar*) to knock down; (*casa, árbol*) to pull down. **5** (*derramar*) to spill. **6** (*vaso, botella*) to knock over. **7** (*estirar*) to pull. **8** (*imprimir*) to print. **9** (*hacer - foto*) to take; (*línea, plano*) to draw. **10** (*un tiro*) to fire; (*una bomba*) to drop; (*cohete*) to launch. **11** (*beso*) to blow; (*pellizco*) to give; (*patada, coz*) to kick. **12** DEP to take. **13** *fig* (*malgastar*) to waste, squander. **14** *fam fig* (*suspender*) to fail. – **15** *i* (*cuerda, puerta*) to pull (**de**, -). **16** (*carreta, carro*) to draw (**de**, -). **17** (*atraer*) to draw, attract. **18** (*estufa, chimenea*) to draw. **19** (*en juegos*) to be a player's move, be a player's turn: *tira él,* it's his turn. **20** *fam* (*funcionar*) to work, run: *esto ya no tira,* this

doesn't work anymore. **21** *fam* (*durar*) to last: *con esta reparación tirará un par de meses,* after these repairs it'll last for a couple of months. **22** (*quedar estrecho*) to be tight on: *esta camisa me tira de la espalda,* this shirt's tight on me. **23** *fig* (*tender*) to tend (**a**, towards); (*ser un poco*) to be a bit: *tira a verde,* it's greenish in colour; *tira a dulce,* it's a bit sweet. **24** *fam fig* (*atraer*) to attract, appeal: *no le tira la mecánica,* mechanics doesn't appeal to him. **25** *fig* (*inclinarse*) to be attracted (**a/hacia**, to), be drawn (**a/hacia**, to): *esta chica tira hacia las artes,* this girl is drawn to the arts. **26** *fig* (*parecerse*) to take after (**a**, -): *tira a su padre,* she takes after her father. **27** *fig* (*ir*) to go, turn: *tira a la derecha,* turn right. **28** *fig* (*mantenerse*) to get by, get along: *ella tira con poco dinero,* she gets by with little money. **29** (*disparar*) to shoot, fire. **30** DEP (*fútbol*) to shoot; (*ciclismo*) to set the pace. – **31 tirarse**, *p* (*lanzarse*) to throw os., hurl os. **32** (*abalanzarse*) to rush (**sobre**, at), jump (**sobre**, on). **33** (*tumbarse*) to lie down. **34** *fam* (*tiempo*) to spend: *se tiró una hora en la ducha,* he spent an hour in the shower. **35** *arg* (*fornicar*) to lay (**a**, -).
● **a todo tirar,** *fig* at the most, at the latest. ‖ **ir tirando,** (*espabilarse*) to manage, get by; (*tener buena salud*) to be okay. ‖ **tira y afloja,** *fig* give and take. ‖ **tirando,** *fam* so-so. ‖ **tirar abajo,** (*gen*) to demolish, pull down; (*puerta*) to smash in. ‖ **tirar al blanco,** to shoot at a target. ‖ **tirar de,** *fam* to use: *cuando no tiene dinero tira de tarjeta,* when he hasn't got any money he uses his credit card. ‖ **tirar a algn. de la lengua,** *fig* to draw sb. out. ‖ **tirar de cartera,** to dip into one's wallet. ‖ **tirar la casa por la ventana,** *fig* to spare no expense, push the boat out. ‖ **tirar la primera piedra,** *fig* to cast the first stone. ‖ **tirar una moneda al aire,** to toss a coin. ‖ **tirarse de cabeza al agua,** to dive into the water.
tirilla *f* neckband.
tirita *f* sticking plaster, plaster, Elastoplast, Band-aid.
▲ *Registered trademark.*
tiritar *i* (*gen*) to shiver, shake, tremble; (*dientes*) to chatter.
tiritera *f* (*gen*) shivering, shivers *pl*; (*de dientes*) chattering: *nos dio la tiritera,* we started shivering.
tiritona *f* → **tiritera**.
tiro **1** *m* (*lanzamiento*) throw. **2** (*disparo, ruido*) shot. **3** (*galería de tiro*) shooting-gallery. **4** DEP shooting. **5** (*caballerías*) team. **6** COST (*vestido*) shoulder width; (*de pantalón*) distance between waist and crotch. **7** (*de chimenea*) draught (US draft); (*de mina*) mineshaft. **8** (*de escaleras*) flight. **9** (*fútbol etc*) shot.
● **a tiro,** (*de arma*) within range; (*a mano*) within reach. ‖ **a tiro hecho,** with precision; *fig* deliberately. ‖ **a un tiro de piedra,** a stone's throw away. ‖ **dar un tiro / pegar un tiro,** to shoot, fire a shot. ‖ **de tiros largos,** *fig* all dressed up. ‖ **errar el tiro,** to miss the mark, fail. ‖ **ir los tiros,** *fam* to be going on: *acaba de llegar y no sabe por dónde van los tiros,* he's just arrived and he doesn't quite know what's going on; *sabe por dónde van los tiros,* he's sussed out what's going on. ‖ **le salió el tiro por la culata,** *fig* it backfired on him. ‖ **liarse a tiros,** to start shooting. ‖ **ni a tiros,** *fam* not for love nor money. ‖ **pegarse un tiro,** to shoot os.; (*comida*) to make one feel really ill. ‖ **tirar a gol,** to shoot at goal.
■ **animal de tiro,** draught animal. ‖ **tiro al blanco,** target shooting. ‖ **tiro al plato,** trap-shooting, clay-pigeon shooting. ‖ **tiro con arco,** archery. ‖ **tiro de gracia,** coup de grâce. ‖ **tiro de pichón,** pigeon shooting.
tiroideo,-a *adj* thyroid.

tiroides **1** *adj* thyroid. – **2** *m* thyroid, thyroid gland.
▲ *pl* **tiroides**.
Tirol *m* Tyrol.
tirolés,-esa **1** *adj* Tyrolean. – **2** *m,f* Tyrolean.
tirón *m* pull, tug.
● **dar el tirón,** *fam* (*robar*) to snatch sb.'s handbag. ‖ **dar un tirón de orejas a algn.,** to pull sb.'s ear. ‖ **de un tirón,** *fam* in one go.
tirotear *t* to shoot, snipe.
tiroteo *m* shooting, exchange of shots.
tirreno,-a *adj* Tyrrhenian.
■ **el (mar) Tirreno,** the Tyrrhenian (Sea).
tirria *f fam* dislike.
● **tener tirria a,** *fam* to dislike, have it in for.
tisana *f* infusion, tisane.
tísico,-a **1** *adj* tubercular, consumptive. – **2** *m,f* consumptive.
tisis *f* consumption, tuberculosis, phthisis.
▲ *pl* **tisis**.
tisú *m* (*de oro*) gold lamé; (*de plata*) silver lamé.
▲ *pl* **tisúes**.
titán *m* titan.
titánico,-a *adj* titanic.
titanio *m* titanium.
títere **1** *m* (*marioneta*) puppet, marionette. **2** *fig* (*persona*) puppet, dupe. – **3 títeres,** *mpl* puppet show *sing*.
● **no dejar títere con cabeza / no quedar títere con cabeza,** *fam* (*destruir*) to break everything in sight; (*criticar*) to spare nobody.
titi *m arg* (*hombre*) young guy; (*mujer*) young girl.
tití *m* titi.
titilante **1** *adj* (*temblor*) quivering. **2** (*luz*) flickering; (*estrella*) twinkling.
titilar **1** *i* (*temblar*) to quiver. **2** (*luz*) to flicker; (*de estrella*) to twinkle.
titileo **1** *m* (*temblor*) quiver. **2** (*de luz*) flicker; (*de estrella*) twinkle.
titiritar *i* to tremble, shiver.
titiritero,-a **1** *m,f* (*de títeres*) puppeteer. **2** (*volatinero*) tightrope walker. **3** (*saltimbanqui*) travelling acrobat.
tito,-a *m,f fam* (*tío*) uncle; (*tía*) aunt.
titubeante **1** *adj* (*tambaleante*) staggering, shaky. **2** (*al hablar*) stammering. **3** *fig* (*indeciso*) hesitant.
titubear **1** *i* (*tambalearse*) to stagger, totter, shake. **2** (*tartamudear*) to stammer. **3** *fig* (*vacilar*) to hesitate.
titubeo **1** *m* (*temblor*) stagger, staggering, tottering. **2** (*tartamudeo*) stammering. **3** *fig* (*duda*) hesitation.
● **sin titubeo,** *fig* decisively, without hesitation.
titulación *f* qualifications *pl*.
titulado,-a **1** *pp* → **titular**. – **2** *adj* (*llamado*) called. **3** EDUC (*diplomado*) qualified; (*licenciado*) graduate: *es titulado en derecho,* he has a degree in law.
titular **1** *t* to entitle, title, call. – **2** *adj* regular. – **3** *mf* (*poseedor*) holder. **4** (*de un puesto*) office holder; (*de cátedra*) professor. – **5** *m* (*prensa*) headline. – **6 titularse,** *p* (*llamarse*) to be called, be titled. **7** EDUC to graduate (**en**, in).
■ **el titular de la cartera de ...,** POL the minister of ...
titularidad *f* entitlement.
titulillo *m* running title.
título **1** *m* (*de obra*) title. **2** (*de texto legal*) heading. **3** (*dignidad*) title. **4** (*persona noble*) noble (person). **5** EDUC (*licenciatura*) degree; (*diploma*) certificate, diploma. **6** (*documento*) title. **7** (*titular de prensa*) headline. **8** (*banca*) bond, security. – **9 títulos,** *mpl* (*titulación*) qualifications; (*méritos*) qualities.

● **a título de,** (*en calidad de*) as; (*en concepto de*) by way of.

■ **título de nobleza,** nobility title. ‖ **título de propiedad,** deeds *pl.*

tiza *f* chalk: *dame una tiza,* give me a piece of chalk.

tiznado,-a 1 *pp* → **tiznar.** – 2 *adj* sooty, blackened.

tiznadura *f* soot mark, smudge.

tiznar 1 *t* to blacken, soil with soot. 2 *fig* to blacken, soil. – 3 **tiznarse,** *p* to blacken.

tizne *m* soot.

tiznón *m* smudge.

tizón 1 *m* half-burnt stick, brand. 2 *fig* stain.

● **ser negro,-a como un tizón,** *fig* to be as black as soot, be as black as coal.

Tm *sím* metric ton.

TNT *abr* (*trinitrotolueno*) trinitrotoluene; (*abreviatura*) TNT.

toalla *f* towel.

● **arrojar la toalla / tirar la toalla,** *fig* to throw in the towel.

■ **toalla de baño,** bath towel. ‖ **toalla de manos,** hand towel.

toallero *m* towel rail, towel rack.

toba 1 *f* (*piedra*) tufa. 2 (*sarro*) tartar. 3 *fig* (*capa*) layer. 4 (*cardo*) cotton thistle. 5 *fam* (*golpe*) punch.

Tobago *m* Tobago.

tobera 1 *f* (*gen*) nozzle. 2 (*de alto horno*) tuyère, twyer.

tobillera *f* ankle sock, ankle support.

tobillo *m* ankle.

tobogán 1 *m* (*rampa*) slide, chute. 2 (*trineo*) toboggan, sledge.

toca *f* (*sombrero*) head-dress; (*de monja*) wimple.

tocadiscos *m* record-player.
▲ *pl* **tocadiscos.**

tocado[1] 1 *m* (*peinado*) coiffure, hairdo. 2 (*prenda*) head-dress, hat.

tocado,-a[2] 1 *pp* → **tocar.** – 2 *adj* (*fruta*) bad, rotten. 3 *fam* (*perturbado*) crazy, touched. 4 DEP injured.

● **tocado,-a de la cabeza,** touched, not all there.

tocador 1 *m* (*mueble*) dressing-table. 2 (*habitación*) dressing-room, boudoir.

■ **artículos de tocador,** toiletries. ‖ **tocador de señoras,** powder room.

tocante tocante a, *adv* concerning, about.

● **en lo tocante a,** with reference to.

tocar[1] 1 *t* (*gen*) to touch: *no tocar la mercancía,* do not handle the goods. 2 (*sentir por el tacto*) to feel: *tócalo, está frío,* feel it, it's cold. 3 (*revolver*) to rummage amongst, root around: *no toques mis papeles,* leave my papers alone. 4 (*hacer sonar - instrumento, canción*) to play; (*timbre*) to ring; (*bocina*) to blow, honk; (*campanas*) to strike. 5 *fig* (*retocar*) to change, alter: *no toques más la redacción,* don't do anything else to your essay. 6 (*la hora*) to strike. 7 MIL (*diana*) to sound. 8 DEP (*diana*) to hit; (*esgrima*) to touch. 9 *fig* (*mencionar*) to touch on. 10 *fig* (*impresionar*) to touch, reach: *me tocó el corazón,* he touched my heart. – 11 *i* (*ser el turno*) to be one's turn: *le toca a él,* it's his turn. 12 (*corresponder*) to be up to: *le toca a él explicarse,* it's up to him to explain himself. 13 (*ganar*) to win: *nos tocó un premio,* we won a prize. 14 (*en un reparto etc*) to fall: *me tocó a mí hablarle,* it fell to me to speak to him. 15 (*un destino*) to be posted: *le tocó en Cartagena,* he was posted to Cartagena. 16 (*tener que*) to have to: *nos tocó llevarla,* we had to take her. 17 (*afectar*) to concern, affect: *le toca directamente,* it directly concerns you. 18 (*ser parientes*) to be a relative

of, be related. 19 (*barco, avión*) to call (**en,** at), stop over (**en,** at). 20 (*entrar en contacto*) to touch. – 21 **tocarse,** *p* (*uso reflexivo*) to touch os.; (*uso recíproco*) to touch each other.

● **por lo que a mí toca,** as far as I am concerned. ‖ **tocar a muerto,** to toll. ‖ **tocar a su fin,** *fig* to be coming to an end. ‖ **tocar con,** to be next to: *toca con el cine,* it's next to the cinema. ‖ **tocar en,** *fig* to border on, verge on: *sus palabras tocan en grosería,* his words are verging on rudeness. ‖ **tocarse la nariz,** to pick one's nose.

▲ *Conjugation model* |1|, *like* sacar.

tocar[2] 1 *t* (*peinar*) to do the hair of. – 2 **tocarse,** *p* (*cubrirse*) to cover one's head.

▲ *Conjugation model* |1|, *like* sacar.

tocata 1 *f* MÚS toccata. – 2 *m fam* (*tocadiscos*) record-player.

tocateja a tocateja, *loc adv* cash.

● **pagar a tocateja,** to pay on the nail.

tocayo,-a *m,f* namesake.

tocho 1 *m* (*lingote*) iron ingot. 2 *fam* (*libro grande*) tome; (*libro aburrido*) boring book.

tocinería *f* pork butcher's.

tocino 1 *m* (*carne*) bacon. 2 (*grasa*) fat, lard.

■ **tocino ahumado,** smoked bacon. ‖ **tocino entreverado,** streaky bacon. ‖ **tocino de cielo,** sweet made with egg yolk.

tocología *f* tocology, obstetrics.

tocólogo,-a *m,f* tocologist, obstetrician.

tocón[1] *m* (*de tronco*) stump.

tocón,-ona[2] *adj fam* groper: *ése es un tocón,* he's got wandering hands.

todavía 1 *adv* (*a pesar de ello*) still: *es hipócrita y todavía le quiero,* he's a hypocrite but I still love him. 2 (*tiempo*) still, yet: *todavía están allí,* they're still there; *todavía no lo quiere,* he doesn't want it yet. 3 (*para reforzar*) even: *esto todavía está mejor,* this is even better.

todito,-a *adj fam* all.

todo,-a 1 *adj* (*sin excluir nada*) all: *todos los vecinos lo vieron,* all the neighbours saw it; *se bebió todo el vino,* he drank all the wine; *tú responderás por todos nosotros,* you'll answer for all of us. 2 (*verdadero*) real: *era todo un reto,* it was a real challenge; *era toda una mujer,* she was every inch a woman. 3 (*cada*) every: *todo delito,* every crime; *todas las noches,* every night; *todos los días,* every day. 4 (*igual*) like, exactly like, the image of: *era toda su madre,* she was exactly like her mother. – 5 *pron* (*sin excluir nada*) all, everything: *llamaron todos,* they all phoned; *le gusta todo,* she likes everything. 6 (*cualquiera*) anybody: *todo el que yo diga,* anybody I say. – 7 **todo,** *m* (*totalidad*) whole: *si lo consideramos como un todo,* if we take it as a whole. 8 (*en charadas*) all, whole. – 9 *adv* completely, totally, all: *está todo mojado,* it's all wet.

● **así y todo,** in spite of everything. ‖ **a todo esto,** (*por cierto*) by the way; (*mientras*) in the meantime. ‖ **con todo,** in spite of everything. ‖ **de todas formas / después de todo,** anyway, after all. ‖ **del todo,** completely, entirely: *arriba del todo,* right at the top. ‖ **eso es todo,** that's all, that's it. ‖ **estar en todo,** to be really with it, know what's going on. ‖ **fue todo uno,** *fam* it all happened at once. ‖ **hay de todo,** there are all sorts. ‖ **jugarse el todo por el todo,** *fig* to take the plunge. ‖ **por todo,-a,** all over: *por toda Francia,* all over France. ‖ **ser todo uno,** *fam* to be all the same thing. ‖ **todo el mundo,** everybody. ‖ **todo lo contrario,** quite the opposite, quite the contrary. ‖ **todo lo más,** at the most. ‖ **todo quisque** / **todo Dios**, *fam* every Tom, Dick and Harry. ‖ **todos y cada uno**, each and everyone.

todopoderoso,-a 1 *adj* almighty, all-powerful. – **2 el Todopoderoso**, *m* the Almighty.

tofe *m* toffee.

toga 1 *f* (*de romanos*) toga. **2** (*de magistrado etc*) gown, robe.

togado,-a 1 *adj* (*magistrado etc*) robed. – **2** *m,f* (*juez*) judge; (*abogado*) lawyer.

Togo *m* Togo.

togolés,-esa 1 *adj* Togolese. – **2** *m,f* Togolese.

toilette *f* (*tocador*) dressing-table; (*lavabo*) toilet.
● **hacerse la toilette**, to make os. up.

toisón *m* fleece.
■ **Orden del Toisón de Oro**, Order of the Golden Fleece.

tojo *m* furze.

toldo 1 *m* (*cubierta*) awning. **2** (*de camión*) tarpaulin, canvas. **3** (*de playa*) sunshade.

tole *m fig* uproar.

toledano,-a 1 *adj* of Toledo, from Toledo. – **2** *m,f* person from Toledo, inhabitant of Toledo.

tolerable *adj* tolerable.

tolerado,-a 1 *pp* → **tolerar**. – **2** *adj* (*película etc*) suitable for children: *la película es tolerada*, the film is suitable for children.

tolerancia 1 *f* tolerance. **2** (*resistencia*) resistance.

tolerante *adj* tolerant, lenient.

tolerar 1 *t* (*permitir, soportar*) to tolerate, put up with: *no te toleraré esa actitud*, I won't put up with that attitude. **2** (*inconvenientes*) to stand. **3** (*gente*) to put up with. **4** (*comida, bebida*) to take. **5** (*peso*) to bear.

tolondro,-a 1 *adj* scatterbrained. – **2** *m,f* scatterbrain.

tolondrón,-ona *adj-m,f* → **tolondro,-a**.

Tolosa *f* Toulouse.

tolteca 1 *adj* Toltec. – **2** *mf* Toltec.

tolueno *m* toluene.

toma 1 *f* (*acción*) taking. **2** MED dose. **3** MIL capture. **4** (*de aire*) intake, inlet; (*de agua*) outlet, tap; (*de electricidad*) plug, socket. **5** (*grabación*) recording. **6** CINEM take, shot.
■ **toma de conciencia**, awareness. ‖ **toma de corriente**, power point. ‖ **toma de muestras**, sampling. ‖ **toma de posesión**, takeover. ‖ **toma de tierra**, ELEC earth, US ground; (*de avión*) landing, touchdown.

tomado,-a 1 *pp* → **tomar**. – **2** *adj* (*voz*) hoarse.
● **tener la voz tomada**, to have a hoarse voice, be hoarse.

tomador,-ra *mf* (*de letra de cambio*) drawee; (*de seguro*) policy holder.

tomadura **tomadura de pelo**, *f fam fig* (*engaño*) hoax; (*burla*) joke, leg-pull, tease; (*timo*) rip-off.

tomar 1 *t* (*gen*) to take: *tomó una carta*, he took a card; *ese fragmento está tomado de Cervantes*, this passage is taken from Cervantes; *lo tomó en broma,* she took it as a joke; *tomamos un taxi*, we took a taxi; *tomamos aquella calle*, we took that road. **2** (*baño, ducha*) to have, take; (*foto*) to take. **3** (*comer, beber*) to have; (*beber*) to drink; (*comer*) to eat: *tómate la leche*, drink your milk; *¿qué tomarás?*, what would you like? **4** (*el autobús, el tren*) to catch. **5** (*aceptar*) to accept, take. **6** (*comprar*) to buy, get, have: *tomaré manzanas*, I'll get some apples. **7** (*contratar*) to take on, hire: *tomaremos una criada*, we'll take on a servant. **8** (*alquilar*) to take, rent. **9** (*adquirir*) to acquire, get into: *tomar una costumbre*, to acquire a habit. **10** MIL to capture, take. – **11** *i* (*encaminarse*) to go, turn: *tomaron hacia la izquierda y se perdieron*, they turned

left and got lost. – **12 tomarse**, *p* (*gen*) to take: *me tomé una aspirina*, I took an aspirin. **13** (*beber*) to drink; (*comer*) to eat.
● **lo toma o lo deja**, take it or leave it. ‖ **no te lo tomes así**, don't take it like that. ‖ **toma**, (*aquí tienes*) here you are, here. ‖ **¡toma!**, *fam* (*sorpresa*) fancy that!; (*enfado*) it serves you right! ‖ **¡toma castaña!**, *fam* take that! ‖ **toma y daca**, *fig* give and take. ‖ **tomar a algn. de la mano**, to hold sb.'s hand. ‖ **tomar a pecho**, to take to heart. ‖ **tomar afecto** / **tomar cariño**, to become fond of. ‖ **tomar algo a mal**, to take sth. badly. ‖ **tomar aliento**, to catch one's breath. ‖ **tomar decisiones**, to make decisions. ‖ **tomar el fresco**, to get some fresh air. ‖ **tomar el pelo a algn.**, *fig* to pull sb.'s leg. ‖ **tomar el sol**, to sunbathe. ‖ **tomar en cuenta**, to take into account. ‖ **tomar en serio**, to take seriously. ‖ **tomar forma**, to take shape. ‖ **tomar frío**, to catch a cold. ‖ **tomar la costumbre**, to get into the habit. ‖ **tomar la palabra**, to speak. ‖ **tomar las aguas**, to take the waters. ‖ **tomar las de Villadiego**, *fig* to beat it. ‖ **tomar nota**, to take note. ‖ **tomar partido por**, to take sides with. ‖ **tomar por**, (*considerar*) to take for: *me tomó por mi hermana*, he took me for my sister; *me tomó por tonto*, she took me for a fool. ‖ **tomar tierra**, to land. ‖ **tomarla con alguien**, *fam* to have it in for sb. ‖ **tomarse la molestia de**, to take the trouble to. ‖ **tomarse las cosas con calma**, to take it easy.

tomatazo *m* pelt with a tomato.
● **dar un tomatazo a algn.**, to pelt sb. with tomatoes.

tomate 1 *m* (*fruto*) tomato. **2** *fam fig* (*en calcetines etc*) hole. **3** *fam fig* (*jaleo*) fuss, commotion. **4** *fam fig* (*dificultad*) snag, catch.
● **ponerse como un tomate**, *fig* to go as red as a beetroot. ‖ **tener tomate**, *fam* to be difficult.

tomatera *f* → **tomatero,-a**.

tomatero,-a 1 *m,f* tomato seller. – **2 tomatera**, *f* (*planta*) tomato plant. **3** *fam fig* (*vanidad*) vanity, conceit.
■ **pollo tomatero**, spring chicken.

tomavistas *m* cine camera, US movie camera.

tómbola *f* tombola.

tomillo *m* thyme.

tomismo *m* Thomism.

tomo 1 *m* (*volumen*) volume. **2** *fig* (*importancia*) importance.
● **de tomo y lomo**, *fam* utter, out-and-out.

ton **sin ton ni son**, *loc adv* without rhyme or reason.

tonada 1 *f* tune, song. **2** (*acento*) accent.

tonadilla *f* ditty, little tune, popular song.

tonadillero,-a *m,f* (*compositor*) writer of ditties, writer of popular songs; (*cantante*) singer of ditties, singer of popular songs.

tonal *adj* tonal.

tonalidad *f* tonality, tone.

tonar *i* *lit* to thunder.
▲ *Conjugation model* [31], *like* **contar**.

tonel *m* barrel, cask.
● **estar como un tonel**, *fam* to be like a barrel.

tonelada *f* ton.
■ **tonelada métrica**, metric ton, tonne.

tonelaje *m* tonnage.

tonelería 1 *f* (*fabricación*) cooperage, barrel-making. **2** (*tienda*) barrel shop. **3** (*toneles*) barrels *pl*, casks *pl*.

tonelero,-a 1 *adj* barrel, cask. – **2** *m,f* cooper, barrel-maker.

Tonga *f* Tonga.

tongada *f* pile, heap.
tongano,-a 1 *adj* Tongan. – 2 *m,f* (*persona*) Tongan. – 3 tongano, *m* (*idioma*) Tongan.
tongo *m* fix: *en la carrera hubo tongo,* the race was fixed, the race was rigged.
tónica *f* → **tónico,-a**.
tónico,-a 1 *adj* (*sílaba*) tonic, stressed. 2 MÚS MED tonic. – 3 tónico, *m* MED tonic. 4 (*para la piel*) skin tonic. – 5 tónica, *f* (*tendencia*) tendency, trend. 6 (*bebida*) tonic, tonic water. 7 MÚS tonic.
■ **tónica general,** overall trend.
tonificante *adj* invigorating.
tonificar *t* to tone up, invigorate.
▲ *Conjugation model* [1], *like* **sacar**.
tonillo 1 *m* (*sonsonete*) drone, monotone. 2 (*acento*) accent, lilt. 3 (*retintín*) sarcastic tone.
tono 1 *m* (*gen*) tone: *el tono de su discurso,* the tone of her speech; *no me hables en ese tono,* don't speak to me in that tone. 2 (*energía*) energy.
● **a tono con,** in tune with, in harmony with. ‖ **bajar de tono / bajar el tono,** to lower one's voice; *fig* to tone down. ‖ **dar tono / dar buen tono,** *fig* to give class, give prestige. ‖ **darse tono,** *fig* to put on airs. ‖ **de buen tono,** (*elegante*) elegant, stylish; (*cortés*) gentlemanly. ‖ **de mal tono,** *fig* vulgar. ‖ **en tono airado,** in an angry tone. ‖ **fuera de tono,** *fig* inappropiate, out of place. ‖ **sin venir a tono,** *fig* for no good reason. ‖ **subir de tono / subir el tono,** to speak louder; *fig* to warm up.
■ **tono alto,** MÚS high pitch. ‖ **tono bajo,** MÚS low pitch. ‖ **tono mayor,** MÚS major key. ‖ **tono menor,** MÚS minor key.
tonsura *f* tonsure.
tonsurar 1 *t* (*el pelo*) to cut; (*la lana*) to shear. 2 (*clérigo*) to tonsure.
tontada 1 *f* (*bobada*) silly thing, nonsense. 2 (*insignificancia*) trifle.
tontaina 1 *adj fam* foolish, silly. – 2 *mf fam* fool, nitwit.
tontamente *adv* foolishly.
tontear 1 *i* (*decir tonterías*) to act the clown, fool about. 2 (*galantear*) to flirt.
tontería 1 *f* (*calidad de tonto*) stupidity, silliness. 2 (*dicho, hecho*) silly thing, stupid thing. 3 (*insignificancia*) trifle. 4 (*regalito*) little something.
● **decir tonterías,** to talk nonsense. ‖ **dejarse de tonterías,** (*al hablar*) to be serious; (*al actuar*) to stop messing about: *¡déjate de tonterías!,* stop messing about! ‖ **hacer tonterías,** to mess about, fool around.
tonto,-a 1 *adj* silly, stupid, US dumb: *¡qué idea más tonta!,* what a stupid idea! – 2 *m,f* fool, idiot.
● **a tontas y a locas,** without rhyme or reason. ‖ **hacer el tonto / hacer la tonta,** to act the fool. ‖ **hacerse el tonto / hacerse la tonta,** to play dumb. ‖ **ponerse tonto,-a,** *fam* to get stroppy.
■ **tonto,-a de remate / tonto,-a de capirote,** *fam* prize idiot. ‖ **un,-a tonto,-a del bote,** *fam* a right berk, a real twerp.
tontuna *f fam* silliness.
topacio *m* topaz.
topar 1 *i* (*chocar*) to bump into: *el coche topó contra un poste,* the car bumped into a pole. 2 (*encontrar - algo*) to come across, find; (*- alguien*) to bump into, run into. 3 *fig* (*dificultades etc*) to come up against, run into. 4 (*en juego*) to take a bet. – 5 toparse, *p* (*encontrarse alguien*) to meet, bump into: *me topé con tu amigo,* I bumped into your friend. 6 *fig* (*dificultades etc*) to meet with, encounter, run into.

tope 1 *m* (*límite*) limit, end. 2 TÉC stop, check. 3 (*de ferrocarril*) buffer, bumping post, bumper. 4 MAR masthead. – 5 *adj fig* top, maximum: *¡tope!,* smashing! 6 *arg* (*fantástico*) fab, super. – 7 *adv arg* really, absolutely: *la fiesta fue tope divertida,* the party was absolutely brilliant.
● **a tope,** *arg* (*al límite*) flat out; (*lleno*) jam-packed, chock-a-block; (*estupendo*) terrific; (*música*) full blast: *íbamos a tope,* we were going flat out; *la sala estaba a tope,* the hall was jam-packed; *lo pasamos a tope,* we had a terrific time. ‖ **estar hasta los topes,** *fig* to be full up. ‖ **llegar al tope,** *fig* to reach one's limit.
■ **precio tope,** top price. ‖ **tope de puerta,** doorstop.
topetada *f fig* butt, bump.
topetar 1 *t fig* to bump into. – 2 *i fig* to bump.
topetazo 1 *m* (*con la cabeza*) butt, bump. 2 (*de coche etc*) bump, crash.
topetear *t-i fig* → **topetar**.
topetón *m* → **topetazo**.
tópico,-a 1 *adj* MED external: *uso tópico,* external use. – 2 tópico, *m* commonplace, cliché.
topless *m* topless.
● **en topless,** topless.
topo *m* mole.
● **más ciego,-a que un topo,** *fig* as blind as a bat.
topografía *f* topography.
topográfico,-a *adj* topographic, topographical.
topógrafo,-a *m,f* topographer.
topología *f* topology.
toponimia 1 *f* (*ciencia*) toponymy. 2 (*nombres*) place-names *pl*.
toponímico,-a *adj* toponymic, toponymical.
topónimo *m* place-name, toponym.
toque 1 *m* (*acto*) touch. 2 (*de campana*) ringing, peal, pealing; (*de trompeta*) blare, sounding; (*de claxon*) honk; (*de sirena*) hoot; (*de tambor*) beat, beating. 3 (*pincelada*) touch. 4 *fig* (*advertencia*) warning.
● **dar el toque de alarma,** *fig* to sound the alarm. ‖ **dar el último toque,** to put the finishing touch. ‖ **dar un toque a algn.,** (*llamar*) to take sb. to task; (*llamar la atención*) to call sb.'s attention.
■ **toque de alarma,** alarm signal. ‖ **toque de atención,** warning, warning note. ‖ **toque de balón,** ball control. ‖ **toque de diana,** reveille. ‖ **toque de difuntos,** death knell. ‖ **toque de queda,** curfew. ‖ **toque de retreta,** tattoo.
toquetear 1 *t* (*tocar*) to fiddle with, finger. 2 (*acariciar*) to fondle, caress.
toqueteo 1 *m* (*manoseo*) fiddling, handling. 2 (*caricias*) fondling, petting.
toquilla *f* shawl, knitted shawl.
tora *f* Torah.
torácico,-a *adj* thoracic.
■ **caja torácica,** chest cavity.
tórax *m* thorax.
▲ *pl* **tórax**.
torbellino 1 *m* (*de viento*) whirlwind; (*de agua*) whirlpool; (*de polvo*) whirl, cloud. 2 *fig* (*abundancia de cosas*) whirl, turmoil, welter: *un torbellino de sentimientos,* a whirl of emotions. 3 *fig* (*persona*) live wire, human dynamo.
■ **torbellino de ideas,** *fig* brainstorm.
torcecuello *m* wryneck.
torcedura 1 *f* (*acción*) twist, twisting. 2 MED sprain.
torcer 1 *t* (*gen*) to twist. 2 (*doblar*) to bend; (*madera*) to warp. 3 (*desviar*) to change. 4 (*cuadro*) to slant. 5 *fig* (*significado, frase, etc*) to distort. 6 *fig* (*corromper a alguien*) to corrupt, pervert. 7 *fig* (*la cara*) to contort. 8 MED to

sprain. – **9** *i* (*girar*) to turn: *torció a la derecha,* he turned right. – **10 torcerse,** *p* (*gen*) to twist. **11** (*doblarse*) to bend; (*madera*) to warp. **12** (*ladearse*) to become slanted. **13** MED to sprain, twist. **14** *fig* (*plan*) to fall through. **15** *fig* (*una persona*) to go astray. **16** *fig* (*empeorar*) to take a turn for the worse.

● **no dar su brazo a torcer,** *fig* not to give in. ‖ **torcer el gesto,** *fig* to look cross. ‖ **torcer la vista,** to look away.

▲ *Conjugation model* [54], *like cocer.*

torcida *f* → **torcido,-a.**

torcido,-a 1 *adj* (*que no es recto*) twisted. **2** (*madera*) warped; (*metal*) bent. **3** (*ladeado*) slanted, crooked, lopsided: *el cuadro está torcido,* the painting is crooked. **4** MED sprained, strained. **5** *fig* (*mente etc*) twisted. – **6 torcida,** *f* (*mecha*) wick.

tordo,-a 1 *adj* dapple-grey. – **2 tordo,** *m* (*pájaro*) thrush.

torear 1 *t* (*lidiar*) to fight. **2** *fig* (*entretener*) to put off. **3** *fig* (*burlar*) to tease, confuse. **4** *fig* (*asunto etc*) to tackle skilfully, handle well. **5** *fig* (*evitar*) to avoid. – **6** *i* (*lidiar*) to fight: *torea muy bien,* he's a very good bullfighter.

toreo *m* bullfighting.

● **¡se acabó el toreo!,** *fam* no more fooling around!

torera *f* → **torero,-a.**

torero,-a 1 *adj* bullfighting. – **2** *m,f* bullfighter, matador. – **3 torera,** *f* bolero jacket, bolero.

● **saltarse algo a la torera,** *fam* to ignore sth. completely.

toril *m* bullpen.

tormenta *f* storm.

● **una tormenta en un vaso de agua,** a storm in a teacup.

tormento 1 *m* (*tortura*) torture. **2** (*dolor*) torment, torture. **3** (*angustia*) anguish. **4** *fig* (*aflicción*) affliction, suffering.

● **dar tormento,** (*torturar*) to torture; (*molestar*) to torment. ‖ **ser un tormento,** *fam* to be real torture.

tormentoso,-a *adj* stormy.

torna *f* return.

● **volverle a uno las tornas,** to turn the tables on sb.

tornado *m* tornado.

tornar 1 *t* (*devolver*) to give back (**a,** to), return (**a,** to). **2** (*mudar*) to transform (**en,** into), turn (**en,** into). – **3** *i* (*regresar*) to go back (**a,** to), return (**a,** to). **4** (*volver a*) to start again: *tornó a beber,* he started drinking again. – **5 tornarse,** *p* to become, turn.

● **tornar en sí,** to regain consciousness.

tornasol 1 *m* BOT sunflower. **2** (*luz*) iridescense. **3** (*colorante*) litmus.

tornasolado,-a *adj* iridescent.

torneado,-a 1 *pp* → **tornear.** – **2** *adj* TÉC lathed, turned on the lathe. **3** (*cuerpo*) shapely, with soft curves. – **4 torneado,** *m* TÉC turning.

tornear *t* to turn.

torneo 1 *m* (*justa*) tourney, joust. **2** DEP tournament, competition.

tornero,-a *m,f* turner, lathe operator.

tornillo *m* screw, bolt.

● **apretarle los tornillos a algn.,** *fam* to put the screws on sb. ‖ **faltar un tornillo,** *fam* to have a screw loose.

■ **tornillo de banco,** vice (US vise), clamp. ‖ **tornillo de orejas,** thumbscrew.

torniquete 1 *m* (*palanca*) turnstile. **2** MED tourniquet.

torno 1 *m* TÉC lathe. **2** (*elevador*) winch, windlass. **3** (*de convento*) revolving window.

● **en torno a,** (*alrededor de*) around; (*acerca de*) about, concerning.

■ **torno de alfarero,** potter's wheel.

toro 1 *m* (*animal*) bull. – **2 los toros,** *mpl* (*corrida*) bullfight *sing*; (*arte*) bullfighting *sing*.

● **coger al toro por los cuernos,** *fig* to take the bull by the horns. ‖ **estar hecho un toro,** *fam* to be a big strapping man. ‖ **fuerte como un toro,** *fig* as strong as an ox. ‖ **ir a los toros,** to go to a bullfight. ‖ **ver los toros desde la barrera,** *fig* to sit on the fence. ‖

■ **toro bravo / toro de lidia,** fighting bull.

toronja *f* grapefruit.

toronjina *f* lemon balm.

torpe 1 *adj* (*poco hábil*) clumsy. **2** (*de movimiento*) slow, awkward. **3** (*poco inteligente*) dim, thick.

torpedear *t* to torpedo.

torpedero,-a 1 *adj* torpedo. – **2 torpedero,** *m* torpedo boat.

torpedo 1 *m* MIL torpedo. **2** (*pez*) electric ray.

torpemente 1 *adv* (*sin habilidad*) clumsily, awkwardly. **2** (*lentamente*) slowly.

torpeza 1 *f* (*falta de habilidad*) clumsiness, awkwardness. **2** (*mental*) dimness, stupidity. **3** (*de movimiento*) slowness, heaviness. **4** (*error*) blunder.

● **cometer una torpeza,** to make a blunder.

torpón,-ona 1 *adj* fam (*falto de habilidad*) clumsy. **2** *fam* (*tonto*) dim, stupid.

torrar *t* to toast.

torre 1 *f* (*gen*) tower. **2** (*campanario*) bell tower. **3** (*chalé*) country house, house, villa. **4** (*de buque*) turret. **5** (*ajedrez*) rook, castle.

■ **torre de comunicaciones,** communications tower. ‖ **torre de control,** control tower. ‖ **torre de marfil,** *fig* ivory tower. ‖ **torre de perforación,** derrick. ‖ **torre de vigía,** crow's nest.

torrefacto,-a *adj* torrefied, dry-roasted.

torrencial *adj* torrential.

torrente 1 *m* (*de agua*) mountain stream, torrent. **2** (*de sangre*) bloodstream. **3** *fig* (*abundancia*) flood, stream.

■ **torrente de voz,** strong loud voice.

torreón *m* fortified tower.

torrero *m* lighthouse keeper.

torreta 1 *f* (*torre*) turret, small tower. **2** MIL (*de tanque etc*) turret; (*de submarino*) conning tower.

torrezno *m* rasher of fried bacon.

tórrido,-a *adj* torrid.

torrija *f* type of French toast.

torsión 1 *f* (*torcedura*) twist, twisting. **2** TÉC torsion.

■ **momento de torsión,** TÉC torque.

torso 1 *m* ANAT torso. **2** (*estatua*) bust.

torta 1 *f* CULIN cake. **2** *fam* (*golpe*) blow, crack; (*bofetada*) slap, wallop. **3** *fam* (*borrachera*) binge.

● **coger una torta / pillar una torta,** *fig* to get plastered. ‖ **ni torta,** *fam* not a thing: *no ve ni torta,* he can't see a thing. ‖ **pegarse una torta,** *fam* to give so. a bump. ‖ **te va a costar la torta un pan,** *fam* it's more trouble than it's worth.

tortada *f* meat pie, chicken pie.

tortazo 1 *m* *fam* (*golpe*) whack, thump. **2** *fam* (*bofetada*) slap, punch.

● **darse un tortazo / pegarse un tortazo,** *fam* (*accidente*) to crash; (*caerse*) to come a cropper: *se pegó un tortazo contra la valla,* he crashed into the fence.

tortícolis *f* stiff neck, crick in the neck.

▲ *pl tortícolis.*

tortilla 1 *f* omelette (US omelet). **2** AM tortilla, pancake.

● **se volvió la tortilla,** *fig* the tables were turned.

■ **tortilla a la francesa,** omelette, plain omelette. ‖ **tortilla de patatas,** potato omelette, Spanish omelette.

tortillera *f fam* dyke, lesbian.

tortita *f* pancake.

tórtola *f* → **tórtolo,-a.**

tortolear *t* to court, flatter.

tortolito,-a *adj* inexperienced, green.

tórtolo,-a 1 *m.f (macho)* male turtledove; *(hembra)* turtledove. – 2 **tórtolos,** *mpl fig (enamorados)* lovebirds, lovers.

tortuga 1 *f (de tierra)* tortoise. 2 *(marina)* turtle.
● **andar a paso de tortuga / ir a paso de tortuga,** *fig* to walk at a snail's pace.

tortuosidad *f* tortuousness.

tortuoso,-a *adj* tortuous, winding.

tortura 1 *f (tormento)* torture. 2 *fig (padecimiento)* intense suffering, agony.

torturador,-ra *m.f* torturer.

torturar 1 *t* to torture. – 2 **torturarse,** *p* to torture os.

torvo,-a *adj* grim, fierce.

torzal 1 *m (de seda)* silk twist. 2 *fig (de varias cosas)* twist, twine.

tos *f* cough, coughing.
● **tener tos,** to have a cough.
■ **acceso de tos,** coughing fit. ‖ **tos ferina,** whooping cough.
▲ *pl* **toses.**

tosca *f* tufa, tuff.

tosco,-a 1 *adj (basto)* rough, rustic. 2 *(persona)* uncouth.

toser *i* to cough.
● **a mi no me tose nadie,** *fam* no one tells me what to do. ‖ **no hay quien le tosa,** *fam* he's one step ahead of everyone.

tosquedad *f* roughness, crudeness.

tostada *f* → **tostado,-a.**

tostadero *m* roaster.
■ **tostadero de café,** *(máquina)* coffee toaster; *(local)* coffee bar which roasts and sells coffee.

tostado,-a 1 *pp* → **tostar.** – 2 *adj (pan)* toasted; *(café)* roasted. 3 *fig (moreno)* tanned, brown. 4 *(color)* brown. – 5 **tostada,** *f* toast, slice of toast.
● **olerse la tostada,** *fam* to smell a rat.

tostador,-ra *m.f (de pan)* toaster; *(de café)* roaster.

tostar 1 *t (pan)* to toast; *(café)* to roast; *(carnes)* to brown. 2 *fig (piel)* to tan. – 3 **tostarse,** *p (pan)* to toast; *(café)* to roast. 4 *fig (la piel)* to get brown, turn brown, tan.
▲ *Conjugation model* [31], *like* **contar.**

tostón 1 *m (garbanzo)* roasted chick-pea. 2 *(pan frito)* crouton. 3 *fam fig* bore, drag: *la peli fue un tostón,* the film was a drag.
● **dar el tostón,** *fam* to get on everybody's nerves.

total 1 *adj* total, complete, overall: *la imprenta supuso una revolución total,* printing brought about a complete revolution; *anestesia total,* general anaesthetic. – 2 *m (totalidad)* whole: *el total de la población,* the whole population. 3 *(suma)* total, sum. – 4 *adv (en conclusión)* in short, so: *total, fue un fracaso,* in short, it was a failure; *total, que se fueron porque quisieron,* they left because they wanted to. 5 *(al fin y al cabo)* after all: *total, para lo que me sirve ...,* after all, for all the good it is to me ...
● **en total,** in all.

totalidad *f* whole, totality.
● **en su totalidad,** as a whole.

totalitario,-a *adj* totalitarian.

totalitarismo *m* totalitarianism, dictatorship.

totalitarista *adj* totalitarian.

totalizar 1 *t* to total. 2 *(ascender)* to amount to.
▲ *Conjugation model* [4], *like* **realizar.**

totalmente *adv* totally, completely.

tótem *m* totem; *(efigie)* totem pole.
▲ *pl* **tótems** *or* **tótemes.**

tournée *f (gira)* tour; *(viaje)* touring holiday.

touroperador *m* travel firm.

toxicidad *f* toxicity.

tóxico,-a 1 *adj* toxic, poisonous. – 2 **tóxico,** *m* toxicant, poison.

toxicología *f* toxicology.

toxicológico,-a *adj* toxicologic, toxicological.

toxicólogo,-a *m.f* toxicologist.

toxicomanía *f* drug addiction.

toxicómano,-a 1 *adj* addicted to drugs. – 2 *m.f* drug addict.

toxina *f* toxin.

tozudez *f* stubbornness, obstinacy.

tozudo,-a *adj* stubborn, obstinate, headstrong.

traba 1 *f (de caballería)* hobble. 2 *(unión)* bond, tie. 3 *fig (impedimento)* hindrance, obstacle.
● **poner trabas,** *fig* to put obstacles in the way.

trabado,-a 1 *pp* → **trabar.** – 2 *adj (sujeto)* fastened; *(atascado)* jammed. 3 *(salsa)* smooth. 4 *(caballería)* with two white stockings. 5 *fig (robusto)* robust. 6 *fig (coherente)* coherent.

trabajado,-a 1 *pp* → **trabajar.** – 2 *adj* elaborate, carefully worked, painstaking.

trabajador,-ra 1 *adj (que trabaja)* working. 2 *(laborioso)* hard-working, industrious. – 3 *m.f* worker, labourer (us laborer).

trabajar 1 *i (gen)* to work: *trabaja mucho,* she works hard; *trabaja en una cafetería,* she works in a coffee shop. 2 CINEM TEAT to act, perform: *¿quién trabaja en la obra?,* who's in the play? 3 *fig (soportar)* to be under stress: *esta cuerda trabaja mucho,* this rope is under stress. – 4 *t (materiales)* to work (on). 5 *(idea, idioma, etc)* to work on. 6 *(la tierra)* to till. 7 CULIN *(pasta)* to knead. – 8 **trabajarse,** *p (idea, idioma, etc)* to work on. 9 *fig (a alguien)* to persuade.
● **trabajar a algn. para que haga algo,** to talk sb. into doing sth., try to persuade sb. to do sth. ‖ **trabajar a destajo,** to do piecework. ‖ **trabajar como un,-a condenado-a / trabajar como una bestia,** *fam* to slave away. ‖ **trabajar de,** to be, work as: *trabaja de profesor,* he's a teacher. ‖ **trabajar de balde,** to work for nothing. ‖ **trabajar el hierro / trabajar la madera,** to work iron / work wood. ‖ **trabajar en balde,** *fam* to work in vain. ‖ **trabajar por horas,** to be paid by the hour.

trabajo 1 *m (ocupación)* work. 2 *(tarea)* task, job. 3 *(empleo)* job, employment. 4 *(esfuerzo)* effort. 5 EDUC report, paper. – 6 **trabajos,** *mpl fig (penalidades)* hardships.
● **ahorrarse el trabajo,** to save os. the trouble. ‖ **con gran trabajo / con mucho trabajo,** with great effort. ‖ **cuesta trabajo ...,** it's hard to ...: *cuesta trabajo aceptarlo,* it's hard to accept it. ‖ **estar sin trabajo,** to be out of work. ‖ **ir al trabajo,** to go to work. ‖ **sin trabajo,** *(fácilmente)* easily. ‖ **tomarse el trabajo de,** to take the trouble to.
■ **puesto de trabajo,** job. ‖ **trabajo a destajo,** piecework. ‖ **trabajo de chinos,** *fam fig* very intricate work, time-consuming work. ‖ **trabajo de equipo,** teamwork. ‖ **trabajo de media jornada,** part-time job. ‖ **trabajo eventual,** casual labour (us labor). ‖ **trabajo**

intelectual, brainwork. ‖ **trabajo por turno / trabajo por turnos,** shiftwork. ‖ **trabajos forzados / trabajos forzosos,** hard labour (us labor) *sing.* ‖ **trabajos manuales,** arts and crafts, handicrafts.

trabajosamente *adv* laboriously.

trabajoso,-a 1 *adj* hard, laborious. 2 *(difícil)* difficult.

trabalenguas *m* tongue-twister.
▲ *pl* trabalenguas.

trabar 1 *t (unir)* to join, link. 2 *(sujetar)* to lock, fasten. 3 *(mecanismo)* to jam. 4 *(prender a alguien)* to shackle. 5 *(líquido, salsa)* to thicken. 6 *(caballería)* to hobble. 7 *fig (empezar)* to start. 8 *fig (conversación, amistad)* to strike up. 9 *fig (enlazar)* to connect, relate, link: *durante la reunión trabaron ideas,* they gave coherence to their ideas during the meeting. 10 *fig (impedir)* to impede, hinder, shackle. – 11 **trabarse,** *p (enredarse)* to get tangled up. 12 *(mecanismo)* to jam.
● **trabársele la lengua a algn.,** to get tongue-tied.

trabazón 1 *f (enlace)* bond, tie. 2 CULIN *(de masa etc)* thickness. 3 *fig (conexión)* connection, link, bond.

trabilla *f (de pantalón)* trouser-strap; *(de chaqueta)* half-belt.

trabucar 1 *t* to jumble, mix up. – 2 **trabucarse,** *p* to get all mixed up.
▲ *Conjugation model* [1], *like* **sacar.**

trabucazo *m* shot from a blunderbuss.

trabuco *m* blunderbuss.

traca *f* string of firecrackers, jumping jack.

tracción *f* traction.
■ **tracción delantera / tracción trasera,** front-wheel drive / rear-wheel drive. ‖ **tracción en las cuatro ruedas,** four-wheel drive.

Tracia *f* Thrace.

tracio,-a 1 *adj* Thracian. – 2 *m,f (persona)* Thracian. – 3 tracio, *m (idioma)* Thracian.

tractor,-ra 1 *adj* tractor: *hélice tractora,* tractor propeller. – 2 **tractor,** *m* tractor.

tractorista *mf* tractor driver.

tradición *f* tradition.

tradicional *adj* traditional.
● **es lo tradicional,** it's the traditional thing to do.

tradicionalismo 1 *m* traditionalism. 2 POL radical conservatism.

tradicionalista 1 *adj* traditionalist. 2 POL radical conservative. – 3 *mf* traditionalist. 4 POL radical conservative.

tradicionalmente *adv* traditionally.

tradicionista *mf (escritor)* writer on local traditions; *(colector)* collector of items or works related to local traditions.

traducción *f* translation.
■ **traducción automática,** INFORM machine translation. ‖ **traducción directa,** translation from a foreign language. ‖ **traducción inversa,** translation into a foreign language, prose translation. ‖ **traducción simultánea,** simultaneous translation.

traducible *adj* translatable.

traducir 1 *t (gen)* to translate: *lo tradujo del francés al inglés,* she translated it from French into English. 2 *(expresar)* to express, show. – 3 **traducirse,** *p (resulta)* to result in, give: *su mal humor se tradujo en resultados pobres,* his bad mood gave poor results.
● **traducir directamente,** to translate direct.
▲ *Conjugation model* [46], *like* **conducir.**

traductor,-ra 1 *adj* translating. – 2 *m,f* translator.
■ **traductor,-ra jurado,-a,** sworn translator.

traer 1 *t (gen)* to bring: *nos trajo una botella de whisky,* he brought us a bottle of whisky. 2 *(llevar consigo)* to carry: *traía un bolso,* she was carrying a bag. 3 *(vestir)* to wear: *traía una falda verde,* she was wearing a green skirt. 4 *(traer hacia sí)* to pull, draw, attract: *la secta traía a muchos seguidores,* the sect attracted a lot of followers. 5 *(causar)* to cause, bring: *esto le trajo muchos problemas,* it caused him a lot of problems. 6 *(llevar noticias)* to carry, contain: *la revista traía varias fotos,* the magazine contained several pictures. 7 *(contener)* to contain: *el paquete trae un regalo,* the package contains a gift. – 8 **traerse,** *p (llevar consigo)* to bring along: *tráete al bebé,* bring your baby along.
● **¿qué te trae por aquí?,** what brings you here? ‖ **traer buena suerte / traer suerte,** to bring good luck. ‖ **traer como consecuencia,** to result in. ‖ **traer consecuencias,** to have serious consequences. ‖ **traer consigo,** to bring about. ‖ **traer de cabeza a algn.,** *(preocupar)* to worry sb.; *(volver loco)* to drive sb. mad. ‖ **traerse entre manos,** *fig* to be up to. ‖ **traérselas,** *fam* to be really difficult, be really hard: *eso se las trae,* that's really difficult.
▲ *Conjugation model* [88].

traficante 1 *adj* dealing, trading. – 2 *mf* trader, dealer. 3 *(ilegal)* trafficker.
■ **traficante de drogas,** drug trafficker, drug pusher.

traficar 1 *i* to deal. 2 *(de forma ilegal)* to traffic **(en,** in), deal **(en,** in): *trafica en/con drogas,* he traffics in drugs.
▲ *Conjugation model* [1], *like* **sacar.**

tráfico 1 *m* AUTO traffic. 2 COM traffic, trade.
■ **accidente de tráfico,** road accident, us car accident. ‖ **tráfico de drogas,** drug traffic. ‖ **tráfico de influencias,** POL use of inside information for personal gain, sharp practice. ‖ **tráfico rodado,** road traffic.

tragabolas *m* Aunt Sally.
▲ *pl* tragabolas.

tragacanto *m* tragacanth.

tragaderas 1 *fpl fam (faringe)* throat *sing.* 2 *fam fig (credulidad)* gullibility.
● **tener buenas tragaderas,** *fam (ser crédulo)* to be gullible; *(tener pocos escrúpulos)* to be too easy going.

tragadero 1 *m (faringe)* throat. 2 *(agujero)* drain.

tragaldabas *mf fam* glutton, pig.
▲ *pl* tragaldabas.

tragaleguas *mf fam* keen walker.
▲ *pl* tragaleguas.

tragaluz *m* skylight.

tragamillas *mf fam* keen walker.
▲ *pl* tragamillas.

tragaperras **máquina tragaperras,** *f* slot machine.

tragar 1 *t (ingerir)* to swallow. 2 *(comer mucho)* to gobble up, tuck away, put away. 3 *(absorber)* to soak up. 4 *fig (hacer desaparecer)* to swallow up. 5 *fig (gastar, consumir)* to eat up, guzzle: *este coche traga mucha gasolina,* this car guzzles petrol. 6 *fig (creer)* to swallow, believe. 7 *fig (aguantar)* to put up with; *(disimular)* to hide: *tuvo que tragar sus exigencias,* she had to put up with his demands. 8 *fig (soportar a alguien)* to stand, stomach: *no trago a Pedro,* I can't stand Pedro. – 9 *i* to swallow, swallow up. – 10 **tragarse,** *p (ingerir)* to swallow: *se tragó un botón,* he swallowed a button. 11 *(comer mucho)* to gobble up, tuck away, put away. 12 *(absorber)* to soak up. 13 *fig (hacer desaparecer)* to swallow up: *el mar se tragó el barco,* the ship was swallowed up by the sea. 14 *fig (creer)* to swallow, believe: *se traga todo lo que digo,* he swallows whatever I say. 15 *fig (aguantar)* to put up with; *(disimular)* to hide: *se tragó su opinión,* she hid her opinion.

● **tragar la píldora,** *fig* to swallow it, fall for it. ‖ **tragar millas,** *fig* to burn up the miles.
▲ *Conjugation model* |7|, *like* **llegar.**
tragasables *mf* sword-swallower.
▲ *pl* **tragasables.**
tragasantos *mf fam pey* devout person.
▲ *pl* **tragasantos.**
tragedia *f* tragedy.
● **¡qué tragedia!,** *fam* woe is me! ‖ **terminar en tragedia,** to end tragically.
trágicamente *adv* tragically.
trágico,-a I *adj* tragic. - **2** *m,f* (*actor*) tragedian; (*actriz*) tragedienne.
● **ponerse trágico,-a,** *fam* (*persona*) to get all serious; (*situación*) to become tragic, get tragic.
tragicomedia *f* tragicomedy.
tragicómico,-a *adj* tragicomic.
trago I *m* (*sorbo*) swig, drop. **2** *fam* (*bebida*) drink. **3** *fam fig* (*adversidad*) rough time.
● **beberse algo de un trago,** to down sth. in one. ‖ **echar un trago,** (*sorbo*) to take a swig; (*beber algo*) to have a drink. ‖ **pasar un mal trago,** *fig* to have a bad time of it.
tragón,-ona I *adj fam* greedy, piggy. - **2** *m,f fam* glutton, big eater, greedy-guts.
traición *f* treason, betrayal.
● **a traición,** treacherously.
■ **alta traición,** high treason.
traicionar I *t* (*gen*) to betray: *traicionó a su familia,* he betrayed his family. **2** *fig* (*delatar*) to give away, betray: *su expresión traicionó sus pensamientos,* his expression gave away his thoughts.
traicionero,-a *adj* treacherous.
traído,-a I *pp* → **traer.** - **2** *adj fig* (*gastado*) threadbare, worn-out. **3** *fig* (*visto*) hackneyed, trite.
● **traído,-a por los pelos,** *fam* far-fetched. ‖ **traído,-a y llevado,-a,** *fig* hackneyed, well-worn.
traidor,-ra I *adj* treacherous. - **2** *m,f* traitor.
traigo *pres indic* → **traer.**
tráiler I *m* CINEM trailer, preview. **2** AUTO articulated lorry, US trailer truck.
traílla I *f* (*cuerda*) leash **2** (*allanar*) leveller.
traína *f* trawl, trawl-net.
trainera *f* trawler.
traje[1] I *m* (*de hombre*) suit. **2** (*de mujer*) dress. **3** MIL dress.
■ **traje a medida,** tailor-made suit. ‖ **traje camisero,** shirt-waist dress. ‖ **traje cruzado,** double-breasted suit. ‖ **traje de baño,** swimming costume, bathing costume, swimsuit. ‖ **traje de bonito,** *fam* formal dress. ‖ **traje de calle,** town clothes *pl*. ‖ **traje de campaña,** MIL battledress. ‖ **traje de ceremonia,** full dress, formal dress. ‖ **traje de chaqueta,** tailored suit. ‖ **traje de etiqueta,** full dress. ‖ **traje de faena,** MIL fatigue dress, undress. ‖ **traje de luces,** bullfighter's costume. ‖ **traje de noche / traje largo,** evening dress. ‖ **traje de novia,** wedding dress. ‖ **traje de paisano,** civilian clothes *pl*. ‖ **traje espacial,** spacesuit. ‖ **traje pantalón,** trouser suit. ‖ **traje sastre,** skirt and jacket.
traje[2] *pt indef* → **traer.**
trajeado,-a I *pp* → **trajear.** - **2** *adj fam* sharp, dapper.
trajearse *p* to dress up.
trajín *m fam fig* comings and goings *pl*, hustle and bustle.
trajinar I *t* (*acarrear*) to carry. **2** *fam* (*intentar convencer*) to cajole. - **3** *i* (*moverse*) to bustle about, run about. **4** *fam* (*intentar convencer*) to cajole, coax. **5** *fam fig* (*tramar*) to cook up, be up to: *no sé qué trajinaban,* I don't know

what they were up to. - **6** **trajinarse,** *p fam* to cajole, coax: *se trajinó a sus padres para que le dejaran ir de viaje,* he cajoled his parents into letting him go on a trip.
tralla I *f* (*cuerda*) rope. **2** (*látigo*) whip.
trallazo I *m* (*golpe*) lash. **2** (*chasquido*) crack, crack of a whip.
trama I *f* (*textil*) weft, woof. **2** (*argumento*) plot.
tramar I *t* (*tejidos*) to weave. **2** *fig* (*maquinar*) to plot, cook up: *¿qué estás tramando?,* what are you up to?
tramitación *f* JUR procedure, steps *pl*: *para la tramitación del pasaporte necesitas una foto,* if you want to get a passport you'll need a photo.
tramitar I *t* (*gestionar*) to take the necessary steps to obtain, process: *tramitaremos su pasaporte,* we'll get your passport sorted out; *estamos tramitando su solicitud,* we're processing your application. **2** COM JUR FIN to negotiate, transact, carry out: *no podemos tramitar el acuerdo,* we can't negotiate the agreement. **3** *fml* (*despachar*) to transmit, convey: *tramitaron su disconformidad a través del ministro,* they conveyed their disagreement through the minister.
trámite I *m* (*paso*) step. **2** (*formalidad*) formality, requirement. **3** (*negociación*) procedures *pl*.
● **de puro trámite,** *fig* unimportant.
tramo I *m* (*camino etc*) stretch, section. **2** (*de escalera*) flight. **3** (*de terreno*) lot, plot.
tramontana *f* north wind, tramontana.
tramoya I *f* (*máquina*) stage machinery. **2** *fig* (*trama*) plot, scheme.
tramoyista I *mf* TEAT scene-shifter, stagehand. **2** *fig* schemer, trickster.
trampa I *f* (*abertura*) trapdoor, hatch. **2** (*para cazar*) trap, snare. **3** *fig* (*engaño*) fiddle; (*truco*) trick. **4** *fig* (*deuda*) debt. **5** MIL (*emboscada*) ambush.
● **caer en la trampa,** to fall into the trap. ‖ **hacer trampa / hacer trampas,** to cheat. ‖ **sin trampa ni cartón,** *fam* real. ‖ **tender una trampa,** to set a trap, lay a trap. ‖ **tiene trampa,** there's a catch.
trampear I *t fam* (*engañar*) to cheat. - **2** *i* (*estafar*) to be on the fiddle; (*vivir de su ingenio*) to live by one's wits. **3** (*ir viviendo*) to manage, get by: *vamos trampeando,* we get by.
trampero,-a *m,f* trapper.
trampilla *f* trapdoor, hatch.
trampolín I *m* (*de piscina*) springboard, diving-board. **2** (*de esquí*) ski-jump. **3** *fig* (*medio*) springboard, starting point.
tramposo,-a I *adj* deceitful, tricky. - **2** *m,f* trickster, cheat; (*en las cartas*) cardsharp.
tranca I *f* (*palo*) club, cudgel. **2** (*para puertas etc*) bar. **3** *fam* (*borrachera*) binge, skinful. **4** *tabú* (*pene*) prick.
● **a trancas y barrancas,** *fam* with great difficulty. ‖ **coger una tranca / pillar una tranca,** *fam* to get plastered, get drunk.
trancazo I *m* (*golpe*) blow with a cudgel. **2** *fam fig* (*resfriado*) cold; (*gripe*) flu.
● **pegarse un trancazo,** *fam* to come a cropper.
trance I *m* (*momento crítico*) critical moment. **2** (*dificultad*) fix, tight spot. **3** (*éxtasis*) trance.
● **a todo trance,** *fig* at all costs. ‖ **estar en trance de ...,** to be on the point of ..., be in the process of ... ‖ **pasar por un trance,** to hit a bad patch. ‖ **sacar a algn. de un mal trance,** to get sb. out of a fix.
■ **trance mortal / trance de muerte,** death throes *pl*. ‖ **último trance,** last moments *pl* (of life).

tranco *m* stride.
● **a trancos,** *fig* in a hurry. ‖ **en dos trancos,** in a flash.
tranquera *f* palisade.
tranquilamente *adv* calmly.
tranquilidad *f* (*quietud*) calmness, tranquillity (US tranquility); (*sosiego*) peace and quiet.
● **con toda tranquilidad,** (*con calma*) calmly; (*con confianza*) with no qualms: *dilo con toda tranquilidad,* you needn't have any qualms about saying it. ‖ **para mayor tranquilidad,** to be on the safe side. ‖ **para tu tranquilidad,** for your own peace of mind. ‖ **perder la tranquilidad,** to get het up.
■ **paz y tranquilidad,** peace and quiet.
tranquilizador,-ra *adj* calming, reassuring.
tranquilizante **1** *adj* calming, reassuring. – **2** *m* tranquillizer (US tranquilizer).
tranquilizar **1** *t* (*calmar*) to calm down, tranquillize (US tranquilize). **2** (*dar confianza*) to reassure, set one's mind at rest. – **3 tranquilizarse,** *p* (*calmarse*) to calm down. **4** to set one's mind at rest, be reassured.
▲ *Conjugation model* [4], *like realizar.*
tranquillo *m fig* knack.
● **coger el tranquillo a algo,** *fig* to get the knack of sth.
tranquilo,-a **1** *adj* (*sin inquietud*) calm, relaxed, tranquil. **2** (*sin preocupación*) reassured. **3** (*sin movimiento*) calm, still, quiet. **4** (*sin ruidos*) quiet, still, peaceful. **5** (*persona*) calm, easy-going, placid. **6** (*agua*) still; (*conciencia*) clear.
● **déjame tranquilo,-a,** *fam* leave me alone! ‖ **para que estés tranquilo,-a ...,** for your own peace of mind ... ‖ **¡tranquilo,-a!,** (*no te preocupes*) don't you worry!; (*cálmate*) steady on!, calm down!
tranquilón,-ona *adj* sluggish.
transacción *f* transaction, deal.
transalpino,-a *adj* transalpine.
transandino,-a *adj* transandean.
transatlántico,-a **1** *adj* transatlantic. – **2** transatlántico, *m* liner, ocean liner.
transbordador *m* ferry, car ferry.
■ **transbordador aéreo,** cable-car. ‖ **transbordador espacial,** space shuttle.
transbordar **1** *t* to transfer. **2** (*mercancías*) to transship; (*de orilla a orilla*) to ferry across a river. – **3** *i* (*cambiar de tren, metro*) to change trains, US transfer.
transbordo **1** *m* (*de vehículo*) change, US transfer. **2** (*de barco*) transshipment.
● **hacer transbordo,** to change, US transfer.
transcendencia *f* → **trascendencia**.
transcendental *adj* → **trascendental**.
transcendentalismo *m* transcendentalism.
transcendente *adj* → **trascendente**.
transcender *t-i* → **trascender**.
transcontinental *adj* transcontinental.
transcribir *t* to transcribe.
▲ *pp* **transcrito,-a.**
transcripción *f* transcription.
transcrito,-a *pp* → **transcribir**.
transcurrir **1** *i* (*tiempo*) to pass, elapse. **2** (*acontecer*) to take place, go off: *todo aconteció según lo previsto,* it all went off as expected.
transcurso **1** *m* (*paso*) course, passing. **2** (*duración*) space, period: *en el transcurso de dos años,* in the space of two years.
● **con el transcurso de los años,** with the passing of time. ‖ **en el transcurso de los años,** over the course of the years.

transeúnte **1** *mf* (*peatón*) pedestrian. **2** (*residente transitorio*) temporary resident.
transexual **1** *adj* transsexual. – **2** *mf* transsexual.
transexualismo *m* transsexualism.
transferencia **1** *f* (*gen*) transference. **2** FIN transfer.
■ **transferencia bancaria,** banker's order.
transferible *adj* transferable.
transferir **1** *t* (*cambiar de lugar*) to transfer. **2** (*diferir*) to postpone. **3** FIN to transfer, convey.
▲ *Conjugation model* [35], *like hervir.*
transfiguración *f* transfiguration.
transfigurar **1** *t* to transfigure. – **2 transfigurarse,** *p* to become transfigured.
transfixión *f* transfixion.
transformable *adj* transformable.
transformación *f* transformation.
transformador,-ra **1** *adj* transforming. – **2 transformador,** *m* transformer.
transformar **1** *t* to transform, change. – **2 transformarse,** *p* to change, be transformed: *se transformó completamente,* he was completely transformed.
● **transformarse en,** (*persona*) to become; (*objeto*) to convert into: *se transformó en un monstruo,* he became a monster; *se transforma en cama,* it converts into a bed.
transformismo *m* transformism.
transformista **1** *adj* transformist. – **2** *mf* transformist. **3** TEAT quick-change artist.
tránsfuga **1** *mf* MIL deserter. **2** POL turncoat.
transfuguismo *m* POL tendency to change political colours (US colors).
transfundir **1** *t* (*líquido*) to transfuse. **2** (*comunicar*) to spread.
transfusión *f* transfusion.
■ **transfusión de sangre,** blood transfusion.
transgredir *t* to transgress, break.
▲ *Used only in forms which include the letter i in their endings:* transgredía, transgrediré, transgrediendo.
transgresión *f* transgression.
transgresor,-ra *m,f* transgressor, law-breaker.
transiberiano,-a **1** *adj* Trans-Siberian. – **2 el Transiberiano,** *m* (*tren*) the Trans-Siberian Express; (*ferrocarril*) the Trans-Siberian Railway.
transición *f* transition.
● **sin transición,** abruptly.
transido,-a *adj fig* (*angustiado*) distressed.
● **transido,-a de dolor,** racked with pain. ‖ **transido,-a de frío,** chilled to the bone. ‖ **transido,-a de miedo,** panic-stricken.
transigencia **1** *f* (*actitud*) tolerance, lenience. **2** (*concesión*) compromise.
transigente *adj* accommodating, tolerant, lenient.
transigir **1** *i* (*ceder*) to compromise, give in, yield. **2** (*tolerar*) to tolerate, bear.
▲ *Conjugation model* [6], *like dirigir.*
transistor *m* transistor.
transistorizado,-a *adj* transistorized.
transitable *adj* passable.
● **no estar transitable,** (*en malas condiciones*) not to be passable; (*cerrado al tráfico*) to be closed to traffic: *la carretera no está transitable,* the road isn't passable.
transitado,-a **1** *pp* → **transitar**. – **2** *adj* busy.
transitar **1** *i* (*viajar*) to travel, travel about. **2** (*pasar*) to pass, go, walk.
● **transitar por las calles,** to walk around the streets.

transitivo,-a *adj* transitive.
tránsito 1 *m* (*acción*) passage, transit, movement. 2 AUTO traffic. 3 *euf* (*muerte*) death, passing. 4 (*lugar de parada*) stopping place.
● "cerrado al tránsito", "road closed". ‖ **de mucho tránsito,** busy. ‖ **estar de tránsito,** (*de paso*) to be passing through; (*mercancías, viajeros*) to be in transit.
■ **pasajeros en tránsito,** passengers in transit.
transitoriedad *f* transience, transiency.
transitorio,-a *adj* (*pasajero*) transitory; (*de transición*) transitional, interim.
■ **disposición transitoria,** JUR provisional order, provisional ordinance.
translación *f* → **traslación**.
translimitar 1 *t* (*pasar la frontera*) to cross. 2 (*traspasar*) to go beyond.
translúcido,-a *adj* → **traslúcido,-a**.
translucir *t* → **traslucir**.
▲ *Conjugation model* [45], *like* lucir.
transmediterráneo,-a *adj* transmediterranean.
transmigración *f* transmigration.
transmigrar *i* to transmigrate.
transmisión 1 *f* (*propagación*) transmission. 2 JUR transfer, transference. 3 RAD TV broadcast. 4 TÉC drive. – 5 **transmisiones,** *fpl* MIL signals.
■ **cuerpo de transmisiones,** MIL signal corps *sing.* ‖ **derechos de transmisión,** JUR (*de herencia*) succession duty; (*de televisión etc*) broadcasting rights. ‖ **transmisión del pensamiento,** thought transmission. ‖ **transmisión delantera / transmisión trasera,** AUTO front-wheel drive / rear-wheel drive. ‖ **transmisión en directo,** RAD TV live broadcast. ‖ **transmisión del poder,** transfer of power.
transmisor,-ra 1 *adj* transmitting. – 2 *m,f* transmitter.
■ **estación transmisora,** radio station.
transmitir 1 *t* (*gen*) to transmit. 2 RAD TV to broadcast. 3 (*enfermedad*) to transmit, pass on. 4 JUR to transfer, hand down.
transmudar 1 *t* (*trasladar*) to move. 2 (*transmutar*) to transmute.
transmutación *f* transmutation.
transmutar 1 *t* to transmute. – 2 **transmutarse,** *p* to change, transform.
transoceánico,-a *adj* transoceanic.
transpacífico,-a *adj* transpacific.
transparencia 1 *f* transparency, transparence. 2 (*diapositiva*) transparency, slide.
transparentar 1 *t fig* (*emociones etc*) to reveal. – 2 **transparentarse,** *p* (*ser transparente*) to be transparent, show through. 3 *fig* (*emociones etc*) to show, show through.
transparente 1 *adj* (*gen*) transparent. 2 (*tela, vestido*) transparent, see-through. 3 *fig* straight, plain. – 4 *m* (*tela, papel*) transparency. 5 (*visillo*) net curtain. 6 (*pantalla*) shade, blind. 7 (*vidriera*) stained-glass window.
transpiración *f* perspiration, transpiration.
transpirar *i* to perspire, transpire.
transpirenaico,-a *adj* trans-Pyrenean, beyond the Pyrenees.
transplantar 1 *t* (*gen*) to transplant. 2 (*trasladar*) to transfer. – 3 **transplantarse,** *p* to uproot os., emigrate.
transplante *m* transplant, transplantation.
■ **transplante de corazón / riñón / médula ósea,** heart / kidney / bone-marrow transplant.
transponer 1 *t* (*cambiar de sitio*) to move. 2 (*atravesar*) to cross over. 3 (*trasplantar*) to transplant. 4 (*desaparecer*)

to disappear: *transponer la esquina,* to disappear round the corner. – 5 **transponerse,** *p* (*astro*) to set, go down. 6 (*quedarse dormido*) to doze off.
▲ *Conjugation model* [78], *like* poner; *pp* transpuesto,-a.
transportador,-ra 1 *adj* transporting. – 2 transportador, *m* (*de dibujo*) protractor. 3 TÉC transporter, conveyor.
transportar 1 *t* (*gen*) to transport. 2 (*pasajeros*) to carry; (*mercancías en barco*) to ship. 3 MAT to transfer. 4 MÚS to transpose. 5 *fig* (*hacer perder la razón*) to carry away, send into raptures: *la visión de una mujer tan hermosa lo transportó,* the sight of such a beautiful woman sent him into raptures. – 6 **transportarse,** *p fig* to be transported, be enraptured, be carried away.
transporte 1 *m* (*medio*) transport. 2 (*acción*) transport, transportation. 3 COM freight, freightage. 4 MÚS transposition. 5 *fig* transport, ecstasy, bliss.
■ **transporte de mercancías,** freight, transport. ‖ **transporte marítimo,** shipment. ‖ **transporte público / transportes públicos,** public transport.
transportista *mf* carrier.
transposición *f* transposition.
transpuesto,-a *pp* → **transponer**.
transvasar 1 *t* (*líquidos*) to decant. 2 (*entre ríos*) to transfer.
transvase 1 *m* (*de líquidos*) decanting. 2 (*de ríos*) transfer.
transversal *adj* transversal, transverse, crosswise: *una calle transversal,* a cross-street; *sección transversal,* cross-section.
transverso,-a *adj* transverse, crosswise.
tranvía 1 *m* (*sistema*) tramway. 2 (*vehículo*) tram, tramcar, US streetcar.
tranviario,-a 1 *adj* tram, US streetcar. – 2 *m,f* tram driver.
■ **red tranviaria,** tramway.
trapacería *f* trick, fiddle.
trapacero,-a 1 *adj* tricky. – 2 *m,f* trickster, fiddler.
trapajoso,-a 1 *adj* (*ropa*) tattered, ragged. 2 (*persona*) shabby, dowdy. 3 (*habla*) badly articulated.
● **hablar trapajoso,** to slur one's speech.
trápala 1 *f* (*embuste*) lie; (*engaño*) trick. 2 (*ruido, jaleo*) racket, din. – 3 *mf fig* (*parlanchín*) chatterbox. 4 *fig* (*embustero*) cheat.
trapatiesta *f fam* racket.
● **armar una trapatiesta,** *fam* to kick up a rumpus.
trapecio 1 *m* DEP trapeze. 2 (*geometría*) trapezium, US trapezoid. 3 ANAT (*hueso*) trapezium; (*músculo*) trapezius.
trapecista *mf* trapeze artist.
trapense 1 *adj* Trappist. – 2 *m* Trappist.
trapería *f* old-clothes shop.
trapero,-a *m,f* (*hombre*) rag-and-bone man, US junkman; (*mujer*) rag-and-bone woman.
trapezoide *m* trapezoid, US trapezium.
trapichear 1 *i fam* (*ilegal*) to fiddle, be on the fiddle. 2 *fam* (*maquinar*) to plot. 3 *fam* (*al por menor*) to buy and sell retail.
trapicheo *m fam* fiddling, jiggery-pokery.
● **andar con trapicheos / andarse con trapicheos,** *fam* to be involved in shady dealings, be on the fiddle.
trapillo **de trapillo,** *loc* casually dressed.
trapío *f* elegance, charm.
● **tener buen trapío,** to carry os. well, move elegantly.
trapisonda 1 *f fam* (*bulla*) fuss, commotion, to-do. 2 *fam* (*enredo*) plot, scheme.
trapitos *mpl fam* clothes, rags.
● **hablar de trapitos,** *fam* to talk about clothes.

trapo 1 *m* (*tela vieja*) rag. **2** (*paño, bayeta*) cloth. **3** MAR sails *pl.* **4** (*telón*) curtain. **5** (*del torero*) red cape. – **6** trapos, *mpl* clothes, rags.
● **a todo trapo,** MAR at full sail; *fig* flat out. ‖ **estar hecho,-a un trapo,** to be worn out. ‖ **lavar los trapos sucios en casa,** not to wash one's dirty linen in public. ‖ **poner a algn. como un trapo (sucio),** *fam* to tear sb. apart. ‖ **sacar los trapos sucios a relucir,** *fam* to dig up the past.
■ **trapo de cocina,** dishcloth. ‖ **trapo del polvo,** duster.

traque 1 *m* (*estallido*) bang. **2** (*guía*) fuse.

tráquea *f* trachea, windpipe.

traqueal *adj* tracheal.

traqueotomía *f* tracheotomy.

traquetear 1 *i* (*hacer ruido*) to clatter, rattle. – **2** *t* (*agitar*) to shake, bang about.

traqueteo 1 *m* (*ruido*) rattle, clatter. **2** (*movimiento*) jolting, bumping.

traquido *m* crack, bang.

tras 1 *prep* (*después de*) after: *tras la salida del avión,* after the departure of the plane. **2** (*detrás*) behind: *tras el muro,* behind the wall. **3** (*en pos de*) after, in pursuit of: *iba siempre tras el éxito,* he was always in pursuit of success.
● **día tras día,** day after day.

trasalpino,-a *adj* transalpine.

trasandino,-a *adj* transandean.

trasañejo,-a *adj* over three years old.

trasatlántico,-a *adj-m* → **transatlántico,-a**.

trasbordador *m* ferry, car ferry.

trasbordar *t-i* → **transbordar**.

trasbordo *m* → **transbordo**.

trascendencia 1 *f* (*importancia*) significance, importance. **2** (*filosofía*) transcendence, transcendency.
● **de gran trascendencia,** of great importance. ‖ **sin trascendencia,** of little significance.

trascendental 1 *adj* (*importante*) significant, very important, consequential; (*de gran alcance*) far-reaching. **2** (*filosofía*) transcendent, transcendental.

trascendentalismo *m* transcendentalism.

trascendente *adj* → **trascendental**.

trascender 1 *i* (*olor - despedir*) to smell; (*- llegar hasta*) to reach: *aquel olor trascendía hasta la sala,* that smell reached the hall. **2** (*darse a conocer*) to become known, leak out: *el resultado trascendió,* the result leaked out. **3** (*extenderse*) to spread, have a wide effect. – **4** *t* (*averiguar*) to discover, bring to light.
● **trascender a la opinión pública,** to become common knowledge.
▲ *Conjugation model* |28|, *like entender*.

trascribir *t* to transcribe.
▲ *pp trascrito,-a*.

trascripción *f* transcription.

trascrito,-a *pp* → **trascribir**.

trascurrir *i* → **transcurrir**.

trascurso *m* → **transcurso**.

trasegar 1 *t* (*mudar*) to move about, shuffle. **2** (*líquidos*) to decant. **3** *fam fig* (*beber mucho*) to swill.
▲ *Conjugation model* |48|, *like regar*.

trasero,-a 1 *adj* back, rear. – **2 trasero,** *m fam euf* bottom, bum.
● **en la parte trasera,** at the back.

trasferencia *f* → **transferencia**.

trasferible *adj* transferable.

trasferir *t* → **transferir**.
▲ *Conjugation model* |35|, *like hervir*.

trasfiguración *f* transfiguration.

trasfigurar *t-p* → **transfigurar**.

trasfondo 1 *m* background. **2** *fig* undertone: *un trasfondo de amargura,* an undertone of sorrow.

trasformable *adj* transformable.

trasformación *f* transformation.

trasformador,-ra *adj-m* → **transformador,-ra**.

trasformar *t-p* → **transformar**.

trasformista *adj-mf* → **transformista**.

trásfuga *mf* → **tránsfuga**.

trasfuguismo *m* → **transfuguismo**.

trasfundir *t* → **transfundir**.

trasfusión *f* → **transfusión**.

trasgo *m* goblin, imp.

trasgredir *t* → **transgredir**.

trasgresión *f* transgression.

trasgresor,-ra *m,f* transgressor, law-breaker.

trashumancia *f* transhumance, seasonal migration.

trashumante *adj* transhumant.

trashumar *i* to move new pastures according to the season.

trasiego *m* comings and goings *pl,* hustle and bustle.
■ **trasiego de personal,** reshuffle.

traslación 1 *f* ASTRON passage, movement. **2** MAT translation. **3** LIT metaphor.

trasladar 1 *t* (*cambiar de sitio*) to move. **2** (*de cargo etc*) to transfer. **3** (*aplazar*) to postpone, put off. **4** (*traducir*) to translate. – **5 trasladarse,** *p* (*ir*) to go. **6** (*cambiar de residencia*) to move.
● **trasladar al papel,** *fig* to put down in writing.

traslado 1 *m* (*cambio de lugar*) move, moving; (*de residencia*) removal. **2** (*de cargo etc*) transfer. **3** (*copia*) copy. **4** JUR notification.

traslapar *t* to overlap.

traslúcido,-a *adj* translucent, semitransparent.

traslucir 1 *t fig* to show, reveal, betray. – **2 traslucirse,** *p* (*material*) to be translucent. **2** *fig* (*dejar ver*) to show, show through; (*revelarse*) to be revealed.
▲ *Conjugation model* |45|, *like lucir*.

trasluz *m* diffused light, reflected light.
● **mirar algo al trasluz,** to look at sth. against the light.

trasmano *mf* second hand.
● **a trasmano,** (*objeto*) out of reach; (*lugar*) out of one's way.

trasmigración *f* transmigration.

trasmigrar *i* to transmigrate.

trasmisión *f* → **transmisión**.

trasmisor *adj-m* → **transmisor,-ra**.

trasmitir *t* → **transmitir**.

trasmudar *t* → **transmudar**.

trasmutación *f* transmutation.

trasmutar *t-p* → **transmutar**.

trasnochado,-a 1 *pp* → **trasnochar**. – **2** *adj fig* (*viejo*) old, hackneyed. **3** *fig* (*desmejorado*) haggard, bleary-eyed.

trasnochador,-ra 1 *adj* who stays up late, who stays up until the early hours. – **2** *m,f* night bird, nighthawk.

trasnochar *i* to stay up late, stay up until the early hours.

traspapelado,-a 1 *pp* → **traspapelar**. – **2** *adj* mislaid, misplaced.

traspapelar 1 *t* to mislay, misplace. – **2 traspapelarse,** *p* to get mislaid, get misplaced.

trasparencia *f* → **transparencia**.

trasparentar *t-p* → **transparentar**.

trasparente *adj-m* → **transparente**.

traspasar 1 *t* (*atravesar*) to go through, cross. 2 (*cambiar de lugar*) to move: *traspasó la mesa al salón,* he moved the table into the hall. 3 (*perforar*) to go through, pierce. 4 (*dar, pasar*) to transfer; (*vender*) to sell. 5 *fig* (*exceder*) to exceed, go beyond. 6 *fig* (*dolor físico, moral*) to penetrate, transfix: *el dolor le traspasó el costado,* the pain went through his side. – 7 **traspasarse,** *p* to exceed os.
● "se traspasa", "for sale".

traspaso 1 *m* (*de negocio etc*) transfer, sale. 2 (*precio*) transfer fee.

traspié 1 *m* (*tropezón*) stumble, trip. 2 *fig* (*equivocación*) blunder.
● **dar un traspié,** to trip; *fig* to slip up.
▲ *pl* **traspiés**.

traspiración *f* → **transpiración**.

traspirar *i* → **transpirar**.

traspirenaico,-a *adj* → **transpirenaico,-a**.

trasplantar *t-p* → **transplantar**.

trasplante *m* → **transplante**.

trasponer *t-p* → **transponer**.
▲ *Conjugation model* [78], *like* **poner**; *pp* **traspuesto,-a**.

trasportador,-ra *adj-m* → **transportador,-ra**.

trasportar *t-p* → **transportar**.

trasporte *m* → **trasporte**.

trasportista *mf* carrier.

trasposición *f* transposition.

traspuesto,-a *pp* → **trasponer**.
● **quedarse traspuesto,-a,** to nod off, doze off.

trasquilado,-a 1 *pp* → **trasquilar**. – 2 *adj* (*oveja*) sheared; (*pelo*) hacked, unevenly cut. 3 *fam fig* curtailed, cut down.
● **ir a por lana y salir trasquilado,-a,** *fig* to come out the loser, end up worse off.

trasquilar 1 *t* (*animales*) to shear. 2 (*pelo*) to hack, cut unevenly. 3 *fig* to curtail.

trasquilón 1 *m fam* (*de pelo*) hacked cut, chop. 2 *fam fig* (*de dinero*) loot, catch.
● **a trasquilones / con trasquilones,** unevenly cut, hacked.

trastabillar 1 *i* (*dar traspiés*) to stumble, trip. 2 (*tambalearse*) to stagger, totter. 3 (*tartamudear*) to stammer, stutter.

trastada *f fam* (*mala pasada*) dirty trick; (*broma pesada*) prank.

trastazo *m fam* whack, wallop, thump.
● **darse un trastazo / pegarse un trastazo,** *fam* to come a cropper: *se dio un trastazo contra la pared,* he bumped into the wall.

traste *m* MÚS fret.
● **dar al traste con algo,** *fig* to spoil sth., ruin sth. ‖ **irse al traste,** *fig* to fall through.

trastear 1 *t* MÚS to play. 2 (*revolver*) to rummage in. 3 (*toro*) to play with the cape. 4 *fig* (*manejar*) to twist around one's little finger. – 5 *i* (*revolver*) to rummage. 6 (*mover*) to move from one place to another.

trastera *f* → **trastero,-a**.

trastero,-a 1 *adj* junk. – 2 **trastero,** *m* junk room. – 3 **trastera,** *f* junk room.

trastienda 1 *f* (*de tienda*) back room. 2 *fig* (*astucia*) cunning.
● **por trastienda,** *fig* under the counter. ‖ **tener mucha trastienda,** *fam* to be canny, be a shrewd customer.

trasto 1 *m* (*algo inútil*) piece of junk. 2 *fam* (*cosa cualquiera*) thing, thingumajig, whatnot. 3 (*mueble*) piece of furniture. 4 *fam* (*niño*) little devil. 5 *fam* (*persona*) useless person, good-for-nothing, dead loss. – 6 **trastos,** *mpl* (*utensilios*) tackle *sing,* gear *sing.* 7 *fam* (*pertenencias*) belongings, things.
● **coger los trastos / liar los trastos,** to pack up and leave. ‖ **ser un trasto viejo,** to be a dead loss. ‖ **tirarse los trastos a la cabeza,** *fig* to have a blazing row.

trastocamiento *m* switch, reversal.

trastocar 1 *t* (*cambiar*) to change. – 2 **trastocarse,** *p* (*trastornarse*) to go mad.
▲ *Conjugation model* [1], *like* **sacar**.

trastornado,-a 1 *pp* → **trastornar**. – 2 *adj* (*preocupado*) upset. 3 (*loco*) mad. 4 (*mente*) unbalanced.

trastornar 1 *t* (*revolver*) to turn round, turn upside down. 2 (*alterar - planes*) to disrupt; (*- paz, orden*) to disturb. 3 (*estómago*) to upset. 4 *fig* (*molestar*) to bother, trouble, annoy. 5 *fig* (*enloquecer*) to drive crazy. – 6 **trastornarse,** *p* (*perturbarse*) to go mad, go out of one's mind.

trastorno 1 *m* (*desorden*) confusion. 2 (*molestia*) trouble, inconvenience. 3 (*perturbación*) disruption, upheaval, upset. 4 MED upset.
■ **trastorno estomacal / trastorno mental,** stomach upset / mental disorder.

trastrocar 1 *t* (*gen*) to switch around, change around. 2 (*orden*) to invert, reverse; (*significado*) to change.
▲ *Conjugation model* [49], *like* **trocar**.

trasunto 1 *m* (*copia*) copy. 2 (*representación*) representation.

trasvasar *t* → **transvasar**.

trasvase *m* → **transvase**.

trasversal *adj* → **transversal**.

trasverso,-a *adj* → **transverso,-a**.

trata *f* slave-trade, slave-traffic.
■ **trata de blancas,** white-slave trade.

tratable *adj* friendly, congenial, easy to get along with.

tratadista *mf* treatise writer, essayist.

tratado 1 *m* (*pacto*) treaty. 2 (*estudio*) treatise.

tratamiento 1 *m* (*gen*) treatment. 2 TÉC INFORM processing. 3 (*título*) title, form of address.
● **dar a algn. tratamiento de ...,** to address sb. as. ‖ **un tratamiento a base de...,** MED a course of...
■ **tratamiento de datos,** data processing. ‖ **tratamiento de textos,** word processing.

tratante *mf* dealer.

tratar 1 *t* (*gen - objeto*) to treat, handle; (*- persona*) to treat: *trató la caja con cuidado,* she handled the box with care; *nos trató bien,* he treated us well. 2 (*asunto, tema*) to discuss, deal with. 3 (*gestionar*) to handle, run. 4 (*dar tratamiento*) to address as. 5 (*calificar, considerar*) to consider, call: *lo trató de idiota,* she called him an idiot. 6 MED to treat. 7 INFORM TÉC to process. 8 QUÍM to treat. – 9 *i* (*relacionarse*) to be acquainted (**con,** with), know (**con,** -). 10 (*tener tratos*) to deal (**con,** with). 11 (*negociar*) to negotiate (**con,** with). 12 (*intentar*) to try (**de,** to): *trata de hacerlo,* try to do it. 13 (*versar*) to be about: *trata de/sobre espías,* it's about spies. 14 COM to deal (**en,** in): *trata en pieles,* he deals in furs. – 15 **tratarse,** *p* (*relacionarse*) to talk to each other, be on speaking terms: *no se tratan,* they're not on speaking terms. 16 (*llamarse*) to address each other as, call each other. 17 (*referirse*) to be about: *se trataba de un atraco,* it was about a robbery.
● **se trata de ...,** it's a question of ..., it's a matter of ...: *se trata de averiguar cómo lo hicieron,* it's a question of working out how they did it.

trato 1 *m* (*acción*) treatment. 2 (*modales*) manner. 3 (*contacto*) contact; *pey* dealings *pl*. 4 (*acuerdo*) agreement. 5 COM deal. 6 (*tratamiento*) title.
● **cerrar un trato,** to close a deal. ‖ **dar a algn. el trato de ...,** to address sb. as ... ‖ **estar en tratos con algn.,** to be negotiating with sb. ‖ **tener trato de gentes,** to have a good way with people. ‖ **tener un trato agradable,** to have a pleasant manner. ‖ **¡trato hecho!,** it's a deal!
■ **malos tratos,** ill-treatment *sing*. ‖ **trato carnal,** sexual intercourse. ‖ **trato diario,** daily contact.
trauma *m* trauma.
traumático,-a *adj* traumatic.
traumatismo *m* traumatism.
traumatizar 1 *t* MED to traumatize. 2 *fam* to shock.
▲ *Conjugation model* [4], *like realizar*.
traumatología *f* traumatology.
travelín *m* travelling (US traveling) shot.
través 1 *m* (*inclinación*) slant. 2 (*pieza de madera*) crosspiece, crossbeam. 3 MAR beam. 4 *fig* (*desgracia*) misfortune.
● **al través,** crossways. ‖ **a través de,** (*de un lado a otro*) across, over; (*por dentro*) through; (*mediante*) through, from. ‖ **cortar al través,** COST to cut on the bias. ‖ **de través,** (*transversalmente*) crosswise; (*de lado*) sideways. ‖ **mirar de través,** (*de reojo*) to look out of the corner of one's eye; (*con desaprobación*) to look askance at; (*defecto*) to squint.
travesaño 1 *m* ARQ crosspiece. 2 DEP crossbar.
travesía 1 *f* (*viaje*) crossing; (*por mar*) voyage, crossing. 2 (*calle*) cross-street, passage. 3 (*distancia*) distance.
travesti *mf* transvestite.
travestí *mf* transvestite.
travestido,-a 1 *pp* → **travestirse**. – 2 *m,f* transvestite.
travestirse *p* to wear drag, wear clothes of the opposite sex; (*hombre*) to dress up as a woman; (*mujer*) to dress up as a man.
▲ *Conjugation model* [34], *like servir*.
travestismo *m* transvestism.
travesura *f* piece of mischief, childish prank.
● **hacer travesuras,** to get into mischief.
traviesa *f* → **travieso,-a**.
travieso,-a 1 *adj* mischievous, naughty. – 2 **traviesa,** *f* (*de ferrocarril*) sleeper, US tie. 3 (*en construcción*) trimmer.
● **a campo traviesa,** across country.
trayecto 1 *m* (*distancia*) distance, way. 2 (*recorrido*) route, itinerary.
■ **final de trayecto / final del trayecto,** terminus, end of the line.
trayectoria 1 *f* trajectory. 2 *fig* line, course, path.
traza 1 *f* *fig* (*apariencia*) looks *pl*, appearance. 2 *fig* (*mañas*) skill, knack. 3 ARQ plan, design.
● **darse trazas para algo,** *fig* to manage to do sth., find a way to do sth. ‖ **no llevar trazas de / no tener trazas de,** *fig* not to look as if: *esto no tiene trazas de acabar bien,* it doesn't look as if it's going to work out. ‖ **tener traza para algo,** to be good at sth.
trazado 1 *m* (*plano*) layout, plan. 2 (*dibujo*) drawing, sketch. 3 (*de carretera, ferrocarril*) route, course.
trazar 1 *t* (*línea, plano, dibujo*) to draw, draw up. 2 (*parque*) to lay out; (*edificio*) to design. 3 (*itinerario*) to trace. 4 *fig* (*plan etc*) to outline, draft. – 5 *i* (*describir*) to sketch.
● **trazar una semblanza de algn.,** *fig* to describe sb., depict sb.
▲ *Conjugation model* [4], *like realizar*.
trazo 1 *m* (*línea*) line. 2 (*de una letra*) stroke. 3 *fig* (*rasgo facial*) feature.

trebejo *m fam* gear, stuff.
▲ *Generally used in plural.*
trébol 1 *m* (*planta*) clover, trefoil. 2 (*naipes*) club. 3 (*de carreteras*) cloverleaf interchange.
trece 1 *adj* (*cardinal*) thirteen; (*ordinal*) thirteenth. – 2 *m* (*número*) thirteen; (*fecha*) thirteenth.
● **mantenerse en sus trece / seguir en sus trece,** *fig* to stick to one's guns.
■ **martes y trece,** Friday 13th.
▲ *See also* **seis**.
treceavo,-a 1 *adj* thirteenth. – 2 *m,f* thirteenth.
▲ *See also* **sexto,-a**.
trecho 1 *m* (*espacio*) distance, way; (*tiempo*) while, time. 2 (*de camino, ruta*) stretch. 3 AGR plot, patch. 4 *fam* (*parte*) piece, bit.
● **a trechos,** in parts, in places. ‖ **de trecho en trecho,** at intervals.
tregua 1 *f* truce. 2 *fig* respite, rest.
treinta 1 *adj* (*cardinal*) thirty; (*ordinal*) thirtieth. – 2 *m* (*número*) thirty; (*fecha*) thirtieth.
▲ *See also* **seis**.
treintañero,-a 1 *adj* thirty-year-old. – 2 *m,f* thirty-year-old person.
treintavo,-a 1 *adj* thirtieth. – 2 *m,f* thirtieth.
▲ *See also* **sexto,-a**.
treintena *f* (*exacto*) thirty; (*aproximado*) about thirty.
tremebundo,-a *adj* terrible, dreadful.
tremendista *adj* sensationalist.
tremendo,-a 1 *adj* (*terrible*) terrible, dreadful, frightful. 2 (*muy grande*) huge, terrible; *fig* tremendous.
● **tomarse algo por la tremenda,** *fig* to make a great fuss about sth.
trementina *f* turpentine.
■ **esencia de trementina,** oil of turpentine, spirits of turpentine.
tremolar 1 *t* to wave. – 2 *i* to wave, flutter.
tremolina *f fam fig* uproar, fuss, shindy.
trémolo *m* tremolo.
trémulo,-a 1 *adj* (*tembloroso*) tremulous, quivering. 2 (*luz, llama*) flickering.
tren 1 *m* (*ferrocarril*) train. 2 MIL convoy. 3 (*conjunto de máquinas*) convoy, line. 4 *fig* (*ritmo, modo*) speed, pace.
● **cambiar de tren,** to change, change train, US transfer. ‖ **coger el tren / tomar el tren,** to catch a train. ‖ **estar como un tren / estar como para parar un tren,** *fam* to be a bit of all right. ‖ **ir en tren,** to go by train. ‖ **perder el train,** *fig* to miss the boat. ‖ **vivir a todo tren,** *fig* to live a life of luxury.
■ **tren correo,** mail train. ‖ **tren de alta velocidad,** high-speed train. ‖ **tren de aterrizaje,** undercarriage. ‖ **tren de cercanías,** suburban train. ‖ **tren de lavado,** car wash. ‖ **tren de mercancías / tren de carga,** goods train, US freight train. ‖ **tren de pasajeros,** passenger train. ‖ **tren de vida,** lifestyle, way of life. ‖ **tren directo,** through train.
trena *f arg* clink, prison.
trenca 1 *f* (*palo*) crosspiece. 2 (*abrigo*) duffel coat, duffle coat.
trencilla *f* braided ribbon.
trenza 1 *f* (*peluquería*) plait, US braid. 2 COST braid.
■ **trenza postiza,** (*de pelo*) switch, hairpiece.
trenzado 1 *m* (*trenza - de pelo*) plait, US braid; (- *de costura*) braid. 2 (*en danza*) entrechat. 3 (*de caballo*) crossover step.
trenzar 1 *t* to plait, braid. 2 (*peluquería*) to plait, US braid. – 3 *i* (*en danza*) to weave in and out. 4 (*caballo*) to caper, frisk.

▲ Conjugation model [4], like *realizar*.
trepa *mf fam pey* go-getter, social climber.
trepador,-ra 1 *adj (planta)* climbing. – 2 *m,f fam pey* go-getter, social climber.
■ **ave trepadora,** creeper.
trepanación *f* trepanation, trepanning.
trepanar *i* to trepan, trephine.
trépano 1 *m* MED trephine. 2 TÉC bit.
trepar¹ 1 *t (escalar)* to climb. – 2 *i (escalar)* to climb.
trepar² 1 *t (taladrar)* to drill. 2 *(un bordado)* to trim.
trepidación *f* vibration, shaking.
trepidante 1 *adj* vibrating, shaking. 2 *fig (vida etc)* hectic, frantic.
trepidar *i* to vibrate, shake.
tres 1 *adj (cardinal)* three; *(ordinal)* third. – 2 *m (número)* three; *(fecha)* third.
● **como tres y dos son cinco,** *fam* as sure as eggs are eggs. ‖ **ni a la de tres,** *fam* there was no way.
■ **tres en raya,** noughts and crosses, US tick-tack-toe.
▲ In 2, *pl* **treses**; *see also* **seis**.
trescientos,-as 1 *adj (cardinal)* three hundred; *(ordinal)* three hundredth. – 2 *m (número)* three hundred.
▲ *See also* **seis**.
tresillo 1 *m (mueble)* suite, three-piece suite. 2 MÚS triplet. 3 *(juego de naipes)* ombre.
treta *f* trick, ruse.
tríada *f* triad.
trial *m* trial.
triangular *adj* triangular.
triángulo,-a 1 *adj* triangular. – 2 **triángulo,** *m* triangle.
■ **triángulo amoroso,** *fig* eternal triangle. ‖ **triángulo equilátero,** equilateral triangle. ‖ **triángulo isósceles,** isosceles triangle. ‖ **triángulo rectángulo,** right-angled triangle.
tribal *adj* tribal, tribe.
tribu *f* tribe.
tribulación *f* tribulation.
tribuna 1 *f (plataforma)* rostrum, dais. 2 DEP grandstand.
■ **tribuna de la prensa,** press box.
tribunal 1 *m* JUR court. 2 *(de examen)* board of examiners.
● **llevar a los tribunales,** to take to court.
■ **Tribunal Constitucional,** Constitutional Court. ‖ **tribunal de apelación,** court of appeal. ‖ **Tribunal de Cuentas,** National Audit Office, US Committee on Public Accounts. ‖ **Tribunal Supremo,** High Court, US Supreme Court. ‖ **tribunal tutelar de menores,** juvenile court.
tribuno *m* tribune.
tributable *adj* subject to tax, liable to tax.
tributación *f* taxation, levy.
tributante 1 *adj* taxpaying. – 2 *mf* taxpayer.
tributar *t* to pay.
● **tributar cariño,** to show affection. ‖ **tributar respeto,** to pay respect.
tributario,-a 1 *adj* tributary, tax. – 2 *m,f* taxpayer.
■ **sistema tributario,** tax system.
tributo 1 *m (impuesto)* tax. 2 *(a cambio de algo)* tribute. 3 *fig (carga)* price. 4 *fig (de sentimiento)* token.
■ **tributo de amistad,** token of friendship.
tricéfalo,-a *adj* tricephalous.
tricentenario *m* tricentennial.
tríceps *m* triceps.
▲ *pl* **tríceps**.
triciclo *m* tricycle.
tricolor *adj* tricolour (US tricolor), tricoloured (US tricolored).

tricornio 1 *m (sombrero)* three-cornered hat, tricorn. 2 *arg (guardia civil)* member of the civil guard.
tricot *m* woollen-knit (US woolen-knit), knit, tricot.
tricotar *t* to knit.
tricotosa *f* knitting-machine.
tridente *m* trident.
tridimensional *adj* three-dimensional.
triedro *m* trihedron.
trienal *adj* triennial.
trienio *m* triennium.
trifásico,-a 1 *adj* ELEC three-phase. – 2 **trifásico,** *m arg* white coffee with brandy.
trifulca *f fig* rumpus, row, squabble.
trifurcarse *p* to divide into three.
▲ Conjugation model [1], like *sacar*.
trigal *m* wheat field.
trigémino,-a 1 *adj* trigeminal. – 2 **trigémino,** *m* trigeminal.
trigésimo,-a 1 *adj* thirtieth. – 2 *m,f* thirtieth.
▲ *See also* **sexto,-a**.
triglifo *m* triglyph.
trigo 1 *m (cereal)* wheat. 2 *fam fig (dinero)* dough.
● **meterse en trigo ajeno,** *fig* to meddle in sb. else's affairs. ‖ **no ser trigo limpio,** *(persona)* not to be totally above-board; *(asunto)* to be dodgy, be shady.
■ **trigo duro,** hard wheat. ‖ **trigo sarraceno,** buckwheat.
trigonometría *f* trigonometry.
trigonométrico,-a *adj* trigonometric, trigonometrical.
trigueño,-a 1 *adj (pelo)* corn-coloured (US corn-colored), dark blonde. 2 *(piel)* dark, swarthy. 3 *(persona)* olive-skinned.
triguero,-a 1 *adj* wheat. – 2 **triguero,** *m (ave)* corn-bunting.
trilateral *adj* three-sided, trilateral.
trilátero,-a *adj* three-sided, trilateral.
trilero,-a *m,f arg* person who runs a three-card trick racket.
triles *mpl arg* fraudulent three-card trick played in the street.
trilingüe *adj* trilingual.
trilita *f* TNT, trinitrotoluene.
trilla *f* threshing.
trillado,-a 1 *pp* → **trillar.** – 2 *adj (camino)* beaten, well-trodden. 3 *fig (expresión etc)* overworked, well-worn.
trillador,-ra 1 *adj* threshing. – 2 **trilladora,** *f* threshing-machine.
■ **trilladora segadora,** combine harvester.
trillar 1 *t* to thresh. 2 *fig* to wear out.
trillizo,-a *m,f* triplet.
trillo *m* thresher.
trillón *m* trillion.
trilogía *f* trilogy.
trimestral *adj* quarterly, three-monthly, trimestral.
■ **examen trimestral,** end-of-term examination.
trimestralmente *adv* quarterly.
trimestre 1 *m* quarter, trimester. 2 EDUC term.
trimotor *m* three-engined aircraft.
trinar 1 *i (ave)* to warble, trill. 2 MÚS to trill. 3 *fam (enfadarse)* to rage, fume: *Pedro está que trina,* Pedro is fuming.
trinca *f* trio, threesome.
trincar 1 *t fam (robar)* to steal. 2 *fam (atrapar)* to catch. 3 *arg (beber)* to drink. – 4 **trincarse,** *p arg (beberse)* to drink, put away. 5 *arg (tirarse)* to screw.

trinchante I *m* (*para trinchar*) carving knife. **2** (*para sujetar*) meat fork.

trinchar *t* to carve, slice (up).

trinchera *f* trench.

trinchero *m* serving table, side-table.

trineo *m* sleigh, sled, sledge.

trinidad *f* trinity.

■ **la Santísima Trinidad,** the Blessed Trinity, the Holy Trinity.

Trinidad *f* Trinidad.

■ **Trinidad y Tobago,** Trinidad and Tobago.

trinitario,-a I *adj* Trinitarian. – **2** *m,f* Trinitarian.

trinitrotolueno *m* trinitrotoluene.

trino I *m* (*ave*) warble, trill. **2** MÚS trill.

trino,-a I *adj* trine. **2** REL triune.

trinomio *m* trinomial.

trinquete[1] *m* (*lengüeta*) pawl, ratchet.

trinquete[2] I *m* (*frontón*) pelota court. **2** MAR (*palo*) foremast; (*vela*) foresail.

trinquis *m fam* swig, drink: *le gusta el trinquis,* he likes drinking.

▲ *pl trinquis.*

trío *m* trio.

trip *m arg* trip.

tripa I *f* (*intestino*) gut, intestine; *fam* tummy. **2** (*de vasija*) belly. **3** *fam* (*embarazo*) belly. – **4 tripas,** *fpl fam* (*interior*) innards. **5** (*de fruta*) core *sing.* **6** (*documentos*) dossier *sing.*

● **echar las tripas,** *fam* to throw up. ‖ **echar tripa / tener tripa,** *fam* to get a paunch / have a paunch. ‖ **hacer de tripas corazón,** *fig* to pluck up courage. ‖ **revolver las tripas,** *fig* to turn one's stomach.

■ **dolor de tripas,** *fam* stomachache.

tripartito,-a *adj* tripartite.

tripi I *m arg* (*viaje*) trip. **2** (*droga*) tab of acid.

triple I *adj* triple. **2** (*tres veces*) three times: *pagamos el triple del precio real,* we paid three times the real price. – **3** *m* triple.

triplicado *m* triplicate.

● **por triplicado,** in triplicate.

triplicar *t* to triple, treble.

▲ *Conjugation model* |1|, *like* ***sacar.***

triplicidad *f* triplicity.

trípode *m* tripod.

Trípoli *m* Tripoli.

tripón,-ona *m,f fam* pot-bellied person.

tríptico *m* triptych.

triptongo *m* triphthong.

tripudo,-a *adj fam* paunchy, pot-bellied.

tripulación *f* crew.

tripulante *m* crew member.

tripular *t* to man.

triquina *f* trichina.

triquinosis *f* trichinosis.

▲ *pl triquinosis.*

triquiñuela I *f fam* trick, dodge.

● **andar(se) con triquiñuelas,** *fam* to be a slippery customer. ‖ **saberse las triquiñuelas,** *fam* to know all the dodges.

triquitraque *m* clackety-clack, clatter.

tris *m fam fig* bit; (*sonido*) crack.

● **en un tris,** *fam* in a jiffy: *lo hizo en un tris,* he did it in a jiffy. ‖ **estar en un tris de,** to be on the point of: *estaba en un tris de marcharse,* he was on the point of leaving; *estuve en un tris de ir allí,* I very nearly went there. ‖ **por un tris,** *fam* by skin of one's teeth, by a

hair's breadth: *no lo atropellaste por un tris,* you missed running him over by a hair's breadth.

trisca I *f* (*ruido*) crunch. **2** (*estruendo*) rumpus, uproar.

trisílabo,-a I *adj* trisyllabic. – **2** trisílabo, *m* trisyllable.

triste I *adj* (*infeliz*) sad, unhappy; (*futuro*) bleak. **2** (*oscuro, sombrío*) gloomy, dismal. **3** (*único*) single, only: *ni un triste libro,* not a single book. **4** (*insignificante*) poor, humble.

● **es triste que ...,** it's a pity ...: *es triste que no los podamos ayudar,* it's a pity we can't help them. ‖ **hacer un triste papel,** to cut a sorry figure. ‖ **poner triste a algn.,** to make sb. sad. ‖ **ponerse triste,** to become sad.

■ **triste futuro,** bleak future.

tristemente *adv* sadly.

tristeza I *f* sadness. – **2 tristezas,** *fpl* problems, sufferings.

tristón,-ona *adj fam* gloomy, sad, melancholy.

tritón I *m* (*anfibio*) newt. **2** Tritón, (*mitología*) Triton.

trituración *f* grinding, crushing, trituration.

triturado,-a I *pp* → **triturar.** – **2** *adj* ground, crushed. **3** *fig* crumpled up.

triturador,-ra I *adj* grinding, crushing, triturating. – **2** triturador, *m* waste-disposal unit, US garbage-disposal unit. – **3** trituradora, *f* grinder, crushing machine.

■ **trituradora de papel,** paper shredder.

triturar I *t* to grind (up), crush; (*papel*) to shred. **2** *fig* (*físicamente*) to beat (up); (*moralmente*) to tear apart.

triunfador,-ra I *adj* winning. – **2** *m,f* winner.

triunfal *adj* triumphant.

● **salir triunfal,** to come out the winner, come out on top.

triunfalismo I *m* boastfulness. – **2** *adj* POL jingoism.

triunfalista I *adj* boastful. **2** POL jingoistic.

triunfalmente *adv* triumphantly.

triunfar *i* to triumph, win.

● **triunfar en la vida,** to succeed in life.

triunfo I *m* (*victoria*) triumph, victory. **2** DEP win. **3** (*éxito*) success. **4** (*naipes*) trump.

triunvirato *m* triumvirate.

trivalente *adj* trivalent, tervalent.

trivial *adj* trivial, petty.

trivialidad *f* triviality, pettiness.

trivializar *t* to trivialize, minimize.

triza *f* bit, fragment.

● **hacer trizas,** (*destrozar*) to tear to shreds; (*gastar*) to wear out. ‖ **hacer trizas a algn.,** *fam* to tear sb. to pieces. ‖ **estar hecho,-a trizas,** *fam* to feel washed out.

trocar I *t* (*permutar*) to exchange, swap: *trocar un lápiz por un bolígrafo,* to exchange a pencil for a biro. **2** (*transformar*) to turn (**en,** into), convert (**en,** into). – **3** trocarse, *p* (*mudarse*) to change (**en,** into), turn (**en,** to): *su risa se trocó en llanto,* her smile turned to tears.

▲ *Conjugation model* |49|.

trocear *t* to cut up.

trochemoche **a trochemoche,** *loc adv fam* pell-mell, helter-skelter.

trofeo *m* trophy.

troglodita *mf* troglodyte.

trola *f fam* lie, fib.

trole *m* trolley pole.

trolebús *m* trolley bus, US trolley-car.

trolero,-a I *adj fam* lying. – **2** *mf fam* liar, fibber.

tromba *f* waterspout.

■ **tromba de agua,** downpour.

trombo m thrombus.

trombón 1 m MÚS trombone. **– 2** mf trombonist.
■ trombón de pistones / trombón de llaves, valve trombone. ‖ trombón de varas, slide trombone.

trombosis f thrombosis.
▲ pl *trombosis*.

trompa 1 f MÚS horn. **2** (de elefante) trunk. **3** (de insecto) proboscis. **4** ANAT tube. **5** fam fig (nariz) hooter, snout. **6** fam (borrachera) drunkenness. **– 7** mf MÚS horn player.
● estar trompa / coger una trompa / llevar una trompa, fam to be plastered.
■ trompa de Eustaquio, Eustachian tube. ‖ trompa de Falopio, Fallopian tube.

trompada 1 f fam (puñetazo) thump, punch. **2** fam (encontrón) bump, collision. **3** arg (drogas) hit.

trompazo m bump.
● darse un trompazo / pegarse un trompazo, to have a bump, have a crash.

trompeta 1 f MÚS trumpet. **– 2** mf trumpet player.

trompetazo m trumpet-blast.

trompetilla f ear-trumpet.

trompetista mf trumpet player, trumpeter.

trompicar 1 i to trip, trip up, stumble. **– 2** t to trip, trip up, make stumble.
▲ Conjugation model [1], like **sacar**.

trompicón 1 m (tropezón) trip, stumble. **2** (golpe) blow, hit.
● a trompicones, in fits and starts.

trompo m spinning-top.

tronada f → **tronado,-a**.

tronado,-a 1 pp → **tronar**. **– 2** adj fam (deteriorado) old, broken-down. **3** fam (arruinado) broke. **– 4** tronada, f thunderstorm.

tronar 1 i (trueno) to thunder. **2** (cañón etc) to thunder. **3** fam fig (blasfemar) to swear, curse.
▲ Conjugation model [31], like **contar**; in **1**, used only in the 3rd person; it does not take a subject.

tronchante adj fam hilarious, uproarious.

tronchar 1 t (árboles) to cut down, fell. **2** fig to destroy.
● troncharse de risa, fam to split one's sides with laughter.

troncho adj stem, stalk.

tronco 1 m ANAT trunk, torso. **2** BOT (tallo de árbol) trunk; (leño) log. **3** fig (linaje) family stock. **4** fig (persona inútil) blockhead. **5** (geometría) frustum. **6** arg (compañero) mate, pal, chum.
● dormir como un tronco, fam to sleep like a log.
■ tronco de cono, truncated cone.

tronera 1 f (de fortificación) loophole, slit. **2** (de barco) porthole. **3** (de billar) pocket. **– 4** mf fam fig (hombre) rake; (mujer) slut, loose woman.

tronido 1 m thunderclap. **2** fig (ruina) fall, downfall.

trono m throne.

tronzar 1 t (cortar) to cut up. **2** COST to pleat. **3** fig to exhaust.
▲ Conjugation model [4], like **realizar**.

tropa 1 f MIL troops pl, soldiers pl. **2** (muchedumbre) crowd. **– 3** tropas, fpl MIL troops, fighting soldiers.
■ tropas de asalto, storm troops, shock troops.

tropel m throng, mob.
● en tropel, in a mad rush.

tropelía 1 f (atropello) outrage. **2** (tropel) throng, mob. **3** (delito) crime.

tropezar 1 i (trompicar) to trip, stumble: tropezó con mi pie, he tripped over my foot. **2** fig (encontrar a alguien) to come (**con**, across), bump (**con**, into). **3** fig (encontrar dificultades etc) to come up (**con**, against), run (**con**, into). **4** fig (estar en desacuerdo) to disagree (**con**, with).
▲ Conjugation model [47], like **empezar**.

tropezón 1 m (traspié) trip, stumble. **2** fig (error) slip-up, faux pas. **3** fam (de comida) chunk of food.
● a tropezones, fig in fits and starts. ‖ dar un tropezón, to trip.

tropical adj tropical.

trópico 1 m tropic. **– 2** trópicos, mpl tropics.
■ Trópico de Cáncer/Capricornio, Tropic of Cancer/Capricorn.

tropiezo 1 m (obstáculo) trip. **2** fig (error) blunder, faux pas; (revés) setback, mishap. **3** (riña) quarrel. **– 4** pres indic → **tropezar**.

tropismo m tropism.

tropo m trope.

troposfera f troposphere.

troquel m die.

troqueladora f stamping-press.

troquelar t to stamp.

trotaconventos f lit procuress, go-between.
▲ pl *trotaconventos*.

trotador,-ra adj trotting.

trotamundos mf globe-trotter; (mochilero) back-packer.
▲ pl *trotamundos*.

trotar 1 i to trot. **2** fig (andar) to bustle, run, run about.

trote 1 m (de caballo) trot. **2** fam fig (actividad) chasing about, hustle and bustle, bustle.
● al trote, at a trot. ‖ de todo trote / para todo trote, fig for everyday use, for everyday wear. ‖ no estar para trotes, fam not to be up to that: yo ya no estoy para estos trotes, I cannot keep up the pace any more.

trotón,-ona adj trotting.

trotskista 1 adj Trotskyist. **– 2** mf Trotskyist.

troupe f troupe.

trova f poem.

trovador,-ra m,f troubadour.

trovadoresco,-a adj troubadourish, of a troubadour.

trovar i to write poetry, write verses.

trovero,-a m,f trouvère.

Troya f Troy.
● aquí fue Troya, fig that's where the trouble began. ‖ arda Troya, come what may.
■ caballo de Troya, Trojan Horse.

troyano,-a 1 adj Trojan. **– 2** m,f Trojan.

trozo m piece, chunk.

trucaje m trick photography.

trucar 1 t (foto etc) to doctor, alter, tamper with. **2** AUTO to soup up.
▲ Conjugation model [1], like **sacar**.

trucha f trout.

truco 1 m (ardid) trick. **2** CINEM TV trick effect, trick camera shot. **3** (tranquillo) knack.
● coger el truco a algo, fam to get the knack of sth., get the hang of sth. ‖ tener truco, to be tricky.
■ truco publicitario, advertising stunt, advertising gimmick.

truculencia 1 f cruelty. **2** fig sensationalism.

truculento,-a 1 adj (cruel) cruel. **2** fig (excesivo) sensationalistic.

trueno 1 m thunder, thunderclap. **2** fam (joven) hare brain.

trueque m exchange, swap.

trufa 1 f (hongo) truffle. **2** (de chocolate) chocolate truffle.

trufar 1 t to stuff with truffles. **– 2** i fig to tell lies.

truhán,-ana *m,f* rogue, crook.
trulla *f* uproar, racket.
trullo *m arg* clink.
truncado,-a 1 *pp* → **trucar**. – 2 *adj* (*geometría*) truncated.
truncar 1 *t* (*cortar*) to truncate. 2 *fig* (*ilusiones, esperanzas*) to shatter, cut short. 3 *fig* (*escrito*) to leave unfinished; (*sentido*) to upset. – 4 **truncarse**, *p fig* (*ilusiones etc*) to cut short.
▲ Conjugation model [1], *like* **sacar**.
trust *m* trust, cartel.
▲ *pl* **trusts**.
tse-tsé *f* tsetse-fly.
tu 1 *adj* your: *tu coche,* your car; *tus coches,* your cars. 2 REL Thy.
tú 1 *pron* you. 2 REL Thou.
● **de tú a tú**, on equal terms. ‖ **tratar de tú**, to address as *tú*. ‖ **¡tú!**, hey you!
tuareg 1 *adj* Tuareg. – 2 *m* Tuareg.
tuba *f* tuba.
tuberculina *f* tuberculin.
tubérculo 1 *m* BOT tuber. 2 MED tubercle.
tuberculosis *f* tuberculosis.
▲ *pl* **tuberculosis**.
tuberculoso,-a 1 *adj* BOT tuberous. 2 MED tubercular, tuberculous.
tubería 1 *f* (*de agua*) piping, pipes *pl*, plumbing. 2 (*de gas, petróleo*) pipeline.
tuberosidad *f* tuberosity.
tuberoso,-a *adj* tuberous.
tubo 1 *m* (*de ensayo etc*) tube. 2 (*tubería*) pipe. 3 ANAT tube.
● **alucinar por un tubo**, *arg* to flip, freak out. ‖ **hacer pasar por un tubo. por el tubo**, *fig* to put the screws on sb. ‖ **pasar por el tubo**, *fig* to knuckle under. ‖ **tener algo por un tubo**, *arg* to have loads of, have tons of: *tiene videojuegos por un tubo,* he's got loads of videogames. ■ **falda tubo / vestido tubo**, tight skirt / tight dress. ‖ **tubo de ensayo**, test-tube. ‖ **tubo de escape**, exhaust pipe, exhaust. ‖ **tubo digestivo**, alimentary canal.
tubular 1 *adj* tubular. – 2 *m* bicycle tyre.
tucán *m* toucan.
tuerca *f* nut.
tuerto,-a 1 *adj* one-eyed, blind in one eye. – 2 *m,f* one-eyed person. – 3 **tuerto**, *m* (*agravio*) wrong, injustice.
● **quedarse tuerto,-a**, to go blind in one eye, become blind in one eye.
tuerzo *pres indic* → **torcer**.
tuétano 1 *m* marrow. 2 *fig* essence, core.
● **calado,-a hasta los tuétanos / mojado,-a hasta los tuétanos**, *fig* soaked to the skin. ‖ **hasta los tuétanos**, *fig* through and through.
tufarada *f* strong smell.
tufo 1 *m* (*mal olor*) pong, foul smell, stink. 2 (*emanación*) fume, vapour (*us* vapor).
tugurio 1 *m* (*choza*) shepherd's hut. 2 (*casucha*) hovel, shack. 3 *fig* hole, dive.
tul *m* tulle.
tulipa 1 *f* (*bot*) small tulip. 2 (*lámpara*) tulip-shaped lampshade.
tulipán *m* tulip.
tullidez *f* paralysis; (*incapacidad*) disability, disablement.
tullido,-a 1 *pp* → **tullir**. – 2 *adj* crippled, disabled. – 3 *m,f* cripple.
tullir 1 *t* (*maltratar*) to cripple. 2 (*de cansancio*) to wear out, tire out. – 3 **tullirse**, *p* to become crippled.

▲ Conjugation model [41], *like* **mullir**.
tumba *f* tomb, grave.
● **a tumba abierta**, at full speed. ‖ **ser una tumba**, *fig* not to breathe a word.
tumbado,-a 1 *pp* → **tumbar**. – 2 *adj* (*estirado*) lying, stretched out: *tumbado al sol*, lying in the sun.
tumbar 1 *t* (*derribar*) to knock out, knock over. 2 EDUC *fam* to fail. 3 *fig* (*perder el sentido*) to knock out: *el vino nos tumbó,* the wine knocked us out. – 4 *i* (*caer a tierra*) to fall down. 5 *fam* (*matar*) to bump off. – 6 **tumbarse**, *p* (*acostarse*) to lie down, stretch out. 7 (*arrellanarse*) to lounge, lie back.
● **tumbarse a la bartola**, *fam* to laze around.
tumbo *m* jolt, bump.
● **dar tumbos**, to jolt, bump along.
tumbona 1 *f* (*hamaca*) deck-chair. 2 (*silla extensible*) lounger.
tumefacción *f* swelling, tumefaction.
tumefacto,-a *adj* swollen.
tumor *m* tumour (*us* tumor).
■ **tumor cerebral**, brain tumour (*us* tumor).
túmulo 1 *m* (*montecillo*) tumulus, burial mound, barrow. 2 (*catafalco*) catafalque.
tumulto *m* tumult, commotion.
tumultuoso,-a *adj* tumultuous, riotous.
tuna *f* student minstrel group.
tunante,-a 1 *adj* rascal, rogue. – 2 *m,f* rascal, rogue. – 3 **tunanta**, *f* (*prostituta*) prostitute.
tunantear *i* to be roguish.
tunda 1 *f fam* thrashing, beating. 2 *fig* (*trabajo agotador*) exhausting job, drag.
tundir[1] *t* (*pieles etc*) to shear.
tundir[2] *t* (*golpear*) to thrash.
tundra *f* tundra.
tunear *i* to lead a vagrant life.
tunecino,-a 1 *adj* Tunisian. – 2 *m,f* Tunisian.
túnel *m* tunnel.
● **hacer un túnel**, DEP to slip the ball between an opposing player's legs.
■ **túnel aerodinámico**, wind-tunnel.
Túnez 1 *m* (*ciudad*) Tunis. 2 (*país*) Tunisia.
tungsteno *m* tungsten.
túnica *f* tunic.
tuno[1] *m* BOT prickly pear.
tuno,-a[2] 1 *m* (*copete*) rogue, crook. – 2 **tuno**, *m* (*de la tuna*) member of a *tuna*.
tuntún **al tuntún**, *loc adv fam* haphazardly, any old how.
● **al buen tuntún**, *fam* → **al tuntún**.
tupé 1 *m* (*copete*) tuft of hair, quiff. 2 *fam fig* (*atrevimiento*) nerve, cheek.
tupí 1 *adj* Tupi. – 2 *m,f* Tupi. – 3 *m* (*idioma*) Tupi.
tupido,-a 1 *pp* → **tupir**. – 2 *adj* dense, thick. 3 *fig* (*torpe*) clumsy, dense.
tupir 1 *i* (*apretar*) to pack tight, press down. – 2 **tupirse**, *p* (*comiento*) to stuff os. 3 (*ofuscarse*) to get muddled up, get in a muddle.
turba[1] 1 *f* (*combustible*) peat, turf. 2 (*abono*) peat, peat moss.
turba[2] *f* (*muchedumbre*) mob, crowd.
turbación 1 *f* (*alteración*) disturbance. 2 (*preocupación*) anxiety, worry. 3 (*desconcierto*) confusion, uneasiness.
turbado,-a 1 *pp* → **turbar**. – 2 *adj* (*alterado*) disturbed, unsettled. 3 (*preocupado*) worried, upset. 4 (*desconcertado*) confused.
turbador,-ra 1 *adj* (*que altera*) disturbing, unsettling. 2 (*preocupante*) worrying, upsetting. 3 (*desconcertante*) confusing, disconcerting.

turbamulta *f fam* mob.
turbante *m* turban.
turbar 1 *t* (*alterar*) to unsettle, disturb. 2 (*enturbiar*) to stir up. 3 (*preocupar*) to upset, worry. 4 (*desconcertar*) to baffle, put off. – 5 **turbarse**, *p* (*preocuparse*) to be upset, become upset. 6 (*desconcertarse*) to be confused, be baffled.
turbina *f* turbine.
turbio,-a 1 *adj* (*oscurecido*) cloudy, muddy, turbid. 2 *fig* (*dudoso*) shady, dubious. 3 *fig* (*turbulento*) turbulent. 4 *fig* (*confuso*) confused. 5 *fig* (*vista*) blurred.
turboalternador *m* turboalternator.
turbocompresor *m* turbocompressor.
turbodinamo *m* turbodynamo.
turbogenerador *m* turbogenerator.
turbonada *f* stormy downpour, squall.
turborreactor *m* turbojet, turbojet engine.
turbulencia *f* turbulence.
turbulento,-a *adj* turbulent, troubled.
turco,-a 1 *adj* Turkish. – 2 *m,f* (*persona*) Turk. – 3 **turco**, *m* (*idioma*) Turkish. – 4 **turca**, *f fam* (*borrachera*) drunkenness.
● **coger una turca,** *fam* to be plastered.
■ **cabeza de turco,** *fig* scapegoat.
turcomano,-a 1 *adj* Turkoman, Turcoman. – 2 *m,f* Turkoman, Turcoman. – 3 **turcomano**, *m* (*idioma*) Turkoman, Turcoman.
turgencia *f* turgidity, turgidness.
turgente *adj* turgid.
túrgido,-a *adj* turgid.
turismo 1 *m* (*gen*) tourism. 2 (*industria*) tourist trade, tourist industry. 3 AUTO private car, saloon.
● **hacer turismo,** (*país*) to go touring; (*ciudad, pueblo*) to go sightseeing.
turista *mf* tourist.
● **hacer el turista / hacer la turista,** *fig* to get taken in.
turístico,-a *adj* tourist.
● **de interés turístico,** of interest to tourists.
turmalina *f* tourmaline.
túrmix *m* liquidizer, blender.
▲ *Registered trademark; pl* **túrmix**.
turnar 1 *i* to alternate. – 2 **turnarse**, *p* to take turns.
turnedó *m* turnedos.
turno 1 *m* (*tanda*) turn, go: *es mi turno,* it's my turn; *¿a quién le toca el turno?,* who's next? 2 (*período de trabajo*) shift.
● **estar de turno,** to be on duty.
■ **turno de día / turno de noche,** day shift / night shift.

turolense 1 *adj* from Teruel, of Teruel. – 2 *mf* person from Teruel, inhabitant of Teruel.
turón *m* polecat.
turquesa 1 *adj* turquoise. – 2 *f* (*piedra*) turquoise. – 3 *m* (*color*) turquoise.
Turquestán *m* Turkestan, Turkistan.
Turquía *f* Turkey.
turrar *t* to roast, toast.
turrón *m type of* nougat.
turronería *f* shop selling nougat.
turulato,-a *adj fam* flabbergasted, flummoxed.
tururú *interj fam* certainly not!, no way!: *intenté convencerlo pero me dijo que tururú,* I tried to persuade him but he said no way.
● **estar tururú,** *fam* to be touched in the head.
turuta *adj fam* crazy, mad.
tute 1 *m* (*naipes*) card game. 2 *fig* (*esfuerzo*) beating, thrashing.
● **darse un tute,** *fam* to wear os. out.
tutear 1 *t* to address as *tú*. 2 *fig* to be on familiar terms with. – 3 **tutearse**, *p* (*uso recíproco*) to address each other as *tú*.
tutela 1 *f* JUR guardianship, tutelage. 2 *fig* protection, guidance.
● **bajo la tutela de,** under the protection of.
■ **pupilo,-a bajo tutela judicial,** ward of court.
tutelar *adj* tutelary.
tuteo *m* use of the *tú* form of address.
tutiplén a tutiplén, *loc adv fam* galore.
tutor,-ra 1 *m,f* JUR guardian. 2 *fig* protector, guide. 3 EDUC tutor. – 4 tutor, *m* AGR stake, prop.
tutoría 1 *f* JUR guardianship, tutelage. 2 EDUC post of tutor.
tutti frutti *adj* tutti-frutti.
tutú *m* tutu.
Tuvalu *m* Tuvalu.
tuve *pret indic* → **tener**.
tuyo,-a 1 *adj* of yours, one of your: *¿es primo tuyo?,* is he a cousin of yours?, is he one of your cousins? 2 REL thy, of thine. – 3 *pron* yours, your own: *el tuyo está allí,* yours is there. 4 REL thine, thine own. – 5 **lo tuyo,** *m* (*lo que es tuyo*) what is yours; (*lo que te concierne*) your business, your own business. – 6 **los tuyos,** *mpl* (*familiares*) your family *sing;* (*amigos*) your friends.
TV *abr* (*televisión*) television; (*abreviatura*) TV.
TVE *abr* (*Televisión Española*) Spanish national broadcasting corporation.

U

U, u *f* (*la letra*) U, u.
  ▲ *pl* úes.
u *conj or: diez u once,* ten or eleven.
  ▲ Used *before words beginning with* o *or* ho; *see also* o.
Uagadugú *m* Ouagadougou.
uau *interj* wow!
ubérrimo,-a *adj fml* very fertile, rich; (*vegetación*) luxuriant.
ubicación *f* location, position.
ubicar 1 *i* to be, be situated. – 2 *t* AM (*situar*) to locate, situate, place.
  ▲ Conjugation model |1|, *like sacar.*
ubicuidad *f* ubiquity.
ubicuo,-a *adj* ubiquitous, omnipresent.
ubre *f* udder.
UCD *abr* POL (*Unión de Centro Democrático*) Union of the Democratic Centre (*Spanish centre party*).
UCI *abr* MED (*Unidad de Cuidados Intensivos*) intensive care unit; (*abreviatura*) ICU.
ucraniano,-a 1 *adj* Ukranian. – 2 *m,f* (*persona*) Ukranian.
ucranio,-a 1 *adj* Ukranian. – 2 *m,f* (*persona*) Ukranian. – 3 *ucranio, m* (*idioma*) Ukranian.
Ud. *abr* (*usted*) you.
UDC *abr* POL (*Unió Democràtica de Catalunya*) Catalan centre party.
Uds. *abr* (*ustedes*) you.
UE *abr* (*Unión Europea*) European Union; (*abreviatura*) EU.
UEFA *abr* (*Unión de Asociaciones Europeas de Fútbol*) Union of European Football Associations; (*abreviatura*) UEFA.
UEO *abr* (*Unión de la Europa Occidental*) Western European Union; (*abreviatura*) WEU.
uf 1 *interj* (*alivio, calor, cansancio*) phew! 2 (*asco*) ugh!
ufanamente 1 *adv* (*con orgullo*) proudly. 2 (*con satisfacción*) happily.
ufanarse *p* to boast (**con/de,** of).
ufanía *f* conceit, arrogance.
ufano,-a 1 *adj* (*engreído*) conceited, arrogant. 2 (*satisfecho*) satisfied, happy. 3 (*desenvuelto*) confident.
ufología *f* ufology.
Uganda *f* Uganda.
ugandés,-esa 1 *adj* Ugandan. – 2 *m,f* Ugandan.
ugetista 1 *adj* related to the UGT. – 2 *mf* member of the UGT.
UGT *abr* (*Unión General de Trabajadores*) Socialist-led trade union.
uh 1 *interj* (*desilusión*) ah!, aw! 2 (*desdén*) ooh!
UIMP *abr* EDUC (*Universidad Internacional Menéndez y Pelayo*) Menéndez y Pelayo International University.
ujier *m* usher.
ukelele *m* ukelele.
úlcera *f* ulcer.
  ■ **úlcera de estómago,** stomach ulcer.

ulceración *f* ulceration.
ulcerar 1 *t* to ulcerate. – 2 **ulcerarse,** *p* to ulcerate.
ulceroso,-a *adj* ulcerous.
ulmáceas *fpl* ulmaceae.
ulterior 1 *adj* (*más allá*) further. 2 (*siguiente*) subsequent; (*posterior*) later, further.
ulteriormente *adv* subsequently, afterwards.
ultimación *f* completion, conclusion.
últimamente *adv* lately, recently.
ultimar *t* to finish, complete, conclude.
ultimátum 1 *m* ultimatum. 2 *fam* final word.
  ▲ *pl* ultimátum.
último,-a 1 *adj* last. 2 (*más reciente*) latest; (*de dos*) latter. 3 (*más alejado*) furthest; (*más abajo*) bottom, lowest; (*más arriba*) top; (*más atrás*) back. 4 (*definitivo*) final.
  ● **a la última,** up to date. ‖ **a últimos de,** towards the end of. ‖ **por último,** finally. ‖ **ser lo último,** *fam* (*el colmo*) to be just too much. ‖ **estar en las últimas,** (*moribundo*) to be at death's door; (*arruinado*) to be down and out.
ultra- 1 *pref* ultra. – 2 **ultra,** *adj fam* extreme right-wing. – 3 *mf fam* extreme right-winger.
ultraconservador,-ra 1 *adj* ultraconservative. – 2 *m,f* ultraconservative.
ultracorrección *f* hypercorrection.
ultracorto,-a *adj* ultrashort.
ultraderecha *f* extreme right (wing).
ultraderechista 1 *adj* extreme right-wing. – 2 *mf* extreme right-winger.
ultraísmo *m* ultraism.
ultrajante *adj* outrageous, insulting, offensive.
ultrajar *t* to outrage, insult, offend.
ultraje *m* outrage, insult, offence (US offense).
ultraligero,-a 1 *adj* ultralight, microlight. – 2 **ultraligero,** *m* ultralight, microlight.
ultramar *m* overseas: *viene de ultramar,* it comes from overseas, it's imported.
ultramarino,-a 1 *adj* overseas. – 2 **ultramarino,** *m* (*tienda*) grocer's (shop), US grocery (store). – 3 **ultramarinos,** *mpl* (*comestibles*) groceries.
ultramicroscopio *m* ultramicroscope.
ultramoderno,-a *adj* ultramodern.
ultranza 1 **a ultranza,** *loc adv* (*a muerte*) to the death. 2 (*a todo trance*) at all costs, at any price. 3 (*acérrimo*) out-and-out, extreme.
ultrapasar *t* to surpass, go beyond.
ultrarrápido,-a *adj* extra-fast.
ultrarrojo,-a *adj* infrared.
ultrasensible *adj* hypersensitive.
ultrasónico,-a *adj* ultrasonic.
ultrasonido *m* ultrasound.
ultratumba 1 *adv* beyond the grave. – 2 *f* afterlife.
ultravioleta *adj* ultraviolet.
  ▲ *pl* ultravioleta.

ulular 1 *i* (*animal*) to howl; (*búho*) to hoot. **2** *fig* to howl.
umbilical *adj* umbilical.
umbral 1 *m* threshold. **2** *fig* threshold, outset.
● **en el umbral de la muerte,** at death's door.
umbrela *f* umbrella.
umbría *f* → **umbrío,-a.**
umbrío,-a 1 *adj* shady. − **2 umbría,** *f* shady place.
umbroso,-a *adj* shady.
un,-na 1 *art indef* a, an: *un libro,* a book; *un ojo,* an eye. −
2 *adj* (*numeral*) one: *tiene un año,* he's one year old. **3**
(*indef*) some: *un día volverá,* he'll come some day.
▲ In **2** and **3**, *used before singular masculine noun. See uno,-a.*
unánime *adj* unanimous.
unanimidad *f* unanimity.
● **por unanimidad,** unanimously.
unción 1 *f* unction. **2** *fig* (*devoción*) devotion, fervour.
uncir *t* to yoke.
▲ *Conjugation model* |3|, *like zurcir.*
undécimo,-a 1 *adj* eleventh. − **2** *m,f* (*ordinal, partitivo*)
eleventh.
▲ *See also* **sexto,-a.**
undulación *f* undulation; (*agua*) ripple.
undular 1 *t* (*rizar*) to wave. − **2** *i* (*moverse*) to undulate.
UNED *abr* EDUC (*Universidad Nacional de Educación a Distancia*) ≈ Open University; (*abreviatura*) OU.
ungir *t* to anoint.
▲ *Conjugation model* |6|, *like dirigir.*
ungüento *m* ointment.
unguiculado,-a *adj* unguiculate.
unguis *m* orbit.
ungulado,-a 1 *adj* ungulate, hoofed. − **2 ungulado,** *m*
ungulate, hoofed animal.
únicamente *adv* only.
unicameral *adj* unicameral, single-chamber.
unicelular *adj* unicellular, single-cell.
unicidad *f* uniqueness.
único,-a 1 *adj* (*solo*) only, sole: *la única persona,* the only
person; *lo único es que ...,* the thing is ... **2** (*extraordinario*) unique.
unicolor *adj* of one colour, single-coloured.
unicornio *m* unicorn.
unidad 1 *f* unit. **2** (*barco*) vessel; (*avión*) aircraft; (*de tren*)
carriage, coach: *el tren se componía de once unidades,*
the train was made up of eleven carriages. **3** (*cohesión*)
unity.
■ **unidad de cuidados intensivos,** intensive care
unit. ‖ **unidad de vigilancia intensiva,** intensive care
unit. ‖ **unidad móvil,** outside broadcasting unit.
unidimensional *adj* one-dimensional.
unidireccional *adj* unidirectional.
unido,-a 1 *pp* → **unir.** − **2** *adj* (*junto*) united. **3** (*avenido*)
attached: *estar muy unidos,* to be very close.
unifamiliar **vivienda unifamiliar,** *f* detached house.
unificación *f* unification.
unificador,-ra 1 *adj* unifying. − **2** *m,f* unifier.
unificar *t* to unify.
▲ *Conjugation model* |1|, *like sacar.*
uniformado,-a 1 *pp* → **uniformar.** − **2** *adj* in uniform,
uniformed.
uniformar 1 *t* (*igualar*) to make uniform, standardize. **2**
(*poner un uniforme*) to put into uniform, give a uniform.
uniforme 1 *adj* uniform. **2** (*superficie*) even. − **3** *m* (*prenda*)
uniform.
uniformemente 1 *adv* uniformly. **2** (*superficie*) evenly.
uniformidad 1 *f* (*igualdad*) uniformity. **2** (*de superficie*)
evenness.

uniformizar *t* to standardize.
▲ *Conjugation model* |4|, *like realizar.*
unigénito,-a 1 *adj* only-begotten. − **2 el Unigénito,** *m*
the Son of God, Jesus Christ.
unilateral *adj* unilateral.
unilateralmente *adv* unilaterally.
unión 1 *f* union. **2** TÉC (*acoplamiento*) joining; (*junta*) joint.
● **en unión de,** together with. ‖ **la unión hace la fuerza,** there is strength in numbers.
unionismo *m* unionism.
unionista *adj* unionist.
uníparo,-a *adj* uniparous.
unipersonal 1 *adj* single, individual. **2** GRAM unipersonal.
unir 1 *t* (*juntar*) to unite, join, join together. **2** (*combinar*)
to combine (**a,** with). **3** (*enlazar*) to link (**a,** to).
● **unirse en matrimonio,** *fml* to unite in marriage.
unisex *adj* unisex.
▲ *pl* **unisex.**
unisexual *adj* unisexual.
unisón *adj-m* → **unísono,-a.**
unisonancia *f* unison.
unísono,-a 1 *adj* unisonous, in harmony. − **2 unísono,**
m harmony, unison.
● **al unísono,** in unison.
unitario,-a *adj* unitary.
■ **precio unitario,** unit price.
Univ. *abr* (*Universidad*) university; (*abreviatura*) univ,
Univ.
univalvo,-a *adj* univalve.
universal 1 *adj* universal: *la historia universal,* world history. − **2 universales,** *mpl* (*filosofía, lingüística, etc*) uni-
versals.
universalidad *f* universality.
universalización *f* universalization.
universalizar *t* to universalize.
universalmente *adv* universally.
universidad *f* university.
■ **universidad a distancia,** Open University. ‖ **universidad laboral,** technical college.
universitario,-a 1 *adj* university. − **2** *m,f* (*que está estudiando*) university student; (*licenciado*) university graduate.
universo *m* universe.
unívoco,-a *adj* univocal.
uno,-a 1 *adj* (*numeral*) one: *el número uno,* number one.
− **2** *pron* one (*de ellos*), one of them. **3** (*impersonal*)
one, you: *uno tiene que velar por sus intereses,* one has
to look after one's own interests. **4** *fam* (*persona*) someone, somebody: *estaba hablando con una,* he was
talking to some woman. − **5** uno, *m* (*número*) one. **6**
la una, *f* (*hora*) one o'clock. − **7** unos,-as, *adj* (*indefinido*)
some; (*aproximado*) about, around: *unas cajas,* some
boxes; *habrá unos treinta,* there must be around thirty.
● **a (la) una,** together. ‖ **de uno,-a en uno,-a,** one by
one. ‖ **hacerle una a algn.,** to play a dirty trick on sb.
‖ **me dieron una buena,** I got a really good thrashing.
‖ **uno,-a a uno,-a,** one by one. ‖ **una de dos,** it's either
one thing or the other. ‖ **uno,-a y no más (Santo Tomás),** once bitten, twice shy.
untadura 1 *f* (*acción*) greasing, smearing. **2** (*sustancia*)
grease, ointment.
untar 1 *t* to grease, smear: *untar pan con mantequilla,* to
spread butter on bread. **2** *fam* (*sobornar*) to bribe. − **3**
untarse, *p fam* (*enriquecerse*) to line one's pockets,
feather one's nest.

● **untarse de algo,** to get sth. all over one: *se había untado de grasa,* he'd got grease all over him.

unto *m* grease, ointment.

untuosidad *f* greasiness, oiliness.

untuoso,-a *adj* unctuous, greasy, oily.

untura *f* ointment.

uña 1 *f* nail; (*del dedo*) fingernail; (*del dedo del pie*) toenail. 2 (*garra*) claw; (*pezuña*) hoof.
● **arreglarse las uñas,** to manicure one's nails. ‖ **estar de uñas,** *fig* to be at daggers drawn. ‖ **hacerse las uñas,** to do one's nails. ‖ **ser uña y carne,** to be inseparable.

uñada *f* scratch (with nail).

uñero 1 *m* (*inflamación*) whitlow. 2 (*uña clavada*) ingrowing nail.

upa *interj* up you go!

úpala *interj* up you go!

upar *t* to lift (up).

uperización *f* Ultra-Heat Treatment.

uperizar *t* to treat at an ultrahigh temperature.
■ **leche uperizada,** UHT milk.
▲ *Conjugation model* |4|, *like realizar.*

Urales los Urales, *mpl* the Urals.

uralita *f* uralite.
▲ *Registered trademark.*

uranio *m* uranium.

Urano *m* Uranus.

urbanidad *f* urbanity, politeness.

urbanismo *m* town planning.

urbanista *mf* town planner.

urbanístico,-a *adj* town-planning, urban.

urbanización 1 *f* (*proceso*) urbanization. 2 (*conjunto residencial*) housing development, housing estate.

urbanizar *t* to urbanize, develop.
■ **zona urbanizada,** built-up area.
▲ *Conjugation model* |4|, *like realizar.*

urbano,-a 1 *adj* urban, city: *la vida urbana,* city life. – 2 *m,f fam* (*hombre*) (traffic) policeman; (*mujer*) (traffic) policewoman.

urbe *f* large city, metropolis.

urca 1 *f* (*embarcación*) hooker. 2 (*animal*) orc.

urchilla *f* archil.

urdimbre 1 *f* (*textil*) warp. 2 *fig* (*trama*) intrigue.

urdir 1 *t* (*textil*) to warp. 2 *fig* (*tramar*) to plot, scheme.

urea *f* urea.

uremia *f* uraemia, *us* uremia.

uréter *m* ureter.

uretra *f* urethra.

urgencia 1 *f* urgency. 2 (*necesidad*) urgent need, pressing need. 3 (*emergencia*) emergency. – 4 *fpl* (*servicio*) casualty department *sing,* casualty *sing, us* emergency room.
● **en (un) caso de urgencia,** in an emergency.

urgente 1 *adj* urgent. 2 (*correo*) express (post, *us* mail), first-class (post, *us* mail).

urgentemente *adv* urgently.

urgir *i* to be urgent, be pressing: *¿te urge?,* is it urgent?; *¿te urge tenerlo?,* do you need it urgently?
▲ *Conjugation model* |6|, *like dirigir.*

úrico,-a *adj* uric.

urinario,-a 1 *adj* urinary. – 2 urinario, *m* (*retrete*) urinal.

urna 1 *f* POL ballot box. 2 (*vasija*) urn. 3 (*caja*) glass case.
● **acudir a las urnas,** *fig* to vote.

uro *m* aurochs, urus.

urogallo *m* capercaillie.

urogenital *adj* urogenital.

urología *f* urology.

urólogo,-a *m,f* urologist.

urraca 1 *f* magpie. 2 *fig* (*cotorra*) chatterbox.

URSS *abr* (*Unión de Repúblicas Socialistas Soviéticas*) Union of Socialist Soviet Republics; (*abreviatura*) USSR.

ursulina 1 *f* Ursuline nun. 2 (*mujer recatada*) prudish woman.

urticáceas *fpl* urticaceae.

urticaria *f* hives *pl,* urticaria.

Uruguay *m* Uruguay.

uruguayo,-a 1 *adj* Uruguayan. – 2 *m,f* Uruguayan.

usado,-a 1 *pp →* **usar.** – 2 *adj* (*gastado*) worn out, old. 3 (*de segunda mano*) secondhand, used: *un coche usado,* a secondhand car.

usanza *f lit* fashion, custom.
● **a la antigua usanza,** in the old style.

usar 1 *t* to use. 2 (*prenda*) to wear. – 3 *i* to use (**de,** -): *usó de sus encantos para conseguir el trabajo,* he used his charm to get the job. 4 **usarse,** *p* (*estar de moda*) to be used, be in fashion: *esta palabra ya no se usa,* this word is no longer used.
● **de usar y tirar,** throwaway. ‖ **sin usar,** brand-new.

usía *pron fml* (*hombre*) Your Lordship; (*mujer*) Your Ladyship.

uso 1 *m* use. 2 (*ejercicio*) exercise: *el uso de un privilegio,* the exercise of a privilege. 3 (*de prenda*) wearing. 4 (*costumbre*) usage, custom. 5 GRAM usage.
● **al uso,** in the style of, after the fashion of: *al uso francés,* in the French style. ‖ **estar en buen uso,** to be in good working order. ‖ **estar fuera de uso,** to be out of use, be obsolete. ‖ **hacer uso de la palabra,** to take the floor.
■ **usos y costumbres,** ways and customs.

USO *abr* (*Unión Sindical Obrera*) *professional worker's union.*

usted *pron fml* you.
● **tratar a algn. de usted,** to use the polite form of address with sb.
▲ *pl* **ustedes.**

usual *adj* usual, common.

usualmente *adv* usually.

usuario,-a *m,f* user.

usufructo *m* usufruct, use.

usufructuar *t* to have the usufruct of, usufruct.
▲ *Conjugation model* |11|, *like actuar.*

usufructuario,-a 1 *adj* usufructuary. – 2 *m,f* usufructuary.

usura *f* usury.

usurario,-a *adj* usurious.

usurero,-a *m,f* usurer.

usurpación *f* usurpation.

usurpador,-ra 1 *adj* usurping. – 2 *m,f* usurper.

usurpar *t* to usurp.

utensilio 1 *m* (*herramienta*) tool, utensil. 2 (*aparato*) device, implement.

uterino,-a *adj* uterine.

útero *m* uterus, womb.

útil[1] *adj* useful.
■ **día útil,** working day.

útil[2] *m* (*herramienta*) tool, instrument.
■ **útiles de escritorio,** writing materials. ‖ **útiles de labranza,** agricultural implements.

utilería *f* (stage) props *pl.*

utilidad 1 *f* utility, usefulness: *de gran utilidad,* very useful. 2 (*beneficio*) profit.

utilitario,-a 1 *adj* utilitarian. – 2 **utilitario,** *m* (*coche*) utility vehicle.

utilitarismo *m* utilitarianism.
utilitarista 1 *adj* utilitarian. – **2** *mf* utilitarian.
utilizable *adj* usable, fit for use.
utilización *f* use.
utilizar *t* to use, make use of.
  ▲ Conjugation model [4], *like realizar.*
utillaje *m* tools *pl*, equipment.
útilmente *adv* usefully.
utopía *f* Utopia.
utópico,-a 1 *adj* Utopian. – **2** *m,f* Utopian.
utrero,-a *m,f* young bull.
utrículo *m* utricle.
uuuu *interj* ooh!
UV *abr* POL (*Unión Valenciana*) Valencian regional party.
uva *f* grape.
  ● **estar de mala uva,** *fam* to be in a bad mood. ‖ **tener mala uva,** *fam* (*de mal humor*) to be in a bad mood; (*mal*

carácter) to be a nasty piece of work, be bad-tempered. ‖ **de uvas a peras,** once in a blue moon.
  ■ **uva de mesa,** dessert grape. ‖ **uva moscatel,** muscatel grape. ‖ **uva pasa,** raisin.
uve *f name of the letter v.*
  ● **en forma de uve,** V-shaped.
  ■ **uve doble,** *name of the letter w.*
UVI *abr* MED (*unidad de vigilancia intensiva*) intensive care unit; (*abreviatura*) ICU.
úvula *f* uvula.
uvular *adj* uvular.
uxoricida *m* wife-murderer.
uxoricidio *m* uxoricide.
uy 1 *interj* (*dolor*) ow!, ouch! **2** (*calor, frío, miedo*) ooh!
uzbeco,-a 1 *adj* Uzbek. – **2** *m,f* (*persona*) Uzbek. – **3** uzbeco, *m* (*idioma*) Uzbek.
Uzbekistán *m* Uzbekistan.

V

V, v f (la letra) V, v.
V¹ abr (usted) you.
V² sím (voltio) volt; (símbolo) V.
v.¹ abr (véase) see; (abreviatura) s.
v.² abr (vide) vide; (abreviatura) v.
v.³ abr (verso) verse; (abreviatura) v.
V/ abr (visto) approved.
V.A. abr (Vuestra Alteza) Your Highness.
vaca I f cow. 2 (carne) beef. 3 (cuero) cowhide.
● ponerse como una vaca, fam to stuff one's face. ‖ ya vendrán las vacas gordas, the good times will come.
■ las vacas flacas, the lean years. ‖ las vacas gordas, the years of plenty. ‖ vaca lechera, dairy cow. ‖ vaca marina, sea cow. ‖ vaca sagrada, sacred cow.
vacación f holiday, holidays pl, us vacation: *se fueron de vacaciones a Mallorca,* they went to Majorca for their holidays.
● estar de vacaciones, to be on holiday. ‖ irse de vacaciones, to go on holiday.
■ vacaciones a la sombra, fam time spent in jail. ‖ vacaciones de verano, summer holidays. ‖ vacaciones escolares, school holidays. ‖ vacaciones pagadas, paid holidays.
▲ Generally used in plural.
vacacional adj holiday, us vacation.
vacada f herd of cows.
vacante I adj vacant. – 2 f vacancy.
● cubrir las vacantes, to fill the vacancies.
■ puesto vacante, vacant position.
vacar I i (quedar vacante) to fall vacant. 2 (estar vacante) to be vacant.
▲ Conjugation model [1], like *sacar.*
vaciadero I m (conducto) sewer. 2 (vertedero) dumping ground, rubbish tip.
vaciado I m (fabricación en molde) casting, moulding (us molding). 2 (de un documento) extraction of information. 3 (dejar vacío) emptying; (dejar hueco) hollowing out. 4 INFORM dumping.
■ vaciado de yeso, plaster casting. ‖ vaciado en molde, casting in a mould.
vaciante f ebb tide.
vaciar I t (recipiente) to empty; (local) to empty, clear. 2 (contenido) to pour away, pour out. 3 (dejar hueco) to hollow out. 4 (moldear) to cast, mould (us mold). 5 (afilar) to sharpen. 6 (escrito) to take information from: *hemos vaciado las revistas para hacer un índice de materias,* we've taken information from the magazines to make a table of contents. – 7 i (ríos etc) to flow (en, into). – 8 vaciarse, p (dejar vacío) to empty. 9 fam fig (desahogarse) to let it all out.
▲ Conjugation model [13], like *desviar.*
vacilación I f (duda) hesitation, wavering. 2 (falta de decisión) irresolution. 3 (oscilación) swaying, vacillation.

● sin vacilaciones, without hesitation.
vacilante I adj (dubitativo) hesitating, irresolute. 2 (voz) hesitant, faltering; (luz) flickering; (paso, mesa, etc) unsteady, shaky.
vacilar I i (oscilar) to sway, vacillate. 2 (estar poco firme) to wobble. 3 (al andar) to sway, stagger, wobble; (al hablar) to falter. 4 (luz) to flicker. 5 fig (dudar) to hesitate, waver. 6 fam (tomar el pelo) to joke, tease: *¡no me vaciles!,* don't tease me! 7 fam (presumir) to show off.
● hacer vacilar, fig to shake. ‖ sin vacilar, without hesitation.
■ memoria que vacila, shaky memory.
vacile m fam teasing.
vacilón,-ona m,f fam teaser, joker.
vacío,-a I adj (gen) empty: *el cine está vacío,* the cinema is empty; *la botella está vacía,* the bottle is empty. 2 (no ocupado) vacant, unoccupied; (sin muebles) unfurnished. 3 (hueco) hollow. 4 fig (vano) vain, conceited. 5 fig (palabras, conversación) empty. – 6 vacío, m (gen) emptiness, void. 7 (hueco) gap; (espacio) space, space; (espacio en blanco) blank space. 8 (vacante) vacancy. 9 FÍS vacuum. 10 fig (falta) emptiness, void.
● caer en el vacío, fig to fall on deaf ears. ‖ en vacío, FÍS in a vacuum. ‖ envasar al vacío, to vacuum-pack. ‖ hacer el vacío a algn., fig to cold-shoulder sb., send sb. to Coventry. ‖ sentir un gran vacío, fig to feel empty. ‖ tener el estómago vacío, fig to feel hungry. ‖ tener la cabeza vacía, fig to be empty-headed. ‖ volver con las manos vacías, fig to come back empty-handed. ‖ volver de vacío, (vehículo) to come back empty; (persona) to come back empty-handed.
vacuidad f vacuity, emptiness.
vacuna f → **vacuno,-a.**
vacunación f MED vaccination.
vacunar I t MED to vaccinate (**contra,** against). 2 fig to inure. – 3 vacunarse, p to be vaccinated.
vacuno,-a I adj bovine. – 2 vacuna, f MED vaccine. 3 (de la vaca) cowpox.
vacuo,-a adj vacuous, empty.
vacuola f vacuole.
vadeable I adj (río) fordable. 2 fig surmountable.
vadear I t (río) to ford. 2 fig (dificultad) to overcome.
vademécum m handbook, vademecum.
▲ pl **vademécum.**
vado I m (de río) ford. 2 (de acera) dropped kerb.
■ "vado permanente", "keep clear".
Vaduz m Vaduz.
vagabundear I i (vagar) to wander, roam. 2 (holgazanear) to idle, laze around.
vagabundeo I m (merodeo) wandering, roaming. 2 (holgazanería) idling, lazing around.
vagabundo,-a I adj wandering, roving; pey vagrant. – 2 m,f (trotamundos) wanderer, rover; pey vagrant, tramp, us hobo. 3 (sin casa) tramp, us hobo.

■ **perro vagabundo,** stray dog.
vagamente *adv* vaguely.
vagancia 1 *f* (*estar ocioso,-a*) idleness, laziness. 2 DER vagrancy.
vagar[1] *i* (*estar ocioso*) to idle about, loaf around.
▲ *Conjugation model* |7|, *like* **llegar.**
vagar[2] *i* (*errar*) to wander (**por,** about), roam (**por,** about): *pasa su tiempo vagando por el pueblo,* he spends his time wandering about town.
▲ *Conjugation model* |7|, *like* **llegar.**
vagido *m* cry of a newborn baby.
vagina *f* vagina.
vaginal *adj* vaginal.
vago,-a[1] 1 *adj* (*vacío*) empty; (*desocupado*) vacant. 2 (*holgazán*) lazy, idle. – 3 *m,f* (*holgazán*) idler, layabout, slacker. 4 JUR vagrant: *ley de vagos y maleantes,* vagrancy act.
● **hacer el vago,** to laze around.
vago,-a[2] *adj* (*impreciso*) vague: *idea vaga,* vague idea.
vagón 1 *m* (*para pasajeros*) carriage, coach, US car. 2 (*para mercancías*) wagon, goods van, truck, US boxcar, freight car.
■ **vagón cama,** sleeping-car. ‖ **vagón cisterna,** tanker. ‖ **vagón de mercancías,** goods van, goods wagon, US freight car. ‖ **vagón restaurante,** dining car.
vagoneta *f* small open wagon.
vaguada *f* lowest part of a valley, stream bed.
vaguear *i* → **vagar**[1] **and**[2].
vaguedad 1 *f* (*imprecisión*) vagueness: *la vaguedad de sus pensamientos,* the vagueness of his thoughts. 2 (*expresión imprecisa*) vague remark: *no dijo más que vaguedades,* he only made vague remarks.
● **hablar sin vaguedades,** to get straight to the point.
vaharada *f* puff, breath.
vaharina *f fam* breath, steam.
vahído *m* dizzy spell, fainting spell: *me dio un vahído,* I had a dizzy spell.
vaho 1 *m* (*vapor*) vapour (US vapor), steam: *hay vaho en el espejo,* the mirror's steamed up. 2 (*aliento*) breath. – 3 vahos, *mpl* MED inhalation *sing.*
vaina 1 *f* (*de espada etc*) sheath, scabbard. 2 (*de instrumento etc*) case. 3 BOT pod, husk. – 4 *mf fam fig* (*botarate*) good-for-nothing.
vainica *f* hemstitch.
vainilla *f* vanilla.
vaivén 1 *m* (*oscilación*) swaying, swinging, to-and-fro movement; (*balanceo*) rocking. 2 (*ir y venir*) coming and going, bustle. 3 *fig* (*cambio*) fluctuation, change. 4 *fig* (*intercambio*) exchange.
● **los vaivenes de la vida,** *fig* life's ups and downs.
vajilla *f* tableware, dishes *pl,* crockery.
● **lavar la vajilla,** to wash up.
■ **una vajilla,** a dinner service. ‖ **vajilla de porcelana,** chinaware. ‖ **vajilla de plata,** silverware.
valdepeñas *m* Valdepeñas wine.
▲ *pl* **valdepeñas.**
valdré *fut* → **valer.**
vale 1 *m* (*comprobante*) voucher; (*recibo*) receipt. 2 (*pagaré*) IOU, promissory note. – 3 *interj fam* OK!
■ **vale de devolución,** credit note.
valedero,-a *adj* valid.
valedor,-ra *m,f* protector, patron.
valencia *f* valency.
valenciano,-a 1 *adj* Valencian. – 2 *m,f* (*persona*) Valencian. – 3 **valenciano,** *m* (*idioma*) Valencian.
valentía 1 *f* (*valor*) bravery, courage. 2 (*acto*) heroic deed, bold act.

valentón,-ona 1 *adj pey* arrogant, boastful, bragging. – 2 *m,f pey* braggart.
valentonada *f pey* boast, boasting, bragging.
valer 1 *t* (*tener un valor de*) to be worth: *eso no vale más de 500 pesetas,* that's not worth more than 500 pesetas; *no vale nada,* it is worthless. 2 (*costar*) to cost, be: *vale mil pesetas el kilo,* it costs a thousand pesetas a kilo; *¿cuánto vale?,* how much is it? 3 (*hacer merecedor*) to win, earn, get: *el suspenso le valió un rapapolvo,* failing the exam earned him a good ticking-off. 4 (*ocasionar*) to cause: *me ha valido muchos problemas,* he's caused me a lot of problems. 5 MAT to equal. 6 (*proteger*) to protect: *le valió el casco,* his helmet protected him. – 7 *i* (*tener un valor de*) to be worth. 8 (*ser útil, adecuado*) to be useful, be of use, be good for: *¿te vale este libro?,* is this book any use (to you)?; *no valdrá para director,* he'll be useless as a manager, he won't make a good manager. 9 (*costar*) to cost, be worth. 10 (*ser válido, contar*) to count: *la primera tirada no vale, es de prueba,* the first throw doesn't count, it's a practice one. 11 (*tener validez*) to be valid; (*monedas*) to be legal tender: *esa billete aún vale,* that ticket is still valid. 12 (*ser suficiente, bastar*) to do, be enough: *con esto ya me vale,* this will be enough for me. 13 (*estar permitido*) to be allowed, be permitted: *no vale mirar las cartas de los demás,* looking at other people's cards isn't allowed; *vale todo,* anything goes, there are no holds barred. – 14 *m* (*valía*) value. – 15 **valerse,** *p* (*utilizar*) to use (**de,** of), make use (**de,** of): *se valió de un bastón,* he used a stick. 16 (*espabilarse*) to manage, cope.
● **hacer valer,** (*derechos*) to exercise; (*opinión*) to assert. ‖ **hacerse valer,** to assert os. ‖ **más vale / vale más,** it's better that way. ‖ **más vale que ... / vale más que ...,** you'd better ... ‖ **más vale prevenir que curar,** prevention is better than cure. ‖ **más vale tarde que nunca,** better late than never. ‖ **no hay excusa que valga,** no excuses. ‖ **no hay pero que valga,** no ifs and buts. ‖ **no vale,** it's no good. ‖ **no valer nada,** (*sin valor*) not to be worth a thing; (*ser inútil*) to be useless. ‖ *¿vale?,* *fam* all right?, O.K.? ‖ *¡vale!,* *fam* that's enough! ‖ *¡vale ya de ...!,* stop ...!: *¡vale ya de molestar!,* stop being a nuisance! ‖ **valer la pena,** to be worth it: *vale la pena ir,* it's worth going. ‖ *¡válgame Dios!,* Good heavens!, good help me! ‖ **valerse de todos los medios,** to try everything. ‖ **valerse por sí mismo,** to be able to manage on one's own.
▲ *Conjugation model* |89|.
valeriana *f* BOT valerian.
valeroso,-a *adj* courageous, brave.
Valetta La Valetta, *f* Valletta.
valgo *pres indic* → **valer.**
valía 1 *f* (*objeto*) value, worth. 2 (*persona*) worth, merit.
validadora *f* ticket stamping machine.
validar *t* to validate, make valid.
validez *f* validity.
valido[1] 1 *adj* favourite (US favorite). – 2 *m* favourite (US favorite).
válido,-a *adj* valid.
valiente 1 *adj* (*valeroso*) brave, courageous, bold. 2 (*fuerte*) strong, vigorous. 3 *fam fig* (*excelente*) fine, excellent: *¡valiente ayudante estás hecho!,* a fine assistant you are! 4 *pey* (*bravucón*) boastful, bragging. – 5 *mf* (*valeroso*) brave person. 6 (*bravucón*) boaster, braggart.
valientemente *adv* bravely, courageously.
valija 1 *f* (*maleta*) suitcase, case. 2 (*de correos*) mailbag.
■ **valija diplomática,** diplomatic bag.

valimiento *m* favour (us favor), protection.
● tener valimiento con, to be in favor with.
valioso,-a *adj* valuable, precious.
valla 1 *f (cerca)* fence; *(construcción)* wall. 2 MIL stockade, fortification. 3 DEP hurdle: *100 metros vallas,* 100 metres hurdles. 4 *(para publicidad)* hoarding, us billboard. 5 *fig* obstacle, hindrance.
■ valla publicitaria, hoarding, us billboard.
valladar 1 *m fig (obstáculo)* obstacle, hindrance. 2 *fig (defensa)* defence (us defense).
vallado 1 *m (cerca)* fence. 2 MIL stockade.
vallar 1 *t* to fence (in), build a fence around.
valle *m* valley.
■ valle de lágrimas, *fig* vale of tears, valley of tears.
vallisoletano,-a 1 *adj* of Valladolid, from Valladolid. – 2 *m,f* person from Valladolid, inhabitant of Valladolid.
vallista *mf* hurdler.
valón,-ona 1 *adj* Walloon. – 2 *m,f* Walloon. – 3 **valón,** *m (idioma)* Walloon.
valor 1 *m (valía)* value, worth, merit: *una persona de gran valor,* a person of great merit. 2 *(precio)* price. 3 *(validez)* value: *estos billetes dejarán de tener valor muy pronto,* these tickets won't be valid soon. 4 *(importancia)* importance. 5 *(coraje)* courage, valour (us valor). 6 *(desvergüenza)* cheek, nerve: *tuvo valor para pedirle más,* she had the nerve to ask him for more. 7 *(talento)* talent: *es un actor de gran valor,* he's a very talented actor. 8 MAT MÚS value. – 9 **valores,** *mpl* FIN securities, bonds. 10 *(principios)* values.
● armarse de valor, to pluck up courage. ‖ dar valor a algo, to attach importance to sth. ‖ de valor, valuable. ‖ por el valor de, to the value of: *artículos por el valor de mil libras,* goods to the value of a thousand pounds. ‖ ¡qué valor!, what a nerve! ‖ quitar valor a algo, to reduce the value of sth. ‖ sin valor / sin ningún valor, worthless.
■ escala de valores, scale of values. ‖ objetos de valor, valuables. ‖ valor adquisitivo, purchasing power. ‖ valor alimenticio, food value, nutritional value. ‖ valor de mercado, market value. ‖ valor nominal, *(de cheque)* face value. ‖ valores en cartera, investments. ‖ valores inmuebles, real estate *sing.*
valoración 1 *f (tasación)* valuation, valuing. 2 *(revalorización)* appreciation.
valorar 1 *t (tasar)* to value, calculate the value of. 2 *(aumentar el valor)* to raise the value of.
● valorar a algn. en mucho, *fig* to hold sb. in high esteem.
valorización 1 *f (tasación)* valuation, valuing. 2 *(revalorización)* appreciation.
valorizar 1 *t (tasar)* to value. 2 *(revalorizar)* to raise the value of.
▲ Conjugation model |4|, *like realizar.*
valquiria *f* Valkyrie.
vals *m* waltz.
● bailar el vals, to waltz.
valuar *t* to value.
▲ Conjugation model |11|, *like actuar.*
valva *f* BOT ZOOL valve.
válvula *f* valve.
■ válvula de cierre, stopcock. ‖ válvula de seguridad, safety valve.
vampiresa *f fam* vamp, femme fatale.
vampirismo *m* vampirism.
vampiro 1 *m (espectro)* vampire. 2 *(mamífero)* vampire bat. 3 *fig* leech, parasite.

vanadio *m* vanadium.
vanagloria *f* vainglory.
vanagloriarse *p* to boast (**de,** of).
▲ Conjugation model |12|, *like cambiar.*
vanamente *adv* in vain, vainly: *la buscaron vanamente,* they searched for her in vain.
vandalismo *m* vandalism.
vándalo,-a 1 *adj* Vandal. – 2 *m,f* Vandal. 3 *fig* vandal.
vanguardia 1 *f* ART LIT avant-garde, vanguard. 2 MIL vanguard, van.
● ir a la vanguardia de, *fig* to be at the forefront of.
vanguardismo *m* avant-garde movement.
vanguardista 1 *adj* avant-garde. – 2 *mf* avant-gardist.
vanidad *f* vanity, conceit.
vanidoso,-a 1 *adj* vain, conceited. – 2 *m,f* vain person.
vanilocuencia *f* verbosity.
vano,-a 1 *adj (inútil)* vain, useless. 2 *(ilusorio)* illusory, futile. 3 *(frívolo)* frivolous. 4 *(arrogante)* vain, conceited. 5 *(infundado)* unfounded, groundless. – 6 *m* opening, bay.
● en vano, in vain.
Vanuatu *m* Vanuatu.
vapor 1 *m (gas)* vapour (us vapor), steam. 2 *(barco)* steamship, steamer. – 3 **vapores,** *mpl* MED arc hysteria *sing.*
● a todo vapor, at full steam, at great speed. ‖ al vapor, CULIN steamed.
■ barco de vapor, steamship, steamer. ‖ vapor de agua, water vapour (us vapor).
vaporización *f* vaporization.
vaporizador *m* vaporizer, spray, atomizer.
vaporizar 1 *t* to vaporize. – 2 **vaporizarse,** *p* to vaporize.
▲ Conjugation model |4|, *like realizar.*
vaporoso,-a 1 *adj* vaporous. 2 *fig (tejido)* sheer.
vapulear 1 *t (azotar)* to beat, thrash. 2 *fig (criticar)* to criticize, slate.
vapuleo 1 *m (zurra)* beating, thrashing. 2 *fig (crítica)* slating, hammering.
vaquería 1 *f (establo)* cowshed. 2 *(lechería)* dairy.
vaqueriza *f →* **vaquerizo,-a.**
vaquerizo,-a 1 *adj* cattle. – 2 *m,f* cowherd. – 3 **vaqueriza,** *f* cowshed.
■ corral vaquerizo, cattle pen.
vaquero,-a 1 *adj* cow, cattle. – 2 *m,f (pastor)* cowherd, us cowboy; *(pastora)* cowherd, us cowgirl. – 3 **vaqueros,** *mpl (pantalones)* jeans, pair of jeans.
vaqueta *f* cowhide.
vaquilla *f* heifer.
V.A.R. *abr (Vuestra Alteza Real)* Your Royal Highness.
vara 1 *f (palo)* staff, rod, pole. 2 *(de mando)* staff, mace. 3 *(medida de longitud)* unit of length equal to approximately 33 inches. 4 *(tauromaquia)* lance, pike.
● poner varas, *(tauromaquia)* to thrust at the bull. ‖ tener vara alta, *fig* to hold sway.
varadero *m* shipyard, dry dock.
varado,-a 1 *pp →* **varar.** – 2 *adj (anclado)* at anchor. 3 *(encallado)* stranded.
● estar varado,-a, to run aground.
varal 1 *m (vara larga)* staff, pole. 2 TEAT batten. 3 *fig (persona)* beanpole.
varapalo 1 *m (palo)* long pole. 2 *(golpe)* blow with a pole. 3 *fam fig (daño)* blow, setback.
varar 1 *i* MAR *(encallar)* to run aground. 2 *fig (un negocio)* to come to a standstill. – 3 *t* MAR *(sacar a la playa)* to beach.

varazo *m* blow with a pole.
varear 1 *t* (*golpear*) to beat with a pole. 2 (*fruta*) to knock down (with a pole). 3 (*toro*) to jab with the lance.
varec *m* BOT kelp.
vareo *m* knocking down (fruit from trees).
vareta 1 *f* (*para cazar*) lime-twig. 2 (*de color*) stripe.
● **irse de vareta,** *fam fig* to have diarrhoea.
variabilidad *f* variability.
variable 1 *adj* variable, changeable. – 2 *f* MAT variable.
variación *f* variation, change.
● **sin variación,** unchanged.
■ **variación magnética,** magnetic declination.
variado,-a 1 *pp →* **variar.** – 2 *adj* varied, mixed. 3 (*galletas, helados*) assorted.
variante 1 *adj* variable. – 2 *f* (*versión*) variant. 3 (*diferencia*) difference.
variar 1 *t* (*cambiar*) to change. 2 (*dar variedad*) to vary, give some variety to: *tendrían que variar la carta,* they should vary the menu. – 3 *i* (*cambiar*) to change: *han variado de planes,* they have changed their plans. 4 (*diferir*) to be different (**de,** to), differ (**de,** from): *lo que dices varía de tus primeras declaraciones,* what you're saying differs from your first statement. 5 MAT to vary.
● **para variar,** *irón* as usual, just for a change.
▲ *Conjugation model* |13|, *like* **desviar.**
varice *f* varicose vein.
varicela *f* MED chickenpox, varicella.
varicoso,-a 1 *adj* varicose. – 2 *m,f* person suffering from varicose veins.
variedad 1 *f* variety, diversity: *una gran variedad de productos,* a wide variety of products. 2 BOT ZOOL variety. – 3 **variedades,** *fpl* TEAT variety show *sing.*
● **en la variedad está el gusto,** variety is the spice of life.
varilla 1 *f* (*vara*) stick, rod. 2 (*de paraguas, abanico*) rib; (*de corsé*) stay.
varillaje *m* ribs *pl,* ribbing.
vario,-a 1 *adj* (*diverso*) different, diverse. 2 (*variado*) varied, assorted. 3 (*mudable*) changeable, variable. – 4 **varios,** *mpl* (*algunos*) some, several, a number of: *varios de ellos están sobre la mesa,* some of them are on the table; *surgieron varios problemas,* a number of problems arose.
variopinto,-a 1 *adj* (*diverso*) diverse, assorted. 2 (*mezclado*) mixed, varied: *público variopinto,* mixed audience.
varita *f* small stick.
■ **varita mágica,** magic wand.
variz *f* varicose vein.
▲ *pl* **varices.**
varón 1 *m* (*hombre*) man; (*chico*) boy. 2 (*sexo*) male.
● **ser un santo varón,** *fam* to be a kind soul.
■ **hijo varón,** male child, boy.
varonil *adj* manly, virile, male.
Varsovia *f* Warsaw.
■ **Pacto de Varsovia,** Warsaw Pact.
vas *pres indic →* **ir.**
vasallaje 1 *m* HIST vassalage. 2 *fig* servitude, subjection, serfdom.
● **rendir vasallaje,** to pay homage.
vasallo,-a 1 *adj* HIST vassal. 2 (*súbdito*) subject. – 3 *m,f* HIST vassal. 4 (*súbdito*) subject.
vasar *m* kitchen shelf.
vasco,-a 1 *adj* Basque. – 2 *m,f* (*persona*) Basque. – 3 **vasco,** *m* (*idioma*) Basque.
■ **País Vasco,** Basque Country.
vascón,-ona 1 *adj* of the Vascons, pertaining to the Vascons. – 2 *m,f* Vascon.

vascongado,-a 1 *adj* Basque. – 2 *m,f* Basque. – 3 **vascongado,** *m* (*idioma*) Basque. – 4 **Vascongadas,** *fpl* the Basque Country.
vascuence *m* Basque.
vascular *adj* vascular.
vascularización *f* vascularization.
vasectomía *f* vasectomy.
vaselina 1 *f* (*sustancia*) vaseline. 2 DEP chip.
● **dar vaselina a algn.,** *fam* to soft-soap sb.
▲ *Registered trademark.*
vasija *f* vessel, pot, jar.
vaso 1 *m* (*para beber*) glass. 2 (*para flores*) vase. 3 ANAT vessel.
■ **vaso capilar,** capillary. ‖ **vasos comunicantes,** communicating vessels. ‖ **vasos sanguíneos,** blood vessels.
vasoconstricción *f* vasoconstriction.
vasodilatación *f* vasodilatation.
vástago 1 *m* BOT shoot, bud. 2 *fig* (*descendencia*) offspring. 3 TÉC rod, stem.
vastedad *f* vastness, immensity.
vasto,-a *adj* vast, immense, huge.
vate 1 *m* lit (*adivino*) prophet. 2 lit (*poeta*) poet.
váter *m fam* toilet.
vaticano,-a 1 *adj* Vatican. – 2 **el Vaticano,** *m* the Vatican.
■ **Concilio Vaticano,** Vatican Council. ‖ **la Ciudad Vaticana,** the Vatican City.
vaticinador,-ra 1 *adj* prophesying, predicting. – 2 *m,f* prophet, seer.
vaticinar *t* to predict, foretell, prophesy.
vaticinio *m* prophecy, prediction.
vatio *m* watt.
vaya[1] *pres subj & imperat →* **ir.**
vaya[2] *interj* what a: *¡vaya idea!,* what an idea!
● **¡vaya, vaya!,** well, well!
VºBº *abr* (*visto bueno*) approval, OK.
Vd. *abr* (*usted*) you.
Vdo, -a. *abr* (*viudo,-a - hombre*) widower; (*- mujer*) widow.
ve[1] *pres indic →* **ver.**
ve[2] *imperat →* **ir.**
V.E. *abr* (*Vuestra Excelencia*) Your Excellency.
vecinal *adj* local.
■ **camino vecinal,** country road.
vecindad 1 *f* (*lugar*) neighbourhood (US neighborhood), vicinity. 2 (*vecinos*) neighbours *pl* (US neighbors *pl*), residents *pl,* community.
■ **casa de vecindad,** block of flats.
vecindario 1 *m* (*lugar*) neighbourhood (US neighborhood). 2 (*vecinos*) neighbours *pl* (US neighbors *pl*), community, residents *pl.* – 3 *f* (*población*) residents *pl,* inhabitants *pl.*
vecino,-a 1 *adj* nearby, next, neighbouring (US neighboring). – 2 *m,f* (*del barrio*) neighbour (US neighbor). 3 (*residente*) resident. 4 (*habitante*) inhabitant: *los vecinos de Manresa,* the inhabitants of Manresa.
■ **asociación de vecinos,** resident's association.
vector *m* vector.
vectorial *adj* vectorial.
veda 1 *f* (*prohibición*) prohibition. 2 (*de caza*) close season, US closed season.
● **levantar la veda,** to open the season.
vedado,-a 1 *pp →* **vedar.** – 2 *adj* forbidden, prohibited. – 3 **vedado,** *m* game preserve.
● **cazar en vedado,** to poach.

■ **coto vedado,** game preserve.
vedar 1 *t* (*prohibir*) to prohibit, forbid, ban. **2** (*impedir*) to prevent. **3** (*proyecto, idea*) to veto.
vedette *f* TEAT (*variedades*) star.
vega *f* fertile lowland, fertile plain.
vegetación 1 *f* vegetation. – **2 vegetaciones,** *fpl* MED adenoids.
vegetal 1 *adj* vegetable. – **2** *m* vegetable, plant. **3** (*persona*) vegetable.
vegetar 1 *i* (*plantas*) to vegetate, grow. **2** *fig* (*persona*) to vegetate.
vegetarianismo *m* vegetarianism.
vegetariano,-a 1 *adj* vegetarian. – **2** *m,f* vegetarian.
vegetativo,-a *adj* vegetative.
■ **estado vegetativo,** *fam* coma.
vehemencia *f* vehemence.
vehemente *adj* vehement.
vehículo 1 *m* (*gen*) vehicle. **2** (*coche*) car. **3** *fig* vehicle: *vehículo de intercambio,* vehicle for exchange. **4** *fig* (*enfermedades*) transmitter, carrier.
veinte 1 *adj* (*cardinal*) twenty; (*vigésimo*) twentieth. – **2** *m* (*número*) twenty; (*fecha*) twentieth.
■ **los locos años veinte,** the roaring twenties.
▲ *In 2, pl **veintes**. See also **seis**.*
veinteavo,-a 1 *adj* twentieth. – **2** *m,f* twentieth.
▲ *See also **sexto,-a**.*
veintena *f* (*exacto*) twenty; (*aproximado*) about twenty.
veinticinco 1 *adj* (*cardinal*) twenty-five; (*ordinal*) twenty-fifth. – **2** *m* (*número*) twenty-five; (*fecha*) twenty-fifth.
veinticuatro 1 *adj* (*cardinal*) twenty-four; (*ordinal*) twenty-fourth. – **2** *m* (*número*) twenty-four; (*fecha*) twenty-fourth.
veintidós 1 *adj* (*cardinal*) twenty-two; (*ordinal*) twenty-second. – **2** *m* (*número*) twenty-two; (*fecha*) twenty-second.
veintinueve 1 *adj* (*cardinal*) twenty-nine; (*ordinal*) twenty-ninth. – **2** *m* (*número*) twenty-nine; (*fecha*) twenty-ninth.
veintiocho 1 *adj* (*cardinal*) twenty-eight; (*ordinal*) twenty-eighth. – **2** *m* (*número*) twenty-eight; (*fecha*) twenty-eighth.
veintiséis 1 *adj* (*cardinal*) twenty-six; (*ordinal*) twenty-sixth. – **2** *m* (*número*) twenty-six; (*fecha*) twenty-sixth.
veintisiete 1 *adj* (*cardinal*) twenty-seven; (*ordinal*) twenty-seventh. – **2** *m* (*número*) twenty-seven; (*fecha*) twenty-seventh.
veintitantos,-as 1 *adj* (*cantidad*) twenty-odd, about twenty: *veintitantas personas,* about twenty-odd people. **2** (*fecha*) about the twentieth: *hacia el veintitantos de febrero,* on about the twentieth of February.
veintitrés 1 *adj* (*cardinal*) twenty-three; (*ordinal*) twenty-third. – **2** *m* (*número*) twenty-three; (*fecha*) twenty-third.
veintiún *adj* twenty-one.
▲ *Used only before masculine nouns; see also **veintiuno,-a**.*
veintiuno,-a 1 *adj* (*cardinal*) twenty-one; (*ordinal*) twenty-first. – **2** *m* (*número*) twenty-one; (*fecha*) twenty-first.
vejación 1 *f* (*maltrato*) vexation. **2** (*humillación*) humiliation.
vejamen *m* → **vejación**.
vejar 1 *t* (*molestar*) to vex, annoy. **2** (*humillar*) to humiliate.
vejatorio,-a 1 *adj* (*molesto*) vexatious, annoying. **2** (*humillante*) humiliating.
vejestorio *m fam pey* old dodderer, old crock.
vejete *m fam* old man.
vejez *f* old age.
● **a la vejez viruelas,** there's no fool like an old fool.

vejiga *f* bladder.
■ **vejiga de la bilis,** gall bladder.
vela¹ 1 *f* (*vigilia*) watch, vigil; (*de muerto*) wake. **2** (*desvelo*) wakefulness. **3** (*candela*) candle. – **4 velas,** *fpl fam fig* (*mocos*) snot *sing*.
● **encender una vela a Dios y otra al diablo,** *fam fig* to have a foot in both camps. || **estar a dos velas,** *fam fig* to be broke. || **pasar la noche en vela,** to have a sleepless night. || **¿quién te ha dado vela en este entierro?,** *fam fig* who gave you any say in the matter?
vela² 1 *f* (*de barco*) sail. **2** DEP sailing. **3** *fig* (*barco de vela*) sailing ship.
● **a toda vela / a velas desplegadas,** under full sail, at full speed. || **alzar las velas / largar las velas,** to set sail. || **recoger velas,** *fig* to back down.
■ **vela mayor,** mainsail.
velada 1 *f* (*de música etc*) evening, soirée: *velada musical,* musical soirée. **2** (*fiesta*) soirée.
velado,-a 1 *pp* → **velar**². – **2** *adj* (*oculto*) veiled, hidden. **3** (*fotografía*) blurred.
velador,-ra 1 *adj* watching, guarding. – **2 velador,** *m* (*vigilante*) watchman, guard. **3** (*candelero*) candlestick. **4** (*mesita*) pedestal table.
veladura 1 *f* (*en pintura*) glaze. **2** (*en fotografía*) fog. **3** *fig* (*disimulo*) pretence (US pretense).
velaje *m* sails *pl*.
velamen *m* sails *pl*.
velar¹ 1 *i* (*no dormir*) to stay awake; (*no acostarse*) to stay up. **2** *fig* (*cuidar*) to watch (**por,** over), look (**por,** after): *velaron por él,* they looked after him. **3** (*hacer guardia*) to keep watch. **4** REL to keep vigil. – **5** *t* (*enfermo*) to sit up with, watch over; (*muerto*) to keep vigil over: *velaron a su hija,* they sat up with their daughter.
velar² 1 *t* LING velar. – **2** *t* LING velar. – **3** *t* (*cubrir con velo*) to veil. **4** *fig* (*cubrir*) to hide, cover, veil. **5** (*fotografía*) to fog, expose. **6** (*pintura*) to glaze. – **7 velarse,** *p* (*fotografía*) to become fogged, get exposed.
velarización *f* velarization.
velarizar *t* to velarize.
▲ *Conjugation model* |4|, *like **realizar**.*
velatorio *m* wake, vigil.
veleidad 1 *f* (*capricho*) caprice, whim. **2** (*inconstancia*) inconstancy, fickleness.
veleidoso,-a *adj* inconstant, fickle.
velero,-a 1 *adj* sailing. – **2** *m,f* (*fabricante de velas*) sailmaker. – **3 velero,** *m* sailing ship, sailing boat.
veleta 1 *f* (*para el viento*) weathercock, weather vane. – **2** *mf fam fig* (*persona*) fickle person, changeable person.
vello 1 *m* (*de persona - pelusa*) down; (*- en las piernas etc*) hair. **2** (*de fruta, planta*) down, bloom.
vellocino *m* fleece.
■ **Vellocino de Oro,** Golden Fleece.
vellón *m* fleece.
vellosidad 1 *f* (*vello*) down. **2** (*abundancia - de pelusa*) downiness; (*en las piernas etc*) hairiness.
velloso,-a *adj* downy, hairy, fluffy.
velludillo *m* velveteen.
velludo,-a *adj* downy, hairy, fluffy.
velo 1 *m* (*gen*) veil. **2** ANAT velum.
● **correr un (tupido) velo sobre algo / echar un (tupido) velo sobre algo,** *fig* to draw a veil over sth., keep sth. quiet. || **tomar el velo,** *fam* to take the veil.
■ **velo del paladar,** soft palate, velum.
velocidad 1 *f* (*rapidez*) speed, velocity. **2** AUTO (*marcha*) gear.
● **a toda velocidad,** at full speed. || **cambiar de ve-**

locidad, AUTO to change gear. ‖ cobrar velocidad / ganar velocidad, to gather speed. ‖ con la velocidad del rayo, *fig* as quick as a flash. ‖ de alta velocidad, high-speed. ‖ disminuir la velocidad, to slow down. ■ caja de velocidades, gear box. ‖ Europa de dos velocidades, two-speed Europe. ‖ exceso de velocidad, speeding, exceeding the speed limit: *le multaron por exceso de velocidad,* they fined him for speeding. ‖ velocidad de crucero, cruising speed. ‖ velocidad de la luz, speed of light. ‖ velocidad de transmisión, INFORM bit rate. ‖ velocidad máxima, speed limit. ‖ velocidad operativa, INFORM operating speed.

velocímetro *m* speedometer.

velocípedo *m* velocipede.

velocista *mf* DEP sprinter.

velódromo *m* cycle track, US velodrome.

velomotor *m* moped.

velón *m* oil lamp.

velorio[1] I *m* (*fiesta*) evening party. 2 (*velatorio*) wake.

velorio[2] *m* REL. taking of the veil.

veloz I *adj* fast, quick, swift, rapid. – 2 *adv* fast, quickly, swiftly.

velozmente *adv* quickly, fast.

vena I *f* ANAT vein. 2 (*yacimiento*) vein, seam. 3 BOT vein. 4 (*en mármol etc*) vein, streak. 5 *fig* (*disposición*) mood. ● coger a algn. en vena / coger a algn. de vena, *fig* to catch sb. in the right mood. ‖ coger a algn. la vena / dar a algn. la vena, *fig* to take sth. into one's head: *le ha dado la vena de cantar,* she has taken it into her head to sing. ‖ estar en vena para, *fig* to be in the mood for. ‖ tener una vena de loco, *fig* to have a crazy streak. ‖ tener vena de ...*, to have a gift for ...: *tiene vena de cantante,* he has a gift for singing.

venablo *m* javelin, dart. ● echar venablos, *fig* to blow one's top, explode with anger.

venado I *m* ZOOL. stag, deer. 2 CULIN venison.

venal I *adj* (*vendible*) venal, purchasable. 2 *fig* (*sobornable*) venal, corrupt.

venalidad *f* venality.

venatorio,-a *adj* hunting.

vencedor,-ra I *adj* (*equipo etc*) winning. 2 MIL. conquering, victorious. – 3 *m,f* (*equipo etc*) winner, victor. 4 MIL. conqueror, victor.

vencejo[1] *m* (*ave*) swift. ■ vencejo real, alpine swift.

vencejo[2] *f* (*atadura*) bond.

vencer I *t* DEP to beat. 2 MIL. to defeat, conquer, vanquish: *vencieron al enemigo,* they defeated the enemy. 3 (*exceder*) to outdo, surpass: *la vence en belleza,* she surpasses her in beauty. 4 (*problema etc*) to overcome, surmount. 5 (*ser dominado*) to overcome: *la venció el cansancio,* she was overcome by tiredness. 6 (*romper*) to break; (*doblar*) to bend. – 7 *i* (*ganar*) to win. 8 (*deuda etc*) to fall due, be payable. 9 (*plazo*) to expire. 10 (*torcer*) to go off to: *el camino vence a la derecha,* the path goes off to the right. – 11 vencerse, *p* (*romperse*) to break; (*doblarse*) to bend, incline. 12 *fig* (*reprimir*) to control os. ▲ *Conjugation model* |2|, *like mecer.*

vencido,-a I *pp* → **vencer.** – 2 *adj* (*derrotado*) defeated, beaten. 3 (*deuda*) due, payable. 4 (*plazo*) expired. ● a la tercera va la vencida, *fam fig* third time lucky. ‖ darse por vencido,-a, *fig* to give up, accept defeat.

vencimiento I *m* (*pago etc*) maturity. 2 (*plazo*) expiry, maturity. 3 (*torcimiento*) bend, inclination. 4 *fig* (*problema etc*) overcoming.

venda *f* bandage. ● quitar a algn. la venda de los ojos, to open sb.'s eyes. ‖ tener una venda en los ojos, *fig* to be blind, go around with one's eyes closed.

vendaje *m* dressing.

vendar *t* to bandage. ● vendar los ojos a algn., to blindfold sb.

vendaval *m* strong wind, gale.

vendedor,-ra I *adj* selling. – 2 *m,f* (*gen*) seller; (*hombre*) salesman; (*mujer*) saleswoman. 3 (*dependiente*) shop assistant. ■ vendedor ambulante, street seller, hawker.

vendeja *f* public sale.

vender I *t* (*gen*) to sell: *vende enciclopedias,* he sells encyclopedias; *lo vendieron por un millón de dólares,* they sold it for a million dollars. 2 *fig* (*traicionar*) to betray: *sería capaz de vender a su propia familia,* he would even betray his own family. – 3 venderse, *p* (*uso impersonal*) to be on sale, be sold: *se vende en farmacias,* on sale at your chemist's; *se vende a 40 pesetas el kilo,* it's sold at 40 pesetas a kilo. 4 (*dejarse sobornar*) to sell os. ● "se vende", "for sale". ‖ sin vender, unsold. ‖ vender a plazos, to sell on credit. ‖ vender al contado, to sell for cash. ‖ vender al por mayor, to sell wholesale, wholesale. ‖ vender al por menor, to sell retail, retail. ‖ vender caro, to sell at a high price. ‖ venderse caro,-a, to play hard to get.

vendible *adj* saleable, marketable.

vendido,-a I *pp* → **vender.** – 2 *adj* sold.

vendimia I *f* (*cosecha*) grape harvest. 2 (*año*) vintage, year.

vendimiador,-ra *m,f* grape picker.

vendimiar *t* to harvest. ▲ *Conjugation model* |12|, *like cambiar.*

vendré *fut* → **venir.**

Venecia *f* Venice.

veneciano,-a I *adj* Venetian. – 2 *m,f* Venetian.

veneno I *m* (*química, vegetal*) poison; (*animal*) venom. 2 *fig* spite, venom.

venenoso,-a I *adj* poisonous, venomous. 2 *fig* spiteful, venomous.

venerable *adj* venerable.

veneración *f* veneration, worship.

venerar *t* to venerate, worship, revere.

venéreo,-a *adj* venereal. ■ enfermedad venérea, venereal disease.

venero I *m* (*manantial*) spring. 2 *fig* (*origen*) origin, source. 3 (*mina*) vein, seam.

venezolano,-a I *adj* Venezuelan. – 2 *m,f* Venezuelan.

Venezuela *f* Venezuela.

venga *pres subj & imperat* → **venir.**

vengador,-ra I *adj* avenging. – 2 *m,f* avenger.

venganza *f* revenge, vengeance. ● tomar venganza de algn., to take revenge on sb.

vengar I *t* to avenge. – 2 vengarse, *p* to avenge os., take revenge (**de**, on). ▲ *Conjugation model* |7|, *like llegar.*

vengativo,-a *adj* vengeful, vindictive.

vengo *pres indic* → **venir.**

venia I *f fml* (*licencia*) permission, consent. 2 *fml* (*perdón*) pardon. 3 *fml* (*saludo*) greeting.

venial *adj* venial.

venialidad *f* veniality.

venida *f* coming, arrival. ■ idas y venidas, comings and goings.

venidero,-a adj future, coming.
● **en lo venidero**, in the future.
venir 1 i (gen) to come: *Antonio no vino,* Antonio didn't come; *el mes que viene,* next month; *voy y vengo,* I'll be right back. 2 (*llegar*) to arrive: *vino tarde,* he arrived late. 3 (*proceder*) to come (**de,** from): *viene de París,* it comes from Paris; *viene del latín,* it comes from the Latin. 4 (*estar, aparecer*) to be, come: *las explicaciones vienen en español,* the instructions are in Spanish. 5 (*ser*) to be: *eso te viene grande,* that's too big for you. – 6 **venir a + inf,** aux (*aproximación*) to be about; (*alcanzar, llegar a*) to arrive at; (*terminar por*) to end up: *viene a hacer dos metros de alto,* it's about two metres high; *finalmente vinimos a coincidir,* we finally agreed; *vino a parar a la cárcel,* he ended up in jail. 7 **venir + ger,** (*acción durativa*): *lo venía avisando desde hace tiempo,* he has been warning us about it for a long time. 8 **venir + pp,** (*ser, estar*) to be: *eso viene motivado por la inflación,* it's caused by inflation. – 9 **venirse,** p to come back, go back.
● **¿a qué viene ...?,** what is the point of ...?: *¿a qué viene reír?,* what's the point of laughing? ‖ **de ahí viene que ...,** so it is that ..., that's why ... ‖ **lo veía venir,** I could see it coming, I was expecting it. ‖ **ni te va ni te viene,** fig it's not your business. ‖ **¡venga ya!,** fam (*basta*) stop it!, that's quite enough!; (*incredulidad*) come off it!; (*vamos*) come on! ‖ **venir a cuento / no venir a cuento,** to be relevant / be beside the point. ‖ **venir a la cabeza,** to come to mind. ‖ **venir a la memoria,** fig to remember. ‖ **venir a menos,** fig to come down in the world. ‖ **venir a parar,** to come to, end up. ‖ **venir abajo,** to collapse. ‖ **venir al caso / no venir al caso,** to be relevant / be beside the point. ‖ **venir al mundo,** fig to be born. ‖ **venir al pelo,** fam to suit down to the ground. ‖ **venir bien,** (*favorecer*) to suit; (*prenda*) to fit; (*ser conveniente*) to be suitable, be convenient. ‖ **venir con cuentos,** to tell stories. ‖ **venir con historias,** to come with excuses. ‖ **venir de perlas,** fam to suit down to the ground. ‖ **venir en gana,** to feel like. ‖ **venir motivado,-a por,** to be caused by. ‖ **venir que ni pintado,** fam to suit down to the ground. ‖ **venir rodado,-a,** to come at the right time, happen at the right time. ‖ **venirse abajo,** (*edificio etc*) to collapse, fall down; (*planes*) to fall through; (*persona*) to go to pieces; (*país*) to go to the dogs; (*relación etc*) to be on the skids.
▲ *Conjugation model* [90].
venoso,-a 1 adj (*sangre*) venous. 2 (*manos etc*) veined, veiny. 3 (*hoja*) veined, ribbed.
venta 1 f (*acción*) sale, selling. 2 (*hostal*) country inn; (*restaurante*) restaurant.
● **"en venta",** "for sale". ‖ **estar a la venta,** to be on sale. ‖ **poner a la venta,** (*gen*) to put on sale; (*casa*) to put up for sale.
■ **contrato de venta,** bill of sale. ‖ **departamento de ventas,** sales department. ‖ **precio de venta,** selling price. ‖ **precio de venta al público,** retail price. ‖ **venta a domicilio,** door-to-door selling. ‖ **venta a plazos,** hire purchase, us instalment plan. ‖ **venta al contado,** cash sale. ‖ **venta al por mayor /venta al por menor,** wholesale / retail. ‖ **venta de pisos,** flats for sale. ‖ **venta postbalance,** clearance sale, us post-inventory sale.
ventaja 1 f (gen) advantage: *ganó con dos hora de ventaja,* he won by two hours. 2 (*provecho*) profit; (*beneficio*) benefit.
● **llevar ventaja a algn.,** to have the advantage over

sb. ‖ **sacar ventaja a algn.,** to be ahead of sb. ‖ **sacar ventaja de algo,** to profit from sth., take advantage of sth., benefit from sth. ‖ **ventaja para ...,** (*tenis*) advantage to ...
ventajista 1 adj opportunist. – 2 mf opportunist.
ventajoso,-a 1 adj advantageous. 2 (*beneficioso*) profitable.
ventana 1 f ARQ window. 2 (*de la nariz*) nostril.
● **tirar algo por la ventana,** fig to waste sth.
■ **ventana de guillotina,** sash window. ‖ **ventana vidriera,** picture window.
ventanal m large window.
ventanilla 1 f (*banco, coche, sobre, etc*) window. 2 (*barco*) porthole. 3 (*de taquilla*) window, ticket window. 4 (*de nariz*) nostril.
ventanillo m small window.
ventanuco m small window.
ventarrón m strong wind, gale.
ventear 1 i (*soplar*) to be windy. – 2 t (*husmear*) to sniff. 3 (*airear*) to air, air out. 4 fig (*indagar*) to snoop.
▲ In 1, *used only in the third person; it does not take a subject.*
ventero,-a m,f innkeeper.
ventilación f ventilation.
■ **sin ventilación,** unventilated.
ventilador m ventilator, fan.
ventilar 1 t (*lugar*) to air, ventilate. 2 (*agitar al viento*) to air. 3 fig (*dar a conocer*) to air. 4 fig (*discutir*) to discuss, clear up. 5 fig (*matar*) to kill. – 6 **ventilarse,** p (*lugar*) to be ventilated. 7 (*objeto*) to be aired. 8 fig (*saberse*) to be aired. 9 fig (*discutirse*) to be discussed, be cleared up. 10 (*tomar el aire*) to get some fresh air. 11 fam (*terminar*) to finish off: *se ventiló el pastel en un minuto,* he finished off the cake in a minute.
ventisca f snowstorm, blizzard.
ventiscar 1 i (*nevar*) to blow a blizzard. 2 (*levantarse la nieve*) to swirl.
▲ *Conjugation model* [1], *like* **sacar***; in 1, used only in the third person; it does not take a subject.*
ventisquero 1 m (*ventisca*) snowstorm, blizzard. – 2 f (*zona de la montaña*) part of a mountain above the snow line.
ventolera 1 f (*golpe*) gust of wind. 2 fig caprice, whim.
● **darle a uno la ventolera de hacer algo,** to take it into one's head to do sth. ‖ **darle a uno la ventolera por,** to take a fancy to.
ventorro m small inn.
ventosa 1 f (*pieza cóncava*) suction cup. 2 (*de animal*) sucker. 3 MED cupping glass. 4 (*abertura*) vent, air hole.
ventosear i to break wind.
ventosidad f wind, flatulence.
ventoso,-a adj windy.
ventrículo m ventricle.
ventrílocuo,-a 1 adj ventriloquistic. – 2 m,f ventriloquist.
ventriloquia f ventriloquy, ventriloquism.
ventrudo,-a adj fam pot-bellied.
ventura 1 f (*felicidad*) happiness. 2 (*casualidad*) fortune, chance; (*suerte*) luck. 3 (*hazar*) hazard, risk.
● **a la buena ventura,** with no fixed plan. ‖ **echar la buena ventura a algn.,** to tell sb.'s fortune. ‖ **por ventura,** (*por casualidad*) by chance; (*por suerte*) fortunately. ‖ **probar ventura,** to try one's luck.
venturosamente adv fortunately.
venturoso,-a adj lucky, fortunate.
Venus 1 m Venus. – 2 f Venus.
veo-veo m fam I-spy.

ver 1 *t* (*gen*) to see: *veamos,* let's see; *no te veo,* I can't see you. 2 (*mirar*) to look (at). 3 (*televisión*) to watch. 4 *fig* (*entender*) to see, understand: *no veo por qué lo hizo,* I can't understand why she did it. 5 (*visitar*) to visit, see: *ven a verme,* come and see me. 6 JUR to try, hear. 7 (*parecer*) to look: *te veo triste,* you look sad. – 8 *m* (*vista*) sight, vision. 9 (*apariencia*) looks *pl,* appearance. – 10 verse, *p* (*ser visto*) to be seen: *no se ve el coche,* I can't see the car. 11 (*con algn.*) to meet, see each other. 12 (*en una situación etc*) to find os., be: *se vio en un apuro,* he was in a fix. 13 (*imaginarse*) to imagine os.
● a mi ver, in my opinion. ‖ a ver, let's see, let me see. ‖ a ver si ..., (*deseo*) I hope ... ‖ de buen ver, good-looking. ‖ dejar ver, to let see: *¡déjame verlo!,* let me see it! ‖ dejarse ver, *fig* to appear, become apparent. ‖ es de ver, it is worth seeing. ‖ eso está por ver, that remains to be seen. ‖ ¡hábrase visto!, did you ever!: *¡hábrase visto qué descaro!,* did you ever see such cheek! ‖ hacer ver, to pretend. ‖ ¡hasta más ver!, *fam* see you! ‖ hay que ver lo ... que ..., you should see ...: *hay que ver lo bonita que es,* you should see how beautiful she is. ‖ ¡hay que ver!, *fam* it just goes to show! ‖ ¿lo ves?, see! ‖ mire a ver, have a look. ‖ no poder ver, *fig* to detest: *no le puede ver,* she can't stand him. ‖ no tener nada que ver con, to have nothing to do with. ‖ no ver ni jota / no ver tres en un burro, *fam* to be as blind as a bat. ‖ por lo que veo ..., apparently ..., it seems ... ‖ ... que no veo, *fam* terribly, terrible: *tengo una sed que no veo,* I'm dying of thirst. ‖ ... que no veas, *fam* terribly, terrible: *hacía un calor que no veas,* it was absolutely roasting; *armaron un escándalo que no veas,* they kicked up a terrible fuss. ‖ se ve que ..., apparently ..., it seems ... ‖ ser digno,-a de verse, to be worth seeing. ‖ si no lo veo no lo creo, I would never have believed it. ‖ véase ..., see ... ‖ ver venir algo, *fig* to expect sth. to happen, see sth. coming. ‖ ver venir a algn., *fig* to see sb. coming. ‖ verlas venir, *fig* to catch on quickly. ‖ verse obligado,-a a, to be obliged to. ‖ vérselas con algn., *fig* to deal with sb., have it out with sb. ‖ ya se ve, of course.
▲ *Conjugation model* |91|; *pp* visto,-a.
vera *f* edge, side.
● a la vera de, beside, next to. ‖ a mi vera, beside me.
veracidad *f* veracity, truthfulness.
veranda *f* veranda.
veraneante 1 *mf* (*que hace vacaciones*) holidaymaker, US vacationist. 2 (*que la pasa en un lugar*) summer resident.
veranear *i* to spend the summer (holiday) (**en,** in/at).
veraneo *m* summer holiday.
● ir de veraneo, to go on holiday.
■ lugar de veraneo, summer holiday resort, holiday resort.
veraniego,-a *adj* summer, summery.
veranillo *m* Indian summer.
■ veranillo de San Martín, Indian summer.
verano *m* summer.
veras de veras, *adv* really, seriously: *va de veras,* it's serious.
veraz *adj* truthful, veracious.
verbal *adj* verbal, oral.
verbalismo *m* verbalism.
verbalmente *adv* orally.
verbena 1 *f* BOT verbena. 2 (*fiesta*) night party.
■ verbena de San Juan, night party held on the eve of Saint John's Day.

verbigracia *adv fml* for example, for instance.
verbo *m* verb.
■ verbo auxiliar, auxiliary verb. ‖ verbo copulativo, attributive verb. ‖ verbo intransitivo, intransitive verb. ‖ verbo irregular, irregular verb. ‖ verbo transitivo, transitive verb.
verborrea *f fam* verbosity.
● tener mucha verborrea, to be verbose.
verbosidad *f* verbosity, wordiness.
verdad 1 *f* truth, truthfulness: *es verdad,* it's true. 2 (*confirmación*): *es bonita, ¿verdad?,* she's pretty, isn't she?; *vendrás, ¿verdad?,* you'll come, won't you?; *hay tres, ¿verdad?,* there are three, aren't there?
● a decir verdad, to tell the truth. ‖ de verdad, (*realmente*) really, truly, seriously; (*real*) real: *un amigo de verdad,* a real friend. ‖ de verdad que ..., I swear ...: *de verdad que no fui,* I swear I didn't go. ‖ decir a algn. cuatro verdades, *fam* to give sb. a piece of one's mind. ‖ en verdad, really. ‖ faltar a la verdad, to lie. ‖ la verdad sea dicha, to tell the truth. ‖ ¿no es verdad?, isn't that so? ‖ tan verdad como que es de día / tan verdad como que Dios existe, *fam* it's as true as I'm standing here.
■ la pura verdad, the plain truth. ‖ verdad a medias, a half truth.
verdaderamente 1 *adv* (*en verdad*) really, truly. 2 (*de hecho*) in fact, actually.
verdadero,-a *adj* true, real.
verdal *adj* green.
verde 1 *adj* (*color*) green. 2 (*fruta*) unripe, green; (*madera*) unseasoned. 3 *fig* (*persona*) green, immature. 4 *fam* (*chiste*) blue, dirty. – 5 *m* (*color*) green. 6 (*hierba*) grass. 7 POL green: *los verdes,* the Greens.
● poner verde a algn., *fam* to call sb. every name under the sun.
verdear 1 *i* (*mostrar color*) to look green. 2 (*brotar*) to turn green.
verdecer *i* to grow green.
▲ *Conjugation model* |43|, *like* agradecer.
verdecillo *m* serin.
verdemar 1 *adj* sea-green. – 2 *m* sea-green.
verderón *m* greenfinch.
verdín 1 *m* (*de plantas*) verdure, fresh green. 2 (*capa - de algas*) green slime; (- *de paredes, frutas*) green mould (US mold). 3 (*capa - de óxido*) verdigris. 4 (*mancha*) green stain, grass stain.
verdinegro,-a 1 *adj* dark green. 2 dark green.
verdor 1 *m* (*color*) verdure, greenness. 2 *fig* (*vigor*) vigour (US vigor). 3 *fig* (*mocedad*) youth.
verdoso,-a *adj* greenish.
verdugo 1 *m* (*persona*) executioner. 2 (*prenda*) Balaclava, Balaclava hood. 3 (*azote*) whip. 4 (*roncha*) weal. – 5 *mf fig* tyrant.
verdugón *m* weal.
verduguillo 1 *m* (*en las plantas*) swelling. 2 (*navaja*) razor. 3 (*tauromaquia*) stiletto.
verdulería *f* greengrocer's (shop).
verdulero,-a 1 *m,f* greengrocer. – 2 verdulera, *f fig* coarse woman, foul-mouthed woman.
verdura 1 *f* (*hortaliza*) vegetables *pl,* greens *pl.* 2 (*color*) greenness, greenery.
verdusco,-a *adj* greenish, darkish green.
vereda *f* footpath, path.
● meter en vereda, *fam fig* to bring sb. into line.
veredicto *m* verdict.
■ veredicto de culpabilidad / veredicto de inculpabilidad, verdict of guilty / verdict of not guilty.

verga 1 *f* (*genital*) penis. **2** (*palo*) thin stick. **3** MAR yard.
vergajo *m* pizzle whip.
vergel *m* orchard.
verglás *m* sheet ice, black ice.
vergonzante *adj* shamefaced.
vergonzoso,-a 1 *adj* (*acto*) shameful, shocking: *un asunto vergonzoso,* a shocking business. **2** (*persona*) bashful, shy.
vergüenza 1 *f* (*deshonor etc*) shame, sense of shame: *sus palabras me dan vergüenza,* her words make me feel ashamed. **2** (*timidez*) bashfulness, shyness; (*turbación*) embarrassment: *me da vergüenza bailar,* I'm too shy to dance; *pasó mucha vergüenza cuando salió la noticia,* he was really embarrassed when the news came out. **3** (*escándalo*) disgrace, shame: *lo que han hecho es una vergüenza,* what they did is a disgrace. – **4 vergüenzas,** *fpl fam euf* private parts.
● **caerse la cara de vergüenza,** *fig* to die of embarrassment. ‖ **¡qué vergüenza!,** it's a disgrace!, how disgraceful! ‖ **¿no te da vergüenza?,** aren't you ashamed of yourself? ‖ **no tener vergüenza,** to be a shameless person, have no shame. ‖ **pasar vergüenza,** (*humillación*) to be ashamed; (*turbación*) to be embarrassed. ‖ **pasar vergüenza ajena,** to feel embarrassed for somebody. ‖ **perder la vergüenza,** to lose all sense of shame. ‖ **¡qué poca vergüenza!,** how shameful! ‖ **sacar a algn. a la vergüenza,** to hold sb. up to shame. ‖ **sentir vergüenza,** to be ashamed. ‖ **tener vergüenza de hacer algo,** to be ashamed to do sth.
vericueto *m* rough path, dirt track.
verídico,-a *adj* truthful, true: *es verídico,* it is a fact.
verificación 1 *f* (*comprobación*) verification, checking. **2** (*cumplimiento*) carrying out, conducting.
■ **verificación de cuentas,** FIN audit.
verificador,-ra 1 *adj* verifying, checking. – **2** *m,f* tester.
verificar 1 *t* (*comprobar*) to verify, check. **2** (*probar*) to prove. **3** (*efectuar*) to carry out, perform. – **4 verificarse,** *p* (*comprobarse*) to come true. **5** (*efectuarse*) to take place.
▲ *Conjugation model* |1|, *like* **sacar.**
verja 1 *f* (*reja*) grating, grille. **2** (*cerca*) railing, railings *pl.* **3** (*puerta*) iron gate.
■ **la Verja de Gibraltar,** the frontier with Gibraltar.
vermú 1 *m* (*bebida*) vermouth. **2** (*aperitivo*) aperitive.
▲ *pl* **vermús.**
vermut *m* → **vermú.**
▲ *pl* **vermús.**
vernáculo,-a *adj* vernacular.
■ **lengua vernácula,** vernacular.
verónica 1 *f* BOT veronica. **2** (*tauromaquia*) type of pass with the cape.
verosímil *adj* (*probable*) likely, probable; (*creíble*) credible.
verosimilitud *f* (*probabilidad*) probability, likeliness; (*credibilidad*) credibility, verisimilitude.
verosímilmente *adv* probably.
verraco *m* boar, hog.
verruga *f* wart.
versado,-a 1 *pp* → **versar.** – **2** *adj* versed (**en,** in), proficient (**en,** in).
versal 1 *adj* capital. – **2** *f* capital, capital letter.
versalita 1 *adj* small capital. – **2** *f* small capital letter, small capital.
versallesco,-a *adj fam fig* (*galante*) chivalrous; (*afectado*) affected.
versar 1 *i* (*tratar*) to deal (**sobre,** with), be (**sobre,** about/on): *la conferencia versó sobre la lingüística,* the

lectura was on linguistics. **2** (*dar vueltas*) to revolve, turn.
versátil 1 *adj* (*gen*) versatile. **2** *fig* (*voluble*) changeable, fickle.
versatilidad 1 *f* (*gen*) versatility. **2** *fig* changeableness, fickleness.
versículo *m* verse, versicle.
versificación *f* versification.
versificador,-ra 1 *adj* versifier. – **2** *m,f* versifier.
versificar 1 *t* to versify. – **2** *i* to write in verse.
▲ *Conjugation model* |1|, *like* **sacar.**
versión 1 *f* (*gen*) version, account. **2** (*traducción*) translation. **3** (*adaptación*) adaptation.
● **en versión original,** in the original language. ‖ **en versión española,** dubbed into Spanish.
verso 1 *m* (*de hoja*) verso. **2** LIT verse. **3** *fam* (*poema*) poem.
● **en verso,** in verse. ‖ **hacer versos,** to write poems. ‖ **poner en verso,** to put into verse.
■ **verso blanco / verso libre,** blank verse / free verse.
vértebra *f* vertebra.
vertebrado,-a 1 *adj* vertebrate. – **2** *m,f* vertebrate. – **3 los vertebrados,** *mpl* the vertebrates.
vertebral *adj* vertebral, spinal.
vertebrar *t fig* to be the backbone of, structure: *la base de datos vertebra toda la empresa,* the database is the backbone of the firm.
vertedera *f* mouldboard (US moldboard).
vertedero *m* rubbish dump, rubbish tip.
verter 1 *t* (*líquido - voluntariamente*) to pour, pour out. **2** (*derramar*) to spill; (*lágrimas, sangre*) to shed: *vertió el té sobre la moqueta,* he spilt his tea on the carpet. **3** (*vaciar*) to empty, empty out. **4** (*basura*) to dump: *siguen vertiendo residuos tóxicos en el mar,* they're still dumping toxic waste into the sea. **5** (*traducir*) to translate: *verter al inglés,* to translate into English. **6** *fig* (*conceptos, ideas, etc*) to express, voice. – **7** *i* (*corriente, río*) to run (**a,** into), flow (**a,** into).
▲ *Conjugation model* |28|, *like* **entender.**
vertical 1 *adj* vertical: *lo puso vertical,* she put it upright. – **2** *f* vertical, vertical line. – **3** *m* vertical.
verticalmente *adv* vertically.
vértice *m* vertex.
vertiente 1 *f* (*gen*) slope. **2** *fig* (*aspecto*) angle.
● **desde otra vertiente,** *fig* from a different angle.
vertiginosamente *adv* dizzily, giddily.
vertiginoso,-a *adj* dizzy, giddy.
● **a velocidad vertiginosa,** *fig* at breakneck speed.
vértigo 1 *m* MED vertigo. **2** (*mareo*) dizziness, giddiness: *me da vértigo,* it makes me feel dizzy. **3** *fig* frenzy.
● **de vértigo,** *fig* frenzied. ‖ **tener vértigo,** to feel dizzy, feel giddy.
vesania *f* (*locura*) insanity; (*furia*) fury, rage.
vesícula *f* vesicle.
■ **vesícula biliar,** gall-bladder.
vesicular *adj* vesicular.
vespa *f* scooter, motor scooter.
▲ *Registered trademark.*
vespertino,-a 1 *adj* evening. – **2 vespertino,** *m* evening newspaper.
vespino *m* moped.
▲ *Registered trademark.*
vestal 1 *adj* vestal. – **2** *f* vestal virgin.
vestíbulo 1 *m* (*de casa*) hall, entrance. **2** (*de hotel etc*) hall, lobby, vestibule, foyer. **3** ANAT (*del oído*) vestibule.
vestido,-a 1 *pp* → **vestir.** – **2** *adj* dressed: *vestida de blanco,* dressed in white; *vestida de hombre,* in man's

clothes. **– 3 vestido,** *m* (*indumentaria*) clothes *pl*, dress, costume. **4** (*de mujer*) dress; (*de hombre*) suit.
■ **vestido de etiqueta / vestido de noche,** evening dress.
vestidor *m* dressing room.
vestidura I *f* (*gen*) clothing, clothes *pl*. **2** REL vestments *pl*.
▲ *Generally used in plural.*
vestigio *m* vestige, trace, remains *pl*.
vestimenta *f* clothes *pl*, garments *pl*.
vestir I *t* (*llevar*) to wear, be dressed in: *vestía un vestido rojo,* she was wearing a red dress. **2** (*ayudar a vestirse*) to dress; (*hacer vestidos*) to make clothes for; (*proporcionar vestido*) to clothe, keep in clothes: *la vistió su madre,* her mother dressed her; *esta modista viste a muchas mujeres famosas,* this dressmaker makes clothes for many famous women; *mis padres me han alimentado y me han vestido hasta que he acabado mis estudios,* my parents fed and clothed me until I finished my studies. **3** (*cubrir*) to cover (**de,** with). **4** (*paredes*) to hang (**de,** with). **– 5** i to dress: *vestir de negro,* to dress in black. **6** (*ser elegante, lucir*) to be classy, look smart: *esa falda viste mucho,* that skirt is very classy. **– 7 vestirse,** *p* (*uso reflexivo*) to dress os., get dressed. **8** (*comprarse la ropa*) to buy one's clothes: *se viste en Milán,* she buys her clothes in Milan. **9** (*ir vestido*) to wear (**de,** -), dress (**de,** in); (*disfrazarse*) to disguise os. (**de,** as), dress up (**de,** as): *se vistió de un traje azul,* he wore a blue suit.
● **de vestir / de mucho vestir,** formal. ‖ **el mismo que viste y calza,** *fam* the very same, none other. ‖ **vestirse de punta en blanco,** *fig* to dress up to the nines. ‖ **vestirse de verano,** to put on one's summer clothes. ‖ **vísteme despacio que tengo prisa,** more haste less speed.
▲ *Conjugation model* |34|, *like servir.*
vestuario I *m* (*ropas*) wardrobe, clothes *pl*. **2** MIL uniform. **3** TEAT (*ropa*) wardrobe, costumes *pl*; (*camerino*) dressing room. **4** DEP changing room. **5** (*de fábrica etc*) cloakroom.
veta I *f* (*de mármol, roca*) seam, vein; (*de madera*) streak. **2** *fig* streak.
vetar *t* to veto, put a veto on: *vetaron la reunión,* they vetoed the meeting.
veteado,-a I *pp* → **vetear. – 2** *adj* (*mármol etc*) veined, streaked; (*madera*) grained.
vetear *t* to grain, streak.
veteranía I *f* seniority, long experience. **2** MIL long service.
veterano,-a I *adj* veteran. **– 2** *m,f* veteran. **3** *fig* old hand.
veterinaria *f* → **veterinario,-a.**
veterinario,-a I *adj* veterinary. **– 2** *m,f* veterinary surgeon, vet, US veterinarian. **– 3 veterinaria,** *f* veterinary medicine, veterinary science.
veto *m* veto.
● **poner el veto a,** to put a veto on, veto.
■ **derecho a veto,** power of veto, right of veto.
vetustez *f fml* (*antigüedad*) antiquity; (*vejez*) great age.
vetusto,-a *adj fml* (*antiguo*) ancient; (*viejo*) very old.
vez I *f* time: *fue la única vez que la vi,* it was the only time I saw her; *una vez,* once; *dos veces,* twice; *cuatro veces,* four times. **2** (*turno*) turn; (*ocasión*) occasion.
● **a la vez,** at the same time, at once: *todos llegaron a la vez,* they all arrived at the same time. ‖ **a su vez,** in turn. ‖ **a veces,** sometimes. ‖ **alguna que otra vez,** on the odd occasion. ‖ **alguna vez,** sometimes; (*en pregunta*) ever: *¿has estado alguna vez allí?,* have you ever been there? ‖ **algunas veces,** sometimes. ‖ **cada vez,** every time, each time. ‖ **cada vez más,** more and more, increasingly: *el edificio está cada vez más degradado,* the building is getting more and more dilapidated. ‖ **cada vez peor,** worse and worse: *sus libros están cada vez peores,* his books are getting worse and worse. ‖ **de una vez,** (*de un acto*) in one go; (*definitivamente*) once and for all: *terminó el cuadro de una vez,* she finished the painting in one go; *¡acabémoslo de una vez!,* let's get it over with! ‖ **de una vez para siempre,** once and for all. ‖ **de vez en cuando,** from time to time, now and again, every now and then, every so often: *lo encuentro por la calle de vez en cuando,* I see him in the street now and again. ‖ **en vez de,** instead of. ‖ **érase una vez ... / había una vez ...,** (*en cuentos*) once upon a time ... ‖ **hacer las veces de,** to act as. ‖ **muchas veces,** often. ‖ **otra vez,** again: *tócala otra vez, Sam,* play it again, Sam. ‖ **perder la vez,** to lose one's turn.
v.g. *abr* (*verbigracia*) for instance, for example; (*abreviatura*) eg.
v.gr. *abr* (*verbigracia*) for instance, for example; (*abreviatura*) eg.
vía I *f* (*camino*) road, way; (*calle*) street; (*carril*) lane. **2** (*de tren*) track, line; (*en la estación*) platform: *el tren de la vía uno,* the train at platform one. **3** ANAT passage, canal, track. **4** *fig* (*modo*) way, manner, means. **5** JUR procedure. **6** (*rumbo, dirección*) via, through: *Barcelona-Singapur vía Frankfurt,* Barcelona-Singapore via Frankfurt.
● **dar vía libre a,** to leave the way open for. ‖ **de vía doble,** double-track. ‖ **de vía estrecha,** (*ferrocarril*) narrow-gauge; *fig* mediocre. ‖ **en vías de,** in the process of: *países en vías de desarrollo,* developing countries. ‖ **por vía aérea,** (*gen*) by air; (*correo*) airmail. ‖ **por vía marítima,** by sea. ‖ **por vía oficial,** through official channels. ‖ **por vía oral,** to be taken orally. ‖ **por vía terrestre,** overland.
■ **transmisión vía satélite,** satellite transmission. ‖ **vía contenciosa,** JUR legal action. ‖ **vía de acceso,** slip road. ‖ **vía de agua,** leak. ‖ **vía de circunvalación,** bypass. ‖ **vía de comunicación,** communication channel. ‖ **vía férrea,** railway track, US railroad track. ‖ **vía judicial,** legal procedure. ‖ **Vía Láctea,** Milky Way. ‖ **vía muerta,** (*ferrocarril*) siding; *fig* impasse. ‖ **vía pública,** public thoroughfare. ‖ **vía oficial,** official channel. ‖ **vías urinarias,** urinary tract *sing*.
viabilidad *f* viability.
■ **plan de viabilidad,** viability study.
viable *adj* viable.
vía crucis I *m* Way of the Cross, Stations *pl* of the Cross. **2** *fig* great suffering.
viaducto *m* viaduct.
viajante *m* commercial traveller (US traveler), travelling (US traveling) salesman.
viajar i to travel: *ha viajado por el mundo entero,* she's travelled all over the world; *siempre viaja en coche,* he always travels by car.
● **haber viajado mucho,** to be widely travelled.
viaje[1] I *m* (*gen*) journey, trip. **2** (*en coche*) drive, journey. **3** (*travesía por mar*) voyage. **4** (*concepto de viajar*) travel. **5** (*carga*) load. **6** *arg* (*drogas*) trip.
● **¡buen viaje!,** bon voyage!, have a good trip! ‖ **de un viaje,** *fam* in one go. ‖ **estar de viaje,** to be away, be away on a trip. ‖ **irse de viaje / marcharse de viaje,** to go on a journey, go on a trip. ‖ **para este viaje no se necesitan alforjas,** *fam* it was hardly worth bothering about.

■ **cheque de viaje,** traveller's cheque (US traveler's check). ‖ **el último viaje,** *fig* one's journey's end. ‖ **libro de viajes,** travel book. ‖ **viaje de ida,** outward journey. ‖ **viaje de ida y vuelta,** return trip, US round trip. ‖ **viaje de negocios,** business trip. ‖ **viaje de novios,** honeymoon. ‖ **viaje en barco,** boat trip. ‖ **viaje en tren,** train journey.
▲ In 4, generally used in plural.

viaje² *m fam* (*herida*) slash.

viajero,-a 1 *adj* travelling (US traveling). – 2 *m,f* traveller (US traveler). 3 (*en transporte público*) passenger.
● **¡viajeros al tren!,** all aboard!

vial¹ 1 *adj* road. – 2 *m* (*camino*) road.
■ **seguridad vial,** road safety.

vial² *m* (*frasquito*) phial.

vianda *f* food, victuals *pl*.

viandante *mf* pedestrian, passer-by.

viario,-a *adj* road, highway.
■ **red viaria,** road network.

viático *m* REL viaticum.

víbora *f* viper.
■ **lengua de víbora,** *fig* spiteful tongue, venomous tongue.

vibración 1 *f* vibration. 2 LING rolling, trilling.

vibrador *m* vibrator.

vibrante 1 *adj* (*enérgico*) vibrant, vigorous; (*emocionante*) exciting, stirring: *habló con la voz vibrante de emoción,* she spoke in a voice vibrant with emotion; *un partido vibrante,* an exciting match. 2 LING rolled, trilled. – 3 *f* LING vibrant.

vibrar 1 *t* to vibrate. 2 LING to roll, trill. – 3 *i* (*gen*) to vibrate; (*pulsar*) to throb, pulsate: *los cristales vibran cada vez que pasa un tren,* the windows vibrate every time a train goes past; *su voz vibraba de ira,* his voice vibrated with anger; *toda la cuidad vibraba de actividad,* the whole city throbbed with activity. 4 *fig* (*conmoverse*) to be moved, be overcome with emotion: *vibró de la emoción cuando cogió el bebé por primera vez,* he was overcome with emotion when he picked up the baby for the first time; *el cantante hizo vibrar al público,* the singer thrilled the audience. 5 LING to roll, trill.

vibrátil *adj* vibratile, vibratory.

vibratorio,-a *adj* vibratory.

vicaría 1 *f* (*dignidad*) vicarship, vicariate. 2 (*lugar*) vicarage.
● **pasar por la vicaría,** *fam* to get married, get married in church.

vicario,-a 1 *adj* vicarial. – 2 *m,f* vicar.
■ **el Vicario de Cristo,** the Vicar of Christ.

vicealmirante *m* vice-admiral.

vicecanciller *m* vice-chancellor.

vicecónsul *m* vice-consul.

vicegobernador,-ra *m,f* vice-governor.

vicepresidencia 1 *f* (*gen*) vice-chairmanship. 2 POL vice-presidency.

vicepresidente,-a 1 *m,f* (*gen*) vice-chairperson; (*hombre*) vice-chairman; (*mujer*) vice-chairwoman. 2 POL vice-president.

vicerrector,-ra *m,f* EDUC vice-chancellor.

vicesecretario,-a *m,f* assistant secretary.

vicetiple *f* chorus girl.

viceversa *adv* vice versa.

vichy *m* gingham.

viciado,-a 1 *pp* → **viciar.** – 2 *adj* (*corrompido*) corrupt. 3 (*aire - mal olor*) foul, foul-smelling; (- *cargado*) stuffy; (- *contaminado*) polluted.

viciar 1 *t* (*corromper*) to corrupt, lead astray. 2 (*aire*) to pollute. 3 JUR to vitiate, nullify. 4 (*estropear*) to spoil. 5 *fig* (*tergiversar*) to twist, distort. – 6 **viciarse,** *p* (*enviciarse*) to take to vice, become corrupted. 7 (*objeto*) to go out of shape; (*madera*) to warp.
▲ Conjugation model [12], like *cambiar*.

vicio 1 *m* (*corrupción*) vice, corruption. 2 (*mala costumbre*) bad habit; (*inmoralidad*) vice. 3 (*del lenguaje*) incorrect usage. 4 (*defecto*) defect.
● **de vicio / por vicio,** for no reason at all, for the sake of it. ‖ **quejarse de vicio,** to complain for the sake of it.

vicioso,-a 1 *adj* (*cosa*) faulty, defective. 2 (*persona*) depraved, perverted. – 3 *m,f* depraved person. 4 (*niño mimado*) spoiled child, spoilt child.

vicisitud *f* vicissitude.
■ **las vicisitudes de la vida,** life's ups and downs.

víctima *f* victim, casualty: *hubo dos víctimas en el accidente,* there were two casualties in the accident; *las víctimas del atentado,* the victims of the bombing.
■ **víctima propiciatoria,** scapegoat.

victoria *f* victory, triumph.
● **alzarse con la victoria,** to win. ‖ **cantar victoria,** to proclaim a victory.

victoriano,-a *adj* Victorian.

victoriosamente *adv* triumphantly.

victorioso,-a *adj* victorious, triumphant.

vicuña *f* ZOOL vicuna, vicuña.

vid *f* grapevine, vine.

vid. *abr* (*vide, véase*) see; (*abreviatura*) s.

vida 1 *f* (*gen*) life. 2 (*viveza*) liveliness. 3 (*tiempo*) lifetime, life. 4 (*modo de vivir*) life, way of life. 5 (*medios*) living, livelihood.
● **amargarle la vida a algn.,** to make sb.'s life a misery. ‖ **¡así es la vida!,** such is life!, that's life! ‖ **cambiar de vida,** to change one's lifestyle. ‖ **como si le fuera la vida en ello,** as if his life depended on it. ‖ **costarle algo la vida a algn.,** to pay with one's life. ‖ **dar la vida por,** to give one's life for, give one's right arm for. ‖ **dar vida a,** (*parir*) to give birth to; (*realizar*) to bring to life. ‖ **darse la gran vida / pegarse la gran vida / darse la vida padre,** *fam* to live it up. ‖ **debatirse entre la vida y la muerte,** to fight for one's life. ‖ **de por vida,** for life. ‖ **de toda la vida,** lifelong: *un amigo de toda la vida,* a lifelong friend. ‖ **echarse a la vida,** *fam fig* to go on the game, become a prostitute. ‖ **en la flor de la vida,** in the prime of life. ‖ **en mi** *(tu, su, etc)* **vida,** never in my (your, his, etc) life. ‖ **en vida de,** during the life of. ‖ **escapar con vida / salir con vida,** to come out alive, survive. ‖ **estar con vida / estar sin vida,** to be alive / be dead. ‖ **¡esto es vida! / ¡esto sí que es vida!,** this is the life! ‖ **ganarse la vida,** to earn one's living. ‖ **hacerle la vida imposible a algn.,** to make life impossible for sb. ‖ **llevar una vida agitada / llevar una vida tranquila,** to lead a busy life / lead a quiet life. ‖ **pagar algn. con su vida,** to pay with one's life. ‖ **pasar a mejor vida,** *euf* to pass away. ‖ **perder la vida,** to die. ‖ **¿qué es de tu vida?,** how are things? ‖ **quitarle la vida a algn.,** to take sb.'s life. ‖ **¡vida mía! / ¡mi vida!,** my love!, darling!
■ **la otra vida,** *euf* the next life. ‖ **nivel de vida,** standard of living. ‖ **señales de vida,** signs of life. ‖ **vida de perros,** *fam fig* dog's life. ‖ **vida familiar,** family life. ‖ **vida íntima,** private life. ‖ **vida sentimental,** love life.

vidente 1 *mf* (*persona que ve*) sighted person. 2 (*persona que adivina*) clairvoyant.

vídeo *m* (*aparato*) video, video recorder; (*cinta*) video, videotape.
● grabar algo en video, to record sth. on video.
videocámara *f* video camera.
videocasete *f* videocassette.
videocinta *f* video tape.
videoclub *m* video club.
videodisco *m* videodisc.
videojuego *m* video game.
videoteca *f* video library.
videoteléfono *m* videophone.
videotexto *m* videotex.
vidorra *f fam* easy life.
● darse la gran vidorra / pegarse la gran vidorra, *fam* to live like a king.
vidriado,-a I *pp* → vidriar. – 2 *adj* glazed. – 3 vidriado, *m* (*cerámica*) glazed earthenware. 4 (*barniz*) glaze. 5 (*acción*) glazing.
vidriar I *t* (*cerámica*) to glaze. – 2 vidriarse, *p* (*cerámica*) to become glazed, become glassy. 3 *fig* (*ojos*) to become glazed. 4 *fig* (*asunto etc*) to become tricky.
▲ *Conjugation model* |14|, *like auxiliar.*
vidriera I *f* (*ventana*) picture window. 2 (*puerta*) glass door. 3 (*de balcón, galería*) French window. 4 (*vitral*) stained-glass window. 5 (*escaparate*) shop window.
vidriería I *f* (*fábrica*) glassworks *sing*. 2 (*tienda*) glazier's.
vidriero,-a I *m,f* (*fabricante*) picture-maker. 2 (*colocador*) glazier.
vidrio I *m* (*material*) glass. 2 (*objeto*) glass object.
● pagar los vidrios rotos, *fig* to carry the can.
■ fibra de vidrio, fibreglass. ‖ vidrio mate, frosted glass. ‖ vidrio plano, sheet glass.
vidrioso,-a I *adj* (*gen*) glassy; (*quebradizo*) brittle, glass-like. 2 (*resbaladizo*) slippery. 3 (*ojos*) glazed, glassy. 4 *fig* (*asunto etc*) touchy, delicate.
vieira *f* scallop.
viejales *mf fam* (*hombre*) old buffer; (*mujer*) old girl.
▲ *pl viejales.*
viejo,-a I *adj* (*gen*) old: *una mujer vieja,* an old woman; *un coche viejo,* an old car; *es más viejo que tú,* he's older than you. 2 (*desgastado*) old, worn-out. 3 (*antiguo*) old, ancient. – 4 *m,f* (*hombre*) old man; (*mujer*) old woman. – 5 los viejos, *mpl* elderly people.
● caerse de viejo,-a, *fig* to be falling apart with age. ‖ estar viejo,-a, to look old. ‖ hacer la cuenta a la vieja, to count on one's fingers. ‖ hacerse viejo,-a, to grow old. ‖ más viejo,-a que Matusalén / más viejo,-a que ir a pie, *fam* as old as the hills. ‖ mi viejo,-a, *fam* (*hombre*) my old man, the old man; (*mujer*) my old woman, my old lady, the old lady. ‖ mis viejos, *fam* my folks, my parents. ‖ morir de viejo, to die of old age. ‖ ser gato viejo / ser perro viejo, *fam fig* to be a sly old fox.
■ viejo verde, *fam* dirty old man.
Viena *f* Vienna.
vienés,-esa I *adj* Viennese. – 2 *m,f* Viennese.
viento I *m* (*gen*) wind. 2 (*rumbo*) direction. 3 (*de caza*) scent. 4 (*cuerda*) rope, guy. 5 *fam* (*flatulencia*) wind, flatulence.
● beber los vientos por algn., *fig* to be crazy about sb. ‖ contra viento y marea, *fig* come hell or high water. ‖ corren malos vientos, *fig* the time is not right. ‖ gritar algo a los cuatro vientos, *fig* to shout sth. from the rooftops. ‖ hacer viento / soplar viento, to be windy. ‖ ir como el viento, *fig* to fly like the wind. ‖ ir viento en popa, MAR to sail before the wind; *fig* to

do very well. ‖ mandar a algn. a tomar viento (fresco), *fam fig* to tell sb. where to go. ‖ ¿qué viento te trae por aquí?, *fam* what brings you here? ‖ quien siembra vientos recoge tempestades, *fig* you reap what you sow.
■ la rosa de los vientos, the wind rose. ‖ vientos alisios, trade winds.
vientre I *m* ANAT belly, abdomen. 2 (*vísceras*) bowels *pl*. 3 (*de embarazada*) womb. 4 (*de objeto*) belly.
● hacer de vientre, *euf* to have a bowel movement.
■ bajo vientre, lower abdomen. ‖ dolor de vientre, stomachache; *fam* bellyache.
viernes *m* Friday.
■ Viernes Santo, Good Friday.
▲ *pl viernes; see also jueves.*
Vietnam *m* Vietnam.
vietnamita I *adj* Vietnamese. – 2 *m,f* (*persona*) Vietnamese. – 3 vietnamita, *m* (*idioma*) Vietnamese.
viga I *f* (*de madera*) beam, rafter. 2 (*de acero etc*) girder.
■ viga maestra, main beam. ‖ viga transversal, crossbeam.
vigencia *f* validity.
● entrar en vigencia, to come into effect, come into force, become valid. ‖ estar en vigencia / tener vigencia, to be in force, be valid.
vigente *adj* in force, valid.
vigésimo,-a I *adj* twentieth: *vigésimo primero,* twenty-first. – 2 *m,f* twentieth.
▲ *See also sexto,-a.*
vigía I *f* (*atalaya*) watchtower, lookout post. – 2 *mf* lookout.
vigilancia I *f* (*acción*) surveillance: *está bajo vigilancia,* he's under surveillance. 2 (*cuidado*) vigilance, watchfulness.
■ torre de vigilancia, lookout post.
vigilante I *adj* (*que vigila*) vigilant, watchful. 2 (*alerta*) alert. – 3 *mf* (*hombre*) guard, watchman; (*mujer*) guard.
■ vigilante jurado, security guard. ‖ vigilante nocturno, night watchman.
vigilar I *t* (*cuidar*) to watch (over), look after: *vigila al niño,* look after the baby. 2 (*con armas etc*) to guard. 3 (*supervisar*) to oversee. 4 (*estar atento*) to keep an eye on, take care of: *vigila la puerta, que no entre nadie,* keep an eye on the door and see nobody gets in. – 5 *i* (*gen*) to keep watch.
● vigilar por algo, to watch over sth., look after sth.: *vigilar por el bien público,* to guarantee public law and order. ‖ vigilar sobre algn., to watch over sb., look after sb.
vigilia I *f* (*estado de no dormir*) wakefulness, sleeplessness. 2 (*víspera*) eve. 3 (*comida sin carne*) meat-free meal. 4 (*trabajo*) time spent working at night: *el libro es fruto de sus vigilias,* the book is the product of many sleepless nights. 5 REL vigil.
● guardar la vigilia, to abstain from eating meat. ‖ pasar la noche de vigilia, to stay awake all night.
■ día de vigilia, day of abstinence.
vigor I *m* (*fuerza*) vigour (US vigor), strength. 2 (*validez*) force, effect.
● en vigor, in force. ‖ poner en vigor, to put into effect.
vigorizador,-ra *adj* invigorating, fortifying.
vigorizar I *t* to invigorate, fortify. 2 *fig* to encourage, stimulate.
▲ *Conjugation model* |4|, *like realizar.*
vigoroso,-a *adj* vigorous, strong.

viguería f (*de madera*) beams pl; (*de metal*) girders pl.
vigués,-esa 1 adj of Vigo, from Vigo. – **2** m,f person from Vigo, inhabitant of Vigo.
vigueta f (*de madera*) small beam; (*de metal*) small girder.
VIH abr MED (*Virus de inmunodeficiencia Humana*) Human Immune Deficiency Virus; (*abreviatura*) HIV.
vihuela f vihuela, *type of* guitar.
vikingo,-a 1 adj Viking. – **2** m,f Viking.
vil adj vile, base, despicable.
vileza 1 f (*cualidad*) vileness, baseness. **2** (*acto*) vile act, despicable deed.
vilipendiar 1 t (*ofender*) to revile, insult. **2** (*despreciar*) to despise.
▲ *Conjugation model* [12], *like* **cambiar**.
vilipendio 1 m (*ofensa*) offence (US offense); (*humillación*) humiliation. **2** (*desprecio*) scorn, contempt.
vilipendioso,-a 1 adj (*ofensivo*) vilifying. **2** (*despreciable*) despicable.
villa 1 f (*casa*) villa, country house. **2** (*pueblo*) small town; (*ciudad*) town.
Villadiego tomar las de Villadiego, *loc fam* to clear off, beat it.
villancico m carol, Christmas carol.
villanía 1 f (*bajeza*) vileness, baseness. **2** *fig* (*acción*) vile deed, despicable act. **3** *fig* (*expresión*) coarse remark.
villano,-a 1 adj (*ni noble ni hidalgo*) common, peasant. **2** *fig* (*rústico*) rustic. **3** *fig* (*ruin*) villainous. – **4** m,f HIST villein, serf. **5** *fig* (*persona ruin*) villain.
villorrio m *pey* one-horse town.
vilo. 1 en vilo, *loc adv* (*supendido*) in the air, suspended. **2** *fig* (*indeciso*) in suspense, on tenterhooks.
● tener a algn. con el alma en vilo, *fig* to keep sb. in suspense.
vilordo,-a adj lazy.
vinagre 1 m vinegar. **2** *fig* sourpuss.
vinagrera 1 f vinegar bottle. – **2** vinagreras, *fpl* cruet sing, cruet set sing.
vinagreta f vinaigrette sauce.
vinajera f altar cruet.
vinatería 1 f (*comercio*) wine trade. **2** (*tienda*) wine shop.
vinatero,-a 1 adj wine. – **2** m,f wine merchant.
vinaza f poor-quality wine, plonk.
vinculación 1 f (*acción*) linking, binding. **2** (*vínculo*) link, bond. **3** (*relación*) relation.
vincular 1 t (*unir*) to link (**a**, to), bind (**a**, to). **2** (*relacionar*) to relate (**con**, to), connect (**con**, with), link (**con**, with): *estaba vinculada con la secta*, she was connected with the sect. **3** *fig* (*sujetar*) to tie (**a**, to), attach (**a**, to): *están vinculados a la empresa*, they are tied to the firm. **4** JUR to entail. – **5** vincularse, p to link os. (**a**, to).
● vincular sus esperanzas en, to found one's hopes on.
vínculo 1 m tie, bond, link. **2** JUR entail. **3** *fig* link.
■ vínculos familiares, family ties.
vindicación 1 f (*defensa*) vindication. **2** (*venganza*) revenge, vengeance.
vindicar 1 t (*defender*) to vindicate. **2** (*vengar*) to avenge. – **3** vindicarse, pron (*defenderse*) to vindicate os. **4** (*vengarse*) to avenge os.
▲ *Conjugation model* [1], *like* **sacar**.
vindicativo,-a 1 adj (*que defiende*) vindicatory. **2** (*vengativo*) vindictive. **3** JUR punitive.
vindicatorio,-a adj vindicatory.
vine pt indef → **venir**.
vinícola adj wine-producing.

vinicultor,-ra m,f wine producer.
vinicultura f wine production, wine growing.
vinificación f wine-making process.
vinílico,-a adj vinyl.
vinilo m vinyl.
vino m wine.
● ahogar las penas en vino, *fam* *fig* to drown one's sorrows. ‖ bautizar el vino, *fig* to water down wine. ‖ dormir el vino, to sleep it off. ‖ ir de vinos, to go out for a few drinks. ‖ tener mal vino, *fig* to become aggressive when drunk.
■ vino a granel, wine from the barrel. ‖ vino abocado, fortified wine. ‖ vino añejo, vintage wine. ‖ vino blanco, white wine. ‖ vino clarete, dark rosé wine. ‖ vino de aguja, slightly sparkling wine. ‖ vino de Jerez, sherry. ‖ vino de la casa, house wine. ‖ vino de mesa, table wine. ‖ vino dulce, sweet wine. ‖ vino espumoso, sparkling wine. ‖ vino generoso, full-bodied wine. ‖ vino peleón, *fam* plonk. ‖ vino rosado, rosé. ‖ vino seco, dry wine. ‖ vino tinto, red wine.
vinoso,-a adj wine, wine-like.
viña f vineyard.
● de todo hay en la viña del señor, *fig* it takes all sorts to make a world.
viñador,-ra m,f vine grower, viticulturist.
viñedo m vineyard.
viñeta 1 f (*en impresión*) vignette. **2** (*dibujo humorístico*) cartoon.
viola 1 f viola. – **2** mf viola player.
violáceo,-a adj violaceous, violet.
violación 1 f (*transgresión*) violation, infringement. **2** (*de persona*) rape.
violado,-a 1 adj violaceous, violet. – **2** violado, m violet.
violador,-ra 1 m,f (*de leyes etc*) violator. **2** (*lugar*) violator, trespasser; (*tumba*) desecrator. – **3** violador, m rapist.
violar 1 t (*transgredir*) to violate, infringe. **2** (*lugar*) to violate, trespass; (*tumba*) to desecrate. **3** (*persona*) to rape.
violencia 1 f (*fuerza*) violence. **2** (*embarazo*) embarrassment. **3** (*situación embarazosa*) embarrassing situation. **4** (*violación*) rape. **5** (*injusticia*) outrage.
violentar 1 t (*forzar algo*) to force, break open. **2** (*obligar a alguien*) to force, use force on. **3** *fig* (*entrar*) to break into, enter by force. **4** *fig* (*dicho, escrito*) to twist, distort. – **5** violentarse, p *fig* (*obligarse*) to force os. (**en**, to): *se violentó en comerlo*, he forced himself to eat it. **6** *fig* (*molestarse*) to get annoyed. **7** *fig* (*avergonzarse*) to feel ashamed; (*pasar vergüenza*) to be ashamed.
violento,-a 1 adj (*gen*) violent. **2** (*vergonzoso*) embarrassing, awkward. **3** (*molesto*) embarrassed, awkward, ill at ease. **4** (*dicho, escrito*) twisted, distorted. **5** (*postura*) forced, unnatural. **6** DEP rough.
violeta 1 adj (*color*) violet. – **2** m (*color*) violet. – **3** f BOT violet.
violetera f violet seller.
violín 1 m violin; *fam* fiddle. – **2** mf violinist.
violinista mf violinist.
violón 1 m double bass. – **2** mf double bass player.
violoncelista mf celllist, violoncello.
violoncelo m cello.
violonchelista mf cellist, violoncello.
violonchelo m cello.
viperino,-a 1 adj viperine, viperous. **2** *fig* venomous.
■ lengua viperina, *fig* venomous tongue, spiteful tongue.
vira 1 f (*saeta*) dart. **2** (*de zapato*) welt.

virada *f* MAR tack, tacking.
virago *f* virago.
viraje 1 *m* (*curva*) turn, bend. 2 (*en coche*) turn. 3 MAR tack. 4 (*fotografía*) toning. 5 *fig* (*de ideas etc*) change in direction, about-face, volte-face.
virar 1 *i* MAR to tack, put about. 2 AUTO to turn round. 3 *fig* to change. – 4 *t* (*en fotografía*) to tone.
● virar en redondo, *fig* to change completely.
virgen 1 *adj* (*persona*) virgin. 2 (*puro*) virgin, pure. 3 *fig* (*intacto*) unspoiled. 4 (*reputación*) unsullied. – 5 *mf* virgin.
● ser un viva la Virgen, *fam* to be a devil-may-care person.
■ aceite de oliva virgen, virgen olive oil. ‖ cinta virgen, blank tape. ‖ la Santísima Virgen, the Blessed Virgin. ‖ selva virgen, virgin forest.
Vírgenes las Islas Vírgenes, *fpl* the Virgin Islands.
virginal 1 *adj* virginal. 2 REL of the Virgin.
Virginia *f* Virginia.
■ enredadera de Virginia, Virginia creeper. ‖ Virginia Occidental, Western Virginia.
virginidad *f* virginity.
virgo 1 *m* (*virginidad*) virginity. 2 (*himen*) hymen. 3 Virgo, (*astronomía, astrología*) Virgo.
▲ In *3, pl* Virgo.
virguería 1 *f arg* (*habilidad*) gem, marvel. 2 *arg* (*adorno*) frill.
● hacer virguerías, *fam* to work wonders, be a dab hand.
virguero,-a *adj arg* great, brill.
vírgula *f* → **virgulilla**.
virgulilla 1 *f* (*gen*) small punctuation mark. 2 (*acento*) accent. 3 (*coma*) comma; (*comillas*) inverted commas; (*apóstrofo*) apostrophe. 4 (*cedilla*) cedilla. 5 (*rayita*) line, dash.
vírico,-a *adj* viral.
viril *adj* virile, manly.
virilidad *f* virility.
virreina 1 *f* (*mujer del virrey*) viceroy's wife. 2 (*que gobierna*) vicereine, female viceroy.
virreinato *m* viceroyalty.
virrey *m* viceroy.
virtual *adj* virtual.
virtualmente *adv* virtually.
virtud 1 *f* (*cualidad*) virtue. 2 (*propiedad, eficacia*) property, quality: *con virtudes curativas,* with medicinal properties.
● en virtud de, by virtue of.
virtuosismo *m* virtuosity.
virtuoso,-a 1 *adj* virtuous. – 2 *m,f* virtuous person. 3 ART virtuoso.
viruela 1 *f* MED smallpox. 2 (*marca*) pockmark.
● picado,-a de viruelas, pockmarked.
viruji *m fam* fresh air.
virulé 1 a la virulé, *loc adv fam* (*estropeado*) damaged, broken; (*torcido*) crooked, twisted. 2 *fam* (*chiflado*) mad, nuts, crazy.
● tener un ojo a la virulé, *fam* to have a black eye.
virulencia *f* virulence.
virulento,-a *adj* virulent.
virus *m* virus.
▲ *pl* virus.
viruta *f* shaving.
vis vis cómica, *f* comic sense, humour (US humor).
visa *f* AM visa.

visado,-a 1 *pp* → **visar**. – 2 *adj* endorsed with a visa. – 3 visado, *m* visa.
visaje *m* grimace.
visar 1 *t* (*pasaporte*) to endorse with a visa. 2 (*documento*) to endorse, approve.
víscera 1 *f* internal organ. – 2 vísceras, *fpl* viscera, entrails.
visceral 1 *adj* visceral. 2 *fig* profound, deep-rooted.
viscosidad *f* viscosity.
viscoso,-a *adj* viscous.
visera 1 *f* (*de gorra*) peak; (*de casco*) visor. 2 (*suelta*) eyeshade. 3 AUTO sun visor.
● calarse la visera, to pull down one's visor.
■ gorra de visera, peaked cap.
visibilidad *f* visibility: *curva con mala visibilidad,* blind bend.
visible 1 *adj* (*que se ve*) visible. 2 (*evidente*) evident.
● estar visible, *fig* to be decent.
visiblemente 1 *adv* (*perceptiblemente*) visibly. 2 (*claramente*) clearly, evidently.
visigodo,-a 1 *adj* Visigothic. – 2 *m,f* Visigoth.
visigótico,-a *adj* Visigothic.
visillo *m* small lace curtain.
visión 1 *f* (*acción*) vision. 2 (*vista*) sight. 3 (*ilusión*) vision. 4 *fig* (*persona fea*) fright, sight.
● quedarse como quien ve visiones, *fam fig* to look as if one has seen a ghost. ‖ ver visiones, to dream, see things.
■ visión de conjunto, *fig* overall view.
visionario,-a 1 *adj* visionary. – 2 *m,f* visionary.
visir *m* vizir, vizier.
■ gran visir, grand vizier.
visita 1 *f* (*acción*) visit. 2 (*invitado*) visitor, guest; (*invitados*) visitors *pl*, guests *pl*.
● estar de visita en, to be visiting. ‖ hacer una visita a algn., to pay sb. a visit. ‖ ir de visita a casa de algn., to pay sb. a visit. ‖ tener visita, (*uno*) to have a visitor; (*varios*) to have visitors.
■ horas de visita, MED surgery hours. ‖ visita de cortesía / visita de cumplido, courtesy visit. ‖ visita de médico, *fam* short visit. ‖ visita relámpago, flying visit, lightning visit.
visitación *f* visitation.
visitador,-ra 1 *adj* fond of visiting. – 2 *m,f* (*representante - hombre*) pharmaceutical salesman; (*- mujer*) pharmaceutical saleswoman. 3 (*inspector*) inspector.
visitante 1 *adj* visiting. – 2 *mf* visitor.
visitar 1 *t* (*ir a ver a alguien*) to visit, pay a visit to, call on, go and see: *vamos a ver a la abuela,* let's go and visit grandma. 2 (*lugar*) to visit, see: *visitaron la Sagrada Familia,* they visited the Sagrada Familia. 3 (*inspeccionar*) to inspect, visit, examine.
vislumbrar 1 *t* (*ver*) to glimpse, catch a glimpse of, make out. 2 *fig* (*conjeturar*) to begin to see: *vislumbraron una solución al problema,* they began to see a solution to the problem.
vislumbre 1 *f* (*de luz*) glimmer. 2 (*atisbo*) glimpse. 3 *fig* glimmer.
● tener vislumbres de, *fig* to have an inkling of.
viso 1 *m* (*reflejo*) sheen, shimmer. 2 (*ropa interior*) underskirt. 3 *fig* (*apariencia*) appearance.
● de viso, important. ‖ tener visos de, to seem, appear.
visón *m* mink.
visor 1 *m* (*de arma*) sight. 2 (*de máquina fotográfica*) viewfinder.

víspera 1 *f* (*día anterior*) day before. 2 (*de fiesta*) eve. – 3 **vísperas,** *fpl* REL vespers.
● **día de mucho, víspera de nada,** *fig* nothing lasts forever. ‖ **en vísperas de,** on the eve of.
vista *f* → **visto,-a.**
vistavisión *f* wide screen.
vistazo *m* glance.
● **dar un vistazo a algo / echar un vistazo a algo,** (*mirar*) to have a look at sth.; (*vigilar*) to keep an eye on.
visto,-a 1 *pp* → **ver.** – 2 *adj* (*anticuado*) old-fashioned. 3 (*dado*) in view of, considering. 4 (*corriente*) common. 5 (*ladrillo, viga, obra*) exposed. 6 JUR (*dictaminado*): *el caso está visto para sentencia,* the case has been heard and a verdict may be decided upon. – 7 **visto,** *m* approval. – 8 **vista,** *f* (*visión*) sight, vision. 9 (*ojo*) eye, eyes *pl.* 10 (*panorama*) view. 11 (*aspecto*) appearance, aspect, look. 12 (*dibujo, cuadro, foto*) view. 13 (*intención*) intention. 14 (*propósito*) outlook, prospect. 15 JUR trial, hearing. – 16 **vistas,** *fpl* view *sing: la habitación tiene vistas al mar,* the room has a view of the sea.
● **a la vista,** at sight, on sight: *pagadero a la vista,* payable at sight. ‖ **a la vista de todos,** (*públicamente*) in full view of everyone; (*abiertamente*) openly. ‖ **a primera vista / a simple vista,** at first sight: *a primera vista parecía más complicado,* at first sight it looked more complicated. ‖ **a tantos días vista,** so many days after sight. ‖ **ver algo a vista de pájaro,** to have a a bird's-eye view of sth.: *Londres a vista de pájaro,* a bird's-eye view of London. ‖ **actuar con mucha vista,** *fig* to act with great foresight. ‖ **alzar la vista,** to raise one's eyes, look up. ‖ **apartar la vista de algo/algn.,** to look away from sth./sb. ‖ **bajar la vista,** to look down. ‖ **clavar la vista en algo / fijar la vista en algo,** to stare at sth. ‖ **comerse algo/algn. con la vista,** *fig* to devour sth./sb. with one's eyes. ‖ **con vistas a,** (*hacia*) overlooking; (*pensando en*) with a view to, in anticipation of. ‖ **conocer a algn. de vista,** to know sb. by sight. ‖ **dar el visto bueno a algo,** to approve sth., O.K. sth. ‖ **en vista de,** in view of, considering. ‖ **está visto que ...,** it's obvious that. ‖ **estar a la vista,** to be evident, be obvious: *está a la vista que no lo conseguirán,* it's obvious they won't manage it. ‖ **estar algo muy visto,-a,** (*pasado de moda*) to be old-fashioned; (*poco original*) not to be very original, be old hat; (*corriente*) to be very common: *esas botas están muy vistas,* everyone's wearing those boots now; *es un truco muy visto,* it's an old trick. ‖ **estar bien visto,-a,** to be well looked upon, be considered acceptable. ‖ **estar mal visto,-a,** to be frowned upon. ‖ **hacer la vista gorda,** *fam* to turn a blind eye. ‖ **lo nunca visto,** something extraordinary, something quite out of the ordinary: *esto es lo nunca visto,* this is unheard of. ‖ **ni visto ni oído,** *fig* in a flash. ‖ **no quitar la vista de encima,** *fig* not to take one's eyes off: *no pudo quitarle la vista de encima,* he couldn't take his eyes off her. ‖ **poner a la vista,** to put on show. ‖ **por lo visto,** apparently. ‖ **quitar de la vista,** to take away. ‖ **ser agradable a la vista,** to be pleasing to the eye. ‖ **ser corto,-a de vista,** to be short-sighted. ‖ **tener la vista cansada,** to be suffering from eyestrain. ‖ **tener mala vista,** to have poor eyesight. ‖ **tener mucha vista,** *fig* to be far-sighted. ‖ **tener vista de lince,** *fig* to be eagle-eyed, have eyes like a hawk. ‖ **visto que ...,** in view of the fact that ..., given that ..., seeing that ... ‖ **volver la vista atrás,** to look back.
■ **visto bueno,** approval, O.K.
vistosamente 1 *adv* (*de forma llamativa*) showily, flashily. 2 (*con colorido*) colourfully (US colorfully).

vistoso,-a 1 *adj* (*llamativo*) showy, flashy. 2 (*colorido*) bright, colourful (US colorful).
visual 1 *adj* visual. – 2 *f* (*línea*) line of vision, line of sight. 3 *arg* (*vistazo*) look.
visualizar 1 *t* to visualize. 2 INFORM to display.
▲ *Conjugation model* [4], *like realizar.*
vital 1 *adj* (*de la vida*) vital. 2 *fig* (*esencial*) essential, vital. 3 (*persona*) lively, full of vitality.
■ **órgano vital,** vital organ.
vitalicio,-a 1 *adj* life, for life. – 2 **vitalicio,** *m* (*pensión*) life annuity. 3 (*seguro*) life insurance policy.
■ **cargo vitalicio,** post held for life. ‖ **pensión vitalicia / renta vitalicia,** life annuity.
vitalidad *f* vitality.
vitalismo *m* vitalism.
vitalizar *t* to vitalize.
▲ *Conjugation model* [4], *like realizar.*
vitamina *f* vitamin.
vitaminado,-a *adj* vitamin-enriched, enriched with vitamins.
vitamínico,-a *adj* vitamin.
vitando,-a 1 *adj* (*que se debe evitar*) to be avoided. 2 *fml* (*abominable*) hateful, odious.
vitela *f* vellum.
vitelina *f* → **vitelino,-a.**
vitelino,-a 1 *adj* vitelline. – 2 **vitelina,** *f* vitelline membrane.
vitelo *m* vitellus.
vitícola *adj* wine-growing, wine-producing, viticultural.
viticultor,-ra *m,f* wine grower, viticulturist.
viticultura *f* wine-growing, viticulture.
vito *m* Andalusian dance and song.
Vito baile de San Vito, *m* St. Vitus' dance.
vitola 1 *f* (*para calibrar balas*) calibrator. 2 (*de cigarro*) cigar band. 3 *fig* (*facha*) appearance.
vítor 1 *m* acclamation, cheer. – 2 *interj* bravo!, hurrah!
● **dar vítores,** to cheer, acclaim.
▲ *Generally used in plural.*
vitorear *t* (*aclamar*) to cheer, acclaim; (*aplaudir*) to applaud.
vitoriano,-a 1 *adj* of Vitoria, from Vitoria. – 2 *m,f* person from Vitoria, inhabitant of Vitoria.
vitral *m* stained-glass window.
vítreo,-a *adj* vitreous.
vitrificar 1 *t* to vitrify. – 2 **vitrificarse,** *p* to vitrify.
▲ *Conjugation model* [1], *like sacar.*
vitrina 1 *f* (*armario*) glass cabinet, display cabinet. 2 (*de exposición*) glass case, showcase. 3 (*escaparate*) shop window.
vitriolo *m* vitriol.
vitro, *loc* in vitro.
■ **fecundación in vitro,** in vitro fertilization.
vitrocerámica encimera **vitrocerámica,** *f* ceramic hob.
vitualla *f* provisions *pl,* food.
▲ *Generally used in plural.*
vituperable *adj* reprehensible, reproachable.
vituperación *f* vituperation.
vituperar *t* to vituperate, censure, condemn.
vituperio *m* vituperation, censure, condemnation.
viudedad 1 *f* (*estado*) widowhood. 2 (*pensión - hombre*) widower's pension; (- *mujer*) widow's pension.
viudez *f* widowhood.
viudo,-a 1 *adj* widowed. – 2 *m,f* (*hombre*) widower; (*mujer*) widow.

● **quedar viudo / quedar viuda,** to be left a widower / be left a widow.
viva *m* → **vivo,-a**.
vivac *m* bivouac.
▲ *pl vivaques.*
vivacidad *f* vivacidad, liveliness, vivaciousness.
vivalavirgen *mf fam* devil-may-care person.
▲ *pl vivalavirgen.*
vivales *mf fam* crafty devil, smooth operator, sly one.
vivamente 1 *adv (con viveza)* vividly. **2** *(intensamente)* strongly, intensely. **3** *(profundamente)* deeply. **4** *(sinceramente)* sincerely.
vivaque *m* bivouac.
vivaquear *i* to bivouac.
vivar 1 *m (de conejos)* warren. **2** *(de peces)* fish farm, fish hatchery.
vivaracho,-a 1 *adj fam* vivacious, lively, sprightly. **2** *fam (ojos)* sparkling.
vivaz 1 *adj (vivo)* vivacious, lively. **2** *(perspicaz)* sharp, quick-witted. **3** *(que dura)* long-lived. **4** *(planta)* perennial.
vivencia *f* personal experience.
víveres *mpl* food *sing*, provisions, supplies.
vivero 1 *m (de plantas)* nursery. **2** *(de peces)* fish farm, fish hatchery; *(de moluscos)* bed. **3** *fig* breeding ground, hotbed.
viveza 1 *f (persona)* liveliness, vivacity. **2** *(color, relato)* vividness. **3** *(al hablar)* vehemence. **4** *(agudeza)* sharpness, quick-wittedness. **5** *(ardor)* passion, force. **6** *(en ojos)* sparkle.
vivido,-a 1 *pp* → **vivir**. **- 2** *adj (real)* real, real-life, true-life. **3** *(de la propia experiencia)* based on personal experience.
vívido,-a *adj* vivid.
vividor,-ra 1 *adj (vivaz)* living, alive. **2** *(laborioso)* capable, shrewd. **- 3** *m,f (persona que sabe vivir)* person who makes the most of life. **4** *pey (aprovechado)* sponger, scrounger.
vivienda 1 *f (gen)* housing, accommodation. **2** *(morada)* dwelling. **3** *(casa)* house. **4** *(piso)* flat.
■ **bloque de viviendas,** block of flats. ‖ **vivienda de protección oficial,** council house, council flat. ‖ **vivienda unifamiliar,** detached house.
viviente *adj* living, alive.
● **todo bicho viviente,** *fam* every living creature.
vivificador,-ra *adj* life-giving, vivifying.
vivificante *adj* life-giving, vivifying.
vivificar *t* to vivify, give life to, enliven.
▲ *Conjugation model* |1|, *like* **sacar.**
vivíparo,-a *adj* viviparous.
vivir 1 *i (tener vida)* to live; *(estar vivo)* to be alive: *vivió hasta los ochenta años,* he lived until he was eighty; *¿vive aún?,* is she still alive? **2** *(habitar)* to live: *vive en Barcelona,* she lives in Barcelona. **3** *(mantenerse)* to live, live on, make a living: *ese trabajo no le da para vivir,* he can't live on what that job pays. **4** *fig (durar)* to last, live on. **- 5** *t (pasar por, experimentar)* to live through, go through, experience: *mi abuelo vivió la guerra,* my grandfather lived through the war. **- 6** *m* living, life.
● **hay que seguir viviendo,** life must go on. ‖ **ir viviendo,** to get by, manage. ‖ **no dejar vivir a algn.,** *fig* to give sb. a hard time. ‖ **saber vivir,** to enjoy life. ‖ **viven de milagro,** *fig* it's a wonder they're still alive. ‖ **vivir a cuerpo de rey,** *fig* to live like a king. ‖ **vivir a lo grande,** *fam* to live it up, live in style. ‖ **vivir de,** to live on: *viven de su pensión,* they live on his pension. ‖ **vivir de ilusiones,** to live in a dreamworld. ‖ **vivir de**

sus ahorros, to live off one's savings. ‖ **vivir del aire,** *fig* to live on fresh air. ‖ **vivir del cuento,** *fam* not to know what hard work is, never to have earned an honest penny. ‖ **¡viva el rey!,** long live the king! ‖ **¡vivan los novios!,** three cheers for the bride and groom! ‖ **y vivieron felices y comieron perdices,** and they all lived happily ever after. ‖ **vivir para algo,** to live for sth.: *vive para la música,* he lives for music, music is his whole life.
■ **gente de mal vivir,** shady characters.
vivisección *f* vivisection.
vivito,-a *adj fam* alive.
● **vivito,-a y coleando,** *fam* alive and kicking.
vivo,-a 1 *adj (que tiene vida)* living; *(que está)* alive: *materia viva,* living matter; *Pepe está vivo,* Pepe is alive. **2** *(fuego, llama)* live, burning. **3** *(lengua)* living. **4** *fig (color etc)* bright, vivid. **5** *fig (animado)* lively, vivacious. **6** *fig (dolor, emoción, etc)* acute, deep, intense. **7** *fig (descripción etc)* lively, graphic. **8** *fig (carácter)* quick, irritable. **9** *fig (listo)* quick-witted. **10** *fig (astuto)* shrewd, sly. **11** *fig (llaga, herida)* open. **- 12** *m,f* living person: *los vivos,* the living. **13** *fam fig (astuto)* quick-witted person. **- 14** vivo, *m* COST trimming, border. **15** viva, *f* cheer, shout.
● **dar vivas,** to cheer. ‖ **a lo vivo,** vividly. ‖ **de viva voz,** verbally, by word of mouth. ‖ **en carne viva,** raw, red raw; *fig* fresh. ‖ **en vivo,** TV live. ‖ **al rojo vivo,** red-hot. ‖ **herir a algn. en lo más vivo / tocar a algn. en lo más vivo,** *fig* to cut sb. to the quick. ‖ **¿quién vive?,** MIL who goes there? ‖ **ser el vivo retrato de / ser la viva imagen de,** *fam* to be the spitting image of. ‖ **tener el genio vivo,** to be quick-tempered.
■ **fuerzas vivas,** *fig* driving forces.
vizcaíno,-a 1 *adj* of Vizcaya, from Vizcaya. **- 2** *m,f* person from Vizcaya, inhabitant of Vizcaya.
Vizcaya *f* Vizcaya.
■ **golfo de Vizcaya,** Bay of Biscay.
vizcondado 1 *m (territorio)* viscounty. **2** *(título)* viscountcy, viscountship.
vizconde *m* viscount.
vizcondesa *f* viscountess.
V.M. *abr (Vuestra Majestad)* Your Majesty.
VO *abr* CINEM *(Versión Original)* original language version.
vocablo *m* word, term.
vocabulario *m* vocabulary.
vocación *f* vocation, calling.
vocacional *adj* vocational.
vocal 1 *adj* vocal. **- 2** *f* vowel. **- 3** *mf (de junta etc)* member.
vocálico,-a *adj* vocalic.
vocalismo *m* vowel system.
vocalista *mf* vocalist, singer.
vocalización *f* vocalization.
vocalizar 1 *i* to vocalize. **- 2** *t* to vocalize.
▲ *Conjugation model* |4|, *like* **realizar.**
vocativo *m* vocative.
voceador,-ra 1 *adj* vociferous, loud-mouthed. **- 2** *m,f* shouter. **- 3** **voceador,** *m* town crier.
vocear 1 *i (dar voces)* to shout, cry out. **- 2** *t (divulgar)* to publish. **3** *(gritar)* to shout, cry out. **4** *(divulgar)* to publish, proclaim. **5** *(aclamar)* to cheer, acclaim.
voceras *mf fam* loudmouth.
vocerío *m* shouting, uproar.
vocero,-a *m,f (gen)* spokesperson; *(hombre)* spokesman; *(mujer)* spokeswoman.
vociferador,-ra *adj* vociferous.
vociferante *adj* vociferous.
vociferar 1 *i* to vociferate, shout. **- 2** *t* to vociferate, shout.

vocinglero,-a *adj* loud-mouthed.
vodevil *m* vaudeville, music hall.
vodevilesco,-a *adj* vaudevillian, music-hall.
vodka *m* vodka.
vol. *abr* (*volumen*) volume; (*abreviatura*) vol.
voladizo,-a 1 *adj* projecting, jutting out. – 2 **voladizo,** *m* projection.
volado,-a 1 *pp* → **volar.** – 2 *adj* (*en impresión*) superior. 3 ARQ projecting.
● **dar un beso volado a algn.,** *fam* to blow sb. a kiss.
‖ **estar volado,-a,** *fam* (*intranquilo*) to feel uneasy; (*impaciente*) to be in a hurry; (*molesto*) to feel embarrassed.
volador,-ra 1 *adj* flying. – 2 **volador,** *m* (*cohete*) rocket. 3 (*pez*) flying fish. 4 (*molusco*) type of squid.
voladura 1 *f* (*gen*) blowing up, demolition. 2 (*en mina*) blasting.
volandas en volandas, *loc adv* (*por el aire*) in the air, flying through the air; (*muy rápidamente*) swiftly, rapidly.
● **llevar a algn. en volandas,** to rush sb.: *la llevó en volandas al aeropuerto,* he rushed her to the airport.
volandeira *f* (*marisco*) queen.
volandera *f* → **volandero,-a.**
volandero,-a 1 *adj* (*volantón*) ready to fly. 2 (*que cuelga*) hanging; (*que está suelto*) loose. 3 *fig* (*imprevisto*) unexpected, unforeseen. 4 *fig* (*que vagabundea*) wandering, restless. – 5 **volandera,** *f* (*piedra del molino*) millstone.
volante 1 *adj* (*que vuela*) flying. 2 (*que se desplaza*) flying, mobile. – 3 *m* COST flounce; (*adorno*) frill, ruffle. 4 AUTO steering wheel. 5 TÉC flywheel. 6 (*de reloj*) balance wheel. 7 (*aviso, orden*) note, order. 8 DEP shuttlecock.
● **ir al volante,** to be driving.
volantín *m* type of fishing line.
volantón,-ona *adj* fledged, ready to fly.
volapié *m* method used in killing the bull.
volar 1 *i* (*ir por el aire*) to fly. 2 *fig* (*papeles etc*) to be blown away. 3 *fig* (*ir deprisa*) to fly: *el tiempo vuela,* time flies. 4 *fam fig* (*desaparecer*) to disappear, vanish. 5 *fig* (*sobresalir de un edificio*) to jut out, project. 6 *fig* (*noticia etc*) to spread rapidly. – 7 *t fig* (*hacer explotar - edificio*) to blow up, demolish; (- *caja fuerte*) to blow open; (- *en minería*) to blast. 8 *fig* (*en impresión*) to raise. 9 (*en caza*) to flush. – 10 **volarse,** *p* (*papeles etc*) to be blown away. 11 *fig* (*irritarse*) to blow up, lose one's temper.
● **echarse a volar,** to fly away, fly off. ‖ **hacer algo volando,** *fam fig* to do sth. as quick as a flash, do sth. in a jiffy: *limpió la casa volando,* he cleaned the house in a jiffy; *pasó volando,* she flew past. ‖ **¡volando!,** *fam fig* jump to it!
▲ *Conjugation model* |31|, *like* **contar.**
volatería 1 *f* (*caza*) falconry. 2 (*aves*) fowl *sing,* birds.
volátil *adj* volatile.
volatilidad *f* volatility.
volatilizar 1 *t* to volatilize. – 2 **volatilizarse,** *p* to volatilize. 3 *fig* to vanish into thin air.
▲ *Conjugation model* |4|, *like* **realizar.**
volatín 1 *m* (*acrobacia*) acrobatics *pl.* 2 (*acróbata*) acrobat.
volatinero,-a *m,f* acrobat.
volcán *m* volcano.
volcánico,-a *adj* volcanic.
volcanismo *m* volcanism.
volcar 1 *i* (*coche etc*) to turn over, overturn. 2 MAR to capsize. – 3 *t* (*gen*) to turn over, knock over, upset. 4 (*vaciar*) to empty out, pour out. 5 *fig* (*hacer cambiar de parecer*) to make change one's mind. 6 *fig* (*molestar*) to annoy, irritate, upset. 7 *fig* (*turbar la cabeza*) to make feel dizzy. – 8 **volcarse,** *p* (*objeto*) to fall over, tip over; (*coche*) to turn

over, overturn; (*barco*) to capsize. **9** *fig* (*entregarse*) to do one's utmost.
▲ *Conjugation model* |49|, *like* **trocar.**
volea 1 *f* (*palo*) whippletree, swingletree. 2 DEP volley.
volear *t* to volley.
voleibol *m* volleyball.
voleo 1 *m* DEP volley. 2 (*en danza*) high kick. 3 (*bofetón*) slap.
● **a voleo / al voleo,** *fig* at random, haphazardly. ‖ **de un voleo,** *fig* very quickly, in one go.
volframio *m* wolfram.
volitivo,-a *adj* volitive.
volován *m* vol-au-vent.
volquete *m* dumper, tipcart.
voltaje *m* voltage.
voltear 1 *t* (*dar vueltas*) to whirl, twirl. 2 (*poner al revés*) to turn over, toss. 3 (*campanas*) to peal, ring out. 4 (*a una persona*) to toss up in the air.
voltense 1 *adj* Voltaic. – 2 *m* Voltaic.
voltereta *f* somersault.
● **dar volteretas,** to do somersaults.
volterianismo *m* Voltairianism.
volteriano,-a 1 *adj* Voltairian, Voltairean. – 2 *m,f* Voltairian, Voltairean.
voltímetro *m* voltmeter.
voltio *m* volt.
volubilidad 1 *f* changeability, fickleness. 2 BOT volubility.
voluble 1 *adj* changeable, fickle. 2 BOT voluble, twining.
volumen 1 *m* (*gen*) volume. 2 (*tamaño*) size.
● **bajar el volumen / subir el volumen,** to turn the volume down / turn the volume up. ‖ **de mucho volumen,** sizeable, important.
■ **volumen de negocios,** turnover.
volumetría *f* volumetry.
voluminoso,-a 1 *adj* voluminous. 2 (*enorme*) bulky, massive.
voluntad 1 *f* (*cualidad*) will. 2 (*fuerza de voluntad*) willpower: *tiene mucha voluntad,* she's very strong-willed. 3 (*deseo*) wish. 4 (*propósito*) intention, purpose: *tiene buena voluntad,* her intentions are good. 5 (*afecto*) affection.
● **a voluntad,** at will. ‖ **ganarse la voluntad de algn.,** to win sb. over. ‖ **hacer uno su santa voluntad,** *fam* to have one's way, do as one likes. ‖ **hágase tu voluntad,** REL Thy will be done. ‖ **por causas ajenas a nuestra voluntad,** due to reasons beyond our control. ‖ **¿qué quiere? -la voluntad, ¿**what do you want? -whatever you think right. ‖ **buena voluntad,** goodwill.
■ **última voluntad,** last wish. ‖ **voluntad de Dios,** God's will. ‖ **voluntad de hierro / voluntad férrea,** will of iron, iron will.
voluntariado 1 *m* MIL voluntary enlistment. 2 (*civil*) group of volunteers.
voluntariamente *adv* voluntarily.
voluntario,-a 1 *adj* voluntary. – 2 *m,f* volunteer.
● **ofrecerse voluntario,-a,** to volunteer.
voluntarioso,-a 1 *adj* (*con voluntad*) willing. 2 *pey* (*testarudo*) wilful, headstrong.
voluptuosidad *f* voluptuousness.
voluptuoso,-a *adj* voluptuous.
voluta 1 *f* ARQ volute, scroll. 2 (*espiral*) spiral, column. 3 (*de humo*) ring.
volver 1 *t* (*dar vuelta a*) to turn, turn over; (*hacia abajo*) to turn upside down; (*de dentro afuera*) to turn inside out; (*lo de atrás hacia delante*) to turn back to front: *volver la*

tortilla, to turn the omelette. **2** (*convertir*) to turn, make, change: *el dinero ha vuelto tonto a Paco,* money has made Paco foolish; *volvió el agua en vino,* he changed water into wine. **3** (*devolver*) to give back; (*a su lugar*) to put back. **4** (*torcer*) to turn: *al volver la esquina,* on turning the corner. – **5** *i* (*regresar*) to return; (*ir*) to go back; (*venir*) to come back: *volvió de la guerra,* he returned form the war; *volvieron a casa después de cenar,* they went back home after dinner; *vuelve cuando quieras,* come back whenever you want. **6** (*a un tema etc*) to return, revert. **7** *volver a,* (*hacer otra vez*) to do again: *volver a leer,* to read again. – **8** **volverse,** *p* (*regresar - ir*) to go back; (*- venir*) to come back. **9** (*darse la vuelta*) to turn. **10** (*convertirse*) to turn, become.

● **volver a algn. a la vida,** to revive sb., bring sb. back to life. ‖ **volver a las andadas,** to fall back into one's old habits. ‖ **volver del revés,** to turn inside out. ‖ **volver en sí,** to regain consciousness, come round. ‖ **volver los ojos hacia,** to turn one's eyes towards. ‖ **volver sobre sus pasos,** to retrace one's steps. ‖ **volverle la espalda a algn.,** *fig* to turn one's back on sb. ‖ **volverse atrás,** *fig* to go back on one's word, back out. ‖ **volverse en contra de algn.,** to turn against sb.

▲ Conjugation model [32], *like mover; pp* **vuelto,-a.**

vomitar I *t* to vomit, bring up. **2** *fig* to belch, spew out. – **3** *i* to be sick, vomit: *tengo ganas de vomitar,* I feel sick.

● **vomitar injurias,** *fig* to hurl insults. ‖ **vomitar sangre,** to cough up blood.

vomitivo,-a I *adj* emetic. – **2 vomitivo,** *m* emetic.

vómito I *m* (*resultado*) vomit. **2** (*acción*) vomiting.

vomitona *f* vomit.

● **echar la vomitona,** *fam* to be violently sick.

voracidad *f* voracity, voraciousness.

vorágine *f* vortex, whirlpool.

voraz I *adj* voracious. **2** *fig* fierce, raging.

vorazmente I *adv* voraciously. **2** *fig* fiercely.

vórtice I *f* vortex, whirlpool. **2** (*de ciclón*) centre (US center) of a cyclone.

vos I *pron arc* (*usted*) thou, you; (Dios) Thou. **2** AM (*tú*) you.

Vos.E *abr* CINEM (*Versión Original Subtitulada en Español*) film in the original language version with Spanish subtitles.

vosear *t* to address as *vos.*

voseo *m* use of *vos.*

Vosgos los **Vosgos,** *mpl* the Vosges.

vosotros,-as *pron* (*sujeto*) you; (*objeto*) you, yourselves: *con vosotros,* with you; *entre vosotros,* among yourselves; *¿cómo lo sabéis vosotros?,* how do you know?

● **de vosotros,** your, yours: *¿estos libros son de vosotros?,* are these your books?; *creo que esto es de vosotros,* I think this is yours.

votación I *f* (*voto*) vote, ballot. **2** (*acto*) vote, voting.

● **poner algo a votación / someter algo a votación,** to put sth. to the vote, take a ballot on sth. ■ **votación a mano alzada,** voting by a show of hands.

votante I *adj* voting. – **2** *mf* voter.

votar I *i* (*dar el voto*) to vote. **2** (*blasfemar*) to swear. **3** REL to vow. – **4** *t* (*proponer para aprobar*) to pass. **5** REL to vow.

voto I *m* (*gen*) vote: *tres votos a favor,* three votes for. **2** REL vow. **3** (*deseo*) wish. **4** (*blasfemia*) curse, oath.

● **formular votos por el éxito de / hacer votos por el éxito de,** to express one's wishes for the success of. ‖ **hacer voto de castidad,** to take a vow of chastity. ‖ **por mayoría de votos,** by a majority vote. ‖ **tener**

voto, to have the right to vote. ‖ **no tener ni voz ni voto,** to have no say in the matter.

■ **derecho al voto,** the right to vote. ‖ **voto de censura,** vote of no confidence. ‖ **voto de confianza,** vote of confidence. ‖ **voto de silencio,** vow of silence. ‖ **voto por correo,** postal vote. ‖ **voto secreto,** secret ballot.

vox ser **vox pópuli,** *loc fam* to be common knowledge.

voy *pres indic* → **ir.**

voz I *f* (*sonido*) voice. **2** (*grito*) shout. **3** (*vocablo, palabra*) word. **4** GRAM voice: *voz activa,* active voice. **5** MÚS (*de instrumento*) tone; (*cantante*) voice: *canción a tres voces,* three-part song. **6** *fig* (*rumor*) rumour (US rumor). **7** *fig* (*en asamblea - facultad de hablar*) voice, say; (*- voto*) vote.

● **a media voz,** in a low voice, softly. ‖ **a voces,** shouting. ‖ **a voz en cuello / a voz en grito,** at the top of one's voice. ‖ **aclararse la voz,** to clear one's throat. ‖ **alzar la voz / levantar la voz,** to raise one's voice. ‖ **corre la voz que ...,** rumour has it that ... ‖ **dar la voz de alarma,** to raise the alarm. ‖ **dar una voz a algn.,** to give sb. a shout. ‖ **dar voces,** to shout. ‖ **en voz alta,** aloud. ‖ **en voz baja,** in a low voice. ‖ **estar pidiendo algo a voces,** *fig* to be crying out for sth. ‖ **llevar la voz cantante,** to sing the leading part; *fig* to rule the roost. ‖ **mudarle la voz,** to break: *se le está mudando la voz,* his voice is breaking. ‖ **ser voz pública,** to be common knowledge. ‖ **tener voz y voto,** *fam* to have a say; POL to be a voting member.

vozarrón,-ona *m,f* powerful voice, booming voice.

V.R. *abr* (*Vuestra Reverencia*) Your Reverence.

V.S. *abr* (*Vuestra Señoría, Usía*) Your Honour.

vudú *m* voodoo.

vuelapluma a **vuelapluma,** *loc adv* in a jiffy.

vuelco I *m* (*gen*) tumble, upset. **2** (*barco*) capsizing. **3** *fig* change.

● **dar un vuelco,** (*coche*) to overturn; (*empresa*) to go to ruin. ‖ **me dio un vuelco el corazón,** my heart missed a beat.

vuelo I *m* (*acto, espacio, etc*) flight. **2** (*acción*) flying. **3** (*vestido*) fullness, flare: *un vestido de vuelo,* a full dress. **4** (*plumas*) flight feathers *pl*; (*alas*) wings *pl*. **5** ARQ (*voladizo*) projection.

● **al vuelo,** in flight. ‖ **alzar el vuelo / emprender el vuelo / levantar el vuelo,** to take flight. ‖ **cazarlas al vuelo / cogerlas al vuelo,** *fig* to be quick on the uptake. ‖ **cortarle los vuelos a algn.,** *fig* to clip sb.'s wings. ‖ **de alto vuelo,** *fig* important, far-reaching. ‖ **de mucho vuelo,** (*vestido*) full; (*persona*) important, high-flying. ‖ **de un vuelo,** *fig* in a flash. ‖ **remontar el vuelo,** to soar up. ‖ **tener muchas horas de vuelo,** *fam* *fig* to be an old hand at sth. ‖ **tomar vuelo,** to take off, grow.

■ **personal de vuelo,** flight crew. ‖ **vuelo chárter / vuelo regular,** charter flight / scheduled flight. ‖ **vuelo espacial,** space flight. ‖ **vuelo libre,** hang-gliding. ‖ **vuelo sin escala,** non-stop flight. ‖ **vuelo sin motor,** gliding.

vuelta *f* → **vuelto,-a.**

vuelto,-a I *pp* → **volver.** – **2** *adj* (*cuello*) roll: *jersey de cuello vuelto,* roll-neck sweater. – **3 vuelta,** *f* (*giro*) turn. **4** (*en un circuito*) lap, circuit. **5** (*paseo*) walk, stroll: *vamos a dar una vuelta,* let's go for a walk. **6** (*regreso, retorno*) return; (*viaje de regreso*) return journey, journey back: *a la vuelta de las vacaciones,* after the holidays. **7** (*dinero de cambio*) change: *quédese con la vuelta,* keep the change. **8** (*curva*) bend, curve. **9** (*reverso*) back, reverse. **10** (*de torneo etc*) round. **11** (*cambio*) change, alteration.

12 COST (*de pantalón*) turn-up; (*forro*) lining. **13** (*al hacer punto*) row. **14** ARQ vault. **15** *fam* (*de bebidas*) round.
● **a la vuelta,** on the way back. ‖ **a vuelta de correo,** by return of post. ‖ **andar a vueltas con algo,** *fig* to deal with sth., sort sth. out: *anda a vueltas con la compra del piso,* she's sorting out the purchase of the flat. ‖ **buscarle las vueltas a algn.,** *fam fig* to find fault with sb. ‖ **cerrar con dos vueltas,** to double-lock. ‖ **cogerle las vueltas a algn.,** *fam fig* to have sb. figured out. ‖ **dar la vuelta a,** (*alrededor*) to go round; (*girar*) to turn (round); (*de arriba abajo*) to turn upside down; (*de dentro a fuera*) to turn inside out; (*cambiar de lado*) to turn over. ‖ **dar la vuelta al mundo,** to go round the world. ‖ **dar una vuelta en coche,** to go for a drive, go for a spin. ‖ **dar vueltas,** to turn round, go round, rotate, spin: *llevo toda la tarde dando vueltas por el centro buscando ese disco,* I've been walking round town all afternoon looking for that record. ‖ **dar vueltas a,** (*alrededor*) to go around; (*girar*) to turn; (*mover*) to stir. ‖ **dar vueltas a algo,** *fig* to worry about sth.: *¡no lo des más vueltas!,* don't worry about it! ‖ **darle cien vueltas a algn.,** *fig* to run rings round sb. ‖ **darse una vuelta por casa de algn.,** to drop by and see sb. ‖ **dar media vuelta,** to turn round. ‖ **estar a la vuelta de la esquina,** to be just around the corner. ‖ **estar de vuelta,** to be back; *fig* not to have been born yesterday. ‖ **¡hasta la vuelta!,** see you when I get back! ‖ **la cabeza me da vueltas,** *fig* my head is spinning. ‖ **la vida da muchas vueltas,** *fam* life is full of ups and downs. ‖ **no tener vuelta de hoja,** *fig* to be beyond doubt. ‖ **poner a algn. de vuelta y media,** *fig* to pull sb. to pieces.
■ **la vuelta al colegio,** (*en publicidad*) "back to school"; (*primer día*) first day back at school. ‖ **la vuelta ciclista a España,** the Tour of Spain. ‖ **la vuelta al ruedo,** (*en los toros*) lap of honour (US honor). ‖ **partido de vuelta,** return match. ‖ **vuelta de campana,** somersault.

vuelvepiedras *m* turnstone.
▲ *pl* **vuelvepiedras**.
vuestro,-a 1 *adj* your, of yours: *vuestra casa,* your house; *un amigo vuestro,* a friend of yours. – **2** *pron* yours: *éstas son las vuestras,* these are yours. – **3** **lo vuestro,** *m* what is yours, what belongs to you.
vulcanismo *m* vulcanism.
vulcanología *f* volcanology, vulcanology.
vulcanólogo,-a *m,f* volcanologist, vulcanologist.
vulgar 1 *adj* (*grosero*) vulgar, coarse, common: *lenguaje vulgar,* coarse language. **2** (*general*) common, general. **3** (*banal*) banal, ordinary; (*idea*) commonplace. **4** (*no técnico*) lay: *término vulgar,* lay term.
vulgaridad 1 *f* (*grosería*) vulgarity, coarseness. **2** (*banalidad*) banality, triviality.
● **decir vulgaridades,** (*groserías*) to use bad language; (*banalidades*) to talk in platitudes.
vulgarismo *m* vulgarism.
vulgarización *f* vulgarization, popularization.
vulgarizar 1 *t* (*popularizar*) to popularize, vulgarize. **2** (*hacer vulgar*) to make common. – **3 vulgarizarse,** *p* (*popular*) to become popular, become common; (*grosero*) to become vulgar, become common.
▲ Conjugation model |4|, like *realizar*.
vulgarmente 1 *adv* (*con vulgaridad*) vulgarly. **2** (*generalmente*) generally, commonly.
vulgata *f* Vulgate.
vulgo *m* *pey* common people *pl,* masses *pl.*
vulnerabilidad *f* vulnerability.
vulnerable *adj* vulnerable.
vulneración 1 *f* (*gen*) violation. **2** *fig* (*reputación*) damaging, harming.
vulnerar 1 *t* (*ley etc*) to violate. **2** *fig* (*honor etc*) to damage, harm.
vulva *f* vulva.
VV *abr* (*ustedes*) you.

W

W, w f (la letra) W, w.
W sím (vatio) watt; (símbolo) W.
walkman m walkman.
   ▲ Registered trademark; pl **walkmans**.
wáter m fam toilet.
   ▲ pl **wáteres**.
waterpolo m water polo.
watt m watt.
   ▲ pl **watts**. See also **vatio**.
W.C. abr (retrete) water-closet; (abreviatura) WC.

wélter m welterweight.
whiskería f whisky bar.
whisky m whisky; (irlandés) whiskey.
windsurf m windsurfing.
windsurfing m windsurfing.
windsurfista mf windsurfer.
wolfram m wolfram.
wolframio m wolfram.

X

X, x *f (la letra)* X, x.
xenofilia *f* xenophilia.
xenófilo,-a **1** *adj* xenophilous. – **2** *m,f* xenophile.
xenofobia *f* xenophobia.
xenofobo,-a **1** *adj* xenophobic. – **2** *m,f* xenophobe.
xenón *m* xenon.
xerografía *f* xerography.

xileno *m* xylene.
xilofonista *mf* xylophonist.
xilófono *m* xylophone.
xilografía **1** *f (arte)* xylography. **2** *(impresión)* xylograph.
xilográfico,-a *adj* xylographic.
xilógrafo,-a *m,f* xylographer.

Y

Y, y *f* (*la letra*) Y, y.

y 1 *conj* and: *Alberto y María*, Alberto and Maria; *un chico joven y apuesto,* a handsome young boy; *¡y no chilles!,* and don't shout!; *hay amigos y amigos,* there are friends and friends. 2 (*hora*) past: *son las tres y cuarto,* it's a quarter past three. 3 (*en pregunta*) what about: *¿y Pepe, se viene?,* what about Pepe, is he coming?. 4 (*repetición*) after: *veces y veces,* time after time, time and time again.
 ● **y eso que,** even though: *no lo encontré, y eso que lo busqué en todas partes,* I couldn't find it even though I looked everywhere for it; *me asusté, y eso que yo no soy miedoso,* it gave me a fright, and I'm not easily frightened, you know. ‖ **¿y (qué)?,** so (what)?. ‖ **¿y si ... ?,** what if ... ?. ‖ **¡y tanto!,** you bet!, and how!
 ▲ See also **e**.

ya 1 *adv* already: *esa película ya la he visto,* I've already seen that film; *¿que ya se han casado?,* what! they've got married already?; *el domingo ya no estaremos aquí,* we'll already have left by Sunday; *eso ya no lo veré yo,* I won't live to see that. 2 (*más tarde*) later: *ya lo haré,* I'll do it later; *ya te llamaré,* I'll give you a ring. 3 (*ahora mismo*) at once, right now, straightaway: *tienes que mandarlo ya,* you must send it at once; *¡ya voy!,* I'm coming! 4 (*ahora*) now: *ya viven en el piso nuevo,* they're living in the new flat now. 5 (*uso enfático*) *ya lo sé,* I know that; *es facilísimo, ya verás,* it's dead easy, you'll see; *y ya no es por el dinero ...,* and it's not the money that matters ... 6 (*denota satisfacción*): *¡ya tenemos coche nuevo!,* we've got the new car!; *¡ya están aquí!,* they're here! 7 (*con tono amenazante*): *¡ya verás ya!,* just you wait! 8 (*con indignación*): *¡ya está bien!,* enough is enough! 9 (*para tranquilizar*): *ya encontrarás trabajo, ya verás como sí,* you'll find a job, you'll see. 10 (*para afirmar*) I know, yes: *tienes que estudiar – ya, pero ...,* you have to study – I know, but ... – 11 *interj irón* oh yes!
 ● **ya ... ya ...,** now ... now ...: *ya ríe, ya llora,* now she laughs, now she weeps; *fantasmas que ya surgen, ya se esfuman,* ghosts which first appear and then vanish; *ya fueran católicos, ya protestantes,* whether they be Catholic or Protestant. ‖ **ya entiendo,** I see. ‖ **ya era hora,** about time too. ‖ **¡ya está!,** there we are!, all done! ‖ **ya nos veremos,** see you soon. ‖ **ya que,** since, seeing that: *ya que estás aquí, quédate a cenar,* seeing that you're here, why don't you stay for supper?.

yaacabó *m* ORN South American hawk.

yac *m* yak.

yacente *adj* lying.
 ■ **estatua yacente,** recumbent statue.

yacer 1 *i* (*estar enterrado*) to lie. 2 *fml* (*hallarse*) to lie. 3 *lit* (*dormir*) to be lying; (*acostarse*) to lie (**con,** with): *Aquí yace ...,* Here lies ...
 ▲ Conjugation model [92].

yacimiento *m* bed, deposit.
 ■ **yacimiento petrolífero,** oilfield.

yago *pres indic* → **yacer**.

yaguar *m* jaguar.

yak *m* ZOOL yak.

Yakarta *m* Djakarta, Jakarta.

yámbico,-ca *adj* iambic.

yambo *m* iamb.

yanqui 1 *mf* HIST Yankee. 2 *pey* Yank. – 3 *adj* HIST Yankee; *pey* Yankee.

yanqui 1 *adj* Yankee. – 2 *mf* Yankee.

yantar 1 *m arc* fare, viands *pl*. – 2 *i arc* to eat.

yarda *f* yard.

yaro *m* arum.

yate *m* yacht.

Yaundé *m* Yaoundé.

yayo,-a *m,f fam* (*abuelo*) grandad; (*abuela*) grandma.

yaz *m* → **jazz**.

yazgo *pres indic* → **yacer**.

yedra *f* ivy.

yegua *f* mare.

yeguada *f* herd of horses.

yeguar *adj* of mares.

yegüero,-a *m,f* keeper of a herd of horses.

yeísmo *m* pronunciation of *ll* as *y*.

yelmo *m arc* helmet.

yema 1 *f* (*de huevo*) yolk. 2 BOT bud. 3 (*del dedo*) fingertip. 4 CULIN sweet made from sugar and egg yolk.
 ■ **yema de huevo,** egg yolk.

Yemen *m* Yemen.

yemení 1 *adj* Yemeni. – 2 *mf* Yemeni.

yen *m* yen.

yendo *ger* → **ir**.

yerba *f* → **hierba**.

yergo *pres indic* → **erguir**.

yermo,-a 1 *adj* (*estéril*) barren. 2 (*despoblado*) deserted, uninhabited. – 3 *m* (*terreno inculto*) wasteland.

yerno *m* son-in-law.

yernocracia *f fam* nepotism.

yerro 1 *m desus* error. – 2 *pres indic* → **errar**.

yerto,-a *adj* rigid, stiff: *yerto de frío,* rigid with cold.

yesal *m* gypsum quarry.

yesar *m* → **yesal**.

yesca *f* tinder.
 ■ **mechero de yesca,** wick lighter.

yesería 1 *f* plasterwork, plastering. 2 (*fábrica*) gypsum kiln. – 3 **yeserías,** *fpl* ART plasterwork.

yesero,-a 1 *m,f* (*fabricante*) plaster manufacturer. 2 (*trabajador*) plasterer.

yeso 1 *m* (*mineral*) gypsum. 2 (*para la construcción*) plaster. 3 (*tiza*) chalk. 4 (*escultura*) plaster cast.

yesoso,-a *adj* chalky.

yesquero *m* wick lighter.

yeti 1 *m* yeti. 2 **el Yeti,** the Abominable Snowman.

yeyé *adj* (*música etc*) sixties.

yeyuno *m* jejunum.
yiddish *m* Yiddish.
yiddish 1 *adj* Yiddish. – **2** *m* (*idioma*) Yiddish.
yiu-yitsu *m* jiujitsu.
yo 1 *pron* I: *el jefe soy yo*, I'm the boss; *soy yo*, it's me; *fui yo quien se lo dijo*, it was me who told him; *entre tú y yo*, between you and me; *yo en tu lugar* ..., if I were you ...; *yo que tú* ..., if I were you ... – **2 el yo,** *m* the ego, the self.
yod *f* yod.
yodado,-a *adj* iodized.
yodo *m* iodine.
yoduro *m* iodide.
yoga *m* yoga.
yogui *mf* yogi.
yogur *m* yoghurt, yogurt.
■ **yogur de fresa,** strawberry yoghurt. ‖ **yogur natural,** plain yoghurt.
▲ *pl* **yogures**.
yogurtera *f* yoghurt maker.
yoin *m* arg joint.
yola *f* yawl.
yonqui *mf* arg junkie.
yóquey *m* jockey.
yoqui *m* jockey.

yoyó *m* yo-yo.
yubarta *f* ZOOL finback, rorqual.
yuca 1 BOT yucca. **2** CULIN cassava, manioc.
yucal *m* yucca plantation.
yudo *m* judo.
yudoka *mf* judoka.
yugo *m* yoke.
● **bajo el yugo de,** under the yoke of.
Yugoslavia *f* Yugoslavia.
yugular 1 *adj* ANAT jugular. – **2** *f* jugular vein.
● **saltarle a algn. a la yugular,** to go for sb.'s jugular.
yuju *interj fam* → **yupi**.
yunque *m* anvil.
yunta *f* team of oxen, yoke.
yuntero *m* ploughman, US plowman.
yupi *interj fam* whoopee!, yippee!
yuppie 1 *adj* yuppie. – **2** *mf* yuppie.
yute *m* jute.
yuto,-a 1 *adj* Jutish. – **2** *m,f* Jute.
yuxtaponer *t* to juxtapose.
▲ *Conjugation model* [78], *like poner*; *pp* **yuxtapuesto,-a**.
yuxtaposición *f* juxtaposition.
yuxtapuesto,-a *pp* → **yuxtaponer**.

Z

Z, z f (la letra) Z, z.

zafarrancho 1 m MIL clearing for action. 2 (jaleo) commotion. 3 (desorden) mess.
● ¡zafarrancho de combate!, action stations!

zafarse p to get away (**de**, from), free os. (**de**, from), escape (**de**, from): logró zafarse de la policía, he managed to get away from the police.

zafiedad f uncouthness.

zafio,-a 1 adj uncouth. 2 fig gauche.

zafiro m sapphire.

zaga f rear.
● a la zaga, behind. ‖ no irle a la zaga a algn., not to lag behind sb.: es muy travieso, pero su hermano no le va a la zaga, he's really naughty, but his brother's every bit as bad 2 f DEP defence (us defense).

zagal,-la 1 m,f (muchacho) lad; (muchacha) lass. 2 (pastor) shepherd; (pastora) shepherdess.

zaguán m hall, hallway.

zaguero,-a m,f DEP back, defender.

zaherir 1 t to wound, hurt. 2 (sentimientos) to hurt.
▲ Conjugation model [35], like hervir.

zahones mpl chaps.

zahorí 1 mf (adivino) seer, clairvoyant; (buscador de agua) water diviner. 2 fig mindreader.
▲ pl zahoríes.

zahúrda f hovel, pigsty.

zaino,-a 1 adj (traidor) treacherous. 2 (caballo) chestnut; (res vacuna) black.

Zaire m Zaire.

zaireño,-a 1 adj Zairean. – 2 m,f Zairean.

zalamería f winning ways pl.

zalamero,-a 1 adj charming, winning. – 2 m,f charmer.
● ponerse zalamero,-a, to turn on the charm.

zalema 1 f (reverencia) salaam, curtsy. – 2 zalemas, fpl (zalamería) charm.

zamarra f sheepskin jacket.

Zambesi el Zambesi, m the Zambesi.

Zambia f Zambia.

zambiano,-a 1 adj Zambian. – 2 m,f Zambian.

zambo,-a 1 adj knock-kneed. – 2 m ZOOL spider monkey.

zambomba 1 f zambomba, rustic drum-like instrument played by rubbing a stick attached to the drumskin. – 2 interj fam gosh!

zambombazo m fam bang.

zambra f (jaleo) racket.
■ zambra gitana, gypsy party.

zambullida f plunge, dive.
● darse una zambullida, to take a dip.

zambullir t to plunge.

zambullirse 1 p (en el agua) to plunge in, dive in: se zambulló en el agua, he plunged into the water. 2 (en una actividad) to throw os. (**en**, into).

zampabollos mf fam greedy-guts.

zampar i fam to stuff oneself.

zamparse p fam to wolf down.

zampatortas mf fam greedy-guts.

zampoña f MÚS panpipe.

zampullín m ORN little grebe.

zanahoria f carrot.

zanca f (de pájaro) leg; (de persona) long leg.

zancada f stride.
● en dos zancadas, in two shakes.

zancadilla 1 f trip. 2 fam (engaño) ruse, trick.
● ponerle la zancadilla a algn., to trip sb. up.

zanco m stilt.

zancudo,-a 1 adj long-legged. 2 (ave) wading. – 3 m AM mosquito. – 4 zancudas, fpl waders, wading birds.
■ aves zancudas, waders, wading birds.

zanganear i to loaf around.

zángano,-a 1 m,f fam (persona) loafer. – 2 m (insecto) drone.

zangolotear 1 i (persona) to roam around. 2 (puerta) to rattle.

zangolotino niño zangolotino, adj desus big baby.

zanja f trench.
● abrir una zanja, to dig a trench.

zanjar t fig (asunto) to settle.

zanquilargo,-a 1 adj long-legged, leggy. – 2 m,f long-legged person.

zapa 1 f trenching. 2 (pala) spade.

zapador,-ra m,f sapper.

zapata 1 f (arandela) washer. 2 TÉC shoe. 3 (de cámara fotográfica) hot shoe.
■ zapata de freno, brake shoe.

zapatazo 1 m (a alguien) blow with a shoe. 2 (en el suelo) stamp.
● dar zapatazos, to stamp one's feet.

zapateado m zapateado, Spanish stamping dance.

zapatear i (bailar) to stamp one's feet rhythmically.

zapateo m rhythmic stamping.

zapatería 1 f (tienda) shoe shop. 2 (taller de reparación) shoe-repairer's; (taller de fabricación) shoemaker's. 3 (oficio) shoemaking.

zapatero,-a 1 m,f (que arregla) shoe repairer, cobbler. 2 (que fabrica) shoemaker. 3 (que vende) shoe seller.
● ¡zapatero a tus zapatos!, the cobbler should stick to his last.
■ zapatero remendón, cobbler.

zapatiesta f fam hurly-burly.

zapatilla 1 f (de estar en casa) slipper. 2 (de loneta) plimsoll.
■ zapatilla de ballet, ballet shoe. ‖ zapatilla de deporte, trainer, running shoe. ‖ zapatilla de puntas, toe shoe.

zapato m shoe.
■ zapatos de tacón, high-heeled shoes.

zape interj fam (asombro) gosh!; (al gato) shoo!

zapoteca 1 adj Zapotec. – **2** mf (persona) Zapotec. – **3** zapoteca, m (idioma) Zapotec.
zapoteca 1 adj Zapotecan. – **2** mf Zapotec.
zapping m TV channel-zapping, channel-hopping: *se pasa la vida haciendo zapping,* he spends all day channel-hopping.
zar m tsar, czar.
zarabanda 1 f MÚS saraband. **2** fam (jaleo) bustle, confusion.
zaragata f rumpus.
Zaragoza f Saragossa.
zaragüelles 1 mpl (calzones) breeches. **2** (pantalones) baggy trousers.
zaranda f sieve.
zarandajas fpl fam trifles.
zarandear 1 t (sacudir) to shake; (empujar) to jostle, knock about. **2** (cribar) to sieve.
zarandearse 1 p (ajetrearse) to bustle about, rush about. **2** (contonearse) to swagger, strut.
zarandeo 1 m (sacudida) shaking; (empujones) jostling about. **2** (criba) sieving. **3** (contoneo) swaggering, strutting.
zarapito m ORN curlew.
zarcero m ORN melodious warbler.
zarcillo 1 m (pendiente) earring. **2** BOT tendril.
zarco,-a adj blue.
zarigüeya f opossum.
zarina f tsarina, czarina.
zarismo m tsarism, czarism.
zarista 1 adj tsarist, czarist. – **2** mf tsarist, czarist.
zarpa f claw, paw.
● **echarle la zarpa a algo,** (animal) to pounce on sth.; (persona) to grab sth.
zarpar i to weigh anchor, set sail.
zarpazo m (marca) claw mark.
● **dar un zarpazo, pegar un zarpazo,** to claw.
zarrapastroso,-a 1 adj fam scruffy. – **2** m,f scruff.
zarza f bramble, blackberry bush.
zarzal m bramble patch.
zarzamora f (zarza) blackberry bush; (fruto) blackberry.
zarzaparrilla f sarsaparilla.
zarzuela 1 f MÚS zarzuela, Spanish operetta. **2** CULIN fish stew.
zarzuelero,-a adj in the style of an operetta.
zarzuelístico,-a adj MÚS to do with zarzuela.
zas interj woosh!
▲ See also **zis**.
zascandil 1 m (alocado) madcap, featherbrain. **2** (entrometido) busybody, meddler.
zascandilear i to meddle.
zeda f → **zeta**.
zéjel m LIT zéjel Spanish stanza, usually octosyllabic.
zenit m zenith.
zepelín m zeppelin.
zeta 1 f zed, US zee. – **2** m arg police car.
zeta f (letra) zed, US zee.
zigzag m zigzag.
▲ pl zigzags or zigzagues.
zigzagueante adj zigzag.
zigzaguear i to zigzag.
zimbabuo,-a adj-m,f → **zimbabwense**.
Zimbabwe m Zimbabwe.
zimbabwense 1 adj Zimbabwean. – **2** mf Zimbabwean.
zinc m zinc.

zíngaro, -a 1 m,f Tzigane, Hungarian gypsy. – **2** adj Tzigane.
zipizape m fam rumpus: *se armó un zipizape tremendo,* there was a hell of a rumpus.
zis zis, zas, interj (espada) swish-swash; (mano) slap-slap.
zócalo 1 m (de habitación) skirting board; (de edificio) plinth course, plinth. **2** (pedestal) plinth, socle.
zoco m souk, suq, open-air marketplace in some Arab countries.
zodiacal adj zodiacal.
zodiaco m zodiac.
▲ also **zodíaco**.
zombi mf zombie.
● **estar zombi,** fam (atontado) to be groggy; (loco) to be loopy.
zona 1 f area. **2** (fronteriza, militar) zone. – **3** m MED (herpes) shingles.
■ **zona azul,** parking meter zone. ‖ **zona edificada,** built-up area. ‖ **zona fronteriza,** border zone. ‖ **zona glacial,** frigid zone. ‖ **zona templada,** temperate zone. ‖ **zona tórrida,** torrid zone. ‖ **zonas verdes,** parks and gardens: *este solar será zona verde,* this piece of land is going to be a park.
zonzo,-a adj AM silly.
zoo m zoo.
zoología f zoology.
zoológico,-a 1 adj zoological. – **2** m zoo.
zoólogo,-a m,f zoologist.
zoom m zoom, zoom lens.
zopenco,-a 1 m,f fam oaf. – **2** adj fam oafish.
zoquete m fam nincompoop, numskull.
zorcico m MÚS Basque song and dance.
zorongo m MÚS Andalusian song and dance.
zorra f → **zorro,-a**.
zorrera 1 f (madriguera) fox hole. **2** fam smoke-filled room.
zorrería f fam dirty trick: *¡qué zorrería!,* what a rotten thing to do!
zorrillo m ZOOL zorilla.
zorro,-a 1 adj (astuto) cunning, sly. – **2** zorro, m (animal) fox; (macho) dog-fox. **3** (piel) fox-fur, fox-skin. **4** (persona) old fox. – **5** zorros, mpl (para el polvo) duster sing. – **6** zorra, f (animal) vixen. **7** tabú (mujer) bitch.
● **estar hecho,-a unos zorros,** fam to be bushed. ‖ **ni zorra,** fam sod all. ‖ **no tener ni zorra idea,** fam not to have a clue.
■ **zorro azul,** blue fox. ‖ **zorro viejo,** sly old fox.
zorrupia f fam trollop.
zorzal m ORN thrush.
■ **zorzal alirrojo,** redwing. ‖ **zorzal charlo,** mistle thrush. ‖ **zorzal real,** fieldfare.
zote 1 adj dim-witted. – **2** mf dimwit.
zozobra 1 f (de un barco) sinking, capsizing. **2** fig (congoja) anguish, anxiety.
zozobrar 1 i (barco) to sink, capsize. **2** (persona) to worry, be anxious. **3** (proyecto) to fail, be ruined.
zueco m clog.
zulo m hideout.
zumaya f tawny owl.
zumba 1 f (burla) teasing. **2** (paliza) thrashing.
zumbado,-a adj fam barmy, zany.
zumbar 1 i (abejorro, oídos) to buzz: *me zumban los oídos,* my ears are buzzing. – **2** t fam (pegar) to thrash. **3** zumbarse de, (burlarse de) to make fun of, to tease.
● **salir zumbando,** fam to zoom off.

zumbido *m* buzzing.
zumbón,-ona 1 *adj* teasing, joking. – **2** *m,f* teaser, joker.
zumo *m* juice: *zumo de naranja*, orange juice.
zurcido 1 *m* darn, mend. **2** (*acción*) darning.
zurcir *t* to darn, mend.
 ● ¡que te zurzan!, get lost!
 ▲ *Conjugation model* [3].
zurdo,-a 1 *adj* (*persona*) left-handed; (*mano*) left. – **2** *m,f* left-hander, left-handed person. – **3** *f* (*mano*) left hand: *un golpe con la zurda*, a left-handed blow.
zurear *i* (*palomas*) to bill and coo.
zureo *m* billing and cooing.
zurra *f fam* thrashing.

zurrapa 1 *f* (*de posos*) dregs *pl*. **2** *tabú* (*de excrementos*) skid mark.
zurrar 1 *t fam* to thrash. **2** *fam* (*cuero*) to tan.
 ● zurrarle la badana a algn., to tan sb.'s hide.
zurriagazo 1 *m* (*latigazo*) lash, stroke. **2** *fam* (*desgracia*) blow, stroke of bad luck.
zurriago *m* whip.
zurriburri 1 *m fam* (*mezcla de gente*) hotchpotch, mishmash. **2** (*grupo ruidoso*) rowdy bunch, noisy crowd.
zurrón *m* shepherd's pouch, shepherd's bag.
zurullo 1 *m* (*grumo*) lump. **2** *tabú* turd.
zutano,-a *m,f fam* → **fulano,-a**.